THE AUTHORITY SINCE 1868

THE
WORLD
ALMANAC
& BOOK OF FACTS
1985

Published Annually by
NEWSPAPER ENTERPRISE ASSOCIATION, INC.
New York

THE WORLD ALMANAC & BOOK OF FACTS 1985

Publisher: Jane D. Flatt
Editor: Hana Umlauf Lane
Managing Editor: Mark S. Hoffman
Senior Assistant Editors: June Foley, Thomas J. McGuire

Assistant to the Publisher: Constance M. Fidler
Editorial Assistant: Marie P. Wagner
Canadian Editor: John Filion
Indexer: Deborah G. Felder
Chronology: Donald Young

Paperback cover design: Barbara Wilhelm, Elke Raedisch

The editors acknowledge with thanks the many letters of helpful comment and criticism from users of THE WORLD ALMANAC, and invite further suggestions and observations. Because of the volume of mail directed to the editorial offices, it is not possible personally to reply to each letter writer. However, every communication is read by the editors and all comments and suggestions receive careful attention. Inquiries regarding contents should be sent to: The World Almanac, 200 Park Avenue, New York, NY 10166.

THE WORLD ALMANAC is published annually in November. Purchase orders should be sent to: World Almanac Education Division, 1278 W. 9th St., Cleveland, OH 44113.

THE WORLD ALMANAC does not decide wagers.

The first edition of THE WORLD ALMANAC, a 120-page volume with 12 pages of advertising, was published by the New York World in 1868, 117 years ago. Annual publication was suspended in 1876. Joseph Pulitzer, publisher of the New York World, revived THE WORLD ALMANAC in 1886 with the goal of making it a "compendium of universal knowledge." It has been published annually since then. In 1931, it was acquired by the Scripps-Howard Newspapers; until 1951, it bore the imprint of the New York World-Telegram and thereafter, until 1967, that of the New York World-Telegram and Sun. It is now published in paper and clothbound editions by Newspaper Enterprise Association, Inc., a Scripps-Howard company.

NEWSPAPER ENTERPRISE ASSOCIATION, INC.
200 Park Avenue, New York, NY 10166

1985 HIGHLIGHTS

GENERAL INDEX

Addenda, Late News, Changes

Aerospace (p. 203)

Joe W. Kittinger set a world distance record for a solo balloon flight. His helium-filled balloon, *Rosie O'Grady's* began in Caribou, Me. and landed 3,535 miles and nearly 84 hours later in the mountains of the Italian Riviera.

Awards

Nobel Prizes (pp. 407-409)

The Nobel Prizes in literature, medicine, physics and chemistry were established under the will of Alfred B. Nobel, the Swedish industrialist and inventor of dynamite, who died in 1896. The Bank of Sweden added an economics prize in 1969. The 1984 Nobel Prizes consisted of diplomas, gold medals, and cash prizes of approximately $190,000 in each field.

Nobel Prize in Physics: Carlo Rubbia, an Italian on the Harvard University faculty, and Simon van der Meer of the Netherlands shared the award for their part in discovering three sub-atomic particles, considered a crucial step in developing a single theory to account for all natural forces. (p. 407)

Nobel Prize in Chemistry: R. Bruce Merrifield of Rockefeller University won the award for research revolutionizing the study of proteins and leading to the development of significant new drugs. (p. 407)

Nobel Prize in Medicine or Physiology: Cesar Milstein, of the British Medical Research Council's laboratory in Cambridge; George J. F. Kohler, of the Basel Institute of Immunology in Switzerland; and Niels K. Jerne, professor emeritus at the Basel Institute, were awarded the prize. Jerne was cited in particular for three important theories of immunology, Milstein and Kohler for their discovery of a laboratory technique for anti-body production that is now used virtually universally. (p. 408)

Nobel Prize in Literature: Jaroslav Seifert, considered Czechoslovakia's national poet, became the first of his countrymen to win the Nobel Prize for literature. (p. 408)

Nobel Peace Prize: Bishop Desmond Tutu, the general secretary of the South African Council of Churches and a leading voice for nonviolent efforts to end apartheid, was cited. (p. 409)

Nobel Memorial Prize in Economics: Sir Richard Stone, a retired Cambridge University professor, won the prize for his work in developing systems for measuring the performance of national economies that are now used widely and are pivotal in the work of such organizations as the United Nations, International Monetary Fund, and World Bank. (p. 408)

Books, Allied Arts (pp. 414-415)

New York Times Book Review's best illustrated children's books, 1983: *Twelve Cats for Christmas,* written and illustrated by Martin Leman; *Round Trip,* written and illustrated by Ann Jonas; *Little Red Cap,* by the Brothers Grimm, illustrated by Lisbeth Zwerger; *Leonard Baskin's Miniature Natural History: First Series,* written and illustrated by Leonard Baskin; *The Wreck of the Zephyr,* written and illustrated by Chris Van Allsburg; *Simon's Book,* written and illustrated by Henrik Drescher; *Tools,* written and photographed by Ken Robbins; *The Favershams,* written and illustrated by Roy Gerrard; *Up a Tree,* illustrated by Ed Young.

Broadcasting and Theater (pp. 415-416)

Emmy Awards, by Academy of Television Arts and Sciences, for nighttime programs, 1983-84: Dramatic series: *Hill Street Blues;* actor: Tom Selleck, *Magnum, P.I.;* actress: Tyne Daly, *Cagney and Lacey;* supporting actor: Bruce Weitz, *Hill Street Blues;* supporting actress: Alfre Woodard, *Hill Street Blues;* directing: Corey Allen, *Hill Street Blues;* writing: *St. Elsewhere.* Comedy series: *Cheers;* actor: John Ritter, *Three's Company;* actress: Jane Curtin, *Kate & Allie;* supporting actor: Pat Harrington, *One Day at a Time;* supporting actress: Rhea Perlman, *Cheers;* directing: Bill Persky, *Kate & Allie;* writing: David Angell, *Cheers.* Limited series: *Concealed Enemies;* actor: Laurence Olivier, *Laurence Olivier's King Lear;* actress: Jane Fonda, *The Dollmaker;* supporting actor: Art Carney, *Terrible Joe Moran;* supporting actress: Roxanna Zal, *Something About Amelia;* directing: Jeff Bleckner, *Concealed Enemies;* writing: William Hanley, *Something About Amelia;* drama special: *Something About Amelia.* Variety, music, or comedy program: *The Sixth Annual Kennedy Center Honors;* directing: Dwight Hemion, *Here's Television Entertainment;* writing: *Late Night With David Letterman.* Children's program: *He Makes Me Feel Like Dancin'.* Animated program: *Garfield on the Town.* Information special: *America Remembers John F. Kennedy;* series: *A Walk through the 20th Century with Bill Moyers.* Classical program: *Placido Domingo Celebrates Seville.*

Miscellaneous (p. 416)

Einstein Peace Prize, by Albert Einstein Foundation, for working to promote disarmament ($50,000): Pierre Elliott Trudeau, prime minister of Canada.

Kennedy Center awards, for distinguished achievement in the performing arts: singer Lena Horne, comedy actor Danny Kaye, composer Gian Carlo Menotti, playwright Arthur Miller, violinist Isaac Stern.

MacArthur Foundation fellowships, for exceptionally talented individuals ($176,000 to $300,000 each, over five years): Shelly Bernstein, molecular biologist, clinical fellow in pediatrics at Harvard Medical School; Peter Bickel, statistician, divisional dean of physical sciences at the University of California, Berkeley; William Drayton, Jr., attorney, chairman of the American Environmental Safety Council, chairman of the Ashoka Society Fellowships program; Sidney Drell, theoretical physicist, deputy director of Stanford's Linear Accelerator Center, co-director of the Center for International Security and Arms Control at Stanford; Mitchell Feigenbaum, mathematical physicist at Cornell University, on leave to Rockefeller Institute, New York, and the Institute for Advanced Study, Princeton, N.J.; Michael Freedman, professor of mathematics at the University of California, San Diego; Curtis Hames, Sr., country doctor from Claxton, Ga., researcher in epidemiology; Shirley Brice Heath, associate professor of education, specialist in anthropology and linguistics at Stanford University; Bette Howland, novelist; Bill Irwin, actor and mime in theater and television; Fritz John, retired professor of mathematics from New York University; Galway Kinnel, writer, poet, and translator; Henry Kraus, art historian and author; Peter Mathews, archeologist, specialist in Mayan hieroglyphics, research assistant at the Peabody Museum of Archeology and Ethnology; Beaumont Newhall, photography historian, professor of art at the University of New Mexico; Roger Payne, research scientist with the World Wildlife Fund; Edward Roberts, founder, World Institute of Disability; Elliot Sperling, specialist in Medieval and modern Sino-Tibetan relations teaching at the University of Southern Mississippi, Hattiesburg; Frank J. Sulloway, science historian in the department of psychology and social relations, Harvard University; Alar Toomre, astronomer, professor in the department of mathematics, MIT; Amos Tversky, professor of psychology at Stanford University, currently visiting professor at Hebrew University, Jerusalem; John Kirk Train Varnedoe, art historian at the New York University Institute of Fine Arts, co-director of current exhibit on primitivism in 20th-century art at the Museum of Modern Art; Bret

Wallach, geographer, essayist, associated professor of geography at the University of Oklahoma; Arthur T. Winfree, mathematical biologist and professor of biological sciences at Purdue University; Billie Jean Young, organizer in developing leadership among Southern black women through the Southern Rural Women's Movement.

1985 Calendar
(Inside Front Cover)

The second Thursday in October should read 10, not 19. The second Tuesday in December should read 10, not 19.

Chronology (p. 917)

The UAW and Ford Motor Company reached an agreement on a new contract, Oct. 15, that closely paralleled the settlement between the union and GM. The union also reported, Oct. 15, that the agreement with GM had been ratified by 57 percent of the rank and file.

Nations of the World (pp. 515-600)

France: Laurent Fabius became prime minister following the resignation of Pierre Mauroy.

Israel: The Knesset installed Labor leader Shimon Peres as prime minister for the first 25 months of the 51-month term. Likud leader Yitshak Shamir became deputy prime minister and foreign minister. Their roles will be reversed for the second part of the term.

Upper Volta: The former French colony changed its name to Bourkina Fasso.

Postal Rates (pp. 772-777)

On Sept. 7, 1984 the independent Postal Rates Commission recommended raising the price of a first-class stamp to 22 cents from 20 cents as part of a $2.2 billion rate increase affecting most classes of mail. The Postal Service board of governors was expected to accept the recommendation, the higher rates to take effect in early 1985.

Other recommended changes included: postcards—a one-cent increase from 13 to 14 cents; a one-cent greater discount for first-class mail presorted by ZIP code, from 3 to 4 cents; a 13 percent increase for third-class mail; a 14 percent increase for second-class mail; and a 15 percent increase for express mail.

Religion (p. 367)

Josyf Cardinal Slipyj, the Major Archbishop of The Ukrainians died in Rome at age 92 on September 8. Cardinal Slipyj had spent 18 years in Soviet prison camps until Pope John XXIII obtained his release from the Soviet leader, Nikita S. Krushchev, in 1963, one of the first important results of the early phase of detente between Moscow and the Vatican.

Sports (pp. 795-890)

Baseball: Rick Sutcliffe of the Chicago Cubs won the 1984 National League Cy Young Award.

Relief pitcher Willie Hernandez of the Detroit Tigers won the 1984 American League Cy Young Award.

Hernandez was also chosen as the 1984 American League Most Valuable Player.

Golf: Ryder Cup—United States 14$\frac{1}{4}$, Great Britain-Ireland 13$\frac{1}{4}$. Curtis Cup—United States 9$\frac{1}{2}$, Great Britain 8$\frac{1}{2}$.

Boston Marathon: Geoff Smith won the 88th annual Boston Marathon in 2:10.34. Lorraine Moller was first among the women with a time of 2:29.28.

New York Marathon: Orlando Pizzolato of Italy won the New York Marathon in 2:14:53. Grete Waitz of Norway was first among the women in 2:29:30. Waitz became the women's champion for the 6th time in 7 years. Pizzolato and Waitz each won $25,000.

Supreme Court (pp. 921-924)

The Supreme Court opened its 1984-85 term on October 1. From a list of more than 1,000 appeals, the justices added 29 cases to the court's calendar. These included cases involving the definition of obscenity, the right to speak in favor of homosexuality, and the right of lawyers to seek clients for specific cases. Among the cases the court refused to review were those involving the court-supervised desegregation of the St. Louis schools and a challenge to a Miami ordinance setting aside public works contracts for black construction firms.

Ten Most Dramatic Sports Events, Nov. 1983—Oct. 1984

Selected by The World Almanac Sports Staff

—Miami upsets number 1 ranked Nebraska 31-30 in the Orange Bowl game. The Cornhuskers, who had a 22-game winning streak, failed in their attempt at a two-point conversion in the final seconds of the game.

—Carl Lewis won four track and field gold medals at the Olympic games. He equaled the record set by Jesse Owens in 1936.

—Walter Payton of the Chicago Bears rushed for a 6-yard gain to become the National Football League's all-time leading rusher. Payton passed Jim Brown who rushed for 12,312 yards from 1957 to 1965.

—Mike Witt of the California Angels pitched a perfect game defeating the Texas Rangers 1-0 on the final day of the season. It was the first major league perfect game in 3 years and the 10th since 1900.

—The San Diego Padres defeated the Chicago Cubs 6-3 to become the first team to win the best-of-five National League championship series after losing the first two games.

—Mary Lou Retton scored a perfect 10 on the vault, her final event, to win the Olympic gold medal in the all-around gymnastics event. She defeated Romania's Ecaterina Szabo by .05 points.

—The Boston Celtics defeated the Los Angeles Lakers 111-102 in game seven to win the National Basketball Association championship. It was the 15th NBA championship for the Celtics.

—Georgetown Univ. won their first NCAA basketball championship by defeating Houston Univ. 84-75 in the championship game. The Hoyas' 34 victories were the most since the 36 registered by the Univ. of Kentucky in 1947-48.

—The Edmonton Oilers defeated the N.Y. Islanders 4 games to 1 to win their first Stanley Cup championship. The Islanders had won the National Hockey League title for 4 consecutive years.

—Lee Trevino, at age 44, won the Professional Golfers Assn. championship by 4 strokes. He shot a 273, the lowest subpar effort in the 66-year history of the PGA championship.

The World Almanac

and Book of Facts for 1985

The Top 10 News Stories

Hampering drastically prospects for a permanent peace in Lebanon, a suicide terrorist driving a truck laden with TNT blew up the U.S. Marine headquarters at Beirut International Airport, killing 241 Americans, most of them Marines.

Evoking mixed reactions at home and abroad, the United States invaded Grenada, citing a formal request for help from the Organization of East Caribbean States to restore order and democracy, and to rescue Americans considered to be in danger.

Leaving tradition behind, Walter Mondale selected a woman, New York Representative Geraldine Ferraro, as his running mate; Ferraro was enthusiastically endorsed by the Democratic National Convention as the first women to be nominated for vice president by a major political party.

Emergency surgery failed to save the life of Indian Prime Minister Indira Gandhi after she was shot outside her home by 2 Sikh gunmen who were members of her security guard; Gandhi had been at the center of a controversy over the handling of a Sikh campaign for greater autonomy in the Punjab.

Not even a year and one-half after coming to power, Soviet Communist Party Leader Yuri Andropov died after a lengthy illness; Konstantin U. Chernenko, a close Brezhnev ally, succeeded to the top post in the USSR.

Positive economic news dominated most of the past year, indicating a continuation of the economic recovery, until August when the first signs appeared that the recovery was slowing down.

Assailing planned security precautions in Los Angeles, the Soviet Union and most of the East European nations pulled their athletes out of the Summer Olympics, leaving a clear field to the American athletes who swept the medals in the quadrennial competition.

Uncertainty over the stability of the Persian Gulf grew as the Iran-Iraq war continued, especially with Iranian attacks on commercial shipping in the gulf and Saudi Arabia's downing of Iranian jet fighters.

Leading Democrats criticized the $180.4 billion deficit projected in President Reagan's 1985 budget, especially the proposed increase of $33 billion in defense spending; the deficit and its roots became a major issue in the presidential election campaign.

House and Senate members voted, amid furor, to condemn U.S. participation in the CIA-directed mining of Nicaraguan ports, following the disclosure that the U.S. role had been larger than previously believed.

Ronald Reagan Wins Landslide Re-election;
Democrats Retain House, Win 2 Seats in Senate

Pres. Ronald Reagan's record-breaking Maine-to-California landslide re-election victory, Nov. 6, was a strong national affirmation of his personal popularity. It also established that a majority of American voters wanted to stay on the conservative path that he had followed since 1981. Had Reagan lost in 1984, his first national victory in 1980 might have been written off by future historians merely as a rejection of an unpopular president, Jimmy Carter. But his 49-state sweep in 1984 reflected voter approval of the strong economic recovery and of Reagan's military build-up.

Needing only 270 electoral votes to retain the presidency, Reagan captured 525, more than anyone ever had. Former Vice Pres. Walter Mondale, the candidate of the Democratic Party, carried his home state of Minnesota and the District of Columbia, for a total of 13 electoral votes, 4 less than McGovern's total in 1972. Reagan's lead in the nationwide popular vote was also decisive, though not a record; he received 52.7 million votes (59 percent) to 36.5 million votes (41 percent) for Mondale.

The Republicans picked up about 13 seats in the U.S. House of Representatives, not enough to bring them up to even an ideological majority. The Democrats retained the House by about 255 to 180. The Republicans won 17 of 33 Senate races for a net loss of 2, and emerged with a 54-46 majority.

Victory Covers Major Political Bases

Reagan's victory crossed all regional and most demographic lines. Indeed, the Democrats, losing for the fourth time in the last 5 presidential contests, appeared to have no remaining regional base of support. Certainly it was not in their once "Solid South," where every state went for Reagan, usually by decisive majorities. In the West, the continuation of the Sun Belt that the Republicans had identified as their own emerging base, Reagan easily won everywhere. He beat back a vigorous effort by Mondale in his home state of California.

The Northeast, once a stronghold of the GOP when moderate Republicans controlled their party, and the principal home of Democratic liberalism in more recent years, stayed in the Reagan column for the second time. Mondale did not even come close in New York, Pennsylvania, and New Jersey. Elsewhere in the East, Mondale salvaged only the District of Columbia, which is predominantly black. Reagan also handily swept the industrial states of the Great Lakes, even though recovery from the 1981–1982 economic recession was not yet complete. Despite displeasure among farmers with Reagan's agricultural policies, the president won all of the upper Midwest and farm states aside from Minnesota.

Reagan, who had come close to casting himself as an Uncle Sam figure and who had spoken of the Republicans as "America's party," got an endorsement from people from all walks of life. All age groups supported him, including the youngest voters, many of whose older brothers and sisters had been strongly, even vociferously, in the Democratic column during the era of Vietnam and Watergate. Members of the "baby boom" generation, now in their late 20s and 30s, also voted for the president. Many of them had voted for Sen. Gary Hart (Col.) when he challenged Mondale for the Democratic nomination. Hart had argued that Mondale represented old ideas which Hart had predicted would be rejected in November. Older voters also backed Reagan, though some retired Americans were concerned by his past statements about the need to make adjustments in Social Security and Medicare, either to keep the systems going or to help reduce federal budget deficits.

The vote in union households was watched closely because this segment of the population had been wavering in its support for Democrats in recent years. For Mondale, the results represented the worst of both worlds. Before the Democratic convention, he had received the endorsement of the AFL-CIO, and primarily for that reason he had thereafter been tagged by his rivals as the candidate of the "special interests." Then, in the election itself, he received only about half of the union vote.

The defection of white southerners, especially those Protestants who called themselves born-again Christians, further weakened the coalition that had elected all Democratic presidents since Franklin D. Roosevelt. As recently as 1976 and 1980, Jimmy Carter had drawn heavily from this group of which he was a member, but such was not to happen in 1984. These religious and political conservatives turned overwhelmingly to Reagan, who had articulated their values eloquently and who had supported constitutional amendments forbidding abortions and permitting prayer in the public schools. Roman Catholics, another component of Democratic coalitions in years past, gave a majority of their votes to Reagan.

Less Affluent Vote Democratic

Middle class and wealthy Americans supported Reagan, while less affluent voters stayed in the Democratic column. Blacks, among whom unemployment was still high, remained strongly Democratic—by about 90 percent. Commanding greater attention because their votes were less predictable and their ranks growing more rapidly, were the nation's Hispanic voters. Although they gave a maority to Mondale, many of them, particularly those with ties to Cuba and Central America, supported Reagan—in part because of his outspoken warnings about, and actions against, the Communist threat in the Carribbean and Central America. Hispanics, who now constitute a large bloc in a number of big states, had helped defeat an immigration bill in Congress in 1984, and they emerged from the election as a much stronger force in American politics.

The large turnout among blacks, Hispanics, white southern Protestants, and other groups had been the result of unusually aggressive voter-registration drives by both parties. Frank Fahrenkopf, the Republican national chairman, said his party had signed up 4 million Reagan supporters. The Rev. Jesse Jackson, the first serious black candidate for president, had been in the vanguard of the Democratic effort to recruit new voters.

Debate about the "gender gap" had continued throughout the campaign. For several years, voting results and public-opinion polls had shown that men gave much more support than women did to Reagan and other Republicans. Weaker backing for Reagan among women had been attributed to his opposition to the Equal Rights Amendment and to concern among many women over his economic policies and his saber-rattling in foreign affairs. The nomination of Rep. Geraldine Ferraro of New York as the Democratic candidate for vice president—the first woman to be named to a major-party ticket—intentisfied competition for the women's vote in November. Again, Reagan prevailed as women nationwide supported him. But men continued to support the president even more strongly.

The Congressional voting did not strengthen Reagan's claim of a mandate for his second term. Both Fahrenkopf and Ed Rollins, the president's campaign manager, had said that the "Reagan Revolution" would be over if the GOP failed to make significant gains in the House. But the Republicans recovered only about half of the 26 House seats lost to the Democrats in the 1982 off-year election. Reagan would begin his second term with fewer Republican senators and representatives than he had had behind him 4 years earlier.

Reagan Coattails Weak in Congress

As in most House elections in recent years, the vast majority of incumbent representatives in both parties were returned to office. Prominent Democrats targeted for defeat by the Republicans were successful in defending their seats. These included James Jones (Okla.), chairman of the House budget committee, who had been a formidable opponent of the president's economic policies. Clarence Long (Md.), a consistent thorn in Reagan's side on Central American policy, prevailed again at the age of 75.

Two representatives who had been censured by the House in 1983 for having had sexual relationships with teen-age House pages, had different re-election luck. Gerry Studds

was returned to office in his Massachusetts district, but Daniel Crane lost in Illinois. George Hansen of Idaho, a Republican, who had been convicted of violating the Ethics in Government act, lost by an extremely slim margin.

Reagan had carried a Republican Senate into office in 1980 on his coattails, and this majority had remained essentially unchanged. The Senate would be expected to play a key role in his second term should he submit an arms-control treaty with the Soviet Union for ratification. The Senate would also be important if, as expected, Reagan had an opportunity to nominate several U.S. Supreme Court justices to replace those expected to retire soon. Reagan had made no secret of his desire to establish a firm and longlasting conservative majority on the high court as well as on other federal benches.

Although only one third of the Senate (33 seats) was contested in 1984, the Democrats had believed that they could wipe out the 55-45 Republican majority. With the election in Tennessee of Albert Gore, Jr., whose father had once served in the Senate, they picked up the seat of Howard Baker, the Senate majority leader, who retired, presumably to prepare for a race for president in 1988. The Democrats took another seat from the GOP in Iowa, where Rep. Tom Harkin defeated the conservative Republican incumbent, Roger Jepson. A GOP veteran of 18 years, Charles Percy of Illinois, chairman of the powerful Foreign Relations Committee, lost his bid for a fourth term to Rep. Paul Simon. Another Democrat won in Massachusetts, where Lt. Gov. John Kerry, a Vietnam veteran, defeated conservative businessman Raymond Shamie for the seat being vacated by the retiring Paul Tsongas, a Democrat. But Democratic Gov. James Hunt was unable to unseat the ultraconservative Jesse Helms in North Carolina in what was by all odds the most bitter and expensive ($21 million) contest of the year. Phil Gramm, a Reagan supporter who had quit the Democratic Party, won the Senate seat in Texas vacated by John Tower, a Republican. The Democrats suffered their only loss of a seat in Kentucky, where A. Mitchell McConnell upset the incumbent Walter Huddleston by a few thousand votes.

Prominent Republicans who won re-election included Strom Thurmond (S.C.), Mark Hatfield (Ore.), and Nancy Landon Kassebaum (Kan.). Democrats re-elected included Sam Nunn (Ga.), Joseph Biden, Jr. (Del.), and Claiborne Pell (R. I.), and Bill Bradley (N. J.). Gov. John D. Rockefeller 4th of West Virginia, who spent $7 million of his own money to get elected, was the best known of the new Democratic senators.

Democrats went into the election with a commanding 35-15 majority among the nation's governors. With only 13 state houses being contested, the Republicans had little chance to improve their position, but they did make a gain in North Carolina, where James Martin was an upset winner as part of the statewide GOP sweep. Former Gov. Arch Moore retook the West Virginia state house for the Republicans. Edward DiPriete added a third in the usually Democratic state of Rhode Island, and Utah also elected a Republican, Norman Bangerter, to succeed the popular Scott Matheson, who retired.

But the Republicans lost ground in North Dakota, where George Sinner surprised the incumbent Gov. Allen Olson. And Booth Gardner turned out another Republican governor, John Spellman, in Washington, and Madeleine Kunin defeated Republican John Easton in Vermont.

The Democrats continued to hold a majority of the state legislatures, further evidence that the political realignment, if any, had occurred only at the presidential level.

Economy Key to Reagan Win

In retrospect, it did not seem likely that any Democrat could have beaten Ronald Reagan. Public-opinion surveys showed that a majority of Americans believed that they were much better off economically than they had been 4 years earlier, and history showed that national elections were almost inevitably decided on the basis of the voters' economic well-being, or lack of it. Reagan had pounded home the fact that unemployment and inflation had declined during his administration, though it was also true that the jobless rate had soared in his first two years. Just as skillfully, he had brushed aside Mondale's warning that huge

Reaganite budget deficits would ultimately cause the economic house of cards to collapse. Unable to demonstrate how deficits were affecting the daily lives of the voters, Mondale was reduced to a shrill voice warning of future doom. Reagan, in any case, argued that economic growth would generate sufficient tax revenue to wipe out the deficits, a cornerstone of the economic theory known as supply-side economics. Mondale had "promised" the voters a tax increase, which he said would be concentrated on wealthy tax payers and corporations, but the credit he got for being candid failed to overcome the unpopularity of the plan. Reagan, by insisting that he would not raise taxes, had run the considerable risk of painting himself into a corner.

Mondale tried a variety of issues, to no avail. He suggested that Reagan was unable or unwilling to take command of his own office, but the 73-year-old president quashed that matter with a self-assured performance in the second debate between the two men on Oct. 21. Mondale also charged that Reagan had tied himself too closely to religious fundamentalists and their social agenda. Reagan had declared during the Republican convention in Dallas that religion and politics are "necessarily related," but Mondale appeared unable to persuade many voters that Reagan contemplated knocking down the wall between church and state that had stood for 200 years.

In foreign affairs, Reagan's relentless insistence that America was back and standing tall had overridden a spotty record that had included a near debacle in the Middle East. Lebanon had apparently passed under the influence of Syria, and in the process several hundred U.S. servicemen, mostly Marines in a peacekeeping force, had been killed in terrorist bombings. In Central America, Reagan's firmness did not seem excessive to most voters in the face of the rise of the leftist Sandinista regime in Nicaragua and the guerrilla movement against the noncommunist regime in El Salvador. The not-so-secret covert war in Nicaragua—involving anticommunist "contras"—run under the supervision of the U.S. Central Intelligence Agency, did not seem greatly out of line with similar activities by that agency during administrations of both parties since World War II. On the most serious concern of all, arms control, Reagan could point to the fact that he had toned down his anti-Soviet rhetoric and to the revolving-door leadership in the Soviet gerontocracy, which had not provided much of an opportunity for setting up summit conferences.

Mondale Lacked Strong Theme

In these circumstances, Mondale had seemed unable to settle upon a theme, certainly nothing that could be captured in a single snappy phrase such as New Deal or Fair Deal. He did argue that the recovery in the economy had not been felt equally by all economic groups, and he argued a lack of "fairness" in the president's policies. Emphasizing what he felt was a callousness on the part of the president and his supporters, Mondale had been at his most eloquent when he had said in the first televised debate, "I'd rather lose a campaign about decency than win one about self-interest."

In defeat, the Democrats had made history twice. Jackson had been the first black to bid seriously for a major party presidential nomination, and Ferraro had broken the sex barrier on the national ticket. And yet, these were ideas whose time had not yet quite come. Bert Lance, a leader of the Democrats in the South, observed, in reference to Ferraro, that "the pioneers take all the arrows." Ferraro was the first national candidate forced to defend the business activities of a spouse who happened to be a man—few wives of candidates had come under the scrutiny of the Ethics in Government act in the past. As a woman, and as a Roman Catholic, she was also compelled to defend, in the most personal terms, her views on abortion. Although she said she would not have an abortion, Ferraro had declared that she would not impose her views on others—that other women must make their own choice.

As for Jackson, his campaign had been far too divisive to permit the creation of a political base much beyond his own race. And yet the campaign ended with the suspicion that in the near future, with precisely the right candidate and under more favorable circumstances, a black or a woman would be taking an oath of office on the steps of the Capitol on January 20th.   Donald Young

America's 25 Most Influential Women in 1984

The following women were chosen in a World Almanac poll by editors at daily newspapers across the United States. First place balloting went to Geraldine Ferraro, the first female Democratic vice-presidential candidate in U.S. history.

Arts

Beverly Sills, general director of the New York City Opera.
Cathy Guisewite, cartoonist, "Cathy."

Business

Katharine Graham, Washington Post Co. board chairman.
Mary Kay Ash, founder and chair of Mary Kay Cosmetics.

Education, Scholarship, Science

Sally Ride, America's first female astronaut.
Barbara Jordan, professor, former U.S. representative (D., Tex.).
Barbara Tuchman, author and historian.

Entertainment

Jane Fonda, actress, author of bestselling exercise book, videotape.
Shirley MacLaine, winner of 1983 best actress Oscar, bestselling author.
Katharine Hepburn, actress, 4-time winner of Academy Award.

Government

Geraldine Ferraro, Democratic nominee for U.S. vice president.
Sandra Day O'Connor, U.S. Supreme Court justice.

Elizabeth Dole, U.S. Secretary of Health and Human Services.
Dianne Feinstein, mayor of San Francisco.
Nancy Reagan, U.S. First Lady.
Jeane Kirkpatrick, U.S. representative to the United Nations.

Media

Ellen Goodman, syndicated Boston Globe columnist.
Ann Landers, advice columnist.
Erma Bombeck, humorist, author of syndicated column and best-selling books.

Social Activists

Gloria Steinem, women's rights leader, editor of Ms. magazine.
Betty Ford, former First Lady, advocate of drug/alcohol abuse treatment.
Phyllis Schlafly, anti-ERA activist, conservative author, lecturer.

Sports

Martina Navratilova, tennis champion, 1983-84 U.S. Open singles champion, and 5-time Wimbledon singles champion.
Mary Decker, long-distance runner.
Chris Evert Lloyd, tennis player, 6-time U.S. singles champion.

National Spelling Bee Champions

The Scripps-Howard National Spelling Bee, conducted by Scripps-Howard Newpapers and other leading newpapers since 1939, was instituted by the Louisville (Ky.) Courier-Journal in 1925. Children under 16 years of age and not beyond the eighth grade are eligible to compete for cash prizes at the finals, which are held annually in Washington, D.C.

In the 1984 spelldown, the runner-up missed "towhee" (a North American finch). The winner spelled it correctly, and also the final word, "luge" (a type of sled). **Recent winners are:**

1983 — 1. Blake Giddens, 14, Alamogordo, N.M. (El Paso Herald-Post). 2. Eric Rauchway, 13, St. Petersburg, Fl. (St. Petersburg Times). 3. Tanya Zahava Soloman, 11, Kansas City, Mo. (Independence Examiner & Blue Springs Examiner, Independence, Mo.).

1984 — 1. Dan Greenblatt, 13, Sterling Va. (Loudoun Times-Mirror, Leesburg, Va.). 2. Amy McWhirter, 13, St. Joseph, Mich. (Herald Palladium, Benton Harbor/St. Joseph, Mich.). 3. Jennifer Poole, 13, Alexandria, Va. (Journal Newspapers, Wash. D.C.).

Heroes of Young America: The Fifth Annual Poll

High school students across America have picked pop singer Michael Jackson as their Top Hero. For the fifth year in succession, The World Almanac has turned to America's youth to select those individuals in public life they admire most. The selection was made in 9 categories.

Students in grades 8 through 12 voted in their classrooms in selected schools across the United States. The schools, chosen to participate through The World Almanac cosponsoring newspapers, represented a geographic cross-section of the United States in both suburban and intercity schools.

Some Surprises in Top Hero Vote

Although the choice of Michael Jackson was by no means a surprise, the other winning vote-getters in the Top Hero category were somewhat unexpected. Whereas five years ago, in the first annual Heroes of Young America poll, almost all the top "heroes" were youthful entertainment or sports figures, the final results in the 1984 voting in the top hero category showed Ronald Reagan, Pope John Paul II, and Katharine Hepburn running strong.

A glance at the winners in the other 9 categories reinforces the indication that America's youth is looking toward mature, well-established individuals as their role models. Walter Cronkite, Barbara Walters, Chris Evert-Lloyd, Joan Rivers, Katharine Hepburn, and Neil Armstrong certainly fit that description.

Male vs. Female Voting

Do males and females vote for the same heroes? Generally not. The only winners selected by a fairly even male-female mix were Eddie Murphy and Steven Spielberg. Julius Erving was selected on the strength of male support, with females voting in greater numbers for runnersup Tony Dorsett and Sugar Ray Leonard.

The female voting patterns in general showed greater consistency in selecting one hero, while the male vote was scattered among many individuals. Female consistency helped to select Tom Cruise, Tom Selleck, Debbie Allen, Barbara Walters, and Sally Ride.

What about the voting for Michael Jackson? In the Music and Dance category, voting ran 4-to-3 female-male, with the females giving Jackson the edge needed to win. In the runnerups for top male in this category, females voted in strength for Lionel Ritchie, while the males voted for Eddie Van Halen.

Continuity in Winners

Another interesting element in this year's list is the continuity from previous years. Tom Selleck, Pat Benatar, Walter Cronkite, Barbara Walters, and Neil Armstrong made their third appearance as category winners. Judy Blume, Steven Spielberg, Debbie Allen, Michael Jackson, and Eddie Murphy appear as category winners for the second year in a row. During the first two years of polling, there were no categories. Past top hero winners include Burt Reynolds, Alan Alda, and Sylvester Stallone.

Top Hero

Michael Jackson, pop singer.

Movie Performers/Non-comedy

Tom Cruise, actor, star of *Risky Business* and *All the Right Moves.*
Katharine Hepburn, actress, most recently starred in *On Golden Pond.*

Television Performers/Non-comedy

Tom Selleck, actor, stars in the weekly TV series, "Magnum, P.I."
Debbie Allen, actress, dancer, star of the TV series, "Fame."

Comedy

Eddie Murphy, actor, TV comic on "Saturday Night Live," starred in *Trading Places.*
Joan Rivers, comedian, often hosts "The Tonight Show."

Music and Dance

Michael Jackson, pop singer.
Pat Benatar, pop singer.

Sports

Julius Erving, basketball player for the Philadelphia 76ers.
Chris Evert-Lloyd, tennis player.

News and Sports Media

Walter Cronkite, former anchorman, "CBS Evening News."
Barbara Walters, TV journalist, ABC News.

Artists and Writers

Steven Spielberg, director of *E.T.* and *Raiders of the Lost Ark.*
Judy Blume, author, primarily of children's and young adult novels, including *Superfudge* and *Tiger Eyes.*

Newsmakers

Neil Armstrong, former astronaut, the first man to walk on the moon.
Sally Ride, astronaut, the first U.S. woman in space.

OMNI Forecasts: 1986 and Beyond

When *OMNI* magazine debuted in October 1978, its editors described their creation as "the magazine of the future." Since then, *OMNI*'s unchanging focus on the future has made it one of the most widely read and influential magazines now published. Here the editors of *OMNI* offer their view of things to come.

1986

Uranus unveiled by spectacular *Voyager* photos — The *Voyager 2* space probe, launched on September 20, 1977, will arrive at Uranus on January 24 to take the first close-up portraits of this little-known planet, its five known moons, and nine faint rings. Given the probe's dramatic revelations of Saturn in August 1981, the least we can expect to see are some new moons. Still to come, a Neptune flyby in the 1990s—if NASA budgets permit.

Spray protects against smoking, air pollution — Just reaching the drug stores is an inhaler that can shield your lungs from damage caused by smoking and living in the city. Much of the destruction is caused by "free radicals," highly reactive chemicals found in tobacco smoke and air pollution. Vitamin E is a potent "quencher" that can destroy free radicals before they have a chance to attack delicate lung tissues. Breathe in the new spray—vitamin E in mineral oil—and you are protected for up to five days, say its developers at UCLA.

1987

U.S. bans drugs in meat and poultry — The federal Food and Drug Administration bars farmers from adding antibiotics to feed for meat animals. Tetracycline and other drugs were used for 30 years to speed growth of farm animals; in

1983, about 60 percent of the feedlot cattle, 80 percent of the pigs, 30 percent of the chickens, and all turkeys grown in the United States were given the drugs. But the practice also promoted the growth of bacteria immune to antibiotics. Drug-resistant *Salmonella* infections kill up to 2,000 Americans a year, and many of these deaths, public health officials believe, were due to meat from drugged farm animals.

1989

Voyager 2 reaches Neptune — Scientists at Pasadena's Jet Propulsion Laboratory should begin receiving detailed photographs of Neptune this August 24. According to plan, the probe will dive to within 7,500 miles of the planet's surface, then pass near Neptune's largest moon, Triton. After that, its next stop is the star Sirius, which it will pass at one light-year's distance 358,000 years from now.

1990

"Mermen" spend two weeks in sea off California — Four divers wearing artificial gills complete two weeks underwater near San Diego. Based on a hemoglobin-containing plastic developed at Duke University, the gills extract oxygen directly from sea water, allowing divers to stay submerged indefinitely. When not diving, the mermen lived in an ocean-floor habitat with a scaled-up gill as their only source of air.

1991

Biochip computer linked to human brain — A tiny research firm in Bethesda, MD, announces that they have used a tiny computer made of protein to restore sight to a child blinded in an auto accident. One part of the device replaces the visual receptors of the damaged eye; the other couples with the optic nerve, feeding natural-seeming nerve pulses to the brain. The company predicts that within 15 years a more advanced chip will make it possible to feed computer data directly to the brain.

Practical life-extension arrives — Three factors are crucial to the advance: One is thymosin, a natural hormone crucial to the body's immune defenses. Its production falls off dramatically as we age, and supplements greatly strengthen resistance to disease. The second is a mixture of drugs that shield proteins and DNA from damage by environmental hazards—the ultimate limit on human survival. Most important is a blocker for a hormone known as DECO. Produced in growing quantities with age, DECO interferes with the thyroid hormone needed for most bodily activities; in effect, it slowly turns us off. The anti-aging treatments are expected to add at least 30 years to the average life span, and further extensions are in the offing.

1992

First 3-D TV — Not one, but two electronics firms announce plans to introduce 3-D televisions this model year. Both systems can use normal television signals, and both require special glasses to view the effect. The first practical product is a $150 add-on that makes 3-D home movies using ordinary video recorders.

1993

Doctor's heal paralyzed girl's severed spine — Surgeons at New York City's Columbia-Presbyterian Hospital announce that they have used weak electrical pulses to reunite the spinal nerves of a 13-year-old accident victim. The pulses mimic the natural communication system used by the body to direct growth of its tissues. Electrohealing has been used since the 1970s to mend broken bones that would not heal under standard treatments. Researchers at the Syracuse (NY) Veterans Administration Hospital, where the natural electrical system was discovered, predict that it will be possible to regrow a lost limb within five years.

1994

Fusion power demonstrated — Scientists at Princeton's Plasma Physics Laboratory announce that their latest experiment in nuclear fusion actually produced slightly more power than it consumed. This "first" is, in theory, the last scientific breakthrough needed for fusion generators. However, the physicists point out that the net energy gain was far smaller than required for a practical power source and that many years of engineering and design are needed before construction of even a small test power plant can begin.

1995

Cancer vaccine debuts — The first vaccine against a human cancer wins approval for distribution. The vaccine defends against Epstein-Barr virus (EBV). Best known in the United States as the cause of mononucleosis, EBV also produces Burkitt's lymphoma, one of the most common cancers of children in Africa, as well as tumors of the nose and throat. A vaccine against hepatitis B virus, which is believed to cause liver cancer, was developed earlier but is still being tested in China.

1996

Artificial liver perfected — Unlike the heart and lung, the liver proves far too complex to duplicate in plastic and metal. Instead, doctors settle for a technique first tried in the early 1980s: They trap liver cells from an ape in a plastic container and implant them in a patient's body. Shielded from the host's immune system, they are not destroyed by antibodies and white blood cells as a simple transplant would be, yet they can still absorb toxins from the blood, release bile, and allow the patient to carry on a normal life. The device is used for only a few years; then electrohealing allows doctors to regenerate the natural liver.

1999

Robots displace human workers — Japan has in excess of 10 million robots this year, the United States about 7 million. Each does the work of at least four people. As a result, manufacturing jobs, which represented nearly 25 percent of employment in the U.S. as recently as 1975, have become a thing of the past. Human secretaries and receptionists are quickly becoming a prestige "perk" for high-level executives. Even fast-food workers, pegged by the U.S. Department of Labor as the most rapidly growing industry segment in the last 20 years of the century, have been largely replaced by hamburger-making robots. Only creative professions, such as music and writing, remain immune to the trend, and music-composing computers are gaining fans.

Small cars average 100 mpg — Two factors win credit for the advance: careful streamlining to cut wind resistance and computerized fuel and engine controls, which eliminate incomplete combustion. The added efficiency also cuts air pollution to half its 1980 level.

2000

Revival of atomic power — Shrinking oil reserves, fears that air pollution could soon warm the Earth enough to destroy American farming, and a changed political climate at last weaken resistance to nuclear power. Because practical fusion generators still appear at least ten years off, the U.S. Department of Energy begins large-scale tests of three reactor designs: the High Temperature Gas, Process Inherent Ultimate Safe, and Actinide-Nitride reactors. Available for 20 years or more, but shelved because light-water models were cheaper, the systems work only under hard-to-meet conditions; if anything goes wrong, they simply shut down. Most likely to be adopted is the actinide-nitride reactor, which "burns" all but 1 percent of the nuclear fuel, leaving almost no radwaste.

Neptune and Pluto switch positions — Though most of us think of it as the most distant planet, Pluto has such a flattened orbit that it has been closer to the sun than Neptune since 1979. This year it regains its traditional position.

2002

U.N. cites Mexico City as most polluted — With a population of 35 million, Mexico City is the largest city in the world. Thanks to its 6 million cars and heavy industrialization, it is also the most polluted. Mountains that circle the city trap the poisoned air, aggravating the problem. With 16 million people and nearly that many cars, Los Angeles is nearly as polluted as Mexico City. Even healthy individuals must stay indoors and avoid strenuous exercise two days out of three.

PRESIDENTIAL ELECTIONS

Popular and Electoral Vote, 1980 and 1984

(1984 results are preliminary)

Source: News Election Service

States	1980 Electoral Vote Carter	1980 Electoral Vote Reagan	Democrat Carter	Republican Reagan	Indep. Anderson	1984 Electoral Vote Mondale	1984 Electoral Vote Reagan	Democrat Mondale	Republican Reagan
Ala. . . .	0	9	636,730	654,192	16,481	0	9	540,445	844,299
Alas. . .	0	3	41,842	86,112	11,156	0	3	51,169	115,390
Ariz.. . .	0	6	246,843	529,688	76,952	0	7	325,924	669,353
Ark.. . .	0	6	398,041	403,164	22,468	0	6	325,185	505,562
Cal.. . .	0	45	3,083,652	4,524,835	739,832	0	47	3,803,913	5,291,747
Col. . . .	0	7	368,009	652,264	130,633	0	8	434,560	768,711
Conn.. .	0	8	541,732	677,210	171,807	0	8	560,712	883,486
Del.. . .	0	3	105,754	111,252	16,288	0	3	100,632	151,494
D.C.. . .	3	0	130,231	23,313	16,131	3	0	172,459	26,805
Fla. . . .	0	17	1,419,475	2,046,951	189,692	0	21	1,373,137	2,512,318
Ga. . . .	12	0	890,733	654,168	36,055	0	12	696,181	1,050,852
Ha. . . .	4	0	135,879	130,112	32,021	0	4	145,975	183,998
Ida. . . .	0	4	110,192	290,699	27,058	0	4	108,447	296,687
Ill.	0	26	1,981,413	2,358,094	346,754	0	24	2,036,337	2,667,721
Ind. . . .	0	13	844,197	1,255,656	111,639	0	12	814,659	1,332,679
Ia.. . . .	0	8	508,672	676,026	115,633	0	8	601,946	698,239
Kan. . .	0	7	326,150	566,812	68,231	0	7	321,010	649,423
Ky. . . .	0	9	617,417	635,274	31,127	0	9	535,704	816,644
La. . . .	0	10	708,453	792,853	26,345	0	10	648,040	1,030,091
Me.. . .	0	4	220,974	238,522	53,327	0	4	212,190	336,113
Md. . . .	10	0	726,161	680,606	119,537	0	10	757,635	836,295
Mass.. .	0	14	1,053,802	1,056,223	382,539	0	13	1,219,513	1,293,367
Mich. . .	0	21	1,661,532	1,915,225	275,223	0	20	1,468,512	2,147,147
Minn. . .	10	0	954,173	873,268	174,997	10	0	971,648	941,609
Miss. . .	0	7	429,281	441,089	12,036	0	7	351,195	577,378
Mo.. . .	0	12	931,182	1,074,181	77,920	0	11	808,601	1,242,678
Mon.. .	0	4	118,032	206,814	29,281	0	4	131,975	207,163
Neb.. .	0	5	166,424	419,214	44,854	0	5	183,838	446,938
Nev.. .	0	3	66,666	155,017	17,651	0	4	91,654	188,794
N.H.. . .	0	4	108,864	221,705	49,693	0	4	110,268	244,790
N.J.. . .	0	17	1,147,364	1,546,557	234,632	0	16	1,229,206	1,861,774
N.M. . .	0	4	167,826	250,779	29,459	0	5	199,671	302,932
N.Y.. . .	0	41	2,728,372	2,893,831	467,801	0	36	3,013,521	3,525,266
N.C.. . .	0	13	875,635	915,018	52,800	0	13	809,876	1,314,802
N.D.. . .	0	3	79,189	193,695	23,640	0	3	80,839	155,856
Oh.. . .	0	25	1,352,414	2,206,545	254,472	0	23	1,804,870	2,653,691
Okla.. . .	0	8	402,026	695,570	38,284	0	8	362,771	793,258
Ore.. . .	0	6	456,890	571,044	112,389	0	7	496,237	618,824
Pa. . . .	0	27	1,933,540	2,261,872	292,921	0	25	2,209,137	2,564,273
R.I. . . .	4	0	198,342	154,393	59,819	0	4	191,914	204,450
S.C.. . .	0	8	428,220	439,277	13,868	0	8	312,911	555,314
S.D.. . .	0	4	103,855	198,343	21,431	0	3	114,967	198,119
Tenn.. .	0	10	783,051	787,361	35,991	0	11	705,719	1,002,307
Tex.. . .	0	26	1,881,147	2,510,705	111,613	0	29	1,873,499	3,301,024
Ut. . . .	0	4	124,266	439,687	30,284	0	5	154,239	464,535
Vt.. . . .	0	3	81,952	94,628	31,761	0	3	94,518	134,252
Va.. . .	0	12	752,174	989,609	95,418	0	12	793,711	1,325,516
Wash. .	0	9	650,193	865,244	185,073	0	10	731,440	939,124
W.Va.. .	6	0	367,462	334,206	31,691	0	6	322,142	396,332
Wis.. . .	0	11	981,584	1,088,845	160,657	0	11	992,807	1,208,379
Wyo.. .	0	3	49,427	110,700	12,072	0	3	53,154	131,998
Total . .	49	489	35,481,435	43,899,248	5,719,437	13	525	36,450,613	52,609,797

40

Presidential Election Returns by Counties

All results are preliminary. Results for New England states are for selected cities or towns due to unavailability of county results. Totals are always statewide.

Source: News Election Service

Alabama

County	1980 Carter (D)	1980 Reagan (R)	1980 Anderson (I)	1984 Mondale (D)	1984 Reagan (R)
Autauga	4,295	6,292	125	3,320	8,000
Baldwin	8,448	18,652	414	6,943	24,000
Barbour	4,458	4,171	65	4,428	5,192
Bibb	3,097	2,491	22	1,003	1,557
Blount	5,656	6,819	75	3,737	8,506
Bullock	3,960	1,446	29	3,537	1,697
Butler	4,156	3,810	59	3,636	4,938
Calhoun	17,017	17,475	433	12,356	22,246
Chambers	6,649	4,864	122	5,400	7,520
Cherokee	3,764	2,482	63	2,984	3,118
Chilton	4,706	6,615	60	2,809	7,954
Choctaw	3,680	2,859	22	2,668	3,721
Clarke	5,249	5,059	55	4,452	6,332
Clay	2,858	2,764	34	1,456	3,432
Cleburne	2,050	2,389	34	1,238	3,259
Coffee	6,140	6,760	189	4,260	10,016
Colbert	12,550	6,619	209	11,008	9,527
Conecuh	3,102	2,948	29	2,609	3,362
Coosa	2,383	1,714	19	1,781	2,585
Covington	6,305	7,014	110	3,728	9,579
Crenshaw	2,704	2,478	39	1,904	3,257
Cullman	11,525	10,212	228	7,822	14,214
Dale	4,936	7,247	134	3,214	10,293
Dallas	9,770	7,647	131	10,374	9,038
DeKalb	8,820	9,673	107	7,067	11,877
Elmore	5,947	8,688	171	4,197	11,693
Escambia	5,148	6,513	87	3,841	8,685
Etowah	20,790	16,177	358	19,171	19,349
Fayette	3,389	3,315	47	2,533	4,649
Franklin	6,136	4,448	51	4,601	5,304
Geneva	4,703	4,747	67	2,330	6,306
Greene	3,474	1,034	16	3,551	1,314
Hale	3,583	2,074	56	3,287	2,690
Henry	2,973	2,813	18	2,231	3,952
Houston	7,848	14,884	184	6,709	20,772
Jackson	8,776	4,897	156	7,359	6,312
Jefferson	113,069	132,612	3,509	105,391	156,656
Lamar	3,366	2,778	16	1,910	3,947
Lauderdale	15,379	10,467	431	12,619	14,741
Lawrence	6,112	2,456	64	4,802	4,402
Lee	9,606	10,982	643	9,072	16,750
Limestone	8,180	4,574	183	5,407	8,318
Lowndes	3,577	1,524	15	3,566	1,629
Macon	7,028	1,259	36	7,856	1,543
Madison	30,469	30,604	2,246	26,602	43,293
Marengo	5,170	4,048	35	4,822	5,263
Marion	5,450	5,182	61	3,918	6,771
Marshall	10,854	8,159	283	7,704	12,326
Mobile	46,180	67,515	1,333	45,282	74,116
Monroe	4,262	4,615	43	3,328	5,294
Montgomery	28,018	35,745	985	29,704	47,004
Morgan	14,703	13,214	457	10,499	22,523
Perry	4,208	2,262	28	3,731	2,600
Pickens	4,504	3,582	61	3,680	4,672
Pike	4,417	5,220	83	3,540	6,227
Randolph	3,378	3,279	58	2,439	4,940
Russell	8,123	4,485	137	7,618	6,653
St. Clair	5,236	7,768	121	3,972	9,984
Shelby	7,396	14,957	407	5,554	20,299
Sumter	5,015	2,104	45	4,477	2,492
Talladega	10,159	9,902	140	10,030	12,823
Tallapoosa	7,260	5,958	96	4,447	9,062
Tuscaloosa	19,103	19,750	789	15,645	27,788
Walker	13,616	8,795	82	9,912	11,887
Washington	3,520	3,045	24	3,081	4,434
Wilcox	4,951	2,280	13	3,404	2,243
Winston	3,368	4,981	29	2,624	6,845
Totals	636,730	654,192	16,481	540,180	843,771

Alabama Vote Since 1932

1932 (Pres.), Roosevelt, Dem., 207,910; Hoover, Rep., 34,675; Foster, Com., 406; Thomas, Soc. 2,030; Upshaw, Proh., 13.

1936 (Pres.), Roosevelt, Dem., 238,195; Landon, Rep., 35,358; Colvin, Proh., 719; Browder, Com., 679; Lemke, Union, 549; Thomas, Soc., 242.

1940 (Pres.), Roosevelt, Dem., 250,726; Willkie, Rep., 42,174; Babson, Proh., 698; Browder, Com., 509; Thomas, Soc., 100.

1944 (Pres.), Roosevelt, Dem., 198,918; Dewey, Rep., 44,540; Watson, Proh., 1,095; Thomas, Soc., 190.

1948 (Pres.), Thurmond, States' Rights, 171,443; Dewey, Rep., 40,930; Wallace, Prog., 1,522; Watson, Proh., 1,085.

1952 (Pres.), Eisenhower, Rep., 149,231; Stevenson, Dem., 275,075; Hamblen, Proh., 1,814.

1956 (Pres.), Stevenson, Dem., 290,844; Eisenhower, Rep. 195,694; Independent electors, 20,323.

1960 (Pres.), Kennedy, Dem., 324,050; Nixon, Rep., 237,981; Faubus, States' Rights, 4,367; Decker, Proh., 2,106; King, Afro-Americans, 1,485; scattering, 236.

1964 (Pres.), Dem. 209,848 (electors unpledged); Goldwater, Rep., 479,085; scattering, 105.

1968 (Pres.), Nixon, Rep., 146,923; Humphrey, Dem., 196,579; Wallace, 3d party, 691,425; Munn, Proh., 4,022.

1972 (Pres.), Nixon, Rep., 728,701; McGovern, Dem., 219,108 plus 37,815 Natl. Demo. Party of Alabama; Schmitz, Conservative, 11,918; Munn., Proh., 8,551.

1976 (Pres.), Carter, Dem., 659,170; Ford, Rep., 504,070; Maddox, Am. Ind., 9,198; Bubar, Proh., 6,669; Hall, Com., 1,954; MacBride, Libertarian, 1,481.

1980 (Pres.), Reagan, Rep., 654,192; Carter, Dem., 636,730; Anderson, Independent, 16,481; Rarick, Amer. Ind., 15,010; Clark, Libertarian, 13,318; Bubar, Statesman, 1,743; Hall, Com., 1,629; DeBerry, Soc. Work., 1,303; McReynolds, Socialist, 1,006, Commoner, Citizens, 517.

Alaska

Election District	1980 Carter (D)	1980 Reagan (R)	1980 Anderson (I)	1984 Mondale (D)	1984 Reagan (R)
No. 1	1,772	3,473	440	NA	NA
No. 2	1,256	1,612	329	NA	NA
No. 3	1,354	2,019	346	NA	NA
No. 4	3,899	5,345	1,282	NA	NA
No. 5	973	2,847	288	NA	NA
No. 6	1,316	5,008	402	NA	NA
No. 7	2,620	4,311	676	NA	NA
No. 8	2,860	7,432	737	NA	NA
No. 9	1,164	2,363	342	NA	NA
No. 10	2,778	7,659	849	NA	NA
No. 11	3,308	9,741	1,016	NA	NA
No. 12	2,456	7,450	829	NA	NA
No. 13	1,806	6,170	479	NA	NA
No. 14	044	1,473	254	NA	NA
No. 15	710	832	213	NA	NA
No. 16	1,083	869	204	NA	NA
No. 17	1,623	720	280	NA	NA
No. 18	1,327	769	193	NA	NA
No. 19	1,168	2,255	267	NA	NA
No. 20	5,310	11,673	1,304	NA	NA
No. 21	1,022	1,010	223	NA	NA
No. 22	1,193	1,081	202	NA	NA
Totals	41,842	86,112	11,155	51,169	115,390

Alaska Vote Since 1960

1960 (Pres.), Kennedy, Dem., 29,809; Nixon, Rep. 30,953.

1964 (Pres.), Johnson, Dem., 44,329; Goldwater, Rep., 22,930.

1968 (Pres.), Nixon, Rep., 37,600; Humphrey, Dem., 35,411; Wallace, 3d party, 10,024.

1972 (Pres.), Nixon, Rep., 55,349; McGovern, Dem., 32,967; Schmitz, American, 6,903.

1976 (Pres.), Carter, Dem., 44,058; Ford, Rep., 71,555; MacBride, Libertarian, 6,785.

1980 (Pres.), Reagan, Rep., 86,112; Carter, Dem., 41,842; Clark, Libertarian, 18,479; Anderson, Ind., 11,155; Write-in, 857.

Arizona

County	1980 Carter (D)	1980 Reagan (R)	1980 Anderson (I)	1984 Mondale (D)	1984 Reagan (R)
Apache	3,917	5,991	495	3,962	4,620
Cochise	7,028	13,351	1,656	9,671	16,405
Coconino	7,832	14,613	2,815	11,525	17,576
Gila	5,068	7,405	656	6,509	8,543
Graham	2,801	4,765	268	3,078	5,246
Greenlee	2,043	1,537	150	1,963	1,801

La Paz	—	—	—	1,502	2,757	Jefferson	17,292	10,697	802	18,077	14,509
Maricopa	119,752	316,287	38,975	154,506	410,539	Johnson	3,709	3,619	187	3,055	4,710
Mohave	4,900	13,809	978	5,123	10,992	Lafayette	1,947	1,756	47	1,638	2,234
Navajo	5,110	10,790	710	8,017	11,379	Lawrence	3,547	3,245	117	2,594	4,037
Pima	64,418	93,055	25,294	89,681	120,636	Lee	3,103	1,711	47	2,541	2,101
Pinal	9,207	12,195	1,346	11,857	16,354	Lincoln	2,517	1,243	56	2,406	1,860
Santa Cruz	2,089	2,674	482	2,463	3,855	Little River	2,631	2,272	41	2,090	3,155
Yavapai	6,664	19,823	1,754	9,609	24,802	Logan	4,098	4,511	166	2,265	3,866
Yuma	6,014	13,393	1,373	6,458	13,848	Lonoke	5,605	5,619	246	4,212	8,124
Totals	246,843	529,688	76,952	325,924	669,353	Madison	2,434	3,180	126	2,133	3,506

County					
Marion	2,046	3,059	160	1,944	3,544
Miller	5,996	6,770	105	3,057	4,993
Mississippi	8,908	7,170	234	6,556	8,558
Monroe	2,686	2,027	82	2,412	2,505
Montgomery	1,878	1,585	86	1,497	2,219
Nevada	2,631	1,697	50	1,783	2,352
Newton	1,436	2,423	100	1,414	2,749
Ouachita	7,152	4,329	248	5,856	6,698
Perry	1,606	1,459	73	1,404	2,044
Phillips	6,642	4,270	163	5,942	4,680
Pike	2,094	1,916	58	1,182	2,164
Poinsett	4,894	4,040	153	3,905	5,614
Polk	2,617	3,993	139	2,101	5,178
Pope	6,364	7,217	471	4,810	9,868
Prairie	1,928	1,855	64	1,437	2,407
Pulaski	54,839	52,125	4,657	52,856	74,441
Randolph	3,070	2,579	125	2,505	3,186
St. Francis	5,816	4,485	132	4,775	5,364
Saline	10,368	8,330	643	6,976	11,704
Scott	2,236	2,228	92	1,609	3,065
Searcy	1,536	2,459	101	1,313	2,818
Sebastian	10,141	23,403	1,023	5,638	17,555
Sevier	2,854	2,502	97	1,942	3,301
Sharp	2,774	3,420	160	2,491	4,387
Stone	1,968	1,793	133	1,966	1,401
Union	6,852	9,401	313	6,204	12,326
Van Buren	2,968	3,090	153	2,378	3,813
Washington	12,276	20,788	1,737	11,316	24,981
White	8,750	8,079	309	6,602	12,562
Woodruff	2,452	1,204	74	2,055	1,666
Yell	3,702	3,187	181	2,679	4,051
Totals	398,041	403,164	22,468	325,185	505,562

Arizona Vote Since 1932

1932 (Pres.), Roosevelt, Dem., 79,264; Hoover, Rep., 36,104; Thomas, Soc., 2,618; Foster, Com., 256.

1936 (Pres.), Roosevelt, Dem., 86,722; Landon, Rep., 33,433; Lemke, Union, 3,307; Colvin, Proh., 384; Thomas, Soc., 317.

1940 (Pres.), Roosevelt, Dem., 95,267; Willkie, Rep., 54,030; Babson, Proh., 742.

1944 (Pres.), Roosevelt, Dem., 80,926; Dewey, Rep., 56,287; Watson, Proh., 421.

1948 (Pres.), Truman, Dem., 95,251; Dewey, Rep., 77,597; Wallace, Prog., 3,310; Watson, Proh., 786; Teichert, Soc. Labor, 121.

1952 (Pres.), Eisenhower, Rep., 152,042; Stevenson, Dem., 108,528.

1956 (Pres.), Eisenhower, Rep., 176,990; Stevenson, Dem., 112,880; Andrews, Ind. 303.

1960 (Pres.), Kennedy, Dem., 176,781; Nixon, Rep., 221,241; Hass, Soc. Labor, 469.

1964 (Pres.), Johnson, Dem., 237,753; Goldwater, Rep., 242,535; Hass, Soc. Labor, 482.

1968 (Pres.), Nixon, Rep., 266,721; Humphrey, Dem., 170,514; Wallace, 3d party, 46,573; McCarthy, New Party, 2,751; Halstead, Soc. Worker, 85; Cleaver, Peace and Freedom, 217; Blomen, Soc. Labor, 75.

1972 (Pres.), Nixon, Rep., 402,812; McGovern, Dem., 198,540; Schmitz, Amer., 21,208; Soc. Workers, 30,945. (Due to ballot peculiarities in 3 counties (particularly Pima), thousands of voters cast ballots for the Socialist Workers Party *and* one of the major candidates. Court ordered both votes counted as official.

1976 (Pres.), Carter, Dem., 295,602; Ford, Rep., 418,642; McCarthy, Ind., 19,229; MacBride, Libertarian, 7,647; Camejo, Soc. Workers, 928; Anderson, Amer., 564; Maddox, Am. Ind., 85.

1980 (Pres.), Reagan, Rep., 529,688; Carter, Dem., 246,843; Anderson, Ind., 76,952; Clark, Libertarian, 18,784; De Berry, Soc. Workers, 1,100; Commoner, Citizens, 551; Hall, Com., 25; Griswold, Workers World, 2.

Arkansas

	1980			1984	
County	Carter (D)	Reagan (R)	Anderson (I)	Mondale (D)	Reagan (R)
Arkansas	4,303	3,409	193	2,998	4,609
Ashley	4,552	3,960	130	3,373	5,675
Baxter	4,789	9,684	494	4,370	10,328
Benton	9,231	18,830	1,018	7,305	24,283
Boone	4,576	6,778	429	3,356	7,956
Bradley	3,139	1,650	66	2,313	2,690
Calhoun	1,438	896	52	979	1,371
Carroll	2,977	4,273	298	1,967	4,290
Chicot	3,445	2,239	26	3,407	2,500
Clark	6,122	2,743	215	4,465	4,105
Clay	3,985	3,091	121	3,279	3,764
Cleburne	4,021	4,042	204	3,172	5,768
Cleveland	1,856	1,124	36	1,379	1,772
Columbia	4,445	5,259	107	3,580	6,526
Conway	4,698	4,145	232	3,716	4,979
Craighead	9,231	11,010	708	9,032	14,036
Crawford	3,948	8,542	245	3,126	9,589
Crittenden	7,022	6,248	185	6,499	7,663
Cross	3,471	2,895	89	2,701	3,916
Dallas	2,838	1,596	74	2,035	2,360
Desha	3,748	2,057	77	2,918	2,696
Drew	3,757	2,272	117	2,638	3,407
Faulkner	8,528	7,544	769	7,175	11,597
Franklin	2,716	3,448	197	2,399	4,381
Fulton	2,037	2,101	83	544	927
Garland	12,515	15,739	1,042	11,482	21,199
Grant	3,078	2,007	102	2,148	3,167
Greene	5,996	4,514	219	4,730	6,177
Hempstead	4,671	3,852	72	3,017	4,353
Hot Spring	6,897	3,561	244	4,871	4,496
Howard	2,564	2,386	63	1,530	2,918
Independence	5,683	5,076	276	4,169	6,904
Izard	2,750	2,266	160	971	1,045
Jackson	4,651	3,191	174	3,935	3,819

Arkansas Vote Since 1932

1932 (Pres.), Roosevelt, Dem., 189,602; Hoover, Rep., 28,467; Thomas, Soc., 1,269; Harvey, Ind., 1,049; Foster, Com., 175.

1936 (Pres.), Roosevelt, Dem. 146,765; Landon, Rep., 32,039; Thomas, Soc., 446; Browder, Com., 164; Lemke, Union, 4.

1940 (Pres.), Roosevelt, Dem., 158,622; Willkie, Rep., 42,121; Babson, Proh., 793; Thomas, Soc., 305.

1944 (Pres.), Roosevelt, Dem., 148,965; Dewey, Rep., 63,551; Thomas, Soc. 438.

1948 (Pres.), Truman, Dem., 149,659; Dewey, Rep., 50,959; Thurmond, States' Rights, 40,068; Thomas, Soc., 1,037; Wallace, Prog., 751; Watson, Proh., 1.

1952 (Pres.), Eisenhower, Rep., 177,155; Stevenson, Dem., 226,300; Hamblen, Proh., 886; MacArthur, Christian Nationalist, 458; Hass, Soc. Labor, 1.

1956 (Pres.), Stevenson, Dem., 213,277; Eisenhower, Rep., 186,287; Andrews, Ind., 7,008.

1960 (Pres.), Kennedy, Dem., 215,049; Nixon, Rep., 184,508; Nat'l. States' Rights, 28,952.

1964 (Pres.), Johnson, Dem., 314,197; Goldwater, Rep., 243,264; Kasper, Nat'l. States Rights, 2,965.

1968 (Pres.), Nixon, Rep., 189,062; Humphrey, Dem., 184,901; Wallace, 3d party, 235,627.

1972 (Pres.), Nixon, Rep., 445,751; McGovern, Dem., 198,899; Schmitz, Amer., , 3,016.

1976 (Pres.), Carter, Dem., 498,604; Ford, Rep., 267,903; McCarthy, Ind., 639; Anderson, Amer., 389.

1980 (Pres.), Reagan, Rep., 403,164; Carter, Dem., 398,041; Anderson, Ind., 22,468; Clark, Libertarian, 8,970; Commoner, Citizens, 2,345; Bubar, Statesman, 1,350; Hall, Comm., 1,244.

California

	1980			1984	
County	Carter (D)	Reagan (R)	Anderson (I)	Mondale (D)	Reagan (R)
Alameda	201,720	158,531	40,834	277,225	188,947
Alpine	133	254	50	194	264
Amador	3,191	5,401	788	4,166	6,970
Butte	19,520	38,188	6,108	25,126	44,836
Calaveras	3,076	6,054	776	3,919	7,339
Colusa	1,605	2,897	325	1,715	3,362
Contra Costa	107,398	144,112	28,209	137,941	167,797
Del Norte	2,338	4,016	486	324	585
El Dorado	10,765	21,238	3,287	13,969	26,900

Fresno	65,254	82,515	10,727	83,416	101,156
Glenn	2,227	5,386	537	2,483	6,017
Humboldt	17,113	24,047	5,440	24,870	27,495
Imperial	7,961	12,068	1,203	8,231	13,816
Inyo	2,080	5,201	515	2,348	5,811
Kern	41,097	72,842	5,799	44,523	85,872
Kings	7,299	10,531	901	7,317	13,357
Lake	5,978	8,934	1,157	8,292	10,291
Lassen	2,941	4,464	543	3,253	5,338
Los Angeles	979,830	1,224,533	175,882	1,113,204	1,369,630
Madera	7,783	10,599	1,013	9,067	13,890
Marin	39,231	49,678	13,805	56,796	55,845
Mariposa	1,889	3,082	458	2,121	3,571
Mendocino	10,784	12,432	2,747	14,172	16,107
Merced	15,886	18,043	2,316	16,875	25,003
Modoc	1,046	2,579	293	1,219	2,995
Mono	865	2,132	302	944	2,630
Monterey	29,086	47,452	8,008	39,676	54,440
Napa	14,898	23,632	4,218	18,234	25,715
Nevada	7,605	15,207	2,235	10,941	19,440
Orange	176,704	529,797	55,299	200,477	615,099
Placer	17,311	28,179	4,356	20,527	36,565
Plumas	2,911	4,182	783	3,709	5,079
Riverside	76,650	145,642	16,362	99,853	178,397
Sacramento	130,031	153,721	29,655	152,457	196,415
San Benito	2,749	4,054	552	3,454	5,530
San Bernardino	91,790	172,957	19,106	114,710	217,556
San Diego	195,410	435,910	67,491	251,134	487,362
San Francisco	133,184	80,967	29,365	189,421	88,091
San Joaquin	41,551	64,718	8,416	53,440	81,083
San Luis Obispo	20,508	38,631	8,407	26,626	48,331
San Mateo	87,335	116,491	27,985	120,853	133,912
Santa Barbara	40,650	69,629	14,786	49,505	85,458
Santa Clara	166,995	229,048	65,481	224,032	280,425
Santa Cruz	32,346	37,347	10,590	47,240	39,862
Shasta	15,364	27,547	3,220	19,178	32,854
Sierra	651	855	156	823	1,078
Siskiyou	5,664	9,331	1,269	7,130	10,544
Solano	30,952	40,919	6,713	41,435	50,867
Sonoma	45,596	60,722	14,068	68,839	73,499
Stanislaus	33,683	41,595	7,134	32,056	47,309
Sutter	5,103	11,778	1,089	5,936	15,797
Tehama	4,832	9,140	1,014	6,511	11,536
Trinity	1,734	3,048	506	2,204	3,525
Tulare	25,155	41,317	3,244	27,707	50,262
Tuolumne	5,449	8,810	1,390	7,212	10,376
Ventura	56,311	114,930	14,887	64,623	146,647
Yolo	21,527	19,603	6,669	25,264	23,604
Yuba	4,896	7,942	878	4,996	9,265
Totals	3,083,661	4,524,858	739,833	3,803,913	5,291,747

California Vote Since 1932

1932 (Pres.), Roosevelt, Dem., 1,324,157; Hoover, Rep., 847,902; Thomas, Soc., 63,299; Upshaw, Proh., 20,637; Harvey, Liberty, 9,827; Foster, Com., 1,023.

1936 (Pres.), Roosevelt, Dem., 1,766,836; Landon, Rep., 836,431; Colvin, Proh., 12,917; Thomas, Soc., 11,325; Browder, Com., 10,877.

1940 (Pres.), Roosevelt, Dem., 1,877,618; Willkie, Rep., 1,351,419; Thomas, Prog., 16,506; Browder, Com., 13,586; Babson, Proh., 9,400.

1944 (Pres.), Roosevelt, Dem., 1,988,564; Dewey, Rep., 1,512,965; Watson, Proh., 14,770; Thomas, Soc., 3,923; Teichert, Soc. Labor, 327.

1948 (Pres.), Truman, Dem., 1,913,134; Dewey, Rep., 1,895,269; Wallace, Prog., 190,381; Watson, Proh., 16,926; Thomas, Soc., 3,459; Thurmond, States' Rights, 1,228; Teichert, Soc. Labor, 195; Dobbs, Soc. Workers, 133.

1952 (Pres.), Eisenhower, Rep., 2,897,310; Stevenson, Dem., 2,197,548; Hallinan, Prog., 24,106; Hamblen, Proh., 15,653; MacArthur, (Tenny Ticket), 3,326; (Kellems Ticket) 178; Hass, Soc. Labor, 273; Hoopes, Soc., 206; scattered, 3,249.

1956 (Pres.), Eisenhower, Rep., 3,027,668; Stevenson, Dem., 2,420,136; Holtwick, Proh., 11,119; Andrews, Constitution, 6,087; Hass, Soc. Labor, 300; Hoopes, Soc., 123; Dobbs, Soc. Workers, 96; Smith, Christian Nat'l., 8.

1960 (Pres.), Kennedy, Dem., 3,224,099; Nixon, Rep., 3,259,722; Decker, Proh., 21,706; Hass, Soc. Labor, 1,051.

1964 (Pres.), Johnson, Dem., 4,171,877; Goldwater, Rep., 2,879,108; Hass, Soc. Labor, 489; DeBerry, Soc. Worker, 378; Munn, Proh., 305; Hensley, Universal, 19.

1968 (Pres.), Nixon, Rep., 3,467,664; Humphrey, Dem., 3,244,318; Wallace, 3d party, 487,270; Peace and Freedom party, 27,707; McCarthy, Alternative, 20,721; Gregory, write-in, 3,230; Mitchell, Com., 260; Munn, Proh., 59; Blomen, Soc. Labor, 341; Soeters, Defense, 17.

1972 (Pres.), Nixon, Rep., 4,602,096; McGovern, Dem., 3,475,847; Schmitz, Amer., 232,554; Spock, Peace and Freedom, 55,167; Hall, Com., 373; Hospers, Libertarian, 980; Munn, Proh., 53; Fisher, Soc. Labor, 197; Jenness, Soc. Workers, 574; Green, Universal, 21.

1976 (Pres.), Carter, Dem., 3,742,284; Ford, Rep., 3,882,244; MacBride, Libertarian, 56,388; Maddox, Am. Ind., 51,098; Wright, People's, 41,731; Camejo, Soc. Workers, 17,259; Hall, Com., 12,766; write-in, McCarthy, 58,412; other write-in, 4,935.

1980 (Pres.) Reagan, Rep. 4,524,858; Carter, Dem., 3,083,661; Anderson, Ind., 739,833; Clark, Libertarian, 148,434; Commoner, Ind. 61,063; Smith, Peace & Freedom, 18,116; Rarick, Amer. Ind., 9,856.

Colorado

	1980			1984	
County	Carter (D)	Reagan (R)	Anderson (I)	Mondale (D)	Reagan (R)
Adams	31,357	42,916	8,342	34,153	52,625
Alamosa	1,821	2,601	289	1,642	2,676
Arapahoe	30,148	79,594	15,329	37,966	100,659
Archuleta	532	1,252	83	542	1,377
Baca	551	1,999	106	548	1,724
Bent	1,206		164	798	1,170
Boulder	28,422	40,698	13,712	39,589	49,597
Chaffee	1,583	3,327	432	1,603	3,292
Cheyenne	322	816	76	289	808
Clear Creek	837	1,784	402	1,006	1,966
Conejos	1,503	1,597	90	1,491	1,530
Costilla	1,036	489	38	865	524
Crowley	472	926	57	522	993
Custer	231	674	59	213	696
Delta	2,348	6,179	455	2,509	5,984
Denver	85,900	80,398	28,610	109,758	105,044
Dolores	157	615	32	173	667
Douglas	2,108	8,126	1,058	2,808	11,090
Eagle	1,608	3,061	906	2,032	4,501
Elbert	698	2,107	238	770	2,394
El Paso	27,463	66,199	7,886	26,221	80,587
Fremont	3,952	7,162	731	3,621	7,463
Garfield	2,639	5,416	978	2,864	6,419
Gilpin	441	694	175	573	773
Grand	820	2,133	413	937	2,560
Gunnison	1,297	2,576	704	1,222	2,679
Hinsdale	76	232	13	98	310
Huerfano	1,574	1,258	146	1,602	1,581
Jackson	283	673	80	168	660
Jefferson	41,525	97,008	19,530	51,056	116,845
Kiowa	331	754	61	232	747
Kit Carson	790	2,622	185	798	2,762
Lake	1,213	1,375	289	1,209	1,221
La Plata	3,034	7,291	1,537	3,744	7,856
Larimer	17,072	36,240	8,887	22,502	46,190
Las Animas	4,117	2,917	278	3,324	2,617
Lincoln	602	1,535	175	538	1,546
Logan	2,332	5,238	588	1,942	5,391
Mesa	7,549	22,686	2,004	9,146	21,354
Mineral	125	271	41	102	276
Moffat	1,079	3,344	329	1,140	3,319
Montezuma	1,467	4,120	275	1,530	4,278
Montrose	2,232	6,685	635	2,622	6,398
Morgan	2,246	5,209	693	2,231	6,097
Otero	3,294	4,801	572	2,737	4,781
Ouray	237	813	129	329	771
Park	674	1,623	293	713	1,807
Philips	640	1,488	193	615	1,539
Pitkin	1,760	2,153	1,128	1,974	2,635
Prowers	1,569	3,115	340	1,341	3,058
Pueblo	21,874	20,770	3,102	25,723	22,670
Rio Blanco	462	1,971	143	440	1,926
Rio Grande	1,370	2,844	185	1,036	2,821
Routt	1,944	3,574	920	1,879	3,795
Saguache	893	1,124	71	597	1,035
San Juan	146	268	94	155	257
San Miguel	651	774	297	533	725
Sedgwick	438	1,151	100	403	1,060
Summit	1,285	2,027	845	1,449	2,924
Teller	802	2,457	322	956	3,169
Washington	568	2,007	160	541	1,951
Weld	11,433	23,901	4,309	13,321	29,446
Yuma	1,043	3,220	319	1,058	3,146
Total	367,973	652,264	130,633	434,560	768,711

Colorado Vote Since 1932

1932 (Pres.), Roosevelt, Dem., 250,877; Hoover, Rep., 189,617; Thomas, Soc., 14,018; Upshaw, Proh., 1,928

1936 (Pres.), Roosevelt, Dem., 295,081; Landon, Rep., 181,267; Lemke, Union, 9,962; Thomas, Soc., 1,593; Browder, Com., 497; Aiken, Soc. Labor, 336.

1940 (Pres.), Roosevelt, Dem., 265,554; Willkie, Rep., 279,576; Thomas, Soc., 1,899; Babson, Proh., 1,597; Browder, Com., 378.

1944 (Pres.), Roosevelt, Dem., 234,331; Dewey, Rep., 268,731; Thomas, Soc., 1,977.

1948 (Pres.), Truman, Dem., 267,288; Dewey, Rep., 239,714; Wallace, Prog., 6,115; Thomas, Soc., 1,678; Dobbs, Soc. Workers, 228; Teichert, Soc. Labor, 214.

1952 (Pres.), Eisenhower, Rep., 379,782; Stevenson, Dem., 245,504; MacArthur, Constitution, 2,181; Hallinan, Prog., 1,919; Hoopes, Soc., 365; Hass, Soc. Labor, 352.

1956 (Pres.), Eisenhower, Rep., 394,479; Stevenson, Dem., 263,997; Hass, Soc. Lab., 3,308; Andrews, Ind., 759; Hoopes, Soc., 531.

1960 (Pres.), Kennedy, Dem., 330,629; Nixon, Rep., 402,242; Hass, Soc. Labor, 2,803; Dobbs, Soc. Workers, 572.

1964 (Pres.), Johnson, Dem., 476,024; Goldwater, Rep., 296,767; Hass, Soc. Labor, 302; DeBerry, Soc. Worker, 2,537; Munn, Proh., 1,356.

1968 (Pres.), Nixon, Rep., 409,345; Humphrey, Dem., 335,174; Wallace, 3d party, 60,813; Blomen, Soc. Labor, 3,016; Gregory, New-party, 1,393; Munn, Proh., 275; Halstead, Soc. Worker, 235.

1972 (Pres.), Nixon, Rep., 597,189; McGovern, Dem., 329,980; Fisher, Soc. Labor, 4,361; Hospers, Libertarian, 1,111; Hall, Com., 432; Jenness, Soc. Workers, 555; Munn, Proh., 467; Schmitz, Amer., 17,269; Spock, Peoples, 2,403.

1976 (Pres.), Carter, Dem., 460,353; Ford, Rep., 584,367; McCarthy, Ind., 26,107; MacBride, Libertarian, 5,330; Bubar, Proh., 2,882.

1980 (Pres.), Reagan, Rep., 652,264; Carter, Dem., 367,973; Anderson, Ind., 130,633; Clark, Libertarian, 25,744; Commoner, Citizens, 5,614; Bubar, Statesman, 1,180; Pulley, Socialist, 520; Hall, Com., 487.

Connecticut

County	1980 Carter (D)	Reagan (R)	Anderson (I)	1984 Mondale (D)	Reagan (R)
Bridgeport	23,505	19,185	2,793	24,332	24,256
Hartford	27,657	8,138	3,441	28,647	11,645
New Britain	15,649	10,292	3,203	14,610	13,723
New Haven	26,648	14,388	3,930	26,827	14,785
Norwalk	11,785	16,696	3,284	12,509	22,447
Stamford	17,633	23,250	4,669	19,432	29,167
Waterbury	17,992	19,461	3,853	18,217	24,764
West Hartford	14,662	16,590	6,807	16,882	20,517
Totals	541,732	677,210	171,807	560,712	883,486

Connecticut Vote Since 1932

1932 (Pres.), Roosevelt, Dem., 281,632; Hoover, Rep., 288,420; Thomas, Soc., 22,767.

1936 (Pres.), Roosevelt, Dem., 382,129; Landon, Rep., 278,685; Lemke, Union, 21,805; Thomas, Soc., 5,683; Browder, Com., 1,193.

1940 (Pres.), Roosevelt, Dem., 417,621; Willkie, Rep., 361,021; Browder, Com., 1,091; Aiken, Soc. Labor, 971; Willkie, Union, 798.

1944 (Pres.), Roosevelt, Dem., 435,146; Dewey, Rep., 390,527; Thomas, Soc., 5,097; Teichert, Soc. Labor, 1,220.

1948 (Pres.), Truman, Dem., 423,297; Dewey, Rep., 437,754; Wallace, Prog., 13,713; Thomas, Soc., 6,964; Teichert, Soc. Labor, 1,184; Dobbs, Soc. Workers, 606.

1952 (Pres.), Eisenhower, Rep., 611,012; Stevenson, Dem., 481,649; Hoopes, Soc., 2,244; Hallinan, Peoples, 1,466; Hass, Soc. Labor, 535; write-in, 5.

1956 (Pres.), Eisenhower, Rep., 711,837; Stevenson, Dem., 405,079; scattered, 205.

1960 (Pres.), Kennedy, Dem., 657,055; Nixon, Rep., 565,813.

1964 (Pres.), Johnson, Dem., 826,269; Goldwater, Rep., 390,996; scattered, 1,313.

1968 (Pres.), Nixon, Rep., 556,721; Humphrey, Dem., 621,561; Wallace, 3d party, 76,650; scattered, 1,300.

1972 (Pres.), Nixon, Rep., 810,763; McGovern, Dem., 555,498; Schmitz, Amer., 17,239; scattered, 777.

1976 (Pres.), Carter, Dem., 647,895; Ford, Rep., 719,261; Maddox, George Wallace Party, 7,101; LaRouche, U.S. Labor, 1,789.

1980 (Pres.), Reagan, Rep., 677,210; Carter, Dem., 541,732; Anderson, Ind., 171,807; Clark, Libertarian, 8,570; Commoner, Citizens, 6,130; scattered, 836.

Delaware

County	1980 Carter (D)	Reagan (R)	Anderson (I)	1984 Mondale (D)	Reagan (R)
Kent	12,884	14,882	1,831	11,789	21,537
New Castle	76,897	76,898	12,828	75,246	101,774
Sussex	15,973	19,472	1,629	13,597	28,183
Totals	105,754	111,252	16,288	100,632	151,494

Delaware Vote Since 1932

1932 (Pres.), Hoover, Rep., 57,074; Roosevelt, Dem., 54,319; Thomas, Soc., 1,376; Foster, Com., 133.

1936 (Pres.), Roosevelt, Dem., 69,702; Landon, Rep. 54,014; Lemke, Union, 442; Thomas, Soc., 179; Browder, Com., 52.

1940 (Pres.), Roosevelt, Dem., 74,559; Willkie, Rep., 61,440; Babson, Proh., 220; Thomas, Soc., 115.

1944 (Pres.), Roosevelt, Dem., 68,166; Dewey, Rep., 56,747; Watson, Proh., 294; Thomas, Soc., 154.

1948 (Pres.), Truman, Dem., 67,813; Dewey, Rep., 69,688; Wallace, Prog., 1,050; Watson, Proh., 343; Thomas, Soc., 250; Teichert, Soc. Labor, 29.

1952 (Pres.), Eisenhower, Rep., 90,059; Stevenson, Dem., 83,315; Hass, Soc. Labor, 242; Hamblen, Proh., 234; Hallinan, Prog., 155; Hoopes, Soc., 20.

1956 (Pres.), Eisenhower, Rep., 98,057; Stevenson, Dem., 79,421; Oltwick, Proh., 400; Hass, Soc. Labor, 110.

1960 (Pres.), Kennedy, Dem., 99,590; Nixon, Rep., 96,373; Faubus, States' Rights, 354; Decker, Proh., 284; Hass, Soc. Labor, 82.

1964 (Pres.), Johnson, Dem., 122,704; Goldwater, Rep., 78,078; Hass, Soc. Labor, 113; Munn, Proh., 425.

1968 (Pres.), Nixon, Rep., 96,714; Humphrey, Dem., 89,194; Wallace, 3d party, 28,459.

1972 (Pres.), Nixon, Rep., 140,357; McGovern, Dem., 92,283; Schmitz, Amer., 2,638; Munn, Proh., 238.

1976 (Pres.), Carter, Dem., 122,596; Ford, Rep., 109,831; McCarthy, non-partisan, 2,437; Anderson, Amer., 645; LaRouche, U.S. Labor, 136; Bubar, Proh., 103; Levin, Soc. Labor, 86.

1980 (Pres.), Reagan, Rep., 111,252; Carter, Dem., 105,754; Anderson, Ind., 16,288; Clark, Libertarian, 1,974; Greaves, American, 400.

District of Columbia

County	1980 Carter (D)	Reagan (R)	Anderson (I)	1984 Mondale (D)	Reagan (R)
Totals	130,231	23,313	16,131	172,459	26,805

District of Columbia Vote Since 1964

1964 (Pres.), Johnson, Dem., 169,796; Goldwater, Rep., 28,801.

1968 (Pres.), Nixon, Rep., 31,012; Humphrey, Dem., 139,566.

1972 (Pres.), Nixon, Rep., 35,226; McGovern, Dem., 127,627; Reed, Soc. Workers, 316; Hall, Com., 252.

1976 (Pres.), Carter, Dem., 137,818; Ford, Rep., 27,873; Camejo, Soc. Workers, 545; MacBride, Libertarian, 274; Hall, Com., 219; LaRouche, U.S. Labor, 157.

1980 (Pres.), Reagan, Rep., 23,313; Carter, Dem., 130,231; Anderson, Ind., 16,131; Commoner, Citizens, 1,826; Clark, Libertarian, 1,104; Hall, Com., 369; De Berry, Soc. Work., 173; Griswold, Workers World, 52; write-ins, 690.

Florida

County	1980 Carter (D)	Reagan (R)	Anderson (I)	1984 Mondale (D)	Reagan (R)
Alachua	26,817	19,771	4,167	25,111	28,190
Baker	2,606	2,271	56	1,381	3,485
Bay	12,338	20,815	720	8,601	24,933
Bradford	3,340	2,771	89	2,500	3,550
Brevard	38,915	69,228	5,820	21,249	54,158
Broward	146,322	229,693	31,553	183,215	236,753
Calhoun	2,295	1,504	52	1,262	2,378
Charlotte	9,750	20,433	1,204	10,132	24,847
Citrus	9,148	14,276	784	10,463	20,754
Clay	7,589	15,497	679	5,488	21,545
Collier	7,735	23,878	1,675	9,065	33,603

Columbia	5,677	5,638	246	4,023	8,212
Dade	210,683	265,550	44,723	213,915	306,640
De Soto	2,709	3,340	155	2,302	4,792
Dixie	2,007	1,098	45	1,224	2,204
Duval	90,330	98,389	5,153	74,029	116,231
Escambia	33,378	51,443	2,595	25,427	57,860
Flaglor	2,494	2,876	153	2,999	4,907
Franklin	1,772	1,500	53	1,089	2,218
Gadsden	8,207	3,708	201	7,170	5,308
Gilchrist	1,625	1,089	55	1,051	2,056
Glades	1,203	1,096	61	1,070	1,987
Gulf	2,680	2,116	56	1,603	3,209
Hamilton	1,921	1,301	40	1,284	1,724
Hardee	2,597	2,595	83	1,536	3,956
Hendry	2,540	2,696	130	1,841	4,104
Hernando	8,835	12,099	852	10,484	17,602
Highlands	6,685	11,914	531	6,774	15,212
Hillsborough	88,221	106,080	8,939	83,052	148,255
Holmes	2,767	3,208	68	1,179	4,290
Indian River	7,748	15,545	1,184	8,114	21,168
Jackson	7,549	6,331	158	4,762	8,371
Jefferson	2,366	1,621	96	2,055	2,244
Lafayette	1,034	795	22	682	1,513
Lake	13,121	26,775	1,240	11,505	32,422
Lee	28,007	60,717	4,191	30,011	85,006
Leon	28,420	24,840	3,181	28,404	33,791
Levy	4,170	3,203	175	2,964	5,161
Liberty	1,111	895	24	649	1,404
Madison	3,129	2,275	65	1,989	2,587
Manatee	21,660	40,506	2,921	19,646	51,130
Marion	15,362	23,668	1,173	16,221	37,796
Martin	8,078	20,493	1,317	8,976	28,597
Monroe	7,875	11,546	1,914	7,046	13,887
Nassau	5,051	5,414	178	3,483	8,033
Okaloosa	10,738	27,665	1,080	6,508	30,500
Okeechobee	3,226	2,778	156	2,021	4,027
Orange	48,732	87,375	5,389	45,805	108,576
Osceola	6,594	10,839	560	6,627	18,344
Palm Beach	91,932	143,491	15,178	116,071	186,755
Pasco	34,045	50,080	3,565	38,915	62,052
Pinellas	138,307	185,482	17,789	128,490	240,461
Polk	43,291	59,600	2,618	33,908	78,767
Putnam	8,898	8,258	410	7,821	11,424
St. Johns	6,879	11,179	546	6,209	15,011
St. Lucie	10,341	18,107	1,109	13,039	28,189
Santa Rosa	6,964	13,802	606	4,322	18,816
Sarasota	25,557	67,946	4,773	28,199	79,524
Seminole	17,431	39,970	2,451	12,755	38,447
Sumter	4,378	3,666	141	3,270	5,816
Suwannee	4,345	3,894	135	2,788	6,079
Taylor	2,955	2,772	78	1,572	3,679
Union	1,235	1,120	45	761	1,804
Volusia	44,476	52,598	3,296	41,534	62,598
Wakulla	2,078	2,014	111	1,388	2,917
Walton	4,323	4,651	194	2,330	6,373
Washington	3,095	3,222	92	1,778	4,086
Totals	1,419,475	2,046,951	189,692	1,373,137	2,512,318

Florida Vote Since 1932

1932 (Pres.), Roosevelt, Dem., 206,307; Hoover, Rep., 69,170; Thomas, Soc., 775.

1936 (Pres.), Roosevelt, Dem., 249,117; Landon, Rep., 78,248.

1940 (Pres.), Roosevelt, Dem., 359,334; Willkie, Rep., 126,158.

1944 (Pres.), Roosevelt, Dem., 339,377; Dewey, Rep., 143,215.

1948 (Pres.), Truman, Dem., 281,988; Dewey, Rep., 194,280; Thurmond, States' Rights, 89,755; Wallace, Prog., 11,620.

1952 (Pres.), Eisenhower, Rep., 544,036; Stevenson, Dem., 444,950; scattered, 351.

1956 (Pres.), Eisenhower, Rep., 643,849; Stevenson, Dem., 480,371.

1960 (Pres.), Kennedy, Dem., 748,700; Nixon, Rep., 795,476.

1964 (Pres.), Johnson, Dem., 948,540; Goldwater, Rep., 905,941.

1968 (Pres.), Nixon, Rep., 886,804; Humphrey, Dem., 676,794; Wallace, 3d party, 624,207.

1972 (Pres.), Nixon, Rep., 1,857,759; McGovern, Dem., 718,117; scattered, 7,407.

1976 (Pres.), Carter, Dem., 1,636,000; Ford, Rep., 1,469,531; McCarthy, Ind., 23,643; Anderson, Amer., 21,325.

1980 (Pres.), Reagan, Rep., 2,046,951; Carter, Dem., 1,419,475; Anderson, Ind., 189,692; Clark, Libertarian, 30,524; write-ins, 285.

Georgia

County	1980 Carter (D)	1980 Reagan (R)	1980 Anderson (I)	1984 Mondale (D)	1984 Reagan (R)
Appling	2,985	1,961	41	1,958	2,959
Atkinson	1,449	747	16	901	944
Bacon	1,622	1,427	32	779	1,258
Baker	1,035	510	11	691	675
Baldwin	4,368	3,639	230	3,853	5,717
Banks	2,091	746	18	1,063	1,549
Barrow	3,876	2,284	99	2,367	4,123
Bartow	7,490	3,136	135	4,780	7,104
Ben Hill	2,544	1,459	41	1,859	2,313
Berrien	2,869	1,487	24	1,592	2,323
Bibb	31,770	15,175	848	25,023	23,979
Bleckley	2,014	1,261	47	1,408	1,819
Brantley	2,066	882	17	1,517	1,499
Brooks	2,230	1,546	39	1,567	2,089
Bryan	1,966	1,212	51	1,398	2,265
Bulloch	4,921	3,750	160	3,644	6,117
Burke	3,047	1,871	56	3,006	2,789
Butts	2,574	1,210	38	1,820	2,141
Calhoun	1,414	652	16	1,077	776
Camden	2,924	1,439	62	2,164	2,841
Candler	1,358	1,030	24	1,014	1,497
Carroll	8,202	5,815	294	5,590	11,436
Catoosa	4,921	5,962	121	2,727	6,768
Charlton	1,469	779	26	1,111	1,368
Chatham	28,635	26,499	1,244	27,429	36,151
Chattahoochee	476	256	16	428	459
Chattooga	4,279	1,946	61	1,609	2,982
Cherokee	6,020	5,250	230	3,499	11,146
Clarke	10,519	8,094	1,060	10,132	11,503
Clay	909	316	9	758	419
Clayton	17,540	19,160	923	11,763	31,553
Clinch	1,325	513	18	625	861
Cobb	39,157	51,977	3,229	28,414	97,429
Coffee	4,038	2,499	58	2,633	4,200
Colquitt	5,353	3,593	80	3,100	5,479
Columbia	5,335	6,293	248	3,727	12,294
Cook	2,461	1,188	25	1,510	1,860
Coweta	5,697	4,480	161	3,650	7,971
Crawford	1,673	642	35	1,423	1,298
Crisp	3,403	1,861	54	2,128	2,895
Dade	1,735	2,114	62	1,053	2,580
Dawson	1,072	729	23	643	1,322
Decatur	3,242	2,919	54	2,504	3,854
DeKalb	82,743	74,904	7,241	77,329	104,697
Dodge	4,635	1,719	56	2,593	2,765
Dooly	2,364	1,083	31	1,726	1,435
Dougherty	13,430	12,726	326	11,817	14,261
Douglas	6,807	6,945	304	4,446	12,355
Early	2,110	1,538	23	1,494	2,239
Echols	515	259	8	227	453
Effingham	2,783	2,528	38	2,055	4,266
Elbert	4,014	1,967	50	2,068	2,691
Emanuel	3,971	2,199	45	2,378	3,920
Evans	1,456	1,090	20	1,193	1,601
Fannin	2,526	3,196	61	1,679	3,602
Fayette	3,798	6,351	272	2,862	12,575
Floyd	13,710	9,220	398	8,390	14,434
Forsyth	4,325	3,157	160	2,275	6,841
Franklin	3,528	1,387	30	1,685	2,910
Fulton	118,748	64,909	6,738	125,567	95,149
Gilmer	2,246	2,170	72	1,336	3,189
Glascock	614	510	7	151	291
Glynn	7,540	7,214	296	6,574	11,722
Gordon	5,199	3,107	141	2,607	5,566
Grady	3,023	2,018	56	2,177	3,654
Greene	2,571	961	29	1,731	1,860
Gwinnett	21,958	27,185	1,497	13,589	52,313
Habersham	4,394	2,224	100	2,125	4,647
Hall	12,124	7,760	463	7,431	15,176
Hancock	2,205	573	23	2,109	690
Haralson	3,606	2,229	71	1,938	3,945
Harris	2,807	2,001	100	2,038	2,980
Hart	4,539	1,577	59	2,352	2,636
Heard	1,348	875	35	810	1,492
Henry	5,635	5,326	163	4,096	9,142
Houston	10,915	9,005	536	9,219	14,245
Irwin	1,555	1,056	11	905	1,316
Jackson	4,591	2,209	107	2,717	4,202
Jasper	1,546	879	38	1,181	1,431
Jeff Davis	2,059	1,191	40	1,380	2,233
Jefferson	3,305	1,605	44	2,816	2,999
Jenkins	1,632	824	24	1,108	1,399
Johnson	1,854	1,123	20	1,199	1,733
Jones	3,239	1,828	112	2,679	3,218
Lamar	2,453	1,298	42	1,605	2,198
Lanier	1,116	470	9	741	852
Laurens	7,860	4,392	147	5,471	7,181
Lee	1,670	1,942	26	1,075	1,957
Liberty	3,099	1,507	49	2,717	3,040
Lincoln	1,617	806	10	1,033	1,195
Long	1,202	514	23	816	1,099
Lowndes	5,989	6,622	214	6,167	10,437

	1980 Carter (D)	1980 Reagan (R)	Anderson (I)	1984 Mondale (D)	1984 Reagan (R)
Lumpkin	1,951	1,024	83	1,110	1,991
McDuffie	2,667	1,928	59	2,006	3,256
McIntosh	2,104	876	38	1,796	1,512
Macon	3,025	894	39	2,419	1,435
Madison	2,980	2,330	59	1,690	3,768
Marion	1,174	567	16	951	846
Meriwether	3,876	1,838	59	2,617	2,814
Miller	1,127	900	19	526	1,348
Mitchell	3,566	2,231	40	2,791	2,736
Monroe	2,542	1,242	43	2,189	2,420
Montgomery	1,663	948	23	950	1,365
Morgan	2,276	1,323	57	1,714	2,301
Murray	3,094	1,538	42	1,557	3,382
Muscogee	23,272	15,203	811	20,835	23,816
Newton	5,611	3,206	150	3,388	5,810
Oconee	2,141	2,065	106	1,467	3,471
Oglethorpe	1,611	1,187	44	112	258
Paulding	4,686	2,845	97	2,621	6,048
Peach	3,415	1,642	68	3,228	3,282
Pickens	2,358	1,612	73	1,194	2,583
Pierce	1,918	1,027	21	1,501	1,978
Pike	1,755	1,271	45	1,203	2,090
Polk	5,421	2,949	116	3,262	5,435
Pulaski	1,997	1,153	54	1,440	1,509
Putnam	1,951	1,166	35	1,336	1,830
Quitman	589	240	2	490	361
Rabun	2,327	1,070	67	1,267	2,191
Randolph	1,861	879	1	1,454	1,578
Richmond	24,104	19,619	887	21,208	29,869
Rockdale	4,395	5,300	219	3,309	10,121
Schley	613	453	9	403	614
Screven	2,117	1,490	36	1,747	2,583
Seminole	1,794	1,117	16	1,350	1,636
Spalding	7,176	4,809	248	4,878	8,571
Stephens	4,529	2,045	69	2,272	4,057
Stewart	1,440	611	23	1,308	805
Sumter	4,956	2,957	103	3,527	4,211
Talbot	1,635	572	20	1,568	870
Taliaferro	670	270	8	550	318
Tattnall	2,864	2,082	37	1,971	3,606
Taylor	1,845	815	19	1,340	1,292
Telfair	2,700	1,173	41	2,049	1,980
Terrell	2,010	1,378	21	1,598	1,744
Thomas	5,695	4,294	117	4,039	6,427
Tift	4,572	3,280	99	2,736	4,429
Toombs	3,255	2,835	68	2,542	4,360
Towns	1,510	1,475	57	858	1,696
Treutlen	1,307	668	21	843	1,086
Troup	7,716	5,398	191	5,277	9,340
Turner	1,990	898	16	1,216	1,251
Twiggs	2,213	747	8	1,914	1,652
Union	1,700	1,546	43	1,112	1,914
Upson	4,713	2,788	77	2,943	4,803
Walker	6,809	7,088	171	4,983	10,733
Walton	4,525	2,618	112	2,531	4,995
Ware	6,307	3,715	77	4,435	5,547
Warren	1,517	779	20	1,528	1,087
Washington	3,452	1,822	60	2,917	2,671
Wayne	3,843	2,213	52	2,434	3,698
Webster	608	312	8	534	402
Wheeler	1,599	550	28	774	833
White	2,017	1,175	58	1,090	2,369
Whitfield	9,691	6,404	229	5,084	11,310
Wilcox	1,780	827	13	1,212	1,218
Wilkes	2,350	1,212	31	1,586	1,837
Wilkinson	2,365	1,116	31	2,102	1,756
Worth	2,567	2,076	35	1,685	2,910
Totals	**890,955**	**654,168**	**36,055**	**696,181**	**1,050,852**

Georgia Vote Since 1932

1932 (Pres.), Roosevelt, Dem., 234,118; Hoover, Rep., 19,863; Upshaw, Proh., 1,125; Thomas, Soc., 461; Foster, Com., 23.

1936 (Pres.), Roosevelt, Dem., 255,364; Landon, Rep., 36,942; Colvin, Proh., 660; Lemke, Union, 141; Thomas, Soc., 68.

1940 (Pres.), Roosevelt, Dem., 265,194; Willkie, Rep., 23,934; Ind. Dem., 22,428; total, 46,362; Babson, Proh., 983.

1944 (Pres.), Roosevelt, Dem., 268,187; Dewey, Rep., 56,506; Watson, Proh., 36.

1948 (Pres.), Truman, Dem., 254,646; Dewey, Rep., 76,691; Thurmond, States' Rights, 85,055; Wallace, Prog., 1,636; Watson, Proh., 732.

1952 (Pres.), Eisenhower, Rep., 198,979; Stevenson, Dem., 456,823; Liberty Party, 1.

1956 (Pres.), Stevenson, Dem., 444,388; Eisenhower, Rep., 222,778; Andrews, Ind., write-in, 1,754.

1960 (Pres.), Kennedy, Dem., 458,638; Nixon, Rep., 274,472; write-in, 239.

1964 (Pres.), Johnson, Dem., 522,557; Goldwater, Rep., 616,600.

1968 (Pres.), Nixon, Rep., 380,111; Humphrey, Dem., 334,440; Wallace, 3d party, 535,550; write-in, 162.

1972 (Pres.), Nixon, Rep., 881,496; McGovern, Dem., 289,529; Schmitz, Amer., 2,288; scattered.

1976 (Pres.), Carter, Dem., 979,409; Ford, Rep., 483,743; write-in, 4,306.

1980 (Pres.), Reagan, Rep., 654,168; Carter, Dem., 890,955; Anderson, Ind., 36,055; Clark, Libertarian, 15,627.

Hawaii

County	1980 Carter (D)	1980 Reagan (R)	Anderson (I)	1984 Mondale (D)	1984 Reagan (R)
Hawaii	17,630	14,247	3,091	17,866	20,707
Oahu	96,472	99,596	25,331	107,460	140,374
Kauai	9,081	5,883	1,352	8,562	9,249
Maui	12,674	10,359	2,237	12,966	14,720
Absentees	22	27	10	NA	NA
Totals	**135,879**	**130,112**	**32,021**	**145,975**	**183,998**

Hawaii Vote Since 1960

1960 (Pres.), Kennedy, Dem., 92,410; Nixon, Rep., 92,295.

1964 (Pres.), Johnson, Dem., 163,249; Goldwater, Rep., 44,022.

1968 (Pres.), Nixon, Rep., 91,425; Humphrey, Dem., 141,324; Wallace, 3d party, 3,469.

1972 (Pres.), Nixon, Rep., 168,865; McGovern, Dem., 101,409.

1976 (Pres.), Carter, Dem., 147,375; Ford, Rep., 140,003; MacBride, Libertarian, 3,923.

1980 (Pres.), Reagan, Rep., 130,112; Carter, Dem., 135,879; Anderson, Ind., 32,021; Clark, Libertarian, 3,269; Commoner, Citizens, 1,548; Hall, Com., 458.

Idaho

County	1980 Carter (D)	1980 Reagan (R)	Anderson (I)	1984 Mondale (D)	1984 Reagan (R)
Ada	21,324	55,205	7,987	21,760	60,036
Adams	590	1,189	88	540	1,381
Bannock	8,639	18,477	1,896	9,399	18,742
Bear Lake	508	2,941	63	481	2,760
Benewah	1,361	2,111	286	1,447	2,039
Bingham	2,933	11,781	489	2,986	11,630
Blaine	1,840	2,716	775	1,970	3,603
Boise	518	1,134	86	436	1,249
Bonner	4,060	6,727	880	4,628	6,889
Bonneville	5,052	24,715	1,355	4,878	24,392
Boundary	1,087	2,088	225	1,158	2,159
Butte	424	1,275	35	439	1,245
Camas	145	360	16	123	364
Canyon	9,172	24,375	1,798	7,506	24,546
Caribou	481	3,234	106	535	3,032
Cassias	1,369	6,511	212	1,036	6,503
Clark	87	379	11	59	353
Clearwater	1,699	2,178	291	1,608	2,176
Custer	398	1,398	64	461	1,653
Elmore	1,760	3,994	311	1,458	4,595
Franklin	511	3,669	61	439	3,261
Fremont	926	4,167	108	818	4,006
Gem	1,613	3,766	218	1,607	3,644
Gooding	1,481	3,897	218	1,247	3,819
Idaho	2,078	4,425	409	1,996	4,219
Jefferson	833	5,860	135	743	5,410
Jerome	1,368	4,962	178	1,284	4,813
Kootenai	7,521	17,022	1,808	9,005	17,330
Latah	5,037	6,967	2,465	5,571	7,709
Lemhi	794	2,646	167	852	2,810
Lewis	774	1,088	160	648	1,000
Lincoln	462	1,294	83	386	1,211
Madison	728	6,555	64	531	6,899
Minidoka	1,689	6,035	260	1,398	5,938
Nez Perce	6,565	7,495	1,344	5,981	8,153
Oneida	434	1,461	50	370	1,538
Owyhee	732	2,257	93	574	2,132
Payette	1,828	4,508	253	1,410	4,605
Power	727	2,235	119	678	2,298
Shoshone	3,102	3,994	407	3,033	3,156
Teton	360	1,227	67	380	1,242
Twin Falls	4,835	17,425	976	4,524	16,833
Valley	926	2,041	245	945	2,299
Washington	1,421	2,915	172	1,919	3,015
Totals	**110,192**	**290,699**	**27,058**	**108,447**	**296,687**

Idaho Vote Since 1932

1932 (Pres.), Roosevelt, Dem., 109,479; Hoover, Rep., 71,312; Harvey, Lib., 4,712; Thomas, Soc., 526; Foster, Com., 491.

1936 (Pres.), Roosevelt, Dem., 125,683; Landon, Rep., 66,256; Lemke, Union, 7,684.

1940 (Pres.), Roosevelt, Dem., 127,842; Willkie, Rep., 106,553; Thomas, Soc., 497; Browder, Com., 276.

1944 (Pres.), Roosevelt, Dem., 107,399; Dewey, Rep., 100,137; Watson, Proh., 503; Thomas, Soc., 282.

1948 (Pres.), Truman, Dem., 107,370; Dewey, Rep., 101,514; Wallace, Prog., 4,972; Watson, Proh., 628; Thomas, Soc., 332.

1952 (Pres.), Eisenhower, Rep., 180,707; Stevenson Dem., 95,081; Hallinan, Prog., 443; write-in, 23.

1956 (Pres.), Eisenhower, Rep., 166,979; Stevenson, Dem., 105,868; Andrews, Ind., 126; write-in, 16.

1960 (Pres.), Kennedy, Dem., 138,853; Nixon, Rep., 161,597.

1964 (Pres.), Johnson, Dem., 148,920; Goldwater, Rep., 143,557.

1968 (Pres.), Nixon, Rep., 165,369; Humphrey, Dem., 89,273; Wallace, 3d party, 36,541.

1972 (Pres.), Nixon, Rep., 199,384; McGovern, Dem., 80,826; Schmitz, Amer., 28,869; Spock, Peoples, 903.

1976 (Pres.), Carter, Dem., 126,549; Ford, Rep., 204,151; Maddox, Amer., 5,935; MacBride, Libertarian, 3,558; LaRouche, U.S. Labor, 739.

1980 (Pres.), Reagan, Rep., 290,699; Carter, Dem., 110,192; Anderson, Ind., 27,058; Clark, Libertarian, 8,425; Rarick, Amer., 1,057.

Illinois

County	1980 Carter (D)	1980 Reagan (R)	1980 Anderson (I)	1984 Mondale (D)	1984 Reagan (R)
Adams	10,606	19,842	1,202	10,336	20,225
Alexander	2,925	2,650	74	2,872	2,574
Bond	2,834	4,398	244	2,870	4,240
Boone	3,175	6,697	1,578	3,717	7,536
Brown	950	1,660	59	959	1,478
Bureau	5,753	11,484	1,093	6,925	11,740
Calhoun	1,208	1,591	76	1,443	1,648
Carroll	2,154	5,084	705	2,398	5,237
Cass	2,543	3,965	199	2,937	3,435
Champaign	21,017	33,329	9,972	27,266	39,224
Christian	6,625	8,770	499	7,541	8,534
Clark	2,855	5,476	243	3,032	5,010
Clay	2,587	4,447	187	2,524	4,562
Clinton	4,470	8,500	528	4,577	9,016
Coles	6,743	11,994	1,726	7,156	14,044
Cook	1,124,584	856,574	149,712	1,060,854	1,033,292
Crawford	3,372	5,894	341	3,130	6,261
Cumberland	1,892	3,159	190	2,709	3,980
DeKalb	8,913	16,370	4,526	10,942	20,294
DeWitt	2,262	4,648	368	2,352	4,530
Douglas	2,564	5,330	344	2,886	5,691
DuPage	68,991	182,308	29,810	71,080	225,962
Edgar	3,394	6,639	400	3,241	6,821
Edwards	1,041	2,556	118	1,057	2,778
Effingham	4,229	9,104	393	3,841	9,617
Fayette	3,614	6,523	229	3,844	6,607
Ford	1,803	5,024	328	1,763	4,871
Franklin	9,425	9,731	558	10,604	9,615
Fulton	7,481	10,316	838	9,131	9,147
Gallatin	1,678	1,700	78	2,164	1,939
Greene	2,607	4,224	220	2,562	4,053
Grundy	3,970	8,397	701	4,671	9,595
Hamilton	1,990	3,254	171	2,100	2,937
Hancock	3,522	6,597	383	3,713	6,251
Hardin	1,314	1,721	56	1,205	1,699
Henderson	1,609	2,443	143	1,969	2,289
Henry	7,977	14,506	1,440	10,678	14,504
Iroquois	3,362	11,247	592	3,300	11,327
Jackson	10,291	10,505	2,526	12,105	13,609
Jasper	1,846	3,548	157	1,750	3,673
Jefferson	6,761	8,972	506	7,200	9,642
Jersey	3,324	5,266	314	3,762	5,146
JoDaviess	2,678	5,186	983	3,348	5,877
Johnson	1,586	3,201	84	1,647	3,424
Kane	29,015	64,106	9,179	31,874	72,652
Kankakee	14,626	23,810	1,802	15,150	23,603
Kendall	3,143	10,028	979	3,789	10,872
Knox	8,719	14,907	2,069	12,027	14,974
Lake	48,287	96,350	17,726	53,947	118,401
LaSalle	16,818	27,323	3,041	20,532	27,388
Lawrence	3,030	4,453	293	2,924	4,686
Lee	3,170	11,373	781	3,779	10,705
Livingston	4,111	11,544	980	4,567	12,291
Logan	3,916	9,681	650	4,052	9,932
McDonough	4,093	8,995	1,230	4,561	9,383
McHenry	14,540	40,045	5,871	14,420	47,282
McLean	13,587	30,096	4,961	11,170	22,069
Macon	22,325	28,298	2,804	25,463	30,457
Macoupin	9,116	12,131	901	10,602	12,282
Madison	43,860	51,160	4,206	58,352	57,021
Marion	6,990	10,969	567	7,599	11,300
Marshall	1,903	4,349	336	2,386	4,060
Mason	2,680	4,644	267	3,354	4,109
Massac	2,821	4,284	124	3,192	3,847
Menard	1,589	3,622	274	1,826	3,925
Mercer	3,361	5,144	540	3,976	4,902
Monroe	3,121	6,315	405	3,093	6,434
Montgomery	5,721	8,947	611	6,360	8,191
Morgan	5,483	10,406	900	5,335	10,629
Moultrie	2,332	3,495	280	2,458	3,591
Ogle	4,067	12,533	2,042	4,803	13,503
Peoria	28,276	47,815	6,169	36,796	45,406
Perry	4,337	5,888	319	4,584	5,852
Piatt	2,421	4,867	447	2,840	5,000
Pike	3,695	5,301	303	3,966	5,287
Pope	880	1,501	58	940	1,545
Pulaski	1,955	2,083	49	1,724	1,923
Putnam	1,158	1,959	235	1,487	1,912
Randolph	6,052	8,810	514	6,355	9,415
Richland	2,463	5,241	358	2,182	5,665
Rock Island	30,045	34,788	5,818	40,208	35,121
St. Clair	50,046	46,063	3,879	48,737	46,417
Saline	5,683	7,157	321	6,038	7,176
Sangamon	29,354	49,372	5,439	34,059	54,086
Schuyler	1,445	2,799	155	1,533	2,515
Scott	941	1,990	80	943	1,976
Shelby	3,988	6,441	381	4,317	6,372
Stark	806	2,358	147	1,072	2,228
Stephenson	6,195	10,779	3,145	6,723	14,237
Tazewell	16,924	35,481	3,206	23,095	33,782
Union	3,781	4,289	291	3,815	4,721
Vermilion	14,498	22,579	2,110	16,530	22,932
Wabash	1,975	3,571	230	1,795	3,639
Warren	2,756	5,667	489	3,318	5,846
Washington	2,158	5,354	205	2,363	5,129
Wayne	3,258	6,013	222	2,621	6,298
White	3,463	5,279	274	3,457	5,500
Whiteside	7,191	17,309	1,242	11,226	16,743
Will	41,975	69,310	7,855	45,193	78,684
Williamson	10,779	14,451	793	11,614	14,930
Winnebago	32,384	48,825	22,596	44,629	64,203
Woodford	3,552	10,791	711	4,425	10,758
Totals	1,981,413	2,358,049	346,754	2,036,337	2,667,721

Illinois Vote Since 1932

1932 (Pres.), Roosevelt, Dem., 1,882,304; Hoover, Rep., 1,432,756; Thomas, Soc., 67,258; Foster, Com., 15,582; Upshaw, Proh., 6,388; Reynolds, Soc. Labor, 3,638.

1936 (Pres.), Roosevelt, Dem., 2,282,999; Landon, Rep., 1,570,393; Lemke, Union, 89,439; Thomas, Soc., 7,530; Colvin, Proh., 3,439; Aiken, Soc. Labor, 1,921.

1940 (Pres.), Roosevelt, Dem., 2,149,934; Willkie, Rep., 2,047,240; Thomas, Soc., 10,914; Babson, Proh., 9,190.

1944 (Pres.), Roosevelt, Dem., 2,079,479; Dewey, Rep., 1,939,314; Teichert, Soc. Labor, 9,677; Watson, Proh., 7,411; Thomas, Soc., 180.

1948 (Pres.), Truman, Dem., 1,994,715; Dewey, Rep., 1,961,103; Watson, Proh., 11,959; Thomas, Soc., 11,522; Teichert, Soc. Labor, 3,118.

1952 (Pres.), Eisenhower, Rep., 2,457,327; Stevenson, Dem., 2,013,920; Hass, Soc. Labor, 9,363; write-in, 448.

1956 (Pres.), Eisenhower, Rep., 2,623,327; Stevenson, Dem., 1,775,682; Hass, Soc. Labor, 8,342; write-in, 56.

1960 (Pres.), Kennedy, Dem., 2,377,846; Nixon, Rep., 2,368,988; Hass, Soc. Labor, 10,560; write-in, 15.

1964 (Pres.), Johnson, Dem., 2,796,833; Goldwater, Rep., 1,905,946; write-in, 62.

1968 (Pres.), Nixon, Rep., 2,174,774; Humphrey, Dem., 2,039,814; Wallace, 3d party, 390,958; Blomen, Soc. Labor, 13,878; write-in, 395.

1972 (Pres.), Nixon, Rep. 2,788,179; McGovern, Dem., 1,913,472; Fisher, Soc. Labor, 12,344; Schmitz, Amer., 2,471; Hall, Com., 4,541; others, 2,229.

1976 (Pres.), Carter, Dem., 2,271,295; Ford, Rep., 2,364,269; McCarthy, Ind., 55,939; Hall, Com., 9,250; MacBride, Libertarian, 8,057; Camejo, Soc. Workers, 3,615; Levin, Soc. Labor, 2,422; LaRouche, U.S. Labor, 2,018; write-in, 1,968.

1980 (Pres.), Reagan, Rep., 2,358,049; Carter, Dem., 1,981,413; Anderson, Ind., 346,754; Clark, Libertarian, 38,939; Commoner, Citizens, 10,692; Hall, Com., 9,711; Griswold, Workers World, 2,257; DeBerry, Socialist Workers, 1,302; write-ins, 604.

Indiana

County	1980 Carter (D)	1980 Reagan (R)	1980 Anderson (I)	1984 Mondale (D)	1984 Reagan (R)
Adams	4,673	6,368	767	3,923	7,958
Allen	37,765	68,524	10,368	36,508	70,647
Bartholomew	9,260	15,801	1,604	8,075	18,704
Benton	1,520	3,189	187	1,357	3,281
Blackford	2,431	3,168	258	2,420	3,843
Boone	4,535	10,484	681	3,982	11,790
Brown	2,014	2,884	237	1,941	3,517
Carroll	2,966	5,262	338	2,774	5,524
Cass	5,838	11,500	696	5,521	12,455
Clark	14,137	15,508	1,102	14,318	19,419
Clay	4,363	6,980	311	3,707	6,957
Clinton	5,258	8,158	427	4,329	8,969
Crawford	2,130	2,554	124	2,256	2,633
Daviess	4,057	7,022	345	3,545	7,721
Dearborn	5,135	7,467	464	4,920	9,149
Decatur	3,646	5,819	377	2,766	6,551
Dekalb	4,911	7,886	883	4,536	8,769
Delaware	20,923	28,342	2,743	19,791	30,092
Dubois	6,700	6,775	578	5,423	9,473
Elkhart	14,883	30,081	3,256	13,240	34,621
Fayette	4,304	6,004	293	4,122	7,142
Floyd	11,543	12,456	1,047	10,616	15,466
Fountain	2,845	5,289	280	2,897	5,450
Franklin	2,834	4,551	234	2,225	5,202
Fulton	2,788	5,458	349	2,527	6,057
Gibson	6,834	7,643	591	7,082	8,618
Grant	10,390	19,078	1,043	9,969	20,458
Greene	6,027	7,452	299	4,734	8,153
Hamilton	7,036	26,218	1,736	6,364	30,254
Hancock	5,124	12,093	746	4,550	12,874
Harrison	4,865	6,287	341	4,364	7,255
Hendricks	7,412	19,366	1,048	6,659	21,307
Henry	7,626	12,724	562	7,064	11,926
Howard	12,916	21,272	1,325	10,458	22,386
Huntington	5,415	9,497	824	4,598	10,805
Jackson	6,425	8,903	430	5,163	9,879
Jasper	2,544	6,316	283	2,821	6,535
Jay	3,256	5,351	484	3,174	5,975
Jefferson	5,496	6,831	477	4,781	7,117
Jennings	3,931	5,498	281	3,264	6,356
Johnson	8,445	20,018	1,348	7,715	23,482
Knox	7,829	10,083	617	6,417	10,872
Kosciusko	5,684	15,633	1,164	4,877	17,560
LaGrange	2,095	4,259	377	1,884	4,772
Lake	101,145	95,408	8,275	117,984	94,870
LaPorte	15,387	22,424	2,080	15,904	23,346
Lawrence	5,826	10,846	380	5,608	11,440
Madison	23,554	35,582	2,389	22,254	36,510
Marion	126,103	168,680	15,709	125,885	175,912
Marshall	5,113	10,209	836	4,931	11,100
Martin	2,479	3,082	149	1,937	3,363
Miami	4,927	8,672	508	4,067	9,126
Monroe	13,316	18,233	3,921	14,719	21,772
Montgomery	4,158	9,936	622	3,626	11,119
Morgan	5,439	13,321	498	4,627	14,884
Newton	1,649	3,850	194	1,596	3,560
Noble	4,721	7,624	749	4,237	8,459
Ohio	1,074	1,264	57	1,068	1,503
Orange	3,228	5,073	181	2,571	5,909
Owen	2,325	3,632	188	2,082	4,204
Parke	2,432	4,595	194	1,714	4,232
Perry	4,540	4,350	448	4,760	4,835
Pike	3,346	3,343	190	3,231	3,689
Porter	12,869	30,055	3,061	17,862	32,505
Posey	4,465	6,096	667	4,452	6,472
Pulaski	2,092	3,916	175	1,909	3,941
Putnam	3,996	7,090	501	3,392	7,820
Randolph	4,025	7,762	426	3,805	7,793
Ripley	4,022	5,770	303	3,448	7,038
Rush	2,388	4,829	224	2,307	5,429
St. Joseph	44,218	50,607	6,962	47,526	52,280
Scott	3,694	3,432	139	3,460	4,130
Shelby	5,861	10,496	614	5,357	10,860
Spencer	4,153	5,284	196	4,005	5,816
Starke	3,615	5,035	297	3,674	5,104
Steuben	2,606	5,670	602	2,441	6,424
Sullivan	4,335	4,465	212	4,006	4,771
Switzerland	1,704	1,584	38	1,484	1,857
Tippecanoe	14,636	27,589	5,141	15,789	29,706
Tipton	2,547	5,150	285	2,268	5,687
Union	898	1,766	92	816	1,970
Vanderburgh	29,930	36,248	4,150	30,675	40,802
Vermillion	3,793	4,195	269	3,666	4,428
Vigo	19,261	24,133	2,484	NA	NA
Wabash	4,620	8,738	797	4,077	9,862
Warren	1,287	2,665	145	1,309	2,525
Warrick	6,845	8,681	890	6,845	10,202
Washington	3,663	5,234	191	3,334	5,874
Wayne	9,599	16,981	1,174	10,173	18,955
Wells	3,760	5,864	717	3,274	7,579
White	3,247	6,999	466	3,157	7,279
Whitley	4,497	7,146	928	3,690	7,763
Totals	**844,197**	**1,255,656**	**111,639**	**814,659**	**1,332,679**

Indiana Vote Since 1932

1932 (Pres.), Roosevelt, Dem., 862,054; Hoover, Rep., 677,184; Thomas, Soc., 21,388; Upshaw, Proh., 10,399; Foster, Com., 2,187; Reynolds, Soc. Labor, 2,070.

1936 (Pres.), Roosevelt, Dem., 943,974; Landon, Rep., 691,570; Lemke, Union, 19,407; Thomas, Soc., 3,856; Browder, Com., 1,090.

1940 (Pres.), Roosevelt, Dem., 874,063; Willkie, Rep., 899,466; Babson, Proh., 6,437; Thomas, Soc., 2,075; Aiken, Soc. Labor, 706.

1944 (Pres.), Roosevelt, Dem., 781,403; Dewey, Rep., 875,891; Watson, Proh., 12,574; Thomas, Soc., 2,223.

1948 (Pres.), Truman, Dem., 807,833; Dewey, Rep., 821,079; Watson, Proh., 14,711; Wallace, Prog., 9,649; Thomas, Soc., 2,179; Teichert, Soc. Labor, 763.

1952 (Pres.), Eisenhower, Rep., 1,136,259; Stevenson, Dem., 801,530; Hamblen, Proh., 15,335; Hallinan, Prog., 1,222; Hass, Soc. Labor, 979.

1956 (Pres.), Eisenhower, Rep., 1,182,811; Stevenson, Dem., 783,908; Holtwick, Proh., 6,554; Hass, Soc. Labor, 1,334.

1960 (Pres.), Kennedy, Dem., 952,358; Nixon, Rep., 1,175,120; Decker, Proh., 6,746; Hass, Soc. Labor, 1,136.

1964 (Pres.), Johnson, Dem. 1,170,848; Goldwater, Rep., 911,118; Munn, Proh., 8,266; Hass, Soc. Labor, 1,374.

1968 (Pres.), Nixon, Rep., 1,067,885; Humphrey, Dem., 806,659; Wallace, 3d party, 243,108; Munn, Proh., 4,616; Halstead, Soc. Worker, 1,293; Gregory, write-in, 36.

1972 (Pres.), Nixon, Rep., 1,405,154; McGovern, Dem., 708,568; Reed, Soc. Workers, 5,575; Fisher, Soc. Labor, 1,688; Spock, Peace & Freedom, 4,544.

1976 (Pres.), Carter, Dem., 1,014,714; Ford, Rep., 1,185,958; Anderson, Amer., 14,048; Camejo, Soc. Workers, 5,695; LaRouche, U.S. Labor, 1,947.

1980 (Pres.) Reagan, Rep., 1,255,656; Carter, Dem., 844,197; Anderson, Ind., 111,639; Clark, Libertarian, 19,627; Commoner, Citizens, 4,852; Greaves, American, 4,750; Hall, Com., 702; DeBerry, Soc., 610.

Iowa

County	1980 Carter (D)	1980 Reagan (R)	1980 Anderson (I)	1984 Mondale (D)	1984 Reagan (R)
Adair	1,454	2,821	356	1,979	2,610
Adams	940	1,779	214	1,221	1,706
Allamakee	2,170	4,000	343	2,281	3,896
Appanoose	2,769	3,544	353	3,288	3,407
Audubon	1,546	2,523	251	1,852	2,301
Benton	4,223	5,329	948	4,993	5,565
Black Hawk	27,443	29,627	5,847	29,522	29,404
Boone	5,126	5,732	1,081	8,479	6,741
Bremer	3,527	6,706	970	4,081	6,881
Buchanan	3,605	5,041	689	3,965	4,792
Buena Vista	3,468	5,272	771	4,099	5,173
Butler	1,990	4,730	392	2,323	4,570
Calhoun	2,150	3,633	407	2,540	3,306
Carroll	3,885	5,017	736	5,057	5,011
Cass	2,176	5,391	475	2,414	4,951
Cedar	2,589	4,398	697	3,103	4,609
Cerro Gordo	9,363	11,189	2,024	11,567	11,154
Cherokee	2,719	4,087	599	3,340	4,039
Chickasaw	2,935	3,929	500	3,176	3,742
Clarke	1,614	2,417	310	2,035	2,276
Clay	3,179	4,479	991	3,773	4,434
Clayton	3,297	5,115	669	3,441	5,022
Clinton	9,698	13,025	2,140	10,375	13,893
Crawford	2,500	4,883	509	3,391	4,546
Dallas	5,310	6,296	1,200	6,561	6,075
Davis	1,689	2,003	200	1,993	1,804
Decatur	2,048	2,212	318	2,098	2,103
Delaware	2,671	4,316	727	3,157	4,765
Des Moines	9,977	9,158	1,041	11,165	9,533
Dickinson	2,620	4,028	687	3,024	4,059
Dubuque	18,689	18,649	3,708	21,847	19,192
Emmet	2,153	3,062	446	2,736	2,932
Fayette	4,377	6,374	647	4,668	6,649
Floyd	3,634	4,665	728	4,078	4,250
Franklin	1,920	3,290	406	2,347	3,130
Fremont	1,203	2,693	191	1,423	2,683
Greene	2,210	3,154	510	2,927	2,867
Grundy	1,869	4,644	440	1,859	4,527
Guthrie	1,866	3,214	384	2,345	2,503
Hamilton	2,741	4,745	679	3,322	4,273
Hancock	1,918	3,681	462	2,535	3,352
Hardin	3,757	5,329	730	4,364	5,180
Harrison	2,152	4,502	311	2,493	4,351
Henry	3,317	4,430	629	3,374	4,509

Howard	2,214	2,975	336	2,128	2,708
Humboldt	1,840	3,575	394	2,404	3,387
Ida	1,235	2,825	254	1,559	2,615
Iowa	2,606	4,153	667	2,815	4,347
Jackson	3,518	4,479	622	4,400	4,809
Jasper	7,258	8,286	1,221	8,028	8,573
Jefferson	2,577	4,099	505	2,960	4,723
Johnson	20,122	13,642	8,101	25,935	18,621
Jones	3,521	4,506	759	3,830	5,016
Keokuk	2,390	3,145	369	2,649	2,911
Kossuth	3,810	5,568	775	4,805	4,920
Lee	8,204	8,793	1,047	8,902	8,733
Linn	31,950	36,254	8,773	38,039	40,489
Louisa	1,700	2,530	291	1,927	2,622
Lucas	1,989	2,593	291	2,420	2,630
Lyon	1,431	4,349	375	1,348	4,160
Madison	2,496	3,320	505	3,063	3,160
Mahaska	3,968	5,650	603	4,109	6,079
Marion	5,490	6,665	1,232	6,274	7,255
Marshall	7,114	10,707	1,541	8,800	10,820
Mills	1,244	3,581	281	1,432	3,990
Mitchell	2,040	3,401	361	2,528	3,141
Monona	1,660	3,268	275	2,159	2,745
Monroe	1,866	2,003	216	2,346	1,926
Montgomery	1,556	4,115	301	1,656	4,222
Muscatine	5,597	7,829	1,522	5,970	9,058
O'Brien	2,210	4,937	536	2,479	5,018
Osceola	1,051	2,177	234	1,144	2,285
Page	1,772	5,618	356	1,913	5,922
Palo Alto	2,463	3,025	412	3,015	2,706
Plymouth	2,965	6,515	756	3,459	6,474
Pocahontas	1,959	3,194	397	2,479	2,624
Polk	61,984	64,156	15,819	74,872	71,234
Pottawattamie	10,709	20,222	1,870	12,318	21,286
Poweshiek	3,529	4,598	821	4,097	4,706
Ringgold	1,150	1,884	191	1,593	1,522
Sac	1,976	3,725	467	2,371	3,298
Scott	26,301	94,701	5,760	32,613	37,993
Shelby	1,892	4,147	372	2,287	4,150
Sioux	2,698	10,768	610	2,584	11,659
Story	13,529	15,829	7,252	17,781	19,143
Tama	3,049	4,840	593	4,064	4,798
Taylor	1,226	2,715	240	1,499	2,494
Union	2,182	3,372	368	2,552	3,567
Van Buren	1,311	2,142	183	1,604	2,133
Wapello	8,923	7,475	1,050	10,543	7,095
Warren	6,610	7,360	1,369	8,165	8,268
Washington	2,877	3,967	703	3,078	4,610
Wayne	1,627	2,221	218	1,926	2,060
Webster	9,001	10,438	1,386	9,922	9,597
Winnebago	2,208	3,808	417	2,662	3,607
Winneshiek	3,201	5,033	938	3,658	5,195
Woodbury	15,930	23,553	3,184	18,932	22,868
Worth	1,721	2,247	301	2,262	1,983
Wright	2,645	3,936	497	2,979	3,672
Totals	508,672	676,026	115,633	601,946	698,239

Iowa Vote Since 1932

1932 (Pres.), Roosevelt, Dem., 598,019; Hoover, Rep., 414,433; Thomas, Soc., 20,467; Upshaw, Proh., 2,111; Coxey, Farm-Lab., 1,094; Foster, Com., 559.

1936 (Pres.), Roosevelt, Dem., 621,756; Landon, Rep., 487,977; Lemke, Union, 29,687; Thomas, Soc., 1,373; Colvin, Proh., 1,182; Browder, Com., 506; Aiken, Soc. Labor, 252.

1940 (Pres.), Roosevelt, Dem., 578,800; Willkie, Rep., 632,370; Babson, Proh., 2,284; Browder, Com., 1,524; Aiken, Soc. Labor, 452.

1944 (Pres.), Roosevelt, Dem., 499,876; Dewey, Rep., 547,267; Watson, Proh., 3,752; Thomas, Soc., 1,511; Teichert, Soc. Labor, 193.

1948 (Pres.), Truman, Dem., 522,380; Dewey, Rep., 494,018; Wallace, Prog., 12,125; Teichert, Soc. Labor, 4,274; Watson, Proh., 3,382; Thomas, Soc., 1,829; Dobbs, Soc. Workers, 26.

1952 (Pres.), Eisenhower, Rep., 808,906; Stevenson, Dem., 451,513; Hallinan, Prog., 5,085; Hamblen, Proh., 2,882; Hoopes, Soc., 219; Hass, Soc. Labor, 139; scattering 29.

1956 (Pres.), Eisenhower, Rep., 729,187; Stevenson, Dem., 501,858; Andrews (A.C.P. of Iowa), 3,202; Hoopes, Soc., 192; Hass, Soc. Labor, 125.

1960 (Pres.), Kennedy, Dem., 550,565; Nixon, Rep., 722,381; Hass, Soc. Labor, 230; write-in, 634.

1964 (Pres.), Johnson, Dem., 733,030; Goldwater, Rep., 449,148; Hass, Soc. Labor, 182; DeBerry, Soc. Worker, 159; Munn, Proh., 1,902.

1968 (Pres.), Nixon, Rep., 619,106; Humphrey, Dem., 476,699; Wallace, 3d party, 66,422; Munn, Proh., 362; Halstead, Soc. Worker, 3,377; Cleaver, Peace and Freedom, 1,332; Blomen, Soc. Labor, 241.

1972 (Pres.), Nixon, Rep., 706,207; McGovern, Dem., 496,206; Schmitz, Amer., 22,056; Jenness, Soc. Workers, 488; Fisher, Soc. Labor, 195; Hall, Com. 272; Green, Universal, 199; scattered, 321.

1976 (Pres.), Carter, Dem., 619,931; Ford, Rep., 632,863; McCarthy, Ind., 20,051; Anderson, Amer., 3,040; MacBride, Libertarian, 1,452.

1980 (Pres.), Reagan, Rep., 676,026; Carter, Dem., 508,672; Anderson, Ind., 115,633; Clark, Libertarian, 13,123; Commoner, Citizens, 2,273; McReynolds, Socialist, 534; Hall Com., 298; DeBerry, Soc. Work., 244; Greaves, American, 189; Bubar, Statesman, 150; scattering, 519.

Kansas

	1980			1984	
County	Carter (D)	Reagan (R)	Anderson (I)	Mondale (D)	Reagan (R)
Allen	2,009	3,811	380	1,779	4,266
Anderson	1,170	2,363	184	1,155	2,462
Atchison	3,063	4,084	345	2,641	4,536
Barber	914	1,872	168	805	2,111
Barton	3,663	9,147	793	2,288	8,827
Bourbon	2,605	4,263	251	2,174	4,856
Brown	1,370	3,598	286	1,214	3,542
Butler	6,875	10,210	1,015	3,958	7,817
Chase	413	1,073	92	393	1,162
Chautauqua	543	1,566	57	497	1,688
Cherokee	3,969	5,296	282	3,663	5,801
Cheyenne	358	1,330	81	356	1,442
Clark	430	901	67	324	1,075
Clay	932	3,449	217	704	2,769
Cloud	1,793	3,581	344	1,878	3,856
Coffey	938	2,491	128	555	2,054
Comanche	393	877	50	285	993
Cowley	5,474	8,749	866	1,601	2,182
Crawford	7,658	8,058	847	4,898	6,441
Decatur	443	1,642	125	467	1,769
Dickinson	2,108	5,654	469	2,288	6,901
Doniphan	1,001	2,523	146	962	2,818
Douglas	9,360	14,106	4,770	12,637	18,302
Edwards	616	1,409	127	606	1,352
Elk	482	1,280	54	452	1,301
Ellis	3,940	5,634	923	3,359	7,239
Ellsworth	886	2,155	167	905	2,353
Finney	2,689	4,831	531	2,398	6,943
Ford	3,194	5,686	622	2,914	6,738
Franklin	2,726	5,525	432	2,524	6,283
Geary	2,357	3,534	332	2,301	4,475
Gove	396	1,263	91	426	1,310
Graham	473	1,450	98	195	516
Grant	683	1,711	150	615	2,043
Gray	583	1,310	123	514	1,580
Greeley	235	600	85	227	699
Greenwood	1,241	2,685	170	1,173	2,900
Hamilton	402	889	66	408	1,037
Harper	990	2,254	182	893	3,696
Harvey	4,173	7,045	1,356	4,599	8,679
Haskell	374	1,014	84	281	1,152
Hodgeman	339	831	69	306	939
Jackson	1,537	3,211	234	1,667	3,464
Jefferson	1,776	4,046	364	1,990	4,524
Jewell	578	2,074	153	583	1,992
Johnson	33,210	78,048	10,947	37,782	101,042
Kearny	375	924	62	321	1,214
Kingman	1,133	2,610	286	1,047	2,826
Kiowa	438	1,433	88	367	1,537
Labette	3,947	5,244	588	3,631	6,542
Lane	321	924	100	282	1,008
Leavenworth	6,354	9,157	955	5,724	9,267
Lincoln	528	1,685	96	551	1,723
Linn	1,157	2,407	103	1,152	2,794
Logan	358	1,261	66	331	1,235
Lyon	4,680	8,431	1,216	4,188	9,796
McPherson	3,340	6,843	1,222	3,185	8,630
Marion	1,569	3,960	488	1,633	4,407
Marshall	1,555	4,127	330	1,813	4,097
Meade	482	1,618	121	491	1,804
Miami	3,071	4,740	368	3,076	5,877
Mitchell	876	2,821	197	919	3,036
Montgomery	5,282	10,856	488	4,933	12,023
Morris	810	1,933	166	820	2,240
Morton	414	1,157	71	322	1,353
Nemaha	1,600	3,546	243	1,761	3,653
Neosho	2,923	4,613	432	2,679	4,968
Ness	616	1,657	136	539	1,779
Norton	666	2,625	151	611	2,515
Osage	2,088	3,817	330	2,072	4,288
Osborne	620	2,188	125	686	2,171
Ottawa	630	2,118	150	698	2,343
Pawnee	1,184	2,170	281	1,092	2,570
Phillips	748	2,731	143	626	2,810
Pottawatomie	1,724	3,895	444	1,586	4,055
Pratt	1,369	2,866	329	1,253	3,240
Rawlins	427	1,524	87	412	1,625
Reno	9,615	13,804	2,225	9,229	16,621

Republic	850	3,031	183	1,000	2,974	Casey	1,298	4,239	38	1,122	4,356
Rice	1,847	3,211	426	1,532	3,551	Christian	7,048	8,209	190	5,432	10,708
Riley	5,224	8,904	2,443	5,644	10,629	Clark	5,071	4,302	242	3,595	6,130
Rooks	725	2,275	144	699	2,604	Clay	2,121	4,594	37	1,634	4,772
Rush	557	1,840	144	718	1,758	Clinton	1,000	3,539	34	838	3,459
Russell	910	3,241	229	1,055	3,673	Crittenden	1,508	2,219	28	1,483	2,167
Saline	6,382	12,758	1,706	6,527	15,242	Cumberland	821	2,216	27	766	2,729
Scott	456	1,829	99	427	2,017	Daviess	14,902	14,643	752	13,347	19,495
Sedgwick	55,105	75,317	10,222	55,060	95,972	Edmonson	1,252	2,913	28	1,200	3,001
Seward	1,460	4,385	250	924	3,836	Elliott	1,668	551	15	1,683	601
Shawnee	24,852	36,290	5,524	26,307	43,435	Estill	1,965	2,818	45	1,593	3,511
Sheridan	391	1,202	68	429	1,274	Fayette	30,511	35,349	4,933	28,898	51,081
Sherman	779	2,315	215	655	2,377	Fleming	2,051	2,189	54	1,616	2,824
Smith	719	2,415	183	684	2,330	Floyd	10,975	4,179	171	10,259	5,218
Stafford	872	1,865	184	844	2,062	Franklin	11,193	6,455	610	7,790	11,057
Stanton	231	672	62	205	783	Fulton	2,016	1,462	31	1,534	1,780
Stevens	478	1,502	67	386	1,862	Gallatin	988	684	20	1,042	1,042
Summer	3,761	6,038	486	3,713	6,942	Garrard	1,774	2,585	62	1,566	3,784
Thomas	1,045	2,789	269	670	2,434	Grant	2,272	1,779	76	1,685	2,840
Trego	523	1,340	138	558	1,350	Graves	6,999	6,556	135	6,759	7,287
Wabaunsee	853	2,255	173	804	2,276	Grayson	2,788	5,084	78	2,115	5,298
Wallace	167	811	36	152	838	Green	1,758	2,775	39	1,611	3,210
Washington	784	3,058	195	889	2,979	Greenup	7,126	6,857	220	6,923	7,451
Wichita	303	880	60	232	916	Hancock	1,530	1,367	52	1,287	1,967
Wilson	1,205	3,328	208	1,343	3,660	Hardin	8,339	9,779	452	6,329	14,293
Woodson	646	1,435	89	596	1,408	Harlan	8,798	5,460	131	7,663	6,959
Wyandotte	32,763	23,012	3,018	35,887	27,267	Harrison	3,319	2,184	107	2,405	3,467
Totals	326,150	566,812	68,231	321,010	649,423	Hart	3,005	3,129	42	2,278	3,065

Henderson	8,082	5,074	354	6,795	7,389
Henry	2,999	1,723	69	2,279	2,802
Hickman	1,456	1,143	28	1,028	1,342
Hopkins	8,810	6,238	213	6,743	9,368
Jackson	702	3,379	29	528	3,699
Jefferson	125,844	127,254	9,686	29,842	40,902
Jessamine	3,310	4,809	278	2,379	7,081
Johnson	3,142	5,039	96	3,078	5,225
Kenton	17,907	25,965	1,583	14,775	34,754
Knott	5,405	1,602	25	4,487	1,728
Knox	3,543	5,539	113	2,932	5,720
Larue	2,183	2,000	43	1,514	2,873
Laurel	3,969	8,868	114	3,267	9,621
Lawrence	2,362	2,564	32	2,223	2,713
Lee	1,017	1,650	41	768	1,862
Leslie	1,327	3,536	40	1,075	3,385
Letcher	4,280	3,426	78	3,752	3,245
Lewis	1,543	2,802	34	1,484	3,445
Lincoln	2,991	3,034	58	2,498	3,996
Livingston	2,287	1,670	30	2,007	1,866
Logan	4,264	3,366	85	3,347	4,889
Lyon	1,496	968	26	1,267	961
McCracken	13,365	10,281	369	12,535	12,903
McCreary	1,377	3,786	40	1,609	4,028
McLean	2,147	1,497	44	1,917	1,942
Madison	8,208	8,437	739	6,307	10,971
Magoffin	2,986	2,265	25	2,942	2,343
Marion	3,577	2,126	87	2,835	3,305
Marshall	6,231	4,403	96	5,725	5,152
Martin	1,567	2,793	51	1,471	3,238
Mason	3,181	2,926	127	2,663	3,751
Meade	3,205	2,740	90	2,503	3,820
Menifee	966	547	11	956	785
Mercer	3,528	3,275	92	2,516	4,592
Metcalfe	1,628	2,013	39	1,575	2,349
Monroe	1,156	4,592	47	975	4,365
Montgomery	3,391	2,869	117	2,490	3,864
Morgan	2,698	1,450	31	2,481	1,834
Muhlenberg	6,616	4,893	148	6,157	6,094
Nelson	5,514	3,349	162	4,199	6,044
Nicholas	1,349	915	56	1,107	1,535
Ohio	3,486	5,272	103	3,255	5,119
Oldham	3,487	5,586	351	2,857	8,112
Owen	2,323	944	43	1,575	1,735
Owsley	437	1,250	7	375	1,466
Pendleton	1,992	1,757	69	1,539	2,767
Perry	6,031	4,226	72	5,258	5,218
Pike	14,878	10,550	204	15,493	11,493
Powell	2,006	1,716	33	1,575	2,269
Pulaski	6,570	12,970	257	4,384	14,434
Robertson	562	416	14	467	567
Rockcastle	1,345	3,543	37	1,089	4,328
Rowen	2,975	2,758	191	2,748	3,698
Russell	1,693	3,804	29	1,148	4,476
Scott	3,531	2,868	197	2,606	4,461
Shelby	4,429	3,423	178	3,326	5,390
Simpson	2,713	2,020	59	2,140	3,073
Spencer	1,216	935	27	910	1,456
Taylor	3,400	4,243	84	3,286	5,927
Todd	1,956	1,945	44	1,505	2,364
Trigg	2,619	1,913	56	1,905	2,512
Trimble	1,478	824	49	1,088	1,389
Union	3,479	1,847	68	3,090	2,524
Warren	9,643	12,184	602	7,937	16,167
Washington	2,147	2,008	43	1,786	2,804
Wayne	2,673	3,972	50	2,277	4,449
Webster	3,506	1,939	52	3,042	2,504
Whitley	3,889	7,007	125	3,575	7,851
Wolfe	1,814	951	19	1,394	1,257

Kansas Vote Since 1932

1932 (Pres.), Roosevelt, Dem., 424,204; Hoover, Rep., 349,498; Thomas, Soc., 18,276.

1936 (Pres.), Roosevelt, Dem., 464,520; Landon, Rep., 397,727; Thomas, Soc., 2,766; Lemke, Union, 494.

1940 (Pres.), Roosevelt, Dem., 364,725; Willkie, Rep., 489,169; Babson, Proh., 4,056; Thomas, Soc., 2,347.

1944 (Pres.), Roosevelt, Dem., 287,458; Dewey, Rep., 442,096; Watson, Proh., 2,609; Thomas, Soc., 1,613.

1948 (Pres.), Truman, Dem., 351,902; Dewey, Rep., 423,039; Watson, Proh., 6,468; Wallace, Prog., 4,603; Thomas, Soc., 2,807.

1952 (Pres.), Eisenhower, Rep., 616,302; Stevenson, Dem., 273,296; Hamblen, Proh., 6,038; Hoopes, Soc., 530.

1956 (Pres.), Eisenhower, Rep., 566,878; Stevenson. Dem., 296,317; Holtwick, Proh., 3,048.

1960 (Pres.), Kennedy, Dem., 363,213; Nixon, Rep., 561,474; Decker, Proh., 4,138.

1964 (Pres.), Johnson, Dem., 464,028; Goldwater, Rep., 386,579; Munn, Proh., 5,393; Hass, Soc. Labor, 1,901.

1968 (Pres.), Nixon, Rep., 478,674; Humphrey, Dem., 302,996; Wallace, 3d, 88,921; Munn, Proh., 2,192.

1972 (Pres.), Nixon, Rep., 619,812; McGovern, Dem., 270,287; Schmitz, Cons., 21,808; Munn, Proh., 4,188.

1976 (Pres.), Carter, Dem., 430,421; Ford, Rep., 502,752; McCarthy, Ind., 13,185; Anderson, Amer., 4,724; MacBride, Libertarian, 3,242; Maddox, Cons., 2,118; Bubar, Proh., 1,403.

1980 (Pres.), Reagan, Rep., 566,812; Carter, Dem., 326,150; Anderson, Ind., 68,231; Clark, Libertarian, 14,470; Shelton, American, 1,555; Hall, Com., 967; Bubar, Statesman, 821; Rarick, Conservative, 789.

Kentucky

	1980			1984	
County	Carter (D)	Reagan (R)	Anderson (I)	Mondale (D)	Reagan (R)
Adair	2,285	4,051	53	1,812	4,500
Allen	2,010	3,186	54	1,521	3,427
Anderson	2,567	2,052	90	1,717	3,425
Ballard	2,583	1,190	23	2,002	1,663
Barren	5,285	6,405	164	4,503	7,717
Bath	2,174	1,463	47	1,781	2,020
Bell	6,362	5,433	150	5,490	7,249
Boone	5,374	8,263	383	4,853	12,690
Bourbon	3,641	2,475	153	2,649	3,836
Boyd	10,702	10,367	496	9,600	10,925
Boyle	4,429	3,848	254	3,379	5,328
Bracken	1,420	1,154	36	1,131	1,804
Breathitt	3,916	1,532	68	3,441	2,855
Breckinridge	3,163	3,629	72	2,669	4,432
Bullitt	5,884	6,364	202	5,005	9,556
Butler	1,274	3,129	28	1,055	3,121
Caldwell	2,924	2,609	66	2,427	3,162
Calloway	6,809	4,498	318	5,028	6,442
Campbell	11,059	16,743	943	9,068	21,473
Carlisle	1,542	975	8	1,277	1,308
Carroll	2,127	1,076	82	1,564	1,824
Carter	3,782	3,934	86	3,985	4,566

Woodford	3,122	3,105	213	2,290	4,746
Totals	616,417	635,274	31,127	535,704	816,644

Kentucky Vote Since 1932

1932 (Pres.), Roosevelt, Dem., 580,574; Hoover, Rep., 394,716; Upshaw, Proh., 2,252; Thomas, Soc., 3,853; Reynolds, Soc. Labor, 1,396; Foster, Com., 272.

1936 (Pres.), Roosevelt, Dem., 541,944; Landon, Rep., 369,702; Lemke, Union, 12,501; Colvin, Proh., 929; Thomas, Soc., 627; Aiken, Soc. Labor, 294; Browder, Com., 204.

1940 (Pres.), Roosevelt, Dem., 557,222; Willkie, Rep., 410,384; Babson, Proh., 1,443; Thomas, Soc., 1,014.

1944 (Pres.), Roosevelt, Dem., 472,589; Dewey, Rep., 392,448; Watson, Proh., 2,023; Thomas, Soc., 535; Teichert, Soc. Labor, 326.

1948 (Pres.), Truman, Dem., 466,756; Dewey, Rep., 341,210; Thurmond, States' Rights, 10,411; Wallace, Prog., 1,567; Thomas, Soc., 1,284; Watson, Proh., 1,245; Teichert, Soc. Labor, 185.

1952 (Pres.), Eisenhower, Rep., 495,029; Stevenson, Dem., 495,729; Hamblen, Proh., 1,161; Hass, Soc. Labor, 893; Hallinan, Proh., 336.

1956 (Pres.), Eisenhower, Rep., 572,192; Stevenson, Dem., 476,453; Byrd, States' Rights, 2,657; Holtwick, Proh., 2,145; Hass, Soc. Labor, 358.

1960 (Pres.), Kennedy, Dem., 521,855; Nixon, Rep., 602,607.

1964 (Pres.), Johnson, Dem., 669,659; Goldwater, Rep., 372,977; John Kasper, Nat'l. States Rights, 3,469.

1968 (Pres.), Nixon, Rep., 462,411; Humphrey, Dem., 397,547; Wallace, 3d p., 193,098; Halstead, Soc. Worker, 2,843.

1972 (Pres.), Nixon, Rep., 676,446; McGovern, Dem., 371,159; Schmitz, Amer., 17,627; Jenness, Soc. Workers, 685; Hall, Com., 464; Spock, Peoples, 1,118.

1976 (Pres.), Carter, Dem., 615,717; Ford, Rep., 531,852; Anderson, Amer., 8,308; McCarthy, Ind., 6,837; Maddox, Amer. Ind., 2,328; MacBride, Libertarian, 814.

1980 (Pres.), Reagan, Rep., 635,274; Carter, Dem., 616,417; Anderson, Ind., 31,127; Clark, Libertarian, 5,531; McCormack, Respect For Life, 4,233; Commoner, Citizens, 1,304; Pulley, Socialist, 393; Hall, Com., 348.

Louisiana

Parish	1980 Carter (D)	Reagan (R)	Anderson (I)	1984 Mondale (D)	Reagan (R)
Acadia	9,948	11,533	416	9,262	14,906
Allen	6,057	3,328	110	4,842	4,474
Ascension	12,381	7,238	286	11,048	11,945
Assumption	4,679	4,001	153	4,660	5,433
Avoyelles	7,174	8,216	190	6,808	9,402
Beauregard	5,556	5,250	163	4,200	7,453
Bienville	4,123	3,508	51	3,530	4,587
Bossier	9,377	16,515	327	7,006	22,458
Caddo	36,422	51,202	1,128	35,727	63,433
Calcasieu	35,446	27,600	1,259	32,988	35,468
Caldwell	1,786	2,653	43	1,348	3,341
Cameron	2,221	1,449	82	1,639	2,354
Catahoula	2,414	2,942	38	1,649	3,640
Claiborne	3,443	3,538	53	2,788	4,349
Concordia	3,956	4,933	52	3,332	6,177
DeSoto	5,861	4,349	49	4,642	5,989
E. Baton Rouge	57,442	71,063	3,312	56,340	95,589
East Carroll	2,283	1,867	24	2,089	1,974
East Feliciana	4,033	2,650	53	4,122	4,166
Evangeline	6,722	7,412	160	6,981	8,680
Franklin	4,177	5,301	65	2,937	6,708
Grant	3,290	3,611	77	2,588	5,334
Iberia	9,681	14,273	410	11,170	17,627
Iberville	9,361	4,463	172	8,587	6,458
Jackson	3,609	3,923	56	2,568	5,034
Jefferson	50,870	99,403	3,578	41,118	124,501
Jefferson Davis	6,140	5,667	201	5,962	8,296
Lafayette	19,694	31,429	1,263	19,265	44,344
Lafourche	14,222	14,951	675	10,186	20,830
LaSalle	2,665	3,792	61	1,318	5,404
Lincoln	5,598	7,515	177	5,556	9,418
Livingston	11,319	10,666	287	8,913	17,465
Madison	3,264	2,531	16	2,906	2,849
Morehouse	4,856	7,254	65	4,829	8,585
Natchitoches	7,102	6,668	158	5,806	8,836
Orleans	106,858	74,302	4,246	119,547	86,003
Ouachita	16,306	29,799	495	15,525	37,070
Plaquemines	4,318	5,489	154	3,261	7,655
Pointe Coupee	6,395	3,667	105	6,732	5,477

Rapides	19,436	25,576	530	15,791	32,564
Red River	2,776	2,147	29	1,876	3,060
Richland	3,745	4,772	48	2,918	5,980
Sabine	5,100	4,265	74	2,980	6,295
St. Bernard	11,367	19,410	616	8,076	24,428
St. Charles	7,898	6,779	283	6,784	10,185
St. Helena	3,183	1,531	42	2,956	2,366
St. James	6,206	3,429	113	5,989	4,627
St. John The Baptist	7,647	5,819	261	7,646	9,093
St. Landry	17,125	14,940	332	17,951	18,855
St. Martin	7,760	6,701	281	8,707	9,698
St. Mary	10,506	10,378	339	5,553	8,805
St. Tammany	14,161	27,214	872	11,719	38,646
Tangipahoa	15,272	15,187	491	12,799	19,440
Tensas	2,046	1,645	25	1,628	1,956
Terrebonne	10,804	16,644	559	9,640	23,706
Union	3,841	5,130	60	2,916	6,585
Vermilion	9,743	10,481	473	9,033	12,721
Vernon	7,198	5,869	167	4,076	9,035
Washington	10,413	8,681	170	7,680	11,185
Webster	8,568	8,865	118	6,508	12,055
W. Baton Rouge	4,739	2,828	117	4,636	4,189
West Carroll	2,118	3,430	38	1,474	3,874
West Feliciana	2,341	1,237	40	2,296	2,097
Winn	3,411	3,944	57	2,633	-4,934
Totals	708,453	792,853	26,345	648,040	1,030,091

Louisiana Vote Since 1932

1932 (Pres.), Roosevelt, Dem., 249,418; Hoover, Rep., 18,863.

1936 (Pres.), Roosevelt, Dem., 292,894; Landon, Rep., 36,791.

1940 (Pres.), Roosevelt, Dem., 319,751; Willkie, Rep., 52,446.

1944 (Pres.), Roosevelt, Dem., 281,564; Dewey, Rep., 67,750

1948 (Pres.), Thurmond, States' Rights, 204,290; Truman, Dem., 136,344; Dewey, Rep., 72,657; Wallace, Prog., 3,035.

1952 (Pres.), Eisenhower, Rep., 306,925, Stevenson, Dem., 345,027.

1956 (Pres.), Eisenhower, Rep., 329,047; Stevenson, Dem., 243,977; Andrews, States' Rights, 44,520.

1960 (Pres.), Kennedy, Dem., 407,339; Nixon, Rep., 230,890; States' Rights (unpledged) 169,572.

1964 (Pres.), Johnson, Dem., 387,068; Goldwater, Rep., 509,225.

1968 (Pres.), Nixon, Rep., 257,535; Humphrey, Dem., 309,615; Wallace, 3d party, 530,300.

1972 (Pres.), Nixon, Rep., 686,852; McGovern, Dem., 298,142; Schmitz, Amer., 52,099; Jenness, Soc. Workers, 14,398.

1976 (Pres.), Carter, Dem., 661,365; Ford, Rep., 587,446; Maddox, Amer., 10,058; Hall, Com., 7,417; McCarthy, Ind., 6,588; MacBride, Libertarian, 3,325.

1980 (Pres.), Reagan, Rep., 792,853; Carter, Dem., 708,453; Anderson, Ind., 26,345; Rarick, Amer. Ind., 10,333; Clark, Libertarian, 8,240; Commoner, Citizens, 1,584; DeBerry, Soc. Work., 783.

Maine

City	1980 Carter (D)	Reagan (R)	Anderson (I)	1984 Mondale (D)	Reagan (R)
Auburn	5,071	4,886	1,136	4,430	6,994
Augusta	4,470	4,271	1,262	4,451	5,995
Bangor	6,032	6,082	1,562	6,155	8,389
Bath	2,173	2,005	398	1,714	2,899
Biddeford	5,788	2,738	888	4,886	3,863
Brewer	1,767	2,526	435	1,461	3,193
Gardiner	1,325	1,265	415	1,216	1,942
Lewiston	11,365	6,205	1,875	9,853	9,480
Old Town	2,454	1,480	466	2,217	2,087
Portland	14,815	9,122	3,325	15,868	13,055
Rockland	1,140	1,366	292	1,051	2,169
Saco	3,240	2,583	695	3,094	3,761
Sanford	4,020	3,124	695	3,518	4,578
South Portland	5,371	4,519	1,280	5,377	6,653
Waterville	4,125	2,952	877	4,075	3,873
Westbrook	3,882	2,952	693	3,345	4,456
Totals	220,974	238,522	53,327	212,190	336,113

Maine Vote Since 1932

1932 (Pres.), Roosevelt, Dem., 128,907; Hoover, Rep., 166,631; Thomas, Soc., 2,439; Reynolds, Soc. Labor, 255; Foster, Com., 162.

1936 (Pres.), Landon, Rep., 168,823; Roosevelt, Dem., 126,333; Lemke, Union, 7,581; Thomas. Soc., 783; Colvin, Proh., 334; Browder, Com., 257; Aiken, Soc. Labor, 129.

1940 (Pres.), Roosevelt, Dem., 156,478; Willkie, Rep., 165,951; Browder, Com., 411.

1944 (Pres.), Roosevelt, Dem., 140,631; Dewey, Rep., 155,434; Teichert, Soc. Labor, 335.

1948 (Pres.), Truman, Dem., 111,916; · Dewey, Rep., 150,234; Wallace, Prog., 1,884; Thomas, Soc., 547; Teichert, Soc. Labor, 206.

1952 (Pres.), Eisenhower, Rep., 232,353; Stevenson, Dem., 118,806; Hallinan, Prog., 332; Hass, Soc. Labor, 156; Hoopes, Soc., 138; scattered, 1.

1956 (Pres.), Eisenhower, Rep., 249,238; Stevenson, Dem., 102,468.

1960 (Pres.), Kennedy, Dem., 181,159; Nixon, Rep., 240,608.

1964 (Pres.), Johnson, Dem., 262,264; Goldwater, Rep., 118,701.

1968 (Pres.), Nixon, Rep., 169,254; Humphrey, Dem., 217,312; Wallace, 3d party, 6,370.

1972 (Pres.), Nixon, Rep., 256,458; McGovern, Dem., 160,584; scattered, 229.

1976 (Pres.), Carter, Dem., 232,279; Ford, Rep., 236,320; McCarthy, Ind., 10,874; Bubar, Proh., 3,495.

1980 (Pres.), Reagan, Rep., 238,522; Carter, Dem., 220,974; Anderson, Ind., 53,327; Clark, Libertarian, 5,119; Commoner, Citizens, 4,394; Hall, Com., 591; write-ins, 84.

Maryland

County	1980 Carter (D)	Reagan (R)	Anderson (I)	1984 Mondale (D)	Reagan (R)
Allegany	12,167	17,512	1,486	10,658	18,764
Anne Arundel	50,780	69,443	10,020	46,054	89,993
Baltimore	121,280	132,490	23,096	102,914	166,685
Calvert	4,745	5,440	590	5,272	7,958
Caroline	2,833	3,582	291	2,109	4,702
Carroll	10,393	19,859	2,243	8,626	23,977
Cecil	7,937	9,673	1,037	5,904	9,934
Charles	8,887	11,807	1,153	9,967	15,493
Dorchester	4,908	5,160	360	3,079	6,467
Frederick	13,629	22,033	2,891	12,370	28,409
Garrett	2,708	5,475	270	2,370	6,652
Harford	20,042	26,713	3,761	16,518	35,812
Howard	20,702	24,272	6,028	24,565	33,921
Kent	2,986	2,889	371	2,272	3,683
Montgomery	105,822	125,515	32,730	137,304	137,775
Prince George's	98,757	78,977	14,574	132,197	91,002
Queen Anne's	3,820	4,749	480	2,860	6,542
St. Mary's	6,773	8,267	892	6,196	10,614
Somerset	3,342	3,312	215	2,373	4,222
Talbot	3,995	6,044	570	3,029	7,597
Washington	14,118	22,901	1,689	12,813	25,687
Wicomico	9,431	11,229	1,092	7,750	15,358
Worcester	4,195	5,362	586	3,589	7,686
BALTIMORE CITY	191,911	57,902	13,112	196,365	77,362
Totals	726,161	680,606	119,537	757,635	836,295

Maryland Vote Since 1932

1932 (Pres.), Roosevelt, Dem., 314,314; Hoover, Rep., 184,184; Thomas, Soc., 10,489; Reynolds, Soc. Labor, 1,036; Foster, Com., 1,031.

1936 (Pres.), Roosevelt, Dem., 389,612; Landon, Rep., 231,435; Thomas, Soc., 1,629; Aiken, Soc. Labor, 1,305; Browder, Com., 915.

1940 (Pres.), Roosevelt, Dem., 384,546; Willkie, Rep., 269,534; Thomas, Soc., 4,093; Browder, Com., 1,274; Aiken, Soc. Labor, 657.

1944 (Pres.), Roosevelt, Dem., 315,490; Dewey, Rep., 292,949.

1948 (Pres.), Truman, Dem., 286,521; Dewey, Rep., 294,814; Wallace, Prog., 9,983; Thomas, Soc., 2,941; Thurmond, States' Rights, 2,476; Wright, write-in, 2,294.

1952 (Pres.), Eisenhower, Rep., 499,424; Stevenson, Dem., 395,337; Hallinan, Prog., 7,313.

1956 (Pres.), Eisenhower, Rep., 559,738; Stevenson, Dem., 372,613.

1960 (Pres.), Kennedy, Dem., 565,800; Nixon, Rep., 489,538.

1964 (Pres.), Johnson, Dem., 730,912; Goldwater, Rep., 385,495; write-in, 50.

1968 (Pres.), Nixon, Rep., 517,995; Humphrey, Dem., 538,310; Wallace, 3d party, 178,734.

1972 (Pres.), Nixon, Rep., 829,305; McGovern, Dem., 505,781; Schmitz, Amer., 18,726.

1976 (Pres.), Carter, Dem., 759,612; Ford, Rep., 672,661.

1980 (Pres.), Reagan, Rep., 680,606; Carter, Dem.. 726,161; Anderson, Ind., 119,537; Clark, Libertarian, 14,192.

Massachusetts

County	1980 Carter (D)	Reagan (R)	Anderson (I)	1984 Mondale (D)	Reagan (R)
Boston	95,133	58,656	22,577	131,015	74,281
Brockton	12,751	15,350	4,633	13,983	17,011
Cambridge	24,337	7,952	6,694	32,409	9,937
Fall River	19,644	9,958	3,694	20,898	11,651
Framingham	12,275	11,979	4,940	14,368	15,074
Lawrence	12,145	8,020	2,341	10,986	9,871
Lowell	16,353	12,668	3,791	15,033	16,825
Lynn	15,777	11,966	3,911	17,099	14,470
New Bedford	18,014	13,217	3,843	22,067	13,143
Newton	20,173	15,621	7,778	27,299	16,176
Quincy	17,977	18,038	5,328	19,275	20,118
Somerville	16,931	9,533	4,143	21,056	11,315
Springfield	26,414	17,694	6,327	29,379	21,441
Worcester	31,146	23,305	8,411	31,100	26,267
Totals	1,053,802	1,057,631	382,539	1,219,513	1,293,367

Massachusetts Vote Since 1932

1932 (Pres.), Roosevelt, Dem., 800,148; Hoover, Rep., 736,959; Thomas, Soc., 34,305; Foster, Com., 4,821; Reynolds, Soc. Labor, 2,668; Upshaw, Proh., 1,142.

1936 (Pres.), Roosevelt, Dem., 942,716; Landon, Rep., 768,613; Lemke, Union, 118,639; Thomas, Soc., 5,111; Browder, Com., 2,930; Aiken, Soc. Labor, 1,305; Colvin, Proh., 1,032.

1940 (Pres.), Roosevelt, Dem., 1,076,522; Willkie, Rep., 939,700; Thomas, Soc., 4,091; Browder, Com., 3,806; Aiken, Soc. Labor, 1,492; Babson, Proh., 1,370.

1944 (Pres.), Roosevelt, Dem., 1,035,296; Dewey, Rep., 921,350; Teichert, Soc. Labor, 2,780; Watson, Proh., 973.

1948 (Pres.), Truman, Dem., 1,151,788; Dewey, Rep., 909,370; Wallace, Prog., 38,157; Teichert, Soc. Labor, 5,535; Watson, Proh., 1,663.

1952 (Pres.), Eisenhower, Rep., 1,292,325; Stevenson, Dem., 1,083,525; Hallinan, Prog., 4,636; Hass, Soc. Labor, 1,957; Hamblen, Proh., 886; scattered, 69; blanks, 41,150.

1956 (Pres.), Eisenhower, Rep., 1,393,197; Stevenson, Dem., 948,190; Hass, Soc. Labor, 5,573; Holtwick, Proh., 1,205; others, 341.

1960 (Pres.), Kennedy, Dem., 1,487,174; Nixon, Rep., 976,750; Hass, Soc. Labor, 3,892; Decker, Proh., 1,633; others, 31; blank and void, 26,024.

1964 (Pres.), Johnson, Dem., 1,786,422; Goldwater, Rep., 549,727; Hass, Soc. Labor, 4,755; Munn, Proh., 3,735; scattered, 159; blank, 48,104.

1968 (Pres.), Nixon, Rep., 766,844; Humphrey, Dem., 1,469,218; Wallace, 3d party, 87,088; Blomen, Soc. Labor, 6,180; Munn, Proh., 2,369; scattered, 53; blanks, 25,394.

1972 (Pres.), Nixon, Rep., 1,112,078; McGovern, Dem., 1,332,540; Jenness, Soc. Workers, 10,600; Fisher, Soc. Labor, 129; Schmitz, Amer., 2,877; Spock, Peoples, 101; Hall, Com., 46; Hospers, Libertarian, 43; scattered, 342.

1976 (Pres.), Carter, Dem., 1,429,475; Ford, Rep., 1,030,276; McCarthy, Ind., 65,637; Camejo, Soc. Workers, 8,138; Anderson, Amer., 7,555; La Rouche, U.S. Labor, 4,922; MacBride, Libertarian, 135.

1980 · (Pres.), Reagan, Rep., 1,057,631; Carter, Dem., 1,053,802; Anderson, Ind., 382,539; Clark, Libertarian, 22,038; DeBerry, Soc. Workers, 3,735; Commoner, Citizens, 2,056; McReynolds, Socialist, 62; Bubar, Statesman, 34; Griswold, Workers World, 19; scattered, 2,382.

Michigan

County	1980 Carter (D)	Reagan (R)	Anderson (I)	1984 Mondale (D)	Reagan (R)
Alcona	1,857	2,905	247	1,616	3,223
Alger	2,242	2,059	263	2,018	2,175
Allegan	9,877	20,560	1,984	8,389	23,762
Alpena	5,834	6,901	913	5,154	8,262
Antrim	2,909	4,706	602	2,507	5,731
Arenac	2,547	3,436	333	2,410	3,438

Baraga	1,609	2,046	201	1,818	1,965
Barry	6,857	12,006	1,399	5,948	14,245
Bay	24,517	25,331	3,886	22,914	26,402
Benzie	1,842	3,054	455	1,866	3,590
Berrien	22,152	41,458	3,422	21,167	43,093
Branch	4,635	10,224	1,102	3,800	11,004
Calhoun	23,022	30,912	4,468	20,194	34,446
Cass	7,058	11,206	1,156	6,456	11,219
Charlevoix	3,741	5,053	816	3,178	6,433
Cheboygan	3,938	5,221	638	2,380	4,337
Chippewa	5,268	7,059	951	4,575	8,134
Clare	4,164	5,719	663	3,763	6,584
Clinton	7,539	14,968	1,736	6,261	17,468
Crawford	1,826	2,652	390	1,558	3,303
Delta	8,475	8,146	849	7,934	8,951
Dickinson	5,694	6,614	596	5,614	6,880
Eaton	12,742	22,927	3,533	10,290	27,520
Emmet	3,724	5,930	1,134	3,254	7,760
Genesee	90,393	78,572	12,274	89,491	92,943
Gladwin	3,733	4,509	463	3,368	5,401
Gogebic	5,254	4,388	493	5,584	4,026
Grand Traverse	7,150	14,484	2,568	6,375	15,820
Gratiot	4,916	9,294	1,193	4,017	10,507
Hillsdale	4,375	10,951	882	3,626	12,088
Houghton	6,858	7,926	1,423	6,434	8,644
Huron	4,434	10,553	976	3,967	11,073
Ingham	48,278	56,777	17,139	46,403	68,747
Ionia	7,039	12,040	1,539	5,735	14,164
Iosco	4,255	6,680	739	3,572	7,341
Iron	3,742	3,507	371	3,558	3,466
Isabella	7,293	10,407	2,511	6,236	11,803
Jackson	23,685	33,749	4,165	17,840	39,606
Kalamazoo	34,528	48,669	10,833	32,333	58,363
Kalkaska	1,807	2,802	260	965	2,261
Kent	72,790	112,604	17,913	66,212	137,433
Keweenaw	570	583	87	628	599
Lake	2,041	1,730	187	1,845	2,125
Lapeer	9,671	15,996	1,868	7,800	19,222
Leelanau	2,348	4,585	839	2,498	5,356
Lenawee	12,935	20,366	2,230	11,029	22,454
Livingston	12,626	25,012	3,247	10,720	31,846
Luce	992	1,659	177	833	1,715
Mackinac	2,262	3,021	415	1,238	2,208
Macomb	120,125	154,155	18,975	80,025	155,701
Manistee	4,164	5,662	699	3,917	6,328
Marquette	13,312	13,181	2,481	14,074	14,194
Mason	4,134	7,137	825	3,803	8,202
Mecosta	5,228	7,754	1,322	4,065	9,085
Menominee	4,962	6,170	452	4,425	6,617
Midland	12,019	17,828	3,152	10,769	21,521
Missaukee	1,563	3,221	230	1,256	3,970
Monroe	20,578	25,612	3,111	19,622	29,419
Montcalm	6,706	10,822	1,309	5,613	13,351
Montmorency	1,654	2,400	195	1,387	2,913
Muskegon	26,645	36,512	4,094	25,364	39,445
Newaygo	5,236	8,918	850	4,513	10,676
Oakland	164,869	253,211	38,273	149,455	303,446
Oceana	3,386	5,465	570	2,576	5,897
Ogemaw	3,426	4,169	425	3,096	4,824
Ontonagon	2,375	2,569	237	1,350	2,464
Osceola	2,650	4,902	466	2,127	5,923
Oscoda	1,325	1,915	183	951	2,239
Otsego	2,666	3,771	493	2,149	4,680
Ottawa	18,435	51,217	4,903	15,000	60,142
Presque Isle	2,952	3,486	382	2,481	4,207
Roscommon	3,763	5,280	508	3,309	6,259
Saginaw	41,650	45,233	5,677	29,666	40,189
St. Clair	20,410	31,021	3,592	4,160	8,774
St. Joseph	6,318	13,631	1,283	5,304	13,912
Sanilac	4,898	12,158	863	4,125	12,640
Schoolcraft	1,964	2,097	243	1,929	2,139
Shiawassee	11,985	15,756	2,121	9,514	18,756
Tuscola	7,632	13,306	1,266	5,933	14,325
Van Buren	9,248	14,451	1,691	8,859	16,426
Washtenaw	51,013	48,699	13,463	55,009	58,369
Wayne	522,024	315,532	43,608	481,926	353,637
Wexford	4,173	6,027	752	3,329	7,341
Totals	1,661,532	1,915,225	275,223	1,468,512	2,147,147

Michigan Vote Since 1932

1932 (Pres.), Roosevelt, Dem., 871,700; Hoover, Rep., 739,894; Thomas, Soc., 39,025; Foster, Com., 9,318; Upshaw, Proh., 2,893; Reynolds, Soc. Labor, 1,041; Harvey, Lib., 217.

1936 (Pres.), Roosevelt, Dem., 1,016,794; Landon, Rep., 699,733; Lemke, Union, 75,795; Thomas, Soc., 8,208; Browder, Com., 3,384; Aiken, Soc. Labor, 600; Colvin, Proh., 579.

1940 (Pres.), Roosevelt, Dem., 1,032,991; Willkie, Rep., 1,039,917; Thomas, Soc., 7,593; Browder, Com., 2,834; Babson, Proh., 1,795; Aiken, Soc. Labor, 795.

1944 (Pres.), Roosevelt, Dem., 1,106,899; Dewey, Rep., 1,084,423; Watson, Proh., 6,503; Thomas, Soc., 4,598; Smith, America First, 1,530; Teichert, Soc. Labor, 1,264.

1948 (Pres.), Truman, Dem., 1,003,448; Dewey, Rep., 1,038,595; Wallace, Prog., 46,515; Watson, Proh., 13,052; Thomas, Soc. 6,063; Teichert, Soc. Labor, 1,263; Dobbs, Soc. Workers, 672.

1952 (Pres.), Eisenhower, Rep., 1,551,529; Stevenson, Dem., 1,230,657; Hamblen, Proh., 10,331; Hallinan, Prog., 3,922; Hass, Soc. Labor, 1,495; Dobbs, Soc. Workers, 655; scattering, 3.

1956 (Pres.), Eisenhower, Rep., 1,713,647; Stevenson, Dem., 1,359,898; Holtwick, Proh., 6,923.

1960 (Pres.), Kennedy, Dem., 1,687,269; Nixon, Rep., 1,620,428; Dobbs, Soc. Workers, 4,347; Decker, Proh., 2,029; Daly, Tax Cut, 1,767; Hass, Soc. Labor, 1,718; Ind. American, 539.

1964 (Pres.), Johnson, Dem., 2,136,615; Goldwater, Rep., 1,060,152; DeBerry, Soc. Workers, 3,817; Hass, Soc. Labor, 1,704; Proh. (no candidate listed), 699, scattering, 145.

1968 (Pres.), Nixon, Rep., 1,370,665; Humphrey, Dem., 1,593,082; Wallace, 3d party, 331,968; Halstead, Soc. Worker, 4,099; Blomen, Soc. Labor, 1,762; Cleaver, New Politics, 4,585; Munn, Proh., 60; scattering, 29.

1972 (Pres.), Nixon, Rep., 1,961,721; McGovern, Dem., 1,459,435; Schmitz, Amer., 63,321; Fisher, Soc. Labor, 2,437; Jenness, Soc. Workers, 1,603; Hall, Com., 1,210.

1976 (Pres.), Carter, Dem., 1,696,714; Ford, Rep., 1,893,742; McCarthy, Ind., 47,905; MacBride, Libertarian, 5,406; People's, 3,504, Camejo, Soc. Workers, 1,804; LaRouche, U.S. Labor, 1,366; Levin, Soc. Labor, 1,148; scattering, 2,160.

1980 (Pres.), Reagan, Rep., 1,915,225; Carter, Dem., 1,661,532; Anderson, Ind., 275,223; Clark, Libertarian, 41,597; Commoner, Citizens, 11,930; Hall, Com., 3,262; Griswold, Workers World, 30; Greaves, American, 21; Bubar, Statesman, 9.

Minnesota

	1980			1984	
County	Carter (D)	Reagan (R)	Anderson (I)	Mondale (D)	Reagan (R)
Aitkin	3,677	3,396	380	3,943	3,422
Anoka	45,532	33,100	6,828	47,855	43,683
Becker	5,221	6,848	866	5,451	7,534
Beltrami	7,432	6,481	1,254	7,477	7,411
Benton	5,272	5,513	646	4,922	6,826
Big Stone	1,814	1,950	249	1,994	1,820
Blue Earth	10,930	11,966	2,698	11,877	14,298
Brown	4,915	8,051	842	4,469	8,398
Carlton	8,822	4,760	883	9,008	4,509
Carver	6,621	9,909	1,496	6,728	11,964
Cass	4,717	6,119	434	3,742	5,386
Chippewa	3,164	4,252	532	3,047	3,960
Chisago	6,240	5,017	939	6,683	6,278
Clay	8,940	10,447	2,773	9,888	10,937
Clearwater	1,955	1,919	185	1,917	2,066
Cook	871	1,174	182	1,129	1,218
Cottonwood	2,958	4,258	535	2,761	3,404
Crow Wing	9,323	10,844	1,046	8,639	11,276
Dakota	43,433	40,708	8,588	47,593	53,565
Dodge	2,698	3,900	367	2,780	4,428
Douglas	5,530	7,778	844	5,741	9,002
Faribault	3,620	6,206	525	3,993	5,690
Fillmore	4,010	6,452	650	4,351	6,340
Freeborn	8,212	8,475	808	9,338	8,413
Goodhue	8,566	9,329	1,964	8,675	11,161
Grant	1,822	2,054	333	1,867	2,111
Hennepin	239,592	194,998	56,390	236,582	205,505
Houston	3,218	5,582	477	3,512	5,643
Hubbard	2,840	4,172	365	2,806	4,621
Isanti	5,457	4,480	641	4,040	4,094
Itasca	12,138	8,368	1,080	11,214	9,036
Jackson	3,062	3,391	463	3,437	3,131
Kanabec	2,654	2,500	269	2,660	3,026
Kandiyohi	8,038	8,480	1,244	8,402	9,537
Kittson	1,407	1,875	243	1,610	1,716
Koochiching	4,181	3,433	496	4,236	3,458
LacQuiParle	2,457	2,981	334	2,685	2,731
Lake	3,864	2,414	443	3,984	1,621
Lake O'Woods	763	1,052	128	824	1,094
Le Sueur	5,161	5,478	731	5,069	6,033
Lincoln	1,640	2,122	295	1,827	1,904
Lyon	5,626	5,852	1,129	5,343	7,078
McLeod	4,987	7,819	852	4,864	8,788
Mahnomen	1,175	1,275	153	1,241	1,327
Marshall	2,636	3,638	397	2,705	4,750
Martin	4,301	7,057	751	4,463	7,262
Meeker	4,238	5,032	668	4,161	5,508
Mille Lacs	4,443	3,860	550	4,013	4,306
Morrison	6,930	6,296	559	4,419	5,812
Mower	10,538	7,908	1,465	12,497	8,050
Murray	2,714	3,004	359	2,841	2,778
Nicollet	5,400	6,436	1,519	5,784	7,472

Nobles	4,703	4,706	657	4,618	4,876
Norman	2,253	2,192	369	2,204	2,189
Olmsted	13,983	22,704	3,638	16,107	27,543
Otter Tail	9,108	15,091	1,538	9,714	15,653
Pennington	3,101	3,715	472	2,913	3,536
Pine	5,121	3,899	467	5,222	4,491
Pipestone	2,392	3,207	561	2,390	3,042
Polk	7,151	9,036	1,207	7,033	8,615
Pope	2,527	3,159	354	2,757	3,064
Ramsey	124,774	78,860	23,222	151,231	95,356
Red Lake	1,318	1,223	116	1,294	1,184
Redwood	2,952	5,993	548	2,323	4,474
Renville	4,058	5,544	653	3,971	5,571
Rice	9,531	8,168	2,414	10,504	9,947
Rock	2,089	3,164	397	2,188	2,970
Roseau	2,616	3,358	259	2,319	3,445
St. Louis	69,403	33,407	8,719	74,739	33,294
Scott	9,115	9,018	1,475	6,830	11,564
Sherburne	6,229	6,035	985	1,191	1,197
Sibley	2,521	4,460	509	2,761	4,638
Stearns	21,862	24,888	3,555	20,069	29,206
Steele	5,095	7,805	1,087	4,726	8,177
Stevens	2,559	3,283	524	2,451	3,250
Swift	3,245	2,943	511	3,530	2,891
Todd	4,975	6,451	451	4,657	6,578
Traverse	1,258	1,574	159	1,331	1,399
Wabasha	3,712	4,886	549	3,870	5,296
Wadena	2,635	4,089	265	2,454	4,404
Waseca	3,535	4,801	777	3,527	5,509
Washington	25,634	22,718	5,050	13,590	14,018
Watonwan	2,442	3,629	415	1,254	1,760
Wilkin	1,496	2,224	318	1,409	2,367
Winona	9,814	10,332	1,780	9,565	11,975
Wright	12,383	12,293	1,692	10,843	13,198
Yellow Med	2,833	4,004	456	2,776	3,551
Totals	954,173	873,268	174,997	971,648	941,609

Minnesota Vote Since 1932

1932 (Pres.), Roosevelt, Dem., 600,806; Hoover, Rep., 363,959; Thomas, Soc., 25,476; Foster, Com., 6,101; Coxey, Farm.-Lab., 5,731; Reynolds, Ind., 770.

1936 (Pres.), Roosevelt, Dem., 698,811; Landon, Rep., 350,461; Lemke, Union, 74,296; Thomas, Soc., 2,872; Browder, Com., 2,574; Aiken, Soc. Labor, 961.

1940 (Pres.), Roosevelt, Dem., 644,196; Willkie, Rep., 596,274; Thomas, Soc., 5,454; Browder, Com., 2,711; Aiken, Ind., 2,553.

1944 (Pres.), Roosevelt, Dem., 589,864; Dewey, Rep., 527,416; Thomas, Soc., 5,073; Teichert, Ind. Gov't., 3,176.

1948 (Pres.), Truman, Dem., 692,966; Dewey, Rep., 483,617; Wallace, Prog., 27,866; Thomas, Soc., 4,646; Teichert, Soc. Labor, 2,525; Dobbs, Soc. Workers, 606.

1952 (Pres.), Eisenhower, Rep., 763,211; Stevenson, Dem., 608,458; Hallinan, Prog., 2,666; Hass, Soc. Labor, 2,383; Hamblen, Proh., 2,147; Dobbs, Soc. Workers, 618.

1956 (Pres.), Eisenhower, Rep., 719,302; Stevenson, Dem., 617,525; Hass, Soc. Labor (Ind. Gov.), 2,080; Dobbs, Soc. Workers, 1,098.

1960 (Pres.), Kennedy, Dem., 779,933; Nixon, Rep., 757,915; Dobbs, Soc. Workers, 3,077; Industrial Gov., 962.

1964 (Pres.), Johnson, Dem., 991,117; Goldwater, Rep., 559,624; DeBerry, Soc. Workers, 1,177; Hass, Industrial Gov., 2,544.

1968 (Pres.), Nixon, Rep., 658,643; Humphrey, Dem., 857,738; Wallace, 3d party, 68,931; scattered, 2,443; Halstead, Soc. Worker, 808; Blomen, Ind. Gov't., 285; Mitchell, Com., 415; Cleaver, Peace, 935; McCarthy, write-in, 585; scattered, 170.

1972 (Pres.), Nixon, Rep., 898,269; McGovern, Dem., 802,346; Schmitz, Amer., 31,407; Spock, Peoples, 2,805; Fisher, Soc. Labor, 4,261; Jenness, Soc. Workers, 940; Hall, Com., 662; scattered, 962.

1976 (Pres.), Carter, Dem., 1,070,440; Ford, Rep., 819,395; McCarthy, Ind., 35,490; Anderson, Amer., 13,592; Camejo, Soc. Workers, 4,149; MacBride, Libertarian, 3,529; Hall, Com., 1,092.

1980 (Pres.), Reagan, Rep., 873, 268; Carter, Dem., 954,173; Anderson, Ind., 174,997; Clark, Libertarian, 31,593; Commoner, Citizens, 8,406; Hall, Com., 1,117; DeBerry, Soc. Workers, 711; Griswold, Workers World, 698; McReynolds, Socialist, 536; write-ins, 281.

Mississippi

	1980			1984	
	Carter	Reagan	Anderson	Mondale	Reagan
County	(D)	(R)	(I)	(D)	(R)
Adams	7,228	7,523	151	7,835	9,414
Alcom	6,242	5,196	898	4,747	7,197
Amite	3,229	2,653	43	2,554	3,443
Attala	4,117	3,975	71	3,291	4,839
Benton	2,094	1,254	35	1,717	1,737
Bolivar	8,839	5,148	280	8,761	6,937
Calhoun	3,295	2,579	64	1,748	3,571
Carroll	2,037	2,153	22	1,462	2,823
Chickasaw	3,622	2,540	71	2,329	3,605
Choctaw	1,729	1,927	26	1,168	2,491
Claiborne	3,032	1,129	22	3,178	1,293
Clarke	3,303	3,303	41	2,260	4,547
Clay	4,275	3,439	124	4,046	4,112
Coahoma	7,030	4,592	256	6,873	5,697
Copiah	5,517	4,461	76	4,591	5,706
Covington	2,956	3,471	39	2,247	4,177
DeSoto	6,344	9,655	237	4,369	12,576
Forrest	8,274	12,656	275	6,773	15,694
Franklin	2,040	2,026	23	1,477	2,550
George	2,757	3,052	64	1,655	4,346
Greene	1,740	1,772	23	1,297	2,744
Grenada	4,182	3,993	59	3,325	5,181
Hancock	3,544	5,088	159	2,637	7,606
Harrison	16,318	25,175	822	12,387	33,704
Hinds	39,369	48,135	1,414	43,051	55,067
Holmes	5,463	2,693	57	5,528	3,194
Humphreys	2,970	1,841	68	2,587	2,403
Issaquena	598	349	5	501	512
Itawamba	4,852	2,906	57	2,673	4,584
Jackson	12,226	22,498	653	8,821	29,585
Jasper	3,813	2,781	34	3,038	3,713
Jefferson	2,871	751	41	1,898	532
Jefferson Davis	3,831	2,280	24	2,635	2,871
Jones	11,117	12,900	155	7,113	17,484
Kemper	2,601	1,822	12	2,089	2,355
Lafayette	4,887	4,366	243	3,638	5,993
Lamar	3,005	5,395	84	1,953	7,919
Lauderdale	9,918	14,727	784	7,555	19,083
Lawrence	2,692	2,781	49	2,210	3,893
Leake	4,033	3,624	40	2,844	4,663
Lee	10,047	8,326	321	6,198	13,283
Leflore	7,498	5,798	166	7,145	7,596
Lincoln	5,213	7,286	75	4,363	8,710
Lowndes	6,187	9,973	140	6,061	12,049
Madison	7,621	6,024	276	7,813	9,090
Marion	5,366	5,218	62	3,757	7,355
Marshall	7,153	3,455	121	5,835	4,383
Monroe	6,998	4,793	177	4,437	7,387
Montgomery	2,730	2,479	42	1,869	3,093
Neshoba	3,872	5,165	72	2,648	6,717
Newton	3,455	4,317	86	2,127	5,911
Noxubee	3,434	1,970	47	2,924	2,123
Oktibbeha	6,039	6,300	258	5,079	7,555
Panola	6,179	4,219	149	5,817	5,432
Pearl River	5,028	6,822	161	3,063	9,893
Perry	1,957	2,255	25	1,415	3,098
Pike	6,694	6,661	129	6,137	8,254
Pontotoc	4,499	3,198	58	2,612	4,728
Prentiss	4,832	3,264	40	2,890	4,823
Quitman	2,926	1,691	83	2,343	2,198
Rankin	8,047	16,650	296	5,643	21,151
Scott	4,043	4,645	72	3,274	5,663
Sharkey	1,957	996	28	1,723	1,487
Simpson	4,015	5,190	70	2,894	5,983
Smith	2,474	3,772	46	1,573	5,116
Stone	1,821	1,888	53	1,185	2,980
Sunflower	5,035	3,728	82	4,876	5,142
Tallahatchie	3,467	2,183	45	2,726	2,898
Tate	3,892	3,343	80	2,846	4,787
Tippah	3,878	3,338	116	2,568	4,707
Tishomingo	4,595	2,489	79	2,879	3,527
Tunica	2,198	954	24	2,221	1,595
Union	5,001	3,545	94	2,778	5,837
Walthall	2,960	2,703	34	2,219	3,332
Warren	7,489	10,151	274	7,896	12,798
Washington	10,722	8,978	186	10,751	12,362
Wayne	3,494	3,844	26	2,818	5,000
Webster	2,178	2,386	75	1,395	3,384
Wilkinson	2,981	1,442	25	2,633	1,725
Winston	4,416	3,998	65	3,543	5,192
Yalobusha	3,432	2,224	78	2,337	2,934
Yazoo	5,464	4,819	99	5,023	6,259
Totals	429,281	441,089	12,036	351,195	577,378

Mississippi Vote Since 1932

1932 (Pres.), Roosevelt, Dem., 140,168; Hoover, Rep., 5,180; Thomas, Soc., 686.

1936 (Pres.), Roosevelt, Dem., 157,318; Landon, Rep.,
Howard faction, 2,760; Rowlands faction, 1,675 total
4,435; Thomas, Soc., 329.

1940 (Pres.), Roosevelt, Dem., 168,252; Willkie, Ind. Rep.,
4,550; Rep., 2,814; total, 7,364; Thomas, Soc., 103.

1944 (Pres.), Roosevelt, Dem., 158,515; Dewey, Rep., 3,742;
Reg. Dem., 9,964; Ind. Rep., 7,859.

1948 (Pres.), Thurmond, States' Rights, 167,538; Truman,
Dem., 19,384; Dewey, Rep., 5,043; Wallace, Prog., 225.

1952 (Pres.), Eisenhower, Ind. vote pledged to Rep. candidate, 112,966; Stevenson, Dem., 172,566.

1956 (Pres.), Stevenson, Dem., 144,498; Eisenhower, Rep.,
56,372; Black and Tan Grand Old Party, 4,313; total,
60,685; Byrd, Ind., 42,966.

1960 (Pres.), Democratic unpledged electors, 116,248;
Kennedy, Dem., 108,362; Nixon, Rep., 73,561. Mississippi's victorious slate of 8 unpledged Democratic electors
cast their votes for Sen. Harry F. Byrd (D-Va.).

1964 (Pres.), Johnson, Dem., 52,618; Goldwater, Rep.,
356,528.

1968 (Pres.), Nixon, Rep., 88,516; Humphrey, Dem.,
150,644; Wallace, 3d party, 415,349.

1972 (Pres.), Nixon, Rep., 505,125; McGovern, Dem.,
126,782; Schmitz, Amer., 11,598; Jenness, Soc. Workers,
2,458.

1976 (Pres.), Carter, Dem., 381,309; Ford, Rep., 366,846;
Anderson, Amer., 6,678; McCarthy, Ind., 4,074; Maddox,
Ind., 4,049; Camejo, Soc. Workers, 2,805; MacBride, Lib-
ertarian, 2,609.

1980 (Pres.), Reagan, Rep., 441,089; Carter, Dem., 429,281;
Anderson, Ind., 12,036; Clark, Libertarian, 5,465; Griswold, Workers World, 2,402; Pulley, Soc. Worker, 2,347.

Missouri

| | 1980 | | | 1984 | |
County	Carter (D)	Reagan (R)	Anderson (I)	Mondale (D)	Reagan (R)
Adair	3,507	5,513	414	3,119	6,430
Andrew	2,575	3,690	245	2,457	4,252
Atchison	1,273	2,096	151	1,219	2,277
Audrain	5,168	6,347	233	4,667	7,281
Barry	4,193	7,038	150	3,292	6,983
Barton	1,901	3,337	115	1,350	4,001
Bates	3,297	4,061	114	2,889	4,223
Benton	2,241	3,451	126	2,251	3,805
Bollinger	2,160	2,863	35	1,923	2,778
Boone	18,527	16,313	3,519	19,364	26,599
Buchanan	16,967	16,551	1,301	14,393	18,202
Butler	5,605	8,342	181	4,696	8,722
Caldwell	1,541	2,551	108	1,382	2,678
Callaway	5,560	6,755	420	4,769	9,685
Camden	3,416	6,541	218	3,088	8,057
Cape Girardeau	8,625	14,861	873	7,346	17,404
Carroll	2,130	3,201	130	1,900	0,465
Carter	1,087	1,218	37	916	1,402
Cass	8,198	10,105	667	7,517	14,456
Cedar	1,703	3,469	86	1,440	3,539
Chariton	2,250	2,641	63	2,244	2,744
Christian	3,502	6,487	205	3,223	7,634
Clark	1,494	2,042	56	1,562	2,042
Clay	24,250	28,521	2,782	20,925	33,582
Clinton	3,001	3,599	184	2,778	4,226
Cole	9,210	16,373	691	6,702	20,366
Cooper	2,687	3,996	130	2,200	4,599
Crawford	2,710	4,081	170	2,610	4,716
Dade	1,283	2,410	61	858	2,126
Dallas	2,011	3,297	114	1,902	3,577
Daviess	1,770	2,125	61	1,526	2,414
DeKalb	1,677	2,062	111	1,464	2,088
Dent	2,528	3,477	86	2,544	3,496
Douglas	1,677	3,440	93	1,536	3,662
Dunklin	6,120	5,253	128	4,967	6,103
Franklin	10,480	15,210	863	8,319	18,669
Gasconade	1,550	4,481	136	1,130	4,678
Gentry	1,720	2,005	117	1,600	2,047
Greene	30,498	43,116	3,261	27,965	57,250
Grundy	2,064	2,890	110	1,861	3,156
Harrison	1,732	2,734	140	2,011	3,359
Henry	4,648	4,807	238	3,761	5,399
Hickory	1,248	1,893	52	1,212	2,190
Holt	1,119	1,993	59	1,028	2,087
Howard	2,243	2,179	114	2,044	2,406
Howell	4,472	7,149	211	3,301	7,053
Iron	2,226	2,205	94	2,008	2,322
Jackson	135,805	106,156	12,260	135,089	132,270
Jasper	11,953	21,664	785	9,007	22,586
Jefferson	24,042	28,546	1,753	20,026	34,525
Johnson	5,441	6,449	571	4,238	8,413
Knox	1,187	1,475	36	1,097	1,510

Laclede	3,443	5,642	153	2,665	6,406
Lafayette	5,792	7,271	339	3,937	7,211
Lawrence	4,670	7,921	184	3,720	8,370
Lewis	2,314	2,350	102	1,926	2,337
Lincoln	4,110	4,963	182	3,290	6,137
Linn	3,467	3,585	139	2,758	3,312
Livingston	3,368	3,654	205	2,704	4,364
McDonald	2,485	4,114	124	2,109	4,521
Macon	3,578	4,430	135	2,670	3,968
Madison	2,231	2,618	70	1,862	2,808
Maries	1,732	1,985	39	1,388	2,267
Marion	5,890	6,036	192	4,666	6,831
Mercer	821	1,266	54	875	1,229
Miller	2,469	5,560	115	2,052	6,699
Mississippi	3,040	2,459	64	2,524	2,502
Moniteau	2,284	3,430	98	1,614	3,821
Monroe	2,445	2,026	53	2,022	2,163
Montgomery	2,007	3,061	124	1,665	3,263
Morgan	2,460	3,577	114	2,169	4,392
New Madrid	4,171	4,041	64	3,776	4,323
Newton	5,621	10,515	341	4,721	11,708
Nodaway	4,257	4,544	414	3,615	5,441
Oregon	2,326	1,523	26	2,026	1,979
Osage	2,045	3,679	72	1,343	4,381
Ozark	1,242	2,434	63	1,105	2,614
Pemiscot	4,140	3,519	52	3,293	3,733
Perry	2,416	5,053	178	1,837	4,493
Pettis	6,475	8,833	435	5,403	10,956
Phelps	5,470	7,366	620	5,074	9,012
Pike	3,454	3,932	158	3,313	3,933
Platte	7,342	10,092	1,107	7,668	12,859
Polk	3,336	4,842	135	2,819	5,477
Pulaski	3,707	3,998	128	3,045	5,330
Putnam	871	1,722	44	798	1,550
Ralls	2,009	1,900	75	2,011	2,007
Randolph	4,884	5,141	213	4,471	5,745
Ray	4,518	4,064	215	4,004	4,875
Reynolds	1,919	1,271	44	2,026	1,330
Ripley	2,156	2,524	61	1,883	2,926
St. Charles	20,668	36,050	2,494	15,469	41,366
St. Clair	1,706	2,419	60	1,655	2,667
St. Francois	7,495	8,914	397	7,137	9,787
Ste. Genevieve	3,324	2,768	151	2,723	3,245
St. Louis	192,796	263,518	25,032	173,203	307,947
Saline	4,943	5,218	353	4,281	6,041
Schuyler	1,114	1,386	48	1,141	1,250
Scotland	1,200	1,592	63	739	1,838
Scott	6,854	8,227	203	5,569	8,722
Shannon	1,818	1,523	44	1,580	1,779
Shelby	1,849	2,151	60	1,573	2,242
Stoddard	5,128	6,199	132	4,171	6,433
Stone	2,210	4,780	180	2,119	5,726
Sullivan	1,824	2,412	76	1,784	2,306
Taney	3,389	6,230	195	2,912	7,082
Texas	4,261	4,879	125	3,662	5,591
Vernon	3,704	4,391	285	2,439	4,128
Warren	2,132	4,366	192	1,989	5,150
Washington	2,873	3,439	89	2,997	3,853
Wayne	2,549	2,823	44	1,999	2,452
Webster	3,409	5,121	149	2,982	5,529
Worth	760	833	47	734	921
Wright	2,182	4,451	56	1,973	4,687
ST. LOUIS CITY	113,697	50,333	5,656	80,127	45,049
Totals	931,182	1,074,181	77,920	808,601	1,242,678

Missouri Vote Since 1932

1932 (Pres.), Roosevelt, Dem., 1,025,406; Hoover, Rep.,
564,713; Thomas, Soc., 16,374; Upshaw, Proh., 2,429;
Foster, Com., 568; Reynolds, Soc. Labor, 404.

1936 (Pres.), Roosevelt, Dem., 1,111,403; Landon, Rep.,
697,891; Lemke, Union, 14,630; Thomas, Soc., 3,454; Colvin, Proh., 908; Browder, Com., 417; Aiken, Soc. Labor,
292.

1940 (Pres.), Roosevelt, Dem., 958,476; Willkie, Rep.,
871,009; Thomas, Soc., 2,226; Babson, Proh., 1,809; Aiken, Soc. Labor, 209.

1944 (Pres.), Roosevelt, Dem., 807,357; Dewey, Rep.,
761,175; Thomas, Soc., 1,750; Watson, Proh., 1,175; Teichert, Soc. Labor, 221.

1948 (Pres.), Truman, Dem., 917,315; Dewey, Rep.,
655,039; Wallace, Prog., 3,998; Thomas, Soc., 2,222.

1952 (Pres.), Eisenhower, Rep., 959,429; Stevenson, Dem.,
929,830; Hallinan, Prog., 987; Hamblen, Proh., 885;
MacArthur, Christian Nationalist, 302; America First,
233; Hoopes, Soc., 227; Hass, Soc. Labor, 169.

1956 (Pres.), Stevenson, Dem., 918,273; Eisenhower, Rep.,
914,299.

1960 (Pres.), Kennedy, Dem., 972,201; Nixon, Rep.,
962,221.

1964 (Pres.), Johnson, Dem., 1,164,344; Goldwater, Rep.,
653,535.

1968 (Pres.), Nixon, Rep., 811,932; Humphrey, Dem., 791,444; Wallace, 3d party, 206,126.

1972 (Pres.), Nixon, Rep., 1,154,058; McGovern, Dem., 698,531.

1976 (Pres.), Carter, Dem., 999,163; Ford, Rep., 928,808; McCarthy, Ind., 24,329.

1980 (Pres.), Reagan, Rep., 1,074,181; Carter, Dem., 931,182; Anderson, Ind., 77,920; Clark, Libertarian, 14,422; DeBerry, Soc. Workers, 1,515; Commoner, Citizens, 573; write-ins, 31.

Montana

County	1980 Carter (D)	Reagan (R)	Anderson (I)	1984 Mondale (D)	Reagan (R)
Beaverhead	842	2,955	205	793	2,335
Big Horn	1,644	1,730	308	2,679	2,316
Blaine	1,107	1,686	163	1,232	1,736
Broadwater	401	1,052	69	458	1,345
Carbon	1,468	2,471	331	1,645	2,856
Carter	237	766	37	197	823
Cascade	11,105	17,664	2,655	13,016	17,377
Chouteau	853	2,448	216	906	2,433
Custer	1,822	3,533	369	1,984	3,867
Daniels	483	1,086	77	473	984
Dawson	1,543	3,045	424	1,776	3,467
Deer Lodge	3,077	1,905	474	3,538	1,899
Fallon	512	1,286	94	569	1,237
Fergus	1,840	4,455	388	1,801	4,580
Flathead	6,349	15,102	1,621	8,242	16,899
Gallatin	5,747	12,738	2,432	8,134	15,579
Garfield	169	760	29	134	770
Glacier	1,394	2,283	297	2,167	2,228
Golden Valley	155	362	28	211	384
Granite	439	811	76	417	880
Hill	2,875	4,448	604	3,498	4,575
Jefferson	1,055	1,841	216	1,324	2,226
Judith Basin	480	1,030	93	603	930
Lake	2,615	5,083	573	2,653	4,136
Lewis & Clark	6,815	12,128	1,793	8,945	13,361
Liberty	283	872	71	323	894
Lincoln	2,422	4,202	485	1,733	2,036
Madison	676	2,220	174	701	2,294
McCone	349	1,000	86	459	1,015
Meagher	247	689	41	161	418
Mineral	660	800	138	718	941
Missoula	13,115	16,161	3,847	8,437	9,698
Musselshell	784	1,279	106	700	1,540
Park	1,663	3,929	459	2,373	4,091
Petroleum	90	225	15	86	258
Phillips	745	1,723	146	174	553
Pondera	897	2,270	207	1,057	2,156
Powder River	336	985	94	328	965
Powell	883	1,770	198	1,166	1,433
Prairie	283	580	57	289	698
Ravalli	3,063	7,268	743	3,823	8,155
Richland	1,252	3,348	343	1,280	3,632
Roosevelt	1,504	2,298	304	1,939	2,301
Rosebud	1,167	1,875	265	1,914	2,405
Sanders	1,395	2,194	291	1,635	2,407
Sheridan	955	1,658	247	896	1,335
Silver Bow	9,721	7,301	1,752	11,091	6,628
Stillwater	919	1,828	181	1,100	2,118
Sweet Grass	440	1,169	98	378	1,417
Teton	902	2,415	186	1,102	2,257
Toole	634	2,000	154	781	1,927
Treasure	181	321	34	209	352
Valley	1,567	3,242	264	1,849	3,122
Wheatland	381	742	88	407	753
Wibaux	219	450	45	216	423
Yellowstone	15,272	27,332	4,590	17,255	29,718
Totals	**118,032**	**206,814**	**29,281**	**131,975**	**207,163**

Montana Vote Since 1932

1932 (Pres.), Roosevelt, Dem., 127,286; Hoover, Rep., 78,078; Thomas, Soc., 7,891; Foster, Com., 1,775; Harvey, Lib., 1,449.

1936 (Pres.), Roosevelt, Dem., 159,690; Landon, Rep., 63,598; Lemke, Union, 5,549; Thomas, Soc., 1,066; Browder, Com., 385; Colvin, Proh., 224.

1940 (Pres.), Roosevelt, Dem., 145,698; Willkie, Rep., 99,579; Thomas, Soc., 1,443; Babson, Proh., 664; Browder, Com., 489.

1944 (Pres.), Roosevelt, Dem., 112,556; Dewey, Rep., 93,163; Thomas, Soc., 1,296; Watson, Proh., 340.

1948 (Pres.), Truman, Dem., 119,071; Dewey, Rep., 96,770; Wallace, Prog., 7,313; Thomas, Soc., 695; Watson, Proh., 429.

1952 (Pres.), Eisenhower, Rep., 157,394; Stevenson, Dem., 106,213; Hallinan, Prog., 723; Hamblen, Proh., 548; Hoopes, Soc., 159.

1956 (Pres.), Eisenhower, Rep., 154,933; Stevenson, Dem., 116,238.

1960 (Pres.), Kennedy, Dem., 134,891; Nixon, Rep., 141,841; Decker, Proh., 456; Dobbs, Soc. Workers, 391.

1964 (Pres.), Johnson, Dem., 164,246; Goldwater, Rep., 113,032; Kasper, Nat'l States Rights, 519; Munn, Proh., 499; DeBerry, Soc. Worker, 332.

1968 (Pres.), Nixon, Rep., 138,835; Humphrey, Dem., 114,117; Wallace, 3d party, 20,015; Halstead, Soc. Worker, 457; Munn, Proh., 510; Caton, New Reform, 470.

1972 (Pres.), Nixon, Rep., 183,976; McGovern, Dem., 120,197; Schmitz, Amer., 13,430.

1976 (Pres.), Carter, Dem., 149,259; Ford, Rep., 173,703; Anderson, Amer., 5,772.

1980 (Pres.), Reagan, Rep., 206,814; Carter, Dem., 118,032; Anderson, Ind., 29,281; Clark, Libertarian, 9,825.

Nebraska

County	1980 Carter (D)	Reagan (R)	Anderson (I)	1984 Mondale (D)	Reagan (R)
Adams	3,361	8,469	879	2,922	9,032
Antelope	659	3,192	150	693	3,214
Arthur	55	242	9	33	248
Banner	33	481	14	58	450
Blaine	63	361	15	46	336
Boone	769	2,598	176	686	2,493
Box Butte	1,206	3,898	307	1,292	3,729
Boyd	376	1,261	62	301	1,150
Brown	341	1,614	105	310	1,500
Buffalo	3,162	9,764	1,028	3,022	11,122
Burt	814	2,806	232	1,049	2,637
Butler	1,112	2,596	159	1,133	2,389
Cass	2,007	5,180	487	2,479	5,403
Cedar	1,265	3,257	273	1,200	3,286
Chase	324	1,593	91	364	1,672
Cherry	489	2,517	105	458	2,628
Cheyenne	776	3,073	196	853	3,149
Clay	840	2,739	150	809	2,902
Colfax	892	3,259	230	979	2,978
Cuming	803	3,999	266	756	3,686
Custer	1,011	4,562	285	1,084	4,347
Dakota	1,928	3,165	317	2,500	3,434
Dawes	703	3,281	228	858	3,301
Dawson	1,462	6,687	357	1,536	6,391
Deuel	192	943	63	197	951
Dixon	822	2,328	200	981	2,231
Dodge	3,556	9,514	988	4,242	10,124
Douglas	51,504	96,741	13,198	57,063	107,967
Dundy	192	1,135	55	225	983
Fillmore	1,025	2,435	221	1,004	2,462
Franklin	441	1,672	109	523	1,589
Frontier	259	1,345	84	256	1,347
Furnas	536	2,483	113	551	2,244
Gage	2,258	6,072	722	2,695	6,093
Garden	202	1,297	63	175	1,144
Garfield	238	811	42	207	874
Gosper	181	783	47	201	796
Grant	76	373	13	51	405
Greeley	495	1,028	78	484	940
Hall	4,391	12,083	981	4,423	12,363
Hamilton	777	3,199	245	797	3,192
Harlan	486	1,690	109	492	1,684
Hayes	82	617	21	100	590
Hitchcock	328	1,471	115	336	1,388
Holt	1,016	4,488	243	877	4,490
Hooker	63	386	18	54	430
Howard	788	1,969	170	883	1,889
Jefferson	1,125	3,090	297	1,361	3,103
Johnson	623	1,716	180	818	1,531
Kearney	726	2,510	227	722	2,497
Keith	710	3,373	199	623	3,385
Keya Paha	130	524	27	127	506
Kimball	385	1,615	97	329	1,709
Knox	1,057	3,404	245	1,086	3,191
Lancaster	27,040	38,630	9,221	32,509	48,257
Lincoln	3,762	9,631	841	4,446	10,582
Logan	71	442	17	63	444
Loup	74	368	21	78	319
McPherson	49	285	5	57	294
Madison	1,924	9,715	552	1,745	9,744
Merrick	712	2,710	212	814	2,685
Morrill	512	1,887	96	440	1,784
Nance	561	1,439	100	516	1,382
Nemaha	929	2,693	221	1,002	2,744
Nuckolls	899	2,180	159	946	2,129
Otoe	1,471	4,611	391	1,865	4,667
Pawnee	431	1,418	122	552	1,299
Perkins	313	1,338	81	301	1,410
Phelps	734	3,465	192	705	3,486
Pierce	517	2,935	155	535	2,950
Platte	2,385	8,781	546	1,971	9,545

Polk.	538	2,206	149	622	2,145
Red Willow. . . .	892	4,019	254	971	3,893
Richardson. . . .	1,350	3,634	264	1,347	3,396
Rock	145	855	39	141	833
Saline.	1,900	2,934	480	2,384	2,885
Sarpy.	5,678	15,523	1,685	6,683	19,404
Saunders. . . .	2,034	5,222	516	2,455	5,186
Scotts Bluff. . .	2,851	9,485	677	3,033	10,593
Seward	1,799	3,525	533	1,871	3,893
Sheridan	369	2,747	121	376	2,645
Sherman	576	1,253	116	699	1,140
Sioux	120	759	32	121	731
Stanton	361	1,942	118	411	2,075
Thayer	925	2,514	178	943	2,567
Thomas.	65	306	26	72	295
Thurston	724	1,454	140	1,074	1,404
Valley	654	2,100	124	733	2,039
Washington . . .	1,445	4,560	356	1,410	4,482
Wayne	733	2,844	300	826	3,058
Webster	547	1,676	138	608	1,609
Wheeler	93	371	22	97	362
York.	1,118	5,065	323	1,112	4,997
Totals	**166,424**	**419,214**	**44,854**	**183,838**	**446,938**

Nebraska Vote Since 1932

1932 (Pres.), Roosevelt, Dem., 359,082; Hoover, Rep., 201,177; Thomas, Soc., 9,876.

1936 (Pres.), Roosevelt, Dem., 347,454; Landon, Rep., 248,731; Lemke, Union, 12,847.

1940 (Pres.), Roosevelt, Dem., 263,677; Willkie, Rep., 352,201.

1944 (Pres.), Roosevelt, Dem., 233,246; Dewey, Rep., 329,880.

1948 (Pres.), Truman, Dem., 224,165; Dewey, Rep., 264,774.

1952 (Pres.), Eisenhower, Rep., 421,603; Stevenson Dem., 188,057.

1956 (Pres.), Eisenhower, Rep., 378,108; Stevenson Dem., 199,029.

1960 (Pres.), Kennedy, Dem., 232,542; Nixon, Rep., 380,553.

1964 (Pres.), Johnson, Dem., 307,307; Goldwater, Rep., 276,847.

1968 (Pres.), Nixon, Rep., 321,163; Humphrey, Dem., 170,784; Wallace, 3d party, 44,904.

1972 (Pres.), Nixon, Rep., 406,298; McGovern, Dem., 169,991; scattered 817.

1976 (Pres.), Carter, Dem., 233,287; Ford, Rep., 359,219; McCarthy, Ind., 9,383; Maddox, Amer. Ind., 3,378; Mac-Bride, Libertarian, 1,476.

1980 (Pres.), Reagan, Rep., 419,214; Carter, Dem., 166,424; Anderson, Ind., 44,854; Clark, Libertarian, 9,041.

Nevada

	1980			1984	
County	Carter (D)	Reagan (R)	Anderson (I)	Mondale (D)	Reagan (R)
Churchill	1,055	3,841	257	1,304	4,479
Clark	38,313	76,194	8,702	53,386	94,133
Douglas.	1,352	5,254	511	1,877	6,385
Elko	1,296	4,393	301	1,566	5,110
Esmeralda	110	311	29	158	453
Eureka	103	430	13	124	439
Humboldt. . . .	684	1,950	128	862	2,498
Lander	361	935	64	301	1,222
Lincoln	396	1,087	38	397	1,175
Lyon	1,288	3,709	271	1,673	4,370
Mineral	631	1,628	147	766	1,645
Nye	973	2,387	204	1,269	3,573
Pershing	311	877	60	333	956
Storey	222	460	62	251	568
Washoe.	15,621	41,276	5,705	22,321	50,418
White Pine . . .	1,181	1,896	195	1,276	1,893
CARSON CITY . .	2,769	8,389	964	3,790	9,477
Totals	**66,666**	**155,017**	**17,651**	**91,654**	**188,794**

Nevada Vote Since 1932

1932 (Pres.), Roosevelt, Dem., 28,756; Hoover, Rep., 12,674.

1936 (Pres.), Roosevelt, Dem., 31,925; Landon, Rep., 11,923.

1940 (Pres.), Roosevelt, Dem., 31,945; Willkie, Rep., 21,229.

1944 (Pres.), Roosevelt, Dem., 29,623; Dewey, Rep., 24,611.

1948 (Pres.), Truman, Dem., 31,291; Dewey, Rep., 29,357; Wallace, Prog., 1,469.

1952 (Pres.), Eisenhower, Rep., 50,502; Stevenson Dem., 31,688.

1956 (Pres.), Eisenhower, Rep., 56,049; Stevenson, Dem., 40,640.

1960 (Pres.), Kennedy, Dem., 54,880; Nixon, Rep., 52,387.

1964 (Pres.), Johnson, Dem., 79,339; Goldwater, Rep., 56,094.

1968 (Pres.), Nixon, Rep., 73,188; Humphrey, Dem., 60,598; Wallace, 3d party, 20,432.

1972 (Pres.), Nixon, Rep., 115,750; McGovern, Dem. 66,016.

1976 (Pres.), Carter Dem., 92,479; Ford, Rep., 101,273; MacBride, Libertarian, 1,519; Maddox, Amer. Ind., 1,497; scattered 5,108.

1980 (Pres.), Reagan, Rep., 155,017; Carter, Dem., 66,666; Anderson, Ind., 17,651; Clark, Libertarian, 4,358.

New Hampshire

	1980			1984	
County	Carter (D)	Reagan (R)	Anderson (I)	Mondale (D)	Reagan (R)
Berlin City	2,202	2,847	347	1,862	3,261
Claremont	2,171	2,365	506	2,006	2,868
Concord	4,330	6,092	2,204	5,171	7,189
Dover.	3,344	4,497	1,517	NA	NA
Keene.	2,875	4,317	1,650	3,236	4,967
Laconia	1,635	3,529	628	1,237	3,285
Manchester . . .	10,919	23,557	3,178	9,154	22,459
Nashua	9,156	13,874	3,391	9,299	16,936
Portsmith	3,666	4,023	1,467	4,112	4,469
Rochester	2,566	4,495	650	2,622	5,453
Totals	**108,864**	**221,705**	**49,693**	**110,268**	**244,790**

New Hampshire Vote Since 1932

1932 (Pres.), Roosevelt, Dem., 100,680; Hoover, Rep., 103,629; Thomas, Soc., 947; Foster, Com., 264.

1936 (Pres.), Roosevelt, Dem., 108,640; Landon, Rep., 104,642; Lemke, Union, 4,819; Browder, Com., 193.

1940 (Pres.), Roosevelt, Dem., 125,292; Willkie, Rep., 110,127.

1944 (Pres.), Roosevelt, Dem., 119,663; Dewey, Rep., 109,916; Thomas, Soc., 46.

1948 (Pres.), Truman, Dem., 107,995; Dewey, Rep., 121,299; Wallace, Prog., 1,970; Thomas, Soc., 86; Teichert, Soc. Labor, 83; Thurmond, States' Rights, 7.

1952 (Pres.), Eisenhower, Rep., 166,287; Stevenson, Dem., 106,663.

1956 (Pres.), Eisenhower, Rep., 176,519; Stevenson, Dem., 90,364; Andrews, Const., 111.

1960 (Pres.), Kennedy, Dem., 137,772; Nixon, Rep., 157,989.

1964 (Pres.), Johnson, Dem., 182,065; Goldwater, Rep., 104,029.

1968 (Pres.), Nixon, Rep., 154,903; Humphrey, Dem., 130,589; Wallace, 3d party, 11,173; New Party, 421; Halstead, Soc. Worker, 104.

1972 (Pres.), Nixon, Rep., 213,724; McGovern, Dem., 116,435; Schmitz, Amer., 3,386; Jenness, Soc. Workers, 368; scattered, 142.

1976 (Pres.), Carter, Dem., 147,645; Ford, Rep., 185,935; McCarthy, Ind., 4,095; MacBride, Libertarian, 936; Reagan, write-in, 388; La Rouche, U.S. Labor, 186; Camejo, Soc. Workers, 161; Levin, Soc. Labor, 66; scattered, 215.

1980 (Pres.), Reagan, Rep., 221,705; Carter, Dem., 108,864; Anderson, Ind., 49,693; Clark, Libertarian, 2,067; Commoner, Citizens, 1,325; Hall, Com., 129; Griswold, Workers World, 76; DeBerry, Soc. Workers, 72; scattered, 68.

New Jersey

	1980			1984	
County	Carter (D)	Reagan (R)	Anderson (I)	Mondale (D)	Reagan (R)
Atlantic	31,286	37,973	5,582	32,576	46,195
Bergen	139,474	232,043	38,242	147,730	255,655
Burlington	50,083	68,415	11,314	55,608	85,648
Camden	80,033	87,939	16,125	87,033	105,033
Cape May	12,708	22,729	2,550	12,717	26,751
Cumberland . . .	19,356	23,242	3,253	20,425	28,152
Essex	145,281	117,222	21,271	179,183	133,345
Gloucester	29,804	40,306	7,533	32,702	54,041
Hudson	95,622	91,207	8,941	88,413	106,887
Hunterdon	10,029	21,403	3,610	11,058	29,501
Mercer	60,888	53,450	12,117	64,409	68,578
Middlesex	97,304	122,354	17,463	104,993	159,940
Monmouth	71,328	120,173	17,444	75,217	139,597

Morris	48,965	105,260	17,181	50,444	130,765
Ocean	46,923	98,433	10,073	49,360	118,427
Passaic	61,486	82,531	9,385	62,610	97,278
Salem	10,209	13,000	1,800	8,935	17,368
Somerset	29,470	52,591	8,346	31,924	66,303
Sussex	10,531	27,063	3,988	11,513	35,709
Union	86,074	112,288	15,586	91,709	134,663
Warren	10,510	16,935	2,828	10,647	21,938
Totals	1,147,364	1,546,557	234,632	1,229,206	1,861,774

New Jersey Vote Since 1932

1932 (Pres.), Roosevelt, Dem., 806,630; Hoover, Rep., 775,684; Thomas, Soc., 42,998; Foster, Com., 2,915; Reynolds, Soc. Labor, 1,062; Upshaw, Proh., 774.

1936 (Pres.), Roosevelt, Dem., 1,083,549; Landon, Rep., 719,421; Lemke, Union, 9,405; Thomas, Soc., 3,895; Browder, Com., 1,590; Colvin, Proh., 916; Aiken, Soc. Labor, 346.

1940 (Pres.), Roosevelt, Dem., 1,016,404; Willkie, Rep., 944,876; Browder, Com., 8,814; Thomas, Soc., 2,823; Babson, Proh., 851; Aiken, Soc. Labor, 446.

1944 (Pres.), Roosevelt, Dem., 987,874; Dewey, Rep., 961,335; Teichert, Soc. Labor, 6,939; Watson, Nat'l. Proh., 4,255; Thomas, Soc., 3,385.

1948 (Pres.), Truman, Dem., 895,455; Dewey, Rep., 981,124; Wallace, Prog., 42,683; Watson, Proh., 10,593; Thomas, Soc., 10,521; Dobbs, Soc. Workers, 5,825; Teichert, Soc. Labor, 3,354.

1952 (Pres.), Eisenhower, Rep., 1,373,613; Stevenson, Dem., 1,015,902; Hoopes, Soc., 8,593; Hass, Soc. Labor, 5,815; Hallinan, Prog., 5,589; Krajewski, Poor Man's, 4,203; Dobbs, Soc. Workers, 3,850; Hamblen, Proh., 989.

1956 (Pres.), Eisenhower, Rep., 1,606,942; Stevenson Dem., 850,337; Holtwick, Proh., 9,147; Hass, Soc. Labor, 6,736; Andrews, Conservative, 5,317; Dobbs, Soc. Workers, 4,004; Krajewski, American Third Party, 1,829.

1960 (Pres.), Kennedy, Dem., 1,385,415; Nixon, Rep., 1,363,324; Dobbs, Soc. Workers, 11,402; Lee, Conservative, 8,708; Hass, Soc. Labor, 4,262.

1964 (Pres.), Johnson, Dem., 1,867,671; Goldwater, Rep., 963,843; DeBerry, Soc. Workers, 8,181; Hass, Soc. Labor, 7,075.

1968 (Pres.), Nixon, Rep., 1,325,467; Humphrey, Dem., 1,264,206; Wallace, 3d party, 262,187; Halstead, Soc. Worker, 8,667; Gregory, Peace Freedom, 8,084; Blomen, Soc. Labor, 6,784.

1972 (Pres.), Nixon, Rep., 1,845,502; McGovern, Dem., 1,102,211; Schmitz, Amer., 34,378; Spock, Peoples, 5,355; Fisher, Soc. Labor, 4,544; Jenness, Soc. Workers, 2,233; Mahalchik, Amer. First, 1,743; Hall, Com., 1,263.

1976 (Pres.), Carter, Dem., 1,444,653; Ford, Rep., 1,509,688; McCarthy, Ind., 32,717; MacBride, Libertarian, 9,449; Maddox, Amer., 7,716; Levin, Soc. Labor, 3,686; Hall, Com., 1,662; LaRouche, U.S. Labor, 1,650; Camejo, Soc. Workers, 1,184; Wright, People's, 1,044; Bubar, Proh., 554; Zeidler, Soc., 469.

1980 (Pres.), Reagan, Rep., 1,546,557; Carter, Dem., 1,147,364; Anderson, Ind., 234,632; Clark, Libertarian, 20,652; Commoner, Citizens, 8,203; McCormack, Right to Life, 3,927; Lynen, Middle Class, 3,694; Hall, Com., 2,555; Pulley, Soc. Workers, 2,198; McReynolds, Soc., 1,973; Gahres, Down With Lawyers, 1,718; Griswold, Workers World, 1,288; Wendelken, Ind., 923.

New Mexico

	1980			1984	
County	Carter (D)	Reagan (R)	Anderson (I)	Mondale (D)	Reagan (R)
Bernalillo	54,841	83,956	15,118	67,373	103,496
Catron	466	906	40	418	970
Chaves	5,350	12,502	543	5,332	15,150
Cibola				3,024	3,492
Colfax	2,266	2,537	199	2,434	2,967
Curry	3,622	8,132	183	2,933	9,083
De Baca	484	655	14	387	756
Dona Ana	10,839	15,539	1,863	13,886	21,952
Eddy	7,028	9,817	326	7,343	11,827
Grant	4,600	4,628	349	5,745	4,977
Guadalupe	980	1,065	58	946	990
Harding	225	356	14	224	401
Hidalgo	840	1,059	59	860	1,282
Lea	5,006	10,727	298	4,558	14,343
Lincoln	1,127	3,009	172	1,134	3,992
Los Alamos	2,368	5,460	1,388	2,595	6,245
Luna	2,443	3,636	157	2,557	4,145

McKinley	4,869	7,329	498	7,439	6,516
Mora	1,274	1,037	44	1,235	1,017
Otero	4,111	7,210	478	4,064	9,214
Quay	1,422	2,499	58	1,370	2,842
Rio Arriba	6,245	3,794	379	6,927	4,047
Roosevelt	2,240	3,950	208	1,696	4,598
Sandoval	4,740	6,762	789	6,703	8,409
San Juan	6,705	15,579	741	8,963	18,680
San Miguel	4,514	3,292	416	5,227	3,405
Santa Fe	12,658	12,361	3,123	18,372	15,906
Sierra	1,169	2,222	117	1,335	2,663
Socorro	2,226	2,685	387	2,541	3,403
Taos	4,346	3,584	482	5,140	4,154
Torrance	1,261	1,907	101	1,256	2,327
Union	675	1,407	32	488	1,503
Valencia	6,886	11,177	825	5,166	8,180
Totals	167,826	250,779	29,459	199,671	302,932

New Mexico Vote Since 1932

1932 (Pres.), Roosevelt, Dem., 95,089; Hoover, Rep., 54,217; Thomas, Soc., 11,776; Harvey, Lib., 389; Foster, Com., 135.

1936 (Pres.), Roosevelt, Dem., 105,838; Landon, Rep., 61,710; Lemke, Union, 942; Thomas, Soc., 343; Browder, Com., 43.

1940 (Pres.), Roosevelt, Dem., 103,699; Willkie, Rep., 79,315.

1944 (Pres.), Roosevelt, Dem., 81,389; Dewey, Rep., 70,688; Watson, Proh., 148.

1948 (Pres.), Truman, Dem., 105,464; Dewey, Rep., 80,303; Wallace, Prog., 1,037; Watson, Proh., 127; Thomas, Soc., 83; Teichert, Soc. Labor, 49.

1952 (Pres.), Eisenhower, Rep., 132,170; Stevenson, Dem., 105,661; Hamblen, Proh., 297; Hallinan, Ind. Prog., 225; MacArthur, Christian National, 220; Hass, Soc. Labor, 35.

1956 (Pres.), Eisenhower, Rep., 146,788; Stevenson, Dem., 106,098; Holtwick, Proh., 607; Andrews, Ind., 364; Hass, Soc. Labor, 69.

1960 (Pres.), Kennedy, Dem., 156,027; Nixon, Rep., 153,733; Decker, Proh., 777; Hass, Soc. Labor, 570.

1964 (Pres.), Johnson, Dem., 194,017; Goldwater, Rep., 131,838; Hass, Soc. Labor, 1,217; Munn, Proh., 543.

1968 (Pres.), Nixon, Rep., 169,692; Humphrey, Dem., 130,081; Wallace, 3d party, 25,737; Chavez, 1,519; Halstead, Soc. Worker, 252.

1972 (Pres.), Nixon, Rep., 235,606; McGovern, Dem., 141,084; Schmitz, Amer., 8,767; Jenness, Soc. Workers, 474.

1976 (Pres.), Carter, Dem., 201,148; Ford, Rep., 211,419; Camejo, Soc. Workers, 2,462; MacBride, Libertarian, 1,110; Zeidler, Soc., 240; Bubar, Proh., 211.

1980 (Pres.), Reagan, Rep., 250,779; Carter, Dem., 167,826; Anderson, Ind., 29,459; Clark, Libertarian, 4,365; Commoner, Citizens, 2,202; Bubar, Statesman, 1,281; Pulley, Soc. Worker, 325.

New York

	1980			1984	
County	Carter (D)	Reagan (R-C**)	Anderson (L)	Mondale (D)	Reagan (R)
Albany	74,429	52,354	14,563	74,165	70,512
Allegany	5,879	10,423	973	4,749	14,229
Broome	37,013	39,275	11,388	36,144	54,735
Cattaraugus	12,917	17,222	1,848	10,161	23,988
Cayuga	11,708	17,945	2,539	11,582	20,006
Chautauqua	22,871	30,081	4,699	23,643	36,779
Chemung	14,565	19,674	2,465	14,566	24,701
Chenango	6,917	10,400	1,908	5,951	13,159
Clinton	11,498	13,120	1,904	10,951	19,792
Columbia	9,500	13,946	2,204	8,916	18,580
Cortland	6,176	9,885	1,603	6,349	13,446
Delaware	6,333	10,609	1,865	5,647	13,799
Dutchess	28,616	53,616	8,824	29,570	63,944
Erie	215,283	169,209	29,580	232,298	218,144
Essex	6,443	9,025	1,213	5,096	11,835
Franklin	7,281	7,620	1,182	6,151	10,109
Fulton	10,675	11,448	1,566	7,587	14,736
Genesee	10,677	11,650	1,651	8,357	16,118
Greene	6,488	11,286	1,338	5,477	13,031
Hamilton	925	2,038	176	688	2,480
Herkimer	11,497	14,105	1,830	9,654	17,545
Jefferson	13,271	16,455	2,834	10,896	23,235
Lewis	3,973	4,937	716	2,623	6,642
Livingston	9,030	11,193	1,694	7,283	16,031
Madison	7,843	13,309	2,122	8,215	17,337
Monroe	142,423	128,615	29,118	126,454	176,375
Montgomery	9,645	11,917	2,080	9,271	14,234

Niagara	40,405	38,760	6,014	41,257	51,118
Oneida	44,292	51,968	6,929	37,357	56,774
Onondaga	73,453	97,887	18,805	79,233	115,535
Ontario	14,477	17,036	3,147	12,193	23,245
Orange	30,022	51,268	7,656	32,004	70,200
Orleans	5,767	7,536	977	4,419	10,467
Oswego	15,343	22,816	3,333	13,702	30,657
Otsego	8,795	11,814	2,874	9,386	16,725
Putnam	8,691	20,193	2,340	7,839	25,074
Rensselaer	29,880	32,005	6,443	26,465	43,093
Rockland	35,277	59,068	8,709	43,537	68,109
St. Lawrence	17,006	18,437	3,544	15,929	25,913
Saratoga	23,641	34,184	6,201	21,996	46,769
Schenectady	29,932	32,003	7,146	30,622	42,494
Schoharie	4,715	6,382	940	3,796	8,211
Schuyler	2,514	3,838	476	2,361	5,088
Seneca	5,010	7,174	1,205	4,546	8,903
Steuben	12,826	22,418	2,257	9,383	25,783
Sullivan	9,553	15,089	2,095	5,507	10,227
Tioga	6,690	10,291	1,851	5,928	14,680
Tompkins	11,970	12,448	4,081	18,241	17,234
Ulster	22,179	36,709	5,995	25,415	45,152
Warren	6,971	13,264	1,766	5,399	16,143
Washington	7,144	12,835	1,501	5,457	15,477
Wayne	12,590	16,498	2,623	9,541	23,715
Wyoming	5,234	8,108	855	4,269	11,105
Yates	2,828	4,694	690	2,657	6,305
Outside N.Y. Metro					
Area	**1,188,511**	**1,386,140**	**244,336**	**1,160,883**	**2,079,798**
Nassau	207,602	333,567	44,758	238,489	388,475
Suffolk	149,945	256,294	34,743	167,378	325,282
Westchester	130,136	190,552	30,119	142,654	202,613
N.Y. Suburban	**487,683**	**788,413**	**109,620**	**548,521**	**916,370**
Bronx	181,090	86,843	11,286	218,249	106,121
Kings	288,893	200,306	24,341	360,667	226,215
New York	275,742	115,911	38,597	363,415	138,303
Queens	269,147	251,333	32,566	319,404	278,000
Richmond	37,306	64,885	7,055	42,382	80,459
N.Y. Metro Area	**1,052,178**	**719,278**	**113,845**	**1,304,117**	**829,098**
N.Y. Metro					
Area	**1,539,861**	**1,507,691**	**223,465**	**1,852,638**	**1,445,468**
D/R Total	**2,728,372**	**2,637,700**	**—**	**2,894,654**	**3,247,503**
2d party (Con)	**—**	**256,131**	**—**		
Totals	**2,728,372**	**2,893,831**	**467,801**	**3,013,521**	**3,525,266**

New York Vote Since 1932

1932 (Pres.), Roosevelt, Dem., 2,534,959; Hoover, Rep., 1,937,963; Thomas, Soc., 177,397; Foster, Com., 27,956; Reynolds, Soc. Labor, 10,339.

1936 (Pres.), Roosevelt, Dem., 3,018,298; American Lab., 274,924; total 3,293,222; Landon, Rep., 2,180,670; Thomas, Soc., 86,879; Browder, Com., 35,609.

1940 (Pres.), Roosevelt, Dem., 2,834,500; American Lab., 417,418; total, 3,251,918; Willkie, Rep., 3,027,478; Thomas, Soc., 18,950; Babson, Proh., 3,250.

1944 (Pres.), Roosevelt, Dem., 2,478,598; American Lab., 496,405; Liberal, 329,325; total, 3,304,238; Dewey, Rep., 2,987,647; Teichert, Ind. Gov't., 14,352; Thomas, Soc., 10,553.

1948 (Pres.), Truman, Dem., 2,557,642; Liberal, 222,562; total, 2,780,204; Dewey, Rep., 2,841,163; Wallace, Amer. Lab., 509,559; Thomas, Soc., 40,879; Teichert, Ind. Gov't., 2,729; Dobbs, Soc. Workers, 2,675.

1952 (Pres.), Eisenhower, Rep., 3,952,815; Stevenson, Dem., 2,687,890, Liberal, 416,711; total, 3,104,601; Hallinan, American Lab., 64,211; Hoopes, Soc., 2,664; Dobbs, Soc. Workers, 2,212; Hass, Ind. Gov't., 1,560; scattering, 178; blank and void, 87,813.

1956 (Pres.), Eisenhower, Rep., 4,340,340; Stevenson, Dem., 2,458,212; Liberal, 292,557; total, 2,750,769; write-in votes for Andrews, 1,027; Werdel, 492; Hass, 150; Hoopes, 82; others, 476.

1960 (Pres.), Kennedy, Dem., 3,423,909; Liberal, 406,176; total, 3,830,085; Nixon, Rep., 3,446,419; Dobbs, Soc. Workers, 14,319; scattering, 256; blank and void, 88,896.

1964 (Pres.), Johnson, Dem., 4,913,156; Goldwater, Rep., 2,243,559; Hass, Soc. Labor, 6,085; DeBerry, Soc. Workers, 3,215; scattering, 188; blank and void, 151,383.

1968 (Pres.), Nixon, Rep., 3,007,932; Humphrey, Dem., 3,378,470; Wallace, 3d party, 358,864; Blomen, Soc. Labor, 8,432; Halstead, Soc. Worker, 11,851; Gregory, Freedom and Peace, 24,517; blank, void, and scattering, 171,624.

1972 (Pres.), Nixon, Rep., 3,824,642; Conservative, 368,136; McGovern, Dem., 2,767,956; Liberal, 183,128; Reed, Soc. Workers, 7,797; Fisher, Soc. Labor, 4,530; Hall, Com., 5,641; blank, void, or scattered, 161,641.

1976 (Pres.), Carter, Dem., 3,389,558; Ford, Rep., 3,100,791; MacBride, Libertarian, 12,197; Hall, Com., 10,270; Camejo, Soc. Workers, 6,996; LaRouche, U.S. Labor, 5,413; blank, void, or scattered, 143,037.

1980 (Pres.), Reagan, Rep., 2,893,831; Carter, Dem., 2,728,372; Anderson, Lib., 467,801; Clark, Libertarian, 52,648; McCormack, Right To Life, 24,159; Commoner, Citizens, 23,186; Hall, Com., 7,414; DeBerry, Soc. Workers, 2,068; Griswold, Workers World, 1,416; scattering, 1,064.

North Carolina

	1980			1984	
County	Carter (D)	Reagan (R)	Anderson (I)	Mondale (D)	Reagan (R)
Alamance	15,042	18,077	760	11,227	26,063
Alexander	4,546	6,376	137	3,584	8,498
Alleghany	2,198	1,995	91	2,096	2,586
Anson	4,973	1,968	111	5,015	3,719
Ashe	4,461	5,643	154	4,009	6,606
Avery	1,527	3,480	147	1,158	4,678
Beaufort	6,024	6,773	186	5,975	9,492
Bertie	3,863	1,695	45	3,953	2,879
Bladen	6,104	2,745	64	4,895	4,353
Brunswick	6,761	5,897	265	6,774	9,673
Buncombe	24,837	26,124	2,153	23,333	37,698
Burke	11,680	12,956	558	10,348	18,761
Cabarrus	9,768	15,143	562	8,477	22,528
Caldwell	8,738	12,965	440	6,727	15,526
Camden	1,212	813	45	1,075	1,281
Carteret	6,485	7,733	460	5,539	10,924
Caswell	3,529	2,156	66	4,157	4,092
Catawba	13,873	22,873	886	11,646	31,184
Chatham	7,144	5,414	481	7,456	8,594
Cherokee	3,114	3,849	80	2,774	4,894
Chowan	2,146	1,424	71	1,685	2,171
Clay	1,324	2,136	53	1,339	2,251
Cleveland	12,219	10,828	333	10,073	16,237
Columbus	10,212	5,522	148	8,728	9,150
Craven	7,781	8,534	356	7,134	12,801
Cumberland	22,073	21,540	1,261	22,351	30,814
Currituck	1,980	1,668	97	1,676	2,876
Dare	2,497	2,794	260	1,739	4,738
Davidson	14,579	22,794	679	11,452	30,432
Davie	3,289	6,302	223	2,911	8,201
Duplin	7,524	5,403	109	7,041	7,892
Durham	24,969	19,276	3,052	32,154	29,109
Edgecombe	7,945	5,916	148	10,537	9,627
Forsyth	38,870	42,389	2,897	36,800	59,201
Franklin	5,427	3,508	104	4,766	5,984
Gaston	19,016	25,139	823	14,129	38,812
Gates	2,435	957	61	2,223	1,694
Graham	1,608	1,961	36	1,494	2,514
Granville	5,556	3,513	133	5,217	6,302
Greene	2,835	2,221	34	2,772	3,195
Guilford	44,516	53,291	4,019	46,402	75,141
Halifax	8,364	6,033	180	9,378	8,832
Harnett	8,791	7,284	165	6,646	10,684
Haywood	9,814	7,217	349	8,011	10,377
Henderson	7,578	13,573	901	7,192	18,964
Hertford	4,102	1,854	80	4,498	3,176
Hoke	3,376	1,168	56	3,213	2,449
Hyde	1,221	807	37	1,004	1,195
Iredell	12,067	14,926	624	8,136	17,742
Jackson	4,857	4,140	246	4,375	5,582
Johnston	9,601	10,444	271	7,831	16,207
Jones	2,198	1,401	18	2,025	2,062
Lee	5,426	4,847	251	3,997	8,092
Lenoir	7,546	9,832	263	8,560	13,317
Lincoln	7,796	9,009	299	5,994	12,481
McDowell	4,703	5,680	175	4,076	7,639
Macon	4,105	4,727	153	3,570	6,661
Madison	3,202	2,629	108	2,983	2,661
Martin	4,750	2,564	81	3,868	4,263
Mecklenburg	66,995	68,384	6,560	60,780	101,098
Mitchell	1,765	4,322	146	1,286	4,737
Montgomery	4,129	3,587	99	3,830	5,099
Moore	8,084	10,158	563	6,995	14,282
Nash	8,184	11,043	293	8,926	17,405
New Hanover	13,670	17,243	1,114	12,572	23,723
Northampton	4,933	1,847	62	5,124	3,130
Onslow	7,371	8,861	400	5,713	13,922
Orange	15,226	9,261	3,364	19,715	15,071
Pamlico	2,224	1,504	48	2,152	2,681
Pasquotank	4,128	3,340	179	3,650	4,603
Pender	4,382	3,018	103	4,649	5,105
Perquimans	1,560	1,210	63	1,441	1,935
Person	4,111	3,281	104	3,528	5,958
Pitt	12,590	12,816	827	13,474	18,975
Polk	2,375	3,021	160	2,167	4,046
Randolph	10,107	19,881	563	7,249	24,801
Richmond	7,416	3,911	224	7,494	6,807
Robeson	17,618	6,982	331	15,064	12,816

Rockingham	11,708	11,205	463	6,722	11,405
Rowan	11,671	18,566	707	10,643	25,207
Rutherford	8,315	8,363	203	6,858	11,365
Sampson	9,090	8,097	308	9,112	10,665
Scotland	4,446	2,133	155	4,028	4,077
Stanly	7,784	9,734	248	6,138	12,504
Stokes	5,764	7,275	151	4,950	9,313
Surry	8,987	10,065	256	7,188	13,339
Swain	1,987	1,457	70	2,000	2,012
Transylvania	4,008	4,826	274	3,390	6,235
Tyrrell	887	466	14	807	774
Union	10,073	9,012	487	7,024	16,801
Vance	5,415	4,217	101	5,880	6,836
Wake	49,003	49,768	5,455	48,008	77,451
Warren	3,750	1,582	74	3,854	2,557
Washington	3,008	1,943	68	3,114	2,731
Watauga	5,022	6,149	645	5,163	9,090
Wayne	9,586	12,860	322	9,583	17,008
Wilkes	8,184	14,462	282	6,852	18,670
Wilson	8,042	8,329	243	8,223	11,959
Yadkin	3,850	7,530	136	3,073	8,975
Yancey	4,010	3,363	110	3,259	4,079
Totals	875,635	915,018	52,800	809,876	1,314,802

North Carolina Vote Since 1932

1932 (Pres.), Roosevelt, Dem., 497,566; Hoover, Rep., 208,344; Thomas, Soc., 5,591.

1936 (Pres.), Roosevelt, Dem., 616,141; Landon, Rep., 223,283; Thomas, Soc., 21; Browder, Com., 11; Lemke, Union 2.

1940 (Pres.), Roosevelt, Dem., 609,015; Willkie, Rep., 213,633.

1944 (Pres.), Roosevelt, Dem., 527,399; Dewey, Rep., 263,155.

1948 (Pres.), Truman, Dem., 459,070; Dewey, Rep., 258,572; Thurmond, States' Rights, 69,652; Wallace, Prog., 3,915.

1952 (Pres.), Eisenhower, Rep., 558,107; Stevenson, Dem., 652,803.

1956 (Pres.), Eisenhower, Rep., 575,062; Stevenson, Dem., 590,530.

1960 (Pres.), Kennedy, Dem., 713,136; Nixon, Rep., 655,420.

1964 (Pres.), Johnson, Dem., 800,139; Goldwater Rep., 624,844.

1968 (Pres.), Nixon, Rep., 627,192; Humphrey, Dem., 464,113; Wallace, 3d party, 496,188.

1972 (Pres.), Nixon, Rep., 1,054,889; McGovern, Dem., 438,705; Schmitz, Amer., 25,018.

1976 (Pres.), Dem., 927,365; Ford, Rep., 741,960; Anderson, Amer., 5,607; MacBride, Libertarian, 2,219; LaRouche, U.S. Labor, 755.

1980 (Pres.), Reagan, Rep., 915,018; Carter, Dem., 875,635; Anderson, Ind., 52,800; Clark, Libertarian, 9,677; Commoner, Citizens, 2,287; DeBerry, Soc. Workers, 416.

North Dakota

County	1980 Carter (D)	Reagan (R)	Anderson (I)	1984 Mondale (D)	Reagan (R)
Adams	470	1,334	107	295	717
Barnes	2,128	4,392	705	2,500	4,337
Benson	1,119	2,149	262	916	1,155
Billings	122	524	33	95	388
Bottineau	1,090	3,394	267	938	2,483
Bowman	454	1,507	142	364	995
Burke	418	1,442	82	327	637
Burleigh	6,129	18,437	2,109	8,764	19,876
Cass	13,562	23,886	5,421	7,851	12,521
Cavalier	1,105	2,582	238	876	2,069
Dickey	917	2,455	161	666	1,657
Divide	509	1,267	109	431	807
Dunn	532	1,706	115	645	1,573
Eddy	539	1,153	145	637	792
Emmons	502	2,369	132	456	1,151
Foster	586	1,534	152	630	1,130
Golden Valley	259	1,006	62	253	822
Grand Forks	6,997	14,257	2,932	3,866	6,022
Grant	317	1,891	110	219	518
Griggs	636	1,342	158	833	1,259
Hettinger	434	1,699	104	396	1,168
Kidder	326	1,474	85	504	1,237
La Moure	850	2,136	254	1,088	1,977
Logan	283	1,474	69	401	1,221
McHenry	939	2,922	190	957	1,778
McIntosh	308	2,471	72	375	1,835
McKenzie	867	2,265	182	424	1,294
McLean	1,613	4,234	318	2,058	3,662
Mercer	1,209	3,224	204	611	842
Morton	2,861	7,659	742	3,962	7,088
Mountrail	1,183	2,165	182	1,331	1,564

Nelson	726	1,611	226	1,023	1,441
Oliver	270	966	55	419	917
Pembina	1,239	3,101	303	1,365	2,889
Pierce	517	2,273	168	690	1,881
Ramsey	1,607	4,078	514	2,302	4,142
Ransom	974	1,883	237	1,220	1,699
Renville	570	1,154	98	591	1,161
Richland	2,698	5,711	750	3,043	5,973
Rolette	1,660	1,599	265	2,177	1,477
Sargent	1,048	1,565	174	1,294	1,383
Sheridan	208	1,326	65	267	856
Sioux	383	620	72	655	442
Slope	128	462	45	174	417
Stark	2,016	6,312	512	2,752	7,626
Steele	617	997	229	781	940
Stutsman	2,573	6,545	960	3,487	6,578
Towner	568	1,375	152	629	830
Traill	1,428	3,092	512	1,578	3,036
Walsh	1,850	4,488	485	2,262	4,339
Ward	5,554	14,997	1,234	7,314	16,026
Wells	746	2,660	148	679	1,562
Williams	2,545	6,530	592	2,468	5,666
Totals	79,189	193,695	23,640	80,839	155,856

North Dakota Vote Since 1932

1932 (Pres.), Roosevelt, Dem., 178,350; Hoover, Rep., 71,772; Harvey, Lib., 1,817; Thomas, Soc., 3,521; Foster, Com., 830.

1936 (Pres.), Roosevelt, Dem., 163,148; Landon, Rep., 72,751; Lemke, Union, 36,708; Thomas, Soc., 552; Browder, Com., 360; Colvin, Proh., 197.

1940 (Pres.), Roosevelt, Dem., 124,036; Willkie, Rep., 154,590; Thomas, Soc., 1,279; Knutson, Com., 545; Babson, Proh., 325.

1944 (Pres.), Roosevelt, Dem., 100,144; Dewey, Rep., 118,535; Thomas, Soc., 943, Watson, Proh., 549.

1948 (Pres.), Truman, Dem., 95,812; Dewey, Rep., 115,139; Wallace, Prog., 8,391; Thomas, Soc., 1,000, Thurmond, States' Rights, 374.

1952 (Pres.), Eisenhower, Rep., 191,712; Stevenson, Dem., 76,694; MacArthur, Christian Nationalist, 1,075; Hallinan, Prog., 344; Hamblen, Proh., 302.

1956 (Pres.), Eisenhower, Rep., 156,766; Stevenson, Dem., 96,742; Andrews, Amer., 483.

1960 (Pres.), Kennedy, Dem., 123,963; Nixon, Rep., 154,310; Dobbs, Soc. Workers, 158.

1964 (Pres.), Johnson, Dem., 149,784; Goldwater, Rep., 108,207; DeBerry, Soc. Worker, 224; Munn, Proh., 174.

1968 (Pres.), Nixon, Rep., 138,669; Humphrey, Dem., 94,769; Wallace, 3d party, 14,244; Halstead, Soc. Worker, 128; Munn, Prohibition, 38; Troxell, Ind., 34.

1972 (Pres.), Nixon, Rep., 174,109; McGovern, Dem., 100,384; Jenness, Soc. Workers, 288; Hall, Com., 87; Schmitz, Amer., 5,646.

1976 (Pres.), Carter, Dem., 136,078; Ford, Rep., 153,470; Anderson, Amer., 3,698; McCarthy, Ind., 2,952; Maddox, Amer. Ind., 269; MacBride, Libertarian, 256; scattering, 371.

1980 (Pres.), Reagan, Rep., 193,695; Carter, Dem., 79,189; Anderson, Ind., 23,640; Clark, Libertarian, 3,743; Commoner, Libertarian, 429; McLain, Nat'l People's League, 296; Greaves, American, 235; Hall, Com., 93; DeBerry, Soc. Workers, 89; McReynolds, Soc., 82; Bubar, Statesman, 54.

Ohio

County	1980 Carter (D)	Reagan (R)	Anderson (I)	1984 Mondale (D)	Reagan (R)
Adams	4,161	5,336	303	3,633	6,112
Allen	13,140	29,070	1,439	12,163	33,486
Ashland	5,142	11,691	1,128	4,802	14,079
Ashtabula	17,363	19,847	2,481	19,322	21,660
Athens	9,514	8,170	1,544	10,173	11,507
Auglaize	5,022	11,537	785	4,100	14,764
Belmont	16,653	13,601	1,432	19,450	15,162
Brown	4,706	6,065	339	4,068	8,215
Butler	31,796	61,231	4,717	27,611	76,021
Carroll	3,476	5,806	406	3,963	6,882
Champaign	4,109	7,356	596	3,543	9,925
Clark	22,630	27,237	3,414	21,103	35,800
Clermont	13,199	26,674	1,697	11,710	35,301
Clinton	3,967	7,675	608	3,332	9,599
Columbiana	17,459	20,798	2,320	20,148	24,537
Coshocton	4,725	8,359	525	4,383	9,764
Crawford	6,058	12,424	411	4,920	14,004
Cuyahoga	307,448	254,883	40,750	361,856	283,812
Darke	7,635	12,773	1,198	5,903	16,372

efiance	5,096	9,358	896	4,994	10,937
elaware	6,417	14,740	1,278	5,624	18,814
rie	12,343	15,628	1,908	13,477	19,157
airfield	13,144	24,096	1,689	9,817	30,826
ayette	2,810	5,827	327	2,126	6,836
ranklin	143,932	200,948	21,269	130,534	248,718
ulton	3,972	9,519	1,026	4,216	11,410
allia	4,406	6,469	401	4,246	8,187
eauga	9,542	17,762	2,359	9,721	22,331
reene	20,068	24,922	3,160	16,975	34,012
uernsey	5,121	8,180	604	4,963	10,247
amilton	129,114	206,979	17,898	140,153	245,838
lancock	6,843	18,264	1,467	5,760	22,178
ardin	3,863	7,457	528	3,813	8,718
arrison	2,848	3,639	331	3,369	4,275
enry	3,059	7,584	691	2,778	9,316
ighland	4,363	7,359	454	3,784	8,997
ocking	3,765	4,588	312	3,275	6,070
olmes	2,094	3,860	329	1,736	5,143
uron	6,537	11,173	1,110	6,534	14,238
ackson	4,409	5,902	274	4,361	7,393
efferson	20,382	15,777	1,797	22,853	17,136
nox	6,586	10,384	987	5,729	13,987
ake	35,246	43,485	5,925	36,683	54,483
awrence	11,366	13,799	813	9,949	12,696
icking	17,208	28,425	2,419	13,991	37,544
ogan	4,319	9,727	718	3,642	12,226
orain	40,919	51,034	7,324	52,242	56,801
ucas	85,341	86,653	16,636	97,170	100,069
adison	3,565	7,166	438	2,924	8,977
ahoning	63,677	50,153	9,490	75,501	52,797
arion	9,419	14,605	1,255	8,825	17,380
edina	13,573	24,723	2,965	15,559	30,035
eigs	3,827	4,911	294	3,548	6,305
ercer	5,506	8,673	941	4,422	11,540
iami	12,893	19,928	2,429	9,693	26,296
onroe	3,166	2,870	266	3,609	3,303
ontgomery	105,110	101,443	13,817	93,989	136,986
organ	1,875	3,236	156	1,864	3,995
orrow	3,239	6,179	383	2,839	8,114
uskingum	12,584	17,921	1,329	10,203	21,920
oble	1,944	3,025	208	1,777	3,854
ttawa	6,753	8,641	1,281	7,051	10,912
aulding	2,778	4,971	550	2,729	5,376
erry	4,383	5,725	369	3,950	7,533
ckaway	5,052	9,289	515	4,068	11,840
ke	4,938	4,426	257	4,874	6,295
ortage	20,570	22,829	3,798	21,716	29,519
eble	5,416	8,376	687	4,198	11,061
utnam	3,742	9,752	533	3,194	11,929
ichland	18,253	29,213	2,586	16,130	35,271
oss	9,355	13,251	812	7,898	16,173
andusky	8,482	13,420	1,851	8,551	17,205
cioto	15,552	15,881	816	14,116	18,808
eneca	7,303	14,172	1,415	7,903	16,512
helby	6,425	8,988	895	4,314	13,505
ark	59,005	87,769	8,030	64,704	97,926
ummit	102,459	92,299	15,002	96,062	100,862
umbull	44,366	41,056	6,281	56,885	45,607
uscarawas	12,117	15,708	1,779	13,121	19,332
nion	3,038	7,576	421	2,578	9,335
an Wert	4,070	7,866	741	3,339	9,570
nton	2,381	2,484	138	1,990	3,038
arren	11,306	22,430	1,348	9,027	29,841
ashington	7,936	14,310	1,121	7,916	16,504
ayne	12,129	18,962	2,313	11,315	24,462
illiams	4,015	9,146	872	3,624	10,801
ood	14,139	23,315	4,156	15,845	29,632
yandot	2,757	5,786	407	2,313	7,095
otals	**1,752,414**	**2,206,545**	**254,472**	**1,804,870**	**2,653,691**

Ohio Vote Since 1932

932 (Pres.), Roosevelt, Dem., 1,301,695; Hoover, Rep., 1,227,679; Thomas, Soc., 64,094; Upshaw, Proh., 7,421; Foster, Com., 7,221; Reynolds, Soc. Labor, 1,968.

936 (Pres.), Roosevelt, Dem., 1,747,122; Landon, Rep., 1,127,709; Lemke, Union, 132,212; Browder, Com., 5,251; Thomas, Soc., 117; Aiken, Soc. Labor, 14.

940 (Pres.), Roosevelt, Dem., 1,733,139; Willkie, Rep., 1,586,773.

944 (Pres.), Roosevelt, Dem., 1,570,763; Dewey, Rep., 1,582,293.

948 (Pres.), Truman, Dem., 1,452,791; Dewey, Rep., 1,445,684; Wallace, Prog., 37,596.

952 (Pres.), Eisenhower, Rep., 2,100,391; Stevenson, Dem., 1,600,367.

956 (Pres.), Eisenhower, Rep., 2,262,610; Stevenson, Dem., 1,439,655.

960 (Pres.), Kennedy, Dem., 1,944,248; Nixon, Rep., 2,217,611.

964 (Pres.), Johnson, Dem., 2,498,331; Goldwater, Rep., 1,470,865.

968 (Pres.), Nixon, Rep., 1,791,014; Humphrey, Dem., 1,700,586; Wallace, 3d party, 467,495; Gregory, 372;

Munn, Proh., 19; Blomen, Soc. Labor, 120; Halstead, Soc. Worker, 69; Mitchell, Com., 23.

1972 (Pres.), Nixon, Rep., 2,441,827; McGovern, Dem., 1,558,889; Fisher, Soc. Labor, 7,107; Hall, Com., 6,437; Schmitz, Amer., 80,067; Wallace, Ind., 460.

1976 (Pres.), Carter, Dem., 2,011,621; Ford, Rep., 2,000,505; McCarthy, Ind., 58,258; Maddox, Amer. Ind., 15,529; MacBride, Libertarian, 8,961; Hall, Com., 7,817; Camejo, Soc. Workers, 4,717; LaRouche, U.S. Labor, 4,335; scattered, 130.

1980 (Pres.), Reagan, Rep., 2,206,545; Carter, Dem., 1,752,414; Anderson, Ind., 254,472; Clark, Libertarian, 49,033; Commoner, Citizens, 8,564; Hall, Com., 4,729; Congress, Ind. 4,029; Griswold, Workers World, 3,790; Bubar, Statesman, 27.

Oklahoma

	1980			1984	
County	Carter (D)	Reagan (R)	Anderson (I)	Mondale (D)	Reagan (R)
Adair	2,761	3,429	107	2,346	4,323
Alfalfa	899	2,628	86	866	2,715
Atoka	2,505	1,613	66	2,047	2,361
Beaver	696	2,430	58	536	2,689
Beckham	3,298	3,637	123	2,336	4,312
Blaine	1,399	3,708	103	1,484	4,037
Bryan	6,410	3,980	129	5,475	6,246
Caddo	4,695	5,945	232	4,463	6,811
Canadian	4,889	15,272	642	5,245	20,929
Carter	6,509	9,262	258	5,386	9,763
Cherokee	5,215	5,594	362	5,307	7,614
Choctaw	3,507	2,394	73	2,801	3,155
Cimarron	373	1,404	23	359	1,420
Cleveland	14,536	31,178	3,910	16,512	42,806
Coal	1,442	926	47	1,284	1,259
Comanche	9,972	16,609	1000	8,890	21,382
Cotton	1,410	1,702	63	1,264	1,796
Craig	2,801	2,956	156	2,203	3,276
Creek	7,339	11,749	460	6,327	12,545
Custer	3,008	6,469	290	2,730	8,191
Delaware	4,244	5,302	177	3,157	5,646
Dewey	826	1,943	70	664	2,098
Ellis	561	1,908	54	562	1,881
Garfield	5,718	17,989	846	5,576	18,381
Garvin	5,033	5,520	210	4,215	7,505
Grady	5,330	8,131	351	3,785	7,940
Grant	927	2,411	84	825	2,470
Greer	1,492	1,535	48	1,220	1,664
Harmon	961	676	21	321	1,550
Harper	517	1,652	40	282	1,299
Haskell	2,874	2,024	65	2,535	2,417
Hughes	3,211	2,170	85	2,147	2,096
Jackson	4,031	4,327	144	2,996	5,773
Jefferson	1,812	1,440	55	1,496	1,656
Johnston	2,066	1,701	57	1,820	2,205
Kay	6,449	15,004	665	6,044	16,731
Kingfisher	1,282	4,962	122	1,125	5,528
Kiowa	2,372	2,636	88	2,016	2,951
Latimer	2,105	1,737	71	1,858	2,210
Le Flore	6,668	6,807	174	5,307	7,321
Lincoln	3,231	6,064	204	2,854	6,590
Logan	3,246	6,311	259	2,741	6,166
Love	1,578	1,449	31	1,357	1,833
McClain	2,990	4,284	185	2,549	6,056
McCurtain	5,953	5,189	149	3,718	5,785
McIntosh	3,654	2,925	118	2,843	2,904
Major	584	3,059	62	619	3,385
Marshall	2,157	1,961	52	2,039	2,488
Mayes	5,344	6,633	256	4,049	6,781
Murray	2,384	2,494	126	2,229	3,073
Muskogee	13,341	11,511	633	12,221	13,054
Noble	1,398	3,663	124	997	3,205
Nowata	1,694	2,640	75	1,687	3,030
Okfuskee	2,177	2,126	58	1,687	2,443
Oklahoma	58,765	139,538	9,190	58,921	154,729
Okmulgee	7,236	6,652	286	7,380	8,704
Osage	5,687	8,044	363	5,059	9,208
Ottawa	6,143	6,362	317	5,062	10,633
Pawnee	2,020	3,902	161	2,165	4,699
Payne	7,466	15,955	1,812	7,053	19,093
Pittsburg	8,292	7,062	339	6,563	9,198
Pontotoc	5,942	6,232	335	5,526	8,301
Pottawatomie	8,526	12,466	625	5,960	13,997
Pushmataha	2,666	1,989	65	2,079	2,499
Roger Mills	877	1,221	50	680	1,550
Rogers	6,399	11,581	461	4,317	11,311
Seminole	4,726	5,067	224	3,957	6,009
Sequoyah	4,983	5,987	178	4,252	7,042
Stephens	7,191	10,199	310	6,359	12,871
Texas	1,451	5,503	93	1,033	5,968
Tillman	2,144	2,450	69	1,674	2,637
Tulsa	53,438	124,643	7,802	53,021	132,750
Wagoner	5,235	8,969	369	5,121	11,815
Washington	5,854	16,553	851	4,541	13,855
Washita	2,044	3,206	71	1,547	3,847

Woods	1,364	3,592	191	1,231	3,741
Woodward	1,703	5,318	175	1,868	5,056
Totals	402,026	695,570	38,284	362,771	793,258

Oklahoma Vote Since 1932

1932 (Pres.), Roosevelt, Dem., 516,468; Hoover, Rep., 188,165.

1936 (Pres.), Roosevelt, Dem., 501,069; Landon, Rep., 245,122; Thomas, Soc., 2,221; Colvin, Proh., 1,328.

1940 (Pres.), Roosevelt, Dem., 474,313; Willkie, Rep., 348,872; Babson, Proh., 3,027.

1944 (Pres.), Roosevelt, Dem., 401,549; Dewey, Rep., 319,424; Watson, Proh., 1,663.

1948 (Pres.), Truman, Dem., 452,782; Dewey, Rep., 268,817.

1952 (Pres.), Eisenhower, Rep., 518,045; Stevenson, Dem., 430,939.

1956 (Pres.), Eisenhower, Rep., 473,769; Stevenson, Dem., 385,581.

1960 (Pres.), Kennedy, Dem., 370,111; Nixon, Rep., 533,039.

1964 (Pres.), Johnson, Dem., 519,834; Goldwater, Rep. 412,665.

1968 (Pres.), Nixon, Rep., 449,697; Humphrey, Dem., 301,658; Wallace, 3d party, 191,731.

1972 (Pres.), Nixon, Rep. 759,025; McGovern, Dem., 247,147; Schmitz, Amer., 23,728.

1976 (Pres.), Carter, Dem., 532,442; Ford, Rep., 545,708; McCarthy, Ind., 14,101.

1980 (Pres.), Reagan, Rep., 695,570; Carter, Dem., 402,026; Anderson, Ind., 38,284; Clark, Libertarian, 13,828.

Oregon

	1980			1984	
County	Carter (D)	Reagan (R)	Anderson (I)	Mondale (D)	Reagan (R)
Baker	2,515	4,747	487	1,433	2,644
Benton	13,150	14,982	4,950	15,965	17,754
Clackamas	40,462	54,111	11,386	42,054	60,150
Clatsop	6,482	6,124	1,854	7,525	7,522
Columbia	7,124	6,623	1,158	9,162	7,811
Coos	11,817	13,041	2,428	13,681	13,658
Crook	2,162	3,113	435	2,471	4,041
Curry	2,656	4,910	652	2,287	3,352
Deschutes	9,641	15,186	2,909	11,679	19,340
Douglas.	12,564	23,101	2,529	14,412	25,065
Gilliam	394	622	85	369	700
Grant	1,274	2,519	273	1,250	2,425
Harney	1,110	2,313	255	1,102	1,909
Hood River. . . .	2,924	3,450	530	3,021	4,530
Jackson	19,903	32,879	4,019	22,003	35,402
Jefferson	1,654	2,523	431	1,166	1,796
Josephine	7,116	16,827	1,401	8,530	19,453
Klamath	7,371	16,060	1,427	7,027	16,374
Lake	1,147	2,234	201	1,175	2,446
Lane	52,240	54,750	12,076	60,418	56,688
Lincoln	7,009	7,637	1,637	8,637	9,111
Linn	13,516	18,943	2,823	16,161	23,461
Malheur.	2,937	7,705	472	1,996	6,453
Marion	32,134	42,191	8,755	36,365	54,399
Morrow	1,077	1,728	239	1,021	1,385
Multnomah	120,487	101,606	27,572	135,797	109,851
Polk.	7,833	10,006	2,026	8,569	12,419
Sherman	389	677	62	398	828
Tillamook	4,521	4,123	931	4,987	5,267
Umatilla.	7,382	12,950	1,531	8,245	14,195
Union	3,677	6,514	763	NA	NA
Wallowa	995	2,485	216	1,204	2,619
Wasco	4,336	4,703	819	4,563	5,610
Washington . . .	37,915	57,165	13,076	41,913	69,638
Wheeler	282	442	62	253	504
Yamhill	8,694	12,054	1,919	8,374	14,446
Totals	456,890	571,044	112,389	505,632	633,246

Oregon Vote Since 1932

1932 (Pres.), Roosevelt, Dem., 213,871; Hoover, Rep., 136,019; Thomas, Soc., 15,450; Reynolds, Soc. Labor, 1,730; Foster, Com., 1,681.

1936 (Pres.), Roosevelt, Dem., 266,733; Landon, Rep., 122,706; Lemke, Union, 21,831; Thomas, Soc., 2,143; Aiken, Soc. Labor, 500; Browder, Com., 104; Colvin, Proh., 4.

1940 (Pres.), Roosevelt, Dem., 258,415; Willkie, Rep., 219,555; Aiken, Soc. Labor, 2,487; Thomas, Soc., 398; Browder, Com., 191; Babson, Proh., 154.

1944 (Pres.), Roosevelt, Dem., 248,635; Dewey, Rep., 225,365; Thomas, Soc., 3,785; Watson, Proh., 2,362.

1948 (Pres.), Truman, Dem., 243,147; Dewey, Rep. 260,904; Wallace, Prog., 14,978; Thomas, Soc., 5,051.

1952 (Pres.), Eisenhower, Rep., 420,815; Stevenson, Dem., 270,579; Hallinan, Ind., 3,665.

1956 (Pres.), Eisenhower, Rep., 406,393; Stevenson, Dem., 329,204.

1960 (Pres.), Kennedy, Dem., 367,402; Nixon, Rep., 408,060.

1964 (Pres.), Johnson, Dem., 501,017; Goldwater, Rep., 282,779; write-in, 2,509.

1968 (Pres.), Nixon, Rep., 408,433; Humphrey, Dem., 358,866; Wallace, 3d party, 49,683; write-in, McCarthy, 1,496; N. Rockefeller, 69; others, 1,075.

1972 (Pres.), Nixon, Rep., 486,686; McGovern, Dem., 392,760, Schmitz, Amer., 46,211; write-in, 2,289.

1976 (Pres.), Carter, Dem., 490,407; Ford, Rep., 492,120; McCarthy, Ind., 40,207; write-in, 7,142.

1980 (Pres.), Reagan, Rep., 571,044; Carter, Dem., 456,890; Anderson, Ind., 112,389; Clark, Libertarian, 25,838; Commoner, Citizens, 13,642; scattered, 1,713.

Pennsylvania

	1980			1984	
County	Carter (D)	Reagan (R)	Anderson (I)	Mondale (D)	Reagan (R)
Adams	7,266	13,760	1,139	7,074	16,3
Allegheny	297,464	271,850	38,710	369,887	282,3
Armstrong	12,718	12,955	1,153	14,525	13,7
Beaver	43,955	30,496	4,549	54,195	31,2
Bedford.	4,950	10,930	416	5,411	13,0
Berks	36,449	60,576	8,863	37,843	74,5
Blair.	15,014	28,931	2,011	15,614	29,9
Bradford	6,439	13,139	1,068	5,469	14,5
Bucks	59,120	100,536	18,107	74,465	129,8
Butler	19,711	28,821	3,453	24,704	31,5
Cambria	36,121	33,072	2,398	39,694	31,7
Cameron	1,112	1,795	92	991	2,0
Carbon	8,009	10,042	956	8,935	10,6
Centre	15,987	20,605	5,247	16,155	27,7
Chester.	34,307	73,046	10,911	38,870	92,2
Clarion	5,472	8,812	678	5,743	10,1
Clearfield.	11,647	15,299	944	11,974	18,6
Clinton	4,842	6,288	733	4,526	6,6
Columbia	9,449	12,426	1,197	8,254	14,3
Crawford	11,778	16,552	2,095	13,771	20,0
Cumberland . . .	19,789	41,152	5,437	21,328	48,9
Dauphin.	27,252	44,039	6,034	33,567	54,3
Delaware	88,314	143,282	20,907	98,769	163,2
Elk.	5,898	7,175	472	5,374	8,5
Erie	45,946	48,918	6,349	51,897	55,4
Fayette	27,963	19,252	1,348	34,982	21,3
Forest.	819	1,206	93	839	1,4
Franklin.	12,061	22,716	1,724	11,480	27,2
Fulton.	1,342	2,740	107	1,319	3,2
Greene	8,193	5,336	450	9,033	5,9
Huntingdon	5,094	8,140	567	4,465	10,1
Indiana	13,828	15,607	1,708	14,923	17,8
Jefferson	6,296	9,628	687	5,862	11,2
Juniata	2,696	4,139	280	2,524	5,0
Lackawanna . . .	45,257	44,242	4,209	44,348	44,3
Lancaster.	30,026	79,963	7,442	31,225	98,4
Lawrence.	19,506	18,404	1,908	23,727	19,0
Lebanon	8,281	24,495	2,314	10,519	26,8
Lehigh	34,827	50,782	8,977	41,044	61,3
Luzerne.	59,976	67,822	4,947	58,187	69,1
Lycoming	14,609	23,415	2,034	13,122	28,3
McKean.	5,064	9,229	661	4,803	11,1
Mercer	19,716	22,372	3,247	23,135	21,6
Mifflin	5,226	7,541	578	5,173	9,1
Monroe	7,551	12,357	1,967	8,139	16,1
Montgomery . . .	84,289	156,996	26,133	100,422	181,8
Montour	2,272	3,399	375	2,055	4,1
Northampton . . .	31,920	35,787	6,823	37,609	44,2
Northumberland .	13,750	20,608	1,515	13,557	21,7
Perry	3,681	8,026	717	3,685	9,3
Philadelphia . . .	421,253	244,108	42,967	490,655	262,7
Pike	2,132	5,249	452	2,502	6,2
Potter.	2,299	4,073	225	1,786	5,1
Schuylkill	24,968	36,273	3,079	25,803	37,1
Snyder	2,418	7,634	451	2,370	9,0
Somerset.	11,695	17,729	815	13,657	19,0
Sullivan	1,074	1,676	130	960	1,9
Susquehanna . .	4,660	8,994	786	4,457	10,8
Tioga	4,273	8,770	664	4,055	10,4
Union	2,687	6,798	628	2,746	7,1
Venango	7,800	11,547	1,015	8,985	13,3
Warren	5,560	9,165	922	6,308	10,3
Washington . . .	45,295	32,532	3,413	50,839	34,4
Wayne	3,375	8,408	490	3,255	10,1
Westmoreland . .	68,627	63,140	5,985	79,739	70,1
Wyoming	2,766	5,919	384	2,530	7,1

York.	33,406	61,098	5,779	33,278	74,749
Totals	1,937,540	2,261,872	292,921	2,209,137	2,564,273

Pennsylvania Vote Since 1932

1932 (Pres.), Roosevelt, Dem., 1,295,948; Hoover, Rep., 1,453,540; Thomas, Soc., 91,119; Upshaw, Proh., 11,319; Foster, Com., 5,658; Cox, Jobless, 725; Reynolds, Indust., 659.

1936 (Pres.), Roosevelt, Dem., 2,353,788; Landon, Rep., 1,690,300; Lemke, Royal Oak, 67,467; Thomas, Soc., 14,375; Colvin, Proh., 6,691; Browder, Com., 4,060; Aiken, Ind. Lab., 1,424.

1940 (Pres.), Roosevelt, Dem., 2,171,035; Willkie, Rep., 1,889,848; Thomas, Soc., 10,967; Browder, Com., 4,519; Aiken, Ind. Gov., 1,518.

1944 (Pres.), Roosevelt, Dem., 1,940,479; Dewey, Rep., 1,835,054; Thomas, Soc., 11,721; Watson, Proh., 5,750; Teichert, Ind. Gov., 1,789.

1948 (Pres.), Truman, Dem., 1,752,426; Dewey, Rep., 1,902,197; Wallace, Prog., 55,161; Thomas, Soc., 11,325; Watson, Proh., 10,338; Dobbs, Militant Workers, 2,133; Teichert, Ind. Gov., 1,461.

1952 (Pres.), Eisenhower, Rep., 2,415,789; Stevenson, Dem., 2,146,269; Hamblen, Proh., 8,771; Hallinan, Prog., 4,200; Hoopes, Soc., 2,684; Dobbs, Militant Workers, 1,502; Hass, Ind. Gov., 1,347; scattered, 155.

1956 (Pres.), Eisenhower, Rep., 2,585,252; Stevenson, Dem., 1,981,769; Hass, Soc. Labor, 7,447; Dobbs, Militant Workers, 2,035.

1960 (Pres.), Kennedy, Dem., 2,556,282; Nixon, Rep., 2,439,956; Hass, Soc. Labor, 7,185; Dobbs, Soc. Workers, 2,678; scattering, 440.

1964 (Pres.), Johnson, Dem., 3,130,954; Goldwater, Rep., 1,673,657; DeBerry, Soc. Workers, 10,456; Hass, Labor, 5,092; scattering, 2,531.

1968 (Pres.), Nixon, Rep., 2,090,017; Humphrey, Dem., 2,259,405; Wallace, 3d party, 378,582; Blomen, Soc. Labor, 4,977; Halstead, Soc. Workers, 4,862; Gregory, 7,821; others, 2,264.

1972 (Pres.), Nixon, Rep., 2,714,521; McGovern, Dem., 1,796,951; Schmitz, Amer., 70,593; Jenness, Soc. Workers, 4,639; Hall, Com., 2,686; others, 2,715.

1976 (Pres.), Carter, Dem., 2,328,677; Ford, Rep., 2,205,604; McCarthy, Ind., 50,584; Maddox, Constitution, 25,344; Camejo, Soc. Workers, 3,009; LaRouche, U.S. Labor, 2,744; Hall, Com., 1,891; others, 2,934.

1980 (Pres.), Reagan, Rep., 2,261,872; Carter, Dem., 1,937,540; Anderson, Ind., 292,921; Clark, Libertarian, 33,263; DeBerry, Soc. Workers, 20,291; Commoner, Consumer, 10,430; Hall, Com., 5,184.

Rhode Island

	1980			1984	
County	Carter (D)	Reagan (R)	Anderson (I)	Mondale (D)	Reagan (R)
Cranston	17,293	14,781	5,420	17,151	18,895
East Providence. .	11,440	7,566	3,094	10,778	9,947
Pawtucket	14,455	8,402	3,644	13,988	12,156
Providence	36,249	16,689	7,932	35,368	19,163
Warwick	18,424	15,890	6,498	18,827	21,605
Totals	198,342	154,793	59,819	191,914	204,450

Rhode Island Vote Since 1932

1932 (Pres.), Roosevelt, Dem., 146,604; Hoover, Rep., 115,266; Thomas, Soc., 3,138; Foster, Com., 546; Reynolds, Soc. Labor, 433; Upshaw, Proh., 183.

1936 (Pres.), Roosevelt, Dem., 165,238; Landon, Rep., 125,031; Lemke, Union, 19,569; Aiken, Soc. Labor, 929; Browder, Com., 411.

1940 (Pres.), Roosevelt, Dem., 182,182; Willkie, Rep., 138,653; Browder, Com., 239; Babson, Proh., 74.

1944 (Pres.), Roosevelt, Dem., 175,356; Dewey, Rep., 123,487; Watson, Proh., 433.

1948 (Pres.), Truman, Dem., 188,736; Dewey, Rep., 135,787; Wallace, Prog., 2,619; Thomas, Soc., 429; Teichert, Soc. Labor, 131.

1952 (Pres.), Eisenhower, Rep., 210,935; Stevenson, Dem., 203,293; Hallinan, Prog., 187; Hass, Soc. Labor, 83.

1956 (Pres.), Eisenhower, Rep., 225,819; Stevenson, Dem., 161,790.

1960 (Pres.), Kennedy, Dem., 258,032; Nixon, Rep., 147,502.

1964 (Pres.), Johnson, Dem., 315,463; Goldwater, Rep., 74,615.

1968 (Pres.), Nixon, Rep., 122,359; Humphrey, Dem., 246,518; Wallace, 3d party, 15,678; Halstead, Soc. Worker, 383.

1972 (Pres.), Nixon, Rep., 220,383; McGovern, Dem., 194,645; Jenness, Soc. Workers, 729.

1976 (Pres.), Carter, Dem., 227,636; Ford, Rep., 181,249; MacBride, Libertarian, 715; Camejo, Soc. Workers, 462; Hall, Com., 334; Levin, Soc. Labor, 188.

1980 (Pres.), Reagan, Rep., 154,793; Carter, Dem., 198,342; Anderson, Ind., 59,819; Clark, Libertarian, 2,458; Hall, Com., 218; McReynolds, Socialist, 170; DeBerry, Soc. Worker, 90; Griswold, Workers World, 77.

South Carolina

	1980			1984	
County	Carter (D)	Reagan (R)	Anderson (I)	Mondale (D)	Reagan (R)
Abbeville	4,049	2,261	111	3,051	3,798
Aiken	13,014	18,568	601	1,078	2,891
Allendale	2,775	1,181	18	2,170	1,570
Anderson	18,796	15,666	474	9,629	22,844
Bamberg	3,294	2,098	18	2,892	2,908
Barnwell	3,399	3,228	64	2,811	4,346
Beaufort	7,415	8,620	513	7,344	13,661
Berkeley	9,850	12,790	17	9,339	17,091
Calhoun	2,043	1,767	31	2,308	2,737
Charleston	32,744	44,006	2,213	25,195	44,769
Cherokee	6,891	5,378	86	4,101	8,733
Chester	5,145	3,104	87	3,547	4,415
Chesterfield	6,393	3,477	65	4,616	5,466
Clarendon	5,980	4,158	28	5,591	5,102
Colleton	5,745	4,719	58	1,993	2,650
Darlington	9,009	8,289	219	7,450	11,099
Dillon	4,518	3,384	59	3,360	4,646
Dorchester	7,237	10,893	140	3,834	7,970
Edgefield	3,465	2,415	30	1,209	1,041
Fairfield	4,153	2,098	37	5,560	3,753
Florence	16,391	17,069	348	14,513	24,194
Georgetown	6,701	5,151	148	8,196	9,461
Greenville	32,135	46,168	1,600	24,137	66,766
Greenwood	9,283	7,287	230	6,505	10,813
Hampton	4,329	2,217	35	3,736	3,464
Horry	13,885	14,322	530	8,916	20,345
Jasper	3,316	1,617	33	3,505	2,691
Kershaw	5,103	6,652	145	4,213	8,449
Lancaster	8,282	6,409	331	5,803	10,311
Laurens	7,858	6,034	129	5,620	9,728
Lee	4,816	2,952	18	3,909	3,548
Lexington	12,334	28,313	762	8,820	38,615
McCormick	5,378	2,585	52	1,525	1,159
Marion	1,774	797	22	5,013	4,698
Marlboro	5,377	3,318	80	4,290	3,950
Newberry	4,825	5,568	80	3,790	7,179
Oconee	7,677	5,652	188	3,330	8,619
Orangeburg	16,178	11,313	141	14,453	13,743
Pickens	7,789	9,574	402	4,479	15,151
Richland	33,298	35,843	1,808	32,170	46,724
Saluda	2,649	2,451	38	1,962	3,515
Spartanburg	27,238	28,820	933	20,128	41,790
Sumter	9,205	10,655	250	NA	NA
Union	6,274	4,035	93	2,911	4,397
Williamsburg	8,135	5,110	64	4,904	4,660
York	12,075	11,261	539	9,035	19,854
Totals	428,220	439,277	13,868	312,911	555,314

South Carolina Vote Since 1932

1932 (Pres.), Roosevelt, Dem., 102,347; Hoover, Rep., 1,978; Thomas, Soc., 82.

1936 (Pres.), Roosevelt, Dem., 113,791; Landon, Rep., Tolbert faction 953, Hambright faction 693, total, 1,646.

1940 (Pres.), Roosevelt, Dem., 95,470; Willkie, Rep., 1,727.

1944 (Pres.), Roosevelt, Dem., 90,601; Dewey, Rep., 4,547; Southern Democrats, 7,799; Watson, Proh., 365; Rep. Tolbert faction, 63.

1948 (Pres.), Thurmond, States' Rights, 102,607; Truman, Dem., 34,423; Dewey, Rep., 5,386; Wallace, Prog., 154; Thomas, Soc., 1.

1952 (Pres.), Eisenhower ran on two tickets. Under state law vote cast for two Eisenhower slates of electors could not be combined. Eisenhower, Ind., 158,289; Rep., 9,793; total, 168,082; Stevenson, Dem., 173,004; Hamblen, Proh., 1.

1956 (Pres.), Stevenson, Dem., 136,372; Byrd, Ind., 88,509; Eisenhower, Rep., 75,700; Andrews, Ind., 2.

1960 (Pres.), Kennedy, Dem., 198,129; Nixon, Rep., 188,558; write-in, 1.

1964 (Pres.), Johnson, Dem., 215,700; Goldwater, Rep., 309,048; write-ins: Nixon, 1, Wallace, 5; Powell, 1; Thurmond, 1.

1968 (Pres.), Nixon, Rep., 254,062; Humphrey, Dem., 197,486; Wallace, 3d party, 215,430.

1972 (Pres.), Nixon, Rep., 477,044; McGovern, Dem., 184,559, United Citizens, 2,265; Schmitz, Amer., 10,075; write-in, 17.

1976 (Pres.), Carter, Dem., 450,807; Ford, Rep., 346,149; Anderson, Amer., 2,996; Maddox, Amer. Ind., 1,950; write-in, 681.

1980 (Pres.), Reagan, Rep., 439,277; Carter, Dem., 428,220; Anderson, Ind., 13,868; Clark, Libertarian, 4,807; Rarick, Amer. Ind., 2,086.

South Dakota

County	1980 Carter (D)	Reagan (R)	Anderson (I)	1984 Mondale (D)	Reagan (R)
Aurora	709	1,251	125	840	1,029
Beadle	3,521	5,921	545	3,533	5,877
Bennett	350	919	42	453	856
Bon Homme	1,191	2,794	214	1,408	2,475
Brookings	3,934	5,727	1,169	2,967	4,636
Brown	6,050	10,550	1,143	6,852	10,541
Brule	925	1,674	153	961	1,578
Buffalo	147	272	26	336	253
Butte	843	2,850	150	784	2,865
Campbell	182	1,271	39	214	1,035
Chas. Mix	1,741	2,608	203	1,877	2,661
Clark	774	1,963	151	960	1,748
Clay	2,271	3,004	906	2,711	3,057
Codington	3,353	5,903	638	3,527	6,109
Corson	708	1,233	82	792	955
Custer	708	2,057	129	858	2,183
Davison	3,107	4,743	568	3,248	4,783
Day	1,720	2,507	259	1,932	2,150
Deuel	891	1,657	169	941	1,537
Dewey	600	1,045	109	772	941
Douglas	508	1,855	91	536	1,713
Edmunds	883	1,881	125	1,007	1,553
Fall River	982	2,831	184	1,135	2,748
Faulk	520	1,300	110	579	1,124
Grant	1,602	2,691	254	1,606	2,738
Gregory	883	2,283	121	780	1,777
Haakon	255	1,162	38	237	1,168
Hamlin	903	1,885	197	963	1,782
Hand	803	2,066	159	846	2,030
Hanson	598	1,015	93	625	898
Harding	205	727	28	186	723
Hughes	1,751	4,652	554	2,072	4,985
Hutchinson	1,145	3,789	228	1,237	3,372
Hyde	273	864	60	350	797
Jackson	354	929	50	365	903
Jerauld	595	1,018	103	542	1,012
Jones	189	689	37	198	689
Kingsbury	1,132	2,376	258	1,249	2,121
Lake	2,207	3,093	504	2,367	3,027
Lawrence	2,259	5,306	574	2,565	5,949
Lincoln	2,261	3,848	524	2,626	3,988
Lyman	486	1,256	106	478	1,120
McCook	1,223	2,014	269	1,447	1,901
McPherson	287	2,056	54	571	1,812
Marshall	1,120	1,710	147	1,111	1,529
Meade	1,721	5,349	342	2,093	5,908
Mellette	279	624	46	303	616
Miner	833	1,172	148	960	1,004
Minnehaha	20,008	26,256	4,658	23,052	29,899
Moody	1,364	1,807	279	1,586	1,633
Pennington	7,121	18,991	1,650	8,221	21,947
Perkins	595	1,931	93	701	1,674
Potter	436	1,633	81	482	1,551
Roberts	1,829	2,904	235	2,063	2,767
Sanborn	628	1,178	107	611	1,024
Shannon	1,132	438	91	1,231	299
Spink	1,572	2,915	294	1,675	2,627
Stanley	339	892	55	351	942
Sully	220	852	60	266	836
Todd	972	803	112	1,022	679
Tripp	947	2,669	130	935	2,483
Turner	1,369	3,343	281	1,486	3,086
Union	1,830	2,788	359	2,221	2,431
Walworth	753	2,675	139	779	2,396
Yankton	2,698	5,355	553	2,932	5,160
Ziebach	246	523	30	353	429
Totals	103,855	198,343	21,431	114,967	198,119

South Dakota Vote Since 1932

1932 (Pres.), Roosevelt, Dem., 183,515; Hoover, Rep., 99,212; Harvey, Lib., 3,333; Thomas, Soc., 1,551; Upshaw, Proh., 463; Foster, Com., 364.

1936 (Pres.), Roosevelt, Dem., 160,137; Landon, Rep., 125,977; Lemke, Union, 10,338.

1940 (Pres.), Roosevelt, Dem., 131,862; Willkie, Rep., 177,065.

1944 (Pres.), Roosevelt, Dem., 96,711; Dewey, Rep., 135,365.

1948 (Pres.), Truman, Dem., 117,653; Dewey, Rep., 129,651; Wallace, Prog., 2,801.

1952 (Pres.), Eisenhower, Rep., 203,857; Stevenson, Dem., 90,426.

1956 (Pres.), Eisenhower, Rep., 171,569; Stevenson, Dem., 122,288.

1960 (Pres.), Kennedy, Dem., 128,070; Nixon, Rep., 178,417.

1964 (Pres.), Johnson, Dem., 163,010; Goldwater, Rep., 130,108.

1968 (Pres.), Nixon, Rep., 149,841; Humphrey, Dem., 118,023; Wallace, 3d party, 13,400.

1972 (Pres.), Nixon, Rep., 166,476; McGovern, Dem., 139,945; Jenness, Soc. Workers, 994.

1976 (Pres.), Carter, Dem., 147,068; Ford, Rep., 151,505; MacBride, Libertarian, 1,619; Hall, Com., 318; Camejo, Soc. Workers, 168.

1980 (Pres.), Reagan, Rep., 198,343; Carter, Dem., 103,855; Anderson, Ind., 21,431; Clark, Libertarian, 3,824; Pulley, Soc. Workers, 250.

Tennessee

County	1980 Carter (D)	Reagan (R)	Anderson (I)	1984 Mondale (D)	Reagan (R)
Anderson	10,194	14,235	1,161	10,421	16,764
Bedford	5,987	3,377	159	4,734	4,935
Benton	3,811	2,281	71	3,398	2,481
Bledsoe	1,585	1,970	26	1,316	1,950
Blount	9,412	17,959	620	9,188	20,158
Bradley	7,638	11,869	316	6,085	16,382
Campbell	4,752	5,537	120	4,690	5,687
Cannon	2,351	1,403	41	1,746	1,669
Carroll	5,277	5,681	125	4,578	6,017
Carter	6,006	11,648	326	4,827	13,140
Cheatham	3,771	2,296	90	2,992	4,112
Chester	2,123	2,751	52	1,854	2,893
Claiborne	2,844	4,289	94	2,870	4,474
Clay	1,376	1,344	27	1,281	1,328
Cocke	2,139	6,802	139	2,067	6,657
Coffee	7,612	5,454	239	5,690	7,700
Crockett	2,422	2,117	27	1,937	2,479
Cumberland	3,775	6,354	227	3,612	7,183
Davidson	103,741	65,772	4,834	89,115	98,038
Decatur	2,139	2,095	35	2,031	2,390
De Kalb	2,948	1,841	48	2,645	2,337
Dickson	6,622	3,636	157	5,809	5,828
Dyer	5,713	5,475	158	3,966	6,473
Fayette	4,141	2,944	75	3,634	3,733
Fentress	1,543	2,493	49	1,755	2,922
Franklin	6,760	3,995	251	5,845	5,705
Gibson	9,829	6,792	227	8,333	9,566
Giles	4,653	2,757	85	3,812	3,873
Grainger	1,495	3,254	66	1,565	3,212
Greene	5,822	10,704	338	4,771	13,122
Grundy	2,837	1,139	33	2,596	1,396
Hamblen	5,890	9,741	336	4,922	11,144
Hamilton	41,913	57,575	2,087	41,448	69,624
Hancock	704	1,734	32	644	1,493
Hardeman	4,153	2,931	73	3,797	3,632
Hardin	3,164	4,152	76	3,040	4,736
Hawkins	5,283	7,836	310	4,802	9,863
Haywood	3,445	2,435	49	3,308	2,839
Henderson	2,702	5,108	78	2,426	5,162
Henry	6,601	4,299	200	5,407	5,378
Hickman	3,225	1,903	78	2,941	2,370
Houston	1,757	738	31	1,716	882
Humphreys	3,974	1,897	74	3,768	2,249
Jackson	2,480	995	27	2,893	1,544
Jefferson	3,180	6,944	201	3,185	7,721
Johnson	1,141	3,716	66	999	3,853
Knox	45,634	66,153	4,801	43,297	96,763
Lake	1,718	823	11	1,041	762
Lauderdale	4,318	2,818	73	3,506	3,566
Lawrence	6,082	6,532	212	5,292	6,794
Lewis	2,190	1,076	33	1,556	1,733
Lincoln	5,387	2,856	119	4,098	3,988
Loudon	3,699	6,382	235	3,227	7,113
McMinn	5,460	7,825	200	5,141	9,605
McNairy	3,801	4,603	76	3,825	4,776
Macon	1,947	2,925	65	1,747	3,330
Madison	12,986	13,667	363	6,878	11,677
Marion	4,623	3,902	93	3,942	4,337
Marshall	4,277	2,282	78	2,939	3,411

County	7,957	6,637	225	6,950	9,000
aury	7,957	6,637	225	6,950	9,000
eigs	999	1,278	31	1,003	1,575
onroe	4,612	6,246	125	4,223	6,665
ontgomery	11,573	8,503	490	9,939	13,198
oore	993	551	34	808	863
organ	2,094	2,823	70	2,121	2,903
bion	5,766	5,397	138	4,769	6,389
verton	3,343	1,869	38	2,749	2,165
erry	1,401	783	32	1,316	948
ckett	758	1,319	12	716	1,246
olk	2,470	2,414	45	1,990	2,630
utnam	8,084	6,235	342	7,443	9,000
hea	3,070	4,689	93	2,804	5,689
oane	6,473	11,096	481	6,623	11,680
obertson	7,381	3,560	127	5,746	5,444
utherford	15,213	11,208	703	11,741	18,963
cott	1,724	3,014	63	1,810	3,107
equatchie	1,509	1,512	23	1,238	1,785
evier	3,450	10,576	338	3,385	12,524
helby	159,240	140,157	7,180	165,747	170,066
mith	3,674	1,755	69	3,258	2,393
tewart	2,274	985	42	2,174	1,285
ullivan	22,341	25,963	1,874	16,925	35,816
umner	14,150	11,876	540	11,526	18,542
ipton	4,934	4,339	109	3,895	5,945
rousdale	1,674	629	30	1,142	781
nicoi	1,880	3,828	97	1,497	3,889
nion	1,435	2,453	45	1,475	2,459
an Buren	886	499	11	810	718
Varren	6,021	3,680	148	4,813	4,811
Vashington	11,599	17,457	934	9,459	21,762
Vayne	1,633	3,418	78	1,533	3,332
Veakley	5,910	5,668	136	4,752	6,480
Vhite	3,415	2,100	64	3,032	2,897
Villiamson	8,815	11,597	551	6,926	17,508
Vilson	11,248	7,535	380	8,433	12,891
otals	783,051	787,761	35,991	705,719	1,002,307

Tennessee Vote Since 1932

1932 (Pres.), Roosevelt, Dem., 259,817; Hoover, Rep., 126,806; Upshaw, Proh., 1,995; Thomas, Soc., 1,786; Foster, Com., 234.

1936 (Pres.), Roosevelt, Dem., 327,083; Landon, Rep., 146,516; Thomas, Soc., 685; Colvin, Proh., 632; Browder, Com., 319; Lemke, Union, 296.

1940 (Pres.), Roosevelt, Dem., 351,601; Willkie, Rep., 169,153; Babson, Proh., 1,606; Thomas, Soc., 463.

1944 (Pres.), Roosevelt, Dem., 308,707; Dewey, Rep., 200,311; Watson, Proh., 882; Thomas, Soc., 892.

1948 (Pres.), Truman, Dem., 270,402; Dewey, Rep., 202,914; Thurmond, States' Rights, 73,815; Wallace, Prog., 1,864; Thomas, Soc., 1,288.

1952 (Pres.), Eisenhower, Rep., 446,147; Stevenson, Dem., 443,710; Hamblen, Proh., 1,432; Hallinan, Prog., 885; MacArthur, Christian Nationalist, 379.

1956 (Pres.), Eisenhower, Rep., 462,288; Stevenson, Dem., 456,507; Andrews, Ind., 19,820; Holtwick, Proh., 789.

1960 (Pres.), Kennedy, Dem., 481,453; Nixon, Rep., 556,577; Faubus, States' Rights, 11,304; Decker, Proh., 2,458.

1964 (Pres.), Johnson, Dem. 635,047; Goldwater, Rep., 508,965; write-in, 34.

1968 (Pres.), Nixon, Rep., 472,592; Humphrey, Dem., 351,233; Wallace, 3d party, 424,792.

1972 (Pres.), Nixon, Rep., 813,147; McGovern, Dem., 357,293; Schmitz, Amer., 30,373; write-in, 369.

1976 (Pres.), Carter, Dem., 825,879; Ford, Rep., 633,969; Anderson, Amer., 5,769; McCarthy, Ind., 5,004; Maddox, Am. Ind., 2,303; MacBride, Libertarian, 1,375; Hall, Com., 547; LaRouche, U.S. Labor, 512; Bubar, Proh., 442; Miller, Ind., 316; write-in, 230.

1980 (Pres.), Reagan, Rep., 787,761; Carter, Dem., 783,051; Anderson, Ind., 35,991; Clark, Libertarian, 7,116; Commoner, Citizens, 1,112; Bubar, Statesman, 521; McReynolds, Socialist, 519; Hall, Com., 503; DeBerry, Soc. Worker, 490; Griswold, Workers World, 400; write-ins, 152.

Texas

County	1980			1984	
	Carter (D)	Reagan (R)	Anderson (I)	Mondale (D)	Reagan (R)
anderson	5,163	5,970	137	4,643	8,161
ndrews	1,155	2,800	39	820	3,918
ngelina	10,140	9,900	232	9,054	14,655
ansas	1,800	3,081	134	1,696	4,352
cher	1,444	1,804	30	1,089	2,487
mstrong	333	709	9	238	791
ascosa	3,980	4,364	93	3,345	4,248
Austin	1,893	3,734	87	1,941	4,872
Bailey	800	1,809	26	684	1,888
Bandera	894	2,373	64	771	3,152
Bastrop	4,716	3,768	205	4,744	6,439
Baylor	1,183	1,098	14	1,019	1,314
Bee	3,606	4,171	125	3,659	5,377
Bell	15,823	20,729	934	13,322	31,022
Bexar	137,729	159,578	9,467	136,957	202,966
Blanco	794	1,434	52	701	1,957
Borden	131	279	3	140	325
Bosque	2,431	2,908	62	2,048	3,927
Bowie	11,339	13,942	244	10,077	18,224
Brazoria	18,253	27,614	1,205	18,609	39,166
Brazos	9,856	17,798	1,453	12,348	34,733
Brewster	1,271	1,496	89	1,462	2,066
Briscoe	561	562	13	471	538
Brooks	2,488	780	43	2,702	846
Brown	4,867	6,515	102	4,070	8,468
Burleson	2,615	1,943	33	2,578	3,076
Burnet	3,711	4,033	132	2,983	5,895
Caldwell	3,155	2,879	112	3,224	3,905
Calhoun	3,034	3,312	136	2,541	4,395
Callahan	2,002	2,284	29	1,260	3,486
Cameron	23,200	22,041	801	25,649	24,935
Camp	2,052	1,531	19	1,917	2,237
Carson	1,006	1,888	26	826	2,412
Cass	5,578	4,993	60	4,989	6,605
Castro	1,199	1,955	44	1,009	2,026
Chambers	2,517	3,140	96	2,632	4,322
Cherokee	5,726	5,629	92	4,494	8,187
Childress	1,222	1,443	33	900	1,574
Clay	2,233	1,824	40	1,800	2,537
Cochran	513	1,064	23	557	1,117
Coke	838	708	10	532	1,060
Coleman	1,719	2,228	33	1,429	2,789
Collin	15,187	36,559	1,559	13,604	61,095
Collingsworth	798	1,020	18	689	1,383
Colorado	2,377	3,520	58	2,657	4,782
Comal	3,554	9,758	324	4,179	13,452
Comanche	2,550	1,977	40	2,258	2,688
Concho	702	700	8	580	821
Cooke	3,842	6,760	129	3,278	8,265
Coryell	4,097	5,494	228	3,064	8,979
Cottle	732	511	9	623	507
Crane	607	1,310	23	392	1,473
Crockett	595	885	10	589	824
Crosby	1,408	1,361	17	1,212	1,376
Culberson	423	541	7	406	478
Dallam	632	965	33	496	1,594
Dallas	190,459	306,682	14,271	203,218	405,046
Dawson	1,867	3,267	55	1,781	3,788
Deaf Smith	1,666	4,073	77	1,485	4,762
Delta	1,347	767	18	973	1,024
Denton	17,381	29,908	1,953	16,772	52,865
DeWitt	2,044	3,450	66	1,882	4,401
Dickens	912	554	13	692	594
Dimmit	2,102	1,173	25	2,546	1,338
Donley	751	1,106	22	529	1,297
Duval	3,706	1,012	28	3,748	1,201
Eastland	3,346	3,442	37	2,522	4,841
Ector	9,069	26,188	636	8,913	31,228
Edwards	237	575	11	159	626
Ellis	9,219	10,046	214	7,932	16,720
El Paso	40,082	53,276	5,096	34,574	47,437
Erath	4,156	3,981	92	3,222	6,119
Falls	3,328	2,606	51	2,834	3,133
Fannin	5,284	3,196	74	4,399	4,692
Fayette	2,590	4,104	77	2,379	5,711
Fisher	1,564	838	23	1,384	965
Floyd	1,477	2,043	24	1,023	2,092
Foard	617	349	7	448	472
Fort Bend	11,583	25,366	1,005	18,546	39,912
Franklin	1,487	1,105	14	1,104	1,836
Freestone	2,739	2,468	33	2,529	3,624
Frio	2,849	1,753	47	2,594	1,992
Gaines	1,182	2,390	46	797	2,714
Galveston	30,778	29,527	1,955	32,639	36,222
Garza	677	1,188	22	521	1,219
Gillespie	1,170	4,736	90	1,137	5,496
Glasscock	116	416	2	128	403
Goliad	1,081	1,170	22	815	1,528
Gonzales	2,896	2,931	61	2,196	3,962
Gray	2,786	7,187	103	2,003	8,955
Grayson	13,807	16,811	532	11,803	22,554
Gregg	10,219	23,399	311	10,653	29,696
Grimes	2,440	2,087	42	2,370	3,365
Guadalupe	5,049	9,901	407	5,060	14,382
Hale	3,610	7,277	123	3,202	7,670
Hall	1,057	1,141	13	684	1,058
Hamilton	1,526	1,683	30	1,130	2,116
Hansford	518	2,046	17	259	2,213
Hardeman	1,174	1,056	28	927	1,238
Hardin	7,358	6,087	200	6,782	8,380
Harris	274,061	416,555	22,917	332,605	535,687
Harrison	7,746	9,328	125	7,868	12,649
Hartley	470	1,248	28	361	1,410
Haskell	1,951	1,447	22	1,434	1,701
Hays	6,013	6,517	590	6,663	12,470
Hemphill	592	1,152	21	413	1,650
Henderson	8,199	7,903	134	7,302	12,725

County					
Hidalgo	34,542	25,808	1,063	40,461	26,923
Hill	4,688	4,113	73	2,501	3,696
Hockley	2,447	4,599	90	2,044	5,462
Hood	3,001	3,755	109	2,695	6,211
Hopkins	4,344	3,834	93	3,707	5,772
Houston	4,181	2,889	47	3,275	4,542
Howard	4,451	6,658	158	4,115	7,519
Hudspeth	394	471	14	362	557
Hunt	8,773	9,283	327	4,946	10,922
Hutchinson	2,935	7,439	170	2,052	9,078
Irion	239	427	2	198	619
Jack	1,349	1,482	29	946	1,825
Jackson	1,826	2,540	66	1,804	3,661
Jasper	5,707	4,396	98	5,835	5,951
Jeff Davis	300	409	10	299	511
Jefferson	45,642	36,763	1,664	54,846	45,124
Jim Hogg	1,437	535	23	1,703	608
Jim Wells	7,267	4,606	102	7,795	5,896
Johnson	10,542	11,411	333	9,148	18,354
Jones	3,043	2,765	45	2,348	4,017
Karnes	2,284	2,719	52	1,802	3,068
Kaufman	6,266	5,852	110	4,809	8,221
Kendall	1,075	3,890	88	938	4,568
Kenedy	106	76	2	111	96
Kent	351	339	0	253	332
Kerr	3,387	9,090	259	2,999	11,672
Kimble	608	1,011	22	442	1,333
King	55	144	5	53	141
Kinney	472	543	23	392	745
Kleberg	5,125	4,608	231	4,924	5,712
Knox	1,163	783	17	921	1,027
Lamar	7,178	6,094	148	4,917	8,194
Lamb	2,132	3,723	51	1,919	3,892
Lampasas	1,979	2,323	56	1,331	3,278
LaSalle	1,442	773	19	1,504	1,006
Lavaca	2,678	3,254	54	2,117	4,248
Lee	1,581	1,803	59	1,659	2,967
Leon	2,190	1,821	19	1,517	2,601
Liberty	6,810	6,470	163	5,689	9,382
Limestone	3,403	2,835	45	3,104	4,012
Lipscomb	338	1,343	28	241	1,461
Live Oak	1,380	2,193	32	1,260	2,481
Llano	2,130	2,866	72	1,894	4,004
Loving	22	50	0	16	57
Lubbock	18,732	46,711	1,952	18,793	57,151
Lynn	1,236	1,603	28	1,009	1,617
McCulloch	1,750	1,522	24	1,433	2,060
McLennan	26,305	31,968	964	23,206	42,132
McMullen	122	271	4	60	313
Madison	1,583	1,389	32	1,281	1,795
Marion	2,015	1,666	28	786	1,032
Martin	605	1,093	15	512	1,218
Mason	630	966	17	570	1,168
Matagorda	4,585	5,545	146	4,851	7,876
Maverick	2,932	1,370	39	3,063	1,783
Medina	3,034	4,742	84	3,053	5,737
Menard	489	548	11	394	725
Midland	6,839	25,027	586	6,348	33,195
Milam	4,230	3,251	111	3,734	4,384
Mills	1,028	985	24	688	1,262
Mitchell	1,446	1,455	12	1,332	2,007
Montague	3,233	3,143	59	2,216	3,682
Montgomery	12,593	26,237	819	13,353	41,240
Moore	1,743	3,736	67	1,129	4,649
Morris	3,105	2,133	27	2,925	2,778
Motley	341	573	7	282	533
Nacogdoches	5,981	8,626	422	5,689	13,063
Navarro	6,988	5,400	126	5,572	7,633
Newton	3,284	1,379	24	3,296	2,115
Nolan	2,796	2,781	87	2,524	3,608
Nueces	43,424	40,586	2,045	46,886	54,940
Ochiltree	594	3,032	52	419	3,492
Oldham	290	557	9	226	762
Orange	14,928	12,389	395	16,816	15,386
Palo Pinto	4,244	4,068	98	3,061	4,935
Panola	3,637	4,022	58	3,179	5,676
Parker	7,336	8,505	189	6,050	13,645
Parmer	707	2,640	30	567	2,524
Pecos	1,602	2,723	37	1,596	3,451
Polk	4,213	3,771	80	3,898	5,987
Potter	9,633	16,327	545	8,365	20,396
Presidio	1,039	723	22	992	837
Rains	1,174	813	18	1,038	1,565
Randall	7,323	23,136	677	6,044	30,249
Reagan	414	917	14	243	1,079
Real	603	832	14	360	1,004
Red River	3,501	2,225	31	2,518	2,979
Reeves	2,138	2,315	52	2,396	2,461
Refugio	2,224	1,944	57	1,559	2,421
Roberts	150	482	4	106	539
Robertson	3,572	1,661	33	3,339	2,663
Rockwall	1,985	4,036	113	1,639	6,688
Runnels	1,648	2,532	36	1,179	2,968
Rusk	5,582	8,705	116	4,599	11,081
Sabine	1,983	1,387	15	1,940	2,065
San Augustine	1,674	1,397	14	1,583	1,937
San Jacinto	2,376	1,726	42	1,993	2,630
San Patricio	8,627	8,326	280	8,836	11,074
San Saba	1,405	948	23	1,070	1,566
Schleicher	444	672	6	326	854
Scurry	2,003	3,745	53	1,564	5,028
Shackelford	606	959	9	415	1,181
Shelby	4,215	3,500	71	3,538	4,853
Sherman	286	1,128	28	246	1,269
Smith	14,838	28,236	414	15,227	40,740
Somervell	1,015	792	21	635	1,422
Starr	4,782	1,389	50	5,047	1,658
Stephens	1,372	2,161	34	1,040	2,885
Sterling	218	364	2	129	577
Stonewall	719	488	6	643	599
Sutton	485	1,000	13	465	1,251
Swisher	1,854	1,450	50	1,642	1,611
Tarrant	121,068	173,466	7,818	102,886	214,377
Taylor	13,245	22,961	620	9,628	34,444
Terrell	260	411	14	289	407
Terry	1,945	3,178	45	1,535	3,581
Throckmorton	455	444	7	388	574
Titus	3,872	3,747	44	3,576	5,052
Tom Green	9,892	16,555	661	8,981	23,847
Travis	75,028	73,151	9,796	83,482	107,421
Trinity	2,510	1,503	32	2,115	2,599
Tyler	3,540	2,545	70	2,831	3,310
Upshur	4,894	4,836	78	4,614	7,325
Upton	485	1,169	13	380	1,603
Uvalde	2,402	3,887	62	2,482	4,690
Val Verde	4,116	5,055	145	3,857	5,909
Van Zandt	5,707	5,495	78	4,506	8,474
Victoria	7,382	13,392	347	7,037	18,681
Walker	4,869	5,657	274	4,263	8,811
Waller	3,329	3,019	76	3,828	4,119
Ward	1,405	2,912	50	1,188	3,474
Washington	2,518	4,821	95	2,483	6,506
Webb	11,856	5,421	242	12,084	8,462
Wharton	5,138	6,598	160	5,050	8,436
Wheeler	1,090	1,626	16	805	2,251
Wichita	17,657	22,884	847	16,009	28,932
Wilbarger	2,347	3,031	53	2,011	3,644
Willacy	3,047	1,995	38	3,037	2,340
Williamson	10,408	15,035	946	1,198	1,521
Wilson	3,097	3,443	73	2,829	4,588
Winkler	1,021	2,160	35	752	2,213
Wise	4,674	4,350	108	3,835	6,952
Wood	4,033	4,515	74	3,454	7,154
Yoakum	715	1,937	28	456	2,204
Young	2,740	4,153	84	1,814	4,193
Zapata	1,218	874	19	1,577	1,214
Zavala	2,621	831	69	2,937	924
Totals	1,881,147	2,510,705	111,613	1,873,499	3,301,024

Texas Vote Since 1932

1932 (Pres.), Roosevelt, Dem., 760,348; Hoover, Rep., 97,959; Thomas, Soc., 4,450; Harvey, Lib., 324; Foster Com., 207; Jackson Party, 104.

1936 (Pres.), Roosevelt, Dem., 734,485; Landon, Rep. 103,874; Lemke, Union, 3,281; Thomas, Soc., 1,075; Colvin, Proh., 514; Browder, Com., 253.

1940 (Pres.), Roosevelt, Dem., 840,151; Willkie, Rep. 199,152; Babson, Proh., 925; Thomas, Soc., 728; Browder Com., 212.

1944 (Pres.), Roosevelt, Dem., 821,605; Dewey, Rep. 191,425; Texas Regulars, 135,439; Watson, Proh., 1,017; Thomas, Soc., 594; America First, 250.

1948 (Pres.), Truman, Dem., 750,700; Dewey, Rep. 282,240; Thurmond, States' Rights, 106,909; Wallace Prog., 3,764; Watson, Proh., 2,758; Thomas, Soc., 874.

1952 (Pres.), Eisenhower, Rep., 1,102,878; Stevenson, Dem 969,228; Hamblen, Proh., 1,983; MacArthur, Christian Nationalist, 833; MacArthur, Constitution, 730; Hallinan Prog., 294.

1956 (Pres.), Eisenhower, Rep., 1,080,619; Stevenson, Dem 859,958; Andrews, Ind., 14,591.

1960 (Pres.), Kennedy, Dem., 1,167,932; Nixon, Rep 1,121,699; Sullivan, Constitution, 18,169; Decker, Proh 3,870; write-in, 15.

1964 (Pres.), Johnson, Dem., 1,663,185; Goldwater, Rep 958,566; Lightburn, Constitution, 5,060.

1968 (Pres.), Nixon, Rep., 1,227,844; Humphrey, Dem 1,266,804; Wallace, 3d party, 584,269; write-in, 489.

1972 (Pres.), Nixon, Rep., 2,298,896; McGovern, Dem 1,154,289; Schmitz, Amer., 6,039; Jenness, Soc. Workers 8,664; others, 3,393.

1976 (Pres.), Carter, Dem., 2,082,319; Ford, Rep 1,953,300; McCarthy, Ind., 20,118; Anderson, Amer 11,442; Camejo, Soc. Workers, 1,723; write-in, 2,982.

1980 (Pres.), Reagan, Rep., 2,510,705; Carter, Dem 1,881,147; Anderson, Ind., 111,613; Clark, Libertarian 37,643; write-in, 528.

Utah

County	1980 Carter (D)	Reagan (R)	Anderson (I)	1984 Mondale (D)	Reagan (R)
Beaver	621	1,477	43	708	1,515
Box Elder	2,142	12,500	306	1,981	13,216
Cache	3,639	20,251	1,494	4,119	22,090
Carbon	4,317	4,320	309	4,347	4,361
Daggett	109	290	10	225	294
Davis	9,065	45,695	2,253	11,602	49,391
Duchesne	854	3,827	87	746	4,427
Emery	1,315	3,076	90	1,310	3,049
Garfield	375	1,578	50	310	1,555
Grand	703	2,362	205	876	2,462
Iron	1,242	6,207	240	1,342	6,843
Juab	720	1,872	51	915	1,881
Kane	256	1,492	59	294	1,700
Millard	795	3,620	72	1,191	4,340
Morgan	373	1,985	42	481	1,934
Piute	157	551	3	151	606
Rich	143	762	18	129	792
Salt Lake	58,472	169,411	19,547	78,317	182,938
San Juan	763	2,774	72	989	2,498
Sanpete	1,260	5,143	112	1,226	5,504
Sevier	1,112	5,614	117	1,059	5,733
Summit	1,184	3,330	480	1,610	4,079
Tooele	3,132	6,024	391	3,579	6,423
Uintah	1,049	6,045	155	1,036	6,080
Utah	12,166	71,859	1,264	14,845	71,908
Wasatch	994	2,799	113	1,013	2,789
Washington	1,678	10,181	185	1,846	12,038
Wayne	226	835	15	224	930
Weber	15,404	43,807	2,501	17,768	43,159
Totals	**124,266**	**439,687**	**30,284**	**154,239**	**464,535**

Utah Vote Since 1932

932 (Pres.), Roosevelt, Dem., 116,750; Hoover, Rep., 84,795; Thomas, Soc., 4,087; Foster, Com., 947.

1936 (Pres.), Roosevelt, Dem., 150,246; Landon, Rep., 64,555; Lemke, Union, 1,121; Thomas, Soc., 432; Browder, Com., 280; Colvin, Proh., 43.

1940 (Pres.), Roosevelt, Dem., 154,277; Willkie, Rep., 93,151; Thomas, Soc., 200; Browder, Com., 191.

1944 (Pres.), Roosevelt, Dem., 150,088; Dewey, Rep., 97,891; Thomas, Soc., 340.

1948 (Pres.), Truman, Dem., 149,151; Dewey, Rep., 124,402; Wallace, Prog., 2,679; Dobbs, Soc. Workers, 73.

1952 (Pres.), Eisenhower, Rep., 194,190; Stevenson, Dem., 135,364.

1956 (Pres.), Eisenhower, Rep., 215,631; Stevenson, Dem., 118,364.

1960 (Pres.), Kennedy, Dem., 169,248; Nixon, Rep., 205,361; Dobbs, Soc. Workers, 100.

1964 (Pres.), Johnson, Dem., 219,628; Goldwater, Rep., 181,785.

1968 (Pres.), Nixon, Rep., 238,728; Humphrey, Dem., 156,665; Wallace, 3d party, 26,906; Halstead, Soc. Worker, 89; Peace and Freedom, 180.

1972 (Pres.), Nixon, Rep., 323,643; McGovern, Dem., 126,284; Schmitz, Amer., 28,549.

1976 (Pres.), Carter, Dem., 182,110; Ford, Rep., 337,908; Anderson, Amer., 13,304; McCarthy, Ind., 3,907; Mac-Bride, Libertarian, 2,438; Maddox, Am. Ind., 1,162; Camejo, Soc. Workers, 268; Hall, Com., 121.

1980 (Pres.), Reagan, Rep., 439,687; Carter, Dem., 124,266; Anderson, Ind., 30,284; Clark, Libertarian, 7,226; Commoner, Citizens, 1,009; Greaves, American, 965; Rarick, Amer. Ind., 522; Hall, Com., 139; DeBerry, Soc. Worker, 124.

Vermont

County	1980 Carter (D)	Reagan (R)	Anderson (I)	1984 Mondale (D)	Reagan (R)
Barre City	1,857	1,603	461	1,867	2,163
Bennington	2,528	2,059	828	2,879	3,237
Battleboro	1,877	1,890	1,021	2,741	2,645
Burlington	6,752	4,506	2,796	10,080	7,857
Montpelier	1,575	1,824	656	2,120	2,257
Rutland City	3,284	2,921	991	2,970	3,568
St. Albans City	1,395	1,381	299	1,346	1,748
St. Johnsbury	1,055	1,918	300	915	2,152
South Burlington	2,044	2,324	1,025	2,729	3,445
Winooski	1,425	686	251	1,361	1,264
Totals	**81,891**	**94,598**	**31,760**	**94,518**	**134,252**

Vermont Vote Since 1932

1932 (Pres.), Roosevelt, Dem., 56,266; Hoover, Rep., 78,984; Thomas, Soc., 1,533; Foster, Com., 195.

1936 (Pres.), Landon, Rep., 81,023; Roosevelt, Dem., 62,124; Browder, Com., 405.

1940 (Pres.), Roosevelt, Dem., 64,269; Willkie, Rep., 78,371; Browder, Com., 411.

1944 (Pres.), Roosevelt, Dem., 53,820; Dewey, Rep., 71,527.

1948 (Pres.), Truman, Dem., 45,557; Dewey, Rep., 75,926; Wallace, Prog., 1,279; Thomas, Soc., 585.

1952 (Pres.), Eisenhower, Rep., 109,717; Stevenson, Dem., 43,355; Hallinan, Prog., 282; Hoopes, Soc., 185.

1956 (Pres.), Eisenhower, Rep., 110,390; Stevenson, Dem., 42,549; scattered, 39.

1960 (Pres.), Kennedy, Dem., 69,186; Nixon, Rep., 98,131.

1964 (Pres.), Johnson, Dem., 107,674; Goldwater, Rep., 54,868.

1968 (Pres.), Nixon, Rep., 85,142; Humphrey, Dem., 70,255; Wallace, 3d party, 5,104; Halstead, Soc. Worker, 295; Gregory, New Party, 579.

1972 (Pres.), Nixon, Rep., 117,149; McGovern, Dem., 68,174; Spock, Liberty Union, 1,010; Jenness, Soc. Workers, 296; scattered, 318.

1976 (Pres.), Carter, Dem., 77,798; Carter, Ind. Vermonter, 991; Ford, Rep., 100,387; McCarthy, Ind., 4,001; Camejo, Soc. Workers, 430; LaRouche, U.S. Labor, 196; scattered, 99.

1980 (Pres.), Reagan, Rep., 94,598; Carter, Dem., 81,891; Anderson, Ind., 31,760; Commoner, Citizens, 2,316; Clark, Libertarian, 1,900; McReynolds, Liberty Union, 136; Hall, Com. 118; DeBerry, Soc. Worker, 75; scattering, 413.

Virginia

County	1980 Carter (D)	Reagan (R)	Anderson (I)	1984 Mondale (D)	Reagan (R)
Accomack	4,872	5,371	292	4,376	8,072
Albemarle	7,293	10,424	1,435	7,577	13,487
Alleghany	2,411	2,185	116	1,932	3,067
Amelia	1,643	1,969	52	1,432	2,336
Amherst	3,476	5,088	208	3,409	7,004
Appomattox	1,492	2,548	85	1,498	3,386
Arlington	26,502	30,854	8,042	37,031	34,848
Augusta	5,202	11,011	539	3,895	15,274
Bath	999	921	70	727	1,434
Bedford	4,721	6,608	336	4,754	10,371
Bland	1,002	1,278	35	863	1,805
Botetourt	3,698	4,408	329	3,243	6,059
Brunswick	3,430	2,310	70	3,039	2,948
Buchanan	5,768	4,554	95	7,840	5,083
Buckingham	1,933	1,864	77	1,879	2,627
Campbell	4,473	9,592	396	4,380	13,388
Caroline	2,924	2,071	116	2,434	1,951
Carroll	3,437	5,905	183	2,906	7,032
Charles City	1,564	506	39	1,776	776
Charlotte	2,108	2,322	59	1,816	3,004
Chesterfield	13,060	37,908	2,182	12,576	53,015
Clarke	1,156	1,876	177	1,215	2,529
Craig	946	768	41	845	1,173
Culpeper	2,519	4,312	231	2,253	5,600
Cumberland	1,355	1,515	51	1,237	2,027
Dickenson	4,177	3,687	77	4,870	3,934
Dinwiddie	3,475	3,369	107	3,485	4,547
Essex	1,280	1,581	76	1,300	2,120
Fairfax	73,734	137,620	24,605	57,541	95,076
Fauquier	4,119	6,782	548	4,056	10,319
Floyd	1,642	2,447	131	1,597	3,431
Fluvanna	1,424	1,605	108	1,332	2,247
Franklin	5,685	4,993	304	4,903	7,674
Frederick	2,948	7,293	455	2,671	9,541
Giles	3,627	2,978	211	3,047	4,340
Gloucester	3,138	4,261	354	2,830	7,109
Goochland	2,290	2,423	113	2,178	3,404
Grayson	2,875	3,494	106	2,319	4,508
Greene	925	1,702	105	760	2,216
Greensville	2,142	1,583	39	2,352	2,304
Halifax	4,528	5,088	125	4,269	6,676
Hanover	5,383	14,262	589	4,830	18,799
Henrico	21,023	50,505	2,976	21,336	63,859
Henry	8,800	8,258	355	6,976	12,693
Highland	487	751	25	398	997
Isle of Wight	3,951	3,526	197	3,659	5,699
James City	3,068	4,289	551	3,482	7,103
King George	1,318	1,784	185	1,450	2,355
King and Queen	1,128	949	43	1,201	1,449

County					
King William	1,446	2,036	80	1,448	2,803
Lancaster	1,567	2,780	106	1,559	3,416
Lee	4,758	4,417	137	5,083	5,314
Loudoun	6,694	12,076	1,312	8,225	17,765
Louisa	2,809	2,633	160	2,703	3,789
Lunenburg	1,958	2,045	59	1,754	2,712
Madison	1,351	1,959	156	1,302	2,723
Mathews	1,300	2,204	148	1,106	2,868
Mecklenburg	3,790	4,853	142	3,439	6,759
Middlesex	1,395	1,810	90	1,196	2,572
Montgomery	7,455	8,222	1,400	7,148	12,351
Nelson	2,410	1,866	143	1,948	2,777
New Kent	1,204	1,739	68	1,204	2,679
Northampton	2,363	2,165	114	2,226	2,906
Northumberland	1,551	2,598	109	1,407	3,166
Nottoway	2,593	2,813	113	2,292	3,418
Orange	2,420	3,381	241	2,285	4,481
Page	2,607	4,297	161	2,437	5,022
Patrick	2,382	3,436	105	1,908	4,703
Pittsylvania	7,653	12,022	250	7,785	15,829
Powhatan	1,484	2,933	98	1,381	3,921
Prince Edward	2,553	2,774	137	2,589	3,452
Prince George	2,310	3,389	130	2,136	4,999
Prince William	12,787	23,061	2,676	13,412	29,910
Pulaski	5,769	5,747	343	4,364	8,242
Rappahannock	1,055	1,179	99	999	1,696
Richmond	854	1,567	49	830	1,869
Roanoke	12,114	17,182	1,286	10,569	23,348
Rockbridge	2,475	2,784	296	2,098	4,067
Rockingham	5,294	11,397	771	4,219	13,425
Russell	5,764	4,778	125	6,760	5,738
Scott	4,314	4,744	153	3,904	5,807
Shenandoah	3,137	7,517	385	2,771	9,049
Smyth	5,335	6,033	224	4,101	8,592
Southampton	3,347	2,997	163	3,296	4,643
Spotsylvania	4,039	5,385	464	4,012	8,210
Stafford	4,211	7,106	623	2,344	5,704
Surry	1,756	962	63	1,875	1,469
Sussex	2,447	1,664	86	2,408	2,183
Tazewell	7,003	7,021	225	8,008	9,644
Warren	2,597	3,861	297	2,551	5,016
Washington	6,390	8,402	382	5,044	10,517
Westmoreland	2,271	2,510	133	2,363	3,219
Wise	6,779	5,767	258	7,303	7,908
Wythe	3,677	4,758	164	3,041	6,749
York	4,532	6,744	723	4,063	10,209
Total	445,151	665,012	63,068		

CITIES

City					
Alexandria	17,134	17,865	4,546	23,551	21,165
Bedford	1,149	1,145	75	997	1,553
Bristol	2,889	3,432	160	2,429	5,011
Buena Vista	1,031	942	59	724	1,335
Charlottesville	6,866	5,907	1,377	7,319	6,947
Chesapeake	17,155	17,888	1,189	16,345	26,363
Clifton Forge	1,012	716	68	896	965
Colonial Heights	1,692	5,012	219	1,218	6,387
Covington	1,813	1,187	101	1,391	1,722
Danville	6,138	10,665	296	5,846	12,141
Emporia	855	988	41	807	1,252
Fairfax	2,614	4,475	800	3,738	6,234
Falls Church	1,703	2,485	497	2,398	2,684
Franklin	1,324	1,045	62	1,537	1,561
Fredericksburg	2,174	2,502	245	2,439	3,500
Galax	1,061	1,188	31	813	1,548
Hampton	18,517	17,023	1,598	17,484	24,192
Harrisonburg	1,896	3,388	403	2,384	5,223
Hopewell	3,102	4,423	178	2,563	5,661
Lexington	963	956	129	946	1,197
Lynchburg	7,783	15,245	854	6,939	12,398
Manassas	1,565	3,009	318	1,719	4,296
Manassas Park	447	729	52	NA	NA
Martinsville	3,337	3,433	162	2,938	4,234
Newport News	22,066	22,423	2,068	21,825	33,613
Norfolk	35,118	27,506	3,333	38,869	36,316
Norton	762	572	42	842	806
Petersburg	7,931	5,001	254	9,247	6,050
Poquoson	877	2,338	158	647	3,667
Portsmouth	20,900	13,660	1,124	21,085	18,092
Radford	2,225	1,964	233	1,781	2,855
Richmond	47,975	34,629	3,502	48,577	37,410
Roanoke	18,139	15,164	1,350	16,705	17,949
Salem	4,091	4,862	359	3,347	6,419
South Boston	971	1,615	51	973	1,899
Staunton	2,658	4,819	311	2,012	6,639
Suffolk	9,064	7,179	360	8,823	10,125
Virginia Beach	24,895	47,936	4,830	23,726	68,346
Waynesboro	1,926	3,697	255	1,579	4,465
Williamsburg	1,199	1,344	340	1,468	1,913
Winchester	2,006	4,240	320	2,064	5,054
Total	307,023	324,597	32,350		
Aggregate	752,174	989,609	95,418	793,711	1,325,516

Virginia Vote Since 1932

1932 (Pres.), Roosevelt, Dem., 203,979; Hoover, Rep., 89,637; Thomas, Soc., 2,382; Upshaw, Proh., 1,843; Foster, Com., 86; Cox, Ind. 15.

1936 (Pres.), Roosevelt, Dem., 234,980; Landon, Rep., 98,366; Colvin, Proh., 594; Thomas, Soc., 313; Lemke, Union, 233; Browder, Com., 98.

1940 (Pres.), Roosevelt, Dem., 235,961; Willkie, Rep., 109,363; Babson, Proh., 882; Thomas, Soc., 282; Browder Com., 71; Aiken, Soc. Labor, 48.

1944 (Pres.), Roosevelt, Dem., 242,276; Dewey, Rep., 145,243; Watson, Proh., 459; Thomas, Soc., 417; Teichert Soc. Labor, 90.

1948 (Pres.), Truman, Dem., 200,786; Dewey, Rep., 172,070; Thurmond, States' Rights, 43,393; Wallace Prog., 2,047; Thomas, Soc., 726; Teichert, Soc. Labor 234.

1952 (Pres.), Eisenhower, Rep., 349,037; Stevenson, Dem., 268,677; Hass, Soc. Labor, 1,160; Hoopes, Social Dem. 504; Hallinan, Prog., 311.

1956 (Pres.), Eisenhower, Rep., 386,459; Stevenson, Dem., 267,760; Andrews, States' Rights, 42,964; Hoopes, Soc. Dem., 444; Hass, Soc. Labor, 351.

1960 (Pres.), Kennedy, Dem., 362,327; Nixon, Rep., 404,521; Coiner, Conservative, 4,204; Hass, Soc. Labor 397.

1964 (Pres.), Johnson, Dem., 558,038; Goldwater, Rep., 481,334; Hass, Soc. Labor, 2,895.

1968 (Pres.), Nixon, Rep., 590,319; Humphrey, Dem., 442,387; Wallace, 3d party, *320,272; Blomen, Soc. Labor, 4,671; Munn, Proh., 601; Gregory, Peace and Freedom, 1,680.

*10,561 votes for Wallace were omitted in the count.

1972 (Pres.), Nixon, Rep., 988,493; McGovern, Dem., 438,887; Schmitz, Amer., 19,721; Fisher, Soc. Labor 9,918.

1976 (Pres.), Carter, Dem., 813,896; Ford, Rep., 836,554; Camejo, Soc. Workers, 17,802; Anderson, Amer., 16,686; LaRouche, U.S. Labor, 7,508; MacBride, Libertarian, 4,648.

1980 (Pres.), Reagan, Rep., 989,609; Carter, Dem., 752,174; Anderson, Ind., 95,418; Commoner, Citizens, 14,024; Clark, Libertarian, 12,821; DeBerry, Soc. Worker, 1,986.

Washington

	1980			1984	
County	Carter (D)	Reagan (R)	Anderson (I)	Mondale (D)	Reagan (R)
Adams	1,223	3,248	255	1,289	3,365
Asotin	2,724	3,275	539	2,982	3,788
Benton	11,561	28,728	3,301	12,016	28,321
Chelan	6,483	11,299	1,608	5,954	11,522
Clallam	8,029	11,515	2,172	9,312	13,056
Clark	30,584	33,223	6,445	33,807	38,751
Columbia	587	1,349	119	662	1,352
Cowlitz	12,560	13,154	2,336	13,417	12,973
Douglas	2,833	5,171	564	2,796	5,618
Ferry	802	1,108	127	804	1,014
Franklin	3,719	7,327	699	3,633	6,635
Garfield	509	875	122	483	896
Grant	5,673	11,152	1,091	5,371	11,008
Grays Harbor	11,290	10,226	3,267	12,532	9,528
Island	5,422	10,926	1,800	6,366	11,934
Jefferson	3,279	3,645	876	3,586	3,444
King	235,046	272,567	76,119	278,064	308,124
Kitsap	20,893	29,420	8,525	25,780	30,688
Kittitas	4,075	5,359	1,066	4,249	5,588
Klickitat	2,596	3,113	423	1,727	2,462
Lewis	6,962	13,636	1,603	6,562	13,604
Lincoln	1,597	3,324	357	1,604	3,339
Mason	5,241	6,745	1,353	6,592	7,841
Okanogan	4,634	6,460	1,030	5,079	7,101
Pacific	3,727	3,132	945	4,565	3,479
Pend Oreille	1,399	2,136	221	1,227	1,798
Pierce	64,444	90,247	18,345	64,935	89,734
San Juan	1,666	2,363	728	1,258	1,391
Skagit	11,299	15,520	2,854	12,928	17,477
Skamania	1,373	1,416	218	1,413	1,526
Snohomish	52,003	66,153	14,465	63,027	85,052
Spokane	49,263	78,096	11,258	54,443	78,817
Stevens	3,584	7,094	601	3,829	7,194
Thurston	20,508	26,369	5,993	24,216	30,758
Wahkiakum	751	828	148	840	686
Walla Walla	5,825	11,223	1,591	6,447	11,171
Whatcom	18,430	21,371	4,906	19,421	23,118
Whitman	5,726	8,636	2,331	6,453	9,744
Yakima	21,873	33,815	4,672	21,771	34,291
Totals	650,193	865,244	185,073	731,440	939,124

Washington Vote Since 1932

1932 (Pres.), Roosevelt, Dem., 353,260; Hoover, Rep., 208,645; Harvey, Lib., 30,308; Thomas, Soc., 17,080; Foster, Com., 2,972; Upshaw, Proh., 1,540; Reynolds, Soc. Labor, 1,009.

1936 (Pres.), Roosevelt, Dem., 459,579; Landon, Rep., 206,892; Lemke, Union, 17,463; Thomas, Soc., 3,496; Browder, Com., 1,907; Pellsy, Christian, 1,598; Colvin, Proh., 1,041; Aiken, Soc. Labor, 362.

1940 (Pres.), Roosevelt, Dem., 462,145; Willkie, Rep., 322,123; Thomas, Soc., 4,586; Browder, Com., 2,626; Babson, Proh., 1,686; Aiken, Soc. Labor, 667.

1944 (Pres.), Roosevelt, Dem., 486,774; Dewey, Rep., 361,689; Thomas, Soc., 3,824; Watson, Proh., 2,396; Teichert, Soc. Labor, 1,645.

1948 (Pres.), Truman, Dem., 476,165; Dewey, Rep., 386,315; Wallace, Prog., 31,692; Watson, Proh., 6,117; Thomas, Soc., 3,534; Teichert, Soc. Labor, 1,133; Dobbs, Soc. Workers, 103.

1952 (Pres.), Eisenhower, Rep., 599,107; Stevenson, Dem., 492,845; MacArthur, Christian Nationalist, 7,290; Hallinan, Prog., 2,460; Hass, Soc. Labor, 633; Hoopes, Soc., 254; Dobbs, Soc. Workers, 119.

1956 (Pres.), Eisenhower, Rep., 620,430; Stevenson, Dem., 523,002; Hass, Soc. Labor, 7,457.

1960 (Pres.), Kennedy, Dem., 599,298; Nixon, Rep., 629,273; Hass, Soc. Labor, 10,895; Curtis, Constitution, 1,401; Dobbs, Soc. Workers, 705.

1964 (Pres.), Johnson, Dem., 779,699; Goldwater, Rep., 470,366; Hass, Soc. Labor, 7,772; DeBerry, Freedom Soc., 537.

1968 (Pres.), Nixon, Rep., 588,510; Humphrey, Dem., 616,037; Wallace, 3d party, 96,990; Blomen, Soc. Labor, 488; Cleaver, Peace and Freedom, 1,609; Halstead, Soc. Worker, 270; Mitchell, Free Ballot, 377.

1972 (Pres.), Nixon, Rep., 837,135; McGovern, Dem., 568,334; Schmitz, Amer., 58,906; Spock, Ind., 2,644; Fisher, Soc. Labor, 1,102; Jenness, Soc. Worker, 623; Hall, Com., 566; Hospers, Libertarian, 1,537.

1976 (Pres.), Carter, Dem., 717,323; Ford, Rep., 777,732; McCarthy, Ind., 36,986; Maddox, Amer. Ind., 8,585; Anderson, Amer., 5,046; MacBride, Libertarian, 5,042; Wright, People's, 1,124; Camejo, Soc. Workers, 905; LaRouche, U.S. Labor, 903; Hall, Com., 817; Levin, Soc. Labor, 713; Zeidler, Soc., 358.

1980 (Pres.), Reagan, Rep., 865,244; Carter, Dem., 650,193; Anderson, Ind., 185,073; Clark, Libertarian, 29,213; Commoner, Citizens, 9,403; DeBerry, Soc. Worker, 1,137; McReynolds, Socialist, 956; Hall, Com., 834; Griswold, Workers World, 341.

West Virginia

County	1980 Carter (D)	Reagan (R)	Anderson (I)	1984 Mondale (D)	Reagan (R)
Barbour	3,451	3,311	292	3,089	3,861
Berkeley	6,783	9,955	625	3,923	7,699
Boone	7,515	4,164	268	7,036	4,590
Braxton	3,795	2,403	173	3,322	2,876
Brooke	6,430	4,622	634	6,627	4,808
Cabell	17,732	19,482	2,146	15,315	21,475
Calhoun	1,717	1,606	92	1,449	1,723
Clay	2,185	1,452	102	2,112	1,663
Doddridge	1,043	1,888	120	842	2,339
Fayette	13,175	5,784	725	11,600	7,305
Gilmer	1,854	1,452	153	1,486	1,948
Grant	1,041	3,452	87	823	3,679
Greenbrier	7,128	6,221	546	5,592	7,322
Hampshire	2,522	2,879	157	2,102	4,065
Hancock	8,784	6,610	917	8,696	7,321
Hardy	2,052	2,329	99	1,637	2,931
Harrison	18,813	14,251	1,339	14,929	19,342
Jackson	4,120	6,041	352	4,131	7,091
Jefferson	4,679	4,454	572	4,146	5,771
Kanawha	42,829	42,604	5,838	37,060	50,478
Lewis	3,455	3,747	359	2,672	5,326
Lincoln	5,317	4,009	128	5,210	3,934
Logan	12,024	4,945	381	10,765	6,407
McDowell	9,822	3,862	216	8,032	4,289
Marion	14,189	10,952	1,171	13,290	13,067
Marshall	7,832	7,252	725	7,860	8,486
Mason	5,683	6,040	312	5,476	6,294
Mercer	11,804	12,273	563	9,123	13,871
Mineral	4,671	6,125	386	3,815	7,241
Mingo	9,328	3,716	208	8,433	4,268
Monongalia	12,883	11,972	2,745	13,180	14,899
Monroe	2,877	2,999	166	2,326	3,590
Morgan	1,594	2,833	172	1,447	3,428
Nicholas	5,265	3,885	322	4,538	4,619
Ohio	10,973	11,414	1,334	10,128	13,363
Pendleton	1,724	1,677	80	1,462	2,042
Pleasants	1,494	1,852	84	1,458	2,255
Pocahontas	2,170	2,011	150	1,903	2,476
Preston	4,317	5,828	515	4,048	6,943
Putnam	6,409	7,561	632	5,178	9,180
Raleigh	16,955	10,713	1,046	14,270	14,351
Randolph	5,937	4,374	518	4,799	6,031
Ritchie	1,450	3,081	128	1,231	3,347
Roane	2,408	3,219	184	2,454	3,726
Summers	3,114	2,456	201	2,618	2,950
Taylor	3,216	3,010	233	2,743	4,003
Tucker	1,862	1,798	153	1,765	2,237
Tyler	1,482	2,707	163	1,394	3,166
Upshur	2,867	4,751	415	2,455	5,896
Wayne	8,687	7,541	441	8,437	8,813
Webster	2,578	1,262	117	2,352	1,562
Wetzel	4,035	3,588	327	3,544	4,617
Wirt	1,058	1,176	44	866	1,445
Wood	13,622	20,080	1,536	11,271	24,566
Wyoming	6,624	4,537	299	5,682	5,357
Totals	367,462	334,206	31,691	322,142	396,332

West Virginia Vote Since 1932

1932 (Pres.), Roosevelt, Dem., 405,124; Hoover, Rep., 330,731; Thomas, Soc., 5,133; Upshaw, Proh., 2,342; Foster, Com., 444.

1936 (Pres.), Roosevelt, Dem., 502,582; Landon, Rep., 325,358; Colvin, Prog., 1,173; Thomas, Soc., 832.

1940 (Pres.), Roosevelt, Dem., 495,662; Willkie, Rep., 372,414.

1944 (Pres.), Roosevelt, Dem., 392,777; Dewey, Rep., 322,819.

1948 (Pres.), Truman, Dem., 429,188; Dewey, Rep., 316,251; Wallace, Prog., 3,311.

1952 (Pres.), Eisenhower, Rep., 419,970; Stevenson, Dem., 453,578.

1956 (Pres.), Eisenhower, Rep., 449,297; Stevenson, Dem., 381,534.

1960 (Pres.), Kennedy, Dem., 441,786; Nixon, Rep., 395,995.

1964 (Pres.), Johnson, Dem., 538,087; Goldwater, Rep., 253,953.

1968 (Pres.), Nixon, Rep., 307,555; Humphrey, Dem., 374,091; Wallace, 3d party, 72,560.

1972 (Pres.), Nixon, Rep., 484,964; McGovern, Dem., 277,435.

1976 (Pres.), Carter, Dem., 435,864; Ford, Rep., 314,726.

1980 (Pres.), Reagan, Rep., 334,206; Carter, Dem., 367,462; Anderson, Ind., 31,691; Clark, Libertarian, 4,356.

Wisconsin

County	1980 Carter (D)	Reagan (R)	Anderson (I)	1984 Mondale (D)	Reagan (R)
Adams	2,773	3,304	318	2,693	3,645
Ashland	4,469	3,262	685	4,669	3,510
Barron	8,654	8,791	883	8,060	9,583
Bayfield	3,705	3,278	554	4,034	3,474
Brown	29,796	47,067	4,680	30,186	51,161
Buffalo	3,276	3,569	404	2,921	3,325
Burnet	3,200	3,027	393	3,328	3,528
Calumet	5,036	7,885	1,064	4,735	8,969
Chippewa	9,836	10,531	1,160	10,200	10,983
Clark	6,091	7,921	679	5,646	8,101
Columbia	8,715	10,478	1,373	8,125	11,658
Crawford	3,392	3,934	371	3,435	4,411
Dane	85,609	57,545	19,772	94,637	74,005
Dodge	11,966	19,435	1,709	10,961	20,321
Door	4,961	7,170	655	3,760	7,946
Douglas	11,703	7,258	1,728	14,295	7,167
Dunn	7,743	7,428	1,565	7,710	8,372
Eau Claire	17,602	17,304	3,486	19,315	20,303
Florence	943	1,187	86	870	1,227
Fond duLac	15,293	24,196	2,191	13,982	26,067
Forest	2,402	2,070	141	2,211	2,296
Grant	8,406	13,298	1,690	7,890	13,427
Green	5,336	7,714	947	4,367	7,826
Green Lake	2,851	5,868	368	2,441	6,198
Iowa	4,154	4,068	546	3,842	4,982
Iron	1,941	1,811	219	1,970	1,667
Jackson	3,629	4,327	413	3,427	4,383
Jefferson	11,335	16,174	1,925	10,788	17,780
Juneau	3,884	5,591	463	3,151	5,627
Kenosha	26,738	24,481	3,802	29,232	26,102
Kewaunee	3,706	5,577	318	3,444	5,705
La Crosse	17,304	23,427	3,652	17,787	25,718
La Fayette	3,598	4,421	450	2,959	4,582
Langlade	4,498	4,866	369	3,678	5,628
Lincoln	5,438	6,473	630	5,352	6,681
Manitowoc	17,330	18,591	2,014	17,249	29,635
Marathon	23,281	25,868	3,257	20,126	27,077
Marinette	7,718	10,444	683	6,798	11,436
Marquette	2,180	3,166	270	2,031	3,404
Menominee	544	302	57	904	392

Milwaukee	240,174	183,450	34,281	257,292	195,094
Monroe	6,521	8,136	780	5,624	8,227
Oconto	5,352	8,292	440	5,288	8,613
Oneida	7,008	8,602	832	6,421	9,792
Outagamie	21,284	31,500	5,735	19,313	38,887
Ozaukee	10,779	21,371	2,463	10,763	23,895
Pepin	1,673	1,541	183	1,629	1,554
Pierce	7,312	6,209	1,752	7,281	7,611
Polk	7,607	7,207	1,102	8,036	8,101
Portage	16,443	10,465	2,851	14,399	13,603
Price	3,595	4,028	394	3,479	4,385
Racine	33,565	39,683	5,167	36,953	42,084
Richland	3,413	4,601	413	2,844	4,863
Rock	24,740	30,960	4,408	26,146	32,265
Rusk	3,584	3,704	340	3,761	3,997
St. Croix	10,203	9,265	1,867	10,130	11,365
Sauk	8,456	9,992	1,405	7,157	11,067
Sawyer	3,065	3,548	323	2,981	3,911
Shawano	5,410	9,922	652	5,469	10,635
Sheboygan	20,974	23,036	3,859	21,111	26,243
Taylor	3,739	4,596	403	3,271	4,918
Trempealeau	5,390	5,992	558	5,410	6,007
Vernon	5,501	6,528	494	5,043	6,476
Vilas	3,293	6,034	421	2,940	5,963
Walworth	11,344	19,194	2,581	9,814	20,518
Washburn	3,172	3,193	355	3,188	3,848
Washington	12,944	23,213	2,654	12,969	25,275
Waukesha	46,612	81,059	9,778	47,308	92,505
Waupaca	6,401	12,568	1,072	5,894	13,097
Waushara	2,987	5,576	335	2,782	5,768
Winnebago	24,203	34,286	4,779	22,785	38,985
Wood	13,804	17,987	2,010	12,117	20,525
Totals	**981,584**	**1,088,845**	**160,657**	**992,807**	**1,208,379**

Wisconsin Vote Since 1932

1932 (Pres.), Roosevelt, Dem., 707,410; Hoover, Rep., 347,741; Thomas, Soc. 53,379; Foster, Com., 3,112; Upshaw Proh., 2,672; Reynolds, Soc. Labor, 494.

1936 (Pres.), Roosevelt, Dem., 802,984; Landon, Rep., 380,828; Lemke, Union, 60,297; Thomas, Soc., 10,626; Browder, Com., 2,197; Colvin, Proh., 1,071; Aiken, Soc. Labor, 557.

1940 (Pres.), Roosevelt, Dem., 704,821; Willkie, Rep., 679,260; Thomas, Soc., 15,071; Browder, Com., 2,394; Babson, Proh., 2,148; Aiken, Soc. Labor, 1,882.

1944 (Pres.), Roosevelt, Dem., 650,413; Dewey, Rep., 674,532; Thomas, Soc., 13,205; Teichert, Soc. Labor, 1,002.

1948 (Pres.), Truman, Dem., 647,310; Dewey, Rep., 590,959; Wallace, Prog., 25,282; Thomas, Soc., 12,547; Teichert, Soc. Labor, 399; Dobbs, Soc. Workers, 303.

1952 (Pres.), Eisenhower, Rep., 979,744; Stevenson, Dem., 622,175; Hallinan, Ind., 2,174; Dobbs, Ind., 1,350; Hoopes, Ind., 1,157; Hass, Ind., 770.

1956 (Pres.), Eisenhower, Rep., 954,844; Stevenson, Dem., 586,768; Andrews, Ind., 6,918; Hoopes, Soc., 754; Hass, Soc. Labor, 710; Dobbs, Soc. Workers, 564.

1960 (Pres.), Kennedy, Dem., 830,805; Nixon, Rep., 895,175; Dobbs, Soc. Workers, 1,792; Hass, Soc. Labor, 1,310.

1964 (Pres.), Johnson, Dem., 1,050,424; Goldwater, Rep., 638,495; DeBerry, Soc. Worker, 1,692; Hass, Soc. Labor, 1,204.

1968 (Pres.), Nixon, Rep., 809,997; Humphrey, Dem., 748,804; Wallace, 3d party, 127,835; Blomen, Soc. Labor, 1,338; Halstead, Soc. Worker, 1,222; scattered, 2,342.

1972 (Pres.) Nixon, Rep., 989,430; McGovern, Dem., 810,174; Schmitz, Amer., 47,525; Spock, Ind., 2,701; Fisher, Soc. Labor, 998; Hall, Com., 663; Reed, Ind., 506; scattered, 893.

1976 (Pres.), Carter, Dem., 1,040,232; Ford, Rep., 1,004,987; McCarthy, Ind., 34,943; Maddox, Amer. Ind., 8,552; Zeidler, Soc., 4,298; MacBride, Libertarian, 3,814; Camejo, Soc. Workers, 1,691; Wright, People's, 943; Hall Com., 749; LaRouche, U.S. Lab., 738; Levin, Soc. Labor 389; scattering, 2,839.

1980 (Pres.), Reagan, Rep., 1,088,845; Carter, Dem. 981,584; Anderson, Ind., 160,657; Clark, Libertarian, 29,135; Commoner, Citizens, 7,767; Rarick, Constitution 1,519; McReynolds, Socialist, 808; Hall, Com., 772; Griswold, Workers World, 414; DeBerry, Soc. Workers, 383 scattering, 1,337.

Wyoming

County	1980 Carter (D)	Reagan (R)	Anderson (I)	1984 Mondale (D)	Reagan (R)
Albany	3,772	5,830	1,630	4,708	7,451
Big Horn	1,212	3,709	209	1,175	4,019
Campbell	1,400	5,613	460	1,314	7,326
Carbon	2,272	4,337	493	2,295	4,557
Converse	922	2,987	215	929	3,543
Crook	413	1,909	70	550	2,300
Fremont	3,307	9,077	731	3,969	9,883
Goshen	1,373	3,572	269	1,364	3,776
Hot Springs	745	1,602	136	672	1,943
Johnson	635	2,291	139	558	2,634
Laramie	9,512	15,361	2,225	10,110	19,348
Lincoln	1,063	3,412	120	1,021	3,854
Natrona	7,111	16,801	1,768	7,598	18,488
Niobrara	270	1,075	38	239	1,097
Park	1,718	6,435	496	1,964	7,993
Platte	1,555	2,642	262	1,232	2,813
Sheridan	3,034	5,649	641	3,642	7,441
Sublette	357	1,538	139	389	1,976
Sweetwater	4,728	6,265	826	5,132	8,136
Teton	1,361	3,004	664	1,565	3,487
Uinta	1,138	2,738	189	1,276	4,075
Washakie	945	2,634	230	970	3,245
Weston	583	2,219	122	482	2,614
Totals	**49,427**	**110,700**	**12,072**	**53,154**	**131,998**

Wyoming Vote Since 1932

1932 (Pres.), Roosevelt, Dem., 54,370; Hoover, Rep., 39,583; Thomas, Soc. 2,829; Foster, Com., 180.

1936 (Pres.), Roosevelt, Dem., 62,624; Landon, Rep., 38,739; Lemke, Union, 1,653; Thomas, Soc., 200; Browder, Com., 91; Colvin, Proh., 75.

1940 (Pres.), Roosevelt, Dem., 59,287; Willkie, Rep., 52,633; Babson, Proh., 172; Thomas, Soc., 148.

1944 (Pres.), Roosevelt, Dem., 49,419; Dewey, Rep., 51,921.

1948 (Pres.), Truman, Dem., 52,354; Dewey, Rep., 47,947; Wallace, Prog., 931; Thomas, Soc., 137; Teichert, Soc. Labor, 56.

1952 (Pres.), Eisenhower, Rep., 81,047; Stevenson, Dem., 47,934; Hamblen, Proh., 194; Hoopes, Soc., 40; Haas, Soc. Labor, 36.

1956 (Pres.), Eisenhower, Rep., 74,573; Stevenson, Dem., 49,554.

1960 (Pres.), Kennedy, Dem., 63,331; Nixon, Rep., 77,451.

1964 (Pres.), Johnson, Dem., 80,718; Goldwater, Rep., 61,998.

1968 (Pres.), Nixon, Rep., 70,927; Humphrey, Dem., 45,173; Wallace, 3d party, 11,105.

1972 (Pres.), Nixon, Rep., 100,464; McGovern, Dem., 44,358; Schmitz, Amer., 748.

1976 (Pres.), Carter, Dem., 62,239; Ford, Rep., 92,717; McCarthy, Ind., 624; Reagan, Ind., 307; Anderson, Amer., 290; MacBride, Libertarian, 89; Brown, Ind., 47; Maddox, Amer. Ind., 30.

1980 (Pres.), Reagan, Rep., 110,700; Carter, Dem., 49,427; Anderson, Ind., 12,072; Clark, Libertarian, 4,514.

Washington Lobbies

Source: Congressional Record

The following organizations had the highest lobbying expenditures for the first quarter of 1984.

Organization	Expenditures
American Arts Alliance	$79,944
American Farm Bureau Federation	102,359
AFL-CIO	126,116
American Petrochemical Consumers	131,164
American Petroleum Institute	218,365
Citizen Comm. for the Right to Keep & Bear Arms	108,808
Citizen Political Action Comm.	245,648
Citizens for Sensible Control of Acid Rain (Oscar)	226,775
Common Cause	$637,1
Disabled American Veterans	148,1
Gun Owners of America	327,5
Home Recording Rights Coalition	224,5
National Assn. of Manufacturers	70,6
Natural Gas Supply Assn.	362,9
U.S. League of Savings Institutions	142,8

Major Parties' Popular and Electoral Vote for President

(F) Federalist; (D) Democrat; (R) Republican; (DR) Democrat Republican; (NR) National Republican;
(W) Whig; (P) People's; (PR) Progressive; (SR) States' Rights; (LR) Liberal Republican; Asterisk (*)—See notes.

Year	President elected	Popular	Elec.	Losing candidate	Popular	Elec.
1789	George Washington (F)	Unknown	69	No opposition.		
1792	George Washington (F)	Unknown	132	No opposition.		
1796	John Adams (F).	Unknown	71	Thomas Jefferson (DR)	Unknown	68
1800*	Thomas Jefferson (DR)	Unknown	73	Aaron Burr (DR)	Unknown	73
1804	Thomas Jefferson (DR)	Unknown	162	Charles Pinckney (F)	Unknown	14
1808	James Madison (DR). . . .≈. .	Unknown	122	Charles Pinckney (F)	Unknown	47
1812	James Madison (DR).	Unknown	128	DeWitt Clinton (F)	Unknown	89
1816	James Monroe (DR)	Unknown	183	Rufus King (F)	Unknown	34
1820	James Monroe (DR)	Unknown	231	John Quincy Adams (DR). . . .	Unknown	1
1824*	John Quincy Adams (DR) . . .	105,321	84	Andrew Jackson (DR)	155,872	99
				Henry Clay (DR)	46,587	37
				William H. Crawford (DR). . . .	44,282	41
1828	Andrew Jackson (D)	647,231	178	John Quincy Adams (NR). . . .	509,097	83
1832	Andrew Jackson (D)	687,502	219	Henry Clay (NR)	530,189	49
1836	Martin Van Buren (D).	762,678	170	William H. Harrison (W)	548,007	73
1840	William H. Harrison (W)	1,275,017	234	Martin Van Buren (D)	1,128,702	60
1844	James K. Polk (D)	1,337,243	170	Henry Clay (W). . . .	1,299,068	105
1848	Zachary Taylor (W).	1,360,101	163	Lewis Cass (D)	1,220,544	127
1852	Franklin Pierce (D)	1,601,474	254	Winfield Scott (W)	1,386,578	42
1856	James C. Buchanan (D)	1,927,995	174	John C. Fremont (R). . . .	1,391,555	114
1860	Abraham Lincoln (R)	1,866,352	180	Stephen A. Douglas (D)	1,375,157	12
				John C. Breckinridge (D)	845,763	72
				John Bell (Const. Union). . . .	589,581	39
1864	Abraham Lincoln (R)	2,216,067	212	George McClellan (D)	1,808,725	21
1868	Ulysses S. Grant (R)	3,015,071	214	Horatio Seymour (D). . . .	2,709,615	80
1872*	Ulysses S. Grant (R)	3,597,070	286	Horace Greeley (D-LR)	2,834,079	. . .
1876*	Rutherford B. Hayes (R)	4,033,950	185	Samuel J. Tilden (D)	4,284,757	184
1880	James A. Garfield (R)	4,449,053	214	Winfield S. Hancock (D)	4,442,030	155
1884	Grover Cleveland (D)	4,911,017	219	James G. Blaine (R)	4,848,334	182
1888*	Benjamin Harrison (R)	5,444,337	233	Grover Cleveland (D)	5,540,050	168
1892	Grover Cleveland (D)	5,554,414	277	Benjamin Harrison (R)	5,190,802	145
				James Weaver (P)	1,027,329	22
1896	William McKinley (R)	7,035,638	271	William J. Bryan (D-P)	6,467,946	176
1900	William McKinley (R)	7,219,530	292	William J. Bryan (D)	6,358,071	155
1904	Theodore Roosevelt (R)	7,628,834	336	Alton B. Parker (D)	5,084,491	140
1908	William H. Taft (R)	7,679,006	321	William J. Bryan (D)	6,409,106	162
1912	Woodrow Wilson (D)	6,286,214	435	Theodore Roosevelt (PR)	4,216,020	88
				William H. Taft (R)	3,483,922	8
1916	Woodrow Wilson (D)	9,129,606	277	Charles E. Hughes (R). . . .	8,538,221	254
1920	Warren G. Harding (R)	16,152,200	404	James M. Cox (D)	9,147,353	127
1924	Calvin Coolidge (R).	15,725,016	382	John W. Davis (D)	8,385,586	136
				Robert M. LaFollette (PR)	4,822,856	13
1928	Herbert Hoover (R).	21,392,190	444	Alfred E. Smith (D)	15,016,443	87
1932	Franklin D. Roosevelt (D) . . .	22,821,857	472	Herbert Hoover (R)	15,761,841	59
				Norman Thomas (Socialist) . . .	884,781	. . .
1936	Franklin D. Roosevelt (D) . . .	27,751,597	523	Alfred Landon (R)	16,679,583	8
1940	Franklin D. Roosevelt (D) . . .	27,243,466	449	Wendell Willkie (R)	22,304,755	82
1944	Franklin D. Roosevelt (D) . . .	25,602,505	432	Thomas E. Dewey (R)	22,006,278	99
1948	Harry S Truman (D)	24,105,812	303	Thomas E. Dewey (R)	21,970,065	189
				J. Strom Thurmond (SR)	1,169,021	39
				Henry A. Wallace (PR)	1,157,172	. . .
1952	Dwight D. Eisenhower (R) . . .	33,936,252	442	Adlai E. Stevenson (D)	27,314,992	89
1956*	Dwight D. Eisenhower (R) . . .	35,585,316	457	Adlai E. Stevenson (D)	26,031,322	73
1960*	John F. Kennedy (D)	34,227,096	303	Richard M. Nixon (R). . . .	34,108,546	219
1964	Lyndon B. Johnson (D).	43,126,506	486	Barry M. Goldwater (R)	27,176,799	52
1968	Richard M. Nixon (R)	31,785,480	301	Hubert H. Humphrey (D)	31,275,166	191
				George C. Wallace (3d party) . . .	9,906,473	46
1972*	Richard M. Nixon (R)	47,165,234	520	George S. McGovern (D)	29,170,774	17
1976*	Jimmy Carter (D)	40,828,929	297	Gerald R. Ford (R)	39,148,940	240
1980	Ronald Reagan (R).	43,899,248	489	Jimmy Carter (D).	35,481,435	49
				John B. Anderson (independent)	5,719,437	. . .

1800—Elected by House of Representatives because of tied electoral vote.

1824—Elected by House of Representatives. No candidate polled a majority. In 1824, the Democrat Republicans had become a loose coalition of competing political groups. By 1828, the supporters of Jackson were known as Democrats, and the J.Q. Adams and Henry Clay supporters as National Republicans.

1872—Greeley died Nov. 29, 1872. His electoral votes were split among 4 individuals.

1876—Fla., La., Ore., and S. C. election returns were disputed. Congress in joint session (Mar. 2, 1877) declared Hayes and Wheeler elected President and Vice-President.

1888—Cleveland had more votes than Harrison but the 233 electoral votes cast for Harrison against the 168 for Cleveland elected Harrison president.

1956—Democrats elected 74 electors but one from Alabama refused to vote for Stevenson.

1960—Sen. Harry F. Byrd (D-Va.) received 15 electoral votes.

1972—John Hospers of Cal. and Theodora Nathan of Ore. received one vote from an elector of Virginia.

1976—Ronald Reagan of Cal. received one vote from an elector of Washington.

CONGRESS

The Ninety-Ninth Congress
With 1984 Election Results

The Senate

Terms are for 6 years and end Jan. 3 of the year preceding name. Annual salary $72,600. To be eligible for the U.S. Senate a person must be at least 30 years of age, a citizen of the United States for at least 9 years, and a resident of the state from which he is chosen. The Congress must meet annually on Jan. 3, unless it has, by law, appointed a different day.

Senate officials (98th Congress; pre-1984 election): President Pro Tempore Strom Thurmond; Majority Leader Howard H. Baker Jr.; Majority Whip Ted Stevens; Minority Leader Robert C. Byrd; Minority Whip Alan Cranston.

Rep., 54; Dem., 46; Total, 100. *Incumbent. Bold face denotes winner.

Preliminary Returns (Source: News Election Service)

Term ends	Senator (Party, home)	1984 Election	Term ends	Senator (Party, home)	1984 Election
	Alabama			**Kansas**	
1987	Jeremiah Denton* (R, Mobile)		1987	Robert J. Dole* (R, Russell)	
1991	**Howell Heflin*** (D, Tuscumbia)	780,922	1991	**Nancy Landon Kassebaum*** (R, Wichita)	735,080
	Albert Lee Smith (R, Birmingham) . .	464,095		James Maher (D, Overland Pk.) . . .	206,187
	Alaska			**Kentucky**	
1987	Frank Murkowski* (R, Anchorage)		1987	Wendell H. Ford* (D, Owensboro)	
1991	**Ted Stevens*** (R, Anchorage)	121,879	1991	**Mitch McConnell** (R, Louisville) . . .	638,816
	John E. Havelock (D, Anchorage). . .	49,237		Walter D. Huddleston* (D, Elizabeth-town)	635,441
	Arizona			**Louisiana**	
1987	Barry M. Goldwater* (R, Scottsdale)		1987	Russell B. Long* (D, Baton Rouge)	
1989	Dennis DeConcini* (D, Tuscon)		1991	**J. Bennett Johnston*** (D, Shreve-port)	Unopposed
	Arkansas			**Maine**	
1987	Dale Bumpers* (D, Charleston)		1989	George J. Mitchell* (D, Waterville)	
1991	**David Pryor*** (D, Little Rock)	481,943	1991	**William S. Cohen*** (R, Bangor). . . .	400,953
	Ed Bethune (R, Searcy)	354,147		Elizabeth Mitchell (D, Vassalboro) . .	142,312
	California			**Maryland**	
1987	Alan Cranston* (D, Palm Springs)		1987	Charles McC. Mathias Jr.* (R, Frederick)	
1989	Pete Wilson (R, San Diego)		1989	Paul S. Sarbanes* (D, Baltimore)	
	Colorado			**Massachusetts**	
1987	Gary Hart* (D, Denver)		1989	Edward M. Kennedy* (D, Barnstable)	
1991	**William L. Armstrong*** (R, Aurora) .	780,554	1991	**John Kerry** (D, Boston)	1,369,295
	Nancy Dick (D, Aspen)	428,803		Raymond Shamie (R, Walpole) . . .	1,123,235
	Connecticut			**Michigan**	
1987	Christopher J. Dodd* (D, Norwich)		1989	Donald W. Riegle Jr.* (D, Flint)	
1989	Lowell P. Weicker Jr.* (R, Mystic)		1991	**Carl Levin*** (D, Detroit)	1,837,499
	Delaware			Jack Lousma (R, Ann Arbor)	1,650,426
1989	William V. Roth Jr.* (R, Wilmington)			**Minnesota**	
1991	**Joseph R. Biden Jr.*** (D, Wilmington)	147,056	1989	David Durenberger* (R, Minneapolis)	
	John M. Burris (R, Milford)	97,903	1991	**Rudolph E. Boschwitz*** (R, Way-zata)	1,099,063
	Florida			Joan Growe (D, Minneapolis)	791,809
1987	Paula Hawkins* (R, Winter Park)			**Mississippi**	
1989	Lawton Chiles* (D, Holmes Beach)		1989	John C. Stennis* (D, DeKalb)	
	Georgia		1991	**Thad Cochran*** (R, Jackson)	575,963
1987	Mack Mattingly* (R, St. Simons Is.)			William F. Winter (D, Jackson)	369,962
1991	**Sam Nunn*** (D, Perry)	1,316,400		**Missouri**	
	Mike Hicks (R, Riverdale)	327,620	1987	Thomas F. Eagleton* (D, St. Louis)	
	Hawaii		1989	John C. Danforth* (R, Newburg)	
1987	Daniel K. Inouye* (D, Honolulu)			**Montana**	
1989	Spark M. Matsunaga* (D, Honolulu)		1989	John Melcher* (D, Forsyth)	
	Idaho		1991	**Max Baucus*** (D, Helena)	193,061
1987	Steven D. Symms* (R, Boise)			Chuck Cozzens (R, Billings)	139,121
1991	**James A. McClure***(R, McCall) . . .	293,416		**Nebraska**	
	Peter Busch (D, Lewiston)	105,487	1989	Edward Zorinsky* (D, Omaha)	
	Illinois		1991	**J. James Exon*** (D, Lincoln)	334,271
1987	Alan J. Dixon* (D, Belleville)			Nancy Hoch (R, Nebraska City). . . .	299,781
1991	**Paul Simon** (D, Makanda).	2,334,580		**Nevada**	
	Charles H. Percy* (R, Wilmette) . . .	2,273,043	1987	Paul Laxalt* (R, Carson City)	
	Indiana		1989	Chic Hecht (R, Las Vegas)	
1987	Dan Quayle* (R, Huntington)			**New Hampshire**	
1989	Richard G. Lugar* (R, Indianapolis)		1987	Warren Rudman* (R, Nashua)	
	Iowa		1991	**Gordon J. Humphrey*** (R, Chiches-ter).	208,431
1987	Charles E. Grassley* (R, New Hart-ford)			Norman D'Amours (D, Manchester) .	142,311
1991	**Tom Harkin** (D, Cumming)	713,286			
	Roger W. Jepsen* (R, Eldridge). . . .	559,176			

Term ends	Senator (Party, home)	1984 Election
	New Jersey	
1989	Frank R. Lautenburg (D, Montclair)	
1991	**Bill Bradley*** (D, Denville)	1,917,391
	Mary Mochary (R, Montclair)	1,043,984
	New Mexico	
1989	Jeff Bingaman (D, Santa Fe)	
1991	**Pete V. Domenici*** (R, Albuquerque)	357,987
	Judith A. Pratt (D, Albuquerque)	140,252
	New York	
1987	Alfonse M. D'Amato* (R, C, RTL, Island Park)	
1989	Daniel Patrick Moynihan* (D, Oneonta)	
	North Carolina	
1987	John P. East* (R, Greenville)	
1991	**Jesse Helms*** (R, Raleigh)	1,133,221
	James B. Hunt (D, Lucama)	1,050,386
	North Dakota	
1987	Mark Andrews* (R, Mapleton)	
1989	Quentin N. Burdick* (D, Fargo)	
	Ohio	
1987	John Glenn* (D, Grandview Hts.)	
1989	Howard M. Metzenbaum* (D, Lyndhurst)	
	Oklahoma	
1987	Don Nickles* (R, Ponca City)	
1991	**David Boren*** (D, Seminole)	842,556
	Bill Crozier (R, Minco)	257,731
	Oregon	
1987	Bob Packwood* (R, Lake Oswego)	
1991	**Mark O. Hatfield*** (R, Portland)	748,952
	Margie Hendriksen (D, Eugene)	382,121
	Pennsylvania	
1987	Arlen Specter* (R, Philadelphia)	
1989	John Heinz* (R, Pittsburgh)	
	Rhode Island	
1989	John H. Chafee* (R, Warwick)	
1991	**Claiborne deB. Pell*** (D, Newport)	277,022
	Barbara M. Leonard (R, Providence)	104,074
	South Carolina	
1987	Ernest Fritz Hollings* (D, Columbia)	
1991	**Strom Thurmond*** (R, Aiken)	577,587
	Melvin Purvis (D, Florence)	271,820

Term ends	Senator (Party, home)	1984 Election
	South Dakota	
1987	James Abdnor* (R, Mitchell)	
1991	**Larry Pressler*** (R, Humboldt)	232,356
	George V. Cunningham (D, Watertown)	79,680
	Tennessee	
1989	James R. Sasser* (D, Nashville)	
1991	**Albert Gore Jr.** (D, Carthage)	990,906
	Victor Ashe (R, Knoxville)	553,202
	Texas	
1989	Lloyd Bentsen* (D, Houston)	
1991	**Phil Gramm** (R, Bryan)	2,988,346
	Lloyd Doggett (D, Austin)	2,110,834
	Utah	
1987	Jake Garn* (R, Salt Lake City)	
1989	Orrin G. Hatch* (R, Salt Lake City)	
	Vermont	
1987	Patrick J. Leahy* (D, Burlington)	
1989	Robert T. Stafford* (R, Rutland)	
	Virginia	
1989	Paul S. Trible Jr. (R, Newport News)	
1991	**John William Warner*** (R, Richmond)	1,387,473
	Edythe C. Harrison (D, Norfolk)	599,849
	Washington	
1987	Slade Gorton* (R, Olympia)	
1989	Daniel J. Evans* (R, Olympia)	
	West Virginia	
1989	Robert C. Byrd* (D, Sophia)	
1991	**Jay Rockefeller** (D, Charleston)	368,216
	John R. Raese (R, Morgantown)	336,656
	Wisconsin	
1987	Robert W. Kasten Jr.* (R, Thiensville)	
1989	William Proxmire* (D, Madison)	
	Wyoming	
1989	Malcolm Wallop* (R, Big Horn)	
1991	**Alan Kooi Simpson*** (R, Cody)	145,527
	Victor A. Ryan (D, Laramie)	40,246

The House of Representatives

Members' terms to Jan. 3, 1987. Annual salary $72,600; house speaker $94,600. To be eligible for membership, a person must be at least 25, a U.S. citizen for at least 7 years, and a resident of the state from which he or she is chosen.

House Officials (98th Congress; pre-1984 election): Speaker Thomas P. O'Neill; Majority Leader James Wright; Majority Whip Thomas S. Foley; Minority Leader Robert H. Michel; Minority Whip Trent Lott.

C-Conservative; Com-Communist; COP-Concerns of People; D-Democrat; I-Independent; L-Liberal; Libert- Libertarian; PF-Peace and Freedom; PBP-People Before Profits; R-Republican; RTL-Right to Life; SW-Socialist Workers.

Dem., 255, Rep., 180. Total 435. *Incumbent. Bold face denotes winner.

Preliminary Returns (Source: News Election Service)

Dist.	Representative (Party, Home)	1984 Election
	Alabama	
1.	**Sonny Callahan** (R, Mobile)	85,520
	Frank McWright (D, Mobile)	81,228
2.	**William L. Dickinson*** (R, Montgomery)	113,005
	Larry Lee (D, Montgomery)	71,981
3.	**Bill Nichols*** (D, Sylacauga)	111,785
	Mark Thornton (Libert., Auburn)	4,302
4.	**Tom Bevel*** (D, Jasper)	Unopposed
5.	**Ronnie G. Flippo*** (D, Florence)	138,692
	D. M. Samsil (Libert., Birmingham)	5,883

Dist.	Representative (Party, Home)	1984 Election
6.	**Ben Erdreich** (D, Birmingham)	128,323
	J. T. Waggoner (R, Birmingham)	86,549
7.	**Richard C. Shelby*** (D, Tuscaloosa)	130,373
	Charles Ewing (Libert., Birmingham)	4,369
	Alaska At Large	
	Don Young* (R, Fort Yukon)	93,846
	Pegge Begich (D, Anchorage)	72,442
	Arizona	
1.	**John McCain** (R, Tempe)	162,002
	Harry W. Braun III (D, Tempe)	45,505

Dist.	Representative (Party, Home)	1984 Election
2.	**Morris K. Udall*** (D, Tucson)	**105,194**
	Lorenzo Torrez (PBP, Tucson)	13,727
3.	**Bob Stump*** (R, Tolleson)	**149,664**
	Bob Schuster (D, Kingman)	55,451
4.	**Eldon Rudd*** (R, Scottsdale)	**Unopposed**
5.	**Jim Kolbe** (R, Tucson)	**113,754**
	Jim McNulty (R, Tucson)	108,205

Arkansas

Dist.	Representative (Party, Home)	1984 Election
1.	**Bill Alexander*** (D, Osceola)	**Unopposed**
2.	**Tommy Robinson** (D, Little Rock)	**99,067**
	M. Petty (R, Little Rock)	86,632
3.	**John Paul Hammerschmidt*** (R, Harrison)	**Unopposed**
4.	**Beryl Anthony Jr.*** (D, El Dorado)	**Unopposed**

California

Dist.	Representative (Party, Home)	1984 Election
1.	**Douglas H. Bosco** (D, Santa Rosa)	**149,575**
	David Redick (R, Fulton)	90,470
2.	**Gene Chappie*** (R, Chico)	**158,224**
	Harry Cozad (D, Chico)	69,324
3.	**Robert T. Matsui*** (D, Sacramento)	**Unopposed**
4.	**Vic Fazio*** (D, Woodland)	**126,872**
	Roger Canfield (R, Sacramento)	75,269
5.	**Sala Burton*** (D, San Francisco)	**137,067**
	Tom Spinosa (R, San Francisco)	44,796
6.	**Barbara Boxer*** (D, San Rafael)	**158,955**
	Douglas Bindcrup (R, Mill Valley)	69,217
7.	**George Miller*** (D, Martinez)	**148,221**
	Rosemary Thakar (R, Alamo)	74,074
8.	**Ronald V. Dellums*** (D, Oakland)	**141,245**
	Charles Conner (R, Oakland)	92,687
9.	**Fortney H. (Pete) Stark*** (D, Hayward)	**134,270**
	J. T. Eager Beaver (R, San Leandro)	50,331
10.	**Don Edwards*** (D, San Jose)	**100,368**
	Robert P. Herriott (R, Milpitas)	55,238
11.	**Tom Lantos*** (D, Burlingame)	**146,131**
	John Hickey (R, Redwood City)	59,125
12.	**Ed Zschau*** (R, Los Altos)	**150,144**
	Martin Carnoy (D, Menlo Pk.)	88,368
13.	**Norman Y. Mineta*** (D, San Jose)	**136,936**
	John D. Williams (R, San Jose)	69,180
14.	**Norm Shumway*** (R, Stockton)	**176,840**
	Ruth "Paula" Carlson (D, Penryn)	57,325
15.	**Tony Coelho*** (D, Merced)	**99,287**
	Carol Harner (R, Mariposa)	49,357
16.	**Leon E. Panetta*** (D, Carmel Valley)	**149,252**
	Patricia Smith Ramsey (R, Carmel)	58,385
17.	**Charles "Chip" Pashayan Jr.*** (R, Fresno)	**121,153**
	Simon Lakritz (D, Hanford)	43,813
18.	**Richard H. Lehman*** (D, Sanger)	**125,577**
	Dale L. Ewen (R, Groveland)	60,774
19.	**Robert J. Lagomarsino*** (R, Ventura)	**146,161**
	James C. Carey Jr. (D, Santa Barbara)	67,938
20.	**William M. Thomas*** (R, Bakersfield)	**122,586**
	Mike LeSage (D, Paso Robles)	50,185
21.	**Bobbi Fiedler*** (R, Chatsworth)	**168,765**
	Charlie Davis (D, Thousand Oaks)	60,655
22.	**Carlos J. Moorhead*** (R, Glendale)	**178,785**
	Michael B. Yauch (Libert., Pasadena)	30,988
23.	**Anthony C. Beilenson*** (D, Los Angeles)	**135,926**
	Claude Parrish (R, Los Angeles)	80,394
24.	**Henry A. Waxman*** (D, Los Angeles)	**93,811**
	Jerry Zerg (R, Los Angeles)	41,751
25.	**Edward R. Roybal*** (D, Los Angeles)	**71,756**
	Roy D. Bloxom (R, Los Angeles)	23,717
26.	**Howard L. Berman*** (D, Panorama City)	**113,722**
	Miriam Ojeda (R, Mission Hills)	66,896
27.	**Mel Levine*** (D, Santa Monica)	**101,128**
	Robert B. Scribner (R, Pacific Palisades)	83,210
28.	**Julian C. Dixon*** (D, Inglewood)	**109,252**
	Beatrice M. Jett (R, Los Angeles)	32,001
29.	**Augustus F. "Gus" Hawkins*** (D, Los Angeles)	**106,494**
	Echo Y. Gotto (R, Los Angeles)	16,289
30.	**Matthew G. "Marty" Martinez** (D, Montebello)	**62,837**
	Richard Gomez (R, Montebello)	52,205
31.	**Mervyn M. Dymally** (D, Compton)	**97,972**
	Henry C. Minturn (R, Hawthorne)	40,440
32.	**Glenn M. Anderson*** (D, Hawthorne)	**99,472**
	Roger E. Fiola (R, Downey)	59,860
33.	**David Dreier*** (R, Covina)	**142,501**
	Claire K. McDonald (D, Claremont)	52,799
34.	**Esteban E. Torres** (D, Norwalk)	**85,033**
	Paul R. Jackson (R, Pico Rivera)	56,786
35.	**Jerry Lewis*** (R, Apple Valley)	**172,651**
	Kevin Akin (P&F, Riverside)	29,480
36.	**George E. Brown Jr.*** (D, Colton)	**103,076**
	John Paul Stark (R, San Bernardino)	78,904
37.	**Al McCandless** (R, Palm Desert)	**146,196**
	David E. "Dave" Skinner (D, Riverside)	83,932
38.	**Robert K. Dornan** (R, Buena Park)	**84,131**
	Jerry M. Patterson (D, Santa Ana)	71,288
39.	**William E. Dannemeyer*** (R, Fullerton)	**170,250**
	Robert E. Ward (D, Fullerton)	53,546
40.	**Robert E. Badham*** (R, Newport Beach)	**158,455**
	Carol Ann Bradford (D, Newport Beach)	84,622
41.	**Bill Lowery*** (R, San Diego)	**156,554**
	Robert Simmons (D, San Diego)	83,552
42.	**Dan Lungren*** (R, Long Beach)	**171,142**
	Mary Lou Brophy (D, Seal Beach)	58,161
43.	**Ron Packard** (R, Carlsbad)	**159,315**
	Lois E. Humphreys (D, Carlsbad)	49,525
44.	**Jim Bates*** (D, San Diego)	**97,467**
	Neill Campbell (R, San Diego)	38,961
45.	**Duncan Hunter*** (R, El Cajon)	**145,014**
	David W. Guthrie (D, San Diego)	44,420

Colorado

Dist.	Representative (Party, Home)	1984 Election
1.	**Patricia Schroeder*** (D, Denver)	**126,166**
	Mary Downs (R, Denver)	73,900
2.	**Timothy E. Wirth*** (D, Boulder)	**112,756**
	Michael J. Norton (R, Lakewood)	95,503
3.	**Mike Strang** (R, Carbondale)	**110,837**
	W. Mitchell (D, Crested Butte)	84,036
4.	**Hank Brown*** (R, Greeley)	**136,343**
	Mary Fagan Bates (D, Ft. Collins)	53,866
5.	**Ken Kramer*** (R, Colorado Springs)	**150,472**
	William Geffen (D, Colorado Springs)	41,556
6.	**Daniel Schaefer*** (R, Lakewood)	**161,231**
	John Heckman (COP, Lakewood)	19,031

Connecticut

Dist.	Representative (Party, Home)	1984 Election
1.	**Barbara B. Kennelly*** (D, Hartford)	**147,108**
	Herschel A. Klein (R, Windsor)	90,513
2.	**Samuel Gejdenson*** (D, Bozrah)	**123,122**
	Roberta F. Koontz (R, Coventry)	102,210
3.	**Bruce A. Morrison*** (D, Hamden)	**123,506**
	Lawrence J. DeNardis* (R, Hamden)	114,669
4.	**Stewart B. McKinney*** (R, Westport)	**165,657**
	John M. Orman (D, Fairfield)	69,666
5.	**John G. Rowland** (R, Waterbury)	**130,568**
	William R. Ratchford (D, Danbury)	109,822
6.	**Nancy L. Johnson** (R, New Britain)	**150,890**
	Arthur House (D, E. Granby)	85,254

Delaware At Large

Dist.	Representative (Party, Home)	1984 Election
	Thomas R. Carper (D, New Castle)	**141,472**
	Elise du Pont (R, Dover)	100,142

Florida

Dist.	Representative (Party, Home)	1984 Election
1.	**Earl Hutto*** (D, Panama City)	**Unopposed**
2.	**Don Fuqua*** (D, Altha)	**Unopposed**
3.	**Charles E. Bennett*** (D, Jacksonville)	**Unopposed**

Dist.	Representative (Party, Home)	1984 Election
4.	**Bill Chappell*** (D, Daytona Beach) .	**127,665**
	Alton Starling (R, Jacksonville)	67,635
5.	**Bill McCollum*** (R, Altamonte Springs)	**Unopposed**
6.	**Kenneth H. "Buddy" MacKay*** (D, Ocala)	**Unopposed**
7.	**Sam Gibbons*** (D, Tampa)	**95,320**
	Michael Kavouklls (R, Tampa)	65,889
8.	**C. W. Bill Young*** (R, Madeira Beach)	**184,421**
	Robert Kent (D, Treasure Island) . . .	45,340
9.	**Michael Bilirakis*** (R, Palm Harbor).	**185,900**
	Jack Wilson (D, Clearwater)	50,511
10.	**Andy Ireland*** (R, Winter Haven) . .	**94,954**
	Patricia M. Glass (D, Sarasota)	60,071
11.	**Bill Nelson*** (D, Melbourne)	**102,282**
	Rob Quartel (R, Orlando)	66,629
12.	**Tom Lewis*** (R, North Palm Beach) .	**Unopposed**
13.	**Connie Mack*** (R, Cape Coral) . . .	**Unopposed**
14.	**Daniel A. Mica*** (D, Boynton Beach).	**151,424**
	Don Ross (R, Boca Raton)	122,550
15.	**Clay Shaw Jr.*** (R, Fort Lauderdale)	**118,170**
	Bill Humphrey (D, Oakland Park) . . .	62,834
16.	**Larry Smith*** (D, Hollywood)	**102,660**
	Tom Bush (R, Ft. Lauderdale).	79,681
17.	**William Lehman*** (D, Biscayne Park)	**Unopposed**
18.	**Claude Pepper*** (D, Miami).	**71,744**
	Ricardo Nunez (R, Coral Gables) . . .	47,365
19.	**Dante B. Fascell*** (D, Miami).	**109,033**
	Bill Flanagan (R, Coral Gables)	59,012

Georgia

1.	**Lindsay Thomas*** (D, Screven) . . .	**120,505**
	Erie Lee Downing (R, Savannah) . . .	27,018
2.	**Charles Hatcher*** (D, Albany) . . .	**Unopposed**
3.	**Richard Ray** (D, Perry)	**106,422**
	Mitchell Cantu (R, Columbus)	24,321
4.	**Patrick Swindall** (R, Dunwoody) . . .	**120,441**
	Elliott H. Levitas (D, Atlanta)	106,336
5.	**Wyche Fowler Jr.*** (D, Atlanta) . . .	**Unopposed**
6.	**Newt Gingrich*** (R, Jonesboro) . . .	**116,592**
	Gerald Johnson (D, Carrollton) . . .	52,046
7.	**George Darden*** (D, Marietta) . . .	**101,814**
	Bill Bronson (R, Marietta)	83,851
8.	**J. Roy Rowland** (D, Dublin)	**Unopposed**
9.	**Ed Jenkins*** (D, Jasper)	**102,777**
	Frank Cofer (R, Hoschton)	50,096
10.	**Doug Barnard Jr.*** (D, Augusta) . . .	**Unopposed**

Hawaii

1.	**Cecil (Cec) Heftel*** (D, Honolulu) . .	**113,978**
	Willard Beard (R, Honolulu)	20,376
2.	**Daniel K. Akaka*** (D, Honolulu) . . .	**112,086**
	A. D. (Al) Shipley (R, Kailua)	19,908

Idaho

1.	**Larry E. Craig*** (R, Midvale)	**139,021**
	Bill Heller (D, Coeve d'Alene).	63,567
2.	**Richard Stallings** (D, Rexburg) . . .	**101,099**
	George Hansen* (R, Pocatello)	101,032

Illinois

1.	**Charles Hayes*** (D, Chicago)	**157,379**
	Eddie L. Warren (SW, Chicago). . . .	7,040
2.	**Gus Savage*** (D, Chicago)	**140,307**
	Dale Harman (R, Chicago)	30,870
3.	**Marty Russo*** (D, South Holland) . .	**140,046**
	Richard D. Murphy (R, Chicago) . . .	78,060
4.	**George M. O'Brien*** (R, Joliet) . . .	**121,325**
	Dennis Marlow (D, Calumet City) . . .	68,435
5.	**William O. Lipinski*** (D, Chicago) . .	**104,373**
	John Paczkowski (R, Chicago)	60,588
6.	**Henry J. Hyde*** (R, Bensenville) . .	**156,523**
	Robert Renshaw (D, Lombard)	51,922
7.	**Cardiss Collins*** (D, Chicago)	**130,177**
	James Bevel (R, Chicago).	36,699
8.	**Dan Rostenkowski*** (D, Chicago) . .	**110,945**
	Spiro F. Georgeson (R, Chicago) . . .	44,895
9.	**Sidney R. Yates*** (D, Chicago) . . .	**138,013**
	Herbert Sohn (R, Skokie)	66,812

Dist.	Representative (Party, Home)	1984 Election
10.	**John E. Porter*** (R, Winnetka)	**149,997**
	Ruth Braver (D, Highland Park)	56,908
11.	**Frank Annunzio*** (D, Chicago). . . .	**135,015**
	Charles Teusch (R, Chicago)	80,820
12.	**Philip M. Crane*** (R, Mt. Prospect) .	**158,860**
	Edward LaFlamme (D, Round Lake Beach)	45,283
13.	**Harris Fawell** (R, Naperville)	**156,639**
	Michael Donahue (R, Naperville) . . .	76,951
14.	**John Grotberg** (R, St. Charles) . . .	**133,584**
	Dan McGrath (D, Ottowa)	81,768
15.	**Edward R. Madigan*** (R, Lincoln) . .	**135,780**
	John Hoffman (D, Bloomington)	50,459
16.	**Lynn Martin*** (R, Rockford)	**127,239**
	Carl R. Schwerdtfeger (D, Elizabeth) .	90,673
17.	**Lane Evans*** (D, Rock Island) . . .	**128,266**
	Kenneth G. McMillan (R, Bushnell) . .	98,065
18.	**Robert H. Michel*** (R, Peoria) . . .	**135,938**
	Gerald Bradley (D, Bloomington) . . .	86,839
19.	**Terry Bruce** (D, Olney)	**118,185**
	Daniel B. Crane (R, Danville)	108,304
20.	**Richard J. Durbin*** (D, Springfield) .	**145,088**
	Dick Austin (R, Springfield)	91,820
21.	**Melvin Price*** (D, East St. Louis) . .	**123,584**
	Robert H. Gaffner (R, Greenville) . . .	54,773
22.	**Ken Gray** (D, W. Frankfort)	**116,134**
	Randy Patchett (R, Marion)	114,713

Indiana

1.	**Peter Viclosky** (D, Merrillville)	**147,035**
	Joe Grendhik (R, Whiting)	59,986
2.	**Philip R. Sharp*** (D, Muncie)	**118,426**
	Ken Mackenzie (R, Muncie)	102,236
3.	**John Hiler*** (R, LaPorte)	**113,898**
	Michael Barnes (D, South Bend) . . .	102,312
4.	**Dan R. Coats*** (R, Fort Wayne) . . .	**124,692**
	Michael Barnard (D, Fort Wayne). . .	79,660
5.	**Elwood Hillis*** (R, Kokomo)	**142,878**
	Allen B. Maxwell (D, Kokomo)	66,486
6.	**Dan Burton*** (R, Indianapolis) . . .	**165,026**
	Howard Campbell (D, Indianapolis) . .	64,806
7.	**John T. Myers*** (R, Covington) . . .	**117,899**
	Arthur E. Smith (D, Lafayette)	52,555
8.	**Richard McIntyre** (R, Bedford). . . .	**116,451**
	Francis X. McCloskey (D, Blooming- ton)	116,261
9.	**Lee H. Hamilton*** (D, Nashville) . . .	**139,216**
	Floyd E. Coates (R, Lexington)	74,261
10.	**Andrew Jacobs Jr.*** (D, Indianapolis)	**110,836**
	Joseph P. Watkins (R, Indianapolis) .	75,780

Iowa

1.	**Jim Leach*** (R, Davenport)	**131,101**
	Kevin Ready (D, Bettendorf)	64,224
2.	**Thomas J. Tauke*** (R, Dubuque) . .	**136,364**
	Joe Welch (D, Dubuque).	76,930
3.	**Cooper Evans*** (R, Grundy Center).	**130,081**
	Joe Johnston (D, Tiffin)	84,950
4.	**Neal Smith*** (D, Altoona)	**136,500**
	Bob Lockart (R, Des Moines)	87,985
5.	**James Lightfoot** (R, Shenandoah) . .	**104,247**
	Jerry Fitzgerald (D, Ft. Dodge)	101,087
6.	**Berkley Bedell*** (D, Okoboji).	**128,689**
	Darrel Rensink (R, Sioux Center) . . .	77,839

Kansas

1.	**Pat Roberts*** (R, Dodge City)	**154,567**
	Darrell Ringer (D, Quinter)	47,689
2.	**Jim Slattery*** (D, Topeka)	**107,903**
	James Van Slyke (R, Topeka)	68,440
3.	**Jan Meyers** (R, Overland Park) . . .	**116,060**
	Jack Reardan (D, Kansas City)	84,838
4.	**Dan Glickman*** (D, Wichita)	**138,619**
	William Krause (R, Wichita)	47,355
5.	**Bob Whittaker*** (R, Augusta)	**133,728**
	John Barnes (D, Cherryvale)	46,229

Dist.	Representative (Party, Home)	1984 Election

Kentucky

Dist.	Representative (Party, Home)	1984 Election
1.	Carroll Hubbard Jr.* (D, Mayfield)	Unopposed
2.	William H. Natcher* (D, Bowling Green)	91,500
	Timothy Morrison (R, Philpot)	56,056
3.	Romano L. Mazzoli* (D, Louisville)	143,931
	Susanne Warner (R, Louisville)	67,409
4.	Gene Snyder* (R, Brownsboro Farm)	102,608
	Patrick Mulloy (D, Louisville)	92,043
5.	Harold Rogers* (R, Somerset)	124,478
	Sherman McIntosh (D, Williamsburg)	40,015
6.	Larry J. Hopkins* (R, Lexington)	125,972
	Jerry Hammond (D, Versailles)	47,339
7.	Carl C. Perkins* (D, Leburn)	122,072
	Aubrey Russel* (R, Ashland)	43,612

Louisiana

1. Bob Livingston* (R, Metairie)
2. Lindy (Mrs. Hale) Boggs* (D, New Orleans)
3. W.J. "Billy" Tauzin (D, Thibodaux)
4. Buddy Roemer (D, Bossier City)
5. Jerry Huckaby* (D, Ringgold)
6. W. Henson Moore* (R, Baton Rouge)
7. John B. Breaux* (D, Crowley)
8. Gillis W. Long* (D, Alexandria)

In Louisiana, all candidates of all parties run against each other in an open primary. All candidates who receive more than 50 percent of the primary vote run unopposed in the general election. If no candidate wins a majority, the top two finishers regardless of party oppose each other in a November runoff. This year, all eight incumbents won majorities in the primary and thus were elected to Congress.

Maine

Dist.	Representative (Party, Home)	1984 Election
1.	John R. McKernan Jr.* (R, Cumberland)	180,702
	Barry Hobbins (D, Saco)	102,588
2.	Olympia J. Snowe* (R, Auburn)	192,231
	Chipman Bull (D, Presque Isle)	57,220

Maryland

Dist.	Representative (Party, Home)	1984 Election
1.	Roy Dyson* (D, Great Mills)	91,045
	Harley Williams (R, Elkton)	64,758
2.	Helen D. Bentley (R, Lutherville)	108,077
	Clarence D. Long* (D, Ruxton)	102,325
3.	Barbara A. Mikulski* (D, Baltimore)	126,459
	Ross Pierpont (R, Baltimore)	59,567
4.	Majorie S. Holt* (R, Severna Park)	108,857
	Howard Greenebaum (D, Arnold)	56,418
5.	Steny H. Hoyer* (D, Berkshire)	112,390
	John Ritchie (R, Laurel)	42,945
6.	Beverly B. Byron* (D, Frederick)	117,116
	Robin Ficker (R, Potomac)	62,746
7.	Parren J. Mitchell* (D, Baltimore)	Unopposed
8.	Michael D. Barnes* (D, Kensington)	170,890
	Albert Ceccone (R, Chevy Chase)	66,238

Massachusetts

Dist.	Representative (Party, Home)	1984 Election
1.	Silvio O. Conte* (R, Pittsfield)	158,864
	Mary Wentworth (D, Amherst)	63,091
2.	Edward P. Boland* (D, Springfield)	140,773
	Thomas P. Swank (R, West Brookfield)	60,059
3.	Joseph D. Early* (D, Worcester)	146,497
	Kenneth Redding (R, Uxbridge)	71,369
4.	Barney Frank* (D, Newton)	172,396
	Jim Forte (R, Newton)	60,096
5.	Chester Atkins (D, Concord)	120,224
	Greg Hyatt (R, Methuen)	103,731
6.	Nicholas Mavroules* (D, Peabody)	167,206
	Frederick Leber (R, Manchester)	63,330
7.	Edward J. Markey* (D, Malden)	149,379
	Lester Ralph (R, Reading)	61,954
8.	Thomas P. O'Neill Jr.* (D, Cambridge)	179,130
	Laura Ross (Com., Boston)	15,674
9.	John Joseph Moakley* (D, Boston)	Unopposed
10.	Gerry E. Studds* (D, Cohasset)	142,914
	Lew Crompton (R, Plymouth)	113,619
11.	Brian J. Donnelly* (D, Boston)	Unopposed

Michigan

Dist.	Representative (Party, Home)	1984 Election
1.	John Conyers Jr.* (D, Detroit)	147,763
	Edward Mack (R, Detroit)	16,832
2.	Carl D. Pursell* (R, Plymouth)	136,527
	Mike McCauley (D, Plymouth)	60,747
3.	Howard Wolpe* (D, Lansing)	106,634
	Jackie McGregor (R, Lansing)	93,334
4.	Mark D. Siljander* (R, Three Rivers)	126,052
	Charles Rodebaugh (D, Vicksburg)	72,615
5.	Paul Henry (R, Grand Rapids)	139,969
	Gary McInerney (D, Grand Rapids)	85,192
6.	Tom Ritter (R, Clarkston)	94,857
	Bob Carr* (D, East Lansing)	92,958
7.	Dale E. Kildee* (D, Flint)	Unopposed
8.	Bob Traxler* (D, Bay City)	104,452
	John Heussner (R, Marlette)	61,384
9.	Guy Vander Jagt* (R, Luther)	150,181
	Mike Senger (D, Traverse City)	61,110
10.	Bill Schuette (R, Sanford)	102,553
	Donald Joseph Albosta* (D, St. Charles)	100,984
11.	Robert W. Davis* (R, Gaylord)	122,494
	Tom Stewart (D, Harbor Springs)	86,993
12.	David E. Bonior* (D, Mt. Clemens)	65,598
	Eugene Tyza (R, Mt. Clemens)	44,759
13.	George W. Crockett Jr.* (D, Detroit)	130,403
	Robert Murphy (R, Detroit)	20,299
14.	Dennis M. Hertel* (D, Detroit)	113,277
	John Lauve (R, Grosse Pte. Woods)	77,779
15.	William D. Ford* (D, Taylor)	93,272
	Gerald Carlson (R, Wayne)	61,852
16.	John D. Dingell* (D, Trenton)	120,399
	Frank Grzywacki (R, Monroe)	67,621
17.	Sander Levin* (D, Southfield)	Unopposed
18.	William S. Broomfield* (R, Birmingham)	179,760
	Vivian Smargon (D, Franklin)	44,602

Minnesota

Dist.	Representative (Party, Home)	1984 Election
1.	Timothy J. Penny* (D, New Richland)	133,767
	Keith Spicer (R, Rochester)	100,117
2.	Vin Weber* (R, Slayton)	149,349
	Todd Lundquist (D, No. Mankato)	87,831
3.	Bill Frenzel* (R, Golden Valley)	176,085
	David Peterson (D, Golden Valley)	64,418
4.	Bruce F. Vento* (D, St. Paul)	166,341
	Mary Jane Rachner (R, St. Paul)	56,657
5.	Martin Olav Sabo* (D, Minneapolis)	156,532
	Richard Weiblen (R, Minneapolis)	53,823
6.	Gerry Sikorski* (D, Stillwater)	121,318
	Patrick Trueman (R, Buffalo)	72,213
7.	Arlan Stangeland* (R, Barnesville)	129,779
	Collin Peterson (D, Detroit Lakes)	97,956
8.	James L. Oberstar* (D, Duluth)	156,872
	Dave Rueof (R, Aitkin)	75,147

Mississippi

Dist.	Representative (Party, Home)	1984 Election
1.	Jamie L. Whitten* (D, Charleston)	135,956
	John Hargett (I., Tupelo)	17,824
2.	Webb Franklin* (R, Greenwood)	91,390
	Robert G. Clark (D, Greenville)	87,049
3.	G. V. (Sonny) Montgomery* (D, Meridian)	Unopposed
4.	Wayne Dowdy* (D, McComb)	112,969
	David Armstrong (R, Natchez)	89,757
5.	Trent Lott* (R, Pascagoula)	142,224
	Arlon (Blackie) Coate (D, Ocean Springs)	25,814

Missouri

Dist.	Representative (Party, Home)	1984 Election
1.	William (Bill) Clay* (D, St. Louis)	124,539
	Eric Rathbone (R, St. Louis)	66,331
2.	Robert A. Young* (D, Maryland Heights)	137,044
	Jack Buechner (R, Kirkwood)	126,678
3.	Richard A. Gephardt* (D, St. Louis)	Unopposed

Dist.	Representative (Party, Home)	1984 Election
4.	Ike Skelton* (D, Lexington)	147,666
	Carl Russell (R, Russelville)	73,508
5.	Alan Wheat* (D, Kansas City)	150,691
	Jim Kenworthy (R, Kansas City)	72,477
6.	E. Thomas Coleman* (R, Kansas City)	145,524
	Kenneth Hensley (D, Gallatin)	79,345
7.	Gene Taylor* (R, Sarcoxie)	162,867
	Ken Young (D, Point Lookout)	72,548
8.	Bill Emerson* (R, Cape Girardeau)	133,491
	Bill Blue (D, Rolla)	70,237
9.	Harold L. Volkmer* (D, Hannibal)	121,386
	Carrie Francke (R, Columbia)	108,695

Montana

Dist.	Representative (Party, Home)	1984 Election
1.	Pat Williams* (D, Helena)	110,836
	Gary Carlson (R, Hamilton)	53,251
2.	Ron Marlenee* (R, Great Falls)	108,360
	Chet Blaylock (D, Laurel)	56,275

Nebraska

Dist.	Representative (Party, Home)	1984 Election
1.	Douglas K. Bereuter* (R, Utica)	157,088
	Monica Bauer (D, Crete)	54,955
2.	Hal Daub* (R, Omaha)	133,704
	Thomas Cavanaugh (D, Omaha)	72,818
3.	Virginia Smith* (R, Chappell)	179,570
	Tom Vickers (D, Farnham)	35,892

Nevada

Dist.	Representative (Party, Home)	1984 Election
1.	Harry Reid* (D, Las Vegas)	73,242
	Peggy Cavnar (R, Las Vegas)	55,391
2.	Barbara Vucanovich (R, Reno)	99,675
	Andy Barbano (D, Reno)	36,130

New Hampshire

Dist.	Representative (Party, Home)	1984 Election
1.	Robert C. Smith (R, Tuftonboro)	93,500
	Dudley Dudley (D, Durham)	63,625
2.	Judd Gregg* (R, Greenfield)	138,900
	Larry Converse (D, Claremont)	42,556

New Jersey

Dist.	Representative (Party, Home)	1984 Election
1.	James J. Florio* (D, Pine Hill)	148,818
	Fred Busch (R, Clementon)	57,228
2.	William J. Hughes* (D, Ocean City)	127,194
	Ray Massie (R, Brigantine)	74,048
3.	James J. Howard* (D, Spring Lake Heights)	120,072
	Brian Kennedy (R, Bradley Beach)	82,019
4.	Christopher H. Smith* (R, Hamilton Square)	130,852
	James Hedden (D, Trenton)	86,291
5.	Marge Roukema* (R, Ridgewood)	163,905
	Rose Brunetto (D, Ridgewood)	66,863
6.	Bernard J. Dwyer* (D, Edison)	127,228
	Dennis Adams (R, Edison)	89,274
7.	Matthew J. Rinaldo* (R, Union)	165,220
	John Feely (D, Roselle Park)	56,637
8.	Robert A. Roe* (D, Pompton Lakes)	112,922
	Marguerite Page (R, Passaic)	66,431
9.	Robert G. Torricelli* (D, Hackensack)	148,521
	Neil Romano (R, Englewood Cliffs)	85,753
10.	Peter W. Rodino Jr.* (D, Newark)	104,999
	Howard Berkeley (R, Irvington)	19,725
11.	Dean Gallo (R, Morris Plains)	120,146
	Joseph G. Minish* (D, West Orange)	91,353
12.	Jim Courter* (R, Hackettstown)	144,785
	Peter Bearse (D, Princeton)	76,819
13.	Jim Saxton (R, Bordentown)	133,093
	Jim Smith (D, Mt. Holly)	86,613
14.	Frank J. Guarini* (D, Jersey City)	111,713
	Edward Magee (R, Jersey City)	56,642

New Mexico

Dist.	Representative (Party, Home)	1984 Election
1.	Manuel Lujan Jr.* (R, Albuquerque)	114,740
	Ted Asbury (D, Albuquerque)	60,016
2.	Joe Skeen* (R, Picacho)	115,221
	Peter York (D, Roswell)	40,255
3.	Bill Richardson* (D, Santa Fe)	99,729
	Lour Gallegos (R, Sena)	59,191

New York

Dist.	Representative (Party, Home)	1984 Election
1.	William Carney* (R, C, RTL, Hauppauge)	103,489
	George Hochbrueckner (D)	91,533
2.	Thomas J. Downey* (D, I, West Islip)	94,651
	Paul Aniboli (R, I, Amityville)	81,378
3.	Robert J. Mrazek* (D, Huntington)	116,667
	Robert Quinn (R, C, Locust Valley)	110,226
4.	Norman F. Lent* (R, C, Baldwin)	152,669
	Sheldon Englehart (D, L, Oceanside)	65,065
5.	Raymond J. McGrath* (R, C, Valley Stream)	137,755
	Michael D'Innocenzo (D, Uniondale)	78,033
6.	Joseph P. Addabbo* (D, L, Ozone Park)	118,389
	Philip Veltre (R, C, RTL, Queens)	21,661
7.	Gary Ackerman* (D, L, Queens)	94,527
	Gustave Reifenkugel (R, C, Queens)	42,060
8.	James H. Scheuer* (D, L, Queens)	99,948
	Bob Brandofino (R, C, So. Ozone)	59,980
9.	Thomas Manton* (D, Queens)	68,920
	Serphin Maltese (R, C, RTL, Queens)	61,967
10.	Charles E. Schumer* (D, L, Brooklyn)	112,187
	John H. Fox (R, C, Brooklyn)	43,209
11.	Edolphus Towns* (D, L, Brooklyn)	78,448
	Nathaniel Hendricks (R, Brooklyn)	12,035
12.	Major R. Owens* (D, L, Brooklyn)	78,640
	Joseph Caesar (R, C, RTL, Brooklyn)	8,613
13.	Stephen J. Solarz* (D, L, Brooklyn)	80,215
	Yehuda Levin (R, C, RTL, Brooklyn)	42,789
14.	Guy V. Molinari* (R, C, RTL, Staten Island)	112,485
	Kevin Sheehy (D, Staten Island)	48,054
15.	Bill Green* (R, Manhattan)	100,372
	Andrew Stein (D, Mahattan)	78,748
16.	Charles B. Rangel (D, R, Manhatten)	114,487
	Michael T. Berns (C, Manhattan)	2,560
17.	Ted Weiss* (D, L, Manhattan)	152,641
	Kenneth Katzman (R, Bronx)	31,114
18.	Robert Garcia* (D, L, Bronx)	82,700
	Curtis Johnson (R, Bronx)	9,008
19.	Mario Biaggi* (D, R, L, Bronx)	147,616
	Alice Farrell (C, Bronx)	8,120
20.	Joe Dioguardi (R, C, Scarsdale)	97,208
	Orel Teicher (D, White Plains)	91,068
21.	Hamilton Fish Jr.* (R, C, Millbrook)	152,668
	Lawrence Grunberger (D, Peekskill)	39,786
22.	Benjamin A. Gilman* (R, Middletown)	133,357
	Bruce Levine (D, L, Spring Valley)	53,666
23.	Samuel S. Stratton* (D, Schenectady)	176,839
	Frank Wicks (R, Nuclear Freeze, Schenectady)	50,323
24.	Gerald B. H. Solomon* (R, C, RTL, Glen Falls)	157,555
	Edward Bloch (D, Latham)	60,463
25.	Sherwood L. Boehlert* (R, Utica)	129,348
	James Ball (D, Meridale)	49,116
26.	David O'B. Martin* (R, C, Canton)	126,466
	Bernard Lammers (D, Canton)	55,253
27.	George C. Wortley* (R, C, Fayetteville)	116,112
	Tom Buckel (D, L, Syracuse)	90,709
28.	Matthew F. McHugh* (D, Ithaca)	115,012
	Connie Cook (R, Ithaca)	84,386
29.	Frank Horton* (R, Rochester)	127,970
	James R. Toole (D, Rochester)	47,716
30.	Fred Eckert (R, C, Stafford)	117,265
	Doug Call (D, Stafford)	96,760
31.	Jack F. Kemp* (R, C, Hamburg)	163,653
	Peter Martinelli (D, L, Amherst)	55,511
32.	John J. LaFalce* (D, L, Kenmore)	137,690
	Anthony Murty (R, C, RTL, Niagara Falls)	61,359

Dist.	Representative (Party, Home)	1984 Election
33.	Henry J. Nowak* (D, L, Buffalo) . . .	151,691
	David Lewandowski (R, C, RTL, Depew)	43,915
34.	Stanley N. Lundine* (D, Jamestown)	111,422
	Jill Emery (R, C, Geneseo)	87,165

North Carolina

Dist.	Representative (Party, Home)	1984 Election
1.	Walter B. Jones* (D, Farmville) . . .	120,920
	Herbert Lee (R, Greenville)	59,413
2.	I.T. "Tim" Valentine Jr.* (D, Nashville)	122,501
	Frank Hill, Jr. (D, Durham).	58,324
3.	Charles O. Whitley* (D, Mt. Olive) .	99,529
	Danny Moody (R, Fuquay-Varina) .	54,817
4.	William Cobey Jr. (R, Chapel Hill). .	111,748
	Ike Andrews* (D, Cary)	109,478
5.	Stephen L. Neal* (D, Winston-Salem)	105,302
	Stuart Epperson (R, Winston-Salem).	101,620
6.	J. Howard Coble (R, Greensboro). .	103,912
	Charles Robin Britt* (D, Greensboro)	100,061
7.	Charles Rose*(D, Fayetteville). . . .	89,504
	Tommy Rhodes (R, Wilmington) . .	61,130
8.	W. G. (Bill) Hefner* (D, Concord) . .	99,816
	Harris D. Blake (R, Pinehurst). . . .	95,813
9.	David Martin (D, Charlotte).	102,196
	Alex McMillan (R, Charlotte)	99,405
10.	James T. Broyhill* (R, Lenoir). . . .	138,498
	Ted Poovey (D, Granite Falls).	50,736
11.	William M. (Bill) Hendon (R, Asheville)	112,006
	James McClure Clarke* (D, Fairview)	107,828

North Dakota At Large

	Byron L. Dorgan* (D, Bismarck). . .	190,275
	Lois Altenburg (R, Fargo)	50,193

Ohio

Dist.	Representative (Party, Home)	1984 Election
1.	Thomas A. Luken* (D, Cincinnati) . .	121,392
	Norm Murdock (R, Cincinnati).	88,713
2.	Bill Gradison* (R, Cincinnati).	149,603
	Thomas Porter (D, Cincinnati). . . .	68,251
3.	Tony P. Hall* (D, Dayton).	Unopposed
4.	Michael Oxley* (R, Findlay)	161,267
	William Sutton (D, St. Marys)	47,062
5.	Delbert L. Latta* (R, Bowling Green)	132,218
	James R. Sherck (D, Fremont City) .	78,636
6.	Bob McEwen* (R, Hillsboro)	149,985
	Bob Smith (D, Portsmouth)	52,648
7.	Michael Dewine* (R, Cedarville) . .	141,678
	Donald E. Scott (D, St. Paris)	45,908
8.	Thomas N. Kindness* (R, Hamilton)	154,972
	John Francis (D, Greenville).	46,610
9.	Marcy Kaptur* (D, Toledo).	117,536
	Frank Venner (R, Toledo).	92,605
10.	Clarence E. Miller* (R, Lancaster). .	144,556
	John M. Buchanan (D, Newark). . . .	54,538
11.	Dennis E. Eckart* (D, Mentor). . . .	133,019
	Dean Beagle (R, Farmdale).	66,240
12.	John R. Kasich* (R, Columbus) . . .	148,083
	Richard Sloan (D, Columbus)	65,105
13.	Donald J. Pease* (D, Oberlin)	130,523
	William Schaffner (R, Brunswick) . .	58,830
14.	John F. Seiberling* (D, Akron) . . .	136,129
	Jean Bender (R, Akron)	54,136
15.	Chalmers P. Wylie* (R, Columbus) .	147,647
	Duane Jager (D, Columbus).	59,180
16.	Ralph Regula* (R, Navarre)	152,134
	James Gwin (D, Canton).	58,149
17.	James Traficant (D, Poland)	122,426
	Lyle Williams* (R, Warren)	104,861
18.	Douglas Applegate* (D, Steubenville)	155,223
	Kenneth Burt Jr. (R, E. Liverpool). . .	49,255
19.	Edward F. Feighan (D, Lakewood) . .	139,413
	Matt Hatchadorian (R, Highland Heights)	107,844
20.	Mary Rose Oakar* (D, Cleveland). .	Unopposed

Dist.	Representative (Party, Home)	1984 Election
21.	Louis Stokes* (D, Warrensville Hts.)	164,714
	Robert Woodall (R, Cleveland)	29,442

Oklahoma

Dist.	Representative (Party, Home)	1984 Election
1.	James R. Jones* (D, Tulsa)	93,815
	Frank Keating (R, Tulsa). . . . . *. . . .	85,227
2.	Mike Synar* (D, Muskogee)	135,511
	Gary Rice (R, Broken Arrow)	47,716
3.	Wes Watkins* (D, Ada).	129,136
	Patrick M. Miller (R, Snow)	36,695
4.	Dave McCurdy* (D, Norman)	107,409
	Jerry Smith (R, Lindsay)	58,884
5.	Mickey Edwards* (R, Oklahoma City)	124,069
	Alan Greeson (D, Guthrie).	36,328
6.	Glenn English* (D, Cordell)	94,361
	Craig Dodd (R, Enid)	65,699

Oregon

Dist.	Representative (Party, Home)	1984 Election
1.	Les AuCoin* (D, Portland).	131,812
	Bill Moshofsky (R, Portland).	114,145
2.	Bob Smith* (R, Burns)	116,415
	Larryann Willis (D, Vale).	89,185
3.	Ron Wyden* (D, Portland)	161,815
	Drew Davis (R, Lake Oswego)	60,625
4.	James Weaver* (D, Eugene).	127,611
	Bruce Long (R, Roseburg).	91,316
5.	Denny Smith* (R, Salem)	124,005
	J. Ruth McFarland (D, Boring).	104,206

Pennsylvania

Dist.	Representative (Party, Home)	1984 Election
1.	Thomas M. Foglietta* (D, Philadelphia).	145,166
	Carmine DiBiase (R, Philadelphia) . . .	49,865
2.	William H. Gray III* (D, Philadelphia)	177,225
	Ronald Sharper (R, Philadelphia). . . .	17,375
3.	Robert A. Borski* (D, Philadelphia) .	143,175
	Flora Becker (R, Philadelphia)	80,505
4.	Joseph P. Kolter* (D, New Brighton)	112,354
	Jim Kunder (R, Beaver Falls)	85,055
5.	Richard T. Schulze* (R, Paoli)	141,636
	Louis Fanti (D, Coatesville)	53,092
6.	Gus Yatron* (D, Reading)	Unopposed
7.	Robert W. Edgar* (D, Springfield). .	124,054
	Curt Weldon (R, Aston)	123,573
8.	Peter H. Kostmayer (D, New Hope)	112,435
	Dave Christian (R, Washington Crossing)	108,651
9.	Bud Shuster* (R, Everett)	117,070
	Nancy Kulp (D, Port Royal)	60,969
10.	Joseph M. McDade* (R, Clarks Summit)	145,086
	Gene Basalyga (D, Olyphant)	44,465
11.	Paul Kanjorski (D, Nanticoke)	110,737
	Bob Hudock (R, Hazleton)	77,163
12.	John P. Murtha* (D, Johnstown). . .	133,149
	Thomas Fullard (R, Acme).	56,626
13.	Lawrence Coughlin* (R, Villanova) .	133,642
	Joseph Hoeffel (D, Abington)	103,840
14.	William J. Coyne* (D, Pittsburgh) . .	162,468
	John R. Clark (R, Pittsburgh)	42,540
15.	Don Ritter* (R, Allentown)	109,336
	Jane Wells-Schooley (D, Allentown) .	79,110
16.	Robert S. Walker* (R, E. Petersburg)	138,323
	Martin Bard (D, Manheim)	43,488
17.	George W. Gekas* (R, Harrisburg) .	129,348
	Steven Anderson (D, Williamsport) .	48,470
18.	Doug Walgren* (D, Pittsburgh)	149,172
	John Maxwell (R, Mt. Lebanon) . . .	87,240
19.	William F. Goodling* (R, York)	138,989
	John Rahrig (D, Orrtanna)	43,468
20.	Joseph M. Gaydos* (D, McKeesport)	157,999
	Daniel Lloyd (R, Homestead)	50,055
21.	Thomas J. Ridge (R, Erie)	122,006
	Jim Young (D, Edinboro).	68,099
22.	Austin J. Murphy* (D, Charleroi) . .	151,958
	Nancy Pryor (R, Washington)	40,557
23.	William F. Clinger Jr.* (R, Warren) .	94,976
	William Wachob (D, State College). .	88,655

Dist.	Representative (Party, Home)	1984 Election
	Rhode Island	
1.	**Fernand J. St Germain*** (D, Woonsocket)	**126,510**
	Alfred Rego (R, Bristol)	57,694
2.	**Claudine Schneider*** (R, Narragansett)	**130,274**
	Richard Sinapi (D, Warwick)	61,837
	South Carolina	
1.	**Thomas F. Hartnett*** (R, Charleston)	**83,924**
	Ed Pendarvis (D, Charleston)	51,529
2.	**Floyd Spence*** (R, Lexington)	**107,389**
	Ken Mosely (D, Orangeburg)	63,321
3.	**Butler Derrick*** (D, Edgefield)	**68,505**
	Clarence Taylor (R, Seneca)	43,949
4.	**Carroll A. Campbell Jr.*** (R, Fountain Inn)	**102,966**
	Jeff Smith (D, Greer)	56,362
5.	**John Spratt** (D, York)	**81,345**
	Linda Blevins (Libert., Kings Creek)	3,265
6.	**Robert M. Tallon Jr.** (D, Florence)	**97,054**
	Lois Eargle (R, Florence)	64,532
	South Dakota At Large	
1.	**Thomas A. Daschle*** (D, Aberdeen)	**179,244**
	Dale Bell (R, Spearfish)	133,200
	Tennessee	
1.	**James H. Quillen*** (R, Kingsport)	**Unopposed**
2.	**John J. Duncan*** (R, Knoxville)	**132,153**
	John Bowen (D, Knoxville)	38,779
3.	**Marilyn Lloyd*** (D, Chattanooga)	**99,306**
	John Davis (R, Harriman)	90,116
4.	**Jim Cooper*** (D, Shelbyville)	**95,449**
	James Seigneur (R, Shelbyville)	31,193
5.	**Bill Boner*** (D, Nashville)	**Unopposed**
6.	**Bart Gordon** (D, Murfreesboro)	**101,790**
	Joe Simpkins (R, Franklin)	60,586
7.	**Don Sundquist*** (R, Memphis)	**Unopposed**
8.	**Ed Jones*** (D, Yorkville)	**Unopposed**
9.	**Harold E. Ford*** (D, Memphis)	**132,814**
	William Thompson Jr. (R, Memphis)	53,072
	Texas	
1.	**Sam B. Hall Jr.*** (D, Marshall)	**Unopposed**
2.	**Charles Wilson*** (D, Lufkin)	**110,628**
	Louis Dugas (R, Orange)	76,145
3.	**Steve Bartlett*** (R, Dallas)	**228,819**
	James Westbrook (D, Dallas)	46,890
4.	**Ralph M. Hall*** (D, Rockwall)	**114,458**
	Thomas Blow (R, Tyler)	84,367
5.	**John Bryant*** (D, Dallas)	**Unopposed**
6.	**Joe Barton** (R, Ennis)	**124,472**
	Dan Kubiak (D, College Station)	96,579
7.	**Bill Archer*** (R, Houston)	**210,545**
	Billy Willbey (D, Houston)	32,365
8.	**Jack Fields*** (R, Humble)	**114,845**
	Don Buford (D, Houston)	62,259
9.	**Jack Brooks*** (D, Beaumont)	**116,200**
	Jim Mahan (R, Galveston)	81,336
10.	**J. J. "Jake" Pickle*** (D, Austin)	**Unopposed**
11.	**Marvin Leath*** (D, Waco)	**Unopposed**
12.	**Jim Wright*** (D, Fort Worth)	**Unopposed**
13.	**Beau Boulter*** (R, Amarillo)	**107,564**
	Jack Hightower* (D, Vernon)	95,316
14.	**Mac Sweeney** (R, Victoria)	**89,341**
	William N. "Bill" Patman* (D, Ganado)	86,507
15.	**E. "Kika" de la Garza*** (D, Mission)	**Unopposed**
16.	**Ronald Coleman*** (D, El Paso)	**54,274**
	Jack Hammond (R, El Paso)	42,638
17.	**Charles W. Stenholm*** (D, Stamford)	**Unopposed**
18.	**Mickey Leland*** (D, Houston)	**108,819**
	Glen E. Beaman (R, Houston)	26,379
19.	**Larry Combest** (R, Lubbock)	**102,844**
	Don Richards (D, Lubbock)	73,499
20.	**Henry B. Gonzalez*** (D, San Antonio)	**Unopposed**

Dist.	Representative (Party, Home)	1984 Election
21.	**Tom Loeffler*** (R, Hunt)	**199,320**
	Joe Sullivan (D, San Antonio)	46,901
22.	**Tom DeLay** (R, Sugar Land)	**122,660**
	Douglas Williams (D, Missouri City)	67,539
23.	**Albert Bustamente** (D, San Antonio)	**Unopposed**
24.	**Martin Frost*** (D, Dallas)	**150,210**
	Robert Burk (R, Irving)	71,703
25.	**Mike Andrews*** (D, Houston)	**112,145**
	Jerry Patterson (R, Houston)	64,679
26.	**Dick Armey** (R, Denton)	**119,384**
	Tom Vandergriff* (D, Arlington)	109,697
27.	**Solomon P. Ortiz*** (D, Corpus Christi)	**103,278**
	Richard Moore (R, Corpus Christi)	57,141
	Utah	
1.	**James V. Hansen*** (R, Farmington)	**141,203**
	Milton Abrams (D, Logan)	55,702
2.	**Dave Monson** (R, Salt Lake City)	**104,847**
	Frances Farley (D, Salt Lake City)	104,704
3.	**Howard C. Nielson*** (R, Provo)	**136,950**
	Bruce Baird (D, Murray)	46,016
	Vermont At Large	
1.	**James M. Jeffords*** (R, Montpelier)	**146,091**
	Anthony Pollina (D, Montpelier)	59,686
	Virginia	
1.	**Herbert Bateman*** (R, Newport News)	**117,146**
	John J. McGlennon (D, Williamsburg)	79,024
2.	**G. William Whitehurst*** (R, Norfolk)	**Unopposed**
3.	**Thomas J. Bliley Jr.*** (R, Richmond)	**182,206**
	Roger L. Coffey (I., Richmond)	28,424
4.	**Norman Sisisky*** (D, Petersburg)	**Unopposed**
5.	**Dan Daniel*** (D, Danville)	**Unopposed**
6.	**James Olin*** (D, Roanoke)	**103,388**
	Ray Garland (R, Roanoke)	96,185
7.	**French Slaughter** (R, Culpepper)	**107,393**
	Lewis Costello (D, Winchester)	76,569
8.	**Stan Parris*** (R, Woodbridge)	**122,185**
	Richard Saslaw (D, Annandale)	95,900
9.	**Frederick Boucher*** (D, Abingdon)	**102,366**
	Jefferson Stafford (R, Pearisburg)	93,562
10.	**Frank R. Wolf*** (R, Falls Church)	**163,853**
	John Flannery (D, Arlington)	98,742
	Washington	
1.	**John Miller** (R, Seattle)	**136,712**
	Brock Evans (D, Seattle)	106,989
2.	**Al Swift*** (D, Bellingham)	**128,278**
	Jim Klauder (R, Eastsound)	84,540
3.	**Don Bonker*** (D, Vancouver)	**137,254**
	Herb Elder (R, Olympia)	55,415
4.	**Sid Morrison*** (R, Zillah)	**128,320**
	Mark Epperson (D, Golendale)	40,316
5.	**Thomas S. Foley*** (D, Spokane)	**142,997**
	Jack Hebner (R, Spokane)	61,922
6.	**Norman D. Dicks*** (D, Bremerton)	**99,352**
	Mike Lonergan (R, Tacoma)	47,713
7.	**Mike Lowry*** (D, Renton)	**163,059**
	Bob Dorse (R, Seattle)	65,838
8.	**Rodney Chandler*** (R, Redmond)	**136,206**
	Bob Lamson (D, Mercer Island)	82,985
	West Virginia	
1.	**Alan B. Mollohan*** (D, Fairmont)	**104,252**
	Jim Altmeyer (R, Wheeling)	86,927
2.	**Harley O. Staggers Jr.*** (D, Keyser)	**96,728**
	Cleve Benedict (R, Lewisburg)	74,712
3.	**Bob Wise*** (D, Charleston)	**122,933**
	Peggy Miller (R, So. Charleston)	55,964
4.	**Nick J. Rahall II *** (D, Beckley)	**98,490**
	Jess Shumate (R, Beckley)	49,221
	Wisconsin	
1.	**Les Aspin*** (D, East Troy)	**127,105**
	Peter N. Jansson (R, Racine)	99,105

Dist.	Representative (Party, Home)	1984 Election	Dist.	Representative (Party, Home)	1984 Election
2.	**Robert Kastenmeier*** (D, Sun Prairie).	**159,919**		**Wyoming At Large**	
				Richard B. Cheney* (R, Casper). .	**136,662**
	Albert Wiley (R, Stoughton).	91,334		Hugh McFadden (D, Laramie).	45,570
3.	**Steven Gunderson*** (R, Osseo). . .	**160,376**		**Non-Voting Delegates**	
	Charles Dahl (D, Viroqua)	74,416		District of Columbia	
4.	**Gerry Kleczka** (D, Milwaukee). . . .	**156,767**		Walter E. Fauntroy* (D)	
	Robert Nolan (R, So. Milwaukee). . .	77,705		Guam	
5.	**Jim Moody*** (D, Milwaukee)	**172,241**		Antonio Borja Won Pat* (D, Agana)	
	William C. Breihan (SW, Milwaukee) .	4,208		Ben Garrido Blaz (R, Agana)	
6.	**Thomas E. Petri*** (R, Fond du Lac) .	**170,216**		Virgin Islands	
	David Iaquinta (D, Oshkosh).	54,522		Ron de Lugo (D, St. Croix)	
7.	**David R. Obey*** (D, Wausau).	**145,659**		Janet Watlington (I, Charlotte Amalie)	
	Mark Michaelson (R, Marshfield) . . .	92,637		American Samoa	
8.	**Toby Roth*** (R, Appleton).	**159,728**		Fofo I. F. Sunia (D, Pago Pago)	
	Paul Willems (D, Green Bay)	72,623		Aumoeulogo Salanoa Soli (I, Pago Pago)	
9.	**F. James Sensenbrenner Jr.*** (R, Menomonee Falls).	**179,518**		Puerto Rico	
	John Krause (D, Germantown)	65,441		Nelson Famadas (D, Hato Rey)	

Top Congressional Fund-Raisers

Source: Federal Election Commission (Senate), Common Cause

(money raised through Sept. 30, 1984)

Senate			House		
	Total	Political Action Committees		Total	Political Action Committees
Jesse Helms* (R-N.C.) . . . . . :	$14,144,047	$650,775	James Jones (D-Okla.)	$1,072,584	$471,555
Jim Hunt (D-N.C.)	8,021,089	706,908	Andrew Stein (D-N.Y.).	828,062	12,700
Jay Rockefeller (D-W. Va.).	8,010,636	410,285	Joseph Addabbo (D-N.Y.)	817,525	298,808
Phil Gramm (R-Tex.)	6,863,291	899,572	Bruce Morrison (D-Conn.)	761,670	314,482
Rudy Boschwitz* (R-Minn.)	6,092,689	817,100	Jack Fields (R-Tex.)	757,768	267,525
Charles H. Percy* (R-Ill.)	5,094,082	794,416	Stan Parris (R-Va.)	724,162	197,577
Bill Bradley* (D-N.J.)	5,082,929	567,978	Robert Dornan (R-Calif.)	718,255	86,082
Lloyd Doggett (D-Tex.)	4,602,026	681,186	Tommy Robinson (D-Ark.)	696,264	20,550
Ray Shamie (R-Mass.)	3,264,051	0	Ronald Dellums (D-Calif.)	692,218	51,021
Paul Simon (D-Ill.)	3,244,576	667,516	Bill Green (R-N.Y.).	679,580	100,597

*Starting point for Senate incumbents measured from Jan. 1, 1979. For others, it is Jan. 1, 1983.

98th Congress: Bills Turned Down

The following bills were not passed during the final session of the 98th Congress, but are likely to resurface when the 99th convenes:

Immigration reform. House and Senate appeared deadlocked over new measures to deal with aliens entering the U.S. illegally.

Tuition tax credits. Senate killed bill allowing tax deductions for parents with children in private schools.

Abortion. Efforts to extend medicaid to cover abortions for needy victims of rape and incest failed in Senate.

Budget. Constitutional amendment requiring a balanced federal budget stalled in both houses.

Line-item veto. Effort to give President power to veto individual budget items failed in Senate.

Bank deregulation. Bill to permit bank affiliates to enter new marketing areas died in House committee.

School prayer. Amendment allowing silent prayer in public school classrooms killed by Senate.

School busing. Amendment to restrict court-ordered school busing killed by Senate.

Natural gas. Measure to delay scheduled January 1 lifting of price controls blocked in both houses.

Drinking water. Bill to require tougher standards of drinking water stalled in Senate.

Superfund. Effort to extend and expand hazardous-waste-cleanup program was set aside by Senate until next year.

Gun control. Proposal to weaken federal firearm regulations failed in Senate.

Voting for President

Source: Federal Election Commission; Commission for Study of American Electorate

	Candidates	Voter Participation (% of voting-age population)		Candidates	Voter Participation (% of voting-age population)
1932	Roosevelt-Hoover	52.4	1960	Kennedy-Nixon	62.8
1936	Roosevelt-Landon	56.0	1964	Johnson-Goldwater.	61.9
1940	Roosevelt-Wilkie	58.9	1968	Humphrey-Nixon	60.9
1944	Roosevelt-Dewey.	56.0	1972	McGovern-Nixon	55.2
1948	Truman-Dewey	51.1	1976	Carter-Ford	53.5
1952	Stevenson-Eisenhower.	61.6	1980	Carter-Reagan	54.0
1956	Stevenson-Eisenhower.	59.3			

Political Divisions of the U.S. Senate and House of Representatives
From 1859 (36th Cong.) to 1983-1985 (98th Cong.)

Source: Clerk of the House of Representatives; News Election Service

		Senate					House of Representatives				
Congress	Years	Number of Senators	Democrats	Republicans	Other parties	Vacant	Number of Representatives	Democrats	Republicans	Other parties	Vacant
36th....	1859-61	66	38	26	2		237	101	113	23	
37th....	1861-63	50	11	31	7	1	178	42	106	28	2
38th....	1863-65	51	12	39			183	80	103		
39th....	1865-67	52	10	42			191	46	145		
40th....	1867-69	53	11	42			193	49	143		1
41st....	1869-71	74	11	61		2	243	73	170		
42d....	1871-73	74	17	57			243	104	139		
43d....	1873-75	74	19	54		1	293	88	203		2
44th....	1875-77	76	29	46		1	293	181	107	3	2
45th....	1877-79	76	36	39	1		293	156	137		
46th....	1879-81	76	43	33			293	150	128	14	1
47th....	1881-83	76	37	37	2		293	130	152	11	
48th....	1883-85	76	36	40			325	200	119	6	
49th....	1885-87	76	34	41		1	325	182	140	2	1
50th....	1887-89	76	37	39			325	170	151	4	
51st....	1889-91	84	37	47			330	156	173	1	
52d....	1891-93	88	39	47	2		333	231	88	14	
53d....	1893-95	88	44	38	3	3	356	220	126	10	
54th....	1895-97	88	39	44	5		357	104	246	7	
55th....	1897-99	90	34	46	10		357	134	206	16	1
56th....	1899-1901	90	26	53	11		357	163	185	9	
57th....	1901-03	90	29	56	3	2	357	153	198	5	1
58th....	1903-05	90	32	58			386	178	207		1
59th....	1905-07	90	32	58			386	136	250		
60th....	1907-09	92	29	61		2	386	164	222		
61st....	1909-11	92	32	59		1	391	172	219		
62d....	1911-13	92	42	49		1	391	228	162	1	
63d....	1913-15	96	51	44	1		435	290	127	18	
64th....	1915-17	96	56	39	1		435	231	193	8	3
65th....	1917-19	96	53	42	1		435	210	216	9	
66th....	1919-21	96	47	48	1		435	191	237	7	
67th....	1921-23	96	37	59			435	132	300	1	2
68th....	1923-25	96	43	51	2		435	207	225	3	
69th....	1925-27	96	40	54	1	1	435	183	247	5	
70th....	1927-29	96	47	48	1		435	195	237	3	
71st....	1929-31	96	39	56	1		435	163	267	1	4
72d....	1931-33	96	47	48	1		435	²216	218	1	
73d....	1933-35	96	59	36	1		435	313	117	5	
74th....	1935-37	96	69	25	2		435	322	103	10	
75th....	1937-39	96	75	17	4		435	333	89	13	
76th....	1939-41	96	69	23	4		435	262	169	4	
77th....	1941-43	96	66	28	2		435	267	162	6	
78th....	1943-45	96	57	38	1		435	222	209	4	
79th....	1945-47	96	57	38	1		435	243	190	2	
80th....	1947-49	96	45	51			435	188	246	1	
81st....	1949-51	96	54	42			435	263	171	1	
82d....	1951-53	96	48	47	1		435	234	199	2	
83d....	1953-55	96	46	48	2		435	213	221	1	
84th....	1955-57	96	48	47	1		435	232	203		
85th....	1957-59	96	49	47			435	234	201		
86th....	1959-61	98	64	34			³436	283	153		
87th....	1961-63	100	64	36			⁴437	262	175		
88th....	1963-65	100	67	33			435	258	176		1
89th....	1965-67	100	68	32			435	295	140		
90th....	1967-69	100	64	36			435	248	187		
91st....	1969-71	100	58	42			435	243	192		
92d....	1971-73	100	54	44	2		435	255	180		
93d....	1973-75	100	56	42	2		435	242	192	1	
94th....	1975-77	100	61	37	2		435	291	144		
95th....	1977-79	100	61	38	1		435	292	143		
96th....	1979-81	100	58	41	1		435	277	158		
97th....	1981-83	100	46	53	1		435	242	190		3
98th⁵	1983-85	100	45	55			435	267	166		2

(1) Democrats organized House with help of other parties. (2) Democrats organized House due to Republican deaths. (3) Proclamation declaring Alaska a State issued Jan. 3, 1959. (4) Proclamation declaring Hawaii a State issued Aug. 21, 1959. (5) Totals are based on preliminary results of Nov. 4, 1984 election.

Senate Standing Committees

(As of Mar. 26, 1984)

Agriculture, Nutrition, and Forestry
Chairman: Jesse Helms, N.C.
Ranking Dem.: Walter D. Huddleston, Ky.
Appropriations
Chairman: Mark O. Hatfield, Ore.
Ranking Dem.: John C. Stennis, Miss.
Armed Services
Chairman: John Tower, Tex.
Ranking Dem.: Sam Nunn, Ga.
Banking, Housing, and Urban Affairs
Chairman: Jake Garn, Utah
Ranking Dem.: William Proxmire, Wis.
Budget
Chairman: Pete V. Domenici, N.M.
Ranking Dem.: Lawton Chiles, Fla.
Commerce, Science, and Transportation
Chairman: Bob Packwood, Ore.
Ranking Dem.: Ernest F. Hollings, S.C.
Energy and Natural Resources
Chairman: James A. McClure, Idaho
Ranking Dem.: J. Bennett Johnston, La.
Environment and Public Works
Chairman: Robert T. Stafford, Vt.
Ranking Dem.: Jennings Randolph, W.Va.
Finance
Chairman: Robert Dole, Kans.
Ranking Dem.: Russell B. Long, La.
Foreign Relations
Chairman: Charles H. Percy, Ill.
Ranking Dem.: Claiborne Pell, R.I.
Governmental Affairs
Chairman: William V. Roth, Del.
Ranking Dem.: Thomas F. Eagleton, Mo.
Judiciary
Chairman: Strom Thurmond, S.C.
Ranking Dem.: Joseph R. Biden, Del.
Labor and Human Resources
Chairman: Orrin G. Hatch, Utah
Ranking Dem.: Edward M. Kennedy, Mass.
Rules and Administration
Chairman: Charles McC. Mathias, Jr., Md.
Ranking Dem.: Wendell H. Ford, Ky.
Small Business
Chairman: Lowell P. Weicker, Conn.
Ranking Dem.: Dale Bumpers, Ark.
Veterans' Affairs
Chairman: Alan K. Simpson, Wyo.
Ranking Dem.: Alan Cranston, Calif.

Senate Select and Special Committees

Aging
Chairman: John Heinz, Pa.
Ranking Dem.: John Glenn, Ohio
Ethics
Chairman: Ted Stevens, Alas.
Ranking Dem.: Howell Heflin, Ala.
Indian Affairs
Chairman: Mark Andrews, N.D.
Ranking Dem.: John Melcher, Mont.
Intelligence
Chairman: Barry Goldwater, Ariz.
Ranking Dem.: Daniel Patrick Moynihan, N.Y.
Security and Cooperation in Europe
Chairman: Robert Dole, Kan.
V. Chairman: Dennis DeConcini, Ariz.

Joint Committees of Congress

Economic Committee
Chairman: Sen. Roger W. Jepsen (R), Iowa
V. Chairman: Rep. Lee H. Hamilton (D), Ind.
Committee on the Library
Chairman: Sen. Charles McC. Mathias, Jr. (R), Md.
V. Chairman: Rep. Augustus F. Hawkins (D), Calif.
Committee on Printing
Chairman: Rep. Augustus F. Hawkins (D), Calif.
V. Chairman: Sen. Charles McC. Mathias, Jr. (R), Md.
Committee on Taxation
Chairman: Sen. Robert Dole (R), Kan.
V. Chairman: Rep. Dan Rostenkowski (D), Ill.

House Standing Committees

(As of Aug. 15, 1984)

Agriculture
Chairman: E de la Garza, Tex.
Ranking Rep.: Edward R. Madigan, Ill.
Appropriations
Chairman: Jamie L. Whitten, Miss.
Ranking Rep.: Silvio O. Conte, Mass.
Armed Services
Chairman: Melvin Price, Ill.
Ranking Rep.: William L. Dickinson, Ala.
Banking, Finance, and Urban Affairs
Chairman: Fernand J. St. Germain, R.I.
Ranking Rep.: Chalmers P. Wylie, Ohio
Budget
Chairman: James R. Jones, Okla.
Ranking Rep.: Delbert L. Latta, Ohio
District of Columbia
Chairman: Ronald V. Dellums, Calif.
Ranking Rep.: Stewart B. McKinney, Conn.
Education and Labor
Chairman: Carl D. Perkins, Ky.
Ranking Rep.: John N. Erlenborn, Ill.
Energy and Commerce
Chairman: John D. Dingell, Mich.
Ranking Rep.: James T. Broyhill, N.C.
Foreign Affairs
Chairman: Dante B. Fascell, Fla.
Ranking Rep.: William S. Broomfield, Mich.
Government Operations
Chairman: Jack Brooks, Tex.
Ranking Rep.: Frank Horton, N.Y.
House Administration
Chairman: Augustus F. Hawkins, Calif.
Ranking Rep.: Bill Frenzel, Minn.
Interior and Insular Affairs
Chairman: Morris K. Udall, Ariz.
Ranking Rep.: Manuel Lujan, Jr., N. M.
Judiciary
Chairman: Peter W. Rodino, Jr., N.J.
Ranking Rep.: Hamilton Fish, Jr., N.Y.
Merchant Marine and Fisheries
Chairman: Walter B. Jones, N.C.
Ranking Rep.: Joel Pritchard, Wash.
Post Office and Civil Service
Chairman: William D. Ford, Mich.
Ranking Rep.: Gene Taylor, Mo.
Public Works and Transportation
Chairman: James J. Howard, N.J.
Ranking Rep.: Gene Snyder, Ky.
Rules
Chairman: Claude Pepper, Fla.
Ranking Rep.: James H. Quillen, Tenn.
Science and Technology
Chairman: Don Fuqua, Fla.
Ranking Rep.: Larry Winn, Jr., Kans.
Small Business
Chairman: Parren J. Mitchell, Md.
Ranking Rep.: Joseph M. McDade, Pa.
Standards of Official Conduct
Chairman: Louis Stokes, Ohio
Ranking Rep.: Floyd Spence, S.C.
Veterans' Affairs
Chairman: G.V. Montgomery, Miss.
Ranking Rep.: John Paul Hammerschmidt, Ark.
Ways and Means
Chairman: Dan Rostenkowski, Ill.
Ranking Rep.: Barber B. Conable, Jr., N.Y.

House Select Committees

Aging
Chairman: Edward R. Roybal, Calif.
Ranking Rep.: Matthew J. Rinaldo, N.J.
Children, Youth, and Families
Chairman: George Miller, Calif.
Ranking Rep.: Dan Marriott, Utah
Hunger
Chairman: Mickey Leland, Tex.
Ranking Rep.: Margo Roukema, N.J.

(continued)

Intelligence
Chairman: Edward P. Boland, Mass.
Ranking Rep.: J. Kenneth Robinson, Va.

Narcotics Abuse and Control
Chairman: Charles B. Rangel, N.Y.
Ranking Rep.: Benjamin A. Gilman, N.Y.

Governors of States and Possessions

Reflecting preliminary results of Nov. 6, 1984 Elections

State	Capital	Governor	Party	Term years	Term expires	Annual salary
Alabama	Montgomery	George C. Wallace	Dem.	4	Jan. 1987	$63,838
Alaska	Juneau	William Sheffield	Dem.	4	Dec. 1986	81,648
Arizona	Phoenix	Bruce Babbitt	Dem.	4	Jan. 1987	62,500
Arkansas	Little Rock	Bill Clinton	Dem.	2	Jan. 1987	35,000
California	Sacramento	George Deukmejian	Rep.	4	Jan. 1987	49,100
Colorado	Denver	Richard D. Lamm	Dem.	4	Jan. 1987	60,000
Connecticut	Hartford	William A. O'Neill	Dem.	4	Jan. 1987	65,000
Delaware	Dover	Michael Castle	Rep.	4	Jan. 1989	70,000
Florida	Tallahassee	Robert Graham	Dem.	4	Jan. 1987	69,550
Georgia	Atlanta	Joe Frank Harris	Dem.	4	Jan. 1987	71,314
Hawaii	Honolulu	George R. Ariyoshi	Dem.	4	Dec. 1986	59,000
Idaho	Boise	John V. Evans	Dem.	4	Jan. 1987	50,000
Illinois	Springfield	James R. Thompson	Rep.	4	Jan. 1987	58,000
Indiana	Indianapolis	Robert D. Orr	Rep.	4	Jan. 1989	66,000
Iowa	Des Moines	Terry Branstad	Rep.	4	Jan. 1987	64,000
Kansas	Topeka	John Carlin	Dem.	4	Jan. 1987	54,784
Kentucky	Frankfort	Martha L. Collins	Dem.	4	Dec. 1987	60,000
Louisiana	Baton Rouge	Edwin W. Edwards	Dem.	4	May 1988	73,440
Maine	Augusta	Joseph E. Brennan	Dem.	4	Jan. 1987	35,000
Maryland	Annapolis	Harry Hughes	Dem.	4	Jan. 1987	75,000
Massachusetts	Boston	Michael S. Dukakis	Dem.	4	Jan. 1987	75,000
Michigan	Lansing	James J. Blanchard	Dem.	4	Jan. 1987	80,000
Minnesota	St. Paul	Rudy Perpich	Dem.	4	Jan. 1987	66,500
Mississippi	Jackson	William A. Allain	Dem.	4	Jan. 1988	63,000
Missouri	Jefferson City	John Ashcroft	Rep.	4	Jan. 1989	55,000
Montana	Helena	Ted Schwinden	Dem.	4	Jan. 1989	47,963
Nebraska	Lincoln	Robert Kerrey	Dem.	4	Jan. 1987	40,000
Nevada	Carson City	Richard Bryan	Dem.	4	Jan. 1987	65,000
New Hampshire	Concord	John H. Sununu	Rep.	2	Jan. 1987	44,520
New Jersey	Trenton	Thomas H. Kean	Rep.	4	Jan. 1986	85,000
New Mexico	Santa Fe	Toney Anaya	Dem.	4	Jan. 1987	60,000
New York	Albany	Mario Cuomo	Dem.	4	Jan. 1987	100,000
North Carolina	Raleigh	James G. Martin	Rep.	4	Jan. 1989	60,768
North Dakota	Bismarck	George Sinner	Dem.	4	Jan. 1989	60,862
Ohio	Columbus	Richard Celeste	Dem.	4	Jan. 1987	60,000
Oklahoma	Oklahoma City	George Nigh	Dem.	4	Jan. 1987	70,000
Oregon	Salem	Victor Atiyeh	Rep.	4	Jan. 1987	52,092
Pennsylvania	Harrisburg	Dick Thornburgh	Rep.	4	Jan. 1987	75,000
Rhode Island	Providence	Edward DiPrete	Rep.	2	Jan. 1987	49,500
South Carolina	Columbia	Richard W. Riley	Dem.	4	Jan. 1987	60,000
South Dakota	Pierre	William J. Janklow	Rep.	4	Jan. 1987	49,025
Tennessee	Nashville	Lamar Alexander	Rep.	4	Jan. 1987	68,226
Texas	Austin	Mark White Jr.	Dem.	4	Jan. 1987	88,900
Utah	Salt Lake City	Wayne Bangerter	Rep.	4	Jan. 1989	52,000
Vermont	Montpelier	Madeleine Kunin	Dem.	2	Jan. 1987	50,000
Virginia	Richmond	Charles S. Robb	Dem.	4	Jan. 1986	75,000
Washington	Olympia	Booth Gardner	Dem.	4	Jan. 1989	63,000
West Virginia	Charleston	Arch A. Moore	Rep.	4	Jan. 1989	60,000
Wisconsin	Madison	Anthony S. Earl	Dem.	4	Jan. 1987	75,337
Wyoming	Cheyenne	Ed Herschler	Dem.	4	Jan. 1987	70,000
Amer. Samoa	Pago Pago	Peter Coleman	Rep.	4	Jan. 1989	—
Guam	Agana	Ricardo Bordallo	Dem.	4	Jan. 1989	50,000
N. Mariana Isls.	Saipan	Pedro Tenorio	Rep.	4	Jan. 1986	20,000
Puerto Rico	San Juan	Rafael Hernandez Colon	P.D.	4	Jan. 1989	36,200
Virgin Islands	Charlotte Amalie	Juan Luis	Ind.	4	Jan. 1987	52,000

The Race for Governor

State	Republican	Vote	Democrat	Vote
Arkansas	Woody Freeman	312,089	Bill Clinton	527,364
Delaware	Michael Castle	133,892	William T. Quillen	107,736
Indiana	Robert Orr	1,097,897	Wayne Townsend	994,966
Missouri	John Ashcroft	1,165,159	Kenneth Rothman	870,817
Montana	Pat Goodover	90,128	Ted Schwinden	239,568
New Hampshire	John Sununu	234,714	Chris Spirou	115,850
North Carolina	James Martin	1,177,753	Rufus Edmisten	994,551
North Dakota	Allen Olson	108,078	George Sinner	137,065
Rhode Island	Edward DiPrete	237,160	Anthony Solomon	157,814
Utah	Norman Bangerter	348,585	Wayne Owens	273,307
Vermont	John Easton	111,809	Madeleine Kunin	115,500
Washington	John Spellman	792,547	Booth Gardner	906,928
West Virginia	Arch Moore	385,116	Clyde See	342,036

Mayors and City Managers of Larger North American Cities

Reflecting Nov. 6, 1984 Elections

*Asterisk before name denotes city manager. All others are mayors. For mayors, dates are those of next election; for city managers, they are dates of appointment.

D, Democrat; R, Republican; N-P, Non-Partisan

City	Name	Term	City	Name	Term
Abilene, Tex.	David Stubbeman, N-P	1988, Apr.	Brownsville, Tex.	*Kenneth Lieck	1981, Apr.
Abington, Pa.	*Albert Herrmann	1978, May	Bryan, Tex.	*Ernest R. Clark	1979, Feb.
Akron, Oh.	Thomas C. Sawyer, D	1987, Nov.	Buffalo, N.Y.	James D. Griffin, D	1985, Nov.
Alameda, Cal.	Anne B. Diament, N-P.	1987, May.	Burbank, Cal.	*Andrew Lazzaretto Jr.	1983, Mar.
Albany, Ga.	*Carl Leavy	1980, Feb.	Burlington, Vt.	Bernard Sanders, N-P	1985, Mar.
Albany, N.Y.	Thomas M. Whalen,3d,D	1985, Nov.	Calumet City, Ill.	Robert C. Stefaniak, D	1985, Apr.
Albuquerque, N.M.	Harry Kinney, R	1985, Nov.	Cambridge, Mass.	*Robert Healy,	1974, May
Alexandria, La.	John K. Snyder, D	1986, Sept.	Camden, N.J.	Melvin Primas Jr., D.	1985, May
Alexandria, Va.	*Douglas Harman	1975, Nov.	Canton, Oh.	Sam Purses, D.	1987, Nov.
Alhambra, Cal.	*Kevin J. Murphy.	1983, May	Cape Girardeau, Mo.	*Gary A. Eide	1981, Mar.
Allen Park, Mich.	Frank J. Lada, D	1985, Nov.	Carson, Cal.	*Raymond Meador	1982, May
Allentown, Pa.	Joseph S. Daddona, D	1985, Nov.	Casper, Wyo.	*Kenneth Erickson	1969, Oct.
Alton, Ill.	Paul A. Lenz, N-P	1985, Apr.	Cedar Rapids, Ia.	Donald J. Canney, N-P	1985, Nov.
Altoona, Pa.	David Jannetta, D	1987, Nov.	Champaign, Ill.	*John Bloomberg	1984, Apr.
Amarillo, Tex.	*John Ward	1983, June	Charleston, S.C.	Joseph P. Riley Jr., D	1987, Nov.
Ames, Ia.	*Steven L. Schainker	1982, Oct.	Charleston, W. Va.	James E. Roark, R	1987, Apr.
Anaheim, Cal.	*William O. Talley	1976, July	Charlotte, N.C.	Harvey Gantt, D	1985, Nov.
Anchorage, Alas.	Tony Knowles, N-P	1986, Oct.	Charlottesville, Va.	*Cole Hendrix	1970, Jan.
Anderson, Ind.	Thomas McMahan, R	1987, Nov.	Chattanooga, Tenn.	Gene Roberts, R	1987, Mar.
Anderson, S.C.	*Richard Burnette	1976, Sept.	Chesapeake, Va.	*John T. Maxwell	1978, Sept.
Ann Arbor, Mich.	*Godfrey Collins	1982, Dec.	Chester, Pa.	Joseph Battle, R	1987, Nov.
Appleton, Wis.	Dorothy Johnson, N-P	1988, Apr.	Cheyenne, Wyo.	Donald Erickson, R	1988, Nov.
Arcadia, Cal.	*George J. Watts	1981, Feb.	Chicago, Ill.	Harold Washington, D	1987, Apr.
Athens, Ga.	Lauren Coile, D	1985, Nov.	Chicago Hts., Ill.	Charles Panici, R	1987, Apr.
Arlington, Mass.	*Donald R. Marquis	1966, Nov.	Chicopee, Mass.	Richard S. Lak, D	1985, Nov.
Arlington, Tex.	*William Kirchhoff	1984, Oct.	Chino, Cal.	*Roger A. Storey	1982, Nov.
Arlington, Va.	*W.V. Ford	1976, Mar.	Chula Vista, Cal.	*John Goss	1983, Jan.
Arlington Hts., Ill.	James Ryan, N-P	1985, Apr.	Cicero, Ill.	Henry J. Klosak, R	1985, Apr.
Arvada, Col.	*Craig Kocian	1977, Mar.	Cincinnati, Oh.	*Sylvester Murray	1979, Sept.
Asheville, N.C.	*Neal Creighton	1984, Oct.	Clearwater, Fla.	*Anthony Shoemaker	1977, June
Athens, Ga.	Lauren Coile, D	1985, Nov.	Cleveland, Oh.	George Voinovich, R	1985, Nov.
Atlanta, Ga.	Andrew Young, D	1985, Nov.	Cleveland Hgts., Oh.	*Richard Robinson	1978, July
Atlantic City, N.J.	James L. Usry, R	1986, June	Clifton, N.J.	*Joseph J. Lynn	1983, June
Auburn, N.Y.	*Bruce Clifford.	1966, Aug.	Col. Spgs., Col.	*George H. Fellows	1966, July
Augusta, Ga.	Charles Devaney, D	1988, Oct.	Columbia, Mo.	*Richard Gray	1980, Nov.
Aurora, Col.	*James Griesemer	1984, Jan.	Columbia, S.C.	*Graydon V. Olive Jr.	1970, Mar.
Aurora, Ill.	Jack Hill, N-P	1985, Apr.	Columbus, Ga.	J. W. Feighner, N-P	1986, Nov.
Austin, Tex.	Ron Mullen, N-P	1985, Apr.	Columbus, Oh.	Dana Rinehart, R	1987, Nov.
Bakersfield, Cal.	*George Caravalho	1984, May	Commerce, Cal.	*Robert Hinderliter	1973, Aug.
Baldwin Park, Cal.	*Ralph Webb	1981, Apr.	Compton, Cal.	*Laventa Montgomery	1983, Apr.
Baltimore, Md.	William Schaefer, D	1987, Nov.	Concord, Cal.	*F.A. Stewart	1960, Apr.
Bangor, Me.	*John W. Flynn	1977, Feb.	Coon Rapids., Minn.	*Richard Thistle	1979, July
Baton Rouge, La.	Pat Screen, D	1988, Nov.	Coral Gables, Fla.	*Donald E. Leburn	1982, Mar.
Battle Creek, Mich.	*Gordon Jaeger	1976, Mar.	Corpus Christi, Tex.	*Edward A. Martin.	1982, Mar.
Bay City, Mich.	*David D. Barnes	1979, May	Corvallis, Ore.	*Gary F. Pokorny	1978, Nov.
Bayonne, N.J.	Dennis P. Collins, D	1986, May	Costa Mesa, Cal.	*Fred Sorsabel	1970, Nov.
Baytown, Tex.	*Fritz Lanham	1972, May	Council Bluffs, Ia.	*Michael G. Miller	1978, Aug.
Beaumont, Tex.	*Karl Nollenberger	1983, June	Covington, Ky.	Tom Behan, N-P	1987, Nov.
Belleville, Ill.	Richard Brauer, N-P.	1985, Apr.	Cranston, R.I.	Edward DiPrete, R	1986, Nov.
Bellevue, Wash.	*Andrea Beatty	1980, May	Crystal, Minn.	*John Irving	1963, Jan.
Bellflower, Cal.	John Ansdell, D	1986, Apr.	Culver City, Cal.	*Dale Jones	1969, Aug.
Beloit, Wis.	*H. Herbert Holt	1971, Mar.	Cuyahoga Falls, Oh.	Robert Quirk, D	1985, Nov.
Berkeley, Cal.	*Daniel Boggan Jr.	1982, Jan.	Dallas, Tex.	*Charles S. Anderson	1981, Oct.
Berwyn, Ill.	Joseph Lanzillotti, D	1985, Apr.	Daly City, Cal.	*David R. Rowe	1969, July
Bessemer, Ala.	Ed Porter, D	1986, July	Danbury, Conn.	James Dyer, D.	1985, Nov.
Bethlehem, Pa.	Paul M. Marcincin, D	1985, Nov.	Danville, Va.	*Charles Church	1981, June
Beverly Hills, Cal.	*Edward Kreins	1979, Oct.	Davenport, Ia.	Charles Peart, R.	1985, Nov.
Billings, Mont.	*Al Thelen	1979, Nov.	Dayton, Oh.	*Richard Helwig, act.	1984, June
Biloxi, Miss.	Gerald Blessey, D	1985, May	Daytona Bch., Fla.	*Howard D. Tipton	1978, Oct.
Binghamton, N.Y.	Juanita M. Crabb, D	1985, Nov.	Dearborn, Mich.	John O'Reilly, N-P.	1985, Nov.
Birmingham, Ala.	Richard Arrington Jr., D.	1987, Oct.	Dearborn Hts., Mich.	Wesley Tennant, D	1985, Nov.
Bismarck, N.D.	Bus Leary, D	1986, Apr.	Decatur, Ill.	*Leslie T. Allen	1972, Sept.
Bloomfield, Minn.	*John Pidgeon	1967, Dec.	Denton, Tex.	*G. C. Hartung.	1977, Sept.
Bloomfield, N.J.	John W. Kinder, R	1985, Nov.	Denver, Col.	Federico Pena, D	1987, May
Bloomington, Ill.	Richard Buchanan, R	1985, Apr.	Des Moines, Ia.	*Richard Wilkey	1984, Mar.
Bloomington, Ind.	Tomilea Allison, D	1987, Nov.	Des Plaines, Ill.	John Seitz, R.	1985, Apr.
Bloomington, Minn.	*John Pidgeon	1967, Sept.	Detroit, Mich.	Coleman A. Young, N-P	1987, Nov.
Boca Raton, Fla.	*James Rutherford	1984, Apr.	Dotham, Ala.	Kenneth Everett, N-P	1985, July
Boise, Ida.	Dick Eardley, N-P	1985, Nov.	Dover, Del.	Crawford J. Carroll, N-P	1986, Apr.
Bossier City, La.	Don E. Jones, D	1985, Mar.	Downers Grove, Ill.	*James R. Griesemer.	1972, Sept.
Boston, Mass.	Raymond L. Flynn, D	1987 Nov.	Downey, Cal.	Robert Ovrom	1983, May
Boulder, Col.	*James W. Piper	1984, May	Dubuque, Ia.	*W. Kenneth Gearhart	1979, Aug.
Bowie, Md.	*G. Charles Moore	1976, Aug.	Duluth, Minn.	John Fedo, N-P	1987, Nov.
Bowling Green, Ky.	*Charles W. Coates.	1977, Feb.	Durham, N.C.	*Orville Powell	1983, Mar.
Bridgeport, Conn.	Leonard Paoletta, R	1985, Nov.	E. Chicago, Ind.	Robert A. Pastrick, D	1987, Nov.
Bristol, Conn.	John Leone, D.	1985, Nov.	E. Cleveland, Oh.	*Frank Wise	1979, Jan.
Brockton, Mass.	Carl Pitaro, D	1985, Nov.	E. Hartford, Conn.	George Dagon, D	1985, Nov.
Brooklyn Center, Minn.	*Gerald G. Splinter	1977, Oct.	E. Lansing, Mich.	*Jerry Coffman	1977, Jan.
			E. Orange, N.J.	Thomas H. Cooke Jr., D	1985, Nov.

City	Name	Term
E. Providence, R.I.	*Earl Sandquist	1979, Sept.
Eau Claire, Wis.	*Eric Anderson	1984, Jan.
Edina, Minn.	*Kenneth Rosland	1977, Nov.
Edison, N.J.	Anthony Yelencsics, D	1985, Nov.
El Cajon, Cal.	*Robert Acker	1982, July
El Monte, Cal.	*Don McMillen, R	1986, Apr.
El Paso, Tex.	Johnathan W. Rogers, N-P	1985, Apr.
Elgin, Ill.	*Robert Malm	1984, May
Elizabeth, N.J.	Thomas G. Dunn, D	1988, Nov.
Elkhart, Ind.	James Perron, D	1987, Nov.
Elmhurst, Ill.	Abner Ganet, N-P	1985, Apr.
Elmira, N.Y.	*Joseph E. Sartori	1972, June
Elyria, Oh.	Michael Keys, D	1987, Nov.
Enfield, Conn.	*Robert J. MacReady	1983, Feb.
Enid, Okla.	*Lyle Smith	1979, Feb.
Erie, Pa.	Louis J. Tullio, D	1985, Nov.
Escondido, Cal.	*Vernon Hazen	1982, July
Euclid, Oh.	Anthony Giunta, D	1987, Nov.
Eugene, Ore.	*Michael Gleason	1981, Jan.
Evanston, Ill.	*Joel Asprooth	1981, Mar.
Evansville, Ind.	Michael Vandeveer, D	1987, Nov.
Everett, Mass.	Edward Connolly, D	1985, Nov.
Everett, Wash.	William Moore, N-P	1985, Nov.
Fairborn, Oh.	*William Burns	1977, Feb.
Fairfield, Cal.	*B. Gale Wilson	1956, Mar.
Fair Lawn, N.J.	*Joseph Garger	1979, Oct.
Fall River, Mass.	*Alan Silva	1981, Apr.
Fargo, N.D.	Jon Lindgren, D	1986, Apr.
Farmington Hills, Mich.	*Lawrence Savage	1979, Feb.
Fayetteville, Ark.	*Donald Grimes	1972, Apr.
Fayetteville, N.C.	*John P. Smith	1981, Jan.
Fitchburg, Mass.	Bernard Chartrand, D	1985, Nov.
Flagstaff, Ariz.	*Frank Abeyta	1981, Jan.
Flint, Mich.	James Sharp Jr., N-P	1987, Nov.
Florissant, Mo.	James J. Eagan, N-P	1987, Apr.
Fond du Lac, Wis.	*Daniel Thompson	1983, Dec.
Ft. Collins, Col.	*John Arnold	1977, Oct.
Ft. Lauderdale, Fla.	*Constance Hoffmann	1980, Oct.
Ft. Lee, N.J.	Nicholas Corbiscello, R	1987, Nov.
Ft. Smith, Ark.	*William Faught	1981, July
Ft. Wayne, Ind.	Win Moses, D	1987, Nov.
Ft. Worth, Tex.	*Robert Herchert	1978, Aug.
Fountain Valley, Cal.	*Judy Kelsey	1984, May
Fremont, Cal.	*Charles Kent McClain	1981, May
Fresno, Cal.	*Robert Christofferson	1983, Nov.
Fullerton, Cal.	*William C. Winter	1979, Oct.
Gadsden, Ala.	Steve Means, D	1986, July
Gainesville, Fla.	*W.D. Higginbotham Jr.	1984, Sept.
Galesburg, Ill.	*Lawrence Asaro	1979, Sept.
Galveston, Tex.	*Stephen Huffman	1980, Apr.
Gardena, Cal.	Mardi Reagan	1983, Feb.
Garden Grove, Cal.	*Dolbert L. Powers	1900, July
Garfield Hts., Oh.	Thomas Longo, D	1985, Nov.
Garland, Tex.	*Fred Greene	1979, July
Gary, Ind.	Richard G. Hatcher, D	1987, Nov.
Gastonia, N.C.	*Gary Hicks	1973, Dec.
Glendale, Ariz.	*John Maltbie	1982, July
Glendale, Cal.	*James M. Rez	1983, Dec.
Grand Forks, N.D.	H.C. Wessman, R	1988, Nov.
Grand Island, Neb.	Bill Wright, N-P	1986, Nov.
Gr. Prairie, Tex.	*Bob Blodgett	1984, Aug.
Gr. Rapids, Mich.	*G. Stevens Bernard	1982, June
Great Falls, Mont.	*G. Allen Johnson	1981, Jan.
Greeley, Col.	*Peter Morrell	1973, Dec.
Green Bay, Wis.	Samuel Halloin, N-P	1987, Apr.
Greensboro, N.C.	*T.Z. Osborne	1973, Feb.
Greenville, Miss.	William Burnley Jr., D	1987, Oct.
Greenville, S.C.	*John Dullea	1971, Oct.
Greenwich, Conn.	Roger Pierson, D, first selectman	1985, Nov.
Groton, Conn.	Catherine Kolnaski, D	1985, May
Gulfport, Miss.	Jack Barnett, R	1985, June
Hackensack, N.J.	*Joseph J. Squillace	1964, Oct.
Hagerstown, Md.	Donald Frush, R	1985, Mar.
Hamilton, Oh.	*William Tallman	1983, Sept.
Hammond, Ind.	Thomas McDermott, R	1987, Nov.
Hampton, Va.	*Thomas Miller	1981, Mar.
Harlingen, Tex.	*G.D. Sotelo	1981, July
Harrisburg, Pa.	Stephen Reed, D	1985, Nov.
Hartford, Conn.	Thirman L. Milner, D	1985, Nov.
Harvey, Ill.	David Johnson, N-P	1987, Apr.
Hattiesburg, Miss.	Bobby L. Chain, D	1985, June
Haverhill, Mass.	William H. Ryan, R	1985, Nov.
Hawthorne, Cal.	*R. Kenneth Jue	1977, Jan.
Hayward, Cal.	*Donald Blubaugh	1979, Nov.
Hialeah, Fla.	Raul Martinez, D	1985, Nov.
High Point, N.C.	*H. Lewis Price	1983, July
Hoboken, N.J.	Steve Cappiello, D	1985, May
Hollywood, Fla.	*James Chandler	1976, Nov.
Holyoke, Mass.	Ernest Proulx, D	1985, Nov.
Honolulu, Ha.	Frank Fasi, R	1988, Nov.
Hot Springs, Ark.	Jim Randall, N-P	1986, Nov.
Houston, Tex.	Kathryn Whitmire, N-P	1985, Nov.
Huntington, W. Va.	*Stephen Williams	1984, July
Huntington Beach, Cal.	*Charles Thompson	1981, Oct.
Huntsville, Ala.	Joe W. Davis, N-P	1988, Oct.
Hutchinson, Kan.	*George Pyle	1967, Sept.
Idaho Falls, Ida.	Thomas Campbell, N-P	1985, Nov.
Independence, Mo.	Barbara Potts, N-P	1986, Apr.
Indianapolis, Ind.	William Hudnut, R	1987, Nov.
Inglewood, Cal.	*Paul Eckles	1975, Nov.
Inkster, Mich.	*Gregory Knowles	1984, June
Iowa City, Ia.	*Neal Berlin	1975, Feb.
Irving, Tex.	*Jack Huffman	1974, Jan.
Irvington, N.J.	Anthony T. Blasi, D	1988, May
Jackson, Mich.	*S.W. McAllister Jr.	1974, Mar.
Jackson, Miss.	Dale Danks, D	1985, May
Jackson, Tenn.	Bob Conger, D	1987, June
Jacksonville, Fla.	Jake Godbold, D	1987, May
Jamestown, N.Y.	Steve Carlson, D	1985, Nov.
Janesville, Wis.	*Philip L. Deaton	1976, Mar.
Jefferson City, Mo.	George Hartsfield, D	1987, Apr.
Jersey City, N.J.	Gerald McCann, N-P	1985, May
Johnson City, Tenn.	*John G. Campbell	1984, June
Johnstown, Pa.	Herbert Pfuhl Jr., R	1985, Nov.
Joliet, Ill.	*Paul A. Flynn	1984, Sept.
Joplin, Mo.	*Stribling Boynton	1983, Sept.
Kalamazoo, Mich.	*Sheryl Sculley	1984, Apr.
Kansas City, Kan.	John Reardon, D	1987, Apr.
Kansas City, Mo.	*A.J. Wilson	1983, Oct.
Kenosha, Wis.	John Bilotti, D	1988, Apr.
Kettering, Oh.	*Robert Walker	1982, Oct.
Key West, Fla.	*Joel L. Koford	1982, Oct.
Killeen, Tex.	*Robert M. Hopkins	1982, Apr.
Knoxville, Tenn.	Kyle C. Testerman, N-P	1987, Nov.
Kokomo, Ind.	Stephen Daily, D	1987, Nov.
LaCrosse, Wis.	Patrick Zielke, N-P	1985, Apr.
La Habra, Cal.	*Lee Risner	1970, Nov.
La Mesa, Cal.	*Ronald Bradley	1980, May
La Mirada, Cal.	*Gary K. Sloan	1981, Apr.
Lafayette, Ind.	James Riehle, D	1987, Nov.
Lafayette, La.	Dud Lastrapes, R	1988, May
Lake Charles, La.	Paul Savoie, D	1985, Apr.
Lakeland, Fla.	*Robert V. Youkey	1960, Jan.
Lakewood, Cal.	*Howard L. Chambers	1976, June
Lakewood, Col.	*Bill Kirchhoff	1980, Nov.
Lakewood, Oh	Anthony Sinagra, R	1987, Nov.
Lancaster, Pa.	Arthur E. Morris, R	1985, Nov.
Lansing, Mich.	Terry John McKane, N-P	1985, Nov.
Largo, Fla.	*D. Russell Barr	1979, Dec.
Las Cruces, N.M.	*Dana Miller	1983, Feb.
Las Vegas, Nev.	William Briare, N-P	1987, June
Lawrence, Kan.	*Buford M. Watson Jr.	1970, Jan.
Lawrence, Mass.	John J. Buckley, D	1985, Nov.
Lawton, Okla.	Wayne Gilley, N-P	1985, Apr.
Lewiston, Me.	*Lucien Gosselin	1980, July
Lexington, Ky.	Scotty Baesler, D	1985, Nov.
Lima, Oh.	Harry Moyer, N-P	1985, Nov.
Lincoln, Neb.	Roland Luedtke, R	1987, Apr.
Linden, N.J.	*George Hudak, D	1986, Nov.
Little Rock, Ark.	*Mahlon Martin	1980, July
Livermore, Cal.	*Leland Horner	1978, Oct.
Lombard, Ill.	*Paul Sharon	1979, Nov.
Long Beach, Cal.	*John Dever	1977, Jan.
Longmont, Col.	*William Swenson, N-P	1983, Nov.
Longview, Tex.	*C. Ray Jackson	1980, Apr.
Lorain, Oh.	Joseph Zahorec, D	1987, Nov.
Los Angeles, Cal.	Thomas Bradley, N-P	1985, June
Louisville, Ky.	Harvey Sloane, D	1985, Nov.
Lowell, Mass.	*B. Joseph Tully	1979, June
L. Merion, Pa.	*Thomas B. Fulweiler	1968, Jan.
Lubbock, Tex.	*Larry Cunningham	1976, Sept.
Lynchburg, Va.	*E. Allen Culverhouse	1979, June
Lynn, Mass.	Antonio J. Marino, D	1985, Nov.
Lynwood, Cal.	*Charles Gomez	1981, Dec.
Macon, Ga.	George Israel, R	1987, Nov.
Madison, Wis.	F.T. Sensenbrenner Jr., D	1985, Apr.
Malden, Mass.	Thomas Fallon, D	1985, Nov.
Manchester, Conn.	Barbara Weinberg, D	1985, Nov.
Manchester, N.H.	Robert Shaw, R	1985, Nov.
Manitowoc, Wis.	Anthony V. Dufek, D	1985, Apr.
Mansfield, Oh.	Edward Meehan, D	1987, Nov.
Marion, Oh.	Ronald Malone, D	1987, Nov.

City	Name	Term
McAllen, Tex.	*Jose Escamilla	1983, Oct.
McKeesport, Pa.	Lou Washowich, D	1987, Nov.
Medford, Mass.	*Carroll P. Sheehan.	1980, Aug.
Melbourne, Fla.	*Samuel Halter	1978, July
Memphis, Tenn.	Richard C. Hackett, N-P	1987, Nov.
Mentor, Oh.	*Edward Podojil	1977, Nov.
Meriden, Conn.	*Terry Sprenkel	1983, Feb.
Meridian, Miss.	*Wallace Heggie	1984, June
Mesa, Ariz.	*C.K. Luster	1979, June
Mesquite, Tex.	*C.K. Duggins	1976, Feb.
Miami, Fla.	*Howard V. Gary	1981, Apr.
Miami Beach, Fla.	*vacant	…
Middletown, Conn.	Sebastian Garafalo, R	1985, Nov.
Middletown, Oh.	*Dale F. Helsel	1970, Oct.
Midland, Tex.	G. Thane Akins, R	1985, Apr.
Midwest City, Okla.	*vacant	…
Milford, Conn.	Alberta Jagoe, D	1985, Nov.
Milwaukee, Wis.	Henry W. Maier, D	1988, Nov.
Minneapolis, Minn.	Donald Fraser, D	1985, Nov.
Minnetonka, Minn.	*James F. Miller	1979, Jan.
Minot, N.D.	Charles Reiten, R	1986, Apr.
Mobile, Ala.	Lambert C. Mims, D	1985, July
Modesto, Cal.	*Garth Lipsky	1974, Jan.
Monroe, La.	Robert Powell, D	1988, Apr.
Montclair, N.J.	*Bertrand Kendall	1980, Sept.
Montebello, Cal.	*Joseph Goeden	1980, May
Monterey Park, Cal.	*Lloyd de Llamas	1976, Sept.
Montgomery, Ala.	Emory Folmar, R	1987, Nov.
Mt. Lebanon, Pa.	*James Cain	1982, Apr.
Mt. Prospect, Ill.	*Terrance Burghard.	1978, Nov.
Mt. Vernon, N.Y.	Thomas E. Sharpe, D	1987, Nov.
Mountain View, Cal.	*Bruce Liedstrand	1976, June
Muncie, Ind.	James Carey, D	1987, Nov.
Muskegon, Mich.	*Robert Hagemann	1983, Sept.
Muskogee, Okla.	*C. Clay Harrell	1979, June
Napa, Cal.	*William Bopf	1977, Dec.
Naperville, Ill.	*George Smith	1978, June
Nashua, N.H.	Maurice Arel, D	1987, Nov.
Nashville, Tenn.	Richard Fulton, D	1987, Aug.
National City, Cal.	*Tom McCabe	1979, Feb.
New Bedford, Mass.	Brian Lawler, N-P	1985, Oct.
New Britain, Conn.	William J. McNamara, D	1985, Nov.
New Brunswick, N.J.	John Lynch, D	1986, Nov.
New Castle, Pa.	Dale W. Yoho, R.	1987, Nov.
New Haven, Conn.	Biagio DiLieto, D	1985, Nov.
New London, Conn.	*C.F. Driscoll.	1969, May
New Orleans, La.	Ernest Morial, D	1986, Feb.
New Rochelle, N.Y.	*C. Samuel Kissinger	1975, Apr.
New York, N.Y.	Edward Koch, D	1985, Nov.
Newark, N.J.	Kenneth Gibson, D	1986, May
Newark, Oh.	William Moore, R	1985, Nov.
Newport, R.I.	*John Connors Jr.	1981, Mar.
Newport Beach, Cal.	*Robert L. Wynn	1971, Aug.
Newport News, Va.	*Robert T. Williams	1981, Feb.
Newton, Mass.	Theodore Mann, R	1985, Nov.
Niagara Falls, N.Y.	*Nicholas Merchelos	1984, June
Norfolk, Va.	*Julian Hirst	1976, Apr.
Norman, Okla.	*James D. Crosby	1976, Feb.
Norristown, Pa.	John Marberger, R	1985, Nov.
North Charleston, S.C.	John Bourne Jr., R	1986, May
North Chicago, Ill.	Bobby E. Thompson, D	1985, Apr.
North Las Vegas.	*Michael Dyal	1982, May
No. Little Rock, Ark.	Reed Thompson, N-P	1988, May
Norwalk, Cal.	*Ray Gibbs.	1984, Feb.
Norwalk, Conn.	William Collins, D	1985, Nov.
Norwich, Conn.	*Charles Whitty	1973, Feb.
Novato, Cal.	*Phillip J. Brown	1974, May
Oak Lawn, Ill.	*Richard E. O'Neill	1976, May
Oak Park, Ill.	*Ralph De Santis	1980, Apr.
Oak Ridge, Tenn.	*M. Lyle Lacy 3d	1978, July
Oakland, Cal.	*Henry L. Gardner	1981, June
Oceanside, Cal.	*Suzanne Foucault	1983, Jan.
Odessa, Tex.	*John Harrison	1982, Aug.
Ogden, Ut.	Robert A. Madsen, R	1985, Nov.
Oklahoma City, Okla.	*Scott Johnson	1982, Nov.
Omaha, Neb.	Michael Boyle, N-P	1985, May
Ontario, Cal.	R.E. Ellingwood, N-P	1986, Apr.
Orange, Cal.	*J. William Little	1984, Jan.
Orange, N.J.	Paul Monacelli, D	1988, July
Orlando, Fla.	Bill Frederick, D	1988, Sept.
Oshkosh, Wis.	*W. O. Frueh.	1976, Aug.
Overland Park, Kan.	*Donald Pipes	1977, June
Owensboro, Ky.	*Max Rhoads	1983, July
Oxnard, Cal.	*James Frandsen	1984, Aug.
Pacifica, Cal.	*David Finigan	1981, May
Palm Springs, Cal.	*Norman R. King	1979, Dec.
Palo Alto, Cal.	*William Zaner.	1979, Sept.
Park Ridge, Ill.	*George E. Hagman	1984, July
Parkersburg, W. Va.	Pat S. Pappas, R	1985, Nov.
Pasadena, Cal.	*Donald F. McIntyre.	1973, June
Pasadena, Tex.	Johnny Isbell, N-P	1985, Apr.
Passaic, N.J.	Robert Hare, N-P	1985, May
Paterson, N.J.	Frank X. Graves Jr., D	1986, May
Pawtucket, R.I.	Henry Kinch, D	1985, Nov.
Peabody, Mass.	Peter Torigian, D	1985, Nov.
Pekin, Ill.	Willard Birkmeier, D	1987, Apr.
Pensacola, Fla.	*Steve Garman	1978, May
Peoria, Ill.	*James B. Daken	1979, Jan.
Perth Amboy, N.J.	George J. Otlowski, D	1988, May
Petersburg, Va.	*vacant	…
Philadelphia, Pa.	W. Wilson Goode, D.	1987, Nov.
Phoenix, Ariz.	*Marvin Andrews	1976, Oct.
Pico Rivera, Cal.	*Robert L. Williams	1981, Aug.
Pittsburgh, Pa.	Richard S. Caliguiri, D	1985, Nov.
Pittsfield, Mass.	Charles Smith, N-P	1985, Nov.
Plainfield, N.J.	Everett C. Lattimore, D	1985, Nov.
Plano, Tex.	*David Griffin	1971, Sept.
Pocatello, Ida.	*Charles W. Moss.	1970, Sept.
Pomona, Cal.	*Ora E. Lampman.	1978, July
Pompano Beach, Fla.	*James Soderlund	1984, Feb.
Pontiac, Mich.	Wallace Holland, N-P	1985, Nov.
Port Huron, Mich.	*Gerald R. Bouchard	1965, June
Portage, Mich.	*Donald Ziemke	1974, Aug.
Portland, Me.	David Brenerman, D	1985, May
Portland, Ore.	Bud Clark, N-P	1988, Nov.
Portsmouth, Oh.	*Barry Feldman	1977, Jan.
Portsmouth, Va.	*George Hanbury	1982, June
Poughkeepsie, N.Y.	*William J. Theysohn	1982, Mar.
Providence, R.I.	Joseph Paolino Jr., D	1986, Nov.
Provo, Ut.	Jim Ferguson, D	1985, Nov.
Pueblo, Col.	*John Bramble.	1984, Apr.
Quincy, Ill.	C. David Neussen, R	1985, Apr.
Quincy, Mass.	Francis X. McCauley, R	1985, Nov.
Racine, Wis.	Stephen Olson, N-P	1985, Apr.
Raleigh, N.C.	*Dempsey Benton.	1983, Dec.
Rapid City, S.D.	Arthur La Croix, R	1985, Apr.
Reading, Pa.	Karen Miller, D.	1987, Nov.
Redding, Cal.	*Robert E. Courtney	1982, Nov.
Redlands, Cal.	*John E. Holmes	1983, Apr.
Redondo Beach, Cal.	*Timothy Casey	1981, Nov.
Redwood City, Cal.	*James M. Fales Jr.	1971, Aug.
Reno, Nev.	*Chris Cherches.	1980, Nov.
Revere, Mass.	George V. Colella, D	1985, Nov.
Richfield, Minn.	*John Cartwright	1983, Oct.
Richmond, Cal.	*James M. Fales Jr.	1983, May
Richmond, Ind.	Frank Waltermann, D	1987, Apr.
Richmond, Va.	*Manuel Deese	1979, Jan.
Riverside, Cal.	*Douglas Weiford	1980, Mar.
Roanoke, Va.	Noel Taylor, R	1988, May
Rochester, Minn.	*Steven Kvenvold	1979, June
Rochester, N.Y.	*Peter Korn	1980, Mar.
Rock Hill, S.C.	*Joe Lanford	1979, July
Rockford, Ill.	John McNamara, D	1985, Apr.
Rockville, Md.	John Freeland, N-P	1985, Nov.
Rome, N.Y.	Carl Eilenberg, R	1987, Nov.
Rosemead, Cal.	*Frank Tripepi	1974, Oct.
Roseville, Mich.	*Thomas Van Damme	1983, Dec.
Roseville, Minn.	*James Andre	1974, May
Roswell, N.M.	*James Whitford Jr.	1982, Aug.
Royal Oak, Mich.	*William Baldridge.	1975, Sept.
Sacramento, Cal.	*Walter Slipe.	1976, Mar.
Saginaw, Mich.	*Thomas Dalton.	1978, Nov.
St. Clair Shores, Mich.	*Roy Stype.	1982, May
St. Cloud, Minn.	Robert Huston, N-P	1989, Nov.
St. Joseph, Mo.	*Hal Kooistra	1983, Sept.
St. Louis, Mo.	Vincent Schoemehl, D	1985, Apr.
St. Louis Park, Minn.	*James Brimeyer	1980, Aug.
St. Paul, Minn.	George Latimer, D	1985, Nov.
St. Petersburg, Fla.	*Alan Harvey	1980, Mar.
Salem, Mass.	Anthony V. Salvo, D.	1985, Nov.
Salem, Ore.	*Russ Abolt	1983, Jan.
Salina, Kan.	*Rufus L. Nye	1979, May
Salinas, Cal.	*William Carlson.	1984, Apr.
Salt Lake City, Ut.	Ted Wilson, N-P	1987, Nov.
San Angelo, Tex.	*Stephen Brown.	1982, Jan.
San Antonio, Tex.	*Louis J. Fox.	1982, Jan.
San Bernardino, Cal.	W. R. Holcomb, N-P.	1985, Mar.
San Bruno, Cal.	*Gerald Minford	1971, Dec.
San Diego, Cal.	*Ray Blair Jr.	1978, May
San Francisco, Cal.	Dianne Feinstein, D	1987, Nov.
San Jose, Cal.	*Gerald Newfarmer.	1983, July
San Leandro, Cal.	*Lee Riordan.	1976, Jan.
San Mateo, Cal.	*Richard Delong.	1976, Sept.
San Rafael, Cal.	*Hobert Beyer.	1980, Nov.
Sandusky, Oh.	*Frank Link.	1972, Jan.
Sandy, Ut.	Lawrence P. Smith, R.	1985, Nov.

City	Name	Term
Santa Ana, Cal.	*A. J. Wilson	1980, July
Santa Barbara, Cal.	*Richard Thomas	1977, Jan.
Santa Clara, Cal.	*Donald Von Raesfeld	1962, Feb.
Santa Cruz, Cal.	*Richard Wilson	1981, June
Santa Fe, N.M.	Louis Montano, D	1986, Mar.
Santa Maria, Cal.	*Robert Grogan	1963, Jan.
Santa Monica, Cal.	*John Alschuler	1981, Nov.
Santa Rosa, Cal.	*Kenneth Blackman	1970, July
Sarasota, Fla.	*Kenneth Thompson	1950, Feb.
Savannah, Ga.	*Arthur A. Mendonsa	1962, July
Schenectady, N.Y.	Karen Johnson, D	1987, Nov.
Scottsdale, Ariz.	*Roy Pederson	1980, Mar.
Scranton, Pa.	James McNulty, D	1985, Nov.
Seattle, Wash.	Charles Royer, D	1985, Nov.
Shaker Heights, Oh.	Stephen Alfred, N-P	1987, Nov.
Sheboygan, Wis.	Richard Suscha, N-P	1985, Apr.
Shreveport, La.	John Hussey, D	1986, Nov.
Simi Valley, Cal.	*Lin Koester	1979, June
Sioux City, Ia.	*J.R. Castner	1982, Sept.
Sioux Falls, S.D.	Joe Cooper, R	1989, Apr.
Skokie, Ill.	*Robert Eppley	1979, Jan.
Somerville, Mass.	Eugene Brune, D	1985, Nov.
South Bend, Ind.	Roger Parent, D	1987, Nov.
South Gate, Cal.	Herbert Cranton, N-P	1986, Apr.
Southfield, Mich.	*Del Borgsdorf	1980, June
Sparks, Nev.	*Patricia Thompson	1983, Sept.
Spartanburg, S.C.	*Wayne Bowers	1984, Sept.
Spokane, Wash.	*Terry Novak	1978, July
Springfield, Ill.	J. Michael Houston, R	1987, Apr.
Springfield, Mass	Richard Neal	1985, Nov.
Springfield, Mo.	*Don G. Busch	1971, Oct.
Springfield, Oh.	*Thomas Bay	1978, Sept.
Springfield, Ore.	*Steven Burkett	1980, Feb.
Stamford, Conn.	Thom Seriana, D	1985, Nov.
Sterling Hts., Mich.	*Barry Feldman	1982, Nov.
Stillwater, Okla.	*Carl Weinaug	1983, Apr.
Stockton, Cal.	*S.E. Griffith, act.	1984, Sept.
Stratford, Conn.	*Ronald Owens	1984, July
Suffolk, Va.	*John Rowe Jr.	1981, Mar.
Sunnyvale, Cal.	*Thomas Lewcock	1980, Apr.
Syracuse, N.Y.	Lee Alexander, D	1985, Nov.
Tacoma, Wash.	*Erling O. Mork	1975, June
Tallahassee, Fla.	*Daniel A. Kleman	1974, Aug.
Tampa, Fla.	Bob Martinez, N-P	1987, Mar.
Taunton, Mass.	Richard Johnson, D	1985, Nov.
Taylor, Mich.	Cameron Priebe, D	1985, Nov.
Teaneck, N.J.	*Werner H. Schmid	1959, Mar.
Tempe, Ariz.	Harry E. Mitchell, D	1986, May
Temple, Tex.	*Barney Knight	1978, Dec.
Terre Haute, Ind.	P. Pete Chalos, D	1985, Nov.
Thornton, Col.	*John Harrington	1984, July
Thousand Oaks, Cal.	*Grant Brimhall	1978, Jan.
Titusville, Fla.	*Norman Hickey	1974, June
Toledo, Oh.	*David A. Boston	1981, Sept.
Topeka, Kan.	Douglas Wright, N-P	1985, Apr.
Torrance, Cal.	*Leroy J. Jackson	1983, Jan.
Trenton, N.J.	Arthur Holland, N-P	1986, May
Troy, Mich.	*Frank Gerstenecker	1970, Feb.
Troy, N.Y.	*John P. Buckley	1972, June
Tucson, Ariz.	*Joel Valdez	1974, May
Tulsa, Okla.	Terry Young	1986, Apr.
Tuscaloosa, Ala.	Alvin DuPont, N-P	1985, July
Tyler, Tex.	*Gary Gwyn	1982, May
Union City, N.J.	William Musto, D	1986, May
Univ. City, Mo.	*Frank Ollendorff	1980, Mar.
Upland, Cal.	*S. Lee Travers	1974, June
Upper Arlington, Oh.	*H. W. Hyrne	1968, May
Urbana, Ill.	Jeffrey Markland, R	1985, Apr.
Utica, N.Y.	Louis La Polla, R	1985, Nov.
Vallejo, Cal.	*Ted McDonell	1979, Jan.
Vancouver, Wash.	*Paul Grattet	1980, Aug.
Victoria, Tex.	*James J. Miller	1980, June
Vineland, N.J.	James E. Romano, R	1988, May
Virginia Beach, Va.	*Thomas Muelhenbeck	1982, June
Waco, Tex.	*David F. Smith Jr.	1971, Sept.
Walnut Creek, Cal.	*Thomas Dunne	1972, May
Waltham, Mass.	Arthur J. Clark, N-P	1985, Nov.
Warren, Mich.	James Randlett, N-P	1985, Nov.
Warren, Oh.	Daniel Sferra, D	1987, Nov.
Wash., D.C.	Marion Barry, D	1987, Nov.
Waterbury, Conn.	Edward Bergin, D	1985, Nov.

City	Name	Term
Waterloo, Ia.	Delman L. Bowers, R	1985, Nov.
Waukegan, Ill.	Bill Morris, D	1985, Apr.
Waukesha, Wis.	Paul Keenan, N-P	1986, Apr.
Wausau, Wis.	John Kannenberg, N-P	1988, Apr.
W. Covina, Cal.	*Herman Fast	1976, Aug.
W. Hartford, Conn.	*William Brady	1977, Sept.
W. Haven, Conn.	Lawrence Minichino, R	1985, Nov.
W New York, N.J.	Anthony DeFino, D	1987, May
W. Orange, N.J.	Samuel Spina, D	1986, May
W. Palm Beach, Fla.	*Richard Simmons	1969, Nov.
Westland, Mich.	Charles Pickering Jr., N-P	1985, Nov.
Westminster, Cal.	*Chris Christiansen	1983, June
Westminster, Col.	*Bill Christopher	1978, June
Wheaton, Ill.	*Donald Rose	1980, Nov.
Wheeling, W. Va.	*F. Wayne Barte	1979, Nov.
White Plains, N.Y.	Alfred Del Vecchio, R	1985, Nov.
Whittier, Cal.	*Tom Mauk	1980, Sept.
Wichita, Kan.	*E. H. Denton	1976, July
Wichita Falls, Tex.	*James Berzina	1983, June
Wilkes-Barre, Pa.	Thomas McLaughlin, D	1987, Nov.
Williamsport, Pa.	Stephen Lucasi, R	1987, Nov.
Wilmington, Del.	Daniel Frawley, D	1986, Nov.
Wilmington, N.C.	*William B. Farris	1983, May
Winston-Salem, N.C.	*Bryce A. Stuart	1980, Jan.
Woonsocket, R.I.	Gaston Ayotte Jr., D	1985, Nov.
Worcester, Mass.	*Francis J. McGrath	1951, Apr.
Wyandotte, Mich.	James Wagner, N-P	1985, Apr.
Wyoming, Mich.	*James Sheeran	1976, Nov.
Yakima, Wash.	*Richard Zais Jr.	1979, Jan.
Yonkers, N.Y.	*Rodney H. Irwin	1984, Feb.
York, Pa.	William Althaus, R	1985, Nov.
Youngstown, Oh.	George Vukovich, D	1985, Nov.
Yuma, Ariz.	Philip Clark, R	1985, Oct.
Zanesville, Oh.	Donald Lewis Mason, R	1987, Nov.

Canadian Cities

(as of Oct. 22, 1984)

City	Name	Term
Calgary, Alta.	Ralph Klein	1986, Oct.
Charlottetown, P.E.I.	Frank Moran	1985, Nov.
Edmonton, Alta.	Laurence Decore	1986, Oct.
Fredericton, N.B.	Elbridge Wilkins	1986, May
Guelph, Ont.	Norman Jary	1985, Nov.
Halifax, N.S.	Ronald Wallace	1985, Oct.
Hamilton, Ont.	Robert Morrow	1985, Nov.
Hull, Que.	Michel Legere	1985, Nov.
Kingston, Ont.	John Gerretsen	1985, Nov.
Kitchener, Ont.	Domenic P. D. Cardillo	1985, Nov.
London, Ont.	Al Gleeson	1985, Nov.
Mississauga, Ont.	Hazel McCallion	1985, Nov.
Moncton, N.B.	J. S. Rideout	1986, May
Montreal, Que.	Jean Drapeau	1985, Nov.
North York, Ont.	Mel Lastman	1985, Nov.
Oshawa, Ont.	Allan Pilkey	1985, Nov.
Ottawa, Ont.	Mrs. Marion Dewar	1985, Nov.
Peterborough, Ont.	Robert J. Barker	1985, Nov.
Quebec, Que.	Jean Pelletier	1985, Nov.
Regina, Sask.	Larry Schneider	1985, Oct.
Saint John, N.B.	Elsie Wayne	1986, May
St. John's, Nfld.	John Murphy	1985, Nov.
Saskatoon, Sask.	Clifford Wright	1985, Oct.
Sherbrooke, Que.	Jacques O'Bready	1985, Nov.
Sudbury, Ont.	Peter Wong	1985, Nov.
Toronto, Ont.	Art Eggleton	1985, Nov.
Vancouver, B.C.	Michael Harcourt	1984, Nov.
Victoria, B.C.	Peter Pollen	1985, Nov.
Waterloo, Ont.	Mrs. Marjorie Carroll	1985, Nov.
Windsor, Ont.	Mrs. Elizabeth Kishkon	1985, Nov.
Winnipeg, Man.	Bill Norrie	1986, Nov.

CONSUMER SURVIVAL KIT
Your Federal Income Tax: Facts on Filing

Who Must File

Generally, every individual under 65 years of age who resided in the United States and had a gross income of $3,300 or more during the year must file a federal income tax return. Generally, anyone 65 or older on the last day of the tax year is not required to file a return unless he or she had gross income of $4,300 or more during the year. A married couple, living together at the end of the year, both 65 or older, filing a joint return, need not file unless their gross income is $7,400 or more.

A taxpayer with gross income of less than $3,300 (or less than $4,300 if 65 or older) should file a return to claim the refund of any taxes withheld, even if he or she is listed as a dependent by another taxpayer.

If you are married, you must file a tax return if your combined gross income was $5,400 or more, provided you are eligible to file a joint return and are living together at the close of the tax year. The requirement is $6,400 if one spouse is 65 or older, and $7,400 if both of you are 65 or older. If you are married and your spouse files a separate return, or you did not share the same household at the end of the year, you must file a tax return if your gross income was $1,000 or more.

If you are a qualifying widow or widower with a dependent child, you must file a return if your gross income was $4,400 or more ($5,400 or more if you are 65 or older).

Forms to Use

A taxpayer may, at his or her election, use form 1040, form 1040A or form 1040EZ. However, those taxpayers who choose to itemize deductions must use the longer form 1040 and the 1040EZ can be used only by qualifying single taxpayers.

New Tax Changes for 1984 and After

The Tax Reform Act of 1984, signed by President Reagan on July 18, 1984, is a massive piece of legislation. Some of the changes incorporated in the Act that are most likely to affect millions of taxpayers include:

- **Net Interest Exclusion.** Beginning in 1985 individuals would have been able to exclude 15% of interest income, to the extent it exceeded certain interest deductions, up to a maximum of $450.00 per year ($900.00 for married couples filing a joint return). This interest exclusion has been repealed.

- **Earned Income Credit.** Beginning in 1985, the earned income credit is increased from 10% to 11%, thus increasing the maximum credit from $500 to $550. Further, the income range over which the credit is phased out will increase to $6,500 to $11,000 (from the present range of $6,000 to $10,000).

- **Communication Services.** The 3% excise tax imposed for local telephone service, toll telephone service and teletypewriter exchange service, which had been scheduled to expire after 1985, is extended through calendar year 1987.

- **Distilled Spirits.** The excise tax on distilled spirits is $10.50 per proof gallon. Beginning rate of tax October 1, 1985, has been increased to $12.50 per proof gallon.

- **Alimony.** Alimony is generally deductible by the payor and includible in the income of the payee. Beginning in 1985, only cash payments pursuant to a divorce or separation agreement that will terminate upon the death of the payee made between former spouses not living in the same household will qualify as alimony.

Deductions

Generally, a taxpayer may either itemize deductions choose the zero bracket amount. For single taxpayers t zero bracket amount is $2,300. For married taxpayers fil a joint return it is $3,400. For married taxpayers filing sep rate returns the deduction is $1,700 each. Some taxpaye are required to itemize deductions.

Dates for Filing Returns

For individuals using the calendar year, Apr. 15 is the nal date (unless it falls on a Saturday, Sunday, or a leg holiday) for filing income tax returns and paying any ta due, and for paying the first quarterly installment of the est mated tax. Other installments of estimated tax are to be pai by June 15, Sept. 15, and Jan. 15.

Instead of paying the 4th installment by Jan. 15, a fin income tax return, with payment of any tax due, may b filed by Jan. 31. Farmers may file a final return by Mar. with payment of any tax due, to satisfy estimated tax r quirements.

Joint Return

A husband and wife may file a joint return, even if or has no income.

One provision stipulates that if one spouse dies, the surv vor may compute his or her tax using joint return rates fc the first two taxable years following the year of death, pro vided the survivor was also entitled to file a joint retur with the decedent for the year of the death, and he or sh furnishes over half the cost of maintaining in his or he household a home for a dependent child or stepchild. If th taxpayer remarries before the end of the taxable year, thes privileges are lost but he or she is permitted to file a joir return with his or her new spouse.

Estimated Tax

Generally, if total tax exceeds withheld tax by at lea $400 in 1984 ($500 in 1985 and thereafter), estimated ta installments are required from (1) single individuals, head of a household or surviving spouses, or a married person en titled to file a joint return whose spouse does not receiv wages, who expects a gross income over $20,000; (2) marrie individuals with over $10,000 where both spouses receiv wages; (3) married individuals with over $5,000 not entitle to file a joint return; and (4) individuals whose gross incom can reasonably be expected to include more than $500 fro sources other than income subject to withholding.

Exemptions

Personal exemption is $1,000.

Every individual has an exemption of $1,000, to be d ducted from gross income. A husband and a wife are eac entitled to a $1,000 exemption. A taxpayer or spouse who 65 or over on the last day of the year gets another exem tion of $1,000. A husband or wife who is blind on the la day of the year gets another exemption of $1,000.

Exemption for dependents, over one-half of whose tot support comes from the taxpayer and for whom the oth dependency tests have been met, is $1,000. This applies to child, stepchild, or adopted child as well as certain other re atives with less than $1,000 gross income; also to a chil stepchild, or adopted child of the taxpayer who is under at the end of the year or was a full-time student during months of the year even if the child makes $1,000 or mo A dependent can be a non-relative if a member of the tax payer's household and living there all year.

Taxpayer gets the exemption for his child who is a stude regardless of the student's age or earnings, provided the ta payer provides over half of the student's total support. If t student gets a scholarship, this is not counted as support.

Child and Disabled Dependent Care

To qualify, a taxpayer must be employed or looking for work, and provide over one-half the cost of maintaining a household for a dependent child under 15, a dependent of any age who is mentally or physically unable to care for himself or herself; or a spouse unable to care for himself or herself.

Taxpayers may be allowed a credit based on a percentage of employment related expenses. The credit may be up to $720 if there is one qualifying dependent or spouse, and up to $1,440 for two or more. Employment related expenses are expenses that allowed the taxpayer to work (or look for work) and that are paid for household services or for the care of the qualifying dependent or spouse.

For further information consult your local IRS office or the instructional material attached to your return form.

Dividends

The first $100 in dividends can be excluded from income. A husband and wife may exclude up to $200 on their joint return. It does not matter which spouse receives the dividend income. An individual is also entitled to exclude up to $750 ($1,500 on a joint return) for certain dividends received from qualifying domestic public utilities.

The $100 ($200) dividend exclusion does not apply to dividends from tax-exempt corporations, mutual savings banks, building and loan associations, and several others.

Dividends paid in stock or in stock rights are generally exempt from tax, except: (1) when the stockholder has an option to take stock or property, or (2) when the stock distribution is disproportionate, or (3) when the distribution is in convertible preferred stock and has the same result as (2), or (4) when the distribution gives preferred stock to some common stock shareholders and common stock to other common shareholders, or (5) when the distribution is on preferred stock, except for an increase in the conversion ratio of convertible preferred stock solely to take into account a stock dividend or stock split on the stock into which the convertible preferred stock may be converted.

Deductible Medical Expenses

Expenses for medical care, not compensated for by insurance or other payment for taxpayer, spouse, and dependents, in excess of 5% of adjusted gross income are deductible. There is no limit to the maximum amount of medical expenses that can be deducted.

Medical care includes diagnosis, treatment and prevention of disease or for the purpose of affecting any structure or function of the body, and amounts paid for insurance to reimburse for hospitalization, surgical fees and other medical expenses.

Beginning in 1984 subject to certain limits, you may be able to deduct lodging expenses (but not meals) that are not provided in a hospital or similar institution, if the lodging is primarily to enable you to receive medical care.

Medical expenses for a decedent paid by his estate within one year after his death may be treated as expenses of the decedent taxpayer.

Medical and hospital benefits provided by the employer may be exempt from individual income tax.

Deductions for Contributions

Deductions up to 50% of taxpayers' adjusted gross income may be taken for contribution to most publicly supported charitable organizations, including churches or associations of churches, tax-exempt educational institutions, tax-exempt hospitals, and medical research organizations associated with a hospital. The deduction is limited to 20% or gifts of long-term capital gain appreciated property to private nonoperating foundations, and 30% for contributions to such organizations as veterans organizations, fraternal societies, and non-profit cemetery companies.

Taxpayers also are permitted to carry over for five years certain contributions, generally to publicly supported organizations, which exceed the 50% allowable deduction the year the contribution was made.

Also permissible is the deduction as a charitable contribution of unreimbursed amounts up to $50 a school month spent to maintain an elementary or high school student, other than a dependent or relative, in taxpayer's home. There must be a written agreement between you and a qualified organization.

Deductions for Interest Paid

Interest paid by the taxpayer is deductible.

To deduct interest on a debt, you must be legally liable for that debt. No deduction will be allowed for payments you make for another person if you were not legally liable to make them.

Prizes and Awards

All prizes and awards must be reported in gross income, except when received without action by the recipient and recipient is not expected to perform any future services. To be exempt, awards must be received primarily in recognition of religious, charitable, scientific, educational, artistic, literary, or civic achievement. Examples of prizes that do not have to be included in income are Nobel and Pulitzer prizes.

Deductions for Employees

An employee may use the zero bracket amount and deduct as well the following if in connection with his employment: transportation, including automobile expenses, such as gas, oil, and depreciation; however, meals and lodging are deductible as traveling expense only if the employee is away from home overnight. Commuting expenses to and from work are not deductible.

An outside salesman—a salesman who works fulltime outside the office, using the latter only for incidentals—may use the zero bracket amount and deduct all his business expenses.

Don't Forget These Changes from Prior Years

The following tax code provisions that affected prior year returns are still in effect:

• **Sale of a Home.** Two provisions, both of which apply to the sale of a principal residence only, may shield some of the gains made on the sale from taxes.

1. For those 55 or older, the tax exclusion on profit on selling a home is $125,000 on all sales made after July 20, 1981.

2. The period during which payment of income tax on the profit from selling a home can be delayed if the profit is reinvested in another principal residence in 2 years.

• **Capital Gains Tax Reduced.** The tax rate on long-term capital gains (profits from the sale of an asset such as stocks or real estate held for more than a year) decreases from a maximum of 28 percent to no more than 20 percent on sales and exchanges that took place after June 9, 1981.

• **Windfall Profit Tax Credit.** Up through 1984 royalty holders are exempt from windfall profits tax liability on up to two barrels of crude oil production per day. Beginning in 1985 and thereafter, the exemption is increased to three barrels.

• **Tougher Penalties.** In addition to the normal penalties for late filing and late payment, recent tax law changes provide new penalties for substantial understatement of tax liability and for "frivolous" tax returns. If you face the possibility of paying your taxes late, closely examine the new rules for interest rates—the IRS can charge the full prime lending rate (the rate banks often charge their best customers) on taxes paid late. Interest is now compounded daily.

An employee who is reimbursed and is required to account to his employer for his business expenses will not be required to report either the reimbursement or the expenses on his tax return. Any allowance to the employee in excess of his expenses must be included in gross income. If he claims a deduction for an excess of expenses over reimbursement he will have to report the reimbursement and claim actual expenses.

An employee who is not required to account to his employer must report on his return the total amounts of reimbursements and expenses for travel, transportation, entertainment, etc., that he incurs under a reimbursement arrangement with his employer.

The expense of moving to a new place of employment may be deducted under certain circumstances regardless of whether the taxpayer is a new or continuing employee, or whether he pays his own expenses or is reimbursed by his employer. Reimbursement must be reported as income.

Tax Credit for the Elderly and the Permanently and Totally Disabled

Subject to certain rules or exclusions, taxpayers 65 or older may claim a credit which varies according to filing status. Taxpayers should read IRS instructions carefully for full details. You may also be eligible for this credit if you are under age 65, you retired on permanent and total disability, and you received taxable disability benefits.

The credit is limited to 15% of $5,000 for single taxpayers; 15% of $5,000 for married taxpayers filing a joint return when only one taxpayer is either 65 or older or under 65 and retired on permanent and total disability; 15% of $7,500 for married taxpayers filing a joint return if both are 65 or older, or one is 65 or older and the other is under 65 and retired on permanent and total disability, or both are under 65 and both are retired on permanent and total disability; and 15% of $3,750 for a married taxpayer filing a separate return. If you are under 65 and retired on permanent and total disability and your taxable disability income is less than these amounts, the credit is limited to 15% of your taxable disability income.

Net Capital Losses

An individual taxpayer may deduct capital losses up to $3,000 against his ordinary income. However, it takes $2 of net long-term capital loss to get $1 of offset against other income. He may carry the rest over to subsequent years at the same rate, no legal limit on the number of years.

Income Averaging

Individuals with a large increase in taxable income in a particular year may be able to take advantage of income averaging provisions. Generally, a taxpayer is eligible to income average if his or her taxable income in a given year exceeds 140% if his or her average income for the prior 3 years, if the excess is more than $3,000.

Individual Income Tax Returns for 1982

(money amounts are in thousands of dollars)

Size of adjusted gross income	Number of returns	Adjusted gross income less deficit	Total income tax			
			Number of returns	Percent of all returns	Amount	Average (dollars)
All returns, total	95,297,502	1,847,801,109	76,704,684	80.5	278,473,358	3,630
No adjusted gross income. . . .	822,704	− 23,553,456	20,726	2.5	342,002	16,501
$1 under $1,000	2,570,474	1,403,760	4,811	.2	3,089	642
$1,000 under $2,000	3,849,025	5,783,608	238,753	6.2	13,200	55
$2,000 under $3,000	3,804,230	9,277,659	137,882	3.6	32,995	239
$3,000 under $4,000	3,450,462	11,899,350	1,682,176	48.8	122,845	73
$4,000 under $5,000	3,559,628	15,838,548	2,358,616	66.3	354,832	150
$5,000 under $6,000	3,528,420	19,169,415	2,436,633	69.1	647,720	266
$6,000 under $7,000	3,149,038	20,181,699	2,078,369	66.0	815,219	392
$7,000 under $8,000	3,426,978	25,329,243	2,438,223	71.2	1,133,763	465
$8,000 under $9,000	3,777,790	31,658,006	3,209,319	85.0	1,842,311	574
$9,000 under $10,000	3,204,184	30,076,025	2,904,779	90.7	2,001,128	689
$10,000 under $11,000	3,236,887	33,947,872	3,068,718	94.8	2,464,842	803
$11,000 under $12,000	2,849,178	32,778,161	2,736,544	96.1	2,613,154	955
$12,000 under $13,000	2,776,049	34,701,704	2,665,868	96.0	3,058,051	1,147
$13,000 under $14,000	2,732,764	36,873,238	2,663,127	97.5	3,331,575	1,251
$14,000 under $15,000	2,647,804	38,356,511	2,603,549	98.3	3,666,002	1,408
$15,000 under $16,000	2,491,767	38,662,125	2,458,869	98.7	3,911,522	1,591
$16,000 under $17,000	2,234,620	36,813,496	2,199,501	98.4	3,863,760	1,757
$17,000 under $18,000	2,014,453	35,243,476	1,977,949	98.2	4,005,987	2,025
$18,000 under $19,000	1,933,220	35,771,454	1,902,672	98.4	3,959,119	2,081
$19,000 under $20,000	1,828,372	35,599,846	1,803,693	98.7	3,963,453	2,197
$20,000 under $25,000	8,766,489	197,077,045	8,666,330	98.9	24,141,676	2,786
$25,000 under $30,000	7,589,962	208,643,698	7,543,932	99.4	27,918,968	3,701
$30,000 under $40,000	9,809,629	338,176,424	9,763,586	99.5	49,678,204	5,088
$40,000 under $50,000	4,691,587	207,926,018	4,666,658	99.5	35,000,016	7,500
$50,000 under $75,000	3,104,158	182,060,231	3,048,573	98.2	36,033,923	11,820
$75,000 under $100,000	699,982	59,533,561	689,112	98.5	14,620,998	21,217
$100,000 under $200,000	574,621	75,632,449	565,307	98.4	22,015,282	38,944
$200,000 under $500,000	142,798	40,702,278	140,612	98.5	14,297,671	101,682
$500,000 under $1,000,000 . . .	22,026	14,685,249	21,711	99.6	5,693,938	262,261
$1,000,000 or more	8,203	17,552,416	8,086	98.6	6,926,111	856,556
Taxable returns, total	76,704,684	1,796,257,429	76,704,684	100.0	278,473,358	3,630
Nontaxable returns, total	18,592,818	51,543,680	—	—	—	—

Selected Income and Taxes by State, 1982

(money amounts are in thousands of dollars)

State	All returns	Adjusted income less deficit	Total income tax		Average total income tax (dollars)	State	All returns	Adjusted income less deficit	Total income tax		Average total income tax (dollars)
			Number of returns	Amount					Number of returns	Amount	
United States, Total	95,297,502	1,847,801,109	76,704,684	278,473,356	3,630	Ariz.	1,169,558	21,771,393	937,751	3,035,649	3,237
Ala.	1,393,231	23,764,869	1,063,446	3,183,780	2,994	Ark.	820,173	12,748,096	612,951	1,681,955	2,744
Alas.	219,899	5,326,141	201,096	1,071,965	5,331	Cal.	10,526,521	217,635,548	8,515,743	31,723,359	3,725
						Col.	1,357,408	27,730,961	1,144,434	4,239,502	3,704

(continued)

State	All returns	Adjusted income less deficit	Number of returns	Amount	Average total income tax (dollars)	State	All returns	Adjusted income less deficit	Number of returns	Amount	Average total income tax (dollars)
Conn.	1,464,919	32,393,702	1,229,024	5,594,842	4,552	N.H.	423,794	7,811,894	343,545	1,149,406	3,346
Del.	260,392	5,345,415	227,503	831,652	3,656	N.J.	3,266,893	70,638,855	2,734,915	11,440,195	4,183
D.C.	314,090	6,128,882	244,301	1,002,700	4,104	N.M.	546,320	9,267,530	411,550	1,289,061	3,132
Fla.	4,459,690	81,117,660	3,560,514	12,573,441	3,531	N.Y.	7,200,449	148,765,176	5,905,442	22,654,418	3,836
Ga.	2,192,677	38,143,859	1,737,195	5,245,523	8,020	N.C.	2,379,318	39,267,324	1,826,973	5,143,002	2,815
Ha.	444,673	8,336,770	351,506	1,140,006	3,243	N.D.	278,843	4,762,230	201,715	695,714	3,449
Ida.	361,102	6,087,612	279,764	801,465	2,865	Oh.	4,344,591	83,073,330	3,595,001	12,531,924	3,486
Ill.	4,760,305	98,948,775	3,911,553	16,141,950	4,127	Okla.	1,282,967	24,835,788	1,008,906	3,921,171	3,887
Ind.	2,165,944	40,524,399	1,700,693	6,173,586	3,630	Ore.	1,063,417	19,317,864	794,157	2,635,056	3,318
Ia.	1,164,625	21,416,865	904,195	3,083,199	3,410	Pa.	4,857,511	92,066,956	3,983,912	13,948,352	3,501
Kan.	995,986	19,355,178	801,241	3,000,217	3,744	R.I.	408,590	7,135,572	333,504	998,182	2,993
Ky.	1,310,291	22,606,035	1,026,412	3,136,184	3,055	S.C.	1,202,461	19,842,782	959,342	2,552,777	2,661
La.	1,632,253	31,585,571	1,288,020	5,146,608	3,996	S.D.	277,590	4,172,994	191,677	547,835	2,858
Me.	465,136	7,354,078	364,934	944,166	2,587	Tenn.	1,752,884	29,495,823	1,311,700	4,140,518	3,157
Md.	1,878,838	40,112,861	1,619,553	6,119,056	3,778	Tex.	6,251,060	128,964,322	5,033,277	21,948,479	4,361
Mass.	2,580,841	49,805,315	2,133,221	7,620,759	3,572	Ut.	555,240	10,284,951	422,314	1,253,253	2,968
Mich.	3,531,786	72,124,666	2,829,607	10,712,706	3,786	Vt.	214,449	3,472,220	172,484	461,487	2,676
Minn.	1,720,058	32,370,873	1,346,017	4,581,143	3,403	Va.	2,271,779	45,142,440	1,861,676	6,743,029	3,622
Miss.	861,949	13,530,671	633,483	1,810,671	2,858	Wash.	1,781,654	36,620,807	1,489,424	5,797,208	3,892
Mo.	1,981,263	36,404,060	1,581,657	5,452,220	3,447	W.Va.	665,179	11,750,054	512,845	1,715,533	3,345
Mont.	335,324	5,559,488	252,391	754,629	2,990	Wis.	1,943,052	36,336,802	1,512,647	5,044,039	3,335
Neb.	663,159	11,508,131	517,892	1,624,734	3,137	Wyo.	213,210	4,551,215	174,290	755,615	4,335
Nev.	404,007	7,817,591	337,249	1,243,774	8,688						

State Individual Income Taxes: Rates, Exemptions

Source. Tax Foundation, Inc. Data as of Sept. 1, 1984
Footnotes at end of table.

State	Taxable income	Percentage rates	Taxable income	Percentage rates	Personal exemp. Single	Married family head	Credit per depend.
Alabama[1]	First $1,000	2	Over $6,000	5	$1,500	$3,000	$300
	1,001-6,000	4					
Arizona[1][2][4]	First 1,000	2	3,001-4,000	5	1,729	3,518	1,056
	1,001-2,000	3	4,001-5,000	6			
	2,001-3,000	4	5,001-6,000	7	Over 6,000	8	
Arkansas[3]	First 2,999	1	9,000-14,999	4.5	17.50	35	6
	3,000-5,999	2.5	15,000-24,999	6	(tax credit)		
	6,000-8,999	3.5	25,000 and over	7			
California[1][2][4][6]	First 3,120	1	12,500-14,850	6	(tax credit)		
	3,120-5,450	2	14,850-17,170	7	38	76	12
	5,450-7,790	3	17,170-19,520	8	Heads of households have slightly lower		
	7,790-10,160	4	19,520-21,860	9	tax rates		
	10,100-12,500	5	21,860-24,200	10	Over 24,200	11	
Colorado[1][4][6]	First 1,415	2.5	8,492-9,907	5.5	850	1,700	850
	1,415-2,831	3	9,907-11,322	6			
	2,831-4,246	3.5	11,322-12,738	6.5	Surtax on intangible income over $5,000,		
	4,246-5,661	4	12,738-14,153	7.5	2%. A credit equal to ½ of 1% of net		
	5,661-7,076	4.5	14,153 and over	8	taxable income is allowed for income under		
$9,000.							
	7,076-8,492	5					
Connecticut.	\[colspan\] 7% capital gains tax; tax on dividends earned if federal adjusted gross income is greater than or equal to $50,000; tax ranges from 6% on $50,000 through 13% on $100,000 and over.				100	200	
Delaware[3]	First 1,000	1.4	10,001-15,000	8.2	Exemptions apply only to adjusted gross		
	1,001-2,000	2.0	15,001-20,000	8.4	incomes of more than $20,000 and net		
	2,001-3,000	3.0	20,001-25,000	8.8	capital gains more than $100 (or $200 on		
	3,001-4,000	4.2	25,001-30,000	9.4	joint returns).		
	4,001-5,000	5.2	30,001-40,000	11.0	600	1,200	600
	5,001-6,000	6.2	40,001-50,000	12.2			
	6,001-8,000	7.2	Over 50,000	13.5			
	8,000-10,000	8.0					
Dist. of Col.[1][4]	First 1,000	2	5,001-10,000	7	750	1,500	750
	1,001-2,000	3	10,001-13,000	8			
	2,001-3,000	4	13,001-17,000	9			
	3,001-4,000	5	17,001-25,000	10			
	4,001-5,000	6	Over 25,000	11			
Georgia[3][5]	First 1,000	1	5,000-6,999	4	1,500	3,000	700
	1,001-2,999	2	7,000-10,000	5			
	3,000-4,999	3	Over 10,000	6	For married persons filing separately,		

rates range from 1% on the first $500 to 6% on $5,000 or more. For single persons rates range from 1% on first $750 to 6% on $7,000 or more.

State	Taxable income	Percentage rates	Taxable income	Percentage rates	Personal exemp. Single	Married family head	Credit per depend
Hawaii[1] . . . . . First	$1000	0	$5,001-7,000	6.5	$1,000	$2,000	$1,00
	1,001-2,000	2.25	7,001-11,000	7.5	Special tax rates for heads of households.		
	2,001-3,000	3.25	11,001-21,000	8.5			
	3,001-4,000	4.5	21,001-29,000	9.5	41,001-61,000	10.5	
	4,001-5,000	5	29,001-41,000	10	Over 61,000	11	
Idaho[2][3][4] . . . . . First	1,000	2	3,001-4,000	5.5	Federal exemptions		
	1,001-2,000	4	4,001-5,000	6.5	Each person (husband and wife filing joint*		
	2,001-3,000	4.5	Over 5,000	7.5	are deemed one person) filing return pay additional $10.		
Illinois	Total net income			2.5	1,000	2,000	1,00
Indiana[4]	Adjusted gross	3			1,000	*2,000	50
*Lesser of $1,000 or adjusted gross income of each spouse, but not less than $500.							
Iowa[3][6]. . . . . . . First	1,023	0.5	3,070-4,092	3.5	(tax credit) 20	40	1
	1,024-2,046	1.25	4,093-7,161	5	Net incomes $5,000 or less are not taxable		
	2,047-3,069	2.75	7,162-9,207	6	On up to 13% over $76,725		
Kansas[2][4] . . . . . First	2,000	2	5,001-7,000	5	1,000	2,000	1,00
	2,001-3,000	3.5	7,001-10,000	6.5	20,001-25,000	8.5	
	3,001-5,000	4	10,001-20,000	7.5	Over 25,000	9.0	
Kentucky[3]. . . . . First	3,000	2	4,001-5,000	4	(tax credit)		
	3,001-4,000	3	5,001-8,000	5	20	40	2
			Over 8,000	6			
Louisiana[1][2]. . . .	First 10,000	2	Over 50,000	6	4,500	9,000	1,00
	10,001-50,000	4					
Additional $100 credit for blindness allowed for dependents.							
Maine[1][3] . . . . . . First	2,000	1	8,200-10,200	7	1,000	2,000	1,00
	2,001-4,100	2	10,200-15,300	8			
	4,101-6,100	3	15,300-25,000	9.2			
	6,100-8,200	6	Over 25,000	10			
Maryland[1][3][4]. . . First	1,000	2	2,001-3,000	4	800	1,600	8C
	1,001-2,000	3	Over 3,000	5			
	An additional exemption of $800 is allowed for each dependent 65 or over.						
Massachusetts	Earned and business income:	5*			2,200	4,400	70
	Interest, divs., capital gains on intangibles:	10*	The exemptions shown are those allowed against business income, including salaries and wages. A specific exemption of $2,200 is allowed for each taxpay er. In addition, a dependency exemption of $800 is allowed for a depende spouse who has income from all sources of less than $2,200. In the case of a				
joint return, the exemption is the smaller of (1) $4,400 or (2) $2,200 plus the income of the spouse having the smaller income. *Plus 7.5% surtax.							
Michigan[4]	All taxable income	6.1 (1984)			1,500	3,000	1,5C
Minnesota[1][3][4][6] . First	672	1.6	6,716-9,401	10.2	67	134	
	672-1,344	2.2	9,401-12,086	11.5			
	1,344-2,687	3.5	12,086-16,785	12.8			
	2,687-4,030	5.8	16,785-26,855	14			
	4,030-5,373	7.3	26,855-36,925	15	An additional tax credit of $67 is allowe		
	5,373-6,716	8.8	Over 36,925	16	for each unmarried taxpayer aged 65 older.		
Mississippi[3] . . . . First	5,000	3	Next 5,000	4	6,000	9,500	1,5(
			Over 10,000	5			
Missouri[4] . . . . . First	1,000	1.5	5,001- 6,000	4	1,200	2,400	4(
	1,001-2,000	2	6,001- 7,000	4.5			
	2,001-3,000	2.5	7,001- 8,000	5	An additional $800 exemption is allow		
	3,001-4,000	3	8,001-9,000	5.5	unmarried head of household.		
	4,001-5,000	3.5	Over 9,000	6			
Montana[3] . . . . . First	1,200	2	9,601-12,000	7	960	1,920	9(
effective	1,200-2,400	3	12,001-16,800	8			
12/82-1/84	2,401-4,800	4	16,801-24,000	9	Additional surtax of 10% on tax liabil.		
	4,801-7,200	5	24,001-42,000	10			
	7,201-9,600	6	Over 42,000	11			

Nebraska[3][4]   Federal exemptions
The tax is imposed as a % of the taxpayer's Fed. income tax liability (not including surtax) before credits, with limited adjustmen
The rate is 18%.

State	Taxable income	Percentage rates	Taxable income	Percentage rates	Single	Married family head	Credit per depend.
ew Hampshire	Interest and dividends (except interest on savings accounts).	5	4% commuter tax				

New Hampshire: Interest and dividends (except interest on savings accounts). 5   4% commuter tax

$1,200 each income is exempt; additional $1,200 exemptions are allowed to persons who are 65 or older, blind or handicapped and unable to work.

---

ew Jersey[3] . . .

Taxable income	Percentage rates
First $20,000	2
Next 30,000	2.5
Over 50,000	3.5

$1,000 $2,000 $1,000
Additional credit of $1,000 allowed for the elderly, and disabled.

ommuter tax from 2% on net income under $1,000 to 14% on income over $23,000. (Will cease after 12/31/90)

---

ew Mexico[2, 3, 4] . . .

Taxable income	Percentage rates	Taxable income	Percentage rates
First 2,000	0.7	12,001-14,000	3.6
2,001-3,000	0.8	14,001-16,000	4.2
3,001-4,000	1.0	16,001-18,000	4.9
4,001-5,000	1.1	18,001-20,000	5.5
5,001-6,000	1.3	20,001-25,000	6.1
6,001-7,000	1.6	25,001-35,000	6.5
7,001-8,000	2.0	35,001-50,000	6.9
8,001-10,000	2.5	50,001-100,000	7.4
10,000-12,000	3.0	Over 100,000	7.8

Federal exemptions

The income classes reported are for individuals. For joint returns and heads of households, a separate rate schedule is provided. A credit is allowed for state and local taxes for gross income of less than $9,000

---

ew York[1, 4] . . .

Taxable income	Percentage rates	Taxable income	Percentage rates
First 1,000	2	13,001-15,000	9
1,001-3,000	3	15,001-17,000	10
3,001-5,000	4	17,001-19,000	11
5,001-7,000	5	19,001-21,000	12
7,001-9,000	6	21,001-23,000	13
9,001-11,000	7	Over 23,000	14
11,001-13,000	8		

800   1,600   800
Income from unincorporated business is taxed at 4½%.
The maximum tax rate on personal service income is 10%.

---

orth Carolina[3,4]

Taxable income	Percentage rates	Taxable income	Percentage rates
First 2,000	3	6,001-10,000	6
2,001-4,000	4	Over 10,000	7
4,001-6,000	5		

1,100   2,200*   800

*An additional exemption of $1,100 is allowed the spouse having the lower income; joint returns are not permitted.

---

orth Dakota[3] .

Taxable income	Percentage rates	Taxable income	Percentage rates
First 3,000	2	25,001-35,000	7
3,001-5,000	3	35,001-50,000	8
5,001-8,000	4	Over 50,000	9
8,000-15,000	5		
15,001-25,000	6		

Federal exemptions

---

hio[4] . . . . . .

Taxable income	Percentage rates	Taxable income	Percentage rates
First 5,000	0.5	20,001-40,000	3
5,001-10,000	1	40,001-80,000	3.5
10,001-15,000	2	80,001-100,000	4
15,001-20,000	2.5	Over 100,000	5

650   1,300   650

xpayers age 65 or older are allowed a $50 credit, or if they have received a lump sum distribution from a pension, retirement or ofit sharing plan during the tax year, they are allowed a credit equal to $50 times the taxpayer's expected remaining life. Credit may exceed tax otherwise due. Credit is also allowed for an amount paid during the school year for elementary and secondary ucation or instruction or training of dependents who do not have a high school diploma.

---

lahoma[1,4] . .

Taxable income	Percentage rates	Taxable income	Percentage rates
First 2,000	0.5	10,001-12,500	4
2,001-5,000	1	12,501-15,000	5
5,001-7,500	2	Over 15,000	6
7,501-10,000	3		

1,000   2,000   1,000
Rates for single persons, married couples filing separately, and estates and trusts range from .5% on the first $1,000 to 6% over $7,500.

n-resident aliens are taxed at a flat rate of 8% of Oklahoma taxable income.

---

egon[3,4] . . . .

Taxable income	Percentage rates	Taxable income	Percentage rates
First 500	4.2	3,001-4,000	8.7
501-1,000	5.3	4,001-5,000	9.8
1,001-2,000	6.5	Over 5,000	10.8
2,001-3,000	7.6		

1,000   2,000   1,000
A credit is provided in an amount and equal to 25% of the federal retirement income tax credit to the extent that such a credit is based on Oregon taxable income.

---

nnsylvania .   2.35% of specified classes of taxable income

---

ode Island .   24.9% of modified federal income tax liability

Federal Exemptions

---

uth Carolina[1]

Taxable income	Percentage rates	Taxable income	Percentage rates
First 2,000	2	6,001-8,000	5
2,001-4,000	3	8,001-10,000	6
4,001-6,000	4	Over 10,000	7

800   1,600   800

---

nnessee | Interest and dividends | 6 | Dividends from corporations, 75% of whose property is taxable in Tenn., are taxed at 4%.

---

ah[1] . . . . . .

Taxable income	Percentage rates	Taxable income	Percentage rates
First 1,500	2.25	4,501-6,000	5.75
1,501-3,000	3.75	6,001-7,500	6.75
3,001-4,500	4.75	Over 7,500	7.75

Federal Exemptions
Married taxpayers filing separately, single taxpayers, estates and trusts, pay rates ranging from 2.75% on first $750 of taxable income to 7.75% on taxable income over $3,750.

---

rmont[4] . . . .   Federal exemptions.
tax is imposed at a rate of 26% of the fed. income tax liability of the taxpayer for the taxable year after certain credits (retirement me, investment, foreign tax, child and dependent care, and tax-free covenant bonds) but before any surtax on fed. liability, uced by a % equal to the % of the taxpayer's adjusted gross income for the taxable year which is not Vermont income.

State		Taxable Income	Percentage rates	Taxable income	Percentage rates	Personal exemp.		
						Single	Married family head	Cre depe
Virginia[3]	First	$3,000	2	$5,001-12,000	5	$600	$1,200	$6
		3,001-5,000	3	Over 12,000	5.75			
West Virginia[1,3]	First	2,000	2.1	18,001-20,000	7.4	800	1,600	6
		2,001-4,000	2.3	20,001-22,000	8.2	For joint returns and a return of a surviv		
		4,001-6,000	2.8	22,001-26,000	9.2	spouse, a separate rate schedule is p		
		6,001-8,000	3.2	26,001-32,000	10.5	vided.		
		8,001-10,000	3.5	32,001-38,000	11.6			
		10,001-12,000	4	38,001-44,000	12.6			
		12,001-14,000	5.3	44,001-60,000	12.9			
		14,001-16,000	5.9	Over 60,000	13.0			
		16,001-18,000	6.8					
Wisconsin[1,4]	First	3,900	3.74	15,500-19,400	9.57	(Tax Credit)		
		3,900-7,700	5.72	19,400-25,800	10.01	20	40	
		7,700-11,700	7.70	25,800-51,600	10.45			
		11,700-15,500	9.02	Over $51,600	11.00			

(1) A standard deduction and optional tax table are provided. In Louisiana, standard deduction is incorporated in tax bles. (2) Community property state in which, in general, one-half of the community income is taxable to each spouse. (3) standard deduction is allowed. (4) A limited general tax credit for taxpayers filing joint returns and a credit for home i provements is allowed in Ohio; a limited tax credit is allowed for sales taxes in Colorado, Massachusetts, Nebraska, and V mont; for property taxes and city income taxes in Michigan; for personal property taxes in Maryland and Wisconsin; property taxes in D.C. if household income is less than $10,000, and in N.Y. if household income is less than $12,000; for stallation of solar energy devices in Arizona, California, Kansas, New Mexico, North Carolina, and Oregon; for prope taxes paid on pollution control property in Colorado; for installation of insulation in residences in Idaho; and for making existing building accessible to the handicapped in Kansas. (5) Tax credits are allowed: $15 for single person or married p son filing separately if AGI is $3,000 or less. (For each dollar by which the federal AGI exceeds $3,000 the credit is redu by $1 until no credit is allowed if federal AGI is $3,015 or more.) $30 for heads of households or married persons fil jointly with $6,000 or less AGI. (For each dollar by which federal AGI exceeds $6,000, credit is reduced by $1 until no cre is allowed if federal AGI is $6,030 or more.) (6) Tax bracket adjusted for inflation.

State Estate Tax Rates and Exemptions

Source: Compiled by Tax Foundation from Commerce Clearing House data

As of August 1984. *See index for state inheritance tax rates and exemptions.*

State (a)	Rates (on net estate after exemptions) (b)	Maximum rate applies above	Exemptic
Alabama	Maximum federal credit (c, d)	$10,040,000	$60,000
Alaska	Maximum federal credit (c, d)	10,040,000	60,000
Arizona	Maximum federal credit (c, d)	10,000,000	60,000 (e)
Arkansas	Maximum federal credit (c, d)	10,040,000	60,000 (e)
California	Maximum federal credit (c, d)	10,040,000	60,000
Colorado	Maximum federal credit (c, d)	10,040,000	60,000
Florida	Maximum federal credit (c, d)	10,040,000	60,000
Georgia	Maximum federal credit (c, d)	10,040,000	60,000
Illinois	Maximum Federal credit (c, d)	10,040,000	60,000
Massachusetts	5% on first $50,000 to 16%	4,000,000	30,000 (e,
Minnesota	7% on first $25,000 to 12%	10,000,000	225,000 (e)
Mississippi	1% on first $60,000 to 16% (g)	10,000,000	175,625 (e)
Missouri	Maximum federal credit (c, d)	10,040,000	60,000
New Mexico	Maximum federal credit (c, d)	10,040,000	60,000
New York	2% on first $50,000 to 21% (g, h)	10,100,000	(e,i,j)
North Dakota	Maximum federal credit (c, d)	10,040,000	60,000 (e)
Ohio	2% on first $40,000 to 7% (g)	500,000	10,000 (e,
Oklahoma	.5% on first $10,000 to 15% (g)	10,000,000	60,000 (e,
Rhode Island	2% on first $25,000 to 9% (c, g)	1,000,000	25,000 (e,
South Carolina	6% on first $40,000 to 8% (g)	100,000	120,000 (e,
Texas	Maximum federal credit (c, d)	10,040,000	60,000
Utah	Maximum federal credit (c, d)	10,040,000	60,000 (e)
Vermont	Maximum federal credit (c, d)	10,040,000	60,000 (e)
Virginia	Maximum federal credit (c, d)	10,040,000	60,000 (e)
Washington	Maximum federal credit (c, d)	10,040,000	60,000
Wyoming	Maximum federal credit (c, d)	10,040,000	60,000

(a) Excludes states shown in table on page 97 which levy an estate tax, in addition to their inheritance taxes, to assure full absorptic the federal credit. (b) The rates generally are in addition to graduated absolute amounts. (c) Maximum federal credit allowed unde 1954 code for state estate taxes paid is expressed as a percentage of the taxable estate (after $60,000 exemption) in excess of $40,000, p graduated absolute amount. In Rhode Island on net estates above $250,000. (d) A tax on nonresident estates is imposed on the propor ate share of the net estate which the property located in the state bears to the entire estate wherever situated. (e) Transfers to relig charitable, educational, and municipal corporations generally are fully exempt. Limited in Mississippi to those located in United Stat its possessions. (f) Applies to net estates above $60,000. Otherwise, exemption is equal to Massachusetts net estate. (g) An additional e tax is imposed to assure full absorption of the federal credit. In New York, this applies only to residents. In Rhode Island on net es above $250,000. (h) On net estate before exemption. Marital deduction is one-half of adjusted gross estate or $250,000, whichev greater. Orphans under age 21 receive deduction. (i) Insurance receives special treatment. (j) The specific exemptions are $20,000 of th estate transferred to spouse and $5,000 to lineal ancestors and descendants and certain other named relatives. The credit is variable, ra from the full amount of tax if estate tax is $2,750 or less to $500 if estate tax is $5,000 or more. (k) Property is exempt to the extent t ferred to surviving spouse, not exceeding $60,000; for a child under 18, $14,000; and for each child 18 years of age and older, $6,000. (l) estate valued at $100 or less is exempt. (m) Exemption is a total aggregate of $175,000 for father, mother, child, and named relative Marital deduction is $175,000 in Rhode Island. In South Carolina, marital deduction is one-half of adjusted gross estate up to $250,00

State Retail Sales Taxes: Types and Rates

January 1, 1984

State	Tangible personal property	Admissions	Selected service			Rates on other services and nonretail business
			Rest. meals	Transient lodging	Public utilities	
Alabama[2]	4%[3]	4%	4%	4%	...	Gross rcpts of amus't operators, 4%, agric., mining and mfg. mach., 1.5%
Arizona[2]	5	4	4	3	4	Timbering, 1.5%; storage, apt., office rental, 3%.
Arkansas[2]	4	3	3	3	3	Printing, photographic services; rcpts. from coin-operated dev.; repair services incl. auto and elect., 3%.
California[2]	4.75[5]	...	4.75	...	[14]	Renting, leasing, producing, fabricating, processing, pringting, 4.75%
Colorado[2]	3.5	...	3	3[10]	3	
Connecticut	7.5	...	7[7]	7[10]	7[13]	Storing for use or consumption of personal property items, 7%.
D. of C.	6	5	6	6	5	Duplicating, mailing, addressing and public stenographic services, 5%; sales of food for off-premise consumption, nonprescription medicines, 2%.
Florida	5	5	5	5	...	Rental income of amus't mach., 5%.
Georgia	3	3	3	3 / 3		Levies on amus's dev., 3%.
Hawaii[1]	4	4	4	4	...	Sugar processors, pineapple farmers and selected businesses, 0.5%; insur. solicitors, 2% contractors, sales rep., professions, radio stations, 4%.
Idaho[6]	4	4	4	4	...	Closed circuit TV boxing, wrestling, 5%.
Illinois[2]	5	...	4	...	...	Property sold in connection with a sale of service, 4%, remodeling repairing and reconditioning of tangible personal property, 4%.
Indiana	5	...	5	5	5	
Iowa	4	4	4	4	4	Laundry, dry cleaning, automobile and cold storage, photography, printing, repairs, barber and beauty parlor services, advt., dry cleaning equip. rentals and gross rcpts. from amus't dev., 4%.
Kansas[2]	3	3	3	3	3	Gross rcpts. from operation of coin-operated devices; commer. amus't, 3%.
Kentucky[2]	5	5	5	5	5	Storage, sewer services, photog. and photo fin., 5%; ticket sales to boxing or wrestling on closed circuit TV, 5% of gross rcpts; tax also applies to pay'ts for right to broadcast matches
Louisana[2]	4	3	3	3	...	Food and prescpt'n. drugs, exempt.
Maine	5	...	5	5	5	Proceeds from closed circuit TV, 5%.
Maryland[2]	5[3]	[11]	5[7]	5	5	Farm equip., 2%; mfg. equip., including that used in generation of electricity or in R.&S. sold to mfrs., 2%; watercraft, 3%
Mass.	5	...	[7]	5.7[9]	...	
Michigan	4	...	4	4	4	
Minnesota[2]	6[3]	6	6	6	6	Food, medicines and clothing are exempt; coin-operated vending mach., 3% of gross sales.
Mississippi[1]	6[3]	...	5	5	5	Wholesaling, 0.125% (0.5% on sales of meat for human consumption; 5% on beer, alc. bevs., soft drinks and motor fuel); extracting or mining of minerals, specified miscellaneous bus. incl. bowling, pool halls, warehouses, laundry and dry cleaning, pest control services, specified repair services, 5%; cotton ginning, 15c per bale; sales of materials to railroads for use in track structures, 3%; tractors, indust. fuel and mfg. mach. sales over $500, 1%.
Missouri[2]	4.125	4.125	4.125	4.125	4.125	
Nebraska[2]	4	3.5	3.5	3.5	3.5	
Nevada[2]	5.75[10]	...	5.75	...	...	
New Jersey[1] [2]	6	6[11]	6	6[9]	...	
New Mexico[1] [2]	3.75[3]	3.5	3.5	3.5	3.5	
New York[2]	4	4[11]	4[7]	4[9]	4	Safe deposit rentals, 4%.
North Carolina[2]	3[3]	...	3	3	...	Farm and industrial machinery, 1% ($80 max.); airplanes, boats and locomotives, 2% ($120 max.); sales of horses and mules, 1%.

State	Tangible personal property	Admissions	Rest. meals	Selected service Transient lodging	Public utilities	Rates on other services and nonretail business
North Dakota	4[3]	3	3	3	3	Severance of sand or gravel from the soil, 3%.
Ohio[2]	5	...	5	5	...	
Oklahoma[2]	3[3]	2	2	2	2	Advert. (exclusive of newspapers, periodicals, billboards), printing, auto storage, gross proceeds from amusement dev., 2%.
Pennsylvania[2]	6	...	6[7]	6	6	Cleaning, polishing, lubr. and insp. mot. vehicles, rental income of coin-operated amuse. dev. 6%.
Rhode Island	6	...	6	6	6	
South Carolina	5	...	4	4	4	
South Dakota[1][2]	4	4	4	3	3	Farm mach. and agric. irrigation equip. 2%; gross rcpts. from professions (other than medical), 4%
Tennessee[2]	4.5	...	4.5	4.5	4.5	Vending machines, 1.5% (except tobacco products, 2.5%); industrial, farm equipment and machinery, 1%
Texas[2]	4[3]	...	4	...	4	
Utah[2]	4.625	4	4	4	4	
Vermont	4	4	12	12	4	
Virginia[2]	3[3]	...	3	3	...	
Washington[1][2]	6.5	6.5	6.5	6.5	...	Rentals, auto, parking, other specific services, amusements, recreations, 4.5% (unless subject to county or city adm. taxes, when they remain taxable und. the state business, occupation levy, 1%).
West Virginia[1]	5[3]	5	5	5	...	All services except public util. and personal and professional services, 5%.
Wisconsin[2]	5	5[11]	5	5	5	
Wyoming[2]	3	3	3	3	3	

(1) All but a few states levy sales taxes of the single-stage retail type. Ha. and Miss. levy multiple-stage sales taxes. The N.M. and S.D. taxes have broad bases with respect to taxable services but they are not multiple-stage taxes. Wash. and W.Va. levy gross receipts taxes on all business, distinct from their sales taxes. Alaska also levies a gross receipts tax on businesses. The rates applicable to retailers, with exceptions, under these gross receipts taxes are as follows: Alaska 0.5% on gross receipts of $20,000-$100,000 and 0.25% on gross receipts in excess of $100,000; Wash., 0.44%, plus a 6% surtax; and W.Va. 0.55%. N.J. imposes a tax of 0.05% on retail stores with income in excess of $150,000, and an unincorporated business tax the rate of 0.25% of 1% if gross receipts exceed $5,000.

(2) In addition to the State tax, sales taxes are also levied by certain cities and/or counties.

(3) Motor vehicles are taxed at the general sales tax rates with the following exceptions: Ala., 1.5%; Miss., 3%; and N.J. 2% ($120 maximum). Motor vehicles are exempt from the general sales and use taxes but are taxed under motor vehicle t laws in Md., 4%; Minn., 4%; N.M., 2%; N.D. 4%; Okla., 2%; S.D. and W.Va., 3%; Tex., 4%; Va., 2%; and the D.C., 4%.

(4) Ariz. and Miss. also tax the transportation of oil and gas by pipeline. Ga., Mo., Okla., and Utah do not tax transportation of property. Miss. taxes taxicab transportation at the rate of 2%. Okla. does not tax fares of 15¢ or less on local transportation. Utah does not tax street railway fares.

(5) "Lease" excludes the use of tangible personal property for a period of less than one day for a charge of less than $5 when the privilege of using the property is restricted to use on the premises or at a business location of the grantor.

(6) A limited credit (or refund) in the form of a flat dollar amount per personal exemption is allowed against the person income tax to compensate for (1) sales taxes paid on food in Col., D.C.; and Neb.; and (2) all sales taxes paid in Ida., Mass. and Vt. Low-income taxpayers (adjusted gross income not over $6,000) are allowed a credit against D.C. tax liability rangi from $2 to $6 per personal exemption, depending on taxpayer's income bracket. A refund is allowed if credit exceeds tax l bility.

(7) Restaurant meals below a specified price are exempt: Conn. and Md. less than $1; N.Y. less than $1 (when alcoho beverages are sold, meals are taxable regardless of price); and Pa., 50¢ or less. In Mass., restaurant meals ($1 or more) whi are taxed at 8% under the meals excise tax are exempt.

(8) Conn., exempts clothing for children under 10 years of age. Pa. and Wisc. exempt clothing with certain exceptions.

(9) In Col. and Conn., the first 30 consecutive days of rental or occupancy of rooms is taxable. Over 30 days is exempt. Mass., transient lodging (in excess of $2 a day) is subject to a 5.7% (5% plus 14% surtax) room occupancy excise tax. In N and N.Y., rooms which rent for $2 a day or less are exempt.

(10) Includes a statewide mandatory 1% county sales tax collected by the state and paid to the counties for support of loc school districts.

(11) Md. taxes at 0.5% gross receipts derived from charges for rentals of sporting or recreational equipment, and adm sions, cover charges for tables, services or merchandise at any roof garden or cabaret. In N.J., admissions to a place of amu ment are taxable if the charge is in excess of 75¢. N.Y. taxes admissions when the charge is over 10¢; exempt are participati sports (such as bowling and swimming), motion picture theaters, race tracks, boxing, wrestling, and live dramatic or music performances. In Wis., admissions to motion picture theaters costing 75¢ or less are exempt.

(12) Meals and rooms are exempt from sales tax, but are subject to a special excise tax of 5%.

(13) Gas, water, electricity, telephone and telegraph services provided to consumers through mains, lines or pipes are empt. Gas and electric energy used for domestic heating are exempt. Interstate telephone calls are exempt, as are calls from coin-operated telephones.

(14) Beginning Jan. 1, 1975, a surcharge for efficiency is imposed at the rate of 1/10th mill ($0.0001) per kwh.

State Inheritance Tax Rates and Exemptions

Source: Compiled by Tax Foundation from Commerce Clearing House data.
August 1984

State (a)	Rates (b) (percent)			Max. rate applies above ($1,000)	Exemptions (c) ($1,000)			
	Spouse, child, or parent	Brother or sister	Other than relative		Spouse	Child or parent	Brother or sister	Other than relative
Connecticut (d)	2-8	4-10	8-14	1,000	100	20	6	1
Delaware	1-6	5-10	10-16	200	70	3	1	None
District of Columbia	1-8	5-23	5-23	1,000	5	5	1	1
Idaho	2-15	4-20	8-30	500	All	30(f)	10	10
Indiana	1-10	7-15	10-20	1,500(g)	All	10(f)	0.5	0.1
Iowa	1-8	5-10	10-15	150	180	15	None	None
Kansas	1-5	3-12.5	10-15	500	All	30	5	None
Kentucky	2-10	4-16	6-16	500	50	5	1	0.5
Louisiana	2-3	5-7	5-10	25	5(e)	5	1	0.5
Maine (h)	5-10	8-14	14-18	250(j)	50	25	1	1
Maryland (k)	1	10	10	(h)	.15	.15	0.15	0.15
Michigan	2-10 (m)	2-10 (m)	12-17 (m)	750	65(f)	10	10	None
Montana	2-8	4-16	8-32	100	All	7	1.0	None
Nebraska	1	1	6-18	60	All	10	10	0.5
New Hampshire	(o)	15	15	(h)	(o)	(o)	None	None
New Jersey	2-16	11-16	15-16	3,200	15	15	0.5	0.5
North Carolina	1-12	4-16	8-17	3,000	3.15(p)	(q)	None	None
Oregon	12	12	12	(h)	(r,s)	(r,s)	(r)	None
Pennsylvania	6	15	15	(h)	None	None	None	None
South Dakota (u)	1.5-15	4-20	6-30	100	All	30(f)	0.5	0.1
Tennessee	5.5-9.5	5.5-9.5	6.5-16	440	120(w)	120	120	10
West Virginia	3-13	4-18	10-30	1,000	30	10	None	None
Wisconsin	2.5-12.5	5-25	10-30(u)	500	All	10	1	0.5

(a) In addition to an inheritance tax, all states listed also levy an estate tax, generally to assure full absorption of the federal credit. Exception is S.D.

(b) Rates generally apply to excess above graduated absolute amounts.

(c) Generally, transfers to governments or to solely charitable, educational, scientific, religious, literary, public, and other similar organizations in the U.S. are wholly exempt. Some states grant additional exemptions either for insurance, homestead, joint deposits, support allowance, disinherited minor children, orphaned, incompetent or blind children, and for previously or later taxed transfers. In many states, exemptions are deducted from the first bracket only.

(d) There is a marital deduction equal to the greater of $250,000 or 50% of the value of the gross estate.

(e) Community property state in which, in general, either all community property to the surviving spouse is exempt, or only one-half of the community property is taxable on the death of either spouse.

(f) Exemption for child (in thousands); $20 in Iowa; and $30 in S.D.; $10 in Indiana ($5,000 per parent). Exemption for minor child is (in thousands): $50 in Idaho; $20 in Ky. In Mich. a widow receives $5,000 for every minor child to whom no property is transferred in addition to the normal exemption for a spouse.

(g) Additional credit of $1,200

(h) For persons dying after 6/30/81 but before 7/1/82 tax liability is 85% of calculated tax; 75% between 6/30/82 and 7/1/83; 65% between 6/30/83 and 7/1/84; 55% between 6/30/84 and 7/1/85; 45% between 6/30/85 and 7/1/86. Tax is scheduled to be replaced after 6/30/86.

(i) On estates an additional inheritance tax equal to 30% of the basic tax is imposed.

(j) In Maine the maximum rate for any other relative applies above $150,000.

(k) Where property of a decedent subject to administration in Md. is $7,500 or less, no inheritance taxes are due.

(l) Rate applies to entire share.

(m) No exemption if share exceeds amounts stated.

(n) There is no tax on the share of any beneficiary if the value of the share is less than $100.

(o) Spouse entitled to another $10,000 exemption.

(p) Spouses, minor children, parents, and minor adopted children in the decedent's line of succession are entirely exempt.

(q) Credit.

(r) Credits allowed on pro rata basis according to tax liability on the amount of credit unused by surviving spouse or beneficiaries.

(s) Net taxable estates are allowed an exemption of $100,000 if the decedent died in 1982, $200,000 if death occurs in 1983 or 1984 and $500,000 if death occurs in 1985 or 1986.

(t) Credit is allowed to surviving spouse, child or stepchild under 18 years who is incapable of self support. The credit is $48,000 in 1982, $36,000 in 1983 and 1984 and zero thereafter. Estates of decedents dying after 1/1/87 are not subject to inheritance tax.

(u) Primary rate. If value of share exceeds $15,000 but less than $50,000, the tax liability is 2½ times the primary rate; between $50,000 and $100,000, 4 times the primary rate; over $100,000, 5 times the primary rate.

(v) However, the $2,000 family exemption is specifically allowed as a deduction.

(w) The rates range from 3-6% for a spouse or a child and from 3-12% for parents. Parent exemption is $3,000. Spouses exempt from tax.

Federal Estate and Gift Tax

Source: Tax Foundation, Inc.

Estate Tax

As a result of the Economic Recovery Tax Act of 1981, the lifetime unified credit against combined estate and gift taxes is increased in steps from $47,000 in 1981 to $62,800 in 1982, $79,300 in 1983, $96,300 in 1984, $121,800 in 1985, $155,800 in 1986, and $192,800 in 1987. Thus, cumulative transfers exempt from estate and gift taxes are increased from $175,625 in 1981, to $225,000 in 1982, $275,000 in 1983, $325,000 in 1984, $400,000 in 1985, $500,000 in 1986, and $600,000 in 1987 and thereafter. The act also reduced the maximum estate and gift tax rate over a four-year period from 70 percent in 1981, decreasing to 50 percent in 1985 and thereafter. The schedules for 1983 through 1985 are shown below.

Estate taxes are computed by applying the unified rate schedule, shown below, to the total estate minus allowable deductions, such as funeral expenses, administrative expenses, debts and charitable contributions, plus taxable gifts made after 1976. Gift taxes paid are subtracted from tax due, and credit also may be taken for state death taxes. The amount of the state tax credit is determined by the schedule shown in the table below or the actual state taxes paid, whichever is less. No state tax credit is available to an adjustable taxable estate (i.e., taxable estate minus $60,000) smaller than $40,000. Transfers to a surviving spouse are generally tax exempt.

The law provides for real property passed on to family members for use in a closely held business, such as farming, to be valued in basis of such use, rather than fair market value on basis of highest and best use. In no case may th special valuation reduce the gross estate by more th $600,000 in 1981, $700,000 in 1982, and $750,000 in 19 and thereafter.

Generation-skipping transfers that occur after April 1976, in general are now subject to taxes substantially equi alent to those that would have been imposed had the pro erty been transferred outright to each successive generatio However, an exclusion is provided for transfers to grandch dren up to $250,000 for each child of the decedent wh serves as a conduit for the transfer (not for each grandchild

A return must be filed for the estate of every U.S. citize or resident whose gross estate exceeds $225,000 in 19 ($60,000 for the estate of a nonresident not a citizen). T return is due nine months after death unless an extension granted.

Gift Tax

Any citizen or resident alien whose gifts to any one pe son exceed $3,000 ($10,000 after 1981) within a calend year will be liable for payment of a gift tax, at rates dete mined under the unified estate and gift tax schedule. Gift ta returns are filed on an annual basis and ordinarily are du by April 15 of the following year.

Gifts made by a husband and wife to a third party may l considered as having been made one-half by each, provide both spouses consent to such division.

Unified Rate Schedule for Estate and Gift Tax for 1984

If the amount with respect to which the tentative tax to be computed is:			**The tentative tax is:**		
Not over $10,000			18 percent of such amount.		
Over	$10,000	but not over	$20,000.	$1,800, plus 20%	of the excess over	$10,00
Over	$20,000	but not over	$40,000.	$3,800, plus 22%	of the excess over	$20,00
Over	$40,000	but not over	$60,000.	$8,200, plus 24%	of the excess over	$40,00
Over	$60,000	but not over	$80,000.	$13,000, plus 26%	of the excess over	$60,00
Over	$80,000	but not over	$100,000.	$18,200, plus 28%	of the excess over	$80,00
Over	$100,000	but not over	$150,000.	$23,800, plus 30%	of the excess over	$100,00
Over	$150,000	but not over	$250,000.	$38,800, plus 32%	of the excess over	$150,00
Over	$250,000	but not over	$500,000.	$70,800, plus 34%	of the excess over	$250,00
Over	$500,000	but not over	$750,000.	$155,800, plus 37%	of the excess over	$500,00
Over	$750,000	but not over	$1,000,000.	$248,300, plus 39%	of the excess over	$750,00
Over	$1,000,000	but not over	$1,250,000.	$345,800, plus 41%	of the excess over	$1,000,00
Over	$1,250,000	but not over	$1,500,000.	$448,300, plus 43%	of the excess over	$1,250,00
Over	$1,500,000	but not over	$2,000,000.	$555,800, plus 45%	of the excess over	$1,500,00
Over	$2,000,000	but not over	$2,500,000.	$780,800, plus 49%	of the excess over	$2,000,00
Over	$2,500,000	but not over	$3,000,000.	$1,025,800, plus 53%	of the excess over	$2,500,00
Over	$3,000,000	. . . .		$1,290,800, plus 55%	of the excess over	$3,000,00

Rates remain the same for 1985 and thereafter except for the maximum:

			Over $2,500,000.	$1,025,800, plus 50%	of the excess over	$2,500,00

State Death Tax Credit for Estate Tax

Adjusted taxable estate from	to	Credit = +	%	Of excess over	Adjusted taxable estate from	to	Credit = +	%	Of exce over
$ 0	$ 40,000	0	0	$ 0	2,540,000	3,040,000	146,800	8.8	2,540,0
40,000	90,000	0	.8	40,000	3,040,000	3,540,000	190,800	9.6	3,040,0
90,000	140,000	400	1.6	90,000	3,540,000	4,040,000	238,800	10.4	3,540,0
140,000	240,000	1,200	2.4	140,000	4,040,000	5,040,000	290,800	11.2	4,040,0
240,000	440,000	3,600	3.2	240,000	5,040,000	6,040,000	402,800	12	5,040,0
440,000	640,000	10,000	4	440,000	6,040,000	7,040,000	522,800	12.8	6,040,0
640,000	840,000	18,000	4.8	640,000	7,040,000	8,040,000	650,800	13.6	7,040,0
840,000	1,040,000	27,600	5.6	840,000	8,040,000	9,040,000	786,800	14.4	8,040,0
1,040,000	1,540,000	38,800	6.4	1,040,000	9,040,000	10,040,000	930,800	15.2	9,040,0
1,540,000	2,040,000	70,800	7.2	1,540,000	10,040,000		1,082,800	16	10,040,0
2,040,000	2,540,000	106,800	8	2,040,000					

(1) The unified credit for estates of decedents dying during 1984 is $96,300.

City Income Tax in U.S. Cities over 50,000

Compiled by Tax Foundation from Commerce Clearing House data and other sources.

City	Rates % 1984	Orig.	Year began	City	Rates % 1984	Orig.	Year began
Cities with 500,000 or more inhabitants				Youngstown, Oh.	2.0	0.3	1948
altimore, Md.	(50% of state tax)	1.0	1966	**Cities with 50,000 to 99,999 Inhabitants**			
eveland, Oh.	2.0	0.5	1967	Altoona, Pa.	1.0	1.0	1948
olumbus, Oh.	2.0	0.5	1947	Bethlehem, Pa.	1.0	1.0	1957
etroit, Mich.	2.0	1.0	1965	Chester, Pa.	2.0	1.0	1956
ew York, N.Y.	.9-4.3	0.4-2.0	1966	Covington, Ky.	2.5	1.0	1956
iladelphia, Pa.	4.96	1.5	1939	Euclid, Oh.	2.0	0.5	1967
Cities with 100,000 to 499,999 inhabitants				Gadsden, Ala.	2.0	1.0	1956
kron, Oh.	2.0	1.0	1962	Hamilton, Oh.	1.5	0.8	1960
llentown, Pa.	1.0	1.0	1958	Harrisburg, Pa.	1.0	1.0	1966
rmingham, Ala.	1.0	1.0	1970	Lakewood, Oh.	1.5	1.0	1968
anton, Oh.	2.0	0.6	1954	Lancaster, Pa.	1.0	0.5	1959
incinnati, Oh.	2.0	1.0	1954	Lima, Oh.	1.5	.75	1959
ayton, Oh.	2.25	0.5	1949	Lorain, Oh.	1.0	0.5	1967
rie, Pa.	1.0	1.0	1948	Parma, Oh.	2.0	0.5	1967
int, Mich.	1.0	1.0	1965	Pontiac, Mich.	1.0	1.0	1968
rand Rapids, Mich.	1.0	1.0	1967	Reading, Pa.	1.0	1.0	1969
ansas City, Mo.	1.0	0.5	1964	Saginaw, Mich.	1.0	1.0	1965
ansing, Mich.	1.0	1.0	1968	Scranton, Pa.	2.5	1.0	1948
exington, Ky.	2.0	1.0	1952	Springfield, Oh.	2.0	1.0	1948
ouisville, Ky.'	2.2	0.75	1948	Warren, Oh.	1.5	0.5	1952
ttsburgh, Pa.	2.125	1.0	1954	Wilkes-Barre, Pa.	3.0	1.0	1966
t Louis, Mo	1.0	.25	1948	Wilmington, Del.	1.25	0.5	1970
oledo, Oh.	2.25	1.0	1946	York, Pa.	1.0	1.0	1965

(1) Includes rates for Jefferson County and school board.

Understanding the Economy: A Glossary of Terms

Balance of payments: The difference between all payments made to foreign countries and all payments coming in from abroad over a set period of time. A *favorable* balance exists when more payments are coming in than going out and an *unfavorable* balance exists when the reverse is true. Payments include gold, the cost of merchandise and services, interest and dividend payments, money spent by travelers, and repayment of principal on loans.

Balance of trade (trade gap): The difference between exports and imports, both in actual funds and credit. A nation's balance of trade is *favorable* when exports exceed imports and *unfavorable* when the reverse is true.

Cost of living: The cost of maintaining a particular standard of living measured in terms of purchased goods and services. The rise in the cost of living is the same as the rate of inflation.

Cost-of-living benefits: Benefits that go to those persons whose money receipts increase automatically as prices rise.

Credit crunch (liquidity crisis): The period when cash for lending to business and consumers is in short supply.

Deficit spending: The practice whereby a government goes into debt to finance some of its expenditures.

Depression: A long period of little business activity when prices are low, unemployment is high, and purchasing power decreases sharply.

Devaluation: The official lowering of a nation's currency, decreasing its value in relations to foreign currencies.

Disposable income: Income after taxes which is available to persons for spending and saving.

Federal Reserve System: The entire banking system of the U.S., incorporating 12 Federal Reserve banks (one in each of 12 Federal Reserve districts), and 24 Federal Reserve branch banks, all national banks and state-chartered commercial banks and trust companies that have been admitted to its membership. The system wields a great deal of influence on the nation's monetary and credit policies.

Gross National Product (GNP): The total dollar value of all goods that have been bought for final use and services during a year. The GNP is generally considered to be the most comprehensive measure of a nation's economic activity. The *Real* GNP is the GNP adjusted for inflation.

GNP price deflator: A statistical measure that shows changes, both up and down, in the price level of the GNP over a span of years. It covers a larger segment of the economy than is usually covered by other price indexes.

Inflation: An increase in the average level of prices; double-digit inflation occurs when the percent increase rises above 10.

Key leading indicators: A series of a dozen indicators from different segments of the economy used by the Commerce Department to try to foretell what will happen in the economy in the near fu-ture.

Money supply: The currency held by the public plus checking accounts in commercial banks and savings institutions.

National debt: The debt of the central government as distinguished from the debts of the political subdivisions of the nation and private business and individuals.

National debt ceiling:—Limit set by Congress beyond which the national debt cannot rise. This limit is periodically raised by Congressional vote.

Per capita income: The nation's total income divided by the number of people in the nation.

Prime interest rate: The rate charged by banks on short-term loans to their large commercial customers with the highest credit rating.

Producer price index (formerly the wholesale price index): A statistical measure of the change in the price of wholesale goods. It is reported for 3 different stages of the production chain: crude, intermediate, and finished goods.

Public debt: The total of the nation's debts owed by state, local, and national government. This is considered a good measure of how much of the nation's spending is financed by borrowing rather than taxation.

Recession: A mild decrease in economic activity marked by a decline in real GNP, employment, and trade, usually lasting 6 months to a year, and marked by widespread decline in many sectors of the economy. Not as severe as a depression.

Seasonal adjustment: Statistical changes made to compensate for regular fluctuations in data that are so great they tend to distort the statistics and make comparisons meaningless. For instance, seasonal adjustments are made in mid-winter for a slowdown in housing construction and for the rise in farm income in the fall after the summer crops are harvested.

Stagflation (slumpflation): The combination in the economy in which a high rate of inflation coincides with a high rate of unemployment.

Supply-side economics: The school of economic thinking which stresses the importance of the costs of production as a means of revitalizing the economy. Advocates policies that raise capital and labor output by increasing the incentives to produce.

Wage-price controls: A policy under which the level of wages, salaries and prices are set by law or the administration.

Wage-price spiral: The phenomenon that takes place when workers succeed in obtaining pay raises greater than their increase in productivity. Since the higher wages mean increased cost to the employers, prices tend to increase; the resulting higher prices give workers an incentive to bargain for even higher wages.

Windfall profits tax: A tax on the profits received by oil producers as a result of the decontrol of oil prices and their resulting rise.

How Much Do You Really Make?
Is Your Salary Keeping Up With Inflation?

The Consumer Price Index (CPI) is a measure of the average change in prices over time in a fixed market basket of goods and services. From Jan. 1978, the Bureau of Labor Statistics began publishing CPI's for two population groups: (1) a new CPI for All Urban Consumers (CPI-U) which covers about 80% of the total noninstitutional civilian population; and (2) a revised CPI for Urban Wage Earners and Clerical Workers (CPI-W) which represents about half the population covered by the CPI-U. The CPI-U includes, in addition to wage earners and clerical workers, groups that had been excluded from CPI coverage, such as professional, managerial, and technical workers, the self-employed, retirees and others not in the labor force.

The CPI is based on prices of food, clothing, shelter, and fuels, transportation fares, charges for doctors' and dentists' services, drugs, and the other goods and services bought for day-to-day living. The index measures price changes from a designated reference date—1967—which equals 100.0. An increase of 122%, for example, is shown as 222.0. This change can also be expressed in dollars as follows: The price of a base period "market basket" of goods and services in the CPI has risen from $10 in 1967 to $22.00.

Which Index For You?

Which index should you use to calculate the impact of inflation on your life? If your income is near the poverty level, or if you are retired on a moderate income, you should probably use the new CPI-U. Otherwise, even if you are moderately rich, the CPI-W will probably be the best indicator for you.

The CPI (W and U) emerges each month as single numbers. At the end of the year an average is computed from the monthly figures. (Averaging does away with fluctuations caused by special situations that have nothing to do with inflation.)

For example, the average CPI for 1983 was 298.4. This means that the value of goods and services, which was set at 100% in 1967, cost 198.4% more in 1983.

Changes in prices and how they affect you can be calculated by comparing the CPI of one period against another. The 1983 CPI reading of 298.4 can be compared to the 1982 reading of 289.1 Dividing by 289.1, the excess over 1 is the percentage increase for the year 1981; in this case, 3.2%.

Did your income increase by enough to keep up with this inflation? To make the comparison, dig out your old W-2 or income tax return forms, or find your old paycheck stubs. Both gross and takehome pay comparisons will be of interest to you, but take care to compare equals. Overtime pay should not be counted. Also, watch out for changes in deductions such as those for tax exemptions, credit union payments, payroll bonds, and the like. These have nothing to do with inflation and should be added back to your take home pay.

Measuring Your Paycheck

A. To compare year-to-year earnings in percent form, divide your 1983 earnings by those of 1982 and express the result as a percentage. For example, if you earned the gross wages of the average U.S. worker, your paychecks in 1984 showed about $267.26 per week as compared with $280.76 per week in 1983, an increase of 10.5%. Since prices rose by 3.2% during 1983, the average worker gained 7.3% in real gross income that year. You can do the same kind of calculation on your total 1982 and 1983 earnings by using your total annual income figures in place of weekly earnings figures.

B. Another way to handle the same figures takes a dollar form. For this calculation, assume your wage was $267.26 at the end of 1982. During 1983, prices increased by 3.2. To match that price increase, your wages should have gone up to $275.8 (267.26 times 3.2) by the end of 1983.

While readings on a monthly basis may be misleading, you may want a rough idea of how much you are being affected by inflation right now. For example, if you had weekly earnings of $291.46 in May of 1984, compared to earnings of $289.68 in December, 1983, your income went up 0.006% (The difference, $1.78, divided by 289.68). The CPI-W went from 296.3 to 293.3 during the same period, decrease of 3.0%. This means you more than kept pace with inflation in the first 5 months of 1984. You can make the same calculation for any month by using the latest CPI figures as they are issued by the Department of Labor and published in your local newspaper.

Consumer Price Indexes, 1984

Source: Bureau of Labor Statistics, U.S. Labor Department

(1967=100)	March CPI-U	CPI-W	May CPI-U	CPI-W	July CPI-U	CPI-W
Food, beverages	293.9	294.1	293.1	293.3	294.4	294.
Housing . . . . —	331.2	323.0	334.1	325.0	336.7	327.
Apparel, upkeep	198.6	197.8	198.6	197.3	199.0	197.
Transportation	309.4	311.6	312.7	315.1	311.1	313.
Medical care	373.5	370.2	377.3	372.2	381.1	379.
Entertainment	251.2	247.3	253.0	249.2	255.5	251.
Other goods, services	302.7	301.1	305.0	302.1	309.8	306
Services	356.7	350.1	359.9	353.4	364.0	357
Rent, for home	105.9	244.1	106.9	246.5	108.1	249
Household, less rent . . .	105.8	410.9	107.4	414.9	109.7	420
Transportation	315.1	311.3	317.5	313.7	321.4	317.
Medical care	404.0	401.3	408.1	405.5	412.1	409.
Other services	290.9	287.8	293.7	290.5	297.0	293.
All items less food	307.1	302.8	309.7	305.0	311.2	306
Commodities	279.1	278.6	280.1	279.4	294.4	294
Commodities less food . . .	265.1	264.9	267.2	266.4	266.0	265
Nondurables	285.8	286.7	285.5	286.3	285.7	286
Energy[1]	421.8	422.1	425.4	425.3	421.2	420
All items less energy[1]	299.4	294.2	301.2	295.8	303.2	297

(1) Excludes motor oil, coolant, and other products as of January, 1983.

Average Consumer Price Indexes

Source: Bureau of Labor Statistics, U.S. Labor Department

The Consumer Price Index (CPI-W) measures the average change in prices of goods and services purchased by urban wage earners and clerical workers (1967 = 100). NA = Not available.

	1977 Index	%+	1978 Index	%+	1979 Index	%+	1980 Index	%+	1981 Index	%+	1982 Index	%+	1983 Index	%+
All items	181.5	6.5	195.3	7.6	217.7	11.5	247.0	13.5	273.3	10.2	288.6	6.0	NA	NA
Food, drink	188.0	6.0	206.2	9.7	228.7	10.9	248.7	8.7	267.8	7.7	278.5	4.0	284.7	2.2
Housing	186.5	6.8	202.6	8.6	227.5	12.3	263.2	12.3	293.2	11.4	314.7	7.3	322.0	2.3
Apparel, upkeep	154.2	4.5	159.5	3.4	166.4	4.3	177.4	6.6	186.6	5.2	190.9	2.3	195.6	2.5
Transportation	177.2	7.1	185.8	4.9	212.8	14.5	250.5	17.7	281.3	12.3	293.1	4.2	300.0	2.4
Medical care	202.4	9.6	219.4	8.4	240.1	9.4	267.2	11.3	295.1	10.4	326.9	10.8	355.1	8.6
Entertainment	167.7	4.9	176.2	5.1	187.7	6.5	203.7	8.5	219.0	7.5	232.4	6.1	242.4	4.3
Other	172.2	5.8	183.2	6.4	196.3	7.2	213.6	8.8	233.3	9.2	257.0	10.2	286.3	11.4

Consumer Price Index by Cities

(CPI-W; 1967-100, except Anchorage and Miami)

City[1]	March 1984	April 1984	May 1984	May 1983	Percent change to May 1984 from— March 1984	April 1984
Anchorage, Alas. (10/67 = 100)	265.9	—	265.7	4.3	—.1	—
Atlanta, Ga.	—	009.0	—		—	—
Baltimore, Md.	307.2	—	309.4	4.3	.7	—
Boston, Mass.	298.2	—	300.8	5.2	.9	—
Buffalo, N.Y.	—	286.6	—		—	—
Chicago, Ill-Northwest Ind.	296.0	296.3	296.3	.5	.1	.0
Cincinnati, Ohio-Ky.-Ind.	313.8	—	312.3	.9	—.5	—
Cleveland, Ohio	—	320.7	—		—	—
Dallas-Ft. Worth, Tex.	—	316.5	—		—	—
Denver-Boulder, Col.	341.7	—	340.8	2.7	—.3	—
Detroit, Mich.	302.9	298.6	298.3	—.2	—1.5	—.1
Honolulu-Ha.	—	289.0	—		—	—
Houston, Tex.	—	324.9	—		—	—
Kansas City, Mo.-Kan.	—	299.7	—		—	—
Los Angeles-Long Beach, Anaheim, Cal.	297.9	298.9	303.1	3.8	1.7	1.4
Miami, Fla. (11/77 = 100)	166.3	—	167.2	3.6	.5	—
Milwaukee, Wis.	335.3	—	338.2	7.2	.9	—
Minneapolis-St. Paul, Minn.-Wis.	—	321.1	—		—	—
New York, N.Y.-Northeast N.J.	289.9	291.2	291.6	2.7	.6	.1
Northeast Pa. (Scranton)	294.0	—	295.5	4.5	.5	—
Philadelphia, Pa.-N.J.	298.8	299.0	300.5	4.9	.6	.5
Pittsburgh, Pa.	—	301.5	—		—	—
Portland, Ore.-Wash.	292.2	—	297.5	4.8	1.8	—
St. Louis, Mo.-Ill.	297.3	—	297.3	1.1	.0	—
San Diego, Cal.	326.6	—	328.2	4.3	.5	—
San Francisco, Oakland, Cal.	—	310.8	—		—	—
Seattle-Everett, Wash.	299.9	—	302.7	4.2	.9	—
Washington, D.C.-Md.-Va.	308.2	—	308.9	3.7	.2	—

(1) The area listed includes the entire Standard Metropolitan Statistical Area, except New York and Chicago, which include the Standard Consolidated Area.

Annual Percent Change in Productivity and Related Data, 1972-83

Source: Bureau of Labor Statistics, U.S. Labor Department

Item	1972	1973	1974	1975	1976	1977	1978	1979	1980	1981	1982	1983
Business sector:												
Output per hour of all persons	3.5	2.6	-2.4	2.2	3.3	2.4	0.6	-1.2	-0.5	2.4	-0.1	2.7
Real compensation per hour	3.1	1.6	-1.4	0.5	2.6	1.2	0.9	-1.7	-2.6	-0.6	1.5	1.1
Unit labor cost	2.9	5.3	12.1	7.3	5.1	5.1	8.0	10.7	11.1	7.1	7.9	1.6
Unit nonlabor payments	4.5	5.9	4.4	15.1	4.0	6.4	6.7	5.8	5.5	14.4	0.5	6.3
Implicit price deflator	3.4	5.5	9.5	9.8	4.7	5.6	7.5	9.0	9.2	9.4	5.4	3.0
Nonfarm business sector:												
Output per hour of all persons	3.7	2.4	-2.5	2.0	3.2	2.2	0.6	-1.5	-0.7	1.9	-0.1	3.5
Real compensation per hour	3.3	1.3	-1.4	0.4	2.2	1.0	0.9	-2.0	-2.8	-0.6	1.6	1.6
Unit labor cost	2.8	5.0	12.2	7.5	4.8	5.2	8.0	10.7	11.1	7.7	7.9	1.4
Unit nonlabor payments	3.2	1.3	5.9	16.7	5.7	6.9	5.3	4.8	7.4	13.9	1.4	7.4
Implicit price deflator	3.0	3.8	10.2	10.3	5.1	5.7	7.1	8.8	10.0	9.6	5.8	3.2
Manufacturing:												
Output per hour of all persons	5.0	5.4	-2.4	2.9	4.4	2.5	0.8	0.7	0.2	3.5	1.2	4.3
Real compensation per hour	2.0	0.9	-0.3	2.5	2.1	1.8	0.6	-1.4	-1.6	-0.4	2.2	0.2
Unit labor cost	0.3	1.7	13.3	8.8	3.4	5.7	7.4	9.0	11.5	6.1	7.2	-0.8
Unit nonlabor payments	0.8	-3.3	-1.8	25.9	7.4	6.7	2.5	-2.6	-2.2	12.8	-0.9	16.5
Implicit price deflator	0.5	0.3	9.0	13.1	4.6	6.0	6.0	5.7	7.9	7.7	5.2	3.3

Consumer Price Index by Region and City Size

Source: Bureau of Labor Statistics, U.S. Labor Department

(City sizes: A=1.25 million or more; B=385,000 to 1.25 million; C=75,000 to 385,000; D=75,000 or less.)

(Dec. 1977 = 100)	Feb. 1984	CPI-U % change, Feb. 1984 to Apr. 1984	Apr. 1984	% change, Apr. 1983 to Apr. 1984	Feb. 1984	CPI-W % change, Feb. 1984 to Apr. 1984	Apr. 1984	% change, Apr. 1983 to Apr. 1984
Northeast								
Size A	159.5	0.8	160.7	5.0	156.0	0.3	156.5	3.2
Size B	165.9	0.2	166.3	4.6	162.7	0.6	163.6	4.1
Size C	170.5	0.2	170.9	4.5	170.9	−0.6	169.8	4.3
Size D	164.9	0.8	166.3	5.1	163.8	0.7	164.9	4.1
North Central								
Size A	168.7	0.7	169.9	3.9	166.8	−0.2	166.5	1.8
Size B	165.2	1.0	166.8	3.5	161.9	0.5	162.7	0.7
Size C	162.5	0.6	163.4	3.9	159.1	0.9	160.6	3.7
Size D	163.7	0.5	164.5	4.0	163.5	1.8	166.5	3.4
South								
Size A	165.7	0.4	166.3	4.5	166.2	0.1	166.4	3.8
Size B	166.9	0.8	168.2	4.5	165.1	−0.4	164.5	2.2
Size C	165.3	1.0	166.9	4.2	165.3	−0.1	165.1	2.5
Size D	166.6	0.9	168.1	4.5	165.2	0.7	166.4	3.7
West								
Size A	165.7	0.9	167.2	5.0	164.1	0.1	164.2	3.7
Size B	165.3	0.9	166.8	4.6	165.5	0.6	166.5	4.8
Size C	157.6	1.0	159.1	4.5	155.5	1.0	157.0	4.1
Size D	164.8	1.0	166.5	6.1	162.9	0.4	163.6	2.2

The Northeast region includes cities from Boston to Pittsburgh; the North Central, cities from Cleveland to Grand Island, Neb. and from Minneapolis to St. Louis and Cincinnati; the South, cities from Baltimore to Dallas; the West, cities from Alamogordo, N. Mex., to Butte, Mont. Anchorage, and Honolulu.

Annual Average Purchasing Power of the Dollar

Source: Bureau of Labor Statistics, U.S. Labor Department

Obtained by dividing the index for 1967 (100.00) by the index for the given period and expressing the result in dollars and cents. Beginning 1961, wholesale prices include data for Alaska and Hawaii; beginning 1964, consumer prices include them. NA = Not available.

Year	As measured by— Wholesale prices	Consumer prices	Year	Wholesale prices	Consumer prices	Year	Wholesale prices	Consumer prices
1940	$2.469	$2.381	1970	$ .906	$ .860	1977	$ .515	$ .551
1950	1.222	1.387	1971	.878	.824	1978	.478	.493
1955	1.139	1.247	1972	.840	.799	1979	.463	.461
1960	1.054	1.127	1973	.744	.752	1980	.405	.406
1965	1.035	1.058	1974	.625	.677	1981	.371	367
1968	.976	.960	1975	.572	.620	1982	NA	.347
1969	.939	.960	1976	.546	.587	1983	NA	.285

Average Weekly Earnings of Production Workers[1]

Source: Bureau of Labor Statistics, U.S. Labor Department

Year and month	Manufacturing workers Gross average weekly earnings Current dollars	1977 dollars	Spendable average weekly earnings[2] Worker with no dependents Current dollars	1977 dollars	Worker with 3 dependents Current dollars	1977 dollars	Private nonagricultural workers Gross average weekly earnings Current dollars	1977 dollars	Spendable average weekly earnings[2] Worker with no dependents Current dollars	1977 dollars	Worker with 3 dependents Current dollars	1977 dollars
1974	176.80	217.20	140.19	172.22	151.56	186.19	154.76	190.12	124.37	152.79	151.56	165.37
1975	190.79	214.85	151.61	170.73	166.29	187.26	163.53	184.16	132.49	149.20	166.29	164.02
1976	209.32	222.92	167.83	178.73	181.32	193.10	175.45	186.85	143.30	152.61	181.32	166.00
1977	228.90	228.90	183.80	183.80	200.06	200.06	189.00	189.00	155.19	155.19	200.06	169.93
1978	249.27	231.66	197.40	183.46	214.87	199.69	203.70	189.31	165.39	153.71	214.87	167.95
1979	268.94	224.64	212.77	177.40	232.38	193.81	219.91	183.41	178.00	148.46	194.82	162.49
1980	288.62	212.64	225.79	165.90	247.01	181.49	235.10	172.74	188.82	138.74	206.40	151.65
1981	318.00	212.00	244.09	163.73	267.36	178.24	255.20	170.13	202.00	134.67	220.57	147.05
1982	330.65	207.96	—	—	—	—	266.92	167.87	—	—	—	—
1983	354.08	216.03	—	—	—	—	280.70	171.26	—	—	—	—
1984 Jan..	368.65	221.01	—	—	—	—	289.10	173.32	—	—	—	—
Feb..	368.74	220.67	—	—	—	—	288.40	172.59	—	—	—	—
Mar..	369.96	221.40	—	—	—	—	288.40	172.59	—	—	—	—
Apr..	372.60	222.45	—	—	—	—	292.64	174.71	—	—	—	—
May..	369.87	219.77	—	—	—	—	291.46	173.18	—	—	—	—
June	372.91p	221.05p	—	—	—	—	294.65p	174.66p	—	—	—	—
July..	370.47p	—	—	—	—	—	297.74p	—	—	—	—	—

(1) Data relate to production workers in mining and manufacturing; to construction workers in contract construction; and to nonsupervisory workers in transportation and public utilities; wholesale and retail trade; finance, insurance, and real estate; and services. (2) Spendable average weekly earnings are based on gross average weekly earnings less the estimated amount of the worker's Federal, social security, and income taxes. Figures are no longer available after 1981. (p)—preliminary.

Interest Laws and Consumer Finance Loan Rates

Source: Revised by Christian T. Jones. Editor, Consumer Finance Law Bulletin, San Diego, Ca.

Most states have laws regulating interest rates. These laws fix a legal or conventional rate which applies when there is no contract for interest. They also fix a general maximum contract rate, but in many states there are so many exceptions that the general contract maximum actually applies only to exceptional cases. Also, federal law has preempted state limits on first home mortgages, subject to each state's right to reinstate its own law and given depository institutions parity with other state lenders.

Legal rate of interest. The legal or conventional rate of interest applies to money obligations when no interest rate is contracted for and also to judgments. The rate is usually somewhat below the general interest rate.

General maximum contract rates. General interest laws in most states set the maximum rate between 8% and 16% per year. The general maximum is fixed by the state constitution at 5% over the Federal Reserve Discount rate in Arkansas. Loans to corporations are frequently exempted or subject to a higher maximum. In recent years, it has also been common to provide special rates for home mortgage loans and variable usury rates that are indexed to federal rates.

Specific enabling acts. In many states special statutes permit industrial loan companies, second mortgage lenders, and banks to charge 1.5% a month or more. Laws regulating revolving loans, charge accounts and credit cards generally limit charges between 1.5% and 2% per month plus annual fees for credit cards. Rates for installment sales contracts in most states are somewhat higher. Credit unions may generally charge 1% to 1½% a month. Pawnbrokers' rates vary widely. Savings and loan associations, and loans insured by federal agencies, are also specially regulated. A number of states allow regulated lenders to charge any rate agreed to with the customer.

Consumer finance loan statutes. Most consumer finance loan statutes are based on early models drafted by the Russell Sage Foundation (1916-42) to provide small loans to wage earners under license and other protective regulations. Since 1969 the model has frequently been the Uniform Consumer Credit Code which applies to credit sales and loans for consumer purposes. In general, licensed lenders may charge 3% a month for loans of smaller amounts and reduced rates for additional amounts. A few states permit add-on rates of 17% to 20% to $300 and lower rates for additional amounts. An add-on of 17% ($17 per $100) per year yields about 2.5% per month if paid in equal monthly installments. Discount rates produce higher yields than add-on rates of the same amount. In the table below unless otherwise stated, monthly and annual rates are based on reducing principal balances, annual add-on rates are based on the original principal for the full term, and two or more rates apply to different portions of balance or original principal.

States with consumer finance loan laws and the rates of charge as of Oct. 1, 1984:

Maximum monthly rates computed on unpaid balances, unless otherwise stated.

Ala. . . . Annual add-on: 15% to $750, 10% to $2,000, 8% over $2,000 (min. 1.5% on unpaid balances), plus 2% fee (max. $20). Higher rates for loans up to $749. Over $2,000, any agreed rate.

Alas. . . 3% to $850, 2% to $10,000, flat rate to $25,000. Over $10,000, any agreed rate.

Ariz. . . To $1,000: 3%. Over $1,000: 3% to $500, 2% to $10,000. Over $10,000, any agreed rate.

Cal . . . 2.5% to $225, 2% to $900, 1.5% to $1,650, 1% to $5,000 (1.6% min.). Over $5,000, any agreed rate. 5% fee (max. $50) to $2,500

Colo. . . 36% per year to $630, 21% to $2,100, 15% to $25,000 (21% min.).

Conn. . Annual Add-on: 17% to $600, 11% to $5,000; 11% over $1,800 to $5,000 for certain secured loans.

Del. . . . Any agreed rate.

Fla. . . . 30% per year to $500, 24% to $1,000, 18% to $2,500; 18% per year on any amount over $2,500 to $25,000.

Ga. . . . 10% per year discount to 18 months, add-on to 36½ months; 8% fee to $600, 4% on excess plus $2 per month; max. $3,000. Over $3,000, any agreed rate.

Ha. . . . 3.5% to $100, 2.5% to $300; 2% on entire balance over $300.

Ida. . . . Any agreed rate.

Ill. . . . . Any agreed rate.

Ind. . . . 36% per year to $720, 21% to $2,400, 15% to $60,000 (21% min.).

Ia. . . . 3% to $500, 2% to $1,200, 1.5% to $2,000; or equivalent flat rate. Over $2,000, 10% per year discount.

Kan. . . 36% per year to $570, 21% to $1,900, 14.45% to $25,000 (21% min.).

Ky. . . . 3% to $1,000, 2% to $3,000. Over $3,000, 2%.

La. . . . 36% per year to $1,400, 27% to $4,000, 24% to $7,000, 21% over $7,000, plus $25 fee.

Me. . . . 30% per year to $690, 21% to $1,900, 15% to $55,000 (18% min.).

Md. . . . 2.75% to $500, 2% to $2,000. Over $2,000, 2%.

Mass. . 23% per year plus $20 fee to $6,000.

Mich. . . 31% per year to $500, 13% to $3,000 (18% min.).

Minn. . . 33% per year to $385, 19% to $38,500 (21.75% min.).

Miss. . . 36% per year to $800, 33% to $1,800, 24% to $4,500, 12% over $4,500.

Mo. . . . 2.218% to $800, 1.25% to $2,500, 10% per year over $2,500, plus 5% fee (max. $15).

Mont. . . Annual add-on: 20% to $550, 16% to $1,100, 12% to $8,750. 2% per mo. over $7,500 to $25,000.

Neb. . . 24% per year to $1,000. 21% over, plus fee of 7% to $2,000 and 5% over (max. $500).

Nev. . . Any agreed rate.

N.H. . . 2% to $600, 1.5% to $1,500; Any agreed rate to $10,000.

N.J. . . . 30% per year to $5,000.

N.M. . . Any agreed rate.

N.Y. . . . Any agreed rate.

N.C. . . 3% to $600, 1.25% to $3,000.

N.D. . . 2.5% to $250, 2% to $500, 1.75% to $750, 1.5% to $1,000; any agreed rate on entire amount over $1,000 to $15,000.

Ohio . . 28% per year to $1,000, 22% to $3,000; 25% on entire amount over $3,000.

Okla. . . 30% per annum to $630, 21% to $2,100, 15% to $47,500. (21% min.). Special rates to $100.

Ore. . . Any agreed rate.

Pa. . . . 9.5% per year discount to 36 months, 6% for remaining time plus 2% fee (min. 2%) to $5,000.

P.R. . . 27% per year.

R.I. . . . 3% to $300, 2.5% for loans between $300 and $800; 2% for larger loans to $2,500.

S.C. . . Any agreed rate.

S.D. . . Any agreed rate.

Tenn. . . Over $100, 24% per year plus fees.

Texas . Annual add-on: 18% to $870, 8% to $7,200 or formula rate (max. 24% per year on unpaid balances.)

Utah . . 36% per year to $840, 21% to $2,800, 15% to $55,000 (18% min.) or, by rule, 19.6%.

Vt. . . . 2% to $1,000, 1% to $3,000 (min. 1.5%).

Va. . . . 3% to $600, 2.25% to $1,800, 1.5% to $2,800; or annual add-on of 21% to $600, 17% to $1,800, 13% to $2,800; 2% fee.

Wash. . 2.5% to $500, 1.5% to $1,000, 1% to $2,500.

W.Va. . 36% per year to $500, 24% to $1,500, 18% to $2,000.

Wis. . . 23% per year to $3,000; 21% on entire balance over $3,000; any agreed rate, 11/1/84 to 10/31/87.

Wyo. . . 36% per year to $1,000, 21% to $25,000 (21% min.).

Shopping for Credit: Ask the Right Questions
Source: New York State Banking Department

Under federal law, all institutions that extend or arrange for the extension of consumer credit must give the borrower meaningful information about the cost of each loan. The cost must be expressed as the dollar amount of the interest or finance charge, and as the annual percentage rate computed on the amount financed.

To be sure the loan or credit agreement you are considering suits both your budget and your individual needs, shop around. And ask questions to compare and evaluate a lender's rate and services. For instance:

1. What is the annual percentage rate?
2. What is the total cost of the loan in dollars?

3. How long do you have to pay off the loan?
4. What are the number, amounts, and due dates of payments?
5. What is the cost of deferring or extending the time period of the loan?
6. What is the cost of late charges for overdue payments?
7. If you pay the loan off early, are there any prepayment penalties?
8. Does the loan have to be secured? If so, what collateral is required?
9. What is the cost of credit life or other insurance that is being offered or may be required?
10. Are there any other charges you may have to pay?

Fair Credit: What You Should Know
Source: Federal Trade Commission

Federal legislation has made it easier for you to be treated fairly in credit-related areas:

Billing. Don't let the anonymous computer get you down. The Fair Credit Billing Act states that, if you find an error in the amount of $50 or more in your credit card statement or department store revolving charge statement and you write to the company about it (on a separate sheet of paper, not the bill), the company must acknowledge your letter within 30 days and must resolve the dispute within 90 days.

Equal Credit. The Equal Credit Opportunity Act (ECOA) bans any discrimination according to sex or marital status in the granting of credit. Discrimination is also prohibited on the basis of age, race, color, religion, national origin, or receipt of public assistance payments.

However, the creditor may ask questions relating to these areas if they have bearing on your credit worthiness. The creditor does have the right to determine whether you are willing and able to repay your debts. For instance, the creditor can ask you if you are "married," "unmarried," or "separated" if, and only if, (1) you are applying jointly with your

spouse; (2) your spouse will be an authorized user of the account; (3) you live in a community property state or you list assets located in a community property state. Similarly, a creditor may ask about alimony, child support, and separate maintenance if, and only if, you are depending on these as sources to establish your ability to repay your debts. In this case, the creditor may ask whether there is a court order that requires the payments or may inquire about the length of time and regularity of the payments, as well as your exspouse's credit history.

The ECOA also requires that if you are turned down for credit, the creditor must tell you the reason you were turned down.

Mail-Order Merchandise. By law, you have the right to receive merchandise ordered through the mail within 30 days, unless another deadline has been specified. Promises such as "one week" or "4 to 6 weeks" must be met. If either the seller's or the FTC's deadline is missed, you have the right to cancel and have all your money returned. If you run into a problem with late or non-delivery, contact the Federal Trade Commission for help.

Managing Credit: How Much Debt is Safe?
Source: Citibank

With the current rate of inflation, it is extremely important for consumers to keep close track of their individual use of credit and debt.

Before you make any new purchases, which involve moving income from the optional spending part of your budget to your fixed budget as a loan to be repaid, you must be sure you have those extra dollars and that you can do without them each month.

How Much Average Debt is Safe?

Once you've decided to apply for credit, you face the most-asked question about consumer debt: how much is safe?

There is no simple answer that applies to each consumer's situation. Most experts, today, avoid general rules of thumb. Don't be misled by the percents of gross income that lenders may use to decide how much institutional risk they run in any specific application for a loan. The lending institution can use only gross income and loan-commitment averages to estimate its own average risk, and cannot know how any individual consumer will actually repay. Only you can gauge that, based on your own habits, values, and needs.

How do you determine what you can handle? To help decide, you must know at a given time how many dollars you have for optional spending, and then how many of those

dollars you can move into fixed repayments.

Here's one technique for determining how many optional dollars you have:

1. Write down your annual take-home income after deductions (for taxes, etc.) and divide by 12 to get your monthly take-home income.
2. From the monthly figure, subtract all your current monthly fixed expenses—those to which you are currently committed or must cover over the next year. Include your gasoline and car costs, other transportation, heating, utilities, food, rent, or mortgage (but no other loan repayments), real estate taxes, insurance, etc.
3. Next, total your monthly nonmortgage loan repayments and subtract them from the previous amount.

The total figure you're left with is your monthly optional spending amount. Now you must consider how comfortably you're managing with this amount. Consider that amount less the new monthly repayment. Can you still manage on the remaining amount, or should you wait until your take-home income goes up or your present debt loan goes down?

Are You Headed for Financial Trouble?

Although there is no dependable formula for determining your individual debt ratio, there are certain clear warning signals that you may have reached or have already passed it consider the following signals and, if several of them describe your financial situation, it may be time to look for help.

. Your checkbook balance is getting lower and lower each month.

. You don't seem to be able to make it from month to month without writing overdrafts on your checking account.

. You pay only the minimum due or even less on your charge accounts each month.

. You have borrowed on your life insurance and see little possibility of paying it back soon.

. Your savings account is slowly disappearing or has completely disappeared, and you're not able to put any of your regular income into savings.

. You manage to get through each month by depending on undependable extra income like overtime or odd jobs.

. You find yourself depending on credit cards for day-to-day living expenses and using cash advances to pay off other debts.

. You are behind on one or more of your installment payments.

. You don't really know how much money you owe.

10. You are receiving overdue notices or phone calls from creditors.

1. Family disputes over money are growing.

2. You occasionally juggle paying bills, paying one creditor while giving excuses to another.

3. You've had to ask creditors for extensions on due dates.

4. You've taken out loans to pay debts, or taken out a debt consolidation loan.

5. You are at or near the limit on the credit lines allowed on your credit cards.

6. When you use credit, you try to get it for the longest time period and the lowest payments without considering how much more this will cost you in interest.

17. You must borrow money to pay bills you can anticipate, like quarterly property taxes.

18. Although you regularly pay all of your debts, you are forced to continue living on credit and, as a result, your debt loan never really shrinks or is even increasing.

What can you do if you find yourself in financial trouble? The first step is to drastically cut your optional spending. Put yourself and your family on a crash tight-cash program until you can stabilize your financial situation. Also, you may need to turn some assets into cash and apply it to your debts.

If these attempts fail, get in touch with your creditors. Candidly, explain your situation. Some of them may agree to a longer repayment schedule which will insure that they get their money back and that they will keep you as a customer. You may pay more in interest, but you'll have a better credit record.

If you're still in trouble, you probably need good financial counseling.

How to Find Credit Counseling

In the U.S., there are hundreds of free volunteer-staffed credit counseling sources. Others, staffed by professionals, charge a fee.

Look up Consumer Credit Counseling in your local phone book. Call the Consumer Affairs Department of your city for referrals. Contact community-centered organizations, church, local banks, consumer finance company, credit union, labor union, or your employer's personnel department.

If you can't find a local agency, write to the Family Service Association of America (44 E. 23rd St., New York, NY 10010) or the National Foundation for Consumer Credit (1819 H Street N.W., Washington, DC 20006).

Consumer Installment Credit

Source: Federal Reserve System (estimates of amounts outstanding, millions of dollars, not seasonally adjusted)

| End of year month | Total | By holder | | | | | By type | | | |
		Commercial banks	Finance companies	Credit unions	Retailers	Savings-loans and other	Automobile	Mobile homes	Revolving	All others
'76	193,525	93,728	38,918	31,169	19,260	10,450	67,707	14,573	17,189	94,056
'77	230,564	112,373	44,868	37,605	23,490	12,228	82,911	14,945	39,274	93,434
'78	273,645	136,016	54,298	44,334	25,987	13,010	101,647	15,235	48,309	108,454
'79	312,024	154,177	68,318	46,517	28,119	14,893	116,362	16,838	56,937	121,887
'80	313,472	147,013	76,756	44,041	28,448	17,214	116,838	17,322	58,352	120,960
'81	331,697	147,622	89,818	45,954	29,551	18,752	125,331	18,373	62,819	125,174
'82	344,798	152,069	94,322	47,253	30,202	20,952	130,227	18,988	67,184	128,399
'83	396,082	171,978	102,862	53,471	35,911	31,860	142,449	23,680	80,823	149,130
'84, June .	360,605	191,519	104,460	59,893	34,206	37,487	155,937	24,427	84,598	162,603

Investment: A Basic Glossary

Source: Merrill, Lynch, Pierce, Fenner & Smith, Inc.

The investment possibilities in securities for you as an individual are extremely varied. If you are beginning to consider what is best for your personal needs and find the world of securities somewhat bewildering, we hope the following glossary may offer some help.

Bear Market: A market in which prices are falling.

Bond: A written promise or IOU by the issuer to repay a fixed amount of borrowed money on a specified date and to pay a set annual rate of interest in the meantime, generally at semi-annual intervals. Bonds are generally considered safe because the borrower (whether a company or the government) must make interest payments before their money is

spent on anything else. Some of the most common bonds include:

Commercial Paper: An extremely short-term corporate IOU, generally due in 270 days or less. Available in face amounts of $100,000, $250,000, $500,000, $1,000,000 and combinations thereof. Yield in recent years has averaged from 12 to 17 percent.

Convertible Bond: A corporate bond (see below) which may be converted into a stated number of shares of the corporations common stock. Its price tends to fluctuate along with fluctuations in the price of the stock as well as with changes in interest rates. Average yield in recent years has ranged from 8 to 12 percent.

Corporate Bond: Evidence of debt by a corporation. Differs from a municipal bond in various ways, but particularly in taxability of interest. Considered safer than the common or preferred stock of the same company. Yield has averaged in recent years from 12 to 17 percent.

Government Bond: An IOU of the U.S. Treasury, considered the safest security in the investment world. They are divided into two categories, those that are not marketable and those that are. *Savings Bonds* cannot be bought and sold once the original purchase is made. These include the familiar Series E bonds. You buy them at 75 percent of their face value and when they mature, 5 years later, they will pay you back 100 percent of face value if you cash them in. Recently they have been paying about 6 percent interest compounded semiannually to maturity. Another type, Series H, are not discounted, but issued in amounts of $500, $1,000, $5,000, and $10,000 and pay their interest in semiannual checks. They pay 8 percent the first year of their 10-year life, 5.8 percent for the next 4 years, and 6 percent for the last 5 years. Marketable bonds fall into 3 categories. *Treasury Bills* are short-term U.S. obligations, maturing in 3, 6, or 12 months. They are sold at a discount of the face value, and the minimum denomination is $10,000. Yield in recent years has ranged from 7½ percent to 16½ percent. *Treasury Notes* mature in up to 10 years. Denominations range from $500, $1,000 to $5,000, $10,000 and up. In recent years the yield has ranged from 8¼ percent to 15 percent. *Treasury Bonds* mature in 10 to 30 years. The minimum investment is $1,000 and yield has ranged from 8⅜ to 14 percent in recent years.

Municipal Bond: Issued by governmental units such as states, cities, local taxing authorities and other agencies. Interest is exempt from U.S. — and sometimes state and local — income tax. Yield in recent years has averaged from 9 to 13 percent. *Municipal Bond Unit Investment Trusts* allow you to invest with as little as $1,000 in a portfolio of many different municipal bonds chosen by professionals. The income is paid either monthly or semiannually and is exempt from Federal income taxes.

Bull Market: A market in which prices are on the rise.

Stock: *Common Stocks* are shares of ownership in a corporation; they are the most direct way to participate in the fortunes of a company. The sometimes wide swings in the prices of this kind of stock may mean a chance for big profits (or equally big losses). *Preferred Stock* is a type of stock on which a fixed dividend must be paid before holders of common stock are issued their share of the issuing corporation's earnings. Prices are higher and yields lower than comparable bonds and are, consequently, not the best invest-

ment for individuals. Payments are usually made quarterl. They are especially attractive to corporate investors becaus 85 percent of preferred dividends are tax exempt to corpor tions. Many high-grade preferreds currently pay about 10½ percent to 11¾ percent interest. *Convertible Preferred Sto* can be converted into the common stock of the compan that issued the preferred. This stock has the advantage producing a higher yield than common stock and it also ha appreciation potential. *Over-the-Counter Stock* is not trade on the major or regional exchanges, but rather through dea ers from whom you buy directly. These stocks tend to b long to smaller companies. Prices of OTC stocks are base on the dealer's supply, what he paid for them, the deman for them, and the prices of competitive dealers. *Blue Ch* stocks are so called because they have been leading stock for a long time. They do not show dramatic growth, bi yield good dividends over time. *Growth* stocks are stock which grow yearly by a growing percentage; they do we even in bad times.

Dow-Jones Industrial Average: A measure of stock ma ket prices, based on the 30 leading manufacturing compani on the New York Stock Exchange.

Mutual Fund: A portfolio, or selection, of professional bought and managed stocks in which you pool your mon along with thousands of other people. A share price is base on net asset value, or the value of all the investments own by the funds, less any debt, and divided by the total numb of shares. The major advantage is less risk — it is spread o over many stocks and, if one or two do badly, the remain may shield you from the losses. *Bond Funds* are mutu funds that deal in the bond market exclusively. *Money Ma ket Mutual Funds* buy in the so-called "Money Market" institutions that need to borrow large sums of money f short terms. Usually the individual investor cannot affo the denominations required in the "Money Market" (i treasury bills, commercial paper, certificates of deposit), b through a money market mutual fund he can take advanta of these money makers when interest rates are high. The funds offer special checking account advantages, as you c generally write a check against your investment at any tim in amounts of $500 or more. The minimum investment generally $1,000. Average yield over recent years has be from 9 to 15 percent.

Unit Investment Trust: A portfolio of many different c porate bonds, preferred stocks, government-backed secu ties or utility common stocks in which you can invest wi as little as $1,000. Professional managers choose the secu ties, arrange for safe-keeping and collect the income. Y receive your pro rata share of income every month.

Year-End Assets and Liabilities of Individuals in the U.S.[1]

Source: Federal Reserve System
(billions of dollars)

	1960	1965	1970	1975	1980	1981	1982	198
Total financial assets	1002.4	1499.8	1966.4	2611.3	4612.8	4913.8	5470.5	6158
Checkable deposits & curr.	91.5	107.3	137.2	190.0	283.9	319.5	336.0	376
Time & savings deposits	164.0	288.4	426.3	766.0	1282.2	1348.9	1460.8	1659
Money market fund shares	—	—	—	3.7	74.4	181.9	206.6	162
Securities	512.1	766.9	928.3	925.4	1600.5	1566.8	1745.4	2021
U.S. savings bonds	45.6	49.7	52.1	67.4	72.5	68.2	68.3	71
Other U.S. Treasury secur.	25.9	26.3	32.8	58.9	115.6	140.0	157.9	197
U.S. Govt. agency secur.	2.3	3.7	20.9	12.5	52.1	56.5	51.1	59
Tax-exempt obligations	30.8	36.4	46.0	68.1	89.9	100.8	132.8	173
Corporate & foreign bonds	10.0	9.5	36.2	60.9	58.3	50.4	45.7	45
Open-market paper	2.0	5.6	11.7	10.9	23.8	16.5	14.7	7
Mutual fund shares	17.0	35.2	46.8	43.0	63.5	63.8	89.5	129
Private life insurance res.	78.8	98.9	123.3	158.5	207.4	216.3	223.3	231
Private insured pension res.	18.9	27.3	41.0	72.3	172.0	199.8	242.9	286
Private noninsured pen. res.	38.1	73.6	110.4	186.6	412.7	431.0	518.1	607
Govt. insurance & pen. res.	40.2	60.8	95.2	154.7	283.6	319.7	371.2	437
Miscellaneous finan. assets	58.8	76.6	104.7	154.1	296.2	329.9	366.1	376
Total liabilities	280.5	444.9	650.2	1107.4	2069.6	2256.3	2397.1	2663
Mtg. debt on nonfarm homes.	137.4	214.4	290.4	482.9	967.5	1051.0	1096.9	1200
Other mortgage debt[2]	35.7	65.3	118.7	248.8	412.5	445.5	479.0	540
Consumer credit	65.1	103.2	143.1	223.2	389.7	416.4	441.7	493
Security credit	5.4	9.1	10.4	12.1	27.2	25.6	28.8	48
Policy loans	6.7	8.3	17.0	25.5	42.6	50.0	54.2	55
Other debt[2]	31.2	44.6	70.4	114.9	230.1	267.9	298.5	321

(1) Combined statement for households, farm business, and nonfarm noncorporate business. (2) Includes corporate farms.

Directory of Consumer and Information Offices

Source: U.S. Office of Consumer Affairs.

For best results, consult your local telephone directory under U.S. Government, then the specific categories below. If a category does not appear, contact the Federal Information Center (FIC) nearest you. If the FIC is unable to help you, write or call as listed below.

Aging:
Public Inquiries Office, Administration on Aging, Office of Human Development Services, Dept. of Health and Human Services, Washington, DC 20201; (202) 245-0188.

AIDS Hotline: (800) 342-AIDS; (202) 646-8182 in DC

Alcoholism:
Bureau of Alcohol, Tobacco and Firearms, Room 4216, 1200 Pennsylvania Ave., NW, Washington, DC 20226; (202) 566-9100.

Appliances:
Public Inquiries Office, Consumer Product Safety Commission, 5401 W. Bard Ave., Bethesda, MD 20207; (800) 638-2772; (202) 492-6800 in DC.

Automobiles:
Auto Safety Hotline: National Highway Traffic Safety Administration, Dept. of Transportation, Washington, DC 20590; (800) 424-9393; (202) 426-0123 in DC.
Fuel-saving devices and additives
Fuel-Saving Device Evaluation Coordinator, Vehicle Emission Lab., Environmental Protection Agency, 2565 Plymouth Rd., Ann Arbor, MI 48105; (313) 668-4299.

Cancer Hotline: (800) 4-CANCER; (202) 636-5700 in DC; (800) 638-6070 in Alaska; (800) 524-1234 in Hawaii; (212) 794-7982 NYC.

Child Abuse:
National Center on Child Abuse and Neglect, P.O. Box 1182, Washington, DC 20013; (202) 245-2640.
Parents Anonymous, Suite 208, 22330 Hawthorne Blvd., Torrance, CA 90505; (800) 352-9386 in California.

Child Support:
Office of Child Support Enforcement, Dept. of Health and Human Services, 6110 Executive Blvd., Rockville, MD 20852; (301) 443-4442.

Civil Rights:
Asst. Staff Director, U.S. Commission on Civil Rights, 1121 Vermont Ave. NW, Room 500, Washington, DC 20425; (202) 254-6345.
Employment
Office of Exec. Director, Equal Employment Opportunity Commission, Washington, DC 20507; (202) 632-6814.

Consumer Information:
For a free Consumer Information Catalog, a listing of more than 200 Federal consumer publications, write or call: Consumer Information Center, Pueblo, CO 81009; (303) 948-3334.

Copyrights:
Information and Publication Section, Copyright Office, Library of Congress, Washington, DC 20559; (202) 287-8700.

Credit Counseling:
Executive Director, National Foundation for Consumer Credit, 8701 Georgia Ave., Silver Springs, MD 20910.

Drug Abuse:
Director, Natl. Center for Alcohol and Drug Abuse, 5600 Fishers Lane, Rockville, MD 20857, (301) 443-3673.

Education:
Natl. Education Association, 1201 16th St. NW, Washington, DC 20036; (202) 833-4000.

Employment:
Safety and Health
Office of Information, Occupational Safety and Health Administration, Dept. of Labor, Washington, DC 20210; (202) 523-8151.
Training
Director, Office of Public Affairs, Employment and Training Administration, Dept. of Labor, Washington, DC 20530; (202) 376-6270.

Energy:
Conservation and Renewable Energy Referral Service, P.O. Box 8900 Silver Spring, MD 20907; (800) 523-2929; (800) 462-4983 in PA.

Federal Regulations:
Office of the Federal Register, General Information, Washington, D.C. 20405; (202) 523-5240. The *Federal Register,* published 5 days a week, lists new and proposed government regulations, and Presidential documents. It may be ordered from the Superintendent of Documents, U.S. Govt. Printing Office, Washington, DC 20402 for $1.50 per copy, $150 for six months, or $300 per year.

Food:
General inquiries and labeling, quality, and safety (all foods except meat and poultry products)
Office of Consumer Affairs, Food and Drug Administration, Dept. of Health and Human Services, 5600 Fishers Lane, Rockville, MD 20857; (301) 443-3170.
Meat and Poultry Hotline: Food and Safety Inspection

Service, Dept. of Agriculture, Washington, DC 20250; (202) 472-4485.

Freight Shipments:
Community and Consumer Liaison Division, Federal Aviation Administration, Dept. of Transportation, Washington, DC 20591; (202) 426-1960.

Handicapped:
Clearinghouse on the Handicapped, Dept. of Education, Washington, DC 20202; (202) 245-0080. Handicapped Infants Hotline: (800) 368-1019; (202) 863-0100 in DC.

Health:
Natl. Health Information Clearinghouse, Dept. of Health and Human Services, P.O. Box 1133, Washington, DC 20013; (800) 336-4797; (703) 522-2590 in DC, Virginia, Alaska, and Hawaii.

Housing:
Information Center, Dept. of Housing and Urban Development, Washington, DC 20410; (202) 755-6420.
Real Estate Settlement Procedures
Office of Single-Family Housing, Dept. of Housing and Urban Development, Washington, DC 20410; (202) 426-0070.

Insurance:
Insurance Information Institute, 1025 Vermont Ave., Washington, DC 20005; (202) 347-3929.

Mail:
Fraud
Check with your local postmaster, or Consumer Advocate, U.S. Postal Service, Washington, DC 20260; (202) 245-4514.
Mail orders
Mail Order Action Line, 6 E. 43rd St., New York, NY 10017; (212) 689-4977.
Unordered merchandise and *late delivery*
Check with your local postmaster, or Enforcement, Federal Trade Commission, Washington, DC 20580.
Unsolicited mail
Mail Preference Service, Name-Removal Program, 6 E. 43rd St., New York, NY 10017; (212) 689-4977.

Medicaid:
Contact your local Welfare or Social Services offices.

Medicare:
Contact your local Social Security Office, or your area Medicare carrier. Or contact Medicare Inquiries, Health Care Financing Administration, Dept. of Health and Human Services, 6325 Security Blvd., Baltimore, MD 21207; (301) 594-9086.

Nursing Homes:
Division of Long-Term Care, Health Care Financing Administration, Dept. of Health and Human Services, 1849 Gwyn Oak Ave., Dogwood East Bldg., Baltimore, MD 21207; (301) 594-3642.

Passports:
Citizens Counselor Services, Dept. of State, Room 481 Washington, DC 20005; (202) 833-2050.

Patents and Trademarks:
Commissioner of Patents and Trademarks, Washington DC 20231; (703) 557-3158.

Pensions:
Pension Benefit Guaranty Corp., Dept. of Labor, 2020 St. NW, Washington, DC 20006; (202) 254-4817.

Stocks and Bonds:
Director, Office of Consumer Affairs, Securities and Exchange Commission, Washington, DC 20549; (20 272-7450.

Taxes:
The Internal Revenue Service (IRS) has 58 district offic that provide tax assistance by toll-free telephone. Toll-free numbers are listed in local telephone directories. Taxpayers may also use the toll-free network to clarify problems

Veterans:
Medical Care
Inquiries Unit, Veterans Administration, Washington DC 20420; (202) 389-3314.
Employment
Employment and Training Office, Asst. Secy. for Veterans Employment and Training, Dept. of Labor, Washington DC 20210; (202) 523-9116.

Warranties:
Federal Trade Commission, 6th and Pennsylvania A NW, Washington, DC 20580; (202) 523-3567.

Canadian Consumer Associations

Consumers' Association of Canada

The Consumers' Association of Canada (CAC) is a voluntary, non-profit organization founded in 1947 to represent consumer interests. It also provides members with information on consumer legislation and the results of its research and tests on consumer goods and services. The national office is at 2660 Southvale Cres., Level 3, Ottawa, Ont. K 5C4; branch offices are in each province and territory. CAC publishes monthly, bilingual magazines, *Canadian Consumer* and *Le Consommateur Canadien* (circulation 160,000). A nual membership fee is $18.

Automobile Protection Association

The Automobile Protection Association (APA) is a no profit, independently-financed consumer group founded 1969 to advise motorists on the quality of automotive products and services, to publicize and encourage legal acti against what it considers dishonest or dangerous practices the automobile industry, and to press federal and provinc governments for protective legislation. For a $25 annual members receive periodic APA bulletins as well as free le consultation when needed. Accredited garage service is p vided in Montreal and Toronto. Headquarters are at 2 St-Joseph West, Montreal, Quebec H2V 2N7. Branch off at 100 Granby St., Toronto, Ont. M5B 1J1.

Options for Savers

	Minimum Deposit	Maturity	Comments
Passbook savings	None	None	Low interest rate; money can be withdrawn at any time.
NOW accounts	Varies	None	Checks can be written; minimum balance may be required.
Super NOW accounts	$2,500*	None	High rate paid on readily available cash; no limit on checking.
7-to-31-day time deposits	$2,500*	7-31 days	Savings earn market yields; checking privileges; penalty for early withdrawal.
Money-market deposit accounts	$2,500*	None	Money-market rate paid on savings; six automatic monthly transfers allowed, of which three can be checks.
3-month certificates	Varies	3 months	Market yields; no checking privileges; penalty for early withdrawal.
6-month money-market time deposits	Varies	6 months	Savings earn market yields; penalty for early withdrawal; no compounding of interest.
12-month small-savers certificates	Varies	12 months	High yields for small deposits
Long-term certificates	Varies	2½ years +	Savings locked up for long time; savers can shop around for best yields. Interest compounded.
IRA certificates	Varies	Varies	Both deposits and interest income are deferred from federal income taxes until money is withdrawn; $2,000 maximum contribution.
Money-market mutual funds	$100-$1,000	None	Market yields paid on funds that can be withdrawn at any time; checks can be written; no federal deposit insurance.
Bond funds	Varies	None	Shares can be easily resold but lose value if interest rates rise.
Tax-exempt bond funds	Varies	None	Interest income is exempt from federal taxes; shares lose value if interest rates rise.
Stock funds	Varies	None	Small investors can diversify their holdings; shares lose value if stock prices fall.
Treasury bills	$10,000	6 months	Market yields and safety; easily sold; not subject to state and local income taxes.
U.S. savings bonds	$25	10 years	Safe; long term.
Corporate bonds	$1,000	10-30 years	Market yields plus liquidity; investment will lose value if interest rates rise.
Common stocks	—	None	Potential for dividends, long-term capital gains; risk of capital loss.
Zero-coupon bonds	$1,000 is usual minimum	6 months to 10 years +	Yields fixed for term of investment; backed by U.S. securities and sold at a deep discount; no interest is received until notes mature and are redeemed at face value.

*None if account is an IRA or Keogh Plan.

Individual Retirement Accounts

All wage earners under the age of 70 1/2 became eligible to set up their own tax-sheltered Individual Retirement Account (IRA) in 1982. Those who elect to open an IRA can choose from a wide variety of investment options offered by banks, insurance companies, credit unions, mutual funds, brokerage firms, etc. Investment in life insurance and collectibles such as gems, art works, antiques, stamps, etc. are prohibited.

What is an IRA?

An IRA is a tax-deferred investment plan that allows almost anyone who earns wages to save a portion of their income for retirement and to legally shelter that income from taxes. Each individual employee can set aside in an IRA any portion of his income up to a maximum of $2,000, or $2,250 if he or she has a non-working spouse: A married couple, when both are wage earners, can set aside $4,000. The couple may then apportion the money between them in any way they choose, so long as neither one receives more than $2,000.

A person is under no obligation to contribute the maximum $2,000 each year. In fact, if a person chooses, no yearly contribution need be made at all. The money may be invested in different kinds of investment vehicles.

Tax Advantage

The full amount that is contributed to an IRA each year is deducted from the wage earner's taxable income. No taxes are paid on the money invested or the interest it earns until the money is withdrawn from the account. It should be stressed that an IRA is not tax-free, but tax-deferred. The taxes must be paid when the money begins to be withdrawn at retirement, when the wage earner will presumably be in a much lower tax bracket and pay less tax.

Withdrawals from an IRA *may* be made without penalty in the year that a person turns 59 1/2, and *must* be made in the year that a person turns 70 1/2. Withdrawals may be made in installments over a period of years or in a single lump sum.

The minimum amount that *must* be withdrawn from an IRA at age 70 1/2 is based on a person's life expectancy, or the combined life expectancy of both spouses in the case of a married couple. Actuarial tables show that a man at age 70 1/2 has a life expectancy of 12 years; therefore, enough should be taken from his IRA in steady yearly withdrawals to empty the account in 12 years. At age 70 1/2, a women's life expectancy is 14 years.

When a wage earner dies, the money left in an IRA goes to the named beneficiary. The beneficiary may take the money and pay tax on it, or move the money into the beneficiary's own IRA to prolong its tax-deferred status. The $2,000 ceiling does not apply in this situation, nor does it apply to persons who transfer accumulated pension benefits into an IRA.

Establishing an IRA

A person may establish an account at any time during the calendar year up until they file their tax return for that year—no later than April 15, unless an extension has been granted. To start an IRA, a person need only complete a form and provide the money, either in a single sum or in smaller contributions during the year.

While the funds in an IRA cannot be withdrawn before age 59 1/2 without a penalty, they may be moved from one investment vehicle to another. The funds may also be moved from one financial institution to another, if the wage earner is not happy with the earnings performance of the account, or as individual objectives or economic conditions change. However, this may only be done once a year.

Early Withdrawal

If a person decides to remove funds from an IRA before reaching the age of 59 1/2, the amount withdrawn is taxable that year. In addition, the person will be subject to a 10% IRS tax penalty.

Growth or Stability?

Because IRA income can be placed in a wide range of investment vehicles, individuals should give careful consideration to their objectives before committing their money.

Some may feel more comfortable with a highly stable investment with a fixed rate of return. In this case, an investor should shop around for the best rate of return.

Others may feel that they can afford to invest in stocks, corporate bonds, or a mutual fund which may fluctuate and contain an element of risk, but offer the potential for rapid growth.

By 1984, 12.8 million people (16 percent of the 80 million people who returned 1983 tax returns) had claimed an IRA deduction according to the Internal Revenue Service.

Employment and Training Services and Unemployment Insurance

Source: Employment and Training Administration, U.S. Department of Labor

Employment Service

The Federal-State Employment Service consists of the United States Employment Service and affiliated state employment services which make up the Nation's public employment service system. During fiscal year 1982, the public employment service made 4.8 million placements—4.4 million in nonagricultural and .4 million in agricultural industries. Overall, 3.0 million different individuals were placed in employment.

The employment service refers employable applicants to job openings that use their highest skills and helps the unemployed obtain services or training to make them employable. It also provides special attention to handicapped workers, migrants and seasonal farmworkers, workers who lose their jobs because of foreign trade competition, and other worker groups. Veterans receive priority services including referral to jobs and training. During fiscal year 1982, more than 408,000 veterans were placed in jobs.

Job Training

The Job Training Partnership Act (JTPA) of 1982 went into full effect on October 1, 1983, replacing the Comprehensive Employment and Training Act (CETA), with training programs focusing almost entirely on the private sector.

State governors will receive bloc grants from the Labor Department. The funds will be distributed to Service Delivery Areas—areas of 200,000 population or more where local elected officials will work with Private Industry Councils to plan and conduct training projects in local areas.

Key differences in the new act are that at least 70 cents of each training dollar must be used for direct training costs, as compared to CETA's 18 cents. (CETA wound up nine years of existence at a total cost of $58 billion with 27 million enrollees and a 15 percent placement rate for training participants.)

JTPA has provisions for the retraining and job placement of dislocated workers—persons with long attachment to the labor force who have lost their jobs through plant closings and technological change, with little chance of returning to their old jobs. This program has already provided for 30,000 workers with $110 million in fiscal year 1983 and is expected to reach another 70,000 million with $223 million in FY 1984.

For the first time in the history of such programs, specific performance standards have been established and each Service Delivery Area and each state will have to match its performance to the minimum standards initially set by the Employment and Training Administration.

All in all, approximately 1 million unemployed workers are expected to be trained or assisted in obtaining employment through JTPA.

Other sections of JTPA include the Job Corps, which will enroll approximately 88,000 youth between the ages of 16 through 21 in 108 centers throughout the country for job and educational training; the summer jobs for youth program which will provide temporary summer work for nine weeks to approximately 800,000 youth; the migrant and seasonal farmworker program, which will provide job, social, and educational services to thousands of agricultural workers; and the Indian and Native American program which is expected to spend about $80 million on job and training programs, mostly on reservations.

Other National Training Programs

The Work Incentive (WIN) program for employable recipients of Aid to Families of Dependent Children has been placing approximately 350,000 persons, mostly women, in private sector jobs. The Trade Adjustment Act program for workers who have lost their jobs because of foreign trade competition assisted approximately 90,000 workers in fiscal year 1983 with 52 weeks of cash benefits and up to 26 weeks of retraining.

Unemployment Insurance

Unlike old-age and survivors insurance, entirely a federal program, the unemployment insurance program is a Federal-State system that provides insured wage earners with partial replacement of wages lost during involuntary unemployment. The program protects most workers. During calendar year 1982, an estimated 93 million workers in commerce, industry, agriculture, and government, including the armed forces, were covered under the Federal-State system. In addition, an estimated 500,000 railroad workers were insured against unemployment by the Railroad Retirement Board.

Each state, as well as the District of Columbia, Puerto Rico, and the Virgin Islands, has its own law and operates its own program. The amount and duration of the weekly benefits are determined by state laws, based on prior wages and length of employment. States are required to extend the duration of benefits when unemployment rises to and remains above specified state levels; costs of extended benefits are shared by the state and federal governments.

Under the Federal Unemployment Tax Act, as amended in 1976, the tax rate is 3.4% on the first $6,000 paid to each employee of employers with one or more employees in 20 weeks of the year or a quarterly payroll of $1,500. A credit of up to 2.7% is allowed for taxes paid under state unemployment insurance laws that meet certain criteria, leaving the federal share at 0.7% of taxable wages.

Social Security Requirement

The Social Security Act requires, as a condition of such grants, prompt payment of due benefits. The Federal Unemployment Tax Act provides safeguards for workers' right to benefits if they refuse jobs that fail to meet certain labor standards. Through the Unemployment Insurance Service of the Employment and Training Administration, the Secretary of Labor determines whether states qualify for grants and for tax offset credit for employers.

Benefits are financed solely by employer contributions, except in Alaska, Alabama, and New Jersey, where employees also contribute. Benefits are paid through the states' public employment offices, at which unemployed workers must register for work and to which they must report regularly for referral to a possible job during the time when they are drawing weekly benefit payments. During the 1982 calendar year, $20.4 billion in benefits was paid under state unemployment insurance programs to 11.7 million beneficiaries. They received an average weekly payment of $119.34 for total unemployment for an average of 15.9 weeks.

Unemployment Insurance and Benefits

Selected unemployment insurance data by state. Calendar year 1982, state programs only.

	Insured claimants[1] (1,000)	Bene- fici- aries[2] (1,000)	Exhaus- tions[3] (1,000)	Initial claims[4] (1,000)	Benefits paid[5] (1,000)	Avg. weekly benefit for total unemployment[6]	Funds avail- able for benefits Dec. 31, 1982[5] (millions)	Employers subject to state law Dec. 31, 1982 (1,000)
Alabama	263	240	71	632	$224,143	$80.24	$9	66
Alaska	42	40	16	75	71,159	130.25	131	13
Arizona	146	108	37	247	163,525	100.10	210	56
Arkansas	151	121	36	336	137,122	96.06	0	44
California	1,662	1,327	528	3,573	2,233,015	99.87	2,642	601
Colorado	149	115	47	231	193,527	140.83	1	78
Connecticut	199	175	34	386	261,193	122.47	18	77
Delaware	34	32	7	78	41,376	98.04	19	14
District of Columbia	38	31	16	44	80,099	141.15	0	19
Florida	330	277	105	557	335,289	95.28	843	225
Georgia	368	318	101	840	305,109	96.39	387	104
Hawaii	50	41	12	93	70,974	129.82	105	22
Idaho	59	50	28	146	91,929	116.45	28	22
Illinois	771	614	289	1,391	1,576,263	146.01	0	264
Indiana	361	307	123	776	389,443	94.24	62	93
Iowa	169	152	58	315	282,277	137.26	0	64
Kansas	124	114	43	219	207,251	128.05	139	55
Kentucky	235	192	72	507	327,805	116.01	0	62
Louisiana	270	204	78	422	482,187	144.75	0	83
Maine	74	51	28	173	69,527	101.40	17	31
Maryland	191	177	61	413	321,995	116.14	215	80
Massachusetts	344	285	87	705	492,139	115.36	426	121
Michigan	473	604	250	1,785	1,524,401	154.38	0	160
Minnesota	215	194	82	380	399,664	137.08	0	87
Mississippi	148	130	40	353	136,146	79.72	251	43
Missouri	279	238	89	678	301,768	93.72	26	114
Montana	40	41	17	83	61,597	122.11	9	23
Nebraska	64	54	19	103	65,393	96.73	70	38
Nevada	65	59	21	120	103,764	116.00	119	21
New Hampshire	63	54	5	96	46,031	95.37	73	24
New Jersey	490	418	199	827	806,780	120.09	97	167
New Mexico	51	42	15	92	68,140	105.49	99	29
New York	734	634	230	1,708	1,131,938	98.88	800	392
North Carolina	544	432	89	1,709	448,630	104.01	391	104
North Dakota	30	28	10	59	45,655	127.61	11	18
Ohio	697	616	256	1,641	1,495,839	143.59	0	196
Oklahoma	140	120	43	241	179,978	137.22	106	67
Oregon	188	171	70	469	335,596	117.48	157	66
Pennsylvania	867	765	210	2,154	1,823,688	146.38	0	202
Puerto Rico	161	53	23	375	135,499	65.92	19	55
Rhode Island	88	69	25	182	106,529	107.67	25	23
South Carolina	247	227	61	885	238,869	93.83	50	54
South Dakota	17	15	3	39	19,128	109.53	8	18
Tennessee	311	262	85	859	323,996	87.02	15	77
Texas	667	422	110	904	634,462	126.91	0	288
Utah	75	65	24	133	121,853	129.68	10	30
Vermont	35	30	7	70	42,691	107.42	4	14
Virginia	225	210	57	577	239,521	108.17	14	96
Virgin Islands	5	4	2	8	6,528	87.01	30	2
Washington	263	250	91	614	525,967	130.68	147	95
West Virginia	134	123	35	180	233,902	129.58	0	33
Wisconsin	319	311	123	762	335,121	136.62	0	87
Wyoming	50	29	9	48	61,407	136.56	45	17
TOTAL	**13,715**	**11,650**	**4,177**	**30,293**	**$20,357,827**	**$119.34**	**$7,828**	**4,834**

(p.) Preliminary. (1) Claimants whose base-period earnings or whose employment — covered by the unemployment insurance program — was sufficient to make them eligible for unemployment insurance benefits as provided by state law. (2) Based on number of first payments. (3) Based on final payments. Some claimants shown, therefore, actually experienced their final week of compensable unemployment toward the end of the previous calendar year but received their final payments in the current calendar year. Similarly, some claimants who served their last week of compensable unemployment toward the end of the current calendar year did not receive their final payment in this calendar year and hence are not shown. A final week of compensable unemployment in a benefit year results in the exhaustion of benefit rights for the benefit year. Claimants who exhaust their benefit rights in one benefit year may be entitled to further benefits in the following benefit year. (4) Excludes intrastate transitional claims to reflect more nearly instances of new unemployment. Includes claims filed by interstate claimants in the Virgin Islands. (5) Adjusted for voided benefit checks and transfers under interstate combined wage plan. (6) Sum of balance in state clearing accounts, benefit payment accounts, and unemployment trust fund accounts in the U.S. Treasury.

Jobs: Job Openings to 1990 and Current Earnings

Source: Bureau of Labor Statistics, U.S. Labor Department. For more detailed information on job categories, see the Occupational Outlook Handbook, 1982-83 Edition.

Occupation	Est. no. of Jobs, 1981 (000)	% Change 1980-90 (est.)	Median Earnings[3] (dollars)
Industrial			
Assemblers	1,145	19-31	236
Blue-collar worker supv.	1,790	16-25	394
Compositors	128[1]	−2 to −10	394
Machine tool oper.	1,020[3]	18-21	274
Machinist, all-round	557	16-29	356
Photographic process workers	85	6-16	230
Printing press oper.	163	9-17	320
Tool-and-die makers	170	8-24	433
Welders	709	22-37	334
Office			
Accountants	1,096	25-34	379
Bank officers, mgrs.	680	26-33	411
Bank tellers	558	25-29	189
Bookkeepers	1,922	15-24	227
Cashiers	1,621	28-36	168
Collection workers	90	22-34	233
Computer operating pers.	551	22-30	260
Computer programmers	357	49-60	422
Computer systems analysts	209	68-80	519
Insurance claim reps.	186	39-43	270
Lawyers	548	25-39	546
Librarians	276	3-5	320
Library assistants	149	3-4	203
Personnel & labor relations	432	15-22	402
Postal clerks	263	−29	400
Purchasing agents	260	16-24	390
Receptionists	660	22-31	200
Secretaries	3,587	28-37	229
Stenographers	72	−2 to −8	275
Telephone operators	301	4-15	240
Typists	1,011	18-25	213
Service Occupations			
Barbers	106	7-22	327[4]
Bartenders	309	19-26	195
Correction officers	103[1]	47-49	313[5]
Cooks and chefs	1,360	22-28	171
Cosmetologists	564	14-29	179
Firefighters	210	17-19	362
Food counter workers	460	48	141
Guards	593	23-24	232
Meatcutters	173	11-18	316
Police officers	503	17-19	363
Waiters and waitresses	1,442	21-28	150
Educational and related occupations			
K-6 teachers	1,389	18-19	322
Second. school teach.	1,213	−14	351
Coll., univ. faculty	691	−9	444
Sales occupations			
Advertising workers	126	NA	334
Auto. sales workers	157[1]	26-36	179
Real estate agents, brokers	546	34-46	326
Retail trade sales workers	2,380	19-27	178
Construction occupations			
Carpenters	1,082[2]	18-27	325
Constr. laborers	768[2]	NA	250
Electricians (constrs.)	628[2]	20-28	419
Painters	473[2]	14-25	271
Plumbers, pipefitters	482[2]	20-28	404
Roofers	133[2]	15-24	267
Transportation occupations			
Airplane mechanics	119	15-22	427
Airplane pilots	80	15-23	530
Airline reser. agts.	86[1]	0-7	339[42]
Flight attendants	56[1]	15-22	365[4]
Busdrivers (local)	355	27-29	298
Truckdrivers (local)	1,843	23-31	314
Truckdrivers (long-dist.)	575	23-31	517
Scientific and technical occupations			
Aerospace engineers	68[1]	43-52	NA
Chemical engineers	65	23-32	575
Chemists	134	18-24	467
Civil engineers	183	26-31	505
Drafters	332	20-39	343
Electrical engineers	370	35-47	549
Industrial engineers	231	26-38	530
Mathematicians	40[1]	11-14	508[6]
Mechanical engineers	247	29-41	540
Mechanics and repairers			
Appliance repairers	77[1]	16-29	385[7]
Automobile mechanics	1,013	24-33	285
Bus. machine operators	73	60-74	327
Computer serv. technicians	97	93-112	395
Indust. machinery repairers	507[1]	17-26	334[7]
Shoe repairers	16[1]	12-17	200[4]
Telephone, PBX installers and repairers	318	15-30	412
TV, radio serv. technicians	83[1]	31-43	336
Health and medical occupations			
Dentists	127	23	352
Dental assistants	139	38-42	183
Dental hygienists	54	67	351
Dietitians	62	38-46	291
Health serv. administrators	216	43-53	431
Medical laboratory workers	205[1]	35-43	304[8]
Nurses, registered	1,311	40-47	332
Nurses, licensed practical	395	42	227
Operating room technicians	31.5[1]	39-45	
Pharmacists	147	10-20	463
Physical therapists	244	51-59	305
Physicians, osteopaths	436	32	501
Radiologic technologists	102	36-43	290
Veterinarians	36[1]	31-43	656[5]
Social scientists			
Economists	157	26-32	536
Political scientists	15[1]	14	413[9]
Psychologists	115	22-27	394
Sociologists	21[1]	6-8	500[10]
Social service occupations			
School counselors	53[1]	0	396
Social workers	383	20-24	309
Design occupations			
Architects	91	33-41	428
Interior designers	35[1]	25	(11)
Communications occupations			
Newspaper reporters	57[1]	22-32	351
Public relations workers	121	18-26	402

(1) 1980 estimate. (2) 1982 estimate. (3) Average median weekly earnings of wage and salary workers employed full-time, annual averages in 1981. (4) 1980 annual average based on reports in Occupational Outlook Handbook, 1982-83 edition. (5) 1980 average for federal government workers. (6) Average starting salary for Ph.D. holders in 1980. (7) 1980 average salary based on 35-hour week. (8) 1980 average salary for medical technologists working in hospitals, medical centers, and medical schools. (9) 1979-80 average salary for associate professors. (10) 1979 average salary for doctoral sociologists. (11) 1980 average salary ranged from $15,000 to $25,000 for moderately experienced workers.

Quality of Life in U.S. Metropolitan Areas: A Comparative Table

Source: For personal per capita income, *Survey of Current Business*, April 1984; for unemployment rate, Bureau of Labor Statistics; for projected growth in employment and in personal income, Chase Econometrics Regional Forecasting Service; for weather data, *Comparative Climatic Data for the United States Through 1982*, National Oceanic and Atmospheric Administration. Data given are for Standard Metropolitan Statistical Area (SMSAs) whenever possible; in all other cases, data given are for segment of SMSA for which data are available.

	Per capita personal income 1982	% Job-less April 1984[P]	Projected annual % growth in jobs 1979-1993	Projected annual % growth in income 1979-1993	Mean no. of days[4] clr.— cldy.	Mean no. of days temp. below 32°F	Normal daily max. temp. August[5] °F
Anaheim-Santa Ana Garden Gr., Cal.	$13,927	4.3	3.1	3.5	NA	NA	NA
Atlanta, Ga.	11,590	4.8	2.6	3.4	108—149	58	86.4
Baltimore, Md.	11,560	5.9	1.0	2.2	107—149	99	85.1
Birmingham, Ala.	9,941	10.1	1.0	1.6	99—155	60	89.7
Boston-Lowell-Brockton Lawrence-Haverhill, Mass.-N.H.	13,087	4.3[1]	1.7	2.7	100—160	99	79.3
Bridgeport-Stamford-Norwalk-Danbury, Ct.	16,878	4.8[2]	1.6	2.5	103—160	135	80.4
Buffalo, N.Y.	11,160	8.5	—	1.0	55—208	132	77.6
Chicago, Ill.	13,069	8.7	0.6	1.6	86—173	99	82.3
Cincinnati, Oh., Ky., Ind.	11,224	NA	0.6	1.6	NA	125	85.8
Cleveland, Oh.	12,757	9.3	0.2	1.1	68—199	121	80.4
Columbus, Oh.	10,629	7.8	1.5	2.3	73—186	121	83.7
Dallas-Ft. Worth, Tex.	13,846	3.9	2.7	3.6	138—132	41	96.1
Dayton, Oh.	11,579	8.4	3.8	1.4	80—184	118	83.4
Denver-Boulder, Col.	13,964	4.1	2.5	3.2	117—120	157	85.8
Detroit, Mich.	12,092	NA	0.2	1.1	80—177	139	81.6-82.0
Ft. Lauderdale-Hollywood, Fla.	13,091	4.6	2.9	4.1	NA	NA	NA
Hartford-New Britain-Bristol, Ct.	13,416	3.9	1.6	2.5	81—175	136	81.9
Honolulu, Ha.	12,130	4.7	1.8	2.4	86—100	0	87.4
Houston, Tex.	14,128	7.3	2.3	3.2	97—157	24	94.3
Indianapolis,Ind.	11,226	7.9	1.7	1.8	90—177	121	84.0
Kansas City, Mo.-Kan.	10,994	6.1	0.7	1.9	120—154	109	88.7
Los Angeles-Long Beach, Cal.	13,080	7.3	1.4	2.6	185—74	0	75.8-84.0
Louisville, Ky.-Ind.	10,579	NA	3.6	1.4	93—169	92	86.8
Memphis, Tenn.-Ark.-Miss.	9,968	7.5	0.9	2.1	120—149	58	90.6
Miami, Fla.	11,717	6.7	2.2	3.4	74—117	0	89.9
Milwaukee, Wis.	12,597	6.6	0.7	1.6	94—172	144	79.7
Minneapolis-St. Paul, Minn.-Wis.	12,811	4.7	1.5	2.5	99—165	156	80.8
Nashville-Davidson, Tenn.	10,229	5.7	1.6	2.6	103—157	78	89.2
Newark, N.J.	13,671	6.1	0.9	1.8	96—158	87	83.7
New Orleans, La.	11,680	7.8	1.3	2.8	108—139	13	90.6
New York, N.Y.-N.J.	12,874	7.1	1.1	2.1	107—133	81	82.5
Philadelphia, Pa.-N.J.	11,946	6.7	0.9	1.9	93—161	99	84.8
Phoenix, Ariz.	11,086	3.9	2.9	3.6	213—71	10	102.2
Pittsburgh, Pa.	11,762	11.3	—	1.4	59—203	124	80.9
Portland, Ore.-Wash.	11,793	8.3	0.9	2.5	69—227	44	78.1
Providence-Warwick-Pawtucket, R.I.	10,748	6.8	0.9	1.9	101—161	121	79.8
Riverside-San Bernadino-Ontario, Cal.	10,092	8.7	2.9	4.0	NA	NA	NA
Rochester, N.Y.	12,463	5.9	0.7	1.7	61—196	135	80.1
Sacramento, Cal.	11,176	8.4	2.4	3.2	191—101	17	91.3
St. Louis, Mo.-Ill.	12,338	8.8	0.8	1.8	105—160	105	87.2
Salt Lake City-Ogden, Ut.	9,670	6.1	1.7	2.6	127—135	128	90.2
San Antonio, Tex.	10,131	5.1	3.1	3.8	107—141	23	95.9
San Diego, Cal.	11,638	6.0	3.2	3.5	147—100	0	77.3
San Francisco-Oakland, Cal.	17,131	6.2	1.4	2.3	162—104	0	68.2
San Jose, Cal.	14,998	5.0	3.0	3.6	NA	NA	NA
Seattle-Everett, Wash.	13,239	8.4	1.5	3.0	71—201	16	74
Tampa-St. Petersburg, Fla.	10,675	5.1	3.2	3.9	97—126	4	90.4
Washington D.C.-Md.-Va.	14,960	4.0	1.5	2.2	100—161	117	86

(1) Boston only; (2) Bridgeport only; (3) Hartford only; (4) Daylight only; clear = 0 to 0.3 sky cover, cloudy = 0.8 to complete sky cover; (5) 1941-1970. P = preliminary

Personal Computers

If the last two decades of the 20th century are to be called the age of technology, then nothing in this "high tech" world will affect the average family more than the personal computer. Computers are now in about 6.3 million homes, less than 6 percent of all households, but it is estimated that most homes will have some type of computer by the year 2000. Sales of personal computers reached $2.4 billion in 1983 and are expected to climb to $7 billion by 1988. However, the expected boom in home computers failed to materialize in 1984. Sales of home computers priced below $1,000 fell some 30% from 1983 levels. Nevertheless, one clear sign of the industry's growth is the more than 75 magazines presently available for computerphiles. Some provide general information while others cater to special features of selected hardware and/or software. In addition, the number of books concerning microcomputers or related topics has doubled in the past two years to over 3,500 as of early 1984.

Many who initially purchased computers to play video games, are now buying more expensive equipment as they have come to rely on their equipment to perform more sophisticated tasks, and to insure that their children are not left behind by the electronic revolution. Some are spending as much as $3,000 for their computer, peripheral devices, and software. Many are attending computer-club meetings, and spending as much as $1,200 to send their kids to a computer camp for 2 weeks.

Most youngsters will get their introduction to computers through their school or library. School systems throughout the nation are investing hundreds of thousands of dollars for computer equipment. Thousands of teachers are receiving instruction in computer usage, and curriculums are undergoing major revisions, with some schools imposing a requirement of "computer literacy" for graduation. According to the National Center for Education Statistics, one third of all public elementary and high schools have one or more microcomputers or terminals available to their students. More then 4.5 million youngsters, mostly high school students, used computers in public schools during the 1982-83 academic year.

Some educators and social activists have voiced their concern about a widening gap in computer literacy between more affluent suburban school districts and poorer urban ones. Some have stated that federal cutbacks in aid to education have added to this discrepancy. It is argued that wealthier school districts will find the means to purchase the necessary technological educational equipment, while less affluent school districts will not, therefore perpetuating the economic status quo.

Although it is too early to draw definitive conclusions, most educators agree that computers help students with their schoolwork. Software programs offer a variety of subjects and skills, using a variety of teaching techniques. Computers can be especially helpful for slow learners who have problems with subjects that require memorization, since drill and practice are the most common types of computer exercises. Studies show that a student's attention span increases when at a computer. In addition, computers teach users how to make decisions and to think logically.

The rapid development and commercialization of the computer has caused educators, sociologists, and psychologists to become concerned with the possible adverse impact on some children. Questions being investigated about the social and emotional effects of computerization in the home and schools are strikingly similar to those raised in response to the influence of television. Studies, just beginning to be undertaken, will examine the influence of computers on child development, as well as on the quality of family life.

Industry Growing Pains

The industry began facing serious financial difficulties toward the end of 1983. Oversupply and severe price competition caused many of the more than 150 companies involved to incur heavy losses. This was especially true for those companies selling lower-priced models. Texas Instruments and Timex Corp. stopped manufacturing PC's and sold off their inventory for as little as $49. Another PC leader, the Osborne Computer Corp., declared bankruptcy.

It was generally accepted that the computer manufacturers themselves were to blame for the poor sales. The industry became so absorbed in building faster and cheaper machines that they failed to communicate to the public the reason they should have a PC in their home.

In contrast, those machines costing $2,500 and up continued to sell well. Their consumer base, office workers and professionals, seemed to know exactly how they wanted to use their PC.

Some experts are predicting that by the end of the decade there will be only 3 or 4 major suppliers in the home computer market, and less than 15 majors in the office desk-top area, with IBM dominating both markets.

Smaller Computers

The market for the battery-powered "lap computer" showed signs of growth in 1984. The computers, which are small enough to slip into a briefcase and powerful enough to communicate with the home office, proved popular with traveling salespeople, executives, and journalists. Some 240,00 were sold in 1984. That number was expected to double in 1985, and by 1988, shipments of one million units are projected.

Software Publishing

In 1983, sales of personal computer software—the basic product for most software publishers—amounted to about one billion dollars, as software became one of the fastest moving segments of the computer industry, with an estimated annual growth rate of 50%.

The major categories of published microcomputer software are: home entertainment, consisting of arcade-style games and more intellectually challenging titles; educational, for home and school, with an emphasis on learning values and "how to" applications; home management, including accounting and word processing; single-application business, with separate programs for graphics, financial analysis, data management, and others; and operating environments and integrated software, which integrate a series of related applications within one large program.

Leading Uses of Home Computers

Source: Gallup Organization

The percentage of home-computer owners surveyed who said that they used their computer for a particular task (owners were able to give multiple responses).

Use	Percent	Use	Percent
Video games	51	Word-processing	18
Business or office homework	46	Mailing lists	16
Child's learning tool	46	Information retrieval[1]	14
Adult's learning tool	42	Appointment calendar	9
Balancing checkbook or budget	37	Storing recipes	9
Business-in-home uses	27	Calorie counting	4

(1) Includes information on investing, travel and account balances, as well as paying bills by phone.

Video Cassette Recorders

Video Cassette Recorders (VCR's), a technology originated in the U.S. in 1961 but today dominated by Japan, continued to change the home entertainment habits of millions of Americans in 1984. It was estimated that VCR's would be in some 15 million homes by the end of 1984. By 1987, one in three U.S. households was expected to have one. Worldwide sales were expected to reach 100 million in 1986.

A major reason for the VCR boom was the steady reduction in the price of the portable recording machines—from more than $1,000 a few years ago to as low as $250 today. In 1984, there were about 15,000 video stores, as well as hundreds of grocery, drug, and other retail stores offering tapes in the U.S. Another boom to the VCR industry was a

January 1984 Supreme Court decision which established that federal copyright laws were not violated by the taping of television broadcasts at home for later viewing. This practice, called "time shifting" in the industry, has been one of the strongest selling points for VCR's.

Every facet of the entertainment industry has been affected by the versatile little machines, and a whole new industry—the sales and rental of prerecorded tapes—has become a $1 billion per year business. The best-selling cassettes were movies, which accounted for about 67% of the market, followed by "adult" entertainment (14%), instruction or informational tapes (7%), and music (4%). It was expected that by 1988, music videos would account for a quarter of the home video market.

Most-Recorded TV Programs

Source: A. C. Nielson Co.
(August 1984)

1. All My Children
2. General Hospital
3. Days of Our Lives
4. As the World Turns
5. Guiding Light

6. One Life to Live
7. Hill Street Blues
8. Dallas
9. The Young and the Restless
10. (tie) Dynasty; Cheers

Top-Selling Cassettes

Source: Billboard Magazine
(August 1984)

Title (Weeks on list)

1. Terms of Endearment (7)
2. Jane Fonda's Workout (116)
3. Raiders of the Lost Ark (33)
4. Cartoon Classics Limited Gold Edition Mickey (6)
5. Scarface (9)
6. Making Michael Jackson's Thriller (31)
7. Cartoon Classics Limited Gold Edition Donald (6)
8. Money Hunt (3)
9. Cartoon Classics Limited Gold Edition Minnie (5)
10. Vertigo (1)

Title (Weeks on list)

11. The Right Stuff (5)
12. Cartoon Classics Limited Gold Edition Disney's Best (4)
13. Culture Club: A Kiss Across the Ocean (3)
14. Star Trek II: The Wrath of Khan (74)
15. Let's Break: A Visual Guide to Break Dancing (6)
16. Silkwood (8)
17. Cartoon Classics Limited Gold Edition Pluto (5)
18. Children of the Corn (2)
19. Trading Places (20)
20. Jane Fonda's Workout Challenge (20)

All-Time Best Selling Cassettes

Source: Video Week
(August 1984)

Title (Units sold)

1. Raiders of the Lost Ark (600,000)
2. Making Michael Jackson's Thriller (450,000)
3. Jane Fonda's Workout (420,000)
4. Flashdance (305,000)
5. An Officer and a Gentleman (220,000)

Title (Units sold)

6. Terms of Endearment (205,000)
7. Star Trek II: The Wrath of Khan (200,000)
8. Trading Places (175,000)
9. Staying Alive (170,000)
10. Star Wars (150,000)

Cable Television

After a decade of red ink, the cable television industry saw three of its services become profitable, while several others hovered near the break-even point. The three moneymakers were Nickelodeon, MTV (Music Television), and CBN Cable Network. Two reasons cited for this progress were growth in the number of cable viewers and the desire of advertising agencies to reach those viewers.

Ten years ago, cable television was envisioned as a technological wonderland that would have 108 channels. It was to provide two-way services, banking, tele-shopping, home security, energy monitoring, video games, and news and sports scores on demand. Most of these high-tech services have been delayed as the immense cost of building the cable systems, especially in the big cities, has placed a heavy burden on the operators. A shortage of programming has made it likely that there will not be more than 40 channels in the forseeable future.

As of mid-1984, cable was in nearly 40 percent of the more than 80 million American TV homes. The average household, however, took only 1.3 pay services, below the average of 2 that the industry had hoped for. Worse, some 40 percent of subscribers disconnected pay services each year. Only half of the disconnections could be explained by a change of address or failure to pay the bill. This indicated that many subscribers were unsatisfied with what was being

offered on pay television.

Many cable viewers expressed disappointment that the same movies were repeated over and over, and that some channels interested relatively few viewers.

Nevertheless, A.C. Nielson reported that American television viewing reached an all-time high in 1983. The average American household watched TV, or at least had the TV on, seven hours and two minutes a day, an increase of 14 minutes over 1982. The average number of households watching TV at any given minute was 33.9 percent in homes with pay-cable, 28.1 percent in homes with basic cable, and 27.2 percent in non-cable households.

The year's prime-time viewing through November 1983 saw 78 percent watching network stations (down from 91 percent a decade ago), 12 percent watching the independents, 6 percent watching pay cable (HBO, Showtime), 4 percent watching cable originated stations, 4 percent watching PBS, and 3 percent watching superstations.

A survey by the National Telemedia Council asking viewers what they would like to see more of on television brought the following response:

Comedy	51.9%	Sports	17.2%
Movies	51.3%	News	9.1%
Drama	33.4%	Religion	6.9%
Music	33.1%		

Computer Language

The following is a glossary of key words or terms that consumers should learn if they are considering buying their own personal computer.

Access: the ability to get information or use a computer or program.

Acoustic coupler: a device that allows other electronic devices to communicate by making, and also listening to sounds made over an ordinary telephone. See **Modem.**

Address: designates the location of an item of information stored in the computer's memory.

ASCII: acronym for American Standard Code for Information Interchange. A 7-bit code used to represent alphanumeric characters.

Assembly language: a machine oriented language in which mnemonics are used to represent each machine-language instruction. Each CPU has its own specific assembly language.

BASIC: a popular computer language that is used by many small and personal computer systems. It means— Beginner's All-purpose Symbolic Instruction Code.

Baud rate: serial-data transmission speed. Originally a telegraph term, expressed in terms of the number of events that take place in one second. One baud is equal to one bit per second.

Binary: refers to the base-2 number system in which the only allowable digits are 0 and 1.

Bit: short for binary digit, the smallest unit of information stored in a computer. It always has the binary value of "O" or "1."

Boot, Booting, or Bootstrap: the program, or set of commands, that gets the computer to move into action.

Bubble memory: a relatively new type of computer memory, it uses tiny magnetic "pockets" or "bubbles" to store data.

Buffer: a place to put information before further processing.

Bug: a mistake that occurs in a program within a computer or in the unit's electrical system. When a mistake is found and corrected, it's called debugging.

Bundling: the practice of selling the hardware and software as a single package.

Byte: an 8-bit sequence of binary digits. Each byte corresponds to 1 character of data, representing a single letter, number, or symbol. Bytes are the most common unit for measuring computer and disk storage capacity.

Cassette: units used to store information for mini and microcomputers. They are similar in size and shape to audio recording cassettes.

Compiler: a program that translates a high-level language, such as BASIC, into machine language.

CPU: the Central Processing Unit within the computer that executes the instructions that the user gives the system.

Chip: a term for the integrated circuit and its package which contains coded signals.

Cursor: the symbol on the computer monitor that marks the place where the operator is working.

Database: a large amount of data stored in a well organized format. A database management system is a program that allows access to the information.

Dedicated: designed for a single use.

Density: the amount of data that can be stored on one sector of one track of a disk.

Disk: a revolving plate on which information and programs are stored. See also **Floppy disk.**

Disk Drive: a peripheral machine that stores information on disks.

Documentation: user or operator instructions that come with some hardware and software that tells how to use the material.

DOS: "Disk Operating System," a collection of programs designed to facilitate the use of a disk drive and floppy disk.

Error Message: a statement by the computer indicating that the user has done something incorrectly.

File: a logical group of pieces of information labelled by a specific name; considered a single unit by the computer. It is used commonly on microcomputers and word processors.

Floppy disk: a small inexpensive disk used to record and store information. It must be used in conjunction with a disk drive.

Format: the arrangement by which information is stored.

Graphics: the pictures or illustrations in the computer program.

Hardware: the physical apparatus or "nuts and bolts" that make up a computer. It includes silicon chips, transformers, boards and wires, etc. Also used to describe various pieces of equipment including the CPU, printer, modem, CRT (cathode ray tube), etc.

Hexadecimal: refers to the base-16 number system. Machine language programs are often written in hexadecimal notation.

Interface: the hardware or software necessary to connect one device or system to another.

K: abbreviation for Kilo-byte used to denote 1,024 units of stored matter.

Language: any set of compiled, unified, or related commands or instructions that are acceptable to a computer.

Load: the actual operation of putting information and data into the computer or memory.

Menu: programs, functions or other choices displayed on the monitor for user selection.

Memory: the internal storage of information.

Microcomputer: a small, complete computer system. Most personal computers now in use are microcomputers.

Minicomputer: an intermediate computer system sized between the very small microcomputer and the large computer.

Modem: short for modulating-demodulating. An acoustic or non-acoustic coupler, used either with a telephone or on a direct-line, for transmitting information from one computer to another.

Monitor: the screen on which the material from the computer appears and can be read. Looks like a small TV screen but produces more vivid characters than a home TV.

Port: a channel through which data is transferred to and from the CPU.

Printer: a computer output device that, when attached to a computer, will produce printed copy on paper.

Program: coded instructions telling a computer how to perform a specific function.

RAM: abbreviation for random-access-memory. A type of microchip, its patterns can be changed by the user and the information it generates stored on tape, disk, or in printed form.

ROM: abbreviation for read-only-memory. A type of microchip that is different from RAM in that it cannot be altered by the user.

Software: the programs, or sets of instructions, procedural rules, and, in some cases, documentation that make the computer function.

Terminal: a work station away from the main computer that allows several people to have access to a single, main computer.

User friendly: hardware or software designed to help people become familiar with their computer. Usually includes simple and easy to follow instructions.

Word: number of bits treated as a single unit by the CPU. In an 8-bit machine, the word length is 8 bits; in a 16-bit machine, it is 16 bits.

Word Processor: a text–editing program or system that allows electronic writing and correcting of articles, books, etc.

Social Security Programs: After the Paychecks Stop

Source: Social Security Administration, U.S. Department of Health and Human Services

Old-Age, Survivors, and Disability Insurance; Medicare; Supplemental Security Income

New Legislation

On April 20, 1983, President Reagan signed into law the Social Security Amendments of 1983 (Public Law 98-21). Among the changes brought about by the new legislation are provisions to:

(1) Cover the President and Vice President, members of Congress, Federal judges, most Federal political appointees, all newly hired Federal civilian employees, and all employees of nonprofit organizations, effective January 1984. (Note: Under the Deficit Reduction Act of 1984 (Public Law 98-369), churches and church-controlled organizations are permitted to make an irrevocable election to have services performed by its employees excluded from employment for Social Secruity purposes. Employees of churches and organizations which make such an election will be treated as self-employed persons (for Social Security purposes.)

(2) Delay the July 1983 cost-of-living adjustment (COLA) to January 1984 and shift future COLA's to a calendar-year basis.

(3) Include up to 50 percent of Social Security benefits in the taxable income of higher-income beneficiaries—those whose incomes, including non-taxable interest income and half of their Social Security benefits exceed $25,000 if they are single and $32,000 if they are married and file a joint return.

(4) Accelerate implementation of scheduled increases in the Social Security tax rates for employees and employers and increase the rates for the self-employed to equal the combined employee/employer rate. The higher rates for the self-employed will be partially offset by income tax credits.

(5) Gradually increase the age of eligibility for full benefits from age 65 to age 66 in 2009 and to age 67 in 2027. (These changes affect persons born in 1938 and after.)

(6) Eliminate windfall benefits for certain workers with pensions from noncovered employment and gradually increase the delayed retirement credit—payable to persons who postpone retirement past the full-benefit retirement age (now 65)—from the current 3 percent to 8 percent a year for workers age 65 after 2007.

(7) Change the method by which Medicare makes payments to hospitals. For hospital fiscal years beginning on or after October 1, 1983, such facilities will no longer be reimbursed on a reasonable-cost basis for their inpatient operating costs but will be paid a prospectively determined amount per discharge using diagnosis-related groups.

Old-Age, Survivors, and Disability Insurance

Old-Age, Survivors, and Disability Insurance covers almost all jobs in which people work for wages or salaries, as well as most work of self-employed persons.

Old-Age, Survivors, and Disability Insurance is paid for by a tax on earnings (for 1984, up to $37,800; the taxable earnings base is now subject to automatic adjustment to reflect increases in average wages). The employed worker and his or her employer share the tax equally. (Cash tips count as covered wages if they amount to $20 or more in a month from one place of employment. The worker reports them to the employer, who includes them in the Social Security tax reports. The worker pays contributions on the full amount of the tips and the employer pays Social Security taxes on an amount that, when added to the employee's wages, equals the minimum wage).

The employer deducts the tax each payday and sends it, with an equal amount (the employer's share), to the District Director of Internal Revenue. The collected taxes are deposited in the Federal Old-Age and Survivors Insurance Trust Fund, the Federal Disability Insurance Trust Fund, and the Federal Hospital Insurance Trust Fund; they can be used only to pay benefits, the cost of rehabilitation services, and administrative expenses.

Social Security Benefits

Social Security benefits are based on a worker's primary insurance amount (PIA), which is related by law to the average indexed monthly earnings (AIME) on which social security contributions have been paid. The full PIA is payable to a retired worker who becomes entitled to benefits at age 65 and to an entitled disabled worker at any age. Spouses and children of retired or disabled workers and survivors of deceased workers receive set proportions of the PIA subject to a family maximum amount. The PIA is calculated by applying varying percentages to succeeding parts of the AIME. The formula is adjusted annually to reflect changes in average annual wages in the economy.

Automatic increases in Social Security benefits are initiated whenever the Consumer Price Index (CPI) of the Bureau of Labor Statistics for the first calendar quarter of a year exceeds by at least 3 percent the CPI for the base quarter, which is either the first calendar quarter of the preceding year or the quarter in which an increase was legislated by Congress. Beginning with the adjustment paid in January 1985, the period for measuring the increase in the CPI will be shifted to a third-quarter measure. The size of the benefit increase is determined by the actual percentage rise of the CPI between the quarters measured. However, beginning with the January 1985 adjustment, if the balance in the combined OASDI trust funds falls below a specified level, the automatic benefit increase will be based on the lesser of the increase in the CPI or the increase in average wages. If one or more benefit increases are based on the increase in average wages, a "catch up" benefit increase will be made in a subsequent year when the combined trust fund balance reaches a higher specified level.

As noted above, the increase originally scheduled for July 1983 was deferred to January 1984.

Average monthly benefits payable to retired workers rose to $442.00 in April 1984. The average amount for disabled workers in that month was $455.00.

Amount of Work Required

To qualify for benefits, the worker must have worked in covered employment long enough to become insured. Just how long depends on when the worker reaches age 62 or, if earlier, when he or she dies or becomes disabled.

A person is fully insured if he or she has one quarter of coverage for every year after 1950 (or year age 21 is reached, if later) up to but not including the year in which the worker reaches age 62, dies, or becomes disabled. In 1984, a person earns one quarter of coverage for each $390 of annual earnings in covered employment, up to a maximum of 4 quarters per year.

The law permits special monthly payments under the Social Security program to certain persons aged 72 and over who are not eligible for regular social security benefits since they had little or no opportunity to earn social security work credits during their working lifetime.

To get disability benefits, in addition to being fully insured, the worker must also have credit for 5 out of 10 years before he or she becomes disabled. A disabled blind worker need meet only the fully insured requirement. Persons disabled before age 31 can qualify with a briefer period of coverage. Certain survivor benefits are payable if the deceased worker had 6 quarters of coverage in the 13 quarters preceding death.

Work credit for survivors and disability benefits

Born after 1929, die or become disabled at age	Born before 1930, die or become disabled before age 62 in	Years needed
32		2½
34		3
36		3½
38		4
40		4½
42		5
44		5½

(continued)

45.	5¾
46.	6
48.	6½
50.	1979 7
52.	1981 . . . . 7½
54.	1983 8
56.	1985 . . . . 8½
58.	1987 9
60.	1989 . . . . 9½
62 or older	1991 or later. . . 10

Work Years Required

The following table shows the number of work years required to be fully insured for Old-Age or Survivors benefits, according to the year worker reaches retirement age or dies.

Work credit for retirement benefits

If you reach 62 in	Years you need	If you reach 62 in	Years you need
1974	6*	1979	7
1975	6	1981	7½
1976	6¼	1983	8
1977	6½	1987	9
1978	6¾	1991 or later.	10

*For 1974 a woman needs only 5¾ years.

Contribution and benefit base

Calendar year	Base
1978	$17,700
1979	22,900
1980	25,900
1981	29,700
1982	32,400
1983	35,700
1984	37,800

Tax-rate schedule
[Percent of covered earnings]

Year	Total Employees and employers, each	OASDI	HI
1979-80	6.13	5.08	1.05
1981	6.65	5.35	1.30
1982-83	6.70	5.40	1.30
1984	7.00	5.70	1.30
1985	7.05	5.70	1.35
1986-87	7.15	5.70	1.45
1988-89	7.51	6.06	1.45
1990 and after.	7.65	6.20	1.45
	Self-employed		
1979-80	8.10	7.05	1.05
1981	9.30	8.00	1.30
1982-83	9.35	8.05	1.30
1984	14.00	11.40	2.60
1985	14.10	11.40	2.70
1986-87	14.30	11.40	2.90
1988-89	15.02	12.12	2.90
1990 and after.	15.30	12.40	2.90

What Aged Workers Get

When a person has enough work in covered employment and reaches retirement age (currently 65 for full benefit, 62 for reduced benefit), he or she may retire and get monthly old-age benefits. The 1983 amendments provided that the age at which unreduced benefits are payable will be increased gradually from 65 to 67 over a 21-year period beginning with workers age 62 in the year 2000. (Reduced benefits will still be available as early as age 62.) If a person aged 65 or older continues to work and has earnings of more than $6,960 in 1984, $1 in benefits will be withheld for every $2 above $6,960. The annual exempt amount for people under age 65 is $5,160 in 1984. The annual exempt amount and the monthly test are raised automatically as the general earnings level rises. The eligible worker who is 70 receives the full benefit regardless of earnings. Beginning in 1990, benefits for persons who reach the normal retirement age will be reduced $1 for each $3 of excess earnings.

For workers who reach age 65 after 1981, the worker's benefit will be raised by 3% for each year for which the worker between 65 and 70 (72 before 1984) did not receive benefits because of earnings from work or because the worker had not applied for benefits. The delayed retirement credit is 1 percent a year for workers reaching age 65 before 1982. Under the 1983 amendments, the delayed retirement credit will gradually rise from the current 3% per year to 8% per year between the years 1990 and 2009.

Effective December 1983, the special benefit for persons aged 72 or over who do not meet the regular coverage requirements is $129.90 a month. Like the monthly benefits, these payments are subject to cost-of-living increases. The special payment is not made to persons on the public assistance or supplemental security income rolls.

Workers retiring before age 65 have their benefits permanently reduced by 5/9 of 1% for each month they receive benefits before age 65. Thus, workers entitled to benefits in the month they reach age 62 receive 80% of the PIA, while a worker retiring at age 65 receives a benefit equal to 100% of the PIA. The nearer to age 65 the worker is when he or she begins collecting a benefit, the larger the benefit will be.

Benefits for Worker's Spouse

The spouse of a worker who is getting Social Security retirement or disability payments may become entitled to a spouse's insurance benefit when he or she reaches 65 of one-half of the worker's PIA. Reduced spouse's benefits are available at age 62 (25/36 of 1% reduction for each month of entitlement before age 65). Benefits are also payable to the divorced spouse of an insured worker if he or she was married to the worker for at least 10 years.

Benefits for Children of Retired or Disabled Workers

If a retired or disabled worker has a child under 18 the child will get a benefit that is half of the worker's unreduced benefit, and so will the worker's spouse, even if he or she is under 62 if he or she is caring for an entitled child of the worker who is under 16 or who became disabled before age 22. Total benefits paid on a worker's earnings record are subject to a maximum and if the total paid to a family exceeds that maximum, the individual dependents' benefits are adjusted downward. (Total benefits paid to the family of a worker who retired in January 1984 at age 65 and who always had the maximum amount of earnings creditable under Social Security can be no higher than $1,232.10.)

When entitled children reach 18, their benefits will generally stop, except that a child disabled before 22 may get a benefit as long as his or her disability meets the definition in the law. Additionally, benefits will be paid to a child until age 19 if the child is in full-time attendance at an elementary or secondary school. Benefits to children age 18 to 22 who are attending post-secondary school are being phased out.

Benefits may now be paid to a grandchild or step-grandchild of a worker or of his or her spouse, in special circumstances.

OASDI	July 1984	July 1983	July 1982
Monthly beneficiaries, total (in thousands)	36,051	35,745	35,375
Aged 65 and over, total	25,754	25,301	24,626
Retired workers	19,223	18,829	18,244
Survivors and dependents	6,486	6,416	6,314
Special age-72 beneficiaries	44	55	68
Under age 65, total	10,297	10,444	10,749
Retired workers	2,421	2,301	2,197
Disabled workers	2,574	2,588	2,681
Survivors and dependents	5,303	5,555	5,871
Total monthly benefits (in millions)	$14,292	$13,482	$13,089

What Disabled Workers Get

If a worker becomes so severely disabled that he or she is unable to work, he or she may be eligible to receive a monthly disability benefit that is the same amount that would have been received for a retired-worker benefit if he or she were 65 at the start of the disability. When he or she reaches 65, the disability benefit becomes a retired-worker benefit.

Benefits generally like those provided for dependents of retired-worker beneficiaries may be paid to dependents of disabled beneficiaries.

Survivor Benefits

If an insured worker should die, one or more types of benefits may be payable to survivors.

1. A cash payment to cover burial expenses that amounts to $255. Payment is made only when there is a spouse who was living with the worker or a spouse or child eligible for immediate monthly survivor benefits.

2. If claiming benefits at 65, the surviving spouse will receive a benefit that is 100% of the deceased worker's PIA. The surviving spouse may choose to get the benefit as early as age 60, but the benefit is then reduced by 19/40 of 1% for each month it is paid before age 65. However, for those aged 62 and over whose spouses claimed their benefits before 65, the benefit is the reduced amount the worker would be getting if alive but not less than 82 1/2% of the worker's PIA.

Disabled widows and widowers may under certain circumstances qualify for benefits after attaining age 50 at the rate of 71.5% of the deceased worker's PIA. (Prior to the 1983 amendments, benefits for disabled widow(er)s age 50-59 were reduced depending upon age at entitlement.) The widow or widower must have become totally disabled before or within 7 years after the spouse's death, the last month in which he or she received mother's or father's insurance benefits, or the last month he or she previously received surviving spouse's benefits.

3. A benefit for each child until the child reaches 18. The monthly benefit of each child of a worker who has died is three-quarters of the amount the worker would have received if he or she had lived and drawn full retirement benefits. A child with a disability that began before age 22 may receive his or her benefit after that age. Also, a child may receive benefits until age 19 if he or she is in full-time attendance at an elementary or secondary school. Benefits to children age 18-22 who are attending post-secondary school are being phased out; no new entitlements have occurred since 1982.

4. A mother's or father's benefit for the widow(er), if children of the worker under 16 are in his or her care. The benefit is 75% of the PIA and he or she draws it until the youngest child reaches 16. Payments stop then even if the child's benefit continues. They may start again when he or she is 60 unless he or she is married. If he or she marries and the marriage is ended, he or she regains benefit rights. If he or she has a disabled child beneficiary aged 16 or over in care, benefits also continue. This benefit is also paid to the divorced spouse, if the marriage lasted for at least 10 years.

5. Dependent parents may be eligible for benefits, if they have been receiving at least half their support from the worker before his or her death, have reached age 62, and (except in certain circumstances) have not remarried since the worker's death. Each parent gets 75% of the worker's PIA; if only one parent survives the benefit is 82 1/2%.

Self-Employed

A self-employed person who has net earnings of $400 or more in a year must report such earnings for social security tax purposes. The person reports net returns from the business. Income from real estate, savings, dividends, loans, pensions or insurance policies may not be included unless they are part of the business.

A self-employed person who has net earnings of $400 or more in a year gets a quarter of coverage for each $390 (for 1984), up to a maximum of 4 quarters of coverage. If earnings are less than $400 in a year they do not count toward Social Security credits. The nonfarm self-employed person must make estimated payments of his or her social security taxes, on a quarterly basis, for 1983, if combined estimated income tax and social security tax amount to at least $300.

The nonfarm self-employed have the option of reporting their earnings as 2/3 of their gross income from self-employment but not more than $1,600 a year and not less than their actual net earnings. This option can be used only if actual net earnings from self-employment income is less than $1,600 and may be used only 5 times. Also, the self-employed person must have actual net earnings of $400 or more in 2 of the 3 taxable years immediately preceding the year in which he or she uses the option.

When a person has both taxable wages and earnings from self-employment, only as much of the self-employment income as will bring total earnings up to the current taxable maximum is subject to tax for social security purposes.

Farm Owners and Workers

Self-employed farmers whose gross annual earnings from farming are $2,400 or less may report 2/3 of their gross earnings instead of net earnings for social security purposes. Farmers whose gross income is over $2,400 and whose net earnings are less than $1,600 can report $1,600. Cash or crop shares received from a tenant or share farmer count if the owner participated materially in production or management. The self-employed farmer pays contributions at the same rate as other self-employed persons.

Agricultural employees. Earnings from farm work count toward benefits (1) if the employer pays $150 or more in cash during the year; or (2) if the employee works on 20 or more days for cash pay figured on a time basis. Under these rules a person gets credit for one calendar quarter for each $390 in cash pay in 1984 up to four quarters.

Foreign farm workers admitted to the United States on a temporary basis are not covered.

Household Workers

Anyone working as maid, cook, laundress, nursemaid, baby-sitter, chauffeur, gardener and at other household tasks in the house of another is covered by Social Security if he or she earns $50 or more in cash in a calendar quarter from any one employer. Room and board do not count, but carfare counts if paid in cash. The job does not have to be regular or fulltime. The employee should get a Social Security card at the social security office and show it to the employer.

The employer deducts the amount of the employee's social security tax from the worker's pay, adds an identical amount as the employer's social security tax and sends the total amount to the federal government, with the employee's social security number.

Medicare

Under Medicare, protection against the costs of hospital care is provided for Social Security and Railroad Retirement beneficiaries aged 65 and over and, for persons entitled for 24 months to receive a social security disability benefit, certain persons (and their dependents) with end-stage renal disease, and, on a voluntary basis with payment of a special premium, persons aged 65 and over not otherwise eligible for hospital benefits; all those eligible for hospital benefits may enroll for medical benefits and pay a monthly premium and so may persons aged 65 and over who are not eligible for hospital benefits.

Persons eligible for both hospital and medical insurance may choose to have their covered services provided through a Health Maintenance Organization.

Hospital insurance.—From October 1981 to September 1982, about $34.9 billion was withdrawn from the hospital insurance trust fund for hospital and related benefits.

As of January 1983, the hospital insurance program paid the cost of covered services for hospital and posthospital care as follows:

- Up to 90 days of hospital care during a benefit period (spell of illness) starting the first day that care as a bed-patient is received in a hospital or skilled-nursing facility and ending when the individual has not been a bed-patient for 60 consecutive days. For the first 60 days, the hospital insurance pays for all but the first $304 of expenses; for the 61st day to 90th day, the program pays all but $76 a day for covered services. In addition, each person has a 60-day lifetime reserve that can be used after the 90 days of hospital care in a benefit period are exhausted, and all but $152 a day of expenses during the reserve days are paid. Once used, the reserve days are not replaced. (Payment for care in a mental hospital is limited to 190 days.)

- Up to 100 days' care in a skilled-nursing facility (skilled-nursing home) in each benefit period. Hospital insurance pays for all covered services for the first 20 days and all but $38 daily for the next 80 days. At least 3 days' hospital stay must precede these services, and the skilled-nursing facility must be entered within 14 days after leaving the hospital. (The 1972 law permits more than 14 days in certain circumstances.)

- Unlimited visits by nurses or other health workers (not doctors) from a home health agency in the 365 days after release from a hospital or extended-care facility.

Medical insurance. Aged persons can receive benefits under this supplementary program only if they sign up for them and agree to a monthly premium ($12.20 beginning July 1982 and continuing through December 1983). The Federal Government pays the rest of the cost.

About 142 million bills were reimbursed under the medical insurance program from October 1981 to September 1982 for a total of $14.9 billion. As of September 1982, about 28.2 million persons were enrolled — 2.7 million of them disabled persons under age 65.

The medical insurance program pays 80% of the reasonable charges (after the first $75 in each calendar year) for the following services:

- Physicians' and surgeons' services, whether in the doctor's office, a clinic, or hospital or at home (but physician's charges for X-ray or clinical laboratory services for hospital bed-patients are paid in full and without meeting the deductible).
- Other medical and health services, such as diagnostic tests, surgical dressings and splints, and rental or purchase of medical equipment. Services of a physical therapist in independent practice, furnished in his office or the patient's home. A hospital or extended-care facility may provide covered outpatient physical therapy services under the medical insurance program to its patients who have exhausted their hospital insurance coverage.
- Physical therapy services furnished under the supervision of a practicing hospital, clinic, skilled nursing facility, or agency.
- Certain services by podiatrists.
- All outpatient services of a participating hospital (including diagnostic tests).
- Outpatient speech pathology services, under the same requirements as physical therapy.
- Services of licensed chiropractors who meet uniform standards, but only for treatment by means of manual manipulation of the spine and treatment of subluxation of the spine demonstrated by X-ray.
- Supplies related to colostomies are considered prosthetic devices and payable under the program.
- Home health services even without a hospital stay (up to 100 visits a year) are paid up to 100%.

To get medical insurance protection, persons approaching age 65 may enroll in the 7-month period that includes 3 months before the 65th birthday, the month of the birthday, and 3 months after the birthday, but if they wish coverage to begin in the month they reach 65 they must enroll in the 3 months **before** their birthday. Persons not enrolling within their first enrollment period may enroll later, during the first 3 months of each year but their premium is 10% higher for each 12-month period elapsed since they first could have enrolled.

The monthly premium is deducted from the cash benefit for persons receiving Social Security, Railroad Retirement, or Civil Service retirement benefits. Income from the medical premiums and the federal matching payments are put in a Supplementary Medical Insurance Trust Fund, from which benefits and administrative expenses are paid.

Medicare card. Persons qualifying for hospital insurance under Social Security receive a health insurance card similar to cards now used by Blue Cross and other health agencies. The card indicates whether the individual has taken out medical insurance protection. It is to be shown to the hospital, skilled-nursing facility, home health agency, doctor, or whoever provides the covered services.

Payments are made only in the 50 states, Puerto Rico, the Virgin Islands, Guam, and American Samoa, except that hospital services may be provided in border areas immediately outside the U.S. if comparable services are not accessible in the U.S. for a beneficiary who becomes ill or is injured in the U.S.

Supplemental Security Income

On Jan. 1, 1974, the Supplemental Security Income (SSI) program established by the 1972 Social Security Act amendments replaced the former federal grants to states for aid to the needy aged, blind, and disabled in the 50 states and the District of Columbia. The program provides both for federal payments based on uniform national standards and eligibility requirements and for state supplementary payments varying from state to state. The Social Security Administration administers the federal payments financed from general funds of the Treasury—and the state supplements as well, if the state elects to have its supplementary program federally administered. The states may supplement the federal payment for all recipients and must supplement it for persons otherwise adversely affected by the transition from the former public assistance programs. In April 1984, the number of persons receiving federal payments and federally administered state payments was 3,948,152 and the amount of these payments was $875 million.

The maximum federal SSI payment for an individual with no other countable income, living in his own household, was $314.00 in July 1984. For a couple it was $472.40.

Minimum and maximum monthly retired-worker benefits payable to individuals who retired at age 65[1]

Year of attainment of age 65[2]	Minimum benefit		Maximum benefit			
	Payable at the time of retirement	Payable effective December 1983	Payable at the time of retirement		Payable effective December 1983	
			Men[3]	Women	Men[3]	Women
1965 . . .	$44.00	$182.30	$131.70	135.90	$505.70	521.80
1970 . . .	64.00	182.30	189.80	196.40	560.40	580.10
1980 . . .	133.90	182.30	572.00	. . .	808.20	. . .
1983 . . .	[4]166.40	172.20	709.50	. . .	734.30	. . .

(1) Assumes retirement at beginning of year. (2) The final benefit amount payable after SMI premium or any other deductions is rounded to next lower $1 (if not already a multiple of $1). (3) Benefit for both men and women are shown in men's columns except where women's benefit appears separately. (4) Derived from transitional guarantee computation based on 1978 PIA table.

Examples of monthly cash benefit awards for selected beneficiary families with first eligibility in 1984, effective January 1984

Beneficiary Family	Career Earnings Level		
	Low Earnings ($6,968 in 1984)	Average Earnings ($16,019 in 1984)[1]	Maximum Earnings ($37,800 in 1984)
Primary Insurance amount (worker retiring at 65)	$361.00	$542.80	$703.00
Maximum family benefit (worker retiring at 65)	574.60	985.70	1,232.10
Disability maximum family benefit (worker disabled at 55)	549.90	814.00	1,048.90
Disabled worker: (worker disabled at 55)			
Worker alone	361.00	542.00	699.00
Worker, spouse, and 1 child	549.00	814.00	1,047.00
Retired worker claiming benefits at age 62:			
Worker alone[2]	289.00	434.00	559.00
Worker with spouse claiming benefits at—			
Age 65 or over	469.00	705.00	908.00
Age 62[2]	424.00	637.00	821.00
Widow or widower claiming benefits at—			
Age 65 or over[3]	361.00	542.00	703.00
Age 60	258.00	388.00	503.00
Disabled widow or widower claiming benefits at age 50-59[4]	258.00	388.00	503.00
1 surviving child	270.00	407.00	527.00
Widow or widower age 65 or over and 1 child	574.00	949.00	1,230.00
Widowed mother or father and 1 child	540.00	814.00	1,054.00
Widowed mother or father and 2 children	574.00	985.00	1,232.00

[1]Estimate. [2]Assumes maximum reduction. [3]A widow(er)'s benefit amount is limited to the amount the spouse would have been receiving if still living but not less than 82.5 percent of the PIA. [4]Effective January 1984, disabled widow(er)s claiming benefit at ages 50-59 will receive benefit equal to 71.5 percent of the PIA (based on 1983 Social Security Amendment provision).

Social Security Trust Funds

Old-Age and Survivors Insurance Trust Fund, 1940-83

[in millions]

Calendar year	Receipts Net contrib. inc., reimbursements from gen'l rev.	Net interest received	Cash benefit payments, rehabilitation services	Expenditures Transfers to Railroad Retirement acct.	Administrative expenses	Total assets at end of year
1940	$325	$43	$35	...	$26	$2,031
1950	2,667	257	961		61	13,721
1960	10,866	516	10,677	$318	203	20,324
1970	30,705	1,515	28,798	579	471	32,454
1980	103,996	1,845	105,082	1,442	1,154	22,823
1981	123,301	2,060	123,804	1,585	1,307	21,490
1982	124,354	845	138,806	1,793	1,519	22,088
1983	143,878	6,706	149,215	2,251	1,534	19,672
Cum., 1937-83	1,297,605	43,861	1,298,879	21,643	18,524	—

Disability Insurance Trust Fund, 1960-83

1960	$1,010	$53	$568	$ −5	$36	$2,289
1970	4,497	277	3,085	10	164	5,614
1980	13,385	485	15,515	12	368	3,629
1981	16,906	172	17,275	29	436	3,049
1982	22,169	546	17,376	26	590	2,691
1983	19,112	1,569	17,485	28	664	—
Cum., 1957-83	173,063	7,501	164,249	492	5,682	5,195

Hospital Insurance Trust Fund, 1970-83

[In thousands]

Fiscal year:	Receipts Net contribution income[1]	Transfers from railroad retirement account[2]	Reimbursements from general revenues[3]	Net interest[4]	Expenditures Net hospital and related service benefits[5]	Administrative expenses[6]	Total assets at end of period
1970	4,784,789	61,307	628,262	139,423	4,804,242	148,660	2,677,401
1975	11,296,773	126,749	529,353	614,989	10,355,390	256,134	9,870,039
1980	23,260,335	221,800	837,906	1,061,433	23,793,420	460,841	14,489,913
1981	30,445,979	246,700	800,000	1,324,834	28,909,081	305,416	18,092,929
1982	34,414,993	308,110	1,015,000	1,872,541	34,343,651	620,360	20,839,552
1983	32,906,678	308,600	—	1,631,010	38,101,524	522,228	13,719,000
Cum., 1966-83	242,736,474	2,310,150	10,864,582	11,011,534	245,024,589	4,836,058	34,558,552

(1) Represents amounts appropriated (estimated tax collections with suitable subsequent adjustments) after deductions for refund of estimated amount of employee-tax overpayment; and, beginning July 1973, premiums for coverage of uninsured individuals aged 65 and over. (2) Transfers (principal only) from the railroad retirement account with respect to contributions for hospital insurance coverage of railroad workers. (3) Represents Federal Government transfers from general funds appropriations to meet costs of benefits for persons not insured for cash benefits under OASDHI or railroad retirement and for costs of benefits arising from military wage credits. (4) Interest and profit on investments after transfers of interest or reimbursed administrative expenses (see footnote 6) and interest on amounts transferred from railroad retirement account (see footnote 3). (5) Represents payment vouchers on letters of credit issued to fiscal intermediaries under sec. 1816 and direct payments to providers of services under sec. 1815 of the Social Security Act. (6) Subject to subsequent adjustment among all four Social Security trust funds for allocated cost of each operation. Fiscal year 1966 includes "tool-up" period from date of enactment of Social Security Amendments of 1965 (July 20).

Supplementary Medical Insurance Trust Fund: Status, 1970-83

[In thousands]

Fiscal year:	Receipts Premium income[1]	Transfers from general revenues[2]	Net interest[3]	Expenditures Net medical service benefits[4]	Administrative expenses[5]	Total assets at end of period
1970	$936,000	$928,151	$11,536	$1,979,287	$216,993	$57,181
1975	1,886,962	2,329,590	105,539	3,765,397	404,458	1,424,413
1980	2,927,711	6,931,713	415,510	10,143,930	593,327	4,531,591
1981	3,319,607	8,747,430	384,348	12,344,913	895,374	3,742,690
1982	3,830,558	13,323,012	473,203	14,806,214	753,255	5,809,993
1983	4,227,379	14,237,991	680,441	17,487,322	819,778	6,646,303
Cum., 1967-83	34,849,548	76,905,698	3,132,416	100,699,873	7,539,082	16,198,986

(1) Represents voluntary premium payments from and in behalf of the insured aged and (beginning July 1973) disabled. (2) Represents Federal Government transfers from general funds appropriations to match aggregate premiums paid. (3) Represents interest and profit on investments, after transfers of interest on reimbursed administrative expenses (see footnote 5). (4) Represents payment vouchers on letters of credit issued to carriers under sec. 1842 of the Social Security Act. (5) Subject to subsequent adjustments among all four Social Security trust funds for allocated cost of each operation. Fiscal year 1966 includes "tool-up" period from date of enactment of Social Security Amendments of 1965 (July 30).

Tips on Cutting Energy Costs in Your Home

Source: Con Edison Conservation Services

Heating

In many homes, in areas where temperatures drop during the winter, more energy is used for heating than anything else. Conservation measures pay off in a home which is losing heat excessively. Installing the right amount of insulation, storm windows and doors, caulking and weatherstripping are important. Also consider the following advice:

- Make sure the thermostat and heating system are in good working order. An annual checkup is recommended.
- Set the thermostat no higher than 68 degrees. When no one is home, or when everyone is sleeping, the setting should be turned down to 60 degrees or lower. An automatic setback thermostat can raise and lower your home's temperature at times you specify.
- Close off and do not heat unused areas.
- If you do not have conventional storm windows or doors use kits to make plastic storm windows.
- Keep the outside doors closed as much as possible.
- Special glass fireplace doors help keep a room's heat from being drawn up the chimney when the fire is burning low. In any case, close the damper when a fireplace is not in use.
- Use the sun's heat by opening blinds and draperies closed at night or on cold cloudy days to reduce heat loss.
- Keep radiators and warm air outlets clean. Do not block them with furniture or draperies.

Water Heater

In many homes, the water heater ranks second only to the heating system in total energy consumption. It pays to keep the water heater operating efficiently, and not to waste hot water.

- Put an insulation blanket on your water heater when you go on vacation, or turn it to a minimum setting if there is danger of freezing pipes.
- If you have a dishwasher, set the water heater thermostat no higher than 140 degrees. If not, or if you have a separate water heater for baths, a setting as low as 110 degrees may be sufficient.
- Run the dishwasher and clothes washer only when you have a full load. Use warm or cold water cycles for laundry when you can.
- Take showers instead of tub baths. About half as much hot water is used for a shower.
- Install a water-saver shower head.
- Do not leave the hot water running when rinsing dishes or shaving. Plug and partially fill the basin, or fill a pan with water.
- Use the right size water heater for your needs. An oversized unit wastes energy heating unneeded water. An undersized unit will not deliver all the hot water you want when you need it.
- When shopping for a water heater, look for the yellow-and-black federal EnergyGuide label to learn the estimated yearly energy cost of a unit.

Air Conditioning

- Clean or replace the filter in an air conditioner at the beginning of the cooling season. Then check it once a month and clean or change the filter if necessary. A dirty filter blocks the flow of air and keeps the air conditioner from doing its best job of cooling.
- Adjust the temperature control setting to provide a room temperature no lower than 78 degrees. Since most air conditioner thermostats are not marked in degrees but by words such as "cold" and "colder," use a good wall thermometer to tell which setting will provide the desired temperature.
- Close windows and doors when the air conditioner is running.
- When the outside temperature is 78 degrees or cooler, turn off the air conditioner and open windows to cool your home.
- Always keep your air conditioner turned off when you are away from home or not using the areas that it cools. An air conditioner timer can be set to turn it off when family members go to work, and to turn it on just before the first one arrives home. These timers are available at hardware stores.
- Close draperies and shades to block out the sun's heat.
- When shopping for a new room air conditioner, look for the yellow-and-black federal EnergyGuide label to learn the Energy Efficiency Rating (EER) and the estimated yearly operating cost. The higher the EER, the less electricity will be used for a cooling job.
- Read the manufacturer's instructions and follow them closely.
- If you have a central air conditioning system, run your hands along the ducts while it is operating to check for air leaks. Repair leaks with duct tape. Make sure the duct system is properly insulated.

Refrigerators and Freezers

The refrigerator operates 24 hours a day, every day, so it is important to make sure your refrigerator is working efficiently. It is one of the biggest users of energy in the home all year round.

- Keep the condenser coils clean. The coils are on the back or at the bottom of the refrigerator. Carefully wipe, vacuum or brush the coils to remove dust and dirt at least once a year.
- Examine door gaskets and hinges regularly for air leaks. The doors should fit tightly. To check, place a piece of paper between the door and the cabinet. Close the door with normal force, then try to pull the paper straight out. There will be a slight resistance. Test all around the door, including the hinge side. If there are any places where the paper slides out easily, you need to adjust the hinges or replace the gasket, or both.
- Pause before opening your refrigerator door. Think of everything you will need before you open the door so you do not have to go back several times. When you open the door, close it quickly to keep the cool air in.
- Adjust the temperature-setting dial of the refrigerator as the manufacturer recommends. Use a thermometer to check the temperature (38 to 40 degrees is usually recommended for the refrigerator; zero degrees for the freezer). Settings that are too cold waste electricity and can ruin foods.
- If you have a manual-defrost refrigerator, do not allow the ice to build up more than $1/4$ inch thick.
- For greatest efficiency, keep your refrigerator well-stocked but allow room for air to circulate around the food.
- The freezer, on the other hand, should be packed full. If necessary, fill empty spaces with bags of ice cubes or fill milk cartons with water and freeze.
- When you are going to be away from home for a week or more, turn off and unplug the refrigerator, empty and clean it, and prop the door open.

- If you are buying a new refrigerator, look for one with a humid-dry ("power-saver") switch. This switch is used to turn off "anti-sweat" heaters in the doors to save electricity when the heaters are not needed.
- When shopping for a new refrigerator or freezer, look for the federal EnergyGuide label to help you select an efficient unit.

Cooking

There are many ways to save electricity or gas by careful use of the range or oven.

- Cook as many dishes in the oven at one time as you can instead of cooking each separately. If recipes call for slightly different temperatures, say 325, 350, and 375 degrees, pick the middle temperature of 350 to cook all 3 dishes and remove each dish as it's done.
- Don't preheat the oven unnecessarily. Usually, any food that takes more than an hour of cooking can be started in a cold oven.
- Turn off your oven or range just before the cooking is finished. The heat that is left will usually finish the cooking.
- Whenever you peek into an oven by opening a door, the temperature drops about 25 degrees. So open the oven door as little as possible.
- Use the lowest possible heat setting to cook foods on top of the range.
- Match the pot to the size of the surface unit. Putting a small pot on a large surface unit wastes energy without cooking the food any faster.
- On gas ranges, the flame should burn in a firm, blue cone. If the flame is not blue, the range is probably not working efficiently. Get a service representative to check it.

Lighting

The first rule is to turn off lights no one is using. There also are ways to improve your home's lighting level and save energy at the same time.

- Get all family members in the habit of turning off lights when they leave a room, even if they will be gone only for a short time.
- During the day, try to get along with as few lights as possible. Let the daylight do the work. White or light-colored walls make a room seem brighter.
- Use bulbs of lower wattage where you don't need strong light.
- When you need strong light, use one large bulb instead of several smaller ones. One 100-watt incandescent bulb produces more light than 2 60-watt bulbs, with 20 percent less energy consumption. But never use bulbs of a higher wattage than a fixture was designed to take.
- Use 3-way bulbs where possible, so you can choose the amount of light you need.
- Modern solid-state dimmer controls let you save energy by reducing your lighting level and wattage. Many are easy to install.
- Consider changing to fluorescent lighting, especially in kitchens, bathrooms, and work areas. Fluorescent tubes give more light at lower energy cost than incandescent bulbs with the same wattage. Plug-in fluorescent fixtures are available at hardware stores, or an electrician can install permanent fixtures.

Fuel Economy in 1985 Autos; Comparative Miles per Gallon

Source: U.S. Environmental Protection Agency

The mileage numbers and rankings below refer to testing completed through September 18, 1984. For the second consecutive year, the top-rated model is the Honda Civic Coupe at 49 in city driving and 54 mpg on the highway. Other top-rated 1985 cars include the Chevrolet Sprint (47 mpg city; 53 mpg highway), Nissan Sentra (45 adn 50 mpg); Ford Escort and Lincoln Lynx (both 43 and 52 mpg).

Make, model, fuel[1]	Cu. in. displcmt.	Cylinders	Trans.[2]	City Mileage	Hwy. Mileage	Make, model, fuel[1]	Cu. in. displcmt.	Cylinders	Trans.[2]	City Mileage	Hwy. Mileage	Make, model, fuel[1]	Cu. in. displcmt.	Cylinders	Trans.[2]	City Mileage	Hwy. Mileage
Alfa Romeo Spider	120	4	m	21-27		Dodge Diplomat	318	8	a	16-22		Olds. Cutlass Sup.	307	8	a	17-22	
Audi Coupe GT	136	5	m	19-25		Dodge Omni	135	4	a	24-28		Oldsmobile 98 Firenza	110	4	m	26-35	
Audi 4000S	109	4	m	24-30		Dodge 600						Peugeot 505	120	4	m	19-24	
Audi 5000S	131	5	a	17-22		Convertible	135	4	a	23-26		Plymouth Colt.	90	4	m	37-41	
BMW 3-Series	108	4	m	23-29		Ford Escort (d)	122	4	m	43-52		Plymouth Conquest	156	4	m	19-24	
Buick Century (d)	263	6	a	26-35		Ford EXP	98	4	m	25-35		Plymouth Horizon	135	4	m	26-37	
Buick Electra	231	6	a	19-26		Ford LTD	140	4	a	16-23		Plymouth Turismo	135	4	m	21-30	
Buick LeSabre	231	6	a	17-21		Ford Mustang	140	4	m	23-29		Pontiac Bonneville	305	8	a	16-22	
Buick Regal	262	6	a	18-27		Ford Tempo	122	4	m	36-44		Pontiac Fiero	151	4	m	25-31	
Buick Riviera	231	6	a	16-24		Ford Thunderbird	231	6	a	19-22		Pontiac Grand Prix	231	6	a	19-24	
Buick Skylark	173	6	m	18-23		Honda Accord	112	4	a	24-30		Pontiac Firebird	305	8	m	15-24	
Cadillac Eldorado,						Honda Civic	82	4	m	38-42		Pontiac 1000 (d)	111	4	m	39-46	
Seville	249	8	a	16-22		Honda Civic Coupe.	91	4	m	49-54		Renault Alliance/					
Chevrolet Celebrity	151	4	m	24-31		Isuzu I-Mark (d)	111	4	m	24-49		Encore	85	4	m	31-35	
Chevrolet Camaro	305	8	m	15-24		Isuzu Impulse	119	4	m	22-28		Renault Fuego	95	4	m	23-31	
Chevrolet Cavalier	173	6	m	18-23		Jaguar XJ	258	6	a	15-19		Rolls Royce					
Chevrolet Chevette						Lincoln-Mercury Lynx						Camargue	412	8	a	8-11	
(d)	111	4	m	39-46		(d)	122	4	m	43-52		Subaru XT	109	4	m	25-32	
Chevrolet Citation II	173	6	a	20-26		Mazda GLC	91	4	m	30-31		Toyota Celica	144	4	m	24-30	
Chevrolet Monte Carlo	229	6	a	18-27		Mazda 626	122	4	m	26-32		Toyota Celica Supra	168	6	m	20-24	
Chevrolet Sprint	61	3	m	47-53		Mercedes-Benz						Toyota Corolla (d)	112	4	m	38-47	
Chrysler LeBaron.	135	4	a	23-26		500SEC	303	8	a	14-16		Toyota Cressida	168	6	a	19-24	
Chrysler New Yorker	135	4	a	20-23		Mercury Cougar	231	6	a	19-22		Toyota Tercel.	89	4	m	35-39	
Datsun Nissan Sentra						Mercury Lynx (d)	122	4	m	43-52		Volkswgn Golf (d)	97	4	m	37-46	
(d)	103	4	m	45-50		Mercury Mark VII	302	8	a	16-23		Volkswgn Jetta (d)	97	4	m	37-46	
Datsun Nissan Pulsar	98	4	m	31-37		Mercury Marquis	140	4	a	21-25		Volkswgn Cabriolet	109	4	m	24-29	
Dodge Aries	135	4	a	24-29		Mitsubishi Cordia	122	4	m	25-39		Volkswgn Scirocco	109	4	m	24-29	
Dodge Colt	90	4	m	37-41		Mitsubishi Mirage	90	4	m	37-41		Volvo 740/760	174	6	a	18-23	
Dodge Charger	97	4	m	28-33		Mitsubishi Tredia	122	4	m	25-32							

(1) Type of fuel: (d) = diesel; all others are gasoline-powered. (2) Type of transmission: a = automatic; m = manual.

Measuring Energy

Source: Energy Information Administration, U.S. Energy Dept.

The following tables of equivalents contain those figures commonly used to compare different types of energy sources and their various measurements.

Btu — a British thermal unit — the amount of heat required to raise one pound of water one degree Fahrenheit. Equivalent to 1,055 joules or about 252 gram calories. A therm is usually 100,000 Btu but is sometimes used to refer to other units.

Calorie — The amount of heat required to raise one gram of water one degree Centigrade; abbreviated cal.; equivalent to about .003968 Btu. More common is the kilogram calorie, also called a kilocalorie and abbreviated Cal. or Kcal; equivalent to about 3.97 Btu. (One Kcal is equivalent to one food calorie.)

Btu Values of Energy Sources

(These are conventional or average values, not precise equivalents.)

Coal (per 2,000 lb. ton of U.S. production):
Anthracite = 22.9×10^6 Btu
Bituminous coal and lignite = 22.6×10^6
Average heating value of coal used to generate electricity in 1979 was 21.4×10^6 Btu per metric ton.

Natural Gas:
Dry (per cubic foot) = 1,021 Btu
Liquefied Natural Gas (Methane) (per barrel) = 3.0×10^6
Electricity — 1 kwh = 3,412 Btu
Petroleum (per barrel):
Crude oil = 5.80×10^6 Btu
Residual fuel oil = 6.29×10^6
Distillate fuel oil = 5.83×10^6
Gasoline (including aviation gas) = 5.25×10^6
Jet fuel (kerosene) = 5.67×10^6
Jet fuel (naphtha) = 5.36×10^6
Kerosene = 5.67×10^6
Nuclear — (per kilowatt hour) = 10,769

The Btu and calorie, being small amounts of energy, are usually expressed as follows when large numbers are involved.

1×10^3 Btu = 1,000
1×10^6 = 1,000,000
1×10^9 = 1,000,000,000

1×10^{12} = 1 trillion
1×10^{15} = 1 quadrillion
1×10^{18} = 1 quintillion or 1 Q unit
One Q unit = 44.3 billion short tons of coal
= 172.4 billion tons of oil
= 980 trillion cubic feet of natural gas

Other Conversion Factors

Electricity — 1 kwh = 0.3 pounds of coal
= 0.25 gallon of crude oil
= 3.3 cubic feet of natural gas

Natural gas — 1 tcf (trillion cubic feet) = 45×10^6 short tons of bituminous and lignite coal produced
= 176×10^6 barrels of crude oil

Coal — 1 mstce (million short tons of coal equivalent) = 3.9×10^6 barrels of crude oil
= 1.7×10^6 short tons of crude oil
= 22.1×10^9 cubic feet of natural gas

Oil — 1 million short tons (6.65×10^6 barrels) = 4×10^9 kwh of electricity (when used to generate power)
= 12×10^9 kwh uncoverted
= 1.7×10^6 short tons of coal
= 37×10^6 cubic feet of natural gas

Approximate Conversion Factors for Oils

To convert	Barrels to metric tons	Metric tons to barrels	Barrels/ day to tons/ year	Tons/year to barrels/ day
	Multiply by:			
Crude oil[1] . . .	.136	7.33	49.8	.0201
Gasoline . .	.118	8.45	43.2	.0232
Kerosene . .	.128	7.80	46.8	.0214
Diesel fuel . .	.133	7.50	48.7	.0205
Fuel oil . . .	.149	6.70	54.5	.0184

(1) Based on world average gravity (excluding natural gas liquids).

Removing Common Spots and Stains

By Polly Fisher, Syndicated Columnist, "Polly's Pointers," Newspaper Enterprise Association

Precaution: The following stain removal techniques are primarily intended for use on washable fabrics and surfaces, unless otherwise noted. If your fabric is labeled "dry clean only," consult a professional dry cleaner for safe treatment of the stain. Before treating any stain, be sure the remedy is safe for the fabric or finish of the stained surface. Always test the recommended cleaning solution at the recommended temperature (and this includes water, soap, and detergent) on a hidden part of the garment or other item: a seam allowance, a collar facing, a turned-under hem. While these remedies are all considered reasonably safe for most fabrics, the colorfastness of commercial dyes varies greatly. Be especially alert for any bleeding or change of color when you make your test. Above all, follow the care-label instructions and use common sense when dealing with any cleaning method. All products mentioned here can be obtained at local supermarkets, drug stores, or hardware stores.

Beverages (Alcoholic Drinks, Coffee, Fruit Juice, Soda, Tea, Wine)

When spills first occur, pour, sponge, or otherwise wet the fabric with ordinary club soda or any unflavored carbonated or sparkling water. Blot with a clean cloth, napkin, tissue, or paper towel. In most cases, this will clean up the spot without leaving any stain.

When such stains have set, stretch the stained area of fabric over a large bowl and hold it taut with a large rubber band. Then pour boiling water over the stain. If any stain remains, sponge with lemon juice. If the fabric is white, leave the lemon juice-treated fabric out in the sun to dry and

bleach.

Blood

Wash fresh blood stains in cold water and a mild soap or detergent. Hand soap or dishwashing liquid is fine. Never wash blood stains with warm or hot water.

If stains have dried and set, sponge with a little hydrogen peroxide until the stain disappears.

On mattresses and other large items that are difficult to wash, spread a thick paste of cornstarch and water over the stained area. Let dry thoroughly, then vacuum off.

Candle Wax

With a dull knife, gently scrape off as much wax as possi

ble. Sandwich the fabric between two thick layers of paper towels and iron over the spot with a hot iron. Frequently change the towels for fresh ones as the wax melts and soaks into the paper. If any colored stain remains after all wax has been removed, sponge with rubbing alcohol.

Chewing Gum

On flat, smooth fabrics, harden gum by rubbing with an ice cube, then peel gum off. If any stain remains, sponge with alcohol or dry cleaning fluid (often sold as "spot remover.")

On knits, particularly fuzzy, loose sweaters, massage vegetable shortening into the gummy area. This will loosen the gum and lift it from the fibers. Wash out with cool water and mild soap or detergent. Repeat if necessary until all gum is gone.

Chocolate

Rub with a mild detergent and warm water. If stain remains, sponge lightly with dry cleaning fluid.

Glue

To remove plastic cement, apply nail-polish remover (acetone) sparingly. This will dissolve the cement. Blot with a clean cloth. Nail-polish remover and other acetone-based products will also dissolve "super" glues. Do not use on acetates and acetate blends.

White all-purpose glue should be soaked in warm water, then sponged with ammonia. Rinse, then launder.

The glue left by price tags and labels on bottles, plastics, or almost any surface, can be easily removed by rubbing with vegetable oil and a clean cloth. Rinse or wash the oil off after removing the glue. (Not recommended for use on fabrics.)

Grease and Oil Stains

Rub fresh stains with hand soap and wash vigorously with warm water.

On fabrics that cannot be washed, sprinkle fresh grease stains liberally with cornstarch. Let set for fifteen minutes, then brush or vacuum thoroughly. The cornstarch will absorb the grease. Safe for velvets and furs if brushed out gently.

Apply waterless handcleaner to grease, oil, or tar stains. Rub in gently, then launder as usual. Place paper towels un-

der the fabric to absorb the grease as you're working the handcleaner into the fabric.

Greying (All-Over)

Greying of fabrics may be caused by soap left in the fabric after laundering. Add one cup of white vinegar to the final rinse water of your machine's cycle. This will break up and rinse away soap buildup and soften the fabric.

Ink

Ballpoint pen ink on fabrics and vinyl can be sprayed with hairspray. The hairspray will dissolve the ink which should be blotted up and wiped away with a clean cloth or paper towels.

Sponge stains caused by printer's ink or carbon paper with rubbing alcohol, then rinse.

Mildew

Saturate light mildew stains on white and pastel fabrics with lemon juice and bleach in the sun for several hours. (Don't apply the juice to any other part of the fabric.) Launder as usual.

If mildew stains are heavy or remain after treating with lemon juice, sponge with hydrogen peroxide. Again, launder afterwards.

Paint

Dab paint spots with turpentine. When paint softens, blot up with clean paper towels. Rinse, then launder.

To remove paint from your skin, rub the spots with ordinary vegetable oil.

Perspiration

Soak stained fabric in warm white vinegar for thirty minutes, then launder as usual.

Yellowing (All-Over)

Use chlorine bleach (on cottons and other bleachable fabrics only) in laundering, according to bottle directions. Do not use chlorine bleach on nylon fabrics. Chlorine bleach can *cause* yellowing on nylon.

Restore whiteness to delicate fabrics and items that you don't want to treat with harsh chemicals by soaking in a cream of tartar solution. Add one tablespoon cream of tartar to one gallon of hot water, then soak garments overnight. Good for baby clothes, diapers, linen handkerchiefs, and delicate synthetic knits.

Life Insurance: Facts You Need to Know

Source: American Council of Insurance

One of the most important purchases you can make—and one you need to be well-informed about—is life insurance.

Most insurance companies are currently simplifying their life insurance plans in order that consumers might have a better idea of what they're really buying. In addition to making policies easier to read and understand, the companies are developing new premium payment methods to lower the financial burden of insurance purchase. Since almost one-third of all life insurance is bought by people aged 25-43, with over 60% paying more than $260 annually for insurance, such innovations as monthly payment plans (instead of annual or semi-annual, lump sum payments) are becoming common.

There are 3 basic types of insurance policies: (1) whole life—a policy that continues in effect as long as you pay the fixed premium; (2) endowment—a policy that will pay you or your beneficiary its face amount after a designated time; and (3) term—the policy pays your beneficiary the face amount if you die while the policy is in force.

Life Insurance as an Investment?

There's a good deal of controversy about the value of insurance as an investment, especially in times of double-digit inflation. Whole life policies, with their fixed premiums and cash value that grows over the course of the years (that can be collected when you decide to terminate the policy or bor-

rowed against up to the current value of the policy) are considered by many to be an effective way to protect a family financially, while also having money wisely invested. Term insurance, on the other hand, is a much less expensive type of insurance, and achieves much the same purpose as whole life (of course, only during the "term" of its existence). But there is no cash surrender value or borrowing privilege.

Since both current protection and a good future investment are necessary, the consumer must carefully weigh the advantages of life insurance before making a purchase.

How to Read a Life Insurance Policy

All life insurance policies, regardless of type, can be divided into 3 parts:

1. **Summary**—This is the basic agreement of the policy. It includes the name of the insured, the face amount of the policy, the beneficiary's name, and premium amount, as well as the type of policy, any riders (additions to the policy you might have bought), and whether or not the cost of the insurance has been figured on a guaranteed basis or a participating basis.

2. **Details**—Approximately 10 clauses giving the specifics of the policy's operation, such as due date of premium, value of the policy when you surrender it for either cash or a loan, the amount paid on your death, options for how your beneficiary can receive that money.

3. **Application**—A two-fold section that gives personal information about you and it lets you make some decisions about how the policy will work. Among typical items covered are what happens in the event of your suicide, whether you engage in dangerous sports or occupations, what your rights are under the policy, etc.

As with any legal document, it is important to read and understand what you are purchasing. If you need further information, a good source is the American Council of Insurance, 1850 K St. N.W., Washington, DC 20006.

How Is Your Life Insurance Dollar Used?

Source: American Council of Life Insurance, 1982 figures.

Of each dollar of income received by U.S. insurance companies, $ .715 omes from premiums and $ .285 from net investment earning and other income.

The following breakdown shows how each premium dollar received from insurance purchasers is spent:

Benefit payments to policy holders	$ .466	Home and field office expenses	$ .096
Additions to policy reserve funds	$ .324	Taxes	$ .023
Additions to special reserves & surplus funds	$ .019	Dividends to shareholders	$ .011
Commissions to agents	$ .061	**Total**	$ 1.000

Stress: How Much Can Affect Your Health?

Source: Reprinted with permission from the *Journal of Psychosomatic Research*, Vol. 11, pp. 213-218, T.H. Holmes, M.D.; The Social Readjustment Rating Scale © 1967, Pergamon Press, Ltd.

Change, both good and bad, can create stress and stress, if sufficiently severe, can lead to illness. Drs. Thomas Holmes and Minoru Masudu, psychiatrists at the University of Washington in Seattle, have developed the Social Readjustment Rating Scale. In their study, they gave a point value to stressful events. The psychiatrists discovered that in 79 percent of the persons studied major illness followed the accumulation of stress-related changes totaling over 300 points in one year. The scale follows:

The Social Readjustment Rating Scale

Life Event	Value
Death of Spouse	100
Divorce	73
Marital separation from mate	65
Detention in jail or other institution	63
Death of a close family member	63
Major personal injury or illness	53
Marriage	50
Being fired at work	47
Marital reconciliation with mate	45
Retirement from work	45
Major change in the health or behavior of a family member	44
Pregnancy	40
Sexual difficulties	39
Gaining a new family member (e.g., through birth, adoption, oldster moving in, etc.)	39
Major business readjustment (e.g., merger, reorganization, bankruptcy, etc.)	39
Major change in financial state (e.g., a lot worse off or a lot better off than usual)	38
Death of a close friend	37
Changing to a different line of work	36
Major change in the number of arguments with spouse (e.g., either a lot more or a lot less than usual regarding child-rearing, personal habits, etc.)	35
Taking out a mortgage or loan for a major purchase (e.g. for a home, business, etc.)	31
Foreclosure on a mortgage or loan	30
Major change in responsibilities at work (e.g., promotion, demotion, lateral transfer)	29
Son or daughter leaving home (e.g., marriage, attending college, etc.)	29
In-law troubles	29
Outstanding personal achievement	28
Wife beginning or ceasing work outside the home	26
Beginning or ceasing formal schooling	26
Major change in living conditions (e.g., building a new home, remodeling, deterioration of home or neighborhood)	25
Revision of personal habits (dress, manners, association, etc.)	24
Troubles with the boss	23
Major change in working hours or conditions	20
Change in residence	20
Changing to a new school	20
Major change in usual type and/or amount of recreation	19
Major change in church activities (e.g., a lot more or a lot less than usual)	19
Major change in social activities (e.g., clubs, dancing, movies, visiting, etc.)	18
Taking out a mortgage or loan for a lesser purchase (e.g., for a car, TV, freezer, etc.)	17
Major change in sleeping habits (a lot more or a lot less sleep, or change in part of day when asleep)	16
Major change in number of family get-togethers (e.g., a lot more or a lot less than usual)	15
Major change in eating habits (a lot more or a lot less food intake, or very different meal hours or surroundings)	15
Vacation	13
Christmas	12
Minor violations of the law (e.g., traffic tickets, jaywalking, disturbing the peace, etc.)	11

Effects of Commonly Abused Drugs

Source: National Institute on Drug Abuse

Tobacco

Effects and dangers: Nicotine, the active ingredient in tobacco, acts as a stimulant on the heart and nervous system. When tobacco smoke is inhaled the immediate effects on the body are a faster heart beat and elevated blood pressure. These effects, however, are quickly dissipated. Tar (in the smoke) contains many carcinogens. These compounds, many of which are in polluted air but are found in vastly greater quantities in cigarette smoke, have been identified as major causes of cancer and respiratory difficulties. Even relatively young smokers can have shortness of breath, nagging cough, or develop cardiovascular and respiratory difficulties. A third principal component of cigarette smoke, carbon monoxide, is also a cause of some of the more serious health effects of smoking. Carbon monoxide can reduce the blood's ability to carry oxygen to body tissues and can promote the development of arteriosclerosis (hardening of the arteries). Long-term effects of smoking cigarettes are emphysema, chronic bronchitis, heart disease, lung cancer, and cancer in other parts of the body.

Risks during pregnancy: Women who smoke during pregnancy are more likely to have babies that weigh less, and more frequently lose their babies through stillbirth or death soon after birth.

Alcohol

Effects: Like sedatives, it is a central nervous system depressant. In small doses, it has a tranquilizing effect on most people, although it appears to stimulate others. Alcohol first acts on those parts of the brain which affect self-control and other learned behaviors; lowered self-control often leads to the aggressive behavior associated with some people who drink.

Dangers: In large doses, alcohol can dull sensation and impair muscular coordination, memory, and judgment. Taken in larger quantities over a long period time, alcohol can damage the liver and heart and can cause permanent brain damage. A large dose of alcohol, which can be as little as a pint or less of whiskey consumed at once, can interfere with the part of the brain that control breathing. The respiratory failure which results can bring death. Delirium tremens, the most extreme manifestation of alcohol withdrawal, can also cause death. On the average, heavy drinkers shorten their life span by about 10 years.

Risks during pregnancy: Women who drink heavily during pregnancy (more than 3 ounces of alcohol per day or about 2 mixed drinks) run a higher risk than other women of delivering babies with physical, mental and behavioral abnormalities.

Dependence: Repeated drinking produces tolerance to the drug's effects and dependence. The drinker's body then needs alcohol to function. Once dependent, drinkers experience withdrawal symptoms when they stop drinking.

Marijuana ("grass", "pot", "weed")

What is it?: A common plant (*Cannabis sativa*), its chief psychoactive ingredient is delta-9-tetrahydrocannabinol, or THC. The amount of THC in the marijuana cigarette (joint) primarily determines its psychoactive potential.

Effects: Most users experience an increase in heart rate, reddening of the eyes, and dryness in the mouth and throat. Studies indicate the drug temporarily impairs short-term memory, alters sense of time, and reduces the ability to perform tasks requiring concentration, swift reactions, and coordination. Many feel that their hearing, vision, and skin sensitivity are enhanced by the drug, but these reports have not been objectively confirmed by research. Feelings of euphoria, relaxation, altered sense of body image, and bouts of exaggerated laughter are also commonly reported.

Dangers: Scientists believe marijuana can be particularly harmful to lungs because users typically inhale the filtered smoke deeply and hold it in their lungs for prolonged periods of time. Marijuana smoke has been found to have more cancer-causing agents than are found in cigarette smoke (see above). Because marijuana use increases heart rate as much as 50% and brings on chest pain in people who have a poor blood supply to the heart (and more rapidly than tobacco smoke does), doctors believe people with heart conditions or

who are at high risk for heart ailments, should not use marijuana. Findings also suggest that regular use may reduce fertility in women and that men with marginal fertility or endocrine functioning should avoid marijuana use and that it is especially harmful during adolescence, a period of rapid physical and sexual development.

Risks during pregnancy: Research is limited, but scientists believe marijuana which crosses the placential barrier, may have a toxic effect on embryos and fetuses.

Dependence: Tolerance to marijuana, the need to take more and more of the drug over time to get the original effect, has been proven in humans and animals. Physical dependence has been demonstrated in research subjects who ingested an amount equal to smoking 10 to 20 joints a day. When the drug was discontinued, subjects experienced withdrawal symptoms—irritability, sleep disturbances, loss of appetite and weight, sweating, and stomach upset.

Bad reactions: Most commonly reported immediate adverse reaction to marijuana use is the "acute panic anxiety reaction," usually described as an exaggeration of normal marijuana effects in which intense fears of losing control and going crazy accompany severe anxiety. The symptoms often disappear in a few hours when the acute drug effects have worn off.

Hallucinogens ("psychodelics")

What are they?: Drugs which affect perception, sensation, thinking, self-awareness, and emotion.

(1) **LSD (lysergic acid diethylamide)**, a synthetic, is converted from lysergic acid which comes from fungus (ergot).

Effects: Vary greatly according to dosage, personality of the user, and conditions under which the drug is used. Basically, it causes changes in sensation. Vision alters; users describe changes in depth perception and in the meaning of the perceived object. Illusions and hallucinations often occur. Physical reactions range from minor changes such as dilated pupils, a rise in temperature and heartbeat, or a slight increase in blood pressure, to tremors. High doses can greatly alter the state of consciousness. Heavy use of the drug may produce flashbacks, recurrences of some features of a previous LSD experience days or months after the last dose.

Dangers: After taking LSD, a person loses control over normal thought processes. Although many perceptions are pleasant, others may cause panic or may make a person believe that he or she cannot be harmed. Longer-term harmful reactions include anxiety and depression, or "breaks from reality" which may last from a few days to months. Heavy users sometimes develop signs of organic brain damage, such as impaired memory and attention span, mental confusion, and difficulty with abstract thinking. It is not known yet whether such mental changes are permanent.

(2) **Mescaline:** Comes from peyote cactus and its effects are similar to those of LSD.

Phencyclidine (PCP or "angel dust")

What is it?: A drug that was developed as a surgical anesthetic for humans in the late 1950s. Because of its unpleasant and unusual side effects, PCP was soon restricted to its only current legal use as a veterinary anesthetic and tranquilizer.

Effects: Vary according to dosage. Low doses may provide the usual releasing effects of many psychoactive drugs. A floaty euphoria is described, sometimes associated with a feeling of numbness (part of the drug's anesthetic effects). Increased doses produce an excited, confused intoxication, which may include muscle rigidity, loss of concentration and memory, visual disturbances, delirium, feelings of isolation, convulsions, speech impairment, violent behavior, fear of death, and changes in the user's perceptions of their bodies.

Dangers: PCP intoxication can produce violent and bizarre behavior even in people not otherwise prone to such behavior. Violent actions may be directed at themselves or others and often account for serious injuries and death. More people die from accidents caused by the erratic behavior produced by the drug than from the drug's direct effect on the body. A temporary, schizophrenic-like psychosis, which can last for days or weeks, has also occurred in users of moderate or higher doses.

Stimulants ("Uppers")

What are they?: A class of drugs which stimulate the central nervous system and produce an increase in alertness and activity.

(1) **Amphetamines** promote a feeling of alertness and increase in speech and general physical activity. Under medical supervision, the drugs are taken to control appetite.

Effects and dangers: Even small, infrequent doses can produce toxic effects in some people. Restlessness, anxiety, mood swings, panic, circulatory and cardiac disturbances, paranoid thoughts, hallucinations, convulsions, and coma have all been reported. Heavy, frequent doses can produce brain damage which results in speed disturbances and difficulty in turning thoughts into words. Death can result from injected amphetamine overdose. Long-term users often have acne resembling a measles rash; trouble with teeth, gums and nails, and dry lifeless hair. As heavy users who inject amphetamines accumulate larger amounts of the drug in their bodies, the resulting toxicity can produce amphetamine psychosis. People in this extremely suspicious, paranoid state, frequently exhibit bizarre, sometimes violent behavior.

Dependence: People with a history of sustained low-dose use quite often become dependent and feel they need the drug to get by.

(2) **Cocaine** is a stimulant drug extracted from the leaves of the coca plant. Street cocaine is a powder that is most commonly inhaled, though some users ingest, inject, or smoke a form of the drug called freebase.

Effect: Increases heart rate and blood pressure.

Dangers: Paranoia is not an uncommon response to heavy doses. Psychosis may be triggered in users prone to mental instability. Repeated inhalation often results in nostril and nasal membrane irritation. Some regular users have reported feelings of restlessness, irritability, and anxiety. Others have experienced hallucinations of touch, sight, taste, or smell. When people stop using cocaine after taking it for a long time, they frequently become depressed. They tend to fight off this depression by taking more cocaine, just as in the up/down amphetamine cycle. Cocaine is toxic. Although few people realize it, overdose deaths, though rare, from injected, oral and even snorted cocaine have occurred. The deaths are a result of seizures followed by respiratory arrest and coma, or sometimes by cardiac arrest.

Dependence: It's not a narcotic; no evidence suggests that it produces a physical dependence, but psychological dependence can clearly result from heavy or continuous use.

Sedatives (Tranquilizers, sleeping pills)

What are they?: Drugs which depress the central nervous system, more appropriately called sedative-hypnotics because they include drugs which calm the nerves (the sedation effect) and produce sleep (the hypnotic effect). Of drugs in this class, barbiturates ("barbs", "downers," "reds") have the highest rate of abuse and misuse. The most commonly abused barbiturates include pentobarbital (Nembutal), secobarbital (Seconal), and amobarbital (Amytal). These all have legitimate use as sedatives or sleeping aids. Among the most commonly abused nonbarbiturate drugs are glutethimide (Doriden), meprobamate (Miltown), methyprylon (Noludar), ethchlorvynol (Placidyl), and methaqualone (Sopor,

Quaalude). These are prescribed to help people sleep. Benzodiazepines, especially diazepam (Valium), prescribed to relieve anxiety, are commonly abused, and their rate of abuse and misuse is increasing.

Dangers: These can kill. Barbiturate overdose is implicated in nearly one-third of all reported drug-induced deaths. Accidental deaths may occur when a user takes an unintended larger or repeated dose of sedatives because of confusion or impairment in judgment caused by initial intake of the drug. With lesser, but still large doses, users can go into coma. Moderately large doses often produce an intoxicated stupor. Users' speech is often slurred, memory vague, and judgment impaired. Taken along with alcohol, the combination can be fatal. Tranquilizers act somewhat differently than other sedatives and are considered less hazardous. But even by themselves, or in combination with other drugs (especially alcohol and other sedatives) they can be quite dangerous.

Dependence: Potential for dependence is greatest with barbiturates, but all sedatives, tranquilizers, can be addictive. Barbiturate withdrawal is often more severe than heroin withdrawal.

Narcotics

What they are?: Drugs that relieve pain and often induce sleep. The opiates, which are narcotics, include opium and drugs derived from opium, such as morphine, codeine, and heroin. Narcotics also include certain synthetic chemicals that have a morphine-like action, such as methadone.

Which are abused?: Heroin ("junk," "smack") accounts for 90% of narcotic abuse in the U.S. Sometimes medicinal narcotics are also abused, including paregoric containing codeine, and methadone, meperidine, and morphine.

Dependence: Anyone can become heroin dependent if he or she takes the drug regularly. Although environmental stress and problems of coping have often been considered as factors that lead to heroin addiction, physicians or psychologists do not agree that some people just have an "addictive personality" and are prone to dependence. All we know for certain is that continued use of heroin causes dependence.

Dangers: Physical dangers depend on the specific drug, its source, and the way it is used. Most medical problems are caused by the uncertain dosage level, use of unsterile needles and other paraphernalia, contamination of the drug, or combination of a narcotic with other drugs, rather than by the effects of the heroin (or another narcotic) itself. The life expectancy of a heroin addict who injects the drug intravenously is significantly lower than that of one who does not. An overdose can result in death. If, for example, an addict obtains pure heroin and is not tolerant of the dose, he or she may die minutes after injecting it. Infections from unsterile needles, solutions, syringes, cause many diseases. Serum hepatitis is common. Skin abscesses, inflammation of the veins and congestion of the lungs also occur.

Withdrawal: When a heroin-dependent person stops taking the drug, withdrawal begins within 4-6 hours after the last injection. Full-blown withdrawal symptoms—which include shaking, sweating, vomiting, a running nose and eyes, muscle aches, chills, abdominal pains, and diarrhea—begin some 12-16 hours after the last injection. The intensity of symptoms depends on the degree of dependence.

Immunization Schedule for Children

Source: American Academy of Pediatrics

Age	Type of Vaccination	Disease Immunized Against	Age	Type of Vaccination	Disease Immunized Against
2 months	D-T-P	Diphtheria, Tetanus (Lockjaw), Pertussis (Whooping Cough)		Mumps Vaccine* (Or a single injection combined vaccine for all three diseases may be given at 15 months.)	Mumps
	Oral Polio Vaccine	Polio Myelitis			
4 months	D-T-P				
	Oral Polio Vaccine				
6 months	D-T-P		18 months	D-T-P Booster	
15 months	Measles Vaccine	Measles		Oral Polio Booster	
	Rubella Vaccine*	German Measles	School Entry	D-T-P Booster Oral Polio Booster	

*Rubella or mumps vaccine alone may be given as early as 12 months.

Heart Disease

Warning Signs

Source: American Heart Association

Of Heart Attack
- Prolonged, oppressive pain or unusual discomfort in the center of the chest
- Pain may radiate to the shoulder, arm, neck or jaw
- Sweating may accompany pain or discomfort
- Nausea and vomiting may also occur
- Shortness of breath may accompany other signs

The American Heart Association advises immediate action at the onset of these symptoms. The Association points out that over half of heart attack victims die before they reach the hospital and that the average victim waits 3 hours before seeking help.

Of Stroke
- Sudden temporary weakness or numbness of face or limbs on one side of the body
- Temporary loss of speech, or trouble speaking or understanding speech
- Temporary dimness or loss of vision, particularly in one eye
- An episode of double vision
- Unexplained dizziness or unsteadiness
- Change in personality, mental ability
- New or unusual pattern of headaches

Major Risk Factors

Blood pressure— systolic pressure under 120 is normal; systolic pressure over 150
= 2 times the risk of heart attack
= 4 times the risk of stroke

Cholesterol— level under 194 is normal;
level of 250 or over
= 3 times the risk of heart attack or stroke

Cigarettes— with non-smoking considered normal;
smoking one pack a day
= 2 times the risk of heart attack
= 4 times the risk of stroke

U.S. DEATHS DUE TO CARDIOVASCULAR DISEASES BY MAJOR TYPE OF DISORDER, 1981

* Rheumatic Fever and Rheumatic Heart Disease
Source National Center for Health Statistics
U.S. Department of Health and Human Services

ESTIMATED ECONOMIC COSTS IN BILLIONS OF DOLLARS OF CARDIOVASCULAR DISEASES BY TYPE OF EXPENDITURE, 1984

Source American Heart Association

Cardiovascular Disease Statistical Summary

Cost — $64.4 billion (AHA est.) in 1984.

Prevalence — 42,330,000 Americans have some form of heart and blood vessel disease.
- hypertension — 37,330,000 (nearly one in 4 adults).
- coronary heart disease — 4,600,000
- rheumatic heart disease — 2,010,000.
- stroke — 1,870,000.

Mortality — 989,610 in 1981 (50% of all deaths). 1980: 1,012,150 (51%).
- over one-fifth of all persons killed by CVD are under age 65.

Congenital or inborn heart defects — 35 recognizable types of defects.
- about 25,000 babies are born every year with heart defects.
- post-natal mortality from heart defects was estimated to be 6,500 in 1981.

Heart attack — caused 559,000 deaths in 1981.
- 4,600,000 alive today have history of heart attack and/or angina pectoris.
- 350,000 a year die of heart attack before they reach hospital.
- As many as 1,500,000 Americans will have a heart attack this year and about 550,000 of them will die.

Stroke — killed 164,300 in 1981; afflicts 870,000.

CCU — most of the 7,000 general hospitals in U.S. have coronary care capability.
Hypertension (high blood pressure) — 37,330,000 adults.
- easily detected and usually controllable, but only a minority have it under adequate control.

Rheumatic heart disease — 100,000 children; 910,000 adults.
- killed 13,402 in 1978, 7,700 in 1981.
Note: 1980 mortality data are estimates based on 1980 provisional data as published by USDHHS.

Cancer Information

Source: American Cancer Society

Cancer Warnings

Site	Warning signal— see your doctor	Comment
Breast	Lump or thickening in the breast, or unusual discharge from nipple.	The leading cause of cancer death in women.
Colon and rectum	Change in bowel habits; bleeding.	Considered a highly curable disease when digital and procto-scopic examinations are included in routine checkups.
Lung	Persistent cough, or lingering respiratory ailment.	The leading cause of cancer death among men and rising mortality among women.
Oral (including pharynx)	Sore that does not heal; difficulty in swallowing.	Many more lives should be saved because the mouth is easily accessible to visual examination by physicians and dentists.
Skin	Sore that does not heal, or change in wart or mole.	Skin cancer is readily detected by observation, and diagnosed by simple biopsy.
Uterus	Unusual bleeding or discharge.	Uterine cancer mortality has declined 70% during the last 40 years with wider application of the Pap test. Postmenopausal women with abnormal bleeding should be checked.
Kidney and bladder	Urinary difficulty, bleeding.	Protective measures for workers in high-risk industries are helping to eliminate one of the important causes of these cancers.
Larynx	Hoarseness, difficulty in swallowing.	Readily curable if caught early.
Prostate	Urinary diffculty.	Occurs mainly in men over 60, the disease can be detected by palpation at regular checkup.
Stomach	Indigestion.	An 80% decline in mortality in 50 years, for reasons yet unknown.
Leukemia	Leukemia is a cancer of blood-forming tissues and is characterized by the abnormal production of immature white blood cells. Acute lymphocytic leukemia strikes mainly children and is treated by drugs which have extended life from a few months to as much as 10 years. Chronic leukemia strikes usually after age 25 and progresses less rapidly.	
Lymphomas (including multiple myeloma)	These cancers arise in the lymph system and include Hodgkin's disease and lymphosarcoma. Some patients with lymphatic cancers can lead normal lives for many years. Five-year survival rate for Hodgkin's disease increased from 25% to 54% in 20 years.	

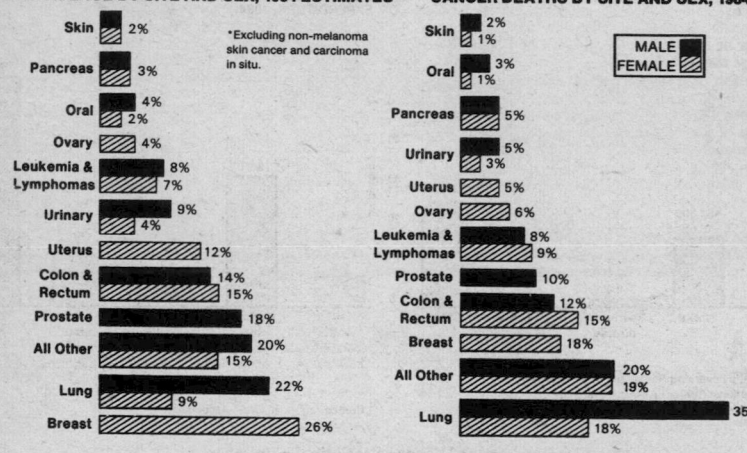

CANCER INCIDENCE BY SITE AND SEX, 1984 ESTIMATES*

*Excluding non-melanoma skin cancer and carcinoma in situ.

Site	Male	Female
Skin	2%	
Pancreas	3%	
Oral	4%	2%
Ovary		4%
Leukemia & Lymphomas	8%	7%
Urinary	9%	4%
Uterus		12%
Colon & Rectum	14%	15%
Prostate	18%	
All Other	20%	15%
Lung	22%	9%
Breast		26%

CANCER DEATHS BY SITE AND SEX, 1984 ESTIMATES

MALE / FEMALE

Site	Male	Female
Skin	2%	1%
Oral	3%	1%
Pancreas	5%	
Urinary	5%	3%
Uterus		5%
Ovary		6%
Leukemia & Lymphomas	8%	9%
Prostate	10%	
Colon & Rectum	12%	15%
Breast		18%
All Other	20%	19%
Lung	35%	18%

Basic First Aid

First aid experts stress that knowing what to do for an injured person until a doctor or trained person gets to an accident scene can save a life, especially in cases of stoppage of breath, severe bleeding, and shock.

People with special medical problems, such as diabetes, cardiovascular disease, epilepsy, or allergy, are also urged to wear some sort of emblem identifying it, as a safeguard against use of medication that might be injurious or fatal in an emergency. Emblems may be obtained from Medic Alert Foundation, Turlock, CA 95380.

Most accidents occur in homes. National Safety Council figures show that home accidents annually far outstrip those in other locations, such as in autos, at work, or in public places.

In all cases, get medical assistance as soon as possible.

Animal bites — Wounds should be washed with soap under running water and animal should be caught alive for ra-

bies test.

Asphyxiation — Start mouth-to-mouth resuscitation imme diately after getting patient to fresh air.

Bleeding — Elevate the wound above the heart if possible Press hard on wound with sterile compress until bleedin stops. Send for doctor if it is severe.

Burns — If mild, with skin unbroken and no blisters, plung into ice water until pain subsides. Apply mild burn oin ment or petroleum jelly if pain persists. Send for physicia if burn is severe. Apply sterile compresses and keep pa tient quiet and comfortably warm until doctor's arriva Do not try to clean burn, or to break blisters.

Chemicals in eye — With patient lying down, pour cupfu of water immediately into corner of eye, letting it run t other side to remove chemicals thoroughly. Cover wit sterile compress.

Choking — Get behind the victim, wrap your arms abou

him above his waist. Make a fist with one hand and place it, with large thumb knuckle pressing inward, just below the point of the "V" of the rib cage. Grasp the fist with the other hand and give several hard upward thrusts or hugs. As last resort, lean victim forward and slap back between shoulder blades. Start mouth-to-mouth resuscitation if breathing stops.

Convulsions — Place person on back on bed or rug so he can't hurt himself. Loosen clothing. Turn head to side. Put thick wad of cloth between jaws so patient can't bite tongue. Raise and pull lower jaw forward. Sponge head and neck with cool water if convulsions do not stop.

Cuts (minor) — Apply mild antiseptic and sterile compress after washing with soap under warm running water.

Drowning — (See Mouth-to-Mouth Resuscitation) Artificial breathing must be started at once, before victim is out of the water, if possible. If the victim's stomach is bloated with water, put victim on stomach, place hands under stomach, and lift. If no pulse is felt, begin cardiac compression. This should only be done by those professionally trained. If necessary, treat for shock. (See Shock)

Electric shock — If possible, turn off power. Don't touch victim until contact is broken; pull him from contact with rope, wooden pole, or loop of dry cloth. Start artificial respiration if breathing has stopped.

Foreign body in eye — Touch object with moistened corner of handkerchief if it can be seen. If it cannot be seen or does not come out after a few attempts, take patient to doctor. Do not rub eye.

Fainting — Seat patient and fan his face if he feels faint. Lower head to knees. Lay him down with head turned to side if he becomes unconscious. Loosen clothing and open windows. Wave aromatic spirits of ammonia or smelling salts under nose. Keep patient lying quietly for at least 15 minutes after he regains consciousness. Call doctor if faint lasts for more than a few minutues.

Falls — Send for physician if patient has continued pain. Cover wound with sterile dressing and stop any severe bleeding. Do not move patient unless absolutely necessary — as in case of fire — if broken bone is suspected. Keep patient warm and comfortable.

Loss of Limb — If a limb is severed, it is important to properly protect the limb so that it can possibly be reattached to the victim. After the victim is cared for, the limb should be placed in a clean plastic bag, garbage can or other suitable container. Pack ice around the limb on the OUTSIDE of the bag to keep the limb cold. Call ahead to the hospital to alert them of the situation.

Poisoning — Call doctor. Use antidote listed on label if container is found. Call local Poison Control Center if possible. Except for lye, other caustics, and petroleum products, induce vomiting unless victim is unconscious. Give milk if poision or antidote is unknown.

Shock (injury-related) — Keep the victim lying down; if uncertain as to his injuries, keep the victim flat on his back. Maintain the victim's normal body temperature; if the weather is cold or damp, place blankets or extra clothing over and under the victim; if weather is hot, provide shade.

Snakebites — Immediately get victim to a hospital. If there is mild swelling or pain, apply a consticting band 2 to 4 inches above the bite.

Stings from insects — If possible, remove stinger and apply solution of ammonia and water, or paste of baking soda. Call physician immediately if body swells or patient collapses.

Unconsciousness — Send for doctor and place person on his back. Start resuscitation if he stops breathing. Never give food or liquids to an unconscious person.

Mouth-to-Mouth Resuscitation

Stressing that your breath can save a life, the American Red Cross gives the following directions for mouth-to-mouth resuscitation if the victim is not breathing:

- Turn victim on his back and begin artificial respiration at once.
- Wipe out quickly any foreign matter visible in the mouth, using your fingers or a cloth wrapped around your fingers.
- Tilt victim's head back.
- Pull or push jaw into jutting-out position.
- If victim is a small child, place your mouth tightly over his mouth and nose and blow gently into his lungs about 20 times a minute. If victim is adult, cover the mouth with the mouth, pinch his nostrils shut, and blow vigorously about 12 times a minute.
- If unable to get air into lungs of victim, and if head and jaw positions are correct, suspect foreign matter in the throat. To remove it, suspend a small child momentarily by the ankles or hold child with head down for a moment and slap sharply between shoulder blades.
- If victim is an adult, turn him on his side and use same procedure.
- Again, wipe mouth to remove foreign matter.
- Repeat breathing, removing mouth each time to allow for escape of air. Continue until victim breathes for himself.

A Patient's Bill of Rights

Source: American Hospital Association, © copyright 1972.

Often, as a hospital patient, you feel you have little control over your circumstances. You do, however, have some important rights. They have been enumerated by the American Hospital Association.

1. The patient has the right to considerate and respectful care.

2. The patient has the right to obtain from his physician complete current information concerning his diagnosis, treatment, and prognosis in terms that can be reasonably expected to understand. When it is not medically advisable to give such information to the patient, the information should be made available to an appropriate person in his behalf. He has the right to know, by name, the physician responsible for coordinating his care.

3. The patient has the right to receive from his physician information necessary to give informed consent prior to the start of any procedure and/or treatment. Except in emergencies, such information for informed consent should include but not necessarily be limited to the specific procedure and/or treatment, the medically significant risks involved, and the probable duration of incapacitation. Where medically significant alternatives for care or treatment exist, or when the patient requests information concerning medical alternatives, the patient has the right to such information. The patient also has the right to know the name of the person responsible for the procedures and/or treatment.

4. The patient has the right to refuse treatment to the extent permitted by law and to be informed of the medical consequences of his action.

5. The patient has the right to every consideration of his privacy concerning his own medical care program. Case discussion, consultation, examination, and treatment are confidential and should be conducted discreetly. Those not directly involved in his care must have the permission of the patient to be present.

6. The patient has the right to expect that all communications and records pertaining to his care should be treated as confidential.

7. The patient has the right to expect that within its capacity a hospital must make reasonable response to the request of a patient for services. The hospital must provide evaluation, service, and/or referral as indicated by the urgency of the case. When medically permissable, a patient may be transferred to another facility only after he has received complete information and explanation concerning the need for and alternatives to such a transfer. The institution to which the patient is to be transferred must first have accepted the patient for transfer.

8. The patient has the right to obtain information as to any relationship of his hospital to other health care and edu-

cation institutions insofar as this care is concerned. The patient has the right to obtain information as to the existence of any professional relationships among individuals, by name, who are treating him.

9. The patient has the right to be advised if the hospital proposes to engage in or perform human experimentation affecting his care or treatment. The patient has the right to refuse to participate in such research projects.

10. The patient has the right to expect reasonable continuity of care. He has the right to know in advance what appointment times and physicians are available and where. The patient has the right to expect that the hospital will provide a mechanism whereby he is informed by his physician of the patient's continuing health care requirements following discharge.

11. The patient has the right to examine and receive an explanation of his bill, regardless of the source of payment.

12. The patient has the right to know what hospital rules and regulations apply to his conduct as a patient.

Common Food Additives: How Safe Are They?

Source: Reprinted from "Chemical Cuisine" which is available from Center for Science in the Public Interest, 1755 S St., N.W., Washington, D.C. 20009, for $2.50, copyright 1978.

Avoid

Artificial Colorings: Most are synthetic chemicals not found in nature. Some are safer than others, but names of colorings are not listed on label. Used mostly in foods of low nutritional value, usually indicating that fruit or natural ingredient omitted.

Additive	Use	Comment
Citrus Red No. 2	Skin of some Florida oranges.	May cause cancer. Does not seep through into pulp.
Orange B	Hot dogs.	Causes cancer in animals.
Red No. 3	Cherries in fruit cocktail, candy, baked goods.	May cause cancer.
Yellow No. 5	Gelatin dessert, candy, pet food, baked goods.	Poorly tested; may cause cancer. Some people allergic to it. Widely used.
Butylated Hydroxyanisole (BHA)	Antioxidant. Cereals, chewing gum, potato chips, oils.	Appears safer than BHT but needs better testing. Safer substitutes available.
Brominated Vegetable Oil (BVO)	Emulsifier, clouding agent. Citrus-flavored soft drinks.	Residue found in body fat; safer substitutes available.
Butylated Hydroxytoluene (BHT)	Antioxidant. Cereals, chewing gum, potato chips, oils, etc.	May cause cancer; stored in body fat; can cause allergic reaction. Safer alternatives.
Caffeine	Stimulant. Naturally in coffee, tea cocoa; added to soft drinks.	Causes sleeplessness; may cause miscarriages or birth defects.
Propyl Gallate	Antioxidant. Oil, meat products, potato stocks, chicken soup base, chewing gum.	Not adequately tested, use in frequently unnecessary.
Quinine	Flavoring. Tonic water, quinine water, bitter lemon.	Poorly tested; may cause birth defects.
Saccharin	Noncaloric sweetener. "Diet" products.	Causes cancer in animals.
Sodium Nitrite	Preservative, coloring, flavoring. Bacon, ham, frankfurters, luncheon meats, smoked fish, corned beef.	Prevents growth of botulism bacteria but can lead to formation of small amounts of cancer-causing nitrosamines, particularly in fried bacon.
Sulfur Dioxide Sodium Bisulfite	Preservative, bleach. Sliced fruit, wine, grape juice, dried potatoes, dried fruit.	Can destroy vitamin B-1, but otherwise safe.

Caution

Artificial Flavoring	Soda, candy, breakfast cereals, gelatin desserts.	Hundreds of chemicals used to mimic natural flavors, almost exclusively in "junk" foods; indicates "real thing" is left out. May cause hyperactivity in some children.
Blue No. 1	In beverages, candy, baked goods.	Very poorly tested.
Blue No. 2	Pet food, beverages, candy.	Very poorly tested.
Green No. 3	Candy, beverages.	Needs better testing.
Heptyl Paraben	Preservative. Beer.	Probably safe, has not been tested in presence of alcohol.
Monosodium Glutamate (MSG)	Flavor enhancer. Soup, seafood, poultry, cheese, sauces, stews, etc.	Damages brain cells in infant mice, causes "Chinese restaurant syndrome" (headache and burning or tightness in head, neck, arms) in some sensitive people.
Phosphoric Acid; Phosphates	Acidifier, chelating agent, buffer, emulsifier, nutrient, discoloration inhibitor. Baked goods, cheese, powdered foods, cured meat, soda, breakfast cereals, dried potatoes.	Useful chemicals that are not toxic, but their widespread use creates dietary imbalance that may be causing osteoporosis.
Red No. 40	Soda, candy, gelatin, desserts, pastry, pet food, sausage.	Causes cancer in mice. Widely used.

Safe

The following common food additives are rated as safe by the Center for Science in the Public Interest. Space restrictions prohibit a detailed description of each additive. The additives are: Alginate, Propylene & Glycol Alginate, Alpha Tocopherol, Ascorbic Acid, Erythorbic Acid, Beta Carotene, Calcium (Sodium) Propionate, Calcium (or Sodium) Stearoyl Lactylate, Carrageenan, Casein, Sodium Caseinate, Citric Acid, Sodium Citrate, EDTA, Ferrous Gluconate, Fumaric Acid, Gelatin, Glycerin (Glycerol), gums (Locust Bean, Guar, Furcelleran, Arabic, Karaya, Tragacanth, Ghatti), Hydrolyzed Vegetable Protein (HVP), Lactic Acid, Lactose, Lecithin, Mannitol, Mon-and-Diglycerides, Polysorbate 60, 65 and 80, Sodium Benzoate, Sodium Carboxymethylcellulose (CMC), Sorbic Acid, Potassium Sorbate, Sorbitan Monostearate, Sorbitol, Starch and Modified Starch, Vanillin, Ethyl Vanillan.

Special Considerations

Artificial Coloring: Yellow No. 6	Beverages, sausage, baked goods, candy, gelatin.	Appears safe, but can cause allergic reactions.
Salt (Sodium chloride)	Flavoring. Most processed foods: soup, potato chips, crackers, cured meat, etc.	Large amounts of sodium may cause high blood pressure in susceptible persons and increase risk of heart attack and stroke.
Sugars: Corn Syrup, Dextrose, Glucose, Invert Sugar, Sugar	Sweeteners. Candy, soft drinks, cookies, syrups, toppings, sweetened cereals and many other foods.	Mostly in foods with low, if any, nutritional value. Excess sugars may promote tooth decay and precipitate diabetes in susceptible persons; condensed sources of calories.

Food and Nutrition

Food contains proteins, carbohydrates, fats, water, vitamins and minerals. Nutrition is the way your body takes in and uses these ingredients to maintain proper functioning. If you aren't eating foods that your body needs, you suffer from poor nutrition and, sooner or later, your health will deteriorate.

Protein

Proteins are composed of amino acids and are indispensable in the diet. They build, maintain, and repair the body. Best sources: eggs, milk, fish, meat, poultry, soybeans, nuts. High quality proteins such as eggs, meat, or fish supply all 8 amino acids needed in the diet. Low quality proteins such as nuts and grain do not.

Fats

Fats provide energy by furnishing calories to the body, and by carrying vitamins A, D, E, and K. They are the most concentrated source of energy in the diet. Best sources: butter, margarine, salad oils, nuts, cream, egg yokes, most cheeses, lard, meat.

Carbohydrates

Carbohydrates provide energy for body function and activity by supplying immediate calories. The carbohydrate group includes sugars, starches, fiber, and starchy vegetables. Best sources: grains, legumes, nuts, potatoes, fruits.

Water

Water dissolves and transports other nutrients throughout the body aiding the process of digestion, absorption, circulation, and excretion. It also helps regulate body temperature. We get water from all foods.

Vitamins

Vitamin A—promotes good eyesight and helps keep the skin and mucous membranes resistant to infection. Best sources: liver, carrots, sweet potatoes, kale, collard greens, turnips, fortified milk.

Vitamin B1 (thiamine)—prevents beriberi. Essential to carbohydrate metabolism and health of nervous system.

Vitamin B2 (riboflavin)—protects skin, mouth, eye, eyelids, and mucous membranes. Essential to protein and energy metabolism. Best sources; liver, milk, meat, poultry, broccoli, mushrooms.

Vitamin B6 (pyridoxine)—important in the regulation of the central nervous system and in protein metabolism. Best

sources: whole grains, meats, nuts, brewers' yeast.

Vitamin B12 (cobalamin)—necessary for the formation of red blood cells. Best sources: liver, meat, fish, eggs, soybeans.

Niacin—maintains the health of skin, tongue, and digestive system. Best sources: poultry, peanuts, fish, organ meats, enriched flour and bread.

Other B vitamins are—biotin, choline, folic acid (folacin), inositol, PABA (para-aminobenzoic acid), and pantothenic acid.

Vitamin C (ascorbic acid)—maintains collagen, a protein necessary for the formation of skin, ligaments, and bones. It helps heal wounds and mend fractures, and aids in resisting some types of virus and bacterial infections. Best sources: citrus fruits and juices, turnips, broccoli, Brussels sprouts, potatoes and sweet potatoes, tomatoes, cabbage.

Vitamin D—important for bone development. Best sources: sunlight, fortified milk and milk products, fish-liver oils, egg yolks, organ meats.

Vitamin E (tocopherol)—helps protect red blood cells. Best sources: vegetable oils, wheat germ, whole grains, eggs, peanuts, organ meats, margarine, green leafy vegetables.

Vitamin K—necessary for formation of prothrombin, which helps blood to clot. Also made by intestinal bacteria. Best dietary sources: green leafy vegetables, tomatoes.

Minerals

Calcium—the most abundant mineral in the body, works with phosphorus in building and maintaining bones and teeth. Best sources: milk and milk products, cheese, and blackstrap molasses.

Phosphorus—the 2d most abundant mineral, performs more functions than any other mineral, and plays a part in nearly every chemical reaction in the body. Best source: whole grains, cheese, milk.

Iron—Necessary for the formation of myoglobin, which transports oxygen to muscle tissue, and hemoglobin, which transports oxygen in the blood. Best sources: organ meats, beans, green leafy vegetables, and shellfish.

Other minerals—chromium, cobalt, copper, fluorine, iodine, magnesium, manganese, molybdenum, potassium, selenium, sodium, sulfur, and zinc.

Recommended Daily Dietary Allowances

Source: Food and Nutrition Board, National Academy of Sciences—National Research Council

The allowances are amounts of nutrients recommended as adequate for maintenance of good nutrition in almost all healthy persons in the U.S. Diets should be based on a variety of common foods in order to provide other nutrients for which human requirements have been less well defined.

	Age (years)	Weight (lbs.)	Protein (grams)	Vitamin A[1]	Vitamin D[2]	Vitamin E[3]	Vitamin C (mg.)	Thiamin (mg.)	Riboflavin (mg.)	Niacin (mg.)[4]	Vitamin B6 (mg.)	Folacin (micrograms)	Vitamin B12 (micrograms)	Calcium (mg.)	Phosphorus (mg.)	Magnesium (mg.)	Iron (mg.)	Zinc (mg.)	Iodine (micrograms)
Infants...	to 6 mos.	13 kg × 2.2		420	10	3	35	0.3	0.4	6	0.3	30	0.5	360	240	50	10	3	40
	to 1 yr.	20 kg × 2.0		400	10	4	35	0.5	0.6	8	0.6	45	1.5	540	360	70	15	5	50
Children..	1-3	29	23	400	10	5	45	0.7	0.8	9	0.9	100	2.0	800	800	150	15	10	70
	4-6	44	30	500	10	6	45	0.9	1.0	11	1.3	200	2.5	800	800	200	10	10	90
	7-10	62	34	700	10	7	45	1.2	1.4	16	1.6	300	3.0	800	800	250	10	10	120
Males..	11-14	99	45	1000	10	8	50	1.4	1.6	18	1.8	400	3.0	1200	1200	350	18	15	150
	15-18	145	56	1000	10	10	60	1.4	1.7	18	2.0	400	3.0	1200	1200	400	18	15	150
	19-22	154	56	1000	7.5	10	60	1.5	1.7	19	2.2	400	3.0	800	800	350	10	15	150
	23-50	154	56	1000	5	10	60	1.4	1.6	18	2.2	400	3.0	800	800	350	10	15	150
	51+	154	56	1000	5	10	60	1.2	1.4	16	2.2	400	3.0	800	800	350	10	15	150
Females.	11-14	101	46	800	10	8	50	1.1	1.3	15	1.8	400	3.0	1200	1200	300	18	15	150
	15-18	120	46	800	10	8	60	1.1	1.3	14	2.0	400	3.0	1200	1200	300	18	15	150
	19-22	120	44	800	7.5	8	60	1.1	1.3	14	2.0	400	3.0	800	800	300	18	15	150
	23-50	120	44	800	5	8	60	1.0	1.2	13	2.0	400	3.0	800	800	300	18	15	150
	51+	120	44	800	5	8	60	1.0	1.2	13	2.0	400	3.0	800	800	300	10	15	150
Pregnant			+30	+200	+5	+2	+20	+0.4	+0.3	+2	+0.6	+400	+1.0	+400	+400	+150	[5]	+5	+25
Lactating			+20	+400	+5	+3	+40	+0.5	+0.5	+5	+0.5	+100	+1.0	+400	+400	+150	[5]	+10	+50

(1) Retinol equivalents. (2) Micrograms of cholecalciferol. (3) Milligrams alpha-tocopherol equivalents. (4) Niacin equivalents. (5) The use of 30-60 milligrams of supplemental iron is recommended.

Nutritive Value of Food (Calories, Proteins, etc.)

Source: Home and Garden Bulletin No. 72; available from Supt. of Documents, U. S. Government Printing Office, Washington, DC 20402

Food	Measure	Food Energy (calories)	Protein (grams)	Fat (grams)	Saturated fats (grams)	Carbohydrate (grams)	Calcium (milligrams)	Iron (milligrams)	Vitamin A (I.U.)	Thiamin (milligrams)	Riboflavin (milligrams)	Niacin (milligrams)	Ascorbic acid (milligrams)
Dairy products													
Cheese, cheddar	1 oz.	115	7	9	6.1	T	204	.2	300	.01	.11	T	0
Cheese, cottage, small curd	1 cup	220	26	9	6.0	6	126	.3	340	.04	.34	.3	T
Cheese, cream	1 oz.	100	2	10	6.2	1	23	.3	400	T	.06	T	0
Cheese, Swiss	1 oz.	105	8	8	5.0	1	272	T	240	.01	.10	T	0
Cheese, pasteurized process spread, American	1 oz.	82	5	6	3.8	2	159	.1	220	.01	.12	T	0
Half-and-Half	1 tbsp.	20	T	2	1.1	1	16	T	20	.01	.02	T	T
Cream, sour	1 tbsp.	25	T	3	1.6	1	14	T	90	T	.02	T	T
Milk, whole	1 cup	150	8	8	5.1	11	291	.1	310	.09	.40	.2	2
Milk, nonfat (skim)	1 cup	85	8	T	.3	12	302	.1	500	.09	.37	.2	2
Buttermilk	1 cup	100	8	2	1.3	12	285	.1	80	.08	.38	.1	2
Milkshake, chocolate	10.6 oz.	355	9	8	5.0	63	396	.9	260	.14	.67	.4	0
Ice Cream, hardened	1 cup	270	5	14	8.9	32	176	.1	540	.05	.33	.1	1
Sherbet	1 cup	270	2	4	2.4	59	103	.3	190	.03	.09	.1	4
Yogurt, fruit-flavored	8 oz.	230	10	3	1.8	42	343	.2	120	.08	.40	.2	1
Eggs													
Fried in butter	1	85	5	6	2.4	1	26	.9	290	.03	.13	T	0
Hard-cooked	1	80	6	6	1.7	1	28	1.0	260	.04	.14	T	0
Scrambled in butter (milk added)	1	95	6	7	2.8	1	47	.9	310	.04	.16	T	0
Fats & oils													
Butter	1 tbsp.	100	T	12	7.2	T	3	T	430	T	T	T	0
Margarine	1 tbsp.	100	T	12	2.1	T	3	T	470	T	T	T	0
Salad dressing, blue cheese	1 tbsp.	75	1	8	1.6	1	12	T	30	T	.02	T	T
Salad dressing, French	1 tbsp.	65	T	6	1.1	3	2	1	-	-	-	-	-
Salad dressing, Italian	1 tbsp.	85	T	9	1.6	1	2	T	T	T	T	T	-
Mayonnaise	1 tbsp.	100	T	11	2.0	T	3	.1	40	T	.01	T	-
Meat, poultry, fish													
Bluefish, baked with butter or margarine	3 oz.	135	22	4	-	0	25	0.6	40	.09	.08	1.6	-
Clams, raw, meat only	3 oz.	65	11	1	-	2	59	5.2	90	.08	.15	1.1	8
Crabmeat, white or king, canned	1 cup	135	24	3	.6	1	61	1.1	-	.11	.11	2.6	-
Fish sticks, breaded, cooked, frozen	1 oz.	50	5	3	-	2	3	.1	0	.01	.02	.5	-
Salmon, pink, canned	3 oz.	120	17	5	.9	0	167	.7	60	.03	.16	6.8	-
Sardines, Atlantic, canned in oil	3 oz.	175	20	9	3.0	0	372	2.5	190	.02	.17	4.6	-
Shrimp, French fried	3 oz.	190	17	9	2.3	9	61	1.7	-	.03	.07	2.3	-
Tuna, canned in oil	3 oz.	170	24	7	1.7	0	7	1.6	70	.04	.10	10.1	-
Bacon, broiled or fried crisp	2 slices	85	4	8	2.5	T	2	.5	0	.08	.05	.8	-
Ground beef, broiled, 10% fat	3 oz.	185	23	10	4.0	0	10	3.0	20	.08	.20	5.1	-
Roast beef, relatively lean	3 oz.	165	25	7	2.8	0	11	3.2	10	.06	.19	4.5	-
Beef steak, lean and fat	3 oz.	330	20	27	11.3	0	9	2.5	50	.05	.15	4.0	-
Beef & vegetable stew	1 cup	220	16	11	4.9	15	29	2.9	2,400	.15	.17	4.7	17
Lamb, chop, lean and fat	3.1 oz.	360	18	32	14.8	0	8	1.0	-	.11	.19	4.1	-
Liver, beef	3 oz.	195	22	9	2.5	5	9	7.5	45,390	.22	3.56	14.00	23
Ham, light cure, lean and fat	3 oz.	245	18	19	6.8	0	8	2.2	0	.40	.15	3.1	-
Pork, chop, lean and fat	2.7 oz	305	19	25	8.9	0	9	2.7	0	.75	.22	4.5	-
Bologna	1 slice	85	3	8	3.0	T	2	.5	-	.05	.06	.7	-
Frankfurter, cooked	1	170	7	15	5.6	1	3	.8	-	.08	.11	1.4	-
Sausage, pork link, cooked	1 link	60	2	6	2.1	T	1	.3	0	.10	.04	.5	-
Veal, cutlet, braised or boiled	3 oz.	185	23	9	4.0	0	9	2.7	-	.06	.21	4.6	-
Chicken, drumstick, fried, bones removed	1.3 oz.	90	12	4	1.1	1	6	.9	50	.03	.15	2.7	-
Chicken, half broiler, broiled, bones removed	6.2 oz.	240	42	7	2.2	0	16	3.0	160	.09	.34	15.5	-
Chicken a la king	1 cup	470	27	34	12.7	12	127	2.5	1,130	.10	.42	5.4	12
Chicken potpie, baked, 1/3 of 9 in. diam. pie	1 piece	545	23	31	11.3	42	70	3.0	3,090	.34	.31	5.5	5
Fruits & products													
Apple, raw, 2-3/4 in. diam.	1	80	T	1	-	20	10	.4	120	.04	.03	.1	6
Applejuice	1 cup	120	T	T	-	30	15	1.5	-	.02	.05	.2	2
Applesauce, canned, sweetened	1 cup	230	T	T	-	61	10	1.3	100	.05	.03	.1	3
Apricots, raw	3	55	1	T	-	14	18	.5	2,890	.03	.04	.6	11
Banana, raw	1	100	1	T	-	26	10	.8	230	.06	.07	.8	12
Cherries, sweet, raw	10	45	1	T	-	12	15	.3	70	.03	.04	.3	7
Fruit cocktail, canned, in heavy syrup	1 cup	195	1	T	-	50	23	1.0	360	.05	.03	1.0	5
Grapefruit, raw, medium, white	1/2	45	1	T	-	12	19	.5	10	.05	.02	.2	44
Grapes, Thompson seedless	10	35	T	T	-	9	6	.2	50	.03	.02	.2	2
Lemonade, frozen, diluted	1 cup	105	T	T	-	28	2	.1	10	.01	.02	.2	17
Cantaloupe, 5-in. diam.	1/2	80	2	T	-	20	38	1.1	9,240	.11	.08	1.6	90
Orange, 2-5/8 in. diam.	1	65	1	T	-	16	54	.5	260	.13	.05	.5	66
Orange juice, frozen, diluted	1 cup	120	2	T	-	29	25	.2	540	.23	.03	.9	120
Peach, raw, 2-1/2 in. diam.	1	40	1	T	-	10	9	.5	1,330	.02	.05	1.0	7
Peaches, canned in syrup	1	200	1	T	-	51	10	.8	1,100	.03	.05	1.5	8
Pear, raw, Bartlett, 2-1/2 in. diam.	1	100	1	1	-	25	13	.5	30	.03	.07	.2	7
Pineapple, heavy syrup pack, crushed, chunks	1 cup	190	1	T	-	49	28	.8	130	.20	.05	.5	18
Raisins, seedless	1 cup	420	4	T	-	112	90	5.1	30	.16	.12	.7	1
Strawberries, whole	1 cup	55	1	1	-	13	31	1.5	90	.04	.10	.9	88
Watermelon, 4 by 8 in. wedge	1 wedge	110	2	1	-	27	30	2.1	2,510	.13	.13	.9	30
Grain products													
Bagel, egg	1	165	6	2	.5	28	9	1.2	30	.14	.10	1.2	0
Biscuit, 2 in. diam., from home recipe	1	105	2	5	1.2	13	34	.4	T	.08	.08	.7	T
Bread, raisin	1 slice	65	2	1	-	13	18	.6	T	.09	.06	.6	T
Bread, white, enriched, soft-crumb	1 slice	70	2	1	.2	13	21	.6	T	.10	.06	.8	T
Bread, whole wheat, soft-crumb	1 slice	65	3	1	.1	14	24	.8	T	.09	.03	.8	T
Oatmeal or rolled oats	1 cup	130	5	2	.4	23	22	1.4	0	.19	.05	.2	0
Bran flakes (40% bran), added sugar, salt, iron, vitamins	1 cup	105	4	1	-	28	19	12.4	1,650	.41	.49	4.1	12
Corn flakes, added sugar, salt, iron, vitamins	1 cup	95	2	T	-	21	*	0.6	1,180	.29	.35	2.9	9
Rice, puffed, added iron, thiamin, niacin	1 cup	60	1	T	-	13	3	.3	0	.07	.01	.7	0

(continued)

(continued)

Food	Measure	Food Energy (calories)	Protein (grams)	Fat (grams)	Saturated fats (grams)	Carbohydrate (grams)	Calcium (milligrams)	Iron (milligrams)	Vitamin A (I.U.)	Thiamin (milligrams)	Riboflavin (milligrams)	Niacin (milligrams)	Ascorbic acid (milligrams)
Wheat, shredded, plain, 1 biscuit or 1/2 cup	1 serving	90	2	1	-	20	11	.9	0	.06	.03	1.1	0
Cake, angel food, 1/12 of cake	1	135	3	T	-	32	50	.2	0	.03	.08	.3	0
Coffeecake, 1/6 cake	1	230	5	7	2.0	38	44	1.2	120	.14	.15	1.3	T
Cupcake, 2-1/2 in. diam., with chocolate icing	1	130	2	5	2.0	21	47	.4	60	.05	.06	.4	T
Boston cream pie with custard filling, 1/12 of cake	1	210	3	6	1.9	34	46	.7	140	.09	.11	.8	T
Fruitcake, dark, 1/30 of loaf	1	55	1	2	.5	9	11	.4	20	.02	.02	.2	T
Cake, pound, 1/17 of loaf	1	160	2	10	2.5	16	6	.5	80	.05	.06	.4	0
Brownies, with nuts, from commercial recipe	1	85	1	4	.9	13	9	.4	20	.03	.02	.2	T
Cookies, chocolate chip, from home recipe	4	205	2	12	3.5	24	14	.8	40	.06	.06	.5	T
Vanilla wafers	10	185	2	6	-	30	16	.6	50	.10	.09	.8	0
Crackers, graham	2	55	1	1	.3	10	6	.5	0	.02	.08	.5	0
Crackers, saltines	4	50	1	1	.3	8	2	.5	0	.05	.05	.4	0
Danish pastry, round piece	1	275	5	15	4.7	30	33	1.2	200	.18	.19	1.7	T
Doughnut, cake type	1	100	1	5	1.2	13	10	.4	20	.05	.05	.4	T
Macaroni and cheese, from home recipe	1 cup	430	17	22	8.9	40	362	1.8	860	.20	.40	1.8	T
Muffin, corn	1	125	3	4	1.2	19	42	.7	120	.10	.10	.7	T
Noodles, enriched, cooked	1 cup	200	7	2	-	37	16	1.4	110	.22	.13	1.9	0
Pancake, plain, from home recipe	1	60	2	2	.5	9	27	.4	30	.06	.07	.5	T
Pie, apple, 1/7 of pie	1	345	3	15	3.9	51	11	.9	40	.15	.11	1.3	2
Pie, banana cream, 1/7 of pie	1	285	6	12	3.8	40	86	1.0	330	.11	.22	1.0	1
Pie, cherry, 1/7 of pie	1	350	4	15	4.0	52	19	.9	590	.16	.12	1.4	T
Pie, lemon meringue, 1/7 of pie	1	305	4	12	3.7	45	17	1.0	200	.09	.12	.7	4
Pie, pecan, 1/7 of pie	1	495	6	27	4.0	61	55	3.7	190	.26	.14	1.0	T
Pie, pumpkin, 1/7 of pie	1	275	5	15	5.4	32	66	1.0	3,210	.11	.18	1.0	T
Pizza, cheese, 1/8 of 12 in. diam. pie	1	145	6	4	1.7	22	86	1.1	230	.16	.18	1.6	4
Popcorn, popped, plain	1 cup	25	1	T	T	5	1	.2	-	-	.01	.1	0
Pretzels, stick	10	10	T	T	-	2	1	T	0	.01	.01	.1	0
Rice, white, enriched, instant, cooked	1 cup	180	4	T	T	40	5	1.3	0	.21	**	1.7	0
Rolls, enriched, brown & serve	1	85	2	2	-	14	20	.5	T	.10	.06	.9	T
Rolls, frankfurter & hamburger	1	120	3	2	.5	21	30	.8	T	.16	.10	1.3	T
Spaghetti with meat balls & tomato sauce, from home recipe	1 cup	330	19	12	3.3	39	124	3.7	1,590	.25	.30	4.0	22
Legumes, nuts, seeds													
Beans, Great Northern, cooked	1 cup	210	14	1	-	38	90	4.9	0	.25	.13	1.3	0
Peanuts, roasted in oil, salted	1 cup	840	37	72	13.7	27	107	3.0	-	.46	.19	24.8	0
Peanut butter	1 tbsp.	95	4	8	1.5	3	9	.3	-	.02	.02	2.4	0
Sunflower seeds	1 cup	810	35	69	8.2	29	174	10.3	70	2.84	.33	7.8	-
Sugars & sweets													
Candy, caramels	1 oz.	115	1	3	1.6	22	42	.4	T	.01	.05	.1	T
Candy, milk chocolate	1 oz.	145	2	9	5.5	16	65	.3	80	.02	.10	.1	T
Fudge, chocolate	1 oz.	115	1	3	1.3	21	22	.3	T	.01	.03	.1	T
Candy, hard	1 oz.	110	0	T	-	28	6	.5	0	0	0	0	0
Honey	1 tbsp.	65	T	0	0	17	1	.1	0	T	.01	.1	T
Jams & Preserves	1 tbsp.	55	T	T	-	14	4	.2	T	T	.01	T	T
Sugar, white, granulated	1 tbsp.	45	0	0	0	12	0	T	0	0	0	0	0
Vegetables													
Asparagus, canned, spears	4 spears	15	2	T	-	3	15	1.5	640	.05	.08	.6	12
Beans, lima, thick-seeded	1 cup	170	10	1	-	32	34	2.9	390	.12	.09	1.7	29
Beans, green, from frozen, cuts	1 cup	35	2	1	-	8	54	.9	780	.09	.12	.5	7
Beets, canned, diced or sliced	1 cup	65	2	T	-	15	32	1.2	30	.02	.05	.2	5
Broccoli, cooked	1 stalk	45	6	1	-	8	158	1.4	4,500	.16	.36	1.4	162
Cabbage, raw, coarsely shredded or sliced	1 cup	15	1	T	-	4	34	.3	90	.04	.04	.2	33
Carrots, raw, 7-1/2 by 1-1/8 in.	1	30	1	T	-	7	27	.5	7,930	.04	.04	.4	6
Cauliflower, raw	1 cup	31	3	T	-	6	29	1.3	70	.13	.12	.8	90
Celery, raw	1 stalk	5	T	T	-	2	16	.1	110	.01	.01	.1	4
Collards, cooked	1 cup	65	7	1	-	10	357	1.5	14,820	.21	.38	2.3	144
Corn, sweet, cooked	1 ear	70	2	1	-	16	2	.5	310	.09	.08	1.1	7
Corn, cream style	1 cup	210	5	2	-	51	8	1.5	840	.08	.13	2.6	13
Cucumber, with peel	6-8 slices	5	T	T	-	1	7	.3	70	.01	.01	.1	3
Lettuce, iceberg, chopped	1 cup	5	T	T	-	2	11	.3	180	.03	.03	.2	3
Mushrooms, raw	1 cup	20	2	T	-	3	4	.6	T	.07	.32	2.9	2
Onions, raw, chopped	1 cup	65	3	T	-	15	46	.9	T	.05	.07	.3	17
Peas, frozen, cooked	1 cup	110	8	T	-	19	30	3.0	960	.43	.14	2.7	21
Potatoes, baked, peeled	1	145	4	T	-	33	14	1.1	T	.15	.07	2.7	31
Potatoes, frozen, French fried	10	110	2	4	1.1	17	5	.9	T	.07	.01	1.3	11
Potatoes, mashed, milk added	1 cup	135	4	2	.7	27	50	.8	40	.17	.11	2.1	21
Potato chips	10	115	1	8	2.1	10	8	.4	T	.04	.01	1.0	3
Potato salad	1 cup	250	7	7	2.0	41	80	1.5	350	.20	.18	2.8	28
Sauerkraut, canned	1 cup	40	2	T	-	9	85	1.2	120	.07	.09	.5	33
Spinach, chopped, from frozen	1 cup	45	6	1	-	8	232	4.3	16,200	.14	.31	.8	39
Squash, summer, cooked	1 cup	30	2	T	-	7	53	.8	820	.11	.17	1.7	21
Sweet potatoes, baked in skin, peeled	1	160	2	1	-	37	46	1.0	9,230	.10	.08	.8	25
Tomatoes, raw	1	25	1	T	-	6	16	.6	1,110	.07	.05	.9	28
Tomato catsup	1 tbsp.	15	T	T	-	4	3	.1	210	.01	.01	.2	2
Tomato juice	1 cup	45	2	T	-	10	17	2.2	1,940	.12	.07	1.9	39
Miscellaneous													
Beer	12 fl. oz.	150	1	0	0	14	18	T	-	.01	.11	2.2	-
Gin, rum, vodka, whisky, 86 proof	1-1/2 fl. oz.	105	0	0	0	T	-	-	-	-	-	-	-
Wine, table	3-1/2 fl. oz.	85	T	0	0	4	9	.4	-	T	.01	.1	-
Cola-type beverage	12 fl. oz.	145	0	0	0	37	-	-	0	0	0	0	0
Ginger ale	12 fl. oz	115	0	0	0	29	-	-	0	0	0	0	0
Gelatin dessert	1 cup	140	4	0	0	34	-	-	-	-	-	-	-
Mustard, prepared	1 tsp.	5	T	T	-	T	4	.1	-	-	-	-	-
Olives, pickled, green	4 medium	15	T	2	.2	T	8	.2	40	-	-	-	-
Pickles, dill, whole	1	5	T	T	-	1	17	.7	70	T	.01	T	4
Popsicle, 3 fl. oz.	1	70	0	0	0	18	0	T	0	0	0	0	0
Soup, cream of chicken, prepared with milk	1 cup	180	7	10	4.2	15	172	.5	610	.05	.27	.7	2
Soup, cream of mushroom, prepared with milk	1 cup	215	7	14	5.4	16	191	.5	250	.05	.34	.7	1
Soup, tomato, prepared with water	1 cup	90	2	3	.6	16	15	.7	1,000	.05	.05	1.2	12

T — Indicates trace   * — Varies by brand

Birthstones

Source: Jewelry Industry Council

Month	Ancient	Modern	Month	Ancient	Modern
January	Garnet	Garnet	July	Onyx	Ruby
February	Amethyst	Amethyst	August	Carnelian	Sardonyx or Peridot
March	Jasper	Bloodstone or Aquamarine	September	Chrysolite	Sapphire
April	Sapphire	Diamond	October	Aquamarine	Opal or Tourmaline
May	Agate	Emerald	November	Topaz	Topaz
June	Emerald	Pearl, Moonstone, or Alexandrite	December	Ruby	Turquoise or Zircon

Wedding Anniversaries

The traditional names for wedding anniversaries go back many years in social usage. As such names as wooden, crystal, silver, and golden were applied it was considered proper to present the married pair with gifts made of these products or of something related. The list of traditional gifts, with a few allowable revisions in parentheses, is presented below, followed by modern gifts in **bold face**.

1st-Paper, **clocks**
2d-Cotton, **china**
3d-Leather, **crystal & glass**
4th-Linen (silk), **electrical appliances**
5th-Wood, **silverware**
6th-Iron, **wood**
7th-Wool (copper), **desk sets**
8th-Bronze, **linens & lace**
9th-Pottery (china), **leather**

10th-Tin (aluminum), **diamond jewelry**
11th-Steel, **fashion jewelry, accessories**
12th-Silk, **pearls or colored gems**
13th-Lace, **textiles & furs**
14th-Ivory, **gold jewelry**
15th-Crystal, **watches**
20th-China, **platinum**
25th-Silver, **sterling silver jubliee**

30th-Pearl, **diamond**
35th-Coral (jade), **jade**
40th-Ruby, **ruby**
45th-Sapphire, **sapphire**
50th-Gold, **gold**
55th-Emerald, **emerald**
60th-Diamond, **diamond**

Canadian Marriage Information

Source: Compiled from information provided by the various provincial government departments and agencies concerned.

Marriageable age, by provinces, for both males and females with and without consent of parents or guardians. In some provinces, the court has authority, given special circumstances, to marry young couples below the minimum age. Most provinces waive the blood test requirement and the waiting period varies across the provinces.

Province	With consent		Without consent		Blood test Required	other province Accepted	Wait for license	Wait after license
	Men	Women	Men	Women				
Newfoundland	16	16	19	19	None	None	4 days	4 days
Prince Edward Island	16	16	18	18	Yes	Yes	5 days	None
Nova Scotia	(1)	(1)	19	19	None	None	5 days	None
New Brunswick	16	14	18	18	None	None	5 days	None
Quebec	14	12	18	18	None	—	—	None
Ontario	16	16	18	18	None	—	None[2]	3 days
Manitoba	16	16	18	18	Yes	Yes	None	24 hours
Saskatchewan	15	15	18	18	Yes	Yes	None	24 hours
Alberta	16[8]	16[8]	18	18	Yes[3]	Yes[4]	None[5]	None
British Columbia	16[6]	16[6]	19	19	None	None	2 days[7]	None
Yukon Territory	15	15	19	19	None	None	None	24 hours
Northwest Territories	15	15[9]	19	19	None	Yes	None	None

(1) There is no statutory minimum age in the province. Anyone under the age of 19 years must have consent for marriage and no person under the age of 16 may be married without authorization of a Family Court judge and in addition must have the necessary consent of the parent or guardian. (2) Special requirements applicable to nonresidents. (3) Applies only to applicants under 60 years of age. (4) This is upon filing of negative lab report indicating blood test was taken within 14 days preceding date of application for license. (5) Exception where consent is required by mail; depending receipt of divorce documents, etc. (6) Persons under 16 years of age (no minimum age specified) may also be married if they have obtained, in addition to the usual consent from parents or guardian, an order from a judge of the Supreme or County Court in this province. (7) Including day of application, e.g., a license applied for on a Monday cannot be issued until Wednesday. (8) Under 16 allowed if pregnant or the mother of a living child. (9) Under 15 allowed if pregnant or with the written permission of the Commissioner of the NWT.

Grounds for Divorce in Canada

Source: Government of Canada Divorce Act

The grounds for divorce in Canada are the same for all the provinces and its territories. There are two categories of offense:

A. Marital Offense:
  Adultery
  Sodomy
  Bestiality
  Rape
  Homosexual act
  Subsequent marriage
  Physical cruelty
  Mental cruelty

B. Marriage breakdown by reason of:
  Imprisonment for aggregate period of not less than 3 years
  Imprisonment for not less than 2 years on sentence of death or sentence of 10 years or more
  Addiction to alcohol
  Addiction to narcotics
  Whereabouts of spouse unknown
  Non-consummation
  Separation for not less than 3 years
  Desertion by petitioner for not less than 5 years

Residence time: Domicile in Canada. Time between interlocutory and final decree: normally 3 months before final can be applied for.

Marriage Information

Source: Compiled by William E. Mariano, Council on Marriage Relations, Inc.,
110 E. 42d St., New York, NY 10017 (as of Aug. 24, 1982)

Marriageable age, by states, for both males and females with and without consent of parents or guardians. In most states, the court has authority to marry young couples below the ordinary age of consent, where due regard for their morals and welfare so requires. In many states, under special circumstances, blood test and waiting period may be waived.

State	With consent		Without consent		Blood test*		Wait for license	Wait after license
	Men	Women	Men	Women	Required	Other state accepted		
Alabama(b)	14	14	18	18	Yes	Yes	none	none
Alaska	16	16	18	18	Yes	No	3 days	none
Arizona	16(g)	16	18	18	Yes	Yes	none	none
Arkansas	17	16(h)	18	18	Yes	No	3 days	none
California	18(g)	18	18	18	Yes	Yes	none	none
Colorado	16	16	18	18	Yes	...	none	none
Connecticut	16	16(j)	18	18	Yes	Yes	4 days	none
Delaware	18	16(k)	18	18	Yes	Yes	none	24 hrs. (c)
District of Columbia	16	16	18	18	Yes	Yes	3 days	none
Florida	16	16	18	18	Yes	Yes	3 days	none
Georgia	16(g)	16(g)	18	18	Yes	Yes	none (k)	none
Hawaii	16	16	18	18	Yes	Yes	none	none
Idaho	16	16	18	18	Yes	Yes	none	none
Illinois (a)	16	16	18	18	Yes	Yes	none	1 day
Indiana	17(k)	17(k)	18	18	Yes	No	72 hours	none
Iowa	— (k)	— (k)	18	18	Yes	Yes	3 days	none
Kansas	14	12	18	18	Yes	Yes	3 days	none
Kentucky	— (k)	— (k)	18	18	Yes	No	3 days	none
Louisiana (a)	18(k)	16(h)	18	16	Yes	No	none	72 hours
Maine	16(h)	16(h)	18	18	No	No	5 days	none
Maryland	16	16	18	18	none	none	48 hours	none
Massachusetts	— (k)	— (k)	18	18	Yes	Yes	3 days	none
Michigan (a)	16	16	18	18	Yes	No	3 days	none
Minnesota	16(e)	16(e)	18	18	none	...	5 days	none
Mississippi (b)	17(l)	15(l)	21	21	Yes	...	3 days	none
Missouri	15	15	18	18	none	Yes	3 days	none
Montana	15	15	18	18	Yes	Yes	none	3 days
Nebraska	17	17	18	18	Yes	Yes	2 days	none
Nevada	16	16	18	18	none	none	none	none
New Hampshire (a)	14(e)	13(e)	18	18	Yes	Yes	5 days	none
New Jersey (a)	— (g)	12	18	18	Yes	Yes	72 hours	none
New Mexico	16	16	18	18	Yes	Yes	none	none
New York	16	14(e)	18	18	Yes	No	none	24 hrs.(f)
North Carolina (a)	16	16	18	18	Yes	No	none	none
North Dakota (a)	16	16	18	18	Yes	...	none	none
Ohio (a)	18	16	18	18	Yes	Yes	5 days	none
Oklahoma	16	16	18	18	Yes	No	none	none
Oregon	17	17	18	18	Yes	No	3 days	none
Pennsylvania	16	16	18	18	Yes	No	3 days	none
Rhode Island (a) (b)	14	12	18	18	Yes	Yes	none	none
South Carolina	14	12	18	18	none	none	24 hrs.	none
South Dakota	16	16	18	18	Yes	Yes	none	none
Tennessee (b)	16	16	18	18	Yes	Yes	3 days	none
Texas	14(k)	14(k)	18	18	Yes	Yes	none	none
Utah (a)	14	14	18	18	none	Yes	none	none
Vermont (a)	16	16	18	18	Yes	...	none	5 days
Virginia (a)	16	16	18	18	Yes	Yes	none	none
Washington	17	17	18	18	(d)	...	3 days	none
West Virginia	16	16	18	18	Yes	No	3 days	none
Wisconsin	16	16	18	18	Yes	Yes	5 days	none
Wyoming	16	16	19	19	Yes	Yes	none	none
Puerto Rico	18	16	21	21	Yes	none	none	8 days
Virgin Islands	16	16	18	18	none	none	none	none

*Many states have additional special requirements; contact individual state. (a) Special laws applicable to non-residents. **(b)** Special laws applicable to those under 21 years; Ala., bond required if male is under 18, female under 18. **(c)** 24 hours if one or both parties resident of state; 96 hours if both parties are non-residents. **(d)** None, but both must file affidavit. **(e)** Parental consent plus court's consent required. **(f)** Marriage may not be solemnized within 10 days from date of blood test. **(g)** Statute provides for obtaining license with parental or court consent with no state minimum age. **(h)** Under 16, with parental and court consent. **(j)** If either under 18, wait 3 full days. **(j)** If under stated age, court consent required. **(k)** If under 18, parental and/or court consent required. **(l)** Both parents' consent required for men age 17, women age 15; one parent's consent required for men 18-20 years, women ages 16-20 years.

How to Obtain Birth, Marriage, Death Records

The United States government has published a series of inexpensive booklets entitled: Where to Write for Birth & Death Records; Where to Write for Marriage Records; Where to Write for Divorce Records; Where to Write for Birth and Death Records of U. S. Citizens Who were Born or Died Outside of the U. S.; Birth Certifications for Alien Children Adopted by U. S. Citizens; You May Save Time Proving Your Age and Other Birth Facts. They tell where to write to get a certified copy of an original vital record. Supt. of Documents, Government Printing Office, Washington, DC 20402.

Grounds for Divorce

Source: Compiled by William E. Mariano, Council on Marriage Relations, Inc., 110 E. 42d St., New York, NY 10017 (as of Aug. 24, 1982)

Persons contemplating divorce should study latest decisions or secure legal advice before initiating proceedings since different interpretations or exceptions in each case can change the conclusion reached.

State	Breakdown of marriage/ incompatibility	Cruelty	Desertion	Non-support	Alcohol &/or drug addiction	Felony	Impotency	Insanity[1]	Living separate and apart	Other grounds	Residence time	Time between interlocut'y and final decrees
Alabama	X	X	X	X	X	X	X	X	2 yrs.	A-B-E	6 mos.	none-M
Alaska	X									B-C-F	1 yr.	none
Arizona	X										90 days	none
Arkansas	...	X	X	X	X	X	X	X	3 yrs.	C-I	3 mos.	none
California[2]	X							X			6 mos.	6 mos.
Colorado[2]	X										90 days	none
Connecticut	X	X	X	X	X	X		X	18 mos.	B	1 yr.	none
Delaware	X[4]								6 mos.		6 mos.	none
Dist. of Columbia									6 mos.-1 yr.		6 mos.	none
Florida	X							X			6 mos.	none
Georgia	X	X	X		X	X	X	X		A-B-F	6 mos.	L
Hawaii	X	X	X						2 yrs.	K	3 mos.	none
Idaho	X	X	X	X	X	X		X	5 yrs.	H	6 wks.	none
Illinois		X	X	X	X	X				I-J	90 days	none
Indiana	X					X	X	X			6 mos.	none
Iowa	X										1 yr.	none-N
Kansas	X									H	60 days	none-M
Kentucky	X								1 yr.		180 days	none
Louisiana	...	X	X	X	X	X			1 yr.	C-J-K	12 mos.	none-N
Maine	X	X	X	X	X		X			H	6 mos.	none
Maryland	...	X	X			X	X	X	1-3 yrs.	D-I	1 yr.	none
Massachusetts	X[4]	X	X	X	X	X	X		6 mos.-1 yr.		1 yr.	6 mos.
Michigan	X										180 days	none
Minnesota	X										180 days	none-O
Mississippi	X	X	X		X	X	X	X		A	6 mos.	none-P
Missouri	X[4]										90 days	none
Montana	X										90 days	none
Nebraska	X										1 yr.	6 mos.
Nevada	X							X	1 yr.		6 wks.	none
New Hampshire[3]	X	X	X	X	X	X	X		2 yrs.	K	1 yr.	none
New Jersey	...	X	X		X	X		X	18 mos.	E-K	1 yr.	none
New Mexico	X	X	X								6 mos.	none
New York		X	X			X			1 yr.	K	1 yr.	none
North Carolina								X	1 yr.	A-E	6 mos.	none
North Dakota	X	X	X	X	X	X	X	X		H-K	12 mos.	none
Ohio	X	X	X	X	X	X	X	X	2 yrs.	B-G-H-I	6 mos.	none
Oklahoma	X	X	X	X	X	X	X	X		A-B-G-H	6 mos.	none
Oregon[2]	X									B	6 mos.	30 days
Pennsylvania	X	X	X		X	X	X		3 yrs.	C-D-I	6 mos.	none
Rhode Island	X	X	X	X	X	X	X	...	3 yrs.		1 yr.	3 mos.
South Carolina	X	X	X		X				1 yr.		3 mos.	none
South Dakota	...	X	X	X	X	X					none	none
Tennessee	X	X	X	X	X	X	X			A-H-I-J-K	6 mos.	none-O
Texas	X	X	X		X			X	3 yrs.		6 mos.	none-O
Utah	X	X	X	X	X	X	X	X		K	3 mos.	3 mos.
Vermont	X	X	X	X		X			6 mos.		6 mos.	3 mos.
Virginia		X	X			X			6 mos.-1 yr.	E	6 mos.	none-P
Washington	X										none	none-R
West Virginia	X	X	X	X	X			X	1 yr.	U	1 yr.	none
Wisconsin	X								1 yr.	K	6 mos.	none-O
Wyoming	X							X	2 yrs.		60 days	none

Adultery is either grounds for divorce or evidence of irreconcilable differences and a breakdown of the marriage in all states. The plaintiff can invariably remarry in the same state where he or she procured a decree of divorce or annulment. Not so the defendant, who is barred in certain states for some offenses. After a period of time has elapsed even the offender can apply for permission.

(1) Generally 5 yrs. insanity but: permanent insanity in Ut.; incurable insanity in Col.; 1 yr. Wis.; 18 mos. Alas.; 2 yrs. Ga., Ha., Ind., Nev., N.J., Ore., Wash., Wy.; 3 yrs. Ark., Cal., Fla., Md., Minn., Miss., N.C., Tex., W. Va.; 6 yrs. Ida.; Kan: Incompability by reason of mental illness or incapacity. (2) Cal., Colo., and Ore., have procedures whereby a couple can obtain a divorce without an attorney and without appearing in court provided certain requirements are met. (3) Other grounds existing only in N.H. are: Joining a religious order disbelieving in marriage, treatment which injures health or endangers reason, wife without the state for 10 years, and wife in state 2 yrs. husband never in state and intends to become a citizen of a foreign country. (4) Provable only by fault grounds, separation for some period, generally a year, proof of marital discord or commitment for mental illness. (A) Pregnancy at marriage. (B) Fraudulent contract. (C) Indignities. (D) Consanguinity. (E) Crime against nature. (F) Mental incapacity at time of marriage. (G) Procurement of out-of-state divorce. (H) Gross neglect of duty. (I) Bigamy. (J) Attempted homocide. (K) Separation by decree in Conn.; after decree: one yr. in La., N.Y., Wis.; 18 mos. in N.H.; 2 yrs. in Ala., Ha., Minn., N.C. Tenn.; 3 yrs. in Ut.; 4 yrs. in N.J., N.D.; 5 yrs. in Md. (L) Determined by court order. (N) 60 days to remarry. (N) One yr. to remarry except Ha. one yr. with minor child; La. 90 days. (O) 6 mos. to remarry. (P) Adultery cases, remarriage in court's discretion. (Q) Plaintiff, 6 mos.; defendant 2 yrs. to remarry. (R) No remarriage if an appeal is pending. (S) Actual domicile in adultery cases. (U) Abuse and neglect of child; physical or mental injury to child. **Enoch Arden Laws.** disappearance and unknown to be alive - Conn., S.C., Va., Vt., 7 yrs. absence; Ala., Ark., N.Y. 5 yrs. (called dissolution); N.H. 2 yrs.

N.B. Grounds not recognized for divorce may be recognized for separation or annulment. Local laws should be consulted.

Who Owns What: Familiar Consumer Products

The following is a list of familiar consumer products and their parent companies. If you wish to register a complaint beyond the local level, the address of the parent company can be found on pages 140-146.

Admiral appliances: Magic Chef
Ajax cleanser: Colgate-Palmolive
Allstate Insurance Co.: Sears, Roebuck
Anacin: American Home Products
Aqua Velva: Nabisco
Arby's restaurants: Royal Crown
Arrid anti-perspirant: Carter-Wallace
Baggies: Colgate-Palmolive
Ban anti-perspirant: Bristol-Myers
Bayer aspirin: Sterling Drug
Beech Aircraft: Raytheon
Benson & Hedges cigarettes; Philip Morris
Betty Crocker products: General Mills
Birds Eye frozen foods: General Foods
Brooks Brothers stores: Allied Stores
Brut toiletries: Faberge
Budweiser beer: Anheuser-Busch
Bufferin: Bristol-Myers
Burger King restaurants: Pillsbury
Business Week magazine: McGraw-Hill
Buster Brown shoes: Brown Group
Cabbage Patch Kids dolls: Coleco
Cap'n Crunch cereal: Quaker Oats
Carrier air conditioners: United Technologies
Celeste Pizza: Quaker Oats
Chap Stick: A.H. Robins
Chef Boy-ar-dee products: American Home Products
Cheerios cereal: General Mills
Clairol hair products: Bristol-Myers
Cold Power detergent: Colgate-Palmolive
Colt 45 malt liquor: Heileman Brewing
Columbia Pictures: Coca Cola
Copenhagen snuff: U.S. Tobacco
Cover Girl cosmetics: Noxell
Cracker Jack: Borden
Crest toothpaste: Procter & Gamble
Crisco shortening: Procter & Gamble
Cycle dog food: General Foods
Dash detergent: Procter & Gamble
Del Monte foods: R.J. Reynolds
Diet Rite Cola: Royal Crown
Doritos chips: PepsiCo
Dristan: American Home Products
Duracell batteries: Dart & Kraft
Easy-Off oven cleaner: American Home Products
Elizabeth Arden cosmetics: Eli Lilly
Esquire shoe polish: Papercraft
Ethan Allen furniture: Interco
Eveready batteries: Union Carbide
Excedrin: Bristol-Myers
Fab detergent: Colgate-Palmolive
Family Circle magazine: New York Times
Fisher Price toys: Quaker Oats
Flagg Bros. shoe stores: Genesco
Foamy shaving cream: Gillette
Folger coffee: Procter & Gamble
Formula 409 spray cleaner: Clorox
Franco-American foods: Campbell Soup
Friendly Ice Cream restaurants: Hershey Foods
Friskies pet foods: Carnation
Frito-Lay snacks: PepsiCo
Gatorade: Quaker Oats
Geritol: Nabisco
Gleem toothpaste: Procter & Gamble
Good Seasons salad dressing: General Foods
Green Giant vegetables: Pillsbury
Haagen-Dazs ice cream: Pillsbury
Hamilton Beach appliances: Scovill
Handy Wipes: Colgate-Palmolive
Harrah's resorts, casinos: Holiday Inns
Head and Shoulders shampoo: Procter & Gamble
Hellman's mayonnaise: CPC International
Hertz car rental: RCA
Hi-C fruit drinks: Coca Cola
Ivory soap products: Procter & Gamble
Jack in the Box restaurants: Ralston Purina
Jack Daniels bourbon: Brown-Forman
Jantzen swimwear: Blue Bell
Jell-o: General Foods
Jim Beam whiskey: American Brands
Karastan rugs: Fieldcrest Mills
Ken-L-Ration pet foods: Quaker Oats
Kentucky Fried Chicken: R.J. Reynolds
Kinney shoe stores: F.W. Woolworth

Knorr soups: CPC International
Kool Aid soft drinks: General Foods
La Menu frozen dinners: Campbell Soup
Lee jeans: VF Corp.
Lestoil: Noxell
Life Savers candy: Nabisco
Log Cabin syrup: General Foods
Lucite paints: Clorox
Magnavox products: North American Philips
Marlboro cigarettes: Philip Morris
Maxwell House coffee: General Foods
Mazola oil: CPC International
Michelob beer: Anheuser-Busch
Miller beer: Philip Morris
Minute Rice: General Foods
Mountain Dew soda: PepsiCo
NBC broadcasting: RCA
National Car Rental: Household International
Newsweek magazine: Washington Post
9-Lives cat food: H.J. Heinz
Norelco products: North American Philips
Norge appliances: Magic Chef
Noxzema skin products: Noxell
Oil of Olay: Richardson-Vicks
Ore-Ida frozen foods: H.J. Heinz
Oreo cookies: Nabisco
Oscar Mayer meats: General Foods
Pall Mall cigarettes: American Brands
Pampers: Procter & Gamble
Paper Mate pens: Gillette
Paul Masson wines: Seagram
People magazine: Time
Pepto-Bismol: Procter & Gamble
Pepperidge Farms products: Campbell Soup
Pizza Hut restaurants: PepsiCo
Planters peanuts: Nabisco
Playtex products: Esmark
Prego spaghetti sauce: Campbell Soup
Prell shampoo: Procter & Gamble
Prince Matchabelli fragrances: Chesebrough-Pond's
Q-Tips: Chesebrough-Pond's
Radio Shack retail outlets: Tandy
Ragu foods: Chesebrough-Pond's
Ramblin root beer: Coca Cola
Red Devil paints: Insilco
Red Lobster Inns: General Mills
Right Guard deodorant: Gillette
Rise shave lathers: Carter-Wallace
Ritz crackers: Nabisco
Roy Rogers restaurants: Marriott
Samsonite luggage: Beatrice Foods
Sanka coffee: General Foods
Sergeant's pet care products: A.H. Robins
7-Eleven stores: Southland
Seven-Up: Philip Morris
Soft and Dri deodorant: Gillette
Sports Illustrated magazine: Time
Steak and Ale restaurants: Pillsbury
Sugartwin: Alberto Culver
Sunkist orange soda: General Cinema
Taco Bell restaurants: PepsiCo
Tang soft drink: General Foods
Thom McAn shoe stores: Melville
Tide detergent: Procter & Gamble
Tiparillo's: Culbro
Tropicana foods: Beatrice Foods
Tropicana hotels & casinos: Ramada Inns
Tupperware products: Dart & Kraft
Ty-D-Bol toilet cleaner: Papercraft
Tylenol: Johnson & Johnson
Ultra Brite toothpaste: Colgate-Palmolive
V-8 vegetable juice: Campbell Soup
Vanity Fair apparel: VF Corp.
Vidal Sassoon hair products: Richardson-Vicks
Virginia Slims cigarettes: Philip Morris
Wall Street Journal: Dow Jones
Weight Watchers: H.J. Heinz
Wheaties cereal: General Mills
White Owl cigars: Culbro
White Rain shampoo: Gillette
Wizard air freshener: American Home Products
Wyler's drink mixes: Borden
Yuban coffee: General Foods

Business Directory

Listed below are major U.S. corporations, and major foreign corporations with their U.S. headquarters, whose operations—products and services—directly concern the American consumer. At the end of each listing is a representative sample of some of the company's products.

Should you, as a dissatisfied consumer, wish to register a complaint beyond the local level, address your correspondence to the attention of the Consumer Complaint Office of the individual company. Be as specific as possible about the dealer's name and address, purchase date or date of service, price, name and serial number (if any) of the product, and places you may have sought relief, with dates. Include copies of receipts and guarantees and/or warranties. Don't forget your name and complete address and telephone number with area code.

Company. . .Address. . .Phone Number. . .Chief executive officer. . .Business.

AMF Inc.. . .777 Westchester Ave., White Plains, NY 10604. . .(914) 694-9000. . .W.T. York. . .producer bowling equip., industrial prods.

AMR Corp.. . .PO Box 61616, Dallas/Ft. Worth Airport, TX 75261. . .(214) 355-1234. . Albert V. Casey. . .Air transportation (American Airlines).

Abbott Laboratories.. . Abbott Park, No. Chicago, IL 60064. . .(312) 937-6100. . .R.A. Schoellhorn. . health care prods.

Aetna Life & Casualty Co.. . .151 Farmington Ave., Hartford, CT 06156 . . .(203) 273-0123. . .James T. Lynn. . .insurance.

Alberto-Culver Co.. . .2525 Armitage Ave., Melrose Park, IL 60160. . .(312) 450-3000. . .Leonard H. Lavin. . .hair care preparations, feminine hygiene products, household and grocery items.

Albertson's Inc.. . .250 Parkchester Blvd., Boise, ID 83726. . .(208) 344-7441. . .D.I. Connolly. . .supermarkets

Alcan Aluminium Ltd.. . .P.O. Box 6077 Montreal, Que., Canada H3C 3A7. . .(514) 848-8050. . .D.M. Culver. . .aluminum producer.

Allied Corp.. . . Box 2245R, Morristown, NJ 07960. . .(201) 455-2000. . .Edward L. Hennessy Jr.. . .oil, gas, chemicals, fibers & plastics, electrical products, auto safety restraints.

Allied Stores Corp.. . .1114 Ave. of the Americas, N.Y., NY 10036. . .(212) 764-2000. . .Thomas M. Macioce. . .dept. stores incl. Bonwit Teller; Plymouth Shops; Gertz; Garfinckel's, Stern's; Brooks Brothers.

Allis Chalmers Corp.. . .1205 S. 70th St., West Allis, WI 53214. . .(414) 475-3752. . .W.F. Bueche. . .manuf. of processing equip., electrical power equip., industrial trucks, farm machinery.

Aluminum Co. of America.. .1501 Alcoa Bldg., Pittsburgh, PA 15219. . .(412) 533-4707. . .C.W. Parry. . .mining, refining, & processing of aluminum.

AMAX Inc.. . .AMAX Center, Greenwich, CT 06836. . .(203) 629-6000. . .P. Gousseland. . .natural resources and mineral development.

Amerada Hess Corp.. . .1185 Ave. of the Americas, N.Y., NY 10036. . .(212) 977-8500. . .P. Kramer. . .integrated petroleum co.

American Bakeries Co.. . .111 E. 58th St., N.Y., NY 10022. . .(212) 486-9800. . .E.G. Bewkes Jr.. . .wholesale bakery goods.

American Brands, Inc.. . .245 Park Ave., N.Y., NY 10017. . .(212) 880-4200. . .E.H. Whittemore. . .tobacco (Pall Mall, Lucky Strike cigarettes; Half and Half, Paledon pipe tobacco); whiskey (Jim Beam); snack foods (Sunshine Biscuits); golf equipment, office supplies, toiletries, insurance.

American Broadcasting Companies Inc.. . .1330 Ave. of the Americas, N.Y., NY 10019. . .(212) 887-7777. . .L.H. Goldenson. . .broadcasting, publishing.

American Can Co.. . . American Lane, Greenwich, CT 06836. . .(203) 552-2000. . .William S. Woodside. . .manuf. containers and packaging prods; financial services.

American Cyanamid Co.. . . One Cyanamid Plaza, Wayne, NJ 07470. . .(201) 831-2000. . .G.J. Sella Jr.. . .medical, agricultural prods., specialty chemicals.

American Express Co.. . . American Express Plaza, N.Y., NY 10004 . . .(212) 323-2000 . . .J.D. Robinson 3d . . .travelers checks; credit card services; insurance; investment services (Shearson Loeb Rhodes).

American Greetings Corp.. . .10500 American Rd., Cleveland, OH 44144. . .(216) 252-7300. . .Irving I. Stone. . .greeting cards.

American Hoist & Derrick Co.. . .63 S. Robert, St. Paul, MN 55107. . .(612) 293-4567. . .R.H. Nassau. . .heavy equip.

American Home Products Corp.. . .685 3d Ave., N.Y., NY 10017. . .(212) 986-1000. . .J.W. Culligan. . .prescription drugs, household prods. (Woolite, Easy-Off oven cleaner); food (Chef Boy-ar-dee); drugs (Anacin, Dristan).

American Motors Corp.. . .2777 Franklin Rd., Southfield, MI 48034. . .(313) 827-1000. . .W.P. Tippett Jr.. . .passenger vehicles, service parts; Jeep Corp.

American Sterilizer Co.. . .2222 W. Grandview Blvd., Erie, PA 16514. . .(814) 452-3100. . .H.E. Fish. . .health care equip.

American Stores Co.. . .709 East South Temple, Salt Lake City, UT 84127. . .(801) 539-0112. . .J.S. Skaggs. . .retail food markets, dept. & drug stores.

American Telephone & Telegraph Co.. . .550 Madison Ave. N.Y., NY 10022. . .(212) 605-5500. . .Charles L. Brown. . .communications. . .Western Electric.

Anheuser-Busch, Inc.. . . One Busch Place, St. Louis, MO 63118. . .(314) 577-2000. . .A.A. Busch 3d. . .brewing (Budweiser, Michelob, Natural Light).

Armstrong Rubber Co.. . .500 Sargent Dr., New Haven, CT 06507. . .(203) 562-1161. . .James A. Walsh. . .tires.

Armstrong World Industries.. .W. Liberty St., Lancaster, PA 17604. . .(717) 397-0611. . .J.L. Jones. . .interior furnishings.

Arvin Industries, Inc.. . .1531 13th St., Columbus, IN 47201. . .(812) 372-7271. . .J.K. Baker. . .auto exhaust systems, record players.

Ashland Oil, Inc.. . .1401 Westchester Ave., Ashland, KY 41114. . .(606) 329-3333. . .J.R. Hall. . .petroleum refiner; chemicals, coal, insurance.

Associated Dry Goods Corp.. . .417 5th Ave., N.Y., NY 10016. . .(212)679-8700. . .W.P. Arnold. . .department stores incl. Lord & Taylor; Caldor; Loehmann's; Horne's.

Atlantic Richfield Co.. . .515 S. Flower St., Los Angeles, CA 90071. . .(213) 486-3511. . .Robert O. Anderson. . .petroleum, chemicals.

Avco Corp.. . .1275 King St., Greenwich, CT 06830. . .(203) 531-2800. . .R.P. Bauman. . .consumer finance, insurance and management services.

Avery International Corp.. . .150 N. Orange Grove Blvd., Pasadena, CA 91103. . .(213) 304-2000. . .Charles D. Miller. . .self-adhesive labels.

Avon Products, Inc.. . .9 West 57th St., N.Y., NY 10019. . .(212) 546-6015. . .Hicks B. Walderon. . .cosmetics, fragrances, toiletries, jewelry.

Bally Manufacturing Corp.. . .8700 W. Bryn Mawr Ave., Chicago, IL 60631. . .(312) 399-1300. . .R.E. Mullane. . .coin-operated amusement and gaming equip.; hotel-casino operator; theme park operator.

Bausch & Lomb.. . One Lincoln First Square, Rochester, NY 14601. . .(716) 338-6000. . .D.E. Gill. . .manuf. of vision care products, accessories.

Baxter Travenol Labs Inc.. . . One Baxter Pky., Deerfield, IL. 60015. . .(312) 948-2000. . .Vernon R. Loucks Jr.. . .medical care prods.

Beatrice Cos.. . .2 LaSalle St., Chicago, IL 60602. . .(302) 782-3820. . .James L. Dutt. . .foods (Tropicana, Meadow Gold, La Choy); recreational, travel (Samsonite luggage), home prods.(Stiffel Lamps).

Bell & Howell Co.. . .7100 McCormick Rd., Chicago, IL 60645.. .(312) 673-3300. . .D.N. Frey. . .audio-visual instruments, business equip., educational & training equip.

Best Products Co.. . . Box 26303, Richmond, VA 23260. . .(804) 261-2000. . .Sydney Lewis. . .catalog/showroom merchandiser.

Bethlehem Steel Corp.. . .8th & Eaton Ave., Bethlehem, PA 18016. . .(215) 694-2424. . .D.H. Trautlein. . .steel & steel prods.

Beverly Enterprises.. .873 S. Fair Oaks Ave., Pasadena, CA 91105. . .(213) 577-6111. . .R. Van Tuyle. . .provides health care through retirement centers, home health services.

Black & Decker Mfg. Co.. . .701 E. Joppa Rd., Towson, MD 21204. . .(301) 583-3900. . .L.J. Farley. . .manuf. power tools.

H & R Block, Inc...4410 Main St., Kansas City, MO 64111...(816) 753-6900...Henry W. Bloch...tax preparation.

Blue Bell, Inc...335 Church Ct., Greensboro, NC 27420...(919) 373-3400...E.J. Bauman...manuf. western wear (Wrangler), sports and swim wear (Jantzen).

Boeing Company...7755 E. Marginal Way So., Seattle, WA 98108...(206) 655-2121...T.A. Wilson...aircraft manuf.

Boise Cascade Corp...One Jefferson Square, Boise, ID 83728...(208) 384-6161...J.B. Fery...timber, paper, wood prod.

Borden, Inc...277 Park Ave., N.Y., NY 10172...(212) 573-4000...E.J. Sullivan...food, cheese and cheese products, snacks (Cracker Jack), beverages.

Borg-Warner Corp...200 S. Michigan Ave., Chicago, IL 60604...(312) 322-8500...J.F. Bere...air conditioning, plastics, chemicals, industrial prods., financial & protection services.

Bristol-Myers Co...345 Park Ave., N.Y., NY 10154...(212) 644-2100...Richard L. Gelb...toiletries (Ban anti-perspirant), hair items (Clairol), drugs (Bufferin, Excedrin), household prods.(Drano), infant formula (Enfamil).

Brown-Forman Distillers Corp...850 Dixie Hwy., Louisville, KY 40210...(502) 585-1100...W.L.L. Brown Jr...distilled spirits (Jack Daniel); wines (Bolla, Cella), champagne (Korbel).

Brown Group, Inc...8400 Maryland Ave., St. Louis, MO 63166...(314) 854-4000...B.A. Brightwater Jr...manuf. and wholesaler of women's and children's shoes (Buster Brown).

Brunswick Corp...One Brunswick Plaza, Skokie, IL 60077...(312) 470-4700...J.F. Reichert...marine, recreation prods.

Bucyrus-Erie Co...P.O. Box 56, S. Milwaukee, WI 53172...(414) 768-4000...N.K. Ekstrom...mining, construction equip.

Burlington Industries, Inc...3330 W. Friendly Ave., Greensboro, NC 27470...(919) 379-2000...W. A. Klopman...largest U.S. textile mfg.

Burlington Northern Inc...999 3d Ave., Seattle, WA 98104...(206) 467-3838...R.M. Bressler...rail transportation, natural resources.

Burroughs Corp...Burroughs Place, Detroit, MI 48232...(313) 972-7000...W.M. Blumenthal...business equipment.

CBS Inc...51 W. 52d St., N.Y., NY 10019...(212) 975-6075...T.H. Wyman...broadcasting, publishing, recorded music, leisure prods.

CPC International, Inc...International Plaza, Englewood Cliffs, NJ 07632...(201) 894-4000...J.W. McKee Jr...branded food items (Hellman's; Best Foods; Mazola; Skippy; Knorr Soups), corn wet milling prods.

Campbell Soup Co...Campbell Pl., Camden, NJ 08101...(609) 964-4000...R. G. McGovern...canned soups, spaghetti (Franco-American), vegetable juice (V-8), pork and beans; pet foods, restaurants, confections; Le Menu frozen dinners; Prego spaghetti sauce; Mrs. Pauls frozen fish.

Capital Cities Communications, Inc...485 Madison Ave., New York, NY 10022...(212) 421-9595...T.S. Murphy...operates television and radio stations, newspapers.

Carnation Co...5045 Wilshire Blvd., Los Angeles, CA 90036...(213) 932-6001...H.E. Olson...canned evaporated milk, tomato prods., pet foods (Friskies).

Carter-Wallace, Inc...767 5th Ave., New York, NY 10153...(212) 758-4500...H.H. Hoyt Jr...personal care items, anti-perspirant (Arrid), shave lathers (Rise), laxative (Carter's Pills), pet products.

Castle & Cooke, Inc...Financial Plaza of the Pacific, P.O. Box 2990, Honolulu, HI 96802...(808) 548-6611...I.R. Wilson...food processing...Dole, Bumble Bee.

Caterpillar Tractor Co...100 N.E. Adams St., Peoria, IL 61629...(309) 675-1000...Robert E. Gilmore...heavy duty earth-moving equip., diesel engines.

Cessna Aircraft Co...5800 East Pawnee Rd., Wichita, KS 67201...(316) 685-9111...Russell W. Meyer Jr...general aviation aircraft, accessories, fluid power systems.

Champion International Corp...1 Champion Plaza, Stamford, CT 06921...(203) 358-7000...A.C. Sigler...forest prods.

Champion Spark Plug Co...900 Upton Ave., Toledo, OH 43661...(419) 535-2567...R.A. Stranahan Jr...ignition devices.

Chesebrough-Pond's Inc...33 Benedict Pl., Greenwich, CT 06830...(203) 661-2000...Ralph E. Ward...cosmetics, toiletries, clothing, food prods., footwear...Adolph's; Health-Tex; Vaseline; Q-Tips; Pertussin; Prince Matchabelli; Ragu.

Chevron Corp...225 Bush St., San Francisco, CA 94104...(415)894-7700...J.R. Grey...integrated oil co.

Chrysler Corp...1200 Lynn Townsend Dr., Detroit, MI 48231...(313) 956-5252...Lee Iacocca...cars, trucks.

Church's Fried Chicken, Inc...355A Spencer Lane, San Antonio, TX 78284...(512) 735-9392...J.D. Bamberger...fried chicken restaurants.

Cincinnati Milacron Inc...4701 Marburg Ave., Cincinnati, OH 45209...(513) 841-8100...J.D. Bamberger...machine tools.

Citicorp...399 Park Ave., N.Y., NY 10043...(212)559-1000...W.B. Wriston...largest U.S. commercial bank.

Clorox Co...1221 Broadway, Oakland, CA 94612...(415) 271-7000...C.S. Hatch...retail consumer prods (Formula 409; Jifoam; Twice As Fresh; Lucite paints; Kingsford charcoal briquets).

Cluett, Peabody & Co...510 5th Ave., New York, NY 10036...(212) 930-3000...H.H. Henley Jr...apparel (Arrow shirts; Gold Toe socks).

Coachman Industries Inc...P.O. Box 30, Middlebury, IN 46540...(219)825-5821...T.H. Corson...manuf. recreational vehicles.

Coca-Cola Co...310 North Ave., Atlanta, GA 30313...(404) 676-2121...R.C. Goizueta...soft drink (Coca Cola; MelloYellow; Ramblin root beer), syrups, citrus and fruit juices (Minute Maid, Hi-C), films (Columbia Pictures).

Coleco Industries, Inc...999 Quaker Lane S., Hartford, CT 06110...A.C. Greenberg...consumer electronics, games, toys (Cabbage Patch Kids).

Coleman Co., Inc...250 N. St. Francis Ave., Wichita, KS 67202...(316) 261-3211...S. Coleman...outdoor recreation prods., heating & air conditioning equip.

Colgate-Palmolive Co...300 Park Ave., N.Y., NY 10022...(212) 310-2000. Keith Crane...soaps (Palmolive; Irish Spring), detergents (Fab; Ajax; Cold Power), tooth paste (Colgate; Ultra Brite), household prods. (Baggies; Handy Wipes; Curad bandages), restaurants (Ranch House; Lum's).

Collins & Aikman Corp...210 Madison Ave., N.Y., NY 10016...(212) 953-4100...Donald F. McCullough...textiles.

Consolidated Foods Corp...3 First National Plaza, Chicago, IL 60602...(312) 726-2600...John H. Bryan Jr...foods, housewares, appliances, clothing...Electrolux; Fuller Brush; Hanes; Gant; Popsicle; Sara Lee; Shasta; Tyco.

Continental Group, Inc...One Harbor Plaza, Stamford, CT 06904...(203) 964-6000...S. B. Smart Jr...natural resources, financial services, packaging, insurance.

Adolph Coors Co...East of Town, Golden, CO 80401...(303) 279-6565...W. K. Coors...brewery.

Corning Glass Works...Houghton Park, Corning, NY 14831...(607) 974-9000...J.R. Houghton...glass mfg.

Cox Communications, Inc...1400 Lake Hearn Dr., Atlanta, GA 30319...(404) 843-5126...W.A. Schwartz...broadcasting, publishing.

Crane Co...300 Park Ave., N.Y., NY 10022...(212) 980-3600...R.J. Slater...fluid & pollution controls, steel, aircraft and aerospace, building prods.

A.T. Cross Co...One Albion Rd., Lincoln, RI 02865...(401) 333-1200...B.R. Boss...writing instruments.

Crown Cork & Seal Co...9300 Ashton Rd., Phila., PA 19136...(215) 698-5100...J.F. Connelly...cans, packaging machinery & equip.

Crown Zellerbach Corp...One Bush St., San Francisco, CA 94104...(415) 823-5000...W.T. Creson...forest products.

Culbro Corp...605 3d Ave., New York, NY 10016...(212) 687-7575...E. M. Cullman...cigars (Corina; Robert Burns; White Owl; Tiparillo's), snack foods.

Dana Corp...4500 Dorr St., Toledo, OH 43697...(419) 535-4500...Gerald B. Mitchell...truck and auto parts supplies.

Dart & Kraft, Inc...2211 Sansters Rd., Northbrook, IL 60062...(312) 498-8000...J. R. Richman...food prods. (cheese, mayonnaise), direct selling (Tupperware), consumer products (Duracell batteries; West Bend appliances).

Data General Corp...Southboro, MA 01772...(617) 485-9100...E. D. deCastro...digital computers.

Dayton-Hudson Corp...777 Nicollet Mall, Minneapolis, MN 55402...(612) 370-6948...W. A. Andres...department, specialty, book stores; B. Dalton; Mervyn's; Target.

Deere & Company...John Deere Rd., Moline, IL 61265...(309) 752-8000...Robert A. Hanson...farm, industrial, and outdoor power equip.

Delta Air Lines, Inc...Hartsfield Atlanta Intl. Airport, Atlanta, GA 30320...(404) 346-6622...David C. Garrett Jr...air transportation.

Denny's, Inc. . . .16700 Valley View Ave., La Mirada, CA 90637. . .(714) 739-8100. . .V.O. Curtis. . .restaurants.

Diamond Shamrock Corp. . . .717 North Harwood St., Dallas, TX 75201. . .(214) 745-2000. . .W.H. Bricker. . .energy, chemicals.

Diebold, Inc. . . .Canton, OH 44711. . .(216) 489-4000. . .R. Koontz. . .equip. for financial insts.

Digital Equipment Corp. . . .146 Main St., Maynard, MA 01754. . .(617) 897-5111. . .Kenneth H. Olsen. . .mini- computers.

Walt Disney Productions. . .500 S. Buena Vista St., Burbank, CA 91521. . .(213) 840-1000. . .R.W. Miller. . .motion pictures, CATV, amusement parks. . .Disneyland, Walt Disney World, Epcot Center.

Donnelly & Sons Co. . . .2223 Martin Luther King Drive, Chicago, IL 60616. . .(312) 326-8000. . .J.B. Schwemm. . .largest commercial printer.

Dow Chemical Co. . . .2030 Dow Center, Midland, MI 48640. . .(517) 636-1000. . .P.F. Oreffice. . .chemicals, plastics, metals, consumer prods.

Dow Jones & Co. . . .22 Cortlandt St., New York, NY 10007. . .(212) 285-5000. . .W. H. Phillips. . .financial news service, publishing (Wall Street Journal; Barron's; Ottaway Newspapers).

Dresser Industries, Inc. . . .The Dresser Bldg., Dallas, TX 75201. . .(214) 746-6000. . .J.J. Murphy . . .supplier of technology and services to energy related industries.

E.I. du Pont de Nemours & Co. . . .1007 Market St., Wilmington, DE 19898. . .(302) 774-1000. . .E. G. Jefferson. . .chemicals, petroleum, consumer prods., coal.

Dun & Bradstreet Corp. . . .299 Park Ave., New York, NY 10171. . .(212) 593-6800. . .H. Drake. . .business information and computer services, publishing, broadcasting.

Eastman Kodak Co. . . .343 State St., Rochester, NY 14650. . .(716) 724-4000. . .C.H. Chandler. . .photographic prods.

(Jack) Eckerd Corp. . . .8333 Bryan Dairy Rd., Clearwater, FL 33518. . .(813) 397-7461. . .S. Turley. . .drug store chain, department stores, optical & video equip. stores.

Emerson Electric Co. . . .8100 W. Florissant Ave., St. Louis, MO 63136. . .(314) 553-2197. . .C.F. Knight. . .electrical/electronics products & systems

Emery Air Freight Corp. . . .Old Danbury Rd., Wilton, CT 06897. . .(203) 762-8601. . .John C. Emery Jr.. . .air freight forwarder.

Ethyl Corp. . . .330 S. 4th St., Richmond, VA 23217. . .(804) 788-5000. . .Floyd D. Gottwald Jr.. . .petroleum and industrial chemicals, plastics, aluminum.

Exxon Corp. . . .1251 Ave. of the Americas, N.Y., NY 10020. . .(212) 398-3093. . .C.C. Garvin Jr.. . .world's largest oil co.

Fabergé,Inc. . . .1345 Ave. of the Americas, N.Y., NY 10105. . .(212) 581-3500. . .D.J. Manella. . .cosmetics, toiletries (Brut; Babe; Farrah Fawcett).

Fairchild Industries, Inc. . . .Germantown, MD 20874. . .(301) 428-6000. . .E.G. Uhl. . .aircraft manuf.

Family Dollars Stores, Inc. . . .10401 Old Monroe Rd., Charlotte, NC 28212. . .(704)847-6961. . .L.E. Levine. . .discount variety stores.

Federal Express Corp. . . .2990 Airways Blvd., Memphis, TN 38194. . .(901) 369-3600. . .F.W. Smith. . .small package delivery service.

Federated Department Stores, Inc. . . .7 W. 7th St., Cincinnati, OH 45202. . .(513) 579-7000. . .H. Goldfeder. . .dept. stores. . . Abraham & Straus; Bloomingdale's; Boston Store; Burdines; Foley's; Lazarus; Rich's; Children's Place.

Fieldcrest Mills, Inc. . . .326 East Stadium Dr., Eden, NC 27288. . .(919) 623-2123. . .F.X. Larkin. . .household textile prods., rugs (Karastan, Laurelcrest).

Firestone Tire & Rubber Co. . . .1200 Firestone Pkwy., Akron, OH 44317. . .(216) 379-7000. . .J.J. Nevin. . .tires, rubber and metal prods.

Fleetwood Enterprises, Inc. . . .3125 Myers St., Riverside, CA 92523. . .(714) 351-3500. . .John C. Crean. . .mobile homes, recreational vehicles.

Fluor Corp. . . .3333 Michelson Dr., Irvine, CA 92730. . .(714) 975-2000. . .J. R. Fluor. . .engineering and construction.

Ford Motor Co. . . .The American Rd., Dearborn, MI 48121. . .(313) 322-8540. . .Philip Caldwell. . .motor vehicles, Ford Tractor; Lincoln-Mercury.

Fort Howard Paper Co. . . .1919 S. Broadway, Green Bay, WI 54305. . .(414) 435-8821. . .P.J. Schierl. . .disposable paper prods.

GAF Corp. . . .140 W. 51st St., New York, NY 10020. . .(212) 621-5000. . .Jesse Werner. . .chemicals, bldg. materials.

GTE Corp. . . .One Stamford Forum, Stamford, CT 06904. . .(203) 965-2000. . .Theodore F. Brophy. . .operates largest U.S. independent telephone system.

Gannett Co., Inc. . . .Lincoln Tower, Rochester, NY 14604. . .(716) 546-8600. . .A.H. Neuharth. . .newspaper publishing (USA TODAY), TV stations, outdoor advertising.

Gencorp. . . .One General St., Akron, OH 44329. . .(216) 798-3000. . .M.G. O'Neil. . .tires, rubber prods.

General Cinema Corp. . . .27 Boylston St., Chestnut Hill, MA 02167. . .(617) 232-8200. . .R. A. Smith. . .movie exhibitor, soft drinks (Sunkist).

General Dynamics Corp. . . .Pierre Laclede Ctr., St. Louis, MO 63105. . .(314) 889-8200. . .D. S. Lewis. . .military and commercial aircraft, tactical missiles.

General Electric Co. . . .3135 Easton Ave., Fairfield, CT 06431. . .(203) 373-2431. . .J. F. Welch Jr.. . .electrical, electronic equip.

General Foods Corp. . . .250 North, White Plains, NY 10625. . .(914) 683-2500. . .J.L. Ferguson. . .packaged foods (Maxwell House; Yuban; Sanka; Jell-O; Post cereals; Birds Eye frozen foods; Gaines, Cycle dog foods; Tang, Kool Aid soft drinks; Minute Rice; Oscar Mayer meats.

General Instruments Corp. . . .1775 Broadway, New York, NY 10019. . .(212) 708-7800. . .F. G. Hickey. . .race track betting systems, CATV, semiconductors, electronic equip.

General Mills, Inc. . . .9200 Wayzatta Blvd., Minneapolis, MN 55440 . . .(612) 540-2311. . .H.B. Atwater Jr.. . .foods, toys, restaurants, fashion and specialty retailing. . .Wheaties; Cheerios; Betty Crocker; Red Lobster Inns).

General Motors Corp. . . .Gen. Motors Bldg., Detroit, MI 48202. . .(313) 556-5000. . .R. B. Smith. . .world's largest auto manuf.

Genesco Inc. . . .Genesco Park, Nashville, TN 37202. . .(615) 367-7000. . .R.W. Hanselman. . .footwear and men's clothing. . .Hardy; Cover Girl; Jarman; Flagg Bros.; Bell Bros.; Johnston & Murphy.

Georgia-Pacific Corp. . . .133 Peachtree St., NE, Atlanta, GA 30303. . .(404) 521-4720. . .T.M. Hahn Jr.. . .building prods., pulp, paper, chemicals.

Gerber Products Co. . . .445 State St., Fremont, MI 49412. . .(616) 928-2000. . .L.D. Goulet. . .baby foods, clothing, nursery accessories; life insurance.

Gillette Co. . . .Prudential Tower Bldg., Boston, MA 02199. . .(617) 421-7000. . .Colman M. Mockler Jr.. . .razors, pens (Paper Mate; Flair), toiletries (Right Guard, Dri, Soft deodorants; Foamy shaving cream; Earth Born shampoo), hair products (Toni; Adorn; White Rain).

Golden Nugget, Inc. . . .129 Freemont St., Las Vegas, NV 89101. . .(702) 385-7111. . .Steve Wynn. . .operates casino-hotels.

B.F. Goodrich Company. . .500 S. Main St., Akron, OH 44318. . .(216) 374-2632. . .John D. Ong. . .rubber, chemical, plastic prods.

Goodyear Tire & Rubber Co. . . .1144 E. Market St., Akron, OH 44316. . .(216) 794-4436. . .Charles J. Pilliod Jr.. . .tires, rubber prods.

Gordon Jewelry Corp. . . .820 Fannin St., Houston TX 77002. . .(713) 222- 8080. . .A.S. Gordon. . .jewelry retailer.

Gould Inc. . . .10 Gould Center, Rolling Meadows, IL 60008. . .(312) 640-4000. . .W.T. Ylvisaker. . .electrical and industrial prods.

W.R. Grace & Co. . . .Grace Plaza, 1114 Ave. of the Americas, N.Y., NY 10036. . .(212) 819-5500. . .J. Peter Grace. . .chemicals, natural resources, consumer prods. and services, restaurants. . .Channel Home Centers; Herman's World of Sporting Goods.

Great Atlantic & Pacific Tea Co. . . .2 Paragon Dr., Montvale, NJ 07645. . .(201) 573-9700. . .James Wood. . .retail food stores.

Greyhound Corp. . . .Greyhound Tower, Phoenix, AZ 85077. . .(602) 248-4000. . .John W. Teets. . .bus transportation, soap (Dial), food, financial services.

Grumman Corp. . . .111 Stewart, Bethpage, NY 11714. . .(516) 575-7474. . .John C. Bierwirth. . .aerospace, truck bodies.

Gulf Corp. . . .P.O. Box 1166, Pittsburgh, PA 15230. . .(412) 263-5000. . .J.E. Lee. . . production and marketing of petroleum and related products.

Gulf + Western Industries, Inc. . . .One Gulf + Western Plaza, N.Y., NY 10023. . .(212) 333-7000. . .M.S. Davis. . .diversified manufacturing, financial services, consumer and food products, home furnishings, entertainment (Paramount Pictures; Madison Square Garden).

Halliburton Co....2600 Southland Center, Dallas, TX 75201...(214) 748-7261...J. P. Harbin...oil field services, engineering, construction.

Harcourt Brace Jovanovich, Inc....757 3d Ave., New York, NY 10017...(212) 888-4444...W. Jovanovich...textbook publisher, entertainment (Sea World).

Hartmarx...101 N. Wacker Dr., Chicago, IL 60606...(312) 372-6300...Jerome S. Gore...apparel manufacturer and retailer (Hickey-Freeman).

Heileman (G.) Brewing Co....100 Harborview Plaza, La Crosse, WI 54601...(608) 785-1000...R. G. Cleary...brewery (Schmidt; Blatz; Colt 45 Malt Liquor).

H.J. Heinz Co....P.O. Box 57, Pittsburgh, PA 15230...(412) 237-5757...Anthony J.F. O'Reilly...foods (Star-Kist; Ore-Ida; '57 Varieties), 9-Lives cat food, Weight Watchers.

Hershey Foods Corp....100 Manson Rd., Hershey, PA 17033...(717) 534-4000...R.A. Zimmerman...chocolate & confectionery prods., pasta (San Giorgio); restaurants (Friendly Ice Cream).

Hewlett-Packard Co....1501 Page Mill Rd., Palo Alto, CA 94304...(415) 856-1501...John A. Young...electronic instruments.

Hillenbrand Industries, Inc...Highway 46, Batesville, IN 47006...(812) 934-7000...D.A. Hillenbrand...manuf. burial caskets, electronically operated hospital beds.

Hilton Hotels Corp....9880 Wilshire Blvd., Beverly Hills, CA 90210...(213) 278-4321...Barron Hilton...hotels, casinos.

Holiday Inns, Inc...3742 Lamar Ave., Memphis, TN 38195...(901) 364-4001...M.D. Rose...hotels, motels, casinos (Harrah's).

Honda Motor Co., LTD...1270 Ave. of the Americas, N.Y., NY 10020...(212) 765-3804...Tadashi Kume...manuf. autos, motorcycles.

Honeywell, Inc...Honeywell Plaza, Minneapolis, MN 55408...(612) 870-5200...E.W. Spencer...industrial systems & controls, aerospace guidance systems, information systems.

Hoover Co...101 E. Maple St., No. Canton, OH 44720...(216) 499-9200...M. R. Rawson...manuf. vacuum cleaners, washing machines, dryers.

Geo. A. Hormel & Co...501 16th Ave. N.E., Austin, MN 55912...(507) 437-5611...R.L. Knowlton...meat packaging, pork and beef prods.

Household International Inc...2700 Sanders Rd., Prospect Heights, IL 60070...(312) 564-5000...D.C. Clark...financial and insurance services, merchandising, manufacturing, transportation...National Car Rental; Household Finance.

Hughes Tool Co...6500 Texas Commerce Tower, Houston, TX 77002...(713) 222-0686...J.R. Lesch...supplier of products and services to the oil, gas, & mining industries; mfg. of rock drilling bits & tool joints.

Humana, Inc...P.O. Box 1438, Louisville, KY 40201...(502) 561-2000...D. A. Jones...operates hospitals.

IC Industries, Inc...One Illinois Ctr., 111 E. Wacker Dr., Chicago, IL 60601...(312) 565-3000...William B. Johnson...diversified prods. and services...railroads, consumer products, food, auto products.

ITT Corp...320 Park Ave., N.Y., NY 10022...(212) 752-6000...R.V. Araskog...world's largest manuf. of telecommunications equip.

Imperial Oil Ltd...111 St. Clair Ave. W., Toronto, Ont., Canada...(416) 924-4111...D.M. Ivor...Canada's largest oil co.

Insilco Corp...1000 Research Pkwy., Meriden, CT 06450...(203) 634-2000...D.J. Harper...diversified manufacturer...Red Devil Paints and Chemicals; Rolodex; Taylor Publishing; International Silver.

Intel Corp...3065 Bowers Ave., Santa Clara, CA 95051...(408) 987-8080...G. E. Moore...semiconductor memory components.

Interco Inc...P.O. Box 8777, St. Louis, MO 63102...(314) 231-1100...H. Saligman...apparel, footwear mfg.; specialty apparel shops, home furnishings (Ethan Allen).

International Business Machines Corp...Old Orchard Rd., Armonk, NY 10504...(914) 765-1900...J.F. Akers...information-handling systems, equip., and services.

International Harvester Co...401 N. Michigan Ave., Chicago, IL 60611...(312) 636-2000...J.D. Rutherford...manuf. farm tractors and machinery, truck and construction equip.

International Paper Co...77 W. 45th St., New York, NY 10036...(212) 536-6000...E. A. Gee...paper, wood prods.

Johnson & Johnson...One Johnson & Johnson Plaza, Brunswick, NJ 08903...(201) 524-0400...James E. Burke...surgical dressings, pharmaceuticals, health and baby prods.

Jonathan Logan, Inc...50 Terminal Rd., Secaucus, NJ 07094...Richard W. Schwartz...female apparel.

Jostens, Inc...5501 Norman Center Dr., Minneapolis, MN 55437...(612) 830-3336...H. W. Lurton...school rings, yearbooks.

Kaiser Aluminum & Chemical Corp...300 Lakeside Dr., Oakland, CA 94643...(415) 271-3300...Cornell C. Maier...aluminum, chemicals.

Kaufman and Broad, Inc...11601 Wilshire Blvd., Los Angeles, CA 90025...(213) 312-5000...Eli Broad...home builder.

Kellogg Co...235 Porter, Battle Creek, MI 49016...(616) 966-2000...William E. LaMothe...ready to eat cereals & other food prods...Mrs. Smith's Pie Co.; Salada Foods.

Kerr-McGee Corp...P.O. Box 25861, Oklahoma City, OK 73125...(405) 263-1313...F.A. McPherson...oil, natural gas, uranium, coal.

Kidde, Inc...Park 80 West-Plaza Two, Box 5555, Saddle Brook, NJ 07622...(201) 368-9000...Fred R. Sullivan...mfgr. safety, security, protection, industrial, commercial, consumer and recreation prods. and services.

Kimberly-Clark Corp...N. Lake St., Neenah, WI 54956...(414) 721-2000...Darwin E. Smith...paper and lumber prods.

K mart Corp...3300 W. Big Beaver Rd., Troy, MI 48084...(313) 643-1000...B. M. Fauber...largest U.S. chain of discount stores.

Knight-Ridder Newspapers, Inc...One Harold Plaza, Miami, FL 33101...(305) 350-2650...A.H. Chapman Jr...largest U.S. newspaper co.; broadcasting, publishing.

Kroger Co...1014 Vine St., Cincinnati, OH 45201...(513) 762-4000...Lyle Everingham...grocery chain, drugstores (SupeRx).

LTV Corporation...P.O. Box 225003, Dallas, TX 75265...(214) 746-7711...R.A. Hay...steel, aerospace, meat & food prods., shipping, energy-oriented prods.

Levi Strauss & Co...1155 Battery St., San Francisco, CA 94120...(415) 544-6000...R. D. Haas...blue denim jeans, other apparel.

Levitz Furniture Corp...1317 NW 167th St., Miami, FL 33169...(305) 625-6421...Robert M. Elliott...furniture stores.

Libbey-Owens-Ford Co...811 Madison Ave., Toledo, OH 43695...(419) 247-4856...Don T. Mc Kone...automotive glass and fabricated prods.

Eli Lilly & Company...307 E. McCarty St., Indianapolis, IN 46285...(317) 261-2000...Richard D. Wood...mfg. human health and agricultural products, cosmetics (Elizabeth Arden).

The Limited, Inc...One Limited Pkwy., Columbus, OH 43216...(614) 475-4000...L.H. Wexner...women's apparel stores...Lane Bryant.

Litton Industries, Inc...360 N. Crescent, Beverly Hills, CA 90210...(213) 859-5000...O.C. Hoch...industrial systems & services, advanced electronic systems, electronic & electrical prods., marine engineering, printing & publishing.

Lockheed Corp...2555 N. Hollywood Way, Burbank, CA 91520...(213) 847-6121...R.A. Anderson...commercial and military aircraft, missiles.

Loews Corp...666 5th Ave., N.Y., NY 10019...(212) 841-1000...Laurence A. Tisch...tobacco prods., motion picture theaters, hotels, real estate, insurance.

Lucky Stores, Inc...6300 Clark Ave., Dublin, CA 94566...(415) 828-1000...S. D. Ritchie...supermarkets, restaurants, dept., fabric, and automotive stores.

MCA Inc...100 Universal City Plaza, Universal City, CA 91608...(213) 985-4321...Lew R. Wasserman...motion pictures, television; music publishing, mail order, novelty, and gift merchandise.

MEI Corp...710 Marquette Ave., Minneapolis, MN 55402...(362) 339-8853...Donald E. Benson...soft drink bottler, distributor.

MacMillan, Inc...866 3d Ave., New York, NY 10022...(212) 702-2000...E. P. Evans...book printing and publishing; education (Berlitz; Katharine Gibbs).

R. H. Macy & Co. Inc...151 W. 34th St., New York, NY 10001...(212) 560-3600...E. S. Finkelstein...department stores.

Magic Chef, Inc...740 King Edward Ave., Cleveland, TN 37311...(615) 472-3371...S.B. Rymer Jr...major household appliances, heating and air conditioning equip., soft drink vending equip.. . .Admiral; Norge; Gaffers & Sattler; Johnson; Dixie-Narco; Toastmaster.

Manor Care, Inc.. . .10750 Columbia Pike, Silver Spring, MD 20901. . .S. Bainum. . .nursing homes.

MAPCO, Inc.. . .1800 South Baltimore Ave., Tulsa, OK 74119. . .(918) 584-4471. . .J. E. Barnes. . .coal, gas, natural gas liquids.

Marriott Corp.. . .Marriott Dr., Wash., DC 20058. . .(301) 897-9000. . .J. Willard Marriott Jr.. . .restaurants (Roy Rogers; Big Boy), hotels, food services, theme parks.

Martin Marietta Corp.. . .6801 Rockledge Dr., Bethesda, MD 20817. . .(301) 897-6000. . .T.G. Pownall. . .aluminum, aerospace, chemicals.

Mary Kay Cosmetics, Inc.. . .8787 Stemmon Freeway, Dallas, TX 75247. . .(214) 630-8787. . .Mary Kay Ash. . .cosmetics, toiletries.

Mattel, Inc.. . .5150 Rosecrans Ave., Hawthorne, CA 90250. . .(213) 978-5150. . .A. S. Spear. . .toy & hobby prods.

Maytag Co.. . .403 W. 4th St. N., Newton, IA 50208. . .(515) 792-7000. . .Daniel J. Krumm. . .manuf. home laundry equip.

McCormick & Co., Inc.. . .11350 McCormick Rd., Hunt Valley, MD 21031. . .(301) 667-7301. . .H. K. Wells. . .world's leading manuf. of seasoning & flavoring prods.

McDonald's Corp.. . .McDonald's Plaza, Oak Brook, IL 60521. . .(312) 887-3200. . .F. L. Turner. . .fast service restaurants.

McDonnell Douglas Corp.. . .P.O. Box 516, St. Louis, MO 63131. . .(314) 232-0232. . .Sanford N. McDonnell. . .commercial & military aircraft, space systems & missiles.

McGraw-Hill, Inc.. . .1221 Ave. of the Americas, New York, NY 10020. . .(212) 512-2000. . .J.L. Dionne. . .book, magazine publishing (Business Week), information & financial services (Standard and Poor's), TV stations.

Medtronic, Inc.. . .3055 Hwy 8, Minneapolis, MN 55440. . .(612) 574-4000. . .D. R. Olseth. . .heart pacemakers and support systems.

Melville Corp.. . .3000 Westchester Ave., Harrison, NY 10528. . .(914) 253-8000. . .Francis C. Rooney Jr.. . .shoe stores (Thom McAn), apparel (Marshalls); drug stores.

Merck & Co., Inc.. . .P.O. Box 2000, Rahway, NJ 07065. . .(201) 574-4000. . .J.J. Horan. . .human & animal health care prods.

Merrill Lynch & Co., Inc.. . .One Liberty Plaza, N.Y., NY 10080. . .(212) 637-7455. . .W.A Schreyer. . .securities broker, financial services, real estate.

Metromedia, Inc.. . .One Harmon Plaza, Secaucus, NJ 07094. . .(201) 348-3244. . .J. W. Kluge. . .television & radio broadcasting, publishing, entertainment (Ice Capades; Harlem Globetrotters).

Milton Bradley Co.. . .111 Maple St., Springfield, MA 01105. . .(413) 525-6411. . .James J. Shea Jr.. . .board and card games, electronic games, toys (Playskool), educational materials.

Minnesota Mining & Manuf. Co.. . .3M Center, St. Paul, MN 55144. . .(612) 733-1100. . .L.W. Lehr. . .abrasives, adhesives, building services & chemicals, electrical, health care, photographic, printing, recording materials.

Mobil Corp.. . .150 E. 42d St., N.Y., NY 10017. . .(212) 883-4242. . .Rawleigh Warner Jr.. . .international oil co.; chemicals, dept. stores (Montgomery Ward).

Mohasco Corp.. . .57 Lyon St., Amsterdam, NY 12010. . .(518) 841-2211. . .H. J. Broner. . .interior furnishings.

Monsanto Company.. . .800 N. Lindbergh Blvd., St. Louis, MO 63166. . .(314) 694-1000. . .R. J. Mahoney. . .chemicals, plastics, agricultural prods., textiles.

Morton Thiokol, Inc.. . .110 N. Wacker Dr., Chicago, IL 60606. . .(312) 621-5200. . .Charles S. Locke. . .salt (Morton), household cleaning prods. (Fantastik; Spray 'n Wash), specialty chemicals.

Motorola, Inc.. . .1303 E. Algonquin Rd., Schaumburg, IL 60196. . .(312) 397-5000. . .R. W. Galvin. . .electronic equipment and components.

Murray Ohio Manuf. Co.. . .219 Franklin Rd., Brentwood, TN 37027. . .(615) 373-6500. . .W. M. Hannon. . .bicycles, power mowers.

NCR Corp.. . .1700 S. Patterson Blvd., Dayton, OH 45479. . .(513) 449-2000. . .Charles E. Exley Jr.. . .business information processing systems.

Nabisco Brands, Inc.. . .Nabisco Brands Plaza, Parsippany, NJ 07054. . .(201) 898-7100. . .Robert M. Schaeberle. . .crackers (Ritz; Premium), cookies (Oreo; Fig Newton, Almost Home) toiletries (Aqua Velva), pharmaceutical prods. (Geritol), candy

(Baby Ruth; Butter Finger, Life Savers), Gum (Carefree, Sugarless).

National Distillers & Chemical Corp.. . .99 Park Ave., N.Y., NY 10016. . .(212) 949-5000. . .Drummond C. Bell. . .wines and liquors, chemicals, insurance. . .Almaden Vineyards.

National Medical Care, Inc.. . .Hancock Tower, Boston, MA 02116. . .(617) 262-1200. . .C. L. Hampers. . .medical services and prods.

National Semiconductor Corp.. . .2900 Semiconductor Dr., Santa Clara, CA 95051. . .(408) 721-5000. . .Charles E. Sporck. . .manuf. of semiconductors.

New York Times Co.. . .229 W. 43rd St., N.Y., NY 10036. . .(212) 556-1234. . .A. O. Sulzberger. . .newspapers, radio, CATV stations, magazines (Family Circle; Golf Digest).

North American Philips Corp.. . .100 E. 42d St., N.Y., NY 10017. . .(212) 697-3600. . .P. C. Vink. . .consumer prods., electrical, electronic prods., professional equip.. . .Magnavox; Norelco.

Northrop Corp.. . .1800 Century Park E., Los Angeles, CA 90067. . .(213) 553-6262. . .Thomas V. Jones. . .aircraft, electronics, communications.

Northwest Airlines, Inc.. . .Minneapolis-St. Paul Intl. Airport, St. Paul, MN 55111. . .(612) 726-2111. . .M. J. Lapensky. . .air transportation.

Noxell Corp.. . .11050 York Rd., Cockeysville, MD. . .(301) 628-7300. . .G. L. Bunting Jr.. . .toiletry, household, consumer prods. (Noxzema; Rain Tree; Lestoil; Cover Girl).

Occidental Petroleum Corp.. . .10889 Wilshire Blvd., Los Angeles, CA 90024. . .(213) 879-1700. . .Dr. Armand Hammer. -.oil, gas, chemicals, coal.

Ogden Corp.. . .277 Park Ave., New York NY 10017. . .(212) 754-4000. . .R. E. Ablon. . .transportation, foods, metals.

Olin Corp.. . .120 Long Ridge Rd., Stamford, CT 06904. . .(203) 356-2000. . .John M. Henske. . .chemicals, metals, paper, sporting and defense ammunition.

Outboard Marine Corp.. . .100 Sea Horse Dr., Waukegan, IL 60085. . .(312) 689-6200. . .C.D. Strang. . .outboard motors, mowers (Lawn Boy).

Owens-Corning Fiberglas Corp.. . .Fiberglas Tower, Toledo, OH 43659. . .(419) 248-8000. . .W.W. Boeschenstein. . .glass fiber and related prods.

Owens-Illinois, Inc.. . .One SeaGate Toledo, OH 43666. . .(419) 247-5000. . .R.J. Lanigan. . .glass, corrugated, and plastic containers.

Pan American World Airways.. . .Pan Am Bldg., 200 Park Ave., N.Y., NY 10166. . .(212) 880-1234. . .C. Edward Acker. . .air transportation.

Papercraft Corp.. . .Papercraft Park, Pittsburgh, PA 15238. . .M. P. Katz. . .gift wrapping paper, ribbons, artificial Christmas trees; household products (Ty-D-Bol toilet cleaner; Esquire shoe polish).

Parker Pen Co.. . .1 Parker Place, Janesville, WI 53545. . .(608) 755-7000. . .J. R. Peterson. . .writing instruments, recreational equip., temp. help service (Manpower, Inc.).

J.C. Penney Co.. . .1301 Ave. of the Americas, N.Y., NY 10019. . .(212) 957-4321. . .W. R. Howell, chmn.. . .dept. stores, catalog sales, food, drugs, insurance.

Pennzoil Co.. . .Pennzoil Pl., Houston, TX 77252. . .(713) 236-7878. . .B. P. Kerr. . .Integrated oil and gas co.

PepsiCo, Inc.. . .Anderson Hill Rd., Purchase, NY 10577. . .(914) 253-2000. . .D. M. Kendall. . .soft drinks, (Pepsi-Cola; Mountain Dew), snack foods (Frito-Lay; Doritos) restaurants (Pizza Hut; Taco Bell), sporting goods (Wilson), transportation (North American Van Lines).

Pfizer Inc.. . .235 E. 42d St. N.Y., NY 10017. . .(212) 573-2323. . .E.T. Pratt Jr.. . .pharmaceutical, hospital, agricultural, chemical prods.

Philip Morris, Inc.. . .100 Park Ave., N.Y., NY 10017. . .(212) 880-5000. . .George Weissman. . .cigarettes (Marlboro, Benson & Hedges, Merit, Virginia Slims); beer (Miller High Life, Lite; Lowenbrau brand); soft drinks (Seven-up); specialty chemicals, paper, packaging materials, real estate.

Phillips-Van Heusen Corp.. . .1290 Ave. of the Americas, New York, NY 10104. . .(212) 541-5200. . .L. S. Phillips. . .men, boys apparel.

Pillsbury Co.. . .200 S. 6th St., Minneapolis, MN 55402. . .(612) 330-4966. . .W. H. Spoor. . .canned & frozen vegetables (Green Giant), bakery, flour mixes, ice cream (Haagen Dazs); restaurants (Burger King; Steak and Ale).

tney Blowes, Inc....Walter H. Wheeler Dr., Stamford, CT 06904. . .(203) 356-5000. . .G. B. Harvey. . .postage meters, mail handling equip., office equipment, retail systems.

ayboy Enterprises, Inc....919 N. Michigan Ave., Chicago, IL 60691. . .(312) 751-8000. . .Hugh Hefner. . .magazine publishing, night clubs, CATV.

laroid Corp....549 Technology Sq., Cambridge, MA 02139. . .(617) 577-2000. . .W. J. McCune Jr.. .photographic equip., supplies and optical goods.

nderosa, Inc....P.O. Box 578, Dayton, OH 45401. . .(513) 890-6400. . .G. S. Office Jr.. . .steakhouse restaurants.

entice-Hall, Inc....Sylvan Ave., Englewood, NJ 07632. . .(201) 592-2000. . .D. A. Schaefer. .publishes college, high and elementary school textbooks.

octer & Gamble Co....301 E. 6th St., Cincinnati, OH 45202. . .(513) 562-1100. . .J. G. Smale. . .soap & detergent (Ivory; Dash; Tide; Spic and Span), shortenings (Crisco; Fluffo),toiletries (Crest and Gleem toothpastes; Prell, and Head and Shoulders shampoos), pharmaceuticals (Pepto-Bismol), Pampers disposable diapers, Folger coffee.

rolator Courier Corp....255 Old New Brunswick Rd., Piscataway, NJ 08854. . .(201) 885-1100. . .F. H. Cook. . .auto equip., courier and guard services.

aker Oats Co....Merchandise Mart Plaza, Chicago, IL 60654. . .(312) 222-7111. . .William D. Smithburg. . .foods, cereal (Life; Cap'n Crunch; Puffed Wheat; Puffed Rice), foods Aunt Jemima; Celeste pizza; Van Camp's pork and beans; Gatorade), pet foods (Ken-L-Ration; Puss 'Boots), Fisher Price oys, Magic Pan restaurants.

aker State Oil Refining Corp....255 Elm St., Oil City, PA 16301. . .(814) 676-7676. . .Q.E. Wood. . .refining, marketing etroleum prods., filters, mining & marketing coal.

A Corp....30 Rockefeller Plaza, N.Y., NY 10020. . .(212) 21-6000. . .T. F. Bradshaw. . .radio, television (NBC), electronics, communications, financial services, auto rental Hertz).

ston Purina Co....Checkerboard Sq., St. Louis, MO 63164. . .(314) 982-1000. . .W. R. Stritz. . .pet and livestock ood, Jack In the Box restaurants.

mada Inns, Inc....3838 E. Van Buren, Phoenix, AZ 85008. . .(602) 273-4000. . .Richard Snell. . .hotel operation, asinos (Tropicana).

rtheon Company...141 Spring St., Lexington, MA 02173. . .(617) 862-6600. . .Thomas L. Phillips. . .electronics, aviation, appliances. . .Amana Refrigeration; Beech Aircraft.

vlon, Inc....767 5th Ave., N.Y., NY 10153. . .(212) 572-5000. . .Michael C. Bergerac. . .cosmetics, pharmaceuticals.

ynolds Metals Co....6601 W. Broad St., Richmond, VA 23261. . .(804) 281-2000. . .D P Reynolds. . .aluminum prods.

Heynolds Industries, Inc....Reynolds Blvd., Winston-Salem, NC 27102. . .(919) 773-2000. . .J. Tylee Wilson. . .crude l, petroleum, transportation, tobacco (Camels; More), food, nd beverage prods. (Del Monte); restaurants (Kentucky Fried hicken).

hardson-Vicks Inc....10 Westport Rd., Wilton, CT 06897. . .(203) 762-2222. . .J.S. Scott. . .health and personal are prods. (NyQuil; Oil of Olay), drugs, specialty chemicals.

Aid Corp....Shiremanstown, PA 17011. . .(717) 761-633. . .A. Grass. . .discount drug stores.

Robins Co., Inc....1407 Cummings Dr., Richmond, VA 23261. . .(804) 257-2000. . .E.C. Robins Jr.. . .health care, consumer prods. (Chap Stick; Quencher), Sergeant's pet care ods.

kwell Intl. Corp....600 Grant St., Pittsburgh, PA 5219. . .(412) 565-2000. . .R. Anderson. . .aerospace, electronic, automotive prods.

er Corp....1905 W. Court St., Kankakee, IL 60901. . .(815) 37-6000. . .C.M. Hoover. . .appliances, home and lawn prods.

er Group Inc....500 Virginia Dr., Ft. Washington, PA 19034. . .(215) 628-6000. . .J. W. Eckman. . .pharmaceuticals Maalox; Ascriptin; Emetrol).

al Crown Cos., Inc....41 Perimeter Center East, Atlanta, A 30346. . .(404) 394-6120. . .D.A. McMahon. . .soft drinks ehi; RC Cola; Diet Rite Cola), restaurants (Arby's), citrus ods., home furnishings.

bermaid Inc....1147 Akron Rd., Wooster, OH 44691. . .(216) 264-6464. . .S. C. Gault. . .rubber and plastic nsumer prods.

er System, Inc....3600 NW 82d Ave., Miami, FL 33166. . .(305) 593-3726. . .M. A. Burns. . .truck leasing service.

SCM Corp....299 Park Ave., N.Y., NY 10171. . .(212) 752-2700. . .Paul H. Elicker. . .typewriters, appliances, food, chemicals, paper prods.. . .Smith Corona; Proctor-Silex.

Safeway Stores, Inc....4th & Jackson Sts., Oakland, CA 94660. . .(415) 891-3000. . .P. A. Magowan. . .retail food stores.

Santa Fe Southern Pacific Corp....224 S. Michigan Ave., Chicago, IL 60604. . .(312) 427-4900. . .J. J. Schmidt. . .railroad, real estate, construction, natural resources.

Schering-Plough Corp....One Giralda Farms, Madison, NJ 07940. . .(201) 822-7000. . .R. P. Luciano. . .pharmaceuticals, consumer prods; radio stations.

Schlumberger Ltd....277 Park Ave., New York, NY 10172. . .(212) 350-9400. . .Jean Riboud. . .oilfield services, electronics, measurement and control devices.

Scott Paper Co....Scott Plaza, Phila., PA 19113. . .(215) 521-5000. . .P. E. Lippincott. . .paper prods.

Scovill Inc....500 Chase Pkwy., Waterbury, CT 06708. . .(203) 757-6061. . .W. F. Andrews. . .automotive, security, housing prods., sewing aids, small appliances (Hamilton Beach).

Seagram Co. Ltd....1430 Peel St., Montreal, Que., Canada H3A 1S9. . .(514) 849-5271. . .E.M. Bronfman. . .distilled spirits & wine (Crown Royal; Chivas Regal; Calvert; Wolfschmidt Vodka; Paul Masson; Christian Brothers; Gold Seal; Myer's Jamaica Rum).

G.D. Searle & Co....P.O. Box 1045, Skokie, IL 60076. . .(312) 982-7000. . .Donald Rumsfeld. . .pharmaceutical/consumer, medical, optical prods., vision centers.

Sears, Roebuck & Co....Sears Tower, Chicago, IL 60684. . .(312) 875-2500. . .Edward R. Telling. . .merchandising, insurance (Allstate), financial services (Dean Winter).

Shaklee Corp....444 Market St., San Francisco, CA 94111. . .(415) 954-3000. . .J. G. Shansby. . .manuf. nutritional, personal care, household prods.

Shell Oil Co....P.O. Box 2463, Houston, TX 77001. . .(713) 241-4083. . .John F. Bookout. . .oil, gas, chemicals.

Sherwin-Williams Co....101 Prospect Ave. N.W., Cleveland, OH 44115. . .(216) 566-2000. . .John G. Breen. . .world's largest paint producer; drug stores.

Simplicity Pattern Co., Inc....200 Madison Ave., New York, NY 10016. . .(212) 576-0500. . .C. Hurwitz. . .paper patterns for home sewing.

Singer Co....8 Stanford Forum, Stanford, CT 06904. . .(203) 356-4200. . .Joseph B. Flavin. . .electronics, sewing prods., power tools.

Skyline Corp....2520 By-Pass Rd., Elkhart, IN 46515. . .(219) 294-6521. . .Arthur J. Decio. . .mfg housing and recreational vehicles.

Smithkline Beckman Corp....One Franklin Plaza, Phila., PA 19101. . .(215) 751-4000. . .H. Wendt. . .pharmaceuticals, animal health prods., diagnostic instruments.

Smucker (J.M.) Co....Strawberry Lane, Orville, OH 44667. . .(216) 682-0015. . .P. H. Smucker. . .preserves, jams, jollies, toppings.

Snap-on Tools Corp....2801 80th St., Kenosha, WI 53141. . .(414) 656-5200. . .W. B. Rayburn. . .manuf. mechanic's tools, equip.

Sony Corp....Tokyo, Japan. . .A. Morita. . .manuf. televisions, radios, tape recorders, audio equip., video tape recorders.

Southland Corp....2828 N. Haskell Ave., Dallas, TX 75221. . .(214) 828-7011. . .J.P. Thompson. . .convenience stores (7-Eleven; Gristede's), auto parts stores.

Sperry Corp....1290 Ave. of the Americas, N.Y., NY 10104. . .(212) 956-2121. . .G. G. Probst. . .computers and data processing, farm, guidance & control equip.

Squibb Corp....P.O. Box 4000, Princeton, NJ 08540. . .(609) 921-4000. . .Richard M. Furlaud. . .drugs, confectionary, household prods. . . .Charles of the Ritz.

A.E. Staley Manufacturing Co....2200 E. Eldorado St., Decatur, IL 62525. . .(217) 423-4411. . .Donald E. Nordlund. . .corn and soybean processing, consumer prods (Sta-Puff softeners).

Standard Oil Co. (Indiana)....200 E. Randolph Dr., Chicago, IL 60601. . .(312) 856-6111. . .R. M. Morrow. . .oil and gas exploitation & prod., chemicals, fertilizers.

Standard Oil Co. (Ohio)....Midland Bldg., Cleveland, OH 44115. . .(216) 575-4141. . .Alton W. Whitehouse Jr.. . .oil & natural gas.

Stanley Works....195 Lake St., New Britain, CT 06050. . .(203) 225-5111. . .D.W. Davis. . .hand tools, hardware, door opening equipment.

Sterling Drug Inc....90 Park Ave., N.Y., NY 10016...(212) 907-2000...W. Clarke Wescoe...pharmaceuticals, cosmetics & toiletries, household, proprietary prods., chemicals (Bayer Aspirin, Lysol, Dorothy Gray; Parfums Givenchy).

J.P. Stevens & Co., Inc....1185 Ave. of the Americas, N.Y., NY 10036...(212) 930-2000...W. Stevens...fabrics, carpets, other textile home furnishings.

Storer Communications, Inc....1200 Biscayne Blvd., Miami, FL 33261...(305) 652-9900...P. Storer...television broadcasting, CATV.

Sun Company, Inc....100 Matsonford Rd., Radnor, PA 19087...(215) 293-6000...R. McClements...petroleum.

Supermarkets General Corp....301 Blair Rd., Woodbridge, NJ 07095...(201) 499-3000...L. Lieberman...supermarkets (Pathmark); Rickel Home Centers.

Taft Broadcasting Co....1718 Young St., Cincinnati, OH 45210...(513) 721-1414...C.S. Mechem Jr...radio, TV broadcasting, TV cartoons (Hanna-Barbera), amusement parks.

Tambrands Inc....10 Delaware Dr., Lake Success, NY 11042...(516) 437-8800...E. H. Shutt Jr...menstrual tampons (Tampax).

Tandy Corp....1800 One Tandy Center, Fort Worth, TX 76102...(817) 390-3700...J.V. Roach...consumer electronics retailing & mfg...Radio Shack.

Teledyne, Inc....1901 Ave. of the Stars, Los Angeles, CA 90067...(213) 277-3311...H. E. Singleton...electronics, aerospace prods., industrial prods., insurance, finance.

Tenneco Inc....P.O. Box 2511, Houston, TX 77001...(713) 757-2131...J. L. Ketelsen...oil, natural gas pipelines, construction and farm equip.

Texaco Inc....2000 Westchester Ave., White Plains, NY 10650...(914) 253-4000...John K. McKinley...petroleum and petroleum prods.

Texas Instruments Inc....P.O. Box 225474, Dallas, TX 75265...(214) 238-2011...J. F. Bucy...electrical & electronics prods.

Textron, Inc....40 Westminster St., Providence, RI 02903...(401) 421-2800...Robert P. Straetz...aerospace, consumer, industrial, metal prods.

Tidewater Inc....1440 Canal St., New Orleans, LA 70112...(504) 568-1010...J.P. Laborde...marine equip. and services for oil industry.

Time Inc....Time & Life Bldg., New York, NY 10020...(212) 586-1212...J.R. Munro...magazine publisher (Time; Sports Illustrated; Fortune; Money; People), CATV (Home Box Office), forest prods.

Toys "R" Us....395 W. Passaic St., Rochelle Park, NJ 07662...(201) 845-5033...Charles Lazarus...toy retailer.

Transamerica Corp....600 Montgomery St., San Francisco, CA 94111...(415) 983-4180...J.R. Harvey...insurance, financial, leisure, business services (Occidental Life Ins.; Budget Rent A Car).

Trans World Corp....605 3d Ave., N.Y., NY 10116...(212) 557-3000...L. Edwin Smart...holding co...Trans World Airlines; Hilton International; Spartan Food Systems, Century 21 real estate corp.

Travelers Corp....One Tower Sq., Hartford, CT 06115...(203) 277-0111...E. H. Budd...insurance.

UAL, Inc....1200 Algonquin Rd., Elk Grove Township, IL 60007...(312) 952-4000...R. J. Ferris...holding co. United Airlines, Westin Hotels.

Union Carbide Corp....Old Ridgebury Rd., Danbury, CT 06817...(203) 794-2000...W. M. Anderson...chemicals.

Union Pacific Corp....345 Park Ave., N.Y., NY 10154...(212) 418-7800...W.S. Cook...railroad, natural resources.

Uniroyal, Inc....Middlebury, CT 06749...(203) 573-2000...Joseph P. Flannery...tires, chemical, plastic prods.

United States Gypsum Co....101 S. Wacker Dr., Chicago, IL 60606...(312) 321-4000...E. W. Duffy...largest U.S. producer of gypsum & related prods.

United States Shoe Corp....One Eastwood Dr., Cincinnati, OH 45227...(513) 527-7000...P. G. Branch...apparel, retailer (Casual Corner; J. Riggins), shoes (Red Cross; Joyce).

United States Steel Corp....600 Grant St., Pittsburgh, PA 15230...(412) 433-1121...David M. Roderick...largest U.S. steel co., chemicals, transportation, oil.

United States Tobacco Co....100 W. Putnam Ave., Greenwich, CT 06830...(203) 661-1100...L.F. Bantle...smokeless tobacco (Copenhagen; Skoal; Happy Days), pipes (Dr. Grabow), pipe tobacco.

United Technologies Corp....United Technologies Bldg., Hartford, CT 06101...(203) 728-7000...Harry J. Gray...aerospace, industrial prods. & services...Carrier Corp.; Otis Elevator; Pratt & Whitney, Sikorsky Aircraft.

Upjohn Co....7000 Portage Rd., Kalamazoo, MI 49001...(616) 323-4000...R.T. Parfet Jr...pharmaceuticals, chemicals, agricultural and health care prods.

U.S. Home Corp....1177 West Loop South, Houston, TX 77252...(713) 877-2311...G. R. Odom...manuf. single family homes.

VF Corp....1047 No. Park Rd., Wyomissing, PA 19610...(215) 378-1151...L.R. Pugh...apparel...Vanity Fair; Lee jeans.

Vulcan Materials Co....One Metroplex Dr., Birmingham, AL 35209...(205) 877-3000...W.H. Blount...construction materials, chemicals, metals.

Wal-Mart Stores Inc....702 W. 8th St., Bentonville, AR 72712...(501) 273-4000...S.M. Walton...discount dept. stores.

Walgreen Co....200 Wilmot Rd., Deerfield, IL 60015...(312) 940-2500...Charles R. Walgreen 3d...retail drug chain, restaurants (Wags).

Wang Laboratories, Inc....One Industrial Ave., Lowell, MA 01851...A. Wang...word processors.

Warnaco Inc....350 Lafayette St., Bridgeport, CT 06601...(203) 579-8272...R.J. Matura...apparel...Hathway, Puritan, Rosanna, White Stag.

Warner Communications Inc....75 Rockefeller Plaza, N.Y., NY 10019...(212) 484-8000...Steven J. Ross...filmed entertainment, records & music publishing, book publishing, CATV system, consumer prods.

Warner-Lambert Co....201 Tabor Rd., Morris Plains, NJ 07950...(201) 540-2000...Ward S. Hagan...health care, optical prods., candy.

Washington Post Co....1150 15th St., N.W., Washington, DC 20071...(202) 223-6000...Katharine Graham...newspaper, magazines (Newsweek), TV stations.

Wendy's Intl., Inc....PO Box 256, Dublin, OH 43017...(614) 764-3100...R. L. Barney...quick service hamburger restaurants.

West Point-Pepperell Inc....400 W. 10th St., West Point, GA 31833...J. L. Lanier Jr...apparel, industrial & household fabrics.

Western Union Corp....One Lake St., Upper Saddle River, NJ 07458...(201) 825-5000...T. Roland Berner...telecommunications.

Westinghouse Electric Corp....Westinghouse Bldg., Gateway Center, Pittsburgh, PA 15222...(412) 255-3800...D. D. Danforth...manuf. electrical, mechanical equip., radio and television stations.

Weyerhaeuser Co....Tacoma, WA 98477...(206) 924-2345...George H. Weyerhaeuser...manuf., distribution of forest prods.

Whirlpool Corp....Administrative Center, Benton Harbor, MI 49022...(616) 926-5000...J.D. Sparks...major home appliances.

White Consolidated Industries, Inc....11770 Berea Rd., Cleveland, OH 44111...(216) 252-3700...R.H. Holdt...major home appliances (Kelvinator, Frigidaire), industrial equip. & machinery.

Willamette Industries, Inc....3800 1st Interstate Tower, Portland, OR 97201...(503) 227-5581...William Swindells Jr...building materials and paper prods.

Williams Cos....One Williams Center, Tulsa, OK 74172...(918) 588-2000...J. H. Williams...fertilizer, energy, metals.

Winn-Dixie Stores, Inc....5050 Edgewood Ct., Jacksonville, FL 32203...(904) 783-5000...A.D. Davis...retail grocery chain.

F.W. Woolworth Co....233 Broadway, N.Y., NY 10007...(212) 553-2000...J.W. Lynn...variety stores, shoe stores (Kinney).

Wm. Wrigley Jr. Co....410 N. Michigan Ave., Chicago, IL 60611...(312) 644-2121...William Wrigley...chewing gum.

Xerox Corp....Stamford, CT 06904...(203) 329-8700...D. Kearns...equip. for reproduction, reduction, and transmission of printed information.

Zale Corp....3000 Diamond Park, Dallas TX 75247...(214) 634-4011...D. Zale...jewelry retailer.

Zayre Corp....Framingham, MA 01701...(617) 620-5000...M. Segall...self-service discount dept. stores, specialty shops (Hit or Miss; T. J. Maxx).

Zenith Electronics Corp....1000 Milwaukee Ave., Glenview, IL 60025...(312) 391-7000...Jerry K. Pearlman...consumer electronic prods.

ECONOMICS

U.S. Budget Receipts and Outlays—1980-1983

Source: U.S. Treasury Department, Bureau of Govt. Financial Operations
(Fiscal years end Sept. 30)
(1980-81 in thousands; 1982-83 in millions)

Classification	Fiscal 1980	Fiscal 1981	Fiscal 1982	Fiscal 1983
Net Receipts				
Individual income taxes	$244,068,898	$285,550,802	$298,111	288,938
Corporation income taxes	64,599,673	61,137,136	49,207	37,022
Social insurance taxes and contributions:				
Federal old-age and survivors insurance	95,580,645	117,757,091	122,840	128,972
Federal disability insurance	16,639,155	12,418,490	20,626	18,348
Federal hospital insurance	23,233,135	30,360,679	34,301	35,641
Railroad retirement taxes	2,311,977	2,457,238	2,917	2,805
Total employment taxes and contributions	**138,764,911**	**162,993,498**	**180,686**	**185,766**
Other insurance and retirement:				
Unemployment	15,335,788	15,398,386	16,234	18,799
Federal supplementary medical insurance	2,927,711	3,319,094	NA	NA
Federal employees retirement	3,659,505	3,908,270	4,140	4,358
Civil service retirement and disability	59,228	76,148	72	78
Total social insurance taxes and contributions	**160,747,143**	**186,426,256**	**201,131**	**209,001**
Excise taxes	24,329,156	40,839,143	36,311	35,300
Estate and gift taxes	6,389,480	6,786,537	7,991	6,053
Customs duties	7,173,836	8,082,808	8,854	8,655
Deposits of earnings-Federal Reserve Banks	11,767,143	12,833,713	15,186	15,594
All other miscellaneous receipts	980,682	955,899	976	1,102
Net Budget Receipts	**$520,056,012**	**$602,612,295**	**$617,766**	**600,563**
Net Outlays				
Legislative Branch	$1,217,983	$1,208,819	$1,362	$1,435
The Judiciary	564,144	637,279	705	780
Executive Office of the President:				
The White House Office	18,967	21,078	20	20
Office of Management and Budget	34,963	35,122	37	37
Total Executive Office	**95,385**	**95,635**	**95**	**95**
Funds appropriated to the President:				
Appalachian regional development	340,531	336,795	312	264
Disaster relief	573,760	400,547	115	202
Foreign assistance-security	3,903,034	3,546,682	3,052	NA
Foreign assistance-bilateral	1,372,452	1,489,325	1,578	NA
Int. narcotics control assistance	26,875	NA	NA	NA
Total funds appropriated to the President	**7,507,055**	**7,009,908**	**6,073**	**5,417**
Agriculture Department:				
Food stamp program	9,117,136	11,252,902	11,014	11,839
Child Nutrition Program	3,377,056	3,438,238	3,020	3,278
Total Agriculture Department	**24,554,916**	**26,029,802**	**36,213**	**46,372**
Commerce Department	3,103,596	2,226,045	2,045	1,913
Defense Department:				
Military personnel	30,841,732	36,408,884	42,341	45,523
Retired military personnel	11,919,776	13,729,065	14,938	15,945
Operation and maintenance	44,770,126	51,863,633	59,674	64,915
Procurement	29,020,667	35,191,231	43,271	43,274
Research and development	13,126,878	15,277,593	17,729	20,554
Military construction	2,449,521	2,458,186	2,922	2,922
Family housing	1,680,174	1,720,887	1,993	2,126
Corps of Engineers and civil functions	3,204,436	3,124,375	2,944	2,899
Total Defense Department	**136,137,929**	**159,183,160**	**185,821**	**205,012**
Education Department	13,124,205	15,087,770	14,081	14,555
Energy Department	6,463,498	11,631,087	7,705	8,348
Health and Human Services Department:				
Food and Drug Administration	325,736	337,167	343	364
National Institutes of Health	33,222,304	3,603,805	3,665	3,750
Public Health Service	7,817,750	8,378,623	8,334	7,856
Old-age and survivors benefits	100,621,850	119,413,467	134,661	148,642
Social Security Administration	134,353,608	159,500,955	176,265	214,012
Human Development Services	5,343,312	5,090,101	5,104	5,344
Total Health and Human Services Dept.	**194,690,800**	**230,303,851**	**251,268**	**274,131**
Housing and Urban Development Department	12,582,279	14,032,380	14,491	15,312
Interior Department	4,376,994	4,427,690	3,793	4,485
Justice Department:				
Federal Bureau of Investigation	609,181	691,176	737	824
Total Justice Department	**2,631,677**	**2,682,472**	**2,584**	**2,832**
Labor Department:				
Unemployment Trust Fund	16,440,284	18,739,096	24,282	32,655
Total Labor Department	**29,724,001**	**30,083,819**	**30,736**	**38,176**
State Department	1,938,405	1,897,364	2,185	2,263
Transportation Department	19,614,572	22,554,054	19,929	20,591
Treasury Department:				
Internal Revenue Service	4,331,945	5,033,188	5,749	6,391
Interest on the public debt	74,860,250	95,589,367	117,404	128,813
General revenue sharing	6,828,835	5,136,892	4,569	4,614
Total Treasury Department	**76,690,723**	**92,632,962**	**110,521**	**116,787**
Environmental Protection Agency	5,601,883	5,231,851	5,004	4,301

Classification Net Outlays (cont'd)	Fiscal 1980	Fiscal 1981	Fiscal 1982	Fiscal 1983
General Services Administration.	$169,331	$185,562	$229	$127
National Aeronautics and Space Administration . . .	4,849,924	5,421,388	6,026	6,657
Veterans Administration	21,134,538	22,904,006	23,927	24,805
Independent agencies:				
ACTION.	133,319	150,164	136	126
Arms Control and Disarmament Agency	17,256	15,888	NA	NA
Board for International Broadcasting.	98,372	88,199	83	91
Civil Aeronautics Board	116,657	147,151	110	78
Commission on Civil Rights	12,035	12,137	NA	NA
Community Services Administration	2,166,279	689,228	132	NA
Consumer Product Safety Commission	44,177	40,861	34	34
Corporation for Public Broadcasting	152,000	162,000	172	137
District of Columbia	424,694	492,231	439	427
Equal Employment Opportunity Commission . .	130,788	134,212	138	152
Export-Import Bank of the United States	1,836,003	2,066,222	1,173	578
Federal Communications Commission.	75,804	80,892	80	80
Federal Deposit Insurance Corporation	— 922,130	— 1,725,994	— 1,440	— 613
Federal Emergency Management Agency	660,106	372,135	279	NA
Federal Home Loan Bank Board.	552,046	70,081	— 588	— 452
Federal Trade Commission	68,474	70,081	68	65
Intragovernmental Agencies	104,927	69,152	69	55
International Communications Agency	432,752	436,926	485	NA
Interstate Commerce Commission	155,682	74,190	11	25
Legal Services Corporation	320,308	324,314	259	234
Merit Systems Protection Board	13,086	20,569	20	24
National Foundation on the Arts and Humanities	320,702	314,172	298	260
National Labor Relations Board	108,867	114,450	119	122
National Science Foundation	911,907	975,009	1,099	1,055
National Transportation Safety Board	17,754	18,296	17	NA
Nuclear Regulatory Commission.	377,872	416,844	442	515
Office of Personnel Management	15,052,426	18,088,914	19,973	21,275
Postal Service	1,676,878	1,343,217	707	785
Railroad Retirement Board	4,788,046	5,307,621	5,721	6,236
Securities and Exchange Commission	74,140	78,025	79	9
Small Business Administration	1,898,932	1,912,527	631	479
Smithsonian Institution.	138,758	166,875	181	194
Tennessee Valley Authority	1,869,233	1,927,758	1,527	826
U.S. Railway Association	672,055	191,250	28	4
Other Independent agencies	287,139	464,643	449	305
Total independent agencies	34,931,166	35,567,788	33,110	34,291
Undistributed offsetting receipts	— 21,932,702	— 30,306,097	— 29,261	— 35,564
Net Budget Outlays	579,602,970	660,544,033	728,424	795,917
Less net receipts	520,056,012	602,612,295	617,766	600,563
Deficit	— $59,546,958	— $57,931,739	— $110,658	— 195,354

(NA) Not available.

U.S. Net Receipts and Outlays

Source: U.S. Treasury Department; annual statements for year ending June 30[1] (thousands of dollars)

Yearly average	Receipts	Expenditures	Yearly average	Receipts	Expenditures	Yearly average	Receipts	Expenditure
1789-1800[1]	5,717	5,776	1871-1875	336,830	287,460	1916-1920[6]	3,483,652	8,065,3..
1801-1810[2]	13,056	9,086	1876-1880	288,124	255,598	1921-1925	4,306,673	3,578,9..
1811-1820[2]	21,032	23,943	1881-1885	366,961	257,691	1926-1930	4,069,138	3,182,8..
1821-1830[2]	21,928	16,162	1886-1890	375,448	279,134	1931-1935[4]	2,770,973	5,214,8..
1831-1840[2]	30,461	24,495	1891-1895	352,891	363,599	1936-1940[4]	4,960,614	10,192,3..
1841-1850[2]	28,545	34,097	1896-1900	434,877	457,451	1941-1945[4]	25,951,137	66,037,9..
1851-1860	60,237	60,163	1901-1905	559,481	535,559	1946-1950[5] [7]	39,047,243	42,334,5..
1861-1865	160,907	683,785	1906-1910	628,507	639,178			
1866-1870	447,301	377,642	1911-1915	710,227	720,252			

Fiscal year	Receipts	Expenditures	Fiscal year	Receipts	Expenditures	Fiscal year	Receipts	Expenditure
1955	60,389,744	64,569,973	1972[8]	215,262,639	238,285,907	1978	401,997,000	450,758,..
1960	77,763,460	76,539,413	1973	232,191,842	246,603,359	1979	465,954,656	493,607,..
1964	89,458,664	97,684,375	1974	264,847,484	268,342,957	1980	520,056,012	579,602,..
1965	93,071,797	96,506,904	1975	281,037,466	324,641,586	1981	602,612,295	660,544,..
1968[9]	153,675,705	172,803,186	1976	300,005,077	365,610,129	1982	617,766,000	728,424,..
1970	193,843,791	194,968,258	1976 Trans[3]. .	81,772,766	94,472,996	1983	600,563,000	795,917,..
1971	188,332,129	210,652,667	1977[3]	356,861,331	401,896,376			

(1) Average for period March 4, 1789, to Dec. 31, 1800. (2) Years ended Dec. 31, 1801 to 1842; average for 1841-1850 is for period Jan. 1, 1841, to June 30, 1850. (3) Effective fiscal year 1977, fiscal year is reckoned Oct. 1-Sept. 30; transition quarter covers July 1, 1976-Sept. 30, 1976. (4) Expenditures for years 1932 through 1946 have been revised to include Government corps. (wholly owned) etc. (net). (5) Effective January 3, 1949, amounts refunded by the Government, principally for the overpayment of taxes, are being reported as deductions from total receipts rather than as expenditures. Also, effective July 1, 1948, payments to the Treasury principally by wholly owned Government corporations for retirement of capital stock and for disposition of earnings, are excluded in reporting both budget receipts and expenditures. Neither of these changes affects the size of the budget surplus or deficit. Beginning 1931 figures in each case have been adjusted accordingly for comparative purposes. (6) Figures for 1918 through 1946 are revised to exclude statutory debt retirement (sinking fund, etc.). (7) Excludes $3 billion transferred to Foreign Economics Corporation Trust Fund and includes $3 billion representing expenditures made from the FEC Trust Fund. (8) Effective fiscal year 1972 loan repayments and loan disbursements will be netted against expenditures and known as outlays. (9) From 1968, figures include trust funds (e.g. Social Security).

Summary of U.S. Receipts by Source and Outlays by Function
Source: U.S. Treasury Department, Bureau of Govt. Financial Operations

(in millions)

Net Receipts	Fiscal 1980	Fiscal 1981	Fiscal 1982	Fiscal 1983
Individual income taxes	$244,069	$285,551	$298,111	$288,938
Corporation income taxes	64,600	61,137	49,207	49,207
Social insurance taxes and contributions	160,747	183,086	201,132	208,999
Excise taxes	24,329	40,839	36,311	35,300
Estate and gift taxes	6,389	6,787	7,991	6,053
Customs duties	7,174	8,083	8,854	8,655
Miscellaneous receipts	12,748	13,790	16,161	15,594
Total	**$520,056**	**$599,272**	**$617,766**	**$600,563**
Net outlays				
National defense	$135,880	$159,736	$187,397	$210,461
International affairs	10,472	11,052	9,983	8,927
General science, space, and technology	5,999	6,422	7,096	7,777
Energy	6,623	10,351	4,844	4,035
Natural resources and environment	14,130	13,764	13,086	12,676
Agriculture	4,951	5,598	14,808	22,173
Commerce and housing credit	7,795	3,995	3,843	4,721
Transportation	20,840	23,312	20,589	21,231
Community and regional development	9,917	9,538	7,410	7,302
Education, training, employment and social services	31,399	30,533	25,411	25,726
Health	58,165	65,984	74,018	81,157
Income security	192,133	225,599	248,807	280,244
Veterans benefits and services	21,167	22,937	23,973	24,845
Administration of justice	4,554	4,720	4,648	5,014
General government	4,641	4,759	4,833	4,991
General purpose fiscal assistance	8,306	6,621	6,161	6,287
Interest	64,564	82,590	100,777	103,916
Undistributed offsetting receipts	−21,933	−30,306	−29,261	−35,566
Total	**$579,603**	**$657,204**	**$728,424**	**$795,917**

U.S. Direct Investment Abroad, Countries and Industries
Source: Bureau of Economic Analysis, U.S. Commerce Department

(millions of dollars)

	Direct investment position		Equity and intercompany account outflows (inflows (−))		Reinvested earnings		Fees and royalties		Income	
	1982	1983	1982	1983	1982	1983	1982	1983	1982	1983
All areas	221,512	226,117	−4,756	4,881	6,375	9,090	5,516	6,275	22,268	20,757
Petroleum	56,642	59,785	3,145	2,719	1,141	2,155	345	546	10,059	9,172
Manufacturing	90,582	90,124	542	423	669	1,670	3,640	4,056	4,987	5,789
Other	74,287	76,208	−8,443	1,739	4,564	5,265	1,575	1,673	7,223	5,797
Developed countries	164,157	169,582	−1,229	5,862	2,422	5,855	4,596	5,073	13,269	14,844
Petroleum	37,077	38,879	−504	1,460	15	1,670	330	315	4,821	5,484
Manufacturing	71,385	71,744	507	1,250	968	2,178	3,303	3,665	4,282	5,342
Other	55,695	58,959	−1,233	3,152	1,439	2,007	964	1,092	4,166	4,108
Canada	46,183	47,538	−1,616	1,413	852	3,664	962	991	2,879	5,157
Petroleum	10,354	10,874	105	500	493	943	78	37	1,076	1,337
Manufacturing	19,724	19,849	1	260	39	1,920	699	762	895	2,645
Other	16,106	16,815	−1,722	653	320	800	185	192	908	1,175
Europe	99,459	102,461	783	3,224	1,517	1,666	2,981	3,315	8,987	7,929
Petroleum	22,526	23,640	−605	656	−516	550	207	229	3,228	3,577
Manufacturing	44,130	43,959	1,034	564	940	91	2,224	2,475	2,931	2,087
Other	32,803	34,862	353	2,005	1,093	1,026	550	611	2,829	2,265
Other	18,515	19,583	−397	1,224	54	526	653	766	1,402	1,758
Petroleum	4,197	4,365	−5	304	38	177	44	50	518	570
Manufacturing	7,532	7,936	−528	426	−11	167	380	428	455	610
Other	6,787	7,282	136	495	26	181	229	289	429	579
Developing countries	52,441	50,978	−3,790	−1,510	3,574	2,683	1,173	1,278	8,262	5,164
Petroleum	15,929	16,572	3,237	641	743	−63	226	308	4,558	2,963
Manufacturing	19,198	18,380	35	−827	−299	−508	337	390	705	447
Other	17,315	16,026	−7,062	−1,324	3,129	3,254	609	580	2,999	1,754
Latin America	32,546	29,501	−6,500	−3,066	2,137	1,712	590	514	2,706	690
Petroleum	6,606	6,839	1,298	215	295	42	70	67	975	623
Manufacturing	15,630	14,749	−48	−891	−498	−915	187	143	250	−215
Other	10,310	7,913	−7,750	−2,391	2,341	2,585	333	304	1,480	282
Other	19,895	21,477	2,710	1,556	1,436	971	583	764	5,556	4,474
Petroleum	9,322	9,733	1,939	426	448	−106	156	241	3,583	2,340
Manufacturing	3,568	3,631	82	64	200	407	151	247	455	662
Other	7,005	8,113	688	1,066	788	669	276	276	1,518	1,472
International	4,913	5,557	264	530	379	552	−208	−76	738	749

Third World Debt
The following is a list of debt owed by Third World nations to Western banks and financial institutions as of mid-1984.

Country	Dollars	Country	Dollars	Country	Dollars
Brazil	93 billion	Indonesia	25 billion	Algeria	15 billion
Mexico	89 billion	Philippines	24 billion	Malaysia	12 billion
Argentina	44 billion	Chile	18 billion	Nigeria	12 billion
Venezuela	34 billion	Turkey	17 billion		

U.S. Federal Budget Deficits Since 1946

(In Billions of Dollars)

Fiscal Year	President	Surplus = + Deficit = −	% of GNP	Fiscal Year	President	Surplus = + Deficit = −	% of GNP
1946	Truman	$15.9 −	7.8%	1966	"	3.8 −	0.5
1947	"	3.9 +	Surplus	1967	"	8.7 −	1.1
1948	"	12.0 +	Surplus	1968	"	25.2 −	3.0
1949	"	0.6 +	Surplus	1969	"	3.2 +	Surplus
1950	"	3.1 −	1.2	1970	Nixon	2.8 −	0.3
1951	"	6.1 +	Surplus	1971	"	23.0 −	2.2
1952	"	1.5 −	0.4	1972	"	23.4 −	2.1
1953	"	6.5 −	1.8	1973	"	14.8 −	1.2
1954	Eisenhower	1.2 −	0.3	1974	"	4.7 −	0.3
1955	"	3.0 −	0.8	1975	Ford	45.2 −	3.1
1956	"	4.1 +	Surplus	1976	"	79.4 −	4.0
1957	"	3.2 +	Surplus	1977	Carter	44.9 −	2.4
1958	"	2.9 −	0.7	1978	"	48.8 −	2.3
1959	"	12.9 −	2.7	1979	"	27.7 −	1.2
1960	"	0.3 +	Surplus	1980	"	59.6 −	2.3
1961	"	3.4 −	0.7	1981	Reagan	57.9 −	2.0
1962	Kennedy	7.1 −	1.3	1982	"	110.6 −	3.6
1963	"	4.8 −	0.8	1983	"	195.4 −	6.1
1964	Johnson	5.9 −	1.0	1984	"	183.7 est.	5.2 est.
1965	"	1.6 −	0.2	1985	"	180.4 est.	4.6 est.

Note: Fiscal year ends Sept. 30 (June 30 prior to 1977).

U.S. Balance of International Payments

Source: Bureau of Economic Analysis, U.S. Commerce Department
(millions of dollars)

	1955	1960	1965	1970	1975	1978	1980	1982	1983
Exports of goods and services . . .	19,948	28,861	41,086	65,673	155,729	221,036	344,667	348,324	332,20
Merchandise, adjusted	14,424	19,650	26,461	42,469	107,088	142,054	223,966	211,217	200,25
Transfers under U.S. military agency sales contracts	200	335	830	1,501	4,049	8,240	8,231	4,131	4,83
Receipts of income on U.S. investments abroad	2,817	4,616	7,436	11,746	25,351	42,972	75,936	85,338	72,17
Other services.	2,507	4,261	6,359	9,957	19,242	27,772	36,534	52,961	54,94
Imports of goods and services . . .	−17,795	−23,729	−32,801	−60,050	−132,836	−230,240	−333,888	−351,502	−365,11
Merchandise, adjusted	−11,527	−14,758	−21,510	−39,866	−98,041	−175,813	−249,308	−247,606	−261,31
Direct defense expenditures.	−2,901	−3,087	−2,952	−4,855	−4,795	−7,354	−10,746	—	—
Payments of income on foreign investments in the U.S.	−520	−1,237	−2,088	−5,516	−12,564	−22,073	−43,174	−56,678	−56,49
Other services.	−2,847	−4,646	−6,251	−9,815	−17,436	−25,001	−30,660	−52,981	−50,30
Unilateral transfers, net	−2,498	−2,308	−2,854	−3,294	−4,613	−5,055	−7,056	−8,034	−8,65
U.S. official reserve assets, net	182	2,145	1,225	2,481	−849	−732	−8,155	−4,965	−1,1
U.S. Government assets, other than official reserve assets, net	−310	−1,100	−1,605	−1,589	−3,474	−4,644	−5,165	−5,732	−5,0
U.S. private assets, net	−1,255	−5,144	−5,335	−10,228	−35,380	−57,279	−71,456	−100,348	−43,2
Foreign official assets in the U.S., net .		1,473	134	6,908	7,027	33,293	−15,492	3,172	5,3
Other foreign assets in the U.S., net. .		821	607	−550	8,643	30,804	34,769	84,694	76,3
Statistical discrepancy.	371	−1,019	−458	−219	5,753	11,354	29,640	41,390	9,3
Memoranda:									
Balance on merchandise trade . . .	2,897	4,892	4,951	2,603	9,047	−33,759	−25,342	−36,389	−61,0
Balance on goods and services . . .	2,153	5,132	8,284	5,624	22,893	−9,204	10,779	−3,177	−32,9
Balance on goods, services, and remittances	1,556	4,496	7,238	4,066	21,175	−11,088	8,382	5,799	−35,5
Balance on current account	−345	2,824	5,431	2,330	18,280	−14,259	3,723	11,211	−41,5

Note.—Details may not add to totals because of rounding.

Public Debt of the U.S.

Source: U.S. Treasury Department, Bureau of Govt. Financial Operations; Bureau of the Census

Fiscal year	Gross debt	Per cap.	Fiscal year	Gross debt	Per cap.	Fiscal year	Gross debt	Per c
1870	$2,436,453,269	$61.06	1930	$16,185,309,831	$131.51	1975	$533,188,976,772	$2,49(
1880	2,090,908,872	41.60	1940	42,967,531,038	325.23	1977	698,839,928,356	3,21!
1890	1,132,396,584	17.80	1950	256,087,352,351	1,688.30	1979	826,519,096,841	3,73(
1900	1,263,416,913	16.60	1960	284,092,760,848	1,572.31	1980	907,701,290,900	3,96!
1910	1,146,939,969	12.41	1965	313,818,898,984	1,612.70	1981	997,854,525,000	4,32!
1920	24,299,321,467	228.23	1970	370,093,706,950	1,807.09	1982	1,142,035,000,000	4,86;
						1983	1,377,211,000,000	5,81!

Note: Through 1976 the fiscal year ended June 30. From 1977 on, fiscal year ends Sept. 30.

Gross National Product, National Income, and Personal Income

Source: Bureau of Economic Analysis, U.S. Commerce Department
includes Alaska and Hawaii beginning in 1960 (millions of dollars)

	1950	1960	1970	1975	1980	1983[1]
Gross national product	286,172	505,978	982,419	1,528,833	2,631,688	3,304.8
Less: Capital consumption allowances.	23,853	47,712	90,827	161,954	293,160	377.1
Equals: Net national product	262,319	458,266	894,592	1,366,879	2,338,528	2,927.7
Less: Indirect business tax and nontax liability .	23,422	45,389	94,027	139,246	213,387	280.4
Business transfer payments	778	1,974	3,983	7,599	11,677	15.6
Statistical discrepancy	2,030	−683	−2,076	7,371	2,291	.5
Plus: Subsidies minus current surplus of						
government enterprises	114	422	2,716	2,339	5,471	15.6
Equals: National income	236,203	412,008	798,374	1,215,002	2,116,644	2,646.7
Less: Corporate profits and inventory						
valuation adjustment	2,272	9,760	37,549	95,902	175,429	225.2
Net interest	. . .	. . .	. . .	78,615	192,624	256.6
Contributions for social insurance	7,058	21,058	58,712	110,579	203,661	272.7
Wage accruals less disbursement	24	0	0	0	−40	−.4
Plus: Government transfer payment to persons.	14,404	26,966	75,898	170,567	285,893	389.3
Personal interest income.	8,929	23,284	64,284	115,529	265,968	376.3
Dividends.	8,803	12,890	22,884	31,885	56,807	70.3
Business transfer payments	778	1,974	3,983	7,599	11,677	15.6
Equals: Personal income	226,102	399,724	801,271	2,578,622	2,165,315	2,744.2

(1) Billions of dollars. .

National Income by Type of Income

(millions of dollars)

	1960	1965	1970	1975	1980	1981	1983[1]
Compensation of employees	294,932	396,543	609,150	931,079	1,599,630	1,769,248	1,984.9
Wages and salaries	271,932	362,005	546,453	805,872	1,356,645	1,439,241	1,658.8
Private.	222,782	292,145	430,481	630,431	1,096,391	1,208,785	1,331.1
Government.	49,150	69,860	115,972	175,441	260,254	284,456	327.7
Supplements to wages, salary	23,000	34,538	62,697	125,207	242,985	276,007	326.2
Employer contrib. for social ins.. . .	11,780	16,698	30,680	60,079	114,984	132,466	153.1
Other labor income.	11,220	17,840	32,017	65,128	128,001	143,541	173.1
Proprietors' income.	46,978	56,674	65,140	86,980	117,446	120,166	100.4
Business and professional	35,558	44,106	51,208	63,509	95,634	89,700	-.8
Inventory valuation adj..	91	-198	-506	-1,164	-3,104	-1,545	13.8
Farm.	11,420	12,568	13,932	23,471	21,812	30,466	58.3
Rental income of persons	13,758	17,117	18,644	22,426	31,515	41,385	225.2
Corp. prof., with inv. adjust.	46,580	77,096	67,891	95,902	175,429	192,334	203.2
Corp. profits before tax	48,540	75,209	71,485	120,378	234,614	226,959	75.8
Corp. profits tax liability	22,696	30,876	34,477	49,811	84,785	82,842	127.4
Corp. profits after tax	25,844	44,333	37,008	70,567	149,829	144,117	72.9
Dividends	12,890	19,120	22,884	31,885	58,589	64,658	54.5
Undistributed profits	12,954	25,213	14,124	38,682	91,240	79,459	-11.2
Inventory valuation adj.	327	-1,865	-5,067	-12,432	-42,872	-23,620	33.2
Net interest	9,760	18,529	37,549	78,615	192,624	249,893	256.6
National income	412,008	565,959	798,374	1,215,002	2,116,644	2,373,026	2,446.7

(1) Billions of dollars.

Appropriations by the Federal Government

Source: U.S. Treasury Department, Bureau of Govt. Financial Operations (fiscal year)

Year	Appropriations	Year	Appropriations	Year	Appropriations	Year	Appropriations
1890	$395,430,284.26	1940	$13,349,202,681.73	1959	$82,055,863,758.58	1972	$247,638,104,722.57
1895	492,477,759.97	1944	118,411,173,965.24	1960	80,169,728,902.87	1973	275,554,945,383.88
1900	698,912,982.83	1945	73,067,712,071.39	1961	89,229,575,129.94	1974	311,728,034,120.95
1905	781,288,215.95	1950	52,867,672,466.21	1962	91,447,827,731.00	1975	374,124,469,875.62
1910	1,044,433,622.64	1952	127,788,153,262.97	1963	102,149,886,566.52	1976	403,740,395,600.61
1915	1,122,471,919.12	1953	94,916,821,231.67	1965	107,555,087,612.62	1977	466,559,809,964.06
1920	6,454,596,649.56	1954	74,744,844,304.88	1967	140,861,235,376.56	1978	507,782,291,489.99
1925	3,748,651,750.35	1955	54,761,172,461.58	1969	203,049,351,090.91	1979	563,960,833,788.25
1930	4,665,236,678.04	1956	63,857,731,203.86	1970	222,200,021,901.52	1980	690,391,124,920.77
1935	7,527,559,327.66	1958	77,145,934,082.25	1971	247,623,820,964.75	1981	744,409,241,781.90

Note: Through 1976 the fiscal year ended June 30. From 1977 on, fiscal year ends Sept. 30.

U.S. Customs and Internal Revenue Receipts

Source: U.S. Treasury Department, Bureau of Govt. Financial Operations

Gross. Not reduced by appropriations to Federal old-age and survivors insurance trust fund or refunds of receipts.

Fiscal year	Customs	Internal Revenue	Fiscal year	Customs	Internal Revenue	Fiscal year	Customs	Internal Revenue
930	$587,000,903	$3,039,295,014	1955	$606,396,634	$66,288,691,586	1978	$6,728,612,000	$399,776,000,000
935	343,353,034	3,277,690,028	1960	1,123,037,579	91,774,802,823	1979	7,639,620,000	460,412,185,000
940	348,590,635	5,303,133,988	1965	1,477,548,820	114,428,991,753	1980	7,481,593,000	519,375,273,000
945	354,775,542	43,902,001,929	1970	2,429,799,000	195,700,000,000	1981	8,523,275,124	606,799,103,000
950	422,650,329	39,448,607,109	1975	3,675,532,000	293,800,000,000	1982	9,277,790,149	632,240,506,000
						1983	9,059,594,659	627,246,793,000

Note: Through 1976 the fiscal year ended June 30. From 1977 on, fiscal year ends Sept. 30.

National Income by Industry

Source: Bureau of Economic Analysis, U.S. Commerce Department
(millions of dollars)

	1960	1965	1970	1975	1980	1982	1983
Agricul., forestry, fisheries	17,468	20,366	24,455	42,827	61,355	69,533	60,888
Farms	16,452	18,805	22,191	39,379	54,060	61,514	52,329
Agri. services, forestry, fisheries	1,016	1,561	2,264	3,448	7,295	8,039	8,559
Mining	5,613	6,013	7,810	18,149	38,512	46,473	39,997
Metal mining	807	856	1,179	1,635	2,817	1,974	2,051
Coal mining	1,286	1,372	2,231	6,228	8,783	9,907	8,157
Crude petroleum, natural gas	2,606	2,670	3,099	8,075	23,289	31,291	26,457
Nonmetallic min. & quar.	914	1,115	1,301	2,211	3,623	3,301	3,332
Contract construction	20,972	29,840	43,821	61,795	107,237	107,836	112,268
Manufacturing	125,448	170,361	215,388	312,467	526,514	549,644	579,863
Nondurable goods	51,818	65,416	88,088	127,942	214,563	238,274	250,354
Food, kindred products	12,150	14,232	19,579	30,020	41,329	46,207	46,898
Tobacco manufactures	1,020	1,096	1,696	2,155	4,139	4,703	5,301
Textile mill products	4,484	5,872	7,525	8,754	13,387	13,478	15,440
Apparel, other fabric prod.	4,933	6,494	8,722	10,773	16,102	17,477	19,194
Paper, allied products	4,706	6,005	7,968	11,833	19,568	20,345	22,632
Printing, pub., allied industry	6,666	8,725	11,883	16,672	28,131	32,328	36,922
Chemicals, allied products	9,106	12,398	16,042	23,820	36,990	42,328	44,829
Petroleum and coal products	4,396	4,811	6,632	12,893	36,285	40,219	36,634
Rubber, misc. plastic products	2,751	3,939	5,804	8,661	14,854	16,704	18,534
Leather, leather products	1,606	1,844	2,237	2,361	3,778	4,027	3,970
Durable goods	73,630	104,945	127,300	184,525	311,951	311,370	329,509
Lumber, wood, except furn.	3,362	4,534	5,537	8,936	15,129	11,974	15,461
Furniture and fixtures	2,098	2,904	3,715	4,588	7,885	8,325	9,460
Stone, clay, glass products	4,620	5,654	6,891	9,858	16,424	14,410	16,588
Primary metal industries	11,066	14,491	15,757	24,231	37,554	27,975	28,622
Fabricated metal products	8,124	11,475	14,812	24,300	40,595	40,013	41,225
Machinery, except electrical	11,919	18,239	24,353	36,801	68,403	68,545	64,324
Electric and electronic equipment	10,496	14,855	20,132	26,646	49,879	53,733	57,491
Transport equip. exc. autos.	8,266	11,330	14,480	15,715	29,030	24,830	34,428
Motor vehicles and equipment.	8,399	14,455	12,086	19,045	21,863	31,519	31,570
Instruments	2,948	4,128	5,797	9,006	17,383	21,048	21,729
Misc. manufacturing	2,332	2,880	3,740	5,399	7,806	8,998	8,611
Transportation	18,141	23,069	30,308	44,455	80,425	83,326	87,679
Railroad	6,710	7,016	7,612	9,987	17,382	15,871	15,873
Local; interurban passenger transit	1,619	1,897	2,308	2,933	4,328	4,555	4,641
Motor freight trans., warehousing	5,886	8,396	11,830	18,935	33,044	34,929	36,714
Water transportation	1,635	1,982	2,503	3,323	5,877	6,057	5,818
Air transportation	1,370	2,636	4,358	7,062	13,290	14,317	16,395
Pipeline transportation	350	390	528	820	1,765	1,556	1,772
Transportation service	571	752	1,169	1,935	4,739	6,041	6,466
Communication	8,228	11,497	17,600	27,066	48,181	59,287	60,080
Telephone and telegraph	7,293	10,255	15,887	24,358	42,838	52,759	52,944
Radio broadcasting, television.	935	1,242	1,713	2,708	5,343	6,528	7,136
Electric, gas, sanitary services	8,923	11,442	14,864	24,302	42,651	57,675	64,263
Wholesale and retail trade.	64,737	84,662	122,213	194,227	316,630	358,933	386,363
Wholesale trade	23,420	30,469	44,860	80,564	137,572	152,967	161,208
Retail trade	41,317	54,193	77,353	113,663	179,058	205,966	255,155
Finance, ins. and real estate	48,608	63,987	92,625	140,375	290,851	355,102	393,955
Banking	7,255	8,943	16,448	20,109	45,051	42,202	44,710
Credit agencies, other than banks	-1,076	-1,617	-1,981	-4,729	2,300	4,947	8,246
Security, commodity brokers	1,219	1,942	2,733	4,144	8,229	12,618	16,736
Insurance carriers	4,816	5,880	9,269	12,751	29,278	26,655	30,092
Insurance agents, brokers, service	2,070	2,957	4,223	6,704	12,267	14,121	15,372
Real estate	33,940	45,741	61,812	100,078	195,760	250,408	273,289
Holding and other investment cos.	384	141	121	1,318	-2,034	4,151	5,510
Services.	44,648	64,142	103,304	168,516	310,008	387,029	426,636
Hotels, other lodging places	2,114	2,964	4,659	6,952	13,826	15,799	17,381
Personal services	4,608	5,965	7,436	8,329	13,278	15,049	16,381
Misc. business services	5,091	8,399	14,051	23,928	53,027	69,119	77,860
Automobile repair, serv., garages	1,746	2,402	3,616	5,944	11,242	12,843	13,685
Misc. repair services	1,094	1,494	2,149	3,478	6,813	7,262	7,495
Motion pictures	891	1,201	1,581	1,842	3,841	4,507	5,249
Amusement, recreation services	1,662	2,201	3,321	5,268	9,033	10,705	11,856
Medical, other health services.	10,636	15,790	29,472	54,075	99,625	130,993	144,913
Legal services.	2,695	4,197	6,691	11,828	21,310	18,065	32,514
Education services	2,419	4,145	6,688	10,014	15,438	18,514	19,750
Social Services	—	—	—	5,003	9,455	10,932	11,895
Nonprofit membership org..	4,176	5,787	8,912	11,016	15,494	29,173	31,422
Misc. professional services	3,719	5,629	9,673	15,030	31,041	37,406	40,362
Private households	3,797	3,968	5,055	5,809	6,585	7,594	7,768
Government, government enterprises	52,707	75,374	127,421	199,875	306,343	364,131	391,653
Federal	25,303	33,303	53,093	72,007	102,767	124,282	132,768
General Government	21,676	28,298	44,723	58,976	82,947	101,162	107,777
Government enterprises.	3,627	5,005	8,370	13,031	19,820	23,120	24,991
State & local.	27,404	42,071	74,328	127,868	2,128,707	239,849	258,885
General Government	25,470	39,294	69,964	119,641	82,947	223,746	241,399
Government enterprises	1,934	2,777	4,364	8,227	19,820	16,103	17,48
Domestic income	415,493	560,753	799,809	1,234,054	2,128,707	2,438,989	2,603,64
Rest of the world	2,477	4,681	4,616	10,534	45,310	47,955	48,297
All industries, total	417,970	565,434	804,425	1,244,588	2,174,017	2,486,944	2,651,94

Producer Price Indexes

Source: Bureau of Labor Statistics, U.S. Labor Department

Producer Price Indexes measure average changes in prices received in primary markets of the U.S. by producers of commodities in all stages of processing.

Commodity group (1967 = 100)	Annual Avg.		1983		1984	
	1981	1983	Jan.	June	Jan.	June
commodities.	293.4	303.1	299.9	302.4	308.0	311.4
rm products processed foods and feeds.	251.5	253.9	245.8	252.5	264.4	262.7
Farm products	254.9	248.2	233.2	247.4	263.4	257.1
Processed foods and feeds	248.7	255.9	251.7	254.3	263.8	264.8
dustrial commodities	304.1	315.7	313.9	315.3	319.1	323.9
Textile products and apparel.	199.7	205.1	202.7	204.7	208.2	210.3
Hides, skins, leathers, and related products	260.9	271.1	266.7	271.2	279.1	290.3
Fuels and related products and power	694.5	664.7	683.6	665.5	652.1	667.9
Chemicals and allied products	287.6	293.0	289.3	290.8	298.1	302.5
Rubber and plastic products	232.6	243.2	242.9	243.1	244.8	247.3
Lumber and wood products	292.8	307.1	293.3	314.8	309.1	307.1
Pulp, paper, and allied products	273.8	298.1	293.6	297.0	309.1	317.6
Metals and metal products	300.4	307.2	306.3	306.3	312.9	317.2
Machinery and equipment	263.3	286.4	283.3	286.2	289.7	293.1
Furniture and household durables	198.5	214.0	210.9	214.0	216.8	219.2
Nonmetallic mineral products	309.5	325.2	321.5	324.5	330.1	338.4
Transportation equipment (Dec. 1968 = 100)	235.4	256.7	256.3	256.1	261.5	262.6
Miscellaneous products.	265.7	289.6	285.7	288.0	294.5	295.6

Indexes of Manufacturing, Industrial Countries

Source: Bureau of Labor Statistics, U.S. Labor Department (1977 = 100)

Output per hour

untry	1960	1965	1970	1975	1978	1980	1981	1982	1983[1]
ited States	60.0	74.5	79.1	93.4	100.8	101.7	104.6	103.6	113.1
Foreign countries[2]	37.7	50.3	70.2	89.8	103.9	111.4	115.5	118.8	NA
anada	50.4	62.9	77.0	91.2	101.7	102.3	103.1	100.3	109.0
pan	22.0	33.1	61.4	85.3	107.9	125.4	126.3	127.6	155.2
lgium	32.2	39.8	58.8	85.1	105.0	115.4	121.8	130.0	NA
nmark	36.4	47.4	65.3	94.4	102.4	109.8	116.0	119.5	125.6
ance.	39.8	51.2	70.1	87.9	105.7	112.6	114.4	122.3	129.1
est Germany	40.0	53.8	68.2	89.0	103.3	109.8	112.8	114.7	118.5
ly	36.5	52.9	72.7	91.1	103.0	116.9	121.0	122.6	124.8
therlands.	31.7	41.3	63.0	85.1	106.6	114.2	117.2	121.4	NA
rway	54.6	64.4	81.7	96.8	101.8	109.3	110.4	109.7	116.3
eden	43.0	59.4	82.0	100.5	104.3	114.4	114.5	117.9	123.9
ited Kingdom	55.6	67.0	80.5	94.8	103.3	108.1	114.2	118.2	118.0

Unit Labor Costs in U.S. dollars

	1960	1965	1970	1975	1978	1980	1981	1982	1983
ited States	61.1	57.5	72.7	91.5	107.4	130.6	140.0	153.4	147.4
Foreign countries[2]	36.3	41.6	48.0	93.3	115.6	138.4	130.8	124.3	NA
nada	59.3	51.0	62.0	90.3	97.8	114.9	123.5	136.9	143.6
pan	30.2	37.4	41.3	90.4	126.2	113.8	123.8	112.0	102.7
gium	30.5	38.6	41.9	90.6	117.3	135.5	109.4	91.5	NA
nmark	30.1	37.0	44.5	89.8	117.3	132.6	108.8	99.3	94.6
nce.	40.7	49.0	48.3	100.6	116.5	151.7	134.0	122.0	114.7
st Germany	26.3	32.7	43.2	89.2	121.6	147.5	124.2	119.5	113.3
ly	32.5	41.2	50.6	104.3	115.6	141.4	126.2	122.9	127.7
therlands.	24.9	35.0	41.4	93.5	115.8	133.1	108.4	104.7	NA
rway	21.7	26.9	34.5	81.4	109.7	126.2	120.0	118.0	107.4
eden	29.6	34.9	40.5	82.9	105.6	123.2	116.4	96.7	81.2
ted Kingdom	44.8	51.7	55.0	101.9	124.0	212.7	203.3	185.1	164.5

Preliminary estimates. (2) Trade-weighted geometric average reflecting the relative importance of each country as a manufactur-trade competitor of the U.S.

Index of Leading Economic Indicators

Source: Bureau of Economic Analysis, U.S. Dept. of Commerce

The index of leading economic indicators, which is issued to project the economy's performance six months or a year ad, fell eight-tenths of 1 percent in July 1984. The June index had fallen 1.3 percent, breaking a string of twenty-one con-utive increases, the longest since the end of World War II. It was the first time this index had declined two consecutive nths since the beginning of 1982.

he index is made up of twelve measurements of economic activity that tend to change direction long before the overall nomy does. The volatility of the index, caused, in part, by the fact that many of the statistics covered do not reach the mmerce Department until weeks after the initial report, usually results in at least one revision after the initial reporting.

wo companion indexes—those of coincident and lagging indicators—rose in July by eight-tenths of 1 percent and nine-hs of 1 percent, respectively. The coincident index reflects current economic conditions. Its components are: employees on agricultural payrolls; personal income less transfer payments; industrial production; and manufacturing and trade sales. lagging index consists of items that tend to lag behind the business cycle.

t the end of July 1984, the index of leading indicators stood at 165.3, with the level in 1967 providing the base of 100. coincident index was reported at 156.5 and the lagging index at 118.1.

Leading Indicators: Component Analysis

Components	Contribution to change June to July 1984	Components	Contribution to change June to July 1984	Components	Contribution to change June to July 1984
Average workweek of production workers in manufacturing	+0.09	Index of net business formation	+0.01	Index of stock prices	−0.10
Average weekly claims for State unemployment insurance[1]	−0.14	Contracts and orders for plant and equipment, adjusted for inflation	−0.15	Money supply: M-2, adjusted for inflation	+0.05
New orders for consumer goods and materials, adjusted for inflation	+0.25	New building permits issued	−0.43	Change in credit (business and consumer borrowing)	NA
Vendor performance (companies receiving slower deliveries from suppliers)	−0.29	Change in inventories on hand and on order, adjusted for inflation	NA		
		Change in sensitive materials prices	−0.24	Leading indicators index, percent change	−0.8

(1) Series is inverted in computing index; that is, a decrease in the series is considered upward movement. (NA) Not available.

State Finances

Revenues, Expenditures, Debts, Taxes, U.S. Aid, Military Contracts

For fiscal 1982 (year ending June 30, 1982, except: Alabama and Michigan, Sept. 30; New York, Mar. 31; Texas, Aug. 31) *Military prime contracts. Taxes are State income and sales (or gross receipts) taxes, and vehicle, etc., fees.

Sources: Census Bureau, U.S. Treasury and Defense Depts.

State	Receipts (thousands)	Outlays (thousands)	Total debt (thousands)	Per cap. debt	Per cap. taxes	Per cap. U.S. aid	Military contracts (thousands)
Alabama	$4,823,344	$4,666,822	$1,958,569	$502.97	$563.90	$362.42	$930,00*
Alaska	5,888,850	3,280,885	3,700,774	9,205.91	6,316.40	963.29	327,00*
Arizona.	3,500,695	3,245,103	240,258	88.40	682.86	279.44	1,490,00*
Arkansas. . . .	2,506,361	2,362,381	554,540	242.58	552.82	368.30	452,00*
California. . . .	42,247,431	40,443,843	10,330,999	436.50	921.86	364.65	22,578,00*
Colorado	3,804,808	3,635,365	741,305	256.51	584.79	317.48	1,072,00*
Connecticut . .	4,300,183	3,993,741	4,620,575	1,486.67	752.74	355.26	5,897,00*
Delaware. . . .	1,189,869	1,083,992	1,359,539	2,288.79	1,001.37	464.06	239,00*
Florida	9,363,821	9,322,355	2,993,388	307.14	570.07	274.49	4,046,00*
Georgia	6,143,878	6,007,075	1,645,941	301.29	600.60	387.53	1,596,00*
Hawaii	2,146,401	1,994,359	2,109,692	2,186.21	1,104.90	410.05	511,00*
Idaho	1,237,053	1,208,724	427,178	452.52	612.94	362.53	77,00*
Illinois.	14,441,250	14,138,237	7,470,299	653.74	650.15	358.36	1,210,00*
Indiana	5,657,182	5,694,016	1,024,784	186.66	558.04	284.84	2,004,00*
Iowa	3,884,709	3,903,183	458,042	157.19	685.30	307.46	339,00*
Kansas	2,751,183	2,634,443	397,481	168.14	610.29	293.33	1,442,00*
Kentucky	4,885,352	4,725,792	2,659,592	726.66	680.62	388.43	247,00*
Louisiana. . . .	6,453,026	6,462,588	4,146,609	985.88	743.52	364.84	1,455,00*
Maine.	1,571,826	1,527,076	860,782	765.14	649.76	464.94	784,00*
Maryland. . . :	6,280,701	6,260,305	4,212,457	998.92	757.19	237.90	3,082,00*
Massachusetts	8,752,196	8,631,490	6,420,794	1,119.19	837.31	420.33	5,301,00*
Michigan	14,586,994	13,996,829	3,859,420	416.69	680.97	474.90	1,572,00*
Minnesota . . .	7,059,552	6,924,688	2,659,518	652.48	932.13	398.95	1,434,00*
Mississippi . . .	3,229,576	3,038,846	748,192	296.78	580.04	428.08	1,161,00*
Missouri	4,744,705	4,409,964	1,836,490	373.50	470.42	427.57	5,294,00*
Montana	1,331,090	1,134,840	399,215	507.26	672.36	333.62	36,00*
Nebraska . . .	1,658,315	1,646,185	295,479	188.20	548.11	476.45	140,00*
Nevada.	1,551,591	1,413,147	648,313	810.39	931.82	330.25	109,00*
New Hampshire	1,051,492	1,005,092	1,270,612	1,379.60	353.44	392.96	538,00*
New Jersey . .	11,341,194	11,151,579	8,795,893	1,194.28	757.26	333.36	2,858,00*
New Mexico . .	3,020,298	2,391,761	823,500	632.00	941.32	365.48	455,00*
New York . . .	33,395,716	30,159,759	25,813,504	1,470.18	879.26	535.12	7,741,00*
North Carolina.	7,128,334	6,850,703	1,591,067	270.50	644.34	525.94	828,00*
North Dakota .	1,285,713	1,190,922	324,836	497.45	815.67	307.76	68,00*
Ohio	15,308,028	13,742,322	4,999,271	462.98	538.94	449.98	3,300,00*
Oklahoma . . .	4,691,617	4,162,348	1,171,937	387.42	896.85	334.68	563,00*
Oregon.	4,381,937	4,209,686	6,220,641	2,362.57	589.56	311.99	168,00*
Pennsylvania .	16,290,149	15,328,386	6,244,149	526.31	689.95	440.77	3,052,00*
Rhode Island .	1,686,047	1,628,042	1,987,036	2,098.24	712.56	390.16	285,00*
South Carolina	4,209,113	4,110,192	3,077,471	985.74	627.55	491.60	379,00*
South Dakota .	872,639	828,962	708,707	1,025.63	475.81	325.61	51,00*
Tennessee. . .	4,521,319	4,298,381	1,587,121	345.70	467.49	470.00	672,00*
Texas.	16,365,057	14,151,809	2,587,117	181.82	639.53	345.59	6,747,00*
Utah	2,323,913	1,994,176	722,510	494.53	650.83	243.80	562,00*
Vermont	832,212	888,330	673,362	1,317.73	650.31	389.07	202,00*
Virginia	6,614,492	6,298,334	2,614,239	488.92	605.17	524.53	4,050,00*
Washington . . .	7,446,082	7,255,537	2,492,091	603.12	853.91	295.59	2,817,00*
West Virginia . .	3,100,465	2,841,679	1,804,135	925.20	753.27	372.19	101,00*
Wisconsin . . .	7,533,059	6,894,524	2,647,931	562.67	836.06	396.10	863,00*
Wyoming	1,558,599	1,123,329	532,745	1,133.50	1,622.41	251.53	89,00*
United States. Total or average	330,949,417	310,292,127	147,470,100	652.78	720.01	402.46	$115,280,0*

Civilian Employment of the Federal Government

Source: Workforce Analysis and Statistics Division, U.S. Office of Personnel Management as of March 1984
(Payroll in thousands of dollars)

Agency	All Areas		United States		Overseas		Wash., D.C.
	Employment	Payroll	Employment	Payroll	Employment	Payroll	Employment
Total, all agencies[1]	**2,895,587**	**7,071,813**	**2,756,493**	**6,847,638**	**139,094**	**224,175**	**351,805**
Legislative branch	**39,013**	**100,961**	**38,945**	**100,679**	**68**	**282**	**36,675**
Congress	19,854	41,945	19,854	41,945	—	—	19,854
Senate	7,242	15,505	7,242	15,505	—	—	7,242
House of Representatives	12,598	26,396	12,598	26,396	—	—	12,598
Comm. on Security and Coop. in Europe	14	44	14	44	—	—	14
Architect of the Capitol	2,172	6,146	2,172	6,146	—	—	2,172
General Accounting Office	5,260	21,010	5,198	20,754	62	256	3,369
Government Printing Office	5,685	19,016	5,685	19,016	—	—	5,244
Library of Congress	5,294	10,735	5,288	10,709	6	26	5,288
Tax Court	261	678	261	678	202	442	261
Judicial branch	**16,867**	**36,462**	**16,665**	**36,020**	—	—	**1,654**
United States Courts	330	731	330	731	202	442	1,324
Supreme Court	16,537	35,731	16,335	35,289	138,824	223,451	33ʃ
Executive branch	**2,839,707**	**6,934,390**	**2,700,883**	**6,710,939**	**6**	**34**	**313,476**
Executive Office of the President	1,570	6,665	1,564	6,631	—	—	1,564
White House Office	366	1,501	366	1,501	—	—	366
Office of the Vice President	20	92	20	92	—	—	20
Office of Management and Budget	589	2,744	589	2,744	—	—	589
Council of Economic Advisors	32	150	32	150	—	—	32
Council on Environmental Quality	10	62	10	62	—	—	10
Domestic Policy Staff	41	200	41	200	—	—	10
Executive Mansions and Grounds	—	—	—	—	—	—	—
Office of Special Representatives Trade Negotiations	141	660	135	626	6	34	135
Office of Science and Technology Policy	28	85	28	85	—	—	28
National Security Council	61	255	61	255	—	—	61
Executive departments	**1,749,685**	**3,945,831**	**1,632,976**	**3,764,581**	**116,709**	**181,250**	**231,223**
State	24,180	54,233	8,148	24,351	15,762	29,882	7,162
Treasury	134,544	377,434	133,481	373,103	1,063	4,331	18,648
Defense	1,045,710	1,989,961	951,168	1,857,017	94,542	132,944	86,954
Department of the Army	376,622	598,659	333,332	529,670	—	—	28,626
Department of the Navy	338,931	719,883	314,656	697,087	24,275	22,796	36,650
Department of the Air Force	245,323	493,663	230,490	475,027	14,833	18,636	6,294
Defense Logistics Agency	47,569	91,460	47,131	90,729	438	731	2,685
Other Defense Activities	37,265	86,296	25,559	64,504	11,706	21,792	12,699
Justice	60,179	148,776	59,204	146,047	975	2,729	17,276
Interior	74,240	163,617	73,863	162,586	377	1,031	9,791
Agriculture	113,661	301,807	112,210	298,933	1,451	2,874	12,479
Commerce	34,837	109,274	34,009	107,383	828	1,891	18,548
Labor	19,143	67,107	19,062	66,888	81	219	6,798
Health and Human Services	145,906	423,411	144,951	420,557	955	2,854	31,593
Housing and Urban Development	12,584	45,588	12,445	45,082	139	506	3,467
Transportation	62,243	189,501	61,710	187,531	533	1,970	8,987
Department of Energy	17,197	60,750	17,194	60,731	3	19	6,049
Department of Education	5,261	14,372	5,261	14,372	—	—	3,471
Independent agencies	**1,088,452**	**2,981,894**	**1,066,343**	**2,939,727**	**22,109**	**42,167**	**80,689**
Action	515	1,993	512	1,982	3	11	270
Board of Governors, Fed. Res. System	1,580	4,266	1,580	6,266	—	—	1,580
Committee on Civil Rights	233	630	223	630	—	—	168
Environmental Protection Agency	12,707	28,680	12,692	28,664	15	36	4,475
Federal Communications Comm.	1,979	7,094	1,970	7,012	9	82	1,418
Federal Trade Commission	1,339	6,267	1,339	6,267	—	—	1,140
General Services Admin.	29,462	59,107	29,363	58,810	99	297	10,208
International Trade Commission	443	1,196	443	1,196	—	—	443
Interstate Commerce Commission	1,182	3,402	1,182	3,402	—	—	845
National Aeronautics and Space Admin.	22,400	70,547	22,386	70,485	14	62	4,831
National Labor Relations Board	2,758	10,598	2,742	10,543	16	55	861
Nuclear Regulatory Comm.	3,580	12,110	3,580	12,110	19	25	2,575
Office of Personnel Mgmt.	6,427	12,324	6,408	12,299	8,143	12,783	2,642
Panama Canal Commission	8,157	12,812	1,839	29	—	—	5
Securities and Exchange Comm.	1,839	4,801	301	4,801	3	2	1,224
Selective Service System	304	519	4,849	517	110	315	126
Small Business Admin.	4,959	16,453	670,278	16,138	—	—	1,453
Tennessee Valley Authority	33,961	85,612	33,961	85,612	—	—	12
U.S. Postal Service	673,214	2,091,394	237,537	2,082,393	2,936	9,001	17,907
Veterans Administration	239,956	439,478	—	435,551	2,419	3,927	6,589

(1) Excludes employees of Central Intelligence Agency, National Security Agency (not reported to the Office of Personnel Management) and uncompensated employees. June 1981 total includes 40,742 employees exempted from personnel ceilings in the Youth Programs and Worker Trainee Opportunities Program.

U.S. Labor Force, Employment and Unemployment

Source: Bureau of Labor Statistics, U.S. Labor Department

(numbers in thousands; monthly data are seasonally adjusted)

Employment status	Annual averages			1984					
	1979	1981	1983	Jan.	Feb.	March	April	May	June
Civilian labor force	104,962	108,670	111,550	112,215	112,693	112,912	113,245	113,803	113,877
Employed	98,824	100,397	100,834	103,190	103,892	104,140	104,402	105,288	105,748
Agriculture	3,347	3,368	3,383	3,271	3,395	3,281	3,393	3,389	3,403
Nonagricultural industries	95,477	97,030	97,450	99,918	100,496	100,859	101,009	101,899	102,344
Unemployed	6,137	8,273	10,717	9,026	8,801	8,772	8,843	8,514	8,130
Long term, 15 weeks & over	1,241	2,285	4,210	3,201	2,984	2,873	2,855	2,851	2,619

Unemployment rates (unemployment in each group as a percent of the groups' civilian labor force)

Total, 16 years and over	5.8	7.6	9.6	8.0	7.8	7.8	7.8	7.5	7.1
Men, 20 years and over	4.2	6.3	8.9	7.3	7.0	6.8	6.9	6.5	6.3
Women, 20 years and over	5.7	6.8	8.1	7.1	6.9	6.9	7.0	6.8	6.4
Both sexes, 16 to 19 years	16.1	19.6	22.4	19.4	19.3	19.9	19.4	19.0	17.6
White, total	5.1	6.7	8.4	6.9	6.7	6.7	6.7	6.4	6.1
Men, 20 years and over	3.6	5.6	7.9	6.3	6.1	5.8	5.9	5.6	5.2
Women, 20 years and over	5.0	5.9	6.9	6.0	5.8	5.9	6.0	5.8	5.4
Both sexes, 16 to 19 years	14.0	17.3	19.3	16.2	16.5	17.1	16.2	16.2	15.8
Black, total	12.3	15.6	19.5	16.7	16.2	16.6	16.8	15.8	15.6
Men, 20 years and over	9.3	13.5	18.1	14.8	14.1	15.4	16.0	14.1	14.
Women, 20 years and over	10.9	13.4	16.5	14.3	14.4	13.5	13.4	13.6	12.
Both sexes, 16 to 19 years	36.5	41.4	48.5	47.9	43.5	46.7	44.8	44.1	34.
Married men, spouse present	2.8	4.3	6.5	5.0	4.9	4.7	4.7	4.5	4.
Married women, spouse present	5.1	6.0	7.0	6.0	5.9	5.8	5.8	5.8	5.
Women who head families	8.3	10.4	12.2	10.7	11.0	11.0	10.5	9.8	9.
Full-time workers	5.3	7.3	9.5	7.8	7.5	7.5	7.6	7.2	6.
Part-time workers	8.8	9.4	10.4	9.2	9.3	9.2	9.1	9.3	10
Nonagricultural w/s workers	5.4	7.2	9.1	7.5	7.3	7.1	7.2	6.8	6.
Construction	10.3	15.6	18.4	15.0	15.1	13.3	14.3	14.8	14
Manufacturing	5.6	8.3	11.2	8.4	7.5	7.5	7.7	7.1	7
Durable goods	5.0	8.2	12.1	8.0	7.3	7.8	7.5	7.0	7
Nondurable goods	6.5	8.4	10.0	8.9	7.8	7.2	8.0	7.1	7
Wholesale & retail trades	6.5	8.1	10.0	8.4	8.3	8.3	8.7	7.9	7
Finance & service industries	4.9	5.9	7.2	6.3	6.3	6.4	6.1	5.5	5
Government workers	3.7	4.7	5.3	5.0	4.5	4.4	4.4	4.7	4

Note: Pre-1982 data have been revised to reflect 1980 census population controls.

Employed Persons by Major Occupational Groups and Sex

1983 Annual Averages	Thousands of persons			Percent distribution		
Occupational group	Both sexes	Males	Females	Both sexes	Males	Female
Total Employed	100,834	56,787	44,047	100.0	100.0	100.0
Managerial and professional specialty	23,592	13,933	9,659	23.4	24.5	21.9
Executive, administration and managerial	10,772	7,282	3,490	10.7	12.8	7.9
Professional specialty	12,280	6,651	6,169	12.7	11.7	14.0
Technical, sales and administrative support	31,265	11,078	20,187	31.0	19.5	45.8
Technicians and related support	3,053	1,582	1,471	3.0	2.8	3.3
Sales occupations	11,818	6,201	5,617	11.7	10.9	12.8
Administrative support, including clerical	16,395	3,295	13,100	16.3	5.8	29.7
Service occupations	13,857	5,330	8,326	13.7	9.7	18.9
Private household	980	38	942	1.0	.1	2.1
Protective service	1,672	1,457	215	1.7	2.6	.5
Service, except private household and protective	11,205	4,035	7,170	11.1	7.1	16.3
Precision production, craft, and repair	12,328	11,328	1,000	12.2	19.9	2.3
Mechanics and repairers	4,158	4,033	125	4.1	7.1	.3
Construction trades	4,289	4,210	79	4.3	7.4	.2
Other precision production, craft, and repair	3,881	3,085	795	3.8	5.4	1.8
Operators, fabricators, and laborers	16,091	11,809	4,282	16.0	20.8	9.7
Machine operators, assemblers, and inspectors	7,744	4,484	3,259	7.7	7.9	7.4
Transportation and material moving occupations	4,201	3,875	326	4.2	6.8	.7
Handlers, equipment cleaners, helpers, and laborers	4,147	3,450	697	4.1	6.1	1.6
Farming, forestry, and fishing	3,700	3,108	592	3.7	5.5	1.3

Note: Pre-1982 data have been revised to reflect 1980 census population controls.

Employment and Unemployment in the U.S.

Civilian labor force, persons 16 years of age and over (in thousands)

Year	Civilian labor force	Employed	Unemployed	Year	Civilian labor force	Employed	Unemployed
1940[1]	55,640	47,520	8,120	1976	96,158	88,752	7,4
1950	62,208	58,918	3,288	1977	99,009	92,017	6,9
1960	69,628	65,778	3,852	1978	102,251	96,048	6,2
1965	74,455	71,088	3,366	1980	106,940	99,303	7,6
1970	82,771	78,678	4,093	1981	108,670	100,397	8,2
1974	91,949	86,794	5,156	1982	110,204	99,526	10,6
1975	93,775	85,846	7,929	1983	111,550	100,834	10,7

[1] Persons 14 years of age and over

Gold Reserves of Central Banks and Governments

Source: IMF. *International Financial Statistics*
(Million fine troy ounces)

Year end	All countries¹	Int'l Monetary Fund	United States	Canada	Japan	Belgium	France	Fed. Rep. of Germany	Italy	Netherlands	Switzerland	United Kingdom
1968	1,107.37	65.37	311.20	24.66	10.17	43.53	110.77	129.69	83.52	48.51	74.97	42.09
1969	1,112.90	66.00	338.83	24.92	11.81	43.40	101.34	116.56	84.46	49.16	75.49	42.06
1970	1,057.89	123.97	316.34	22.59	15.22	42.01	100.91	113.70	82.48	51.06	78.03	38.52
1971	1,028.44	135.20	291.60	22.69	19.42	44.12	100.66	116.47	82.40	54.53	83.11	22.18
1972	1,019.68	153.43	275.97	21.95	21.10	43.08	100.69	117.36	82.37	54.17	83.11	21.08
1973	1,022.24	153.43	275.97	21.95	21.11	42.17	100.91	117.61	82.48	54.33	83.20	21.01
1974	1,020.24	153.40	275.97	21.95	21.11	42.17	100.93	117.61	82.48	54.33	83.20	21.03
1975	1,018.71	153.43	274.71	21.95	21.11	42.17	100.93	117.61	82.48	54.33	83.20	21.03
1976	1,014.23	149.51	274.68	21.62	21.11	42.17	101.02	117.61	82.48	54.33	83.28	21.03
1977	1,029.19	131.57	277.55	22.01	21.62	42.45	101.67	118.30	82.91	54.63	83.28	22.23
1978	1,036.82	118.20	276.41	22.13	23.97	42.59	101.99	118.64	83.12	54.78	83.28	22.83
1979	944.44	106.83	264.60	22.18	24.23	34.21	81.92	95.25	66.71	43.97	83.28	18 25
1980	952.40	103.44	264.32	20.98	24.23	34.18	81.85	95.18	66.67	43.94	83.28	18.84
1981	951.54	103.44	264.11	20.46	24.23	34.18	81.85	95.18	66.67	43.94	83.28	19.03
1982	947.07	103.44	264.03	20.26	24.23	34.18	81.85	95.18	66.67	43.94	83.28	19.01
1983	945.67	103.44	263.39	20.17	24.23	34.18	81.85	95.18	66.67	43.94	83.28	19.01

(1) Covers IMF members with reported gold holdings, Switzerland and Netherlands Antilles. For countries not listed above, see *International Financial Statistics*, a monthly publication of the International Monetary Fund.

World Gold Production

(Troy Ounces)

Year	Estimated world prod.	Africa South Africa	Ghana	Zaire	North and South America United States	Canada	Mexico	Nicaragua	Colombia	Australia	India	Other Japan	Philippines	All other
1972	44,843,374	29,245,273	724,051	140,724	1,449,943	2,078,567	146,061	112,340	188,137	754,866	105,776	243,027	606,730	9,047,879
1973	43,296,755	27,494,603	722,531	133,642	1,175,750	1,954,340	132,557	85,051	215,876	554,278	105,390	188,274	572,250	9,962,213
1974	40,124,290ⁱ	24,388,203	ⁱ614,007	130,603	1,126,886	1,698,392	134,454	82,639	265,195	ⁱ512,611	101,114	ⁱ139,719	ⁱ537,615	ⁱ10,392,852
1975	38,476,371ⁱ	22,937,820	523,889	103,217	1,052,252	ⁱ1,653,611	144,710	70,281	³308,864	ⁱ526,821	ⁱ90,826	ⁱ143,503	ⁱ502,577	ⁱ10,418,000
1976	39,024,485ⁱ	22,936,018	532,473	91,093	1,048,037	1,691,806	162,811	75,841	300,307	502,741	100,696	ⁱ137,643	501,210	10,943,809
1977	38,906,145ⁱ	22,501,886	480,884	80,418	1,100,347	1,733,609	212,709	65,764	²257,070	ⁱ624,270	ⁱ96,902	ⁱ149,004	ⁱ558,554	ⁱ11,044,728
1978	38,983,019ⁱ	22,648,558	402,034	76,077	998,832	1,735,077	202,003	ⁱ73,947	²246,446	647,579	89,186	145,240	586,531	ⁱ11,131,509
1979	38,768,978ⁱ	22,617,179	362,000	69,992	ⁱ964,390	1,644,265	ⁱ190,364	61,086	269,369	596,910	ⁱ84,781	ⁱ227,626	ⁱ535,166	ⁱ11,245,850
1980	39,197,315	21,669,468	ⁱ353,000	39,963	ⁱ969,782	ⁱ1,627,477	ⁱ195,991	59,994	ⁱ510,439	547,591	78,834	ⁱ102,339	753,452	12,398,632
1981	41,249,456	21,121,157	341,000	64,430	1,379,161	1,672,893	203,160	62,000	529,214	590,737	79,875	99,242	753,451	14,353,136
1982ᵖ	43,056,674	21,355,111	331,000	62,233	1,465,683	2,081,230	196,248	51,849	481,846	866,815	71,935	104,136	834,439	15,154,149
1983ʳ	44,533,309	21,847,310	303,000	60,000	1,957,379	2,274,480	209,000	46,742	428,779	1,035,250	69,000	100,921	801,710	15,399,738

(e) estimated (p) preliminary (r) revised

U.S. and World Silver Production

Source: Bureau of Mines, U.S. Interior Department

Largest production of silver in the United States in 1915—74,961,075 fine ounces.

Year (Cal.)	United States Fine ozs.	Value	World Fine ozs.	Year (Cal.)	United States Fine ozs.	Value	World Fine ozs.
1930	50,748,127	$19,538,000	248,708,426	1965	39,806,033	51,469,201	257,415,000
1935	45,924,454	33,008,000	220,704,231	1970	45,006,000	79,697,000	310,891,000
1940	69,585,734	49,483,000	275,387,000	1975	34,938,000	154,424,000	303,112,000
1945	29,063,255	20,667,000	162,000,000	1980	32,329,000	667,278,000	339,382,000
1950	43,308,739	38,291,545	203,300,000	1981	40,683,000	427,921,000	361,781,000
1955	36,469,610	33,006,839	224,000,000	1982ᵖ	40,248,000	319,975,000	383,766,000
1960	36,000,000	$33,305,858	241,300,000	1983ᵉ	43,415,000	496,671,000	390,618,000

(e) estimated (p) preliminary

Dow Jones Industrial Average Since 1954

High		Year	Low		High		Year	Low	
Dec. 31	404.39	1954	Jan. 11	279.87	Dec. 29	842.00	1970	May 6	631.16
Dec. 30	488.40	1955	Jan. 17	388.20	Apr. 28	950.82	1971	Nov. 23	797.97
Apr. 6	521.05	1956	Jan. 23	462.35	Dec. 11	1036.27	1972	Jan. 26	889.15
July 12	520.77	1957	Oct. 22	419.79	Jan. 11	1051.70	1973	Dec. 5	788.31
Dec. 31	583.65	1958	Feb. 25	436.89	Mar. 13	891.66	1974	Dec. 6	577.60
Dec. 31	679.36	1959	Feb. 9	574.46	July 15	881.81	1975	Jan. 2	632.04
Jan. 5	685.47	1960	Oct. 25	566.05	Sept. 21	1014.79	1976	Jan. 2	858.71
Dec. 13	734.91	1961	Jan. 3	610.25	Jan. 3	999.75	1977	Nov. 2	800.85
Jan. 3	726.01	1962	June 26	535.76	Sept. 8	907.74	1978	Feb. 28	742.12
Dec. 18	767.21	1963	Jan. 2	646.79	Oct. 5	897.61	1979	Nov. 7	796.67
Nov. 18	891.71	1964	Jan. 2	766.08	Nov. 20	1000.17	1980	Apr. 21	759.13
Dec. 31	969.26	1965	June 28	840.59	Apr. 27	1024.05	1981	Sept. 25	824.01
Feb. 9	995.15	1966	Oct. 7	744.32	Dec. 27	1070.55	1982	Aug. 12	776.92
Sept. 25	943.08	1967	Jan. 3	786.41	Nov. 29	1287.20	1983	Jan. 3	1027.04
Dec. 3	985.21	1968	Mar. 21	825.13	Jan. 6	1286.64	1984*	June 15	1086.90
May 14	968.85	1969	Dec. 17	769.93				*As of	8/15/84.

Components of Dow Jones Industrial Average

Allied Corp.	General Electric	Owens-Illinois
Aluminum Co. of Amer.	General Foods	Procter & Gamble
American Brands	General Motors	Sears Roebuck
American Can	Goodyear	Standard Oil of Cal.
American Express	Inco	Texaco
AT&T	IBM	Union Carbide
Bethlehem Steel	International Harvester	United Technologies
DuPont	International Paper	U.S. Steel
Eastman Kodak	Merck	Westinghouse
Exxon	Minn. Mining & Manuf.	Woolworth

Bull Market of the 1980s

One of the major upward moves in stock prices began in August 1982. Below is the performance of the major market indexes since that bull market began.

Market index	8-12-82	8-15-84	Change
Amex market value	118.65[1]	210.87	77.7%
NYSE composite	58.80	95.96	63.2
S&P 500 stocks	102.42	167.06	63.1
NASDAQ composite	159.84	253.86	58.8
Dow 30 industrials	776.92	1231.77	58.5

(1) Adjusted for split

Stocks Exchanges

N.Y. Stock Exchange Transactions and Seat Prices

Year	Yearly volumes Stock shares	Bonds par values	Seat price High	Low	Year	Yearly volumes Stock shares	Bonds par values	Seat price High	Low
1900	138,981,000	$579,293,000	$47,500	$37,500	1950	524,799,621	$1,112,425,170	$54,000	$46,000
1905	260,569,000	1,026,254,000	85,000	72,000	1960	766,693,818	1,346,419,750	162,000	135,000
1910	163,705,000	634,863,000	94,000	65,000	1970	2,937,359,448	4,494,864,600	320,000	130,000
1915	172,497,000	961,700,000	74,000	38,000	1975	4,693,427,000	5,178,300,000	138,000	55,000
1920	227,636,000	3,868,422,000	115,000	85,000	1979	8,155,914,000	4,087,890,000	210,000	82,000
1925	459,717,623	3,427,042,210	150,000	99,000	1980	11,352,294,000	5,190,304,000	275,000	175,000
1929	1,124,800,410	2,996,398,000	625,000	550,000	1981	11,853,740,659	5,733,071,000	285,000	220,000
1930	810,632,546	2,720,301,800	480,000	205,000	1982	16,458,036,768	7,155,443,000	340,000	190,000
1935	381,635,752	3,339,458,000	140,000	65,000	1983	21,589,576,997	7,572,315,000	NA	NA
1940	207,599,749	1,669,438,000	60,000	33,000					

A 1983 survey by the New York Stock Exchange found that 42.4 million Americans owned individual stock or stock mutual funds in U.S. corporations. The median age of these investors was 34, and 57% of them were women. NA = Not available.

American Stock Exchange Transactions

Year	Yearly volumes Stock shares	Bonds[1] princ. amts.	Year	Yearly volumes Stock shares	Bonds[1] princ. amts.	Year	Yearly volumes Stock shares	Bonds[1] princ. amts.
1929	476,140,375	$513,551,000	1950	107,792,340	47,549,000	1981	1,343,400,220	301,226,000
1930	222,270,065	863,541,000	1960	286,039,982	$32,670,000	1982	1,485,831,536	325,240,000
1940	42,928,337	303,902,000	1970	843,116,260	641,270,000	1983	2,081,270,000	395,190,000
1945	143,309,392	167,333,000	1980	1,626,072,625	355,723,000			

(1) corporate

NASDAQ Reports Record Volume

NASDAQ, The National Association of Securities Dealers Automated Quotations, reported turnover volume of 15.9 billion shares in 1983. This was an increase of 88.7% over 1982. The number of companies with shares traded in this market grew to 3,901 by the end of 1983, making NASDAQ the third-largest market in the world, after the New York and Tokyo exchanges.

Federal Deposit Insurance Corporation (FDIC)

The primary purpose of the Federal Deposit Insurance Corporation (FDIC) is to insure deposits in all banks approved for insurance coverage benefits under the Federal Deposit Insurance Act. The major functions of the FDIC are to pay off depositors of insured banks closed without adequate provision having been made to pay depositors' claims, to act as receiver for all national banks placed in receivership and for state banks placed in receivership when appointed receiver by state authorities, and to prevent the continuance or development of unsafe and unsound banking practices. The FDIC's entire income consists of assessments on insured banks and income from investments; it receives no appropriations from Congress. It may borrow from the U.S. Treasury not to exceed $3 billion outstanding, but has made no such borrowings since it was organized in 1933. The FDIC surplus (Deposit Insurance Fund) as of Dec. 31, 1983 was $15.4 billion.

Federal Reserve System

The Federal Reserve System is the central bank for the United States. The system was established on December 23, 1913, originally to give the country an elastic currency, to provide facilities for discounting commercial paper, and to improve the supervision of banking. Since then, the System's responsibilities have been broadened and, through the monitoring of money and credit growth, it helps work toward sustainable economic growth and price stability.

The Federal Reserve System consists of the Board of Governors; the 12 District Reserve Banks and their branch offices; the Federal Open Market Committee; and, the member banks. Several advisory councils help the Board meet its varied responsibilities.

The hub of the System is the seven member Board of Governors in Washington. The members of the Board are appointed by the President and confirmed by the Senate, to serve 14-year terms. The President also appoints the Chairman and Vice-Chairman of the Board from among the board members for 4-year terms that may be renewed. Currently, the board members are: Paul A. Volcker, Chairman; Preston Martin, Vice Chairman; Henry C. Wallich; J. Charles Partee; Martha R. Seger; Emmett J. Rice; and Lyle E. Gramley.

The Board is the policy-making body. In addition to its policy making responsibilities, it supervises the budget and operations of the Reserve Banks, approves the appointments of their presidents and appoints 3 of each District Bank's directors, including the chairman and vice chairman of each Reserve Bank's board.

The 12 Reserve Banks and their branch offices serve as the decentralized portion of the System, carrying out day-to-day operations such as circulating currency and coin, providing fiscal agency functions and payments mechanism services. The District Banks are located in Boston, New York, Philadelphia, Cleveland, Richmond, Atlanta, Chicago, St. Louis, Minneapolis, Kansas City, Dallas and San Francisco.

The System's principal function is monetary policy, which it controls using three tools: reserve requirements, the discount rate and open market operations. Uniform reserve requirements, set by the Board, are applied to the transaction accounts and nonpersonal time deposits of all depository institutions. Responsibility for setting the discount rate (the interest rate at which depository institutions can borrow money from the Reserve Banks) is shared by the Board of Governors and the Reserve Banks. Changes in the discount rate are recommended by the individual Boards of Directors of the Reserve Banks and are subject to approval by the Board of Governors. The most important tool of monetary policy is open market operations (the purchase and sale of government securities). Responsibility for influencing the cost and availability of money and credit through the purchase and sale of government securities lies with the Federal Open Market Committee (FOMC). This committee is composed of the 7 members of the Board of Governors, the president of the Federal Reserve Bank of New York, and 4 other Federal Reserve Bank presidents, who serve on a rotating basis as voting members of the committee. The committee bases its decisions on current economic and financial developments and outlook, setting yearly growth objectives for key measures of money supply and credit. The decisions of the committee are carried out by the Domestic Trading Desk of the Federal Reserve Bank of New York.

The Federal Reserve Act prescribes a Federal Advisory Council, consisting of one member from each Federal Reserve District, elected annually by the Board of Directors of each of the 12 Federal Reserve Banks. They meet with the Federal Reserve Board at least four times a year to discuss business and financial conditions and to make advisory recommendations.

The Consumer Advisory Council is a statutory body, including both consumer and creditor representatives, which advises the Board of Governors on its implementation of consumer regulations and other consumer-related matters. Following the passage of the Monetary Control Act of 1980, the Board of Governors established the Thrift Institutions Advisory Council to provide information and views on the special needs and problems of thrift institutions. The group is comprised of representatives of mutual savings banks, savings and loan associations, and credit unions.

This piece of legislation also extended access to Federal Reserve discount and borrowing privileges and other services to all depository institutions. The act required the Federal Reserve to set a schedule of fees for its services. And, it was through this act that the Depository Institutions Deregulations Committee (DIDC) was formed to provide for the orderly elimination of the limitations on the maximum rate of interest and dividends which may be paid on deposits by commercial banks, mutual savings banks, and savings and loan associations. Congress intended that the phase-out be completed by March 31, 1986. DIDC consists of the Secretary of the Treasury, the Chairman of the Board of Governors of the Federal Reserve System, the Chairman of the Board of Directors of the Federal Deposit Insurance Corporation, the Chairman of the Federal Home Loan Bank Board, and the Chairman of the National Credit Union Administration Board, each of whom has one vote, and the Comptroller of the Currency who is a nonvoting members.

Largest Banks Outside the U.S.

Source: 500 Largest Banks in the Free World, compiled by the American Banker, New York. (Copyright 1984) Based on deposits Dec. 31, 1983, or nearest fiscal year-end.

(thousands of U.S. dollars)

Bank, country	Deposits	Bank, country	Deposits
Dai-Ichi Kangyo Bank Ltd., Tokyo, Japan	88,431,682	Long-Term Credit Bank Of Japan Ltd., Tokyo, Japan	52,625,535
Banque Nationale de Paris, France	86,787,611	Mitsubishi Trust & Banking Corp., Tokyo, Japan	51,832,142
Barclays Bank Plc, London, United Kingdom	82,692,050	Bank of Tokyo, Ltd., Japan	51,550,594
Fuji Bank, Ltd., Tokyo, Japan	81,048,392	Lloyds Bank Plc, London, United Kingdom	51,508,350
Sumitomo Bank Ltd., Osaka, Japan	79,532,516	Westdeutsche Landesbank Girozentrale, Duesseldorf, Germany	49,069,024
Mitsubishi Bank Ltd., Tokyo, Japan	77,747,226	Canadian Imperial Bank of Commerce, Toronto, Canada	48,859,971
Credit Lyonnais, Paris, France	77,621,655	Barclays Bank International Ltd., London, United Kingdom	47,457,050
National Westminster Bank Plc, London, United Kingdom	77,215,400	Sumitomo Trust & Banking Co., Ltd., Osaka, Japan	47,374,686
Societe Generale, Paris, France	75,927,079	Union Bank of Switzerland, Zurich, Switzerland	45,066,888
Sanwa Bank Ltd., Osaka, Japan	74,233,780	Bank of Montreal, Canada	44,847,668
Credit Agricole Mutuel, Paris, France	73,559,520	Mitsui Trust & Banking Co., Ltd., Tokyo, Japan	44,058,721
Deutsche Bank, Frankfurt, Germany	70,828,507	Taiyo Kobe Bank, Ltd., Kobe, Japan	43,871,203
Midland Pank Plc, London, United Kingdom	69,900,150	Swiss Bank Corp., Basle, Switzerland	43,361,513
Industrial Bank of Japan, Ltd., Tokyo, Japan	65,992,979	Daiwa Bank, Ltd., Osaka, Japan	40,476,125
Norinchukin Bank, Tokyo, Japan	65,281,706	Bank of Nova Scotia, Toronto, Canada	39,436,629
Royal Bank of Canada, Montreal, Canada	60,307,330	Commerzbank, Duesseldorf, Germany	39,256,176
Mitsui Bank Ltd., Tokyo, Japan	56,769,898		
Dresdner Bank, Frankfurt, Germany	55,404,155		
Hongkong and Shanghai Banking Corp., Hong Kong, Hong Kong	52,890,608		
Tokai Bank Ltd., Nagoya, Japan	52,858,252		

Largest U.S. Commercial Banks

Source: Largest Commercial Banks in U.S., compiled by the American Banker, New York. (Copyright 1984) Based on deposits Dec. 31, 1983.

(thousands)

Rank	Deposits	Rank	Deposits
Bank of America NT&SA, San Francisco . . .	90,250,018	InterFirst Bank Dallas NA	7,577,289
Citibank NA, New York	78,392,000	Republic National Bank, New York	7,263,260
Chase Manhattan Bank NA, New York	59,824,598	Metropolitan Savings Bank FSB, Brooklyn,	
Manufacturers Hanover Trust Co., New York.	42,186,468	New York	7,084,514
Morgan Guaranty Trust Co., New York	39,419,026	NCNB National Bank of North Carolina, Char-	
Chemical Bank, New York	33,355,815	lotte.	6,608,873
Continental Illinois NB&T Co., Chicago	30,082,230	Valley National Bank, Phoenix	6,568,084
First National Bank, Chicago	27,854,663	Southeast Bank NA, Miami	6,434,788
Security Pacific National Bank, Los Angeles .	27,763,181	Seattle-First National Bank	6,311,056
Bankers Trust Co., New York.	24,506,971	Texas Commerce Bank NA, Houston	6,243,431
Wells Fargo Bank NA, San Francisco	20,554,485	Dime Savings Bank of New York FSB, Brook-	
Crocker National Bank, San Francisco	19,045,237	lyn.	6,125,183
Marine Midland Bank NA, Buffalo, N.Y.	16,409,827	Union Bank, Los Angeles	6,068,815
First Interstate Bank of California, Los Angeles	15,266,068	Wachovia B&T Co. NA, Winston-Salem, N.C..	5,825,768
Mellon Bank NA, Pittsburgh.	12,924,800	National Westminster Bank USA, New York .	5,746,245
First National Bank, Boston	11,180,445	Sovran Bank NA, Richmond, VA	5,576,104
Irving Trust Co., New York	10,701,228	Anchor Savings Bank FSB, Northport, NY . .	5,187,381
American Express Intl. Banking Corp., New		Bowery Savings Bank, New York	5,087,682
York.	10,505,000	Rainier National Bank, Seattle	4,811,956
Philadelphia Saving Fund Society	9,987,139	BancOhio National Bank, Columbus	4,763,410
Goldome FSB, Buffalo, NY	9,834,219	Harris Trust & Savings Bank, Chicago.	4,735,607
Bank of New York	9,564,834	Dollar-Dry Dock Savings Bank, Bronx, N.Y.. .	4,733,109
RepublicBank Dallas NA	8,754,883	European American B&T Co., New York . . .	4,674,868
First City National Bank, Houston	7,974,072	Pittsburgh National Bank	4,625,620
National Bank of Detroit.	7,638,307		

Bank Suspensions

Source: Federal Deposit Insurance Corp. Deposits in thousands of dollars. The figures represent banks which, during the periods shown, closed temporarily or permanently on account of financial difficulties; does not include failed banks whose deposit liabilities were assumed by other banks.

Year	Susp.	Deposits	Year	Susp.	Deposits	Year	Susp.	Deposits	Year	Susp.	Deposits
1929 . .	659	230,643	1938	50	10,296	1964	7	23,438	1975	1	18,248
1930 . .	1,352	853,363	1939	32	32,738	1965	3	42,889	1976	3	18,859
1931 . .	2,294	1,690,669	1940	19	5,657	1966	1	774	1978	1	1,284
1932 . .	1,456	715,626	1955(a) . .	4	6,503	1967	4	10,878	1979	3	12,795
1933* .	4,004	3,598,975	1958	3	4,156	1969	4	9,011	1980	3	15,500
1934	9	1,968	1959	3	2,593	1970	4	34,040	1981	2	45,700
1935	24	9,091	1960	1	6,930	1971	5	74,605	1982	7	530,400
1936	42	11,241	1961	5	8,936	1972	1	20,482	1983	9	160,988
1937	50	14,960	1963	2	23,444	1973	3	25,811			

*Figures for 1933 comprise 628 banks with deposits of $360,413,000 suspended before or after the banking holiday (the holiday began March 6 and closed March 15) or placed in receivership during the holiday; 2,124 banks with deposits of $2,520,391,000 which were not licensed following the banking holiday and were placed in liquidation or receivership; and 1,252 banks with deposits of $718,171,000 which had not been licensed by June 20, 1933. (a) No suspensions in years 1945-1954, 1962, 1968, 1974, 1977.

All Banks in U.S.—Number, Deposits

Source: Federal Reserve System

Comprises all national banks in the United States and all state commercial banks, trust companies, mutual stock savings banks, private and industrial banks, and special types of institutions that are treated as banks by the federal bank supervisory agencies.

Year (As of June 30)	Total all banks	Number of banks					Total deposits (millions of dollars)				
		F.R.S. members		Nonmembers			Total all banks	F.R.S. members		Nonmembers	
		Total	Nat'l	State	Mutual savings	Other		Total	Nat'l	State	Mutual savings	Other
1925.	26,479	9,538	8,066	1,472	621	18,320	51,641	32,457	19,912	12,546	7,089	12,095
1930.	23,855	8,315	7,247	1,068	604	14,936	59,828	38,069	23,235	14,834	9,117	12,642
1935.	16,047	6,410	5,425	985	569	9,068	51,149	34,938	22,477	12,461	9,830	6,381
1940.	14,955	6,398	5,164	1,234	551	8,008	70,770	51,729	33,014	18,715	10,631	8,410
1945.	14,542	6,840	5,015	1,825	539	7,163	151,033	118,378	76,534	41,844	14,413	18,242
1950.	14,674	6,885	4,971	1,914	527	7,262	163,770	122,707	82,430	40,277	19,927	21,137
1955.	14,309	6,611	4,744	1,867	525	7,173	208,850	154,670	98,636	56,034	27,310	26,870
1960.	14,006	6,217	4,542	1,675	513	7,276	249,163	179,519	116,178	63,341	35,316	34,328
1965.	14,295	6,235	4,803	1,432	504	7,556	362,611	259,743	171,528	88,215	50,980	51,889
1970.	14,167	5,805	4,638	1,167	496	7,866	502,542	346,289	254,322	91,967	69,285	86,968
1975, Dec. 31 . .	15,108	5,787	4,741	1,046	475	8,846	896,879	590,999	447,590	143,409	110,569	195,311
1080, Dec. 31 . .	15,145	5,422	4,425	997	400	9,263	1,333,399	843,030	651,848	191,182	150,000	340,369
1982, Dec. 31 . .	14,934	5,632	4,580	1,052	386	8,916	1,541,015	995,230	779,110	216,120	146,524	399,261
1983, Dec. 31 . .	14,922	5,821	4,755	1,066	366	8,735	1,688,817	1,085,930	864,399	221,531	161,543	441,343

Bank Rates on Short-term Business Loans

Source: Federal Reserve System

Percent per annum. Short-term loans mature within one year.

			All size loans						Size of loan in $1,000				
	Ave. 35 cities	N.Y. C.	7 Other N.E.	8 No. Cent.	7 S.E.	8 S.W.	4 West	1-9	10-99	100 to 499	500 to 999	1,000 and over
1967 Aug. 1-15	5.95	5.66	6.29	5.92	5.92	6.01	6.02	6.58	6.46	6.16	5.89	5.72
1970 Aug. 1-15	8.50	8.24	8.89	8.47	8.49	8.53	8.54	9.15	9.07	8.75	8.46	8.25
1974 May	11.15	11.08	11.65	11.09	10.88	10.82	11.19	10.50	11.06	11.41	11.32	11.06
1975 May	8.16	7.88	8.37	8.00	8.70	8.34	8.33	9.57	9.10	8.52	8.18	7.90
1976 Aug.	7.80	7.48	8.18	7.70	7.95	7.75	8.15	8.85	9.41	8.65	9.33	9.26
Nov.	7.28	6.88	7.62	7.28	7.51	7.33	7.52	8.56	9.22	8.45	9.13	8.69

		All sizes	1-24	25-49	50-99	100-499	500-999	1,000 and over
				Size of Loan in $1,000[1]				
1980 Feb.		15.67	15.06	15.54	15.91	16.23	16.34	15.50
May		17.75	17.90	18.78	18.95	18.49	19.13	17.10
1981 Feb.		19.91	19.59	19.53	19.77	20.18	20.87	19.83
May		19.99	19.45	19.87	19.10	19.93	19.58	20.14
1982 Feb.		17.13	18.34	17.88	18.20	17.65	17.31	16.99
May		17.11	18.51	18.56	18.06	17.77	17.98	16.94
1983 Feb.		10.20	14.44	13.57	13.40	12.71	11.59	9.81
May		10.30	13.86	13.68	12.62	11.87	11.34	9.87
1984 Feb.		11.06	14.13	13.45	13.33	12.66	11.09	10.75
May		12.45	14.93	14.46	14.41	13.86	13.37	12.12

(1) In Feb. 1977, The Quarterly Interest Rate Survey was replaced by the Survey of Terms of Bank Lending (STBL). The STBL is conducted in the middle month of each quarter at about 340 member and nonmember banks. The regional breakdown was discontinued at that time. The last previous revision began with the survey period of Feb. 1971. It incorporated a number of technical changes in coverage, sampling, and interest rate calculations.

U.S. Industrial Corporations with Largest Sales in 1983

Source: FORTUNE Magazine

Company	Sales (thousands)	Income (or loss) (thousands)	Company	Sales (thousands)	Income (or loss) (thousands)
xon	$88,561,134	$4,977,957	AT&T	$11,154,700	$50,700
neral Motors	74,581,600	3,730,200	Boeing	11,129,000	355,000
bil	54,607,000	1,503,000	Dow Chemical	10,951,000	334,000
rd Motor	44,454,600	1,866,900	Allied	10,351,000	98,000
M.	40,180,000	5,485,000	Eastman Kodak	10,170,000	565,000
xaco	40,068,000	1,233,000	Unocal	10,065,600	625,900
Pont	35,378,000	1,127,000	Goodyear	9,735,800	305,500
andard Oil (Indiana)	27,635,000	1,868,000	Dart & Kraft	9,714,000	435,100
evron	27,342,000	1,590,000	Westinghouse	9,532,600	449,000
neral Electric	26,797,000	2,024,000	Philip Morris	9,465,600	903,500
lf Oil	26,581,000	978,000	Beatrice Foods	9,188,200	43,200
antic Richfield	25,147,036	1,547,875	Union Carbide	9,001,100	79,200
ell Oil	19,678,000	1,633,000	Xerox	8,463,500	466,400
cidental Petroleum	19,115,700	566,700	Amerada Hess	8,368,946	205,347
S. Steel	16,869,000	(1,161,000)	Union Pacific	8,352,585	296,886
llips Petroleum	15,249,000	721,000	General Foods	8,256,433	288,525
n	14,730,000	453,000	McDonnell Douglas	8,111,000	274,900
ited Technologies	14,669,265	509,173	Rockwell International	8,097,900	389,100
neco	14,353,000	716,000	PepsiCo	7,895,936	284,111
	14,155,408	674,510	Ashland Oil	7,852,299	102,833
rysler	13,240,399	700,900	General Dynamics	7,146,300	286,600
cter & Gamble	12,452,000	866,000	Minnesota Mininh & Manuf.	7,039,000	667,000
. Reynolds Industries	11,957,000	881,000	Coca-Cola	6,990,992	558,787
ty Oil	11,600,024	494,314	Consolidated Foods	6,572,298	171,255
ndard Oil (Ohio)	11,599,000	1,512,000	Lockheed	6,490,300	262,800

Total Value of Canadian Construction Work

Source: Statistics Canada (thousands of Canadian dollars)

rovince	1982 New	1982 Repair	1982 Total	1983 New	1983 Repair	1983 Total
wfoundland	1,054,389	142,040	1,196,429	1,281,468	158,585	1,440,053
ce Edward Island	114,705	47,275	161,980	99,469	46,691	146,160
a Scotia	1,202,046	309,822	1,511,868	1,448,503	316,885	1,765,388
w Brunswick	850,322	218,619	1,068,941	776,988	237,684	1,014,672
bec	8,111,000	2,237,483	10,348,483	8,142,453	2,334,397	10,476,850
ario	11,312,725	3,031,761	14,344,486	10,735,710	3,225,460	13,961,170
nitoba	1,047,000	378,317	1,425,317	1,091,976	397,916	1,489,892
katchewan	2,207,075	425,180	2,452,255	1,999,827	458,408	2,458,235
berta	12,458,274	1,544,292	14,002,566	11,751,855	1,679,160	13,431,015
sh Columbia	8,030,560	1,200,310	9,230,870	8,077,187	1,282,996	9,360,183
al	46,208,096	9,535,099	55,743,195	45,406,436	10,138,182	55,543,618

Per Capita Personal Income, by States and Regions

Source: Bureau of Economic Analysis. U.S. Commerce Department (dollars)

State and Region	1970	1975	1980	1982	1983
United States	**3,893**	**5,861**	**9,503**	**11,107**	**11,685**
New England	**4,245**	**6,030**	**9,989**	**11,916**	**13,005**
Connecticut	4,871	6,779	11,536	13,748	14,895
Maine	3,250	4,766	7,672	9,042	9,847
Massachusetts	4,276	6,077	10,089	12,088	13,264
New Hampshire	3,720	5,417	9,010	10,729	12,021
Rhode Island	3,878	5,709	9,174	10,723	11,670
Vermont	3,447	4,924	7,832	9,507	9,979
Mideast	**4,384**	**6,380**	**10,190**	**12,087**	**12,794**
Delaware	4,468	6,547	10,066	11,731	12,665
District of Columbia	4,644	7,262	12,269	14,550	15,744
Maryland	4,267	6,403	10,385	12,238	12,994
New Jersey	4,684	6,794	10,976	13,089	14,122
New York	4,605	6,519	10,283	12,314	12,990
Pennsylvania	3,879	5,841	9,389	10,955	11,488
Great Lakes	**4,050**	**6,047**	**9,734**	**11,055**	**11,517**
Illinois	4,446	6,735	10,471	12,100	12,405
Indiana	3,709	5,609	8,896	10,021	10,476
Michigan	4,041	5,991	9,872	10,956	11,466
Ohio	3,949	5,778	9,430	10,677	11,216
Wisconsin	3,712	5,616	9,347	10,774	11,352
Plains	**3,657**	**5,719**	**9,234**	**10,789**	**11,332**
Iowa	3,643	5,894	9,336	10,791	10,705
Kansas	3,725	5,958	9,942	11,765	12,247
Minnesota	3,819	5,779	9,688	11,175	11,913
Missouri	3,654	5,476	8,720	10,170	10,969
Nebraska	3,657	5,882	9,137	10,883	11,212
North Dakota	3,077	5,888	8,759	10,876	11,666
South Dakota	3,108	5,009	8,028	9,666	9,847
Southeast	**3,208**	**5,028**	**8,137**	**9,602**	**10,216**
Alabama	2,892	4,635	7,477	8,649	9,242
Arkansas	2,791	4,510	7,166	8,479	8,967
Florida	3,698	5,631	9,201	10,978	11,593
Georgia	3,300	5,029	8,061	9,583	10,379
Kentucky	3,076	4,887	7,648	8,934	9,397
Louisiana	3,023	4,803	8,525	10,231	10,270
Mississippi	2,547	4,047	6,680	7,778	8,098
North Carolina	3,200	4,940	7,753	9,044	9,787
South Carolina	2,951	4,665	7,298	8,502	9,187
Tennessee	3,079	4,804	7,662	8,906	9,549
Virginia	3,677	5,772	9,357	11,095	12,116
West Virginia	3,038	4,962	7,665	8,769	9,159
Southwest	**3,465**	**5,469**	**9,298**	**11,122**	**11,330**
Arizona	3,614	5,391	8,832	10,173	10,656
New Mexico	3,045	4,843	7,891	9,190	9,640
Oklahoma	3,341	5,280	9,187	11,370	10,963
Texas	3,507	5,584	9,538	11,419	11,685
Rocky Mountain	**3,540**	**5,571**	**9,092**	**10,754**	**11,069**
Colorado	3,838	5,987	10,042	12,302	12,770
Idaho	3,243	5,179	8,044	9,029	9,555
Montana	3,395	5,388	8,361	9,580	9,949
Utah	3,169	4,900	7,566	8,875	8,993
Wyoming	3,672	6,123	11,042	12,372	11,911
Far West	**4,310**	**6,474**	**10,689**	**12,238**	**12,892**
California	4,423	6,575	10,920	12,567	13,257
Nevada	4,583	6,625	10,761	11,981	12,451
Oregon	3,677	5,769	9,356	10,335	10,740
Washington	3,997	6,298	10,198	11,560	12,177
Alaska	4,638	9,636	12,916	16,257	17,194
Hawaii	4,599	6,708	10,222	11,652	12,114

Effective Federal Minimum Hourly Wage Rates, 1950 to 1981, and Coverage in 1982

Source: U.S. Department of Labor.

(Employee estimates as of **September 1982**, except as indicated. The Fair Labor Standards Act of 1938 and subsequent amendments provide for minimum wage coverage applicable to specified nonsupervisory employment categories. Exempt from coverage are executives and administrators or professionals).

Effective Date	Laws prior to 1966[1]	Percent, avg earnings[2]	1966 and later[3]	Minimum rates for farm workers[4]
Jan. 25, 1950	$.75	54	(X)	(X)
Mar. 1, 1956	1.00	52	(X)	(X)
Sept. 3, 1961	1.15	50	(X)	(X)
Sept. 3, 1963	1.25	51	(X)	(X)
Feb. 1, 1967	1.40	50	$1.00	$1.00
Feb. 1, 1968	1.60	54	1.15	1.15
Feb. 1, 1969	(5)	(5)	1.30	1.30
Feb. 1, 1970	(5)	(5)	1.45	(5)
Feb. 1, 1971	(5)	(5)	1.60	(5)
May 1, 1974	2.00	46	1.90	1.60
Jan. 1, 1975	2.10	45	2.00	1.80
Jan. 1, 1976	2.30	46	2.20	2.00
Jan. 1, 1977	(5)	(5)	2.30	2.20
Jan. 1, 1978	2.65	44	2.65	2.65
Jan. 1, 1979	2.90	45	2.90	2.90
Jan. 1, 1980	3.10	45	3.10	3.10
Jan. 1, 1981	3.35	43	3.35	3.35

Sex, Race, and Industry	Total (1,000)	Total (1,000)	Percent of total	Prior to 1966[6,7] (1,000)	1966 and later[3,6,7] (1,000)
Total	75,779	59,208	78.1	42,423	16,785
Male	40,799	31,839	78.0	24,666	7,173
Female	34,980	27,369	78.2	17,757	9,612
White	66,602	52,054	78.2	37,916	14,138
Black and other	9,177	7,154	78.0	4,507	2,647
Black only	8,367	6,538	78.1	4,119	2,419
Private Industry	66,185	56,617	85.5	42,423	14,194
Agriculture	1,539	593	38.5	—	593
Mining	941	937	99.6	937	—
Construction	3,698	3,677	99.4	3,115	562
Manufacturing	16,611	16,151	97.2	16,052	99
Transp., public utilities	4,499	4,468	99.3	4,386	82
Wholesale trade	4,521	3,604	79.7	3,369	235
Retail trade	13,762	11,475	83.4	6,115	5,360
Finance, insurance, real estate	4,593	3,483	75.8	3,347	136
Service	14,498	11,239	77.5	5,102	6,137
Private households	1,523	990	65.0	—	990
Government[8]	**9,594**	**2,591**	**27.0**	**—**	**2,591**

(X) Not applicable. (1) Applies to workers covered prior to 1961 Amendments and, after Sept. 1965, to workers covered by 1961 Amendments. Rates set by 1961 Amendments were: Sept. 1961, $1.00; Sept. 1964, $1.15; and Sept. 1965, $1.25. (2) Percent of gross average hourly earnings of production workers in manufacturing. (3) Applies to workers newly covered by Amendments of 1966, 1974, and 1977, and Title IX of Education Amendments of 1972. (4) Included in coverage as of 1966, 1974, and 1977 Amendments. (5) No change in rate. (6) Currently employed workers subject to criteria in effect prior to 1966 Amendments, except workers in retail-service establishments with less than $250,000, who otherwise would have been exempt prior to the 1966 Amendments, are included if part of enterprises subject to criteria established prior to the 1966 Amendments. (7) Currently employed workers subject to provisions. (8) Federal, State, and local employees.

U.S. Currency and Coin

Source: U.S. Treasury Department (June 30, 1983)

Amounts in Circulation and Outstanding

Currency	Amounts in circulation	Add amounts held by: United States Treasury	Federal Reserve Banks	Amounts outstanding
Federal Reserve Notes[1]	$147,543,697,969	$4,551,132	$18,848,878,513	$166,397,127,614
United States Notes	299,924,176	22,614,839	1	322,539,016
Currency No Longer Issued	274,315,132	259,659	61,044	274,635,835
Total	$148,117,937,277	$27,425,630	$18,848,939,558	$166,994,302,465
Coin[2]				
Dollars[3]	$1,512,665,103	$361,124,075	$150,914,720	$2,024,703,898
Fractional Coin	12,396,464,169	142,315,344	231,497,487	12,770,277,000
Total	13,909,129,272	503,439,419	382,412,207	14,794,980,898
Total currency and coin	$162,027,066,549	$530,865,049	$19,231,351,765	$181,789,283,363

Currency in Circulation by Denominations

Denomination	Total currency in circulation	Federal Reserve Notes[1]	United States Notes	Currency no longer issued
1 Dollar	$3,559,494,891	$3,405,491,900	$143,480	$153,859,511
2 Dollars	686,493,604	552,868,554	133,611,966	13,084
5 Dollars	4,646,303,800	4,493,558,455	113,181,410	39,563,935
10 Dollars	11,424,726,160	11,399,183,120	5,950	25,537,090
20 Dollars	46,795,148,820	46,774,836,540	3,380	20,308,900
50 Dollars	17,870,026,700	17,858,244,000	......	11,782,700
100 Dollars	62,788,198,200	62,712,524,400	52,977,900	22,695,900
500 Dollars	158,196,500	158,004,000	......	192,500
1,000 Dollars	184,033,000	183,822,000	......	211,000
5,000 Dollars	1,835,000	1,785,000	......	50,000
10,000 Dollars	3,480,000	3,380,000	......	100,000
Fractional parts	487	......	......	487
Partial notes[4]	115	......	90	25
Total currency	$148,117,937,277	$147,543,697,969	$299,924,176	$274,315,132

Comparative Totals of Money in Circulation — Selected Dates

Date	Amounts (in millions)	Per capita[5]	Date	Amounts (in millions)	Per capita[5]	Date	Amounts (in millions)	Per capita[5]
June 30, 1983	[6]$162,027.1	$691.74	June 30, 1960	32,064.6	177.47	June 30, 1930	$4,522.0	$36.74
June 30, 1982	148,170.0	638.77	June 30, 1955	$30,229.3	$182.90	June 30, 1925	4,815.2	41.56
June 30, 1981	138,080.2	600.86	June 30, 1950	27,156.3	179.03	June 30, 1920	5,467.6	51.36
June 30, 1975	81,196.4	380.08	June 30, 1945	26,746.4	191.14	June 30, 1915	3,319.6	33.01
June 30, 1970	54,351.0	265.39	June 30, 1940	7,847.5	59.40	June 30, 1910	3,148.7	34.07
June 30, 1965	39,719.8	204.14	June 30, 1935	5,567.1	43.75			

(1) Issued on and after July 1, 1929. (2) Excludes coin sold to collectors at premium prices. (3) Includes $481,781,898 in standard silver dollars. (4) Represents value of certain partial denominations not presented for redemption. (5) Based on Bureau of the Census estimates of population. (6) Highest amount to date.

The requirement for a gold reserve against U.S. notes was repealed by Public Law 90-269 approved Mar. 18, 1968. Silver certificates issued on and after July 1, 1929 became redeemable from the general fund on June 24, 1968. The amount of security after those dates has been reduced accordingly.

U.S. Money in Circulation, by Denominations

Source: U.S. Treasury Department, Bureau of Governmental Financial Operations
Outside Treasury and Federal Reserve Banks. (millions of dollars)

End of year	Total in circulation	Coin and small denomination Total	Coin	$1	$2	$5	$10	$20	Large denomination currency Total	$50	$100	$500	$1,000	$5,000	$10,000
1950	27,741	19,305	1,554	1,113	64	2,049	5,998	8,529	8,438	2,422	5,043	368	588	4	12
1960	32,869	23,521	2,427	1,533	88	2,246	6,691	10,536	9,348	2,815	5,954	249	316	3	10
1970	57,093	39,639	6,281	2,310	136	3,161	9,170	18,581	17,454	4,896	12,084	215	252	3	4
1975	86,547	54,866	8,959	2,809	135	3,841	10,777	28,344	31,681	8,157	23,139	175	204	2	4
1978	114,645	66,693	10,739	3,194	661	4,393	11,661	36,045	47,952	11,279	36,306	167	194	2	4
1979	125,600	70,693	11,658	3,308	671	4,549	11,924	38,613	54,907	12,585	41,960	164	192	2	4
1980	137,244	73,893	12,419	3,499	677	4,635	11,924	40,739	63,352	13,731	49,264	163	189	2	3

Seigniorage on Coin and Silver Bullion

Source: U.S. Treasury Department, Bureau of Govt. Financial Operations

Seigniorage is the profit from coining money; it is the difference between the monetary value of coins and their cost, including the manufacturing expense.

Fiscal year	Total		Total
Jan. 1, 1935–June 30, 1965, cumulative	$2,525,927,763.84	1978	367,156,260.25
1968	383,141,339.00[1]	1979	991,909,496.55
1970	274,217,884.01	1980	662,814,791.48
1972	580,586,683.00	1981	450,174,439.26
1974	320,706,638.49	1982	390,407,804.91
1975	660,898,070.69	1983	477,479,387.58
(1) Revised to include seigniorage on clad coins.		Cumulative Jan. 1, 1935–Sept. 30, 1982	10,914,690,323.14

United States Mint

Source: United States Mint, U.S. Treasury Department

The first United States Mint was established in Philadelphia, Pa., then the nation's capital, by the Act of April 2, 1792, which provided for gold, silver, and copper coinage. Originally, supervision of the Mint was a function of the secretary of state, but in 1799 it became an independent agency reporting directly to the president. When the Coinage Act of 1873 was passed, all mint and assay office activities were placed under a newly organized Bureau of the Mint in the Department of the Treasury.

The Mint manufactures all U.S. coins and distributes them through the Federal Reserve banks and branches. The Mint also maintains physical custody of the Treasury's monetary stocks of gold and silver, moving, storing and releasing from custody as authorized. Functions performed by the Mint on a reimbursable basis include: the manufacture and sale of medals of a national character, the production and sale of numismatic coins and coin sets and, as scheduling permits, the manufacture of foreign coins.

The traditional 90% silver coinage was gradually phased out and cupronickel clad coinage introduced when the Coinage Act of 1965 removed all silver from the dime and quarter and reduced the silver content of the half dollar to 40%. P.L. 91-607, approved Dec. 31, 1970, removed the remaining silver from the half dollar, and in providing for the resumption of dollar coinage, directed that both denominations produced for circulation also be cupronickel clad metal. P.L. 95-447, approved Oct. 10, 1978, further amended the Coinage Act of 1965 to provide for changes in the design, weight and size of the $1 coin. Beginning in January 1979, the likeness of Susan B. Anthony has appeared on the obverse with the Apollo II Moon Landing on the reverse. The new small dollar weighs 8.1 grams and has a diameter of 26.5 millimeters.

The composition of the 5-cent coin continues to be 75% copper and 25% nickel. The traditional 95% copper cent has been replaced with a copper-plated zinc coin. Production commenced early in 1982. Both types are circulating simultaneously. The new cents are identical in size, shape, color and design to the predominantly copper cents but are somewhat lighter, having a standard weight of 2.50 grams as opposed to the 3.11 gram standard weight of the copper cent. They contain 2.4% copper and 97.6% zinc. The core is an alloy of zinc with 0.8% copper. The outer surface is barrel electroplated with copper.

P.L. 97-104, approved December 23, 1981, directed the production for public sale of up to 10 million 90% silver half dollars commemorating the 250th anniversary, in 1982, of the birth of George Washington. This is the first time a special commemorative coin has been issued for the government's own account in a design reserved solely for the commemorative issue and not intended for general circulation. It is also the first time since 1964 that a 90% silver coin has been produced by the U.S. Mint.

Calendar year coinage production for 1983 follows:

Domestic Coinage Executed During Calendar Year 1983

Denomination Dollars—non-silver	Philadelphia	Denver	San Francisco	Total value	Total Pieces
Subsidiary	–0–	–0–	–0–	–0–	–0–
Half dollars	$ 17,069,500.00	$ 16,236,122.00	-0-	$ 33,305,622.00	66,611,244
Quarter dollars	168,383,750.00	154,451,611.50	-0-	322,835,361.50	1,291,341,466
Dimes	64,702,500.00	73,012,922.40	-0-	137,715,422.40	1,377,154,224
Total subsidiary	**$250,155,750.00**	**$243,700,655.90**	**-0-**	**$493,856,405.90**	**2,735,106,914**
Minor					
Five-cent pieces	$ 28,080,750.00	$ 26,836,313.80	-0-	$ 54,917,063.80	1,098,341,276
One-cent pieces[1]	75,715,900.00	64,671,994.28	$ 1,807,650.00	142,195,544.28	14,219,554,428
Total minor,	**$103,796,650.00**	**$ 91,508,308.08**	**$ 1,807,650.00**	**$197,112,608.08**	**15,317,895,704**
Total domestic coinage	**$353,952,400.00**	**$335,208,963.98**	**$ 1,807,650.00**	**$690,969,013.98**	**18,053,002,618**

Deliveries of Numismatic Items

1983 Proof Sets (regular)	3,138,765
Bicentennial Proof Sets	26,784
Bicentennial Uncirculated Sets	16,264
George Washington Proof Sets	1,226,888
George Washington Uncirculated Sets	342,840
1983 Olympic Proof Dollars	915,466
1984 Olympic Proof Dollars	184,500
1983 Olympic Uncirculated Dollars (S)	302,000
1983 Olympic Uncirculated Dollars (D)	255,478
1983 Olympic Uncirculated Dollars (P)	206,862
1984 Olympic Uncirculated Dollars (P)	31,000
1983 Prestige Sets	89,883

Coinage Executed for Foreign Governments

Country	No. of Pieces
Panama	25,500,000

(1) Manufactured at West Point Depository—$19,900,050 (pieces). (2) Set adjustment (6 sets) from 3,917 to 3,911 October report. (3) Piece adjustment (500,000 pieces) from 4,500,000 to 4,000,000 May report.

Portraits on U.S. Treasury Bills, Bonds, Notes and Savings Bonds

Denomination	Savings bonds	Treas. bills	Treas. bonds	Treas. notes
25	Washington			
50	F.D. Roosevelt		Jefferson	
75	Truman			
100	Eisenhower		Jackson	
200	Kennedy			
500	Wilson		Washington	
1,000	T. Roosevelt	H. McCulloch	Lincoln	Lincoln
5,000	McKinley	J.G. Carlisle	Monroe	Monroe
10,000	Cleveland	J. Sherman	Cleveland	Cleveland
50,000		C. Glass		
100,000		A Gallatin	Grant	Grant
1,000,000		O. Wolcott	T. Roosevelt	T. Roosevelt
100,000,000				Madison
500,000,000				McKinley

Large Denominations of U.S. Currency Discontinued

The largest denomination of United States currency now being issued is the $100 bill. Issuance of currency in denominations of $500, $1000, $5,000 and $10,000 was discontinued in 1969 because their use had declined sharply over the previous two decades.

As large denomination bills reach the Federal Reserve Bank they are removed from circulation.

Because some of the discontinued currency is expected to be in the hands of holders for many years, the description of the various denominations below is continued:

Amt.	Portrait	Embellishment on back	Amt.	Portrait	Embellishment on back
$ 1	Washington	Great Seal of U.S.	$ 100	Franklin	Independence Hall
2	Jefferson	Signers of Declaration	500	McKinley	Ornate denominational marking
5	Lincoln	Lincoln Memorial	1,000	Cleveland	Ornate denominational marking
10	Hamilton	U.S. Treasury	5,000	Madison	Ornate denominational marking
20	Jackson	White House	10,000	Chase	Ornate denominational marking
50	Grant	U.S. Capitol	100,000*	Wilson	Ornate denominational marking

*For use only in transactions between Federal Reserve System and Treasury Department.

MANUFACTURES AND MINERALS

General Statistics for Major Industry Groups

Source: Bureau of the Census

The estimates for 1981 in the following table are based upon reports from a representative sample of about 56,000 manufacturing establishments.

Industry	All employees		Production workers			Value added by mfr. (millions)
	Number (1,000)	Payroll (millions)	Number (1,000)	Manhours (millions)	Wages (millions)	
Food and kindred products	1,511.2	24,695.7	1,068.7	2,115.0	15,707.1	80,794.7
Tobacco products	61.1	1,219.2	49.1	91.5	891.4	6,429.6
Textile mill products	785.2	9,574.0	678.5	1,333.2	7,439.0	19,463.2
Apparel, oth. textile prods.	1,251.1	11,804.6	1,078.6	1,929.2	8,734.4	25,639.9
Lumber and wood products	649.4	8,990.9	543.8	1,035.4	6,752.9	17,321.0
Furniture and fixtures	459.8	5,982.8	374.1	715.8	4,189.1	12,668.7
Paper and allied products	635.8	12,643.7	486.6	993.5	8,820.4	32,366.7
Printing and publishing	1,270.1	20,609.3	719.7	1,342.6	10,454.0	49,351.6
Chemicals, allied products	892.3	19,772.8	532.6	1,066.9	10,230.1	80,032.3
Petroleum and coal products	152.2	4,076.3	101.0	209.0	2,522.1	26,740.3
Rubber, misc. plastics prod.	691.2	11,047.1	541.9	1,049.5	7,392.7	26,005.9
Leather, leather products	227.6	2,363.3	196.8	347.3	1,766.0	5,230.3
Stone, clay, glass products	589.7	10,574.5	462.5	910.3	7,568.6	24,853.9
Primary metal industries	1,062.8	25,322.2	825.9	1,600.1	18,564.1	49,550.6
Fabricated metal products	1,567.6	28,531.4	1,182.8	2,336.8	19,134.0	61,558.2
Machinery, except electric	2,379.7	48,642.9	1,561.0	3,086.3	27,762.2	111,393.7
Electric, electronic equip.	1,959.0	35,988.9	1,278.1	2,453.2	19,192.4	79,720.4
Transportation equipment	1,749.4	42,335.6	1,185.3	2,319.8	26,096.6	82,938.2
Instruments, related prods.	611.5	11,564.6	368.3	716.8	5,536.7	31,493.8
Misc. manufacturing indus.	413.1	5,630.0	307.5	580.9	3,447.1	13,953.5
Administrative and auxiliary[1]	1,344.2	37,894.6				
All industries, total	**20,264.0**	**379,214.4**	**13,542.8**	**26,233.1**	**212,200.9**	**837,506.5**

(1) In addition to the employment and payroll for operating manufacturing establishments, manufacturing concerns reported separately for central administrative offices or auxiliary units (e.g., research laboratories, storage warehouses, power plants, garages, repair shops, etc.) which serve the manufacturing establishments of a company rather than the public.

Manufacturing Production Worker Statistics

Source: Bureau of Labor Statistics, U.S. Labor Department (p — preliminary)

Year	All employees	Production workers	Payroll index 1977=100	Avg. weekly earnings	Avg. hourly earnings	Avg. hrs. per wk.
1955	16,882,000	13,288,000	31.5	$75.30	$1.85	40.7
1960	16,796,000	12,586,000	35.4	89.72	2.26	39.7
1965	18,062,000	13,434,000	45.1	107.53	2.61	41.2
1970	19,367,000	14,044,000	58.6	133.33	3.35	39.8
1975	18,323,000	13,043,000	76.8	190.79	4.83	39.5
1978	20,505,000	14,734,000	113.6	249.27	6.17	40.4
1979	21,040,000	15,068,000	125.2	269.34	6.70	40.2
1980	20,285,000	14,214,000	126.8	288.62	7 27	39.7
1981	20,170,000	14,020,000	137.8	318.00	7.99	39.8
1982	18,781,000	12,742,000	130.1	330.26	8.49	38.9
1983	18,497,000	12,581,000	137.7	354.08	8.83	40.1
1984 Jan.	19,034,000	13,034,000	148.2	368.65	9.08	40.6
Feb.	19,181,000	13,163,000	149.9	368.74	9.06	40.7
Mar.	19,323,000	13,280,000	151.7	369.96	9.09	40.7
Apr.	19,432,000	13,368,000	153.8	372.60	9.11	40.9
May[p]	19,552,000	13,455,000	153.8	370.37	9.10	40.7
June[p]	19,768,000	13,630,000	157.2	373.42	9.13	40.9

Personal Consumption Expenditures for the U.S.

Source: Bureau of Economic Analysis, U.S. Commerce Department
(billions of dollars)

	1978	1979	1980	1981	1982	1983
Durable goods	**200.2**	**213.4**	**214.7**	**235.4**	**245.1**	**279.8**
Motor vehicles and parts	95.7	96.6	90.7	101.9	108.7	129.3
Furniture and household equipment	72.8	81.8	86.3	92.3	94.4	104.1
Other	31.7	35.1	37.7	41.2	42.1	46.4
Nondurable goods	**528.2**	**600.0**	**668.8**	**730.7**	**757.5**	**801.7**
Food	275.9	311.6	345.1	373.9	392.8	416.5
Clothing and shoes	92.4	99.1	104.6	114.3	118.8	127.0
Gasoline and oil	51.2	66.6	84.8	94.6	90.4	90.0
Other nondurable goods	108.8	122.8	134.3	147.9	155.6	168.2
Fuel oil and coal	11.9	16.1	18.6	20.7	20.6	21.0
Other	96.9	106.6	115.7	127.1	135.0	147.2
Services	**618.0**	**693.7**	**784.5**	**883.0**	**982.2**	**1,074.4**
Housing	209.6	236.0	266.2	302.0	333.8	363.3
Household operation	90.1	99.3	113.0	127.5	143.4	153.8
Electricity and gas	42.9	47.8	57.6	65.8	75.2	81.3
Other	47.2	51.5	55.4	61.7	68.2	72.5
Transportation	51.2	56.3	61.1	65.0	68.2	72.5
Other	267.1	302.0	344.3	388.5	436.8	484.8
Total personal consumption expenditures	**1,346.5**	**1,507.2**	**1,668.1**	**1,849.1**	**1,984.9**	**2,155.9**

U.S. Nonfuel Mineral Production

Source: Bureau of Mines, U.S. Interior Department

Production as measured by mine shipments, sales, or marketable production (including consumption by producers)

Metals	1982 Quantity	1982 Value (thousands)	1983 Quantity	1983 Value (thousands)
Antimony ore and concentrate . . . . . short tons, antimony content	503	W	838	W
Bauxite . . . . thousand metric tons, dried equivalent	732	$12,334	679	11,309
Copper (recoverable content of ores, etc.) . . . . metric tons	ʳ1,146,975	ʳ1,840,856	1,038,098	1,751,476
Gold (recoverable content of ores, etc.). . . . . troy ounces	ʳ1,465,686	ʳ550,968	1,957,379	829,929
Iron ore, usable (excluding byproduct iron sinter) thousand long tons, gross weight	35,751	1,491,705	44,295	1,938,496
Iron oxide pigments, crude . . . . short tons	67,294	2,702	40,023	2,368
Lead (recoverable content of ores, etc.) . . . . metric tons	ʳ512,516	ʳ288,579	449,038	214,623
Manganiferous ore (5% to 35% Mn). . . . . short tons, gross weight	31,509	293	33,523	216
Mercury . . . . 76-pound flasks	25,760	W	25,070	W
Molybdenum (content of concentrate). . . . . thousand pounds	ʳ76,135	ʳ504,089	49,163	167,164
Nickel (content of ore and concentrate). . . . . short tons	3,203	W	—	—
Silver (recoverable content of ores, etc.) . . . thousand troy ounces	ʳ40,248	ʳ319,975	43,415	496,671
Titanium concentrate:				
Ilmenite . . . . short tons, gross weight	233,063	19,093	W	W
Tungsten ore and concentrate . . . . thousand pounds contained W	3,473	22,062	1,016	10,528
Vanadium (recoverable in ore and concentrate) . . . . . short tons	4,098	52,577	2,171	30,675
Zinc (recoverable content of ores, etc.) . . . . metric tons	ʳ303,160	ʳ257,116	275,294	251,204
Combined value of beryllium, magnesium chloride for magnesium metal, platinum-group metals (1980), rare-earth metals, tin, titanium (rutile), zircon concentrate, and values indicated by symbol W	XX	154,917	XX	161,100
Total metals	XX	ʳ5,517,000	XX	5,866,000

Nonmetals (except fuels)				
Abrasive stones[2] . . . . short tons	1,285	553	1,101	482
Asbestos. . . . . metric tons	63,515	24,917	W	W
Asphalt and related bitumens, native:				
bituminous limestone, sandstone, gilsonite . . thousand short tons	W	W	W	W
Barite. . . . . do	1,845	69,522	754	29,203
Boron minerals . . . . do	1,234	384,597	1,303	439,181
Bromine. . . . . thousand pounds	401,100	102,600	370,000	91,000
Calcium chloride . . . . short tons	ᵉ616,513	ᵉ61,483	W	W
Cement:				
Masonry. . . . . thousand short tons	2,364	145,172	2,921	186,240
Portland . . . . do	61,080	3,084,439	67,183	3,315,690
Clays. . . . . do	35,345	825,064	40,858	931,091
Diatomite. . . . . do	613	107,619	619	114,279
Feldspar . . . . do	615,000	20,300	710,000	22,500
Fluorspar . . . . do	77,017	13,293	61,000	10,000
Garnet (abrasive) . . . . do	27,303	2,321	29,767	2,533
Gem stones(e).	NA	7,150	NA	7,425
Gypsum . . . . thousand short tons	10,538	89,131	12,884	101,361
Helium:				
Crude . . . . million cubic feet	175	2,100	W	W
Grade-A. . . . . do	³1,248	³42,432	³1,299	³45,465
Lime . . . . thousand short tons	14,075	696,207	14,867	757,611
Magnesium compounds . . . . short tons	—	—	556,113	145,084
Mica:				
Scrap. . . . . do	106	ʳ6,398	140	6,479
Peat . . . . do	ʳ769	ʳ16,871	725	18,667
Perlite . . . . short tons	506,000	16,044	474,000	15,664
Phosphate rock . . . . thousand metric tons	37,414	950,326	42,573	1,020,901
Potassium salts . . . . thousand metric tons, K O equivalent	1,784	265,600	1,513	220,800
Pumice . . . . thousand short tons	416	3,750	449	4,486
Pyrites . . . . thousand metric tons	676	41,943	W	W
Salt. . . . . thousand short tons	ʳ37,894	ʳ671,424	34,573	597,081
Sand and gravel (construction) . . . . do	ʳ594,000	ʳ1,674,000	655,100	1,935,000
Sand and gravel (industrial) . . . . do	ʳ27,400	ʳ323,800	26,620	335,200
Sodium sulfate (natural) . . . . do	W	W	423	39,425
Stone[4](crushed). . . . . do	ᵖ790,030	ᵖ2,918,300	862,700	3,337,300
Stone[4](dimension) . . . . do	ᵖ1,330	ᵖ145,113	1,186	149,483
Sulfur, Frasch process . . . . thousand metric tons	3,598	434,660	4,111	445,131
Talc and pyrophyllite . . . . thousand short tons	1,135	ʳ20,671	1,066	20,280
Tripoli . . . . short tons	112,928	653	111,020	649
Vermiculite . . . . thousand short tons	316	28,508	282	27,170
Combined value of aplite, emery, graphite, iodine, kyanite, lithium minerals, magnesite, magnesium compounds, greensand marl, olivine, staurolite, wollastonite, and values indicated by symbol W	XX	ʳ959,269	XX	895,921
Total nonmetals	XX	ʳ14,158,000	XX	15,268,000
Grand total	XX	ʳ19,675,000	XX	21,134,000

(e) Estimate. (r) Revised. (W) Withheld to avoid disclosing company proprietary data; included in "Combined value" figures. (XX) Not applicable.
(1) Production as measured by mine shipments, sales, or marketable production (including consumption by producers).
(2) Grindstones, pulpstones, grinding pebbles, sharpening stones, and tube mill liners.
(3) Excludes output in New Mexico, withheld to avoid disclosing company proprietary data; included in nonmetals combined value figure for 1982-83.
(4) Excludes abrasive stone, bituminous limestone, bituminous sandstone; all included elsewhere in table.

Sales and Profits of Manufacturing Corporations by Industry Groups

Source: Bureau of the Census—Economic Surveys Division
(millions of dollars)

Industry Group	Sales			Net profits after taxes		
	1Q 1983	4Q 1983	1Q 1984	1Q 1983	4Q 1983	1Q 1984
All manufacturing corporations	490,836	561,633	565,870	15,527	25,009	26,463
Nondurable manufacturing corporations	270,281	296,227	295,458	10,951	15,828	14,727
Food and kindred products	68,360	75,348	72,416	1,504	3,001	2,368
Tobacco manufactures	6,099	5,326	5,410	552	668	581
Textile mill products	10,592	12,961	12,452	249	396	413
Paper and allied products	15,329	16,873	17,459	446	655	629
Printing and publishing	20,221	24,000	23,580	949	1,543	1,316
Chemicals and allied products	47,512	51,759	53,628	2,722	2,691	3,706
Industrial chemicals and synthetics	22,126	24,569	25,093	744	650	1,418
Drugs	7,072	7,612	7,666	971	1,077	1,037
Petroleum and coal products	75,944	79,569	79,919	3,679	5,638	4,476
Rubber and miscellaneous plastics products	11,913	13,737	14,057	388	509	605
Other nondurable manufacturing corporations	15,312	16,654	16,537	462	727	633
Durable manufacturing corporations . .	220,555	265,406	270,412	4,576	9,181	11,735
Stone, clay and glass products . . .	9,365	11,615	11,293	-260	382	162
Primary metal industries	22,844	26,990	28,728	-901	-1,972	433
Iron and steel.	14,125	17,337	18,396	-759	-1,801	214
Nonferrous metals.	8,719	9,653	10,332	-142	-171	219
Fabricated metal products	23,246	26,966	27,850	322	853	966
Machinery, except electrical	40,140	49,049	49,544	1,256	2,769	2,159
Electrical and electronic equipment .	38,015	45,470	44,981	1,325	2,181	2,228
Transportation equipment.	55,011	66,582	70,722	1,661	2,273	2,278
Motor vehicles and equipment	31,178	40,267	45,451	1,139	2,498	3,318
Aircraft, guided missiles and parts . .	19,848	21,161	19,918	485	840	832
Instruments and related products . .	12,334	14,429	13,666	786	949	971
Other durable manufacturing corporations	19,600	24,306	23,628	387	746	539
All mining corporations.	10,222	10,637	10,504	385	-10	580
All retail trade corporations	85,788	113,765	N/A	1,523	4,467	N/A
All wholesale trade corporations	111,920	129,787	130,593	588	1,226	1,596

Retail Store Sales

Source: Bureau of the Census, U.S. Department of Commerce
(millions of dollars)

Kind of business	1982	1983	Kind of business	1982	1983
Retail trade, total	1,074,561	1,173,966	Nondurable goods stores, total	750,072	788,825
Durable goods stores, total. . .	324,489	385,141	Apparel and accessory stores . .	51,387	54,005
Automotive dealers	182,607	221,687	Men's, boys' clothing, furnishings stores.	8,045	8,170
Motor vehicle, other miscellaneous automotive dealers.	162,931	200,209	Women's clothing, specialty stores, furriers.	19,440	21,256
Auto and home supply stores .	19,676	21,478	Shoe stores	8,903	9,266
Furniture, home furnishings, equipment stores	46,106	51,774	Food stores	249,257	259,441
Furniture, home furnishings stores	26,863	30,595	Grocery stores.	233,327	243,913
			General merchandise group stores	132,581	142,997
Household appliance, radio, and TV stores	15,237	17,288	Department stores.	107,863	116,658
			Variety stores	8,818	9,312
Building materials, hardware, garden supply, and mobile home dealers.	51,301	59,873	Eating and drinking places.	104,715	115,710
			Gasoline service stations	103,547	103,121
Building materials and supply stores	35,573	43,143	Drug stores	35,967	38,776
Hardware stores.	9,135	9,680	Liquor stores	19,394	19,690

Total retail stores sales (millions of dollars) — (1955) 183,851; (1958) 200,353; (1959) 215,413; (1960) 219,529; (1961) 218,992; (1962) 235,563; (1963) 246,666; (1964) 261,870; (1965) 284,128; (1966) 303,956; (1967) 292,956; (1968) 324,358; (1969) 346,717; (1970) 368,403; (1971) 406,234; (1972) 449,069; (1973) 509,538; (1974) 540,988; (1975) 588,146; (1976) 657,375; (1977) 725,220; (1978) 806,898; (1979) 899,379; (1980) 960,767; (1981) 1,043,524.

Employees in Non-Agricultural Establishments

Source: Bureau of Labor Statistics, U.S. Labor Department (thousands)

Annual Average by Industry Division

Year	Total	Mining	Contr./ construction	Manu- facturing	Trans. and public utilities	Whole- retail trade	Finance, insur., real estate	Service, miscel- laneous	Govern- ment
1955	50,641	792	2,839	16,882	4,141	10,535	2,298	6,240	6,914
1960	54,189	712	2,926	16,796	4,004	11,391	2,629	7,378	8,353
1965	60,765	632	3,232	18,062	4,036	12,716	2,977	9,036	10,074
1970	70,880	623	3,588	19,367	4,515	15,040	3,645	11,548	12,554
1975	76,945	752	3,525	18,323	4,542	17,060	4,165	13,892	14,686
1980	90,406	1,027	4,346	20,285	5,146	20,310	5,160	17,890	16,241
1981	91,156	1,139	4,188	20,170	5,165	20,547	5,298	18,619	16,031
1982	89,566	1,128	3,905	18,781	5,082	20,457	5,341	19,036	15,837
1983	90,138	957	3,940	18,497	4,958	20,804	5,467	19,665	15,851

Offstream Water Use

Source: Geological Survey, U.S. Interior Department
(millions of gallons per day, except as noted)

1980 State	Population, in thousands	Per Capita use, fresh water in gpd	Withdrawals (includes irrigation conveyance losses)				Total, excluding reclaimed sewage	Consumptive use, fresh water
			Ground water Fresh	Saline	Surface water Fresh	Saline		
Alabama	3,890	2,700	350	1.4	10,000	73	11,000	570
Alaska	403	550	49	0	170	0	220	35
Arizona	2,718	2,900	4,200	0	3,700	0	8,000	4,500
Arkansas	2,290	6,800	4,000	0	12,000	0	16,000	3,600
California	23,669	1,900	21,000	250	23,000	9,800	54,000	25,000
Colorado	2,889	5,400	2,800	0	13,000	0	16,000	4,000
Connecticut	3,108	420	140	1.0	1,200	2,400	3,700	160
Delaware	595	230	82	0.3	57	1,100	1,200	11
D.C.	638	530	0.8	0	340	0	340	23
Florida	9,740	750	3,800	42	3,600	14,000	21,000	2,400
Georgia	5,464	1,200	1,200	0	5,500	200	6,900	1,000
Hawaii	965	1,400	800	0	510	1,200	2,500	680
Idaho	944	19,000	6,300	0	12,000	0	18,000	5,900
Illinois	11,418	1,600	930	38	17,000	0	18,000	590
Indiana	5,396	2,600	1,300	0	13,000	0	14,000	690
Iowa	2,913	1,500	760	0	3,500	0	4,300	290
Kansas	2,363	2,800	5,600	0	980	0	6,600	4,700
Kentucky	3,661	1,300	250	0	4,600	0	4,800	290
Louisiana	4,199	2,900	1,800	19	11,000	390	13,000	3,500
Maine	1,125	750	80	0	770	710	1,600	53
Maryland	4,216	270	150	0	970	6,600	7,700	100
Massachusetts	5,737	430	320	0	2,100	3,500	5,900	90
Michigan	9,258	1,600	530	420	14,000	0	15,000	460
Minnesota	4,061	760	670	0	2,400	0	3,100	450
Mississippi	2,521	1,100	1,500	0	1,400	660	3,500	710
Missouri	4,888	1,400	470	0	6,400	0	6,900	670
Montana	786	14,000	260	2.1	11,000	0	11,000	2,700
Nebraska	1,570	7,700	7,200	0	4,900	0	12,000	7,600
Nevada	799	4,500	710	9.0	2,900	0	3,600	1,700
New Hampshire	921	420	65	0	320	620	1,000	17
New Jersey	7,360	390	730	0	2,100	7,500	10,000	380
New Mexico	1,300	3,000	1,800	0.9	2,100	0	3,900	1,900
New York	17,557	450	780	12	7,200	8,600	17,000	590
North Carolina	5,874	1,400	770	0	7,300	42	8,100	760
North Dakota	652	2,000	120	0.2	1,200	0	1,300	330
Ohio	10,797	1,300	980	0	13,000	0	14,000	550
Oklahoma	3,025	570	960	95	760	0	1,800	1,000
Oregon	2,614	2,600	1,100	0	5,700	0	6,800	3,200
Pennsylvania	11,824	1,300	1,000	0	15,000	93	16,000	920
Rhode Island	947	180	37	0	140	330	500	15
South Carolina	3,119	2,000	230	0	5,900	38	6,200	280
South Dakota	695	990	330	3.4	360	0	690	460
Tennessee	4,591	2,200	450	0	9,600	0	10,000	270
Texas	14,013	1,000	8,000	0	6,300	6,600	21,000	10,000
Utah	1,462	3,100	1,000	4.0	3,500	56	4,600	2,900
Vermont	511	660	45	0	290	0	340	41
Virginia	5,346	1,000	390	0.2	5,200	4,100	9,700	−230
Washington	4,127	2,000	770	0	7,500	42	8,300	2,900
West Virginia	1,950	2,900	220	0	5,400	0	5,600	200
Wisconsin	4,710	1,200	610	0	5,200	0	5,800	310
Wyoming	471	11,000	540	24	4,800	0	5,400	2,600
Puerto Rico	3,400	240	310	5.0	500	2,400	3,200	300
Virgin Islands	100	63	4.0	0	2.2	32	38	2.1
Total	**229,592**	**1,600**	**88,000**	**930**	**290,000**	**71,000**	**450,000**	**100,000**

Note: Figures may not add to totals because of independent rounding.

Canadian Pulpwood, Wood Pulp, and Newsprint

Source: Statistics Canada (thousands of metric tons)

Year	Pulpwood production[1] (1,000 cu. meters)	Wood pulp production[2] Total	Mechanical	Chemical	Wood pulp exports[3]	Newsprint production	Newsprint shipments Total	Domestic	Exports[4]
1980	50,386	19,970.2	7,506.0	12,438.7	7,990	8,625	8,621	982	7,639
1981	52,688	19,303.7	7,630.6	11,654.3	7,433	8,947	8,917	1,041	7,877
1982	41,337	17,008.6	6,815.9	10,175.2	6,741	8,117	8,074	934	7,139
1983	43,027	19,101.7	7,705.1	11,381.9	7,521	8,494	8,441	972	7,471

(1) Pulpwood produced for domestic use, excluding exports, but including receipts of purchased roundwood. (2) Total pulp production covers "screenings" which are already included in exports. "Screenings" are excluded throughout from mechanical and chemical pulp. (3) Customs exports. (4) Mill shipments destined for export.

Mineral Distribution, Reserves and Resources

Source: Bureau of Mines, U.S. Interior Department

Mineral	Distribution of reserves (% of world total)	Reserves[1] (million metric tons)	Resources[2]	Ratio of reserves to 1981 primary demand	Ratio of reserves to cumulative primary demand 1981-2000
Aluminum	Guinea(27) Australia(21) Brazil(11) Jamaica(9) India(5)	21,000[3]	40,400[4]	289	9.7
Chromium	Republic of South Africa(91) Philippines(2) Zimbabwe(2) Finland(2) USSR(2)	275	10,000	143	200
Cobalt	Zaire(50) Zambia(13) New Caledonia(8) Cuba(7) Indonesia(7)	2.72	11	171	4.5
Columbium	Brazil(79) USSR(17) Canada(3)	4	17	241	10
Copper	Chile(23) United States(16) Zambia(9) Zaire(7) Mexico(5)	350	2,300[5]	34	1.8
Gold	Republic of South Africa(53) USSR(18) United States(8) Canada(4) Brazil(2)	0.034	0.075	32	1.4
Iron	USSR(34) Brazil(15) Australia(14) India(7) Canada(7)	66,000	240,000	132	5.5
Lead	United States(20) Australia(15) USSR(14) Canada(12) Republic of South Africa(4)	100	1,500[5]	32	1.3
Manganese	Republic of South Africa(41) USSR(37) Gabon(11) Australia(5) India(2)	907	over 4,000	106	4.4
Nickel	New Caledonia(26) Canada(15) USSR(15) Philippines(10) Australia(10)	49	130	69	2.6
Platinum-Group Metals[6]	Republic of South Africa(79) USSR(19)	0.03	0.10	147	7
Silver	Canada(19) USSR(19) United States(18) Mexico(13) Australia(12)	0.26	0.77[7]	30	1.2
Tantalum	Thailand(27) USSR(17) Australia(17) Nigeria(12)	0.03	0.3	30	1.1
Titanium	Brazil(19) Republic of South Africa(17) Norway(14) Australia(9) China, People's Republic of(9)	200[8]	653[8]	125	5.2
Vanadium	USSR(60) Republic of South Africa(20) China, People's Republic of(14) United States(4)	4	64	112	4.4
Zinc	Canada(15) Australia(13) United States(8) Republic of South Africa(7) USSR(7)	168	1,800	29	1.2

(1) Mineral Commodity Profiles-1983. Unless otherwise stated, reserves are that portion of the resources that can be economically extracted or produced at the time of determination. (2) Mineral Commodity Summaries-1984. Unless otherwise stated, resources are identified resources derived in collaboration with the U.S. Geological Survey whose location, grade, quality, and quantity are known or estimated from geologic evidence, including economic, marginally economic, and subeconomic components. (3) Bauxite. Convert to aluminum equivalent by multiplying by 0.212. (4) Includes undiscovered deposits. (5) Includes seabed deposits. (6) Includes platinum, palladium, rhodium, ruthenium, iridium, and osmium. (7) From Mineral Commodity Profiles-1983. (8) Includes ilmenite, rutile, and anatase.

U.S. Nonfuel Mineral Production—Leading States

Source: Bureau of Mines, U.S. Interior Department

State	1983 Value (thousands)	Percent of U.S. total	Principal minerals, in order of value
California	$1,764,401	8.35	Bromine, cement, sand and gravel (construction), stone (crushed).
Texas	1,568,557	7.42	Cement, stone (crushed), sulfur, sand and gravel (construction).
Arizona	1,510,878	7.15	Copper, cement, molybdenum, sand and gravel (construction).
Minnesota.	1,455,030	6.88	Iron ore, sand and gravel (construction), stone (crushed and industrial).
Florida.	1,274,979	6.03	Phosphate rock, stone (crushed), cement, clays.
Michigan	1,160,691	5.49	Iron ore, cement, magnesium compounds, salt.
Georgia	850,224	4.02	Clays, stone (crushed), cement, stone (dimension).
Missouri.	725,809	3.43	Lead, cement, stone (crushed), lime.
Utah.	656,579	3.11	Copper, gold, silver, cement.
Pennsylvania	635,141	3.01	Cement, stone (crushed), lime, sand and gravel (construction).

U.S. Pig Iron and Steel Output

Source: American Iron and Steel Institute (net tons)

Year	Total pig iron	Pig iron and ferro-alloys	Raw steel	Year	Total pig iron	Pig iron and ferro-alloys	Raw steel
1940.	46,071,666	47,398,529	66,982,686	1975	101,208,000	103,345,000	116,642,000
1945	53,223,169	54,919,029	79,701,648	1977	81,328,000	83,082,000	125,333,000
1950	64,586,907	66,400,311	96,836,075	1978	87,679,000	89,351,000	137,031,000
1955	76,857,417	79,263,865	117,036,085	1980	68,721,000	70,329,000	111,835,000
1960	66,480,648	68,566,384	99,281,601	1981	73,570,000	75,096,000	120,828,000
1965	88,184,901	90,918,040	131,461,601	1982.	43,309,000	44,147,000	74,577,000
1970	91,435,000	93,851,000	131,514,000	1983.	48,706,000	49,491,000	84,615,000

Steel figures include only that portion of the capacity and production of steel for castings used by foundries which were operated by companies producing steel ingots.

Value of U.S. Mineral Production

(millons of dollars)

Production as measured by mine shipments sales or marketable production.

Year[1]	Fuels	Nonme-tallic	Metals	Total[2]	Year[1]	Fuels	Nonme-tallic	Metals	Total[2]
1930 . . .	2,500	973	501	3,980	1974 . . .	40,889	8,687	5,501	55,077
1940 . . .	2,662	784	752	4,198	1975 . . .	47,505	9,570	5,191	62,266
1950 . . .	8,689	1,882	1,351	11,862	1976 . . .	52,484	10,616	6,086	69,186
1960 . . .	12,142	3,868	2,022	18,032	1977 . . .	59,575	11,701	5,810	77,086
1965 . . .	14,047	4,933	2,544	21,524	1979 . . .	NA	15,438	8,536	NA
1970 . . .	20,152	5,712	3,928	29,792	1980 . . .	NA	16,213	8,921	NA
1972 . . .	22,061	6,482	3,642	32,185	1981 . . .	NA	16,385	8,842	NA
1973 . . .	24,949	7,476	4,362	36,787	1982 . . .	NA	14,147	5,544	NA

(1) Excludes Alaska and Hawaii, 1930-53. (2) Data may not add to total because of rounding figures.

U.S. Copper, Lead, and Zinc Production

Source: Bureau of Mines, U.S. Interior Department

Year	Copper Mil. lbs.	Copper $1,000	Lead[1] Short tons	Lead[1] $1,000	Zinc Short tons	Zinc Mil. dol.	Year	Copper Mil. lbs.	Copper $1,000	Lead[1] Metric tons	Lead[1] $1,000	Zinc Metric tons	Zinc Mil. dol.
1950	1,823	379,122	418,809	113,078	591,454	167	1977	3,008	2,009,297	537,499	363,789	407,889	309
1960	2,286	733,708	228,899	53,562	334,101	87	1980	2,604	2,666,931	550,366	515,189	317,103	262
1965	2,703	957,028	301,147	93,959	611,153	178	1981	3,391	2,886,440	445,535	358,821	312,418	307
1970	3,439	1,984,484	571,767	178,609	534,136	164	1982	2,529	1,840,856	512,516	288,579	303,160	257
1975	2,827	1,814,763	563,783	267,230	425,792	366	1983	2,289	1,751,476	449,038	214,623	275,294	251

(1) Production from domestic ores.

Cotton, Wool, Silk, and Man-Made Fibers Production

Source: Economics, Statistics, and Cooperatives Service, U.S. Agriculture Department

Cotton and wool from reports of the Agriculture Department; silk, rayon, and non-cellulosic man-made fibers from Textile Organon, a publication of the Textile Economics Bureau, Inc.

Year	Cotton[1] U.S. (million bales)[5]	Cotton[1] World (million bales)[5]	Wool[2] U.S. (million pounds)	Wool[2] World (million pounds)	Silk World (mil. lbs.)	Cellulosic U.S. (million pounds)	Cellulosic World (million pounds)	Non-cellulosic[4] U.S.[4] (million pounds)	Non-cellulosic[4] World[6] (million pounds)
1940	12.6	31.2	434.0	4,180	130	471.2	2,485.3	4.6	4.6
1950	10.0	30.6	249.3	4,000	42	1,259.4	3,552.8	145.9	177.4
1960	14.2	46.2	298.9	5,615	68	1,028.5	5,749.1	854.2	1,779.1
1965	15.0	55.0	224.8	5,731	72	1,527.0	7,359.4	2,062.4	4,928.9
1970	10.2	53.6	176.8	6,107	90	1,373.2	7,573.9	4,053.5	10,361.7
1975	8.3	54.0	125.5	5,911	104	749.0	6,523.2	6,432.2	17,344.6
1980	11.1	64.3	106.4	6,283	123	806.0	7,147.8	8,759.8	23,095.4
1981	15.6	70.5	110.7	6,362	126	770.1	7,063.8	9,047.0	23,869.2
1982	12.0	67.2	106.6	6,360	121	584.4	6,485.3	7,359.1	22,354.6
1983	11.8	66.7	101.3	6,285	121	630.3	6,618.8	8,706.9	24,475.5

(1) Year beginning Aug. 1. (2) Grease basis. (3) Includes filament yarn and staple and tow fiber. (4) Includes textile glass fiber. (5) 480-pound net weight bales, U.S. beginning 1960 and world beginning 1965. (6) 1966 to date, excludes Olefin.

Work Stoppages (Strikes) in the U.S.

(involving 1,000 workers or more)

Source: Bureau of Labor Statistics, U.S. Labor Department

Year	Number stoppages[1]	Workers involved[1] (thousands)	Man days idle[1] (thousands)	Year	Number stoppages[1]	Workers involved[1] (thousands)	Man days idle[1] (thousands)
1952	470	2,746	48,820	1968	392	1,855	35,567
1953	437	1,623	18,130	1969	412	1,576	29,397
1954	265	1,075	16,630	1970	381	2,468	52,761
1955	363	2,055	21,180	1971	298	2,516	35,538
1956	287	1,370	26,840	1972	250	975	16,764
1957	279	887	10,340	1973	317	1,400	16,260
1958	332	1,587	17,900	1974	424	1,796	31,809
1959	245	1,381	60,850	1975	235	965	17,563
1960	222	896	13,260	1976	231	1,519	23,962
1961	195	1,031	10,140	1977	298	1,212	21,258
1962	211	793	11,760	1978	219	1,006	23,774
1963	181	512	10,020	1979	235	1,021	20,409
1964	246	1,183	16,220	1980	187	795	20,844
1965	268	999	15,140	1981	145	729	16,908
1966	321	1,300	16,000	1982	96	656	9,061
1967	381	2,192	31,320	1983	81	909	17,461

[1]The number of stoppages and workers relate to stoppages that began in the year. Days of idleness include all stoppages in effect. Workers are counted more than once if they were involved in more than one stoppage during the year.

Labor Union Directory

Source: Bureau of Labor Statistics; World Almanac Questionnaire
(*) Independent union; all others affiliated with AFL-CIO.

Actors and Artistes of America, Associated (AAAA), 165 W. 46th St., New York, NY 10036; founded 1919; Frederick O'-Neal, Pres. (since 1971); no individual members, 9 National Performing Arts Unions are affiliates

Actors' Equity Association, 165 W. 46th St., New York, NY 10036; founded 1913; Ellen Burstyn, Pres.; 34,000 members.

Air Line Pilots Association, 1625 Massachusetts Ave. NW, Washington, DC 20036. Henry A. Duffy, Pres.; 34,000 members.

Aluminum Brick & Glass Workers International Union (AWIU), 3362 Hollenberg Drive, Bridgeton, MO 63044; founded 1953; Lawrence A. Holley, Pres. (since 1977); 55,000 members, 415 locals.

Automobile, Aerospace & Agricultural Implement Workers of America, International Union (UAW), 8000 E. Jefferson Ave., Detroit, MI 48214; founded 1935; Owen Bieber, Pres. (since 1983); 1,151,086 members, 1,517 locals.

Bakery, Confectionery & Tobacco Workers International Union (BC&T), 10401 Connecticut Ave., Kensington, MD 20895; founded 1886; John DeConcini, Pres. (since 1978); 170,000 members, 200 locals.

Boilermakers, Iron Shipbuilders, Blacksmiths, Forgers and Helpers, International Brotherhood of (BSF), 570 New Brotherhood Bldg., Kansas City, KS 66101; founded 1880; Charles W. Jones, Pres. (since 1983) 125,000 members, 400 locals.

Bricklayers and Allied Craftsmen, International Union of, 815 15th St. NW, Washington, DC 20005; John T. Joyce, Pres.; 130,000 members, 585 locals.

Carpenters and Joiners of America, United Brotherhood of, 101 Constitution Ave. NW, Washington, DC 20001; Patrick S. Campbell, Pres.; 820,000 members, 2,301 locals.

Cement, Lime Gypsum and Allied Workers International Union, United (UCLGAWIU), 2500 Brickdale Drive, Elk Grove Village, IL 60007; founded 1939; Richard A. Northrip, Vice Pres. (since 1984); 29,500 members, 296 locals. Merged with Boilermakers (BSF) April 1, 1984.

Chemical Workers Union, International (ICWU), 1655 West Market St., Akron, OH 44313; founded 1944; Frank D. Martino, Pres. (since 1975); 70,000 members, 400 locals.

Clothing and Textile Workers Union, Amalgamated (ACTWU), 15 Union Square, New York, NY 10003; founded 1914; Murray H. Finley, Pres. (since 1972); 349,000 members, 900 locals.

Communications Workers of America, 1925 K St. NW, Washington, DC 20006; Glenn E. Watts, Pres.; 650,000 members, 900 locals.

Distillery, Wine & Allied Workers International Union (DWU), 66 Grand Ave., Englewood, NJ 07631; founded 1940; George J. Oneto, Pres. (since 1974); 25,000 members, 67 locals.

*Education Association, National, 1201 16th St. NW, Washington, DC 20036; Mary H. Futrell, Pres.; 1,700,000 members, 12,000 affiliates.

*Electrical, Radio & Machine Workers of America, United (UE), 11 E. 51st St. New York, NY 10022; founded 1936; James Kane, Gen. Pres. (since 1981); 165,000 members, 200 locals.

Electrical Workers, International Brotherhood of (IBEW), 1125 15th St., NW, Washington, DC 20005; founded 1891; Charles H. Pillard, Pres. (since 1968); 1,000,000 members, 1,421 locals.

Electronic, Electrical, Technical, Salaried and Machine Workers, International Union of (IUE), 1126 16th St. NW, Washington, DC 20036; founded 1949; William H. Bywater, Pres. (since 1982); 200,000 members, 520 locals.

Farm Workers of America, United (UFW), La Paz, Keene, CA 93531; founded 1962; Cesar E. Chavez, Pres. (since 1973); 100,000 members.

*Federal Employees, National Federation of (NFFE), 1016 16th St. NW, Washington, DC 20036; founded 1917; James M. Peirce Jr., Pres. (since 1976); 172,000 members, 450 locals.

Fire Fighters, International Association of, 1750 New York Ave. NW, Washington, DC 20006; John A. Gannon, Pres.; 172,401 members, 1,943 locals.

Firemen and Oilers, International Brotherhood of, VFW Bldg., 200 Maryland Ave. NE, Washington, DC 20002; George J. Francisco, Pres.; 32,000 members.

Food and Commercial Workers International Union, United,

1775 K St., NW, Washington, DC 20006; William H. Wynn, Pres.; 1.3 million members, 790 locals.

Garment Workers of America, United (UGWA), 200 Park Ave. So., New York, NY 10003; founded 1891; William O'Donnell, Gen. Pres. (since 1977); 25,000 members, 155 locals.

Glass, Pottery, Plastics & Allied Workers Intl. Union (GPPAW), 608 E. Baltimore Pike, P.O. Box 607, Media, PA 19063; founded 1842; James E. Hatfield, Pres.; 95,000 members, 314 locals.

Glass and Ceramic Workers of North America, United, 556 E. Town St., Columbus, OH 43215; Joseph Roman, Pres.; 30,000 members, 181 locals.

Glass Workers Union, American Flint (AFGWU), 1440 So. Byrne Rd., Toledo, OH 43614; founded 1878; George M. Parker, Pres. (since 1961); 31,000 members, 238 locals.

Government Employees, American Federation of (AFGE), 1325 Massachusetts Ave. NW, Washington, DC 20005; founded 1932; Kenneth T. Blaylock, Natl. Pres. (since 1976); 300,000 members, 1,500 locals.

Grain Millers, American Federation of (AFGM), 4949 Olson Memorial Hwy., Minneapolis, MN 55422; founded 1948; Robert W. Willis, Gen. Pres.; 35,000 members, 210 locals.

Graphic Arts International Union (GAIU), 1900 L St., NW, Washington, DC 20036; founded 1882; Kenneth J. Brown, Pres. (since 1959); 120,000 members, 220 locals.

Hotel Employees and Restaurant Employees International Union, 120 E. 4th St., Cincinnati, OH 45202; Edward T. Hanley, Pres.; 400,000 members, 225 locals.

Industrial Workers of America, International Union, Allied (AIW), 3520 W. Oklahoma Ave., Milwaukee, WI 53215; founded 1935; Dominick D'Ambrosio, Intl. Pres. (since 1975); 75,000 members, 405 locals.

Iron Workers, International Association of Bridge Structural and Ornamental, 1750 New York Ave. NW, Washington, DC 20006; John H. Lyons, Pres.; 181, 647 members, 318 locals.

Laborers' International Union of North America (LIUNA), 905 16th St. NW, Washington, DC 20006; founded 1903; Angelo Fosco, Gen. Pres. (since 1976); 430,000 members, 800 locals.

Ladies Garment Workers Union, International (ILGWU), 1710 Broadway, New York, NY 10019; founded 1900; Sol C. Chaikin, Pres. (since 1975); 264,227 members, 393 locals.

Leather Goods, Plastic and Novelty Workers' Union, International, 265 W. 14th St., New York, NY 10011; Ralph Cennamo, Gen. Pres.; 40,000 members, 97 locals.

Letter Carriers, National Association of (NALC), 100 Indiana Ave. NW, Washington, DC 20001; founded 1889; Vincent R. Sombrotto, Pres. (since 1979); 256,000 members, 4,190 locals.

*Locomotive Engineers, Brotherhood of (BLE), 1365 Ontario Ave., Cleveland, OH 44114; founded 1863; John F. Sytsma, Pres. (since 1976); 62,888 members, 727 divisions.

Longshoremen's Association, International, 17 Battery Pl., New York, NY 10004; Thomas W. Gleason, Pres.; 76,579 members, 367 locals.

*Longshoremen's & Warehousemen's Union, International (ILWU), 1188 Franklin St., San Francisco, CA 94109; founded 1937; James R. Herman, Pres. (since 1977); 58,000 members, 78 locals.

Machinists and Aerospace Workers, International Association of, 1300 Connecticut Ave. NW, Washington, DC 20036; William W. Winpisinger, Pres.; 943,280 members, 1,904 locals.

Maintenance of Way Employes, Brotherhood of, 12050 Woodward Ave., Detroit, MI 48203; O. M. Berge, Pres.; 80,000 members, 955 locals.

Marine & Shipbuilding Workers of America, Industrial Union of (IUMSWA), 8121 Georgia Ave., Silver Springs, MD 20910; founded 1934; Arthur E. Batson Jr., Pres. (since 1982); 25,000 members, 40 locals.

Maritime Union of America, National, 346 W. 17th St., New York NY 10011; Shannon Wall, Pres.; 35,000 members.

*Mine Workers of America, United (UMWA), 900 15th St. NW, Washington, DC 20005; founded 1890; Rich Trumka, Pres.; 250,000 members, 878 locals.

Molders' and Allied Workers' Union, International, 1225 E. McMillan St., Cincinnati, OH 45206; Bernard Butsavage, Pres.; 50,000 members, 224 locals.

Musicians of the United States and Canada, American Federation of (AF of M), 1500 Broadway, New York, NY 10036;

founded 1896; Victor W. Fuentealba, Pres. (since 1978); 250,000 members, 558 locals.

Newspaper Guild, The (TNG), 1125 15th St. NW, Washington, DC; founded 1933; Charles A. Perlik Jr., Pres.5(since 1969); 32,000members, 80 locals.

Novelty & Production Workers, Intl. Union of Allied, 147-149 E. 26th St., New York, NY 10010; Julius Isaacson, Pres. 30,000 members, 18 locals.

*****Nurses Association, American,** 2420 Pershing Rd., Kansas City, MO 64108; Eunice Cole, Pres.; 53 constituent assns.

Office and Professional Employees International Union, 265 W. 14th St., New York, NY 10011; John Kelly, Pres.; 125,000 members, 275 locals.

Oil, Chemical and Atomic Workers International Union, PO Box 2812, Denver, CO 80201; Joseph M. Misbrener Pres.; 130,000 members, 460 locals.

Operating Engineers, International Union of (IUOE), 1125 17th St. NW, Washington, DC 20036; founded 1896; J.C. Turner, Gen. Pres.; 400,000 members, 210 locals.

Painters and Allied Trades, International Brotherhood of (IBPAT), 1750 New York Ave. NW, Washington, DC 20006; founded 1887; William A. Duval, Gen. Pres. (since 1984); 167,569 members, 709 locals.

Paperworkers International Union, United (UPIU), 702 Church St., P.O. Box 1475, Nashville, TN 37202; founded 1884; Wayne E. Glenn, Pres. (since 1978); 265,000 members, 1,250 locals.

*****Plant Guard Workers of America, International Union, United (UPGWA),** 25510 Kelly Rd., Roseville, MI 48066; founded 1948; James C. McGahey, Pres. (since 1948); 29,243 members, 162 locals.

Plasterers' and Cement Mason's International Association of the United States & Canada; Operative, 1125 17th St. NW, Washington, DC 20036; Melvin H. Roots, Pres.; Robert J. Holton, Secy.-Treas.; 65,000 members, 365 locals.

Plumbing and Pipe Fitting Industry of the United States and Canada, United Association of Journeymen and Apprentices of the, 901 Massachusetts Ave. NW, Washington, DC 20001; Martin Ward, Pres.; 350,000 members.

*****Police, Fraternal Order of,** 5613 Belair Rd., Baltimore, MD 21206; Richard A. Boyd, Pres.; 105,000 members, 1,482 affiliates.

*****Postal Supervisors, National Association of,** 490 L'Enfant Plaza SW, Suite 3200, Washington, DC 20024; Donald N. Ledbetter, Pres.; 37,500 members, 460 locals.

Postal Workers Union, American (APWU), 817 14th St. NW, Washington, DC 20005; founded 1971; Moe Biller, Gen. Pres. (since 1980); 320,000 members, 3,900 locals.

Printing and Graphic Communications Union, International, 1730 Rhode Island Ave. NW, Washington, DC 20036; Sol Fishko, Pres.; 110,000 members, 556 locals.

Railway, Airline and Steamship Clerks, Freight Handlers, Express and Station Employees; Brotherhood of, 3 Research Place, Rockville, MD 20850; R. I. Kilroy, Pres.; 200,000 members, 800 locals.

Railway Carmen of the United States and Canada, Brotherhood, 4929 Main St., Kansas City, MO 64112; founded 1890; C.E. Wheeler, Gen. Pres.; 91,000 members, 600 locals.

Retail, Wholesale and Department Store Union, 30 E. 29th St., New York, NY 10016; Alvin E. Heaps, Pres.; 250,000 members, 315 locals.

Roofers, Waterproofers & Allied Workers, United Union of, 1125 17th St. NW, Washington, DC 20036; Roy Johnson, Pres.; 30,000 members, 157 locals.

Rubber, Cork, Linoleum and Plastic Workers of America, United, 87 South High St., Akron, OH 44308; Milan Stone, Pres.; 120,000 members, 490 locals.

*****Rural Letter Carriers' Association, National,** Suite 100, 1448 Duke St., Alexandria, VA 22314; Tom W. Griffith Pres.; 66,000 members.

Seafarers International Union of North America (SIUNA), 5201 Auth Way, Camp Springs, MD 20746; founded 1938; Frank Drozak, Pres.; 90,000 members.

Service Employees International Union (SEIU), 2020 K St. NW, Washington, DC 20006; founded 1921; John J. Sweeney, Pres. (since 1980); 850,000 members, 328 locals.

Sheet Metal Workers' International Association (SMWIA), 1750 New York Ave. NW, Washington, DC 20006; founded 1888; Edward J. Carlough, Gen. Pres. (since 1970); 160,000 members, 352 locals.

State, County and Municipal Employees, American Federation of, 1625 L St. NW, Washington, DC 20036; Gerald McEntee, Pres.; 1,000,000 members, 2,991 locals.

Steelworkers of America, United (USWA), 5 Gateway Center, Pittsburgh, PA 15222; founded 1942; Lynn Williams, Pres. (since 1983); 1,000,000 members, 4,689 locals.

Teachers, American Federation of (AFT), 555 New Jersey Ave. NW, Washington, DC 20001; founded 1916; Albert Shanker, Pres. (since 1974); 580,000 members, 2,010 locals.

*****Teamsters, Chauffeurs, Warehousemen and Helpers of America, International Brotherhood of (IBT),** 25 Louisiana Ave. NW, Washington, DC 20001; founded 1903; Jackie Presser, Gen. Pres.; 2,000,000 members, 694 locals.

Television and Radio Artists, American Federation of, 1350 Ave. of the Americas, New York, NY; founded 1937; Bill Hillman, Pres.; 60,000 members, 38 locals.

Textile Workers of America, United (UTWA), 420 Common St., Lawrence, MA 01840; founded 1901; Francis Schaufenbil, Intl. Pres. (since 1972); 50,000 members, 221 locals.

Theatrical Stage Employees and Moving Picture Operators of the United States and Canada, International Alliance of, 1515 Broadway, New York, NY 10036; Walter Diehl, Pres.; 61,471 members, 870 locals.

Transit Union, Amalgamated (ATU), 5025 Wisconsin Ave. NW, Washington, DC 20016; founded 1892; John W. Rowland, Intl. Pres. (since 1981); 160,000 members, 295 locals.

Transport Workers Union of America, 1980 Broadway, New York, NY 10023; William G. Lindner, Pres.; 100,000 members, 105 locals.

Transportation Union, United (UTU), 14600 Detroit Ave., Cleveland, OH 44107; founded 1969; Fred A. Hardin, Pres. (since 1979); 210,000 members.

*****Treasury Employees Union, National (NTEU),** 1730 K St. NW, Washington, DC 20006; founded 1938; Robert M. Tobias, Natl. Pres. (since 1966); 125,000 represented, 230 chapters.

Typographical Union, International (ITU), PO Box 157, Colorado Springs, CO 80901; founded 1852; Joe Bingel, Pres. (since 1978); 82,931 members, 503 locals.

*****University Professors, American Association of (AAUP),** 1012-14th St., Washington, DC 20005; founded 1915; Paul H. L. Walter, Pres.; 60,500 members, 1,300 locals.

Upholsterers' International Union of North America (UIU), 25 N. 4th St., Philadelphia, PA 19106; founded 1882; John Serembus, Pres.; 31,827 members, 133 locals.

Utility Workers Union of America (UWUA), 815 16th St. NW, Washington, DC 20006; founded 1946; James Joy Jr., Natl. Pres. (since 1980); 60,000 members, 220 locals.

Woodworkers of America, International (IWA), 1622 N. Lombard St., Portland, OR 97217; founded 1937; Keith Johnson, Intl. Pres. (since 1973); 100,000 members, 200 locals.

Canadian Unions

Source: Labour Canada

Independent Unions (1984)

Hospital Employees Union, Local 180	25,000
Nurses' Association, Ontario	36,800
Quebec Govt. Employees' Union	55,242
Teachers' Association, Alberta	37,381
Teachers' Associations of Ontario, Fed. of Women	30,232
Teachers' Federation, British Columbia	29,780
Teachers' Federation, Ontario Secondary School	36,072
Teaching Congress, Quebec	86,200
Teamsters, Chauffeurs, Warehousemen and Helpers of America, International Brotherhood of	91,500

Canadian Labor Congress (CLC) (1984)

Automobile, Aerospace and Agricultural Implement Workers of America, International Union, United	110,000
Communications Workers of Canada	40,000
Govt. Employees, National Union of Provincial	242,286
Paperworkers Union, Canadian	63,180
Postal Workers, Canadian Union of	24,000
Public Employees, Canadian Union of	293,709
Public Service Alliance of Canada	181,192
Railway, Transport and General Workers, Canadian Brotherhood of	37,359

Confederation of National Trade Unions (CNTU) (1984)

Federation of Public Service Employees Inc.	28,000
National Federation of Building and Woodworkers Inc.	19,000
Social Affairs Federation	93,000

ENERGY

Nuclear Construction

Source: State regulatory agencies, individual utilities, Atomic Industrial Forum, as of Mar. 1, 1984.

Under Construction

	Percent complete	Due in service	First cost estimate	Current estimate
Bellefonte 1 (Scottsboro), Ala.	83	4/88-4/89	$725 million	$5.2-5.6 million
Bellefonte 2, Ala.	63	4/90-4/91	for both	for both
Palo Verde 1 (Wintersburg), Ariz.	99	12/84	$2.8 billion	$5.7 billion
Palo Verde 2, Ariz.	98	9/85	for three	for three
Palo Verde 3, Ariz.	81	1987		
Diablo Canyon 1 (Avila Beach), Cal.	100*	3/84	$620 million	$4.5 billion
Diablo Canyon 2, Cal.	99	5/85	for both	for both
Millstone 3 (Waterford), Conn.	80	5/86	$400 million	$3.54 billion
Alvin W. Vogtle 1 (Waynesboro), Ga.	61	3/87	$2.5 billion	$6.6 billion
Alvin W. Vogtle 2, Ga.	20	Fall, 1988	for both	for both
Braidwood 1 (Braidwood), Ill.	70	4/86	$934 million	$3.575 billion
Braidwood 2, Ill.	54	4/87	for both	for both
Clinton 1 (Clinton), Ill.	82	11/86	$430 million	$2.85 billion
Wolf Creek (Burlington), Kan.	90	3/85	$783 million	$2.67 billion
River Bend 1 (St. Francisville), La.	80	12/85	$350 million	$2.5 billion
Waterford 3 (Taft), La.	99	12/84	$230 million	$2.6 billion
Midland 2 (Midland), Mich.	83	Mid-1986	$350 million	$4.43 billion
Enrico Fermi 2 (Newport), Mich.	98	12/84	$229 million	$3.075 billion
Grand Gulf 1 (Port Gibson), Miss.	100*	Late 1984	$400-$500 million	$3 billion
Callaway 1 (Callaway County), Mo.	95	12/84	$550 million	$2.85 billion
Seabrook 1 (Seabrook), N.H. (Future of Unit 2 uncertain)	86	7/85	$900 million for both	$5.8 billion for both
Hope Creek 1 (Lower Alloways Twp.), N.J.	76	12/86	$600 million for twin units	$3.79 billion for one
Shoreham (Shoreham, L.I.), N.Y.	100*	7/85	$261 million	$4.1 billion
Nine Mile Point 2 (Scriba), N.Y.	81	10/86	$382 million	$4.2 billion
Shearon Harris 1 (New Hill), N.C.	85	10/86	$1 billion for four units	$2.8 billion for one
Perry 1 (North Perry), Oh.	92	5/85	$632 million	$5.2 billion
Perry 2, Oh.	44	5/88	for both	for both
Beaver Valley 2 (Shippingport), Pa.	76	5/86	$321 million	$3.07 billion
Susquehanna 2 (Berwick), Pa. (Unit 1 in service 6/83)	98	12/84	$1.1 billion for two units	$4.1 billion for two units
Limerick 1 (Limerick Twp.), Pa. (Future of Unit 2 uncertain)	92	4/85	$1.7 billion for two units	$6.45 billion for two units
Catawba 1 (York County)	99	Early 1985	$320 million	$1.95 billion
Catawba 2, S.C.	65	Early 1985	$320 million	$1.95 billion
Watts Bar 1 (Spring City), Tenn.	96	Fall 1984	$621 million	$3.4 billion
Watts Bar 2, Tenn.	61	Mid-1986	for both	for both
South Texas Project 1 (Matagorda County), Tex.	50	6/87	$1 billion	$5.5 billion
South Texas Project 2, Tex.	25	6/89	for both	for both
Comanche Peak 1 (Somervell County), Tex.	97	1985	$780 million	$3.89 billion
Comanche Peak 2, Tex.	65	Mid-1986	for both	for both

*Testing not completed.

Work delayed or stopped

	Percent complete	Current status
Limerick 2 (Limerick Twp., Pa)	30	On hold by order of Pennsylvania Public Utility Commission until Unit 1 is done
Grand Gulf 2 (Port Gibson, Miss.)	32	On hold while Mississippi Public Service Commission reconsiders economic viability and need for plant
Midland 1 (Midland, Mich.)	83	On hold because of dispute with Dow Chemical on cost
Carroll County 1 (Savanna, Ill.)	0	Both ordered in 1978; no construction begun because of changes in demand projections
Carroll County 2		
Yellow Creek 1 (Iuka, Miss.)	35	No completion date set because of changing construction costs and demand forecasts.
Yellow Creek 2	3	
Seabrook 2 (Seabrook, N.H.)	28	Work delayed because of cost and demand changes
WPPSS 1 (Richland, Wash.)	63	Stopped because of financing difficulties
WPPSS 3 (Satsop, Wash.)	75	

Operating license denied

Byron 1 (Byron, Ill.)	90	Operating license denied 1/84 for safety reasons. Unit 1 due in
Byron 2	72	service 1/85 and Unit 2 due 4/86, according to Commonwealth Edison, at $3.768 billion for two. Was to cost $902 million.

World Nuclear Power: Current and Projected Capacities

(Net GWe; as of Dec. 31, 1982)

Country[1]	1982[2]	1990[3] Low Case	1990[3] Mid-Case	1990[3] High Case	2000[3] Low Case	2000[3] Mid-Case	2000[3] High Case
OECD Countries[4]							
Belgium	2.6	5.5	5.5	5.5	5.5	8.4	9.4
Canada	5.6	11.8	12.7	12.7	15.5	18.7	21.0
Finland	2.2	2.2	2.2	2.2	2.6	3.4	3.8
France	21.8	48.7	54.4	58.0	54.4	67.7	79.9
West Germany	9.8	17.9	19.2	21.7	19.5	23.8	29.1
Italy	1.3	3.3	3.3	3.3	6.6	7.8	9.2
Japan	16.6	26.9	27.9	32.7	36.9	46.1	59.5
Netherlands	0.5	0.5	0.5	0.5	0.5	2.3	2.7
Spain	2.0	6.5	7.5	8.4	7.5	9.6	11.9
Sweden	6.4	8.4	9.4	9.4	9.4	10.4	11.4
Switzerland	1.9	2.9	2.9	2.9	2.9	3.8	3.8
United Kingdom	7.0	10.3	11.8	12.5	14.4	17.3	19.9
United States	57.3	112.0	114.0	121.0	110.0	130.0	140.0
Total OECD	135.0	257.0	271.0	291.0	286.0	349.0	407.0
Non-OECD Countries							
Argentina	0.3	1.6	1.6	1.6	1.6	2.8	3.0
Brazil	0.6	0.6	1.9	3.1	4.5	8.4	10.5
India	0.8	1.5	1.7	1.9	4.5	6.6	8.2
South Korea	0.6	7.4	8.5	9.4	11.1	15.3	19.1
Mexico	0	0.6	0.6	1.3	3.4	5.3	9.1
South Africa	0	1.8	1.8	1.8	4.5	5.6	6.3
Taiwan	3.1	5.8	5.8	6.8	7.5	8.6	11.3
Total Non-OECD	6.2	21.0	23.0	29.0	41.0	57.0	75.0
Total World	141.2	278.0	294.0	320.0	327.0	406.0	482.0

(1) OECD countries Austria, Greece, Portugal, and Turkey, and non-OECD countries Egypt, Israel, Pakistan, the Phillipines, and Yugoslavia have less than 1.0 current capacity and are projected for less than 5.0 in 2000, high case. (2) Total does not equal sum of components, due to independent rounding. (3) Totals are rounded to the nearest whole number. (4) OECD = Organization for Economic Cooperation and Development.

U.S. Total Energy Production and Consumption

	Production	Consumption (Quadrillion (10[15]) Btu	Imports[1]	Exports	Net Imports		Production	Consumption (Quadrillion (10[15]) Btu	Imports[1]	Exports	Net Imports
1975	59.801	70.485	14.113	2.361	11.753	1983	61.174	70.638	11.990	3.727	8.264
1980	64.708	75.900	15.972	3.726	12.246	Jan., 1984	5.563	7.300	1.087	0.245	0.842
1981	64.376	73.940	13.974	4.331	9.643	Feb., 1984	5.354	6.160	1.047	0.217	0.830
1982	63.851	70.822	12.110	4.637	7.473	Mar., 1984	5.677	6.593	1.044	0.314	0.730

Totals may not equal sum of components due to independent rounding. (1) The sum of domestic energy and net imports of energy does not equal domestic energy consumption due to stock changes; losses and gains in conversion, transportation, distribution; the addition of blending compounds; shipments of anthracite to U.S. Armed Forces, and other adjustments.

Production of Energy by Type

	Coal[1]	Crude oil[2]	NGPL[3]	Natural gas (dry)	Hydro-electric power[4]	Nuclear electric power	Other[5]	Total energy produced
				Quadrillion (10[15]) Btu				
1975 Total	14.931	17.729	2.374	19.640	3.155	1.900	0.072	59.801
1980	18.544	18.249	2.254	19.907	2.900	2.739	0.114	64.708
1981	18.331	18.146	2.307	19.699	2.758	3.008	0.127	64.376
1982	18.603	18.309	2.191	18.255	3.271	3.115	0.108	63.851
1983	17.286	18.392	2.195	16.419	3.511	3.235	0.135	61.174

Geographic coverage: the 50 United States and District of Columbia. Totals may not equal sum of components due to independent rounding. (1) Includes bituminous coal, lignite, and anthracite. (2) Includes lease condensate. (3) Natural gas plant liquids. (4) Includes industrial and utility production of hydropower. (5) Includes geothermal power and electricity produced from wood and waste.

Consumption of Energy by Type

	Coal[1]	Natural gas (dry)	Petroleum	Hydro-electric power[2]	Nuclear electric power	Net imports of coal coke[3]	Other[4]	Total Energy consumed
				Quadrillion (10[15]) Btu				
1975 Total	12.601	19.948	32.731	3.219	1.900	0.014	0.072	70.485
1980	15.373	20.391	34.202	3.118	2.739	0.114	0.114	75.900
1981	15.860	19.926	31.931	3.105	3.008	(0.017)	0.127	73.940
1982	15.291	18.507	30.232	3.592	3.115	(0.023)	0.108	70.822
1983	15.877	17.475	30.076	3.857	3.235	(0.016)	0.135	70.638

Geographic coverage: the 50 United States and District of Columbia. Totals may not equal sum of components due to independent rounding. (1) Includes bituminous coal, lignite, and anthracite. (2) Includes industrial and utility production, and net imports of electricity (3) Parentheses indicate exports are greater than imports. (4) Includes geothermal power and electricity produced from wood and waste.

World Production of Crude Oil

(thousands of barrels per day)

Year	USSR	Saudi Arabia	U.S.	All Arab OPEC Nations[1]	All OPEC Nations[2]	World Total
1973[3]	8,465	7,569	9,208	18,009	30,989	55,674
1974	9,000	8,480	8,774	17,724	30,729	55,852
1975	9,625	7,075	8,375	15,986	27,155	55,880
1976	10,143	8,577	8,135	18,578	30,738	57,312
1977	10,682	9,245	8,245	19,221	31,298	59,685
1978	11,185	8,301	8,707	18,457	29,805	60,057
1979	11,460	9,532	8,552	21,094	30,928	62,535
1980	11,773	9,900	8,597	19,050	26,891	59,538
1981	11,909	9,815	8,572	15,764	22,646	55,900
1982	12,000	6,470	8,649	11,680	18,784	53,162
1983	12,035	5,085	8,688	10,345	17,575	52,885

(1) Algeria, Iraq, Kuwait, Libya, Qatar, Saudi Arabia, United Arab Emirates. (2) Arab OPEC nations plus Ecuador, Gabon, Indonesia, Iran, Nigeria, Venezuela. (3) Average per day.

U.S. Total Fuel Supply and Demand

(thousands of 42-gallon barrels)

Year	Gasoline[1] Production	Gasoline[1] Total demand	Kerosene[2] Production	Kerosene[2] Total demand	Distillate fuel oil Production	Distillate fuel oil Total demand	Residual fuel oil Production	Residual fuel oil Total demand
1950[3] . . .	1,024,181	1,019,011	118,512	119,922	398,912	75,435	425,217	570,021
1960	1,522,497	1,525,126	136,842	133,188	667,050	695,165	332,147	577,934
1965	1,733,258	1,756,419	201,788	219,932	765,430	779,644	268,567	601,893
1970	2,135,838	2,165,598	313,544	358,146	897,097	928,109	257,510	824,073
1971 . . .	2,231,157	2,246,025	306,847	365,308	912,097	974,077	274,684	851,262
1972	2,352,310	2,384,734	313,554	379,984	963,625	1,067,321	292,519	937,707
1974	2,371,004	2,436,681	290,780	346,706	974,025	1,076,771	390,491	968,185
1976	2,549,627	2,597,305	323,114	350,565	1,070,209	1,146,695	503,953	1,025,148
1977	2,565,950	2,625,080	355,145	376,680	1,192,090	1,213,990	635,100	1,111,425
1978	2,612,670	2,702,095	354,415	386,900	1,153,765	1,242,825	615,390	1,103,395
1979	2,494,655	2,566,128	368,707	391,650	1,148,778	1,207,278	614,806	1,029,913
1980	2,374,690	2,401,335	369,380	392,740	971,630	1,046,090	576,700	915,420
1981	2,337,825	2,404,620	434,350	463,550	953,745	1,032,585	482,165	762,120
1982	2,313,370	2,386,735	557,720	547,135	951,190	974,915	390,550	626,340
1983	2,314,100	2,417,030	599,330	550,785	896,440	981,850	310,980	518,665

Demand usually exceeds the production; the difference is made up by dipping into stocks or imports. (1) Includes special naphtha production. (2) Includes kerosene type jet fuel. (3) 1950 figures are on a 48-state basis.

U.S. Crude Petroleum Production by Chief States

(thousands of 42-gallon barrels)

Year	Alas.	Cal.	Col.	Fla.	Kan.	La.	Miss.	N.M.	Okla.	Tex.	Wyo.
1950 . .	0	327,607	23,303	487	107,586	208,965	38,236	47,367	164,599	829,874	61,631
1960 . .	559	305,352	47,469	369	113,453	400,832	51,673	107,380	192,913	927,479	133,910
1965 . .	11,128	316,428	33,511	1,462	104,733	594,853	56,183	119,166	203,441	1,000,749	138,314
1970 . .	83,616	372,191	24,723	12,999	84,853	906,907	65,119	128,184	223,574	1,249,697	160,345
1975 . .	69,834	322,199	38,089	41,877	59,106	650,840	46,614	95,063	163,123	1,221,929	135,943
1976 . .	63,398	326,021	38,992	44,460	58,714	606,501	46,072	92,130	161,426	1,189,523	134,149
1977 . .	169,201	349,609	39,460	46,641	57,496	562,905	43,022	87,223	156,382	1,137,880	136,472
1978 . .	448,620	347,181	36,797	47,536	56,586	532,740	39,494	83,365	150,456	1,074,050	137,385
1979 . .	511,538	352,465	32,251	47,170	56,995	494,462	38,286	79,379	143,642	1,013,255	124,553
1980 . .	591,684	356,644	29,565	42,846	60,152	466,964	36,533	75,456	151,960	975,239	214.161
1981 . .	828,300	544,100	14,700	10,900	37,100	298,500	20,900	55,500	95,000	809,300	84,000
1982 . .	627,000	394,000	30,000	26,000	63,000	388,000	30,000	69,000	138,000	866,000	110,000

Other chief states in 1982 were North Dakota, Michigan, Montana, and Illinois.

Coal Production and Consumption in the U.S.

(Thousand short tons)

Bituminous Coal, Lignite, and Anthracite

	Production	Domestic Consumption	Imports[1]	Exports[2]	Stocks[3]
1973	598,568	562,584	127	53,587	104,335
1974	610,023	558,402	2,080	60,661	96,323
1975	654,641	562,641	940	66,309	128,050
1976	684,913	603,790	1,203	60,021	134,438
1977	697,205	625,291	1,647	54,312	157,098
1978	670,164	625,225	2,953	40,714	145,551
1979	781,134	680,524	2,059	66,042	181,646
1980	829,700	702,729	1,194	91,742	204,028
1981	823,775	723,627	1,043	112,541	NA
1982	838,112	706,911	742	106,277	NA
1983	784,865	736,672	1,271	77,772	NA

(1) Bituminous coal was the only type of coal imported during the years shown above. (2) Excludes shipments of anthracite to U.S. Armed Forces overseas (335,000 short tons in 1982). (3) Stocks held by electric utilities, coke plants, and general industry, not stocks at retail dealers consumed by residential, commercial sector. NA = Not available.

U.S. Petroleum Imports by Source

(thousands of barrels per day)

Nation	1973	1978	1979	1980	1981	1982	1983
Algeria	136	649	636	488	311	170	240
Indonesia	213	573	420	348	366	248	338
Iran	223	555	304	9	0	35	48
Libya	164	654	658	554	319	26	0
Nigeria	459	919	1,080	857	620	514	302
Saudi Arabia	486	1,144	1,356	1,261	1,129	552	337
United Arab Emirates	71	385	281	172	81	92	30
Venezuela	1,135	645	690	481	406	412	422
Other OPEC[1]	106	226	212	130	90	97	144
Total OPEC	**2,993**	**5,751**	**5,637**	**4,300**	**3,323**	**2,146**	**1,862**
Arab OPEC Members[2]	915	2,963	3,056	2,551	1,848	854	632
Bahamas	174	160	147	78	74	65	125
Canada	1,325	467	538	455	447	482	547
Neth'lands Antilles	585	229	231	225	197	175	189
Puerto Rico	99	94	92	88	62	50	40
Trinidad/Tobago	255	253	190	176	133	112	96
Virgin Islands	329	429	431	388	327	316	282
Mexico	16	318	439	533	523	685	826
Other non-OPEC	465	484	548	491	534	627	701
Total non-OPEC	**3,263**	**2,613**	**2,819**	**2,609**	**2,672**	**2,968**	**3,189**
Total imports (avg.)[3]	**6,256**	**8,363**	**8,456**	**6,909**	**5,995**	**5,113**	**5,051**

(1) Includes Ecuador, Gabon, Iraq, Kuwait, Qatar. (2) Includes Algeria, Libya, Saudi Arabia, United Arab Emirates, Iraq, Kuwait, Qatar. (3) Imports do not add to totals because OPEC figures include petroleum transshipped through, and usually refined in, other countries and counted again as imports from those countries.

U.S. Dependence on Petroleum Imports

(thousands of barrels per day average)

Year	Net Imports[1] Arab OPEC[2] Nations	Net Imports[1] All OPEC[3] Nations	Net Imports[1] All Nations	Petroleum Products Supplied	Net Imports as Percent of U.S. Petroleum Products Supplied Arab OPEC[2] Nations	Net Imports as Percent of U.S. Petroleum Products Supplied All OPEC[3] Nations (percent)	Net Imports as Percent of U.S. Petroleum Products Supplied All Nations
1973	914	2,991	6,025	17,308	5.3	17.3	34.8
1974	752	3,277	5,892	16,653	4.5	19.7	35.4
1975	1,382	3,599	5,846	16,322	8.5	22.0	35.8
1976	2,423	5,063	7,090	17,461	13.9	29.0	40.6
1977	3,184	6,190	8,565	18,431	17.3	33.6	46.5
1978	2,962	5,747	8,002	18,847	15.7	30.5	42.5
1979	3,054	5,633	7,985	18,513	16.5	30.4	43.1
1980	2,549	4,293	6,365	17,056	14.9	25.2	37.3
1981	1,844	3,315	5,401	16,058	11.5	20.6	33.6
1982	852	2,136	4,298	15,296	5.6	14.0	28.1
1983	630	1,843	4,312	15,231	4.1	12.1	28.3

(1) Net imports are imports minus exports. (2) Algeria, Iraq, Kuwait, Libya, Qatar, Saudi Arabia, United Arab Emirates. (3) Arab OPEC nations plus Ecuador, Gabon, Indonesia, iran, Nigeria, Venezuela.

U.S. Crude Oil, Natural Gas, and Natural Gas Liquids Reserves

Year	Extensions to Old Reservoirs	New Field Discoveries	New Reservoir Discoveries In Old Fields	Total Discoveries	Production	Proved Reserves 12/31	Net Change from Prior Year
Crude Oil[1]							
1976	—	—	—	—	—	33,502	—
1977	496	168	130	794	2,862	31,780	−1,722
1978	444	267	116	827	3,008	31,355	−425
1979	424	108	104	636	2,955	29,810	−1,545
1980	572	143	147	862	2,975	29,805	−5
1981	750	254	157	1,161	2,949	29,426	−379
1982	634	204	193	1,031	2,950	27,858	−1,568
Natural Gas[2]							
1976	—	—	—	—	—	213,278	—
1977	8,129	3,173	3,301	14,603	18,843	207,413	−5,865
1978	9,582	3,860	4,579	18,021	18,805	208,033	+620
1979	8,950	3,188	2,566	14,704	19,257	200,997	−7,036
1980	9,357	2,539	2,577	14,473	18,699	199,021	−1,976
1981	10,491	3,731	2,998	17,220	18,737	201,730	+2,709
1982	8,349	2,687	3,419	14,455	17,506	201,512	−218
Natural Gas Liquids[1]							
1978	—	—	—	—	—	6,772	—
1979	364	94	97	555	727	6,615	−157
1980	418	90	79	587	731	6,728	+113
1981	542	131	91	764	741	7,068	+340
1982	375	112	109	596	721	7,221	+153

(1) million 42–gallon barrels. (2) Billion cubic ft., dry, 14.73 psia, 60°F.

Average Consumer Cost of Fuels

(constant 1972 dollars)

Year	Leaded Regular Motor Gasoline		Residential Heating Oil		Residential Natural Gas		Residential Electricity	
	cents per gallon	dollars per million Btu	cents per gallon	dollars per million Btu	cents per thousand cubic ft.	dollars per million Btu	cents per kilowat hour	dollars per million Btu
1973	NA	NA	NA	NA	121.4	1.19	2.39	7.00
1974	45.1	3.61	NA	NA	121.3	1.18	2.63	7.71
1975	44.1	3.53	NA	NA	132.9	1.30	2.73	8.00
1976	43.4	3.47	NA	NA	145.5	1.43	2.74	8.03
1977	42.9	3.43	NA	NA	162.2	1.59	2.80	8.21
1978	40.1	3.21	31.4	2.26	164.2	1.62	2.76	8.09
1979	49.4	3.95	40.6	2.93	171.8	1.69	2.67	7.83
1980	60.5	4.84	49.4	3.56	186.8	1.82	2.72	7.97
1981	60.4	4.83	54.9	3.96	197.3	1.92	2.85	8.35
1982	53.0	4.24	50.3	3.63	224.1	2.19	2.97	8.70
1983	48.6	3.89	45.3	3.27	251.5	2.45	3.01	8.82

Average Retail Prices for Motor Gasoline[1]

Year	Leaded Regular	Unleaded Regular	Unleaded Premium	Average
		(Cents per gallon, including tax)		
1974	53.2	NA	NA	NA
1975	56.7	NA	NA	NA
1976	59.0	61.4	NA	NA
1977	62.2	65.6	NA	NA
1978	62.6	67.0	NA	65.2
1979	85.7	90.3	NA	88.2
1980	119.1	124.5	NA	122.1
1981	131.1	137.8	147.0	135.3
1982	122.2	129.6	141.5	128.1
1983	115.7	124.1	138.3	122.5

1) Prices are for U.S. city. From 1974-1977, 56 urban areas; from 1978, 85 urban areas.

U.S. Motor Fuel Supply and Demand

(thousands of 42-gallon barrels)

Year	Supply Production	Daily average	Demand Domestic	Export	Year	Supply Production	Daily average	Demand Domestic	Export
1945	793,431	2,174	696,333	88,059	1976	2,549,627	6,966	2,597,305	1,095
1950	1,024,481	2,806	994,290	24,721	1977	2,566,315	7,031	2,619,605	730
1955	1,373,950	3,764	1,329,788	34,521	1978	2,615,955	7,167	2,706,840	365
1960*	1,522,497	4,171	1,511,670	13,456	1979	2,513,937	6,837	2,580,080	(s)
1965	1,733,258	4,749	1,750,028	6,391	1980	2,374,690	6,506	2,401,335	365
1970	2,135,838	5,852	2,162,642	2,956	1981	2,337,825	6,405	2,404,620	730
1971	2,231,157	6,113	2,242,921	3,104	1982	2,313,370	6,338	2,386,735	7,300
1972	2,352,310	6,445	2,382,569	2,165	1983	2,314,000	6,340	2,417,030	3,600
1973	2,434,943	6,671	2,484,262	1,907					
1974	2,371,004	6,496	2,434,368	730					
1975	2,420,962	6,633	2,477,786	730					

(*) Beginning with 1960 Alaska and Hawaii are included; (s) Less than 500 barrels.

U.S. Passenger Car Efficiency

Year	Average fuel consumed per car		Average miles traveled per car		Average miles traveled per gallon of fuel consumed	
	Gallons	Index	Miles	Index	Miles	Index
67	684	100.0	9,531	100.0	13.93	100.0
70	735	107.5	9,978	104.7	13.57	97.4
72	755	110.4	10,184	106.9	13.49	96.8
74	704	102.9	9,448	99.1	13.43	96.4
75	712	104.1	9,634	101.1	13.53	97.1
76	711	103.9	9,763	102.4	13.72	98.5
77	706	103.2	9,839	103.2	13.94	100.1
78	715	104.5	10,046	105.4	14.06	100.9
79	664	97.1	9,485	99.5	14.29	102.6
80	603	88.2	9,135	95.8	15.15	108.8
81	579	84.6	9,002	94.4	15.54	111.6
82	561	82.0	9,167	96.2	16.33	117.2

Major U.S. Public and Private Dams and Reservoirs

Source: Corps of Engineers, U.S. Army

Heights over 350 feet.

Height—Difference in elevation in feet, between lowest point in foundation and top of dam, exclusive of parapet or other projections. **Length**—Overall length of barrier in feet, main dam and its integral features as located between natural abutments. **Volume**—Total volume in cubic yards of all material in main dam and its appurtenant works. **Year**—Date structure was originally completed for use. (UC) Under construction subject to revision. **River**—Mainstream. **Purpose**—I-Irrigation; C-Flood Control; H-Hydroelectric; N-Navigation; S-Water Supply; R-Recreation; D-Debris Control; O-Other. **Parentheses** after name indicate type of dam as follows: (RE)-Earth; (PG)-Gravity; (ER)-Rockfill; (CB)-Buttress; (VA)-Arch; (MV)-Multi-arch; (OT)-Other.

Name of dam	State	River	Ht.	Lgth.	Vol. (1,000)	Purpose	Year
Oroville (RE)	Cal.	Feather River	756	6800	78000	IRCSH	1968
Hoover (VA)	Nev.	Colorado River	726	1242	4400	IHCO	1936
Dworshak (PG)	Ida.	North Fork of Clearwater	717	3287	6450	HCR	1973
Glen Canyon (VA)	Ariz.	Colorado River	710	1560	4901	HCSR	1966
New Bullards Bar (VA)	Cal.	North Yuba River	635	2200	2600	SH	1970
New Melones (ER)	Cal.	Stanislaus River	625	1560	16000	IHCR	1979
Swift (RE)	Wash.	North Fork Lewis River	610	2100	15400	HRC	1958
Mossyrock (VA)	Wash.	Cowlitz River	606	1648	1270	HCR	1968
Shasta (PG)	Cal.	Sacramento River	602	3460	8711	ISHN	1945
Don Pedro (RE)	Cal.	Tuolumne River	568	1800	16000	H	1971
Hungry Horse (VA)	Mon.	South Fork of Flathead River	564	2115	3086	IHCN	1953
Grand Coulee (PG)	Wash.	Columbia River	550	4173	10585	IHCN	1942
Ross (RE)	Wash.	Skagit River	540	1300	919	HR	1949
Trinity (RE)	Cal.	Trinity River	537	2450	29410	IHCR	1962
Yellowtail (VA)	Mon.	Bighorn River	525	1480	1546	ICHR	1966
Cougar (ER)	Ore.	South Fork McKenzie River	519	1600	13000	HCIR	1964
Flaming Gorge (VA)	Ut.	Green River	502	1285	987	HCSR	1964
Fontana (PG)	N.C.	Little Tennessee River	480	2365	3576	H	1944
New Exchequer (ER)	Cal.	Merced River	479	1240	5169	H	1926
Little Blue Run (RE)	Penn.	Little Blue Run	400	2100	13000	—	1977
Morrow Point (VA)	Col.	Gunnison River	468	741	365	HCR	1968
Carters (ER)	Ga.	Coosawattee River	464	1950	15000	CHR	1974
Detroit (PG)	Ore.	North Santiam River	463	1580	1500	HCRI	1953
Anderson Ranch (RE)	Ida.	South Fork Boise River	456	1350	9653	IHCR	1950
Union Valley (RE)	Cal.	Silver Creek	453	1800	10000	S	1963
Round Butte (RE)	Ore.	Deschutes River	440	1450	9600	HR	1964
Pine Flat Lake (PG)	Cal.	Kings River	440	1840	2400	CIRH	1954
Jocassee (ER)	S.C.	Keowee River	435	1800	11600	H	1973
O'Shaughnessy (PG)	Cal.	Moccasin Creek	430	900	663	HS	1923
Mud Mountain (ER)	Wash.	White River	425	700	2300	C	1948
Libby (PG)	Mon.	Kootenai River	422	2890	3760	HCR	1973
Pacoima (VA)	Cal.	Pacoima Creek	420	640	226	C	1929
Owyhee (VA)	Ore.	Owyhee River	417	833	538	ICR	1932
Lower Hell Hole (ER)	Cal.	Rubicon River	410	1550	8315	SH	1966
Castaic (RE)	Cal.	Castaic Creek	410	5200	44000	IRS	1973
Mammoth Pool (RE)	Cal.	San Joaquin River	406	820	5355	HS	1960
San Gabriel No. 1 (ER)	Cal.	San Gabriel River	405	1520	10600	CS	1939
Navajo (RE)	N.M.	San Juan River	402	3648	26840	IR	1963
No name (RE)	S.C.	Jocassee River	400	1000		H	1973
Pyramid (ER)	Cal.	Piru Creek	400	1080	6952	IRSH	1973
Bath County Upper (ER,RE)	Va.	Little Bush Creek	470	2398	23544	H	198
Brownlee (ER)	Ida.	Snake River	395	1380	6000	HCR	1958
Summersville (ER)	W.Va.	Gauley River	390	2280	13565	CRS	1966
Blue Mesa (REER)	Col.	Gunnison River	390	785	3080	HCR	1966
Diablo (VA)	Wash.	Skagit River	386	1180	350	HR	1929
San Luis (RE)	Cal.	San Luis Creek	382	18500	77900	ISHR	1967
Green Peter (PG)	Ore.	Middle Santiam River	378	1517	1142	CHRI	1967
Merriman (RE)	N.Y.	Roundout Creek	375	2400	5800	S	194
Arrowrock (VA)	Ida.	Boise River	350	1150	636	ICR	1915

Production of Electricity in the U.S. by Source[1]

Includes both privately-owned and publicly-owned utilities.

(million kilowatt hours)

Amount and Percentage Produced by Source

Year	Total Production	Coal	%	Oil	%	Gas	%	Nuclear	%	Hydro	%
1975	1,917,649	852,786	44.5	289,095	15.1	299,778	15.6	172,505	9.0	300,047	15
1980	2,286,439	1,161,562	50.8	245,994	10.8	346,240	15.1	251,116	11.0	276,021	12
1981	2,294,812	1,203,203	52.4	206,421	9.0	345,777	15.1	272,674	11.9	260,684	11
1982	2,241,211	1,192,004	53.2	146,797	6.5	305,260	13.6	282,773	12.6	309,213	13
1983	2,310,285	1,259,424	54.5	144,499	6.3	274,098	11.9	293,677	12.7	332,130	14

(1) Other sources, representing less than one percent of production, include geothermal power, wood, and waste.

U.S. Electricity Sales

	Commercial	Industrial	Residential	Other[1]	Total[2]		Commercial	Industrial	Residential	Other[1]	Total
1975	403,049	687,680	588,140	68,222	1,747,091	1981	514,338	825,742	722,265	84,756	2,147,1
1980	488,156	815,067	717,495	73,732	2,094,449	1982	526,397	744,949	729,512	85,575	2,086,4
						1983	543,788	775,999	750,948	80,219	2,150,0

(1) Includes sales to government, railways, street lighting authorities. (2) Totals may not equal sum of components due to independent rounding.

World's Largest Hydroelectric Plants

Source: Bureau of Reclamation, U.S. Dept. of The Interior

Rank order	Name, country	Rated capacity (present) MW	(ultimate) MW	Year of initial operation	Rank order	Name, country	Rated Capacity (present) MW	(ultimate) MW	Year of initial operation
1.	Itaipu, Brazil/ Paraguay	—	12600	UC(1983)	29.	Itaparica, Brazil	—	2500	UC(1985)
2.	Grand Coulee, U.S.A.	6430	10080	1942	30.	Bennett W.A.C.,			
3.	Guri (Raul Leoni),					Canada	2116	2416	1969
	Venezuela	2800	10060	1968	31.	Chicoasén, Mexico	—	2400	1980
4.	Tucuruí, Brazil	—	6480	UC(1982)	32.	Atatürk, Turkey	—	2400	UC(1990)
5.	Sayano-Shushensk,				33.	LaGrande 3, Canada	—	2304	UC(1982)
	USSR	—	6400	1980	34.	Volga-V.I. Lenin, USSR	2300	2300	1955
6.	Corpus-Christi,				35.	Iron Gates I,			
	Argentina/Paraguay	—	6000	UC(1990)		Romania/Yugoslavia	2300	2300	1970
7.	Krasnoyarsk, USSR	6096	6096	1968	36.	Fos do Areia, Brazil	2250	2250	UC(1983)
8.	LaGrande 2, Canada	—	5328	UC(1982)	37.	Itumbiara, Brazil	—	2124	UC(1982)
9.	Churchill Falls, Canada	5225	5225	1971	38.	Bath County, U.S.A.	—	2100	UC(1985)
10.	Bratsk, USSR	4100	4600	1964	39.	High Aswan			
11.	Ust'-Ilimsk, USSR	3675	4500	1974		(Saad-el-Aali), Egypt	2100	2100	1967
12.	Cabora Bassa,				40.	Tarbella, Pakistan	1400	2100	1977
	Mozambique	2075	4150	1974	41.	Piedra de Aquila,			
13.	Yacyretá-Apipe,					Argentina	—	2100	UC(1989)
	Argentina/Paraguay	—	4050	UC(1986)	42.	Chief Joseph, U.S.A.	2069	2069	1956
14.	Rogun, USSR	—	3600	UC(1985)	43.	Salto Santiago, Brazil	—	2031	1980
15.	Randolph-Hunting,				44.	McNary, U.S.A.	980	2030	1954
	U.S.A.	—	3575	UC(1991)	45.	Green River, U.S.A.	—	2000	1980
16.	Paulo Afonso, Brazil	1524	3409	1955	46.	Tehri, India	—	2000	UC(1990)
17.	Pati (Chapéton),				47.	Cornwall, U.S.A.	—	2000	1978
	Argentina	—	3300	UC(1990)	48.	Ludington, U.S.A.	1979	1979	1973
18.	Brumley Gap, U.S.A.	3200	3200	1973	49.	Robert Moses-			
19.	Inga I, Zaire	360	2820	1974		Niagara, U.S.A.	1950	1950	1961
20.	Gezhouba, China	—	2715	UC(1986)	50.	Salto Grande,			
21.	John Day, U.S.A.	2160	2700	1969		Argentina/Uruguay	—	1890	1979
22.	Nurek, USSR	900	2700	1976	51.	Saunders-Moses,			
23.	Revelstoke, Canada	—	2700	UC(1983)		Canada/U.S.A.	1824	1824	1958
24.	Sao Simao, Brazil	2680	2680	1979	52.	The Dalles, U.S.A.	1119	1807	1957
25.	Ilha Solteira, Brazil	2650	2650	1973	53.	Karakaya, Turkey	—	1800	UC(1985)
26.	LaGrande 4, Canada	—	2637	UC(1984)	54.	Dinorwic, Great Britain	—	1800	UC(1982)
27.	Mica, Canada	1736	2610	1976	55.	Grand'Maison, France	—	1800	1984
28.	Volgograd-22nd				56.	Kayalaan, Philippines	—	1800	UC(1983)
	Congress, USSR	2560	2560	1958	57.	Inga II, Zaire	180	1750	1979

Largest Hydroelectric Plants in U.S.

(Capacities as of Aug. 21, 1984)

Plant Name	State	Owner	Installed Capacity (KW)
Coulee Dam	Washington	USBR-Pacific NW Region	6,494,000
John Day	Oregon	USCE-North Pacific Div	2,160,000
Chf Joseph	Washington	USCE-North Pacific Div	2,069,000
LD Pump St	Michigan	Consumers Power Co	1,978,800
Moses Niag	New York	Power Authy of St of NY	1,950,000
Dalles Dam	Oregon	USCE-North Pacific Div	1,806,800
Raccoon Mt	Tennessee	Tennessee Valley Auth	1,530,000
Castaic	California	Los Angeles (city of)	1,331,000
Rocky Reach	Washington	Chelan Pub Util Dist #1	1,213,950
Bonneville	Oregon	USCE-North Pacific Div	1,076,000
Blenheim G	New York	Power Authy of St of NY	1,000,000
McNary	Oregon	USCE-North Pacific Div	980,000
Glen Canyon	Arizona	USBR-Upper Colorado Reg	950,000
Moses Pr Dm	New York	Power Authy of St of NY	912,000
Northfld Mt	Massachusetts	W Massachusetts Elec Co	846,000
Wanapum	Washington	Grant Pub Util Dist #2	831,250
Little Goose	Washington	USCE-North Pacific Div	810,000
Monumental	Washington	USCE-North Pacific Div	810,000
Lwr Granite	Washington	USCE-North Pacific Div	810,000
Muddy Run	Pennsylvania	Philadelphia Elec Co	800,000
Priest Rpds	Washington	Grant Pub Util Dist #2	788,500
Wells	Washington	Douglas Pub Util Dist #1	774,300
Edwrd Hyatt	California	California (State of)	714,600
Hoover Dam	Nevada	USBR-Lower Colorado Reg	672,500
Hoover Dam	Arizona	USBR-Lower Colorado Reg	667,500
Boundary	Washington	Seattle (city of)	634,600
Wilson Dam	Alabama	Tennessee Valley Auth	629,840
Rock Island	Washington	Chelan Pub Util Dist #1	622,500
Jocassee	South Carolina	Duke Power Co	610,000
Ice Harbor	Washington	USCE-North Pacific Div	603,000
Bear Swamp	Massachusetts	New England Elec System	600,000
Oahe	South Dakota	USCE-Omaha District	595,000
Brownlee	Idaho	Idaho Power Co	585,400
Smith Mt	Virginia	Appalachian Power Co	547,250
Shasta Dam	California	USBR-Mid Pacific Region	535,000
Fairfield	South Carolina	So Carolina Elec & Gas Co	511,200
Carters	Georgia	USCE-Alt-Buf-Cart Prj	500,000

Major World Dams

Source: Int'l Commission on Large Dams. (1) Bureau of Reclamation, U.S. Interior Dept. *Replaces existing dam.
Volume in cubic yards. Capacity (gross) in acre feet. Year of completion. U.C. under construction.
Type: A—Arch. B—Buttress. E—Earthfill. G—Gravity. R—Rockfill. MA—Multi-arch.

Name of dam	Type	Year	River and basin	Country	Height Feet	Crest Length Feet	Vol- ume (1,000 C.Y.)	Res. cap. (1,000 A.F.)
Afsluitdijk	E	1932	Zuider Zee	Netherlands	62	105,000	82,927	4,864
Akosombo-Main	R	1965	Volta	Ghana	463	2,100	10,333	120,000
Almendra	A	1970	Turmes-Douro	Spain	662	1,860	2,188	2,148
Alpe Gera	G	1965	Comor-Adda-Po	Italy	584	1,710	2,252	53
Bagdad Tailings	E	1973	Maroney Gulch	U.S.A.	121	6,601	37,303	40
Beas	G	1974	Beas-Indus	India	436	6,400	46,325	6,600
W.A.C. Bennett*	E	1967	Peace-Mackenzie	Canada	600	6,700	57,201	57,006
Bhakra	G	1963	Sutlend-Indus	India	741	1,700	5,400	8,002
Bratsk	GE	1964	Angara	USSR	410	16,864	18,283	137,220
Brouwershavense Gat.	E	1972	.	Netherlands	118	20,341	35,315	466
Castaic	E	1973	Castaic Cr.	U.S.A.	340	5,200	44,000	350
Charvak	E	1970	Chirchik-Sir Darya	USSR	552	2,507	28,252	1,620
Chirkey	A	1975	Sulak-Caspian Sea	USSR	764	1,093	1,776	2,252
Chivor	R	1975	Bata	Colombia	778	919	14,126	661
Cochiti (1).	E	1975	Rio Grande	U.S.A.	250	28,000	62,128	596
Copper Cities Tailing 2	E	1973	Tinhorn Wash.	U.S.A.	325	7,598	30,002	4
Cougar	R	1964	S.F. McKenzie	U.S.A.	518	1,601	13,001	219
Dartmouth	R	1978	Mitta-Mitta	Australia	591	2,200	18,312	3,243
Dneprodzerzhinsk	GE	1964	Dnieper	USSR	112	116,306	28,502	1,994
Don Pedro*	R	1971	Tuolume-San Joaquin	U.S.A.	584	1,900	16,761	2,030
Dworshak	G	1974	N. Fork Clearwater	U.S.A.	717	3,287	6,500	3,453
El Chocon	E	1974	Limay	Argentina	282	7,546	17,003	17,025
Emosson	A	1974	Barberine	Switz.	590	1,821	1,426	184
Esperanza Tailings	E	1973	Santa Cruz	U.S.A.	121	10,600	39,704	5
Fort Peck (1)	E	1940	Missouri	U.S.A.	250	21,026	125,628	19,100
Fort Randall (1)	E	1956	Missouri	U.S.A.	160	10,700	50,200	6,100
Gardiner*	E	1968	South Saskatchewan	Canada	223	16,700	85,592	8,000
Garrison (1).	E	1956	Missouri	U.S.A.	210	12,000	66,500	24,400
Gepatsch	R	1965	Faggenbach-Inn.	Austria	502	1,908	9,286	113
Glen Canyon (1)	A	1964	Colorado	U.S.A.	710	1,560	4,901	27,000
Goscheneralp	E	1960	Goschenerreuss	Switz.	508	1,771	12,230	62
Grand Coulee (1)	G	1942	Columbia	U.S.A.	550	5,673	11,976	9,386
Grande Dixence	G	1962	Dixence-Rhone	Switz.	935	2,280	7,792	324
Guri (Raul Leoni)	GE	1986U.C.	Caroni-Orinoco	Venezuela	348	22,966	102,014	110,256
Haringvliet	E	1970	Haringvliet	Netherlands	79	18,044	26,159	527
High Aswan (Saad-el-Aali)	ER	1970	Nile	Egypt	364	12,565	55,745	137,000
Hirakud	GE	1956	Mahandi	India	194	15,748	32,830	6,571
Hoover (1)	AG	1936	Colorado	U.S.A.	726	1,244	3,246	28,537
Hungry Horse (1)	AG	1953	S. Fork Flathead	U.S.A.	564	2,115	3,086	3,468
Ilha Solteira.	EG	1973	Parana Rio de la Plata	Brazil.	243	20,292	34,368	17,159
Irkutsk	GE	1956	Angara	USSR	144	8,989	16,219	37,290
Iroquois	G	1958	St. Lawrence	Canada	75	2,665	175	24,288
Ivankovo	EG	1937	Volga-Caspian S.	USSR	74	31,837	19,881	908
Jari	E	1967	Jhelum	Pakistan	233	5,500	42,900	400
Daniel Johnson*	MA	1968	Manicouagan-St. Lawrence	Canada	703	4,311	2,949	115,000
Kakhovka	EG	1955	Dnieper	USSR	121	5,380	46,617	14,755
Kanev	E	1976	Dnieper	USSR	82	52,950	49,520	2,125
Kapshagay	E	1970	Ili	USSR	164	1,542	5,078	22,813
Kariba	A	1959	Zambezi	Zimbabwe-Zambia	417	2,025	1,33	147,218
Kárun	A	1975	Karoun	Iran.	656	1,247	1,570	2,351
Keban	ERG	1974	Firat (Euphrates)	Turkey	656	3,599	19,619	25,110
Kiev	E	1964	Dnieper	USSR	72	177,448	56,034	3,021
Kremasta (King Paul)	ER	1965	Acheloüs.	Greece.	541	1,510	10,686	3,850
Kremenchug	EG	1961	Dnieper	USSR	108	39,844	41,190	10,945
Kurobe No. 4	A	1964	Kurobe	Japan	610	1,603	1,782	162
Lauwerszee	E	1969	Lauwerszee	Netherlands	75	42,650	46,532	40
Ludington	E	1973	Lake Michigan	U.S.A.	170	29,301	37,703	83
Luzzone	A	1963	Brenno di Luzzone	Switz.	682	1,738	1,739	71
Mangla	E	1967	Jhelum	Pakistan	453	11,000	85,872	5,154
Marimbondo	E	1975	Grande	Brazil	295	11,811	18,965	4,986
Mauvoisin	A	1957	Drance de Bagnes	Switz.	777	1,706	2,655	146
Mica	E	1973	Columbia	Canada	794	2,600	42,001	20,000
Mingechaur	E	1953	Kura	USSR	262	5,085	20,404	12,971
Navajo (1)	E	1963	San Juan.	U.S.A.	402	3,648	26,841	1,709
New Bullards Bar	A	1968	North Yuba-Sacramento	U.S.A.	637	2,064	2,700	960
New Cornelia Tailings	E	1973	Ten Mile Wash, Ariz.	U.S.A.	98	35,600	274,015	20
New Melones (1).	R	1979	Stanislaus	U.S.A.	625	1,650	15,708	2,400
Oahe (1)	E	1963	Missouri	U.S.A.	246	9,300	92,000	23,600
Okutadami	G	1961	Tadami.	Japan	515	1,575	2,145	487
Oroville	E	1968	Feather-Sacramento	U.S.A.	770	6,920	78,008	3,538
Owen Falls	G	1954	Lake Victoria-Nile.	Uganda	100	2,725	.	166,000
Place Moulin	AG	1965	Buthier-Dora Baltea	Italy	502	2,181	1,962	84
Rybinsk	GE	1941	Volga-Caspian S.	USSR	98	2,060	3,329	20,595
Sakuma	G	1956	Tenryu	Japan	510	963	1,465	265
San Luis (1).	E	1967	San Luis	U.S.A.	382	18,600	77,670	2,041
Saratov	E	1967	Volga-Caspian S.	USSR	131	37,204	52,843	10,452
Shasta (1)	AG	1945	Sacramento	U.S.A.	602	3,460	8,430	4,552
Swift	E	1958	Lewis-Columbia	U.S.A.	610	2,100	15,800	755
Tabka	E	1976	Euphrates	Syria	197	14,764	60,168	11,357
Talbingo	R	1971	Tamut	Australia	531	2,300	18,950	742
Tarbela	ER	1976	Indus	Pakistan	469	8,999	159,203	11,098
Trinity (1)	E	1962	Trinity.	U.S.A.	537	2,450	29,400	2,448
Tsimlyansk	EG	1952	Don	USSR	128	43,412	44,323	17,717
Tuttle Creek	E	1962	Big Blue-Missouri	U.S.A.	154	7,500	22,936	41
Twin Buttes (1)	E	1963	Mid and So. Concho R., Spring Cr.	U.S.A.	240	42,460	21,407	64
Twin Buttes Tailings	E	1973	Santa Cruz	U.S.A.	239	11,299	38,604	20
Vilyuy	E	1967	Vilyuy.	USSR	246	2,297	3,793	29,102
Volga-22d Congress.	ERG	1958	Volga-Caspian S.	USSR	144	13,108	33,918	25,496
Volga-V. I. Lenin	EG	1955	Volga-Caspian S.	USSR	148	12,405	44,299	47,020
Yellowtail (1)	A	1966	Bighorn.	U.S.A.	525	1,480	1,546	1,375
Zeya.	G	1975	Zeya	USSR	377	2,343	3,139	55,450

ENVIRONMENT

Environmental Quality Index

Source: Copyright 1984 by the National Wildlife Federation.
Reprinted with permission from the Feb.-Mar., 1984 issue of NATIONAL WILDLIFE Magazine.

The first Environmental Quality Index was published by NATIONAL WILDLIFE in 1969. This article discusses the changes that have taken place in the environment over the past 15 years and recounts important events of 1983.

Wildlife: Several endangered and threatened U.S. animals have staged comebacks because of a proliferation of refuges and a steady infusion of money into many state management programs. The wild turkey has been restored to 43 states, and the Atlantic salmon successfully reintroduced to New England waters that were totally devoid of the fish for more than a century. In many parts of the East, the bald eagle is steadily increasing its numbers yearly as a result of protective laws and aggressive reintroduction programs.

Other lesser-known or non-game animals have not done as well. The blue pike was declared officially extinct in 1983, a victim of over-fishing and pollution. An estimated two to three million ducks and geese die each year from lead poisoning after ingesting lead shot. In Colorado, brown trout only live half as long as they used to, because of pollution from mining. The poisoning affects other species along the food chain.

Although 28 states have adopted income tax checkoff programs to help increase funding for non-game wildlife programs, many programs have suffered from a lack of federal funds. In 1983, the Interior Department sought budget cuts for its endangered species program. Little money was available for research or habitat purchases needed to carry out required recovery plans for imperiled creatures. Interior also pushed to open up several dozen National Wildlife Refuges to oil and gas development. The National Wildlife Federation filed suit to stop the plan.

Congress approved nearly $50 million for wetlands and refuge acquisitions for 1984, but it also appropriated more funds for the controversial Garrison Diversion Project in North Dakota—a massive system of irrigation canals and lakes that will drain, thus destroy, more than 70,000 acres of wetlands and portions of 12 National Wildlife Refuges.

Air: A cleaner fleet of U.S. automobiles has improved the quality of the nation's air considerably in the past 15 years in many areas. Air quality has held steady in other areas despite increases in population, urban density, industry and traffic.

In 1970, the President's Council on Environmental Quality estimated the nation's air was polluted with more than 200 million tons of potentially dangerous substances, including 110 million tons of carbon monoxide, 30 million tons of sulfur dioxide, and 20 million tons of soot and other particulate matter. By 1980, carbon monoxide emissions were reduced to 85 million tons a year, sulfur dioxide was down to 27 million tons, and particulates were cut to 8 million tons.

Today's vehicles emit 90 percent less carbon monoxide than their 1970 counterparts. All but 11 states have implemented required vehicle inspection programs.

However, ozone, a pollutant created by a combination of industrial and automobile emissions, is harder to control. In 1983, more than 90 million Americans were exposed to ozone levels above the national standard intended to protect human health. Scientists are concerned now about the effects of sulfates, minute particles produced when sulfur dioxide emissions from industries and power plants react in the air. Their fine particles are proving far more hazardous to humans than are many other pollutants. These same sulfates, swept along on high winds, are coming down in the form of unwelcome acid rain, damaging aquatic life and buildings and threatening forests and crops throughout much of the country. In 1983, the National Academy of Sciences reported a direct link between the sulfur dioxide spewing from smokestacks and the death of aquatic life in parts of the U.S. and Canada.

Water: Though toxic waste contamination and nonpoint pollution are still severe problems, the Council on Environmental Quality reports that most U.S. surface waterways are meeting the Clean Water Act's 1983 goal of being "fishable and swimmable."

Progress has been expensive, however. During the past decade, the federal government has spent more than $37 billion on the problem, much of it for sewer plant construction. Many of those plants are not operating properly or are incapable of handling many chemical wastes, leaving large metropolitan areas still releasing billions of gallons of untreated sewage.

Nonpoint pollution, created by runoff from farms, city streets and construction sites, continues to be a pressing clean-water problem. Some estimates state this uncontrolled runoff accounts for more than half the water pollution in the U.S.

Conservationists are also concerned about the depletion and contamination of subsurface waters. In the last 30 years, withdrawals from the nation's groundwater supplies have nearly tripled, outstripping nature's ability to recharge aquifers in some areas. Even where underground water is plentiful, pollution is seeping downward at an alarming rate, poisoning drinking water supplies for millions of Americans. In virtually every state, wells have been closed because of dangerous levels of toxics.

Although the full extent of such pollution is not known, EPA has increased the number of abandoned hazardous waste dumps receiving top priority for cleanup.

Soil: The steady loss of topsoil from America's farmlands continued in 1983, despite dramatic increases in the use of conservation tillage practices. Even though Uncle Sam has spent more than $20 billion in recent years to reverse the trend, erosion continues.

The average acre of cropland currently loses about 6.8 tons of soil a year to the wind and water, about the same as in 1977. The amount of land being cultivated has remained relatively stable, but more and more fragile hillsides and highly erodible prairies are being farmed as developments gobble up more desirable farmland.

Minerals: Americans have made major strides in reducing their consumption of electric power and gasoline over the past 15 years. Jolted by the Arab oil embargo of 1973, the nation began to think seriously about conservation. However, energy "independence" remains elusive, and the country now seems to be relaxing its conservation efforts. In 1983, for the first time in several years, the gasoline efficiency of new U.S. automobiles declined.

The administration continued to press for nuclear power in 1983, funneling 61 percent of the Department of Energy's energy technologies budget into nuclear research, compared to 4 percent for energy conservation. To keep programs for renewable energy sources, such as solar power, from disappearing, Congress had to step in by approving funds the administration had not requested.

Congress accused the Interior Department of raiding the national savings account with its "fire sales" of coal leases on U.S. lands. Conservationists were also concerned about the government's ability to safeguard the environment under the speed of energy development. Under Interior's accelerated five-year program of offshore oil leasing, virtually the entire U.S. coastline will be offered for lease by 1987.

Living space: Americans are moving to the country, reversing a trend almost as old as the nation itself. This "outmigration," means the nation will have to eventually re-examine policies based on the idea that pollution would continue to be concentrated primarily in traditional urban areas.

In New Hampshire, Colorado, Virginia and other havens for thousands of people fleeing from the crowded industrial cities, clear air is becoming dim from increased energy and automobile use, and rolling valleys are being subdivided into "farmettes."

By the year 2000, the U.S. Census Bureau predicts, six of every 10 U.S. residents will live either in the South or the West. The greatest population growth is expected to occur in the arid Southwest, putting more pressure on already limited water supplies. The move to the country also increases the competition between people and wildlife for the limited natural resources of the land.

Americans are continuing to place added strain on the nation's parklands. Visits to national park facilities have increased by nearly 400 percent since 1960, to more than 300 million visits a year. In 1983, Congress allocated more than $114 million for new federal parkland acquisitions. By the end of the fiscal year, the Interior Department had spent less than 70 percent of the funds Congress had earlier committed for new parklands.

Forests: Although forests still cover a third of the nation's land, and Americans continue to grow more wood than they cut, the amount of U.S. forestland is decreasing slightly. Along the Pacific Coast, harvesting of lumber-quality "saw timber" has exceeded the annual growth rate for 30 years.

Because large, commercially owned timber tracts have been heavily harvested in many areas, publicly owned forests have come under increasing pressure. Although the amount of timber sold on National Forest land was down slightly last year, the actual harvest in federal woodlands was up by 25 percent.

Because so much of the timber on accessible National Forest land has already been harvested, timber is now being taken from environmentally sensitive regions. As harvests increase, wildlife habitat declines.

In addition to increasing timbering on public lands last year, the Forest Service also processed nearly 3,400 new mineral leases in its domain, opening up additional acreage to mineral development.

Hazardous Waste Sites

Source: Environmental Protection Agency

As of August, 1984 there were 546 abandoned hazardous waste sites (including 133 scheduled to be finalized in Sept.) on the EPA's "national priority list" of sites requiring remedial action for posing the gravest threats to public health and the environment. The map shows the number of locations given priority for cleanup, by state. New Jersey has the most—85 sites. The EPA has identified more than 17,000 hazardous waste sites around the country, and by 1985 the priority list is expected to include at least 1,000 sites.

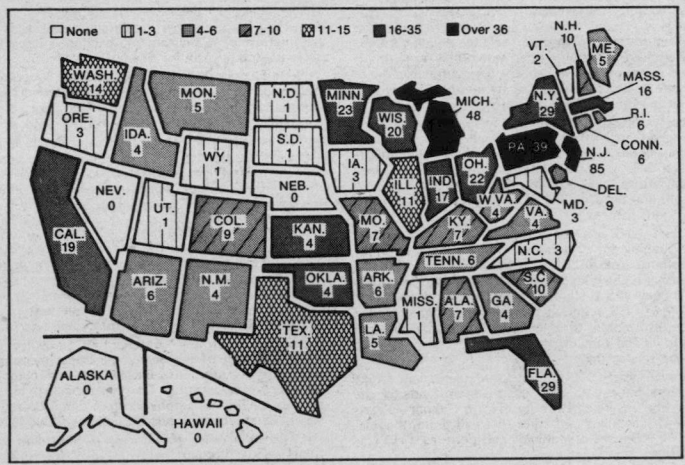

Investment for Pollution Control by U.S. Industries

Source: Bureau of Economic Analysis, U.S. Commerce Department
(billions of dollars)

New plant and equipment expenditures by U.S. nonfarm business: total and for pollution abatement

	1983ᵖ Pollution abatement					Planned 1984 Pollution abatement				
	Total expenditures[1]	Total	Air	Water	Solid waste	Total expenditures[1]	Total	Air	Water	Solid waste
Total nonfarm business	302.50	7.24	3.66	2.90	.68	343.57	7.64	3.79	2.85	1.00
Manufacturing	111.53	4.01	1.72	1.94	.36	129.72	4.31	1.75	2.07	.49
Durable goods	51.78	1.33	.65	.55	.13	62.78	1.62	.76	.68	.18
Primary metals[2]	6.39	.36	.19	.15	.02	7.23	.50	.26	.20	.04
Blast furnaces, steel works	2.97	.19	.08	.11	(*)	3.27	.29	.12	.16	.01
Nonferrous metals	2.44	.13	.10	.02	(*)	2.73	.17	.13	.03	.01
Fabricated metals	2.22	.03	.01	.02	.01	2.57	.05	.01	.03	(*)
Electrical machinery	10.90	.14	.04	.08	.01	13.48	.15	.04	.10	.01
Machinery, except elec.	12.35	.26	.08	.15	.04	14.73	.28	.09	.15	.04
Transportation equipment[3]	13.02	.30	.17	.10	.03	16.65	.33	.17	.13	.04
Motor vehicles	7.17	.24	.15	.07	.02	9.61	.24	.13	.09	.02
Aircraft	4.93	.05	.02	.02	.01	5.93	.08	.03	.04	.01
Stone, clay, and glass	2.45	.07	.04	.02	.01	2.81	.12	.09	.02	.02
Other durables[3]	4.45	.17	.12	.03	.01	5.30	.19	.10	.06	.03
Nondurable goods	59.75	2.68	1.06	1.39	.23	66.93	2.69	.98	1.39	.31
Food including beverage	6.60	.25	.13	.10	.02	6.76	.20	.10	.08	.02
Textiles	1.39	.03	.01	.02	(*)	1.78	.03	.01	.01	(*)
Paper	6.18	.25	.16	.07	.02	7.13	.39	.22	.10	.07
Chemicals	13.28	.57	.21	.28	.05	14.34	.55	.18	.32	.05
Petroleum	23.48	1.55	.51	.91	.12	26.51	1.50	.47	.88	.15
Rubber	1.91	.01	(*)	(*)	(*)	2.21	.01	(*)	.01	(*)
Other nondurables[4]	6.91	.04	.02	.02	.01	8.20	.02	.01	(*)	.01
Nonmanufacturing	190.97	3.23	1.94	.96	.32	213.86	3.33	2.04	.78	.50
Mining	11.83	.26	.08	.14	.05	14.34	.26	.08	.12	.07
Transportation	11.20	.06	.02	.05	(*)	12.00	.08	.02	.05	(*)
Railroad	3.92	.03	(*)	.02	(*)	4.73	.04	(*)	.03	(*)
Air	3.77	(*)	(*)	.00	.00	2.78	.01	.01	.00	.00
Other	3.50	.04	.01	.03	(*)	4.49	.04	.01	.02	(*)
Public utilities	42.00	2.77	1.78	.75	.24	44.79	2.85	1.88	.58	.39
Electric	34.99	2.69	1.74	.72	.23	35.54	2.64	1.82	.46	.37
Gas and other	7.00	.07	.04	.03	(*)	9.24	.21	.06	.12	.02
Trade and services	87.94	.10	.05	.02	.03	100.25	.12	.05	.03	.04
Communication and other[5]	38.02	.03	.02	.01	(*)	42.47	.02	.01	.01	(*)

ᵖ Preliminary (1) Consists of final estimates taken from the quarterly surveys of total new plant and equipment and, for 1983, plans based on the 1982 fourth-quarter survey taken in late January and February 1983. (2) Includes industries not shown separately. (3) Consists of lumber, furniture, instruments, and miscellaneous. (4) Consists of apparel, tobacco, leather, and printing-publishing. (5) Consists of communication; construction; social services and membership organizations; and forestry, fisheries, and agricultural services. *Less than $5 million.

U.S. Forest Land by State and Region

Source: Forest Service, U.S. Agriculture Department, 1979.

State or region	Land area (1,000 acres)	Area forested	Percent forested	State or region	Land area (1,000 acres)	Area forested	Percent forested
Connecticut	3,081	1,861	60	Arkansas	33,091	18,282	55
Maine	19,729	17,718	90	Florida	33,994	17,040	50
Massachusetts	5,007	2,952	59	Georgia	36,796	25,256	69
New Hampshire	5,731	5,013	87	Louisiana	28,409	14,558	51
Rhode Island	664	404	61	Mississippi	29,930	16,716	56
Vermont	5,907	4,512	76	North Carolina	30,956	20,043	65
New England	**40,119**	**32,460**	**81**	Oklahoma	43,728	8,513	19
Delaware	1,233	392	32	South Carolina	19,143	12,249	64
Maryland	6,289	2,653	42	Tennessee	26,290	13,161	50
New Jersey	4,775	1,928	40	Texas	167,283	23,279	14
New York	30,357	17,218	57	Virginia	25,286	16,417	65
Pennsylvania	28,592	16,826	59	**South**	**474,906**	**185,514**	**39**
West Virginia	15,334	11,669	76	Alaska	362,485	119,145	33
Mid Atlantic	**87,813**	**50,686**	**58**	California	99,847	40,152	48
Michigan	30,634	19,270	63	Hawaii	4,109	1,986	40
Minnesota	50,382	16,709	33	Oregon	61,356	29,810	49
North Dakota	43,939	422	1	Washington	42,456	23,181	55
South Dakota	48,381	1,702	4	**Pacific Coast**	**570,253**	**214,274**	**38**
Wisconsin	34,616	14,908	43	Arizona	72,580	18,494	25
Lake States	**207,952**	**53,011**	**25**	Colorado	66,283	22,271	34
Illinois	35,442	3,810	11	Idaho	52,676	21,726	41
Indiana	22,951	3,943	17	Montana	92,826	22,559	24
Iowa	35,634	1,561	4	Nevada	70,295	7,683	11
Kansas	52,127	1,344	3	New Mexico	77,669	18,060	23
Kentucky	25,282	12,161	48	Utah	52,505	15,557	30
Missouri	43,868	12,876	29	Wyoming	62,055	10,028	16
Nebraska	48,828	1,029	2	**Rocky Mountain**	**546,959**	**136,378**	**25**
Ohio	26,121	6,147	24				
Central	**241,425**	**42,871**	**18**	**Total U.S.**	**2,169,427**	**'715,194**	**33**
Alabama	32,231	21,361	66				

(1) Of this total, 482,486,000 acres are of commercial quality (137 million acres are government owned); 20,664,000 acres are productive but reserved (land set aside by statute); 4,626,000 acres are deferred for possible reserve status; and 228,782,000 acres are unproductive or awaiting survey.

Major U.S. and Canadian Public Zoological Parks

Source: World Almanac questionnaire, 1984; budget, metro population, and attendance in millions. (A) park has not provided up-to-date data.

Zoo	Budget	Attendance	Acres	Species	Major Attractions
Albuquerque (A)	$2.0	0.4	50	281	Rain forest exhibit, reptile house.
Arizona-Sonora Desert Museum (Tucson)	2.5	0.5	12	300	Earth science center, Sonora Desert exhibit.
Bronx (N.Y.C.)	22.0	2.0	265	699	Wild Asia, children's zoo, World of Birds.
Brookfield (Chicago) (A)	14.5	1.8	200	500	Porpoise show, predator ecology, baboon island.
Buffalo (A)	2.3	0.4	24	234	Rhino yard, tropical gorilla exhibit, children's zoo.
Calgary (A)	6.5	0.75	220	325	Exotic vertebrates, prehistoric park, tropical conservatory.
Cincinnati	4.3	0.9	64	780	Gorilla World, Insect World, World of Cats.
Cleveland	3.5	0.7	130	300	Birds of the World, African Plains.
Columbia, S.C.	1.5	0.4	50	162	Natural habitat exhibits, rain forest exhibit.
Dallas	2.4	0.6	50	507	Okapi, bongo antelope, Grevy's zebra.
Denver	3.0	1.0	76	400	Bird world, Bighorn and Dall sheep exhibit.
Detroit	6.2	0.8	122	430	Aviary, Penguinarium, Marine mammals.
Houston	2.5	2.2	46	881	Gorilla habitat, tropical bird house, Kipp aquarium.
Lincoln Park (Chicago)	3.5	4.0	35	417	Great Ape House, farm in the zoo.
Los Angeles	4.0	1.5	73	500	Koalas, white tigers, children's zoo.
Memphis	2.1	0.9	36	356	Zoo rides, aquarium, waterfowl.
Miami Metrozoo	5.4	0.7	225	193	Open air paddocks, crocodile breeding program.
Milwaukee	7.8	1.6	185	625	Monkey island, moose yard, predator/prey exhibit, Great Ape Escape.
Minnesota	7.0	0.9	467	300	Whale, animals and plants from Asia, Minnesota exhibit, children's zoo.
National (Wash. D.C.) (A)	9.2	3.3	168	395	Lion/Tiger complex, Beaver Valley, giant pandas.
New Orleans (Audubon)	6.0	1.2	58	268	Asian Domain, Tropical Bird House, primates.
Oklahoma City	4.8	5.5	110	500	African plains, Patagonian cliffs, Galapagos Isl.
Philadelphia (A)	5.5	1.1	42	525	Reptiles, African plains, hummingbirds.
Phoenix (A)	2.6	0.7	125	275	Arabian oryx herd, Orangutans, Arizona exhibit.
St. Louis	6.0	2.0	83	630	Big cat country, herpetarium, primate house.
San Antonio	4.3	1.0	49	610	Antelopes, whooping cranes, children's zoo.
San Diego	27.8	3.0	100	777	Loalas, pygmy chimps, Skyfari aerial tramway, parrots, koalas (breeding colony), red pandas.
San Diego (Wild Animal Park)	11.5	1.5	1,800	140	Wgasa Bush Line monorail-African & Asian exhibits.
San Francisco	4.7	0.9	125	259	Gorilla World, insect zoo, white tigers, wolf woods.
Toledo	2.9	0.5	30	352	Aquarium, greenhouse, botanical gardens, children's zoo.
Toronto (A)	9.4	1.1	710	413	Canadian Domain ride, polar bears, gorillas.
Washington Pk (Portland)	15.3	0.7	60	114	Asian elephants, penguinarium, Cascade Mts. exhibit.
Woodland Pk (Seattle)	3.3	0.8	90	305	African savanna, swamp & marsh exhibit.

Mammals: Orders and Major Families

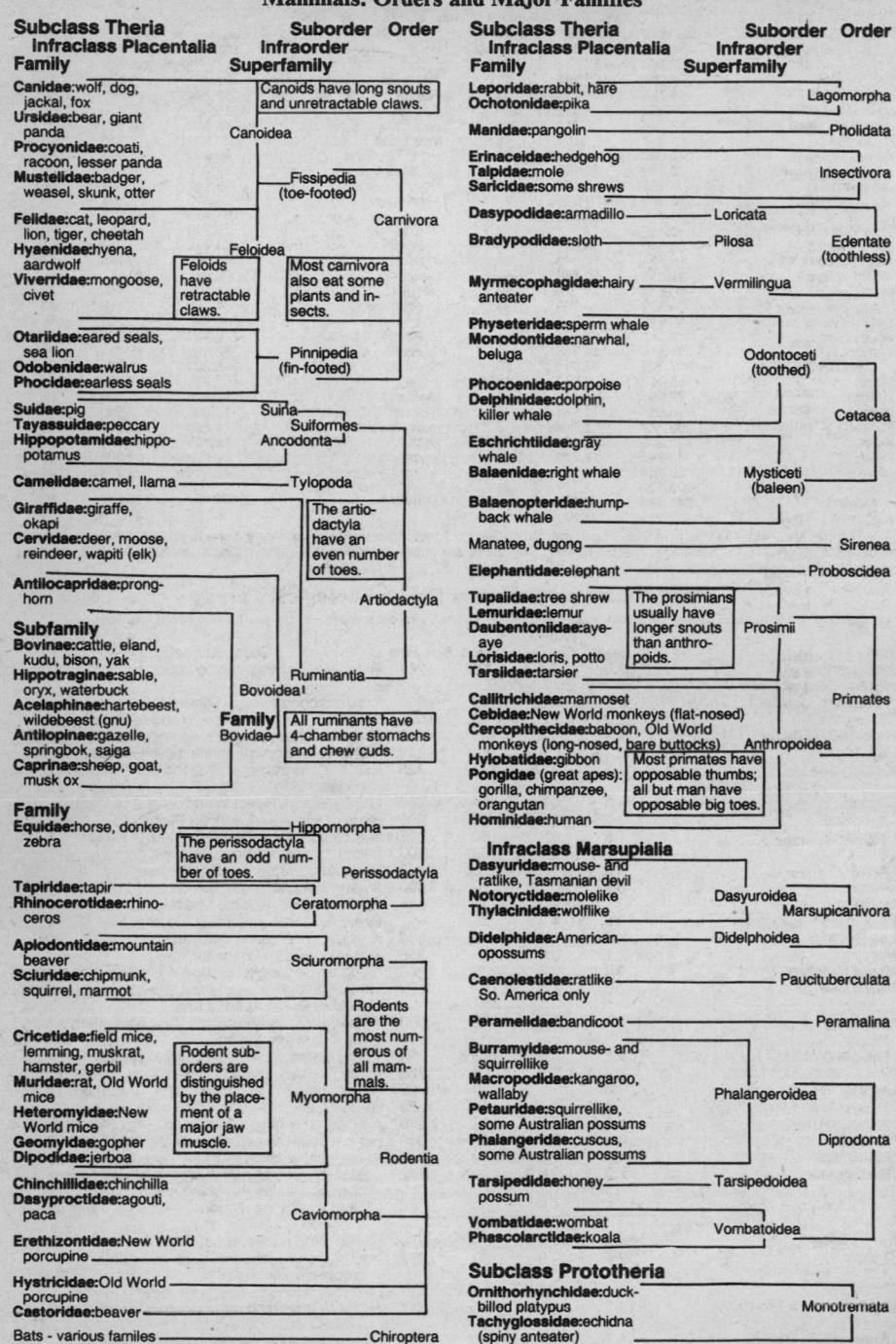

Subclass Theria
Infraclass Placentalia
Family — **Superfamily** — **Infraorder** — **Suborder** — **Order**

Canidae:wolf, dog, jackal, fox | Canoids have long snouts and unretractable claws.
Ursidae:bear, giant panda
Procyonidae:coati, racoon, lesser panda
Mustelidae:badger, weasel, skunk, otter
— Canoidea
— Fissipedia (toe-footed)

Felidae:cat, leopard, lion, tiger, cheetah
Hyaenidae:hyena, aardwolf | Feloids have retractable claws.
Viverridae:mongoose, civet
— Feloidea
— Carnivora
Most carnivora also eat some plants and insects.

Otariidae:eared seals, sea lion
Odobenidae:walrus
Phocidae:earless seals
— Pinnipedia (fin-footed)

Suidae:pig — Suina
Tayassuidae:peccary — Suiformes
Hippopotamidae:hippopotamus — Ancodonta

Camelidae:camel, llama — Tylopoda

Giraffidae:giraffe, okapi
Cervidae:deer, moose, reindeer, wapiti (elk)
The artiodactyla have an even number of toes.

Antilocapridae:pronghorn
— Artiodactyla

Subfamily
Bovinae:cattle, eland, kudu, bison, yak
Hippotraginae:sable, oryx, waterbuck
Acelaphinae:hartebeest, wildebeest (gnu)
Antilopinae:gazelle, springbok, saiga
Caprinae:sheep, goat, musk ox
— Ruminantia
— Bovoidea

Family — Bovidae | All ruminants have 4-chamber stomachs and chew cuds.

Family
Equidae:horse, donkey, zebra — Hippomorpha
The perissodactyla have an odd number of toes.
— Perissodactyla

Tapiridae:tapir
Rhinocerotidae:rhinoceros
— Ceratomorpha

Aplodontidae:mountain beaver
Sciuridae:chipmunk, squirrel, marmot
— Sciuromorpha

Cricetidae:field mice, lemming, muskrat, hamster, gerbil
Muridae:rat, Old World mice
Heteromyidae: New World mice
Geomyidae:gopher
Dipodidae:jerboa
Rodent suborders are distinguished by the placement of a major jaw muscle.
— Myomorpha
Rodents are the most numerous of all mammals.
— Rodentia

Chinchillidae:chinchilla
Dasyproctidae:agouti, paca
— Caviomorpha

Erethizontidae: New World porcupine

Hystricidae: Old World porcupine
Castoridae:beaver

Bats - various families — Chiroptera

Subclass Theria
Infraclass Placentalia
Family — **Superfamily** — **Infraorder** — **Suborder** — **Order**

Leporidae:rabbit, hare
Ochotonidae:pika
— Lagomorpha

Manidae:pangolin — Pholidata

Erinaceidae:hedgehog
Talpidae:mole
Saricidae:some shrews
— Insectivora

Dasypodidae:armadillo — Loricata
Bradypodidae:sloth — Pilosa
— Edentate (toothless)

Myrmecophagidae:hairy anteater — Vermilingua

Physeteridae:sperm whale
Monodontidae:narwhal, beluga
Phocoenidae:porpoise
Delphinidae:dolphin, killer whale
— Odontoceti (toothed)
— Cetacea

Eschrichtidae:gray whale
Balaenidae:right whale
Balaenopteridae:humpback whale
— Mysticeti (baleen)

Manatee, dugong — Sirenea
Elephantidae:elephant — Proboscidea

Tupaiidae:tree shrew
Lemuridae:lemur
Daubentoniidae:aye-aye
Lorisidae:loris, potto
Tarsiidae:tarsier
The prosimians usually have longer snouts than anthropoids.
— Prosimii
— Primates

Callitrichidae:marmoset
Cebidae: New World monkeys (flat-nosed)
Cercopithecidae:baboon, Old World monkeys (long-nosed, bare buttocks)
Hylobatidae:gibbon
Pongidae (great apes): gorilla, chimpanzee, orangutan
Hominidae:human
Most primates have opposable thumbs; all but man have opposable big toes.
— Anthropoidea

Infraclass Marsupialia
Dasyuridae:mouse- and ratlike, Tasmanian devil
Notoryctidae:molelike
Thylacinidae:wolflike
— Dasyuroidea
— Marsupicanivora

Didelphidae: American opossums — Didelphoidea

Caenolestidae:ratlike So. America only — Paucituberculata

Peramelidae:bandicoot — Peramalina

Burramyidae:mouse- and squirrellike
Macropodidae:kangaroo, wallaby
Petauridae:squirrellike, some Australian possums
Phalangeridae:cuscus, some Australian possums
— Phalangeroidea
— Diprodonta

Tarsipedidae:honey possum — Tarsipedoidea

Vombatidae:wombat
Phascolarctidae:koala
— Vombatoidea

Subclass Prototheria
Ornithorhynchidae:duck-billed platypus
Tachyglossidae:echidna (spiny anteater)
— Monotremata

Some Other Endangered Species in the World

Source: U.S. Fish and Wildlife Service, U.S. Interior Department

Common name	Scientific name	Range
Mammals		
Giant sable antelope	Hippotragus niger variani	Angola
African elephant*	Loxodonta africana	Africa
Saudi Arabian gazelle	Gazella dorcas saudiya	Israel, Iraq, Jordan, Syria, Arabian Peninsula
Brown hyena	Hyaena brunnea	Southern Africa
Red kangaroo*	Macropus (=Megaleia rufus)	Australia
Leopard**	Panthera pardus	Africa, Asia
Black howler monkey*	Alouatta pigra	Mexico, Guatemala, Belize
Thin-spined porcupine	Chaetomys subspinosus	Brazil
Tiger	Panthera tigris	Asia
Banded hare wallaby	Lagostrophus fasciatus	Australia
Gray whale	Eschrichtius robustus	N. Pacific Ocean
Wild yak	Bos grunniens	China (Tibet), India
Mountain zebra	Equus zebra zebra	South Africa
Birds		
Indigo macaw	Anodorhynchus leari	Brazil
West African ostrich	Struthio camelus spatzi	Spanish Sahara
Anjouan scops owl	Otus rutilus capnodes	Indian Ocean: Comoro Island
Golden parakeet	Aratinga guarouba	Brazil
Australian parrot	Geopsittacus occidentalis	Australia

*Threatened rather than endangered.   **Threatened in South Africa.

Some Endangered Species in North America

Source: U.S. Fish and Wildlife Service, U.S. Interior Department

Common name	Scientific name	Range
Mammals		
Virginia big-eared bat	Plecotus townsendii virginianus	U.S. (Ky., W.V., Va.)
Columbian white-tailed deer	Odocoileus virginianus leucurus	U.S. (Wash., Ore.)
San Joaquin kit fox	Vulpes macrotis mutica	U.S. (Cal.)
Salt marsh harvest mouse	Reithrodontomys raviventris	U.S. (Cal.)
Ocelot	Felis pardalis	U.S. (Tex., Ariz.) C. and S. America
Florida panther	Felis concolor coryi	U.S. (La., Ark. east to S.C., Fla.)
Utah prairie dog*	Cynomys parvidens	U.S. (Ut.)
Morro Bay kangaroo rat	Dipodomys heermanni morroensis	U.S. (Cal.)
Delmarva Peninsula fox squirrel	Sciurus niger cinereus	U.S. (DelMarVa Peninsula to SE Pa.)
West Indian manatee	Trichechus manatus	U.S. (SE), Caribbean, So. Amer.
Red wolf	Canis rufus	U.S. (Southeast to central Tex.)
Birds		
Masked bobwhite (quail)	Colinus virginianus ridgwayi	U.S. (Ariz.), Mexico (Sonora)
California condor	Gymnogyps californianus	U.S. (Ore., Cal.), Mexico (Baja Calif.)
Whooping crane	Grus americana	U.S. (Rky. Mntns. east to Carolinas), Canada, Mexico
Eskimo curlew	Numenius borealis	Alaska and N. Canada to Argentina
Bald eagle**	Haliaeetus leucocephalus	U.S. (most states), Canada
American peregrine falcon	Falco peregrinus anatum	Canada to Mexico
Aleutian Canada goose	Branta canadensis leucopareia	U.S. (Alaska, Cal., Ore., Wash.), Japan
Brown pelican	Pelecanus occidentalis	U.S. (Carolinas to Tex., Cal.), West Indies, C. and S. America
Attwater's greater prairie-chicken	Tympanuchus cupido attwateri	U.S. (Tex.)
Bachman's warbler (wood)	Vermivora bachmanii	U.S. (Southeastern), Cuba
Kirtland's warbler (wood)	Dendroica kirtlandii	U.S., Canada, Bahama Is.
Ivory-billed woodpecker	Campephilus principalis	U.S. (Southcentral and Southeast), Cuba
Reptiles		
American alligator**	Alligator mississippiensis	U.S. (Southeast)
American crocodile	Crocodylus acutus	U.S. (Fla.), Mexico, South and Central America, Caribbean
Island night lizard*	Xantusia (=Klauberina) riversiana	U.S. (Cal.)
Eastern indigo snake*	Drymarchon corais couperi	U.S. (Ala., Fla., Ga., Miss., S.C.)

*Threatened rather than endangered.   **Endangered except where listed as threatened.

Young of Animals Have Special Names

The young of many animals, birds and fish have come to be called by special names. A young eel, for example, is an elver. Many young animals, of course, are often referred to as infants, babies, younglets, or younglings.

bunny: rabbit.
calf: cattle, elephant, antelope, rhino, hippo, whale, etc.

cheeper: grouse, partridge, quail.
chick, chicken: fowl.
cockerel: rooster.

codling, sprag: codfish.
colt: horse (male).
cub: lion, bear, shark, fox, etc.

cygnet: swan.
duckling: duck.
eaglet: eagle.
elver: eel.
eyas: hawk, others.
fawn: deer.
filly: horse (female).
fingerling: fish generally.
flapper: wild fowl.
fledgling: birds generally.
foal: horse, zebra, others.
fry: fish, generally.

gosling: goose.
heifer: cow.
joey: kangaroo, others.
kid: goat.
kit: fox, beaver, rabbit, cat.
kitten, kitty, catling: cats, other fur-bearers.
lamb, lambkin, cosset, hog: sheep.
leveret: hare.
nestling: birds generally.
owlet: owl.
parr, smolt, grilse: salmon.

piglet, shoat, farrow, suckling: pig.
polliwog, tadpole: frog.
poult: turkey.
pullet: hen.
pup: dog, seal, sea lion, fox.
puss, pussy: cat.
spike, blinker, tinker: mackerel.
squab: pigeon.
squeaker: pigeon, others.
whelp: dog, tiger, beasts of prey.
yearling: cattle, sheep, horse, etc.

Speeds of Animals

Source: Natural History magazine, March 1974.
Copyright © The American Museum of Natural History, 1974.

Animal	Mph	Animal	Mph	Animal	Mph
Cheetah	70	Mongolian wild ass	40	Human	27.89
Pronghorn antelope	61	Greyhound	39.35	Elephant	25
Wildebeest	50	Whippet	35.50	Black mamba snake	20
Lion	50	Rabbit (domestic)	35	Six-lined race runner	18
Thomson's gazelle	50	Mule deer	35	Wild turkey	15
Quarterhorse	47.5	Jackal	35	Squirrel	12
Elk	45	Reindeer	32	Pig (domestic)	11
Cape hunting dog	45	Giraffe	32	Chicken	9
Coyote	43	White-tailed deer	30	Spider (Tegenaria atrica)	1.17
Gray fox	42	Wart hog	30	Giant tortoise	0.17
Hyena	40	Grizzly bear	30	Three-toed sloth	0.15
Zebra	40	Cat (domestic)	30	Garden snail	0.03

Most of these measurements are for maximum speeds over approximate quarter-mile distances. Exceptions are the lion and elephant, whose speeds were clocked in the act of charging; the whippet, which was timed over a 200-yard course; the cheetah over a 100-yard distance; man for a 15-yard segment of a 100-yard run (of 13.6 seconds); and the black mamba, six-lined race runner, spider, giant tortoise, three-toed sloth, and garden snail, which were measured over various small distances.

Gestation, Longevity, and Incubation of Animals

Longevity figures were supplied by Ronald T. Reuther. They refer to animals in captivity; the potential life span of animals is rarely attained in nature. Maximum longevity figures are from the Biology Data Book, 1972. Figures on gestation and incubation are averages based on estimates by leading authorities.

Animal		Gestation (day)	Average longevity (years)	Maximum longevity (yrs., mos.)	Animal	Gestation (day)	Average longevity (years)	Maximum longevity (yrs., mos.)
Ass		365	12	35-10	Leopard	98	12	19-4
Baboon		187	20	35-7	Lion	100	15	25-1
Bear:	Black	219	18	36-10	Monkey (rhesus)	164	15	—
	Grizzly	225	25	—	Moose	240	12	—
	Polar	240	20	34-8	Mouse (meadow)	21	3	—
Beaver		122	5	20-6	Mouse (dom. white)	19	3	3-6
Buffalo (American)		278	15	—	Opossum (American)	14-17	1	—
Bactrian camel		406	12	29-5	Pig (domestic)	112	10	27
Cat (domestic)		63	12	28	Puma	90	12	19
Chimpanzee		231	20	44-6	Rabbit (domestic)	31	5	13
Chipmunk		31	6	8	Rhinoceros (black)	450	15	—
Cow		284	15	30	Rhinoceros (white)	—	20	—
Deer (white-tailed)		201	8	17-6	Sea lion (California)	350	12	28
Dog (domestic)		61	12	20	Sheep (domestic)	154	12	20
Elephant (African)		—	35	60	Squirrel (gray)	44	10	—
Elephant (Asian)		645	40	70	Tiger	105	16	26-3
Elk		250	15	26-6	Wolf (maned)	63	5	—
Fox (red)		52	7	14	Zebra (Grant's)	365	15	—
Giraffe		425	10	33-7				
Goat (domestic)		151	8	18	**Incubation time** (days)			
Gorilla		257	20	39-4	Chicken 21			
Guinea pig		68	4	7-6	Duck 30			
Hippopotamus		238	25	—	Goose 30			
Horse		330	20	46	Pigeon 18			
Kangaroo		42	7	—	Turkey 26			

A Collection of Animal Collectives

The English language boasts an abundance of names to describe groups of things, particularly pairs or aggregations of animals. Some of these words have fallen into comparative disuse, but many of them are still in service, helping to enrich the vocabularies of those who like their language to be precise, who tire of hearing a group referred to as "a bunch of," or who enjoy the sound of words that aren't overworked.

band of gorillas
bed of clams, oysters
bevy of quail, swans
brace of ducks
brood of chicks
cast of hawks
cete of badgers
charm of goldfinches
chattering of choughs
cloud of gnats

clowder of cats
clutch of chicks
clutter of cats
colony of ants
congregation of plovers
covey of quail, partridge
cry of hounds
down of hares
drift of swine
drove of cattle, sheep

exaltation of larks
flight of birds
flock of sheep, geese
gaggle of geese
gam of whales
gang of elks
grist of bees
herd of elephants
hive of bees
horde of gnats

husk of hares
kindle or **kendle** of kittens
knot of toads
leap of leopards
leash of greyhounds, foxes
litter of pigs
mob of kangaroos
murder of crows
muster of peacocks
mute of hounds

nest of vipers	school of fish	sounder of boars, swine	troop of kangaroos,
nest, nide of pheasants	sedge or siege of cranes	span of mules	monkeys
pack of hounds, wolves	shoal of fish, pilchards	spring of teals	volery of birds
pair of horses	skein of geese	swarm of bees	watch of nightingales
pod of whales, seals	skulk of foxes	team of ducks, horses	wing of plovers
pride of lions	sleuth of bears	tribe or trip of goats	yoke of oxen

Major Venomous Animals

Snakes

Coral snake - 2 to 4 ft. long, in Americas south of Canada; bite is nearly painless; very slow onset of paralysis, difficulty breathing; mortality high without antivenin.

Rattlesnake - 2 to 8 ft. long, throughout W. Hemisphere. Rapid onset of symptoms of severe pain, swelling; mortality low, but amputation of affected limb is sometimes necessary; antivenin. Probably high mortality for Mojave rattler.

Cottonmouth water moccasin - less than 6 ft. long, wetlands of southern U.S. from Virginia to Texas. Rapid onset of symptoms of severe pain, swelling; mortality low, but tissue destruction, caused by the venom's effect on the blood, can be extensive; antivenin.

Copperhead - less than 4 ft. long, from New England to Texas; pain and swelling; very seldom fatal.

Fer-de-lance - up to 7 ft. long, Martinique only; venom attacks nerves and blood; probably high mortality.

Bushmaster - up to 9 ft. long, jungles of C. and S. America; few bites recorded; probably low mortality.

Barba Amarilla - up to 7 ft. long, from tropical Mexico to Brazil; severe tissue damage common; low mortality; antivenin.

Asian pit vipers - from 2 to 5 ft. long throughout Asia; reactions and mortality vary but most bites cause tissue damage and mortality is generally low.

Sharp-nosed pit viper - up to 5 ft. long, in eastern China and Indo-China; the most toxic of Asian pit vipers; very rapid onset of swelling and tissue damage, internal bleeding; moderate mortality; antivenin.

Boomslang - under 6 ft. long, in African savannahs; rapid onset of nausea and dizziness, often followed by slight recovery and then sudden death from internal hemorrhaging; bites rare, mortality high; antivenin.

European vipers - from 1 to 3 ft. long; bleeding and tissue damage; mortality low; antivenins.

Puff adder - up to 5 ft. long, fat; south of the Sahara and throughout the Middle East; rapid large swelling, great pain, dizziness; moderate mortality often from internal bleeding; antivenin.

Gaboon viper - over 6 ft. long, fat; 2-inch fangs; south of the Sahara; massive tissue damage, internal bleeding; mortality rate not clear.

Saw-scaled or carpet viper - up to 2 ft. long, in dry areas from India to Africa; severe bleeding, fever; high mortality, venom 3 times more toxic than common cobra's; antivenin.

Desert horned viper - in dry areas of Africa and western Asia; swelling and tissue damage; low mortality; antivenin.

Russell's viper or tic-palonga - over 5 ft. long, throughout Asia; internal bleeding; mortality rate not clear; bite reports common; antivenin.

Black mamba - up to 14 ft. long, fast-moving; S. and C. Africa; rapid onset of dizziness, difficulty breathing, erratic heart-beat; mortality high, nears 100% without antivenin.

Kraits - in S. Asia; rapid onset of sleepiness; numbness; up to 50% mortality even with antivenin treatment.

Common or Asian cobra - 4 to 8 ft. long, throughout S. Asia; considerable tissue damage, sometimes paralysis; mortality probably not more than 10%; antivenin.

King cobra - up to 16 ft. long, throughout S. Asia; rapid swelling, dizziness, loss of consciousness, difficulty breathing, erratic heart-beat; mortality varies sharply with amount of venom involved, most bites involve non-fatal amounts; antivenin.

Yellow or Cape cobra - 7 ft. long, in southern Africa; most toxic venom of any cobra; rapid onset of swelling, breathing and cardiac difficulties; mortality high without treatment; antivenin.

Ringhals, or spitting, cobra - 5 ft. and 7 ft. long; southern Africa; squirt venom through holes in front of fangs as a defense; venom is severely irritating and can cause blindness.

Australian brown snakes - very slow onset of symptoms of cardiac or respiratory distress; moderate mortality; antivenin.

Tiger snake - 2 to 6 ft. long, S. Australia; pain, numbness, mental disturbances with rapid onset of paralysis; may be the most deadly of all land snakes though antivenin is quite effective.

Death adder - less than 3 ft. long, Australia; rapid onset of faintness, cardiac and respiratory distress; at least 50% mortality without antivenin.

Taipan - up to 11 ft. long, in Australia and New Guinea; rapid paralysis with severe breathing difficulty; mortality nears 100% without antivenin.

Sea snakes - throughout Pacific, Indian oceans except NE Pacific; almost painless bite, variety of muscle pain, paralysis; mortality rate about 15%, many bites are not envenomed; some antivenins.

Notes: Not all snake bites by venomous snakes are actually envenomed; for a various reasons, the snake may be temporarily lacking in venom or fail to inject it. Any animal bite, however, carries the danger of tetanus and no bite by a venomous snake should go untreated. Antivenins are not certain cures; they are only an aid in the treatment of bites. Mortality rates above are for envenomed bites; low mortality, up to 5% result in death; moderate, up to 15%; high, over 15%. Even when the victim recovers fully, prolonged hospitalization and extensive medical procedures are usually required.

Lizards

Gila monster - up to 30 inches long with heavy body and tail, in high desert in southwest U.S. and N. Mexico; immediate severe pain followed by vomiting, thirst, difficulty swallowing, weakness approaching paralysis; mortality very low.

Mexican beaded lizard - similar to Gila monster, Mexican westcoast; reaction and mortality rate similar to Gila monster.

Insects

Ants, bees, wasps, hornets, etc. Global distribution. Usual reaction is piercing pain in area of sting. Not directly fatal, except in cases of massive multiple stings. Many people suffer allergic reactions - swelling, rashes, partial paralysis –and a few may die within minutes from severe sensitivity to the venom (anaphylactic shock).

Spiders, scorpions

Black widow - small, round-bodied with hour-glass marking; the widow and its relatives are found around the world in tropical and temperate zones; sharp pain, weakness, clammy skin, muscular rigidity, breathing difficulty and, in small children, convulsions; low mortality; antivenin.

Brown recluse or fiddleback - small, oblong body; throughout U.S.; slow onset of pain and severe ulceration at place of bite; in severe cases fever, nausea, and stomach cramps; ulceration may last months; very low mortality.

Atrax spiders - several varieties, often large, in Australia; slow onset of breathing, circulation difficulties; low mortality.

Tarantulas - large, hairy spiders found around the world; American tarantulas, and probably all others, are **harmless**, though their bite may cause some pain and swelling.

Scorpions - crab-like body with stinger in tail, various sizes, many varieties throughout tropical and subtropical areas; various symptoms may include severe pain spreading from the wound, numbness, severe emotional agitation, cramps; severe reactions include vomiting, diarrhea, respiratory failure; moderate to high mortality, particularly in children; antivenins.

Sea Life

Sea wasps - jellyfish, with tentacles up to 30 ft. long, in the S. Pacific; very rapid onset of circulatory problems; high mortality largely because of speed of toxic reaction; antivenin.

Portuguese man-of-war - jellyfish-like, with tentacles up to 70 ft. long, in most warm water areas; immediate severe pain; not fatal, though shock may cause death in a rare case.

Octopi - global distribution, usually in warm waters; all varieties produce venom but only a few can cause death; rapid onset of paralysis with breathing difficulty.

Stingrays - several varieties of differing sizes, found in tropical and temperate seas and some fresh water; severe pain, rapid onset of nausea, vomiting, breathing difficulties; wound area may ulcerate, gangrene may appear; seldom fatal.

Stonefish - brownish fish which lies motionless as a rock on bottom in shallow water; throughout S. Pacific and Indian oceans; extraordinary pain, rapid paralysis; low mortality.

Cone-shells - molluscs in small, beautiful shells in the S. Pacific and Indian oceans; shoot barbs into victims; paralysis; low mortality.

Stonefish - brownish fish which lies motionless as a rock on bottom in shallow water; throughout S. Pacific and Indian oceans; extraordinary pain, rapid paralysis; low mortality.

Cone-shells - molluscs in small, beautiful shells in the S. Pacific and Indian oceans; shoot barbs into victims; paralysis; low mortality.

American Kennel Club Registrations

	Rank 1983	1983	Rank 1982	1982		Rank 1983	1983	Rank 1982	1982
Cocker Spaniels	1	92,836	2	87,218	English Setters	70	1,012	65	1,205
Poodles	2	90,250	1	88,650	Bullmastiffs	71	997	71	966
Labrador Retrievers	3	67,389	4	62,465	Bearded Collies	72	895	73	763
Doberman Pinschers	4	66,184	3	73,180	Giant Schnauzers	73	771	77	634
German Shepherd Dogs	5	65,073	5	60,445	Australian Terriers	74	747	72	774
Golden Retrievers	6	52,525	6	51,045	Tibetan Spaniels	75	743	—	—
Beagles	7	39,992	8	35,548	Welsh Terriers	76	724	75	656
Miniature Schnauzers	8	37,820	7	36,502	Portuguese Water Dogs	77	721	—	—
Dachshunds	9	33,514	9	32,835	Papillons	78	714	74	696
Shetland Sheepdogs	10	33,375	10	30,512	Australian Cattle Dogs	79	709	82	558
Yorkshire Terriers	11	28,350	11	26,205	Belgian Sheepdogs	80	677	78	605
Chow Chows	12	27,815	13	22,623	Pharaoh Hounds	81	673	—	—
Lhasa Apsos	13	27,087	12	25,945	Standard Schnauzers	82	650	76	653
Shih Tzu	14	23,308	16	20,556	Salukis	83	649	78	605
English Springer Span.	15	22,626	14	22,296	Kerry Blue Terriers	84	648	80	593
Siberian Huskies	16	21,237	15	20,654	Italian Greyhounds	85	640	81	569
Collies	17	20,789	17	20,084	Tibetan Terriers	86	514	84	495
Pomeranians	18	19,691	18	18,456	Manchester Terriers	87	510	83	519
Basset Hounds	19	19,042	19	17,871	Belgian Tervuren	88	501	85	446
Brittanys	20	18,433	21	17,349	Bernese Mountain Dogs	89	482	86	424
Pekingese	21	17,611	20	17,434	Pointers	90	434	87	419
Boxers	22	17,365	22	16,301	Japanese Chin	91	426	89	386
Chihuahuas	23	16,946	23	15,867	Cardigan Welsh Corgis	92	360	88	393
Rottweilers	24	13,265	27	9,269	American Water Span.	93	339	91	331
Boston Terriers	25	11,855	25	11,361	Bedlington Terriers	94	334	90	379
Great Danes	26	11,352	24	12,092	Kuvaszok	95	311	100	235
German Shorthaired Pointers	27	10,126	26	10,019	Pulik	96	300	92	326
Maltese	28	8,796	30	8,050	Briards	97	288	96	277
Samoyeds	29	7,918	31	7,862	Flat-Coated Retrievers	98	273	95	283
Old English Sheepdogs	30	7,658	28	8,332	Border Terriers	99	265	97	272
West Highland White Terriers	31	7,540	32	7,397	Black and Tan Coon-hounds	100	240	94	284
Airedale Terriers	32	7,149	34	6,876	Lakeland Terriers	101	239	101	229
Alaskan Malamutes	33	7,044	33	7,209	Staffordshire Bull Terriers	102	238	99	236
Bulldogs	34	6,943	35	6,657	Brussels Griffons	103	237	104	199
Pugs	35	6,544	37	6,058	Irish Terriers	104	228	93	312
Keeshonden	36	6,214	38	5,977	Welsh Springer Spaniels	105	227	103	200
Cairn Terriers	37	6,154	36	6,108	Norwich Terriers	106	216	98	243
Irish Setters	38	6,114	29	8,183	French Bulldogs	107	201	105	182
Dalmatians	39	6,032	40	5,409	Skye Terriers	108	186	102	223
Scottish Terriers	40	5,857	39	5,834	Dandie Dinmont Terriers	109	175	107	152
Weimaraners	41	4,578	41	4,586	Scottish Deerhounds	110	162	106	171
Chesapeake Bay Retr.	42	4,512	44	4,243	Norfolk Terriers	111	151	108	134
Norwegian Elkhounds	43	4,308	43	4,368	Komondorok	112	138	109	128
Afghan Hounds	44	4,063	42	4,484	English Toy Spaniels	113	134	118	56
St. Bernards	45	4,052	45	4,296	Clumber Spaniels	114	126	115	77
Bichons Frises	47	4,038	48	3,632	Greyhounds	115	125	111	127
Fox Terriers (Smooth & Wire)	46	3,878	47	3,815	Wirehaired Pointing Griffons	116	113	109	128
Akitas	48	3,865	46	3,257	Ibizan Hounds	117	109	113	93
Pembroke Welsh Corgis	49	2,757	50	2,575	Sealyham Terriers	118	107	116	73
Silky Terriers	50	2,641	49	2,627	Affenpinschers	119	98	112	97
Miniature Pinschers	51	2,554	52	2,193	Curly-Coated Retrievers	120	86	119	50
Newfoundlands	52	2,428	51	2,394	Irish Water Spaniels	121	79	114	85
Bouviers des Flandres	53	1,903	55	1,632	Belgian Malinois	122	64	120	45
Vizslas	54	1,859	53	1,847	Field Spaniels	123	53	123	27
Schipperkes	55	1,758	56	1,569	American Foxhounds	124	38	117	57
American Staffordshire Terriers	56	1,630	57	1,550	Otter Hounds	125	27	121	34
Rhodesian Ridgebacks	57	1,614	63	1,368	Sussex Spaniels	125	27	124	22
Great Pyrenees	58	1,590	54	1,684	Harriers	127	26	121	34
Mastiffs	59	1,580	60	1,419	English Foxhounds	128	18	125	12
Basenjis	60	1,473	58	1,517	**Total Registrations:**		1,085,248		1,037,149
English Cocker Spaniels	61	1,393	62	1,391					
Borzois	62	1,383	64	1,366					
Whippets	63	1,348	61	1,392					
Bloodhounds	64	1,336	59	1,503					
Bull Terriers	65	1,195	66	1,162					
Soft-Coated Wheaten Terriers	66	1,159	68	1,111					
Gordon Setters	67	1,142	69	1,082					
Irish Wolfhounds	68	1,109	67	1,131					
German Wirehaired Pointers	69	1,098	70	1,049					

Dogs Registered by Groups	1983	1982
Sporting breeds	287,400	275,600
Hound breeds	111,249	104,800
Working breeds	161,950	289,650
Terrier breeds	77,150	75,250
Toy breeds	128,700	119,449
Non-sporting breeds	183,450	172,500
Herding breeds	135,349	

Cat Breeds

There are 27 cat breeds recognized: abyssinian, american shorthair, balinese, birman, bombay, burmese, colorpoint shorthair, egyptian mau, exotic shorthair, havana brown, himalayan, japanese bobtail, korat, leopard cat, lilac foreign shorthair, maine coon cat, manx, ocicat, oriental shorthair, persian, rex, russian blue, scottish fold, siamese, sphynx, turkish angora, wirehair shorthair.

TRADE AND TRANSPORTATION
Notable Steamships and Motorships
Source: Lloyd's Register of Shipping as of June 1984

Gross tonnage is a measurement of enclosed space (1 gross ton = 100 cu. ft.) Deadweight tonnage is the weight (in tons of 1,000 kg) of cargo, fuel, etc., which a vessel is designed to carry safely.

Name, registry	Dwght. ton.	Lgth. ft.	Bdth. ft.	Name, registry	Dwght. ton.	Lgth. ft.	Bdth. ft.
Oil Tankers				**Container, Liquefied Gas, Misc. Ships**			
Seawise Giant, Liber.	564,739	1504.0	209.0	Senshu Maru, Jap.	106,500	928.0	147.0
Prairial, Fr.	555,051	1359.0	206.0	Banshu Maru, Jap.	104,121	928.0	146.0
Bellamya, Fr.	553,662	1359.0	206.0	Echigo Maru, Jap.	102,390	928.0	147.0
Batillus, Fr.	553,662	1358.0	206.0	Bishu Maru, Jap.	100,295	925.0	145.0
Esso Atlantic, Bahamas.	516,893	1333.0	233.0	Kotowaka Maru, Jap.	97,788	921.0	145.0
Esso Pacific, Liber.	516,423	1333.0	233.0	Hoegh Gandria, Nor.	95,683	943.0	142.0
Nanny, Swed.	491,120	1194.0	259.0	LNG Libra, U.S.	95,084	936.0	149.0
Nissei Maru, Jap.	484,276	1242.0	203.0	LNG Taurus, U.S.	95,084	936.0	149.0
Globtik London, Liber.	483,933	1243.0	203.0	LNG Virgo, U.S.	95,084	936.0	149.0
Globtik Tokyo, Liber.	483,662	1243.0	203.0	LNG Capricorn, U.S.	95,084	936.0	149.0
Burmah Enterprise, U.K.	457,927	1241.0	224.0	LNG Gemini, U.S.	95,084	936.0	149.0
Burmah Endeavour, U.K.	457,841	1241.0	223.0	LNG Leo, U.S.	95,084	936.0	149.0
Robinson, Liber.	431,232	1236.0	226.0	LNG Aquarius, U.S.	95,084	936.0	143.0
Coraggio, It.	423,798	1240.0	226.0	LNG Aries, U.S.	95,084	936.0	149.0
Berge Empress, Nor.	423,700	1252.0	223.0	Golar Spirit, Liber.	93,815	948.0	146.0
Berge Emperor, Nor.	423,700	1285.0	223.0	Golar Freeze, Liber.	85,158	943.0	142.0
Hilda Knudsen, Nor.	423,639	1240.0	226.0	Khannur, Liber.	84,855	961.0	136.0
Esso Deutschland, W. Ger.	421,681	1240.0	226.0	Gimi, Liber.	84,855	963.0	136.0
Jinko Maru, Jap.	413,553	1200.0	229.0	Hilli, Liber.	84,855	961.0	136.0
Chevron South America, Liber.	413,158	1200.0	229.0	Lake Charles, U.S.	83,743	936.0	149.0
David Packard, Liber.	413,115	1200.0	229.0	Louisiana, U.S.	83,743	936.0	149.0
Aiko Maru, Jap.	412,941	1200.0	229.0	Mostefa Ben-Boulaid, Alger.	82,243	914.0	134.0
Chevron No. Amer., Liber.	412,612	1200.0	229.0	Rhenania, W. Ger.	80,946	941.0	137.0
World Petrobras, Liber.	411,508	1187.0	229.0	LNG 564, Swed.	80,912	941.0	137.0
Nai Superba, It.	409,400	1253.0	207.0	Bachir Chihani, Alger.	80,328	924.0	136.0
Nai Genova, It.	409,400	1253.0	207.0	Larbi Ben M'Hidi, Alger.	80,328	924.0	136.0
Al Rekkah, Kuw.	407,822	1200.0	229.0	Ben Franklin, Pan.	80,070	894.0	134.0
Esso Japan, Liber.	406,640	1187.0	229.0	Nestor, Bermuda	78,915	902.0	138.0
Esso Tokyo, Liber.	406,258	1187.0	229.0	Methania, Belg.	78,511	918.0	136.0
U.S.T. Pacific, U.S.	404,531	1188.0	228.0	Edouard L.D., Fr.	78,212	920.0	136.0
U.S.T. Atlantic, U.S.	404,531	1188.0	228.0	Pollenger, U.K.	76,496	857.0	131.0
				Norman Lady, Liber.	76,416	818.0	131.0
Bulk, Ore, Bulk Oil, & Ore Oil Carriers				Mourad Didouche, Alger.	74,741	900.0	137.0
World Gala, Liber.	282,462	1109.0	179.0	Ramdane Abane, Alger.	74,741	900.0	137.0
Weser Ore, Liber.	278,734	1099.0	170.0	Columbia, U.S.	72,000	931.0	140.0
Docecanyon, Liber.	275,588	1113.0	180.0	Southern, U.S.	69,472	948.0	135.0
Mary R. Koch, Liber.	274,999	1099.0	170.0	Gamma, U.S.	69,472	948.0	135.0
Jose Bonifacio, Braz.	270,358	1106.0	179.0	Arzew, U.S.	69,472	948.0	135.0
Usa Maru, Jap.	269,110	1105.0	179.0	Gastor, Pan.	68,246	902.0	138.0
Castor, Liber.	268,728	1101.0	176.0	Tenaga Dua, Malays.	68,085	920.0	136.0
Hitachi Venture, Liber.	267,889	1063.0	180.0	Tenaga Lima, Malays.	68,085	920.0	136.0
Rhine Ore, Pan.	264,999	1099.0	170.0	Tenaga Empat, Malays.	68,085	920.0	136.0
Licorne Atlantique, Fr.	262,596	1101.0	176.0	Tenaga Tiga, Malays.	68,085	920.0	136.0
Alkisma Alarabia, Saud. Arab.	264,591	1101.0	176.0	El Paso Consolidated, Liber.	66,807	920.0	136.0
Hoegh Hill, Nor.	249,259	1069.0	170.0	Al Rawdatain, Kuw.	66,807	920.0	136.0
World Truth, Liber.	249,223	1069.0	170.0	El Paso Paul Kayser, Liber.	66,807	920.0	136.0
Hoegh Hood, Nor.	248,604	1069.0	170.0	Esso Westernport, Bah.	63,495	838.0	116.0
Seiko Maru, Jap.	247,867	1069.0	170.0	Palace Tokyo, Jap.	63,204	807.0	131.0
Konkar Dinos, Gr.	234,752	1075.0	160.0	Kurama Maru, Jap.	59,407	949.0	105.0
World Recovery, Liber.	231,054	1075.0	161.0	Nedlloyd Dejima, Neth.	58,613	941.0	106.0
Berge Brioni, Nor.	227,558	1030.0	165.0	Nedlloyd Delft, Neth.	58,613	941.0	106.0
Berge Adria, Nor.	227,558	1030.0	164.0	Cardigan Bay, U.K.	58,497	950.0	106.0
Rimula, U.K.	227,412	1091.0	149.0	Kowloon Bay, U.K.	58,496	950.0	106.0
Rapana, U.K.	227,400	1091.0	149.0	Tokyo Bay, U.K.	58,496	950.0	106.0
Ruhr Ore, Liber.	227,086	1096.0	149.0	Liverpool Bay, U.K.	58,496	950.0	106.0
Konkar Theodoros, Gr.	225,162	1028.0	164.0	Osaka Bay, U.K.	58,496	950.0	106.0
Alva Sea U.K.	225,010	1090.0	149.0	Kasuga Maru, Jap.	58,440	948.0	105.0
Chishirokawa Maru, Jap.	224,666	1033.0	164.0	Frankfurt Express, W. Ger.	58,384	943.0	106.0
Frontier Maru, Jap.	224,222	1023.0	164.0	City of Edinburgh, U.K.	58,284	950.0	106.0
Andros Atlas, Gr.	224,074	1061.0	158.0	Benavon, U.K.	58,283	950.0	106.0
Andros Antares, Liber.	223,888	1061.0	158.0	Benalder, U.K.	58,283	950.0	106.0
Andros Aries, Gr.	223,605	1061.0	158.0	Hamburg Express, W. Ger.	58,087	943.0	106.0
World Lady, Liber.	219,080	1075.0	164.0	Tokio Express, W. Ger.	57,995	943.0	106.0
Donau Ore, Liber.	218,957	1075.0	164.0	Bremen Express, W. Ger.	57,495	949.0	106.0
Tantalus, U.K.	218,035	1075.0	164.0	Hongkong Express, W. Ger.	57,495	949.0	106.0
				Korrigan, Fr.	57,304	946.0	105.0
World's Largest Passenger Ships				Esso Fuji, Pan.	55,896	807.0	131.0
Norway, Nor.	70,202	1035.0	110.0	City of Durban, U.K.	53,790	848.0	106.0
Queen Elizabeth 2, U.K.	67,139	963.0	105.0				
Canberra, U.K.	44,807	818.0	102.0				
Oriana, U.K.	41,920	804.0	97.0				
Rotterdam, Neth. Ant.	38,644	748.0	94.0				
United States, U.S.	38,216	990.0	101.0	**Nuclear Powered Merchant Ships**			
Song of America, Nor.	37,584	703.0	107.0				
Nieuw Amsterdam, Neth. Ant.	33,930	704.0	89.0	Leonid Ilich Brezhnev, USSR.	18,172	485.0	98.0
Europa, W. Ger.	33,819	654.0	98.0	Norasia Susan, W. Ger.	16,291	564.0	77.0
Noordam, Neth.	32,300	704.0	89.0	Lenin, USSR.	13,366	439.0	90.0
Eugenio C, It.	30,567	713.0	96.0	Mutsu, Jap.	8,214	428.0	62.0

U.S. Foreign Trade with Leading Countries

Source: Office of Industry and Trade Information, U.S. Commerce Department

(millions of dollars)

Exports from the U.S. to the following areas and countries and imports into the U.S. from those areas and countries:	Exports			Imports		
	1980	1982	1983	1980	1982	1983
Total	**220,705**	**212,275**	**200,538**	**240,834**	**243,952**	**258,048**
Western Hemisphere	**74,114**	**67,312**	**63,970**	**78,489**	**84,467**	**93,873**
Canada	35,395	33,720	38,244	41,455	46,477	52,130
20 Latin American Republics	36,030	30,086	22,618	29,851	32,513	35,683
Central American Common Market	1,951	1,405	1,494	1,849	1,467	1,585
Dominican Republic	795	664	632	786	629	814
Panama	699	1,803	748	330	255	337
Bahamas	396	590	452	1,382	1,050	1,687
Jamaica	305	468	452	383	294	273
Netherlands Antilles	448	659	553	2,564	2,117	2,291
Trinidad and Tobago	680	894	728	2,378	1,627	1,318
Europe	**71,372**	**63,664**	**59,590**	**47,849**	**53,413**	**55,243**
OECD countries (excludes depend. and Yugo.)	66,654	59,378	55,261	45,952	51,966	53,468
Western Europe	67,512	60,054	55,980	46,416	52,346	53,884
European Economic Community	53,679	47,932	44,311	35,958	42,509	43,892
Belgium and Luxembourg	6,661	5,229	5,049	1,914	2,396	2,412
Denmark	863	732	24,953	725	905	1,067
France	7,485	7,110	5,961	5,247	5,545	6,025
Germany, Federal Republic of	10,960	9,291	8,737	11,681	11,975	12,695
Ireland	836	983	1,115	411	556	560
Italy	5,511	4,616	3,908	4,313	5,301	5,455
Netherlands	8,669	8,604	7,767	1,910	2,494	2,970
United Kingdom	12,694	10,645	10,621	9,755	13,095	12,470
Austria	448	371	371	388	491	447
Finland	505	489	413	439	414	496
Iceland	79	77	53	200	184	219
Norway	843	950	813	2,632	1,973	1,358
Portugal	911	838	1,212	256	283	280
Sweden	1,767	1,689	1,581	1,617	1,993	2,429
Switzerland	3,781	2,707	2,960	2,787	2,340	2,494
Greece	922	721	503	292	242	238
Spain	3,179	3,456	2,763	1,209	1,505	1,533
Turkey	540	868	783	175	274	320
Yugoslavia	756	494	572	446	360	386
Eastern Europe	3,860	3,610	2,891	1,433	1,067	1,359
USSR	1,513	2,587	2,003	453	228	347
Asia	**60,168**	**64,822**	**63,813**	**78,848**	**85,170**	**91,464**
Near East	**11,900**	**15,950**	**13,796**	**17,280**	**11,812**	**7,135**
Iran	23	122	190	339	585	1,130
Iraq	724	846	512	352	39	59
Israel	2,045	2,271	2,071	943	1,164	1,255
Jordan	407	620	436	3	7	5
Kuwait	886	941	741	472	40	130
Lebanon	303	294	484	33	19	17
Saudi Arabia	5,769	9,026	7,903	12,509	7,443	3,627
Syria	239	138	102	26	10	8
Japan	**20,790**	**20,966**	**21,894**	**30,701**	**37,744**	**41,183**
East and South Asia	**27,478**	**27,907**	**28,123**	**30,867**	**35,615**	**43,146**
Bangladesh	292	227	190	85	70	88
China, People's Republic of	3,755	2,912	2,173	1,054	2,284	2,244
China, Republic of	4,337	4,367	4,667	6,850	8,893	11,204
Hong Kong	2,686	2,453	2,564	4,736	5,540	6,394
India	1,689	1,599	1,828	1,098	1,404	2,191
Indonesia	1,545	2,025	1,466	5,183	4,224	5,285
Korea, Republic of	4,685	5,529	5,925	4,147	5,637	7,148
Malaysia	1,337	1,736	1,684	2,577	1,885	2,124
Pakistan	642	700	812	128	165	167
Philippines	1,999	1,854	1,807	1,730	1,806	2,001
Singapore	3,033	3,214	3,759	1,920	2,195	2,868
Thailand	1,263	915	1,063	816	884	967
Oceania	**4,876**	**5,700**	**4,827**	**3,392**	**3,131**	**3,044**
Australia	4,093	4,535	3,954	2,509	2,287	2,222
New Zealand and Samoa	599	900	625	703	777	737
Africa	**9,060**	**10,271**	**8,768**	**32,251**	**17,770**	**14,425**
Algeria	542	909	594	6,577	2,673	3,551
Canary Islands	158	127	142	6	3	3
Egypt	1,874	2,875	2,813	458	547	303
Gabon	48	110	63	278	610	657
Ghana	127	116	119	206	362	120
Ivory Coast	185	97	61	288	303	343
Kenya	141	98	69	54	71	65
Liberia	113	113	110	128	91	91
Libya	509	301	191	7,124	512	1
Morocco	344	397	440	35	45	31
Nigeria	1,150	1,295	864	10,905	7,045	3,736
South Africa, Rep. of	2,464	2,368	2,129	3,321	1,967	2,027
Sudan	143	270	157	17	16	19
Tunisia	174	213	216	60	59	33
Zaire	155	91	83	361	407	366

U.S. Exports and Imports of Leading Commodities

Source: Office of Industry and Trade Information, U.S. Commerce Department (millions of dollars)

Commodity	Exports			Imports		
	1980	1982	1983	1980	1982	1983
Food and live animals	**27,744**	**23,950**	**24,166**	**15,763**	**144538**	**15,412**
Cattle, except for breeding	...	...	...	228	289	301
Meat and preparations	1,293	1,285	1,191	2,346	2,075	2,034
Dairy products and eggs	255	409	373	318	371	403
Fish	915	995	917	2,612	3,143	3,594
Grains and preparations	18,079	14,747	15,123	...	...	...
Wheat, including flour	6,586	6,869	6,508	...	...	...
Rice	1,285	997	926	...	...	...
Grains and animal feed	2,878	2,473	2,802	331	437	483
Fruits and nuts	2,930	2,716	2,444	859	1,094	1,172
Vegetables	...	...	...	1,188	1,722	1,748
Sugar	...	...	...	1,988	863	1,047
Coffee, crude	...	...	...	3,872	2,730	2,590
Cocoa or cacao beans	...	...	...	395	323	349
Tea	...	...	...	131	129	132
Beverages and Tobacco	**2,663**	**3,026**	**2,813**	**2,772**	**3,364**	**3,408**
Alcoholic beverages	...	...	...	2,220	2,513	2,626
Tobacco, unmanufactured	2,390	...	1,462	422	445	464
Crude materials, inedible, except fuels	**23,791**	**19,248**	**18,596**	**10,496**	**8,589**	**9,590**
Hides and skins	694	778	807	88	71	64
Soybeans, oilseeds, peanuts	5,883	6,240	5,925	...	73	92
Synthetic rubber	695	553	543	...	...	...
Rubber, including latex	...	...	...	816	535	655
Lumber and rough wood	2,675	2,095	2,104	2,134	1,737	2,719
Wood pulp and pulpwood	2,454	1,964	1,916	1,725	1,485	1,508
Textile fibers and wastes	2,864	1,955	1,817	242	264	312
Ores and metal scrap	4,518	2,174	2,276	3,696	2,684	2,500
Mineral fuels and related mat'ls	**7,932**	**12,729**	**9,500**	**79,058**	**65,409**	**57,952**
Coal	4,523	6,072	4,115	...	...	....
Petroleum and products	2,833	5,947	4,557	73,771	59,396	52,325
Natural gas	NA	...	...	5,155	5,934	5,530
Animal and vegetable oils and fats	**1,946**	**1,541**	**1,459**	**533**	**406**	**495**
Chemicals	**20,740**	**19,891**	**19,751**	**8,583**	**9,494**	**10,779**
Medicines and pharmaceuticals	1,932	2,275	2,494	508	563	703
Fertilizers, manufactured	2,265	1,386	1,267	1,104	963	997
Plastic materials and resins	3,884	3,650	3,732	...	...	...
Machinery and transport equip.	**84,629**	**87,148**	**82,578**	**60,546**	**73,320**	**86,131**
Machinery	55,790	59,324	54,309	31,904	39,457	46,975
Aircraft engines and parts	1,915	2,570	2,788	...	...	...
Auto engines and parts	1,688	1,955	2,082	...	...	...
Agricultural machinery	3,104	2,389	1,589	682	1,042	1,196
Tractors and parts	1,809	1,262	757	NA	778	711
Office machines and computers	8,709	10,206	11,669	2,929	4,299	6,759
Transport equipment	28,839	27,824	28,269	28,642	33,863	39,156
Road motor vehicles and parts	14,590	13,907	14,463	24,134	25,246	46,247
Aircraft and parts except engines	12,816	11,775	12,189	1,885	2,481	2,051
Other manufactured goods	**42,714**	**37,818**	**34,666**	**55,900**	**61,209**	**66,539**
Tires and tubes	511	372	304	1,143	1,239	1,406
Wood and manufactures, exc. furniture	2,675	2,095	...	632	544	754
Paper and manufactures	2,831	2,654	2,553	3,587	3,848	4,215
Glassware and pottery	...	...	...	1,224	1,351	1,602
Diamonds, excl. industrial	...	...	...	2,252	1,917	2,275
Nonmetallic mineral manuf.	2,209	1,805	1,770	...	...	...
Metal manufactures	4,205	3,981	3,444	...	4,294	4,504
Pig iron and ferroalloys	3,123	2,168	1,478	...	...	...
Iron and steel-mill products	2,998	2,101	1,415	6,686	9,184	6,338
Nonferrous base metals	2,964	1,768	1,606	7,623	5,321	7,422
Textiles, other than clothing	3,632	2,784	2,368	2,493	2,808	3,225
Clothing	1,203	952	818	6,427	8,165	9,583
Footwear	...	...	...	2,808	3,438	4,010
Furniture	521	639	593	...	...	...
Scientific and photo equip., photo supplies	6,763	7,399	7,221	...	...	...
Printed matter	1,097	1,341	1,324	613	664	739
Clocks and watches	133	125	90	1,097	991	1,058
Toys, games, sporting goods	1,012	957	878	1,914	2,786	2,506
Artworks and antiques	...	...	...	2,672	2,024	2,017
Other transactions	**8,496**	**6,924**	**7,009**	**7,183**	**7,708**	**7,742**
Total	**220,705**	**212,275**	**200,538**	**240,834**	**243,952**	**258,048**

Value of U.S. Exports, Imports, and Merchandise Balance

(millions of dollars)

Year	U.S. exports and reexports excluding military grant-aid	Principal Census trade totals — U.S. general imports f.a.s. transaction values[1]	U.S. merchandise balance f.a.s.[1]	U.S. general imports c.i.f.	U.S. balance exports f.a.s. imports c.i.f.	Other Census totals — Military grant-aid shipments	Exports of domestic merchandise	Re-exports
1950	9,997	8,954	1,043	—	—	282	10,146	133
1955	14,298	11,566	2,732	—	—	1,256	15,426	128
1960	19,659	15,073	4,586	—	—	949	20,408	201
1965	26,742	21,520	5,222	—	—	779	27,178	343
1970	42,681	40,356	2,325	42,833	−152	565	42,612	634
1975	107,652	98,503	9,149	105,935	1,716	461	106,622	1,490
1980	220,626	244,871	−24,245	256,984	−36,358	156	216,668	4,115
1982	212,193	243,952[2]	−31,759	254,885	−42,691	82	207,158	5,117
1983	200,486	258,048[2]	−57,562	269,878	−69,392	52	195,969	4,568

Note: Export values include both commercially-financed shipments and shipments under government-financed programs such as AID and PL-480. (1) Prior to 1974, imports are customs values, i.e. generally at prices in principal foreign markets. (2) In 1981 import value changes back to customers value.

U.S. Foreign Trade, by Economic Classes

(millions of dollars)

Economic class	1965	1970	1975	1980	1981	1982	1983
Exports, total	29,128	45,114	106,622	216,672	228,961	207,158	195,969
Excluding military grant-aid	...	...	106,161	216,515	228,899	207,076	195,918
Crude foods	2,587	2,748	11,804	9,695	10,662	9,077	8,969
Manufactured foods	1,590	1,921	4,221	13,197	13,064	12,618	11,936
Crude materials	2,887	4,492	10,883	18,776	20,314	15,710	15,817
Agricultural	1,942	2,524	5,747	...	...	...	...
Semimanufactures	4,114	6,866	12,815	37,312	44,836	40,545	37,059
Finished manufactures	16,008	26,563	66,379	126,518	140,086	129,208	122,188
Excluding military grant-aid	...	...	65,918	126,362	140,023	129,127	122,136
Imports, total[1]	22,293	40,748	99,305	245,262	260,982	243,952	258,048
Crude foods	2,008	2,579	3,642	7,737	7,318	7,318	7,664
Manufactured foods	1,877	3,519	5,953	10,385	10,841	9,832	10,549
Crude materials	3,709	4,126	23,570	76,380	75,475	57,704	48,293
Agricultural	864	797	1,280	2,336	2,425	2,109	2,291
Semimanufactures	4,964	7,263	17,326	34,072	37,712	33,264	39,797
Finished manufactures	8,871	22,464	46,411	112,620	129,636	135,833	151,745

(1) Customs values are shown for imports.

Total Exports and Exports Financed by Foreign Aid

(millions of dollars)

	1965	1970	1975	1980	1981	1982	1983
Exports, total	27,530	43,224	107,592	220,783	233,739	212,275	200,538
Agricultural commodities	6,306	7,349	22,097	41,757	43,815	37,011	36,456
Nonagricultural commodities	20,445	35,310	85,094	178,948	189,924	175,264	164,082
Manufactured goods (domestic)	17,439	29,343	70,950	143,971	154,335	139,738	132,427
Military grant—aid	779	565	461	156	62	82	52
Export financed under P.L.-480	1,323	1,021	1,181	1,094	1,276	956	1,043
Sales for foreign currency	899	276	—	—	—	—	—
Donations, including disaster relief	253	255	257	329	504	228	286
Long-term dollar credit sales	152	490	924	765	772	727	758
AID expend. for U.S. goods for export	—	—	665	673	588	567	580

Value of Principal Agricultural Exports

(millions of dollars)

Commodity	Avg. 1961-65	Avg. 1966-70	1965	1970	1975	1980	1982	1983
Wheat and wheat products	1,268	1,197	1,214	1,144	5,292	6,660	6,927	6,561
Feed grains	841	1,082	1,162	1,099	5,492	9,759	6,444	7,266
Rice	178	311	244	314	858	1,288	997	926
Fodders and feeds	179	386	278	496	987	1,126	1,037	1,230
Oilseeds and products	774	1,182	1,029	1,642	NA	9,393	9,141	8,716
Cotton, raw	639	408	495	377	991	2,864	1,955	1,817

Public Transportation Usage

Source: U.S. Bureau of the Census

(percentage of workers 16 years and older in each region or SMSA.)

	1970	1980		1970	1980		1970	1980
United States	**9.0**	**6.4**	Los Angeles	5.6	7.0	St. Louis	8.0	5.7
			San Francisco	15.5	16.4	Minneapolis	8.5	8.7
Northeast	**19.1**	**14.2**	Anaheim	0.4	2.1	Cleveland	13.4	10.6
New York	52.5	45.1	San Diego	4.3	3.3	**South**	**5.0**	**3.3**
Philadelpha	20.7	14.0	Denver	4.4	6.1	Washington, D.C.	16.3	15.5
Boston	19.7	15.6	**North Central**	**6.7**	**4.9**	Dallas	5.1	3.4
Nassau-Suffolk, N.Y.	15.5	12.5	Chicago	23.3	18.0	Houston	5.4	3.0
Pittsburgh	14.6	11.5	Detroit	7.9	3.7	Baltimore	13.8	10.3
West	**4.6**	**5.0**				Atlanta	8.4	7.6

Merchant Fleets of the World

Source: Maritime Administration, U.S. Commerce Department

Oceangoing steam and motor ships of 1,000 gross tons and over as of Jan. 1, 1984, excludes ships operating exclusively on the Great Lakes and inland waterways and special types such as channel ships, icebreakers, cable ships, etc., and merchant ships owned by any military force. Tonnage is in thousands. Gross tonnage is a volume measurement; each cargo gross ton represents 100 cubic ft. of enclosed space. Deadweight tonnage is the carrying capacity of a ship in long tons (2,240 lbs.).

Country of registry	Total no.	Total gross tons	Dwt. tons	Freighters Number	Freighters Dwt. tons	Bulk Carriers Number	Bulk Carriers Dwt. tons	Tankers Number	Tankers Dwt. tons
Total-All Countries . . .	25,579	395,325	666,404	14,268	125,646	5,384	216,468	5,548	322,617
United States [1]	788	15,713	24,409	437	6,591	24	1,016	289	16,508
Privately-Owned	538	13,386	21,569	233	4,290	24	1,016	274	16,205
Government-Owned . .	250	2,328	2,840	204	2,301	—	—	15	302
Algeria	64	1,301	1,909	35	281	6	127	22	1,498
Argentina	195	2,292	3,446	103	1,083	19	774	72	1,586
Australia	82	1,900	2,964	31	380	34	1,714	17	870
Belgium.	76	2,063	3,420	29	409	32	2,351	14	645
Brazil	344	5,453	8,988	192	1,676	76	4,004	72	3,303
British Colonies	309	6,247	10,200	141	1,131	139	7,112	27	1,951
*Bulgaria	114	1,201	1,781	50	338	43	885	17	538
*China (People's Rep.)	861	8,293	12,628	599	6,036	138	4,570	114	1,959
China (Republic of) . . .	166	3,083	4,854	98	1,099	51	2,835	16	920
Cyprus	480	4,731	8,110	356	2,281	63	1,611	58	4,209
Denmark	261	4,583	7,444	162	1,889	17	767	79	4,785
Finland	156	2,177	3,595	75	502	35	650	43	2,434
France	314	9,483	16,532	161	1,953	49	2,988	99	11,578
*German Dem. Rep. . . .	158	1,236	1,647	131	1,076	20	456	5	111
Germany (Fed. Rep.) . .	437	5,716	8,869	314	3,173	30	1,741	88	3,925
Greece	2,454	39,090	68,612	1,110	11,709	920	30,596	381	26,169
India	375	6,068	9,847	208	2,617	118	4,938	42	2,251
Indonesia.	317	1,472	2,200	237	1,284	13	330	57	521
Iran	80	1,667	2,847	43	565	17	499	20	1,783
Iraq	48	1,429	2,526	25	386	—	—	22	2,138
Italy	601	8,955	14,964	233	1,591	123	6,490	231	6,816
Japan	1,712	36,933	61,191	692	6,660	490	23,247	525	31,271
Korea (Republic of) . . .	499	6,253	10,585	256	1,895	170	6,348	73	2,342
Kuwait	71	2,527	4,056	39	794	—	—	32	3,262
Liberia	2,019	68,093	131,545	449	5,261	810	42,797	752	83,427
Malaysia	139	1,394	1,979	93	564	17	747	26	659
Mexico	81	1,235	1,959	25	205	6	206	50	1,548
Nassau Bahamas	50	1,944	3,567	16	130	9	292	21	3,127
Netherlands	448	4,408	7,040	350	2,267	29	1,249	65	3,494
Norway	529	18,458	32,470	125	1,332	135	9,332	248	21,737
Panama	3,290	34,617	57,781	2,100	17,566	730	22,526	430	17,498
Philippines	301	2,814	4,601	177	1,189	70	2,289	40	1,086
Poland	306	3,223	4,576	209	1,746	82	2,019	11	799
Portugal	76	1,463	2,630	46	333	6	222	22	2,068
*Romania	242	2,444	3,709	179	1,181	54	1,841	8	685
Saudi Arabia	230	4,781	8,370	127	1,578	23	910	77	5,874
Singapore	556	6,920	11,634	364	3,624	85	3,525	103	4,473
Spain	611	6,023	10,765	323	1,583	75	2,245	112	6,936
Sweden	216	2,941	4,688	119	1,337	22	608	71	2,734
Turkey	260	2,465	4,116	162	802	47	1,605	44	1,693
*USSR	2,497	17,299	23,157	1,804	11,380	192	4,106	455	7,564
United Kingdom	685	16,921	27,251	250	3,010	138	7,233	287	16,948
Yugoslavia	263	2,562	3,923	197	1,949	52	1,593	10	372

*Source material limited. (1) Excludes 56 non-merchant type and/or Navy-owned vessels currently in the Natl. Defense Reserve Fleet.

Commerce at Principal U.S. Ports

Source: Corps of Engineers, Department of the Army (short tons per year, 1983)

Port	Short tons	Port	Short tons
New Orleans, La.	177,302,387	Newport News, Va.	20,911,877
New York, N.Y.	149,255,276	Port Arthur, Tex.	19,945,958
Houston, Tex.	94,649,549	Pascagoula, Miss.	19,157,414
Valdez Hrbr., Alas.	90,138,462	Lake Charles, La.	18,876,295
Baton Rouge, La.	68,556,268	Paulsboro, N.J.	18,756,325
Norfolk Hrbr., Va.	55,294,916	Cincinnati, Ohio.	18,120,151
Long Beach, Calif.	42,010,254	Seattle, Wash.	17,805,168
Baltimore, Hrbr., Md.	40,830,961	Boston, Mass, Port Of.	17,593,627
Tampa Harbor, Fla.	38,079,856	Toledo Hrbr., Ohio.	16,394,148
Corpus C. Ship. Chnl., Tex.	37,974,192	Richmond, Calif.	15,394,697
Corpus Christi, Tex.	36,186,072	Freeport, Tex.	14,989,683
Texas City, Tex.	33,370,791	Huntington, W. Va.	13,748,329
Beaumont, Tex.	33,286,791	Tacoma Hrbr., Wash.	13,246,939
Los Angeles, Calif.	33,099,929	Detroit, Mich.	13,176,099
Mobile, Ala.	32,320,845	Jacksonville, Fla.	12,707,273
Philadelphia, Pa.	31,936,235	Indiana, Ind.	12,303,783
Pittsburgh, Pa.	28,251,436	Everglades, Fla.	11,487,539
Duluth-Supr., Minn.	27,436,085	Savannah, Ga.	10,975,740
Chicago, Ill.	26,819,783	Conneaut Hrbr., Ohio.	10,968,273
Portland, Ore.	25,129,278	Portland, Me.	10,455,784
Marcus Hook, Pa.	23,880,652	Cleveland, Ohio.	8,941,232
St. Louis, Metro., Mo.	22,398,160	Lorain Hrbr., Ohio.	5,672,469

Commerce on U.S. Inland Waterways

Source: Corps of Engineers, Department of the Army 1982

Mississippi River System and Gulf Intracoastal Waterway

Waterway	Tons
Mississippi River, Minneapolis to the Gulf	407,598,656
Mississippi River, Minneapolis to St. Louis	74,660,831
Mississippi River, St. Louis to Cairo	90,495,924
Mississippi River, Cairo to Baton Rouge	143,100,665
Mississippi River, Baton Rouge to New Orleans	296,392,659
Mississippi River, New Orleans to Gulf	260,319,463
Gulf Intracoastal Waterway	82,980,463
Mississippi River System	539,645,354

Ton-Mileage of Freight Carried on Inland Waterways

System	Ton-miles
Atlantic Coast waterways	25,400,557
Gulf Coast waterways	31,844,154
Pacific Coast waterways	12,822,003
Mississippi River System, including Ohio River and tributaries	217,980,716
Great Lakes system, U.S. commerce only	63,232,461
Total:	**351,279,891**

Important Waterways and Canals

The St. Lawrence & Great Lakes Waterway, the largest inland navigation system on the continent, extends from the Atlantic Ocean to Duluth at the western end of Lake Superior, a distance of 2,342 miles. With the deepening of channels and locks to 27 ft., ocean carriers are able to penetrate to ports in the Canadian interior and the American midwest.

The major canals are those of the St. Lawrence Great Lakes waterway — the 3 new canals of the St. Lawrence Seaway, with their 7 locks, providing navigation for vessels of 26-foot draught from Montreal to Lake Ontario; the Welland Ship Canal by-passing the Niagara River between Lake Ontario and Lake Erie with its 8 locks, and the Sault Ste. Marie Canal and lock between Lake Huron and Lake Superior. These 16 locks overcome a drop of 580 ft. from the head of the lakes to Montreal. From Montreal to Lake Ontario the former bottleneck of narrow, shallow canals and of slow passage through 22 locks has been overcome, giving faster and safer movement for larger vessels. The new locks and linking channels now accommodate all but the largest ocean-going vessels and the upper St. Lawrence and Great Lakes are open to 80% of the world's saltwater fleet.

Subsidiary Canadian canals or branches include the St. Peters Canal between Bras d'Or Lakes and the Atlantic Ocean in Nova Scotia; the St. Ours and Chambly Canals on the Richelieu River, Quebec; the Ste. Anne and Carillon Canals on the Ottawa River; the Rideau Canal between the Ottawa River and Lake Ontario, the Trent and Murray Canals between Lake Ontario and Georgian Bay in Ontario and the St. Andrew's Canal on the Red River. The commercial value of these canals is not great but they are maintained to control water levels and permit the passage of small vessels and pleasure craft. The Canso Canal, completed 1957, permits shipping to pass through the causeway connecting Cape Breton Island with the Nova Scotia mainland.

The Welland Canal overcomes the 326-ft. drop of Niagara Falls and the rapids of the Niagara River. It has 8 locks, each 859 ft. long, 80 ft. wide and 30 ft. deep. Regulations permit ships of 730-ft. length and 75-ft. beam to transit.

Shortest Navigable Distances Between Ports

Source: Distances Between Ports, Defense Mapping Agency Hydrographic/Topographic Center

Distances shown are in nautical miles (1.852 meters or about 6,076.115 feet) To get statute miles, multiply by 1.15.

TO	FROM New York	Montreal	Colon[1]
Algiers, Algeria	3,618	3,592	4,737
Amsterdam, Netherlands	3,411	3,318	4,829
Baltimore, Md.	410	1,820	1,904
Barcelona, Spain	3,721	3,695	4,840
Boston, Mass.	378	1,309	2,136
Buenos Aires, Argentina	5,845	6,440	5,344
Cape Town, S. Africa[2]	6,789	7,115	6,425
Cherbourg, France	3,127	3,034	4,545
Cobh, Ireland	2,878	2,780	4,320
Copenhagen, Denmark	3,934	3,841	5,352
Dakar, Senegal	3,336	3,562	3,689
Galveston, Tex.	1,862	3,224	1,485
Gibraltar[3]	3,210	3,184	4,329
Glasgow, Scotland	3,324	3,231	4,742
Halifax, N.S.	593	958	2,298
Hamburg, W. Germany	3,636	3,543	5,054
Hamilton, Bermuda	697	1,621	1,644
Havana, Cuba	1,167	2,528	990
Helsinki, Finland	4,484	4,391	5,902
Istanbul, Turkey	5,006	4,980	6,125
Kingston, Jamaica	1,472	2,690	555
Lagos, Nigeria	4,870	5,130	5,033
Lisbon, Portugal	2,980	2,941	4,155
Marseille, France	3,896	3,870	5,015
Montreal, Quebec	1,516		3,190
Naples, Italy	4,185	4,159	5,304
Nassau, Bahamas	961	2,274	1,165
New Orleans, La.	1,707	3,069	1,403
New York, N.Y.		1,516	1,972
Norfolk, Va.	287	1,697	1,781
Oslo, Norway	3,888	3,795	5,306
Piraeus, Greece	4,687	4,661	5,806
Port Said, Egypt	5,119	5,093	6,238
Rio de Janeiro, Brazil	4,743	5,342	4,246
St. John's, Nfld.	1,097	1,038	2,697
San Juan, Puerto Rico	1,399	2,445	992
Southampton, England	3,156	3,063	4,514

TO	FROM San. Fran.	Vancouver	Panama[1]
Acapulco, Mexico	1,834	2,612	1,426
Anchorage, Alas.	1,892	1,347	5,127
Bombay, India	9,791	9,513	12,930
Calcutta, India	9,006	8,728	12,145
Colon, Panama[1]	3,290	4,065	44
Jakarta, Indonesia	7,657	7,413	10,570
Haiphong, Vietnam	6,657	6,358	9,806
Hong Kong	6,044	5,756	9,196
Honolulu, Hawaii	2,095	2,419	4,688
Los Angeles, Cal.	369	1,162	2,912
Manila, Philippines	6,223	5,946	9,355
Melbourne, Australia	6,966	7,342	7,916
Pusan, S. Korea	4,922	4,623	8,074
Ho Chi Min City, Vietnam	6,890	6,606	9,822
San Francisco, Cal.		812	3,246
Seattle, Wash.	796	126	4,005
Shanghai, China	5,398	5,110	8,571
Singapore	7,356	7,078	10,495
Suva, Fiji	4,760	5,183	6,312
Valparaiso, Chile	5,146	5,915	2,615
Vancouver, B.C.	812		4,021
Vladivostok, USSR	4,554	4,262	7,738
Yokohama, Japan	4,547	4,260	7,687

TO	FROM	Port Said	Cape Town[2]	Singapore
Bombay, India		3,046	4,599	2,435
Calcutta, India		4,691	5,489	1,650
Dar es Salaam, Tanzania		3,129	2,369	4,041
Jakarta, Indonesia		5,276	5,184	527
Hong Kong		6,474	7,071	1,460
Kuwait		3,306	5,169	3,845
Manila, Philippines		6,355	6,952	1,341
Melbourne, Australia		7,837	6,104	3,842
Ho Chi Min City, Vietnam		5,660	6,263	646
Singapore		5,014	5,611	
Yokohama, Japan		7,906	8,503	2,891

(1) Colon on the Atlantic is 44 nautical miles from Panama (port) on the Pacific. (2) Cape Town is 35 nautical miles northwest of the Cape of Good Hope. (3) Gibraltar (port) is 24 nautical miles east of the Strait of Gibraltar.

Notable Ocean Passages by Ships

Compiled by N.R.P. Bonsor

Sailing Vessels

Date	Ship		From	To	Nautical miles	Time D. H. M	Speed (knots)†
1846	Yorkshire		Liverpool	New York	3150	16. 0. 0	8.46†
1853	Northern Light		San Francisco	Boston	—	76. 6. 0	—
1854	James Baines		Boston Light	Light Rock	—	12. 6. 0	—
1854	Flying Cloud		New York	San Francisco	15091	89. 0. 0	7.07†
1868-9	Thermopylae		Liverpool	Melbourne	—	63.18.15	—
—	Red Jacket		New York	Liverpool	3150	13. 1.25	10.05†
—	Starr King		50 S. Lat	Golden Gate	—	36. 0. 0	—
—	Golden Fleece		Equator	San Francisco	—	12.12. 0	—
1905	Atlantic		Sandy Hook	England	3013	12. 4. 0	10.32

Atlantic Crossing by Passenger Steamships

Date	Ship		From	To	Nautical miles	Time D. H. M	Speed (knots)†
1819 (5/22 - 6/20)	Savannah (a)	US	Savannah	Liverpool	—	29. 4. 0	—
1838 (5/7 - 5/22)	Great Western	Br	New York	Avonmouth	3218	14.15.59	9.14
1840 (8/4 - 8/14)	Britannia (b)	Br	Halifax	Liverpool	2610	9.21.44	10.98†
1854 (6/28 - 7/7)	Baltic	US	Liverpool	New York	3037	9.16.52	13.04
1856 (8/6 - 8/15)	Persia	Br	Sandy Hook	Liverpool	3046	8.23.19	14.15†
1876 (12/16-12/24)	Britannic	Br	Sandy Hook	Queenstown	2882	7.12.41	15.94
1895 (5/18 - 5/24)	Lucania	Br	Sandy Hook	Queenstown	2897	5.11.40	22.00
1898 (3/30 - 4/5)	Kaiser Wilhelm der Grosse	Ger	Needles	Sandy Hook	3120	5.20. 0	22.29
1901 (7/10 - 7/17)	Deutschland	Ger	Sandy Hook	Eddystone	3082	5.11. 5	23.51
1907 (10/6 - 10/10)	Lusitania	Br	Queenstown	Sandy Hook	2780	4.19.52	23.99
1924 (8/20 - 8/25)	Mauretania	Br	Ambrose	Cherbourg	3198	5. 1.49	26.25
1929 (7/17 - 7/22)	Bremen*	Ger	Cherbourg	Ambrose	3164	4.17.42	27.83
1933 (6/27 - 7/2)	Europa	Ger	Cherbourg	Ambrose	3149	4.16.48	27.92
1933 (8/11 - 8/16)	Rex	It	Gibraltar	Ambrose	3181	4.13.58	28.92
1935 (5/30 - 6/3)	Normandie*	Fr	Bishop Rock	Ambrose	2971	4. 3. 2	29.98
1938 (8/10 - 8/14)	Queen Mary	Br	Ambrose	Bishop Rock	2938	3.20.42	31.69
1952 (7/11 - 7/15)	United States	US	Bishop Rock	Ambrose	2906	3.12.12	34.51
1952 (7/3 - 7/7)	United States* (e)	US	Ambrose	Bishop Rock	2942	3.10.40	35.59

Other Ocean Passages

Date	Ship		From	To	Nautical miles	Time D. H. M	Speed (knots)†
1928 (June)	USS Lexington		San Pedro	Honolulu	2226	3. 0.36	30.66
1944 (Jul-Sep)	St. Roch (c) (Can)		Halifax	Vancouver	7295	86. 0. 0	—
1945 (7/16-7/19)	USS Indianapolis (d)		San Francisco	Oahu, Hawaii	2091	3. 2.20	28.07
1945 (11/26)	USS Lake Champlain		Gibraltar	Newport News	3360	4. 8.51	32.04
1950 (Jul-Aug)	USS Boxer		Japan	San Francisco	5000	7.18.36	26.80†
1951 (6/1-6/9)	USS Philippine Sea		Yokohama	Alameda	5000	7.13. 0	27.62†
1958 (2/25-3/4)	USS Skate (f)		Nantucket	Portland, Eng	3161	8.11. 0	15.57
1958 (3/23-3/29)	USS Skate (f)		Lizard, Eng	Nantucket	—	7. 5. 0	—
1958 (7/23-8/7)	USS Nautilus (g)		Pearl Harbor	Iceland (via N. Pole)	—	15. 0. 0	—
1960 (2/16-5/10)	USS Triton (h)		New London	Rehoboth, Del	41500	84. 0. 0	20.59†
1960 (8/15-8/20)	USS Seadragon (i)		Baffin Bay	NW Passage, Pac	850	6. 0. 0	—
1962 (10/30-11/11)	African Comet* (US)		New York	Cape Town	6786	12.16.22	22.03
1973 (8/20)	Sea-Land Exchange (k) (US)		Bishop Rock	Ambrose	2912	3.11.24	34.92
1973 (8/24)	Sea-Land Trade (US)		Kobe	Race Rock, BC	4126	5. 6. 0	32.75

† The time taken and/or distance covered is approximate and so, therefore, is the average speed.

* Maiden voyage. (a) The Savannah, a fully rigged sailing vessel with steam auxiliary (over 300 tons, 98.5 ft. long, beam 25.8 ft., depth 12.9 ft.) was launched in the East River in 1818. It was the first ship to use steam in crossing any ocean. It was supplied with engines and detachable iron paddle wheels. On its famous voyage it used steam 105 hours. (b) First Cunard liner. (c) First ship to complete NW Passage in one season. (d) Carried Hiroshima atomic bomb in World War II. (e) Set world speed record; average speed eastbound on maiden voyage 35.59 knots (about 41 m.p.h.). (f) First atomic submarine to cross Atlantic both ways submerged. (g) World's first atomic submarine also first to make undersea voyage under polar ice cap, 1,830 mi. from Point Barrow, Alaska, to Atlantic Ocean, Aug. 1-4, 1958, reaching North Pole Aug. 3. Second undersea transit of the North Pole made by submarine USS Skate Aug. 11, 1958, during trip from New London, Conn., and return. (h) World's largest submarine. Nuclear-powered Triton was submerged during nearly all its voyage around the globe. It duplicated the route of Ferdinand Magellan's circuit (1519-1522) 30,708 mi., starting from St. Paul Rocks off the NE coast of Brazil, Feb. 24-Apr. 25, 1960, then sailed to Cadiz, Spain, before returning home. (i) First underwater transit of Northwest Passage. (k) Fastest freighter crossing of Atlantic.

Fastest Scheduled Train Runs in U.S. and Canada

Source: Donald M. Steffee, figures are based on 1984 timetables

Passenger—(80 mph and over)

Railroad	Train	From	To	Dis. miles	Time min.	Speed mph.
Amtrak	Two trains	Newark'	Trenton	48.1	31	93.1
Amtrak	Nineteen Metroliners	Wilmington'	Baltimore	68.4	45	91.2
Amtrak	Four trains	Baltimore	Wilmington	68.4	46	89.2
Amtrak	Metroliner 101	Metro Park	Trenton	33.9	23	88.4
Amtrak	Four trains	Rensselaer	Hudson	28.0	19	88.4
Amtrak	Garden State Special	Aberdeen	Wilmington	38.3	26	88.4
Amtrak	Seven Metroliners	Newark	Philadelphia	80.5	55	87.8
Amtrak	Two trains	Wilmington	Baltimore	68.4	47	87.3
Amtrak	Eleven trains	Wilmington'	Baltimore	68.4	48	85.5
Amtrak	Nite Owl	Wilmington	Aberdeen	38.3	27	85.1
Amtrak	Three trains	Trenton	Newark	48.1	34	84.9
Amtrak	Two Metroliners	Metro Park	Philadelphia	66.4	47	84.8
Amtrak	Two Metroliners	Philadelphia	Newark	80.5	57	84.7
Via Rail Canada	Renaissance	Kingston	Dorval	165.8	118	84.3
Via Rail Canada	Exec	Brockville	Kingston	50.5	36	84.2
Amtrak	Three trains	Wilmington	Baltimore	68.4	49	83.7

Railroad	Train	From	To	Dis. miles	Time min.	Speed mph.
Amtrak	Four trains	Philadelphia	Newark	80.5	58	83.3
Via Rail Canada	Exec	Guildwood	Kingston	145.1	105	82.9
Amtrak	Embassy	Newark(Del.)	Baltimore	56.4	41	82.5
Amtrak	Four trains	Trenton	Newark	48.1	35	82.5
Amtrak	Two trains	Baltimore	Aberdeen	30.1	22	82.1
Amtrak	Four trains	Baltimore	Wilmington	68.4	50	82.1
Amtrak	Two trains	Wilmington¹	Aberdeen	38.3	28	82.1
Via Rail Canada	Renaissance	Dorval	Kingston	165.8	122	81.5
Amtrak	Four trains	Metro Park¹	Trenton	33.9	25	81.4
Amtrak	Three Metroliners	Philadelphia	Metro Park	66.4	49	81.3
Amtrak	Southwest Limited	Garden City¹	Lamar	99.9	74	81.0
Amtrak	Clocker Service	Princeton Jct	Metro Park	24.3	18	81.0
Amtrak	Merchants Limited	Wilmington	Baltimore	68.4	51	80.5
Amtrak	Two trains	Newark	Trenton	48.1	36	80.2
Via Rail Canada	York	Cornwall	Kingston	108.1	81	80.1

Freight — (62 mph and over)

Railroad	Train	From	To	Dis. miles	Time min.	Speed mph.
Union Pacific	BASV	North Platte	Cheyenne	225.4	205	66.0
Union Pacific	Super Van	North Platte	Cheyenne	225.4	215	62.9
Santa Fe	Seven trains	Gallup	Winslow	125.8	120	62.9
Santa Fe	No. 199	Seligman	Kingman	88.1	85	62.9

Fastest Scheduled Passenger Train Runs in Japan and European Countries

Country	Train	From	To	Dis. miles	Time min.	Speed mph.
France	TGV trains (4 runs)	Paris	Macon	225.5	101	134.0
Japan	Hikari train	Nagoya	Yokohama	196.5	105	112.3
Great Britain	High Speed trains (2)	Peterborough	Stevenage	48.8	29	101.0
West Germany	Six trains	Hamm	Bielefeld	41.7	26	96.2
Italy	Two trains	Rome¹	Chiusi	91.9	66	83.5
Spain	Two trains	Albacete¹	Ea Encina	60.7	48	75.8
Sweden	Two trains	Skvode¹	Hallsberg	70.8	56	75.8
Holland	No. 715	Amersfoort²	Zwolle	41.4	33	75.4

(1) Runs listed in both directions   (2) Mondays only

French Open Northern Section of Paris-Lyon High Speed Line

On September 25th, 1983, the northern section (Combs-la-ville to St. Florentin) of the new high speed line was opened to traffic. As a result, the distance between Paris and Lyon is further shortened to 264.7 miles and train time was cut to two hours—calling for an overall speed of 132.4 mph.

Passenger Car Production, U.S. Plants

Source: Motor Vehicle Manufacturers Association of the U.S., Inc.

	1982	1983	1984 5 mos.		1982	1983	1984 5 mos.
Concord	17,143	3	—	Mark	29,959	34,143	15,141
Eagle	21,672	4,068	—	Continental	20,052	13,513	15,744
Renault Alliance	57,752	153,878	46,364	**Total Lincoln-**			
Renault Encore	—	42,436	40,094	**Mercury**	413,409	538,881	265,338
Total American				**Total Ford Motor Co.**	1,104,054	1,547,680	767,586
Motors Corp.	109,549	200,385	86,458	Chevrolet	42,648	91,228	51,636
Horizon	77,572	117,744	68,397	Corvette	22,838	28,174	14,321
Reliant	162,097	186,496	86,493	Monte Carlo	81,181	124,925	55,556
Caravelle (K)	565	1,999	995	Celebrity/Malibu	169,868	244,480	130,256
Caravelle (E)	990	3,285	2,085	Camaro	214,107	193,118	114,735
Caravelle (M)	—	45	968	Citation	159,068	86,878	48,042
Gran Fury	—	1,255	8,446	Cavalier	96,124	308,461	178,708
Total Plymouth	241,225	310,824	167,384	Chevette	208,417	201,841	94,691
Laser	—	23,656	34,672	**Total Chevrolet**	994,251	1,279,106	687,945
LeBaron	95,361	86,261	57,097	Pontiac	—	12,457	8,589
Fifth Avenue	—	19,733	49,947	Grand Prix	63,509	41,797	9,391
E Class	19,083	73,597	19,421	Bonneville/LeMans			
New Yorker (E)	—	31,402	28,802	& 6000	97,814	55,560	10,612
Total Chrysler-				Firebird	127,861	100,225	48,355
Plymouth	355,669	545,473	357,323	Phoenix	45,469	25,060	9,766
Omni	72,456	126,443	64,594	Fiero	—	29,630	52,526
Daytona	—	19,428	26,289	2000	41,834	117,013	64,946
Aries	129,213	144,042	68,060	1000	44,830	48,178	19,060
Dodge 400	30,458	18,478	—	**Total Pontiac**	421,317	429,920	223,245
Dodge 600 (K)	12,706	8,104	14,625	Oldsmobile	284,440	365,554	177,927
Dodge 600 (E)	—	41,077	22,046	Toronado	35,077	43,135	20,149
Diplomat	—	1,241	15,231	Supreme/Ciera	328,087	527,391	255,762
Total Dodge	244,833	358,813	210,845	Omega	71,394	59,966	22,883
Total Chrysler Corp.	600,502	904,286	568,168	Firenza	40,639	54,800	34,593
Ford	2,034	93,768	34,157	**Total Oldsmobile**	759,637	1,050,846	511,314
Thunderbird	29,326	186,566	70,549	Buick	183,325	249,838	110,221
LTD	—	179,192	98,008	Riviera	43,882	52,503	23,261
Fairmont	57,983	23,728	—	Century/Regal	320,766	411,255	193,770
Tempo	—	106,977	72,611	Skylark	137,810	112,843	42,516
Escort	270,299	290,045	155,279	Skyhawk	65,555	79,169	70,332
EXP	1,062	4,298	13,752	**Total Buick**	751,338	905,608	440,100
Mustang	127,371	124,255	57,892	Cadillac	156,618	180,654	84,730
Total Ford	690,645	1,008,799	502,248	Eldorado	56,638	73,026	34,152
Grand Marquis/Marquis	88,404	90,805	41,351	Seville	22,716	34,873	18,381
Cougar/XR7	10,580	126,395	44,235	Cimarron	10,630	21,258	8,130
Marquis	24,858	77,147	48,542	**Total Cadillac**	246,602	309,811	145,393
Zephyr	40,406	—	—	**Total General**			
Topaz	—	31,005	18,945	**Motors Corp.**	3,173,145	3,975,291	2,007,997
Lynx	82,475	73,413	30,107	Honda	—	55,335	54,132
LN 7	409	290	—	Volkswagen of America	84,246	98,207	50,395
Capri	32,704	24,697	8,327				
Lincoln	47,609	58,872	42,946	**Total Passenger Cars**	5,073,496	6,781,184	3,534,736

Motor Vehicle Registrations, Taxes, Motor Fuel, Drivers' Ages

Source: Federal Highway Adm.; National Transportation Safety Board

State, 1983	Driver's age Jan. 1, 1984 (1) Regular	(2) Juvenile	Minimum age for purchase alcoholic beverage	Licensed drivers[7] (1,000)	Registered autos, buses & trucks[7] (1,000)	State gas tax per gal. cents	Motor fuel adjusted net total tax receipts $1,000	Motor fuel consumption[8] Highway 1,000 gallons	Non-highway 1,000 gallons
Alabama	16		19	2,330	3,078	11	231,914	1,789,845	39,336
Alaska	16		21	343	340	8	18,773	192,852	38,783
Arizona	16		21[3]	2,140	2,308	12	130,063	1,300,264	41,351
Arkansas	16		21	1,594	1,466	9.5	127,574	1,082,402	27,625
California	16/18	14	21	16,656	17,798	9	811,734	10,400,394	260,140
Colorado	18	16	18/21[4]	2,189	2,516	12	138,012	1,443,232	55,243
Connecticut	16/18		20	2,252	2,280	14	151,766	1,249,142	29,813
Delaware	16/18		21	436	423	11	33,761	275,895	5,881
Dist. of Col.	18	16	18/21[4]	383	229	14.8	21,680	167,651	2,991
Florida	16		19	8,255	8,954	9.7	416,761	4,740,741	139,779
Georgia	16		19	3,654	3,972	7.5	246,889	2,754,747	58,680
Hawaii	15		18	569	593	8.5	27,422	299,352	14,471
Idaho	16	14	19	671	890	14.5	60,335	408,350	31,419
Illinois	16/18		21	6,970	7,256	11	365,778	4,284,689	190,455
Indiana	16/18		21	3,349	3,882	11.1	312,797	2,336,250	67,701
Iowa	16/18	14	19	1,932	2,356	13	173,576	1,280,262	127,217
Kansas	16	14	18/21[4]	1,714	2,097	10	117,391	1,147,316	74,832
Kentucky	16		21	2,159	2,633	10	197,454	1,673,670	31,670
Louisiana	15/17	15	18	2,586	2,818	8	192,355	2,076,371	75,117
Maine	15/17		20	785	770	14	49,598	490,251	12,717
Maryland	16/18	15¾	21	2,786	2,933	13.5	207,026	1,849,402	29,946
Massachusetts	17/18	16½	20	3,657	3,749	11	257,564	2,173,346	38,890
Michigan	16/18	14	21	6,465	6,338	13	424,433	3,629,611	121,571
Minnesota	16/18	15	19	2,414	3,327	13	258,428	1,750,093	160,815
Mississippi	15		18/21[4]	1,745	1,610	9	123,243	1,103,696	23,444
Missouri	16		21	3,336	3,439	7	190,572	2,368,597	94,632
Montana	15/16		19	496	783	15	47,278	406,462	40,371
Nebraska	16	14	21[5]	1,094	1,229	15.5	115,974	713,345	67,409
Nevada	16	14	21	661	719	12	61,501	463,627	21,691
New Hampshire	16/18	16	20	686	781	14	56,303	382,003	7,713
New Jersey	17	16	21	5,385	4,940	8	288,300	3,061,619	58,603
New Mexico	15/16		21	965	1,234	11	83,863	715,758	17,703
New York	17/18	16	19	9,022	8,277	8	454,406	5,338,859	184,868
North Carolina	16/18		19/21[4]	3,948	4,588	12	367,899	2,717,239	87,089
North Dakota	16	14	21	434	665	13	33,754	334,727	63,431
Ohio	16/18	14	19/21[4]	7,670	7,596	12	576,225	4,395,587	117,856
Oklahoma	16		21	2,073	2,840	6.5	130,140	1,796,621	53,378
Oregon	16	14	21	1,900	2,085	8	95,479	1,161,783	49,084
Pennsylvania	17/18	16	21	7,356	6,736	12	708,656	4,242,313	103,039
Rhode Island	16/18		21	603	585	13	42,830	346,636	11,908
South Carolina	16	15	18/21[4]	1,907	2,045	13	218,070	1,473,121	36,942
South Dakota	16	14	19/21[4]	495	627	13	54,351	330,997	58,292
Tennessee	16	14	19	2,921	3,353	9	250,975	2,263,193	59,034
Texas	16/18	15	19	10,348	11,627	5	498,729	7,969,555	162,808
Utah	16/18		21	922	1,048	11	80,436	652,228	21,636
Vermont	18	16	18	356	353	11	26,957	229,768	5,868
Virginia	16/18		19/21[4]	3,711	3,689	11	339,834	2,424,216	59,468
Washington	16/18		21	2,767	3,217	16	240,799	1,787,621	56,009
West Virginia	16/18	16	19[6]	1,416	1,142	15.3	98,552	793,277	12,730
Wisconsin	16/18	14	19	3,054	3,203	15	287,045	1,885,665	79,095
Wyoming	16	14	19	398	522	8	37,744	324,240	29,342
Total				**152,038**	**161,939**	**—**	**10,483,799**	**98,478,881**	**3,259,886**

(1) Unrestricted operation of private passenger car. When 2 ages are shown, license is issued at lower age upon completion of approved driver education course. (2) Juvenile license issued with consent of parent or guardian. (3) Effective Jan. 1, 1985. (4) Limited purchase of alcohol, such as beer, is permitted at 18 or 19. (5) Effective Jul. 1, 1985. (6) Age is 21 for nonresidents. (7) Estimated. (8) 1982.

Automobile Factory Sales

Source: Motor Vehicle Manufacturers Association, Detroit, Mich.—wholesale values

Year	Passenger cars Number	Value	Motor trucks, buses Number	Value	Total Number	Value
900	4,192	$4,899,433	—	—	4,190	$4,899,443
910	181,000	215,340,000	6,000	9,660,000	187,000	225,000,000
920	1,905,560	1,809,170,963	321,789	423,249,410	2,227,349	2,232,420,373
930	2,787,456	1,644,083,152	575,364	390,752,061	3,362,820	2,034,853,213
940	3,717,385	2,370,654,083	754,901	567,820,414	4,472,286	2,938,474,497
950	6,665,863	8,468,137,000	1,337,193	1,707,748,000	8,003,056	10,175,885,000
970	6,546,817	14,630,217,000	1,692,440	4,819,752,000	8,239,257	19,449,969,000
981	6,255,340	—	1,700,908		7,956,248	—
982	5,049,184	—	1,906,455		6,955,639	—
983	6,739,223	—	2,413,897		9,153,120	—

After July 1, 1964 all tactical vehicles are excluded. Federal excise taxes are excluded in all years.

Road Mileage Between Selected U.S. Cities

	Atlanta	Boston	Chicago	Cincin-nati	Cleve-land	Dallas	Denver	Des Moines	Detroit	Houston
Atlanta, Ga.	....	1,037	674	440	672	795	1,398	870	699	789
Boston, Mass.. . .	1,037	....	963	840	628	1,748	1,949	1,280	695	1,804
Chicago, Ill.	674	963	....	287	335	917	996	327	266	1,067
Cincinnati, Oh. . .	440	840	287	....	244	920	1,164	571	259	1,029
Cleveland, Oh. . .	672	628	335	244	....	1,159	1,321	652	170	1,273
Dallas, Tex.	795	1,748	917	920	1,159	....	781	684	1,143	243
Denver, Col.. . . .	1,398	1,949	996	1,164	1,321	781	....	669	1,253	1,019
Detroit, Mich. . . .	699	695	266	259	170	1,143	1,253	584	....	1,265
Houston, Tex.. . .	789	1,804	1,067	1,029	1,273	243	1,019	905	1,265	....
Indianapolis, Ind. .	493	906	181	106	294	865	1,058	465	278	987
Kansas City, Mo. .	798	1,391	499	591	779	489	600	195	743	710
Los Angeles, Cal.	2,182	2,979	2,054	2,179	2,367	1,387	1,059	1,727	2,311	1,538
Memphis, Tenn.. .	371	1,296	530	468	712	452	1,040	599	713	561
Milwaukee, Wis. .	761	1,050	87	374	422	991	1,029	361	353	1,142
Minneapolis, Minn.	1,068	1,368	405	692	740	936	841	252	671	1,157
New Orleans, La..	479	1,507	912	786	1,030	496	1,273	978	1,045	356
New York, N.Y.. .	841	206	802	647	473	1,552	1,771	1,119	637	1,608
Omaha, Neb. . . .	986	1,412	459	693	784	644	537	132	716	865
Philadelphia, Pa. .	741	296	738	567	413	1,452	1,691	1,051	573	1,508
Pittsburgh, Pa. .	687	561	452	287	129	1,204	1,411	763	287	1,313
Portland, Ore.. . .	2,601	3,046	2,083	2,333	2,418	2,009	1,238	1,786	2,349	2,205
St. Louis, Mo.. . .	541	1,141	289	340	529	630	857	333	513	779
San Francisco . .	2,496	3,095	2,142	2,362	2,467	1,753	1,235	1,815	2,399	1,912
Seattle, Wash. . .	2,618	2,976	2,013	2,300	2,348	2,078	1,307	1,749	2,279	2,274
Tulsa, Okla.	772	1,537	683	736	925	257	681	443	909	478
Washington, D.C..	608	429	671	481	346	1,319	1,616	984	506	1,375

	Indiana-polis	Kansas City	Los Angeles	Louis-ville	Memphis	Mil-waukee	Minnea-polis	New Orleans	New York	Omaha
Atlanta, Ga.	493	798	2,182	382	371	761	1,068	479	841	986
Boston, Mass.. . .	906	1,391	2,979	941	1,296	1,050	1,368	1,507	206	1,412
Chicago, Ill.	181	499	2,054	292	530	87	405	912	802	459
Cincinnati, Oh. . .	106	591	2,179	101	468	374	692	786	647	693
Cleveland, Oh. . .	294	779	2,367	345	712	422	740	1,030	473	784
Dallas, Tex.	865	489	1,387	819	452	991	936	496	1,552	644
Denver, Col.. . . .	1,058	600	1,059	1,120	1,040	1,029	841	1,273	1,771	537
Detroit, Mich. . . .	278	743	2,311	360	713	353	671	1,045	637	716
Houston, Tex.. . .	987	710	1,538	928	561	1,142	1,157	356	1,608	865
Indianapolis, Ind. .	....	485	2,073	111	435	268	586	796	713	587
Kansas City, Mo. .	485	....	1,589	520	451	537	447	806	1,198	201
Los Angeles, Cal.	2,073	1,589	....	2,108	1,817	2,087	1,889	1,883	2,786	1,595
Memphis, Tenn.. .	435	451	1,817	367	....	612	826	390	1,100	652
Milwaukee, Wis. .	268	537	2,087	379	612	....	332	994	889	493
Minneapolis, Minn.	586	447	1,889	697	826	332	....	1,214	1,207	357
New Orleans, La..	796	806	1,883	685	390	994	1,214	....	1,311	1,007
New York, N.Y.. .	713	1,198	2,786	748	1,100	889	1,207	1,311	....	1,251
Omaha, Neb. . . .	587	201	1,595	687	652	493	357	1,007	1,251	....
Philadelphia, Pa. .	633	1,118	2,706	668	1,000	825	1,143	1,211	100	1,183
Pittsburgh, Pa. .	353	838	2,426	388	752	539	857	1,070	368	895
Portland, Ore.. . .	1,227	1,809	959	2,320	2,259	2,010	1,678	2,505	2,885	1,654
St. Louis, Mo.. . .	235	257	1,845	263	285	363	552	673	948	449
San Francisco . .	2,256	1,835	379	2,349	2,125	2,175	1,940	2,249	2,934	1,683
Seattle, Wash. . .	2,194	1,839	1,131	2,305	2,290	1,940	1,608	2,574	2,815	1,638
Tulsa, Okla.	631	248	1,452	659	401	757	695	647	1,344	387
Washington, D.C..	558	1,043	2,631	582	867	758	1,076	1,078	233	1,116

	Phila-delphia	Pitts-burgh	Port-land	St. Louis	Salt Lake City	San Fran-cisco	Seattle	Toledo	Tulsa	Washing-ton
Atlanta, Ga.	741	687	2,601	541	1,878	2,496	2,618	640	772	608
Boston, Mass.. . .	296	561	3,046	1,141	2,343	3,095	2,976	739	1,537	429
Chicago, Ill.	738	452	2,083	289	1,390	2,142	2,013	232	683	671
Cincinnati, Oh. . .	567	287	2,333	340	1,610	2,362	2,300	200	736	481
Cleveland, Oh. . .	413	129	2,418	529	1,715	2,467	2,348	111	925	346
Dallas, Tex.	1,452	1,204	2,009	630	1,242	1,753	2,078	1,084	257	1,319
Denver, Col.. . . .	1,691	1,411	1,238	857	504	1,235	1,307	1,218	681	1,616
Detroit, Mich. . . .	573	287	2,349	513	1,647	2,399	2,279	59	909	506
Houston, Tex.. . .	1,508	1,313	2,205	779	1,438	1,912	2,274	1,206	478	1,375
Indianapolis, Ind. .	633	353	2,227	235	1,504	2,256	2,194	219	631	558
Kansas City, Mo. .	1,118	838	1,809	257	1,086	1,835	1,839	687	248	1,043
Los Angeles, Cal.	2,706	2,426	959	1,845	715	379	1,131	2,276	1,452	2,631
Memphis, Tenn.. .	1,000	752	2,259	285	1,535	2,125	2,290	654	401	867
Milwaukee, Wis. .	825	539	2,010	363	1,423	2,175	1,940	319	757	758
Minneapolis, Minn.	1,143	857	1,678	552	1,186	1,940	1,608	637	695	1,076
New Orleans, La..	1,211	1,070	2,505	673	1,738	2,249	2,574	986	647	1,078
New York, N.Y.. .	100	368	2,885	948	2,182	2,934	2,815	578	1,344	233
Omaha, Neb. . . .	1,183	895	1,654	449	931	1,683	1,638	681	387	1,116
Philadelphia, Pa. .	....	288	2,821	868	2,114	2,866	2,751	514	1,264	133
Pittsburgh, Pa. . .	288	....	2,535	588	1,826	2,578	2,465	228	984	221
Portland, Ore.. . .	2,821	2,535	....	2,060	767	636	172	2,315	1,913	2,754
St. Louis, Mo.. . .	868	588	2,060	....	1,337	2,089	2,081	454	396	793
San Francisco . .	2,866	2,578	636	2,089	752	....	808	2,364	1,760	2,799
Seattle, Wash. . .	2,751	2,465	172	2,081	836	808	....	2,245	1,982	2,684
Tulsa, Okla.	1,264	984	1,913	396	1,172	1,760	1,982	850	....	1,189
Washington, D.C..	133	221	2,754	793	2,047	2,799	2,684	447	1,189	....

Memorable Manned Space Flights

Sources: National Aeronautics and Space Administration and The World Almanac.

Crew, date	Mission name	Orbits[1]	Duration	Remarks
Yuri A. Gagarin (4/12/61)	Vostok 1	1	1h 48m.	First manned orbital flight.
Alan B. Shepard Jr. (5/5/61)	Mercury-Redstone 3	(2)	15m 22s . .	First American in space.
Virgil I. Grissom (7/21/61)	Mercury-Redstone 4	(2)	15m 37s . .	Spacecraft sank. Grissom rescued.
Gherman S. Titov (8/6-7/61).	Vostok 2	16	25h 18m.	First space flight of more than 24 hrs.
John H. Glenn Jr. (2/20/62)	Mercury-Atlas 6	3	4h 55m 23s . .	First American in orbit.
M. Scott Carpenter (5/24/62)	Mercury-Atlas 7	3	4h 56m 05s . .	Manual retrofire error caused 250 mi. landing overshoot.
Andrian G. Nikolayev (8/11-15/62)	Vostok 3	64	94h 22m.	Vostok 3 and 4 made first group flight.
Pavel R. Popovich (8/12-15/62)	Vostok 4	48	70h 57m.	On first orbit it came within 3 miles of Vostok 3.
Walter M. Schirra Jr. (10/3/62)	Mercury-Atlas 8	6	9h 13m 11s . .	Closest splashdown to target to date (4.5 mi.).
L. Gordon Cooper (5/15-16/63)	Mercury-Atlas 9	22	34h 19m 49s . .	First U.S. evaluation of effects on man of one day in space.
Valery F. Bykovsky (6/14-6/19/63)	Vostok 5	81	119h 06m.	Vostok 5 and 6 made 2d group flight.
Valentina V. Tereshkova (6/16-19/63)	Vostok 6	48	70h 50m.	First woman in space.
Vladimir M. Komarov, Konstantin P. Feoktistov, Boris B. Yegorov (10/12/64)	Voskhod 1	16	24h 17m.	First 3-man orbital flight; first without space suits.
Pavel I. Belyayev, Aleksei A. Leonov (3/18/65)	Voskhod 2	17	26h 02m.	Leonov made first "space walk" (10 min.)
Virgil I. Grissom, John W. Young (3/23/65)	Gemini-Titan 3	3	4h 53m 00s . .	First manned spacecraft to change its orbital path.
James A. McDivitt, Edward H. White 2d, (6/3-7/65)	Gemini-Titan 4	62	97h 56m 11s . .	White was first American to "walk in space" (20 min.).
L. Gordon Cooper Jr., Charles Conrad Jr. (8/21-29/65)	Gemini-Titan 5	120	190h 55m 14s . .	First use of fuel cells for electric power; evaluated guidance and navigation system.
Frank Borman, James A. Lovell Jr. (12/4-18/65)	Gemini-Titan 7	206	330h 35m 31s . .	Longest duration Gemini flight
Walter M. Schirra Jr., Thomas P. Stafford (12/15-16/65)	Gemini-Titan 6-A	16	25h 51m 24s . .	Completed world's first space rendezvous with Gemini 7.
Neil A. Armstrong, David R. Scott (3/16-17/66)	Gemini-Titan 8	6.5	10h 41m 26s . .	First docking of one space vehicle with another; mission aborted, control malfunction.
John W. Young, Michael Collins (7/18-21/66)	Gemini-Titan 10	43	70h 46m 39s . .	First use of Agena target vehicle's propulsion systems; rendezvoused with Gemini 8.
Charles Conrad Jr., Richard F. Gordon Jr. (9/12-15/66)	Gemini-Titan 11	44	71h 17m 08s . .	Docked, made 2 revolutions of earth tethered; set Gemini altitude record (739.2 mi.).
James A. Lovell Jr., Edwin E. Aldrin Jr. (11/11-15/66)	Gemini-Titan 12	59	94h 34m 31s . .	Final Gemini mission; record 5½ hrs. of extravehicular activity.
Vladimir M. Komarov (4/23/67)	Soyuz 1	17	26h 40m.	Crashed after re-entry killing Komarov.
Walter M. Schirra Jr., Donn F. Eisele, R. Walter Cunningham (10/11-22/68)	Apollo-Saturn 7	163	260h 09m 03s . .	First manned flight of Apollo spacecraft command-service module only.
Georgi T. Beregovoi (10/26-30/68)	Soyuz 3	64	94h 51m.	Made rendezvous with unmanned Soyuz 2.
Frank Borman, James A. Lovell Jr., William A. Anders (12/21-27/68) . .	Apollo-Saturn 8	10[3]	147h 00m 42s	First flight to moon (command-service module only); views of lunar surface televised to earth.
Vladimir A. Shatalov (1/14-17/69)	Soyuz 4	45	71h 14m.	Docked with Soyuz 5.
Boris V. Volyanov, Aleksei S. Yeliseyev, Yevgeny V. Khrunov (1/15-18/69)	Soyuz 5	46	72h 46m.	Docked with Soyuz 4; Yeliseyev and Khrunov transferred to Soyuz 4.
James A. McDivitt, David R. Scott, Russell L. Schweickart (3/3-13/69) .	Apollo-Saturn 9	151	241h 00m 54s . .	First manned flight of lunar module.

Crew, date	Mission name	Orbits[1]	Duration	Remarks
Thomas P. Stafford, Eugene A. Cernan, John W. Young (5/18-26/69)	Apollo-Saturn 10	31[4]	192h 03m 23s	First lunar module orbit of moon.
Neil A. Armstrong, Edwin E. Aldrin Jr., Michael Collins (7/16-24/69)	Apollo-Saturn 11	30[3]	195h 18m 35s	First lunar landing made by Armstrong and Aldrin; collected 48.5 lbs. of soil, rock samples; lunar stay time 21 h, 36m, 21 s.
Georgi S. Shonin, Valery N. Kubasov (10/11-16/69)	Soyuz 6	79	118h 42m.	First welding of metals in space. Space lab construction tests made; Soyuz 6, 7 and 8 — first time 3 spacecraft 7 crew orbited earth at once.
Anatoly V. Filipchenko, Vladislav N. Volkov, Viktor V. Gorbatko (10/12-17/69)	Soyuz 7	79	118h 41m.	
Charles Conrad Jr., Richard F. Gordon, Alan L. Bean (11/14-24/69)	Apollo-Saturn 12	45[3]	244h 36m 25s	Conrad and Bean made 2d moon landing; collected 74.7 lbs. of samples, lunar stay time 31 h, 31 m.
James A. Lovell Jr., Fred W. Haise Jr., John L. Swigart Jr. (4/11-17/70)	Apollo-Saturn 13	...	142h 54m 41s	Aborted after service module oxygen tank ruptured; crew returned safely using lunar module oxygen and power.
Alan B. Shepard Jr., Stuart A. Roosa, Edgar D. Mitchell (1/31-2/9/71)	Apollo-Saturn 14	34[3]	216h 01m 57s	Shepard and Mitchell made 3d moon landing, collected 96 lbs. of lunar samples; lunar stay 33 h, 31 m.
Georgi T. Dobrovolsky, Vladislav N. Volkov, Viktor I. Patsayev (6/6-30/71)	Soyuz 11	360	569h 40m.	Docked with Salyut space station; and orbited in Salyut for 23 days; crew died during re-entry from loss of pressurization.
David R. Scott, Alfred M. Worden, James B. Irwin (7/26-8/7/71)	Apollo-Saturn 15	74[3]	295h 11m 53s	Scott and Irwin made 4th moon landing; first lunar rover use; first deep space walk; 170 lbs. of samples; 66 h, 55 m, stay.
Charles M. Duke Jr., Thomas K. Mattingly, John W. Young (4/16-27/72)	Apollo-Saturn 16	64[3]	265h 51m 05s	Young and Duke made 5th moon landing; collected 213 lbs. of lunar samples; lunar stay line 71 h, 2 m.
Eugene A. Cernan, Ronald E. Evans, Harrison H. Schmitt (12/7-19/72)	Apollo-Saturn 17	75[3]	301h 51m 59s	Cernan and Schmitt made 6th manned lunar landing; collected 243 lbs. of samples; record lunar stay of 75 h.
Charles Conrad Jr., Joseph P. Kerwin, Paul J. Weitz (5/25-6/22/73)	Skylab 2	...	672h 49m 49s	First American manned orbiting space station; made long-flights tests, crew repaired damage caused during boost.
Alan L. Bean, Jack R. Lousma, Owen K. Garriott (7/28-9/25/73)	Skylab 3	...	1,427h 09m 04s	Crew systems and operational tests, exceeded pre-mission plans for scientific activities; space walk total 13h, 44 m.
Gerald P. Carr, Edward G. Gibson, William Pogue (11/16/73-2/8/74)	Skylab 4	...	2,017h 16m 30s	Final Skylab mission; record space walk of 7 h, 1 m., record space walks total for a mission 22 h, 21 m.
Alexi Leonov, Valeri Kubason (7/15-7/21/75)	Soyuz 19	96	143h 31m	
Vance Brand, Thomas P. Stafford, Donald K. Slayton (7/15-7/24/75)	Apollo 18	136	217h 30m.	U.S.-USSR joint flight. Crews linked-up in space, conducted experiments, shared meals, and held a joint news conference.
Anatoly Berezovnoy, Valentin Lebedev (5/3-12/10/82)	Soyuz T-5	...	211 days	Set space endurance record.

U.S. Space Shuttles

Name, date	Crew
Columbia (4/12-14/81)	Robert L. Crippen, John W. Young.
Columbia (11/12-14/81)	Joe Engle, Richard Truly.
Columbia (3/22-30/82)	Jack Lousma, C. Gordon Fullerton.
Columbia (6-27/7-4/82)	Thomas Mattingly 2d, Henry Hartsfield Jr.
Columbia (11/11-16/82)	Vance Brand, Robert Overmyer, William Lenoir Joseph Allen.
Challenger (4/4-9/83)	Paul Weitz, Karol Bobko, Story Musgrave, Donald Peterson.
Challenger (6/18-24/83)	Robert L. Crippen, Norman Thagard, John Fabian, Frederick Hauck, Sally K. Ride (1st U.S. woman in space).
Challenger (8/30-9/5/83)	Richard Truly, Daniel Brandenstein, William Thornton, Guion Bluford (1st U.S. black in space), Dale Gardner.
Columbia (11/28-12/8/83)	John Young, Brewster Shaw Jr., Robert Parker, Owen

Name, date	Crew	Name, date	Crew
	Garriott, Byron Lichtenberg, Ulf Merbold.	Challenger (4/6-13/84) . . .	Robert Stewart. Robert L. Crippen, Francis R. Scobee, George D. Nelson, Terry J. Hart, James D. Van Hoften
Challenger (2/3-11/84) . . .	Vance Brand, Robert Gibson, Ronald McNair, Bruce McCandless,		

(1) The U.S. measures orbital flights in revolutions while the Soviets use "orbits." (2) Suborbital. (3) Moon orbits in command module. (4) Moon orbits.

Fire aboard spacecraft Apollo I on the ground at Cape Kennedy, Fla. killed Virgil I. Grissom, Edward H. White and Roger B. Chaffee on Jan. 27, 1967. They were the only U.S. astronauts killed in space tests.

Notable Ocean and Intercontinental Flights

(Certified by the Federation Aeronautique Internationale as of Jan., 1984)

	From	To	Miles	Time	Date
		Dirigible Balloons			
British R-34(1).	East Fortune, Scot.	Mineola, N.Y.	.....	108 hrs.	July 2-6, 1919
	Mineola, N.Y.	Pulham, Eng.	.....	75 hrs.	July 9-13, 1919
Amundsen-Ellsworth-Nobile expedition . . .	Spitsbergen	Teller, Alas.	.....	80 hrs.	May 11-14, 1926
Graf Zeppelin	Friedrichshafen	Lakehurst, N.J. . . .	6,630	4d 15h 46m	Oct. 11-15, 1928
Hindenburg Zeppelin . .	Germany	Lakehurst, N.J. . . .	.....	51h 17m	June 30-July 2, 1936
	Lakehurst, N.J.	Frankfort, Ger.	.....	42h 53m	Aug. 9-11, 1936
USN ZPG-2 Blimp . . .	S. Weymouth, Mass.	Africa			
	Africa	Key West, Fla.	7,000	275h	Mar. 4-16, 1957
		Airplanes			
John Alcock-A.W. Brown (2)	St. John's, Nfld.	Clifden, Ireland . . .	1,960	16h 12m	June 14-15, 1919
Richard E. Byrd (3) . .	Spitsbergen	North Pole	1,545	15h 30m	May 9, 1926
Charles Lindbergh (4) . .	Mineola, N.Y.	Paris	3,610	33h 29m 30s	May 20-21, 1927
C. Levin- C. Chamberlin (5) . .	Roosevelt Field, N.Y. . . . . Mineola, N.Y.	Isleben, Germany . . .	3,911	42h 31m	June 4-6, 1927
Baron G. von Huenefeld, crew (6) . .	Dublin	Greenly Isl., Lab. . . .	.....	37 hrs.	Apr. 12-13, 1928
Sir Hubert Wilkins (9)	Point Barrow, Alaska . . .	Spitsbergen	......	....	Apr. 16, 1928
Sir Chas. Kingsford-Smith, crew (7) . .	Oakland, Cal.	Brisbane, Aust.	.....	....	May 31-June 8, 1928
Amelia Earhart Putnam, W. Stultz, L. Gordon.	Trepassy, Nfld.	Burry Port, Wales . . .	.....	20h 40m	June 17-18, 1928
Richard E. Byrd (8) . .	Bay of Whales.	South Pole	......	....	Nov. 28-29, 1929
D. Coste-M. Bellonte .	Paris.	Valley Stream, N.Y. . .	4,100	37h 18m 30s	Sept. 1-2, 1930
Wiley Post-Harold Gatty	Harbor Grace, Nfld. . . .	England	2,200	16h 17m	June 23-24, 1931
Clyde Pangborn-Hugh Herndon Jr. (10) . . .	Tokyo	Wenatchee, Wash. . . .	4,458	41h 34m	Oct. 3-5, 1931
Amelia Earhart Putnam (11).	Harbor Grace, Nfld. . . .	Ireland	2,026	14h 56m	May 20-21, 1932
James A. Mollison (12)	Portmarnock, Ire.	Pennfield, N.B.	.....	....	Aug. 18, 1932
China Clipper (Pan Am. Airways) (13) . .	San Francisco . . . . . . Manila, P.I.	Manila, P.I San Francisco	....	....	Nov. 22-28, 1935 Dec. 1-6, 1935
Douglas C. Corrigan .	New York.	Dublin, Ire.	.....	28h 13m	July 17-18, 1938
B-29 (C.J. Miller) . .	Honolulu	Washington, D.C. . . .	4,640	17h 21m	Sept. 1, 1945
C-54 (Maj. G.E. Cain)	Tokyo	Washington, D.C. . . .	.....	31h 24m	Sept. 3, 1945
Col. David C. Schilling, USAF (14)	England	Limestone, Me.	3,300	10h 01m	Sept. 22, 1950
Chas. F. Blair Jr. . . .	New York	London.	3,500	7h 48m	Jan 31, 1951
Chas. F. Blair Jr. (15). .	Bardufoss, Norway	Fairbanks, Alas. . . .	3,300	10h 29m	May 29, 1951
Chas. F. Blair Jr. . . .	Fairbanks, Alaska	New York	3,450	9h 31m	May 30, 1950
Canberra Bomber . . .	England	Australia	.....	20h 20m	Mar. 16, 1952
Two U.S. S-55 Helicopters (16)	Westover AFB, Mass. . . .	Prestwick, Scotland . .	3,410	42h 30m	July 15-31, 1952
Canberra Bomber (17)	Aldergrove, N.Ire. . . .	Gander, Nfld. . . .	2,073	4h 34m	Aug. 26, 1952
	Gander, Nfld.	Aldergrove, N.Ire. . .	2,073	3h 25m	Aug. 26, 1952
British Comet	London-Tokyo	Tokyo-London. . . .	20,400	74h 52m	Apr. 3-7, 1953
British Comet	London	Rio de Janeiro . . .	6,000	12h 30m	Sept. 13-14, 1953
Max Conrad (solo) . .	New York.	Paris	.....	22h 23m	Nov. 7, 1954
Canberra Bomber . . .	London (round trip)	New York	6,920	14h 21m 45.4s	Aug. 23, 1955
Capt. William F. Judd .	New York.	Paris	.....	24h 11m	Jan. 29-30, 1956
Spirit of St. Louis II (USAF F-100F jet) . .	McGuire AFB, N.J. . . .	Le Bourget, Paris . . .	.....	6h 38m	May 21, 1957
Max Conrad (solo) . .	New York	Palermo, Sicily . . .	4,440	32h 55m	June 22-23, 1958
Max Conrad (solo) . .	Chicago	Rome.	5,000	34h 3m	Mar. 5-6, 1959
Max Conrad (solo) . .	Casablanca, Mor.	Los Angeles	7,700	58h 36m	June 2-4, 1959
USSR TU-114 (18) . .	Moscow	New York	5,092	11h 6m	June 28, 1959
Boeing 707 airliner . .	San Francisco	Sydney, Australia . . .	7,630	16h 10m	July 2, 1959
Boeing 707-320	New York.	Moscow	c.5,090	8h 54m	July 23, 1959
Max Conrad (solo) . .	Casablanca, Mor.	El Paso, Tex.	6,911	56h 26m	Nov. 22-26, 1959
Col. J.B. Swindal . .	Washington, D.C. . . .	Moscow	5,004	8h 39m 02.2s	May 19, 1963
Concorde GB	London	Washington, D.C. . .	1,023 mph	3h 34m 48s	May 29, 1976
Concorde.	Paris.	Washington, D.C. . .	1,071.86 mph	3h 35m 15s	Aug. 18, 1978
Concorde.	Paris.	New York	1,037.50 mph	3h 30m 11s	Aug. 22, 1978

Notable first flights: (1) Atlantic aerial round trip. (2) Non-stop transatlantic flight. (3) Polar flight. (4) Solo transatlantic flight in the Ryan monoplane the "Spirit of St. Louis." (5) Transatlantic passenger flight. (6) East-West transatlantic crossing. (7) U.S. to Australia flight. (8) South Pole flight. (9) Trans-Arctic flight. (10) Non-stop Pacific flight. (11) Woman's transoceanic solo flight. (12) Westbound transatlantic solo flight. (13) Pacific airmail and U.S. to Philippines crossing. (14) Non-stop jet transatlantic flight. (15) Solo across North Pole. (16) Transatlantic helicopter flight. (17) Transatlantic round trip on same day. (18) Non-stop between Moscow and New York.

International Aeronautical Records

Source: The National Aeronautic Association, 821 15th St. NW, Washington, DC 20005, representative in the United States of the Federation Aeronautique Internationale, certifying agency for world aviation and space records. The International Aeronautical Federation was formed in 1905 by representatives from Belgium, France, Germany, Great Britain, Spain, Italy, Switzerland, and the United States, with headquarters in Paris. Regulations for the control of official records were signed Oct. 14, 1905. World records are defined as maximum performance, regardless of class or type of aircraft used. Records to June, 1984.

World Air Records—Maximum Performance in Any Class

Speed over a straight course — 3,529.56 kph. (2,193.16 mph) — Capt. Elden W. Joersz, USAF, Lockheed SR-71; Beale AFB, Cal., July 28, 1976.

Speed over a closed circuit — 3,367.221 kph. (2,092.294 mph) — Maj. Adolphus H. Bledsoe Jr., USAF, Lockheed SR-71; Beale AFB, Cal., July 27, 1976.

Distance in a straight line — 20,168.78 kms (12,532.28 mi.) — Maj. Clyde P. Evely, USAF, Boeing B52-H; Kadena, Okinawa to Madrid, Spain, Jan. 11, 1962.

Distance over a closed circuit — 18,245.05 kms (11,336.92 mi.) — Capt. William Stevenson, USAF, Boeing B52-H; Seymour-Johnson, N.C., June 6-7, 1962.

Altitude — 37,650 meters (123,523.58 feet) — Alexander Fedotov, USSR, E-266M; Podmoskovnoye, USSR, Aug. 31, 1977.

Altitude in horizontal flight — 25,929.031 meters (85,068.997 ft.) — Capt. Robert C. Helt, USAF, Lockheed SR-71; Beale AFB, Cal., July 28, 1976.

Class K Spacecraft

Duration — 211 days, 9 hrs., 4 min., 32 sec. — Anatoly Berezovnoy & Valentin Lebedev, USSR, Salyut 7, Soyuz T5, Soyuz T7; May 13-Dec. 10, 1982.

Altitude — 377,668.9 kms (234,672.5 mi.) — Frank Borman, James A. Lovell Jr., William Anders, Apollo 8; Dec. 21-27, 1968.

Greatest mass lifted — 127,980 kgs. (282,197 lbs.) — Frank Borman, James S. Lovell Jr., William Anders, Apollo 8; Dec. 21-27, 1968.

Distance — 140,800,200 kms. (87,436,800 mi.) — Anatoly Berezovnoy & Valentin Lebedev, USSR, Salyut 7, Soyuz T5, Soyuz T7; May 13-Dec. 10, 1982.

World "Class" Records

All other records, international in scope, are termed World "Class" records and are divided into classes: airships, free balloons, airplanes, seaplanes, amphibians, gliders, and rotorplanes. Airplanes (Class C) are sub-divided into four groups: Group I — piston engine aircraft, Group II — turboprop aircraft, Group III — jet aircraft, Group IV — rocket powered aircraft. A partial listing of world records follows:

Airplanes (Class C-I, Group I—piston engine)

Distance, closed circuit — 16,104.0 kms (10,007 mi.) — Jerry Mullens; BD-2; Oklahoma City, Okla.—Jacksonville, Fla. course; Dec. 5-8, 1981.

Distance, straight line — 18,081.99 kms. (11,235.6 miles) — Cmdr. Thomas D. Davies, USN; Cmdr. Eugene P. Rankin, USN; Cmdr. Walter S. Reid, USN, and Lt. Cmdr. Ray A. Tabeling, USN; Lockheed P2V-1; from Pearce Field, Perth, Australia to Columbus, Oh., Sept. 29-Oct. 1, 1946.

Speed over 3-kilometer measured course — 803.138 kph. (499.04 mph) — Steve Hinton; P-51D; Tonopah, Nev., Aug. 14, 1979.

Speed for 100 kilometers (62.137 miles) without payload — 755.668 kph. (469.549 mph.) — Jacqueline Cochran, U.S.; North American P-51; Coachella Valley, Cal., Dec. 10, 1947.

Speed for 1,000 kilometers (621.369 miles) without payload — 693.78 kph. (431.09 mph.) — Jacqueline Cochran, U.S.; North American P-51; Santa Rosasummit, Cal. — Flagstaff, Ariz. course, May 24, 1948.

Speed for 5,000 kilometers (3,106.849 miles) without payload — 544.59 kph. (338.39 mph.) — Capt. James Bauer, USAF, Boeing B-29; Dayton, Oh., June 28, 1946.

Speed around the world — 327.73 kph (203.64 mph) — D.N. Dalton, Australia; Beechcraft Duke; Brisbane, Aust., July 20-25, 1975. Time: 5 days, 2 hours, 19 min., 57 sec.

Light Airplanes—(Class C-1.d)

Distance in a straight line — 12,341.26 kms. (7,668.48 miles) — Max Conrad, U.S.; Piper Comanche; Casablanca, Morocco to Los Angeles, June 2-4, 1959.

Speed for 100 kilometers — (62.137 miles) in a closed circuit — 519.480 kph. (322.780 mph.) — Ms. R. M. Sharpe, Great Britain; Vickers Supermarine Spitfire 5-B; Wolverhampton, June 17, 1950.

Helicopters (Class E-1)

Distance in a straight line — 3,561.55 kms. (2,213.04 miles) — Robert G. Ferry, U.S.; Hughes YOH-6A helicopter; Culver City, Cal., to Ormond Beach, Fla., Apr. 6-7, 1966.

Speed over 3-km. course — 348.971 kph. (216.839 mph.) — Byron Graham, U.S.; Sikorsky S-67 helicopter; Windsor Locks, Conn., Dec. 14, 1970.

Speed around the world —56.97 kph. (35.40 mph) — H. Ross Perot Jr.; Bell 206 L-11 Long Ranger N39112; Dallas, Tex.–Dallas, Tex.; Sept. 1-30, 1982; 29 days, 3 hrs., 8 min., 13 sec.

Gliders (Class D-I—single place)

Distance, straight line — 1,460.8 kms. (907.7 miles) — Hans Werner Grosse, West Germany; ASK12 sailplane; Luebeck to Biarritz, Apr. 25, 1972.

Altitude above sea level — 14,102 meters (46,267 feet) — Paul F. Bikle, U.S.; Sailplane Schweizer SGS-123-E; Mojave, Lancaster, Cal., Feb. 25, 1961.

Airplanes (Class C-I, Group II—Turboprop)

Distance in a straight line — 14,052.95 kms. (8,732.09 miles) — Lt. Col. Edgar L. Allison Jr., USAF, Lockheed HC-130 Hercules aircraft; Taiwan to Scott AFB, Ill.; Feb. 20, 1972.

Altitude — 15,549 meters (51,014 ft.) — Donald R. Wilson, U.S.; LTV L450F aircraft; Greenville, Tex., Mar. 27, 1972.

Speed for 1,000 kilometers (621.369 miles) without payload — 871.38 kph. (541.449 mph.) — Ivan Soukhomline, USSR; TU-114 aircraft; Sternberg, USSR; Mar. 24, 1960.

Speed for 5,000 kilometers (3,106.849 miles) without payload — 877.212 kph. (545.072 mph.) — Ivan Soukhomline, USSR; TU-114 aircraft, Sternberg, USSR; Apr. 9, 1960.

Airplanes (Class C-1, Group III—Jet-powered)

Distance in a straight line — 20,168.78 kms. (12,532.28 mi.) — Maj. Clyde P. Evely, USAF, Boeing B-52-H, Kadena, Okinawa, to Madrid, Spain, Jan. 10-11, 1962.

Distance in a closed circuit — 18,245.05 kms. (11,336.92 mi.) — Capt. William Stevenson, USAF, Boeing B-52-H, Seymour-Johnson, N.C., June 6-7, 1962.

Altitude — 36,650 meters (123,523.58 ft.) — Alexander Fedotov, USSR; E-226M airplane; Podmoskovnoye, USSR, Aug. 31, 1977.

Speed over a 3-kilometer course — 1,590.45 kph (988.26 mph) — Darryl G. Greenamyer, U.S.; F-104; Tonopah, Nev., Oct. 24, 1977.
Speed for 100 kilometers in a closed circuit — 2,605 kph. (1,618.7 mph.) — Alexander Fedotov, USSR; E-266 airplane, Apr. 8, 1973.
Speed for 500 kilometers in a closed circuit — 2,981.5 kph. (1,852.61 mph.) — Mikhail Komarov, USSR; E-266 airplane, Oct. 5, 1967.
Speed for 1,000 kilometers in a closed circuit — 3,367.221 kph (2,092.294 mph) — Maj. Adolphus H. Bledsoe Jr., USAF; Lockheed SR-71; Beale AFB, Cal., July 27, 1976.
Speed for 2,000 kilometers in closed circuit — 2,012,257 kph. (1,250.42 mph.) — S. Agapov, USSR; Podmoscovnde, USSR; July 20, 1983.
Speed around the world — 825.32 kph. (512.853 mph) — Brooke Knapp, U.S., Gulfstream III; Washington, D.C., Feb. 13-15, 1984.

Balloons-Class A

Altitude — 34,668 meters (113,739.9 feet) — Cmdr. Malcolm D. Ross, USNR; Lee Lewis Memorial Winzen Research Balloon; Gulf of Mexico, May 4, 1961.
Distance — 8,382.4 kms.(5,208.67 mi.) — Ben Abruzzo; Raven Experimental; Nagashima, Japan to Covello, Cal., Nov. 9-12, 1981.

Duration — 137 hr., 5 min., 50 sec. — Ben Abruzzo and Maxie Anderson; Double Eagle II; Presque Isle, Maine to Miserey, France (3,107.61 mi.); Aug. 12-17, 1978.

FAI Course Records

Los Angeles to New York — 1,954.79 kph (1,214.65 mph) — Capt. Robert G. Sowers, USAF; Convair B-58 Hustler; elapsed time: 2 hrs. 58.71 sec., Mar. 5, 1962.
New York to Los Angeles — 1,741 kph (1,081.80 mph) — Capt. Robert G. Sowers, USAF; Convair B-58 Hustler; elapsed time: 2 hrs. 15 min. 50.08 sec., Mar. 5, 1962.
New York to Paris — 1,753.068 kph (1,089.36 mph) — Maj. W. R. Payne, U.S.; Convair B-58 Hustler; elapsed time: 3 hrs 19 min. 44 sec., May 26, 1961.
London to New York — 945.423 kph (587.457 mph) — Maj. Burl Davenport, USAF; Boeing KC-135; elapsed time: 5 hrs. 53 min. 12.77 sec.; June 27, 1958.
Baltimore to Moscow, USSR — 906.64 kph (563.36 mph) — Col. James B. Swindal, USAF; Boeing VC-137 (707); elapsed time: 8 hrs. 33 min. 45.4 sec., May 19, 1963.
New York to London — 2,908.026 kph (1,806.964 mph) — Maj. James V. Sullivan, USAF; Lockheed SR-71; elapsed time 1 hr. 54 min. 56.4 sec., Sept. 1, 1974.
London to Los Angeles — 2,310.353 kph (1,435.587 mph) — Capt. Harold B. Adams, USAF; Lockheed SR-71; elapsed time: 3 hrs. 47 min. 39 sec., Sept. 13, 1974.

National Aviation Hall of Fame

The National Aviation Hall of Fame at Dayton, Oh., is dedicated to honoring the outstanding pioneers of air and space.

Allen, William M.
Armstrong, Neil A.
Arnold, Henry H. "Hap"
Atwood, John Leland

Balchen, Bernt
Baldwin, Thomas S.
Beachley, Lincoln
Beech, Olive A.
Beech, Walter H.
Bell, Alexander Graham
Bell, Lawrence D.
Boeing, William E.
Borman, Frank
Boyd, Albert
Byrd, Richard E.

Cessna, Clyde V.
Chamberlin, Clarence D.
Chanute, Octave
Chennault, Claire L.
Cochran (Odlum), Jacqueline
Conrad Jr., Charles
Crossfield, A. Scott
Cunningham, Alfred A.
Curtiss, Glenn H.

deSeversky, Alexander P.
Doolittle, James H.
Douglas, Donald W.
Draper, Charles S.

Eaker, Ira C.
Earhart, (Putnam), Amelia
Ellyson, Theodore G.
Ely, Eugene B.

Fairchild, Sherman M.
Fleet, Reuben H.
Fokker, Anthony H.G.
Ford, Henry
Foss, Joseph
Foulois, Benjamin D.

Gabreski, Francis S.
Glenn Jr., John H.
Goddard, George W.
Goddard, Robert H.
Goldwater, Barry M.
Gross, Robert E.
Grumman, Leroy R.
Guggenheim, Harry F.

Hegenberger, Albert F.
Heinemann, Edward H.
Hughes, Howard R.

Ingalls, David S.

Johnson, Clarence L.

Kenney, George C.
Kettering, Charles F.
Kindelberger, James H.

Knabenshue, A. Roy

Lahm, Frank P.
Langley, Samuel P.
Lear, William P. Sr.
LeMay, Curtis E.
LeVier, Anthony W.
Lindbergh, Anne M.
Lindbergh, Charles A.
Link, Edwin A.
Loening, Grover
Luke Jr., Frank

Macready, John A.
Martin, Glenn L.
Mcdonnell, James S.
Mitchell, William "Billy"
Montgomery, John J.
Moss, Sanford A.

Northrop, John K.

Patterson, William A.
Piper Sr., William T.
Post, Wiley H.

Read, Albert C.
Reeve, Robert C.
Rentschler, Frederick B.
Richardson, Holden C.
Rickenbacker, Edward V.

Rodgers, Calbraith P.
Rogers, Will
Ryan, T. Claude

Schriever, Bernard A.
Selfridge, Thomas E.
Shepard Jr., Alan B.
Sikorsky, Igor I.
Six, Robert F.
Smith, C.R.
Spaatz, Carl A.
Sperry Sr., Elmer A
Sperry Sr., Lawrence B.

Taylor, Charles E.
Towers, John H.
Trippe, Juan T.
Turner, Roscoe
Twining, Nathan F.

von Braun, Wernher
von Karman, Theodore

Wade, Leigh
Walden, Henry W.
Wilson, Thornton A.
Wright, Orville
Wright, Wilbur

Yeager, Charles

The Busiest U.S. Airports in 1983

Source: Federal Aviation Administration; (Total take-offs and landings)

Chicago O'Hare International	671,724	St. Louis International	361,724
Atlanta International	612,791	Oakland International	356,799
Los Angeles International	506,076	Denver Arapahoe County	353,877
Van Nuys	494,273	Boston Logan	351,474
Denver Stapleton International	458,060	La Guardia (N.Y. City)	350,214
Santa Ana	457,805	J.F. Kennedy International (N.Y. City)	347,801
Dallas/Ft. Worth Regional	435,533	Phoenix Sky Harbor	346,722
Long Beach	422,196	Miami International	341,619
Seattle Boeing	392,031	Honolulu	335,928
San Francisco	364,791	Anchorage Merrill	335,509

Notable Trips Around the World

(Certified by Federation Aeronautique Internationale as of Jan., 1984)

Fast circuits of the earth have been a subject of wide interest since Jules Verne, French novelist, described an imaginary trip by Phileas Fogg in Around the World in 80 Days, assertedly occurring Oct. 2 to Dec. 20, 1872.

	Terminal	Miles	Time	Date
Nellie Bly	New York, N.Y.		72d 06h 11m	1889
George Francis Train	New York, N.Y.		67d 12h 03m	1890
Charles Fitzmorris	Chicago		60d 13h 29m	1901
J. W. Willis Sayre	Seattle		54d 09h 42m	1903
Col. Burnlay-Campbell			40d 19h 30m	1907
Andre Jaeger-Schmidt			39d 19h 42m 38s	1911
John Henry Mears			35d 21h 36m	1913
Two U.S. Army airplanes	Seattle (57 hops, 21 countries)	26,103	35d 01h 11m	1924
Edward S. Evans and Linton Wells (New York World) (1)	New York	18,400	28d 14h 36m 05s	June 16-July 14, 1926
John H. Mears and Capt. C.B.D. Collyer	New York		23d 15h 21m 03s	June 29-July 22, 1928
Graf Zeppelin	Friedrichshafen, Ger. via Tokyo, Los Angeles, Lakehurst, N.J.	21,700	20d 04h	Aug. 14-Sept. 4, 1929
Wiley Post and Harold Gatty (Monoplane Winnie Mae)	Roosevelt Field, N.Y. via Arctic Circle	15,474	8d 15h 51m	June 23-July 1, 1931
Wiley Post (Monoplane Winnie Mae) (2)	Floyd Bennett Field, N.Y. via Arctic Circle	15,596	115h 36m 30s	July 15-22, 1933
H. R. Ekins (Scripps-Howard Newspapers in race) (Zeppelin Hindenburg to Germany air planes from Frankfurt)	Lakehurst, N.J., via Frankfurt, Germany	25,654	18d 11h 14m 33s	Sept. 30-Oct. 19, 1936
Howard Hughes and 4 assistants	New York, Paris, Moscow, Siberia, Fairbanks	14,824	3d 19h 08m 10s	July 10-13, 1938
Mrs. Clara Adams (Pan American Clipper)	Port Washington, N.Y., return Newark, N.J.		16d 19h 04m	June 28-July 15, 1939
Globester, U.S. Air Transport Command	Washington, D.C.	23,279	149h 44m	Sept. 28-Oct. 4, 1945
Capt. William P. Odom (A-26 Reynolds Bombshell)	New York, via Paris, Cairo, Tokyo, Alaska	20,000	78h 55m 12s	Apr. 12-16, 1947
America, Pan American 4-engine Lockheed Constellation (3)	New York	22,219	101h 32m	June 17-30, 1947
Col. Edward Eagan	New York	20,559	147h 15m	Dec. 13, 1948
USAF B-50 Lucky Lady II (Capt. James Gallagher) (4)	Fort Worth, Tex.	23,452	94h 01m	Feb. 26-Mar. 2, 1949
Jean-Marie Audibert	Paris		4d 19h 38m	Dec. 11-15, 1952
Pamela Martin	Midway Airport, Chicago		90h 59m	Dec. 5-8, 1953
Three USAF B-52 Stratofortresses (5)	Merced, Cal., via Nfld., Morocco, Saudi Arabia, India, Ceylon, P.I., Guam	24,325	45h 19m	Jan. 15-18, 1957
Joseph Cavoli	Cleveland, Oh.		89h 13m 37s	Jan. 31-Feb. 4, 1958
Peter Gluckmann (solo)	San Francisco	22,800	29d	Aug. 22-Sept. 20, 1959
Milton Reynolds	San Francisco		51h 45m 22s	Jan. 12-14, 1960
Sue Snyder	Chicago	21,219	62h 59m	June 22-24, 1960
Max Conrad (solo)	Miami, Fla.	25,946	8d 18h 35m 57s	Feb. 28-Mar. 8, 1961
Sam Miller & Louis Fodor	New York		46h 28m	Aug. 3-4, 1963
Robert & Joan Wallick	Manila, Philippines	23,129	5d 6h 17m 10s	June 2-7, 1966
Arthur Godfrey, Richard Merrill Fred Austin, Karl Keller	New York	23,333	86h 9m 01s	June 4-7, 1966
Trevor K. Brougham	Darwin, Australia	24,800	5d 05h 57m	Aug. 5-10, 1972
Walter H. Mullikin, Albert Frink, Lyman Watt, Frank Cassaniti, Edward Shields	New York	23,137	1d 22h 50s	May 1-3, 1976
Arnold Palmer	Denver, Col.	22,985	57h 25m 42s	May 17-19, 1976
Boeing 747 (6)	San Francisco	26,382	54h 7m 12s	Oct. 28-31, 1977

(1) Mileage by train and auto, 4,110; by plane, 6,300; by steamship, 8,000. (2) First to fly solo around northern circumference of the world, also first to fly twice around the world. (3) Inception of regular commercial global air service. (4) First non-stop round-the-world flight, refueled 4 times in flight. (5) First non-stop global flight by jet planes; refueled in flight by KC-97 aerial tankers; average speed approx. 525 mph. (6) Speed record around the world over both the earth's poles.

U.S. Scheduled Airline Traffic

Source: Air Transport Association of America (thousands)

	1981	1982	1983
Passenger traffic			
Revenue passengers enplaned	285,976	294,102	317,905
Revenue passenger miles	248,887,801	259,643,870	281,305,274
Available seat miles	424,897,230	440,119,206	463,375,756
Cargo traffic (ton miles)	7,060,028	6,885,973	7,565,519
Freight	5,618,113	5,424,233	6,020,527
Express	67,974	57,965	66,142
U.S. Mail	1,348,030	1,374,572	1,374,572
Overall traffic and service			
Nonscheduled traffic—total ton miles	1,974,626	2,200,552	2,205,927
Total revenue ton miles—all services	33,923,495	35,050,938	37,901,864
Total available ton miles—all services	64,244,767	65,769,930	68,561,441

AGRICULTURE

World Wheat, Rice and Corn Production, 1981

Source: UN Food and Agriculture Organization

(thousands of metric tons)

Country	Wheat	Rice	Corn	Country	Wheat	Rice	Corn
World, total	**458,195**	**413,785**	**451,704**	Italy	8,921	931	7,250
United States	76,026	8,408	208,314	Japan	612	12,824	3
Afghanistan	3,000	475	798	Kampuchea	NA	1,160	98'
Argentina	8,100	286	13,500	Korea, Dem. Peo. Rep.'	400	4,900	2,200'
Australia	16,400	761	118	Korea, Republic of	57	7,032	145
Austria	1,025	NA	1,374	Laos	NA	1,155'	33
Bangladesh	1,093	20,000'	1'	Madagascar	—	1,999	126
Belgium	943²	NA	25²	Malaysia	NA	2,147	8
Brazil	2,207	8,261	21,098	Mexico	3,189	644	14,766
Bulgaria	4,429	71	2,477	Nepal	440	2,407	720'
Burma	80'	14,636	100'	Netherlands	892	NA	2
Canada	24,519	NA	6,214	New Zealand	373	NA	177
Chile	686	100	518	Pakistan	11,340	5,093	1,004
China: Mainland'	57,003	146,087	61,061	Panama	NA	192	68
Colombia	62	1,799	880	Peru	117	684	628
Cuba	NA	518'	95'	Philippines	NA	7,720	3,176
Czechoslovakia	4,400'	NA	800	Poland	4,229	NA	79
Denmark	792	NA	NA	Portugal	310	112	417
Ecuador	41	402	246	Romania	5,800'	65	11,200'
Egypt	1,850	2,500	2,700	South Africa	2,090	3'	14,650
Ethiopia	491	NA	1,100'	Soviet Union	88,000'	2,400'	8,000'
Finland	235	NA	NA	Spain	3,356	441	2,151
France	22,782	21	9,100	Sri Lanka	NA	2,020	25'
German Dem. Rep.	3,000'	NA	2'	Sweden	1,034	NA	NA
Germany, Fed. Rep.	8,314	NA	832	Switzerland	391	NA	117
Greece	2,750	74	1,250	Syria	2,086	NA	89
Hungary	4,800'	35'	6,500	Thailand	NA	19,000	3,700
India	36,460	82,000'	7,000'	Turkey	17,040	290	1,100
Indonesia	NA	33,000	3,991	United Kingdom	8,465	NA	1'
Iran	5,800	1,400	50'	Uruguay	400	326	196
Iraq	1,100	250'	90'	Venezuela	1	708	486
Ireland	240	NA	NA	Vietnam	NA	12,570	540'
Israel	215	NA	15'	Yugoslavia	4,270	40'	9,800

(1) FAO estimate. (2) Includes Luxembourg. (NA) Not available.

Wheat, Rice and Corn—Exports and Imports of 10 Leading Countries

Source: U.S Agriculture Department

(In thousands of metric tons.)

Leading Exporters	Exports			Leading Importers	Imports		
	1975	1980	1981		1975	1980	1981
Wheat				**Wheat**			
United States	30,967	35,756	43,909	Soviet Union	9,146	14,700	16,500
Canada	11,065	16,760	15,472	China: Mainland	3,893	12,255	13,038
France	6,281	9,889	12,785	Japan	5,654	5,682	5,633
Australia	7,860	14,876	10,552	Brazil	2,098	4,755	4,360
Argentina	1,758	4,495	3,758	Egypt	2,681	4,417	3,949
Soviet Union	2,681	1,270	1,600	Poland	1,477	3,466	3,448
United Kingdom	217	1,057	1,450	Italy	1,613	3,134	3,016
Hungary	952	814	1,298	Morocco	1,352	1,652	2,368
Netherlands	1,537	525	626	Iran	1,440	1,330	2,060
Spain	—	45	538	Korea, Rep. of	1,519	1,868	1,957
Rice				**Rice**			
Thailand	951	2,797	3,138	Korea, Rep. of	483	899	2,585
United States	2,139	3,054	3,133	Soviet Union	279	694	1,283
Pakistan	478	1,087	1,244	Nigeria	7	400	600
India	18	575	953	Indonesia	693	2,012	538
Japan	11	689	855	Iran	286	470	500
Burma	286	653	700	Saudi Arabia	69	356	427
China: Mainland	1,968	1,311	692	Hong Kong	344	359	360
Italy	439	577	572	Iraq	151	345	350
Korea, Dem. Peo. Rep.	340	300	300	Malaysia	165	168	342
Australia	174	457	281	Senegal	102	279	321
Corn				**Corn**			
United States	33,503	63,152	54,856	Soviet Union	5,548	10,000	14,630
Argentina	3,887	3,481	9,112	Japan	7,470	12,830	13,590
South Africa	3,218	3,317	4,400	Spain	4,182	4,532	4,830
Thailand	2,072	2,175	2,549	China: Mainland	1,538	4,405	3,261
France	2,552	3,181	2,355	Korea, Rep. of	541	2,351	3,051
Belgium-Luxembourg	232	1,357	1,486	Mexico	2,637	3,713	2,844
Canada	17	771	1,207	Portugal	1,221	2,624	2,644
Romania	458	1,000	1,000	Netherlands	5,236	3,010	2,622
Netherlands	2,553	490	459	Belgium-Luxembourg	1,468	2,570	2,576
Yugoslavia	52	273	220	Italy	4,499	2,931	2,556

Agricultural Products — U.S. and World Production and Exports

Source: Foreign Agricultural Service. U.S. Agriculture Department

1983/84 Commodity	Unit	Production U.S.	Production World	% U.S.	Exports[6] U.S.	Exports[6] World	% U.S.
Wheat[1]	MMT	65.9	489.7	13.5	38.1	107.7	35.4
Oats[1]	MMT	6.9	45.9	15.0	0.05	2.1	2.4
Corn[1]	MMT	105.8	346.8	30.5	50.2	69.3	72.4
Barley[1]	MMT	11.1	170.4	6.5	2.0	18.9	10.6
Rice[1]	MMT	4.5	448.9	1.0	2.0	11.9	16.8
Sorghum[1]	MMT	12.2	61.3	19.9	5.7	12.5	45.6
Soybeans[1]	MMT	42.6	79.7	53.4	22.5	26.4	85.2
Tobacco, unmfd.[1]	MMT	0.65	6.0	10.8	0.24	1.4	17.2
Edible, Veg. Oils[1]	MMT	5.4	41.7	13.0	1.0	6.9	14.5
Cotton[1]	MB[2]	7.8	67.6	11.5	5.5	19.2	28.6

(1) Standard Trade Years Wheat: July-June (83/84); Oats: Oct-Sept (83/84); Corn: Oct-Sept (83/84); Barley: Oct-Sept (83/84); Rice: Aug-July (83/84); Sorghum: Oct-Sept (83/84); Soybeans: Sept-Oct (83/84); Tobacco: Jan-Dec (83); Edible Veg. Oils: Jan-Dec (83); Cotton: Aug-July (83/84). (2) Million Bales.

Grain, Hay, Potato, Cotton, Soybean, Tobacco Production

Source: Economic Research Service. U.S. Agriculture Department

1983 State	Barley 1,000 bushels	Corn, grain 1,000 bushels	Cotton lint 1,000 bales	All hay 1,000 tons	Oats 1,000 bushels	Potatoes 1,000 cwt.	Soybeans 1,000 bushels	Tobacco 1,000 pounds	All wheat 1,000 bushels
Alabama	—	17,995	180	1,040	1,960	1,536	27,550	—	15,180
Alaska	—	—	—	—	—	—	—	—	—
Arizona	4,104	2,448	—	98	—	1,274	—	—	11,094
Arkansas	—	2,640	320	1,279	3,600	—	69,660	—	58,500
California	29,400	33,280	1,960	1,272	2,610	19,949	—	—	47,900
Colorado	19,125	76,250	—	1,248	3,355	17,764	—	—	122,103
Connecticut[2]	—	—	—	138	—	266	—	3,517	—
Delaware	2,915	11,100	—	26	—	999	7,105	—	1,716
Florida	—	8,576	17	550	—	5,840	10,250	17,940	—
Georgia	—	55,125	115	1,000	5,185	—	42,000	95,400	33,320
Hawaii	—	—	—	—	—	—	—	—	—
Idaho	65,650	7,021	—	897	3,648	83,590	—	—	91,710
Illinois	—	632,000	—	799	12,600	552	255,200	—	65,800
Indiana	—	346,910	—	798	4,560	788	122,450	11,250	49,470
Iowa	—	743,850	—	1,100	38,250	176	270,640	—	1,900
Kansas	4,500	83,600	—	2,100	5,820	—	23,550	—	448,200
Kentucky	825	46,080	—	2,080	308	—	23,630	311,790	17,920
Louisiana	—	5,040	540	735	—	50	66,820	—	7,500
Maine[2]	—	—	—	355	2,294	22,090	—	—	—
Maryland	4,950	37,740	—	389	896	304	9,250	29,700	5,166
Massachusetts[2]	—	—	—	230	—	589	—	752	—
Michigan	1,518	172,040	—	540	15,600	8,825	30,550	—	35,770
Minnesota	41,340	367,080	—	2,046	76,950	11,369	147,200	—	78,960
Mississippi	—	3,520	900	1,350	76,950	—	57,720	—	20,400
Missouri	—	74,360	75	4,480	2,484	—	101,400	5,800	70,300
Montana	77,700	1,365	—	1,470	5,280	1,800	—	—	136,930
Nebraska	3,042	475,200	—	2,520	13,640	2,235	59,450	—	98,900
Nevada	2,720	—	—	405	—	3,720	—	—	1,260
New Hampshire[2]	—	—	—	144	—	—	—	—	—
New Jersey	1,007	6,120	—	140	255	1,501	3,059	—	1,800
New Mexico	1,425	7,000	76	108	—	1,408	—	—	13,630
New York	—	54,000	—	2,680	11,400	9,710	—	—	7,360
North Carolina	2,744	76,800	44	504	42,000	2,529	33,000	544,570	16,320
North Dakota	124,200	29,145	—	2,088	63,630	20,460	14,575	—	194,595
Ohio	—	232,400	—	1,680	15,360	2,096	101,680	17,635	58,650
Oklahoma	1,496	4,144	140	2,320	3,920	—	3,910	—	150,500
Oregon	16,380	5,346	—	1,273	6,000	20,710	—	—	65,570
Pennsylvania	3,850	72,450	—	2,240	16,200	4,300	2,730	22,800	8,580
Rhode Island[2]	—	—	—	16	—	644	—	—	—
South Carolina	920	17,050	55	387	2,120	—	23,595	112,050	10,500
South Dakota	23,100	103,400	—	2,210	79,200	2,079	24,778	—	89,729
Tennessee	—	26,010	150	1,694	387	175	30,225	119,790	21,120
Texas	2,475	104,760	2,391.5	6,670	24,000	3,324	9,660	—	161,000
Utah	11,088	1,540	—	270	884	1,242	—	—	8,027
Vermont[2]	—	—	—	722	—	132	—	—	—
Virginia	5,900	14,880	3	1,330	1,100	1,001	10,370	98,456	14,280
Washington	54,400	17,050	—	950	2,046	53,560	—	—	169,320
West Virginia	540	4,290	—	594	520	—	—	3,300	378
Wisconsin	1,680	223,100	—	1,540	44,200	18,910	13,430	16,118	5,812
Wyoming	10,032	7,072	—	952	3,381	954	—	—	8,238
Total U.S.	**519,026**	**4,203,777**	**7,724.8**	**59,457**	**477,303**	**325,721**	**1,595,437**	**1,410,868**	**2,425,408**

(1) Equiv. to 480 lbs. (2) All harvested corn acreage is for silage.

Production of Chief U.S. Crops

Source: Economics, Statistics, and Cooperatives Service: U.S. Agriculture Department

Year	Corn for grain 1,000 bushels	Oats 1,000 bushels	Barley 1,000 bushels	Sorghums for grain 1,000 bushels	All wheat 1,000 bushels	Rye 1,000 bushels	Flax-seed 1,000 bushels	Cotton lint 1,000 bales	Cotton seed 1,000 tons
1970 ..	4,152,243	915,236	416,091	683,179	1,351,558	36,840	29,416	10,192	4,068
1976 ..	6,828,061	642,042	374,386	763,046	2,122,450	15,058	15,550	8,302	3,210
1978 ..	7,267,927	581,657	454,759	731,270	1,775,524	24,065	8,614	10,855	4,269
1980 ..	6,644,841	458,263	360,956	579,197	2,374,306	16,483	7,928	11,122	4,470
1981 ..	8,201,598	509,167	479,333	879,222	2,798,738	18,222	7,799	15,733	6,397
1982 ..	8,359,364	620,509	522,387	841,369	2,812,297	20,954	11,635	11,963	4,744
1983 ..	4,203,777	477,303	519,026	483,056	2,425,408	28,152	7,363	7,725	3,105

Year	Tobacco 1,000 lbs.	All hay 1,000 tons	Beans dry edible 1,000 cwt.	Peas dry edible 1,000 cwt.	Peanuts 1,000 lbs.	Soy-beans 1,000 bushels	Pota-toes 1,000 cwt.	Sweet pota-toes 1,000 cwt.
1970	1,906,453	126,969	17,399	3,315	2,983,121	1,127,100	325,716	13,164
1975	2,181,775	132,210	17,442	2,731	3,857,122	1,547,383	322,254	13,225
1978	2,024,820	143,817	18,935	3,601	3,952,384	1,868,754	366,314	13,115
1980	1,786,192	131,027	26,395	3,285	2,307,847	1,792,062	302,857	10,953
1981	2,063,611	143,201	32,183	2,290	3,981,850	2,000,145	338,591	12,752
1982	1,982,245	152,534	25,049	—	3,438,330	2,229,486	351,822	14,290
1983	1,410,868	142,979	15,254	—	3,273,495	1,595,437	325,721	11,786

Year	Five seed crops* 1,000 lbs.	Sugar and seed 1,000 tons	Sugar beets 1,000 tons	'Pecans million lbs.	Al-monds million lbs.	'Wal-nuts 1,000 tons	'Fil-berts 1,000 tons	Oranges** 1,000 boxes	Grape-fruit** 1,000 boxes
1970	251,934	23,996	26,378	77.6	124.0	111.8	9.3	189,970	53,910
1975	161,609	28,344	29,704	124.2	160.0	199.3	12.1	243,060	61,610
1978	143,817	25,997	25,788	249.9	82.1	160	14.1	225,320	74,660
1980	131,070	26,963	23,502	183.5	322.0	197	15.4	280,010	73,200
1981	159,195	27,408	27,538	339.1	407.0	225	14.7	244,580	67,860
1982	—	29,770	20,894	107.6	283.5	234.0	18.8	176,690	70,400
1983	—	29,643	21,111	141.8	195.8	190.0	7.7	225,080	60,600

*Fine seed crops include alfalfa, red clover, lespedeza, and timothy. **Crop year ending in year cited. (1) In shells.

Harvested Acreage of Principal U.S. Crops

Source: Economics, Statistics, and Cooperatives Service: U.S. Agriculture Department (thousands of acres)

State	1983	1982	1981	State	1983	1982	1981
Alabama	3,446	4,603	4,642	Nevada	584	570	534
Arizona	688	965	1,226	New Hampshire	119	117	117
Arkansas	7,926	9,327	9,612	New Jersey	453	521	547
California	4,919	6,298	6,903	New Mexico	1,127	1,391	1,402
Colorado	6,281	6,553	6,672	New York	3,907	4,172	4,240
Connecticut	142	148	146	North Carolina	4,721	5,686	5,674
Delaware	525	572	547	North Dakota	19,070	22,603	22,926
Florida	1,280	1,508	1,552	Ohio	9,011	10,955	10,883
Georgia	5,289	6,417	6,327	Oklahoma	7,328	10,091	10,030
Hawaii	98	95	105	Oregon	2,659	2,712	2,753
Idaho	4,490	4,733	4,879	Pennsylvania	4,301	4,584	4,647
Illinois	19,807	23,783	24,116	Rhode Island	17	17	18
Indiana	10,698	13,019	13,040	South Carolina	2,608	3,292	3,148
Iowa	20,028	25,404	25,851	South Dakota	13,443	16,253	15,810
Kansas	19,100	22,814	21,791	Tennessee	5,014	5,818	5,738
Kentucky	4,949	5,882	5,872	Texas	17,304	22,680	24,364
Louisiana	4,533	5,471	5,565	Utah	1,063	1,141	1,140
Maine	393	408	407	Vermont	574	572	540
Maryland	1,538	1,691	1,649	Virginia	2,892	3,135	3,167
Massachusetts	166	166	164	Washington	4,652	4,872	5,037
Michigan	6,110	7,345	7,362	West Virginia	764	762	754
Minnesota	17,568	21,758	22,225	Wisconsin	8,502	9,670	9,507
Mississippi	5,588	6,869	6,702	Wyoming	1,804	1,822	1,877
Missouri	12,962	14,706	14,823	**Total U.S.**	**294,408**	**352,548**	**355,731**
Montana	8,709	9,658	9,719				
Nebraska	15,268	18,919	18,981				

Crop acreages included are corn, sorghum, oats, barley, wheat, rice, rye, soybeans, flaxseed, peanuts, sunflower, popcorn, cotton, all hay, dry edible beans, dry edible peas, potatoes, sweet potatoes, tobacco, sugarcane and sugar beets; harvested acreages for winter wheat, rye, all hay, tobacco and sugarcane are used in computing total planted acreage.

Farms—Number and Acreage, by States

Source: U.S. Dept. of Agriculture

State	Farms (1,000) 1980	1983	Acreage (mil.) 1980	1983	Acreage per farm 1980	1983	State	Farms (1,000) 1980	1983	Acreage (mil.) 1980	1983	Acreage per farm 1980	1983
U.S.	2,428	2,370	1,042	1,035	429	437	Mont.	24	24	62	62	2,609	2,588
Ala.	58	54	13	12	219	224	Nebr.	65	63	48	48	734	756
Alaska . . .	(z)	(z)	2	2	4,108	3,422	Nev.	3	3	9	9	3,100	3,296
Ariz.	7	7	39	39	5,557	5,557	N.H.	3	3	1	1	160	169
Ark.	59	56	17	16	280	289	N.J.	9	10	1	1	109	108
Calif.	80	78	34	34	424	432	N. Mex. . . .	14	14	47	47	3,467	3,481
Colo.	27	25	37	36	1,377	1,411	N.Y.	48	50	9	10	196	190
Conn.	4	5	(z)	(z)	117	111	N.C.	93	85	12	11	126	127
Del.	4	3	1	1	186	191	N. Dak. . . .	40	38	42	42	1,043	1,112
Fla.	39	41	13	13	344	312	Ohio	95	92	16	16	172	175
Ga.	59	55	16	15	263	273	Okla.	72	71	35	34	481	479
Hawaii . . .	4	4	2	2	458	445	Oreg.	35	37	18	18	517	492
Idaho	24	24	15	15	639	619	Pa.	62	59	9	9	145	147
Ill.	107	101	29	29	269	284	R.I.	1	1	(z)	(z)	87	100
Ind.	88	87	17	17	191	193	S.C.	35	31	6	6	183	190
Iowa.	119	115	34	34	284	293	S. Dak. . . .	39	37	45	45	1,169	1,219
Kans.	75	75	48	49	644	647	Tenn.	96	95	14	13	142	141
Ky.	102	103	15	16	143	141	Tex.	186	184	139	138	746	752
La.	37	37	10	10	273	277	Utah	13	13	13	12	969	961
Maine	8	8	2	2	195	193	Vt.	8	8	2	2	226	227
Md.	18	18	3	3	157	150	Va.	58	58	10	10	169	169
Mass.	6	5	1	1	115	113	Wash.	38	38	16	16	424	429
Mich.	66	65	11	12	173	177	W. Va. . . .	20	21	4	4	210	203
Minn.	104	103	30	30	288	295	Wis.	93	90	19	18	200	202
Miss.	55	51	15	14	265	280	Wyo.	9	9	35	35	3,846	3,837
Mo.	120	117	32	31	163	268							

(z) Less than 500 farms or 500,000 acres.

Farms—Number and Acreage: 1930 to 1983

Source: U.S. Dept. of Agriculture

Year	Farms Number (1,000)	Annual change[1] (1,000)	Land in farms Total (mil. acres)	Average per farm (acres)	Year	Farms Number (1,000)	Annual change[1] (1,000)	Land in farms Total (mil. acres)	Average per farm (acres)
1930[2] . . .	6,546	15	987	151	1969	3,000	-71	1,108	369
1935	6,814	54	1,055	155	1970	2,949	-51	1,102	374
1940	6,350	-93	1,061	167	1971	2,902	-47	1,097	378
1945	5,967	-77	1,142	191	1972	2,860	-42	1,092	382
1950	5,648	-64	1,202	213	1973	2,823	-37	1,088	385
1954	4,798	-213	1,206	251	1974	2,795	-28	1,084	388
1959[3] . . .	4,105	-139	1,183	288	1975[4] . . .	2,521	(x)	1,059	420
1960	3,963	-142	1,176	297	1976	2,497	-24	1,054	422
1961	3,825	-138	1,168	305	1977	2,456	-41	1,048	427
1962	3,692	-133	1159	314	1978	2,436	-20	1,045	429
1963	3,572	-120	1,152	322	1979	2,430	-6	1,043	429
1964	3,457	-115	1,146	332	1980	2,428	-2	1,042	429
1965	3,356	-101	1,140	340	1981	2,434	6	1,042	428
1966	3,257	-99	1,132	348	1982	2,400	-34	1,039	433
1967	3,162	-95	1,123	355	1983, prel. .	2,370	-30	1,035	437
1968	3,071	-91	1,115	363					

(x) Not applicable. (1) Average annual change from preceding year shown. For 1930, change from 1925. (2) Estimated prior to 1959, excludes Alaska and Hawaii. (3) For 1959-1974, places of less than 10 acres were counted as farms if estimated sales of agricultural products for the year amounted to at least $250, and places of 10 or more acres if such sales amounted to at least $50. (4) 1975-1983, all land on which agricultural operations were conducted under the day-to-day control of an individual management and from which $1,000 or more of agricultural products were, or potentially could be, sold during the census year.

Livestock on Farms in the U.S.

Source: Economics, Statistics, and Cooperatives Service; U.S. Dept. of Agriculture (thousands)

Year (On Jan. 1)	All cattle	Milk cows	All sheep	Hogs	Horses* and mules	Year (On Jan. 1)	All cattle	Milk cows	All sheep	Hogs
1890. . . .	60,014	15,000	44,518	48,130	18,054	1970	112,369	12,091	20,423	[3]57,046
1900. . . .	59,739	16,544	48,105	51,055	21,004	1971	114,578	11,909	19,731	[3]67,285
1910. . . .	58,993	19,450	50,239	48,072	24,211	1972	117,862	11,776	18,739	[3]62,412
1920. . . .	70,400	21,455	40,743	60,159	25,742	1973	121,539	11,622	17,641	[3]59,017
1925. . . .	63,373	22,575	38,543	55,770	22,569	1974	127,788	11,297	16,310	[3]60,614
1930. . . .	61,003	23,032	51,565	55,705	19,124	1975	132,028	11,220	14,515	[3]54,693
1935. . . .	68,846	26,082	51,808	39,066	16,683	1976	127,980	11,071	13,311	[3]49,267
1940. . . .	68,039	24,940	52,107	61,165	14,478	1978	116,375	10,896	12,421	[3]56,539
1945. . . .	85,573	27,770	46,520	59,373	11,950	1980	111,192	10,779	12,687	[3]67,353
1950. . . .	77,963	23,853	29,826	58,937	7,781	1981	114,321	10,860	12,936	[3]64,512
1955. . . .	96,592	23,462	31,582	50,474	4,309	1982[1]	115,604	11,012	12,966	[3]58,688
1960. . . .	96,236	19,527	33,170	59,026	3,089	1983[3]	115,199	11,176	12,026	[3]53,935
1965. . . .		109,000	[2]15,380	25,127	57,030	1984[3]	114,400	11,140	11,411	[3]55,819

*Discontinued in 1960. (1) Total estimated value on farms as of Jan. 1, 1982, was as follows (avg. value per head in parentheses): cattle and calves $47,978,582 ($415); sheep and lambs $746,520,000 ($56.90); hogs and pigs $4,115,148,000 ($70.10). (2) New series, milk cows and heifers that have calved, beginning 1965. (3) As of Dec. 1 of preceding year.

Wool Production

Source: Economic Research Service U.S. Agriculture Department (Statistics for "pulled wool" are no longer being collected as of 1982.)

	Sheep shorn (1,000)	Shorn wool (1,000 lbs.)	Value ($1,000)	Price per lb. (cents)	Pulled wool (1,000 lbs.)	Total wool (1,000 lbs)
1970	19,163	161,587	57,162	35.4	15,200	176,787
1975	14,403	119,535	53,505	44.8	6,000	125,535
1976	13,536	111,100	73,332	66.0	4,850	115,950
1978	12,719	102,942	76,690	74.5	1,000	103,942
1979	13,068	104,860	90,531	86.3	900	105,760
1980	13,255	105,367	92,799	88.1	1,050	106,417
1981	13,477	109,689	103,578	94.4	NA	109,689
1982	13,152	105,596	72,349	68.5	NA	105,596
1983	12,640	100,265	61,460	61.3	NA	100,265

U.S. Meat and Lard Production and Consumption

Source: Economic Research Service U.S. Agriculture Department (million lbs.)

Year	Beef Production	Beef Consumption	Veal Production	Veal Consumption	Lamb and mutton Production	Lamb and mutton Consumption	Pork (exclud. lard) Production	Pork (exclud. lard) Consumption	All meats Production	All meats Consumption	Lard Production	Lard Consumption
1940	7,175	7,257	981	981	876	873	10,044	9,701	19,076	18,812	2,288	1,901
1950	9,534	9,529	1,230	1,206	597	596	10,714	10,390	22,075	21,721	2,631	1,891
1960	14,753	15,147	1,109	1,093	768	852	13,905	13,838	30,535	30,930	2,562	1,358
1970	21,685	22,926	588	581	551	657	14,699	14,661	37,523	38,825	1,913	939
1980	21,664	23,321	400	412	318	350	16,615	16,562	38,979	40,645	1,207	540
1981	22,389	23,756	435	437	338	361	15,873	15,927	39,035	40,483	1,158	572
1982	22,536	23,998	448	457	365	381	14,229	14,425	37,578	39,261	1,011	585

Grain Receipts at U.S. Grain Centers

Source: Chicago Board of Trade Market Information Department (thousands bushels)

1983	Wheat	Corn	Oats	Rye	Barley	Soybeans	Total
Chicago	6,008	79,263	5,703	0	260	29,772	121,006
Duluth**	—	—	—	—	—	—	—
Enid*	—	—	—	—	—	—	—
Hutchinson*	—	—	—	—	—	—	—
Indianapolis	26	686	0	0	0	281	993
Kansas*	—	—	—	—	—	—	—
Milwaukee	2,937	26,070	3	0	5,335	627	34,972
Minneapolis	197,977	18,382	22,845	3,014	0	2,013	244,231
Omaha	33,962	44,515	350	0	0	9,945	88,772
Peoria	0	2,013	0	0	0	221	2,234
Sioux City	0	26	90	0	0	76	192
St. Joseph	1,360	3,560	1,748	0	0	510	7,178
St. Louis	1,435	82	0	0	0	935	2,452
Toledo	15,643	73,585	3,794	0	0	40,933	133,955
Witchita	28,744	2	0	0	0	1,398	30,144
Total	**288,092**	**248,184**	**34,533**	**3,014**	**5,595**	**86,711**	**666,129**

*Not available **Duluth included in Minnesota figures.

Grain Storage Capacity at Principal Grain Centers in U.S.

Source: Chicago Board of Trade Market Information Department (bushels)

Cities	Capacity	Cities	Capacity
Atlantic Coast	36,800,000	Texas High Plains	76,800,000
Great Lakes		Enid	66,100,000
Toledo	4,330,000	Gulf Points	
Buffalo	8,200,000	South Mississippi	43,600,000
Chicago	48,835,000	North Texas Gulf	28,200,000
Milwaukee	9,100,000	South Texas Gulf	14,000,000
Duluth	75,800,000	Plains	
River Points		Wichita	60,300,000
Minneapolis	124,200,000	Topeka	61,600,000
Peoria	6,600,000	Salina	45,000,000
St. Louis	25,500,000	Hutchinson	42,000,000
Sioux City	11,600,000	Hastings-Grand Island	24,100,000
Omaha-Council Bluffs	35,300,000	Lincoln	39,600,000
Atchison	24,500,000	Pacific N.W.	
St. Joseph	20,600,000	Puget Sound	9,500,000
Kansas City, Mo.	72,400,000	Portland	24,900,000
Southwest		California Ports	14,300,000
Fort Worth	57,600,000		

Atlantic Coast — Albany. N.Y., Philadelphia. Pa., Baltimore. Md., Norfolk. Va. **Gulf Points** — New Orleans. Baton Rouge. Ama. Belle Chase. La., Mobile. Ala. **North Texas Gulf** — Houston. Galveston. Beaumont. Port Arthur. Texas. **South Texas Gulf** — Corpus Christi. Brownsville. Texas. **Pacific N.W.** — Seattle. Tacoma. Wash., Portland. Oreg., Columbia River **Calif. Ports** — San Francisco. Stockton. Sacramento. Los Angeles. **Texas High Plains** — Amarillo. Lubbock. Hereford. Plainview. Texas.

U.S. Egg Production

Source: Economic Research Service: U.S. Agriculture Department (millions of eggs)

State	1983	1982	1981	1980	State	1983	1982	1981	1980	State	1983	1982	1981	1980
Ala...	2,813	2,879	3,095	3,354	La...	417	457	510	553	Oh..	2,980	2,755	2,431	2,333
Alas..	15.6	8.8	6.7	4.4	Me...	1,395	1,430	1,607	1,793	Okla..	841	814	839	839
Ariz..	102	114	98	.11	Md...	836	658	547	381	Ore..	630	620	665	638
Ark...	3,768	4,064	3,996	4,153	Mass..	265	314	321	326	Pa...	4,716	4,324	4,268	4,251
Cal...	8,173	8,288	8,400	8,796	Mich..	1,454	1,525	1,541	1,459	R.I...	62	74	88	84
Col...	618	627	552	464	Minn..	2,508	2,432	2,355	2,223	S.C...	1,594	1,656	1,613	1,679
Conn..	1,073	1,057	990	1,004	Miss..	1,285	1,524	1,717	1,584	S.D...	374	428	461	464
Del..	142	137	175	138	Mo...	1,336	1,456	1,431	1,460	Tenn..	822	879	922	962
Fla..	2,959	2,963	2,802	3,044	Mont..	193	188	174	170	Tex..	3,089	3,113	3,224	3,092
Ga...	4,671	5,419	5,578	5,637	Neb..	792	809	802	847	Ut. ..	456	439	459	416
Ha...	197.3	202.2	221.3	229	Nev..	1.8	1.8	1.8	1.8	Vt..	69	79	81	100
Ida...	240	238	202	202	N.H...	142	147	157	182	Va. ..	840	929	947	913
Ill...	1,004	1,158	1,262	1,267	N.J...	242	276	291	279	Wash..	1,232	1,334	1,332	1,295
Ind...	4,619	4,464	4,093	3,697	N.M...	287	302	347	378	W.Vir..	136	142	155	149
Ia...	1,826	1,985	1,920	1,784	N.Y...	1,732	1,859	1,858	1,776	Wis..	904	991	951	946
Kan..	481	462	416	427	N.C...	3,149	3,065	3,078	3,174	Wyo. .	8.6	8.2	8.1	10.5
Ky..	457	484	509	536	N.D..	119	102	80	82	Total.	68,108	69,680	69,603	69,683

Note: The egg and chicken production year runs from Dec. 1 of the previous year through Nov. 30. (1) Included are eggs destroyed because of possible PCB contamination.

Net Income per Farm by States

Source: Economic Research Service. U.S. Agriculture Department (dollars)

State	1981	1982	1983	State	1981	1982	1983
Alabama	9,845	8,568	7,923	Nebraska	18,712	11,358	6,110
Alaska	6,513	2,126	4,507	Nevada	9,177	5,747	9,444
Arizona	45,065	15,173	12,768	New Hampshire	3,612	3,439	3,373
Arkansas	13,029	8,630	8,356	New Jersey	9,826	13,513	11,885
California	54,495	41,312	38,354	New Mexico	5,219	2,856	3,938
Colorado	16,238	11,091	17,683	New York	7,287	4,398	3,027
Connecticut	11,710	14,614	11,575	North Carolina	12,978	11,508	9,439
Delaware	26,799	31,099	42,770	North Dakota	19,775	9,983	17,377
Florida	36,289	31,954	36,322	Ohio	3,302	5,122	1,310
Georgia	9,642	11,210	10,914	Oklahoma	5,795	7,226	2,930
Hawaii	22,210	20,040	28,412	Oregon	11,417	7,932	9,777
Idaho	20,978	11,490	15,282	Pennsylvania	10,871	8,307	6,630
Illinois	17,676	8,989	-5,786	Rhode Island	4,555	5,073	1,043
Indiana	7,457	5,418	-1,490	South Carolina	4,064	4,128	-596
Iowa	17,680	7,376	-1,890	South Dakota	15,583	11,311	12,824
Kansas	11,353	12,180	7,958	Tenneesse	4,410	4,342	1,595
Kentucky	10,283	9,679	4,358	Texas	9,946	5,106	5,400
Louisiana	5,755	6,225	10,407	Utah	4,377	2,119	2,998
Maine	11,899	126	-3,404	Vermont	10,842	13,207	9,086
Maryland	12,463	11,172	9,122	Virginia	5,467	2,147	819
Massachusetts	15,649	19,033	19,362	Washington	20,894	20,239	25,963
Michigan	7,594	6,608	5,348	West Virginia	-374	-1,941	-923
Minnesota	14,325	9,627	7,132	Wisconsin	15,504	12,914	10,805
Mississippi	2,629	5,505	3,541	Wyoming	-189	-7,847	-6,764
Missouri	6,942	2,937	-509	Total. U.S.	12,722	93,018	67,913
Montana	8,142	2,325	2,153				

Note: Data based on the 1974 Census of Agriculture definition of a farm (sales of $1,000 or more).

Farm Income—Cash Receipts from Marketings

Source: Economic Research Service: U.S. Agriculture Department ($1,000)

1983 State	Crops	Live-stock	Gov't pay'ts	Total	1983 State	Crops	Live-stock	Gov't pay'ts	Total
Alabama	853,887	1,258,461	64,280	2,176,628	Nebraska	2,007,223	4,003,129	762,251	6,772,603
Alaska	11,074	7,504	240	18,818	Nevada	71,125	153,052	4,251	228,428
Arizona	928,120	715,510	111,402	1,755,032	New Hampshire	39,950	78,115	642	114,707
Arkansas	1,499,184	1,500,283	294,997	3,294,464	New Jersey	406,760	136,358	4,287	547,405
California	9,333,761	4,159,970	372,278	13,866,009	New Mexico	327,336	634,719	57,076	1,019,131
Colorado	926,571	2,000,417	163,970	3,090,958	New York	742,552	1,929,463	37,922	2,709,937
Connecticut	118,316	202,327	541	321,184	North Carolina	2,127,468	1,656,457	67,565	3,851,490
Delaware	139,249	315,875	3,885	459,009	North Dakota	2,028,479	662,654	578,760	3,269,893
Florida	3,332,605	992,765	13,040	4,338,410	Ohio	2,135,849	1,537,815	170,749	3,844,413
Georgia	1,604,531	1,705,568	82,240	3,392,339	Oklahoma	1,003,405	1,688,110	364,703	3,056,218
Hawaii	450,156	86,488	6,743	543,387	Oregon	1,145,071	555,044	66,786	1,766,901
Idaho	1,132,490	883,033	136,397	2,151,920	Pennsylvania	755,574	2,220,814	29,110	3,005,498
Illinois	5,849,047	2,294,569	542,745	8,686,361	Rhode Island	19,033	12,280	107	31,420
Indiana	2,180,237	1,829,205	264,619	4,274,061	South Carolina	652,591	405,348	47,613	1,105,552
Iowa	3,939,756	5,395,117	899,484	10,234,357	South Dakota	930,181	1,655,967	267,132	2,853,280
Kansas	2,201,807	3,196,060	598,239	5,996,106	Tennessee	1,023,386	906,922	68,235	1,998,543
Kentucky	1,322,886	1,475,261	60,095	2,858,242	Texas	3,448,249	5,522,150	1,127,875	10,098,274
Louisiana	1,369,916	483,190	157,649	2,010,755	Utah	145,960	432,747	19,136	597,843
Maine	153,260	259,802	2,679	415,741	Vermont	35,899	391,138	1,526	428,563
Maryland	330,503	701,951	12,571	104,025	Virginia	581,799	857,738	28,875	1,468,412
Massachusetts	230,859	136,089	710	367,658	Washington	2,104,329	958,680	158,995	3,222,004
Michigan	1,758,474	1,242,987	140,936	3,142,397	West Virginia	54,771	172,877	3,895	231,543
Minnesota	2,949,075	3,328,332	610,934	6,888,341	Wisconsin	1,062,484	4,140,446	160,053	5,362,983
Mississippi	1,364,511	926,608	230,089	2,512,208	Wyoming	114,742	478,145	19,658	612,545
Missouri	1,728,714	2,259,288	236,918	4,224,920	U.S.	69,516,144	69,203,192	9,294,293	148,013,629
Montana	846,939	656,364	239,410	1,742,713	(1) Not official.				

Average Prices Received by U.S. Farmers

Source: Statistical Reporting Service; U.S. Agriculture Department

The figures represent dollars per 100 lbs. for hogs, beef cattle, veal calves, sheep, lamb, and milk (wholesale), dollars per head for milk cows; cents per lb. for milk fat (in cream), chickens, broilers, turkeys, and wool; cents for eggs per dozen.

Weighted calendar year prices for livestock and livestock products other than wool, 1943 through 1963, wool prices are weighted on marketing year basis. The marketing year has been changed (1964) from a calendar year to a Dec.-Nov. basis for hogs, chickens, broilers and eggs.

Year	Hogs	Cattle (beef)	Calves (veal)	Sheep	Lambs	Cows (milk)	All Milk	Milk fat (in cream)	Chickens (excl. broilers)	Broilers	Turkeys	Eggs	Wool
1930	8.84	7.71	9.68	4.74	7.76	74	2.21	34.5	....	...	20.2	23.7	19.5
1940	5.39	7.56	8.83	3.95	8.10	61	1.82	28.0	13.0	17.3	15.2	18.0	28.4
1950	18.00	23.30	26.30	11.60	25.10	198	3.89	62.0	22.2	27.4	32.8	36.3	62.1
1960	15.30	20.40	22.90	5.61	17.90	223	4.21	60.5	12.2	16.9	25.4	36.1	42.0
1970	22.70	27.10	34.50	7.51	26.40	332	5.71	70.0	9.1	13.6	22.6	39.1	35.4
1975	46.10	32.20	27.20	11.30	42.10	412	8.75	71.0	9.9	26.3	34.8	54.5	44.8
1979	41.80	66.10	88.80	26.30	66.70	1,040	12.00	119.0	14.4	25.9	41.3	58.3	86.3
1980	38.00	62.40	76.80	21.10	63.60	1,190	13.00	—	11.0	27.7	41.3	56.3	88.1
1982	52.30	56.70	59.80	19.50	53.10	1,110	13.60	—	10.3	26.9	39.5	59.5	68.4
1983	46.80	55.70	61.70	15.70	53.90	1,030	13.60	—	12.7	28.6	38.0	61.1	61.3

The figures represent cents per lb. for cotton, apples, and peanuts; dollars per bushel for oats, wheat, corn, barley, and soybeans; dollars per 100 lbs. for rice, sorghum, and potatoes; dollars per ton for cottonseed and baled hay.

Weighted crop year prices. Crop years are as follows: apples, June-May; wheat, oats, barley, hay and potatoes, July-June; cotton, rice, peanuts and cottonseed, August-July; soybeans, September-August; and corn and sorghum grain, October-September.

Crop year	Corn	Wheat	Upland cotton[1]	Oats	Barley	Rice	Soybeans	Sorghum	Peanuts	Cotton-seed	Hay	Potatoes	Apples
1930	.598	.663	9.46	0.311	420	1.74	1.34	1.02	5.01	22.00	11.00	1.47	
1940	6·8	.674	9.83	0.298	393	1.80	892	.873	3.72	21.70	9.78	.850	
1950	1.52	2.00	39.90	0.788	1.19	5.09	2.47	1.88	10.9	86.60	21.10	1.50	
1960	1.00	1.74	30.08	0.599	840	4.55	2.13	1.49	10.0	42.50	21.70	2.00	2.72
1970	1.33	1.33	21.86	0.623	973	5.17	2.85	2.04	12.8	56.40	26.10	2.21	6.52
1975	2.54	3.55	51.10	1.45	2.42	8.35	4.92	4.21	19.6	97.00	52.10	4.48	8.80
1979	2.52	3.78	62.3	1.36	2.29	10.50	6.28	4.18	20.6	121.00	59.50	3.43	15.40
1980	3.11	3.91	74.4	1.79	2.86	12.80	7.57	5.25	25.1	129.00	71.00	6.55	12.1
1982	2.68	3.55	59.1	1.48	2.23	8.11	5.69	4.50	25.1	77.00	68.80	4.45	13.2
1983	3.30	3.54	66.4	1.69	2.56	8.92	7.87	5.16	24.1	166.00	76.20	5.69	14.9

(1) Beginning 1964, 480 lb. net weight bales. (2) Series discontinued in 1980.

Index Numbers of Prices Received by Farmers

Source: Statistical Reporting Service; U.S. Agriculture Department (index 1910-14 = 100 per cent)

Year	All farm products	All crops	Livestock	Food grains	Feed grains and hay	Cotton	Tobacco	Oil-bearing crops	Fruit	Commercial vegetables	Potatoes sweetpot.[1]	Meat animals	Dairy products	Poultry and eggs	Ratio of prices[2] received to prices paid by farmers — Year	ratio
1910	104	105	102	109	96	118	84	120	100	...	83	101	100	104	1968	79
1920	211	235	190	249	202	262	233	208	188	...	294	171	202	222	1969	79
1930	125	115	134	93	106	104	140	111	149	128	162	133	142	128	1970	77
1940	100	90	109	84	85	83	134	103	81	122	89	108	120	98	1971	75
1950	258	233	280	224	193	282	402	276	194	211	166	340	249	186	1972	79
1960	239	222	253	203	152	254	500	214	244	256	204	296	259	160	1973	94
1970	274	225	325	162	179	183	604	265	217	292	218	405	350	147	1975	76
1980	614	539	691	452	417	583	1,219	664	458	562	469	878	798	254	1980	65
1982	609	525	696	401	378	469	1,501	575	648	631	455	876	831	252	1982	58
1983	614	551	679	407	453	534	1,429	663	467	650	445	831	830	269	1983	58

(1) Including dry edible beans. (2) Ratio of the index prices received by farmers, adjusted to reflect government payments to the index of prices paid, for commodities and services, interest, taxes and wage rates.

Food Stamps—Costs and Benefits

Fiscal year	Average persons participating per month	Value per year		Avg. bonus per participant per month
		Total purchase	Bonus	
1965	424,652	$ 85,471,989	$ 32,505,096	6.38
1970	4,340,030	1,089,960,761	549,663,811	10.55
1975	17,064,196	7,265,641,706	4,385,501,248	21.41
1981	22,430,562	NA[1]	10,629,972,724	39.49
1982	20,355,136	NA[1]	9,538,292,623[2]	39.05
1983(p)	21,630,443	NA[1]	11,155,071,470[2]	42.98

(p) preliminary. (1) Not Applicable. The elimination of the purchase requirement began January 1979. The Food Stamp Program enables low-income families to buy more food of greater variety to improve their diets. If a household meets eligibility requirements it receives food stamps based on its net income and the number of people in the household. Over the past few years major reform measures went into effect. These include changes in the allowable deductions; eliminate the food stamp purchase requirement; streamline administration; and reduce the potential for fraud or abuse. County and city welfare departments administer the program locally. (2) Excludes Puerto Rico's nutrition assistance program which initiated operations in July 1982. Puerto Rican benefits totaled $200 million for July-September 1982 at an average participation of 1.66 million persons.

Government Payments by Programs, by States

Source: Economic Research Service. U.S. Agriculture Department ($1.000)

1982 State	Conservation[1]	Feed grain program	Wheat program	Cotton program	Rice program	Drought & flood program	Misc. program[2]	Total
Alabama	4,167	1,651	1,478	22,511	0	0	1,630	31,437
Alaska	148	248	1	0	0	0	14	411
Arizona	1,492	823	1,183	54,733	0	0	1,216	59,447
Arkansas	3,312	6,708	9,063	36,939	61,620	0	1,703	119,345
California	4,869	4,280	9,524	86,731	23,697	0	5,400	134,501
Colorado	5,210	12,233	23,678	0	0	0	27,643	68,764
Connecticut	472	6	0	0	0	0	25	503
Delaware	182	129	51	0	0	0	350	712
Florida	3,223	1,256	158	1,271	90	0	1,495	7,493
Georgia	4,756	4,941	3,966	11,651	0	0	4,028	29,342
Hawaii	607	0	0	0	0	0	48	655
Idaho	2,626	10,724	24,372	0	0	0	13,845	51,567
Illinois	6,041	35,956	7,070	0	0	7	69,084	118,158
Indiana	3,681	21,588	3,992	0	0	0	28,283	57,544
Iowa	6,463	81,366	467	0	0	5	127,568	215,869
Kansas	5,020	93,149	94,329	3	0	0	87,763	280,264
Kentucky	4,349	4,640	2,252	0	0	0	1,676	12,917
Louisiana	3,132	1,106	889	48,787	27,731	0	1,474	83,119
Maine	1,940	94	3	0	0	0	250	2,287
Maryland	900	722	280	0	0	0	678	2,580
Massachusetts	543	11	0	0	0	0	86	640
Michigan	4,181	13,562	3,970	0	0	0	18,704	40,417
Minnesota	4,974	47,033	32,958	0	0	0	97,892	182,857
Mississippi	4,085	1,320	2,053	83,477	11,693	0	1,301	103,929
Missouri	6,536	33,256	16,794	10,499	2,284	0	10,456	79,825
Montana	3,559	18,230	66,805	0	0	0	28,322	116,916
Nebraska	3,965	97,817	19,922	0	0	7	155,767	277,478
Nevada	931	287	409	76	0	0	2,727	4,430
New Hampshire	591	2	0	0	0	0	66	659
New Jersey	485	245	146	0	0	0	200	1,076
New Mexico	2,143	7,396	6,183	8,188	0	0	8,029	31,939
New York	4,397	4,751	1,186	0	0	0	3,433	13,767
North Carolina	3,944	2,998	1,541	4,815	0	0	3,166	16,464
North Dakota	2,491	22,055	105,430	0	0	0	70,150	200,176
Ohio	4,197	19,935	6,543	0	0	0	11,723	42,398
Oklahoma	4,347	12,785	53,944	30,169	10	0	26,472	127,727
Oregon	3,558	2,612	15,838	0	0	0	8,614	30,622
Pennsylvania	3,766	1,528	334	0	0	0	1,810	7,438
Rhode Island	92	0	0	0	0	0	13	105
South Carolina	2,530	1,927	1,797	8,050	0	0	2,849	17,153
South Dakota	2,311	20,972	30,684	0	0	0	38,754	92,721
Tennessee	4,364	2,909	3,811	16,032	0	0	962	28,078
Texas	15,793	87,724	52,291	376,262	28,785	0	82,743	643,598
Utah	2,985	1,081	1,762	0	0	0	3,351	9,179
Vermont	1,126	40	0	0	0	0	454	1,620
Virginia	2,642	1,649	998	17	0	0	2,151	7,457
Washington	4,366	10,366	41,545	0	0	0	20,696	76,973
West Virginia	1,810	126	8	0	0	0	524	2,468
Wisconsin	4,467	18,536	603	0	0	0	22,857	46,463
Wyoming	1,463	542	1,907	0	0	0	6,565	10,477
Total	165,232	713,315	652,268	800,211	155,910	19	1,005,010	3,491,965

(1) Includes amounts paid under Agricultural and Conservation Programs. (2) Includes Sugar Act. National Wool Act. Milk Indemnity Program. Beekeepers Indemnity Program. Hay and Cattle Transportation Program. Cropland Adjustment Program. Forest Incentive Program. Water Bank Program. Emergency Livestock Feed Program. Great Plains and other miscellaneous programs.

Hired Farmworkers—Workers and Earnings: 1970 to 1981

Represents persons 14 years old and over in the civilian noninstitutional population who did hired farmwork at any time during the year.

Source: Economic Research Service. U.S. Dept. of Agriculture

	Workers (1,000)							Median Earnings Per Day		
				1981 Duration of farmwork						
	1970	1975	Total	Under 25 days	25-74 days	75-149 days	150-249 days	250 days and over	1970	1975	1981
All workers	2,488	2,638	2,492	969	538	310	281	394	$9.30	$14.80	$23.83
White[1]	1,940	1,907	1,824	781	409	198	150	285	9.70	14.75	21.79
Black and other[1]	547	446	340	119	73	40	61	48	8.00	13.90	23.92
Hispanic	NA	285	328	69	57	72	70	61	NA	17.10	29.46
Male	1,889	2,036	1,918	658	390	247	254	369	9.75	15.45	24.64
Female	599	602	574	312	149	63	26	24	7.65	12.35	20.44
Region:											
Northeast	241	227	204	63	50	24	22	44	9.95	14.00	20.13
North Central	590	674	688	345	136	86	48	74	9.20	14.45	23.68
South	1,093	1,074	1,004	398	221	110	120	155	8.35	14.10	20.76
West	564	664	595	163	132	90	90	121	11.75	18.00	29.90
Migratory	196	188	115	24	37	12	28	15	NA	NA	NA
Nonmigratory	2,291	2,450	2,377	945	501	299	253	379	NA	NA	NA

(1) Beginning 1975, excludes persons of Hispanic origin. 1970 data not comparable with later years. (NA) Not available.

Federal Food Program Costs[1]

Source: Management Information Division. Food and Nutrition Service. USDA (millions of dollars)

Fiscal year	Food stamps Bonus	Food distribution[4]				Child nutrition (Cash payments)					Total food costs
		WIC[3]	Needy persons[5]	Schools	Institutions	School lunch	School breakfast	Child care	Summer food	Special milk	
1975	4,386	77	58	431	20	1,289	86	49	50	123	6,569
1977	5,067	212	49	554	18	1,570	149	109	110	150	7,988
1978	5,139	312	69	629	28	1,808	181	135	96	135	8,532
1979	6,480	429	93	760	54	1,984	231	164	106	134	10,435
1980	8,685	584	115	919	71	2,282	288	212	85	145	13,386
1981	10,630	708	154	907	132	2,381	332	297	103	101	15,745
1982	9,538[4]	756	349[5]	779	111	2,185	317	268	100	18	14,421
1983[p]	11,155[2]	903	1,183[5]	867	151	2,401	336	306	96	18	17,416

(1) Cost data are direct federal benefits to recipients: they exclude federal administrative payments and applicable State and local contributions. (2) Excludes Puerto Rico Nutrition Assistance Program. (3) Special Supplemental Food Program for Women, Infants and Children. (4) Includes cost of commodity entitlements, cash-in-lieu of commodities and bonus foods. (5) Includes Food Distribution Program on Indian Reservations, Needy Family Program in Trust Territory, Commodity Supplemental Food Program and Nutrition Program for the Elderly. (6) Includes Temporary Emergency Food Assistance Program. (7) Includes Child Care and Summer Feeding foods. (p) Preliminary.

Consumption of Major Food Commodities per Person

Source: Economic Research Service: U.S. Agriculture Department

Commodity[1]	1981	1982	1983	Commodity[1]	1981	1982	1983
Meats	144.5	139.4	176.4	Processed:			
Beef	77.2	77.3	106.51	Canned fruit	16.6	13.0	13.0
Veal	1.6	1.6	1.97	Canned juice	19.1	13.8	16.2
Lamb and mutton	1.4	1.5	1.67	Frozen (including juices)	12.9	14.1	15.0
Pork	64.3	59.0	56.24	Chilled citrus juices	4.2	3.5	N.A.
Fish (edible weight)	13.0	16.4	12.90	Dried	2.4	2.8	2.9
Poultry products:				Vegetables:			
Eggs	33.6	33.8	261.00	Fresh	95.2	150.9	109.0
Chicken (ready-to-cook)	51.7	52.9	53.90	Canned (excluding potatoes and			
Turkey (ready-to-cook)	10.7	10.8	11.20	sweet potatoes)	45.9	45.7	45.3
Dairy products:				Frozen (excluding potatoes)	11.3	10.7	11.1
Cheese	18.0	N.A.	22.4	Potatoes	110.1	N.A.	N.A.
Condensed and evaporated milk	3.9	N.A.	3.9	Sweet potatoes[3]	4.7	N.A.	N.A.
Fluid milk and cream (product weight)	245	N.A.	24.0	Grains:			
Ice cream (product weight)	17.2	N.A.	17.9	Wheat flour[4]	117	108.6	116.0
Fats and Oils—Total fat content	57.3	56.8	59.6	Rice	11.0	11.8	9.8
Butter (actual weight)	4.3	4.7	5.1	Other:			
Margarine (actual weight)	11.2	11.1	10.4	Coffee	7.1	7.5	10.2
Lard	2.5	4.1	1.8	Tea	.8	.8	.7
Shortening	18.5	18.8	18.6	Cocoa	2.9	3.0	40.0
Other edible fats and oils	23.5	23.3	24.8	Peanuts (shelled)	6.1	N.A.	6.7
Fruits:				Dry edible beans	4.2	N.A.	5.6
Fresh	87.3	81.4	94.8	Melons	18.9	24.4	N.A.
Citrus	24.6	24.0	31.7	Sugar (refined)	79.4	N.A.	71.0
Noncitrus	62.7	57.4	N.A.				

(1) Quantity in pounds, retail weight unless otherwise shown. Data on calendar year basis except for dried fruits, fresh citrus fruits, peanuts, and rice which are on a crop-year basis, and eggs which are on a marketing year basis. Data are as of August 1983. (2) Commercial production for sale as fresh produce. (3) Including fresh equivalent of processed. (4) White, whole wheat, and semolina flour including use in bakery products.

Farm-Real Estate Debt Outstanding by Lender Groups

Source: Economic Research Service. U.S. Agriculture Department

Jan. 1	Total farm-real estate debt[1]	Amounts held by principal lender groups				
		Federal land banks[1]	Farmers Home Administration[2]	Life insurance companies[3]	All commercial banks	Other[4]
	$1,000	$1,000	$1,000	$1,000	$1,000	$1,000
1955	8,245,278	1,279,787	378,108	2,051,784	1,161,308	3,374,291
1960	12,082,409	2,335,124	676,224	2,819,542	1,523,051	4,728,468
1965	18,894,240	3,686,755	1,284,913	4,287,671	2,416,634	7,218,267
1970	29,182,766	6,671,222	2,279,620	5,733,900	3,545,024	10,953,000
1975	44,637,780	13,402,441	3,214,657	6,297,400	5,966,282	15,757,000
1978	63,307,877	21,391,162	3,982,054	8,819,400	7,780,261	21,335,000
1979	71,412,951	24,619,184	4,121,038	10,478,200	8,556,542	23,638,000
1980	85,420,978	29,641,784	7,110,613	12,165,300	8,623,281	27,880,000
1981	95,512,462	35,944,492	7,714,928	12,927,800	8,745,242	30,180,000
1982	105,539,132	43,563,819	8,744,181	13,073,900	8,387,232	31,770,000
1983[5]	109,507,332	47,180,392	9,084,694	12,801,546	8,440,700	32,000,000
1984[5]	110,635,126	47,947,976	9,328,750	12,717,600	9,320,800	32,320,000

(1) Includes data for joint stock land banks and Federal Farm Mortgage Corporations. (2) Includes loans made directly by FmHA for farm ownership, soil and water loans to individuals, recreation loans to individuals, Indian tribe land acquisition, grazing associations, and irrigation drainage and soil conservation associations. Also includes loans for rural housing on farm tracts and labor housing. (3) American Council of Life Insurance. (4) Estimated by ERS. USDA. (5) Preliminary.

Giant Trees of the U.S.

Source: The American Forestry Association

There are approximately 748 different species of trees native to the continental U.S., including a few imports that have become naturalized to the extent of reproducing themselves in the wild state.

The oldest living trees in the world are reputed to be the bristlecone pines, the majority of which are found growing on the arid crags of California's White Mts. Some of them are estimated to be more than 4,600 years old. The largest known bristlecone pine is the "Patriarch," believed to be 1,500 years old. The oldest known redwoods are about 3,500 years old.

Recognition as the National Champion of each species is determined by total mass of each tree, based on this formula: the circumference in inches as measured at a point 4 1/2 feet above the ground plus the total height of the tree in feet plus 1/4 of the average crown spread in feet. Trees are compared on the basis of this formula. Trees, within five points of each other are declared co-champions. The Giant Sequoia champion has the largest circumference, 83 ft. 2 in.. Gallberry Holly the smallest, 5 in. Following is a small selection of the 661 trees registered with the American Forestry Assn.

(Figure in parentheses is year of most recent measurement)

Species	Height (ft.)	Location
Acacia, Koa (1969)	140	Kau, Ha.
Ailanthus, Tree-of-Heaven (1972)	60	Long Island, N.Y.
Alder, European (1982)	70	Princeton, Ill.
Apple, Southern Crab (1981)	35.5	Swannanoa, N.C.
Ash, Blue (1970)	86	Danville, Ky.
Bald Cypress, Common (1981)	83	St. Francisville, La.
Basswood, American (1983)	101	Grand Traverse Co., MI
Bayberry, Pacific (1972)	38	Siuslaw Natl. Forest, Ore.
Beech, American (1984)	130	Ashtabula Co., OH
Birch, River (1983)	86	Anne Arundel Co., Md.
Birch, Yellow (1983)	76	Deer Isle, Me.
Blackbead, Catclaw (1976)	88	Sarasota, Fla.
Blackhaw, Rusty (1961)	25	nr. Washington, Ark
Bladdernut, American (1972)	36	nr. Utica, Mich.
Boxelder (1976)	110	Lenawee Co., Mich.
Buckeye, Painted (1972)	144	Union County, Ga.
Buckthorn, Cascara (1977)	35	Coos County, Ore.
Buckthorn, Cascara (1977)	37	Seaside, Ore.
Buckwheat-tree (1981)	44	Wash. County, Fla.
Buffaloberry, Silver (1975)	22	Malheur Co., Ore.
Bumelia, Gum (1977)	80	Robertson Co., Tex.
Buttonbush, Common (1977)	23	nr. High Springs, Fla.
Cajeput Tree (1983)	83	Davie, FL
Camphor-tree (1977)	72	Hardee Co., Fla.
Casuarina, Horsetail (1968)	89	Olowalo, Maui, Ha.
Catalpa, Northern (1984)	98	Lansing, MI
Cedar, Port-Orford (1972)	219	Siskiyou Natl. Forest, Ore.
Cercocarpus, Birchleaf (1972)	34	Central Point, Ore.
Cherry, Black (1984)	93	Allegan Co., MI
Chestnut, American (1979)	82	Oregon City, Ore.
Chinaberry (1967)	75	Koahe, So. Kuona, Ha.
Chinkapin, Giant (1979)	75	Cottage Grove, Ore.
Chokecherry, Common (1982)	67	Ada, Mich.
Coconut (1979)	92.5	Hilo, Ha.
Coffeetree, Kentucky (1976)	110	Van Buren Co., Mich.
Cottonwood, Black (1982)	148	Rainbow Falls St. Park, Wash.
Cypress, Monterey (1975)	97	Brookings, Ore.
Dahoon (1972)	72	Osceola For., Fla.
Desert-Willow (1976)	56	Gila Co., Ariz.
Devil's-walkingstick (1982)	51	San Felasco Hammock, Fla.
Devilwood (1972)	37	Mayo, Fla.
Dogwood, Pacific (1975)	50	nr. Clatskanie, Ore.
Douglas-fir, Coast (1975)	221	Olympic National Park, Wash.
Doveplum (1965)	45	Miami, Fla.
False-Mastic (1975)	70	Lignumvitae Key, Fla.
Fig, Florida Strangler (1973)	80	Old Cutler Hammock, Fla.
Fir, Noble (1972)	278	Gifford Pinchot Natl. Forest, Wash.
Gumbo-limbo (1973)	50	Homestead, Fla.
Hackberry, Common (1972)	118	Allegany Co., Mich.
Hawthorn, Scarlet, (1980)	37	Clinton, New York
Hemlock, Western (1978)	195	Tillamook, Ore.
Hercules-club (1961)	38	Little Rock, Ark.
Hickory, Pignut (1972)	125	nr. Brunswick, Ga.
Holly, American (1983)	50	St. Mary's City, Md.
Honeylocust, Thornless (1976)	130	Washtenaw Co., Mich.
Hophornbeam, Eastern (1976)	73	Grand Traverse Co., Mich.
Hoptree, Common (1982)	35	Ada, Mich.
Hornbeam, American (1982)	69	Milton, N.Y.

Species	Height (ft.)	Location
Joshua-tree (1967)	32	San Bernardino Natl. Forest, Cal.
Juniper, Western (1983)	86	Stanislaus Natl. Forest, CA
Larch, Western (1980)	175	Libby, Mont.
Laurelcherry, Carolina (1972)	44	Dellwood, Fla.
Lebbek (1968)	65	Lahaina, Maui, Ha.
Loblolly-Bay (1983)	94	Ocala Natl. Forest, FL
Locust, Black (1974)	96	Dansville, N.Y.
Lysiloma, Bahama (1973)	79	Homestead, Fla.
Madrone, Pacific (1955)	79	Ettersburg, CA
Magnolia, Cucumber tree (1982)	94	North Canton, Oh.
Mangrove, Red (1975)	75	Everglades Natl. Pk., Fla.
Maple, Red (1984)	179	St. Clair Co., MI
Mesquite, Velvet (1952)	55	Coronado Nat!. Forest, Ariz.
Mountain-Ash, Showy (1982)	58	nr. Gould City, Mich.
Mountain-Laurel (1981)	28	Oconee County, S.C.
Mulberry, White (1982)	55	Leavenworth, Ks.
Oak, Pin (1978)	134	Smithland, Ky.
Oak, Scarlet (1978)	150	Maud, Ala.
Osage-Orange (1969)	51	nr. Brookneal, VA
Palmetto, Cabbage (1978)	90	Highlands Hammock State Pk., Fla.
Paloverde, Blue (1976)	53	Riverside Co., Cal.
Paulownia, Royal (1969)	105	Philadelphia, Pa.
Pawpaw, Common (1981)	56	Pickens County, S.C.
Pear (1976)	57	Clawson, Mich.
Pecan (1983)	130	Warren Co., Miss.
Peppertree (1973)	47	San Juan Capistrano, Cal.
Pinckneya (1982)	32	nr. Orange Springs, Fla.
Pine, Ponderosa (1974)	223	Plumas, Cal.
Plum, American (1972)	35	Oakland Co., Mich.
Poison Sumac (1972)	20	Robin's Island, N.Y.
Pondcypress (1972)	135	nr. Newton, Ga.
Poplar, Balsam (1982)	98	South Egremont, Mass.
Possumhaw (1981)	42	Congaree Swamp, S.C.
Redbay (1972)	58	Randolph City, Ga.
Redwood, Coast (1972)	362	Humboldt Redwoods State Park, Cal.
Royalpalm, Florida (1973)	80	Homestead, Fla.
Sassafras (1972)	100	Owensboro, Ky.
Seagrape (1972)	57	Miami, Fla.
Sequoia, Giant (1975)	275	Sequoia Natl. Pk., Cal.
Serviceberry, Downy (1984)	63	Barry Co., MI
Silktree (1971)	41	Gilmer, Tex.
Silverbell, Two-wing (1982)	66.5	Ashville, S.C.
Smoketree, American (1984)	35	West Lafayette, IN
Soapberry, Western (1984)	72	Coyle, OK
Sourwood (1972)	118	nr. Robbinsville, N.C.
Sparkleberry Tree (1977)	30	Pensacola, Fla.
Spruce, Sitka (1973)	216	Seaside, Ore.
Sugarberry (1976)	78	Society Hills, S.C.
Sumac, Shining (1974)	55	Grenada Co., Miss.
Sweetleaf (1972)	55	Tallahassee, Fla.
Sycamore, Cal. (1945)	116	nr. Santa Barbara, Cal.
Tamarisk (1981)	34	Columbus, N.M.
Tesota (1972)	32	nr. Quartzsite, Ariz.
Trifoliate-Orange (1984)	14	Aiken Co., SC
Tupelo, Black (1969)	117	Harrison Co., Tex.
	(1971)	139	nr. Houston, Tex.
Walnut, Cal. (1973)	116	nr. Chico, Cal.
Willow, Crack (1972)	112	nr. Utica, Mich.
Winterberry, Common (1971)	40	Wildwood, Fla.
Yaupon (1972)	45	nr. Devers, Tex.
Yellow-Poplar (1972)	124	Bedford, Va.
Yew, Pacific (1969)	60	nr. Mineral, Wash.
Yucca, Aloe (1972)	15	Lakeland, Fla.

EDUCATION

American Colleges and Universities

General Information for the 1983-84 Academic Year

Source: Peterson's Guides

The word college is part of the name unless another designation is given. All institutions are coeducational unless the zip code is followed by: (1) men only; (2) primarily men; (3) women only; (4) primarily women; or (5) coordinate (separate colleges or campuses for men and women with shared facilities and courses).

Year is that of founding.

Governing official is president or chancellor unless otherwise designated. NA designates colleges that have not provided up-to-date information.

Affiliation: Private—0-Independent (nonprofit); 1-Independent-religious; 2-Proprietary (profit-making). Public—3-Federal; 4-State; 5-Province (Canada); 6-Commonwealth (Puerto Rico); 7-Territory (U.S. Territories); 8-County; 9-District; 10-City; 11-State and Local; 12-State-related.

Highest degree offered: A-Associate's; B-Bachelor's; M-Master's; D-Doctorate.

Each institution listed has an enrollment of at least 600 students of college grade.

Number of teachers is the total number of individuals on teaching staff.

Four-Year Schools

Name, address	Year	Governing official affiliation, and highest degree offered		Stu-dents	Teach-ers
Abilene Christian Univ., Abilene, TX 79699	1906	William J. Teague	1-M	4,656	251
Acad. of Aeronautics, Flushing, NY 11371 (2)	1932	George W. Bush	0-B	1,450	68
Acad. of Art, San Francisco, CA 94102	1929	Donald Haight	2-M	1,800	120
Adams State, Alamosa, CO 81102	1921	William M. Fulkerson Jr.	4-M	2,087	91
Adelphi Univ., Garden City, NY 11530	1896	Timothy W. Costello	0-D	11,087	857
Adrian, Adrian, MI 49221	1859	Donald S. Stanton	1-B	1,192	102
Alabama A&M Univ., Normal, AL 35762	1875	Richard D. Morrison	4-M	4,310	500
Alabama Christian, Montgomery, AL 36193	1942	Ernest A. Clevenger Jr.	1-B	1,635	93
Alabama State Univ., Montgomery, AL 36195	1874	Leon Howard	4-M	4,050	247
Alaska Pacific Univ., Anchorage, AK 99508	1957	Glenn A. Olds	1-M	668	65
Albany State, Albany, GA 31705	1903	Billy C. Black	4-M	1,865	127
Albion, Albion, MI 49224	1835	Melvin L. Vulgamore	1-B	1,710	122
Albright, Reading, PA 19603	1856	David G. Ruffer	1-B	1,413	126
Alcorn State Univ., Lorman, MS 39096	1871	Walter Washington	4-M	2,442	162
Alderson-Broaddus, Philippi, WV 26416	1871	W. Christian Sizemore	1-B	817	81
Alfred Univ., Alfred, NY 14802	1836	Edward G. Coll Jr.	0-D	2,448	176
Allegheny, Meadville, PA 16335	1815	David B. Harned	1-M	1,955	161
Allentown Coll. of St. Francis de Sales, Center Valley, PA 18034	1962	Rev. Daniel G. Gambet	1-B	742	66
Alma, Alma, MI 48801	1886	Oscar E. Remick	1-B	1,033	76
Alvernia, Reading, PA 19607	1958	Sr. M. Dolorey	1-B	706	80
Alverno, Milwaukee, WI 53215 (3)	1936	Sr. Joel Read	0-B	1,330	138
Amber Univ., Garland, TX 75041	1971	Douglas W. Warner	0-M	1,050	55
American Coll. of Puerto Rico, Bayamon, PR 00619	1963	Juan B. Nazario Negron	0-B	3,789	138
American International, Springfield, MA 01109	1885	Harry J. Courniotes	0-D	2,280	123
American Univ., Washington, DC 20016	1893	Richard Berendzen	1-D	11,322	1,057
Amherst, Amherst, MA 01002	1821	G. Armour Craig	0-B	1,522	171
Anderson, Anderson, IN 46012	1917	Robert H. Reardon	1-M	2,070	163
Andrews Univ., Berrien Springs, MI 49104	1874	W. Richard Lesher	1-D	2,878	240
Angelo State Univ., San Angelo, TX 76909	1928	Lloyd Drexell Vincent	4-M	6,345	227
Anna Maria Coll. for Men and Women, Paxton, MA 01612	1946	Sr. Bernadette Madore	1-M	1,500	78
Antillian, Mayaguez, PR 00708	1957	Angel M. Rodriguez	1-B	894	75
Antioch Univ., Philadelphia, Philadelphia, PA 19130	1852	David Allen Frisby III, Dean	0-M	662	82
Antioch Univ., West, San Francisco, CA 94118	1852	Linda Dunne, Provost	0-M	982	151
Appalachian State Univ., Boone, NC 28608	1899	John E. Thomas	4-M	10,222	584
Aquinas, Grand Rapids, MI 49506	1886	Norbert J. Hruby	1-M	2,805	122
Arizona State Univ., Tempe, AZ 85287	1885	J. Russell Nelson	4-D	40,239	1,687
Arkansas, Batesville, AR 72501	1872	Dan C. West	1-B	653	59
Arkansas State Univ., State University, AR 72467	1909	Eugene W. Smith	4-M	8,358	310
Arkansas Tech Univ., Russellville, AR 72801	1909	Kenneth G. Kersh	4-M	3,362	150
Armstrong State, Savannah, GA 31406	1935	Robert A. Burnett	4-M	2,988	160
Art Center Coll. of Design, Pasadena, CA 91103	1930	Donald R. Kubly	0-M	1,208	175
Asbury, Wilmore, KY 40390	1890	John N. Oswalt	0-B	1,075	109
Ashland, Ashland OH 44805	1878	Joseph Shultz	1-M	3,110	122
Assumption, Worcester, MA 01609	1904	Joseph H. Hagan	1-M	2,000	148
Athens State, Athens, AL 35611	1822	James R. Chasteen	4-B	1,110	78
Atlantic Christian, Wilson, NC 27893	1902	James B. Hemby	1-B	1,526	110
Auburn Univ., Auburn, AL 36849	1856	James E. Martin	4-D	18,426	1,105
Auburn Univ. at Montgomery, Montgomery, AL 36193	1967	James O. Williams	4-M	5,366	350
Augsburg, Minneapolis, MN 55454	1869	Charles S. Anderson	1-B	1,250	183
Augusta, Augusta, GA 30910	1925	George A. Christenberry	4-M	4,252	189
Augustana, Rock Island, IL 61201	1860	Thomas Tredway	1-B	2,352	144
Augustana, Sioux Falls, SD 57197	1860	William C. Nelson	1-M	1,957	163
Aurora, Aurora, IL 60506	1893	Alan J. Stone	1-M	1,490	88
Austin, Sherman, TX 75090	1849	Harry E. Smith	1-M	1,162	111
Austin Peay State Univ., Clarksville, TN 37044	1927	Robert O. Riggs	4-M	5,393	257
Averett, Danville, VA 24541	1859	Howard W. Lee	1-M	1,000	54
Avila, Kansas City, MO 64145	1916	Sr. Olive L. Dallavis, CSJ	1-M	1,765	214
Azusa Pacific Univ., Azusa, CA 91702	1899	Paul E. Sago	1-M	2,425	128
Babson, Babson Park, MA 02157	1919	William R. Dill	0-M	3,137	129
Baker Univ., Baldwin City, KS 66006	1858	Ralph M. Tanner	1-M	826	55

Name, address	Year	Governing official affiliation, and highest degree offered		Stu-dents	Teach-ers
Baldwin-Wallace, Berea, OH 44017	1845	Neal Malicky	1-M	3,651	209
Ball State Univ., Muncie, IN 47306	1918	John E. Worthen	4-D	18,359	1,220
Baltimore Hebrew, Baltimore, MD 21215	1919	Leivy Smolar	1-D	637	17
Baptist Bible, Springfield, MO 65802	1950	A. V. Henderson	1-B	1,538	58
Baptist Bible of Pennsylvania, Clarks Summit, PA 18411	1932	Mark E. Jackson	1-M	761	49
Baptist Coll. at Charleston, Charleston, SC 29411	1964	John A. Hamrick	1-M	1,966	102
Barat, Lake Forest, IL 60045 (4)	1858	Richard P. Soter	1-B	732	72
Bard College, Annandale-on-Hudson, NY 12504	1860	Leon Botstein	0-M	745	90
Barnard, New York, NY 10027 (5)	1889	Ellen Futter	0-B	2,250	246
Barry Univ., Miami Shores, FL 33161	1940	Sr. Jeanne O'Laughlin	1-D	3,218	205
Bartlesville Wesleyan, Bartlesville, OK 74006	1909	Paul R. Mills	1-B	802	59
Bates, Lewiston, ME 04240	1855	Thomas H. Reynolds	0-B	1,425	134
Bayamon Central Univ., Bayamon, PR 00619	1970	Rev. Vincent A. M. Van Rooij, OP	0-B	1,600	78
Baylor Coll. of Dentistry, Dallas, TX 75246	1905	Richard E. Bradley	0-D	665	229
Baylor Univ., Waco, TX 76798	1845	Herbert H. Reynolds	1-D	10,818	585
Beaver, Glenside, PA 19038	1853	Bruce L. Wilson	1-M	2,210	160
Belhaven, Jackson, MS 39202	1883	Verne R. Kennedy	1-B	875	82
Bellarmine, Louisville, KY 40205	1950	Eugene V. Petrik	1-M	2,870	112
Bellevue, Bellevue, NE 68005	1966	Richard D. Winchell	0-B	2,697	102
Belmont Abbey, Belmont, NC 28012	1876	John R. Dempsey	1-B	840	64
Belmont, Nashville, TN 37203	1951	William E. Troutt	1-B	2,041	181
Beloit, Beloit, WI 53511	1846	Roger H. Hull	1-M	1,079	97
Bemidji State Univ., Bemidji, MN 56601	1919	Lowell R. Gillett	4-M	4,153	229
Benedict, Columbia, SC 29204	1870	Henry Ponder	1-B	1,457	97
Benedictine, Atchison, KS 66002	1971	Rev. Gerard Senecal	1-B	965	94
Bennington, Bennington, VT 05201	1932	Michael K. Hooker	0-M	640	80
Bentley, Waltham, MA 02254	1917	Gregory H. Adamian	0-M	8,104	296
Berea, Berea, KY 40404	1855	John B. Stephenson	0-B	1,600	127
Berklee Coll. of Music, Boston, MA 02215	1945	Lee Eliot Berk	0-B	2,487	210
Berry, Mount Berry, GA 30149	1902	Gloria M. Shatto	0-M	1,403	115
Bethany, Lindsborg, KS 67456	1881	Peter J. Ristuben	1-B	770	86
Bethany, Bethany, WV 26032	1840	Todd H. Bullard	1-B	823	79
Bethany Nazarene, Bethany, OK 73008	1899	John A. Knight	1-M	1,320	100
Bethel, North Newton, KS 67117	1887	Harold J. Schultz	1-B	671	60
Bethel, St. Paul, MN 55112	1871	George K. Brushaber	1-B	1,931	194
Bethune-Cookman, Daytona Beach, FL 32015	1904	Oswald P. Bronson	1-B	1,724	122
Biola Univ., La Mirada, CA 90639	1908	Clyde Cook	1-D	3,083	253
Birmingham-Southern, Birmingham, AL 35254	1856	Neal R. Berte	1-M	1,587	135
Bishop, Dallas TX 75241	1881	Harry S. Wright	1-B	1,196	61
Black Hills State, Spearfish, SD 57783	1883	Gilbert Hause	4-M	2,218	104
Bloomfield, Bloomfield, NJ 07003	1868	Merle F. Allshouse	1-B	1,730	134
Bloomsburg, Univ. of Pennsylvania, Bloomsburg, PA 17815	1839	Larry W. Jones	4-M	6,316	340
Bluefield State, Bluefield, WV 24701	1895	Jerold O. Dugger	4-B	2,380	145
Bluffton, Bluffton, OH 45817	1899	Elmer Neufeld	1-B	610	59
Bob Jones Univ., Greenville, SC 29614	1927	Bob Jones III	1-D	4,619	329
Boise State Univ., Boise ID 83725	1932	John H. Keiser	4-M	11,236	453
Boricua, New York, NY 10032	1974	Victor G. Alicea	0-B	904	106
Boston Architectural Center, Boston, MA 02115	1889	Bernard P. Spring	0-B	653	142
Boston, Chestnut Hill, MA 02167	1863	Rev. J. Donald Monan, SJ.	1-D	14,059	857
Boston Univ., Boston, MA 02215	1839	John R. Silber	0-D	27,724	2,600
Bowdoin, Brunswick, ME 04011	1794	A. LeRoy Greason	0-B	1,371	116
Bowie State, Bowie, MD 20715	1865	Marcellina Brooks	4-M	2,366	138
Bowling Green State Univ., Bowling Green, OH 43403	1910	Paul J. Olscamp	4-D	16,886	848
Bradley, Univ., Peoria, IL 61625	1897	Martin G. Abegg	0-M	5,604	377
Brandeis Univ., Waltham, MA 02254	1948	Evelyn E. Handler	0-D	3,245	448
Brenau, Gainesville, GA 30501 (4)	1878	James T. Rogers	0-M	1,786	149
Brescia, Owensboro, KY 42301	1950	Sr. George Ann Cecil	1-B	930	78
Brewton-Parker, Mt. Vernon, GA 30445	1904	Y. Lynn Holmes	1-B	1,207	32
Briar Cliff, Sioux City, IA 51104	1930	Charles J. Bensman	1-B	1,307	75
Bridgeport Engineering, Inst., Bridgeport, CT 06606	1924	William J. Owens III	0-B	900	80
Bridgewater, Bridgewater, VA 22812	1880	Wayne F. Geisert	1-B	873	70
Bridgewater State, Bridgewater, MA 02324	1840	Adrian Rondileau	4-M	4,990	302
Brigham Young Univ., Provo, UT 84602	1875	Jeffrey R. Holland	1-D	26,963	1,536
Brigham Young Univ., Hawaii Campus, Laie, Oahu, HI 96762	1955	J. Elliot Cameron	1-B	1,820	116
Brooks Inst., Santa Barbara, CA 93108	1945	Ernest H. Brooks II	2-M	682	34
Brown Univ., Providence, RI 02912	1764	Howard R. Swearer	0-D	6,869	523
Bryant, Smithfield RI 02917	1863	William T. O'Hara	0-M	6,763	164
Bryn Mawr, Bryn Mawr, PA 19010 (3)	1885	Mary P. McPherson	0-D	1,590	199
Bucknell Univ., Lewisburg, PA 17837	1846	Gary A. Sojka	0-M	3,338	252
Buena Vista, Storm Lake, IA 50588	1891	Keith G. Briscoe	1-B	904	70
Butler Univ., Indianapolis, IN 46208	1855	John G. Johnson	0-M	4,058	340
Cabrini, Radnor, PA 19087	1957	Sr. Eileen Currie	1-M	800	75
Caguas City, Caguas, PR 00626	1966	Alex A. DeJorge	2-B	909	25
Caldwell, Caldwell, NJ 07006 (3)	1939	Sr. Vivien Jennings	1-B	718	71
California Baptist, Riverside, CA 92504	1950	Russell R. Tuck.	1-M	678	70
California Coll. of Arts and Crafts, Oakland, CA 94618	1907	Harry X. Ford	0-M	1,001	143
California Inst. of Technology, Pasadena, CA 91125	1891	Marvin L. Goldberger	0-D	1,765	337
California Inst. of the Arts, Valencia, CA 91355	1961	Robert J. Fitzpatrick	0-M	866	168
California Lutheran, Thousand Oaks, CA 91360	1959	Jerry H. Miller	1-M	2,467	166
California Polytechnic State Univ., San Luis Obispo, CA 93407	1901	Warren J. Baker	4-M	15,623	958
California State, Bakersfield, Bakersfield, CA 93309	1970	Tomas A. Arciniega	4-M	3,380	205
California State, San Bernardino, San Bernardino, CA 92407	1962	Anthony H. Evans	4-M	5,450	272
California State, Stanislaus, Turlock, CA 95380	1957	Walter Olson	4-M	4,448	232
California State Polytechnic Univ., Pomona, CA 91768	1938	Hugh O. La Bounty	4-M	16,701	989
California State Univ., Chico, Chico, CA 95929	1887	Robin Wilson	4-M	14,129	944
California State Univ., Dominguez Hills, Carson, CA 90747	1960	NA	4-M	8,271	489
California State Univ., Fresno, Fresno, CA 93740	1911	Harold H. Haak	4-M	16,293	1,090
California State Univ., Fullerton, Fullerton, CA 92634	1957	Jewel Plummer Cobb	4-M	23,234	1,388
California State Univ., Hayward, Hayward, CA 94542	1957	Ellis E. McCune	4-M	11,978	615
California State Univ., Long Beach, Long Beach, CA 90840	1949	Stephen Horn	4-M	31,492	1,686
California State Univ., Los Angeles, Los Angeles, CA 90032	1947	James M. Rosser	4-D	21,000	1,150
California State Univ., Northridge, Northridge, CA 91330	1958	James Cleary	4-M	27,736	1,500
California State Univ., Sacramento, Sacramento, CA 95819	1947	Donald R. Gerth	4-M	21,636	1,163

Name, address	Year	Governing official affiliation, and highest degree offered		Stu-dents	Teach-ers
California Univ. of Pennnsylvania, California, PA 15419	1852	John Pierce Watkins	4-M	4,877	305
Calumet, Whiting, IN 46394	1951	Rev. Louis Osterhage	1-B	1,297	83
Calvin, Grand Rapids, MI 49506	1876	Anthony J. Diekema	1-M	3,942	255
Cameron Univ., Lawton, OK, 73505	1927	Don Davis	4-B	5,194	325
Campbellsville, Campbellsville, KY 42718	1906	W. R. Davenport	1-B	731	56
Campbell Univ., Buies Creek, NC 27506	1887	Norman A. Wiggins	1-D	3,500	120
Canisius, Buffalo, NY 14208	1870	Rev. James M. Demske, SJ.	0-M	4,567	271
Capital Univ., Columbus, OH 43209	1850	Rev. Harvey Stegmoeller	1-M	2,537	192
Capitol Inst. of Technology, Laurel, MD 20708	1964	G. William Troxler	0-B	1,076	57
Cardinal Stritch, Milwaukee, WI 53217	1937	Sr. M. Camille Kliebhan	1-M	1,763	147
Caribbean, Univ., Bayamon, PR 00619	1969	Angel E. Juan-Ortega	0-B	2,706	116
Carleton, Northfield, MN 55057	1866	Robert H. Edwards	0-B	1,857	142
Carlow, Pittsburgh, PA 15213 (4)	1929	Mary Louise Fennell, RSM	1-M	991	117
Carnegie-Mellon Univ., Pittsburgh, PA 15213	1900	Richard M. Cyert	0-D	5,818	511
Carroll, Waukesha, WI 53186	1846	Robert V. Cramer	1-B	1,194	107
Carroll Coll. of Montana, Helena, MT 59625	1909	Francis J. Kerins	1-B	1,533	117
Carson-Newman, Jefferson City, TN 37760	1851	J. Cordell Maddox	1-B	1,763	113
Carthage, Kenosha, WI 53141	1847	Erno J. Dahl	1-M	1,410	97
Case Western Reserve Univ., Cleveland, OH 44106	1826	David V. Ragone	0-D	8,698	1,535
Castleton State, Castleton, VT 05735	1787	Thomas K. Meier	4-M	2,200	113
Catawba, Salisbury, NC 28144	1851	Stephen H. Wurster	1-B	961	64
Catholic Univ. of America, Washington, DC 20064	1887	Rev. William J. Byron, SJ	1-D	7,258	616
Catholic Univ. of Puerto Rico, Ponce, PR 00732	1948	Rev. F. Tosello Giangiacomo	1-M	13,816	632
Catholic Univ. of Puerto Rico, Arecibo Center, PR 00612	1964	NA	1-B	1,453	56
Catholic Univ. of Puerto Rico, Mayaguez Center, PR 00708	1975	NA	1-B	1,007	82
Cedar Crest, Allentown, PA 18104 (4)	1867	Gene S. Cesari	1-B	1,142	123
Cedarville, Cedarville, OH 45314	1887	Paul H. Dixon	1-B	1,793	121
Centenary, Hackettstown, NJ 07804 (3)	1867	Kenneth G. Powell	0-B	694	67
Centenary Coll. of Louisana, Shreveport, LA 71134	1825	Donald A. Webb	1-M	1,387	108
Center for Creative Studies & Coll. of Art and Design, Detroit, MI 48202	1926	Jerome Grove	0-B	904	152
Central Bible, Springfield, MO 65803	1922	H. Maurice Lednicky	1-B	909	51
Central Connecticut State Univ., New Britain, CT 06050	1849	F. Don James	4-M	13,209	638
Central Methodist, Fayette, MO 65248	1854	Joseph A. Howell	1-B	623	62
Central Michigan Univ., Mount Pleasant, MI 48859	1892	Harold Abel	4-D	16,315	740
Central Missouri State Univ., Warrensburg, MO 64093	1871	James M. Harmon	4-M	9,601	452
Central New England, Worcester, MA 01610	1888	Edward Paul Mattar III	0-B	2,146	129
Central State Univ., Wilberforce, OH 45384	1887	Lionel H. Newsom	4-B	2,390	154
Central State Univ., Edmond, OK 73034	1890	Bill J. Lillard	4-M	12,309	430
Central Univ. of Iowa, Pella, IA 50219	1853	Kenneth J. Weller	1-B	1,535	93
Central Washington Univ., Ellersburg, WA 98926	1891	Donald L. Garrity	4-M	7,121	304
Centre, Danville, KY 40422	1819	Richard L. Morrill	1-B	759	70
Chadron State, Chadron, NE 69337	1911	Edwin C. Nelson	4-M	1,977	104
Chaminade Univ. of Honolulu, Honolulu, HI 96816	1955	Rev. Raymond A. Roesch, SM	1-M	2,421	65
Chapman, Orange CA 92666	1861	G. T. Smith	1-M	1,699	193
Charter Oak, Hartford, CT 06106	1973	Bernard Shea	4-B	1,200	55
Chatham, Pittsburgh, PA 15232 (3)	1869	Rebecca Stafford	0-B	610	70
Chestnut Hill, Philadelphia, PA 19118 (4)	1924	Sr. Matthew Anita MacDonald	1-M	819	100
Cheyney Univ. of Pennsylvania, Cheyney, PA 19319	1837	C. T. Enus Wright	4-M	1,992	163
Chicago State Univ., Chicago, IL 60628	1867	George E. Ayers	4-M	7,510	430
Christian Brothers, Memphis, TN 38104	1871	Br. Theodore Drahmann	1-B	1,493	150
Cincinnati Bible, Cincinnati, OH 45204	1924	John E. Anderson	4-B	4,398	120
The Citadel, Charleston, SC 29409 (1)	1842	Harvey C. Bream Jr	1-B	612	45
City Univ., Bellevue, WA 98008	1973	Maj. Gen. James A. Grimsley	4-M	3,123	150
City Univ. of New York, Bernard M. Baruch Coll., New York, NY 10010	1968	Michael A. Pastore	0-M	2,838	220
City Univ. of New York, Brooklyn Coll., Brooklyn, NY 11210	1930	Joel Segall	11-M	15,368	800
City Univ. of New York, City Coll., New York, NY 10031	1847	Robert Hess	11-M	12,271	1,045
City Univ. of New York, Coll. of Staten Island, NY 10301	1955	Bernard W. Harleston	11-M	13,129	1,013
City Univ. of New York, Herbert H. Lehman Coll., Bronx, NY 10468	1931	Edmond L. Volpe	11-M	11,100	379
City Univ. of New York, Hunter Coll., New York, NY 10021	1870	Leonard Lief	11-M	10,500	820
City Univ. of New York, John Jay Coll. of Criminal Justice, New York, NY 10019	1964	Donna E. Shalala	11-M	17,784	1,122
City Univ. of New York, Medgar Evers Coll., Brooklyn, NY 11225	1969	Gerald Lynch	11-D	6,369	406
City Univ. of New York, New York City Tech. Coll., Brooklyn, NY 11201	1946	Jay Carrington Chunn	11-B	2,536	323
City Univ. of New York, Queens Coll., Flushing, NY 11367	1937	Ursula C. Schwerin	11-B	12,077	1,030
City Univ. of New York, York Coll., Jamaica, NY 11451	1967	Saul Bernard Cohen	11-M	17,179	1,435
Claflin, Orangeburg, SC 29115	1869	Milton G. Bassin	11-B	4,200	200
Claremont McKenna, Claremont, CA 91711	1946	Oscar A. Rogers Jr	1-B	633	65
Clarion Univ. of Pennsylvania, Clarion, PA 16214	1867	Jack L. Stark	0-B	844	99
Clark, Atlanta, Ga 30314	1869	Thomas A. Bond	4-M	4,841	320
Clarke, Dubuque, IA 52001	1843	Elias Blake Jr	1-B	1,936	157
Clarkson Univ., Potsdam, NY 13676	1896	Meneve Dunham	1-M	906	79
Clark Univ., Worcester, MA 01610	1887	Robert A. Plane	0-D	4,080	231
Cleary, Ypsilanti, MI 48197	1883	Richard P. Traina	0-D	2,700	175
Clemson Univ., Clemson, SC 29631	1889	Harry Howard	0-B	1,089	62
Cleveland State Univ., Cleveland, OH 44115	1964	Bill L. Atchley	4-D	12,459	1,005
Clinch Valley Coll. of the Univ. of Virginia, Wise, VA 24293	1954	Walte B. Waetjen	4-D	18,942	710
Coe, Cedar Rapids, IA 52402	1851	Joseph C. Smiddy	4-B	1,037	58
Colby, Waterville, ME 04901	1813	John E. Brown	1-B	1,371	101
Coleman, La Mesa, CA 92041	1963	William R. Cotter	0-B	1,675	154
Colgate Univ., Hamilton, NY 13346	1819	NA	0-M	802	41
Coll. Misericordia, Dallas, PA 18612	1924	George D. Langdon Jr.	0-M	2,594	208
Coll. of Boca Raton, Boca Raton, FL 33431	1963	Joseph R Fink	1-M	1,303	128
Coll. of Charleston, Charleston, SC 29424	1770	Donald E. Ross	0-B	700	57
Coll. of Great Falls, Great Falls, MT 59405	1932	Edward Collins Jr.	4-M	5,323	326
Coll. of Idaho, Caldwell, ID 83605	1891	William A. Shields	1-M	1,192	87
Coll. of Insurance, New York, NY 10007	1962	Arthur H. DeRosier Jr.	1-M	885	104
Coll. of Mt. St. Joseph on the Ohio, OH 45051	1920	Linda H. Lamel	0-M	602	255
Coll. of Mt. St. Vincent, Riverdale, NY 10471 (4)	1847	Sr. Jean Patrice Harrington	1-M	1,753	116
Coll. of New Rochelle, NY 10801 (4)	1904	Sr. Doris Smith	0-B	1,108	83
		Sr. Dorothy A. Kelly	0-M	2,041	135

Name, address	Year	Governing official affiliation, and highest degree offered		Stu-dents	Teach-ers
Coll. of New Rochelle, New Resources Div., New Rochelle, NY 10801	1973	Sr. Dorothy Ann Kelly	0-B	3,030	429
Coll. of Notre Dame, Belmont, CA 94002	1868	Sr. Veronica Skillin	1-M	1,254	141
Coll. of St. Benedict, St. Joseph, MN 56374 (5)	1913	Sr. Emmanuel Renner	1-B	1,747	136
Coll. of St. Catherine, St. Paul, MN 55105 (3)	1905	Anita Pampusch	1-M	2,291	178
Coll. of St. Elizabeth, Convent Station, NJ 07961 (4)	1899	Sr. Jacqueline Burns	1-B	671	93
Coll. of St. Francis, Joliet, IL 60435	1920	John C. Orr	1-M	1,062	87
Coll. of St. Mary, Omaha, NE 68124 (4)	1923	Kenneth Nielson	1-B	1,207	114
Coll. of St. Rose, Albany, NY 12203	1920	Louis C. Vaccaro	0-M	2,378	187
Coll. of St. Scholastica, Duluth, MN 55811	1906	Daniel H. Pilon	1-M	1,307	120
Coll. of St. Thomas, St. Paul, MN 55105	1885	Msgr. Terrence J. Murphy	1-M	5,959	350
Coll. of Santa Fe, Santa Fe, NM 87501	1947	Br. Donald Mouton	1-B	857	90
Coll. of the Holy Cross, Worcester, MA 01610	1843	Rev. John E. Brooks, SJ.	1-B	2,536	214
Coll. of the Ozarks, Clarksville, AR 72830	1834	Fritz Ehren	1-B	708	40
Coll. of the Virgin Islands, Charlotte Amalie, St. Thomas VI, 00802	1962	Arthur A. Richards	7-M	2,864	165
Coll. of William and Mary, Williamsburg, VA 23185	1693	Thomas A. Graves Jr.	4-D	6,607	537
Coll. of Wooster, Wooster, OH 44691	1866	Henry J. Copeland	1-B	1,612	142
Colorado Coll., Colorado Springs, CO 80903	1874	Gresham Riley	0-M	1,906	175
Colorado School of Mines, Golden CO 80401	1874	George S. Ansell	4-D	2,931	210
Colorado State Univ., Fort Collins, CO 80523	1870	Philip E. Austin	4-D	18,295	1,158
Colorado Tech. Coll., Colorado Springs, CO 80907	1965	Marilyn O. Sullivan	2-B	634	65
Columbia Bible, Columbia, SC 29230	1923	J. Robertson McQuilkin	1-M	923	49
Columbia, Chicago, IL 60605	1890	Mirron Alexandroff	0-M	4,754	473
Columbia, Columbia, MO 65216	1851	Donald B. Ruthenberg	0-B	681	61
Columbia, New York, NY 10027	1754	NA	0-B	2,900	560
Columbia, Columbia, SC 29203 (3)	1854	Ralph T. Mirse	1-M	1,100	71
Columbia Union, Takoma Park, MD 20912	1904	William A. Loveless	1-B	874	80
Columbia Univ., School of Engineering and Applied Science, New York, NY 10027	1864	Robert A. Gross, Dean	0-D	2,200	143
Columbia Univ., School of General Studies, New York, NY 10027	1947	NA	0-B	2,096	420
Columbus, Columbus, GA 31993	1958	Francis J. Brooke	4-M	4,283	219
Columbus Coll. of Art and Design, Columbus, OH 43215	1879	Joseph V. Canzani	0-B	941	65
Concord, Athens, WV 24712	1872	Meredith N. Freeman	4-B	2,176	121
Concordia, River Forest, IL 60305	1864	Eugene, L. Krentz	1-M	1,322	111
Concordia, Moorhead, MN 56560	1891	Paul J. Dovre	1-B	2,505	180
Concordia, St. Paul, MN 55104	1893	Gerhadt W. Hyatt.	1-B	779	77
Concordia Coll., Wisconsin, Mequon, WI 53092	1881	R. John Buuck	1-B	784	57
Concordia Teachers, Seward, NE 68434	1894	Alan Harre	1-M	959	101
Connecticut, New London, CT 06320	1911	Oakes Ames	0-M	1,806	230
Consortium of the California State Univ., Long Beach, CA 90802	1973	David H. Elliott	4-M	3,000	100
Converse, Spartanburg, SC 29301 (3)	1889	Robert T. Coleman Jr.	0-M	1,083	80
Cooper Union for the Advancement of Science and Art, New York, NY 10003	1859	Bill N. Lacy	0-M	1,035	188
Coppin State, Baltimore, MD 21216	1900	Calvin W. Burnett.	4-M	2,650	140
Cornell, Mt. Vernon, IA 52314	1853	David G. Marker	1-B	961	95
Cornell Univ., Ithaca, NY 14853	1865	Frank H. T. Rhodes	0-D	17,146	1,555
Corpus Christi State Univ., Corpus Christi, TX 78412	1971	B. Alan Sugg	4-M	3,567	157
Creighton Univ., Omaha, NE 68178	1878	Rev. Michael G. Morrison	1-D	5,864	988
Culver-Stockton, Canton, MO 63435	1853	Robert Brown	0-B	719	57
Cumberland, Williamsburg, KY 40769	1889	James Taylor	1-M	1,956	111
Cumberland Coll. of Tennessee, Lebanon, TN 37087	1842	Robert N. Clement	0-B	617	55
Curry, Milton, MA 02186	1879	William L. Boyle Jr.	0-M	1,189	111
Daeman, Amherst, NY 14226	1947	Robert S. Marshall	0-B	1,623	127
Dakota State, Madison, SD 57042	1881	NA	4-B	1,246	77
Dallas Baptist, Dallas, TX 75211	1965	W. Marvin Watson	1-M	1,437	47
Dartmouth, Hanover, NH 03755	1769	David T. McLaughlin	0-D	5,000	1,313
David Lipscomb, Nashville, TN 37203	1891	Willard Collins	1-M	2,360	147
Davidson, Davidson, NC 28036	1837	John W. Kuykendall	1-B	1,371	117
Davis & Elkins, Elkins, WV 26241	1904	C. Brent DeVore	1-B	1,085	77
Defiance, Defiance, OH 43512	1850	Marvin Ludwig	1-B	917	77
Delaware State, Dover, DE 19901	1891	Luna I. Mishoe	4-M	2,128	140
Delaware Valley Coll. of Science and Agriculture, Doylestown, PA 18901	1896	Joshua Feldstein	0-B	1,305	71
Delta State, Cleveland, MS 38733	1925	F. Kent Wyatt	4-D	3,713	17
Denison Univ., Granville, OH 43023	1831	Andrew G. De Rocco	0-B	2,138	17
DePaul Univ., Chicago, IL 60604	1898	Rev. John T. Richardson, CM.	1-D	12,447	97
DePauw Univ., Greencastle, IN 46135	1837	Richard F. Rosser	1-M	2,381	22
Detroit Coll. of Business, Dearborn, MI 48126	1962	Frank Paone	0-B	2,658	12
DeVry Inst. of Tech., Phoenix, AZ 85016	1967	Harry Overton	2-B	4,615	22
DeVry Inst. of Tech., City of Industry, CA 91744	1983	NA	2-B	873	
DeVry Inst. of Tech., Atlanta, GA 30341	1969	William N. Weaver	2-B	2,759	
DeVry Inst. of Tech., Chicago, IL 60618	1931	Lee H. Bishop.	2-B	4,838	1
DeVry Inst. of Tech., Lombard, IL 60148	1982	NA	2-B	2,865	1
DeVry Inst. of Tech., Kansas City, MO 64131	1931	Charles R. Levalley	2-B	2,141	1
DeVry Inst. of Tech., Columbus, OH 43209	1952	Richard A. Czerniak	2-B	4,440	2
DeVry Inst. of Tech., Irving, TX 75062	1969	David L. Moffatt.	2-B	2,306	
Dickinson, Carlisle, PA 17013	1773	Samuel Alston Banks	1-B	1,776	1
Dickinson State, Dickinson, ND 58601	1918	Albert A. Watrel	4-B	1,234	
Dillard Univ., New Orleans, LA 70122	1869	Samuel Du Bois Cook	1-B	1,142	
Doane, Crete, NE 68333	1872	Philip R. Heckman	1-B	688	
Dr. Martin Luther, New Ulm, MN 56073	1884	Rev. Lloyd O. Huebner	1-B	627	
Dr. William M. Scholl Coll. of Chicago Podiatric Medicine, Chicago, IL 60610	1912	George B. Geppner	0-D	650	
Dominican Coll. of Blauvelt, Orangeburg, NY 10962	1952	Sr. Mary E. O'Brien	0-B	1,729	1
Dominican Coll. of San Rafael, San Rafael, CA 94901	1890	Barbara K. Bundy	1-M	710	1
Dordt, Sioux Center, IA 51250	1955	John B. Hulst	1-B	1,113	
Dowling, Oakdale, NY 11769	1959	Victor P. Meskill	0-M	2,260	
Drake Univ., Des Moines, IA 50311	1881	Wilbur C. Miller	0-D	6,008	3
Drew Univ., Madison, NJ 07940	1866	Paul Hardin	0-D	2,397	2
Drexel Univ., Philadelphia, PA 19104	1891	William S. Gaither	0-D	12,687	3
Drury, Springfield, MO 65802	1873	John E. Moore Jr.	0-M	1,212	

Name, address	Year	Governing official affiliation, and highest degree offered	Students	Teachers
Duke Univ*, Durham, NC 27706	1838	Terry Sanford 0-D	9,285	1,442
Duquesne Univ., Pittsburgh, PA 15282	1878	Donald S. Nesti 1-D	6,340	492
Dyke, Cleveland, OH 44115	1848	John C. Corfias 0-B	1,482	128
D'Youville, Buffalo, NY 14201	1908	Sr. Denise Roche 0-M	1,270	102
Earlham, Richmond, IN 47374	1847	NA 1-M	1,058	97
East Carolina Univ., Greenville, NC 27834	1907	John M. Howell 4-D	13,358	864
East Central Oklahoma State Univ., Ada, OK 74820	1909	Stanley P. Wagner 4-M	4,268	210
Eastern, St. Davids, PA 19087	1932	Robert A. Seiple 1-M	907	77
Eastern Connecticut State Univ., Willimantic, CT 06226	1889	Charles R. Webb Jr. 4-M	3,754	212
Eastern Illinois Univ., Charleston, IL 61920	1895	Stanley Rives 4-M	10,028	549
Eastern Kentucky Univ., Richmond, KY 40475	1906	J. C. Powell 4-M	12,661	739
Eastern Mennonite, Harrisonburg, VA 22801	1917	Richard C. Detweiler 1-B	891	84
Eastern Michigan Univ., Ypsilanti, MI 48197	1849	John W. Porter 4-M	19,809	843
Eastern Montana, Billings, MT 59101	1927	Bruce H. Carpenter 4-M	4,424	218
Eastern Nazarene, Quincy, MA 02170	1918	Stephen W. Nease 1-M	888	66
Eastern New Mexico Univ., Portales, NM 88130	1934	Robert Matheny 4-M	3,748	200
Eastern Oregon State, La Grande, OR 97850	1929	David E. Gilbert 4-M	1,674	126
Eastern Washington Univ., Cheney, WA 99004	1882	H. George Frederickson 4-M	8,493	390
East Stroudsburg Univ. of Pennsylvania, PA 18301	1893	Dennis Bell 4-M	4,065	217
East Tennessee State Univ., Johnson City, TN 37614	1911	Ronald E. Beller 4-D	9,805	429
East Texas Baptist Univ., Marshall, TX 75670	1912	Jerry F. Dawson 1-B	814	56
East Texas State Univ., Commerce, TX 75428	1889	Charles J. Austin 4-M	7,578	363
East Texas State Univ. at Texarkana, Texarkana, TX 75501	1971	John F. Moss 4-M	1,138	55
Eckerd, St. Petersburg, FL 33733	1958	Peter H. Armacost 1-B	1,058	91
Edgewood, Madison, WI 53711	1927	Sr. Mary Ewens 1-B	797	71
Edinboro Univ. of Pennsylvania, Edinboro, PA 16444	1857	Foster F. Diebold 4-M	5,913	339
Edward Waters, Jacksonville, FL 32209	1866	Cecil W. Cone 1-B	877	43
Electronic Data Processing Coll. of Puerto Rico, Hato Rey, PR 00918	1968	Anibal Nieves 2-B	2,600	91
Elizabeth City State Univ., Elizabeth City, NC 27909	1891	Jimmy R. Jenkins 4-B	1,600	114
Elizabethtown, Elizabethtown, PA 17022	1899	Mark C. Ebersole 1-B	1,864	135
Elmhurst, Elmhurst, IL 60126	1871	Ivan Frick 1-B	3,605	184
Elmira, Elmira, NY 14901	1855	Leonard T. Grant 0-M	2,088	258
Elms, Chicopee, MA 01013 (3)	1928	Sr. Mary A. Dooley 1-B	741	75
Elon, Elon College, NC 27244	1889	J. Fred Young 1-M	2,715	149
Embry-Riddle Aeronautical Univ., Daytona Beach, FL 32014	1926	NA 0-M	4,994	270
Embry-Riddle Aeronautical Univ., Intl. Campus, Bunnell, FL 32010	1926	Charles S. Williams, Provost . . 0-M	4,404	1,104
Embry-Riddle Aeronautical Univ., Prescott Campus, AZ 86302	1978	Paul Daly, V.P. 0-B	884	53
Emerson, Boston, MA 02116	1880	Allen E. Koenig 0-M	2,251	167
Emmanuel, Boston, MA 02115 (3)	1919	Sr. Janet Eisner 1-M	1,259	95
Emory & Henry, Emory, VA 24327	1836	Charles W. Sydnos Jr. 1-B	789	66
Emory Univ., Atlanta, GA 30322	1836	James T. Laney 1-D	8,052	1,309
Emporia State Univ., Emporia, KS 66801	1863	John E. Visser 4-M	5,358	284
Evangel, Springfield, MO 65802	1955	Robert H. Spence 1-B	1,811	115
Evergreen State, Olympia, WA 98505	1967	Richard N. Schwartz 4-M	2,717	165
Fairfield Univ., Fairfield, CT 06430	1942	Rev. Aloysius P. Kelley 1-M	5,242	323
Fairleigh Dickinson Univ., Florham-Madison Campus, NJ 07940	1958	James V. Griffo, Provost. . . . 0-M	4,603	239
Fairleigh Dickinson Univ., Rutherford Campus, NJ 07070	1942	Robert E. Wall, Provost 0-M	3,576	246
Fairleigh Dickinson Univ., Teaneck-Hackensack Campus, Teaneck, NJ 07666	1954	Ralph S. Kaslick, Acting Provost 0-D	7,347	688
Fairmont State, Fairmont, WV 26554	1865	Wendell G. Hardway. 4-B	4,844	312
Fashion Inst. of Tech., New York, NY 10001	1944	Marvin J. Feldman 11-B	3,930	650
Fayetteville State Univ., Fayetteville, NC 28301	1867	Charles Lyons Jr 4-M	2,666	183
Felician, Lodi, NJ 07644 (4)	1942	Sr. Theresa Mary Martin. . . . 1-B	678	78
Ferris State, Big Rapids, MI 49307	1884	Robert L. Ewigleben 4-D	10,767	650
Ferrum, Ferrum, VA 24088	1913	Joseph T. Hart 1-B	1,577	95
Findlay, Findlay, OH 45840	1882	Kenneth E. Zirkle 1-B	1,157	99
Fisk Univ., Nashville, TN 37203	1866	NA 1-M	694	77
Fitchburg State, Fitchburg, MA 01420	1894	Vincent J. Mara 4-M	6,574	512
Flagler, St. Augustine, FL 32084	1968	William L. Proctor 0-B	1,009	83
Florida A&M Univ., Tallahassee, FL 32307	1887	Walter L. Smith 4-M	5,175	327
Florida Atlantic Univ., Boca Raton, FL 33431	1961	Helen Popovich 4-D	7,287	508
Florida Inst. of Tech., Melbourne, FL 32901	1958	Jerome P. Keuper 0-D	7,018	392
Florida Inst. of Tech., School of Applied Technology, Jensen Beach, FL 33457	1972	Marion Rice, Provost. 0-M	971	80
Florida Int. Univ., Miami, FL 33199	1965	Gregory B. Wolfe 4-D	10,732	704
Florida Memorial, Miami, FL 33054	1879	W. C. Robinson 1-B	1,750	94
Florida Southern, Lakeland, FL 33802	1885	Robert A. Davis 1-M	1,960	135
Florida State Univ., Tallahassee, FL 32306	1857	Bernard F. Sliger. 4-D	19,877	1,489
Fontbonne, St. Louis, MO 63105	1917	Sr. Jane Kehoe Hassett 1-M	940	129
Fordham Univ. at Lincoln Center, New York, NY 10023	1841	NA 1-D	3,983	898
Fordham Univ., Rose Hill Campus, Bronx, NY 10458	1841	NA 1-D	6,037	930
Fort Hays State Univ., Hays, KS 67601	1902	Gerald W. Tomanek 4-M	5,476	264
Fort Lauderdale, Fort Lauderdale, FL 33301	1940	Douglas D. Devaux 2-B	720	40
Fort Lewis, Durango, CO 81301	1911	Rexer Berndt 4-B	3,685	158
Fort Valley State, Fort Valley, GA 31030	1895	Walter Wade Sullivan 4-M	1,870	142
Framingham State, Framingham, MA 01701	1839	D. Justin McCarthy 4-M	3,732	214
Francis Marion, Florence, SC 29501	1970	Thomas C. Stanton 4-M	3,131	137
Franklin and Marshall, Lancaster, PA 17604	1787	James L. Powell 0-B	2,010	164
Franklin Coll. of Indiana, Franklin, IN 46131	1834	NA 1-B	662	59
Franklin Pierce, Rindge, NH 03461	1962	Walter Peterson 0-B	991	145
Franklin Univ., Columbus, OH 43215	1902	Frederick J. Bunte 0-B	4,857	218
Freed-Hardeman, Henderson, TN 38340	1869	E. C. Gardner 1-B	1,146	80
Fresno Pacific, Fresno, CA 93702	1944	Edmund Janzen 1-M	890	63
Friends Univ., Wichita, KS 67213	1898	Richard Felix 1-B	761	58
Frostburg State, Frostburg, MD 21532	1898	Nelson P. Guild 4-M	3,400	185
Furman Univ., Greenville, SC 29613	1826	John E. Johns 1-M	2,625	163
Gallaudet, Washington, DC 20002	1856	Jerry C. Lee 0-D	1,680	280
Gannon Univ., Erie, PA 16541	1944	Joseph P. Scottino 1-M	3,600	251
Gardner-Webb, Boiling Springs, NC 28017	1905	Craven E. Williams 1-M	1,878	152
Geneva, Beaver Falls, PA 15010	1848	Joe McFarland 1-B	1,290	101

Name, address	Year	Governing official affiliation, and highest degree offered		Stu-dents	Teach-ers
George Fox, Newberg, OR 97132	1891	Edward F. Stevens	1-B	653	73
George Mason Univ., Fairfax, VA 22030	1957	George W. Johnson	4-D	14,545	756
Georgetown, Georgetown, KY 40324	1829	W. Morgan Patterson	1-M	1,302	85
Georgetown Univ., Washington, DC 20057	1789	Rev. Timothy S. Healy	1-D	11,237	1,475
George Washington Univ., Washington, DC 20052	1821	Lloyd H. Elliott	0-D	14,482	1,769
George Williams, Downers Grove, IL 60515	1890	John W. Kessler	0-M	1,036	103
Georgia, Milledgeville, GA 31061	1889	Edwin G. Speir	4-M	3,554	179
Georgia Inst. of Tech., Atlanta, GA 30332	1885	Joseph M. Pettit	4-D	10,918	603
Georgian Court, Lakewood, NJ 08701 (4)	1908	Sr. Barbara Williams	1-M	1,468	124
Georgia Southern, Statesboro, GA 30460	1906	Dale W. Lick	4-M	7,018	400
Georgia Southwestern, Americus, GA 31709	1906	William H. Capitan	4-M	2,344	116
Georgia State Univ., Atlanta, GA 30303	1913	Noah Langdale Jr.	4-D	21,512	924
Gettysburg, Gettysburg, PA 17325	1832	Charles E. Glassick	1-B	1,850	132
Glassboro State, Glassboro, NJ 08028	1923	Mark M. Chamberlain	4-M	9,500	534
Glenville State, Glenville, WV 26351	1872	William K. Simmons	4-B	1,807	96
GMI Engineering & Management Inst., Flint, MI 48502	1919	William B. Cottingham	0-M	2,638	148
Golden Gate Univ., San Francisco, CA 94105	1901	Otto W. Butz	0-D	11,083	768
Goldey Beacom, Wilmington, DE 19808	1886	William R. Baldt	0-B	1,993	92
Gonzaga Univ., Spokane, WA 99258	1887	Rev. Bernard J. Coughlin	1-D	3,464	281
Gordon, Wenham, MA 01984	1889	Richard F. Gross	1-B	1,095	72
Goshen, Goshen, IN 46526	1894	Victor Stoltzfus	1-B	1,088	90
Goucher, Towson, MD 21204 (3)	1885	Rhoda M. Dorsey	0-M	1,041	25
Governors State Univ., University Park, IL 60466	1969	Leo Goodman Malamuth II	4-M	4,546	32
Grace, Winona Lake, IN 46590	1948	Homer A. Kent Jr.	1-B	915	4
Graceland, Lamoni, IA 50140	1895	Joe E. Hanna	0-B	1,059	10
Grambling State Univ., Grambling, LA 71245	1901	Joseph B. Johnson	4-M	4,593	20
Grand Canyon, Phoenix, AZ 85061	1949	William Williams	1-B	1,305	9
Grand Rapids Baptist Coll. and Seminary, MI 49505	1941	Charles Wagner	1-M	1,028	6
Grand Valley State, Allendale, MI 49401	1960	Arend D. Lubbers	4-M	5,158	22
Grand View, Des Moines, IA 50316	1896	Karl F. Langrock	1-B	1,307	9
Grantham Coll. of Engineering, Los Angeles, CA 90035	1951	D. J. Grantham	2-B	931	
Greenville, Greenville, IL 62246	1892	W. Richard Stephens	1-B	688	7
Griffin, Seattle, WA 98121	1909	J. Michael Griffin	3-B	712	7
Grinnell, Grinnell, IA 50112	1846	George A. Drake	0-B	1,107	11
Grove City, Grove City, PA 16127	1876	Charles S. Mackenzie	1-B	2,186	12
Guilford, Greensboro, NC 27410	1837	William R. Rogers	1-B	1,112	12
Gustavus Adolphus, St. Peter, MN 56082	1862	John S. Kendall	1-B	2,180	20
Gwynedd-Mercy, Gwynedd Valley, PA 19437 (4)	1948	Sr. Isabelle Keiss	1-M	2,191	21
Hahnemann Univ., Philadelphia, PA 19102	1848	Bertram S. Brown	0-D	2,036	35
Hamilton, Clinton, NY 13323	1812	J. Martin Carovano	0-B	1,620	14
Hamline Univ., St. Paul, MN 55104	1854	Charles J. Graham	1-M	1,866	12
Hampden-Sydney, Hampden-Sydney, VA 23943	1776	Josiah Bunting III	1-B	800	6
Hampshire, Amherst, MA 01002	1965	Adele S. Simmons	0-B	1,100	9
Hampton Inst., Hampton, VA 23668	1868	William H. Harvey	0-M	4,063	23
Hanover, Hanover, IN 47243	1827	John E. Horner	1-B	1,000	
Harding Univ., Searcy, AR 72143	1924	Clifton L. Ganus Jr.	1-M	2,885	16
Hardin-Simmons Univ., Abilene, TX 79698	1891	Jesse C. Fletcher	1-M	1,927	12
Harris-Stowe State, St. Louis, MO 63103	1857	Henry Givens Jr.	4-B	1,287	6
Hartwick, Oneonta, NY 13820	1928	Philip S. Wilder Jr.	0-B	1,440	1
Harvard and Radcliffe, Cambridge, MA 02138	1636	Derek C. Bok	0-D	6,537	65
Hastings, Hastings, NE 68901	1882	Clyde B. Matters	1-B	792	
Haverford, Haverford, PA 19041	1833	Robert B. Stevens	0-B	1,020	
Hawaii Pacific, Honolulu, HI 96813	1966	Chatt Wright	0-B	3,108	1
Hawthorne, Antrim, NH 03440	1962	Kenneth F. McLaughlin	0-B	621	
Heidelberg, Tiffin, OH 44883	1850	William C. Cassell	1-B	843	
Henderson State Univ., Arkadelphia, AR 71923	1890	Martin B. Garrison	4-M	2,824	1
Hendrix, Conway, AR 72032	1876	Joe B. Hatcher	1-B	990	
High Point, High Point, NC 27262	1924	Charles R. Lucht	1-B	1,359	
Hillsdale, Hillsdale, MI 49242	1844	George C. Roche III	0-B	1,010	
Hiram, Hiram, OH 44234	1850	Elmer Jagow	1-B	1,209	
Hobart, Geneva, NY 14456 (5)	1822	Carroll Brewster	1-B	1,050	1
Hofstra Univ., Hempstead, NY 11550	1935	James M. Shuart	0-D	11,535	6
Hollins, Hollins College, VA 24020 (3)	1842	Paula P. Brownlee	0-M	970	
Holy Family, Philadelphia, PA 19114 (4)	1954	Sr. M. Francesca	1-B	1,506	
Holy Names, Oakland, CA 94619	1868	Sr. Lois MacGillivray	1-M	632	1
Hood, Frederick, MD 21701 (4)	1893	Martha E. Church	1-M	1,750	1
Hope, Holland, MI 49423	1851	Gordon Van Wylen	1-B	2,530	2
Houghton, Houghton, NY 14744	1883	Daniel R. Chamberlain	1-B	1,214	
Houston Baptist Univ., Houston, TX 77004	1960	William H. Hinton	1-M	3,522	1
Howard Payne Univ., Brownwood, TX 76801	1889	Ralph A. Phelps Jr	1-B	1,067	
Howard Univ., Washington, DC 20059	1867	James E. Cheek	0-D	11,594	1,9
Humboldt State Univ., Arcata, CA 95521	1913	Alistair W. McCrone	4-M	7,359	4
Huntingdon, Montgomery, AL 36194	1854	Allen K. Jackson	1-B	742	
Husson, Bangor, ME 04401	1898	Delmont N. Merrill	0-M	1,475	
Idaho State Univ., Pocatello, ID 83209	1901	Myron L. Coulter	4-D	6,041	5
Illinois Benedictine, Lisle, IL 60532	1887	Richard C. Becker	1-M	2,345	
Illinois, Jacksonville, IL 62650	1829	Donald C. Mundinger	1-B	764	
Illinois Inst. of Tech., Chicago, IL 60616	1892	Thomas L. Martin Jr.	0-D	4,784	5
Illinois State Univ., Normal, IL 61761	1857	Lloyd I. Watkins	4-D	19,817	1,0
Illinois Wesleyan Univ., Bloomington, IL 16702	1850	Robert S. Eckley	1-B	1,634	1
Immaculata, Immaculata, PA 19345 (4)	1920	Sr. Marian William	1-M	1,918	1
Incarnate Word, San Antonio, TX 78209	1881	Sr. Margaret P. Slattery	1-M	1,321	1
Indiana Central Univ., Indianapolis, IN 46227	1902	Gene E. Sease	1-M	3,323	
Indiana Inst. of Tech., Fort Wayne, IN 46803	1930	Thomas F. Scully	0-B	850	
Indiana State Univ., Terre Haute, IN 47809	1865	Richard D. Landini	4-D	11,587	
Indiana State Univ., Evansville, Evansville, IN 47712	1965	David L. Rice	4-M	3,806	
Indiana Univ. at Kokomo, Kokomo, IN 46901	1945	Hugh L. Thompson	4-M	2,735	
Indiana Univ. at South Bend, South Bend, IN 46634	1922	Lester M. Wolfson	4-M	5,610	
Indiana Univ., Bloomington, Bloomington, IN 47405	1820	Kenneth R. R. Gros Louis, V.P.	4-D	33,109	1,5
Indiana Univ., Northwest, Gary, IN 46408	1959	Peggy G. Elliott	4-M	5,116	
Indiana Univ. of Pennsylvania, Indiana, PA 15705	1875	John E. Welty	4-D	12,526	
Indiana Univ. & Purdue Univ. at Fort Wayne, IN 46805	1917	Joseph P. Giusti	4-M	10,476	
Indiana Univ. & Purdue Univ. at Indianapolis, IN 46202	1969	Glenn W. Irwin Jr., V.P.	4-D	23,514	1,

Name, address	Year	Governing official affiliation, and highest degree offered	Students	Teachers
Indiana Univ., Southeast, New Albany, IN 47150	1941	Edwin W. Crooks ... 4-M	4,671	250
Inter American Univ. of Puerto Rico, Arecibo Regional Coll., Arecibo, PR 00612	1957	Maria delos A. Ortiz deLeon, Dir. ... 0-B	3,517	156
Inter American Univ. of Puerto Rico, Metropolitan Campus, Hato Rey, PR 00919	1960	Rafael Cartagena ... 0-M	15,421	571
Inter American Univ. of Puerto Rico, San German Campus, San German, PR 00753	1912	Federico Matheu ... 0-M	8,216	NA
International, Los Angeles, CA 90024	1970	Linden G. Leavitt ... 0-D	600	NA
International Inst. of the Americas of World Univ., Hato Rey, PR 00620	1965	Ronald C. Bauer ... 0-M	4,723	279
Iona, New Rochelle, NY 10801	1940	Br. John G. Driscoll ... 0-M	6,200	353
Iowa State Univ., Ames, IA 50011	1858	W. Robert Parks ... 4-D	26,020	2,098
Iowa Wesleyan, Mount Pleasant, IA 52641	1842	Jerry Richards ... 1-B	721	55
Ithaca, Ithaca, NY 14850	1892	James J. Whalen ... 0-M	5,252	415
Jackson State Univ., Jackson, MS 39217	1877	John A. Peoples Jr. ... 4-D	6,503	344
Jacksonville State Univ., Jacksonville, AL 36265	1883	Theron E. Montgomery ... 4-M	6,522	529
Jacksonville Univ., Jacksonville, FL 32211	1934	Frances B. Kinne ... 0-M	2,270	181
James Madison Univ., Harrisonburg, VA 22807	1908	Ronald E. Carrier ... 4-M	9,242	548
Jersey City State, Jersey City, NJ 07305	1927	William J. Maxwell ... 4-M	7,464	469
John Brown Univ., Siloam Springs, AR 72761	1919	John E. Brown III ... 1-B	768	51
John Carroll Univ., University Heights, OH 44118	1886	Rev. Thomas P. O'Malley ... 1-M	3,900	223
John F. Kennedy Univ., Orinda CA 94563	1964	Robert M. Fisher ... 0-D	1,853	262
Johns Hopkins Univ., Baltimore, MD 21218	1876	Steven Muller ... 0-D	3,155	332
Johnson & Wales, Providence, RI 02903	1914	Morris J. Gaebe ... 0-B	4,250	125
Johnson C. Smith Univ., Charlotte, NC 28216	1867	Mack L. Davidson ... 1-B	1,130	95
Johnson State, Johnson, VT 05656	1828	Eric R. Gilbertson ... 4-M	1,237	101
Jones, Jacksonville, FL 32211	1918	James M. Patch ... 0-B	1,719	61
Jordan, Cedar Springs, MI 49319	1967	De Wayne A. Coxon ... 1-B	1,050	100
Juilliard School, New York, NY 10023	1905	Joseph Olisi ... 0-D	917	220
Juniata, Huntingdon, PA 16652	1876	Frederick M. Binder ... 1-B	1,274	97
Kalamazoo, Kalamazoo, MI 49007	1833	David Breneman ... 1-B	1,130	96
Kansas Newman, Wichita, KS 67213	1933	Robert J. Giroux ... 1-B	901	72
Kansas State Univ., Manhattan, KS 66506	1863	Duane C. Acker ... 4-D	18,470	1,544
Kean Coll. of New Jersey, Union, NJ 07083	1855	Nathan Weiss ... 4-M	10,561	587
Kearney State, Kearney, NE 68849	1903	William R. Nester ... 4-M	7,939	330
Keene State, Keene, NH 03431	1909	Barbara J. Seelye ... 4-M	2,967	194
Kennesaw, Marietta, GA 30061	1966	Betty L. Siegel ... 4-B	5,383	196
Kent State Univ., Kent, OH 44242	1910	Michael Schwartz ... 4-D	19,687	1,188
Kentucky State Univ., Frankfort, KY 40601	1886	Raymond M. Burse ... 12-M	2,431	144
Kentucky Wesleyan, Owensboro, KY 42301	1858	Luther W. White ... 1-B	942	85
Kenyon, Gambier, OH 43022	1824	Philip H. Jordan Jr ... 0-B	1,408	120
King's, Briarcliff Manor, NY 10510	1938	Robert A. Cook ... 1-B	760	64
King's, Wilkes-Barre, PA 18711	1946	Rev. James Lackenmier ... 1-B	2,309	151
Knox, Galesburg, IL 61401	1837	John P. McCall ... 0-B	919	86
Kutztown Univ. of Pennsylvania, Kutztown, PA 19530	1866	Lawrence M. Stratton ... 4-M	6,453	303
Lafayette, Easton, PA 18042	1826	David W. Ellis ... 1-B	2,050	205
LaGrange, LaGrange, GA 30240	1831	Walter Y. Murphy ... 1-M	987	62
Lake Erie, Painesville, OH 44077, (4)	1859	Charles E. P. Simmons ... 0-M	1,171	78
Lake Forest, Lake Forest, IL 60045	1857	Eugene Hotchkiss III ... 0-M	1,030	93
Lake Superior State, Sault Sainte Marie, MI 49783	1946	Kenneth F. Light ... 4-M	2,820	136
Lamar Univ., Beaumont, TX 77710	1923	C. Robert Kemble ... 4-D	14,638	572
Lambuth, Jackson, TN 38301	1843	Harry W. Gilmer ... 1-B	820	77
Lander, Greenwood, SC 29646	1872	Larry A. Jackson ... 4-M	2,136	113
Lane, Jackson, TN 38301	1882	Herman Stone ... 1-B	687	47
Langston Univ., Langston OK 73050	1897	Ernest L. Holloway ... 4-B	2,100	168
Laredo State Univ., Laredo, TX 78040	1969	Billy F. Cowart ... 4-M	932	50
La Roche, Pittsburgh, PA 15237	1963	Sr. Margaret Huber ... 1-M	1,723	111
La Salle Univ., Philadelphia, PA 19141	1863	Br. Patrick Ellis ... 1-M	6,725	289
Lawrence Inst. of Tech., Southfield, MI 48075	1932	Richard E. Marburger ... 0-B	6,230	323
Lawrence Univ., Appleton, WI 54912	1847	Richard Warch ... 0-B	1,066	112
Lebanon Valley, Annville, PA 17003	1866	Frederick P. Sample ... 1-B	946	90
Lee, Cleveland, TN 37311	1918	Ray H. Hughes ... 1-B	1,060	70
Lehigh Univ., Bethlehem, PA 18015	1865	Peter W. Likins ... 0-D	6,042	422
Le Moyne, Syracuse, NY 13214	1946	Rev. Frank R Haig, SJ ... 1-B	1,855	176
LeMoyne-Owen, Memphis, TN 38126	1870	Walter L. Walker ... 1-B	950	77
Lenoir-Rhyne, Hickory, NC 28603	1891	Albert Allran ... 1-M	1,382	112
Lesley, Cambridge, MA 02238, (3)	1909	Don A. Orton ... 0-M	1,916	334
LeTourneau, Longview, TX 75607, (2)	1946	Richard H. LeTourneau ... 1-B	1,045	72
Lewis and Clark, Portland, OR 97219	1867	James A. Gardner ... 1-M	3,037	165
Lewis-Clark State, Lewiston, ID 83501	1894	Lee A. Vickers ... 4-B	2,165	120
Lewis Univ., Romeoville, IL 60441	1932	Br. David Delahanty, FSC ... 1-M	2,811	140
Liberty Baptist, Lynchburg, VA 24506	1971	A. Pierre Guillermin ... 1-M	4,207	207
Limestone, Gaffney, SC 29340	1845	William J. Briggs ... 0-B	1,536	75
Lincoln Memorial Univ., Harrogate, TN 37752	1897	Gary J. Burchett ... 0-M	1,418	80
Lincoln Univ., Jefferson City, MO 65102	1866	Thomas Miller Jenkins ... 4-M	2,895	169
Lincoln Univ., Lincoln University, PA 19352	1854	Herman R. Branson ... 12-M	1,250	88
Lindenwood, St. Charles, MO 63301	1827	James I. Spainhower ... 0-M	1,865	108
Linfield, McMinnville, OR 97128	1849	Charles U. Walker ... 1-M	1,180	112
Livingstone, Salisbury, NC 28144	1879	James W. Young ... 1-B	618	77
Livingston Univ., Livingston, AL 35470	1835	Asa N. Green ... 4-M	1,517	83
Lock Haven Univ. of Pennsylvania, Lock Haven, PA 17745	1870	Craig Dean Willis ... 4-B	2,661	173
Loma Linda Univ., Riverside, CA 92515	1915	R. Dale McCune, Provost ... 1-D	4,853	1,794
Long Island Univ., Brooklyn Campus, Brooklyn, NY 11201	1926	Edward A. Clark ... 0-D	4,974	406
Long Island Univ., C.W. Post Campus, Greenvale, NY 11548	1954	Edward J. Cook ... 0-M	10,488	705
Long Island Univ., Southampton Campus, NY 11968	1963	Edward J. Cook ... 0-M	1,279	107
Longwood, Farmville, VA 23901	1839	Janet D. Greenwood ... 4-M	2,590	158
Loras, Dubuque, IA 52001	1839	Pasquale Di Pasquale Jr. ... 1-M	2,003	125
Loretto Heights, Denver, CO 80236	1918	Thomas K. Craine ... 0-B	800	97
Louisiana, Pineville LA 71359	1906	Robert L. Lynn ... 1-B	1,302	93
Louisiana State Univ. and A&M College, Baton Rouge, LA 70803	1860	James H. Wharton ... 4-D	29,863	1,485

Name, address	Year	Governing official affiliation, and highest degree offered		Stu-dents	Teach-ers
Louisiana State Univ. in Shreveport, LA 71115	1965	E. Grady Bogue	4-M	4,625	196
Louisiana Tech. Univ., Ruston, LA 71272	1894	F. Jay Taylor	4-D	11,172	466
Lourdes, Sylvania, OH 43560	1958	Sr. Ann Francis Klimkowski, OSF	1-B	762	38
Loyola, Baltimore, MD 21210	1852	Rev. Joseph A. Sellinger	1-M	6,168	296
Loyola Marymount Univ., Los Angeles, CA 90045	1911	Rev. James N. Loughran, SJ	1-D	6,448	348
Loyola Univ., of New Orleans, LA 70118	1912	Rev. James C. Carter, SJ	1-M	4,588	309
Loyola Univ., Chicago, IL 60611	1870	Rev. Raymond C. Baumhart	1-D	13,215	1,322
Lubbock Christian, Lubbock, TX 79407	1957	Steven S. Lemley	1-B	1,000	97
Luther, Decorah, IA 52101	1861	H. George Anderson	1-B	2,136	163
Lycoming, Williamsport, PA 17701	1812	Frederick E. Blumer	1-B	1,205	75
Lynchburg, Lynchburg, VA 24501	1903	George N. Rainsford	1-M	2,207	152
Lyndon State, Lyndonville, VT 05851	1911	Clive C. Veri	4-M	1,052	86
Macalester, St. Paul, MN 55105	1874	Robert M. Gavin Jr.	1-B	1,682	149
MacMurray, Jacksonville, IL 62650	1846	B. G. Stephens	1-B	626	71
Madonna, Livonia, MI 48150	1947	Sr. Mary Francilene	1-M	3,924	198
Maharishi Intl. Univ., Fairfield, IA 52556	1971	Bevan Morris	0-M	708	78
Maine Maritime Academy, Castine, ME 04420	1941	RADM Edward A. Rodgers, Supt.	4-M	671	64
Malone, Canton, OH 44709	1892	Gordon R. Werkema	1-B	876	65
Manchester, North Manchester, IN 46962	1889	A. Blair Helman	1-M	1,036	92
Manhattan, Riverdale, NY 10471.	1853	Br. J. Stephen Sullivan FSC	0-M	4,928	415
Manhattan School of Music, New York, NY 10027	1917	John O. Crosby	0-D	668	155
Manhattanville, Purchase, NY 10577	1841	Barbara K. Debs	0-M	1,300	176
Mankato State Univ., Mankato, MN 56001	1867	Margaret R. Preska	4-M	12,700	587
Mansfield Univ. of Pennsylvania, Mansfield, PA 16933	1857	Rod C. Kelchner	4-M	2,900	201
Marian, Indianapolis, IN 46222	1851	Louis C. Gatto	1-B	948	91
Marietta, Marietta, OH 45750	1835	Sherrill Cleland	0-M	1,250	101
Marion, Marion, IN 46952	1920	B. Gray Allison	1-M	1,159	91
Marist, Poughkeepsie, NY 12601	1949	Dennis J. Murray	0-M	2,631	121
Marquette Univ., Milwaukee, WI 53233	1881	Rev. John P. Raynor, SJ	1-D	11,722	932
Marshall Univ., Huntington, WV 25701	1837	Dale F. Nitzchke	4-D	11,657	51
Mars Hill, Mars Hill, NC 28754	1856	Fred B. Bentley	1-B	1,481	95
Mary Baldwin, Staunton, VA 24401 (3)	1842	Virgina L. Lester	1-B	660	7
Mary, Bismarck, ND 58501	1959	Sr. Thomas Welder	1-M	1,122	7
Marycrest, Davenport, IA 52804	1939	A. Lynn Bryant	1-M	1,200	9
Marygrove, Detroit, MI 48221	1910	John E. Shay Jr.	1-M	1,135	5
Maryland Inst., Coll. of Art, Baltimore, MD 21217	1826	Fred Lazarus	0-M	884	9
Marylhurst Coll. for Lifelong Learning, Marylhurst, OR 97036	1893	Veronica Ann Baxter, SNJM	1-M	892	14
Marymount, Tarrytown, NY 10591 (4)	1907	Sr. Brigid Driscoll	0-B	755	12
Marymount Coll. of Kansas, Salina, KS 67401	1922	John Murry	1-B	709	6
Marymount Coll. of Virginia, Arlington, VA 22207	1950	Sr. M. Majella Berg	1-M	1,868	9
Marymount Manhattan, New York, NY 10021 (4)	1936	Sr. Colette Mahoney	0-B	2,052	17
Maryville, Maryville, TN 37801	1819	Wayne W. Anderson	1-B	651	9
Maryville Coll. & Saint Louis, St. Louis, MO 63141	1872	Claudius H. Pritchard Jr.	0-M	2,050	14
Mary Washington, Fredericksburg, VA 22401	1908	William M. Anderson Jr.	4-M	2,990	16
Marywood, Scranton, PA 18509 (4)	1915	Sr. M. Coleman Nee	1-M	3,116	19
Massachusetts Coll. of Art, Boston, MA 02115.	1873	Jack F. Nolan.	4-M	1,104	9
Massachusetts Coll. of Pharmacy and Allied Health Sciences, Boston, MA 02115	1823	Raymond A. Gosselin	0-D	987	8
Massachusetts Inst. of Tech., Cambridge, MA 02139	1861	Paul E. Gray	0-D	8,935	1,70
Massachusetts Maritime Acad., Buzzards Bay, MA 02532 (2)	1891	RADM John F. Aylmer	4-B	850	7
Mayville State, Mayville, ND 58257	1889	James A. Schobel	4-B	759	5
McKendree, Lebanon, IL 62254	1828	Gerrit J. TenBrink	1-B	1,000	7
McMurry, Abilene, TX 79697	1923	Thomas K. Kim	1-B	1,602	12
McNeese State Univ., Lake Charles, LA 70609	1939	Jack V. Doland	4-M	8,026	33
Medaille, Buffalo, NY 14214	1875	Leo R. Downey	0-B	755	9
Medical Coll. of Georgia, Augusta, GA 30912	1828	Jesse L. Steinfeld	4-D	1,820	6
Memphis State Univ., Memphis, TN 38152	1912	Thomas G. Carpenter	4-D	22,040	9
Menlo, Atherton, CA 94025.	1927	Richard F O'Brien	0-B	629	7
Mercer Univ., Macon, GA 31207	1833	R. Kirby Godsey	1-D	2,886	2
Mercer Univ. in Atlanta, Atlanta, GA 30341	1968	R. Kirby Godsey	1-M	1,868	1
Mercy, Dobbs Ferry, NY 10522	1951	Donald Grunewald	0-M	9,206	6
Mercy Coll. of Detroit, Detroit, MI 48219	1941	Maureen A. Fay, OP	1-M	2,257	2
Mercyhurst, Erie, PA 16546	1926	William P. Garvey	1-M	1,654	1
Meredith, Raleigh, NC 27607 (3)	1891	John E. Weems	1-M	1,507	1
Merrimack, North Andover, MA 01845	1947	Rev. John E. Deegan, OSA	1-B	2,159	1
Mesa, Grand Junction, CO 81502	1925	John U. Tomlinson	4-B	4,621	1
Messiah, Grantham, PA 17027	1909	D. Ray Hostetter	1-B	1,612	1
Methodist, Fayetteville, NC 28301	1956	M. Elton Hendricks	1-B	643	
Metropolitan State, Denver, CO 80204	1965	Brage Golding	4-B	16,408	7
Metropolitan State Univ., St. Paul, MN 55101	1971	Reatha Clark King	4-M	3,529	4
Miami Univ., Oxford, OH 45056	1809	Paul G. Pearson	4-M	14,870	7
Michigan State Univ., East Lansing, MI 48824	1855	Cecil Mackey	4-D	41,765	2,5
Michigan Technological Univ., Houghton, MI 49931	1885	Dale F. Stein	4-D	7,414	3
Mid-America Nazarene, Olathe, KS 66061	1966	R. Curtiss Smith	1-B	1,219	
Middlebury, Middlebury, VT 05753.	1800	Olin C. Robison	0-D	1,900	
Middle Tennessee State Univ., Murfreesboro, TN 37132	1911	Sam H. Ingram	4-D	11,369	4
Midland Lutheran, Fremont, NE 68025	1883	Carl L. Hansen	1-B	855	
Midwestern State Univ., Wichita Falls, TX 76308.	1922	Louis J. Rodriguez	4-M	5,125	2
Miles, Birmingham, AL 35208	1905	W. Clyde Williams	1-D	687	
Millersville Univ. of Pennsylvania, Millersville, PA 17551	1854	Joseph A. Caputo	4-M	6,721	3
Milligan, Milligan College, TN 37682	1866	Marshall J. Leggett.	1-B	694	
Millikin Univ., Decatur, IL 62522	1901	J. Roger Miller	1-B	1,529	
Millsaps, Jackson, MS 39210	1890	George M. Harmon	1-M	1,246	
Mills, Oakland, CA 94613 (3).	1852	Mary S. Metz	0-M	900	
Milwaukee School of Engineering, Milwaukee, WI 53201 (2)	1903	Robert R. Spitzer	0-M	1,925	
Minot State, Minot, ND 58701	1913	Gordon B. Olson	4-M	2,985	1
Mississippi, Clinton, MS 39058	1826	Lewis Nobles	1-M	2,592	1
Mississippi State Univ., Mississippi State, MS 39762	1878	James D. McComas	4-D	12,325	
Mississippi Univ. for Women, Columbus, MS 39701 (4)	1884	James W. Strobel	4-M	2,278	
Mississippi Valley State Univ., Itta Bena, MS 38941	1946	Joe L. Boyer	4-M	2,575	
Missouri Southern State, Joplin, MO 64801	1937	Julio Leon	4-B	4,305	
Missouri Western State, St. Joseph, MO 64507	1915	Janet Gorman Murphy	4-B	4,233	

ame, address	Year	Governing official affiliation, and highest degree offered	Stu-dents	Teach-ers
ohile, Mobile, AL 36613	1961	Michael A. Magnoli . . 1-M	1,002	74
olloy, Rockville Centre, NY 11570	1955	Janet A. Fitzgerald, OP . 1-B	1,690	174
onmouth, Monmouth, IL 61462	1853	Bruce Haywood . 1-B	692	72
onmouth, West Long Branch, NJ 07764	1933	Samuel H. Magill . 0-M	4,135	279
ontana Coll. of Mineral Science and Tech., Butte, MT 59701	1893	Fred W. De Money . 4-M	2,334	134
ontana State Univ., Bozeman, MT 59717	1893	William J. Tietz . 4-D	11,447	681
ontclair State, Upper Montclair, NJ 07043	1908	David W. D. Dickson . 4-M	14,949	720
oody Bible Inst., Chicago, IL 60610	1886	George Sweeting . 1-B	1,365	96
oore Coll. of Art, Philadelphia, PA 19103	1844	Edward C. McGuire . 0-B	628	80
oorhead State Univ., Moorhead, MN 56560	1887	Roland Dille . 4-M	7,334	343
oravian, Bethlehem, PA 18018	1742	Herman E. Collier Jr. . 0-B	1,233	146
orehead State Univ., Morehead, KY 40351	1922	Morris L. Norfleet . 4-M	6,505	319
orehouse, Atlanta, GA 30314 (1).	1867	Hugh M. Gloster . 0-B	2,001	132
organ State Univ., Baltimore, MD 21239	1867	Earl Richardson . 4-D	4,555	356
orningside, Sioux City, IA 51106	1894	Miles Tommeraasen . 1-M	1,246	94
orris Brown, Atlanta, GA 30314	1881	Robert Threatt . 1-B	1,268	84
ount Holyoke, South Hadley, MA 01075 (3)	1837	Elizabeth Topham Kennan . 0-M	1,920	230
ount Ida, Newton Centre, MA 02159 (4)	1899	Bryan E. Carlson . 0-B	835	92
ount Marty, Yankton, SD 57078	1936	NA . 1-M	650	58
ount Mary, Milwaukee, WI 53222 (3)	1913	Sr. Ellen Lorenz . 1-M	1,144	119
ount Mercy, Cedar Rapids, IA 52402	1928	Thomas R. Feld . 1-B	1,262	81
ount Saint Mary, Newburgh, NY 12550	1930	Sr. Ann V. Sakac . 0-M	1,079	86
ount St. Mary's, Los Angeles CA 90049 (4)	1925	Sr. Magdalen Coughlin . 1-M	1,252	142
ount Saint Mary's, Emmitsburg, MD 21727	1808	Robert J. Wickenheiser . 1-M	1,625	103
ount Union, Alliance, OH 44601	1846	G. Benjamin Lantz Jr. . 1-B	989	94
ount Vernon Nazarene, Mt. Vernon, OH 43050	1968	William J. Prince . 1-B	1,052	72
uhlenberg, Allentown, PA 18104	1848	Jonathan C. Messerli . 1-B	1,530	140
ultnomah School of the Bible, Portland OR 97220.	1936	Joseph C. Aldrich . 1-M	682	52
undelein, Chicago, IL 60660 (4)	1930	John Richert . 1-M	1,282	137
urray State Univ., Murray, KY 42071	1922	Constantine W. Curris . 4-M	7,600	381
skingum, New Concord, OH 43762	1837	Arthur J De Jong . 1-B	1,017	83
tional, Rapid City, SD 57709	1941	John W. Hauer . 2-B	1,033	63
tional Coll. of Chiropractic, Lombard, IL 60148	1906	Joseph Janse . 0-D	961	87
tional Coll. of Education, Evanston, IL 60201	1886	Orley R. Herron . 0-M	1,050	118
tional Univ., San Diego, CA 92108	1971	David Chigos . 0-D	7,855	612
azareth, Nazareth, MI 49074	1924	Patrick D. Smith . 1-B	671	69
azareth Coll. of Rochester, Rochester, NY 14610	1924	Rose Marie Beston . 0-M	1,836	151
ebraska Wesleyan Univ., Lincoln, NE 68504	1887	John W. White Jr. . 1-B	1,246	104
eumann, Aston, PA 19014	1965	Sr. M. Margarella O'Neill . 1-M	1,006	84
ewberry, Newberry, SC 29108	1856	John Ammarell . 1-B	630	76
ew Coll. of California, San Francisco, CA 94110	1971	Mildred Henry . 0-M	617	27
ew England, Henniker, NH 03242	1946	K. Roald Bergethon . 0-M	1,180	109
ew England Conservatory of Music, Boston, MA 02115	1867	Laurence Lesser . 0-M	683	168
ew England Inst. of Tech., Providence, RI 02907 (2).	1940	Richard I. Gouse . 0-M	1,471	69
ew Hampshire, Manchester, NH 03104	1932	Edward M. Shapiro . 0-M	2,763	74
ew Jersey Inst. of Tech., Newark, NJ 07102	1881	Saul K. Fenster . 12-D	7,285	433
ew Mexico Highlands Univ., Las Vegas, NM 87701	1893	John Aragon . 4-M	2,326	126
ew Mexico Inst. of Mining and Tech., Socorro, NM 87801,	1889	Laurence H. Lattman . 4-D	1,345	94
ew Mexico State Univ., Las Cruces, NM 88003	1888	James E. Halligan . 4-D	12,926	712
ew York Inst. of Tech., Old Westbury, NY 11568.	1955	NA . 0-D	12,621	987
ew York School of Interior Design, New York, NY 10022	1916	Arthur Satz . 0-B	783	75
ew York Univ., New York, NY 10003	1831	John Brademas . 0-D	23,000	5,422
iagara Univ., Niagara University, NY 14109	1856	Rev. John G. Nugent . 4-M	3,600	240
icholls State Univ., Thibodaux, LA 70310	1948	Donald J. Ayo . 4-M	7,445	257
ichols, Dudley, MA 01570	1815	Lowell C. Smith . 0-M	990	39
orfolk State Univ., Norfolk, VA 23504	1935	Harrison B. Wilson . 4-M	7,400	410
orth Adams State, North Adams, MA 01247	1894	James R. Roach . 4-M	2,500	190
orth Carolina A&T State Univ., Greensboro, NC 27411	1891	Edward B. Fort . 4-M	5,622	376
orth Carolina Central Univ., Durham, NC 27707	1910	Leroy T. Walker . 4-M	5,228	379
orth Carolina State Univ., at Raleigh, Raleigh, NC 27695	1862	Bruce R. Poulton . 4-D	22,632	1,606
orth Carolina Wesleyan, Rocky Mount, NC 27801	1956	S. Bruce Petteway . 1-B	1,157	40
orth Central Bible, Minneapolis, MN 55404	1930	Don H. Argue . 1-B	1,082	51
orth Central, Naperville, IL 60566	1861	Gael D. Swing . 1-B	1,628	116
orth Dakota State Univ., Fargo, ND 58105	1890	Laurel D. Loftsgard . 4-D	9,477	571
ortheastern Illinois Univ., Chicago, IL 60625	1961	Ronald Williams . 4-M	10,404	455
ortheastern Oklahoma State Univ., Tahlequah, OK 74464	1846	W. Roger Webb . 4-D	7,444	220
ortheastern Univ., Boston, MA 02115	1898	Kenneth Ryder . 0-D	36,559	2,420
ortheast Louisiana Univ., Monroe, LA 71209	1931	Dwight D. Vines . 4-D	11,586	478
ortheast Missouri State Univ., Kirksville, MO 63501	1867	Charles J. McClain . 4-M	6,990	351
orthern Arizona Univ., Flagstaff, AZ 86011	1899	Eugene M. Hughes . 4-D	11,501	652
orthern Illinois Univ., De Kalb, IL 60115	1895	William R. Monat . 4-D	24,524	1,207
orthern Kentucky Univ., Highland Heights, KY 41076	1968	Leon E. Boothe . 4-M	9,377	487
orthern Michigan Univ., Marquette, MI 49855	1899	James B. Appleberry . 4-M	8,283	360
orthern Montana, Havre, MT 59501	1929	James Erickson . 4-M	1,859	122
orthern State, Aberdeen, SD 57401	1901	Terence Brown . 4-M	2,718	110
orth Georgia, Dahlonega, GA 30597	1873	John H. Owen . 4-M	1,990	140
oshland, Ashland, WI 54806	1892	Malcolm McLean . 1-B	657	46
orth Park, Chicago, IL 60625	1891	Lloyd H. Ahlem . 1-B	1,137	106
orthrop Univ., Inglewood, CA 90306	1942	B. J. Shell . 0-D	1,522	43
orth Texas State Univ., Denton, TX 76203	1890	Alfred F. Hurley . 4-D	20,234	840
orthwest Coll. of the Assemblies of God, Kirkland, WA 98033	1934	D. V. Hurst . 1-B	719	46
orthwestern, Orange City, IA 51041	1882	Friedhelm Radandt . 1-B	866	71
orthwestern, Roseville, MN 55113	1902	William B. Berntsen . 1-B	949	73
orthwestern Oklahoma State Univ., Alva, OK 73717	1897	Joe J. Struckle . 4-M	1,863	82
orthwestern State Univ. of Louisiana, Natchitoches, LA 71497	1884	Joseph J. Orze . 4-D	6,272	225
orthwestern Univ., Evanston, IL 60201	1851	Robert H. Strotz . 0-D	15,890	1,783
orthwestern Univ., Chicago Campus, Chicago, IL 60611	1858	NA . 0-D	2,000	50
orthwest Missouri State Univ., Maryville, MO 64468	1905	NA . 4-M	5,243	255
orthwest Nazarene, Nampa, ID 83651	1913	A. Gordon Wetmore . 1-M	1,111	85
orwood Univ., Midland, MI 48640	1959	David E. Fry . 0-B	1,850	67
orwich Univ., The Military Coll. of Vermont, Northfield, VT 05663.	1819	Lt. Gen. W. Russell Todd . 0-M	1,594	162
orwich Univ., Vermont Coll., Montpelier, VT 05602.	1834	Maureen Lippincott, V.P. . 0-M	880	56
otre Dame, Manchester, NH 03104 (4)	1950	Sr. Jeannette Vezeau . 1-M	741	70

Name, address	Year	Governing official affiliation, and highest degree offered	Stu-dents	Teach-ers
Notre Dame Coll. of Ohio, Cleveland, OH 44121 (3)	1922	Sr. Mary Marthe	1-B	750	6
Nova Univ., Fort Lauderdale, FL 33314	1964	Abraham S. Fischler	0-D	6,159	40
Nyack, Nyack, NY 10960	1882	David L. Rambo	1-M	870	5
Oakland City, Oakland City, IN 47660	1885	James W. Murray	1-M	645	5
Oakland Univ., Rochester, MI 48063	1957	Joseph E. Champagne	4-D	12,084	52
Oakwood, Huntsville, AL 35896	1896	Calvin B. Rock	1-B	1,465	10
Oberlin, Oberlin, OH 44074	1833	S. Frederick Starr	0-M	2,898	22
Occidental, Los Angeles, CA 90041	1887	Richard C. Gilman	0-M	1,586	13
Oglala Lakota, Kyle, SD 57752	1970	Elgin Badwound	11-B	643	5
Oglethorpe Univ., Atlanta, GA 30319	1835	Manning M. Pattillo Jr.	0-M	1,030	8
Ohio Dominican, Columbus, OH 43219	1911	Sr. Mary Andrew Matesich	1-B	1,020	8
Ohio Northern Univ., Ada, OH 45810	1871	De Bow Freed	1-D	2,474	19
Ohio State Univ., Columbus, OH 43210	1870	Edward Jennings	4-D	53,757	3,26
Ohio State Univ.-Lima Campus, Lima, OH 45804	1959	James S. Biddle, Dean and Dir.	4-B	985	3
Ohio State Univ.-Mansfield Campus, Mansfield, OH 44906	1958	David W. Kramer, Dean and Dir.	4-B	1,124	3
Ohio State Univ.-Marion Campus, Marion, OH 43302	1957	Francis E. Hazard, Dir.	4-B	830	2
Ohio State Univ.-Newark Campus, Newark, OH 43055	1957	Julius S. Greenstein, Dean	4-B	924	2
Ohio Univ., Athens, OH 45701	1804	Charles J. Ping	4-D	14,646	75
Ohio Univ.-Chillicothe, Chillicothe, OH 45601	1946	Ann Jones, Dean	4-B	1,168	7
Ohio Univ.-Ironton, Ironton, OH 45638	1956	Bill Dingus, Dir.	4-B	880	8
Ohio Univ.-Lancaster, Lancaster, OH 43130	1968	Raymond Wilkes, Dean	4-M	1,550	10
Ohio Univ.-Zanesville, Zanesville, OH 43701	1946	Craig D. Laubenthal, Dean	4-B	904	6
Ohio Wesleyan Univ., Delaware, OH 43015	1842	David L. Warren	1-B	1,546	16
Oklahoma Baptist Univ., Shawnee, OK 74801	1910	Bob R. Agee	1-B	1,527	1
Oklahoma Christian, Oklahoma City, OK 73111	1950	Terry Johnson	1-B	1,539	
Oklahoma City Univ., Oklahoma City, OK 73106	1904	Jerald C. Walker	1-M	3,264	2
Oklahoma Panhandle State Univ., Goodwell, OK 73939	1909	Thomas L. Palmer	4-B	1,354	
Oklahoma State Univ., Stillwater, OK 74078	1890	Lawrence L. Boger	4-D	22,823	1,92
Old Dominion Univ., Norfolk, VA 23508	1930	Alfred B. Rollins Jr.	4-D	14,966	7
Olivet, Olivet, MI 49076	1844	Donald A. Morris	1-B	616	7
Olivet Nazarene, Kankakee, IL 60901	1907	Leslie A. Parrott	1-M	1,773	1
Oral Roberts Univ., Tulsa, OK 74171	1963	G. Oral Roberts	1-D	4,507	5
Oregon Inst. of Tech., Klamath Falls, OR 97601	1947	Larry J. Blake	4-B	2,698	1
Oregon State Univ., Corvallis, OR 97331	1868	Robert W. MacVicar	4-D	16,119	1,1
Orlando, Orlando, FL 32810	1918	Ovida B. Kirby, V.P.	0-B	906	
Otis Art Inst. of Parsons-School of Design, Los Angeles, CA 90057	1917	NA	0-M	710	1
Otterbein, Westerville, OH 43081	1847	C. Brent DeVore	1-B	1,594	1
Ouachita Baptist Univ., Arkadelphia, AR 71923	1885	Daniel R. Grant	1-M	1,591	1
Our Lady of Holy Cross, New Orleans, LA 70114	1916	Walter Maestri	1-B	621	
Our Lady of the Lake Univ. of San Antonio, TX 78285	1911	Sr. Elizabeth Sueltenfuss	1-M	1,758	
Pace Univ., New York, NY 10038	1906	Edward J. Mortola	0-D	10,498	7
Pace Univ., Coll. of White Plains, White Plains, NY 10603	1923	Frank S. Falcone, Exec. V.P.	0-M	3,455	1
Pace Univ.-Pleasantville/Briarcliff, Pleasantville, NY 10570	1963	Frank S. Falcone, Exec.	0-D	4,138	5
Pacific Lutheran Univ., Tacoma, WA 98447	1890	William O. Rieke	1-M	3,533	2
Pacific Union, Angwin, CA 94508	1882	D. Malcolm Maxwell	1-M	1,443	1
Pacific Univ., Forest Grove, OR 97116	1849	Robert F. Duvall	0-D	1,071	
Paine, Augusta, GA 30910	1882	William H. Harris	1-B	816	
Palm Beach Atlantic, West Palm Beach, FL 33401	1968	Claude Rhea	1-B	711	
Pan American Univ., Edinburg, TX 78539	1927	Miguel A. Nevarez	4-M	9,622	4
Parks Coll. of Saint Louis, Cahokia, IL 62206	1927	Paul A. Whelan, V.P.	1-B	1,072	
Parsons School of Design, New York, NY 10011	1896	John R. Everett	0-M	1,670	2
Pembroke State Univ., Pembroke, NC 28372	1887	Paul R. Givens	4-M	2,122	1
Pennsylvania State Univ.-Behrend Coll., Erie, PA 16563	1926	John M. Lilley, Dean	12-M	1,972	1
Pennsylvania State Univ.-Capitol Campus, Middletown, PA 17057	1966	Ruth Leventhal, Provost	12-M	2,452	1
Pennsylvania State Univ.-University Park Campus, University Park, PA 16802	1855	Bryce Jordan	12-D	33,445	1,7
Pepperdine Univ., Malibu, CA 90265	1937	Howard A. White	1-D	2,622	2
Pepperdine Univ., Pepperdine Plaza, Los Angeles, CA 90034	1937	Howard A. White	1-D	3,411	2
Peru State, Peru, NE 68421	1867	Jerry L. Gallentine	4-B	1,306	1
Pfeiffer, Misenheimer, NC 28109	1885	Cameron P. West	1-B	821	
Philadelphia Coll. of Art, Philadelphia, PA 19102	1876	Thomas F. Schutte	0-M	1,659	1
Philadelphia Coll. of Pharmacy and Science, PA 19104	1821	Allen Misher	0-D	1,119	1
Philadelphia Coll. of Textiles and Science, PA 19144	1884	James P. Gallagher	0-M	1,851	1
Philander Smith, Little Rock, AR 72203	1877	Grant S. Shockley	1-B	637	
Phillips, Gulfport, MS 39501	1927	NA	2-B	821	
Phillips Univ., Enid, OK 73702	1906	Joe Jones	1-D	1,284	1
Pittsburg State Univ., Pittsburg, KS 66762	1903	Donald W. Wilson	4-M	4,959	3
Pitzer, Claremont, CA 91711	1963	Frank L. Ellsworth	0-B	740	
Plymouth State Coll. of the Univ. System of New Hampshire, Plymouth, NH 03264	1871	William J. Fanell	4-M	3,400	
Point Loma Nazarene, San Diego, CA 92106	1902	Jim L. Bond	1-M	1,873	1
Point Park, Pittsburgh, PA 15222	1960	John V. Hopkins	0-M	2,665	1
Polytechnic Inst. of New York, Brooklyn Campus, NY 11201	1854	George Bugliarello	0-D	3,191	2
Polytechnic Inst. of New York, Farmingdale Campus, Farmingdale, NY 11735	1854	James J. Conti, Dir.	0-D	1,383	1
Pomona, Claremont, CA 91711	1887	David Alexander	0-B	1,358	1
Portland State Univ., Portland, OR 92707	1946	Joseph C. Blumel	4-D	14,497	1
Post, Waterbury, CT 06708	1890	Douglas R. Picht	0-B	1,438	1
Prairie View A&M Univ., Prairie View, TX 77445	1878	Alvin I. Thomas	4-M	4,495	2
Pratt Inst., Brooklyn, NY 11205	1887	Richardson Pratt Jr.	0-M	4,062	1
Presbyterian, Clinton, SC 29325	1880	Kenneth B. Orr	1-B	895	
Princeton Univ., Princeton, NJ 08544	1756	William G. Bowen	0-D	6,036	1
Principia, Elsah, IL 62028	1910	John E. G. Boyman	1-B	748	
Providence, Providence, RI 02918	1917	Rev. Thomas R. Peterson	1-D	4,735	3
Purdue Univ., West Lafayette, IN 47907	1869	Steven C. Beering	4-D	31,856	3
Purdue Univ.-Calumet, Hammond, IN 46323	1951	Richard J. Combs	4-M	7,830	3
Purdue Univ.-North Central, Westville, IN 46391	1967	Dale W. Alspaugh	4-B	2,560	
Queens, Charlotte, NC 28274 (4)	1857	Billy O. Wireman	1-M	1,175	
Quincy, Quincy, IL 62301	1860	Rev. James Toal	1-M	1,759	1
Quinnipiac, Hamden, CT 06518	1929	Richard A. Terry	0-M	2,745	1

Name, address	Year	Governing official affiliation, and highest degree offered	Students	Teachers
adford Univ., Radford, VA 24142	1910	Donald N. Dedmon	4-M	6,285	290
amapo Coll. of New Jersey, Mahwah, NJ 07430	1969	Thomas A. Porter	4-B	4,303	210
andolph-Macon, Ashland, VA 23005	1830	Ladell Payne	1-B	925	84
andolph-Macon Woman's, Lynchburg, VA 24503 (3)	1891	Robert Atwood Spivey	1-B	750	83
eed, Portland, OR 97202	1910	Paul E. Bragdon	0-M	1,140	117
egis, Denver, CO 80221	1877	Rev. David M. Clarke	1-M	1,220	95
egis, Weston, MA 02193 (3)	1927	Sr. Therese Higgins	1-M	1,250	91
ensselaer Polytechnic Inst., Troy, NY 12181	1824	Daniel Berg	0-D	6,667	638
hode Island, Providence, RI 02908	1854	David E. Sweet	4-M	9,178	506
hode Island School of Design, Providence, RI 02903	1877	Lee Hall	0-M	1,775	213
hodes, Memphis, TN 38112	1848	James H. Daughdrill Jr.	1-B	985	117
ce Univ., Houston, TX 77251	1891	Norman Hackerman	0-D	3,719	421
der, Lawrenceville, NJ 08648	1865	Frank N. Elliott	0-M	5,349	285
o Grande Community Coll., Rio Grande, OH 45674	1876	Paul C. Hayes	0-B	1,553	92
pon, Ripon, WI 54971	1851	Bernard S. Adams	0-B	900	94
vier, Nashua, NH 03060 (4)	1933	Sr. Jeanne Perreault	1-M	2,285	170
oanoke, Salem, VA 24153	1842	Norman D. Fintel	1-B	1,378	91
obert Morris, Coraopolis, PA 15108	1921	Charles L. Sewall	0-M	5,522	223
oberts Wesleyan, Rochester, NY 14624	1866	William C. Crothers	1-B	668	85
ochester Inst. of Tech., Rochester, NY 14623	1829	M. Richard Rose	0-M	16,005	1,170
ockford, Rockford, IL 61101	1847	Norman L. Stewart	0-M	1,452	136
ockhurst, Kansas City, MO 64110	1910	Rev. Robert F. Weiss, SJ	1-M	3,325	180
oger Williams, Bristol, RI 02809	1948	William H. Rizzini	0-B	2,500	120
ollins, Winter Park, FL 32789	1885	Thaddeus Seymour	0-M	2,241	134
oosevelt Univ., Chicago, IL 60605	1945	Rolf A. Weil	0-M	6,374	476
osary, River Forest, IL 60305	1848	Sr. Jean Murray	1-M	1,734	136
ose-Hulman Inst. of Tech., Terre Haute, IN 47803 (1)	1874	Samuel F. Hulbert	0-M	1,329	96
ush Univ., Chicago, IL 60612	1969	Leo M. Henikoff	0-D	1,171	211
ussell Sage, Troy, NY 12180 (3)	1916	William F. Kahl	0-M	1,430	130
ust, Holly Springs, MS 38635	1866	William A. McMillan	1-B	851	40
tgers Univ., Camden Coll. of Arts and Sciences, NJ 08102	1950	Walter K. Gordon, Provost	4-B	2,672	161
tgers Univ., Coll. of Engineering, New Brunswick, NJ 08903	1864	NA	4-B	2,728	107
tgers Univ., Coll. of Pharmacy, New Brunswick, NJ 08903	1927	NA	4-B	697	34
tgers Univ., Cook Coll., New Brunswick, NJ 08903	1921	George H. Nieswand, Dean	4-B	2,998	223
tgers Univ., Douglass Coll., New Brunswick, NJ 08903 (3)	1918	Mary S. Hartman, Dean	4-B	3,428	NA
tgers Univ., Livingston Coll., New Brunswick, NJ 08903	1969	W. Robert Jenkins, Dean	4-B	3,474	NA
tgers Univ., Newark Coll. of Arts and Sciences, NJ 07102	1946	NA	4-B	3,485	221
tgers Univ., Rutgers Coll., New Brunswick, NJ 08903	1766	NA	4-B	8,057	NA
tgers Univ., Univ. Coll.-Camden, Camden, NJ 08102	1934	NA	4-B	1,193	16
tgers Univ., Univ. Coll.-Newark, Newark, NJ 07102	1934	NA	4-B	1,784	40
tgers Univ., Univ. Coll.-New Brunswick, NJ 08903	1934	NA	4-B	3,411	NA
cred Heart Univ., Bridgeport, CT 06606	1963	Thomas P. Melady	1-M	4,660	333
ginaw Valley State, University Center, MI 48710	1963	Jack M. Ryder	4-M	4,650	259
Ambrose, Davenport, IA 52803	1882	William J. Bakrow	1-M	2,161	144
Andrews Presbyterian, Laurinburg, NC 28352	1958	Alvin P. Perkinson	1-B	724	57
Augustine's, Raleigh, NC 27611	1867	Prezell R. Robinson	1-B	1,641	84
Bonaventure Univ., St. Bonaventure, NY 14778	1854	Rev. Mathias Doyle	1-D	2,740	185
Cloud State Univ., St. Cloud, MN 56301	1869	Brenda McDonald	4-M	9,846	587
Edward's Univ., Austin, TX 78704	1885	Patricia Hayes	1-M	2,557	141
Francis, Fort Wayne, IN 46808	1890	Sr. M. JoEllen Scheetz	1-M	1,267	90
Francis, Brooklyn, NY 11201	1858	Br. Donald Sullivan OSF	1-B	2,631	125
Francis, Loretto, PA 15940	1847	Rev. Christian R. Oravec	1-M	1,600	87
John Fisher, Rochester, NY 14618	1948	Patrick O. Braden	0-M	1,853	182
John's Univ., Collegeville, MN 56321 (5)	1857	Fr. Hilary Thimmesh, OSB	1-M	2,019	158
John's Univ., Jamaica, NY 11439	1870	Rev. Joseph T. Cahill	1-D	19,287	930
Joseph, West Hartford, CT 06117 (3)	1932	Sr. M. Paton Ryan	1-M	1,289	96
Joseph's, Rensselaer, IN 47978	1889	Fr. Charles Banet	1-M	991	67
Joseph's, Brooklyn, NY 11205	1916	Sr. George A. O'Connor	0-B	1,050	113
Joseph's, Suffolk Campus, Patchogue, NY 11772	1916	Virginia Therese Callahan, V.P.	0-B	1,397	110
Joseph's Univ., Philadelphia, PA 19131	1851	Rev. Donald I. Maclean	1-M	6,251	190
awrence Univ., Canton, NY 13617	1856	W. Lawrence Gulick	0-M	2,384	180
eo, Saint Leo, FL 33574	1889	Thomas B. Southard	1-B	1,108	91
ouis Coll. of Pharmacy, St. Louis, MO 63110	1864	Sumner M. Robinson	0-B	664	43
ouis Univ., St. Louis, MO 63103	1818	Rev. Thomas R. Fitzgerald	1-D	10,059	2,236
Mary, Leavenworth, KS 66048 (4)	1923	Sr. M. Janet McGilley	1-B	1,008	80
Mary of the Plains, Dodge City, KS 67801	1952	Michael J. McCarthy	1-B	675	46
Mary-of-the-Woods, Saint Mary-of-the-Woods, IN 47876 (3)	1840	Barbara Doherty, SP	1-B	650	73
Mary's, Notre Dame, IN 46556 (4)	1844	John M. Duggan	1-B	1,776	173
Mary's, Winona, MN 55987	1912	Br. Louis DeThomasis, FSC	1-M	1,425	102
Mary's Coll. of California, Moraga, CA 94575	1863	Br. Mel Anderson	1-M	2,675	174
Mary's Coll. of Maryland, St. Mary's City, MD 20686	1839	Edward T. Lewis	4-B	1,330	107
Mary's Univ. of San Antonio, San Antonio, TX 78284	1852	Rev. David J. Paul	1-D	3,233	187
Michael's, Winooski, VT 05404	1904	Edward L. Henry	1-M	1,930	131
Norbert, De Pere, WI 54115	1898	Thomas A. Manion	1-M	1,706	108
Olaf, Northfield, MN 55057	1874	Harlan F. Foss	1-B	2,939	312
aul Bible, Bible College, MN 55375	1916	L. John Eagen	1-B	658	42
aul's, Lawrenceville, VA 23868	1888	S. Dallas Simmons	1-B	701	49
eter's, Jersey City, NJ 07306	1872	Rev. Edward Glynn, SJ	1-M	2,730	315
homas Aquinas, Sparkill, NY 10976	1958	Donald T. McNelis	0-B	1,566	67
homas of Villanova Univ., Miami, FL 33054	1961	Rev. Patrick H. O'Neill	1-B	3,401	250
incent, Latrobe, PA 15650	1846	Rev. Augustine J. Flood, OSB	1-B	901	84
avier, Chicago, IL 60655	1847	R. Champagne	1-M	2,367	160
m, Salem, WV 26426	1888	Ronald Ohl	0-M	1,289	96
m State, Salem, MA 01970	1854	James T. Amsler	4-M	8,551	297
sbury State, Salisbury, MD 21801	1925	Thomas A. Bellavance	4-M	4,506	243
e Regina-The Newport, Newport, RI 02840	1934	Sr. M. Lucille McKillop	1-M	2,120	176
ford Univ., Birmingham, AL 35229	1841	Thomas E. Corts	1-M	4,121	291
Houston State Univ., Huntsville, TX 77341	1879	Elliott T. Bowers	4-D	10,580	754
Diego State Univ., San Diego, CA 92182	1897	Thomas B. Day	4-D	32,194	1,935
Francisco Art Inst., San Francisco, CA 94133	1871	Stephen J. Goldstine	0-D	641	68
Francisco State Univ., San Francisco, CA 94132	1899	Paul F. Romberg	4-M	23,966	1,882
amon State Univ., Springfield, IL 62708	1969	Durward Long	4-M	3,197	222

Name, address	Year	Governing official affiliation, and highest degree offered		Stu-dents	Teach-ers
San Jose State Univ., San Jose, CA 95192	1857	Gail Fullerton	4-M	25,081	1,674
Sarah Lawrence, Bronxville, NY 10708	1926	Alice Stone Ilchman	0-M	987	132
Savannah Coll. of Art and Design, Savannah, GA 31401	1976	Richard G. Rowan	0-B	770	48
Savannah State Coll., Savannah, GA 31404	1890	Wendell G. Rayburn	4-M	2,180	15
School for Intl. Training, Brattleboro, VT 05301	1964	Charles MacCormack	0-M	656	38
School for Lifelong Learning of the Univ. System of New Hampshire, Durham, NH 03824	1972	Thomas Flygare, Dean	11-B	1,250	30
School of the Art Inst. of Chicago, Chicago, IL 60603	1866	Neil J. Hoffman	0-M	1,541	168
School of the Museum of Fine Arts, Boston, MA 02115	1948	Bruce K. MacDonald, Dean	0-M	602	65
School of the Ozarks, Point Lookout, MO 65726	1906	Stephen G. Jennings	0-B	1,260	93
School of Visual Arts, New York, NY 10010	1947	David Rhodes	2-M	2,506	603
Scripps, Claremont, CA 91711 (3)	1926	John H. Chandler	0-B	625	7
Seattle Pacific Univ., Seattle, WA 98119	1891	David C. LeShana	1-M	2,869	199
Seattle Univ., Seattle, WA 98122	1891	Rev. William J. Sullivan	1-D	4,686	300
Seton Hall Univ., South Orange, NJ 07079	1856	Msgr. John J. Petillo	1-D	8,241	53
Seton Hill, Greensburg, PA 15601 (3)	1882	Eileen Farrell	1-B	968	8
Shaw Univ., Raleigh, NC 27611	1865	Stanley H. Smith	1-B	1,922	8
Shenandoah Coll. and Conservatory of Music, Winchester, VA 22601	1875	Robert P. Parker	1-M	927	12
Shepherd, Shepherdstown, WV 25443	1871	James A. Butcher	4-B	3,507	13
Shippensburg Univ. of Pennsylvania, Shippensburg, PA 17257	1871	Anthony F. Ceddia	4-M	6,033	31
Shorter, Rome, GA 30161	1873	George Balentine	1-B	781	5
Siena, Loudonville, NY 12211	1938	Fr. Hugh F. Hines	1-B	2,939	21
Siena Heights, Adrian, MI 49221	1919	James A. Ebben	1-M	1,483	11
Simmons, Boston, MA 02115 (3)	1899	William J. Holmes	0-D	2,188	27
Simpson, Indianola, IA 50125	1860	Robert E. McBride	1-B	1,122	6
Sioux Falls, Sioux Falls, SD 57105	1883	Owen P. Halleen	1-M	872	6
Skidmore, Saratoga Springs, NY 12866	1922	Joseph C. Palamountain Jr.	0-B	2,142	22
Slippery Rock Univ. of Pennsylvania, Slippery Rock, PA 16057	1889	Herb F. Reinhard Jr.	4-M	5,782	34
Smith, Northampton, MA 01063 (3)	1871	Jill K. Conway	0-D	2,684	28
Sonoma State Univ., Rohnert Park, CA 94928	1961	Peter Diamandopoulos	4-M	5,380	37
South Carolina State, Orangeburg, SC 29117	1896	M. Maceo Nance Jr.	4-M	4,187	25
South Dakota School of Mines and Tech., Rapid City, SD 57701	1885	Richard A. Schleusener	4-D	2,908	13
South Dakota State Univ., Brookings, SD 57007	1881	Sherwood O. Berg	4-D	7,026	40
Southeastern Coll. of the Assemblies of God, Lakeland, FL 33801	1935	Rev. James Hennesy	1-B	1,023	5
Southeastern Louisiana Univ., Hammond, LA 70402	1925	J. Larry Crain	4-M	9,019	29
Southeastern Massachusetts Univ., North Dartmouth, MA 02747	1895	John R. Brazil	4-M	5,531	36
Southeastern Oklahoma State, Univ., Durant, OK 74701	1909	Leon Hibbs	4-M	4,340	18
Southeastern Univ., Washington, DC 20024	1879	W. Robert Higgins	0-M	1,206	15
Southeast Missouri State Univ., Cape Girardeau, MO 63701	1873	Bill W. Stacy	4-M	9,018	44
Southern Arkansas Univ., Magnolia, AR 71753	1909	Harold T. Brinson	4-M	2,165	1
Southern California, Costa Mesa, CA 92626	1920	Wayne E. Kraiss	1-M	858	
Southern Coll. of Seventh-Day Adventists, Collegedale, TN 37315	1892	John Wagner	1-B	1,625	1
Southern Connecticut State Univ., New Haven, CT 06515	1893	Frank Harrison	4-M	10,000	6
Southern Illinois Univ. at Carbondale, Carbondale, IL 62901	1869	Albert Somit	4-D	23,383	1,4
Southern Illinois Univ. at Edwardsville, Edwardsville, IL 62026	1957	Earl E. Lazerson	4-D	10,360	6
Southern Methodist Univ., Dallas, TX 75275	1911	L. Donald Shields	0-D	9,149	6
Southern Oregon State, Ashland, OR 97520	1926	Natale Sicuro	4-M	4,535	2
Southern Tech. Inst., Marietta, GA 30060	1948	Stephen R. Cheshier	4-B	3,499	1
Southern Univ. and A&M Coll., Baton Rouge, LA 70813	1880	James J. Prestage	4-M	9,500	4
Southern Univ. in New Orleans, New Orleans, LA 70126	1959	Emmett W. Bashful	4-B	2,700	1
Southern Utah State, Cedar City, UT 84720	1897	Gerald R. Sherratt	4-M	2,543	1
Southern Vermont, Bennington, VT 05201	1926	William A. Glasser	1-B	650	
Southwest Baptist Univ., Bolivar, MO 65613	1878	Charles L. Chaney	1-M	1,752	
Southwestern Adventist, Keene, TX 76059	1894	Marvin E. Anderson	1-B	708	
Southwestern, Winfield, KS 67156	1885	Bruce Blake	1-B	668	
Southwestern Oklahoma State Univ., Weatherford, OK 73096	1903	Leonard G. Campbell	4-M	5,116	2
Southwestern Univ., Georgetown, TX 78626	1840	Roy B. Shilling Jr.	1-B	998	
Southwest Missouri State Univ., Springfield, MO 65804	1906	Marshall Gordon	4-M	15,156	6
Southwest State Univ., Marshall, MN 56258	1963	Robert L. Carothers	4-B	1,922	1
Southwest Texas State Univ., San Marcos, TX 78666	1899	Robert L. Hardesty	4-M	18,317	1
Spalding Univ., Louisville, KY 40203	1814	Sr. Eileen Egan	1-D	1,115	1
Spelman, Atlanta, GA 30314 (3)	1881	Donald M. Stewart	0-B	1,642	1
Spring Arbor, Spring Arbor, MI 49283	1873	Kenneth H. Coffman	1-B	633	
Springfield, Springfield, MA 01109	1885	Wilbert E. Locklin	0-D	2,378	1
Spring Garden, Philadelphia, PA 19118	1851	Daniel N. DeLucca	0-B	1,450	1
Spring Hill, Mobile, AL 36608	1830	Rev. Paul S. Tipton, SJ	1-M	1,200	1
Stanford Univ., Stanford, CA 94305	1891	Donald Kennedy	0-D	12,341	1,2
State Univ. of New York at Albany, Albany, NY 12222	1844	Vincent I. O'Leary	4-D	16,000	1
State Univ. of New York at Binghamton, NY 13901	1946	Clifford D. Clark	4-D	10,701	1
State Univ. of New York at Buffalo, Buffalo, NY 14260	1846	Steven B. Sample	4-D	26,406	1,9
State Univ. of New York at Stony Brook, NY 11794	1957	John H. Marburger III	4-D	14,982	1,3
State Univ. of New York Coll. at Brockport, NY 14420	1867	John Van de Wetering	4-M	7,234	1
State Univ. of New York Coll. at Buffalo, Buffalo, NY 14222	1871	D. Bruce Johnstone	4-M	11,660	1
State Univ. of New York Coll. at Cortland, Cortland, NY 13045	1868	James M. Clark	4-M	6,260	1
State Univ. of New York Coll. at Fredonia, Fredonia, NY 14063	1867	Dallas K. Beal	4-M	5,161	1
State Univ. of New York Coll. at Geneseo, Geneseo, NY 14454	1867	Edward B. Jakubauskas	4-M	5,314	1
State Univ. of New York Coll. at New Paltz, NY 12561	1828	Alice Chandler	4-M	7,515	1
State Univ. of New York Coll. at Old Westbury, NY 11568	1968	Clyde J. Wingfield	4-B	3,865	1
State Univ. of New York Coll. at Oneonta, Oneonta, NY 13820	1889	Clifford J. Craven	4-M	5,972	1
State Univ. of New York Coll. at Oswego, Oswego, NY 13126	1861	Virginia L. Radley	4-M	7,832	1
State Univ. of New York Coll. at Plattsburgh, NY 12901	1889	Joseph C. Burke	4-M	5,917	1
State Univ. of New York Coll. at Potsdam, Potsdam, NY 13676	1816	Humphrey Tonkin	4-M	4,860	1
State Univ. of New York Coll. at Purchase, NY 10577	1972	Sheldon Grebstein	4-M	2,188	
State Univ. of New York Coll. of Environmental Science and Forestry, Syracuse, NY 13210	1911	Ross S. Whaley	4-D	1,555	
State Univ. of New York Coll. of Tech. at Utica/Rome, Utica, NY 13502	1973	Peter J. Cayan	4-B	2,552	
State Univ. of New York Empire State Coll., Saratoga Springs, NY 12866	1971	NA		4,735	
State Univ. of New York Maritime Coll., Bronx, NY 10465	1874	RADM Sheldon H. Kinney	4-M	1,060	

Name, address	Year	Governing official affiliation, and highest degree offered	Students	Teachers
State Univ. of New York Upstate Medical Center, Syracuse. NY 13210	1950	Richard P. Schmidt. 4-D	898	233
Stephen F. Austin State Univ., Nacogdoches, TX 75962	1923	William R. Johnson. 4-D	12,500	470
Stephens, Columbia, MO 65215 (3)	1833	Patsy H. Sampson 0-B	1,141	120
Stetson Univ., DeLand, FL 32720	1883	Pope A. Duncan 1-M	2,900	138
Stevens Inst. of Tech., Hoboken, NJ 07030.	1870	Kenneth C. Rogers. 0-D	3,062	240
Stillman, Tuscaloosa, AL 35403	1876	Cordell Wynn. 1-B	627	34
Stockton State, Pomona, NJ 08240	1971	Vera King Farris 4-B	4,923	215
Stonehill, North Easton, MA 02357	1948	Rev. Bartley MacPhaidin 1-B	1,741	132
Strayer, Washington, DC 20005	1898	Charles B. Harrington 2-B	1,723	75
Suffolk Univ., Boston, MA 02114.	1906	Daniel H. Perlman 0-D	6,294	251
Sul Ross State Univ., Alpine, TX 79832	1917	C. R. Richardson. 4-M	2,448	150
Susquehanna Univ., Selinsgrove, PA 17870	1858	Joel L. Cunningham 1-B	1,445	117
Swarthmore, Swarthmore, PA 19081	1864	David W. Fraser 0-B	1,280	150
Sweet Briar, Sweet Briar, VA 24595 (3).	1901	Nenah E. Fry 0-B	738	87
Syracuse Univ., Syracuse, NY 13210	1870	Melvin A. Eggers. 0-D	21,288	1,233
Tampa, Tampa, FL 33614	1890	Donald C. Jones 0-B	1,413	65
Tarleton State Univ., Stephenville, TX 76402	1899	Barry B. Thompson 4-M	4,430	166
Taylor Univ., Upland, IN 46989	1846	Gregg O. Lehman 1-B	1,559	105
Temple Univ., Philadelphia, PA 19122.	1884	Peter Liacouras. 12-D	24,786	2,564
Temple Univ., Ambler Campus, Ambler, PA 19002 . . .	1910	Walter J. Gershenfeld, Dean . . 12-D	4,140	205
Tennessee State Univ., Nashville, TN 37203	1912	Frederick S. Humphries 4-D	8,131	522
Tennessee Tech. Univ., Cookeville, TN 38505	1915	Arliss L. Roaden 4-D	7,848	400
Tennessee Temple Univ., Chattanooga, TN 37404 . . .	1946	Lee E. Roberson 1-D	2,909	139
Texas A&I Univ., Kingsville, TX 78363	1925	Billy J. Franklin 4-D	5,560	226
Texas A&M Univ., College Station, TX 77843	1876	Frank E. Vandiver 4-D	36,846	2,182
Texas Christian Univ., Fort Worth, TX 76129	1873	William Tucker 1-D	6,878	519
Texas Lutheran, Seguin, TX 78155	1891	Charles H. Oestreich 1-B	978	78
Texas Southern Univ., Houston, TX 77004	1947	Leonard H. O. Spearman 4-D	9,002	600
Texas Tech Univ., Lubbock, TX 79409	1923	Lauro F. Cavazos 4-D	23,704	1,571
Texas Wesleyan, Fort Worth, TX 76105	1891	Jerry G. Bawcomng, Int. C.E.O. 1-M	1,629	113
Texas Woman's Univ., Denton, TX 76204 (4).	1901	Mary Evelyn Blagg Huey 4-D	8,483	648
Thiel Coll., Greenville, PA 16125.	1866	Louis T. Almen 1-B	921	82
Thomas A. Edison State, Trenton, NJ 08625	1972	George A. Pruitt 4-B	4,112	NA
Thomas, Waterville, ME 04901.	1894	Paul G. Jenson 0-M	1,018	45
Thomas Jefferson Univ., Philadelphia, PA 19107 . . .	1824	Lewis W. Bluemle Jr.. . . . . 0-D	1,434	73
Thomas More, Crestview Hills, KY 41017.	1921	Thomas A. Coffey 1-B	1,335	117
Toccoa Falls, Toccoa Falls, GA 30598	1907	Paul L. Alford 1-B	613	46
Tougaloo, Tougaloo, MS 39174	1869	George A. Owens 0-B	653	86
Touro, New York, NY 10036	1971	Bernard Lander. 0-D	3,200	253
Towson State Univ., Towson, MD 21204	1866	Hoke L. Smith. 4-M	15,155	883
Transylvania Univ., Lexington, KY 40508	1780	Charles L. Shearer. 1-B	701	72
Trenton State, Trenton, NJ 08625	1855	Harold Eickhoff 4-M	10,000	500
Trevecca Nazarene, Nashville, TN 37203.	1901	Homer J. Adams 1-M	987	104
Trinity, Hartford, CT 01606	1823	James F. English Jr.. . . . . . 0-M	1,982	154
Trinity, Washington, DC 20017 (3)	1897	Sr. Donna M. Jurick 1-M	670	86
Trinity, Burlington, VT 05401 (4)	1925	Sr. Janice Ryan 1-B	953	65
Trinity Univ., San Antonio, TX 78284.	1869	Ronald K. Calgaard 0-M	3,027	274
Troy State Univ., Angola, IN 46703	1884	Beaumont Davison 0-B	1,049	77
Troy State Univ., Troy, AL 36082	1887	Ralph W. Adams 4-M	7,019	388
Troy State Univ. at Dothan, Dothan/Fort Rucker, AL 36301	1962	Robert Paul, V.P. 4-M	1,631	73
Troy State Univ. in Montgomery, Montgomery, AL 36195. .	1957	Millard E. Elrod, V.P. 4-M	2,004	142
Tufts Univ., Medford, MA 02155.	1852	Jean Mayer 0-D	7,074	445
Tulane Univ., New Orleans, LA 70118.	1834	Eamon M. Kelly. 0-D	10,700	879
Tulane Univ., Newcomb Coll., New Orleans, LA 70118 (5) .	1886	NA 0-B	1,594	163
Tuskegee Inst., Tuskegee Institute, AL 36088	1881	Benjamin F. Payton 0-M	3,400	337
Union, Barbourville, KY 40906	1879	Jack C. Phillips 1-M	794	72
Union, Lincoln, NE 68506	1891	Dean L. Hubbard 1-B	1,040	86
Union, Schenectady, NY 12308	1795	John S. Morris 1-B	2,749	205
Union, Jackson, TN 38305	1825	Robert E. Craig. 1-B	1,431	91
U.S. Air Force Acad., USAF Academy, CO 80840. . . .	1954	Lt. Gen. Winfield W. Scott Jr., Supt. 3-B	4,502	575
U.S. Coast Guard Acad., New London, CT 06320 . . .	1876	RADM E. Nelson Jr., Supt. . . 3-B	850	114
U.S. Intl. Univ., San Diego, CA 92131	1952	William C. Rust 0-D	3,275	334
U.S. Merchant Marine Acad., Kings Point, NY 11024 . .	1943	RADM Thomas A. King, Supt. . . 3-B	1,043	80
U.S. Military Acad., West Point, NY 10996	1802	Lt. Gen. W. W. Scott Jr., Supt. . 3-B	4,500	591
U.S. Naval Acad., Annapolis, MD 21402 (2)	1845	RADM Charles R. Larson, Supt. 3-B	4,500	494
Universidad del Turabo, Caguas, PR 00626	1972	NA 0-M	6,800	190
Universidad Politecnica de Puerto Rico, Hato Rey, PR 00918	1974	Ernesto Vazquez-Torres. . . . 0-B	893	55
Univ. of Akron, Akron, OH 44325	1870	Dominic J. Guzetta 4-D	27,022	1,487
Univ. of Alabama, University, AL 35486	1831	Joab L. Thomas 4-D	15,497	919
Univ. of Alabama in Birmingham, Birmingham, AL 35294 . .	1966	S. Richardson Hill 4-D	14,679	1,654
Univ. of Alabama in Huntsville, Huntsville, AL, 35899 . . .	1950	John C. Wright 4-D	6,116	351
Univ. of Alaska, Anchorage, Anchorage, AK 99508 . . .	1976	David L. Outcalt 4-M	4,088	224
Univ. of Alaska, Fairbanks, Fairbanks, AK 99701	1917	Donald O'Dowd 4-D	4,622	427
Univ. of Alaska, Juneau, Juneau, AK 99801	1972	Michael E. Paradise 4-M	2,361	130
Univ. of Albuquerque, Albuquerque, NM 87140	1920	Rev. Alfred McBride 1-B	1,800	148
Univ. of Arizona, Tucson, AZ 85721	1885	Henry Koffler 4-D	33,006	1,678
Univ. of Arkansas, Fayetteville, AR 72701	1871	Ray Thornton 4-D	13,483	843
Univ. of Arkansas at Little Rock, Little Rock, AR 72204 . .	1927	James H. Young 4-M	10,091	643
Univ. of Arkansas at Monticello, Monticello, AR 71655 . .	1909	Fred J. Taylor 4-B	1,915	107
Univ. of Arkansas at Pine Bluff, Pine Bluff, AR 71601 . . .	1873	Lloyd V. Hackley 4-B	2,545	151
Univ. of Arkansas for Medical Sciences, Little Rock, AR, 72205	1879	Harry P. Ward 4-D	1,421	555
Univ. of Baltimore, Baltimore, MD 21201	1925	H. Mebane Turner 4-M	5,128	266
Univ. of Bridgeport, Bridgeport, CT 06601	1927	Leland H. Miles 0-D	6,413	523
Univ. of California, Berkeley, Berkeley, CA 94720 . . .	1868	Ira M. Heyman 4-D	30,010	1,700
Univ. of California, Davis, Davis, CA 95616	1906	James H. Meyer 4-D	18,971	1,366
Univ. of California, Irvine, Irvine, CA 92717	1960	Jack W. Peltason. 4-D	11,909	584
Univ. of California, Los Angeles, Los Angeles, CA 90024 . .	1919	Charles E. Young. 4-D	34,754	3,000
Univ. of California, Riverside, Riverside, CA 92521 . . .	1954	Daniel G. Aldrich Jr. 4-D	4,706	369
Univ. of California, San Diego, La Jolla, CA 92093 . . .	1964	William C. Atkinson. 4-D	13,670	880
Univ. of California, San Francisco, San Francisco, CA 94143	1873	Francis A. Sooy 4-D	3,739	1,126
Univ. of California, Santa Barbara, Santa Barbara, CA 93106	1891	Robert A. Huttenback 4-D	15,489	1,112

Name, address	Year	Governing official affiliation, and highest degree offered	Students	Teachers
Univ. of California, Santa Cruz, Santa Cruz, CA 95064	1965	Robert L. Sinsheimer	4-D	6,893	64
Univ. of Central Arkansas, Conway, AR 72032	1907	Jefferson D. Farris Jr.	4-M	5,992	31
Univ. of Central Florida, Orlando, FL 32816	1963	Trevor Calbourn	4-D	15,648	65
Univ. of Charleston, Charleston, WV 25304	1888	Thomas G Voss	0-M	2,316	13
Univ. of Chicago, Chicago, IL 60637	1890	Hanna Holborn Gray	0-D	7,833	1,13
Univ. of Cincinnati, Cincinnati, OH 45221	1819	Henry Winkler	4-D	31,734	2,60
Univ. of Colorado at Boulder, Boulder, CO 80309	1876	Harrison Shull	4-D	22,180	1,15
Univ. of Colorado at Colorado Springs, CO 80933	1965	Neal F. Lane	4-M	5,560	33
Univ. of Colorado at Denver, Denver, CO 80202	1912	Gene M. Nordby	4-D	11,365	34
Univ. of Colorado Health Sciences Center, Denver, CO 80262	1898	John Cowee	4-M	1,338	3,23
Univ. of Connecticut, Storrs, CT 06268	1881	John A. DiBiaggio	4-D	16,184	1,25
Univ. of Connecticut at Stamford, Stamford, CT 06903	NA	Yakira H. Frank, Dir.	4-M	1,700	7
Univ. of Dallas, Irving, TX 75061	1956	Robert F. Sasseen	1-D	2,600	18
Univ. of Dayton, Dayton, OH 45469	1850	Br. Raymond L. Fitz, SM.	1-D	10,577	68
Univ. of Delaware, Newark, DE 19716	1743	E. Arthur Trabant	12-D	15,260	92
Univ. of Denver, Denver, CO 80208	1864	Dwight Smith	0-D	8,472	48
Univ. of Detroit, Detroit, MI 48221	1877	Rev. Robert A. Mitchell, SJ	1-D	6,310	43
Univ. of Dubuque, Dubuque, IA 52001	1852	Walter F. Peterson	1-M	1,229	7
Univ. of Evansville, Evansville, IN 47702	1854	Wallace B. Graves	1-M	4,626	28
Univ. of Florida, Gainesville, FL 32611	1853	Marshall M. Criser	4-D	34,694	2,74
Univ. of Georgia, Athens, GA 30602	1785	Fred C. Davison	4-D	25,042	1,90
Univ. of Guam, Mangilao, GU 96913	1952	Jose Q. Cruz	7-M	2,774	19
Univ. of Hartford, West Hartford, CT 06117	1877	Stephen J. Trachtenberg	0-D	8,062	62
Univ. of Hawaii at Hilo, Hilo, HI 96720	1970	Stephen R. Mitchell	4-B	3,557	24
Univ. of Hawaii at Manoa, Honolulu, HI 96822	1907	Marvin J. Anderson	4-D	21,112	1,61
Univ. of Houston-Clear Lake, Houston, TX 77058	1971	Thomas M. Stauffer	4-M	6,498	22
Univ. of Houston-Downtown, Houston, TX 77002	1974	Alexander F. Schilt	4-B	6,323	27
Univ. of Houston-University Park, Houston, TX 77004	1927	Charles E. Bishop	4-D	31,500	2,33
Univ. of Idaho, Moscow, ID 83843	1889	Dr. Richard D Gibb	4-D	9,237	57
Univ. of Illinois at Chicago, University Center, IL 60680	1965	Donald N. Langenberg	4-D	24,651	1,20
Univ. of Illinois at Urbana-Champaign, Urbana, IL 61801	1867	Thomas E. Everhart	4-D	34,632	2,38
Univ. of Iowa, Iowa City, IA 52242	1847	James O. Freedman	4-D	29,599	1,95
Univ. of Kansas, Lawrence, KS 66045	1866	Gene A. Budig	4-D	24,219	1,31
Univ. of Kansas Coll. of Health Sciences and Hospital, Kansas City, KS 66103	1905	D. Kay Clawson, Exec. V. Chanc.	4-D	2,560	68
Univ. of Kentucky, Lexington, KY 40536	1865	Otis A. Singletary	4-D	21,616	1,8
Univ. of La Verne, La Verne, CA 91750	1891	Richard Landis	0-D	2,476	11
Univ. of Louisville, Louisville, KY 40292	1798	Donald C. Swain	4-D	19,750	1,42
Univ. of Lowell, Lowell, MA 01854	1894	William T. Hogan	4-D	15,977	77
Univ. of Maine at Augusta, Augusta, ME 04330	1965	Byron Skinner	4-B	3,420	2
Univ. of Maine at Farmington, Farmington, ME 04938	1864	Judith A. Sturnick	4-B	2,053	1
Univ. of Maine at Fort Kent, Fort Kent, ME 04743	1878	Richard J. Spath	4-B	678	
Univ. of Maine at Machias, Machias, ME 04654	1909	Frederic A. Reynolds	4-B	806	
Univ. of Maine at Orono, Orono, ME 04469	1865	Arthur M. Johnson	4-D	11,507	6
Univ. of Maine at Presque Isle, Presque Isle, ME 04769	1903	Constance H. Carlson	4-B	1,187	
Univ. of Mary Hardin-Baylor, Belton, TX 76513	1845	Bobby E. Parker	1-M	1,270	
Univ. of Maryland at Baltimore, Baltimore, MD 21201	1807	John M. Dennis	4-D	4,682	1,2
Univ. of Maryland at College Park, College Park, MD 20742	1856	John B. Slaughter	4-D	37,413	2,3
Univ. of Maryland, Baltimore County, Catonsville, MD 21228	1966	John W. Dorsey	4-D	7,966	4
Univ. of Maryland, Eastern Shore, Princess Anne, MD 21853	1886	William P. Hytche	4-D	1,223	
Univ. of Maryland, University College, College Park, MD 20742	1947	John B. Slaughter	4-M	11,567	6
Univ. of Massachusetts at Amherst, Amherst, MA 01003	1863	Joseph Duffey	4-D	24,500	1,4
Univ. of Massachusetts at Boston, Boston, MA 02125	1965	Robert A. Corrigan	4-D	11,370	5
Univ. of Miami, Coral Gables, FL 33124	1925	Edward T. Foote II	0-D	18,145	1,5
Univ. of Michigan, Ann Arbor, MI 48109	1817	Harold T. Shapiro	4-D	34,289	2,7
Univ. of Michigan-Dearborn, Dearborn, MI 48128	1959	William A. Jenkins	4-M	5,649	3
Univ. of Michigan-Flint, Flint, MI 48502	1956	Clinton B. Jones	4-M	5,707	2
Univ. of Minnesota, Duluth, Duluth, MN 55812	1948	Robert L. Heller, Provost	4-M	7,525	4
Univ. of Minnesota, Morris, Morris, MN 56267	1959	John Q. Imholte, Provost	4-B	1,603	1
Univ. of Minnesota, Twin Cities Campus, Minneapolis, MN 55455	1851	C. Peter Magrath	4-D	46,445	5,8
Univ. of Mississippi, University, MS 38677	1844	R. Gerald Turner	4-D	9,236	
Univ. of Mississippi, Medical Center, Jackson, MS 39216	1955	Norman C. Nelson, V. Chanc.	4-D	1,733	
Univ. of Missouri-Columbia, Columbia, MO 65211	1839	Barbara S. Uehling	4-D	24,059	1,5
Univ. of Missouri-Kansas City, Kansas City, MO 64110	1933	George A. Russell	4-D	11,496	1,0
Univ. of Missouri-Rolla, Rolla, MO 65401	1870	Joseph M. Marchello	4-D	7,566	3
Univ. of Missouri-St. Louis, St. Louis, MO 63121	1963	Arnold B. Grobman	4-D	11,558	4
Univ. of Montana, Missoula, MT 59812	1893	Neil S. Bucklew	4-D	9,350	4
Univ. of Montevallo, Montevallo, AL 35115	1896	James F. Vickrey Jr.	4-M	2,461	
Univ. of Nebraska at Omaha, Omaha, NE 68182	1908	Del D. Weber	4-M	14,531	4
Univ. of Nebraska-Lincoln, Lincoln, NE 68588	1869	Martin A. Massengale	4-D	24,336	1,0
Univ. of Nebraska Medical Center, Omaha, NE 68105	1869	Charles E. Andrews	4-D	2,265	6
Univ. of Nevada, Las Vegas, Las Vegas, NV 89154	1957	Robert Maxson	4-D	9,112	4
Univ. of Nevada Reno, Reno, NV 89557	1874	Joseph N. Crowley	4-D	8,937	7
Univ. of New England, Biddeford, ME 04005	1939	Jack S. Ketchum	0-D	750	
Univ. of New Hampshire, Durham, NH 03824	1866	Gordon A Haaland	4-D	10,300	
Univ. of New Haven, West Haven, CT 06516	1920	Phillip S. Kaplan	0-M	7,201	
Univ. of New Mexico, Albuquerque, NM 87131	1889	John Perovich	4-D	23,897	1,6
Univ. of New Orleans, New Orleans, LA 70148	1958	Cooper R. Mackin	4-M	16,317	
Univ. of North Alabama, Florence, AL 35632	1872	Robert M. Guillot	4-M	5,323	
Univ. of North Carolina at Asheville, Asheville, NC 28814	1927	David G. Brown	4-B	2,648	
Univ. of North Carolina at Chapel Hill, Chapel Hill, NC 27514	1795	Christopher C. Fordham III	4-D	21,757	1,
Univ. of North Carolina at Charlotte, Charlotte, NC 28223	1946	Elbert K. Fretwell Jr.	4-M	10,347	
Univ. of North Carolina at Greensboro, Greensboro, NC 27412	1891	William E. Moran	4-D	9,924	
Univ. of North Carolina at Wilmington, Wilmington, NC 28403	1947	William H. Wagoner	4-M	5,432	
Univ. of North Dakota, Grand Forks, ND 58202	1883	Thomas J. Clifford	4-D	11,053	
Univ. of Northern Colorado, Greeley, CO 80639	1890	Robert C. Dickeson	4-D	9,784	
Univ. of Northern Iowa, Cedar Falls, IA 50613	1876	Constantine W. Curris	4-D	13,900	
Univ. of North Florida, Jacksonville, FL 32216	1965	Curtis L. McCray	4-M	5,651	
Univ. of Notre Dame, Notre Dame, IN 46556	1842	Rev. Theodore M. Hesburgh	1-D	9,400	
Univ. of Oklahoma, Norman, OK 73019	1890	William S. Banowski	4-D	21,493	
Univ. of Oklahoma Health Sciences Center, Oklahoma City, OK 73190	1890	Clayton Rich, Provost	4-D	3,236	
Univ. of Oregon, Eugene, OR 97403	1876	Paul Olum	4-D	15,478	1

Name, address	Year	Governing official affiliation, and highest degree offered		Stu-dents	Teach-ers
Univ. of Osteopathic Medicine and Health Sciences, Des Moines, IA 50312	1898	J. Leonard Azneer	0-D	770	70
Univ. of Pennsylvania, Philadelphia, PA 19104	1740	F. Sheldon Hackney	0-D	22,000	2,500
Univ. of Phoenix, Phoenix, AZ 85004	1976	John G. Sperling	2-M	2,500	242
Univ. of Pittsburgh, Pittsburgh, PA 15260	1787	Wesley W. Posvar	12-D	29,425	2,683
Univ. of Pittsburgh at Bradford, Bradford, PA 16701	1963	Richard E. McDowell	12-B	1,100	59
Univ. of Pittsburgh at Greensburg, Greensburg, PA 15601	1963	George F. Chambers	12-B	1,400	51
Univ. of Pittsburgh at Johnstown, Johnstown, PA 15904	1927	Frank H. Blackington III	12-B	3,319	133
Univ. of Portland, Portland, OR 97203	1901	Rev. Thomas C. Oddo	1-M	2,847	176
Univ. of Puerto Rico, Arecibo Tech. Univ. Coll., Arecibo, PR 00613	1967	Marcos Morell, Dir.-Dean	6-B	3,569	171
Univ. of Puerto Rico, Cayey Univ. Coll., Cayey, PR 00633	1967	Jose L. Monserrate-Vila	6-B	2,565	139
Univ. of Puerto Rico, Humacao Univ. Coll., Humacao, PR 00661	1962	Lillian C. Morales, Dean	6-B	3,134	221
Univ. of Puerto Rico, Mayaguez, Mayaguez, PR 00708	1911	Salvador E. Alencang	6-D	8,808	553
Univ. of Puerto Rico Medical Sciences Campus, San Juan, PR 00936	1950	Norman Maldonado	6-D	3,391	683
Univ. of Puerto Rico, Ponce Tech. Univ. Coll., Ponce, PR 00732	1970	NA	6-B	1,867	118
Univ. of Puerto Rico, Rio Piedras, Rio Piedras, PR 00931	1903	Antonio-Miro Montilla	6-D	18,864	1,102
Univ. of Puget Sound, Tacoma, WA 98416	1888	Philip Monford Phibbs	1-M	4,021	183
Univ. of Redlands, Redlands, CA 92374	1907	Douglas R. Moore	0-M	1,236	184
Univ. of Rhode Island, Kingston, RI 02881	1892	Edward Eddy	4-D	10,239	857
Univ. of Richmond, Richmond, VA 23173	1830	E. Bruce Heilman	1-M	4,300	364
Univ. of Rochester, Rochester, NY 14627	1850	G. Dennis O'Brien	0-D	6,969	662
Univ. of St. Thomas, Houston, TX 77006	1947	Rev. William J. Young	1-D	2,068	167
Univ. of San Diego, San Diego, CA 92110	1949	Author E. Hughes	1-D	5,077	314
Univ. of San Francisco, San Francisco, CA 94117	1855	Rev. John J. Lo Schiavo, SJ	1-D	5,339	418
Univ. of Santa Clara, Santa Clara, CA 95053	1851	Rev. William J. Rewak, SJ	1-D	7,420	444
Univ. of Scranton, Scranton, PA 18510	1888	Rev. J. A. Panuska, SJ	1-M	4,801	269
Univ. of South Alabama, Mobile, AL 36688	1964	Frederick P. Whiddon	4-D	9,380	583
Univ. of South Carolina, Columbia, SC 29208	1801	James B. Holderman	4-D	24,296	1,253
Univ. of South Carolina at Aiken, Aiken, SC 29801	1961	Robert E. Alexander	4-B	1,932	150
Univ. of South Carolina at Spartanburg, SC 29303	1967	Olin B. Sansbury Jr.	4-B	2,728	189
Univ. of South Carolina-Coastal Carolina Coll., Conway, SC 29526	1954	Fred W. Hicks	4-B	2,470	140
Univ. of South Dakota, Vermillion, SD 57069	1862	Joseph M. McFadden	4-D	6,001	440
Univ. of Southern California, Los Angeles, CA 90089	1880	James H. Zumberge	0-D	29,411	2,441
Univ. of Southern Colorado, Pueblo, CO 81001	1933	Lyle C. Wilcox	4-M	4,982	269
Univ. of Southern Maine, Portland, ME 04103	1878	Robert L. Woodbury	4-M	8,700	607
Univ. of Southern Mississippi, Hattiesburg, MS 39406	1910	Aubrey K. Lucus	4-D	11,333	655
Univ. of South Florida, Tampa, FL 33620	1956	John Lott Brown	4-D	27,301	1,192
Univ. of Southwestern Louisiana, Lafayette, LA 70504	1898	Ray P. Authement	4-D	16,266	621
Univ. of Steubenville, Steubenville, OH 43952	1946	Rev. Michael Scanlan	1-M	934	66
Univ. of Tampa, Tampa, FL 33606	1931	Richard D. Cheshire	0-M	2,069	161
Univ. of Tennessee at Chattanooga, Chattanooga, TN 37402	1886	Frederick N. Obear	4-M	7,834	415
Univ. of Tennessee at Martin, Martin, TN 38238	1927	Charles E. Smith	4-M	5,696	255
Univ. of Tennessee Center for the Health Sciences, Memphis, TN 38163	1911	James C. Hunt	4-D	1,988	686
Univ. of Tennessee, Knoxville, Knoxville, TN 37996	1794	Jack E. Reese	4-D	27,018	1,334
Univ. of Texas at Arlington, Arlington, TX 76019	1895	Wendell H. Nedderman	4-D	23,175	940
Univ. of Texas at Austin, Austin, TX 78712	1883	Peter T. Flawn	4-D	47,631	2,100
Univ. of Texas at Dallas, Richardson, TX 75080	1969	Robert H. Rutford	4-D	7,455	382
Univ. of Texas at El Paso, El Paso, TX 79968	1913	Haskell M. Monroe	4-D	15,268	595
Univ. of Texas at San Antonio, San Antonio, TX 78285	1969	James W. Wagener	4-M	11,890	579
Univ. of Texas at Tyler, Tyler, TX 75701	1972	George F. Hamm	4-M	3,142	199
Univ. of Texas Health Science Center at Dallas, TX 75235	1972	Charles C. Sprague	4-D	1,368	263
Univ. of Texas Health Science Center at Houston, TX 77225	1943	Roger J. Bulger	4-D	2,679	874
Univ. of Texas Health Science Center at San Antonio, San Antonio, TX 78284	1976	Frank Harrison	4-M	624	64
Univ. of Texas Medical Branch at Galveston, TX 77550	1891	William C. Levin	4-D	1,766	450
Univ. of Texas of the Permian Basin, Odessa, TX 79762	1973	Duane M. Leach	4-M	1,983	102
Univ. of the District of Columbia, Washington, DC 20008	1976	Lisle C. Carter Jr.	9-M	13,576	905
Univ. of the Pacific, Stockton, CA 95211	1851	Stanley E. McCaffrey	0-D	5,877	341
Univ. of the Sacred Heart, Santurce, PR 00914	1939	Pedro Gonzalez Ramos	1-B	7,985	330
Univ. of the South, Sewanee, TN 37375	1858	Robert M. Ayres Jr.	1-D	1,163	116
Univ. of the State of New York Regents External Degree Program, Albany, NY 12230	1970	NA	12-B	18,242	NA
Univ. of Toledo, Toledo, OH 43606	1872	Glen R. Driscoll	4-D	21,652	1,194
Univ. of Tulsa, Tulsa, OK 74104	1894	J. Paschal Twyman	1-D	5,769	449
Univ. of Utah, Salt Lake City, UT 84112	1850	Chase N. Peterson	4-D	24,911	2,734
Univ. of Vermont, Burlington, VT 05405	1791	Lattie F. Coor	4-D	8,717	857
Univ. of Virginia, Charlottesville, VA 22903	1819	Frank L. Hereford Jr.	12-D	16,379	1,579
Univ. of Washington, Seattle, WA 98195	1861	William P. Gerberding	4-D	34,308	2,600
Univ. of West Florida, Pensacola, FL 32514	1963	James A. Robinson	4-M	6,092	342
Univ. of Wisconsin-Eau Claire, Eau Claire, WI 54701	1916	Larry Schnack	4-M	11,072	577
Univ. of Wisconsin-Green Bay, Green Bay, WI 54302	1968	Edward W. Weidner	4-M	4,880	243
Univ. of Wisconsin-La Crosse, La Crosse, WI 54601	1909	Noel J. Richards	4-M	9,849	425
Univ. of Wisconsin-Madison, Madison, WI 53706	1849	Irving Shain	4-D	43,075	2,269
Univ. of Wisconsin-Milwaukee, Milwaukee, WI 53201	1956	Frank E. Horton	4-D	26,468	1,200
Univ. of Wisconsin-Oshkosh, Oshkosh, WI 54901	1871	Edward M. Penson	4-M	11,200	600
Univ. of Wisconsin-Parkside, Kenosha, WI 53141	1968	Alan E. Guskin	4-M	5,990	280
Univ. of Wisconsin-Platteville, Platteville, WI 53818	1866	William W. Chmurny	4-M	5,480	244
Univ. of Wisconsin-River Falls, River Falls, WI 54022	1874	George R. Field	4-M	5,368	279
Univ. of Wisconsin-Stevens Point, Stevens Point, WI 54481	1894	Philip R. Marshall	4-M	8,906	455
Univ. of Wisconsin-Stout, Menomonie, WI 54751	1893	Robert S. Swanson	4-M	7,470	383
Univ. of Wisconsin-Superior, Superior, WI 54880	1893	Karl W. Meyer	4-M	2,219	144
Univ. of Wisconsin-Whitewater, Whitewater, WI 53190	1868	James R. Connor	4-D	10,493	617
Univ. of Wyoming, Laramie, WY 82071	1886	Donald L. Veal	4-D	10,270	868
Upsala, East Orange, NJ 07019	1893	Rodney Felder	1-M	1,198	140
Ursinus, Collegeville, PA 19426	1869	Richard P. Richter	1-B	1,104	100
Ursuline, Pepper Pike, OH 44124 (4)	1871	Sr. Mary Kenan Dulzer	1-M	1,318	90
Utah State Univ., Logan, UT 84322	1888	Stanford Cazier	4-D	11,849	504
Utica Coll. of Syracuse Univ., Utica, NY 13502	1946	Lansing G. Baker	0-B	1,336	175
Valdosta State, Valdosta, GA 31698	1906	Hugh C. Bailey	4-M	5,835	245

Name, address	Year	Governing official affiliation, and highest degree offered	Students	Teachers
Valley City State, Valley City, ND 58072	1890	Charles B. House Jr.	4-B	1,167	66
Valparaiso Univ., Valparaiso, IN 46383	1859	Robert V. Schnabel	1-D	3,783	356
Vanderbilt Univ., Nashville, TN 37240	1873	Joe B. Wyatt	0-D	8,500	1,985
Vassar, Poughkeepsie, NY 12601	1861	Virginia B. Smith	0-M	2,358	240
Villa Julie, Stevenson, MD 21153	1952	Carolyn Manuszak	0-B	1,031	120
Villa Maria, Erie, PA 16505	1925	Sr. M. Lawrence Antoun	1-B	609	72
Villanova Univ., Villanova, PA 19085.	1842	Rev. John M. Driscoll, OSA	1-D	11,190	493
Virginia Commonwealth Univ., Richmond, VA 23284	1838	Edmund F. Ackell	4-D	20,402	1,960
Virginia Military Inst., Lexington, VA 24450 (1)	1839	Gen. Samuel S. Walker, Supt.	4-B	1,309	98
Virginia Polytechnic Inst. and State Univ., Blacksburg, VA 24061.	1872	William E. Lavery	12-D	21,357	1,846
Virginia State Univ., Petersburg, VA 23803	1882	Wilbert Greenfield	4-M	3,956	266
Virginia Union Univ., Richmond, VA 23220	1865	David T. Shannon	1-M	1,333	102
Virginia Wesleyan, Norfolk, VA 23502.	1960	Lambuth M. Clarke.	1-B	926	72
Viterbo, La Crosse, WI 54601	1890	Robert E. Gibbons	1-B	1,173	120
Wabash, Crawfordsville, IN 47933 (1)	1832	Lewis S. Salter	0-B	774	77
Wagner, Staten Island, NY 10301	1883	Sam Frank	1-M	2,500	216
Wake Forest Univ., Winston-Salem, NC 27109.	1834	Thomas K. Hearn Jr.	1-D	4,818	1,128
Walla Walla, College Place, WA 99324	1892	N. Clifford Sorensen	1-M	1,660	151
Walsh, Canton, OH 44720	1958	Br. Francis Blouin.	1-M	1,205	108
Walsh Coll. of Accountancy & Business Administration, Troy, MI 48007	1922	Jeffery W. Barry	0-M	2,072	76
Wartburg, Waverly, IA 50677	1852	Robert Vogel	1-B	1,141	86
Washburn Univ. of Topeka, Topeka, KS 66621	1865	John L. Green Jr.	10-D	6,987	260
Washington and Jefferson, Washington, PA 15301	1781	Howard J. Burnett	0-B	1,030	97
Washington and Lee Univ., Lexington, VA 24450 (1)	1749	John D. Wilson	0-D	1,694	147
Washington, Chestertown, MD 21620	1782	Douglass Cater.	0-M	797	73
Washington State Univ., Pullman, WA 99164.	1892	Glenn Terrell	4-D	16,403	976
Washington Univ., St. Louis, MO 63130	1853	William H. Danforth	0-D	10,769	2,515
Wayland Baptist Univ., Plainview, TX 79072	1908	Roy C. McClung	1-M	1,695	92
Waynesburg, Waynesburg, PA 15370.	1849	J. Thomas Mills Jr.	1-M	780	64
Wayne State, Wayne, NE 68787	1910	Eddie M. Elliot	4-M	2,405	126
Wayne State Univ., Detroit, MI 48202	1868	Thomas N. Bonner	4-D	29,639	2,148
Weber State, Ogden, UT 84408	1889	Rodney H. Brady	4-M	10,348	476
Webster Univ., St. Louis, MO 63119.	1915	Leigh Gerdine.	0-M	5,218	621
Wellesley, Wellesley, MA 02181 (3)	1875	Nannerl Keohane.	0-B	2,170	311
Wentworth Inst. of Tech., Boston, MA 02115.	1904	Edward T. Kirkpatrick	0-B	3,300	170
Wesleyan Univ., Middletown, CT 06457.	1831	Colin Campbell.	0-D	2,625	269
Wesley, Dover, DE 19901	1873	Reed M. Stewart	1-B	1,229	77
West Chester Univ. of Pennsylvania, West Chester, PA 19383	1871	Kenneth L. Perrin.	4-M	9,586	529
West Coast Univ., Los Angeles, CA 90020	1909	Robert M. Baicer Jr.	0-M	1,400	250
Western Carolina Univ., Cullowhee, NC 28723.	1889	H. F. Robinson	4-M	6,027	359
Western Connecticut State Univ., Danbury, CT 06810	1903	Stephen Feldman	4-M	5,908	220
Western Illinois Univ., Macomb, IL 61455	1899	Leslie F. Malpass.	3-M	12,411	693
Western Intl. Univ., Phoenix, AZ 85021	1978	Ronald C. Bauer	0-M	850	50
Western Kentucky Univ., Bowling Green, KY 42101	1906	Donald W. Zacharias.	0-M	12,666	631
Western Maryland, Westminster, MD 21157	1867	Robert H. Chambers.	1-M	1,765	133
Western Michigan Univ., Kalamazoo, MI 49008	1903	John T. Bernhard.	4-D	18,542	1,171
Western Montana, Dillon, MT 59725.	1893	Robert H. Thomas	12-M	960	52
Western New England, Springfield, MA 01119	1919	Beverly W. Miller	0-D	4,716	268
Western New Mexico Univ., Silver City, NM 88061	1893	Mervyn L. Cadwallader	4-M	1,805	75
Western Oregon State, Monmouth, OR 97361.	1856	Richard S. Meyers	4-M	2,881	200
Western State Coll. of Colorado, Gunnison, CO 81230	1911	John P. Mellon	4-M	2,850	134
Western State Univ., Coll. of Law of Orange County, Fullerton, CA 92631	1966	NA	2-D	1,423	56
Western State Univ., Coll. of Law of San Diego, CA 92110.	1969	William B. Lawless	2-D	719	51
Western Washington Univ., Bellingham, WA 98225	1893	G. Robert Ross	4-M	9,617	504
Westfield State, Westfield, MA 01085	1838	Francis J. Pilecki	4-M	3,200	195
West Georgia, Carrollton, GA 30118	1933	Maurice K. Townsend	4-M	6,352	305
West Liberty State, West Liberty, WV 26074	1837	NA	4-B	2,540	131
Westminster, Fulton, MO 65251	1851	J. Harvey Saunders	1-B	647	57
Westminster, New Wilmington, PA 16172.	1852	Allen P. Splete	1-M	1,542	143
Westminster Coll. of Salt Lake City, Salt Lake City, UT 84105.	1875	James E. Petersen.	0-M	1,291	79
Westmont, Santa Barbara, CA 93108	1940	David K. Winter	1-B	992	104
West Texas State Univ., Canyon, TX 79016	1909	Gail Shannon	4-M	6,805	364
West Virginia Inst. of Tech., Montgomery, WV 25136	1895	Leonard C. Nelson	4-M	3,439	185
West Virginia State, Institute, WV 25112	1891	Thomas W. Cole Jr.	4-B	4,731	210
West Virginia Univ., Morgantown, WV 26506	1867	E. Gordon Gee	4-D	20,624	2,367
West Virginia Wesleyan, Buckhannon, WV 26201	1890	Hugh A. Latimer	1-M	1,497	114
Wheaton, Wheaton, IL 60187.	1860	NA	1-M	2,378	150
Wheaton, Norton, MA 02766 (3)	1834	Alice F. Emerson.	0-B	1,204	130
Wheeling, Wheeling, WV 26003	1954	Fr. Thomas S. Acker, SJ	1-M	1,046	72
Wheelock, Boston, MA 02215 (4)	1888	Daniel S. Cheever Jr.	0-M	630	135
Whitman, Walla Walla, WA 99362	1859	Robert A. Skotheim	0-B	1,238	113
Whittier, Whittier, CA 90608	1901	Eugene S. Mills.	0-M	1,750	105
Whitworth, Spokane, WA 99251	1890	Robert H. Mounce	1-M	1,884	90
Wichita State Univ., Wichita, KS 67208	1895	Warren B. Armstrong	4-D	20,252	703
Widener Univ., Delaware Campus, Wilmington, DE 19803	1965	NA	0-B	1,180	55
Widener Univ., Pennsylvania Campus, Chester, PA 19013	1821	NA	0-D	5,425	202
Wilberforce Univ., Wilberforce, OH 45384	1856	Charles E. Taylor.	1-B	881	71
Wilkes, Wilkes-Barre, PA 18766	1933	Christopher N. Breiseth	0-M	2,808	198
Willamette Univ., Salem, OR 97301	1842	Jerry E. Hudson	1-D	1,850	172
William Carey, Hattiesburg, MS 39401	1906	James R. Noonkester	1-M	1,728	110
William Jewell, Liberty, MO 64068.	1849	J. Gordon Kingsley.	1-B	1,399	120
William Paterson Coll. of New Jersey, Wayne, NJ 07470.	1855	Seymour C. Hyman	4-M	12,491	601
Williams, Williamstown, MA 01267.	1793	John W. Chandler	0-M	2,023	232
William Smith, Geneva, NY 14456 (5).	1908	NA	0-B	750	143
William Woods, Fulton, MO 65251.	1870	John M. Bartholomy	1-B	796	69
Wilmington, New Castle, DE 19720	1967	Audrey K. Doberstein	0-M	1,038	79
Wilmington Coll. of Ohio, Wilmington, OH 45177.	1870	Neil Thorburn.	1-B	857	59
Wingate, Wingate, NC 28174.	1895	Paul R. Corts.	1-B	1,500	78
Winona State Univ., Winona, MN 55987.	1858	Thomas Stark.	4-M	5,300	270
Winston-Salem State Univ., Winston-Salem, NC 27110.	1892	H. Douglas Covington	4-B	2,224	145
Winthrop, Rock Hill, SC 29733	1886	Philip Lader	4-M	4,999	313

Name, address	Year	Governing official affiliation, and highest degree offered	Stu-dents	Teach-ers
Wittenberg Univ., Springfield, OH 45501	1845	William A. Kinnison 1-B	2,142	75
Wofford, Spartanburg, SC 29301	1854	Joab M. Lesesne 1-B	1,046	174
Woodbury Univ., Los Angeles, CA 90017	1884	Wayne Miller 0-M	1,003	85
Worcester Polytechnic Inst., Worcester, MA 01609	1865	Edmund T. Cranch 0-D	3,895	322
Worcester State, Worcester, MA 01602	1874	Philip P. Vairo 4-M	4,700	171
Wright State Univ., Dayton, OH 45435	1964	Robert J. Kegerreis 4-D	15,452	878
Xavier Univ., Cincinnati, OH 45207	1831	Rev. Charles L. Currie, SJ . . . 1-M	6,950	343
Xavier Univ. of Louisiana, New Orleans, LA 70125	1925	Norman C. Francis 1-M	2,243	180
Yale Univ., New Haven, CT 06520	1701	A. Bartlett Giamatti 0-D	10,448	1,741
Yeshiva Univ., Yeshiva Coll. & Stern Coll. for Women, New York, NY 10033 (5)	1886	Norman Lamm 0-B	1,210	168
York Coll. of Pennsylvania, York, PA 17405	1787	Robert V. Iosue 0-M	4,533	230
Youngstown State Univ., Youngstown, OH 44555	1908	John J. Coffelt 4-M	15,849	785

Two-Year Schools

The highest degree offered for all two year schools is an Associate's degree.

Name, address	Year	Governing official	Stu-dents	Teach-ers
Abraham Baldwin Agricultural, Tifton, GA 31793	1933	Stanley R. Anderson 4	2,215	140
Adirondack Comm., Glens Falls, NY 12801	1960	Gordon C. Blank 11	3,019	150
Aiken Technical, Aiken SC 29801	1972	Ashley J. Little 11	1,023	135
Aims Comm., Greeley, CO 80632	1967	George R. Conger 9	5,356	260
Alabama Aviation and Tech., Ozark, AL 36360	1960	James G. Sasser 4	653	41
Alabama Tech., East Gadsden, AL 35999	1925	Robert W. Howard 4	921	45
Albany Jr., Albany, GA 31707	1965	Bill R. Tilley 4	1,911	100
Alexander City State Jr., Alexander City, AL 35010	1965	W. Byron Causey. 4	1,284	88
Alexandria Area Vocational Tech. Inst., Alexandria, MN 56308	1961	V. R. Maack, Dir. 4	1,600	114
Allan Hancock, Santa Maria, CA 93454	1920	Gary R. Edelbrock 11	8,733	290
Allegany Comm., Cumberland, MD 21502	1961	Donald L. Alexander 11	2,191	135
Allen County Comm., Iola, KS 66749	1923	Paul Hines. 8	1,035	92
Alpena Comm., Alpena, MI 49707	1952	Charles B. Donnelly 4	1,738	122
Alvin Comm., Alvin, TX 77511	1949	A. R. Allbright. 11	3,723	150
Amarillo, Amarillo, TX 79178	1929	H. D. Yarbrough 11	5,682	315
American Academy of Art, Chicago, IL 60604	1923	Clinton E. Frank, Exec. Dir. . . . 2	887	26
American Inst. of Business, Des Moines, IA 50321	1921	Keith Fenton 0	1,131	47
American River, Sacramento, CA 95841	1955	Robert D. Jensen. 9	22,800	693
American Samoa Comm., Pago Pago, AS 96799	1969	Saeuteuga Scanlan 7	986	65
Anderson, Anderson, SC 29621	1911	Mark L. Hopkins 1	972	62
Angelina, Lufkin, TX 75902	1968	Jack W. Hudgins 11	2,200	141
Anne Arundel Comm., Arnold, MD 21012	1961	Thomas E. Florestano 11	8,276	386
Anoka-Ramsey Comm., Coon Rapids, MN 55433	1965	Neil Christenson 4	3,880	137
Anson Tech., Ansonville, NC 28007	1962	Edwin R. Chapman. 4	624	46
Antelope Valley, Lancaster, CA 93534	1929	C. W. Stine 4	7,369	250
Arapahoe Comm., Littleton, CO 80120	1965	James F. Weber 4	6,200	354
Arizona Western, Yuma, AZ 85364	1962	Kenneth E. Borland 11	4,120	201
Arkansas State Univ., Beebe Branch, Beebe, AR 72012	1927	William H. Owen Jr. 4	915	32
Art Inst. of Atlanta, Atlanta, GA 30326	1949	Gerald A. Murphy 2	746	40
Art Inst. of Ft. Lauderdale, Ft. Lauderdale, FL 33316	1968	Mark K. Wheeler 2	1,221	62
Art Inst. of Philadelphia, Philadelphia, PA 19103	1966	Philip Trachtman 2	850	72
Art Inst. of Pittsburgh, Pittsburgh, PA 15222	1921	John R. Knepper 2	1,952	90
Asnuntuck Comm., Enfield, CT 06082	1972	Daniel R. McLaughlin 4	1,796	37
Atlanta Jr., Atlanta, GA 30310	1974	Edwin A. Thompson. 4	1,585	91
Atlantic Comm., Mays Landing, NJ 08330	1966	Ronald W. Bush 8	3,700	190
Austin Comm., Austin, MN 55912	1940	James Flannery 4	887	53
Austin Comm., Austin, TX 78768	1972	NA 9	15,929	695
Bailey Tech. School, St. Louis, MO 63108 (2)	1936	NA 2	786	25
Bainbridge Jr., Bainbridge, GA 31717	1972	Edward D. Mobley 4	639	45
Baker Jr. Coll. of Business, Flint, MI 48507	1911	Edward J. Kurtz 0	1,763	76
Barstow, Barstow, CA 92311	1962	Edwin Spear 4	1,500	75
Barton County Comm., Great Bend, KS 67530	1969	Jimmie L. Downing. 11	2,640	121
Bay de Noc Comm., Escanaba, MI 49829	1963	Edwin E. Wuehle 4	1,687	87
Bay Path Jr., Longmeadow, MA 01106	1897	Jeanette T. Wright 0	680	35
Bay State Jr., Boston, MA 02116	1934	George Brennan Jr. 0	617	27
Beaufort County Comm., Washington, NC 27889	1968	James P. Blanton. 4	1,127	72
Beaufort Tech., Beaufort, SC 29902	1972	George W. Goldsmith Jr. 4	1,080	150
Becker Jr.-Worcester Campus, Worcester, MA 01609	1887	Lloyd H. Van Buskirk. 0	710	38
Beckley, Beckley, WV 25801	1933	John W. Saunders 0	1,407	59
Bee County, Beeville, TX 78102	1965	Norman Wallace 8	2,154	102
Belleville Area, Belleville, IL 62221	1946	Bruce R. Wisore 9	12,773	483
Bellevue Comm., Bellevue, WA 98007	1966	Paul N. Thompson 4	3,979	426
Belmont Tech., St. Clairsville, OH 43950	1971	Paul R. Ohm 4	1,004	75
Bergen Comm., Paramus, NJ 07652	1965	Jose Lopez-Isa 8	11,432	517
Berkeley School, White Plains, NY 10604	1945	Robert V. Maher 2	650	28
Berkshire Comm., Pittsfield, MA 01202	1960	Jonathan M. Daube 4	1,973	96
Big Bend Comm., Moses Lake, WA 98837	1962	Peter D. DeVries 4	2,307	159
Bismarck Jr., Bismarck, ND 58501	1939	Kermit Lidstrom. 9	2,325	109
Black Hawk-East Campus, Kewanee, IL 61443	1967	Ronald F. Williams 11	1,200	101
Black Hawk-Quad-Cities Campus, Moline, IL 61265	1946	Richard J. Puffer 11	5,766	283
Blackhawk Tech. Inst., Janesville, WI 53547	1968	O. L. Johnson, Dir. 9	2,144	174
Blair Jr., Colorado Springs, CO 80915	1897	NA 2	600	43
Blinn, Brenham, TX 77833	1883	James H. Atkinson 4	3,163	123
Blue Mountain Comm., Pendleton, OR 97801	1962	Ronald L. Daniels 8	2,061	152
Blue Ridge Comm., Weyers Cave, VA 24486	1965	James A. Armstrong 4	2,046	102
Blue Ridge Tech., Flat Rock, NC 28731	1969	William D. Killian 4	1,127	76
Bossier Parish Comm., Bossier City, LA 71111	1967	NA 11	1,463	54
Bowling Green State Univ.-Firelands Coll., Huron, OH 44839	1968	Algalee Adams, Dean 4	1,256	63
Brazosport, Lake Jackson, TX 77566	1948	Wilbur A. Bass 11	3,617	190
Brevard, Brevard, NC 28712	1853	Jacob C. Martinson Jr. 1	749	90
Brevard Comm., Cocoa, FL 32922	1960	Maxwell C. King 4	10,513	818
Brewer State Jr., Fayette, AL 35555	1969	Tommy M. Boothe 4	603	29
Bristol Comm., Fall River, MA 02720	1965	Eileen Farley 4	2,547	127

Name, address	Year	Governing official affiliation, and highest degree offered		Stu-dents	Teach-ers
Brookdale Comm., Lincroft, NJ 07738	1967	B. A. Barringer	8	12,533	438
Brookhaven, Farmers Branch, TX 75234	1978	Patsy J. Fulton	8	6,010	211
Brooks, Long Beach, CA 90804	1971	Steve Sotraidis, Exec. Dir.	2	779	60
Broome Comm., Binghamton, NY 13902	1946	Donald W. Beattie	11	6,841	563
Broward Comm., Fort Lauderdale, FL 33301	1960	A. Hugh Adams	4	29,665	705
Brunswick Jr., Brunswick, GA 31520	1961	John W. Teel	4	1,197	64
Bryant and Stratton Business Inst., Buffalo, NY 14202	1854	Francis J. Gustina Jr.	2	2,596	182
Bryant and Stratton Business Inst., Rochester, NY 14604 (4)	1973	Paul Hossenlopp, Mgr. Dir.	2	606	24
Bryant and Stratton Business Inst., Eastern Hills Campus, Clarence, NY 14031	1978	NA	2	670	30
Bucks County Comm., Newtown, PA 18940	1964	Charles E. Rollins	4	9,296	337
Bunker Hill Comm., Boston, MA 02129	1973	Harold E. Shively	4	3,193	141
Burlington County, Pemberton, NJ 08068	1966	Harmon B. Pierce	4	6,981	242
Butler County Comm., El Dorado, KS 67042	1927	Carl L. Heinrich	11	3,300	202
Butler County Comm., Butler, PA 16001	1965	Thomas Ten Hoeve Jr.	8	1,100	65
Butte, Oroville, CA 95965	1966	Wendell L. Reeder	9	1,000	330
Cabrillo, Aptos, CA 95003	1959	John C. Petersen	9	11,223	300
Caldwell Comm. and Tech. Inst., Lenoir, NC 28645	1964	Eric B. McKeithan	4	1,722	137
Camden County, Blackwood, NJ 08012	1967	Otto R. Mauke	11	8,725	375
Canada, Redwood City, CA 94061	1968	D. Robert Stiff	9	7,996	270
Cape Cod Comm., West Barnstable, MA 02668	1961	James F. Hall	4	1,896	141
Cape Fear Tech. Inst., Wilmington, NC 28401	1959	Malcolm J. McLeod	4	1,550	67
Capital City Jr., Little Rock, AR 72203	1927	Kenneth Sullivan	2	641	20
Carl Albert Jr., Poteau, OK 74953	1934	Joe White	4	2,126	66
Carl Sandburg, Galesburg, IL 61401	1967	Robert K. Luther	11	4,000	117
Carteret Tech., Morehead City, NC 28557	1963	Donald W. Bryant	4	1,025	58
Casper, Casper, WY 82601	1945	Lloyd H. Loftin	9	1,587	190
Catawba Valley Tech., Hickory, NC 28601	1960	Robert E. Paap	11	2,400	186
Catonsville Comm., Catonsville, MD 21228	1957	John M. Kingsmore	8	10,274	561
Cayuga County Comm., Auburn, NY 13021	1953	Helena Howe	4	3,308	144
Cecil Comm., North East, MD 21901	1968	Robert L. Gell	4	1,450	92
Cedar Valley, Lancaster, TX 75134	1977	Floyd S. Elkins	4	2,348	105
Central Arizona, Coolidge, AZ 85228	1969	James M. Kraby	8	5,175	328
Central Carolina Tech., Sanford, NC 27330	1962	Marvin R. Joyner	11	2,039	130
Central City Business Inst., Syracuse, NY 13203	1904	Donald J. Nelli	2	727	57
Central Comm. Coll.-Grand Island Campus, NE 68802	1975	Larry L. Keller, Dir.	11	1,476	46
Central Comm. Coll.-Hastings Campus, Hastings, NE 68901	1966	Edwin Minnick, Dir.	11	1,975	86
Central Comm. Coll.-Platte Campus, Columbus, NE 68601	1968	Jerry A. Lee	11	990	55
Central Florida Comm., Ocala, FL 32670	1957	Henry E. Goodlett	4	2,709	100
Centralia, Centralia, WA 98531	1925	Jerry Young	4	3,248	270
Central Ohio Tech., Newark, OH 43055	1971	Julius S. Greenstein	4	1,230	91
Central Oregon Comm., Bend, OR 97701	1949	Frederick H. Boyle	9	2,019	142
Central Pennsylvania Business School, Summerdale, PA 17093	1922	Bart A. Milano	2	729	48
Central Piedmont Comm., Charlotte, NC 28235	1963	Richard H. Hagemeyer	11	17,774	1,111
Central Texas, Killeen, TX 76541	1967	Luis M. Morton	11	4,779	131
Central Virginia Comm., Lynchburg, VA 24502	1966	J. E. Merritt	4	4,000	142
Central Wyoming, Riverton, WY 82501	1966	Edward L. Donovan	11	778	45
Century, Huntington, WV 25701	1947	Philip G. Niebergall	2	600	37
Cerritos, Norwalk, CA 90650	1956	Wilford Michael	11	22,976	700
Cerro Coso Comm., Ridgecrest, CA 93555	1973	Raymond McCue	4	3,995	201
Chabot, Hayward, CA 94545	1961	William J. Moore	4	18,986	1,060
Chaffey, Alta Loma, CA 91701	1883	Samuel A. Ferguson	9	12,649	400
Chamberlayne Jr., Boston, MA 02116	1892	Matthew J. Malloy	0	853	55
Champlain, Burlington, VT 05402	1878	Robert A. Skiff	0	1,124	77
Charles County Comm., La Plata, MD 20646	1958	John Sine	11	3,942	218
Charles Stewart Mott, Flint, MI 48503	1923	Robert N. Rue	8	10,600	NA
Chattahoochee Valley State, Phenix City, AL 36867	1974	James E. Owen	4	1,447	65
Chattanooga State Tech. Comm., Chattanooga, TN 37406	1965	Charles W. Branch	4	5,347	158
Chemeketa Comm., Salem, OR 97309	1955	William Segura	9	6,523	573
Chesapeake, Wye Mills, MD 21679	1967	Robert C. Schleiger	11	1,906	126
Chesterfield-Marlboro Tech., Cheraw, SC 29520	1967	Ronald W. Hampton	11	665	42
Chipola Jr., Marianna, FL 32446	1947	James R. Richburg	4	1,402	71
Chowan, Murfreesboro, NC 27855	1848	Bruce E. Whitaker	1	1,078	72
Cincinnati Tech., Cincinnati, OH 45223	1966	Frederick B. Schlimm	4	3,839	203
Cisco Jr., Cisco, TX 76437	1940	Henry E. McCullough	11	1,592	113
Citrus, Azusa, CA 91702	1915	Dan Angel	11	10,052	320
City Coll. of San Francisco, San Francisco, CA 94112	1935	Harry W. Frustuck	11	28,485	1,087
City Coll. of Chicago, Chicago City-Wide, Chicago, IL 60601	1975	Mark Warden	11	10,852	205
City Coll. of Chicago, Harry S. Truman, Chicago, IL 60640	1956	Wallace B. Appelson	11	13,942	336
City Coll. of Chicago, Kennedy-King, Chicago, IL 60621	1935	Ewen M. Akin	11	9,968	358
City Coll. of Chicago, Loop, Chicago, IL 60601	1962	NA	11	9,138	190
City Coll. of Chicago, Malcolm X, Chicago, IL 60612	1911	James C. Griggs	11	4,195	339
City Coll. of Chicago, Olive-Harvey, Chicago, IL 60628	1970	Homer D. Franklin	11	9,283	237
City Coll. of Chicago, Richard J. Daley, Chicago, IL 60652	1960	William P. Conway	11	11,386	229
City Coll. of Chicago, Wilbur Wright, Chicago, IL 60634	1934	Ernest V. Clements	11	10,548	344
City Univ. of New York, Borough of Manhattan Comm., New York, NY 10007	1963	Joshua L. Smith	10	9,867	623
City Univ. of New York, Bronx Comm., Bronx, NY 10453	1959	Roscoe C. Brown	10	6,802	400
City Univ. of New York, Fiorello H. LaGuardia Comm., Long Island City, NY 11101	1971	Joseph Shenker	11	6,582	368
City Univ. of New York, Hostos Comm., Bronx, NY 10451	1968	Flora M. Edwards	10	3,607	192
City Univ. of New York, Kingsborough Comm., Brooklyn, NY 11235	1963	Leon M. Goldstein	11	9,212	683
City Univ. of New York, Queensborough Comm., Bayside, NY 11364	1958	Kurt R. Schmeller	10	12,970	785
Clackamas Comm., Oregon City, OR 97045	1966	John W. Hakanson	8	4,650	353
Clarendon, Clarendon, TX 79226	1898	Kenneth D. Vaughan	4	686	48
Clark, Vancouver, WA 98663	1933	Earl P. Johnson	4	8,200	300
Clark County Comm., North Las Vegas, NV 89030	1971	Paul Meacham	4	10,075	451
Clark Tech., Springfield, OH 45501	1962	George H. Robertson	4	2,652	166
Clatsop Comm., Astoria, OR 97103	1958	Philip L. Bainer	8	2,800	159
Clayton Jr., Morrow, GA 30260	1969	Harry S. Downs	4	3,692	148
Cleveland Inst. of Electronics, Cleveland, OH 44114 (2)	1934	NA	2	25,608	63

Name, address	Year	Governing official affiliation, and highest degree offered	Stu-dents	Teach-ers
Cleveland State Comm., Cleveland, TN 37311	1967	L. Quentin Lane ... 4	3,544	141
Cleveland Tech., Shelby, NC 28150	1965	James B. Petty ... 4	1,373	03
Clinton Comm., Clinton, IA 52732	1946	Charles Spence ... 4	1,131	68
Clinton Comm., Plattsburgh, NY 12901	1969	Alfred Light ... 11	1,500	82
Cloud County Comm., Concordia, KS 66901	1965	James P. Ihrig ... 4	2,087	248
Coastal Carolina Comm., Jacksonville, NC 28540	1964	James L. Henderson Jr. ... 11	2,744	122
Coastline Comm., Fountain Valley, CA 92708	1976	Edward Decker ... 9	21,483	634
Cochise, Douglas, AZ 85607	1962	Andrew S. Moreland ... 8	4,083	320
Coffeyville Comm., Coffeyville, KS 67337	1923	Russell H. Graham ... 11	1,692	50
Colby Comm., Colby, KS 67701	1964	James H. Tangeman ... 11	898	109
Coll. of DuPage, Glen Ellyn, IL 60137	1966	Harold D. McAninch ... 11	24,034	1,220
Coll. of Eastern Utah, Price, UT 84501	1937	James R. Randolph ... 4	1,134	60
Coll. of Lake County, Grayslake, IL 60030	1967	John O. Hunter ... 11	12,187	657
Coll. of San Mateo, San Mateo, CA 94402	1922	Lois A. Callahan ... 11	15,063	750
Coll. of Southern Idaho, Twin Falls, ID 83301	1964	Gerald R. Meyerhoeffer ... 11	2,658	107
Coll. of the Albemarle, Elizabeth City, NC 27909	1960	Parker Chesson Jr. ... 4	1,451	81
Coll. of the Canyons, Valencia, CA 91355	1969	Ramon F. La Grandeur ... 11	3,496	95
Coll. of the Desert, Palm Desert, CA 92260	1959	F. D. Stout. ... 11	11,200	270
Coll. of the Mainland, Texas City, TX 77591	1967	Larry L. Stanley ... 11	2,630	182
Coll. of the Redwoods, Eureka, CA 95501	1964	D. Donald D. Weichert ... 11	10,964	720
Coll. of the Sequoias, Visalia, CA 93277	1925	Ivan C. Crookshanks ... 11	7,371	160
Coll. of the Siskiyous, Weed, CA 96094	1957	Eugene Schumacher ... 11	2,862	142
Colorado Mountain, Spring Valley Campus, Glenwood Springs, CO 81601	1965	F. Dean Lillie ... 11	741	58
Colorado Mountain, Timberline Campus, Leadville, CO 80461	1967	F. Dean Lillie ... 9	612	55
Columbia Basin, Pasco, WA 99301	1955	Fred L. Esvelt ... 4	5,000	310
Columbia, Columbia, CA 95310	1968	Dean Cunningham ... 4	2,714	91
Columbia-Greene Comm., Hudson, NY 12534	1969	Robert K. Luther ... 11	1,300	59
Columbia Jr. Coll. of Business, Columbia, SC 29203	1935	Michael Gorman ... 2	700	30
Columbus Tech. Inst., Columbus, OH 43216	1963	Harold M. Nestor ... 4	9,550	465
Comm. Coll. of Allegheny County-Allegheny Campus, Pittsburgh, PA 15212	1966	Julius R. Brown, V.P. ... 8	6,800	415
Comm. Coll. of Allegheny, County-Boyce Campus, Monroeville, PA 15146	1966	James L. Evanko, V.P. ... 11	3,571	80
Comm. Coll. of Allegheny, County-Coll. Center North, Pittsburgh, PA 15237	1972	Emma L. Watson, Exec. Dean ... 11	3,616	196
Comm. Coll. of Baltimore, Baltimore, MD 21215	1947	Charles G. Tildon Jr. ... 11	8,278	585
Comm. Coll. of Beaver County, Monaca, PA 15061	1966	Terry L. Dicianna ... 4	2,200	87
Comm. Coll. of Philadelphia, Philadelphia, PA 19107	1964	Judith S. Eaton ... 11	10,431	756
Comm. Coll. of Rhode Island, Flanagan Campus, Lincoln, RI 02865	1964	Edward J. Liston ... 4	3,120	179
Comm. Coll. of Rhode Island, Knight Campus, Warwick, RI 02886	1964	Edward Liston ... 4	4,483	519
Comm. Coll. of the Air Force, Maxwell Air Force Base, AL 36112	1972	Col. Rodney V. Cox Jr. ... 3	159,697	10,000
Comm. Coll. of the Finger Lakes, Canandaigua, NY 14424	1965	Charles J. Meder ... 11	1,933	209
Comm. Coll. of Vermont, Montpelier, VT 05602	1970	Ken Kalb ... 4	602	396
Compton Comm., Compton, CA 90221	1927	Jean Larson ... 11	6,500	338
Connors State, Warner, OK 74469	1908	Carl O. Westbrook ... 4	1,389	62
Contra Costa, San Pablo, CA 94806	1948	H. Rex Craig ... 11	8,287	301
Cooke County, Gainesville, TX 76240	1924	Alton Laird ... 4	1,754	90
Copiah-Lincoln Jr., Wesson, MS 39191	1928	Billy B. Thames ... 9	1,475	94
Corning Comm., Corning, NY 14830	1956	Donald H. Hangen ... 11	2,100	131
Cosumnes River, Sacramento, CA 95823	1970	Vincent P. Padilla. ... 9	6,625	194
County Coll. of Morris, Randolph, NJ 07869	1966	Sherman H. Masten ... 8	12,012	558
Cowley County Comm., Arkansas City, KS 67005.	1922	Gwendel Nelson ... 8	2,014	82
Crafton Hills, Yucaipa, CA 92399	1972	Donald L. Singer ... 11	4,296	155
Craven Comm., New Bern, NC 28560	1965	Thurman E. Brock ... 4	1,816	124
Crowder, Neosho, MO 64850	1963	Dell Reed ... 11	1,252	70
Cuesta, San Luis Obispo, CA 93403	1964	Frank R. Martinez ... 9	5,893	181
Culinary Inst. of America, Hyde Park, NY 12538	1946	Ferdinand E. Metz ... 0	1,800	94
Cumberland County, Vineland, NJ 08360	1963	Philip S. Phelon ... 11	2,419	94
Cuyahoga Comm., Eastern Campus, Warrensville Township, OH 44122	1971	David C. Mitchell, Provost ... 8	5,929	215
Cuyahoga Comm., Western Campus, Parma, OH 44130.	1966	Paul E. Shumaker, Provost ... 11	11,996	436
Cuyamaca, El Cajon, CA 92020	1978	Samuel M. Ciciati. ... 4	3,041	136
Cypress, Cypress, CA 90630	1966	Jack Scott. ... 11	15,320	418
Dabney S. Lancaster Comm., Clifton Forge, VA 24422	1967	John F. Backels ... 4	1,224	79
Dalton Jr., Dalton, GA 30720	1963	Derrell C. Roberts ... 4	1,755	70
Danville Area Comm., Danville, IL 61832	1946	Ronald K. Lingle ... 11	3,287	219
Danville Comm., Danville, VA 24541	1967	Walter S. Delany ... 4	2,617	112
Davenport Coll. of Business, Grand Rapids, MI 49503	1866	Donald W. Maine ... 0	4,511	123
Davidson County Comm., Lexington, NC 27292	1958	J. Bryan Brooks ... 11	2,592	111
Dawson Comm., Glendive, MT 59330	1940	Donald H. Kettner ... 11	690	32
Daytona Beach Comm., Daytona Beach, FL 32015	1958	Charles H. Polk. ... 4	7,793	639
Dean Jr., Franklin, MA 02038	1865	Richard E. Crockford ... 0	1,013	82
De Anza, Cupertino, CA 95014.	1967	A. Robert Dehart ... 11	26,979	855
DeKalb Comm., Clarkston, GA 30021.	1964	Marvin M. Cole ... 8	17,322	819
Delaware Comm., Media, PA 19063.	1967	Richard D. De Cosmo ... 9	7,209	498
Delaware Tech. and Comm., Southern Campus, Georgetown, DE 19947	1967	Jack Owens, Dir. ... 4	900	128
Delaware Tech. and Comm., Stanton/Wilmington Campus, Newark, DE 19702	1966	William A. Faucett, Dir. ... 4	4,569	248
Delaware Tech. and Comm., Terry Campus, Dover, DE 19901	1972	William C. Pfeifer, V.P. and Dir. ... 4	1,216	52
Delgado Comm., New Orleans, LA 70119	1921	Harry J. Boyer ... 4	8,733	550
Del Mar, Corpus Christi, TX 78404	1935	Edwin Biggerstaff. ... 11	7,407	330
Delta, University Center, MI 48710	1961	Donald J. Carlyon ... 8	9,898	603
Denmark Tech., Denmark, SC 29042	1948	John W. Henry Jr. ... 4	743	44
Denver Auraria Comm., Denver, CO 80204	1970	Myer L. Titus ... 4	3,793	249
Denver Inst. of Tech., Denver, CO 80221 (2).	1953	R. Wade Murphree ... 2	843	43
Des Moines Area Comm., Ankeny, IA 50021	1966	Joseph Borgen ... 11	6,483	377
District One Tech. Inst., Eau Claire, WI 54701	1912	Norbert K. Wurtzel, Dir. ... 9	3,142	175
Dixie, St. George, UT 84770	1912	Alton L. Wade. ... 4	1,904	80
Dodge City Comm., Dodge City, KS 67801	1935	Jean Thomas-Sims ... 8	1,376	73

Name, address	Year	Governing official affiliation, and highest degree offered		Stu-dents	Teach-ers
Draughons Jr., Savannah, GA 31406	1899	John T. South III	2	678	48
Draughons Jr., Memphis, TN 38116	1890	Jerry F. Daly	2	1,000	37
Draughons Jr., Nashville, TN 37217	1884	Dave Davidson	2	631	42
Dundalk Comm., Baltimore, MD 21222	1970	Philip R. Day Jr.	8	2,709	166
Durham Tech. Inst., Durham, NC 27703	1963	Phail Wynn Jr.	4	3,867	120
Dutchess Comm., Poughkeepsie, NY 12601	1957	Jerry Lee	11	4,995	421
Dyersburg State Comm., Dyersburg, TN 38024	1969	Carl Christian Andersen	4	1,571	81
East Arkansas Comm., Forrest City, AR 72335	1974	Horace E. Hartsell	4	1,155	69
East Central, Union, MO 63084	1968	Donald D. Shook	9	2,100	120
East Central Jr., Decatur, MS 39327	1928	Charles V. Wright	11	921	59
Eastern Arizona, Thatcher, AZ 85552	1888	Gherald L. Hoopes Jr.	11	3,900	290
Eastern Maine Vocational-Tech. Inst., Bangor, ME 04401	1966	Alan R. Campbell, Dir.	4	606	55
Eastern New Mexico Univ.-Roswell, Roswell, NM 88201	1958	Loyd R. Hughes, Provost	4	1,525	70
Eastern Oklahoma State, Wilburton, OK 74578	1907	James M. Miller	4	2,504	72
Eastern Wyoming, Torrington, WY 82240	1948	Charles Rogers	11	761	47
Eastfield, Mesquite, TX 75150	1970	Eleanor Ott	11	8,969	316
East Los Angeles, Monterey Park, CA 91754	1945	Arthur Avila	9	17,772	639
Edgecombe Tech., Tarboro, NC 27886	1968	Charles B. McIntyre	11	1,140	68
Edison Comm., Fort Myers, FL 33907	1962	David G. Robinson	11	5,649	218
Edison State Comm., Piqua, OH 45356	1973	James E. Seitz	4	2,285	122
Edmonds Comm., Lynnwood, WA 98036	1967	Thomas C. Nielsen	11	6,364	230
El Camino, Torrance, CA 90506	1947	Rafael L. Cortada	9	30,820	691
El Centro, Dallas, TX 75202	1966	Wueen F. Randall	8	7,004	308
Elgin Comm., Elgin, IL 60120	1949	Searle Charles	11	6,610	364
Elizabeth Seton, Yonkers, NY 10701	1960	Sr. Mary Ellen Brosnan	0	1,536	101
Ellsworth Comm., Iowa Falls, IA 50126	1890	Duane R. Lloyd, Dean	11	980	53
El Paso Comm., El Paso, TX 79998	1969	Robert E. Shepack	8	11,209	695
El Reno Jr., El Reno, OK 73036	1938	Bill S. Cole	11	1,425	44
Endicott, Beverly, MA 01915 (3)	1939	Carol A. Hawkes	0	783	75
Enterprise State Jr., Enterprise, AL 36331	1965	J. D. Talmadge	4	1,938	84
Erie Comm., City Campus, Buffalo, NY 14203	1971	John R. Birkholz	11	1,328	103
Erie Comm., South Campus, Orchard Park, NY 14127	1974	Vincent Rolletta, Dean	11	3,786	103
Essex A&T Inst., Hathorne, MA 01937	1912	Raymond F. Potter, Dir.	8	750	37
Essex Comm., Baltimore, MD 21237	1957	John E. Ravekes	11	9,951	392
Essex County, Newark, NJ 07102	1967	Zachary Yamba	8	5,647	310
Everett Comm., Everett, WA 98201	1941	NA	4	5,848	304
Evergreen Valley, San Jose, CA 95135	1975	Gerald H. Strelitz	11	8,363	269
Fairleigh Dickinson Univ., Edward Williams, Hackensack, NJ 07601	1964	Kenneth T. Vehrkens, Dean	0	1,117	54
Fashion Inst. of Design & Merchandising, Los Angeles Campus, Los Angeles, CA 90017	1969	Tonian Hohberg	2	2,201	179
Fayetteville Tech. Inst., Fayetteville, NC 28303	1961	Craig Allen	4	5,688	218
Feather River, Quincy, CA 95971	1968	Joseph Brennan	9	854	58
Fergus Falls Comm., Fergus Falls, MN 56537	1960	Dan F. True, Provost	4	677	44
Fisher Jr., Boston, MA 02116	1903	Richard A. Boudreau	0	640	45
Flathead Valley Comm., Kalispell, MT 59901	1967	Howard L. Fryett	11	1,771	127
Florence-Darlington Tech., Florence, SC 29501	1963	Fred C. Fore	4	2,324	178
Florida Career, Miami, FL 33126	1974	NA	2	1,288	26
Florida Jr. at Jacksonville, Jacksonville, FL 32202	1966	Benjamin R. Wygal	4	15,661	1,761
Florida Keys Comm., Key West, FL 33040	1965	William A. Seeker	4	1,860	54
Foothill, Los Altos Hills, CA 94022	1958	Thomas H. Clements	11	14,026	376
Forsyth Tech. Inst., Winston-Salem, NC 27103	1964	Bob H. Greene	4	2,979	174
Fort Scott Comm., Fort Scott, KS 66701	1921	Richard D. Hedges	4	1,292	72
Fort Steilacoom Comm., Tacoma, WA 98498	1967	Robert H. Stauffer	4	8,138	196
Fox Valley Tech. Inst., Appleton, WI 54913	1967	William M. Sirek, Dir.	11	4,700	800
Frank Phillips, Borger, TX 79007	1948	Andy Hicks	11	1,000	81
Frederick Comm., Frederick, MD 21701	1957	Jack Kussmaul	11	3,150	183
Fresno City, Fresno, CA 93741	1910	Clyde C. McCully	9	13,183	378
Front Range Comm., Westminster, CO 80030	1968	John H. Swenson	4	5,679	337
Fullerton, Fullerton, CA 92634	1913	Philip W. Borst	9	19,733	600
Fulton-Montgomery Comm., Johnstown, NY 12095	1964	John G. Boshart	11	1,816	85
Gadsden State Jr., Gadsden, AL 35999	1965	Arthur W. Dennis	4	3,572	165
Gainesville Jr., Gainesville, GA 30503	1964	J. Foster Watkins	4	1,679	65
Galveston, Galveston, TX 77550	1967	John E. Pickelman	11	1,649	99
Garden City Comm., Garden City, KS 67846	1919	Thomas F. Saffell	9	1,780	75
Garland County Comm., Hot Springs, AR 71913	1973	Gerald H. Fisher	11	1,809	90
Garrett Comm., McHenry, MD 21541	1966	Donald L. Ruhl	11	650	60
Gaston, Dallas, NC 28034	1963	W. Wayne Scott	11	3,318	151
Gateway Tech. Inst., Kenosha, WI 53140	1912	Keith W. Stoehr	11	7,002	93
Gateway Tech. Inst., Racine, WI 53403	1911	Rolland Graf, Deputy Dir.	11	2,503	218
Gavilan, Gilroy, CA 95020	1919	Rudolph Melone	11	3,150	164
Genesee Comm., Batavia, NY 14020	1966	Stuart Steiner	11	2,338	99
George Corley Wallace State Comm., Selma, AL 36701	1966	Charles L. Byrd	4	1,000	95
George C. Wallace State Comm., Dothan, AL 36303	1949	Nathan L. Hodges	4	3,050	130
Germanna Comm., Locust Grove, VA 22508	1970	William P. Briley	4	1,666	84
Glendale Comm., Glendale, CA 91208	1927	H. Rex Craig	11	11,536	509
Glen Oaks Comm., Centreville, MI 49032	1965	Philip G. Ward	9	1,454	73
Gloucester County, Sewell, NJ 08080	1967	Gary L. Reddig	8	3,743	138
Gogebic Comm., Ironwood, MI 49938	1932	C. Robert Bennett	11	1,517	85
Golden West, Huntington Beach, CA 92647	1966	Lee A. Stevens	4	20,960	246
Gordon Jr., Barnesville, GA 30204	1852	Jerry M. Williamson	4	1,400	60
Grand Rapids Jr., Grand Rapids, MI 49503	1914	Richard Calkins	10	9,800	465
Grays Harbor, Aberdeen, WA 98520	1930	Joseph A. Malik	4	1,075	205
Grayson County, Denison, TX 75020	1964	Jim M. Williams	11	4,923	201
Greater Hartford Comm., Hartford, CT 06105	1967	Arthur C. Banks Jr.	4	3,700	72
Greater New Haven State Tech., North Haven, CT 06473	1977	Thomas J. Sullivan	4	1,057	70
Greenfield Comm., Greenfield, MA 01301	1962	Theodore L. Provo	4	1,570	92
Green River Comm., Auburn, WA 98002	1965	James F. Chadbourne	4	6,082	167
Greenville Tech., Greenville, SC 29606	1962	Thomas E. Barton Jr.	4	6,385	400
Grossmont, El Cajon, CA 92020	1961	Donald E. Walker, Supt.	11	15,536	719
Guilford Tech. Comm., Jamestown, NC 27282	1958	Ray Needham	11	4,141	244
Gulf Coast Comm., Panama City, FL 32401	1957	Lawrence W. Tyree	4	4,000	140

Name, address	Year	Governing official affiliation, and highest degree offered		Stu-dents	Teach-ers
Hagerstown Jr., Hagerstown, MD 21740	1946	Atlee C. Kepler	8	2,456	141
Halifax Comm., Weldon, NC 27890	1967	Phillip W. Taylor	11	1,231	68
Harcum Jr., Bryn Mawr, PA 19010 (4)	1915	Norma F. Furst	0	890	72
Harford Comm., Bel Air, MD 21014	1957	Alfred C. O'Connell	11	4,706	301
Harrisburg Area Comm., Harrisburg, PA 17110	1964	Kenneth B. Woodbury	11	6,459	277
Harry M. Ayers State Tech., Anniston, AL 36201	1966	Pierce C. Cain	4	625	34
Hartford State Tech., Hartford, CT 06106	1946	Kenneth DeRego	4	1,871	51
Hartnell, Salinas, CA 93901	1920	James R. Haledt	9	7,560	260
Haskell Indian Jr., Lawrence, KS 66044	1884	Gerald E. Gipp	3	925	65
Hawkeye Inst. of Tech., Waterloo, IA 50704	1967	John E. Hawse, Supt.	11	2,047	132
Haywood Tech., Clyde, NC 28721	1964	Joseph H. Nanney	11	958	77
Heald Business, San Francisco, CA 94109	1863	NA	0	750	20
Heald Coll. Tech. Div., San Francisco, CA 94103	1863	James Deitz, V.P.	0	1,080	70
Henderson County Jr., Athens, TX 75751	1946	William C. Campion	11	2,743	125
Henry Ford Comm., Dearborn, MI 48128	1938	Stuart M. Bundy	9	17,364	810
Herkimer County Comm., Herkimer, NY 13350	1966	Robert McLaughlin	11	1,890	88
Hesser, Manchester, NH 03101	1900	Kenneth W. Galeucia	2	1,708	83
Hesston, Hesston, KS 67062	1909	Kirk Alliman	1	657	60
Hibbing Comm., Hibbing, MN 55746	1917	Orville A. Olson, Provost	4	794	49
Highland Comm., Freeport, IL 61032	1962	Joseph C. Piland	9	2,480	103
Highland Comm., Highland, KS 66035	1858	Bill R. Spencer	4	1,250	59
Highland Park Comm., Highland Park, MI 48203	1918	Chrystine R. Shack.	11	2,875	112
Highline Comm., Midway, WA 98032	1961	Shirley B. Gordon	4	10,460	426
Hilbert, Hamburg, NY 14075	1957	Sr. Edmunette Paczesny	0	677	66
Hill Jr., Hillsboro, TX 76645.	1923	W. R. Auvenshine	9	1,234	55
Hillsborough Comm., Tampa, FL 33622.	1968	Barbara D. Holmes.	4	11,340	508
Hiwassee, Madisonville, TN 37354	1849	NA	1	720	32
Hocking Tech., Nelsonville, OH 45764	1968	John J. Light	4	2,625	147
Holyoke Comm., Holyoke, MA 01040	1946	David M. Bartley	4	3,218	179
Housatonic Comm., Bridgeport, CT 06608	1966	Vincent S. Darnowski	4	2,693	112
Houston Comm. Coll. System, Houston, TX 77270	1971	J. B. Whiteley	11	31,996	1,400
Howard Coll. at Big Spring, Big Spring, TX 79720	1945	Charles D. Hays	11	1,085	80
Howard Comm., Columbia, MD 21044	1966	Dwight A. Burrill	11	3,650	221
Hudson County Comm., Jersey City, NJ 07306	1974	Walter N. Sheil	11	2,882	187
Hudson Valley Comm., Troy, NY 12180	1953	Joseph J. Bulmer	11	8,167	396
Hutchinson Comm., Hutchinson, KS 67501	1928	James H. Stringer	11	3,224	210
ICM School of Business, Pittsburgh, PA 15222	1963	NA	2	750	60
ICS Center for Degree Studies, Scranton, PA 18515	1975	David Crowther	2	6,000	40
Illinois Central, East Peoria, IL 61635	1967	Leon H. Perley	11	14,469	639
Illinois Eastern Comm., Frontier Comm. Fairfield, IL 62837	1976	Richard Mason	11	3,756	515
Illinois Eastern Comm., Lincoln Trail, Robinson, IL 62454	1969	Richard L. Sanders.	11	2,017	116
Illinois Eastern Comm., Olney Central, Olney, IL 62450	1960	Charles Novak	11	2,077	130
Illinois Eastern Comm., Wabash Valley, Mount Carmel, IL 62863	1960	Jim Benedict	11	2,709	142
Illinois Valley Comm., Oglesby, IL 61348	1924	Alfred E. Wisgoski	9	4,520	184
Imperial Valley, Imperial, CA 92251	1922	John A. DePaoli	11	5,200	323
Independence Comm., Independence, KS 67301	1925	Leon Foster	11	945	67
Indiana Univ. East, Richmond, IN 47374.	1971	Glenn A. Goerke	4	1,448	105
Indiana Vocational Tech.-Central Indiana, Indianapolis, IN 46202	1963	Meredith L. Carter, V.P./Dean	4	4,253	215
Indiana Vocational Tech.-Columbus, Columbus, IN 47201	1963	Harvey Poling, V.P./Dean	4	1,845	108
Indiana Vocational Tech.-Eastcentral, Muncie, IN 47302	1968	Richard L. Davidson, V.P./Dean	4	2,194	116
Indiana Vocational Tech.-Kokomo, Kokomo, IN 46901	1968	James B. Lansinger, V.P./Dean	4	1,494	98
Indiana Vocational Tech.-Northcentral, South Bend, IN 46619	1968	Carl F. Lutz, V.P./Dean	4	2,374	118
Indiana Vocational Tech.-Northeast, Fort Wayne, IN 46805.	1969	Jon L. Rupright, V.P./Dean	4	3,375	141
Indiana Vocational Tech.-Northwest, Gary, IN 46409	1963	Donald P. Belec, V.P./Dean.	4	3,176	125
Indiana Vocational Tech.-Southcentral, Sellersburg, IN 47172	1968	Carl F. Scott, V.P./Dean.	4	1,395	106
Indiana Vocational Tech.-Southwest, Evansville, IN 47710	1963	Jack J. Bainter, V.P./Dean	4	1,706	85
Indiana Vocational Tech.-Wabash Valley, Terre Haute, IN 47802	1966	Samuel Borden, V.P./Dean	4	1,559	80
Indiana Vocational Tech.-Whitewater, Richmond, IN 47374.	1963	Judith A. Redwine, V.P.	11	905	56
Indian Hills Comm., Ottumwa, IA 52501	1966	Lyle A. Hellyer	11	2,105	68
Indian River Comm., Fort Pierce, FL 33450	1960	Herman A. Heise	4	6,200	200
Indian Valley, Novato, CA 94947	1971	Constance Carroll	9	3,403	145
Instituto Comercial de Puerto Rico Jr., Hato Rey, PR 00919	1946	Enrique Pineiro	2	1,687	85
Instituto Technico Comercial Jr, Rio Piedras, PR 00926.	1948	NA	2	1,320	46
Inter American Univ. of Puerto Rico, Aguadilla Regional, Aguadilla, PR 00603	1957	Juan Colon, Dir.	0	2,379	118
Inter American Univ. of Puerto Rico, Barranquitas Regional, Barranquitas, PR 00615	1957	Vidal Rivera-Garcia, Dir.	0	1,249	53
Inter American Univ. of Puerto Rico, Fajardo Regional, Fajardo, PR 00648	1965	NA	0	1,750	76
Inter American Univ. of Puerto Rico, Guayama Regional, Guayama, PR 00654	1958	Maria Ortiz, Dir.	0	1,162	70
Inter American Univ. of Puerto Rico, Ponce Regional, Ponce, PR 00731	1962	Jose I. Correa, Dir.	0	1,951	97
Interboro Inst., New York, NY 10003	1888	Mischa Lazoff	2	1,100	40
Inver Hills Comm., Inver Grove Heights, MN 55075	1969	NA	4	4,000	186
Iowa Central Comm, Fort Dodge, IA 50501.	1966	Harvey D. Martin, Supt.	11	2,833	103
Iowa Lakes Comm., North Attendance Center, Estherville, IA 51334	1967	Richard H. Blacker	11	886	43
Iowa Lakes Comm., South Attendance Center, Emmetsburg, IA 50536	1967	Richard H. Blacker	11	875	57
Iowa Western Comm.-Council Bluffs Center, IA 51502	1966	Robert D. Looft	9	2,929	201
Isothermal Comm., Spindale, NC 28160	1965	Ben E. Fountain Jr.	4	2,650	162
Itasca Comm., Grand Rapids, MN 55744	1922	Lawrence N. Dukes, Provost	4	943	110
Itawamba Jr., Fulton, MS 38843	1947	W. O. Benjamin.	11	2,441	151
ITT Tech. Inst., Portland, OR 97266	1971	NA	2	726	25
Jackson Comm., Jackson, MI 49201	1928	Clyde LeTarte	8	8,000	300
Jackson State Comm., Jackson, TN 38301.	1967	James A. Hefner	4	2,981	112
James Sprunt Tech., Kenansville, NC 28349	1964	Carl D. Price	4	853	45
Jamestown Comm., Jamestown, NY 14701	1950	Paul A. Benke	11	4,371	229

Name, address	Year	Governing official affiliation, and highest degree offered		Stu-dents	Teach-ers
Jefferson, Hillsboro, MO 63050	1963	B. Ray Henry	11	2,361	123
Jefferson Comm., Watertown, NY 13601	1961	John T. Henderson	11	1,805	85
Jefferson Davis State Jr., Brewton, AL 36427	1965	George R. McCormick	4	846	47
Jefferson State Jr., Birmingham, AL 35215	1965	Judy M. Merritt	4	6,587	305
Jefferson Tech., Steubenville, OH 43952	1966	Fred S. Robie	11	1,654	108
J. F. Drake State Tech., Huntsville, AL 35811	1961	Johnny L. Harris	4	818	45
John A. Logan, Carterville, IL 62918	1967	Harold R. O'Neil	11	2,530	67
John C. Calhoun State Comm., Decatur, AL 35602	1965	James R. Chasteen	4	6,021	220
John M. Patterson State Tech., Montgomery, AL 36116	1962	J. L. Taunton	4	934	51
Johnson County Comm., Overland Park, KS 66210	1967	Charles J. Carlsen	11	7,698	343
Johnston Tech., Smithfield, NC 27577	1969	John L. Tart	4	1,850	125
John Tyler Comm., Chester, VA 23831	1967	Freddie W. Nicholas	11	4,020	163
John Wood Comm., Quincy, IL 62301	1974	Paul R. Heath	9	4,043	102
Joliet Jr., Joliet, IL 60436	1901	NA	11	11,078	600
Jones County Jr., Ellisville, MS 39437	1928	T. Terrell Tisdale	11	2,239	119
J. Sargeant Reynolds Comm., Richmond, VA 23241	1972	S. A. Burnette	4	10,560	488
Junior Coll. of Albany, Albany, NY 12208	1957	William F. Kahl	0	970	78
Kalamazoo Valley Comm., Kalamazoo, MI 49009	1966	Marilyn J. Schlack	11	7,895	245
Kankakee Comm., Kankakee, IL 60901	1966	Lilburn H. Horton Jr.	11	3,300	109
Kansas City Kansas Comm., Kansas City, KS 66112	1923	Alton L. Davies	8	3,300	222
Kansas Tech. Inst., Salina, KS 67401	1965	Thomas F. Creech	4	628	37
Kaskaskia, Centralia, IL 62801	1966	Paul L. Blowers	11	3,185	95
Kellogg Comm., Battle Creek, MI 49016	1956	Richard F. Whitmore	11	4,941	200
Kent State Univ., Ashtabula Campus, Ashtabula, OH 44004	1958	Paul A. Reichert, Dean	4	1,030	59
Kent State Univ., East Liverpool Campus, OH 43920	1967	Richard Q. King, Dean	4	653	40
Kent State Univ., Stark Campus, Canton, OH 44720	1967	William G. Bittle, Dean	4	1,776	98
Kent State Univ., Trumbull Campus, Warren, OH 44483	1910	Dennis L. Smith, Dean	4	1,540	85
Kent State Univ., Tuscarawas Campus, New Philadelphia, OH 44663	1962	Francis E. Hazard, Dir.	4	944	51
Keystone Jr., La Plume, PA 18440	1868	John B. Hibbard	0	697	74
Kilgore, Kilgore, TX 75662	1935	Stewart H. McLaurin	11	4,389	181
King's River Comm., Reedley, CA 93654	1926	Richard J. Giese	11	3,308	122
Kirkwood Comm., Cedar Rapids, IA 52406	1966	Bill F. Stewart	11	5,917	461
Kirtland Comm., Roscommon, MI 48653	1966	Raymond D. Homer	11	1,335	69
Kishwaukee, Malta, IL 60150	1967	Norman L. Jenkins	11	3,707	270
Labette Comm., Parsons, KS 67357	1923	Gery C. Hochanadel	8	2,270	171
Lackawanna Jr., Scranton, PA 18505	1894	John X. McConkey	0	1,132	97
Lake City Comm., Lake City, FL 32055	1962	Charles M. Greene	4	2,874	232
Lake Land, Mattoon, IL 61938	1966	Robert D. Webb	11	3,517	285
Lakeland Comm., Mentor, OH 44060	1967	James Catanzaro	11	9,234	390
Lake Michigan, Benton Harbor, MI 49022	1946	Walter F. Browe	4	3,324	250
Lake Region Comm., Devils Lake, ND 58301	1941	William L. Taylor	11	602	39
Lakeshore Tech. Inst., Cleveland, WI 53015	1967	Frederick J. Nierode, Dir.	11	3,415	105
Lake-Sumter Comm., Leesburg, FL 32748	1961	Robert S. Palinchak	11	1,344	114
Lake Tahoe Comm., South Lake Tahoe, CA 95702	1975	James W. D ke	9	1,491	82
Lakewood Comm., White Bear Lake, MN 55110	1967	Carl Gerber	4	4,440	100
Lane Comm., Eugene, OR 97405	1964	Eldon G. Schafer	11	7,920	343
Laney, Oakland, CA 94607	1953	Lawrence A. Davis	4	11,687	329
Lansing Comm., Lansing, MI 48901	1957	Philip J. Gannon	11	20,407	1,000
Laramie County Comm., Cheyenne, WY 82001	1968	Harlan L. Heglar	8	2,661	162
Laredo Jr., Laredo, TX 78040	1946	Domingo Arechiga	11	3,100	160
Lasell Jr., Newton, MA 02166 (3)	1851	Peter T. Mitchell	0	650	77
Lassen, Susanville, CA 96130	1925	Warren Sorenson	11	2,605	200
Latter-Day Saints Business, Salt Lake City, UT 84111	1886	R. F. Kirkham	1	622	35
Lawson State Comm., Birmingham, AL 35221	1965	Jesse J. Lewis	4	1,057	47
Lee, Baytown, TX 77520	1934	Robert C. Cloud	9	4,832	202
Lees-McRae, Banner Elk, NC 28604	1900	NA	1	710	40
Lehigh County Comm., Schnecksville, PA 18078	1967	Robert L. Barthlow	11	3,140	120
Lenoir Comm., Kinston, NC 28501	1960	Jesse L. McDaniel	4	2,119	105
Lewis and Clark Comm., Godfrey, IL 62035	1970	Wilbur R. L. Trimpe	9	5,593	300
Lima Tech., Lima, OH 45804	1971	James S. Biddle	4	2,323	115
Lincoln Land Comm., Springfield, IL 62708	1967	Robert L. Poorman	11	7,067	391
Lockyear, Indianapolis Campus, Indianapolis, IN 46202	1893	Tony Payne	2	1,300	15
Long Beach City, Long Beach, CA 90808	1927	John T. McCuen	4	32,327	1,320
Longview Comm., Lee's Summit, MO 64063	1969	Aldo W. Leker	9	5,410	178
Lorain County Comm., Elyria, OH 44035	1963	Omar L. Olson	11	6,692	311
Lord Fairfax Comm., Middletown, VA 22645	1969	William H. McCoy	11	1,762	74
Los Angeles City, Los Angeles, CA 90029	1929	Stelle Feuers	9	20,169	810
Los Angeles Harbor, Wilmington, CA 90744	1949	James L. Heinselman	11	12,500	436
Los Angeles Metropolitan, Los Angeles, CA 90015 (2)	1972	NA	9	10,000	200
Los Angeles Mission, San Fernando, CA 91340	1974	Lowell J. Erickson	11	4,589	127
Los Angeles Pierce, Woodland Hills, CA 91371	1947	Herbert W. Ravetch	4	23,721	596
Los Angeles Southwest, Los Angeles, CA 90047	1967	Walter C. McIntosh	4	7,165	203
Los Angeles Trade-Tech., Los Angeles, CA 90015	1925	Thomas L. Stevens Jr.	9	18,000	558
Los Angeles Valley, Van Nuys, CA 91401	1949	NA	11	26,610	618
Louisburg, Louisburg, NC 27549	1787	J. Allen Norris Jr.	1	710	45
Louisiana State Univ. at Alexandria, Alexandria, LA 71301	1960	James W. Firnberg	4	1,713	91
Louisiana State Univ. at Eunice, Eunice, LA 70535	1967	Anthony Mumphrey	4	1,528	71
Lower Columbia, Longview, WA 98632	1934	Vernon R. Pickett	4	4,000	145
Lurleen B. Wallace State Jr., Andalusia, AL 36420	1969	William H. McWhorter	4	860	49
Luzerne County Comm., Nanticoke, PA 18634	1966	Thomas J. Moran	8	3,940	213
MacCormac Jr., Chicago, IL 60604	1904	Gordon C. Borchardt	0	709	50
Macomb Comm., Warren, MI 48093	1954	Albert L. Lorenzo	11	29,090	1,011
Macon Jr., Macon, GA 31297	1911	William W. Wright Jr.	4	2,962	101
Madison Area Tech., Madison, WI 53703	1968	Norman P. Mitby, Dir.	9	6,889	350
Manatee Jr., Bradenton, FL 33507	1957	Stephen J. Korcheck	4	6,604	218
Manchester Comm., Manchester, CT 06040	1963	William E. Vincent	4	5,000	200
Maple Woods Comm., Kansas City, MO 64156	1969	Stephen R. Brainard	11	2,826	122
Maria, Albany, NY 12208	1958	Sr. Laureen Fitzgerald	0	785	59
Maricopa Tech Comm., Phoenix, AZ 85034	1968	Charles A. Green	8	3,729	165
Marion Tech., Marion, OH 43302	1971	John Richard Bryson	12	1,516	80
Marshalltown Comm., Marshalltown, IA 50158	1927	Paul Kegel, Dean	9	1,435	77

Name, address	Year	Governing official affiliation, and highest degree offered		Stu-dents	Teach-ers
Martin Comm., Williamston, NC 27892	1968	W. Travis Martin	4	704	51
Mary Holmes, West Point, MS 39773	1892	Joseph A. Gore	1	655	30
Massachusetts Bay Comm., Wellesley Hills, MA 02181	1961	Roger A. Van Winkle	4	4,360	231
Massasoit Comm., Brockton, MA 02402	1968	Gerard F. Burke	4	2,689	138
Mattatuck Comm., Waterbury, CT 06708	1967	Richard L. Sanders	4	3,597	148
Mayland Tech., Spruce Pine, NC 28777	1971	O.M. Blake	11	720	46
McCook Comm., McCook, NE 69001	1926	Harold Deselms	11	630	55
McDowell Tech., Marion, NC 28752	1964	John A. Price	4	648	41
McHenry County, Crystal Lake, IL 60014	1967	Robert C. Bartlett	11	3,979	143
McIntosh, Dover, NH 03820	1896	Richard F. Waldo	2	612	27
McLennan Comm., Waco, TX 76708	1965	Wilbur A. Ball	8	4,091	208
Mendocino, Ukiah, CA 95482	1973	Leroy R. Lowery	11	3,603	160
Merced, Merced, CA 95340	1962	Tom K. Harris Jr.	11	8,500	380
Mercer County Comm., West Windsor, NJ 08520	1966	John P. Hanley	8	5,372	322
Meridian, Jr., Meridian, MS 39301	1937	William F. Scaggs	11	2,800	151
Merritt, Oakland, CA 94619	1953	Norma J. Tucker	11	9,129	325
Mesabi Comm., Virginia, MN 55792	1918	Richard Kohlase, Provost	4	933	35
Metropolitan Tech. Comm., Omaha, NE 68103	1974	J. Richard Gilliland	11	6,632	296
Miami-Dade Comm., Miami, FL 33176	1960	Robert McCabe	11	42,226	2,299
Miami-Jacobs Jr. Coll. of Business, Dayton, OH 45401	1860	Charles G. Campbell	2	615	34
Miami Univ.-Hamilton Campus, Hamilton, OH 45011	1968	M. Douglas Reed, Dir.	4	1,777	51
Miami Univ.-Middletown Campus, Middletown, OH 45042	1966	C. Eugene Bennett, Exec. Dir.	4	1,689	143
Middle Georgia, Cochran, GA 31014	1884	Louis C. Alderman Jr.	4	1,395	105
Middlesex Comm., Middletown, CT 06457	1966	Robert A. Chapman	4	2,306	75
Middlesex Comm., Bedford, MA 01730	1970	James E. Houlihan Jr.	4	1,440	100
Middlesex County, Edison, NJ 08818	1964	Rose M. Channing	8	12,590	500
Midland, Midland, TX 79701	1969	Jess H. Parrish	11	3,255	151
Midlands Tech., Columbia, SC 29202	1974	James R. Morris	11	5,943	457
Mid Michigan Comm., Harrison, MI 48625	1965	Eugene W. Gillaspy	11	2,018	85
Mid Plains Comm., North Platte, NE 69101	1965	Kenneth L. Aten	9	1,800	74
Mid State Tech. Inst., Wisconsin Rapids, WI 54494	1967	M. H. Schneeberg, Dir.	11	2,020	89
Miles Comm., Miles City, MT 59301	1939	Judson H. Flower	11	1,032	54
Milwaukee Area Tech., Milwaukee, WI 53203	1912	Rus F. Slicker, Dir.	9	12,499	1,991
Mineral Area, Flat River, MO 63601	1922	Dixie Kohn	9	1,604	70
Minneapolis Comm., Minneapolis, MN 55403	1965	Earl. W. Bowman	4	3,050	161
MiraCosta, Oceanside, CA 92056	1934	H. Deon Holt	4	8,515	358
Mission, Santa Clara, CA 95054	1977	NA	11	9,433	375
Mississippi County, Blytheville, AR 72315	1975	John P. Sullins	4	1,180	65
Mississippi Delta Jr., Moorhead, MS 38761	1926	J. T. Hall	9	1,698	110
Mississippi Gulf Coast Jr., Jackson County Campus, Gautier, MS 39553	1965	Curtis L. Davis, Dean	9	1,550	122
Mississippi Gulf Coast Jr., Jefferson Davis Campus, Gulfport, MS 39501	1965	Glen W. Cadle, Exec. Dean	11	2,200	165
Mississippi Gulf Coast Jr., Perkinston Campus, MS 39573	1925	Clyde E. Strickland, V.P.	11	802	55
Mitchell, New London, CT 06320	1938	Robert C. Weller	0	910	38
Mitchell Comm., Statesville, NC 28677	1852	Charles C. Poindexter	4	1,453	76
Moberly Area Jr., Moberly, MO 65270	1927	Andrew Komar Jr.	11	1,200	68
Modesto Jr., Modesto, CA 95350	1921	Louis E. Zellers	11	10,996	454
Mohave Comm., Kingman, AZ 86401	1971	Charles W. Hall	4	3,297	216
Mohawk Valley Comm., Utica, NY 13501	1946	Michael I. Schafer	4	6,000	427
Mohegan Comm., Norwich, CT 06360	1969	Myrna R. Miller	4	2,023	97
Monroe Business Inst., Bronx, NY 10468	1933	Stephen J. Jerome	2	1,091	49
Monroe Comm., Rochester, NY 14623	1961	Peter A. Spina	11	11,138	547
Monroe County Comm., Monroe, MI 48161	1964	Ronald Campbell	8	2,706	98
Montcalm Comm., Sidney, MI 48885	1963	Herbert N. Stoutenburg	11	1,207	63
Monterey Peninsula, Monterey, CA 93940	1947	Max R. Tadlock	4	8,405	225
Montgomery-Germantown Campus, Germantown, MD 20874	1975	Stanley M. Dahlman, Provost	11	2,561	104
Montgomery-Rockville Campus, Rockville, MD 20850	1965	Antoinette P. Hastings, Provost	11	13,060	529
Montgomery-Takoma Park Campus, Takoma Park, MD 20912	1946	O. Robert Brown Jr., Provost	11	4,345	174
Montgomery County Comm., Blue Bell, PA 19422	1964	Edmond A. Watters III	8	7,993	347
Moorpark, Moorpark, CA 93021	1967	W. Ray Hearon	8	8,557	415
Moraine Park Tech. Inst., Fond du Lac Campus, WI 54935	1967	John J. Shanahan, Dir.	9	3,011	247
Moraine Valley Comm., Palos Hills, IL 60465	1967	Fred Gaskin	11	11,474	447
Morgan Comm., Fort Morgan, CO 80701	1967	Larry D. Carter	4	643	72
Morton, Cicero, IL 60650	1924	Robert V. Moriarty	4	4,345	200
Motlow State Comm., Tullahoma, TN 37388	1969	Harry D. Wagner	4	2,244	96
Mountain Empire Comm., Big Stone Gap, VA 24219	1972	Victor Ficker	4	2,700	90
Mt. Hood Comm., Gresham, OR 97030	1966	R. Stephen Nicholson	11	7,691	566
Mt. San Antonio, Walnut, CA 91789	1946	John D. Randall	9	22,934	681
Mt. San Jacinto, San Jacinto, CA 92383	1963	Dennis M. Mayer	9	3,678	156
Mount Wachusett Comm., Gardner, MA 01440	1963	Arthur F. Haley	4	1,684	87
Murray State, Tishomingo, OK 73460	1908	Clyde R. Kindell	4	1,501	60
Muscatine Comm., Muscatine, IA 52761	1929	Lee J. Betts	4	850	45
Muskegon Business, Muskegon, MI 49442	1888	Robert D. Jewell	0	1,259	50
Muskegon Comm., Muskegon, MI 49442	1926	John G. Thompson	8	4,611	195
Napa Valley, Napa, CA 94558	1940	William H. Feddersen	11	6,371	294
Nash Tech., Rocky Mount, NC 27801	1968	J. Reid Parrott Jr.	4	1,554	90
Nashville State Tech. Inst., Nashville, TN 37209	1970	Howard J. Lawrence	4	5,879	251
Nassau Comm., Garden City, NY 11530	1959	Sean Fanelli	11	21,961	1,285
Natl. Education Center-Arkansas Coll. of Tech. Campus, Little Rock, AR 72207	1969	Lyle R. Groth, Dir.	2	650	26
Natl. Education Center-Brown Inst. Campus, Minneapolis, MN 55406	1946	NA	2	1,500	69
Natl. Education Center-Kentucky Coll. of Tech. Campus, Louisville, KY 40216	1946	NA	2	979	39
Natl. Education Center-Tampa Tech. Inst. Campus, FL 33610	1948	NA	2	1,511	56
Natl. School of Health Tech., Philadelphia, PA 19103	1963	NA	2	600	24
Navajo Comm., Tsaile, AZ 86556	1968	Dean Jackson	3	1,418	148
Navarro, Corsicana, TX 75110	1946	Kenneth P. Walker	11	2,363	118
Nebraska Western, Scottsbluff, NE 69361	1926	John N. Harms	11	1,398	72
Neosho County Comm., Chanute, KS 66720	1936	J. C. Sanders	8	892	83
Newbury Jr., Boston, MA 02115	1962	Edward J. Tassinari	0	1,134	61
New Mexico Jr., Hobbs, NM 88240	1965	Robert A. Anderson Jr.	11	2,309	96
New Mexico State Univ.-Alamogordo, Alamogordo, NM 88310	1958	Charles R. Reidlinger, Dir.	4	1,296	28

Name, address	Year	Governing official affiliation, and highest degree offered		Students	Teachers
New Mexico State Univ.-Carlsbad, Carlsbad, NM 88220	1950	Shelton W. Marlow, Dir.	4	706	55
New River Comm., Dublin, VA 24084	1969	H. Randall Edwards	4	3,180	168
Niagra County Comm., Sanborn, NY 14132	1962	Donald J. Donato	11	4,327	317
Nicolet Coll. and Tech. Inst., Rhinelander, WI 54501	1968	Richard J. Brown, Dir.	11	1,265	92
Normandale Comm., Bloomington, MN 55431	1968	Dale A. Lorenz	4	6,275	220
Northampton County Area Comm., Bethlehem, PA 18017	1967	Robert J. Kopecek	11	4,608	221
North Arkansas Comm., Harrison, AR 72601	1974	Bill Baker	11	881	75
North Central Michigan, Petoskey, MI 49770	1958	Alfred D. Shankland	8	1,681	87
North Central Tech., Mansfield, OH 44906	1961	Byron E. Kee	4	1,962	113
North Central Tech. Inst., Wausau, WI 54401	1912	Dwight, E. Davis, Dir.	9	3,983	139
North Country Comm., Saranac Lake, NY 12983	1967	David W. Petty	11	1,448	75
North Dakota State School of Science, Wahpeton, ND 58075	1903	Clair T. Blikre	4	3,398	185
Northeast Alabama State Jr., Rainsville, AL 35986	1963	Charles M. Pendley	4	998	63
Northeastern Jr., Sterling, CO 80751	1941	Marvin W. Weiss	11	1,537	72
Northeastern Oklahoma A&M, Miami, OK 74354	1919	Bobby R. Wright	4	3,044	110
Northeast Iowa Tech. Inst.-South Center, Peosta, IA 52068	1970	Donald L. Roby, Asst. Supt.	11	625	49
Northeast Mississippi Jr., Booneville, MS 38829	1948	Harold T. White	9	3,300	120
Northeast Tech. Comm., Norfolk, NE 68701	1973	Robert P. Cox.	4	1,686	115
Northern Essex Comm., Haverhill MA 01830	1960	John R. Dimitry	4	4,047	367
Northern Nevada Comm., Elko, NV 89801	1967	William J. Berg	4	1,746	125
Northern New Mexico Comm., El Rito, NM 87530	1909	Frank A. Serrano III	4	1,846	140
Northern Oklahoma, Tonkawa, OK 74653	1901	Edwin E. Vineyard	4	1,731	79
Northern Virginia Comm., Annandale, VA 22003	1965	Richard J. Ernst	4	34,482	1,410
North Florida Jr., Madison, FL 32340	1958	Robert Ramsay.	4	915	42
North Harris County, Houston, TX 77073	1972	Joe A. Airola	11	9,495	350
North Hennepin Comm., Minneapolis, MN 55445	1966	John Heiling.	4	4,950	175
North Iowa Area Comm., Mason City, IA	1918	David Buettner, Supt.	11	2,208	166
North Lake, Irving, TX 75038	1977	James F. Horton Jr.	8	5,151	206
Northland Comm., Thief River Falls, MN 56701	1965	T. A. Easton.	4	617	33
Northland Pioneer, Holbrook, AZ 86025	1974	Marvin L. Vasher	11	6,377	492
North Seattle Comm., Seattle, WA 98103	1970	Cecil Baxter Jr..	4	7,352	272
North Shore Comm., Beverly, MA 01915	1965	George Traicoff.	4	2,737	120
Northwest Comm., Powell, WY 82435	1946	Sinclair Orendorff	11	1,370	140
Northwestern Business-Tech. Center, Lima, OH 45805	1920	Loren R. Jarvis.	2	710	70
Northwestern Connecticut Comm., Winsted, CT 06098	1965	Regina M. Duffy	4	2,371	85
Northwestern Electronics Inst., Columbia Heights, MN 55421	1930	David Arneson	0	958	65
Northwestern Michigan, Traverse City, MI 49684	1951	George T. Miller	11	3,432	123
Northwest Mississippi Jr., Senatobia, MS 38668	1927	Henry B. Koon	4	3,008	164
Northwest Tech., Archbold, OH 43502	1968	James O Miller	4	920	79
Norwalk Comm., Norwalk, CT 06854	1961	William H. Schwab	4	3,511	105
Norwalk State Tech., Norwalk, CT 06854.	1961	William M. Krummel	4	800	100
Oakland Comm., Bloomfield Hills, MI 48013	1964	Robert F. Roelofs	11	25,682	642
Oakton Comm., Des Plaines, IL 60016	1969	William A. Koehnline	9	8,639	392
Ocean County, Toms River, NJ 08753	1964	Milton Shaw.	8	3,718	225
Odessa, Odessa, TX 79762	1946	Philip T. Speegle	9	4,098	224
Ohio State Univ. Agricultural Tech. Inst., Wooster, OH 44691	1970	Dan D. Garrison, Dir.	4	705	33
Ohlone, Fremont, CA 94539	1967	Peter Blomerley	11	8,294	300
Okaloosa-Walton Jr., Niceville, FL 32578	1963	J. E. McCracken	11	3,825	170
Oklahoma City Comm., Oklahoma City, OK 73159	1969	Donald L. Newport	4	7,721	282
Oklahoma State Univ. School of Tech. Training, Okmulgee, OK 74447.	1946	Robert Klabenes, Dir.	4	3,100	160
Oklahoma State Univ. Tech. Inst., Oklahoma City, OK 73107	1961	Philip P. Chandler, Dir..	4	2,800	146
Olympia Tech. Comm., Olympia, WA 98502	1970	Kenneth Minnaert	4	3,394	175
Olympic, Bremerton, WA 98310	1946	Henry M. Milander	4	6,009	259
Onondaga Comm., Syracuse, NY 13215	1962	Andreas A. Paloumpis	11	7,642	300
Orangeburg-Calhoun Tech., Orangeburg, SC 29115	1966	M. Rudolph Groomes	11	976	177
Orange Coast, Costa Mesa, CA 92626	1947	S. Arthur Martinez	11	26,691	877
Orange County Comm., Middletown, NY 10940	1950	Mary M. Norman	11	5,425	260
Otero Jr., La Junta, CO 81050	1941	W. L. McDivitt	4	850	52
Owens Tech., Toledo, OH 43699	1966	Jacob H. See	4	4,351	250
Oxnard, Oxnard, CA 93033	1975	Edward W. Robings	8	5,749	255
Palm Beach Jr., Lake Worth, FL 33461	1933	Edward M. Eissey	4	11,600	467
Palomar, San Marcos, CA 92069	1946	Omar M. Scheidt	11	17,344	651
Palo Verde, Blythe, CA 92225	1947	Kirk Avery	9	620	37
Panola Jr., Carthage, TX 75633	1947	Gary McDaniel	8	1,094	47
Paris Jr., Paris, TX 75460	1924	Dennis F. Michaelis	11	2,186	128
Parkersburg Comm., Parkersburg, WV 26101	1971	Eldon L. Miller	4	3,419	166
Parkland, Champaign, IL 61821	1967	William M. Staerkel	9	9,199	529
Parks, Denver CO 80221	1895	Morgan Landry, C.E.O.	2	629	26
Pasadena City, Pasadena, CA 91106	1924	John W. Casey	9	19,991	845
Pasco-Hernando Comm., Dade City, FL 33525	1972	Milton O. Jones.	4	3,332	247
Passaic County, Paterson, NJ 07509	1968	Gustavo A. Mellander	8	2,894	198
Patrick Henry Comm., Martinsville, VA 24112	1962	Max F. Wingett.	4	1,489	80
Patrick Henry State Jr., Monroeville, AL 36460	1965	James A. Allen	4	671	32
Paul D. Camp Comm., Franklin, VA 23851	1971	Michael B. McCall	4	1,118	65
Paul Smith's, Paul Smiths, NY 12970	1937	Harry K. Miller Jr.	0	920	80
Pearl River Jr., Poplarville, MS 39470	1909	Marvin R. White.	4	1,692	107
Peirce Jr., Philadelphia, PA 19102	1865	Raymond C. Lewin.	0	2,118	98
Peninsula, Port Angeles, WA 98362	1961	Paul G. Cornaby	4	870	47
Pennsylvania State Univ.-Altoona Campus, Altoona, PA 16603	1929	Robert L. Smith.	12	1,967	110
Pennsylvania State Univ.-Beaver Campus, Monaca, PA 15061	1964	David B. Otto, Exec. Officer.	12	1,096	53
Pennsylvania State Univ.-Berks Campus, Reading, PA 19608	1924	Frederick H. Gaige.	12	959	53
Pennsylvania State Univ.-Delaware County Campus, Media, PA 19063	1966	John D. Vairo, Exec. Officer.	12	1,203	67
Pennsylvania State Univ.-DuBois Campus, DuBois, PA 15801	1935	Jacqueline Schoch.	12	655	41
Pennsylvania State Univ.-Fayette Campus, Uniontown, PA 15401.	1934	Albert Skomra, Exec. Officer.	12	845	50
Pennsylvania State Univ.-Hazelton Campus, PA 18201	1934	William J. David, Exec. Officer.	12	1,056	52
Pennsylvania State Univ.-McKeesport Campus, PA 15132	1947	Herbert G. McGibbeny,	12	1,246	58
Pennsylvania State Univ.-Mont Alto Campus, PA 17237	1929	Vernon L. Shockley	12	848	48
Pennsylvania State Univ. New Kensington Campus, New Kensington, PA 15068	1958	Robert D. Arbuckle.	12	1,071	44
Pennsylvania State Univ.-Ogontz Campus, Abington, PA 19001	1950	Robert A. Bernoff, Exec. Officer	12	2,140	115

Name, address	Year	Governing official, affiliation, and highest degree offered	Stu-dents	Teach-ers
Pennsylvania State Univ.-Schuylkill Campus, Schuylkill Haven, PA 17972	1934	Wayne Lammie, Exec. Officer . 12	808	36
Pennsylvania State Univ.-Shenango Valley Campus, Sharon, PA 16146	1965	Vincent De Sanctis 12	762	47
Pennsylvania State Univ.-Wilkes-Barre Campus, PA 18708	1916	James H. Ryan, Exec. Officer . 12	689	38
Pennsylvania State Univ.-Worthington Scranton Campus, Dunmore, PA 18512	1923	James D. Gallagher 12	1,082	62
Pennsylvania State Univ.-York Campus, York, PA 17403	1926	Edward M. Elias, Exec. Officer . 12	1,067	59
Penn Valley Comm., Kansas City, MO 64111	1969	Andrew V. Stevenson 9	5,917	208
Pensacola Jr., Pensacola, FL 32504	1948	Horace E. Hartsell 4	16,673	600
Phillips Coll. of New Orleans, New Orleans, LA 70121	1970	Jessy Adams 2	1,000	51
Phillips County Comm., Helena AR 72342	1965	John W. Easley 11	1,557	90
Piedmont Tech., Roxboro, NC 27573	1970	Edward W. Cox 4	757	50
Piedmont Tech., Greenwood, SC 29646	1966	Lex D. Walters 4	1,700	175
Piedmont Virginia Comm., Charlottesville, VA 22901	1972	George B. Vaughan 4	3,348	160
Pikes Peak Comm., Colorado Springs, CO 80906	1969	Donald W. McInnis 4	6,025	200
Pima Comm., Tucson, AZ 85709	1966	S. James Manilla 4	21,780	1,026
Pitt Comm., Greenville, NC 27835	1961	Charles E. Russell 11	2,771	110
Pittsburgh Inst. of Aeronautics, Pittsburgh, PA 15236	1929	Ivan D. Livi 0	600	28
Polk Comm., Winter Haven, FL 33880	1964	Maryly VanLeer Peck 4	5,400	250
Porterville, Porterville, CA 93257	1927	Paul D. Alcantra 4	2,435	110
Portland Comm., Portland, OR 97219	1961	John H. Anthony 11	20,271	1,647
Potomac State Coll. of West Virginia Univ., Keyser, WV 26726	1901	James L. McBee Jr. 4	1,105	60
Prairie State, Chicago Heights, IL 60411	1958	Richard C. Creal 11	6,400	410
Prince George's Comm., Largo, MD 20772	1958	Robert I. Bickford. 8	15,354	645
Pueblo Comm., Pueblo, CO 81004	1979	Ron Meek 4	941	43
Quincy Jr., Quincy, MA 02169	1958	Lawrence P. Creedon 10	1,332	173
Quinebaug Valley Comm., Danielson, CT 06239	1971	Robert E. Miller 4	936	46
Quinsigamond Comm., Worcester, MA 01606	1963	Clifford Peterson 4	2,266	174
Randolph Tech., Asheboro, NC 27203	1962	Merton H. Branson 4	1,189	55
Ranger Jr., Ranger, TX 76470	1926	Jack M. Elsom 12	800	55
Rappahannock Comm., Glenns, VA 23149	1970	John H. Upton 11	712	59
Reading Area Comm., Reading, PA 19603	1971	Lewis W. Ogle 9	1,353	76
Red Rocks Comm., Golden, CO 80401	1967	Richard E. Wilson 4	5,559	247
Rend Lake, Ina, IL 62846	1967	Harry J. Braun 4	3,114	215
RETS Electronic Inst., Birmingham, AL 35234	1974	Gene Smythe 2	839	18
Richard Bland, Petersburg, VA 23805	1961	Clarence Maze Jr. 4	1,090	60
Richland, Dallas, TX 75243	1972	Stephen Mittelstet 11	13,902	570
Richland Comm., Decatur, IL 62526	1971	John M. Kirk. 9	3,200	191
Richmond Tech., Hamlet, NC 28345	1964	R. Kenneth Melvin 4	1,092	111
Ricks, Rexburg, ID 83440	1888	Bruce C. Hafen. 1	6,614	310
Rio Hondo Comm., Whittier, CA 90608	1960	Herbert M. Sussman. 11	11,850	347
Riverside City, Riverside, CA 92506	1916	Charles A. Kane 11	15,738	471
Roane State Comm., Harriman, TN 37748	1971	Cuyler A. Dunbar 4	3,550	115
Roanoke-Chowan Tech., Ahoskie, NC 27910	1967	David W. Sink Jr. 4	650	53
Robert Morris, Carthage Campus, Carthage, IL 62321	1965	J. R. McCartan 0	650	30
Robert Morris, Chicago Campus, Chicago, IL 60601	1965	Richard D. Pickett 0	867	46
Rochester Comm., Rochester, MN 55904	1915	Geraldine A. Evans. 4	3,278	160
Rockingham Comm., Wentworth, NC 27375	1965	N. J. Owens Jr. 4	2,094	138
Rockland Comm., Suffern, NY 10901	1959	Seymour Eskow 11	7,798	366
Rock Valley, Rockford, IL 61101	1964	Karl J. Jacobs 9	8,460	555
Rogers State, Claremore, OK 74017	1971	Richard H. Mosier 4	2,558	106
Rogue Comm., Grants Pass, OR 97526	1971	Howard D. Sims 4	2,842	267
Rose State, Midwest City, OK 73110	1971	Joe T. Packnett. 11	9,250	272
Rowan Tech., Salisbury, NC 28144	1963	Richard L. Brownell 4	2,100	130
Roxbury Comm., Boston, MA 02115	1973	Kenneth W. Haskins 4	625	41
Saddleback Comm., Mission Viejo, CA 92692	1967	William O. Jay 11	23,431	725
St. Augustine Comm., Chicago, IL 60640	1980	NA 1	892	70
St. Bernard Parish Comm., Chalmette, LA 70043	1967	NA 11	616	21
St. Johns River Comm., Palatka, FL 32077	1958	R. L. McLendon Jr. 4	1,654	96
St. Louis Comm. Coll. at Florissant Valley, St. Louis, MO 63135	1963	David Harris. 9	12,069	241
St. Louis Comm. at Forest Park, St. Louis, MO 63110	1962	Vernon O. Crawley 9	7,905	371
St. Louis Comm. at Meramec, Kirkwood, MO 63122	1963	Ralph R. Doty. 9	12,784	410
St. Mary's Coll. of O'Fallon, O'Fallon, MO 63366	1921	Sr. Elizabeth Weiman 1	617	59
St. Mary's Jr., Minneapolis, MN 55454	1964	Sr. Anne Joachim Moore 1	890	90
St. Petersburg Jr., St. Petersburg, FL 33733	1927	Carl M. Kuttler Jr. 11	16,358	447
St. Philip's, San Antonio, TX 78203	1898	Gloria Jackson 9	6,920	464
Sampson Tech., Clinton, NC 28328	1965	Clifton W. Paderick. 11	876	66
San Antonio, San Antonio, TX 78284	1925	Max Castillo. 11	21,198	1,022
San Bernardino Valley, San Bernardino, CA 92403	1926	Arthur M. Jensen 11	15,256	413
Sandhills Comm., Carthage, NC 28327	1963	Raymond A. Stone 11	1,937	105
San Diego City., San Diego, CA 92101	1914	Allen J. Repashy 11	19,924	960
San Diego Mesa, San Diego, CA 92111	1962	Allen Brooks 9	23,000	1,110
San Diego Miramar, San Diego, CA 92126	1969	George F. Yee 11	3,681	303
San Jacinto-Central Campus, Pasadena, TX 77505	1961	Monte Blue 11	9,591	238
San Jacinto-North Campus, Houston, TX 77049	1974	Edwin E. Lehr. 11	3,650	165
San Jacinto-South Campus, Houston, TX 77089	1979	Parker Williams 11	3,101	122
San Joaquin Delta, Stockton, CA 95207	1935	Lawrence A. DeRicco 9	17,772	534
San Jose City, San Jose, CA 95128.	1921	Theodore I. Murguia 9	13,253	541
San Juan, Farmington, NM 87401	1958	James C. Henderson 8	1,868	105
Santa Ana, Santa Ana, CA 92706	1915	J. William Wenrich 9	25,772	1,056
Santa Barbara City, Santa Barbara, CA 93109	1908	Peter R. MacDougall. 9	10,823	391
Santa Fe Comm., Gainesville, FL 32601	1966	Alan J. Robertson 11	7,304	419
Santa Monica, Santa Monica, CA 90405	1929	Richard L. Moore 11	20,096	743
Santa Rosa Jr., Santa Rosa, CA 95401.	1918	Roy Mikalson 11	22,448	334
Sauk Valley, Dixon, IL 61021	1965	Hal Garner 9	3,500	180
Schenectady County Comm., Schenectady, NY 12305	1968	Wright L. Lassiter Jr. 11	1,913	168
Schoolcraft, Livonia, MI 48152	1961	Richard W. McDowell 9	8,220	350
Scott Comm., Bettendorf, IA 45722	1966	John T. Blong 11	2,244	121
S. D. Bishop State Jr., Mobile, AL 36690	1965	Yvonne Kennedy 4	1,619	51
Seattle Central Comm., Seattle, WA 98122	1966	Ernest Martinez. 4	8,483	345
Seminole Comm., Sanford, FL 32771	1966	Earl S. Weldon 11	5,172	349

Name, address	Year	Governing official affiliation, and highest degree offered		Stu-dents	Teach-ers
Seminole Jr., Seminole, OK 74868	1931	Gregory G. Fitch	4	1,437	67
Seward County Comm., Liberal, KS 67901	1969	James E. Hooper	4	1,418	71
Shawnee State Comm., Portsmouth, OH 45662	1975	Frank C. Taylor	4	1,910	167
Shelby State Comm., Memphis, TN 38104	1970	Raymond C. Bowen	4	5,009	286
Shelton State Comm., Tuscaloosa, AL 35404	1979	Leo Sumner	4	2,898	31
Sheridan, Sheridan WY 82801	1948	Gordon A. Ward	11	1,188	133
Shoreline Comm., Seattle, WA 98133	1964	Ronald E. Bell	4	5,735	285
Sinclair Comm., Dayton, OH 45402	1887	David H. Ponitz	11	18,662	829
Skagit Valley, Mount Vernon, WA 98273	1926	James M. Ford	4	1,818	241
Skyline, San Bruno, CA 94066	1969	Donald J. MacIntyre	8	7,868	267
Snead State Jr., Boaz, AL 35957	1935	William H. Osborn	4	1,170	50
Snow, Ephraim, UT 84627	1888	Steven D. Bennion	4	1,411	60
Solano Comm., Suisun City, CA 94585	1945	William H. Wilson Sr.	8	9,799	152
Somerset County, Somerville, NJ 08876	1965	S. Charles Irace	8	4,952	185
South Central Comm., New Haven, CT 06511	1968	Richard M. Turner III	4	2,318	101
Southeast Comm., Lincoln Campus, Lincoln, NE 68520	1973	Jack Huck, Dir.	9	4,093	660
Southeast Comm., Milford Campus, Milford, NE 68405	1941	Thomas Stone, Dir.	9	1,100	120
Southeastern Comm., Whiteville, NC 28472	1966	Dan W. Moore	4	1,911	212
Southeastern Comm., North Campus, West Burlington, IA 52655	1968	Carlton W. Callison, Supt.	11	1,650	135
Southeastern Illinois, Harrisburg, IL 62946	1960	Harry W. Abell	4	2,715	183
Southern Arkansas Univ. Tech., East Camden, AR 71701	1968	George J. Brown	4	691	43
Southern Jr. Coll. of Business, Birmingham, AL 35203	1969	NA	2	1,077	41
Southern Maine Vocational-Tech. Inst., South Portland, ME 04106	1946	Wayne H. Ross, Dir.	4	1,200	144
Southern Ohio, Cincinnati Campus, Cincinnati, OH 45237	1927	Elmer Smith	2	1,300	75
Southern Ohio, Fairfield Campus, Fairfield, OH 45014	1927	Burton Lipson, Dir.	2	947	67
Southern State Comm., Hillsboro, OH 45133	1975	Lewis C. Miller	4	1,365	116
Southern Union State Jr., Wadley, AL 36276	1922	L. Ray Jones	4	1,574	41
Southern Univ., Shreveport-Bossier City Campus, LA 71107	1964	Leonard C. Barnes	4	696	41
Southern West Virginia Comm., Logan, WV 25601	1971	Gregory D. Adkins	4	2,059	127
South Georgia, Douglas, GA 31533	1906	Edward O. Jackson Jr.	4	1,244	71
South Mountain Comm., Phoenix, AZ 85040	979	Raul Cardenas	8	1,481	120
South Plains, Levelland, TX 79336	1958	Marvin L. Baker	11	3,399	200
South Seattle Comm., Seattle, WA 98106	1970	Jerry M. Brockey	4	4,973	248
Southside Virginia Comm., Alberta, VA 23821	1969	John Cavan	4	1,275	105
Southwestern, Chula Vista, CA 92010	1961	Jewell E. Stindt	11	12,907	565
Southwestern Michigan, Dowagiac, MI 49047	1964	David C. Briegel	4	3,000	170
Southwestern Oregon Comm., Coos Bay, OR 97420	1961	Jack E. Brookins	4	3,879	270
Southwestern Tech., Sylva, NC 28779	1964	Norman K. Myers.	4	1,190	72
Southwest Mississippi Jr., Summit, MS 39666	1918	Horace C. Holmes	4	1,313	53
Southwest State Tech., Mobile, AL 36690	1954	Donald S. Jefferies	4	942	43
Southwest Texas Jr., Uvalce, TX 78801	1946	Jimmy Goodson	4	2,179	135
Southwest Virginia Comm., Richlands, VA 24641	1968	Charles R. King	4	2,831	150
Southwest Wisconsin Vocational-Tech. Inst., Fennimore, WI 53809	1967	Ronald H. Anderson, Dir.	11	1,450	123
Spartanburg Methodist, Spartanburg, SC 29301	1911	George D. Fields	1	1,072	76
Spartanburg Tech., Spartanburg, SC 29303	1961	Joe D. Gault	4	2,025	180
Spokane Comm., Spokane, WA 99207	1963	F. William McMulkin	4	4,855	247
Spokane Falls Comm., Spokane, WA 99204	1967	Phyllis Everest	4	4,844	193
Spoon River, Canton, IL 61520	1959	NA	4	2,362	135
Springfield Tech. Comm., Springfield, MA 01105	1967	Leonard J. Collamore	4	3,647	187
Stanly Tech., Albemarle, NC 28001	1971	Charles H. Byrd	4	1,022	52
Stark Tech., Canton, OH 44720	1970	John J. McGrath	11	3,125	146
State Fair Comm., Sedalia, MO 65301	1966	Fred E. Davis	9	1,528	113
State Tech. Inst. at Knoxville, Knoxville, TN 37919	1974	J. L. Goins.	4	2,828	151
State Tech. Inst. at Memphis, Memphis, TN 38134	1967	Charles Temple	4	7,385	347
State Univ. of New York, A&T Coll. at Alfred, Alfred, NY 14802	1948	David H. Huntington	4	4,173	250
State Univ. of New York, A&T Coll. at Canton, NY 13617	1906	Earl W. MacArthur	4	2,638	122
State Univ. of New York A&T Coll. at Cobleskill, NY 12043	1916	Walton A. Brown	4	2,762	142
State Univ. of New York A & T Coll. at Delhi, Delhi, NY 13753	1913	Seldon M. Kruger	4	2,228	121
State Univ. of New York A&T Coll. at Farmingdale, NY 11735	1912	Frank A. Cipriani	4	6,252	404
State Univ. of New York A&T Coll. at Morrisville, NY 13408	1908	Donald G. Butcher	4	3,046	150
Stautzenberger, Toledo, OH 43623	1923	NA	2	1,645	133
Suffolk County Comm.-Eastern Campus, Riverhead, NY 11901	1977	R. David Cox, Exec. Dean	11	2,242	38
Suffolk County Comm.-Selden Campus, Selden, NY 11784	1962	Robert T. Kreiling	11	21,000	435
Suffolk County Comm.-Western Campus, Brentwood, NY 11717	1974	B. Wayne Peuey, Exec. Dean.	11	2,117	259
Sullivan County Comm., Loch Sheldrake, NY 12759	1962	John F. Walter	11	1,750	75
Sullivan Jr. Coll. of Business, Louisville, KY 40232	1864	David P. Higley, V.P./Dir.	2	1,357	62
Sumter Area Tech., Sumter, SC 29150	1963	James L. Hudgins	4	1,754	231
Surry Comm., Dobson, NC 27017	1965	Swanson Richards	4	2,243	75
Tacoma Comm, Tacoma, WA 98465	1965	Carleton Opgard	4	4,100	310
Taft, CA 93268	1922	David Cothrun	4	1,211	80
Tallahasee Comm., Tallahassee, FL 32304	1966	James H. Hinson Jr.	11	4,871	174
Tarrant County Jr., Fort Worth, TX 76102	1967	Joe B. Rushing	8	25,746	840
Taylor Business Inst., New York, NY 10119	1961	William N. Wildish	2	1,500	85
Technical Career Inst., New York, NY 10001	1974	George Leelike	2	2,000	70
Technical Coll. of Alamance, Haw River, NC 27258	1959	W. Ronald McCarter	4	2,200	50
Temple Jr., Temple, TX 76501	1926	Marvin R. Felder	9	2,400	104
Terra Tech., Fremont, OH 43420	1968	Richard M. Simon	4	2,228	110
Texarkana Comm., Texarkana, TX 75501	1927	Carl M. Nelson	4	3,203	200
Texas Southmost, Brownsville, TX 78520	1926	Albert A. Besteiro	9	4,500	100
Texas State Tech. Inst.-Amarillo Campus, Amarillo, TX 79111	1970	Ronald DeSpain	4	1,166	115
Texas State Tech. Inst.-Harlingen Campus, TX 78550	1967	J. Gilbert Leal.	4	1,903	127
Texas State Tech. Inst.-Sweetwater Campus, TX 79556	1970	Herbert C. Robbins	4	735	76
Texas State Tech. Inst.-Waco Campus, Waco, TX 76705	1965	Jack E. Tompkins	4	5,133	319
Thames Valley State Tech., Norwich, CT 06360	1963	Donald R. Welter	4	840	42
Thomas Nelson Comm., Hampton, VA 23670	1968	Thomas S. Kubala	4	6,284	258
Thornton Comm., South Holland, IL 60473	1927	Nathan A. Ivey	4	8,500	313
Three Rivers Comm., Poplar Bluff, MO 63901	1966	Jack L. Bottenfield	4	1,389	62
Tidewater Comm., Chesapeake Campus, VA 23320	1968	George B. Pass.	4	1,980	95
Tidewater Comm., Frederick Campus, Portsmouth, VA 23703	1968	George B. Pass.	4	4,653	234
Tidewater Comm., Virginia Beach Campus, VA 23456	1968	George B. Pass.	4	8,417	386

Name, address	Year	Governing official affiliation, and highest degree offered	Students	Teachers
Tompkins Cortland Comm., Dryden, NY 13053	1968	Hushang BahanLibby Jr. 4	3,450	100
Treasure Valley Comm., Ontario, OR 97914	1062	Glenn Maybo 11	1,993	75
Trenholm State Tech., Montgomery, AL 36108	1965	Tad McClammy 4	891	60
Trenton Jr., Trenton, MO 64683	1925	Robert M. Webb 9	744	51
Tri-Cities State Tech., Blountville, TN 37617	1966	H. James Owen 4	1,700	120
Tri-County Comm., Murphy, NC 28906	1964	Vincent W. Crisp 4	761	35
Tri-County Tech., Pendleton, SC 29670	1062	Don C. Garrison 4	2,615	150
Trinidad State Jr., Trinidad, CO 81082	1925	Thomas E. Sullivan 4	1,784	115
Triton, River Grove, IL 60171	1964	Daniel F. Moriarty 4	14,746	1,039
Trocaire, Buffalo, NY 14220	1958	Sr. Mary Carmina Coppola 0	901	109
Truckee Meadows Comm., Reno, NV 89512	1971	V. James Eardley 4	8,248	368
Tulsa Jr., Tulsa, OK 74119	1968	Alfred M. Philips 4	15,153	650
Tunxis Comm., Farmington, CT 06032	1969	Eduardo Marti, Exec. Dean 4	1,603	110
Tyler Jr., Tyler, TX 75711	1926	Raymond M. Hawkins 11	7,411	300
Ulster County Comm., Stone Ridge, NY 12484	1962	Robert T. Brown 11	3,133	160
Umpqua Comm., Roseburg, OR 97470	1964	Bud Hakanson 11	1,650	250
Union County, Cranford, NJ 07016	1933	Derek Nunney 11	9,531	395
United Coll. of Business-Hollywood, Hollywood, CA 90028	1969	Alan D. Mentzer 2	600	35
United Electronics Inst., Tampa, FL 33607	1967	George E. Glenn 2	956	27
Univ. of Akron, Wayne General and Tech., Orrville, OH 44667	1972	D. J. Guzzetta 4	905	81
Univ. of Alaska, Anchorage Comm., Anchorage, AK 99508	1954	Edwin Biggerstaff. 4	9,893	450
Univ. of Alaska, Islands Comm., Sitka, AK 99835	1954	Jerry L. Harris 4	766	45
Univ. of Alaska, Kenai Peninsula Comm., Soldotna, AK 99669	1964	Les Vierra. 4	1,112	79
Univ. of Alaska, Ketchikan Comm., Ketchikan, AK 99901	1954	John C. Menzie 4	824	72
Univ. of Alaska, Kodiak Comm., Kodiak, AK 99615	1968	Carolyn Floyd. 4	1,115	53
Univ. of Alaska, Kuskokwim Comm., Bethel, AK 99559	1972	NA 4	634	38
Univ. of Alaska, Matanuska-Susitna Comm., Palmer, AK 99645	1958	Alvin S. Okeson 4	913	58
Univ. of Alaska, Tanana Valley Comm., Fairbanks, AK 99701	1974	Michael Metty. 4	2,183	203
Univ. of Cincinnati, Raymond Walters General and Tech., Cincinnati, OH 45236.	1967	Ernest G. Muntz, Dean. 4	3,600	100
Univ. of Hawaii-Honolulu Comm., Honolulu, HI 96817	1920	Peter R. Kessinger, Provost. 4	5,325	248
Univ. of Hawaii-Kapiolani Comm., Honolulu, HI 96814.	1964	John F. Morton, Provost. 4	5,555	198
Univ. of Hawaii-Kauai Comm., Lihue, HI 96766.	1965	David Iha, Provost 4	1,266	64
Univ. of Hawaii-Leeward Comm., Pearl City, HI 96782	1968	Melvyn K. Sakaguchi, Provost 4	6,195	236
Univ. of Hawaii-Maui Comm., Kahului, HI 96732	1967	Alma Cooper, Provost. 4	2,287	107
Univ. of Hawaii-Windward Comm., Kaneohe, HI 96744	1972	Peter T. Dyer, Provost. 4	1,548	68
Univ. of Kentucky, Ashland Comm., Ashland, KY 41101	1937	Robert L. Goodpaster, Dir. 4	1,573	72
Univ. of Kentucky, Elizabethtown Comm., KY 42701	1964	James S. Owen, Dir. 4	2,187	86
Univ. of Kentucky, Henderson Comm., Henderson, KY 42420	1963	Marshall Arnold, Dir. 4	1,052	49
Univ. of Kentucky, Hopkinsville Comm., Hopkinsville, KY 42240	1965	Thomas L. Riley, Dir. 4	1,164	64
Univ. of Kentucky, Lexington Tech. Inst., Lexington, KY 40506	1965	William N. Price, Dir. 4	2,462	138
Univ. of Kentucky, Madisonville Comm., KY 42431	1968	Arthur D. Stumpf, Dir. 4	1,266	56
Univ. of Kentucky, Paducah Comm., Paducah, KY 42001	1932	D. J. Clemens, Chief Admin. 4	1,885	73
Univ. of Kentucky, Prestonsburg Comm., KY 41653	1964	Henry A. Campbell Jr., Dir. 4	919	43
Univ. of Kentucky, Somerset Comm., Somerset, KY 42501	1965	Roscoe D. Kelley, Dir. 4	1,132	75
Univ. of Kentucky, Southeast Comm., Cumberland, KY 40823	1960	Vivian B. Blevins, Dir. 4	816	48
Univ. of Minnesota Tech. Coll., Crookston, MN 56716	1966	Stanley D. Sahlstrom, Provost 4	1,149	75
Univ. of Minnesota Tech. Coll., Waseca, Waseca, MN 56093	1971	Edward C. Frederick, Provost. 4	774	76
Univ. of New Mexico Gallup Branch, Gallup, NM 87301	1968	John M Phillips, Dir. 4	1,250	80
Univ. of North Dakota-Williston Center, Williston, ND 58801	1957	Garvin L. Stevens, Dean. 11	624	50
Univ. of Puerto Rico, Aguadilla Regional, Ramey, PR 00604	1972	Ruth Burgos-Sasscer, Dean 6	1,067	69
Univ. of Puerto Rico, Carolina Regional, Carolina, PR 00630	1974	Gilberto Moreno-Rodriguez, Dir. 6	1,464	87
Univ. of South Carolina at Sumter, Sumter, SC 29150	1966	J. C. Anderson Jr., Dir. 4	1,189	44
Univ. of Wisconsin Center-Fond du Lac, Fond du Lac, WI 54935	1966	Willard J. Henken, Dean. 4	609	42
Univ. of Wisconsin Center-Fox Valley, Menasha, WI 54952	1935	Rue C. Johnson, Dean. 4	1,175	50
Univ. of Wisconsin Center-Marathon County, Wausau, WI 54401.	1947	Stephen R. Portch, Dean 4	1,268	66
Univ. of Wisconsin Center-Marshfield/Wood County, Marshfield, WI 54449	1964	Norbert E. Koopman, Dean 4	665	37
Univ. of Wisconsin Center-Rock County, Janesville, WI 53545	1966	Thomas W. Walterman, Dean. 4	850	36
Univ. of Wisconsin Center-Sheboygan County, WI 53081	1933	Kenneth M. Bailey, Dean 4	695	42
Univ. of Wisconsin Center-Washington County, West Bend, WI 53095.	1968	Robert Thompson, Dean 4	758	37
Univ. of Wisconsin Center-Waukesha County, WI 53186	1966	Mary S. Knudten, Dean 4	2,200	90
Utah Tech. Coll. at Provo, Provo, UT 84603	1941	J. Marvin Higbee 4	5,593	237
Utah Tech. Coll. at Salt Lake, Salt Lake City, UT 84131	1948	Orville D. Carnahan 4	8,200	205
Valencia Comm., Orlando, FL 32802	1967	Paul C. Gianini Jr. 4	11,123	663
Vance-Granville Comm., Henderson, NC 27536	1969	Ben F. Currin 11	1,131	85
Ventura, Ventura, CA 93003	1925	Richard A. Glenn 11	14,000	776
Vermont Tech., Randolph Center, VT 05061	1957	Robert G. Clarke 4	801	61
Vernon Regional Jr., Vernon, TX 76384	1972	Jim M. Williams. 11	1,594	103
Victoria, Victoria, TX 77901	1925	Roland E. Bing 8	2,649	120
Victor Valley, Victorville, CA 92392	1961	Burton W. Wadsworth 4	5,200	135
Villa Maria Coll. of Buffalo, Buffalo, NY 14225	1960	Sr. Marcella Maria Garus 1	776	65
Vincennes Univ., Vincennes, IN 47591	1801	Phillip M. Summers. 4	4,506	182
Virginia Highlands Comm., Abingdon, VA 24210	1968	N. DeWitt Moore Jr. 4	1,027	76
Virginia Western Comm., Roanoke, VA 24038	1966	Charles L. Downs 4	3,200	230
Vista, Berkeley, CA 94704	1974	John J. Holleman. 11	10,290	250
Volunteer State Comm., Gallatin, TN 37066	1970	NA 4	4,072	177
Wake Tech., Raleigh, NC 27603	1963	Bruce I. Howell 11	3,354	120
Walker, Jasper, AL 35501	1938	David J. Rowland. 0	712	35
Wallace State Comm., Hanceville, AL 35077.	1966	James C. Bailey 4	2,588	133
Walla Walla Comm., Walla Walla, WA 99362	1967	Wayland DeWitt 4	4,800	252
Walters State Comm., Morristown, TN 37814	1970	Jack E. Campbell 4	3,920	220
Washtenaw Comm., Ann Arbor, MI 48106	1965	Gunder A. Myran 11	8,733	525
Waterbury State Tech., Waterbury, CT 06708	1964	Charles A. Ekstrom 4	1,902	97
Watterson, Louisville, KY 40218	1962	O'Neal Briel. 2	989	90
Waubonsee Comm, Sugar Grove, IL 60554	1966	John J. Swalec 9	6,510	306
Wayne Comm., Goldsboro, NC 27530	1957	Clyde A. Erwin Jr. 11	2,330	142
Wayne County Comm., Detroit, MI 48226.	1967	George Bell 11	21,000	850
Weatherford, Weatherford, TX 76086	1869	E. W. Mince 4	1,596	74
Wenatchee Valley, Wenatchee, WA 98801	1939	James R. Davis. 11	2,765	190

Name, address	Year	Governing official affiliation, and highest degree offered		Students	Teachers
Westark Comm., Fort Smith, AR 72913	1928	Joel R. Stubblefield	11	3,698	170
Westchester Comm., Valhalla, NY 10595	1946	Joseph N. Hankin	11	8,764	403
Western Iowa Tech Comm., Sioux City, IA 51102	1966	Robert H. Kiser, Supt.	4	1,214	790
Western Nevada Comm., Carson City, NV 89701	1971	J. Clark Davis, Exec. V.P.	4	2,842	100
Western Oklahoma State, Altus, OK 73521	1926	W. C. Burris	4	1,984	66
Western Piedmont Comm., Morganton, NC 28655	1964	Jim A. Richardson	4	1,752	99
Western Texas, Snyder, TX 79549	1969	Don Newbury	11	1,164	75
Western Wisconsin Tech. Inst., La Crosse, WI 54601	1911	Charles G. Richardson, Dir.	9	2,431	883
Western Wyoming Comm., Rock Springs, WY 82901	1959	Bert S. Slafter	11	1,350	81
West Hills, Coalinga, CA 93210	1932	Joseph M. Conte	4	2,400	185
West Los Angeles, Culver City, CA 90230	1969	Gerhardt W. Riedel	9	11,675	375
Westmoreland County Comm., Youngwood, PA 15697	1970	Norman P. Shea	8	3,242	165
West Shore Comm., Scottville, MI 49454	1967	John M. Eaton	9	1,075	67
West Valley, Saratoga, CA 95070	1963	Frank C. Pearce	11	16,012	500
West Virginia Northern Comm., Wheeling, WV 26003	1972	Daniel B. Crowder	4	3,814	221
Wharton County Jr., Wharton, TX 77488	1946	Theodore Nicksick Jr.	11	2,466	139
Wilkes Comm., Wilkesboro, NC 28697	1965	David E. Daniel	4	2,781	158
William Rainey Harper, Palatine, IL 60067	1965	James J. McGrath	11	18,630	762
Williamsport Area Comm., Williamsport, PA 17701	1965	Robert Breuder	11	3,599	188
Willmar Comm., Willmar, MN 56201	1961	John W. Torgelson	4	761	58
Wilson County Tech. Inst., Wilson, NC 27893	1959	Frank L. Eagles	4	1,425	59
Wisconsin Indianhead Tech. Inst., New Richmond Campus, New Richmond, WI 54017	1972	Marilyn McCarty, Admin.	9	814	27
Wisconsin Indianhead Tech. Inst., Rice Lake Campus, Rice Lake, WI 54868	1941	NA	9	782	45
Wisconsin Indianhead Tech. Inst., Superior Campus, Superior, WI 54880	1912	Richard Parish, Admin.	9	970	43
Worthington Comm., Worthington, MN 56187	1936	Paul D. Walker	4	750	48
Wor-Wic Tech. Comm., Salisbury, MD 21801	1976	Arnold H. Maner	11	642	60
Wright State Univ., Western Ohio Branch Campus, Celina, OH 45822	1969	Thomas A. Knapke, Dean	4	950	36
Wytheville Comm., Wytheville, VA 24382	1967	William F. Snyder	4	1,714	106
Yakima Valley Comm., Yakima, WA 98907	1928	Terrance R. Brown	4	5,262	312
Yavapai, Prescott, AZ 86301	1966	Joseph F. Russo	11	5,844	396
York Tech., Rock Hill, SC 29730	1961	Baxter Hood	11	2,189	111
Yuba, Marysville, CA 95901	1927	Daniel G. Walker	11	8,463	270

Tuition and College Costs

According to a survey by the College Board, the total annual cost for living in a dormitory at a four-year college in 1984 will be $4,881 at a public institution and $9,022 at a private institution.

The most expensive universitites, including costs for room, board, tuition, books, transportation, and related expenses for an undergraduate, will be: Massachusetts Institute of Technology, $16,130; Bennington, $16,040; Harvard, $15,750; Princeton, $15,625; Barnard, $15,558; Yale, $15,500; Brandeis, $15,250; Tufts, $15,236; Brown, $15,190; and Sarah Lawrence, $15,180. Bennington's tuition of $11,770 will be the highest in the nation.

Students who commute from home and attend two-year community colleges face the lowest costs, totaling an average of $3,423 when all the expenses related to living and eating at home are included. Average tuition for such students will be $598, lower than any other type of institution of higher education.

Just 10 years ago, the average annual cost to an undergraduate at a four-year institution was $2,365 at a public college and $3,860 at a private college.

Public Libraries

Source: World Almanac questionnaire (1983)

First figure in parentheses denotes number of branches-2d figure indicates number of bookmobiles. (*) indicates county library system; (†) indicates state library system; (C) Canadian dollars; (A) library has not provided up-to-date information.

City	No. bound volumes	Circulation	Cost of operation	City	No. bound volumes	Circulation	Cost of operation
Akron, Oh.* (18-2)	1,102,970	2,014,701	$ 4,991,407	New Haven, Conn. (8-0)	550,000	450,000	1,600,000
Albuquerque, N.M. (8-2)	(A)	1,630,000	2,568,716	New Orleans, La. (11-0)	802,934	1,176,304	3,735,693
Atlanta, Ga.* (24-3)	1,100,000	2,500,000	(A)	New York (resrch)	7,271,592	780,171	3,575,281
Austin, Tex. (15-0)	726,500	2,066,326	6,309,173	N.Y.C. brches (82-2)	3,450,969	8,107,362	(A)
Baltimore, Md.† (33-2)	1,900,197	2,124,114	10,890,029	Brooklyn* (58-0)	3,885,530	6,970,799	18,759,885
Baton Rouge, La. (10-0)	443,983	1,429,408	2,364,151	Queens* (59-0)	4,260,930	6,877,351	25,434,000
Boston, Mass. (25-2)	4,916,277	1,454,414	11,500,000	Norfolk, Va. (11-1)	700,513	1,158,565	2,038,747
Buffalo, N.Y.* (52-3)	3,299,943	5,849,765	13,703,848	Okla. City, Okla.* (10-5)	600,000	1,800,000	5,000,000
Cincinnati, Oh.* (39-2)	3,332,926	6,166,548	12,678,623	Omaha, Neb. (9-0)	557,237	1,771,537	3,118,831
Cleveland, Oh. (31-2)	2,484,947	3,605,627	15,300,000	Philadelphia, Pa. (51-0)	2,947,727	4,960,439	20,304,476
Columbus, Oh.* (20-1)	1,209,858	3,856,356	9,507,762	Phoenix, Ariz. (9-1)	1,208,624	3,607,506	6,878,000
Corpus Christi, Tex. (4-0)	355,949	614,641	1,226,976	Pittsburgh, Pa. (21-3)	1,907,373	2,837,534	8,539,756
Dallas, Tex. (18-0)	1,730,807	3,739,164	11,801,745	Portland, Ore.* (14-1)	1,161,710	3,142,016	5,257,709
Dayton, Oh.* (19-1)	1,368,923	4,859,877	5,925,992	Richmond, Va. (7-2)	659,068	1,031,353	1,767,384
Detroit, Mich. (24-3)	2,500,000	1,500,000	14,000,000	Rochester, N.Y. (10-2)	927,750	1,402,934	5,684,514
Des Moines, la. (6-0)	844,256	1,245,575	2,487,760	St. Louis, Mo.* (15-20)	1,695,046	7,369,219	8,952,219
El Paso, Tex. (9-3)	701,000	1,400,000	2,800,000	St. Paul, Minn. (10-1)	683,489	1,872,891	4,063,165
Ft. Worth, Tex. (8-0)	798,608	1,650,930	3,784,161	San Antonio, Tex.* (13-3)	1,200,000	2,217,603	6,672,424
Honolulu, Ha.† (47-6)	2,118,238	5,267,042	9,871,991	San Diego, Cal. (30-1)	1,733,387	4,191,538	7,391,165
Indianapolis, Ind.* (22-2)	2,736,395	3,829,511	7,961,974	San Fran., Cal. (26-1)	1,749,129	2,470,091	9,146,080
Jacksonville, Fla.* (11-1)	1,013,497	2,026,528	3,808,000	San Jose, Cal. (17-1)	1,250,000	2,800,000	5,800,000
Long Beach, Cal. (12-0)	709,815	1,986,085	7,501,378	St. Petersburg, Fla. (5-0)	453,162	1,160,442	1,424,820
Louisville, Ky.* (20-3)	1,119,771	2,626,808	5,356,478	Syracuse, N.Y. (10-1)	524,649	1,063,057	4,435,336
Memphis, Tenn.* (22-3)	1,560,872	2,400,000	7,327,863	Tucson, Ariz.* (15-2)	710,000	3,700,000	5,943,900
Miami, Fla.* (25-6)	2,000,000	3,700,000	(A)	Tulsa, Okla.* (20-1)	525,000	1,760,922	5,942,647
Minneapolis, Minn. (14-0)	1,641,546	2,573,358	8,939,819	Wash. D.C. (20-0)	1,346,723	1,487,009	10,707,700
Mobile, Ala. (5-1)	380,626	830,756	1,890,732	Wichita, Kan. (10-0)	531,200	1,152,438	2,588,257
Nashville, Tenn.* (15-2)	568,824	1,505,810	4,267,443	Yonkers, N.Y. (3-1)	293,165	802,855	3,425,000

Educational Attainment by Age, Race, and Sex

Source: U.S. Bureau of the Census unpublished data as of March. 1983 (Number of persons in thousands)

Race, age, and sex	Years of school completed					Percent				
	All persons	Less than high school, 4 years	High school, 4 years	College, 1 to 3 years	College, 4 years or more	All persons	Less than high school, 4 years	High school, 4 years	College, 1 to 3 years	College, 4 years or more
March 1983										
All races										
18 to 24 years.	29,047	6,344	13,158	7,528	2,018	100.0	21.8	45.3	25.9	6.9
25 years and over	138,020	38,514	52,060	21,531	25,915	100.0	27.9	37.7	15.6	18.8
25 to 34 years	39,342	5,364	15,804	8,569	9,605	100.0	13.6	40.2	21.8	24.4
35 to 44 years	28,750	5,315	11,564	5,040	6,831	100.0	18.5	40.2	17.5	23.8
45 to 54 years	22,205	6,013	9,223	3,005	3,964	100.0	27.1	41.5	13.5	17.9
55 to 64 years	21,985	7,957	8,480	2,554	2,993	100.0	36.2	38.6	11.6	13.6
65 years and over	25,738	13,865	6,989	2,362	2,521	100.0	53.9	27.2	9.2	9.8
Male. 25 years and over. . .	65,004	17,720	22,048	10,310	14,926	100.0	27.3	33.9	15.9	23.0
Female, 25 years and over .	73,016	20,794	30,012	11,220	10,990	100.0	28.5	41.1	15.4	15.1
White										
18 to 24 years.	24,389	4,981	11,158	6,449	1,803	100.0	20.4	45.8	26.4	7.4
25 years and over	120,610	31,628	46,370	19,145	23,466	100.0	26.2	38.4	15.9	19.5
25 to 34 years	33,514	4,249	13,422	7,310	8,533	100.0	12.7	40.0	21.8	25.5
35 to 44 years	24,874	4,157	10,131	4,477	6,110	100.0	16.7	40.7	18.0	24.6
45 to 54 years	19,366	4,770	8,289	2,687	3,620	100.0	24.6	42.8	13.9	18.7
55 to 64 years	19,622	6,515	7,880	2,403	2,824	100.0	33.2	40.2	12.2	14.4
65 years and over	23,234	11,937	6,648	2,268	2,379	100.0	51.4	28.6	9.8	10.2
Male. 25 years and over . . .	57,263	14,686	19,654	9,207	13,715	100.0	25.6	34.3	16.1	24.0
Female, 25 years and over .	63,347	16,941	26,716	9,939	9,752	100.0	26.7	42.2	15.7	15.4
Black										
18 to 24 years.	3,875	1,193	1,734	816	130	100.0	30.8	44.7	21.1	3.4
25 years and over	13,940	6,019	4,722	1,868	1,331	100.0	43.2	33.9	13.4	9.5
25 to 34 years	4,621	957	2,031	1,004	628	100.0	20.7	44.0	21.7	13.6
35 to 44 years	2,976	1,004	1,218	426	326	100.0	33.7	40.9	14.3	11.0
45 to 54 years	2,261	1,100	745	233	182	100.0	48.7	33.0	10.3	8.0
55 to 64 years	1,960	1,263	475	124	98	100.0	64.4	24.2	6.3	5.0
65 years and over	2,124	1,693	254	81	95	100.0	79.7	12.0	3.8	4.5
Male. 25 years and over. . . .	6,139	2,674	2,017	835	614	100.0	43.6	32.9	13.6	10.0
Female, 25 years and over .	7,801	3,346	2,705	1,034	717	100.0	42.9	34.7	13.3	9.2
Spanish Origin[1]										
18 to 24 years.	1,972	856	747	323	45	100.0	43.4	37.9	16.4	2.3
25 years and over	6,885	3,703	1,884	751	547	100.0	53.8	27.4	10.9	7.9
25 to 34 years	2,608	1,092	872	377	266	100.0	41.9	33.4	14.5	10.2
35 to 44 years	1,729	880	509	197	143	100.0	50.9	29.4	11.4	8.3
45 to 54 years	1,181	712	286	114	69	100.0	60.3	24.2	9.7	5.8
55 to 64 years	771	537	148	40	46	100.0	69.6	19.2	5.2	6.0
65 years and over	596	480	69	23	23	100.0	80.5	11.6	3.9	3.9
Male. 25 years and over . . .	3,190	1,640	871	384	295	100.0	51.4	27.3	12.0	9.2
Female. 25 years and over .	3,694	2,062	1,014	367	252	100.0	55.8	27.4	9.9	6.8

110 Years of Public Schools

	1869-70	1899-1900	1909-10	1919-20	1929-30	1939-40	1949-50	1959-60	1969-70	1979-80
Pupils and teachers (thousands) .										
Total U.S. population	39,818	75,995	90,492	104,512	121,770	130,880	148,665	179,323	203,212	226,546
Population 5-17 years of age	12,055	21,573	24,009	27,556	31,417	30,150	30,168	43,881	52,490	47,406
Percent aged 5-17 years	30.3	28.4	26.5	26.4	25.8	23.0	20.3	24.5	25.8	20.9
Enrollment (thousands)										
Elementary and secondary	6,872	15,503	17,814	21,578	25,678	25,434	25,111	36,087	45,619	41,654[2]
Percent pop. 5-17 enrolled	57.0	71.9	74.2	78.3	81.7	84.4	83.2	82.2	86.9	87.8
Percent in high schools	1.2	.3	5.1	10.2	17.1	26.0	22.7	23.5	28.5	32.9
High school graduates.	....	62	111	231	592	1,143	1,063	1,627	2,589	2,757
Average school term (in days). . . .	132.2	144.3	157.5	161.9	172.7	175.0	177.9	178.0	178.9	178.5[4]
Total instructional staff	....	....	....	678	880	912	962	1,464	2,253	2,441
Teachers, librarians: Men	78	127	110	93	140	195	195	402	691	782[4]
Women	123	296	413	565	703	681	719	985	1,440	1,518[4]
Percent men	38.7	29.9	21.1	14.1	16.6	22.2	21.3	29.0	33.4	34.0[4]
Revenue & expenditures (millions)										
Total revenue	....	$219	$433	$970	$2,088	$2,260	$5,437	$14,746	$40,267	$96,881
Total expenditures	$63	214	426	1,036	2,316	2,344	5,837	15,613[1]	40,683	95,962
Current elem. and secondary. . .	....	....	179	356	861	1,843	1,941	4,687	12,329	34,218	86,984
Capital outlay	....	....	35	69	153	370	257	1,014	2,661	4,659	6,506
Interest on school debt	....	....	....	....	18	92	130	100	489	1,171	1,874
Other	....	....	....	....	3	9	13	35	132	636	598
Salaries and pupil cost			(Data in unadjusted dollars)							
Average annual teacher salary[2] . . .	$189	$325	$485	$2,130	$3,869	$3,894	$5,928	$8,213	$10,917	$16,780[4]
Expenditure per capita total pop. .	1.59	2.83	4.71	24.24	51.85	48.40	77.34	138.21	247.23	423.59
Current expenditure per pupil ADA[3].	....	16.67	27.85	130.41	236.25	238.05	411.29	595.50	1,007.65	2,271.78

(1) Because of a modification of the scope, "current expenditures for elementary and secondary schools" data for 1959-60 and later years are not entirely comparable with data for prior years. (2) Includes supervisors, principals, teachers and other nonsupervisory instructional staff. (3) "ADA" means average daily attendance in elementary and secondary day schools. (4) Estimated.

Fall Enrollment and Teachers in Full-time Day Schools
Elementary and Secondary Day Schools, Fall 1982
Source: National Center for Education Statistics, U.S. Education Dept.

	Local school districts			Enrollment			Instruc-
	Total	Operating	Nonoperating	Total	Pupils per teacher	Classroom teachers	tional aides
United States.	15,840	15,517	323	39,643,476	—	2,118,963	310,728
Alabama	128	128	0	724,037	20.3	35,619	2,930
Alaska	53	53	0	89,413	13.2	6,793	998
Arizona	220	208	12	510,296	19.5	26,190	3,671
Arkansas	371	371	0	432,565	18.2	23,713	2,260
California	1,033	1,033	0	4,065,486	23.3	174,674	95,900
Colorado	181	181	0	545,209	18.6	29,380	4,271
Connecticut	165	165	0	486,470	14.8	32,760	68
Delaware	19	19	0	92,646	17.5	5,296	710
District of Columbia . . .	1	1	0	91,105	17.2	5,305	13,210
Florida	67	67	0	1,484,734	17.8	83,301	9,108
Georgia	187	187	0	1,053,689	18.6	56,510	91
Hawaii	1	1	0	162,024	22.9	7,077	768
Idaho	115	115	0	202,973	20.7	9,790	9,05
Illinois	1,010	1,008	2	1,880,289	18.0	104,619	5,853
Indiana	306	304	2	999,542	19.8	50,528	2,621
Iowa	441	441	0	504,983	15.7	32,110	1,99
Kansas	306	306	0	407,074	15.6	26,056	2,84
Kentucky	180	180	0	651,084	20.2	32,237	4,794
Louisiana	66	66	0	775,666	18.4	42,214	1,784
Maine	284	233	51	211,986	19.5	10,852	5,00
Maryland	24	24	0	699,201	18.3	38,120	2,51
Massachusetts	404	351	53	908,984	16.1	56,498	10,48
Michigan	574	572	2	1,761,521	21.9	80,364	6,45
Minnesota	437	435	2	715,190	18.0	39,775	2,47
Mississippi	153	153	0	468,294	18.6	25,176	3,41
Missouri	548	548	0	802,535	17.4	46,047	1,03
Montana	569	561	8	152,335	16.0	9,517	2,12
Nebraska	1,014	968	46	269,000	15.5	17,381	1,27
Nevada	17	17	0	151,104	20.9	7,222	4,62
New Hampshire	169	158	11	160,197	16.4	9,758	2,67
New Jersey	607	582	25	1,172,520	15.8	74,303	17,80
New Mexico	89	89	0	268,632	18.6	14,323	16,02
New York	722	715	7	2,718,678	18.8	144,591	60
North Carolina	143	143	0	1,096,815	19.8	55,261	5,77
North Dakota	327	292	35	117,078	16.6	7,071	3,37
Ohio	615	615	0	1,860,245	19.8	94,126	3,46
Oklahoma	619	619	0	593,825	17.0	34,960	9,03
Oregon	310	309	1	448,184	18.6	24,074	
Pennsylvania	500	500	0	1,783,969	17.2	103,855	4,11
Rhode Island	40	40	0	139,362	15.7	8,854	1,00
South Carolina	92	92	0	608,518	18.9	32,244	4,17
South Dakota	195	187	8	123,897	15.5	7,974	24,58
Tennessee	147	146	1	828,264	20.9	39,660	1,58
Texas	1,075	1,075	0	2,985,659	17.9	166,961	98
Utah	40	40	0	370,183	24.3	15,227	3,85
Vermont	273	247	26	91,454	13.9	6,591	2,61
Virginia	139	135	4	975,727	17.4	56,038	4,46
Washington	300	300	0	739,215	21.7	34,056	79
West Virginia	55	55	0	375,115	16.9	22,159	18
Wisconsin	460	433	27	784,830	17.4	45,047	1,37
Wyoming	49	49	0	101,665	15.2	6,706	40

Federal Funds for Education, 1983
Source: National Center for Education Statistics, U.S. Department of Education

Federal funds obligated for major programs administered by the Dept. of Education (thousands of dollars).

Total	**14,562,040**	Interest subsidy grants	24,18
Elementary-secondary education.	**$3,884,092**	College housing loans	136,63
Educationally disadvantaged	3,200,520	**Vocational education**	**640,16**
Special programs and populations	545,515	Basic programs	516,11
Bilingual education	138,057	Consumer and homemaking	27,64
School asst.—federally affected areas .	**544,350**	Program improvement and support	88,41
Maintenance and operation	467,222	State advisory councils	7,99
Construction	77,128	**Education personnel training**	**78,51**
Higher education.	**7,365,042**	Grants to institutions and individuals . .	29,21
College library resources	1,920	Special education	49,30
Library training	880	**Public library services**	**100,01**
Strengthening institutions	157,282	Public library services	60,00
Educational opportunity grants	3,287,555	Interlibrary cooperation	11,52
Work-study and coop. education	600,579	**Education for the handicapped**	**994,17**
Direct loans to students	203,879	State grant programs	908,67
Guaranteed student loans	2,942,072	Early childhood education	35,10
Special programs for the disadvantaged.	158,740	Special centers, projects, and research .	38,40
Other.	12,135	Captioned films and media services . . .	12,00
Higher education facilities	199,927	**Adult basic and secondary education** . .	**95,56**
Construction loans and insurance	39,109	**Department salaries and expenditures** .	**291,59**

The Principal Languages of the World

Source: Sidney S. Culbert. Guthrie Hall NI-25 — University of Washington

Total number of speakers of languages spoken by at least one million persons (midyear 1984)

Language	Millions	Language	Millions	Language	Millions
Achinese (Indonesia)	2	Ijaw (W. Africa)	2	Pashto (see Pushtu)	
Afrikaans (S. Africa)	9	Ilocano (Philippines)	4	Pedi (see Sotho, Northern)	
Albanian	4	Iloko (see Ilocano)		Persian (Iran, Afghanistan)	29
Amharic (Ethiopia)	10	Indonesian (see Malay-Indonesian)		Polish	39
Arabic	166	Italian	62	Portuguese	157
Armenian	4			Provencal (Southern France)	4
Assamese[1] (India)	15	Japanese	121	Punjabi[1] (India; Pakistan)	69
Aymara (Bolivia; Peru)	2	Javanese	50	Pushtu (mainly Afghanistan)	19
Azerbaijani (USSR; Iran)	8	Kamba (E. Africa)	1		
		Kanarese (see Kannada)		Quechua (S. America)	7
Bahasa (see Malay-Indonesian)		Kannada[1] (India)	36		
Balinese	3	Kanuri (W. and Central Africa)	3	Romanian	24
Baluchi (Pakistan; Iran)	3	Kashmiri[1]	3	Ruanda (S. Central Africa)	7
Batak (Indonesia)	2	Kazakh (USSR)	6	Rundi (S. Central Africa)	5
Bemba (S. Central Africa)	2	Khalkha (Mongolia)	2	Russian (Great Russian only)	280
Bengali[1] (Bangladesh; India)	160	Khmer (Kampuchea)	6		
Berber[2] (N. Africa)		Kikongo (see Kongo)		Samar-Leyte (Philippines)	2
Bhili (India)	4	Kikuyu (or Gekoyo)(Kenya)	3	Sango (Central Africa)	2
Bikol (Philippines)	2	Kimbundu (see Mbundu-Kimbundu)		Santali (India)	4
Bisaya (see Cebuano, Panay-Hiligaynon,		Kirghiz (USSR)	2	Sepedi (see Sotho, Northern)	
and Samar-Leyte)		Kituba (Congo River)	3	Serbo-Croatian (Yugoslavia)	20
Bugi (Indonesia)	3	Kongo (Congo River)	2	Shan (Burma)	2
Bulgarian	9	Konkani (India)	2	Shona (S.E. Africa)	5
Burmese	28	Korean	63	Siamese (see Thai)	
Buyi (China)	1	Kurdish (S.W. of Caspian Sea)	7	Sindhi[1] (India; Pakistan)	11
Byelorussian (mainly USSR)	9	Kurukh (or Oraon)(India)	1	Sinhalese (Sri Lanka)	12
				Slovak	5
Cambodian (see Khmer)		Lao[5] (Laos, Asia)	3	Slovene (Yugoslavia)	2
Canarese (see Kannada)		Latvian (or Lettish)	2	Somali (E. Africa)	5
Cantonese (China)	57	Lingala (see Ngala)		Sotho, Northern (S. Africa)	2
Catalan (Spain; France; Andorra)	6	Lithuanian	3	Sotho, Southern (S. Africa)	3
Cebuano (Philippines)	9	Luba-Lulua (Zaire)	3	Spanish	275
Chinese[3]		Luganda (see Ganda)		Sundanese (Indonesia)[3]	17
Chuang[7] (China)		Luhya (or Luhia)(Kenya)	1	Swahili (E. Africa)	35
Chuvash (USSR)	2	Luo (Kenya)	2	Swedish	9
Czech	11	Luri (Iran)	2		
				Tagalog (Philippines)	28
Danish	5	Macedonian (Yugoslavia)	2	Tajiki (USSR)	3
Dayak (Borneo)	1	Madurese (Indonesia)	9	Tamil[1] (India; Sri Lanka)	60
Dutch (see Netherlandish)		Makua (S.E. Africa)	3	Tatar (or Kazan-Turkic)(USSR)	7
		Malagasy (Madagascar)	9	Telugu[1] (India)	60
Edo (W. Africa)	1	Malay-Indonesian	122	Thai[5]	42
Efik	3	Malayalam[1] (India)	31	Thonga (S.E. Africa)	1
English	409	Malinke-Bambara-Dyula (Africa)	7	Tibetan	6
Esperanto	1	Mandarin (China)	755	Tigrinya (Ethiopia)	4
Estonian	1	Marathi[1] (India)	59	Tiv (E. Central Nigeria)	2
Ewe (W. Africa)	3	Mazandarani (Iran)	2	Tong (China)	1
		Mbundu (Umbundu group)(S.Angola)	3	Tswana (S. Africa)	3
Fang-Bulu (W. Africa)	2	Mbundu (Kimbundu group)(Angola)	2	Tulu (India)	1
Finnish	5	Mende (Sierra Leone)	1	Turkish	48
Flemish (see Netherlandish)		Meo (see Miao)		Turkoman (USSR)	2
French	110	Miao (and Meo)(S.E.Asia)	4	Twi-Fante (or Akan)(W.Africa)	6
Fula (W. Africa)	10	Min (China)	44		
		Minankabau (Indonesia)	4	Uighur (Sinkiang, China)	6
Galician (Spain)	3	Moldavian (inc. with Romanian)		Ukrainian (mainly USSR)	42
Galla (see Oromo)		Mongolian (see Khalkha)		Umbundu (see Mbundu-Umbundu)	
Ganda (or Luganda)(E. Africa)	3	Mordvin (USSR)	1	Urdu[1] (Pakistan; India)	77
Georgian (USSR)	4	Moré (see Mossi)		Uzbek (USSR)	10
German	118	Mossi (or Moré)(W. Africa)	3		
Gilaki (Iran)	2			Vietnamese	48
Gondi (India)	2	Ndongo (see Mbundu-Kimbundu)		Visayan (see Cebuano, Panay-	
Greek	11	Nepali (Nepal; India)	11	Hiligaynon, and Samar-Leyte)	
Guarani (mainly Paraguay)	3	Netherlandish (Dutch and Flemish)	20	White Russian (see Byelorussian)	
Gujarati[1] (India)	35	Ngala (or Lingala)(Africa)	3	Wolof (W. Africa)	3
		Norwegian	5	Wu (China)	54
Hakka (China)	25	Nyamwezi-Sukuma (S.E. Africa)	2		
Hani (S.E. Asia)	1	Nyanja (S.E. Africa)	3	Xhosa (S. Africa)	5
Hausa (W. and Central Africa)	27				
Hebrew	3	Oraon (see Kurukh)		Yi (China)	5
Hindi[1,4]	275	Oriya[1] (India)	28	Yiddish[6]	3
Hindustani[4]		Oromo (Ethiopia)	8	Yoruba (W. Africa)	15
Hungarian (or Magyar)	13				
Ibibio (see Efik)		Panay-Hiligaynon (Philippines)	4	Zhuang[7] (China)	
Ibo (or Igbo)(W. Africa)	13	Panjabi (see Punjabi)		Zulu (S. Africa)	6

(1) One of the fifteen languages of the Constitution of India. (2) Here considered a group of dialects. (3) See Mandarin, Cantonese, Wu, Min and Hakka. The "national language" (Guoyu) or "common speech" (Putonghua) is a standardized form of Mandarin as spoken in the area of Peking. (4) Hindi and Urdu are essentially the same language, Hindustani. As the official language of India it is written in the Devanagari script and called Hindi. As the official language of Pakistan it is written in a modified Arabic script and called Urdu. (5) Thai includes Central, Southwestern, Northern and Northeastern Thai. The distinction between Northeastern Thai and Lao is political rather than linguistic. (6) Yiddish is usually considered a variant of German, though it has its own standard grammar, dictionaries, a highly developed literature, and is written in Hebrew characters. (7) A group of Thai-like dialects with about 10 million speakers.

UNITED STATES POPULATION

Demographic Patterns Reflect Changing Society

By John G. Keane
Director, U.S. Bureau of the Census

On January 1, 1984, the estimated resident population was 235.1 million people—a 3.8 percent increase over the 1980 census count of 226.5 million.

During 1983, the Nation's population increased by 2.1 million, the net result of 3.6 million births, 2 million deaths, and 517,000 in net immigration. This compares with a net gain of 2.2 million in 1982.

The annual total fertility rate in 1982 was estimated to be 1.8, which is substantially below that required for natural replacement of the population, that is, 2.1 children per woman.

Number of One-Parent Families Rises Sharply

The increase in the number of one-parent families has been one of the most important changes in family composition since 1970. One-parent families rose by 107 percent between 1970 and 1983, although there was no significant change in the number between 1982 and 1983. Two-parent families declined by 5 percent during the same period, and the overall number of families with children under 18 years increased by 8 percent.

Divorce and separation, and a rise in the number of never-married parents have been the major contributors to increases in one-parent families. Nine out of 10 were maintained by the mother in both 1970 and 1983.

Number of Persons Per Household Stabilizes

The average number of persons per household began to decline in the mid-1960s, dropping from 3.33 persons in 1964 to 2.73 persons in 1981. However, with no statistically significant change in 1982 and 1983, average household size appears to have stabilized. Factors contributing to the earlier decline were relatively low birth rates, high levels of separation and divorce, and a substantial increase in the number of persons living alone.

About 23 percent of households contained one person in 1983, 32 percent two persons, 18 percent three persons, 16 percent four persons, and 12 percent five or more.

Nation's Age Structure Changing

The population continued to age between 1980 and 1983, the median age rising by 0.9 years to 30.9. The trend is expected to continue as the early baby boom generations head toward middle age.

The under 5 population increased by 9 percent, caused almost entirely by an increase in the number of women in their prime childbearing years, rather than a rise in fertility. However, the next three age groups decreased—the 5 to 13 year-olds by 3.3 percent, the 14 to 17 year-olds by 9.9 percent, and the 18 to 24 year-olds by 0.5 percent.

Adults 25 to 44 years old increased by 10.9 percent (8.3 percent for 25-34 year-olds and 14.8 percent for 35-44 year olds). Those 65 years and older grew by 7.2 percent, from 25.5 million to 27.4 million.

Young Adults, Blacks Made Most Notable Gains in Schooling

The proportion of adults (persons 25 years and older) completing high school rose sharply between 1970 and 1982, climbing from 55 to 71 percent within the 12 year period. This increase resulted from both continued replacement of older, less educated cohorts by younger, more educated cohorts, and the steady improvement in high school graduation rates. Young adults, those 25-34 years old, went from 74 percent in 1970 to 86 percent in 1982.

Blacks gained more rapidly than whites in rate of high school completion during the same period. A significantly higher proportion of black young adults (79 percent) were high school graduates in 1982 than in 1970 (53 percent). Whites increased from 76 to 87 percent over the same time.

The proportion of young adults who completed four or more years of college rose from 17 to 25 percent of whites and from 6 to 13 percent of blacks during the same span of years.

Voting-Age Population Expands and Gets Younger

The voting-age population is expected to total nearly 174 million in November 1984, up by 10 million over the previous presidential election year (1980) and 33 million more than in November 1972, another sign of the baby boom generation moving into adulthood.

The median age of the voting-age population dropped from 42 years in 1970 to 40 in 1980. In November 1984, 2 out of 5 voting-age persons were expected to be 25 to 44 years old and somewhat fewer than 1 in 5 will be under 25.

In 1984, blacks are expected to comprise 11 percent (about 19 million) of the total electorate. In 1980, the most recent year for state-level black voting-age population estimates, southern states had the highest black proportions; about one-third of the voting-age population in both Mississippi and South Carolina were black. The greatest numbers were in New York, California, Texas, and Illinois.

In 1980, nearly 70 percent of the 9 million Spanish-origin electorate was in California, Texas, New York, and Florida; the first two states had about half of the nation's Hispanic voters.

Taxes Take Nearly One-Fourth of Household Incomes

Nearly one-fourth —23.6 percent— of household income went to pay taxes in 1981—federal and state income taxes, social security, and property taxes. Average household income after taxes was $17,500, a 2.6 percent decrease from 1980 after adjusting for inflation. Taxes reduced household income by about $442 billion in 1981, of which $271 billion was in federal income taxes.

Households headed by those 65 years and older paid about 14 percent of their income toward taxes in 1981, reducing their average income from $14,250 to $12,320.

More Women Are Managers and Family Breadwinners

The proportion of executives, administrators, and managers who were women rose from 19 to 31 percent between 1970 and 1980. The increase was much greater than the overall growth of women in the labor force. Women also improved their share in other job categories during the 1970s: professional (44 to 49 percent), technical (34 to 44 percent), and sales (41 to 49 percent).

In 1981, nearly 6 million wives (12 percent of all American couples) earned more than their husbands. The wife was the sole earner for 2 million couples. Both spouses earned income among the other 4 million couples, but the wife's share was larger. The wife was the primary earner for one of five black couples compared with one in 10 white or Hispanic couples.

Most Working Mothers Used Childcare Outside the Home

More than half (55 percent) of working mothers with preschool children in 1982 had them cared for outside the home. Another 40 percent used other homes, while 15 percent used group care centers.

Working mothers most likely to use group care services were black, those whose youngest child was at least three years old, well-educated women, and those working full time.

In 23 percent of the families, one parent provided the care—14 percent by fathers at home and 9 percent by mothers while at work. Nearly one fourth of fathers providing primary child care were unemployed.

Americans Move Less Frequently

About 17 percent of the population changed residence between 1981 and 1982 compared with about 18 percent in 1970-71 and 20 percent in 1960-61. The decline occurred even though the most frequent movers, those 20 to 29 year old, increased their proportion of the population from 1 percent in 1961 to 18 percent in 1982. Some reasons are a steady drop in average family size since the mid-1960s, reducing the need for larger homes; increases in homeownership (renters are four to five times more likely to move a homeowners); more two-earner families, which curtails long distance moving; and difficulty in purchasing homes because

246

of increased housing costs, which tend to reduce the desire or ability to move.

Most 1981-82 moves were for short distances—about 62 percent within the same county, 82 percent within the same state, and 90 percent within the same region. The Northeast and North Central regions had net outmigrations (212,000 and 370,000), but the South showed a net inmigration of 470,000.

Central cities of metropolitan areas had a loss of 2.5 million, 2.7 million moving in but 5.2 million moving out. Of those moving from central cities, three times as many went to the suburbs (4 million) as to nonmetropolitan areas (1.2 million).

Means of Transportation and Travel Time to Work

According to the 1980 Census of Population, nearly two-thirds of the 97 million persons 16 years and over at work in 1980 drove to the jobsite alone. One-fifth rode in carpools, 6 percent used public transportation, 6 percent walked to work, 2 percent used other means, and 2 percent worked at home.

Average travel time to work was 22 minutes, ranging from 13 minutes in South Dakota to 29 minutes in New York. The average was 23 minutes for residents within a metropolitan area and 19 minutes for those living farther out. Generally, the greater the rate of use of public transportation, the longer the average travel time.

Population of the U.S., 1970-1980

Source: U.S. Bureau of the Census

Region, division, and state	1980 Census	1970 Census	Pct. + or −	1980 Urban	1980 Rural	Pct. urban	Rank 1980	Rank 1970
United States.	226,545,805	203,302,031	11.4	167,050,992	59,494,813	73.7	...	...
Regions:								
Northeast	49,135,283	49,060,514	0.2	38,905,545	10,229,738	79.2	...	...
North Central	58,865,670	56,590,294	4.0	41,519,746	17,345,924	70.5	...	...
South.	75,372,362	62,812,980	20.0	50,414,258	24,958,104	66.9	...	...
West	43,172,490	34,838,243	23.9	36,211,443	6,961,047	83.9	...	...
New England	12,348,493	11,847,245	4.2	9,269,249	3,079,244	75.1	...	...
Maine.	1,124,660	993,722	13.2	534,072	590,588	47.5	38	38
New Hampshire.	920,610	737,681	24.8	480,325	440,285	52.2	42	41
Vermont	511,456	444,732	15.0	172,735	338,721	33.8	48	48
Massachusetts	5,737,037	5,689,170	0.8	4,808,339	928,698	83.8	11	10
Rhode Island	947,154	949,723	-0.3	824,004	123,150	87.0	40	39
Connecticut	3,107,576	3,032,217	2.5	2,449,774	657,802	78.8	25	24
Middle Atlantic	36,786,790	37,213,269	-1.1	29,636,296	7,150,494	80.6	...	...
New York	17,558,072	18,241,391	-3.7	14,858,068	2,700,004	84.6	2	2
New Jersey	7,364,823	7,171,112	2.7	6,557,377	807,446	89.0	9	8
Pennsylvania	11,863,895	11,800,766	0.5	8,220,851	3,643,044	69.3	4	3
East North Central	41,682,217	40,262,747	3.5	30,533,879	11,148,338	73.3	...	...
Ohio	10,797,630	10,657,423	1.3	7,918,259	2,879,371	73.3	6	6
Indiana	5,490,224	5,195,392	5.7	3,525,298	1,964,926	64.2	12	11
Illinois	11,426,518	11,110,285	2.8	9,518,039	1,908,479	83.3	5	5
Michigan	9,262,078	8,881,826	4.3	6,551,551	2,710,527	70.7	8	7
Wisconsin	4,705,767	4,417,821	6.5	3,020,732	1,685,035	64.2	16	16
West North Central	17,183,453	16,327,547	5.2	10,985,867	6,197,586	63.9	...	...
Minnesota	4,075,970	3,806,103	7.1	2,725,202	1,350,768	66.9	21	19
Iowa	2,913,808	2,825,368	3.1	1,708,232	1,205,576	58.6	27	25
Missouri	4,916,686	4,677,623	5.1	3,349,588	1,567,098	68.1	15	13
North Dakota	652,717	617,792	5.7	318,310	334,407	48.8	46	45
South Dakota	690,768	666,257	3.7	320,777	369,991	46.4	45	44
Nebraska	1,569,825	1,485,333	5.7	987,859	581,966	62.9	35	35
Kansas	2,363,679	2,249,071	5.1	1,575,899	787,780	66.7	32	28
South Atlantic	36,959,123	30,678,826	20.5	24,813,020	12,146,103	67.1	...	...
Delaware	594,338	548,104	8.4	419,819	174,519	70.6	47	46
Maryland.	4,216,975	3,923,897	7.5	3,386,555	830,420	80.3	18	18
District of Columbia.	638,333	756,668	-15.6	638,333	—	100.0	...	...
Virginia	5,346,818	4,651,448	14.9	3,529,423	1,817,395	66.0	14	14
West Virginia	1,949,644	1,744,237	11.8	705,319	1,244,325	36.2	34	34
North Carolina.	5,881,766	5,084,411	15.7	2,822,852	3,058,914	48.0	10	12
South Carolina	3,121,820	2,590,713	20.5	1,689,253	1,432,567	54.1	24	26
Georiga	5,463,105	4,587,930	19.1	3,409,081	2,054,024	62.4	13	15
Florida	9,746,324	6,791,418	43.5	8,212,385	1,533,939	84.3	7	9
East South Central	14,666,423	12,808,077	14.5	8,166,274	6,500,149	55.7	...	...
Kentucky.	3,660,777	3,320,711	13.7	1,862,183	1,798,594	50.9	23	23
Tennessee.	4,591,120	3,926,018	16.9	2,773,573	1,817,547	60.4	17	17
Alabama.	3,893,888	3,444,354	13.1	2,337,713	1,556,175	60.0	22	21
Mississippi	2,520,638	2,216,994	13.7	1,192,805	1,327,833	47.3	31	29
West South Central	23,746,816	19,326,077	22.9	17,434,964	6,311,852	73.4	...	...
Arkansas.	2,286,435	1,923,322	18.9	1,179,556	1,106,879	51.6	33	32
Louisiana.	4,205,900	3,644,637	15.4	2,887,309	1,318,591	68.6	19	20
Oklahoma	3,025,290	2,559,463	18.2	2,035,082	990,208	67.3	26	27
Texas.	14,229,191	11,198,655	27.1	11,333,017	2,896,174	79.6	3	4
Mountain	11,372,785	8,289,901	37.2	8,685,310	2,687,475	76.4	...	...
Montana	786,690	694,409	13.3	416,402	370,288	52.9	44	43
Idaho	943,935	713,015	32.4	509,702	434,233	54.0	41	42
Wyoming.	469,557	332,416	41.3	294,639	174,918	62.7	49	49
Colorado.	2,889,964	2,209,596	30.8	2,329,869	560,095	80.6	28	30
New Mexico	1,302,894	1,017,055	28.1	939,963	362,931	72.1	37	37
Arizona.	2,718,215	1,775,399	53.1	2,278,728	439,487	83.8	29	33
Utah	1,461,037	1,059,273	37.9	1,233,060	227,977	84.4	36	36
Nevada.	800,493	488,738	63.8	682,947	117,546	85.3	43	47
Pacific	31,799,705	26,548,342	19.8	27,526,133	4,273,572	86.6	...	...
Washington	4,132,156	3,413,244	21.1	3,037,014	1,095,142	73.5	20	22
Oregon.	2,633,105	2,091,533	25.9	1,788,354	844,751	67.9	30	31
California.	23,667,902	19,971,069	18.5	21,607,606	2,060,296	91.3	1	1
Alaska	401,851	302,583	32.8	258,567	143,284	64.3	50	50
Hawaii	964,691	769,913	25.3	834,592	130,099	86.5	39	40
Puerto Rico	3,196,520	2,712,033	17.9	2,134,365	1,062,155	66.8	...	...

U.S. Population by Official

(Members of the Armed Forces overseas or

State	1790	1800	1810	1820	1830	1840	1850	1860	1870	1880
Ala. . .	....	1,250	9,046	127,901	309,527	590,756	771,623	964,201	996,992	1,262,505
Alas.. .	....	....	....	....	....	....	....	....	....	33,426
Ariz.. .	....	....	....	....	....	....	....	....	9,658	40,440
Ark.. .	....	....	1,062	14,273	30,388	97,574	209,897	435,450	484,471	802,525
Cal.. .	....	....	....	....	....	....	92,597	379,994	560,247	864,694
Col.. .	....	....	....	....	....	....	....	34,277	39,864	194,327
Conn. .	237,946	251,002	261,942	275,248	297,675	309,978	370,792	460,147	537,454	622,700
Del.. .	59,096	64,273	72,674	72,749	76,748	78,085	91,532	112,216	125,015	146,608
D.C.. .	....	8,144	15,471	23,336	30,261	33,745	51,687	75,080	131,700	177,624
Fla.. .	....	....	....	....	34,730	54,477	87,445	140,424	187,748	269,493
Ga.. .	82,548	162,686	252,433	340,989	516,823	691,392	906,185	1,057,286	1,184,109	1,542,180
Ha.. .	....	....	....	....	....	....	....	....	....	....
Ida.. .	....	....	....	....	....	....	....	....	14,999	32,610
Ill.. .	....	....	12,282	55,211	157,445	476,183	851,470	1,711,951	2,539,891	3,077,871
Ind.. .	....	5,641	24,520	147,178	343,031	685,866	988,416	1,350,428	1,680,637	1,978,301
Ia.. .	....	....	....	....	....	43,112	192,214	674,913	1,194,020	1,624,615
Kan.. .	....	....	....	....	....	....	....	107,206	364,399	996,096
Ky.. .	73,677	220,955	406,511	564,317	687,917	779,828	982,405	1,155,684	1,321,011	1,648,690
La.. .	....	....	76,556	153,407	215,739	352,411	517,762	708,002	726,915	939,946
Me.. .	96,540	151,719	228,705	298,335	399,455	501,793	583,169	628,279	626,915	648,936
Md.. .	319,728	341,548	380,546	407,350	447,040	470,019	583,034	687,049	780,894	934,943
Mass.. .	378,787	422,845	472,040	523,287	610,408	737,699	994,514	1,231,066	1,457,351	1,783,085
Mich.. .	....	....	4,762	8,896	31,639	212,267	397,654	749,113	1,184,059	1,636,937
Minn.. .	....	....	....	....	....	....	6,077	172,023	439,706	780.773
Miss.. .	....	7,600	31,306	75,448	136,621	375,651	606,526	791,305	827,922	1,131,597
Mo.. .	....	....	19,783	66,586	140,455	383,702	682,044	1,182,012	1,721,295	2,168,380
Mon.. .	....	....	....	....	....	....	....	....	20,595	39,159
Neb.. .	....	....	....	....	....	....	....	28,841	122,993	452,402
Nev.. .	....	....	....	....	....	....	....	6,857	42,491	62,266
N.H.. .	141,885	183,858	214,460	244,161	269,328	284,574	317,976	326,073	318,300	346,991
N.J.. .	184,139	211,149	245,562	277,575	320,823	373,306	489,555	672,035	906,096	1,131,116
N.M.. .	....	....	....	....	....	....	61,547	93,516	91,874	119,565
N.Y.. .	340,120	589,051	959,049	1,372,812	1,918,608	2,428,921	3,097,394	3,880,735	4,382,759	5,082,871
N.C.. .	393,751	478,103	555,500	638,829	737,987	753,419	869,039	992,622	1,071,361	1,399,750
N.D.. .	....	....	....	....	....	....	....	....	*2,405	36,909
Oh.. .	....	45,365	230,760	581,434	937,903	1,519,467	1,980,329	2,339,511	2,665,260	3,198,062
Okla.. .	....	....	....	....	....	....	....	....	....	....
Ore.. .	....	....	....	....	....	....	12,093	52,465	90,923	174,768
Pa.. .	434,373	602,365	810,091	1,049,458	1,348,233	1,724,033	2,311,786	2,906,215	3,521,951	4,282,891
R.I.. .	68,825	69,122	76,931	83,059	97,199	108,830	147,545	174,620	217,353	276,531
S.C.. .	249,073	345,591	415,115	502,741	581,185	594,398	668,507	703,708	705,606	995,577
S.D.. .	....	....	....	....	....	....	....	*4,837	*11,776	98,268
Tenn.. .	35,691	105,602	261,727	422,823	681,904	829,210	1,002,717	1,109,801	1,258,520	1,542,359
Tex.. .	....	....	....	....	....	....	212,592	604,215	818,579	1,591,749
Ut.. .	....	....	....	....	....	....	11,380	40,273	86,786	143,963
Vt.. .	85,425	154,465	217,895	235,981	280,652	291,948	314,120	315,098	330,551	332,286
Va.. .	691,737	807,557	877,683	938,261	1,044,054	1,025,227	1,119,348	1,219,630	1,225,163	1,512,565
Wash.. .	....	....	....	....	....	....	1,201	11,594	23,955	75,116
W. Va.. .	55,873	78,592	105,469	136,808	176,924	224,537	302,313	376,688	442,014	618,457
Wis.. .	....	....	....	....	....	30,945	305,391	775,881	1,054,670	1,315,497
Wy.. .	....	....	....	....	....	....	....	....	9,118	20,789
U.S. . . .	3,929,214	5,308,483	7,239,881	9,638,453	12,860,702	17,063,353	23,191,876	31,443,321	38,558,371	50,189,209

Note: Where possible, population shown is that of 1980 area of state.
*1860 figure is for Dakota Territory; 1870 figures are for parts of Dakota Territory. (1) U.S. total includes persons (5,318 in 1830 and 6,100 in 1840) on public ships in the service of the United States not credited to any region, division, or state.

Density of Population by States

(Per square mile, land area only)

State	1920	1960	1970	1980	State	1920	1960	1970	1980	State	1920	1960	1970	1980
Ala.. .	45.8	64.2	67.9	76.6	La. . .	39.6	72.2	81.0	94.5	Okla.. .	29.2	33.8	37.2	44.1
Alas.*	0.1	0.4	0.5	0.7	Me. . .	25.7	31.3	32.1	36.3	Ore. .	8.2	18.4	21.7	27.4
Ariz. .	2.9	11.5	15.6	23.9	Md. . .	145.8	313.5	396.6	428.7	Pa. . .	194.5	251.4	262.3	264.3
Ark.. .	33.4	34.2	37.0	43.9	Mass. .	479.2	657.3	727.0	733.3	R.I. . .	566.4	819.3	902.5	897.8
Cal.. .	22.0	100.4	127.6	151.4	Mich.. .	63.8	137.7	156.2	162.6	S.C. . .	55.2	78.7	85.7	103.4
Col.. .	9.1	16.9	21.3	27.9	Minn.. .	29.5	43.1	48.0	51.2	S.D. . .	8.3	9.0	8.8	9.1
Conn.. .	286.4	520.6	623.6	637.8	Miss.. .	38.6	46.0	46.9	53.4	Tenn.. .	56.1	86.2	94.9	111.6
Del.. .	113.5	225.2	276.5	307.6	Mo.. .	49.5	62.6	67.8	71.3	Tex.. .	17.8	36.4	42.7	54.3
D.C. . .	7,292.9	12,523.9	12,401.8	10,132.3	Mon.. .	3.8	4.6	4.8	5.4	Ut.. .	5.5	10.8	12.9	17.8
Fla.. .	17.7	91.5	125.5	180.0	Neb.. .	16.9	18.4	19.4	20.5	Vt.. .	38.6	42.0	47.9	55.2
Ga.. .	49.3	67.8	79.0	94.1	Nev.. .	.7	2.6	4.4	7.3	Va.. .	57.4	99.6	116.9	134.7
Ha.* .	39.9	98.5	119.6	150.1	N. H.. .	49.1	67.2	81.7	102.4	Wash.. .	20.3	42.8	51.2	62.1
Ida.. .	5.2	8.1	8.6	11.5	N. J.. .	420.0	805.5	953.1	986.2	W. Va.. .	60.9	77.2	72.5	80.8
Ill.. .	115.7	180.4	199.4	205.3	N. M.. .	2.9	7.8	8.4	10.7	Wis.. .	47.6	72.6	81.1	86.5
Ind.. .	81.3	128.8	143.9	152.8	N. Y.. .	217.9	350.6	381.3	370.6	Wy.. .	2.0	3.4	3.4	4.9
Ia.. .	43.2	49.2	50.5	52.1	N. C.. .	52.5	93.2	104.1	120.4	U.S. . .	*29.9	50.6	57.4	64.0
Kan.. .	21.6	26.6	27.5	28.9	N. D.. .	9.2	9.1	8.9	9.4					
Ky. . .	60.1	76.2	81.2	92.3	Oh.. .	141.4	236.6	260.0	263.3					

*For purposes of comparison, Alaska and Hawaii included in above tabulation for 1920, even though not states then.

Census from 1790 to 1980

other U.S. nationals overseas are not included.)

1890	1900	1910	1920	1930	1940	1950	1960	1970	1980[1]
1,513,401	1,828,697	2,138,093	2,348,174	2,646,248	2,832,961	3,061,743	3,266,740	3,444,354	3,893,888
32,052	63,592	64,356	55,036	59,278	72,524	128,643	226,167	302,583	401,851
88,243	122,931	204,354	334,162	435,573	499,261	749,587	1,302,161	1,775,399	2,718,215
1,128,211	1,311,564	1,574,449	1,752,204	1,854,482	1,949,387	1,909,511	1,786,272	1,923,322	2,286,435
1,213,398	1,485,053	2,377,549	3,426,861	5,677,251	6,907,387	10,586,223	15,717,204	19,971,069	23,667,902
413,249	539,700	799,024	939,629	1,035,791	1,123,296	1,325,089	1,753,947	2,209,596	2,889,964
746,258	908,420	1,114,756	1,380,631	1,606,903	1,709,242	2,007,280	2,535,234	3,032,217	3,107,576
168,493	184,735	202,322	223,003	238,380	266,505	318,085	446,292	548,104	594,338
230,392	278,718	331,069	437,571	486,869	663,091	802,178	763,956	756,668	638,333
391,422	528,542	752,619	968,470	1,468,211	1,897,414	2,771,305	4,951,560	6,791,418	9,746,324
1,837,353	2,216,331	2,609,121	2,895,832	2,908,506	3,123,723	3,444,578	3,943,116	4,587,930	5,463,105
......	154,001	191,874	255,881	368,300	422,770	499,794	632,772	769,913	964,691
88,548	161,772	325,594	431,866	445,032	524,873	588,637	667,191	713,015	943,935
3,826,352	4,821,550	5,638,591	6,485,280	7,630,654	7,897,241	8,712,176	10,081,158	11,110,285	11,426,518
2,192,404	2,516,462	2,700,876	2,930,390	3,238,503	3,427,796	3,934,224	4,662,498	5,195,392	5,490,224
1,912,297	2,231,853	2,224,771	2,404,021	2,470,939	2,538,268	2,621,073	2,757,537	2,825,368	2,913,808
1,428,108	1,470,495	1,690,949	1,769,257	1,880,999	1,801,028	1,905,299	2,178,611	2,249,071	2,363,679
1,858,635	2,147,174	2,289,905	2,416,630	2,614,589	2,845,627	2,944,806	3,038,156	3,220,711	3,660,777
1,118,588	1,381,625	1,656,388	1,798,509	2,101,593	2,363,880	2,683,516	3,257,022	3,644,637	4,205,900
661,086	694,466	742,371	768,014	797,423	847,226	913,774	969,265	993,722	1,124,660
1,042,390	1,188,044	1,295,346	1,449,661	1,631,526	1,821,244	2,343,001	3,100,689	3,923,897	4,216,975
2,238,947	2,805,346	3,366,416	3,852,356	4,249,614	4,316,721	4,690,514	5,148,578	5,689,170	5,737,037
2,093,890	2,420,982	2,810,173	3,668,412	4,842,325	5,256,106	6,371,766	7,823,194	8,881,826	9,262,078
1,310,283	1,751,394	2,075,708	2,387,125	2,563,953	2,792,300	2,982,483	3,413,864	3,806,103	4,075,970
1,289,600	1,551,270	1,797,114	1,790,618	2,009,821	2,183,796	2,178,914	2,178,141	2,216,994	2,520,638
2,679,185	3,106,665	3,293,335	3,404,055	3,629,367	3,784,664	3,954,653	4,319,813	4,677,623	4,916,686
142,924	243,329	376,053	548,889	537,606	559,456	591,024	674,767	694,409	786,690
1,062,656	1,066,300	1,192,214	1,296,372	1,377,963	1,315,834	1,325,510	1,411,330	1,485,333	1,569,825
47,355	42,335	81,875	77,407	91,058	110,247	160,083	285,278	488,738	800,493
376,530	411,588	430,572	443,083	465,293	491,524	533,242	606,921	737,681	920,610
1,444,933	1,883,669	2,537,167	3,155,900	4,041,334	4,160,165	4,835,329	6,066,782	7,171,112	7,364,823
160,282	195,310	327,301	360,350	423,317	531,818	681,187	951,023	1,017,055	1,302,894
6,003,174	7,268,894	9,113,614	10,385,227	12,588,066	13,479,142	14,830,192	16,782,304	18,241,391	17,558,072
1,617,949	1,893,810	2,206,287	2,559,123	3,170,276	3,571,623	4,061,929	4,556,155	5,084,411	5,881,766
190,983	319,146	577,056	646,872	680,845	641,935	619,636	632,446	617,792	652,717
3,672,329	4,157,545	4,767,121	5,759,394	6,646,697	6,907,612	7,946,627	9,706,397	10,657,423	10,797,630
258,657	790,391	1,657,155	2,028,283	2,396,040	2,336,434	2,233,351	2,328,284	2,559,463	3,025,290
317,704	413,536	672,765	783,389	953,786	1,089,684	1,521,341	1,768,687	2,091,533	2,633,105
5,258,113	6,302,115	7,665,111	8,720,017	9,631,350	9,900,180	10,498,012	11,319,366	11,800,766	11,863,895
345,506	428,556	542,610	604,397	687,497	713,346	791,896	859,488	949,723	947,154
1,151,149	1,340,316	1,515,400	1,683,724	1,738,765	1,899,804	2,117,027	2,382,594	2,590,713	3,121,820
348,600	401,570	583,888	636,547	692,849	642,961	652,740	680,514	666,257	690,768
1,767,518	2,020,616	2,184,789	2,337,885	2,616,556	2,915,841	3,291,718	3,567,089	3,926,018	4,591,120
2,235,527	3,048,710	3,896,542	4,663,228	5,824,715	6,414,824	7,711,194	9,579,677	11,198,655	14,229,191
210,779	276,749	373,351	449,396	507,847	550,310	688,862	890,627	1,059,273	1,461,037
332,422	343,641	355,956	352,428	359,611	359,231	377,747	389,881	444,732	511,456
1,655,980	1,854,184	2,061,612	2,309,187	2,421,851	2,677,773	3,318,680	3,966,949	4,651,448	5,346,818
357,232	518,103	1,141,990	1,356,621	1,563,396	1,736,191	2,378,963	2,853,214	3,413,244	4,132,156
762,794	958,800	1,221,119	1,463,701	1,729,205	1,901,974	2,005,552	1,860,421	1,744,237	1,949,644
1,693,330	2,069,042	2,333,860	2,632,067	2,939,006	3,137,587	3,434,575	3,951,777	4,417,821	4,705,767
62,555	92,531	145,965	194,402	225,565	250,742	290,529	330,066	332,416	469,557
62,979,766	76,212,168	92,228,496	106,021,537	123,202,624	132,164,569	151,325,798	179,323,175	203,302,031	226,545,805

U.S. Center of Population, 1790-1980

Center of Population is that point which may be considered as center of population gravity of the U.S. or that point upon which the U.S. would balance if it were a rigid plane without weight and the population distributed thereon with each individual being assumed to have equal weight and to exert an influence on a central point proportional to his distance from that point.

Year	N. Lat.			W.Long.			Approximate location
1790	39	16	30	76	11	12	23 miles east of Baltimore, Md.
1800	39	16	6	76	56	30	18 miles west of Baltimore, Md.
1810	39	11	30	77	37	12	40 miles northwest by west of Washington, D.C. (in Va.)
1820	39	5	42	78	33	0	16 miles east of Moorefield, W. Va.'
1830	38	57	54	79	16	54	19 miles west-southwest of Moorefield, W. Va.'
1840	39	2	0	80	18	0	16 miles south of Clarksburg, W. Va.'
1850	38	59	0	81	19	0	23 miles southeast of Parkersburg, W. Va.'
1860	39	0	24	82	48	48	20 miles south by east of Chillicothe, Oh.
1870	39	12	0	83	35	42	48 miles east by north of Cincinnati, Oh.
1880	39	4	8	84	39	40	8 miles west by south of Cincinnati, Oh. (in Ky.)
1890	39	11	56	85	32	53	20 miles east of Columbus, Ind.
1900	39	9	36	85	48	54	6 miles southeast of Columbus, Ind.
1910	39	10	12	86	32	20	In the city of Bloomington, Ind.
1920	39	10	21	86	43	15	8 miles south-southeast of Spencer, Owen County, Ind.
1930	39	3	45	87	8	6	3 miles northeast of Linton, Greene County, Ind.
1940	38	56	54	87	22	35	2 miles southeast by east of Carlisle, Sullivan County, Ind.
1950 (Inc. Alaska & Hawaii)	38	48	15	88	22	8	3 miles northeast of Louisville, Clay County, Ill.
1960	38	35	58	89	12	35	6 1/2 miles northwest of Centralia, Ill.
1970	38	27	47	89	42	22	5 miles east southeast of Mascoutah, St. Clair County, Ill.
1980	38	8	13	90	34	26	1/4 mile west of DeSoto, Mo.

(1) West Virginia was set off from Virginia Dec. 31, 1862, and admitted as a state June 20, 1863.

Congressional Apportionment

	1980	1970		1980	1970		1980	1970		1980	1970		1980	1970
Ala..	7	7	Ida..	2	2	Minn..	8	8	N. D..	1	1	Vt...	1	1
Alas.	1	1	Ill...	22	24	Miss...	5	5	Oh...	21	23	Va....	10	10
Ariz.	5	4	Ind...	10	11	Mo...	9	10	Okla..	6	6	Wash..	8	7
Ark..	4	4	Ia....	6	6	Mon..	2	2	Ore..	5	4	W. Va.	4	4
Cal..	45	43	Kan..	5	5	Neb..	3	3	Pa...	23	25	Wis...	9	9
Col..	6	5	Ky...	7	7	Nev..	2	1	R. I...	2	2	Wy....	1	1
Conn..	6	6	La....	8	8	N. H..	2	2	S. C..	6	6			
Del..	1	1	Me...	2	2	N. J...	14	15	S. D..	1	2	Totals.	435	435
Fla..	19	15	Md..	8	8	N. M..	3	2	Tenn..	9	8			
Ga..	10	10	Mass..	11	12	N. Y...	34	39	Tex...	27	24			
Ha..	2	2	Mich..	18	19	N. C...	11	11	Ut...	3	2			

The chief reason the Constitution provided for a census of the population every 10 years was to give a basis for apportionment of representatives among the states. This apportionment largely determines the number of electoral votes allotted to each state.

The number of representatives of each state in Congress is determined by the state's population, but each state is entitled to one representative regardless of population. A Congressional apportionment has been made after each decennial census except that of 1920.

Under provisions of a law that became effective Nov. 15, 1941,

apportionment of representatives is made by the method of equal proportions. In the application of this method, the apportionment is made so that the average population per representative has the least possible variation between one state and any other. The first House of Representatives, in 1789, had 65 members, as provided by the Constitution. As the population grew, the number of representatives was increased but the total membership has been fixed at 435 since the apportionment based on the 1910 census.

U.S. Area and Population: 1790 to 1980

Source: U.S. Bureau of the Census

	Area (square miles)				Population			
Census date	Gross	Land	Water	Number	Per sq. mile of land	Increase over preceding census Number	%
1980 (Apr. 1).........	3,618,770	3,539,289	79,481	226,545,805	64.0	23,243,774	11.4
1970 (Apr. 1).........	3,618,770	3,536,855	81,915	203,302,031	57.5	23,978,856	13.4
1960 (Apr. 1).........	3,618,770	3,540,911	77,859	179,323,175	50.6	27,997,377	18.5
1950 (Apr. 1).........	3,618,770	3,552,206	66,564	151,325,798	42.6	19,161,229	14.5
1940 (Apr. 1).........	3,618,770	3,554,608	64,162	132,164,569	37.2	8,961,945	7.3
1930 (Apr. 1).........	3,618,770	3,551,608	67,162	123,202,624	34.7	17,181,087	16.2
1920 (Jan. 1).........	3,618,770	3,546,931	71,839	106,021,537	29.9	13,793,041	15.0
1910 (Apr. 15)........	3,618,770	3,547,045	71,725	92,228,496	26.0	16,016,328	21.0
1900 (June 1)........	3,618,770	3,547,314	71,456	76,212,168	21.5	13,232,402	21.0
1890 (June 1)........	3,612,299	3,540,705	71,594	62,979,766	17.8	12,790,557	25.5
1880 (June 1)........	3,612,299	3,540,705	71,594	50,189,209	14.2	11,630,838	30.2
1870 (June 1)........	3,612,299	3,540,705	71,594	38,558,371	10.9	7,115,050	22.6
1860 (June 1)........	3,021,295	2,969,640	51,655	31,443,321	10.6	8,251,445	35.6
1850 (June 1)........	2,991,655	2,940,042	51,613	23,191,876	7.9	6,122,423	35.9
1840 (June 1)........	1,792,552	1,749,462	43,090	17,069,453	9.8	4,203,433	32.7
1830 (June 1)........	1,792,552	1,749,462	43,090	12,866,020	7.4	3,227,567	33.5
1820 (June 1)........	1,792,552	1,749,462	43,090	9,638,453	5.5	2,398,572	33.1
1810 (Aug. 6)........	1,722,685	1,681,828	40,857	7,239,881	4.3	1,931,398	36.4
1800 (Aug. 4)........	891,364	864,746	26,618	5,308,483	6.1	1,379,269	35.1
1790 (Aug. 2)........	891,364	864,746	26,618	3,929,214	4.5	—	—

NOTE: Percent changes are computed on basis of change in population since preceding census date, and period covered therefore is not always exactly 10 years.

Population density figures given for various years represent the area within the boundaries of the United States which was under the jurisdiction on date in question, including in some cases considerable areas not organized or settled and not covered by the census. In 1870, for example, Alaska was not covered by the census.

Revised figure of 39,818,449 for the 1870 population includes adjustments for undernumeration in the Southern states. On the basis of the revised figure, the population increased by 8,375,128, or 26.6 percent between 1860 and 1870, and by 10,370,760, or 26.1 percent between 1870 and 1880.

Black and Hispanic Population by States

Source: U.S. Bureau of the Census (1980)

	Black	Hispanic		Black	Hispanic		Black	Hispanic
Ala.	996,335	33,299	La.	1,238,241	99,134	Okla.	204,674	57,419
Alas.	13,643	9,507	Me.	3,128	5,005	Ore.	37,060	65,847
Ariz.	74,977	440,701	Md.	958,150	64,746	Pa.	1,046,810	153,961
Ark.	373,768	17,904	Mass.	221,279	141,043	R.I.	27,584	19,707
Cal.	1,819,281	4,544,331	Mich.	1,199,023	162,440	S.C.	948,623	33,426
Col.	101,703	339,717	Minn.	53,344	32,123	S.D.	2,144	4,023
Conn.	217,433	124,499	Miss.	887,206	24,731	Tenn.	725,942	34,077
Del.	95,845	9,661	Mo.	514,276	51,653	Tex.	1,710,175	2,985,824
D.C.	448,906	17,679	Mon.	1,786	9,974	Ut.	9,225	60,302
Fla.	1,342,688	858,158	Neb.	48,390	28,025	Vt.	1,135	3,304
Ga.	1,465,181	61,260	Nev.	50,999	53,879	Va.	1,008,668	79,868
Ha.	17,364	71,263	N.H.	3,990	5,587	Wash.	105,574	120,016
Ida.	2,716	36,615	N.J.	925,066	491,883	W.Va.	65,051	12,707
Ill.	1,675,398	635,602	N.M.	24,020	477,222	Wis.	182,592	62,972
Ind.	414,785	87,047	N.Y.	2,402,006	1,659,300	Wy.	3,364	24,499
Ia.	41,700	25,536	N.C.	1,318,857	56,667	Total	26,495,025	14,608,673
Kan.	126,127	63,339	N.D.	2,568	3,902			
Ky.	259,477	27,406	Oh.	1,076,748	119,883			

Rankings of U.S. Standard Metropolitan Statistical Areas
Source: U.S. Bureau of the Census

Metropolitan areas are ranked by 1980 provisional population size based on new SMSA definitions and compared with a ranking of areas as defined in the 1970 census. Included are 141 of the 323 Standard Metropolitan Statistical Areas (SMSAs) as defined through June 30, 1981 by the Office of Federal Statistical Policy and Standards.

SMSA	1980 Rank	1980 Pop.	1970 Rank	1970 Pop.
New York, NY-NJ	1	9,120,346	1	9,973,716
Los Angeles-Long Beach, CA	2	7,477,503	2	7,041,980
Chicago, IL	3	7,103,624	3	6,974,755
Philadelphia, PA-NJ	4	4,716,818	4	4,824,110
Detroit, MI	5	4,353,413	5	4,435,051
San Francisco-Oakland, CA	6	3,250,630	6	3,109,249
Washington, DC-MD-VA	7	3,060,922	7	2,910,111
Dallas-Fort Worth, TX	8	2,974,805	12	2,377,623
Houston, TX	9	2,905,353	16	1,999,316
Boston, MA	10	2,763,357	8	2,899,101
Nassau-Suffolk, NY	11	2,605,813	9	2,555,868
St. Louis, MO-IL	12	2,356,460	10	2,410,884
Pittsburgh, PA	13	2,263,894	11	2,401,362
Baltimore, MD	14	2,174,023	13	2,071,016
Minneapolis-St. Paul, MN-WI	15	2,113,533	17	1,965,391
Atlanta, GA	16	2,029,710	18	1,595,517
Newark, NJ	17	1,965,969	15	2,057,468
Anaheim-Santa Ana-Garden Grove, CA	18	1,932,709	20	1,421,233
Cleveland, OH	19	1,898,825	14	2,063,729
San Diego, CA	20	1,861,846	23	1,357,854
Miami, FL	21	1,625,781	26	1,267,792
Denver-Boulder, CO	22	1,620,902	27	1,239,545
Seattle-Everett, WA	23	1,607,469	19	1,424,605
Tampa-St. Petersburg, FL	24	1,569,134	30	1,088,549
Riverside-San Bernardino-Ontario, CA	25	1,558,182	28	1,139,149
Phoenix, AZ	26	1,509,052	35	971,228
Cincinnati, OH-KY-IN	27	1,401,491	22	1,387,207
Milwaukee, WI	28	1,397,143	21	1,403,884
Kansas City, MO-KS	29	1,327,106	25	1,273,926
San Jose, CA	30	1,295,071	31	1,065,313
Buffalo, NY	31	1,242,826	24	1,349,211
Portland, OR-WA	32	1,242,594	34	1,007,130
New Orleans, LA	33	1,187,073	32	1,046,470
Indianapolis, IN	34	1,166,575	29	1,111,352
Columbus, OH	35	1,093,316	33	1,017,847
San Juan, PR	36	1,086,376	—	936,693
San Antonio, TX	37	1,071,954	38	888,179
Fort Lauderdale-Hollywood, FL	38	1,018,200	58	620,100
Sacramento, CA	39	1,014,002	42	803,793
Rochester, NY	40	971,230	36	961,516
Salt Lake City-Ogden, UT	41	936,255	49	705,458
Providence-Warwick-Pawtucket, RI-MA	42	919,216	37	908,887
Memphis, TN-AR-MS	43	913,472	41	834,103
Louisville, KY-IN	44	906,152	39	867,330
Nashville-Davidson, TN	45	850,505	50	699,271
Birmingham, AL	46	847,487	44	767,230
Oklahoma City, OK	47	834,088	51	699,092
Dayton, OH	48	830,070	40	852,531
Greensboro-Winston-Salem-High Point, NC	49	827,252	47	724,129
Norfolk-Virginia Beach-Portsmouth, VA-NC	50	806,951	46	732,600
Albany-Schenectady-Troy, NY	51	795,019	43	777,977
Toledo, OH-MI	52	791,599	45	762,658
Honolulu, HI	53	762,565	55	630,528
Jacksonville, FL	54	737,541	57	621,827
Hartford, CT	55	726,114	48	720,581
Orlando, FL	56	700,055	74	453,270
Tulsa, OK	57	689,434	63	549,154
Akron, OH	58	660,328	52	679,239
Syracuse, NY	59	642,971	53	636,596
Gary, Hammond, E. Chicago, IN	60	642,781	54	633,367
Northeast Pennsylvania	61	640,396	56	621,882
Charlotte-Gastonia, NC	62	637,218	62	557,785
Allentown-Bethlehem-Easton, PA-NJ	63	635,481	60	594,382
Richmond, VA	64	632,015	64	547,542
Grand Rapids, MI	65	601,680	67	539,225
New Brunswick-Perth Amboy-Sayreville, NJ	66	595,893	61	583,813
West Palm Beach, FL	67	576,863	96	348,993
Omaha, NE-IA	68	569,614	65	542,646
Greenville-Spartanburg, SC	69	569,066	71	473,454
Jersey City, NJ	70	556,972	59	607,839
Austin, TX	71	536,688	93	360,463
Tucson, AZ	72	531,443	95	351,667
Youngstown-Warren, OH	73	531,350	68	537,124
Raleigh-Durham, NC	74	531,167	76	419,254
Springfield-Chicopee-Holyoke, MA	75	530,668	66	541,752
Oxnard-Simi Valley-Ventura, CA	76	529,174	85	378,497
Wilmington, DE-NJ-MD	77	523,221	70	499,493
Flint, MI	78	521,589	69	508,664
Fresno, CA	79	514,621	77	413,329
Long Branch-Asbury Park, NJ	80	503,173	72	461,849
Baton Rouge, LA	81	494,151	87	375,628
Tacoma, WA	82	485,643	78	412,344
El Paso, TX	83	479,899	94	359,291
Knoxville, TN	84	476,517	81	409,409
Lansing-East Lansing, MI	85	471,565	75	424,271
Las Vegas, NV	86	463,087	123	273,288
Albuquerque, NM	87	454,499	102	333,266
Paterson-Clifton-Passaic, NJ	88	447,585	73	460,782
Harrisburg, PA	89	446,576	80	410,505
Mobile, AL	90	443,536	86	376,690
Johnson City-Kingsport-Bristol, TN-VA	91	433,638	88	373,591
Charleston-North Charleston, SC	92	430,462	100	336,125
Chattanooga, TN-GA	93	426,540	90	370,857
New Haven, CT	94	417,592	79	411,287
Wichita, KS	95	411,313	84	389,352
Columbia, SC	96	410,088	107	322,880
Canton, OH	97	404,421	83	393,789
Bakersfield, CA	98	403,089	104	330,234
Bridgeport, CT	99	395,455	82	401,752
Little Rock, AR	100	393,774	106	323,296
Davenport-Rock I.-Moline, IA-IL	101	383,958	91	362,638
Fort Wayne, IN	102	382,961	92	361,984
York, PA	103	381,255	105	329,540
Shreveport, LA	104	376,710	101	336,000
Beaumont-Port Arthur-Orange, TX	105	375,497	97	347,568
Worcester, MA	106	372,940	89	372,144
Peoria, IL	107	365,864	98	341,979
Newport News-Hampton, VA	108	364,449	103	333,140
Lancaster, PA	109	362,346	108	320,079
Stockton, CA	110	347,342	113	291,073
Spokane, WA	111	341,835	115	287,487
Des Moines, IA	112	338,048	109	313,562
Vallejo-Fairfield, Napa, CA	113	334,402	135	251,129
Augusta, GA-SC	114	327,372	122	275,787
Corpus Christi, TX	115	326,228	118	284,832
Madison, WI	116	323,545	114	290,272
Lakeland-Winter Haven, FL	117	321,652	143	228,515
Jackson, MS	118	320,425	130	258,906
Utica-Rome, NY	119	320,180	99	340,477
Lexington-Fayette, KY	120	317,629	125	266,701
Colorado Springs, CO	121	317,458	139	239,288
Reading, PA	122	312,509	112	296,382
Huntington-Ashland, WV-KY-OH	123	311,350	116	286,935
Evansville, IN-KY	124	309,408	117	284,959
Huntsville, AL	125	308,593	119	282,450
Trenton, NJ	126	307,863	110	304,116
Binghamton, NY	127	301,336	111	302,672
Santa Rosa, CA	128	299,681	156	204,885
Santa Barbara-Santa Maria-Lompoc, CA	129	298,694	127	264,324
Appleton-Oshkosh, WI	130	291,369	121	276,948
Salinas-Seaside-Monterey, CA	131	290,444	136	247,450
Pensacola, FL	132	289,782	137	243,075
McAllen-Pharr-Edinburg, TX	133	283,229	162	181,535
Lawrence-Haverhill, MA-NH	134	281,981	131	258,564
South Bend, IN	135	280,772	120	279,813
Erie, PA	136	279,780	128	263,654
Rockford, IL	137	279,514	124	272,063
Kalamazoo-Portage, MI	138	279,192	132	257,723
Eugene-Springfield, OR	139	275,226	151	215,401
Lorain-Elyria, OH	140	274,909	134	256,843
Melbourne-Titusville-Cocoa, FL	141	272,959	142	230,006

Cities—Growth and Decline

Source: U.S. Bureau of the Census (cities over 170,000 ranked by 1980 population)

Rank	City	1980	1970	1960	1950	1900	1850	1790
1	New York, N.Y.	7,071,639	7,895,563	7,781,984	7,891,957	3,437,202	696,115	49,401
2	Chicago, Ill.	3,005,072	3,369,357	3,550,404	3,620,962	1,698,575	29,963	...
3	Los Angeles, Cal.	2,966,850	2,811,801	2,479,015	1,970,358	102,479	1,610	...
4	Philadelphia, Pa.	1,688,210	1,949,996	2,002,512	2,071,605	1,293,697	121,376	28,522
5	Houston, Tex.	1,595,138	1,233,535	938,219	596,163	44,633	2,396	...
6	Detroit, Mich.	1,203,339	1,514,063	1,670,144	1,849,568	285,704	21,019	...
7	Dallas, Tex.	904,078	844,401	679,684	434,462	42,638	...	...
8	San Diego, Cal.	875,538	697,471	573,224	334,387	17,700	...	...
9	Phoenix, Ariz.	789,704	584,303	439,170	106,818	5,544	...	...
10	Baltimore, Md.	786,775	905,787	939,024	949,708	508,957	169,054	13,503
11	San Antonio, Tex.	785,880	654,153	587,718	408,442	53,321	3,488	...
12	Honolulu Co., Ha.	762,874	630,528	294,194	248,034	39,306	...	...
13	Indianapolis, Ind.	700,807	736,856	476,258	427,173	169,164	8,091	...
14	San Francisco, Cal.	678,974	715,674	740,316	775,357	342,782	34,776	...
15	Memphis, Tenn.	646,356	623,988	497,524	396,000	102,320	8,841	...
16	Washington, D.C.	638,333	756,668	763,956	802,178	278,718	40,001	...
17	Milwaukee, Wis.	636,212	717,372	741,324	637,392	285,315	20,061	...
18	San Jose, Cal.	629,442	459,913	204,196	95,280	21,500	...	...
19	Cleveland, Oh.	573,822	750,879	876,050	914,808	381,768	17,034	...
20	Columbus, Oh.	564,871	540,025	471,316	375,901	125,560	17,882	...
21	Boston, Mass.	562,994	641,071	697,197	801,444	560,892	136,881	18,320
22	New Orleans, La.	557,515	593,471	627,525	570,445	287,104	116,375	...
23	Jacksonville, Fla.	540,920	504,265	201,030	204,517	28,429	1,045	...
24	Seattle, Wash.	493,846	530,831	557,087	467,591	80,671	...	...
25	Denver, Col.	492,365	514,678	493,887	415,786	133,859	...	...
26	Nashville-Davidson, Tenn.	455,651	426,029	170,874	174,307	80,865	10,165	...
27	St. Louis, Mo.	453,085	622,236	750,026	856,796	575,238	77,860	...
28	Kansas City, Mo.	448,159	507,330	475,539	456,622	163,752	...	...
29	El Paso, Tex.	425,259	322,261	276,687	130,485	15,906	...	...
30	Atlanta, Ga.	425,022	495,039	487,455	331,314	89,872	2,572	...
31	Pittsburgh, Pa.	423,938	520,089	604,332	676,806	321,616	46,601	...
32	Oklahoma City, Okla.	403,213	368,164	324,253	243,504	10,037	...	...
33	Cincinnati, Oh.	385,457	453,514	502,550	503,998	325,902	115,435	...
34	Fort Worth, Tex.	385,164	393,455	356,268	278,778	26,688	...	...
35	Minneapolis, Minn.	370,951	434,400	482,872	521,718	202,718	...	...
36	Portland, Ore.	366,383	379,967	372,676	373,628	90,426	...	...
37	Long Beach, Cal.	361,334	358,879	344,168	250,767	2,252	...	...
38	Tulsa, Okla.	360,919	330,350	261,685	182,740	1,390	...	...
39	Buffalo, N.Y.	357,870	462,768	532,759	580,132	352,387	42,261	...
40	Toledo, Oh.	354,635	383,062	318,003	303,616	131,822	3,829	...
41	Miami, Fla.	346,865	334,859	291,688	249,276	1,681	...	...
42	Austin, Tex.	345,496	253,539	186,545	132,459	22,258	629	...
43	Oakland, Cal.	339,337	361,561	367,548	384,575	66,960	...	...
44	Albuquerque, N.M.	331,767	244,501	201,189	96,815	6,238	...	...
45	Tucson, Ariz.	330,537	262,933	212,892	45,454	7,531	...	...
46	Newark, N.J.	329,248	381,930	405,220	438,776	246,070	38,894	...
47	Charlotte, N.C.	314,447	241,420	201,564	134,042	18,091	1,065	...
48	Omaha, Neb.	314,255	346,929	301,598	251,117	102,555	...	...
49	Louisville, Ky.	298,451	361,706	390,639	369,129	204,731	43,194	200
50	Birmingham, Ala.	284,413	300,910	340,887	326,037	38,415	...	...
51	Wichita, Kan.	279,272	276,554	254,698	168,279	24,671	...	...
52	Sacramento, Cal.	275,741	257,105	191,667	137,572	29,282	6,820	...
53	Tampa, Fla.	271,523	277,714	274,970	124,681	15,839	...	...
54	St. Paul, Minn.	270,230	309,866	313,411	311,349	163,065	1,112	...
55	Norfolk, Va.	266,979	307,951	304,869	213,513	46,624	14,326	2,959
56	Virginia Beach, Va.	262,199	172,106	8,091	5,390	...	...	...
57	Rochester, N.Y.	241,741	295,011	318,611	332,488	162,608	36,403	...
58	St. Petersburg, Fla.	238,647	216,159	181,298	96,738	1,575	...	...
59	Akron, Oh.	237,177	275,425	290,351	274,605	42,728	3,266	...
60	Corpus Christi, Tex.	231,999	204,525	167,690	108,287	4,703	...	...
61	Jersey City, N.J.	223,532	260,350	276,101	299,017	206,433	6,856	...
62	Baton Rouge, La.	219,419	165,921	152,419	125,629	11,269	3,905	...
63	Anaheim, Cal.	219,311	166,408	104,184	14,556	1,456	...	...
64	Richmond, Va.	219,214	249,332	219,958	230,310	85,050	27,570	3,761
65	Fresno, Cal.	218,202	165,655	133,929	91,669	12,470	...	...
66	Colorado Springs, Col.	215,150	135,517	70,194	45,472	21,085	...	...
67	Shreveport, La.	205,820	182,064	164,372	127,206	16,013	1,728	...
68	Lexington-Fayette, Ky.	204,165	108,137	62,810	55,534	26,369	8,159	834
69	Santa Ana, Cal.	203,713	155,710	100,350	45,533	4,933	...	...
70	Dayton, Oh.	203,371	243,023	262,332	243,872	85,333	10,977	...
71	Jackson, Miss.	202,895	153,968	144,422	98,271	7,816	1,881	...
72	Mobile, Ala.	200,452	190,026	194,856	129,009	38,469	20,515	...
73	Yonkers, N.Y.	195,351	204,297	190,634	152,798	47,931	...	...
74	Des Moines, Ia.	191,003	201,404	208,982	177,965	62,139	...	...
75	Grand Rapids, Mich.	181,843	197,649	177,313	176,515	87,565	2,686	...
76	Montgomery, Ala.	177,857	133,386	134,393	106,525	30,346	8,728	...
77	Knoxville, Tenn.	175,030	174,587	111,827	124,769	32,637	2,076	...
78	Anchorage, Alas.	174,431	48,081	44,237	11,254	...	...	...
79	Lubbock, Tex.	173,979	149,101	128,691	71,747	...	...	...
80	Fort Wayne, Ind.	172,196	178,269	161,776	133,607	45,115	4,282	...
81	Lincoln, Neb.	171,932	149,518	128,521	98,884	40,169	...	...
82	Spokane, Wash.	171,300	170,516	181,608	161,721	36,848	...	...
83	Riverside, Cal.	170,876	140,089	84,332	46,764	7,973	...	...
84	Madison, Wis.	170,616	171,809	126,706	96,056	19,164	1,525	...
85	Huntington Beach, Cal.	170,505	115,960	11,492	5,237	...	...	...
86	Syracuse, N.Y.	170,105	197,297	216,038	220,583	108,374	22,271	...

City Population by Race and Spanish Origin

Source: U.S. Bureau of the Census

This table presents a summary of the final 1980 census population counts for cities over 200,000, classified by race and Spanish origin. Counts of the population by race as well as Spanish origin in this table are provisional.

	Total	White	Black	Am. Indian Eskimo & Aleut.	Asian & Pacific Islander[1]	Other	Spanish origin[2]
Akron, Oh.	237,177	182,114	52,719	368	858	1,118	1,534
Albuquerque, NM	331,767	268,731	8,361	7,341	3,162	44,172	112,084
Anaheim, CA	219,311	190,679	2,557	1,686	8,913	18,012	38,015
Atlanta, GA	425,022	137,878	282,912	422	2,000	1,810	5,842
Austin, TX	345,496	261,166	42,118	1,003	3,642	37,567	64,766
Baltimore, MD	786,775	345,113	431,151	2,108	4,949	3,454	7,641
Baton Rouge, LA	219,419	135,766	80,119	288	1,603	1,710	3,985
Birmingham, AL	284,413	124,730	158,223	185	793	482	2,227
Boston, MA	562,994	393,937	126,229	1,302	15,150	26,376	36,068
Buffalo, NY	357,870	252,365	95,116	2,383	1,322	6,684	9,499
Charlotte, NC	314,447	211,980	97,627	1,039	2,367	1,434	3,418
Chicago, IL	3,005,072	1,490,217	1,197,000	6,072	69,191	242,592	422,061
Cincinnati, OH	385,457	251,144	130,467	425	2,216	1,205	2,988
Cleveland, OH	573,822	307,264	251,347	1,094	3,384	10,733	17,772
Colorado Springs, CO	215,150	189,113	11,961	1,100	3,144	9,832	18,268
Columbus, OH	564,871	430,678	124,880	924	4,714	3,675	4,651
Corpus Christi, TX	231,999	188,279	11,889	662	1,277	29,892	108,175
Dallas, TX	904,078	555,270	265,594	3,732	7,678	71,804	111,082
Dayton, OH	203,371	126,389	75,031	300	869	999	1,748
Denver, CO	492,365	367,344	59,252	3,847	7,007	53,946	91,937
Detroit, MI	1,203,339	413,730	758,939	3,420	6,621	20,629	28,970
El Paso, TX	425,259	249,214	13,466	1,251	3,544	157,784	265,819
Fort Worth, TX	385,164	265,428	87,723	1,227	2,340	28,423	48,696
Fresno, CA	218,202	156,501	20,665	2,097	6,111	32,828	51,489
Honolulu, HI (county)	762,874	252,293	16,831	2,182	456,873	34,695	54,777
Houston, TX	1,595,138	977,530	440,257	3,228	32,898	140,173	281,224
Indianapolis, IN	700,807	540,294	152,626	994	3,792	3,101	6,145
Jackson, MS	202,895	106,285	95,357	142	621	490	1,508
Jacksonville, FL	540,920	394,734	137,324	1,198	5,240	2,402	9,775
Jersey City, NJ	223,532	127,699	61,954	261	9,793	23,825	41,672
Kansas City, MO	448,159	312,836	122,699	1,622	3,499	7,503	14,703
Lexington-Fayette, KY	204,165	174,605	27,121	225	1,360	854	1,488
Long Beach, CA	361,334	269,953	40,732	2,982	19,609	28,058	50,700
Los Angeles, CA	2,966,850	1,816,683	505,208	16,595	196,024	432,253	815,989
Louisville, KY	298,451	212,102	84,080	336	931	1,002	2,005
Memphis, TN	646,356	333,789	307,702	530	2,701	1,634	5,225
Miami, FL	346,865	231,069	87,110	329	1,861	26,562	194,087
Milwaukee, WI	636,212	466,620	146,940	5,018	3,600	14,034	26,111
Minneapolis, MN	370,951	323,832	38,433	8,932	4,104	5,650	4,684
Mobile, AL	200,452	125,786	72,568	368	972	758	2,265
Nashville-Davidson, TN	455,651	344,886	105,942	529	2,202	2,092	3,627
New Orleans, LA	557,515	236,967	308,136	524	7,332	4,523	19,219
New York, NY	7,071,639	4,293,695	1,784,124	11,824	231,505	749,882	1,405,957
Newark, NJ	329,248	101,417	191,743	551	2,366	33,171	61,254
Norfolk, VA	266,979	162,300	93,987	885	7,149	2,658	6,074
Oakland, CA	339,337	129,690	159,234	2,199	26,341	21,824	32,491
Oklahoma City, OK	403,213	322,374	58,702	10,405	4,167	7,565	11,295
Omaha, NE	314,255	266,070	37,852	1,792	1,734	4,233	7,304
Philadelphia, PA	1,688,210	983,084	638,878	2,325	17,764	46,159	63,570
Phoenix, AZ	789,704	642,059	37,682	10,771	6,979	67,420	115,572
Pittsburgh, PA	423,938	316,694	101,813	482	2,596	2,353	3,196
Portland, OR	366,383	316,993	27,734	3,526	10,636	7,494	7,807
Richmond, VA	219,214	104,743	112,357	357	976	781	2,210
Rochester, NY	241,741	168,102	62,332	1,014	1,536	8,757	13,153
Sacramento, CA	275,741	186,477	36,866	3,322	24,017	25,059	39,160
St. Louis, MO	453,085	242,576	206,386	642	1,696	1,785	5,531
St. Paul, MN	270,230	243,226	13,305	2,538	2,695	8,466	7,864
St. Petersburg, FL	238,647	193,277	41,000	331	1,272	1,013	4,210
San Antonio, TX	785,880	617,636	57,654	1,782	5,086	103,252	421,774
San Diego, CA	875,538	666,829	77,700	5,065	57,207	68,703	130,610
San Francisco, CA	678,974	395,082	86,414	3,548	147,426	46,504	83,373
San Jose, CA	629,442	470,013	29,157	4,826	52,448	80,106	140,574
Santa Ana, CA	203,713	132,072	8,232	1,627	10,631	51,151	90,646
Seattle, WA	493,846	392,766	46,755	6,253	36,613	11,459	12,646
Shreveport, LA	205,820	119,529	84,627	292	773	594	2,769
Tampa, FL	271,523	200,741	63,835	545	1,903	4,499	35,982
Toledo, OH	354,635	283,920	61,750	661	1,653	6,651	10,667
Tucson, AZ	330,537	270,188	12,301	4,341	3,523	40,184	82,189
Tulsa, OK	360,919	298,114	42,594	13,740	2,813	3,658	6,189
Virginia Beach, VA	262,199	226,788	26,291	633	6,570	1,917	5,160
Washington, DC	638,333	171,796	448,229	1,031	6,635	9,960	17,652
Wichita, KA	279,272	235,818	30,200	2,579	3,895	6,780	9,902

(1) excludes other Asian and Pacific Islander groups identified in sample tabulations
(2) Persons of Spanish origin may be of any race

Immigration by Country of Last Residence 1820-1981

Source: U.S. Immigration and Naturalization Service (thousands)

Country	Total 1820-1981	Total 1961-1970	Total 1971-1980	1977	1978	1979	1980[11]	1981[11]	Percent 1820-1981	Percent 1961-1970	Percent 1971-1980
All countries*	50,253	3,321.7	4,493.3	462.3	601.4	460.3	530.6	596.6	100.0	100.0	100.0
Europe	36,407	1,123.4	800.3	74.0	76.2	64.2	72.1	66.7	72.4	33.8	17.8
Austria	4,319	20.6	9.5	0.5	0.5	0.5	0.4	0.4	8.6	.6	.2
Hungary		5.4	6.6	0.5	0.6	0.5	0.8	0.6		.2	.1
Belgium	204	9.2	5.1	0.5	0.6	0.6	0.4	0.5	.4	.3	.1
Czechoslovakia	140	3.3	6.1	0.3	0.4	0.5	1.1	0.8	.3	.1	.1
Denmark	366	9.2	4.4	0.4	0.4	0.4	0.5	0.5	.7	.3	.1
Finland	35	4.2	2.7	0.2	0.3	0.3	0.4	0.3	.1	.1	.1
France	757	45.2	24.6	2.7	2.7	2.9	1.9	1.7	1.5	1.4	.5
Germany	6,998	190.8	74.5	7.4	7.6	7.2	6.6	6.6	13.9	5.7	1.7
Great Britain	4,979	214.5	137.4	14.0	16.4	15.5	15.5	15.0	9.9	6.5	3.1
Greece	670	86.0	92.4	7.8	7.0	5.9	4.7	4.4	1.3	2.6	2.1
Ireland	4,693	37.5	11.6	1.0	0.9	0.8	1.0	0.9	9.3	1.1	.3
Italy	5,310	214.1	129.4	7.4	7.0	6.0	5.5	4.7	10.6	6.4	2.9
Netherlands	363	30.6	10.7	1.0	1.2	1.2	1.2	1.0	.7	.9	.2
Norway	858	15.5	3.9	0.3	0.4	0.4	0.4	0.3	1.7	.5	.1
Poland	528	53.5	37.2	3.3	4.5	3.9	4.7	5.0	1.1	1.6	.8
Portugal	467	76.1	101.7	10.0	10.5	7.1	8.4	7.0	.9	2.3	2.3
Spain	267	44.7	39.3	5.6	4.3	3.3	1.9	1.7	.5	1.3	.9
Sweden	1,275	17.1	6.6	0.6	0.6	0.8	0.8	0.8	2.5	.5	.1
Switzerland	351	18.5	8.4	0.8	0.9	0.8	0.7	0.6	.7	.6	.2
USSR	3,395	2.3	38.9	5.4	4.7	1.9	10.5	9.2	6.8	.1	.9
Yugoslavia	119	20.4	30.6	2.3	2.2	1.9	2.1	2.0	.2	.6	.7
Other Europe	313	4.7	18.7	2.0	2.5	1.8	2.6	2.7	.6	.1	.4
Asia	3,538	427.8	1,588.2	150.8	243.6	183.0	236.1	264.3	7.0	12.9	35.3
China	594	34.8	124.4	12.5	14.5	12.3	27.7	25.8	1.2	1.0	2.8
Hong Kong	208	75.0	113.4	12.3	11.1	16.8	3.9	4.1	.4	2.3	2.5
India	226	27.2	164.0	16.8	19.1	18.6	22.6	21.5	.4	.8	3.6
Iran	70	10.3	45.3	4.2	5.9	8.3	10.4	11.1	.1	.3	1.0
Israel	97	29.6	37.7	4.4	4.5	4.3	3.5	3.5	.2	.9	.8
Japan	419	40.0	49.6	4.5	4.5	4.5	4.2	3.9	.8	1.2	1.1
Jordan	48	11.7	27.3	2.9	3.2	3.2	3.3	3.8	.1	.4	.6
Korea	341	34.5	267.7	30.7	28.8	28.7	32.3	32.7	.7	1.0	6.0
Lebanon	66	15.2	41.4	5.5	4.8	4.8	4.1	4.0	.1	.5	.9
Philippines	517	98.4	355.0	38.5	36.6	40.8	42.3	43.8	1.0	3.0	7.9
Turkey	392	10.1	13.3	1.0	1.0	1.3	2.2	2.8	.8	.3	.3
Vietnam	233	4.3	172.8	3.4	87.6	19.1	43.5	55.6	.5	.1	3.8
Other Asia	327	36.7	176.4	14.1	22.0	20.3	36.1	51.7	.7	.1	3.9
America	9,699	1,716.4	1,982.8	223.2	266.5	197.1	204.5	246.3	19.3	51.7	44.1
Argentina	102	49.7	30.0	3.1	4.1	3.1	2.8	2.2	.2	1.5	.7
Brazil	62	29.3	18.0	1.9	2.2	1.8	1.6	1.6	.1	.9	.4
Canada	4,150	413.3	169.8	18.0	23.5	20.2	13.6	11.2	8.3	12.4	3.8
Colombia	178	72.0	77.3	8.2	10.9	10.5	11.3	10.3	.4	2.2	1.7
Cuba	565	208.5	264.8	66.1	27.5	14.0	15.1	10.9	1.1	6.3	5.9
Dominican Rep.	270	93.3	148.0	11.6	19.5	17.5	17.2	18.2	.5	2.8	3.3
Ecuador	102	36.8	50.1	5.2	5.7	4.4	6.1	5.1	.2	1.1	1.1
El Salvador	64	15.0	34.5	4.4	5.9	4.5	6.1	8.2	.1	.5	.8
Guatemala	52	15.9	26.0	3.7	4.1	2.6	3.8	3.9	.1	.5	.6
Haiti	102	34.5	56.3	5.2	6.1	6.1	6.5	6.7	.2	1.0	1.3
Honduras	42	15.7	17.4	1.6	2.7	2.5	2.6	2.4	.1	.5	.4
Mexico	2,334	453.9	640.4	44.6	92.7	52.5	56.7	101.3	4.6	13.7	14.3
Panama	59	19.4	23.4	2.5	3.3	3.5	3.6	4.6	.1	.6	.5
Peru	61	19.1	29.1	3.9	5.1	4.0	4.0	4.7	.1	.6	.6
West Indies	967	133.9	271.9	27.1	34.6	33.5	34.5	37.5	1.9	4.0	6.1
Other America	589	106.2	125.9	16.1	18.6	16.4	19.0	17.5	1.2	3.2	2.8
Africa	172	29.0	80.7	9.6	10.3	11.2	14.0	15.0	.3	.9	1.8
Australia and New Zealand	125	19.6	23.8	2.5	2.7	2.5	2.2	1.9	.2	.6	.5
Other Oceania	313	5.7	17.4	2.1	2.2	2.4	1.7	2.3	.6	.2	.4

* Figures may not add to total due to rounding. (1) 1938-1945, Austria included with Germany; 1899-1919, Poland included with Austria-Hungary, Germany, and USSR. (2) Beginning 1952, includes data for United Kingdom not specified, formerly included with "Other Europe". (3) Comprises Eire and Northern Ireland. (4) Europe and Asia. (5) Beginning 1957, includes Taiwan. (6) Prior to 1951, included with "Other Asia". (7) Prior to 1951, Philippines included with "All other". (8) Prior to 1953, data for Vietnam not available. (9) Prior to 1951, included with "Other America". (10) Prior to 1951, included with "West Indies". (11) Data on immigration by country of last residence for 1980 and 1981 are not available; data based on country of birth.

Poverty by Family Status, Sex, and Race

Source: U.S. Bureau of the Census. Current Population Reports
By thousands

	1983 No.[1]	1983 %[2]	1982 No.[1]	1982 %[2]	1979 No.[1]	1979 %[2]	1978 No.[1]	1978 %[2]
Total poor	35,266	15.2	34,398	15.0	26,072	11.7	24,497	11.4
In families	27,804	13.8	27,349	13.6	19,964	10.2	19,062	10.0
Head	7,641	12.3	7,512	12.2	5,461	9.2	5,280	9.1
Related children	13,326	21.7	13,139	21.3	9,993	16.0	9,722	15.7
Other relatives	6,837	8.8	6,698	8.7	4,509	6.1	4,059	5.7
Unrelated individuals	6,832	23.4	6,458	23.1	5,743	21.9	5,435	22.1
In female-head families	12,020	40.2	11,701	40.6	10,563	34.9	9,269	35.6
Head	3,557	36.0	3,434	36.3	2,816	30.4	2,654	31.4
Related children	6,709	55.4	6,696	56.0	4,358	48.6	5,687	50.6
Other relatives	1,755	22.1	1,571	21.2	3,389	16.9	928	14.6
Unrelated female individuals	4,213	26.2	4,110	26.6	1,972	26.0	3,611	26.0
In male-head families	15,784	9.2	15,649	9.1	9,400	6.3	9,793	5.9
Head	4,084	7.8	4,079	7.9	2,645	5.5	2,626	5.3
Related children	6,617	13.4	6,443	13.0	5,635	8.5	4,035	7.9
Other relatives	5,083	7.3	5,127	7.3	1,120	5.1	3,131	4.8
Unrelated male individuals	2,619	19.9	2,347	18.8	3,771	16.9	1,824	17.1
Total white poor	23,074	12.1	23,517	12.0	17,214	9.0	16,259	8.7
In families	18,269	10.1	18,015	10.6	12,495	7.4	12,050	7.3
Head	5,223	9.7	5,118	9.6	3,581	6.9	3,523	6.9
Female	1,920	28.3	1,813	27.9	1,350	22.3	1,391	23.5
Related children	8,456	16.9	8,282	16.5	5,909	11.4	5,674	11.0
Other relatives	4,590	6.8	4,615	6.9	3,006	4.7	2,852	4.5
Unrelated individuals	5,291	20.9	5,041	20.7	4,452	19.7	4,209	19.8
Total black poor	9,885	35.7	9,697	35.6	8,050	31.0	7,625	30.6
In families	8,381	34.7	8,355	34.9	6,800	30.0	6,493	29.5
Head	2,162	32.4	2,158	33.0	1,722	27.8	1,622	27.5
Female	1,545	53.8	1,535	56.2	1,234	49.4	1,208	50.6
Related children	4,258	46.3	4,388	47.3	3,745	40.8	3,781	41.2
Other relatives	1,961	23.7	1,809	22.2	1,333	18.2	1,094	15.7
Unrelated individuals	1,334	40.8	1,229	40.3	1,168	37.3	1,132	38.6

[1] Beginning in 1979, total includes members of unrelated subfamilies not shown separately. For earlier years, unrelated subfamily members are included in the "in family" category.
[2] Percent of total population in that general category who fell below poverty level. For example, of all black female heads of households in 1978, 50.6% were poor.

Poverty Level by Family Size 1982, 1983
By thousands

	1983	1982		1983	1982
1 persons	$ 5,061	$ 4,901	3 persons	$ 7,983	$ 7,693
Under 65 years	5,180	5,019	4 persons	10,178	9,862
65 years and over	4,775	4,626	5 persons	12,049	11,684
2 persons	6,483	6,281	6 persons	13,630	13,207
Householder under 65 years	6,697	6,487	7 persons	15,500	15,036
Householder 65 years and			8 persons	17,170	16,719
over	6,023	5,836	9 persons or more	20,310	19,698

Income Distribution by Population Fifths

Families, 1983 Race	Top income of each fifth					Percent distribution of total income					
	Lowest	Second	Third	Fourth	Top 5%	Lowest fifth	Second fifth	Third fifth	Fourth fifth	Highest fifth	Top 5%
Total	$11,629	$20,060	$29,204	$41,824	$67,326	4.7	11.1	17.1	24.4	42.7	15.8
White	12,878	21,288	30,255	42,915	69,342	5.2	11.5	17.2	24.2	42.0	15.8
Black and other	6,206	12,000	20,120	32,011	52,712	3.6	8.8	15.6	25.3	46.8	17.0
Black	5,915	11,025	18,300	29,100	47,610	3.7	9.0	15.9	25.5	45.9	16.0
Region											
Northeast	$12,580	$22,000	$31,325	$43,887	$70,226	4.8	11.5	17.6	24.6	41.6	15.0
North Central	12,000	20,484	29,200	41,000	64,200	4.8	11.5	17.4	24.3	41.9	15.6
South	10,600	18,220	27,200	39,922	65,500	4.5	10.6	16.6	24.3	43.9	16.6
West	12,306	21,000	30,100	43,862	70,000	4.9	11.2	17.1	24.5	42.4	15.5

Persons Below Poverty Level, 1959-1983

Year	Number Below Poverty Level (mil.)				Percent Below Poverty Level				Average income cutoffs for non-farm family of 4[3] at poverty level
	All races[1]	White	Black	Spanish origin[2]	All races[1]	White	Black	Spanish origin[2]	
1960	39.9	28.3	NA	NA	22.2	17.8	NA	NA	3,022
1965	33.2	22.5	NA	NA	17.3	13.3	NA	NA	3,223
1970	25.4	17.5	7.5	NA	12.6	9.9	33.5	NA	3,968
1975	25.9	17.8	7.5	3.0	12.3	9.7	31.3	26.9	5,500
1980[4]	29.3	19.7	8.6	3.5	13.0	10.2	32.5	25.7	8,414
1981[4]	31.8	21.6	9.2	3.7	14.0	11.1	34.2	26.5	9,287.
1982[4]	34.4	23.5	9.7	4.3	15.0	12.0	35.6	29.9	9,862
1983[4]	35.3	23.9	9.8	4.2	15.2	12.1	35.7	28.4	10,178

NA = Not Available. (1) Includes other races not shown separately. (2) Persons of Spanish origin may be of any race. (3) Beginning in 1981, income cutoffs for nonfarm families are applied to both farm and nonfarm families. (4) Data based on revised poverty definition.

Aid to Families with Dependent Children

Source: Office of Research and Statistics. Social Security Administration
(thousands)

1983 State	Total Assistance Payments	Ave. Monthly Caseload	Ave. Monthly Recipients	Ave. Payment Per Family	Ave. Payment Per Person
Alabama	$73,168	55,022	154,547	$110.82	$39.45
Alaska	30,039	4,644	11,026	538.99	227.04
Arizona	62,513	24,163	67,463	215.60	77.22
Arkansas	34,460	22,455	63,761	127.89	45.04
California	2,986,330	538,848	1,579,695	461.84	157.54
Colorado	99,017	29,208	85,194	282.51	96.85
Connecticut	217,422	43,903	127,980	412.70	141.57
Delaware	27,236	9,576	26,505	237.00	85.63
Dist. of Columbia	80,073	23,838	62,362	279.92	107.00
Florida	239,576	103,344	281,308	193.19	70.97
Georgia	189,307	89,168	239,945	176.92	65.75
Hawaii	86,414	17,719	54,607	406.40	131.87
Idaho	21,434	6,960	18,944	256.62	94.28
Illinois	824,339	237,123	734,882	289.70	93.48
Indiana	145,694	57,070	164,546	212.74	73.79
Iowa	144,761	37,164	103,263	324.60	116.82
Kansas	91,050	24,769	72,228	306.33	105.05
Kentucky	126,737	57,545	152,487	183.53	69.26
Lousiana	133,196	65,944	200,306	168.32	55.41
Maine	63,377	17,029	48,925	310.14	107.95
Maryland	224,514	70,429	192,364	265.65	97.26
Massachusetts	416,357	91,483	256,431	379.27	135.31
Michigan	1,132,177	240,069	751,634	393.00	125.52
Minnesota	257,723	47,718	138,661	450.08	154.89
Mississippi	56,595	51,814	151,177	91.02	31.20
Missouri	187,202	64,799	181,495	240.75	85.95
Montana	23,714	6,536	17,951	302.34	110.09
Nebraska	54,328	14,213	40,956	318.54	110.54
Nevada	10,868	4,685	12,971	193.33	69.82
New Hampshire	23,689	7,024	18,947	281.05	104.19
New Jersey	497,916	132,595	397,082	312.93	104.49
New Mexico	43,261	17,626	48,031	204.53	75.06
New York	1,737,668	360,372	1,089,780	401.82	132.88
North Carolina	152,964	69,647	174,245	183.02	73.16
North Dakota	14,891	4,009	10,957	309.56	113.25
Ohio	652,861	211,418	634,440	257.33	85.75
Oklahoma	77,065	25,027	72,264	256.61	88.87
Oregon	100,065	27,622	73,638	301.69	113.24
Pennsylvania	733,780	194,097	579,399	315.04	105.54
Rhode Island	67,559	15,938	45,159	353.24	124.67
South Carolina	75,846	49,569	134,145	127.51	47.12
South Dakota	17,573	5,995	16,746	244.26	87.45
Tennessee	81,190	58,367	152,625	115.92	44.33
Texas	156,266	102,266	307,045	127.34	42.41
Utah	53,916	12,892	38,050	348.50	118.08
Vermont	36,479	7,280	21,389	417.58	142.12
Virginia	168,523	60,449	160,809	232.32	87.33
Washington	261,579	54,539	144,868	399.68	150.47
West Virginia	56,607	28,395	79,400	166.13	59.41
Wisconsin	457,114	87,799	266,390	450.95	148.63
Wyoming	11,181	2,954	7,679	315.40	121.34
Guam	4,224	1,500	5,410	234.66	65.07
Puerto Rico	63,976	54,795	183,385	97.30	29.07
Virgin Islands	2,995	1,301	3,748	191.93	66.60
Total	**$13,606,809**	**3,650,713**	**10,659,245**	**$310.60**	**$106.38**

Welfare Recipients and Payments, 1955-1982

Category		1955, Dec.	1965, Dec.	1970, Dec.	1975, Dec. (b)	1980, Dec.	1981, Dec.	1982, Dec.
Old age:	Recipients	2,538,000	2,087,000	2,082,000	2,333,685	1,807,776	1,678,090	1,548,741
	Total amt.	$127,003,000	$131,674,000	$161,642,000	$217,002,000	$221,303,000	$231,274,000	$225,637,000
	Avg. amt.	$50.05	$63.10	$77.65	$92.99	$128.20	$137.81	$145.69
	(a)Avg. real $	$62.41	$66.75	$66.78	$57.65	$49.56	$49.03	$49.89
AFDC:	Recipients	2,192,000	4,396,000	9,659,000	11,389,000	11,101,556	10,612,943	10,503,918
	Total amt.	$51,472,000	$144,355,000	$485,877,000	$824,648,000	$1,105,777,000	$1,109,068,000	$1,101,149,000
	Avg. amt.	$23.50	$32.85	$50.30	$72.40	$99.61	$103.09	$104.83
	(a)Avg. real $	$29.30	$34.76	$43.26	$44.89	$38.55	$36.62	$35.85
Blind:	Recipients	104,000	85,100	81,000	75,315	78,401	78,570	77,356
	Total amt.	$5,803,000	$6,922,000	$8,446,000	$11,220,000	$16,381,000	$17,891,000	$18,689,000
	Avg. amt.	$55.55	$81.35	$104.35	$148.97	$213.23	$227.70	$241.60
	(a)Avg. real $	$69.27	$86.07	$89.74	$92.36	$82.42	$81.00	$82.73
Disabled:	Recipients	241,000	557,000	935,000	1,950,625	2,255,840	2,262,215	2,231,493
	Total amt.	$11,750,000	$37,035,000	$91,325,000	$279,073,000	$444,322,000	$485,235,000	$511,114,000
	Avg. amt.	$48.75	$66.50	$97.65	$143.07	$197.90	$214.49	$229.04
	(a)Avg. real $	$60.79	$70.36	$83.98	$88.70	$76.50	$79.36	$78.44

(a) Dollar amounts adjusted to represent actual purchasing power in terms of average value of dollar during 1967. (b) Administration of the public assistance programs of Old-age Assistance. Aid to the Blind. and Aid to the Disabled was transferred to the Social Security Administration by Public Law 92-603 effective 1/1/74.

U.S. Places of 5,000 or More Population—With ZIP and Area Codes

Source: U.S. Bureau of the Census; U.S. Postal Service; N.Y. Telephone Co.

The listings below show the official urban population of the United States. "Urban population" is defined as all persons living in (a) places of 5,000 inhabitants or more, incorporated as cities, villages, boroughs (except Alaska), and towns (except in New England, New York, New Jersey, Pennsylvania and Wisconsin), but excluding those persons living in the rural portions of extended cities; (b) unincorporated places of 5,000 inhabitants or more; and (c) other territory, incorporated or unincorporated, included in urbanized areas.

The non-urban portion of an extended city contains one or more areas, each at least 5 square miles in extent and with a population density of less than 100 persons per square mile. The area or areas constitute at least 25 percent of the legal city's land area of a total of 25 square miles or more.

In New England, New York, New Jersey, Pennsylvania, and Wisconsin, minor civil divisions called "towns" often include rural areas and one or more urban areas. Only the urban areas of these "towns" are included here, except in the case of New England where entire town populations, which may include some rural population, are shown; these towns are indicated by italics. Boroughs in Alaska may contain one or more urban areas which are included here. Population in Hawaii is counted by county subdivisions.

(u) means place is unincorporated.

The ZIP Code of each place appears before the name of that place, if it is obtainable. Telephone Area Code appears in parentheses after the name of the state or, if a state has more than one number, after the name of the place.

CAUTION—Where an asterisk (*) appears before the ZIP Code, ask your local postmaster for the correct ZIP Code for a specific address within the place listed.

ZIP code	Place	1980	1970		ZIP code	Place	1980	1970
	Alabama (205)				36067	Prattville	18,647	13,116
					36610	Prichard	30,541	41,578
35007	Alabaster	7,079	2,642		35901	Rainbow City	6,299	3,099
35950	Albertville	12,039	9,963		35809	Redstone Arsenal(u)	5,728	
35010	Alexander City	13,807	12,358		36274	Roanoke	5,896	5,251
36420	Andalusia	10,415	10,092		35653	Russellville	8,195	7,814
36201	Anniston	29,135	31,533		36201	Saks(u)	11,118	
35016	Arab	5,967	4,399		36571	Saraland	9,833	7,840
35611	Athens	14,558	14,360		35768	Scottsboro	14,758	9,324
36502	Atmore	8,789	8,293		36701	Selma	26,684	27,379
35954	Attalla	7,737	7,510		36701	Selmont-West Selmont(u)	5,255	2,270
36830	Auburn	28,471	22,767		35660	Sheffield	11,903	13,115
36507	Bay Minette	7,455	6,727		35901	Southside	5,141	983
35020	Bessemer	31,729	33,428		35150	Sylacauga	12,708	12,255
*35203	Birmingham	284,413	300,910		35160	Talladega	19,128	17,662
35957	Boaz	7,151	5,635		35217	Tarrant City	8,148	6,835
36426	Brewton	6,680	6,747		36582	Theodore(u)	6,392	
35020	Brighton	5,308	2,277		36619	Tillman's Corner(u)	15,941	
35215	Center Point(u)	23,317	15,675		36081	Troy	12,587	11,482
36611	Chickasaw	7,402	8,447		35401	Tuscaloosa	75,143	65,773
35044	Childersburg	5,084	4,831		35674	Tuscumbia	9,137	8,828
35045	Clanton	5,832	5,868		36083	Tuskegee	12,716	11,028
35055	Cullman	13,084	12,601		35216	Vestavia Hills	15,733	12,250
35601	Decatur	42,002	38,044		36201	West End-Cobb(u)	5,189	5,515
36732	Demopolis	7,678	7,651					
36301	Dothan	48,750	36,733					
36330	Enterprise	18,033	15,591			**Alaska (907)**		
36027	Eufaula	12,097	9,102					
35064	Fairfield	13,242	14,369		*99502	Anchorage	173,017	48,081
36532	Fairhope	7,286	5,720		99702	Eielson AFB(u)	5,232	6,149
35555	Fayette	5,287	4,568		99701	Fairbanks	22,645	14,771
35630	Florence	37,029	34,031		99801	Juneau	19,528	6,050
35214	Forestdale(u)	10,814	6,091		99611	Kenai Peninsula borough	25,282	16,586
35967	Fort Payne	11,485	8,435		99901	Ketchikan	7,198	6,994
36360	Fort Rucker(u)	8,932	14,242		99835	Sitka	7,803	3,370
35068	Fultondale	6,217	5,163					
*35901	Gadsden	47,565	53,928					
35071	Gardendale	8,005	6,537			**Arizona (602)**		
36037	Greenville	7,807	8,033					
35976	Guntersville	7,041	6,491		85321	Ajo(u)	5,189	5,881
35565	Haleyville	5,306	4,190		85220	Apache Junction	9,935	2,443
35640	Hartselle	8,858	7,355		85323	Avondale	8,134	6,626
35209	Homewood	21,271	21,245		85603	Bisbee	7,154	8,328
35226	Hoover	15,064	688		86430	Bullhead City-Riviera(u)	10,364	
35020	Hueytown	13,452	7,095		85222	Casa Grande	14,971	10,536
*35804	Huntsville	142,513	139,282		85224	Chandler	29,673	13,763
35210	Irondale	6,521	3,166		85228	Coolidge	6,851	5,314
36545	Jackson	6,073	5,957		85707	Davis-Monthan AFB(u)	6,279	
36265	Jacksonville	9,735	7,715		85607	Douglas	13,058	12,462
35501	Jasper	11,894	10,798		85205	Dreamland-VeldaRose(u)	5,969	
36863	Lanett	6,897	6,908		85231	Eloy	6,240	5,381
35094	Leeds	8,638	6,991		86001	Flagstaff	34,641	26,117
35228	Midfield	6,182	6,621		85613	Fort Huachuca(u)	NA	6,659
*36601	Mobile	200,452	190,026		85234	Gilbert	5,717	1,971
36460	Monroeville	5,674	4,846		*85301	Glendale	96,988	36,228
*36104	Montgomery	178,157	133,386		85501	Globe	6,886	7,333
35223	Mountain Brook	17,400	19,474		85614	Green Valley(u)	7,999	
35660	Muscle Shoals	8,911	6,907		86025	Holbrook	5,785	4,759
35476	Northport	14,291	9,435		86401	Kingman	9,257	7,312
36801	Opelika	21,896	19,027		86403	Lake Havasu City	15,737	4,111
36467	Opp	7,204	6,493		85301	Luke(u)	NA	5,047
36203	Oxford	8,939	4,361		*85201	Mesa	152,453	63,049
36360	Ozark	13,188	13,555		85621	Nogales	15,683	8,946
35124	Pelham	6,759	931		86040	Page(u)	NA	1,439
35125	Pell City	6,616	5,602		85253	Paradise Valley	10,832	6,637
36867	Phenix City	26,928	25,281		85345	Peoria	12,307	4,792
36272	Piedmont	5,544	5,063		*85001	Phoenix	764,911	584,303
35127	Pleasant Grove	7,102	5,090		86301	Prescott	20,055	13,631
					85546	Safford	7,010	5,493

ZIP code	Place	1980	1970
85631	San Manuel(u)	5,443	....
*85251	Scottsdale	88,622	67,823
85635	Sierra Vista	25,968	6,689
85350	Somerton	5,761	2,225
85713	South Tucson	6,554	6,220
85351	Sun City(u)	40,505	13,670
*85282	Tempe	106,919	63,550
86045	Tuba City(u)	5,045	....
*85726	Tucson	330,537	262,933
85364	West Yuma(u)	NA	5,552
86047	Winslow	7,921	8,066
85364	Yuma	42,481	29,007

Arkansas (501)

ZIP code	Place	1980	1970
71923	Arkadelphia	10,005	9,841
72501	Batesville	8,447	7,209
72015	Benton	17,437	16,499
72712	Bentonville	8,756	5,508
72315	Blytheville	24,314	24,752
71701	Camden	15,356	15,147
72830	Clarksville	5,237	4,616
72032	Conway	20,375	15,510
71635	Crossett	6,706	6,191
71639	Dumas	6,091	4,600
71730	El Dorado	26,685	25,283
72701	Fayetteville	36,604	30,729
71742	Fordyce	5,175	4,837
72335	Forrest City	13,803	12,521
72901	Fort Smith	71,384	62,802
72601	Harrison	9,567	7,239
72342	Helena	9,598	10,415
71801	Hope	10,290	8,830
71901	Hot Springs	35,166	35,631
72076	Jacksonville	27,589	19,832
72401	Jonesboro	31,530	27,050
*72201	Little Rock	158,915	132,483
71753	Magnolia	11,909	11,303
72104	Malvern	10,163	8,739
72360	Marianna	6,220	6,196
71654	McGehee	5,671	4,683
71953	Mena	5,154	4,530
71655	Monticello	8,259	5,085
72110	Morrilton	7,355	6,814
72653	Mountain Home	7,447	3,936
72112	Newport	8,339	7,725
*72114	North Little Rock	64,388	60,040
72370	Osceola	8,881	7,892
72450	Paragould	15,214	10,639
71601	Pine Bluff	56,576	57,389
72455	Pocahontas	5,995	4,544
72756	Rogers	17,429	11,050
72801	Russellville	14,000	11,750
72143	Searcy	13,612	9,040
72116	Sherwood	10,423	2,754
72761	Siloam Springs	7,940	6,009
72764	Springdale	23,458	16,783
72160	Stuttgart	10,941	10,477
75501	Texarkana	21,459	21,682
72472	Trumann	6,395	6,023
72956	Van Buren	12,020	8,373
71671	Warren	7,646	6,433
72390	West Helena	11,367	11,007
72301	West Memphis	28,138	26,070
72396	Wynne	7,805	6,696

California

ZIP code	Place		1980	1970
94501	Alameda	(415)	63,852	70,968
94507	Alamo(u)	(415)	8,505	14,059
94706	Albany	(415)	15,130	15,561
*91802	Alhambra	(818)	64,767	62,125
90249	Alondra Park(u)	(213)	12,096	12,193
92001	Alpine(u)	(619)	5,368	1,570
91001	Altadena(u)	(213)	40,510	42,415
95116	Alum Rock(u)	(408)	17,471	18,355
94590	American Canyon(u)	(707)	5,712	....
*92803	Anaheim	(714)	219,494	166,408
96007	Anderson	(916)	7,381	5,492
94509	Antioch	(415)	43,559	28,060
92307	Apple Valley(u)	(714)	14,305	6,702
95003	Aptos(u)	(408)	7,039	8,704
91006	Arcadia	(818)	45,993	45,138
95521	Arcata	(707)	12,849	8,985
95825	Arden-Arcade(u)	(916)	87,570	82,492
93420	Arroyo Grande	(805)	11,290	7,454
90701	Artesia	(213)	14,301	14,757
93203	Arvin	(805)	6,863	5,199
94577	Ashland(u)	(415)	13,893	14,810
93422	Atascadero	(805)	15,930	10,290
94025	Atherton	(415)	7,797	8,085
95301	Atwater	(209)	17,530	11,640
95603	Auburn	(916)	7,540	6,570
92505	August(u)	(209)	5,445	6,293
91746	Avocado Heights(u)	(213)	11,721	9,810
91702	Azusa	(818)	29,300	25,217
*93302	Bakersfield	(805)	105,611	69,515
91706	Baldwin Park	(818)	50,554	47,285

ZIP code	Place		1980	1970
92220	Banning	(714)	14,020	12,034
92311	Barstow	(619)	17,690	17,442
93402	Baywood-Los Osos(u)	(805)	10,933	3,487
95903	Beale AFB East(u)	(916)	6,329	7,029
92223	Beaumont	(714)	6,818	5,484
90201	Bell	(213)	25,450	21,836
90706	Bellflower	(213)	53,441	52,334
90201	Bell Gardens	(213)	34,117	29,308
94002	Belmont	(415)	24,505	23,538
94510	Benicia	(707)	15,376	7,349
95005	Ben Lomond(u)	(408)	7,238	2,793
*94704	Berkeley	(415)	103,328	114,091
*90213	Beverly Hills	(213)	32,646	33,416
92314	Big Bear(u)	(714)	11,151	5,268
92316	Bloomington(u)	(714)	6,674	11,957
92225	Blythe	(619)	6,805	7,047
92002	Bonita(u)	(714)	6,257	....
95006	Boulder Creek(u)	(408)	5,662	1,806
92227	Brawley	(619)	14,946	13,746
92621	Brea	(714)	27,913	18,447
95605	Broderick-Bryte(u)	(916)	10,194	12,782
*90620	Buena Park	(714)	64,165	63,646
*91505	Burbank	(818)	84,625	88,871
94010	Burlingame	(415)	26,173	27,320
92231	Calexico	(714)	14,412	10,625
93725	Calwa(u)	(209)	6,640	5,191
93010	Camarillo	(805)	37,732	19,219
93010	Camarillo Heights(u)	(805)	6,341	5,892
95682	Cameron Park(u)	(916)	5,607	....
95008	Campbell	(408)	26,910	23,797
91351	Canyon Country(u)	(805)	15,728	....
92055	Camp Pendleton South(u)	(714)	7,952	13,692
92624	Capistrano Beach(u)	(714)	6,168	4,149
95010	Capitola	(408)	9,095	5,080
92007	Cardiff-by-the-Sea(u)	(714)	10,054	5,724
92008	Carlsbad	(619)	35,490	14,944
95608	Carmichael(u)	(916)	43,108	37,625
93013	Carpinteria	(805)	10,835	6,982
90744	Carson	(213)	81,221	71,150
92077	Casa De Oro-Mt. Helix(u)	(714)	19,651	....
92010	Castle Park-Otay(u)	(714)	21,049	15,445
94546	Castro Valley(u)	(415)	44,011	44,760
95307	Ceres	(209)	13,281	6,029
90701	Cerritos	(213)	52,756	15,856
91724	Charter Oak(u)	(213)	6,840	....
94541	Cherryland(u)	(415)	9,425	9,969
92223	Cherry Valley(u)	(714)	5,012	3,165
95926	Chico	(916)	26,716	19,580
95926	Chico North(u)	(916)	11,739	6,656
95926	Chico West(u)	(916)	6,378	4,787
91710	Chino	(714)	40,165	20,411
93610	Chowchilla	(209)	5,122	4,349
*92010	Chula Vista	(619)	83,927	67,901
95610	Citrus(u)	(916)	12,450	....
95610	Citrus Heights(u)	(916)	85,911	21,760
91711	Claremont	(714)	31,028	24,776
93612	Clovis	(209)	33,021	13,856
92236	Coachella	(714)	9,129	8,353
93210	Coalinga	(209)	6,593	6,161
92324	Colton	(714)	27,419	20,016
90022	Commerce	(213)	10,509	10,635
*90220	Compton	(213)	81,230	78,547
*94520	Concord	(415)	103,763	85,164
93212	Corcoran	(209)	6,454	5,249
91720	Corona	(714)	37,791	27,519
92118	Coronado	(619)	18,790	20,020
94925	Corte Madera	(415)	8,074	8,464
*92626	Costa Mesa	(714)	82,291	72,660
	Country Club(u)	(209)	9,585	....
*91722	Covina	(818)	32,746	30,395
92325	Crestline(u)	(714)	6,715	....
90201	Cudahy	(213)	18,275	16,998
90230	Culver City	(213)	38,139	34,451
95014	Cupertino	(408)	34,297	17,895
90630	Cypress	(714)	40,391	31,569
*94017	Daly City	(415)	78,519	66,922
94526	Danville(u)	(415)	26,446	....
92629	Dana Point(u)	(714)	10,602	4,745
95616	Davis	(916)	36,640	23,488
90250	Del Aire(u)	(213)	8,487	11,930
93215	Delano	(805)	16,491	14,559
92014	Del Mar	(619)	5,017	3,956
92240	Desert Hot Springs	(619)	5,941	2,738
91765	Diamond Bar(u)	(714)	28,045	10,576
93618	Dinuba	(209)	9,907	7,917
95620	Dixon	(916)	7,541	4,432
*90241	Downey	(213)	82,602	88,573
91010	Duarte	(818)	16,766	14,981
94566	Dublin(u)	(415)	13,496	13,641
90220	East Compton(u)	(213)	6,435	5,853
92343	East Hemet(u)	(714)	14,712	8,598
90638	East La Mirada(u)	(213)	9,688	12,339
90022	East Los Angeles(u)	(213)	110,017	104,881
94303	East Palo Alto(u)	(415)	18,191	18,727
93257	East Porterville(u)	(209)	5,218	4,042
92508	Edgemont(u)	(714)	5,215	....
93523	Edwards AFB(u)	(805)	8,554	10,331
*92020	El Cajon	(619)	73,892	52,273
92243	El Centro	(619)	23,996	19,272
94530	El Cerrito	(415)	22,731	25,190
95624	Elk Grove(u)	(916)	10,959	3,721

ZIP code	Place		1980	1970
*91734	El Monte	(818)	79,494	69,892
93446	El Paso de Robles	(213)	9,163	7,168
93030	El Rio(u)	(805)	5,674	6,173
90245	El Segundo	(213)	13,752	15,620
94803	El Sobrante(u)	(415)	10,535	
92630	El Toro(u)	(714)	38,153	8,654
92709	El Toro Station(u)	(714)	7,632	6,970
92024	Encinitas(u)	(619)	10,796	5,375
*92025	Escondido	(619)	62,480	36,792
95501	Eureka	(707)	24,153	24,337
93221	Exeter	(209)	5,619	4,475
94930	Fairfax	(415)	7,391	7,661
94533	Fairfield	(707)	58,099	44,146
95628	Fair Oaks(u)	(916)	20,235	11,256
92028	Fallbrook(u)	(619)	14,041	6,945
93223	Farmersville	(209)	5,544	3,456
93015	Fillmore	(805)	9,602	6,285
90001	Florence-Graham(u)	(213)	48,662	42,900
95828	Florin(u)	(916)	16,523	9,646
95630	Folsom	(916)	11,003	5,810
92335	Fontana	(714)	37,105	20,673
95841	Foothill Farms(u)	(916)	13,700	
95437	Fort Bragg	(707)	5,019	4,455
95540	Fortuna	(707)	7,591	4,203
94404	Foster City	(415)	23,287	9,522
92708	Fountain Valley	(714)	55,080	31,886
95019	Freedom(u)	(408)	6,416	5,563
*94536	Fremont	(415)	131,945	100,869
*93706	Fresno	(209)	217,346	165,655
*92631	Fullerton	(714)	102,246	85,987
95632	Galt	(209)	5,514	3,200
*90247	Gardena	(213)	45,165	41,021
95205	Garden Acres(u)	(213)	7,361	7,870
*92640	Garden Grove	(714)	123,351	121,155
92392	George AFB(u)	(714)	7,061	7,404
95020	Gilroy	(408)	21,641	12,684
92509	Glen Avon(u)	(714)	8,444	5,759
*91209	Glendale	(818)	139,060	132,664
91740	Glendora	(818)	38,500	32,143
92324	Grand Terrace	(714)	8,498	5,901
95945	Grass Valley	(916)	6,697	5,149
93308	Greenacres(u)	(805)	5,381	2,116
93433	Grover City	(805)	8,827	5,939
91745	Hacienda Heights	(213)	49,422	35,969
94019	Half Moon Bay	(415)	7,282	4,023
93230	Hanford	(209)	20,958	15,179
90716	Hawaiian Gardens	(213)	10,548	9,052
90250	Hawthorne	(213)	56,437	53,304
*94544	Hayward	(415)	93,585	93,058
95448	Healdsburg	(707)	7,217	5,438
92343	Hemet	(714)	23,211	12,252
94547	Hercules	(415)	5,963	252
90254	Hermosa Beach	(213)	18,070	17,412
92345	Hesperia(u)	(714)	13,540	4,592
92346	Highland(u)	(714)	10,908	12,669
94010	Hillsborough	(415)	10,372	8,753
95023	Hollister	(408)	11,488	7,663
91720	Home Gardens(u)	(714)	5,783	5,116
*92647	Huntington Beach	(714)	170,505	115,960
90255	Huntington Park	(213)	45,932	33,744
92032	Imperial Beach	(619)	22,689	20,244
92201	Indio	(619)	21,611	14,459
*90306	Inglewood	(213)	94,162	89,985
*92711	Irvine	(714)	62,134	7,381
94707	Kensington(u)	(415)	5,342	5,823
93930	King City	(408)	5,495	3,717
93631	Kingsburg	(209)	5,115	3,843
91011	La Canada-Flintridge	(818)	20,153	20,714
91214	La Crescenta-Montrose(u)	(213)	16,531	19,620
90045	Ladera Heights(u)	(213)	6,647	6,079
94549	Lafayette	(415)	20,837	20,484
*92651	Laguna Beach	(714)	17,858	14,550
92653	Laguna Hills(u)	(714)	33,600	13,676
92677	Laguna Niguel(u)	(714)	12,237	4,644
90631	La Habra	(213)	45,232	41,350
92352	Lake Arrowhead(u)	(714)	6,272	2,682
92040	Lakeside(u)	(714)	23,921	11,991
92330	Lake Elsinore	(714)	5,982	3,530
*90714	Lakewood	(213)	74,654	83,025
92041	La Mesa	(619)	50,342	39,178
90638	La Mirada	(213)	40,986	30,808
93241	Lamont(u)	(805)	9,616	7,007
93534	Lancaster	(805)	48,027	32,728
90624	La Palma	(213)	15,663	9,687
91747	La Puente	(818)	30,882	31,092
	La Riviera(u)	(916)	10,906	
94939	Larkspur	(415)	11,064	10,487
91750	La Verne	(714)	23,508	12,965
90260	Lawndale	(213)	23,460	24,825
92045	Lemon Grove	(619)	20,780	19,794
93245	Lemoore	(209)	8,832	4,219
93245	Lemoore Station(u)	(209)	5,888	9,210
90304	Lennox(u)	(213)	18,445	16,121
92024	Leucadia(u)	(714)	9,478	
95207	Lincoln Village(u)	(916)	6,476	6,112
95901	Linda(u)	(916)	10,225	7,112
93247	Lindsay	(209)	6,936	5,206
95062	Live Oak(u) (Santa Cruz)	(916)	11,482	6,443
94550	Livermore	(415)	48,349	37,703
95334	Livingston	(209)	5,326	2,588
95240	Lodi	(209)	35,221	28,691
92354	Loma Linda	(714)	10,694	7,651
90717	Lomita	(213)	17,191	19,784
93436	Lompoc	(805)	26,267	25,284
*90801	Long Beach	(213)	361,355	358,879
90720	Los Alamitos	(213)	11,529	11,346
94022	Los Altos	(415)	25,769	25,062
94022	Los Altos Hills	(415)	7,421	6,871
*90052	Los Angeles	(213)	2,968,579	2,811,801
93635	Los Banos	(209)	10,341	9,188
95030	Los Gatos	(408)	26,593	22,613
94903	Lucas Valley-Marinwood(u)	(415)	6,409	
90262	Lynwood	(213)	48,409	43,354
93637	Madera	(209)	21,732	16,044
90266	Manhattan Beach	(213)	31,542	35,352
95336	Manteca	(209)	24,925	13,845
93933	Marina	(408)	20,647	*8,343
90291	Marina Del Rey(u)	(213)	8,065	
94553	Martinez	(415)	22,582	16,506
95901	Marysville	(916)	9,898	9,353
95655	Mather AFB(u)	(916)	5,245	7,027
91016	Mayflower Village(u)	(213)	5,017	
90270	Maywood	(213)	21,810	16,996
93250	Mc Farland	(805)	5,151	4,177
95521	McKinleyville(u)	(707)	7,772	
93023	Meiners Oaks-Mira Monte(u)	(805)	9,512	7,025
93640	Mendota	(209)	5,038	2,705
94025	Menlo Park	(415)	26,438	26,826
95340	Merced	(209)	36,499	22,670
94030	Millbrae	(415)	20,058	20,920
94941	Mill Valley	(415)	12,967	12,942
95035	Milpitas	(408)	37,820	26,561
91752	Mira Loma(u)	(714)	8,707	8,482
92675	Mission Viejo(u)	(714)	48,384	11,933
*95350	Modesto	(209)	106,963	61,712
91016	Monrovia	(818)	30,531	30,562
91763	Montclair	(714)	22,628	22,546
90640	Montebello	(213)	52,929	42,807
93940	Monterey	(408)	27,558	26,302
91754	Monterey Park	(213)	54,338	49,166
94556	Moraga	(415)	15,014	14,205
95037	Morgan Hill	(408)	17,060	5,579
93442	Morro Bay	(805)	9,064	7,109
*94042	Mountain View	(415)	58,655	54,132
92405	Muscoy(u)	(714)	6,188	7,091
94558	Napa	(707)	50,879	36,103
92050	National City	(619)	48,772	43,184
94560	Newark	(415)	32,126	27,153
91321	Newhall(u)	(805)	12,029	9,651
*92660	Newport Beach	(714)	63,475	49,582
93444	Nipomo(u)	(805)	5,247	3,642
91760	Norco	(714)	19,732	14,511
95603	North Auburn(u)	(916)	7,619	
94025	North Fair Oaks(u)	(415)	10,294	9,740
95660	North Highlands(u)	(916)	37,825	31,854
90650	Norwalk	(213)	84,901	90,164
94947	Novato	(415)	43,916	31,006
95361	Oakdale	(209)	8,474	6,594
*94615	Oakland	(415)	339,288	361,561
92054	Oceanside	(619)	76,698	40,494
93308	Oildale(u)	(805)	23,382	20,879
93023	Ojai	(805)	6,816	5,591
95961	Olivehurst(u)	(916)	8,929	8,100
*91761	Ontario	(714)	88,820	64,118
95060	Opal Cliffs(u)	(408)	5,041	5,425
*92667	Orange	(714)	91,450	77,365
95662	Orangevale(u)	(916)	20,585	16,493
94563	Orinda(u)	(415)	16,825	6,790
95965	Oroville	(916)	8,683	7,536
93030	Oxnard	(805)	108,195	71,225
94044	Pacifica	(415)	36,866	36,020
93950	Pacific Grove	(408)	15,755	13,505
93550	Palmdale	(805)	12,277	8,511
92260	Palm Desert	(619)	11,801	6,171
92262	Palm Springs	(619)	32,359	20,936
94302	Palo Alto	(415)	55,225	56,040
90274	Palos Verdes Estates	(213)	14,376	13,631
95969	Paradise	(916)	22,571	14,539
90723	Paramount	(213)	36,407	34,734
95823	Parkway-Sacramento So.(u)	(916)	26,815	28,574
*91109	Pasadena	(818)	118,072	112,951
92370	Perris	(714)	6,740	4,228
94952	Petaluma	(707)	33,834	24,870
90660	Pico Rivera	(213)	53,387	54,170
94611	Piedmont	(415)	10,498	10,917
94564	Pinole	(415)	14,253	13,266
93449	Pismo Beach	(805)	5,364	4,043
94565	Pittsburg	(415)	33,465	21,423
92670	Placentia	(714)	35,041	21,948
95667	Placerville	(916)	6,739	5,416
94523	Pleasant Hill	(415)	25,547	24,610
94566	Pleasanton	(415)	35,160	18,328
91766	Pomona	(714)	92,742	87,384
93257	Porterville	(209)	19,707	12,602
93041	Port Hueneme	(805)	17,803	14,295
92064	Poway(u)	(619)	32,263	9,422
93534	Quartz Hill(u)	(213)	7,421	4,935
92065	Ramona(u)	(714)	8,173	3,554
95670	Rancho Cordova(u)	(916)	42,881	30,451
91730	Rancho Cucamonga	(714)	55,250	19,484

ZIP code	Place		1980	1970
92270	Rancho Mirage	(714)	6,281	2,767
90274	Rancho Palos Verdes	(213)	35,227	33,285
96080	Red Bluff	(916)	9,490	7,676
96001	Redding	(916)	41,995	16,659
92373	Redlands	(714)	43,619	36,355
*90277	Redondo Beach	(213)	57,102	57,451
*94064	Redwood City	(415)	54,965	55,686
93654	Reedley	(209)	11,071	8,131
92376	Rialto	(714)	37,862	28,370
*94802	Richmond	(415)	74,676	79,043
93555	Ridgecrest	(714)	15,929	7,629
95003	Rio Del Mar(u)	(408)	7,067	....
95673	Rio Linda(u)	(916)	7,359	7,524
95367	Riverbank	(209)	5,695	3,949
*92502	Riverside	(714)	170,591	140,089
95677	Rocklin	(916)	7,344	3,039
94572	Rodeo(u)	(415)	8,286	5,356
94928	Rohnert Park	(707)	22,965	6,133
90274	Rolling Hills Estates	(213)	9,412	6,735
95401	Roseland(u)	(707)	7,915	5,105
91770	Rosemead	(818)	42,604	40,972
95826	Rosemont(u)	(916)	18,888	....
95678	Roseville	(916)	24,347	18,221
90720	Rossmoor(u)	(213)	10,457	12,922
91745	Rowland Heights(u)	(818)	28,252	16,881
92509	Rubidoux(u)	(714)	16,763	13,969
*95813	Sacramento	(916)	275,741	257,105
93901	Salinas	(408)	80,479	58,896
94960	San Anselmo	(415)	12,067	13,031
*92403	San Bernardino	(714)	118,794	106,869
94066	San Bruno	(415)	35,417	36,254
	San Buenaventura (*see* Ventura)	(805)		
94070	San Carlos	(415)	24,710	26,053
92672	San Clemente	(714)	27,325	17,063
*92109	San Diego	(619)	875,504	697,471
91773	San Dimas	(714)	24,014	15,692
*91340	San Fernando	(818)	17,731	16,571
*94101	San Francisco	(415)	678,974	715,674
91776	San Gabriel	(818)	30,072	29,336
93657	Sanger	(209)	12,558	10,088
92383	San Jacinto	(714)	7,098	4,385
95101	San Jose	(408)	629,400	459,913
92375	San Juan Capistrano	(714)	18,959	3,781
94577	San Leandro	(415)	63,952	68,698
94580	San Lorenzo(u)	(415)	20,545	24,633
93401	San Luis Obispo	(805)	34,252	28,036
92069	San Marcos	(619)	17,479	3,896
91108	San Marino	(213)	13,307	14,177
*94402	San Mateo	(415)	77,640	78,991
94806	San Pablo	(415)	19,750	21,461
*94901	San Rafael	(415)	44,700	38,977
94583	San Ramon(u)	(415)	22,356	4,084
*92711	Santa Ana	(714)	204,023	155,710
*93102	Santa Barbara	(805)	74,542	70,215
*95050	Santa Clara	(408)	87,700	86,118
95060	Santa Cruz	(408)	41,483	32,076
90670	Santa Fe Springs	(213)	14,559	14,750
93454	Santa Maria	(805)	39,685	32,749
*90406	Santa Monica	(213)	88,314	88,289
93060	Santa Paula	(805)	20,658	18,001
*95402	Santa Rosa	(707)	83,205	50,006
92071	Santee(u)	(619)	47,080	21,107
95070	Saratoga	(408)	29,261	26,810
91350	Saugus-Bouquet Canyon(u)	(805)	16,283	....
94965	Sausalito	(415)	7,090	6,158
95066	Scotts Valley	(408)	6,891	3,621
90740	Seal Beach	(213)	25,975	24,441
93955	Seaside	(408)	36,567	36,883
95472	Sebastopol	(707)	5,500	3,993
93662	Selma	(209)	10,942	7,459
93263	Shafter	(805)	7,010	5,327
91024	Sierra Madre	(818)	10,837	12,140
90806	Signal Hill	(213)	5,734	5,588
93065	Simi Valley	(805)	77,500	59,832
92075	Solana Beach(u)	(714)	13,047	5,023
93960	Soledad	(408)	5,928	4,222
95476	Sonoma	(707)	6,054	4,259
95073	Soquel(u)	(408)	6,212	5,795
91733	South El Monte	(213)	16,623	13,443
90280	South Gate	(213)	66,784	56,909
92677	South Laguna(u)	(714)	6,013	2,566
95705	South Lake Tahoe	(916)	20,681	12,921
95350	South Modesto(u)	(209)	12,492	7,889
95965	South Oroville(u)	(916)	7,246	4,111
91030	South Pasadena	(213)	22,681	22,979
94080	South San Francisco	(415)	49,393	46,646
91770	South San Gabriel(u)	(213)	5,421	5,051
91744	South San Jose Hills(u)	(213)	16,049	12,386
90605	South Whittier(u)	(213)	43,815	46,641
95991	South Yuba(u)	(916)	7,530	5,352
*92077	Spring Valley(u)	(714)	40,191	29,742
94305	Stanford(u)	(415)	11,045	8,691
90680	Stanton	(714)	21,144	18,186
*95204	Stockton	(209)	149,779	109,963
94585	Suisun City	(707)	11,087	2,917
92381	Sun City(u)	(714)	8,460	5,519
92388	Sunnymead(u)	(714)	11,554	6,708
*94086	Sunnyvale	(408)	106,618	95,976
96130	Susanville	(916)	6,520	6,608
93268	Taft	(805)	5,316	4,285
94806	Tara Hills-Montalvin Manor(u)	(415)	9,471	....
94941	Tamalpais-Homestead Valley(u)	(415)	8,511	....
91780	Temple City	(818)	28,972	31,034
*91360	Thousand Oaks	(805)	77,797	35,873
94920	Tiburon	(415)	6,685	6,209
*90510	Torrance	(213)	131,497	134,968
*95386	Tracy	(209)	18,428	14,724
93274	Tulare	(209)	22,530	16,235
95380	Turlock	(209)	26,291	13,992
92680	Tustin	(714)	32,256	22,313
92705	Tustin-Foothills(u)	(714)	26,174	26,699
92277	Twentynine Palms(u)	(619)	7,465	5,667
92278	Twentynine Palms Base(u)	(619)	7,079	5,647
95482	Ukiah	(707)	12,035	10,095
94587	Union City	(415)	39,406	14,724
91786	Upland	(714)	47,647	32,551
95688	Vacaville	(707)	43,367	21,690
91355	Valencia(u)	(805)	12,163	4,243
91744	Valinda(u)	(213)	18,700	18,837
94590	Vallejo	(707)	80,188	71,710
92343	Valle Vista(u)	(714)	5,474	....
93437	Vandenberg AFB(u)	(805)	8,136	13,193
93436	Vandenberg Village(u)	(805)	5,839	....
*93001	Ventura	(805)	73,774	57,964
92392	Victorville	(619)	14,220	10,845
90043	View Park-Windsor Hills(u)	(213)	12,101	12,268
92667	Villa Park	(714)	7,137	2,723
94553	Vine Hill-Pacheco(u)	(415)	6,129	....
*93277	Visalia	(209)	49,729	27,130
92083	Vista	(619)	35,834	24,688
91789	Walnut	(714)	9,978	5,992
*94596	Walnut Creek	(415)	54,410	39,844
94596	Walnut Creek West(u)	(415)	5,893	8,330
90255	Walnut Park(u)	(213)	11,811	8,925
93280	Wasco	(805)	9,613	8,269
95076	Watsonville	(408)	23,662	14,719
90044	West Athens(u)	(213)	8,531	13,311
90502	West Carson(u)	(213)	17,997	15,501
90247	West Compton(u)	(213)	5,907	5,748
*91793	West Covina	(213)	80,292	68,034
90069	West Hollywood(u)	(213)	35,703	34,622
92683	Westminster	(714)	71,133	60,076
95351	West Modesto(u)	(209)	NA	6,135
90047	Westmont(u)	(213)	27,916	29,310
94565	West Pittsburg(u)	(415)	8,773	5,969
91746	West Puente Valley(u)	(213)	20,445	20,733
95691	West Sacramento(u)	(916)	10,875	12,002
*90606	West Whittier-Los Nietos(u)	(213)	20,962	20,845
*90605	Whittier	(213)	68,558	72,863
90222	Willowbrook(u)	(213)	30,845	28,705
93286	Woodlake	(209)	5,375	3,371
95695	Woodland	(916)	30,235	20,677
94062	Woodside	(415)	5,291	4,734
92686	Yorba Linda	(714)	28,254	11,856
96097	Yreka City	(916)	5,916	5,394
95991	Yuba City	(916)	18,736	13,986
92399	Yucaipa(u)	(714)	23,345	19,284
92284	Yucca Valley(u)	(619)	8,294	3,893

Colorado (303)

ZIP code	Place	1980	1970
80840	Air Force Academy	8,655	....
81101	Alamosa	6,830	6,985
80401	Applewood(u)	12,040	8,214
*80001	Arvada	84,576	49,844
80010	Aurora	158,588	74,974
*80302	Boulder	76,685	66,870
80601	Brighton	12,773	8,309
80020	Broomfield	20,730	7,261
81212	Canon City	13,037	9,206
	Castlewood	16,413	....
80110	Cherry Hills Village	5,127	4,605
81220	Cimarron Hills	6,597	....
81520	Clifton	5,223	....
*80901	Colorado Springs	215,105	135,517
80120	Columbine	23,523	....
80022	Commerce City	16,234	17,407
81321	Cortez	7,095	6,032
81625	Craig	8,133	4,205
*80202	Denver	492,686	514,678
80022	Derby(u)	8,576	10,206
81301	Durango	11,649	10,333
80110	Englewood	30,021	33,695
80620	Evans	5,063	2,570
80439	Evergreen	6,376	2,321
80221	Federal Heights	7,846	1,502
80913	Fort Carson(u)	13,219	19,399
80521	Fort Collins	64,632	43,337
80701	Fort Morgan	8,768	7,594
80017	Fountain	8,324	3,515
80401	Golden	12,237	9,817
81501	Grand Junction	27,956	20,170
80631	Greeley	53,006	38,902
80110	Greenwood Village	5,729	3,095
80501	Gunbarrel	5,172	....
81230	Gunnison	5,785	4,613

ZIP code	Place	1980	1970
.....	Ken Caryl	10,661	.....
80026	Lafayette.	8,985	3,498
81050	La Junta	8,338	8,205
80215	Lakewood	113,808	92,743
81052	Lamar	7,713	7,797
80120	Littleton.	28,631	26,466
80120	Littleton Southeast(u).	33,029	22,899
80501	Longmont	42,942	23,209
80027	Louisville	5,593	2,409
80537	Loveland	30,215	16,220
81401	Montrose.	8,722	6,496
80233	Northglenn.	29,847	27,785
*81003	Pueblo	101,686	97,774
80911	Security-Widefield(u)	18,768	15,297
80110	Sheridan	5,377	4,787
80221	Sherrelwood(u)	17,629	18,868
80122	Southglenn.	37,787	.....
80477	Steamboat Springs	5,098	2,340
80751	Sterling	11,385	10,636
80906	Stratmoor	5,519	.....
80229	Thornton	40,343	13,326
81082	Trinidad.	9,663	9,901
80229	Welby(u)	9,668	6,875
80030	Westminster	50,211	19,512
80221	Westminster East(u)	6,002	7,576
80033	Wheat Ridge.	30,293	29,778

Connecticut (203)

See Note on Page 257

06401	Ansonia	19,039	21,160
06001	Avon	11,201	8,352
06037	Berlin	15,121	14,149
06801	Bethel	16,004	10,945
06002	Bloomfield.	18,608	18,301
06405	Branford	23,363	20,444
*06602	Bridgeport	142,546	156,542
06010	Bristol.	57,370	55,487
06804	Brookfield	12,872	9,688
06013	Burlington	5,660	4,070
06234	Brooklyn	5,691	4,965
06019	Canton	7,635	6,868
06410	Cheshire	21,788	19,051
06413	Clinton	11,195	10,267
06415	Colchester	7,761	6,603
06340	Conning Towers-Nautilus Park(u) .	9,665	9,791
06238	Coventry	8,895	8,140
06416	Cromwell.	10,265	7,400
06810	Danbury	60,470	50,781
06820	Darien	18,892	20,336
06418	Derby	12,346	12,599
06422	Durham	5,143	4,489
06423	East Haddam	5,621	4,676
06424	East Hampton	8,572	7,078
06108	East Hartford	52,563	57,583
06512	East Haven	25,028	25,120
06333	East Lyme	13,870	11,399
06425	Easton	5,962	4,885
06016	East Windsor	8,925	8,513
06029	Ellington	9,711	7,707
06082	Enfield	42,695	46,189
06426	Essex	5,078	4,911
06430	Fairfield	54,849	56,487
06032	Farmington	16,407	14,390
06033	Glastonbury	24,327	20,651
06035	Granby	7,956	6,150
06830	Greenwich	59,578	59,755
06351	Griswold	8,967	7,763
06340	Groton	41,062	38,244
06340	Groton Borough	10,086	8,933
06437	Guilford.	17,375	12,033
06438	Haddam	6,383	4,934
06514	Hamden	51,071	49,357
*06101	Hartford	136,392	158,017
06082	Hazardville(u)	5,436	.....
06248	Hebron	5,453	3,815
06037	Kensington(u)	7,502	.....
06239	Killingly	14,519	13,573
06339	Ledyard	13,735	14,837
06759	Litchfield.	7,605	7,399
06443	Madison	14,031	9,768
06040	Manchester	49,761	47,994
06250	Mansfield.	20,634	19,994
06450	Meriden	57,118	55,959
06762	Middlebury	5,995	5,542
06457	Middletown	39,040	36,924
06460	Milford	50,898	50,858
06468	Monroe.	14,010	12,047
06353	Montville	16,455	15,662
06770	Naugatuck	26,456	23,034
*06050	New Britain	73,840	83,441
06840	New Canaan	17,931	17,451
06810	New Fairfield	11,260	6,991
*06510	New Haven	126,089	137,707
06111	Newington	28,841	26,037
06320	New London	28,842	31,630
06776	New Milford	19,420	14,601

06470	Newtown.	19,107	16,942
06471	North Branford	11,554	10,778
06473	North Haven	22,080	22,194
06856	Norwalk	77,767	79,288
06360	Norwich	38,074	41,739
06779	Oakville(u)	8,737	.....
06371	Old Lyme	6,159	4,964
06475	Old Saybrook	9,287	8,468
06477	Orange.	13,237	13,524
02891	Pawcatuck(u)	5,216	5,255
06374	Plainfield	12,774	11,957
06062	Plainville	16,401	16,733
06782	Plymouth.	10,732	10,321
06480	Portland	8,383	8,812
06712	Prospect	6,807	6,543
06260	Putnam.	6,855	6,918
.....	Putnam.	8,580	8,598
06875	Redding	7,272	5,590
06877	Ridgefield Center(u)	6,066	5,878
.....	Ridgefield	20,120	18,188
06067	Rocky Hill	14,559	11,103
06483	Seymour	13,434	12,776
06484	Shelton	31,314	27,165
06082	Sherwood Manor(u)	6,303	.....
06070	Simsbury	21,161	17,475
06071	Somers	8,473	6,893
06488	Southbury	14,156	7,852
06489	Southington	36,879	30,946
06074	South Windsor	17,198	15,553
06082	Southwood Acres(u)	9,779	.....
06075	Stafford	9,268	8,680
*06904	Stamford	102,466	108,798
06378	Stonington	16,220	15,940
06268	Storrs(u)	11,394	10,691
06430	Stratford-Brooklawn(u).	8,890	.....
06497	Stratford	50,541	49,775
06078	Suffield	9,294	8,634
06786	Terryville(u)	5,234	.....
06787	Thomaston.	6,272	6,233
06277	Thompson	8,141	7,580
06084	Tolland	9,694	7,857
06790	Torrington	30,987	31,952
06611	Trumbull	32,989	31,394
06060	Vernon	27,974	27,237
06492	Wallingford.	37,274	35,714
*06701	Waterbury	103,266	108,033
06385	Waterford	17,843	17,227
06795	Watertown	19,489	18,610
06498	Westbrook	5,216	3,820
06107	West Hartford	61,301	68,031
06516	West Haven	53,184	52,851
06880	Weston	8,284	7,417
06880	Westport.	25,290	27,318
06109	Wethersfield	26,013	26,662
06226	Willimantic	14,652	14,402
06897	Wilton.	15,351	13,572
06094	Winchester.	10,841	11,106
06280	Windham	21,062	19,626
06095	Windsor	25,204	22,502
06096	Windsor Locks.	12,190	15,080
06098	Winsted	8,092	8,954
06716	Wolcott	13,008	12,495
06525	Woodbridge	7,761	7,673
06798	Woodbury	6,942	5,869
06281	Woodstock.	5,117	4,311

Delaware (302)

19711	Brookside(u)	15,255	7,856
19703	Claymont(u)	10,022	6,584
19901	Dover.	23,507	17,488
19802	Edgemoor(u).	7,397	.....
19805	Elsmere	6,493	8,415
19963	Milford	5,366	5,314
19711	Newark.	25,247	21,298
19973	Seaford	5,256	5,537
19804	Stanton(u)	5,495	.....
19803	Talleyville(u)	6,880	.....
19899	Wilmington	70,195	80,386
19720	Wilmington Manor —Chelsea—Leedom	9,233	10,134

District of Columbia (202)

*20013	Washington	638,432	756,668

Florida

32701	Altamonte Springs	(305)	21,114	4,391
32703	Apopka	(305)	6,019	4,045
33821	Arcadia	(813)	6,002	5,658
32233	Atlantic Beach	(904)	7,847	6,132
33823	Auburndale	(813)	6,501	5,386
.....	Aventura(u)	(305)	10,162	.....
33825	Avon Park	(813)	8,026	6,712
32807	Azalea Park(u)	(305)	8,304	7,367
33830	Bartow	(813)	14,780	12,891
.....	Bay Crest(u)	(813)	5,927	.....

ZIP code	Place		1980	1970
....	Bayonet Point(u)	(813)	16,455	....
33542	Bay Pines(u)	(813)	5,757	....
33505	Bayshore Gardens(u)	(813)	14,945	9,255
33589	Beacon Square(u)	(813)	6,513	2,927
32073	Bellair-Meadowbrook Terrace(u)	(904)	12,144	
33430	Belle Glade	(305)	16,535	15,949
32506	Belleview(u)	(904)	15,439	916
32661	Beverly Hills(u)	(904)	5,024	....
33432	Boca Raton	(305)	49,447	28,506
33923	Bonita Springs(u)	(813)	5,435	1,932
33435	Boynton Beach	(305)	35,624	18,115
*33506	Bradenton	(813)	30,228	21,040
33511	Brandon(u)	(813)	41,826	12,749
32525	Brent(u)	(904)	21,872	....
33314	Broadview Park(u)	(305)	6,022	6,049
33313	Broadview-Pompano Park(u)	(305)	5,256	....
33512	Brooksville	(904)	5,582	4,060
33311	Browardale(u)	(305)	7,571	17,444
33142	Browns Village(u)	(305)	NA	23,442
33142	Brownsville(u)	(305)	18,058	....
33054	Bunche Park(u)	(305)	NA	5,773
32401	Callaway	(904)	7,154	3,240
32920	Cape Canaveral	(305)	5,733	4,258
33904	Cape Coral	(813)	32,103	11,470
33055	Carol City(u)	(305)	47,349	27,361
32707	Casselberry	(305)	15,247	9,438
33401	Century Village(u)	(305)	10,619	2,679
32324	Chattahoochee	(904)	5,332	7,944
*33515	Clearwater	(813)	85,450	52,074
32711	Clermont	(904)	5,461	3,661
33440	Clewiston	(813)	5,219	3,896
32922	Cocoa	(305)	16,096	16,110
32931	Cocoa Beach	(305)	10,926	9,952
32922	Cocoa West(u)	(305)	6,432	5,779
33066	Coconut Creek	(305)	6,288	1,359
33060	Collier City(u)	(305)	7135	....
33064	Collier Manor-Cresthaven(u)	(305)	7,045	7,202
33801	Combee Settlement(u)	(813)	5,400	4,963
32809	Conway(u)	(305)	23,940	8,642
33314	Cooper City	(305)	10,140	2,535
33134	Coral Gables	(305)	43,241	42,494
33065	Coral Springs	(305)	37,349	1,489
....	Coral Terrace(u)	(305)	22,702	....
32536	Crestview	(904)	7,617	7,952
33803	Crystal Lake(u)	(813)	6,827	6,227
33157	Cutler(u)	(305)	15,593	....
33157	Cutler Ridge(u)	(305)	20,886	17,441
33880	Cypress Gardens(u)	(813)	8,043	3,757
....	Cypress Lake(u)	(813)	8,721	....
33004	Dania	(305)	11,796	9,013
33314	Davie	(305)	20,515	5,859
*32015	Daytona Beach	(904)	54,176	45,327
33441	Deerfield Beach	(305)	39,193	16,662
32433	DeFuniak Springs	(904)	5,563	4,966
32720	De Land	(904)	15,354	11,641
33444	Delray Beach	(305)	34,329	19,915
33617	Del Rio(u)	(813)	7,409	....
32725	Deltona(u)	(904)	15,710	4,868
33528	Dunedin	(813)	30,203	17,639
33610	East Lake-Orient Park (u)	(813)	5,612	5,697
33940	East Naples(u)	(813)	12,127	6,152
32032	Edgewater	(904)	6,726	3,348
32542	Eglin AFB(u)	(904)	7,574	7,769
33614	Egypt Lake(u)	(813)	11,932	7,556
33531	Elfers(u)	(813)	11,396	....
33533	Englewood(u)	(813)	10,242	5,108
32504	Ensley(u)	(904)	14,422	....
32726	Eustis	(904)	9,453	6,722
32804	Fairview Shores(u)	(305)	10,174	....
32034	Fernandina Beach	(904)	7,224	6,955
32730	Fern Park(u)	(305)	8,890	....
32504	Ferry Pass(u)	(904)	16,910	....
33030	Florida City	(305)	6,174	5,133
32751	Forest City(u)	(305)	6,819	....
*33310	Fort Lauderdale	(305)	153,256	139,590
33841	Fort Meade	(813)	5,546	4,374
33920	Fort Myers	(813)	36,638	27,351
33931	Fort Myers Beach(u)	(813)	5,753	4,305
33450	Fort Pierce	(305)	33,802	29,721
33452	Fort Pierce NW(u)	(305)	5,929	3,269
32548	Fort Walton Beach	(904)	20,829	19,994
*32601	Gainesville	(904)	81,371	64,510
33801	Gibsonia(u)	(813)	5,011	....
32960	Gifford(u)	(305)	6,240	5,772
....	Gladeview(u)	(305)	18,919	....
33143	Glenvar Heights(u)	(305)	13,216	....
33055	Golden Glades(u)	(305)	23,154	....
32733	Goldenrod(u)	(305)	13,681	....
32560	Gonzalez(u)	(904)	6,084	....
32503	Goulding(u)	(904)	5,352	....
33170	Goulds(u)	(305)	7,078	6,690
33463	Greenacres City	(305)	8,780	1,731
32561	Gulf Breeze	(904)	5,478	4,190
33581	Gulf Gate Estates(u)	(813)	9,248	5,874
33737	Gulfport	(813)	11,180	9,976
33844	Haines City	(813)	10,799	8,956
33009	Hallandale	(305)	36,517	23,849
*33010	Hialeah	(305)	145,254	102,452
33455	Hobe Sound(u)	(305)	6,822	2,029
32805	Holden Heights(u)	(305)	13,840	6,206
33590	Holiday(u)	(813)	18,392	....
32017	Holly Hill	(904)	9,953	8,191
*33022	Hollywood	(305)	117,188	106,873
33030	Homestead	(305)	20,668	13,674
33030	Homestead Base(u)	(305)	7,594	8,257
33568	Hudson(u)	(813)	5,799	2,278
33934	Immokalee(u)	(813)	11,038	3,764
32937	Indian Harbour Beach	(305)	5,967	5,371
33880	Inwood(u)	(813)	6,668	....
33162	Ives Estates(u)	(305)	12,623	....
*32201	Jacksonville	(904)	540,898	504,265
32250	Jacksonville Beach	(904)	15,462	12,779
33568	Jasmine Estates(u)	(813)	11,995	2,967
33457	Jensen Beach(u)	(305)	6,639	....
33458	Jupiter	(305)	9,868	3,136
....	Kendale Lakes(u)	(305)	32,769	....
33156	Kendall(u)	(305)	73,758	35,497
....	Kendall Green(u)	(305)	6,768	....
33149	Key Biscayne(u)	(305)	6,313	....
33037	Key Largo(u)	(305)	7,447	2,866
33040	Key West	(305)	24,292	29,312
32303	Killearn(u)	(904)	8,700	....
....	Kings Point(u)	(305)	8,724	....
32741	Kissimmee	(305)	15,487	7,119
33618	Lake Carroll(u)	(813)	13,012	5,577
32055	Lake City	(904)	9,257	10,575
*33802	Lakeland	(813)	47,406	42,803
33801	Lakeland Highlands(u)	(813)	10,426	....
....	Lake Lorraine(u)	(904)	5,427	....
33054	Lake Lucerne(u)	(305)	9,762	....
33612	Lake Magdalene(u)	(813)	13,331	9,266
33403	Lake Park	(305)	6,909	6,993
....	Lakeside(u)	(904)	10,534	....
33853	Lake Wales	(813)	8,466	8,240
33460	Lake Worth	(305)	27,048	23,714
33460	Lantana	(305)	8,048	7,126
33540	Largo	(813)	58,977	24,230
33313	Lauderdale Lakes	(305)	25,426	10,577
33313	Lauderhill	(305)	37,271	8,465
33545	Laurel(u)	(813)	6,368	....
33717	Lealman(u)	(813)	19,873	....
32748	Leesburg	(904)	13,191	11,869
33936	Lehigh Acres(u)	(813)	9,604	4,394
33033	Leisure City(u)	(305)	17,905	....
33614	Leto(u)	(904)	9,003	8,458
33064	Lighthouse Point	(305)	11,488	9,071
....	Lindgren Acres(u)	(305)	11,986	....
32060	Live Oak	(904)	6,732	6,830
32810	Lockhart(u)	(305)	10,571	5,809
33548	Longboat Key	(813)	8,221	2,850
32750	Longwood	(305)	10,029	3,203
33549	Lutz(u)	(813)	5,555	....
32444	Lynn Haven	(904)	6,239	4,044
32751	Maitland	(305)	8,763	7,157
33550	Mango-Seffner(u)	(813)	6,493	....
33060	Marathon(u)	(305)	7,568	4,397
33063	Margate	(305)	35,900	8,867
32446	Marianna	(904)	7,074	7,282
*32901	Melbourne	(305)	46,536	40,236
33314	Melrose Park(u)	(904)	5,725	6,111
33561	Memphis(u)	(813)	5,501	3,207
32952	Merritt Island(u)	(305)	30,708	29,233
*33152	Miami	(305)	346,931	334,859
33139	Miami Beach	(305)	96,298	87,072
33023	Miami Gardens—Utopia-Carver(u)	(305)	9,025	....
33014	Miami Lakes(u)	(305)	9,809	....
33153	Miami Shores	(305)	9,244	9,425
33166	Miami Springs	(305)	12,350	13,279
32570	Milton	(904)	7,206	5,360
32754	Mims(u)	(305)	7,583	8,309
33023	Miramar	(305)	32,813	23,997
32757	Mount Dora	(904)	5,883	4,646
32506	Myrtle Grove(u)	(904)	14,238	16,186
33940	Naples	(813)	17,581	12,042
33940	Naples Park(u)	(813)	5,438	1,522
33032	Naranja-Princeton(u)	(305)	10,381	....
32233	Neptune Beach	(904)	5,248	4,281
33552	New Port Richey	(813)	11,196	6,098
33552	New Port Richey East(u)	(813)	6,627	2,758
32069	New Smyrna Beach	(904)	13,557	10,580
32578	Niceville	(904)	8,543	4,155
33169	Norland(u)	(305)	19,471	....
33308	North Andrews Gardens(u)	(305)	8,967	7,082
33903	North Fort Myers(u)	(813)	22,808	8,798
33068	North Lauderdale	(305)	18,653	1,213
33161	North Miami	(305)	42,566	34,767
33160	North Miami Beach	(305)	36,481	30,544
33940	North Naples(u)	(813)	7,950	3,201
33408	North Palm Beach	(305)	11,344	9,035
33596	North Port	(813)	6,205	2,244
33169	Norwood(u)	(305)	NA	14,973
33308	Oakland Park	(305)	22,944	16,261
33860	Oak Ridge(u)	(813)	15,477	....
32670	Ocala	(904)	37,170	22,583
32548	Ocean City(u)	(904)	5,582	5,267
32761	Ocoee	(813)	7,803	3,937
33163	Oius(u)	(305)	17,344	....
33165	Olympia Heights(u)	(305)	33,112	....

ZIP code	Place		1980	1970
33558	Oneco(u)	(813)	6.417	3.246
33054	Opa-Locka	(305)	14.460	11.902
33054	Opa-Locka North(u)	(305)	5.721	
32073	Orange Park	(904)	8.766	5.019
*32802	Orlando	(305)	128.394	99.006
32811	Orlovista(u)	(305)	6.474	
32074	Ormond Beach	(904)	21.438	14.063
32074	Ormond By-The-Sea(u)	(904)	7.665	6.002
32570	Pace(u)	(904)	5.006	1.776
33476	Pahokee	(305)	6.346	5.663
32077	Palatka	(904)	10.175	9.444
33505	Palma Sola(u)	(813)	5.297	1.745
32905	Palm Bay	(305)	18.560	7.176
33480	Palm Beach	(305)	9.729	9.086
33403	Palm Beach Gardens	(305)	14.407	6.102
33561	Palmetto	(813)	8.637	7.422
33157	Palmetto Estates(u)	(305)	11.116	
33563	Palm Harbor(u)	(813)	5.215	
33619	Palm River-Clair Mel(u)	(813)	14.447	8.536
33460	Palm Springs	(305)	8.166	4.340
33012	Palm Springs North(u)	(305)	5.838	
32401	Panama City	(904)	33.346	32.096
33866	Pembroke Park	(305)	5.326	2.949
33023	Pembroke Pines	(305)	35.776	15.496
32502	Pensacola	(904)	57.619	59.507
33157	Perrine(u)	(305)	16.129	10.257
32347	Perry	(904)	8.254	7.701
32809	Pine Castle(u)	(305)	9.992	
32808	Pine Hills(u)	(305)	35.771	13.882
33565	Pinellas Park	(813)	32.811	22.287
33168	Pinewood(u)	(305)	16.216	
33566	Plant City	(813)	17.064	15.451
33314	Plantation	(813)	48.653	23.523
*33060	Pompano Beach	(305)	52.618	38.587
33064	Pompano Beach Highlands(u)	(305)	16.154	5.014
33950	Port Charlotte(u)	(813)	25.730	10.769
32019	Port Orange	(904)	18.756	3.781
33452	Port St. Lucie	(305)	14.690	330
*33950	Punta Gorda	(813)	6.797	3.879
32351	Quincy	(904)	8.591	8.334
33156	Richmond Heights(u)	(305)	8.577	6.663
33312	Riverland(u)	(305)	5.919	5.512
33404	Riviera Beach	(305)	26.596	21.401
33314	Rock Island(u)	(813)	5.022	
32955	Rockledge	(305)	11.877	10.523
33570	Ruskin(u)	(813)	5.117	2.414
33572	Safety Harbor	(813)	6.461	3.103
32084	St. Augustine	(904)	11.985	12.352
32769	St. Cloud	(305)	7.840	5.041
*33730	St. Petersburg	(813)	236.893	216.159
33706	St. Petersburg Beach	(813)	9.354	8.024
33508	Samoset(u)	(813)	5.747	4.070
33432	Sandalfoot Cove(u)	(305)	5.299	
32771	Sanford	(305)	23.176	17.393
*33578	Sarasota	(813)	48.868	40.237
33577	Sarasota Springs(u)	(813)	13.860	4.405
32937	Satellite Beach	(305)	9.163	6.558
	Scott Lake(u)	(305)	14.154	
33870	Sebring	(813)	8.736	7.223
33578	Siesta Key(u)	(813)	7.010	4.460
32809	Sky Lake(u)	(305)	6.692	
32703	South Apopka(u)	(305)	5.687	2.293
33505	South Bradenton(u)	(813)	14.297	
32021	South Daytona	(904)	9.608	4.979
33579	Southgate(u)	(813)	7.322	6.885
33143	South Miami	(305)	10.895	11.780
33157	South Miami Heights(u)	(305)	23.559	10.395
32937	South Patrick Shores(u)	(305)	9.816	10.313
33595	South Venice(u)	(813)	8.075	4.680
32401	Springfield	(904)	7.220	5.949
33512	Spring Hill(u)	(813)	6.468	
32091	Starke	(904)	5.306	4.848
33494	Stuart	(305)	9.467	4.820
33570	Sun City Center(u)	(813)	5.605	2.143
33160	Sunny Isles(u)	(305)	12.564	
33304	Sunrise	(305)	39.681	7.403
33139	Sunset(u)	(305)	13.531	
33144	Sweetwater	(305)	8.251	3.357
33614	Sweetwater Creek(u)	(813)	NA	19.453
*32303	Tallahassee	(904)	81.548	72.624
33313	Tamarac	(305)	29.142	5.193
33144	Tamiami(u)	(305)	17.607	
*33602	Tampa	(813)	271.598	277.714
	Tanglewood(u)	(813)	8.229	
33589	Tarpon Springs	(813)	13.251	7.118
33617	Temple Terrace	(813)	11.097	7.347
33905	Tice(u)	(813)	6.645	7.254
32780	Titusville	(305)	31.910	30.515
32505	Town 'n' Country(u)	(904)	37.834	
33740	Treasure Island	(813)	6.316	6.120
32807	Union Park(u)	(305)	19.175	2.595
33620	University (Hillsborough)(u)	(813)	24.514	10.039
32580	Valparaiso	(904)	6.142	6.504
33595	Venice	(813)	12.153	6.648
33595	Venice Gardens(u)	(813)	6.568	
32960	Vero Beach	(305)	16.176	11.908
32960	Vero Beach South(u)	(305)	12.636	7.330
33901	Villas(u)	(813)	8.724	
32507	Warrington(u)	(904)	15.792	15.848

ZIP code	Place		1980	1970
33314	Washington Park(u)	(305)	7.240	
32703	Wekiva Springs(u)	(305)	13.386	
33505	West Bradenton(u)	(813)	NA	6.162
33155	Westchester(u)	(305)	29.272	
32446	West End(u)	(904)	NA	5.289
33138	West Little River(u)	(305)	32.492	
32901	West Melbourne	(305)	5.078	3.050
33144	West Miami	(305)	6.076	5.494
*33401	West Palm Beach	(305)	62.530	57.375
32505	West Pensacola(u)	(904)	24.371	20.924
33168	Westview(u)	(305)	9.102	
33880	West Winter Haven(u)	(813)	NA	7.716
33165	Westwood Lakes(u)	(305)	11.478	12.811
33305	Wilton Manors	(305)	12.742	10.948
33803	Winston(u)	(813)	9.315	4.505
32787	Winter Garden	(305)	6.789	5.153
33880	Winter Haven	(813)	21.119	16.136
32708	Winter Park	(305)	22.314	21.895
32707	Winter Springs	(305)	10.475	1.161
32548	Wright(u)	(904)	13.011	
33599	Zephyrhills	(813)	5.742	3.369

Georgia

ZIP code	Place		1980	1970
31620	Adel	(912)	5.592	4.972
*31701	Albany	(912)	74.425	72.623
31709	Americus	(912)	16.120	16.091
*30601	Athens	(404)	42.549	44.342
*30304	Atlanta	(404)	425.022	495.039
*30901	Augusta	(404)	47.532	59.864
31717	Bainbridge	(912)	10.553	10.887
30032	Belvedere Park(u)	(404)	17.766	
31723	Blakely	(912)	5.880	5.267
31520	Brunswick	(912)	17.605	19.585
30518	Buford	(404)	6.578	4.640
31728	Cairo	(912)	8.777	8.061
30701	Calhoun	(404)	5.335	4.748
31730	Camilla	(912)	5.414	4.987
30032	Candler-McAfee(u)	(404)	27.306	
30117	Carrollton	(404)	14.078	13.520
30120	Cartersville	(404)	9.247	10.138
30125	Cedartown	(404)	8.619	9.253
30341	Chamblee	(404)	7.137	9.127
31014	Cochran	(912)	5.121	5.161
30337	College Park	(404)	24.632	18.203
*31902	Columbus	(404)	169.441	155.028
30027	Conley(u)	(404)	6.033	
30207	Conyers	(404)	6.567	4.809
31015	Cordele	(912)	11.184	10.733
30209	Covington	(404)	10.586	10.267
30720	Dalton	(404)	20.548	18.872
31742	Dawson	(912)	5.699	5.383
*30030	Decatur	(404)	18.404	21.943
31520	Dock Junction(u)	(912)	6.189	6.009
30340	Doraville	(404)	7.414	9.157
31533	Douglas	(912)	10.980	10.195
30134	Douglasville	(404)	7.641	5.472
30333	Druid Hills(u)	(404)	12.700	
31021	Dublin	(912)	16.083	15.143
30338	Dunwoody(u)	(404)	17.768	
31023	Eastman	(912)	5.330	5.416
30344	East Point	(404)	37.486	39.315
30635	Elberton	(404)	5.686	6.438
30060	Fair Oaks(u)	(404)	8.486	
30535	Fairview(u)	(404)	6.558	
31750	Fitzgerald	(912)	10.187	8.187
30050	Forest Park	(404)	18.782	19.994
31905	Fort Benning South(u)	(404)	15.074	27.495
30905	Fort Gordon(u)	(404)	14.069	15.589
30741	Fort Oglethorpe	(404)	5.443	3.869
31313	Fort Stewart(u)	(912)	15.031	4.467
31030	Fort Valley	(912)	9.000	9.251
30501	Gainesville	(404)	15.280	15.459
31408	Garden City	(912)	6.895	5.790
30316	Gresham Park(u)	(404)	6.232	
30223	Griffin	(404)	20.728	22.734
30354	Hapeville	(404)	6.166	9.567
31313	Hinesville	(912)	11.309	4.115
31545	Jesup	(912)	9.418	9.091
30144	Kennesaw	(404)	5.095	3.548
30728	La Fayette	(404)	6.517	6.044
30240	La Grange	(404)	24.204	23.301
30245	Lawrenceville	(404)	8.928	5.207
30057	Lithia Springs(u)	(404)	9.145	
30059	Mableton(u)	(404)	25.111	
*31201	Macon	(912)	116.860	122.423
30060	Marietta	(404)	30.805	27.216
30907	Martinez(u)	(404)	16.472	
31034	Midway-Hardwick(u)	(912)	8.977	14.047
31061	Milledgeville	(912)	12.176	11.601
30655	Monroe	(404)	8.854	8.071
31768	Moultrie	(912)	15.105	14.400
30075	Mountain Park(u)	(404)	9.425	268
30263	Newnan	(404)	11.449	11.205
30319	North Atlanta(u)	(404)	30.521	
30033	North Decatur(u)	(404)	11.830	
30033	North Druid Hills(u)	(404)	12.438	
30032	Panthersville(u)	(404)	11.366	
30269	Peachtree City	(404)	6.429	793
31069	Perry	(912)	9.453	7.771
31643	Quitman	(912)	5.188	4.818

ZIP code	Place		1980	1970
*30274	Riverdale	(404)	7,121	2,521
30161	Rome	(404)	29,928	30,759
30075	Roswell	(404)	23,337	5,430
31522	St. Simons(u)	(912)	6,566	5,346
31082	Sandersville	(912)	6,137	5,546
30328	Sandy Springs(u)	(404)	46,877	.....
*31401	Savannah	(912)	141,654	118,349
30079	Scottdale(u)	(404)	8,770	.....
30080	Smyrna	(404)	20,312	19,157
30278	Snellville	(404)	8,514	1,990
30901	South Augusta(u)	(404)	51,072	.....
30458	Statesboro	(912)	14,866	14,616
30401	Swainsboro	(912)	7,602	7,325
31791	Sylvester	(912)	5,860	4,226
30286	Thomaston	(404)	9,682	10,024
31792	Thomasville	(912)	18,463	18,155
30824	Thomson	(404)	7,001	6,503
31794	Tifton	(912)	13,749	12,179
30577	Toccoa	(404)	8,805	6,971
30084	Tucker(u)	(404)	25,399	.....
31601	Valdosta	(912)	37,596	32,303
30474	Vidalia	(912)	10,393	9,507
31093	Warner Robins	(912)	39,893	33,491
31501	Waycross	(912)	19,371	18,996
30830	Waynesboro	(404)	5,760	5,530
30901	West Augusta(u)	(404)	24,242	.....
31410	Wilmington Island(u)	(912)	7,546	3,284
30680	Winder	(404)	6,705	6,605

Hawaii (808)

See Note on Page 257

96706	Ewa		190,037	132,299
96720	Hilo		37,017	28,412
*96815	Honolulu		365,048	324,871
96732	Kahului		13,026	8,287
96749	Keaau-Mountain View		7,055	3,802
96752	Kekaha-Waimea		5,256	4,159
96753	Kihei		6,035	1,636
.....	Koolauloa		14,195	10,562
.....	Koolaupoko		109,373	92,219
96790	Kula		5,077	2,124
96761	Lahaina		10,284	5,524
96768	Makawao-Paia		10,361	5,788
.....	North Kona		13,748	4,832
96781	Papaikou-Wailea		5,261	5,503
.....	South Kona		5,914	4,004
96786	Wahiawa		41,562	37,329
96791	Waialua		9,849	9,171
96792	Waianae		32,810	24,077
96703	Wailua-Anahola		6,030	3,599
96793	Wailuku		10,674	9,084

Idaho (208)

83221	Blackfoot		10,065	8,716
*83708	Boise City		102,249	74,990
83318	Burley		8,761	8,279
83605	Caldwell		17,699	14,219
83201	Chubbuck		7,052	2,924
83814	Coeur D'Alene		19,913	16,228
83401	Idaho Falls		39,734	35,776
83338	Jerome		6,891	4,183
83501	Lewiston		27,986	26,068
83642	Meridian		6,658	2,616
83843	Moscow		16,513	14,146
83647	Mountain Home		7,540	6,451
83648	Mountain Home AFB(u)		6,403	6,038
83651	Nampa		25,112	20,768
83661	Payette		5,448	4,521
83201	Pocatello		46,340	40,036
83854	Post Falls		5,736	2,371
83440	Rexburg		11,559	8,272
83350	Rupert		5,476	4,563
83301	Twin Falls		26,209	21,914

Illinois

60101	Addison	(312)	29,826	24,482
60102	Algonquin	(312)	5,834	3,515
60658	Alsip	(312)	17,134	11,608
62002	Alton	(618)	34,171	39,700
62906	Anna	(618)	5,408	4,766
*60004	Arlington Heights	(312)	66,116	65,058
*60507	Aurora	(312)	81,293	74,389
60010	Barrington	(312)	9,029	8,581
60103	Bartlett	(312)	13,254	3,501
61607	Bartonville	(309)	6,110	7,221
60510	Batavia	(312)	12,574	9,060
62618	Beardstown	(217)	6,338	6,222
*62220	Belleville	(618)	42,150	41,223
60104	Bellwood	(312)	19,811	22,096
61008	Belvidere	(815)	15,176	14,061
60106	Bensenville	(312)	16,106	12,956
62812	Benton	(618)	7,778	6,833
60162	Berkeley	(312)	5,467	6,152

60402	Berwyn	(312)	46,849	52,502
62010	Bethalto	(618)	8,630	7,074
60108	Bloomingdale	(312)	12,659	2,974
61701	Bloomington	(309)	44,189	39,992
60406	Blue Island	(312)	21,855	22,629
60439	Bolingbrook	(312)	37,261	7,651
60538	Boulder Hill(u)	(312)	9,333	.....
60914	Bourbonnais	(815)	13,280	5,909
60915	Bradley	(815)	11,015	9,881
60455	Bridgeview	(312)	14,155	12,506
60153	Broadview	(312)	8,618	9,623
60513	Brookfield	(312)	19,395	20,284
60090	Buffalo Grove	(312)	22,230	12,333
60459	Burbank	(312)	28,462	26,726
62206	Cahokia	(618)	18,904	20,649
62914	Cairo	(618)	5,931	6,277
60409	Calumet City	(312)	39,673	33,107
60643	Calumet Park	(312)	8,788	10,069
61520	Canton	(309)	14,626	14,217
62901	Carbondale	(618)	26,414	22,816
62626	Carlinville	(217)	5,439	5,675
62821	Carmi	(618)	6,264	6,033
60187	Carol Stream	(312)	15,472	4,434
60110	Carpentersville	(312)	23,272	24,059
60013	Cary	(312)	6,640	4,358
62801	Centralia	(618)	15,126	15,966
62206	Centreville	(618)	9,747	11,378
61820	Champaign	(217)	58,267	56,837
61920	Charleston	(217)	19,355	16,421
62629	Chatham	(217)	5,597	2,788
62233	Chester	(618)	8,027	5,310
*60607	Chicago	(312)	3,005,072	3,369,357
60411	Chicago Heights	(312)	37,026	40,900
60415	Chicago Ridge	(312)	13,473	9,187
61523	Chillicothe	(309)	6,176	6,052
60650	Cicero	(312)	61,232	67,058
60514	Clarendon Hills	(312)	6,857	6,750
61727	Clinton	(217)	8,014	7,581
62234	Collinsville	(618)	19,613	18,224
60477	Country Club Hills	(312)	14,076	6,920
60525	Countryside	(312)	6,242	2,864
60435	Crest Hill	(815)	9,252	7,460
60445	Crestwood	(312)	10,712	5,770
60417	Crete	(312)	5,417	4,656
61611	Creve Coeur	(309)	6,851	6,440
60014	Crystal Lake	(815)	18,590	14,541
61832	Danville	(217)	38,985	42,570
60559	Darien	(312)	14,968	7,789
*62521	Decatur	(217)	93,939	90,397
60015	Deerfield	(312)	17,432	18,876
60115	De Kalb	(815)	33,157	32,949
*60016	Des Plaines	(312)	53,568	57,239
61021	Dixon	(815)	15,710	18,147
60419	Dolton	(312)	24,766	25,990
60515	Downers Grove	(312)	42,691	32,544
62832	Du Quoin	(618)	6,594	6,691
62024	East Alton	(618)	7,096	7,309
60411	East Chicago Heights	(312)	5,347	5,000
61244	East Moline	(309)	20,907	20,956
61611	East Peoria	(309)	22,385	18,671
*62201	East St. Louis	(618)	55,200	70,169
62025	Edwardsville	(618)	12,460	11,070
62401	Effingham	(217)	11,270	9,458
62930	Eldorado	(618)	5,198	3,876
60120	Elgin	(312)	63,668	55,691
60007	Elk Grove Village	(312)	28,679	20,346
60126	Elmhurst	(312)	44,251	46,392
60635	Elmwood Park	(312)	24,016	26,160
*60204	Evanston	(312)	73,706	80,113
60642	Evergreen Park	(312)	22,260	25,921
62837	Fairfield	(618)	5,954	5,897
62208	Fairview Heights	(618)	12,414	10,050
62839	Flora	(618)	5,379	5,283
60422	Flossmoor	(312)	8,423	7,846
60130	Forest Park	(312)	15,177	15,472
60020	Fox Lake	(312)	6,831	4,511
60131	Franklin Park	(312)	17,507	20,348
61032	Freeport	(815)	26,406	27,736
60030	Gages Lake-Wildwood(u)	(312)	5,848	5,337
61401	Galesburg	(309)	35,305	36,290
61254	Geneseo	(309)	6,373	5,840
60134	Geneva	(312)	9,881	9,049
62034	Glen Carbon	(618)	5,197	1,897
60022	Glencoe	(312)	9,200	10,542
60137	Glendale Heights	(618)	23,163	11,406
60137	Glen Ellyn	(312)	23,743	21,909
60025	Glenview	(312)	30,842	24,880
60425	Glenwood	(312)	10,538	7,416
62040	Granite City	(618)	36,815	40,685
60030	Grayslake	(312)	5,260	4,907
62246	Greenville	(618)	5,271	4,631
60031	Gurnee	(312)	7,179	2,738
60103	Hanover Park	(312)	28,719	11,735
62946	Harrisburg	(618)	9,322	9,535
60033	Harvard	(815)	5,126	5,177
60426	Harvey	(312)	35,810	34,636
60656	Harwood Heights	(312)	8,228	9,060
60429	Hazel Crest	(312)	13,973	10,329
62948	Herrin	(618)	10,708	9,623
60457	Hickory Hills	(312)	13,778	13,176
62249	Highland	(618)	7,122	5,981

ZIP code	Place		1980	1970
60035	Highland Park	(312)	30,599	32,263
60040	Highwood	(312)	5,455	4,973
60162	Hillside	(312)	8,279	8,888
60521	Hinsdale	(312)	16,726	15,918
60172	Hoffman Estates	(312)	38,258	22,238
60456	Hometown	(312)	5,324	6,729
60430	Homewood	(312)	19,724	18,871
60942	Hoopeston	(217)	6,411	6,461
60143	Itasca	(312)	7,948	4,638
62650	Jacksonville	(217)	20,284	20,553
62052	Jerseyville	(618)	7,506	7,446
*60431	Joliet	(815)	77,956	78,827
60458	Justice	(312)	10,552	9,473
60901	Kankakee	(815)	29,635	30,944
61443	Kewanee	(309)	14,508	15,762
60525	La Grange	(312)	15,693	17,814
60525	La Grange Park	(312)	13,359	15,459
60045	Lake Forest	(312)	15,245	15,642
60102	Lake in the Hills	(312)	5,651	3,240
60047	Lake Zurich	(312)	8,225	4,082
60438	Lansing	(312)	29,039	25,805
61301	La Salle	(815)	10,347	10,736
62439	Lawrenceville	(618)	5,652	5,863
60439	Lemont	(312)	5,640	5,080
60048	Libertyville	(312)	16,520	11,684
62656	Lincoln	(217)	16,327	17,582
60645	Lincolnwood	(312)	11,921	12,929
60046	Lindenhurst	(312)	6,220	3,141
60532	Lisle	(312)	13,638	5,329
62056	Litchfield	(217)	7,204	7,190
60441	Lockport	(815)	9,192	9,861
60148	Lombard	(312)	36,879	34,043
61111	Loves Park	(815)	13,192	12,390
60534	Lyons	(312)	9,925	11,124
61455	Macomb	(309)	19,632	19,643
62060	Madison	(618)	5,301	7,042
62959	Marion	(618)	14,031	11,724
60426	Markham	(312)	15,172	15,907
60443	Matteson	(312)	10,223	4,741
61938	Mattoon	(217)	19,293	19,681
60153	Maywood	(312)	27,998	29,019
60050	McHenry	(815)	10,908	6,772
*60160	Melrose Park	(312)	20,735	22,716
61342	Mendota	(815)	7,134	6,902
62960	Metropolis	(618)	7,171	6,940
60445	Midlothian	(312)	14,274	14,422
61264	Milan	(309)	6,371	4,873
61265	Moline	(309)	46,407	46,237
61462	Monmouth	(309)	10,706	11,022
60450	Morris	(815)	8,833	8,194
61550	Morton	(309)	14,178	10,811
60053	Morton Grove	(312)	23,747	26,369
62863	Mount Carmel	(618)	8,908	8,096
60056	Mount Prospect	(312)	52,634	34,995
62864	Mount Vernon	(618)	16,995	16,270
60060	Mundelein	(312)	17,053	16,128
62966	Murphysboro	(618)	9,866	10,013
60540	Naperville	(312)	42,601	22,794
60451	New Lenox	(815)	5,792	2,855
60648	Niles	(312)	30,363	31,432
61761	Normal	(309)	35,672	26,396
60656	Norridge	(312)	16,483	17,113
60542	North Aurora	(312)	5,205	4,833
60062	Northbrook	(312)	30,735	25,422
60064	North Chicago	(312)	38,774	47,275
60164	Northlake	(312)	12,166	14,191
61111	North Park(u)	(815)	15,806	15,679
60546	North Riverside	(312)	6,764	8,097
60521	Oak Brook	(312)	6,676	4,164
60452	Oak Forest	(312)	26,096	19,271
*60454	Oak Lawn	(312)	60,590	60,305
*60301	Oak Park	(312)	54,887	62,511
62269	O'Fallon	(618)	12,173	7,268
62450	Olney	(618)	9,026	8,974
60462	Orland Park	(312)	23,045	6,391
61350	Ottawa	(815)	18,166	18,716
60067	Palatine	(312)	32,166	26,050
60463	Palos Heights	(312)	11,096	8,544
60465	Palos Hills	(312)	16,654	6,629
62557	Pana	(217)	6,040	6,326
61944	Paris	(217)	9,885	9,971
60466	Park Forest	(312)	26,222	30,638
60466	Park Forest South	(312)	6,245	1,748
60068	Park Ridge	(312)	38,704	42,614
61554	Pekin	(309)	33,967	31,375
*61601	Peoria	(309)	124,160	126,963
61614	Peoria Heights	(309)	7,453	7,943
61354	Peru	(815)	10,886	11,772
61764	Pontiac	(815)	11,227	10,595
61356	Princeton	(815)	7,342	6,959
60070	Prospect Heights	(312)	11,823	13,333
62301	Quincy	(217)	42,352	45,288
61866	Rantoul	(217)	20,161	25,562
60471	Richton Park	(312)	9,403	2,558
60627	Riverdale	(312)	13,233	15,806
60305	River Forest	(312)	12,392	13,402
60171	River Grove	(312)	10,368	11,465
60546	Riverside	(312)	9,236	10,357
60472	Robbins	(312)	8,119	9,641
62454	Robinson	(618)	7,285	7,178
61068	Rochelle	(815)	8,982	8,594
61071	Rock Falls	(815)	10,624	10,287
*61125	Rockford	(815)	139,712	147,370
61201	Rock Island	(309)	46,821	50,166
60008	Rolling Meadows	(312)	20,167	19,178
60441	Romeoville	(815)	15,519	12,888
60172	Roselle	(312)	17,034	6,207
62024	Rosewood Heights(u)	(217)	5,085	3,391
60073	Round Lake Beach	(312)	12,921	5,717
60174	St. Charles	(312)	17,492	12,945
62881	Salem	(618)	7,813	6,187
60548	Sandwich	(815)	5,365	5,056
60411	Sauk Village	(312)	10,906	7,479
60172	Schaumburg	(312)	53,355	18,531
60176	Schiller Park	(312)	11,458	12,712
62225	Scott AFB(u)	(618)	8,648	7,871
62565	Shelbyville	(217)	5,259	4,887
61282	Silvis	(309)	7,130	5,907
60076	Skokie	(312)	60,278	68,322
60177	South Elgin	(312)	5,970	4,289
60473	South Holland	(312)	24,977	23,931
*62703	Springfield	(217)	100,054	91,753
61362	Spring Valley	(815)	5,822	5,605
60475	Steger	(312)	9,269	8,104
61081	Sterling	(815)	16,273	16,113
60402	Stickney	(312)	5,893	6,601
60103	Streamwood	(312)	23,456	18,176
61364	Streator	(815)	14,795	15,600
60501	Summit	(312)	10,110	11,569
62221	Swansea	(618)	5,347	5,432
60178	Sycamore	(815)	9,219	7,843
62568	Taylorville	(217)	11,386	10,644
60477	Tinley Park	(312)	26,178	12,572
*61801	Urbana	(217)	35,978	33,976
62471	Vandalia	(618)	5,338	5,160
60061	Vernon Hills	(312)	9,827	1,056
60181	Villa Park	(312)	23,155	25,891
60555	Warrenville	(312)	7,519	3,281
01571	Washington	(309)	10,364	6,790
62204	Washington Park	(618)	8,223	9,524
60970	Watseka	(815)	5,543	5,294
60084	Wauconda	(312)	5,688	5,460
60085	Waukegan	(312)	67,653	65,134
60153	Westchester	(312)	17,730	20,033
60185	West Chicago	(312)	12,550	9,988
60558	Western Springs	(312)	12,876	13,029
62896	West Frankfort	(618)	9,437	8,854
60559	Westmont	(312)	17,353	8,832
61604	West Peoria(u)	(309)	5,219	6,873
60187	Wheaton	(312)	43,043	31,138
60090	Wheeling	(312)	23,266	13,243
60091	Wilmette	(312)	28,221	32,134
60093	Winnetka	(312)	12,772	14,131
60096	Winthrop Harbor	(312)	5,427	4,794
60097	Wonder Lake(u)	(312)	5,917	4,806
60191	Wood Dale	(312)	11,251	8,831
60515	Woodridge	(312)	21,763	11,028
62095	Wood River	(618)	12,446	13,186
60098	Woodstock	(815)	11,725	10,226
60482	Worth	(312)	11,592	11,999
60099	Zion	(312)	17,865	17,268

Indiana

ZIP code	Place		1980	1970
46001	Alexandria	(317)	6,028	5,600
46011	Anderson	(317)	64,695	70,787
46703	Angola	(219)	5,486	5,117
46706	Auburn	(219)	8,122	7,388
47421	Bedford	(812)	14,410	13,087
46107	Beech Grove	(317)	13,196	13,559
47401	Bloomington	(812)	51,646	43,262
46714	Bluffton	(219)	8,705	8,297
47601	Boonville	(812)	6,300	5,736
47834	Brazil	(812)	7,852	8,163
46112	Brownsburg	(317)	6,242	5,751
46032	Carmel	(317)	18,272	6,691
46303	Cedar Lake	(219)	8,754	7,589
47111	Charlestown	(812)	5,596	5,933
46304	Chesterton	(219)	8,531	6,177
47130	Clarksville	(812)	15,164	13,298
47842	Clinton	(317)	5,267	5,340
46725	Columbia City	(219)	5,091	4,911
47201	Columbus	(812)	30,292	26,457
47331	Connersville	(317)	17,023	17,604
47933	Crawfordsville	(317)	13,325	13,842
46307	Crown Point	(219)	16,455	10,931
46733	Decatur	(219)	8,649	8,445
46514	Dunlap(u)	(219)	5,397	
46311	Dyer	(219)	9,555	4,906
46312	East Chicago	(219)	39,786	46,982
46514	Elkhart	(219)	41,305	43,152
46036	Elwood	(317)	10,867	11,196
*47708	Evansville	(812)	130,496	138,764
*46802	Fort Wayne	(219)	172,391	178,269
46041	Frankfort	(317)	15,168	14,956
46131	Franklin	(317)	11,563	11,477
*46401	Gary	(219)	151,968	175,415
46933	Gas City	(317)	6,370	5,742
46526	Goshen	(219)	19,665	17,871
46135	Greencastle	(317)	8,403	8,852

ZIP code	Place		1980	1970
46140	Greenfield	(317)	11,299	9,986
47240	Greensburg	(812)	9,254	8,620
46142	Greenwood	(317)	19,327	11,869
46319	Griffith	(219)	17,026	18,168
*46320	Hammond	(219)	93,714	107,983
47348	Hartford City	(317)	7,622	8,207
46322	Highland	(219)	25,935	24,947
46342	Hobart	(219)	22,987	21,485
47542	Huntingburg	(812)	5,376	4,794
46750	Huntington	(219)	16,202	16,217
46206	Indianapolis	(317)	700,807	736,856
47546	Jasper	(812)	9,097	8,641
47130	Jeffersonville	(812)	21,220	20,008
46755	Kendallville	(219)	7,299	6,838
46901	Kokomo	(317)	47,808	44,042
*47901	Lafayette	(317)	43,011	44,955
46405	Lake Station	(219)	15,087	9,858
46350	La Porte	(219)	21,796	22,140
46226	Lawrence	(317)	25,591	16,353
46052	Lebanon	(317)	11,456	9,766
47441	Linton	(812)	6,315	5,450
46947	Logansport	(219)	17,731	19,255
46356	Lowell	(219)	5,827	3,839
47250	Madison	(812)	12,472	13,081
46952	Marion	(317)	35,874	39,607
46151	Martinsville	(317)	11,311	9,723
46410	Merrillville	(219)	27,677	15,918
46360	Michigan City	(219)	36,850	39,369
46544	Mishawaka	(219)	40,224	36,060
47960	Monticello	(219)	5,162	4,869
46158	Mooresville	(317)	5,349	5,000
47620	Mount Vernon	(812)	7,656	6,770
*47302	Muncie	(317)	77,216	69,082
46321	Munster	(219)	20,671	16,514
47150	New Albany	(812)	37,103	38,402
47362	New Castle	(317)	20,056	21,215
46774	New Haven	(219)	6,714	5,346
46060	Noblesville	(317)	12,056	7,548
46962	North Manchester	(219)	5,998	5,791
47265	North Vernon	(812)	5,768	4,582
47130	Oak Park(u)	(812)	5,871	....
46970	Peru	(317)	13,764	14,139
46168	Plainfield	(317)	9,191	8,211
46563	Plymouth	(219)	7,693	7,661
46368	Portage	(219)	27,409	19,127
47371	Portland	(219)	7,074	7,115
47670	Princeton	(812)	8,976	7,431
47374	Richmond	(317)	41,349	43,999
46975	Rochester	(219)	5,050	4,631
46173	Rushville	(317)	6,113	6,686
47167	Salem	(812)	5,290	5,041
46375	Schererville	(219)	13,209	3,663
47170	Scottsburg	(812)	5,068	4,791
47274	Seymour	(812)	15,050	13,352
46176	Shelbyville	(317)	14,989	15,094
*46624	South Bend	(219)	109,727	125,580
46383	South Haven(u)	(219)	6,679	....
46224	Speedway	(317)	12,641	14,523
47586	Tell City	(812)	8,704	7,933
*47808	Terre Haute	(812)	61,125	70,335
46072	Tipton	(317)	5,004	5,313
46383	Valparaiso	(219)	22,247	20,020
47591	Vincennes	(812)	20,857	19,867
46992	Wabash	(219)	12,985	13,379
46580	Warsaw	(219)	10,647	7,506
47501	Washington	(812)	11,325	11,358
47906	West Lafayette	(317)	21,247	19,157
46394	Whiting	(219)	5,630	7,054
47394	Winchester	(317)	5,659	5,493

Iowa

50511	Algona	(515)	6,289	6,032
50009	Altoona	(515)	5,764	2,883
50010	Ames	(515)	45,775	39,505
50021	Ankeny	(515)	15,429	9,151
50022	Atlantic	(712)	7,789	7,306
52722	Bettendorf	(319)	27,381	22,126
50036	Boone	(515)	12,602	12,468
52601	Burlington	(319)	29,529	32,366
51401	Carroll	(712)	9,705	8,716
50613	Cedar Falls	(319)	36,322	29,597
*52401	Cedar Rapids	(319)	110,243	110,642
52544	Centerville	(515)	6,558	6,531
50049	Chariton	(515)	5,116	5,009
50616	Charles City	(515)	8,778	9,268
51012	Cherokee	(712)	7,004	7,272
51632	Clarinda	(712)	5,458	5,420
50428	Clear Lake City	(515)	7,458	6,430
52732	Clinton	(319)	32,828	34,719
50053	Clive	(515)	5,906	3,005
52240	Coralville	(319)	7,687	6,130
51501	Council Bluffs	(712)	56,449	60,348
50801	Creston	(515)	8,429	8,234
*52802	Davenport	(319)	103,264	98,469
52101	Decorah	(319)	7,991	7,237
51442	Denison	(712)	6,675	6,218
*50318	Des Moines	(515)	191,003	201,404
52001	Dubuque	(319)	62,321	62,374

51334	Estherville	(712)	7,518	8,108
52556	Fairfield	(515)	9,428	8,715
50501	Fort Dodge	(515)	29,423	31,263
52627	Fort Madison	(319)	13,520	13,996
51534	Glenwood	(712)	5,280	4,421
50112	Grinnell	(515)	8,868	8,402
51537	Harlan	(712)	5,357	5,049
50644	Independence	(319)	6,392	5,910
50125	Indianola	(515)	10,843	8,852
52240	Iowa City	(319)	50,508	46,850
50126	Iowa Falls	(515)	6,174	6,454
52632	Keokuk	(319)	13,536	14,631
50138	Knoxville	(515)	8,143	7,755
51031	Le Mars	(712)	8,276	8,159
52060	Maquoketa	(319)	6,313	5,677
52302	Marion	(319)	19,474	18,028
50158	Marshalltown	(515)	26,938	26,219
50401	Mason City	(515)	30,144	30,379
52641	Mount Pleasant	(319)	7,322	7,007
52761	Muscatine	(319)	23,467	22,405
50201	Nevada	(515)	5,912	4,952
50208	Newton	(515)	15,292	15,619
50662	Oelwein	(319)	7,564	7,735
52577	Oskaloosa	(515)	10,629	11,224
52501	Ottumwa	(515)	27,381	29,610
50219	Pella	(515)	8,349	6,668
50220	Perry	(515)	7,053	6,906
51566	Red Oak	(712)	6,810	6,210
51201	Sheldon	(712)	5,003	4,535
51601	Shenandoah	(712)	6,274	5,968
*51101	Sioux City	(712)	82,003	85,925
51301	Spencer	(712)	11,726	10,278
50588	Storm Lake	(712)	8,814	8,591
50322	Urbandale	(515)	17,869	14,434
52349	Vinton	(319)	5,040	4,845
52353	Washington	(319)	6,584	6,317
*50701	Waterloo	(319)	75,985	75,533
50677	Waverly	(319)	8,444	7,205
50595	Webster City	(515)	8,572	8,488
50265	West Des Moines	(515)	21,894	16,441
50311	Windsor Heights	(515)	5,632	6,303

Kansas

67410	Abilene	(913)	6,572	6,661
67005	Arkansas City	(316)	13,201	13,216
66002	Atchison	(913)	11,407	12,565
67010	Augusta	(316)	6,968	5,977
66012	Bonner Springs	(913)	6,266	3,884
66720	Chanute	(316)	10,506	10,341
67337	Coffeyville	(316)	15,185	15,116
67701	Colby	(913)	5,544	4,658
66901	Concordia	(913)	6,847	7,221
67037	Derby	(316)	9,786	7,947
67801	Dodge City	(316)	18,001	14,127
67042	El Dorado	(316)	11,555	12,308
66801	Emporia	(316)	25,287	23,327
66442	Fort Riley North(u)	(913)	16,086	12,469
66701	Fort Scott	(316)	8,893	8,967
67846	Garden City	(316)	18,256	14,790
67735	Goodland	(913)	5,708	5,510
67530	Great Bend	(316)	16,608	16,133
67601	Hays	(913)	16,301	15,396
67060	Haysville	(316)	8,006	6,531
67501	Hutchinson	(316)	40,284	36,885
67301	Independence	(316)	10,598	10,347
66749	Iola	(316)	6,938	6,493
66441	Junction City	(913)	19,305	19,018
*66110	Kansas City	(913)	161,148	168,213
66043	Lansing	(913)	5,307	3,797
66044	Lawrence	(913)	52,738	45,698
66048	Leavenworth	(913)	33,656	25,147
66206	Leawood	(913)	13,360	10,645
66215	Lenexa	(913)	18,639	5,549
67901	Liberal	(316)	14,911	13,862
67460	McPherson	(316)	11,753	10,851
66502	Manhattan	(913)	32,644	27,575
66203	Merriam	(913)	10,794	10,955
66222	Mission	(913)	8,643	8,125
67114	Newton	(316)	16,332	15,439
66061	Olathe	(913)	37,258	17,917
66067	Ottawa	(913)	11,016	11,036
66204	Overland Park	(913)	81,784	77,934
67357	Parsons	(316)	12,898	13,015
66762	Pittsburg	(316)	18,770	20,171
66208	Prairie Village	(913)	24,657	28,378
67124	Pratt	(316)	6,885	6,736
66203	Roeland Park	(913)	7,962	9,760
67665	Russell	(913)	5,427	5,371
67401	Salina	(913)	41,843	37,714
*66203	Shawnee	(913)	29,653	20,946
*66603	Topeka	(913)	118,690	125,011
67152	Wellington	(316)	8,212	8,072
*67202	Wichita	(316)	279,835	276,554
67156	Winfield	(316)	10,736	11,405

Kentucky

41101	Ashland	(606)	27,064	29,245
40004	Bardstown	(502)	6,155	5,816

ZIP code	Place		1980	1970
41073	Bellevue	(606)	7,678	8,847
40403	Berea	(606)	8,226	6,956
42101	Bowling Green	(502)	40,450	36,705
40218	Buechel(u)	(502)	6,912	5,359
42718	Campbellsville	(502)	8,715	7,598
42330	Central City	(502)	5,250	5,450
40701	Corbin	(606)	8,075	7,474
*41011	Covington	(606)	49,567	52,535
41031	Cynthiana	(606)	5,881	6,356
40422	Danville	(606)	12,942	11,542
41074	Dayton	(606)	6,979	8,751
41017	Edgewood	(606)	7,243	4,139
42701	Elizabethtown	(502)	15,380	11,748
41018	Elsmere	(606)	7,203	5,161
41018	Erlanger	(606)	14,466	12,676
40118	Fairdale(u)	(502)	7,315	....
40291	Fern Creek(u)	(502)	16,866	....
41139	Flatwoods	(606)	8,354	7,380
41042	Florence	(606)	15,586	11,661
42223	Fort Campbell North(u)	(502)	17,211	13,616
40121	Fort Knox(u)	(502)	31,035	37,608
41017	Fort Mitchell	(606)	7,310	6,982
41075	Fort Thomas	(606)	16,012	16,338
40601	Frankfort	(502)	25,973	21,902
42134	Franklin	(502)	7,738	6,553
40324	Georgetown	(502)	10,972	8,629
42141	Glasgow	(502)	12,958	11,301
40330	Harrodsburg	(502)	7,265	6,741
41701	Hazard	(606)	5,429	5,459
42420	Henderson	(502)	24,834	22,976
40228	Highview(u)	(502)	13,286	....
40229	Hillview	(502)	5,196	....
42240	Hopkinsville	(502)	27,318	21,395
41051	Independence	(606)	7,998	1,715
40299	Jeffersontown	(502)	15,795	9,701
40342	Lawrenceburg	(502)	5,167	3,579
40033	Lebanon	(502)	6,590	5,528
*40511	Lexington-Fayette	(000)	204,165	108,137
*40201	Louisville	(502)	298,694	361,706
42431	Madisonville	(502)	16,979	15,332
42066	Mayfield	(502)	10,705	10,724
41056	Maysville	(606)	7,983	7,411
40965	Middlesborough	(606)	12,251	11,878
42633	Monticello	(606)	5,677	3,618
40351	Morehead	(606)	7,789	7,191
40353	Mount Sterling	(606)	5,820	5,083
42071	Murray	(502)	14,248	13,537
40218	Newburg(u)	(502)	24,612	....
*41071	Newport	(606)	21,587	25,998
40356	Nicholasville	(606)	10,400	5,829
40219	Okolona(u)	(502)	20,039	17,643
42301	Owensboro	(502)	54,450	50,329
42001	Paducah	(502)	29,315	31,627
40361	Paris	(606)	7,935	7,823
40258	Pleasure Ridge Park(u)	(502)	27,332	28,566
42445	Princeton	(502)	7,073	6,292
40160	Radcliff	(502)	14,519	8,426
40475	Richmond	(606)	21,705	16,861
42276	Russellville	(502)	7,520	6,456
40207	St. Matthews	(502)	13,519	13,152
40065	Shelbyville	(502)	5,308	4,182
40216	Shively	(502)	16,645	19,139
42501	Somerset	(606)	10,649	10,436
40272	Valley Station(u)	(502)	24,474	24,471
40383	Versailles	(606)	6,427	5,679
41101	Westwood(u)	(606)	5,973	777
40769	Williamsburg	(606)	5,560	3,687
40391	Winchester	(606)	15,216	13,402

Louisiana

ZIP code	Place		1980	1970
70510	Abbeville	(318)	12,391	10,996
71301	Alexandria	(318)	51,565	41,811
70032	Arabi(u)	(504)	10,248	....
70094	Avondale(u)	(504)	6,699	....
70714	Baker	(504)	12,865	8,281
71220	Bastrop	(318)	15,527	14,713
70821	Baton Rouge	(504)	220,394	165,921
70360	Bayou Cane(u)	(504)	15,723	9,077
70380	Bayou Vista(u)	(504)	5,805	5,121
70037	Belle Chasse(u)	(504)	5,412	....
70427	Bogalusa	(504)	16,976	18,412
71010	Bossier City	(318)	49,969	43,769
70517	Breaux Bridge	(318)	5,922	4,942
	Broadmoor(u)	(318)	7,051	....
71291	Brownsville-Bawcomville(u)	(318)	7,252	....
71322	Bunkie	(318)	5,364	5,395
70043	Chalmette(u)	(504)	33,847	....
71291	Claiborne(u)	(318)	6,278	....
70433	Covington	(504)	7,892	7,170
70526	Crowley	(318)	16,036	16,104
70345	Cut Off(u)	(504)	5,049	....
70726	Denham Springs	(504)	8,412	6,752
70634	De Ridder	(318)	11,057	8,030
70346	Donaldsonville	(504)	7,901	7,367
70072	Estelle(u)	(504)	12,724	....
70535	Eunice	(318)	12,479	11,390
70538	Franklin	(318)	9,584	9,325
70354	Galliano(u)	(504)	5,159	....
70737	Gonzales	(504)	7,287	4,512
70053	Gretna	(504)	20,615	24,875
70401	Hammond	(504)	15,043	12,487
70123	Harahan	(504)	11,384	13,037
70058	Harvey(u)	(504)	22,709	6,347
70360	Houma	(504)	32,602	30,922
70544	Jeanerette	(318)	6,511	6,322
70121	Jefferson(u)	(504)	15,550	16,489
70546	Jennings	(318)	12,401	11,783
71251	Jonesboro	(318)	5,061	5,072
70548	Kaplan	(318)	5,016	5,540
70062	Kenner	(504)	66,382	29,858
70445	Lacombe(u)	(504)	5,146	....
70501	Lafayette	(318)	80,584	68,908
70601	Lake Charles	(318)	75,051	77,998
71254	Lake Providence	(318)	6,361	6,183
70068	Laplace(u)	(504)	16,112	5,953
70373	Larose(u)	(504)	5,234	4,267
71446	Leesville	(318)	9,054	8,928
70123	Little Farms(u)	(504)	NA	15,713
70448	Mandeville	(504)	6,076	2,571
71052	Mansfield	(318)	6,485	6,432
71351	Marksville	(318)	5,113	4,519
70072	Marrero(u)	(504)	36,548	29,015
*70004	Metairie(u)	(504)	164,160	136,477
71055	Minden	(318)	15,074	13,996
71201	Monroe	(318)	57,597	56,374
70380	Morgan City	(504)	16,114	16,586
70601	Moss Bluff(u)	(318)	7,004	....
71457	Natchitoches	(318)	16,664	15,974
70560	New Iberia	(318)	32,766	30,147
*70113	New Orleans	(504)	557,927	593,471
71463	Oakdale	(318)	7,155	7,301
70570	Opelousas	(318)	18,903	20,387
71360	Pineville	(318)	12,034	8,951
70764	Plaquemine	(504)	7,521	7,739
70454	Ponchatoula	(504)	5,469	4,545
70767	Port Allen	(504)	6,114	5,728
70055	Poydras(u)	(504)	5,722	....
70601	Prien(u)	(318)	6,224	....
70394	Raceland(u)	(504)	6,302	4,880
70578	Rayne	(318)	9,066	9,510
70084	Reserve(u)	(504)	7,288	6,381
70123	River Ridge(u)	(504)	17,146	....
71270	Ruston	(318)	20,585	17,365
70582	St. Martinville	(318)	7,965	7,153
70807	Scotlandville(u)	(504)	15,113	22,599
*71102	Shreveport	(318)	205,815	182,064
70458	Slidell	(504)	26,718	16,101
71459	South Fort Polk(u)	(318)	12,498	15,600
71075	Springhill	(318)	6,516	6,496
70663	Sulphur	(318)	19,709	14,959
71282	Tallulah	(318)	11,341	9,643
71285	Terrytown(u)	(504)	23,548	13,382
70301	Thibodaux	(504)	15,810	15,028
70053	Timberlane(u)	(504)	11,579	....
71373	Vidalia	(318)	5,936	5,538
70586	Ville Platte	(318)	9,201	9,692
70002	Violet(u)	(504)	11,678	....
70094	Waggaman(u)	(504)	9,004	....
70669	Westlake	(318)	5,246	4,082
71291	West Monroe	(318)	14,993	14,868
70094	Westwego	(504)	12,663	11,402
71483	Winnfield	(318)	7,311	7,142
71295	Winnsboro	(318)	5,921	5,349
70791	Zachary	(504)	7,297	4,964

Maine (207)

See Note Page 257

ZIP code	Place	1980	1970
04210	Auburn	23,128	24,151
04330	Augusta	21,819	21,945
04401	Bangor	31,643	33,168
04530	Bath	10,246	9,679
04915	Belfast	6,243	5,957
04005	Biddeford	19,638	19,983
04412	Brewer	9,017	9,300
04011	Brunswick Center(u)	10,990	10,867
04011	Brunswick	17,366	16,195
04093	Buxton	5,775	3,135
04107	Cape Elizabeth	7,838	7,873
04736	Caribou	9,916	10,419
04021	Cumberland	5,284	4,096
04605	Ellsworth	5,179	4,603
04937	Fairfield	6,113	5,684
04105	Falmouth	6,853	6,291
04938	Farmington	6,730	5,657
04032	Freeport	5,863	4,781
04345	Gardiner	6,485	6,685
04038	Gorham	10,101	7,839
04444	Hampden	5,250	4,693
04730	Houlton Center(u)	5,730	6,760
04730	Houlton	6,766	8,111
04239	Jay	5,080	3,954
04043	Kennebunk	6,621	5,646
03904	Kittery Center(u)	5,465	7,363
03904	Kittery	9,314	11,028
04240	Lewiston	40,481	41,779

ZIP code	Place	1980	1970
04750	Limestone	8,719	10,360
04457	Lincoln	5,066	4,759
04250	Lisbon	8,769	6,544
04750	Loring(u)	6,572	7,881
04756	Madawaska	5,282	5,585
04462	Millinocket Center(u)	7,567	7,558
04462	Millinocket	7,567	7,742
04062	North Windham(u)	5,492	....
04963	Oakland	5,162	3,535
04064	Old Orchard Beach Ctr.(u)	6,023	5,273
04064	Old Orchard Beach	6,291	5,404
04468	Old Town	8,422	8,741
04473	Orono Center(u)	9,891	9,146
04473	Orono	10,578	9,989
*04101	Portland	61,572	65,116
04769	Presque Isle	11,172	11,452
04841	Rockland	7,919	8,505
04276	Rumford Compact(u)	6,256	6,198
04276	Rumford	8,240	9,363
04072	Saco	12,921	11,678
04073	Sanford Center(u)	10,268	10,457
04073	Sanford	18,020	15,812
04074	Scarborough	11,347	7,845
04976	Skowhegan Center(u)	6,517	6,571
04976	Skowhegan	8,098	7,601
04106	South Portland	22,712	23,267
04084	Standish	5,946	3,122
04086	Topsham	6,431	5,022
04901	Waterville	17,779	18,192
04090	Wells	8,211	4,448
04092	Westbrook	14,976	14,444
04082	Windham	11,282	6,593
04901	Winslow Center(u)	5,903	5,389
04901	Winslow	8,057	7,299
04364	Winthrop	5,889	4,335
04096	Yarmouth	6,585	4,854
03909	York	8,465	5,690

Maryland (301)

ZIP code	Place	1980	1970
21001	Aberdeen	11,533	7,403
21005	Aberdeen Proving Ground(u)	5,772	7,403
20783	Adelphi(u)	12,530	....
20331	Andrews(u)	10,064	6,418
*21401	Annapolis	31,740	30,095
21227	Arbutus(u)	20,163	22,745
21012	Arnold(u)	12,285	....
20906	Aspen Hill(u)	47,455	16,887
*21233	Baltimore	786,741	905,787
21014	Bel Air	7,814	6,307
21050	Bel Air North(u)	5,043	....
21014	Bel Air South(u)	8,461	....
20705	Beltsville(u)	12,760	8,912
20815	Bethesda(u)	63,022	71,621
20710	Bladensburg	7,691	7,977
20715	Bowie	33,695	35,028
21225	Brooklyn Park(u)	11,508	....
20731	Cabin John-Brookmont(u)	5,135	....
20619	California(u)	5,770	....
21613	Cambridge	11,703	11,595
20748	Camp Springs(u)	16,118	22,776
21401	Cape St. Clair(u)	6,022	....
20027	Carmody Hills-Pepper Mill(u)	5,571	6,245
21234	Carney(u)	21,488	....
21228	Catonsville(u)	33,208	54,812
20785	Cheverly	5,751	6,808
20815	Chevy Chase(u)	12,232	16,424
20783	Chillum(u)	32,775	35,656
20735	Clinton(u)	16,438	....
20904	Cloverly(u)	5,153	....
21030	Cockeysville(u)	17,013	....
20904	Colesville(u)	14,359	9,455
20740	College Park	23,614	26,156
21043	Columbia(u)	52,518	8,815
20027	Coral Hills(u)	11,602	9,058
21114	Crofton(u)	12,009	4,478
21502	Cumberland	25,933	29,724
20747	District Heights	6,799	7,846
20785	Dodge Park(u)	5,275	....
21222	Dundalk(u)	71,293	85,377
21601	Easton	7,536	6,809
20840	East Riverdale(u)	14,117	....
21219	Edgemere(u)	9,078	10,352
21040	Edgewood	19,455	8,551
21921	Elkton	6,468	5,362
*21043	Ellicott(u)	21,784	9,435
21221	Essex(u)	39,614	38,193
20904	Fairland(u)	5,154	....
21047	Fallston(u)	5,572	....
21061	Ferndale(u)	14,314	9,929
21050	Forestville(u)	16,401	16,188
20755	Fort Meade(u)	14,083	16,699
21701	Frederick	27,557	23,641
.....	Friendly(u)	8,848	....
21532	Frostburg	7,715	7,327
20877	Gaithersburg	26,424	8,344
20874	Germantown(u)	9,721	....
.....	Glassmanor(u)	7,751	....
21061	Glen Burnie(u)	37,263	38,608
20769	Glenn Dale(u)	5,106	....
20771	Goddard(u)	6,147	....
20770	Greenbelt	16,000	18,199
21122	Green Haven(u)	6,577	....
21740	Hagerstown	34,132	35,862
21740	Halfway(u)	8,659	6,106
21204	Hampton(u)	5,220	....
21078	Havre De Grace	8,763	9,791
20903	Hillandale(u)	9,686	....
20031	Hillcrest Heights	17,021	24,037
*20780	Hyattsville	12,709	14,998
21085	Joppatowne(u)	11,348	9,092
20785	Kentland(u)	8,596	9,649
20870	Kettering(u)	6,972	....
21122	Lake Shore(u)	10,181	....
20785	Landover(u)	5,374	5,597
20787	Langley Park(u)	14,038	11,564
20706	Lanham-Seabrook(u)	15,814	13,244
21227	Lansdowne-Baltimore Highlands(u)	16,759	17,770
.....	Largo(u)	5,557	....
20810	Laurel	12,103	10,525
21502	La Vale-Narrows Park(u)	5,523	3,971
20653	Lexington Pk.(u)	10,361	9,136
21090	Linthicum(u)	7,457	9,775
21207	Lochearn(u)	26,908	....
21037	Londontowne(u)	6,052	3,864
21093	Lutherville-Timonium(u)	17,854	24,055
20031	Marlow Heights(u)	5,824	....
20810	Maryland City(u)	6,949	7,102
.....	Mays Chapel(u)	5,213	....
21220	Middle River(u)	26,756	19,935
.....	Milford Mill(u)	20,354	....
20879	Montgomery Village(u)	18,725	....
20822	Mount Rainier	7,361	8,180
21402	Naval Academy(u)	5,367	....
20784	New Carrollton	12,632	14,870
20014	North Bethesda(u)	22,671	....
20795	North Kensington(u)	9,039	....
20810	North Laurel(u)	6,093	....
21113	Odenton(u)	13,270	5,989
20832	Olney(u)	13,026	2,138
21206	Overlea(u)	12,965	13,124
21117	Owings Mills(u)	9,526	7,360
20745	Oxon Hill(u)	36,267	11,974
20785	Palmer Park(u)	7,986	8,172
21234	Parkville	35,159	33,589
21122	Pasadena(u)	7,439	....
21128	Perry Hall(u)	13,455	5,446
21208	Pikesville(u)	22,555	25,395
20854	Potomac(u)	40,402	....
21227	Pumphrey(u)	5,666	6,425
20760	Quince Orchard(u)	5,107	....
21133	Randallstown(u)	25,927	33,683
.....	Redland(u)	10,759	....
21136	Reisterstown(u)	19,385	12,568
21122	Riviera Beach(u)	8,812	7,464
*20850	Rockville	43,811	42,739
21237	Rosedale(u)	19,956	19,417
21221	Rossville(u)	8,646	....
20601	St. Charles(u)	13,921	....
21801	Salisbury	16,429	15,252
20027	Seat Pleasant	5,217	7,217
21740	Security(u)	29,453	....
21144	Severn(u)	20,147	....
21146	Severna Park	21,253	16,358
*20907	Silver Spring(u)	72,893	77,411
21061	South Gate(u)	24,185	9,356
20795	South Kensington(u)	9,344	10,281
20810	South Laurel(u)	18,034	13,345
20023	Sutland-Silver Hills(u)	32,164	30,351
20912	Takoma Park	16,231	18,507
.....	Tantallon(u)	9,945	....
20748	Temple Hills(u)	6,630	....
21204	Towson(u)	51,083	77,768
20601	Waldorf(u)	9,782	7,363
20028	Walker Mill(u)	10,651	7,102
21157	Westminster	8,808	7,207
20902	Wheaton Glenmont(u)	48,598	66,280
20903	White Oak(u)	13,700	19,769
20695	White Plains(u)	5,167	....
21207	Woodlawn(u)	5,306	....

Massachusetts

See Note on Page 257

ZIP code	Place	Area Code	1980	1970
02351	Abington	(617)	13,517	12,33
01720	Acton	(617)	17,544	14,77
02743	Acushnet	(617)	8,704	7,76
01220	Adams Center(u)	(413)	6,857	11,25
.....	Adams	(413)	10,381	11,77
01001	Agawam	(413)	26,271	21,71
01913	Amesbury Center(u)	(617)	12,236	10,08
.....	Amesbury	(617)	13,971	11,38
01002	Amherst Center	(413)	17,773	17,92
.....	Amherst	(413)	33,229	26,33
01810	Andover	(617)	26,370	23,69
02174	Arlington	(617)	48,219	53,5
01721	Ashland	(617)	9,165	8,88

ZIP code	Place		1980	1970
01331	Athol Center(u)	(617)	8,708	9,723
.....	Athol	(617)	10,634	11,185
02703	Attleboro	(617)	34,196	32,907
01501	Auburn	(617)	14,845	15,347
02322	Avon	(617)	5,026	5,295
*01432	Ayer	(617)	6,993	8,325
02630	Barnstable	(617)	30,898	19,842
01730	Bedford	(617)	13,067	13,513
01007	Belchertown	(413)	8,339	5,936
02019	Bellingham	(617)	14,300	13,967
02178	Belmont	(617)	26,100	28,285
01915	Beverly	(617)	37,655	38,348
01821	Billerica	(617)	36,727	31,648
01504	Blackstone	(617)	6,570	6,566
*02109	Boston	(617)	562,994	641,071
02532	Bourne	(617)	13,874	12,636
01921	Boxford	(617)	5,374	4,032
02184	Braintree	(617)	36,337	35,050
02631	Brewster	(617)	5,226	1,790
02324	Bridgewater	(617)	17,202	12,911
*02403	Brockton	(617)	95,172	89,040
02146	Brookline	(617)	55,062	58,689
01803	Burlington	(617)	23,486	21,980
*02138	Cambridge	(617)	95,322	100,361
02021	Canton	(617)	18,182	17,100
02330	Carver	(617)	6,988	2,420
01507	Charlton	(617)	6,719	4,654
02633	Chatham	(617)	6,071	4,554
01824	Chelmsford	(617)	31,174	31,432
02150	Chelsea	(617)	25,431	30,625
*01021	Chicopee	(413)	55,112	66,676
01510	Clinton	(617)	12,771	13,383
01778	Cochituate(u)	(617)	6,126	
02025	Cohasset	(617)	7,174	6,954
01742	Concord	(617)	16,293	16,148
01226	Dalton	(413)	6,797	7,505
01923	Danvers	(617)	24,100	26,151
02714	Dartmouth	(617)	23,966	18,800
02026	Dedham	(617)	25,298	26,938
02638	Dennis	(617)	12,360	6,454
02715	Dighton	(617)	5,352	4,667
01826	Dracut	(617)	21,249	18,214
01570	Dudley	(617)	8,717	8,087
02332	Duxbury	(617)	11,807	7,636
02333	East Bridgewater	(617)	9,945	8,347
02536	East Falmouth(u)	(617)	5,181	2,971
01027	Easthampton	(413)	15,580	13,012
01028	East Longmeadow	(413)	12,905	13,029
02334	Easton	(617)	16,623	12,157
01249	Everett	(617)	37,195	42,485
02719	Fairhaven	(617)	15,759	16,332
*02722	Fall River	(617)	92,574	96,898
*02540	Falmouth Center(u)	(617)	5,720	5,806
.....	Falmouth	(617)	23,640	15,942
01420	Fitchburg	(617)	39,580	43,343
01433	Fort Devens(u)	(617)	9,546	12,915
02035	Foxborough	(617)	14,148	14,218
01701	Framingham	(617)	65,113	64,048
02038	Franklin Center(u)	(617)	9,296	8,863
.....	Franklin	(617)	18,217	17,830
02702	Freetown	(617)	7,058	4,270
01440	Gardner	(617)	17,900	19,748
01833	Georgetown	(617)	5,687	5,290
01930	Gloucester	(617)	27,768	27,941
01519	Grafton	(617)	11,238	11,659
01033	Granby	(413)	5,380	5,473
01230	Great Barrington	(413)	7,405	7,537
01301	Greenfield Center(u)	(413)	14,198	14,642
.....	Greenfield	(413)	18,436	18,116
01450	Groton	(617)	6,154	5,109
01834	Groveland	(617)	5,040	5,382
02338	Halifax	(617)	5,513	3,537
01936	Hamilton	(617)	6,960	6,373
02339	Hanover	(617)	11,358	10,107
02341	Hanson	(617)	8,617	7,148
01451	Harvard	(617)	12,170	12,494
02645	Harwich	(617)	8,971	5,892
01830	Haverhill	(617)	46,865	46,120
02043	Hingham	(617)	20,339	18,845
.....	Holbrook	(617)	11,140	11,775
01520	Holden	(617)	13,336	12,564
01746	Holliston	(617)	12,622	12,069
01040	Holyoke	(413)	44,678	50,112
01748	Hopkinton	(617)	7,114	5,981
01749	Hudson Center(u)	(617)	14,156	14,283
.....	Hudson	(617)	16,408	16,084
02045	Hull	(617)	9,714	9,961
02601	Hyannis(u)	(617)	9,118	6,847
01938	Ipswich(u)	(617)	NA	5,022
.....	Ipswich	(617)	11,158	10,750
02364	Kingston	(617)	7,362	5,999
02346	Lakeville	(617)	5,931	4,376
01523	Lancaster	(617)	6,334	6,095
01842	Lawrence	(617)	63,175	66,915
01238	Lee	(413)	6,247	6,426
01524	Leicester	(617)	9,446	9,140
01240	Lenox	(413)	6,523	5,804
01453	Leominster	(617)	34,508	32,939
02173	Lexington	(617)	29,479	31,886
01773	Lincoln	(617)	7,098	7,567
01460	Littleton	(617)	6,970	6,380
01106	Longmeadow	(413)	16,301	15,630
*01853	Lowell	(617)	92,418	94,239
01056	Ludlow	(413)	18,150	17,580
01462	Lunenburg	(617)	8,405	7,419
*01901	Lynn	(617)	78,471	90,294
01940	Lynnfield	(617)	11,267	10,826
02148	Malden	(617)	53,386	56,127
01944	Manchester	(617)	5,424	5,151
02048	Mansfield	(617)	13,453	9,939
01945	Marblehead	(617)	20,126	21,295
01752	Marlborough	(617)	30,617	27,936
02050	Marshfield	(617)	20,916	15,223
02739	Mattapoisett	(617)	5,597	4,500
01754	Maynard	(617)	9,590	9,710
02052	Medfield	(617)	10,220	9,821
02155	Medford	(617)	58,076	64,397
02053	Medway	(617)	8,447	7,938
02176	Melrose	(617)	30,055	33,180
01844	Methuen	(617)	36,701	35,456
02346	Middleborough Center(u)	(617)	7,012	6,259
.....	Middleborough	(617)	16,404	13,607
01757	Milford Center(u)	(617)	NA	13,740
.....	Milford	(617)	23,390	19,352
01527	Millbury	(617)	11,808	11,987
02054	Millis	(617)	6,908	5,686
02186	Milton	(617)	25,860	27,190
01057	Monson	(413)	7,315	7,355
01351	Montague	(413)	8,011	8,451
02554	Nantucket	(617)	5,087	3,774
01760	Natick	(617)	29,461	31,057
02192	Needham	(617)	27,901	29,748
*02741	New Bedford	(617)	98,478	101,777
01950	Newburyport	(617)	15,900	15,807
02158	Newton	(617)	83,622	91,263
02056	Norfolk	(617)	6,363	4,656
01247	North Adams	(413)	18,063	19,195
01002	North Amherst(u)	(413)	5,616	2,054
01060	Northampton	(413)	29,286	29,664
01845	North Andover	(617)	20,129	16,284
*02760	North Attleborough	(617)	21,095	18,665
01532	Northborough	(617)	10,568	9,218
01534	Northbridge	(617)	12,246	11,795
01864	North Reading	(617)	11,455	11,264
02060	North Scituate(u)	(617)	5,221	5,507
02766	Norton	(617)	12,690	9,487
02061	Norwell	(617)	9,182	7,796
02062	Norwood	(617)	29,711	30,815
01364	Orange	(617)	6,844	6,104
02653	Orleans	(617)	5,306	3,055
01253	Otis(u)	(413)	NA	5,596
01540	Oxford Center(u)	(617)	6,369	6,109
.....	Oxford	(617)	11,680	10,345
01069	Palmer	(413)	11,389	11,680
01960	Peabody	(617)	45,976	48,080
02359	Pembroke	(617)	13,487	11,193
01463	Pepperell	(617)	8,061	5,887
01866	Pinehurst(u)	(617)	6,568	
01201	Pittsfield	(413)	51,974	57,020
02762	Plainville	(617)	5,857	4,953
*02360	Plymouth Center(u)	(617)	7,232	6,940
.....	Plymouth	(617)	35,913	18,606
02169	Quincy	(617)	84,743	87,966
02368	Randolph	(617)	28,218	27,035
02767	Raynham	(617)	9,085	6,705
01867	Reading	(617)	22,678	22,539
02769	Rehoboth	(617)	7,570	6,512
02151	Revere	(617)	42,423	43,159
02370	Rockland	(617)	15,695	15,674
01966	Rockport	(617)	6,345	5,636
01970	Salem	(617)	38,276	40,556
01950	Salisbury	(617)	5,973	4,179
02563	Sandwich	(617)	8,727	5,239
01906	Saugus	(617)	24,746	25,110
02066	Scituate	(617)	17,317	16,973
02771	Seekonk	(617)	12,269	11,116
02067	Sharon	(617)	13,601	12,367
01464	Shirley	(61*7)	5,124	4,909
01545	Shrewsbury	(617)	22,674	19,196
02725	Somerset	(617)	18,813	18,088
02143	Somerville	(617)	77,372	88,779
01772	Southborough	(617)	6,193	5,798
01550	Southbridge Center(u)	(617)	12,882	14,261
.....	Southbridge	(617)	16,665	17,057
01075	South Hadley	(413)	16,399	17,033
01077	Southwick	(413)	7,382	6,330
02664	South Yarmouth(u)	(617)	7,525	5,380
01562	Spencer Center(u)	(617)	6,350	5,895
.....	Spencer	(617)	10,774	8,779
*01101	Springfield	(413)	152,319	163,905
01564	Sterling	(617)	5,440	4,247
02180	Stoneham	(617)	21,424	20,725
02072	Stoughton	(617)	26,710	23,459
01775	Stow	(617)	5,144	3,984
01566	Sturbridge	(617)	5,976	4,878
01776	Sudbury	(617)	14,027	13,506
01527	Sutton	(617)	5,855	4,590
01907	Swampscott	(617)	13,837	13,578
02777	Swansea	(617)	15,461	12,640
02780	Taunton	(617)	45,001	43,756

ZIP code	Place		1980	1980
01468	Templeton	(617)	6,070	5,863
01876	Tewksbury	(617)	24,635	22,755
01983	Topsfield	(617)	5,709	5,225
01469	Townsend	(617)	7,201	4,281
01376	Turners Falls(u)	(413)	NA	5,168
01879	Tyngsborough	(617)	5,683	4,204
01569	Uxbridge	(617)	8,374	8,253
01880	Wakefield	(617)	24,895	25,402
02081	Walpole	(617)	18,859	18,149
02154	Waltham	(617)	58,200	61,582
01082	Ware Center(u)	(413)	6,806	6,509
.....	Ware	(413)	8,953	8,187
02571	Wareham	(617)	18,457	11,492
02172	Watertown	(617)	34,384	39,307
01778	Wayland	(617)	12,170	13,461
01570	Webster Center(u)	(617)	11,175	12,432
.....	Webster	(617)	14,480	14,917
02181	Wellesley	(617)	27,209	28,051
01581	Westborough	(617)	13,619	12,594
01583	West Boylston	(617)	6,204	6,369
02379	West Bridgewater	(617)	6,359	6,070
01742	West Concord(u)	(617)	5,331	....
01085	Westfield	(413)	36,465	31,433
01886	Westford	(617)	13,434	10,368
01473	Westminster	(617)	5,139	4,273
02193	Weston	(617)	11,169	10,870
02790	Westport	(617)	13,763	9,791
01089	West Springfield	(413)	27,042	28,461
02090	Westwood	(617)	13,212	12,570
02188	Weymouth	(617)	55,601	54,610
01588	Whitinsville(u)	(617)	5,379	5,210
02382	Whitman	(617)	13,534	13,059
01095	Wilbraham	(413)	12,053	11,984
01267	Williamstown	(413)	8,741	8,454
01887	Wilmington	(617)	17,471	17,102
01475	Winchendon	(617)	7,019	6,635
01890	Winchester	(617)	20,701	22,269
02152	Winthrop	(617)	19,294	20,335
01801	Woburn	(617)	36,626	37,406
*01613	Worcester	(617)	161,799	176,572
02093	Wrentham	(617)	7,580	7,315
02675	Yarmouth	(617)	18,449	12,033

Michigan

ZIP code	Place		1980	1980
49221	Adrian	(517)	21,276	20,382
49224	Albion	(517)	11,059	12,112
48101	Allen Park	(313)	34,196	40,747
48801	Alma	(517)	9,652	9,611
49707	Alpena	(517)	12,214	13,805
*48106	Ann Arbor	(313)	107,969	100,035
48063	Avon(u)	(313)	40,779	....
*49016	Battle Creek	(616)	35,724	38,931
48706	Bay City	(517)	41,593	49,449
48505	Beecher(u)	(313)	17,178	....
48809	Belding	(616)	5,634	5,121
49022	Benton Harbor	(616)	14,707	16,481
49022	Benton Heights(u)	(616)	6,787	....
48072	Berkley	(313)	18,637	21,879
48009	Beverly Hills	(313)	11,598	13,598
49307	Big Rapids	(616)	14,361	11,995
*48012	Birmingham	(313)	21,689	26,170
48013	Bloomfield(u)	(313)	42,876	....
49107	Buchanan	(616)	5,142	4,645
*48502	Burton	(313)	29,976	32,540
49601	Cadillac	(616)	10,199	9,990
48724	Carrollton(u)	(517)	7,482	7,300
48015	Center Line	(313)	9,293	10,379
48813	Charlotte	(517)	8,251	8,244
49721	Cheboygan	(616)	5,106	5,553
48017	Clawson	(313)	15,103	17,617
48043	Clinton(u)	(313)	72,400	1,677
49036	Coldwater	(517)	9,461	9,155
49321	Comstock Park(u)	(616)	5,506	5,766
49508	Cutlerville(u)	(616)	8,256	6,267
48423	Davison	(313)	6,087	5,259
*48120	Dearborn	(313)	90,660	104,199
48127	Dearborn Heights	(313)	67,706	80,069
*48233	Detroit	(313)	1,203,368	1,514,053
49047	Dowagiac	(616)	6,307	6,583
48021	East Detroit	(313)	38,280	45,920
49506	East Grand Rapids	(616)	10,914	12,565
48823	East Lansing	(517)	48,309	47,540
49001	Eastwood(u)	(517)	7,186	9,682
48229	Ecorse	(313)	14,447	17,515
49829	Escanaba	(906)	14,355	15,368
49022	Fair Plain(u)	(616)	8,289	3,680
48024	Farmington	(313)	11,022	10,329
48024	Farmington Hills	(313)	58,056	48,694
48430	Fenton	(313)	8,098	8,284
48220	Ferndale	(313)	26,227	30,850
48134	Flat Rock	(313)	6,853	5,643
*48502	Flint	(313)	159,611	193,317
48433	Flushing	(313)	8,624	7,190
48026	Fraser	(313)	14,560	11,868
48135	Garden City	(313)	35,640	41,864
48439	Grand Blanc	(313)	6,848	5,132
49417	Grand Haven	(616)	11,763	11,844
48837	Grand Ledge	(517)	6,920	6,032
*49501	Grand Rapids	(616)	181,843	197,649
49418	Grandville	(616)	12,412	10,764
48838	Greenville	(616)	8,019	7,493
48138	Grosse Ile(u)	(313)	9,320	8,306
48236	Grosse Pointe	(313)	5,901	6,637
48236	Grosse Pointe Farms	(313)	10,551	11,701
48236	Grosse Pointe Park	(313)	13,562	15,641
48236	Grosse Pointe Woods	(313)	18,886	21,878
48212	Hamtramck	(313)	21,300	26,783
49930	Hancock	(906)	5,122	4,820
48236	Harper Woods	(313)	16,361	20,186
48625	Harrison(u)	(517)	23,649	....
48840	Haslett(u)	(517)	7,025	....
49058	Hastings	(616)	6,418	6,501
48030	Hazel Park	(313)	20,914	23,784
48203	Highland Park	(313)	27,909	35,444
49242	Hillsdale	(517)	7,432	7,728
49423	Holland	(616)	26,281	26,479
48842	Holt(u)	(517)	10,097	6,980
49931	Houghton	(906)	7,512	6,067
48843	Howell	(517)	6,976	5,224
48070	Huntington Woods	(313)	6,937	8,536
48141	Inkster	(313)	35,190	38,595
48846	Ionia	(616)	5,920	6,361
49801	Iron Mountain	(906)	8,341	8,702
49938	Ironwood	(906)	7,741	8,711
49849	Ishpeming	(906)	7,538	8,245
*49201	Jackson	(517)	39,739	45,484
49428	Jenison(u)	(616)	16,330	11,266
*49001	Kalamazoo	(616)	79,722	85,555
49508	Kentwood	(616)	30,438	20,310
49801	Kingsford	(906)	5,290	5,276
49843	K.I. Sawyer(u)	(906)	7,345	8,224
49015*	Lakeview(u)	(517)	13,345	11,391
48144	Lambertville(u)	(313)	6,341	5,711
*48924	Lansing	(517)	130,414	131,403
48446	Lapeer	(313)	6,225	6,314
48146	Lincoln Park	(313)	45,105	52,984
*48150	Livonia	(313)	104,814	110,109
49431	Ludington	(616)	8,937	9,021
48071	Madison Heights	(313)	35,375	38,599
49660	Manistee	(616)	7,665	7,723
49855	Marquette	(906)	23,288	21,967
49068	Marshall	(616)	7,201	7,253
48040	Marysville	(313)	7,345	5,610
48854	Mason	(517)	6,019	5,468
48122	Melvindale	(313)	12,322	13,862
49858	Menominee	(906)	10,099	10,748
49254	Michigan Center(u)	(517)	5,244	....
48640	Midland	(517)	37,269	35,176
48042	Milford	(313)	5,041	4,699
48161	Monroe	(313)	23,531	23,894
48043	Mount Clemens	(313)	18,991	20,476
48858	Mount Pleasant	(517)	23,746	20,524
*49440	Muskegon	(616)	40,823	44,631
49444	Muskegon Heights	(616)	14,611	17,304
49866	Negaunee	(906)	5,189	5,248
48047	New Baltimore	(313)	5,439	4,132
49120	Niles	(616)	13,115	12,988
.....	Northview(u)	(313)	11,662	....
48167	Northville	(313)	5,698	5,400
49441	Norton Shores	(616)	22,025	22,271
48050	Novi	(313)	22,525	9,668
48237	Oak Park	(313)	31,537	36,762
48864	Okemos(u)	(517)	8,882	7,770
48867	Owosso	(517)	16,455	17,179
49770	Petoskey	(616)	6,097	6,342
48170	Plymouth	(313)	9,986	11,758
*48053	Pontiac	(313)	76,715	85,279
49081	Portage	(616)	38,157	33,590
48060	Port Huron	(313)	33,981	35,794
48239	Redford(u)	(313)	58,441	....
48218	River Rouge	(313)	12,912	15,947
48192	Riverview	(313)	14,569	11,342
48063	Rochester	(313)	7,203	7,054
48174	Romulus	(313)	24,857	22,879
48066	Roseville	(313)	54,311	60,529
*48068	Royal Oak	(313)	70,893	86,238
*48605	Saginaw	(517)	77,508	91,849
*48083	St. Clair Shores	(313)	76,210	88,093
48879	St. Johns	(517)	7,376	6,672
49085	St. Joseph	(616)	9,622	11,042
48176	Saline	(313)	6,483	4,811
49783	Sault Ste. Marie	(906)	14,448	15,136
*48075	Southfield	(313)	75,568	69,285
48198	Southgate	(313)	32,058	33,909
49090	South Haven	(616)	5,943	6,471
48178	South Lyon	(313)	5,214	2,675
49015	Springfield	(616)	5,917	3,999
*48078	Sterling Heights	(313)	108,999	61,365
49091	Sturgis	(616)	9,468	9,295
48473	Swartz Creek	(313)	5,013	4,927
48180	Taylor	(313)	77,568	70,020
49286	Tecumseh	(517)	7,320	7,120
49093	Three Rivers	(616)	7,015	7,355
49684	Traverse City	(616)	15,516	18,048
48183	Trenton	(313)	22,762	24,127
48084	Troy	(313)	67,102	39,419
48087	Utica	(313)	5,282	3,504
49504	Walker	(616)	15,088	11,498

ZIP code	Place		1980	1970
*48089	Warren	(313)	161,134	179,260
48095	Waterford(u)	(313)	64,250	....
48184	Wayne	(313)	21,159	21,054
48033	West Bloomfield(u)	(313)	41,962	....
48185	Westland	(313)	84,603	86,749
49007	Westwood(u)	(616)	8,519	9,143
48019	White Lake-Seven Harbors(u)	(313)	7,557	....
48096	Wixom	(313)	6,705	2,010
48183	Woodhaven	(313)	10,902	3,566
48753	Wurtsmith(u)	(517)	5,168	6,932
*48192	Wyandotte	(313)	34,006	41,061
49509	Wyoming	(616)	59,616	56,560
48197	Ypsilanti	(313)	24,031	29,538

Minnesota

ZIP code	Place		1980	1970
56007	Albert Lea	(507)	19,190	19,418
56308	Alexandria	(612)	7,608	6,973
55303	Andover	(612)	9,387	....
55303	Anoka	(612)	15,634	13,298
55068	Apple Valley	(612)	21,818	8,502
55912	Austin	(507)	23,020	26,210
56601	Bemidji	(218)	10,949	11,490
55433	Blaine	(612)	28,558	20,573
55420	Bloomington	(612)	81,831	81,970
56401	Brainerd	(218)	11,489	11,667
55429	Brooklyn Center	(612)	31,230	35,173
55429	Brooklyn Park	(612)	43,332	26,230
55337	Burnsville	(612)	35,674	19,940
55316	Champlin	(612)	9,006	2,275
55317	Chanhassen	(612)	6,359	4,879
55318	Chaska	(612)	8,346	4,352
55719	Chisholm	(218)	5,930	5,913
55720	Cloquet	(218)	11,142	8,699
55421	Columbia Heights	(612)	20,029	23,997
55433	Coon Rapids	(612)	35,826	30,505
55016	Cottage Grove	(612)	18,994	13,419
55716	Crookston	(218)	8,628	8,312
55428	Crystal	(612)	25,543	30,925
56501	Detroit Lakes	(218)	7,106	5,797
55806	Duluth	(218)	92,811	100,578
55121	Eagan	(612)	20,532	10,398
55005	East Bethel	(612)	6,626	2,586
56721	East Grand Forks	(218)	8,537	7,607
55343	Eden Prairie	(612)	16,263	6,938
55424	Edina	(612)	46,073	44,046
55330	Elk River	(612)	6,785	2,252
55734	Eveleth	(218)	5,042	4,721
56031	Fairmont	(507)	11,506	10,751
55113	Falcon Heights	(507)	5,291	5,530
55021	Faribault	(507)	16,241	16,595
56537	Fergus Falls	(218)	12,519	12,443
55421	Fridley	(612)	30,228	29,233
55427	Golden Valley	(612)	22,775	24,246
55744	Grand Rapids	(218)	7,934	7,247
55303	Ham Lake	(612)	7,832	3,327
55033	Hastings	(612)	12,827	12,195
55811	Hermantown	(218)	6,759	....
55746	Hibbing	(218)	21,193	16,104
55343	Hopkins	(612)	15,336	13,428
55350	Hutchinson	(612)	9,244	8,031
56649	International Falls	(218)	5,611	6,439
55075	Inver Grove Heights	(612)	17,171	12,148
55042	Lake Elmo	(612)	5,296	3,565
55044	Lakeville	(612)	14,790	7,556
55355	Litchfield	(612)	5,904	5,262
55110	Little Canada	(612)	7,102	3,481
56345	Little Falls	(218)	7,250	7,467
56001	Mankato	(507)	28,646	30,895
55369	Maple Grove	(612)	20,525	6,275
55109	Maplewood	(612)	26,990	25,186
56258	Marshall	(507)	11,161	9,886
55118	Mendota Heights	(612)	7,288	6,565
55401	Minneapolis	(612)	370,951	434,400
55343	Minnetonka	(612)	38,683	35,776
56265	Montevideo	(612)	5,845	5,661
56560	Moorhead	(218)	29,998	29,687
56267	Morris	(612)	5,367	5,366
55364	Mound	(612)	9,280	7,572
55112	Mounds View	(612)	12,593	10,599
55112	New Brighton	(612)	23,269	19,507
55112	New Hope	(612)	23,087	23,180
56073	New Ulm	(507)	13,755	13,051
55057	Northfield	(507)	12,562	10,235
56001	North Mankato	(507)	9,145	7,347
55109	North St. Paul	(612)	11,921	11,950
55119	Oakdale	(612)	12,123	7,795
55323	Orono	(612)	6,845	6,787
55060	Owatonna	(507)	18,632	15,341
55427	Plymouth	(612)	31,615	18,077
55372	Prior Lake	(612)	7,284	1,114
55303	Ramsey	(612)	10,093	....
55066	Red Wing	(612)	13,736	10,441
56283	Redwood Falls	(507)	5,210	4,774
55423	Richfield	(612)	37,851	47,231
55422	Robbinsdale	(612)	14,422	16,845
55901	Rochester	(507)	57,906	53,766
55068	Rosemount	(612)	5,083	1,337
55113	Roseville	(612)	35,820	34,438
55418	St. Anthony	(612)	7,981	9,239
56301	St. Cloud	(612)	42,566	39,691
55426	St. Louis Park	(612)	42,931	48,883
*55101	St. Paul	(612)	270,230	309,866
55082	St. Peter	(507)	9,056	8,339
56379	Sauk Rapids	(612)	5,793	5,051
55379	Shakopee	(612)	9,941	6,876
55112	Shoreview	(612)	17,300	10,978
55075	South St. Paul	(612)	21,235	25,016
55432	Spring Lake Park	(612)	6,477	6,417
55082	Stillwater	(612)	12,290	10,191
56701	Thief River Falls	(218)	9,105	8,618
55110	Vadnais Heights	(612)	5,111	3,411
55792	Virginia	(218)	11,056	12,450
56093	Waseca	(507)	8,219	6,789
55118	West St. Paul	(612)	18,527	18,802
55110	White Bear Lake	(612)	22,538	23,313
56201	Willmar	(612)	15,895	12,869
55987	Winona	(507)	25,075	26,438
55119	Woodbury	(612)	10,297	6,184
56187	Worthington	(507)	10,243	9,916

Mississippi (601)

ZIP code	Place	1980	1970
39730	Aberdeen	7,184	6,507
38821	Amory	7,307	7,236
38606	Batesville	5,162	3,796
39520	Bay St. Louis	7,850	6,752
*39530	Biloxi	49,311	48,486
38829	Booneville	6,199	5,895
39042	Brandon	9,626	2,685
39601	Brookhaven	10,800	10,700
39046	Canton	11,116	10,503
38614	Clarksdale	21,137	21,673
38732	Cleveland	14,524	13,327
39056	Clinton	14,660	7,289
39429	Columbia	7,733	7,587
39701	Columbus	27,503	25,795
38834	Corinth	13,180	11,581
39532	D'Iberville(u)	13,369	7,288
39552	Escatawpa(u)	5,367	1,579
39074	Forest	5,229	4,085
39553	Gautier(u)	8,917	2,087
38701	Greenville	40,613	39,648
38930	Greenwood	20,115	22,400
39501	Grenada	12,641	9,944
39401	Gulfport	39,676	40,791
38635	Hattiesburg	40,829	38,277
38751	Holly Springs	7,285	5,728
38751	Indianola	8,221	8,947
*39205	Jackson	202,895	153,968
39090	Kosciusko	7,415	7,266
39440	Laurel	21,897	24,145
38756	Leland	6,667	6,000
39560	Long Beach	14,199	6,170
39339	Louisville	7,323	6,626
39648	McComb	12,331	11,851
39301	Meridian	46,577	45,083
39563	Moss Point	18,998	19,321
39120	Natchez	22,209	19,704
38652	New Albany	7,072	6,426
39501	North Gulfport(u)	6,660	6,996
39560	North Long Beach(u)	7,063	....
39564	Ocean Springs	14,504	19,160
39567	Orange Grove(u)	13,476	....
38655	Oxford	9,882	8,519
39567	Pascagoula	29,318	27,264
39571	Pass Christian	5,014	2,979
39208	Pearl	18,602	9,623
39465	Petal	8,476	6,986
39350	Philadelphia	6,434	6,274
39466	Picayune	10,361	9,780
39157	Ridgeland	5,461	1,650
38668	Senatobia	5,013	4,247
38671	Southaven(u)	16,071	8,931
39759	Starkville	16,139	11,369
38801	Tupelo	23,905	20,471
39180	Vicksburg	25,434	25,478
39367	Waynesboro	5,349	4,368
39773	West Point	8,811	8,714
38967	Winona	6,177	5,521
39194	Yazoo City	12,092	11,688

Missouri

ZIP code	Place		1980	1970
63123	Affton(u)	(314)	23,181	24,264
63010	Arnold	(314)	19,141	17,381
65605	Aurora	(417)	6,437	5,359
63011	Ballwin	(314)	12,750	10,656
63137	Bellefontaine Neighbors	(314)	12,082	14,084
64012	Belton	(816)	12,708	12,270
63134	Berkeley	(314)	15,922	19,743
63031	Black Jack	(314)	5,293	4,145
64015	Blue Springs	(816)	25,936	6,779
65613	Bolivar	(417)	5,919	4,769
65233	Boonville	(816)	6,959	7,514
63114	Breckenridge Hills	(816)	5,666	7,011
63144	Brentwood	(314)	8,209	11,248
63044	Bridgeton	(314)	18,445	19,992

ZIP code	Place		.1980	1970
64628	Brookfield	(816)	5,555	5,491
63701	Cape Girardeau	(314)	34,361	31,282
64836	Carthage	(417)	11,104	11,035
63830	Caruthersville	(314)	7,958	7,350
63834	Charleston	(314)	5,230	5,131
64601	Chillicothe	(816)	9,089	9,519
63105	Clayton	(314)	14,306	16,100
64735	Clinton	(816)	8,366	7,504
65201	Columbia	(314)	62,061	58,812
63128	Concord(u)	(314)	20,896	21,217
63126	Crestwood	(314)	12,815	15,123
63141	Creve Coeur	(314)	11,743	8,967
63136	Dellwood	(314)	6,200	7,137
63020	De Soto	(314)	5,993	5,984
63131	Des Peres	(314)	7,953	5,333
63841	Dexter	(314)	7,043	6,024
63011	Ellisville	(314)	6,233	4,681
64024	Excelsior Springs	(816)	10,424	9,411
63640	Farmington	(314)	8,270	6,590
63135	Ferguson	(314)	24,549	28,759
63028	Festus	(314)	7,574	7,530
*63033	Florissant	(314)	55,372	65,908
65473	Fort Leonard Wood(u)	(314)	21,262	33,799
65251	Fulton	(314)	11,046	12,248
64118	Gladstone	(816)	24,990	23,422
63122	Glendale	(314)	6,035	6,981
64030	Grandview	(816)	24,561	17,456
63401	Hannibal	(314)	18,811	18,609
64701	Harrisonville	(816)	6,372	5,052
*63042	Hazelwood	(314)	12,935	14,082
*64051	Independence	(816)	111,797	111,630
63755	Jackson	(314)	7,827	5,896
65101	Jefferson City	(314)	33,619	32,407
63136	Jennings	(314)	17,247	19,379
64801	Joplin	(417)	39,023	39,256
*64108	Kansas City	(816)	448,028	507,330
63857	Kennett	(314)	10,145	10,090
63501	Kirksville	(816)	17,167	15,560
63122	Kirkwood	(314)	27,987	31,679
63124	Ladue	(314)	9,369	10,306
65536	Lebanon	(417)	9,507	8,616
64063	Lee's Summit	(816)	28,741	16,230
63125	Lemay(u)	(314)	35,424	40,529
64067	Lexington	(816)	5,063	5,388
64068	Liberty	(816)	16,251	13,704
63552	Macon	(816)	5,680	5,301
63863	Malden	(314)	6,096	5,374
63011	Manchester	(314)	6,351	5,031
63143	Maplewood	(314)	10,960	12,785
65340	Marshall	(816)	12,781	12,051
63043	Maryland Heights(u)	(314)	5,676	8,805
64468	Maryville	(816)	9,558	9,970
65265	Mexico	(314)	12,276	11,807
65270	Moberly	(816)	13,418	12,988
65708	Monett	(417)	6,148	5,937
63026	Murphy(u)	(314)	8,121	....
64850	Neosho	(417)	9,493	7,517
64772	Nevada	(417)	9,044	9,736
63121	Normandy	(314)	5,174	6,236
63121	Northwoods	(314)	5,831	4,607
63366	O'Fallon	(314)	8,654	7,018
63124	Olivette	(314)	7,952	9,156
63114	Overland	(314)	19,620	24,819
63775	Perryville	(314)	7,343	5,149
63120	Pine Lawn	(314)	6,570	5,745
63901	Poplar Bluff	(314)	17,139	16,653
64133	Raytown	(816)	31,831	33,306
64085	Richmond	(816)	5,499	4,948
63117	Richmond Heights	(314)	11,516	13,802
63124	Rock Hill	(314)	5,702	6,815
65401	Rolla	(314)	13,303	13,571
63074	St. Ann	(314)	15,523	18,215
63301	St. Charles	(314)	37,379	31,834
63114	St. John	(314)	7,854	8,960
*64501	St. Joseph	(816)	76,691	72,748
*63155	St. Louis	(314)	452,801	622,236
63376	St. Peters	(314)	15,700	486
63126	Sappington(u)	(314)	11,388	10,603
65301	Sedalia	(816)	20,927	22,847
63119	Shrewsbury	(314)	5,077	5,896
63801	Sikeston	(314)	17,431	14,699
63138	Spanish Lake(u)	(314)	20,632	15,647
*65801	Springfield	(417)	133,119	120,096
63080	Sullivan	(314)	5,461	5,111
64683	Trenton	(816)	6,811	6,063
63084	Union	(314)	5,506	5,183
63130	University City	(314)	42,690	47,527
64093	Warrensburg	(816)	13,807	13,125
63090	Washington	(314)	9,251	8,499
64870	Webb City	(417)	7,309	6,923
63119	Webster Groves	(314)	23,097	27,457
65775	West Plains	(417)	7,741	6,893

Montana (406)

59711	Anaconda-Deer Lodge County		12,518	9,771
*59101	Billings		66,842	61,581
59101	Billings Heights(u)		8,480	....
59715	Bozeman		21,645	18,670
59701	Butte-Silver Bow		37,205	23,368
59330	Glendive		5,978	6,305
*59401	Great Falls		56,725	60,091
59501	Havre		10,891	10,558
59601	Helena		23,938	22,730
59901	Kalispell		10,695	10,526
59044	Laurel		5,481	4,454
59457	Lewistown		7,104	6,437
59047	Livingston		6,994	6,883
59402	Malmstrom AFB(u)		6,675	8,374
59301	Miles City		9,602	9,023
59801	Missoula		33,351	29,497
59801	Missoula South(u)		5,557	4,886
59801	Orchard Homes(u)		10,837	
59270	Sidney		5,726	4,543

Nebraska

69301	Alliance	(308)	9,920	6,862
68310	Beatrice	(402)	12,891	12,389
68005	Bellevue	(402)	21,813	21,953
68008	Blair	(402)	6,418	6,106
69337	Chadron	(308)	5,933	5,921
68601	Columbus	(402)	17,328	15,471
68355	Falls City	(402)	5,374	5,444
68025	Fremont	(402)	23,979	22,962
69341	Gering	(308)	7,760	5,639
68801	Grand Island	(308)	33,180	32,358
68901	Hastings	(402)	23,045	23,580
68949	Holdrege	(308)	5,624	5,635
68847	Kearney	(308)	21,158	19,181
68128	La Vista	(402)	9,588	4,858
68850	Lexington	(308)	6,898	5,654
*68501	Lincoln	(402)	171,932	149,518
69001	McCook	(308)	8,404	8,285
68410	Nebraska City	(402)	7,127	7,441
68701	Norfolk	(402)	19,449	16,607
69101	North Platte	(308)	24,509	19,447
68113	Offutt AFB West(u)	(402)	8,787	8,445
69153	Ogallala	(308)	5,638	4,976
*68108	Omaha	(402)	313,939	346,929
68046	Papillion	(402)	6,399	5,606
68048	Plattsmouth	(402)	6,295	6,371
68127	Ralston	(402)	5,143	4,731
69361	Scottsbluff	(308)	14,156	14,507
68434	Seward	(402)	5,713	5,294
69162	Sidney	(308)	6,010	6,403
68776	South Sioux City	(402)	9,339	7,920
68787	Wayne	(402)	5,240	5,379
68467	York	(402)	7,723	6,778

Nevada (702)

89005	Boulder City		9,590	5,223
89701	Carson City		32,022	15,468
89112	East Las Vegas(u)		6,449	6,501
89801	Elko		8,758	7,621
89015	Henderson		24,363	16,395
89450	Incline Village-Crystal Bay(u)		6,225	....
*89114	Las Vegas		164,674	125,787
89110	Nellis AFB(u)		6,205	6,449
89030	North Las Vegas		42,739	46,067
89109	Paradise(u)		84,818	24,477
*89501	Reno		100,756	72,863
89431	Sparks		40,780	24,187
89110	Sunrise Manor(u)		44,155	9,684
89431	Sun Valley(u)		8,822	2,414
89109	Vegas Creek(u)		NA	8,970
89101	Winchester(u)		19,728	13,981

New Hampshire (603)

See note on page 257

03031	Amherst		8,243	4,605
03102	Bedford		9,481	5,859
03570	Berlin		13,084	15,256
03743	Claremont		14,557	14,221
03301	Concord		30,400	30,022
03818	Conway		7,158	4,865
03038	Derry Compact(u)		12,248	6,099
	Derry		18,875	11,712
03820	Dover		22,377	20,850
03824	Durham Compact(u)		8,448	7,222
	Durham		10,652	8,869
03833	Exeter Compact(u)		8,947	6,430
	Exeter		11,024	8,892
03235	Franklin		7,901	7,292
03045	Goffstown		11,315	9,284
03842	Hampton Compact(u)		6,779	5,403
	Hampton		10,493	8,011
03755	Hanover Compact(u)		6,861	6,144
	Hanover		9,119	8,494
03106	Hooksett		7,303	5,564
03061	Hudson		14,022	10,638
03431	Keene		21,449	20,467
03246	Laconia		15,575	14,888
03766	Lebanon		11,134	9,725

ZIP code	Place		1980	1970
03516	Littleton		5,558	5,290
03053	Londonderry		13,598	5,346
*03101	Manchester		90,936	87,754
03054	Merrimack		15,406	8,595
03055	Milford		8,685	6,622
03060	Nashua		67,865	55,820
03773	Newport		6,229	5,899
03076	Pelham		8,090	5,408
03865	Plaistow		5,609	4,712
03801	Portsmouth		26,254	25,717
03077	Raymond		5,453	3,003
03867	Rochester		21,560	17,938
03079	Salem		24,124	20,142
03874	Seabrook		5,917	3,053
03878	Somersworth		10,350	9,026
03087	Windham		5,664	3,008

New Jersey

ZIP code	Place		1980	1970
07747	Aberdeen(u)	(201)	17,235	
08201	Absecon	(609)	6,859	6,094
07401	Allendale	(201)	5,901	6,240
07712	Asbury Park	(201)	17,015	16,533
*08401	Atlantic City	(609)	40,199	47,859
08106	Audubon	(609)	9,533	10,802
08007	Barrington	(609)	7,418	8,409
07002	Bayonne	(201)	65,047	72,743
08722	Beachwood	(201)	7,687	4,390
07109	Belleville	(201)	35,367	37,629
08031	Bellmawr	(609)	13,721	15,618
07719	Belmar	(201)	6,771	5,782
07621	Bergenfield	(201)	25,568	29,000
07922	Berkeley Hts. Twp.	(201)	12,549	13,078
08009	Berlin	(609)	5,786	4,997
07924	Bernardsville	(201)	6,715	6,652
08012	Blackwood(u)	(609)	5,219	
07003	Bloomfield	(201)	47,792	52,029
07403	Bloomingdale	(201)	7,867	7,797
07603	Bogota	(201)	8,344	8,960
07005	Boonton	(201)	8,620	9,261
08805	Bound Brook	(201)	9,710	10,450
08723	Brick Twp	(201)	53,629	35,057
08302	Bridgeton	(609)	18,795	20,435
08203	Brigantine	(609)	8,318	6,741
08015	Browns Mills(u)	(609)	10,568	7,144
07828	Budd Lake	(201)	6,523	
08016	Burlington	(609)	10,246	12,010
07405	Butler	(201)	7,616	7,051
07006	Caldwell	(201)	7,624	8,677
*08101	Camden	(201)	84,910	102,551
08701	Candlewood(u)	(201)	6,750	5,629
07072	Carlstadt	(201)	6,166	6,724
08069	Carney's Point	(609)	7,574	
07008	Carteret	(201)	20,598	23,137
07009	Cedar Grove Twp.	(201)	12,600	15,582
07928	Chatham	(201)	8,537	9,566
*08002	Cherry Hill Twp.	(609)	68,785	64,395
08077	Cinnaminson Twp.	(609)	16,072	16,962
07066	Clark Twp.	(201)	16,699	18,829
08312	Clayton	(609)	6,013	5,193
08021	Clementon	(609)	5,764	4,492
07010	Cliffside Park	(201)	21,464	18,891
07721	Cliffwood-Cliffwood Beach(u)	(201)	NA	7,056
*07015	Clifton	(201)	74,388	82,437
07624	Closter	(201)	8,164	8,604
08108	Collingswood	(609)	15,838	17,422
07016	Cranford Twp.	(201)	24,573	27,391
07626	Cresskill	(201)	7,609	8,298
	Crestwood Village	(201)	7,965	
08075	Delran Twp.	(609)	14,811	10,065
07834	Denville Twp.	(201)	14,380	14,045
08096	Deptford Twp.	(609)	23,473	24,232
07801	Dover	(201)	14,681	15,039
07628	Dumont	(201)	18,334	20,155
08812	Dunellen	(201)	6,593	7,072
08816	East Brunswick Twp.	(201)	37,711	34,166
07936	East Hanover	(201)	9,319	
07019	East Orange	(201)	77,878	-75,471
07073	East Rutherford	(201)	7,849	8,536
08520	East Windsor Twp.	(609)	21,041	11,736
07724	Eatontown	(201)	12,703	14,619
08010	Edgewater Park	(609)	9,273	
08817	Edison Twp.	(201)	70,193	67,120
07201	Elizabeth	(201)	106,201	112,654
07407	Elmwood Park	(201)	18,377	20,511
07630	Emerson	(201)	7,793	8,428
07631	Englewood	(201)	23,701	24,985
07632	Englewood Cliffs	(201)	5,698	5,938
08053	Evesham Twp.	(609)	21,659	13,477
08618	Ewing Twp.	(609)	34,842	32,831
*07006	Fairfield	(201)	7,987	6,731
*07701	Fair Haven	(201)	5,679	6,142
07410	Fair Lawn	(201)	32,229	38,040
07022	Fairview	(201)	10,519	10,698
07023	Fanwood	(201)	7,767	8,920
08518	Florence-Roebling(u)	(609)	7,677	7,551
07932	Florham Park	(201)	9,359	9,373
08640	Fort Dix(u)	(609)	14,297	26,290
07024	Fort Lee	(201)	32,449	30,631
07417	Franklin Lakes	(201)	8,769	7,550
07728	Freehold	(201)	10,020	10,545
07026	Garfield	(201)	26,803	30,797
08753	Gilford Park	(201)	6,528	4,007
08026	Glassboro	(609)	14,674	12,938
08029	Glendora	(609)	5,632	
07028	Glen Ridge	(201)	7,855	8,518
07452	Glen Rock	(201)	11,497	13,011
08030	Gloucester City	(609)	13,121	14,707
	Gordon's Corner	(201)	6,320	
07093	Guttenberg	(201)	7,340	5,754
*07602	Hackensack	(201)	36,039	36,008
07840	Hackettstown	(201)	8,850	9,472
08108	Haddon Twp.	(609)	15,875	18,192
08033	Haddonfield	(609)	12,337	13,118
08035	Haddon Heights	(609)	8,361	9,365
07508	Haledon	(201)	6,607	6,767
08037	Hammonton	(609)	12,298	11,464
07981	Hanover Twp.	(201)	11,846	10,700
07029	Harrison	(201)	12,242	11,811
07604	Hasbrouck Heights	(201)	12,166	13,651
07506	Hawthorne	(201)	18,200	19,173
07730	Hazlet Twp.	(201)	23,013	22,239
08904	Highland Park	(201)	13,396	14,385
07732	Highlands	(201)	5,187	3,916
07642	Hillsdale	(201)	10,495	11,768
07205	Hillside Twp.	(201)	21,440	21,636
07030	Hoboken	(201)	42,460	45,380
08753	Holiday City-Berkeley	(201)	9,019	
07843	Hopatcong	(201)	15,531	9,052
08560	Hopewell Twp. (Mercer)	(609)	10,893	10,030
07111	Irvington	(201)	61,493	59,743
08527	Jackson Twp.	(201)	25,644	18,276
*07303	Jersey City	(201)	223,532	260,350
07734	Keansburg	(201)	10,613	9,720
07032	Kearny	(201)	35,735	37,585
08824	Kendall Park(u)	(201)	7,419	7,412
07033	Kenilworth	(201)	8,221	9,165
07735	Keyport	(201)	7,413	7,205
07405	Kinnelon	(201)	7,770	7,600
07034	Lake Hiawatha(u)	(201)	NA	11,389
07871	Lake Mohawk(u)	(201)	8,498	6,262
07054	Lake Parsippany(u)	(201)	NA	7,488
08701	Lakewood(u)	(201)	22,863	17,874
08879	Laurence Harbor(u)	(201)	6,737	6,715
07605	Leonia	(201)	8,027	8,847
07035	Lincoln Park	(201)	8,806	9,034
07036	Linden	(201)	37,836	41,409
08021	Lindenwold	(609)	18,196	12,199
08221	Linwood	(609)	6,144	6,159
07424	Little Falls Twp.	(201)	11,496	11,727
07643	Little Ferry	(201)	9,399	9,064
07739	Little Silver	(201)	5,548	6,010
07039	Livingston Twp.	(201)	28,040	30,127
07644	Lodi	(201)	23,956	25,163
07740	Long Branch	(201)	29,819	31,774
07071	Lyndhurst Twp.	(201)	20,326	22,729
07940	Madison	(201)	15,357	16,710
08859	Madison Park	(201)	7,447	
07430	Mahwah Twp.	(201)	12,127	10,800
08736	Manasquan	(201)	5,354	4,971
08835	Manville	(201)	11,278	13,029
08052	Maple Shade Twp.	(609)	20,525	16,464
07040	Maplewood Twp.	(201)	22,950	24,932
08402	Margate City	(609)	9,179	10,576
07746	Marlboro Twp.	(201)	17,560	12,273
08053	Marlton(u)	(609)	9,411	10,180
07747	Matawan	(201)	8,837	9,136
07607	Maywood	(201)	9,895	11,087
08641	McGuire AFB(u)	(201)	7,853	10,933
08619	Mercerville-Hamilton Sq.(u)	(609)	25,446	24,465
08840	Metuchen	(201)	13,762	16,031
08846	Middlesex	(201)	13,480	15,038
07748	Middletown Twp.	(201)	61,615	54,623
07432	Midland park	(201)	7,381	8,159
07041	Milburn Twp.	(201)	19,543	21,089
08850	Milltown	(201)	7,136	6,470
08332	Millville	(609)	24,815	21,366
08094	Monroe Twp. (Gloucester)	(609)	21,639	14,071
*07042	Montclair	(201)	38,321	44,043
07645	Montvale	(201)	7,318	7,327
07045	Montville Twp.	(201)	14,290	11,846
08057	Moorestown-Lenola(u)	(609)	13,695	14,179
07950	Morris Plains	(201)	5,305	5,540
07960	Morristown	(201)	16,614	17,662
07092	Mountainside	(201)	7,118	7,520
08060	Mount Holly Twp.	(609)	10,818	12,713
07753	Neptune Twp.	(201)	28,366	27,863
07753	Neptune City	(201)	5,276	5,502
*07102	Newark	(201)	329,248	381,930
*08901	New Brunswick	(201)	41,442	41,885
08511	New Hanover	(201)	14,248	27,410
07646	New Milford	(201)	16,876	19,149
07974	New Providence	(201)	12,426	13,796
07860	Newton	(201)	7,748	7,297
07032	North Arlington	(201)	16,587	18,096
07047	North Bergen Twp.	(201)	47,019	47,751
08902	North Brunswick Twp.	(201)	22,220	16,691
07006	North Caldwell	(201)	5,832	6,733
08225	Northfield	(609)	7,795	8,646
07508	North Haledon	(201)	8,177	7,614

ZIP code	Place		1980	1970
07060	North Plainfield	(201)	19,108	21,796
07647	Northvale	(201)	5,046	5,177
07110	Nutley	(201)	28,998	31,913
07755	Oakhurst(u)	(201)	NA	5,558
07436	Oakland	(201)	13,443	14,420
08226	Ocean City	(609)	13,949	10,575
07757	Oceanport	(201)	5,888	7,503
08758	Ocean Twp	(201)	23,570	....
08857	Old Bridge	(201)	21,815	25,176
08857	Old Bridge Twp	(201)	51,515	48,715
07649	Oradell	(201)	8,658	8,903
*07050	Orange	(201)	31,136	32,566
07650	Palisades Park	(201)	13,732	13,351
08065	Palmyra	(609)	7,085	6,969
07652	Paramus	(201)	26,474	28,381
07656	Park Ridge	(201)	8,515	8,709
07054	Parsippany-Troy Hills	(201)	49,868	....
*07055	Passaic	(201)	52,463	55,124
*07510	Paterson	(201)	137,970	144,824
08066	Paulsboro	(609)	6,944	8,084
08110	Pennsauken Twp	(609)	33,775	36,394
08069	Penns Grove	(609)	5,760	5,727
08070	Pennsville Center(u)	(609)	12,467	11,014
07440	Pequannock Twp	(201)	13,776	14,350
*08861	Perth Amboy	(201)	38,951	38,798
08865	Phillipsburg	(201)	16,647	17,849
08021	Pine Hill	(201)	8,684	5,132
08854	Piscataway Twp	(201)	42,223	36,418
08071	Pitman	(609)	9,744	10,257
*07061	Plainfield	(201)	45,555	46,862
08232	Pleasantville	(609)	13,435	14,007
08742	Point Pleasant	(201)	17,747	15,968
08742	Point Pleasant Beach	(201)	5,415	4,882
07442	Pompton Lakes	(201)	10,660	11,397
08540	Princeton	(609)	12,035	12,311
08540	Princeton North(u)	(609)	NA	5,488
07508	Prospect Park	(201)	5,142	5,176
*07065	Rahway	(201)	26,723	29,114
08057	Ramblewood(u)	(609)	6,475	5,556
07446	Ramsey	(201)	12,899	12,571
07869	Randolph Twp	(201)	17,828	13,296
08869	Raritan	(201)	6,128	6,691
07701	Red Bank	(201)	12,031	12,847
07657	Ridgefield	(201)	10,294	11,308
07660	Ridgefield Park	(201)	12,738	13,990
*07451	Ridgewood	(201)	25,208	27,547
07456	Ringwood	(201)	12,625	10,393
07661	River Edge	(201)	11,111	12,850
08075	Riverside Twp	(609)	7,941	8,591
07675	River Vale	(201)	9,489	....
07726	Robertsville	(201)	8,461	....
07662	Rochell Park Twp	(201)	5,603	6,380
07866	Rockaway	(201)	6,852	6,383
07068	Roseland	(201)	5,330	4,453
07203	Roselle	(201)	20,641	22,585
07204	Roselle Park	(201)	13,377	14,277
07760	Rumson	(201)	7,623	7,421
08078	Runnemede	(609)	9,461	10,475
*07070	Rutherford	(201)	19,068	20,802
07662	Saddle Brook Twp	(201)	14,084	15,910
08079	Salem	(609)	6,959	7,648
08872	Sayreville	(201)	29,969	32,508
07076	Scotch Plains Twp	(201)	20,774	22,279
07094	Secaucus	(201)	13,719	13,228
08753	Silverton	(201)	7,236	....
08083	Somerdale	(609)	5,900	6,510
08873	Somerset	(201)	21,731	....
08244	Somers Point	(609)	10,330	7,919
08876	Somerville	(201)	11,973	13,652
08879	South Amboy	(201)	8,322	9,338
07079	South Orange Vill. Twp	(201)	15,864	....
07080	South Plainfield	(201)	20,521	21,142
08882	South River	(201)	14,361	15,428
07871	Sparta Twp	(201)	13,333	10,819
08884	Spotswood	(201)	7,840	7,891
07081	Springfield Twp	(201)	13,955	15,740
07762	Spring Lake Heights	(201)	5,424	4,602
08084	Stratford	(609)	8,005	9,801
07747	Strathmore(u)	(609)	NA	7,674
07876	Succasunna-Kenvil	(201)	10,931	....
07901	Summit	(201)	21,071	23,620
07666	Teaneck Twp	(201)	39,007	42,355
07670	Tenafly	(201)	13,552	14,827
07724	Tinton Falls	(201)	7,740	8,395
08753	Toms River(u)	(201)	7,465	7,303
07512	Totowa	(201)	11,448	11,580
*08608	Trenton	(609)	92,124	104,786
08520	Twin Rivers	(609)	7,742	....
07083	Union Twp	(201)	50,184	53,077
07735	Union Beach	(201)	6,354	6,472
07087	Union City	(201)	55,593	57,305
07458	Upper Saddle River	(201)	7,958	7,949
08406	Ventnor City	(609)	11,704	10,385
07044	Verona	(201)	14,166	15,067
08251	Villas	(609)	5,909	3,155
08360	Vineland	(609)	53,753	47,399
07463	Waldwick	(201)	10,802	12,313
07057	Wallington	(201)	10,741	10,284
07465	Wanaque	(201)	10,025	8,636

ZIP code	Place		1980	1970
07882	Washington	(201)	6,429	5,943
07675	Washington Twp. (Bergen)	(201)	9,550	10,577
07060	Watchung	(201)	5,290	4,750
07470	Wayne Twp	(201)	46,474	49,141
07087	Weehawken Twp	(201)	13,168	13,383
07006	West Caldwell	(201)	11,407	11,913
*07091	Westfield	(201)	30,447	33,720
07728	West Freehold	(201)	9,929	....
07764	West Long Branch	(201)	7,380	6,845
07480	West Milford Twp	(201)	22,750	17,304
07093	West New York	(201)	39,194	40,627
07052	West Orange	(201)	39,510	43,715
07424	West Paterson	(201)	11,293	11,692
07675	Westwood	(201)	10,714	11,105
07885	Wharton	(201)	5,485	5,535
08610	White Horse	(609)	10,098	....
07886	White Meadow Lake(u)	(201)	8,429	8,499
08004	Williamstown	(609)	5,768	4,075
08046	Willingboro Twp	(609)	39,912	43,386
08095	Winslow Twp	(609)	20,034	11,202
07095	Woodbridge Twp	(201)	90,074	98,944
08096	Woodbury	(609)	10,353	12,408
07675	Woodcliff Lake	(201)	5,644	5,506
07075	Wood-Ridge	(201)	7,929	8,311
07481	Wyckoff Twp	(201)	15,500	16,039
08620	Yardville-Groveville	(609)	9,414	....
.....	Yorketown	(201)	5,330	....

New Mexico (505)

ZIP code	Place	1980	1970
88310	Alamogordo	24,024	23,035
*87101	Albuquerque	332,336	244,501
88210	Artesia	10,385	10,315
87410	Aztec	5,512	3,354
87002	Belen	5,617	4,823
88101	Cannon(u)	NA	5,461
88220	Carlsbad	25,496	21,297
88101	Clovis	31,194	28,495
88030	Deming	9,964	8,343
87532	Espanola	6,803	4,528
87401	Farmington	30,729	21,979
87301	Gallup	18,167	14,596
87020	Grants	11,451	8,768
88240	Hobbs	28,794	26,025
88330	Holloman AFB(u)	7,245	8,001
88001	Las Cruces	45,086	37,857
88701	Las Vegas	14,322	7,528
87544	Los Alamos(u)	11,039	11,310
88260	Lovington	9,727	8,915
87107	North Valley(u)	13,006	10,366
87114	Paradise Hills	5,096	....
88130	Portales	9,940	10,554
87740	Raton	8,225	6,962
87124	Rio Rancho Estates	9,985	....
88201	Roswell	39,676	33,908
87115	Sandia(u)	5,288	6,867
87501	Santa Fe	49,160	41,167
87420	Shiprock	7,237	....
88061	Silver City	9,887	8,557
87801	Socorro	7,576	5,849
87105	South Valley(u)	38,916	29,389
87901	Truth or Consequences	5,219	4,656
88401	Tucumcari	6,765	7,189
87544	White Rock	6,560	3,861
87327	Zuni Pueblo	5,551	3,958

New York

ZIP code	Place		1980	1970
*12207	Albany	(518)	101,727	115,781
11507	Albertson(u)	(516)	5,561	6,825
11701	Amityville	(516)	9,076	9,794
12010	Amsterdam	(518)	21,872	25,524
12603	Arlington(u)	(914)	11,305	11,203
13021	Auburn	(315)	32,548	34,599
*11702	Babylon	(516)	12,388	12,897
11510	Baldwin(u)	(516)	31,630	34,525
13027	Baldwinsville	(315)	6,446	6,298
14020	Batavia	(716)	16,703	17,338
14810	Bath	(607)	6,042	6,053
13088	Bayberry-Lynelle Meadows(u)	(315)	14,813	....
11705	Bayport(u)	(516)	9,282	8,235
11706	Bay Shore(u)	(516)	10,784	11,119
11709	Bayville	(516)	7,034	6,141
12508	Beacon	(914)	12,937	13,255
11710	Bellmore(u)	(516)	18,106	18,431
11714	Bethpage(u)	(516)	16,840	18,555
*13902	Binghamton	(201)	55,860	64,123
10913	Blauvelt(u)	(914)	NA	5,427
11716	Bohemia(u)	(516)	9,308	8,928
11717	Brentwood(u)	(516)	44,321	28,322
10510	Briarcliff Manor	(914)	7,115	6,521
14610	Brighton(u)	(716)	35,776	....
14420	Brockport	(716)	9,776	7,878
10708	Bronxville	(914)	6,267	6,627
*14240	Buffalo	(716)	357,870	462,768
14424	Canandaigua	(716)	10,419	10,488

ZIP code	Place		1980	1970
13617	Canton	(315)	7,055	6,398
11514	Carle Place(u)	(516)	5,470	6,326
11516	Cedarhurst	(516)	6,162	6,941
11720	Centereach(u)	(516)	30,136	9,427
11934	Center Moriches(u)	(516)	5,703	3,802
11721	Centerport(u)	(516)	6,576	....
11722	Central Islip(u)	(516)	19,734	36,391
14225	Cheektowaga(u)	(716)	92,145	....
12065	Clifton Knolls(u)	(518)	5,636	5,771
12043	Cobleskill	(518)	5,272	4,368
12047	Cohoes	(518)	18,144	18,653
11724	Cold Spring Harbor(u)	(516)	5,336	5,509
12205	Colonie	(518)	8,869	8,701
11725	Commack(u)	(516)	34,719	24,138
10920	Congers(u)	(914)	7,123	5,928
11726	Copiague(u)	(516)	20,132	19,632
11727	Coram(u)	(516)	24,752	....
14830	Corning	(607)	12,953	15,792
13045	Cortland	(607)	20,138	19,621
10520	Croton-on-Hudson	(914)	6,889	7,523
11729	Deer Park(u)	(516)	30,394	32,274
12054	Delmar(u)	(518)	8,423	....
14043	Depew	(716)	19,819	22,158
13214	DeWitt(u)	(315)	9,024	10,032
11746	Dix Hills(u)	(516)	26,693	10,050
10522	Dobbs Ferry	(914)	10,053	10,353
14048	Dunkirk	(716)	15,310	16,855
14052	East Aurora	(716)	6,803	7,033
10709	Eastchester(u)	(914)	20,305	23,750
11735	East Farmingdale(u)	(516)	5,522	....
12302	East Glenville(u)	(518)	6,537	5,898
11746	East Half Hollow Hills(u)	(516)	NA	9,691
11576	East Hills	(516)	7,160	8,624
11730	East Islip(u)	(516)	13,852	6,861
11758	East Massapequa(u)	(516)	13,987	15,926
11554	East Meadow(u)	(516)	39,317	46,290
11743	East Neck(u)	(516)	NA	5,221
11731	East Northport(u)	(516)	20,187	12,392
11772	East Patchogue(u)	(516)	18,139	8,092
14445	East Rochester	(716)	7,596	8,347
11518	East Rockaway	(516)	10,917	11,795
13902	East Vestal(u)	(607)	NA	10,472
*14901	Elmira	(607)	35,327	39,945
11003	Elmont(u)	(516)	27,592	29,363
11731	Elwood(u)	(516)	11,847	15,031
13760	Endicott	(607)	14,457	16,556
13760	Endwell(u)	(607)	13,745	15,999
13219	Fairmount(u)	(315)	13,415	15,317
14450	Fairport	(716)	5,970	6,474
12601	Fairview(u)	(914)	5,852	8,517
11735	Farmingdale	(516)	7,946	9,297
11738	Farmingville(u)	(516)	13,398	....
*11001	Floral Park	(516)	16,805	18,466
11768	Fort Salonga(u)	(516)	9,550	....
11010	Franklin Square(u)	(516)	29,051	32,156
14063	Fredonia	(716)	11,126	10,326
11520	Freeport	(516)	38,272	40,374
13069	Fulton	(315)	13,312	14,003
11530	Garden City	(516)	22,927	25,373
11040	Garden City Park(u)	(516)	7,712	7,488
14624	Gates-North Gates(u)	(716)	15,244	....
14454	Geneseo	(716)	6,746	5,714
14456	Geneva	(315)	15,133	16,793
11542	Glen Cove	(516)	24,618	25,770
12801	Glens Falls	(518)	15,897	17,222
12801	Glens Falls North(u)	(518)	6,956	NA
12078	Gloversville	(518)	17,836	19,677
*11022	Great Neck	(516)	9,168	10,798
11020	Great Neck Plaza	(516)	5,604	6,043
14616	Greece(u)	(716)	16,177	....
11740	Greenlawn(u)	(516)	13,869	8,493
12083	Greenville(u)	(518)	8,706	....
11746	Half Hollow Hills(u)	(516)	NA	12,081
14075	Hamburg	(716)	10,582	10,215
11946	Hampton Bays(u)	(516)	7,256	1,862
14221	Harris Hill(u)	(716)	5,087	....
10528	Harrison	(914)	23,046	21,544
10530	Hartsdale(u)	(914)	10,216	12,226
10706	Hastings-on-Hudson	(914)	8,573	9,479
11787	Hauppauge(u)	(516)	20,960	13,957
10927	Haverstraw	(914)	8,800	8,198
10532	Hawthorne(u)	(914)	5,010	....
11551	Hempstead	(516)	40,404	39,411
13350	Herkimer	(315)	8,383	8,960
11040	Herricks(u)	(516)	8,123	9,112
11557	Hewlett(u)	(516)	6,986	6,796
11802	Hicksville(u)	(516)	43,245	49,820
10977	Hillcrest(u)	(914)	5,733	5,357
11741	Holbrook(u)	(516)	24,382	....
11742	Holtsville(u)	(516)	13,515	....
14843	Hornell	(607)	10,234	12,144
14845	Horseheads	(607)	7,348	7,989
12534	Hudson	(518)	7,986	8,940
12839	Hudson Falls	(518)	7,419	7,917
11743	Huntington(u)	(516)	21,727	12,601
11746	Huntington Station(u)	(516)	28,769	28,817
13357	Ilion	(315)	9,450	9,808
11696	Inwood(u)	(516)	8,228	8,433
14617	Irondequoit(u)	(716)	57,648	....
10533	Irvington	(914)	5,774	5,878
11751	Islip(u)	(516)	13,438	7,692
11752	Islip Terrace(u)	(516)	5,588	....
14850	Ithaca	(607)	28,732	26,226
14701	Jamestown	(716)	35,775	39,795
10535	Jefferson Valley-Yorktown(u)	(914)	13,380	9,008
11753	Jericho(u)	(516)	12,739	14,010
13790	Johnson City	(607)	17,126	18,025
12095	Johnstown	(518)	9,360	10,045
14217	Kenmore	(716)	18,474	20,980
11754	Kings Park(u)	(516)	16,131	5,555
11024	Kings Point	(516)	5,234	5,614
12401	Kingston	(914)	24,481	25,544
14218	Lackawanna	(716)	22,701	28,657
10512	Lake Carmel(u)	(914)	7,295	4,796
11755	Lake Grove	(516)	9,692	8,133
11779	Lake Ronkonkoma(u)	(516)	38,336	7,284
11552	Lakeview(u)	(516)	5,276	5,471
14086	Lancaster	(716)	13,056	13,365
10538	Larchmont	(914)	6,308	7,203
12110	Latham(u)	(914)	11,182	9,661
11559	Lawrence	(516)	6,175	6,566
11756	Levittown(u)	(516)	57,045	65,440
11757	Lindenhurst	(516)	26,919	28,359
13365	Little Falls	(315)	6,156	7,629
14094	Lockport	(716)	24,844	25,399
11791	Locust Grove(u)	(516)	9,670	11,626
11561	Long Beach	(516)	34,073	33,127
12211	Loudonville(u)	(518)	11,480	9,299
11563	Lynbrook	(516)	20,424	23,151
13208	Lyncourt(u)	(315)	5,129	....
10541	Mahopac(u)	(914)	7,681	5,265
12953	Malone	(518)	7,668	8,049
11565	Malverne	(516)	9,262	10,036
10543	Mamaroneck	(914)	17,616	18,909
11030	Manhasset(u)	(516)	8,485	8,541
13104	Manlius	(315)	5,241	4,295
11050	Manorhaven	(516)	5,384	5,488
11758	Massapequa(u)	(516)	24,454	26,821
11762	Massapequa Park	(516)	19,779	22,112
13662	Massena	(315)	12,851	14,042
11950	Mastic(u)	(516)	10,413	....
11951	Mastic Beach(u)	(516)	8,318	4,870
13211	Mattydale(u)	(315)	7,511	8,292
12118	Mechanicville	(518)	5,500	6,247
11763	Medford(u)	(516)	20,418	....
14103	Medina	(716)	6,392	6,415
11746	Melville(u)	(516)	8,139	6,641
11566	Merrick(u)	(516)	24,478	25,904
11953	Middle Island(u)	(516)	5,703	....
10940	Middletown	(914)	21,454	22,607
11764	Miller Place(u)	(516)	7,877	....
11501	Mineola	(516)	20,757	21,845
10950	Monroe	(914)	5,996	4,439
10952	Monsey(u)	(914)	12,380	8,797
12701	Monticello	(914)	6,306	5,991
10549	Mt. Kisco	(914)	8,025	8,172
11766	Mount Sinai(u)	(516)	6,591	....
*10551	Mount Vernon	(914)	66,713	72,788
12590	Myers Corner(u)	(914)	5,180	2,826
10954	Nanuet(u)	(914)	12,578	10,447
11767	Nesconset(u)	(516)	10,706	10,048
14513	Newark	(315)	10,017	11,644
12550	Newburgh	(914)	23,438	26,219
11590	New Cassel(u)	(516)	9,635	8,721
10956	New City(u)	(914)	35,859	27,344
11040	New Hyde Park	(516)	9,801	10,116
*10802	New Rochelle	(914)	70,794	75,385
12550	New Windsor Center(u)	(914)	7,812	8,803
*10001	New York	(212)	7,071,639	7,895,563
*10451	Bronx	(718)	1,168,972	1,471,701
*11201	Brooklyn	(718)	2,230,936	2,602,102
*10001	Manhattan	(212)	1,428,285	1,539,233
*(Q)	Queens	(718)	1,891,325	1,987,174

(Q) There are 4 P.O.s for Queens: 11101 for L.I. City; 11690 Far Rockaway; 11351 Flushing; and 11431 Jamaica.

*10314	Staten Island	(212)	352,121	295,443
14301	Niagara(u)	(716)	9,648	....
*14302	Niagara Falls	(716)	71,384	85,615
12309	Niskayuna(u)	(518)	5,223	6,186
11701	North Amityville(u)	(516)	13,140	11,936
11703	North Babylon(u)	(516)	19,019	39,526
11706	North Bay Shore(u)	(516)	35,020	....
11710	North Bellmore(u)	(516)	20,630	22,893
11713	North Bellport(u)	(516)	7,432	5,903
11752	North Great River(u)	(516)	11,416	12,080
11757	North Lindenhurst(u)	(516)	11,511	11,117
11758	North Massapequa(u)	(516)	21,385	23,123
11566	North Merrick(u)	(516)	12,848	13,650
11040	North New Hyde Park(u)	(516)	15,114	18,154
11772	North Patchogue(u)	(516)	7,126	5,232
11768	Northport	(516)	7,651	7,494
13212	North Syracuse	(315)	7,970	8,687
10591	North Tarrytown	(914)	7,994	8,334
14120	North Tonawanda	(716)	35,760	36,012
11580	North Valley Stream(u)	(516)	14,530	14,881
11793	North Wantagh(u)	(516)	12,677	15,053
13815	Norwich	(607)	8,082	8,843
10960	Nyack	(914)	6,428	6,659
11769	Oakdale(u)	(516)	8,090	7,334

ZIP code	Census Division		1980	1970
11572	Oceanside(u)	(516)	33,639	35,372
13669	Ogdensburg	(315)	12,375	14,554
11804	Old Bethpage(u)	(516)	6,215	7,084
14760	Olean	(716)	18,207	19,169
13421	Oneida	(315)	10,810	11,658
13820	Oneonta	(607)	14,933	16,030
12550	Orange Lake(u)	(914)	5,120	4,348
10562	Ossining	(914)	20,196	21,659
13126	Oswego	(315)	19,793	20,913
11771	Oyster Bay(u)	(516)	6,497	6,822
11772	Patchogue	(516)	11,291	11,582
10965	Pearl River(u)	(914)	15,893	17,146
10566	Peekskill	(914)	18,236	19,283
10803	Pelham	(914)	6,848	2,076
10803	Pelham Manor	(914)	6,130	6,673
14527	Penn Yan	(315)	5,242	5,293
13212	Pitcher Hill	(315)	6,063	
11714	Plainedge(u)	(516)	9,629	10,759
11803	Plainview(u)	(516)	28,037	31,695
12901	Plattsburgh	(518)	21,057	18,715
12903	Plattsburgh AFB(u)	(518)	5,905	7,078
10570	Pleasantville	(914)	6,749	7,110
10573	Port Chester	(914)	23,565	25,803
11777	Port Jefferson	(516)	6,731	5,515
11776	Port Jefferson Station(u)	(516)	17,009	7,403
12771	Port Jervis	(914)	8,699	8,852
11050	Port Washington(u)	(516)	14,521	15,923
13676	Potsdam	(315)	10,635	10,303
*12601	Poughkeepsie	(914)	29,757	32,029
12603	Red Oaks Mill(u)	(914)	5,236	3,919
12144	Rensselaer	(518)	9,047	10,136
11961	Ridge(u)	(516)	8,977	
11901	Riverhead(u)	(516)	6,339	7,585
11901	Riverside-Flanders(u)	(516)	5,400	
*14603	Rochester	(716)	241,741	295,011
*11570	Rockville Centre	(516)	25,412	27,444
11778	Rocky Point(u)	(516)	7,012	
12205	Roessleville(u)	(518)	11,685	5,476
13440	Rome	(315)	43,826	50,148
11575	Roosevelt(u)	(516)	14,109	15,008
11577	Roslyn Heights(u)	(516)	6,546	7,242
12303	Rotterdam(u)	(518)	22,933	25,214
10580	Rye	(914)	15,083	15,869
11780	St. James(u)	(516)	12,122	10,500
14779	Salamanca	(716)	6,890	7,877
12983	Saranac Lake	(518)	5,578	6,086
12866	Saratoga Springs	(518)	23,906	18,845
11782	Sayville(u)	(516)	12,013	11,680*
10583	Scarsdale	(914)	17,650	19,229
*12301	Schenectady	(518)	67,972	77,958
10940	Scotchtown(u)	(914)	7,352	2,119
12302	Scotia	(518)	7,280	7,370
11579	Sea Cliff	(516)	5,364	5,890
11783	Seaford(u)	(516)	16,117	17,379
11784	Selden(u)	(516)	17,259	11,613
13148	Seneca Falls	(315)	7,466	7,794
11733	Setauket-East Setauket(u)	(516)	10,176	6,857
11967	Shirley(u)	(516)	18,072	6,280
11787	Smithtown(u)	(516)	30,906	
13209	Solvay	(315)	7,140	8,280
11789	South Beach(u)	(516)	8,071	
11735	South Farmingdale(u)	(516)	16,439	20,464
14850	South Hill(u)	(607)	5,276	
11746	South Huntington(u)	(516)	14,854	9,115
14904	Southport(u)	(607)	8,329	8,685
11581	South Valley Stream(u)	(516)	5,462	6,595
11590	South Westbury(u)	(516)	9,732	10,978
10977	Spring Valley	(914)	20,537	18,112
11790	Stony Brook(u)	(516)	16,155	6,391
10980	Stony Point(u)	(914)	8,686	8,270
10901	Suffern	(914)	10,794	8,273
11791	Syosset(u)	(516)	9,818	10,084
*13201	Syracuse	(315)	170,105	197,297
10983	Tappan(u)	(914)	8,267	7,424
10591	Tarrytown	(914)	10,648	11,115
10594	Thornwood(u)	(914)	7,197	6,874
14150	Tonawanda	(716)	18,693	21,898
*12180	Troy	(518)	56,638	62,918
10707	Tuckahoe	(914)	6,076	6,236
11553	Uniondale(u)	(516)	20,016	22,077
*13503	Utica	(315)	75,632	91,373
10989	Valley Cottage(u)	(914)	8,214	6,007
*11580	Valley Stream	(516)	35,769	40,413
10901	Viola(u)	(914)	5,340	5,136
12586	Walden	(914)	5,659	5,277
11793	Wantagh(u)	(516)	19,817	21,783
12590	Wappingers Falls	(914)	5,110	5,607
13165	Waterloo	(315)	5,303	5,418
13601	Watertown	(315)	27,861	30,787
12189	Watervliet	(518)	11,354	12,404
14580	Webster	(716)	5,499	5,037
14895	Wellsville	(716)	5,769	5,815
11758	West Amityville(u)	(516)	6,623	6,424
11704	West Babylon(u)	(516)	41,699	12,893
11706	West Bay Shore(u)	(516)	5,118	
11590	Westbury	(516)	13,871	15,362
14905	West Elmira(u)	(607)	5,485	5,901
12801	West Glens Falls(u)	(518)	5,331	3,363
10993	West Haverstraw	(914)	9,181	8,558
11552	West Hempstead(u)	(516)	18,536	20,375
11743	West Hills(u)	(516)	6,071	....
11795	West Islip(u)	(516)	29,533	17,374
12203	Westmere(u)	(518)	6,881	6,364
10994	West Nyack(u)	(914)	8,553	5,510
10996	West Point(u)	(914)	8,105	....
11796	West Sayville(u)	(516)	8,185	7,386
14224	West Seneca(u)	(716)	51,210	....
13219	Westvale(u)	(315)	6,169	7,253
*10602	White Plains	(914)	46,999	50,346
14221	Williamsville	(716)	6,017	6,878
11596	Williston Park	(516)	8,216	9,154
11797	Woodbury(u)	(516)	7,043	....
11598	Woodmere(u)	(516)	17,205	19,831
11798	Wyandach(u)	(516)	13,215	15,716
*10701	Yonkers	(914)	195,351	204,297
10598	Yorktown Heights(u)	(914)	7,696	6,805

North Carolina

ZIP code	Census Division		1980	1970
28001	Albemarle	(704)	15,110	11,126
27263	Archdale	(919)	5,326	4,874
27203	Asheboro	(919)	15,252	10,797
*28801	Asheville	(704)	53,281	57,820
28303	Bonnie Doone(u)	(919)	5,950	....
28607	Boone	(704)	10,191	8,754
28712	Brevard	(704)	5,323	5,243
27215	Burlington	(919)	37,266	35,930
28542	Camp Le Jeune(u)	(919)	30,764	34,549
27510	Carrboro	(919)	7,517	5,058
27511	Cary	(919)	21,612	7,640
27514	Chapel Hill	(919)	32,421	26,199
*28202	Charlotte	(704)	315,474	241,420
27012	Clemmons(u)	(919)	7,401	....
28328	Clinton	(919)	7,552	7,157
28025	Concord	(704)	16,942	18,464
28334	Dunn	(919)	8,962	8,302
*27701	Durham	(919)	100,538	95,438
28379	East Rockingham(u)	(919)	5,190	2,858
27288	Eden	(919)	15,672	15,871
27932	Edenton	(919)-	5,264	4,956
27909	Elizabeth City	(919)	13,784	14,381
28728	Enka(u)	(704)	5,567	....
*28302	Fayetteville	(919)	59,507	53,510
28043	Forest City	(704)	7,688	7,179
28307	Fort Bragg(u)	(919)	37,834	46,995
27529	Garner	(919)	9,556	4,923
28052	Gastonia	(704)	47,333	47,322
27530	Goldsboro	(919)	31,871	26,960
27253	Graham	(919)	8,415	8,172
*27420	Greensboro	(919)	155,642	144,076
27834	Greenville	(919)	35,740	29,063
28532	Havelock	(919)	17,718	3,012
27536	Henderson	(919)	13,522	13,896
28739	Hendersonville	(704)	6,862	6,443
28601	Hickory	(704)	20,757	20,569
*27260	High Point	(919)	64,107	63,229
28348	Hope Mills	(919)	5,412	1,866
28540	Jacksonville	(919)	18,237	16,289
28081	Kannapolis(u)	(704)	34,564	36,293
27284	Kernersville	(919)	5,875	4,815
27021	King(u)	(919)	8,757	1,033
	Kings Grant(u)	(919)	6,652	....
28086	Kings Mountain	(704)	9,080	8,465
28501	Kinston	(919)	25,234	23,020
28352	Laurinburg	(919)	11,480	8,859
28645	Lenoir	(704)	13,748	14,705
27292	Lexington	(704)	15,711	17,205
28358	Lumberton	(919)	18,340	16,961
28212	Mint Hill	(704)	9,830	
28110	Monroe	(704)	12,639	11,282
28115	Mooresville	(704)	8,575	8,808
28655	Morganton	(704)	13,763	13,625
27030	Mount Airy	(919)	6,862	7,325
28560	New Bern	(919)	14,557	14,660
27604	New Hope (Wake)(u)	(919)	6,768	
	New Hope (Wayne)(u)	(919)	6,685	
28540	New River Station(u)	(919)	5,401	
28658	Newton	(704)	7,624	7,857
28012	North Belmont(u)	(704)	10,762	10,677
27565	Oxford	(919)	7,580	7,177
	Piney Green-White Oak(u)	(919)	6,058	
*27611	Raleigh	(919)	149,771	122,830
27320	Reidsville	(919)	12,492	13,636
27870	Roanoke Rapids	(919)	14,702	13,500
28379	Rockingham	(919)	8,300	5,852
27801	Rocky Mount	(919)	41,283	34,284
27573	Roxboro	(919)	7,532	5,370
28601	St. Stephens(u)	(704)	10,797	
28144	Salisbury	(704)	22,677	22,515
27330	Sanford	(919)	14,773	11,716
28150	Shelby	(704)	15,310	16,328
27577	Smithfield	(919)	7,288	6,677
28387	Southern Pines	(919)	8,620	5,937
28390	Spring Lake	(919)	6,273	3,968
27045	Stanleyville(u)	(919)	5,039	2,368
28677	Statesville	(704)	18,622	20,007
28778	Swannanoa(u)	(704)	5,586	1,945
27886	Tarboro	(919)	8,634	9,425
27360	Thomasville	(919)	14,144	15,230

ZIP code	Place		1980	1970
27370	Trinity(u)	(919)	6,726	....
27889	Washington	(919)	8,418	8,961
28786	Waynesville	(704)	6,765	6,488
28025	West Concord(u)	(704)	5,859	5,347
28472	Whiteville	(919)	5,565	4,195
27892	Williamston	(919)	6,159	6,570
28401	Wilmington	(919)	44,000	46,169
27893	Wilson	(919)	34,424	29,347
*27102	Winston-Salem	(919)	131,885	133,683

North Dakota (701)

58501	Bismarck		44,485	34,703
58301	Devils Lake		7,442	7,078
58601	Dickinson		15,924	12,405
58102	Fargo		61,308	53,365
58237	Grafton		5,293	5,946
58201	Grand Forks(u)		43,765	39,008
58201	Grand Forks AFB(u)		9,390	10,474
58401	Jamestown		16,280	15,385
58554	Mandan		15,513	11,093
58701	Minot		32,843	32,290
58701	Minot AFB(u)		9,880	12,077
58072	Valley City		7,774	7,843
58075	Wahpeton		9,064	7,076
58078	West Fargo		10,099	5,161
58801	Williston		13,336	11,280

Ohio

45810	Ada	(419)	5,669	5,309
*44309	Akron	(216)	237,177	275,425
44601	Alliance	(216)	24,315	26,547
44001	Amherst	(216)	10,638	9,902
44805	Ashland	(419)	20,326	19,872
44004	Ashtabula	(216)	23,449	24,313
45701	Athens	(614)	19,743	24,168
44202	Aurora	(216)	8,177	6,549
44515	Austintown(u)	(216)	33,636	29,393
44011	Avon	(216)	7,241	7,214
44012	Avon Lake	(216)	13,222	12,261
44203	Barberton	(216)	29,751	33,052
44140	Bay Village	(216)	17,846	18,163
44122	Beachwood	(216)	9,983	9,631
45385	Beavercreek	(513)	31,589	
44146	Bedford	(216)	15,056	17,552
44146	Bedford Heights	(216)	13,214	13,063
43906	Bellaire	(614)	8,241	9,655
45305	Bellbrook	(513)	5,174	1,268
43311	Bellefontaine	(513)	11,888	11,255
44811	Bellevue	(419)	8,187	8,604
45714	Belpre	(614)	7,193	7,189
44017	Berea	(216)	19,567	22,466
43209	Bexley	(614)	13,405	14,888
43004	Blacklick Estates(u)	(614)	11,223	8,351
45242	Blue Ash	(513)	9,510	8,324
44512	Boardman(u)	(216)	39,161	30,852
43402	Bowling Green	(419)	25,728	14,656
44141	Brecksville	(216)	10,132	9,137
45231	Brentwood(u)	(513)	5,508	....
45211	Bridgetown(u)	(513)	11,460	13,352
44141	Broadview Heights	(216)	10,920	11,463
44144	Brooklyn	(216)	12,342	13,142
44142	Brook Park	(216)	26,195	30,774
44212	Brunswick	(216)	27,689	15,852
43506	Bryan	(419)	7,879	7,008
44820	Bucyrus	(419)	13,433	13,111
43725	Cambridge	(614)	13,573	13,656
44405	Campbell	(216)	11,619	12,577
44406	Canfield	(216)	5,535	4,997
*44711	Canton	(216)	93,077	110,053
45822	Celina	(419)	9,137	8,072
45459	Centerville	(513)	18,886	10,333
45211	Cheviot	(513)	9,888	11,135
45601	Chillicothe	(614)	23,420	24,842
*45234	Cincinnati	(513)	385,409	453,514
43113	Circleville	(614)	11,700	11,687
*44101	Cleveland	(216)	573,822	750,879
44118	Cleveland Heights	(216)	56,438	60,767
43410	Clyde	(419)	5,489	5,503
*43216	Columbus	(614)	565,032	540,025
44030	Conneaut	(216)	13,835	14,552
44410	Cortland	(216)	5,011	2,525
43812	Coshocton	(614)	13,405	13,747
45238	Covedale(u)	(513)	5,830	6,639
44827	Crestline	(419)	5,406	5,965
*44222	Cuyahoga Falls	(216)	43,710	49,815
*45401	Dayton	(513)	193,536	243,023
45236	Deer Park	(513)	6,745	7,415
43512	Defiance	(419)	16,810	16,281
43015	Delaware	(614)	18,780	15,008
45238	Delhi Hills(u)	(513)	27,647	
45833	Delphos	(419)	7,314	7,608
44622	Dover	(216)	11,526	11,516
44112	East Cleveland	(216)	36,957	39,600
44094	Eastlake	(216)	22,104	19,690
43920	East Liverpool	(216)	16,687	20,020
44413	East Palestine	(216)	5,306	5,604
45320	Eaton	(513)	6,839	6,020
*44035	Elyria	(216)	57,504	53,427
45322	Englewood	(513)	11,329	7,885
44117	Euclid	(216)	59,999	71,552
45324	Fairborn	(513)	29,702	32,267
45014	Fairfield	(513)	30,777	14,680
44313	Fairlawn	(216)	6,100	6,102
44126	Fairview Park	(216)	19,311	21,699
45840	Findlay	(419)	35,594	35,800
45405	Forest Park	(513)	10,566	15,139
45426	Fort McKinley(u)	(513)	10,161	11,536
44830	Fostoria	(419)	15,743	16,037
45005	Franklin	(513)	10,711	10,075
43420	Fremont	(419)	17,834	18,490
43230	Gahanna	(614)	18,001	12,400
44833	Galion	(419)	12,391	13,123
45631	Gallipolis	(614)	5,576	7,490
44125	Garfield Heights	(216)	33,380	41,417
44041	Geneva	(216)	6,655	6,449
45327	Germantown	(513)	5,015	4,088
44420	Girard	(216)	12,517	14,119
43212	Grandview Heights	(614)	7,420	8,460
45123	Greenfield	(513)	5,150	4,780
45331	Greenville	(513)	12,999	12,380
45239	Groesbeck(u)	(513)	9,594	
43123	Grove City	(614)	16,793	13,911
*45012	Hamilton	(513)	63,189	67,865
45030	Harrison	(513)	5,855	4,408
43055	Heath	(614)	6,969	6,768
44124	Highland Heights	(216)	5,739	5,926
43026	Hilliard	(614)	8,008	8,369
45133	Hillsboro	(513)	6,356	5,584
44484	Howland(u)	(216)	7,441	
44425	Hubbard	(216)	9,245	8,583
45424	Huber Heights(u)	(513)	31,731	18,943
43081	Huber Ridge(u)	(614)	5,835	
44839	Huron	(419)	7,123	6,896
44131	Independence	(216)	8,165	7,034
45638	Ironton	(614)	14,290	15,030
45640	Jackson	(614)	6,675	6,843
44240	Kent	(216)	26,164	28,183
43326	Kenton	(419)	8,605	8,315
45236	Kenwood(u)	(513)	9,928	15,789
45429	Kettering	(513)	61,186	71,864
44094	Kirtland	(216)	5,969	5,530
44107	Lakewood	(216)	61,963	70,173
43130	Lancaster	(614)	34,953	32,911
45036	Lebanon	(513)	9,636	7,934
*45802	Lima	(419)	47,827	53,734
45215	Lincoln Heights	(513)	5,259	6,099
43228	Lincoln Village(u)	(614)	10,548	11,215
43138	Logan	(614)	6,557	6,269
43140	London	(614)	6,958	6,481
*44052	Lorain	(216)	75,416	78,185
44641	Louisville	(216)	7,996	6,298
45140	Loveland	(513)	9,100	7,120
44124	Lyndhurst	(216)	18,092	19,749
44056	Macedonia	(216)	6,571	6,375
45243	Madeira	(513)	9,341	6,713
*44901	Mansfield	(419)	53,927	55,047
44137	Maple Heights	(216)	29,735	34,093
45750	Marietta	(614)	16,467	16,861
43302	Marion	(614)	37,040	38,646
43935	Martins Ferry	(614)	9,331	10,757
43040	Marysville	(513)	7,414	5,744
45040	Mason	(513)	8,692	5,677
44646	Massillon	(216)	30,557	32,539
43537	Maumee	(419)	15,747	15,937
44124	Mayfield Heights	(216)	21,550	22,139
44256	Medina	(216)	15,268	10,913
44060	Mentor	(216)	42,065	36,912
44060	Mentor-on-the-Lake	(216)	7,919	6,517
45342	Miamisburg	(513)	15,304	14,797
44130	Middleburg Heights	(216)	16,218	12,367
45042	Middletown	(513)	43,719	48,767
45042	Middletown South(u)	(513)	5,260	
45150	Milford	(513)	5,232	4,826
45239	Monfort Heights(u)	(513)	9,745	
45242	Montgomery	(513)	10,084	5,683
45439	Moraine	(513)	5,325	4,898
45231	Mount Healthy	(513)	7,562	7,446
43050	Mount Vernon	(614)	14,380	13,373
43545	Napoleon	(419)	8,614	7,791
43055	Newark	(614)	41,200	41,836
45344	New Carlisle	(513)	6,498	6,112
43764	New Lexington	(614)	5,179	4,921
44663	New Philadelphia	(216)	16,883	15,184
44446	Niles	(216)	23,088	21,581
45239	Northbrook(u)	(513)	8,357	
44720	North Canton	(216)	14,228	15,228
45239	North College Hill	(513)	10,990	12,363
44057	North Madison(u)	(216)	8,741	6,882
44070	North Olmsted	(216)	36,486	34,861
45502	Northridge(u) (Clark)	(513)	5,559	12
45414	Northridge(u) (Montgomery)	(513)	9,720	10,084
44039	North Ridgeville	(216)	21,522	13,152
44133	North Royalton	(216)	17,671	12,807
	Northview(u)	(513)	9,973	
43619	Northwood	(419)	5,495	4,222

ZIP code	Place		1980	1970
44203	Norton	(216)	12,242	12,308
44857	Norwalk	(419)	14,358	13,386
45212	Norwood	(513)	26,342	30,420
45873	Oakwood	(419)	9,372	10,095
44074	Oberlin	(216)	8,660	8,761
44138	Olmsted Falls	(216)	5,868	2,504
43616	Oregon	(419)	18,675	16,563
44667	Orrville	(216)	7,511	7,408
45431	Overlook-Page Manor(u).	(513)	14,825	19,719
45056	Oxford	(513)	17,655	15,868
44077	Painesville	(216)	16,391	16,536
45344	Park Layne(u)	(513)	5,372	....
44129	Parma	(216)	92,548	100,216
44130	Parma Heights	(216)	23,112	27,192
44124	Pepper Pike	(216)	6,177	5,382
44646	Perry Heights(u).	(216)	9,206	....
43551	Perrysburg.	(419)	10,215	7,693
45356	Piqua	(513)	20,480	20,741
45069	Pisgah(u).	(513)	15,660	....
44319	Portage Lakes(u)	(216)	11,310	....
43452	Port Clinton	(419)	7,223	7,202
45662	Portsmouth	(614)	25,943	27,633
44266	Ravenna	(216)	11,987	11,780
45215	Reading	(513)	12,879	14,617
43068	Reynoldsburg	(614)	20,661	13,921
44143	Richmond Heights	(213)	10,095	9,220
44270	Rittman	(216)	6,063	6,308
44116	Rocky River	(216)	21,084	22,958
43460	Rossford	(419)	5,978	5,302
45217	St. Bernard	(513)	5,396	6,131
43950	St. Clairsville	(614)	5,452	4,754
45885	St. Marys	(419)	8,414	7,699
44460	Salem	(216)	12,869	14,186
44870	Sandusky	(419)	31,360	32,674
44870	Sandusky South(u)	(419)	6,548	8,501
44672	Sebring	(216)	5,078	4,954
44131	Seven Hills	(216)	13,650	12,700
44120	Shaker Heights	(216)	32,487	36,306
45241	Sharonville	(513)	10,108	11,393
44054	Sheffield Lake	(216)	10,484	8,734
44875	Shelby	(419)	9,645	9,847
45415	Shiloh(u)	(419)	11,735	11,368
45365	Sidney	(513)	17,657	16,332
45236	Silverton	(513)	6,172	6,588
44139	Solon	(216)	14,341	11,147
44121	South Euclid	(216)	25,713	29,579
45246	Springdale	(216)	10,111	8,127
*45501	Springfield	(513)	72,563	81,941
43952	Steubenville	(614)	26,400	30,771
44224	Stow	(216)	25,303	20,061
44240	Streetsboro	(216)	9,055	7,966
44136	Strongsville	(216)	28,577	15,182
44471	Struthers	(216)	13,624	15,343
43560	Sylvania	(419)	15,527	12,031
44278	Tallmadge	(216)	15,269	15,274
45243	The Village of Indian Hill	(513)	5,521	5,651
44883	Tiffin	(419)	19,549	21,596
45371	Tipp City	(513)	5,595	5,090
*43601	Toledo	(419)	354,635	383,062
43964	Toronto	(614)	6,934	7,705
45067	Trenton.	(513)	6,401	5,278
45426	Trotwood	(513)	7,802	6,997
45373	Troy	(513)	19,086	17,186
44087	Twinsburg	(216)	7,632	6,432
44683	Uhrichsville	(614)	6,130	5,731
45322	Union	(513)	5,219	3,654
44118	University Heights.	(216)	15,401	17,055
43221	Upper Arlington	(614)	35,648	38,727
43351	Upper Sandusky	(419)	5,967	5,645
43078	Urbana	(513)	10,762	11,237
45377	Vandalia	(513)	13,161	10,796
45891	Van Wert	(419)	11,035	11,320
44089	Vermilion	(216)	11,012	9,872
44281	Wadsworth	(216)	15,166	13,142
45895	Wapakoneta	(419)	8,402	7,324
*44481	Warren	(216)	56,629	63,494
44122	Warrensville Heights	(216)	16,565	18,925
43160	Washington	(513)	12,682	12,495
43567	Wauseon	(419)	6,173	4,932
45692	Wellston	(614)	6,016	5,410
43968	Wellsville	(216)	5,095	5,891
45449	West Carrollton	(513)	13,148	10,748
43081	Westerville	(614)	23,414	12,530
44145	Westlake	(216)	19,483	15,689
43213	Whitehall	(614)	21,299	25,263
45239	White Oak(u)	(513)	9,563	....
44092	Wickliffe	(216)	16,790	20,632
44890	Willard	(419)	5,674	5,510
44094	Willoughby	(216)	19,329	18,634
44094	Willoughby Hills	(216)	8,612	5,969
44094	Willowick	(216)	17,834	21,237
45177	Wilmington	(513)	10,431	10,051
45459	Woodbourne-Hyde Park(u)	(513)	8,826	....
44691	Wooster	(216)	19,289	18,703
43085	Worthington	(614)	15,016	15,326
45215	Wyoming	(513)	8,282	9,089
45385	Xenia	(513)	24,653	25,373
*44501	Youngstown	(216)	115,436	140,909
43701	Zanesville	(614)	28,655	33,045

Oklahoma

ZIP code	Place		1980	1970
74820	Ada	(405)	15,902	14,859
73521	Altus	(405)	23,101	23,302
73717	Alva	(405)	6,416	7,440
73005	Anadarko	(405)	6,378	6,682
73401	Ardmore	(405)	23,689	20,881
74003	Bartlesville	(918)	34,568	29,683
73008	Bethany	(405)	22,130	22,694
74008	Bixby	(918)	6,969	3,973
74631	Blackwell	(405)	8,400	8,645
74728	Broken Arrow	(918)	35,761	11,018
73018	Chickasha	(405)	15,828	14,194
73020	Choctaw	(405)	7,520	4,750
74017	Claremore	(918)	12,085	9,084
73601	Clinton	(405)	8,796	8,513
74023	Cushing	(918)	7,720	7,529
73115	Del City	(405)	28,523	27,133
73533	Duncan	(405)	22,517	19,718
74701	Durant	(405)	11,972	11,118
73034	Edmond	(405)	34,637	16,633
73644	Elk City	(405)	9,579	7,323
73036	El Reno	(405)	15,486	14,510
73701	Enid	(405)	50,363	44,986
73503	Fort Sill(u)	(405)	15,924	21,217
73542	Frederick	(405)	6,153	6,132
73044	Guthrie	(405)	10,312	9,575
73942	Guymon	(405)	8,492	7,674
74437	Henryetta	(918)	6,432	6,430
74848	Holdenville	(405)	5,469	5,181
74743	Hugo	(405)	7,172	6,585
74745	Idabel	(405)	7,622	5,946
74037	Jenks	(918)	5,876	2,685
73501	Lawton	(405)	80,054	74,470
73055	Marlow	(405)	5,017	3,995
74501	McAlester	(918)	17,255	18,802
74354	Miami	(918)	14,237	13,880
73110	Midwest City	(405)	49,559	48,212
73060	Moore	(405)	35,063	18,761
74401	Muskogee	(918)	40,011	37,331
73064	Mustang	(405)	7,496	2,637
73069	Norman	(405)	68,020	52,117
*73125	Oklahoma City	(405)	404,014	368,164
74447	Okmulgee	(918)	16,263	15,180
74055	Owasso	(918)	6,149	3,491
73075	Pauls Valley	(405)	5,664	5,769
73077	Perry	(405)	5,796	5,341
74601	Ponca City	(405)	26,238	25,940
74953	Poteau	(918)	7,089	5,500
74361	Pryor Creek	(918)	8,483	7,057
74955	Sallisaw	(918)	6,403	4,888
74063	Sand Springs	(918)	13,121	10,565
74066	Sapulpa	(918)	15,853	15,159
74868	Seminole	(405)	8,590	7,878
74801	Shawnee	(405)	26,506	25,075
74074	Stillwater	(405)	38,268	31,126
73086	Sulphur	(405)	5,516	5,158
74464	Tahlequah	(918)	9,708	9,254
74873	Tecumseh	(405)	5,123	4,451
73120	The Village	(918)	11,114	13,695
*74101	Tulsa	(918)	360,919	330,350
74156	Turley(u)	(918)	6,336	....
74301	Vinita	(918)	6,740	5,847
74467	Wagoner	(918)	6,191	4,959
73132	Warr Acres	(405)	9,940	9,887
73096	Weatherford	(405)	9,640	7,959
74884	Wewoka	(405)	5,472	5,284
73801	Woodward	(405)	13,610	9,563
73099	Yukon	(405)	17,112	8,411

Oregon (503)

ZIP code	Place	1980	1970
97321	Albany	26,511	18,181
97005	Aloha(u)	28,353	....
97601	Altamont(u)	19,805	15,746
97520	Ashland	14,943	12,342
97103	Astoria	9,998	10,244
97814	Baker	9,471	9,354
97005	Beaverton	31,926	18,577
97701	Bend	17,263	13,710
97013	Canby	7,659	3,813
97225	Cedar Hills(u)	9,619	....
	Centennial(u)	22,118	....
97502	Central Point	6,357	4,004
97420	Coos Bay	14,424	13,466
97330	Corvallis	40,960	35,056
97424	Cottage Grove	7,148	6,004
	Cully(u)	10,569	....
97338	Dallas	8,530	6,361
97266	Errol Heights(u)	10,487	....
*97401	Eugene	105,664	79,028
97116	Forest Grove	11,499	8,275
97301	Four Corners(u)	11,331	5,823
97223	Garden Home-Whitford(u)	6,926	....
97027	Gladstone	9,500	6,254
97526	Grants Pass	14,997	12,455
97030	Gresham	33,005	10,030
97303	Hayesville(u)	9,213	5,518
97230	Hazelwood(u)	25,541	....
97838	Hermiston	9,408	4,893

ZIP code	Place	1980	1970
97123	Hillsboro	27,664	14,675
97303	Keizer(u)	18,592	11,405
97601	Klamath Falls	16,661	15,775
97850	La Grande	11,354	9,645
97034	Lake Oswego	22,527	14,615
97355	Lebanon	10,413	6,636
97367	Lincoln City	5,469	4,198
97128	McMinnville	14,080	10,125
97501	Medford	39,603	28,973
97223	Metzger(u)	5,544	....
97862	Milton-Freewater	5,086	4,105
97222	Milwaukie	17,931	16,444
97361	Monmouth	5,594	5,237
97132	Newberg	10,394	6,507
97365	Newport	7,519	5,188
97459	North Bend	9,779	8,553
....	North Springfield(u)	6,140	....
97268	Oak Grove(u)	11,640	....
97914	Ontario	8,814	6,523
97045	Oregon City	14,673	9,176
97220	Parkrose(u)	21,108	....
97801	Pendleton	14,521	13,197
*97208	Portland	368,139	379,967
97236	Powellhurst(u)	20,132	....
97754	Prineville	5,276	4,101
97225	Raleigh Hills(u)	6,517	....
97756	Redmond	6,452	3,721
97404	River Road(u)	10,370	....
97470	Roseburg	16,644	14,461
97051	St. Helens	7,064	6,212
*97301	Salem	89,233	68,725
97401	Santa Clara(u)	14,288	....
97138	Seaside	5,193	4,402
97381	Silverton	5,168	4,301
97477	Springfield	41,621	26,874
97386	Sweet Home	6,921	3,799
97058	The Dalles	10,820	10,423
97223	Tigard	14,799	6,499
97060	Troutdale	5,908	1,661
97062	Tualatin	7,483	750
97068	West Linn	11,358	7,091
97225	West Slope(u)	5,364	....
97501	White City(u)	5,445	....
97233	Wilkes-Rockwood(u)	23,216	....
97071	Woodburn	11,196	7,495

Pennsylvania

ZIP code	Place		1980	1970
19001	Abington Township(u)	(215)	59,084	63,625
15001	Aliquippa	(412)	17,094	22,277
*18101	Allentown	(215)	103,758	109,871
*16603	Altoona	(814)	57,078	63,115
19002	Ambler	(215)	6,628	7,800
15003	Ambridge	(412)	9,575	11,324
18403	Archbald	(717)	6,295	6,118
19003	Ardmore(u)	(215)	NA	5,131
15068	Arnold	(412)	6,853	8,174
19014	Aston Township(u)	(215)	14,530	13,704
15202	Avalon	(412)	6,240	7,010
15005	Baden	(412)	5,318	5,536
19004	Bala-Cynwyd(u)	(215)	NA	6,483
15234	Baldwin	(412)	24,714	26,729
18013	Bangor	(215)	5,006	5,425
15009	Beaver	(412)	5,441	6,100
15010	Beaver Falls	(412)	12,525	14,635
16823	Bellefonte	(814)	6,300	6,828
15202	Bellevue	(412)	10,128	11,586
19020	Bensalem Township(u)	(215)	52,399	33,038
18603	Berwick	(717)	12,189	12,274
15102	Bethel Park	(412)	34,755	34,758
*18016	Bethlehem	(215)	70,419	72,686
18447	Blakely	(717)	7,438	6,391
17815	Bloomsburg	(717)	11,717	11,652
15104	Braddock	(412)	5,634	8,795
16701	Bradford	(814)	11,211	12,672
15227	Brentwood	(412)	11,859	13,732
15017	Bridgeville	(412)	6,154	6,717
19007	Bristol	(215)	10,867	12,085
19007	Bristol Twp(u)	(215)	58,733	67,498
19015	Brookhaven	(215)	7,912	7,370
16001	Butler	(412)	17,026	18,691
15419	California	(412)	5,703	6,635
17011	Camp Hill	(717)	8,422	9,931
15317	Canonsburg	(412)	10,459	11,439
18407	Carbondale	(717)	11,255	12,478
17013	Carlisle	(717)	18,314	18,079
15106	Carnegie	(412)	10,099	10,864
15108	Carnot-Moon(u)	(412)	11,102	13,093
15234	Castle Shannon	(412)	10,164	12,036
18032	Catasauqua	(215)	7,944	5,702
17201	Chambersburg	(717)	16,174	17,315
15022	Charleroi	(412)	5,717	6,723
19012	Cheltenham Twp(u)	(215)	35,509	40,238
*19003	Chester	(215)	45,794	56,331
19013	Chester Twp(u)	(215)	5,687	5,708
15025	Clairton	(412)	12,188	15,051
16214	Clarion	(814)	6,198	6,095
18411	Clarks Summit	(717)	5,272	5,376

ZIP code	Place		1980	1970
16830	Clearfield	(814)	7,580	8,176
19018	Clifton Heights	(215)	7,320	8,348
19320	Coatesville	(215)	10,698	12,331
19023	Collingdale	(215)	9,539	10,605
17512	Columbia	(717)	10,466	11,237
15425	Connellsville	(412)	10,319	11,643
19428	Conshohocken	(215)	8,591	10,195
15108	Coraopolis	(412)	7,308	8,435
16407	Corry	(814)	7,149	7,435
15205	Crafton	(412)	7,623	8,233
17821	Danville	(717)	5,239	6,176
19023	Darby	(215)	11,513	13,729
19036	Darby Twp(u)	(215)	12,264	....
19333	Devon-Berwyn(u)	(215)	5,246	....
18519	Dickson City	(717)	6,699	7,698
15033	Donora	(412)	7,524	8,825
15216	Dormont	(412)	11,275	12,856
19335	Downingtown	(215)	7,650	7,437
18901	Doylestown	(215)	8,717	8,270
15801	Du Bois	(814)	9,290	10,112
18512	Dunmore	(717)	16,781	18,168
15110	Duquesne	(412)	10,094	11,410
18642	Duryea	(717)	5,415	5,264
19401	East Norriton(u)	(215)	12,711	....
18042	Easton	(215)	26,027	29,450
18301	East Stroudsburg	(717)	8,039	7,894
15005	Economy	(412)	9,538	7,176
16412	Edinboro	(814)	6,324	4,871
18704	Edwardsville	(717)	5,729	5,633
17022	Elizabethtown	(717)	8,233	8,072
16117	Ellwood City	(412)	9,998	10,857
18049	Emmaus	(215)	11,001	11,511
17522	Ephrata	(717)	11,095	9,662
*16501	Erie	(814)	119,123	129,265
18643	Exeter	(717)	5,493	4,670
19054	Falls Twp(u)	(215)	36,083	35,830
16121	Farrell	(412)	8,645	11,000
19032	Folcroft	(215)	8,231	9,610
15221	Forest Hills	(412)	8,198	9,561
18704	Forty Fort	(717)	5,590	6,114
15238	Fox Chapel	(412)	5,049	4,684
17931	Frackville	(717)	5,308	5,445
16323	Franklin	(814)	8,146	8,629
15143	Franklin Park	(412)	6,135	5,310
18052	Fullerton(u)	(215)	8,055	7,908
17325	Gettysburg	(717)	7,194	7,275
15045	Glassport	(412)	6,242	7,450
19036	Glenolden	(215)	7,633	8,697
15601	Greensburg	(412)	17,558	17,077
15220	Green Tree	(412)	5,722	6,441
16125	Greenville	(412)	7,730	8,704
16127	Grove City	(412)	8,162	8,312
17331	Hanover	(717)	14,890	15,623
*17105	Harrisburg	(717)	53,264	68,061
19040	Hatboro	(215)	7,579	8,880
19083	Haverford Twp(u)	(215)	52,349	55,132
18201	Hazleton	(717)	27,318	30,426
18055	Hellertown	(215)	6,025	6,615
17033	Hershey(u)	(717)	13,249	7,407
18042	Highland Park (Northampton)(u)	(717)	5,922	5,500
16648	Hollidaysburg	(814)	5,892	6,262
16001	Homeacre-Lyndora(u)	(412)	8,333	8,415
15120	Homestead	(412)	5,092	6,309
18431	Honesdale	(717)	5,128	5,224
19044	Horsham(u)	(215)	9,900	....
17036	Hummelstown	(717)	6,159	4,723
16652	Huntingdon	(814)	7,042	6,987
15701	Indiana	(412)	16,051	16,100
15644	Jeannette	(412)	13,106	15,209
15344	Jefferson	(412)	8,643	8,512
18229	Jim Thorpe	(717)	5,263	5,456
*15901	Johnstown	(814)	35,496	42,476
15108	Kennedy Twp(u)	(412)	7,159	6,859
18704	Kingston	(717)	15,681	18,325
16201	Kittanning	(412)	5,432	6,231
*17604	Lancaster	(717)	54,725	57,690
19446	Lansdale	(215)	16,526	18,451
19050	Lansdowne	(215)	11,891	14,090
15650	Latrobe	(412)	10,799	11,749
17042	Lebanon	(717)	25,711	28,572
18235	Lehighton	(717)	5,826	6,095
17837	Lewisburg	(717)	5,407	5,718
17044	Lewistown	(717)	9,830	11,098
17543	Lititz	(717)	7,590	7,072
17745	Lock Haven	(717)	9,617	11,427
15068	Lower Burrell	(412)	13,200	13,654
19003	Lower Merion Twp(u)	(215)	59,651	63,392
19006	Lower Moreland Twp(u)	(215)	12,472	11,746
19047	Lower Southampton Twp(u)	(215)	18,305	17,578
19008	Marple Twp(u)	(215)	23,642	25,040
15237	McCandless Twp(u)	(412)	26,250	22,404
*15134	McKeesport	(412)	31,012	37,977
15136	McKees Rocks	(412)	8,742	11,901
17948	Mahanoy City	(717)	6,167	7,257
17545	Manheim	(717)	5,015	5,434
16335	Meadville	(814)	15,544	16,573
17055	Mechanicsburg	(717)	9,487	9,385
*19063	Media	(215)	6,119	6,444
17057	Middletown (Dauphin)	(717)	10,122	9,080
18017	Middletown (Northampton)(u)	(215)	5,801	....

ZIP code	Place		1980	1970
17057	Middletown Twp			
	(Delaware)(u)	(215)	12,463	12,878
17551	Millersville	(717)	7,668	6,396
17847	Milton	(717)	6,730	7,723
17954	Minersville	(717)	5,635	6,012
15061	Monaca	(412)	7,661	7,486
15062	Monessen	(412)	11,928	15,216
15063	Monongahela	(412)	5,950	7,113
15146	Monroeville	(412)	30,977	29,011
17754	Montoursville	(717)	5,403	5,985
18507	Moosic	(717)	6,068	4,646
19067	Morrisville	(215)	9,845	11,309
17851	Mount Carmel	(717)	8,190	9,317
17552	Mount Joy	(717)	5,680	5,041
15666	Mount Pleasant	(412)	5,354	5,895
15228	Mount Lebanon(u)	(412)	34,414	39,157
15120	Munhall	(412)	14,535	16,574
15668	Murrysville	(412)	16,036	12,661
18634	Nanticoke	(717)	13,044	14,638
18064	Nazareth	(215)	5,443	5,815
	Nether Providence Twp(u)	(215)	12,730	13,644
15066	New Brighton	(412)	7,364	7,637
*16101	New Castle	(412)	33,621	38,559
17070	New Cumberland	(717)	8,051	9,803
15068	New Kensington	(412)	17,660	20,312
*19401	Norristown	(215)	34,684	38,169
18067	Northampton	(215)	8,240	8,389
15104	North Braddock	(412)	8,711	10,838
15137	North Versailles(u)	(412)	13,294	....
16421	Northwest Harbor-Creek(u)	(814)	7,485	....
19074	Norwood	(215)	6,647	7,229
15139	Oakmont	(412)	7,039	7,550
16301	Oil City	(814)	13,881	15,033
18518	Old Forge	(717)	9,304	9,522
18447	Olyphant	(717)	5,204	5,422
18071	Palmerton	(215)	5,455	5,620
17078	Palmyra	(717)	7,228	7,615
19301	Paoli(u)	(215)	6,698	5,835
17333	Parkville(u)	(717)	5,009	5,120
15235	Penn Hills(u)	(412)	57,632	....
18944	Perkasie	(215)	5,241	5,451
*19104	Philadelphia	(215)	1,688,210	1,949,996
19460	Phoenixville	(215)	14,165	14,823
*15219	Pittsburgh	(412)	423,959	520,089
*18640	Pittston	(717)	9,930	11,113
18705	Plains(u)	(717)	5,455	6,606
15236	Pleasant Hills	(412)	9,676	10,409
15239	Plum	(412)	25,390	21,932
18651	Plymouth	(717)	7,605	9,536
19462	Plymouth Twp(u)	(215)	17,168	16,876
15133	Port Vue	(412)	5,316	5,862
19464	Pottstown	(215)	22,729	25,355
17901	Pottsville	(717)	18,195	19,715
19076	Prospect Park	(215)	6,593	7,250
15767	Punxsutawney	(814)	7,479	7,792
18951	Quakertown	(215)	8,867	7,276
19087	Radnor Twp(u)	(215)	27,676	27,459
*19603	Reading	(215)	78,686	87,643
17356	Red Lion	(717)	5,824	5,645
18954	Richboro(u)	(215)	5,141	....
15853	Ridgway	(814)	5,604	6,022
19078	Ridley Park	(215)	7,889	9,025
19033	Ridley Twp(u)	(215)	33,771	39,085
15237	Ross Twp(u)	(412)	35,102	32,892
15857	St. Marys	(814)	6,417	7,470
18840	Sayre	(717)	6,951	7,473
17972	Schuylkill Haven	(717)	5,977	6,125
15683	Scottdale	(412)	5,833	5,818
15106	Scott Twp(u)	(412)	20,413	21,856
*18503	Scranton	(717)	88,117	102,696
17870	Selinsgrove	(717)	5,227	5,116
15116	Shaler Twp(u)	(412)	33,712	33,369
17872	Shamokin	(717)	10,357	11,719
16146	Sharon	(412)	19,057	22,653
19079	Sharon Hill	(215)	6,221	7,464
16150	Sharpsville	(412)	5,375	6,126
17976	Shenandoah	(717)	7,589	8,287
19607	Shillington	(215)	5,601	6,249
17404	Shiloh(u)	(717)	5,315	....
17257	Shippensburg	(717)	5,261	6,536
15501	Somerset	(814)	6,474	6,269
18964	Souderton	(215)	6,657	6,366
17701	South Williamsport	(717)	6,581	7,153
19064	Springfield(u)	(215)	25,326	....
19118	Springfield Twp(u)	(215)	20,344	22,394
16801	State College	(814)	36,130	32,833
17113	Steelton	(717)	6,484	8,556
15136	Stowe Twp(u)	(412)	9,202	10,119
18360	Stroudsburg	(717)	5,148	5,451
16323	Sugar Creek(u)	(717)	5,954	5,944
17801	Sunbury	(717)	12,292	13,025
19081	Swarthmore	(215)	5,950	6,156
17111	Swatara Twp(u)	(717)	18,796	17,178
15218	Swissvale	(412)	11,345	13,819
18704	Swoyersville	(717)	5,795	6,786
18252	Tamaqua	(717)	8,843	9,246
15084	Tarentum	(412)	6,419	7,379
18517	Taylor	(717)	7,246	6,977
16354	Titusville	(814)	6,884	7,331

ZIP code	Place		1980	1970
19401	Trooper(u)	(215)	7,370	
15145	Turtle Creek	(412)	6,959	8,308
16686	Tyrone	(814)	6,346	7,072
15401	Uniontown	(412)	14,510	16,282
19061	Upper Chichester Twp(u)	(215)	14,377	11,414
19082	Upper Darby(u)	(215)	84,054	95,910
19034	Upper Dublin Twp(u)	(215)	22,348	19,449
19406	Upper Merion Twp(u)	(215)	26,138	23,699
19090	Upper Moreland Twp(u)	(215)	25,874	24,866
19063	Upper Providence Twp(u)	(215)	9,477	9,234
15241	Upper St. Clair(u)	(412)	19,023	....
19006	Upper Southampton Twp(u)	(215)	15,806	13,936
15690	Vandergrift	(412)	6,823	7,889
18974	Warminster(u)	(215)	35,543	....
16365	Warren	(814)	12,146	12,998
15301	Washington	(412)	18,363	19,827
17268	Waynesboro	(717)	9,726	10,011
	Weigelstown(u)	(717)	5,213	....
19380	West Chester	(215)	17,435	19,301
19380	West Goshen(u)	(215)	7,998	....
15122	West Mifflin	(412)	26,322	28,070
19401	West Norriton(u)	(215)	14,034	....
15905	Westmont	(814)	6,113	6,673
18643	West Pittston	(717)	5,980	7,074
15229	West View	(412)	7,648	8,312
18052	Whitehall	(215)	15,143	16,450
19428	Whitemarsh Twp(u)	(215)	15,101	15,886
15131	White Oak	(717)	9,480	9,304
*18701	Wilkes-Barre	(717)	51,551	58,856
15221	Wilkinsburg	(412)	23,669	26,780
15145	Wilkins Twp(u)	(412)	8,472	8,749
17701	Williamsport	(717)	33,401	37,918
15025	Wilson	(412)	7,564	8,406
15963	Windber	(814)	5,585	6,332
19610	Wyomissing	(215)	6,551	7,136
19050	Yeadon	(215)	11,727	12,136
*17405	York	(717)	44,619	50,335

Rhode Island (401)

See Note on Page 257

		1980	1970
02806	Barrington	16,174	17,554
02809	Bristol	20,128	17,860
02830	Burrillville	13,164	10,087
02863	Central Falls	16,995	18,716
02816	Coventry	27,065	22,947
02910	Cranston	71,992	74,287
02864	Cumberland	27,069	26,605
02864	Cumberland Hill(u)	5,421	....
02818	East Greenwich	10,211	9,577
02914	East Providence	50,980	48,207
02814	Glocester	7,550	5,160
02828	Greenville(u)	7,576	....
02833	Hopkinton	6,406	5,392
02919	Johnston	24,907	22,037
02881	Kingston(u)	5,479	5,601
02865	Lincoln	16,949	16,182
02840	Middletown	17,216	29,290
02882	Narragansett	12,088	7,138
02840	Newport	29,259	34,562
02843	Newport East(u)	11,030	10,285
02852	North Kingstown	21,938	29,793
02908	North Providence	29,188	24,337
02876	North Smithfield	9,972	9,349
*02860	Pawtucket	71,204	76,984
02871	Portsmouth	14,257	12,521
*02904	Providence	156,804	179,116
02857	Scituate	8,405	7,489
02917	Smithfield	16,886	13,468
02879	South Kingstown	20,414	16,913
02878	Tiverton	13,526	12,559
02864	Valley Falls(u)	10,892	....
*02880	Wakefield-Peacedale(u)	6,474	6,331
02885	Warren	10,640	10,523
*02887	Warwick	87,123	83,694
02891	Westerly	18,580	17,248
02891	Westerly Center(u)	14,093	13,654
02893	West Warwick	27,026	24,323
02895	Woonsocket	45,914	46,820

South Carolina (803)

		1980	1970
29620	Abbeville	5,863	5,515
29801	Aiken	14,978	13,436
29621	Anderson	27,628	27,556
29407	Avondale-Moorland(u)	5,355	5,236
29812	Barnwell	5,572	4,439
29902	Beaufort	8,634	9,434
29627	Belton	5,312	5,257
29841	Belvedere(u)	6,859	....
29512	Bennettsville	8,774	7,468
29611	Berea(u)	13,164	7,180
	Brookdale(u)	6,123	....
29020	Camden	7,462	8,532
29209	Capitol View(u)	9,962	....
29033	Cayce	11,701	9,967
*29401	Charleston	69,855	66,945
29404	Charleston Base(u)	NA	6,230

ZIP code	Place	1980	1970
29408	Charleston Yard(u)	NA	13,565
29520	Cheraw	5,654	5,627
29706	Chester	6,820	7,045
29631	Clemson	8,118	6,690
29325	Clinton	8,596	8,138
29201	Columbia	101,229	113,542
29526	Conway	10,240	8,151
20532	Darlington	7,989	6,990
29204	Dentsville(u)	13,579	
29536	Dillon	7,042	6,391
29405	Dorchester Terrace-Brentwood(u)	7,862	
29601	Dunean(u)	5,146	1,266
29640	Easley	14,264	11,175
29501	Florence	29,842	25,997
29206	Forest Acres	6,062	6,808
29340	Gaffney	13,453	13,131
29605	Gantt(u)	13,719	11,386
29440	Georgetown	10,144	10,449
29445	Goose Creek	17,811	3,825
29602	Greenville	58,242	61,436
29203	Greenview(u)	5,515	
29646	Greenwood	21,613	21,069
29651	Greer	10,525	10,642
29410	Hanahan	13,224	9,118
29550	Hartsville	7,631	8,017
29928	Hilton Head Island(u)	11,344	
29621	Homeland Park(u)	6,720	
29412	James Island(u)	24,124	
29456	Ladson(u)	13,246	
29560	Lake City	5,636	6,247
29720	Lancaster	9,703	9,186
29902	Laurel Bay(u)	5,238	
29360	Laurens	10,587	10,298
29571	Marion	7,700	7,435
29662	Mauldin	8,143	3,797
29464	Mount Pleasant	14,209	6,879
29574	Mullins	6,068	6,006
29577	Myrtle Beach	18,758	9,035
29108	Newberry	9,866	9,218
29841	North Augusta	13,593	12,883
29406	North Charleston	62,504	21,211
	North Trenholm(u)	10,962	
29565	Oak Grove(u)	7,092	
29115	Orangeburg	14,933	13,252
29905	Parris Island(u)	7,752	8,868
29483	Pinehurst-Sheppard Park(u)	6,956	1,711
29730	Rock Hill	35,327	33,846
29407	St. Andrews (Charleston)(u)	9,908	9,202
29210	St. Andrews (Richland)(u)	20,245	
29609	Sans Souci(u)	8,393	
29678	Seneca	7,436	6,573
	Seven Oaks(u)	16,604	
29152	Shaw AFB(u)	6,939	5,819
29681	Simpsonville	9,037	3,308
	South Sumter(u)	7,096	
29301	Spartanburg	43,826	44,546
29483	Summerville	6,706	3,839
29150	Sumter	24,921	24,555
29687	Taylors(u)	15,801	6,831
29379	Union	10,523	10,775
29205	Valencia Heights(u)	5,328	
29607	Wade-Hampton(u)	20,180	17,152
29488	Walterboro	6,036	6,257
29405	Wando Woods(u)	5,266	
29611	Welcome(u)	6,922	
29169	West Columbia	10,409	7,838
29206	Woodfield(u)	9,588	
29388	Woodruff	5,171	4,690
29745	York	6,412	5,081

South Dakota (605)

ZIP code	Place	1980	1970
57401	Aberdeen	25,851	26,476
57006	Brookings	14,951	13,717
57350	Huron	13,000	14,299
57042	Madison	6,210	6,315
57301	Mitchell	13,916	13,425
57501	Pierre	11,973	9,699
57701	Rapid City	46,492	43,836
57101	Sioux Falls	81,343	72,488
57785	Sturgis	5,184	4,536
57069	Vermillion	9,582	9,128
57201	Watertown	15,649	13,388
57078	Yankton	12,011	11,919

Tennessee

ZIP code	Place		1980	1970
37701	Alcoa	(615)	6,870	7,739
37303	Athens	(615)	12,080	11,790
38134	Bartlett	(901)	17,170	1,150
37660	Bloomingdale(u)	(615)	12,088	3,120
38008	Bolivar	(901)	6,597	6,674
37027	Brentwood	(615)	9,431	4,099
37620	Bristol	(615)	23,986	20,064
38012	Brownsville	(901)	9,307	7,011
37401	Chattanooga	(615)	169,728	119,923
37040	Clarksville	(615)	54,777	31,719
37311	Cleveland	(615)	26,415	21,446
37716	Clinton	(615)	5,245	4,794
38017	Collierville	(901)	7,839	3,651
37663	Colonial Heights(u)	(615)	6,744	3,027
38401	Columbia	(615)	26,571	21,471
37022	Concord (Knox)(u)	(615)	8,569	
38501	Cookeville	(615)	20,350	14,403
38019	Covington	(901)	6,065	5,801
38555	Crossville	(615)	6,394	5,381
37321	Dayton	(615)	5,913	4,361
37055	Dickson	(615)	7,040	5,665
38024	Dyersburg	(901)	15,856	14,523
37801	Eagleton Village(u)	(615)	5,331	5,345
37412	East Ridge	(615)	21,236	21,799
37643	Elizabethton	(615)	12,431	12,269
37334	Fayetteville	(615)	7,559	7,691
37064	Franklin	(615)	12,407	9,497
37066	Gallatin	(615)	17,191	13,253
38138	Germantown	(901)	21,482	3,474
37072	Goodlettsville	(615)	8,327	6,168
37075	Greater Hendersonville(u)	(615)	25,029	11,996
37743	Greeneville	(615)	14,097	13,722
37918	Halls(u)	(615)	10,363	
37748	Harriman	(615)	8,303	8,734
37341	Harrison(u)	(615)	6,206	
37075	Hendersonville	(615)	26,561	412
38343	Humboldt	(901)	10,209	10,066
38301	Jackson	(901)	49,258	39,996
37760	Jefferson City	(615)	5,612	5,124
37601	Johnson City	(615)	39,753	33,770
*37662	Kingsport	(615)	32,027	31,938
*37901	Knoxville	(615)	175,045	174,587
37766	La Follette	(615)	8,176	6,902
37086	LaVergne	(615)	5,495	5,220
38464	Lawrenceburg	(615)	10,175	8,889
37087	Lebanon	(615)	11,872	12,492
37771	Lenoir City	(615)	5,180	5,324
37091	Lewisburg	(615)	8,760	7,207
38351	Lexington	(901)	5,934	5,024
37665	Lynn Garden(u)	(615)	7,213	
38201	McKenzie	(901)	5,405	4,873
37110	McMinnville	(615)	10,683	10,662
37355	Manchester	(615)	7,250	6,208
38237	Martin	(901)	8,898	7,781
37801	Maryville	(615)	17,480	13,808
*38101	Memphis	(901)	646,174	623,988
37343	Middle Valley(u)	(615)	11,420	
38358	Milan	(901)	8,083	7,313
38053	Millington	(901)	20,236	21,177
37814	Morristown	(615)	19,570	20,318
37130	Murfreesboro	(615)	32,845	26,360
*37202	Nashville-Davidson	(615)	455,651	**426,029
37821	Newport	(615)	7,580	7,328
37830	Oak Ridge	(615)	27,662	28,319
38242	Paris	(901)	10,728	9,892
37849	Powell(u)	(615)	7,220	
38478	Pulaski	(615)	7,184	6,989
37415	Red Bank White Oak	(615)	13,129	12,715
38063	Ripley	(901)	6,366	4,794
37854	Rockwood	(615)	5,767	5,259
38372	Savannah	(901)	6,992	5,576
37160	Shelbyville	(615)	13,530	12,262
37377	Signal Mountain	(615)	5,818	4,839
37167	Smyrna	(615)	8,839	5,698
37379	Soddy-Daisy	(615)	8,388	7,569
37172	Springfield	(615)	10,814	9,720
37363	Summit (Hamilton)(u)	(615)	8,345	
37388	Tullahoma	(615)	15,800	15,311
38261	Union City	(901)	10,436	11,925
37398	Winchester	(615)	5,821	5,256

**Comprises the Metropolitan Government of Nashville and Davidson County.

Texas

ZIP code	Place		1980	1970
*79604	Abilene	(915)	98,315	89,653
75001	Addison	(214)	5,553	593
78516	Alamo	(512)	5,831	4,291
78209	Alamo Heights	(512)	6,252	6,933
77039	Aldine(u)	(713)	12,623	
78332	Alice	(512)	20,961	20,121
75002	Allen	(214)	8,314	1,940
79830	Alpine	(915)	5,465	5,971
77511	Alvin	(713)	16,515	10,671
*79105	Amarillo	(806)	149,230	127,010
79714	Andrews	(915)	11,061	8,625
77515	Angleton	(409)	13,929	9,906
78336	Aransas Pass	(512)	7,173	5,813
*76010	Arlington	(817)	160,123	90,229
75751	Athens	(214)	10,197	9,582
75551	Atlanta	(214)	6,272	5,007
*78710	Austin	(512)	345,890	253,539
76020	Azle	(817)	5,822	4,493
75149	Balch Springs	(214)	13,746	10,464
77414	Bay City	(409)	17,837	13,445
77520	Baytown	(713)	56,923	43,980
*77704	Beaumont	(409)	118,102	117,548
76021	Bedford	(817)	20,821	10,049
78102	Beeville	(512)	14,574	13,506
77401	Bellaire	(713)	14,950	19,009

ZIP code	Place		1980	1970
76704	Bellmead	(817)	7,569	7,698
76513	Belton	(817)	10,660	8,696
76126	Benbrook	(817)	13,579	8,169
79720	Big Spring	(915)	24,804	28,735
75418	Bonham	(214)	7,338	7,698
79007	Borger	(806)	15,837	14,195
76230	Bowie	(817)	5,610	5,185
76825	Brady	(915)	5,969	5,557
76024	Breckenridge	(817)	6,921	5,944
77833	Brenham	(409)	10,966	8,922
77611	Bridge City	(713)	7,667	8,164
79316	Brownfield	(806)	10,387	9,647
78520	Brownsville	(512)	84,997	52,522
76801	Brownwood	(915)	19,203	17,368
77801	Bryan	(409)	44,337	33,719
76354	Burkburnett	(817)	10,668	9,230
76028	Burleson	(817)	11,734	7,713
76520	Cameron	(817)	5,721	5,546
79015	Canyon	(806)	10,724	8,333
78834	Carrizo Springs	(512)	6,886	5,374
75006	Carrollton	(214)	40,591	13,855
75633	Carthage	(214)	6,447	5,392
75104	Cedar Hill	(214)	6,849	2,610
75935	Center	(409)	5,827	4,989
.....	Champions(u)	(713)	14,692	
77530	Channelview(u)	(713)	17,471	
79201	Childress	(817)	5,817	5,408
76031	Cleburne	(817)	19,218	16,015
77327	Cleveland	(713)	5,977	5,627
77015	Clover Leaf(u)	(713)	17,317	
77531	Clute	(409)	9,577	6,023
76834	Coleman	(915)	5,960	5,608
77840	College Station	(409)	37,272	17,676
76034	Colleyville	(817)	6,700	3,342
79512	Colorado City	(915)	5,405	5,227
75428	Commerce	(214)	8,136	9,534
77301	Conroe	(409)	18,034	11,969
78109	Converse	(512)	5,150	1,383
76522	Copperas Cove	(817)	19,469	10,818
*78408	Corpus Christi	(512)	231,134	204,525
75110	Corsicana	(214)	21,712	19,972
75835	Crockett	(713)	7,405	6,616
76036	Crowley	(817)	5,852	2,662
78839	Crystal City	(512)	8,334	8,104
77954	Cuero	(512)	7,124	6,956
79022	Dalhart	(806)	6,854	5,705
*75260	Dallas	(214)	904,570	844,401
77536	Deer Park	(713)	22,648	12,773
78840	Del Rio	(512)	30,034	21,330
75020	Denison	(214)	23,884	24,923
76201	Denton	(817)	48,063	39,874
75115	De Soto	(214)	15,538	6,617
75941	Diboll	(713)	5,227	3,557
77539	Dickinson	(713)	7,505	10,776
79027	Dimmitt	(806)	5,019	4,327
78537	Donna	(512)	9,952	7,365
79029	Dumas	(806)	12,194	9,771
75116	Duncanville	(214)	27,781	14,105
78852	Eagle Pass	(512)	21,407	15,364
78539	Edinburg	(512)	24,075	17,163
77957	Edna	(512)	5,650	5,332
77437	El Campo	(619)	10,462	9,332
79910	El Paso	(915)	425,259	322,261
78543	Elsa	(512)	5,061	4,400
75119	Ennis	(214)	12,110	11,046
76039	Euless	(817)	24,002	19,316
76140	Everman	(817)	5,387	4,570
78355	Fallurrias	(512)	6,103	6,355
75234	Farmers Branch	(214)	24,863	27,492
76119	Forest Hill	(817)	11,684	8,236
79906	Fort Bliss(u)	(915)	12,687	13,288
76544	Fort Hood(u)	(817)	31,250	32,597
79735	Fort Stockton	(915)	8,688	8,283
76101	Fort Worth	(817)	385,141	393,455
78624	Fredericksburg	(512)	6,412	5,326
77541	Freeport	(409)	13,444	11,997
77546	Friendswood	(713)	10,719	5,675
76240	Gainesville	(817)	14,081	13,830
77547	Galena Park	(713)	9,879	10,479
77550	Galveston	(409)	61,902	61,809
*75040	Garland	(214)	138,857	81,437
76528	Gatesville	(817)	6,260	4,683
78626	Georgetown	(512)	9,468	6,395
75644	Gilmer	(214)	5,167	4,196
75647	Gladewater	(214)	6,548	5,574
78629	Gonzales	(512)	7,152	5,854
76046	Graham	(817)	9,055	7,477
75050	Grand Prairie	(214)	71,462	50,904
76051	Grapevine	(817)	11,801	7,049
75401	Greenville	(214)	22,161	22,043
77619	Groves	(713)	17,090	18,067
76117	Haltom City	(817)	29,014	28,127
76541	Harker Heights	(817)	7,345	4,216
78550	Harlingen	(512)	43,543	33,503
77859	Hearne	(713)	5,418	4,982
75652	Henderson	(214)	11,473	10,187
79045	Hereford	(806)	15,853	13,414
76643	Hewitt	(817)	5,247	569
75205	Highland Park	(214)	8,909	10,133
77562	Highlands	(713)	6,467	3,462
76645	Hillsboro	(817)	7,397	7,224
77563	Hitchcock	(713)	6,103	5,565
78861	Hondo	(512)	6,057	5,487
*77013	Houston	(713)	1,594,086	1,233,535
77338	Humble	(713)	6,729	3,272
77340	Huntsville	(409)	23,936	17,610
76053	Hurst	(817)	31,420	27,215
78362	Ingleside	(512)	5,436	3,763
76367	Iowa Park	(817)	6,184	5,796
*75061	Irving	(214)	109,943	97,260
77029	Jacinto City	(713)	8,953	9,563
75766	Jacksonville	(214)	12,264	9,734
75951	Jasper	(409)	6,959	6,251
77450	Katy	(713)	5,660	2,923
79745	Kermit	(915)	8,015	7,884
78028	Kerrville	(512)	15,276	12,672
75662	Kilgore	(214)	11,331	9,495
76541	Killeen	(817)	46,296	35,507
78363	Kingsville	(512)	28,808	28,915
.....	Kingwood	(713)	16,261	
78219	Kirby	(512)	6,435	3,238
78236	Lackland AFB(u)	(512)	14,459	19,141
77566	Lake Jackson	(409)	19,102	13,376
77568	La Marque	(409)	15,372	16,131
79631	Lamesa	(806)	11,790	11,559
76550	Lampasas	(512)	6,165	5,922
75146	Lancaster	(214)	14,807	10,522
77571	La Porte	(713)	14,062	7,149
78040	Laredo	(512)	91,449	69,024
77573	League City	(713)	16,578	10,818
78238	Leon Valley	(512)	9,088	2,487
79336	Levelland	(806)	13,809	11,445
75067	Lewisville	(214)	24,273	9,264
77575	Liberty	(713)	7,945	5,531
79339	Littlefield	(806)	7,409	6,738
78233	Live Oak	(512)	8,183	2,779
78644	Lockhart	(512)	7,953	6,489
75601	Longview	(214)	62,762	45,547
*79408	Lubbock	(806)	173,979	149,101
75901	Lufkin	(409)	28,562	23,049
78648	Luling	(512)	5,039	4,719
78501	McAllen	(512)	67,042	37,636
75069	McKinney	(214)	16,249	15,193
76063	Mansfield	(817)	8,092	3,658
76661	Marlin	(817)	7,099	6,351
75670	Marshall	(214)	24,921	22,937
78368	Mathis	(512)	5,667	5,351
78570	Mercedes	(512)	11,851	9,355
75149	Mesquite	(214)	67,053	55,131
76667	Mexia	(817)	7,094	5,943
79701	Midland	(915)	70,525	59,463
76067	Mineral Wells	(817)	14,468	18,411
78572	Mission	(512)	22,653	13,043
77459	Missouri City	(713)	24,423	4,136
79756	Monahans	(915)	8,397	8,333
75455	Mount Pleasant	(214)	11,003	9,459
75961	Nacogdoches	(409)	27,149	22,544
77868	Navasota	(409)	5,971	5,111
77627	Nederland	(409)	16,855	16,810
78130	New Braunfels	(512)	22,402	17,859
76118	North Richland Hills	(817)	30,592	16,514
*79760	Odessa	(915)	90,027	78,380
77630	Orange	(409)	23,628	24,457
75801	Palestine	(214)	15,948	14,525
79065	Pampa	(806)	21,396	21,726
75460	Paris	(214)	25,498	23,441
*77501	Pasadena	(713)	112,560	89,956
77581	Pearland	(713)	13,248	6,444
78061	Pearsall	(512)	7,383	5,545
79772	Pecos	(915)	12,855	12,682
79070	Perryton	(806)	7,991	7,810
78577	Pharr	(512)	21,381	15,829
79072	Plainview	(806)	22,187	19,096
75074	Plano	(214)	72,331	17,872
78064	Pleasanton	(512)	6,346	5,407
77640	Port Arthur	(409)	61,195	57,371
78374	Portland	(512)	12,023	7,302
77979	Port Lavaca	(512)	10,911	10,491
77651	Port Neches	(713)	13,944	10,894
78580	Raymondville	(512)	9,493	7,987
75080	Richardson	(214)	72,496	48,400
76118	Richland Hills	(817)	7,977	8,865
77469	Richmond	(713)	9,692	5,777
78582	Rio Grande City(u)	(512)	8,930	5,676
77019	River Oaks	(817)	6,890	8,193
78701	Robinson	(817)	6,074	3,807
78380	Robstown	(512)	12,100	11,217
75567	Rockdale	(512)	5,611	4,655
75087	Rockwall	(214)	5,939	3,121
77471	Rosenberg	(713)	17,840	12,098
78664	Round Rock	(512)	12,740	2,811
75088	Rowlett	(214)	7,522	2,224
76179	Saginaw	(817)	5,736	2,382
76901	San Angelo	(915)	73,240	63,884
*78284	San Antonio	(512)	785,940	654,153
78586	San Benito	(512)	17,988	15,176
78384	San Diego	(512)	5,225	4,490
78589	San Juan	(512)	7,608	5,070
78666	San Marcos	(512)	23,420	18,860
77550	Santa Fe	(713)	5,413	

ZIP code	Place		1980	1970
78154	Schertz	(512)	7,262	4,061
75159	Seagoville	(214)	7,304	4,390
78155	Seguin	(512)	17,854	15,934
79360	Seminole	(915)	6,080	5,007
75090	Sherman	(214)	30,413	29,061
77656	Silsbee	(713)	7,684	7,271
78387	Sinton	(512)	6,044	5,563
79364	Slaton	(806)	6,804	6,583
79549	Snyder	(915)	12,705	11,171
77587	South Houston	(713)	13,293	11,527
76401	Stephenville	(817)	11,881	9,277
77478	Sugar Land	(713)	8,826	3,318
75482	Sulphur Springs	(214)	12,804	10,642
79556	Sweetwater	(915)	12,242	12,020
76574	Taylor	(512)	10,619	9,616
76501	Temple	(817)	42,354	33,431
75160	Terrell	(214)	13,269	14,182
75501	Texarkana	(214)	31,271	30,497
77590	Texas City	(409)	41,201	38,908
*75056	The Colony	(214)	11,586	....
77380	The Woodlands	(713)	8,443	....
79088	Tulia	(806)	5,033	5,294
75701	Tyler	(214)	70,508	57,770
78148	Universal City	(512)	10,720	7,613
76308	University Park	(214)	22,254	23,498
78801	Uvalde	(512)	14,178	10,764
76384	Vernon	(817)	12,695	11,454
77901	Victoria	(512)	50,695	41,349
77662	Vidor	(713)	11,834	9,738
*76701	Waco	(817)	101,261	95,326
76148	Watauga	(817)	10,284	3,778
75165	Waxahachie	(214)	14,624	13,452
76086	Weatherford	(817)	12,049	11,750
78596	Weslaco	(512)	19,331	15,313
77005	West University Place	(713)	12,010	13,317
77488	Wharton	(713)	9,033	7,881
76108	White Settlement	(817)	13,508	13,449
*76307	Wichita Falls	(817)	94,201	96,265
78239	Windcrest	(512)	5,332	3,371
76710	Woodway	(817)	7,091	4,819
77995	Yoakum	(512)	6,148	5,755

Utah (801)

ZIP code	Place	1980	1970
84003	American Fork	12,417	7,713
84118	Bennion(u)	9,632	....
84010	Bountiful	32,877	27,751
84302	Brigham City	15,596	14,007
84720	Cedar City	10,972	8,946
84014	Centerville	8,069	3,268
84015	Clearfield	17,982	13,316
84015	Clinton	5,777	1,768
84121	Cottonwood(u)	11,554	8,431
84121	Cottonwood Heights(u)	22,665	....
84020	Draper	5,530	....
84109	East Millcreek(u)	24,150	26,579
84106	Granite Park(u)	5,554	9,573
84117	Holladay(u)	22,189	23,014
84037	Kaysville	9,811	6,192
84118	Kearns(u)	21,353	17,247
84041	Layton	22,862	13,603
84043	Lehi	6,848	4,659
84321	Logan	26,844	22,333
84044	Magna(u)	13,138	5,509
84047	Midvale	10,144	7,840
84532	Moab	5,333	4,793
84117	Mount Olympus(u)	6,068	5,909
84107	Murray	25,750	21,206
84404	North Ogden	9,309	5,257
84054	North Salt Lake	5,548	2,143
*84401	Ogden	64,407	69,478
84057	Orem	52,399	25,729
84651	Payson	8,246	4,501
84062	Pleasant Grove	10,669	5,327
84501	Price	9,086	6,218
84601	Provo	74,111	53,131
84701	Richfield	5,482	4,471
84065	Riverton	7,032	2,820
84067	Roy	19,694	14,356
84770	St. George	11,350	7,097
*84101	Salt Lake City	163,034	175,885
84070	Sandy City	52,210	6,438
84121	South Cottonwood(u)	11,117	....
84065	South Jordan	7,492	2,942
84403	South Ogden	11,366	9,991
84115	South Salt Lake	10,413	7,810
84660	Spanish Fork	9,825	7,284
84663	Springville	12,101	8,790
84015	Sunset	5,733	6,268
84107	Taylorsville(u)	17,448	....
84074	Tooele	14,335	12,539
84047	Union-East Midvale(u)	9,663	....
84010	Val Verda(u)	6,422	....
84078	Vernal	6,600	3,908
84403	Washington Terrace	8,212	7,241
84084	West Jordan	27,325	4,221
84119	West Valley(u)	72,299	....
84070	White City(u)	7,180	6,402

Vermont (802)

See Note on Page 257

ZIP code	Place	1980	1970
05641	Barre	9,824	10,209
.....	Barre	7,090	6,509
05201	Bennington(u)	15,815	14,586
.....	Bennington(u)	9,349	7,950
05301	Brattleboro Center(u)	8,596	9,055
.....	Brattleboro	11,886	12,239
05401	Burlington	37,712	38,633
05446	Colchester	12,629	8,776
05451	Essex	14,392	10,951
05452	Essex Junction	7,033	6,511
05753	Middlebury	7,574	6,532
05602	Montpelier	8,241	8,609
05701	Rutland	18,436	19,293
05478	St. Albans	7,308	8,082
05819	St. Johnsbury	7,938	8,409
05401	South Burlington	10,679	10,032
05156	Springfield Center(u)	5,603	5,632
.....	Springfield	10,190	10,063
05404	Winooski	6,318	7,309

Virginia

ZIP code	Place		1980	1970
*22313	Alexandria	(703)	103,217	110,927
22003	Annandale(u)	(703)	49,524	27,405
*22210	Arlington(u)	(703)	152,599	174,284
22041	Bailey's Crossroads(u)	(703)	12,564	7,295
24523	Bedford	(703)	5,991	6,011
22307	Belle Haven(u)	(703)	6,520	....
23234	Bellwood(u)	(804)	6,439	....
23234	Bensley(u)	(804)	5,299	....
24060	Blacksburg	(703)	30,638	9,384
24605	Bluefield	(703)	5,946	5,286
23235	Bon Air(u)	(804)	16,224	10,771
24201	Bristol	(703)	19,042	14,857
24416	Buena Vista	(703)	6,717	6,425
22015	Burke(u)	(703)	33,835	....
24018	Cave Spring(u)	(703)	21,682	....
22020	Centreville(u)	(703)	7,473	....
23227	Chamberlayne(u)	(804)	5,136	....
22021	Chantilly(u)	(703)	12,259	....
*22906	Charlottesville	(804)	45,010	38,880
*23320	Chesapeake	(804)	114,226	89,580
23831	Chester(u)	(804)	11,728	5,556
24073	Christiansburg	(703)	10,345	7,857
24422	Clifton Forge	(703)	5,046	5,501
24078	Collinsville(u)	(703)	7,517	6,015
23834	Colonial Heights	(804)	16,509	15,097
24426	Covington	(703)	9,063	10,060
22701	Culpeper	(703)	6,621	6,056
22191	Dale City(u)	(703)	33,127	13,857
24541	Danville	(804)	45,642	46,391
23228	Dumbarton(u)	(804)	8,149	....
22027	Dunn Loring(u)	(703)	6,077	....
23222	East Highland Park(u)	(804)	11,797	....
22030	Fairfax	(703)	19,390	22,727
*22046	Falls Church	(703)	9,515	10,772
23901	Farmville	(804)	6,067	4,331
22060	Fort Belvoir(u)	(703)	7,726	14,591
22308	Fort Hunt(u)	(703)	14,294	10,415
23801	Fort Lee(u)	(804)	9,784	12,435
22310	Franconia(u)	(703)	8,476	....
23851	Franklin	(804)	7,308	6,880
22401	Fredericksburg	(703)	15,322	14,450
22630	Front Royal	(703)	11,126	8,211
24333	Galax	(703)	6,524	6,278
23060	Glen Allen(u)	(804)	6,202	....
23062	Gloucester Point(u)	(804)	5,841	....
22306	Groveton(u)	(703)	18,860	11,761
*23660	Hampton	(804)	122,617	120,779
22801	Harrisonburg	(703)	19,671	14,605
22070	Herndon	(703)	11,449	4,301
23075	Highland Springs(u)	(804)	12,146	7,345
24019	Hollins(u)	(703)	12,187	....
23860	Hopewell	(804)	23,397	23,471
22303	Huntington(u)	(703)	5,813	5,559
23306	Hybla Valley(u)	(703)	15,533	....
22043	Idylwood(u)	(703)	11,982	....
22042	Jefferson(u)	(804)	24,342	25,432
22041	Lake Barcroft(u)	(703)	8,725	11,605
22191	Lake Ridge(u)	(703)	11,072	....
23228	Lakeside(u)	(804)	12,289	11,137
23060	Laurel(u)	(804)	10,569	....
22075	Leesburg	(703)	8,357	4,821
24450	Lexington	(703)	7,292	7,597
22312	Lincolnia(u)	(703)	10,350	10,355
22079	Lorton(u)	(703)	5,813	....
*24505	Lynchburg	(804)	66,743	54,083
24572	Madison Heights(u)	(804)	14,146	....
22110	Manassas	(703)	15,438	9,164
22110	Manassas Park	(703)	6,524	6,844
22030	Mantua(u)	(703)	6,523	6,911
24354	Marion	(703)	7,287	8,158
24112	Martinsville	(703)	18,149	19,653
22101	McLean(u)	(703)	35,664	17,698
23111	Mechanicsville(u)	(804)	9,269	5,189
22116	Merrifield(u)	(703)	7,525	....

ZIP code	Place		1980	1970
23231	Montrose(u)	(804)	5,349	....
22121	Mount Vernon(u)	(703)	24,058	....
22122	Newington(u)	(703)	8,313	....
*23607	Newport News	(804)	144,903	138,177
*23501	Norfolk	(804)	266,979	307,951
22151	North Springfield(u)	(703)	9,538	8,631
22124	Oakton(u)	(703)	19,150	....
23803	Petersburg	(804)	41,055	36,103
22043	Pimmit Hills(u)	(703)	6,658	....
23662	Poquoson	(804)	8,726	5,441
*23705	Portsmouth	(804)	104,577	110,963
24301	Pulaski	(703)	10,106	10,279
22134	Quantico Station(u)	(703)	7,121	6,213
24141	Radford	(703)	13,225	11,596
22090	Reston(u)	(703)	36,407	5,723
24641	Richlands	(703)	5,796	4,843
*23232	Richmond	(804)	219,214	249,332
*24001	Roanoke	(703)	100,427	92,115
22310	Rose Hill(u)	(703)	11,926	14,492
24153	Salem	(703)	23,958	21,982
22044	Seven Corners(u)	(703)	6,058	5,590
24592	South Boston	(804)	7,093	6,889
*22150	Springfield	(703)	21,435	11,613
24401	Staunton	(703)	21,857	24,504
22170	Sterling Park(u)	(703)	16,080	8,321
23434	Suffolk	(804)	47,621	9,858
22170	Sugarland Run(u)	(703)	6,258	....
24502	Timberlake(u)	(804)	9,697	....
23229	Tuckahoe(u)	(804)	39,868	....
22101	Tysons Corner(u)	(703)	10,065	....
22180	Vienna	(703)	15,469	17,146
24179	Vinton	(703)	8,027	6,347
*23458	Virginia Beach	(804)	262,199	172,106
22980	Waynesboro	(703)	15,329	16,707
22110	West Gate(u)	(703)	7,119	....
22152	West Springfield(u)	(703)	25,012	14,143
23185	Williamsburg	(804)	9,870	9,069
22601	Winchester	(703)	20,217	14,643
24592	Wolf Trap(u)	(804)	9,875	....
22191	Woodbridge(u)	(703)	24,004	25,412
24382	Wytheville	(703)	7,135	6,069

Washington

ZIP code	Place		1980	1970
98520	Aberdeen	(206)	18,739	18,489
98036	Alderwood Manor(u)	(206)	16,524	....
98221	Anacortes	(206)	9,013	7,701
98002	Auburn	(206)	26,417	21,653
*98009	Bellevue	(206)	73,903	61,196
98225	Bellingham	(206)	45,794	39,375
98390	Bonney Lake	(206)	5,328	2,700
98011	Bothell	(206)	7,943	5,420
	Boulevard Park(u)	(206)	8,382	....
98310	Bremerton	(206)	36,208	35,307
98178	Bryn Mawr-Skyway(u)	(206)	11,754	....
98166	Burien(u)	(206)	23,189	....
98607	Camas	(206)	5,681	5,790
98055	Cascade-Fairwood(u)	(206)	16,939	....
98531	Centralia	(206)	10,809	10,054
98532	Chehalis	(206)	6,100	5,727
99004	Cheney	(509)	7,630	6,358
99403	Clarkston	(509)	6,903	6,312
99324	College Place	(509)	5,771	4,510
98188	Des Moines	(206)	7,378	3,951
99213	Dishman(u)	(509)	10,169	9,079
	Dumas Bay-Twin Lakes(u)	(206)	14,535	....
98004	Eastgate(u)	(206)	8,341	....
	East Renton Highlands(u)	(206)	12,033	....
98801	East Wenatchee Bench(u)	(509)	11,410	2,446
98020	Edmonds	(206)	27,526	23,684
98926	Ellensburg	(509)	11,752	13,568
98022	Enumclaw	(206)	5,427	4,703
98823	Ephrata	(509)	5,359	5,255
99210	Esperance(u)	(509)	11,120	....
*98201	Everett	(206)	54,413	53,622
99011	Fairchild AFB(u)	(509)	5,353	6,754
98201	Fairmont-Intercity(u)	(206)	6,997	....
98055	Fairwood(u)	(206)	5,337	....
98466	Fircrest	(206)	5,477	5,651
98433	Fort Lewis(u)	(206)	23,761	38,054
98930	Grandview	(509)	5,615	3,605
98660	Hazel Dell(u)	(206)	15,386	....
98550	Hoquiam	(206)	9,719	10,466
98011	Inglewood(u)	(206)	12,467	....
98027	Issaquah	(206)	5,536	4,313
98033	Juanita(u)	(206)	17,232	....
98626	Kelso	(206)	11,129	10,296
98028	Kenmore(u)	(206)	7,281	....
99336	Kennewick	(509)	34,397	15,212
98031	Kent	(206)	22,961	17,711
98033	Kingsgate(u)	(206)	12,652	....
98033	Kirkland	(206)	18,785	14,970
98503	Lacey	(206)	13,940	9,696
98155	Lake Forest North(u)	(206)	7,995	....
	Lakeland North(u)	(206)	11,451	....
	Lakeland South(u)	(206)	5,225	....
	Lake Stickney(u)	(206)	6,135	....
98632	Lakes District(u)	(206)	54,533	48,195
98632	Longview	(206)	31,052	28,373
98036	Lynnwood	(206)	21,937	17,381
	Martha Lake(u)	(206)	7,022	....
98270	Marysville	(206)	5,080	4,343
98438	McChord AFB(u)	(206)	5,746	6,515
98040	Mercer Island	(206)	21,522	19,047
98837	Moses Lake	(509)	10,629	10,310
98043	Mountlake Terrace	(206)	16,534	16,600
98273	Mount Vernon	(206)	13,009	8,804
98006	Newport Hills(u)	(206)	12,245	....
98155	North City-Ridgecrest(u)	(206)	13,551	....
	North Hill(u)	(206)	10,170	....
98270	North Marysville(u)	(206)	15,159	....
98277	Oak Harbor	(206)	12,271	9,167
*98501	Olympia	(206)	27,447	23,296
99214	Opportunity(u)	(509)	21,241	16,604
98662	Orchards(u)	(206)	8,828	....
98444	Parkland(u)	(206)	23,355	21,012
99301	Pasco	(509)	18,428	13,920
98362	Port Angeles	(206)	17,311	16,367
98368	Port Townsend	(206)	6,067	5,241
	Poverty Bay(u)	(206)	8,353	....
99163	Pullman	(509)	23,579	20,509
98371	Puyallup	(206)	18,251	14,742
98052	Redmond	(206)	23,318	11,020
98055	Renton	(206)	31,031	25,878
99352	Richland	(509)	33,578	26,290
98160	Richmond Beach-Innis Arden(u)	(206)	6,700	....
98113	Richmond Highlands(u)	(206)	24,463	....
98188	Riverton(u)	(206)	14,182	....
98033	Rose Hill(u)	(206)	7,616	....
*98109	Seattle	(206)	493,846	530,831
98284	Sedro Woolley	(206)	6,110	4,598
98584	Shelton	(206)	7,629	6,515
98155	Sheridan Beach(u)	(206)	6,873	....
98201	Silver Lake-Fircrest(u)		10,299	....
98290	Snohomish	(206)	5,294	5,174
98387	Spanaway(u)	(206)	8,868	5,768
*99210	Spokane	(509)	171,300	170,516
98944	Sunnyside	(509)	9,225	6,751
*98402	Tacoma	(206)	158,501	154,407
98501	Tanglewilde-Thompson Place(u)	(206)	5,910	3,423
98948	Toppenish	(509)	6,517	5,744
99268	Town and Country(u)	(509)	5,578	6,484
98502	Tumwater	(206)	6,705	5,373
98406	University Place(u)	(206)	20,381	13,230
	Valley Ridge(u)	(206)	17,961	....
*98660	Vancouver	(206)	42,834	41,859
99037	Veradale(u)	(509)	7,256	....
99362	Walla Walla	(509)	25,618	23,619
98801	Wenatchee	(509)	17,257	16,912
98003	West Federal Way(u)	(206)	16,872	....
99301	West Pasco(u)	(509)	6,210	....
98166	White Center-Shorewood(u)	(206)	19,362	....
*98901	Yakima	(509)	49,826	45,588
98188	Zenith-Saltwater(u)	(206)	8,982	....

West Virginia (304)

ZIP code	Place	1980	1970
25801	Beckley	20,492	19,884
24701	Bluefield	16,060	15,921
26330	Bridgeport	6,604	4,777
26201	Buckhannon	6,820	7,261
*25301	Charleston	63,968	71,505
26301	Clarksburg	22,371	24,864
25064	Dunbar	9,285	9,151
26241	Elkins	8,536	8,287
26554	Fairmont	23,863	26,093
26354	Grafton	6,845	6,433
*25701	Huntington	63,684	74,315
26726	Keyser	6,569	6,586
25401	Martinsburg	13,063	14,626
26505	Morgantown	27,605	29,431
26041	Moundsville	12,419	13,560
26155	New Martinsville	7,109	6,528
25143	Nitro	8,074	8,019
25901	Oak Hill	7,120	4,738
26101	Parkersburg	39,946	44,208
25550	Point Pleasant	5,682	6,122
24740	Princeton	7,538	7,253
25177	St. Albans	12,402	14,356
25303	South Charleston	15,968	16,333
26105	Vienna	11,618	11,549
26062	Weirton	25,371	27,131
26452	Weston	6,250	7,323
26003	Wheeling	43,070	48,188
25661	Williamson	5,219	5,831

Wisconsin

ZIP code	Place		1980	1970
54301	Allouez(u)	(414)	14,882	13,753
54409	Antigo	(715)	8,653	9,005
54911	Appleton	(414)	58,913	56,377
54806	Ashland	(715)	9,115	9,615

ZIP code	Place		1980	1970
54304	Ashwaubenon	(414)	14,486	9,323
53913	Baraboo	(608)	8,081	7,931
53916	Beaver Dam	(414)	14,149	14,265
53511	Beloit	(608)	35,207	35,729
53511	Beloit North(u)	(608)	5,457	
54923	Berlin	(414)	5,478	5,338
53005	Brookfield	(414)	34,035	31,761
53209	Brown Deer	(414)	12,921	12,582
53105	Burlington	(414)	8,385	7,479
53012	Cedarburg	(414)	9,005	7,697
54729	Chippewa Falls	(715)	11,845	12,351
53110	Cudahy	(414)	19,547	22,078
53115	Delavan	(414)	5,684	5,526
54115	De Pere	(414)	14,892	13,309
54701	Eau Claire	(715)	51,509	44,619
53122	Elm Grove	(414)	6,735	7,201
54935	Fond Du Lac	(414)	35,863	35,515
53538	Fort Atkinson	(414)	9,785	9,164
53217	Fox Point	(414)	7,649	7,939
53132	Franklin	(414)	16,871	12,247
53022	Germantown	(414)	10,729	6,974
53209	Glendale	(414)	13,882	13,426
53024	Grafton	(414)	8,381	5,998
*54305	Green Bay	(414)	87,899	87,809
53129	Greendale	(414)	16,928	15,089
53220	Greenfield	(414)	31,353	24,424
53130	Hales Corners	(414)	7,110	7,771
53027	Hartford	(414)	7,159	6,499
53029	Hartland	(414)	5,559	2,763
54303	Howard	(414)	8,240	4,911
54016	Hudson	(715)	5,434	5,049
53545	Janesville	(608)	51,071	46,426
53549	Jefferson	(414)	5,647	5,429
54130	Kaukauna	(414)	11,310	11,308
53140	Kenosha	(414)	77,685	78,805
54136	Kimberly	(414)	5,881	6,131
54601	La Crosse	(608)	48,347	50,286
53147	Lake Geneva	(414)	5,612	4,890
54140	Little Chute	(414)	7,907	5,522
*53701	Madison	(608)	170,616	171,809
54220	Manitowoc	(414)	32,547	33,430
54143	Marinette	(715)	11,965	12,696
54449	Marshfield	(715)	18,290	15,619
54952	Menasha	(414)	14,728	14,836
53051	Menomonee Falls	(414)	27,845	31,697
54751	Menomonie	(715)	12,769	11,112
53092	Mequon	(414)	16,193	12,150
54452	Merrill	(715)	9,578	9,502
53562	Middleton	(608)	11,851	8,246
*53203	Milwaukee	(414)	636,297	717,372
53716	Monona	(608)	8,809	10,420
53566	Monroe	(608)	10,027	8,654
53150	Muskego	(414)	15,277	11,573
54956	Neenah	(414)	23,272	22,902
53151	New Berlin	(414)	30,529	26,910
54961	New London	(414)	6,210	5,801
53154	Oak Creek	(414)	16,932	13,928
53066	Oconomowoc	(414)	9,909	8,741
54650	Onalaska	(608)	9,249	4,909
54901	Oshkosh	(414)	49,678	53,082
53818	Platteville	(608)	9,580	9,599
54467	Plover	(715)	5,310	
53073	Plymouth	(414)	6,027	5,810
53901	Portage	(608)	7,896	7,821
53074	Port Washington	(414)	8,612	8,752
53821	Prairie du Chien	(608)	5,859	5,540
*53401	Racine	(414)	85,725	95,162
53959	Reedsburg	(608)	5,038	4,585
54501	Rhinelander	(715)	7,873	8,218
54868	Rice Lake	(715)	7,691	7,278
54971	Ripon	(414)	7,111	7,053
54022	River Falls	(715)	9,019	7,238
53207	St. Francis	(414)	10,095	10,489
54166	Shawano	(715)	7,013	6,488
53081	Sheboygan	(414)	48,085	48,484
53085	Sheboygan Falls	(414)	5,253	4,771
53211	Shorewood	(414)	14,327	15,576
53172	South Milwaukee	(414)	21,069	23,297
54656	Sparta	(608)	6,934	6,258
54481	Stevens Point	(715)	22,970	23,479
53589	Stoughton	(608)	7,589	6,096
54235	Sturgeon Bay	(414)	8,847	6,776
53590	Sun Prairie	(608)	12,931	9,935
54880	Superior	(715)	29,571	32,237
54660	Tomah	(608)	7,204	5,647
54241	Two Rivers	(414)	13,354	13,732
53094	Watertown	(414)	18,113	15,683
53186	Waukesha	(414)	50,365	39,695
53963	Waupun	(414)	8,132	7,946
54401	Wausau	(715)	32,426	32,806
54401	Wausau West Rib Mt.(u)	(715)	6,005	
53213	Wauwatosa	(414)	51,308	58,676
53214	West Allis	(414)	63,982	71,649
53095	West Bend	(414)	21,484	16,555
54476	Weston(u)	(715)	8,775	3,375
53217	Whitefish Bay	(414)	14,930	17,402
53190	Whitewater	(414)	11,520	12,038
54494	Wisconsin Rapids	(715)	17,995	18,587

Wyoming (307)

82601	Casper		51,016	39,361
82001	Cheyenne		47,283	41,254
82414	Cody		6,599	5,161
82633	Douglas		6,030	2,677
82930	Evanston		6,265	4,462
82716	Gillette		12,134	7,194
82335	Green River		12,807	4,196
82520	Lander		9,126	7,125
82070	Laramie		24,410	23,143
82435	Powell		5,310	4,807
82301	Rawlins		11,547	7,855
82501	Riverton		9,562	7,995
82901	Rock Springs		19,458	11,657
82801	Sheridan		15,146	10,856
82240	Torrington		5,441	4,237
02201	Wheatland		5,016	2,400
82401	Worland		6,391	5,055

Census and Areas of Counties and States

Source: U.S. Bureau of the Census
With names of county seats or court houses

Population figures listed below are final counts in the 1980 census, conducted on Apr. 1, 1980, and updated in March 1984, for all counties and states. Figures are subject to change pending the outcome of various lawsuits dealing with the census counts.

Alabama

(67 counties, 50,767 sq. mi. land; pop., 3,894,046)

County	Pop.	County seat or court house	Land area sq. mi.
Autauga	32,259	Prattville	597
Baldwin	78,440	Bay Minette	1,589
Barbour	24,756	Clayton	884
Bibb	15,723	Centreville	625
Blount	36,459	Oneonta	643
Bullock	10,596	Union Springs	625
Butler	21,680	Greenville	779
Calhoun	116,936	Anniston	611
Chambers	39,191	Lafayette	596
Cherokee	18,760	Centre	553
Chilton	30,612	Clanton	695
Choctaw	16,839	Butler	909
Clarke	27,702	Grove Hill	1,230
Clay	13,703	Ashland	605
Cleburne	12,595	Heflin	561
Coffee	38,533	Elba	680
Colbert	54,519	Tuscumbia	589
Conecuh	15,884	Evergreen	854
Coosa	11,377	Rockford	657
Covington	36,850	Andalusia	1,038
Crenshaw	14,110	Luverne	611
Cullman	61,642	Cullman	738
Dale	47,821	Ozark	561
Dallas	53,981	Selma	975
De Kalb	53,658	Fort Payne	778
Elmore	43,390	Wetumpka	622
Escambia	38,392	Brewton	951
Etowah	103,057	Gadsden	542
Fayette	18,809	Fayette	630
Franklin	28,350	Russellville	643
Geneva	24,253	Geneva	578
Greene	11,021	Eutaw	631
Hale	15,604	Greensboro	661
Henry	15,302	Abbeville	557
Houston	74,632	Dothan	577
Jackson	51,407	Scottsboro	1,070
Jefferson	671,392	Birmingham	1,119
Lamar	16,453	Vernon	605
Lauderdale	80,504	Florence	661
Lawrence	30,170	Moulton	693
Lee	76,283	Opelika	609
Limestone	46,005	Athens	559
Lowndes	13,253	Hayneville	714
Macon	26,829	Tuskegee	614
Madison	196,966	Huntsville	806
Marengo	25,047	Linden	982
Marion	30,041	Hamilton	743
Marshall	65,622	Guntersville	567
Mobile	364,379	Mobile	1,238
Monroe	22,651	Monroeville	1,019
Montgomery	197,038	Montgomery	793
Morgan	90,231	Decatur	575
Perry	15,012	Marion	718
Pickens	21,481	Carrollton	890
Pike	28,050	Troy	672
Randolph	20,075	Wedowee	584

County	Pop.	County Seat or court house	Land area sq. mi.
Russell	47,356	Phenix City	634
St. Clair	41,205	Ashville & Pell City	646
Shelby	66,298	Columbiana	800
Sumter	16,908	Livingston	907
Talladega	73,826	Talladega	753
Tallapoosa	38,766	Dadeville	701
Tuscaloosa	137,473	Tuscaloosa	1,336
Walker	68,660	Jasper	804
Washington	16,821	Chatom	1,081
Wilcox	14,755	Camden	883
Winston	21,953	Double Springs	613

Alaska

(23 divisions, 570,833 sq. mi. land; pop., 401,851)

Census area	Pop.	Land area sq. mi.
Aleutian Islands	7,768	10,890
Anchorage Borough	173,017	1,732

Census division	Pop.	Land area sq. mi.
Bethel	10,999	36,104
Bristol Bay Borough	1,094	531
Dillingham	4,616	46,042
Fairbanks North Star Borough	53,983	7,404
Haines Borough	1,680	2,374
Juneau Borough	19,528	2,626
Kenai Peninsula Borough	25,282	16,056
Ketchikan Gateway Borough	11,316	1,242
Kobuk	4,831	31,593
Kodiak Island Borough	9,939	4,796
Matanuska-Susitna Borough	17,766	24,502
Nome	6,537	23,871
North Slope Borough	4,199	90,955
Prince of Wales-Outer Ketchikan	3,822	7,660
Sitka Borough	7,803	2,938
Skagway-Yakutat-Angoon	3,478	13,239
Southeast Fairbanks	5,770	24,169
Valdez-Cordova	8,348	39,229
Wade Hampton	4,665	17,816
Wrangell-Petersburg	6,167	5,965
Yukon-Koyukuk	7,873	159,099

Arizona

(14 counties, 113,508 sq. mi. land; pop. 2,718,425)

County	Pop.	County seat or court house	Land area sq. mi.
Apache	52,083	Saint Johns	11,211
Cochise	86,717	Bisbee	6,218
Coconino	74,947	Flagstaff	18,608
Gila	37,080	Globe	4,752
Graham	22,862	Safford	4,630
Greenlee	11,406	Clifton	1,837
Maricopa	1,509,262	Phoenix	9,127
Mohave	55,693	Kingman	13,285
Navajo	67,709	Holbrook	9,955
Pima	531,263	Tucson	9,187
Pinal	90,918	Florence	5,343
Santa Cruz	20,459	Nogales	1,238
Yavapai	68,145	Prescott	8,123
Yuma	90,554	Yuma	9,994

Arkansas

(75 counties, 52,078 sq. mi. land; pop. 2,286,414)

County	Pop.	County seat or court house	Land area sq. mi.
Arkansas	24,175	DeWitt & Stuttgart	1,006
Ashley	26,538	Hamburg	934
Baxter	27,409	Mountain Home	546
Benton	78,115	Bentonville	843
Boone	26,067	Harrison	584
Bradley	13,803	Warren	654
Calhoun	6,079	Hampton	628
Carroll	16,203	Berryville and Eureka Sp.	634
Chicot	17,793	Lake Village	649
Clark	23,326	Arkadelphia	867
Clay	20,616	Corning; Piggott	641
Cleburne	16,909	Heber Springs	551
Cleveland	7,868	Rison	599
Columbia	26,644	Magnolia	767
Conway	19,505	Morrilton	558
Craighead	63,218	Jonesboro and Lake City	713
Crawford	36,892	Van Buren	594
Crittenden	49,097	Marion	599
Cross	20,434	Wynne	622
Dallas	10,515	Fordyce	668
Desha	19,760	Arkansas City	746
Drew	17,910	Monticello	831
Faulkner	46,192	Conway	645
Franklin	14,705	Charleston and Ozark	609
Fulton	9,975	Salem	616
Garland	69,916	Hot Spgs. Nat'l Pk.	657
Grant	13,008	Sheridan	633
Greene	30,744	Paragould	579
Hempstead	23,635	Hope	725
Hot Spring	26,819	Malvern	615
Howard	13,459	Nashville	574
Independence	30,147	Batesville	763
Izard	10,768	Melbourne	581
Jackson	21,646	Newport	633
Jefferson	90,718	Pine Bluff	882
Johnson	17,423	Clarksville	676
Lafayette	10,213	Lewisville	518
Lawrence	18,447	Walnut Ridge	589
Lee	15,539	Marianna	602
Lincoln	13,369	Star City	562
Little River	13,952	Ashdown	516
Logan	20,144	Booneville & Paris	717
Lonoke	34,518	Lonoke	783
Madison	11,373	Huntsville	837
Marion	11,334	Yellville	587
Miller	37,766	Texarkana	619
Mississippi	59,517	Blytheville and Osceola	896
Monroe	14,052	Clarendon	609
Montgomery	7,771	Mount Ida	774
Nevada	11,097	Prescott	620
Newton	7,756	Jasper	823
Ouachita	30,541	Camden	737
Perry	7,266	Perryville	550
Phillips	34,772	Helena	685
Pike	10,373	Murfreesboro	598
Poinsett	27,032	Harrisburg	762
Polk	17,007	Mena	860
Pope	39,003	Russellville	820
Prairie	10,140	Des Arc and De Valls Bluff	656
Pulaski	340,597	Little Rock	767
Randolph	16,834	Pocahontas	656
St. Francis	30,858	Forrest City	638
Saline	53,156	Benton	725
Scott	9,685	Waldron	896
Searcy	8,847	Marshall	668
Sebastian	94,930	Fort Smith; Greenwood	535
Sevier	14,060	De Queen	560
Sharp	14,607	Ash Flat	606
Stone	9,022	Mountain View	606
Union	49,988	El Dorado	1,053
Van Buren	13,357	Clinton	709
Washington	99,735	Fayetteville	951
White	50,835	Searcy	1,040
Woodruff	11,222	Augusta	592
Yell	17,026	Danville and Dardanelle	930

California

(58 counties, 156,299 sq. mi. land; pop. 23,668,049)

County	Pop.	County seat or court house	Land area sq. mi.
Alameda	1,105,379	Oakland	736
Alpine	1,097	Markleeville	738
Amador	19,314	Jackson	589
Butte	143,851	Oroville	1,646
Calaveras	20,710	San Andreas	1,021
Colusa	12,791	Colusa	1,152
Contra Costa	656,331	Martinez	730
Del Norte	18,217	Crescent City	1,007
El Dorado	85,812	Placerville	1,715
Fresno	515,013	Fresno	5,978
Glenn	21,350	Willows	1,319
Humboldt	108,525	Eureka	3,579
Imperial	92,110	El Centro	4,173
Inyo	17,895	Independence	10,223
Kern	403,089	Bakersfield	8,130
Kings	73,738	Hanford	1,392
Lake	36,366	Lakeport	1,262
Lassen	21,661	Susanville	4,553
Los Angeles	7,477,421	Los Angeles	4,070
Madera	63,116	Madera	2,145
Marin	222,592	San Rafael	523
Mariposa	11,108	Mariposa	1,456
Mendocino	66,738	Ukiah	3,512
Merced	134,558	Merced	1,944
Modoc	8,610	Alturas	4,064
Mono	8,577	Bridgeport	3,018
Monterey	290,444	Salinas	3,303
Napa	99,199	Napa	744
Nevada	51,645	Nevada City	960
Orange	1,932,921	Santa Ana	798
Placer	117,247	Auburn	1,416
Plumas	17,340	Quincy	2,573
Riverside	663,199	Riverside	7,214
Sacramento	783,381	Sacramento	971
San Benito	25,005	Hollister	1,388
San Bernardino	893,157	San Bernardino	20,064
San Diego	1,861,846	San Diego	4,212
San Francisco	678,974	San Francisco	47
San Joaquin	347,342	Stockton	1,415
San Luis Obispo	155,345	San Luis Obispo	3,308
San Mateo	588,164	Redwood City	447
Santa Barbara	298,660	Santa Barbara	2,748
Santa Clara	1,295,071	San Jose	1,293
Santa Cruz	188,141	Santa Cruz	446
Shasta	115,715	Redding	3,786
Sierra	3,073	Downieville	959
Siskiyou	39,732	Yreka	6,281
Solano	235,203	Fairfield	834
Sonoma	299,827	Santa Rosa	1,604
Stanislaus	265,902	Modesto	1,506
Sutter	52,246	Yuba City	602
Tehama	38,888	Red Bluff	2,953
Trinity	11,858	Weaverville	3,190

County	Pop.	County seat or court house	Land area sq. mi.
Tulare	245,751	Visalia	4,808
Tuolumne	33,920	Sonora	2,234
Ventura	529,899	Ventura	1,862
Yolo	113,374	Woodland	1,014
Yuba	49,733	Marysville	640

Colorado
(63 counties, 103,595 sq. mi. land; pop. 2,889,735)

County	Pop.	County seat	Land area sq. mi.
Adams	245,944	Brighton	1,235
Alamosa	11,799	Alamosa	719
Arapahoe	293,300	Littleton	800
Archuleta	3,664	Pagosa Springs	1,353
Baca	5,419	Springfield	2,554
Bent	5,945	Las Animas	1,517
Boulder	189,625	Boulder	742
Chaffee	13,227	Salida	1,008
Cheyenne	2,153	Cheyenne Wells	1,783
Clear Creek	7,308	Georgetown	396
Conejos	7,794	Conejos	1,284
Costilla	3,071	San Luis	1,227
Crowley	2,988	Ordway	790
Custer	1,528	Westcliffe	740
Delta	21,225	Delta	1,141
Denver	492,365	Denver	111
Dolores	1,658	Dove Creek	1,064
Douglas	25,153	Castle Rock	841
Eagle	13,171	Eagle	1,690
Elbert	6,850	Kiowa	1,851
El Paso	309,424	Colorado Springs	2,129
Fremont	28,676	Canon City	1,538
Garfield	22,514	Glenwood Springs	2,952
Gilpin	2,441	Central City	149
Grand	7,475	Hot Sulphur Springs	1,854
Gunnison	10,689	Gunnison	3,238
Hinsdale	408	Lake City	1,115
Huerfano	6,440	Walsenburg	1,584
Jackson	1,863	Walden	1,614
Jefferson	371,741	Golden	768
Kiowa	1,936	Eads	1,758
Kit Carson	7,599	Burlington	2,160
Lake	8,830	Leadville	379
La Plata	27,195	Durango	1,692
Larimer	149,184	Fort Collins	2,604
Las Animas	14,897	Trinidad	4,771
Lincoln	4,663	Hugo	2,586
Logan	19,800	Sterling	1,818
Mesa	81,530	Grand Junction	3,309
Mineral	804	Creede	877
Moffat	13,133	Craig	4,732
Montezuma	16,510	Cortez	2,038
Montrose	24,352	Montrose	2,240
Morgan	22,513	Fort Morgan	1,276
Otero	22,567	LaJunta	1,247
Ouray	1,925	Ouray	542
Park	5,333	Fairplay	2,192
Phillips	4,542	Holyoke	688
Pitkin	10,338	Aspen	968
Prowers	13,070	Lamar	1,629
Pueblo	125,972	Pueblo	2,377
Rio Blanco	6,255	Meeker	3,222
Rio Grande	10,511	Del Norte	913
Routt	13,404	Steamboat Springs	2,367
Saguache	3,935	Saguache	3,167
San Juan	833	Silverton	388 *
San Miguel	3,192	Telluride	1,287
Sedgwick	3,266	Julesburg	540
Summit	8,848	Breckenridge	607
Teller	8,034	Cripple Creek	559
Washington	5,304	Akron	2,520
Weld	123,438	Greeley	3,990
Yuma	9,682	Wray	2,365

Connecticut
(8 counties, 4,872 sq. mi. land; pop. 3,107,564)

County	Pop.	County seat	Land area sq. mi.
Fairfield	807,143	Bridgeport	632
Hartford	807,766	Hartford	739
Litchfield	156,769	Litchfield	921
Middlesex	129,017	Middletown	373
New Haven	761,325	New Haven	610
New London	238,409	Norwich	669
Tolland	114,823	Rockville	412
Windham	92,312	Putnam	515

Delaware
(3 counties, 1,932 sq. mi. land; pop. 594,338)

County	Pop.	County seat	Land area sq. mi.
Kent	98,219	Dover	595
New Castle	399,002	Wilmington	396
Sussex	98,004	Georgetown	942

District of Columbia
(63 sq. mi. land; pop. 638,432)

Florida
(67 counties, 54,153 sq. mi. land; pop. 9,747,197)

County	Pop.	County seat	Land area sq. mi.
Alachua	151,369	Gainesville	901
Baker	15,289	Macclenny	585
Bay	97,740	Panama City	758
Bradford	20,023	Starke	293
Brevard	272,959	Titusville	995
Broward	1,018,257	Fort Lauderdale	1,211
Calhoun	9,294	Blountstown	568
Charlotte	59,115	Punta Gorda	690
Citrus	54,703	Inverness	629
Clay	67,052	Green Cove Spgs	592
Collier	85,791	Naples	1,994
Columbia	35,399	Lake City	796
Dade	1,625,724	Miami	1,955
De Soto	19,039	Arcadia	636
Dixie	7,751	Cross City	701
Duval	570,981	Jacksonville	776
Escambia	233,794	Pensacola	660
Flagler	10,913	Bunnell	491
Franklin	7,661	Apalachicola	545
Gadsden	41,674	Quincy	518
Gilchrist	5,767	Trenton	354
Glades	5,992	Moore Haven	763
Gulf	10,658	Port St. Joe	559
Hamilton	8,761	Jasper	517
Hardee	20,357	Wauchula	637
Hendry	18,599	La Belle	1,163
Hernando	44,469	Brooksville	477
Highlands	47,526	Sebring	1,029
Hillsborough	646,960	Tampa	1,053
Holmes	14,723	Bonifay	488
Indian River	59,896	Vero Beach	497
Jackson	39,154	Marianna	942
Jefferson	10,703	Monticello	609
Lafayette	4,035	Mayo	545
Lake	104,870	Tavares	954
Lee	205,266	Fort Myers	803
Leon	148,655	Tallahassee	676
Levy	19,870	Bronson	1,100
Liberty	4,260	Bristol	837
Madison	14,894	Madison	710
Manatee	148,445	Bradenton	747
Marion	122,488	Ocala	1,610
Martin	64,014	Stuart	555
Monroe	63,098	Key West	1,034
Nassau	32,894	Fernandina Beach	649
Okaloosa	109,920	Crestview	936
Okeechobee	20,264	Okeechobee	770
Orange	470,865	Orlando	910
Osceola	49,287	Kissimmee	1,350
Palm Beach	576,758	West Palm Beach	1,993
Pasco	193,661	Dade City	738
Pinellas	728,409	Clearwater	280
Polk	321,652	Bartow	1,823
Putnam	50,549	Palatka	733
St. Johns	51,303	Saint Augustine	617
St. Lucie	87,182	Fort Pierce	581
Santa Rosa	55,988	Milton	1,024
Sarasota	202,251	Sarasota	573
Seminole	179,752	Sanford	298
Sumter	24,272	Bushnell	561
Suwannee	22,287	Live Oak	690
Taylor	16,532	Perry	1,058
Union	10,166	Lake Butler	246
Volusia	258,762	De Land	1,113
Wakulla	10,887	Crawfordville	601
Walton	21,300	De Funiak Springs	1,066
Washington	14,509	Chipley	590

Georgia
(159 counties, 58,056 sq. mi. land; pop. 5,462,892)

County	Pop.	County seat	Land area sq. mi.
Appling	15,565	Baxley	510
Atkinson	6,141	Pearson	344
Bacon	9,379	Alma	286
Baker	3,808	Newton	347
Baldwin	34,686	Milledgeville	257
Banks	8,702	Homer	234
Barrow	21,293	Winder	163
Bartow	40,760	Cartersville	456
Ben Hill	16,000	Fitzgerald	254
Berrien	13,525	Nashville	456
Bibb	151,085	Macon	253
Bleckley	10,767	Cochran	219
Brantley	8,701	Nahunta	445
Brooks	15,255	Quitman	491
Bryan	10,175	Pembroke	441
Bulloch	35,785	Statesboro	678
Burke	19,349	Waynesboro	833
Butts	13,665	Jackson	187
Calhoun	5,717	Morgan	284
Camden	13,371	Woodbine	649
Candler	7,518	Metter	248
Carroll	56,346	Carrollton	501
Catoosa	36,991	Ringgold	162
Charlton	7,343	Folkston	780
Chatham	202,226	Savannah	443
Chattahoochee	21,732	Cusseta	250
Chattooga	21,856	Summerville	313
Cherokee	51,699	Canton	424
Clarke	74,498	Athens	122
Clay	3,553	Fort Gaines	196
Clayton	150,357	Jonesboro	148
Clinch	6,660	Homerville	821
Cobb	297,694	Marietta	343
Coffee	26,894	Douglas	602
Colquitt	35,376	Moultrie	557

County	Pop.	County seat or court house	Land area sq. mi.
Columbia	40,118	Appling	290
Cook	13,490	Adel	233
Coweta	39,268	Newnan	444
Crawford	7,684	Knoxville	328
Crisp	19,489	Cordele	275
Dade	12,318	Trenton	176
Dawson	4,774	Dawsonville	210
Decatur	25,495	Bainbridge	586
De Kalb	483,024	Decatur	270
Dodge	16,955	Eastman	504
Dooly	10,826	Vienna	397
Dougherty	100,710	Albany	330
Douglas	54,573	Douglasville	203
Early	13,158	Blakely	516
Echols	2,297	Statenville	421
Effingham	18,327	Springfield	482
Elbert	18,758	Elberton	367
Emanuel	20,795	Swainsboro	688
Evans	8,428	Claxton	186
Fannin	14,748	Blue Ridge	384
Fayette	29,043	Fayetteville	199
Floyd	79,800	Rome	519
Forsyth	27,958	Cumming	226
Franklin	15,185	Carnesville	264
Fulton	589,904	Atlanta	534
Gilmer	11,110	Ellijay	427
Glascock	2,382	Gibson	144
Glynn	54,981	Brunswick	412
Gordon	30,070	Calhoun	355
Grady	19,845	Cairo	459
Greene	11,391	Greensboro	389
Gwinnett	166,808	Lawrenceville	435
Habersham	25,020	Clarkesville	278
Hall	75,649	Gainesville	379
Hancock	9,466	Sparta	470
Haralson	18,422	Buchanan	283
Harris	15,464	Hamilton	464
Hart	18,585	Hartwell	230
Heard	6,520	Franklin	292
Henry	36,309	McDonough	321
Houston	77,605	Perry	380
Irwin	8,988	Ocilla	362
Jackson	25,343	Jefferson	342
Jasper	7,553	Monticello	371
Jeff Davis	11,473	Hazlehurst	335
Jefferson	18,403	Louisville	529
Jenkins	8,841	Millen	353
Johnson	8,660	Wrightsville	306
Jones	16,579	Gray	394
Lamar	12,215	Barnesville	186
Lanier	5,654	Lakeland	194
Laurens	36,990	Dublin	816
Lee	11,684	Leesburg	358
Liberty	37,583	Hinesville	517
Lincoln	6,949	Lincolnton	196
Long	4,524	Ludowici	402
Lowndes	67,972	Valdosta	507
Lumpkin	10,762	Dahlonega	287
McDuffie	18,546	Thomson	256
McIntosh	8,046	Darien	425
Macon	14,003	Oglethorpe	404
Madison	17,747	Danielsville	285
Marion	5,297	Buena Vista	366
Meriwether	21,229	Greenville	506
Miller	7,038	Colquitt	284
Mitchell	21,114	Camilla	512
Monroe	14,610	Forsyth	397
Montgomery	7,011	Mount Vernon	244
Morgan	11,572	Madison	349
Murray	19,685	Chatsworth	345
Muscogee	170,108	Columbus	218
Newton	34,489	Covington	277
Oconee	12,427	Watkinsville	186
Oglethorpe	8,929	Lexington	442
Paulding	26,042	Dallas	312
Peach	19,151	Fort Valley	152
Pickens	11,652	Jasper	232
Pierce	11,897	Blackshear	344
Pike	8,937	Zebulon	219
Polk	32,382	Cedartown	311
Pulaski	8,950	Hawkinsville	249
Putnam	10,295	Eatonton	344
Quitman	2,357	Georgetown	146
Rabun	10,466	Clayton	370
Randolph	9,599	Cuthbert	431
Richmond	181,629	Augusta	326
Rockdale	36,747	Conyers	132
Schley	3,433	Ellaville	169
Screven	14,043	Sylvania	655
Seminole	9,057	Donalsonville	225
Spalding	47,899	Griffin	199
Stephens	21,761	Toccoa	177
Stewart	5,896	Lumpkin	452
Sumter	29,360	Americus	489
Talbot	6,536	Talbotton	395
Taliaferro	2,032	Crawfordville	196
Tattnall	18,134	Reidsville	484
Taylor	7,902	Butler	382
Telfair	11,445	McRae	444
Terrell	12,017	Dawson	337
Thomas	38,098	Thomasville	551
Tift	32,862	Tifton	268
Toombs	22,592	Lyons	371
Towns	5,638	Hiawassee	165
Treutlen	6,087	Soperton	202
Troup	50,003	La Grange	414
Turner	9,510	Ashburn	289
Twiggs	9,354	Jeffersonville	362
Union	9,390	Blairsville	320
Upson	25,998	Thomaston	326
Walker	56,470	La Fayette	446
Walton	31,211	Monroe	330
Ware	37,180	Waycross	907
Warren	6,583	Warrenton	286
Washington	18,842	Sandersville	684
Wayne	20,750	Jesup	647
Webster	2,341	Preston	210
Wheeler	5,155	Alamo	299
White	10,120	Cleveland	242
Whitfield	65,775	Dalton	291
Wilcox	7,682	Abbeville	382
Wilkes	10,951	Washington	470
Wilkinson	10,368	Irwinton	451
Worth	18,064	Sylvester	575

Hawaii
(4 counties, 6,425 sq. mi. land; pop. 964,691)

County	Pop.	County seat	Land area
Hawaii	92,053	Hilo	4,034
Honolulu	762,874	Honolulu	596
Kauai	39,082	Lihue	620
Maui*	70,991	Wailuku	1,175

*Includes population of Kalawao County (146).

Idaho
(44 counties, 82,412 sq. mi. land; pop. 944,127)

County	Pop.	County seat	Land area
Ada	173,125	Boise	1,052
Adams	3,347	Council	1,362
Bannock	65,421	Pocatello	1,112
Bear Lake	6,931	Paris	990
Benewah	8,292	Saint Maries	784
Bingham	36,489	Blackfoot	2,096
Blaine	9,841	Hailey	2,634
Boise	2,999	Idaho City	1,901
Bonner	24,163	Sandpoint	1,726
Bonneville	65,980	Idaho Falls	1,840
Boundary	7,289	Bonners Ferry	1,268
Butte	3,342	Arco	2,236
Camas	818	Fairfield	1,071
Canyon	83,756	Caldwell	584
Caribou	8,695	Soda Springs	1,763
Cassia	19,427	Burley	2,560
Clark	798	Dubois	1,763
Clearwater	10,390	Orofino	2,236
Custer	3,385	Challis	4,927
Elmore	21,565	Mountain Home	3,071
Franklin	8,895	Preston	664
Fremont	10,813	Saint Anthony	1,852
Gem	11,972	Emmett	558
Gooding	11,874	Gooding	728
Idaho	14,769	Grangeville	8,497
Jefferson	15,304	Rigby	1,093
Jerome	14,840	Jerome	601
Kootenai	59,770	Coeur d'Alene	1,240
Latah	28,749	Moscow	1,077
Lemhi	7,460	Salmon	4,564
Lewis	4,118	Nezperce	478
Lincoln	3,436	Shoshone	1,205
Madison	19,480	Rexberg	468
Minidoka	19,718	Rupert	757
Nez Perce	33,220	Lewiston	845
Oneida	3,258	Malad City	1,200
Owyhee	8,272	Murphy	7,643
Payette	15,825	Payette	405
Power	6,844	American Falls	1,403
Shoshone	19,226	Wallace	2,641
Teton	2,897	Driggs	448
Twin Falls	52,927	Twin Falls	1,944
Valley	5,604	Cascade	3,670
Washington	8,803	Weiser	1,454

Illinois
(102 counties, 55,645 sq. mi. land; pop. 11,427,409)

County	Pop.	County seat	Land area
Adams	71,622	Quincy	852
Alexander	12,264	Cairo	236
Bond	16,224	Greenville	377
Boone	28,630	Belvidere	282
Brown	5,411	Mount Sterling	306
Bureau	39,114	Princeton	869
Calhoun	5,867	Hardin	254
Carroll	18,779	Mount Carroll	444
Cass	15,084	Virginia	376
Champaign	168,392	Urbana	998
Christian	36,446	Taylorville	710
Clark	16,913	Marshall	501
Clay	15,283	Louisville	468
Clinton	32,617	Carlyle	474
Coles	52,992	Charleston	508

County	Pop.	County seat or court house	Land area sq. mi.
Cook	5,253,628	Chicago	958
Crawford	20,818	Robinson	446
Cumberland	11,062	Toledo	346
De Kalb	74,628	Sycamore	634
De Witt	18,108	Clinton	397
Douglas	19,774	Tuscola	417
Du Page	658,858	Wheaton	337
Edgar	21,725	Paris	623
Edwards	7,961	Albion	223
Effingham	30,944	Effingham	478
Fayette	22,167	Vandalia	709
Ford	15,265	Paxton	486
Franklin	43,201	Benton	414
Fulton	43,687	Lewiston	871
Gallatin	7,590	Shawneetown	325
Greene	16,661	Carrollton	543
Grundy	30,582	Morris	423
Hamilton	9,172	McLeansboro	436
Hancock	23,877	Carthage	796
Hardin	5,383	Elizabethtown	181
Henderson	9,114	Oquawka	373
Henry	57,968	Cambridge	824
Iroquois	32,976	Watseka	1,118
Jackson	61,649	Murphysboro	590
Jasper	11,318	Newton	496
Jefferson	36,558	Mount Vernon	570
Jersey	20,538	Jerseyville	373
Jo Daviess	23,520	Galena	603
Johnson	9,624	Vienna	346
Kane	278,405	Geneva	524
Kankakee	102,926	Kankakee	679
Kendall	37,202	Yorkville	322
Knox	61,607	Galesburg	720
Lake	440,388	Waukegan	454
La Salle	109,139	Ottawa	1,139
Lawrence	17,807	Lawrenceville	374
Lee	36,328	Dixon	725
Livingston	41,381	Pontiac	1,046
Logan	31,802	Lincoln	619
McDonough	37,236	Macomb	590
McHenry	147,724	Woodstock	606
McLean	119,149	Bloomington	1,185
Macon	131,375	Decatur	581
Macoupin	49,384	Carlinville	865
Madison	247,661	Edwardsville	728
Marion	43,523	Salem	573
Marshall	14,479	Lacon	388
Mason	19,492	Havana	536
Massac	14,990	Metropolis	241
Menard	11,700	Petersburg	315
Mercer	19,286	Aledo	559
Monroe	20,117	Waterloo	388
Montgomery	31,686	Hillsboro	705
Morgan	37,502	Jacksonville	568
Moultrie	14,546	Sullivan	325
Ogle	46,338	Oregon	759
Peoria	200,466	Peoria	621
Perry	21,714	Pinckneyville	443
Piatt	16,581	Monticello	439
Pike	18,896	Pittsfield	830
Pope	4,404	Golconda	374
Pulaski	8,840	Mound City	203
Putnam	6,085	Hennepin	160
Randolph	35,566	Chester	583
Richland	17,587	Olney	360
Rock Island	166,759	Rock Island	423
St. Clair	265,469	Belleville	672
Saline	27,360	Harrisburg	385
Sangamon	176,070	Springfield	866
Schuyler	8,365	Rushville	436
Scott	6,142	Winchester	251
Shelby	23,923	Shelbyville	747
Stark	7,389	Toulon	288
Stephenson	49,536	Freeport	564
Tazewell	132,078	Pekin	650
Union	16,851	Jonesboro	414
Vermilion	95,222	Danville	900
Wabash	13,713	Mt. Carmel	224
Warren	21,943	Monmouth	543
Washington	15,472	Nashville	563
Wayne	18,059	Fairfield	715
White	17,864	Carmi	497
Whiteside	65,970	Morrison	682
Will	324,460	Joliet	844
Williamson	56,538	Marion	427
Winnebago	250,884	Rockford	516
Woodford	33,320	Eureka	527

Indiana
(92 counties, 35,932 sq. mi. land; pop. 5,490,212)

County	Pop.	County seat	Land area
Adams	29,619	Decatur	340
Allen	294,335	Fort Wayne	659
Bartholomew	65,088	Columbus	409
Benton	10,218	Fowler	407
Blackford	15,570	Hartford City	166
Boone	36,446	Lebanon	423
Brown	12,377	Nashville	312
Carroll	19,722	Delphi	372
Cass	40,936	Logansport	414
Clark	88,838	Jeffersonville	376
Clay	24,862	Brazil	360
Clinton	31,545	Frankfort	405
Crawford	9,820	English	307
Daviess	27,836	Washington	432
Dearborn	34,291	Lawrenceburg	307
Decatur	23,841	Greensburg	373
DeKalb	33,606	Auburn	364
Delaware	128,587	Muncie	392
Dubois	34,238	Jasper	429
Elkhart	137,330	Goshen	466
Fayette	28,272	Connersville	215
Floyd	61,205	New Albany	150
Fountain	19,033	Covington	398
Franklin	19,612	Brookville	385
Fulton	19,335	Rochester	369
Gibson	33,156	Princeton	490
Grant	80,934	Marion	415
Greene	30,416	Bloomfield	546
Hamilton	82,381	Noblesville	398
Hancock	43,939	Greenfield	307
Harrison	27,276	Corydon	486
Hendricks	69,804	Danville	409
Henry	53,336	New Castle	394
Howard	86,896	Kokomo	293
Huntington	35,596	Huntington	366
Jackson	36,523	Brownstown	513
Jasper	26,138	Rensselaer	561
Jay	23,239	Portland	384
Jefferson	30,419	Madison	363
Jennings	22,854	Vernon	378
Johnson	77,240	Franklin	321
Knox	41,838	Vincennes	520
Kosciusko	59,555	Warsaw	540
Lagrange	25,550	Lagrange	380
Lake	522,917	Crown Point	501
La Porte	108,632	La Porte	600
Lawrence	42,472	Bedford	452
Madison	139,336	Anderson	453
Marion	765,233	Indianapolis	396
Marshall	39,155	Plymouth	444
Martin	11,001	Shoals	339
Miami	39,820	Peru	369
Monroe	98,387	Bloomington	385
Montgomery	35,501	Crawfordsville	505
Morgan	51,999	Martinsville	409
Newton	14,844	Kentland	401
Noble	35,443	Albion	413
Ohio	5,114	Rising Sun	87
Orange	18,677	Paoli	408
Owen	15,840	Spencer	386
Parke	16,372	Rockville	444
Perry	19,346	Cannelton	382
Pike	13,465	Petersburg	341
Porter	119,816	Valparaiso	418
Posey	26,414	Mount Vernon	409
Pulaski	13,258	Winamac	435
Putnam	29,163	Greencastle	482
Randolph	29,997	Winchester	454
Ripley	24,398	Versailles	447
Rush	19,604	Rushville	408
St. Joseph	241,617	South Bend	459
Scott	20,422	Scottsburg	191
Shelby	39,887	Shelbyville	413
Spencer	19,361	Rockport	400
Starke	21,997	Knox	309
Steuben	24,694	Angola	308
Sullivan	21,107	Sullivan	452
Switzerland	7,153	Vevay	223
Tippecanoe	121,702	Lafayette	502
Tipton	16,819	Tipton	260
Union	6,860	Liberty	162
Vanderburgh	167,515	Evansville	236
Vermillion	18,229	Newport	260
Vigo	112,385	Terre Haute	405
Wabash	36,640	Wabash	398
Warren	8,976	Williamsport	366
Warrick	41,474	Boonville	391
Washington	21,932	Salem	516
Wayne	76,058	Richmond	404
Wells	25,401	Bluffton	370
White	23,867	Monticello	506
Whitley	26,215	Columbia City	336

Iowa
(99 counties; 55,965 sq. mi. land; pop. 2,913,387)

County	Pop.	County seat	Land area
Adair	9,509	Greenfield	570
Adams	5,731	Corning	425
Allamakee	15,108	Waukon	633
Appanoose	15,511	Centerville	498
Audubon	8,559	Audubon	444
Benton	23,649	Vinton	718
Black Hawk	137,961	Waterloo	573
Boone	26,184	Boone	573
Bremer	24,820	Waverly	439
Buchanan	22,900	Independence	572
Buena Vista	20,774	Storm Lake	575
Butler	17,668	Allison	582
Calhoun	13,542	Rockwell City	571

County	Pop.	County seat or court house	Land area sq. mi.
Carroll	22,951	Carroll	570
Cass	16,932	Atlantic	565
Cedar	18,635	Tipton	582
Cerro Gordo	48,458	Mason City	569
Cherokee	16,238	Cherokee	577
Chickasaw	15,437	New Hampton	505
Clarke	8,612	Osceola	431
Clay	19,576	Spencer	569
Clayton	21,098	Elkader	779
Clinton	57,122	Clinton	695
Crawford	18,935	Denison	714
Dallas	29,513	Adel	591
Davis	9,104	Bloomfield	504
Decatur	9,794	Leon	535
Delaware	18,933	Manchester	578
Des Moines	46,203	Burlington	414
Dickinson	15,629	Spirit Lake	381
Dubuque	93,745	Dubuque	607
Emmet	13,336	Estherville	394
Fayette	25,488	West Union	731
Floyd	19,597	Charles City	501
Franklin	13,036	Hampton	583
Fremont	9,401	Sidney	515
Greene	12,119	Jefferson	571
Grundy	14,366	Grundy Center	501
Guthrie	11,983	Guthrie Center	590
Hamilton	17,862	Webster City	576
Hancock	13,833	Garner	571
Hardin	21,776	Eldora	569
Harrison	16,348	Logan	697
Henry	18,890	Mount Pleasant	436
Howard	11,114	Cresco	473
Humboldt	12,246	Dakota City	436
Ida	8,908	Ida Grove	432
Iowa	15,429	Marengo	587
Jackson	22,503	Maquoketa	638
Jasper	36,425	Newton	731
Jefferson	16,316	Fairfield	440
Johnson	81,717	Iowa City	614
Jones	20,401	Anamosa	576
Keokuk	12,921	Sigourney	580
Kossuth	21,891	Algona	974
Lee	43,106	Fort Madison and Keokuk	522
Linn	169,775	Cedar Rapids	724
Louisa	12,055	Wapello	402
Lucas	10,313	Chariton	432
Lyon	12,896	Rock Rapids	588
Madison	12,597	Winterset	563
Mahaska	22,507	Oskaloosa	571
Marion	29,669	Knoxville	560
Marshall	41,652	Marshalltown	573
Mills	13,406	Glenwood	439
Mitchell	12,329	Osage	470
Monona	11,692	Onawa	697
Monroe	9,209	Albia	434
Montgomery	13,413	Red Oak	424
Muscatine	40,436	Muscatine	442
O'Brien	16,972	Primghar	574
Osceola	8,371	Sibley	399
Page	19,063	Clarinda	535
Palo Alto	12,721	Emmetsburg	562
Plymouth	24,743	Le Mars	864
Pocahontas	11,369	Pocahontas	577
Polk	303,170	Des Moines	582
Pottawattamie	86,500	Council Bluffs	953
Poweshiek	19,306	Montezuma	585
Ringgold	6,112	Mount Ayr	535
Sac	14,118	Sac City	576
Scott	160,022	Davenport	459
Shelby	15,043	Harlan	591
Sioux	30,813	Orange City	769
Story	72,326	Nevada	574
Tama	19,533	Toledo	721
Taylor	8,353	Bedford	537
Union	13,858	Creston	426
Van Buren	8,626	Keosauqua	484
Wapello	40,241	Ottumwa	434
Warren	34,878	Indianola	573
Washington	20,141	Washington	570
Wayne	8,199	Corydon	526
Webster	45,953	Fort Dodge	718
Winnebago	13,010	Forest City	401
Winneshiek	21,876	Decorah	690
Woodbury	100,884	Sioux City	873
Worth	9,075	Northwood	401
Wright	16,319	Clarion	579

Kansas

(105 counties, 81,778 sq. mi. land; pop. 2,364,236)

County	Pop.	County seat or court house	Land area sq. mi.
Allen	15,654	Iola	505
Anderson	8,749	Garnett	584
Atchison	18,397	Atchison	431
Barber	6,548	Medicine Lodge	1,136
Barton	31,343	Great Bend	895
Bourbon	15,969	Fort Scott	638
Brown	11,955	Hiawatha	572
Butler	44,782	El Dorado	1,443
Chase	3,309	Cottonwood Falls	77
Chautauqua	5,016	Sedan	64
Cherokee	22,304	Columbus	59
Cheyenne	3,678	Saint Francis	1,02
Clark	2,599	Ashland	97
Clay	9,802	Clay Center	63
Cloud	12,494	Concordia	71
Coffey	9,370	Burlington	61
Comanche	2,554	Coldwater	78
Cowley	36,824	Winfield	1,12
Crawford	37,916	Girard	59
Decatur	4,509	Oberlin	89
Dickinson	20,175	Abilene	85
Doniphan	9,268	Troy	38
Douglas	67,640	Lawrence	46
Edwards	4,271	Kinsley	62
Elk	3,918	Howard	65
Ellis	26,098	Hays	90
Ellsworth	6,640	Ellsworth	71
Finney	23,825	Garden City	1,30
Ford	24,315	Dodge City	1,09
Franklin	21,813	Ottawa	57
Geary	29,852	Junction City	37
Gove	3,726	Gove	1,07
Graham	3,995	Hill City	89
Grant	6,977	Ulysses	57
Gray	5,138	Cimarron	86
Greeley	1,845	Tribune	77
Greenwood	8,764	Eureka	1,13
Hamilton	2,514	Syracuse	99
Harper	7,778	Anthony	80
Harvey	30,531	Newton	54
Haskell	3,814	Sublette	57
Hodgeman	2,269	Jetmore	86
Jackson	11,644	Holton	65
Jefferson	15,207	Oskaloosa	53
Jewell	5,241	Mankato	91
Johnson	270,269	Olathe	47
Kearny	3,435	Lakin	86
Kingman	8,960	Kingman	86
Kiowa	4,046	Greensburg	72
Labette	25,682	Oswego	65
Lane	2,472	Dighton	71
Leavenworth	54,809	Leavenworth	46
Lincoln	4,145	Lincoln	72
Linn	8,234	Mound City	60
Logan	3,478	Oakley	1,07
Lyon	35,108	Emporia	84
McPherson	26,855	McPherson	90
Marion	13,522	Marion	94
Marshall	12,720	Marysville	87
Meade	4,788	Meade	97
Miami	21,618	Paola	59
Mitchell	8,117	Beloit	71
Montgomery	42,281	Independence	64
Morris	6,419	Council Grove	69
Morton	3,454	Elkhart	73
Nemaha	11,211	Seneca	71
Neosho	18,967	Erie	57
Ness	4,498	Ness City	1,07
Norton	6,689	Norton	87
Osage	15,319	Lyndon	69
Osborne	5,959	Osborne	88
Ottawa	5,971	Minneapolis	72
Pawnee	8,065	Larned	75
Phillips	7,406	Phillipsburg	88
Pottawatomie	14,782	Westmoreland	82
Pratt	10,275	Pratt	73
Rawlins	4,105	Atwood	1,06
Reno	64,983	Hutchinson	1,25
Republic	7,569	Belleville	72
Rice	11,900	Lyons	72
Riley	63,505	Manhattan	59
Rooks	7,006	Stockton	88
Rush	4,516	LaCrosse	71
Russell	8,868	Russell	86
Saline	48,905	Salina	72
Scott	5,782	Scott City	71
Sedgwick	367,088	Wichita	1,00
Seward	17,071	Liberal	64
Shawnee	154,916	Topeka	54
Sheridan	3,544	Hoxie	89
Sherman	7,759	Goodland	1,05
Smith	5,947	Smith Center	89
Stafford	5,539	Saint John	78
Stanton	2,339	Johnson	68
Stevens	4,736	Hugoton	72
Sumner	24,928	Wellington	1,18
Thomas	8,451	Colby	1,07
Trego	4,165	Wakeeney	88
Wabaunsee	6,867	Alma	79
Wallace	2,045	Sharon Springs	91
Washington	8,543	Washington	89
Wichita	3,041	Leoti	72
Wilson	12,128	Fredonia	57
Woodson	4,600	Yates Center	49
Wyandotte	172,335	Kansas City	14

Kentucky

(120 counties, 39,669 sq. mi. land; pop. 3,660,380)

County	Pop.	County seat or court house	Land area sq. mi.
Adair	15,233	Columbia	40

County	Pop.	County seat or court house	Land area sq. mi.
Allen	14,128	Scottsville	338
Anderson	12,567	Lawrenceburg	204
Ballard	8,798	Wickliffe	254
Barren	34,009	Glasgow	482
Bath	10,025	Owingsville	277
Bell	34,330	Pineville	361
Boone	45,842	Burlington	246
Bourbon	19,405	Paris	292
Boyd	55,513	Catlettsburg	160
Boyle	25,066	Danville	182
Bracken	7,738	Brooksville	203
Breathitt	17,004	Jackson	495
Breckinridge	16,861	Hardinsburg	565
Bullitt	43,346	Shepherdsville	300
Butler	11,064	Morgantown	431
Caldwell	13,473	Princeton	347
Calloway	30,031	Murray	386
Campbell	83,317	Alexandria	152
Carlisle	5,487	Bardwell	191
Carroll	9,270	Carrollton	130
Carter	25,060	Grayson	407
Casey	14,818	Liberty	445
Christian	66,878	Hopkinsville	722
Clark	28,322	Winchester	255
Clay	22,752	Manchester	471
Clinton	9,321	Albany	196
Crittenden	9,207	Marion	360
Cumberland	7,289	Burkesville	304
Daviess	85,949	Owensboro	463
Edmonson	9,962	Brownsville	302
Elliott	6,908	Sandy Hook	234
Estill	14,495	Irvine	256
Fayette	204,165	Lexington	285
Fleming	12,323	Flemingsburg	351
Floyd	48,764	Prestonsburg	393
Franklin	41,830	Frankfort	212
Fulton	8,971	Hickman	211
Gallatin	4,842	Warsaw	99
Garrard	10,853	Lancaster	232
Grant	13,308	Williamstown	259
Graves	34,049	Mayfield	557
Grayson	20,854	Leitchfield	493
Green	11,043	Greensburg	289
Greenup	39,132	Greenup	347
Hancock	7,742	Hawesville	189
Hardin	88,917	Elizabethtown	629
Harlan	41,889	Harlan	468
Harrison	15,166	Cynthiana	310
Hart	15,402	Munfordville	412
Henderson	40,849	Henderson	438
Henry	12,740	New Castle	291
Hickman	6,065	Clinton	245
Hopkins	46,174	Madisonville	552
Jackson	11,996	McKee	346
Jefferson	684,688	Louisville	386
Jessamine	26,065	Nicholasville	174
Johnson	24,432	Paintsville	264
Kenton	137,058	Independence	163
Knott	17,940	Hindman	352
Knox	30,239	Barbourville	388
Larue	11,983	Hodgenville	263
Laurel	38,982	London	434
Lawrence	14,121	Louisa	420
Lee	7,754	Beattyville	211
Leslie	14,882	Hyden	402
Letcher	30,687	Whitesburg	339
Lewis	14,545	Vanceburg	484
Lincoln	19,053	Stanford	337
Livingston	9,219	Smithland	312
Logan	24,138	Russellville	556
Lyon	6,490	Eddyville	209
McCracken	61,310	Paducah	251
McCreary	15,634	Whitley City	427
McLean	10,090	Calhoun	256
Madison	53,352	Richmond	443
Magoffin	13,515	Salyersville	310
Marion	17,910	Lebanon	347
Marshall	25,637	Benton	304
Martin	13,925	Inez	230
Mason	17,760	Maysville	241
Meade	22,854	Brandenburg	306
Menifee	5,117	Frenchburg	203
Mercer	19,011	Harrodsburg	250
Metcalfe	9,484	Edmonton	291
Monroe	12,353	Tompkinsville	331
Montgomery	20,046	Mount Sterling	199
Morgan	12,103	West Liberty	382
Muhlenberg	32,238	Greenville	478
Nelson	27,584	Bardstown	424
Nicholas	7,157	Carlisle	197
Ohio	21,765	Hartford	596
Oldham	28,094	La Grange	190
Owen	8,924	Owenton	354
Owsley	5,709	Booneville	198
Pendleton	10,989	Falmouth	281
Perry	33,763	Hazard	341
Pike	81,123	Pikeville	785
Powell	11,101	Stanton	180

County	Pop.	County seat	Land area
Pulaski	45,803	Somerset	660
Robertson	2,270	Mount Olivet	100
Rockcastle	13,973	Mount Vernon	318
Rowan	19,049	Morehead	282
Russell	13,708	Jamestown	250
Scott	21,813	Georgetown	286
Shelby	23,328	Shelbyville	385
Simpson	14,673	Franklin	236
Spencer	5,929	Taylorsville	192
Taylor	21,178	Campbellsville	270
Todd	11,874	Elkton	377
Trigg	9,384	Cadiz	421
Trimble	6,253	Bedford	148
Union	17,821	Morganfield	341
Warren	71,828	Bowling Green	548
Washington	10,764	Springfield	301
Wayne	17,022	Monticello	446
Webster	14,832	Dixon	336
Whitley	33,396	Williamsburg	443
Wolfe	6,698	Campton	223
Woodford	17,778	Versailles	192

Louisiana
(64 parishes, 44,521 sq. mi. land; pop. 4,206,116)

Parish	Pop.	Seat	Land area
Acadia	56,427	Crowley	657
Allen	21,408	Oberlin	765
Ascension	50,068	Donaldsville	296
Assumption	22,084	Napoleonville	342
Avoyelles	41,393	Marksville	846
Beauregard	29,692	De Ridder	1,163
Bienville	16,387	Arcadia	816
Bossier	80,721	Benton	845
Caddo	252,437	Shreveport	894
Calcasieu	167,048	Lake Charles	1,082
Caldwell	10,761	Columbia	541
Cameron	9,336	Cameron	1,417
Catahoula	12,287	Harrisonburg	732
Claiborne	17,095	Homer	765
Concordia	22,981	Vidalia	717
De Soto	25,664	Mansfield	880
East Baton Rouge	366,164	Baton Rouge	458
East Carroll	11,772	Lake Providence	426
East Feliciana	19,015	Clinton	455
Evangeline	33,343	Ville Platte	667
Franklin	24,141	Winnsboro	635
Grant	16,703	Colfax	653
Iberia	63,752	New Iberia	589
Iberville	32,159	Plaquemine	638
Jackson	17,321	Jonesboro	579
Jefferson	454,592	Gretna	348
Jefferson Davis	32,168	Jennings	655
Lafayette	150,017	Lafayette	270
Lafourche	82,483	Thibodaux	1,141
La Salle	17,004	Jena	638
Lincoln	39,763	Ruston	472
Livingston	58,655	Livingston	661
Madison	15,682	Tallulah	631
Morehouse	34,803	Bastrop	807
Natchitoches	39,863	Natchitoches	1,264
Orleans	557,927	New Orleans	199
Ouachita	139,241	Monroe	627
Plaquemines	26,049	Pointe a la Hache	1,035
Pointe Coupee	24,045	New Roads	566
Rapides	135,282	Alexandria	1,341
Red River	10,433	Coushatta	394
Richland	22,187	Rayville	563
Sabine	25,280	Many	855
St. Bernard	64,097	Chalmette	486
St. Charles	37,259	Hahnville	286
St. Helena	9,827	Greensburg	409
St. James	21,495	Convent	248
St. John The Baptist	31,924	Edgard	213
St. Landry	84,128	Opelousas	936
St. Martin	40,214	Saint Martinville	749
St. Mary	64,395	Franklin	613
St. Tammany	110,554	Covington	873
Tangipahoa	80,698	Amite	783
Tensas	8,525	Saint Joseph	623
Terrebonne	94,393	Houma	1,367
Union	21,167	Farmerville	884
Vermilion	48,458	Abbeville	1,205
Vernon	53,475	Leesville	1,332
Washington	44,207	Franklinton	676
Webster	43,631	Minden	602
West Baton Rouge	19,086	Port Allen	194
West Carroll	12,922	Oak Grove	360
West Feliciana	12,186	Saint Francisville	406
Winn	17,253	Winnfield	953

Maine
(16 counties, 30,995 sq. mi. land; pop. 1,125,043)

County	Pop.	Seat	Land area
Androscoggin	99,509	Auburn	477
Aroostook	91,344	Houlton	6,721
Cumberland	215,789	Portland	876
Franklin	27,447	Farmington	1,699
Hancock	41,781	Ellsworth	1,537
Kennebec	109,889	Augusta	876
Knox	32,941	Rockland	370
Lincoln	25,691	Wiscasset	458
Oxford	49,043	South Paris	2,053

County	Pop.	County seat or court house	Land area sq. mi.
Penobscot	137,015	Bangor	3,430
Piscataquis	17,634	Dover-Foxcroft	3,986
Sagadahoc	28,795	Bath	257
Somerset	45,049	Skowhegan	3,930
Waldo	28,414	Belfast	730
Washington	34,963	Machias	2,586
York	139,739	Alfred	1,008

Maryland
(23 cos., 1 ind. city, 9,837 sq. mi. land; pop. 4,216,941)

County	Pop.	County seat	Land area
Allegany	80,548	Cumberland	421
Anne Arundel	370,775	Annapolis	418
Baltimore	655,615	Towson	598
Calvert	34,638	Prince Frederick	213
Caroline	23,143	Denton	321
Carroll	96,356	Westminster	452
Cecil	60,430	Elkton	360
Charles	72,751	La Plata	452
Dorchester	30,623	Cambridge	593
Frederick	114,263	Frederick	663
Garrett	26,498	Oakland	657
Harford	145,930	Bel Air	448
Howard	118,572	Ellicott City	251
Kent	16,695	Chestertown	278
Montgomery	579,053	Rockville	495
Prince Georges	665,071	Upper Marlboro	487
Queen Annes	25,508	Centreville	372
St. Mary's	59,895	Leonardtown	373
Somerset	19,188	Princess Anne	338
Talbot	25,604	Easton	259
Washington	113,086	Hagerstown	455
Wicomico	64,540	Salisbury	379
Worcester	30,889	Snow Hill	475
Independent City			
Baltimore	786,775	....	80

Massachusetts
(14 counties; 7,824 sq. mi. land; pop. 5,737,093)

County	Pop.	County seat	Land area
Barnstable	147,925	Barnstable	400
Berkshire	145,110	Pittsfield	929
Bristol	474,641	Taunton	557
Dukes	8,942	Edgartown	102
Essex	633,688	Salem	495
Franklin	64,317	Greenfield	702
Hampden	443,018	Springfield	618
Hampshire	138,813	Northampton	528
Middlesex	1,367,034	Cambridge	822
Nantucket	5,087	Nantucket	47
Norfolk	606,587	Dedham	400
Plymouth	405,437	Plymouth	655
Suffolk	650,142	Boston	57
Worcester	646,352	Worcester	1,513

Michigan
(83 counties; 56,954 sq. mi. land; pop. 9,262,044)

County	Pop.	County seat	Land area
Alcona	9,740	Harrisville	679
Alger	9,225	Munising	912
Allegan	81,555	Allegan	832
Alpena	32,315	Alpena	567
Antrim	16,194	Bellaire	480
Arenac	14,706	Standish	367
Baraga	8,484	L'Anse	901
Barry	45,781	Hastings	560
Bay	119,881	Bay City	447
Benzie	11,205	Beulah	322
Berrien	171,276	Saint Joseph	576
Branch	40,188	Coldwater	508
Calhoun	141,579	Marshall	712
Cass	49,499	Cassopolis	496
Charlevoix	19,907	Charlevoix	421
Cheboygan	20,649	Cheboygan	720
Chippewa	29,029	Sault Sainte Marie	1,590
Clare	23,822	Harrison	570
Clinton	55,893	Saint Johns	573
Crawford	9,465	Grayling	559
Delta	38,947	Escanaba	1,173
Dickinson	25,341	Iron Mountain	770
Eaton	88,337	Charlotte	579
Emmet	22,992	Petoskey	468
Genesee	450,449	Flint	642
Gladwin	19,957	Gladwin	505
Gogebic	19,686	Bessemer	1,105
Grand Traverse	54,899	City	466
Gratiot	40,448	Ithaca	570
Hillsdale	42,071	Hillsdale	603
Houghton	37,872	Houghton	1,014
Huron	36,459	Bad Axe	830
Ingham	272,437	Mason	560
Ionia	51,815	Ionia	577
Iosco	28,349	Tawas City	546
Iron	13,635	Crystal Falls	1,163
Isabella	54,110	Mount Pleasant	577
Jackson	151,495	Jackson	705
Kalamazoo	212,378	Kalamazoo	562
Kalkaska	10,952	Kalkaska	563
Kent	444,506	Grand Rapids	862
Keweenaw	1,963	Eagle River	543
Lake	7,711	Baldwin	568
Lapeer	70,038	Lapeer	658
Leelanau	14,007	Leland	341
Lenawee	89,948	Adrian	753
Livingston	100,289	Howell	574
Luce	6,659	Newberry	904
Mackinac	10,178	Saint Ignace	1,025
Macomb	694,600	Mount Clemens	482
Manistee	23,019	Manistee	543
Marquette	74,101	Marquette	1,821
Mason	26,365	Ludington	494
Mecosta	36,961	Big Rapids	560
Menominee	26,201	Menominee	1,045
Midland	73,578	Midland	525
Missaukee	10,009	Lake City	565
Monroe	134,659	Monroe	557
Montcalm	47,555	Stanton	713
Montmorency	7,492	Atlanta	550
Muskegon	157,589	Muskegon	507
Newaygo	34,917	White Cloud	847
Oakland	1,011,793	Pontiac	875
Oceana	22,002	Hart	541
Ogemaw	16,436	West Branch	570
Ontonagon	9,861	Ontonagon	1,311
Osceola	18,928	Reed City	569
Oscoda	6,858	Mio	568
Otsego	14,993	Gaylord	516
Ottawa	157,174	Grand Haven	567
Presque Isle	14,267	Rogers City	656
Roscommon	16,374	Roscommon	528
Saginaw	228,059	Saginaw	815
St. Clair	138,802	Port Huron	734
St. Joseph	56,083	Centreville	503
Sanilac	40,789	Sandusky	964
Schoolcraft	8,575	Manistique	1,173
Shiawassee	71,140	Corunna	540
Tuscola	56,961	Caro	812
Van Buren	66,814	Paw Paw	611
Washtenaw	264,740	Ann Arbor	710
Wayne	2,337,843	Detroit	615
Wexford	25,102	Cadillac	566

Minnesota
(87 counties; 79,548 sq. mi. land; pop. 4,075,970)

County	Pop.	County seat	Land area
Aitkin	13,404	Aitkin	1,834
Anoka	195,998	Anoka	430
Becker	29,336	Detroit Lakes	1,312
Beltrami	30,982	Bemidji	2,507
Benton	25,187	Foley	408
Big Stone	7,716	Ortonville	497
Blue Earth	52,314	Mankato	749
Brown	28,645	New Ulm	610
Carlton	29,936	Carlton	864
Carver	37,046	Chaska	351
Cass	21,050	Walker	2,033
Chippewa	14,941	Montevideo	584
Chisago	25,717	Center City	417
Clay	49,327	Moorhead	1,049
Clearwater	8,761	Bagley	999
Cook	4,092	Grand Marais	1,412
Cottonwood	14,854	Windom	640
Crow Wing	41,722	Brainerd	1,008
Dakota	194,111	Hastings	574
Dodge	14,773	Mantorville	439
Douglas	27,839	Alexandria	643
Faribault	19,714	Blue Earth	714
Fillmore	21,930	Preston	862
Freeborn	36,329	Albert Lea	705
Goodhue	38,749	Red Wing	763
Grant	7,171	Elbow Lake	547
Hennepin	941,411	Minneapolis	541
Houston	19,617	Caledonia	564
Hubbard	14,098	Park Rapids	936
Isanti	23,600	Cambridge	440
Itasca	43,006	Grand Rapids	2,661
Jackson	13,690	Jackson	699
Kanabec	12,161	Mora	527
Kandiyohi	36,763	Willmar	784
Kittson	6,672	Hallock	1,104
Koochiching	17,571	International Falls	3,108
Lac qui Parle	10,592	Madison	772
Lake	13,043	Two Harbors	2,053
Lake of the Woods	3,764	Baudette	1,296
Le Sueur	23,434	Le Center	446
Lincoln	8,207	Ivanhoe	538
Lyon	25,207	Marshall	714
McLeod	29,657	Glencoe	489
Mahnomen	5,535	Mahnomen	559
Marshall	13,027	Warren	1,760
Martin	24,687	Fairmont	706
Meeker	20,594	Litchfield	624
Mille Lacs	18,430	Milaca	578
Morrison	29,311	Little Falls	1,124
Mower	40,390	Austin	711
Murray	11,507	Slayton	702
Nicollet	26,929	Saint Peter	440
Nobles	21,840	Worthington	714
Norman	9,379	Ada	538
Olmsted	91,971	Rochester	655
Otter Tail	51,937	Fergus Falls	1,973

County	Pop.	County seat or court house	Land area sq. mi.
Pennington	15,258	Thief River Falls	618
Pine	19,871	Pine City	1,421
Pipestone	11,690	Pipestone	466
Polk	34,844	Crookston	1,982
Pope	11,657	Glenwood	668
Ramsey	459,784	Saint Paul	154
Red Lake	5,471	Red Lake Falls	433
Redwood	19,341	Redwood Falls	882
Renville	20,401	Olivia	984
Rice	46,087	Faribault	501
Rock	10,703	Luverne	483
Roseau	12,574	Roseau	1,677
St. Louis	222,229	Duluth	6,125
Scott	43,784	Shakopee	357
Sherburne	29,908	Elk River	435
Sibley	15,448	Gaylord	593
Stearns	108,161	Saint Cloud	1,338
Steele	30,328	Owatonna	431
Stevens	11,322	Morris	560
Swift	12,920	Benson	743
Todd	24,991	Long Prairie	941
Traverse	5,542	Wheaton	575
Wabasha	19,335	Wabasha	537
Wadena	14,192	Wadena	538
Waseca	18,448	Waseca	422
Washington	113,571	Stillwater	390
Watonwan	12,361	Saint James	435
Wilkin	8,382	Breckenridge	751
Winona	46,256	Winona	630
Wright	58,962	Buffalo	672
Yellow Medicine	13,653	Granite Falls	758

Mississippi

(82 counties, 47,233 sq. mi. land; pop. 2,520,698)

County	Pop.	County seat or court house	Land area sq. mi.
Adams	38,071	Natchez	456
Alcorn	33,036	Corinth	401
Amite	13,369	Liberty	732
Attala	19,865	Kosciusko	737
Benton	8,153	Ashland	407
Bolivar	45,965	Cleveland & Rosedale	892
Calhoun	15,664	Pittsboro	573
Carroll	9,776	Carrollton & Vaiden	634
Chickasaw	17,851	Houston & Okolona	503
Choctaw	8,996	Ackerman	420
Claiborne	12,279	Port Gibson	494
Clarke	16,945	Quitman	692
Clay	21,082	West Point	415
Coahoma	36,918	Clarksdale	559
Copiah	26,503	Hazlehurst	779
Covington	15,927	Collins	416
De Soto	53,930	Hernando	483
Forrest	66,018	Hattiesburg	469
Franklin	8,208	Meadville	566
George	15,297	Lucedale	483
Greene	9,827	Leakesville	718
Grenada	21,043	Grenada	421
Hancock	24,496	Bay Saint Louis	478
Harrison	157,665	Gulfport	581
Hinds	250,998	Jackson & Raymond	875
Holmes	22,970	Lexington	759
Humphreys	13,931	Belzoni	430
Issaquena	2,513	Mayersville	406
Itawamba	20,518	Fulton	540
Jackson	118,015	Pascagoula	731
Jasper	17,265	Bat Springs & Paulding	678
Jefferson	9,181	Fayette	523
Jefferson Davis	13,846	Prentiss	409
Jones	61,912	Ellisville & Laurel	696
Kemper	10,148	De Kalb	766
Lafayette	31,030	Oxford	669
Lamar	23,821	Purvis	499
Lauderdale	77,285	Meridian	705
Lawrence	12,518	Monticello	435
Leake	18,790	Carthage	584
Lee	57,061	Tupelo	451
Leflore	41,525	Greenwood	605
Lincoln	30,174	Brookhaven	587
Lowndes	57,304	Columbus	517
Madison	41,613	Canton	718
Marion	25,708	Columbia	548
Marshall	29,296	Holly Springs	709
Monroe	36,404	Aberdeen	772
Montgomery	13,366	Winona	408
Neshoba	23,789	Philadelphia	572
Newton	19,967	Decatur	580
Noxubee	13,212	Macon	698
Oktibbeha	36,018	Starkville	459
Panola	28,164	Batesville & Sardis	694
Pearl River	33,795	Poplarville	818
Perry	9,864	New Augusta	651
Pike	36,173	Magnolia	410
Pontotoc	20,918	Pontotoc	499
Prentiss	24,025	Booneville	438
Quitman	12,636	Marks	406
Rankin	69,427	Brandon	782
Scott	24,556	Forest	610
Sharkey	7,964	Rolling Fork	435

County	Pop.	County seat or court house	Land area sq. mi.
Simpson	23,441	Mendenhall	591
Smith	15,077	Raleigh	635
Stone	9,716	Wiggins	446
Sunflower	34,844	Indianola	706
Tallahatchie	17,157	Charleston & Sumner	651
Tate	20,119	Senatobia	406
Tippah	18,739	Ripley	458
Tishomingo	18,434	Iuka	434
Tunica	9,652	Tunica	460
Union	21,741	New Albany	416
Walthall	13,761	Tylertown	404
Warren	51,627	Vicksburg	596
Washington	72,344	Greenville	733
Wayne	19,135	Waynesboro	813
Webster	10,300	Walthall	424
Wilkinson	10,021	Woodville	678
Winston	19,474	Louisville	610
Yalobusha	13,183	Coffeeville & Water Valley	478
Yazoo	27,349	Yazoo City	933

Missouri

(114 cos., 1 ind. city, 68,945 sq. mi. land; pop. 4,916,766)

County	Pop.	County seat or court house	Land area sq. mi.
Adair	24,870	Kirksville	567
Andrew	13,980	Savannah	435
Atchison	8,605	Rockport	542
Audrain	26,458	Mexico	697
Barry	24,408	Cassville	773
Barton	11,292	Lamar	596
Bates	15,873	Butler	849
Benton	12,183	Warsaw	729
Bollinger	10,301	Marble Hill	621
Boone	100,376	Columbia	687
Buchanan	87,888	Saint Joseph	409
Butler	37,693	Poplar Buff	698
Caldwell	8,660	Kingston	430
Callaway	32,252	Fulton	842
Camden	19,963	Camdenton	641
Cape Girardeau	58,837	Jackson	577
Carroll	12,131	Carrollton	695
Carter	5,428	Van Buren	509
Cass	51,029	Harrisonville	701
Cedar	11,894	Stockton	470
Chariton	10,489	Keytesville	758
Christian	22,402	Ozark	564
Clark	8,493	Kahoka	507
Clay	136,488	Liberty	403
Clinton	15,916	Plattsburg	423
Cole	56,663	Jefferson City	392
Cooper	14,643	Boonville	567
Crawford	18,300	Steelville	744
Dade	7,383	Greenfield	491
Dallas	12,096	Buffalo	543
Daviess	8,905	Gallatin	568
De Kalb	8,222	Maysville	425
Dent	14,517	Salem	755
Douglas	11,594	Ava	814
Dunklin	36,324	Kennett	547
Franklin	71,233	Union	922
Gasconade	13,181	Hermann	521
Gentry	7,887	Albany	493
Greene	185,302	Springfield	677
Grundy	11,959	Trenton	437
Harrison	9,890	Bethany	725
Henry	19,672	Clinton	729
Hickory	6,367	Hermitage	379
Holt	6,882	Oregon	457
Howard	10,008	Fayette	465
Howell	28,807	West Plains	928
Iron	11,084	Ironton	552
Jackson	629,180	Independence	611
Jasper	86,958	Carthage	641
Jefferson	146,814	Hillsboro	661
Johnson	39,059	Warrensburg	834
Knox	5,508	Edina	507
Laclede	24,323	Lebanon	768
Lafayette	29,925	Lexington	632
Lawrence	28,973	Mount Vernon	613
Lewis	10,901	Monticello	509
Lincoln	22,193	Troy	627
Linn	15,495	Linneus	620
Livingston	15,739	Chillicothe	537
McDonald	14,917	Pineville	540
Macon	16,313	Macon	797
Madison	10,725	Fredericktown	497
Maries	7,551	Vienna	528
Marion	28,638	Palmyra	438
Mercer	4,685	Princeton	454
Miller	18,539	Tuscumbia	593
Mississippi	15,726	Charleston	410
Moniteau	12,068	California	417
Monroe	9,716	Paris	670
Montgomery	11,537	Montgomery City	540
Morgan	13,807	Versailles	594
New Madrid	22,945	New Madrid	658
Newton	40,555	Neosho	627
Nodaway	21,996	Maryville	875
Oregon	10,238	Alton	792
Osage	12,014	Linn	606
Ozark	7,961	Gainesville	731
Pemiscot	24,987	Caruthersville	517
Perry	16,784	Perryville	473

County	Pop.	County seat or court house	Land area sq. mi.
Pettis	36,378	Sedalia	686
Phelps	33,633	Rolla	674
Pike	17,568	Bowling Green	673
Platte	46,341	Platte City	421
Polk	18,822	Bolivar	636
Pulaski	42,011	Waynesville	550
Putnam	6,092	Unionville	520
Ralls	8,984	New London	482
Randolph	25,460	Huntsville	477
Ray	21,378	Richmond	568
Reynolds	7,230	Centerville	809
Ripley	12,458	Doniphan	631
St. Charles	143,455	St. Charles	558
St. Clair	8,622	Osceola	699
St. Francois	42,600	Farmington	451
St. Louis	974,180	Clayton	506
Ste. Genevieve	15,180	Ste. Genevieve	504
Saline	24,919	Marshall	755
Schuyler	4,979	Lancaster	309
Scotland	5,415	Memphis	438
Scott	39,647	Benton	423
Shannon	7,885	Eminence	1,004
Shelby	7,826	Shelbyville	501
Stoddard	29,009	Bloomfield	815
Stone	15,587	Galena	451
Sullivan	7,434	Milan	651
Taney	20,467	Forsyth	608
Texas	21,070	Houston	1,180
Vernon	19,806	Nevada	837
Warren	14,900	Warrenton	429
Washington	17,983	Potosi	762
Wayne	11,277	Greenville	762
Webster	20,414	Marshfield	594
Worth	3,008	Grant City	266
Wright	16,188	Hartville	682
Independent City			
St. Louis	453,085	....	61

Montana
(57 counties, 145,388 sq. mi. land; pop., 786,690)

County	Pop.	County seat	Land area
Beaverhead	8,186	Dillon	5,529
Big Horn	11,096	Hardin	4,983
Blaine	6,999	Chinook	4,257
Broadwater	3,267	Townsend	1,189
Carbon	8,099	Red Lodge	2,056
Carter	1,799	Ekalaka	3,342
Cascade	80,696	Great Falls	2,699
Chouteau	6,092	Fort Benton	3,987
Custer	13,109	Miles City	3,776
Daniels	2,835	Scobey	1,427
Dawson	11,805	Glendive	2,374
Deer Lodge	12,518	Anaconda	740
Fallon	3,763	Baker	1,623
Fergus	13,076	Lewistown	4,340
Flathead	51,966	Kalispell	5,112
Gallatin	42,865	Bozeman	2,510
Garfield	1,656	Jordan	4,491
Glacier	10,628	Cut Bank	2,994
Golden Valley	1,026	Ryegate	1,172
Granite	2,700	Philipsburg	1,729
Hill	17,985	Havre	2,897
Jefferson	7,029	Boulder	1,657
Judith Basin	2,646	Stanford	1,871
Lake	19,056	Polson	1,445
Lewis & Clark	43,039	Helena	3,461
Liberty	2,329	Chester	1,426
Lincoln	17,752	Libby	3,616
McCone	2,702	Circle	2,626
Madison	5,448	Virginia City	3,590
Meagher	2,154	White Sulphur Springs	2,392
Mineral	3,675	Superior	1,216
Missoula	76,016	Missoula	2,582
Musselshell	4,428	Roundup	1,871
Park	12,869	Livingston	1,665
Petroleum	655	Winnett	1,652
Phillips	5,367	Malta	5,130
Pondera	6,731	Conrad	1,632
Powder River	2,520	Broadus	3,288
Powell	6,958	Deer Lodge	2,329
Prairie	1,836	Terry	1,732
Ravalli	22,493	Hamilton	2,384
Richland	12,243	Sidney	2,081
Roosevelt	10,467	Wolf Point	2,357
Rosebud	9,899	Forsyth	5,019
Sanders	8,675	Thompson Falls	2,749
Sheridan	5,414	Plentywood	1,681
Silver Bow	38,092	Butte	718
Stillwater	5,598	Columbus	1,793
Sweet Grass	3,216	Big Timber	1,903
Teton	6,491	Choteau	2,275
Toole	5,559	Shelby	1,931
Treasure	981	Hysham	975
Valley	10,250	Glasgow	4,936
Wheatland	2,359	Harlowton	1,419
Wibaux	1,476	Wibaux	888
Yellowstone	108,035	Billings	2,624
Yellowstone Nat. Park	66	....	245

Nebraska
(93 counties, 76,644 sq. mi. land; pop., 1,569,825)

County	Pop.	County seat	Land area
Adams	30,656	Hastings	564
Antelope	8,675	Neligh	859
Arthur	513	Arthur	711
Banner	918	Harrisburg	747
Blaine	867	Brewster	714
Boone	7,391	Albion	687
Box Butte	13,696	Alliance	1,077
Boyd	3,331	Butte	532
Brown	4,377	Ainsworth	1,214
Buffalo	34,797	Kearney	945
Burt	8,813	Tekamah	486
Butler	9,330	David City	584
Cass	20,297	Plattsmouth	557
Cedar	10,852	Hartington	740
Chase	4,758	Imperial	894
Cherry	6,758	Valentine	5,961
Cheyenne	10,057	Sidney	1,196
Clay	8,106	Clay Center	574
Colfax	9,890	Schuyler	410
Cuming	11,664	West Point	575
Custer	13,877	Broken Bow	2,571
Dakota	16,573	Dakota City	258
Dawes	9,609	Chadron	1,397
Dawson	22,162	Lexington	982
Deuel	2,462	Chappell	437
Dixon	7,137	Ponca	474
Dodge	35,847	Fremont	534
Douglas	397,884	Omaha	333
Dundy	2,861	Benkelman	920
Fillmore	7,920	Geneva	576
Franklin	4,377	Franklin	576
Frontier	3,647	Stockville	976
Furnas	6,486	Beaver City	721
Gage	24,456	Beatrice	858
Garden	2,802	Oshkosh	1,680
Garfield	2,363	Burwell	570
Gosper	2,140	Elwood	461
Grant	877	Hyannis	775
Greeley	3,462	Greeley	570
Hall	47,690	Grand Island	537
Hamilton	9,301	Aurora	543
Harlan	4,292	Alma	555
Hayes	1,356	Hayes Center	713
Hitchcock	4,079	Trenton	709
Holt	13,552	O'Neil	2,406
Hooker	990	Mullen	721
Howard	6,773	Saint Paul	564
Jefferson	9,817	Fairbury	575
Johnson	5,285	Tecumseh	377
Kearney	7,053	Minden	519
Keith	9,364	Ogallala	1,039
Keya Paha	1,301	Springview	769
Kimball	4,882	Kimball	952
Knox	11,457	Center	1,105
Lancaster	192,884	Lincoln	839
Lincoln	36,455	North Platte	2,525
Logan	983	Stapleton	571
Loup	859	Taylor	574
McPherson	593	Tryon	859
Madison	31,382	Madison	575
Merrick	8,945	Central City	478
Morrill	6,085	Bridgeport	1,405
Nance	4,740	Fullerton	439
Nemaha	8,367	Auburn	409
Nuckolls	6,726	Nelson	576
Otoe	15,183	Nebraska City	615
Pawnee	3,937	Pawnee City	433
Perkins	3,637	Grant	885
Phelps	9,769	Holdrege	540
Pierce	8,481	Pierce	575
Platte	28,852	Columbus	669
Polk	6,320	Osceola	437
Red Willow	12,615	McCook	718
Richardson	11,315	Falls City	553
Rock	2,383	Bassett	1,003
Saline	13,131	Wilber	575
Sarpy	86,015	Papillion	238
Saunders	18,716	Wahoo	753
Scotts Bluff	38,344	Gering	725
Seward	15,789	Seward	575
Sheridan	7,544	Rushville	2,453
Sherman	4,226	Loup City	564
Sioux	1,845	Harrison	2,070
Stanton	6,549	Stanton	431
Thayer	7,582	Hebron	575
Thomas	973	Thedford	713
Thurston	7,186	Pender	391
Valley	5,633	Ord	567
Washington	15,508	Blair	386
Wayne	9,858	Wayne	443
Webster	4,858	Red Cloud	575
Wheeler	1,060	Bartlett	575
York	14,798	York	576

Nevada
(16 cos., 1 ind. city, 109,894 sq. mi. land; pop., 800,508)

County	Pop.	County seat	Land area
Churchill	13,917	Fallon	4,990
Clark	461,816	Las Vegas	7,881

County	Pop.	County seat or court house	Land area sq. mi.
Douglas	19,421	Minden	708
Elko	17,269	Elko	17,135
Esmeralda	777	Goldfield	3,587
Eureka	1,198	Eureka	4,175
Humboldt	9,449	Winnemucca	9,698
Lander	4,082	Austin	5,515
Lincoln	3,732	Pioche	10,635
Lyon	13,594	Yerington	2,007
Mineral	6,217	Hawthorne	3,744
Nye	9,048	Tonopah	18,155
Pershing	3,408	Lovelock	6,036
Storey	1,459	Virginia City	264
Washoe	193,623	Reno	6,317
White Pine	8,167	Ely	8.902
Independent City			
Carson City	32,022	Carson City	146

New Hampshire
(10 counties, 8,993 sq. mi. land; pop., 920,610)

County	Pop.	County seat or court house	Land area sq. mi.
Belknap	42,884	Laconia	404
Carroll	27,931	Ossipee	933
Cheshire	62,116	Keene	711
Coos	35,147	Lancaster	1,804
Grafton	65,806	Woodsville	1,719
Hillsborough	276,608	Nashua	876
Merrimack	98,302	Concord	936
Rockingham	190,345	Exeter	699
Strafford	85,408	Dover	370
Sullivan	36,063	Newport	540

New Jersey
(21 counties, 7,468 sq. mi. land; pop., 7,365,011)

County	Pop.	County seat or court house	Land area sq. mi.
Atlantic	194,119	Mays Landing	568
Bergen	845,385	Hackensack	237
Burlington	362,542	Mount Holly	808
Camden	471,650	Camden	223
Cape May	82,266	Cape May Court House	263
Cumberland	132,866	Bridgeton	498
Essex	851,304	Newark	127
Gloucester	199,917	Woodbury	327
Hudson	556,972	Jersey City	46
Hunterdon	87,361	Flemington	426
Mercer	307,863	Trenton	227
Middlesex	595,893	New Brunswick	316
Monmouth	503,173	Freehold	472
Morris	407,630	Morristown	470
Ocean	346,038	Toms River	641
Passaic	447,585	Paterson	187
Salem	64,676	Salem	338
Somerset	203,129	Somerville	305
Sussex	116,119	Newton	526
Union	504,094	Elizabeth	103
Warren	84,429	Belvidere	359

New Mexico
(32 counties, 121,335 sq. mi. land; pop., 1,303,302)

County	Pop.	County seat or court house	Land area sq. mi.
Bernalillo	420,261	Albuquerque	1,169
Catron	2,720	Reserve	6,929
Chaves	51,103	Roswell	6,066
Colfax	13,706	Raton	3,762
Curry	42,019	Clovis	1,400
De Baca	2,454	Fort Sumner	2,323
Dona Ana	96,340	Las Cruces	3,819
Eddy	47,855	Carlsbad	4,184
Grant	26,204	Silver City	3,969
Guadalupe	4,496	Santa Rosa	3,032
Harding	1,090	Mosquero	2,122
Hidalgo	6,049	Lordsburg	3,445
Lea	55,634	Lovington	4,389
Lincoln	10,997	Carrizozo	4,832
Los Alamos	17,599	Los Alamos	109
Luna	15,585	Deming	2,965
McKinley	56,536	Gallup	5,442
Mora	4,205	Mora	1,930
Otero	44,665	Alamogordo	6,626
Quay	10,577	Tucumcari	2,874
Rio Arriba	29,282	Tierra Amarilla	5,856
Roosevelt	15,695	Portales	2,453
Sandoval	34,400	Bernalillo	3,707
San Juan	80,833	Aztec	5,521
San Miguel	22,751	Las Vegas	4,709
Santa Fe	75,519	Santa Fe	1,905
Sierra	8,454	Truth or Consequences	4,178
Socorro	12,969	Socorro	6,625
Taos	18,862	Taos	2,204
Torrance	7,491	Estancia	3,335
Union	4,725	Clayton	3,830
Valencia	60,853	Los Lunas	5,616

New York
(62 counties, 47,377 sq. mi. land; pop., 17,558,165)

County	Pop.	County seat or court house	Land area sq. mi.
Albany	285,909	Albany	524
Allegany	51,742	Belmont	1,032
Bronx	1,168,972	Bronx	42
Broome	213,648	Binghamton	712
Cattaraugus	85,697	Little Valley	1,306
Cayuga	79,894	Auburn	695
Chautauqua	146,925	Mayville	1,064
Chemung	97,656	Elmira	411
Chenango	49,344	Norwich	897
Clinton	80,750	Plattsburgh	1,043
Columbia	59,487	Hudson	638
Cortland	48,820	Cortland	500
Delaware	46,824	Delhi	1,440
Dutchess	245,055	Poughkeepsie	804
Erie	1,015,472	Buffalo	1,046
Essex	36,176	Elizabethtown	1,806
Franklin	44,929	Malone	1,642
Fulton	55,153	Johnstown	497
Genesee	59,400	Batavia	495
Greene	40,861	Catskill	648
Hamilton	5,034	Lake Pleasant	1,721
Herkimer	66,714	Herkimer	1,416
Jefferson	88,151	Watertown	1,273
Kings	2,231,028	Brooklyn	70
Lewis	25,035	Lowville	1,283
Livingston	57,006	Geneseo	633
Madison	65,150	Wampsville	656
Monroe	702,238	Rochester	663
Montgomery	53,439	Fonda	404
Nassau	1,321,582	Mineola	287
New York	1,428,285	New York	22
Niagara	227,354	Lockport	526
Oneida	253,466	Utica	1,219
Onondaga	463,920	Syracuse	784
Ontario	88,909	Canandaigua	644
Orange	259,603	Goshen	826
Orleans	38,496	Albion	391
Oswego	113,901	Oswego	954
Otsego	59,075	Cooperstown	1,004
Putnam	77,193	Carmel	231
Queens	1,891,325	Jamaica	109
Rensselaer	151,966	Troy	655
Richmond	352,029	Saint George	59
Rockland	259,530	New City	175
St. Lawrence	114,347	Canton	2,728
Saratoga	153,759	Ballston Spa	810
Schenectady	149,946	Schenectady	206
Schoharie	29,710	Schoharie	624
Schuyler	17,686	Watkins Glen	329
Seneca	33,733	Ovid & Waterloo	327
Steuben	99,217	Bath	1,396
Suffolk	1,284,231	Riverhead	911
Sullivan	65,155	Monticello	976
Tioga	49,812	Owego	519
Tompkins	87,085	Ithaca	477
Ulster	158,158	Kingston	1,131
Warren	54,854	Lake George	882
Washington	54,795	Hudson Falls	836
Wayne	84,581	Lyons	605
Westchester	866,599	White Plains	438
Wyoming	39,895	Warsaw	595
Yates	21,459	Penn Yan	339

North Carolina
(100 counties, 48,843 sq. mi. land; pop., 5,881,462)

County	Pop.	County seat or court house	Land area sq. mi.
Alamance	99,136	Graham	433
Alexander	24,999	Taylorsville	259
Alleghany	9,587	Sparta	235
Anson	25,562	Wadesboro	533
Ashe	22,325	Jefferson	426
Avery	14,409	Newland	247
Beaufort	40,266	Washington	826
Bertie	21,024	Windsor	701
Bladen	30,448	Elizabethtown	879
Brunswick	35,767	Southport	860
Buncombe	160,934	Asheville	659
Burke	72,504	Morganton	504
Cabarrus	85,895	Concord	364
Caldwell	67,746	Lenoir	471
Camden	5,829	Camden	240
Carteret	41,092	Beaufort	526
Caswell	20,705	Yanceyville	428
Catawba	105,208	Newton	396
Chatham	33,415	Pittsboro	708
Cherokee	18,933	Murphy	452
Chowan	12,558	Edenton	182
Clay	6,619	Hayesville	214
Cleveland	83,435	Shelby	468
Columbus	51,037	Whiteville	938
Craven	71,043	New Bern	701
Cumberland	247,160	Fayetteville	657
Currituck	11,089	Currituck	256
Dare	13,377	Manteo	391
Davidson	113,162	Lexington	548
Davie	24,599	Mocksville	267
Duplin	40,952	Kenansville	819
Durham	152,785	Durham	298
Edgecombe	55,988	Tarboro	506
Forsyth	243,704	Winston-Salem	412
Franklin	30,055	Louisburg	494
Gaston	162,568	Gastonia	357
Gates	8,875	Gatesville	338
Graham	7,217	Robbinsville	289
Granville	33,995	Oxford	534
Greene	16,117	Snow Hill	266

County	Pop.	County seat or court house	Land area sq. mi.
Guilford	317,154	Greensboro	651
Halifax	55,286	Halifax	724
Harnett	59,570	Lillington	601
Haywood	46,495	Waynesville	555
Henderson	58,580	Hendersonville	374
Hertford	23,368	Winton	356
Hoke	20,383	Raeford	391
Hyde	5,873	Swanquarter	624
Iredell	82,538	Statesville	574
Jackson	25,811	Sylva	491
Johnston	70,599	Smithfield	795
Jones	9,705	Trenton	470
Lee	36,718	Sanford	259
Lenoir	59,819	Kinston	402
Lincoln	42,372	Lincolnton	298
McDowell	35,135	Marion	437
Macon	20,178	Franklin	517
Madison	16,827	Marshall	451
Martin	25,948	Williamston	461
Mecklenburg	404,270	Charlotte	528
Mitchell	14,428	Bakersville	222
Montgomery	22,469	Troy	490
Moore	50,505	Carthage	701
Nash	67,153	Nashville	540
New Hanover	103,471	Wilmington	185
Northampton	22,584	Jackson	538
Onslow	112,784	Jacksonville	763
Orange	77,055	Hillsboro	400
Pamlico	10,398	Bayboro	341
Pasquotank	28,462	Elizabeth City	228
Pender	22,262	Burgaw	875
Perquimans	9,486	Hertford	246
Person	29,164	Roxboro	398
Pitt	83,651	Greenville	657
Polk	12,984	Columbus	238
Randolph	91,300	Asheboro	789
Richmond	45,481	Rockingham	477
Robeson	101,571	Lumberton	949
Rockingham	83,426	Wentworth	569
Rowan	99,186	Salisbury	519
Rutherford	53,787	Rutherfordton	568
Sampson	49,687	Clinton	947
Scotland	32,273	Laurinburg	319
Stanly	48,517	Albemarle	396
Stokes	33,086	Danbury	452
Surry	59,449	Dobson	539
Swain	10,283	Bryson City	526
Transylvania	23,417	Brevard	378
Tyrrell	3,975	Columbia	407
Union	70,380	Monroe	639
Vance	36,748	Henderson	249
Wake	300,833	Raleigh	854
Warren	16,232	Warrenton	427
Washington	14,801	Plymouth	332
Watauga	31,678	Boone	314
Wayne	97,054	Goldsboro	554
Wilkes	58,657	Wilkesboro	752
Wilson	63,132	Wilson	374
Yadkin	28,439	Yadkinville	336
Yancey	14,934	Burnsville	314

North Dakota

(53 counties, 69,300 sq. mi. land; pop., 652,717)

County	Pop.	County seat	Land area sq. mi.
Adams	3,584	Hettinger	988
Barnes	13,960	Valley City	1,498
Benson	7,944	Minnewaukan	1,412
Billings	1,138	Medora	1,152
Bottineau	9,338	Bottineau	1,668
Bowman	4,229	Bowman	1,162
Burke	3,822	Bowbells	1,118
Burleigh	54,811	Bismarck	1,618
Cass	88,247	Fargo	1,767
Cavalier	7,636	Langdon	1,507
Dickey	7,207	Ellendale	1,139
Divide	3,494	Crosby	1,288
Dunn	4,627	Manning	1,993
Eddy	3,554	New Rockford	634
Emmons	5,877	Linton	1,499
Foster	4,611	Carrington	640
Golden Valley	2,391	Beach	1,003
Grand Forks	66,100	Grand Forks	1,440
Grant	4,274	Carson	1,660
Griggs	3,714	Cooperstown	708
Hettinger	4,275	Mott	1,133
Kidder	3,833	Steele	1,362
La Moure	6,473	La Moure	1,150
Logan	3,493	Napoleon	1,000
McHenry	7,858	Towner	1,887
McIntosh	4,800	Ashley	984
McKenzie	7,132	Watford City	2,754
McLean	12,288	Washburn	2,065
Mercer	9,378	Stanton	1,044
Morton	25,177	Mandan	1,921
Mountrail	7,679	Stanley	1,837
Nelson	5,233	Lakota	991
Oliver	2,495	Center	723
Pembina	10,399	Cavalier	1,120
Pierce	6,166	Rugby	1,037
Ramsey	13,048	Devils Lake	1,241
Ransom	6,698	Lisbon	862
Renville	3,608	Mohall	874
Richland	19,207	Wahpeton	1,436
Rolette	12,177	Rolla	914
Sargent	5,512	Forman	857
Sheridan	2,819	McClusky	989
Sioux	3,620	Fort Yates	1,099
Slope	1,157	Amidon	1,219
Stark	23,697	Dickinson	1,338
Steele	3,106	Finley	713
Stutsman	24,154	Jamestown	2,263
Towner	4,052	Cando	1,035
Traill	9,624	Hillsboro	861
Walsh	15,371	Grafton	1,290
Ward	58,392	Minot	2,041
Wells	6,979	Fessenden	1,288
Williams	22,237	Williston	2,074

Ohio

(88 counties, 41,004 sq. mi. land; pop., 10,797,603)

County	Pop.	County seat	Land area sq. mi.
Adams	24,328	West Union	586
Allen	112,241	Lima	405
Ashland	46,178	Ashland	424
Ashtabula	104,215	Jefferson	703
Athens	56,399	Athens	508
Auglaize	42,554	Wapakoneta	398
Belmont	82,569	Saint Clairsville	537
Brown	31,920	Georgetown	493
Butler	258,787	Hamilton	470
Carroll	25,598	Carrollton	393
Champaign	33,649	Urbana	429
Clark	150,236	Springfield	398
Clermont	128,483	Batavia	456
Clinton	34,603	Wilmington	410
Columbiana	113,572	Lisbon	534
Coshocton	36,024	Coshocton	566
Crawford	50,075	Bucyrus	403
Cuyahoga	1,498,295	Cleveland	459
Darke	55,096	Greenville	600
Defiance	39,987	Defiance	414
Delaware	53,840	Delaware	443
Erie	79,655	Sandusky	264
Fairfield	93,678	Lancaster	506
Fayette	27,467	Washington C. H.	405
Franklin	869,126	Columbus	543
Fulton	37,751	Wauseon	407
Gallia	30,098	Gallipolis	471
Geauga	74,474	Chardon	408
Greene	129,769	Xenia	416
Guernsey	42,024	Cambridge	522
Hamilton	873,203	Cincinnati	412
Hancock	64,581	Findlay	532
Hardin	32,719	Kenton	471
Harrison	18,152	Cadiz	400
Henry	28,383	Napoleon	415
Highland	33,477	Hillsboro	553
Hocking	24,304	Logan	423
Holmes	29,416	Millersburg	424
Huron	54,608	Norwalk	494
Jackson	30,592	Jackson	420
Jefferson	91,564	Steubenville	410
Knox	46,309	Mount Vernon	529
Lake	212,801	Painesville	231
Lawrence	63,849	Ironton	457
Licking	120,981	Newark	686
Logan	39,155	Bellefontaine	458
Lorain	274,909	Elyria	495
Lucas	471,741	Toledo	341
Madison	33,004	London	467
Mahoning	289,487	Youngstown	417
Marion	67,974	Marion	403
Medina	113,150	Medina	422
Meigs	23,641	Pomeroy	432
Mercer	38,334	Celina	457
Miami	90,381	Troy	410
Monroe	17,382	Woodsfield	457
Montgomery	571,697	Dayton	458
Morgan	14,241	McConnelsville	420
Morrow	26,480	Mount Gilead	406
Muskingum	83,340	Zanesville	654
Noble	11,310	Caldwell	399
Ottawa	40,076	Port Clinton	253
Paulding	21,302	Paulding	419
Perry	31,032	New Lexington	412
Pickaway	43,662	Circleville	503
Pike	22,802	Waverly	443
Portage	135,856	Ravenna	493
Preble	38,223	Eaton	426
Putnam	32,991	Ottawa	484
Richland	131,205	Mansfield	497
Ross	65,004	Chillicothe	692
Sandusky	63,267	Fremont	409
Scioto	84,545	Portsmouth	613
Seneca	61,901	Tiffin	553
Shelby	43,089	Sidney	409
Stark	378,823	Canton	574
Summit	524,472	Akron	412
Trumbull	241,863	Warren	612
Tuscarawas	84,614	New Philadelphia	570

County	Pop.	County seat or court house	Land area sq. mi.
Union	29,536	Marysville	437
Van Wert	30,458	Van Wert	410
Vinton	11,584	McArthur	414
Warren	99,276	Lebanon	403
Washington	64,266	Marietta	640
Wayne	97,408	Wooster	557
Williams	36,369	Bryan	422
Wood	107,372	Bowling Green	619
Wyandot	22,651	Upper Sandusky	406

Oklahoma
(77 counties, 68,655 sq. mi. land; pop., 3,025,487)

County	Pop.	County seat or court house	Land area sq. mi.
Adair	18,575	Stillwell	577
Alfalfa	7,077	Cherokee	864
Atoka	12,748	Atoka	980
Beaver	6,806	Beaver	1,808
Beckham	19,243	Sayre	904
Blaine	13,443	Watonga	920
Bryan	30,535	Durant	902
Caddo	30,905	Anadarko	1,286
Canadian	56,452	El Reno	901
Carter	43,610	Ardmore	828
Cherokee	30,684	Tahlequah	748
Choctaw	17,203	Hugo	762
Cimarron	3,648	Boise City	1,842
Cleveland	133,173	Norman	529
Coal	6,041	Coalgate	520
Comanche	112,456	Lawton	1,076
Cotton	7,338	Walters	656
Craig	15,014	Vinita	763
Creek	59,210	Sapulpa	930
Custer	25,995	Arapaho	981
Delaware	23,946	Jay	720
Dewey	5,922	Taloga	1,007
Ellis	5,596	Arnett	1,232
Garfield	62,820	Enid	1,060
Garvin	27,856	Pauls Valley	813
Grady	39,490	Chickasha	1,106
Grant	6,518	Medford	1,004
Greer	6,877	Mangum	638
Harmon	4,519	Hollis	537
Harper	4,715	Buffalo	1,039
Haskell	11,010	Stigler	570
Hughes	14,338	Holdenville	806
Jackson	30,356	Altus	817
Jefferson	8,294	Waurika	769
Johnston	10,356	Tishomingo	639
Kay	49,852	Newkirk	921
Kingfisher	14,187	Kingfisher	906
Kiowa	12,711	Hobart	1,019
Latimer	9,840	Wilburton	728
Le Flore	40,698	Poteau	1,585
Lincoln	26,601	Chandler	964
Logan	26,881	Guthrie	748
Love	7,469	Marietta	519
McClain	20,291	Purcell	582
McCurtain	36,151	Idabel	1,826
McIntosh	15,495	Eufaula	599
Major	8,772	Fairview	958
Marshall	10,550	Madill	372
Mayes	32,261	Pryor	644
Murray	12,147	Sulphur	420
Muskogee	67,033	Muskogee	815
Noble	11,573	Perry	736
Nowata	11,486	Nowata	540
Okfuskee	11,125	Okemah	628
Oklahoma	568,933	Oklahoma City	708
Okmulgee	39,169	Okmulgee	698
Osage	39,327	Pawhuska	2,265
Ottawa	32,870	Miami	465
Pawnee	15,310	Pawnee	551
Payne	62,435	Stillwater	691
Pittsburg	40,524	McAlester	1,251
Pontotoc	32,598	Ada	717
Pottawatomie	55,239	Shawnee	783
Pushmataha	11,773	Antlers	1,417
Roger Mills	4,799	Cheyenne	1,146
Rogers	46,436	Claremore	683
Seminole	27,465	Wewoka	639
Sequoyah	30,749	Sallisaw	678
Stephens	43,419	Duncan	884
Texas	17,727	Guymon	2,040
Tillman	12,398	Frederick	904
Tulsa	470,593	Tulsa	572
Wagoner	41,801	Wagoner	559
Washington	48,113	Bartlesville	423
Washita	13,798	Cordell	1,006
Woods	10,923	Alva	1,291
Woodward	21,172	Woodward	1,242

Oregon
(36 counties, 96,184 sq. mi. land; pop., 2,633,156)

County	Pop.	County seat or court house	Land area sq. mi.
Baker	16,134	Baker	3,072
Benton	68,211	Corvallis	679
Clackamas	241,911	Oregon City	1,870
Clatsop	32,489	Astoria	805
Columbia	35,646	Saint Helens	651
Coos	64,047	Coquille	1,606
Crook	13,091	Prineville	2,984
Curry	16,992	Gold Beach	1,629
Deschutes	62,142	Bend	3,025
Douglas	93,748	Roseburg	5,044
Gilliam	2,057	Condon	1,213
Grant	8,210	Canyon City	4,525
Harney	8,314	Burns	10,174
Hood River	15,835	Hood River	521
Jackson	132,456	Medford	2,787
Jefferson	11,599	Madras	1,789
Josephine	58,820	Grants Pass	1,640
Klamath	59,117	Klamath Falls	5,954
Lake	7,532	Lakeview	8,251
Lane	275,226	Eugene	4,562
Lincoln	35,264	Newport	980
Linn	89,495	Albany	2,296
Malheur	26,896	Vale	9,861
Marion	204,692	Salem	1,184
Morrow	7,519	Heppner	2,044
Multnomah	562,647	Portland	431
Polk	45,203	Dallas	741
Sherman	2,172	Moro	827
Tillamook	21,164	Tillamook	1,101
Umatilla	58,861	Pendleton	3,218
Union	23,921	La Grande	2,035
Wallowa	7,273	Enterprise	3,150
Wasco	21,732	The Dalles	2,384
Washington	245,860	Hillsboro	725
Wheeler	1,513	Fossil	1,713
Yamhill	55,332	McMinnville	715

Pennsylvania
(67 counties, 44,888 sq. mi. land; pop., 11,864,720)

County	Pop.	County seat or court house	Land area sq. mi.
Adams	68,292	Gettysburg	521
Allegheny	1,450,195	Pittsburgh	727
Armstrong	77,768	Kittanning	646
Beaver	204,141	Beaver	430
Bedford	46,784	Bedford	1,017
Berks	312,509	Reading	861
Blair	136,621	Hollidaysburg	527
Bradford	62,919	Towanda	1,152
Bucks	479,180	Doylestown	610
Butler	147,912	Butler	789
Cambria	183,263	Ebensburg	691
Cameron	6,674	Emporium	398
Carbon	53,285	Jim Thorpe	384
Centre	112,760	Bellefonte	1,106
Chester	316,660	West Chester	758
Clarion	43,362	Clarion	607
Clearfield	83,578	Clearfield	1,149
Clinton	38,971	Lock Haven	891
Columbia	61,967	Bloomsburg	486
Crawford	88,869	Meadville	1,011
Cumberland	179,625	Carlisle	547
Dauphin	232,317	Harrisburg	528
Delaware	555,029	Media	184
Elk	38,338	Ridgeway	830
Erie	279,780	Erie	804
Fayette	160,395	Uniontown	794
Forest	5,072	Tionesta	428
Franklin	113,629	Chambersburg	774
Fulton	12,842	McConnellsburg	438
Greene	40,355	Waynesburg	577
Huntingdon	42,253	Huntingdon	877
Indiana	92,281	Indiana	829
Jefferson	48,303	Brookville	657
Juniata	19,188	Mifflintown	392
Lackawanna	227,908	Scranton	461
Lancaster	362,346	Lancaster	952
Lawrence	107,150	New Castle	363
Lebanon	109,829	Lebanon	363
Lehigh	273,582	Allentown	348
Luzerne	343,079	Wilkes-Barre	891
Lycoming	118,416	Williamsport	1,237
McKean	50,635	Smethport	979
Mercer	128,299	Mercer	672
Mifflin	46,908	Lewistown	413
Monroe	69,409	Stroudsburg	609
Montgomery	643,371	Norristown	486
Montour	16,675	Danville	131
Northampton	225,418	Easton	376
Northumberland	100,381	Sunbury	461
Perry	35,718	New Bloomfield	557
Philadelphia	1,688,210	Philadelphia	136
Pike	18,271	Milford	550
Potter	17,726	Coudersport	1,081
Schuylkill	160,630	Pottsville	782
Snyder	33,584	Middleburg	329
Somerset	81,243	Somerset	1,073
Sullivan	6,349	Laporte	451
Susquehanna	37,876	Montrose	826
Tioga	40,973	Wellsboro	1,131
Union	32,870	Lewisburg	317
Venango	64,444	Franklin	679
Warren	47,449	Warren	885
Washington	217,074	Washington	958
Wayne	35,237	Honesdale	731
Westmoreland	392,294	Greensburg	1,033
Wyoming	26,433	Tunkhannock	399
York	312,963	York	906

County	Pop.	County seat or court house	Land area sq. mi.

Rhode Island
(5 counties, 1,055 sq. mi. land; pop., 947,154)

County	Pop.	County seat	Land area
Bristol	46,942	Bristol	26
Kent	154,163	East Greenwich	172
Newport	81,383	Newport	107
Providence	571,349	Providence	416
Washington	93,317	West Kingston	333

South Carolina
(46 counties, 30,203 sq. mi. land; pop., 3,122,717)

County	Pop.	County seat	Land area
Abbeville	22,627	Abbeville	508
Aiken	105,630	Aiken	1,092
Allendale	10,700	Allendale	413
Anderson	133,235	Anderson	718
Bamberg	18,118	Bamberg	395
Barnwell	19,868	Barnwell	558
Beaufort	65,364	Beaufort	579
Berkeley	94,745	Moncks Corner	1,108
Calhoun	12,206	Saint Matthews	380
Charleston	276,573	Charleston	938
Cherokee	40,983	Gaffney	396
Chester	30,148	Chester	580
Chesterfield	38,161	Chesterfield	802
Clarendon	27,464	Manning	602
Colleton	31,676	Walterboro	1,052
Darlington	62,717	Darlington	563
Dillon	31,083	Dillon	406
Dorchester	59,028	Saint George	575
Edgefield	17,528	Edgefield	490
Fairfield	20,700	Winnsboro	685
Florence	110,163	Florence	804
Georgetown	42,461	Georgetown	822
Greenville	287,895	Greenville	795
Greenwood	57,847	Greenwood	451
Hampton	18,159	Hampton	561
Horry	101,419	Conway	1,143
Jasper	14,504	Ridgeland	655
Kershaw	39,015	Camden	723
Lancaster	53,361	Lancaster	552
Laurens	52,214	Laurens	712
Lee	18,929	Bishopville	411
Lexington	140,353	Lexington	707
McCormick	7,797	McCormick	350
Marion	34,179	Marion	493
Marlboro	31,634	Bennettsville	483
Newberry	31,111	Newberry	634
Oconee	48,611	Walhalla	629
Orangeburg	82,276	Orangeburg	1,111
Pickens	79,292	Pickens	499
Richland	269,600	Columbia	762
Saluda	16,136	Saluda	456
Spartanburg	203,023	Spartanburg	814
Sumter	88,243	Sumter	665
Union	30,764	Union	515
Williamsburg	38,226	Kingstree	934
York	106,720	York	685

South Dakota
(67 counties, 75,952 sq. mi. land; pop., 690,768)

County	Pop.	County seat	Land area
Aurora	3,628	Plankinton	707
Beadle	19,195	Huron	1,259
Bennett	3,236	Martin	1,182
Bon Homme	8,059	Tyndall	552
Brookings	24,332	Brookings	795
Brown	36,962	Aberdeen	1,722
Brule	5,245	Chamberlain	815
Buffalo	1,795	Gannvalley	475
Butte	8,372	Belle Fourche	2,251
Campbell	2,243	Mound City	732
Charles Mix	9,680	Lake Andes	1,090
Clark	4,894	Clark	953
Clay	13,135	Vermillion	409
Codington	20,885	Watertown	694
Corson	5,196	McIntosh	2,467
Custer	6,000	Custer	1,559
Davison	17,820	Mitchell	436
Day	8,133	Webster	1,022
Deuel	5,289	Clear Lake	631
Dewey	5,366	Timber Lake	2,310
Douglas	4,181	Armour	434
Edmunds	5,159	Ipswich	1,149
Fall River	8,439	Hot Springs	1,740
Faulk	3,327	Faulkton	1,004
Grant	9,013	Milbank	681
Gregory	6,015	Burke	1,013
Haakon	2,794	Philip	1,822
Hamlin	5,261	Hayti	512
Hand	4,948	Miller	1,437
Hanson	3,415	Alexandria	433
Harding	1,700	Buffalo	2,678
Hughes	14,220	Pierre	757
Hutchinson	9,350	Olivet	816
Hyde	2,069	Highmore	860
Jackson	3,437	Kadoka	1,872
Jerauld	2,929	Wessington Spgs.	530
Jones	1,463	Murdo	971
Kingsbury	6,679	De Smet	824

County	Pop.	County seat	Land area
Lake	10,724	Madison	560
Lawrence	18,339	Deadwood	800
Lincoln	13,942	Canton	578
Lyman	3,864	Kennebec	1,679
McCook	6,444	Salem	576
McPherson	4,027	Leola	1,148
Marshall	5,404	Britton	848
Meade	20,717	Sturgis	3,481
Mellette	2,249	White River	1,311
Miner	3,739	Howard	570
Minnehaha	109,435	Sioux Falls	810
Moody	6,692	Flandreau	520
Pennington	70,133	Rapid City	2,783
Perkins	4,700	Bison	2,884
Potter	3,674	Gettysburg	869
Roberts	10,911	Sisseton	1,102
Sanborn	3,213	Woonsocket	569
Shannon	11,323	(Attached to Fall River)	2,094
Spink	9,201	Redfield	1,505
Stanley	2,533	Fort Pierre	1,431
Sully	1,990	Onida	972
Todd	7,328	(Attached to Tripp)	1,388
Tripp	7,268	Winner	1,618
Turner	9,255	Parker	617
Union	10,938	Elk Point	453
Walworth	7,011	Selby	707
Washabaugh	—	(Attached to Jackson)	—
Yankton	18,952	Yankton	518
Ziebach	2,308	Dupree	1,969

Tennessee
(95 counties, 41,155 sq. mi. land; pop., 4,591,120)

County	Pop.	County seat	Land area
Anderson	67,346	Clinton	339
Bedford	27,916	Shelbyville	475
Benton	14,901	Camden	392
Bledsoe	9,478	Pikeville	407
Blount	77,770	Maryville	558
Bradley	67,547	Cleveland	327
Campbell	34,841	Jacksboro	479
Cannon	10,234	Woodbury	266
Carroll	28,285	Huntingdon	600
Carter	50,205	Elizabethton	341
Cheatham	21,616	Ashland City	304
Chester	12,727	Henderson	289
Claiborne	24,595	Tazewell	432
Clay	7,676	Celina	227
Cocke	28,792	Newport	432
Coffee	38,311	Manchester	428
Crockett	14,941	Alamo	266
Cumberland	28,676	Crossville	682
Davidson	477,811	Nashville	501
Decatur	10,857	Decaturville	330
De Kalb	13,589	Smithville	291
Dickson	30,037	Charlotte	491
Dyer	34,663	Dyersburg	520
Fayette	25,305	Somerville	705
Fentress	14,826	Jamestown	498
Franklin	31,983	Winchester	543
Gibson	49,467	Trenton	602
Giles	24,625	Pulaski	610
Grainger	16,751	Rutledge	273
Greene	54,406	Greeneville	619
Grundy	13,787	Altamont	361
Hamblen	49,300	Morristown	156
Hamilton	287,740	Chattanooga	539
Hancock	6,887	Sneedville	223
Hardeman	23,873	Bolivar	670
Hardin	22,280	Savannah	578
Hawkins	43,751	Rogersville	486
Haywood	20,318	Brownsville	534
Henderson	21,390	Lexington	520
Henry	28,656	Paris	560
Hickman	15,151	Centerville	610
Houston	6,871	Erin	200
Humphreys	15,957	Waverly	528
Jackson	9,398	Gainesboro	308
Jefferson	31,284	Dandridge	265
Johnson	13,745	Mountain City	297
Knox	319,694	Knoxville	506
Lake	7,455	Tiptonville	169
Lauderdale	24,555	Ripley	474
Lawrence	34,110	Lawrenceburg	617
Lewis	9,700	Hohenwald	282
Lincoln	26,483	Fayetteville	571
Loudon	28,553	Loudon	235
McMinn	41,878	Athens	429
McNairy	22,525	Selmer	562
Macon	15,700	Lafayette	307
Madison	74,546	Jackson	558
Marion	24,416	Jasper	512
Marshall	19,698	Lewisburg	376
Maury	51,095	Columbia	616
Meigs	7,431	Decatur	189
Monroe	28,700	Madisonville	637
Montgomery	83,342	Clarksville	539
Moore	4,510	Lynchburg	129
Morgan	16,604	Wartburg	523
Obion	32,781	Union City	550
Overton	17,575	Livingston	433
Perry	6,111	Linden	412
Pickett	4,358	Byrdstown	159

County	Pop.	County seat or court house	Land area sq. mi.
Polk	13,602	Benton	438
Putnam	47,601	Cookeville	399
Rhea	24,235	Dayton	309
Roane	48,425	Kingston	357
Robertson	37,021	Springfield	476
Rutherford	84,058	Murfreesboro	606
Scott	19,259	Huntsville	528
Sequatchie	8,605	Dunlap	266
Sevier	41,418	Sevierville	590
Shelby	777,113	Memphis	772
Smith	14,935	Carthage	313
Stewart	8,665	Dover	454
Sullivan	143,968	Blountville	415
Sumner	85,790	Gallatin	529
Tipton	32,747	Covington	454
Trousdale	6,137	Hartsville	114
Unicoi	16,362	Erwin	186
Union	11,707	Maynardville	218
Van Buren	4,728	Spencer	273
Warren	32,653	McMinnville	431
Washington	88,755	Jonesboro	326
Wayne	13,946	Waynesboro	734
Weakley	32,896	Dresden	581
White	19,567	Sparta	373
Williamson	58,108	Franklin	584
Wilson	56,064	Lebanon	570

Texas

(254 counties, 262,017 sq. mi. land; pop., 14,227,770)

County	Pop.	County seat or court house	Land area sq. mi.
Anderson	38,381	Palestine	1,077
Andrews	13,323	Andrews	1,501
Angelina	64,172	Lufkin	807
Aransas	14,260	Rockport	280
Archer	7,266	Archer City	907
Armstrong	1,994	Claude	909
Atascosa	25,055	Jourdanton	1,218
Austin	17,726	Bellville	656
Bailey	8,168	Muleshoe	826
Bandera	7,084	Bandera	793
Bastrop	24,726	Bastrop	895
Baylor	4,919	Seymour	862
Bee	26,030	Beeville	880
Bell	157,820	Belton	1,055
Bexar	988,971	San Antonio	1,248
Blanco	4,681	Johnson City	714
Borden	859	Gail	900
Bosque	13,401	Meridian	989
Bowie	75,301	Boston	891
Brazoria	169,587	Angleton	1,407
Brazos	93,588	Bryan	589
Brewster	7,573	Alpine	6,169
Briscoe	2,579	Silverton	887
Brooks	8,428	Falfurrias	942
Brown	33,057	Brownwood	936
Burleson	12,313	Caldwell	669
Burnet	17,803	Burnet	994
Caldwell	23,637	Lockhart	546
Calhoun	19,574	Port Lavaca	540
Callahan	10,992	Baird	899
Cameron	209,680	Brownsville	906
Camp	9,275	Pittsburg	203
Carson	6,672	Panhandle	924
Cass	29,430	Linden	937
Castro	10,556	Dimmitt	899
Chambers	18,538	Anahuac	616
Cherokee	38,127	Rusk	1,052
Childress	6,950	Childress	707
Clay	9,582	Henrietta	1,086
Cochran	4,825	Morton	775
Coke	3,196	Robert Lee	908
Coleman	10,439	Coleman	1,277
Collin	144,490	McKinney	851
Collingsworth	4,648	Wellington	909
Colorado	18,823	Columbus	965
Comal	36,446	New Braunfels	555
Comanche	12,617	Comanche	930
Concho	2,915	Paint Rock	992
Cooke	27,656	Gainesville	893
Coryell	56,767	Gatesville	1,057
Cottle	2,947	Paducah	895
Crane	4,600	Crane	782
Crockett	4,608	4,588 Ozona	2,806
Crosby	8,859	Crosbyton	899
Culberson	3,315	Van Horn	3,815
Dallam	6,531	Dalhart	1,505
Dallas	1,556,549	Dallas	880
Dawson	16,184	Lamesa	903
Deaf Smith	21,165	Hereford	1,497
Delta	4,839	Cooper	278
Denton	143,126	Denton	911
Dewitt	18,903	Cuero	910
Dickens	3,539	Dickens	907
Dimmit	11,367	Carrizo Springs	1,307
Donley	4,075	Clarendon	929
Duval	12,517	San Diego	1,795
Eastland	19,480	Eastland	924
Ector	115,374	Odessa	903
Edwards	2,033	Rocksprings	2,121
Ellis	59,743	Waxahachie	939
El Paso	479,899	El Paso	1,014
Erath	22,560	Stephenville	1,080
Falls	17,946	Marlin	770
Fannin	24,285	Bonham	895
Fayette	18,832	La Grange	950
Fisher	5,801	Roby	807
Floyd	9,834	Floydada	992
Foard	2,158	Crowell	703
Fort Bend	130,962	Richmond	876
Franklin	6,893	Mount Vernon	294
Freestone	14,830	Fairfield	888
Frio	13,785	Pearsall	1,133
Gaines	13,150	Seminole	1,504
Galveston	195,738	Galveston	399
Garza	5,336	Post	895
Gillespie	13,532	Fredericksburg	1,061
Glasscock	1,304	Garden City	900
Goliad	5,193	Goliad	859
Gonzales	16,949	Gonzales	1,068
Gray	26,386	Pampa	921
Grayson	89,796	Sherman	934
Gregg	99,495	Longview	273
Grimes	13,580	Anderson	799
Guadalupe	46,708	Seguin	713
Hale	37,592	Plainview	1,005
Hall	5,594	Memphis	877
Hamilton	8,297	Hamilton	836
Hansford	6,209	Spearman	921
Hardeman	6,368	Quanah	688
Hardin	40,721	Kountze	898
Harris	2,409,544	Houston	1,734
Harrison	52,265	Marshall	908
Hartley	3,987	Channing	1,462
Haskell	7,725	Haskell	901
Hays	40,594	San Marcos	678
Hemphill	5,304	Canadian	903
Henderson	42,606	Athens	888
Hidalgo	283,323	Edinburg	1,569
Hill	25,024	Hillsboro	968
Hockley	23,230	Levelland	908
Hood	17,714	Granbury	425
Hopkins	25,247	Sulphur Springs	789
Houston	22,299	Crockett	1,234
Howard	33,142	Big Spring	901
Hudspeth	2,728	Sierra Blanca	4,567
Hunt	55,248	Greenville	840
Hutchinson	26,304	Stinnett	872
Irion	1,386	Mertzon	1,052
Jack	7,408	Jacksboro	920
Jackson	13,352	Edna	844
Jasper	30,781	Jasper	921
Jeff Davis	1,647	Fort Davis	2,257
Jefferson	250,938	Beaumont	937
Jim Hogg	5,168	Hebbronville	1,136
Jim Wells	36,498	Alice	867
Johnson	67,649	Cleburne	730
Jones	17,268	Anson	931
Karnes	13,593	Karnes City	753
Kaufman	39,038	Kaufman	788
Kendall	10,635	Boerne	663
Kenedy	543	Sarita	1,389
Kent	1,145	Jayton	878
Kerr	28,780	Kerrville	1,107
Kimble	4,063	Junction	1,250
King	425	Guthrie	914
Kinney	2,279	Brackettville	1,359
Kleberg	33,358	Kingsville	853
Knox	5,329	Benjamin	845
Lamar	42,156	Paris	919
Lamb	18,669	Littlefield	1,013
Lampasas	12,005	Lampasas	714
La Salle	5,514	Cotulla	1,517
Lavaca	19,004	Hallettsville	971
Lee	10,952	Giddings	631
Leon	9,594	Centerville	1,079
Liberty	47,088	Liberty	1,174
Limestone	20,224	Groesbeck	930
Lipscomb	3,766	Lipscomb	933
Live Oak	9,606	George West	1,057
Llano	10,144	Llano	939
Loving	91	Mentone	670
Lubbock	211,651	Lubbock	900
Lynn	8,605	Tahoka	888
McCulloch	8,735	Brady	1,071
McLennan	170,755	Waco	1,031
McMullen	789	Tilden	1,163
Madison	10,649	Madisonville	472
Marion	10,360	Jefferson	385
Martin	4,684	Staton	914
Mason	3,683	Mason	934
Matagorda	37,828	Bay City	1,127
Maverick	31,398	Eagle Pass	1,287
Medina	23,164	Hondo	1,331
Menard	2,346	Menard	902
Midland	82,636	Midland	902
Milam	22,732	Cameron	1,019
Mills	4,477	Goldthwaite	748
Mitchell	9,088	Colorado City	912
Montague	17,410	Montague	928
Montgomery	127,222	Conroe	1,047

County	Pop.	County seat or court house	Land area sq. mi.
Moore	16,575	Dumas	905
Morris	14,629	Daingerfield	256
Motley	1,950	Matador	959
Nacogdoches	46,786	Nacogdoches	939
Navarro	35,323	Corsicana	1,068
Newton	13,254	Newton	935
Nolan	17,359	Sweetwater	915
Nueces	268,215	Corpus Christi	847
Ochiltree	9,588	Perryton	919
Oldham	2,283	Vega	1,485
Orange	83,838	Orange	362
Palo Pinto	24,062	Palo Pinto	949
Panola	20,724	Carthage	812
Parker	44,609	Weatherford	902
Parmer	11,038	Farwell	885
Pecos	14,618	Fort Stockton	4,777
Polk	24,407	Livingston	1,061
Potter	98,637	Amarillo	902
Presidio	5,188	Marfa	3,857
Rains	4,839	Emory	243
Randall	75,062	Canyon	917
Reagan	4,135	Big Lake	1,173
Real	2,469	Leakey	697
Red River	16,101	Clarksville	1,054
Reeves	15,801	Pecos	2,626
Refugio	9,289	Refugio	771
Roberts	1,187	Miami	915
Robertson	14,653	Franklin	864
Rockwall	14,528	Rockwall	128
Runnels	11,872	Ballinger	1,056
Rusk	41,382	Henderson	932
Sabine	8,702	Hemphill	486
San Augustine	8,785	San Augustine	524
San Jacinto	11,434	Coldspring	572
San Patricio	58,013	Sinton	693
San Saba	5,693	San Saba	1,136
Schleicher	2,820	Eldorado	1,309
Scurry	18,192	Snyder	900
Shackelford	3,915	Albany	915
Shelby	23,084	Center	791
Sherman	3,174	Stratford	923
Smith	128,366	Tyler	932
Somervell	4,154	Glen Rose	188
Starr	27,266	Rio Grande City	1,226
Stephens	9,926	Breckenridge	894
Sterling	1,206	Sterling City	923
Stonewall	2,406	Aspermont	925
Sutton	5,130	Sonora	1,455
Swisher	9,723	Tulia	902
Tarrant	860,880	Fort Worth	868
Taylor	110,932	Abilene	917
Terrell	1,595	Sanderson	2,357
Terry	14,581	Brownfield	887
Throckmorton	2,053	Throckmorton	912
Titus	21,442	Mount Pleasant	412
Tom Green	84,784	San Angelo	1,515
Travis	419,335	Austin	989
Trinity	9,450	Groveton	692
Tyler	16,223	Woodville	922
Upshur	28,595	Gilmer	587
Upton	4,619	Rankin	1,243
Uvalde	22,441	Uvalde	1,564
Val Verde	35,910	Del Rio	3,150
Van Zandt	31,426	Canton	855
Victoria	68,807	Victoria	887
Walker	41,789	Huntsville	786
Waller	19,798	Hempstead	514
Ward	13,976	Monahans	836
Washington	21,998	Brenham	610
Webb	99,258	Laredo	3,362
Wharton	40,242	Wharton	1,086
Wheeler	7,137	Wheeler	904
Wichita	121,082	Wichita Falls	606
Wilbarger	15,931	Vernon	947
Willacy	17,495	Raymondville	589
Williamson	76,521	Georgetown	1,137
Wilson	16,756	Floresville	807
Winkler	9,944	Kermit	840
Wise	26,525	Decatur	902
Wood	24,697	Quitman	689
Yoakum	8,299	Plains	800
Young	19,001	Graham	919
Zapata	6,628	Zapata	999
Zavala	11,666	Crystal City	1,298

Utah

(29 counties, 82,073 sq. mi. land; pop. 1,461,037

County	Pop.	County seat or court house	Land area sq. mi.
Beaver	4,378	Beaver	2,586
Box Elder	33,222	Brigham City	5,614
Cache	57,176	Logan	1,171
Carbon	22,179	Price	1,479
Daggett	769	Manila	699
Davis	146,540	Farmington	299
Duchesne	12,565	Duchesne	3,233
Emery	11,451	Castle Dale	4,449
Garfield	3,673	Panguitch	5,148
Grand	8,241	Moab	3,689
Iron	17,349	Parowan	3,301
Juab	5,530	Nephi	3,396
Kane	4,024	Kanab	3,898
Millard	8,970	Fillmore	6,818
Morgan	4,917	Morgan	603
Piute	1,329	Junction	759
Rich	2,100	Randolph	1,034
Salt Lake	619,066	Salt Lake City	756
San Juan	12,253	Monticello	7,725
Sanpete	14,620	Manti	1,587
Sevier	14,727	Richfield	1,910
Summit	10,198	Coalville	1,865
Tooele	26,033	Tooele	6,919
Uintah	20,506	Vernal	4,479
Utah	218,106	Provo	2,018
Wasatch	8,523	Heber City	1,191
Washington	26,065	Saint George	2,422
Wayne	1,911	Loa	2,461
Weber	144,616	Ogden	566

Vermont

(14 counties, 9,273 sq. mi. land; pop. 511,456)

County	Pop.	County seat or court house	Land area sq. mi.
Addison	29,406	Middlebury	773
Bennington	33,345	Bennington	677
Caledonia	25,808	Saint Johnsbury	651
Chittenden	115,534	Burlington	540
Essex	6,313	Guildhall	666
Franklin	34,788	Saint Albans	649
Grand Isle	4,613	North Hero	89
Lamoille	16,767	Hyde Park	461
Orange	22,739	Chelsea	690
Orleans	23,440	Newport	697
Rutland	58,347	Rutland	932
Washington	52,393	Montpelier	690
Windham	36,933	Newfane	787
Windsor	51,030	Woodstock	972

Virginia

(95 cos., 41 ind. cities, 39,704 sq. mi. land; pop. 5,346,797)

County	Pop.	County seat or court house	Land area sq. mi.
Accomack	31,268	Accomac	476
Albemarle	50,689	Charlottesville	725
Alleghany	14,333	Covington	446
Amelia	8,405	Amelia, C.H.	357
Amherst	29,122	Amherst	479
Appomattox	11,971	Appomattox	336
Arlington	152,599	Arlington	26
Augusta	53,732	Staunton	989
Bath	5,860	Warm Springs	538
Bedford	34,927	Bedford	747
Bland	6,349	Bland	359
Botetourt	23,270	Fincastle	545
Brunswick	15,632	Lawrenceville	563
Buchanan	37,989	Grundy	504
Buckingham	11,751	Buckingham	583
Campbell	45,424	Rustburg	505
Caroline	17,904	Bowling Green	535
Carroll	27,270	Hillsville	478
Charles City	6,692	Charles City	181
Charlotte	12,266	Charlotte Courthouse	477
Chesterfield	141,372	Chesterfield	434
Clarke	9,965	Berryville	178
Craig	3,948	New Castle	330
Culpeper	22,620	Culpeper	382
Cumberland	7,881	Cumberland	300
Dickenson	19,806	Clintwood	331
Dinwiddie	22,602	Dinwiddie	507
Essex	8,864	Tappahannock	263
Fairfax	596,901	Fairfax	394
Fauquier	35,889	Warrenton	651
Floyd	11,563	Floyd	381
Fluvanna	10,244	Palmyra	290
Franklin	35,740	Rocky Mount	683
Frederick	34,150	Winchester	415
Giles	17,810	Pearisburg	362
Gloucester	20,107	Gloucester	225
Goochland	11,761	Goochland	281
Grayson	16,579	Independence	446
Greene	7,625	Stanardsville	157
Greensville	10,903	Emporia	300
Halifax	30,418	Halifax	816
Hanover	50,398	Hanover	467
Henrico	180,735	Richmond	238
Henry	57,654	Martinsville	382
Highland	2,937	Monterey	416
Isle of Wight	21,603	Isle of Wight	319
James City	22,763	Williamsburg	153
King and Queen	5,968	King and Queen	317
King George	10,543	King George	180
King William	9,327	King William	278
Lancaster	10,129	Lancaster	133
Lee	25,956	Jonesville	437
Loudoun	57,427	Leesburg	521
Louisa	17,825	Louisa	497
Lunenburg	12,124	Lunenburg	432
Madison	10,232	Madison	322
Mathews	7,995	Mathews	87
Mecklenburg	29,444	Boydton	616
Middlesex	7,719	Saluda	134
Montgomery	63,516	Christiansburg	390
Nelson	12,204	Lovingston	474
New Kent	8,781	New Kent	213

County	Pop.	County seat or court house	Land area sq. mi.
Northampton	14,625	Eastville	226
Northumberland	9,828	Heathsville	185
Nottoway	14,666	Nottoway	316
Orange	17,827	Orange	342
Page	19,401	Luray	313
Patrick	17,585	Stuart	481
Pittsylvania	66,147	Chatham	995
Powhatan	13,062	Powhatan	261
Prince Edward	16,456	Farmville	354
Prince George	25,733	Prince George	266
Prince William	144,703	Manassas	339
Pulaski	35,229	Pulaski	318
Rappahannock	6,093	Washington	267
Richmond	6,952	Warsaw	193
Roanoke	72,945	Salem	251
Rockbridge	17,911	Lexington	603
Rockingham	57,038	Harrisonburg	865
Russell	31,761	Lebanon	479
Scott	25,068	Gate City	535
Shenandoah	27,559	Woodstock	512
Smyth	33,345	Marion	452
Southampton	18,731	Courtland	603
Spotsylvania	34,435	Spotsylvania	404
Stafford	40,470	Stafford	271
Surry	6,046	Surry	281
Sussex	10,874	Sussex	491
Tazewell	50,511	Tazewell	520
Warren	21,200	Front Royal	217
Washington	46,487	Abingdon	562
Westmoreland	14,041	Montross	227
Wise	43,863	Wise	405
Wythe	25,522	Wytheville	465
York	35,463	Yorktown	113

Independent cities

City	Pop.	Land area sq. mi.
Alexandria	103,217	15
Bedford	5,991	7
Bristol	19,042	12
Buena Vista	6,717	3
Charlottesville	45,010	10
Chesapeake	114,226	340
Clifton Forge	5,046	3
Colonial Heights	16,509	8
Covington	9,063	4
Danville	45,642	17
Emporia	4,840	2
Fairfax	19,390	6
Falls Church	9,515	2
Franklin	7,308	8
Fredericksburg	15,322	6
Galax	6,524	8
Hampton	122,617	51
Harrisonburg	19,671	6
Hopewell	23,397	10
Lexington	7,292	2
Lynchburg	66,743	50
Manassas	15,438	8
Manassas Park	6,524	2
Martinsville	18,149	11
Newport News	144,903	65
Norfolk	266,979	53
Norton	4,757	7
Petersburg	41,055	23
Poquoson	8,726	17
Portsmouth	104,577	30
Radford	13,225	7
Richmond	219,214	60
Roanoke	100,427	43
Salem	23,958	14
South Boston	7,093	6
Staunton	21,857	9
Suffolk	47,621	409
Virginia Beach	262,199	256
Waynesboro	15,329	8
Williamsburg	9,870	5
Winchester	20,217	9

Washington

(39 counties, 66,511 sq. mi. land; pop., 4,132,353)

County	Pop.	County seat or court house	Land area sq. mi.
Adams	13,267	Ritzville	1,921
Asotin	16,823	Asotin	635
Benton	109,444	Prosser	1,715
Chelan	45,061	Wenatchee	2,916
Clallam	51,648	Port Angeles	1,753
Clark	192,227	Vancouver	627
Columbia	4,057	Dayton	865
Cowlitz	79,548	Kelso	1,140
Douglas	22,144	Waterville	1,817
Ferry	5,811	Republic	2,200
Franklin	35,025	Pasco	1,243
Garfield	2,468	Pomeroy	706
Grant	48,522	Ephrata	2,660
Grays Harbor	66,314	Montesano	1,918
Island	44,048	Coupeville	212
Jefferson	15,965	Port Townsend	1,805
King	1,269,898	Seattle	2,128
Kitsap	146,609	Port Orchard	393
Kittitas	24,877	Ellensburg	2,308
Klickitat	15,822	Goldendale	1,880
Lewis	55,279	Chehalis	2,409
Lincoln	9,604	Davenport	2,310
Mason	31,184	Shelton	961
Okanogan	30,663	Okanogan	5,281
Pacific	17,237	South Bend	908
Pend Oreille	8,580	Newport	1,400
Pierce	485,643	Tacoma	1,675
San Juan	7,838	Friday Harbor	179
Skagit	64,138	Mount Vernon	1,735
Skamania	7,919	Stevenson	1,672
Snohomish	337,016	Everett	2,090
Spokane	341,835	Spokane	1,762
Stevens	28,979	Colville	2,470
Thurston	124,264	Olympia	727
Wahkiakum	3,832	Cathlamet	261
Walla Walla	47,435	Walla Walla	1,261
Whatcom	106,701	Bellingham	2,125
Whitman	40,103	Colfax	2,151
Yakima	172,508	Yakima	4,287

West Virginia

(55 counties, 24,119 sq. mi. land; pop., 1,950,186)

County	Pop.	County seat or court house	Land area sq. mi.
Barbour	16,639	Philippi	343
Berkeley	46,775	Martinsburg	321
Boone	30,447	Madison	503
Braxton	13,894	Sutton	513
Brooke	31,117	Wellsburg	90
Cabell	106,835	Huntington	282
Calhoun	8,250	Grantsville	280
Clay	11,265	Clay	346
Doddridge	7,433	West Union	321
Fayette	57,863	Fayetteville	667
Gilmer	8,334	Glenville	340
Grant	10,210	Petersburg	480
Greenbrier	37,665	Lewisburg	1,025
Hampshire	14,867	Romney	644
Hancock	41,053	New Cumberland	84
Hardy	10,030	Moorefield	585
Harrison	77,710	Clarksburg	417
Jackson	25,794	Ripley	464
Jefferson	30,302	Charles Town	209
Kanawha	231,414	Charleston	901
Lewis	18,813	Weston	389
Lincoln	23,675	Hamlin	439
Logan	50,679	Logan	456
McDowell	49,899	Welch	535
Marion	65,789	Fairmont	312
Marshall	41,608	Moundsville	305
Mason	27,045	Point Pleasant	433
Mercer	73,870	Princeton	420
Mineral	27,234	Keyser	329
Mingo	37,336	Williamson	424
Monongalia	75,024	Morgantown	363
Monroe	12,873	Union	473
Morgan	10,711	Berkeley Springs	230
Nicholas	28,126	Summersville	650
Ohio	61,389	Wheeling	106
Pendleton	7,910	Franklin	698
Pleasants	8,236	St. Marys	131
Pocahontas	9,919	Marlinton	942
Preston	30,460	Kingwood	651
Putnam	38,181	Winfield	346
Raleigh	86,821	Beckley	608
Randolph	28,734	Elkins	1,040
Ritchie	11,442	Harrisville	454
Roane	15,952	Spencer	484
Summers	15,875	Hinton	353
Taylor	16,584	Grafton	174
Tucker	8,675	Parsons	421
Tyler	11,320	Middlebourne	258
Upshur	23,427	Buckhannon	355
Wayne	46,021	Wayne	508
Webster	12,245	Webster Springs	556
Wetzel	21,874	New Martinsville	359
Wirt	4,922	Elizabeth	235
Wood	93,627	Parkersburg	367
Wyoming	35,993	Pineville	502

Wisconsin

(72 counties, 54,426 sq. mi. land; pop., 4,705,642)

County	Pop.	County seat or court house	Land area sq. mi.
Adams	13,457	Friendship	648
Ashland	16,783	Ashland	1,048
Barron	38,730	Barron	865
Bayfield	13,822	Washburn	1,462
Brown	175,280	Green Bay	524
Buffalo	14,309	Alma	699
Burnett	12,340	Grantsburg	818
Calumet	30,867	Chilton	326
Chippewa	51,702	Chippewa Falls	1,017
Clark	32,910	Neillsville	1,218
Columbia	43,222	Portage	771
Crawford	16,556	Prairie du Chien	566
Dane	323,545	Madison	1,205
Dodge	74,747	Juneau	887
Door	25,029	Sturgeon Bay	492
Douglas	44,421	Superior	1,305
Dunn	34,314	Menomonie	853
Eau Claire	78,805	Eau Claire	638
Florence	4,172	Florence	486

County	Pop.	County seat or court house	Land area sq. mi.
Fond Du Lac	88,952	Fond du Lac	725
Forest	9,044	Crandon	1,011
Grant	51,736	Lancaster	1,144
Green	30,012	Monroe	583
Green Lake	18,370	Green Lake	357
Iowa	19,802	Dodgeville	760
Iron	6,730	Hurley	751
Jackson	16,831	Black River Falls	998
Jefferson	66,152	Jefferson	562
Juneau	21,037	Mauston	774
Kenosha	123,137	Kenosha	273
Kewaunee	19,539	Kewaunee	343
La Crosse	91,056	La Crosse	457
Lafayette	17,412	Darlington	634
Langlade	19,978	Antigo	873
Lincoln	26,311	Merrill	886
Manitowoc	82,918	Manitowoc	594
Marathon	111,270	Wausau	1,559
Marinette	39,314	Marinette	1,395
Marquette	11,672	Montello	455
Menominee	3,373	Keshena	359
Milwaukee	964,988	Milwaukee	241
Monroe	35,074	Sparta	904
Oconto	28,947	Oconto	1,002
Oneida	31,216	Rhinelander	1,130
Outagamie	128,726	Appleton	642
Ozaukee	66,981	Port Washington	235
Pepin	7,477	Durand	231
Pierce	31,149	Ellsworth	577
Polk	32,351	Balsam Lake	919
Portage	57,420	Stevens Point	810
Price	15,788	Phillips	1,256
Racine	173,132	Racine	335
Richland	17,476	Richland Center	585
Rock	139,420	Janesville	723
Rusk	15,589	Ladysmith	913
St. Croix	43,872	Hudson	723
Sauk	43,469	Baraboo	838

County	Pop.		Pop.
Sawyer	12,843	Hayward	1,255
Shawano	35,928	Shawano	897
Sheboygan	100,935	Sheboygan	515
Taylor	18,817	Medford	975
Trempealeau	26,158	Whitehall	736
Vernon	25,642	Viroqua	808
Vilas	16,535	Eagle River	867
Walworth	71,507	Elkhorn	556
Washburn	13,174	Shell Lake	815
Washington	84,848	West Bend	430
Waukesha	280,203	Waukesha	554
Waupaca	42,831	Waupaca	754
Waushara	18,526	Wautoma	628
Winnebago	131,772	Oshkosh	449
Wood	72,799	Wisconsin Rapids	801

Wyoming

(23 counties, 96,989 sq. mi. land; pop. 469,557)

County	Pop.		Pop.
Albany	29,062	Laramie	4,268
Big Horn	11,896	Basin	3,139
Campbell	24,367	Gillette	4,796
Carbon	21,896	Rawlins	7,877
Converse	14,069	Douglas	4,271
Crook	5,308	Sundance	2,855
Fremont	40,251	Lander	9,181
Goshen	12,040	Torrington	2,186
Hot Springs	5,710	Thermopolis	2,005
Johnson	6,700	Buffalo	4,166
Laramie	68,649	Cheyenne	2,684
Lincoln	12,177	Kemmerer	4,070
Natrona	71,856	Casper	5,347
Niobrara	2,924	Lusk	2,684
Park	21,639	Cody	6,936
Platte	11,975	Wheatland	2,023
Sheridan	25,048	Sheridan	2,532
Sublette	4,548	Pinedale	4,872
Sweetwater	41,723	Green River	10,352
Teton	9,355	Jackson	4,011
Uinta	13,021	Evanston	2,085
Washakie	9,496	Worland	2,243
Weston	7,106	Newcastle	2,402

Population of Outlying Areas

Source: U.S. Bureau of the Census
Population figures are final counts from the census conducted on Apr. 1, 1980.

Puerto Rico

ZIP code	Municipios	Pop.	Land area sq. mile	ZIP code	Municipios	Pop.	Land area sq. mile	ZIP code	Municipios	Pop.	Land area sq. mile
00601	Adjuntas	18,786	67	00650	Florida	7,232	10	00720	Orocovis	19,332	64
00602	Aguada	31,567	31	00653	Guanica	18,799	37	00723	Patillas	17,774	47
00603	Aguadilla	54,606	37	00654	Guayama	40,183	65	00724	Penuelas	19,116	45
00607	Aguas Buenas	22,429	30	00656	Guayanilla	21,050	42	00731	Ponce	189,046	117
00609	Aibonito	22,167	31	00657	Guaynabo	80,742	27	00742	Quebradillas	19,728	23
00610	Anasco	23,274	40	00658	Gurabo	23,574	28	00743	Rincon	11,788	14
00612	Arecibo	86,766	127	00659	Hatillo	28,958	42	00745	Rio Grande	34,283	62
00615	Arroyo	17,014	15	00660	Hormigueros	14,030	11	00747	Sabana Grande	20,207	36
00617	Barceloneta	18,942	24	00661	Humacao	46,134	45	00751	Salinas	26,438	71
00618	Barranquitas	21,639	34	00662	Isabela	37,435	56	00753	San German	32,922	54
00619	Bayamon	196,206	45	00664	Jayuya	14,722	44	*00936	San Juan	434,849	47
00623	Cabo Rojo	34,045	72	00665	Juana Diaz	43,505	61	00754	San Lorenzo	32,428	53
00625	Caguas	117,959	59	00666	Juncos	25,397	27	00755	San Sebastian	35,690	71
00627	Camuy	24,884	47	00667	Lajas	21,236	60	00757	Santa Isabel	19,854	35
00629	Canovanas	31,880	33	00669	Lares	26,743	62	00758	Toa Alta	31,910	28
00630	Carolina	165,954	48	00670	Las Marias	8,747	46	00759	Toa Baja	78,246	24
00632	Catano	26,243	6	00671	Las Piedras	22,412	34	00760	Trujillo Alto	51,389	21
00633	Cayey	41,099	52	00672	Loiza	20,867	21	00761	Utuado	34,505	115
00635	Ceiba	14,944	27	00673	Luquillo	14,895	26	00762	Vega Alta	28,696	28
00638	Ciales	16,211	67	00701	Manati	36,562	46	00763	Vega Baja	47,115	53
00639	Cidra	28,365	36	00706	Maricao	6,737	37	00765	Vieques	7,662	53
00640	Coamo	30,822	78	00707	Maunabo	11,813	21	00766	Villalba	20,734	37
00642	Comerio	18,212	29	00708	Mayaguez	96,193	77	00767	Yabucoa	31,425	55
00643	Corozal	28,221	43	00716	Moca	29,185	50	00768	Yauco	37,742	69
00645	Culebra	1,265	13	00717	Morovis	21,142	39		Total	3,196,520	3,459
00646	Dorado	25,511	24	00718	Naguabo	20,617	52				
00648	Fajardo	32,087	31	00719	Naranjito	23,633	28				

ZIP code	Area	Pop.	Land area sq. mile	ZIP code	Area	Pop.	Land area sq. mile	ZIP code	Area	Pop.	Land area sq. mile
	American Samoa				Mongmong-Toto-Maite	5,245	2	00820	Christiansted	2,904	
96799	American Samoa	32,297	77		Piti	2,866	7	00840	Frederiksted	1,046	
				96915	Santa Rita	9,183	17		Total	96,569	132
	Guam				Sinajana	2,485	1		**Trust Territory of Pacific Islands**		
96910	Agana	896	1		Talofofo	2,006	17				
	Agana Hts.	3,284	1	96911	Tamuning	13,580	6		Kosrae	NA	42
96915	Agat	3,999	10		Umatac	732	6		Marshall Islands	NA	70
	Asan	2,034	6		Yigo	10,359	35		Palau	NA	192
96913	Barrigada	7,756	9	96914	Yona	4,228	20		Ponape	NA	176
	Chalan-Pago-Ordot	3,120	6		Total	105,979	209		Truk	NA	49
96912	Dededo	23,644	30						Yap	NA	46
96916	Inarajan	2,050	19		**Virgin Islands**				Total	NA	533
	Mangilao	6,840	10		St. Croix	49,725	80				
96916	Merizo	1,663	6		St. John	2,472	20		**No. Mariana Islands**	16,758	184
					St. Thomas	44,372	32				
				00801	Charlotte Amalie	11,671					

BIOGRAPHIES OF U.S. PRESIDENTS

George Washington

George Washington, first president, was born Feb. 22, 1732 (Feb. 11, 1731, old style), the son of Augustine Washington and Mary Ball, at Wakefield on Pope's Creek, Westmoreland Co., Va. His early childhood was spent on the Ferry farm, near Fredericksburg. His father died when George was 11. He studied mathematics and surveying and when 16 went to live with his half brother Lawrence, who built and named Mount Vernon. George surveyed the lands of William Fairfax in the Shenandoah Valley, keeping a diary. He accompanied Lawrence to Barbados, West Indies, contracted small pox, and was deeply scarred. Lawrence died in 1752 and George acquired his property by inheritance. He valued land and when he died owned 70,000 acres in Virginia and 40,000 acres in what is now West Virginia.

Washington's military service began in 1753 when Gov. Dinwiddie of Virginia sent him on missions deep into Ohio country. He clashed with the French and had to surrender Fort Necessity July 3, 1754. He was an aide to Braddock and at his side when the army was ambushed and defeated on a march to Ft. Duquesne, July 9, 1755. He helped take Fort Duquesne from the French in 1758.

After his marriage to Martha Dandridge Custis, a widow, in 1759, Washington managed his family estate at Mount Vernon. Although not at first for independence, he opposed British exactions and took charge of the Virginia troops before war broke out. He was made commander-in-chief by the Continental Congress June 15, 1775.

The successful issue of a war filled with hardships was due to his leadership. He was resourceful, a stern disciplinarian, and the one strong, dependable force for unity. He favored a federal government and became chairman of the Constitutional Convention of 1787. He helped get the Constitution ratified and was unanimously elected president by the electoral college and inaugurated, Apr. 30, 1789, on the balcony of New York's Federal Hall.

He was reelected 1792, but refused to consider a 3d term and retired to Mount Vernon. He suffered acute laryngitis after a ride in snow and rain around his estate, was bled profusely, and died Dec. 14, 1799.

John Adams

John Adams, 2d president, Federalist, was born in Braintree (Quincy), Mass., Oct. 30, 1735 (Oct. 19, o. s.), the son of John Adams, a farmer, and Susanna Boylston. He was a great-grandson of Henry Adams who came from England in 1636. He was graduated from Harvard, 1755, taught school, studied law. In 1765 he argued against taxation without representation before the royal governor. In 1770 he defended the British soldiers who fired on civilians in the "Boston Massacre." He was a delegate to the first Continental Congress, and signed the Declaration of Independence. He was a commissioner to France, 1778, with Benjamin Franklin and Arthur Lee; won recognition of the U.S. by The Hague, 1782; was first American minister to England, 1785-1788, and was elected vice president, 1788 and 1792.

In 1796 Adams was chosen president by the electors. Intense antagonism to America by France caused agitation for war, led by Alexander Hamilton. Adams, breaking with Hamilton, opposed war.

To fight alien influence and muzzle criticism Adams supported the Alien and Sedition laws of 1798, which led to his defeat for reelection. He died July 4, 1826, on the same day as Jefferson (the 50th anniversary of the Declaration of Independence).

Thomas Jefferson

Thomas Jefferson, 3d president, was born Apr. 13, 1743 (Apr. 2, o. s.), at Shadwell, Va., the son of Peter Jefferson, a civil engineer of Welsh descent who raised tobacco, and Jane Randolph. His father died when he was 14, leaving him 2,750 acres and his slaves. Jefferson attended the College of William and Mary, 1760-1762, read classics in Greek and Latin and played the violin. In 1769 he was elected to the House of Burgesses. In 1770 he began building Monticello, near Charlottesville. He was a member of the Virginia Committee of Correspondence and the Continental Congress. Named a member of the committee to draw up a Declaration of Independence, he wrote the basic draft. He was a member of the Virginia House of Delegates, 1776-79, elected governor to succeed Patrick Henry, 1779, reelected 1780, resigned June 1781, amid charges of ineffectual military preparation. During his term he wrote the statute on religious freedom. In the Continental Congress, 1783, he drew up an ordinance for the Northwest Territory, forbidding slavery after 1800; its terms were put into the Ordinance of 1787. He was sent to Paris with Benjamin Franklin and John Adams to negotiate commercial treaties, 1784; made minister to France, 1785.

Washington appointed him secretary of state, 1789. Jefferson's strong faith in the consent of the governed, as opposed to executive control favored by Hamilton, secretary of the treasury, often led to conflict: Dec. 31, 1793, he resigned. He was the Republican candidate for president in 1796; beaten by John Adams, he became vice president. In 1800, Jefferson and Aaron Burr received equal electoral college votes for president. The House of Representatives elected Jefferson. Major events of his administration were the Louisiana Purchase, 1803, and the Lewis and Clark Expedition. He established the Univ. of Virginia and designed its buildings. He died July 4, 1826, on the same day as John Adams.

James Madison

James Madison, 4th president, Republican, was born Mar. 16, 1751 (Mar. 5, 1750, o. s.) at Port Conway, King George Co., Va., eldest son of James Madison and Eleanor Rose Conway. Madison was graduated from Princeton, 1771; studied theology, 1772; sat in the Virginia Constitutional Convention, 1776. He was a member of the Continental Congress. He was chief recorder at the Constitutional Convention in 1787, and supported ratification in the Federalist Papers, written with Alexander Hamilton and John Jay. He was elected to the House of Representatives in 1789, helped frame the Bill of Rights and fought the Alien and Sedition Acts. He became Jefferson's secretary of state, 1801.

Elected president in 1808, Madison was a "strict constructionist," opposed to the free interpretation of the Constitution by the Federalists. He was reelected in 1812 by the votes of the agrarian South and recently admitted western states. Caught between British and French maritime restrictions, the U.S. drifted into war, declared June 18, 1812. The war ended in a stalemate. He retired in 1817 to his estate at Montpelier. There he edited his famous papers on the Constitutional Convention. He became rector of the Univ. of Virginia, 1826. He died June 28, 1836.

James Monroe

James Monroe, 5th president, Republican, was born Apr. 28, 1758, in Westmoreland Co., Va., the son of Spence Monroe and Eliza Jones, who were of Scottish and Welsh descent, respectively. He attended the College of William and Mary, fought in the 3d Virginia Regiment at White Plains, Brandywine, Monmouth, and was wounded at Trenton. He studied law with Thomas Jefferson, 1780, was a member of the Virginia House of Delegates and of Congress, 1783-86. He opposed ratification of the Constitution because it lacked a bill of rights; was U.S. senator, 1790; minister to France, 1794-96; governor of Virginia, 1799-1802, and 1811. Jefferson sent him to France as minister, 1803. He helped R. Livingston negotiate the Louisiana Purchase, 1803. He ran against Madison for president in 1808. He was elected to the Virginia Assembly, 1810-1811; was secretary of state under Madison, 1811-1817.

In 1816 Monroe was elected president; in 1820 reelected

with all but one electoral college vote. Monroe's administration became the "Era of Good Feeling." He obtained Florida from Spain; settled boundaries with Canada, and eliminated border forts. He supported the anti-slavery position that led to the Missouri Compromise. His most significant contribution was the "Monroe Doctrine," which became a cornerstone of U.S. foreign policy. Monroe retired to Oak Hill, Va. Financial problems forced him to sell his property. He moved to New York City to live with a daughter. He died there July 4, 1831.

John Quincy Adams

John Quincy Adams, 6th president, independent Federalist, was born July 11, 1767, at Braintree (Quincy), Mass., the son of John and Abigail Adams. His father was the 2d president. He was educated in Paris, Leyden, and Harvard, graduating in 1787. He served as American minister in various European capitals, and helped draft the War of 1812 peace treaty. He was U.S. Senator, 1803-08. President Monroe made him secretary of state, 1817, and he negotiated the cession of the Floridas from Spain, supported exclusion of slavery in the Missouri Compromise, and helped formulate the Monroe Doctrine. In 1824 he was elected president by the House after he failed to win an electoral college majority. His expansion of executive powers was strongly opposed and he was beaten in 1828 by Jackson. In 1831 he entered Congress and served 17 years with distinction. He opposed slavery, the annexation of Texas, and the Mexican War. He helped establish the Smithsonian Institution. He had a stroke in the House and died in the Speaker's Room, Feb. 23, 1848.

Andrew Jackson

Andrew Jackson, 7th president, was a Jeffersonian-Republican, later a Democrat. He was born in the Waxhaws district, New Lancaster Co., S.C., Mar. 15, 1767, the posthumous son of Andrew Jackson and Elizabeth Hutchinson, who were Irish immigrants. At 13, he joined the militia in the Revolution and was captured.

He read law in Salisbury, N.C., moved to Nashville, Tenn., speculated in land, married, and practiced law. In 1796 he helped draft the constitution of Tennessee and for a year occupied its one seat in Congress. He was in the Senate in 1797, and again in 1823. He defeated the Creek Indians at Horseshoe Bend, Ala., 1814. With 6,000 backwoods fighters he defeated Packenham's 12,000 British troops at the Chalmette, outside New Orleans, Jan. 8, 1815. In 1818 he briefly invaded Spanish Florida to quell Seminoles and outlaws who harassed frontier settlements. In 1824 he ran for president against John Quincy Adams and had the most popular and electoral votes but not a majority; the election was decided by the House, which chose Adams. In 1828 he defeated Adams, carrying the West and South. He was a noisy debater and a duelist and introduced rotation in office called the "spoils system." Suspicious of privilege, he ruined the Bank of the United States by depositing federal funds with state banks. Though "Let the people rule" was his slogan, he at times supported strict constructionist policies against the expansionist West. He killed the Congressional caucus for nominating presidential candidates and substituted the national convention, 1832. When South Carolina refused to collect imports under his protective tariff he ordered army and naval forces to Charleston. Jackson recognized the Republic of Texas, 1836. He died at the Hermitage, June 8, 1845.

Martin Van Buren

Martin Van Buren, 8th president, Democrat, was born Dec. 5, 1782, at Kinderhook, N.Y., the son of Abraham Van Buren, a Dutch farmer, and Mary Hoes. He was surrogate of Columbia County, N.Y., state senator and attorney general. He was U.S. senator 1821, reelected, 1827, elected governor of New York, 1828. He helped swing eastern support to Jackson in 1828 and was his secretary of state 1829-31. In 1832 he was elected vice president. He was a

consummate politician, known as "the little magician," and influenced Jackson's policies. In 1836 he defeated William Henry Harrison for president and took office as the Panic of 1837 initiated a 5-year nationwide depression. He inaugurated the independent treasury system. His refusal to spend land revenues led to his defeat by Harrison in 1840. He lost the Democratic nomination of 1844 to Polk. In 1848 he ran for president on the Free Soil ticket and lost. He died July 24, 1862, at Kinderhook.

William Henry Harrison

William Henry Harrison, 9th president, Whig, who served only 31 days, was born in Berkeley, Charles City Co., Va., Feb. 9, 1773, the 3d son of Benjamin Harrison, signer of the Declaration of Independence. He attended Hampden Sydney College. He was secretary of the Northwest Territory, 1798; its delegate in Congress, 1799; first governor of Indiana Territory, 1800; and superintendent of Indian affairs. With 900 men he routed Tecumseh's Indians at Tippecanoe, Nov. 7, 1811. A major general, he defeated British and Indians at Battle of the Thames, Oct. 5, 1813. He served in Congress, 1816-19; Senate, 1825-28. In 1840, when 68, he was elected president with a "log cabin and hard cider" slogan. He caught pneumonia during the inauguration and died Apr. 4, 1841.

John Tyler

John Tyler, 10th president, independent Whig, was born Mar. 29, 1790, in Greenway, Charles City Co., Va., son of John Tyler and Mary Armistead. His father was governor of Virginia, 1808-11. Tyler was graduated from William and Mary, 1807; member of the House of Delegates, 1811; in congress, 1816-21; in Virginia legislature, 1823-25; governor of Virginia, 1825-26; U.S. senator, 1827-36. In 1840 he was elected vice president and, on Harrison's death, succeeded him. He favored pre-emption, allowing settlers to get government land; rejected a national bank bill and thus alienated most Whig supporters; refused to honor the spoils system. He signed the resolution annexing Texas, Mar. 1, 1845. He accepted renomination, 1844, but withdrew before election. In 1861, he chaired an unsuccessful Washington conference called to avert civil war. After its failure he supported secession, sat in the provisional Confederate Congress, became a member of the Confederate House, but died, Jan. 18, 1862, before it met.

James Knox Polk

James Knox Polk, 11th president, Democrat, was born in Mecklenburg Co., N.C., Nov. 2, 1795, the son of Samuel Polk, farmer and surveyor of Scotch-Irish descent, and Jane Knox. He graduated from the Univ. of North Carolina, 1818; member of the Tennessee state legislature, 1823-25. He served in Congress 1825-39 and as speaker 1835-39. He was governor of Tennessee 1839-41, but was defeated 1841 and 1843. In 1844, when both Clay and Van Buren announced opposition to annexing Texas, the Democrats made Polk the first dark horse nominee because he demanded control of all Oregon and annexation of Texas. Polk reestablished the independent treasury system originated by Van Buren. His expansionist policy was opposed by Clay, Webster, Calhoun; he sent troops under Zachary Taylor to the Mexican border and, when Mexicans attacked, declared war existed. The Mexican war ended with the annexation of California and much of the Southwest as part of America's "manifest destiny." He compromised on the Oregon boundary ("54-40 or fight!") by accepting the 49th parallel and giving Vancouver to the British. Polk died in Nashville, June 15, 1849.

Zachary Taylor

Zachary Taylor, 12th president, Whig, who served only 16 months, was born Nov. 24, 1784, in Orange Co., Va., the son of Richard Taylor, later collector of the port of Louisville, Ky., and Sarah Strother. Taylor was commissioned first lieutenant, 1808; fought in the War of 1812; the Black

Hawk War, 1832; and the second Seminole War, 1837. He was called Old Rough and Ready. He settled on a plantation near Baton Rouge, La. In 1845 Polk sent him with an army to the Rio Grande. When the Mexicans attacked him, Polk declared war. Taylor was successful at Palo Alto and Resaca de la Palma, 1846; occupied Monterrey. Polk made him major general but sent many of his troops to Gen. Winfield Scott. Outnumbered 4-1, he defeated Santa Anna at Buena Vista, 1847. A national hero, he received the Whig nomination in 1848, and was elected president. He resumed the spoils system and though once a slave-holder worked to have California admitted as a free state. He died in office July 9, 1850.

Millard Fillmore

Millard Fillmore, 13th president, Whig, was born Jan. 7, 1800, in Cayuga Co., N.Y., the son of Nathaniel Fillmore and Phoebe Miller. He taught school and studied law; admitted to the bar, 1823. He was a member of the state assembly, 1829-32; in Congress, 1833-35 and again 1837-43. He opposed the entrance of Texas as slave territory and voted for a protective tariff. In 1844 he was defeated for governor of New York. In 1848 he was elected vice president and succeeded as president July 10, 1850, after Taylor's death. Fillmore favored the Compromise of 1850 and signed the Fugitive Slave Law. His policies pleased neither expansionists nor slave-holders and he was not renominated in 1852. In 1856 he was nominated by the American (Know-Nothing) party and accepted by the Whigs, but defeated by Buchanan. He died in Buffalo, Mar. 8, 1874.

Franklin Pierce

Franklin Pierce, 14th president, Democrat, was born in Hillsboro, N. H., Nov. 23, 1804, the son of Benjamin Pierce, veteran of the Revolution and governor of New Hampshire, 1827. He graduated from Bowdoin, 1824. A lawyer, he served in the state legislature 1829-33; in Congress, supporting Jackson, 1833-37; U.S. senator, 1837-42. He enlisted in the Mexican War, became brigadier general under Gen. Winfield Scott. In 1852 Pierce was nominated on the 49th ballot over Lewis Cass, Stephen A. Douglas, and James Buchanan, and defeated Gen. Scott, Whig. Though against slavery, Pierce was influenced by Southern pro-slavery men. He ignored the Ostend Manifesto that the U.S. either buy or take Cuba. He approved the Kansas-Nebraska Act, leaving slavery to popular vote ("squatter sovereignty"), 1854. He signed a reciprocity treaty with Canada and approved the Gadsden Purchase from Mexico, 1853. Denied renomination by the Democrats, he spent most of his remaining years in Concord, N.H., where he died Oct. 8, 1869.

James Buchanan

James Buchanan, 15th president, Federalist, later Democrat, was born of Scottish descent near Mercersburg, Pa., Apr. 23, 1791. He graduated from Dickinson, 1809; was a volunteer in the War of 1812; member, Pennsylvania legislature, 1814-16, Congress, 1820-31; Jackson's minister to Russia, 1831-33; U.S. senator 1834-45. As Polk's secretary of state, 1845-49, he ended the Oregon dispute with Britain, supported the Mexican War and annexation of Texas. As minister to Britain, 1853, he signed the Ostend Manifesto. Nominated by Democrats, he was elected, 1856, over John C. Fremont (Republican) and Millard Fillmore (American Know-Nothing and Whig tickets). On slavery he favored popular sovereignty and choice by state constitutions; he accepted the pro-slavery Dred Scott decision as binding. He denied the right of states to secede. A strict constructionist, he desired to keep peace and found no authority for using force. He died at Wheatland, near Lancaster, Pa., June 1, 1868.

Abraham Lincoln

Abraham Lincoln, 16th president, Republican, was born Feb. 12, 1809, in a log cabin on a farm then in Hardin Co.,

Ky., now in Larue. He was the son of Thomas Lincoln, a carpenter, and Nancy Hanks.

The Lincolns moved to Spencer Co., Ind., near Gentryville, when Abe was 7. Nancy died 1818, and his father married Mrs. Sarah Bush Johnston, 1819; she had a favorable influence on Abe. In 1830 the family moved to Macon Co., Ill. Lincoln lost election to the Illinois General Assembly, 1832, but later won 4 times, beginning in 1834. He enlisted in the militia for the Black Hawk War, 1832. In New Salem he ran a store, surveyed land, and was postmaster.

In 1837 Lincoln was admitted to the bar and became partner in a Springfield, Ill., law office. He was elected to Congress, 1847-49. He opposed the Mexican War. He supported Zachary Taylor, 1848. He opposed the Kansas-Nebraska Act and extension of slavery, 1854. He failed, in his bid for the Senate, 1855. He supported John C. Fremont, 1856.

In 1858 Lincoln had Republican support in the Illinois legislature for the Senate but was defeated by Stephen A. Douglas, Dem., who had sponsored the Kansas-Nebraska Act.

Lincoln was nominated for president by the Republican party on an anti-slavery platform, 1860. He ran against Douglas, a northern Democrat; John C. Breckinridge, southern pro-slavery Democrat; John Bell, Constitutional Union party. When he won the election, South Carolina seceded from the Union Dec. 20, 1860, followed in 1861 by 10 Southern states.

The Civil War erupted when Fort Sumter was attacked Apr. 12, 1861. On Sept. 22, 1862, 5 days after the battle of Antietam, he announced that slaves in territory then in rebellion would be free Jan. 1, 1863, date of the Emancipation Proclamation. His speeches, including his Gettysburg and Inaugural addresses, are remembered for their eloquence.

Lincoln was reelected, 1864, over Gen. George B. McClellan, Democrat. Lee surrendered Apr. 9, 1865. On Apr. 14, Lincoln was shot by actor John Wilkes Booth in Ford's Theatre, Washington. He died the next day.

Andrew Johnson

Andrew Johnson, 17th president, Democrat, was born in Raleigh, N.C., Dec. 29, 1808, the son of Jacob Johnson, porter at an inn and church sexton, and Mary McDonough. He was apprenticed to a tailor but ran away and eventually settled in Greeneville, Tenn. He became an alderman, 1828; mayor, 1830; state representative and senator, 1835-43; member of Congress, 1843-53; governor of Tennessee, 1853-57; U.S. senator, 1857-62. He supported John C. Breckinridge against Lincoln in 1860. He had held slaves, but opposed secession and tried to prevent his home state, Tennessee, from seceding. In Mar. 1862, Lincoln appointed him military governor of occupied Tennessee. In 1864 he was nominated for vice president with Lincoln on the National Union ticket to win Democratic support. He succeeded Lincoln as president April 15, 1865. In a controversy with Congress over the president's power over the South, he proclaimed, May 26, 1865, an amnesty to all Confederates except certain leaders if they would ratify the 13th Amendment abolishing slavery. States doing so added anti-Negro provisions that enraged Congress, which restored military control over the South. When Johnson removed Edwin M. Stanton, secretary of war, without notifying the Senate, thus repudiating the Tenure of Office Act, the House impeached him for this and other reasons. He was tried by the Senate, and acquitted by only one vote, May 26, 1868. He returned to the Senate in 1875. Johnson died July 31, 1875.

Ulysses Simpson Grant

Ulysses S. Grant, 18th president, Republican, was born at Point Pleasant, Oh., Apr. 27, 1822, son of Jesse R. Grant, a tanner, and Hannah Simpson. The next year the family moved to Georgetown, Oh. Grant was named Hiram Ulysses, but on entering West Point, 1839, his name was entered as Ulysses Simpson and he adopted it. he was graduated in 1843; served under Gens. Taylor and Scott in the Mexican War; resigned, 1854; worked in St. Louis until 1860, then went to Galena, Ill. With the start of the Civil War, he was named colonel of the 21st Illinois Vols., 1861, then brigadier general; took Forts Henry and Donelson; fought at Shiloh, took Vicksburg. After his victory at Chattanooga, Lincoln placed him in command of the Union Armies. He accepted Lee's surrender at Appomattox, Apr., 1865. President Johnson appointed Grant secretary of war when he suspended Stanton, but Grant was not confirmed. He was nominated for president by the Republicans and elected over Horatio Seymour, Democrat. The 15th Amendment, amnesty bill, and civil service reform were events of his administration. The Liberal Republicans and Democrats opposed him with Horace Greeley, 1872, but he was reelected. An attempt by the Stalwarts (Old Guard) to nominate him in 1880 failed. In 1884 the collapse of Grant & Ward, investment house, left him penniless. He wrote his personal memoirs while ill with cancer and completed them 4 days before his death at Mt. McGregor, N.Y., July 23, 1885. The book realized over $450,000.

Rutherford Birchard Hayes

Rutherford B. Hayes, 19th president, Republican, was born in Delaware, Oh., Oct. 4, 1822, the posthumous son of Rutherford Hayes, a farmer, and Sophia Birchard. He was raised by his uncle Sardis Birchard. He graduated from Kenyon College, 1842, and Harvard Law School, 1845. He practiced law in Lower Sandusky, Oh., now Fremont; was city solicitor of Cincinnati, 1858-61. In the Civil War, he was major of the 23d Ohio Vols., was wounded several times, and rose to the rank of brevet major general, 1864. He served in Congress 1864-67, supporting Reconstruction and Johnson's impeachment. He was elected governor of Ohio, 1867 and 1869; beaten in the race for Congress, 1872; reelected governor, 1875. In 1876 he was nominated for president and believed he had lost the election to Samuel J. Tilden, Democrat. But a few Southern states submitted 2 different sets of electoral votes and the result was in dispute. An electoral commission, appointed by Congress, 8 Republicans and 7 Democrats, awarded all disputed votes to Hayes allowing him to become president by one electoral vote. Hayes, keeping a promise to southerners, withdrew troops from areas still occupied in the South, ending the era of Reconstruction. He proceeded to reform the civil service, alienating political spoilsmen. He advocated repeal of the Tenure of Office Act. He supported sound money and specie payments. Hayes died in Fremont, Oh., Jan. 17, 1893.

James Abram Garfield

James A. Garfield, 20th president, Republican, was born Nov. 19, 1831, in Orange, Cuyahoga Co., Oh., the son of Abram Garfield and Eliza Ballou. His father died in 1833. He worked as a canal bargeman, farmer, and carpenter; attended Western Reserve Eclectic, later Hiram College, and was graduated from Williams in 1856. He taught at Hiram, and later became principal. He was in the Ohio senate in 1859. Anti-slavery and anti-secession, he volunteered for the war, became colonel of the 42d Ohio Infantry and brigadier in 1862. He fought at Shiloh, was chief of staff for Rosecrans and was made major general for gallantry at Chickamauga. He entered Congress as a radical Republican in 1863; supported specie payment as against paper money (greenbacks). On the electoral commission in 1876 he voted for Hayes against Tilden on strict party lines. He was senator-elect in 1880 when he became the Republican nominee for president. He was chosen as a compromise over Gen. Grant, James G. Blaine, and John Sherman. This alienated the Grant following but Garfield was elected. On July 2, 1881, Garfield was shot by mentally disturbed office-seeker, Charles J. Guiteau, while entering a railroad station in Washington. He died Sept. 19, 1881, at Elberon, N.J.

Chester Alan Arthur

Chester A. Arthur, 21st president, Republican, was born at Fairfield, Vt., Oct. 5, 1829, the son of the Rev. William Arthur, from County Antrim, Ireland, and Malvina Stone. He graduated from Union College, 1848, taught school at Pownall, Vt., studied law in New York. In 1853 he argued

in a fugitive slave case that slaves transported through N.Y. State were thereby freed; in 1885 he obtained a ruling that Negroes were to be treated the same as whites on street cars. He was made collector of the Port of New York, 1871. President Hayes, reforming the civil service, forced Arthur to resign, 1879. This made the New York machine stalwarts enemies of Hayes. Arthur and the stalwarts tried to nominate Grant for a 3d term in 1880. When Garfield was nominated, Arthur received 2d place in the interests of harmony. When Garfield died, Arthur became president. He supported civil service reform and the tariff of 1883. He was defeated for renomination by James G. Blaine. He died in New York City Nov. 18, 1886.

Grover Cleveland

(According to a ruling of the State Dept., Grover Cleveland is both the 22d and the 24th president, because his 2 terms were not consecutive. By individuals, he is only the 22d.)

Grover Cleveland, 22d and 24th president, Democrat, was born in Caldwell, N.J. Mar. 18, 1837, the son of Richard F, Cleveland, a Presbyterian minister, and Ann Neale. He was named Stephen Grover, but dropped the Stephen. He clerked in Clinton and Buffalo, N.Y., taught at the N.Y. City Institution for the Blind; was admitted to the bar in Buffalo, 1859; became assistant district attorney, 1863; sheriff, 1871; mayor, 1881; governor of New York, 1882. He was an independent, honest administrator who hated corruption. He was nominated for president over Tammany Hall opposition, 1884, and defeated Republican James G. Blaine. He enlarged the civil service, vetoed many pension raids on the Treasury. In 1888 he was defeated by Benjamin Harrison, although his popular vote was larger. Reelected over Harrison in 1892, he faced a money crisis brought about by lowering of the gold reserve, circulation of paper and exorbitant silver purchases under the Sherman Act; obtained a repeal of the latter and a reduced tariff. A severe depression and labor troubles racked his administration but he refused to interfere in business matters and rejected Jacob Coxey's demand for unemployment relief. He broke the Pullman strike, 1894. In 1896, the Democrats repudiated his administration and chose silverite William Jennings Bryan as their candidate. Cleveland died in Princeton, N.J., June 24, 1908.

Benjamin Harrison

Benjamin Harrison, 23d president, Republican, was born at North Bend, Oh., Aug. 20, 1833. His great-grandfather, Benjamin Harrison, was a signer of the Declaration of Independence; his grandfather, William Henry Harrison, was 9th President; his father, John Scott Harrison, was a member of Congress. His mother was Elizabeth F. Irwin. He attended school on his father's farm; graduated from Miami Univ. at Oxford, Oh., 1852; admitted to the bar, 1853, and practiced in Indianapolis. In the Civil War, he rose to the rank of brevet brigadier general, fought at Kennesaw Mountain, Peachtree Creek, Nashville, and in the Atlanta campaign. He failed to be elected governor of Indiana, 1876; but became senator, 1881, and worked for the G. A. R. pensions vetoed by Cleveland. In 1888 he defeated Cleveland for president despite having fewer popular votes. He expanded the pension list; signed the McKinley high tariff bill and the Sherman Silver Purchase Act. During his administration, 6 states were admitted to the union. He was defeated for reelection, 1892. He represented Venezuela in a boundary arbitration with Great Britain in Paris, 1899. He died at Indianapolis, Mar. 13, 1901.

William McKinley

William McKinley, 25th president, Republican, was born in Niles, Oh., Jan. 29, 1843, the son of William McKinley, an ironmaker, and Nancy Allison. McKinley attended school in Poland, Oh., and Allegheny College, Meadville, Pa., and enlisted for the Civil War at 18 in the 23d Ohio, in which Rutherford B. Hayes was a major. He rose to captain and in 1865 was made brevet major. He studied law in the Albany, N.Y., law school; opened an office in Canton, Oh.

in 1867, and campaigned for Grant and Hayes. He served in the House of Representatives, 1877-83, 1885-91, and led the fight for passage of the McKinley Tarriff, 1890. Defeated for reelection on the issue in 1890, he was governor of Ohio, 1892-96. He had support for president in the convention that nominated Benjamin Harrison in 1892. In 1896 he was elected president on a protective tariff, sound money (gold standard) platform over William Jennings Bryan, Democratic proponent of free silver. McKinley was reluctant to intervene in Cuba but the loss of the battleship Maine at Havana crystallized opinion. He demanded Spain's withdrawal from Cuba; Spain made some concessions but Congress announced state of war as of Apr. 21. He was reelected in the 1900 campaign, defeating Bryan's anti-imperialist arguments with the promise of a "full dinner pail." McKinley was respected for his conciliatory nature, but conservative on business issues. On Sept. 6, 1901, while welcoming citizens at the Pan-American Exposition, Buffalo, N.Y., he was shot by Leon Czolgosz, an anarchist. He died Sept. 14.

Theodore Roosevelt

Theodore Roosevelt, 26th president, Republican, was born in N.Y. City, Oct. 27, 1858, the son of Theodore Roosevelt, a glass importer, and Martha Bulloch. He was a 5th cousin of Franklin D. Roosevelt and an uncle of Mrs. Eleanor Roosevelt. Roosevelt graduated from Harvard, 1880; attended Columbia Law School briefly; sat in the N.Y. State Assembly, 1882-84; ranched in North Dakota, 1884-86; failed election as mayor of N.Y. City, 1886; member of U.S. Civil Service Commission, 1889; president, N.Y. Police Board, 1895, supporting the merit system; assistant secretary of the Navy under McKinley, 1897-98. In the war with Spain, he organized the 1st U.S. Volunteer Cavalry (Rough Riders) as lieutenant colonel; led the charge up Kettle Hill at San Juan. Elected New York governor, 1898-1900, he fought the spoils system and achieved taxation of corporation franchises. Nominated for vice president, 1900, he became nation's youngest president when McKinley died. As president he fought corruption of politics by big business; dissolved Northern Securities Co. and others for violating, anti-trust laws; intervened in coal strike on behalf of the public, 1902; obtained Elkins Law forbidding rebates to favored corporations, 1903; Hepburn Law regulating railroad rates, 1906; Pure Food and Drugs Act, 1906, Reclamation Act and employers' liability laws. He organized conservation, mediated the peace between Japan and Russia, 1905; won the Nobel Peace Prize. He was the first to use the Hague Court of International Arbitration. By recognizing the new Republic of Panama he made Panama Canal possible. He was reelected in 1904.

In 1908 he obtained the nomination of William H. Taft, who was elected. Feeling that Taft had abandoned his policies, Roosevelt unsuccessfully sought the nomination in 1912. He bolted the party and ran on the Progressive "Bull Moose", ticket against Taft and Woodrow Wilson, splitting the Republicans and insuring Wilson's election. He was shot during the campaign but recovered. In 1916 he supported Charles E. Hughes, Republican. A strong friend of Britain, he fought American isolation in World War I. He wrote some 40 books on many topics; his *Winning of the West* is best known. He died Jan. 6, 1919, at Sagamore Hill, Oyster Bay, N.Y.

William Howard Taft

William Howard Taft, 27th president, Republican, was born in Cincinnati, Oh., Sept. 15, 1857, the son of Alphonso Taft and Louisa Maria Torrey. His father was secretary of war and attorney general in Grant's cabinet; minister to Austria and Russia under Arthur. Taft was graduated from Yale, 1878; Cincinnati Law School, 1880; became law reporter for Cincinnati newspapers; was assistant prosecuting attorney, 1881-83; assistant county solicitor, 1885; judge, superior court, 1887; U.S. solicitor-general, 1890; federal circuit judge, 1892. In 1900 he became head of the U.S. Philippines Commission and was first civil governor of the Philippines, 1901-04; secretary of war, 1904; provisional governor of Cuba, 1906. He was groomed for president by Roosevelt and elected over Bryan, 1908. His administration dissolved Standard Oil and tobacco trusts; instituted Dept. of Labor; drafted direct election of senators and income tax amendments. His tariff and conservation policies angered progressives; though renominated he was opposed by Roosevelt; the result was Democrat Woodrow Wilson's election. Taft, with some reservations, supported the League of Nations. He was professor of constitutional law, Yale, 1913-21; chief justice of the U.S., 1921-30; illness forced him to resign. He died in Washington, Mar. 8, 1930.

Woodrow Wilson

Woodrow Wilson, 28th president, Democrat, was born at Staunton, Va., Dec. 28, 1856, as Thomas Woodrow Wilson, son of a Presbyterian minister, the Rev. Joseph Ruggles Wilson and Janet (Jessie) Woodrow. In his youth Wilson lived in Augusta, Ga., Columbia, S.C., and Wilmington, N.C. He attended Davidson College, 1873-74; was graduated from Princeton, A.B., 1879; A.M., 1882; read law at the Univ. of Virginia, 1881; practiced law, Atlanta, 1882-83; Ph.D., Johns Hopkins, 1886. He taught at Bryn Mawr, 1885-88; at Wesleyan, 1888-90; was professor of jurisprudence and political economy at Princeton, 1890-1910; president of Princeton, 1902-1910; governor of New Jersey, 1911-13. In 1912 he was nominated for president with the aid of William Jennings Bryan, who sought to block James "Champ" Clark and Tammany Hall. Wilson won the election because the Republican vote for Taft was split by the Progressives under Roosevelt.

Wilson protected American interests in revolutionary Mexico and fought for American rights on the high seas. His sharp warnings to Germany led to the resignation of his secretary of state, Bryan, a pacifist. In 1916 he was reelected by a slim margin with the slogan, "He kept us out of war." Wilson's attempts to mediate in the war failed. After 4 American ships had been sunk by the Germans, he secured a declaration of war against Germany on Apr. 6, 1917.

Wilson proposed peace Jan. 8, 1918, on the basis of his "Fourteen Points," a state paper with worldwide influence. His doctrine of self-determination continues to play a major role in territorial disputes. The Germans accepted his terms and an armistice, Nov. 11.

Wilson went to Paris to help negotiate the peace treaty, the crux of which he considered the League of Nations. The Senate demanded reservations that would not make the U.S. subordinate to the votes of other nations in case of war. Wilson refused to consider any reservations and toured the country to get support. He suffered a stroke, Oct., 1919. An invalid for months, he clung to his executive powers while his wife and doctor sought to shield him from affairs which would tire him.

He was awarded the 1919 Nobel Peace Prize, but the treaty embodying the League of Nations was rejected by the Senate, 1920. He died Feb. 3, 1924.

Warren Gamaliel Harding

Warren Gamaliel Harding, 29th president, Republican, was born near Corsica, now Blooming Grove, Oh., Nov. 2, 1865, the son of Dr. George Tyron Harding, a physician, and Phoebe Elizabeth Dickerson. He attended Ohio Central College. He was state senator, 1900-04; lieutenant governor, 1904-06; defeated for governor, 1910; chosen U.S. senator, 1915. He supported Taft, opposed federal control of food and fuel; voted for anti-strike legislation, woman's suffrage, and the Volstead prohibition enforcement act over President Wilson's veto; and opposed the League of Nations. In 1920 he was nominated for president and defeated James M. Cox in the election. The Republicans capitalized on war weariness and fear that Wilson's League of Nations would curtail U.S. sovereignty. Harding stressed a return to "normalcy"; worked for tariff revision and repeal of excess profits law and high income taxes. Two Harding appointees, Albert B. Fall (interior) and Harry Daugherty (attorney general), became involved in the Teapot Dome scandal that embittered Harding's last days. He called the International Conference on Limitation of Armaments, 1921-22. Returning from a trip to Alaska he became ill and died in San Francisco, Aug. 2, 1923.

Calvin Coolidge

Calvin Coolidge, 30th president, Republican, was born in Plymouth, Vt., July 4, 1872, the son of John Calvin Coolidge, a storekeeper, and Victoria J. Moor, and named John

Calvin Coolidge. Coolidge graduated from Amherst in 1895. He entered Republican state politics and served as mayor of Northampton, Mass., state senator, lieutenant governor, and, in 1919, governor. In Sept., 1919, Coolidge attained national prominence by calling out the state guard in the Boston police strike. He declared: "There is no right to strike against the public safety by anybody, anywhere, anytime." This brought his name before the Republican convention of 1920, where he was nominated for vice president. He succeeded to the presidency on Harding's death. He opposed the League of Nations; approved the World Court; vetoed the soldiers' bonus bill, which was passed over his veto. In 1924 he was elected by a huge majority. He reduced the national debt by $2 billion in 3 years. He twice vetoed the McNary-Haugen farm bill, which would have provided relief to financially hard-pressed farmers. With Republicans eager to renominate him he announced, Aug. 2, 1927: "I do not choose to run for president in 1928." He died in Northampton, Jan. 5, 1933.

Herbert Hoover

Herbert C. Hoover, 31st president, Republican, was born at West Branch, Ia., Aug. 10, 1874, son of Jesse Clark Hoover, a blacksmith, and Hulda Randall Minthorn. Hoover grew up in Indian Territory (now Oklahoma) and Oregon; won his A.B. in engineering at Stanford, 1891. He worked briefly with U.S. Geological Survey and western mines; then was a mining engineer in Australia, Asia, Europe, Africa, America. While chief engineer, imperial mines, China, he directed food relief for victims of Boxer Rebellion, 1900. He directed American Relief Committee, London, 1914-15; U.S. Comm. for Relief in Belgium, 1915-1919; was U.S. Food Administrator, 1917-1919; American Relief Administrator, 1918-1923, feeding children in defeated nations; Russian Relief, 1918-1923. He was secy. of commerce, 1921-28. He was elected president over Alfred E. Smith, 1928. In 1929 the stock market crashed and the economy collapsed. During the depression, Hoover opposed federal aid to the unemployed. He was defeated in the 1932 election by Franklin D. Roosevelt. President Truman made him co-ordinator of European Food Program, 1947, chairman of the Commission for Reorganization of the Executive Branch, 1947-49. He founded the Hoover Institution on War, Revolution, and Peace at Stanford Univ. He died in N.Y. City, Oct. 20, 1964.

Franklin Delano Roosevelt

Franklin D. Roosevelt, 32d president, Democrat, was born near Hyde Park, N.Y., Jan. 30, 1882, the son of James Roosevelt and Sara Delano. He graduated from Harvard, 1904; attended Columbia Law School; was admitted to the bar. He went to the N.Y. Senate, 1910 and 1913. In 1913 President Wilson made him assistant secretary of the navy.

Roosevelt ran for vice president, 1920, with James Cox and was defeated. From 1920 to 1928 he was a N.Y. lawyer and vice president of Fidelity & Deposit Co. In Aug., 1921, polio paralyzed his legs. He learned to walk with leg braces and a cane.

Roosevelt was elected governor of New York, 1928 and 1930. In 1932, W. G. McAdoo, pledged to John N. Garner, threw his votes to Roosevelt, who was nominated. The depression and the promise to repeal prohibition insured his election. He asked emergency powers, proclaimed the New Deal, and put into effect a vast number of administrative changes. Foremost was the use of public funds for relief and public works, resulting in deficit financing. He greatly expanded the controls of the central government over business, and by an excess profits tax and progressive income taxes produced a redistribution of earnings on an unprecedented scale. The Wagner Act gave labor many advantages in organizing and collective bargaining. He was the last president inaugurated on Mar. 4 (1933) and the first inaugurated on Jan. 20 (1937).

Roosevelt was the first president to use radio for "fireside chats." When the Supreme Court nullified some New Deal laws, he sought power to "pack" the court with additional justices, but Congress refused to give him the authority. He was the first president to break the "no 3d term" tradition (1940) and was elected to a 4th term, 1944, despite failing health. He was openly hostile to fascist governments before

World War II and launched a lend-lease program on behalf of the Allies. He wrote the principles of fair dealing into the Atlantic Charter, Aug. 14, 1941 (with Winston Churchill), and urged the Four Freedoms (freedom of speech, of worship, from want, from fear) Jan. 6, 1941. When Japan attacked Pearl Harbor, Dec. 7, 1941, the U.S. entered the war. He conferred with allied heads of state at Casablanca, Jan., 1943; Quebec, Aug., 1943; Teheran, Nov.-Dec., 1943; Cairo, Dec., 1943; Yalta, Feb., 1945. He died at Warm Springs, Ga., Apr. 12, 1945.

Harry S Truman

Harry S. Truman, 33d president, Democrat, was born at Lamar, Mo., May 8, 1884, the son of John Anderson Truman and Martha Ellen Young. A family disagreement on whether his middle name was Shippe or Solomon, after names of 2 grandfathers, resulted in his using only the middle initial S. He attended public schools in Independence, Mo., worked for the Kansas City Star, 1901, and as railroad timekeeper, and helper in Kansas City banks up to 1905. He ran his family's farm, 1906-17. He was commissioned a first lieutenant and took part in the Vosges, Meuse-Argonne, and St. Mihiel actions in World War I. After the war he ran a haberdashery, became judge of Jackson Co. Court, 1922-24; attended Kansas City School of Law, 1923-25.

Truman was elected U.S. senator in 1934; reelected 1940. In 1944 with Roosevelt's backing he was nominated for vice president and elected. On Roosevelt's death Truman became president. In 1948 he was elected president.

Truman authorized the first uses of the atomic bomb (Hiroshima and Nagasaki, Aug. 6 and 9, 1945), bringing World War II to a rapid end. He was responsible for creating NATO, the Marshall Plan, and what came to be called the Truman Doctrine (to aid nations such as Greece and Turkey, threatened by Russian or other communist takeover). He broke a Russian blockade of West Berlin with a massive airlift, 1948-49. When communist North Korea invaded South Korea, June, 1950, he won UN approval for a "police action" and sent in forces under Gen. Douglas MacArthur. When MacArthur sought to pursue North Koreans into China, Truman removed him from command.

Truman was responsible for higher minimum-wage, increased social-security, and aid-for-housing laws. Truman died Dec. 26, 1972, in Kansas City, Mo.

Dwight David Eisenhower

Dwight D. Eisenhower, 34th president, Republican, was born Oct. 14, 1890, at Denison, Tex., the son of David Jacob Eisenhower and Ida Elizabeth Stover. The next year, the family moved to Abilene, Kan. He graduated from West Point, 1915. He was on the American military mission to the Philippines, 1935-39 and during 4 of those years on the staff of Gen. Douglas MacArthur. He was made commander of Allied forces landing in North Africa, 1942, full general, 1943. He became supreme Allied commander in Europe, 1943, and as such led the Normandy invasion June 6, 1944. He was given the rank of general of the army Dec. 20, 1944, made permanent in 1946. On May 7, 1945, he received the surrender of the Germans at Rheims. He returned to the U.S. to serve as chief of staff, 1945-1948. In 1948, Eisenhower published *Crusade in Europe*, his war memoirs, which quickly became a best seller. From 1948 to 1953, he was president of Columbia Univ., but took leave of absence in 1950, to command NATO forces.

Eisenhower resigned from the army and was nominated for president by the Republicans, 1952. He defeated Adlai E. Stevenson in the election. He again defeated Stevenson 1956. He called himself a moderate, favored "free market system" vs. government price and wage controls; kept government out of labor disputes; reorganized defense establishment; promoted missile programs. He continued foreign aid; sped end of Korean fighting; endorsed Taiwan and SE Asia defense treaties; backed UN in condemning Anglo-French raid on Egypt; advocated "open skies" policy of mutual inspection to USSR. He sent U.S. troops into Little Rock, Ark., Sept., 1957, during the segregation crisis and ordered Marines into Lebanon July-Aug., 1958.

During his retirement at his farm near Gettysburg, Pa., Eisenhower took up the role of elder statesman, counseling his 3 successors in the White House. He died Mar. 28, 1969, in Washington.

John Fitzgerald Kennedy

John F. Kennedy, 35th president, Democrat, was born May 29, 1917, in Brookline, Mass., the son of Joseph P. Kennedy, financier, who later became ambassador to Great Britain, and Rose Fitzgerald. He entered Harvard, attended the London School of Economics briefly in 1935, received a B.S., from Harvard, 1940. He served in the Navy, 1941-1945, commanded a PT boat in the Solomons and won the Navy and Marine Corps Medal. He wrote *Profiles in Courage*, which won a Pulitzer prize. He served as representative in Congress, 1947-1953; was elected to the Senate in 1952, reelected 1958. He nearly won the vice presidential nomination in 1956.

In 1960, Kennedy won the Democratic nomination for president and defeated Richard M. Nixon, Republican. He was the first Roman Catholic president.

Kennedy's most important act was his successful demand Oct. 22, 1962, that the Soviet Union dismantle its missile bases in Cuba. He established a quarantine of arms shipments to Cuba and continued surveillance by air. He defied Soviet attempts to force the Allies out of Berlin. He made the steel industry rescind a price rise. He backed civil rights, a mental health program, arbitration of railroad disputes, and expanded medical care for the aged. Astronaut flights and satellite orbiting were greatly developed during his administration.

On Nov. 22, 1963, Kennedy was assassinated in Dallas, Tex.

Lyndon Baines Johnson

Lyndon B. Johnson, 36th president, Democrat, was born near Stonewall, Tex., Aug. 27, 1908, son of Sam Ealy Johnson and Rebekah Baines. He received a B.S. degree at Southwest Texas State Teachers College, 1930, attended Georgetown Univ. Law School, Washington, 1935. He taught public speaking in Houston, 1930-32; served as secretary to Rep. R. M. Kleberg, 1932-35. In 1937 Johnson won a contest to fill the vacancy caused by the death of a representative and in 1938 was elected to the full term, after which he returned for 4 terms. He was elected U.S. senator in 1948 and reelected in 1954. He became Democratic leader, 1953. Johnson was Texas' favorite son for the Democratic presidential nomination in 1956 and had strong support in the 1960 convention, where the nominee, John F. Kennedy, asked him to run for vice president. His campaigning helped overcome religious bias against Kennedy in the South.

Johnson became president on the death of Kennedy. Johnson worked hard for welfare legislation, signed civil rights, anti-proverty, and tax reduction laws, and averted strikes on railroads. He was elected to a full term, 1964. The war in Vietnam overshadowed other developments, 1965-68.

In face of increasing division in the nation and his own party over his handling of the war, Johnson announced that he would not seek another term, Mar. 31, 1968.

Retiring to his ranch near Johnson City, Tex., Johnson wrote his memoirs and oversaw the construction of the Lyndon Baines Johnson Library on the campus of the Univ. of Texas in Austin. He died Jan. 22, 1973.

Richard Milhous Nixon

Richard M. Nixon, 37th president, Republican, was the only president to resign without completing an elected term. He was born in Yorba Linda, Cal., Jan. 9, 1913, the son of Francis Anthony Nixon and Hannah Milhous. Nixon graduated from Whittier College, 1934; Duke Univ. Law School, 1937. After practicing law in Whittier and serving briefly in the Office of Price Administration in 1942, he entered the navy, serving in the South Pacific, and was discharged as a lieutenant commander.

Nixon was elected to the House of Representatives in 1946 and 1948. He achieved prominence as the House Un-American Activities Committee member who forced the showdown that resulted in the Alger Hiss perjury conviction. In 1950 Nixon moved to the Senate.

He was elected vice president in the Eisenhower landslides of 1952 and 1956. With Eisenhower's endorsement, Nixon won the Republican nomination in 1960. He was defeated by Democrat John F. Kennedy, returned to Cal. and was defeated in his race for governor, 1962.

In 1968, he won the presidential nomination and went on to defeat Democrat Hubert H. Humphrey.

Nixon became the first U.S. president to visit China and Russia (1972). He and his foreign affairs advisor, Henry A. Kissinger, achieved a detente with China. Nixon appointed 4 new Supreme Court justices, including the chief justice, thus altering the court's balance in favor of a more conservative view.

Reelected 1972, Nixon secured a cease-fire agreement in Vietnam and completed the withdrawal of U.S. troops.

Nixon's 2d term was cut short by a series of scandals beginning with the burglary of Democratic party national headquarters in the Watergate office complex on June 17, 1972. Nixon denied any White House involvement in the Watergate break-in. On July 16, 1973, a White House aide, under questioning by a Senate committee, revealed that most of Nixon's office conversations and phone calls had been recorded. Nixon claimed executive privilege to keep the tapes secret and the courts and Congress sought the tapes for criminal proceedings against former White House aides and for a House inquiry into possible impeachment.

On Oct. 10, 1973, Nixon fired the Watergate special prosecutor and the attorney general resigned in protest. The public outcry which followed caused Nixon to appoint a new special prosecutor and to turn over to the courts a number of subpoenaed tape recordings. Public reaction also brought the initiation of a formal inquiry into impeachment.

On July 24, 1974, the Supreme Court ruled that Nixon's claim of executive privilege must fall before the special prosecutor's subpoenas of tapes relevant to criminal trial proceedings. That same day, the House Judiciary Committee opened debate on impeachment. On July 30, the committee recommended House adoption of 3 articles of impeachment charging Nixon with obstruction of justice, abuse of power, and contempt of Congress.

On Aug. 5, Nixon released transcripts of conversations held 6 days after the Watergate break-in showing that Nixon had known of, approved, and directed Watergate cover-up activities. Nixon resigned from office Aug. 9.

Gerald Rudolph Ford

Gerald R. Ford, 38th president, Republican, was born July 14, 1913, in Omaha, Neb., son of Leslie King and Dorothy Gardner, and was named Leslie Jr. When he was 2, his parents were divorced and his mother moved with the boy to Grand Rapids, Mich. There she met and married Gerald R. Ford, who formally adopted the boy and gave him his own name.

He graduated from the Univ. of Michigan, 1935 and Yale Law School, 1941.

He began practicing law in Grand Rapids, but in 1942 joined the navy and served in the Pacific, leaving the service in 1946 as a lieutenant commander.

He entered congress in 1948 and continued to win elections, spending 25 years in the House, 8 of them as Republican leader.

On Oct. 12, 1973, after Vice President Spiro T. Agnew resigned, Ford was nominated by President Nixon to replace him. It was the first use of the procedures set out in the 25th Amendment.

When Nixon resigned Aug. 9, 1974, Ford became president, the first to serve without being chosen in a national election. On Sept. 8 he pardoned Nixon for any federal crimes he might have committed as president. Ford vetoed 48 bills in his first 21 months in office, saying most would prove too costly. He visited China. In 1976, he was defeated in the election by Democrat Jimmy Carter.

Jimmy (James Earl) Carter

Jimmy (James Earl) Carter, 39th president, Democrat, was the first president from the Deep South since before the Civil War. He was born Oct. 1, 1924, at Plains, Ga., where his parents, James and Lillian Gordy Carter, had a farm and several businesses.

He attended Georgia Tech, and graduated from the U.S. Naval Academy. He entered the Navy's nuclear submarine program as an aide to Adm. Hyman Rickover, and studied nuclear physics at Union College.

His father died in 1953 and Carter left the Navy to take over the family businesses — peanut-raising, warehousing, and cotton-ginning. He was elected to the Georgia state senate, was defeated for governor, 1966, but elected in 1970.

Carter won the Democratic nomination and defeated President Gerald R. Ford in the election of 1976.

In 1979, Carter played a major role in the peace negotiations between Israel and Egypt. In Nov., Iranian student militants attacked the U.S. embassy in Teheran and held members of the embassy staff hostage.

During 1980, Carter was widely criticized for the poor state of the economy and high inflation. He was also viewed as weak in his handling of foreign policy. He reacted to the Soviet invasion of Afghanistan by imposing a grain embargo and boycotting the Moscow Olympic games. His failure to obtain the release of the remaining 52 hostages held in Iran, whose first anniversary of capture fell on Election Day, plagued Carter to the end of his term. He was defeated by Ronald Reagan in the election. Carter finally succeeded in obtaining the release of the hostages on Inauguration Day, as the new president was taking the oath of office.

Ronald Wilson Reagan

Ronald Wilson Reagan, 40th president, Republican, was born Feb. 6, 1911, in Tampico, Ill., the son of John Edward Reagan and Nellie Wilson. Reagan graduated from Eureka (Ill.) College in 1932. Following his graduation, he worked for 5 years as a sports announcer in Des Moines, Ia.

Reagan began a successful career as a film actor in 1937, and starred in numerous movies, and later television, until the 1960s. He was a captain in the Army Air Force during World War II.

He served as president of the Screen Actors Guild from 1947 to 1952, and in 1959.

Once a liberal Democrat, Reagan became active in Republican politics during the 1964 presidential campaign of Barry Goldwater. He was elected governor of California in 1966, and reelected in 1970.

Following his retirement as governor, Reagan became the leading spokesman for the conservative wing of the Republican Party, and made a strong bid for the party's 1976 presidential nomination.

In 1980, he gained the Republican nomination and won a landslide victory over Jimmy Carter.

As president, he successfully forged a bipartisan coalition in Congress which led to enactment of an economic program which included the largest budget and tax cuts in U.S. history, and a Social Security reform bill designed to insure the long-term solvency of the system.

Reagan was plagued by a severe recession which caused a 9.7% unemployment rate in 1982, the highest since 1941.

By early 1984, interest rates and inflation had declined and the economy was making a strong recovery. Reagan's fiscal 1985 budget, with a projected deficit of $180 billion and the proposed 3-year deficit of some $550 billion, drew strong criticism from Congress and many economists who feared that the record deficits would cause interest rates to rise and jeopardize the economic recovery.

In 1983, Reagan sent a task force to lead the invasion of Grenada, and joined 3 European nations in maintaining a peacekeeping force in Beirut, Lebanon. He has strongly supported the El Salvador and other anti-communist governments in Central America while aiding anti-government forces in Nicaragua.

Wives and Children of the Presidents
Listed in order of presidential administrations.

Name	State	Born	Married	Died	Sons	Daughters
Martha Dandridge Custis Washington	Va.	1732	1759	1802	...	...
Abigail Smith Adams	Mass.	1744	1764	1818	3	2
Martha Wayles Skelton Jefferson	Va.	1748	1772	1782	1	5
Dorothea "Dolley" Payne Todd Madison	N.C.	1768	1794	1849	...	...
Elizabeth Kortright Monroe	N.Y.	1768	1786	1830	...(1)	2
Louise Catherine Johnson Adams	Md. (2)	1775	1797	1852	3	1
Rachel Donelson Robards Jackson	Va.	1767	1791	1828	...	...
Hannah Hoes Van Buren	N.Y.	1783	1807	1819	4	...
Anna Symmes Harrison	N.J.	1775	1795	1864	6	4
Letitia Christian Tyler	Va.	1790	1813	1842	3	4
Julia Gardiner Tyler	N.Y.	1820	1844	1889	5	2
Sarah Childress Polk	Tenn.	1803	1824	1891	...	...
Margaret Smith Taylor	Md.	1788	1810	1852	1	5
Abigail Powers Fillmore	N.Y.	1798	1826	1853	1	1
Caroline Carmichael McIntosh Fillmore	N.J.	1813	1858	1881	...	...
Jane Means Appleton Pierce	N.H.	1806	1834	1863	3	...
Mary Todd Lincoln	Ky.	1818	1842	1882	4	...
Eliza McCardle Johnson	Tenn.	1810	1827	1876	3	2
Julia Dent Grant	Mo.	1826	1848	1902	3	1
Lucy Ware Webb Hayes	Oh.	1831	1852	1889	7	1
Lucretia Rudolph Garfield	Oh.	1832	1858	1918	4	1
Ellen Lewis Herndon Arthur	Va.	1837	1859	1880	2	1
Frances Folsom Cleveland	N.Y.	1864	1886	1947	2	3
Caroline Lavinia Scott Harrison	Oh.	1832	1853	1892	1	1
Mary Scott Lord Dimmick Harrison	Pa.	1858	1896	1948	...	1
Ida Saxton McKinley	Oh.	1847	1871	1907	...	2
Alice Hathaway Lee Roosevelt	Mass.	1861	1880	1884	...	1
Edith Kermit Carow Roosevelt	Conn.	1861	1886	1948	4	1
Helen Herron Taft	Oh.	1861	1886	1943	2	1
Ellen Louise Axson Wilson	Ga.	1860	1885	1914	...	3
Edith Bolling Galt Wilson	Va.	1872	1915	1961	...	...
Florence Kling De Wolfe Harding	Oh.	1860	1891	1924	...	...
Grace Anna Goodhue Coolidge	Vt.	1879	1905	1957	2	...
Lou Henry Hoover	Ia.	1875	1899	1944	2	...
Anna Eleanor Roosevelt Roosevelt	N.Y.	1884	1905	1962	4 (1)	1
Bess Wallace Truman	Mo.	1885	1919	...	...	1
Mamie Geneva Doud Eisenhower	Ia.	1896	1916	1979	1 (1)	...
Jacqueline Lee Bouvier Kennedy	N.Y.	1929	1953	...	1 (1)	1
Claudia "Lady Bird" Alta Taylor Johnson	Tex.	1912	1934	...	...	2
Thelma Catherine Patricia Ryan Nixon	Nev.	1912	1940	...	...	2
Elizabeth Bloomer Warren Ford	Ill.	1918	1948	...	3	1
Rosalynn Smith Carter	Ga.	1927	1946	...	3	1
Anne Frances "Nancy" Robbins Davis Reagan	N.Y.	1923	1952	...	1 (3)	1(3)

James Buchanan, 15th president, was unmarried. (1) plus one infant, deceased. (2) Born London, father a Md. citizen. (3) President Reagan has a son and daughter from a former marriage.

Electoral Votes for President

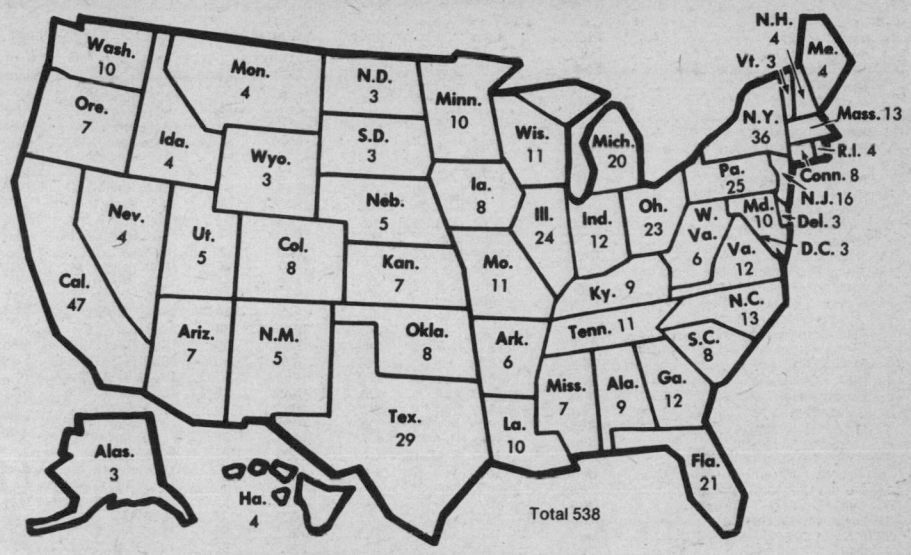

Total 538

Voter Turnout in Presidential Elections
Source: Committee for the Study of the American Electorate

National average of voting age population voting: 1960—62.8; 1964—61.9; 1968—60.6; 1972—55.5; 1976—54.3; 1980—53.9. The sharp drop in 1972 reflects the expansion of eligibility with the enfranchisement of 18 to 21 year olds.

	1980		1976
	Registered voters voting	Voting age population voting	Voting age population voting
Ala.	62.9%	49.7%	47.2%
Alas. . . .	60.7	61.3	48.3
Ariz. . . .	78.0	49.1	48.6
Ark.	70.6	53.6	52.2
Cal	75.6	50.6	51.3
Col.	82.6	57.8	60.4
Conn. . . .	82.4	60.6	62.4
Del.	78.4	56.1	58.4
D.C.	60.2	36.6	33.3
Fla.	76.7	53.6	51.5
Ga.	n/a	43.6	43.3
Ha.	75.3	46.2	48.1
Ida.	75.3	69.0	61.6
Ill.	76.2	59.0	60.6
Ind.	n/a	58.2	61.6
Ia.	76.7	63.0	63.7
Kan. . . .	75.9	55.8	58.4

	1980		1976
	Registered voters voting	Voting age population voting	Voting age population voting
Ky.	71.0	51.2	49.1
La.	76.8	55.7	49.8
Me.	68.8	66.2	65.0
Md.	74.6	50.7	49.9
Mass. . . .	80.1	58.7	61.6
Mich. . . .	68.3	59.6	58.7
Minn. . . .	86.9	69.2	71.4
Miss. . . .	60.2	54.1	49.5
Mo.	73.9	58.8	57.7
Mon. . . .	73.3	65.0	63.7
Neb.	74.7	56.2	56.1
Nev.	81.7	45.7	47.5
N.H.	73.5	58.4	58.8
N.J.	79.0	55.1	58.1
N.M.	69.9	52.5	54.6
N.Y.	n/a	48.1	50.8
N.C.	66.9	45.8	44.1

	1980		1976
	Registered voters voting	Voting age population voting	Voting age population voting
N.D. . . .	n/a	64.3	67.2
Oh.	72.8	55.6	55.4
Okla. . . .	78.2	54.0	55.6
Ore. . . .	75.3	61.9	62.1
Pa.	79.3	52.7	54.7
R.I.	78.4	60.5	61.5
S.C.	71.9	42.9	41.7
S.D.	73.2	67.6	63.8
Tenn. . . .	75.3	50.5	49.6
Tex.	68.4	47.1	47.3
Ut.	77.3	67.1	69.4
Vt.	68.4	59.4	56.9
Va.	81.0	48.9	47.7
Wash. . . .	79.8	62.3	61.1
W.Va. . . .	71.0	54.4	58.1
Wis.	n/a	66.0	65.9
Wy.	80.5	52.8	58.1

n/a—not available.

Party Nominees for President and Vice President
Asterisk (*) denotes winning ticket

	Democratic		Republican	
Year	President	Vice President	President	Vice President
1916	Woodrow Wilson*	Thomas R. Marshall	Charles E. Hughes	Charles W. Fairbanks
1920	James M. Cox	Franklin D. Roosevelt	Warren G. Harding*	Calvin Coolidge
1924	John W. Davis	Charles W. Bryan	Calvin Coolidge*	Charles G. Dawes
1928	Alfred E. Smith	Joseph T. Robinson	Herbert Hoover*	Charles Curtis
1932	Franklin D. Roosevelt*	John N. Garner	Herbert Hoover	Charles Curtis
1936	Franklin D. Roosevelt*	John N. Garner	Alfred M. Landon	Frank Knox
1940	Franklin D. Roosevelt*	Henry A. Wallace	Wendell L. Willkie	Charles McNary
1944	Franklin D. Roosevelt*	Harry S. Truman	Thomas E. Dewey	John W. Bricker
1948	Harry S. Truman*	Alben W. Barkley	Thomas E. Dewey	Earl Warren
1952	Adlai E. Stevenson	John J. Sparkman	Dwight D. Eisenhower*	Richard M. Nixon
1956	Adlai E. Stevenson	Estes Kefauver	Dwight D. Eisenhower*	Richard M. Nixon
1960	John F. Kennedy*	Lyndon B. Johnson	Richard M. Nixon	Henry Cabot Lodge
1964	Lyndon B. Johnson*	Hubert H. Humphrey	Barry M. Goldwater	William E. Miller
1968	Hubert H. Humphrey	Edmund S. Muskie	Richard M. Nixon*	Spiro T. Agnew
1972	George S. McGovern	R. Sargent Shriver Jr.	Richard M. Nixon*	Spiro T. Agnew
1976	Jimmy Carter*	Walter F. Mondale	Gerald R. Ford	Robert J. Dole
1980	Jimmy Carter	Walter F. Mondale	Ronald Reagan*	George Bush

Presidents of the U.S.

No.	Name	Politics	Born . . . . in	Inaug. at age	Died . . . . at age
1	George Washington	Fed.	1732, Feb. 22 Va.	1789 . . . 57	1799, Dec. 14 67
2	John Adams	Fed.	1735, Oct. 30 Mass.	1797 . . . 61	1826, July 4 90
3	Thomas Jefferson	Dem.-Rep.	1743, Apr. 13 Va.	1801 . . . 57	1826, July 4 83
4	James Madison	Dem.-Rep.	1751, Mar. 16 Va.	1809 . . . 57	1836, June 28 . . . 85
5	James Monroe	Dem.-Rep.	1758, Apr. 28 Va.	1817 . . . 58	1831, July 4 73
6	John Quincy Adams	Dem.-Rep.	1767, July 11 Mass.	1825 . . . 57	1848, Feb. 23 . . . 80
7	Andrew Jackson	Dem.	1767, Mar. 15 S.C.	1829 . . . 61	1845, June 8 78
8	Martin Van Buren	Dem.	1782, Dec. 5 N.Y.	1837 . . . 54	1862, July 24 . . . 79
9	William Henry Harrison	Whig	1773, Feb. 9 Va.	1841 . . . 68	1841, Apr. 4 68
10	John Tyler	Whig	1790, Mar. 29 Va.	1841 . . . 51	1862, Jan. 18 . . . 71
11	James Knox Polk	Dem.	1795, Nov. 2 N.C.	1845 . . . 49	1849, June 15 . . . 53
12	Zachary Taylor	Whig	1784, Nov. 24 Va.	1849 . . . 64	1850, July 9 65
13	Millard Fillmore	Whig	1800, Jan. 7 N.Y.	1850 . . . 50	1874, Mar. 8 74
14	Franklin Pierce	Dem.	1804, Nov. 23 N.H.	1853 . . . 48	1869, Oct. 8 64
15	James Buchanan	Dem.	1791, Apr. 23 Pa.	1857 . . . 65	1868, June 1 77
16	Abraham Lincoln	Rep.	1809, Feb. 12 Ky.	1861 . . . 52	1865, Apr. 15 . . . 56
17	Andrew Johnson	(1)	1808, Dec. 29 N.C.	1865 . . . 56	1875, July 31 . . . 66
18	Ulysses Simpson Grant	Rep.	1822, Apr. 27 Oh.	1869 . . . 46	1885, July 23 . . . 63
19	Rutherford Birchard Hayes	Rep.	1822, Oct. 4 Oh.	1877 . . . 54	1893, Jan. 17 . . . 70
20	James Abram Garfield	Rep.	1831, Nov. 19 Oh.	1881 . . . 49	1881, Sept. 19 . . . 49
21	Chester Alan Arthur	Rep.	1829, Oct. 5 Vt.	1881 . . . 50	1886, Nov. 18 . . . 57
22	Grover Cleveland	Dem.	1837, Mar. 18 N.J.	1885 . . . 47	1908, June 24 . . . 71
23	Benjamin Harrison	Rep.	1833, Aug. 20 Oh.	1889 . . . 55	1901, Mar. 13 . . . 67
24	Grover Cleveland	Dem.	1837, Mar. 18 N.J.	1893 . . . 55	1908, June 24 . . . 71
25	William McKinley	Rep.	1843, Jan. 29 Oh.	1897 . . . 54	1901, Sept. 14 . . . 58
26	Theodore Roosevelt	Rep.	1858, Oct. 27 N.Y.	1901 . . . 42	1919, Jan. 6 60
27	William Howard Taft	Rep.	1857, Sept. 15 Oh.	1909 . . . 51	1930, Mar. 8 72
28	Woodrow Wilson	Dem.	1856, Dec. 28 Va.	1913 . . . 56	1924, Feb. 3 67
29	Warren Gamaliel Harding	Rep.	1865, Nov. 2 Oh.	1921 . . . 55	1923, Aug. 2 57
30	Calvin Coolidge	Rep.	1872, July 4 Vt.	1923 . . . 51	1933, Jan. 5 60
31	Herbert Clark Hoover	Rep.	1874, Aug. 10 Ia.	1929 . . . 54	1964, Oct. 20 . . . 90
32	Franklin Delano Roosevelt	Dem.	1882, Jan. 30 N.Y.	1933 . . . 51	1945, Apr. 12 . . . 63
33	Harry S. Truman	Dem.	1884, May 8 Mo.	1945 . . . 60	1972, Dec. 26 . . . 88
34	Dwight David Eisenhower	Rep.	1890, Oct. 14 Tex.	1953 . . . 62	1969, Mar. 28 . . . 78
35	John Fitzgerald Kennedy	Dem.	1917, May 29 Mass.	1961 . . . 43	1963, Nov. 22 . . . 46
36	Lyndon Baines Johnson	Dem.	1908, Aug. 27 Tex.	1963 . . . 55	1973, Jan. 22 . . . 64
37	Richard Milhous Nixon (2)	Rep.	1913, Jan. 9 Cal.	1969 . . . 56	
38	Gerald Rudolph Ford	Rep.	1913, July 14 Neb.	1974 . . . 61	
39	Jimmy (James Earl) Carter	Dem.	1924, Oct. 1 Ga.	1977 . . . 52	
40	Ronald Reagan	Rep.	1911, Feb. 6 Ill.	1981 . . . 69	

(1) Andrew Johnson — a Democrat, nominated vice president by Republicans and elected with Lincoln on National Union ticket. (2) Resigned Aug. 9, 1974.

Presidents, Vice Presidents, Congresses

President	Service	Vice President	Congress
1 George Washington	Apr. 30, 1789—Mar. 3, 1797	1 John Adams	1, 2, 3, 4
2 John Adams	Mar. 4, 1797—Mar. 3, 1801	2 Thomas Jefferson	5, 6
3 Thomas Jefferson	Mar. 4, 1801—Mar. 3, 1805	3 Aaron Burr	7, 8
"	Mar. 4, 1805—Mar. 3, 1809	4 George Clinton	9, 10
4 James Madison	Mar. 4, 1809—Mar. 3, 1813	"(1)	11, 12
"	Mar. 4, 1813—Mar. 3, 1817	5 Elbridge Gerry (2)	13, 14
5 James Monroe	Mar. 4, 1817—Mar. 3, 1825	6 Daniel D. Tompkins	15, 16, 17, 18
6 John Quincy Adams	Mar. 4, 1825—Mar. 3, 1829	7 John C. Calhoun	19, 20
7 Andrew Jackson	Mar. 4, 1829—Mar. 3, 1833	"(3)	21, 22
"	Mar. 4, 1833—Mar. 3, 1837	8 Martin Van Buren	23, 24
8 Martin Van Buren	Mar. 4, 1837—Mar. 3, 1841	9 Richard M. Johnson	25, 26
9 William Henry Harrison (4)	Mar. 4, 1841—Apr. 4, 1841	10 John Tyler	27
10 John Tyler	Apr. 6, 1841—Mar. 3, 1845		27, 28
11 James K. Polk	Mar. 4, 1845—Mar. 3, 1849	11 George M. Dallas	29, 30
12 Zachary Taylor (4)	Mar. 5, 1849—July 9, 1850	12 Millard Fillmore	31
13 Millard Fillmore	July 10, 1850—Mar. 3, 1853		31, 32
14 Franklin Pierce	Mar. 4, 1853—Mar. 3, 1857	13 William R. King (5)	33, 34
15 James Buchanan	Mar. 4, 1857—Mar. 3, 1861	14 John C. Breckinridge	35, 36
16 Abraham Lincoln	Mar. 4, 1861—Mar. 3, 1865	15 Hannibal Hamlin	37, 38
"(4)	Mar. 4, 1865—Apr. 15, 1865	16 Andrew Johnson	39
17 Andrew Johnson	Apr. 15, 1865—Mar. 3, 1869		39, 40
18 Ulysses S. Grant	Mar. 4, 1869—Mar. 3, 1873	17 Schuyler Colfax	41, 42
"	Mar. 4, 1873—Mar. 3, 1877	18 Henry Wilson (6)	43, 44
19 Rutherford B. Hayes	Mar. 4, 1877—Mar. 3, 1881	19 William A. Wheeler	45, 46
20 James A. Garfield (4)	Mar. 4, 1881—Sept. 19, 1881	20 Chester A. Arthur	47
21 Chester A. Arthur	Sept. 20, 1881—Mar. 3, 1885		47, 48
22 Grover Cleveland (7)	Mar. 4, 1885—Mar. 3, 1889	21 Thomas A. Hendricks (8)	49, 50
23 Benjamin Harrison	Mar. 4, 1889—Mar. 3, 1893	22 Levi P. Morton	51, 52
24 Grover Cleveland (7)	Mar. 4, 1893—Mar. 3, 1897	23 Adlai E. Stevenson	53, 54
25 William McKinley	Mar. 4, 1897—Mar. 3, 1901	24 Garret A. Hobart (9)	55, 56
"(4)	Mar. 4, 1901—Sept. 14, 1901	25 Theodore Roosevelt	57
26 Theodore Roosevelt	Sept. 14, 1901—Mar. 3, 1905		57, 58
"	Mar. 4, 1905—Mar. 3, 1909	26 Charles W. Fairbanks	59, 60

President	Service	Vice President	Congress
27 William H. Taft	Mar. 4, 1909—Mar. 3, 1913	27 James S. Sherman (10)	61, 62
28 Woodrow Wilson	Mar. 4, 1913—Mar. 3, 1921	28 Thomas R. Marshall	63, 64, 65, 66
29 Warren G. Harding (4)	Mar. 4, 1921—Aug. 2, 1923	29 Calvin Coolidge	67
30 Calvin Coolidge	Aug. 3, 1923—Mar. 3, 1925		68
"	Mar. 4, 1925—Mar. 3, 1929	30 Charles G. Dawes	69, 70
31 Herbert C. Hoover	Mar. 4, 1929—Mar. 3, 1933	31 Charles Curtis	71, 72
32 Franklin D. Roosevelt (16)	Mar. 4, 1933—Jan. 20, 1941	32 John N. Garner	73, 74, 75, 76
"	Jan. 20, 1941—Jan. 20, 1945	33 Henry A. Wallace	77, 78
"(4)	Jan. 20, 1945—Apr. 12, 1945	34 Harry S. Truman	79
33 Harry S. Truman	Apr. 12, 1945—Jan. 20, 1949		79, 80
"	Jan. 20, 1949—Jan. 20, 1953	35 Alben W. Barkley	81, 82
34 Dwight D. Eisenhower	Jan. 20, 1953—Jan. 20, 1961	36 Richard M. Nixon	83, 84, 85, 86
35 John F. Kennedy (4)	Jan. 20, 1961—Nov. 22, 1963	37 Lyndon B. Johnson	87, 88
36 Lyndon B. Johnson	Nov. 22, 1963—Jan. 20, 1965		88
"	Jan. 20, 1965—Jan. 20, 1969	38 Hubert H. Humphrey	89, 90
37 Richard M. Nixon	Jan. 20, 1969—Jan. 20, 1973	39 Spiro T. Agnew (11)	91, 92, 93
"(12)	Jan. 20, 1973—Aug. 9, 1974	40 Gerald R. Ford (13)	93
38 Gerald R. Ford (14)	Aug. 9, 1974—Jan. 20, 1977	41 Nelson A. Rockefeller (15)	93, 94
39 Jimmy (James Earl) Carter	Jan. 20, 1977—Jan. 20, 1981	42 Walter F. Mondale	95, 96
40 Ronald Reagan	Jan. 20, 1981—	43 George Bush	97, 98

(1) Died Apr. 20, 1812. (2) Died Nov. 23, 1814. (3) Resigned Dec. 28, 1832, to become U.S. Senator. (4) Died in office. (5) Died Apr. 18, 1853. (6) Died Nov. 22, 1875. (7) Terms not consecutive. (8) Died Nov. 25, 1885. (9) Died Nov. 21, 1899. (10) Died Oct. 30, 1912. (11) Resigned Oct. 10, 1973. (12) Resigned Aug. 9, 1974. (13) First non-elected vice president, chosen under 25th Amendment procedure. (14) First non-elected president. (15) 2d non-elected vice president. (16) First president to be inaugurated under 20th Amendment, Jan. 20, 1937.

Vice Presidents of the U.S.

The numerals given vice presidents do not coincide with those given presidents, because some presidents had none and some had more than one.

Name	Birthplace	Year	Home	Inaug.	Politics	Place of death	Year	Age
1 John Adams	Quincy, Mass.	1735	Mass. . .	1789	Fed. . . .	Quincy, Mass.	1826	90
2 Thomas Jefferson	Shadwell, Va. . . .	1743	Va. . . .	1797	Dem.-Rep.	Monticello, Va. . . .	1826	83
3 Aaron Burr	Newark, N.J.	1756	N.Y. . .	1801	Dem.-Rep.	Staten Island, N.Y. . . .	1836	80
4 George Clinton	Ulster Co., N.Y. . .	1739	N.Y. . .	1805	Dem.-Rep.	Washington, D.C. . .	1812	73
5 Elbridge Gerry	Marblehead, Mass. . . .	1744	Mass. . .	1813	Dem.-Rep.	Washington, D.C. . .	1814	70
6 Daniel D. Tompkins . . .	Scarsdale, N.Y.	1774	N.Y. . .	1817	Dem.-Rep.	Staten Island, N.Y. . .	1825	51
7 John C. Calhoun (1) . . .	Abbeville, S.C. . . .	1782	S.C. . . .	1825	Dem.-Rep.	Washington, D.C. . .	1850	68
8 Martin Van Buren . . .	Kinderhook, N.Y. . . .	1782	N.Y. . .	1833	Dem. . .	Kinderhook, N.Y. . .	1862	79
9 Richard M. Johnson . .	Louisville, Ky. . . .	1780	Ky. . . .	1837	Dem. . .	Frankfort, Ky. . . .	1850	70
10 John Tyler	Greenway, Va.	1790	Va. . . .	1841	Whig . .	Richmond, Va. . . .	1862	71
11 George M. Dallas . . .	Philadelphia, Pa. . . .	1792	Pa. . . .	1845	Dem. . .	Philadelphia, Pa. . . .	1864	72
12 Millard Fillmore	Summerhill, N.Y. . . .	1800	N.Y. . .	1849	Whig . .	Buffalo, N.Y.	1874	74
13 William R. King	Sampson Co., N.C. . .	1786	Ala. . . .	1853	Dem. . .	Dallas Co., Ala. . . .	1853	67
14 John C. Breckinridge . .	Lexington, Ky. . . .	1821	Ky. . . .	1857	Dem. . .	Lexington, Ky.	1875	54
15 Hannibal Hamlin . . .	Paris, Me.	1809	Me. . . .	1861	Rep. . . .	Bangor, Me.	1891	81
16 Andrew Johnson	Raleigh, N.C.	1808	Tenn. . .	1865	(2). . .	Carter Co., Tenn. . . .	1875	66
17 Schuyler Colfax . . .	New York, N.Y.	1823	Ind. . . .	1869	Rep. . .	Mankato, Minn. . . .	1885	62
18 Henry Wilson	Farmington, N.H. . . .	1812	Mass. . .	1873	Rep. . .	Washington, D.C. . .	1875	63
19 William A. Wheeler . . .	Malone, N.Y.	1819	N.Y. . .	1877	Rep. . .	Malone, N.Y. . . .	1887	68
20 Chester A. Arthur . . .	Fairfield, Vt.	1829	N.Y. . .	1881	Rep. . .	New York, N.Y. . . .	1886	57
21 Thomas A. Hendricks . .	Muskingum Co., Oh. . .	1819	Ind. . . .	1885	Dem. . .	Indianapolis, Ind. . . .	1885	66
22 Levi P. Morton	Shoreham, Vt. . . .	1824	N.Y. . .	1889	Rep. . .	Rhinebeck, N.Y. . . .	1920	96
23 Adlai E. Stevenson (3) . .	Christian Co., Ky. . . .	1835	Ill. . . .	1893	Dem. . .	Chicago, Ill.	1914	78
24 Garret A. Hobart . . .	Long Branch, N.J. . . .	1844	N.J. . .	1897	Rep. . .	Paterson, N.J. . . .	1899	55
25 Theodore Roosevelt . . .	New York, N.Y.	1858	N.Y. . .	1901	Rep. . .	Oyster Bay, N.Y. . . .	1919	60
26 Charles W. Fairbanks . .	Unionville Centre, Oh. .	1852	Ind. . . .	1905	Rep. . .	Indianapolis, Ind. . . .	1918	66
27 James S. Sherman . . .	Utica, N.Y.	1855	N.Y. . .	1909	Rep. . .	Utica, N.Y.	1912	57
28 Thomas R. Marshall . . .	N. Manchester, Ind. . .	1854	Ind. . . .	1913	Dem. . .	Washington, D.C. . . .	1925	71
29 Calvin Coolidge	Plymouth, Vt. . . .	1872	Mass. . .	1921	Rep. . .	Northampton, Mass. . .	1933	60
30 Charles G. Dawes . . .	Marietta, Oh. . . .	1865	Ill. . . .	1925	Rep. . .	Evanston, Ill.	1951	85
31 Charles Curtis	Topeka, Kan. . . .	1860	Kan. . .	1929	Rep. . .	Washington, D.C. . . .	1936	76
32 John Nance Garner . .	Red River Co., Tex. . .	1868	Tex. . .	1933	Dem. . .	Uvalde, Tex.	1967	98
33 Henry Agard Wallace . .	Adair County, Ia. . . .	1888	Iowa . .	1941	Dem. . .	Danbury, Conn. . . .	1965	77
34 Harry S. Truman	Lamar, Mo.	1884	Mo. . . .	1945	Dem. . .	Kansas City, Mo. . . .	1972	88
35 Alben W. Barkley . . .	Graves County, Ky. . .	1877	Ky. . . .	1949	Dem. . .	Lexington, Va. . . .	1956	78
36 Richard M. Nixon . . .	Yorba Linda, Cal. . . .	1913	Cal. . . .	1953	Rep.			
37 Lyndon B. Johnson . . .	Johnson City, Tex. . .	1908	Tex. . .	1961	Dem. . .	San Antonio, Tex. . . .	1973	64
38 Hubert H. Humphrey . .	Wallace, S.D. . . .	1911	Minn. . .	1965	Dem. . .	Waverly, Minn. . . .	1978	66
39 Spiro T. Agnew	Baltimore, Md. . . .	1918	Md. . . .	1969	Rep.			
40 Gerald R. Ford	Omaha, Neb. . . .	1913	Mich. . .	1973	Rep.			
41 Nelson A. Rockefeller . .	Bar Harbor, Me. . . .	1908	N.Y. . .	1974	Rep. . .	New York, N.Y.	1979	70
42 Walter F. Mondale . . .	Ceylon, Minn. . . .	1928	Minn. . .	1977	Dem.			
43 George Bush	Milton, Mass.	1924	Tex. . .	1981	Rep.			

(1) John C. Calhoun resigned Dec. 28, 1832, having been elected to the Senate to fill a vacancy. (2) Andrew Johnson — a Democrat nominated by Republicans and elected with Lincoln on the National Union Ticket. (3) Adlai E. Stevenson, 23d vice president, was grandfather of Democratic candidate for president, 1952 and 1956.

The Continental Congress: Meetings, Presidents

Meeting places	Dates of meetings	Congress presidents	Date elected
Philadelphia	Sept. 5 to Oct. 26, 1774	Peyton Randolph, Va. (1)	Sept. 5, 1774
"	"	Henry Middleton, S.C.	Oct. 22, 1774
Philadelphia	May 10, 1775 to Dec. 12, 1776	Peyton Randolph, Va.	May 10, 1775
"	"	John Hancock, Mass.	May 24, 1775
Baltimore	Dec. 20, 1776 to Mar. 4, 1777	"	
Philadelphia	Mar. 5 to Sept. 18, 1777	"	
Lancaster, Pa.	Sept. 27, 1777 (one day)	"	
York, Pa.	Sept. 30, 1777 to June 27, 1778	Henry Laurens, S.C.	Nov. 1, 1777(4)
Philadelphia	July 2, 1778 to June 21, 1783	John Jay, N.Y.	Dec. 10, 1778
"	"	Samuel Huntington, Conn.	Sept. 28, 1779
"	"	Thomas McKean, Del.	July 10, 1781
"	"	John Hanson, Md. (2)	Nov. 5, 1781
"	"	Elias Boudinot, N.J.	Nov. 4, 1782
Princeton, N.J.	June 30 to Nov. 4, 1783	Thomas Mifflin, Pa.	Nov. 3, 1783
Annapolis, Md.	Nov. 26, 1783 to June 3, 1784	"	
Trenton, N.J.	Nov. 1 to Dec. 24, 1784	Richard Henry Lee, Va.	Nov. 30, 1784
New York City	Jan. 11 to Nov. 4, 1785	"	
"	Nov. 7, 1785 to Nov. 3, 1786	John Hancock, Mass. (3)	Nov. 23, 1785
"		Nathaniel Gorham, Mass.	June 6, 1786
"	Nov. 6, 1786 to Oct. 30, 1787	Arthur St. Clair, Pa.	Feb. 2, 1787
"	Nov. 5, 1787 to Oct. 21, 1788	Cyrus Griffin, Va.	Jan. 22, 1788
"	Nov. 3, 1788 to Mar. 2, 1789		

(1) Resigned Oct. 22, 1774. (2) Titled "President of the United States in Congress Assembled," John Hanson is considered by some to be the first U.S. President as he was the first to serve under the Articles of Confederation. He was, however, little more than presiding officer of the Congress, which retained full executive power. He could be considered the head of government, but not head of state. (3) Resigned May 29, 1786, without serving, because of illness. (4) Articles of Confederation agreed upon, Nov. 15, 1777; last ratification from Maryland, Mar. 1, 1781.

Cabinets of the U. S.

Secretaries of State

The Department of Foreign Affairs was created by act of Congress July 27, 1789, and the name changed to Department of State on Sept. 15.

President	Secretary	Home	Apptd.	President	Secretary	Home	Apptd.
Washington . .	Thomas Jefferson.	Va.	1789	"	Thomas F. Bayard	Del.	1885
"	Edmund Randolph	"	1794	Harrison, B. . .	"	"	1889
"	Timothy Pickering	Pa.	1795	"	James G. Blaine	Me.	1889
Adams, J. . . .	"	"	1797	"	John W. Foster	Ind.	1892
"	John Marshall	Va.	1800	Cleveland . . .	Walter Q. Gresham	Ill.	1893
Jefferson	James Madison	"	1801	"	Richard Olney	Mass. . . .	1895
Madison	Robert Smith	Md.	1809	McKinley	"	"	1897
"	James Monroe	Va.	1811	"	John Sherman	Oh.	1897
Monroe	John Quincy Adams	Mass. . . .	1817	"	William R. Day	"	1898
Adams, J.Q. . .	Henry Clay	Ky.	1825	"	John Hay	D.C.	1898
Jackson	Martin Van Buren	N.Y.	1829	Roosevelt, T. . .	"	"	1901
"	Edward Livingston	La.	1831	"	Elihu Root	N.Y.	1905
"	Louis McLane	Del.	1833	"	Robert Bacon	"	1909
"	John Forsyth	Ga.	1834	Taft	"	"	1909
Van Buren . . .	"	"	1837	"	Philander C. Knox	Pa.	1909
Harrison, W.H. .	Daniel Webster	Mass. . . .	1841	Wilson	"	"	1913
Tyler	"	"	1841	"	William J. Bryan	Neb.	1913
"	Abel P. Upshur	Va.	1843	"	Robert Lansing	N.Y.	1915
"	John C. Calhoun	S.C.	1844	"	Bainbridge Colby	"	1920
Polk	"	"	1845	Harding	Charles E. Hughes	"	1921
"	James Buchanan	Pa.	1845	Coolidge	"	"	1923
Taylor	"	"	1849	"	Frank B. Kellogg	Minn. . . .	1925
"	John M. Clayton	Del.	1849	Hoover	"	"	1929
Fillmore	"	"	1850	"	Henry L. Stimson	N.Y.	1929
"	Daniel Webster	Mass. . . .	1850	Roosevelt, F.D.	Cordell Hull	Tenn. . . .	1933
"	Edward Everett	"	1852	"	E.R. Stettinius Jr.	Va.	1944
Pierce	William L. Marcy	N.Y.	1853	Truman	"	"	1945
Buchanan . . .	"	"	1857	"	James F. Byrnes	S.C.	1945
"	Lewis Cass	Mich. . . .	1857	"	George C. Marshall	Pa.	1947
"	Jeremiah S. Black	Pa.	1860	"	Dean G. Acheson	Conn. . . .	1949
Lincoln	"	"	1861	Eisenhower . .	John Foster Dulles	N.Y.	1953
"	William H. Seward	N.Y.	1861	"	Christian A. Herter	Mass. . . .	1959
Johnson, A. . . .	"	"	1865	Kennedy	Dean Rusk	N.Y.	1961
Grant	Elihu B. Washburne	Ill.	1869	Johnson, L.B. . .	"	"	1963
"	Hamilton Fish	N.Y.	1869	Nixon	William P. Rogers	N.Y.	1969
Hayes	"	"	1877	"	Henry A. Kissinger	D.C.	1973
"	William M. Evarts	"	1877	Ford	"	"	1974
Garfield	"	"	1881	Carter	Cyrus R. Vance	N.Y.	1977
"	James G. Blaine	Me.	1881	"	Edmund S. Muskie	Me.	1980
Arthur	"	"	1881	Reagan	Alexander M. Haig Jr. . . .	Conn. . . .	1981
"	F.T. Frelinghuysen	N.J.	1881	"	George P. Shultz	Cal.	1982
Cleveland . . .	"	"	1885				

Secretaries of the Treasury

The Treasury Department was organized by act of Congress Sept. 2, 1789.

President	Secretary	Home	Apptd.	President	Secretary	Home	Apptd.
Washington	Alexander Hamilton	N.Y.	1789	Arthur	Charles J. Folger	N.Y.	1881
"	Oliver Wolcott	Conn.	1795	"	Walter Q. Gresham	Ind.	1884
Adams, J.	"	"	1797	"	Hugh McCulloch	"	1884
"	Samuel Dexter	Mass.	1801	Cleveland	Daniel Manning	N.Y.	1885
Jefferson	"	"	1801	Cleveland	Charles S. Fairchild	"	1887
"	Albert Gallatin	Pa.	1801	Harrison, B.	William Windom	Minn.	1889
Madison	"	Pa	1809	"	Charles Foster	Oh.	1891
"	George W. Campbell	Tenn.	1814	Cleveland	John G. Carlisle	Ky.	1893
"	Alexander J. Dallas	Pa.	1814	McKinley	Lyman J. Gage	Ill.	1897
"	William H. Crawford	Ga.	1816	Roosevelt, T.	"	"	1901
Monroe	"	"	1817	"	Leslie M. Shaw	Ia.	1902
Adams, J.Q.	Richard Rush	Pa.	1825	"	George B. Cortelyou	N.Y.	1907
Jackson	Samuel D. Ingham	"	1829	Taft	Franklin MacVeagh	Ill.	1909
"	Louis McLane	Del.	1831	Wilson	William G. McAdoo	N.Y.	1913
"	William J. Duane	Pa.	1833	"	Carter Glass	Va.	1918
"	Roger B. Taney	Md.	1833	"	David F. Houston	Mo.	1920
"	Levi Woodbury	N.H.	1834	Harding	Andrew W. Mellon	Pa.	1921
Van Buren	"	"	1837	Coolidge	"	"	1923
Harrison, W.H.	Thomas Ewing	Oh.	1841	Hoover	"	"	1929
Tyler	"	"	1841	"	Ogden L. Mills	N.Y.	1932
"	Walter Forward	Pa.	1841	Roosevelt, F.D.	William H. Woodin	"	1933
"	John C. Spencer	N.Y.	1843	"	Henry Morgenthau, Jr.	"	1934
Tyler	George M. Bibb	Ky.	1844	Truman	Fred M. Vinson	Ky.	1945
Polk	Robert J. Walker	Miss.	1845	"	John W. Snyder	Mo.	1946
Taylor	William M. Meredith	Pa.	1849	Eisenhower	George M. Humphrey	Oh.	1953
Fillmore	Thomas Corwin	Oh.	1850	"	Robert B. Anderson	Conn.	1957
Pierce	James Guthrie	Ky.	1853	Kennedy	C. Douglas Dillon	N.J.	1961
Buchanan	Howell Cobb	Ga.	1857	Johnson, L.B.	"	"	1963
"	Phillip F. Thomas	Md.	1860	"	Henry H. Fowler	Va.	1965
"	John A. Dix	N.Y.	1861	"	Joseph W. Barr	Ind.	1968
Lincoln	Salmon P. Chase	Oh.	1861	Nixon	David M. Kennedy	Ill.	1969
"	William P. Fessenden	Me.	1864	"	John B. Connally	Tex.	1971
"	Hugh McCulloch	Ind.	1865	"	George P. Shultz	Ill.	1972
Johnson, A.	"	"	1865	"	William E. Simon	N.J.	1974
Grant	George S. Boutwell	Mass.	1869	Ford	"	"	1974
"	William A. Richardson	Mass.	1873	Carter	W. Michael Blumenthal	Mich.	1977
"	Benjamin H. Bristow	Ky.	1874	"	G. William Miller	R.I.	1979
"	Lot M. Morrill	Me.	1876	Reagan	Donald T. Regan	N.Y.	1981
Hayes	John Sherman	Oh.	1877				
Garfield	William Windom	Minn.	1881				

Secretaries of Defense

The Department of Defense, originally designated the National Military Establishment, was created Sept. 18, 1947. It is headed by the secretary of defense, who is a member of the president's cabinet.

The departments of the army, of the navy, and of the air force function within the Department of Defense, and their respective secretaries are no longer members of the president's cabinet.

President	Secretary	Home	Apptd.	President	Secretary	Home	Apptd.
Truman	James V. Forrestal	N.Y.	1947	"	Clark M. Clifford	Md.	1968
"	Louis A. Johnson	W.Va.	1949	Nixon	Melvin R. Laird	Wis.	1969
"	George C. Marshall	Pa.	1950	"	Elliot L. Richardson	Mass.	1973
"	Robert A. Lovett	N.Y.	1951	"	James R. Schlesinger	Va.	1973
Eisenhower	Charles E. Wilson	Mich.	1953	Ford	"	"	1974
"	Neil H. McElroy	Oh.	1957	"	Donald H. Rumsfeld	Ill.	1975
"	Thomas S. Gates Jr.	Pa.	1959	Carter	Harold Brown	Cal.	1977
Kennedy	Robert S. McNamara	Mich.	1961	Reagan	Caspar W. Weinberger	Cal.	1981
Johnson, L.B.	Robert S. McNamara	Mich.	1963				

Secretaries of War

The War (and Navy) Department was created by act of Congress Aug. 7, 1789, and Gen. Henry Knox was commissioned secretary of war under that act Sept. 12, 1789.

President	Secretary	Home	Apptd.	President	Secretary	Home	Apptd.
Washington	Henry Knox	Mass.	1789	Tyler	John Bell	Tenn	1841
"	Timothy Pickering	Pa.	1795	Tyler	John C. Spencer	N.Y.	1841
"	James McHenry	Md.	1796	"	James M. Porter	Pa.	1843
Adams, J.	"	"	1797	"	William Wilkins		1844
"	Samuel Dexter	Mass.	1800	Polk	William L. Marcy	N.Y.	1845
Jefferson	Henry Dearborn	"	1801	Taylor	George W. Crawford	Ga.	1849
Madison	William Eustis	Mass.	1809	Fillmore	Charles M. Conrad	La.	1850
"	John Armstrong	N.Y.	1813	Pierce	Jefferson Davis	Miss.	1853
Madison	James Monroe	Va.	1814	Buchanan	John B. Floyd	Va.	1857
"	William H. Crawford	Ga.	1815	"	Joseph Holt	Ky.	1861
Monroe	John C. Calhoun	S.C.	1817	Lincoln	Simon Cameron	Pa.	1861
Adams, J.Q.	James Barbour	Va.	1825	"	Edwin M. Stanton	Pa.	1862
"	Peter B. Porter	N.Y.	1828	Johnson, A.	"	"	1865
Jackson	John H. Eaton	Tenn.	1829	"	John M. Schofield	Ill.	1868
"	Lewis Cass	Oh.	1831	Grant	John A. Rawlins	Ill.	1869
"	Benjamin F. Butler	N.Y.	1837	"	William T. Sherman	Oh.	1869
Van Buren	Joel R. Poinsett	S.C.	1837	"	William W. Belknap	Ia.	1869
Harrison, W.H.	John Bell	Tenn.	1841	"	Alphonso Taft	Oh.	1876

President	Secretary	Home	Apptd.	President	Secretary	Home	Apptd.
Grant	James D. Cameron	Pa.	1876	Taft	Jacob M. Dickinson	Tenn.	1909
Hayes	George W. McCrary	Ia.	1877	"	Henry L. Stimson	N.Y.	1911
"	Alexander Ramsey	Minn.	1879	Wilson	Lindley M. Garrison	N.J.	1913
Garfield	Robert T. Lincoln	Ill.	1881	"	Newton D. Baker	Oh.	1916
Arthur	"	"	1881	Harding	John W. Weeks	Mass.	1921
Cleveland	William C. Endicott	Mass.	1885	Coolidge	"	"	1923
Harrison, B.	Redfield Proctor	Vt.	1889	"	Dwight F. Davis	Mo.	1925
"	Stephen B. Elkins	W.Va.	1891	Hoover	James W. Good	Ill.	1929
Cleveland	Daniel S. Lamont	N.Y.	1893	Hoover	Patrick J. Hurley	Okla.	1929
McKinley	Russel A. Alger	Mich.	1897	Roosevelt, F.D.	George H. Dern	Ut.	1933
"	Elihu Root	N.Y.	1899	"	Harry H. Woodring	Kan.	1937
Roosevelt, T.	"	"	1901	Roosevelt, F.D.	Henry L. Stimson	N.Y.	1940
"	William H. Taft	Oh.	1904	Truman	Robert P. Patterson	N.Y.	1945
"	Luke E. Wright	Tenn.	1908	"	*Kenneth C. Royall	N.C.	1947

Secretaries of the Navy

The Navy Department was created by act of Congress Apr. 30, 1798.

President	Secretary	Home	Apptd.	President	Secretary	Home	Apptd.
Adams, J.	Benjamin Stoddert	Md.	1798	Lincoln	Gideon Welles	Conn.	1861
Jefferson	"	"	1801	Johnson, A.	"	"	1865
"	Robert Smith	"	1801	Grant	Adolph E. Borie	Pa.	1869
Madison	Paul Hamilton	S.C.	1809	"	George M. Robeson	N.J.	1869
"	William Jones	Pa.	1813	Hayes	Richard W. Thompson	Ind.	1877
"	Benjamin Williams Crowninshield	Mass.	1814	"	Nathan Goff Jr.	W.Va.	1881
Monroe	"	"	1817	Garfield	William H. Hunt	La.	1881
"	Smith Thompson	N.Y.	1818	Arthur	William E. Chandler	N.H.	1882
"	Samuel L. Southard	N.J.	1823	Cleveland	William C. Whitney	N.Y.	1885
Adams, J.Q.	"	"	1825	Harrison, B.	Benjamin F. Tracy	N.Y.	1889
Jackson	John Branch	N.C.	1829	Cleveland	Hilary A. Herbert	Ala.	1893
"	Levi Woodbury	N.H.	1831	McKinley	John D. Long	Mass.	1897
"	Mahlon Dickerson	N.J.	1834	Roosevelt, T.	"	"	1901
Van Buren	"	"	1837	"	William H. Moody	"	1902
"	James K. Paulding	N.Y.	1838	"	Paul Morton	Ill.	1904
Harrison, W.H.	George E. Badger	N.C.	1841	"	Charles J. Bonaparte	Md.	1905
Tyler	"	"	1841	"	Victor H. Metcalf	Cal.	1906
"	Abel P. Upshur	Va.	1841	"	Truman H. Newberry	Mich.	1908
"	David Henshaw	Mass.	1843	Taft	George von L. Meyer	Mass.	1909
"	Thomas W. Gilmer	Va.	1844	Wilson	Josephus Daniels	N.C.	1913
"	John Y. Mason	"	1844	Harding	Edwin Denby	Mich.	1921
Polk	George Bancroft	Mass.	1845	Coolidge	"	"	1923
"	John Y. Mason	Va.	1846	"	Curtis D. Wilbur	Cal.	1924
Taylor	William B. Preston	"	1849	Hoover	Charles Francis Adams	Mass.	1929
Fillmore	William A. Graham	N.C.	1850	Roosevelt, F.D.	Claude A. Swanson	Va.	1933
"	John P. Kennedy	Md.	1852	"	Charles Edison	N.J.	1940
Pierce	James C. Dobbin	N.C.	1853	"	Frank Knox	Ill.	1940
Buchanan	Isaac Toucey	Conn.	1857	"	*James V. Forrestal	N.Y.	1944
				Truman	"	"	1945

*Last members of Cabinet. The War Department became the Department of the Army and it and the Navy Department became branches of the Department of Defense, created Sept. 18, 1947.

Attorneys General

The office of attorney general was organized by act of Congress Sept. 24, 1789. The Department of Justice was created June 22, 1870.

President	Attorney General	Home	Apptd.	President	Attorney General	Home	Apptd.
Washington	Edmund Randolph	Va.	1789	Lincoln	Edward Bates	Mo.	1861
"	William Bradford	Pa.	1794	"	James Speed	Ky.	1864
"	Charles Lee	Va.	1795	Johnson, A.	"	"	1865
Adams, J.	"	"	1797	"	Henry Stanbery	Oh.	1866
Jefferson	Levi Lincoln	Mass.	1801	"	William M. Evarts	N.Y.	1868
"	John Breckenridge	Ky.	1805	Grant	Ebenezer R. Hoar	Mass.	1869
"	Caesar A. Rodney	Del.	1807	"	Amos T. Akerman	Ga.	1870
Madison	"	"	1809	"	George H. Williams	Ore.	1871
"	William Pinkney	Md.	1811	"	Edwards Pierrepont	N.Y.	1875
"	Richard Rush	Pa.	1814	"	Alphonso Taft	Oh.	1876
Monroe	"	"	1817	Hayes	Charles Devens	Mass.	1877
"	William Wirt	Va.	1817	Garfield	Wayne MacVeagh	Pa.	1881
Adams, J.Q.	"	"	1825	Arthur	Benjamin H. Brewster	"	1881
Jackson	John M. Berrien	Ga.	1829	Cleveland	Augustus Garland	Ark.	1885
"	Roger B. Taney	Md.	1831	Harrison, B.	William H. H. Miller	Ind.	1889
"	Benjamin F. Butler	N.Y.	1833	Cleveland	Richard Olney	Mass.	1893
Van Buren	"	"	1837	"	Judson Harmon	Oh.	1895
"	Felix Grundy	Tenn.	1838	McKinley	Joseph McKenna	Cal.	1897
"	Henry D. Gilpin	Pa.	1840	"	John W. Griggs	N.J.	1898
Harrison, W.H.	John J. Crittenden	Ky.	1841	"	Philander C. Knox	Pa.	1901
Tyler	"	"	1841	Roosevelt, T.	"	"	1901
"	Hugh S. Legare	S.C.	1841	"	William H. Moody	Mass.	1904
"	John Nelson	Md.	1843	"	Charles J. Bonaparte	Md.	1906
Polk	John Y. Mason	Va.	1845	Taft	George W. Wickersham	N.Y.	1909
"	Nathan Clifford	Me.	1846	Wilson	J.C. McReynolds	Tenn.	1913
"	Isaac Toucey	Conn.	1848	"	Thomas W. Gregory	Tex.	1914
Taylor	Reverdy Johnson	Md.	1849	"	A. Mitchell Palmer	Pa.	1919
Fillmore	John J. Crittenden	Ky.	1850	Harding	Harry M. Daugherty	Oh.	1921
Pierce	Caleb Cushing	Mass.	1853	Coolidge	"	"	1923
Buchanan	Jeremiah S. Black	Pa.	1857	"	Harlan F. Stone	N.Y.	1924
"	Edwin M. Stanton	Pa.	1860	"	John G. Sargent	Vt.	1925

President	Attorney General	Home	Apptd.	President	Attorney General	Home	Apptd.
Hoover	William D. Mitchell	Minn.	1929	Johnson, L.B.	N. de B. Katzenbach	Ill.	1964
Roosevelt, F.D.	Homer S. Cummings	Conn.	1933	"	Ramsey Clark	Tex.	1967
"	Frank Murphy	Mich.	1939	Nixon	John N. Mitchell	N.Y.	1969
"	Robert H. Jackson	N.Y.	1940	"	Richard G. Kleindienst	Ariz.	1972
"	Francis Biddle	Pa.	1941	"	Elliot L. Richardson	Mass.	1973
Truman	Thomas C. Clark	Tex.	1945	"	William B. Saxbe	Oh.	1974
"	J. Howard McGrath	R.I.	1949	Ford	"	"	1974
"	J.P. McGranery	Pa.	1952	"	Edward H. Levi	Ill.	1975
Eisenhower	Herbert Brownell Jr.	N.Y.	1953	Carter	Griffin B. Bell	Ga.	1977
"	William P. Rogers	Md.	1957	"	Benjamin R. Civiletti	Md.	1979
Kennedy	Robert F. Kennedy	Mass.	1961	Reagan	William French Smith	Cal.	1981
Johnson, L.B.	"	"	1963				

Secretaries of the Interior

The Department of Interior was created by act of Congress Mar. 3, 1849

President	Secretary	Home	Apptd.	President	Secretary	Home	Apptd.
Taylor	Thomas Ewing	Oh.	1849	Taft	Richard A. Ballinger	Wash.	1909
Fillmore	Thomas M. T. McKennan	Pa.	1850	"	Walter L. Fisher	Ill.	1911
Fillmore	Alex H. H. Stuart	Va.	1850	Wilson	Franklin K. Lane	Cal.	1913
Pierce	Robert McClelland	Mich.	1853	"	John B. Payne	Ill.	1920
Buchanan	Jacob Thompson	Miss.	1857	Harding	Albert B. Fall	N.M.	1921
Lincoln	Caleb B. Smith	Ind.	1861	"	Hubert Work	Col.	1923
"	John P. Usher	"	1863	Coolidge	"	"	1923
Johnson, A.	"	"	1865	"	Roy O. West	Ill.	1929
"	James Harlan	Ia.	1865	Hoover	Ray Lyman Wilbur	Cal.	1929
"	Orville H. Browning	Ill.	1866	Roosevelt, F.D.	Harold L. Ickes	Ill.	1933
Grant	Jacob D. Cox	Oh.	1869	Truman	"	"	1945
"	Columbus Delano	"	1870	"	Julius A. Krug	Wis.	1946
"	Zachariah Chandler	Mich.	1875	"	Oscar L. Chapman	Col.	1949
Hayes	Carl Schurz	Mo.	1877	Eisenhower	Douglas McKay	Ore.	1953
Garfield	Samuel J. Kirkwood	Ia.	1881	"	Fred A Seaton	Neb.	1956
Arthur	Henry M. Teller	Col.	1882	Kennedy	Stewart L. Udall	Ariz.	1961
Cleveland	Lucius Q.C. Lamar	Miss.	1885	Johnson, L.B.	"	"	1963
"	William F. Vilas	Wis.	1888	Nixon	Walter J. Hickel	Alas.	1969
Harrison, B.	John W. Noble	Mo.	1889	"	Rogers C.B. Morton	Md.	1971
Cleveland	Hoke Smith	Ga.	1893	Ford	"	"	1974
"	David R. Francis	Mo.	1896	"	Stanley K. Hathaway	Wyo.	1975
McKinley	Cornelius N. Bliss	N.Y.	1897	"	Thomas S. Kleppe	N.D.	1975
"	Ethan A. Hitchcock	Mo.	1898	Carter	Cecil D. Andrus	Ida.	1977
Roosevelt, T.	"	"	1901	Reagan	James G. Watt	Col.	1981
"	James R. Garfield	Oh.	1907	"	William P. Clarke	Cal.	1983

Secretaries of Agriculture

The Department of Agriculture was created by act of Congress May 15, 1862. On Feb. 8, 1889, its commissioner was renamed secretary of agriculture and became a member of the cabinet.

President	Secretary	Home	Apptd.	President	Secretary	Home	Apptd.
Cleveland	Norman J. Colman	Mo.	1889	Roosevelt, F.D.	Henry A. Wallace	Ia.	1933
Harrison, B.	Jeremiah M. Rusk	Wis.	1889	"	Claude R. Wickard	Ind.	1940
Cleveland	J. Sterling Morton	Neb.	1893	Truman	Clinton P. Anderson	N.M.	1945
McKinley	James Wilson	Ia.	1897	"	Charles F. Brannan	Col.	1948
Roosevelt, T.	"	"	1901	Eisenhower	Ezra Taft Benson	Ut.	1953
Taft	"	"	1909	Kennedy	Orville L. Freeman	Minn.	1961
Wilson	David F. Houston	Mo.	1913	Johnson, L.B.	"	"	1963
"	Edwin T. Meredith	Ia.	1920	Nixon	Clifford M. Hardin	Ind.	1969
Harding	Henry C. Wallace	Ia.	1921	"	Earl L. Butz	Ind.	1971
Coolidge	"	"	1923	Ford	"	"	1974
"	Howard M. Gore	W.Va.	1924	"	John A. Knebel	Va.	1976
"	William M. Jardine	Kan.	1925	Carter	Bob Bergland	Minn.	1977
Hoover	Arthur M. Hyde	Mo.	1929	Reagan	John R. Block	Ill.	1981

Secretaries of Commerce and Labor

The Department of Commerce and Labor, created by Congress Feb. 14, 1903, was divided by Congress Mar. 4, 1913, into separate departments of Commerce and Labor. The secretary of each was made a cabinet member.

President	Secretary	Home	Apptd.	President	Secretary	Home	Apptd.
Secretaries of Commerce and Labor				Eisenhower	Martin P. Durkin	Ill.	1953
Roosevelt, T.	George B. Cortelyou	N.Y.	1903	"	James P. Mitchell	N.J.	1953
"	Victor H. Metcalf	Cal.	1904				
"	Oscar S. Straus	N.Y.	1906	Kennedy	Arthur J. Goldberg	Ill.	1961
Taft	Charles Nagel	Mo.	1909	"	W. Willard Wirtz	Ill.	1962
				Johnson, L.B.	"	Ill.	1963
Secretaries of Labor				Nixon	George P. Shultz	Ill.	1969
Wilson	William B. Wilson	Pa.	1913	"	James D. Hodgson	Cal.	1970
Harding	James J. Davis	Pa.	1921	"	Peter J. Brennan	N.Y.	1973
Coolidge	"	"	1923	Ford	"	"	1974
Hoover	"	"	1929	"	John T. Dunlop	Cal.	1975
"	William N. Doak	Va.	1930	"	W.J. Usery Jr.	Ga.	1976
Roosevelt, F.D.	Frances Perkins	N.Y.	1933	Carter	F. Ray Marshall	Tex.	1977
Truman	L.B. Schwellenbach	Wash.	1945	Reagan	Raymond J. Donovan	N.J.	1981
"	Maurice J. Tobin	Mass.	1949				

President	Secretary	Home	Apptd.	President	Secretary	Home	Apptd.
Secretaries of Commerce				Eisenhower	Lewis L. Strauss	N.Y.	1958
Wilson	William C. Redfield	N.Y.	1913	"	Frederick H. Mueller	Mich.	1959
"	Joshua W. Alexander	Mo.	1919	Kennedy	Luther H. Hodges	N.C.	1961
Harding	Herbert C. Hoover	Cal.	1921	Johnson, L.B.	"	"	1963
Coolidge	"	"	1923	"	John T. Connor	N.J.	1965
"	William F. Whiting	Mass.	1928	"	Alex B. Trowbridge	N.J.	1967
Hoover	Robert P. Lamont	Ill.	1929	"	Cyrus R. Smith	N.Y.	1968
"	Roy D. Chapin	Mich.	1932	Nixon	Maurice H. Stans	Minn.	1969
Roosevelt, F.D.	Daniel C. Roper	S.C.	1933	"	Peter G. Peterson	Ill.	1972
"	Harry L. Hopkins	N.Y.	1939	"	Frederick B. Dent	S.C.	1973
"	Jesse Jones	Tex.	1940	Ford	"	"	1974
"	Henry A. Wallace	Ia.	1945	"	Rogers C.B. Morton	Md.	1975
Truman	"	"	1945	"	Elliot L. Richardson	Mass.	1975
"	W. Averell Harriman	N.Y.	1947	Carter	Juanita M. Kreps	N.C.	1977
"	Charles Sawyer	Oh.	1948	"	Philip M. Klutznick	Ill.	1979
Eisenhower	Sinclair Weeks	Mass.	1953	Reagan	Malcolm Baldrige	Conn.	1981

Secretaries of Education, and Health and Human Services

The Department of Health, Education and Welfare, created by Congress Apr. 11, 1953, was divided by Congress Sept. 27, 1979, into separate departments of Education, and Health and Human Services. The secretary of each is a cabinet member.

President	Secretary	Home	Apptd.	President	Secretary	Home	Apptd.
Secretaries of Health, Education, and Welfare				"	Forrest D. Mathews	Ala.	1975
				Carter	Joseph A. Califano, Jr.	D.C.	1977
Eisenhower	Oveta Culp Hobby	Tex.	1953	"	Patricia Roberts Harris	D.C.	1979
"	Marion B. Folsom	N.Y.	1955				
"	Arthur S. Flemming	Oh.	1958	**Secretaries of Health and Human Services**			
Kennedy	Abraham A. Ribicoff	Conn.	1961				
"	Anthony J. Celebrezze	Oh.	1962	Carter	Patricia Roberts Harris	D.C.	1979
Johnson, L.B.	"	"	1963	Reagan	Richard S. Schweiker	Pa.	1981
"	John W. Gardner	N.Y.	1965	"	Margaret M. Heckler	Mass.	1983
Johnson, L.B.	Wilbur J. Cohen	Mich.	1968				
Nixon	Robert H. Finch	Cal.	1969	**Secretaries of Education**			
"	Elliot L. Richardson	Mass.	1970				
"	Caspar W. Weinberger	Cal.	1973	Carter	Shirley Hufstedler	Cal.	1979
Ford	"	"	1974	Reagan	Terrel Bell	Ut.	1981

Secretaries of Housing and Urban Development

The Department of Housing and Urban Development was created by act of Congress Sept. 9, 1965.

President	Secretary	Home	Apptd.	President	Secretary	Home	Apptd.
Johnson, L.B.	Robert C. Weaver	Wash.	1966	"	Carla Anderson Hills	Cal.	1975
"	Robert C. Wood	Mass.	1969	Carter	Patricia Roberts Harris	D.C.	1977
Nixon	George W. Romney	Mich.	1969	"	Moon Landrieu	La.	1979
"	James T. Lynn	Oh.	1973	Reagan	Samuel R. Pierce Jr.	N.Y.	1981
Ford	"	"	1974				

Secretaries of Transportation

The Department of Transportation was created by act of Congress Oct. 15, 1966.

President	Secretary	Home	Apptd.	President	Secretary	Home	Apptd.
Johnson, L.B.	Alan S. Boyd	Fla.	1966	Carter	Brock Adams	Wash.	1977
Nixon	John A. Volpe	Mass.	1969	"	Neil E. Goldschmidt	Ore.	1979
"	Claude S. Brinegar	Cal.	1973	Reagan	Andrew L. Lewis Jr.	Pa.	1981
Ford	Claude S. Brinegar	Cal.	1974	"	Elizabeth Hanford Dole	Kan.	1983
"	William T. Coleman Jr.	Pa.	1975				

Secretaries of Energy

The Department of Energy was created by federal law Aug. 4, 1977.

President	Secretary	Home	Apptd.	President	Secretary	Home	Apptd.
Carter	James R. Schlesinger	Va.	1977	Reagan	James B. Edwards	S.C.	1981
"	Charles Duncan Jr.	Wyo.	1979	"	Donald P. Hodel	Ore.	1982

Burial Places of the Presidents

Washington	Mt. Vernon, Va.	Fillmore	Buffalo, N.Y.
J. Adams	Quincy, Mass.	Pierce	Concord, N.H.
Jefferson	Charlottesville, Va.	Buchanan	Lancaster, Pa.
Madison	Montpelier Station, Va.	Lincoln	Springfield, Ill.
Monroe	Richmond, Va.	A. Johnson	Greeneville, Tenn.
J.Q. Adams	Quincy, Mass.	Grant	New York City
Jackson	Nashville, Tenn.	Hayes	Fremont, Oh.
Van Buren	Kinderhook, N.Y.	Garfield	Cleveland, Oh.
W.H. Harrison	North Bend, Oh.	Arthur	Albany, N.Y.
Tyler	Richmond, Va.	Cleveland	Princeton, N.J.
Polk	Nashville, Tenn.	B. Harrison	Indianapolis, Ind.
Taylor	Louisville, Ky.	McKinley	Canton, Oh.

T. Roosevelt	Oyster Bay, N.Y.
Taft	Arlington Nat'l. Cem'y.
Wilson	Washington Cathedral
Harding	Marion, Oh.
Coolidge	Plymouth, Vt.
Hoover	West Branch, Ia.
F.D. Roosevelt	Hyde Park, N.Y.
Truman	Independence, Mo.
Eisenhower	Abilene, Kan.
Kennedy	Arlington Nat'l. Cem'y.
L.B. Johnson	Stonewall, Tex.

Presidents Pro Tempore of the Senate

Until 1890, presidents "pro tem" were named "for the occasion only." Beginning with that year, they have served "until the Senate otherwise ordered." Sen. John J. Ingalls, chosen under the old rule in 1887, was again elected, under the new rule, in 1890. Party designations are D, Democrat; R, Republican.

Name	Party	State	Elected	Name	Party	State	Elected
John J. Ingalls	R	Kan.	Apr. 3, 1890	Key Pittman	D	Nev.	Mar. 9, 1933
Charles F. Manderson	R	Neb.	Mar. 2, 1891	William H. King	D	Ut.	Nov. 19, 1940
Isham G. Harris	D	Tenn.	Mar. 22, 1893	Pat Harrison	D	Miss.	Jan. 6, 1941
Matt W. Ransom	D	N.C.	Jan. 7, 1895	Carter Glass	D	Va.	July 10, 1941
Isham G. Harris	D	Tenn.	Jan. 10, 1895	Kenneth McKellar	D	Tenn.	Jan. 6, 1945
William P. Frye	R	Me.	Feb. 7, 1896	Arthur H. Vandenberg	R	Mich.	Jan. 4, 1947
Charles Curtis	R	Kan.	Dec. 4, 1911	Kenneth McKellar	D	Tenn.	Jan. 3, 1949
Augustus O. Bacon	D	Ga.	Jan. 15, 1912	Styles Bridges	R	N.H.	Jan. 3, 1953
Jacob H. Gallinger	R	N.H.	Feb. 12, 1912	Walter F. George	D	Ga.	Jan. 5, 1955
Henry Cabot Lodge	R	Mass.	Mar. 25, 1912	Carl Hayden	D	Ariz.	Jan. 3, 1957
Frank R. Brandegee	R	Conn.	May 25, 1912	Richard B. Russell	D	Ga.	Jan. 3, 1969
James P. Clarke	D	Ark.	Mar. 23, 1915	Allen J. Ellender	D	La.	Jan. 22, 1971
Willard Saulsbury	D	Del.	Dec. 14, 1916	James O. Eastland	D	Miss.	July 28, 1972
Albert B. Cummins	R	Ia.	May 19, 1919	Warren G. Magnuson	D	Wash.	Jan. 23, 1979
George H. Moses	R	N.H.	Mar. 6, 1925	Strom Thurmond	R	S.C.	Jan. 5, 1981

Speakers of the House of Representatives

Party designations: A, American; D, Democratic; DR, Democratic Republican; F, Federalist; R, Republican; W, Whig. *Served only one day.

Name	Party	State	Tenure	Name	Party	State	Tenure
Frederick Muhlenberg	F	Pa.	1789-1791	Schuyler Colfax	R	Ind.	1863-1869
Jonathan Trumbull	F	Conn.	1791-1793	*Theodore M. Pomeroy	R	N.Y.	1869-1869
Frederick Muhlenberg	F	Pa.	1793-1795	James G. Blaine	R	Me.	1869-1875
Jonathan Dayton	F	N.J.	1795-1799	Michael C. Kerr	D	Ind.	1875-1876
Theodore Sedgwick	F	Mass.	1799-1801	Samuel J. Randall	D	Pa.	1876-1881
Nathaniel Macon	DR	N.C.	1801-1807	Joseph W. Keifer	R	Oh.	1881-1883
Joseph B. Varnum	DR	Mass.	1807-1811	John G. Carlisle	D	Ky.	1883-1889
Henry Clay	DR	Ky.	1811-1814	Thomas B. Reed	R	Me.	1889-1891
Langdon Cheves	DR	S.C.	1814-1815	Charles F. Crisp	D	Ga.	1891-1895
Henry Clay	DR	Ky.	1815-1820	Thomas B. Reed	R	Me.	1895-1899
John W. Taylor	DR	N.Y.	1820-1821	David B. Henderson	R	Ia.	1899-1903
Philip P. Barbour	DR	Va.	1821-1823	Joseph G. Cannon	R	Ill.	1903-1911
Henry Clay	DR	Ky.	1823-1825	Champ Clark	D	Mo.	1911-1919
John W. Taylor	D	N.Y.	1825-1827	Frederick H. Gillett	R	Mass.	1919-1925
Andrew Stevenson	D	Va.	1827-1834	Nicholas Longworth	R	Oh.	1925-1931
John Bell	D	Tenn.	1834-1835	John N. Garner	D	Tex.	1931-1933
James K. Polk	D	Tenn.	1835-1839	Henry T. Rainey	D	Ill.	1933-1935
Robert M. T. Hunter	D	Va.	1839-1841	Joseph W. Byrns	D	Tenn.	1935-1936
John White	W	Ky.	1841-1843	William B. Bankhead	D	Ala.	1936-1940
John W. Jones	D	Va.	1843-1845	Sam Rayburn	D	Tex.	1940-1947
John W. Davis	D	Ind.	1845-1847	Joseph W. Martin Jr.	R	Mass.	1947-1949
Robert C. Winthrop	W	Mass.	1847-1849	Sam Rayburn	D	Tex.	1949-1953
Howell Cobb	D	Ga.	1849-1851	Joseph W. Martin Jr.	R	Mass.	1953-1955
Linn Boyd	D	Ky.	1851-1855	Sam Rayburn	D	Tex.	1955-1961
Nathaniel P. Banks	A	Mass.	1856-1857	John W. McCormack	D	Mass.	1962-1971
James L. Orr	D	S.C.	1857-1859	Carl Albert	D	Okla.	1971-1977
William Pennington	R	N.J.	1860-1861	Thomas P. O'Neill Jr.	D	Mass.	1977-
Galusha A. Grow	R	Pa.	1861-1863				

National Political Parties

As of Mid-1984

Republican Party

National Headquarters—310 First St., SE, Washington, DC 20003.
Chairman—Frank J. Fahrenkopf Jr.
Co-Chairman—Betty Heitman.
White House Liaison—Frederick K. Beibel.
Dir. of Political Operations—William B. Lacy.
Vice Chairmen—Ranny Riecker, Clarke Reed, Bernard-M. Shanley, Paula F. Hawkins, Shelia Roberge, Edith Holm, John C. McDonald, Jack Londen.
Secretary—Jean G. Birch.

Treasurer—William J. McManus.
General Counsel—Roger Allan Moore.

Democratic Party

National Headquarters—1625 Massachusetts Ave., NW, Washington, DC 20036.
Chairman—Charles T. Manatt.
Vice Chairpersons—Richard Hatcher, Polly Baca, Lynn Cutler.
Secretary—Dorothy V. Bush.
Treasurer—Paul G. Kirk Jr.
Finance Chairman—Peter G. Kelly.

Other Major Political Organizations

American Independent Party
(P.O. Box 3737, Simi Valley, CA 93063)
National Chairman—Tom Goodloe.
Secretary—Patricia Manning.
Treasurer—Lon L. Laymon.

American Party of the United States
(3600 Market St., Salt Lake City, UT 84119)
National Chairman—Earl Jeppson.
Secretary—Doris Feimer.
Treasurer—Dr. R. L. Youngblood.

Americans For Democratic Action
(1411 K St. NW, Washington, DC 20005)
President—Father Robert Drinan.
National Director—Leon Shull.
Chairperson Exec. Comm.—Winn Newman.

Comm. on Political Education, AFL-CIO
(AFL-CIO Building, 815 16th St., Wash., DC 20006)
Chairman—Lane Kirkland.
Secretary-Treasurer—Thomas R. Donahue.

Communist Party U.S.A.
(235 W. 23d St., New York, NY 10011)
National Chairman—Henry Winston.
General Secretary—Gus Hall.

Conservative Party of the State of N.Y.
(45 E. 29th St., New York, NY 10016)
Chairman—J. Daniel Mahoney.
Executive Director—Serphin R. Maltese.
Secretary—A. Terry Anderson.
Treasurer—James E. O'Doherty.

Liberal Party of New York State
(1560 Broadway, New York, NY 10036)
Chairman—Donald S. Harrington.
Treasurer—Alan A. Bailey.
Secretary—James F. Notaro.

Libertarian National Committee
(7887 Katy Freeway #385, Houston, TX 77024.)
Chair—Paul Grant.
Vice-Chair—Mary Gingell.
Secretary—Heide Hartmann-Davis.
Treasurer—David Walter.
National Director—Honey Lanham.

Prohibition National Committee
(P.O. Box 2635, Denver, CO 80201)
National Chairman—Earl F. Dodge.
National Secretary—Rayford G. Feather.

Socialist Party
(1011 N. 3d St. #219, Milwaukee, WI 53203)
Co-Chairs—Margaret Feigin, William Shakalis.
Secretary—Donald J. Doumakes.

Socialist Labor Party
In Minnesota: Industrial Gov't. Party
(914 Industrial Ave., Palo Alto, CA 94303)
National Secretary—Robert Bills.
Financial Secretary—Genevieve Gunderson.

Socialist Workers Party
(14 Charles Lane, New York, NY 10014)
National Secretary—Jack Barnes.
National Co-Chairpersons—Malik Miah, Barry Sheppard, Mary-Alice Waters.

America's Third Parties

Since 1860, there have been only 4 presidential elections in which all third parties together polled more than 10% of the vote: the Populists (James Baird Weaver) in 1892, the National Progressives (Theodore Roosevelt) in 1912, the La Follette Progressives in 1924, and George Wallace's American Party in 1968. In 1948, the combined third parties (Henry Wallace's Progessives, Strom Thurmond's States' Rights party or Dixiecrats, Prohibition, Socialists, and others) received only 5.75% of the vote. In most elections since 1860, fewer than one vote in 20 has been cast for a third party. The only successful third party in American history was the Republican Party in the election of Abraham Lincoln in 1860.

Notable Third Parties

Party	Presidential nominee	Election	Issues	Strength in
Anti-Masonic	William Wirt	1832	Against secret societies and oaths	Pa., Vt.
Liberty	James G. Birney	1844	Anti-slavery	North
Free Soil	Martin Van Buren	1848	Anti-slavery	New York, Ohio
American (Know Nothing)	Millard Fillmore	1856	Anti-immigrant	Northeast, South
Greenback	Peter Cooper	1876	For "cheap money,"	
Greenback	James B. Weaver	1880	labor rights	National
Prohibition	John P. St. John	1884	Anti-liquor	National
Populist	James B. Weaver	1892	For "cheap money," end of national banks	South, West
Socialist	Eugene V. Debs	1900-20	For public ownership	National
Progressive (Bull Moose)	Theodore Roosevelt	1912	Against high tariffs	Midwest, West
Progressive	Robert M. LaFollette	1924	Farmer & labor rights	Midwest, West
Socialist	Norman Thomas	1928-48	Liberal reforms	National
Union	William Lemke	1936	Anti "New Deal"	National
States' Rights	Strom Thurmond	1948	For segregation	South
Progressive	Henry Wallace	1948	Anti-cold war	New York, California
American Independent	George Wallace	1968	For states' rights	South
American	John G. Schmitz	1972	For "law and order"	Far West, Oh., La.
None (Independent)	John B. Anderson	1980	A 3d choice	National

The Electoral College

The president and the vice president of the United States are the only elective federal officials not elected by direct vote of the people. They are elected by the members of the Electoral College, an institution that has survived since the founding of the nation despite repeated attempts in Congress to alter or abolish it. In the elections of 1824, 1876 and 1888 the presidential candidate receiving the largest popular vote failed to win a majority of the electoral votes.

On presidential election day, the first Tuesday after the first Monday in November of every 4th year, each state chooses as many electors as it has senators and representatives in Congress. In 1964, for the first time, the District of Columbia voted for 3 electors. Thus, with 100 senators and 435 representatives, there are 538 members of the Electoral College, with a majority of 270 electoral votes needed to elect the president and vice president.

Political parties customarily nominate their lists of electors at their respective state conventions. An elector cannot be a member of Congress or any person holding federal office.

Some states print the names of the candidates for president and vice president at the top of the November ballot while others list only the names of the electors. In either case, the electors of the party receiving the highest vote are elected. The electors meet on the first Monday after the 2d Wednesday in December in their respective state capitals or in some other place prescribed by state legislatures. By long-established custom they vote for their party nominees, although the Constitution does not require them to do so. All of the state's electoral votes are then awarded to the winners. The only Constitutional requirement is that at least one of the persons each elector votes for shall not be an inhabitant of that elector's home state.

Certified and sealed lists of the votes of the electors in each state are mailed to the president of the U.S. Senate. He opens them in the presence of the members of the Senate and House of Representatives in a joint session held on Jan. 6 (the next day if that falls on a Sunday), and the electoral votes of all the states are then counted. If no candidate for president has a majority, the House of Representatives chooses a president from among the 3 highest candidates, with all representatives from each state combining to cast one vote for that state. If no candidate for vice president has a majority, the Senate chooses from the top 2, with the senators voting as individuals.

UNITED STATES GOVERNMENT

The Reagan Administration

As of mid-1984

Terms of office of the president and vice president, from Jan. 20, 1981 to Jan. 20, 1985. No person may be elected president of the United States for more than two 4-year terms.

President — Ronald Reagan of California receives salary of $200,000 a year taxable; in addition an expense allowance of $50,000 to assist in defraying expenses resulting from his official duties. Also there may be expended not exceeding $100,000, nontaxable, a year for travel expenses and $20,000 for official entertainment available for allocation within the Executive Office of the President. Congress has provided lifetime pensions of $69,630 a year, free mailing privileges, free office space, and up to $96,000 a year for office help for former Presidents except for the first 30 month period during which a former President is entitled to staff assistance for which an amount up to $150,000 a year may be paid, and $20,000 annually for their widows.

Vice President — George Bush of Texas receives salary of $91,000 a year and $10,000 for expenses, all of which is taxable.

For succession to presidency, see Succession in Index.

The Cabinet

(Salary: $80,100 per annum)

Secretary of State — George P. Shultz, Cal.
Secretary of Treasury — Donald T. Regan, N.Y.
Secretary of Defense — Caspar W. Weinberger, Cal.
Attorney General — William French Smith, Cal.
Secretary of Interior — William P. Clark, Cal.
Secretary of Agriculture — John R. Block, Ill.
Secretary of Commerce — Malcoln Baldrige, Conn.
Secretary of Labor — Raymond J. Donovan, N.J.
Secretary of Health and Human Services — Margaret M. Heckler, Mass.
Secretary of Housing and Urban Development — Samuel R. Pierce Jr., N.Y.
Secretary of Transportation — Elizabeth Hanford Dole, Kan.
Secretary of Energy — Donald Paul Hodel, Ore.
Secretary of Education — Terrel H. Bell, Ut.

The White House Staff

1600 Pennsylvania Ave. NW 20500

Counsellor to the President — Edwin Meese 3d.
Chief of Staff — James A. Baker 3d.
Deputy Chief of Staff — Michael K. Deaver.
Press Secretary to the President — James S. Brady.
Counsel to the President — Fred F. Fielding.
Presidential Assistants — Faith Ryan Whittlesey (Public Liaison); M. B. Oglesby (Legislative Affairs); John S. Herrington (Presidential Personnel); Lee J. Verstandig (Intergovernmental Affairs); Craig L. Fuller (Cabinet Affairs); Edward V. Hickey Jr. (Special Support Services).

Executive Agencies

National Security Council — Assistant to the President for Natl. Security Affairs — Robert C. McFarlane.
Council of Economic Advisers — vacant.
Central Intelligence Agency — William J. Casey, dir.
Office of Management and Budget — David A. Stockman, dir.
U.S. Trade Representative — William E. Brock 3d.
Office of Administration — John F. W. Rogers, dir.
Office of Policy Development — Asst. to the President for Policy Development — John A. Svahn.
Office of Science and Technology Policy — George A. Keyworth 2d, dir.
Council on Environmental Quality — A. Alan Hill, chmn.

Department of State

2201 C St. NW 20520

Secretary of State — George P. Shultz.
Deputy Secretary — Kenneth Dam.
Under Sec. for Political Affairs — Michael Armacost.
Under Sec. for Security Assistance, Science and Technology — William Schneider.
Under Sec. for Economic Affairs — W. Allen Wallis.
Under Secretary for Management — Ronald I Spiers.
Counselor — Edward J. Derwinski.
Legal Advisor — Davis Robinson.
Assistant Secretaries for:
  Administration — Robert E. Lamb.
  African Affairs — Chester Crocker.
  Congressional Relations — W. Tapley Bennett.
  East Asian & Pacific Affairs — Paul Wolfowitz.
  Economic & Business Affairs — Richard McCormack.
  European & Canadian Affairs — Richard Burt.
  Human Rights & Humanitarian Affairs — Elliott Abrams.
  Inter-American Affairs — Langhorne A. Motley.
  International Organization Affairs — Gregory J. Newell.
  Near-Eastern & S. Asian Affairs — Richard W. Murphy.
  Public Affairs — John Hughes.
  Oceans, International Environmental & Scientific Affairs — James L. Malone.
Consular Affairs — Joan M. Clark.
Intl. Narcotics Matters — Dominick Di Carlo.
Chief of Protocol — Selwa Roosevelt.
Dir. General, Foreign Service & Dir. of Personnel — Alfred L. Atherton Jr.
Dir. of Intelligence & Research — Hugh Montgomery.
Dir. of Politico-Military Affairs — John T. Chain Jr.
Dir. of Refugee Programs — James Purcell.
Inspector General — William Harrop.
Policy Planning Staff — Peter Rodman.
Related Agencies:
  Arms Control & Disarmament Agency — Kenneth Adelman, dir.
  U.S. Information Agency — Charles Z. Wick, dir.
  Agency for International Development — M. Peter McPherson.
U.S. Rep. to the UN — Jeane J. Kirkpatrick.

Treasury Department

1500 Pennsylvania Ave. NW 20220

Secretary of the Treasury — Donald T. Regan.
Deputy Sec. of the Treasury — R. Tim McNamar.
Under Sec. for Monetary Affairs — Dr. Beryl Sprinkel.
General Counsel — Peter J. Wallison.
Assistant Secretaries: — John Walker, John Chapoton, Manuel Johnson, Carole Dineen; Terence Golden, Alfred D. Kingon, David Mulford, Bruce Thompson, Thomas Dawson.
Bureaus:
  Comptroller of the Currency — C. T. Conover.
  Customs — William von Raab.
  Engraving & Printing — Robert J. Leuver, dir.
  Government Financial Operations — William E. Douglas, comm.
  Internal Revenue Service — Roscoe Egger, comm.
  Mint — Donna Pope, dir.
  Public Debt — W. M. Gregg, act. comm.

Treasurer of the U.S. — Katherine Ortega.
U.S. Secret Service — John R. Simpson, dir.

Department of Defense
The Pentagon 20301
Secretary of Defense — Caspar W. Weinberger.
Deputy Secretary — William H. Taft IV.
Executive Secretariat — Col. John H. Stanford.
Asst. Secretaries of Defense:
  Policy — Fred C. Ikle.
  International Security Affairs — Richard I. Armitage.
  International Security Policy — Richard N. Perle.
  Research and Engineering — Richard DeLauer.
  Atomic Energy — Richard Wagner.
  Comptroller — Vincent Puritano.
  Health Affairs — Dr. William Mayer.
  Manpower, Reserve Affairs and Logistics — Lawrence J. Korb.
  Program Analysis and Evaluation — David S. C. Chu.
  Public Affairs — Michael I. Burch.
  Legislative Affairs — Russell A. Rourke.
Intelligence Oversight — Werner E. Michel.
Chairman, Joint Chiefs of Staff — Gen. John W. Vessey Jr.
European & NATO Policy — Gen. John R. Lasater, USAF.
General Counsel — Leonard Niederlehner, act.

Department of the Army
The Pentagon 20301
Secretary of the Army — John O. Marsh Jr.
Under Secretary — James R. Ambrose.
Assistant Secretaries for:
  Civil Works — William R. Gianelli.
  Installations, Logistics and Financial Management — Pat Hillier.
  Research, Development and Acquisition — Jay R. Sculley.
  Manpower & Reserve Affairs — Delbert L. Spurlock Jr.
Chief of Public Affairs — Maj. Gen. Lyle J. Barker Jr.
Chief of Staff — Gen. John A. Wickham Jr.
General Counsel — Susan Crawford.
Comptroller of the Army — Lt. Gen. Max Noah.
Adjutant General — Gen. Robert M. Joyce.
Inspector General — Lt. Gen. Richard G. Trefry.
Judge Advocate General — Maj. Gen. Hugh Clausen.
Deputy Chiefs of Staff:
  Logistics — Lt. Gen. Benjamin F. Register.
  Operations & Plans — Lt. Gen. F. K. Mahaffey.
  Research, Development, Acquisition — Lt. Gen. Louis C. Wagner Jr.
  Personnel — Lt. Gen. Robert M. Elton.
Commanders:
  U.S. Army Material Development and Readiness Command — Gen. Richard H. Thompson.
  U.S. Army Forces Command — Gen. Robert W. Sennewald.
  U.S. Army Training and Doctrine Command — Gen. William R. Richardson.
  First U.S. Army — Lt. Gen. Charles D. Franklin.
  Second U.S. Army — Lt. Gen. Charles P. Graham.
  Third U.S. Army — Lt. Gen. Theodore G. Jones Jr.
  Fifth U.S. Army — Lt. Gen. Edward Partain.
  Sixth U.S. Army — Lt. Gen. Robert Arter.
  Eighth U.S. Army — Gen. William J. Livsey.
  Military Dist. of Washington — Maj. Gen. John L. Ballantyne 3d.

Department of the Navy
The Pentagon 20350
Secretary of the Navy — John Lehman.
Under Secretary — James F. Goodrich.
Assistant Secretaries for:
  Financial Management — Robert H. Conn.
  Manpower, Reserve Affairs — Chapman B. Cox.

Research, Engineering & Systems — Melvyn Paisley.
Shipbuilding & Logistics — vacant.
Judge Advocate General — RADM James J. McHugh.
Chief of Naval Operations — ADM James D. Watkins.
Chief of Naval Material — ADM Steven A. White.
Chief of Information — COMO Jack A. Garrow.
Naval Military Personnel Command — RADM David L. Harlow.
Military Sealift Command — VADM William H. Rowden.
Chief of Naval Personnel — VADM William P. Lawrence.
Commandants, Naval Bases:
  Philadelphia — RADM James W. Austin.
  Norfolk — RADM Jackson K. Parker.
  Charleston — RADM David W. Cockfield.
  San Diego — COMO "E" Inman Carmichael.
  Seattle — RADM Laverne S. Severance Jr.
  Pearl Harbor — RADM Conrad J. Rorie.
  Naval District Washington — COMO John W. Adams.

U.S. Marine Corps:
(Arlington Annex 20380)
Commandant — Gen. Paul X. Kelley.
Asst. Commandant — Gen. John K. Davis.
Chief of Staff — Lt. Gen. D'Wayne Gray.

Department of the Air Force
The Pentagon 20330
Secretary of the Air Force — Verne Orr.
Under Secretary — Edward C. Aldridge Jr.
Assistant Secretaries for:
  Financial Management — Richard A. Harshman.
  Research, Development & Logistics — Dr. Thomas E. Cooper.
  Manpower, Reserve Affairs & Installations — Tidal W. McCoy.
General Counsel — Eugene R. Sullivan.
Public Affairs — Brig. Gen. Richard F. Abel.
Director of Space Systems — Jimmie D. Hill.
Chief of Staff — Gen. Charles A. Gabriel.
Surgeon General — Lt. Gen. Max B. Bralliar.
Judge Advocate — Maj. Gen. Thomas B. Bruton.
Inspector General — Lt. Gen. Robert Bazley.
Deputy Chiefs of Staff:
  Logistics & Engineering — Lt. Gen. Leo Marquez.
  Programs & Resources — Lt. Gen. Larry D. Welch.
  Manpower & Personnel — Lt. Gen. Kenneth L. Peek Jr.
  Research, Development & Acquisition — Lt. Gen. Robert D. Russ.
  Plans & Operations — Lt. Gen. John T. Chain Jr.
Major Air Commands:
  AF Logistics Command — Gen. James P. Mullins.
  AF Systems Command — Gen. Robert T. Marsh.
  Strategic Air Command — Gen. Bennie L. Davis.
  Tactical Air Command — Gen. W. L. Creech.
  Alaskan Air Command — Lt. Gen. Lynwood E. Clark.
  Pacific Air Forces — Lt. Gen. Jerome F. O'Malley.
  USAF Europe — Gen. Billy M. Minter.
  Electronic Security Command — Maj. Gen. John B. Marks.
  AF Communications Command — Maj. Gen. Robert F. McCarthy.

Department of Justice
Constitution Ave. & 10th St. NW 20530
Attorney General — William French Smith.
Deputy Attorney General — vacant.
Legal Policy — Roger Clegg, act.
Legal Counsel — Theodore B. Olsen.
Intelligence Policy & Review — Mary Lawton.
Professional Responsibility —Michael E. Shaheen Jr.
Solicitor General — Rex E. Lee.
Associate Attorney General — D. Lowell Jensen.

Antitrust Division — J. Paul McGrath.
Civil Division — Richard Willard.
Civil Rights Division — William Bradford Reynolds.
Criminal Division — Stephen Trott.
Drug Enforcement Admin. — Francis Mullen.
Justice Management Division — Kevin D. Rooney.
Land & Natural Resources Division — F. Henry Habicht 3d.
Office of Legislative Affairs — Robert A. McConnell.
Tax Division — Glenn L. Archer Jr.
Fed. Bureau of Investigation — William H. Webster, dir.
Board of Immigr. Appeals — David L. Milhollan, chmn.
Bureau of Prisons — Norman A. Carlson, dir.
Office of Public Affairs — Thomas P. DeCair.
Immigration and Naturalization Service — Alan C. Nelson, comm.
Pardon Attorney — D. C. Stephenson.
U.S. Parole Commission — Benjamin Baer, chmn.
U.S. Marshalls Service — Stanley Morris, dir.

Department of the Interior

C St. between 18th & 19th Sts. NW 20240
Secretary of the Interior — William Clark.
Under Secretary — Ann D. McLaughlin.
Assistant Secretaries for:
  Fish, Wildlife and Parks — G. Ray Arnett.
  Water & Science — Robert Broadbent.
  Land & Minerals Management — Garrey Carruthers.
  Policy, Budget, and Administration — Richard Hite.
  Indian Affairs — Kenneth L. Smith.
  Territorial & Intl. Affairs — Richard Montoya.
Bureau of Land Management — Bob Burford, dir.
Bureau of Mines — Robert C. Horton, dir.
Bureau of Reclamation — vacant.
Fish & Wildlife Service — Robert A. Jantzen, dir.
Geological Survey — Dallas L. Peck, dir.
National Park Service — Russell Dickenson, dir.
Public Affairs — Albert Brashear.
Office of Congressional and Legislative Affairs — Roger Brown.
Solicitor — Frank K. Richardson.

Department of Agriculture

The Mall, 12th & 14th Sts. 20250
Secretary of Agriculture — John R. Block.
Deputy Secretary — Richard E. Lyng.
Executive Assistant — Ray Lett.
Administration — John Franke.
Internat. Affairs & Commodity Programs — Daniel Amstutz.
Food & Consumer Services — Mary C. Jarratt.
Marketing & Inspection Services — C. W. McMillan.
Small Community & Rural Development — Frank Naylor Jr.
Economics — William G. Lesher.
Governmental & Public Affairs — Wilmer D. Mizell.
Natural Resources & Environment — John B. Crowell.
General Counsel — Daniel Oliver.
Science & Education — Orville G. Bentley.

Department of Commerce

14th St. between Constitution & E St. NW 20230
Secretary of Commerce — Malcolm Baldrige.
Deputy Secretary — Clarence J. Brown.
Congressional Affairs — Paul A. Vander Myde.
Inspector General — Sherman M. Funk.
General Counsel — Irving P. Margulies.
Productivity, Technology & Innovation — D. Bruce Merrifield.
Administration — Katherine M. Bulow.
Bureau of the Census — John G. Keane, dir.
Bureau of Economic Analysis — George Jaszi, dir.
Under Secy. for International Trade — Lionel H. Olmer

Under Secy. for Econ. Affairs — Robert Dederick.
Natl. Oceanic & Atmospheric Admin. — John V. Byrne.
Natl. Technical Info. Service — Joseph F. Caponio.
Economic Develop. Admin. — Jane E. Newman.
Natl. Bureau of Standards — Ernest Ambler, dir.
Minority Business Development Agency — James H. Richardson.
Natl. Telecomm. & Information Admin. — David G. Marley, dir.
U.S. Travel & Tourism Adm. — Donna F. Tuttle.
Patent & Trademark Office — Gerald J. Mossinghoff.
Public Affairs — B. Jay Cooper, dir.

Department of Labor

200 Constitution Ave. NW 20210
Secretary of Labor — Raymond J. Donovan.
Under Secretary — Ford B. Ford.
Chief of Staff — vacant.
Assistant Secretaries for:
  Administration and Management — Thomas C. Komarek.
  Employment and Training — vacant.
  Mine Safety & Health — David A. Zegeer.
  Occupational Safety & Health — vacant.
  Policy — vacant.
  Labor Management Relations — vacant.
  Veteran's Employment — William C. Plowden Jr.
Solicitor of Labor — Francis X. Lilly.
Comm. of Labor Statistics — Janet Norwood.
Dep. Under Secy. for Employment Standards — Susan R. Meisinger.
Dep. Under Secy. for Internatl. Affairs — Robert W. Searby.
Dep. Under Secy. for Legislative Affairs — Jonathan W. Sloat.
Office of Information & Public Affairs — Vernon Louviere.
dir. of Women's Bureau — Lenora Cole-Alexander.
Inspector General — J. Brian Hyland.

Department of Health and Human Services

200 Independence Ave. SW 20201
Secretary of HHS — Margaret M. Heckler.
Under Secretary — vacant.
Assistant Secretaries for:
  Management and Budget — John J. O'Shaughnessy.
  Public Affairs — Stephanie Lee Miller.
  Health — Edward Brandt, M.D.
  Planning and Evaluation — vacant.
  Human Development Services — Dorcas Hardy.
  Legislation — John F. Scruggs.
  Personnel Administration — Thomas McFee.
General Counsel — Juan Del Real.
Inspector General — Richard P. Kusserow.
Civil Rights — Betty Lou Dotson.
Health Care Financing Admin. — Carolyn Davis, adm.

Department of Housing and Urban Development

451 7th St. SW 20410
Secretary of Housing & Urban Development — Samuel R. Pierce Jr.
Under Secretary — Philip Abrams.
Assistant Secretaries for:
  Administration — Judith L. Tardy.
  Community Planning & Development — Stephen Bollinger.
  Fair Housing & Equal Opportunity — Antonio Monroig.
  Housing & Federal Housing Commissioner — Maurice Barksdale.
  Legislation & Congressional Relations — Stephen May.
  Policy Development & Research — vacant.
  Public Affairs — vacant.
  Public & Indian Housing — Warren T. Lindquist.
President, Govt. Natl. Mortgage Assn. — Robert W. Karpe.

International Affairs — Theodore Britton Jr.
Labor Relations — Gary Klein, act.
Small & Disadvantaged Business Utilization — Bernice Williams.
General Counsel — John J. Knapp.
Inspector General — Charles L. Dempsey.

Department of Transportation

400 7th St. SW 20590
Secretary of Transportation — Elizabeth Hanford Dole.
Deputy Secretary — James H. Burnley 4th.
Assistant Secretaries — Judith T. Connor (Policy and International Affairs); Donald Derman (Budget and Programs); Robert Fairman (Administration).
National Highway Traffic Safety Admin. — Diane K. Steed.
U. S. Coast Guard Commandant — Adm. James Gracey.
Federal Aviation Admin. — J. Lynn Helms.
Federal Highway Admin. — Ray Barnhart.
Federal Railroad Admin. — John Riley.
Maritime Admin. — Harold E. Shear.
Urban Mass Transportation Admin. — Ralph L. Stanley.
Research & Special Programs Admin. — Howard Duqoff.
Saint Lawrence Seaway Development Corp. — James L. Emery.

Department of Energy

1000 Independence Ave. SW 20585
Secretary of Energy — Donald Paul Hodel.
Deputy Secy. — Danny J. Boggs.
Under Secretary — Pat Collins.
General Counsel — Theodore J. Garrish.

Assistant Secretaries — Martha O. Hesse (Management & Administration); Robert C. Odle Jr. (Congressional, Intergovernmental & Public Affairs); Helmut A. Merklein (International Affairs & Energy Emergencies); Shelby Brewer (Nuclear Energy); Jan W. Mares (Policy Safety & Environment); Herman Roser (Defense Programs); William A. Vaughan (Fossil Energy); vacant (Conservation & Renewable Energy).
Federal Energy Regulatory Comm. — Raymond J. O'Connor.
Off. of Planning & Analysis — Jay Hunter Chiles, dir.
Inspector General — James R. Richards.
Economic Regulatory Admin. — Rayburn Hanzlik, adm.
Energy Information Adm. — J. Erich Evered, adm.
Office of Energy Research — Alvin Trivelpiece, dir.

Department of Education

Wash., D.C. 20202
Secretary of Education — Terrel H. Bell.
Under Secretary — Gary Jones.
Deputy Under Secretaries — Gary Bauer, Ralph Olmo.
General Counsel — Maureen Corcoran.
Assistant Secretaries:
Legislation & Public Affairs — Anne Graham.
Elementary and Secondary Education — Lawrence Davenport.
Postsecondary Education — Ed Elmendorf.
Educational Research and Improvement — Donald J. Senese.
Adult & Vocational Education — Robert Worthington.
Special Education and Rehabilitative Services — Madeline Will.
Civil Rights — Harry M. Singleton.

Judiciary of the U.S.

Data as of mid 1984

Justices of the United States Supreme Court

The Supreme Court comprises the chief justice of the United States and 8 associate justices, all appointed by the president with advice and consent of the Senate. Salaries: chief justice $100,700 annually, associate justice $96,700.

Name; apptd from Chief Justices in italics	Service Term	Yrs.	Born	Died	Name; apptd from Chief Justices in italics	Service Term	Yrs.	Born	Died
John Jay, N. Y.	1789-1795	5	1745	1829	Mass.	1851-1857	6	1809	1874
John Rutledge, S. C.	1789-1791	1	1739	1800	John A. Campbell, Ala.	1853-1861	8	1811	1889
William Cushing, Mass.	1789-1810	20	1732	1810	Nathan Clifford, Me.	1858-1881	23	1803	1881
James Wilson, Pa.	1789-1798	8	1742	1798	Noah H. Swayne, Oh.	1862-1881	18	1804	1884
John Blair, Va.	1789-1796	6	1732	1800	Samuel F. Miller, la.	1862-1890	28	1816	1890
James Iredell, N. C.	1790-1799	9	1751	1799	David Davis, Ill.	1862-1877	14	1815	1886
Thomas Johnson, Md.	1791-1793	1	1732	1819	Stephen J. Field, Cal.	1863-1897	34	1816	1899
William Paterson, N. J.	1793-1806	13	1745	1806	*Salmon P. Chase*, Oh.	1864-1873	8	1808	1873
John Rutledge, S.C.	1795(a)	—	1739	1800	William Strong, Pa.	1870-1880	10	1808	1895
Samuel Chase, Md.	1796-1811	15	1741	1811	Joseph P. Bradley, N. J.	1870-1892	21	1813	1892
Oliver Ellsworth, Conn.	1796-1800	4	1745	1807	Ward Hunt, N. Y.	1872-1882	9	1810	1886
Bushrod Washington, Va.	1798-1829	31	1762	1829	*Morrison R. Waite*, Oh.	1874-1888	14	1816	1888
					John M. Harlan, Ky.	1877-1911	34	1833	1911
Alfred Moore, N. C.	1799-1804	4	1755	1810	William B. Woods, Ga.	1880-1887	6	1824	1887
John Marshall, Va.	1801-1835	34	1755	1835	Stanley Matthews, Oh.	1881-1889	7	1824	1889
William Johnson, S. C.	1804-1834	30	1771	1834	Horace Gray, Mass.	1881-1902	20	1828	1902
Henry B. Livingston, N. Y.	1806-1823	16	1757	1823	Samuel Blatchford, N. Y.	1882-1893	11	1820	1893
					Lucius Q. C. Lamar, Miss.	1888-1893	5	1825	1893
Thomas Todd, Ky.	1807-1826	18	1765	1826	*Melville W. Fuller*, Ill.	1888-1910	21	1833	1910
Joseph Story, Mass.	1811-1845	33	1779	1845	David J. Brewer, Kan.	1889-1910	20	1837	1910
Gabriel Duval, Md.	1811-1835	22	1752	1844	Henry B. Brown, Mich.	1890-1906	15	1836	1913
Smith Thompson, N. Y.	1823-1843	20	1768	1843	George Shiras Jr., Pa.	1892-1903	10	1832	1924
Robert Trimble, Ky.	1826-1828	2	1777	1828	Howell E. Jackson, Tenn.	1893-1895	2	1832	1895
John McLean, Oh.	1829-1861	32	1785	1861	Edward D. White, La.	1894-1910	16	1845	1921
Henry Baldwin, Pa.	1830-1844	14	1780	1844	Rufus W. Peckham, N. Y.	1895-1909	13	1838	1909
James M. Wayne, Ga.	1835-1867	32	1790	1867	Joseph McKenna, Cal.	1898-1925	26	1843	1926
Roger B. Taney, Md.	1836-1864	28	1777	1864	Oliver W. Holmes, Mass.	1902-1932	29	1841	1935
Philip P. Barbour, Va.	1836-1841	4	1783	1841	William R. Day, Oh.	1903-1922	19	1849	1923
John Catron, Tenn.	1837-1865	28	1786	1865	William H. Moody, Mass.	1906-1910	3	1853	1917
John McKinley, Ala.	1837-1852	15	1780	1852	Horace H. Lurton, Tenn.	1909-1914	4	1844	1914
Peter V. Daniel, Va.	1841-1860	19	1784	1860	Charles E. Hughes, N. Y.	1910-1916	5	1862	1948
Samuel Nelson, N. Y.	1845-1872	27	1792	1873	Willis Van Devanter, Wy.	1910-1937	26	1859	1941
Levi Woodbury, N. H.	1845-1851	5	1789	1851	Joseph R. Lamar, Ga.	1910-1916	5	1857	1916
Robert C. Grier, Pa.	1846-1870	23	1794	1870	*Edward D. White*, La.	1910-1921	10	1845	1921
Benjamin R. Curtis,									

Name; apptd from	Service Term	Yrs.	Born	Died
Mahlon Pitney, N. J.	1912-1922	10	1858	1924
James C. McReynolds, Tenn.	1914-1941	26	1862	1946
Louis D. Brandeis, Mass.	1916-1939	22	1856	1941
John H. Clarke, Oh.	1916-1922	5	1857	1945
William H. Taft, Conn.	1921-1930	8	1857	1930
George Sutherland, Ut.	1922-1938	15	1862	1942
Pierce Butler, Minn.	1922-1939	16	1866	1939
Edward T. Sanford, Tenn.	1923-1930	7	1865	1930
Harlan F. Stone, N. Y.	1925-1941	16	1872	1946
Charles E. Hughes, N. Y.	1930-1941	11	1862	1948
Owen J. Roberts, Pa.	1930-1945	15	1875	1955
Benjamin N. Cardozo, N.Y.	1932-1938	6	1870	1938
Hugo L. Black, Ala.	1937-1971	34	1886	1971
Stanley F. Reed, Ky.	1938-1957	19	1884	1980
Felix Frankfurter, Mass.	1939-1962	23	1882	1965
William O. Douglas, Conn.	1939-1975	36	1898	1980
Frank Murphy, Mich.	1940-1949	9	1890	1949
Harlan F. Stone, N. Y.	1941-1946	5	1872	1946
James F. Byrnes, S. C.	1941-1942	1	1879	1972
Robert H. Jackson, N.Y.	1941-1954	12	1892	1954
Wiley B. Rutledge, Ia.	1943-1949	6	1894	1949
Harold H. Burton, Oh.	1945-1958	13	1888	1964

Name; apptd from	Service Term	Yrs.	Born	Died
Fred M. Vinson, Ky.	1946-1953	7	1890	1953
Tom C. Clark, Tex.	1949-1967	18	1899	1977
Sherman Minton, Ind.	1949-1956	7	1890	1965
Earl Warren, Cal.	1953-1969	16	1891	1974
John Marshall Harlan, N. Y.	1955-1971	16	1899	1971
William J. Brennan Jr., N. J.	1956 —		1906	—
Charles E. Whittaker, Mo.	1957-1962	5	1901	1973
Potter Stewart, Oh.	1958-1981	23	1915	—
Byron R. White, Col.	1962 —		1917	—
Arthur J. Goldberg, Ill.	1962-1965	3	1908	—
Abe Fortas, Tenn.	1965-1969	4	1910	1982
Thurgood Marshall, N.Y.	1967 —		1908	—
Warren E. Burger, Va.	1969 —		1907	—
Harry A. Blackmun, Minn.	1970 —		1908	—
Lewis F. Powell Jr., Va.	1972 —		1907	—
William H. Rehnquist, Ariz.	1972 —		1924	—
John Paul Stevens, Ill.	1975 —		1920	—
Sandra Day O'Connor, Ariz.	1981 —	—	1930	

(a) Rejected Dec. 15, 1795.

U.S. Court of International Trade

New York, NY 10007 (Salaries, $73,100)
Chief Judge — Edward D. Re.
Judges — Paul P. Rao, Morgan Ford, James L. Watson, Nils A. Boe, Gregory W. Carman, Jane A. Restani.

U.S. Tax Court

Washington DC 20217 (Salaries, $73,100)
Chief Judge — Harry A. Dawson Jr.
Judges — William M. Fay, Charles R. Simpson, Samuel B. Sterrett, William A. Goffe, Darrell D. Wiles, Richard C. Wilbur, Herbert L. Chabot, Arthur L. Nims 3d, Edna G. Parker, C. Moxley Featherston, Jules J. Korner 3d, Meade Whitaker, Mary Ann Cohen, Perry Shields, Charles E. Clapp 2d, Lapsley W. Hamblen Jr., Stephen J. Swift.

U.S. Courts of Appeals

(Salaries, $77,300. CJ means Chief Judge)

Federal District — Howard T. Markey, CJ; Daniel M. Friedman, Giles S. Rich, Oscar H. Davis, Phillip B. Baldwin, Shiro Kashiwa, Marion T. Bennett, Jack R. Miller, Edward S. Smith, Helen W. Nies, Clerk's Office, Washington, DC 20439.

District of Columbia — Spottswood W. Robinson 3d, CJ; J. Skelly Wright, Edward Allen Tamm, George E. MacKinnon, Malcolm Richard Wilkey, Patricia M. Wald, Abner J. Mikva, Harry T. Edwards, Ruth Bader Ginsburg, Robert H. Bork, Antonin Scalia, Kenneth W. Starr; Clerk's Office, Washington, DC 20001.

First Circuit (Me., Mass., N.H., R.I., Puerto Rico) — Levin H. Campbell, CJ; Frank M. Coffin, Hugh H. Bownes, Stephen Breyer; Clerk's Office, Boston, MA 02109.

Second Circuit (Conn., N.Y., Vt.) — Wilfred Feinberg, CJ; Irving R. Kaufman, James L. Oakes, Ellsworth Van Graafeiland, Thomas J. Meskill, Jon O. Newman, Amalya Lyle Kearse, Richard J. Cardamone, Lawrence W. Pierce, Ralph K. Winter Jr., George C. Pratt; Clerk's Office, New York, NY 10007.

Third Circuit (Del., N.J., Pa., Virgin Is.) — Collins J. Seitz, CJ; Ruggero J. Aldisert, Arlin M. Adams, John J. Gibbons, James Hunter 3d, Joseph F. Weis Jr., Leonard I. Garth, A. Leon Higginbotham Jr., Dolores K. Sloviter, Edward R. Becker; Clerk's Office, Philadelphia, PA 19106.

Fourth Circuit (Md., N.C., S.C., Va., W.Va.) — Harrison L. Winter, CJ; Kenneth K. Hall, Donald Stuart Russell, H. Emory Widener Jr., James D. Phillips Jr., Francis D. Murnaghan Jr., James M. Sprouse, Sam J. Ervin 3d, Robert F. Chapman; Clerk's Office, Richmond, VA 23219.

Fifth Circuit (La., Miss., Tex.) — Charles Clark, CJ; John R. Brown, Thomas G. Gee, Alvin B. Rubin, Thomas M. Reavley, Henry A. Politz, Carolyn D. Randall, Samuel D. Johnson, Albert Tate Jr., Jerre S. Williams, William L. Garwood, E. Grady Jolly, Patrick E. Higginbotham, W. Eugene Davis; Clerk's Office, New Orleans, LA 70130.

Sixth Circuit (Ky., Mich., Ohio, Tenn.) — Pierce Lively, CJ; Albert J. Engel, George Clifton Edwards, Gilbert S. Merritt, Damon J. Keith, Cornelia G. Kennedy, Boyce F. Martin Jr., Nathaniel R. Jones, Leroy J. Contie Jr., Robert B. Krupansky, Harry W. Wellford; Clerk's Office, Cincinnati, OH 45202.

Seventh Circuit (Ill., Ind., Wis.) — Walter J. Cummings, CJ; Wilbur F. Pell Jr., Harlington Wood Jr., William J. Bauer, Richard D. Cudahy, Richard A. Posner, Jesse E. Eschbach, John L. Coffey, Joel M. Flaum; Clerk's Office, Chicago, IL 60604.

Eighth Circuit (Ark., Ia., Minn., Mo., Neb., N.D., S.D.) — Donald P. Lay, CJ; Gerald W. Heaney, Myron H. Bright, Donald R. Ross, Theodore McMillian, Richard S. Arnold, John R. Gibson, George C. Fagg, Pasco M. Bowman 2d; Clerk's Office, St. Louis, MO 63101.

Ninth Circuit (Alaska, Ariz., Cal., Ha., Ida., Mont., Nev., Ore., Wash., Guam, N. Mariana Islands) — James R. Browning, CJ; Herbert Y. C. Choy, J. Clifford Wallace, Alfred T. Goodwin, Anthony M. Kennedy, J. Blaine Anderson, Procter Hug Jr., Thomas Tang, Joseph T. Sneed, Jerome Farris, Betty B. Fletcher, Mary M. Schroeder, Otto R. Skopil Jr., Harry Pregerson, Arthur L. Alarcon, Cecil F. Poole, Warren J. Ferguson, Dorothy W. Nelson, William C. Canby Jr., Robert Boochever, William A. Norris, Stephen Reinhardt; Clerk's Office, San Francisco, CA 94101.

Tenth Circuit (Col., Kan., N.M., Okla., Ut., Wy.) — Oliver Seth, CJ; William J. Holloway Jr., Robert H. McWilliams, James E. Barrett, William E. Doyle, Monroe G. McKay, James K. Logan, Stephanie K. Seymour; Clerk's Office, Denver, CO 80294.

Eleventh Circuit (Ala. Fla., Ga.)— John C. Godbold, CJ; Paul H. Roney, Gerald B. Tjoflat, James C. Hill, Peter T. Fay, Robert S. Vance, Phyllis A. Kravitch, Frank M. Johnson Jr., Albert J. Henderson, Joseph W. Hatchett, R. Lanier Anderson 3d, Thomas C. Clark; Clerk's Office, Atlanta GA 30303.

Temporary Emergency Court of Appeals — J. Skelly Wright, CJ; Clerk's Office, Washington, DC 20001 .

U.S. District Courts

(Salaries, $73,100. CJ means Chief Judge)

Alabama — **Northern:** Sam C. Pointer Jr., CJ; James Hughes Hancock, J. Foy Guin Jr., Robert B. Probst, E. B. Haltom Jr., U. W. Clemon, William M. Acker Jr.; Clerk's Office, Birmingham 35203. **Middle:** Robert E. Varner, CJ; Truman M. Hobbs, Myron H. Thompson; Clerk's Office, Montgomery 36101. **Southern:** William Brevard Hand, CJ; Emmett R. Cox; Clerk's Office, Mobile 36601.

Alaska — James A. von der Heydt, CJ; James M. Fitzgerald; Clerk's Office, Anchorage 99513.

Arizona — C. A. Muecke, CJ; Vlademar A. Cordova, Richard M. Bilby, Charles L. Hardy, Alfredo C. Marquez, Earl H. Carroll; Clerk's Office, Phoenix 85025.

Arkansas — **Eastern:** Garnett Thomas Eisele, CJ; Elsijane Trimble Roy, William Ray Overton, Henry Woods, George Howard Jr.; Clerk's Office, Little Rock 72203. **Western:** H. Franklin Waters, CJ; Elsijane Trimble Roy, George Howard Jr.; Clerk's Office, Fort Smith 72902.

California — **Northern:** Robert F. Peckham, CJ; Lloyd H. Burke, Samuel Conti, Spencer M. Williams, William H. Orrick Jr., William W. Schwarzer, William A. Ingram, Robert P. Aguilar, Thelton E. Henderson, Marilyn H. Patel, Eugene F. Lynch, John P. Vukasin Jr.; Clerk's Office, San Francisco 94102. **Eastern:** Lawrence K. Karlton, CJ; Milton L. Schwartz, Edward Dean Price, Raul A. Ramirez, Robert E. Coyle; Clerk's Office, Sacramento

95814. Central: Manuel L. Real, CJ; Wm. Matthew Byrne Jr., Lawrence T. Lydick, Malcolm M. Lucas, Robert M. Takasugi, Laughlin E. Waters, Mariana R. Pfaelzer, Terry J. Hatter Jr., A. Wallace Tashima, Consuelo Bland Marshall, David V. Kenyon, Cynthia H. Hall, Richard A. Gadbois, Edward Rafeedie, Pamela A. Rymer; Clerk's Office, Los Angeles 90012. **Southern:** Gordon Thompson Jr., CJ; Leland C. Nielsen, William B. Enright, Judith N. Keep, Earl B. Gilliam, J. Lawrence Irving; Clerk's Office, San Diego 92189.

Colorado — Sherman G. Finesilver, CJ; Richard P. Matsch, John L. Kane, Jim R. Carrigan, Zita L. Weinshienk, John P. Moore; Clerk's Office, Denver 80294.

Connecticut — T. F. Gilroy Daly, CJ; Ellen B. Burns, Warren W. Eginton, Jose A. Cabranes, Peter C. Dorsey; Clerk's Office, New Haven 06510.

Delaware — Walter K. Stapleton, CJ; Murray M. Schwartz; Clerk's Office, Wilmington 19801.

District of Columbia — Aubrey E. Robinson Jr., CJ; Gerhard A. Gesell, John H. Pratt, June L. Green, Barrington D. Parker, Charles R. Richey, Thomas A. Flannery, Louis F. Oberdorfer, Harold H. Greene, John Garrett Penn, Joyce Hens Green, Norma H. Johnson, Thomas P. Jackson, Thomas F. Hogan, Stanley S. Harris; Clerk's Office, Washington DC 20001.

Florida — Northern: William H. Stafford Jr. CJ; Maurice M. Paul; Clerk's Office, Tallahassee 32301. **Middle:** William Terrell Hodges, CJ; Howard W. Melton, John A. Reed Jr., George C. Carr, Susan H. Black, William J. Castagna; John H. Moore 2d, Elizabeth A. Kovachevich, George K. Sharp; Clerk's Office, Jacksonville 32201. **Southern:** Joe Eaton, CJ; James Lawrence King, Norman C. Roettger Jr.; Sidney M. Aronovitz, William H. Hoeveler, Jose A. Gonzalez, James W. Kehoe, Eugene P. Spellman, Edward B. Davis, James C. Paine, Alcee L. Hastings, Lenore C. Nesbitt; Clerk's Office, Miami 33101.

Georgia — Northern: Charles A. Moye Jr., CJ; William C.O'-Kelley, Richard C. Freeman, Harold L. Murphy, Marvin H. Shoob, G. Ernest Tidwell, Orinda Dale Evans, Robert L. Vining Jr., Robert H. Hall, Harold T. Ward, J. Owen Forrester; Clerk's Office, Atlanta 30335. **Middle:** Wilbur D. Owens Jr., CJ; J. Robert Elliott; Clerk's Office, Macon 31202. **Southern:** Anthony A. Alaimo, CJ; B. Avant Edenfield, Dudley H. Bowen Jr.; Clerk's Office, Savannah 31412.

Hawaii — Samuel P. King, CJ; Harold M. Fong; Clerk's Office, Honolulu 96850.

Idaho — Marion J. Callister, CJ; Harold L. Ryan; Clerk's Office, Boise, 83724.

Illinois — Northern: Frank J. McGarr, CJ; Thomas R. McMillen, Prentice H. Marshall, John F. Grady, George N. Leighton, Nicholas J. Bua, Stanley J. Roszkowski, James B. Moran, Marvin E. Aspen, Milton I. Shadur, Charles P. Kocoras, Susan Getzendanner, John A. Nordberg, William T. Hart, Paul E. Plunkett; Clerk's Office, Chicago 60604. **Central:** J. Waldo Ackerman, CJ; Michael M. Mihm, Harold A. Baker; Clerk's Office, Peoria 61602. **Southern:** James L. Foreman, CJ; William L. Beatty; Clerk's Office, Benton 62812.

Indiana — Northern: Allen Sharp, CJ; William C. Lee, James T. Moody, Michael S. Kanne; Clerk's Office, South Bend 46601. **Southern:** S. Hugh Dillin, CJ; William E. Steckler, James E. Noland, Gene E. Brooks; Clerk's Office, Indianapolis 46204.

Iowa — Northern: Edward J. McManus, CJ; Donald E. O'-Brien; Clerk's Office, Cedar Rapids 52407. **Southern:** William C. Stuart, CJ; Donald E. O'Brien, Harold D. Vietor; Clerk's Office, Des Moines 50309.

Kansas — Earl E. O'Connor, CJ; Richard Dean Rogers, Dale E. Saffels, Patrick F. Kelly, Sam A. Crow; Clerk's Office, Wichita 67202.

Kentucky — Eastern: Bernard T. Moynahan Jr., CJ; Eugene E. Siler Jr., Scott Reed, William Bertelsman, G. Wix Unthank, Henry R. Wilhoit Jr.; Clerk's Office, Lexington 40586. **Western:** Charles M. Allen, CJ; Eugene E. Siler Jr., Edward H. Johnstone, Thomas A. Ballantine; Clerk's Office, Louisville 40202.

Louisiana — Eastern: Frederick J. R. Heebe, CJ; Fred J. Cassibry, Morey L. Sear, Charles Schwartz Jr., Morley L. Sear, Adrian A. Duplantier, Robert F. Collins, George Arceneaux Jr., Veronica D. Wicker, Patrick E. Carr, Peter Beer, A. J. McNamara, Henry A. Mentz Jr., Martin Feldman; Clerk's Office, New Orleans 70130. **Middle:** John V. Parker, CJ; Frank J. Polozola; Clerk's Office, Baton Rouge 70801. **Western:** Tom Stagg, CJ; Nauman S. Scott, Earl Ernest Veron, John M. Shaw; Clerk's Office, Shreveport 71101.

Maine — Conrad K. Cyr, CJ; Gene Carter; Clerk's Office, Portland 04112.

Maryland — Frank A. Kaufman, CJ; Alexander Harvey 2d,

James R. Miller Jr., Joseph H. Young, Herbert F. Murray, Joseph C. Howard, Norman P. Ramsey, William E. Black Jr.; Clerk's Office, Baltimore 21201.

Massachusetts — Andrew A. Caffrey, CJ; W. Arthur Garrity Jr., Frank H. Freedman, Joseph L. Tauro, Walter Jay Skinner, A. David Mazzone, Robert E. Keeton, John J. McNaught, Rya W. Zobel, David S. Nelson; Clerk's Office, Boston 02109:

Michigan — Eastern: John Feikens, CJ; Philip Pratt, Robert E. DeMascio, Charles W. Joiner, James Harvey, James P. Churchill, Ralph B. Guy Jr., Julian A. Cook, Stewart A. Newblatt, Avern Cohn, Anna Diggs Taylor, Horace W. Gilmore; Clerk's Office, Detroit 48226. **Western:** Wendell A. Miles, CJ; Douglas W. Hillman, Benjamin F. Gibson, Richard A. Enslen; Clerk's Office, Grand Rapids 49503.

Minnesota — Miles W. Lord, CJ; Donald D. Alsop, Harry H. MacLaughlin, Robert G. Renner, Diana E. Murphy, Paul A. Magnuson; Clerk's Office, St. Paul 55101.

Mississippi — Northern: L. T. Senter Jr., CJ; William C. Keady; Clerk's Office, Oxford 38655. **Southern:** Walter L. Nixon Jr., CJ; William H. Barbour Jr.; Clerk's Office, Jackson 39205.

Missouri — Eastern: John F. Nangle, CJ; Edward D. Filippine, William L. Hungate, Clyde S. Cahill Jr., Stephen N. Limbaugh; Clerk's Office, St. Louis 63101. **Western:** Russell G. Clark, CJ; Harold Sachs, Scott O. Wright, Joseph E. Stephens Jr., D. Brook Bartlett, Ross T. Roberts; Clerk's Office, Kansas City 64106.

Montana — James F. Battin, CJ; Paul G. Hatfield; Clerk's Office, Billings 59101.

Nebraska — Warren K. Urbom, CJ; Clarence A. Beam, Albert G. Schatz; Clerk's Office, Omaha 68101.

Nevada — Harry E. Claiborne, CJ; Edward C. Reed Jr.; Clerk's Office, Las Vegas 89101.

New Hampshire — Shane Devine, CJ; Martin F. Loughlin; Clerk's Office, Concord 03301.

New Jersey — Clarkson S. Fisher, CJ; Frederick B. Lacey, Herbert J. Stern, John F. Gerry, Stanley S. Brotman, Anne E. Thompson, D. R. Debevoise, H. Lee Sarokin, Harold A. Ackerman, John W. Bissell, Maryanne Trump Barry; Clerk's Office, Newark 07102.

New Mexico — Howard C. Bratton, CJ; Santiago E. Campos, Juan G. Burciaga, Bobby R. Baldock; Clerk's Office, Albuquerque 87103.

New York — Northern: Howard G. Munson, CJ; Neal P. McCurn, Roger J. Miner; Clerk's Office, Albany 12201. **Eastern:** Jack B. Weinstein, CJ; Mark A. Costantino, Thomas C. Platt Jr., Henry Bramwell, George C. Pratt, Charles P. Sifton, Eugene H. Nickerson, Joseph M. McLaughlin, Israel Leo Glasser, Frank X. Altimari, Leonard D. Wexler; Clerk's Office, Brooklyn 11201. **Southern:** Constance Baker Motley, CJ; David N. Edelstein, Edward Weinfeld, Lee P. Gagliardi, Charles L. Brieant, Whitman Knapp, Charles E. Stewart Jr., Thomas P. Griesa, Robert L. Carter, Robert J. Ward, Kevin Thomas Duffy, William C. Conner, Richard Owen, Leonard B. Sand, Mary Johnson Lowe, Henry F. Werker, Gerard L. Goettel, Charles S. Haight Jr., Vincent L. Broderick, Pierre N. Leval, Robert W. Sweet, Abraham D. Sofaer, John E. Sprizzo, Shirley Wohl Kram, John F. Keenan; Clerk's Office N. Y. City 10007. **Western:** John T. Curtin, CJ; John T. Elfvin, Michael A. Telesca; Clerk's Office, Buffalo 14202.

North Carolina — Eastern: W. Earl Britt, CJ; James C. Fox; Clerk's Office, Raleigh 27611. **Middle:** Hiram H. Ward, CJ; Frank W. Bullock Jr., Richard C. Erwin; Clerk's Office, Greensboro 27402. **Western:** Woodrow Wilson Jones, CJ; James B. McMillan, Robert D. Potter; Clerk's Office Asheville 28802.

North Dakota — Paul Benson, CJ; Bruce M. Van Sickle; Clerk's Office, Bismarck 58501.

Ohio — Northern: Frank J. Battisti, CJ; Thomas D. Lambros, Nicholas J. Walinski, John M. Manos, George W. White, Ann Aldrich, Alvin I. Krenzler, John W. Potter, David D. Dowd Jr., Sam H. Bell; Clerk's Office, Cleveland 44114. **Southern:** Carl B. Rubin, CJ; Joseph P. Kinneary, Robert M. Duncan, John D. Holschuh, Walter H. Rice, S. Arthur Spiegel; Clerk's Office, Columbus 43215.

Oklahoma — Northern: H. Dale Cook, CJ; James O. Ellison, Thomas R. Brett, David L. Russell; Clerk's Office, Tulsa 74103. **Eastern:** Frank H. Shey, CJ; H. Dale Cook, David L. Russell; Clerk's Office, Muskogee 74401. **Western:** Luther B. Eubanks, CJ; H. Dale Cook, Ralph G. Thompson, Lee R. West, David L. Russell; Clerk's Office, Oklahoma City 73102.

Oregon — James M. Burns, CJ; Robert C. Belloni, Owen M. Panner, James A. Redden, Helen J. Frye; Clerk's Office, Portland 97205.

Pennsylvania — Eastern: Alfred L. Luongo, CJ; John P. Fullam, Charles R. Weiner, John B. Hannum, Daniel H. Huyett 3d, Donald W. VanArtsdalen, J. William Ditter Jr., Raymond J. Broderick, Clarence C. Newcomer, Clifford Scott Green, Louis Charles Bechtle, Joseph L. McGlynn Jr., Edward N. Cahn, Louis H. Pollak, Norma L. Shapiro, James T. Giles, James McGirr Kelly; Clerk's Office, Philadelphia 19106. **Middle:** William J. Nealon Jr., CJ; Malcolm Muir, Richard P. Conaboy, Sylvia H. Rambo, William W. Caldwell; Clerk's Office, Scranton 18501. **Western:** Hubert I. Teitelbaum, CJ; Gerald J. Weber, Barron P. McCune, Maurice B. Cohill Jr., Paul A. Simmons, Gustave Diamond, Donald E. Ziegler, Alan N. Bloch, Glenn E. Mencer, Carol Los Mansmann; Clerk's Office, Pittsburgh 15230.

Rhode Island — Francis J. Boyle, CJ; Bruce M. Selya; Clerk's Office, Providence 02903

South Carolina — Charles E. Simons Jr., CJ; Solomon Blatt Jr., C. Weston Houck, Falcon B. Hawkins, Matthew J. Perry Jr., George R. Anderson Jr., William W. Wilkins Jr., Clyde H. Hamilton; Clerk's Office, Columbia 29202.

South Dakota — Andrew A. Bogue, CJ; Donald J. Porter, John Bailey Jones; Clerk's Office, Sioux Falls 57102.

Tennessee — Eastern: Robert L. Taylor, CJ; H. Theodore Milburn, Thomas G. Hill; Clerk's Office, Knoxville 37901. **Middle:** L. Clure Morton, CJ, Thomas A. Wiseman Jr, John T. Nixon; Clerk's Office, Nashville 37203. **Western:** Robert M. McRae Jr., CJ; Odell Horton, Julia S. Gibbons; Clerk's Office, Memphis 38103.

Texas — Northern: Halbert O. Woodward, CJ; Eldon B. Mahon, Robert M. Hill, Robert W. Porter, Mary Lou Robinson, Barefoot Sanders, David O. Belew Jr., Jerry Buchmeyer, A. Joe Fish; Clerk's Office, Dallas 75242. **Southern:** John V. Singleton Jr., CJ; Carl O. Bue Jr., Robert O'Connor Jr., Ross N. Sterling, Norman W. Black, James De Anda, George E. Cire, Gabrielle K. McDonald, George P. Kazen, Hugh Gibson, Filemon R. Vela, Hayden W. Head Jr., Ricardo H. Hinojosa; Clerk's Office, Houston 77208. **Eastern:** William Wayne Justice, CJ; William M. Steger, Robert M. Parker; Clerk's Office, Beaumont 77701. **Western:** William S. Sessions, CJ; Lucius D. Bunton 3d, Harry Lee Hudspeth,

Hipolito F. Garcia, James R. Nowlin; Clerk's Office, San Antonio 78206.

Utah — Aldon J. Anderson, CJ; Bruce S. Jenkins, David K. Winder; Clerk's Office, Salt Lake City 84110.

Vermont — Albert W. Coffrin, CJ; Clerk's Office, Burlington 05402.

Virginia — Eastern: John A. MacKenzie, CJ; Robert R. Merhige Jr., Albert V. Bryan Jr., D. Dortch Warriner, J. Calvitt Clarke, Richard L. Williams, James C. Cacheris, Robert G. Doumar; Clerk's Office, Norfolk 23510. **Western:** James C. Turk, CJ; Glen M. Williams, James H. Michael Jr., Jackson L. Kiser; Clerk's Office; Roanoke 24006.

Washington — Eastern: Robert J. McNichols, CJ; Justin L. Quackenbush; Clerk's Office, Spokane 99210. **Western:** Walter T. McGovern, CJ; Donald S. Voorhees, Jack E. Tanner, Barbara J. Rothstein, John C. Coughenour; Clerk's Office, Seattle 98104.

West Virginia — Northern: Robert Earl Maxwell, CJ; William M. Kidd; Clerk's Office, Elkins 26241. **Southern:** Charles H. Haden 2d, CJ; Robert J. Staker, John T. Copenhaver Jr., Elizabeth V. Hallanan; Clerk's Office, Charleston 25329.

Wisconsin — Eastern: John W. Reynolds, CJ; Robert W. Warren, Terence T. Evans, Thomas J. Curran; Clerk's Office, Milwaukee 53202. **Western:** Barbara B. Crabb, CJ; John C. Shabaz; Clerk's Office, Madison 53701.

Wyoming — Clarence A. Brimmer; Clerk's Office, Cheyenne 82001.

U.S. Territorial District Courts

Guam — Cristobal C. Duenas; Clerk's Office, Agana 96910.
Puerto Rico — Juan R. Torruella, CJ; Juan M. Perez-Gimenez, Gilberto Gierbolini-Ortiz, Carman Consuelo Cerezo, Jaime Pieras Jr., Raymond L. Acosta, Hector M. Laffitte; Clerk's Office, San Juan 00904.
Virgin Islands — Almeric L. Christian, CJ; David V. O'Brien; Clerk's Office, Charlotte Amalie, St. Thomas 00801.

State Officials, Salaries, Party Membership

Compiled from data supplied by state officials, mid-1984

Alabama

Governor — George Wallace, D., $68,838.
Lt. Gov. — Bill Baxley, D., $95 per legislative day, plus annual salary of $600 per month plus $1,500 per month for expenses.
Sec. of State — Don Siegelman, D., $32,940.
Atty. Gen. — Charles Graddick, D., $58,000.
Treasurer — Mrs. Annie Laurie Gunter, D., $45,000.
Legislature: meets annually the 3d Tuesday in Apr. (first year of term of office, first Tuesday in Feb. (2d and 3d years), 2d Tuesday in Jan. (4th year) at Montgomery. Members receive $600 per month, plus $95 per day during legislative sessions, and mileage of 10c per mile.
Senate — Dem., 28; Rep., 4; ind. 3. Total, 35.
House — Dem., 87; Rep., 11; ind. 6; 1 vacancy. Total, 105.

Alaska

Governor — Bill Sheffield, D., $81,648.
Lt. Gov. — Stephen McAlpine, D., $76,188.
Atty. General — Norman Gorsuch, D., $73,620.
Legislature: meets annually in January at Juneau, for as long as may be necessary. First session in odd years. Members receive $46,800 per year plus $4,000 for postage, personal stationery, and other expenses.
Senate — Dem., 11; Rep., 9. Total, 20.
House — Dem., 21; Rep., 19. Total, 40.

Arizona

Governor — Bruce Babbitt, D., $62,500.
Sec. of State — Rose Mofford, D., $35,000.
Atty. Gen. — Bob Corbin, R., $56,250.
Treasurer — Clark Dierks, R., $37,500.
Legislature: meets annually in January at Phoenix. Each member receives an annual salary of $15,000.
Senate — Dem., 12; Rep., 18. Total, 30.
House — Dem., 21; Rep., 39. Total, 60.

Arkansas

Governor — Bill Clinton, D., $35,000.
Lt. Gov. — Winston Bryant, D., $14,000.
Sec. of State — Paul Riviere, D., $22,500.
Atty. Gen. — Steve Clark, D., $26,500.
Treasurer — Jimmie Lou Fisher, D., $22,500.

General Assembly: meets odd years in January at Little Rock. Members receive $7,500 per year, $45 a day while in regular session, plus 13c a mile travel expense.
Senate — Dem., 32; Rep., 3. Total, 35.
House — Dem., 93; Rep., 7. Total, 100.

California

Governor — George Deukmejian, R., $49,100.
Lt. Gov. — Leo T. McCarthy, D., $42,500.
Sec. of State — March Fong Eu, D., $42,500.
Controller — Kenneth Cory, D., $42,500.
Atty. Gen. — John Van de Kamp, D., $47,500.
Treasurer — Jesse M. Unruh, D., $42,500.
Legislature: meets at Sacramento; regular sessions commence on the first Monday in Dec. of every even-numbered year; each session lasts 2 years. Members receive $28,110 per year plus mileage and $65 per diem.
Senate — Dem., 25; Rep., 14; ind 1. Total, 40.
Assembly — Dem., 48; Rep., 32. Total, 80.

Colorado

Governor — Richard D. Lamm, D., $60,000.
Lt. Gov. — Nancy Dick, D., $32,500.
Secy. of State — Natalie Meyer, R., $32,500.
Atty. Gen. — Duane Woodard, R., $40,000.
Treasurer — Roy Romer, D., $32,500.
General Assembly: meets annually in January at Denver. Members receive $14,000 annually.
Senate — Dem., 14; Rep., 21. Total, 35.
House — Dem., 25; Rep., 40. Total, 65.

Connecticut

Governor — William A. O'Neill, D., $65,000.
Lt. Gov. — Joseph J. Fauliso, D., $40,000.
Sec. of State — Julia H. Tashjian, D., $35,000.
Treasurer — Henry E. Parker, D., $35,000.
Comptroller — J. Edward Caldwell, D., $35,000.
Atty. Gen. — Joseph I. Lieberman, D., $50,000.
General Assembly: meets annually odd years in January and even years in February at Hartford. Salary $21,000 per 2-year term plus $2,500 per year for expenses, plus travel allowance.
Senate — Dem., 23; Rep., 13. Total, 36.
House — Dem., 86; Rep., 64; 1 vacancy. Total, 151.

Delaware

Governor — Pierre S. du Pont 4th, R., $70,000.
Lt. Gov. — Michael N. Castle, R., $16,600.
Sec. of State — Glenn C. Kenton, R., $46,700.
Atty. Gen. — Charles Oberly 3d, D., $39,600.
Treasurer — Janet C. Rzewnicki, R., $25,700.
General Assembly: meets annually at Dover from the 2d Tuesday in January to midnight June 30. Members receive $12,255 base salary.
Senate — Dem., 13; Rep., 8. Total, 21.
House — Dem., 24; Rep., 17. Total, 41.

Florida

Governor — Robert Graham, D., $69,550.
Lt. Gov. — Wayne Mixon, D., $60,455.
Sec. of State — George Firestone, D., $59,385.
Comptroller — Gerald Lewis, D., $59,385.
Atty. Gen. — Jim Smith, D., $59,385.
Treasurer — Bill Gunter, D., $59,385.
Legislature: meets annually at Tallahassee. Members receive $12,000 per year plus expense allowance while on official business.
Senate — Dem., 27; Rep., 13. Total, 40.
House — Dem., 80; Rep., 40. Total, 120.

Georgia

Governor — Joe Frank Harris, D., $71,314.
Lt. Gov. — Zell Miller, D., $41,496.
Sec. of State — Max Cleland, D., $51,896.
Comptroller General — Johnnie L. Caldwell, D., $51,896.
Atty. Gen. — Michael J. Bowers, $57,681.
General Assembly: meets annually at Atlanta. Members receive $7,200 per year. During session $59 per day for expenses.
Senate — Dem., 49; Rep., 7. Total, 56.
House — Dem., 156; Rep., 24. Total, 180.

Hawaii

Governor — George R. Ariyoshi, D., $59,000.
Lt. Gov. — John Waihee, D., $53,460.
Atty. Gen. — Tany Hong, $50,490.
Comptroller — Hideo Murakami, $50,490.
Dir. of Budget & Finance — Jensen S. L. Hee, $50,490.
Legislature: meets annually on 3d Wednesday in January at Honolulu. Members receive $13,650 per year plus expenses.
Senate — Dem., 20. Rep., 5. Total, 25.
House — Dem., 43. Rep., 8. Total, 51.

Idaho

Governor — John V. Evans, D., $50,000.
Lt. Gov. — David H. Leroy, R., $14,000.
Sec. of State — Pete T. Cenarrusa, R., $37,500.
Treasurer — Marjorie Ruth Moon, D., $37,500.
Atty. Gen. — Jim Jones, R., $42,000.
Legislature: meets annually on the Monday after the first day in January at Boise. Members receive $4,200 per year, plus $25 per day when authorized, plus travel allowances.
Senate — Dem., 14; Rep., 21. Total, 35.
House — Dem., 19; Rep., 51. Total, 70.

Illinois

Governor — James R. Thompson, R., $58,000.
Lt. Gov. — George H. Ryan, R., $45,500.
Sec. of State — Jim Edgar, R., $50,500.
Comptroller — Roland W. Burris, D., $48,000.
Atty. Gen. — Neil F. Hartigan, D., $50,500.
Treasurer — James H. Donnewald, D., $48,000.
General Assembly: meets annually in January at Springfield. Members receive $28,000 per annum.
Senate — Dem., 33; Rep., 26. Total, 59.
House — Dem., 70; Rep., 48. Total, 118.

Indiana

Governor — Robert D. Orr, R., $66,000 plus discretionary expenses.
Lt. Gov. — John M. Mutz, R., $51,000 plus discretionary expenses.
Sec. of State — Edwin J. Simcox, R., $46,000.
Atty. Gen. — Linley E. Pearson, R., $51,000.
Treasurer — Julian Ridlen, R., $46,000.
General Assembly: meets annually in January. Members receive $11,600 per year plus $65 per day while in session, $15 per day while not in session.
Senate — Dem., 18; Rep., 32. Total, 50.
House — Dem., 43; Rep., 57. Total, 100.

Iowa

Governor — Terry Branstad, R., $64,000 plus $5,724 expenses.
Lt. Gov. — Robert Anderson, R., $21,900 plus personal expenses and travel allowances at same rate as for a senator.
Sec. of State — Mary Jane Odell, R., $41,000.
Atty. Gen. — Tom Miller, D., $54,000.
Treasurer — Michael L. Fitzgerald, D., $41,000.
General Assembly: meets annually in January at Des Moines. Members receive $14,600 annually plus maximum expense allowance of $30 per day for first 120 days of first session, and first 100 days of 2d session; mileage expenses at 20c a mile.
Senate — Dem., 28; Rep., 22. Total, 50.
House — Dem., 60; Rep., 40. Total, 100.

Kansas

Governor — John Carlin, D., $54,784.
Lt. Gov. — Tom Docking, D., $16,436 plus $1,875 for expenses.
Sec. of State — Jack H. Brier, R., $33,480.
Atty. Gen. — Robert T. Stephan, R., $48,697.
Treasurer — Joan Finney, D., $33,480.
Legislature: meets annually in January at Topeka. Members receive $47 a day plus $50 a day expenses while in session, plus $400 per month while not in session.
Senate — Dem., 16; Rep., 24. Total, 40.
House — Dem., 53; Rep., 72. Total, 125.

Kentucky

Governor — Martha L. Collins, D., $60,000.
Lt. Gov. — Steve Beshear, D., $51,008.
Sec. of State — Drexell R. Davis, D., $51,008.
Atty. Gen. — Dave Armstrong, D., $51,008.
Treasurer — Francis J. Mills, D., $51,008.
Auditor — Mary A. Tobin. D., $51,008.
General Assembly: meets even years in January at Frankfort. Members receive $100 per day and $100 per day during session and $950 per month for expenses for interim.
Senate — Dem., 30; Rep., 8. Total, 38.
House — Dem., 77; Rep., 23. Total, 100.

Louisiana

Governor — Edwin W. Edwards, D., $73,440.
Lt. Gov. — Robert L. Freeman, D., $63,367.
Sec. of State — James H. Brown, D., $60,169.
Atty. Gen. — William J. Guste Jr., D., $60,169.
Treasurer — Mary Evelyn Parker, D., $60,169.
Legislature: meets annually for 60 legislative days commencing on 3d Monday in April. Members receive $75 per day and mileage at 21c a mile for 13 round trips, plus $1,400 per month expense allowance.
Senate — Dem., 38; Rep., 1. Total, 39.
House — Dem., 93; Rep., 11; no party 1. Total, 105.

Maine

Governor — Joseph E. Brennan, D., $35,000.
Sec. of State — Rodney Quinn, D., $30,000.
Atty. Gen. — James Tierney, D., $44,431.
Treasurer — Samuel Shapiro, D., $30,000.
Legislature: meets biennially in January at Augusta. Members receive $6,500 for regular sessions, $3,500 for special session plus expenses; presiding officers receive 50% more.
Senate — Dem., 23; Rep., 10. Total, 33.
House — Dem., 93; Rep., 58. Total, 151.

Maryland

Governor — Harry Hughes, D., $75,000.
Lt. Gov. — J. Joseph Curran Jr., D., $62,500.
Comptroller — Louis L. Goldstein, D., $62,500.
Atty. Gen. — Stephen H. Sachs, D., $62,500.
Sec. of State — Lorraine Sheehan, D., $45,000.
Treasurer — William S. James, D., $62,500.
General Assembly: meets 90 days annually on the 2d Wednesday in January at Annapolis. Members receive $22,000 per year.
Senate — Dem., 41; Rep., 6. Total, 47.
House — Dem., 124; Rep., 17. Total, 141.

Massachusetts

Governor — Michael S. Dukakis, D., $75,000.
Lt. Gov. — John Kerry, D., $60,000.
Sec. of State — Michael Joseph Connolly, D., $60,000.
Atty. Gen. — Francis X. Bellotti, D., $65,000.
Treasurer — Robert Q. Crane, D., $60,000.
Auditor — John J. Finnegan, D., $60,000.
General Court (Legislature): meets each January in Boston. Salaries $30,000 per annum.
Senate — Dem., 33; Rep., 7. Total, 40.
House — Dem., 131; Rep., 28; 1 vacancy. Total, 160.

Michigan

Governor — James J. Blanchard, D., $78,000.
Lt. Gov. — Martha W. Griffiths, D., $53,500.
Sec. of State — Richard H. Austin, D., $75,000.
Atty. Gen. — Frank J. Kelley, D., $75,000.
Treasurer — Robert A. Bowman, N-P, $48,400.

Legislature: meets annually in January at Lansing. Members receive $33,200 per year, plus $6,700 expense allowance.
Senate — Dem., 18; Rep., 20. Total, 38.
House — Dem., 62; Rep., 46; 2 vacancies. Total, 110.

Minnesota

Governor — Rudy Perpich, DFL, $66,500.
Lt. Gov. — Marlene Johnson, DFL, $40,000.
Sec. of State — Joan Anderson Growe, DFL., $36,000.
Atty. Gen. — Hubert H. Humphrey 3d, DFL., $56,000.
Treasurer — Robert W. Mattson, DFL., $36,000.
Auditor — Arne H. Carlson, IR, $36,000.
Legislature: meets for a total of 120 days within every 2 years at St. Paul. Members receive $18,500 per year, plus expense allowance during session.
Senate — DFL., 42; IR, 25. Total, 67.
House — DFL., 76; IR, 58. Total, 134.
(DFL means Democratic-Farmer-Labor. IR means Independent Republican.)

Mississippi

Governor — William A. Allain, D., $63,000.
Lt. Gov. — Brad Dye, D., $34,000 per regular legislative session, plus expense allowance.
Sec. of State — Dick Molpus, D., $45,000.
Atty. Gen. — William L. Pittman, D., $51,000.
Treasurer — William J. Cole 3d, D., $45,000.
Legislature: meets annually in January at Jackson. Members receive $8,100 per regular session plus travel allowance, and $210 per month while not in session.
Senate — Dem., 49; Rep., 3. Total, 52.
House — Dem., 117; Rep., 5. Total, 122.

Missouri

Governor — Christopher S. Bond, R., $55,000.
Lt. Gov. — Kenneth J. Rothman, D., $30,000.
Sec. of State — James C. Kirkpatrick, D., $42,500.
Atty. Gen. — John Ashcroft, R., $45,000.
Treasurer — Mel Carnahan, D., $42,500.
General Assembly: meets annually in Jefferson City on the first Wednesday after first Monday in January; adjournment in odd-numbered years by June 30, in even-numbered years by May 15. Members receive $15,000 annually.
Senate — Dem., 22; Rep., 12. Total, 34.
House — Dem., 110; Rep., 53. Total, 163.

Montana

Governor — Ted Schwinden, D., $47,963.
Lt. Gov. — George Turman, D., $34,344.
Sec. of State — Jim Waltermire, R., $31,692.
Atty. Gen. — Mike Greely, D., $43,745.
Legislative Assembly: meets odd years in January at Helena. Members receive $49.50 per day plus $45 per day for expenses while in session.
Senate — Dem., 26; Rep., 24. Total, 50.
House — Dem., 45; Rep., 55. Total, 100.

Nebraska

Governor — Robert Kerrey, D., $40,000.
Lt. Gov. — Donald F. McGinley, D., $32,000.
Sec. of State — Allen J. Beermann, R., $32,000.
Atty. Gen. — Paul Douglas, R., $39,500.
Treasurer — Kay Orr, R., $32,000.
Legislature: meets annually in January at Lincoln. Members receive salary of $4,800 annually plus travelling expenses for one round trip to and from session.
Unicameral body composed of 49 members who are elected on a nonpartisan ballot and are classed as senators.

Nevada

Governor — Richard Bryan, D., $65,000.
Lt. Gov. — Robert Cashell, R., $10,500 plus $104 per day when acting as governor and president of the Senate during legislative sessions.
Sec. of State — William D. Swackhamer, D., $42,500.
Comptroller — Darrel Daines, R., $41,000.
Atty. Gen. — Brian McKay, R., $52,500.
Treasurer — Patty Cafferata, R., $41,000.
Legislature: meets odd years in January at Carson City. Members receive $104 per day for 60 days (20 days for special sessions), plus per diem of $50 per day for entire length of session. Travel allowance of 20c per mile.
Senate — Dem., 17; Rep., 4. Total, 21.
Assembly — Dem., 23; Rep., 19. Total, 42.

New Hampshire

Governor — John H. Sununu, R., $44,520.
Sec. of State — William M. Gardner, D., $31,270.
Atty. Gen. — Gregory H. Smith, $38,690.
Treasurer — Robert W. Flanders, R., $31,270.
General Court (Legislature): meets odd years in January at Concord. Members receive $200; presiding officers $250.
Senate — Dem., 9; Rep., 14; 1 vacancy. Total, 24.
House — Rep., 234; Dem., 158; 2 ind., 6 vacancies. Total, 400.

New Jersey

Governor — Thomas H. Kean, R., $85,000.
Sec. of State — Jane Burgio, R., $66,000.
Atty. Gen. — Irwin I. Kimmelman, R., $70,000.
Treasurer — Michael M. Horn, R., $70,000.
Legislature: meets throughout the year at Trenton. Members receive $25,000 per year, except president of Senate and speaker of Assembly who receive 1/3 more.
Senate — Dem., 23; Rep., 17. Total, 40.
Assembly — Dem., 44; Rep. 36. Total, 80.

New Mexico

Governor — Toney Anaya, D., $60,000.
Lt. Gov. — Mike Runnels, D., $38,500. Acting governor, $150 per day.
Sec. of State — Clara Jones, D., $38,500.
Atty. Gen. — Paul G. Bardacke, D., $44,000.
Treasurer — Earl Edward Hartley, D., $38,500.
Legislature: meets in January at Sante Fe; odd years for 60 days, even years for 30 days. Members receive $75 per day while in session.
Senate — Dem., 23; Rep., 19. Total, 42.
House — Dem., 46; Rep., 24. Total, 70.

New York

Governor — Mario M. Cuomo, D., $100,000.
Lt. Gov. — Alfred B. DelBello, D., $85,000.
Sec. of State — Gail S. Shaffer, D., $65,700.
Comptroller — Edward V. Regan, R., $85,000.
Atty. Gen. — Robert Abrams, D., $85,000.
Legislature: meets annually in January at Albany. Members receive $32,960 per year.
Senate — Dem., 27; Rep., 34. Total, 61.
Assembly — Dem., 98; Rep., 52. Total, 150.

North Carolina

Governor — James B. Hunt, D., $60,768 plus $11,500 per year expenses.
Lt. Gov. — James C. Green, D., $50,328 per year, plus $11,500 per year expense allowance.
Sec. of State — Thad Eure, D., $50,328
Atty. Gen. — Rufus L. Edmisten, D., $53,976.
Treasurer — Harlan E. Boyles, D., $50,328.
General Assembly: meets odd years in January at Raleigh. Members receive $6,936 annual salary and $2,064 annual expense allowance, plus $50 per diem subsistence and travel allowance while in session.
Senate — Dem., 44; Rep., 6. Total, 50.
House — Dem., 102; Rep., 18. Total, 120.

North Dakota

Governor — Allen I. Olson, R., $60,862 plus $13,862 expenses.
Lt. Gov. — Ernest Sands, R., $12,500.
Sec. of State — Ben Meier, R., $43,380 plus $9,880 expenses.
Atty. Gen. — Bob Wefald, R., $49,209 plus $11,206 expenses.
Treasurer — John Lesmeister, R., $43,380 plus $9,880 expenses.
Legislative Assembly: meets odd years in January at Bismarck. Members receive $90 per day expenses during session and $180 per month when not in session.
Senate — Dem., 21; Rep., 32. Total, 53.
House — Dem., 55; Rep., 51. Total, 106.

Ohio

Governor — Richard F. Celeste, D., $60,000.
Lt. Gov. — Myrl H. Shoemaker, D., $35,000.
Sec. of State — Sherrod Brown, D., $50,000.
Atty. Gen. — Anthony J. Celebrezze Jr., D., $50,000.
Treasurer — Mary Ellen Withrow, D., $50,000.
Auditor — Thomas E. Ferguson, D., $50,000.
General Assembly: meets odd years at Columbus on first Monday in January for the 1st session, and no later than Mar. 15th of the following year for the 2d session. Members receive $22,500 per annum.
Senate — Dem., 17; Rep., 16. Total, 33.
House — Dem., 62; Rep., 37. Total, 99.

Oklahoma

Governor — George Nigh, D., $70,000.
Lt. Gov. — Spencer T. Bernard, D., $40,000.
Sec. of State — Jeannette B. Edmondson, D., $37,000.
Atty. Gen. — Mike Turpen, D., $55,000.
Treasurer — Leo Winters, D., $50,000.
Legislature: meets annually in January at Oklahoma City. Members receive $20,000 annually.
Senate — Dem., 34; Rep., 14. Total, 48.
House — Dem., 76; Rep., 25. Total, 101.

Oregon

Governor — Victor Atiyeh, R., $52,092, plus $1,000 monthly expenses.
Sec. of State — Norma Paulus, R., $42,864.
Atty. Gen. — David B. Frohnmayer, R., $50,105.

Treasurer — Bill Rutherford, R., $42,864.
Legislative Assembly: meets odd years in January at Salem. Members receive $658 monthly and $44 expenses per day while in session; $300 per month while not in session.
Senate — Dem., 21; Rep., 9. Total, 30.
House — Dem., 36; Rep., 24. Total, 60.

Pennsylvania

Governor — Dick Thornburgh, R., $75,000.
Lt. Gov. — William W. Scranton 3d, R., $57,500.
Sec. of the Commonwealth — William R. Davis, R., $48,000.
Atty. Gen. — Leroy S. Zimmerman, R., $55,000.
Treasurer — R. Budd Dwyer, R., $48,000.
General Assembly — convenes annually in January at Harrisburg. Members receive $25,000 per year plus $15,000 for expenses.
Senate — Dem., 23; Rep., 27. Total, 50.
House — Dem., 103; Rep., 100. Total, 203.

Rhode Island

Governor — J. Joseph Garrahy, D., $49,500.
Lt. Gov. — Thomas R. DiLuglio, D., $35,500.
Sec. of State — Susan Farmer, R., $35,500.
Atty. Gen. — Dennis J. Roberts 2d, D., $41,875.
Treasurer — Anthony J. Solomon, D., $35,500.
General Assembly: meets annually in January at Providence. Members receive $5 per day for 60 days, and travel allowance of 8c per mile.
Senate — Dem., 29; Rep., 21. Total, 50.
House — Dem., 85; Rep., 15. Total, 100.

South Carolina

Governor — Richard W. Riley, D., $60,000.
Lt. Gov. — Michael Daniel, D., $35,000.
Sec. of State — John T. Campbell, D., $55,000.
Comptroller Gen. — Earle E. Morris Jr., D., $55,000.
Atty. Gen. — T.T. Medlock, D., $55,000.
Treasurer — G.L. Patterson Jr., D., $55,000.
General Assembly: meets annually in January at Columbia. Members receive $10,000 per year and expense allowance of $50 per day, plus travel and postage allowance.
Senate — Dem., 39; Rep., 6; 1 vacancy. Total, 46.
House — Dem. 100; Rep., 22; 2 vacancies. Total, 124.

South Dakota

Governor — William J. Janklow, R., $49,025.
Lt. Gov. — Lowell C. Hansen 2d, R., $6,800 plus $50 per day during legislative session.
Sec. of State — Alice Kundert, R., $33,275.
Treasurer — David Volk, R., $33,275.
Atty. Gen. — Mark Meierhenry, R., $41,675.
Auditor — Vernon Larson, R., $33,275.
Legislature: meets annually in January at Pierre. Members receive $3,200 for 40-day session in odd-numbered years, and $2,800 for 35-day session in even-numbered years, plus $50 per legislative day.
Senate — Dem., 8; Rep., 27. Total, 35.
House — Dem., 16; Rep., 54. Total, 70.

Tennessee

Governor — Lamar Alexander, R., $68,226.
Lt. Gov. — John S. Wilder, D., $8,308.
Sec. of State — Gentry Crowell, D., $51,510.
Comptroller — William Snodgrass, D., $51,510.
Atty. Gen. — William M. Leech, D., $64,494.
General Assembly: meets annually in January at Nashville. Members receive $8,308 yearly plus $66.47 expenses for each day in session, plus mileage and expense allowances.
Senate — Dem., 22; Rep., 11. Total, 33.
House — Dem., 60; Rep., 38; Ind., 1. Total, 99.

Texas

Governor — Mark White Jr., D., $88,900.
Lt. Gov. — Bill Hobby, D., $7,200, plus living quarters. Governor's salary when acting as governor.
Sec. of State — John W. Fainter Jr., D., $61,200.
Comptroller — Bob Bullock, D., $69,000.
Atty. Gen. — Jim Mattox, D., $69,000.
Treasurer — Ann W. Richards, D., $69,000.
Legislature: meets odd years in January at Austin. Members receive annual salary not exceeding $7,200, per diem while in session, and travel allowance.
Senate — Dem., 26; Rep., 5. Total, 31.
House — Dem., 114; Rep., 36. Total, 150.

Utah

Governor — Scott M. Matheson, D., $52,000.
Lt. Gov. — David S. Monson, R., $35,500.
Atty. Gen. — David L. Wilkinson, R., $41,000.
Treasurer — Edward T. Alter, D., $35,500.

Legislature: convenes for 60 days on 2d Monday in January in odd-numbered years; for 20 days in even-numbered years; members receive $25 per day, $15 daily expenses, and mileage.
Senate — Dem., 5; Rep., 24. Total, 29.
House — Dem., 16; Rep., 59. Total, 75.

Vermont

Governor — Richard A. Snelling, R., $50,000.
Lt. Gov. — Peter Smith, R., $22,000.
Sec. of State — James H. Douglas, R., $30,000.
Atty. Gen. — John J. Easton Jr., R., $40,000.
Treasurer — Emory Hebard, R., $30,000.
Auditor of Accounts — Alexander V. Acebo, R., $30,000.
General Assembly: meets odd years in January at Montpelier. Members receive $270 weekly while in session, with a limit of $9,500 for a regular session and $50 per day for special session, plus specified expenses.
Senate — Dem., 13; Rep., 17. Total, 30.
House — Dem., 65; Rep., 84; 1 Ind. Total, 150.

Virginia

Governor — Charles S. Robb, D., $75,000.
Lt. Gov. — Richard J. Davis, D., $20,000.
Atty. Gen. — Gerald L. Baliles, D., $56,000.
Sec. of the Commonwealth — Laurie Naismith, D., $36,410.
Treasurer — C. J. Boehm, $60,632.
General Assembly: meets annually in January at Richmond. Members receive $11,000 annually plus expense and mileage allowances.
Senate — Dem., 32; Rep., 8. Total, 40.
House — Dem., 65; Rep., 34; Ind., 1. Total, 100.

Washington

Governor — John Spellman, R., $63,000.
Lt. Gov. — John A. Cherberg, D., $28,600.
Sec. of State — Ralph Munro, R., $31,000.
Atty. Gen. — Ken Eikenberry, R., $47,100.
Treasurer — Robert S. O'Brien, D., $37,200.
Legislature: meets annually in January at Olympia. Members receive $13,750 annually plus per diem of $44 per day and 10¢ per mile while in session, and $50 per diem for attending meetings during interim.
Senate — Dem., 26; Rep., 23. Total, 49.
House — Dem., 53; Rep., 45. Total, 98.

West Virginia

Governor — Jay Rockefeller, D., $60,000.
Sec. of State — A. James Manchin, D., $36,000.
Atty. Gen. — Chauncey Browning, D., $42,000.
Treasurer — Larrie Bailey, D., $42,000.
Comm. of Agric. — Gus R. Douglass, D., $39,000.
Auditor — Glen B. Gainer Jr., D., $39,000.
Legislature: meets annually in January at Charleston. Members receive $5,136.
Senate — Dem., 31; Rep., 3. Total, 34.
House — Dem., 87; Rep., 13. Total, 100.

Wisconsin

Governor — Anthony S. Earl, D., $75,337.
Lt. Gov. — James T. Flynn, D., $41,390.
Sec. of State — Douglas La Follette, D., $37,334.
Treasurer — Charles P. Smith, D., $37,334.
Atty. Gen. — Bronson C. La Follette, D., $58,139.
Superintendent of Public Instruction — Herbert J. Grover, $58,139.
Legislature: meets in January at Madison. Members receive $22,632 annually plus $41.63 per day expenses.
Senate — Dem., 18; Rep., 14; 1 vacancy. Total, 33.
Assembly — Dem., 58; Rep., 40; 1 vacancy. Total, 99.

Wyoming

Governor — Ed Herschler, D., $70,000.
Sec. of State — Thyra Thomson, R., $52,500.
Atty. Gen. — A.G. McClintock, D., $52,500.
Treasurer — Stan Smith, R., $52,500.
Legislature: meets odd years in January, even years in February, at Cheyenne. Members receive $30 per day while in session, plus $60 per day for expenses.
Senate — Dem., 11; Rep., 19. Total, 30.
House — Dem., 28; Rep. 35; 1 Ind.Total, 64.

Puerto Rico

Governor — Carlos Romero Barceló.
Secretary of State — Carlos S. Quirós.
Secy. of Justice — Nelson Martinez Acosta, act.
These officials belong to the New Progressive Party.
Legislature: composed of a Senate of 27 members and a House of Representatives of 51 members. Majority of the members of both chambers belongs to the Popular Democratic Party. They meet annually on the 2d Monday in January at San Juan.

U.S. Government Independent Agencies

Source: General Services Administration
Address: Washington, DC. Location and ZIP codes of agencies in parentheses; as of mid-1984.

ACTION — Thomas Pauken, dir. (806 Connecticut Ave., NW, 20525).
Administrative Conference of the United States — Loren A. Smith, chmn. (2120 L St., NW, 20037).
American Battle Monuments Commission — Mark W. Clark, chmn. (5127 Pulaski Bldg., 20314).
Appalachian Regional Commission — Winifred A. Pizzano, federal co-chmn.; Gov. Harry R. Hughes of Md., states co-chmn. (1666 Connecticut Ave. NW, 20235).
Arms Control & Disarmament Agency — Kenneth L. Adelman, dir. (320 21st St. NW, 20451).

Board for International Broadcasting — Frank Shakespeare, chmn. (1201 Connecticut Ave., 20005).

Central Intelligence Agency — William J. Casey, dir. (Wash., DC 20505).
Civil Aeronautics Board — Dan McKinnon, chmn. (1825 Connecticut Ave. NW, 20428).
Commission on Civil Rights — Clarence M. Pendleton Jr., chmn. (1121 Vermont Ave. NW, 20425).
Commission of Fine Arts — J. Carter Brown, chmn. (708 Jackson Pl. NW, 20006).
Commodity Futures Trading Commission — Susan M. Phillips, chmn. (2033 K St. NW, 20581).
Consumer Product Safety Commission — Nancy Harvey Steorts, chmn. (1111 18th St. NW, 20207).

Environmental Protection Agency — William Ruckelshaus, adm. (401 M St., SW, 20460).
Equal Employment Opportunity Commission — Clarence Thomas, chmn. (2401 E St., NW, 20507).
Export-Import Bank of the United States — William H. Draper 3d, pres. and chmn. (811 Vermont Ave. NW, 20571).

Farm Credit Administration — John D. Naill, chmn., Federal Farm Credit Board (1501 Farm Credit Drive, McLean, VA 22102).
Federal Communications Commission — Mark S. Fowler, chmn. (1919 M St. NW, 20554).
Federal Deposit Insurance Corporation — William M. Isaac, chmn. (550 17th St. NW, 20429).
Federal Election Commission — Lee Ann Elliott, chmn. (1325 K St. NW, 20463).
Federal Emergency Management Agency — Louis O. Giuffrida, dir. (500 C St. SW, 20472).
Federal Home Loan Bank Board — Edwin J. Gray, chmn. (1700 G St. NW, 20552).
Federal Labor Relations Authority — Barbara J. Mahone, chmn. (500 C St. NW, 20424).
Federal Maritime Commission — Alan Green Jr., chmn. (1100 L St. NW, 20573).
Federal Mediation and Conciliation Service — Kay McMurray, dir. (2100 K St. NW, 20427).
Federal Reserve System — Chairman, board of governors: Paul A. Volcker. (20th St. & Constitution Ave. NW, 20551).
Federal Trade Commission — James C. Miller 3d, chmn. (Pennsylvania Ave. at 6th St. NW, 20580).

General Accounting Office — Comptroller General of the U.S.; Charles A. Bowsher (441 G St. NW, 20548).
General Services Administration — Jack L. Couremanche, adm. (18th & F Sts. NW, 20405).
Government Printing Office — Public printer: William J. Barrett, act. (North Capitol and H Sts. NW, 20401).

Inter-American Foundation — Victor Blanco, chmn. 1515 Wilson Blvd., Rosslyn, VA 22209).
Interstate Commerce Commission — Reese H. Taylor Jr., chmn. (12th St. and Constitution Ave. NW, 20423).

Library of Congress — Daniel J. Boorstin, librarian (10 First St. SE, 20540).

Merit Systems Protection Board — Herbert E. Ellingwood, chmn. (1120 Vermont Ave. NW, 20419).
National Aeronautics and Space Administration — James M. Beggs, adm. (400 Maryland Ave., SW 20546).
National Capital Planning Commission — Glen T. Urquhart, chmn. (1325 G St. NW, 20576).
National Credit Union Administration — Edgar F. Callahan, chmn. (1776 G St. NW, 20456).
National Foundation on the Arts and the Humanities — Frank Hodsoll, chmn. (arts) 1100 Pennsylvania Ave. NW, 20506; William J. Bennett, chmn. (humanities) same address as arts.
National Labor Relations Board — Donald L. Dotson, chmn. (1717 Pennsylvania Ave. NW, 20570).
National Mediation Board — Helen M. Witt, chmn. (1425 K St. NW, 20572).
National Science Foundation — Lewis M. Branscomb, chmn., National Science Board (1800 G St. NW, 20550).
National Transportation Safety Board — James E. Burnett, chmn. (800 Independence Ave. SW, 20594).
Nuclear Regulatory Commission — Nunzio J. Pallidino, chmn. (1717 H St. NW, 20555).

Occupational Safety and Health Review Commission — Robert A. Rowland, chmn. (1825 K St. NW, 20006).
Office of Personnel Management — Donald J. Devine, dir., (1900 E St. NW, 20415).
Overseas Private Investment Corporation — Craig A. Nalen, pres. & CEO (1129 20th St. NW, 20527).

Panama Canal Commission — Dennis P. McAuliffe, adm. (in Panama); Michael Rhode Jr., secy. (in Washington: 425 13th St., NW 20004).
Peace Corps — Loret Miller Ruppe, dir. (806 Connecticut Ave. NW, 20526).
Pennsylvania Avenue Development Corporation — Henry A. Berliner, chmn., board of directors (425 13th St. NW, 20004).
Pension Benefit Guaranty Corporation — Charles Tharp, exec. dir. (2020 K St. NW, 20006).
Postal Rate Commission — Janet D. Steiger, chmn. (2000 L St. NW, 20268).

Railroad Retirement Board — Robert A. Gielow, chmn. (Rm. 630, 425 13th St. NW, 20004), Main Office (844 Rush St., Chicago, IL 60611).

Securities and Exchange Commission — John S.R. Shad, chmn. (450 5th St. NW, 20549).
Selective Service System — Thomas K. Turnage, dir. (National Headquarters, 20435).
Small Business Administration — James C. Sanders, adm. (1441 L St. NW, 20416).
Smithsonian Institution — S. Dillon Ripley, secy. (1000 Jefferson Dr. SW, 20560).

Tennessee Valley Authority — Chairman, board of directors: C.H. Dean Jr. (400 W. Summit Hill Dr., Knoxville, TN 37902 and Capitol Hill Office Bldg., 412 1st St. SE, Washington, DC 20444).

United States Information Agency — Charles Z. Wick, dir. (400 C St. NW, 20547).
United States International Development Cooperation Agency — M. Peter McPherson, act. dir. (320 21st St. NW, 20523).
United States International Trade Commission — Alfred E. Eckes, chmn. (701 E St. NW, 20436).
United States Postal Service — William F. Bolger, postmaster general (475 L'Enfant Plaza West SW, 20260).

Veterans Administration — Harry N. Walters, adm. (810 Vermont Ave. NW, 20420).

NATIONAL DEFENSE
Data as of July, 1984

Chairman, Joint Chiefs of Staff
John W. Vessey Jr. (USA)

The Joint Chiefs of Staff consists of the Chairman of the Joint Chiefs of Staff; the Chief of Staff, U.S. Army; the Chief of Naval Operations; the Chief of Staff, U.S. Air Force; and the Commandant of the Marine Corps.

Army

Chief of Staff—John A. Wickham, Jr.
Generals

	Date of Rank
Gorman, Paul F.	May. 25, 1983
Nutting, Wallace H.	May 25, 1983
Otis, Glenn K.	Aug. 1, 1981
Richardson, William R.	Feb. 28, 1983
Robinson, Roscoe, Jr.	Aug. 30, 1982
Rogers, Bernard W.	Nov. 7, 1974
Sennewald, Robert W.	May 24, 1982
Thurman, Maxwell R.	June 1983
Vessey, John W., Jr.	Nov. 1, 1976
Wickham, John A., Jr.	July 10, 1979

Air Force
Chief of Staff—Charles A. Gabriel
Generals

Creech, Wilbur L.	May 1, 1978
Dalton, James E.	Aug. 1, 1983
Davis, Bennie L.	Apr. 1, 1979
Gabriel, Charles A.	Aug. 1, 1980
Hartinger, James V.	Oct. 1, 1981
Iosue, Andrew P.	July 1, 1983
Lawson, Richard L.	July 1, 1980
Marsh, Robert T.	Feb. 1, 1981
Minter, Billy M.	July 1, 1982
Mullins, James P.	Aug. 1, 1983
O'Malley, Jerome F.	June 1, 1982
Ryan, Thomas M., Jr.	July 31, 1981
Skantze, Lawrence A.	Oct. 6, 1983

Navy

Chief of Naval Operations
Admiral James D. Watkins (submariner)
Admirals

Crowe, William J., Jr. (submariner)	May 30, 1980
Foley, Sylvester R., Jr. (aviator)	May 28, 1982
Hays, Ronald J. (aviator)	April 29, 1983
McDonald, Wesley L. (aviator)	Oct. 1, 1982
McKee, Kinnaird R. (submariner)	Mar. 2, 1982
Small, William N. (aviator)	July 1, 1981
Watkins, James D. (submariner)	Sept. 18, 1979
White, Steven A. (submariner)	Aug. 1, 1983

Marine Corps

Corps Commandant, with rank of General
Paul X. Kelley . . . . July 1, 1983

Asst. Commandant, with rank of General
John K. Davis. . . . . July 1, 1983

Chief of Staff, with rank of Lt. Gen.
D'Wayne Gray . . . . May 20, 1983

Coast Guard

Commandant, with rank of Admiral
James S. Gracey. . . . . May 27, 1982

Vice Commandant, with rank of Vice Admiral
Benedict Stabile. . . . . May 21, 1982

United States Unified and Specified Commands

Atlantic Command—Admiral Wesley L. McDonald, USN
HQ Aerospace Defense Command—Lt. Gen. James V. Hartinger, USAF
U.S. European Command—General Bernard W. Rogers, USA
Pacific Command—Admiral William J. Crowe, USN
U.S. Southern Command—Lt. Gen. Paul F. Gorman, USA
Strategic Air Command—General Bennie L. Davis, USAF

U.S. Central Command—Lt. Gen. Robert C. Kingston, USA
U.S. Readiness Command—General W.A. Nutting, USA
Military Air Lift Command—General Thomas M. Ryan, Jr., USAF
Military Sea Lift Command—Vice Admiral William H. Rowden, USN

North Atlantic Treaty Organization International Commands

Supr. Allied Commander, Europe (SACEUR)—Gen. Bernard W. Rogers, USA
Deputy SACEUR—Air Ch. Marshal Sir Peter Terry (UK), C-in-C SACEUR—Gen. H. J. Mack, Army (Germany)
C-in-C Allied Forces, Northern Europe—Gen. Sir Richard Lawson (UK)
C-in-C Allied Forces, Central Europe—Gen. Leopold Chalupa, Army (Germany)
C-in-C Allied Forces, Southern Europe—Adm. W.J. Small,

USN
Supr. Allied Commander Atlantic (SACLANT)—Adm. Wesley L. McDonald, USN
Deputy SACLANT—V. Adm. Kenneth M. Carr, USN
Commander Strike Force South—V. Adm. E. H. Martin, USN
Allied Commander in Chief, Channel—Adm. William D.M. Staveley, (UK)

Principal U.S. Military Training Centers

Army

Name, P.O. address	Zip	Nearest city	Name, P.O. address	Zip	Nearest city
Aberdeen Proving Ground, MD	21005	Aberdeen	Fort Jackson, SC	29207	Columbia
Carlisle Barracks, PA	17013	Carlisle	Fort Knox, KY	40121	Louisville
Fort Belvoir, VA	22060	Alexandria	Fort Leavenworth, KS	66027	Leavenworth
Fort Benning, GA	31905	Columbus	Fort Lee, VA	23801	Petersburg
Fort Bliss, TX	79916	El Paso	Fort McClellan, AL	36205	Anniston
Fort Bragg, NC	28307	Fayetteville	Fort Monmouth, NJ	07703	Red Bank
Fort Devens, MA	01433	Ayer	Fort Rucker, AL	36362	Dothan
Fort Dix, NJ	08640	Trenton	Fort Sill, OK	73503	Lawton
Fort Eustis, VA	23604	Newport News	Fort Leonard Wood, MO.	65473	Rolla
			National Training Center.	92311	Ft. Irwin
Fort Gordon, GA	30905	Augusta	Redstone Arsenal, AL	35809	Huntsville
Fort Benjamin Harrison, IN	46216	Indianapolis	The Judge Advocate		Charlottes-
Fort Sam Houston, TX.	78234	San Antonio	General School, VA	22901	ville
Fort Huachuca, AZ	85613	Sierra Vista			

Navy Recruit Training Centers

Great Lakes, IL	60088	North Chicago	Orlando, FL	32813	Orlando
San Diego, CA	92133	San Diego			

Major Marine Corps Facilities

Name, P.O. address	Zip	Nearest city	Name, P.O. address	Zip	Nearest city
MCB Camp Lejeune, NC	28542	Jacksonville	MCAS Iwakuni, Japan	FPO Seattle 98764	Iwakuni
MCB Camp Pendleton, CA	92055	Oceanside			
MCB Camp Butler, Okinawa	FPO Seattle 98773	Futenma, Okinawa	MCAS Kaneohe Bay, Oahu, HI	FPO San Francisco 96615	Kailua
MCAGCC Twentynine Palms, CA	92278	Palm Springs			
MCDEC Quantico, VA	22134	Quantico	MCAS (Helo) Futenma, Okinawa	FPO Seattle	Futenma
MCRD Parris Island, SC	29905	Beaufort	MCAS Beaufort, SC	29902	Beaufort
MCRD San Diego, CA	92140	San Diego	MCAS Yuma, AZ	85364	Yuma
MCAS Cherry Point, NC	28533	Cherry Point	MCMWTC Bridgeport, CA	93517	Bridgeport
MCAS El Toro (Santa Ana), CA	92709	Santa Ana	MCLB Albany, GA	31704	Albany
MCAS (Helo) Tustin, CA	92780	Santa Ana	MCLB Barstow, CA	92311	Barstow
MCAS (Helo) New River, NC	28540	Jacksonville			

MCB = Marine Corps Base. MCDEC = Marine Corps Development & Education Command. MCAS = Marine Corps Air Station. Helo = Helicopter. MCAGCC = Marine Corps Air-Ground Combat Center. MCMWTC = Marine Corps Mountain Warfare Training Center. MCLB = Marine Corps Logistics Base.

Air Force

Chanute AFB, IL	61868	Rantoul	Mather AFB, CA	95655	Sacramento
Columbus AFB, MS	39701	Columbus	Maxwell AFB, AL	36112	Montgomery
Goodfellow AFB, TX	76903	San Angelo	Randolph AFB, TX	78150	San Antonio
Gunter AFS, AL	36114	Montgomery	Reese AFB, TX	79489	Lubbock
Keesler AFB, MS	39534	Biloxi	Sheppard AFB, TX	76311	Wichita Falls
Lackland AFB, TX	78236	San Antonio	Vance AFB, OK	73702	Enid
Laughlin AFB, TX	78843	Del Rio	Williams AFB, AZ	85224	Phoenix
Lowry AFB, CO	80230	Denver			

Personal Salutes and Honors

The United States national salute, 21 guns, is also the salute to a national flag. The independence of the United States is commemorated by the salute to the union — one gun for each state — fired at noon on July 4 at all military posts provided with suitable artillery.

A-21-gun salute on arrival and departure, with 4 ruffles and flourishes, is rendered to the President of the United States, to an ex-President and to a President-elect. The national anthem or *Hail to the Chief*, as appropriate, is played for the President, and the national anthem for the others. A 21-gun salute on arrival and departure with 4 ruffles and flourishes, also is rendered to the sovereign or chief of state of a foreign country or a member of a reigning royal family; the national anthem of his or her country is played. The music is considered an inseparable part of the salute and will immediately follow the ruffles and flourishes without pause.

Rank	Salute—guns Arrive—Leave		Ruffles, flourishes	Music
Vice President of United States	19		4	Hail Columbia
Speaker of the House	19		4	March
American or foreign ambassador	19		4	Nat. anthem of official
Premier or prime minister	19		4	Nat. anthem of official
Secretary of Defense, Army, Navy or Air Force	19	19	4	March
Other Cabinet members, Senate President pro tempore, Governor, or Chief Justice of U.S.	19		4	March
Chairman, Joint Chiefs of Staff	19	19	4	
Army Chief of Staff, Chief of Naval Operations, Air Force Chief of Staff, Marine Commandant	19	19	4	General's or Admiral's March
General of the Army, General of the Air Force, Fleet Admiral	19	19	4	
Generals, Admirals	17	17	4	
Assistant Secretaries of Defense, Army, Navy or Air Force	17	17	4	March
Chairman of a Committee of Congress	17	17	4	March

Other salutes (on arrival only) include 15 guns for American envoys or ministers and foreign envoys or ministers accredited to the United States; 15 guns for a lieutenant general or vice admiral; 13 guns for a major general or rear admiral (upper half); 13 guns for American ministers resident and ministers resident accredited to the U.S.; 11 guns for a brigadier general or rear admiral (lower half); 11 guns for American charges d'affaires and like officials accredited to U.S.; and 11 guns for consuls general accredited to U.S.

Military Units, U.S. Army and Air Force

Army units. Squad. In infantry usually ten men under a staff sergeant. **Platoon.** In infantry 4 squads under a lieutenant. **Company.** Headquarters section and 4 platoons under a captain. (Company in the artillery is a battery; in the cavalry, a troop.) **Battalion.** Hdqts. and 4 or more companies under a lieutenant colonel. (Battalion size unit in the cavalry is a squadron.) **Brigade.** Hdqts. and 3 or more battalions under a colonel. **Division.** Hdqts. and 3 brigades with artillery, combat support, and combat service support units under a major general. **Army Corps.** Two or more divisions with corps troops under a lieutenant general. **Field Army.** Hdqts. and two or more corps with field Army troops under a general.

Air Force Units. Flight. Numerically designated flights are the lowest level unit in the Air Force. They are used primarily where there is a need for small mission elements to be incorporated into an organized unit. **Squadron.** A squadron is the basic unit in the Air Force. It is used to designate the mission units in operational commands. **Group.** The group is a flexible unit composed of two or more squadrons whose functions may be either tactical, support or administrative in nature. **Wing.** An operational wing normally has two or more assigned mission squadrons in an area such as combat, flying training or airlift. **Air Division.** The organization of the air division may be similar to that of the numbered air force, though on a much smaller scale. Functions are usually limited to operations and logistics. **Numbered Air Forces.** Normally an operationally oriented agency, the numbered air force is designed for the control of two or more air divisions or units of comparable strength. It is a flexible organization and may be of any size. Its wings may be assigned to air divisions or directly under the numbered air force. **Major Command.** A major subdivision of the Air Force that is assigned a major segment of the USAF mission.

U.S. Army Insignia and Chevrons

Source: Department of the Army

Grade	Insignia

General of the Armies

General John J. Pershing, the only person to have held this rank, was authorized to prescribe his own insignia, but never wore in excess of four stars. The rank originally was established by Congress for George Washington in 1799, and he was promoted to the rank by joint resolution of Congress, approved by Pres. Ford Oct. 19, 1976.

General of Army... Five silver stars fastened together in a circle and the coat of arms of the United States in gold color metal with shield and crest enameled.

General . . . . Four silver stars
Lieutenant General . . . . . Three silver stars
Major General . . . . Two silver stars
Brigadier General . . . . . . One silver star
Colonel . . . . Silver eagle
Lieutenant Colonel . . . . . Silver oak leaf
Major . . . . Gold oak leaf
Captain . . . . Two silver bars
First Lieutenant . . . . One silver bar
Second Lieutenant . . . . . . One gold bar

Warrant officers

Grade Four—Silver bar with 4 enamel black bands.
Grade Three—Silver bar with 3 enamel black bands.
Grade Two—Silver bar with 2 enamel black bands.
Grade One—Silver bar with 1 enamel black band.

Non-commissioned Officers

Sergeant Major of the Army (E-9). Same as Command Sergeant Major (below) but with 2 stars. Also wears distinctive red and white shield on lapel.

Command Sergeant Major (E-9). Three chevrons above three arcs with a 5-pointed star with a wreath around the star between the chevrons and arcs.

Sergeant Major (E-9). Three chevrons above three arcs with a five-pointed star between the chevrons and arcs.

First Sergeant (E-8). Three chevrons above three arcs with a lozenge between the chevrons and arcs.

Master Sergeant (E-8). Three chevrons above three arcs.

Platoon Sergeant or Sergeant First Class (E-7). Three chevrons above two arcs.

Staff Sergeant (E-6). Three chevrons above one arc.

Sergeant (E-5). Three chevrons.

Corporal (E-4). Two chevrons.

Specialists

Specialist Seven (E-7). Three arcs above the eagle device.
Specialist Six (E-6). Two arcs above the eagle device.
Specialist Five (E-5). One arc above the eagle device.
Specialist Four (E-4). Eagle device only.

Other enlisted

Private First Class (E-3). One chevron above one arc.
Private (E-2). One chevron.
Private (E-1). None.

U.S. Army

Source: Department of the Army

Army Military Personnel on Active Duty[1]

June 30[2]	Total strength	Commissioned officers Total	Male	Female[3]	Warrant officers Male[4]	Female	Enlisted personnel Total	Male	Female
1940	267,767	17,563	16,624	939	763	—	249,441	249,441	
1942	3,074,184	203,137	190,662	12,475	3,285	—	2,867,762	2,867,762	
1943	6,993,102	557,657	521,435	36,222	21,919	0	6,413,526	6,358,200	55,325
1944	7,992,868	740,077	692,351	47,726	36,893	10	7,215,888	7,144,601	71,287
1945	8,266,373	835,403	772,511	62,892	56,216	44	7,374,710	7,283,930	90,780
1946	1,889,690	257,300	240,643	16,657	9,826	18	1,622,546	1,605,847	16,699
1950	591,487	67,784	63,375	4,409	4,760	22	518,921	512,370	6,551
1955	1,107,606	111,347	106,173	5,174	10,552	48	985,659	977,943	7,716
1960	871,348	91,056	86,832	4,224	10,141	39	770,112	761,833	8,279
1965	967,049	101,812	98,029	3,783	10,285	23	854,929	846,409	8,520
1969	1,509,637	148,836	143,699	5,137	23,734	20	1,337,047	1,316,326	10,721
1970	1,319,735	143,704	138,469	5,235	23,005	13	1,153,013	1,141,537	11,476
1975	781,316	89,756	85,184	4,572	13,214	22	678,324	640,621	37,703
1978 (May 31)	772,202	96,553	90,749	5,804	13,160	57	662,432	614,961	47,471
1980 (Mar. 31)	762,739	83,117	76,237	6,880	13,093	103	666,426	608,223	58,203
1981 (Jan.)	769,673	85,017	77,179	7,374	13,563	120	671,057	608,293	62,764
1982 (Mar.)	788,026	87,874	79,379	8,495	14,058	143	685,951	618,783	67,168
1983 (Mar.)	774,704	89,012	80,091	8,921	14,481	178	674,033	606,956	67,077
1984 (Mar.)	774,935	90,393	81,046	9,347	14,971	198	669,373	602,702	66,671

(1) Represents strength of the active Army, including Philippine Scouts, retired Regular Army personnel on extended active duty, and National Guard and Reserve personnel on extended active duty; excludes U.S. Military Academy cadets, contract surgeons, and National Guard and Reserve personnel not on extended active duty.

(2) Data for 1940 to 1947 include personnel in the Army Air Forces and its predecessors (Air Service and Air Corps).

(3) Includes: women doctors, dentists, and Medical Service Corps officers for 1946 and subsequent years, women in the Army Nurse Corps for all years, and the Women's Army Corps and Women's Medical Specialists Corps (dieticians, physical therapists, and occupational specialists) for 1943 and subsequent years.

(4) Act of Congress approved April 27, 1926, directed the appointment as warrant officers of field clerks still in active service. Includes flight officers as follows: 1943, 5,700; 1944, 13,615; 1945, 31,117; 1946, 2,580.

The Federal Service Academies

U.S. Military Academy, West Point, N.Y. Founded 1802. Awards B.S. degree and Army commission for a 5-year service obligation. For admissions information, write Admissions Office, USMA, West Point, NY 10996.

U.S. Naval Academy, Annapolis, Md. Founded 1845. Awards B.S. degree and Navy or Marine Corps commission for a 5-year service obligation. For admissions information, write Dean of Admissions, Naval Academy, Annapolis, MD 21402.

U.S. Air Force Academy, Colorado Springs, Colo. Founded 1954. Awards B.S. degree and Air Force commission for a 5-year service obligation. For admissions information, write Registrar, U.S. Air Force Academy, CO 80840.

U.S. Coast Guard Academy, New London, Conn. Founded 1876. Awards B.S. degree and Coast Guard commission for a 5-year service obligation. For admissions information, write Director of Admissions, Coast Guard Academy, New London, CT 06320.

U.S. Merchant Marine Academy, Kings Point, N.Y. Founded 1943. Awards B.S. degree, a license as a deck engineer, or dual officer, and a U.S. Naval Reserve commission. Service obligations vary according to options taken by the graduate. For admissions information, write Admission Office, U.S. Merchant Marine Academy, Kings Point, NY 11024.

U.S. Navy Insignia

Source: Department of the Navy

Navy

Stripes and corps device are of gold embroidery.

Stripes

Fleet Admiral	1 two inch with 4 one-half inch.
Admiral	1 two inch with 3 one-half inch.
Vice Admiral.	1 two inch with 2 one-half inch.
Rear Admiral	1 two inch with 1 one-half inch.
Commodore	1 two inch.
Captain.	4 one-half inch.
Commander	3 one-half inch.
Lieut. Commander . .	2 one-half inch, with 1 one-quarter inch between.
Lieutenant	2 one-half inch.
Lieutenant (j.g.)	1 one-half inch with one-quarter inch above.
Ensign	1 one-half inch.

Warrant Officers—One 1/2" broken with 1/2" intervals of blue as follows:

Warrant Officer W-4—1 break
Warrant Officer W-3—2 breaks, 2" apart
Warrant Officer W-2—3 breaks, 2" apart

The breaks are symmetrically centered on outer face of the sleeve.

Enlisted personnel (non-Commissioned petty officers)...A rating badge worn on the upper left arm, consisting of a spread eagle, appropriate number of chevrons, and centered specialty mark.

Marine Corps

Marine Corps and Army officer insignia are similar. Marine Corps and Army enlisted insignia, although basically similar, differ in color, design, and fewer Marine Corps subdivisions. The Marine Corps' distinctive cap and collar ornament is a combination of the American eagle, globe, and anchor.

Coast Guard

Coast Guard insignia follow Navy custom, with certain minor changes such as the officer cap insignia. The Coast Guard shield is worn on both sleeves of officers and on the right sleeve of all enlisted personnel.

U.S. Navy Personnel on Active Duty

June 30	Officers[1]	Nurses	Enlisted[2]	Off. Cand.	Total
1940	13,162	442	144,824	2,569	160,997
1945	320,293	11,086	2,988,207	61,231	3,380,817
1950	42,687	1,964	331,860	5,037	381,538
1960	67,456	2,103	544,040	4,385	617,984
1970	78,488	2,273	605,899	6,000	692,660
1980	63,100	—	464,100	—	527,200
1983 (Jan.)	66,560	—	482,241	—	548,801
1984 (Jan.)	70,075	—	494,767	—	564,842

(1) Nurses are included after 1973. (2) Officer candidates are included after 1973.

Marine Corps Personnel On Active Duty

Yr.	Officers	Enl.	Total	Yr.	Officers	Enl.	Total	Yr.	Officers	Enl.	Total
1955 . .	18,417	186,753	205,170	1965 . . .	17,258	172,955	190,213	1980. . .	18,198	170,271	188,469
1960 . .	16,203	154,418	170,621	1970 . . .	24,941	234,796	259,737	1983. . .	19,983	174,106	194,089

Armed Services Senior Enlisted Adviser

The U.S. Army, Navy and Air Force in 1966-67 each created a new position of senior enlisted adviser whose primary job is to represent the point of view of his services' enlisted men and women on matters of welfare, morale, and any problems concerning enlisted personnel. The senior adviser will have direct access to the military chief of his branch of service and policy-making bodies.

The senior enlisted adviser for each Dept. is:

Army—Sgt. Major of the Army Glen E. Morrell.
Navy—Master Chief Petty Officer of the Navy Billy C. Sanders.
Air Force—Chief Master Sgt. of the AF Sam E. Parish.
Marines—Sgt. Major of the Marine Corps Robert E. Cleary.

Veteran Population

Source: Veterans Administration

	March 1984
Veterans in civil life, end of month — Total	**28,135,000**
War Veterans — Total	**22,949,000**
Vietnam Era — Total	8,254,000
And service in Korean Conflict	650,000
No service in Korean Conflict.	7,603,000
Korean Conflict — Total	5,266,000
And service in WW II	1,033,000
No service in WW II	4,233,000
World War II	10,840,000
World War I	272,000
Spanish-American War	27
Peacetime Veterans — Total	5,186,000
Post-Vietnam Era	1,729,000
Peacetime service between Korean Conflict and Vietnam Era only	3,045,000
Peacetime Service — other	412,000

Compensation and Pension Case Payments

Fiscal year	Living veteran cases No.	Deceased veteran cases No.	Total cases No.	Total disbursement Dollars	Fiscal year	Living veteran cases No.	Deceased veteran cases No.	Total cases No.	Total disbursement Dollars
1890 . . .	415,654	122,290	537,944	106,093,850	1965 . . .	3,204,275	1,277,009	4,481,284	3,901,598,010
1900 . . .	752,510	241,019	993,529	138,462,130	1970 . . .	3,127,338	1,487,176	4,614,514	5,113,649,490
1910 . . .	602,622	318,461	921,083	159,974,056	1975 . . .	3,226,701	1,628,146	4,854,847	7,600,000,000
1920 . . .	419,627	349,916	769,543	316,418,029	1976 . . .	3,235,778	1,630,830	4,866,608	8,074,488,000
1930 . . .	542,610	298,223	840,833	418,432,808	1979 . . .	3,240,283	1,529,206	4,769,489	10,324,258,000
1940 . . .	610,122	239,176	849,298	429,138,465	1980 . . .	3,195,395	1,450,785	4,646,180	11,045,412,000
1950 . . .	2,368,238	658,123	3,026,361	2,009,462,298	1981 . . .	3,154,030	1,381,280	4,535,310	12,225,027,341
1955 . . .	2,668,786	808,303	3,477,089	2,634,292,537	1982 . . .	3,099,109	1,307,710	4,406,819	13,134,688,679
1960 . . .	3,008,935	950,802	3,959,737	3,314,761,383	1983 . . .	3,043,968	1,241,807	4,285,775	13,697,788,374

Monthly Pay Scale of
Effective

Commissioned Officers

Pay grade	Rank or pay grade Army rank	Navy rank	Cumulative years of service Under 2	2	3	4	6	8
0-10[1]	General*	Admiral	$4,874.40	$5,046.00	$5,046.00	$5,046.00	$5,046.00	$5,239.50
0-9	Lieutenant General	Vice Admiral	4,320.30	4,433.40	4,527.60	4,527.60	4,527.60	4,642.80
0-8	Major General	Rear Admiral	3,912.90	4,030.20	4,125.90	4,125.90	4,125.90	4,433.40
0-7	Brigadier General	Commodore	3,251.40	3,472.50	3,472.50	3,472.50	3,627.90	3,627.90
0-6	Colonel	Captain	2,409.90	2,647.80	2,821.20	2,821.20	2,821.20	2,821.20
0-5	Lieutenant Colonel	Commander	1,927.50	2,263.50	2,419.50	2,419.50	2,419.50	2,419.50
0-4	Major	Lieutenant Comdr.	1,624.50	1,978.20	2,110.50	2,110.50	2,149.20	2,244.60
0-3	Captain	Lieutenant	1,509.90	1,687.80	1,804.20	1,996.50	2,091.90	2,167.50
0-2	First Lieutenant	Lieutenant (J.G.)	1,316.40	1,437.60	1,727.10	1,785.30	1,822.80	1,822.80
0-1	Second Lieutenant	Ensign	1,143.00	1,189.80	1,437.60	1,437.60	1,437.60	1,437.60

Commissioned officers with over 4 years active duty as an enlisted member or warrant officer

0-3E	Captain	Lieutenant	0.00	0.00	0.00	1,996.50	2,091.90	2,167.50
0-2E	First Lieutenant	Lieutenant (J.G.)	0.00	0.00	0.00	1,785.30	1,822.80	1,880.40
0-1E	Second Lieutenant	Ensign	0.00	0.00	0.00	1,437.60	1,535.70	1,592.40

Warrant Officers

W-4	Chief Warrant	Comm. Warrant	1,538.10	1,650.00	1,650.00	1,687.80	1,764.60	1,842.30
W-3	Chief Warrant	Comm. Warrant	1,398.00	1,516.50	1,516.50	1,535.70	1,554.00	1,667.70
W-2	Chief Warrant	Comm. Warrant	1,224.60	1,324.50	1,324.50	1,363.20	1,437.60	1,516.50
W-1	Warrant Officer	Warrant Officer	1,020.30	1,169.70	1,169.70	1,267.20	1,324.50	1,381.50

Enlisted Personnel[2]

E-9[3]	Sergeant Major**	Master C.P.O.	0.00	0.00	0.00	0.00	0.00	0.00
E-8[3]	Master Sergeant	Senior C.P.O.	0.00	0.00	0.00	0.00	0.00	1,500.60
E-7	Sgt. 1st Class	Chief Petty Officer	1,047.60	1,130.70	1,173.00	1,213.80	1,255.50	1,295.10
E-6	Staff Sergeant	Petty Officer 1st Class	901.20	982.50	1,023.60	1,067.10	1,106.40	1,146.90
E-5	Sergeant	Petty Officer 2nd Cl.	791.10	861.00	902.70	942.00	1,003.80	1,044.60
E-4	Corporal	Petty Officer 3rd Cl.	738.00	779.10	824.70	888.90	924.00	924.00
E-3	Private 1st Class	Seaman	695.10	732.90	762.60	792.90	792.90	792.90
E-2	Private	Seaman Apprentice	668.70	668.70	668.70	668.70	668.70	668.70
E-1 > 4	Private	Seaman Recruit	596.40	596.40	596.40	596.40	596.40	596.40
E-1 < 4			573.60	573.60	573.60	573.60	573.60	573.60

The pay scale also applies to: Coast Guard and Marine Corps, National Oceanic and Atmospheric Administration, Public Health Service, National Guard, and the Organized Reserves.

*Basic pay is limited to $5,330.20 by Level V of the Executive Schedule and further limited by Sec. 101C, P.L. 96-86 to $4,176.00 max Four star General or Admiral—personal money allowances of $2,200 per annum, or $4,000 if Chief of Staff of the Army, Chief of Staff of the Air Force, Chief of Naval Operations, Commandant of the Marine Corps, or Commandant of the Coast Guard. Three star General or Admiral—personal money allowance of $500 per annum.

**A new title of Chief Master Sergeant created in 1965 rates E-9 classification.

(1) While serving as Chairman of Joint Chiefs of Staff, Chief of Staff of the Army, Chief of Naval Operations, Chief of Staff of the Air Forces, or Commandant of the Marine Corps, basic pay for this grade is $6,988.50 regardless of years of service.

(2) Air Force enlisted personnel pay grades, E-9, Chief Master Sergeant; E-8, Sr. Master Sergeant; E-7, Master Sergeant; E-6, Technical Sergeant; E-5, Staff Sergeant; E-4, Sergeant; E-3, Airman 1st Class; E-2, Airman; E-1, Basic Airman.

Marine Corps enlisted ranks are as follows: E-9, Sergeant Major and Master Gunnery Sergeant; E-8, First Sergeant and Master Sergeant E-7, Gunnery Sergeant; E-6, Staff Sergeant; E-5, Sergeant; E-4, Corporal; E-3, Lance Corporal; E-2, Private, First Class Marine; E-1, Private.

Marine Corps and Air Force officer ranks are same as Army.

(3) While serving as Sergeant Major of the Army, Master Chief Petty Officer of the Navy, Chief Master Sergeant of the Air Force, or Sergeant Major of the Marine Corps, basic pay for this grade is $2,692.50 regardless of years of service.

U.S. Military Strengths—Worldwide
(As of December 31, 1983)
Source: U.S. Department of Defense

	Ashore	Afloat		Ashore	Afloat
U.S. Territory & Special Locations	1,455,794	169,732	Egypt	1,163	
Western & Southern Europe	316,436	14,248	Saudi Arabia	695	
Germany (Fed. Republic)	246,330[1]		Western Hemisphere	16,774	19,199
United Kingdom	28,256		Panama	9,316	
Italy	13,627		Cuba (Guantanamo)	2,295	
East Asia & Pacific	100,890	19,295	Honduras	2,106	
Japan	45,290		Antarctica	103	
Rep. of Korea	39,610		Eastern Europe	180	
Philippines	14,865		Undistributed	121	
Africa, Near East & South Asia	4,194	23,418	Total Foreign Countries	438,698	59,68
British Indian Ocean Territory	1,506		Total Worldwide	1,894,492	229,41

Note: Ashore includes temporarily shore-based.
(1) Total for individual nations is combined ashore and afloat.

the Uniformed Services
January 1984

Commissioned Officers

\	\	Cumulative years of service	\	\	\	\	\	Without dependents Full Rate	Partial Rate	With Dependents
10	12	14	16	18	20	22	26			
$5,239.50	$5,640.60	$5,640.60	$6,044.10	$6,044.10	$6,448.50	$6,448.50	$6,850.50	$528.90	$50.70	$661.80
4,642.80	4,836.00	4,836.00	5,239.50	5,239.50	5,640.60	5,640.60	6,044.10	528.90	50.70	661.80
4,433.40	4,642.80	4,642.80	4,836.00	5,046.00	5,239.50	5,449.50	5,449.50	528.90	50.70	661.80
3,838.50	3,838.50	4,030.20	4,433.40	4,737.90	4,737.90	4,737.90	4,737.90	528.90	50.70	661.80
2,821.20	2,821.20	2,916.90	3,378.30	3,551.10	3,627.90	3,838.50	4,163.10	474.90	39.60	579.00
2,493.30	2,627.10	2,802.90	3,012.60	3,185.70	3,282.00	3,396.60	3,396.60	437.70	33.00	527.10
2,397.30	2,532.30	2,647.80	2,763.90	2,840.40	2,840.40	2,840.40	2,840.40	389.70	26.70	470.10
2,284.20	2,397.30	2,456.40	2,456.40	2,456.40	2,456.40	2,456.40	2,456.40	342.60	22.20	422.70
1,822.80	1,822.80	1,822.80	1,822.80	1,822.80	1,822.80	1,822.80	1,822.80	297.60	17.70	376.20
1,437.60	1,437.60	1,437.60	1,437.60	1,437.60	1,437.60	1,437.60	1,437.60	232.50	13.20	302.40
2,284.20	2,397.30	2,493.30	2,493.30	2,493.30	2,493.30	2,493.30	2,493.30			
1,978.20	2,053.80	2,110.50	2,110.50	2,110.50	2,110.50	2,110.50	2,110.50			
1,650.00	1,707.30	1,785.30	1,785.30	1,785.30	1,785.30	1,785.30	1,785.30			

Warrant Officers

1,919.70	2,053.80	2,149.20	2,224.80	2,284.20	2,358.30	2,437.20	2,627.10	375.30	25.20	453.30
1,764.60	1,822.80	1,880.40	1,936.80	1,996.50	2,073.90	2,149.20	2,224.80	334.80	20.70	412.80
1,573.80	1,631.40	1,687.80	1,746.90	1,804.20	1,861.50	1,936.80	1,936.80	291.00	15.90	370.80
1,437.60	1,497.30	1,554.00	1,611.30	1,667.70	1,727.10	1,727.10	1,727.10	262.80	13.80	340.50

Enlisted Personnel

1,788.90	1,829.70	1,871.10	1,914.00	1,956.60	1,994.70	2,099.70	2,303.70	283.20	18.60	398.70
1,543.20	1,583.70	1,625.10	1,668.00	1,706.40	1,748.40	1,851.90	2,057.70	261.00	15.30	368.10
1,336.80	1,378.20	1,440.60	1,481.40	1,523.10	1,542.90	1,646.40	1,851.00	222.00	12.00	342.60
1,188.90	1,250.10	1,289.40	1,331.10	1,351.20	1,351.20	1,351.20	1,351.20	201.90	9.90	315.30
1,086.30	1,126.20	1,146.90	1,146.90	1,146.90	1,146.90	1,146.90	1,146.90	194.10	8.70	289.80
924.00	924.00	924.00	924.00	924.00	924.00	924.00	924.00	171.00	8.10	254.70
792.90	792.90	792.90	792.90	792.90	792.90	792.90	792.90	153.00	7.80	222.00
668.70	668.70	668.70	668.70	668.70	668.70	668.70	668.70	135.00	7.20	222.00
596.40	596.40	596.40	596.40	596.40	596.40	596.40	596.40	127.50	6.90	222.00
573.60	573.60	573.60	573.60	573.60	573.60	573.60	573.60	122.70	6.90	213.60

Basic Allowance for Subsistence

This allowance, the quarters allowance, and any other allowance are not subject to income tax.

Officers — Subsistence (food) is paid to all officers regardless of rank $102.10/month
Enlisted members: When on leave or authorized to mess separately $4.87/day
           When rations in kind are not available. $5.50/day
           When assigned to duty under emergency conditions where
           no government messing facilities are available $7.28/day

Family Separation Allowance

Under certain conditions of family separation of more than 30 days, a member in Pay Grades E-4 (with over 4 years' service) and above will be allowed $30 a month in addition to any other allowances to which he is entitled. When separated from family and required to maintain a home for his family and one for himself, the member is entitled to an additional monthly basic allowance for quarters at the "without dependents" rate for his grade.

The Medal of Honor

The Medal of Honor is the highest military award for bravery that can be given to any individual in the United States. The first Army Medals were awarded on March 25, 1863, and the first Navy Medals went to sailors and Marines April 3, 1863.

The Medal of Honor, established by Joint Resolution of Congress, 12 July 1862 (amended by Act of 9 July 1918 and Act of 25 July 1963) is awarded in the name of Congress to a person who, while a member of the Armed Forces, distinguishes himself conspicuously by gallantry and intrepidity at the risk of his life above and beyond the call of duty while engaged in an action against any enemy of the United States; while engaged in military operations involving conflict with an opposing foreign force; or while serving with friendly foreign forces engaged in an armed conflict against an opposing armed force in which the United States is not a belligerent party. The deed performed must have been one of personal bravery or self-sacrifice so conspicuous as to clearly distinguish the individual above his comrades and must have involved risk of life. Incontestable proof of the performance of service is exacted and each recommendation for award of this decoration is considered on the standard of extraordinary merit.

Prior to World War I, the 2,625 Army Medal of Honor awards up to that time were reviewed to determine which past awards met new stringent criteria. The Army removed 911 names from the list, most of them former members of a volunteer infantry group during the Civil War who had been induced to extend their enlistments when they were promised the Medal.

Since that review Medals of Honor have been awarded in the following numbers:

World War I 123   Korean War 131
World War II 433   Vietnam (to date) 233

U.S. Air Force

Source: Department of the Air Force

The Army Air forces were started Aug. 1, 1907, as the Aeronautical Division of the Signal Corps, U.S. Army. The division consisted of one officer and two enlisted men, and it was more than a year before it carried out its first mission in an airplane of its own. When the U.S. entered World War I (April 6, 1917), the Aviation Service, as it was called then, had 55 planes and 65 officers, only 35 of whom were fliers. On the day the Japanese struck at Pearl Harbor (Dec. 7, 1941), the Army Air Forces, as they had been re-

named 6 months previously, had 10,329 planes, of which only 2,846 were suited for combat service. But when the Army's air arm reached its peak during World War II (in July, 1944), it had 79,908 of all types of aircraft and (in May 1945) 43,248 combat aircraft and (in March, 1944) 2,411,294 officers and enlisted men. The Air Force was established under the Armed Services Unification Act of July 26, 1947.

USAF Personnel at Home and Overseas — Officers and Enlisted

June 30	Continental U.S.	Overseas	Total	June 30	Continental U.S.	Overseas	Total
1940	40,229	10,936	51,165	1970	531,386	255,819	787,20
1945	1,153,373	1,128,886	2,282,259	1975	457,484	150,853	608,33
1950	317,816	93,461	411,277	1980	434,646	118,604	553,25
1955	689,635	270,311	959,946	1981	424,504	137,880	562,38
1957[1]	651,674	268,161	919,835	1982	437,184	142,638	578,82
1960[2]	607,383	207,369	814,752	1983	445,790	145,339	591,12
1965	635,430	189,232	824,662	1984	468,344	123,695	592,04

(1) Since 1957 continental U.S. includes Air Force Academy Cadets as follows: (1957) 504; (1960) 1,949; (1964) 2,838; (1965) 2,907; (1966) 3,152; (1967) 3,361; (1968) 3,652; (1969) 3,941; (1970) 4,144; (1971) 2,997; (1972) 2,885; (1973) 4,356; (1974) 4,412; (1975) 4,414; (1976) 4,415; (1977) 4,680; (1978) 4,524; (1979) 4,578; (1980) 4,000; (1981) 4,178; (1982) 4,688; (1983) 4,417; (1984) 4,466.

(2) Since 1960 Overseas includes Alaska and Hawaii. All figures include Mobilized Personnel.

USAF Military Personnel

June 30	Officers & Enlisted	Male commissioned officers				Warrant officers
		USAF	USAFR	ANG	AFUS & AUS	
1955	959,946	23,463	105,587	984	2	3,961
1960	814,752	49,584	72,115	248	3	4,069
1965	824,662	62,076	62,537	280	54	2,532
1970	787,205	63,678	65,852	168	105	639
1975	608,337	57,854	42,131	128	28	39
1980	553,250	54,621	35,454	115	6	1
1982	578,822	58,052	34,251	297	—	0
1984	592,044	93,996	13,674[1]	11,864	—	—

(1) Includes selected and ready reserve.

Female Commissioned Officers, and Enlisted Personnel

June 30	Female commissioned officers				Female WO	Enlisted personnel		
	Total	USAF	Nurses	WMSC		Total	Male	Female
1960	3,858	679	3,020	159	5	685,063	679,412	5,651
1965	4,099	708	3,185	206	1	690,177	685,436	4,741
1970	4,667	1,072	3,407	188	0	657,402	648,415	8,987
1975	4,981	1,542	3,236	203	0	503,176	477,944	25,232
1980	8,060	4,291	3,200	569	0	454,994	404,480	50,514
1982	9,796	5,646	3,414	736	0	476,723	422,240	54,48
1984	10,777	7,086	3,569	122	0	487,660	432,419	55,24

Women in the Armed Forces

Women in the Army, Navy, Air Force, Marines, and Coast Guard are all fully integrated with male personnel. Expansion of military women's programs began in the Department of Defense in fiscal year 1973.

Although women are prohibited by law and directives based on law from serving in combat positions, policy changes in the Department of Defense have made possible the assignment of women to almost all other career fields. Career progression for women is now comparable to that for male personnel. Women are routinely assigned to overseas locations formerly closed to female personnel. Women are in command of activities and units that have missions other than administration of women.

Admission of women to the service academies began in the fall of 1976. The academies provide single-track education, allowing only for minor variations in the cadet program based on physiological differences between men and women.

Army — Information: Chief, Office of Public Affairs, Dept. of Army, Wash., DC 20310; 76,468 women, 66,866 enlisted women, 9,398 officers, 204 warrant officers.

Army Nurse Corps — Brig. Gen. Hazel Johnson, C Army Nurse Corps, Office of the Surgeon General, Dept Army, Wash., DC 20310.

Navy — Information: Chief of Information, Dept. Navy, Wash., DC 20350-1200; 6,605 women officers; 42 enlisted women.

Navy Nurse Corps — Com. Mary J. Nielubowicz, I Navy Nurse Corps, Dept. of Navy, Wash., DC 20372-2 2,855 women officers; 777 men.

Air Force — Information: Office of Public Affairs, D of the Air Force, Wash., DC 20330; 10,560 women offi 54,777 enlisted women.

Air Force Nurse Corps — Brig. Gen. Diann A. F Chief, Air Force Nurse Corps, Office of the Surgeon G USAF, Bolling AFB, Wash., DC 20332.

Marine Corps — Information: Commandant of the rine Corps (Code PA), Headquarters, Marine Corps, W DC 20380; 642 women officers; 8,508 enlisted women.

Coast Guard — Information: Commandant (G-B U.S. Coast Guard, 2100 Second St., SW, Wash., DC 2 163 women officers; 1,700 enlisted women.

Major U.S. Weapons Systems Cost Data

Source: DMS, Inc., Greenwich, Conn.

(millions of dollars)

Designation	Total production	Total cost	Designation	Total production	Total cost
Aircraft			Trident	857	37,392
General Dynamics F-16	2,651	49,920	Tomahawk	3,994	13,017
Grumman F-14A	899	38,257	**Ships**		
Hughes AH-64	524	7,327	CG-47 (DDG-47)	30	28,766
McDonnell Douglas C-17A	210-225	39,754	CVN-72/73	2	7,136
McDonnell Douglas F-15	1,376	38,095	DDG-51	49	14,911
McDonnell Douglas F-18	1,050	39,942	FFG-7	58	9,858
Rockwell International B-1B	100	28,302	SSN-688	64	31,043
Sikorsky UH-60A	1,107	7,314	Trident II Sub	20	15,535
Missiles			**Vehicles**		
AMRAAM	24,504	10,831	FAASV, M992	1,464	11,322
Patriot	6,331	11,862	M-1	7,058	20,050
Peacekeeper	223	21,516			

Strategic Nuclear Armaments: U.S. and USSR

Source: International Institute for Strategic Services, London, England

United States

		Range[2] (km)	Estimated warhead yield[3]	Deployed (July 1984)
Land-based missiles[1]				
ICBM	Titan 2	15,000	9 MT	37
	Minuteman 2	11,300	1-2 MT	450
	Minuteman 3	13,000	3x170 KT	550
Sea-based missiles				
SLBM (nuclear subs)	Poseidon C3	4,600	10x50 KT	304
	Trident C4	7,400	8x100 KT	288

Soviet Union

		Range[2] (km)	Estimated warhead yield[3]	Deployed (July 1984)
Land-based missiles[1]				
ICBM	SS-11 Sego	10,500	1 MT[4]	520
	SS-13 Savage	10,000	1x750 KT	60
	SS-17	10,000	4x750 KT[5]	150
	SS-18	10,000	1x20 MT[6]	308
	SS-19	10,000	66x550 KT	360
Sea-based missiles				
SLBM (nuclear subs)	SS-N-5-Serb	1,400	1x1 MT	45
	SS-N-6-Sawfly	3,000	1x1 MT[7]	368
	SS-N-8	7,800	1x1 MT	292
	SS-NX-17	3,900	1x1 MT	12
	SS-N-18	6,500	7x200 KT MIRV	224
	SS-NX-20	8,300	12 MIRV	40

		Range[9] (km)	Weapons load (lb)	Deployed (July 1984)
Aircraft[8]				
Long-range	B-52G	12,000	70,000	151
	B-52H	16,000	70,000	90
Medium-range	FB-111A	4,700	37,500	56
Strike air-craft:	F-4-E	2,200	16,000	(96)[10]
land-based	F-111E/F	4,700	28,000	(150)[10]
Strike air-craft:	A-6E	3,200	18,000	(60)[10]
carrier-based	A-7E	2,800	20,000	(144)[10]

	Range[9] (km)	Weapons load (lb)	Deployed (July 1984)
Aircraft[8]			
Tu-95 Bear	12,800	40,000	100
Mya-4 Bison	11,200	20,000	43
Tu-16 Badger	4,800	20,000	410
Tu22-Blinder	4,000	12,000	160
Tu22M-26 Backfire	8,000	17,500	235
Su-7 Fitter A	1,400	5,500	130
MiG-21 Fishbed L	1,100	2,000	160
MiG-27 Flogger D S	1,400	7,500	730
Su-17 Fitter D/H	1,800	11,000	850
Su-24 Foncer	4,000	8,000	630
MIC-23 Flogger B/C	3,380	44,000	1,250

(1) ICBM = intercontinental ballistic missile; SLBM = submarine-launched ballistic missile. (2) Operation range depends upon the payload carried; use of maximum payload may reduce missile range by up to 25%. (3) MT = megaton range = 1,000,000 tons of TNT equivalent or over; KT = kiloton range = 1,000 tons of TNT equivalent or more, but less than 1 MT. (4) Some SS-11 missiles carry 3x100 KT warheads. (5) Some SS-17 carry 1x6 MT warheads. (6) Three SS-18 warhead variants: 1x20 MT, 8x900KT. (7) SS-N-6, 1x1 MT or 2x200 KT MIRV warheads. (8) All aircraft listed are dual-capable and many, especially in the categories of strike aircraft, would be more likely to carry conventional than nuclear weapons. (9) Theoretical maximum range, with internal fuel only, at optimum altitude and speed. Ranges for strike aircraft assume no weapons load. Especially in the case of strike aircraft, therefore, range falls sharply for flights at lower altitude, at higher speed, or with full weapons load. (10) Figures in parentheses are estimates of Europe-based systems only.

World Arms Exporters, 1980

Source: U.S. Arms Control and Disarmament Agency, *World Military Expenditures and Arms Transfers 1971-1980* (1983).

Country	Total arms exports ($000,000)	Arms exports as % of total exports	% of total world arms exports	Country	Total arms exports ($000,000)	Arms exports as % of total exports	% of total world arms exports
U.S.S.R.	8,800	11.5	33.7	South Korea	250	1.4	1.0
United States	6,600	3.0	25.2	China	220	1.1	0.8
France	2,900	2.5	11.1	North Korea	190	6.1[1]	0.7
United Kingdom	1,800	1.6	6.9	Netherlands, The	180	0.2	0.7
West Germany	1,300	0.7	5.0	Saudi Arabia	170	0.2	0.7
Czechoslovakia	700	4.4	2.7	Turkey	150	5.4	0.6
Italy	650	0.8	2.5	Belgium	140	0.2	0.5
Yugoslavia	340	2.8[1]	1.3	Israel	140	2.5	0.5
Poland	320	1.9	1.2	Romania	130	0.7	0.5
Switzerland	290	1.0	1.1	Brazil	110	0.5	0.4

(1) 1979.

Casualties in Principal Wars of the U.S.

Data on Revolutionary War casualties is from **The Toll of Independence**, Howard H. Peckham, ed., U. of Chicago Press, 1974. Data prior to World War I are based on incomplete records in many cases. Casualty data are confined to dead and wounded personnel and therefore exclude personnel captured or missing in action who were subsequently returned to military control. Dash (—) indicates information is not available.

Wars	Branch of service	Number serving	Casualties Battle deaths	Casualties Other deaths	Casualties Wounds not mortal[8]	Casualties Total
Revolutionary War	**Total**	—	**6,824**	**18,500**	**8,445**	**33,769**
1775-1783	Army	184,000	5,992	—	7,988	13,980
	Navy &	to	—	—	—	—
	Marines	250,000	832	—	457	1,289
War of 1812	**Total**	**°286,730**	**2,260**	—	**4,505**	**6,765**
1812-1815	Army	—	1,950	—	4,000	5,950
	Navy	—	265	—	439	704
	Marines	—	45	—	66	111
Mexican War	**Total**	**°78,718**	**1,733**	**11,550**	**4,152**	**17,435**
1846-1848	Army	—	1,721	11,500	4,102	17,373
	Navy	—	1	—	3	4
	Marines	—	11	—	47	58
Civil War	**Total**	**°2,213,363**	**140,414**	**224,097**	**281,881**	**646,392**
(Union forces only)	Army	2,128,948	138,154	221,374	280,040	639,568
1861-1865	Navy	—	2,112	2,411	1,710	6,233
	Marines	84,415	148	312	131	591
Confederate forces	**Total**	—	**74,524**	**59,297**	—	**133,821**
(estimate)[1]	Army	600,000	—	—	—	—
1863-1866	Navy	to	—	—	—	—
	Marines	1,500,000	—	—	—	—
Spanish-American	**Total**	**306,760**	**385**	**2,061**	**1,662**	**4,108**
War	Army[4]	280,564	369	2,061	1,594	4,024
1898	Navy	22,875	10	0	47	57
	Marines	3,321	6	0	21	27
World War I	**Total**	**4,743,826**	**53,513**	**63,195**	**204,002**	**320,710**
April 6, 1917-	Army[5]	4,057,101	50,510	55,868	193,663	300,041
Nov. 11, 1918	Navy	599,051	431	6,856	819	8,106
	Marines	78,839	2,461	390	9,520	12,371
	Coast Gd.	8,835	111	81	—	192
World War II	**Total**	**16,353,659**	**292,131**	**115,185**	**670,846**	**1,078,162**
Dec. 7, 1941-	Army[6]	11,260,000	234,874	83,400	565,861	884,135
Dec. 31, 1946[2]	Navy[7]	4,183,466	36,950	25,664	37,778	100,392
	Marines	669,100	19,733	4,778	67,207	91,718
	Coast Gd.	241,093	574	1,343	—	1,917
Korean War	**Total**	**5,764,143**	**33,629**	**20,617**	**103,284**	**157,530**
June 25, 1950-	Army	2,834,000	27,704	9,429	77,596	114,729
July 27, 1953[3]	Navy	1,177,000	458	4,043	1,576	6,077
	Marines	424,000	4,267	1,261	23,744	29,272
	Air Force	1,285,000	1,200	5,884	368	7,452
	Coast Gd.	44,143	—	—	—	—
Vietnam (preliminary)[10]	**Total**	**8,744,000**	**47,318**	**10,694**	**153,303**	**211,315**
Aug. 4, 1964-	Army	4,368,000	30,899	7,267	96,802	134,968
Jan. 27, 1973	Navy	1,842,000	1,605	912	4,178	6,695
	Marines	794,000	13,071	1,747	51,392	66,210
	Air Force	1,740,000	1,738	766	931	3,435
	Coast Gd.	—	5	2	—	7

(1) Authoritative statistics for the Confederate Forces are not available. An estimated 26,000-31,000 Confederate personnel died in Union prisons.

(2) Data are for the period Dec. 1, 1941 through Dec. 31, 1946 when hostilities were officially terminated by Presidential Proclamation, but few battle deaths or wounds not mortal were incurred after the Japanese acceptance of Allied peace terms on Aug. 14, 1945. Numbers serving from Dec. 1, 1941-Aug. 31, 1945 were: Total—14,903,213; Army—10,420,000; Navy—3,883,520; and Marine Corps—599,693.

(3) Tentative final data based upon information available as of Sept. 30, 1954, at which time 24 persons were still carried as missing in action.

(4) Number serving covers the period April 21-Aug. 13, 1898, while dead and wounded data are for the period May 1-Aug. 31, 1898. Active hostilities ceased on Aug. 13, 1898, but ratifications of the treaty of peace were not exchanged between the United States and Spain until April 11, 1899.

(5) Includes Air Service Battle deaths and wounds not mortal include casualties suffered by American forces in Northern Russia to Aug. 25, 1919 and in Siberia to April 1, 1920. Other deaths covered the period April 1, 1917-Dec. 31, 1918.

(6) Includes Army Air Forces.

(7) Battle deaths and wounds not mortal include casualties incurred in Oct. 1941 due to hostile action.

(8) Marine Corps data for World War II, the Spanish-American War and prior wars represent the number of individuals wounded, whereas all other data in this column represent the total number (incidence) of wounds.

(9) As reported by the Commissioner of Pensions in his Annual Report for Fiscal Year 1903.

(10) Number serving covers the period Aug. 4 1964-Jan. 27, 1973 (date of ceasefire). Number of casualties incurred in connection with the conflict in Vietnam from Jan. 1, 1961-Sept. 30, 1977. Includes casualties incurred in Mayaguez Incident. Wounds not mortal exclude 150,375 persons not requiring hospital care.

Nuclear Arms Treaties and Negotiations: An Historical Overview

Aug. 4, 1963—Nuclear Test Ban Treaty, signed in Moscow by the U.S., USSR, and Great Britain, prohibited testing of nuclear weapons in space, above ground, and under water.

1966—Outer Space Treaty banned the introduction of nuclear weapons into space.

1968—Non-proliferation of Nuclear Weapons Treaty, with U.S., USSR, and Great Britain as major signers, limited the spread of military nuclear technology by agreement not to assist nonnuclear nations in getting or making nuclear weapons.

March 26, 1972—SALT I (Strategic Arms Limitations Talks) agreement, in negotiation since Nov. 17, 1969, signed in Moscow by U.S. and USSR. In the area of defensive nuclear weapons, the treaty limited antiballistic missiles to 2 sites of 100 antiballistic missile launchers in each country (amended in 1974 to one site in each country). The treaty also imposed a 5-year freeze on testing and deployment of intercontinental ballistic missiles and submarine-launched ballistic missiles (U.S.: 1,054 ICBMs and 656 SLBMs; USSR: 1,400 ICBMs and 950 SLBMs). An interim short-term agreement putting a ceiling on numbers of offensive nuclear weapons was also signed. SALT I was in effect until Oct. 3, 1977.

July 3, 1974—Protocol on antiballistic missile systems and a treaty and protocol on limiting underground testing of nuclear weapons was signed by U.S. and USSR in Moscow.

Nov. 24, 1974—Vladivostok Agreement announced establishing the framework for a more comprehensive agreement on offensive nuclear arms, setting the guidelines for a second SALT treaty.

Sept. 1977—U.S. and USSR agreed to continue to abide by SALT I, despite its expiration date.

June 18, 1979—SALT II, signed in Vienna by the U.S. and USSR, constrained offensive nuclear weapons, limiting each side to 2,400 missile launchers and heavy bombers with that ceiling to apply until Jan. 1, 1985. The treaty also set a combined total of 1,320 ICBMs and SLBMs with multiple warheads on each side. Although approved by the U.S. Senate Foreign Relations Committee, the treaty never reached the Senate floor because Pres. Jimmy Carter withdrew his support for the treaty following the December 1979 invasion of Afghanistan by Soviet troops.

Nov. 18, 1981—U.S. Pres. Ronald Reagan proposed his controversial "zero option" to cancel deployment of new U.S. intermediate-range missiles in Western Europe in return for Soviet dismantling of comparable forces (600 SS-20, SS-4, and SS-5 missiles already stationed in the European part of its territory).

Nov. 30, 1981—Geneva talks on limiting intermediate nuclear forces based in and around Europe began.

May 9, 1982—U.S. Pres. Ronald Reagan, at Eureka College, proposed 2-step plan for strategic arms reductions and announced that he had proposed to the USSR that START (Strategic Arms Reduction Talks) begin in June. In the first phase of the plan, both the U.S. and USSR would be allowed 850 ballistic missiles, down from 2,350 for the USSR and 1,700 for the U.S. He placed a ceiling of 5,000 on the number of warheads on the missiles, a reduction from about 7,500 on both sides. Half of the warheads could be mounted on land-based missiles (ICBMs). In the second phase, the USSR would eliminate its 3-to-1 advantage in ballistic missile throw weight.

May 18, 1982—Soviet Pres. Leonid Brezhnev rejected Reagan's plan as one-sided, but responded positively to the call for arms reduction talks. He proposed an immediate freeze on nuclear weapons and the modernization of present systems, and proposed that the West agree to a comparable freeze pending completion of an accord. He said that the USSR would stop deployment of mobile medium-range missiles within the range of Europe. The U.S., however, rejected this offer, stating that the USSR already had 300 SS-20s west of the Urals, while it had no similar arms in Europe.

June 29, 1982—START (Strategic Arms Reduction Talks) began in Geneva.

(*For events after Nov. 1, 1983, see Index and Chronology of the Year's Events.*)

U.S. Defense Spending to 1986: Budget Authority vs. Outlays

Source: Office of Management & Budget

(millions of dollars)

Major missions and programs	Budget authority					Outlays				
	1982 actual	1983 estimate	1984 estimate	1985 estimate	1986 estimate	1982 actual	1983 estimate	1984 estimate	1985 estimate	1986 estimate
Department of Defense—Military										
Military personnel.	42,875	45,485	47,927	49,741	51,165	42,341	45,308	47,676	49,548	50,988
Retired military personnel:										
Existing law.	14,986	16,155	17,088	18,080	19,306	14,938	16,130	17,052	18,044	19,267
Proposed legislation	...	...	-282	-667	-830	...	...	-282	-667	-830
Operation and maintenance. .	62,466	66,259	74,002	82,366	90,657	59,674	64,643	71,649	79,080	87,260
Procurement	64,462	80,303	94,088	119,647	136,383	43,271	55,210	68,238	85,905	103,659
Research development test and evaluation	20,060	22,805	29,622	32,206	34,145	17,729	21,430	26,332	29,959	32,604
Military construction	4,916	4,512	5,823	9,901	10,331	2,922	4,124	4,393	5,504	7,619
Family housing	2,203	2,532	2,833	3,464	3,877	1,993	2,358	2,635	3,011	3,375
Revolving funds and other. . .	2,516	932	2,822	1,767	2,287	716	153	1,044	1,804	1,824
Offsetting receipts	-733	-532	-544	-821	-844	-733	-532	-544	-821	-844
Allowance for civilian pay raises	...	...	...	1,420	3,042	...	...	...	1,320	2,974
Allowance for military pay raises and benefits.	...	...	...	4,470	6,862	...	...	...	4,470	6,862
Other legislation	...	...	22	25	18	...	...	22	25	18
Supplemental for later transmittal	...	1,608	...	...	...	...	232	680	466	160
Proposed rescissions for later transmittal	...	-650	...	...	...	...	-124	-295	-148	-38
Atomic energy defense activities	4,737	5,700	6,778	8,037	7,962	4,309	5,471	6,422	7,425	7,714
Defense-related activities										
Existing law	219	371	429	583	738	263	370	387	534	694
Proposed legislation	...	...	-100	-188	-270	...	...	-100	-188	-270
Reductions for offsetting receipts.	-4	-4	-4	-4	-4	-4	-4	-4	-4	-4
Total	218,704	245,474	280,503	330,028	364,826	187,418	214,769	245,305	285,268	323,035

ASSOCIATIONS AND SOCIETIES

Source: World Almanac questionnaire

Arranged according to **key words** in titles. Founding year of organization in parentheses; last figure after ZIP code indicates membership.

Aaron Burr Assn. (1946), R.D. #1, Route 33, Box 429, Hightstown-Freehold, Hightstown, NJ 08520; 500+.

Abortion Federation, Natl. (1977), 900 Pennsylvania Ave. SE, Washington, DC 20003; 270 institutions.

Abortion Rights Action League, Natl. (1969), 1424 K St. NW, Wash., DC 20005; 150,000.

Accountants, Amer. Institute of Certified Public (1887), 1211 Ave. of the Americas, N.Y., NY 10036; 190,000.

Accountants, Natl. Assn. of (1919), 919 Third Ave., N.Y., NY 10022; 95,000.

Accountants, Natl. Soc. of for Cooperatives (1935), 6320 Augusta Dr., Springfield, VA 22150; 2,300.

Accountants, Natl. Society of Public (1945), 1010 N. Fairfax St., Alexandria, VA 22314.

Acoustical Society of America (1929), 335 E. 45 St., N.Y., NY 10017; 5,700.

Actors' Equity Assn. (1913), 165 W. 46 St., N.Y., NY 10036; 34,000.

Actors' Fund of America (1882), 1501 Broadway, N.Y., NY 10036; 3,500.

Actuaries, American Academy of (1965), 1835 K St. NW, Wash., DC 20006; 6,400.

Actuaries, Society of (1949), 500 Park Blvd., Itasca, IL 60143; 9,000.

Adirondack Mountain Club (1922), 172 Ridge St., Glens Falls, NY 12801; 8,000.

Adult Education Assn. of the U.S.A. (1951), 810 18th St. NW, Wash., DC 20006; 3,000.

Advertisers, Assn. of Natl. (1910), 155 E. 44th St., N.Y., NY 10017; 500 cos.

Advertising Agencies, Amer. Assn. of (1917), 666 Third Ave., N.Y., NY 10017; 600 agencies.

Aeronautic Assn. of USA, Inc. (1922), 821 15th St. NW, Wash., DC 20005; 4,095.

Aeronautics and Astronautics, Amer. Institute of (1932), 1633 Broadway, N.Y., NY 10019; 27,152.

Aerospace Industries Assn. of America (1919), 1725 De Sales St. NW, Wash., DC 20036; 59 cos.

Aerospace Medical Assn. (1929), Washington Natl. Airport, Wash., DC 20001; 4,000.

Afro-American Life and History, Assn. for the Study of (1915), 1401 14th St. NW, Wash., DC 20005; 25,000.

Aging Assn., Amer. (1970), Univ. of Nebraska Medical Center, 42d & Dewey Ave., Omaha, NE 68105; 500.

Agnostics, Soc. of Evangelical (1975), Box 515, Auberry, CA 93602; 800+.

Agricultural Chemicals Assn., Natl. (1933), 1155 15th St. NW, Wash., DC 20005; 125 cos.

Agricultural Economics Assn., Amer. (1910), Dept. of Economics, Iowa State Univ., Ames, IA 50011; 4,750.

Agricultural Engineers, Amer. Society of (1907), 2950 Niles Rd., St. Joseph, MI 49085; 11,400.

Agricultural History Society (1919), 500-12th St., SW, Wash., DC 20250; 1,500.

Agronomy, Amer. Society of (1907), 677 S. Segoe Rd., Madison, WI 53711; 12,500.

Aircraft Assn., Experimental (1953), 11311 W. Forest Home Ave., Franklin, WI 53132; 70,000.

Aircraft Owners and Pilots Assn. (1939), 421 Aviation Way, Frederick, MD 21701; 265,000.

Air Force Assn. (1946), 1501 Lee Hwy., Arlington, VA 22209-1198; 200,000.

Air Force Sergeants Assn. (1961), P.O. Box 31050, Temple Hills, MD 20748.

Air Line Employees Assn. (1952), 5600 S. Central Ave., Chicago, IL 60638; 10,000.

Air Line Pilots Assn. (1931), 1625 Massachusetts Ave. NW, Wash., DC 20036; 32,000.

Air Pollution Control Assn. (1906), P.O. Box 2861, Pittsburgh, PA 15230; 7,600.

Air Transport Assn. of America (1936), 1709 New York Ave. NW, Wash., DC 20006; 33 air carriers.

Alcohol Problems, Amer. Council on (1895), 119 Constitution Ave. NE, Wash., DC 20002; 4,000.

Alcoholics Anonymous (1935), 468 Park Ave. So., N.Y., NY 10016; 1,000,000.

Alcoholism, Natl. Council on (1944), 733 Third Ave., N.Y., NY 10017; 220 affiliates.

Allergy and Immunology, Amer. Academy of (1943), 611 E. Wells St., Milwaukee, WI 53202; 3,600.

Alpine Club, Amer. (1902), 113 E. 90th St., N.Y., NY 10028.

Altrusa Intl. (1917), 8 S. Michigan Ave., Chicago, IL 60603.

Amer. Feder. of Labor & Congress of Industrial Organizations (AFL-CIO) (1955, by merging **Amer. Feder. of Labor** estab. 1881 and **Congress of Industrial Organizations** estab. 1935), 815 16th St. NW, Wash., DC 20006; 15,000,000.

Amer. Field Service (1947), 313 E. 43d St., N.Y., NY 10017; 100,000+.

Amer. Indian Affairs, Assn. on (1923), 432 Park Ave. So., N.Y., NY, 10016; 50,000.

American Legion, The (1919), 700 N. Pennsylvania St., Indianapolis, IN 46204; 2,591,789. **American Legion Auxiliary** (1921), 777 N. Meridian St., Indianapolis, IN 46204; 950,000.

Amer. States, Organization of (1948), General Secretariat, Wash., DC 20006; 28 countries.

Amer. Veterans of World War II, Korea & Vietnam (AMVETS), (1944), 4647 Forbes Blvd., Lanham, MD 20706; 200,000. **AMVETS Auxiliary** (1947), Saco Rd., Old Orchard Beach, ME 04064; 60,000.

Amnesty Intl. (1961), 304 W. 58th St., N.Y., NY 10019.

Amputation Foundation, Natl. (1919), 12-45 150th St., Whitestone, NY 11357; 2,000.

Andersonville, Natl. Soc. of (1976), 10 Church St., Andersonville, GA 31711.

Animal Protection Institute of America (1968), 5894 South Land Park Dr., Sacramento, CA 95822; 150,000.

Animal Welfare Institute (1951), P.O. Box 3650, Wash., DC 20007; 8,000.

Animals, Amer. Society for Prevention of Cruelty to (ASPCA) (1866), 441 E. 92d St., N.Y., NY 10028; 75,000.

Animals, Friends of (1957), 11 W. 60th St., N.Y., NY 10023.

Animals, The Fund for (1967), 140 W. 57th St., N.Y., NY 10019; 172,000.

Anthropological Assn., Amer. (1902), 1703 New Hampshire Ave. NW, Wash., DC 20009; 9,000.

Antiquarian Society, Amer. (1812), 185 Salisbury St., Worcester, MA 01609; 425.

Anti-Vivisection Society, Amer. (1883), Suite 204, Noble Plaza, 801 Old York Rd., Jenkintown, PA 19046; 10,000+.

Appalachian Mountain Club (1876), 5 Joy St., Boston, MA 02108; 27,500.

Appalachian Trail Conference (1925), Box 807, Harpers Ferry, WV 25425; 18,000.

Appraisers, Amer. Society of (1936), Dulles Intl Airport, Box 17265, Wash., DC 20041; 5,000.

Arab Americans, Natl. Assn. of (1972), Suite 211, 1825 Connecticut Ave. NW, Wash., DC 20009; 3,000.

Arbitration Assn., Amer. (1926), 140 W. 51st St., N.Y., NY 10020; 5,000.

Arboriculture, Intl. Society of (1924), 5 Lincoln Sq., Urbana IL 61801; 4,000.

Archaeological Institute of America (1879), P.O. Box 1901 Kenmore Station, Boston, MA 02215; 9,700.

Archaeology, Institute of Nautical (1973), Texas A & M University, Drawer AU, College Station, TX 77840; 450.

Archery Assn., Natl. (1879), 1750 E. Boulder St., Colorado Springs, CO 80909; 4,150.

Architects, Amer. Institute of (1857), 1735 New York Ave NW, Wash., DC 20006; 41,000.

Architectural Historians, Society of (1940), 1700 Walnut St., Phila., PA 19103; 4,200.

Archivists, Society of Amer. (1936), 330 S. Wells St., Suite 810, Chicago, IL 60606; 4,000.

Armed Forces Communications and Electronics Assn. (1946), 5641 Burke Centre Pkwy., Burke, VA 22015; 23,000.

Army, Assn. of the United States (1950), 2425 Wilson Blvd., Arlington, VA 22201; 156,714.

Arts, Amer. Council for the (1960), 570 7th Ave., N.Y., NY 10018; 1,200.

Arts, Amer. Federation of (1909), 41 E. 65th St., N.Y., NY 10021; 1,400.

Arts, Associated Councils of the (1969), 570 Seventh Ave. N.Y., NY 10018; 2,000.

Arts, Natl. Endowment for the (1965), 2401 E. St. NW, Wash., DC 20506.

Arts, Action & Consciousness, Comprehensive (1959), P.O. Box 188, Monticello, GA 31064.

Arts and Letters, Amer. Academy and Institute of (1898), 633 W. 155th St., N.Y., NY 10032; 248.

Arts and Letters, Natl. Society of (1944), 9915 Litzsinger Rd., St. Louis, MO 63124; 1,600.

Arts & Psychology, Assn. for the (1976), P.O. Box 160371, Sacramento, CA 95816.

Arts & Sciences, Amer. Academy of (1780), Norton's Woods, 136 Irving St., Cambridge, MA 02138; 3,247.

Assistance League, Natl. (1935), 5627 Fernwood Ave., Los Angeles, CA 90028; 15,000+.

Astrologers, Amer. Federation of (1938), 6535 S. Rural Rd., Tempe, AZ 85282; 4,500+.

Astronautical Society, Amer. (1953), 6060 Duke St., Alexandria, VA 22304; I,000.

Astronomical Society, Amer. (1899), 1816 Jefferson Pl. NW, Wash., DC 20036; 3,900.

Atheist Assn. (1925), 3024 5th Ave., San Diego, CA 92103.

Atheists, Amer. (1963), 2210 Hancock Dr., Austin, TX 78731; 100,000 families.

Athletic Associations, Natl. Federation of State H. S. (1920), 11724 Plaza Circle, Box 20626, Kansas City, MO 64195.

Athletic Union of the U.S., Amateur (1888), 3400 W. 86th St., Indianapolis, IN 46268.

Athletics Congress/USA, The (1979), P.O. Box 120, 155 W. Washington St., Suite 220, Indianapolis, IN 46206; 250,000.

Auctioneers Assn., Natl. (1949), 8880 Ballentine, Overland Park, KS 66214; 6,300.

Audubon Society, Natl. (1905), 950 Third Ave., N.Y., NY 10022; 400,000.

Authors and Composers, Amer. Guild of (1931), 40 W. 57th St., N.Y., NY 10019; 3,000.

Authors League of America (1912), 234 W. 44th St., N.Y., NY 10036; 12,586.

Autistic Children, Natl. Society for, 1234 Massachusetts Ave. NW, Wash., DC 20005; 5,600.

Autograph Collectors Club, Universal. (1965), P.O. Box 467, Rockville Centre, NY 11571-0467; 1,875.

Automobile Assn., Amer. (1902), 8111 Gatehouse Rd., Falls Church, VA 22047; 24 million+.

Automobile Club, Natl. (1924), One Market Plaza, San Francisco, CA 94105; 323,000.

Automobile Club of America, Antique (1935), 501 W. Governor Rd., Hershey, PA 17033; 47,000.

Automobile Dealers Assn., Natl. (1917), 8400 Westpark Dr., McLean, VA 22102; 18,000.

Automobile License Plate Collectors' Assn. (1954), P.O. Box 712, Weston, W. VA 26452; 1,700.

Automotive Booster Clubs Intl. (1921), 5105 Tollview Dr., Rolling Meadows, IL 60008; 3,100.

Automotive Hall of Fame (1939), P.O. Box 1742, Midland, MI 48640; 3,000.

Automotive Organization Team (1939), P.O. Box 1742, Midland, MI 48640; 3,000.

B-24 Liberator Club, Intl. (1968), P.O. Box 841, San Diego, CA 92112; 6,000.

Backpackers' Assn., Intl. (1973), P.O. Box 85, Lincoln Center, ME 04458; 22,861.

Badminton Assn., U.S. (1937), P.O. Box 237, Swartz Creek, MI 48473; 2,500.

Bald-Headed Men of America (1973), 4006 Arendell St., Morehead City, N.C. 28557; 9,500.

Ballplayers of Amer., Assn. of Professional (1924), 12062 Valley View St., #211, Garden Grove, CA 92645; 10,000.

Bankers Assn., Amer. (1875), 1120 Connecticut Ave. NW, Wash., DC 20036; 13,200 banks.

Bankers Assn. of America, Independent (1930), 1625 Massachusetts Ave. NW, Suite 202, Wash. DC 20036; 7,000 banks.

Banks, Natl. Assn. of Mutual Savings (1920), 200 Park Ave., N.Y., NY 10166; 435 banks.

Bar Assn., Amer. (1878), 1155 E. 60th St., Chicago, IL 60637; 300,000.

Bar Assn., Federal (1920), 1815 H St. NW, Wash., DC 20006; 15,000.

Barbershop Quartet Singing in Amer., Soc. for Preservation & Encouragement of (1938), 6315 Third Ave., Kenosha, WI 53141; 38,000.

Baseball Congress, Amer. Amateur (1935), 215 E. Green, Marshall, WI 49068; 7,657 teams.

Baseball Congress, Natl. (1931), 338 S. Sycamore, Wichita, KS 67213.

Baseball Players of America, Assn. of Pro. (1924), 12062 Valley View St., Garden Grove, CA 92645.

Basketball Assn., Natl. (1946), 645 5th Ave., N.Y., NY 0022; 22 teams.

Baton Twirling Assn. of America & Abroad, Intl. (1967), Box 234, Waldwick, NJ 07463; 1,500.

Battleship Assn., Amer. (1963), P.O. Box 11247, San Diego, CA 92111; 1,500.

Beer Can Collectors of America (1970), 747 Merus Ct., Fenton, MO 63026; 4,700.

Beta Gamma Sigma (1913), 605 Old Ballas, Suite 220, St. Louis, MO 63141; 200,000.

Beta Sigma Phi (1931), P.O. Box 8500, Kansas City, MO 64114; 250,000.

Bible Society, Amer. (1816), 1865 Broadway, N.Y., NY 10023; 510,000.

Biblical Literature, Society of (1880), 2201 S. University Blvd., Denver, CO 80231; 5,000.

Bibliographical Society of America (1904), P.O. Box 397, Grand Central Sta., N.Y., NY 10163; 1,300.

Bide-A-Wee Home Assn. (1903), 410 E. 38th St., N.Y., NY 10016; 8,600.

Big Brothers/Big Sisters of America (1903), 117 S. 17th St., Suite 1200, Phila., PA 19103; 80,000.

Biological Chemists, Amer. Society of (1906), 9650 Rockville Pike, Bethesda, MD 20814.

Biological Sciences, Amer. Institute of (1947), 1401 Wilson Blvd., Arlington, VA 22209; 12,500.

Birding Assn., Amer. (1969), Box 4335, Austin, TX 78765.

Blind, Amer. Council of the (1961) 1211 Connecticut Ave. NW, Suite 506, Wash., DC 20036.

Blind, Amer. Foundation for the (1921), 15 W. 16th St., N.Y., NY 10011.

Blind, Natl. Federation of the (1940), 1629 K St., NW, Wash., DC 20006; 50,000.

Blind & Visually Handicpd., Natl. Accred. Cncl. for Agencies Serving (1967), 79 Madison Ave., N.Y., NY 10016.

Blindness, Natl. Society to Prevent (1908), 79 Madison Ave., N.Y., NY 10010.

Blindness, Research to Prevent (1960), 598 Madison Ave., N.Y., NY 10022; 3,000.

Blizzard Club, January 12th, 1888, (1940), 4827 Hillside Ave., Lincoln, NE 68506; 60.

Blue Cross Assn. (1948), 676 St. Clair, Chicago, IL 60611.

Blue Shield Plans, Natl. Assn. of (1946), 676 St. Clair, Chicago, IL 60611; 69 plans.

Blueberry Council, No. Amer. (1965), P.O. Box 166, Marmora, NJ 08223; 45 organizations.

Bluebird Society, No. Amer. (1978), 2 Countryside Ct., Silver Spring, MD 20904; 3,000+.

B'nai B'rith Intl. (1843), 1640 Rhode Island Ave. NW, Wash., DC 20036; 500,000.

Boat Assn., Amer. Power (1903), 17640 E. Nine Mile Rd., E. Detroit, MI 48021; 5,000.

Boat Club, Chris Craft Antique (1974), 217 S. Adams St., Tallahassee, FL 32302; 1,025.

Boat Owners Assn. of the U.S. (1971), 880 S. Pickett St., Alexandria, VA 22304; 115,000.

Bookplate Collectors and Designers, Amer. Soc. of (1922), 605 N. Stoneman Ave. #F, Alhambra, CA 91801; 200.

Booksellers Assn., Amer. (1900), 122 E. 42d St., N.Y., NY 10168; 6,000+.

Botanical Gardens & Arboreta, Amer. Assn. of (1971), P.O. Box 206, Swarthmore, PA 19081; 900+.

Bottle Clubs, Federation of Historical (1969), 5001 Queen Ave. N., Minneapolis, MN 55430; 120 clubs.

Bowling Congress, Amer. (1895), 5301 S. 76th St., Greendale, WI 53129; 4,500,000.

Boys' Brigades of America, United (1893), P.O. Box 8406, Baltimore, MD 21234; 200.

Boys' Clubs of America (1906), 771 First Ave., N.Y., NY 10017; 1,000,000+.

Boy Scouts of America (1910), 1325 Walnut Hill Lane, Irving, TX 75062; 4,688,956.

Brand Names Foundation (1943), 477 Madison Ave., N.Y., NY 10022; 400.

Bread for the World (1974), 32 Union Sq. E., N.Y., NY 10003; 31,000.

Brick Institute of America (1934), 1750 Old Meadow Rd., McLean, VA 22102; 100 cos.

Bridge, Tunnel and Turnpike Assn., Intl. (1932), 2120 L St., Suite 305, Wash., DC 20037; 210 agencies.

Brith Sholom (1905), 3939 Conshohocken Ave., Philadelphia, PA 19131; 6,000.

Broadcasters, Natl. Assn. of (1922), 1771 N St. NW, Wash., DC 20036; 5,000+.

Burroughs Bibliophiles, The (1960), 454 Elaine Dr., Pittsburgh, PA 15236; 254.

Bus Assn., Amer. (1926), 1025 Connecticut Ave. NW, Wash., DC 20036; 700.

Business Bureaus, Council of Better (1970), 1515 Wilson Blvd., Arlington, VA 22209.

Business Clubs, Natl. Assn. of Amer. (1922), 3315 No. Main St., High Point, NC 27262; 6,182.

Business Communication Assn., Amer. (1935), Univ. of Illinois, English Bldg., 608 S. Wright St., Urbana, IL 61801; 2,200.

Business Communicators, Intl. Assn. of (1970), 870 Market St., Suite 928, San Francisco, CA 94102; 7,000+.

Business Education Assn., Natl. (1946), 1906 Association Dr., Reston, VA 22091; 18,000.

Business Real Estate & Law Assn., Amer. (1923), Dept. of Legal Studies, Univ. of Georgia, Athens, GA 30602; 1,050+.

Business-Professional Advertising Assn. (1922), 205 E. 42d St., N.Y., NY 10017; 4,000.

Button Society, Natl. (1938), 2733 Juno Pl., Akron, OH 44313.

Byron Society, The (1971 England, 1973 in U.S.), 259 New Jersey Ave., Collingswood, NJ 08108; 300.

CARE (Cooperative For American Relief Everywhere) (1945), 660 First Ave., N.Y., NY 10016.

CORE (Congress of Racial Equality) (1942), 1916-38 Park Ave., N.Y., NY 10037.

Campers & Hikers Assn., Natl. (1954), 7172 Transit Rd., Buffalo, NY 14221; 38,000 families.

Camp Fire (1910), 4601 Madison Ave., Kansas City, MO 64112; 500,000.

Campers & Hikers Assn., Inc. (1954), 7172 Transit Rd., Buffalo, NY 14221; 30,000.

Camping Assn., Amer. (1910), Bradford Woods, Martinsville, IN 46151; 5,300.

Cancer Council, United (1963), 1803 N. Meridian St., Indianapolis, IN 46202; 32 affiliates.

Cancer Society, Amer. (1913), 777 Third Ave., N.Y., NY 10017; 200.

Canoe Assn., U.S. (1968), 617 South 94, Milwaukee, WI 53214; 1,700.

Carillonneurs in North America, Guild of (1936), 3718 Settle Rd., Cincinnati, OH 45227; 441.

Carnegie Hero Fund Commission (1904), 606 Oliver Bldg., Pittsburgh, PA 15222.

Cartoonists Society, Natl. (1946), 9 Ebony Ct., Brooklyn, NY 11229; 500.

Cat Fanciers' Assn. (1906), 1309 Allaire Ave., Ocean, NJ 07712; 555.

Catholic Bishops, Natl. Conference of/U.S. Cath. Conference (1966), 1312 Massachusetts Ave. NW, Wash., DC 20005; 300.

Catholic Charities, Natl. Conference of (1910), 1346 Connecticut Ave. NW, Wash., DC 20036; 3,000.

Catholic Church Extension Society of the U.S.A. (1905), 35 E. Wacker Dr., Chicago, IL 60601; 60,000.

Catholic Daughters of the Americas (1903), 10 W. 71st St., N.Y., NY 10023; 165,000.

Catholic Educational Assn., Natl. (1904), 1077-30th St. NW, Suite 100, Wash, DC 20007; 15,000.

Catholic Historical Soc., Amer. (1884), 263 S. Fourth St., Philadelphia, PA 19106; 760.

Catholic Library Assn. (1921), 461 W. Lancaster Ave., Haverford, PA 19041; 2,681.

Catholic Press Assn. of U.S. and Canada (1911), 119 N. Park Ave., Rockville Centre, NY 11570; 525.

Catholic Rural Life Conference, Natl. (1923), 4625 NW Beaver Dr., Des Moines, IA 50322; 2,700.

Catholic War Veterans of the U.S.A. (1935), 2 Massachusetts Ave. NW, Wash., DC 20001; 35,000.

Cemetery Assn., Amer. (1887), 5201 Leesburg Pike, Falls Church, VA 22041; 2,504.

Ceramic Society, Amer. (1899), 65 Ceramic Dr., Columbus, OH 43214; 6,000.

Cerebral Palsy Assns., United (1949), 66 E. 34th St., N.Y., NY 10016.

Chamber of Commerce of the U.S.A. (1912), 1615 H St. NW, Wash., DC 20062; 200,000.

Chamber Music Players, Amateur (1947), P.O. Box 547, Vienna, VA 22180; 4,000.

Chaplain's Assn., Intl. (1962), U.S. Box 4266, Norton Air Force Base, CA 92409; 230.

Chaplain's Assn., Natl. (1900), Gatlinburg, TN 37738; 3,782.

Chaplains Assn. of the U.S.A., Military (1930), 6216 Baltimore Ave., P.O. Box 645, Riverdale, MD 20737; 2,046.

Chemical Engineers, Amer. Inst. of (1908), 345 E. 47 St., N.Y., NY 10017; 60,000.

Chemical Manufacturers Assn. (1872), 2501 M St. NW, Wash., DC 20037; 200 cos.

Chemical Society, Amer. (1876), 1155 16th St. NW, Wash., DC 20036; 125,000.

Chemistry, Amer. Assn. for Clinical (1948), 1725 K St. NW, Wash., DC 20006; 6,247.

Chemists, Amer. Institute of (1923), 7315 Wisconsin Ave., Wash., DC 20814; 5,000.

Chemists, Amer. Soc. of Biological (1906), 9650 Rockville Pike, Bethesda, MD 20814; 5,891.

Chemists and Chemical Engineers, Assn. of Consulting (1928), 50 E. 41st St., N.Y. NY 10017; 120.

Chemists Assn., Manufacturing (1872), 1001 Connecticut Ave. NW, Wash., DC 20036.

Chess Federation, U.S. (1939), 186 Rte. 9W, New Windsor, NY 12550; 53,827.

Chess League of Amer., Correspondence (1909), Box 363, Decatur, IL 62525; 1,200.

Child Welfare League of America (1920), 67 Irving Pl., N.Y., NY 10003; 387 agencies.

Childbirth Without Pain Education Assn. (1959), 20134 Snowden, Detroit, MI 48235; 3,000.

Childhood Education Intl., Assn. for (1892), 11141 Georgia Ave., Suite 200, Wheaton, MD 20902; 11,500+.

Children of the Amer. Revolution, Natl. Society (1895), 1776 D St. NW, Wash., DC 20006; 12,000+.

Children's Aid Society (1853), 105 E. 22d St., N.Y., NY 10010.

Children's Book Council (1945), 67 Irving Pl., N.Y., NY 10003; 75 publishing houses.

Chiropractic Assn., Amer. (1963), 1916 Wilson Blvd., Arlington, VA 22201; 18,700.

Chiropractors Assn., Intl. (1926), 1901 L St. NW, Wash., DC 20036; 6,000.

Christian Culture Society (1972), P.O. Box 325, Kokomo, IN 46901; 16,009.

Christian Endeavor, Intl. Society of (1881), 1221 E. Broad St., P.O. Box 1110, Columbus, OH 43216.

Christian Laity Counseling Board (1970), 5901 Plainfield Dr., Charlotte, NC 28215; 38,000,000.

Christians and Jews, Natl. Conference of (1928), 43 W. 57th St., N.Y., NY 10019.

Church Business Administrators, Natl. Assn. of (1956), Suite 324, 7001 Grapevine Hwy., Ft. Worth, TX 76118; 782.

Churches, U.S. Conference for the World Council of (1948), 475 Riverside Dr., N.Y., NY 10115; 27 churches.

Church Women United in the U.S.A. (1941), 475 Riverside Dr., N.Y., NY 10027; 2,000.

Cincinnati, Society of the (1783), 2118 Massachusetts Ave. NW, Wash., DC 20008; 2,800.

Circulation Managers Assn., Intl. (1889), 11600 Sunrise Valley Dr., Reston, VA 22091; 1,400.

Circus Fans Assn. of America (1926), 4 Center Dr., Camp Hill, PA 17011; 2,800.

Cities, Natl. League of (1924), 1301 Pennsylvania Ave. NW, Wash., DC 20004; 15,000 cities.

Citizens Band Radio Patrol (1977), 1100 NE 125th St., N. Miami, FL 33161; 35,000.

City Management Assn., Intl. (1914), 1120 "G" St. NW, Wash., DC 20015; 7,000.

Civil Air Patrol, (1941), Maxwell AFB, AL 36112; 60,000.

Civil Engineers, Amer. Society of (1852), 345 E. 47th St., N.Y., NY 10017; 88,000.

Civil Liberties Union, Amer. (1920), 132 W. 43rd St., N.Y. NY 10036; 250,000.

Civil War Round Table of New York (1951), 820 Carleton Rd., Westfield, NJ 07090; 140.

Civitan Internatl. (1920), P.O. Box 2102, Birmingham, AL 35201; 36,100.

Classical League, Amer. (1919), Miami Univ., Oxford, OH 45056; 3,000.

Clergy, Academy of Parish (1968), 12604 Britton Dr., Cleveland, OH 44120; 500.

Clinical Pastoral Education, Assn. for (1967), 1549 Clairmont Rd., Decatur, GA 30030; 4,000.

Clinical Pathologists, Amer. Society of (1922), 2100 W. Harrison St., Chicago, IL 60612; 34,000.

Coal Association, Natl. (1917), 1130 17th St. NW, Wash. DC 20036; 200+ companies.

Collectors Assn., Amer. (1939), Box 35106, Minneapolis MN 55435; 2,908.

College Athletic Assn., Natl. Junior (1938), 12 E. Second St., P.O. Box 1586, Hutchinson, KS 67501; 1,000.

College Athletic Conference, Eastern (1938), 1311 Craigville Beach Rd., P.O. Box 3, Centerville, MA 02632; 233.

College Board, The (1900), 888 Seventh Ave., N.Y., NY 10106; 2,550 institutions.

College Music Society (1958), Regent Box 44, Univ. of Colorado, Boulder, CO 80309; 5,000.

College Physical Education Assn. for Men, Natl. (1897), 108 Cooke Hall, Univ. of Minnesota, Minneapolis, MN 55455.

College Placement Council (1956), 62 E. Highland Ave. Bethlehem, PA 18017; 2,500.

Colleges, Amer. Assn. of Community and Jr. (1920), One Dupont Circle, Wash., DC 20036; 939 institutions.

Colleges, Assn. of Amer. (1915), 1818 R St. NW, Wash., DC 20009; 653 institutions.

Colleges and Universities, Assn. of the (1973), l301 S. Noland Rd., Independence, MO 64055; 11,000+.

Collegiate Athletic Assn., Natl. (1906), 63rd St. and Nall Ave., Shawnee Mission, KS 66201; 970.

Collegiate Schools of Business, Amer. Assembly of (1916), 11500 Olive Blvd., St. Louis, MO 63141; 650 schools.

Colonial Dames of Amer. (1890), 421 E. 61 St., N.Y., NY 10021.

Colonial Dames XVII Century, Natl. Society (1915), 1300 New Hampshire Ave. NW, Wash., DC 20036; 13,500.

Colonial Wars, Society of (1893), 840 Woodbine Ave., Glendale, OH 45246; 4,300.

Commercial Law League of America (1895), 222 W. Adams St., Chicago, IL 60606; 6,000.

Commercial Travelers of America, Order of United (1888), 632 N. Park St., Columbus, OH 43215; 186,000.

Common Cause (1970), 2030 M St. NW, Wash., DC 20036.

Community Cultural Center Assoc., Amer. (1978), 19 Foothills Dr., Pompton Plains, NJ 07444; 2,000.

Composers/USA, Natl. Assn. of (1929), P.O. Box 49652, Barrington Sta., Los Angeles, CA 90049; 500.

Composers, Authors & Publishers, Amer. Society of (ASCAP) (1914), One Lincoln Plaza, N.Y., NY 10023; 24,000.

Computing Machinery, Assn. for (1947), 11 W. 42nd St., N.Y., NY 10036; 55,000.

Concrete Institute, Amer. (1904), 22400 W. Seven Mile Rd., Detroit, MI 48219; 12,971.

Conscientious Objection, Central Committee for (1948), 2208 South St., Phila., PA 19146.

Conservation Corps Alumni, Natl. Assn. of Civilian (1977), 7245 Arlington Blvd., Falls Church, VA 22042; 11,420.

Conservation Engineers, Assn. of (1961), Missouri Dept. of Conservation, P.O. Box 180, Jefferson City, MO 65101.

Conservation Foundation (1948), 1717 Massachusetts Ave. NW, Wash., DC 20036.

Constantian Society, The (1970), 123 Orr Rd., Pittsburgh, PA 15241; 500.

Construction Industry Manufacturers Assn. (1909), 111 E. Wisconsin Ave., Milwaukee, WI 53202; 165 companies.

Construction Specifications Institute (1948), 1150 17th St. NW, Wash., DC 20036; 11,500.

Consumer Credit Assn., Intl. (1912), 243 N. Lindbergh, St. Louis, MO 63141; 20,000.

Consumer Federation of America (1968), 1314 14th St. NW, Wash., DC 20005; 200+.

Consumer Interests, Amer. Council on (1953), 240 Stanley Hall, Univ. of Missouri, Columbia, MO 65211; 2,000.

Consumer Protection Institute (1970), 5901 Plainfield Dr., Charlotte, NC 28215.

Consumers League, Natl. (1899), 1522 K St. NW, Suite 406, Wash., DC 20005; 600.

Consumers Union of the U.S. (1936), 256 Washington St., Mount Vernon, NY 10553; 193,000.

Contract Bridge League, Amer. (1927), 2200 Democrat Rd., Memphis, TN 38116; 200,000.

Contract Management Assn., Natl. (1959), 6728 Old McLean Village Dr., McLean, VA 22101; 11,580.

Contractors of Amer., General (1918), 1957 E St. NW, Wash., DC 20036; 30,000.

Cooperative League of the U.S.A. (1916), 1828 L St. NW, Wash., DC 20036; 176 co-ops.

Correctional Assn., Amer. (1870), 4321 Hartwick Rd., Suite L-208, College Park, MD 20740; 13,500.

Correctional Officers, Amer. Assn. of (1977), 1474 Willow Ave., Des Plaines, IL 60016.

Cosmopolitan Intl. (1914), 7341 W. 108 Pl., Overland Park, KS 66204; 3,347.

Cotton Council of America, Natl. (1938), 1918 North Parkway, Memphis, TN 38112; 295.

Counseling and Development, Amer. Assn. for (1952), 5999 Stevenson Ave., Alexandria, VA 22304; 41,545.

Country Music Assn. (1958), P.O. Box 22299, Nashville, TN 37202; 6,300.

Creative Children and Adults, Natl. Assn. for (1974), 8080 Springvalley Dr., Cincinnati, OH 45236; 1,000.

Credit Management, Nat. Assn. of (1896), 475 Park Ave. So., N.Y., NY 10016; 45,000.

Credit Union Natl. Assn. (1934), P.O.Box 431, Madison, WI 53701; 52 leagues.

Crime and Delinquency, Natl. Council on (1907), 760 Market St., Suite 433, San Francisco, CA 94102; 2,500.

Criminology, Amer. Assn. of (1953), P.O. Box 1115, North Marshfield, MA 02339; 2,500.

Criminology, Amer. Society of (1940), 1314 Kinnear Rd., Columbus, OH 43212; 1,850.

Crop Science Society of America (1955), 677 S. Segoe Rd., Madison, WI 53711; 5,500.

Cross-Examination Debate Assn. (1971), Dept. of Speech Communication, California State Univ.-Northridge, Northridge, CA 91330; 275 institutions.

Cryptogram Assn., Amer. (1932) 1007 Montrose Ave., Laurel, MD 20707; 900.

Customs Brokers & Forwarders Assn. of Amer. (1897), 1 World Trade Center, Ste. 1109, N.Y., NY 10048; 434.

Cyprus, Sovereign Order of (1192, 1964 in U.S.), 853 Seventh Ave., N.Y., NY 10019; 464.

Dairy Council, Natl. (1915), 6300 N. River Rd., Rosemont, IL 60018; 600.

Dairy and Food Industries Supply Assn. (1919), 6245 Executive Blvd., Rockville, MD 20852.

Dairylea Cooperative (1919), 831 James St., Syracuse, NY13203; 4,000.

Daughters of the American Revolution, Natl. Society, (1890), 1776 D St. NW, Wash., DC 20006; 211,342.

Daughters of the Confederacy, United (1894), 328 N. Blvd., Richmond, VA 23220; 26,000.

Daughters of 1812, Natl. Society, U.S. (1892), 1461 Rhode Island Ave. NW, Wash., DC 20005; 4,300.

Daughters of Union Veterans of the Civil War (1885), 503 S. Walnut St., Springfield, IL 62704; 6,000.

Deaf, Alexander Graham Bell Assn. for the (1890), 3417 Volta Pl. NW, Wash., DC 20007; 5,466.

Deaf, Natl. Assn. of the (1880), 814 Thayer Ave., Silver Spring, MD 20910; 18,000.

Defense Preparedness Assn., Amer. (1919), 1700 N. Moore St., Arlington, VA 22209; 40,000.

Delta Kappa Gamma Society intl. (1929), 416 W. 12th St., Austin, TX 78701; 157,000.

Deltiologists of America (1960), 10 Felton Ave., Ridley Park, PA 19078; 1,250.

Democratic Natl. Committee (1848), 1625 Massachusetts Ave. NW, Wash., DC 20036; 378.

Democratic Socialists of Amer. (1982), 853 Broadway, Suite 801, New York, NY 10003; 7,000.

DeMolay, Intl. Council, Order of (1919), 201 E. Armour Blvd., Kansas City, MO 64111; 100,000.

Dental Assn., Amer. (1859), 211 E. Chicago Ave., Chicago, IL 60611; 145,000.

Descendants of the Colonial Clergy, Society of the (1933), 30 Leewood Rd., Wellesley, MA 02181; 1,400.

Descendants of the Signers of the Declaration of Independence (1907), 1300 Locust St., Phila., PA 19107; 937.

Descendants of Washington's Army at Valley Forge, Society of (1976), Valley Forge, PA 19481; 400.

Desert Protective Council (1953), 85-159 Ave. 66, Thermal, CA 92274; 400.

Diabetes Assn., Amer. (1940), 2 Park Ave., N.Y., NY 10016.

Dialect Society, Amer. (1889), MacMurray College, Jacksonville, IL 62650; 500.

Dietetic Assn., Amer. (1917), 430 N. Michigan Ave., Chicago, IL 60611; 50,000.

Ding-A-Ling Club, Natl. (1971), 3930-D Montclair Rd., Birmingham, AL 35213; 2,000.

Direct Mail/Marketing Assn. (1917), 6 E. 43d St., N.Y., NY 10017; 4,657 companies.

Directors Guild of America (1936), 7950 Sunset Blvd., Los Angeles, CA 90046; 7,000.

Disability Examiners, Natl. Assn. of (1964), P.O. Box 44237, Indianapolis, IN 46244; 1,800.

Disabled Amer. Veterans (1921), P.O. Box 14301, Cincinnati, OH 45214; 850,000.

Disabled Officers Assn. (1919), 927 S. Walter Reed Dr. #6, Arlington, VA 22204; 5,000.

Divorce Reform, U.S. (1961), P.O. Box 243, Kenwood, CA 95452; 6,000.

Dowsers, Amer. Society of (1961), P.O. Box 24, Danville, VT 05828; 3,000.

Dozenal Soc. of America (1944), Math Dept., Nassau Community College, Garden City, NY 11530; 120.

Dracula Society, Count (1962), 334 W. 54th St., Los Angeles, CA 90037; 1,000+.

Drug, Chemical and Allied Trades Assn. (1890), 42-40 Bell Blvd., Suite 604, Bayside, NY 11361; 500 cos.

Ducks Unlimited (1937), One Waterfowl Way at Gilmer Rd., Long Grove, IL 60047; 456,000.

Dulcimer Assn., Southern Appalachian (1972), 5313 Quincy Ave., Birmingham, AL 35208; 189.

Dutch Settlers Soc. of Albany (1924), Box 163, R.D. 2, Troy, NY 12182; 277.

Dwelling Sculpture Institute (1978), 431 Crestvale Dr., Sierra Madre, CA 91024.

Earth, Friends of the (1969), 1045 Sansome St., San Francisco, CA 94111; 31,000.

Easter Seal Society, Natl. (1919), 2023 W. Ogden Ave., Chicago, IL 60612.

Eastern Star, Order of the (1876), 1618 New Hampshire Ave. NW, Wash., DC 20009; 2,500,000.

Economic Assn., Amer. (1885), 1313 21st Ave. So., Nashville, TN 37212; 26,000.

Economic Development, Committee for (1942), 1700 K St. NW, Washington, DC 20006.

Edison Electric Institute (1933), 1111 19th St. NW, Wash., DC 20036; 185 cos.

Education, Amer. Assn. for Adult and Continuing (1982), 1201 16th St. NW, Suite 301, Wash., DC 20036; 4,000.

Education, Amer. Council on (1918), One Dupont Circle NW, Wash., DC 20036; 1,605 schools.

Education, Amer. Soc. for Engineering (1893), 11 Dupont Circle NW, Suite 200, Washington, DC 20036; 10,000.

Education, Council for Advancement & Support of (1974), 11 Dupont Circle NW, Wash., DC 20036; 2,500 schools.

Education, Council for Basic (1956), 725 15th St. NW, Wash., DC 20005; 7,000.

Education, Natl. Committee for Citizens in (1974), 410 Wilde Lake Village Green, Columbia, MD 21044; 1,400.

Education, Natl. Society for the Study of (1902), 5835 Kimbark Ave., Chicago, IL 60637; 4,500.

Education, Society for the Advancement of (1939), 1860 Broadway, N.Y., NY 10023; 3,000.

Education, Institute of Intl. (1919), 809 United Nations Plaza, N.Y., NY 10017; 500 colleges and universities.

Education Assn., Natl. (1857), 1201 16th St. NW, Wash., DC 20036; 1,700,000.

Education Society, Comparative and Intl. (1956), Univ. of S. California, Univ. Park, Los Angeles, CA 90089; 2,500.

Education of Young Children, Natl. Assn. for the (1926), 1834 Connecticut Ave. NW, Wash., DC 20009; 40,000.

Educational Broadcasters, Natl. Assn. of (1925), 1346 Connecticut Ave. NW, Wash., DC 20036; 2,500.

Educational Exchange, Council on Intl. (1947), 205 E. 42d St., N.Y., NY 10017; 162 organizations.

Educational Research Assn., Amer. (1916), 1230 17th St. NW, Wash., DC 20036; 14,000.

Electric Railroaders Assn. (1934), Grand Central Terminal, 89 E. 42d St., N.Y., NY 10017; 1,500.

Electrical and Electronics Engineers, Institute of (1884), 345 E. 47th St., N.Y., NY 10017; 234,875.

Electrical Manufacturers Assn., Natl. (1926), 2101 L St. NW, Wash., DC 20037; 550 companies.

Electrochemical Society (1902), 10 S. Main St., Pennington, NJ 08534; 5,000.

Electronic Industries Assn. (1924), 2001 Eye St. NW, Wash., DC 20006; 1,000.

Electronics, Sales & Service Dealers Assn., Natl. (1973), 2708 W. Berry, Ft. Worth, TX 76109; 1,500.

Electronics Technicians, Intl. Society of Certified (1965), 2708 W. Berry, Ft. Worth, TX 76109; 950.

Electroplaters' Society, Amer. (1909), 1201 Louisiana Ave., Winter Park, FL 32789; 8,695.

Elks of the U.S.A., Benevolent and Protective Order of (1868), 2750 N. Lake View Ave., Chicago, IL 60614; 1,630,000.

Energy, Intl. Assn. for Hydrogen (1974), P.O. Box 24866, Coral Gables, FL 33124; 1,500.

Engine and Boat Manufacturers, Natl. Assn. of (1904), 666 Third Ave., N.Y., NY 10017; 435 firms.

Engineering, Natl. Academy of (1964), 2101 Constitution Ave. NW, Wash., DC 20418; 1,107.

Engineering, Soc. for the Advancement of Material & Process (1944), 843 W. Glentana, P.O. Box 2459, Covina, CA 91722; 4,800.

Engineering Societies, Amer. Assn. of (1979), 345 E. 47th St., N.Y., NY 10017; 38 societies.

Engineering Society of N. America, Illuminating (1907), 345 E. 47th St., N.Y., NY 10017; 8,773.

Engineering Technicians, Amer. Society of Certified (1964), 10401 Holmes Rd., Kansas City, MO 64131; 5,000.

Engineering Trustees, United (1904), 345 E. 47th St., N.Y., NY 10017.

Engineers, Amer. Inst. of Chemical (1908), 345 E. 47th St., N.Y., N.Y. 10017; 55,000.

Engineers, Amer. Society of Lubrication (1944), 838 Busse Hwy., Park Ridge, IL 60068; 3,200.

Engineers, Amer. Soc. of Plumbing (1964), 15233 Ventura Blvd., #811, Sherman Oaks, CA 91403; 4,500.

Engineers, Assn. of Energy (1977), 4025 Pleasantdale Rd., Suite 340, Atlanta, GA 30340; 5,000.

Engineers, Inst. of Industrial (1948), 25 Technology Park, Atlanta, GA 30092; 43,000.

Engineers, Natl. Society of Professional (1934), 2029 K St. NW, Wash., DC 20006; 80,000.

Engineers, Institute of Transportation (1930), 525 School St. SW, Suite 410, Wash., DC 20024; 6,500.

Engineers, Soc. of Logistics (1966), 303 Williams Ave., Suite 922, Huntsville, AL 35801; 6,300.

Engineers, Soc. of Manufacturing (1932), P.O. Box 930, Dearborn, MI 48121; 72,000.

English Assn., College (1939), c/o John Joyce, Nazareth College, 4245 East Ave., Rochester, NY 14610; 2,000.

English-Speaking Union of the U.S. (1921), 16 E. 69th St., N.Y., NY 10021; 30,000.

Entomological Society of America (1889), 4603 Calvert Rd., College Park, MD 20740; 8,500.

Epigraphic Society, Inc., The (1974), 6625 Bamburgh Dr., San Diego, CA 92117; 1,050.

Esperanto League for North America (1952), P.O. Box 1129, El Cerrito, CA 94530; 700.

Euthanasia Foundation, Amer. (1972), 95 N. Birch Rd., Ft. Lauderdale, FL 33304; 40,000.

Exchange Club, Natl. (1911), 3050 Central Ave., Toledo, OH 43606; 46,000.

Experiment in Internatl. Living (1932), Kipling Rd., Brattleboro, VT 05301; 64,000.

Fairs & Expositions, Intl. Assn. of (1919), P.O. Box 985, Springfield, MO 65801; 1,700.

Family Life, Natl. Alliance for, Inc. (1973), Ste. 4, 225 Jericho Tpk., Floral Park, NY 11001; 499.

Family Service Assn. of America (1911), 44 E. 23d St., N.Y., NY 10010; 262 agencies.

Farm Bureau Federation, Amer. (1919), 225 Touhy Ave., Park Ridge, IL 60068; 3,300,000 families.

Farmer Cooperatives, Natl. Council of (1929), 1800 Massachusetts Ave. NW, Wash., DC 20036; 121 co-ops.

Farmers of America, Future (1928), 5632 Mt. Vernon Memorial Hwy., Alexandria, VA 22309; 460,000.

Farmers Educational and Co-Operative Union of America (1902), 12025 E. 45th Ave., Denver, CO 80251; 300,000.

Fat Americans, Natl. Assn. to Aid (NAAFA) (1969), P.O. Box 43, Bellerose, NY 11426; 1,500.

Federal Employees, Natl. Federation of (1917), 1016 16th St. NW, Wash., DC 20036; 150,000.

Federal Employees Veterans Assn. (1953), P.O. Box 183, Merion Sta., PA 19066; 896.

Feminists for Life of America (1972), 1918 Upton Ave. N., Minneapolis, MN 55411.

Fencers League of America, Amateur (1893), 601 Curtis St., Albany, CA 94706; 8,000.

Film Library Assn., Educational (1943), 45 John St., N.Y., NY 10038; 1,600.

Financial Analysts Federation (1947), 1633 Broadway, N.Y., NY 10019; 15,200.

Financial Executives Institute (1931), 10 Madison Ave., P.O. Box 1938, Morristown, NJ 07960, 12,500

Financiers, Intl. Soc. of (1979), 399 Laurel St., Suite 6, San Carlos, CA 94070; 100+.

Fire Chiefs, Intl. Assn. of (1873), 1329 18th St. NW, Wash., DC 20036; 8,894.

Fire Marshals Assn. of No. America (1906), Capital Gallery, Suite 220, 600 Maryland Ave. SW, Wash., DC 20024; 1,000.

Fire Protection Assn., Natl. (1896), Batterymarch Park, Quincy MA 02269; 33,000.

Fire Protection Engineers, Society of (1950), 60 Batterymarch St., Boston, MA 02110; 3,200.

Fish Assn., Intl. Game (1939), 3000 E. Las Olas Blvd., Ft. Lauderdale, FL 33316; 25,000.

Fishes, Soc. for the Protection of Old (1967), School of Fisheries, Univ. of Washington, Seattle, WA 98195; 250.

Fishing Institute, Sport (1949), 608 13th St. NW, Wash., DC 20005; 17,000.

Fishing Tackle Manufacturers Assn., Amer. (1933), 2625 Clearbrook Dr., Arlington Heights, IL 60005; 450 organizations.

Florida Dental Hygienists' Assn., Inc. (1969), 217 S. Adams St., Tallahassee, FL 32302; 1,402.

Fluid Power Society (1959), 3333 N. Mayfair Rd., Milwaukee, WI 53222; 2,500.

Food Processing Machinery and Supplies Assn. (1885), 1828 L St. NW, Wash., DC 20036; 475 organizations.

Food Processors Assn., Natl. (1907), 1133 20th St. NW, Wash., DC 20036.

Football Assn., U.S. Touch and Flag (1976), 2705 Normandy Dr., Youngstown, OH 44511; 20,000.

Footwear Industries Assn., Amer. (1869), 1611 N. Kent St., Arlington, VA 22209; 260.

Foreign Policy Assn. (1918), 205 Loxington Ave., N.Y., NY 10016.

Foreign Relations, Council on (1921), 58 E. 68th St., N.Y., NY 10021; 2,031.

Foreign Student Affairs, Natl. Assn. for (1948), 1860 19th St. NW, Wash., DC 20009; 4,500.

Foreign Study, Amer. Institute for (1964), 102 Greenwich Ave., Greenwich, CT 06830; 300,000.

Foreign Trade Council, Inc., Natl. (1914), 100 E. 42d St., N.Y., NY 10017; 650 companies.

Forensic Sciences, Amer. Academy of (1948), 225 S. Academy Blvd., Colorado Springs, CO 80910; 2,500.

Forest Institute, Amer. (1932), 1619 Massachusetts Ave. NW, Wash., DC 20036; 60 companies.

Forest Products Assn., Natl. (1902), 1619 Massachusetts Ave. NW, Wash., DC 20036; 41.

Forest Products Research Society (1947), 2801 Marshall Ct., Madison, WI 63705; 3,280.

Foresters, Society of Amer. (1900), 5400 Grosvenor La., Bethesda, MD 20814; 21,000

Forestry Assn., Amer. (1875), 1319 18th St. NW, Wash., DC 20036; 55,000.

Fortean Organization, Intl. (1966), P.O. Box 367, Arlington, VA 22210; 2,000.

Foundrymen's Society, Amer. (1896), Golf & Wolf Rds., Des Plaines, IL 60016; 14,000+.

4-H Clubs (1901-1905), Extension Service, U.S. Dept of Agriculture, Wash., DC 20250; 5,800,000.

Franklin D. Roosevelt Philatelic Society (1963), 154 Laguna Ct., St. Augustine Shores, FL 32086; 400+.

Freedom, Young Americans for (1960), Box 1002, Woodland Rd. Sterling, VA 22170; 80,000.

Freedoms Foundation at Valley Forge (1949), Valley Forge, PA 19481; 9,000.

Friedreich's Ataxia Group in Amer. (1969), P.O. Box 11116, Oakland, CA 94611; 2,100.

French Institute (1911), 22 E. 60th St., N.Y., NY 10022.

French-Amer. Chamber of Commerce in the U.S., Inc. (1896), 1350 Ave. of the Americas, NY, NY 10019.

Friends Service Committee, Amer. (1917), 1501 Cherry St., Phila., PA 19102.

Frisbee Assn., Intl. (1967), 900 E. El Monte, San Gabriel, CA 91776; 110,000.

Funeral and Memorial Societies, Continental Assn. of (1963), 2001 S. St. NW, Suite 530, Washington, DC 20009; 900,000.

GASP (Group Against Smokers' Pollution) (1971), P.O. Box 632, College Park, MD 20740; 200 chapters.

Gamblers Anonymous (1957), 1543 W. Olympic, Suite 533, Los Angeles, CA 90015; 10,600.

Garden Club of America (1913), 598 Madison Ave., N.Y., NY 10022.

Garden Clubs, Natl. Council of State (1929), 4401 Magnolia Ave., St. Louis, MO 63110; 310,047.

Garden Clubs of America, Men's (1932), 5560 Merle Hay Rd., Johnston, IA 50323; 9,000.

Gas Appliance Manufacturers Assn. (1935), 1901 N. Ft. Myer Dr., Arlington, VA 22209; 240 companies.

Gas Assn., Amer. (1918), 1515 Wilson Blvd., Arlington, VA 22209; 300 cos.

Gay Academic Union (1973), P.O. Box 82123, San Diego, CA 92138; 1,100.

Gay Task Force, Natl. (1973), 80 Fifth Ave., Suite 1601, N.Y., NY 10011; 10,000.

Genealogical Society, Natl. (1903), 1921 Sunderland Pl. NW, Wash., DC 20036; 6,800.

Genealogical Soc. of Amer. (1888), 3300 Primrose Pl., P.O. Box 9140, Boulder, CO 80301; 14,000.

Genetic Assn., Amer. (1903), 818 18th St. NW, Wash., DC 20006; 1,600.

Geographers, Assn. of Amer. (1904), 1710 16th St. NW, Wash., DC 20009; 5,500.

Geographic Education, Natl. Council for (1914), Western Illinois Univ., Macomb, IL 61455.

Geographic Society, Natl. (1888), Washington, DC 20036; 10,600,000.

Geographical Society, Amer. (1852), 25 W. 39th St., N.Y., NY 10018; 700.

Geolinguistics, Amer. Society of (1964), Bronx Community College, 120 E. 181st St., Bronx, NY 10453; 100.

Geological Institute, Amer. (1948), 5205 Leesburg Pike, Falls Church, VA 22041; 17 societies.

Geological Society of America (1888), 3300 Penrose Pl., Boulder, CO 80301; 13,386.

Geologists, Assn. of Engineering (1963), 5313 Williamsburg Rd., Brentwood, TN 37027; 3,000.

Geologists, Amer. Assn. of Petroleum (1917), 1444 S. Boulder, Tulsa, OK 74101; 40,000.

Geophysicists, Society of Exploration (1930), P.O. Box 3098, Tulsa, OK 74101; 18,000.

George S. Patton, Jr. Historical Society (1970), 11307 Vela Dr., San Diego, CA 92126.

Geriatrics Society, Amer. (1942), 10 Columbus Circle, N.Y., NY 10019; 5,000.

Gideons Intl. (1899), 2900 Lebanon Rd., Nashville, TN 37214; 72,000.

Gifted Children, Amer. Assn. for (1946), 15 Gramercy Park, N.Y., NY 10016.

Gifted Children, Natl. Assn. for (1954), 5100 N. Edgewood Dr., St. Paul, MN 55112; 5,000.

Girls Clubs of America (1945), 205 Lexington Ave., N.Y., NY 10016.

Girl Scouts of the U.S.A. (1912), 830 Third Ave., N.Y., NY 10022; 2,888,000.

Gladiolus Council, No. Amer. (1945), 21 S. Drive, E. Brunswick, NJ 08816; 1,450.

Goat Assn., American Dairy (1904), 209 W. Main St., Spindale, NC 28160; 22,575.

Gold Star Mothers, Amer. (1928), 2128 Leroy Pl. NW, Wash., DC 20008; 6,622.

Golf Association, U.S. (1896), Golf House, Far Hills, NJ 07931; 5,200 clubs.

Goose Island Bird & Girl Watching Society (1960), 301 Arthur Ave., Park Ridge, IL 60068; 946.

Gospel Music Assn. (1964), P.O. Box 23201, Nashville, TN 37202; 3,000.

Government Finance Officers Assn. (1906), 180 N. Michigan Ave., Suite 800, Chicago, IL 60601; 9,207.

Government Funding of Social Services, Greater Wash. Organizations for (1981), 6612 Virginia View Ct. NW, Wash., DC 20816.

Governmental Research Assn. (1914), One Federal St., Boston, MA 02110; 275.

Graduate Schools in the U.S., Council of (1961), One Dupont Circle NW, Wash., DC 20036; 365 institutions.

Grandmother Clubs of America, Natl. Federation of (1938), 203 N. Wabash Ave., Chicago, IL 60601; 20,000.

Grange, Natl. (1867), 1616 H St. NW, Wash., DC 20006.

Graphic Artists, Society of Amer. (1915), 32 Union Sq., 1214, N.Y., NY 10003; 232.

Graphic Arts, Amer. Institute of (1914), 1059 Third Ave., N.Y., NY 10021; 2,200.

Gray Panthers (1970), 3635 Chestnut, Phila., PA 19104.

Greek-Amer. War Veterans in America, Natl. Legion of (1938), 739 W. 186th St., N.Y., NY 10033; 20.

Green Mountain Club, The (1910), 43 State St., Box 889, Montpelier, VT 05602; 4,000.

Grocers, Natl. Assn. of Retail (1893), 11800 Sunrise Valley Dr., Reston, VA 22091; 40,000.

Grocery Manufacturers of America (1908), 1010 Wisconsin Ave., Wash., DC 20007; 130 cos.

Guide Dog Foundation for the Blind (1946), 371 Jericho Tpke., Smithtown, NY 11787; 2,500.

Gyro Intl. (1912), 1096 Mentor Ave., Painesville, OH 44077.

HIAS (Hebrew Immigrant Aid Society) (1880), 200 Park Ave. S, N.Y., NY 10003; 12,000.

Hadassah, the Women's Zionist Organization of America (1912), 50 W. 58th St., N.Y., NY 10019; 370,000+.

Hairdressers and Cosmetologists Assn., Natl. (1921), 3510 Olive St., St. Louis, MO 63103; 58,000.

Handball Assn., U.S. (1951), 4101 Dempster St., Skokie, IL 60076; 15,000.

Handgun, Intl. Metallic Silhouette Assn. (1976), Box 1609, 1409 Benton, Idaho Falls, ID 83401.

Handicapped, Federation of the (1935), 211 W. 14th St., N.Y., NY 10011; 650.

Handicapped, Natl. Assn. of the Physically (1958), 76 Elm St., London, OH 43140; 800.

Hang Gliding Assn., U.S. (1971), 11312 1/2 Venice Blvd., Los Angeles, CA 90066; 8,000.

Health Council, Natl. (1920), 70 W. 40th St., N.Y., NY 10018.

Health Insurance Assn. of America (1957), 1750 K St. NW, Wash., DC 20006; 338 companies.

Health Insurance Institute (1956), 1850 K St. NW, Wash., DC; 325 companies.

Health, Physical Education, Recreation and Dance, Amer. Alliance for (1885), 1900 Association Dr., Reston, VA 22091.

Hearing Aid Society, Natl. (1951), 20361 Middlebelt Rd., Livonia, MI 48152; 3,600.

Hearing and Speech Action, Natl. Assn. for (1919), 814 Thayer Ave., Silver Spring, MD 20910; 12,000.

Heart Assn., Amer. (1924), 7320 Greenville Ave., Dallas TX 75231; 144,000.

Hearts, Mended (1955), 7320 Greenville Ave., Dallas TX 75231; 15,000.

Heating, Refrigerating & Air Conditioning Engineers, Amer. Soc. of (1894), 1791 Tullie Circle NE, Atlanta, GA 30329; 50,000.

Helicopter Assn. Intl. (1948), 1110 Vermont Ave. NW, Wash., DC 20005; 840 companies.

Helicopter Society, Amer. (1943), 217 N. Washington St., Alexandria VA 22314; 6,100.

Hemispheric Affairs, Council on (1975), 1900 L St. NW, Suite 201, Wash., DC 20036; 100.

High School Assns., Natl. Federation of State (1921), 11724 Plaza Circle, Kansas City, MO 64195; 51.

High Twelve Internatl. (1921), 3663 Lindell Blvd., Suite 260, St. Louis, MO 63108; 28,738.

Historians, Organization of Amer. (1907), 112 N. Bryan St., Bloomington, IN 47401; 12,000+.

Historical Assn., Amer. (1884), 400 A St. SE, Wash., DC 20003; 12,000.

Historic Preservation, Natl. Trust for (1949), 1785 Massachusetts Ave. NW, Wash., DC 20009; 125,000.

Hockey Assn. of the U.S., Amateur (1937), 2997 Broadmoor Valley Rd., Colorado Springs, CO 80906; 10,490 teams.

Holiday Institute of Yonkers (1969), Box 414, Yonkers, NY 10710.

Holy Cross of Jerusalem, Order of (1965), 853 Seventh Ave., N.Y., NY 10019; 2,019.

Home Builders, Natl. Assn. of (1942), 15th & M Sts. NW, Wash., DC 20005; 104,000+ firms.

Home Economics Assn., Amer. (1909), 2010 Massachusetts Ave. NW, Wash., DC 20036; 33,000.

Home Improvement Council, Natl. (1956), 11 E. 44th St., N.Y., NY 10017; 3,300.

Homemakers of America, Future (1945), 2010 Massachusetts Ave. NW, Wash., DC 20036; 400,000.

Homemakers Council, Natl. Extension (1936), Route 2, Box 3070, Vale, OR 97918; 500,000.

Horatio Alger Soc. (1961), 4907 Allison Dr., Lansing, MI 48910.

Horse Protection Assn., Amer. (1966), 1312 18th St. NW, Wash., DC 20036; 15,000.

Horse Show Assn. of America Ltd., Natl. (1883), One Penn Plaza, Rm. 4501, N.Y., NY 10001.

Horse Shows Assn., Amer. (1917), 598 Madison Ave., N.Y., NY 10022; 25,000.

Hospital Association, Amer. (1898), 840 N. Lake Shore Dr., Chicago, IL 60611; 5,400 institutions.

Hospital Public Relations, Amer. Society for (1965), 840 N. Lake Shore Dr., Chicago, IL 60611; 2,000.

Hotel & Motel Assn., Amer. (1910), 888 Seventh Ave., N.Y., NY 10019; 8,200 hotels & motels.

Hot Rod Assn., Natl. (1951), 10639 Riverside Dr., N. Hollywood, CA 91602; 37,500.

Humane Society of the U.S. (1954), 2100 L St. NW, Wash., DC 20037; 170,000.

Humanics Foundation, Amer. (1948), 912 Baltimore Ave., Kansas City, MO 64105; 2,000.

Humanities, Natl. Endowment for the (1965), 806 15th St. NW, Wash., DC 20506.

Human Rights and Social Justice, Americans for (1977), P.O. Box 6258, Ft. Worth, TX 76115; 2,100.

Hydrogen Energy, Intl. Assn. for (1974), McArthur Engineering Bldg., Univ. of Miami, Coral Gables, FL 33124; 2,500.

Iceland Veterans (1950), 2101 Walnut St., Phila., PA 19103; 2,000+.

Idaho, U.S.S.(BB-42) Assn. (1957), P.O. Box 11247, San Diego, CA 92111; 750.

Identification, Intl. Assn. for (1915), P.O. Box 376, New Hartford, NY l3413; 2,600.

Illustrators, Society of (1901), 128 E. 63 St., N.Y., NY 10021; 900.

Immigration Reform, Fed. for Amer. (1979), 2028 P St. NW, Wash., DC 20036.

Indian Rights Assn. (1882), 1505 Race St., Phila., PA 19102.

Industrial Democracy, League for (1905), 275 Seventh Ave., N.Y., NY 10001; 1,500.

Industrial Engineers, Amer. Institute of (1948), 25 Technology Park, Norcross, GA 30092; 35,000.

Industrial Health Foundation (1935), 34 Penn Circle West, Pittsburgh, PA 15206; l20 companies.

Industrial Security, Amer. Soc. for (1955), 1655 N. Ft. Myer Dr., Suite 1200, Arlington, VA 22209; 20,000.

Information, Freedom of, Center (1958), P.O. Box 858, Columbia, MO 65205.

Information and Image Management, Assn. for (1942), 1100 Wayne Ave., Silver Spring, MD 20910; 8,000.

Information Managers, Associated (1978), 1776 E. Jefferson St., Rockville, MD 20852; 1,000.

Information Industry Assn. (1969), 316 Pennsylvania Ave. SE, Suite 502, Wash., DC 20003; 300 companies.

Insurance Assn., Amer. (1964), 85 John St., N.Y., NY 10038; 165 companies.

Insurance Seminars, Intl. (1964), P.O. Box J, University, AL 35486; 5,000.

Intelligence Officers, Assn. of Former (1975), 6723 Whittier Ave., Suite 303A, McLean, VA 22101; 3,500.

Intercollegiate Athletics, Natl. Assn. of (1940), 1221 Baltimore Ave., Kansas City, MO 64105; 517 schools.

Interior Designers, Amer. Society of (1975), 1430 Broadway, N.Y., NY 10018; 23,000.

Inventors, Amer. Assn. of (1975), 6562 E. Curtis Rd., Bridgeport, MI 48722; 3,961.

Investors, Natl. Assn. of (1951), 1515 E. Eleven Mile Rd., Royal Oak, MI 48067; 110,000.

Investment Clubs, Natl. Assn. of (1951), 1515 E. Eleven Mile Rd., Royal Oak, MI 48067; 65,000.

Iron Castings Society (1975), 455 State St., Des Plaines, IL 60016; 200 firms.

Iron and Steel Engineers, Assn. of (1907), Three Gateway Center, Suite 2350, Pittsburgh, PA 15222; 11,856.

Iron and Steel Institute, Amer. (1908), 1000 16th St. NW, Wash., DC 20036; 2,500.

Italian Historical Society of America (1949), 111 Columbia Heights, Bklyn., NY 11201; 2,477.

Italy-America Chamber of Commerce (1887), 350 Fifth Ave., N.Y., NY 10118; 650.

Izaak Walton League of America, The (1922), 1701 Ft. Myer Dr., Arlington, VA 22209; 50,000.

JAPOS Study Group (1974), 154 Laguna Ct., St. Augustine Shores, FL 32084; 230.

Jamestowne Society (1936), P.O. Box 14523, Richmond, VA 23221; 2,430.

Japanese Amer. Citizens League (1929), 1765 Sutter St., San Francisco, CA 94115; 30,000.

Jaycees, U.S. (1920), 4 W. 21st St., Tulsa, OK 74104; 275,000.

Jewish Appeal, United (1939), 1290 Ave. of the Americas, N.Y., NY 10019.

Jewish Center Workers, Assn. of (1918), 15 E. 26th St., N.Y., NY 10010; 1,000.

Jewish Committee, Amer. (1906), 165 E. 56th St., N.Y., NY 10022; 40,000.

Jewish Congress, Amer. (1918), 15 E. 84th St., N.Y., NY 10028; 50,000.

Jewish Federations, Council of (1932), 575 Lexington Ave., N.Y., NY 10022; 200 agencies.

Jewish Historical Society, Amer. (1892), 2 Thornton Rd., Waltham, MA 02154; 3,750.

Jewish War Veterans of the U.S.A. (1896), 1712 New Hampshire Ave. NW, Wash., DC 20009; 100,000.

Jewish Welfare Board, Natl. (1917), 15 E. 26th St., N.Y., NY 10010.

Jewish Women, Natl. Council of (1893), 15 E. 26th St., N.Y., NY 10010; 100,000.

Job's Daughters, Internatl. Order of (1921), 119 S. 19th St., Rm. 402, Omaha, NE 68102; 60,000.

Jockey Club (1894), 380 Madison Ave., N.Y., NY 10017; 90.

Jogging Assn., Natl. (1968), 2420 K St. NW, Wash., DC 20037; 35,000.

John Birch Society (1958), 395 Concord Ave., Belmont, MA 02178.

Joseph's Diseases Foundation, Intl. (1977), 1832 Holmes St., Build. E, Livermore, CA 94550; 3,500.

Journalists, Society of Professional (Sigma Delta Chi) (1909), 840 N. Lake Shore Dr., Suite 801, Chicago, IL 60611 24,000.

Journalists and Authors, Amer. Society of (1948), 150 Broadway, Suite 1907, N.Y., NY 10036; 680.

Judaism, Amer. Council for (1943), 298 Fifth Ave., N.Y., NY 10001; 20,000.

Judicature Society, Amer. (1913), 200 W. Monroe, Suite 1606, Chicago, IL 60606; 30,000.

Juggler's Assn., Intl. (1947), 203 Crosby Ave., Kenmore, NY 12417; 3,000.

Junior Achievement (1919), 550 Summer St., Stamford, CT 06901; 300,000.

Junior Colleges, Amer. Assn. of Community and (1920) One Dupont Circle NW, Wash., DC 20036; 900.

Junior Leagues, Assn. of (1921), 825 Third Ave., N.Y., NY 10022; 140,000+.

Kennel Club, Amer. (1884), 51 Madison Ave., N.Y., NY 10010; 438 clubs.

Kiwanis Intl. (1915), 3636 Woodview Trace, Indianapolis, IN 46268.

Knights of Columbus (1882), One Columbus Plaza, New Haven, CT 06507; 1,387,168.

Knights Templar U.S.A., Grand Encampment (1816), 14 E. Jackson Blvd., Suite 1700, Chicago, IL 60604; 330,000.

Krishna Consciousness, Intl. Soc. for (1966), 3764 Watseka Ave., Los Angeles, CA 90034; 2,000,000.

Labor, Amer. Federation of and Congress of Industrial Organizations (1955), 815 16th St. NW, Wash., DC 20006; 13,700,000.

La Leche League Intl. (1956), 9616 Minneapolis, Franklin Park, IL 60131; 50,000.

Lambs, The (1874), 3 W. 51st St., N.Y., NY 10019; 400.

Landscape Architects, Amer. Society of (1899), 1900 M St. NW, Wash., DC 20036; 4,700.

Law, Amer. Society of Intl. (1906), 2223 Massachusetts Ave. NW, Wash., DC 20008; 5,000.

Law Enforcement Officers Assn., Amer. (1966), 1000 Connecticut Ave. NW, Suite 9, Wash., DC 20036; 50,000.

Law Libraries, Amer. Assn. of (1904), 53 W. Jackson Blvd., Chicago, IL 60604; 3,600.

Law and Social Policy, Center for (1969), 1751 N St. NW, Wash., DC 20036.

Learned Societies, Amer. Council of (1919), 800 Third Ave., N.Y., NY 10022; 43 societies.

Lefthanders, League of (1975), P.O. Box 89, New Milford, NJ 07646; 500.

Lefthanders Intl. (1975), 3601 SW 29th St., Topeka, KS 66614; 8,000.

Legal Administrators, Assn. of (1971), 1800 Pickwick Ave., Glenview, IL 60025; 3,000.

Legion of Valor of the U.S.A. (1890), 548 Bellemeade, Gretna, LA 70053; 750.

Leprosy Missions, Amer. (1906), One Broadway, Elmwood Park, NJ 07407.

Lesbian & Gay Academic Union (1979), P.O. Box 82123, San Diego, CA 92138; 3,500.

Leukemia Society of America (1949), 800 Second Ave., N.Y., NY 10017.

Lewis Carroll Society of N. America (1974), 617 Rockford Rd., Silver Spring, MD 20902; 300.

Liberty Lobby (1955), 300 Independence Ave. SE, Wash., DC 20003; 30,000.

Libraries Assn., Special (1909), 235 Park Ave. So., N.Y., NY 10003; 11,500.

Library Assn., Amer. (1876), 50 E. Huron St., Chicago, IL 60611; 40,000.

Library Assn., Medical (1898), 919 N. Michigan Ave., Chicago, IL 60611; 5,000.

Library and Information Assns., Council of Natl. (1942), 461 W. Lancaster Ave., Haverford, PA 19041; 21.

Life, Americans United for (1971), 230 N. Michigan Ave., Suite 915, Chicago, IL 60601.

Life Insurance, Amer. Council of (1976), 1850 K St. NW, Wash., DC 20006; 570 firms.

Life Office Management Assn. (1924), 100 Colony Sq., Atlanta, GA 30361; 700+ companies.

Life Underwriters, Amer. Soc. of Certified (1929), 270 Bryn Mawr Ave., Byrn Mawr, PA 19010; 28,000.

Life Underwriters, Natl. Assn. of (1890), 1922 F St. NW, Wash., DC 20006; 120,000.

Lighter-Than-Air Society (1952), 1800 Triplett Blvd., Akron, OH 44306; 1,200.

Lions Clubs, Intl. Assn. of (1917), 300 22d St., Oak Brook, IL 60570; 1,332,000.

Literacy Volunteers of America (1962), 404 Oak St., Syracuse, NY 13203.

Little League Baseball (1939), P.O. Box 3485, Williamsport, PA 17701; 15,330 leagues.

Little People of America (1957), Box 633, San Bruno, CA 94066; 3,000.

London Club (1975), P.O. Box 4527, Topeka, KS 66604; 100+.

Lung Assn., Amer. (1904), 1740 Broadway, N.Y., NY 10019.

Lutheran Education Assn. (1942), 7400 Augusta St., River Forest, IL 60305; 3,458.

Macaroni Manufacturers Assn., Natl. (1904), 19 S. Bothwell, Box 336, Palatine, IL 60067; 93 firms.

Magazine Publishers Assn. (1919), 575 Lexington Ave., N.Y., NY 10022; 250 publishers.

Magicians, Intl. Brotherhood of (1926), 28 N. Main St., Kenton, OH 43326; 10,500.

Magicians, Society of Amer. (1902), 325 Maple St., Lynn, MA 01904; 5,500.

Magicians Guild of America (1946), 20 W. 40th St., N.Y., NY 10018; 187.

Male Nurse Assn., Natl. (1971), Rush Univ., 1725 W. Harrison St., Chicago, IL 60612; 1,400.

Man Watchers, Inc. (1974), 8033 Sunset, L.A., CA 90046.

Management Assns., Amer. (1923), 135 W. 50th St., N.Y., NY 10020; 85,000.

Management Consultants, Institute of (1968), 19 W. 44th St., N.Y., NY 10036; 1,500.

Management Engineers, Assn. of Consulting (1929), 230 Park Ave., N.Y., NY 10169; 60 firms.

Manufacturers, Natl. Assn. of (1897), 1776 F St. NW, Wash., DC 20006; 13,000 companies.

Manufacturers' Agents Natl. Assn. (1947), P.O. Box 3467, Laguna Hills, CA 92654; 8,500.

March of Dimes Birth Defects Foundation (1938), 1275 Mamaroneck Ave., White Plains, NY 10605; 690 chapters.

Marijuana Laws, Natl. Organization for the Reform of (NORML) (1970), 530 8th St. SE, Wash., DC 20003; 25,000.

Marine Corps League (1923), 956 N. Monroe St., Arlington, VA 22201; 25,000.

Marine Manufacturers Assn., Natl. (1904), 401 N. Michigan Ave., Chicago, IL 60611; 760 companies.

Marine Surveyors, Natl. Assn. of (1960), 86 Windsor Gate Dr., N. Hills, NY 11040; 404.

Marine Technology Society (1963), 1730 M St. NW, Wash., DC 20036; 3,000.

Marketing Assn., Amer. (1937), 250 S. Wacker Dr., Chicago, IL 60606; 40,105.

Masonic Relief Assn. of U.S. and Canada (1885), 32613 Seidel Dr., Burlington, WS 53105; 14,700.

Masonic Service Assn. of the U.S. (1919), 8120 Fenton St., Silver Spring, MD 20910; 43 Grand Lodges.

Masons, Ancient and Accepted Scottish Rite, Southern Jurisdiction, Supreme Council (1801), 1733 16th St. NW, Wash., DC 20009; 654,515.

Masons, Supreme Council 33°, Ancient and Accepted Scottish Rite, Northern Masonic Jurisdiction (1813), 33 Marrett Rd., Lexington, MA 02173; 481,791.

Masons, Royal Arch, General Grand Chapter (1797), P.O. Box 5320, Lexington, KY 40505; 325,000.

Mathematical Assn. of America (1915), 1225 Connecticut Ave. NW, Wash., DC 20036; 18,500.

Mathematical Society, Amer. (1888), 201 Charles St., Providence, RI 02940; 20,165.

Mathematical Statistics, Institute of (1935), 3401 Investment Blvd., 6, Hayward, CA 94545; 3,000.

Mathematics, Society for Industrial and Applied (1952), 117 S. 17th St., Phila., PA 19103; 5,500.

Mayflower Descendants, General Society of (1897), 4 Winslow St., Plymouth, MA 02361; 21,000.

Mayors, U.S. Conference of (1932), 1620 Eye St. NW, Wash., DC 20006; 840 cities.

Mechanical Engineers, Amer. Society of (1880), 345 E. 47th St., N.Y., NY 10017; 114,922.

Mechanics, Amer. Academy of (1969), Dept. of Civil Engineering, Northwestern Univ., Evanston, IL 60201; 1,060.

Mechanics, State Council of VA Jr. Order of Amer. (1853), 170 Railway Rd., Grafton, VA; 1,200.

Medical Assn., Amer. (1847), 535 N. Dearborn St., Chicago, IL 60610.

Medical Assn., Natl. (1895), 1012 Tenth St. NW, Wash., DC 20001.

Medical Record Assn., Amer. (1928), 875 N. Michigan Ave., Chicago, IL 60611; 25,000.

Medical Technicians, Natl. Assn. of Emergency (1975), 621 Main St., Waltham, MA 02154; 12,000.

Medieval Academy of America (1926), 1430 Massachusetts Ave., Cambridge, MA 02138; 3,700.

Medical Technologists, Amer. College of (1942), 5608 Lane, Raytown, MO 64133; 368.

Mensa, Amer. (1960), 1701 W. 3d St., Brooklyn, NY 11223.

Mental Health Assn., Natl. (1950), 1800 N. Kent St., Arlington, VA 22209.

Mental Health Program Directors, Natl. Assn. of State (1963), 1001 3d St. SW, Wash., DC 20024, 54.

Merchant Marine Library Assn., Amer. (1921), One World Trade Center, Suite 2601, N.Y., NY 10048; 1,100.

Merchant Marine Veterans of WWII, U.S. (1944), 1712 Harbor Way, Seal Beach, CA 90740; 5,248.

Merchants Assn., Natl. Retail (1911), 100 W. 31st St., N.Y., NY 10023.

Metal Finishers, Natl. Assn. of (1955), 111 E. Wacker Dr., Chicago, IL 60601; 1,216.

Metallurgy Institute, Amer. Powder (1959), 105 College Rd. East, Princeton, NJ 08540; 2,300.

Metal Powder Industries Federation, (1946), 105 College Rd. East, Princeton, NJ 08540; 260 cos.

Metals, Amer. Society for (1913), Metals Park, OH 44073.

Meteorological Society, Amer. (1919), 45 Beacon St., Boston, MA 02108; 10,000.

Metric Assn., U.S. (1916), 10245 Andasol Ave., Northridge, CA 91325; 3,500.

Microbiology, Amer. Society for (1899), 1913 Eye St. NW, Wash. DC 20006; 32,000.

Micrographics Assn., Natl. (1942), 8719 Colesville Rd., Silver Spring, MD 20910; 9,000.

Mideast Educational and Training Services, America-, (1951), 1717 Massachusetts Ave. NW, Wash., DC 20036.

Military Order of the Loyal Legion of the U.S.A. (1865), 1805 Pine St., Phila., PA 19103; 1,200.

Military Order of the Purple Heart of the USA (1932), 5413-B Backlick Rd., Springfield, VA 22151; 14,000.

Military Order of the World Wars (1920), 1100 17th St. NW, Wash., DC 20036; 14,500.

Mining, Metallurgical and Petroleum Engineers, Amer. Institute of (1871), 345 E. 47th St., N.Y., NY 10017; 90,000.

Mining and Metallurgical Society of America (1908), 230 Park Ave., N.Y., NY 10169; 310.

Ministerial Assn., Amer. (1929), 2210 Wilshire Blvd., Suite 582, Santa Monica, CA 90403.

Ministerial Training, Amer. Commission on (1950), 23820 Arlington, Suite 15, Torrance, CA 90501; 45.

Model Railroad Assn., Natl. (1935), 4121 Cromwell Rd., Chattanooga, TN 37421; 27,000.

Modern Language Assn. of America (1883), 62 Fifth Ave., N.Y., NY 10011; 26,000.

Modern Language Teachers Assns., Natl. Federation of (1916), Gannon Univ., Erie, PA 16541; 6,700.

Moose, Loyal Order of (1888), Mooseheart, IL 60539; 1,303,173.

Mothers, American (1933), 301 Park Ave., N.Y., NY 10022.

Mothers-in-Law Club Intl. (1970), 420 Adelberg Ln., Cedarhurst, NY 11516; 5,000.

Mothers of Twins Clubs, Natl. Organization of (1960), 5402 Amberwood Ln., Rockville, MD 20853; 9,987.

Motion Picture Arts & Sciences, Academy of (1927), 8949 Wilshire Blvd., Beverly Hills, CA 90211; 4,500.

Motion Pictures, Natl. Board of Review of (1909), P.O. Box 589, Lenox Hill Sta., N.Y., NY 10021.

Motion Picture & Television Engineers, Society of (1916), 862 Scarsdale Ave., Scarsdale, NY 10583; 9,604.

Motor Vehicle Administrators, Amer. Assn. of (1933), 1201 Connecticut Ave. NW, Wash., DC 20036; 2,000.

Motor Vehicle Manufacturers Assn. (1913), 300 New Center Building, Detroit, MI 48202; 9 companies.

Motorcyclist Assn., Amer. (1924), 33 Collegeview, Westerville, OH 43081; 133,000.

Multiple Sclerosis Society, Natl. (1946), 205 E. 42d St., N.Y., NY 10017; 321,000.

Municipal Finance Officers Assn. (1906), 180 N. Michigan Ave., Suite 800, Chicago, IL 60601; 9,100.

Municipal League, Natl. (1894), 55 W. 44th St., N.Y., NY 10036; 5,000.

Muscular Dystrophy Assn. (1950), 810 Seventh Ave., N.Y., NY 10019, 1,800,000.

Museums, Amer. Assn. of (1906), 1055 Thomas Jefferson St. NW, Wash., DC 20007; 8,900.

Music Center, Amer. (1940), 250 W. 54th St., N.Y., NY 10019; 1,200.

Music Conference, Amer. (1947), 1000 Skokie Blvd., Wilmette, IL 60091; 400.

Music Council, Natl. (1940), 250 W. 54th St., N.Y., NY 10019; 60 organizations.

Music Educators Natl. Conference (1907), 1902 Association Dr., Reston, VA 22090; 52,000.

Musicians, Amer. Federation of (1896), 1500 Broadway, N.Y., NY 10036; 330,000.

Musicological Society, Amer. (1934), 201 S. 34th St., Phila., PA 19104; 3,600.

Music Publishers' Assn., Natl. (1917), 110 E. 59th St., N.Y., NY 10022; 310.

Music Scholarship Assn., Amer. (1956), 1826 Carew Tower, Cincinnati, OH 45202; 2,500.

Music Teachers Natl. Assn. (1876), 2113 Carew Tower, Cincinnati, OH 45202; 23,000.

Muzzle Loading Rifle Assn., Natl. (1933), P.O. Box 67, Friendship, IN 47021; 25,100.

Mystic Seaport Museum (1929), 30 Greenmanville Ave., Mystic, CT 06355; 17,500.

NAACP (Natl. Assn. for the Advancement of Colored People) (1909), 1790 Broadway, N.Y., NY 10019.

Name Society, Amer. (1951), N. Country Community College, Saranac Lake, NY 12983; 860.

Narcolepsy and Cataplexy Foundation of Amer. (1975), 1410 York Ave., Suite 2D, N.Y. NY 10021; 3,416.

Narcolepsy Assoc., Amer. (1975), P.O. Box 5846, Stanford, CA 94305; 4,000.

National Guard Assn. of the U.S. (1878), One Massachusetts Ave. NW, Wash., DC 20001; 54,000.

Nationalities Service, Amer. Council for (1919), 20 W. 40th St., N.Y., NY 10018; 34 agencies.

Naturalists, Assn. of Interpretive (1961), 6700 Needwood Rd., Derwood, MD 20855; 1,200.

Natural Science for Youth Foundation (1961), 763 Silvermine Rd., New Canaan, CT 06840; 400.

Nature Conservancy (1951), 1800 N. Kent St., Arlington, VA 22209; 193,000.

Nature & Natural Resources, Intl. Union for Conservation of (1948), Avenue du Mont Blanc, 1196 Gland, Switzerland; 502.

Navajo Code Talkers Assn. (1971), Red Rock State Park, P.O. Box 328, Church Rock, NM 87311; 90.

Naval Architects & Marine Engineers, Society of (1893), One World Trade Center, Suite 1369, N.Y., NY 10048; 13,682.

Naval Engineers, Amer. Society of (1888), 1452 Duke St., Alexandria, VA 22152; 7,000.

Naval Institute, U.S. (1873), U.S. Naval Academy, Annapolis, MD 21402; 90,000.

Naval Reserve Assn. (1954), 110 N. Royal St., Suite 307, Alexandria, VA 22314; 23,000.

Navigation, Institute of (1945), 815 15th St. NW, Suite 832, Wash., DC 20005; 2,500.

Navy Club of the U.S.A. Auxiliary (1941), 418 W. Pontiac St., Ft. Wayne, IN 46807; 1,000.

Navy League of the U.S. (1902); 2300 Wilson Blvd., Arlington, VA 22201; 50,000.

Needlework Guild of America (1895), 1342 E. Lincoln Hwy., Langhorne, PA 19047.

Negro College Fund, United (1944), 500 E. 62d St., N.Y., NY 10021; 42 institutions.

Newspaper Editors, Amer. Society of (1922), P.O. Box 17004, Washington, DC 20041; 897.

Newspaper Promotion Assn., Intl. (1930), 11600 Sunrise Valley Dr., Reston, VA 22091; 1,500.

Newspaper Publishers Assn., Amer. (1887), 11600 Sunrise Valley Dr., Reston, VA 22091; 1,400 newspapers.

Ninety-Nines (Intl. Organization of Women Pilots) (1929), P.O. Box 59965; Will Rogers World Airport, Oklahoma City, OK 73159, 6,500.

Non-Commissioned Officers Assn. (1960), 10635 IH 35 No., San Antonio, TX 78233; 170,000.

Non-Parents, Natl. Organization for (1972), 3 N. Liberty, Baltimore, MD 21201.

Notaries, Amer. Society of (1965), 810 18th St. NW, Wash., DC 20006; 17,397.

Nuclear Society, Amer. (1954), 555 N. Kensington Ave., La Grange Park, IL 60525; 15,000.

Numismatic Assn., Amer. (1891), 818 N. Cascade Ave., Colorado Springs, CO 80903; 35,000.

Numismatic Society, Amer. (1858), Broadway at 155th St., N.Y., NY 10032; 2,257.

Nurse Education and Service, Natl. Assn. for Practical (1941), 254 W. 31st St., N.Y., NY 10001; 25,000.

Nurses' Assn., Amer. (1897), 2420 Pershing Rd., Kansas City, MO 64108.

Nursing, Amer. Assembly for Men in (1971), Rush Univ., 600 S. Paulina, Chicago, IL 60617; 1,590.

Nursing, Natl. League for (1952), 10 Columbus Circle, N.Y., NY 10019; 18,000.

Nutrition, Amer. Institute of (1933), 9650 Rockville Pike, Bethesda, MD 20814; 2,140.

ORT Federation, Amer. (Org. for Rehabilitation through Training) (1922), 817 Broadway, N.Y., NY 10003; 20,000.

Odd Fellows, Sovereign Grand Lodge Independent Order of (1819), 422 N. Trade St., Winston Salem, NC 27101; 700,000.

Old Crows, Assn. of (1964), 2300 9th St. S., Arlington, VA 22204; 18,000.

Olympic Committee, U.S. (1920), 1759 E. Boulder St., Colorado Springs, CO 80909; 60 organizations.

Optical Society of America (1916), 1816 Jefferson Pl. NW, Wash., DC 20036; 8,365.

Optimist Intl. (1919), 4494 Lindell Blvd., St. Louis, MO 63108.

Optometric Assn., Amer. (1898), 243 N. Lindbergh Blvd., St. Louis, MO 63141; 23,304.

Oral and Maxillofacial Surgeons, Amer. Assn. of (1918), 211 E. Chicago Ave., Chicago, IL 60611; 4,305.

Organists, Amer. Guild of (1896), 815 Second Ave., Suite 318, N.Y., NY 10017; 25,000.

Oriental Society, Amer. (1842), 329 Sterling Memorial Library, Yale Sta., New Haven, CT 06520; 1,600.

Ornithologists' Union, Amer. (1883), c/o National Museum of Natural History, Smithsonian, Wash., DC 20560; 4,500.

Osteopathic Assn., Amer. (1897), 212 E Ohio St., Chicago, IL 60611; 15,894.

Ostomy Assn., United (1962), 2001 W. Beverly Blvd., Los Angeles, CA 90057; 45,000.

Outlaw and Lawman History, Natl. Assn. for (1974), Univ. of Wyoming, Box 3334, Laramie, WY 82071; 470.

Overeaters Anonymous (1960), 2190 190th St., Torrance, CA 90504; 80,000.

Over-the-Counter Cos., Natl. Assn. of (1973), 1735 K St. NW, Washington, DC 20006; 500+.

PTA (Parent-Teacher Assn.), Natl. (1897), 700 N. Rush St., Chicago, IL 60611; 5,000,000.

Paleontological Research Institution (1932), 1259 Trumansburg Rd., Ithaca, NY 14850; 700+.

Paper Converters Assn. (1934), 1000 Vermont Ave. NW, Wash., DC 20005; 45 companies.

Paper Industry, Technical Assn. of the Pulp and (1916), Technology Park, Atlanta, GA 30348; 23,000.

Paper Institute, Amer. (1966), 260 Madison Ave., N.Y., NY 10016; 170 companies.

Parasitologists, Amer. Society of (1924), 1041 New Hampshire St., Box 368, Lawrence, KS 66044; 1,500.

Parents Without Partners (1958), 7910 Woodmont Ave. NW, Wash., DC 20814; 210,000.

Parkinson's Disease Foundation (1957), Columbia Univ. Medical Center, 650 W. 168th St., N.Y., NY 10032.

Parliamentarians, Amer. Institute of (1958), 229 Army Post Rd., Suite B, Des Moines, IA 50315; 1,200.

Parliamentary Law, Intl. Organization of Professionals in (1977), 3611 Victoria Ave., L.A., CA 90016; 750.

Pasta Assn., Natl. (1904), 19 S. Bothwell St., Palatine, IL 60067; l05 firms.

Pathologists, Amer. Assn. of (1976), 9650 Rockville Pike, Bethesda, MD 20814; 2,400.

Patriotism, Natl. Committee for Responsible (1967), P.O. Box 665, Grand Central Sta., N.Y., NY 10163; 175.

Patriotism, Natl. Council for the Encouragement of (1968), Box 3271, Munster, IN 46321; 1,500.

Pearl Harbor History Associates (1958), P.O. Box 205, Sperryville, VA 22740; 9,000.

Pedestrian Tolls, Committee for (1979), P.O. Box 1578, N.Y., NY l0116; 623.

P.E.N. Amer. Center (1922), 47 Fifth Ave., N.Y., NY 10003.

Pen Women, Natl. League of Amer. (1897), 1300 17th St. NW, Wash., DC 20036; 6,200.

Pennsylvania Society (1899), Suite 1850, Waldorf Astoria Hotel, 301 Park Ave., N.Y., NY 10022; 2,250.

Pension Actuaries, Amer. Society of (1966), 1700 K St. NW, Ste. 404, Wash., DC 20006; 1,800.

P.E.O (Philanthropic Educational Organization) Sisterhood (1869), 3700 Grand Ave., Des Moines, IA 50312; 223,000.

Personnel Administration, Amer. Society for (1948), 606 N. Washington St., Alexandria, VA 22314; 33,000.

Petroleum Geologists, Amer. Assn. of (1917), Box 979, 1444 S. Boulder, Tulsa, OK 74101; 33,000.

Petroleum Equipment Inst. (1951), 3739 E. 31st St., Tulsa, OK 74114; 1,000.

Petroleum Institute, Amer. (1919), 1220 L St. NW, Wash., DC 20005; 6,500.

Petroleum Landmen, Amer. Assn. of (1955), 2408 Continental Life Bldg., Fort Worth, TX 76102; 6,200.

Pharmaceutical Assn., Amer. (1852), 2215 Constitution Ave. NW, Wash., DC 20037; 50,000.

Philatelic Society, Amer. (1886), 100 Oakwood Ave., State College, PA 16803; 53,000.

Philately Assn., Graphics (1975), 1450 Parkchester Rd., Bronx, NY 10462; 100.

Philaticians, Society of (1972), 154 Laguna Ct., St. Augustine Shores, FL 32086; 300+.

Philological Assn., Amer. (1869), 617 Hamilton Hall, Columbia Univ., N.Y., NY 10027; 2,500.

Philosophical Assn., Amer. (1900), Univ. of Delaware, Newark, DE 19710; 6,500.

Philosophical Enquiry, Intl. Society for (1974), P.O. Box 3282, Kingsport, TN 37664; 360.

Philosophical Society, Amer. (1743), 104 S. 5th St., Phila., PA 19106; 625.

Photogrammetry, Amer. Society of (1934), 210 Little Falls St., Falls Church, VA 22046; 8,000.

Photographers of America, Professional (1880), 1090 Executive Way, Des Plaines, IL 60018; 1,500.

Photographic Society of Amer. (1934), 2005 Walnut St., Phila. PA 19103; 14,000.

Physical Therapy Assn., Amer. (1921), 1111 N. Fairfax St., Alexandria, VA 22314; 42,500.

Physicians, Amer. Academy of Family (1947), 1740 W. 92nd St., Kansas City, MO 64114; 56,000.

Physics, Amer. Inst. of (1931), 335 E. 45th St., N.Y., NY 10017.

Physiological Society, Amer. (1887), 9650 Rockville Pike, Bethesda, MD 20814.

Phytopathological Soc., The Amer. (1908), 3340 Pilot Knob Rd., St. Paul, MN 55121; 4,000.

Pilgrim Society (l820), 75 Court St., Plymouth, MA 02360; 700.

Pilgrims of the U.S. (1903), 74 Trinity Pl., N.Y., NY 10006; 1,000.

Pilot Club Intl. (1921), 244 College St., Macon, GA 31213; 21,000.

Pioneer Women, The Women's Labor Zionist Organization of America (1925), 200 Madison Ave., N.Y., NY 10016.

Planetary Society (1980), P.O. Box 91687, Pasadena, CA 91109; 110,000.

Planned Parenthood Federation of America (1916), 810 Seventh Ave., N.Y., NY 10019; 191 affiliates.

Planning Assn., Amer. (1917), 1976 Massachusetts Ave. NW, Wash., DC 20019; 190 affiliates.

Plastic Modelers Society, Intl. (1962), P.O. Box 480, Denver, CO 80201; 6,200.

Plastics Engineers, Society of (1942), 14 Fairfield Dr., Brookfield Cntr., CT 06805; 24,000.

Plastics Industry, Society of (1937), 355 Lexington Ave., N.Y., NY 10017; 1,200 companies.

Platform Assn., Intl. (1831), 2564 Berkshire Rd., Cleveland Heights, OH 44106; 4,700.

Podiatry Assn., Amer. (1912), 20 Chevy Chase Circle NW, Wash., DC 20015; 8,400.

Poetry Day Committee, Natl. (1947), 1110 N. Venetian Dr., Miami, FL 33139; 17,000.

Poetry Society of America (1910), 15 Gramercy Park, N.Y., NY 10003; 1,050.

Poets, Academy of Amer. (1934), 177 E. 87th St., N.Y., NY 10128; 3,000+.

Polar Society, Amer. (1934), c/o Secretary, 98-20 62d Dr., Apt. 7H, Rego Park, NY 11374; 2,088.

Police, Amer. Federation of (1966), 1100 NE 125 St., N. Miami, FL 33161; 47,000.

Police, Internatl. Assn. of Chiefs of (1893), 13 Firstfield Rd., Gaithersburg, MD 20868; 14,500.

Police Reserve Officers Assn., Natl. (1967), 609 W. Main St., Louisville, KY 40202; 11,000.

Polish Army Veterans Assn. of America (1921), 19 Irving Pl., N.Y., NY 10003; 9,762.

Polish Cultural Society of America (1940), 41 John St., N.Y., NY 10038; 91,615.

Polish Legion of American Veterans (1921), 3024 N. Laramie Ave., Chicago, IL 60641; 15,000.

Political Items Collectors, Amer. (1945), 1054 Sharpsburg Dr., Huntsville, AL 35803; 2,300.

Political Science, Academy of (1880), 2852 Broadway, N.Y., NY 10025; 10,500.

Political Science Assn., Amer. (1903), 1527 New Hampshire Ave. NW, Wash., DC 20036; 12,000.

Political & Social Science, Amer. Academy of (1889), 3937 Chestnut St., Phila., PA 19104; 4,900.

Pollution Control, Internatl. Assn. for (1970), 1625 Eye St. NW, Wash. DC 20006; 500.

Polo Assn., U.S. (1898), 1301 W. 22d St., Oak Brook, IL 60521; 2,300.

Population Assn. of America (1931), 806 15th St. NW, Wash., DC 20005; 2,600.

Portuguese Continental Union of the U.S.A. (1925), 899 Boylston St., Boston, MA 02115; 8,226.

Postmasters of the U.S., Natl. Assn. of (1898), 4212 King St., Arlington, VA 22302; 43,000.

Postmasters of the U.S., Natl. League of (1904), 1023 N. Royal St., Alexandria, VA 22314; 21,000.

Poultry Science Assn. (1908), 309 W. Clark, Champaign, IL 61820; 1,900.

Power Boat Assn., Amer. (1903), 17640 E. Nine Mile Rd., E. Detroit, MI 48021; 4,500.

Precancel Collectors, Natl. Assn. of (1950), 5121 Park Blvd., Wildwood, NJ 08260; 7,500.

Press, Associated (1848), 50 Rockefeller Plaza, N.Y., NY 10020; 1,365 newspapers & 3,600 broadcast stations.

Press Club, Natl. (1908), Natl. Press Bldg., Wash., DC 20045; 4,104.

Press Intl., United (1907), 1400 I St. NW, Wash. DC 20005; 7,000.

Press and Radio Club (1948), P.O. Box 7023, Montgomery, AL 36107; 717.

Press Women, Natl. Federation of (1937), 1105 Main St., Blue Springs, MD 64015; 5,000.

Printing Industries of America (1887), 1730 N. Lynn St., Arlington, VA 22209; 11,000 companies.

Procrastinators' Club of America (1956), 1111 Broad-Locust Bldg., Phila., PA 19102; 4,200.

Propeller Club of the U.S. (1927), 1730 M St. NW, Suite 413, Wash., DC 20036; 16,000+.

Psychiatric Assn., Amer. (1844), 1400 K St. NW, Wash., DC 20005; 27,000.

Psychical Research, Amer. Society for (1885), 5 W. 73d St., N.Y., NY 10023; 2,200.

Psychoanalytic Assn., Amer. (1911), One E. 57th St., N.Y., NY 10022; 2,700.

Psychological Assn., Amer. (1892), 1200 17th St. NW, Wash., DC 20036; 65,000.

Psychological Assn. for Psychoanalysis, Natl. (1948), 150 W. 13th St., N.Y., NY 10011; 274.

Psychological Minorities, Society for the Aid of (1953), 42-25 Hampton St., Elmhurst, NY 11373; 523.

Psychotherapy Assn., Amer. Group (1942), 1995 Broadway, N.Y., NY 10023; 3,000.

Public Health Assn., Amer. (1972), 1015 15th St. NW, Wash., DC 20005, 30,000.

Public Relations Soc. of Amer. (1947), 845 Third Ave., N.Y., NY 10022.

Publishers, Assn. of Amer. (1970), One Park Ave., N.Y., NY 10016; 330 publishing houses.

Puppeteers of Amer. (1937), 5 Cricklewood Path, Pasadena, CA 91107; 2,000.

Quality Control, Amer. Society for (1946), 230 W. Wells St., Milwaukee, WI 53203; 37,000.

Rabbinical Alliance of America (1944), 156 5th Ave., N.Y., NY 10010; 502.

Rabbinical Assembly (1900), 3080 Broadway, N.Y., NY 10027.

Rabbis, Central Conference of Amer. (1889), 21 E. 40th St., N.Y., NY 10016; 1,410.

Radio Clubs, Assn. of N. American (1964), 8120 Ripplewood Dr., Austin, TX 78758; 5,000.

Radio Union, Intl. Amateur (1925), P.O. Box AAA, Newington, CT 06111; 113 societies.

Radio and TV Society, Intl. (1939), 420 Lexington Ave., N.Y., NY 10170.

Radio Relay League, Amer. (1914), 225 Main St., Newington, CT 06111; 150,000+.

Railroad Passengers, Natl. Assn. of (1967), 417 New Jersey Ave. SE, Wash., DC 20003; 11,500.

Railroads, Assn. of Amer. (1934), 1920 L St. NW, Wash., DC 20036; 65.

Railway Historical Society, Natl. (1935), P.O. Box 58153, Phila., PA 19102; 11,000.

Railway Progress Institute (1908), 700 N. Fairfax St., Alexandria, VA 22314; 150 companies.

Range Management, Society for (1948), 2760 W. 5th Ave., Denver, CO 80204; 5,000.

Rape, Feminist Alliance Against (1974), P.O. Box 21033, Wash., DC 20009.

Real Estate Appraisers, Natl. Assn. of (1967), 853 Broadway, N.Y., NY 10003; 1,000.

Real Estate Investment Trusts, Natl. Assn. of (1961), 1101 17th St. NW, Wash., DC 20036; 280 associates.

Rebekah Assemblies, Intl. Assn. of (1914), P.O. Box 153, Minneapolis, KS 67467; 338,050.

Reconciliation, Fellowship of (1914), 523 N. Broadway, Nyack, NY 10960; 32,000.

Recording Industry Assn. of America (1951), 888 7th Ave., N.Y., NY 10101; 60.

Records Managers & Administrators, Assn. of (1975), 4200 Somerset Dr., Suite 215, Prairie Village, KS 66208; 7,520.

Recreation and Park Assn., Natl. (1965), 1601 N. Kent St., Arlington, VA 22209; 16,000.

Red Cross, Amer. Natl. (1881), 17th & D Sts. NW, Wash., DC 20006; 2,963 chapters.

Red Men, Improved Order of (1765), 1525 West Ave., P.O. Box 683, Waco, TX 76703; 45,000.

Redwoods League, Save-the- (1918), 114 Sansome St., San Francisco, CA 94104; 42,000.

Reed Organ Society, Inc. (1981), The Musical Museum, Deansboro, NY 13328; 425.

Regional Plan Assn. (1929), 1040 Ave. of the Americas, N.Y., NY 10018; 3,000.

Rehabilitation Assn., Natl. (1925), 1522 K St. NW, Wash., DC 20005; 25,000.

Religion, Amer. Academy of (1909), Dept. of Religion, Syracuse Univ., Syracuse, NY 13210; 4,700.

Renaissance Society of America (1954), 1161 Amsterdam Ave., N.Y., NY 10027; 2,808.

Reserve Officers Assn. of the U.S. (1922), One Constitution Ave., NE, Wash., DC 20002; 123,500.

Restaurant Assn., Natl. (1919), 311 First St. NW, Wash., DC 20001; 18,050.

Retarded Citizens of the U.S., Assn. for (1950), 2501 Ave. J, Arlington, TX 76011; 200,000.

Retired Credit Union People, Natl. Assn. for (1978), P.O. Box 391, 5910 Mineral Pt. Rd., Madison, WI 53701; 61,000.

Retired Federal Employees, Natl. Assn. of (1921), 1533 New Hampshire Ave. NW, Wash., DC 20008; 487,785.

Retired Officers Assn. (1929), 201 N. Washington St., Alexandria, VA 22314; 327,403.

Retired Persons, Amer. Assn. of (1958), 1909 K St. NW, Wash., DC 20049; 16,000,000+.

Retired Teachers Assn., Natl. (1947), 1909 K St. NW, Wash., DC 20049; 540,000.

Retreads (of World War I & II) (1947), 40-07 154th St., Flushing, NY 11354; 1,000.

Revolver Assn., U.S. (1900), 96 W. Union St., Ashland, MA 01721; 1,200.

Reye's Syndrome Foundation, Natl. (1974), 426 N. Lewis, Bryan, OH 43506; 10,000 |.

Richard III Society (1960), P.O. Box 217, Sea Cliff, NY 11579; 600.

Rifle Assn., Natl. (1871), 1600 Rhode Island Ave. NW, Wash., DC 20036; 2,500,000.

Road & Transportation Builders' Assn., Amer. (1902), 525 School St. SW, Wash., DC 20024; 5,400.

Rodeo Cowboys Assn., Professional (1936), 101 Pro Rodeo Dr., Colorado Springs, CO 80919; 10,000.

Roller Skating, U.S. Amateur Confederation of (1973), 7700 A St., Lincoln, NE 68501; 40,000.

Roller Skating Rink Operators Assn. (1937), 7700 A St., Lincoln, NE 68501; 2,000.

Rose Society, Amer. (1899), P.O. Box 30,000, Shreveport, LA 71130; 25,000.

Rosicrucians, Soc. of (1909), 321 W. 101st St., N.Y., NY 10025.

Rotary Intl. (1905), 1600 Ridge Ave., Evanston, IL 60201; 940,000.

Running and Fitness Assn., Amer. (1968), 2420 K St. NW, Wash, DC 20037; 35,000.

Ruritan Natl. (1928), Ruritan Natl. Rd., Dublin, VA 24084.

Safety and Fairness Everywhere, Natl. Assn. Taunting (1980), P.O. Box 5743A, Montecito, CA 93108; 1,036.

Safety Council, Natl. (1913), 444 N. Michigan Ave., Chicago, IL 60611; 12,000.

Safety Engineers, Amer. Society of (1911), 850 Busse Hwy., Park Ridge, IL 60068; 20,000.

Sailors, Tin Can (1976), Battleship Cove, Fall River, MA 02721; 3,500.

St. Dennis of Zante, Sovereign Greek Order of (1096; 1953 in U.S.), 739 W. 186th St., N.Y., NY 10033; 1,011.

St. Luke the Physician, Order of (1880), 2210 Wilshire Blvd., Suite 582, Santa Monica, CA 90403; 720.

St. Paul, Natl. Guild of (1937), 601 Hill 'n Dale, Lexington, KY 40503; 13,652.

Salt Institute (1914), 206 N. Washington St., Alexandria, VA 22314; 33 cos.

Samuel Butler Society (1978), Chaplain Library, Williams College, P.O. Box 426, Williamstown, MA 01267; 100.

Sane Nuclear Policy, A Citizen's Organization for a (1957), 711 G St. SE, Wash., DC 20003; 100,000.

Savings & Loan League, Natl. (1943), 1101 15th St. NW, Wash., DC 20005; 300 associations.

School Administrators, Amer. Assn. of (1865), 1801 N. Moore St., Arlington, VA 22209; 17,500.

School Boards Assn., Natl. (1940), 1055 Thomas Jefferson St. NW, Wash., DC 20007; 52 boards.

School Counselor Assn., Amer. (1953), 5999 Stevenson Ave., Alexandria, VA 22304; 9,000.

Schools of Art, Natl. Assn. of (also: School of Art and Design, School of Dance, Music, and Theater) (1944), 11250 Roger Bacon Dr., #5, Reston, VA 22090.

Schools & Colleges, Amer. Council on (1927), P.O. Box 219, Lomita, CA 90717-0219; 187 institutions.

Science, Amer. Assn. for the Advancement of (1848), 1515 Massachusetts Ave. NW, Wash., DC 20005; 139,000.

Science Fiction, Fantasy and Horror Films, Academy of (1972), 334 W. 54th St., Los Angeles, CA 90037; 2,000+.

Sciences, Natl. Academy of (1863), 2101 Constitution Ave NW, Wash., DC 20418; 1,659.

Science Service (1921), 1719 N St. NW, Wash., DC 20036.

Science Teachers Assn., Natl. (1944), 1742 Connecticut Ave. NW, Wash., DC 20009; 19,272.

Science Writers, Natl. Assn. of (1934), P.O. Box 294, Greenlawn, NY 11740; 1,160.

Scientists, Federation of Amer. (1946), 307 Massachusetts Ave. NE, Wash., DC 20002; 7,000.

Screen Actors Guild (1933), 7750 Sunset Blvd., Hollywood, CA 90046; 54,000.

Sculpture Soc., Natl. (1893), 15 E. 26th St., N.Y., NY 10010; 325.

Seamen's Service, United (1942), One World Trade Ctr., Suite 2601, N.Y., NY 10048.

2d Air Division Assn. (1947), 1 Jeffrey's Neck Rd., Ipswich, MA 01938; 4,186.

Secondary School Principals, Natl. Assn. of (1916), 1904 Association Dr., Reston, VA 22091; 35,000.

Secretaries, Natl. Assn. of **Legal** (1950), 3005 E. Skelly Dr., Tulsa, OK 74105; 23,000.

Secularists of America, United (1947), 377 Vernon St., Oakland, CA 94610.

Securities Industry Assn. (1972), 120 Broadway, N.Y., NY 10271; 520 firms.

Semantics, Institute of General (1938), Office of the Director, 3029 Eastern Ave., Baltimore, MD 21224; 500.

Separation of Church & State, Americans United for (1947), 8120 Fenton St., Silver Spring, MD 20910; 50,000.

Sertoma Internatl. (1912), 1912 E. Meyer Blvd., Kansas City, MO 64132; 34,500.

Sex Information & Education Council of the U.S. (SIECUS) (1964), 80 5th Ave., N.Y., NY 10011; 3,000.

Shakespeare Assn. of America (1973), Box 6328, Vanderbilt Sta., Nashville, TN 37235; 650.

Sheriff's Assn., Natl. (1940), 1250 Connecticut Ave. NW, Wash., DC 20036; 45,000.

Shipbuilders Council of America (1920), 1110 Vermont Ave. NW, Wash., DC 20005.

Ship Society, World (1946), 3319 Sweet Dr., Lafayette, CA 94549; 4,200.

Shoe Retailers Assn., Natl. (1912), 200 Madison Ave., N.Y., NY 10016; 4,000.

Shore & Beach Preservation Assn., Amer. (1926), 412 O'Brien Hall, Univ. of California, Berkeley, CA 94720; 1,100.

Shrine, Ancient Arabic Order of the Nobles of the Mystic (1872), 2900 Rocky Pt. Dr., Tampa, FL 33607; 1,000,000.

Shut-Ins, Natl. Society for (1970), P.O. Box 1392, Reading, PA 19602; 300.

Sierra Club (1892), 530 Bush St., San Francisco, CA 94108.

Signalmen, Society of (1971), P.O. Box 11247, San Diego, CA 92111; 7,500.

Silurians, Society of the (1924), 45 John St., N.Y., NY 10038; 700.

Skating Union of the U.S., Amateur (1928), 4423 W. Deming Pl., Chicago, IL 60639; 2,000.

Skeet Shooting Assn., Natl. (1946), FM 471 at Raft Rd., San Antonio, TX 78228; 15,500.

Ski Assn., U.S. (1904), 1726 Champa St., Denver, CO 80202.

Small Business, Amer. Federation of (1938), 407 S. Dearborn St., Chicago, IL 60605; 5,000.

Small Business Assn., Natl. (1937), 1604 K St. NW, Wash., DC 20006; 50,000.

Smoking & Health, Natl. Clearinghouse for (1965), Center for Disease Control, 1600 Clifton Road NE, Atlanta, GA 30333.

Soaring Society of America (1932), P.O. Box 66071, Los Angeles, CA 90066; 16,000.

Soccer Federation, U.S. (1913), 350 Fifth Ave., N.Y., NY 10001; 700,000.

Social Biology, Society for the Study of (1926), Medical Dept., Brookhaven Natl. Laboratory, Upton, NY 11973; 415.

Social Sciences, Natl. Institute of (1899), 1133 Broadway, Suite 824, N.Y., NY 10010; 800.

Social Service, Intl., Amer. Branch (1923), 291 Broadway, N.Y., NY 10007.

Social Work Education, Council on (1952), 111 8th Ave., N.Y., NY 10017; 4,500.

Social Workers, Natl. Assn. of (1955), 7981 Eastern Ave., Silver Spring, MD 20910; 94,500.

Sociological Assn., Amer. (1905), 1722 N St. NW, Wash., DC 20036; 13,000.

Softball Assn. of America, Amateur (1933), 2801 N.E. 50th St., Oklahoma City, OK 73111; 3,500,000.

Softball League, Cinderella (1958), P.O. Box 1411, Corning, NY 14830.

Soft Drink Assn., Natl. (1919), 1101 16th St. NW, Wash., DC 20036; 1,800.

Soil Conservation Society of America (1945), 7515 N.E. Ankeny Rd., Ankeny, IA 50021; 13,000.

Soil Science Society of America (1936), 677 S. Segoe Rd., Madison, WI 53711; 6,200.

Sojourners, Natl. (1921), 8301 E. Boulevard Dr., Alexandria, VA 22308; 10,000.

Soldier's, Sailor's and Airmen's Club (1919), 283 Lexington Ave., N.Y., NY 10016.

Songwriters Guild, The (1931), 276 Fifth Ave., N.Y., NY 10001; 4000+.

Sons of the Amer. Legion (1932), Box 1055, Indianapolis, IN 46206; 59,577.

Sons of the American Revolution, Natl. Society of (1889), 1000 S. 4th, Louisville, KY 40203; 23,000.

Sons of Confederate Veterans (1896), 3108 Jamestown Rd., Hattiesburg, MS 39401; 7,500.

Sons of the Desert (1965), P.O. Box 8341, Universal City, CA 91608; 3,500.

Sons of Norway (1895), 1455 W. Lake St., Minneapolis, MN 55408; 105,429.

Sons of Poland, Assn. of the (1903), 591 Summit Ave., Jersey City, NJ 07306; 10,000.

Sons of St. Patrick, Society of the Friendly (1784), 80 Wall St., N.Y., NY 10005; 1,000.

Sons of Sherman's March to the Sea (1966), 1725 Farmers Ave., Tempe, AZ 85281; 563.

Sons of Union Veterans of the Civil War (1881), P.O. Box 24, Gettysburg, PA 17325; 3,500.

Soroptimist Intl. of the Americas (1921), 1616 Walnut St., Phila., PA 19103; 40,000.

Southern Christian Leadership Conference (1957), 334 Auburn Ave. NE, Atlanta, GA 30303; 1,000,000.

Southern Regional Council (1944), 75 Marietta St. NW, Atlanta, GA 30303; 120.

Space Education Assoc., U.S. (1973), 746 Turnpike Rd., Elizabethtown, PA 17022; 1,000.

Spanish War Veterans, United (1904), P.O. Box 1915, Washington, DC 20013; 14.

Speech Communication Assn. (1914), 5105 Backlick Rd., Annandale, VA 22003; 5,300.

Speech-Language-Hearing Assn., Amer. (1925), 10801 Rockville Pike, Rockville, MD 20852; 38,500.

Speleological Society, Natl. (1941), 2813 Cave Ave., Huntsville, AL 35810; 5,700.

Sports Car Club of America (1944), 6750 S. Emporia, Englewood, CO 80112; 24,000.

Sports Club, Indoor (1930), 1145 Highland St., Napoleon, OH 43545.

Standards Institute, Amer. Natl. (1918), 1430 Broadway, N.Y., NY 10018; 1,000.

State Communities Aid Assn. (1872), 105 E. 22d St., N.Y., NY 10010; 75.

State Governments, Council of (1933), P.O. Box 11910, Iron Works Pike, Lexington, KY 40578; 50 states.

State & Local History, Amer. Assn. for (1940), 708 Berry Rd., Nashville, TN 37204; 7,600.

Statistical Assn., Amer. (1839), 806 15th St. NW, Wash., DC 20005; 14,000.

Steamship Historical Society of America (1935), 414 Pelton Ave., Staten Island, NY 10310; 3,375.

Steel Construction, Amer. Institute of (1921), 400 N. Michigan Ave., Chicago, IL 60611; 350.

Sterilization, Assn. for Voluntary (1943), 122 E. 42nd St., N.Y., NY 10168; 3,000.

Stock Car Auto Racing, Natl. Assn. for (NASCAR) (1948), 1801 Speedway Blvd., Daytona Beach, FL 32015; 17,000.

Stock Exchange, Amer. (1971), 86 Trinity Pl., N.Y., NY 10006; 611.

Stock Exchange, N.Y. (1792), 11 Wall St., N.Y., NY 10005.

Stock Exchange, Philadelphia (1790), 1900 Market St., Phila., PA 19103; 505.

Structural Stability Research Council (1944), Fritz Engineering Laboratory No. 13, Lehigh Univ., Bethlehem, PA 18015.

Student Assn., U.S. (1947), 1220 G St. SE, Wash., DC 20024; 3,400,000.

Student Councils, Natl. Assn. of (1931), 1904 Association Dr., Reston, VA 22091; 10,000 secondary schools.

Student Consumer Protection Council, Natl. (1972), Villanova Univ., Villanova, PA 19085; 50.

Stuttering Project, Natl. (1977), 1269 7th Ave., San Francisco, CA 94122; 1,000.

Sudden Infant Death Syndrome Foundation, Inc., Natl. (1962), 8240 Professional Pl., Landover, MD 20785.

Sugar Brokers Assn., Natl. (1893), 1 World Trade Center N.Y., NY 10047; 120.

Sunbathing Assn., Amer. (1931), 1703 N. Main St., Kissimmee, FL 32741; 30,000.

Sunday League (1933), 279 Highland Ave., Newark, NJ 07104; 25,000.

Surgeons, Amer. College of (1913), 55 E. Erie St., Chicago IL 60611; 44,847.

Surgeons, Intl. College of (1935), 1516 N. Lake Shore Dr., Chicago IL 60610; 15,000.

Surgeons of the U.S., Assn. of Military (1903), 10605 Concord St., Kensington, MD 20895; 13,000.

Surveying & Mapping, Amer. Congress on (1941), 210 Little Falls, Falls Church, VA 22046; 12,000.

Symphony Orchestra League, Amer. (1942), P.O. Box 669, Vienna, VA 22180; 4,324.

Systems Management, Assn. for (1947), 24587 Bagley Rd., Cleveland, OH 44138; 9,000.

Table Tennis Assn., U.S. (1933), Olympic House, 1750 E. Boulder, Colorado Springs, CO 80909; 6,200.

Tall Buildings and Urban Habitat, Council on (1969), Fritz Engineering Laboratory, Lehigh Univ., Bethlehem, PA 18015.

Tattoo Club of America (1970), 823 Ave. of the Americas, N.Y., NY 10001; 11,500.

Tax Accountants, Natl. Assn. of Enrolled Federal (1960), 6108 N. Harding Ave., Chicago, IL 60659; 500.

Tax Administrators, Federation of (1937), 444 N. Capitol St. NW, Wash., DC 20001; 50 revenue departments.

Tax Assn.-Natl. Tax Institute of America (1907), 21 E. State St., Columbus, OH 43215; 2,000.

Tax Foundation, Inc. (1937), 1 Thomas Circle NW, Wash., DC 20005; 1,081.

Taxpayers for Unitax (1971), 11015 Cumpston St. N., Hollywood, CA 91601; 28,000.

Taxpayers Union, Natl. (1969). 713 Maryland Ave., NE, Washington, DC 20002; 110,000.

Tea Assn. of the U.S.A. (1899), 230 Park Ave., N.Y., NY 10169; 250.

Teachers of English, Natl. Council of (1911), 1111 Kenyon Rd., Urbana, IL 61801; 90,000.

Teachers of English to Speakers of Other Languages (1966), 202 DC Transit Bldg., Georgetown Univ., Wash., DC 20057; 9,700.

Teachers of French, Amer. Assn. of (1927), 57 E. Armory Ave., Champaign, IL 61820; 9,700.

Teachers of German, American Assn. of (1928), 523 Building, Suite 201, Route 38, Cherry Hill, NJ 08034; 7,000+.

Teachers of Mathematics, Natl. Council of (1920), 1906 Association Dr., Reston, VA 22091; 56,000.

Teachers of Singing, Natl. Assn. of (1944), 250 W. 57th St., N.Y., NY 10107; 3,750.

Teachers of Spanish & Portuguese, Amer. Assn. of (1917), Dr. James R. Chatham, Mississippi State Univ., Mississippi State, MS 39762-5720; 12,000.

Teaching of Foreign Languages, Amer. Council on the (1967), 2 Park Ave., N.Y., NY 10016; 10,000.

Telephone Pioneers of Amer. (1911), 195 Broadway, N.Y., NY 10007; 577,000.

Television Arts & Sciences, Natl. Academy of (1947), 291 S. La Cienega Blvd., Beverly Hills, CA 90211; 11,000.

Television Bureau of Advertising (1954), 1345 Ave. of the Americas, N.Y., NY 10019; 560 stations.

Television & Radio Artists, Amer. Federation of (1937), 1350 Ave. of the Americas, N.Y., NY 10019; 60,000.

Telluride Assn. (1910), 217 West Ave., Ithaca, NY 14850.

Tennis Assn., U.S. (1881), 51 E. 42d St., N.Y., NY 10017; 224,000.

Terrain Vehicle Owners Assn., Natl., All- (1972), P.O. Box 574, Feasterville, PA 19047; 1,144.

Tesla Memorial Soc., Inc. (1979), 453 Martin Rd. Lackawanna, NY 14218; 885.

Testing & Materials, Amer. Society for (1898), 1916 Race St., Phila., PA 19103; 30,000.

Textile Assn., Northern (1854), 211 Congress St., Boston, MA 02110.

Textile Manufacturers Institute, Amer. (1949), 2124 Wachovia Ctr., Charlotte, NC 28285; 250 companies.

Theatre Assn., Amer. (1936), 1010 Wisconsin Ave. NW, Suite 620, Wash., DC 20007.

Theatre Organ Society, Amer. (1955), 1930-301 Encinitas Rd., San Marcos, CA 92069; 6,000.

Theodore Roosevelt Assn. (1919), P.O. Box 720, Oyster Bay, NY 11771; 900.

Theological Library Assn., Amer. (1947), 5600 S. Woodlawn Ave., Chicago, IL 60637; 490.

Theological Schools in the U.S. and Canada, Assn. of (1918), 42 E. National Rd., P.O. Box 130, Vandalia, OH 45377.

Theosophical Society (1875), P.O. Box 270, 1926 N. Main St., Wheaton, IL 60187; 5,339.

Thoreau Society (1941), 156 Belknap St., Concord, MA 01742; 2,000.

Thoroughbred Racing Assns. of North America Inc., (1942), 3000 Marcus Ave., Lake Success, NY 11042; 47 racetracks.

Titanic Historical Society (1963), P.O. Box 53, Indian Orchard, MA 01151; 2,500.

Toastmasters Intl. (1924), 2200 N. Grand Ave., Santa Ana,, CA 92701; 103,000.

Toastmistress Clubs, Intl. (1938), 2519 Woodland Dr., Anaheim, CA 92801; 25,000.

Topical Assn., Amer. (1949), P.O. Box 630, Johnstown, PA 15907; 10,000.

Torch Clubs, Internatl. Assn. of (1924), P.O. Box 30578, Lincoln, NE 68503; 4,300.

Toy Manufacturers of America (1916), 200 Fifth Ave., N.Y., NY 10010; 235.

Trade Relations Council of the U.S. (1885), 1001 Connecticut Ave. NW, Wash., DC 20036; 500 companies.

Traffic and Transportation, Amer. Society of (1946), 1816 Norris Pl. #4, Louisville, KY 40205; 2,400.

Trail Association, North Country (1980), 2780 Mundy Ave., White Cloud, MI 49349; 200+.

Training Corps, Amer. (1960), 107-12 Jamaica Ave., Richmond Hill, NY 11418; 60.

Transit Assn., Amer. Public (1974), 1225 Connecticut Ave. NW, Wash., DC 20036; 750.

Translators Assn., Amer. (1959), 109 Croton Ave., Ossining, NY 10562; 2,000+.

Transportation and Logistics, Inc., Amer. Society of (1946), P.O. Box 33095, Louisville, KY 40232; 3,700.

Trapshooting Assn., Amateur (1899), 601 W. National Rd. Vandalia, OH 45377; 100,000.

Travel Agents, Amer. Society of (1931), 711 Fifth Ave., N.Y., NY 10022; 18,000.

Travel Industry Assn. of America (1965), 1899 L St. NW, Wash., DC 20036; 1,600.

Travelers Protective Assn. of America (1890), 3755 Lindell Blvd., St. Louis, MO 63108; 220,000.

Trilateral Commission (1973), 345 E. 46th, N.Y., NY 10017.

Triple Nine Society (1978), 2119 College St., Cedar Falls, IA 50613; 450.

Trucking Assn., Amer. (1933), 1616 P St. NW, Wash., DC.

True Sisters, United Order (1846), 212 Fifth Ave., N.Y., NY 10010; 8,835.

Tuberous Sclerosis Assn. of Amer. (1970), P.O. Box 44, Rockland, MA 02370; 2,100.

UFOs (Unidentified Flying Objects), Natl. Investigations Committee on (1956), 7970 Woodman Ave., Van Nuys, CA 91402; 2,000.

UNICEF, U.S. Committee for (1947), 331 E. 38th St., N.Y., NY 10016.

Uniformed Services, Natl. Assn. for (1968), 5535 Hempstead Way, Springfield, VA 22151; 25,000.

Underwriters, Amer. Soc. of Chartered Life (1927), 270 Bryn Mawr Ave., Bryn Mawr, PA 19010; 28,000.

Underwriters, Amer. Soc. of Chartered Property and Casualty (1944), Kahler Hall, Providence Rd., Malvern, PA 19355; 14,283.

United Nations Assn. of the U.S.A. (1923, as League of Nations Assn.) 300 E. 42d St., N.Y., NY 10017; 25,000.

United Service Organizations (USO) (1941), 237 E. 52d St., N.Y., NY 10022.

U.S., Amer. Assn. for the Study of in World Affairs (1948), 3813 Annandale Rd., Annandale, VA 22003; 1,000.

United Way of America (1918), 801 N. Fairfax St., Alexandria, VA 22309; 1,200.

Universities, Assn. of Amer. (1900), One Dupont Circle NW, Wash., DC 20036; 50 institutions.

Universities & Colleges, Assn. of Governing Boards of (1921), One Dupont Circle NW, Suite 400, Wash., DC 20036; 995 boards.

University Extension Assn., Natl. (1915), One Dupont Circle, Suite 360, NW, Wash., DC 20036; 1,200.

University Foundation, Intl. (1973), 1301 S. Noland Rd., Independence, MO 64055; 10,500+.

University Professors, Amer. Assn. of (1915), One Dupont Circle, Suite 500, NW, Wash., DC 20036; 70,000.

University Professors for Academic Order (1970), 635 SW 4th St., Corvallis, OR 97333; 500.

University Women, Amer. Assn. of (1881), 2401 Virginia Ave. NW, Wash., DC 20037; 190,000.

Urban Coalition, Natl. (1968), 1120 G St. NW, Suite 900 Wash., DC 20005; 42 affiliates.

Urban League, Natl. (1910), 500 E. 62d St., N.Y., NY 10020.

Utility Commissioners, Natl. Assn. of Regulatory (1889) 12th and Constitution Ave. NW, ICC Bldg., Wash., DC 20423 378.

Valley Forge, Society of the Descendants of Washington's Army at (1976) P.O. Box 915, Valley Forge, PA 19481.

Variety Clubs International (1928), 58 W. 58th St., N.Y., NY 10019.

VASA Order of America (1896), 65 Bryant Rd., Cranston R.I. 02910; 34,000.

Ventriloquists, No. Amer. Assn. of (1940), 800 W. Littleton Blvd., Littleton, CO 80120; 1,876.

Ventriloquists, Soc. of Amer. (1976), 414 Oak St., Baltimore, OH 43105; 1,000.

Veterans Assn., Blinded (1945), 1735 DeSales St. NW, Wash., DC 20036; 4,300.

Veterans Assn., China-Burma-India (1947), 750 N. Lincoln Memorial Dr., Milwaukee, WI 53201; 3,221+.

Veterans Committee, Amer. (1944), 1346 Connecticut Ave. NW, Wash., DC 20036; 25,000.

Veterans of Foreign Wars of the U.S. (1899) **& Ladies Auxiliary** (1914), 406 W. 34th St., Kansas City, MO 64111.

Veterans of World War I (1958), 49/801 N. Fairfax St., Alexandria, VA 22314; 140,000.

Veterinary Medical Assn., Amer. (1863), 930 N. Meacham Rd., Schaumburg, IL 60196; 36,636.

Victorian Society in America (1966), 219 S. Sixth St., Phila., PA 19106; 4,000.

Vocational Assn., Amer. (1925), 2020 N. 14th St., Arlington, VA 22201; 56,000.

Volleyball Assn., U.S. (1928), 1750 E. Boulder, Colorado Springs, CO 80909; 22,500.

Walking Assn. (1976), 4113 Lee Hwy., Arlington, VA 22207; 390.

Walking Society Amer. (1980), P.O. Box 1315, Beverly Hills, CA 90213; 103,185.

War of 1812, General Society of the (1814), 1307 New Hampshire Ave. NW, Wash., DC 20036; 1,100.

War Mothers, Amer. (1917), 2615 Woodley Pl. NW, Wash., DC 20008; 7,000.

Warrant and Warrant Officers' Assn., Chief, U.S. Coast Guard (1929), 492 L'Enfant Plaza E., SW, Wash., DC 20024; 3,451.

Watch & Clock Collectors, Natl. Assn. of (1943), 514 Poplar St., Columbia, PA 17512; 32,500.

Watercolor Soc., American (1866), 47 Fifth Ave., N.Y., NY 10003.

Water Pollution Control Federation (1928), 2626 Pennsylvania Ave. NW, Wash., DC 20037; 30,000.

Water Resources Assn., Amer. (1964), 5410 Grosvenor Ln., Suite 220, Bethesda, MD 20814; 2,600.

Water Ski Assn., Amer. (1939), P.O. Box 191, Winter Haven, FL 33882; 16,500.

Water Well Assn., Natl. (1948), 500 W. Wilson Bridge Rd., Worthington, OH 43085; 8,400.

Water Works Assn., Amer. (1881), 6666 W. Quincy Ave., Denver, CO 80235; 34,000.

Watts Family Assn. (1969), 12401 Burton St., N. Hollywood, CA 91605; 12 branches.

Weather Modification Assn. (1969), P.O. Box 8116, Fresno, CA 93727; 250.

Welding Society, Amer. (1919), 550 N.W. LeJeune Rd., Miami, FL 33126; 32,000+.

Wheelchair Athletic Assn., Natl. (1958), Nassau Community College, Garden City, NY 11530; 2,000+.

Wilderness Society (1935), 1901 Pennsylvania Ave. NW, Wash., DC 20006; 65,000.

Wild Horse Organized Assistance (WHOA!) (1971), 140 Greenstone Dr., Reno, NV 89512; 10,000.

Wildlife, Defenders of (1947), 1244 19th St. NW, Wash., DC 20036; 63,000.

Wildlife Federation, Natl. (1936), 1412 16th St. NW, Wash., DC 20036; 4,100,000.

Wildlife Foundation, No. Amer. (1911), 1101-14th St. NW, Suite 725, Wash., DC 20005.

Wildlife Fund, World (1961), 1601 Connecticut Ave. NW, Wash., DC 20009; 85,000.

Wildlife Management Institute (1911), 1101-14th St., Suite 725, NW, Wash., DC 20005.

William Penn Assn. (1886), 100 Wood St., Pittsburgh, PA 15222; 58,290.

Wilsonian Club (1920), 1331 Parkside Dr., Riverside, CA 92506; 150.

Wireless Pioneers, Society of (1968), 3366—15 Mendocino Ave., Santa Rosa, CA 95402; 4,558.

Wizard of Oz Club, Intl. (1957), Box 95, Kinderhook, IL 62345; 1,800.

Women, Natl. Assn. of Bank (1921), 500 No. Michigan Ave., Chicago, IL 60611; 30,000.

Women, Natl. Organization for (NOW) (1966), 425 13th St. NW, Wash., DC 20004; 240,000.

Women, Rural Amer. (1977), 1522 K St. NW, Wash., DC 20005.

Women Artists, Natl. Assn. of (1889), 41 Union Sq., N.Y., NY 10003; 700.

Women Engineers, Society of (1950), 345 E. 47th St., N.Y., NY 10017; 12,500.

Women in Communications (1909), P.O. Box 9561, Austin,

TX 78766; 12,000.

Women in Radio and TV, Inc. (1951), 1321 Connecticut Ave. NW, Washington, DC 20036; 3,000.

Women Geographers, Society of (1925), 1619 New Hampshire Ave. NW, Wash., DC 20009; 500.

Women Marines Assn. (1960), 2545 E. Reno Ave., Las Vegas, NV 89120; 2,700.

Women Strike for Peace (1961), 145 S. 13th St., Phila., PA 19107; 10,000.

Women's Army Corps Veterans Assn. (1946), 1409 E. Euclid Ave., Arlington Heights, IL 60004; 2,400.

Women's Assn., Amer. (1914), 1270 Ave. of the Americas, N.Y., NY 10020; 250.

Women's Assn., Amer. Business (1949), 9100 Ward Pkwy., P.O. Box 8728, Kansas City, MO 64114.

Women's Christian Temperance Union, Natl. (1874), 1730 Chicago Ave., Evanston, IL 60201.

Women's Clubs, General Federation of (1890), 1734 N St. NW., Wash. DC, 20036; 500,000.

Women's Clubs, Natl. Fed. of Business & Professional (1919), 2012 Massachusetts Ave. NW, Wash., DC 20036; 141,000.

Women's Educational & Industrial Union (1877), 356 Boylston St., Boston, MA 02116; 3,000.

Women's Intl. League for Peace & Freedom (1915), 1213 Race St., Phila., PA 19107; 9,000.

Women's Legal Defense Fund (1971), 2000 P St. NW, Suite 400, Washington, DC 20036; 1,700.

Women's Overseas Service League (1921), P.O. Box 39058, Friendship Sta., Wash., DC 20016; 1,500.

Women of the U.S., Natl. Council of (1888), 777 U.N. Plaza, N.Y., NY 10017; 26 organizations.

Women Voters of the U.S., League of (1920), 1730 M St. NW, Wash., DC 20036; 122,000.

Women World War Veterans (1919), 237 Madison Ave., N.Y., NY 10016.

Woodmen of America, Modern (1883), Mississippi River at 17th St., Rock Island, IL 61201; 384,294.

Woodmen of the World (1890), 1450 Speer Blvd., Denver, CO 80204; 28,954.

Woodmen of the World Life Ins. Soc. (1890), 1700 Farnam St., Omaha, NE 68102; 967,500.

Wool Growers Assn., Natl. (1865), 425 13th St., Rm. 548, Wash., DC 20004; 24 state assns.

Workmen's Circle (1900), 45 E. 33d St., N.Y., NY 10016.

World Future Society (1966), 4916 St. Elmo Ave., Bethesda, MD 20814; 30,000.

World Health, Amer. Assn. for (1951), 2121 Virginia Ave. NW, Wash., DC 20037; 700.

World Health, U.S. Committee for (1951), 777 United Nations Plaza, N.Y., NY 10017; 2,017.

World Peace, International Assn. of Educators for (1969), P.O. Box 3282, Blue Spring Station, Huntsville, AL 35810-0282; 18,500.

Writers of America, Western (1953), 1052 Meridian Rd., Victor, MT 59875; 449.

Writers Assn. of America, Outdoor (1927), 4141 W. Bradley Rd., Milwaukee, WI 53209; 1,500.

Writers Guild of America, West (1954), 8955 Beverly Blvd., Los Angeles, CA 90048; 6,000.

Yeoman F. Natl. (1936), 223 El Camino Real, Vallejo, CA 94590; 800.

Young Americans for Freedom (1960), Woodland Rd., Sterling, VA 22170; 55,000.

Young Men's Christian Assns. of the U.S.A., Natl. Council of (1851), 101 N. Wacker Dr., Chicago, IL 60606; 12,195,076.

YM-YMHAs of Greater New York, Associated (1957), 130 E. 59th St., N.Y., NY 10020; 55,100.

Young Women's Christian Assn. of the U.S.A. (1858), 135 W. 50th St., N.Y., NY 10020; 2,300,000.

Young Engineers & Scientists of America Foundation, Inc. (1959), P.O. Box 9066, Phoenix, AZ 85068; 270 chapters.

Youth, Allied (1936), 1556 Wisconsin Ave., Wash., DC 20007.

Youth Hostels, Amer. (1934), 1332 I St. NW, Suite 800, Wash., DC 20005; 100,000.

Zero Population Growth (1968), 1346 Connecticut Ave. NW, Wash., DC 20036; 15,000.

Ziegfeld Club (1936), 3 W. 51st St., N.Y., NY 10019; 399.

Zionist Organization of America (1897), 4 E. 34th St., N.Y., NY 10016; 130,000.

Zonta Intl. (1919), 35 E. Wacker Dr., Chicago, IL 60605.

Zoological Parks & Aquariums, Amer. Assn. of (1924), Oglebay Park, Wheeling, WV 26003; 3,400.

Zoologists, Amer. Society of (1913), Box 2739, California Lutheran College, Thousand Oaks, CA 91360; 4,500.

RELIGIOUS INFORMATION

Census of Religious Groups in the U.S.

Source: 1984 Yearbook of American and Canadian Churches

The 1984 Yearbook of American and Canadian Churches reported a total of 139,603,059 members of religious groups in the U.S.—59.6 percent of the population.

Comparisons of membership statistics from group to group are not necessarily meaningful. Membership definitions vary —e.g., Roman Catholics count members from infancy, but some Protestant groups count only "adult" members, usually 13 years or older; some groups compile data carefully, but others estimate; not all groups report annually.

The number of churches appear in parentheses. Asterisk (*) indicates church declines to publish membership figures; (**) indicates figures date from 1975 or earlier.

Group	Members
Adventist churches:	
Advent Christian Ch. (364)	29,838
Primitive Advent Christian Ch. (10)	566
Seventh-day Adventists (3,826)	606,310
American Rescue Workers (15)	2,140
Anglican Orthodox Church (37)	**2,630
Baha'i Faith (1,650)	100,000
Baptist churches:	
Amer. Baptist Assn. (1,641)	225,000
Amer. Baptist Chs. in U.S.A. (5,939)	1,621,795
Baptist General Conference (721)	120,928
Baptist Missionary Assn. of America (1,140)	225,000
Conservative Baptist Assn. of America (1,095)	237,500
Duck River (and Kindred) Assn. of Baptists (85)	**8,632
Free Will Baptists (2,505)	243,658
Gen. Assn. of General Baptists (870)	75,028
Gen. Assn. of Regular Baptist Chs. (1,571)	300,839
Natl. Baptist Convention of America (11,398)	**2,668,799
Natl. Baptist Convention, U.S.A. (26,000)	**5,500,000
Natl. Primitive Baptist Convention (606)	250,000
No. Amer. Baptist Conference (260)	42,735
Seventh Day Baptist General Conference (63)	5,008
Southern Baptist Convention (36,246)	13,991,709
Brethren (German Baptists):	
Brethren Ch. (Ashland, Ohio) (125)	14,857
Christian Congregation (La Follette, IN) (1,435)	100,694
Ch. of the Brethren (1,063)	168,844
Old German Baptist Brethren (52)	5,254
Brethren, River:	
Brethren in Christ Ch. (167)	16,201
Buddhist Churches of America (62)	100,000
Christadelphians (850)	**15,800
The Christian and Missionary Alliance (1,485)	204,713
Christian Catholic Church (5)	2,500
Christian Church (Disciples of Christ) (4,291)	1,156,458
Christian Churches and Churches of Christ (5,605)	1,063,254
Christian Methodist Episcopal Church (2,883)	786,707
Christian Nation Church U.S.A. (5)	226
Christian Union (108)	5,463
Churches of Christ (12,750)	1,605,000
Churches of Christ in Christian Union (251)	11,954
Churches of God:	
Chs. of God, General Conference (345)	34,241
Church of God (5,284)	463,992
Ch. of God (Anderson, Ind.) (2,275)	184,685
Ch. of God (Seventh Day), Denver, Col. (125)	4,875
Church of Christ, Scientist (3,000)	*
The Church of God by Faith (105)	4,500
Church of the Nazarene (4,902)	498,491
National Council of Community Churches (185)	190,000
Natl. Assn. of Congregational Christian Churches (458)	106,460
Conservative Congregational Christian Conference (140)	26,008
Eastern Orthodox churches:	
Albanian Orth. Diocese of America (10)	5,250
American Carpatho-Russian Orth. Greek Catholic Ch. (70)	100,000
Antiochian Orth. Christian Archdiocese of No. Amer. (110)	152,000
Diocese of the Armenian Ch. of America (66)	450,000
Bulgarian Eastern Orth. Ch. (13)	**86,000
Coptic Orthodox Ch. (29)	100,000
Greek Orth. Archdiocese of N. and S. America (535)	1,950,000
Orthodox Ch. in America (440)	1,000,000
Patriarchal Parishes of the Russian Orth. Ch. in the U.S.A. (41)	**51,500

Group	Members
Romanian Orth. Episcopate of America (34)	40,000
Serbian Eastern Orth. Ch. (75)	97,123
Syrian Orth. Ch. of Antioch (Archdiocese of the U.S.A. and Canada) (13)	30,000
Ukrainian Orth. Ch. in America (Ecumenical Patriarchate) (30)	30,000
Ukrainian Orthodox Church in the U.S.A. (107)	**87,745
The Episcopal Church in the U.S.A. (7,095)	2,794,139
American Ethical Union (Ethical Culture Movement) (25)	4,000
Evangelical Church of North America (143)	13,088
Evangelical Congregational Church (183)	39,710
The Evangelical Covenant Church of America (550)	81,324
Evangelical Free Church of America (853)	110,555
Evangelical associations:	
Apostolic Christian Chs. of America (82)	21,173
Apostolic Christian Ch. (Nazarean) (46)	2,684
Christian Congregation (1,435)	100,694
Friends:	
Evangelical Friends Alliance (217)	24,095
Friends General Conference (233)	**26,184
Friends United Meeting (535)	59,338
Grace Gospel Fellowship (47)	4,250
Independent Fundamental Churches of America (1,019)	120,446
Jehovah's Witnesses (7,752)	619,188
Jewish congregations:	
Agudath Israel of America (Orthodox) (40)	100,000
Union of Amer. Hebrew Congregations (Reformed) (773)	1,300,000
Natl. Council of Young Israel (Orthodox) (167)	250,000+
Union of Orthodox Jewish Congregations of America (1,700)	1,000,000
United Synagogue of America (Conservative) (790)	1,250,000
Latter-day Saints:	
Ch. of Jesus Christ (Bickertonites) (53)	2,654
Ch. of Jesus Christ of Latter-day Saints (Mormon) (7,839)	3,521,000
Reorganized Ch. of Jesus Christ of Latter Day Saints (1,061)	201,460
Lutheran churches:	
American Lutheran Ch. (4,897)	2,346,710
Ch. of the Lutheran Brethren of America (106)	10,580
Ch. of the Lutheran Confession (67)	8,986
Assn. of Evangelical Lutheran Chs. (272)	110,934
Evangelical Lutheran Synod (110)	20,025
Assn. of Free Lutheran Congregations (145)	16,759
Latvian Evangelical Lutheran Church in America (60)	13,526
Lutheran Ch. in America (5,815)	2,925,655
Lutheran Ch.-Missouri Synod (5,752)	2,630,823
Protestant Conference (Lutheran) (10)	1,605
Wisconsin Evangelical Lutheran Synod (1,151)	412,529
Mennonite churches:	
Beachy Amish Mennonite Chs. (79)	5,460
Evangelical Mennonite Ch. (24)	3,832
General Conference of Mennonite Brethren Chs. (124)	17,065
The General Conference Mennonite Ch. (218)	36,644
Hutterian Brethren (220)	31,200
Mennonite Ch. (1,179)	101,501
Old Order Amish Ch. (589)	82,460
Old Order (Wisler) Mennonite Ch. (38)	9,731

Group	Members	Group	Members
Methodist churches:		Pentecostal Assemblies of the World (550) . . .	**4,500
African Methodist Episcopal Ch. (6,200)	2,210,000	Pentecostal Church of God (1,107)	91,008
African Methodist Episcopal Zion Ch. (6,023) . .	1,134,179	United Pentecostal Ch. Intl. (3,300)	465,000
Evangelical Methodist Ch. (139)	**10,502	Pentecostal Free-Will Baptist Ch. (127)	9,280
Free Methodist Ch. of North America (1,012) . .	70,657	**Plymouth Brethren (1,100)**	98,000
Fundamental Methodist Ch. (14)	700	**Polish Natl. Catholic Church of America (162). .**	282,411
Primitive Methodist Ch., U.S.A. (87)	9,978	**Presbyterian churches:**	
Reformed Methodist Union Episcopal Ch. (17) .	**3,800	Associate Reformed Presbyterian Ch. (Gen.	
Southern Methodist Ch. (169)	11,000	Synod) (156)	31,518
United Methodist Ch. (38,298)	9,457,012	Cumberland Presbyterian Ch. (865)	97,813
Moravian churches:		Orthodox Presbyterian Ch. (157)	17,108
Moravian Ch. (Unitas Fratrum), Northern		Presbyterian Ch. in America (797)	149,548
Province (98)	33,092	Presbyterian Ch. in the U.S. (4,250)	814,931
Moravian Ch. in America (Unitas Fratrum),		Reformed Presbyterian Ch. of No. Amer. (67) . .	4,836
Southern Province (56)	21,618	United Presbyterian Ch. in the U.S.A. (8,909) . .	2,342,441
Unity of the Brethren (32)	**6,142		
Muslims	2,000,000+	**Reformed churches:**	
		Christian Reformed Ch. in N. America (648) . . .	223,976
New Apostolic Church of North America (411) .	29,638	Hungarian Reformed Ch. in America (31)	11,000
North American Old Roman Catholic Church		Protestant Reformed Chs. in America (21). . . .	4,544
(130)	62,383	Reformed Ch. in America (915)	346,293
		Reformed Ch. in the U.S. (30)	3,710
Old Catholic churches:		**The Roman Catholic Church (24,071)**	52,088,774
Christ Catholic Ch. (5)	2,500		
Mariavite Old Cath. Ch. Province of North		**The Salvation Army (1,060)**	419,475
America (166).	357,927	**The Schwenkfelder Church (5)**	2,700
No. Amer. Old Roman Cath. Ch. (Schweikert)		**Social Brethren (30)**	1,784
(130)	62,383	**Natl. Spiritualist Assn. of Churches (164)**.	5,168
		Gen. Convention, The Swedenborgian	
Pentecostal churches:		**Church (39)**	1,820
Apostolic Faith (45)	4,100		
Assemblies of God (10,173)	1,879,182	**Unitarian Universalist Assn. (935)**	131,844
Bible Church of Christ (6)	4,350	**United Brethren:**	
Bible Way Church of Our Lord Jesus Christ		Ch. of the United Brethren in Christ (256)	26,869
World Wide (350)	**30,000	United Christian Ch. (11)	430
Church of God (Cleveland, Tenn.) (5,284)	463,992	**United Church of Christ (6,461)**	1,716,723
Church of God of Prophecy (2,026)	74,084	**Universal Fellowship of Metropolitan**	
Congregational Holiness Ch. (174)	8,347	**Community Chs. (185)**	32,000
Gen. Council, Christian Ch. of No. Amer.			
(101)	12,500	**Vedanta Society (13)**	1,000
Intl. Ch. of the Foursquare Gospel (714)	**89,215	**Volunteers of America (607)**	36,634
Open Bible Standard Chs. (277)	46,651		
		The Wesleyan Church (1,725).	105,221

Religious Population of the World

Source: The 1984 Encyclopaedia Britannica Book of the Year

Religion	N. America[1]	S. America	Europe[2]	Asia[3]	Africa	Oceania[4]	Totals
Total Christian. . . .	252,458,670	196,599,780	337,678,150	104,098,695	147,076,000	18,781,550	1,056,692,845
Roman Catholic .	138,875,530	185,251,200	178,032,590	57,265,290	56,999,270	5,215,440	621,639,320
Eastern Orthodox	5,648,620	355,250	47,069,040	2,762,810	9,401,840[6]	407,650	65,645,210
Protestant[5]	107,934,520	10,993,330	112,576,520	44,070,595	80,674,890[7]	13,158,460	369,408,315
Jewish	7,611,940	749,580	4,643,810	4,008,850	231,980	73,980	17,320,140
Muslim[6]	1,580,980	406,190	20,190,500	380,068,940	152,943,570	87,000	555,277,180
Zoroastrian	2,750	2,600	14,000	224,370	900	1,000	245,620
Shinto	50,000	—	—	33,000,000	—	—	33,050,000
Taoist	33,250	12,975	13,500	20,500,000	850	2,900	20,563,475
Confucian	99,750	58,925	450,500	162,500,000	2,550	18,390	163,130,115
Buddhist	336,290	241,090	238,300	250,097,200	15,000	23,700	250,951,580
Hindu.	309,100	637,400	442,890	459,708,450	1,165,600	326,470	462,589,910
Totals.	262,482,730	198,708,540	363,671,650	1,414,206,505	301,436,450	19,314,990	2,559,820,865
Population[7]. . . .	389,914,000	259,644,000	761,195,000	2,771,419,000	516,037,000	23,677,000	4,721,886,000

(1) Includes Central America and West Indies. (2) Includes communist countries where it is difficult to determine religious affiliation. (3) Includes areas in which persons have traditionally enrolled in several religions, as well as China, with an official communist establishment. (4) Includes Australia, New Zealand, and islands of the South Pacific. (5) Protestant figures outside Europe usually include "full members" (adults) rather than all baptized persons and are not comparable to those of ethnic religions or churches counting all adherents. (6) According to the Islamic Center, Wash., D.C., there are 1 billion Muslims worldwide. (7) United Nations data, midyear 1982.

National Council of Churches of Christ

The National Council of the Churches of Christ in the U.S.A. is a cooperative agency of 31 Protestant and Orthodox churches which seeks to advance programs and policies of mutual interest to its members. The NCCC was formed in 1950 by the merger of 14 inter-denominational agencies. The Council's member churches now have an aggregate membership totaling approximately 40 million. The NCCC is not a governing body and has no control over the policies or operations of any church belonging to it. The work of the Council is divided into 3 divisions: Church and Society; Education and Ministry; Overseas Ministries; and 5 commissions — Faith and Order; Regional and Local Ecumenism; Communication; Stewardship; Justice and Liberation. The chief administrative officer of the NCCC is Dr. Claire Randall, 475 Riverside Drive, N.Y., NY 10115.

Headquarters, Leaders of U.S. Religious Groups

See Associations and Societies section for religious organizations. (year organized in parentheses)

Adventist churches:
Advent Christian Church (1854) — Pres., Glennon Balser; exec. v.p., Rev. Adrian B. Shepard, Box 23152, Charlotte, NC 28212.
Primitive Advent Christian Church — Pres., Elza Moss; sec., Hugh W. Good, 395 Frame Rd., Elkview, WV 25071.
Seventh-day Adventists (1863) — Pres., Neal C. Wilson; sec., G. Ralph Thompson, 6840 Eastern Ave. NW, Wash., DC 20012.

Baha'i Faith — Chpsn., Judge James E. Nelson; sec., Dr. Firuz Kazamzadeh, 536 Sheridan Rd., Wilmette, IL 60091.

Baptist churches:
American Baptist Assn. (1905) — Pres., Dr. J. C. James; rec. clk., W E. Norris, 4605 N. State Line, Texarkana, TX 75504.
American Baptist Churches in the U.S.A. (1907) — Pres., Mrs. Margaret Prine; gen. sec., Rev. Dr. Robert C. Campbell, Valley Forge, PA 19481.
Baptist General Conference (1879) — Gen. sec., Dr. Warren Magnuson, 2002 S. Arlington Heights Rd., Arlington Heights, IL 60005.
Baptist Missionary Assn. of America (formerly **North American Baptist Assn.**) (1950) — Pres., Rev. Don Collins, rec. sec., Rev. Ralph Cottrell, Box 2866, Texarkana, AR 75501.
Conservative Baptist Assn. of America (1947) — Gen. Dir., Dr. Russell A. Shive, Box 66, Wheaton, IL 60189.
Free Will Baptists (1727) — Mod., Rev. Bobby Jackson; exec. sec., Dr. Melvin Worthington, Box 1088, Nashville, TN 37202.
General Assn. of General Baptists (1823) — Exec. sec., Rev. Glen Spence, 100 Stinson Dr., Poplar Bluff, MO 63901.
General Assn. of Regular Baptist Churches (1932) — Chpsn., Dr. Mark Jackson; natl. rep., Dr. Paul N. Tassell, 1300 N. Meacham Rd., Schaumburg, IL 60195.
Natl. Baptist Convention, U.S.A. (1880) — Pres., Dr. T.J. Jemison; gen. sec., W. Franklyn Richardson, 52 S. 6th Ave., Mt. Vernon, NY 10550.
North American Baptist Conference (1865) — Mod., Rev. Eugene Kern; exec. dir., Dr. John Binder, 1 S. 210 Summit Ave., Oakbrook Terrace, IL 60181.
Southern Baptist Convention (1945) — Pres., James T. Draper Jr.; exec. sec., exec. comm., Dr. Harold C. Bennett, 460 James Robertson Pkwy., Nashville, TN 37219.
United Free Will Baptist Church (1870) — Vice-Mod., Rev. O.L. Williams, Kingston College, 1101 University St., Kinston, NC 28501.

Brethren in Christ Church (1798) — Mod., Bishop R. Donald Shafer; sec., Dr. Arthur M. Climenhaga, 1125 W. Arrow Highway, Upland, CA 91786.

Brethren (German Baptists):
Brethren Church (Ashland, Oh.) (1882) — Dir., Ronald W. Waters, William Kerner, 524 College Ave., Ashland, OH 44805.
Church of the Brethren (1719) — Mod., Earle W. Fike Jr; gen. sec., Robert Neff, 1451 Dundee Ave., Elgin, IL 60120.

Buddhist Churches of America (1899) — Bishop, Rt. Rev. Seigen H. Yamaoka, 1710 Octavia St., San Francisco, CA 94109.

Calvary Grace Christian Church of Faith (1898) — Intl. gen. supt., Col. Herman Keck Jr., U.S. Box 4266, Norton AFB, San Bernardino, CA 92409.

Calvary Grace Church of Faith (1874) — Intl. gen. supt., Rev. A.C. Spern, Box 333, Rillton, PA 15678.

The Christian and Missionary Alliance (1887) — Pres., Dr. Louis L. King; sec., Dr. Elwood N. Nielsen, 350 N. Highland Ave., Nyack, NY 10960.

Christian Church (Disciples of Christ) (1809) — Gen. minister and pres., Dr. Kenneth L. Teegarden, 222 S. Downey Ave., Box 1986, Indianapolis, IN 46206.

The Christian Congregation (1887) — Gen. supt., Rev. Ora Wilbert Eads, 804 W. Hemlock St., LaFollette, TN 37766.

Christian Methodist Episcopal Church (1870) — Adm. Coord., Rev. Tyrone T. Davis; sec., Rev. Edgar L. Wade, P. O. Box 3403, Memphis, TN 38101.

Churches of Christ in Christian Union (1909) — Gen. supt., Rev. Robert Kline; gen. sec., Rev. Robert Barth, Box, 30, Circleville, OH 43113.

Churches of God:
Churches of God, General Conference (1825) — Admin., Dr. Richard E. Wilkin, Box 926, Findlay, OH 45839.
Church of God (Anderson, Ind.) (1880) — Chpsn., Samuel G. Hines; exec. sec., Paul A. Tanner, Box 2420, Anderson, IN 46018.

Church of Christ, Scientist (1879) — Pres., James K. Kyser; clerk, Allison W. Phinney, Christian Science Center, Boston, MA 02115.

Church of the Nazarene (1908) — Gen. sec., B. Edgar Johnson, 6401 The Paseo, Kansas City, MO 64131.

National Association of Congregational Christian Churches (1955) — Mod., Marion Luenberger; exec. sec., Dr. A. Ray Appelquist, Box 1620, Oak Creek, WI 53154.

Eastern Orthodox churches:
Antiochian Orthodox Christian Archdiocese of North America (formerly **Syrian Antiochian Orthodox Archdiocese**) (1894) — Primate, Metropolitan Archbishop Philip (Saliba); aux., Archbishop Michael (Shaheen), Bishop Antoun (Khouri), 358 Mountain Rd., Englewood, NJ 07631.
Diocese of the Armenian Church of America (1889) — Primate, His Eminence Archbishop Torkom Manoogian; sec., V. Rev. Houssig Bagdasian, 630 2d Ave., N.Y., NY 10016. **Western Diocese** — 1201 N. Vine St., Hollywood, CA 90038.
Coptic Orthodox Ch. — Correspnt., Archpriest Fr. Gabriel Abdelsayed, 427 West Side Ave., Jersey City, NJ 07304.
Greek Orthodox Archdiocese of North and South America (1864) — Primate, Archbishop Iakovos; sec., Peter Kourides, 8-10 E. 79th St., N.Y., NY 10021.
Orthodox Church in America (formerly **Russian Orthodox Greek Catholic Church of North America**) (1792) — Primate, Metropolitan Theodosius; chancellor, V. Rev. Daniel Hubiak, P.O. Box 675, Syosset, NY 11791.
Romanian Orthodox Episcopate of America (1929) — Archbishop, Valerian (D. Trifa); aux. Bishop, Nathaniel (Popp); sec., Rev. Fr. Laurence E. Lazar, 2522 Grey Tower Rd., Jackson, MI 49201.
Serbian Eastern Orthodox Church for the U.S.A. and Canada — Bishops, Rt. Rev. Bishop Firmilian, Rt. Rev. Bishop Gregory; Bishop Christophor; St. Sava Monastery, Libertyville, IL 60048.
Syrian Orthodox Church of Antioch, Archdiocese of the U.S.A. and Canada (1957) — Primate, Archbishop MarAthanasius Y. Samuel; gen. sec., Rev. Fr. John Meno, 45 Fairmount Ave., Hackensack, NJ 07601.
Ukrainian Orthodox Church in America (Ecumenical Patriarchate) (1928) — Primate, Most Rev. Metropolitan Andrei Kuschak; aux., Most Rev. Bishop Nicholas Smisko 90-34 139th St., Jamaica, NY 11435.
Ukrainian Orthodox Church in the U.S.A. (1919) — Metropolitan, Most Rev. Mstyslav S. Skrypnyk, Box 495, South Bound Brook, NJ 08880.

The Episcopal Church (1789) — Presiding bishop, Rt. Rev. John M. Allin; sec., Rev. Canon James R. Gundrum, 815 2d Ave., N.Y., NY 10017.

The Evangelical Covenant Church (1885) — Pres., Dr. Milton B. Engebretson; sec., Rev. Clifford Bjorklund, 5101 N. Francisco Ave., Chicago, IL 60625.

Friends:
Evangelical Friends Alliance (1965) — Pres., Maurice A. Roberts, 2018 Maple, Wichita, KS 67213.
Friends General Conference (1900) — Clk., George N. Webb; gen. sec., Lloyd Lee Wilson, 1520B Race St., Phila., PA 19102.
Friends United Meeting (formerly **Five Years Meeting of Friends**) (1902) — Presiding clerk, Clifford Winslow, 101 Quaker Hill Dr., Richmond, IN 47374.

Independent Fundamental Churches of America (1930) — Pres., Dr. Calvin H.C. Probasco, 5640 Vega Ct., Carmichael, CA 95608.

Federation of Islamic Assns. in U.S. and Canada — 300 E. 44th St., N.Y., NY 10017.

Jehovah's Witnesses (1879) — Watch Tower Pres., Frederick W. Franz, 25 Columbia Heights, Brooklyn, NY 11201.

Jewish congregations:
Union of American Hebrew Congregations (Reform) — Pres., Rabbi Alexander M. Schindler, 838 5th Ave., N.Y., NY 10021.

Union of Orthodox Jewish Congregations of America — Pres., Julius Berman, 116 E. 27th St., N.Y., NY 10016.

United Synagogue of America (Conservative) — Pres., Marshall Wolke, exec. v.p., Rabbi Benjamin Z. Kreitman, 155 5th Ave., N.Y., NY 10010.

Latter-day Saints:

The Church of Jesus Christ of Latter-day Saints (Mormon) (1830) — Pres., Spencer W. Kimball, 50 E. North Temple St., Salt Lake City, UT 84150.

Reorganized Church of Jesus Christ of Latter Day Saints (1830) — Pres., Wallace B. Smith, The Auditorium, P.O. Box 1059, Independence, MO 64051.

Lutheran churches:

The American Lutheran Church (1961) — Pres., Dr. David W. Preus; gen. sec., Dr. Kathryn E. Baerwald, 422 S. 5th St., Minneapolis, MN 55415.

Church of the Lutheran Brethren of America (1900) — Pres., Rev. Everald H. Strom; sec., Rev. George Aase, 1007 Westside Dr., Box 655, Fergus Falls, MN 56537.

Church of the Lutheran Confession (1961) — Pres., Rev. Daniel Fleischer; sec., Rev. Paul F. Nolting, 800 Custer Rd., Apt. 236, Richardson, TX 75080.

Assn. of Evangelical Lutheran Churches (1976) — Bishop, Dr. William H. Kohn; exec. sec., Doctor Elwyn Ewald, 12015 Manchester Rd., St. Louis, MO 63131.

Evangelical Lutheran Synod (1853) — Pres., Rev. George Orvick; sec., Rev. Alf Merseth, 106 13th St. S., Northwood, IA 50459.

Assn. of Free Lutheran Congregations (1962) — Pres., Richard Snipstead; sec., Rev. Bruce Dalager, 3110 E. Medicine Lake Blvd., Minneapolis, MN 55441.

Lutheran Church in America (1962) — Bishop, Rev. Dr. James R. Crumley Jr.; sec., Rev. Dr. Reuben T. Swanson, 231 Madison Ave., N.Y. NY 10016.

Lutheran Church — Missouri Synod (1847) — Pres., Dr. Ralph Bohlmann; sec., Dr. Walter L. Rosin, 1333 S. Kirkwood, St. Louis, MO 63122.

Wisconsin Evangelical Lutheran Synod (1850) — Pres., Rev. Carl H. Mischke; 3512 W. North Ave., Milwaukee, WI 53208; sec., Prof. David Worgull, 1201 W. Tulsa, Chandler, AZ 85224.

Mennonite churches:

The General Conference Mennonite Church (1860) — Pres. Jacob Tilitzky; gen. sec., Norma Weins, 722 Main, Newton, KS 67114.

Mennonite Church (1690) — Mod., James M. Lapp, 528 E. Madison St., Lombard, IL 60148.

Methodist churches:

African Methodist Episcopal Zion Church (1796) — Sr. Bishop, William M. Smith; sec., Bishop Charles H. Foggie, 1200 Windermere Dr., Pittsburgh, PA 15218.

Evangelical Methodist Church (1946) — Gen. supt., John F. Kunkle; gen. sec., Rev. R.D. Driggers, 3000 W. Kellogg Dr., Wichita, KS 67213.

Free Methodist Church of North America (1860) — Bishops R. Andrews, D. Bastian, W. Cryderman, E. Parsons, C. Van Valin, gen. conf. sec., C.T. Denbo, 901 College Ave., Winona Lake, IN 46590.

The United Methodist Church (1968) — Pres. Counc. of Bishops, Bishop Wilbur W. Y. Choy, 223 Fourth Ave., Pittsburgh, PA 15222; sec., gen. conf., Dr. J.B. Holt, Perkins School of Theology, Dallas, TX 75275.

Universal Fellowship of Metropolitan Community Churches —Mod., Rev. Troy D. Perry; clerk, Rev. Nancy L. Wilson, 5300 Santa Monica Blvd., Suite 304, Los Angeles, CA 90029.

Moravian Church (Unitas Fratum) (1740) **Northern Province** — Pres., The Rt. Rev. Wilbur Behrend, 69 W. Church St., Box 1245, Bethlehem, PA 18018. **Southern Province** — Pres., Rev. Graham H. Rights, 459 S. Church St., Winston-Salem, NC 27108.

Old Catholic churches:

Mariavite Old Catholic Church-Province of North America (1932) — Prime bishop, Most Rev. Robert R.J.M. Zaborowski O.M., D.D., 2803 10th St., Wyandotte, MI 48192.

North American Old Roman Catholic Church (1915) — Archbishop, Most Rev. J.E. Schweikert, 4200 N. Kedvale Ave., Chicago, IL 60641.

Pentecostal churches:

Assemblies of God (1914) — Gen. supt., Thomas F. Zimmerman; gen. sec., Joseph R. Flower, 1445 Boonville Ave., Springfield, MO 65802.

Bible Way Church of Our Lord Jesus Christ World Wide (1927) — Presiding bishop, Smallwood E. Williams; gen. sec., Bishop Christal T. Hairston, 1100 New Jersey Ave. NW, Wash., DC 20001.

Gen. Council, Christian Church of No. America (1948) — Gen. overseer; Rev. Carmine Saginario; gen. sec., Rev. John H. King, Box 141-A, RD #1, Rt. 18 & Rutledge Rd., Transfer, PA 16154.

The Church of God (1903) — Gen. overseer, Bishop Voy M. Bullen; gen. sec., Betty Bullen, 2504 Arrow Wood Dr. SE, Huntsville, AL 35803.

Church of God (Cleveland, Tenn.) (1886) — Gen. overseer, C. C. Thomas; gen. sec., Robert J. Hart, Keith at 25th St. NW, Cleveland, TN 37311.

International Church of the Foursquare Gospel (1927) — Pres., Dr. Rolf K. McPherson; sec., Dr. Leland E. Edwards, 1100 Glendale Blvd., Los Angeles, CA 90026.

National Gay Pentecostal Alliance (1980) — Pres., Rev. Wm. H. Carey, P.O. Box 1391, Schenctady, NY 12301.

Open Bible Standard Churches (1919) — Gen. supt., Ray E. Smith; sec., Patrick L. Bowlin, 2020 Bell Ave., Des Moines, IA 50315.

Pentecostal Church of God (1919) — Gen. supt., Dr. Roy M. Chappell; gen. sec., Rev. Ronald R. Minor, 211 Main St., Joplin, MO 64801.

United Pentecostal Church International (1945) — Gen. supt., Nathaniel A. Urshan; gen. sec., Cleveland Becton, 8855 Dunn Rd., Hazelwood, MO 63042.

Pentecostal Free Will Baptist Church (1959) — Gen. supt., Dr. Herbert Carter; gen. sec., Rev. Don Sauls, Box 1568, Dunn, NC 28334.

Presbyterian churches:

Cumberland Presbyterian Church (1810) — Mod., Robert Forester; stated clerk, T.V. Warnick, 1978 Union Ave., Memphis, TN 38104.

The Orthodox Presbyterian Church (1936) — Mod. Glenn T. Black; stated clerk, Richard A. Barker, 7401 Old York Rd., Phila., PA 19126.

Presbyterian Church in America (1973) — Mod., L.B. Austin III; stated clerk, Rev. Morton H. Smith, P.O. Box 1428, Decatur, GA 30031.

Presbyterian Church in the U.S.A. (1865) — Mod., Rev. J. Randolph Taylor; stated clerks, James E. Andrews, William B. Thompson, 475 Riverside Dr., N.Y. NY, 10115.

Reformed Presbyterian Church of No. America (1871) — Mod., Rev. Paul E. Faris, P.O. Box 126-B, Lisbon, NY 13658.

Reformed churches:

Christian Reformed Church in North America (1857) — Stated clerk, Rev. Leonard J. Hoffman, 2850 Kalamazoo Ave., SE, Grand Rapids, MI 49560.

Reformed Church in America (1628) — Pres., Leonard V. Kalkwarf; gen. sec., Edwin G. Mulder, 475 Riverside Dr., N.Y., NY 10115.

Reformed Episcopal Church (1873) — Pres., Rev. Theophilus J. Herter; sec., Rev. Dale H. Crouthamel, 14 Culberson Rd., Basking Ridge, NJ 07920.

Roman Catholic Church — National Conference of Catholic Bishops. Pres., Archbishop James W. Malone; sec., Bishop Thomas C. Kelly, 1312 Massachusetts Ave. NW, Wash., DC 20005.

The Salvation Army (1880) — Natl. cmdr., Commissioner Norman S. Marshall; natl. chief sec., Col. G. Ernest Murray, 799 Bloomfield Ave., Verona, NJ 07044.

Sikh (1972) — Chief adm., Siri Singh Sahib, Harbhajan Singh Khalsa Yogiji; sec. gen., Mukhia Sardarni Sahiba, Sardarni Premka Kaur Khalsa, 1649 S. Robertson Blvd., Los Angeles, CA 90035.

Unitarian Universalist Assn. (1961) — Pres., Rev. Dr. Eugene Pickett; sec., Donald W. Male, 25 Beacon St., Boston, MA 02108.

United Brethren in Christ (1789) — Chpsn., Bishop C. Ray Miller; 302 Lake St., Huntington, IN 46750.

United Church of Christ (1957) — Pres., Rev. Avery D. Post; sec., Rev. Carol Joyce Brun, 105 Madison Ave., N.Y., NY 10016.

Volunteers of America (1896) — Cmdr.-in-chief, Gen. Ray C. Tremont; natl. sec., Maj. John A. Hood, 3939 N. Causeway Blvd., Metairie, LA 70002.

The Wesleyan Church (1968) — Gen. supts., Drs. J. D. Abbott, O.D. Emery, R. McIntyre, V. Mitchell; sec., Ronald Brannon, Box 2000, Marion, IN 46953.

Headquarters of Religious Groups in Canada

(year organized in parentheses)

Anglican Church of Canada (creation of General Synod 1893) - Primate, Most Rev. E.W. Scott; 600 Jarvis St., Toronto, Ont. M4Y 2J6.

Apostolic Church in Canada - H.O. 27 Castlefield Ave., Toronto, Ont. M4R 1G3; Pres., Rev. D.S. Morris, 685 Park St. South, Peterborough, Ont. K9J 3S9.

Baha'is of Canada, The National Spiritual Assembly of the (1949) - Gen. Sec. Douglas Martin, 7200 Leslie St., Thornhill, Ont. L3T 2A1.

Baptist Federation of Canada - Pres., Jerry Zeman; Gen. Sec.-Treasurer, Rev. Michael Steeves, 219 St. George St., Toronto, Ont. M5R 2M2.

Bible Holiness Movement, The (1949) - Pres., Evangelist Wesley H. Wakefield, Box 223, Stn. A, Vancouver, B.C. V6C 2M3.

Canadian Council of Churches, The (1938) - Gen. Sec., Rev. Donald W. Anderson, 40 St. Clair Ave. E., Suite 201, Toronto, Ont. M4T 1M9.

Canadian Jewish Congress (1919) - Pres., Milton Harris; National Exec. Dir. Dr. Jim Archibald; Exec. Vice-Pres., Alan Rose; 1590 Avenue Docteur Penfield, Montreal, Que. H3G 1C5.

Christian and Missionary Alliance in Canada, The (1889) - Pres., Rev. M.P. Sylvester, Box 7900, Stn. B, Willowdale, Ont. M2K 2R3.

Christian Church (Disciples of Christ) (All Canada Committee formed 1922) - Exec. Min. W. Ray Miles 39 Arkell Rd., R.R. 2, Guelph, Ont. N1H 6H8.

Christian Science in Canada - Mr. J. Don Fulton, 339 Bloor St. W., Ste. 214, Toronto, Ont. M5S 1W7.

Church of Jesus Christ of Latter-Day Saints (Mormons) (1830) - Pres. Calgary Stake, R.H. Walker, 930 Prospect Ave. S.W., Calgary Alta. T2T 0W5; Pres. Edmonton Stake, Donald D. Salmon, 11619 48 Ave.., Edmonton, Alta. T6H 0E7; Pres. Toronto Stake, James L. Kirschbaum, 5 Edenbrook Hill, Islington, Ont. M9A 3Z5; Pres. Vancouver Stake, R.W. Komm, 1384 Chartwell Dr., West Vancouver, B.C. V7S 2R5.

Church of the Nazarene (1902) - Dist. Superintendent of Canada Central District, Rev. Lorne MacMillan, 38 Riverhead Dr., Rexdale, Ont. M9W 4G6; Chairman of Exec. Board, Rev. Alexander Ardrey, 2236 Capitol Hill Cres. N.W., Calgary, Alta. T2M 4B9.

Fellowship of Evangelical Baptist Churches in Canada (1953) - Gen. Sec. Dr. Roy W. Lawson, 74 Sheppard Ave. W., Willowdale, Ont. M2N 1M3.

Free Methodist Church in Canada (1880) - Pres., Bishop D.N. Bastian, 96 Elmbrook Cres., Etobicoke, Ont. M9C 5E2; Exec. Sec., Rev. C.A. Horton, 5741 Tunney Dr., Mississauga, Ont. L5M 2G5.

Greek Orthodox Church in Canada - His Grace Bishop Sotirios, 27 Teddington Park Ave., Toronto, Ont. M4N 2C4.

Jehovah's Witnesses (Branch Office estab. in Winnipeg 1918) - Branch Coordinator, Mr. Kenneth A. Little, Watch Tower Bible and Tract Society of Canada, Box 4100, Georgetown, Ont. L7J 4Y4.

Lutheran Council in Canada (a joint body of **The Evangelical Lutheran Church of Canada, Lutheran Church-Canada,** and **Lutheran Church in America - Canada Section**) - Pres., Dr. Roger Nostbakken; Exec. Dir. W.A. Schultz, 500-365 Hargrave St., Winnipeg, Man. R3B 2K3.

Mennonite Brethren Churches of North America, Canadian Conference (inc. 1945) - Mod. John Redekop, 600 Shaftesbury Blvd., Winnipog, Man. R3P 0M4.

Mennonites in Canada, Conference of (1903) - Chairman, Jake Fransen, 298 Ferndale Ave., Waterloo, Ont. N2J 3X9.

Pentecostal Assemblies of Canada, The (inc. 1919) - Gen. Supt., Rev. James MacKnight, 10 Overlea Blvd., Toronto, Ont. M4H 1A5.

Presbyterian Church in Canada, The (1875) - Mod., Dr. D. C. MacDonald, 50 Wynford Dr., Don Mills, Ont. M3C 1J7.

Religious Society of Friends (Quakers), (Canadian Yearly Meeting of the Religious Society of Friends formed 1955) - Presiding Clerk, Isobel Showler, 60 Lowther Ave., Toronto, Ont. M5R 1C7.

Reorganized Church of Jesus Christ of Latter-Day Saints (Canada) (1830) - Ont. Region Pres., Donald H. Comer; Bishop of Canada and Ont. Region, D. Frank Silverthorn, 390 Speedvale Ave. E., Guelph, Ont. N1E 1N5.

Roman Catholic Church in Canada - Canadian Conference of Catholic Bishops, 90 Parent Ave., Ottawa, Ont. K1N 7B1.

Salvation Army, The (1882) - Commissioner Arthur R. Pitcher, P.O. Box 4021, Postal Station A, Toronto, Ont. M5W 2B1.

Seventh-day Adventist Church in Canada - Pres., J.W. Wilson; Sec., P.F. Lemon; 1148 King St. E., Oshawa, Ont. L1H 1H8.

Ukrainian Greek Orthodox Church in Canada - Primate, Metropolitan of Winnipeg and of all Canada, His Beatitude Metropolitan Andrew (Metiuk), 9 St. Johns Ave., Winnipeg, Man. R2W 1G8.

Union of Spiritual Communities of Christ (Orthodox Doukhobors in Canada) (1938) - Administrator, S.W. Babakaiff; Honorary Chmn. of the Exec. Comm., John J. Verigin, Box 760, Grand Forks, B.C. V0H 1H0.

Unitarian Council, Canadian (1961) - Pres., Mrs. Ruth Patrick; Admin. Sec. Mrs. Thelma Peters, 175 St. Clair Ave. W., Toronto, Ont. M4V 1P7.

United Church of Canada, The (1925) - Mod. Rt. Rev. Clarke MacDonald; Sec. of General Council, Rev. Philip A. Cline, 85 St. Clair Ave. E., Toronto, Ont. M4T 1M6.

Episcopal Church Calendar and Liturgical Colors

White—from Christmas Day through the First Sunday after Epiphany; Maundy Thursday (as an alternative to crimson at the Eucharist; from the Vigil of Easter to the Day of Pentecost (Whitsunday); Trinity Sunday; Feasts of the Lord (except Holy Cross Day); the Confession of St. Peter; the Conversion of St. Paul; St. Joseph; St. Mary Magdalene; St. Mary the Virgin; St. Michael and All Angels; All Saint's Day; St. John the Evangelist; memorials of other saints who were not martyred; Independence Day and Thanksgiving Day; weddings and funerals. **Red.**—the Day of Pentecost; Holy Cross Day; feasts of apostles and evangelists (except those listed above); feasts and memorials of martyrs (including Holy Innocents' Day). **Violet**—Advent and Lent. **Crimson** (dark red)—Holy Week. **Green**—the seasons after Epiphany and after Pentecost. **Black**—optional alternative for funerals. Alternative colors used in some churches: **Blue**—Advent; **Lenten White**—Ash Wednesday to Palm Sunday.

Days, etc.	1984		1985		1986		1987		1988		1989	
Golden Number	9		10		11		12		13		14	
Sunday Letter	AG		F		E		D		CB		A	
Sundays after Epiphany	9		6		5		8		6		5	
Ash Wednesday	Mar.	7	Feb.	20	Feb.	12	Mar.	4	Feb.	17	Feb.	8
First Sunday in Lent	Mar.	11	Feb.	24	Feb.	16	Mar.	8	Feb.	21	Feb.	12
Passion/Palm Sunday	Apr.	15	Mar.	31	Mar.	23	Apr.	12	Mar.	27	Mar.	19
Good Friday	Apr.	20	Apr.	5	Mar.	28	Apr.	17	Apr.	1	Mar.	24
Easter Day	Apr.	22	Apr.	7	Mar.	30	Apr.	19	Apr.	3	Mar.	26
Ascension Day	May	31	May	16	May	8	May	28	May	12	May	4
The Day of Pentecost	June	10	May	26	May	18	June	7	May	22	May	14
Trinity Sunday	June	17	June	2	May	25	June	14	May	29	May	21
Numbered Proper of 2 Pentecost	#7		#5		#4		#7		#5		#3	
First Sunday of Advent	Dec.	2	Dec.	1	Nov.	30	Nov.	29	Nov.	27	Dec.	3

In the Episcopal Church the days of fasting are Ash Wednesday and Good Friday. Other days of special devotion (abstinence) are the 40 days of Lent and all Fridays of the year, except those in Christmas and Easter seasons and any Feasts of the Lord which occur on a Friday or during Lent. Ember Days (optional) are days of prayer for the Church's ministry. They fall on the Wednesday, Friday, and Saturday after the first Sunday in Lent, the Day of Pentecost, Holy Cross Day, and the Third Sunday of Advent. Rogation Days (also optional) are the three days before Ascension Day, and are days of prayer for God's blessing on the crops, on commerce and industry, and for the conservation of the earth's resources.

Ash Wednesday and Easter Sunday

Year	Ash Wed.	Easter Sunday	Year	Ash Wed.	Easter Sunday	Year	Ash Wed.	Easter Sunday	Year	Ash Wed.	Easter Sunday
1901	Feb. 20	Apr. 7	1951	Feb. 7	Mar. 25	2001	Feb. 28	Apr. 15	2051	Feb. 15	Apr. 2
1902	Feb. 12	Mar. 30	1952	Feb. 27	Apr. 13	2002	Feb. 13	Mar. 31	2052	Mar. 6	Apr. 21
1903	Feb. 25	Apr. 12	1953	Feb. 18	Apr. 5	2003	Mar. 5	Apr. 20	2053	Feb. 19	Apr. 6
1904	Feb. 17	Apr. 3	1954	Mar. 3	Apr. 18	2004	Feb. 25	Apr. 11	2054	Feb. 11	Mar. 29
1905	Mar. 8	Apr. 23	1955	Feb. 23	Apr. 10	2005	Feb. 9	Mar. 27	2055	Mar. 3	Apr. 18
1906	Feb. 28	Apr. 15	1956	Feb. 15	Apr. 1	2006	Mar. 1	Apr. 16	2056	Feb. 16	Apr. 2
1907	Feb. 13	Mar. 31	1957	Mar. 6	Apr. 21	2007	Feb. 21	Apr. 8	2057	Mar. 7	Apr. 22
1908	Mar. 4	Apr. 19	1958	Feb. 19	Apr. 6	2008	Feb. 6	Mar. 23	2058	Feb. 27	Apr. 14
1909	Feb. 24	Apr. 11	1959	Feb. 11	Mar. 29	2009	Feb. 25	Apr. 12	2059	Feb. 12	Mar. 30
1910	Feb. 9	Mar. 27	1960	Mar. 2	Apr. 17	2010	Feb. 17	Apr. 4	2060	Mar. 3	Apr. 18
1911	Mar. 1	Apr. 16	1961	Feb. 15	Apr. 2	2011	Mar. 9	Apr. 24	2061	Feb. 23	Apr. 10
1912	Feb. 21	Apr. 7	1962	Mar. 7	Apr. 22	2012	Feb. 22	Apr. 8	2062	Feb. 8	Mar. 26
1913	Feb. 5	Mar. 23	1963	Feb. 27	Apr. 14	2013	Feb. 13	Mar. 31	2063	Feb. 28	Apr. 15
1914	Feb. 25	Apr. 12	1964	Feb. 12	Mar. 29	2014	Mar. 5	Apr. 20	2064	Feb. 20	Apr. 6
1915	Feb. 17	Apr. 4	1965	Mar. 3	Apr. 18	2015	Feb. 18	Apr. 5	2065	Feb. 11	Mar. 29
1916	Mar. 8	Apr. 23	1966	Feb. 23	Apr. 10	2016	Feb. 10	Mar. 27	2066	Feb. 24	Apr. 11
1917	Feb. 21	Apr. 8	1967	Feb. 8	Mar. 26	2017	Mar. 1	Apr. 16	2067	Feb. 16	Apr. 3
1918	Feb. 13	Mar. 31	1968	Feb. 28	Apr. 14	2018	Feb. 14	Apr. 1	2068	Mar. 7	Apr. 22
1919	Mar. 5	Apr. 20	1969	Feb. 19	Apr. 6	2019	Mar. 6	Apr. 21	2069	Feb. 27	Apr. 14
1920	Feb. 18	Apr. 4	1970	Feb. 11	Mar. 29	2020	Feb. 26	Apr. 12	2070	Feb. 12	Mar. 30
1921	Feb. 9	Mar. 27	1971	Feb. 24	Apr. 11	2021	Feb. 17	Apr. 4	2071	Mar. 4	Apr. 19
1922	Mar. 1	Apr. 16	1972	Feb. 16	Apr. 2	2022	Mar. 2	Apr. 17	2072	Feb. 24	Apr. 10
1923	Feb. 14	Apr. 1	1973	Mar. 7	Apr. 22	2023	Feb. 22	Apr. 9	2073	Feb. 8	Mar. 26
1924	Mar. 5	Apr. 20	1974	Feb. 27	Apr. 14	2024	Feb. 14	Mar. 31	2074	Feb. 28	Apr. 15
1925	Feb. 25	Apr. 12	1975	Feb. 12	Mar. 30	2025	Mar. 5	Apr. 20	2075	Feb. 20	Apr. 7
1926	Feb. 17	Apr. 4	1976	Mar. 3	Apr. 18	2026	Feb. 18	Apr. 5	2076	Mar. 4	Apr. 19
1927	Mar. 2	Apr. 17	1977	Feb. 23	Apr. 10	2027	Feb. 10	Mar. 28	2077	Feb. 24	Apr. 11
1928	Feb. 22	Apr. 8	1978	Feb. 8	Mar. 26	2028	Mar. 1	Apr. 16	2078	Feb. 16	Apr. 3
1929	Feb. 13	Mar. 31	1979	Feb. 28	Apr. 15	2029	Feb. 14	Apr. 1	2079	Mar. 8	Apr. 23
1930	Mar. 5	Apr. 20	1980	Feb. 20	Apr. 6	2030	Mar. 6	Apr. 21	2080	Feb. 21	Apr. 7
1931	Feb. 18	Apr. 5	1981	Mar. 4	Apr. 19	2031	Feb. 26	Apr. 13	2081	Feb. 12	Mar. 30
1932	Feb. 10	Mar. 27	1982	Feb. 24	Apr. 11	2032	Feb. 11	Mar. 28	2082	Mar. 4	Apr. 19
1933	Mar. 1	Apr. 16	1983	Feb. 16	Apr. 3	2033	Mar. 2	Apr. 17	2083	Feb. 17	Apr. 4
1934	Feb. 14	Apr. 1	1984	Mar. 7	Apr. 22	2034	Feb. 22	Apr. 9	2084	Feb. 9	Mar. 26
1935	Mar. 6	Apr. 21	1985	Feb. 20	Apr. 7	2035	Feb. 7	Mar. 25	2085	Feb. 28	Apr. 15
1936	Feb. 26	Apr. 12	1986	Feb. 12	Mar. 30	2036	Feb. 27	Apr. 13	2086	Feb. 13	Mar. 31
1937	Feb. 10	Mar. 28	1987	Mar. 4	Apr. 19	2037	Feb. 18	Apr. 5	2087	Mar. 5	Apr. 20
1938	Mar. 2	Apr. 17	1988	Feb. 17	Apr. 3	2038	Mar. 10	Apr. 25	2088	Feb. 25	Apr. 11
1939	Feb. 22	Apr. 9	1989	Feb. 8	Mar. 26	2039	Feb. 23	Apr. 10	2089	Feb. 16	Apr. 3
1940	Feb. 7	Mar. 24	1990	Feb. 28	Apr. 15	2040	Feb. 15	Apr. 1	2090	Mar. 1	Apr. 16
1941	Feb. 26	Apr. 13	1991	Feb. 13	Mar. 31	2041	Mar. 6	Apr. 21	2091	Feb. 21	Apr. 8
1942	Feb. 18	Apr. 5	1992	Mar. 4	Apr. 19	2042	Feb. 19	Apr. 6	2092	Feb. 13	Mar. 30
1943	Mar. 10	Apr. 25	1993	Feb. 24	Apr. 11	2043	Feb. 11	Mar. 29	2093	Feb. 25	Apr. 12
1944	Feb. 23	Apr. 9	1994	Feb. 16	Apr. 3	2044	Mar. 2	Apr. 17	2094	Feb. 17	Apr. 4
1945	Feb. 14	Apr. 1	1995	Mar. 1	Apr. 16	2045	Feb. 22	Apr. 9	2095	Mar. 9	Apr. 24
1946	Mar. 6	Apr. 21	1996	Feb. 21	Apr. 7	2046	Feb. 7	Mar. 25	2096	Feb. 29	Apr. 15
1947	Feb. 19	Apr. 6	1997	Feb. 12	Mar. 30	2047	Feb. 27	Apr. 14	2097	Feb. 13	Mar. 31
1948	Feb. 11	Mar. 28	1998	Feb. 25	Apr. 12	2048	Feb. 19	Apr. 5	2098	Mar. 5	Apr. 20
1949	Mar. 2	Apr. 17	1999	Feb. 17	Apr. 4	2049	Mar. 3	Apr. 18	2099	Feb. 25	Apr. 12
1950	Feb. 22	Apr. 9	2000	Mar. 8	Apr. 23	2050	Feb. 23	Apr. 10	2100	Feb. 10	Mar. 28

A lengthy dispute over the date for the celebration of Easter was settled by the first Council of the Christian Churches at Nicaea, in Asia Minor, in 325 A.D. The Council ruled that Easter would be observed on the first Sunday following the 14th day of the Paschal Moon, referred to as the Paschal Full Moon. The Paschal Moon is the first moon whose 14th day comes on or after March 21. Dates of the Paschal Full Moon, which are not necessarily the same as those of the real or astronomical full moon, are listed in the table below with an explanation of how to compute the date of Easter.

If the Paschal Full Moon falls on a Sunday, then Easter is the following Sunday. The earliest date on which Easter can fall is March 22; it fell on that date in 1761 and 1818 but will not do so in the 20th or 21st century. The latest possible date for Easter is April 25; it fell on that date in 1943 and will again in 2038.

For western churches Lent begins on Ash Wednesday, which comes 40 days before Easter Sunday, not counting Sundays. Originally it was a period of but 40 hours. Later it comprised 30 days of fasting, omitting all the Sundays and also all the Saturdays except one. Pope Gregory (590-604) added Ash Wednesday to the fast, together with the remainder of that week.

The last seven days of Lent constitute Holy Week, beginning with Palm Sunday. The last Thursday — Maundy Thursday — commemorates the institution of the Eucharist. The following day, Good Friday, commemorates the day of the Crucifixion.

Easter is the chief festival of the Christian year, commemorating the Resurrection of Christ. It occurs about the same time as the ancient Roman celebration of the Vernal Equinox, the arrival of spring. In the second century, A.D., Easter Day among Christians in Asia Minor was the 14th Nisan, the seventh month of the Jewish calendar. The Christians in Europe observed the nearest Sunday.

Date of Paschal Full Moon, 1900-2199

The Golden Number, used in determining the date of Easter, is greater by unity (one) than the remainder obtained upon dividing the given year by 19. For example, when dividing 1985 by 19, one obtains a remainder of 9. Adding 1 gives 10 as the Golden Number for the year 1985. From the table then the date of the Paschal Full Moon is Apr. 5, 1985. Since this is a Friday, Easter is celebrated on the next Sunday, Apr. 7.

Golden Number	Date	Golden Number	Date	Golden Number	Date	Golden Number	Date
1	Apr. 14	6	Apr. 18	11	Mar. 25	16	Mar. 30
2	Apr. 3	7	Apr. 8	12	Apr. 13	17	Apr. 17
3	Mar. 23	8	Mar. 28	13	Apr. 2	18	Apr. 7
4	Apr. 11	9	Apr. 16	14	Mar. 22	19	Mar. 27
5	Mar. 31	10	Apr. 5	15	Apr. 10		

Jewish Holy Days, Festivals, and Fasts

	1984 (5744-45)		1985 (5745-46)		1986 (5746-47)		1987 (5747-48)		1988 (5748-49)	
Tu B'Shvat	Jan. 19	Thu	Feb. 6	Wed	Jan. 25	Sat	Feb. 14	Sat	Feb. 3	Wed
Ta'anis Esther (Fast of Esther)	Mar. 15	Thu*	Mar. 6	Wed	Mar. 24	Mon	Mar. 12	Thu*	Mar. 2	Wed
Purim	Mar. 18	Sun	Mar. 7	Thu	Mar. 25	Tue	Mar. 15	Sun	Mar. 3	Thu
Passover	April 17	Tue	April 6	Sat	April 24	Thu	April 14	Tue	April 2	Sat
	April 24	Tue	April 13	Sat	May 1	Thu	April 21	Tue	April 9	Sat
Lag B'Omer	May 20	Sun	May 9	Thu	May 27	Tue	May 17	Sun	May 5	Thu
Shavuot	June 6	Wed	May 26	Sun	June 13	Fri	June 3	Wed	May 27	Sun
	June 7	Thu	May 27	Mon	June 14	Sat	June 4	Thu	May 28	Mon
Fast of the 17th Day of Tammuz	July 17	Tue	July 7	Sun*	July 24	Thu	July 14	Tue	July 3	Sun
Fast of the 9th Day of AV	Aug. 7	Tue	July 28	Sun*	Aug. 14	Thu	Aug. 4	Tue	July 24	Sun
Rosh Hashanah	Sep. 27	Thu	Sep. 16	Mon	Oct. 4	Sat	Sep. 24	Thu	Sep. 12	Mon
	Sep. 28	Fri	Sep. 17	Tue	Oct. 5	Sun	Sep. 25	Fri	Sep. 13	Tue
Fast of Gedalya	Sep. 30	Sun*	Sep. 18	Wed	Oct. 6	Mon	Sep. 27	Sun*	Sep. 14	Wed
Yom Kippur	Oct. 6	Sat	Sep. 25	Wed	Oct. 13	Mon	Oct. 3	Sat	Sep. 21	Wed
Sukkot	Oct. 11	Thu	Sep. 30	Mon	Oct. 18	Sat	Oct. 8	Thu	Sep. 26	Mon
	Oct. 17	Wed	Oct. 6	Sun	Oct. 24	Fri	Oct. 14	Wed	Oct. 2	Sun
Shmini Atzeret	Oct. 18	Thu	Oct. 7	Mon	Oct. 25	Sat	Oct. 15	Thu	Oct. 3	Mon
	Oct. 19	Fri	Oct. 8	Tue	Oct. 26	Sun	Oct. 16	Fri	Oct. 4	Tue
Chanukah	Dec. 19	Wed	Dec. 8	Sun	Dec. 27	Sat	Dec. 16	Wed	Dec. 4	Sun
	Dec. 26	Wed	Dec. 15	Sun	Jan. 3	Sat	Dec. 23	Wed	Dec. 11	Sun
Fast of the 10th of Tevet	Jan. 3	Thu	Dec. 22	Sun	Jan. 11	Sun	Dec. 31	Thu	Dec. 18	Sun

The months of the Jewish year are: 1) Tishri; 2) Cheshvan (also Marcheshvan); 3) Kislev; 4) Tebet (also Tebeth); 5) Shebat (also Shebhat); 6) Adar; 6a) Adar Sheni (II) added in leap years; 7) Nisan; 8) Iyar; 9) Sivan; 10) Tammuz; 11) Av (also Abh); 12) Elul. All Jewish holy days, etc., begin at sunset on the day previous.
*Date changed to avoid Sabbath.

Greek Orthodox Church Calendar, 1985

Date		Holy Days	Date		Holy Days
Jan.	1	Circumcision of Jesus Christ; feast day of St. Basil	*June	10	Sunday of Pentecost
Jan.	6	Epiphany: Baptism of Jesus Christ - Sanctification of the Waters	June	29	Feast day of Sts. Peter and Paul
			June	30	Feast day of the Twelve Apostles of Jesus Christ
Jan.	7	Feast day of St. John the Baptist	Aug.	6	Transfiguration of Jesus Christ
Jan.	30	Feast day of the Three Hierarchs: St. Basil the Great, St. Gregory the Theologian, and St. John Chrysostom	Aug.	15	Dormition of the Virgin Mary
			Aug.	29	Beheading of St. John the Baptist
			Sept.	1	Beginning of the Church Year
Feb.	2	Presentation of Jesus Christ in the Temple	Sept.	14	Adoration of the Holy Cross
Feb.	25	Easter Lent begins	Oct.	23	Feast day of St. James
Mar.	25	Annunciation of the Virgin Mary	Oct.	26	Feast day of St. Demetrios the Martyr
Mar.	3	Sunday of Orthodoxy (1st. Sunday of Lent)	Nov.	15	Christmas Lent begins
Apr.	7	Palm Sunday	Nov.	21	Presentation of the Virgin Mary
Apr.	7-14	Holy Week	Nov.	30	Feast day of St. Andrew the Apostle
Apr.	12	Holy (Good) Friday: Burial of Jesus Christ	Dec.	6	Feast day of St. Nicholas, Bishop of Myra
Apr.	14	Easter Sunday: Resurrection of Jesus Christ	Dec.	25	Christmas Day; Nativity of Jesus Christ
*Apr.	23	Feast of St. George			
May	21	Feast day of Sts. Constantine and Helen			
*May	31	Ascension of Jesus Christ			

*Movable holy days dependent upon the date of Easter. (The feast day of St. George is normally celebrated Apr. 23. If this day arrives during Lent, it is then celebrated the day after Easter.) The Greek Orthodox Church celebrates holy days in accordance with the Gregorian Calendar. Some Eastern Orthodox Churches still adhere to the Julian Calendar and observe the holy days (with the exception of the Easter cycle) 13 days later.

Islamic (Muslim) Calendar 1984-1985

The Islamic Calendar is a lunar reckoning from the year of the *hegira*, 622 A.D., when Muhammed moved from Medina to Mecca. It runs in cycles of 30 years, of which the 2d, 5th, 7th, 10th, 13th, 16th, 18th, 21st, 24th, 26th, and 29th are leap years; 1405 is the 25th year of the cycle. Common years have 354 days, leap years 355, the extra day being added to the last month, Zu'lhijjah. Except for this case, the 12 months beginning with Muharram have alternately 30 and 29 days.

Year	Name of month	Month begins	Year	Name of month	Month begins
1405	Muharram (New Year)	Sept. 27, 1984	1405	Rajab	Mar. 23, 1985
1405	Safar	Oct. 27, 1984	1405	Shaban	Apr. 22, 1985
1405	Rabia I	Nov. 25, 1984	1405	Ramadan*	May 21, 1985
1405	Rabia II	Dec. 25, 1984	1405	Shawwai	June 20, 1985
1405	Jumada I	Jan. 23, 1985	1405	Zu'lkadah	July 19, 1985
1405	Jumada II	Feb. 22, 1985	1405	Zu'lhijjah	Aug. 18, 1985

* The date on which Ramadan begins may vary from the calendar date. It actually starts only after the new moon is sighted from the Naval Observatory in Cairo.

Roman Catholic Holy Days of Obligation

Source: 1984 Catholic Almanac

The Holy Days of Obligation, on which Roman Catholics are required to attend mass, vary from country to country. The following are for U.S. Catholics.

Christmas	Dec. 25	Assumption of the Blessed Virgin	Aug. 15
Solemnity of Mary	Jan. 1	All Saint's Day	Nov. 1
Ascension of Jesus Christ	Movable (May 16 in 1985)	Immaculate Conception	Dec. 8

The Major World Religions

Buddhism

Founded: About 525 BC, reportedly near Benares, India.

Founder: Gautama Siddhartha (ca. 563-480), the Buddha, who achieved enlightenment through intense meditation.

Sacred Texts: The *Tripitaka*, a collection of the Buddha's teachings, rules of monastic life, and philosophical commentaries on the teachings; also a vast body of Buddhist teachings and commentaries, many of which are called *sutras*.

Organization: The basic institution is the *sangha* or monastic order through which the traditions are passed to each generation. Monastic life tends to be democratic and anti-authoritarian. Large lay organizations have developed in some sects.

Practice: Varies widely according to the sect and ranges from austere meditation to magical chanting and elaborate temple rites. Many practices, such as exorcism of devils, reflect pre-Buddhist beliefs.

Divisions: A wide variety of sects grouped into 3 primary branches: Therevada (sole survivor of the ancient Hinayana schools) which emphasizes the importance of pure thought and deed; Mahayana, which includes Zen and Soka-gakkai, ranges from philosophical schools to belief in the saving grace of higher beings or ritual practices, and to practical meditative disciplines; and Tantrism, an unusual combination of belief in ritual magic and sophisticated philosophy.

Location: Throughout Asia, from Ceylon to Japan. Zen and Soka-gakkai have several thousand adherents in the U.S.

Beliefs: Life is misery and decay, and there is no ultimate reality in it or behind it. The cycle of endless birth and rebirth continues because of desire and attachment to the unreal "self". Right meditation and deeds will end the cycle and achieve Nirvana, the Void, nothingness.

Hinduism

Founded: Ca. 1500 BC by Aryan invaders of India where their Vedic religion intermixed with the practices and beliefs of the natives.

Sacred texts: The *Veda*, including the *Upanishads*, a collection of rituals and mythological and philosophical commentaries; a vast number of epic stories about gods, heroes and saints, including the *Bhagavadgita*, a part of the *Mahabharata*, and the *Ramayana;* and a great variety of other literature.

Organization: None, strictly speaking. Generally, rituals should be performed or assisted by Brahmins, the priestly caste, but in practice simpler rituals can be performed by anyone. Brahmins are the final judges of ritual purity, the vital element in Hindu life. Temples and religious organizations are usually presided over by Brahmins.

Practice: A variety of private rituals, primarily passage rites (eg. initiation, marriage, death, etc.) and daily devotions, and a similar variety of public rites in temples. Of the latter, the *puja*, a ceremonial dinner for a god, is the most common.

Divisions: There is no concept of orthodoxy in Hinduism, which presents a bewildering variety of sects, most of them devoted to the worship of one of the many gods. The 3 major living traditions are those devoted to the gods Vishnu and Shiva and to the goddess Shakti; each of them divided into further sub-sects. Numerous folk beliefs and practices, often in amalgamation with the above groups, exist side-by-side with sophisticated philosophical schools and exotic cults.

Location: Confined to India, except for the missionary work of Vedanta, the Krishna Consciousness society, and individual *gurus* (teachers) in the West.

Beliefs: There is only one divine principle; the many gods are only aspects of that unity. Life in all its forms is an aspect of the divine, but it appears as a separation from the divine, a meaningless cycle of birth and rebirth (*samsara*) determined by the purity or impurity of past deeds (*karma*). To improve one's *karma* or escape *samsara* by pure acts, thought, and/or devotion is the aim of every Hindu.

Islam (submission)

Founded: 622 AD in Medina, Arabian peninsula.

Founder: Mohammed (ca. 570-632), the Prophet, as a result of visions.

Sacred texts: *Koran*, the words of God, delivered to Mohammed by the angel Gabriel; *Hadith*, collections of the sayings of the Prophet.

Organization: Theoretically the state and religious community are one, administered by a caliph. In practice, Islam is a loose collection of congregations united by a very conservative tradition. Islam is basically egalitarian and non-authoritarian.

Practice: Every Moslem is supposed to make the profession of faith ("There is no god but Allah . . ."), pray 5 times a day, give a regular portion of his goods to charity, fast during the day in the month of Ramadan, and make at least one pilgrimage to Mecca if possible. Additionally saints' days are celebrated and pilgrimages made to shrines.

Divisions: The 2 major sects of Islam are the Sunni (orthodox) and the Shi'ah. The Shi'ah believe in 12 *imams*, perfect teachers, who still guide the faithful from Paradise. Shi'ah practice tends toward the ecstatic, while the Sunni is staid and simple. The Shi'ah sect affirms man's free will; the Sunni is deterministic. The mystic tradition in Islam is Sufism. A Sufi adept believes he has acquired a special inner knowledge direct from Allah.

Location: From the west coast of Africa to the Philipines across a broad band that includes Tanzania, southern USSR and western China, India, Malaysia and Indonesia. Islam has perhaps 100,000 adherents among American blacks.

Beliefs: Strictly monotheistic. God is creator of the universe, omnipotent, just, and merciful. Man is God's highest creation, but limited and sinful. He is misled by Satan, a prideful angel. God gave the *Koran* to Mohammed to guide men to the truth. Those who repent and sincerely submit to God return to a state of sinlessness. In the end, the sinless go to Paradise, a place of physical and spiritual pleasure, and the wicked burn in Hell.

Judaism

Founded: About 1300 BCE.

Founder: Abrahm is regarded as the founding patriarch, but the Torah of Moses is the basic source of the teachings.

Sacred Texts: The five books of Moses constitute the written Torah. Special sanctity is also assigned other writings of the Hebrew Bible—the teachings of oral Torah are recorded in the Talmud, the Midrash, and various commentaries.

Organization: Originally theocratic, Judaism has evolved a congregational polity. The basic institution is the local synagogue, operated by the congregation and led by a rabbi of their choice. Chief Rabbis in France and Great Britain have authority only over those who accept it; in Israel, the 2 Chief Rabbis have civil authority in family law.

Practice: Among traditional practitioners, almost all areas of life are governed by strict religious discipline. Sabbath and holidays are marked by special observances, and attendance at public worship is regarded as especially important then. The chief annual observances are Passover, celebrating the liberation of the Israelites from Egypt and marked by the ritual Seder meal in the home, and the 10 days from Rosh Hashana (New Year) to Yom Kippur (Day of Atonement), a period of fasting and penitence.

Divisions: Judaism is an unbroken spectrum from ultra conservative to ultra liberal, largely reflecting different points of view regarding the binding character of the prohibitions and duties—particularly the dietary and Sabbath observations—prescribed in the daily life of the Jew.

Location: Almost worldwide, with concentrations in Israel and the U.S.

Beliefs: Strictly monotheistic. God is the creator and absolute ruler of the universe. Men are free to choose to rebel against God's rule. God established a particular relationship with the Hebrew people: by obeying a divine law God gave them they would be a special witness to God's mercy and justice. The emphasis in Judaism is on ethical behavior (and, among the traditional, careful ritual obedience) as the true worship of God.

Major Christian Denominations:

Italics indicate that area which, generally speaking, most

Denomination	Origins	Organization	Authority	Special rites
Baptists	In radical Reformation objections to infant baptism, demands for church-state separation; John Smyth, English Separatist in 1609; Roger Williams, 1638, Providence, R.I.	Congregational, *i.e.,* each local church is autonomous.	Scripture; some Baptists, particularly in the South, interpret the Bible literally.	Baptism, after about age 12, by total immersion; Lord's Supper.
Church of Christ (Disciples)	Among evangelical Presbyterians in Ky. (1804) and Penn. (1809), in distress over Protestant factionalism and decline of fervor. Organized 1832.	Congregational.	*"Where the Scriptures speak, we speak; where the Scriptures are silent, we are silent."*	Adult baptism, Lord's Supper (weekly).
Episcopalians	Henry VIII separated English Catholic Church from Rome, 1534, for political reasons. Protestant Episcopal Church in U.S. founded 1789.	*Bishops, in apostolic succession, are elected by diocesan representatives; part of Anglican Communion, symbolically headed by Archbishop of Canterbury.*	Scripture as interpreted by tradition, esp. *39 Articles* (1563); not dogmatic. Triannual convention of bishops, priests, and laymen.	Infant baptism, Holy Communion, others. Sacrament is symbolic, but has real spiritual effect.
Lutherans	Martin Luther in Wittenberg, Germany, 1517, objected to Catholic doctrine of salvation by merit and sale of indulgences; break complete by 1519.	Varies from congregational to episcopal; in U.S. a combination of regional synods and congregational polities is most common.	*Scripture, and tradition as spelled out in Augsburg Confession (1530) and other creeds. These confessions of faith are binding although interpretations vary.*	Infant baptism, Lord's Supper. Christ's true body and blood present "in, with, and under the bread and wine."
Methodists	Rev. John Wesley began movement, 1738, within Church of England. First U.S. denomination Baltimore, 1784.	Conference and superintendent system. *In United Methodist Church, general superintendents are bishops—not a priestly order, only an office—who are elected for life.*	Scripture as interpreted by tradition, reason, and experience.	Baptism of infants or adults, Lord's Supper commanded. Other rites, inc. marriage, ordination, solemnize personal commitments.
Mormons	In visions of the Angel Moroni by Joseph Smith, 1827, in New York, in which he received a new revelation on golden tablets: *The Book of Mormon.*	Theocratic; all male adults are in priesthood which culminates in Council of 12 Apostles and 1st Presidency (1st President, 2 counselors).	*The Bible, Book of Mormon and other revelations to Smith, and certain pronouncements of the 1st Presidency.*	Adult baptism, laying on of hands (which grants gifts of the Spirit), Lord's Supper. Temple rites: baptism for the dead, marriage for eternity, others.
Orthodox	Original Christian proselytizing in 1st century; broke with Rome, 1054, after centuries of doctrinal disputes and diverging traditions.	Synods of bishops in autonomous, usually national, churches elect a patriarch, archbishop or metropolitan. These men, as a group, are the heads of the church.	Scripture, tradition, and the first 7 church councils up to Nicaea II in 787. Bishops in council have authority in doctrine and policy.	Seven sacraments: infant baptism and anointing, Eucharist (both bread and wine), ordination, penance, anointing of the sick, marriage.
Pentecostal	In Topeka, Kansas (1901), and Los Angeles (1906) in reaction to loss of evangelical fervor among Methodists and other denominations.	Originally a movement, not a formal organization, Pentecostalism now has a variety of organized forms and continues also as a movement.	Scripture, individual charismatic leaders, the teachings of the Holy Spirit.	*Spirit baptism, esp. as shown in "speaking in tongues"; healing and sometimes exorcism; adult baptism, Lord's Supper.*
Presbyterians	In Calvinist Reformation in 1500s; differed with Lutherans over sacraments, church government. John Knox founded Scotch Presbyterian church about 1560.	*Highly structured representational system of ministers and laypersons (presbyters) in local, regional and national bodies. (synods).*	Scripture.	Infant baptism, Lord's Supper; bread and wine symbolize Christ's spiritual presence.
Roman Catholics	Traditionally, by Jesus who named St. Peter the 1st Vicar; historically, in early Christian proselytizing and the conversion of imperial Rome in the 4th century.	Hierarchy with supreme power vested in Pope elected by cardinals. Councils of Bishops advise on matters of doctrine and policy.	*The Pope, when speaking for the whole church in matters of faith and morals, and tradition, which is partly recorded in scripture and expressed in church councils.*	Seven sacraments: baptism, contrition and penance, confirmation, Eucharist, marriage, ordination, and anointing of the sick (unction).
United Church of Christ	*By ecumenical union, 1957, of Congregationalists and Evangelical & Reformed, representing both Calvinist and Lutheran traditions.*	Congregational; a General Synod, representative of all congregations, sets general policy.	Scripture.	Infant baptism, Lord's Supper.

How Do They Differ?

distinguishes that denomination from any other.

Practice	Ethics	Doctrine	Other	Denom- ination
Worship style varies from staid to evangelistic. Extensive missionary activity.	Usually opposed to alcohol and tobacco; sometimes tends toward a perfectionist ethical standard.	*No creed; true church is of believers only, who are all equal.*	Since no authority can stand between the believer and God, the Baptists are strong supporters of church-state separation.	Bap- tists
Tries to avoid any rite or doctrine not expli- citly part of the 1st century church. Some congregations may re- ject instrumental music.	Some tendency toward perfectionism; increasing interest in social action programs.	Simple New Testament faith; avoids any elabor- ation not firmly based on Scripture.	Highly tolerant in doctrinal and religious matters; strongly supportive of scholarly education.	Church of Christ (Disci- ples)
Formal, based on *Book of Common Prayer* (1549); services range from austerely simple to highly elaborate.	Tolerant; sometimes permissive; some social action programs.	*Apostles' Creed* is basic; otherwise, considerable variation ranges from rationalist and liberal to acceptance of most Roman Catholic dogma.	Strongly ecumenical, hold- ing talks with all other branches of Christendom.	Epis- copal- ians
Relatively simple formal liturgy with emphasis on the sermon.	Generally, conservative in personal and social ethics; doctrine of "2 kingdoms" (worldly and holy) supports conserva- tism in secular affairs.	Salvation by faith alone through grace. Lutheranism has made major contributions to Protestant theology.	Though still somewhat div- ided along ethnic lines (German, Swede, etc.), main divisions are be- tween funamentalists and liberals.	Luth- erans
Worship style varies widely by denomination, local church, geography.	Originally pietist and perfectionist; always strong social activist elements.	No distinctive theological development; 25 Articles abriged from Church of England's 39 not binding.	In 1968, United Methodist Church joined pioneer English- and German-speaking groups. UMs leaders in ecumenical movement.	Metho- dists
Staid service with hymns, sermon. Secret temple ceremonies may be more elaborate. Strong missionary activity.	Temperance; strict tithing. Combine a strong work ethic with communal self-reliance.	God is a material being; he created the universe out of pre-existing mat- ter; all persons can be saved and many will become divine. Most other beliefs are traditionally Christian.	Mormons regard mainline churches as apostate, cor- rupt. Reorganized Church (founded 1852) rejects most Mormon doctrine and prac- tice except Book of Mormon.	Mor- mons
Elaborate liturgy, usually in the vernacular, though extremely traditional. The liturgy is the essence of Orthodoxy. Veneration of icons.	Tolerant; very little social action; divorce, remarriage permitted in some cases. Priests need not be celibate; bishops are.	Emphasis on Christ's re- surrection, rather than crucifixion; the Holy Spirit proceeds from God the Father only.	Orthodox Church in Amer- ica, orignally under Patriarch of Moscow, was granted autonomy in 1970. Greek Orthodox do not re- cognize this autonomy.	Ortho- dox
Loosely structured service with rousing hymns and sermons, culminating in spirit baptism.	Usually, emphasis on per- fectionism with varying degrees of tolerance.	Simple traditional beliefs, usually Protestant, with emphasis on the immediate presence of God in the Holy Spirit	Once confined to lower- class "holy rollers," Pen- tecostalism now appears in mainline churches and has established middle- class congregations.	Pente- costal
A simple, sober service in which the sermon is central.	Traditionally, a ten- dency toward strictness with firm church- and self-discipline; other- wise tolerant.	Emphasizes the sovereignty and justice of God; no longer doctrinaire.	While traces of belief in predestination (that God has foreordained sal- vation for the "elect") remain, this idea is no longer a central element in Presbyterianism.	Pres- byter- ians
Relatively elaborate ritual; wide variety of public and private rites, eg., rosary recitation, processions, novenas.	Theoretically very strict; tolerant in practice on most issues. Divorce and remarriage not accepted. Celibate clergy, except in Eastern rite.	Highly elaborated. Salvation by merit gained through faith. Unusual development of doctrines surrounding Mary. Dog- matic.	Roman Catholicism is presently in a period of relatively rapid change as a result of Vatican Councils I and II.	Roman Cath- olics
Usually simple services with emphasis on the sermon.	Tolerant; some social action emphasis.	Standard Protestant; *Statement of Faith* (1959) is not binding.	The 2 main churches in the 1957 union represented earlier unions with small groups of almost every Protestant denomin- ation.	United Church of Christ

Roman Catholic Hierarchy

Source: Apostolic Delegation, Washington, D.C.

Supreme Pontiff

At the head of the Roman Catholic Church is the Supreme Pontiff, Pope John Paul II, Karol Wojtyla, born at Wadowice (Krakow), Poland, May 18, 1920; ordained priest Nov. 1, 1946; promoted to Archbishop of Krakow Jan. 13, 1964; proclaimed Cardinal June 26, 1967; elected pope as successor of Pope John Paul I Oct. 16, 1978; solemn commencement as pope Oct. 22, 1978.

College of Cardinals

Members of the Sacred College of Cardinals are chosen by the Pope to be his chief assistants and advisors in the administration of the church. Among their duties is the election of the Pope when the Holy See becomes vacant. The title of cardinal is a high honor, but it does not represent any increase in the powers of holy orders.

In its present form, the College of Cardinals dates from the 12th century. The first cardinals, from about the 6th century, were deacons and priests of the leading churches of Rome, and bishops of neighboring diocese. The title of cardinal was limited to members of the college in 1567. The number of cardinals was set at 70 in 1586 by Pope Sixtus V. From 1959 Pope John XXIII began to increase the number. The greatest membership of the college was 145 under Pope Paul VI in 1973. However, the number of cardinals eligible to participate in papal elections was limited to 120. There were lay cardinals until 1918, when the Code of Canon Law specified that all cardinals must be priests. Pope John XXIII in 1962 established that all cardinals must be bishops. The first age limits were set in 1971 by Pope Paul VI, who decreed that at age 80 cardinals must retire from curial departments and offices and from participation in papal elections. They continue as members of the college, with all other rights and privileges.

Name	Office	Nationality	Born	Named
Alfrink, Bernard		Dutch	1900	1960
Antonelli, Ferdinando		Italian	1896	1973
Aponte Martinez, Luis	Archbishop of San Juan in Puerto Rico	American	1922	1973
Aramburu, Juan	Archbishop of Buenos Aires	Argentinian	1912	1976
Arns, Paulo	Archbishop of Sao Paulo	Brazilian	1921	1973
Bafile, Corrado		Italian	1903	1976
Baggio, Sebastiano	President of the Pontifical Commission for the Vatican City State.	Italian	1913	1969
Ballestrero, Anastasio A.	Archbishop of Turin	Italian	1913	1979
Baum, William	Prefect of the Sacred Congregation for Catholic Education	American	1926	1976
Beras-Rojas, Octavio		Dominican	1906	1983
Bernardin, Joseph Louis	Archbishop of Chicago	American	1928	1983
Bertoli, Paolo	Chamberlain of the Holy Roman Church.	Italian	1908	1969
Brandao Vilela, Avelar	Archbishop of Sao Salvador da Bahia	Brazilian	1912	1973
Bueno y Monreal, Jose		Spanish	1904	1983
Caprio, Giuseppe	President of Administration of Patrimony of the Holy See	Italian	1914	1979
Carberry, John		American	1904	1969
Carpino, Francesco		Italian	1905	1967
Carter, Gerald E.	Archbishop of Toronto	Canadian	1912	1979
Casaroli, Agostino	Secretary of State of His Holiness	Italian	1914	1979
Casoria, Giuseppe		Italian	1908	1983
Cè, Marco	Patriarch of Venice	Italian	1925	1979
Ciappi, O.P., Mario Luigi	Pro-Theologian of Pontifical Household	Italian	1909	1977
Civardi, Ernesto		Italian	1906	1979
Colombo, Giovanni		Italian	1902	1965
Confalonieri, Carlo	Dean of the Sacred College.	Italian	1893	1958
Cooray, Thomas B.		Ceylonese	1901	1965
Cordeiro, Joseph	Archbishop of Karachi	Pakistanian	1918	1973
Corripio Ahumada, Ernesto	Archbishop of Mexico City	Mexican	1919	1979
Danneels, Godfried	Archbiship of Malines-Brussels	Belgian	1933	1983
Darmojuwono, Justinus	Archbishop of Semarang	Indonesian	1914	1967
de Araujo Sales, Eugenio	Archbishop of St. Sebastian of Rio de Janeiro	Brazilian	1920	1969
Dearden, John		American	1907	1969
de Furstenberg, Maximilian		Belgian	1904	1967
Duval, Leon-Etienne	Archbishop of Algiers	Algerian	1903	1965
Ekandem, Dominic	Bishop of Ikot Ekpene	Nigerian	1917	1976
Enrique y Tarancon, Vicente	Archbishop of Madrid.	Spanish	1907	1969
Etchegaray, Roger	President of Justitia et Pax	French	1922	1979
Flahiff, George		Canadian	1905	1983
Florit, Ermenegildo.		Italian	1901	1965
Freeman, James	Archbishop of Sydney	Australian	1907	1973
Gantin, Bernardin	Prefect of the Sacred Congregation for the Bishops	Benin	1922	1977
Garrone, Gabriel-Marie		French	1901	1967
Glemp, Josef	Archbishop of Warsaw, Gniezno	Polish	1928	1983
Gonzalez Martin, Marcelo	Archbishop of Toledo.	Spanish	1918	1973
Gouyon, Paul	Archbishop of Rennes	French	1910	1969
Gray, Gordon	Archbishop of St. Andrews and Edinburgh.	Scottish	1910	1969
Guerri, Sergio		Italian	1905	1981
Guyot, Jean		French	1905	197
Hoffner, Joseph	Archbishop of Cologne.	German	1906	1969
Hume, George Basil	Archbishop of Westminster	English	1923	1976
Jubany Arnau, Narciso	Archbishop of Barcelona.	Spanish	1913	1973

Name	Office	Nationality	Born	Named
Khoraiche, Anthony Peter	Patriarch of Maronites	Lebanese	1907	1983
Kim, Stephan Sou Hwan	Archbishop of Seoul	Korean	1922	1969
Kitbunchu, Michael	Archbishop of Bangkok	Thai	1929	1983
König, Franz	Archbishop of Vienna	Austrian	1905	1958
Krol, John	Archbishop of Philadelphia	American	1910	1967
Kuharic, Franjo	Archbiship of Zagreb	Yugoslavian	1919	1983
Landazuri, Ricketts Juan	Archbishop of Lima	Peruvian	1913	1962
Lebrun-Moratinos, Jose Ali	Archbishop of Caracas	Venezuelan	1919	1983
Léger, Paul		Canadian	1904	1953
Lékai, Laszlo	Archbishop of Esztergom	Hungarian	1910	1976
Lopez-Trujillo, Alphonso	Archbishop Medellin	Colombian	1935	1983
Lorscheider, Aloisio	Archbishop of Fortaleza	Brazilian	1924	1976
deLubac, Henri	Priest of the Society of Jesus, Province of France	French	1896	1983
Lustiger, Jean-Marie	Archbishop of Paris	French	1926	1983
Macharski, Franciszek	Archbishop of Cracow	Polish	1927	1979
Malula, Joseph	Archbishop of Kinshasa	Congolese	1917	1969
Manning, Timothy	Archbishop of Los Angeles	American	1909	1973
Marella, Paolo		Italian	1895	1959
Martini, Carlo Maria	Archbishop of Milan	Italian	1927	1983
Marty, Francois		French	1904	1969
Maurer, Jose	Archbishop of Sucre	Bolivian	1900	1967
McCann, Owen	Archbishop of Cape Town	S. African	1907	1965
Meisner, Joachim	Bishop of Berlin	German	1933	1983
Miranda y Gomez, Miguel		Mexican	1895	1969
Mozzoni, Umberto		Italian	1904	1973
Munoz Duque, Anibal	Archbishop of Bogota	Colombian	1908	1973
Munoz Vega, Paolo	Archbishop of Quito	Ecuadorian	1903	1969
Nasalli Rocca di Corneliano, Mario		Italian	1903	1969
Nasimento, Alexandre do	Archbishop of Lubango	Angolan	1925	1983
Nsubuga, Emmanuel	Archbishop of Kampala	Ugandan	1914	1976
O'Boyle, Patrick		American	1896	1967
Oddi, Silvio	Prefect of Sacred Congregation for the Clergy	Italian	1910	1969
O'Fiaich, Tomás	Archbishop of Armagh, Primate of all Ireland	Irish	1923	1979
Otunga, Maurice	Archbishop of Nairobi	Kenyan	1923	1973
Palazzini, Pietro	Prefect of the Sacred Congregation for the Causes of Saints	Italian	1912	1973
Pappalardo, Salvatore	Archbishop of Palermo	Italian	1918	1973
Parecattil, Joseph	Archbishop of Ernakulam	Indian	1912	1969
Parente, Pietro		Italian	1891	1967
Paupini, Giuseppe		Italian	1907	1969
Pellegrino, Michele		Italian	1903	1967
Picachy, Lawrence	Archbishop of Calcutta	Indian	1916	1976
Pironio, Eduardo	President of the Pontifical Council on the Laity	Argentinian	1920	1976
Poletti, Ugo	Vicar General of His Holiness for the City of Rome	Italian	1914	1973
Poma, Antonio	Archbishop of Bologna	Italian	1910	1969
Primatesta, Raul Francisco	Archbishop of Cordoba	Argentinian	1919	1973
Ratzinger, Joseph	Prefect of Sacred Congregation for the Doctrine of the Faith	German	1927	1977
Razafimahatratra, Victor	Archbishop of Tananarive	Madagascan	1921	1976
Renard, Alexandre		French	1906	1983
Ribeiro, Antonio	Patriarch of Lisbon	Portugese	1928	1973
Righi-Lambertini, Egano		Italian	1906	1979
Rosales, Julio		Filipino	1906	1969
Rossi, Agnelo		Brazilian	1913	1965
Rossi, Opilio		Italian	1910	1976
Roy, Maurice		Canadian	1903	1983
Rubin, Wladyslaw	Prefect of the Sacred Congregation for the Oriental Churches	Polish	1917	1979
Rugambwa, Laurean	Archbishop of Dar-es-Salaam	Tanzanian	1912	1960
Sabattani, Aurelio	Prefect of the Supreme Tribunal of the Apostolic Signatura	Italian	1912	1983
Salazar Lopez, Jose	Archbishop of Guadalajara	Mexican	1910	1973
Satowaki, Joseph A.	Archbishop of Nagasaki	Japanese	1904	1979
Scherer, Alfredo		Brazilian	1903	1969
Sensi, Giuseppe		Italian	1907	1976
Shehan, Lawrence		American	1898	1965
Sidarouss, Stephanos	Coptic Patriarch of Alexandria	Egyptian	1904	1965
Silva Henriquez, Raul		Chilean	1907	1962
Sin, Jaime	Archbishop of Manila	Filipino	1928	1976
Siri, Giuseppe	Archbishop of Genoa	Italian	1906	1953
Slipyj, Josyf	Ukrainian Archbishop of Lwow	Ukrainian	1892	1965
Suenens, Leo		Belgian	1904	1962
Taofinu'u, Pio	Bishop of Samoa and Tokelau	Samoan	1923	1973
Thiandoum, Hyacinthe	Archbishop of Dakar	Senegalese	1921	1976
Tomasek, Frantisek	Archbishop of Prague	Czechoslovakian	1899	1977
Trinh Van Can, Joseph-Marie	Archbishop of Hanoi	Vietnamese	1921	1979
Ursi, Corrado	Archbishop of Naples	Italian	1908	1967
Vaivods, Julijans	Apostolic Administrator of Riga and Liepaja	Latvian	1895	1964
Vilela, Avelar	Archbishop of Sao Salvador	Brazilian	1912	1973
Volk, Hermann		German	1903	1973
Willebrands, John	President of Secretariat for the Union of Christians	Dutch	1909	1969
Yago, Bernard	Archbishop of Abidjan, Ivory Coast	Ivorian	1916	1960
Zoungrana, Paul	Archbishop of Ouagadougou	Upper Voltan	1917	1965

NOTED PERSONALITIES

Widely Known Americans of the Present

Statesmen, authors of nonfiction, military men, and other prominent persons not listed in other categories.

Name (Birthplace)	Birthdate	Name (Birthplace)	Birthdate
Abel, I. W. (Magnolia, Oh.)	8/11/08	Fenwick, Millicent (New York, N.Y.)	2/25/10
Abzug, Bella (New York, N.Y.)	7/24/20	Ferraro, Geraldine (Newburgh, N.Y.)	8/26/35
Agnew, Spiro (Baltimore, Md.)	11/9/18	Foley, Thomas S. (Spokane, Wash.)	3/6/29
Albert, Carl (McAlester, Okla.)	5/10/08	Ford, Elizabeth (Mrs. Gerald) (Chicago, Ill.)	4/8/18
Aldrin, Edwin E. Jr. "Buzz" (Glen Ridge, N.J.)	1/20/30	Ford, Gerald R. (Omaha, Neb.)	7/14/13
Alsop, Joseph W. Jr. (Avon, Conn.)	10/11/10	Fraser, Douglas A. (Glasgow, Scotland)	12/18/16
Arledge, Roone (Forest Hills, N.Y.)	7/8/31	Friedan, Betty (Peoria, Ill.)	2/4/21
Armstrong, William L. (Fremont, Neb.)	1937	Friedman, Milton (Brooklyn, N.Y.)	7/31/12
Anderson, Jack (Long Beach, Cal.)	10/19/22	Fulbright, J. William (Sumner, Mo.)	4/9/05
Armstrong, Neil (Wapakoneta, Oh.)	8/5/30		
		Galbraith, John Kenneth (Ontario, Can.)	10/15/08
Bailey, F. Lee (Waltham, Mass.)	6/10/33	Garvin, Clifton (Portsmouth, Va.)	12/22/21
Baker, Howard (Huntsville, Tenn.)	11/15/25	Gifford, Frank (Santa Monica, Cal.)	8/16/30
Baker, James A. (Houston, Tex.)	4/28/30	Ginsberg, Allen (Paterson, N.J.)	6/3/21
Baker, Russell (Loudoun Co., Va.)	8/14/25	Glenn, John (Cambridge, Oh.)	7/18/21
Belli, Melvin (Sonora, Cal.)	7/29/07	Goldberg, Arthur J. (Chicago, Ill.)	8/8/08
Bentsen, Lloyd (Mission, Tex.)	2/11/21	Goldwater, Barry M. (Phoenix, Ariz.)	1/1/09
Blackmun, Harry (Nashville, Ill.)	11/12/08	Graham, Billy (Charlotte, N.C.)	11/7/18
Blass, Bill (Ft. Wayne, Ind.)	6/22/22	Graham, Katharine (New York, N.Y.)	6/16/17
Bok, Derek (Ardmore, Pa.)	3/22/30	Greenspan, Alan (New York, N.Y.)	3/6/26
Bombeck, Erma (Dauton, Oh.)	2/21/27	Gumble, Bryant (New Orleans, La.)	9/29/48
Bond, Julian (Nashville, Tenn.)	1/14/40		
Borman, Frank (Gary, Ind.)	3/14/28		
Bradley, Bill (Crystal City, Mo.)	7/28/43	Haig, Alexander (Philadelphia, Pa.)	12/2/24
Bradley, Ed (Philadelphia, Pa.)	6/22/41	Harriman, W. Averell (New York, N.Y.)	11/15/91
Bradley, Thomas (Calvert, Tex.)	12/29/17	Hart, Gary (Ottawa, Kan.)	11/28/37
Brennan, William J. (Newark, N.J.)	4/25/06	Hartman, David (Pawtucket, R.I.)	5/19/35
Breslin, Jimmy (Jamaica, N.Y.)	10/17/30	Hatch, Orrin (Homestead, Pa.)	3/22/34
Brinkley, David (Wilmington, N.C.)	7/10/20	Hatfield, Mark O. (Dallas, Ore.)	7/12/22
Brock, William (Chattanooga, Tenn.)	11/23/30	Hawkins, Paula (Salt Lake City, Ut.)	1/24/27
Brokaw, Tom (Webster, S. Dak.)	2/6/40	Heckler, Margaret M. (Flushing, N.Y.)	6/21/31
Brown, Edmund G. Jr. (San Francisco, Cal.)	4/7/38	Hefner, Hugh (Chicago, Ill.)	4/9/26
Brown, Helen Gurley (Green Forest, Ark.)	2/18/22	Heller, Walter (Buffalo, N.Y.)	8/27/15
Brzezinski, Zbigniew (Warsaw, Poland)	3/28/28	Helms, Jesse (Monroe, N.C.)	10/18/21
Buchwald, Art (Mt. Vernon, N.Y.)	10/20/25	Hershey, Lenore (New York, N.Y.)	3/20/20
Buckley, William F. (New York, N.Y.)	11/24/25	Hesburgh, Theodore (Syracuse, N.Y.)	5/25/17
Bumpers, Dale (Charleston, Ark.)	8/12/25	Hiss, Alger (Baltimore, Md.)	11/11/04
Burger, Warren (St. Paul, Minn.)	9/17/07	Hollings, Ernest (Charleston, S.C.)	1/1/22
Burns, Arthur F. (Stanislau, Aust.)	4/27/04		
Bush, George (Milton, Mass.)	6/12/24	Iacocca, Lee A. (Allentown, Pa.)	10/15/24
Byrd, Robert (N. Wilkesboro, N.C.)	11/20/17	Inouye, Daniel (Honolulu, Ha.)	9/7/24
Byrne, Jane M. (Chicago, Ill.)	5/24/34		
		Jackson, Jesse (Greenville, N.C.)	10/8/41
Calderone, Dr. Mary (New York, N.Y.)	7/1/04	Javits, Jacob K. (New York, N.Y.)	5/18/04
Carter, Jimmy (Plains, Ga.)	10/1/24	Jennings, Peter (Toronto, Ont.)	8/29/38
Carter, Rosalynn (Plains, Ga.)	8/18/27	Johnson, Lady Bird (Mrs. Lyndon) (Karnack, Tex.)	12/22/12
Casey, William J. (Queens, N.Y.)	3/13/13	Jordan, Barbara (Houston, Tex.)	2/21/36
Chancellor, John (Chicago, Ill.)	7/14/27		
Chavez, Cesar (Yuma, Ariz.)	3/31/27		
Child, Julia (Pasadena, Cal.)	8/15/12	Kael, Pauline (Petaluma, Calif.)	6/19/19
Chisholm, Shirley (Brooklyn, N.Y.)	11/30/24	Kahn, Alfred E. (Paterson, N.J.)	10/17/17
Chung, Connie (Washington, D.C.)	8/20/46	Kemp, Jack (Los Angeles, Cal.)	7/13/35
Claiborne, Craig (Sunflower, Miss.)	9/4/20	Kennedy, Edward M. (Brookline, Mass.)	2/22/32
Clark, William (Dallas, Tex.)	12/11/30	Kennedy, Rose (Mrs. Joseph P.) (Boston, Mass.)	7/22/90
Collins, Martha (Shelby Cty, Ky.)	12/7/36	Kerr, Walter (Evanston, Ill.)	7/8/13
Commager, Henry Steele (Pittsburgh, Pa.)	10/25/02	King, Coretta (Mrs. Martin L.) (Marion, Ala.)	4/27/27
Commoner, Barry (Brooklyn, N.Y.)	5/28/17	Kirkland, Lane (Camden, S.C.)	3/12/22
Cooney, Joan Ganz (Phoenix, Ariz.)	10/30/29	Kissinger, Henry (Fuerth, Germany)	5/27/23
Cosell, Howard (Winston-Salem, N.C.)	1920	Klein, Calvin (New York, N.Y.)	11/19/42
Cousins, Norman (Union Hill, N.J.)	6/24/12	Koch, Edward I. (New York, N.Y.)	12/12/24
Cranston, Alan (Palo Alto, Cal.)	6/19/14	Koppel, Ted (Lancashire, Eng.)	2/8/40
Crist, Judith (New York, N.Y.)	5/22/22		
Cronkite, Walter (St. Joseph, Mo.)	11/4/16	Laffer, Arthur (Youngstown, Oh.)	8/14/40
Cuomo, Mario (Queens, N.Y.)	6/15/32	Landers, Ann (Sioux City, Ia.)	7/4/18
Curtis, Charlotte (Chicago, Ill.)	1929	Landon, Alfred (West Middlesex, Pa.)	9/9/87
		Lauren, Ralph (Bronx, N.Y.)	10/14/39
Deaver, Michael K. (Bakersfield, Cal.)	4/11/38	Laxalt, Paul (Reno, Nev.)	8/2/22
Dodd, Christopher (Willimantic, Conn.)	5/27/44	LeMay, Curtis (Ohio)	11/15/06
Dole, Elizabeth (Salisbury, N.C.)	7/29/36	Lindbergh, Anne Morrow (Englewood, N.J.)	1906
Dole, Robert (Russell, Kan.)	7/22/23	Long, Russell B. (Shreveport, La.)	11/3/18
Donaldson, Sam (El Paso, Tex.)	3/11/34	Luce, Clare Boothe (New York, N.Y.)	4/10/03
Doolittle, James H. (Alameda, Cal.)	12/14/96		
		Manchester, William (Attleboro, Mass.)	4/1/22
Ephron, Nora (New York, N.Y.)	5/19/41	Mansfield, Mike (New York, N.Y.)	3/16/03
Ervin, Sam (Morganton, N.C.)	9/27/96	Marshall, Thurgood (Baltimore, Md.)	7/2/08
		McCarthy, Eugene (Watkins, Minn.)	3/29/16
Falwell, Jerry (Lynchburg, Va.)	8/11/33	McGovern, George (Avon, S.D.)	7/19/22
Feldstein, Martin (New York, N.Y.)	11/25/39	McNamara, Robert S. (San Francisco, Cal.)	6/9/16

Name (Birthplace)	Birthdate	Name (Birthplace)	Birthdate
Meese, Edwin (Oakland, Cal.)	12/2/31	Shanker, Albert (New York, N.Y.)	9/14/28
Meredith, Don (Mt. Vernon, Tex.)	4/10/38	Shirer, William L. (Chicago, Ill.)	2/23/04
Metzenbaum, Howard (Cleveland, Oh.)	6/4/17	Shriver, R. Sargent (Westminster, Md.)	11/9/15
Michel, Robert H. (Peoria, Ill.)	3/2/23	Shultz, George P. (New York, N.Y.)	12/13/20
Mondale, Walter (Ceylon, Minn.)	1/5/28	Silverstein, Shel (Chicago, Ill.)	1932
Moynihan, Daniel P. (Tulsa, Okla.)	3/16/27	Smeal, Eleanor (Ashtabula, Oh.)	7/30/39
Mudd, Roger (Washington, D.C.)	2/9/28	Smith, Howard K. (Ferriday, La.)	5/12/14
Muskie, Edmund (Rumford, Me.)	3/28/14	Smith, Margaret Chase (Skowhegan, Me.)	12/14/97
		Smith, Roger, B. (Columbus, Oh.)	7/12/25
Nader, Ralph (Winsted, Conn.)	2/27/34	Spock, Benjamin (New Haven, Conn.)	5/2/03
Nixon, Pat (Mrs. Richard) (Ely, Nev.)	3/16/12	Stahl, Leslie (Lynn, Mass.)	12/16/41
Nixon, Richard (Yorba Linda, Cal.)	1/9/13	Stassen, Harold (West St. Paul, Minn.)	4/13/07
Nizer, Louis (London, England)	2/6/02	Steinbrenner, George (Rocky River, Oh.)	7/4/30
Norton, Eleanor Holmes (Washington, D.C.)	6/13/37	Steinem, Gloria (Toledo, Oh.)	3/25/34
Nunn, Sam (Perry, Ga.)	9/8/38	Stennis, John (Kemper City, Miss.)	8/3/01
		Stevens, John Paul (Chicago, Ill.)	4/20/20
O'Connor, Sandra Day (nr. Duncan, Ariz.)	3/26/30	Stockman, David (Ft. Hood, Tex.)	11/10/46
Ogilvy, David (W. Horsley, Eng.)	6/23/11	Sulzberger, Arthur Ochs (New York, N.Y.)	2/5/26
Onassis, Jacqueline (Southampton, N.Y.)	7/28/29		
O'Neill, Thomas P. (Cambridge, Mass.)	12/9/12		
		Taft, Robert Jr. (Cincinnati, Oh.)	2/26/17
Paley, William S. (Chicago, Ill.)	9/28/01	Thomas, Helen (Winchester, Ky.)	8/4/20
Pauley, Jane (Indianapolis, Ind.)	10/31/50	Thomas, Lewis (Flushing, N.Y.)	1/25/13
Pauling, Linus (Portland, Ore.)	2/28/01	Thurmond, J. Strom (Edgefield, S.C.)	12/5/02
Peale, Norman Vincent (Bowersville, Oh.)	5/31/98	Tinker, Grant (Stamford, Conn.)	1/11/26
Pepper, Claude (Dudleyville, Ala.)	9/8/00	Tower, John (Houston, Tex.)	9/29/25
Percy, Charles H. (Pensacola, Fla.)	9/27/19	Trillin, Calvin (Kansas City, Mo.)	12/5/35
Porter, Sylvia (Patchogue, N.Y.)	6/18/13	Truman, Margaret (Independence, Mo.)	2/17/24
Powell, Lewis F. (Suffolk, Va.)	9/19/07	Tuchman, Barbara (New York, N.Y.)	1/30/12
Proxmire, William (Lake Forest, Ill.)	1/11/15	Turner, Ted (Cincinnati, Oh.)	1938
Rather, Dan (Wharton, Tex.)	10/31/31	Udall, Morris K. (St. Johns, Ariz.)	6/15/22
Reagan, Nancy (New York, N.Y.)	7/6/23	Ueberroth, Peter (Chicago, Ill.)	9/2/37
Reagan, Ronald (Tampico, Ill.)	2/6/11		
Reasoner, Harry (Dakota City, Ia.)	4/17/23	Van Buren, Abigail (Sioux City, Ia.)	7/4/18
Regan, Donald T. (Cambridge, Mass.)	12/21/18	Vance, Cyrus R. (Clarksburg, W. Va.)	3/27/17
Rehnquist, William (Milwaukee, Wis.)	10/1/24	Vanderbilt, Gloria (New York, N.Y.)	2/20/24
Reston, James (Clydebank, Scotland)	11/3/09	Veeck, Bill (Chicago, Ill.)	2/9/14
Ribicoff, Abe (New Britain, Conn.)	4/9/10	Volcker, Paul A. (Cape May, N.J.)	9/5/27
Richardson, Elliot L. (Boston, Mass.)	7/20/20		
Rickover, Hyman (Makowa, Poland)	1/27/00		
Ride, Sally K. (Encino, Calif.)	1952	Wallace, George (Clio, Ala.)	8/25/19
Rivlin, Alice (Phila., Pa.)	3/4/31	Wallace, Mike (Brookline, Mass.)	5/9/18
Roberts, Oral (nr. Ada, Okla.)	1/24/18	Walters, Barbara (Boston, Mass.)	9/25/31
Rockefeller, David (New York, N.Y.)	6/12/15	Warhol, Andy (Pittsburgh, Pa.)	—
Rockefeller, John D. 4th "Jay" (New York, N.Y.)	6/18/37	Watt, James G. (Lusk., Wyo.)	1/31/38
Rockefeller, Laurance S. (New York, N.Y.)	5/26/10	Webster, William H. (St. Louis, Mo.)	3/6/24
Rodino, Peter (Newark, N.J.)	6/7/09	Weicker, Lowell (Paris, France)	5/16/31
Rooney, Andy (Albany, N.Y.)	1/14/19	Weinberger, Caspar (San Francisco, Cal.)	8/18/17
Ruckelshaus, William D. (Indianapolis, Ind.)	7/24/32	Westmoreland, William (Spartanburg, S.C.)	3/26/14
Rusk, Dean (Cherokee Co., Ga.)	2/9/09	White, E.B. (Mt. Vernon, N.Y.)	7/11/99
		White, Theodore (Boston, Mass.)	5/6/15
		Wicker, Tom (Hamlet, N.C.)	6/18/26
Safer, Morley (Toronto, Ontario)	11/8/31	Williams, Edward Bennett (Hartford, Conn.)	5/31/20
Safire, William (New York, N.Y.)	12/17/29	Wolfe, Tom (Richmond, Va.)	3/2/31
Sagan, Carl (New York, N.Y.)	11/9/34	Woodcock, Leonard (Providence, R.I.)	2/15/11
Salk, Lee (New York, N.Y.)	12/27/26	Woodruff, Judy (Tulsa, Okla.)	11/20/46
Salk, Jonas (New York, N.Y.)	10/28/14	Woodward, Robert (Geneva, Ill.)	3/26/43
Sawyer, Diane (Glasgow, Ky.)	12/22/45	Wright, James C. Jr. (Ft. Worth, Tex.)	12/22/22
Schlafly, Phyllis (St. Louis, Mo.)	8/15/24	Wriston, Walter (Middletown, Conn.)	8/3/19
Schlesinger, Arthur Jr. (Columbus, Oh.)	10/15/17	Young, Andrew (New Orleans, La.)	3/12/32
Schroeder, Patricia (Portland, Ore.)	7/30/40	Young, Coleman (Tuscaloosa, Ala.)	5/24/18
Schuller, Robert (Alton, Ia.)	9/16/26		
Seaborg, Glenn T. (Ishpeming, Mich.)	4/19/12		
Sevareid, Eric (Velva, N.D.)	11/26/12	Zumwalt, Elmo (San Francisco, Cal.)	11/29/20

Noted Black Americans

Names of black athletes and entertainers are not included here as they are listed elsewhere in The World Almanac.

The Rev. Dr. Ralph David Abernathy, b. 1926, organizer, 1957, and president, 1968, of the Southern Christian Leadership Conference.

Crispus Attucks, c. 1723-1770, agitator led group that precipitated the "Boston Massacre," Mar. 5, 1770.

James Baldwin, b. 1924, author, playwright; *The Fire Next Time, Blues for Mister Charlie, Just Above My Head.*

Benjamin Banneker, 1731-1806, inventor, astronomer, mathematician, and gazeteer; served on commission that surveyed and laid out Washington, D. C.

Imamu Amiri Baraka, b. LeRoi Jones, 1934, poet, playwright.

James P. Beckwourth, 1798-c. 1867, western fur-trader, scout, after whom Beckwourth Pass in northern California is named.

Dr. Mary McCleod Bethune, 1875-1955, adviser to presidents F. D. Roosevelt and Truman; division administrator, National Youth Administration, 1935; founder, president of Bethune-Cookman College.

Henry Blair, 19th century, obtained patents (believed the first issued to a black) for a corn-planter, 1834, and for a cotton-planter, 1836.

Julian Bond, b. 1940, civil rights leader first elected to the Georgia state legislature, 1965; helped found Student Nonviolent Coordinating Committee.

Edward Bouchet, 1852-1918, first black to earn a Ph.D., Yale, 1876; first black elected to Phi Beta Kappa.

Thomas Bradley, b. 1917, elected mayor of Los Angeles, 1973.

Andrew F. Brimmer, b. 1926, first black member, 1966, Federal Reserve Board.

Edward W. Brooke, b. 1919, attorney general, 1962, of Massachusetts; first black elected to U. S. Senate, 1967, since 19th century Reconstruction.

Gwendolyn Brooks, b. 1917, poet, novelist; first black to win a Pulitzer Prize, 1950, for *Annie Allen.*

William Wells Brown, 1815-1884, novelist, dramatist; first American black to publish a novel.

Dr. Ralph Bunche, 1904-1971, first black to win the Nobel Peace Prize, 1950; undersecretary of the UN, 1950.

George E. Carruthers, b. 1940, physicist developed the Apollo 16 lunar surface ultraviolet camera/spectograph.

George Washington Carver, 1861-1943, botanist, chemurgist, and educator; his extensive experiments in soil building and plant diseases revolutionized the economy of the South.

Charles Waddell Chestnutt, 1858-1932, author known primarily for his short stories, including *The Conjure Woman.*

Shirley Chisholm, b. 1924, first black woman elected to House of Representatives, Brooklyn, N. Y., 1968.

Countee Cullen, 1903-1946, poet; won many literary prizes.

Lt. Gen. Benjamin O. Davis Jr. b. 1912, West Point, 1936, first black Air Force general, 1954.

Brig. Gen. Benjamin O. Davis Sr., 1877-1970, first black general, 1940, in U. S. Army.

William L. Dawson, 1886-1970, Illinois congressman, first black chairman of a major House of Representatives committee.

Isaiah Dorman, 19th century, U. S. Army interpreter, killed with Custer, 1876, at Battle of the Little Big Horn.

Aaron Douglas, 1900-1979, painter; called father of black American art.

Frederick Douglass, 1817-1895, author, editor, orator, diplomat; edited the abolitionist weekly, The North Star, in Rochester, N. Y.; U.S. minister and counsul general to Haiti.

Dr. Charles Richard Drew, 1904-1950, pioneer in development of blood banks; director of American Red Cross blood donor project in World War II.

William Edward Burghardt Du Bois, 1868-1963, historian, sociologist; a founder of the National Association for the Advancement of Colored People (NAACP), 1909, and founder of its magazine The Crisis; author, *The Souls of Black Folk.*

Paul Laurence Dunbar, 1872-1906, poet, novelist; won fame with *Lyrics of Lowly Life,* 1896.

Jean Baptiste Point du Sable, c. 1750-1818, pioneer trader and first settler of Chicago, 1779.

Ralph Ellison, b. 1914, novelist, winner of 1952 National Book Award, for *Invisible Man.*

Estevanico, explorer led Spanish expedition of 1538 into the American Southwest.

James Farmer, b. 1920, a founder of the Congress of Racial Equality, 1942; asst. secretary, Dept. of HEW, 1969.

Henry O. Flipper, 1856-1940, first black to graduate, 1877, from West Point.

Charles Fuller, b. 1939, Pulitzer Prize-winning playwright; *A Soldier's Play.*

Marcus Garvey, 1887-1940, founded Universal Negro Improvement Assn., 1911.

Kenneth Gibson, b. 1932, elected Newark, N.J., mayor, 1970.

Charles Gordone, b. 1925, won 1970 Pulitzer Prize in Drama, with *No Place to Be Somebody.*

Vice Adm. Samuel L. Gravely Jr. b. 1922, first black admiral, 1971, served in World War II, Korea, and Vietnam; commander, Third Fleet.

Alex Haley, b. 1921, Pulitzer Prize-winning author; *Roots, The Autobiography of Malcolm X.*

Jupiter Hammon, c. 1720-1800, poet; the first black American to have his works published, 1761.

Lorraine Hansberry, 1930-1965, playwright; won N. Y. Drama Critics Circle Award, 1959, with *Raisin in the Sun.*

Patricia Roberts Harris, b. 1924, U. S. ambassador to Luxembourg, 1965-67, secretary; Dept. of HUD, 1977-1979, Dept. of H.H.S., 1979-1981.

William H. Hastie, 1904-1976 first black federal judge, appointed 1937; governor of Virgin Islands, 1946-49; judge, U.S. Circuit Court of Appeals, 1949.

Matthew A. Henson, 1866-1955, member of Peary's 1909 expedition to the North Pole; placed U.S. flag at the Pole.

Dr. William A. Hinton, 1883-1959, developed the Hinton and Davies-Hinton tests for detection of syphilis; first black professor, 1949, at Harvard Medical School.

Benjamin L. Hooks, b. 1925, first black member, 1972-1979, Federal Communications Comm.; exec. dir., 1977, NAACP.

Langston Hughes, 1902-1967, poet; story, song lyric author.

The Rev. Jesse Jackson, b. 1941, national director, Operation Bread Basket; campaigned for Democratic presidential nomination, 1984.

Maynard Jackson, b. 1938, elected mayor of Atlanta, 1973.

Gen. Daniel James Jr. 1920-1978, first black 4-star general,

1975; Commander, North American Air Defense Command.

Pvt. Henry Johnson, 1897-1929, the first American decorated by France in World War I with the Croix de Guerre.

James Weldon Johnson, 1871-1938, poet, lyricist, novelist; first black admitted to Florida bar; U.S. consul in Venezuela and Nicaragua.

Barbara Jordan, b. 1936, former congresswoman from Texas; member, House Judiciary Committee.

Vernon E. Jordan, b. 1935, exec. dir. Natl. Urban League, 1972.

Ernest E. Just, 1883-1941, marine biologist, studied egg development; author, *Biology of Cell Surfaces,* 1941.

The Rev. Dr. Martin Luther King Jr., 1929-1968, led 382-day, Montgomery, Ala., boycott which brought 1956 U.S. Supreme Court decision holding segregation on buses unconstitutional; founder, president of the Southern Christian Leadership Conference, 1957; won Nobel Peace Prize, 1964.

Lewis H. Latimer, 1848-1928, associate of Edison; supervised installation of first electric street lighting in N.Y.C.

Malcolm X, 1925-1965, leading spokesman for black pride, founded, 1963, Organization of Afro-American Unity.

Thurgood Marshall, b. 1908, first black U.S. solicitor general 1965; first black justice of the U. S. Supreme Court, 1967; as a lawyer led the legal battery that won the historic decision from the Supreme Court declaring racial segregation of public schools unconstitutional, 1954.

Jan Matzeliger, 1852-1889, invented lasting machine, patented 1883, which revolutionized the shoe industry.

Benjamin Mays, 1895-1984, educator, civil rights leader; headed Morehouse College, 1940-1967.

Wade H. McCree Jr., b. 1920, solicitor general of the U.S.

Donald E. McHenry, b. 1936, U.S. ambassador to the United Nations, 1979-1981.

Dorie Miller, 1919-1943, Navy hero of Pearl Harbor attack; awarded the Navy Cross.

Ernest N. Morial, b. 1929, elected first black mayor of New Orleans, 1977.

Toni Morrison, novelist; *Song of Solomon, Tar Baby.*

Willard Motley, 1912-1965, novelist; *Knock on Any Door.*

Elijah Muhammad, 1897-1975, founded Black Muslims, 1931.

Pedro Alonzo Nino, navigator of the Nina, one of Columbus' 3 ships on his first voyage of discovery to the New World, 1492.

Adam Clayton Powell, 1908-1972, early civil rights leader, congressman, 1945-1969; chairman, House Committee on Education and Labor, 1960-1967.

Joseph H. Rainey, 1832-1887, first black elected to House of Representatives, 1869, from South Carolina.

A. Philip Randolph, 1889-1979, organized the Brotherhood of Sleeping Car Porters, 1925; organizer of 1941 and 1963 March on Washington movements; vice president, AFL-CIO.

Charles Rangel, b. 1930, congressman from N.Y.C., 1970; chairman, Congressional Black Caucus.

Hiram R. Revels, 1822-1901, first black U.S. senator, elected in Mississippi, served 1870-1871.

Wilson C. Riles, b. 1917, elected, 1970, California State Superintendent of Public Instruction.

Norbert Rillieux, 1806-1894; invented a vacuum pan evaporator, 1846, revolutionizing the sugar-refining industry.

Carl T. Rowan, b. 1925, prize-winning journalist; director of the U.S. Information Agency, 1964, the first black to sit on the National Security Council; U. S. ambassador to Finland, 1963.

John B. Russwurm, 1799-1851, with **Samuel E. Cornish,** 1793-1858, founded, 1827, the nation's first black newspaper, Freedom's Journal, in N.Y.C.

Bayard Rustin, b. 1910, organizer of the 1963 March on Washington; executive director, A. Philip Randolph Institute.

Peter Salem, at the Battle of Bunker Hill, June 17, 1775, shot and killed British commander Maj. John Pitcairn.

Ntozake Shange, b. Paulette Williams, 1948, playwright, *For Colored Girls Who Have Considered Suicide/When the Rainbow is Enuf.*

Bishop Stephen Spottswood, 1897-1974, board chairman of NAACP from 1966.

Willard Townsend, 1895-1957, organized the United Transport Service Employees, 1935 (redcaps, etc.); vice pres. AFL-CIO.

Sojourner Truth, 1797-1883, born Isabella Baumfree; preacher, abolitionist; raised funds for Union in Civil War; worked for black educational opportunities.

Harriet Tubman, 1823-1913, Underground Railroad conductor served as nurse and spy for Union Army in the Civil War.

Nat Turner, 1800-1831, leader of the most significant of over 200 slave revolts in U.S. history, in Southampton, Va.; he and 16 others were hanged.

Alice Walker, b. 1944, novelist, author of best-selling and award-winning *The Color Purple.*

Booker T. Washington, 1856-1915, founder, 1881, and first president of Tuskegee Institute; author, *Up From Slavery.*

Dr. Robert O. Weaver, b. 1907, first black member of the U.S. Cabinet, secretary, Dept. of HUD, 1966.

Phillis Wheatley, c. 1753-1784, poet; 2d American woman and first black woman to have her works published, 1770.

Walter White, 1893-1955, exec. secretary, NAACP, 1931-1955.

Roy Wilkins, 1901-1981, exec. director, NAACP, 1955-1977.

Dr. Daniel Hale Williams, 1858-1931, performed one of first 2 open-heart operations, 1893; founded Provident, Chicago's first Negro hospital; first black elected a fellow of the American College of Surgeons.

Granville T. Woods, 1856-1910, invented the third-rail system now used in subways, a complex railway telegraph device that holpod roduco train accidents, and an automatic air brake.

Dr. Carter G. Woodson, 1875-1950, historian; founded Assn. for the Study of Negro Life and History, 1915, and Journal of Negro History, 1916.

Richard Wright, 1908-1960, novelist; *Native Son, Black Boy.*

Frank Yerby, b. 1916, first best-selling American black novelist; *The Foxes of Harrow, Vixen.*

Andrew Young, b. 1932, civil rights leader, congressman from Georgia, U.S. ambassador to the United Nations, 1977-79.

Whitney M. Young Jr., 1921-1971, exec. director, 1961, National Urban League; author, lecturer, newspaper columnist.

About 5,000 blacks served in the Continental Army during the **American Revolution,** mostly in integrated units, some in all-black combat units. Some 200,000 blacks served in the Union Army during the **Civil War;** 38,000 gave their lives; 22 won the Medal of Honor, the nation's highest award. Of 367,000 blacks in the armed forces during **World War I,** 100,000 served in France. More than 1,000,000 blacks served in the armed forces during **World War II;** all-black fighter and bomber AAF units and infantry divisions gave distinguished service. In 1954 the policy of all-black units was finally abolished. Of 274,937 blacks who served in the armed forces during the **Vietnam War** (1965-1974), 5,681 were killed in combat.

As of July, 1982, there were 223 black mayors, 1,872 members of municipal governing bodies, 465 county officers, 330 state legislators, and 18 U.S. representatives. There are now 5,160 blacks holding elected office in the U.S. and Virgin Islands, an increase of 2.4% over the previous year, according to a survey by the Joint Center for Political Studies, Washington, D.C.,

Notable American Fiction Writers and Playwrights

Name (Birthplace)	Birthdate	Name (Birthplace)	Birthdate
Albee, Edward (Washington, D.C.)	3/12/28	Kingsley, Sidney (New York, N.Y.)	10/22/06
Anderson, Robert (New York, N.Y.)	4/28/17	Knowles, John (Fairmont, W. Va.)	9/16/26
Asimov, Isaac (Petrovichi, Russia)	1/2/20	Kosinski, Jerzy (Lódz, Poland)	6/14/33
Auchincloss, Louis (Lawrence, N.Y.)	9/27/17		
		L'Amour, Louis (Jamestown, N.D.)	—
Baldwin, James (New York, N.Y.)	8/2/24	Lee, Harper (Alabama)	1926
Barth, John (Cambridge, Md.)	5/27/30	LeGuin, Ursula (Berkeley, Cal.)	10/21/29
Barthelme, Donald (Philadelphia, Pa.)	1931	Levin, Ira (New York, N.Y.)	8/27/29
Bellow, Saul (Quebec, Canada)	7/10/15	Ludlum, Robert (New York, N.Y.)	5/25/27
Benchley, Peter (New York, N.Y.)	5/8/40		
Blume, Judy (Elizabeth, N.J.)	2/12/38	MacDonald, John D. (Sharon, Pa.)	7/24/16
Bradbury, Ray (Waukegan, Ill.)	8/22/20	MacInnes, Helen (Glasgow, Scotland)	10/7/07
Brooks, Gwendolyn (Topeka, Kan.)	6/7/17	Mailer, Norman (Long Branch, N.J.)	1/31/23
Burrows, Abe (New York, N.Y.)	12/18/10	Malamud, Bernard (Brooklyn, N.Y.)	4/26/14
		Mamet, David (Chicago, Ill.)	11/30/47
Caldwell, Erskine (Coweta Co., Ga.)	12/17/03	McCarthy, Mary (Seattle, Wash.)	6/21/12
Caldwell, Taylor (London, England)	1900	McMurtry, Larry (Wichita Falls, Tex.)	6/3/36
Calisher, Hortense (New York, N.Y.)	12/20/11	Michener, James A. (New York, N.Y.)	2/3/07
Capote, Truman (New Orleans, La.)	9/30/24	Miller, Arthur (New York, N.Y.)	10/17/15
Carver, Raymond (Clatskanie, Ore.)	5/25/38	Morris, Wright (Central City, Neb.)	1/6/10
Clavell, James (England)	10/10/24	Morrison, Toni (Lorain, Oh.)	—
Cleary, Beverly (McMinnville, Ore.)	—		
Crews, Harry (Alma, Ga.)	6/6/35	Oates, Joyce Carol (Lockport, N.Y.)	6/16/38
Crichton, Michael (Chicago, Ill.)	10/23/42	Ozick, Cynthia (New York, N.Y.)	4/17/28
De Vries, Peter (Chicago, Ill.)	2/27/10	Paley, Grace (New York, N.Y.)	12/11/22
Dickey, James (Atlanta, Ga.)	2/2/23	Percy, Walker (Birmingham, Ala.)	5/28/16
Didion, Joan (Sacramento, Cal.)	12/5/34	Potok, Chaim (New York, N.Y.)	2/17/29
Doctorow, E. L. (New York, N.Y.)	1/6/31	Puzo, Mario (New York, N.Y.)	10/15/20
Drury, Allen (Houston, Tex.)	9/2/18	Pynchon, Thomas (Glen Cove, N.Y.)	5/8/37
Dunne, John Gregory (Hartford, Conn.)	5/25/32		
		Rabe, David (Dubuque, Ia.)	3/10/40
Elkin, Stanley (New York, N.Y.)	5/11/30	Reed, Ishmael (Chattanooga, Tenn.)	2/22/38
Ellison, Ralph (Oklahoma City, Okla.)	3/1/14	Robbins, Harold (New York, N.Y.)	5/21/12
		Rogers, Rosemary (Panadora, Ceylon)	12/7/32
Fast, Howard (New York, N.Y.)	11/11/14	Roth, Henry (Austria-Hungary)	2/8/06
		Roth, Philip (Newark, N.J.)	3/19/33
Gaddis, William (New York, N.Y.)	1922		
Geisel, Theodore ("Dr. Seuss," Springfield, Mass.)	3/2/04	Salinger, J. D. (New York, N.Y.)	1/1/19
Gibson, William (New York, N.Y.)	11/13/14	Sanders, Lawrence (New York, N.Y.)	1920
Gilroy, Frank (New York, N.Y.)	10/13/25	Scarry, Richard (Boston, Mass.)	6/5/19
Godwin, Gail (Birmingham, Ala.)	6/18/37	Schisgal, Murray (New York, N.Y.)	11/25/26
Goldman, William (Chicago, Ill.)	8/12/31	Schulberg, Budd (New York, N.Y.)	3/27/14
Grau, Shirley Ann (New Orleans, La.)	7/8/29	Segal, Erich (Brooklyn, N.Y.)	6/16/37
		Sendak, Maurice (New York, N.Y.)	6/10/28
Hailey, Arthur (Luton, England)	4/5/20	Shaw, Irwin (New York, N.Y.)	2/27/13
Haley, Alex (Ithaca, N.Y.)	8/11/21	Shepard, Sam (Ft. Sheridan, Fla.)	11/5/42
Hawkes, John (Stamford, Conn.)	8/17/25	Simon, Neil (New York, N.Y.)	7/4/27
Heinlein, Robert (Butler, Mon.)	7/7/07	Singer, Isaac Bashevis (Radzymin, Poland)	7/14/04
Heller, Joseph (Brooklyn, N.Y.)	5/1/23	Slaughter, Frank (Washington, D.C.)	2/25/08
Hellman, Lillian (New Orleans, La.)	6/20/07	Spillane, Mickey (Brooklyn, N.Y.)	3/9/18
Helprin, Mark (New York, N.Y.)	6/28/47	Stegner, Wallace (Lake Mills, Ia.)	2/18/09
Hersey, John (Tientsin, China)	6/17/14	Stone, Irving (San Francisco, Cal.)	7/14/03
Himes, Chester (Jefferson City, Mo.)	7/29/09	Styron, William (Newport News, Va.)	6/11/25
Irving, John (Exeter, N.H.)	3/2/42	Theroux, Paul (Medford, Mass.)	4/10/41
		Tyler, Anne (Minneapolis, Minn.)	10/25/41
Jaffe, Rona (New York, N.Y.)	6/12/32		
Jong, Erica (New York, N.Y.)	3/26/42	Updike, John (Shillington, Pa.)	3/18/32
		Uris, Leon (Baltimore, Md.)	8/3/24
Kerr, Jean (Scranton, Pa.)	7/?/23		
Kesey, Ken (La Junta, Col.)	9/17/35	Vidal, Gore (West Point, N.Y.)	10/3/25
King, Stephen (Portland, Me.)	9/21/47	Vonnegut, Kurt Jr. (Indianapolis, Ind.)	11/11/22

Name, (Birthplace)	Birthdate	Name (Birthplace)	Birthdate
Walker, Alice (Eatonton, Ga.)	1944	Willingham, Calder (Atlanta, Ga.)	12/23/22
Wallace, Irving (Chicago, Ill.)	3/18/16	Wouk, Herman (New York, N.Y.)	5/27/15
Wambaugh, Joseph (East Pittsburgh, Pa.)	1/22/37		
Warren, Robert Penn (Guthrie, Ky.)	4/24/05	Yerby, Frank (Augusta, Ga.)	9/5/16
Welty, Eudora (Jackson, Miss.)	4/13/09		
Wilson, Lanford (Lebanon, Mo.)	4/13/37	Zindel, Paul (New York, N.Y.)	5/15/36

American Architects and Some of Their Achievements

Max Abramovitz, b. 1908, Avery Fisher Hall, Lincoln Center, N.Y.C.
Henry Bacon, 1866-1924, Lincoln Memorial.
Pietro Belluschi, b. 1899, Juilliard School of Music, Lincoln Center, N.Y.C.
Marcel Breuer, 1902-1981, Whitney Museum of American Art, N.Y.C. (with Hamilton Smith).
Charles Bulfinch, 1763-1844, State House, Boston; Capitol, Wash. D.C., (part).
Daniel H. Burnham, 1846-1912, Union Station, Wash. D.C.; Flatiron, N.Y.C.
Ralph Adams Cram, 1863-1942, Cathedral of St. John the Divine, N.Y.C.; U.S. Military Academy (part).
R. Buckminster Fuller, b. 1895, U.S. Pavilion, Expo 67, Montreal (geodesic domes).
Cass Gilbert, 1859-1934, Custom House, Woolworth Bldg., N.Y.C.; Supreme Court bldg., Wash., D.C.
Bertram G. Goodhue, 1869-1924, Capitol, Lincoln, Neb.; St. Thomas, St. Bartholomew, N.Y.C.
Walter Gropius, 1883-1969, Pan Am Building, N.Y.C. (with Pietro Belluschi).
Peter Harrison, 1716-1775, Touro Synagogue, Redwood Library, Newport, R.I.
Wallace K. Harrison, 1895-1981, Metropolitan Opera House, Lincoln Center, N.Y.C.
Thomas Hastings, 1860-1929, Public Library, Frick Mansion, N.Y.C.
James Hoban, 1762-1831, The White House.
William Holabird, 1854-1923, Crerar Library, City Hall, Chicago.
Raymond Hood, 1881-1934, Rockefeller Center, N.Y.C. (part); Daily News, N.Y.C.; Tribune, Chicago.
Richard M. Hunt, 1827-1895, Metropolitan Museum, N.Y.C. (part); Natl. Observatory, Wash., D.C.
William Le Baron Jenney, 1832-1907, Home Insurance, Chicago (demolished 1931).
Philip C. Johnson, b. 1906, N.Y. State Theater, Lincoln Center, N.Y.C.
Albert Kahn, 1869-1942, Athletic Club Bldg., General Motors Bldg., Detroit.
Louis Kahn, 1901-1974, Salk Laboratory, La Jolla, Cal.; Yale Art Gallery.
Christopher Grant LaFarge, 1862-1938, Roman Catholic Chapel, West Point.
Benjamin H. Latrobe, 1764-1820, U.S. Capitol (part).
William Lescaze, 1896-1969, Philadelphia Savings Fund Society; Borg-Warner Bldg., Chicago.
Charles F. McKim, 1847-1909, Public Library, Boston, Columbia Univ., N.Y.C. (part).

Charles M. McKim, b. 1920, KUHT-TV Transmitter Building, Houston; Lutheran Church of the Redeemer, Houston.
Ludwig Mies van der Rohe, 1886-1969, Seagram Building, N.Y.C. (with Philip C. Johnson); National Gallery, Berlin.
Robert Mills, 1781-1855, Washington Monument.
Richard J. Neutra, 1892-1970, Mathematics Park, Princeton; Orange Co. Courthouse, Santa Ana, Cal.
Gyo Obata, b. 1923, Natl. Air & Space Mus., Smithsonian Institution; Dallas-Ft. Worth Airport.
Frederick L. Olmsted, 1822-1903, Central Park, N.Y.C.; Fairmount Park, Philadelphia.
Ieoh Ming Pei, b. 1917, National Center for Atmospheric Research, Boulder, Col.
William Pereira, b. 1909, Cape Canaveral; Transamerica Bldg., San Francisco.
John Russell Pope, 1874-1937, National Gallery.
John Portman, b. 1924, Peachtree Center, Atlanta.
James Renwick Jr., 1818-1895, Grace Church, St. Patrick's Cathedral, N.Y.C.; Smithsonian, Corcoran Galleries, Wash., D.C.
Henry H. Richardson, 1838-1886, Trinity Church, Boston.
Kevin Roche, b. 1922, Oakland Cal. Museum; Fine Arts Center, U. of Mass.
James Gamble Rogers, 1867-1947, Columbia-Presbyterian Medical Center, N.Y.C.; Northwestern Univ., Chicago.
John Wellborn Root, 1887-1963, Palmolive Building, Chicago; Hotel Statler, Washington; Hotel Tamanaco, Caracas.
Paul Rudolph, b. 1918, Jewitt Art Center, Wellesley College; Art & Architecture Bldg., Yale.
Eero Saarinen, 1910-1961, Gateway to the West Arch, St. Louis; Trans World Flight Center, N.Y.C.
Louis Skidmore, 1897-1962, AEC town site, Oak Ridge, Tenn.; Terrace Plaza Hotel, Cincinnati.
Clarence S. Stein, 1882-1975, Temple Emanu-El, N.Y.C.
Edward Durell Stone, 1902-1978, U.S. Embassy, New Delhi, India; (H. Hartford) Gallery of Modern Art, N.Y.C.
Louis H. Sullivan, 1856-1924, Auditorium, Chicago.
Richard Upjohn, 1802-1878, Trinity Church, N.Y.C.
Ralph T. Walker, 1889-1973, N.Y. Telephone Hdqrs., N.Y.C.; IBM Research Lab., Poughkeepsie, N.Y.
Roland A. Wank, 1898-1970, Cincinnati Union Terminal; head architect TVA, 1933-44.
Stanford White, 1853-1906, Washington Arch; first Madison Square Garden, N.Y.C.
Frank Lloyd Wright, 1867 or 1869-1959, Imperial Hotel, Tokyo; Guggenheim Museum, N.Y.C.
William Wurster, 1895-1973, Ghirardelli Sq., San Francisco; Cowell College, U. Cal., Berkeley.
Minoru Yamasaki, b. 1912, World Trade Center, N.Y.C.

Noted American Cartoonists

Charles Addams, b. 1912, noted for macabre cartoons.
Peter Arno, 1904-1968, noted for urban characterizations.
George Baker, 1915-1975, The Sad Sack.
C. C. Beck, b. 1910, Captain Marvel.
Herb Block (Herblock), b. 1909, leading political cartoonist.
Clare Briggs, 1875-1930, Mr. & Mrs.
Dik Browne, b. 1917, Hi & Lois, Hagar the Horrible.
Ernie Bushmiller, 1905-1982, Nancy.
Milton Caniff, b. 1907, Terry & the Pirates; Steve Canyon.
Al Capp, 1909-1979, Li'l Abner.
Paul Conrad, 1924, political cartoonist.
Roy Crane, 1901-1977, Captain Easy; Buz Sawyer.
Robert Crumb, b. 1943, "Underground" cartoonist.
Jay N. Darling (Ding), 1876-1962, political cartoonist.
Jim Davis, b. 1945, Garfield.
Billy DeBeck, 1890-1942, Barney Google.
Rudolph Dirks, 1877-1968, The Katzenjammer Kids.
Walt Disney, 1901-1966, producer of animated cartoons created Mickey Mouse & Donald Duck.
Jules Feiffer, b. 1929, satirical *Village Voice* cartoonist.
Bud Fisher, 1884-1954, Mutt & Jeff.

Ham Fisher, 1900-1955, Joe Palooka.
James Montgomery Flagg, 1877-1960, illustrator created the famous Uncle Sam recruiting poster during WWI.
Hal Foster, 1892-1982, Tarzan; Prince Valiant.
Fontaine Fox, 1884-1964, Toonerville Folks.
Rube Goldberg, 1883-1970, Boob McNutt.
Chester Gould, b. 1900, Dick Tracy.
Harold Gray, 1894-1968, Little Orphan Annie.
Johnny Hart, b. 1931, BC, Wizard of Id.
Jimmy Hatlo, 1898-1963, Little Iodine.
John Held Jr., 1889-1958, "Jazz Age" cartoonist.
George Herriman, 1881-1944, Krazy Kat.
Harry Hershfield, 1885-1974, Abie the Agent.
Burne Hogarth, b. 1911, Tarzan.
Helen Hokinson, 1900-1949, satirized clubwomen.
Walt Kelly, 1913-1973, Pogo.
Hank Ketcham, b. 1920, Dennis the Menace.
Ted Key, b. 1912 Hazel.
Frank King, 1883-1969, Gasoline Alley.
Jack Kirby, b. 1917, Captain America.
Rollin Kirby, 1875-1952, political cartoonist.

Bill Mauldin, b. 1921, depicted squalid life of the G.I. in WWII.
Jeff MacNelly, b. 1947, political cartoonist, and strip Shoe.
Winsor McCay, 1872-1934, Little Nemo.
John T. McCutcheon, 1870-1949, midwestern rural life.
George McManus, 1884-1954, Bringing Up Father (Maggie & Jiggs).
Dale Messick, b. 1906, Brenda Starr.
Bob Montana, 1920-1975, Archie.
Willard Mullin, 1902-1978, sports cartoonist created the Dodgers "Bum" and the Mets "Kid".
Thomas Nast, 1840-1902, political cartoonist instrumental in breaking the corrupt Boss Tweed ring in N.Y. Created the Democratic donkey and Republican elephant.
Pat Oliphant, b. 1935, political cartoonist.
Frederick Burr Opper, 1857-1937, Happy Hooligan.
Richard Outcault, 1863-1928, Yellow Kid; Buster Brown.

Alex Raymond, 1909-1956, Flash Gordon; Jungle Jim.
Charles Schulz, b. 1922, Peanuts.
Elzie C. Segar, 1894-1938, Popeye.
Sydney Smith, 1887-1935, The Gumps.
Otto Soglow, 1900-1975, Little King; Canyon Kiddies.
James Swinnerton, 1875-1974, Little Jimmy.
James Thurber, 1894-1961, New Yorker cartoonist.
Garry Trudeau, b. 1948, Doonesbury.
Mort Walker, b. 1923, Beetle Bailey.
Russ Westover, 1887-1966, Tillie the Toiler.
Frank Willard, 1893-1958, Moon Mullins.
J. R. Williams, 1888-1957, The Willets Family; Out Our Way.
Gahan Wilson, b. 1930, cartoonist of the macabre.
Art Young, 1866-1943, political radical and satirist.
Chic Young, 1901-1973, Blondie.

Noted Political Leaders of the Past

(U.S. presidents and most vice presidents, Supreme Court justices, signers of Declaration of Independence, listed elsewhere.)

Abu Bakr, 573-634, Mohammedan leader, first caliph, chosen successor to Mohammed.
Dean Acheson, 1893-1971, (U.S.) secretary of state, chief architect of cold war foreign policy.
Samuel Adams, 1722-1803, (U.S.) patriot, Boston Tea Party firebrand.
Konrad Adenauer, 1876-1967, (G.) West German chancellor.
Emilio Aguinaldo, 1869-1964, (Philip.) revolutionary, fought against Spain and the U.S.
Akbar, 1542-1605, greatest Mogul emperor of India.
Salvador Allende Gossens, 1908-1973, (Chil.) president, advocate of democratic socialism.
Herbert H. Asquith, 1852-1928, (Br.) Liberal prime minister, instituted an advanced program of social reform.
Atahualpa, ?-1533, Inca (ruling chief) of Peru.
Kemal Atatürk, 1881-1938, (Turk.) founded modern Turkey.
Clement Attlee, 1883-1967, (Br.) Labour party leader, prime minister, enacted national health, nationalized many industries.
Stephen F. Austin, 1793-1836, (U.S.) led Texas colonization.
Mikhail Bakunin, 1814-1876, (R.) revolutionary, leading exponent of anarchism.
Arthur J. Balfour, 1848-1930, (Br.) as foreign secretary under Lloyd George issued Balfour Declaration expressing official British approval of Zionism.
Bernard M. Baruch, 1870-1965, (U.S.) financier, gvt. adviser.
Fulgencio Batista y Zaldivar, 1901-1973, (Cub.) dictator overthrown by Castro.
Lord Beaverbrook, 1879-1964, (Br.) financier, statesman, newspaper owner.
Eduard Benes, 1884-1948, (Czech.) president during interwar and post-WW II eras.
David Ben-Gurion, 1886-1973, (Isr.) first premier of Israel.
Thomas Hart Benton, 1782-1858, (U.S.) Missouri senator, championed agrarian interests and westward expansion.
Lavrenti Beria, 1899-1953, (USSR) Communist leader prominent in political purges under Stalin.
Aneurin Bevan, 1897-1960, (Br.) Labour party leader.
Ernest Bevin, 1881-1951, (Br.) Labour party leader, foreign minister, helped lay foundation for NATO.
Otto von Bismarck, 1815-1898, (G.) statesman known as the Iron Chancellor, uniter of Germany, 1870.
James G. Blaine, 1830-1893, (U.S.) Republican politician, diplomat, influential in launching Pan-American movement.
Léon Blum, 1872-1950, (F.) socialist leader, writer, headed first Popular Front government.
Simón Bolívar, 1783-1830, (Venez.) South American revolutionary who liberated much of the continent from Spanish rule.
William E. Borah, 1865-1940, (U.S.) isolationist senator, instrumental in blocking U.S. membership in League of Nations and the World Court.
Cesare Borgia, 1476-1507, (It.) soldier, politician, an outstanding figure of the Italian Renaissance.
Leonid Brezhnev, 1906-1982, (USSR) leader of the Soviet Union, 1964-82.
Aristide Briand, 1862-1932, (F.) foreign minister, chief architect of Locarno Pact and anti-war Kellogg-Briand Pact.
William Jennings Bryan, 1860-1925, (U.S.) Democratic, populist leader, orator, 3 times lost race for presidency.
Nikolai Bukharin, 1888-1938, (USSR) communist leader.
William C. Bullitt, 1891-1967, (U.S.) diplomat, first ambassador to USSR, ambassador to France.
Ralph Bunche, 1904-1971, (U.S.) a founder and key diplomat of United Nations for more than 20 years.
John C. Calhoun, 1782-1850, (U.S.) political leader, champion of states' rights and a symbol of the Old South.

Robert Castlereagh, 1769-1822, (Br.) foreign secretary, guided Grand Alliance against Napoleon, major figure at the Congress of Vienna, 1814-15.
Camillo Benso Cavour, 1810-1861, (It.) statesman, largely responsible for uniting Italy under the House of Savoy.
Austen Chamberlain, 1863-1937, (Br.) Conservative party leader, largely responsible for Locarno Pact of 1925.
Neville Chamberlain, 1869-1940, (Br.) Conservative prime minister whose appeasement of Hitler led to Munich Pact.
Salmon P. Chase, 1808-1873, (U.S.) public official, abolitionist, jurist, 6th Supreme Court chief justice.
Chiang Kai-shek, 1887-1975, (Chin.) Nationalist Chinese president whose govt. was driven from mainland to Taiwan.
Chou En-lai, 1898-1976, (Chin.) diplomat, prime minister, a leading figure of the Chinese Communist party.
Winston Churchill, 1874-1965, (Br.) prime minister, soldier, author, guided Britain through WW II.
Galeazzo Ciano, 1903-1944, (It.) fascist foreign minister, helped create Rome-Berlin Axis, executed by Mussolini.
Henry Clay, 1777-1852, (U.S.) "The Great Compromiser," one of most influential pre-Civil War political leaders.
Georges Clemenceau, 1841-1929, (F.) twice premier, Wilson's chief antagonist at Paris Peace Conference after WW I.
DeWitt Clinton, 1769-1828, (U.S.) political leader, responsible for promoting idea of the Erie Canal.
Robert Clive, 1725-1774, (Br.) first administrator of Bengal, laid foundation for British Empire in India.
Jean Baptiste Colbert, 1619-1683, (F.) statesman, influential under Louis XIV, created the French navy.
Oliver Cromwell, 1599-1658, (Br.) Lord Protector of England, led parliamentary forces during Civil War.
Curzon of Kedleston, 1859-1925, (Br.) viceroy of India, foreign secretary, major force in dealing with post-WW I problems in Europe and Far East.
Édouard Daladier, 1884-1970, (F.) radical socialist politician, arrested by Vichy, interned by Germans until liberation in 1945.
Georges Danton, 1759-1794, (F.) a leading figure in the French Revolution.
Jefferson Davis, 1808-1889, (U.S.) president of the Confederate States of America.
Charles G. Dawes, 1865-1951, (U.S.) statesman, banker, advanced Dawes Plan to stabilize post-WW I German finances.
Alcide De Gasperi, 1881-1954, (It.) premier, founder of the Christian Democratic party.
Charles DeGaulle, 1890-1970, (F.) general, statesman, and first president of the Fifth Republic.
Eamon De Valera, 1882-1975, (Ir.-U.S.) statesman, led fight for Irish independence.
Thomas E. Dewey, 1902-1971, (U.S.) New York governor, twice loser in try for presidency.
Ngo Dinh Diem, 1901-1963, (Viet.) South Vietnamese president, assassinated in government take-over.
Everett M. Dirksen, 1896-1969, (U.S.) Senate Republican minority leader, orator.
Benjamin Disraeli, 1804-1881, (Br.) prime minister, considered founder of modern Conservative party.
Engelbert Dollfuss, 1892-1934, (Aus.) chancellor, assassinated by Austrian Nazis.
Andrea Doria, 1466-1560, (It.) Genoese admiral, statesman, called "Father of Peace" and "Liberator of Genoa."
Stephen A. Douglas, 1813-1861, (U.S.) Democratic leader, orator, opposed Lincoln for the presidency.
John Foster Dulles, 1888-1959, (U.S.) secretary of state under Eisenhower, cold war policy maker.
Friedrich Ebert, 1871-1925, (G.) Social Democratic move-

ment leader, instrumental in bringing about Weimar constitution.

Sir Anthony Eden, 1897-1977, (Br.) foreign secretary, prime minister during Suez invasion of 1956.

Ludwig Erhard, 1897-1977, (G.) economist, West German chancellor, led nation's economic rise after WW II.

Hamilton Fish, 1808-1893, (U.S.) secretary of state, successfully mediated disputes with Great Britain, Latin America.

James V. Forrestal, 1892-1949, (U.S.) secretary of navy, first secretary of defense.

Francisco Franco, 1892-1975, (Sp.) leader of rebel forces during Spanish Civil War and dictator of Spain.

Benjamin Franklin, 1706-1790, (U.S.) printer, publisher, author, inventor, scientist, diplomat.

Louis de Frontenac, 1620-1698, (F.) governor of New France (Canada) where he encouraged explorations and fought Iroquois.

Hugh Gaitskell, 1906-1963, (Br.) Labour party leader, major force in reversing its stand for unilateral disarmament.

Albert Gallatin, 1761-1849, (U.S.) secretary of treasury who was instrumental in negotiating end of War of 1812.

Léon Gambetta, 1838-1882, (F.) statesman, politician, one of the founders of the Third Republic.

Mohandas K. Gandhi, 1869-1948, (Ind.) political leader, ascetic, led nationalist movement against British rule.

Giuseppe Garibaldi, 1807-1882, (It.) patriot, soldier, a leading figure in the Risorgimento, the Italian unification movement.

Genghis Khan, c. 1167-1227, brilliant Mongol conqueror, ruler of vast Asian empire.

William E. Gladstone, 1809-1898, (Br.) prime minister 4 times, dominant force of Liberal party from 1868 to 1894.

Paul Joseph Goebbels, 1897-1945, (G.) Nazi propagandist, master of mass psychology.

Klement Gottwald, 1896-1953, (Czech.) communist leader ushered communism into his country.

Che (Ernesto) Guevara, 1928-1967, (Arg.) guerilla leader, prominent in Cuban revolution, killed in Bolivia.

Haile Selassie, 1891-1975, (Eth.) emperor, maintained traditional monarchy in face of foreign invasion, occupation, and internal resistance.

Alexander Hamilton, 1755-1804, (U.S.) first treasury secretary, champion of strong central government.

Dag Hammarskjold, 1905-1961, (Swed.) statesman, UN secretary general.

John Hancock, 1737-1793, (U.S.) revolutionary leader, first signer of Declaration of Independence.

John Hay, 1838-1905, (U.S.) secretary of state, primarily associated with Open Door Policy toward China.

Patrick Henry, 1736-1799, (U.S.) major revolutionary figure, remarkable orator.

Édouard Herriot, 1872-1957, (F.) Radical Socialist leader, twice premier, president of National Assembly.

Theodor Herzl, 1860-1904, (Aus.) founder of modern Zionism.

Heinrich Himmler, 1900-1945, (G.) chief of Nazi SS and Gestapo, primarily responsible for the Holocaust.

Paul von Hindenburg, 1847-1934, (G.) field marshal, president.

Adolf Hitler, 1889-1945, (G.) dictator, founder of National Socialism.

Ho Chi Minh, 1890-1969, (Viet.) North Vietnamese president, Vietnamese Communist leader, national hero.

Harry L. Hopkins, 1890-1946, (U.S.) New Deal administrator, closest adviser to FDR during WW II.

Edward M. House, 1858-1938, (U.S.) diplomat, confidential adviser to Woodrow Wilson.

Samuel Houston, 1793-1863, (U.S.) leader of struggle to win control of Texas from Mexico.

Cordell Hull, 1871-1955, (U.S.) secretary of state, initiated reciprocal trade to lower tariffs, helped organize UN.

Hubert H. Humphrey, 1911-1978, (U.S.) Minnesota Democrat, senator, vice president, spent 32 years in public service.

Ibn Saud, c. 1888-1953, (S. Arab.) founder of Saudi Arabia and its first king.

Benito Juarez, 1806-1872, (Mex.) national hero, rallied countrymen against foreign threats, sought to create democratic, federal republic.

Frank B. Kellogg, 1856-1937, (U.S.) secretary of state, negotiated Kellogg-Briand Pact to outlaw war.

Robert F. Kennedy, 1925-1968, (U.S.) attorney general, senator, assassinated while seeking presidential nomination.

Aleksandr Kerensky, 1881-1970, (R.) revolutionary, served as premier after Feb. 1917 revolution until Bolshevik overthrow.

Nikita Khrushchev, 1894-1971, (USSR) communist leader, premier, first secretary of Communist party, initiated de-Stalinization.

Lajos Kossuth, 1802-1894, (Hung.) principal figure in 1848 Hungarian revolution.

Pyotr Kropotkin, 1842-1921, (R.) anarchist, championed the peasants but opposed Bolshevism.

Kublai Khan, c. 1215-1294, Mongol emperor, founder of Yüan dynasty in China.

Béla Kun, 1886-c.1939, (Hung.) communist dictator, member of 3d International, tried to foment worldwide revolution.

Robert M. LaFollette, 1855-1925, (U.S.) Wisconcin public official, leader of progressive movement.

Pierre Laval, 1883-1945, (F.) politician, Vichy foreign minister, executed for treason.

Andrew Bonar Law, 1858-1923, (Br.) Conservative party politician, led opposition to Irish home rule.

Vladimir Ilyich Lenin (Ulyanov), 1870-1924, (USSR) revolutionary, founder of Bolshevism, Soviet leader 1917-1924.

Ferdinand de Lesseps, 1805-1894, (F.) diplomat, engineer, conceived idea of Suez Canal.

Liu Shoa-ch'i, c.1898-1974, (Chin.) communist leader, fell from grace during "cultural revolution."

Maxim Litvinov, 1876-1951, (USSR) revolutionary, commissar of foreign affairs, proponent of cooperation with western powers.

David Lloyd George, 1863-1945, (Br.) Liberal party prime minister, laid foundations for the modern welfare state.

Henry Cabot Lodge, 1850-1924, (U.S.) Republican senator, led opposition to participation in League of Nations.

Huey P. Long, 1893-1935, (U.S.) Louisiana political demagogue, governor, assassinated.

Rosa Luxemburg, 1871-1919, (G.) revolutionary, leader of the German Social Democratic party and Spartacus party.

J. Ramsay MacDonald, 1866-1937, (Br.) first Labour party prime minister of Great Britain.

Joseph R. McCarthy, 1908-1957, (U.S.) senator notorious for his witch hunt for communists in the government.

Makarios III, 1913-1977, (Cypr.) Greek Orthodox archbishop, first president of Cyprus.

Malcolm X (Malcolm Little), 1925-1965, (U.S.) black separatist leader, assassinated.

Mao Tse-tung, 1893-1976, (Chin.) chief Chinese Marxist theorist, soldier, led Chinese revolution establishing his nation as an important communist state.

Jean Paul Marat, 1743-1793, (F.) revolutionary, politician, identified with radical Jacobins, assassinated by Charlotte Corday.

José Marti, 1853-1895, (Cub.) patriot, poet, leader of Cuban struggle for independence.

Jan Masaryk, 1886-1948, (Czech.) foreign minister, died by mysterious suicide following communist coup.

Thomas G. Masaryk, 1850-1937, (Czech.) statesman, philosopher, first president of Czechoslovak Republic.

Jules Mazarin, 1602-1661, (F.) cardinal, statesman, prime minister under Louis XIII and queen regent Anne of Austria.

Tom Mboya, 1930-1969, (Kenyan) political leader, instrumental in securing independence for his country.

Cosimo I de' Medici, 1519-1574, (It.) Duke of Florence, grand duke of Tuscany.

Lorenzo de' Medici, the Magnificent, 1449-1492, (It.) merchant prince, a towering figure in Italian Renaissance.

Catherine de Medicis, 1519-1589, (F.) queen consort of Henry II, regent of France, influential in Catholic-Huguenot wars.

Golda Meir, 1898-1979, (Isr.) prime minister, 1969-74.

Klemens W.N.L. Metternich, 1773-1859, (Aus.) statesman, arbiter of post-Napoleonic Europe.

Anastas Mikoyan, 1895-1978, (USSR) prominent Soviet leader from 1917; president 1964-65.

Guy Mollet, 1905-1975, (F.) social politician, resistance leader.

Henry Morgenthau Jr., 1891-1967, (U.S.) secretary of treasury, raised funds to finance New Deal and U.S. WW II activities.

Gouverneur Morris, 1752-1816, (U.S.) statesman, diplomat, financial expert who helped plan decimal coinage system.

Wayne Morse, 1900-1974, (U.S.) senator, long-time critic of Vietnam War.

Muhammad Ali, 1769?-1849, (Egypt) pasha, founder of dynasty that encouraged emergence of modern Egyptian state.

Benito Mussolini, 1883-1945, (It.) dictator and leader of the Italian fascist state.

Imre Nagy, c. 1895-1958, (Hung.) communist premier, assassinated after Soviets crushed 1956 uprising.

Gamel Abdel Nasser, 1918-1970, (Egypt.) leader of Arab unification, second Egyptian president.

Jawaharlal Nehru, 1889-1964, (Ind.) prime minister, guided India through its early years of independence.

Kwame Nkrumah, 1909-1972, (Ghan.) dictatorial prime minister, deposed in 1966.

Frederick North, 1732-1792, (Br.) prime minister, his inept policies led to loss of American colonies.

Daniel O'Connell, 1775-1847, (Ir.) political leader, known as The Liberator.

Omar, c.581-644, Mohammedan leader, 2d caliph, led Islam to become an imperial power.

Ignance Paderewski, 1860-1941, (Pol.) statesman, pianist, composer, briefly prime minister, an ardent patriot.

Viscount Palmerston, 1784-1865, (Br.) Whig-Liberal prime minister, foreign minister, embodied British nationalism.

George Papandreou, 1888-1968, (Gk.) Republican politician, served three times as prime minister.

Franz von Papen, 1879-1969, (G.) politician, played major role in overthrow of Weimar Republic and rise of Hitler.

Charles Stewart Parnell, 1864-1891, (Ir.) nationalist leader, "uncrowned king of Ireland."

Lester Pearson, 1897-1972, (Can.) diplomat, Liberal party leader, prime minister.

Robert Peel, 1788-1850, (Br.) reformist prime minister, founder of Conservative party.

Juan Perón, 1895-1974, (Arg.) president, dictator.

Joseph Pilsudski, 1867-1935, (Pol.) statesman, instrumental in re-establishing Polish state in the 20th century.

Charles Pinckney, 1757-1824, (U.S.) founding father, his Pinckney plan was largely incorporated into constitution.

William Pitt, the Elder, 1708-1778, (Br.) statesman, called the "Great Commoner," transformed Britain into imperial power.

William Pitt, the Younger, 1759-1806, (Br.) prime minister during French Revolutionary wars.

Georgi Plekhanov, 1857-1918, (R.) revolutionary, social philosopher, called "father of Russian Marxism."

Raymond Poincaré, 1860-1934, (F.) 9th president of the Republic, advocated harsh punishment of Germany after WW I.

Georges Pompidou, 1911-1974, (F.) Gaullist political leader, president from 1969 to 1974.

Grigori Potemkin, 1739-1791, (R.) field marshal, favorite of Catherine II.

Edmund Randolph, 1753-1813, (U.S.) attorney, prominent in drafting, ratification of constitution.

John Randolph, 1773-1833, (U.S.) southern planter, strong advocate of states' rights.

Jeannette Rankin, 1880-1973, (U.S.) pacifist, first woman member of U.S. Congress.

Walter Rathenau, 1867-1922, (G.) industrialist, social theorist, statesman.

Sam Rayburn, 1882-1961, (U.S.) Democratic leader, representative for 47 years, House speaker for 17.

Paul Reynaud, 1878-1966, (F.) statesman, premier in 1940 at the time of France's defeat by Germany.

Syngman Rhee, 1875-1965, (Kor.) first president of the Republic of Korea.

Cecil Rhodes, 1853-1902, (Br.) imperialist, industrial magnate, established Rhodes scholarships in his will.

Cardinal de Richelieu, 1585-1642, (F.) statesman, known as "red eminence," chief minister to Loius XIII.

Maximilien Robespierre, 1758-1794, (F.) leading figure of French Revolution, responsible for much of Reign of Terror.

Nelson Rockefeller, 1908-1979, (U.S.) Republican gov. of N.Y., 1959-73; U.S. vice president, 1974-77.

Eleanor Roosevelt, 1884-1962, (U.S.) humanitarian, United Nations diplomat.

Elihu Root, 1845-1937, (U.S.) lawyer, statesman, diplomat, leading Republican supporter of the League of Nations.

John Russell, 1792-1878, (Br.) Liberal prime minister during the Irish potato famine.

Anwar el-Sadat, 1918-1981, (Egypt) president, 1970-1981, promoted peace with Israel.

Antônio de O. Salazar, 1899-1970, (Port.) statesman, longtime dictator.

José de San Martin, 1778-1850, South American revolutionary, protector of Peru.

Eisaku Sato, 1901-1975, (Jap.) prime minister, presided over Japan's post-WW II emergence as major world power.

Philipp Scheidemann, 1865-1939, (G.) Social Democratic leader, first chancellor of the German republic.

Robert Schuman, 1886-1963, (F.) statesman, founded European Coal and Steel Community.

Carl Schurz, 1829-1906, (U.S.) German-American political leader, journalist, orator, dedicated reformer.

Kurt Schuschnigg, 1897-1977, (Aus.) chancellor, unsuccess-

ful in stopping his country's annexation by Germany.

William H. Seward, 1801-1872, (U.S.) anti-slavery activist, as Lincoln's secretary of state purchased Alaska.

Carlo Sforza, 1872-1952, (It.) foreign minister, prominent Italian anti-fascist.

Alfred E. Smith, 1873-1944, (U.S.) New York Democratic governor, first Roman Catholic to run for presidency.

Jan C. Smuts, 1870-1950, (S.Af.) statesman, philosopher, soldier, prime minister.

Paul Henri Spaak, 1899-1972, (Belg.) statesman, socialist leader.

Joseph Stalin, 1879-1953, (USSR) Soviet dictator from 1924 to 1953.

Edwin M. Stanton, 1814-1869, (U.S.) Lincoln's secretary of war during the Civil War.

Edward R. Stettinius Jr., 1900-1949, (U.S.) industrialist, secretary of state who coordinated aid to WW II allies.

Adlai E. Stevenson, 1900-1865, (U.S.) Democratic leader, diplomat, Illinois governor, presidential candidate.

Henry L. Stimson, 1867-1950, (U.S.) statesman, served in 5 administrations, influenced foreign policy in 1930s and 1940s.

Gustav Stresemann, 1878-1929, (G.) chancellor, foreign minister, dedicated to regaining friendship for post-WW I Germany.

Sukarno, 1901-1970, (Indon.) dictatorial first president of the Indonesian republic.

Sun Yat-sen, 1866-1925, (Chin.) revolutionary, leader of Kuomintang, regarded as the father of modern China.

Robert A. Taft, 1889-1953, (U.S.) conservative Senate leader, called "Mr. Republican."

Charles de Talleyrand, 1754-1838, (F.) statesman, diplomat, the major force of the Congress of Vienna of 1814-15.

U Thant, 1909-1974 (Bur.) statesman, UN secretary-general.

Norman M. Thomas, 1884-1968, (U.S.) social reformer, 6 times unsuccessful Socialist party presidential candidate.

Josip Broz Tito, 1892-1980, (Yug.) president of Yugoslavia from 1953, World War II guerrilla chief, postwar rival of Stalin, leader of 3d world movement.

Palmiro Togliatti, 1893-1964, (It.) major leader of Italian Communist party.

Hideki Tojo, 1885-1948, (Jap.) statesman, soldier, prime minister during most of WW II.

François Toussaint L'Ouverture, c. 1744-1803, (Hait.) patriot, martyr, thwarted French colonial aims.

Leon Trotsky, 1879-1940, (USSR) revolutionary, communist leader, founded Red Army, expelled from party in conflict with Stalin.

Rafael L. Trujillo Molina, 1891-1961, (Dom.) absolute dictator, assassinated.

Moise K. Tshombe, 1919-1969, (Cong.) politician, president of secessionist Katanga, premier of Republic of Congo (Zaire).

William M. Tweed, 1823-1878, (U.S.) politician, absolute leader of Tammany Hall, NYC's Democratic political machine.

Walter Ulbricht, 1893-1973, (G.) communist leader of German Democratic Republic.

Arthur H. Vandenberg, 1884-1951, (U.S.) senator, proponent of anti-communist bipartisan foreign policy after WW II.

Eleutherios Venizelos, 1864-1936, (Gk.) most prominent Greek statesman in early 20th century, considerably expanded Greek Territory through his diplomacy.

Hendrik F. Verwoerd, 1901-1966, (S.Af.) prime minister, rigorously applied apartheid policy despite protest.

Robert Walpole, 1676-1745, (Br.) statesman, generally considered Britain's first prime minister.

Daniel Webster, 1782-1852, (U.S.) orator, politician, enthusiastic nationalist, advocate of business interests during Jacksonian agrarianism.

Chaim Weizmann, 1874-1952, Zionist leader, scientist, first Israeli president.

Wendell L. Wilkie, 1892-1944, (U.S.) Republican who tried to unseat FDR when he ran for his 3d term.

Emiliano Zapata, c. 1879-1919, (Mex.) revolutionary, major influence on modern Mexico.

Notable Military and Naval Leaders of the Past

Creighton Abrams, 1914-1974, (U.S.) commanded forces in Vietnam, 1968-72.

Harold Alexander, 1891-1969, (Br.) led Allied invasion of Italy, 1943.

Ethan Allen, 1738-1789, (U.S.) headed Green Mountain Boys; captured Ft. Ticonderoga, 1775.

Edmund Allenby, 1861-1936, (Br.) in Boer War, WW1; led Egyptian expeditionary force, 1917-18.

Benedict Arnold, 1741-1801, (U.S.) victorious at Saratoga; tied to betray West Point to British.

Henry "Hap" Arnold, 1886-1950, (U.S.) commanded Army Air Force in WW2.

Petr Bagration, 1765-1812, (R.) hero of Napoleonic wars.

John Barry, 1745-1803, (U.S.) won numerous sea battles during revolution.

Pierre Beauregard, 1818-1893, (U.S.) Confederate general ordered bombardment of Ft. Sumter that began the Civil War.

Gebhard v. Blücher, 1742-1819, (G.) helped defeat Napoleon at Waterloo.

Napoleon Bonaparte, 1769-1821, (F.) defeated Russia and Austria at Austerlitz, 1805; invaded Russia, 1812; defeated at Waterloo, 1815.

Edward Braddock, 1695-1755, (Br.) commanded forces in French and Indian War.

Omar N. Bradley, 1893-1981, (U.S.) headed U.S. ground troops in Normandy invasion, 1944.

John Burgoyne, 1722-1792, (Br.) defeated at Saratoga.

Claire Chennault, 1890-1958, (U.S.) headed Flying Tigers in WW2.

Mark Clark, 1896-1984, (U.S.) led forces in WW2 and Korean War.

Karl v. Clausewitz, 1780-1831, (G.) wrote books on military theory.

Henry Clinton, 1738-1795, (Br.) commander of forces in America, 1778-81.

Lucius D. Clay, 1897-1978, (U.S.) led Berlin airlift, 1948-49.

Charles Cornwallis, 1738-1805, (Br.) victorious at Brandywine, 1777; surrendered at Yorktown.

Crazy Horse, 1849-1877, (U.S.) Sioux war chief victorious at Little Big Horn.

George A. Custer, 1839-1876, (U.S.) defeated and killed at Little Big Horn.

Moshe Dayan, 1915-1981, (Isr.) directed campaigns in the 1967, 1973 wars.

Stephen Decatur, 1779-1820, (U.S.) naval hero of Barbary wars, War of 1812.

Anton Denikin, 1872-1947, (R.) led White forces in Russian civil war.

George Dewey, 1837-1917, (U.S.) destroyed Spanish fleet at Manila, 1898.

Hugh C. Dowding, 1883-1970, (Br.) headed RAF, 1936-40.

Jubal Early, 1816-1894, (U.S.) Confederate general led raid on Washington, 1864.

Dwight D. Eisenhower, 1890-1969, (U.S.) commanded Allied forces in Europe, WW2.

David Farragut, 1801-1870, (U.S.) Union admiral captured New Orleans, Mobile Bay.

Ferdinand Foch, 1851-1929, (F.) headed victorious Allied armies, 1918.

Nathan Bedford Forrest, 1821-1877, (U.S.) Confederate general led cavalry raids against Union supply lines.

Frederick the Great, 1712-1786, (G.) led Prussia in The Seven Years War.

Nathanael Greene, 1742-1786, (U.S.) defeated British in Southern campaign, 1780-81.

Charles G. Gordon, 1833-1885, (Br.) led forces in China; killed at Khartoum.

Horatio Gates, 1728-1806, (U.S.) commanded army at Saratoga.

Ulysses S. Grant, 1822-1885, (U.S.) headed Union army, 1864-65; forced Lee's surrender, 1865.

Heinz Guderian, 1888-1953, (G.) tank theorist led panzer forces in Poland, France, Russia.

Douglas Haig, 1861-1928, (Br.) led British armies in France, 1915-18.

William F. Halsey, 1882-1959, (U.S.) defeated Japanese fleet at Leyte Gulf, 1944.

Richard Howe, 1726-1799, (Br.) commanded navy in America, 1776-78; first of June victory against French, 1794.

William Howe, 1729-1814, (Br.) commanded forces in America, 1776-78.

Isaac Hull, 1773-1843, (U.S.) sunk British frigate Guerriere, 1812.

Thomas (Stonewall) Jackson, 1824-1863, (U.S.) Confederate general led forces in the Shenandoah Valley campaign.

Joseph Joffre, 1852-1931, (F.) headed Allied armies, won Battle of the Marne, 1914.

John Paul Jones, 1747-1792, (U.S.) raided British coast; commanded Bonhomme Richard in victory over Serapis, 1779.

Stephen Kearny, 1794-1848, (U.S.) headed Army of the West in Mexican War.

Ernest J. King, 1878-1956, (U.S.) chief naval strategist in WW2.

Horatio H. Kitchener, 1850-1916, (Br.) led forces in Boer War; victorious at Khartoum; organized army in WW1.

Lavrenti Kornilov, 1870-1918, (R.) Commander-in-Chief, 1917; led counter-revolutionary march on Petrograd.

Thaddeus Kosciusko, 1746-1817, (P.) aided American cause in revolution.

Mikhail Kutuzov, 1745-1813, (R.) fought French at Borodino, 1812; abandoned Moscow; forced French retreat.

Marquis de Lafayette, 1757-1834, (F.) aided American cause in the revolution.

Thomas E. Lawrence (of Arabia), 1888-1935, (Br.) organized revolt of Arabs against Turks in WW1.

Henry (Light-Horse Harry) Lee, 1756-1818, (U.S.) cavalry officer in revolution.

Robert E. Lee, 1807-1870, (U.S.) Confederate general defeated at Gettysburg; surrendered to Grant, 1865.

James Longstreet, 1821-1904, (U.S.) aided Lee at Gettysburg.

Douglas MacArthur, 1880-1964, (U.S.) commanded forces in SW Pacific in WW2; headed occupation forces in Japan, 1945-50; UN commander in Korean War.

Francis Marion, 1733-1795, (U.S.) led guerrilla actions in S.C. during revolution.

Duke of Marlborough, 1650-1722, (Br.) led forces against Louis XIV in War of the Spanish Sucession.

George C. Marshall, 1880-1959, (U.S.) chief of staff in WW2; authored Marshall Plan.

George B. McClellan, 1826-1885, (U.S.) Union general commanded Army of the Potomac, 1861-62.

George Meade, 1815-1872; (U.S.) commanded Union forces at Gettysburg.

Billy Mitchell, 1879-1936, (U.S.) air-power advocate; courtmartialed for insubordination, later vindicated.

Helmuth v. Moltke, 1800-1891; (G.) victorious in Austro-Prussian, Franco-Prussian wars.

Louis de Montcalm, 1712-1759, (F.) headed troops in Canada; defeated at Quebec, 1759.

Bernard Law Montgomery, 1887-1976, (Br.) stopped German offensive at Alamein, 1942; helped plan Normandy invasion.

Daniel Morgan, 1736-1802, (U.S.) victorious at Cowpens, 1781.

Louis Mountbatten, 1900-1979, (Br.) Supreme Allied Commander of SE Asia, 1943-46.

Joachim Murat, 1767-1815, (F.) leader of cavalry at Marengo, 1800; Austerlitz, 1805; and Jena, 1806.

Horatio Nelson, 1758-1805, (Br.) naval commander destroyed French fleet at Trafalgar.

Michel Ney, 1769-1815, (F.) commanded forces in Switzerland, Austria, Russia; defeated at Waterloo.

Chester Nimitz, 1885-1966, (U.S.) commander of naval forces in Pacific in WW2.

George S. Patton, 1885-1945, (U.S.) led assault on Sicily, 1943; headed 3d Army invasion of German-occupied Europe.

Oliver Perry, 1785-1819, (U.S.) won Battle of Lake Erie in War of 1812.

John Pershing, 1860-1948, (U.S.) commanded Mexican border campaign, 1916; American expeditionary forces in WW1.

Henri Philippe Pétain, 1856-1951, (F.) defended Verdun, 1916; headed Vichy government in WW2.

George E. Pickett, 1825-1875, (U.S.) Confederate general famed for "charge" at Gettysburg.

Erwin Rommel, 1891-1944, (G.) headed Afrika Korps.

Karl v. Rundstedt, 1875-1953, (G.) supreme commander in West, 1943-45.

Aleksandr Samsonov, 1859-1914, (R.) led invasion of E. Prussia, defeated at Tannenberg, 1914.

Winfield Scott, 1786-1866, (U.S.) hero of War of 1812; headed forces in Mexican war, took Mexico City.

Philip Sheridan, 1831-1888, (U.S.) Union cavalry officer headed Army of the Shenandoah, 1864-65.

William T. Sherman, 1820-1891, (U.S.) Union general sacked Atlanta during "march to the sea," 1864.

Carl Spaatz, 1891-1974, (U.S.) directed strategic bombing against Germany, later Japan, in WW2.

Raymond Spruance, 1886-1969, (U.S.) victorious at Midway Island, 1942.

Joseph W. Stilwell, 1883-1946, (U.S.) headed forces in the China, Burma, India theater in WW2.

J.E.B. Stuart, 1833-1864, (U.S.) Confederate cavalry commander.

George H. Thomas, 1816-1870, (U.S.) saved Union army at Chattanooga, 1863; victorious at Nashville, 1864.

Semyon Timoshenko, 1895-1970, (USSR) defended Moscow, Stalingrad; led winter offensive, 1942-43.

Alfred v. Tirpitz, 1849-1930, (G.) responsible for submarine blockade in WW1.

Jonathan M. Wainwright, 1883-1953, (U.S.) forced to surrender on Corregidor, 1942.

George Washington, 1732-1799, (U.S.) led Continental army, 1775-83.

Archibald Wavell, 1883-1950, (Br.) commanded forces in N. and E. Africa, and SE Asia in WW2.

Anthony Wayne, 1745-1796, (U.S.) captured Stony Point 1779; defeated Indians at Fallen Timbers, 1794.

Duke of Wellington, 1769-1852, (Br.) defeated Napoleon at Waterloo.

James Wolfe, 1727-1759, (Br.) captured Quebec from French, 1759.

Georgi Zhukov, 1895-1974, (USSR) defended Moscow, 1941; led assault on Berlin.

Poets Laureate of England

There is no authentic record of the origin of the office of Poet Laureate of England. According to Warton, there was a Versificator Regis, or King's Poet, in the reign of Henry III (1216-1272), and he was paid 100 shillings a year. Geo frey Chaucer (1340-1400) assumed the title of Poet Laureate, and in 1389 got a royal grant of a yearly allowance of wine. In the reign of Edward IV (1461-1483), John Kay held the post. Under Henry VII (1485-1509), Andrew Bernard was the Poet Laureate, and was succeeded under Henry VIII (1509-1547) by John Skelton. Next came Edmund Spenser, who died in 1599; then Samuel Daniel, appointed 1599, and then Ben Jonson, 1619. Sir William D'Avenant was appointed in 1637. He was a godson of William Shakespeare.

Others were John Dryden, 1670; Thomas Shadwell, 1688; Nahum Tate, 1692; Nicholas Rowe, 1715; the Rev. Laurence Eusden, 1718; Colley Cibber, 1730; William Whitehead, 1757, on the refusal of Gray; Rev. Thomas Warton, 1785, on the refusal of Mason; Henry J. Pye, 1790; Robert Southey, 1813, on the refusal of Sir Walter Scott; William Wordsworth, 1843; Alfred, Lord Tennyson, 1850; Alfred Austin, 1896; Robert Bridges, 1913; John Masefield, 1930; Cecil Day Lewis, 1967; Sir John Betjeman, 1972-1984.

Noted Writers of the Past

Henry Adams, 1838-1918, (U.S.) historian, philosopher. *The Education of Henry Adams.*

George Ade, 1866-1944, (U.S.) humorist. *Fables in Slang.*

Conrad Aiken, 1889-1973, (U.S.) poet, critic.

Louisa May Alcott, 1832-1888, (U.S.) novelist. *Little Women.*

Sholom Aleichem, 1859-1916. (R.) Yiddish writer. *Tevye's Daughter, The Great Fair.*

Horatio Alger, 1832-1899, (U.S.) author of "rags-to-riches" boys' books.

Hans Christian Anderson, 1805-1875, (Den.) author of fairy tales. *The Princess and the Pea, The Ugly Duckling.*

Maxwell Anderson, 1888-1959, (U.S.) playwright. *What Price Glory?, High Tor, Winterset, Key Largo.*

Sherwood Anderson, 1876-1941, (U.S.) author. *Winesburg, Ohio.*

Matthew Arnold, 1822-1888, (Br.) poet, critic. "Thrysis," "Dover Beach."

Jane Austen, 1775-1817, (Br.) novelist. *Pride and Prejudice, Sense and Sensibility, Emma, Mansfield Park.*

Isaac Babel, 1894-1941, (R.) short-story writer, playwright. *Odessa Tales, Red Cavalry.*

Enid Bagnold, 1890-1981, (Br.) playwright, novelist. *National Velvet.*

James M. Barrie, 1860-1937, (Br.) playwright, novelist. *Peter Pan, Dear Brutus, What Every Woman Knows.*

Honoré de Balzac, 1799-1850, (Fr.) novelist. *Le Père Goriot, Cousine Bette, Eugénie Grandet, The Human Comedy.*

Charles Baudelaire, 1821-1867, (Fr.) symbolist poet. *Les Fleurs du Mal.*

L. Frank Baum, 1856-1919, (U.S.) children's author. *Wizard of Oz* series.

Brendan Behan, 1923-1964, (Ir.) playwright. *The Quare Fellow, The Hostage, Borstal Boy.*

Robert Benchley, 1889-1945, (U.S.) humorist. *From Bed to Worse, My Ten Years in a Quandary.*

Stephen Vincent Benét, 1898-1943, (U.S.) poet, novelist. *John Brown's Body.*

John Berryman, 1914-1972, (U.S.) poet. *Homage to Mistress Bradstreet.*

Ambrose Bierce, 1842-1914, (U.S.) short-story writer, journalist. *In the Midst of Life, The Devil's Dictionary.*

William Blake, 1757-1827, (Br.) poet, mystic, artist. *Songs of Innocence, Songs of Experience.*

Giovanni Boccaccio, 1313-1375, (It.) poet, storyteller. *Decameron, Filostrato.*

James Boswell, 1740-1795, (Sc.) author. *The Life of Samuel Johnson.*

Anne Bradstreet, c. 1612-1672, (U.S.) poet. *The Tenth Muse Lately Sprung Up in America.*

Bertolt Brecht, 1898-1956, (G.) dramatist, poet. *The Threepenny Opera, Mother Courage and Her Children.*

Charlotte Brontë, 1816-1855, (Br.) novelist. *Jane Eyre.*

Emily Brontë, 1818-1848, (Br.) novelist. *Wuthering Heights.*

Elizabeth Barrett Browning, 1806-1861, (Br.) poet. *Sonnets from the Portuguese.*

Robert Browning, 1812-1889, (Br.) poet. "My Last Duchess," "Soliloquy of the Spanish Cloister."

Pearl Buck, 1892-1973, (U.S.) novelist. *The Good Earth.*

Mikhail Bulgakov, 1891-1940, (R.) novelist, playwright. *The Heart of a Dog, The Master and Margarita.*

John Bunyan, 1628-1688, (Br.) writer. *Pilgrim's Progress.*

Robert Burns, 1759-1796, (Sc.) poet. "Flow Gently, Sweet Afton," "My Heart's in the Highlands," "Auld Lang Syne."

Edgar Rice Burroughs, 1875-1950, (U.S.) novelist. *Tarzan of the Apes.*

George Gordon Lord Byron, 1788-1824, (Br.) poet. *Don Juan, Childe Harold.*

Albert Camus, 1913-1960, (F.) novelist. *The Plague, The Stranger, Caligula, The Fall.*

Lewis Carroll, 1832-1898, (Br.) writer, mathematician. *Alice's Adventures in Wonderland, Through the Looking Glass.*

Karel Capek, 1890-1938, (Czech.) playwright, novelist, essayist. *R.U.R. (Rossum's Universal Robots).*

Giacomo Casanova, 1725-1798, (It.) Venetian adventurer, author, world famous for his memoirs.

Willa Cather, 1876-1947, (U.S.) novelist, essayist. *O Pio-*

neers!, My Ántonia.

Miguel de Cervantes Saavedra, 1547-1616, (Sp.) novelist, dramatist, poet. *Don Quixote de la Mancha.*

Raymond Chandler, 1888-1959, (U.S.) writer of detective fiction. Philip Marlowe series.

Geoffrey Chaucer, c. 1340-1400, (Br.) poet. *The Canterbury Tales.*

John Cheevers, 1912-1983, (U.S.) short story writer, novelist. *The Wapshot Scandal.*

Anton Chekhov, 1860-1904, (R.) short-story writer, dramatist. *Uncle Vanya, The Cherry Orchard, The Three Sisters.*

G.K. Chesterton, 1874-1936, (Br.) author, Fr. Brown series.

Agatha Christie, 1891-1976, (Br.) mystery writer. *And Then There Were None, Murder on the Orient Express.*

Jean Cocteau, 1889-1963, (F.) writer, visual artist, filmmaker. *The Beauty and the Beast, Enfants Terribles.*

Samuel Taylor Coleridge, 1772-1834, (Br.) poet, man of letters. "Kubla Khan," "The Rime of the Ancient Mariner."

Sidonie Colette, 1873-1954, (F.) novelist. *Claudine, Gigi.*

Joseph Conrad, 1857-1924, (Br.) novelist. *Lord Jim, Heart of Darkness, The Nigger of the Narcissus.*

James Fenimore Cooper, 1789-1851, (U.S.) novelist. *Leather-Stocking Tales.*

Pierre Corneille, 1606-1684, (F.) Dramatist. *Medeé, Le Cid, Horace, Cinna, Polyeucte.*

Hart Crane, 1899-1932, (U.S.) poet. "The Bridge."

Stephen Crane, 1871-1900, (U.S.) novelist. *The Red Badge of Courage.*

e.e. cummings, 1894-1962, (U.S.) poet. *Tulips and Chimneys.*

Gabriele D'Annunzio, 1863-1938, (It.) poet, novelist, dramatist. *The Child of Pleasure, The Intruder, The Victim.*

Dante Alighieri, 1265-1321, (It.) poet. *The Divine Comedy.*

Daniel Defoe, 1660-1731, (Br.) writer. *Robinson Crusoe, Moll Flanders, Journal of the Plague Year.*

Charles Dickens, 1812-1870, (Br.) novelist. *David Copperfield, Oliver Twist, Great Expectations, The Pickwick Papers.*

Emily Dickinson, 1830-1886, (U.S.) poet.

Isak Dinesen (Karen Blixen), 1885-1962, (Dan.) author. *Out of Africa, Seven Gothic Tales, Winter's Tales.*

John Donne, 1573-1631, (Br.) poet. *Songs and Sonnets, Holy Sonnets,* "Death Be Not Proud."

John Dos Passos, 1896-1970, (U.S.) author. *U.S.A.*

Fyodor Dostoyevsky, 1821-1881, (R.) author. *Crime and Punishment, The Brothers Karamazov, The Possessed.*

Arthur Conan Doyle, 1859-1930, (Br.) author, created Sherlock Holmes.

Theodore Dreiser, 1871-1945, (U.S.) novelist. *An American Tragedy, Sister Carrie.*

John Dryden, 1631-1700, (Br.) poet, dramatist, critic. *Fables Ancient and Modern.*

Alexandre Dumas, 1802-1870, (F.) novelist, dramatist. *The Three Musketeers, The Count of Monte Cristo.*

Alexandre Dumas (fils), 1824-1895, (F.) dramatist, novelist. *La Dame aux camélias, Le Demi-Monde.*

Ilya G. Ehrenburg, 1891-1967, (R.) novelist, journalist. *The Thaw.*

George Eliot, 1819-1880, (Br.) novelist. *Adam Bede, Silas Marner, The Mill on the Floss.*

T.S. Eliot, 1888-1965, (Br.) poet, critic. *The Waste Land,* "The Love Song of J. Alfred Prufrock," *Murder in the Cathedral.*

Ralph Waldo Emerson, 1803-1882, (U.S.) poet, essayist. "The Concord Hymn," "Brahma," "The Rhodora."

James T. Farrell, 1904-1979, (U.S.) novelist. *Studs Lonigan* trilogy.

William Faulkner, 1897-1962, (U.S.) novelist. *Sanctuary, Light in August, The Sound and the Fury, Absalom, Absalom!*

Edna Ferber, 1885-1968, (U.S.) novelist, dramatist. *Show Boat, Saratoga Trunk, Giant, Dinner at Eight.*

Henry Fielding, 1707-1754, (Br.) novelist. *Tom Jones.*

F. Scott Fitzgerald, 1896-1940, (U.S.) short-story writer, novelist. *The Great Gatsby, Tender is the Night.*

Gustave Flaubert, 1821-1880, (F.) novelist. *Madame Bovary.*

C.S. Forester, 1899-1966, (Br.) novelist. Horatio Hornblower series.

E.M. Forster, 1879-1970, (Br.) novelist. *A Passage to India, Where Angels Fear to Tread, Maurice.*

Anatole France, 1844-1924. (F.) writer. *Penguin Island, My Friend's Book, Le Crime de Sylvestre Bonnard.*

Robert Frost, 1874-1963, (U.S.) poet. "Birches," "Fire and Ice," "Stopping by Woods on a Snowy Evening."

John Galsworthy, 1867-1933, (Br.) novelist, dramatist. *The Forsyte Saga, A Modern Comedy.*

Erle Stanley Gardner, 1889-1970, (U.S.) author, lawyer. Perry Mason series.

André Gide, 1869-1951, (F.) writer, *The Immoralist, The Pastoral Symphony, Strait is the Gate.*

Jean Giraudoux, 1882-1944, (F.) novelist, dramatist. *Electra, The Madwoman of Chaillot, Ondine, Tiger at the Gate.*

Johann W. von Goethe, 1749-1832, (G.) poet, dramatist, novelist. *Faust.*

Nikolai Gogol, 1809-1852, (R.) short-story writer, dramatist, novelist. *Dead Souls, The Inspector General.*

Oliver Goldsmith, 1730?-1774, (Br.-Ir.) writer. *The Vicar of Wakefield, She Stoops to Conquer.*

Maxim Gorky, 1868-1936, (R.) writer, founder of Soviet realism. *Mother, The Lower Depths.*

Thomas Gray, 1716-1771, (Br.) poet. "Elegy Written in a Country Churchyard."

Zane Grey, 1875-1939, (U.S.) writer of western stories.

Jakob Grimm, 1785-1863, (G.) philologist, folklorist. *German Methodology, Grimm's Fairy Tales.*

Wilhelm Grimm, 1786-1859, (G.) philologist, folklorist. *Grimm's Fairy Tales.*

Edgar A. Guest, 1881-1959, (U.S.) poet. *A Heap of Livin'*

Dashiell Hammett, 1894-1961, (U.S.) writer of detective fiction, created Sam Spade.

Thomas Hardy, 1840-1928, (Br.) novelist, poet. *The Return of the Native, Tess of the D'Urbervilles, Jude the Obscure.*

Joel Chandler Harris, 1848-1908, (U.S.) short-story writer. Uncle Remus series.

Moss Hart, 1904-1961, (U.S.) playwright. *Once in a Lifetime, You Can't Take It With You.*

Bret Harte, 1836-1902, (U.S.) short-story writer, poet. *The Luck of Roaring Camp.*

Jaroslav Hasek, 1883-1923, (Czech.) writer. *The Good Soldier Schweik.*

Nathaniel Hawthorne, 1804-1864, (U.S.) novelist, short story writer. *The Scarlet Letter, The House of the Seven Gables.*

Heinrich Heine, 1797-1856, (G.) poet. *Book of Songs.*

Ernest Hemingway, 1899-1961, (U.S.) novelist, short-story writer. *A Farewell to Arms, For Whom the Bell Tolls.*

O. Henry (W.S. Porter), 1862-1910, (U.S.) short-story writer. "The Gift of the Magi."

Hermann Hesse, 1877-1962, (G.) novelist, poet. *Death and the Lover, Steppenwolf, Siddhartha.*

Oliver Wendell Holmes, 1809-1894, (U.S.) poet, novelist. *The Autocrat of the Breakfast-Table.*

Alfred E. Housman, 1859-1936, (Br.) poet. *A Shropshire Lad.*

William Dean Howells, 1837-1920, (U.S.) novelist, critic, dean of late 19th century American letters.

Langston Hughes, 1902-1967, (U.S.) poet, playwright. *The Weary Blues, One-Way Ticket, Shakespeare in Harlem.*

Victor Hugo, 1802-1885, (F.) poet, dramatist, novelist. *Notre Dame de Paris, Les Misérables.*

Aldous Huxley 1894-1963, (Br.) author. *Point Counter Point, Brave New World.*

Henrik Ibsen, 1828-1906, (Nor.) dramatist, poet. *A Doll's House, Ghosts, The Wild Duck, Hedda Gabler.*

William Inge, 1913-1973, (U.S.) playwright. *Come Back Little Sheba, Bus Stop, The Dark at the Top of the Stairs, Picnic.*

Washington Irving, 1783-1859, (U.S.) essayist, author. "Rip Van Winkle," "The Legend of Sleepy Hollow."

Shirley Jackson, 1919-1965, (U.S.) writer. *The Lottery.*

Henry James, 1843-1916, (U.S.) novelist, critic. *Washington Square, Portrait of a Lady, The American.*

Robinson Jeffers, 1887-1962, (U.S.) poet, dramatist. *Tamar and Other Poems, Medea.*

Samuel Johnson, 1709-1784, (Br.) author, scholar, critic. *Dictionary of the English Language.*

Ben Jonson, 1572-1637, (Br.) dramatist, poet. *Volpone.*

James Joyce, 1882-1941, (Ir.) novelist. *Ulysses, A Portrait of the Artist as a Young Man, Finnegans Wake.*

Franz Kafka, 1883-1924, (G.) novelist, short-story writer. *The Trial, Amerika, The Castle.*

George S. Kaufman, 1889-1961, (U.S.) playwright. *The Man Who Came to Dinner, You Can't Take It With You, Stage Door.*

Nikos Kazantzakis, 1883?-1957, (Gk.) novelist. *Zorba the Greek, A Greek Passion.*

John Keats, 1795-1821, (Br.) poet. *On a Grecian Urn, La Belle Dame Sans Merci.*

Joyce Kilmer, 1886-1918, (U.S.) poet, "Trees."

Rudyard Kipling, 1865-1936, (Br.) author, poet. "The White Man's Burden," "Gunga Din," *The Jungle Book.*

Jean de la Fontaine, 1621-1695, (F.) poet. *Fables choisies.*

Pär Lagerkvist, 1891-1974, (Swed.) poet, dramatist, novelist. *Barabbas, The Sybil.*

Selma Lagerlöf, 1858-1940, (Swed.) novelist. *Jerusalem, The Ring of the Lowenskolds.*

Alphonse de Lamartine, 1790-1869, (F.) poet, novelist, statesman. *Méditations poétiques.*

Charles Lamb, 1775-1834, (Br.) essayist. *Specimens of English Dramatic Poets, Essays of Elia.*

Giuseppe di Lampedusa, 1896-1957, (It.) novelist. *The Leopard.*

Ring Lardner, 1885-1933, (U.S.) short story writer, humorist. *You Know Me, Al.*

D. H. Lawrence, 1885-1930, (Br.) novelist. *Women in Love, Lady Chatterley's Lover, Sons and Lovers.*

Mikhail Lermontov, 1814-1841, (R.) novelist, poet. "Demon," *Hero of Our Time.*

Alain-René Lesage, 1668-1747, (F.) novelist. *Gil Blas de Santillane.*

Gotthold Lessing, 1729-1781, (G.) dramatist, philosopher, critic. *Miss Sara Sampson, Minna von Barnhelm.*

Sinclair Lewis, 1885-1951, (U.S.) novelist, playwright. *Babbitt, Arrowsmith, Dodsworth, Main Street.*

Vachel Lindsay, 1879-1931, (U.S.) poet. *General William Booth Enters into Heaven, The Congo.*

Hugh Lofting, 1886-1947, (Br.) children's author. Dr. Doolittle series.

Jack London, 1876-1916, (U.S.) novelist, journalist. *Call of the Wild, The Sea-Wolf.*

Henry Wadsworth Longfellow, 1807-1882, (U.S.) poet. *Evangeline, The Song of Hiawatha.*

Amy Lowell, 1874-1925, (U.S.) poet, critic. *A Dome of Many-Colored Glass,* "Patterns," "Lilacs."

James Russell Lowell, 1819-1891, (U.S.) poet, editor. *Poems, The Bigelow Papers.*

Robert Lowell, 1917-1977, (U.S.) poet. "Lord Weary's Castle," "For the Union Dead."

Emil Ludwig, 1881-1948, (G.) biographer. *Goethe, Beethoven, Napoleon, Bismarck.*

Niccolò Machiavelli, 1469-1527, (It.) author, statesman. *The Prince, Discourses on Livy.*

Stéphane Mallarmé, 1842-1898, (F.) poet. *The Afternoon of a Faun.*

Thomas Malory, ?-1471, (Br.) writer. *Morte d'Arthur.*

Andre Malraux, 1901-1976, (F.) novelist. *Man's Fate, The Voices of Silence.*

Osip Mandelstam, 1891-1938, (R.) Acmeist poet.

Thomas Mann, 1875-1955, (G.) novelist, essayist. *Buddenbrooks, Death in Venice, The Magic Mountain.*

Katherine Mansfield, 1888-1923, (Br.) short story writer. *Bliss, The Garden Party.*

Christopher Marlowe, 1564-1593, (Br.) dramatist, poet. *Tamburlaine the Great, Dr. Faustus, The Jew of Malta.*

John Masefield, 1878-1967, (Br.) poet. "Sea Fever," "Cargoes," *Salt Water Ballads.*

Edgar Lee Masters, 1869-1950, (U.S.) poet, biographer. *Spoon River Anthology.*

W. Somerset Maugham, 1874-1965, (Br.) author. *Of Human Bondage, The Razor's Edge, The Moon and Sixpence.*

Guy de Maupassant, 1850-1893, (F.) novelist, short-story writer. *A Life, Bel-Ami,* "The Necklace."

François Mauriac, 1885-1970, (F.) novelist, dramatist. *Viper's Tangle, The Kiss to the Leper.*

Vladimir Mayakovsky, 1893-1930, (R.) poet, dramatist. *The Cloud in Trousers.*

Carson McCullers, 1917-1967, (U.S.) novelist. *The Heart is a Lonely Hunter, Member of the Wedding.*

Herman Melville, 1819-1891, (U.S.) novelist, poet. *Moby Dick, Typee, Billy Budd, Omoo.*

H.L. Mencken, 1880-1956, (U.S.) author, critic, editor. *Prejudices, The American Language.*

George Meredith, 1828-1909, (Br.) novelist, poet. *The Ordeal of Richard Feverel, The Egoist.*

Prosper Mérimée, 1803-1870, (F.) author. *Carmen.*

Edna St. Vincent Millay, 1892-1950, (U.S.) poet. *The Harp Weaver and Other Poems, A Few Figs from Thistles.*

A.A. Milne, 1882-1956, (Br.) author. *When We Were Very Young, Winnie-the-Pooh, The House at Pooh Corner.*

John Milton, 1608-1674, (Br.) poet. *Paradise Lost, Samson Agonistes.*

Gabriela Mistral, 1889-1957, (Chil.) poet. *Sonnets of Death, Desolación, Tala, Lagar.*

Margaret Mitchell, 1900-1949, (U.S.) novelist. *Gone With the Wind.*

Jean Baptiste Molière, 1622-1673, (F.) dramatist. *Le Tartuffe, Le Misanthrope, Le Bourgeois Gentilhomme.*

Ferenc Molnár, 1878-1952, (Hung.) dramatist, novelist. *Liliom, The Guardsman, The Swan.*

Michel de Montaigne, 1533-1592, (F.) essayist. *Essais.*

Eugenio Montale, 1896-1981, (It.) poet.

Clement C. Moore, 1779-1863, (U.S.) poet, educator. "A Visit from Saint Nicholas."

Marianne Moore, 1887-1972, (U.S.) poet. *O to Be a Dragon.*

Thomas More, 1478-1535, (Br.) author. *Utopia.*

H.H. Munro (Saki), 1870-1916, (Br.) author. *Reginald, The Chronicles of Clovis, Beasts and Super-Beasts.*

Alfred de Musset, 1810-1857, (F.) poet, dramatist. *Confession d'un enfant du siècle.*

Vladimir Nabokov, 1899-1977, (U.S.) author. *Lolita, Ada.*

Ogden Nash, 1902-1971, (U.S.) poet. *Hard Lines, I'm a Stranger Here Myself, The Private Dining Room.*

Pablo Neruda, 1904-1973, (Chil.) poet. *Twenty Love Poems and One Song of Despair, Toward the Splendid City.*

Sean O'Casey, 1884-1964, (Ir.) dramatist. *Juno and the Paycock, The Plough and the Stars.*

Flannery O'Connor, 1925-1964, (U.S.) novelist, short story writer. *Wise Blood,* "A Good Man Is Hard to Find."

Clifford Odets, 1906-1963, (U.S.) playwright. *Waiting for Lefty, Awake and Sing, Golden Boy, The Country Girl.*

John O'Hara, 1905-1970, (U.S.) novelist. *Butterfield 8, From the Terrace, Appointment in Samarra.*

Omar Khayyam, c. 1028-1122, (Per.) poet. *Rubaiyat.*

Eugene O'Neill, 1888-1953, (U.S.) playwright. *Emperor Jones, Anna Christie, Long Day's Journey into Night, Desire Under the Elms, Mourning Becomes Electra.*

George Orwell, 1903-1950, (Br.) novelist, essayist. *Animal Farm, Nineteen Eighty-Four.*

Thomas (Tom) Paine, 1737-1809, (U.S.) author, political theorist. *Common Sense.*

Dorothy Parker, 1893-1967, (U.S.) poet, short-story writer. *Enough Rope, Laments for the Living.*

Boris Pasternak, 1890-1960, (R.) poet, novelist. *Doctor Zhivago, My Sister, Life.*

Samuel Pepys, 1633-1703, (Br.) public official, author of the greatest diary in the English language.

S. J. Perelman, 1904-1979, (U.S.) humorist. *The Road to Miltown, Under the Spreading Atrophy.*

Francesco Petrarca, 1304-1374, (It.) poet, humanist. *Africa, Trionfi, Canzoniere, On Solitude.*

Luigi Pirandello, 1867-1936, (It.) novelist, dramatist. *Six Characters in Search of an Author.*

Edgar Allan Poe, 1809-1849, (U.S.) poet, short-story writer, critic. "Annabel Lee," "The Raven," "The Purloined Letter."

Alexander Pope, 1688-1744, (Br.) poet. *The Rape of the Lock, An Essay on Man.*

Katherine Anne Porter, 1890-1980, (U.S.) novelist, short story writer. *Ship of Fools.*

Ezra Pound, 1885-1972, (U.S.) poet. *Cantos.*

Marcel Proust, 1871-1922, (F.) novelist. *A la recherche du temps perdu (Remembrance of Things Past).*

Aleksandr Pushkin, 1799-1837, (R.) poet, prose writer. *Boris Godunov, Eugene Onegin, The Bronze Horseman.*

François Rabelais, 1495-1553, (F.) writer, physician. *Gargantua, Pantagruel.*

Jean Racine, 1639-1699, (F.) dramatist. *Andromaque, Phèdre, Bérénice, Britannicus.*

Erich Maria Remarque, 1898-1970, (Ger.-U.S.) novelist. *All Quiet on the Western Front.*

Samuel Richardson, 1689-1761, (Br.) novelist. *Clarissa Harlowe, Pamela; or, Virtue Rewarded.*

James Whitcomb Riley, 1849-1916, (U.S.) poet. "When the Frost is on the Pumpkin," "Little Orphant Annie."

Rainer Maria Rilke, 1875-1926, (G.) poet. *Life and Songs, Divine Elegies, Sonnets to Orpheus.*

Arthur Rimbaud, 1854-1891, (F.) *A Season in Hell,* "Le Bateau ivre."

Edwin Arlington Robinson, 1869-1935, (U.S.) poet. "Richard Cory," "Miniver Cheevy."

Theodore Roethke, 1908-1963, (U.S.) poet. *Open House, The Waking, The Far Field.*

Romain Rolland, 1866-1944, (F.) novelist, biographer. *Jean-Christophe.*

Pierre de Ronsard, 1524-1585, (F.) poet. *Sonnets pour Hélène.*

Edmond Rostand, 1868-1918, (F.) poet, dramatist. *Cyrano de Bergerac.*

Damon Runyon, 1880-1946, (U.S.) short-story writer, journalist. *Guys and Dolls, Blue Plate Special.*

John Ruskin, 1819-1900, (Br.) critic, social theorist. *Modern Painters, The Seven Lamps of Architecture.*

Antoine de Saint-Exupery, 1900-1944, (F.) writer, aviator. *Wind, Sand and Stars, Le Petit Prince.*

George Sand, 1804-1876, (F.) novelist. *Consuelo, The Haunted Pool, Les Maitres sonneurs.*

Carl Sandburg, 1878-1967, (U.S.) poet. *Chicago Poems, Smoke and Steel, Harvest Poems.*

George Santayana, 1863-1952, (U.S.) poet, essayist, philosopher. *The Sense of Beauty, The Realms of Being.*

William Saroyan, 1908-1981, (U.S.) playwright, novelist. *The Time of Your Life, The Human Comedy.*

Friedrich von Schiller, 1759-1805, (G.) dramatist, poet, historian. *Don Carlos, Maria Stuart, Wilhelm Tell.*

Sir Walter Scott, 1771-1832, (Sc.) novelist, poet. *Ivanhoe, Rob Roy, The Bride of Lammermoor.*

William Shakespeare, 1564-1616, (Br.) dramatist, poet. *Romeo and Juliet, Hamlet, King Lear, The Merchant of Venice.*

George Bernard Shaw, 1856-1950, (Ir.) playwright, critic. *St. Joan, Pygmalion, Major Barbara, Man and Superman.*

Mary Wollstonecraft Shelley, 1797-1851, (Br.) author. *Frankenstein.*

Percy Bysshe Shelley, 1792-1822, (Br.) poet. *Prometheus Unbound, Adonais,* "Ode to the West Wind," "To a Skylark."

Richard B. Sheridan, 1751-1816, (Br.) dramatist. *The Rivals, School for Scandal.*

Robert Sherwood, 1896-1955, (U.S.) playwright. *The Petrified Forest, Abe Lincoln in Illinois, Reunion in Vienna.*

Mikhail Sholokhov, 1906-1984 (U.S.S.R.) author. *And Quiet Flows the Don.*

Upton Sinclair, 1878-1968, (U.S.) novelist. *The Jungle.*

Edmund Spenser, 1552-1599, (Br.) poet. *The Faerie Queen.*

Christina Stead, 1903-1983 (Austral.) novelist, short-story writer. *The Man Who Loved Children.*

Richard Steele, 1672-1729, (Br.) essayist, playwright, began the Tatler and Spectator. *The Conscious Lovers.*

Lincoln Steffens, 1866-1936, (U.S.) editor, author. *The Shame of the Cities.*

Gertrude Stein, 1874-1946, (U.S.) author. *Three Lives.*

John Steinbeck, 1902-1968, (U.S.) novelist. *Grapes of Wrath, Of Mice and Men, Winter of Our Discontent.*

Stendhal (Marie Henri Beyle), 1783-1842, (F.) poet, novelist. *The Red and the Black, The Charterhouse of Parma.*

Laurence Sterne, 1713-1768, (Br.) novelist. *Tristram Shandy.*

Wallace Stevens, 1879-1955, (U.S.) poet. *Harmonium, The Man With the Blue Guitar, Transport to Summer.*

Robert Louis Stevenson, 1850-1894, (Br.) novelist, poet, essayist. *Treasure Island, A Child's Garden of Verses.*

Rex Stout, 1886-1975, (U.S.) novelist, created Nero Wolfe.

Harriet Beecher Stowe, 1811-1896, (U.S.) novelist. *Uncle Tom's Cabin.*

Lytton Strachey, 1880-1932, (Br.) biographer, critic. *Eminent Victorians, Queen Victoria, Elizabeth and Essex.*

August Strindberg, 1849-1912, (Swed.) dramatist, novelist. *The Father, Miss Julie, The Creditors.*

Jonathan Swift, 1667-1745, (Br.) author. *Gulliver's Travels.*

Algernon C. Swinburne, 1837-1909, (Br.) poet, critic. *Songs Before Sunrise.*

John M. Synge, 1871-1909, (Ir.) poet, dramatist. *Riders to the Sea, The Playboy of the Western World.*

Rabindranath Tagore, 1861-1941, (Ind.) author, poet. *Sadhana, The Realization of Life, Gitanjali.*

Booth Tarkington, 1869-1946, (U.S.) novelist. *Seventeen, Alice Adams, Penrod.*

Sara Teasdale, 1884-1933, (U.S.) poet. *Helen of Troy and Other Poems, Rivers to the Sea, Flame and Shadow.*

Alfred Lord Tennyson, 1809-1892, (Br.) poet. *Idylls of the King, In Memoriam,* "The Charge of the Light Brigade."

William Makepeace Thackeray, 1811-1863, (Br.) novelist. *Vanity Fair.*

Dylan Thomas, 1914-1953, (Welsh) poet. *Under Milk Wood, A Child's Christmas in Wales.*

James Thurber, 1894-1961, (U.S.) humorist, artist. *The New Yorker, The Owl in the Attic, Thurber Carnival.*

J.R.R. Tolkien, 1892-1973, (Br.) author. *The Hobbit, Lord of the Rings.*

Lev Tolstoy, 1828-1910, (R.) novelist. *War and Peace, Anna Karenina.*

Anthony Trollope, 1815-1882, (Br.) novelist. *The Warden, Barchester Towers, The Palliser novels.*

Ivan Turgenev, 1818-1883, (R.) novelist, short-story writer. *Fathers and Sons, First Love, A Month in the Country.*

Mark Twain (Samuel Clemens), 1835-1910, (U.S.) novelist, humorist. *The Adventures of Huckleberry Finn, Tom Sawyer.*

Sigrid Undset, 1881-1949, (Nor.) novelist, poet. *Kristin Lavransdatter.*

Paul Valéry, 1871-1945, (F.) poet, critic. *La Jeune Parque, The Graveyard by the Sea.*

Jules Verne, 1828-1905, (F.) novelist, originator of modern science fiction. *Twenty Thousand Leagues Under the Sea.*

François Villon, 1431-1463?, (F.) poet. *Le petit et le Grand, Testament.*

Evelyn Waugh, 1903-1966, (Br.) satirist. *The Loved One.*

H.G. Wells, 1866-1946, (Br.) author. *The Time Machine, The Invisible Man, The War of the Worlds.*

Rebecca West, 1893-1983 (Br.) author. *Black Lamb and Grey Falcon.*

Edith Wharton, 1862-1937, (U.S.) novelist. *The Age of Innocence, The House of Mirth.*

T.H. White, 1906-1964, (Br.) author. *The Once and Future King.*

Walt Whitman, 1819-1892, (U.S.) poet. *Leaves of Grass.*

John Greenleaf Whittier, 1807-1892, (U.S.) poet, journalist. *Snow-bound.*

Oscar Wilde, 1854-1900, (Ir.) author, wit. *The Picture of Dorian Gray, The Importance of Being Earnest.*
Thornton Wilder, 1897-1975, (U.S.) playwright. *Our Town, The Skin of Our Teeth, The Matchmaker.*
Tennessee Williams, 1912-1983 (U.S.) playwright. *A Streetcar Named Desire, Cat on a Hot Tin Roof, The Glass Menagerie.*
William Carlos Williams, 1883-1963, (U.S.) poet, physician. *Tempers, Al Que Quiere!, Paterson.*
Edmund Wilson, 1895-1972, (U.S.) author, literary and social critic. *Axel's Castle, To the Finland Station.*
P.G. Wodehouse, 1881-1975, (U.S.) poet, dramatist. The

"Jeeves" novels, *Anything Goes.*
Thomas Wolfe, 1900-1938, (U.S.) novelist. *Look Homeward, Angel, You Can't Go Home Again, Of Time and the River.*
Virginia Woolf, 1882-1941, (Br.) novelist, essayist. *Mrs. Dalloway, To the Lighthouse, The Waves.*
William Wordsworth, 1770-1850, (Br.) poet. "Tintern Abbey," "Ode: Intimations of Immortality."
William Butler Yeats, 1865-1939, (Ir.) poet, playwright. *The Wild Swans at Coole, The Tower, Last Poems.*
Émile Zola, 1840-1902, (F.) novelist. *Nana, The Dram Shop.*

Noted Artists and Sculptors of the Past

Artists are painters unless otherwise indicated.

Washington Allston, 1779-1843, landscapist. Belshazzar's Feast.
Albrecht Altdorfer, 1480-1538, landscapist. Battle of Alexander.
Andrea del Sarto, 1486-1530, frescoes. Madonna of the Harpies.
Fra Angelico, c. 1400-1455, Renaissance muralist. Madonna of the Linen Drapers' Guild.
Alexsandr Archipenko, 1887-1964, sculptor. Boxing Match, Medranos.
John James Audubon, 1785-1851, Birds of America.
Hans Baldung Grien, 1484-1545, Todentanz.
Ernst Barlach, 1870-1938, Expressionist sculptor. Man Drawing a Sword.
Frederic-Auguste Bartholdi, 1834-1904, Liberty Enlightening the World, Lion of Belfort.
Fra Bartolommeo, 1472-1517, Vision of St. Bernard.
Aubrey Beardsley, 1872-1898, illustrator. Salome, Lysistrata.
Max Beckmann, 1884-1950, Expressionist. The Descent from the Cross.
Gentile Bellini, 1426-1507, Renaissance. Procession in St. Mark's Square.
Giovanni Bellini, 1428-1516, St. Francis in Ecstasy.
Jacopo Bellini, 1400-1470, Crucifixion.
George Wesley Bellows, 1882-1925, sports artist. Stag at Sharkey's.
Thomas Hart Benton, 1889-1975, American regionalist. Threshing Wheat, Arts of the West.
Gianlorenzo Bernini, 1598-1680, Baroque sculpture. The Assumption.
Albert Bierstadt, 1830-1902, landscapist. The Rocky Mountains, Mount Corcoran.
George Caleb Bingham, 1811-1879, Fur Traders Descending the Missouri.
William Blake, 1752-1827, engraver. Book of Job, Songs of Innocence, Songs of Experience.
Rosa Bonheur, 1822-1899, The Horse Fair.
Pierre Bonnard, 1867-1947, Intimist. The Breakfast Room.
Paul-Emile Borduas, 1905-1960, Abstractionist. Leeward of the Island, Enchanted Shields.
Gutzon Borglum, 1871-1941, sculptor. Mt. Rushmore Memorial.
Hieronymus Bosch, 1450-1516, religious allegories. The Crowning with Thorns.
Sandro Botticelli, 1444-1510, Renaissance. Birth of Venus.
Constantin Brancusi, 1876-1957, Nonobjective sculptor. Flying Turtle, The Kiss.
Georges Braque, 1882-1963, Cubist. Violin and Palette.
Pieter Bruegel the Elder, c. 1525-1569, The Peasant Dance.
Pieter Bruegel the Younger, 1564-1638, Village Fair, The Crucifixion.
Edward Burne-Jones, 1833-1898, Pre-Raphaelite artist-craftsman. The Mirror of Venus.
Alexander Calder, 1898-1976, sculptor. Lobster Trap and Fish Tail.
Michelangelo Merisi da Caravaggio, 1573-1610, Baroque. The Supper at Emmaus.
Emily Carr, 1871-1945, landscapist. Blunden Harbour, Big Raven.
Carlo Carra, 1881-1966, Metaphysical school. Lot's Daughters.
Mary Cassatt, 1845-1926, Impressionist. Woman Bathing.
George Catlin, 1796-1872, American Indian life. Gallery of Indians.
Benvenuto Cellini, 1500-1571, Mannerist sculptor, goldsmith. Perseus.
Paul Cezanne, 1839-1906, Card Players, Mont-Sainte-Victoire with Large Pine Trees.
Jean Simeon Chardin, 1699-1779, still lifes. The Kiss, The Grace.
Frederic Church, 1826-1900, Hudson River school. Niagara, Andes of Ecuador.
Cimabue, 1240-1302, Byzantine mosaicist. Madonna En-

throned with St. Francis.
Claude Lorrain, 1600-1682, ideal-landscapist. The Enchanted Castle.
Thomas Cole, 1801-1848, Hudson River school. The Ox-Bow.
John Constable, 1776-1837, landscapist. Salisbury Cathedral from the Bishop's Grounds.
John Singleton Copley, 1738-1815, portraitist. Samuel Adams, Watson and the Shark.
Lovis Corinth, 1858-1925, Expressionist. Apocalypse.
Jean-Baptiste-Camille Corot, 1796-1875, landscapist. Souvenir de Mortefontaine, Pastorale.
Correggio, 1494-1534, Renaissance muralist. Mystic Marriages of St. Catherine.
Gustave Courbet, 1819-1877, Realist. The Artist's Studio.
Lucas Cranach the Elder, 1472-1553, Protestant Reformation portraitist. Luther.
Nathaniel Currier, 1813-1888, and **James M. Ives,** 1824-1895, lithographers. A Midnight Race on the Mississippi.
Honore Daumier, 1808-1879, caricaturist. The Third-Class Carriage.
Jacques-Louis David, 1748-1825, Neoclassicist. The Oath of the Horatii.
Arthur Davies, 1862-1928, Romantic landscapist. Unicorns.
Edgar Degas, 1834-1917, The Ballet Class.
Eugene Delacroix, Co. 1400-1455, Romantic. Massacre at Chios.
Paul Delaroche, 1797-1856, historical themes. Children of Edward IV.
Luca Della Robbia, 1400-1482, Renaissance terracotta artist. Cantoria (singing gallery), Florence cathedral.
Donatello, 1386-1466, Renaissance sculptor. David, Gattamelata.
Marcel Duchamp, 1887-1968, Nude Descending a Staircase.
Raoul Dufy, 1877-1953, Fauvist. Chateau and Horses.
Asher Brown Durand, 1796-1886, Hudson River school. Kindred Spirits.
Albrecht Durer, 1471-1528, Renaissance engraver, woodcuts. St. Jerome in His Study, Melancholia I, Apocalypse.
Anthony van Dyck, 1599-1641, Baroque portraitist. Portrait of Charles I Hunting.
Thomas Eakins, 1844-1916, Realist. The Gross Clinic.
Jacob Epstein, 1880-1959, religious and allegorical sculptor. Genesis, Ecce Homo.
Jan van Eyck, 1380-1441, naturalistic panels. Adoration of the Lamb.
Anselm Feuerbach, 1829-1880, Romantic Classicism. Judgement of Paris, Iphigenia.
John Bernard Flannagan, 1895-1942, animal sculptor. Triumph of the Egg.
Jean-Honore Fragonard, 1732-1806, Rococo. The Swing.
Daniel Chester French, 1850-1931, The Minute Man of Concord; seated Lincoln, Lincoln Memorial, Washington, D.C.
Caspar David Friedrich, 1774-1840, Romantic landscapes. Man and Woman Gazing at the Moon.
Thomas Gainsborough, 1727-1788, portraitist. The Blue Boy.
Paul Gauguin, 1848-1903, Post-impressionist. The Tahitians.
Lorenzo Ghiberti, 1378-1455, Renaissance sculptor. Gates of Paradise baptistry doors, Florence.
Alberto Giacometti, 1901-1966, attenuated sculptures of solitary figures. Man Pointing.
Giorgione, c. 1477-1510, Renaissance. The Tempest.
Giotto di Bondone, 1267-1337, Renaissance. Presentation of Christ in the Temple.
Francois Girardon, 1628-1715, Baroque sculptor of classical themes. Apollo Tended by the Nymphs.
Vincent van Gogh, 1853-1890, The Starry Night, L'Arlesienne.
Arshile Gorky, 1905-1948, Surrealist. The Liver Is the Cock's Comb.
Francisco de Goya y Lucientes, 1746-1828, The Naked Maja, The Disasters of War (etchings).

El Greco, 1541-1614, View of Toledo, Burial of the Count of Orgaz.

Horatio Greenough, 1805-1852, Neo-classical sculptor. George Washington.

Matthias Grünewald, 1480-1528, mystical religious themes. The Resurrection.

Frans Hals, c. 1580-1666, portraitist. Laughing Cavalier, Gypsy Girl.

Childe Hassam, 1859-1935, Impressionist. Southwest Wind.

Edward Hicks, 1780-1849, folk painter. The Peaceable Kingdom.

Hans Hofmann, 1880-1966, early Abstract Expressionist. Spring. The Gate.

William Hogarth, 1697-1764, caricaturist. The Rake's Progress.

Katsushika Hokusai, 1760-1849, printmaker. Crabs.

Hans Holbein the Elder, 1460-1524, late Gothic. Presentation of Christ in the Temple.

Hans Holbein the Younger, 1497-1543, portraitist. Henry VIII.

Winslow Homer, 1836-1910, marine themes. Marine Coast, High Cliff.

Edward Hopper, 1882-1967, realistic urban scenes. Sunlight in a Cafeteria.

Jean-Auguste-Dominique Ingres, 1780-1867, Classicist. Valpincon Bather.

George Inness, 1825-1894, luminous landscapist. Delaware Water Gap.

Vasily Kandinsky, 1866-1944, Abstractionist. Capricious Forms.

Paul Klee, 1879-1940, Abstractionist. Twittering Machine.

Kathe Kollwitz, 1867-1945, printmaker, social justice themes. The Peasant War.

Gaston Lachaise, 1882-1935, figurative sculptor. Standing Woman.

John La Farge, 1835-1910, muralist. Red and White Peonies.

Fernand Leger, 1881-1955, machine art. The Cyclists, Adam and Eve.

Leonardo da Vinci, 1452-1519, Mona Lisa, Last Supper, The Annunciation.

Emanuel Leutze, 1816-1868, historical themes. Washington Crossing the Delaware.

Jacques Lipchitz, 1891-1973, Cubist sculptor. Harpist.

Filippino Lippi, 1457-1504, Renaissance. The Vision of St. Bernard.

Fra Filippo Lippi, 1406-1469, Renaissance. Coronation of the Virgin.

Morris Louis, 1912-1962, abstract expressionist. Signa, Stripes.

Aristide Maillol, 1861-1944, sculptor. Night, The Mediterranean.

Edouard Manet, 1832-1883, forerunner of Impressionism. Luncheon on the Grass, Olympia.

Andrea Mantegna, 1431-1506, Renaissance frescoes. Triumph of Caesar.

Franz Marc, 1880-1916, Expressionist. Blue Horses.

John Marin, 1870-1953, expressionist seascapes. Maine Island.

Reginald Marsh, 1898-1954, satirical artist. Tattoo and Haircut.

Masaccio, 1401-1428, Renaissance. The Tribute Money.

Henri Matisse, 1869-1954, Fauvist. Woman with the Hat.

Michelangelo Buonarroti, 1475-1564, Pieta, David, Moses, The Last Judgment, Sistine Ceiling.

Carl Milles, 1875-1955, expressive rhythmic sculptor. Playing Bears.

Jean-Francois Millet, 1814-1875, painter of peasant subjects. The Gleaners, The Man with a Hoe.

David Milne, 1882-1953, landscapist. Boston Corner, Berkshire Hills.

Amedeo Modigliani, 1884-1920, Reclining Nude.

Piet Mondrian, 1872-1944, Abstractionist. Composition.

Claude Monet, 1840-1926, Impressionist. The Bridge at Argenteuil, Haystacks.

Gustave Moreau, 1826-1898, Symbolist. The Apparition, Dance of Salome.

James Wilson Morrice, 1865-1924, landscapist. The Ferry, Quebec, Venice, Looking Over the Lagoon.

Grandma Moses, 1860-1961, folk painter. Out for the Christmas Trees.

Edvard Munch, 1863-1944, Expressionist. The Cry.

Bartolome Murillo, 1618-1682, Baroque religious artist. Vision of St. Anthony. The Two Trinities.

Barnett Newman, 1905-1970, Abstract Expressionist. Stations of the Cross.

Jose Clemente Orozco, 1883-1949, frescoes. House of Tears.

Charles Willson Peale, 1741-1827, American Revolutionary portraitist. Washington, Franklin, Jefferson, John Adams.

Rembrandt Peale, 1778-1860, portraitist. Thomas Jefferson.

Pietro Perugino, 1446-1523, Renaissance. Delivery of the Keys to St. Peter.

Pablo Picasso, 1881-1973, Guernica, Dove, Head of a Woman.

Piero della Francesca, c. 1415-1492, Renaissance. Duke of Urbino, Flagellation of Christ.

Camille Pissarro, 1830-1903, Impressionist. Morning Sunlight.

Jackson Pollock, 1912-1956, Abstract Expressionist. Autumn Rhythm.

Nicolas Poussin, 1594-1665, Baroque pictorial classicism. St. John on Patmos.

Maurice B. Prendergast, c. 1860-1924, Post-impressionist water colorist. Umbrellas in the Rain.

Pierre-Paul Prud'hon, 1758-1823, Romanticist. Crime pursued by Vengeance and Justice.

Pierre Cecile Puvis de Chavannes, 1824-1898, muralist. The Poor Fisherman.

Raphael Sanzio, 1483-1520, Renaissance. Disputa, School of Athens, Sistine Madonna.

Man Ray, 1890-1976, Dadaist. Observing Time, The Lovers.

Odilon Redon, 1840-1916, Symbolist lithographer. In the Dream.

Rembrandt van Rijn, 1606-1669, The Bridal Couple, The Night Watch.

Frederic Remington, 1861-1909, painter, sculptor, portrayer of the American West. Bronco Buster, Cavalry Charge on the Southern Plains.

Pierre-Auguste Renoir, 1841-1919, Impressionist. The Luncheon of the Boating Party.

Ilya Repin, 1844-1918, historical canvases. Zaporozhye Cossacks.

Joshua Reynolds, 1723-1792, portraitist. Mrs. Siddons as the Tragic Muse.

Diego Rivera, 1886-1957, frescoes. The Fecund Earth.

Norman Rockwell, 1894-1978, illustrator. Saturday Evening Post covers.

Auguste Rodin, 1840-1917, sculptor. The Thinker, The Burghers of Calais.

Mark Rothko, 1903-1970, Abstract Expressionist. Light, Earth and Blue.

Georges Rouault, 1871-1958, Expressionist. The Old King.

Henri Rousseau, 1844-1910, primitive exotic themes. The Snake Charmer.

Theodore Rousseau, 1812-1867, landscapist. Under the Birches, Evening.

Peter Paul Rubens, 1577-1640, Baroque. Mystic Marriage of St. Catherine.

Andrey Rublyov, 1370-1430, icon painter. Old Testament Trinity.

Jacob van Ruisdael, c. 1628-1682, landscapist. Jewish Cemetery.

Salomon van Ruysdael, c. 1600-1670, landscapist. River with Ferry-Boat.

Albert Pinkham Ryder, 1847-1917, seascapes and allegories. Toilers of the Sea.

Augustus Saint-Gaudens, 1848-1907, memorial statues. Farragut, Mrs. Henry Adams (Grief).

Andrea Sansovino, 1460-1529, Renaissance sculptor. Baptism of Christ.

Jacopo Sansovino, 1486-1570, Renaissance sculptor. St. John the Baptist.

John Singer Sargent, 1856-1925, Edwardian society portraitist. The Wyndham Sisters, Madam X.

Johann Gottfried Schadow, 1764-1850, monumental sculptor. Quadriga, Brandenburg Gate.

Georges Seurat, 1859-1891, Pointillist. Sunday Afternoon on the Island of Grande Jatte.

Gino Severini, 1883-1966, Futurist and Cubist. Dynamic Hieroglyph of the Bal Tabarin.

Ben Shahn, 1898-1969, social and political themes. Sacco and Vanzetti series, Seurat's Lunch, Handball.

Charles Sheeler, 1883-1965, Abstractionist. Upper Deck, Rolling Power.

David Alfaro Siqueiros, 1896-1974, political muralist. March of Humanity.

John F. Sloan, 1871-1951, depictions of New York City. Wake of the Ferry.

David Smith, 1906-1965, welded metal sculpture. Hudson River Landscape, Zig, Cubi series.

Gilbert Stuart, 1755-1828, portraitist. George Washington.

Thomas Sully, 1783-1872, portraitist. Col. Thomas Handasyd Perkins, The Passage of the Delaware.

Yves Tanguy, 1900-1955, Surrealist. Rose of the Four Winds.

Thomas J. Thomson, 1877-1918, landscapist. Spring Ice.

Giovanni Battista Tiepolo, 1696-1770, Rococo frescoes. The Crucifixion.

Jacopo Tintoretto, 1518-1594, Mannerist. The Last Supper.

Titian, c. 1485-1576, Renaissance. Venus and the Lute Player, The Bacchanal.

Henri de Toulouse-Lautrec, 1864-1901, At the Moulin Rouge.

John Trumbull, 1756-1843, historical themes. The Declaration of Independence.

Joseph Mallord William Turner, 1775-1851, Romantic landscapist. Snow Storm.

Paolo Uccello, 1397-1475, Gothic-Renaissance. The Rout of San Romano.

Maurice Utrillo, 1883-1955, Impressionist. Sacre-Coeur de Montmartre.

John Vanderlyn, 1775-1852, Neo-classicist. Ariadne Asleep on the Island of Naxos.

Diego Velazquez, 1599-1660, Baroque. Las Meninas, Portrait of Juan de Pareja.

Jan Vermeer, 1632-1675, interior genre subjects. Young Woman with a Water Jug.

Paolo Veronese, 1528-1588, devotional themes, vastly peo-pled canvases. The Temptation of St. Anthony.

Andrea del Verrocchio, 1435-1488, Florentine sculptor. Colleoni.

Maurice de Vlaminck, 1876-1958, Fauvist landscapist. The Storm.

Antoine Watteau, 1684-1721, Rococo painter of "scenes of gallantry". The Embarkation for Cythera.

George Frederic Watts, 1817-1904, painter and sculptor of grandiose allegorical themes. Hope, Physical Energy.

Benjamin West, 1738-1820, realistic historical themes. Death of General Wolfe.

James Abbott McNeill Whistler, 1834-1903, Arrangement in Grey and Black, No. 1: The Artist's Mother.

Archibald M. Willard, 1836-1918, The Spirit of '76.

Grant Wood, 1891-1942, Midwestern regionalist. American Gothic, Daughters of Revolution.

Ossip Zadkine, 1890-1967, School of Paris sculptor. The Destroyed City, Musicians, Christ.

Noted Philosophers and Religionists of the Past

Lyman Abbott, 1835-1922, (U.S.) clergyman, reformer; advocate of Christian Socialism.

Pierre Abelard, 1079-1142, (F.) philosopher, theologian, and teacher, used dialectic method to support Christian dogma.

Felix Adler, 1851-1933, (U.S.) German-born founder of the Ethical Culture Society.

St. Augustine, 354-430, Latin bishop considered the founder of formalized Christian theology.

Averroes, 1126-1198, (Sp.) Islamic philosopher.

Roger Bacon, c.1214-1294, (Br.) philosopher and scientist.

Karl Barth, 1886-1968, (Sw.) theologian, a leading force in 20th-century Protestantism.

St. Benedict, c.480-547, (It.) founded the Benedictines.

Jeremy Bentham, 1748-1832, (Br.) philosopher, reformer, founder of Utilitarianism.

Henri Bergson, 1859-1941, (F.) philosopher of evolution.

George Berkeley, 1685-1753, (Ir.) philosopher, churchman.

John Biddle, 1615-1662, (Br.) founder of English Unitarianism.

Jakob Boehme, 1575-1624, (G.) theosophist and mystic.

William Brewster, 1567-1644, (Br.) headed Pilgrims, signed Mayflower Compact.

Emil Brunner, 1889-1966, (Sw.) theologian.

Giordano Bruno, 1548-1600, (It.) philosopher.

Martin Buber, 1878-1965, (G.) Jewish philosopher, theologian, wrote I and Thou.

Buddha (Siddhartha Gautama), c.563-c.483 BC, (Ind.) philosopher, founded Buddhism.

John Calvin, 1509-1564, (F.) theologian, a key figure in the Protestant Reformation.

Rudolph Carnap, 1891-1970, (U.S.) German-born philosopher, a founder of logical positivism.

William Ellery Channing, 1780-1842, (U.S.) clergyman, early spokesman for Unitarianism.

Auguste Comte, 1798-1857, (F.) philosopher, the founder of positivism.

Confucius, 551-479 BC, (Chin.) founder of Confucianism.

John Cotton, 1584-1652, (Br.) Puritan theologian.

Thomas Cranmer, 1489-1556, (Br.) churchman, wrote much of the first Book of Common Prayer; promoter of the English Reformation.

René Descartes, 1596-1650, (F.) philosopher, mathematician.

John Dewey, 1859-1952, (U.S.) philosopher, educator; helped inaugurate the progressive education movement.

Denis Diderot, 1713-1784, (F.) philosopher, creator of first modern encyclopedia.

Mary Baker Eddy, 1821-1910, (U.S.) founder of Christian Science.

Jonathan Edwards, 1703-1758, (U.S.) preacher, theologian.

(Desiderius) Erasmus, c.1466-1536, (Du.) Renaissance humanist.

Johann Fichte, 1762-1814, (G.) philosopher, the first of the Transcendental Idealists.

George Fox, 1624-1691, (Br.) founder of Society of Friends.

St. Francis of Assisi, 1182-1226, (It.) founded the Franciscans.

al Ghazali, 1058-1111, Islamic philosopher.

Georg W. Hegel, 1770-1831, (G.) Idealist philosopher.

Martin Heidegger, 1889-1976, (G.) existentialist philosopher, affected fields ranging from physics to literary criticism.

Johann G. Herder, 1744-1803, (G.) philosopher, cultural historian; a founder of German Romanticism.

David Hume, 1711-1776, (Sc.) philosopher, historian.

Jan Hus, 1369-1415, (Czech.) religious reformer.

Edmund Husserl, 1859-1938, (G.) philosopher, founded Phenomenological movement.

Thomas Huxley, 1825-1895, (Br.) agnostic philosopher, educator.

Ignatius of Loyola, 1491-1556, (Sp.) founder of the Jesuits.

William Inge, 1860-1954, (Br.) theologian, explored the mystic aspects of Christianity.

William James, 1842-1910, (U.S.) philosopher, psychologist; advanced theory of the pragmatic nature of truth.

Karl Jaspers, 1883-1969, (G.) existentialist philosopher.

Immanuel Kant, 1724-1804, (G.) metaphysician, preeminent founder of modern critical philosophy.

Soren Kierkegaard, 1813-1855, (Den.) philosopher, considered the father of Existentialism.

John Knox, 1505-1572, (Sc.) leader of the Protestant Reformation in Scotland.

Lao-Tzu, 604-531 BC, (Chin.) philosopher, considered the founder of the Taoist religion.

Gottfried von Leibniz, 1646-1716, (G.) philosopher, mathematician.

Martin Luther, 1483-1546, (G.) leader of the Protestant Reformation, founded Lutheran church.

Maimonides, 1135-1204, (Sp.) Jewish physician and philosopher.

Jacques Maritain, 1882-1973, (F.) Neo-Thomist philosopher.

Cotton Mather, 1663-1728, (U.S.) defender of orthodox Puritanism; founded Yale, 1703.

Aimee Semple McPherson, 1890-1944, (U.S.) evangelist.

Philipp Melanchthon, 1497-1560, (G.) theologian, humanist; an important voice in the Reformation.

Mohammed, c.570-632, Arab prophet of the religion of Islam.

Dwight Moody, 1837-1899, (U.S.) evangelist.

George E. Moore, 1873-1958, (Br.) ethical theorist.

Elijah Muhammad, 1897-1975, (U.S.) leader of the Black Muslim sect.

Heinrich Muhlenberg, 1711-1787, (G.) organized the Lutheran Church in America.

John H. Newman, 1801-1890, (Br.) Roman Catholic cardinal, led Oxford Movement.

Reinhold Niebuhr, 1892-1971, (U.S.) Protestant theologian, social and political critic.

Friedrich Nietzsche, 1844-1900, (G.) moral philosopher.

Blaise Pascal, 1623-1662, (F.) philosopher and mathematician.

St. Patrick, c.389-c.461, brought Christianity to Ireland.

St. Paul, ?-c.67, a founder of the Christian religion.

Charles S. Peirce, 1839-1914, (U.S.) philosopher, logician; originated concept of Pragmatism, 1878.

Josiah Royce 1855-1916, (U.S.) Idealist philosopher.

Charles T. Russell, 1852-1916, (U.S.) founder of Jehovah's Witnesses.

Fredrich von Schelling, 1775-1854, (G.) philosopher.

Friedrich Schleiermacher, 1768-1834, (G.) theologian, a founder of modern Protestant theology.

Arthur Schopenhauer, 1788-1860, (G.) philosopher.

Joseph Smith, 1805-1844, (U.S.) founded Latter Day Saints (Mormon) movement, 1830.

Herbert Spencer, 1820-1903, (Br.) philosopher of evolution.

Baruch Spinoza, 1632-1677, (Du.) rationalist philosopher.

Billy Sunday, 1862-1935, (U.S.) evangelist.

Daisetz Teitaro Suzuki, 1870-1966, (Jap.) Buddhist scholar.

Emanuel Swedenborg, 1688-1722, (Swed.) philosopher, mystic.

Thomas à Becket, 1118-1170, (Br.) archbishop of Canterbury, opposed Henry II.

Thomas à Kempis, c.1380-1471, (G.) theologian probably wrote Imitation of Christ.

Thomas Aquinas, 1225-1274, (It.) theologian and philosopher.

Paul Tillich, 1886-1965, (U.S.) German-born philosopher and theologian.
John Wesley, 1703-1791, (Br.) theologian, evangelist; founded Methodism.
Alfred North Whitehead, 1861-1947, (Br.) philosopher, mathematician.
William of Occam, c.1285-c.1349 (Br.) philosopher.
Roger Williams, c.1603-1683, (U.S.) clergyman, championed

religious freedom and separation of church and state.
Ludwig Wittgenstein, 1889-1951, (Aus.) philosopher.
John Wycliffe, 1320-1384, (Br.) theologian, reformer.
Brigham Young, 1801-1877, (U.S.) Mormon leader, colonized Utah.
Huldrych Zwingli, 1484-1531, (Sw.) theologian, led Swiss Protestant Reformation.

Noted Social Reformers and Educators of the Past

Jane Addams, 1860-1935, (U.S.) co-founder of Hull House; won Nobel Peace Prize, 1931.
Susan B. Anthony, 1820-1906, (U.S.) a leader in temperance, anti-slavery, and women's suffrage movements.
Henry Barnard, 1811-1900, (U.S.) public school reformer.
Thomas Barnardo, 1845-1905, (Br.) social reformer, pioneered in the care of destitute children.
Clara Barton, 1821-1912, (U.S.) organizer of the American Red Cross.
Henry Ward Beecher, 1813-1887, (U.S.) clergyman, abolitionist.
Amelia Bloomer, 1818-1894, (U.S.) social reformer, women's rights advocate.
William Booth, 1829-1912, (Br.) founded the Salvation Army.
Nicholas Murray Butler, 1862-1947, (U.S.) educator headed Columbia Univ., 1902-45; won Nobel Peace Prize, 1931.
Frances X. (Mother) Cabrini, 1850-1917, (U.S.) Italian-born nun founded numerous charitable institutions; first American to be canonized.
Carrie Chapman Catt, 1859-1947, (U.S.) suffragette, helped win passage of the 19th amendment.
Dorothy Day, 1897-1980, (U.S.) founder of Catholic Worker Movement.
Eugene V. Debs, 1855-1926, (U.S.) labor leader, led Pullman strike, 1894; 4-time Socialist presidential candidate.
Melvil Dewey, 1851-1931, (U.S.) devised decimal system of library-book classification.
Dorothea Dix, 1802-1887, (U.S.) crusader for humane care of mentally ill.
Frederick Douglass, 1817-1895, (U.S.) abolitionist.
W.E.B. DuBois, 1868-1963, (U.S.) Negro-rights leader, educator, and writer.
William Lloyd Garrison, 1805-1879, (U.S.) abolitionist, reformer.
Giovanni Gentile, 1875-1944, (It.) philosopher, educator; reformed Italian educational system.
Samuel Gompers, 1850-1924, (U.S.) labor leader; a founder and president of AFL.
William Green, 1873-1952, (U.S.) president of AFL, 1924-52.
Sidney Hillman, 1887-1946, (U.S.) labor leader, helped organize CIO.
Samuel G. Howe, 1801-1876, (U.S.) social reformer, changed public attitudes toward the handicapped.
Helen Keller, 1880-1968, (U.S.) crusader for better treatment

for the handicapped.
Martin Luther King Jr., 1929-1968, (U.S.) civil rights leader; won Nobel Peace Prize, 1964.
John L. Lewis, 1880-1969, (U.S.) labor leader, headed United Mine Workers, 1920-60.
Horace Mann, 1796-1859, (U.S.) pioneered modern public school system.
William H. McGuffey, 1800-1873, (U.S.) author of Reader, the mainstay of 19th century U.S. public education.
Alexander Meiklejohn, 1872-1964, (U.S.) British-born educator, championed academic freedom and experimental curricula.
Lucretia Mott, 1793-1880, (U.S.) reformer, pioneer feminist.
Philip Murray, 1886-1952, (U.S.) Scotch-born labor leader.
Florence Nightingale, 1820-1910, (Br.) founder of modern nursing.
Emmeline Pankhurst, 1858-1928, (Br.) woman suffragist.
Elizabeth P. Peabody, 1804-1894, (U.S.) education pioneer, founded 1st kindergarten in U.S., 1860.
Walter Reuther, 1907-1970, (U.S.) labor leader, headed UAW.
Jacob Riis, 1849-1914, (U.S.) crusader for urban reforms.
Margaret Sanger, 1883-1966, (U.S.) social reformer, pioneered the birth control movement.
Elizabeth Seton, 1774-1821, (U.S.) established parochial school education in U.S.
Earl of Shaftesbury (A.A. Cooper), 1801-1885, (Br.) social reformer.
Elizabeth Cady Stanton, 1815-1902, (U.S.) women's suffrage pioneer.
Lucy Stone, 1818-1893, (U.S.) feminist, abolitionist.
Harriet Tubman, c.1820-1913, (U.S.) abolitionist, ran Underground Railroad.
Booker T. Washington, 1856-1915, (U.S.) educator, reformer; championed vocational training for blacks.
Walter F. White, 1893-1955, (U.S.) headed NAACP, 1931-55.
William Wilberforce, 1759-1833, (Br.) social reformer, prominent in struggle to abolish the slave trade.
Emma Hart Willard, 1787-1870, (U.S.) pioneered higher education for women.
Frances E. Willard, 1839-1898, (U.S.) temperance, woman's rights leader.
Whitney M. Young Jr., 1921-1971, (U.S.) civil rights leader, headed National Urban League, 1961-71.

Noted Historians, Economists, and Social Scientists of the Past

Brooks Adams, 1848-1927, (U.S.) historian, political theoretician.
Francis Bacon, 1561-1626, (Br.) philosopher, essayist, and statesman.
George Bancroft, 1800-1891, (U.S.) historian, wrote 10-volume History of the United States.
Charles A. Beard, 1874-1948, (U.S.) historian, attacked motives of the Founding Fathers.
Bede (the Venerable), c.673-735, (Br.) scholar, historian.
Ruth Benedict, 1887-1948, (U.S.) anthropologist, studied Indian tribes of the Southwest.
Louis Blanc, 1811-1882, (F.) Socialist leader and historian whose ideas were a link between utopian and Marxist socialism.
Franz Boas, 1858-1942, (U.S.) German-born anthropologist, studied American Indians.
Van Wyck Brooks, 1886-1963, (U.S.) cultural historian, critic.
Edmund Burke, 1729-1797, (Ir.) British parliamentarian and political philosopher; influenced many Federalists.
Thomas Carlyle, 1795-1881, (Sc.) philosopher, historian, and critic.
Edward Channing, 1856-1931, (U.S.) historian wrote 6-volume A History of the United States.
John R. Commons, 1862-1945, (U.S.) economist, labor historian.
Benedetto Croce, 1866-1952, (It.) philosopher, statesman, and historian.
Bernard A. De Voto, 1897-1955, (U.S.) historian, won Pulitzer prize in 1948 for Across the Wide Missouri.
Ariel Durant, 1898-1981, (U.S.) historian, collaborated with husband on 11-volume The Story of Civilization.
Will Durant, 1885-1981, (U.S.) historian. The Story of Civilization, The Story of Philosophy.

Emile Durkheim, 1858-1917, (F.) a founder of modern sociology.
Friedrich Engels, 1820-1895, (G.) political writer, with Marx wrote the Communist Manifesto.
Irving Fisher, 1867-1947, (U.S.) economist, contributed to the development of modern monetary theory.
John Fiske, 1842-1901, (U.S.) historian and lecturer, popularized Darwinian theory of evolution.
Charles Fourier, 1772-1837, (F.) utopian socialist.
Henry George, 1839-1897, (U.S.) economist, reformer, led single-tax movement.
Edward Gibbon, 1737-1794, (Br.) historian, wrote The History of the Decline and Fall of the Roman Empire.
Francesco Guicciardini, 1483-1540, (It.) historian, wrote Storia d'Italia, principal historical work of the 16th-century.
Alvin Hansen, 1887-1975, (U.S.) economist.
Thomas Hobbes, 1588-1679, (Br.) social philosopher.
Richard Hofstadter, 1916-1970, (U.S.) historian, wrote The Age of Reform.
John Maynard Keynes, 1883-1946, (Br.) economist, principal advocate of deficit spending.
Alfred L. Kroeber, 1876-1960, (U.S.) cultural anthropologist, studied Indians of North and South America.
James L. Laughlin, 1850-1933, (U.S.) economist, helped establish Federal Reserve System.
Lucien Lévy-Bruhl, 1857-1939, (F.) philosopher, studied the psychology of primitive societies.
Kurt Lewin, 1890-1947, (U.S.) German-born psychologist, studied human motivation and group dynamics.
John Locke, 1632-1704, (Br.) political philosopher.
Thomas B. Macauley, 1800-1859, (Br.) historian, statesman.
Bronislaw Malinowski, 1884-1942, (Pol.) anthropologist, con-

sidered the father of social anthropology.

Thomas R. Malthus, 1766-1834, (Br.) economist, famed for *Essay on the Principle of Population.*

Karl Mannheim, 1893-1947, (Hung.) sociologist, historian.

Karl Marx, 1818-1883, (G.) political philosopher, proponent of modern communism.

Giuseppe Mazzini, 1805-1872, (It.) political philosopher.

George H. Mead, 1863-1931, (U.S.) philosopher and social psychologist.

Margaret Mead, 1901-1978, (U.S.) cultural anthropologist, popularized field.

James Mill, 1773-1836, (Sc.) philosopher, historian, and economist; a proponent of Utilitarianism.

John Stuart Mill, 1806-1873, (Br.) philosopher, political economist.

Perry G. Miller, 1905-1963, (U.S.) historian, interpreted 17th-century New England.

Theodor Mommsen, 1817-1903, (G.) historian, wrote *The History of Rome.*

Charles-Louis Montesquieu, 1689-1755, (F.) social philosopher.

Samuel Eliot Morison, 1887-1976, (U.S.) historian, chronicled voyages of early explorers.

Allan Nevins, 1890-1971, (U.S.) historian, biographer; twice won Pulitzer prize.

Jose Ortega y Gasset, 1883-1955, (Sp.) philosopher and humanist; advocated control by an elite.

Robert Owen, 1771-1858, (Br.) political philosopher, reformer.

Vilfredo Pareto, 1848-1923, (It.) economist, sociologist.

Francis Parkman, 1823-1893, (U.S.) historian, wrote 8-volume *France and England in North America, 1851-92.*

Marco Polo, c.1254-1324, (It.) narrated an account of his travels to China.

William Prescott, 1796-1859, (U.S.) early American historian.

Pierre Joseph Proudhon, 1809-1865, (F.) social theorist, regarded as the father of anarchism.

Francois Quesnay, 1694-1774, (F.) economic theorist, demonstrated the circular flow of economic activity throughout society.

David Ricardo, 1772-1823, (Br.) economic theorist, advocated free international trade.

James H. Robinson, 1863-1936, (U.S.) historian, educator.

Jean-Jacques Rousseau, 1712-1778, (F.) social philosopher, author.

Hjalmar Schacht, 1877-1970, (G.) economist.

Joseph Schumpeter, 1883-1950, (U.S.) Czech.-born economist, championed big business, capitalism.

Albert Schweitzer, 1875-1965, (Alsatian) social philosopher, theologian, and humanitarian.

George Simmel, 1858-1918, (G.) sociologist, philosopher.

Adam Smith, 1723-1790, (Br.) economist, advocated laissez-faire economy and free trade.

Jared Sparks, 1789-1866, (U.S.) historian, among first to do research from original documents.

Oswald Spengler, 1880-1936, (G.) philosopher and historian, wrote *The Decline of the West.*

William G. Sumner, 1840-1910, (U.S.) social scientist, economist; championed laissez-faire economy, Social Darwinism.

Hippolyte Taine, 1828-1893, (F.) historian.

Frank W. Taussig, 1859-1940, (U.S.) economist, educator.

Alexis de Tocqueville, 1805-1859, (F.) political scientist, historian.

Francis E. Townsend, 1897-1960, (U.S.) author of old-age pension plan.

Arnold Toynbee, 1889-1975, (Br.) historian, wrote 10-volume *A Study of History.*

Heinrich von Treitschke, 1834-1896, (G.) historian, political writer.

George Trevelyan, 1838-1928, (Br.) historian, statesman.

Frederick J. Turner, 1861-1932, (U.S.) historian, educator.

Thorstein B. Veblen, 1857-1929, (U.S.) economist, social philosopher.

Giovanni Vico, 1668-1744, (It.) historian, philosopher.

Voltaire (F.M. Arouet), 1694-1778, (F.) philosopher, historian, and poet.

Izaak Walton, 1593-1683, (Br.) author, wrote first biographical works in English literature.

Sidney J., 1859-1947, and wife **Beatrice,** 1858-1943, **Webb** (Br.) leading figures in Fabian Society and British Labour Party.

Walter P. Webb, 1888-1963, (U.S.) historian of the West.

Max Weber, 1864-1920, (G.) sociologist.

Noted Scientists of the Past

Howard H. Aiken, 1900-1973, (U.S.) mathematician, credited with designing forerunner of digital computer.

Albertus Magnus, 1193-1280, (G.) theologian, philosopher, scientist, established medieval Christian study of natural science.

Andre-Marie Ampère, 1775-1836, (F.) scientist known for contributions to electrodynamics.

Amedeo Avogadro, 1776-1856, (It.) chemist, physicist, advanced important theories on properties of gases.

A.C. Becquerel, 1788-1878, (F.) physicist, pioneer in electrochemical science.

A.H. Becquerel, 1852-1908, (F.) physicist, discovered radioactivity in uranium.

Alexander Graham Bell, 1847-1922, (U.S.) inventor, first to patent and commercially exploit the telephone, 1876.

Daniel Bernoulli, 1700-1782, (Swiss) mathematician, advanced kinetic theory of gases and fluids.

Jöns Jakob Berzelius, 1779-1848, (Swed.) chemist, developed modern chemical symbols and formulas.

Henry Bessemer, 1813-1898, (Br.) engineer, invented Bessemer steel-making process.

Louis Blériot, 1872-1936, (F.) engineer, pioneer aviator, invented and constructed monoplanes.

Niels Bohr, 1885-1962, (Dan.) physicist, leading figure in the development of quantum theory.

Max Born, 1882-1970, (G.) physicist known for research in quantum mechanics.

Robert Bunsen, 1811-1899, (G.) chemist, invented Bunsen burner.

Luther Burbank, 1849-1926, (U.S.) plant breeder whose work developed plant breeding into a modern science.

Vannevar Bush, 1890-1974, (U.S.) electrical engineer, developed differential analyzer, first electronic analogue computer.

Alexis Carrel, 1873-1944, (F.) surgeon, biologist, developed methods of suturing blood vessels and transplanting organs.

George Washington Carver, 1860?-1943, (U.S.) agricultural chemist, experimenter, benefactor of South, a black hero.

Henry Cavendish, 1731-1810, (Br.) chemist, physicist, discovered hydrogen.

James Chadwick, 1891-1974, (Br.) physicist, discovered the neutron.

Jean M. Charcot, 1825-1893, (F.) neurologist known for work on hysteria, hypnotism, sclerosis.

Albert Claude, 1899-1983, (Belg.) a founder of modern cell biology.

John D. Cockcroft, 1897-1967, (Br.) nuclear physicist, constructed first atomic particle accelerator with E.T.S. Walton.

William Crookes, 1832-1919, (Br.) physicist, chemist, discovered thallium, invented a cathode-ray tube, radiometer.

Marie Curie, 1867-1934, (Pol.-F.) physical chemist known for work on radium and its compounds.

Pierre Curie, 1859-1906, (F.) physical chemist known for work with his wife on radioactivity.

Gottlieb Daimler, 1834-1900, (G.) engineer, inventor, pioneer automobile manufacturer.

John Dalton, 1766-1844, (Br.) chemist, physicist, formulated atomic theory, made first table of atomic weights.

Charles Darwin, 1809-1882, (Br.) naturalist, established theory of organic evolution.

Humphry Davy, 1778-1829, (Br.) chemist, research in electrochemistry led to isolation of potassium, sodium, calcium, barium, boron, magnesium, and strontium.

Lee De Forest, 1873-1961, (U.S.) inventor, pioneer in development of wireless telegraphy, sound pictures, television.

Max Delbruck, 1907-1981, (U.S.) pioneer in modern molecular genetics.

Rudolf Diesel, 1858-1913, (G.) mechanical engineer, patented Diesel engine.

Thomas Dooley, 1927-1961, (U.S.) "jungle doctor," noted for efforts to supply medical aid to underdeveloped countries.

Christian Doppler, 1803-1853, (Aus.) physicist, demonstrated Doppler effect (change in energy wavelengths caused by motion).

Thomas A. Edison, 1847-1931, (U.S.) inventor, held over 1,000 patents, including incandescent electric lamp, phonograph.

Paul Ehrlich, 1854-1915, (G.) bacteriologist, pioneer in modern immunology and bacteriology.

Albert Einstein, 1879-1955, (U.S.) theoretical physicist, known for formulation of relativity theory.

Leonhard Euler, 1707-1783, (Swiss) mathematician, physicist, authored first calculus book.

Gabriel Fahrenheit, 1686-1736, (G.) physicist, introduced Fahrenheit scale for thermometers.

Michael Faraday, 1791-1867, (Br.) chemist, physicist, known for work in field of electricity.

Pierre de Fermat, 1601-1665, (F.) mathematician, discovered analytic geometry, founded modern theory of numbers and calculus of probabilities.

Enrico Fermi, 1901-1954, (It.) physicist, one of chief architects of the nuclear age.

Galileo Ferraris, 1847-1897, (It.) physicist, electrical engineer, discovered principle of rotary magnetic field.

Camille Flammarion, 1842-1925, (F.) astronomer, popularized study of astronomy.

Alexander Fleming, 1881-1955, (Br.) bacteriologist, discovered penicillin.

Jean B.J. Fourier, 1768-1830, (F.) mathematician, discovered theorem governing periodic oscillation.

James Franck, 1882-1964, (G.) physicist, proved value of quantum theory.

Sigmund Freud, 1856-1939, (Aus.) psychiatrist, founder of psychoanalysis.

Galileo Galilei, 1564-1642, (It.) astronomer, physicist, a founder of the experimental method.

Luigi Galvani, 1737-1798, (It.) physician, physicist, known as founder of galvanism.

Carl Friedrich Gauss, 1777-1855, (G.) mathematician, astronomer, physicist, made important contributions to almost every field of physical science, founded a number of entirely new fields.

Joseph Gay-Lussac, 1778-1850, (F.) chemist, physicist, investigated behavior of gases, discovered law of combining volumes.

Josiah W. Gibbs, 1839-1903, (U.S.) theoretical physicist, chemist, founded chemical thermodynamics.

Robert H. Goddard, 1882-1945 (U.S.) physicist, father of modern rocketry.

George W. Goethals, 1858-1928, (U.S.) army engineer, built the Panama Canal.

William C. Gorgas, 1854-1920, (U.S.) sanitarian, U.S. army surgeon-general, his work to prevent yellow fever, malaria helped insure construction of Panama Canal.

Ernest Haeckel, 1834-1919, (G.) zoologist, evolutionist, a strong proponent of Darwin.

Otto Hahn, 1879-1968, (G.) chemist, worked on atomic fission.

J.B.S. Haldane, 1892-1964, (Sc.) scientist, known for work as geneticist and application of mathematics to science.

James Hall, 1761-1832, (Br.) geologist, chemist, founded experimental geology, geochemistry.

Edmund Halley, 1656-1742, (Br.) astronomer, calculated the orbits of many planets.

William Harvey, 1578-1657, (Br.) physician, anatomist, discovered circulation of the blood.

Hermann v. Helmholtz, 1821-1894, (G.) physicist, anatomist, physiologist, made fundamental contributions to physiology, optics, electrodynamics, mathematics, meteorology.

William Herschel, 1738-1822, (Br.) astronomer, discovered Uranus.

Heinrich Hertz, 1857-1894, (G.) physicist, his discoveries led to wireless telegraphy.

David Hilbert, 1862-1943, (G.) mathematician, formulated first satisfactory set of axioms for modern Euclidean geometry.

Edwin P. Hubble, 1889-1953, (U.S.) astronomer, produced first observational evidence of expanding universe.

Alexander v. Humboldt, 1769-1859, (G.) explorer, naturalist, propagator of earth sciences, originated ecology, geophysics.

Julian Huxley, 1887-1975, (Br.) biologist, a gifted exponent and philosopher of science.

Edward Jenner, 1749-1823, (Br.) physician, discovered vaccination.

William Jenner, 1815-1898, (Br.) physician, pathological anatomist.

Frederic Joliot-Curie, 1900-1958, (F.) physicist, with his wife continued work of Curies on radioactivity.

Irene Joliot-Curie, 1897-1956, (F.) physicist, continued work of Curies in radioactivity.

James P. Joule, 1818-1889, (Br.) physicist, determined relationship between heat and mechanical energy (conservation of energy).

Carl Jung, 1875-1961, (Sw.) psychiatrist, founder of analytical psychology.

Wm. Thomas Kelvin, 1824-1907, (Br.) mathematician, physicist, known for work on heat and electricity.

Sister Elizabeth Kenny, 1886-1952, (Austral.) nurse, developed method of treatment for polio.

Johannes Kepler, 1571-1630, (G.) astronomer, discovered important laws of planetary motion.

Joseph Lagrange, 1736-1813, (F.) geometer, astronomer, worked in all fields of analysis, and number theory, and analytical and celestial mechanics.

Jean B. Lamarck, 1744-1829, (F.) naturalist, forerunner of Darwin in evolutionary theory.

Irving Langmuir, 1881-1957, (U.S.) physical chemist, his studies of molecular films on solid and liquid surfaces opened new fields in colloid research and biochemistry.

Pierre S. Laplace, 1749-1827, (F.) astronomer, physicist, put forth nebular hypothesis of origin of solar system.

Antoine Lavoisier, 1743-1794, (F.) chemist, founder of modern chemistry.

Ernest O. Lawrence, 1901-1958, (U.S.) physicist, invented the cyclotron.

Louis Leakey, 1903-1972, (Br.) anthropologist, discovered important fossils, remains of early hominids.

Anton van Leeuwenhoek, 1632-1723, (Du.) microscopist, father of microbiology.

Gottfried Wilhelm Leibniz, 1646-1716, (G.) mathematician, developed theories of differential and integral calculus.

Justus von Liebig, 1803-1873, (G.) chemist, established quantitative organic chemical analysis.

Joseph Lister, 1827-1912, (Br.) pioneer of antiseptic surgery.

Percival Lowell, 1855-1916, (U.S.) astronomer, predicted the existence of Pluto.

Guglielmo Marconi, 1874-1937, (It.) physicist, known for his development of wireless telegraphy.

James Clerk Maxwell, 1831-1879, (Sc.) physicist, known especially for his work in electricity and magnetism.

Maria Goeppert Mayer, 1906-1972, (G.-U.S.) physicist, independently developed theory of structure of atomic nuclei.

Lise Meitner, 1878-1968, (Aus.) physicist whose work contributed to the development of the atomic bomb.

Gregor J. Mendel, 1822-1884, (Aus.) botanist, known for his experimental work on heredity.

Franz Mesmer, 1734-1815, (G.) physician, developed theory of animal magnetism.

Albert A. Michelson, 1852-1931, (U.S.) physicist, established speed of light as a fundamental constant.

Robert A. Millikan, 1868-1953, (U.S.) physicist, noted for study of elementary electronic charge and photoelectric effect.

Thomas Hunt Morgan, 1866-1945, (U.S.) geneticist, embryologist, established chromosome theory of heredity.

Isaac Newton, 1642-1727, (Br.) natural philosopher, mathematician, discovered law of gravitation, laws of motion.

J. Robert Oppenheimer, 1904-1967, (U.S.) physicist, director of Los Alamos during development of the atomic bomb.

Wilhelm Ostwald, 1853-1932, (G.) physical chemist, philosopher, chief founder of physical chemistry.

Louis Pasteur, 1822-1895, (F.) chemist, originated process of pasteurization.

Max Planck, 1858-1947, (G.) physicist, originated and developed quantum theory.

Henri Poincaré, 1854-1912, (F.) mathematician, physicist, influenced cosmology, relativity, and topology.

Joseph Priestley, 1733-1804, (Br.) chemist, one of the discoverers of oxygen.

Walter S. Reed, 1851-1902, (U.S.) army pathologist, bacteriologist, proved mosquitoes transmit yellow fever.

Bernhard Riemann, 1826-1866, (G.) mathematician, contributed to development of calculus, complex variable theory, and mathematical physics.

Wilhelm Roentgen, 1845-1923, (G.) physicist, discovered X-rays.

Bertrand Russell, 1872-1970, (Br.) logician, philosopher, one of the founders of modern logic, wrote *Principia Mathematica*.

Ernest Rutherford, 1871-1937, (Br.) physicist, discovered the atomic nucleus.

Giovanni Schiaparelli, 1835-1910, (It.) astronomer, hypothesized canals on the surface of Mars.

Angelo Secchi, 1818-1878, (It.) astronomer, pioneer in classifying stars by their spectra.

Harlow Shapley, 1885-1972, (U.S.) astronomer, noted for his studies of the galaxy.

Charles P. Steinmetz, 1865-1923, (G.-U.S.) electrical engineer, developed fundamental ideas on alternating current systems.

Leo Szilard, 1898-1964, (U.S.) physicist, helped create first sustained nuclear reaction.

Nikola Tesla, 1856-1943, (Croatia-U.S.) electrical engineer, contributed to most developments in electronics.

Rudolf Virchow, 1821-1902, (G.) pathologist, a founder of cellular pathology.

Alessandro Volta, 1745-1827, (It.) physicist, pioneer in electricity.

Alfred Russell Wallace, 1823-1913, (Br.) naturalist, proposed concept of evolution similar to Darwin.

August v. Wasserman, 1866-1925, (G.) bacteriologist, discovered reaction used as test for syphilis.

James E. Watt, 1736-1819, (Sc.) mechanical engineer, inventor, invented modern steam condensing engine.

Alfred L. Wegener, 1880-1930, (G.) meteorologist, geophysicist, postulated theory of continental drift.

Norbert Wiener, 1894-1964, (U.S.) mathematician, founder of the science of cybernetics.

Ferdinand v. Zeppelin, 1838-1917 (G.) soldier, aeronaut, airship designer.

Noted Business Leaders, Industrialists, and Philanthropists of the Past

Elizabeth Arden (F.N. Graham), 1884-1966, (U.S.) Canadian-born businesswoman founded and headed cosmetics empire.

Philip D. Armour, 1832-1901, (U.S.) industrialist, streamlined meat packing.

John Jacob Astor, 1763-1848, (U.S.) German-born fur trader, banker, real estate magnate; at death, richest in U.S.

Francis W. Ayer, 1848-1923, (U.S.) ad industry pioneer.

August Belmont, 1816-1890, (U.S.) German-born financier.

James B. (Diamond Jim) Brady, 1856-1917, (U.S.) financier, philanthropist, legendary bon vivant.

Adolphus Busch, 1839-1913, (U.S.) German-born businessman, established brewery empire.

Asa Candler, 1851-1929, (U.S.) founded Coca-Cola Co.

Andrew Carnegie, 1835-1919, (U.S.) Scots-born industrialist, founded U.S. Steel; financed over 2,800 libraries.

William Colgate, 1783-1857, (U.S.) British-born businessman, philanthropist; founded soap-making empire.

Jay Cooke, 1821-1905, (U.S.) financier, sold $1 billion in Union bonds during Civil War.

Peter Cooper, 1791-1883, (U.S.) industrialist, inventor, philanthropist.

Ezra Cornell, 1807-1874, (U.S.) businessman, philanthropist; headed Western Union, established univ.

Erastus Corning, 1794-1872, (U.S.) financier, headed N.Y. Central.

Charles Crocker, 1822-1888, (U.S.) railroad builder, financier.

Samuel Cunard, 1787-1865, (Can.) pioneered trans-Atlantic steam navigation.

Marcus Daly, 1841-1900, (U.S.) Irish-born copper magnate.

Walt Disney, 1901-1966, (U.S.) pioneer in cinema animation, built entertainment empire.

Herbert H. Dow, 1866-1930, (U.S.) Canadian-born founder of chemical co.

James Duke, 1856-1925, (U.S.) founded American Tobacco, Duke Univ.

Eleuthere I. du Pont, 1771-1834, (U.S.) French-born gunpowder manufacturer; founded one of world's largest business empires.

Thomas C. Durant, 1820-1885, (U.S.) railroad official, financier.

William C. Durant, 1861-1947, (U.S.) industrialist, formed General Motors.

George Eastman, 1854-1932, (U.S.) inventor, manufacturer of photographic equipment.

Marshall Field, 1834-1906, (U.S.) merchant, founded Chicago's largest department store.

Harvey Firestone, 1868-1938, (U.S.) industrialist, founded tire co.

Henry M. Flagler, 1830-1913, (U.S.) financier, helped form Standard Oil; developed Florida as resort state.

Henry Ford, 1863-1947, (U.S.) auto maker, developed first popular low-priced car.

Henry C. Frick, 1849-1919, (U.S.) industrialist, helped organize U.S. Steel.

Jakob Fugger (Jakob the Rich), 1459-1525, (G.) headed leading banking house, trading concern, in 16th-century Europe.

Alfred C. Fuller, 1885-1973, (U.S.) Canadian-born businessman, founded brush co.

Elbert H. Gary, 1846-1927, (U.S.) U.S. Steel head, 1903-27.

Amadeo P. Giannini, 1870-1949, (U.S.) founded Bank of America.

Stephen Girard, 1750-1831, (U.S.) French-born financier, philanthropist; richest man in U.S. at his death.

Jean Paul Getty, 1892-1976, (U.S.) founded oil empire.

Jay Gould, 1836-1892, (U.S.) railroad magnate, financier, speculator.

Hetty Green, 1834-1916, (U.S.) financier, the "witch of Wall St."; richest woman in U.S in her day.

William Gregg, 1800-1867, (U.S.) launched textile industry in the South.

Meyer Guggenheim, 1828-1905, (U.S.) Swiss-born merchant, philanthropist; built merchandising, mining empires.

Edward H. Harriman, 1848-1909, (U.S.) railroad financier, administrator; headed Union Pacific.

William Randolph Hearst, 1863-1951, (U.S.) a dominant figure in American journalism; built vast publishing empire.

Henry J. Heinz, 1844-1919, (U.S.) founded food empire.

James J. Hill, 1838-1916, (U.S.) Canadian-born railroad magnate, financier; founded Great Northern Railway.

Conrad N. Hilton, 1888-1979, (U.S.) intl. hotel chain founder.

Howard Hughes, 1905-1976, (U.S.) industrialist, financier, movie maker.

H.L. Hunt, 1889-1974, (U.S.) oil magnate.

Collis P. Huntington, 1821-1900, (U.S.) railroad magnate.

Henry E. Huntington, 1850-1927, (U.S.) railroad builder, philanthropist.

Howard Johnson, 1896-1972, (U.S.) founded restaurant chain.

Henry J. Kaiser, 1882-1967, (U.S.) industrialist, built empire in steel, aluminum.

Minor C. Keith, 1848-1929, (U.S.) railroad magnate; founded United Fruit Co.

Will K. Kellogg, 1860-1951, (U.S.) businessman, philanthropist, founded breakfast food co.

Richard King, 1825-1885, (U.S.) cattleman, founded half-million acre King Ranch in Texas.

William S. Knudsen, 1879-1948, (U.S.) Danish-born auto industry executive.

Samuel H. Kress, 1863-1955, (U.S.) businessman, art collector, philanthropist; founded "dime store" chain.

Ray A. Kroc, 1902-1984, (U.S.) builder of McDonald's fast food empire; owner, San Diego Padres baseball team.

Alfred Krupp, 1812-1887, (G.) armaments magnate.

Albert Lasker, 1880-1952, (U.S.) businessman, philanthropist.

Thomas Lipton, 1850-1931, (Ir.) merchant, built tea empire.

James McGill, 1744-1813, (Can.) Scots-born fur trader, founded univ.

Andrew W. Mellon, 1855-1937, (U.S.) financier, industrialist; benefactor of National Gallery of Art.

Charles E. Merrill, 1885-1956, (U.S.) financier, developed firm of Merrill Lynch.

John Pierpont Morgan, 1837-1913, (U.S.) most powerful figure in finance and industry at the turn-of-the-century.

Malcolm Muir, 1885-1979, (U.S.) created *Business Week* magazine; headed *Newsweek,* 1937-61.

Samuel Newhouse, 1895-1979, (U.S.) publishing and broadcasting magnate, built communications empire.

Aristotle Onassis, 1900-1975, (Gr.) shipping magnate.

George Peabody, 1795-1869, (U.S.) merchant, financier, philanthropist.

James C. Penney, 1875-1971, (U.S.) businessman, developed department store chain.

William C. Procter, 1862-1934, (U.S.) headed soap co.

John D. Rockefeller, 1839-1937, (U.S.) industrialist, established Standard Oil; became world's wealthiest person.

John D. Rockefeller Jr., 1874-1960, (U.S.) philanthropist, established foundation; provided land for United Nations.

Meyer A. Rothschild, 1743-1812, (G.) founded international banking house.

Thomas Fortune Ryan, 1851-1928, (U.S.) financier, dominated N.Y. City public transportation; helped found American Tobacco.

Russell Sage, 1816-1906, (U.S.) financier.

David Sarnoff, 1891-1971, (U.S.) broadcasting pioneer, established first radio network, NBC.

Richard W. Sears, 1863-1914, (U.S.) founded mail-order co.

(Ernst) Werner von Siemens, 1816-1892, (G.) industrialist, inventor.

Alfred P. Sloan, 1875-1966, (U.S.) industrialist, philanthropist; headed General Motors.

A. Leland Stanford, 1824-1893, (U.S.) railroad official, philanthropist; founded univ.

Nathan Strauss, 1848-1931, (U.S.) German-born merchant, philanthropist; headed Macy's.

Levi Strauss, c.1829-1902, (U.S.) pants manufacturer.

Clement Studebaker, 1831-1901, (U.S.) wagon, carriage manufacturer.

Gustavus Swift, 1839-1903, (U.S.) pioneer meat-packer; promoted refrigerated railroad cars.

Gerard Swope, 1872-1957, (U.S.) industrialist, economist; headed General Electric.

James Walter Thompson, 1847-1928, (U.S.) ad executive.

Theodore N. Vail, 1845-1920, (U.S.) organized Bell Telephone system, headed ATT.

Cornelius Vanderbilt, 1794-1877, (U.S.) financier, established steamship, railroad empires.

Henry Villard, 1835-1900, (U.S.) German-born railroad executive, financier.

Charles R. Walgreen, 1873-1939, (U.S.) founded drugstore chain.

DeWitt Wallace, 1890-1981, (U.S.) and **Lila Wallace,** 1890-1984, (U.S.) co-founders of *Reader's Digest* magazine, philanthropists.

John Wanamaker, 1838-1922, (U.S.) pioneered department-store merchandising.

Aaron Montgomery Ward, 1843-1913, (U.S.) established first mail-order firm.

Thomas J. Watson, 1874-1956, (U.S.) headed IBM, 1924-49.

John Hay Whitney, 1905-1982, (U.S.) publisher, sportsman, philanthropist.

Charles E. Wilson, 1890-1961, (U.S.) auto industry executive; public official.

Frank W. Woolworth, 1852-1919, (U.S.) created 5 & 10 chain.

William Wrigley Jr., 1861-1932, (U.S.) founded chewing gum co.

Composers of the Western World

Carl Philipp Emanuel Bach, 1714-1788, (G.) Prussian and Wurtembergian Sonatas.

Johann Christian Bach, 1735-1782, (G.) Concertos; sonatas.

Johann Sebastian Bach, 1685-1750, (G.) St. Matthew Passion, The Well-Tempered Clavichord.

Samuel Barber, b. 1910, (U.S.) Adagio for Strings, Vanessa.

Bela Bartok, 1881-1945, (Hung.) Concerto for Orchestra, The Miraculous Mandarin.

Ludwig Van Beethoven, 1770-1827, (G.) Concertos (Emperor); sonatas (Moonlight, Pastorale, Pathetique); symphonies (Eroica).

Vincenzo Bellini, 1801-1835, (It.) La Sonnambula, Norma, I Puritani.

Alban Berg, 1885-1935, (Aus.) Wozzeck, Lulu.

Hector Berlioz, 1803-1869, (F.) Damnation of Faust, Symphonie Fantastique, Requiem.

Leonard Bernstein, b. 1918, (U.S.) Jeremiah, West Side Story.

Georges Bizet, 1838-1875, (F.) Carmen, Pearl Fishers.

Ernest Bloch, 1880-1959, (Swiss) Schelomo, Voice in the Wilderness, Sacred Service.

Luigi Boccherini, 1743-1805, (It.) Cello Concerto in B Flat, Symphony in C.

Alexander Borodin, 1834-1887, (R.) Prince Igor, In the Steppes of Central Asia.

Johannes Brahms, 1833-1897, (G.) Liebeslieder Waltzes, Rhapsody in E Flat Major, Opus 119 for Piano, Academic Festival Overture; symphonies; quartets.

Benjamin Britten, 1913-1976, (Br.) Peter Grimes, Turn of the Screw, Ceremony of Carols, War Requiem.

Anton Bruckner, 1824-1896, (Aus.) Symphonies (Romantic), Intermezzo for String Quintet.

Ferruccio Busoni, 1866-1924, (It.) Doctor Faust, Comedy Overture.

Dietrich Buxtehude, 1637-1707, (D.) Cantatas, trio sonatas.

William Byrd, 1543-1623, (Br.) Masses, sacred songs.

Alexis Emmanuel Chabrier, 1841-1894, (Fr.) Le Roi Malgre Lui, Espana.

Gustave Charpentier, 1860-1956, (F.) Louise.

Frederic Chopin, 1810-1849, (P.) Polonaises, mazurkas, waltzes, etudes, nocturnes. Polonaise No. 6 in A Flat Major (Heroic); sonatas.

Aaron Copland, b. 1900, (U.S.) Appalachian Spring.

Claude Achille Debussy, 1862-1918, (F.) Pelleas et Melisande, La Mer, Prelude to the Afternoon of a Faun.

C.P. Leo Delibes, 1836-1891, (F.) Lakme, Coppelia, Sylvia.

Norman Dello Joio, b. 1913, (U.S.), Triumph of St. Joan, Psalm of David.

Gaetano Donizetti, 1797-1848, (It.) Elixir of Love, Lucia Di Lammermoor, Daughter of the Regiment.

Paul Dukas, 1865-1935, (Fr.) Sorcerer's Apprentice.

Antonin Dvorak, 1841-1904, (C.) Symphony in E Minor (From the New World).

Edward Elgar, 1857-1934, (Br.) Pomp and Circumstance.

Manuel de Falla, 1876-1946, (Sp.) La Vide Breve, El Amor Brujo.

Gabriel Faure, 1845-1924, (Fr.) Requiem, Ballade.

Friedrich von Flotow, 1812-1883, (G.) Martha.

Cesar Franck, 1822-1890, (Belg.) D Minor Symphony.

George Gershwin, 1898-1937, (U.S.) Rhapsody in Blue, American in Paris, Porgy and Bess.

Umberto Giordano, 1867-1948, (It.) Andrea Chenier.

Alex K. Glazunoff, 1865-1936, (R.) Symphonies, Stenka Razin.

Mikhail Glinka, 1804-1857, (R.) Ruslan and Ludmilla.

Christoph W. Gluck, 1714-1787, (G.) Alceste, Iphigenie en Tauride.

Charles Gounod, 1818-1893, (F.) Faust, Romeo and Juliet.

Edvard Grieg, 1843-1907, (Nor.) Peer Gynt Suite, Concerto in A Minor.

George Frederick Handel, 1685-1759, (G., Br.) Messiah, Xerxes, Berenice.

Howard Hanson, 1896-1981, (U.S.) Symphonies No. 1 (Nordic) and 2 (Romantic).

Roy Harris, 1898-1979, (U.S.) Symphonies, Amer. Portraits.

Joseph Haydn, 1732-1809, (Aus.) Symphonies (Clock); oratorios; chamber music.

Paul Hindemith, 1895-1963, (U.S.) Mathis Der Maler.

Gustav Holst, 1874-1934, (Br.) The Planets.

Arthur Honegger, 1892-1955, (Swiss) Judith, Le Roi David, Pacific 231.

Alan Hovhaness, b. 1911, (U.S.) Symphonies, Magnificat.

Engelbert Humperdinck, 1854-1921, (G.) Hansel and Gretel.

Charles Ives, 1874-1954, (U.S.) Third Symphony.

Aram Khachaturian, 1903-1978, (R.) Gayane (ballet), symphonies.

Zoltan Kodaly, 1882-1967, (Hung.) Hary Janos, Psalmus Hungaricus.

Fritz Kreisler, 1875-1962, (Aus.) Caprice Viennois, Tambourin Chinois.

Rodolphe Kreutzer, 1766-1831, (F.) 40 etudes for violin.

Edouard V.A. Lalo, 1823-1892, (F.) Symphonie Espagnole.

Ruggiero Leoncavallo, 1858-1919, (It.) I Pagliacci.

Franz Liszt, 1811-1886, (Hung.) 20 Hungarian rhapsodies; symphonic poems.

Edward MacDowell, 1861-1908, (U.S.) To a Wild Rose.

Gustav Mahler, 1860-1911, (Aus.) Lied von der Erde.

Pietro Mascagni, 1863-1945, (It.) Cavalleria Rusticana.

Jules Massenet, 1842-1912, (F.) Manon, Le Cid, Thais.

Mendelssohn-Bartholdy, 1809-1847, (G.) Midsummer Night's Dream, Songs Without Words.

Gian-Carlo Menotti, b. 1911, (It.-U.S.) The Medium, The Consul, Amahl and the Night Visitors.

Giacomo Meyerbeer, 1791-1864, (G.) Robert le Diable, Les Huguenots.

Claudio Monteverdi, 1567-1643, (It.) Opera; masses; madrigals.

Wolfgang Amadeus Mozart, 1756-1791, (Aus.) Magic Flute, Marriage of Figaro; concertos; symphonies, etc.

Modest Moussorgsky, 1835-1881, (R.) Boris Godunov, Pictures at an Exhibition.

Jacques Offenbach, 1819-1880, (F.) Tales of Hoffman.

Carl Orff, 1895-1982, (G.) Carmina Burana.

Ignace Paderewski, 1860-1941, (P.) Minuet in G.

Giovanni P. da Palestrina, 1524-1594, (It.) Masses; madrigals.

Amilcare Ponchielli, 1834-1886, (It.) La Gioconda.

Francis Poulenc, 1899-1963, (F.) Dialogues des Carmelites.

Serge Prokofiev, 1891-1953, (R.) Love for Three Oranges, Lt. Kije, Peter and the Wolf.

Giacomo Puccini, 1858-1924, (It.) La Boheme, Manon Lescaut, Tosca, Madame Butterfly.

Sergei Rachmaninov, 1873-1943, (R.) 24 preludes, E concerti, 4 symphonies. Prelude in C Sharp Minor.

Maurice Ravel, 1875-1937, (Fr.) Bolero, Daphnis et Chloe, Rapsodie Espagnole.

Nikolai Rimsky-Korsakov, 1844-1908, (R.) Golden Cockerel, Capriccio Espagnol, Scheherazade, Russian Easter Overture.

Gioacchino Rossini, 1792-1868, (It.) Barber of Seville, Semiramide, William Tell.

Chas. Camille Saint-Saens, 1835-1921, (F.) Samson and Delilah, Danse Macabre.

Alessandro Scarlatti, 1659-1725, (It.) Cantatas; concertos.

Domenico Scarlatti, 1685-1757, (It.) Harpsichord sonatas.

Arnold Schoenberg, 1874-1951, (Aus.) Pelleas and Melisande, Transfigured Night, De Profundis.

Franz Schubert, 1797-1828, (A.) Lieder; symphonies (Unfinished); overtures (Rosamunde).

William Schuman, b. 1910, (U.S.) Credendum, New England Triptych.

Robert Schumann, 1810-1856, (G.) Symphonies, songs.

Aleksandr Scriabin, 1872-1915, (R.) Prometheus.

Dimitri Shostakovich, 1906-1975, (R.) Symphonies, Lady Macbeth of Mzensk, The Nose.

Jean Sibelius, 1865-1957, (Finn.) Finlandia, Karelia.

Bedrich Smetana, 1824-1884, (Cz.) The Bartered Bride.

Karlheinz Stockhausen, b. 1928, (G.) Kontrapunkte, Kontakte.

Richard Strauss, 1864-1949, (G.) Salome, Elektra, Der Rosenkavalier, Thus Spake Zarathustra.

Igor F. Stravinsky, 1882-1971, (R.-U.S.) Oedipus Rex, Le Sacre du Printemps, Petrushka.

Peter I. Tchaikovsky, 1840-1893, (R.) Nutcracker Suite, Swan Lake, Eugene Onegin.

Ambroise Thomas, 1811-1896, (F.) Mignon.

Virgil Thomson, b. 1896, (U.S.) Opera, ballet; Four Saints in Three Acts.

Ralph Vaughan Williams, 1872-1958, (Br.) Job, London Symphony, Symphony No. 7 (Antartica).

Giuseppe Verdi, 1813-1901, (It.) Aida, Rigoletto, Don Carlo, Il Trovatore, La Traviata, Falstaff, Macbeth.

Heitor Villa-Lobos, 1887-1959, (Brazil) Choros.

Antonio Vivaldi, 1678-1741, (It.) Concerti, The Four Seasons.

Richard Wagner, 1813-1883, (G.) Rienzi, Tannhauser, Lohengrin, Tristan und Isolde.

Karl Maria von Weber, 1786-1826, (G.) Der Freischutz.

Composers of Operettas, Musicals, and Popular Music

Richard Adler, b. 1921, (U.S.) *Pajama Game; Damn Yankees.*

Milton Ager, 1893-1979, (U.S.) I Wonder What's Become of Sally; Hard Hearted Hannah; Ain't She Sweet?

Leroy Anderson, 1908-1975, (U.S.) Syncopated Clock; Blue Tango; Sleigh Ride.

Harold Arlen, b. 1905, (U.S.) Stormy Weather; Over the Rainbow; Blues in the Night; That Old Black Magic.

Burt Bacharach, b. 1928, (U.S.) Raindrops Keep Fallin' on My Head; Walk on By; What the World Needs Now is Love.

Ernest Ball, 1878-1927, (U.S.) Mother Machree; When Irish Eyes Are Smiling.

Irving Berlin, b. 1888, (U.S.) *This is the Army; Annie Get Your Gun; Call Me Madam;* God Bless America; White Christmas.

Eubie Blake, 1883-1983, (U.S.) *Shuffle Along;* I'm Just Wild about Harry.

Jerry Bock, b. 1928, (U.S.) *Mr. Wonderful; Fiorello; Fiddler on the Roof; The Rothschilds.*

Carrie Jacobs Bond, 1862-1946, (U.S.) I Love You Truly.

Nacio Herb Brown, 1896-1964, (U.S.) Singing in the Rain; You Were Meant for Me; All I Do Is Dream of You.

Hoagy Carmichael, 1899-1981, (U.S.) Stardust; Georgia on My Mind; Old Buttermilk Sky.

George M. Cohan, 1878-1942, (U.S.) Give My Regards to Broadway; You're A Grand Old Flag; Over There.

Noel Coward, 1899-1973 (Br.) *Bitter Sweet;* Mad Dogs and Englishmen; Mad About the Boy.

Walter Donaldson, 1893-1947, (U.S.) My Buddy; Carolina in the Morning; You're Driving Me Crazy; Makin' Whoopee.

Vernon Duke, 1903-1969, (U.S.) April in Paris.

Gus Edwards, 1879-1945, (U.S.) School Days; By the Light of the Silvery Moon; In My Merry Oldsmobile.

Sherman Edwards, b. 1919, (U.S.) *See You in September; Wonderful! Wonderful!*

Sammy Fain, b. 1902, Wedding Bells Are Breaking Up That Old Gang of Mine; Let a Smile Be Your Umbrella.

Fred Fisher, 1875-1942, (U.S.) Peg O' My Heart; Chicago; Dardanella.

Stephen Collins Foster, 1826-1864, (U.S.) My Old Kentucky Home; Old Folks At Home.

Rudolf Friml, 1879-1972, (naturalized U.S.) *The Firefly; Rose Marie; Vagabond King; Bird of Paradise.*

John Gay, 1685-1732, (Br.) *The Beggar's Opera.*

Edwin F. Goldman, 1878-1956, (U.S.) marches.

Percy Grainger, 1882-1961, (Br.) Country Gardens.

John Green, b. 1908, (U.S.) Body and Soul; Out of Nowhere; I Cover the Waterfront.

Ferde Grofe, 1892-1972, (U.S.) Grand Canyon Suite.

W. C. Handy, 1873-1958, (U.S.) St. Louis Blues.

Ray Henderson, 1896-1970, (U.S.) *George White's Scandals;* That Old Gang of Mine; Five Foot Two, Eyes of Blue.

Victor Herbert, 1859-1924, (Ir.-U.S.) *Mlle. Modiste; Babes in Toyland; The Red Mill; Naughty Marietta; Sweethearts.*

Jerry Herman, b. 1932, (U.S.) *Milk and Honey; Hello Dolly; Mame; Dear World.*

Al Hoffman, 1902-1960, (U.S.) Heartaches, Mairzy Doats.

Scott Joplin, 1868-1917, (U.S.) *Treemonisha.*

John Kander, b. 1927, (U.S.) *Cabaret; Chicago; Funny Lady.*

Jerome Kern, 1885-1945, (U.S.) *Sally; Sunny; Show Boat; Cat and the Fiddle; Music in the Air; Roberta.*

Burton Lane, b. 1912, (U.S.) *Three's a Crowd; Finian's Rainbow; On A Clear Day You Can See Forever.*

Franz Lehar, 1870-1948, (Hung.) *Merry Widow.*

Mitch Leigh, b. 1928, (U.S.) *Man of La Mancha.*

John Lennon, 1940-1980, (Br.) Hard Day's Night, I Want to Hold Your Hand.

Frank Loesser, 1910-1969, (U.S.) *Guys and Dolls; Where's Charley?; The Most Happy Fella; How to Succeed . . . .*

Frederick Loewe, b. 1901, (Aust.-U.S.) *The Day Before Spring; Brigadoon; Paint Your Wagon; My Fair Lady; Camelot.*

Henry Mancini, b. 1924, (U.S.) Moon River; Days of Wine and Roses; Pink Panther Theme.

Paul McCartney, b. 1942, (Br.) Michelle, Hey Jude, And I Love Her, Yesterday.

Jimmy McHugh, 1894-1969, (U.S.) I Can't Give You Anything But Love; I Feel a Song Coming On.

Joseph Meyer, b. 1894, (U.S.) If You Knew Susie; California, Here I Come; Crazy Rhythm.

Chauncey Olcott, 1860-1932, (U.S.) Mother Machree; My Wild Irish Rose.

Cole Porter, 1893-1964, (U.S.) *Anything Goes; Jubilee; DuBarry Was a Lady; Panama Hattie; Mexican Hayride; Kiss Me Kate; Can Can; Silk Stockings.*

Andre Previn, b. 1929, (U.S.) *Coco.*

Richard Rodgers, 1902-1979, (U.S.) *Garrick Gaieties; Connecticut Yankee; America's Sweetheart; On Your Toes; Babes in Arms; The Boys from Syracuse; Oklahoma!; Carousel; South Pacific; The King and I; Flower Drum Song; The Sound of Music.*

Sigmund Romberg, 1887-1951, (Hung.) *Maytime; The Student Prince; Desert Song; Blossom Time.*

Harold Rome, b. 1908, (U.S.) *Pins and Needles; Call Me Mister; Wish You Were Here; Fanny; Destry Rides Again.*

Vincent Rose, b. 1880-1944, (U.S.) Avalon; Whispering; Blueberry Hill.

Harry Ruby, 1895-1974, (U.S.) Three Little Words; Who's Sorry Now?

Arthur Schwartz, b. 1900, (U.S.) *The Band Wagon; Inside U.S.A.; A Tree Grows in Brooklyn.*

Stephen Sondheim, b. 1930, (U.S.) *A Little Night Music; Company.*

John Philip Sousa, 1854-1932, (U.S.) El Capitan; Stars and Stripes Forever.

Oskar Straus, 1870-1954, (Aus.) *Chocolate Soldier.*

Johann Strauss, 1825-1899, (Aus.) *Gypsy Baron; Die Fledermaus;* waltzes: Blue Danube, Artist's Life.

Charles Strouse, b. 1928, (U.S.) *Bye Bye, Birdie; All American; Golden Boy; Applause; Annie.*

Jule Styne, b. 1905, (b. London-U.S.) *Gentlemen Prefer Blondes; Bells Are Ringing; Gypsy; Funny Girl.*

Arthur S. Sullivan, 1842-1900, (Br.) *H.M.S. Pinafore, Pirates of Penzance; The Mikado.*

Deems Taylor, 1885-1966, (U.S.) *Peter Ibbetson.*

Egbert van Alstyne, 1882-1951, (U.S.) In the Shade of the Old Apple Tree; Memories; Pretty Baby.

James Van Heusen, b. 1913, (U.S.) Moonlight Becomes You; Swinging on a Star.

Albert von Tilzer, 1878-1956, (U.S.) I'll Be With You in Apple Blossom Time; Take Me Out to the Ball Game.

Harry von Tilzer, 1872-1946, (U.S.) Only a Bird in a Gilded Cage; On a Sunday Afternoon.

Harry Warren, 1893-1981, (U.S.) You're My Everything; We're in the Money; I Only Have Eyes for You; September in the Rain.

Kurt Weill, 1900-1950, (G.-U.S.) *Threepenny Opera; Lady in the Dark; Knickerbocker Holiday; One Touch of Venus.*

Percy Wenrich, 1887-1952, (U.S.) When You Wore a Tulip; Moonlight Bay; Put On Your Old Gray Bonnet.

Richard A. Whiting, 1891-1938, (U.S.) Till We Meet Again; Sleepytime Gal; Beyond the Blue Horizon.

Meredith Willson, b. 1902, (U.S.) *The Music Man.*

Vincent Youmans, 1898-1946, (U.S.) *Two Little Girls in Blue; Wildflower; No, No, Nanette; Hit the Deck; Rainbow; Smiles.*

Lyricists

Sammy Cahn, b. 1913, (U.S.) High Hopes; Love and Marriage; The Second Time Around.

Betty Comden, b. 1919 (U.S.) and **Adolph Green,** b. 1915 (U.S.) The Party's Over; Just in Time; New York, New York.

Buddy De Sylva, 1895-1950, (U.S.) When Day is Done; Look for the Silver Lining; April Showers.

Hal David, b. 1921 (U.S.) What the World Needs Now Is Love.

Howard Dietz, b. 1896, (U.S.) Dancing in the Dark; You and the Night and the Music.

Al Dubin, 1891-1945, (U.S.) Tiptoe Through the Tulips; Anniversary Waltz; Lullaby of Broadway.

Dorothy Fields, 1905-1974, (U.S.) On the Sunny Side of the Street; Don't Blame Me; The Way You Look Tonight.

Ira Gershwin, b. 1896, (U.S.) The Man I Love; Fascinating Rhythm; S'Wonderful; Embraceable You.

Wm. S. Gilbert, 1836-1911, (Br.) *The Mikado; H.M.S. Pinafore.*

Oscar Hammerstein II, 1895-1960, (U.S.) Ol' Man River; Oklahoma; Carousel.

E. Y. (Yip) Harburg, 1898-1981, (U.S.) Brother, Can You Spare a Dime; April in Paris; Over the Rainbow.

Lorenz Hart, 1895-1943, (U.S.) Isn't It Romantic; Blue Moon; Lover; Manhattan; My Funny Valentine.

DuBose Heyward, 1885-1940, (U.S.) Summertime; A Woman Is A Sometime Thing.

Gus Kahn, 1886-1941, (U.S.) Memories; Ain't We Got Fun.

Johnny Mercer, 1909-1976, (U.S.) Blues in the Night; Come Rain or Come Shine; Laura; That Old Black Magic.

Jack Norworth, 1879-1959, (U.S.) Take Me Out to the Ball Game; Shine On Harvest Moon.

Jack Yellen, b. 1892, (U.S.) Down by the O-HI-O; Ain't She Sweet; Happy Days Are Here Again.

Noted Jazz Artists

Jazz has been called America's only completely unique contribution to Western culture. The following individuals have made major contributions in this field:

Julian "Cannonball" Adderley, 1928-1975: alto sax.
Louis "Satchmo" Armstrong, 1900-1971: trumpet, singer; originated the "scat" vocal.
Mildred Bailey, 1907-1951: blues singer.
Chet Baker, b. 1929: trumpet.
Count Basie, 1904-1984: orchestra leader, piano.
Sidney Bechet, 1897-1950: early innovator, soprano sax.
Bix Beiderbecke, 1903-1931: cornet, piano, composer.
Bunny Berrigan, 1909-1942: trumpet, singer.
Barney Bigard, b. 1906: clarinet.
Art Blakey, b. 1919: drums, leader.
Jimmy Blanton, 1921-1942: bass.
Charles "Buddy" Bolden, 1868-1931: cornet; formed the first jazz band in the 1890s.
Big Bill Broonzy, 1893-1958: blues singer, guitar.
Clifford Brown, 1930-1956: trumpet.
Ray Brown, b. 1926: bass.
Dave Brubeck, b. 1920: piano, combo leader.
Harry Carney, 1910-1974: baritone sax.
Benny Carter, b. 1907: alto sax, trumpet, clarinet.
Sidney Catlett, 1910-1951: drums.
Charlie Christian, 1919-1942: guitar.
Kenny Clarke, b. 1914: pioneer of modern drums.
Buck Clayton, b. 1911: trumpet, arranger.
Al Cohn, b 1925: tenor sax, composer.
Cozy Cole, 1909-1981: drums.
Ornette Coleman, b. 1930: saxophone; unorthodox style.
John Coltrane, 1926-1967: tenor sax innovator.
Eddie Condon, 1904-1973: guitar, band leader; promoter of Dixieland.
Chick Corea, b. 1941: pianist, composer.
Miles Davis, b. 1926: trumpet; pioneer of cool jazz.
Tadd Dameron, 1917-1965: piano, composer.
Wild Bill Davison, b. 1906: cornet, leader; prominent in early Chicago jazz.
Buddy De Franco, b. 1933: clarinet.
Paul Desmond, 1924-1977: alto sax.
Vic Dickenson, b. 1906: trombone, composer.
Warren "Baby" Dodds, 1898-1959: Dixieland drummer.
Johnny Dodds, 1892-1940: clarinet.
Jimmy Dorsey, 1904-1957: clarinet, alto sax; band leader.
Tommy Dorsey, 1905-1956: trombone; band leader.
Roy Eldridge, b. 1911: trumpet, drums, singer.
Duke Ellington, 1899-1974: piano, band leader, composer.
Bill Evans, 1929-1980: piano.
Gil Evans, b. 1912: composer, arranger, piano.
Ella Fitzgerald, b. 1918: singer.
"Red" Garland, 1923-1984: piano.
Erroll Garner, 1921-1977: piano, composer, "Misty."
Stan Getz, b. 1927: tenor sax.
Dizzy Gillespie, b. 1917: trumpet, composer; bop developer.
Benny Goodman, b. 1909: clarinet, band and combo leader.
Dexter Gordon, b. 1923: tenor sax; bop-derived style.
Stephane Grappelli, b. 1908: violin.
Bobby Hackett, 1915-1976: trumpet, cornet.
Lionel Hampton, b. 1913: vibes, drums, piano, combo leader.
Herbie Hancock, b. 1940: piano, composer.
W. C. Handy, 1873-1958: composer, "St. Louis Blues."
Coleman Hawkins, 1904-1969: tenor sax; 1939 recording of "Body and Soul", a classic.
Roy Haynes, b. 1926: drums.
Fletcher Henderson, 1898-1952: orchestra leader, arranger; pioneered jazz and dance bands of the 30s.
Woody Herman, b. 1913: clarinet, alto sax, band leader.
Jay C. Higginbotham, 1906-1973: trombone.
Earl "Fatha" Hines, 1905-1983: piano, songwriter.
Johnny Hodges, 1906-1971: alto sax.
Billie Holiday, 1915-1959: blues singer, "Strange Fruit."
Sam "Lightnin' " Hopkins, 1912-1982: blues singer, guitar.
Mahalia Jackson, 1911-1972: gospel singer.
Milt Jackson, b. 1923: vibes, piano, guitar.
Illinois Jacquet, b. 1922: tenor sax.
Keith Jarrett, b. 1945: technically phenomenal pianist.
Blind Lemon Jefferson, 1897-1930: blues singer, guitar.
Bunk Johnson, 1879-1949: cornet, trumpet.
James P. Johnson, 1891-1955: piano, composer.
J. J. Johnson, b. 1924: trombone, composer.
Jo Jones, b. 1911: drums.
Philly Joe Jones, 1923: drums.
Quincy Jones, b. 1933: arranger.
Thad Jones, b. 1923: trumpet, cornet.
Scott Joplin, 1868-1917: composer; "Maple Leaf Rag."
Stan Kenton, 1912-1979: orchestra leader, composer, piano.
Barney Kessel, b. 1923: guitar.
Lee Konitz, b. 1927: alto sax.

Gene Krupa, 1909-1973: drums, band and combo leader.
Scott LaFaro, 1936-1961: bass.
Huddie Ledbetter (Leadbelly), 1888-1949: blues singer, guitar.
John Lewis, b. 1920: composer, piano, combo leader.
Jimmie Lunceford, 1902-1947: band leader, sax.
Herbie Mann, b. 1930: flute.
Wynton Marsalis, b. 1961: trumpet.
Jimmy McPartland, b. 1907: trumpet.
Marian McPartland, b. 1920: piano.
Glenn Miller, 1904-1944: trombone, dance band leader.
Charles Mingus, 1922-1979: bass, composer, combo leader.
Thelonious Monk, 1920-1982: piano, composer, combo leader; a developer of bop.
Wes Montgomery, 1925-1971: guitar.
"Jelly Roll" Morton, 1885-1941: composer, piano, singer.
Bennie Moten, 1894-1935: piano; an early organizer of large jazz orchestras.
Gerry Mulligan, b. 1927: baritone sax, arranger, leader.
Turk Murphy, b. 1915: trombone, band leader.
Theodore "Fats" Navarro, 1923-1950: trumpet.
Red Nichols, 1905-1965: cornet, combo leader.
Red Norvo, b. 1908: vibes, band leader.
Anita O'Day, b. 1919: singer.
King Oliver, 1885-1938: cornet, band leader; teacher of Louis Armstrong.
Kid Ory, 1886-1973: trombone, "Muskrat Ramble".
Charlie "Bird" Parker, 1920-1955: alto sax, composer; rated by many as the greatest jazz improviser.
Art Pepper, 1925-1983: alto sax.
Oscar Peterson, b 1925: piano, composer, combo leader.
Oscar Pettiford, 1922-1960: a leading bassist in the bop era.
Bud Powell, 1924-1966: piano; modern jazz pioneer.
Sun Ra, b. 1915?: big band leader, pianist, composer.
Gertrude "Ma" Rainey, 1886-1939: blues singer.
Don Redman, 1900-1964: composer, arranger; pioneer in the evolution of the large orchestra.
Django Reinhardt, 1910-1953: guitar; Belgian gypsy, first European to influence American jazz.
Buddy Rich, b. 1917: drums, band leader.
Max Roach, b. 1925: drums.
Sonny Rollins, b. 1929: tenor sax.
Frank Rosolino, 1926-1978: trombone.
Jimmy Rushing, 1903-1972: blues singer.
George Russell, b. 1923: composer, piano.
Pee Wee Russell, 1906-1969: clarinet.
Artie Shaw, b. 1910: clarinet, combo leader.
George Shearing, b. 1919: piano, composer, "Lullaby of Birdland."
Horace Silver, b. 1928: piano, combo leader.
Zoot Sims, b 1925: tenor, alto sax; clarinet.
Zutty Singleton, 1898-1975: Dixieland drummer.
Bessie Smith, 1894-1937: blues singer.
Clarence "Pinetop" Smith, 1904-1929: piano, singer; pioneer of boogie woogie.
Willie "The Lion" Smith, 1897-1973: stride style pianist.
Muggsy Spanier, 1906-1967: cornet, band leader.
Billy Strayhorn, 1915-67: composer, piano.
Sonny Stitt, 1924-1982: alto, tenor sax.
Art Tatum, 1910-1956: piano; technical virtuoso.
Billy Taylor, b. 1921: piano, composer.
Cecil Taylor, b. 1933: piano, composer.
Jack Teagarden, 1905-1964: trombone, singer.
Dave Tough, 1908-1948: drums.
Lennie Tristano, 1919-1978: piano, composer.
Joe Turner, b. 1911: blues singer.
Joe Turner, b. 1907: stride piano.
McCoy Tyner, b. 1938: piano, composer.
Sarah Vaughan, b. 1924: singer.
Joe Venuti, 1904-1978: first great jazz violinist.
Thomas "Fats" Waller, 1904-1943: piano, singer, composer. "Ain't Misbehavin' ".
Dinah Washington, 1924-1963: singer.
Chick Webb, 1902-1939: band leader, drums.
Ben Webster, b. 1909: tenor sax.
Paul Whiteman, 1890-1967: orchestra leader; a major figure in the introduction of jazz to a large audience.
Charles "Cootie" Williams, b. 1908: trumpet, band leader.
Mary Lou Williams, 1914-1981: piano, composer.
Teddy Wilson, b. 1912: piano, composer.
Kai Winding, 1922-1983: trombone, composer.
Jimmy Yancey, 1894-1951: piano.
Lester "Pres" Young, 1909-1959: tenor sax, composer: a bop pioneer.

Rock & Roll Notables

For more than a quarter of a century, rock & roll has been an important force in American popular culture. The following individuals or groups have made a significant impact. Next to each is an associated single record or record album.

Adam and the Ants: "Goody Two Shoes"
Alabama: "Tennessee River"
The Allman Brothers Band: "Ramblin' Man"
America: "A Horse With No Name"
The Animals: "House of the Rising Sun"
Paul Anka: "Lonely Boy"
The Association: "Cherish"
Frankie Avalon: "Venus"
The Band: "Music from Big Pink"
The Beach Boys: "Surfin' U.S.A."
The Beatles: "Hey Jude"
The Bee Gees: "Stayin' Alive"
Pat Benatar: "Hit Me With Your Best Shot"
Chuck Berry: "Sweet Little Sixteen"
The Big Bopper: "Chantilly Lace"
Blind Faith: "Can't Find My Way Home"
Blondie: "Heart of Glass"
Blood, Sweat and Tears: "Spinning Wheel"
Gary "U.S." Bonds: "Quarter to Three"
Booker T. and the MGs: "Green Onions"
David Bowie: "Space Oddity"
James Brown: "Papa's Got a Brand New Bag"
Jackson Browne: "Doctor My Eyes"
Buffalo Springfield: "For What It's Worth"
Canned Heat: "Going Up the Country"
The Cars: "Shake It Up"
Ray Charles: "Georgia on My Mind"
Cheap Trick: "I Want You to Want Me"
Chubby Checker: "The Twist"
Chicago: "Saturday in the Park"
Eric Clapton: "Layla"
The Clash: "Combat Rock"
The Coasters: "Yakety Yak"
Sam Cooke: "You Send Me"
Alice Cooper: "School's Out"
Elvis Costello: "Less Than Zero"
John Cougar Mellencamp: "Hurt So Good"
Cream: "Sunshine of Your Love"
Credence Clearwater Revival: "Proud Mary"
Jim Croce: "Bad, Bad Leroy Brown"
Crosby, Stills, Nash and Young: "Suite: Judy Blue Eyes"
The Crystals: "Da Doo Ron Ron"
Culture Club: Colour by Numbers
Danny and the Juniors: "At the Hop"
Spencer Davis Group: "Gimme Some Lovin' "
Def Leppard: "Photograph"
Devo: "Whip It"
Bo Diddley: "Who Do You Love?"
Dion and the Belmonts: "A Teenager in Love"
Fats Domino: "Blueberry Hill"
The Doobie Brothers: Minute by Minute
The Doors: "Light My Fire"
The Drifters: "Save the Last Dance for Me"
Duran Duran: "Hungry Like the Wolf"
Bob Dylan: "Like a Rolling Stone"
The Eagles: "Hotel California"
Earth, Wind and Fire: "Shining Star"
The Electric Light Orchestra: "Telephone Line"
Emerson, Lake and Palmer: "From the Beginning"
Everly Brothers: "Wake Up Little Susie"
Jose Feliciano: "Light My Fire"
The Five Satins: "In the Still of the Night"
Fleetwood Mac: Rumours
Dan Fogelberg: The Innocent Age
The Four Seasons: "Sherry"
The Four Tops: "I Can't Help Myself"
Aretha Franklin: "Respect"
Marvin Gaye: "I Heard It through the Grapevine"
The J. Geils Band: Freeze-Frame
Genesis: "Misunderstanding"
Grand Funk Railroad: "We're an American Band"
The Grateful Dead: "Truckin' "
Bill Haley and the Comets: "Rock Around the Clock"
Hall and Oates: "Rich Girl"
Jimi Hendrix: Are You Experienced?
Buddy Holly and the Crickets: "That'll Be the Day"
Janis Ian: "At Seventeen"
The Isley Brothers: "It's Your Thing"
The Jackson 5/The Jacksons: "I'll Be There"
Michael Jackson: "Beat It"
Jay and the Americans: "This Magic Moment"
The Jefferson Airplane/Jefferson Starship: "White Rabbit"
Jethro Tull: Aqualung
Billy Joel: "Uptown Girl"
Elton John: "Your Song"

Janis Joplin: "Me and Bobby McGee"
Carole King: Tapestry
Kiss: "Beth"
Gladys Knight and the Pips: "Midnight Train to Georgia"
Led Zeppelin: "Stairway to Heaven"
Brenda Lee: "I'm Sorry"
Jerry Lee Lewis: "Whole Lotta Shakin' Going On"
Little Anthony and the Imperials: "Tears on My Pillow"
Little Richard: "Tutti Frutti"
Lovin Spoonful: "Do You Believe in Magic?"
Frankie Lymon: "Why Do Fools Fall in Love?"
Lynyrd Skynyrd: "Freebird"
The Mamas and the Papas: "Monday, Monday"
Manfred Mann: "Do Wah Diddy Diddy"
Bob Marley: "Roots, Rock, Reggae"
Martha and the Vandellas: "Dancin' in the Streets"
The Marvelettes: "Please Mr. Postman"
Meat Loaf: "Two Out of Three Ain't Bad"
Men at Work: "Who Can It Be Now?"
Steve Miller Band: "Abracadabra"
Joni Mitchell: Ladies of the Canyon
The Monkees: "I'm a Believer"
Moody Blues: "Nights in White Satin"
Rick Nelson: "Hello Mary Lou"
Roy Orbison: "Oh Pretty Woman"
Ozzy Osbourne: "You Can't Kill Rock 'n' Roll"
Pink Floyd: Dark Side of the Moon
Poco: Deliverin'
The Police: "Every Breath You Take"
Iggy Pop: Zombie Birdhouse
Elvis Presley: "Love Me Tender"
The Pretenders: Learning to Crawl
Lloyd Price: "Stagger Lee"
Procul Harum: "A Whiter Shade of Pale"
Gary Puckett and the Union Gap: "Young Girl"
Queen: "Bohemian Rhapsody"
The Ramones: "Rockaway Beach"
The Rascals: "Good Lovin' "
Otis Redding: "The Dock of the Bay"
Lou Reed: "Walk on the Wild Side"
REO Speedwagon: High-Infidelity
Paul Revere and the Raiders: "Kicks"
Righteous Brothers: "You've Lost that Lovin' Feeling"
Johnny Rivers: "Poor Side of Town"
Smokey Robinson and the Miracles: "Ooh Baby Baby"
The Rolling Stones: "Satisfaction"
The Ronettes: "Be My Baby"
Linda Ronstadt: "You're No Good"
Todd Rundgren: "Hello It's Me"
Sam and Dave: "Soul Man"
Santana: "Soul Sacrifice"
Neil Sedaka: "Breaking Up is Hard to Do"
Bob Seger: "Shame on the Moon"
The Sex Pistols: "God Save the Queen"
Del Shannon: "Runaway"
The Shirelles: "Soldier Boy"
Simon and Garfunkel: "Bridge Over Troubled Water"
Carly Simon: "You're So Vain"
Sly and the Family Stone: "Everyday People"
Patti Smith: "Because the Night"
Southside Johnny and the Asbury Jukes: This Time
Dusty Springfield: "You Don't Have to Say You Love Me"
Bruce Springsteen: Born to Run
Steely Dan: "Rikki Don't Lose That Number"
Steppenwolf: "Born to Be Wild"
Cat Stevens: "Wild World"
Rod Stewart: "Maggie Mae"
Donna Summer: "Bad Girls"
The Supremes: "Stop! In the Name of Love"
Talking Heads: Speaking in Tongues
James Taylor: "You've Got a Friend"
The Temptations: "My Girl"
Three Dog Night: "Joy to the World"
Traffic: "Feelin' Alright"
Ike and Tina Turner: "Proud Mary"
The Turtles: "Happy Together"
Van Halen: "Jump"
Dionne Warwick: "I'll Never Fall in Love Again"
Mary Wells: "My Guy"
The Who: "My Generation"
Jackie Wilson: "That's Why"
Stevie Wonder: "You Are the Sunshine of My Life"
The Yardbirds: "For Your Love"
Yes: "Roundabout"
Frank Zappa/Mothers of Invention: Sheik Yerbouti

Original Names of Selected Entertainers

Edie Adams: Elizabeth Edith Enke
Eddie Albert: Edward Albert Heimberger
Alan Alda: Alphonso D'Abruzzo
Fred Allen: John Sullivan
Woody Allen: Allen Konigsberg
Julie Andrews: Julia Wells
Eve Arden: Eunice Quedens
Beatrice Arthur: Bernice Frankel
Jean Arthur: Gladys Greene
Fred Astaire: Frederick Austerlitz
Lauren Bacall: Betty Joan Perske
Anne Bancroft: Anna Maria Italiano
Brigitte Bardot: Camille Javal
Tony Bennett: Anthony Benedetto
Busby Berkeley: William Berkeley Enos
Jack Benny: Benjamin Kubelsky
Robert Blake: Michael Gubitosi
Dirk Bogarde: Derek Van der Bogaerd
Victor Borge: Borge Rosenbaum
Fanny Brice: Fanny Borach
Charles Bronson: Charles Buchinski
Mel Brooks: Melvin Kaminsky
George Burns: Nathan Birnbaum
Ellen Burstyn: Edna Gilhooley
Richard Burton: Richard Jenkins
Red Buttons: Aaron Chwatt
Michael Caine: Maurice Micklewhite
Maria Callas: Maria Kalogeropoulos
Diahann Carroll: Carol Diahann Johnson
Cyd Charisse: Tula Finklea
Chubby Checker: Ernest Evans
Cher: Cherilyn Sarkisian
Claudette Colbert: Lily Chauchoin
Michael Connors: Kreker Ohanian
Robert Conrad: Conrad Robert Falk
Howard Cosell: Howard Cohen
Alice Cooper: Vincent Furnier
Elvis Costello: Declan Patrick McManus
Joan Crawford: Lucille Le Sueur
Tony Curtis: Bernard Schwartz
Rodney Dangerfield: Jacob Cohen
Bobby Darin: Walden Waldo Cassotto
Doris Day: Doris von Kappelhoff
Yvonne De Carlo: Peggy Middleton
Sandra Dee: Alexandra Zuck
John Denver: Henry John Deutschendorf Jr.
Bo Derek: Cathleen Collins
John Derek: Derek Harris
Angie Dickinson: Angeline Brown
Melvyn Douglas: Melvyn Hesselberg
Bob Dylan: Robert Zimmerman
Barbara Eden: Barbara Huffman
Ron Ely: Ronald Pierce
Chad Everett: Raymond Cramton
Douglas Fairbanks: Douglas Ullman
Morgan Fairchild: Patsy McClenny
Alice Faye: Ann Leppert
W.C. Fields: William Claude Dukenfield
Peter Finch: William Mitchell
Joan Fontaine: Joan de Havilland
John Forsythe: John Freund
Redd Foxx : John Sanford
Anthony Franciosa: Anthony Papaleo
Arlene Francis: Arlene Kazanjian
Connie Francis: Concetta Franconero
Greta Garbo: Greta Gustafsson
Judy Garland: Frances Gumm
James Garner: James Baumgardner
Bobbie Gentry: Roberta Streeter
Stewart Granger: James Stewart
Cary Grant: Archibald Leach
Joel Grey: Joe Katz
Buddy Hackett: Leonard Hacker
Jon Hall: Charles Locher
Jean Harlow: Harlean Carpentier
Helen Hayes: Helen Brown
Rita Hayworth: Margarita Cansino
William Holden: William Beedle
Judy Holliday: Judith Tuvim
Harry Houdini: Ehrich Weiss
Leslie Howard: Leslie Stainer
Rock Hudson: Roy Scherer Jr.
Engelbert Humperdinck: Arnold Dorsey
Kim Hunter: Janet Cole
Betty Hutton: Betty Thornberg
David Janssen: David Meyer
Elton John: Reginald Dwight

Jennifer Jones: Phyllis Isley
Tom Jones: Thomas Woodward
Louis Jourdan: Louis Gendre
Boris Karloff: William Henry Pratt
Diane Keaton: Diane Hall
Carole King: Carole Klein
Ted Knight: Tadeus Wladyslaw Konopka
Cheryl Ladd: Cheryl Stoppelmoor
Veronica Lake: Constance Ockleman
Michael Landon: Eugene Orowitz
Robert Lansing: Robert Broom
Mario Lanza: Alfredo Cocozza
Stan Laurel: Arthur Jefferson
Steve Lawrence: Sidney Leibowitz
Gypsy Rose Lee: Rose Louise Hovick
Peggy Lee: Norma Egstrom
Janet Leigh: Jeanette Morrison
Vivian Leigh: Vivien Hartley
Jerry Lewis: Joseph Levitch
Hal Linden: Harold Lipshitz
Jack Lord: John Joseph Ryan
Sophia Loren: Sophia Scicoloni
Peter Lorre: Laszio Lowenstein
Myrna Loy: Myrna Williams
Shirley MacLaine: Shirley Beaty
Lee Majors: Harvey Lee Yeary 2d
Karl Malden: Malden Sekulovich
Jayne Mansfield: Vera Jane Palmer
Fredric March: Frederick Bickel
Dean Martin: Dino Crocetti
Tony Martin: Alvin Morris
Elaine May: Elaine Berlin
Ethel Merman: Ethel Zimmerman
Ray Milland: Reginald Truscott-Jones
Ann Miller: Lucille Collier
Marilyn Monroe: Norma Jean Mortenson, (later) Baker
Yves Montand: Ivo Levi
Garry Moore: Thomas Garrison Morfit
Harry Morgan: Harry Bratsburg
Mike Nichols: Michael Igor Peschowsky
Sheree North: Dawn Bethel
Hugh O'Brian: Hugh Krampke
Maureen O'Hara: Maureen Fitzsimmons
Jack Palance: Walter Palanuik
Lilli Palmer: Lilli Peiser
Bert Parks: Bert Jacobson
Minnie Pearl: Sarah Ophelia Cannon
Bernadette Peters: Bernadette Lazzaro
Mary Pickford: Gladys Smith
Stephanie Powers: Stefania Federkiewcz
Robert Preston: Robert Preston Meservey
Della Reese: Delloreese Patricia Early
Joan Rivers: Joan Sandra Molinsky
Ginger Rogers: Virginia McMath
Roy Rogers: Leonard Slye
Mickey Rooney: Joe Yule Jr.
Lillian Russell: Helen Leonard
Susan St. James: Susan Miller
Randolph Scott: Randolph Crance
Jane Seymour: Joyce Frankenberg
Omar Sharif: Michael Shalhoub
Martin Sheen: Ramon Estevez
Beverly Sills: Belle Silverman
Suzanne Somers: Suzanne Mahoney
Ann Sothern: Harriette Lake
Kim Stanley: Patricia Reid
Barbara Stanwyck: Ruby Stevens
Jean Stapleton: Jeanne Murray
Ringo Starr: Richard Starkey
Connie Stevens: Concetta Ingolia
Donna Summers: LaDonna Gaines
Robert Taylor: Spangler Arlington Brugh
Danny Thomas: Amos Jacobs
Sophie Tucker: Sophia Kalish
Conway Twitty: Harold Lloyd Jenkins
Rudolph Valentino: Rudolpho D'Antonguolla
Frankie Valli: Frank Castelluccio
Nancy Walker: Myrtle Swoyer
David Wayne: Wayne McMeekan
John Wayne: Marion Morrison
Raquel Welch: Raquel Tejada
Gene Wilder: Jerome Silberman
Shelly Winters: Shirley Schrift
Stevie Wonder: Stevland Morris
Natalie Wood: Natasha Gurdin
Jane Wyman: Sarah Jane Fulks
Gig Young: Byron Barr

Entertainment Personalities — Where and When Born

Actors, Actresses, Dancers, Musicians, Producers, Radio-TV Performers, Singers

Name	Birthplace	Born
Abbott, George	Forestville, N.Y.	6/25/87
Abel, Walter	St. Paul, Minn.	6/6/98
Acuff, Roy	Maynardville, Tenn.	9/15/03
Adams, Don	New York, N.Y.	4/19/26
Adams, Edie	Kingston, Pa.	4/16/29
Adams, Joey	New York, N.Y.	1/6/11
Adams, Julie	Waterloo, Ia.	10/17/28
Adams, Mason	New York, N.Y.	2/26/19
Adams, Maud	Lulea, Sweden	2/12/45
Adler, Larry	Baltimore, Md.	2/10/14
Adler, Luther	New York, N.Y.	5/4/03
Agutter, Jenny	London, England	12/20/52
Aherne, Brian	Worcestershire, England.	5/2/02
Ailey, Alvin	Rogers, Tex.	1/5/31
Aimee, Anouk	Paris, France	4/27/32
Akins, Claude	Nelson, Ga.	5/25/18
Albanese, Licia	Bari, Italy	7/22/13
Alberghetti, Anna Maria	Pesaro, Italy	5/15/36
Albert, Eddie	Rock Island, Ill.	4/22/08
Albert, Edward	Los Angeles, Cal.	2/20/51
Albright, Lola	Akron, Oh.	7/20/24
Alda, Alan	New York, N.Y.	1/28/36
Alda, Robert	New York, N.Y.	2/26/14
Alexander, Jane	Boston, Mass.	10/28/39
Allen, Debbie	Houston, Tex.	1/16/-
Allen, Mel	Birmingham, Ala.	2/14/13
Allen, Peter	Tenderfield, Australia	2/10/44
Allen, Steve	New York, N.Y.	12/26/21
Allen, Woody	Brooklyn, N.Y.	12/1/35
Allison, Fran	LaPorte City, Ia.	—
Allman, Gregg	Nashville, Tenn.	12/7/47
Allyson, June	Lucerne, N.Y.	10/7/17
Alpert, Herb	Los Angeles, Cal.	3/31/35
Altman, Robert	Kansas City, Mo.	2/20/25
Ameche, Don	Kenosha, Wis.	5/31/08
Ames, Ed	Boston, Mass.	7/9/27
Ames, Leon	Portland, Ind.	1/20/03
Amos, John	Newark, N.J.	12/27/39
Amsterdam, Morey	Chicago, Ill.	12/14/14
Anderson, Ian	Dunfermline, Scotland	8/10/47
Anderson, Judith	Adelaide, Australia	2/10/98
Anderson, Loni	St. Paul, Minn.	8/5/45
Anderson, Lynn	Grand Forks, N.D.	9/26/47
Anderson, Marian	Philadelphia, Pa.	2/17/02
Anderson, Mary	Birmingham, Ala.	1922
Anderson, Melissa Sue	Berkeley, Cal.	9/26/62
Anderson, Richard	Long Branch, N.J.	8/8/26
Andersson, Bibi	Stockholm, Sweden	11/11/35
Andress, Ursula	Switzerland	3/19/36
Andrews, Dana	Collins, Miss.	1/1/09
Andrews, Edward	Griffin, Ga.	10/9/15
Andrews, Julie	Walton, England	10/1/35
Andrews, Maxene	Minneapolis, Minn.	1/3/18
Andrews, Patty	Minneapolis, Minn.	2/16/20
Anka, Paul	Ottawa, Ont.	7/30/41
Ann-Margret	Stockholm, Sweden	4/28/41
Arden, Eve	Mill Valley, Cal.	4/30/12
Arkin, Alan	New York, N.Y.	3/26/34
Arnaz, Desi	Santiago, Cuba	3/2/17
Arnaz, Desi Jr.	Los Angeles, Cal.	1/19/53
Arnaz, Lucie	Hollywood, Cal.	7/17/51
Arness, James	Minneapolis, Minn.	5/26/23
Arnold, Eddy	Henderson, Tenn.	5/15/18
Arrau, Claudio	Chillau, Chile	2/6/03
Arroyo, Martina	New York, N.Y.	2/2/37
Arthur, Beatrice	New York, N.Y.	5/13/23
Arthur, Jean	New York, N.Y.	10/17/08
Ashley, Elizabeth	Ocala, Fla.	8/30/41
Asner, Ed	Kansas City, Mo.	11/15/29
Astaire, Fred	Omaha, Neb.	5/10/99
Astin, John	Baltimore, Md.	3/30/30
Astor, Mary	Quincy, Ill.	5/3/06
Atkins, Chet	Luttrell, Tenn.	6/20/24
Attenborough, Richard	Cambridge, England	8/29/23
Auberjonois, Rene	New York, N.Y.	6/1/40
Aumont, Jean-Pierre	Paris, France	1/5/09
Autry, Gene	Tioga, Tex.	9/29/11
Avalon, Frankie	Philadelphia, Pa.	9/8/40
Aykroyd, Dan	Ottawa, Ont.	7/1/52
Ayres, Lew	Minneapolis, Minn.	12/28/08

Name	Birthplace	Born
Aznavour, Charles	Paris, France	5/22/24
Bacall, Lauren	New York, N.Y.	9/16/24
Bach, Catherine	Warren, Oh.	3/1/54
Backus, Jim	Cleveland, Oh.	2/25/13
Baddeley, Hermione	Shropshire, England	11/13/06
Baez, Joan	Staten Island, N.Y.	1/9/41
Bailey, Pearl	Newport News, Va.	3/29/18
Bain, Barbara	Chicago, Ill.	9/13/34
Bain, Conrad	Lethbridge, Alta.	2/4/23
Baio, Scott	Brooklyn, N.Y.	9/22/61
Baird, Bil	Grand Island, Neb.	8/15/04
Baker, Carroll	Johnstown, Pa.	5/28/31
Baker, Joe Don	Groesbeck, Tex.	2/12/36
Baker, Kenny	Monrovia, Cal.	9/30/12
Ball, Lucille	Jamestown, N.Y.	8/6/11
Ballard, Kaye	Cleveland, Oh.	11/20/26
Balsam, Martin	New York, N.Y.	11/4/19
Bancroft, Anne	New York, N.Y.	9/17/31
Barber, Red	Columbus, Miss.	2/17/08
Bardot, Brigitte	Paris, France	9/28/34
Bari, Lynn	Roanoke, Va.	12/18/17
Barker, Bob	Darrington, Wash.	12/12/23
Barnes, Priscilla	Ft. Dix, N.J.	12/7/-
Barrault, Jean-Louis	Vesinet, France	9/8/10
Barrie, Barbara	Chicago, Ill.	5/23/31
Barrie, Mona	London, England	12/18/09
Barry, Gene	New York, N.Y.	6/4/22
Bartholomew, Freddie	London, England	3/28/24
Bartok, Eva	Budapest, Hungary	6/18/29
Baryshnikov, Mikhail	Riga, Latvia	1/28/48
Basehart, Richard	Zanesville, Oh.	8/31/19
Basinger, Kim	Athens, Ga.	12/8/53
Bassey, Shirley	Cardiff, Wales.	1/8/37
Bates, Alan	Allestree, England	2/17/34
Baxter, Anne	Michigan City, Ind.	5/7/23
Baxter-Birney, Meredith	Los Angeles, Cal.	6/21/47
Beal, John	Joplin, Mo.	8/13/09
Bean, Orson	Burlington, Vt.	7/22/28
Beatty, Ned	Louisville, Ky.	7/6/37
Beatty, Robert	Hamilton, Ont.	10/19/09
Beatty, Warren	Richmond, Va.	3/30/37
Bedelia, Bonnie	New York, N.Y.	3/25/46
Bee Gees		
Gibb, Barry	Manchester, England.	9/1/46
Gibb, Robin	" "	12/22/49
Gibb, Maurice	" "	12/22/49
Beery, Noah Jr.	New York, N.Y.	8/10/16
Belafonte, Harry	New York, N.Y.	3/1/27
Bel Geddes, Barbara	New York, N.Y.	10/31/22
Bellamy, Ralph	Chicago, Ill.	6/17/04
Belmondo, Jean-Paul	Neuilly-sur-Seine, France	4/9/33
Benatar, Pat	Brooklyn, N.Y.	1/10/53
Benjamin, Richard	New York, N.Y.	5/22/38
Bennett, Joan	Palisades, N.J.	2/27/10
Bennett, Michael	Buffalo, N.Y.	4/8/43
Bennett, Tony	New York, N.Y.	8/3/26
Benson, George	Pittsburgh, Pa.	3/22/43
Benson, Robby	Dallas, Tex.	1/21/55
Bentley, John	Warwickshire, England.	12/2/16
Bergen, Candice	Beverly Hills, Cal.	5/9/46
Bergen, Polly	Knoxville, Tenn.	7/4/30
Bergerac, Jacques	Biarritz, France	5/26/27
Bergman, Ingmar	Uppsala, Sweden.	7/14/18
Bergner, Elisabeth	Vienna, Austria	8/22/00
Berle, Milton	New York, N.Y.	7/12/08
Berlinger, Warren	Brooklyn, N.Y.	8/31/37
Berman, Shelley	Chicago, Ill.	2/3/26
Bernardi, Herschel	New York, N.Y.	10/20/23
Bernstein, Leonard	Lawrence, Mass.	8/25/18
Berry, Chuck	San Jose, Cal.	1/15/26
Berry, Ken	Moline, Ill.	
Bertinelli, Valerie	Wilmington, Del.	4/23/6
Bikel, Theodore	Vienna, Austria	5/2/2
Birney, David	Washington, D.C.	4/23/3
Bishop, Joey	Bronx, N.Y.	2/3/1
Bisoglio, Val	New York, N.Y.	5/7/2
Bisset, Jacqueline	Weybridge, England	9/13/4
Bixby, Bill	San Francisco, Cal.	1/22/3

Name	Birthplace	Born	Name	Birthplace	Born
Black, Karen	Park Ridge, Ill.	7/1/42	Carlin, George	New York, N.Y.	5/12/37
Blaine, Vivian	Newark, N.J.	11/21/23	Carlisle, Kitty	New Orleans, La.	9/3/15
Blair, Linda	St. Louis, Mo.	1/22/59	Carmen, Eric	Cleveland, Oh.	8/11/49
Blake, Amanda	Buffalo, N.Y.	2/20/31	Carmichael, Ian	Hull, England	6/18/20
Blake, Robert	Nutley, N.J.	9/18/34	Carpenter, John	Carthage, N.Y.	1/16/48
Blanc, Mel	San Francisco, Cal.	5/30/08	Carney, Art	Mt. Vernon, N.Y.	11/4/18
Bloom, Claire	London, England	2/15/31	Carnovsky, Morris	St. Louis, Mo.	9/5/97
Blyth, Ann	Mt. Kisco, N.Y.	8/16/28	Caron, Leslie	Boulogne, France	7/1/31
Bogarde, Dirk	London, England	3/28/20	Carr, Vikki	El Paso, Tex.	7/19/41
Bogdanovich, Peter	Kingston, N.Y.	7/30/39	Carradine, David	Hollywood, Cal.	12/8/36
Bolger, Ray	Dorchester, Mass.	1/10/04	Carradine, John	New York, N.Y.	2/5/06
Bono, Sonny	Detroit, Mich.	2/16/40	Carradine, Keith	San Mateo, Cal.	8/8/49
Booke, Sorrell	Buffalo, N.Y.	1/4/30	Carreras, Jose	Barcelona, Spain	12/5/47
Boone, Debby	Hackensack, N.J.	9/22/56	Carroll, Diahann	Bronx, N.Y.	7/17/35
Boone, Pat	Jacksonville, Fla.	6/1/34	Carroll, Madeleine	W. Bromwich, England	2/26/06
Booth, Shirley	New York, N.Y.	8/30/07	Carroll, Pat	Shreveport, La.	5/5/27
Borge, Victor	Copenhagen, Denmark	1/3/09	Carson, Johnny	Corning, Ia.	10/23/25
Borgnine, Ernest	Hamden, Conn.	1/24/17	Carter, Jack	New York, N.Y.	6/24/23
Bosley, Tom	Chicago, Ill.	10/1/27	Carter, June	Maces Spring, Va.	6/23/29
Bossom, Barbara	Charleroi, Pa.	11/1/39	Carter, Lynda	Phoenix, Ariz.	7/24/51
Bottoms, Joseph	Santa Barbara, Cal.	4/22/54	Carter, Nell	Birmingham, Ala.	9/13/48
Bottoms, Timothy	Santa Barbara, Cal.	8/30/51	Casadesus, Gaby	Marseilles, France	1902
Bowie, David	London, England	1/8/47	Cash, Johnny	Kingsland, Ark.	2/26/32
Boxleitner, Bruce	Elgin, Ill.	5/12/50	Cass, Peggy	Boston, Mass.	5/21/24
Boyle, Peter	Philadelphia, Pa.	10/18/33	Cassavetes, John	New York, N.Y.	12/9/29
Bracken, Eddie	New York, N.Y.	2/7/20	Cassidy, David	New York, N.Y.	4/12/50
Brand, Neville	Kewanee, Ill.	8/13/21	Cassidy, Shaun	Los Angeles, Cal.	9/27/58
Brando, Marlon	Omaha, Neb.	4/3/24	Castellano, Richard	New York, N.Y.	9/4/33
Brazzi, Rossano	Bologna, Italy	9/18/16	Caulfield, Joan	West Orange, N.J.	6/1/22
Brennan, Eileen	Los Angeles, Cal.	9/3/35	Cavallaro, Carmen	New York, N.Y.	5/6/13
Brenner, David	Philadelphia, Pa.	1945	Cavett, Dick	Gibbon, Neb.	11/19/36
Brewer, Teresa	Toledo, Oh.	5/7/32	Chamberlain, Richard	Beverly Hills, Cal.	3/31/35
Brian, David	New York, N.Y.	8/5/14	Champion, Marge	Los Angeles, Cal.	9/2/23
Bridges, Beau	Hollywood, Cal.	12/9/41	Channing, Carol	Seattle, Wash.	1/31/23
Bridges, Jeff	Los Angeles, Cal.	12/4/49	Channing, Stockard	New York, N.Y.	2/13/44
Bridges, Lloyd	San Leandro, Cal.	1/15/13	Chaplin, Geraldine	Santa Monica, Cal.	7/31/44
Bridges, Todd	San Francisco, Cal.	5/27/65	Chaplin, Sydney	Beverly Hills, Cal.	3/31/26
Brisebois, Danielle	New York, N.Y.	6/28/69	Charisse, Cyd	Amarillo, Tex.	3/8/21
Brolin, James	Los Angeles, Cal.	7/18/42	Charles, Ray	Albany, Ga.	9/23/30
Bronson, Charles	Scooptown, Pa.	11/3/22	Charo	Murcia, Spain	1/15/51
Brooks, Louise	Cherryvale, Kan.	11/14/05	Chase, Chevy	New York, N.Y.	10/8/43
Brooks, Mel	New York, N.Y.	6/28/26	Checker, Chubby	Philadelphia, Pa.	10/3/41
Brooks, Stephen	Columbus, Oh.	1942	Cher	El Centro, Cal.	5/20/46
Brosnan, Pierce	Co. Meath, Ireland	5/16/52	Chong, Thomas	Edmonton, Alta.	5/24/38
Brown, James	Pulaski, Tenn.	6/17/28	Christie, Julie	Assam, India	4/14/41
Brown, Jim	St. Simons Island, Ga.	2/17/36	Christopher, Jordan	Youngstown, Oh.	10/23/41
Brown, Les	Reinerton, Pa.	3/14/12	Christopher, William	Evanston, Ill.	10/20/32
Brown, Ray	Pittsburgh, Pa.	10/13/26	Christy, June	Springfield, Ill.	11/20/25
Brown, Tom	New York, N.Y.	1/6/13	Claire, Ina	Washington, D.C.	1892
Browne, Roscoe Lee	Woodbury, N.J.	1925	Clapton, Eric	Surrey, England	3/30/45
Bruce, Carol	Great Neck, N.Y.	11/15/19	Clark, Dane	New York, N.Y.	2/18/15
Bryant, Anita	Barnsdall, Okla.	3/25/40	Clark, Dick	Mt. Vernon, N.Y.	11/30/29
Brynner, Yul	Sakhalin, Japan	7/11/20	Clark, Petula	Ewell, Surrey, England	11/15/32
Bujold, Genevieve	Montreal, Que.	7/1/42	Clark, Roy	Meherrin, Va.	4/15/33
Bumbry, Grace	St. Louis, Mo.	1/4/37	Clark, Susan	Sarnia, Ont.	3/8/44
Burghoff, Gary	Bristol, Conn.	5/24/-	Clayburgh, Jill	New York, N.Y.	4/30/44
Burke, Paul	New Orleans, La.	7/21/26	Clary, Robert	Paris, France	3/1/26
Burnett, Carol	San Antonio, Tex.	4/26/36	Cliburn, Van	Shreveport, La.	7/12/34
Burns, George	New York, N.Y.	1/20/96	Clooney, Rosemary	Maysville, Ky.	5/23/28
Burr, Raymond	New Westminster, B.C.	5/21/17	Close, Glenn	Greenwich, Conn.	1947
Burstyn, Ellen	Detroit, Mich.	12/7/32	Coburn, James	Laurel, Neb.	8/31/28
Burton, LaVar	Landsthul, W. Germany	2/16/57	Coca, Imogene	Philadelphia, Pa.	11/18/08
Burton, Richard	South Wales	11/10/25	Coco, James	New York, N.Y.	3/21/30
Bushell, Anthony	Kent, England	5/19/04	Cohen, Myron	Grodno, Poland	1902
Busey, Gary	Goose Creek, Tex.	6/29/44	Colbert, Claudette	Paris, France	9/18/05
Buttons, Red	New York, N.Y.	2/5/19	Cole, Natalie	Los Angeles, Cal.	2/6/50
Buzzi, Ruth	Westerly, R.I.	7/24/36	Coleman, Dabney	Austin, Tex.	1/3/32
			Coleman, Gary	Zion, Ill.	2/8/68
Caan, James	New York, N.Y.	3/26/39	Collins, Dorothy	Windsor, Ont.	11/18/26
Caballe, Montserrat	Barcelona, Spain	4/12/33	Collins, Joan	London, England	5/23/33
Caesar, Sid	Yonkers, N.Y.	9/8/22	Collins, Judy	Seattle, Wash.	5/1/39
Cagney, James	New York, N.Y.	7/17/99	Colonna, Jerry	Boston, Mass.	9/17/04
Caine, Michael	London, England	3/14/33	Comden, Betty	Brooklyn, N.Y.	5/3/19
Caldwell, Sarah	Maryville, Mo.	3/6/24	Como, Perry	Canonsburg, Pa.	5/18/12
Caldwell, Zoe	Melbourne, Australia	9/14/33	Conklin, Peggy	Dobbs Ferry, N.Y.	11/2/10
Calhoun, Rory	Los Angeles, Cal.	8/8/22	Conner, Nadine	Compton, Cal.	2/20/13
Callas, Charlie	Brooklyn, N.Y.	12/20/-	Connery, Sean	Edinburgh, Scotland	8/25/30
Calloway, Cab	Rochester, N.Y.	12/25/07	Conniff, Ray	Attleboro, Mass.	11/6/16
Campbell, Glen	Billstown, Ark.	4/22/36	Connors, Chuck	Brooklyn, N.Y.	4/10/21
Cannon, Dyan	Tacoma, Wash.	1/4/37	Connors, Mike	Fresno, Cal.	8/15/25
Cantrell, Lana	Sydney, Australia	8/7/43	Conrad, Robert	Chicago, Ill.	3/1/35
Capra, Frank	Palermo, Italy	5/18/97	Constantine, Michael	Reading, Pa.	5/22/27
Carey, Macdonald	Sioux City, Ia.	3/15/13	Conti, Tom	Paisley, Scotland	11/22/41
Carey, Phil	Hackensack, N.J.	7/15/25	Convy, Bert	St. Louis, Mo.	6/23/33
Carey, Ron	Newark, N.J.	12/11/35	Conway, Tim	Willoughby, Oh.	12/15/33
Cariou, Len	Winnipeg, Canada	9/30/39	Cook, Barbara	Atlanta, Ga.	10/25/27
Carle, Frankie	Providence, R.I.	3/25/03	Cook, Peter	Torquay, England	11/17/37

Name	Birthplace	Born
Cooke, Alistair	England	11/20/08
Coolidge, Rita	Nashville, Tenn.	5/1/45
Cooper, Alice	Detroit, Mich.	2/4/48
Cooper, Jackie	Los Angeles, Cal.	9/15/22
Coppola, Francis Ford	Detroit, Mich.	4/7/39
Corby, Ellen	Racine, Wis.	6/3/13
Corelli, Franco	Ancona, Italy	4/8/23
Corey, Jeff	New York, N.Y.	8/10/14
Cosby, Bill	Philadelphia, Pa.	7/12/37
Costello, Elvis	London, England	8/25/54
Cotten, Joseph	Petersburg, Va.	5/15/05
Courtenay, Tom	Hull, England	2/25/37
Craddock, Crash	Greensboro, N.C.	6/16/40
Crain, Jeanne	Barstow, Cal.	5/25/25
Crawford, Broderick	Philadelphia, Pa.	12/9/11
Crenna, Richard	Los Angeles, Cal.	11/30/27
Cronyn, Hume	London, Ont.	7/18/11
Crosby, Bob	Spokane, Wash.	8/25/13
Crosby, Cathy Lee	Los Angeles, Cal.	12/2/-
Crosby, David	Los Angeles, Cal.	8/14/41
Crosby, Kathryn	Houston, Tex.	11/25/33
Crosby, Norm	Boston, Mass.	1/15/27
Cross, Christopher	San Antonio, Tex.	5/3/51
Crothers, Scatman	Terre Haute, Ind.	5/23/10
Crystal, Billy	Long Beach, N.Y.	3/14/47
Cugat, Xavier	Barcelona, Spain	1/1/00
Cullen, Bill	Pittsburgh, Pa.	2/18/20
Cullum, John	Knoxville, Tenn.	3/2/30
Culp, Robert	Oakland, Cal.	8/16/30
Cummings, Constance	Seattle, Wash.	5/15/10
Cummings, Robert	Joplin, Mo.	6/9/10
Curtin, Phyllis	Clarksburg, W.Va.	12/3/30
Curtis, Jamie Lee	Los Angeles, Cal.	11/22/58
Curtis, Keene	Salt Lake City, Ut.	2/15/23
Curtis, Ken	Lamar, Col.	7/2/16
Curtis, Tony	New York, N.Y.	6/3/25
Cusack, Cyril	Durban, S. Africa	11/26/10
Cushing, Peter	Surrey, England	5/26/13
Dahl, Arlene	Minneapolis, Minn.	8/11/28
Dale, Jim	Rothwell, England	8/15/35
Dalrymple, Jean	Morristown, N.J.	9/2/10
Dalton, Abby	Las Vegas, Nev.	8/15/35
Daly, John	Johannesburg, S. Africa	2/20/14
Daly, Tyne	Madison, Wis.	2/21/47
Damone, Vic	Brooklyn, N.Y.	6/12/28
Dangerfield, Rodney	Babylon, N.Y.	1921
Daniels, Charlie	No. Carolina.	10/28/36
Daniels, William	Brooklyn, N.Y.	3/31/27
Danilova, Alexandra	Peterhof, Russia	11/20/07
Danner, Blythe	Philadelphia, Pa.	2/3/43
Danson, Ted	San Diego, Cal.	12/29/-
Danton, Ray	New York, N.Y.	9/19/31
Darby, Kim	Hollywood, Cal.	7/8/48
Darcel, Denise	Paris, France	9/8/25
Darren, James	Philadelphia, Pa.	6/8/36
Darrow, Henry	New York, N.Y.	1933
Da Silva, Howard	Cleveland, Oh.	5/4/09
Dassin, Jules	Middletown, Conn.	12/18/11
Davidson, John	Pittsburgh, Pa.	12/13/41
Davis, Ann B.	Schenectady, N.Y.	5/5/26
Davis, Bette	Lowell, Mass.	4/5/08
Davis, Clifton	Chicago, Ill.	10/4/45
Davis, Mac	Lubbock, Tex.	1/21/42
Davis, Ossie	Cogdell, Ga.	12/18/17
Davis, Sammy Jr.	New York, N.Y.	12/8/25
Davis, Skeeter	Dry Ridge, Ky.	12/30/31
Dawber, Pam	Detroit, Mich.	10/18/51
Dawn, Hazel	Ogden, Ut.	3/23/98
Dawson, Richard	Hampshire, England	11/20/32
Day, Dennis	New York, N.Y.	5/21/17
Day, Doris	Cincinnati, Oh.	4/3/24
Day, Laraine	Roosevelt, Ut.	10/13/20
Dean, Jimmy	Plainview, Tex.	8/10/28
De Camp, Rosemary	Prescott, Ariz.	11/14/10
DeCarlo, Yvonne	Vancouver, B.C.	9/1/22
Dee, Frances	Los Angeles, Cal.	11/26/07
Dee, Ruby	Cleveland, Oh.	10/27/23
Dee, Sandra	Bayonne, N.J.	4/29/42
Defore, Don	Cedar Rapids, Ia.	8/25/17
DeHaven, Gloria	Los Angeles, Cal.	7/23/25
de Havilland, Olivia	Tokyo, Japan	7/1/16
De Niro, Robert	New York, N.Y.	8/17/45
Dell, Gabriel	Barbados, BWI	10/7/19
Della Chiesa, Vivienne	Chicago, Ill.	10/9/20
Delon, Alain	Sceaux, France	11/8/35

Name	Birthplace	Born
DeLuise, Dom	Brooklyn, N.Y.	8/1/33
De Mille, Agnes	New York, N.Y.	1905
Deneuve, Catherine	Paris, France	10/22/43
Denning, Richard	Poughkeepsie, N.Y.	3/27/14
Dennis, Sandy	Hastings, Neb.	4/27/37
Denver, Bob	New Rochelle, N.Y.	1935
Denver, John	Roswell, N.M.	12/31/43
DePalma, Brian	Newark, N.J.	9/11/40
Derek, Bo	Long Beach, Cal.	11/20/56
Derek, John	Hollywood, Cal.	8/12/26
Dern, Bruce	Chicago, Ill.	6/4/36
Desmond, Johnny	Detroit, Mich.	11/14/21
Devane, William	Albany, N.Y.	9/5/37
DeVito, Danny	Neptune, N.J.	11/17/44
Dewhurst, Colleen	Montreal, Que.	6/3/26
DeWitt, Joyce	Wheeling, W.Va.	4/23/49
Dey, Susan	Pekin, Ill.	12/10/52
Diamond, Neil	Brooklyn, N.Y.	1/24/41
Dickinson, Angie	Kulm, N.D.	9/30/31
Dierkop, Charles	La Crosse, Wis.	9/11/36
Dietrich, Marlene	Berlin, Germany	12/27/01
Diller, Phyllis	Lima, Oh.	7/17/17
Dillman, Bradford	San Francisco, Cal.	4/14/30
Dillon, Matt	Westchester Co., N.Y.	2/18/64
Dixon, Ivan	New York, N.Y.	4/6/31
Domingo, Placido	Madrid, Spain	1/21/41
Domino, Fats	New Orleans, La.	2/26/28
Donahue, Phil	Cleveland, Oh.	12/21/35
Donahue, Troy	New York, N.Y.	1/27/36
Donald, James	Aberdeen, Scotland	5/18/17
Donovan	Glasgow, Scotland	5/10/43
d'Orsay, Fifi	Montreal, Que.	4/16/04
Douglas, Kirk	Amsterdam, N.Y.	12/9/18
Douglas, Michael	New Brunswick, N.J.	9/25/44
Douglas, Mike	Chicago, Ill.	8/11/25
Down, Leslie-Ann	London, England	3/17/54
Downey, Morton	Wallingford, Conn.	11/14/01
Downs, Hugh	Akron, Oh.	2/14/21
Doyle, David	Lincoln, Neb.	12/1/29
Dragon, Daryl	Los Angeles, Cal.	8/27/42
Drake, Alfred	Bronx, N.Y.	10/7/14
Drew, Ellen	Kansas City, Mo.	11/23/15
Dreyfuss, Richard	Brooklyn, N.Y.	10/29/47
Dru, Joanne	Logan, W.Va.	1/31/23
Duchin, Peter	New York, N.Y.	7/28/37
Duff, Howard	Bremerton, Wash.	11/24/17
Duffy, Patrick	Townsend, Mont.	3/17/49
Dufour, Val	New Orleans, La.	2/5/27
Duke, Patty	New York, N.Y.	12/14/46
Dullea, Keir	Cleveland, Oh.	5/30/36
Dunaway, Faye	Bascom, Fla.	1/14/41
Duncan, Sandy	Henderson, Tex.	2/20/46
Duncan, Todd	Danville, Ky.	2/12/00
Duncan, Vivian	Los Angeles, Cal.	6/17/02
Dunham, Katherine	Joliet, Ill.	6/22/10
Dunne, Irene	Louisville, Ky.	12/20/04
Dunnock, Mildred	Baltimore, Md.	1/25/04
Durbin, Deanna	Winnipeg, Man.	12/4/21
Durning, Charles	Highland Falls, N.Y.	2/28/23
Dussault, Nancy	Pensacola, Fla.	6/30/36
Duvall, Robert	San Diego, Cal.	1931
Duvall, Shelley	Houston, Tex.	1949
Dylan, Bob	Duluth, Minn.	5/24/41
Easton, Sheena	Glasgow, Scotland	4/27/59
Eastwood, Clint	San Francisco, Cal.	5/31/30
Ebsen, Buddy	Belleville, Ill.	4/2/08
Eckstine, Billy	Pittsburgh, Pa.	7/8/14
Edelman, Herb.	Brooklyn, N.Y.	11/5/33
Eden, Barbara	Tucson, Ariz.	8/23/34
Edwards, Blake	Tulsa, Okla.	7/26/22
Edwards, Ralph	Merino, Col.	6/13/13
Edwards, Vincent	Brooklyn, N.Y.	7/7/28
Egan, Richard	San Francisco, Cal.	7/29/23
Eggar, Samantha	London, England	3/5/39
Eichhorn, Lisa	Reading, Pa.	2/4/52
Ekberg, Anita	Malmo, Sweden	9/29/31
Ekland, Britt	Stockholm, Sweden	1942
Elam, Jack	Miami, Ariz.	11/13/16
Eldridge, Florence	Brooklyn, N.Y.	9/5/01
Elgart, Larry	New London, Conn.	3/20/22
Elgart, Les	New Haven, Conn.	1918
Elliott, Bob	Boston, Mass.	3/26/23
Elliott, Sam	Sacramento, Cal.	8/9/44
Erickson, Leif	Alameda, Cal.	10/27/11
Estrada, Erik	New York, N.Y.	3/16/49

Name	Birthplace	Born	Name	Birthplace	Born
Evans, Dale	Uvalde, Tex.	10/31/12	French, Victor	Santa Barbara, Cal.	12/4/34
Evans, Gene	Holbrook, Ariz.	7/11/24	Frick, Mr. (G. Werner)	Basel, Switzerland	4/21/15
Evans, Linda	Hartford, Conn.	11/18/42	Friedkin, William	Chicago, Ill.	8/29/39
Evans, Maurice	Dorchester, England	6/3/01	Frost, David	Tenterden, England	4/7/39
Evans, Robert	New York, N.Y.	6/29/30	Frye, David	Brooklyn, N.Y.	1934
Everett, Chad	South Bend, Ind.	6/11/37	Funicello, Annette	Utica, N.Y.	10/22/42
Everly, Don	Brownie, Ky.	2/1/37	Funt, Allen	New York, N.Y.	9/16/14
Everly, Phil	Brownie, Ky.	1/19/38			
Ewell, Tom	Owensboro, Ky.	4/29/09	Gabel, Martin	Philadelphia, Pa.	6/19/12
			Gabor, Eva	Hungary	1921
			Gabor, Zsa Zsa	Hungary	—
Fabares, Shelley	Santa Monica, Cal.	1/19/42	Gail, Max	Detroit, Mich.	4/5/43
Fabian (Forte)	Philadelphia, Pa.	2/6/43	Galloway, Don	Brooksville, Ky.	7/27/37
Fabray, Nanette	San Diego, Cal.	10/27/20	Galway, James	Balfast, Ireland	12/8/39
Fairbanks, Douglas Jr.	New York, N.Y.	12/9/09	Gam, Rita	Pittsburgh, Pa.	4/2/27
Fairchild, Morgan	Dallas, Tex.	2/3/50	Garagiola, Joe	St. Louis, Mo.	2/12/26
Falana, Lola	Philadelphia, Pa.	9/11/46	Garbo, Greta	Stockholm, Sweden	9/18/05
Falk, Peter	New York, N.Y.	9/16/27	Gardenia, Vincent	Naples, Italy	1/7/22
Falkenberg, Jinx	Barcelona, Spain	1/21/19	Gardner, Ava	Smithfield, N.C.	12/24/22
Farentino, James	Brooklyn, N.Y.	2/24/38	Garfunkel, Art	New York, N.Y.	10/13/41
Fargo, Donna	Mt. Airy, N.C.	11/10/49	Garland, Beverly	Santa Cruz, Cal.	10/17/29
Farr, Jamie	Toledo, Oh.	7/1/36	Garner, James	Norman, Okla.	4/7/28
Farrell, Charles	Onset Bay, Mass.	1901	Garner, Peggy Ann	Canton, Oh.	2/3/32
Farrell, Eileen	Willimantic, Conn.	2/13/20	Garrett, Betty	St. Joseph, Mo.	5/23/19
Farrell, Mike	St. Paul, Minn.	2/6/39	Garrett, Leif	Hollywood, Cal.	11/8/61
Farrow, Mia	Los Angeles, Cal.	2/9/45	Garson, Greer	Co. Down, N. Ireland	9/29/08
Fawcett, Farrah	Corpus Christi, Tex.	2/2/47	Gatlin, Larry	Seminole, Tex.	5/2/48
Faye, Alice	New York, N.Y.	5/5/15	Gavin, John	Los Angeles, Cal.	4/8/32
Feld, Fritz	Berlin, Germany	10/15/00	Gayle, Crystal	Paintsville, Ky.	1/9/51
Feldon, Barbara	Pittsburgh, Pa.	3/12/41	Gaynor, Janet	Philadelphia, Pa.	10/6/06
Feldshuh, Tovah	New York, N.Y.	12/27/52	Gaynor, Mitzi	Chicago, Ill.	9/4/31
Feliciano, Jose	Lares, Puerto Rico	9/10/45	Gazzara, Ben	New York, N.Y	8/28/30
Fell, Norman	Philadelphia, Pa.	3/24/25	Geary, Anthony	Coalsville, Ut.	5/29/47
Fellini, Federico	Rimini, Italy	1/20/20	Gedda, Nicolai	Stockholm, Sweden	7/11/25
Fellows, Edith	Boston, Mass.	5/20/23	Gennaro, Peter	Metairie, La.	1924
Ferrer, Jose	Santurce, P.R.	1/8/12	Gentry, Bobbie	Chickasaw Co., Miss.	7/27/44
Ferrer, Mel	Elberon, N.J.	8/25/17	Gerard, Gil	Little Rock, Ark.	1/23/43
Ferrigno, Lou	Brooklyn, N.Y.	11/9/52	Gere, Richard	Philadelphia, Pa.	8/31/49
Fetchit, Stepin	Key West, Fla.	5/30/02	Ghostley, Alice	Eve, Mo.	8/14/26
Field, Sally	Pasadena, Cal.	11/6/46	Giannini, Giancarlo	Spezia, Italy	8/1/42
Fields, Kim	Los Angeles, Cal.	5/12/69	Gibb, Andy	Manchester, England.	3/5/58
Finney, Albert	Salford, England	5/9/36	Gibbs, Marla	Chicago, Ill.	6/14/31
Firkusny, Rudolf	Napajedla, Czechoslovakia	2/11/12	Gibson, Henry	Germantown, Pa.	9/21/35
Firth, Peter	Yorkshire, England	10/27/53	Gibson, Mel	New York, N.Y.	1956
Fischer-Dieskau, Dietrich	Berlin, Germany	5/28/25	Gielgud, John	London, England	4/14/04
Fisher, Carrie	Beverly Hills, Cal.	10/21/56	Gilbert, Melissa	Los Angeles, Cal.	5/8/64
Fisher, Eddie	Philadelphia, Pa.	8/10/28	Gilberto, Astrud	Salvador, Brazil	3/30/40
Fitzgerald, Ella	Newport News, Va.	4/25/18	Gilford, Jack	New York, N.Y.	7/25/07
Fitzgerald, Geraldine	Dublin, Ireland.	11/24/13	Gillette, Anita	Baltimore, Md.	8/16/36
Flack, Roberta	Black Mountain, N.C.	2/10/39	Gilley, Mickey	Natchez, Miss.	3/9/36
Flanders, Ed	Minneapolis, Minn.	12/29/34	Gingold, Hermione	London, England	12/9/97
Fleming, Rhonda	Hollywood, Cal.	8/10/23	Ginty, Robert	New York, N.Y.	11/14/48
Fletcher, Louise	Birmingham, Ala.	1936	Gish, Lillian	Springfield, Oh.	10/14/96
Foch, Nina	Leyden, Netherlands	4/20/24	Glaser, Paul Michael	Cambridge, Mass.	3/25/-
Fogelberg, Dan	Peoria, Ill.	8/13/51	Glass, Ron	Evansville, Ind.	7/10/45
Fonda, Jane	New York, N.Y.	12/21/37	Gleason, Jackie	Brooklyn, N.Y.	2/26/16
Fonda, Peter	New York, N.Y.	2/23/40	Gless, Sharon	Los Angeles, Cal.	5/31/43
Fontaine, Joan	Tokyo, Japan	10/22/17	Gobel, George	Chicago, Ill.	5/20/19
Fonteyn, Margot	Reigate, England	5/18/19	Godard, Jean Luc	Paris, France	12/3/30
Ford (Tenn.), Ernie	Bristol, Tenn.	2/13/19	Goddard, Paulette	Great Neck, N.Y.	6/3/11
Ford, Glenn	Quebec, Canada	5/1/16	Goldsboro, Bobby	Marianna, Fla.	1/11/41
Ford, Harrison	Chicago, Ill.	7/13/42	Goodman, Benny	Chicago, Ill.	5/30/09
Ford, Ruth	Hazelhurst, Miss.	1920	Goodman, Dody	Columbus, Oh.	10/28/29
Forrest, Steve	Huntsville, Tex.	9/29/24	Gordon, Gale	New York, N.Y.	2/2/06
Forsythe, John	Penns Grove, N.J.	1/29/18	Gordon, Ruth	Wollaston, Mass.	10/30/96
Fosse, Bob	Chicago, Ill.	6/23/27	Gorin, Igor	Ukraine, Russia	10/26/09
Foster, Jodie	Los Angeles, Cal.	11/19/62	Gorman, Cliff	New York, N.Y.	10/13/36
Foster, Phil	Brooklyn, N.Y.	3/29/14	Gorme, Eydie	Bronx, N.Y.	8/16/32
Fox, James	London, England	5/19/39	Gorshin, Frank	Pittsburgh, Pa.	4/5/34
Fox, Michael J.	Edmonton, Alta.	6/9/61	Gossett Jr., Louis	Brooklyn, N.Y.	5/27/36
Foxx, Redd	St. Louis, Mo.	12/9/22	Gould, Elliott	Brooklyn, N.Y.	8/29/38
Frampton, Peter	Kent, England	4/22/50	Gould, Morton	Richmond Hill, N.Y.	12/10/13
Francescatti, Zino	Marseilles, France	8/9/05	Goulding, Ray	Lowell, Mass.	3/20/22
Franciosa, Anthony	New York, N.Y.	10/25/28	Goulet, Robert	Lawrence, Mass.	11/26/33
Francis, Anne	Ossining, N.Y.	9/16/32	Gowdy, Curt	Green River, Wyo.	7/31/19
Francis, Arlene	Boston, Mass.	10/20/08	Graham, Martha	Pittsburgh, Pa.	5/11/94
Francis, Connie	Newark, N.J.	12/12/38	Graham, Virginia	Chicago, Ill.	7/4/12
Francis, Genie	Los Angeles, Cal.	5/26/62	Granger, Farley	San Jose, Cal.	7/1/25
Franciscus, James	Clayton, Mo.	1/31/34	Granger, Stewart	London, England	5/6/13
Frankenheimer, John	Malba, N.Y.	2/19/30	Granville, Bonita	New York, N.Y.	2/2/23
Franklin, Aretha	Memphis, Tenn.	3/25/42	Grant, Cary	Bristol, England	1/18/04
Franklin, Bonnie	Santa Monica, Cal.	1/6/44	Grant, Lee	New York, N.Y.	10/31/31
Franklin, Joe	New York, N.Y.	1929	Graves, Peter	Minneapolis, Minn.	3/18/26
Freberg, Stan	Pasadena, Cal.	8/7/26	Gray, Coleen	Staplehurst, Neb.	10/23/22
Freed, Bert	New York, N.Y.	11/3/19	Gray, Linda	Santa Monica, Cal.	9/12/40
Freeman Jr., Al	San Antonio, Tex.	3/21/34	Grayson, Kathryn	Winston-Salem, N.C.	2/9/23
			Graziano, Rocky	New York, N.Y.	6/7/22

Name	Birthplace	Born
Greco, Buddy	Philadelphia, Pa.	8/14/26
Greco, Jose	Abruzzi, Italy	12/23/18
Green, Adolph	New York, N.Y.	12/2/15
Green, Al	Forest City, Ark.	4/13/46
Greene, Lorne	Ottawa, Ont.	2/12/15
Greene, Richard	England	1918
Greenwood, Joan	London, England	3/4/21
Greer, Jane	Washington, D.C.	9/9/24
Gregory, Dick	St. Louis, Mo.	10/12/32
Gregory, James	Bronx, N.Y.	12/23/11
Grey, Joel	Cleveland, Oh.	4/11/32
Griffin, Merv	San Mateo, Cal.	7/6/25
Griffith, Andy	Mount Airy, N.C.	6/1/26
Grimes, Tammy	Lynn, Mass.	1/30/36
Grizzard, George	Roanoke Rapids, N.C.	4/1/28
Grodin, Charles	Pittsburgh, Pa.	4/21/35
Grosbard, Ulu	Antwerp, Belgium	1/19/29
Gross, Mary	Chicago, Ill.	3/25/53
Guardino, Harry	New York, N.Y.	12/23/25
Guillaume, Robert	St. Louis, Mo.	11/30/-
Guinness, Alec	London, England	4/2/14
Gunn, Moses	St. Louis, Mo.	10/2/29
Guthrie, Arlo	New York, N.Y.	7/10/47
Hackett, Buddy	Brooklyn, N.Y.	8/31/24
Hackman, Gene	San Bernardino, Cal.	1/30/30
Hagen, Uta	Gottingen, Germany	6/12/19
Haggard, Merle	Bakersfield, Cal.	4/6/37
Haggerty, Dan	Hollywood, Cal.	11/19/41
Hagman, Larry	Ft. Worth, Tex.	9/21/31
Haid, Charles	San Francisco, Cal.	6/2/43
Hale, Barbara	DeKalb, Ill.	4/18/22
Hall, Daryl	Pottstown, Pa.	10/11/49
Hall, Huntz	New York, N.Y.	1920
Hall, Monty	Winnipeg, Man.	8/25/23
Hall, Tom T.	Olive Hill, Ky.	5/25/36
Hamel, Veronica	Philadelphia, Pa.	11/20/43
Hamill, Mark	Oakland, Cal.	9/25/52
Hamilton, George	Memphis, Tenn.	8/12/39
Hamilton, Margaret	Cleveland, Oh.	12/9/02
Hampshire, Susan	London, England	5/12/42
Hampton, Lionel	Birmingham, Ala.	4/12/13
Harmon, Mark	Burbank, Cal.	9/2/51
Harper, Valerie	Suffern, N.Y.	8/22/40
Harrington, Pat Jr.	New York, N.Y.	8/13/29
Harris, Barbara	Evanston, Ill.	7/25/35
Harris, Emmylou	Birmingham, Ala.	4/2/47
Harris, Julie	Grosse Pte. Park, Mich.	12/2/25
Harris, Phil	Linton, Ind.	6/24/06
Harris, Richard	Co. Limerick, Ireland	10/1/33
Harris, Rosemary	Ashby, England	9/19/30
Harrison, George	Liverpool, England	2/25/43
Harrison, Gregory	Avalon, Cal.	5/31/50
Harrison, Rex	Huyton, England	3/5/08
Harry, Deborah	Miami, Fla.	7/1/45
Hartley, Mariette	New York, N.Y.	6/21/40
Hartman, David	Pawtucket, R.I.	5/19/35
Hasselhoff, David	Baltimore, Md.	7/17/52
Hasso, Signe	Stockholm, Sweden	8/15/18
Haver, June	Rock Island, Ill.	6/10/26
Havoc, June	Vancouver, B.C.	11/8/16
Hawn, Goldie	Washington, D.C.	11/21/45
Hayden, Melissa	Toronto, Ont.	4/25/23
Hayden, Sterling	Montclair, N.J.	3/26/16
Hayes, Helen	Washington, D.C.	10/10/00
Hayes, Isaac	Covington, Tenn.	8/20/42
Hayes, Peter Lind	San Francisco, Cal.	6/25/15
Hays, Robert	Bethesda, Md.	7/24/47
Hayward, Louis	Johannesburg, S. Africa	3/19/09
Hayworth, Rita	New York, N.Y.	10/17/18
Healy, Mary	New Orleans, La.	4/14/18
Heatherton, Joey	Rockville Centre, N.Y.	9/14/44
Heckart, Eileen	Columbus, Oh.	3/29/19
Heifetz, Jascha	Vilna, Lithuania	2/2/01
Helpmann, Robert	Mt. Gambier, Australia	4/9/09
Hemingway, Margaux	Portland, Ore.	1955
Hemingway, Mariel	Portland, Ore.	—
Hemmings, David	Guildford, England	11/2/41
Hemsley, Sherman	Philadelphia, Pa.	2/1/38
Henderson, Florence	Dale, Ind.	2/14/34
Henderson, Skitch	Halstad, Minn.	1/27/18
Henner, Marilu	Chicago, Ill.	4/6/52
Henning, Doug	Ft. Garry, Man., Canada	5/3/47
Henreid, Paul	Trieste, Austria	1/10/08
Hensley, Pamela	Los Angeles, Cal.	10/3/50
Henson, Jim	Greenville, Miss.	9/24/36

Name	Birthplace	Born
Hepburn, Audrey	Brussels, Belgium	5/4/29
Hepburn, Katharine	Hartford, Conn.	11/8/09
Herrmann, Edward	Washington, D.C.	7/21/43
Hesseman, Howard	Lebanon, Ore.	2/27/40
Heston, Charlton	Evanston, Ill.	10/4/23
Hildegarde	Adell, Wis.	2/1/06
Hill, Arthur	Melfort, Sask.	8/1/22
Hill, Benny	Southampton, England	1/21/25
Hill, George Roy	Minneapolis, Minn.	12/20/22
Hiller, Wendy	Stockport, England	8/15/12
Hillerman, John	Denison, Tex.	12/30/32
Hines, Jerome	Hollywood, Cal.	11/8/21
Hingle, Pat	Denver, Col.	7/19/24
Hirsch, Judd	Bronx, N.Y.	3/15/35
Hirt, Al	New Orleans, La.	11/7/22
Ho, Don	Kakaako, Oahu, Ha.	8/13/30
Hoffman, Dustin	Los Angeles, Cal.	8/8/37
Holbrook, Hal	Cleveland, Oh.	2/17/25
Holder, Geoffrey	Trinidad	8/1/30
Holliday, Polly	Jasper, Ala.	7/2/37
Holliman, Earl	Delhi, La.	9/11/28
Holloway, Sterling	Cedartown, Ga.	1/4/05
Holm, Celeste	New York, N.Y.	4/29/19
Hooks, Robert	Washington, D.C.	4/18/37
Hope, Bob	London, England	5/29/03
Hopkins, Anthony	Wales	12/31/37
Hopper, Dennis	Dodge City, Kan.	5/17/36
Horne, Lena	Brooklyn, N.Y.	6/30/17
Horne, Marilyn	Bradford, Pa.	1/16/34
Horowitz, Vladimir	Kiev, Russia	10/1/04
Horsley, Lee	Muleshoe, Tex.	5/15/55
Horton, Robert	Los Angeles, Cal.	7/29/24
Houseman, John	Bucharest, Romania	9/22/02
Howard, Ken	El Centro, Cal.	3/28/44
Howard, Ron	Duncan, Okla.	3/1/54
Howard, Trevor	Kent, England	9/29/16
Howes, Sally Ann	London, England	7/20/34
Hudson, Rock	Winnetka, Ill.	11/17/25
Hughes, Barnard	Bedford Hills, N.Y.	7/16/15
Humperdinck, Engelbert	Madras, India	5/3/36
Hunt, Lois	York, Pa.	11/26/25
Hunt, Marsha	Chicago, Ill.	10/17/17
Hunter, Kim	Detroit, Mich.	11/12/22
Hunter, Ross	Cleveland, Oh.	5/6/26
Hunter, Tab	New York, N.Y.	7/11/31
Hurt, John	Chesterfield, England	1/22/40
Hurt, William	Washington, D.C.	3/20/50
Hussey, Olivia	Buenos Aires, Argentina	4/17/51
Hussey, Ruth	Providence, R.I.	10/30/17
Huston, John	Nevada, Mo.	8/5/06
Hutchinson, Josephine	Seattle, Wash.	10/12/09
Hutton, Betty	Battle Creek, Mich.	2/26/21
Hutton, Lauren	Charleston, S.C.	1944
Hutton, Timothy	Los Angeles, Cal.	8/16/60
Hyde-White, Wilfrid	Gloucester, England	5/12/03
Ian, Janis	New York, N.Y.	4/7/51
Ireland, Jill	London, England	4/24/36
Ireland, John	Vancouver, B.C.	1/30/15
Irons, Jeremy	Isle of Wight, England	1950
Irving, Amy	Palo Alto, Cal.	9/10/53
Irving, George S.	Springfield, Mass.	11/1/22
Ives, Burl	Hunt Township, Ill.	6/14/09
Jackson, Anne	Allegheny, Pa.	9/3/26
Jackson, Glenda	Liverpool, England	5/9/38
Jackson, Kate	Birmingham, Ala.	10/29/48
Jackson, Michael	Gary, Ind.	8/29/58
Jacobi, Derek	London, England	10/22/38
Jaeckel, Richard	Long Beach, Cal.	10/10/26
Jagger, Dean	Columbus Grove, Oh.	11/7/05
Jagger, Mick	Dartford, England	7/26/43
Janis, Conrad	New York, N.Y.	2/11/28
Jarreau, Al	Milwaukee, Wis.	5/12/40
Jeanmaire, Renee	Paris, France	4/29/24
Jeffreys, Anne	Goldsboro, N.C.	1/26/23
Jeffries, Fran	San Jose, Cal.	1939
Jenner, Bruce	Mt. Kisco, N.Y.	10/28/49
Jennings, Waylon	Littlefield, Tex.	6/15/37
Jens, Salome	Milwaukee, Wis.	5/8/35
Jepson, Helen	Titusville, Pa.	11/28/07
Jett, Joan	Philadelphia, Pa.	9/22/60
Jillian, Ann	Cambridge, Mass.	1/29/51
Joel, Billy	Bronx, N.Y.	5/9/49
John, Elton	Middlesex, England	3/25/47
Johns, Glynis	Durban, S. Africa	10/5/23

Name	Birthplace	Born
Johnson, Arte	Benton Harbor, Mich.	1/20/34
Johnson, Ben	Foraker, Okla.	6/13/18
Johnson, Van	Newport, R.I.	8/25/16
Jones, Allan	Scranton, Pa.	10/14/08
Jones, Chris	Jackson, Tenn.	1941
Jones, Dean	Morgan City, Ala.	1/25/35
Jones, George	Saratoga, Tex.	9/12/31
Jones, Grandpa	Niagara, Ky.	10/20/13
Jones, Henry	Philadelphia, Pa.	8/1/12
Jones, Jack	Hollywood, Cal.	1/14/38
Jones, James Earl	Tate Co., Miss.	1/17/31
Jones, Jennifer	Tulsa, Okla.	3/2/19
Jones, Shirley	Smithton, Pa.	3/31/34
Jones, Tom	Pontypridd, Wales	6/7/40
Jones, Tommy Lee	San Saba, Tex.	9/15/46
Jourdan, Louis	Marseilles, France	6/19/21
Julia, Raul	San Juan, P.R.	3/9/40
Jurado, Katy	Guadalajara, Mexico	1/16/24
Kahn, Madeline	Boston, Mass.	9/29/42
Kanaly, Steve	Burbank, Cal.	3/14/46
Kane, Carol	Cleveland, Oh.	6/18/52
Kaplan, Gabe	Brooklyn, N.Y.	3/31/45
Karras, Alex	Gary, Ind.	7/15/35
Kavner, Judy	Los Angeles, Cal.	9/7/51
Kaye, Danny	Brooklyn, N.Y.	1/18/13
Kaye, Sammy	Lakewood, Oh.	3/13/13
Kazan, Elia	Constantinople, Turkey	9/7/09
Kazan, Lainie	New York, N.Y.	5/15/42
Keach, Stacy	Savannah, Ga.	6/2/41
Keaton, Diane	Santa Ana, Cal.	1/5/46
Keel, Howard	Gillespie, Ill.	4/13/17
Keeler, Ruby	Halifax, N.S.	8/25/10
Keeshan, Bob	Lynbrook, N.Y.	6/27/27
Keitel, Harvey	Brooklyn, N.Y.	—
Keith, Brian	Bayonne, N.J.	11/14/21
Keith, David	Knoxville, Tenn.	1954
Keller, Marthe	Basel, Switzerland	1945
Kellerman, Sally	Long Beach, Cal.	6/2/37
Kelley, DeForrest	Atlanta, Ga.	1/20/20
Kelly, Gene	Pittsburgh, Pa.	8/23/12
Kelly, Jack	Astoria, N.Y.	9/16/27
Kelly, Nancy	Lowell, Mass.	3/25/21
Kennedy, Arthur	Worcester, Mass.	2/17/14
Kennedy, George	New York, N.Y.	2/18/25
Kennedy, Jayne	Washington, D.C.	11/27/51
Kennedy, Mimi	Rochester, N.Y.	9/25/49
Kent, Allegra	Los Angeles, Cal.	8/11/37
Kercheval, Ken	Wolcottville, Ind.	7/15/35
Kerr, Deborah	Helensburgh, Scotland.	9/30/21
Kerr, John	New York, N.Y.	11/15/31
Kidd, Michael	New York, N.Y.	8/12/25
Kidder, Margot	Yellowknife, N.W.T.	10/17/48
Kiley, Richard	Chicago, Ill.	3/31/22
King, Alan	Brooklyn, N.Y.	12/26/27
King, B. B.	Itta Bena, Miss.	9/16/25
King, Carole	Brooklyn, N.Y.	2/9/42
King, Wayne	Savannah, Ill.	2/16/01
Kingsley, Ben	Yorkshire, England	12/31/43
Kinski, Klaus	Berlin, Germany	1926
Kinski, Nastassia	Berlin, Germany	1/24/60
Kirby, Durward	Covington, Ky.	8/24/12
Kirkland, Gelsey	Bethlehem, Pa.	12/29/52
Kirsten, Dorothy	Montclair, N.J.	7/6/19
Kitt, Eartha	North, S.C.	1/26/28
Klein, Robert	New York, N.Y.	2/8/42
Klemperer, Werner	Cologne, Germany	3/22/20
Kline, Kevin	St. Louis, Mo.	10/24/47
Klugman, Jack	Philadelphia, Pa.	4/27/22
Knight, Gladys	Atlanta, Ga.	5/28/44
Knight, Ted	Terryville, Conn.	12/7/23
Knotts, Don	Morgantown, W. Va.	7/21/24
Knox, Alexander	Strathroy, Ont., Canada	1/16/07
Kopell, Bernie	New York, N.Y.	6/21/33
Korman, Harvey	Chicago, Ill.	2/15/27
Kotto, Yaphet	New York, N.Y.	11/15/37
Kramer, Stanley	New York, N.Y.	9/29/13
Kristofferson, Kris	Brownsville, Tex.	6/22/36
Kubelik, Rafael	Bychori, Czechoslovakia.	6/29/14
Kubrick, Stanley	Bronx, N.Y.	7/26/28
Kulp, Nancy	Harrisburg, Pa.	8/28/21
Kurtz, Swoozie	Omaha, Neb.	9/6/44
Kyser, Kay	Rocky Mount, N.C.	6/18/05
Ladd, Cheryl	Huron, S.D.	7/12/51
Laine, Frankie	Chicago, Ill.	3/30/13

Name	Birthplace	Born
Lamarr, Hedy	Vienna, Austria	9/11/15
Lamas, Lorenzo	Los Angeles, Cal.	1/20/58
Lamb, Gil	Minneapolis, Minn.	6/14/06
Lamour, Dorothy	New Orleans, La.	12/10/14
Lancaster, Burt	New York, N.Y.	11/2/13
Lanchester, Elsa	London, England	10/28/02
Landau, Martin	Brooklyn, N.Y.	1934
Landon, Michael	Forest Hills, N.Y.	—
Lane, Abbe	Brooklyn, N.Y.	1932
Lane, Priscilla	Indianola, Ia.	6/12/17
Lange, Hope	Redding Ridge, Conn.	11/28/31
Lange, Jessica	Cloquet, Minn.	4/20/49
Langella, Frank	Bayonne, N.J.	1/1/46
Langford, Frances	Lakeland, Fla.	4/4/13
Lansbury, Angela	London, England	10/16/25
Lansing, Robert	San Diego, Cal.	6/5/29
Lasser, Louise	New York N.Y.	4/11/39
Laughlin, Tom	Minneapolis, Minn.	1938
Laurie, Piper	Detroit, Mich.	1/22/32
Lavin, Linda	Portland, Me.	10/15/37
Lawford, Peter	London, England	9/7/23
Lawrence, Carol	Melrose Park, Ill.	9/5/34
Lawrence, Steve	Brooklyn, N.Y.	7/8/35
Lawrence, Vicki	Inglewood, Cal.	3/26/49
Leachman, Cloris	Des Moines, Ia.	4/4/26
Lean, David	Croydon, England	3/25/08
Lear, Norman	New Haven, Conn.	7/27/22
Learned, Michael	Washington, D.C.	4/9/39
Lederer, Francis	Prague, Czechoslovakia	11/6/06
Lee, Brenda	Atlanta, Ga.	12/11/44
Lee, Christopher	London, England	5/27/22
Lee, Michele	Los Angeles, Cal.	6/24/42
Lee, Peggy	Jamestown, N.D.	5/26/20
Lee, Pinky	St. Paul, Minn.	—
Le Gallienne, Eva	London, England	1/11/99
Legrand, Michel	Paris, France	2/24/32
Leibman, Ron	New York, N.Y.	10/11/37
Leigh, Janet	Merced, Cal.	7/6/27
Leinsdorf, Erich	Vienna, Austria	2/4/12
Lemmon, Jack	Boston, Mass.	2/8/25
Lennon, Dianne	Los Angeles, Cal.	12/1/39
Lennon, Janet	Culver City, Cal.	11/15/46
Lennon, Kathy	Santa Monica, Cal.	8/22/42
Lennon, Peggy	Los Angeles, Cal.	4/8/41
Leonard, Sheldon	New York, N.Y.	2/22/07
Leontovich, Eugenie	Moscow, Russia	3/21/00
LeRoy, Mervyn	San Francisco, Cal.	10/15/00
Leslie, Joan	Detroit, Mich.	1/26/25
Lester, Jerry	Chicago, Ill.	1911
Letterman, David	Indianapolis, Ind.	4/12/47
Levine, James	Cincinnati, Oh.	6/23/43
Lewis, Jerry	Newark, N.J.	3/16/26
Lewis, Jerry Lee	Ferriday, La.	9/29/35
Lewis, Shari	New York, N.Y.	1/17/34
Liberace	West Allis, Wis.	5/16/19
Lightfoot, Gordon	Orillia, Ont.	11/17/38
Lillie, Beatrice	Toronto, Ont.	5/29/94
Linden, Hal	New York, N.Y.	3/20/31
Lindfors, Viveca	Uppsala, Sweden.	12/29/20
Lindsey, Mort	Newark, N.J.	3/21/23
Linkletter, Art	Saskatchewan, Canada	7/17/12
Lithgow, John	Rochester, N.Y.	1949
Little, Cleavon	Chickasha, Okla.	6/1/39
Little, Rich	Ottawa, Ont.	11/26/38
Little Richard	Macon, Ga.	1935
Lloyd, Christopher	Stamford, Conn.	10/22/38
Locke, Sondra	Shelbyville, Tenn.	5/28/47
Lockhart, June	New York, N.Y.	6/25/25
Locklear, Heather	Los Angeles, Cal.	9/25/-
Lockwood, Margaret	Karachi, India	9/15/16
Loder, John	London, England	1898
Logan, Joshua	Texarkana, Tex.	10/5/08
Loggia, Robert	New York, N.Y.	1/3/30
Loggins, Kenny	Everett, Wash.	1/7/48
Lollobrigida, Gina	Subiaco, Italy	7/4/28
Lom, Herbert	Prague, Czechoslovakia	1917
London, Julie	Santa Rosa, Cal.	9/26/26
Long, Shelley	Ft. Wayne, Ind.	8/23/49
Longet, Claudine	Paris, France	1/29/42
Lopez, Priscilla	New York, N.Y.	2/26/48
Lopez, Trini	Dallas, Tex.	5/15/37
Lord, Jack	New York, N.Y.	—
Loren, Sophia	Rome, Italy	9/20/34
Loudon, Dorothy	Boston, Mass.	9/17/33
Louise, Tina	New York, N.Y.	3/11/34
Love, Bessie	Midland, Tex.	9/10/98
Loy, Myrna	Helena, Mon.	8/2/05

Name	Birthplace	Born
Lucas, George	Modesto, Cal.	5/14/44
Luckinbill, Laurence	Ft. Smith, Ark.	11/21/34
Ludwig, Christa	Berlin, Germany	3/16/28
Luke, Keye	Canton, China.	1904
Lumet, Sidney	Philadelphia, Pa.	6/25/24
Lund, John	Rochester, N.Y.	1913
Lupino, Ida	London, England	2/4/18
LuPone, Patti	Northport, N.Y.	4/21/49
Lynley, Carol	New York, N.Y.	2/13/42
Lynn, Jeffrey	Auburn, Mass.	2/16/09
Lynn, Loretta	Butcher Hollow, Ky.	4/14/35
Lyon, Sue	Davenport, Ia.	7/10/46
Maazel, Lorin	Paris, France	3/6/30
MacArthur, James	Los Angeles, Cal.	12/8/37
MacGraw, Ali	Pound Ridge, N.Y.	4/1/39
MacKenzie, Gisele	Winnipeg, Man.	1/10/27
MacLaine, Shirley	Richmond, Va.	4/24/34
MacLeod, Gavin	Mt. Kisco, N.Y.	2/28/30
MacMurray, Fred	Kankakee, Ill.	8/30/08
MacNeil, Cornell	Minneapolis, Minn.	9/24/22
MacRae, Gordon	East Orange, N.J.	3/12/21
Macy, Bill	Revere, Mass.	5/18/22
Madden, John	Austin, Minn.	4/10/36
Majors, Lee	Wyandotte, Mich.	4/23/40
Makarova, Natalia	Leningrad, USSR	11/21/40
Malbin, Elaine	New York, N.Y.	5/24/32
Malden, Karl	Chicago, Ill.	3/22/13
Malle, Louis	Thumeries, France	10/30/32
Malone, Dorothy	Chicago, Ill.	1/30/25
Manchester, Melissa	Bronx, N.Y.	2/15/51
Mancini, Henry	Cleveland, Oh.	4/16/24
Mandrell, Barbara	Houston, Tex.	12/25/48
Mangione, Chuck	Rochester, N.Y.	11/29/40
Manilow, Barry	New York, N.Y.	6/17/46
Mann, Herbie	New York, N.Y.	4/16/30
Marceau, Marcel	Strasbourg, France	3/22/23
Marchand, Nancy	Buffalo, N.Y.	6/19/28
Margo	Mexico City, Mexico	5/10/18
Margolin, Janet	New York, N.Y.	1943
Marin, Cheech	Los Angeles, Cal.	7/13/46
Markova, Alicia	London, England	12/1/10
Marriner, Neville	Lincoln, England	4/15/25
Marsh, Jean	London, England	7/1/34
Marshall, E. G.	Owatonna, Minn.	6/18/10
Marshall, Penny	New York, N.Y.	10/15/45
Marshall, Peter	Huntington, W.Va.	3/30/-
Martin, Dean	Steubenville, Oh.	6/17/17
Martin, Dick	Detroit, Mich.	1/30/23
Martin, Mary	Weatherford, Tex.	12/1/13
Martin, Pamela Sue	Westport, Conn.	1/5/54
Martin, Steve	Waco, Tex.	1945
Martin, Tony	San Francisco, Cal.	12/25/13
Martino, Al	Philadelphia, Pa.	10/7/27
Marvin, Lee	New York, N.Y.	2/19/24
Mason, Jackie	Sheboygan, Wis.	1931
Mason, James	Huddersfield, England	5/15/09
Mason, Marsha	St. Louis, Mo.	4/3/42
Mason, Pamela	London, England	3/10/22
Mastroianni, Marcello	Rome, Italy	9/28/24
Matheson, Tim	Glendale, Cal.	12/31/47
Mathis, Johnny	San Francisco, Cal.	9/30/35
Matthau, Walter	New York, N.Y.	10/1/20
Mature, Victor	Louisville, Ky.	1/29/16
May, Elaine	Philadelphia, Pa.	4/21/32
Mayo, Virginia	St. Louis, Mo.	11/30/20
Mazurki, Mike	Austria	12/25/09
Mazursky, Paul	Brooklyn, N.Y.	4/25/30
McArdle, Andrea	Philadelphia, Pa.	11/5/63
McBride, Patricia	Teaneck, N.J.	8/23/42
McCallum, David	Glasgow, Scotland	9/19/33
McCambridge, Mercedes	Joliet, Ill.	3/17/18
McCarthy, Kevin	Seattle, Wash.	2/15/14
McCartney, Paul	Liverpool, England	6/18/42
McClure, Doug	Glendale, Cal.	5/11/38
McCord, Kent	Los Angeles, Cal.	9/26/42
McCrary, Tex (John)	Calvert, Tex.	10/13/10
McCrea, Joel	Los Angeles, Cal.	11/5/05
McDowall, Roddy	London, England	9/17/28
McDowell, Malcolm	Leeds, England	6/19/43
McFarland, Spanky	Dallas, Tex.	10/2/28
McGavin, Darren	San Joaquin, Cal.	5/7/22
McGee, Fibber	Peoria, Ill.	11/6/96
McGoohan, Patrick	New York, N.Y.	3/19/28
McGovern, Maureen	Youngstown, Oh.	7/27/49
McGuire, Dorothy	Omaha, Neb.	6/14/19

Name	Birthplace	Born
McIntire, John	Spokane, Wash.	6/27/07
McKechnie, Donna	Pontiac, Mich.	11/16/42
McKellen, Ian	Burnley, England	5/25/39
McKenna, Siobhan	Belfast, Ireland	5/24/23
McLean, Don	New Rochelle, N.Y.	10/2/45
McLerie, Allyn	Grand Mere, Que.	12/1/26
McMahon, Ed	Detroit, Mich.	3/6/23
McNair, Barbara	Racine, Wis.	3/4/39
McNichol, Jimmy	Los Angeles, Cal.	7/2/61
McNichol, Kristy	Los Angeles, Cal.	9/11/62
McQueen, Butterfly	Tampa, Fla.	1/7/11
McRaney, Gerald	Collins, Miss.	8/19/-
Meadows, Audrey	Wu Chang, China	1924
Meadows, Jayne	Wu Chang, China	9/27/26
Meara, Anne	New York, N.Y.	9/20/29
Meeker, Ralph	Minneapolis, Minn.	11/21/20
Mehta, Zubin	Bombay, India	4/29/36
Melanie	New York, N.Y.	1/3/47
Mendes, Sergio	Nitero, Brazil	2/11/41
Menuhin, Yehudi	New York, N.Y.	4/22/16
Mercouri, Melina	Athens, Greece	10/18/25
Meredith, Burgess	Cleveland, Oh.	11/16/08
Merkel, Una	Covington, Ky	12/10/03
Merrick, David	Hong Kong	11/27/12
Merrill, Dina	New York, N.Y.	12/9/25
Merrill, Gary	Hartford, Conn.	8/2/15
Merrill, Robert	Brooklyn, N.Y.	6/4/19
Messina, Jim	Maywood, Cal.	12/5/47
Michaelson, Kari	New York, N.Y.	11/3/61
Midler, Bette	Paterson, N.J.	12/1/45
Milanov, Zinka	Zagreb, Yugoslavia.	5/17/08
Miles, Sarah	Ingatestone, England.	12/31/41
Miles, Vera	near Boise City, Okla.	8/23/30
Milland, Ray	Neath, Wales	1/3/07
Miller, Ann	Houston, Tex.	4/12/23
Miller, Jason	Scranton, Pa.	4/22/39
Miller, Mitch	Rochester, N.Y.	7/4/11
Miller, Roger	Ft. Worth, Tex.	1/2/36
Mills, Donna	Chicago, Ill.	12/11/-
Mills, Hayley	London, England	4/18/46
Mills, John	Suffolk, England	2/22/08
Mills, Juliet	London, England	11/21/41
Mills Brothers:		
Mills, Herbert	Piqua, Oh.	4/12/12
Mills, Donald	Piqua, Oh.	4/29/15
Milner, Martin	Detroit, Mich.	12/28/31
Milnes, Sherrill	Downers Grove, Ill.	1/10/35
Milsap, Ronnie	Robinsville, N.C.	1/16/43
Milstein, Nathan	Odessa, Russia.	12/31/04
Mimieux, Yvette	Hollywood, Cal.	1/8/42
Minnelli, Liza	Los Angeles, Cal.	3/12/46
Mitchell, Cameron	Dallastown, Pa.	11/4/18
Mitchell, Guy	Detroit, Mich.	2/22/25
Mitchell, Joni	McLeod, Alta.	11/7/43
Mitchum, Robert	Bridgeport, Conn.	8/6/17
Moffo, Anna	Wayne, Pa.	6/27/34
Molinaro, Al	Kenosha, Wis.	6/24/19
Montalban, Ricardo	Mexico City, Mexico	11/25/20
Montand, Yves	Monsumagno, Italy	10/13/21
Montgomery, Elizabeth	Hollywood, Cal.	4/15/33
Montgomery, George	Brady, Mon.	8/29/16
Moody, Ron	London, England	1/8/24
Moore, Clayton	Chicago, Ill.	9/14/14
Moore, Constance	Sioux City, Ia.	1/18/22
Moore, Dudley	London, England	4/19/35
Moore, Garry	Baltimore, Md.	1/31/15
Moore, Mary Tyler	Brooklyn, N.Y.	12/29/37
Moore, Melba	New York, N.Y.	10/29/45
Moore, Roger	London, England	10/14/27
Moore, Terry	Los Angeles, Cal.	1/1/32
Moran, Erin	Los Angeles, Cal.	10/18/61
Moreau, Jeanne	Paris, France	1/23/28
Moreno, Rita	Humacao, P.R.	12/11/31
Morgan, Dennis	Prentice, Wis.	12/10/10
Morgan, Harry	Detroit, Mich.	4/10/15
Morgan, Henry	New York, N.Y.	3/31/15
Morgan, Jane	Boston, Mass.	192-
Morgan, Jaye P.	Mancos, Col.	12/3/3
Morgana, Nina	Buffalo, N.Y.	11/15/9
Moriarty, Michael	Detroit, Mich.	4/5/4
Morini, Erika	Vienna, Austria	1/5/1-
Morley, Robert	Wiltshire, England	5/26/0
Morris, Greg	Cleveland, Oh.	9/27/3
Morris, Howard	New York, N.Y.	9/4/2
Morse, Robert	Newton, Mass.	5/18/3
Moss, Arnold	Brooklyn, N.Y.	1/28/1
Mulhare, Edward	Ireland	4/8/2

Name	Birthplace	Born
Mull, Martin	Chicago, Ill.	8/18/43
Mulligan, Richard	New York, N.Y.	11/13/32
Munsel, Patrice	Spokane, Wash.	5/14/25
Murphy, Ben	Jonesboro, Ark.	3/6/42
Murphy, Eddie	Brooklyn, N.Y.	4/3/61
Murphy, George	New Haven, Conn.	7/4/02
Murphy, Michael	Los Angeles, Cal.	5/5/38
Murray, Anne	Springhill, Nova Scotia	6/20/45
Murray, Arthur	New York, N.Y.	4/4/95
Murray, Bill	Evanston, Ill.	9/21/50
Murray, Don	Hollywood, Cal.	7/31/29
Murray, Kathryn	Jersey City, N.J.	9/15/06
Murray, Ken	New York, N.Y.	7/14/03
Musante, Tony	Bridgeport, Conn.	6/30/36
Musburger, Brent	Portland, Ore.	5/26/39
Nabors, Jim	Sylacauga, Ala.	6/12/33
Natwick, Mildred	Baltimore, Md.	6/19/08
Neal, Patricia	Packard, Ky.	1/20/26
Neff, Hildegarde	Ulm, Germany	12/28/25
Negri, Pola	Lipno, Poland	1899
Nelligan, Kate	London, Ontario	3/16/51
Nelson, Barry	San Francisco, Cal.	4/16/20
Nelson, David	New York, N.Y.	10/24/36
Nelson, Ed	New Orleans, La.	12/21/28
Nelson, Gene	Seattle. Wash.	3/24/20
Nelson, Harriet (Hilliard)	Des Moines, Ia.	7/18/14
Nelson, Rick	Teaneck, N.J.	5/8/40
Nelson, Willie	Waco, Tex.	4/30/33
Nero, Peter	New York, N.Y.	5/22/34
Newhart, Bob	Oak Park, Ill.	9/5/29
Newley, Anthony	Hackney, England	9/24/31
Newman, Barry	Boston, Mass.	11/7/38
Newman, Loraine	Los Angeles, Cal.	3/2/-
Newman, Paul	Cleveland, Oh.	1/26/25
Newman, Phyllis	Jersey City, N.J.	3/19/35
Newman, Randy	Los Angeles, Cal.	11/28/43
Newton, Wayne	Roanoke, Va.	4/3/42
Newton-John, Olivia	Cambridge, England	9/26/48
Nichols, Mike	Berlin, Germany	11/6/31
Nicholson, Jack	Neptune, N.J.	4/28/37
Nicks, Stevie	California	5/26/48
Nielsen, Leslie	Regina, Sask.	2/11/26
Nilsson, Birgit	Karup, Sweden	5/17/18
Nimoy, Leonard	Boston, Mass.	3/26/31
Noble, James	Dallas, Tex.	3/5/22
Nolan, Lloyd	San Francisco, Cal.	8/11/02
Nolte, Nick	Omaha, Neb.	1940
Norman, Jessye	Augusta, Ga.	9/15/45
Norris, Chuck	Ryan, Okla.	1942
North, Sheree	Los Angeles, Cal.	1/17/33
Norton-Taylor, Judy	Santa Monica, Cal.	1/29/58
Novak, Kim	Chicago, Ill.	2/18/33
Nureyev, Rudolf	Russia	3/17/38
Oates, John	New York, N.Y.	4/7/48
O'Brian, Hugh	Rochester, N.Y.	4/19/30
O'Brien, Edmond	New York, N.Y.	9/10/15
O'Brien, Margaret	San Diego, Cal.	1/15/37
O'Connell, Helen	Lima, Oh.	1920
O'Connor, Carroll	New York, N.Y.	8/2/24
O'Connor, Donald	Chicago, Ill.	8/28/25
Odetta	Birmingham, Ala.	12/31/30
O'Hara, Maureen	Dublin, Ireland.	8/17/21
O'Herlihy, Dan	Wexford, Ireland	5/1/19
Olivier, Laurence	Dorking, England	5/22/07
Olsen, Merlin	Logan, Ut.	9/15/40
O'Malley, J. Pat	Burnley, England	3/15/01
O'Neal, Patrick	Ocala, Fla.	9/26/27
O'Neal, Ryan	Los Angeles, Cal.	4/20/41
O'Neal, Tatum	Los Angeles, Cal.	11/5/63
O'Neill, Jennifer	Brazil.	2/20/49
Opatoshu, David	New York, N.Y.	1/30/18
Orbach, Jerry	New York, N.Y.	10/20/35
Orlando, Tony	New York, N.Y.	4/3/44
Ormandy, Eugene	Budapest, Hungary	11/18/99
Osbourne, Ozzy	Birmingham, England.	12/3/48
Osmond, Donny	Ogden, Ut.	12/9/57
Osmond, Marie	Ogden, Ut.	10/13/59
O'Sullivan, Maureen	Boyle, Ireland	5/17/11
O'Toole, Annette	Houston, Tex.	4/1/52
O'Toole, Peter	Connemara, Ireland	8/2/32
Owens, Buck	Sherman, Tex.	8/12/29
Owens, Gary	Mitchell, S.D.	5/10/36
Ozawa, Seiji	Shenyang, China	9/1/35

Name	Birthplace	Born
Paar, Jack	Canton, Oh.	5/1/18
Pacino, Al	New York, N.Y.	4/25/40
Page, Geraldine	Kirksville, Mo.	11/22/24
Page, LaWanda	Cleveland, Oh.	10/19/20
Page, Patti	Claremore, Okla.	11/8/27
Paige, Janis	Tacoma, Wash.	9/16/22
Palance, Jack	Lattimer, Pa.	2/18/20
Palmer, Betsy	East Chicago, Ind.	11/1/29
Palmer, Lilli	Posen, Germany	5/24/14
Papas, Irene	Greece.	1926
Papp, Joseph	Brooklyn, N.Y.	6/22/21
Parker, Eleanor	Cedarville, Oh.	6/26/22
Parker, Fess	Ft. Worth, Tex.	8/16/25
Parker, Jameson	Baltimore, Md.	11/18/50
Parker, Jean	Deer Lodge, Mon.	1916
Parks, Bert	Atlanta, Ga.	12/30/14
Parsons, Estelle	Lynn, Mass.	11/20/27
Parton, Dolly	Sevierville, Tenn.	1/19/46
Pasternak, Joseph	Hungary	9/19/01
Patane, Giuseppe	Napoli, Italy	1/1/32
Patinkin, Mandy	Chicago, Ill.	11/30/52
Patterson, Lorna	Whittier, Cal.	7/1/56
Paulsen, Pat	South Bend, Wash.	—
Pavarotti, Luciano	Modena, Italy	10/12/35
Paycheck, Johnny	Greenville, Oh.	5/31/41
Payne, John	Roanoke, Va.	5/23/12
Pearl, Minnio	Contorville, Tenn.	10/25/12
Peck, Gregory	La Jolla, Cal.	4/5/16
Peckinpah, Sam	Fresno, Cal.	2/21/25
Peerce, Jan	New York, N.Y.	6/3/04
Pendergrass, Teddy	Philadelphia, Pa.	3/26/50
Penn, Arthur	Philadelphia, Pa.	9/27/22
Penn, Sean	Santa Monica, Cal.	1961
Peppard, George	Detroit, Mich.	10/1/28
Perkins, Anthony	New York, N.Y.	4/4/32
Perlman, Itzhak	Tel Aviv, Israel	10/31/45
Perlman, Rhea	Brooklyn, N.Y.	3/31/-
Perrine, Valerie	Galveston, Tex.	9/3/43
Persoff, Nehemiah	Jerusalem, Palestine	8/14/20
Peters, Bernadette	New York, N.Y.	2/28/48
Peters, Brock	New York, N.Y.	7/2/27
Peters, Jean	Canton, Oh.	10/15/26
Peters, Roberta	New York, N.Y.	5/4/30
Petit, Pascale	Paris, France	2/27/38
Phillips, MacKenzie	Alexandria, Va.	11/10/59
Phillips, Michelle	Long Beach, Cal.	4/6/44
Piazza, Marguerite	New Orleans, La.	5/6/26
Picon, Molly	New York, N.Y.	6/1/98
Pidgeon, Walter	E. St. John, N.B.	9/23/97
Piscopo, Joe	Passaic, N.J.	6/17/51
Plato, Dana	Maywood, Cal.	11/7/64
Pleasence, Donald	Worksop, England	10/5/21
Pleshette, Suzanne	New York, N.Y.	1/31/37
Plowright, Joan	Brigg, England	10/28/29
Plummer, Christopher	Toronto, Ont.	12/13/29
Poitier, Sidney	Miami, Fla.	2/20/27
Polanski, Roman	Paris, France	8/18/33
Ponti, Carlo	Milan, Italy	12/11/13
Poston, Tom	Columbus, Oh.	10/17/21
Powell, Jane	Portland, Ore.	4/1/28
Powers, Stefanie	Hollywood, Cal.	11/12/42
Preminger, Otto	Vienna, Austria	12/5/06
Prentiss, Paula	San Antonio, Tex.	3/4/39
Preston, Billy	Houston, Tex.	9/9/46
Preston, Robert	Newton, Mass.	6/8/18
Previn, Andre	Berlin, Germany	4/6/29
Price, Leontyne	Laurel, Miss.	2/10/27
Price, Ray	Perryville, Tex.	1/12/26
Price, Vincent	St. Louis, Mo.	5/27/11
Pride, Charlie	Sledge, Miss.	3/18/39
Principal, Victoria	Fulipla, Japan	1/30/50
Provine, Dorothy	Deadwood, S.D.	1/20/37
Prowse, Juliet	Bombay, India.	9/25/37
Pryor, Richard	Peoria, Ill.	12/1/40
Pyle, Denver	Bethune, Col.	5/11/20
Quaid, Dennis	Houston, Tex.	4/9/54
Quaid, Randy	Houston, Tex.	1953
Quayle, Anthony	Lancashire, England	9/7/13
Quillan, Eddie	Philadelphia, Pa.	3/31/07
Quinlan, Kathleen	Pasadena, Cal.	11/19/54
Quinn, Anthony	Chihuahua, Mexico	4/21/15
Rabb, Ellis	Memphis, Tenn.	6/20/30
Rabbitt, Eddie	Brooklyn, N.Y.	11/27/41

Name	Birthplace	Born
Radner, Gilda	Detroit, Mich.	6/28/46
Rae, Charlotte	Milwaukee, Wis.	4/22/26
Raffin, Deborah	Los Angeles, Cal.	3/13/53
Rainer, Luise	Vienna, Austria	1/12/10
Raines, Ella	Snoqualmie Falls, Wash.	8/6/21
Raitt, John	Santa Ana, Cal.	1/19/17
Ralston, Esther	Bar Harbor, Me.	9/19/02
Ralston, Vera Hruba	Prague, Czechoslovakia	6/12/21
Rampal, Jean-Pierre	Marseilles, France	1/7/22
Randall, Tony	Tulsa, Okla.	2/26/20
Rawls, Lou	Chicago, Ill.	12/1/35
Ray, Aldo	Pen Argyl, Pa.	9/25/26
Ray, Gene Anthony	New York, N.Y.	5/24/-
Ray, Johnnie	Dallas, Ore.	1/10/27
Rayburn, Gene	Christopher, Ill.	12/22/17
Raye, Martha	Butte, Mon.	8/27/16
Raymond, Gene	New York, N.Y.	8/13/08
Reddy, Helen	Melbourne, Australia	10/25/41
Redford, Robert	Santa Monica, Cal.	8/18/37
Redgrave, Lynn	London, England	3/8/43
Redgrave, Michael	Bristol, England	3/20/08
Redgrave, Vanessa	London, England	1/30/37
Reed, Donna	Denison, Ia.	1/27/21
Reed, Jerry	Atlanta, Ga.	3/20/37
Reed, Oliver	London, England	2/13/38
Reed, Rex	Ft. Worth, Tex.	10/2/38
Reed, Robert	Highland Park, Ill.	10/19/32
Reese, Della	Detroit, Mich.	7/6/31
Reeve, Christopher	New York, N.Y.	9/25/52
Reeves, Dell	Sparta, N.C.	7/14/33
Regan, Phil	Brooklyn, N.Y.	5/28/06
Reid, Kate	London, England	11/4/30
Reid, Tim	Norfolk, Va.	12/19/44
Reinking, Ann	Seattle, Wash.	11/10/49
Reilly, Charles Nelson	New York, N.Y.	1/13/31
Reiner, Carl	Bronx, N.Y.	3/20/22
Reiner, Rob	Bronx, N.Y.	3/6/45
Remick, Lee	Boston, Mass.	12/14/35
Resnik, Regina	New York, N.Y.	8/30/24
Rey, Alejandro	Buenos Aires, Argentina	2/8/30
Reynolds, Burt	Waycross, Ga.	2/11/36
Reynolds, Debbie	El Paso, Tex.	4/1/32
Reynolds, Marjorie	Buhl, Ida.	8/12/21
Rich, Charlie	Forest City, Ark.	12/14/32
Rich, Irene	Buffalo, N.Y.	10/13/97
Richardson, Tony	Shipley, England	6/5/28
Richie, Lionel	Tuskegee, Ala.	6/20/50
Rickles, Don	New York, N.Y.	5/8/26
Riddle, Nelson	Hackensack, N.J.	6/1/21
Rigg, Diana	Doncaster, England	7/20/38
Ritter, John	Burbank, Cal.	9/17/48
Ritz, Harry	Newark, N.J.	1906
Ritz, Jimmy	Newark, N.J.	1903
Rivera, Chita	Washington, D.C.	1/23/33
Rivers, Joan	Brooklyn, N.Y.	6/8/33
Robards, Jason Jr.	Chicago, Ill.	7/26/22
Robbins, Jerome	New York, N.Y.	10/11/18
Roberts, Doris	St. Louis, Mo.	11/4/30
Roberts, Pernell	Waycross, Ga.	5/18/30
Roberts, Tony	New York, N.Y.	10/22/39
Robertson, Cliff	La Jolla, Cal.	9/9/25
Robertson, Dale	Oklahoma City, Okla.	7/14/23
Robinson, Smokey	Detroit, Mich.	2/19/40
Rodgers, Jimmie	Camas, Wash.	1933
Rodriquez, Johnny	Sabinal, Tex.	12/10/51
Rogers, Chas. (Buddy)	Olathe, Kan.	8/13/04
Rogers, Ginger	Independence, Mo.	7/16/11
Rogers, Kenny	Houston, Tex.	8/21/38
Rogers, Roy	Cincinnati, Oh.	11/5/12
Rogers, Wayne	Birmingham, Ala.	4/7/33
Roland, Gilbert	Juarez, Mexico	12/11/05
Rolle, Esther	Pompano Beach, Fla.	11/8/33
Romero, Cesar	New York, N.Y.	2/15/07
Ronstadt, Linda	Tucson, Ariz.	7/15/46
Rooney, Mickey	Brooklyn, N.Y.	9/23/20
Rose, George	Bicester, England	2/19/20
Rose Marie	New York, N.Y.	8/15/25
Ross, Diana	Detroit, Mich.	3/26/44
Ross, Katharine	Hollywood, Cal.	1/29/43
Ross, Lanny	Seattle, Wash.	1/19/06
Ross, Marion	Albert Lea, Minn.	10/25/28
Rostropovich, Mstislav	Baku, USSR.	3/12/27
Roundtree, Richard	New Rochelle, N.Y.	7/9/37
Rowan, Dan	Beggs, Okla.	7/2/22
Rowlands, Gena	Cambria, Wis.	6/19/36
Rubin, Benny	Boston, Mass.	1899
Rudolf, Max	Frankfurt, Germany	6/15/02

Name	Birthplace	Born
Rule, Janice	Norwood, Oh.	8/15/31
Rush, Barbara	Denver, Col.	1/4/30
Russell, Jane	Bemidji, Minn.	6/21/21
Russell, Ken	Southampton, England.	7/3/27
Russell, Kurt	Springfield, Mass.	3/17/51
Russell, Mark	Buffalo, N.Y.	8/23/32
Russell, Nipsey	Atlanta, Ga.	10/13/24
Rutherford, Ann	Toronto, Ont.	11/2/20
Ryan, Peggy	Long Beach, Cal.	8/28/24
Rydell, Bobby	Philadelphia, Pa.	4/26/42
Sahl, Mort	Montreal, Que.	5/11/27
Saint, Eva Marie	Newark, N.J.	7/4/22
St. James, Susan	Los Angeles, Cal.	8/14/46
St. John, Jill	Los Angeles, Cal.	8/19/40
Sainte-Marie, Buffy	Maine	2/20/41
Saks, Gene	New York, N.Y.	11/8/21
Sales, Soupy	Franklinton, N.C.	1/8/26
Sandy, Gary	Dayton, Oh.	12/25/45
Sanford, Isabel	New York, N.Y.	8/29/17
Santana, Carlos	Mexico	7/20/47
Sarandon, Chris	Beckley, W.Va.	7/24/42
Sarandon, Susan	New York, N.Y.	10/4/46
Sarnoff, Dorothy	New York, N.Y.	5/25/17
Sarrazin, Michael	Quebec City, Que.	5/22/40
Savalas, Telly	Garden City, N.Y.	1/21/24
Saxon, John	Brooklyn, N.Y.	8/5/35
Sayao, Bidu	Rio de Janeiro, Brazil	5/11/02
Sayer, Leo	Sussex, England	5/21/48
Scaggs, Boz	Dallas, Tex.	6/8/44
Schallert, William	Los Angeles, Cal.	7/6/22
Scheider, Roy	Orange, N.J.	11/10/35
Schell, Maria	Vienna, Austria	1/15/26
Schell, Maximilian	Vienna, Austria	12/8/30
Schell, Ronnie	Richmond, Cal.	12/23/31
Schenkel, Chris	Bippus, Ind.	1924
Schnabel, Stefan	Berlin, Germany	2/2/12
Schneider, Alexander	Vilna, Poland	10/21/08
Schneider, John	Mt. Kisco, N.Y.	4/8/54
Schreiber, Avery	Chicago, Ill.	1935
Schroder, Ricky	Staten Island, N.Y.	4/13/70
Schwarzkopf, Elisabeth	Jarotschin, Poland	12/9/15
Scofield, Paul	Hurst, Pierpont, England.	1/21/22
Scorsese, Martin	New York, N.Y.	11/17/42
Scott, George C.	Wise, Va.	10/18/27
Scott, Lizabeth	Scranton, Pa.	9/29/22
Scott, Martha	Jamesport, Mo.	9/22/14
Scott, Randolph	Orange Co., Va.	1/23/03
Scotto, Renata	Savona, Italy	2/24/35
Scully, Vin	New York, N.Y.	11/29/27
Scourby, Alexander	New York, N.Y.	11/13/13
Sebastian, John	New York N.Y.	3/17/44
Sedaka, Neil	New York, N.Y.	3/13/39
Seeger, Pete	New York, N.Y.	5/3/19
Segal, George	Great Neck, N.Y.	2/13/34
Segal, Vivienne	Philadelphia, Pa.	4/19/97
Segovia, Andres	Linares, Spain	2/21/93
Selleck, Tom	Detroit, Mich.	1/29/45
Serkin, Rudolf	Eger, Austria	3/28/03
Severinsen, Doc	Arlington, Ore.	7/7/27
Seymour, Jane	England	2/15/51
Shackelford, Ted	Oklahoma City, Okla.	6/23/46
Shankar, Ravi	India	4/7/20
Sharif, Omar	Alexandria, Egypt.	4/10/32
Shatner, William	Montreal, Que.	3/22/31
Shaw, Robert	Red Bluff, Cal.	4/30/16
Shawn, Dick	Buffalo, N.Y.	12/1/29
Shearer, Moira	Scotland	1/17/26
Sheen, Martin	Dayton, Oh.	8/3/40
Sheldon, Jack	Jacksonville, Fla.	1931
Shelley, Carole	London, England	8/16/39
Shepard, Sam	Ft. Sheridan, Ill.	11/5/43
Shepherd, Cybill	Memphis, Tenn.	2/18/50
Shera, Mark	Bayonne, N.J.	7/10/49
Sherwood, Roberta	St. Louis, Mo.	1913
Shields, Brooke	New York, N.Y.	5/31/65
Shire, Talia	New York, N.Y.	4/25/46
Shirley, Ann	New York, N.Y.	4/17/18
Shore, Dinah	Winchester, Tenn.	3/1/17
Short, Bobby	Danville, Ill.	9/15/24
Sidney, Sylvia	New York, N.Y.	8/8/10
Siepi, Cesare	Milan, Italy	2/10/23
Signoret, Simone	Wiesbaden, Germany	3/25/21
Sills, Beverly	Brooklyn, N.Y.	5/25/29
Silvers, Phil	Brooklyn, N.Y.	5/11/12
Simmons, Jean	London, England	1/31/29

Name	Birthplace	Born	Name	Birthplace	Born
Simon, Carly	New York, N.Y.	6/25/45	Sullivan, Tom	Boston, Mass.	3/27/47
Simon, Paul	Newark, N.J.	—	Sumac, Yma	Ichocan, Peru	9/10/27
Simone, Nina	Tyron, N.C.	2/21/33	Summer, Donna	Boston, Mass.	12/31/48
Sinatra, Frank	Hoboken, N.J.	12/12/15	Susskind, David	New York, N.Y.	12/19/20
Sinatra, Nancy	Jersey City, N.J.	6/8/40	Sutherland, Donald	St. John, New Brunswick	7/17/34
Singer, Lori	Corpus Christie, Tex.	5/6/-	Sutherland, Joan	Sydney, Australia	11/7/26
Singer, Marc	Vancouver, B.C.	—	Suzuki, Pat	Cressey, Cal	1931
Skelton, Red (Richard)	Vincennes, Ind.	7/18/13	Sweet, Blanche	Chicago, Ill.	6/18/95
Slick, Grace	Chicago, Ill.	10/30/39	Swenson, Inga	Omaha, Neb.	12/29/34
Smith, Alexis	Penticton, B.C.	6/8/21	Sweet, Dolph	New York, N.Y.	7/18/20
Smith, Buffalo Bob	Buffalo, N.Y.	11/27/17	Swit, Loretta	Passaic, N.J.	11/4/37
Smith, Connie	Elkhart, Ind.	8/14/41			
Smith, Jaclyn	Houston, Tex.	10/26/48			
Smith, Kate	Greenville, Va.	5/1/07	Mr. T (Lawrence Tero)	Chicago, Ill.	5/21/52
Smith, Keely	Norfolk, Va.	3/9/35	Talbot, Lyle	Pittsburgh, Pa.	2/8/02
Smith, Maggie	Ilford, England.	12/28/34	Tallchief, Maria	Fairfax, Okla.	1/24/25
Smith, Roger	South Gate, Cal.	12/18/32	Tandy, Jessica	London, England	6/7/09
Smothers, Dick	New York, N.Y.	11/20/39	Tarkenton, Fran	Richmond, Va.	2/3/40
Smothers, Tom	New York, N.Y.	2/2/37	Tayback, Vic	New York, N.Y.	1/6/29
Snodgrass, Carrie	Park Ridge, Ill.	10/27/45	Taylor, Elizabeth	London, England	2/27/32
Snow, Hank	Nova Scotia, Canada	5/9/14	Taylor, James	Boston, Mass.	3/12/48
Snyder, Jimmy "Greek"	Steubenville, Oh.	9/9/19	Taylor, Kent	Nashua, Ia.	5/11/07
Snyder, Tom	Milwaukee, Wis.	5/12/36	Taylor, Rod	Sydney, Australia	1/11/29
Solti, Georg	Budapest, Hungary	10/21/12	Tebaldi, Renata	Pesaro, Italy	2/1/22
Somers, Suzanne	San Bruno, Cal.	10/16/46	Temple, Shirley	Santa Monica, Cal.	4/23/28
Somes, Michael	nr. Stroud, England.	9/28/17	Tennille, Toni	Montgomery, Ala.	5/8/43
Sommer, Elke	Berlin, Germany	11/5/41	Terris, Norma	Columbus, Kan.	1904
Sorvino, Paul	Brooklyn, N.Y.	1939	Terry-Thomas	London, England	7/14/11
Sothern, Ann	Valley City, N.D.	1/22/12	Tewes, Lauren	Braddock, Pa.	10/26/-
Soul, David	Chicago, Ill.	8/28/43	Tharp, Twyla	Portland, Ind.	7/1/41
Spacek, Sissy	Quitman, Tex.	12/25/49	Thaxter, Phyllis	Portland, Me.	11/20/21
Spano, Joe	San Francisco, Cal.	7/7/-	Thinnes, Roy	Chicago, Ill.	4/6/38
Spielberg, Stephen	Cincinnati, Oh.	12/18/47	Thomas, B.J.	Houston, Tex.	8/7/42
Springfield, Dusty	London, England	4/16/39	Thomas, Betty	St. Louis, Mo.	7/27/47
Springfield, Rick	Sydney, Australia.	8/23/49	Thomas, Danny	Deerfield, Mich.	1/6/14
Springsteen, Bruce	Freehold, N.J.	9/23/49	Thomas, Heather	Greenwich, Conn.	9/8/57
Stack, Robert	Los Angeles, Cal.	1/13/19	Thomas, Marlo	Detroit, Mich.	11/21/43
Stafford, Jo	Coalinga, Cal.	11/12/18	Thomas, Richard	New York, N.Y.	6/13/51
Stallone, Sylvester	New York, N.Y.	7/6/46	Thompson, Marshall	Peoria, Ill.	11/27/26
Stamp, Terence	Stepney, England.	7/22/39	Thompson, Sada	Des Moines, Ia.	9/27/29
Stander, Lionel	New York, N.Y.	1/11/08	Thulin, Ingrid	Sweden	1/27/29
Stang, Arnold	Chelsea, Mass.	9/28/25	Tiegs, Cheryl	Minnesota	9/27/47
Stanley, Kim	Tularosa, N.M.	2/11/25	Tierney, Gene	Brooklyn, N.Y.	11/20/20
Stanwyck, Barbara	Brooklyn, N.Y.	7/16/07	Tillis, Mel	Tampa, Fla.	8/8/32
Stapleton, Jean	New York, N.Y.	1/19/23	Tillstrom, Burr	Chicago, Ill.	10/13/17
Stapleton, Maureen	Troy, N.Y.	6/21/25	Tilton, Charlene	San Diego, Cal.	12/1/58
Starr, Kay	Dougherty, Okla.	7/21/22	Tiny Tim	New York, N.Y.	4/12/25
Starr, Ringo	Liverpool, England	7/7/40	Todd, Richard	Dublin, Ireland.	6/11/19
Steber, Eleanor	Wheeling, W. Va.	7/17/16	Tomlin, Lily	Detroit, Mich.	9/1/39
Steenburgen, Mary	Newport, Ark.	—	Tomlinson, David	Scotland	5/7/17
Steiger, Rod	W. Hampton, N.Y.	4/14/25	Toomey, Regis	Pittsburgh, Pa.	8/13/02
Steinberg, David	Winnipeg, Man.	8/9/42	Torme, Mel	Chicago, Ill.	9/13/25
Stephens, James	Mt. Kisco, N.Y.	5/18/51	Torn, Rip	Temple, Tex.	2/6/31
Sterling, Jan	New York, N.Y.	4/3/23	Tracy, Arthur	Russia	6/25/03
Sterling, Robert	New Castle, Pa.	11/13/17	Travanti, Daniel J.	Kenosha, Wis.	3/7/40
Stern, Isaac	Kreminiecz, Russia	7/21/20	Travers, Mary	Louisville, Ky.	11/9/36
Sternhagen, Frances	Washington, D.C.	1/13/30	Travolta, John	Englewood, N.J.	2/18/54
Stevens, Andrew	Memphis, Tenn.	6/10/55	Trevor, Claire	New York, N.Y.	3/8/09
Stevens, Cat	London, England	7/21/48	Troyanos, Tatiana	New York, N.Y.	9/12/38
Stevens, Connie	Brooklyn, N.Y.	8/8/38	Truffaut, Francois	Paris, France	2/6/32
Stevens, Kaye	E. Cleveland, Oh.	7/21/35	Tucker, Forrest	Plainfield, Ind.	2/12/19
Stevens, Rise	New York, N.Y.	6/11/13	Tucker, Tanya	Seminole, Tex.	10/10/58
Stevens, Stella	Yazoo City, Miss.	10/1/36	Tune, Tommy	Wichita Falls, Tex.	2/28/39
Stevens, Warren	Clark's Summit, Pa.	11/2/19	Turner, Ike	Clarksdale, Miss.	11/5/31
Stevenson, McLean	Normal, Ill.	11/14/29	Turner, Lana	Wallace, Ida.	2/8/20
Stevenson, Parker	Philadelphia, Pa.	6/4/53	Turner, Tina	Brownsville, Tex.	11/25/41
Stewart, James	Indiana, Pa.	5/20/08	Tushingham, Rita	Liverpool, England	3/14/42
Stewart, Rod	London, England	1/10/45	Twiggy (Leslie Hornby)	London, England	9/19/49
Stickney, Dorothy	Dickinson, N.D.	6/21/00	Twitty, Conway	Friar's Point, Miss.	9/1/33
Stiers, David Ogden	Peoria, Ill.	10/31/42	Tyson, Cicely	New York, N.Y.	12/19/33
Stiller, Jerry	New York, N.Y.	6/8/29			
Stills, Stephen	Dallas, Tex.	1/3/45			
Stockwell, Dean	Hollywood, Cal.	3/5/36	Uggams, Leslie	New York, N.Y.	5/25/43
Storch, Larry	New York, N.Y.	1/8/25	Ullmann, Liv	Tokyo, Japan	12/16/39
Storm, Gale	Bloomington, Tex.	4/5/21	Urich, Robert	Toronto, Ont.	12/19/47
Storrs, Suzanne	Salt Lake City, Ut.	1934	Ustinov, Peter	London, England	4/16/21
Straight, Beatrice	Old Westbury, N.Y.	8/2/18			
Strasberg, Susan	New York, N.Y.	5/22/38	Vaccaro, Brenda	Brooklyn, N.Y.	11/18/39
Stratas, Teresa	Toronto, Ont.	5/26/39	Vale, Jerry	New York, N.Y.	7/8/31
Strauss, Peter	New York, N.Y.	2/20/47	Valente, Caterina	Paris, France	1/14/32
Streep, Meryl	Summit, N.J.	1949	Valentine, Karen	Santa Rosa, Cal.	5/25/47
Streisand, Barbra	Brooklyn, N.Y.	4/24/42	Vallee, Rudy	Island Pond, Vt.	7/28/01
Stritch, Elaine	Detroit, Mich.	2/2/26	Valli, Alida	Pola, Italy	5/31/21
Struthers, Sally	Portland, Ore.	7/28/48	Valli, Frankie	Newark, N.J.	5/3/37
Stuarti, Enzo	Rome, Italy	3/3/25	Van Ark, Joan	New York, N.Y.	6/16/46
Sullivan, Barry	New York, N.Y.	8/29/12	Van Cleef, Lee	Somerville, N.J.	1/9/25
Sullivan, Susan	New York, N.Y.	11/18/-	Van Devere, Trish	Tenafly, N.J.	1945

Name	Birthplace	Born	Name	Birthplace	Born
Van Doren, Mamie	Rowena, S.D.	2/6/33	Widmark, Richard	Sunrise, Minn.	12/26/14
Van Dyke, Dick	West Plains, Mo.	12/13/25	Wilcox, Larry.	San Diego, Cal.	8/8/47
Van Dyke, Jerry	Danville, Ill.	7/27/32	Wilde, Cornel	New York, N.Y.	10/13/18
Van Fleet, Jo.	Oakland, Cal.	12/30/19	Wilder, Billy	Vienna, Austria	6/22/06
Van Pallandt, Nina.	Copenhagen, Denmark	7/15/32	Wilder, Gene.	Milwaukee, Wis.	6/11/35
Van Patten, Dick.	New York, N.Y.	12/9/28	Williams, Andy	Wall Lake, Ia.	12/3/30
Vaughan, Sarah	Newark, N.J.	3/27/24	Williams, Billy Dee	New York, N.Y.	4/6/38
Vaughn, Robert	New York, N.Y.	11/22/32	Williams, Cindy	Van Nuys, Cal.	8/22/47
Venuta, Benay	San Francisco, Cal.	1/27/11	Williams, Emlyn	Mostyn, Wales	11/26/05
Verdon, Gwen	Los Angeles, Cal.	1/13/25	Williams, Esther	Los Angeles, Cal.	8/8/23
Vereen, Ben	Miami, Fla.	10/10/46	Williams Jr., Hank	Shreveport, La.	5/26/49
Verrett, Shirley.	New Orleans, La.	5/31/31	Williams, Joe.	Cordele, Ga.	12/12/18
Vickers, Jon	Prince Albert, Sask.	10/26/26	Williams, JoBeth	Houston, Tex.	1953
Vigoda, Abe	New York, N.Y.	2/24/21	Williams, Paul	Omaha, Neb.	9/19/40
Villechaize, Herve	Paris, France	4/23/43	Williams, Robin	Chicago, Ill.	7/21/52
Villella, Edward	Long Island, N.Y.	10/1/36	Williams, Roger	Omaha, Neb.	1926
Vincent, Jan-Michael	Denver, Col.	7/15/44	Williams, Treat.	Rowayton, Conn.	—
Vinson, Helen	Beaumont, Tex.	9/17/07	Williamson, Nicol	Hamilton, Scotland	9/14/38
Vinton, Bobby	Canonsburg, Pa.	4/16/35	Wilson, Demond	Valdosta, Ga.	—
Voight, Jon	Yonkers, N.Y.	12/29/38	Wilson, Dolores	Philadelphia, Pa.	1929
Von Stade, Frederica	Somerville, N.J.	6/1/45	Wilson, Flip.	Jersey City, N.J.	12/8/33
Von Sydow, Max	Lund, Sweden.	4/10/29	Wilson, Nancy	Chillicothe, Oh.	2/20/37
Voorhees, Donald	Allentown, Pa.	7/26/03	Winchell, Paul	New York, N.Y.	12/21/22
Waggoner, Lyle	Kansas City, Kan.	4/13/35	Windom, William	New York, N.Y.	9/28/23
Wagner, Lindsay.	Los Angeles, Cal.	6/22/49	Winfield, Paul	Los Angeles, Cal.	5/22/41
Wagner, Robert	Detroit, Mich.	2/10/30	Winger, Debra	Columbus, Oh.	5/16/55
Wagoner, Porter.	West Plains, Mo.	8/12/27	Winkler, Henry	New York, N.Y.	10/30/45
Wain, Bea	Bronx, N.Y.	4/30/17	Winters, Jonathan	Dayton, Oh.	11/11/25
Waite, Ralph	White Plains, N.Y.	6/22/29	Winters, Shelley	St. Louis, Mo.	8/18/22
Waldon, Robert	New York, N.Y.	9/25/43	Wiseman, Joseph	Montreal, Que.	5/15/18
Walken, Christopher	New York, N.Y.	3/31/43	Withers, Jane	Atlanta, Ga.	4/12/27
Walker, Clint	Hartford, Ill.	5/30/27	Wonder, Stevie	Saginaw, Mich.	5/13/50
Walker, Jimmy	New York, N.Y.	—	Woodward, Joanne	Thomasville, Ga.	2/27/30
Walker, Nancy	Philadelphia, Pa.	5/10/21	Wopat, Tom	Lodi, Wis.	9/9/51
Wallach, Eli.	Brooklyn, N.Y.	12/7/15	Worth, Irene	Nebraska	6/23/16
Wallis, Hal	Chicago, Ill.	9/14/99	Wray, Fay	Alberta, Canada	9/10/07
Walston, Ray.	Laurel, Miss.	12/2/14	Wright, Martha	Seattle, Wash.	3/23/26
Walter, Jessica	New York, N.Y.	1/31/44	Wright, Teresa	New York, N.Y.	10/27/18
Wanamaker, Sam	Chicago, Ill.	6/14/19	Wrightson, Earl	Baltimore, Md.	1916
Ward, Simon	London, England	10/19/41	Wyatt, Jane	Campgaw, N.J.	8/10/11
Warden, Jack	Newark, N.J.	9/18/20	Wyman, Jane	St. Joseph, Mo.	1/4/14
Warfield, William.	W. Helena, Ark.	1/22/20	Wynette, Tammy	Red Bay, Ala.	5/5/42
Warhol, Andy	Pittsburgh, Pa.	8/6/27	Wynn, Keenan	New York, N.Y.	7/27/16
Waring, Fred	Tyrone, Pa.	6/9/00	Wynter, Dana	London, England	6/8/30
Warren, Michael	So. Bend, Ind.	3/5/46			
Warwick, Dionne.	E. Orange, N.J.	12/12/41			
Watson, Mills.	Oakland, Cal.	7/10/40	Yarborough, Glenn	Milwaukee, Wis.	1/12/30
Watts, Andre	Nuremberg, Germany	6/20/46	Yarrow, Peter	New York, N.Y.	5/31/38
Wayne, David	Traverse City, Mich.	1/30/14	York, Dick	Ft. Wayne, Ind.	9/4/28
Weaver, Dennis	Joplin, Mo.	6/4/24	York, Michael	Fulmer, England	3/27/42
Weaver, Fritz.	Pittsburgh, Pa.	1/19/26	York, Susannah	London, England	1/9/41
Weaver, Sigourney	Los Angeles, Cal.	10/8/49	Young, Alan	Northumberland, England	11/19/19
Welch, Raquel	Chicago, Ill.	9/5/42	Young, Burt	New York, N.Y.	4/30/40
Weld, Tuesday.	New York, N.Y.	8/27/43	Young, Loretta	Salt Lake City, Ut.	1/6/13
Welk, Lawrence	nr. Strasburg, N.D.	3/11/03	Young, Neil.	Toronto, Ont.	11/12/45
Welles, Orson	Kenosha, Wis.	5/6/15	Young, Robert	Chicago, Ill.	2/22/07
Wells, Kitty	Nashville, Tenn.	8/30/19	Youngman, Henny.	Liverpool, England	1906
Wendt, George	Chicago, Ill.	10/17/48			
Werner, Oskar.	Vienna, Austria	11/13/22			
Whelchel, Lisa	Ft. Worth, Tex.	5/29/63	Zappa, Frank.	Baltimore, Md.	12/21/40
White, Barry	Galveston, Tex.	9/12/44	Zeffirelli, Franco	Florence, Italy.	2/12/23
White, Betty	Oak Park, Ill.	1/17/24	Zimbalist, Efrem	Rostov, Russia	4/9/89
White, Jesse	Buffalo, N.Y.	1/3/19	Zimbalist, Efrem Jr.	New York, N.Y.	11/30/23
Whiting, Margaret	Detroit, Mich.	7/22/24	Zimbalist, Stephanie.	New York, N.Y.	10/6/56
Whitman, Stuart	San Francisco, Cal.	2/1/26	Zmed, Adrian	Chicago, Ill.	3/14/-
Whitmore, James	White Plains, N.Y.	10/1/21	Zukerman, Pinchas	Tel Aviv, Israel	7/16/48

Entertainment Personalities of the Past

Born	Died	Name	Born	Died	Name	Born	Died	Name
1895	1974	Abbott, Bud	1883	1950	Allgood, Sara	1890	1956	Arnold, Edward
1872	1953	Adams, Maude	1886	1954	Anderson, John Murray	1905	1974	Arquette, Cliff
1855	1926	Adler, Jacob P.	1915	1967	Andrews, Laverne	1885	1946	Atwill, Lionel
1898	1933	Adoree, Renee	1933	1971	Angeli, Pier	1845	1930	Auer, Leopold
1909	1964	Albertson, Frank	1876	1958	Anglin, Margaret	1905	1967	Auer, Mischa
1910	1981	Albertson, Jack	1887	1933	Arbuckle, Fatty (Roscoe)	1900	1972	Austin, Gene
1885	1952	Alda, Frances	1900	1976	Arlen, Richard	1898	1940	Ayres, Agnes
1894	1956	Allen, Fred	1868	1946	Arliss, George			
1906	1964	Allen, Gracie	1900	1971	Armstrong, Louis	1864	1922	Bacon, Frank

Born	Died	Name
1891	1968	Bainter, Fay
1895	1957	Baker, Belle
1906	1975	Baker, Josephine
1898	1963	Baker, Phil
1904	1983	Balanchine, George
1882	1956	Bancroft, George
1903	1968	Bankhead, Tallulah
1890	1952	Banks, Leslie
1890	1955	Bara, Theda
1810	1891	Barnum, Phineas T.
1912	1978	Barrie, Wendy
1879	1959	Barrymore, Ethel
1882	1942	Barrymore, John
1878	1954	Barrymore, Lionel
1848	1905	Barrymore, Maurice
1897	1963	Barthelmess, Richard
1890	1962	Barton, James
1904	1984	Basie, Count
1873	1951	Bauer, Harold
1893	1951	Baxter, Warner
1880	1928	Bayes, Nora
1904	1965	Beatty, Clyde
1904	1962	Beavers, Louise
1884	1946	Beery, Noah
1889	1949	Beery, Wallace
1901	1970	Begley, Ed
1854	1931	Belasco, David
1949	1982	Belushi, John
1906	1968	Benaderet, Bea
1906	1964	Bendix, William
1904	1965	Bennett, Constance
1873	1944	Bennett, Richard
1894	1974	Benny, Jack
1924	1970	Benzell, Mimi
1899	1966	Berg, Gertrude
1903	1978	Bergen, Edgar
1915	1982	Bergman, Ingrid
1895	1976	Berkeley, Busby
1863	1927	Bernard, Sam
1844	1923	Bernhardt, Sarah
1893	1943	Bernie, Ben
1889	1967	Bickford, Charles
1911	1960	Bjoerling, Jussi
1898	1973	Blackmer, Sidney
1882	1951	Blaney, Charles E.
1900	1943	Bledsoe, Jules
1928	1972	Blocker, Dan
1909	1970	Blondell, Joan
1888	1959	Blore, Eric
1901	1975	Blue, Ben
1899	1957	Bogart, Humphrey
1880	1965	Boland, Mary
1897	1969	Boles, John
1903	1960	Bond, Ward
1892	1981	Bondi, Beulah
1917	1981	Boone, Richard
1833	1893	Booth, Edwin
1796	1852	Booth, Junius Brutus
1894	1953	Bordoni, Irene
1888	1960	Bori, Lucrezia
1905	1965	Bow, Clara
1874	1946	Bowes, Maj. Edward
1928	1977	Boyd, Stephen
1898	1972	Boyd, William
1899	1978	Boyer, Charles
1893	1939	Brady, Alice
1871	1936	Breese, Edmund
1898	1964	Brendel, El
1894	1974	Brennan, Walter
1904	1979	Brent, George
1875	1948	Brian, Donald
1891	1951	Brice, Fanny
1891	1959	Broderick, Helen
1904	1951	Bromberg, J. Edward
1892	1973	Brown, Joe E.
1926	1966	Bruce, Lenny
1895	1953	Bruce, Nigel
1910	1982	Bruce, Virginia
1903	1979	Buchanan, Edgar
1891	1957	Buchanan, Jack
1885	1957	Buck, Gene
1938	1982	Buono, Victor
1885	1970	Burke, Billie
1912	1967	Burnette, Smiley
1896	1956	Burns, Bob
1902	1971	Burns, David
1882	1941	Burr, Henry

Born	Died	Name
1897	1946	Busch, Mae
1883	1966	Bushman, Francis X.
1896	1946	Butterworth, Charles
1893	1971	Byington, Spring
1905	1972	Cabot, Bruce
1918	1977	Cabot, Sebastian
1895	1956	Calhern, Louis
1923	1977	Callas, Maria
1853	1942	Calve, Emma
1933	1976	Cambridge, Godfrey
1865	1940	Campbell, Mrs. Patrick
1892	1964	Cantor, Eddie
1878	1947	Carey, Harry
1950	1983	Carpenter, Karen
1880	1961	Carrillo, Leo
1892	1972	Carroll, Leo G.
1905	1965	Carroll, Nancy
1910	1963	Carson, Jack
1862	1937	Carter, Mrs. Leslie
1873	1921	Caruso, Enrico
1876	1973	Casals, Pablo
1927	1976	Cassidy, Jack
1893	1969	Castle, Irene
1887	1918	Castle, Vernon
1889	1960	Catlett, Walter
1887	1950	Cavanaugh, Hobart
1873	1938	Chaliapin, Feodor
1921	1980	Champion, Gower
1918	1961	Chandler, Jeff
1883	1930	Chaney, Lon
1905	1973	Chaney Jr., Lon
1889	1977	Chaplin, Charles
1093	1940	Chase, Charlie
1893	1961	Chatterton, Ruth
1888	1972	Chevalier, Maurice
1888	1960	Clark, Bobby
1914	1968	Clark, Fred
1887	1950	Clayton, Lou
1920	1966	Clift, Montgomery
1932	1963	Cline, Patsy
1900	1937	Clive, Colin
1892	1967	Clyde, Andy
1911	1976	Cobb, Lee J.
1877	1961	Coburn, Charles
1887	1934	Cody, Lew
1878	1942	Cohan, George M.
1919	1965	Cole, Nat (King)
1878	1955	Collier, Constance
1890	1965	Collins, Ray
1891	1958	Colman, Ronald
1908	1934	Columbo, Russ
1907	1944	Compton, Betty
1887	1940	Connolly, Walter
1915	1982	Conried, Hans
1855	1909	Conried, Henrich
1914	1975	Conte, Richard
1914	1984	Coogan, Jackie
1901	1961	Cooper, Gary
1891	1971	Cooper, Gladys
1896	1973	Cooper, Melville
1914	1968	Corey, Wendell
1893	1974	Cornell, Katherine
1890	1972	Correll, Charles (Andy)
1905	1979	Costello, Dolores
1904	1957	Costello, Helene
1908	1959	Costello, Lou
1877	1950	Costello, Maurice
1899	1973	Coward, Noel
1890	1950	Cowl, Jane
1924	1973	Cox, Wally
1908	1983	Crabbe, Buster
1847	1924	Crabtree, Lotta
1928	1978	Crane, Bob
1875	1945	Craven, Frank
1908	1977	Crawford, Joan
1916	1944	Cregar, Laird
1880	1942	Crews, Laura Hope
1880	1974	Crisp, Donald
1942	1973	Croce, Jim
1910	1960	Cromwell, Richard
1903	1977	Crosby, Bing
1897	1975	Cross, Milton
1878	1968	Currie, Finlay
1816	1876	Cushman, Charlotte
1917	1978	Dailey, Dan

Born	Died	Name
1899	1981	Chief Dan George
1923	1965	Dandridge, Dorothy
1869	1941	Danforth, William
1894	1963	Daniell, Henry
1901	1971	Daniels, Bebe
1860	1935	Daniels, Frank
1936	1973	Darin, Bobby
1921	1965	Darnell, Linda
1879	1967	Darwell, Jane
1866	1949	Davenport, Harry
1897	1961	Davies, Marion
1907	1961	Davis, Joan
1931	1955	Dean, James
1881	1950	DeCordoba, Pedro
1905	1968	Dekker, Albert
1908	1983	Del Rio, Dolores
1881	1959	DeMille, Cecil B.
1891	1967	Denny, Reginald
1901	1974	DeSica, Vittorio
1905	1977	Devine, Andy
1942	1972	De Wilde, Brandon
1907	1974	De Wolfe, Billy
1865	1950	De Wolfe, Elsie
1879	1947	Digges, Dudley
1901	1966	Disney, Walt
1894	1949	Dix, Richard
1856	1924	Dockstader, Lew
1892	1941	Dolly, Jennie
1892	1970	Dolly, Rosie
1905	1958	Donat, Robert
1903	1972	Donlevy, Brian
1901	1981	Douglas, Melvyn
1907	1959	Douglas, Paul
—	1980	Dragonette, Jessica
1889	1956	Draper, Ruth
1881	1965	Dresser, Louise
1869	1934	Dressler, Marie
1820	1897	Drew, Mrs. John
1853	1927	Drew, John (son)
1909	1951	Duchin, Eddy
1890	1965	Dumont, Margaret
1878	1927	Duncan, Isadora
1905	1967	Dunn, James
1893	1980	Durante, Jimmy
1907	1968	Duryea, Dan
1858	1924	Duse, Eleanora
1894	1929	Eagels, Jeanne
1896	1930	Eames, Clare
1865	1952	Eames, Emma
1901	1967	Eddy, Nelson
1897	1971	Edwards, Cliff
1879	1945	Edwards, Gus
1899	1974	Ellington, Duke
1941	1974	Elliot, Cass
1871	1940	Elliott, Maxine
1891	1967	Elman, Mischa
1881	1951	Errol, Leon
1903	1967	Erwin, Stuart
1888	1976	Evans, Edith
1913	1967	Evelyn, Judith
1883	1939	Fairbanks, Douglas
1915	1970	Farmer, Frances
1870	1929	Farnum, Dustin
1876	1953	Farnum, William
1882	1967	Farrar, Geraldine
1904	1971	Farrell, Glenda
1868	1940	Faversham, William
1861	1939	Fawcett, George
1897	1960	Fay, Frank
1895	1962	Fazenda, Louise
1933	1982	Feldman, Marty
1894	1979	Fiedler, Arthur
1918	1973	Field, Betty
1898	1979	Fields, Gracie
1867	1941	Fields, Lew
1879	1946	Fields, W.C.
1931	1978	Fields, Totie
1916	1977	Finch, Peter
1865	1932	Fiske, Minnie Maddern
1888	1961	Fitzgerald, Barry
1895	1962	Flagstad, Kirsten
1900	1971	Flippen, Jay C.
1909	1959	Flynn, Errol
1925	1974	Flynn, Joe
1880	1942	Fokine, Michel

Born	Died	Name
1910	1968	Foley, Red
1905	1982	Fonda, Henry
1920	1978	Fontaine, Frank
1887	1983	Fontanne, Lynn
1853	1937	Forbes-Robertson, J.
1895	1973	Ford, John
1901	1976	Ford, Paul
1899	1966	Ford, Wallace
1806	1872	Forrest, Edwin
1902	1970	Foster, Preston
1857	1928	Foy, Eddie
1903	1968	Francis, Kay
1893	1966	Frawley, William
1885	1938	Frederick, Pauline
1870	1955	Friganza, Trixie
1890	1958	Frisco, Joe
1860	1915	Frohman, Charles
1851	1940	Frohman, Daniel
1885	1947	Fyffe, Will
1901	1960	Gable, Clark
1889	1963	Galli-Curci, Amelita
1877	1967	Garden, Mary
1913	1952	Garfield, John
1922	1969	Garland, Judy
1893	1963	Gaxton, William
1939	1984	Gaye, Marvin
1902	1978	Geer, Will
1904	1954	George, Gladys
1892	1962	Gibson, Hoot
1890	1957	Gigli, Beniamino
1894	1971	Gilbert, Billy
1897	1936	Gilbert, John
1855	1937	Gillette, William
1867	1943	Gillmore, Frank
1879	1939	Gilpin, Charles
1898	1968	Gish, Dorothy
1886	1959	Gleason, James
1884	1938	Gluck, Alma
1903	1983	Godfrey, Arthur
1874	1955	Golden, John
1884	1974	Goldwyn, Samuel
1917	1969	Gorcey, Leo
1884	1940	Gordon, C. Henry
1899	1982	Gosden, Freeman (Amos)
1869	1944	Gottschalk, Ferdinand
1829	1869	Gottschalk, Louis
1916	1973	Grable, Betty
1929	1981	Grahame, Gloria
1901	1959	Gray, Gilda
1879	1954	Greenstreet, Sydney
1874	1948	Griffith, David Wark
1912	1967	Guthrie, Woody
1875	1959	Gwenn, Edmund
1888	1942	Hackett, Charles
1902	1958	Hackett, Raymond
1870	1943	Haines, Robert T.
1892	1950	Hale, Alan
1927	1981	Haley, Bill
1899	1979	Haley, Jack
1847	1919	Hammerstein, Oscar
1879	1955	Hampden, Walter
1924	1964	Haney, Carol
1893	1964	Hardwicke, Sir Cedric
1892	1957	Hardy, Oliver
1883	1939	Hare, T.E. (Ernie)
1911	1937	Harlow, Jean
1872	1946	Harned, Virginia
1844	1911	Harrigan, Edward
1870	1946	Hart, William S.
1907	1955	Hartman, Grace
1928	1973	Harvey, Laurence
1910	1973	Hawkins, Jack
1890	1973	Hayakawa, Sessue
1885	1969	Hayes, Gabby
1918	1980	Haymes, Dick
1902	1971	Hayward, Leland
1917	1975	Hayward, Susan
1896	1937	Healy, Ted
1910	1971	Heflin, Van
1879	1936	Heggie, O.P.
1873	1918	Held, Anna
1942	1970	Hendrix, Jimi
1913	1969	Henie, Sonja
1879	1942	Herbert, Henry
1887	1951	Herbert, Hugh

Born	Died	Name
1886	1956	Hersholt, Jean
1895	1942	Hibbard, Edna
1899	1980	Hitchcock, Alfred
1914	1955	Hodiak, John
1894	1973	Holden, Fay
1918	1981	Holden, William
1922	1965	Holliday, Judy
1936	1959	Holly, Buddy
1888	1951	Holt, Jack
1918	1973	Holt, Tim
1871	1947	Homer, Louise
1898	1978	Homolka, Oscar
1902	1972	Hopkins, Miriam
1858	1935	Hopper, DeWolf
1874	1959	Hopper, Edna Wallace
1888	1970	Horton, Edward Everett
1874	1926	Houdini, Harry
1881	1965	Howard, Eugene
1867	1961	Howard, Joe
1893	1943	Howard, Leslie
1885	1955	Howard, Tom
1885	1949	Howard, Willie
1914	1972	Hudson, Rochelle
1890	1977	Hull, Henry
1886	1957	Hull, Josephine
1895	1958	Humphrey, Doris
1895	1945	Hunter, Glenn
1925	1969	Hunter, Jeffrey
1901	1962	Husing, Ted
1884	1950	Huston, Walter
1892	1950	Ingram, Rex
1895	1969	Ingram, Rex
1895	1980	Iturbi, Jose
1838	1905	Irving, Henry
1871	1944	Irving, Isabel
1872	1914	Irving, Laurence
1875	1942	Jackson, Joe
1911	1972	Jackson, Mahalia
1891	1984	Jaffe, Sam
1889	1956	Janis, Elsie
1886	1950	Jannings, Emil
1930	1980	Janssen, David
1829	1905	Jefferson, Joseph
1859	1923	Jefferson, Thomas
1900	1974	Jenkins, Allen
1898	1981	Jessel, George
1862	1930	Jewett, Henry
1892	1962	Johnson, Chic
1878	1952	Johnson, Edward
1886	1950	Jolson, Al
1889	1942	Jones, Buck
1933	1983	Jones, Carolyn
1911	1965	Jones, Spike
1943	1970	Joplin, Janis
1897	1961	Jordan, Marian
		(Molly McGee)
1905	1981	Joslyn, Allyn
1890	1955	Joyce, Alice
1910	1966	Kane, Helen
1887	1969	Karloff, Boris
1893	1970	Karns, Roscoe
1811	1868	Kean, Charles
1806	1880	Kean, Mrs. Charles
1787	1833	Kean, Edmund
1895	1966	Keaton, Buster
1858	1929	Keenan, Frank
1830	1873	Keene, Laura
1841	1893	Keene, Thomas W.
1899	1960	Keith, Ian
1894	1973	Kellaway, Cecil
1898	1979	Kelly, Emmett
1929	1982	Kelly, Grace
1910	1981	Kelly, Patsy
1899	1956	Kelly, Walter C.
1873	1939	Kelly, Walter C.
1909	1968	Kelton, Pert
1823	1895	Kemble, Agnes
1775	1854	Kemble, Charles
1809	1893	Kemble, Fannie
1848	1935	Kendal, Dame Madge
1843	1917	Kendal, William H.
1926	1959	Kendall, Kay
1890	1948	Kennedy, Edgar
1886	1945	Kent, William

Born	Died	Name
1880	1947	Kerrigan, J. Warren
1886	1956	Kibbee, Guy
1902	1966	Kiepura, Jan
1888	1964	Kilbride, Percy
1863	1933	Kilgour, Joseph
1897	1971	King, Dennis
1901	1980	Kostelanetz, Andre
1919	1962	Kovacs, Ernie
1885	1974	Kruger, Otto
1913	1964	Ladd, Alan
1895	1967	Lahr, Bert
1919	1973	Lake, Veronica
1925	1982	Lamas, Fernando
1919	1948	Landis, Carole
1904	1972	Landis, Jessie Royce
1884	1944	Langdon, Harry
1853	1929	Langtry, Lillie
1921	1959	Lanza, Mario
1870	1950	Lauder, Harry
1899	1962	Laughton, Charles
1890	1965	Laurel, Stan
1898	1952	Lawrence, Gertrude
1890	1929	Lawrence, Margaret
1940	1973	Lee, Bruce
1907	1952	Lee, Canada
1914	1970	Lee, Gypsy Rose
1848	1929	Lehmann, Lilli
1888	1976	Lehmann, Lotte
1896	1950	Lehr, Lew
1913	1967	Leigh, Vivien
1852	1908	Leighton, Margaret
1922	1976	Leighton, Margaret
1894	1931	Leitzel, Lillian
1940	1980	Lennon, John
1900	1981	Lenya, Lotte
1870	1941	Leonard, Eddie
1911	1973	Leonard, Jack E.
1906	1972	Levant, Oscar
1905	1980	Levene, Sam
1911	1980	Levenson, Sam
1881	1955	Levy, Ethel
1902	1971	Lewis, Joe E.
1892	1971	Lewis, Ted
1874	1944	Lhevinne, Josef
1889	1952	Lincoln, Elmo
1820	1887	Lind, Jenny
1889	1968	Lindsay, Howard
1869	1952	Lipman, Clara
1893	1971	Lloyd, Harold
1870	1922	Lloyd, Marie
1891	1957	Lockhart, Gene
1913	1969	Logan, Ella
1909	1942	Lombard, Carole
1902	1977	Lombardo, Guy
1927	1974	Long, Richard
1895	1975	Lopez, Vincent
1888	1968	Lorne, Marion
1904	1964	Lorre, Peter
1914	1962	Lovejoy, Frank
1892	1971	Lowe, Edmund
1892	1947	Lubitsch, Ernst
1882	1956	Lugosi, Bela
1895	1971	Lukas, Paul
1892	1977	Lunt, Alfred
1853	1932	Lupino, George
1893	1942	Lupino, Stanley
1897	1957	Lyman, Abe
1926	1982	Lynde, Paul
1926	1971	Lynn, Diana
1885	1954	Lytell, Bert
1867	1936	Lytton, Henry
1907	1965	MacDonald, Jeanette
1902	1969	MacLane, Barton
1909	1973	Macready, George
1861	1946	Macy, George Carleton
1908	1973	Magnani, Anna
1896	1967	Mahoney, Will
1890	1975	Main, Marjorie
1933	1967	Mansfield, Jayne
1854	1907	Mansfield, Richard
1905	1980	Mantovani, Annunzio
1897	1975	March, Fredric
1865	1950	Marlowe, Julia
1890	1966	Marshall, Herbert
1864	1943	Marshall, Tully

Born	Died	Name	Born	Died	Name	Born	Died	Name
1920	1981	Martin, Ross	1903	1978	Oakie, Jack	1878	1953	Ruffo, Titta
1885	1969	Martinelli, Giovanni	1860	1926	Oakley, Annie	1892	1970	Ruggles, Charles
1888	1964	Marx, Arthur (Harpo)	1911	1979	Oberon, Merle	1864	1936	Russell, Annie
1890	1977	Marx, Julius (Groucho)	1899	1983	O'Brien, Pat	1924	1961	Russell, Gail
1887	1961	Marx, Leonard (Chico)	1908	1981	O'Connell, Arthur	1861	1922	Russell, Lillian
1896	1983	Massey, Raymond	1898	1943	O'Connell, Hugh	1911	1976	Russell, Rosalind
1862	1951	Maude, Cyril	1880	1959	O'Connor, Una	1892	1972	Rutherford, Margaret
1922	1972	Maxwell, Marilyn	1878	1945	O'Hara, Fiske	1902	1973	Ryan, Irene
1879	1948	May, Edna	1908	1968	O'Keefe, Dennis	1909	1973	Ryan, Robert
1885	1957	Mayer, Louis B.	1880	1938	Oland, Warner			
1895	1973	Maynard, Ken	1860	1932	Olcott, Chauncey	1924	1963	Sabu (Dastagir)
1884	1945	McCormack, John	1883	1942	Oliver, Edna May	1877	1968	St. Denis, Ruth
1907	1962	McCormick, Myron	1892	1963	Olsen, Ole	1884	1955	Sakall, S.Z.
1888	1931	McCoy, Bessie	1849	1920	O'Neill, James	1885	1936	Sale (Chic), Charles
1895	1952	McDaniel, Hattie	1876	1949	Ouspenskaya, Maria	1906	1972	Sanders, George
1924	1965	McDonald, Marie	1887	1972	Owen, Reginald	1934	1973	Sands, Diana
1913	1975	McGiver, John				1896	1960	Savo, Jimmy
1899	1981	McHugh, Frank	1860	1941	Paderewski, Ignace	1879	1954	Scheff, Fritzi
1879	1949	McIntyre, Frank J.	1889	1954	Pallette, Eugene	1892	1930	Schenck, Joe
1857	1937	McIntyre, James	1894	1958	Pangborn, Franklin	1895	1964	Schildkraut, Joseph
1879	1937	McKinley, Mabel	1914	1975	Parks, Larry	1865	1930	Schildkraut, Rudolph
1883	1959	McLaglen, Victor	1881	1940	Pasternack, Josef A.	1889	1965	Schipa, Tito
1907	1971	McMahon, Horace	1837	1908	Pastor, Tony	1882	1951	Schnabel, Artur
1930	1980	McQueen, Steve	1843	1919	Patti, Adelina	1938	1982	Schneider, Romy
1920	1980	Medford, Kay	1840	1889	Patti, Carlotta	1910	1949	Schumann, Henrietta
1880	1946	Meek, Donald	1885	1931	Pavlova, Anna	1861	1936	Schumann-Heink, E.
1879	1936	Meighan, Thomas	1900	1973	Paxinou, Katina	1866	1945	Scott, Cyril
1861	1931	Melba, Nellie	1885	1950	Pemberton, Brock	1914	1965	Scott, Zachary
1890	1973	Melchior, Lauritz	1899	1967	Pendleton, Nat	1843	1896	Scott-Siddons, Mrs.
1904	1961	Melton, James	1905	1941	Penner, Joe	1938	1979	Seberg, Jean
1890	1963	Menjou, Adolphe	1892	1937	Perkins, Osgood	1892	1974	Seeley, Blossom
1902	1966	Menken, Helen	1893	1956	Peters, Brandon	1925	1980	Sellers, Peter
1908	1984	Merman, Ethel	1915	1963	Piaf, Edith	1902	1965	Selznick, David O
1904	1944	Miller, Glenn	1893	1979	Pickford, Mary	1858	1935	Sembrich, Marcella
1860	1926	Miller, Henry	1892	1957	Pinza, Ezio	1880	1960	Sennett, Mack
1898	1936	Miller, Marilyn	1898	1963	Pitts, Zasu	1881	1951	Shattuck, Arthur
1895	1927	Mills, Florence	1904	1976	Pons, Lili	1860	1929	Shaw, Mary
1939	1976	Mineo, Sal	1897	1981	Ponselle, Rosa	1927	1978	Shaw, Robert
1903	1955	Minnevitch, Borrah	1903	1969	Portman, Eric	1891	1972	Shawn, Ted
1913	1955	Miranda, Carmen	1904	1963	Powell, Dick	1868	1949	Shean, Al
1892	1962	Mitchell, Thomas	1912	1982	Powell, Eleanor	1902	1983	Shearer, Norma
1880	1940	Mix, Tom	1892	1984	Powell, William	1915	1967	Sheridan, Ann
1845	1909	Modjeska, Helena	1913	1958	Power, Tyrone	1885	1934	Sherman, Lowell
1926	1962	Monroe, Marilyn	1872	1935	Powers, Eugene	1918	1970	Shriner, Herb
1911	1973	Monroe, Vaughn	1935	1977	Presley, Elvis	1875	1953	Shubert, Lee
1875	1964	Monteux, Pierre	1856	1919	Primrose, George	1882	1930	Sills, Milton
1917	1951	Montez, Maria	1954	1977	Prinze, Freddie	1900	1976	Sim, Alastair
1904	1981	Montgomery, Robert	1879	1956	Prouty, Jed	1878	1946	Sis Hopkins (Melville)
1901	1947	Moore, Grace	1871	1942	Pryor, Arthur	1891	1934	Skelly, Hal
1885	1955	Moore, Tom				1858	1942	Skinner, Otis
1876	1962	Moore, Victor	1895	1980	Raft, George	1870	1952	Skipworth, Alison
1906	1974	Moorehead, Agnes	1890	1967	Rains, Claude	1863	1948	Smith, C. Aubrey
1882	1949	Moran, George	1889	1970	Rambeau, Marjorie	1917	1979	Soo, Jack
1884	1952	Moran, Polly	1900	1947	Rankin, Arthur	1826	1881	Sothern, Edward A.
1890	1949	Morgan, Frank	1892	1967	Rathbone, Basil	1859	1933	Sothern, Edward H.
1900	1941	Morgan, Helen	1897	1960	Ratoff, Gregory	1884	1957	Sothern, Harry
1888	1956	Morgan, Ralph	1883	1953	Rawlinson, Herbert	1854	1932	Sousa, John Philip
1901	1970	Morris, Chester	1891	1943	Ray, Charles	1884	1957	Sparks, Ned
1849	1925	Morris, Clara	1941	1967	Redding, Otis	1876	1948	Speaks, Oley
1914	1959	Morris, Wayne	1914	1959	Reeves, George	1890	1970	Spitalny, Phil
1943	1971	Morrison, Jim	1923	1964	Reeves, Jim	1873	1937	Standing, Guy
1915	1977	Mostel, Zero	1860	1916	Rehan, Ada	1900	1941	Stephenson, James
1897	1969	Mowbray, Alan	1892	1923	Reid, Wallace	1883	1939	Sterling, Ford
1895	1967	Muni, Paul	1873	1943	Reinhardt, Max	1882	1928	Stevens, Emily A.
1894	1953	Munn, Frank	1909	1971	Rennie, Michael	1934	1970	Stevens, Inger
1924	1971	Murphy, Audie	1902	1983	Richardson, Ralph	1896	1961	Stewart, Anita
1885	1965	Murray, Mae	1870	1940	Richman, Charles	1882	1977	Stokowski, Leopold
			1895	1972	Richman, Harry	1873	1959	Stone, Fred
1896	1970	Nagel, Conrad	1872	1961	Ring, Blanche	1879	1953	Stone, Lewis
1900	1973	Naish, J. Carroll	1898	1977	Ritchard, Cyril	1904	1980	Stone, Milburn
1898	1961	Naldi, Nita	1907	1974	Ritter, Tex	1898	1959	Sturges, Preston
1888	1950	Nash, Florence	1905	1969	Ritter, Thelma	1911	1960	Sullavan, Margaret
1865	1945	Nash, George	1903	1966	Ritz, Al	1902	1974	Sullivan, Ed
1879	1945	Nazimova, Alla	1925	1982	Robbins, Marty	1903	1956	Sullivan, Francis L.
1846	1905	Neilson, Ada	1898	1976	Robeson, Paul	1892	1946	Summerville, Slim
1848	1880	Neilson, Adelaide	1878	1949	Robinson, Bill	1899	1983	Swanson, Gloria
1868	1957	Neilson-Terry, Julia	1893	1973	Robinson, Edward G.	1904	1969	Swarthout, Gladys
1907	1975	Nelson, Ozzie	1865	1942	Robson, May			
1885	1967	Nesbit, Evelyn	1905	1977	Rochester (E. Anderson)	1893	1957	Talmadge, Norma
1870	1951	Nethersole, Olga	1897	1933	Rodgers, Jimmy	1900	1972	Tamiroff, Akim
1910	1983	Niven, David	1894	1958	Rodzinsky, Artur	1878	1947	Tanguay, Eva
1874	1948	Niblo, Fred	1879	1935	Rogers, Will	1899	1934	Tashman, Lilyan
1890	1950	Nijinsky, Vaslav	1897	1937	Roland, Ruth	1885	1966	Taylor, Deems
1893	1974	Nilsson, Anna Q.	1880	1962	Rooney, Pat	1899	1958	Taylor, Estelle
1898	1930	Normand, Mabel	1899	1966	Rose, Billy	1887	1946	Taylor, Laurette
1879	1959	Norworth, Jack	1910	1980	Roth, Lillian	1911	1969	Taylor, Robert
1905	1968	Novarro, Ramon	1882	1936	Rothafel, S. L. (Roxy)	1878	1938	Tearle, Conway
1893	1951	Novello, Ivor	1887	1982	Rubinstein, Artur			

Born	Died	Name
1884	1953	Tearle, Godfrey
1892	1937	Tell, Alma
1864	1942	Tempest, Marie
1910	1963	Templeton, Alec
1847	1928	Terry, Ellen
1871	1940	Tetrazzini, Luisa
1899	1936	Thalberg, Irving
1857	1914	Thomas, Brandon
1892	1960	Thomas, John Charles
1882	1976	Thorndike, Sybil
		(Three Stooges):
1902	1975	Fine, Larry
1906	1952	Howard, Curly
1897	1975	Howard, Moe
1869	1936	Thurston, Howard
1896	1960	Tibbett, Lawrence
1887	1940	Tinney, Frank
1909	1958	Todd, Michael
1906	1935	Todd, Thelma
1874	1947	Toler, Sidney
1905	1968	Tone, Franchot
1867	1957	Toscanini, Arturo
1898	1968	Tracy, Lee
1900	1967	Tracy, Spencer
1903	1972	Traubel, Helen
1894	1975	Treacher, Arthur
1853	1917	Tree, Herbert Beerbohm
1889	1973	Truex, Ernest
1915	1975	Tucker, Richard
1884	1966	Tucker, Sophie
1874	1940	Turpin, Ben
1908	1959	Twelvetrees, Helen
1894	1970	Ulric, Lenore
1933	1975	Ure, Mary
1895	1926	Valentino, Rudolph
1870	1950	Van, Billy B.
1912	1979	Vance, Vivian
1893	1943	Veidt, Conrad
1926	1981	Vera-Ellen
1885	1957	Von Stroheim, Erich
1906	1981	Von Zell, Harry
1887	1969	Walburn, Raymond
1874	1946	Waldron, Charles D.
1904	1966	Walker, June
1914	1951	Walker, Robert
1898	1983	Wallenstein, Alfred
1887	1980	Walsh, Raoul
1876	1962	Walter, Bruno
1878	1936	Walthall, Henry B.
1872	1952	Ward, Fannie
1866	1951	Warfield, David
1876	1958	Warner, H. B.
1878	1964	Warwick, Robert
1924	1963	Washington, Dinah
1900	1977	Waters, Ethel
1867	1945	Watson, Billy
1907	1979	Wayne, John
1896	1966	Webb, Clifton
1920	1982	Webb, Jack
1867	1942	Weber, Joe
1905	1973	Webster, Margaret
1896	1975	Wellman, William
1892	1980	West, Mae
1895	1968	Wheeler, Bert
1889	1938	White, Pearl
1891	1967	Whiteman, Paul
1865	1948	Whitty, Dame May
1912	1979	Wilding, Michael
1895	1948	William, Warren
1877	1922	Williams, Bert
1867	1918	Williams, Evan
1923	1953	Williams, Hank
1902	1978	Wills, Chill
1917	1972	Wilson, Marie
1884	1969	Winninger, Charles
1904	1959	Withers, Grant
1881	1931	Wolheim, Louis
1907	1961	Wong, Anna May
1938	1981	Wood, Natalie
1892	1978	Wood, Peggy
1888	1963	Woolley, Monty
1881	1956	Wycherly, Margaret
1902	1981	Wyler, William
1886	1966	Wynn, Ed
1906	1964	Wynyard, Diana
1890	1960	Young, Clara Kimball
1917	1978	Young, Gig
1887	1953	Young, Roland
1902	1979	Zanuck, Darryl F.
1869	1932	Ziegfeld, Florenz
1873	1976	Zukor, Adolph

The Theater Hall of Fame

The Theater Hall of Fame was created to honor those who have made outstanding contributions to the New York theater. Members are elected annually by the nation's drama critics and drama editors.

George Abbott
Maude Adams
Viola Adams
Ira Aldridge
Winthrop Ames
Judith Anderson
Maxwell Anderson
Robert Anderson
Margaret Anglin
Harold Arlen
George Arliss
Boris Aronson
Fred & Adele Astaire
Brooks Atkinson
Tallulah Bankhead
Philip Barry
Ethel Barrymore
John Barrymore
Lionel Barrymore
Nora Bayes
S. N. Behrman
David Belasco
Norman Bel Geddes
Richard Bennett
Irving Berlin
Sarah Bernhardt
Leonard Bernstein
Kermit Bloomgarden
Ray Bolger
Edwin Booth
Junius Brutus Booth
Shirley Booth
Alice Brady
Fannie Brice
Peter Brook
John Mason Brown
Billie Burke
Abe Burrows
Mrs. Patrick Campbell
Eddie Cantor
Morris Carnovsky
Mrs. Leslie Carter
Gower Champion
Carol Channing
Ruth Chatterton
Ina Claire
Bobby Clark
Harold Clurman
Lee J. Cobb
George M. Cohan
Constance Collier
Betty Comden & Adolph Green
Marc Connelly
Katharine Cornell
Noel Coward
Jane Cowl
Cheryl Crawford

Hume Cronyn
Russel Crouse
Charlotte Cushman
Augustin Daly
Alfred de Liagre, Jr.
Agnes DeMille
Colleen Dewhurst
Howard Dietz & Arthur Schwartz
Dudley Digges
Alfred Drake
Marie Dressler
Mrs. John Drew
John Drew
Mildred Dunnock
Eleanora Duse
Jeanne Eagles
Florence Eldridge
Lehman Engel
Maurice Evans
Jose Ferrer
W. C. Fields
Minnie Maddern Fiske
Cylde Fitch
Henry Fonda
Lynn Fontanne
Edwin Forrest
Bob Fosse
Rudolf Friml
Charles Frohman
Grace George
George & Ira Gershwin
John Gielgud
William Gillette
Lillian Gish
John Golden
Ruth Gordon
Charlotte Greenwood
Tyrone Guthrie
Uta Hagen
Oscar Hammerstein II
Walter Hampden
Otto Harbach
E. Y. "Yip" Harburg
Harrigan & Hart
Jed Harris
Julie Harris
Sam H. Harris
Rex Harrison
Lorenz Hart
Moss Hart
Helen Hayes
Lillian Hellman
Katharine Hepburn
Victor Herbert
Raymond Hitchcock
Arthur Hopkins
De Wolf Hopper

John Houseman
Leslie Howard
Sidney Howard
Willie & Eugene Howard
Henry Hull
Walter Huston
William Inge
Elsie Janis
Joseph Jefferson
Al Jolson
Robert Edmond Jones
George S. Kaufman
Elia Kazan
George Kelly
Jerome Kern
Walter Kerr
Michael Kidd
Sidney Kingsley
Bert Lahr
Lawrence Langner
Lillie Langtry
Angela Lansbury
Arthur Laurents
Gertrude Lawrence
Eva Le Gallienne
Lotte Lenya
Alan Jay Lerner
Sam Levene
Beatrice Lillie
Howard Lindsay
Frank Loesser
Frederick Loewe
Joshua Logan
Pauline Lord
Alfred Lunt
Ben Hecht & Charles MacArthur
Rouben Mamoulian
Richard Mansfield
Robert B. Mantell
Frederich March
Julia Marlowe
Mary Martin
Helen Menken
Burgess Meredith
Ethel Merman
David Merrick
Jo Mielziner
Arthur Miller
Henry Miller
Marilyn Miller
Helena Modjeska
Ferenc Molnar
Victor Moore
Zero Mostel
Paul Muni
George Jean Nathan
Nazimova

Clifford Odets
Donald Oenslager
Laurence Olivier
Eugene O'Neill
Geraldine Page
Osgood Perkins
Molly Picon
Cole Porter
Harold Prince
Jose Quintero
Ada Rehan
Elmer Rice
Ralph Richardson
Jason Robards
Jerome Robbins
Paul Robeson
Richard Rogers
Will Rogers
Sigmund Romberg
Lillian Russell
William Saroyan
Robert E. Sherwood
Lee & J. J. Shubert
Herman Shumlin
Neil Simon
Otis Skinner
Oliver Smith
Stephen Sondheim
E. A. Sothern
E. H. Sothern
Maureen Stapleton
Fred Stone
Lee Strasberg
Jule Styne
Margaret Sullavan
Jessica Tandy
Laurette Taylor
Ellen Terry
Gwen Verdon
James & Lester Wallack
David Warfield
Ethel Waters
Clifton Webb
Margaret Webster
Weber & Fields
Kurt Weill
Orson Welles
Mae West
Thornton Wilder
Bert Williams
Tennessee Williams
P. G. Wodehouse
Peggy Wood
Irene Worth
Ed Wynn
Vincent Youmans
Stark Young
Florenz Ziegfeld

AWARDS — MEDALS — PRIZES

The Alfred B. Nobel Prize Winners

Alfred B. Nobel, inventor of dynamite, bequeathed $9,000,000, the interest to be distributed yearly to those who had most benefited mankind in physics, chemistry, medicine-physiology, literature, and peace. The first Nobel Memorial Prize in Economics was awarded in 1969. No awards given for years omitted. In 1983, each prize was worth approximately $190,000.

Physics

1983 Subrahmanyan Chandrasekhar, William A. Fowler, both U.S.
1982 Kenneth G. Wilson, U.S.
1981 Nicolass Boembergen, Arthur Schlawlow, both U.S.; Kai M. Siegbahn, Swedish
1980 James W. Cronin, Val L. Fitch, both U.S.
1979 Steven Weinberg, Sheldon L. Glashow, both U.S.; Abdus Salam, Pakistani,
1978 Pyotr Kapitsa, USSR; Arno Penzias, Robert Wilson, both U.S.
1977 John H. Van Vleck, Philip W. Anderson, both U.S.; Nevill F. Mott, British
1976 Burton Richter, U.S. Samuel C.C. Ting, U.S.
1975 James Rainwater, U.S. Ben Mottelson, U.S.-Danish, Aage Bohr, Danish
1974 Martin Ryle, British Antony Hewish, British
1973 Ivar Giaever, U.S. Leo Esaki, Japan Brian D. Josephson, British
1972 John Bardeen, U.S. Leon N. Cooper, U.S. John R. Schrieffer, U.S.
1971 Dennis Gabor, British
1970 Louis Neel, French Hannes Alfven, Swedish
1969 Murray Gell-Mann, U.S.
1968 Luis W. Alvarez, U.S.
1967 Hans A. Bethe, U.S.
1966 Alfred Kastler, French
1965 Richard P. Feynman, U.S. Julian S. Schwinger, U.S. Shinichiro Tomonaga, Japanese
1964 Nikolai G. Basov, USSR Aleksander M. Prochorov, USSR Charles H. Townes, U.S.

1963 Maria Goeppert-Mayer, U.S. J. Hans D. Jensen, German Eugene P. Wigner, U.S.
1962 Lev. D. Landau, USSR
1961 Robert Hofstadter, U.S. Rudolf L. Mossbauer, German
1960 Donald A. Glaser, U.S.
1959 Owen Chamberlain, U.S. Emilio G. Segre, U.S.
1958 Pavel Cherenkov, Ilya Frank, Igor Y. Tamm, all USSR
1957 Tsung-dao Lee, Chen Ning Yang, both U.S.
1956 John Bardeen, U.S. Walter H. Brattain, U.S. William Shockley, U.S.
1955 Polykarp Kusch, U.S. Willis E. Lamb, U.S.
1954 Max Born, British Walter Bothe, German
1953 Frits Zernike, Dutch
1952 Felix Bloch, U.S. Edward M. Purcell, U.S.
1951 Sir John D. Cockroft, British Ernest T. S. Walton, Irish
1950 Cecil F. Powell, British
1949 Hideki Yukawa, Japanese
1948 Patrick M. S. Blackett, British
1947 Sir,Edward V. Appleton, British
1946 Percy Williams Bridgman, U.S.
1945 Wolfgang Pauli, U.S.
1944 Isidor Isaac Rabi, U.S.
1943 Otto Stern, U.S.
1939 Ernest O. Lawrence, U.S.
1938 Enrico Fermi, U.S.
1937 Clinton J. Davisson, U.S. Sir George P. Thomson, British
1936 Carl D. Anderson, U.S. Victor F. Hess, Austrian
1935 Sir James Chadwick, British
1933 Paul A.M. Dirac, British Erwin Schrodinger, Austrian

1932 Werner Heisenberg, German
1930 Sir Chandrasekhara V. Raman, Indian
1929 Prince Louis-Victor de Broglie, French
1928 Owen W. Richardson, British
1927 Arthur H. Compton, U.S. Charles T. R. Wilson, British
1926 Jean B. Perrin, French
1925 James Franck, Gustav Hertz, both German
1924 Karl M. G. Siegbahn, Swedish
1923 Robert A. Millikan, U.S.
1922 Niels Bohr, Danish
1921 Albert Einstein, Ger.-U.S.
1920 Charles E. Guillaume, French
1919 Johannes Stark, German
1918 Max K. E. L. Planck, German
1917 Charles G. Barkla, British
1915 Sir William H. Bragg, British Sir William L. Bragg, British
1914 Max von Laue, German
1913 Heike Kamerlingh-Onnes, Dutch
1912 Nils G. Dalen, Swedish
1911 Wilhelm Wien, German
1910 Johannes D. van der Waals, Dutch
1909 Carl F. Braun, German Guglielmo Marconi, Italian
1908 Gabriel Lippmann, French
1907 Albert A. Michelson, U.S.
1906 Sir Joseph J. Thomson, British
1905 Philipp E. A. von Lenard, Ger.
1904 John W. Strutt, Lord Rayleigh, British
1903 Antoine Henri Becquerel, French Marie Curie, Polish-French Pierre Curie, French
1902 Hendrik A. Lorentz, Pieter Zeeman, both Dutch
1901 Wilhelm C. Roentgen, German

Chemistry

1983 Henry Taube, Canadian
1982 Aaron Klug, S. African
1981 Kenichi Fukui, Japan., Roald Hoffmann, U.S.
1980 Paul Berg , U.S.; Walter Gilbert, U.S., Frederick Sanger, U.K.
1979 Herbert C. Brown, U.S. George Wittig, German
1978 Peter Mitchell, British
1977 Ilya Prigogine, Belgian
1976 William N. Lipscomb, U.S.
1975 John Cornforth, Austral.-Brit., Vladimir Prelog, Yugo.-Switz.
1974 Paul J. Flory, U.S.
1973 Ernst Otto Fischer, W. German Geoffrey Wilkinson, British
1972 Christian B. Anfinsen, U.S. Stanford Moore, U.S. William H. Stein, U.S.
1971 Gerhard Herzberg, Canadian
1970 Luis F. Leloir, Arg.
1969 Derek H. R. Barton, British Odd Hassel, Norwegian
1968 Lars Onsager, U.S.
1967 Manfred Eigen, German Ronald G. W. Norrish, British George Porter, British
1966 Robert S. Mulliken, U.S.
1965 Robert B. Woodward, U.S.
1964 Dorothy C. Hodgkin, British
1963 Giulio Natta, Italian Karl Ziegler, German
1962 John C. Kendrew, British

Max F. Perutz, British
1961 Melvin Calvin, U.S.
1960 Willard F. Libby, U.S.
1959 Jaroslav Heyrovsky, Czech
1958 Frederick Sanger, British
1957 Sir Alexander R. Todd, British
1956 Sir Cyril N. Hinshelwood, British Nikolai N. Semenov, USSR
1955 Vincent du Vigneaud, U.S.
1954 Linus C. Pauling, U.S.
1953 Hermann Staudinger, German
1952 Archer J. P. Martin, British Richard L. M. Synge, British
1951 Edwin M. McMillan, U.S. Glenn T. Seaborg, U.S.
1950 Kurt Alder, German Otto P. H. Diels, German
1949 William F. Giauque, U.S.
1948 Arne W. K. Tiselius, Swedish
1947 Sir Robert Robinson, British
1946 James B. Sumner, John H. Northrop, Wendell M. Stanley, all U.S.
1945 Artturi I. Virtanen, Finnish
1944 Otto Hahn, German
1943 Georg de Hevesy, Hungarian
1939 Adolf F. J. Butenandt, German Leopold Ruzicka, Swiss
1938 Richard Kuhn, German
1937 Walter N. Haworth, British Paul Karrer, Swiss
1936 Peter J. W. Debye, Dutch
1935 Frederic Joliot-Curie, French Irene Joliot-Curie, French

1934 Harold C. Urey, U.S.
1932 Irving Langmuir, U.S.
1931 Friedrich Bergius, German Karl Bosch, German
1930 Hans Fischer, German
1929 Sir Arthur Harden, British Hans von Euler-Chelpin, Swed.
1928 Adolf O. R. Windaus, German
1927 Heinrich O. Wieland, German
1926 Theodor Svedberg, Swedish
1925 Richard A. Zsigmondy, German
1923 Fritz Pregl, Austrian
1922 Francis W. Aston, British
1921 Frederick Soddy, British
1920 Walther H. Nernst, German
1918 Fritz Haber, German
1915 Richard M. Willstatter, German
1914 Theodore W. Richards, U.S.
1913 Alfred Werner, Swiss
1912 Victor Grignard, French Paul Sabatier, French
1911 Marie Curie, Polish-French
1910 Otto Wallach, German
1909 Wilhelm Ostwald, German
1908 Ernest Rutherford, British
1907 Eduard Buchner, German
1906 Henri Moissan, French
1905 Adolf von Baeyer, German
1904 Sir William Ramsay, British
1903 Svante A. Arrhenius, Swedish
1902 Emil Fischer, German
1901 Jacobus H. van't Hoff, Dutch

407

Physiology or Medicine

1982 Sune Bergstrom, Bengt
Samuelsson, both Swedish;
John R. Vane, British.
1981 Roger W. Sperry,
David H. Hubel, Tosten N. Wiesel,
all U.S.
1980 Baruj Benacerraf, George Snell,
both U.S.; Jean Dausset, France
1979 Alian M. Cormack, U.S.
Geoffrey N. Hounsfield, British
1978 Daniel Nathans, Hamilton O. Smith,
both U.S.; Werner Arber, Swiss
1977 Rosalyn S. Yalow, Roger C.L.
Guillemin, Andrew V. Schally, all
U.S.
1976 Baruch S. Blumberg, U.S.
Daniel Carleton Gajdusek, U.S.
1975 David Baltimore, Howard Temin,
both U.S.; Renato Dulbecco,
Ital.-U.S.
1974 Albert Claude, Lux.-U.S.; George
Emil Palade, Rom.-U.S.; Christian
Rene de Duve, Belg.
1973 Karl von Frisch, Ger.; Konrad
Lorenz, Ger.-Austrian; Nikolaas
Tinbergen, Brit.
1972 Gerald M. Edelman, U.S.
Rodney R. Porter, British
1971 Earl W. Sutherland Jr., U.S.
1970 Julius Axelrod, U.S.
Sir Bernard Katz, British
Ulf von Euler, Swedish
1969 Max Delbruck,
Alfred D. Hershey,
Salvador Luria, all U.S.
1968 Robert W. Holley,
H. Gobind Khorana,
Marshall W. Nirenberg, all U.S.
1967 Ragnar Granit, Swedish
Haldan Keffer Hartline, U.S.
George Wald, U.S.
1966 Charles B. Huggins,
Francis Peyton Rous, both U.S.
1965 Francois Jacob, Andre Lwoff,

Jacques Monod, all French
1964 Konrad E. Bloch, U.S.
Feodor Lynen, German
1963 Sir John C. Eccles, Australian
Alan L. Hodgkin, British
Andrew F. Huxley, British
1962 Francis H. C. Crick, British
James D. Watson, U.S.
Maurice H. F. Wilkins, British
1961 Georg von Bekesy, U.S.
1960 Sir F. MacFarlane Bumet,
Australian
Peter B. Medawar, British
1959 Arthur Kornberg, U.S.
Severo Ochoa, U.S.
1958 George W. Beadle, U.S.
Edward L. Tatum, U.S.
Joshua Lederberg, U.S.
1957 Daniel Bovet, Italian
1956 Andre F. Cournand, U.S.
Werner Forssmann, German
Dickinson W. Richards, Jr., U.S.
1955 Alex H. T. Theorell, Swedish
1954 John F. Enders,
Frederick C. Robbins,
Thomas H. Weller, all U.S.
1953 Hans A. Krebs, British
Fritz A. Lipmann, U.S.
1952 Selman A. Waksman, U.S.
1951 Max Theiler, U.S.
1950 Philip S. Hench,
Edward C. Kendall, both U.S.
Tadeus Reichstein, Swiss
1949 Walter R. Hess, Swiss
Antonio Moniz, Portuguese
1948 Paul H. Müller, Swiss
1947 Carl F. Cori,
Gerty T. Cori, both U.S.
Bernardo A. Houssay, Arg.
1946 Hermann J. Muller, U.S.
1945 Ernst B. Chain, British
Sir Alexander Fleming, British
Sir Howard W. Florey, British
1944 Joseph Erlanger, U.S.

Herbert S. Gasser, U.S.
1943 Henrik C. P. Dam, Danish
Edward A. Doisy, U.S.
1939 Gerhard Domagk, German
1938 Corneille J. F. Heymans, Belg.
1937 Albert Szent-Gyorgyi, Hung.-U.S.
1936 Sir Henry H. Dale, British
Otto Loewi, German
1935 Hans Spemann, German
1934 George R. Minot, Wm. P. Murphy,
G. H. Whipple, all U.S.
1933 Thomas H. Morgan, U.S.
1932 Edgar D. Adrian, British
Sir Charles S. Sherrington, Brit.
1931 Otto H. Warburg, German
1930 Karl Landsteiner, U.S.
1929 Christiaan Eijkman, Dutch
Sir Frederick G. Hopkins, British
1928 Charles J. H. Nicolle, French
1927 Julius Wagner-Jauregg, Aus.
1926 Johannes A. G. Fibiger, Danish
1924 Willem Einthoven, Dutch
1923 Frederick G. Banting, Canadian
John J. R. Macleod, Scottish
1922 Archibald V. Hill, British
Otto F. Meyerhof, German
1920 Schack A. S. Krogh, Danish
1919 Jules Bordet, Belgian
1914 Robert Barany, Austrian
1913 Charles R. Richet, French
1912 Alexis Carrel, French
1911 Allvar Gullstrand, Swedish
1910 Albrecht Kossel, German
1909 Emil T. Kocher, Swiss
1908 Paul Ehrlich, German
Elie Metchnikoff, French
1907 Charles L. A. Laveran, French
1906 Camillo Golgi, Italian
Santiago Ramon y Cajal, Sp.
1905 Robert Koch, German
1904 Ivan P. Pavlov, Russian
1903 Niels R. Finsen, Danish
1902 Sir Ronald Ross, British
1901 Emil A. von Behring, German

Literature

1982 Gabriel Garcia Marquez,
Colombian-Mex.
1981 Elias Cenetti, Bulgarian-British
1980 Czeslaw Milosz, Polish-U.S.
1979 Odysseus Elytis, Greek
1978 Isaac Bashevis Singer, U.S.
(Yiddish)
1977 Vicente Aleixandre, Spanish
1976 Saul Bellow, U.S.
1975 Eugenio Montale, Ital.
1974 Eyvind Johnson, Harry Edmund
Martinson, both Swedish
1973 Patrick White, Australian
1972 Heinrich Boll, W. German
1971 Pablo Neruda, Chilean
1970 Aleksandr I. Solzhenitsyn, Russ.
1969 Samuel Beckett, Irish
1968 Yasunari Kawabata, Japanese
1967 Miguel Angel Asturias, Guate.
1966 Samuel Joseph Agnon, Israeli
Nelly Sachs, Swedish
1965 Mikhail Sholokhov, Russian
1964 Jean Paul Sartre, French
(Prize declined)
1963 Giorgos Seferis, Greek
1962 John Steinbeck, U.S.
1961 Ivo Andric, Yugoslavian
1960 Saint-John Perse, French
1959 Salvatore Quasimodo, Italian

1958 Boris L. Pasternak, Russian
(Prize declined)
1957 Albert Camus, French
1956 Juan Ramon Jimenez,
Puerto Rican-Span.
1955 Halldor K. Laxness, Icelandic
1954 Ernest Hemingway, U.S.
1953 Sir Winston Churchill, British
1952 Francois Mauriac, French
1951 Par F. Lagerkvist, Swedish
1950 Bertrand Russell, British
1949 William Faulkner, U.S.
1948 T.S. Eliot, British
1947 Andre Gide, French
1946 Hermann Hesse, Swiss
1945 Gabriela Mistral, Chilean
1944 Johannes V. Jensen, Danish
1939 Frans E. Sillanpaa, Finnish
1938 Pearl S. Buck, U.S.
1937 Roger Martin du Gard, French
1936 Eugene O'Neill, U.S.
1934 Luigi Pirandello, Italian
1933 Ivan A. Bunin, French
1932 John Galsworthy, British
1931 Erik A. Karlfeldt, Swedish
1930 Sinclair Lewis, U.S.
1929 Thomas Mann, German
1928 Sigrid Undset, Norwegian
1927 Henri Bergson, French

1926 Grazia Deledda, Italian
1925 George Bernard Shaw, British
1924 Wladyslaw S. Reymont, Polish
1923 William Butler Yeats, Irish
1922 Jacinto Benavente, Spanish
1921 Anatole France, French
1920 Knut Hamsun, Norwegian
1919 Carl F. G. Spitteler, Swiss
1917 Karl A. Gjellerup, Danish
Henrik Pontoppidan, Danish
1916 Verner von Heidenstam, Swed.
1915 Romain Rolland, French
1913 Rabindranath Tagore, Indian
1912 Gerhart Hauptmann, German
1911 Maurice Maeterlinck, Belgian
1910 Paul J. L. Heyse, German
1909 Selma Lagerlof, Swedish
1908 Rudolf C. Eucken, German
1907 Rudyard Kipling, British
1906 Giosue Carducci, Italian
1905 Henryk Sienkiewicz, Polish
1904 Frederic Mistral, French
Jose Echegaray, Spanish
1903 Bjornsterne Bjornson, Norw.
1902 Theodor Mommsen, German
1901 Rene F. A Sully Prudhomme,
French

Nobel Memorial Prize in Economics

1983 Gerard Debreu, Fr.-U.S.
1982 George J. Stigler, U.S.
1981 James Tobin, U.S.
1980 Lawrence R Klein, U.S.
1979 Theodore W. Schultz, U.S.,
Sir Arthur Lewis, British
1978 Herbert A. Simon, U.S.

1977 Bertil Ohlin, Swedish
James E. Meade, British
1976 Milton Friedman, U.S.
1975 Tjalling Koopmans, Dutch-U.S.,
Leonid Kantorovich, USSR
1974 Gunnar Myrdal, Swed.,
Friedrich A. von Hayek, Austrian

1973 Wassily Leontief, U.S.
1972 Kenneth J. Arrow, U.S.
John R. Hicks, British
1971 Simon Kuznets, U.S.
1970 Paul A. Samuelson, U.S.
1969 Ragnar Frisch, Norwegian
Jan Tinbergen, Dutch

Peace

1983 Lech Walesa, Polish
1982 Alva Myrdal, Swedish; Alfonso
Garcia Robles, Mexican
1981 Office of U.N. High Commissioner
for Refugees
1980 Adolfo Perez Esquivel, Argentine
1979 Mother Theresa of Calcutta,
Albanian-Indian
1978 Anwar Sadat, Egyptian
Menachem Begin, Israeli
1977 Amnesty International
1976 Mairead Corrigan, Betty Williams,
N. Irish
1975 Andrei Sakharov, USSR
1974 Eisaku Sato, Japanese, Sean
MacBride, Irish
1973 Henry Kissinger, U.S.
Le Duc Tho, N. Vietnamese
(Tho declined)
1971 Willy Brandt, W. German
1970 Norman E. Borlaug, U.S.
1969 Intl. Labor Organization
1968 Rene Cassin, French
1965 U.N. Children's Fund (UNICEF)
1964 Martin Luther King Jr., U.S.
1963 International Red Cross,
League of Red Cross Societies
1962 Linus C. Pauling, U.S.
1961 Dag Hammarskjold, Swedish
1960 Albert J. Luthuli, South African
1959 Philip J. Noel-Baker, British

1958 Georges Pire, Belgian
1957 Lester B. Pearson, Canadian
1954 Office of the UN High
Commissioner for Refugees
1053 George C. Marshall, U.S.
1952 Albert Schweitzer, French
1951 Leon Jouhaux, French
1950 Ralph J. Bunche, U.S.
1949 Lord John Boyd Orr of Brechin
Mearns, British
1947 Friends Service Council, Brit.
Amer. Friends Service Com.
1946 Emily G. Balch,
John R. Mott, both U.S.
1945 Cordell Hull, U.S.
1944 International Red Cross
1938 Nansen International Office
for Refugees
1937 Viscount Cecil of Chelwood, Brit.
1936 Carlos de Saavedra Lamas, Arg.
1935 Carl von Ossietzky, German
1934 Arthur Henderson, British
1933 Sir Norman Angell, British
1931 Jane Addams, U.S.
Nicholas Murray Butler, U.S.
1930 Nathan Soderblom, Swedish
1929 Frank B. Kellogg, U.S.
1927 Ferdinand E. Buisson, French
Ludwig Quidde, German
1926 Aristide Briand, French
Gustav Stresemann, German

1925 Sir J. Austen Chamberlain, Brit.
Charles G. Dawes, U.S.
1922 Fridtjof Nansen, Norwegian
1921 Karl H. Branting, Swedish
Christian L. Lange, Norwegian
1920 Leon V.A. Bourgeois, French
1919 Woodrow Wilson, U.S.
1917 International Red Cross
1913 Henri La Fontaine, Belgian
1912 Elihu Root, U.S.
1911 Tobias M.C. Asser, Dutch
Alfred H. Fried, Austrian
1910 Permanent Intl. Peace Bureau
1909 Auguste M. F. Beernaert, Belg.
Paul H. B. B. d'Estournelles de
Constant, French
1908 Klas P. Arnoldson, Swedish
Fredrik Bajer, Danish
1907 Ernesto T. Moneta, Italian
Louis Renault, French
1906 Theodore Roosevelt, U.S.
1905 Baroness Bertha von Suttner,
Austrian
1904 Institute of International Law
1903 Sir William R. Cremer, British
1902 Elie Ducommun,
Charles A. Gobat, both Swiss
1901 Jean H. Dunant, Swiss
Frederic Passy, French

Pulitzer Prizes in Journalism, Letters, and Music

The Pulitzer Prizes were endowed by Joseph Pulitzer (1847-1911), publisher of The World, New York, N.Y., in a bequest to Columbia University, New York, N.Y., and are awarded annually by the president of the university on recommendation of the Pulitzer Prize Board for work done during the preceding year. The administrator is Robert C. Christopher of Columbia Univ. All prizes are $1,000 (originally $500) in each category, except Meritorious Public Service for which a gold medal is given.

Journalism

Meritorious Public Service

For distinguished and meritorious public service by a United States newspaper.

1918—New York Times. Also special award to Minna Lewinson and Henry Beetle Hough.
1919—Milwaukee Journal.
1921—Boston Post.
1922—New York World.
1923—Memphis (Tenn.) Commercial Appeal.
1924—New York World.
1926—Enquirer-Sun, Columbus, Ga.
1927—Canton (Oh.) Daily News.
1928—Indianapolis Times.
1929—Evening World, New York.
1931—Atlanta (Ga.) Constitution
1932—Indianapolis (Ind.) News.
1933—New York World-Telegram.
1934—Medford (Ore.) Mail-Tribune.
1935—Sacramento (Cal.) Bee.
1936—Cedar Rapids (Ia.) Gazette.
1937—St. Louis Post-Dispatch.
1938—Bismarck (N.D.) Tribune.
1939—Miami (Fla.) Daily News.
1940—Waterbury (Conn.) Republican and American.
1941—St. Louis Post-Dispatch.
1942—Los Angeles Times.
1943—Omaha World Herald.
1944—New York Times.
1945—Detroit Free Press.
1946—Scranton (Pa.) Times.
1947—Baltimore Sun.
1948—St. Louis Post-Dispatch.
1949—Nebraska State Journal.
1950—Chicago Daily News; St. Louis Post-Dispatch.
1951—Miami (Fla.) Herald and Brooklyn Eagle.
1952—St. Louis Post-Dispatch.
1953—Whiteville (N.C.) News Reporter; Tabor City (N.C.) Tribune.
1954—Newsday (Long Island, N.Y.)
1955—Columbus (Ga.) Ledger and Sunday Ledger-Enquirer.
1956—Watsonville (Cal.) Register-Pajaronian.
1957—Chicago Daily News.
1958—Arkansas Gazette, Little Rock.
1959—Utica (N.Y.) Observer-Dispatch and Utica Daily Press.
1960—Los Angeles Times.
1961—Amarillo (Tex.) Globe-Times.
1962—Panama City (Fla.) News-Herald.
1963—Chicago Daily News.
1964—St. Petersburg (Fla.) Times.

1965—Hutchinson (Kan.) News.
1966—Boston Globe.
1967—The Louisville Courier-Journal; The Milwaukee Journal.
1968—Riverside (Cal.) Press-Enterprise.
1969—Los Angeles Times.
1970—Newsday (Long Island, N.Y.)
1971—Winston Salem (N.C.) Journal & Sentinel.
1972—New York Times.
1973—Washington Post.
1974—Newsday (Long Island, N.Y.).
1975—Boston Globe.
1976—Anchorage Daily News.
1977—Lufkin (Tex.) News.
1978—Philadelphia Inquirer.
1979—Point Reyes (Cal.) Light.
1980—Gannett News Service.
1981—Charlotte (N.C.) Observer.
1982—Detroit News.
1983—Jackson (Miss.) Clarion-Ledger.
1984—Los Angeles Times.

Reporting

This category originally embraced all fields, local, national, and international. Later separate categories were created for the different fields of reporting.

1917—Herbert Bayard Swope, New York World.
1918—Harold A. Littledale, New York Evening Post.
1920—John J. Leary, Jr., New York World.
1921—Louis Seibold, New York World.
1922—Kirke L. Simpson, Associated Press.
1923—Alva Johnston, New York Times.
1924—Magner White, San Diego Sun.
1925—James W. Mulroy and Alvin H. Goldstein, Chicago Daily News.
1926—William Burke Miller, Louisville Courier-Journal.
1927—John T. Rogers, St. Louis Post-Dispatch.
1929—Paul Y. Anderson, St. Louis Post-Dispatch.
1930—Russell D. Owens, New York Times. Also $500 to W.O. Dapping, Auburn (N.Y.) Citizen.
1931—A.B. MacDonald, Kansas City (Mo.) Star.
1932—W.C. Richards, D.D. Martin, J.S. Pooler, F.D. Webb, J.N.W. Sloan, Detroit Free Press.
1933—Francis A. Jamieson, Associated Press.
1934—Royce Brier, San Francisco Chronicle.
1935—William H. Taylor, New York Herald Tribune.
1936—Lauren D. Lyman, New York Times.
1937—John J. O'Neill, N. Y. Herald Tribune; William L. Laurence, N.Y. Times; Howard W. Blakeslee, A. P.; Gobind Behan Lal, University Service; and David Dietz, Scripps-Howard Newspapers.

1938—Raymond Sprigle, Pittsburgh Post-Gazette.
1939—Thomas L. Stokes, Scripps-Howard Newspaper Alliance.
1940—S. Burton Heath, New York World-Telegram.
1941—Westbrook Pegler, New York World-Telegram.
1942—Stanton Delaplane, San Francisco Chronicle.
1943—George Weller, Chicago Daily News.
1944—Paul Schoenstein, N.Y. Journal-American.
1945—Jack S. McDowell, San Francisco Call-Bulletin.
1946—William L. Laurence, New York Times.
1947—Frederick Woltman, N.Y. World-Telegram.
1948—George E. Goodwin, Atlanta Journal.
1949—Malcolm Johnson, New York Sun.
1950—Meyer Berger, New York Times.
1951—Edward S. Montgomery, San Francisco Examiner.
1952—Geo. de Carvalho, San Francisco Chronicle.

(1) General or Spot; (2) Special or Investigative

1953—(1) Providence (R.I.) Journal and Evening Bulletin; (2) Edward J. Mowery, N.Y. World-Telegram & Sun.
1954—(1) Vicksburg (Miss.) Sunday Post-Herald; (2) Alvin Scott McCoy, Kansas City (Mo.) Star.
1955—(1) Mrs. Caro Brown, Alice (Tex.) Daily Echo; (2) Roland K. Towery, Cuero (Tex.) Record.
1956—(1) Lee Hills, Detroit Free Press; (2) Arthur Daley, New York Times.
1957—(1) Salt Lake Tribune, Salt Lake City, Ut.; (2) Wallace Turner and William Lambert, Portland Oregonian.
1958—(1) Fargo, (N.D.) Forum; (2) George Beveridge, Evening Star, Washington, D.C.
1959—(1) Mary Lou Werner, Washington Evening Star; (2) John Harold Brislin, Scranton (Pa.) Tribune, and The Scrantonian.
1960—(1) Jack Nelson, Atlanta Constitution; (2) Miriam Ottenberg, Washington Evening Star.
1961—(1) Sanche de Gramont, N.Y. Herald Tribune; (2) Edgar May, Buffalo Evening News.
1962—(1) Robert D. Mullins, Deseret News, Salt Lake City; (2) George Bliss, Chicago Tribune.
1963—(1) Shared by Sylvan Fox, William Longgood, and Anthony Shannon, N.Y. World-Telegram & Sun; (2) Oscar Griffin, Jr., Pecos (Tex.) Independent and Enterprise.

(1) General Reporting; (2) Special Reporting.

1964—(1) Norman C. Miller, Wall Street Journal; (2) Shared by James V. Magee, Albert V. Gaudiosi, and Frederick A. Meyer, Philadelphia Bulletin.
1965—(1) Melvin H. Ruder, Hungry Horse News (Columbia Falls, Mon.); (2) Gene Goltz, Houston Post.
1966—(1) Los Angeles Times Staff; (2) John A. Frasca, Tampa (Fla.) Tribune.
1967—(1) Robert V. Cox, Chambersburg (Pa.) Public Opinion; (2) Gene Miller, Miami Herald.
1968—Detroit Free Press Staff; (2) J. Anthony Lukas, N.Y. Times.
1969—(1) John Fetterman, Louisville Courier-Journal and Times; (2) Albert L. Delugach, St. Louis Globe Democrat, and Denny Walsh, Life.
1970—(1) Thomas Fitzpatrick, Chicago Sun-Times; (2) Harold Eugene Martin, Montgomery Advertiser & Alabama Journal.
1971—(1) Akron Beacon Journal Staff, (2) William Hugh Jones, Chicago Tribune.
1972—(1) Richard Cooper and John Máchacek, Rochester Times-Union; (2) Timothy Leland, Gerard M. O'Neill, Stephen A. Kurkjian and Anne De Santis, Boston Globe.
1973—(1) Chicago Tribune; (2) Sun Newspapers of Omaha.
1974—(1) Hugh F. Hough, Arthur M. Petacque, Chicago Sun-Times; (2) William Sherman, N.Y. Daily News.
1975—(1) Xenia (Oh.) Daily Gazette; (2) Indianapolis Star.
1976—(1) Gene Miller, Miami Herald; (2) Chicago Tribune.
1977—(1) Margo Huston, Milwaukee Journal; (2) Acel Moore, Wendell Rawls Jr., Philadelphia Inquirer.
1978—(1) Richard Whitt, Louisville Courier-Journal; (2) Anthony R. Dolan, Stamford (Conn.) Advocate.
1979—(1) San Diego (Cal.) Evening Tribune; (2) Gilbert M. Gaul, Elliot G. Jaspin, Pottsville (Pa.) Republican.
1980—(1) Philadelphia Inquirer; (2) Stephen A. Kurkjian, Alexander B. Hawes Jr., Nils Bruzelius, Joan Vennochi, Robert M. Porterfield, Boston Globe.
1981—(1) Longview (Wash.) Daily News staff; (2) Clark Hallas and Robert B. Lowe, Arizona Daily Star.
1982—(1) Kansas City Star, Kansas City Times; (2) Paul Henderson, Seattle Times.
1983—(1) Fort Wayne (Ind.) News-Sentinel; (2) Loretta Tofani, Washington Post.
1984—(1) Newsday (N.Y.); (2) Boston Globe.

Criticism or Commentary

(1) Criticism; (2) Commentary

1970—(1) Ada Louise Huxtable, N.Y. Times; (2) Marquis W. Childs, St. Louis Post-Dispatch.
1971—(1) Harold C. Schonberg, N.Y. Times; (2) William A. Caldwell, The Record, Hackensack, N.J.
1972—(1) Frank Peters Jr., St. Louis Post-Dispatch; (2) Mike Royko, Chicago Daily News.
1973—(1) Ronald Powers, Chicago Sun-Times; (2) David S. Broder, Washington Post.
1974—(1) Emily Genauer, Newsday, (N.Y.); (2) Edwin A. Roberts, Jr., National Observer.
1975—(1) Roger Ebert, Chicago Sun Times; (2) Mary McGrory, Washington Star.
1976—(1) Alan M. Kriegsman, Washington Post; (2) Walter W. (Red) Smith, N.Y. Times.

1977—(1) William McPherson, Washington Post; (2) George F. Will, Wash. Post Writers Group.
1978—(1) Walter Kerr, New York Times; (2) William Safire, New York Times.
1979—(1) Paul Gapp, Chicago Tribune; (2) Russell Baker, New York Times.
1980—(1) William A. Henry III, Boston Globe; (2) Ellen Goodman, Boston Globe.
1981—(1) Jonathan Yardley, Washington Star; (2) Dave Anderson, New York Times.
1982—(1) Martin Bernheimer, Los Angeles Times; (2) Art Buchwald, Los Angeles Times Syndicate.
1983—(1) Manuela Hoelterhoff, Wall St. Journal; (2) Claude Sitton, Raleigh (N.C.) News & Observer.
1984—Paul Goldberger, New York Times; (2) Vermont Royster, Wall St. Journal

National Reporting

1942—Louis Stark, New York Times.
1944—Dewey L. Fleming, Baltimore Sun.
1945—James B. Reston, New York Times.
1946—Edward A. Harris, St. Louis Post-Dispatch.
1947—Edward T. Folliard, Washington Post.
1948—Bert Andrews, New York Herald Tribune; Nat S. Finney, Minneapolis Tribune.
1949—Charles P. Trussell, New York Times.
1950—Edwin O. Guthman, Seattle Times.
1952—Anthony Leviero, New York Times.
1953—Don Whitehead, Associated Press.
1954—Richard Wilson, Des Moines Register.
1955—Anthony Lewis, Washington Daily News.
1956—Charles L. Bartlett, Chattanooga Times.
1957—James Reston, New York Times.
1958—Relman Morin, AP; Clark Mollenhoff, Des Moines Register & Tribune.
1959—Howard Van Smith, Miami (Fla.) News.
1960—Vance Trimble, Scripps-Howard, Washington, D.C.
1961—Edward R. Cony, Wall Street Journal.
1962—Nathan G. Caldwell and Gene S. Graham, Nashville Tennessean.
1963—Anthony Lewis, New York Times.
1964—Merriman Smith, UPI.
1965—Louis M. Kohlmeier, Wall Street Journal.
1966—Haynes Johnson, Washington Evening Star.
1967—Monroe Karmin and Stanley Penn, Wall Street Journal.
1968—Howard James, Christian Science Monitor; Nathan K. Kotz, Des Moines Register.
1969—Robert Cahn, Christian Science Monitor.
1970—William J. Eaton, Chicago Daily News.
1971—Lucinda Franks & Thomas Powers, UPI.
1972—Jack Anderson, United Features.
1973—Robert Boyd and Clark Hoyt, Knight Newspapers.
1974—James R. Polk, Washington Star-News; Jack White, Providence Journal-Bulletin.
1975—Donald L. Barlett and James B. Steele, Philadelphia Inquirer.
1976—James Risser, Des Moines Register.
1977—Walter Mears, Associated Press.
1978—Gaylord D. Shaw, Los Angeles Times.
1979—James Risser, Des Moines Register.
1980—Charles Stafford, Bette Swenson Orsini, St. Petersburg (Fla.) Times.
1981—John M. Crewdson, New York Times.
1982—Rick Atkinson, Kansas City Times.
1983—Boston Globe.
1984—John Noble Wilford, New York Times

International Reporting

1942—Laurence Edmund Allen, Associated Press.
1943—Ira Wolfert, No. Am. Newspaper Alliance.
1944—Daniel DeLuce, Associated Press.
1945—Mark S. Watson, Baltimore Sun.
1946—Homer W. Bigart, New York Herald Tribune.
1947—Eddy Gilmore, Associated Press.
1948—Paul W. Ward, Baltimore Sun.
1949—Price Day, Baltimore Sun.
1950—Edmund Stevens, Christian Science Monitor.
1951—Keyes Beech and Fred Sparks, Chicago Daily News; Homer Bigart and Marguerite Higgins, New York Herald Tribune; Relman Morin and Don Whitehead, AP.
1952—John M. Hightower, Associated Press.
1953—Austin C. Wehrwein, Milwaukee Journal.
1954—Jim G. Lucas, Scripps-Howard Newspapers.
1955—Harrison Salisbury, New York Times.
1956—William Randolph Hearst, Jr., Frank Conniff, Hearst Newspapers; Kingsbury Smith, INS.
1957—Russell Jones, United Press.
1958—New York Times.
1959—Joseph Martin and Philip Santora, N.Y. News.
1960—A.M. Rosenthal, New York Times.
1961—Lynn Heinzerling, Associated Press.
1962—Walter Lippmann, N.Y. Herald Tribune Synd.
1963—Hal Hendrix, Miami (Fla.) News.
1964—Malcolm W. Browne, AP; David Halberstam, N.Y. Times.
1965—J.A. Livingston, Philadelphia Bulletin.
1966—Peter Arnett, AP.
1967—R. John Hughes, Christian Science Monitor.
1968—Alfred Friendly, Washington Post.
1969—William Tuohy, L.A. Times.

1970—Seymour M. Hersh, Dispatch News Service.
1971—Jimmie Lee Hoagland, Washington Post.
1972—Peter R. Kann, Wall Street Journal.
1973—Max Frankel, N.Y. Times.
1974—Hedrick Smith, N.Y. Times.
1975—William Mullen and Ovie Carter, Chicago Tribune.
1976—Sydney H. Schanberg, N.Y. Times.
1978—Henry Kamm, N.Y. Times.
1979—Richard Ben Cramer, Philadelphia Inquirer.
1980—Joel Brinkley, Jay Mather, Louisville (Ky.) Courier-Journal.
1981—Shirley Christian, Miami Herald.
1982—John Darnton, New York Times.
1983—Thomas L. Friedman, New York Times; Loren Jenkins, Washington Post.
1984—Karen Elliot House, Wall St. Journal

Correspondence

For Washington or foreign correspondence. Category was merged with those in national and international reporting in 1948.

1929—Paul Scott Mowrer, Chicago Daily News.
1930—Leland Stowe, New York Herald Tribune.
1931—H.R. Knickerbocker, Philadelphia Public Ledger and New York Evening Post.
1932—Walter Duranty, New York Times, and Charles G. Ross, St. Louis Post-Dispatch.
1933—Edgar Ansel Mowrer, Chicago Daily News.
1934—Frederick T. Birchall, New York Times.
1935—Arthur Krock, New York Times.
1936—Wilfred C. Barber, Chicago Tribune.
1937—Anne O'Hare McCormick, New York Times.
1938—Arthur Krock, New York Times.
1939—Louis P. Lochner, Associated Press.
1940—Otto D. Tolischus, New York Times.
1941—Bronze plaque to commemorate work of American correspondents on war fronts.
1942—Carlos P. Romulo, Philippines Herald.
1943—Hanson W. Baldwin, New York Times.
1944—Ernest Taylor Pyle, Scripps-Howard Newspaper Alliance.
1945—Harold V. (Hal) Boyle, Associated Press.
1946—Arnaldo Cortesi, New York Times.
1947—Brooks Atkinson, New York Times.

Editorial Writing

1917—New York Tribune.
1918—Louisville (Ky.) Courier-Journal.
1920—Harvey E. Newbranch, Omaha Evening World-Herald.
1922—Frank M. O'Brien, New York Herald.
1923—William Allen White, Emporia Gazette.
1924—Frank Buxton, Boston Herald, Special Prize. Frank I. Cobb, New York World.
1925—Robert Lathan, Charleston (S.C.) News and Courier.
1926—Edward M. Kingsbury, N. Y. Times.
1927—F. Lauriston Bullard, Boston Herald.
1928—Grover C. Hall, Montgomery Advertiser.
1929—Louis Isaac Jaffe, Norfolk Virginian-Pilot.
1931—Chas. Ryckman, Fremont (Neb.) Tribune.
1933—Kansas City (Mo.) Star
1934—E. P. Chase, Atlantic (Ia.) News Telegraph.
1936—Felix Morley, Washington Post. George B. Parker, Scripps-Howard Newspapers.
1937—John W. Owens, Baltimore Sun.
1938—W.W. Waymack, Des Moines (Ia.) Register and Tribune.
1939—Ronald G. Callvert, Portland Oregonian.
1940—Bart Howard, St. Louis Post-Dispatch.
1941—Reuben Maury, Daily News, N.Y.
1942—Geoffrey Parsons, New York Herald Tribune.
1943—Forrest W. Seymour, Des Moines (Ia.) Register and Tribune.
1944—Henry J. Haskell, Kansas City (Mo.) Star.
1945—George W. Potter, Providence (R.I.) Journal-Bulletin.
1946—Hodding Carter, Greenville (Miss.) Delta Democrat-Times.
1947—William H. Grimes, Wall Street Journal.
1948—Virginius Dabney, Richmond (Va.) Times-Dispatch.
1949—John H. Crider, Boston (Mass.) Herald, Herbert Elliston, Washington Post.
1950—Carl M. Saunders, Jackson (Mich.) Citizen-Patriot.
1951—William H. Fitzpatrick, New Orleans States.
1952—Louis LaCoss, St. Louis Globe Democrat.
1953—Vermont C. Royster, Wall Street Journal.
1954—Don Murray, Boston Herald.
1955—Royce Howes, Detroit Free Press.
1956—Lauren K. Soth, Des Moines (Ia.) Register and Tribune.
1957—Buford Boone, Tuscaloosa (Ala.) News.
1958—Harry S. Ashmore, Arkansas Gazette.
1959—Ralph McGill, Atlanta Constitution.
1960—Lenoir Chambers, Norfolk Virginian-Pilot.
1961—William J. Dorvillier, San Juan (Puerto Rico) Star.
1962—Thomas M. Storke, Santa Barbara (Cal.) News-Press.
1963—Ira B. Harkey, Jr., Pascagoula (Miss.) Chronicle.
1964—Hazel Brannon Smith, Lexington (Miss.) Advertiser.
1965—John R. Harrison, The Gainesville (Fla.) Sun.
1966—Robert Lasch, St. Louis Post-Dispatch.
1967—Eugene C. Patterson, Atlanta Constitution.
1968—John S. Knight, Knight Newspapers.
1969—Paul Greenberg, Pine Bluff (Ark.) Commercial.
1970—Philip L. Geyelin, Washington Post.
1971—Horance G. Davis, Jr., Gainesville (Fla.) Sun.
1972—John Strohmeyer, Bethlehem (Pa.) Globe-Times.

1973—Roger B. Linscott, Berkshire Eagle, Pittsfield, Mass.
1974—F. Gilman Spencer, Trenton (N.J.) Trentonian.
1975—John D. Maurice, Charleston (W. Va.) Daily Mail.
1976—Philip Kerby, Los Angeles Times.
1977—Warren L. Lerude, Foster Church, and Norman F. Cardoza, Reno (Nev.) Evening Gazette and Nevada State Journal.
1978—Meg Greenfield, Washington Post.
1979—Edwin M. Yoder, Washington Star.
1980—Robert L. Bartley, Wall Street Journal.
1982—Jack Rosenthal, New York Times.
1983—Editorial board, Miami Herald.
1984—Albert Scardino, Georgia Gazette

Editorial Cartooning

1922—Rollin Kirby, New York World.
1924—Jay N. Darling, Des Moines Register.
1925—Rollin Kirby, New York World.
1926—D. R. Fitzpatrick, St. Louis Post-Dispatch.
1927—Nelson Harding, Brooklyn Eagle.
1928—Nelson Harding, Brooklyn Eagle.
1929—Rollin Kirby, New York World.
1930—Charles Macauley, Brooklyn Eagle.
1931—Edmund Duffy, Baltimore Sun.
1932—John T. McCutcheon, Chicago Tribune.
1933—H. M. Talburt, Washington Daily News.
1934—Edmund Duffy, Baltimore Sun.
1935—Ross A. Lewis, Milwaukee Journal.
1937—C. D. Batchelor, New York Daily News.
1938—Vaughn Shoemaker, Chicago Daily News.
1939—Charles G. Werner, Daily Oklahoman.
1940—Edmund Duffy, Baltimore Sun.
1941—Jacob Burck, Chicago Times.
1942—Herbert L. Block, Newspaper Enterprise Assn.
1943—Jay N. Darling, Des Moines Register.
1944—Clifford K. Berryman, Washington Star.
1945—Bill Mauldin, United Feature Syndicate.
1946—Bruce Alexander Russell, Los Angeles Times.
1947—Vaughn Shoemaker, Chicago Daily News.
1948—Reuben L. (Rube) Goldberg, N. Y. Sun.
1949—Lute Pease, Newark (N.J.) Evening News.
1950—James T. Berryman, Washington Star.
1951—Reginald W. Manning, Arizona Republic.
1952—Fred L. Packer, New York Mirror.
1953—Edward D. Kuekes, Cleveland Plain Dealer.
1954—Herbert L. Block, Washington Post & Times-Herald.
1955—Daniel R. Fitzpatrick, St. Louis Post-Dispatch.
1956—Robert York, Louisville (Ky.) Times.
1957—Tom Little, Nashville Tennessean.
1958—Bruce M. Shanks, Buffalo Evening News.
1959—Bill Mauldin, St. Louis Post-Dispatch.
1961—Carey Orr, Chicago Tribune.
1962—Edmund S. Valtman, Hartford Times.
1963—Frank Miller, Des Moines Register.
1964—Paul Conrad, Denver Post.
1966—Don Wright, Miami News.
1967—Patrick B. Oliphant, Denver Post.
1968—Eugene Gray Payne, Charlotte Observer.
1969—John Fischetti, Chicago Daily News.
1970—Thomas F. Darcy, Newsday.
1971—Paul Conrad, L. A. Times.
1972—Jeffrey K. MacNelly, Richmond News-Leader.
1974—Paul Szep, Boston Globe.
1975—Garry Trudeau, Universal Press Syndicate.
1976—Tony Auth, Philadelphia Inquirer.
1977—Paul Szep, Boston Globe.
1978—Jeffrey K. MacNelly, Richmond News Leader.
1979—Herbert L. Block, Washington Post.
1980—Don Wright, Miami (Fla.) News.
1981—Mike Peters, Dayton (Oh.) Daily News.
1982—Ben Sargent, Austin American-Statesman.
1983—Richard Lochner, Chicago Tribune.
1984—Paul Conrad, Los Angeles Times.

Spot News Photography

1942—Milton Brooks, Detroit News.
1943—Frank Noel, Associated Press.
1944—Frank Filan, AP; Earl L. Bunker, Omaha World-Herald.
1945—Joe Rosenthal, Associated Press, for photograph of planting American flag on Iwo Jima.
1947—Arnold Hardy, amateur, Atlanta, Ga.
1948—Frank Cushing, Boston Traveler.
1949—Nathaniel Fein, New York Herald Tribune.
1950—Bill Crouch, Oakland (Cal.) Tribune.
1951—Max Desfor, Associated Press.
1952—John Robinson and Don Ultang, Des Moines Register and Tribune.
1953—William M. Gallagher, Flint (Mich.) Journal.
1954—Mrs. Walter M. Schau, amateur.
1955—John L. Gaunt, Jr., Los Angeles Times.
1956—New York Daily News.
1957—Harry A. Trask, Boston Traveler.
1958—William C. Beall, Washington Daily News.
1959—William Seaman, Minneapolis Star.
1960—Andrew Lopez, UPI.
1961—Yasushi Nagao, Mainichi Newspapers, Tokyo.
1962—Paul Vathis, Associated Press.
1963—Hector Rondon, La Republica, Caracas, Venezuela.

1964—Robert H. Jackson, Dallas Times-Herald.
1965—Horst Faas, Associated Press.
1966—Kyoichi Sawada, UPI.
1967—Jack R. Thornell, Associated Press.
1968—Rocco Morabito, Jacksonville Journal.
1969—Edward Adams, AP.
1970—Steve Starr, AP.
1971—John Paul Filo, Valley Daily News & Daily Dispatch of Tarentum & New Kensington, Pa.
1972—Horst Faas and Michel Laurent, AP.
1973—Huynh Cong Ut, AP.
1974—Anthony K. Roberts, AP.
1975—Gerald H. Gay, Seattle Times.
1976—Stanley Forman, Boston Herald American.
1977—Neal Ulevich, Associated Press; Stanley Forman, Boston Herald American.
1978—John H. Blair, UPI.
1979—Thomas J. Kelly III, Pottstown (Pa.) Mercury.
1980—UPI.
1981—Larry C. Price, Ft. Worth (Tex.) Star-Telegram.
1982—Ron Edmonds, Associated Press.
1983—Bill Foley, AP.
1984—Stan Grossfeld, Boston Globe.

Feature Photography

1968—Toshio Sakai, UPI.
1969—Moneta Sleet Jr., Ebony.
1970—Dallas Kinney, Palm Beach Post.
1971—Jack Dykinga, Chicago Sun-Times.
1972—Dave Kennerly, UPI.
1973—Brian Lanker, Topeka Capitol-Journal.
1974—Slava Veder, AP.
1975—Matthew Lewis, Washington Post.
1976—Louisville Courier-Journal and Louisville Times.
1977—Robin Hood, Chattanooga News-Free Press.
1978—J. Ross Baughman, AP.
1979—Staff Photographers, Boston Herald American.
1980—Erwin H. Hagler, Dallas Times-Herald.

1981—Taro M. Yamasaki, Detroit Free Press.
1982—John H. White, Chicago Sun-Times.
1983—James B. Dickman, Dallas Times-Herald.
1984—Anthony Suad, Denver Post.

Special Citation

1938—Edmonton (Alberta) Journal, bronze plaque.
1941—New York Times.
1944—Byron Price and Mrs. William Allen White. Also to Richard Rodgers and Oscar Hammerstein 2d, for musical, Oklahoma!
1945—Press cartographers for war maps.
1947—(Pulitzer centennial year.) Columbia Univ. and the Graduate School of Journalism, and St. Louis Post-Dispatch.
1948—Dr. Frank Diehl Fackenthal.
1951—Cyrus L. Sulzberger, New York Times.
1952—Max Kase, New York Journal-American, Kansas City Star.
1953—The New York Times; Lester Markel.
1957—Kenneth Roberts, for his historical novels.
1958—Walter Lippmann, New York Herald Tribune.
1960—Garrett Mattingly, for The Armada.
1961—American Heritage Picture History of the Civil War.
1964—The Gannett Newspapers.
1973—James T. Flexner, for "George Washington," a four-volume biography.
1976—John Hohenberg, for services to American journalism.
1977—Alex Haley, for Roots, $1,000.
1978—Richard Lee Strout, Christian Science Monitor and New Republic.
— E.B. White, for his work.
1984—Theodore Geisel ("Dr. Seuss")

Feature Writing

Category was inaugurated in 1979.
1979—Jon D. Franklin, Baltimore Evening Sun.
1980—Madeleine Blais, Miami Herald Tropic Magazine.
1981—Teresa Carpenter, Village Voice, New York City.
1982—Saul Pett, Associated Press.
1984—Peter M. Rinearson, Seattle Times.

Letters

Fiction

For fiction in book form by an American author, preferably dealing with American life.
1918—Ernest Poole, His Family.
1919—Booth Tarkington, The Magnificent Ambersons.
1921—Edith Wharton, The Age of Innocence.
1922—Booth Tarkington, Alice Adams.
1923—Willa Cather, One of Ours.
1924—Margaret Wilson, The Able McLaughlins.
1925—Edna Ferber, So Big.
1926—Sinclair Lewis, Arrowsmith. (Refused prize.)
1927—Louis Bromfield, Early Autumn.
1928—Thornton Wilder, Bridge of San Luis Rey.
1929—Julia M. Peterkin, Scarlet Sister Mary.
1930—Oliver LaFarge, Laughing Boy.
1931—Margaret Ayer Barnes, Years of Grace.
1932—Pearl S. Buck, The Good Earth.
1933—T. S. Stribling, The Store.
1934—Caroline Miller, Lamb in His Bosom.
1935—Josephine W. Johnson, Now in November.
1936—Harold L. Davis, Honey in the Horn.
1937—Margaret Mitchell, Gone with the Wind.
1938—John P. Marquand, The Late George Apley.
1939—Marjorie Kinnan Rawlings, The Yearling.
1940—John Steinbeck, The Grapes of Wrath.
1942—Ellen Glasgow, In This Our Life.
1943—Upton Sinclair, Dragon's Teeth.
1944—Martin Flavin, Journey in the Dark.
1945—John Hersey, A Bell for Adano.
1947—Robert Penn Warren, All the King's Men.
1948—James A Michener, Tales of the South Pacific.
1949—James Gould Cozzens, Guard of Honor.
1950—A. B. Guthrie Jr., The Way West.
1951—Conrad Richter, The Town.
1952—Herman Wouk, The Caine Mutiny.
1953—Ernest Hemingway, The Old Man and the Sea.
1955—William Faulkner, A Fable.
1956—MacKinlay Kantor, Andersonville.
1958—James Agee, A Death in the Family.
1959—Robert Lewis Taylor, The Travels of Jaimie McPheeters.
1960—Allen Drury, Advise and Consent.
1961—Harper Lee, To Kill a Mockingbird.
1962—Edwin O'Connor, The Edge of Sadness.
1963—William Faulkner, The Reivers.
1965—Shirley Ann Grau, The Keepers of the House.
1966—Katherine Anne Porter, Collected Stories of Katherine Anne Porter.
1967—Bernard Malamud, The Fixer.
1968—William Styron, The Confessions of Nat Turner.
1969—N. Scott Momaday, House Made of Dawn.
1970—Jean Stafford, Collected Stories.
1972—Wallace Stegner, Angle of Repose.
1973—Eudora Welty, The Optimist's Daughter.
1975—Michael Shaara, The Killer Angels.

1976—Saul Bellow, Humboldt's Gift.
1978—James Alan McPherson, Elbow Room.
1979—John Cheever, The Stories of John Cheever.
1980—Norman Mailer, The Executioner's Song.
1981—John Kennedy Toole, A Confederacy of Dunces.
1982—John Updike, Rabbit is Rich.
1983—Alice Walker, The Color Purple.
1984—William Kennedy, Ironweed.

Drama

For an American play, preferably original and dealing with American life.
1918—Jesse Lynch Williams, Why Marry?
1920—Eugene O'Neill, Beyond the Horizon.
1921—Zona Gale, Miss Lulu Bett.
1922—Eugene O'Neill, Anna Christie.
1923—Owen Davis, Icebound.
1924—Hatcher Hughes, Hell-Bent for Heaven.
1925—Sidney Howard, They Knew What They Wanted.
1926—George Kelly, Craig's Wife.
1927—Paul Green, In Abraham's Bosom.
1928—Eugene O'Neill, Strange Interlude.
1929—Elmer Rice, Street Scene.
1930—Marc Connelly, The Green Pastures.
1931—Susan Glaspell, Alison's House.
1932—George S. Kaufman, Morrie Ryskind and Ira Gershwin, Of Thee I Sing.
1933—Maxwell Anderson, Both Your Houses.
1934—Sidney Kingsley, Men in White.
1935—Zoe Akins, The Old Maid.
1936—Robert E. Sherwood, Idiot's Delight.
1937—George S. Kaufman and Moss Hart, You Can't Take It With You.
1938—Thornton Wilder, Our Town.
1939—Robert E. Sherwood, Abe Lincoln in Illinois.
1940—William Saroyan, The Time of Your Life.
1941—Robert E. Sherwood, There Shall Be No Night.
1943—Thornton Wilder, The Skin of Our Teeth.
1945—Mary Chase, Harvey.
1946—Russel Crouse and Howard Lindsay, State of the Union.
1948—Tennessee Williams, A Streetcar Named Desire.
1949—Arthur Miller, Death of a Salesman.
1950—Richard Rodgers, Oscar Hammerstein 2d, and Joshua Logan, South Pacific.
1952—Joseph Kramm, The Shrike.
1953—William Inge, Picnic.
1954—John Patrick, Teahouse of the August Moon.
1955—Tennessee Williams, Cat on a Hot Tin Roof.
1956—Frances Goodrich and Albert Hackett, The Diary of Anne Frank.
1957—Eugene O'Neill, Long Day's Journey Into Night.
1958—Ketti Frings, Look Homeward, Angel.
1959—Archibald MacLeish, J. B.
1960—George Abbott, Jerome Weidman, Sheldon Harnick and Jerry Bock, Fiorello.
1961—Tad Mosel, All the Way Home.

1962—Frank Loesser and Abe Burrows, How To Succeed In Business Without Really Trying.
1965—Frank D. Gilroy, The Subject Was Roses.
1967—Edward Albee, A Delicate Balance.
1969—Howard Sackler, The Great White Hope.
1970—Charles Gordone, No Place to Be Somebody.
1971—Paul Zindel, The Effect of Gamma Rays on Man-in-the-Moon Marigolds.
1973—Jason Miller, That Championship Season.
1975—Edward Albee, Seascape.
1976—Michael Bennett, James Kirkwood, Nicholas Dante, Marvin Hamlisch, Edward Kleban, A Chorus Line.
1977—Michael Cristofer, The Shadow Box.
1978—Donald L. Coburn, The Gin Game.
1979 Sam Shepard, Buried Child.
1980—Lanford Wilson, Talley's Folly.
1981—Beth Henley, Crimes of the Heart.
1982—Charles Fuller, A Soldier's Play.
1983—Marsha Norman, 'night, Mother.
1984—David Mamet, Glengarry Glen Ross.

History

For a book on the history of the United States.

1917—J. J. Jusserand, With Americans of Past and Present Days.
1918—James Ford Rhodes, History of the Civil War.
1920—Justin H. Smith, The War with Mexico.
1921—William Sowden Sims, The Victory at Sea.
1922—James Truslow Adams, The Founding of New England.
1923—Charles Warren, The Supreme Court in United States History.
1924—Charles Howard McIlwain, The American Revolution: A Constitutional Interpretation.
1925—Frederick L. Paxton, A History of the American Frontier.
1926—Edward Channing, A History of the U.S.
1927—Samuel Flagg Bemis, Pinckney's Treaty.
1928—Vernon Louis Parrington, Main Currents in American Thought.
1929—Fred A. Shannon, The Organization and Administration of the Union Army, 1861-65.
1930—Claude H. Van Tyne, The War of Independence.
1931—Bernadotte E. Schmitt, The Coming of the War, 1914.
1932—Gen. John J. Pershing, My Experiences in the World War.
1933—Frederick J. Turner, The Significance of Sections in American History.
1934—Herbert Agar, The People's Choice.
1935—Charles McLean Andrews, The Colonial Period of American History.
1936—Andrew C. McLaughlin, The Constitutional History of the United States.
1937—Van Wyck Brooks, The Flowering of New England.
1938—Paul Herman Buck, The Road to Reunion, 1865-1900.
1939—Frank Luther Mott, A History of American Magazines.
1940—Carl Sandburg, Abraham Lincoln: The War Years.
1941—Marcus Lee Hansen, The Atlantic Migration, 1607-1860.
1942—Margaret Leech, Reveille in Washington.
1943—Esther Forbes, Paul Revere and the World He Lived In.
1944—Merle Curti, The Growth of American Thought.
1945—Stephen Bonsal, Unfinished Business.
1946—Arthur M. Schlesinger Jr., The Age of Jackson.
1947—James Phinney Baxter 3d, Scientists Against Time.
1948—Bernard De Voto, Across the Wide Missouri.
1949—Roy F. Nichols, The Disruption of American Democracy.
1950—O. W. Larkin, Art and Life in America.
1951—R. Carlyle Buley, The Old Northwest: Pioneer Period 1815-1840.
1952—Oscar Handlin, The Uprooted.
1953—George Dangerfield, The Era of Good Feelings.
1954—Bruce Catton, A Stillness at Appomattox.
1955—Paul Horgan, Great River: The Rio Grande in North American History.
1956—Richard Hofstadter, The Age of Reform.
1957—George F. Kennan, Russia Leaves the War.
1958—Bray Hammond, Banks and Politics in America—From the Revolution to the Civil War.
1959—Leonard D. White and Jean Schneider, The Republican Era; 1869-1901.
1960—Margaret Leech, In the Days of McKinley.
1961—Herbert Feis, Between War and Peace: The Potsdam Conference.
1962—Lawrence H. Gibson, The Triumphant Empire: Thunderclouds Gather in the West.
1963—Constance McLaughlin Green, Washington: Village and Capital, 1800-1878.
1964—Sumner Chilton Powell, Puritan Village: The Formation of A New England Town.
1965—Irwin Unger, The Greenback Era.
1966—Perry Miller, Life of the Mind in America.
1967—William H. Goetzmann, Exploration and Empire: the Explorer and Scientist in the Winning of the American West.
1968—Bernard Bailyn, The Ideological Origins of the American Revolution.
1969—Leonard W. Levy, Origin of the Fifth Amendment.
1970—Dean Acheson, Present at the Creation: My Years in the State Department.
1971—James McGregor Burns, Roosevelt: The Soldier of Freedom.
1972—Carl N. Degler, Neither Black Nor White.
1973—Michael Kammen, People of Paradox: An Inquiry Concerning the Origins of American Civilization.
1974—Daniel J. Boorstin, The Americans: The Democratic Experience.
1975—Dumas Malone, Jefferson and His Time.
1976—Paul Horgan, Lamy of Santa Fe.
1977—David M. Potter, The Impending Crisis.

1978 Alfred D. Chandler, Jr., The Visible Hand: The Managerial Revolution in American Business.
1979—Don E. Fehrenbacher, The Dred Scott Case: Its Significance in American Law and Politics.
1980—Leon F. Litwack, Been in the Storm So Long.
1981—Lawrence A. Cremin, American Education: The National Experience, 1783-1876.
1982—C. Vann Woodward, ed., Mary Chestnut's Civil War.
1000—Rhys L. Issac, The Transformation of Virginia, 1740-1790.

Biography or Autobiography

For a distinguished biography or autobiography by an American author.

1917—Laura E. Richards and Maude Howe Elliott, assisted by Florence Howe Hall, Julia Ward Howe.
1918—William Cabell Bruce, Benjamin Franklin, Self-Revealed.
1919—Henry Adams, The Education of Henry Adams.
1920—Albert J. Beveridge, The Life of John Marshall.
1921—Edward Bok, The Americanization of Edward Bok.
1922—Hamlin Garland, A Daughter of the Middle Border.
1923—Burton J. Hendrick, The Life and Letters of Walter H. Page.
1924—Michael Pupin, From Immigrant to Inventor.
1925—M. A. DeWolfe Howe, Barrett Wendell and His Letters.
1926—Harvey Cushing, Life of Sir William Osler.
1927—Emory Holloway, Whitman: An Interpretation in Narrative.
1928—Charles Edward Russell, The American Orchestra and Theodore Thomas.
1929—Burton J. Hendrick, The Training of an American: The Earlier Life and Letters of Walter H. Page.
1930—Marquis James, The Raven (Sam Houston).
1931—Henry James, Charles W. Eliot.
1932—Henry F. Pringle, Theodore Roosevelt.
1933—Allan Nevins, Grover Cleveland.
1934—Tyler Dennett, John Hay.
1935—Douglas Southall Freeman, R. E. Lee
1936—Ralph Barton Perry, The Thought and Character of William James.
1937—Allan Nevins, Hamilton Fish: The Inner History of the Grant Administration.
1938—Divided between Odell Shepard, Pedlar's Progress; Marquis James, Andrew Jackson.
1939—Carl Van Doren, Benjamin Franklin.
1940—Ray Stannard Baker, Woodrow Wilson, Life and Letters.
1941—Ola Elizabeth Winslow, Jonathan Edwards.
1942—Forrest Wilson, Crusader in Crinoline.
1943—Samuel Eliot Morison, Admiral of the Ocean Sea (Columbus).
1944—Carleton Mabee, The American Leonardo: The Life of Samuel F. B. Morse.
1945—Russell Blaine Nye, George Bancroft; Brahmin Rebel.
1946—Linny Marsh Wolfe, Son of the Wilderness.
1947—William Allen White, The Autobiography of William Allen White.
1948—Margaret Clapp, Forgotten First Citizen: John Bigelow.
1949—Robert E. Sherwood, Roosevelt and Hopkins.
1950—Samuel Flag Bemis, John Quincy Adams and the Foundations of American Foreign Policy.
1951—Margaret Louise Coit, John C. Calhoun: American Portrait.
1952—Merlo J. Pusey, Charles Evans Hughes.
1953—David J. Mays, Edmund Pendleton, 1721-1803.
1954—Charles A. Lindbergh, The Spirit of St. Louis.
1955—William S. White, The Taft Story.
1956—Talbot F. Hamlin, Benjamin Henry Latrobe.
1957—John F. Kennedy, Profiles in Courage.
1958—Douglas Southall Freeman (decd. 1953), George Washington, Vols. I-VI: John Alexander Carroll and Mary Wells Ashworth, Vol. VII.
1959—Arthur Walworth, Woodrow Wilson: American Prophet.
1960—Samuel Eliot Morison, John Paul Jones.
1961—David Donald, Charles Sumner and The Coming of the Civil War.
1963—Leon Edel, Henry James: Vol. II. The Conquest of London, 1870-1881; Vol. III, The Middle Years, 1881-1895.
1964—Walter Jackson Bate, John Keats.
1965—Ernest Samuels, Henry Adams.
1966—Arthur M. Schlesinger Jr., A Thousand Days.
1967—Justin Kaplan, Mr. Clemens and Mark Twain.
1968—George F. Kennan. Memoirs (1925-1950).
1969—B. L. Reid, The Man from New York: John Quinn and his Friends.
1970—T. Harry Williams, Huey Long.
1971—Lawrence Thompson, Robert Frost: The Years of Triumph, 1915-1938.
1972—Joseph P. Lash, Eleanor and Franklin.
1973—W. A. Swanberg, Luce and His Empire.
1974—Louis Sheaffer, O'Neill, Son and Artist.
1975—Robert A. Caro, The Power Broker: Robert Moses and the Fall of New York.
1976—R.W.B. Lewis, Edith Wharton: A Biography.
1977—John E. Mack, A Prince of Our Disorder, The Life of T.E. Lawrence.
1978—Walter Jackson Bate, Samuel Johnson.
1979—Leonard Baker, Days of Sorrow and Pain: Leo Baeck and the Berlin Jews.
1980—Edmund Morris, The Rise of Theodore Roosevelt.
1981—Robert K. Massie, Peter the Great: His Life and World.
1982—William S. McFeely, Grant: A Biography.
1983—Russell Baker, Growing Up.
1984—Louis R. Harlan, Booker T. Washington.

American Poetry

Before this prize was established in 1922, awards were made from

gifts provided by the Poetry Society: 1918—Love Songs, by Sara Teasdale. 1919—Old Road to Paradise, by Margaret Widemer; Corn Huskers, by Carl Sandburg.
1922—Edwin Arlington Robinson, Collected Poems.
1923—Edna St. Vincent Millay, The Ballad of the Harp-Weaver; A Few Figs from Thistles; Eight Sonnets in American Poetry, 1922; A Miscellany.
1924—Robert Frost, New Hampshire: A Poem with Notes and Grace Notes.
1925—Edwin Arlington Robinson, The Man Who Died Twice.
1926—Amy Lowell, What's O'Clock.
1927—Leonora Speyer, Fiddler's Farewell.
1928—Edwin Arlington Robinson, Tristram.
1929—Stephen Vincent Benet, John Brown's Body.
1930—Conrad Aiken, Selected Poems.
1931—Robert Frost, Collected Poems.
1932—George Dillon, The Flowering Stone.
1933—Archibald MacLeish, Conquistador.
1934—Robert Hillyer, Collected Verse.
1935—Audrey Wurdemann, Bright Ambush.
1936—Robert P. Tristram Coffin, Strange Holiness.
1937—Robert Frost, A Further Range.
1938—Marya Zaturenska, Cold Morning Sky.
1939—John Gould Fletcher, Selected Poems.
1940—Mark Van Doren, Collected Poems.
1941—Leonard Bacon, Sunderland Capture.
1942—William Rose Benet, The Dust Which Is God.
1943—Robert Frost, A Witness Tree.
1944—Stephen Vincent Benot, Western Star
1945—Karl Shapiro, V-Letter and Other Poems.
1947—Robert Lowell, Lord Weary's Castle.
1948—W. H. Auden, The Age of Anxiety.
1949—Peter Viereck, Terror and Decorum.
1950—Gwendolyn Brooks, Annie Allen.
1951—Carl Sandburg, Complete Poems.
1952—Marianne Moore, Collected Poems.
1953—Archibald MacLeish, Collected Poems.
1954—Theodore Roethke, The Waking.
1955—Wallace Stevens, Collected Poems.
1956—Elizabeth Bishop, Poems, North and South.
1957—Richard Wilbur, Things of This World.
1958—Robert Penn Warren, Promises: Poems 1954-1956.
1959—Stanley Kunitz, Selected Poems 1928-1958.
1960—W. D. Snodgrass, Heart's Needle.
1961—Phyllis McGinley, Times Three: Selected Verse from Three Decades.
1962—Alan Dugan, Poems.
1963—William Carlos Williams, Pictures From Breughel.
1964—Louis Simpson, At the End of the Open Road.
1965—John Berryman, 77 Dream Songs.

1966—Richard Eberhart, Selected Poems.
1967—Anne Sexton, Live or Die.
1968—Anthony Hecht, The Hard Hours.
1969—George Oppen, Of Being Numerous.
1970—Richard Howard, Untitled Subjects.
1971—William S. Merwin, The Carrier of Ladders.
1972—James Wright, Collected Poems.
1973—Maxine Winokur Kumin, Up Country.
1975—Gary Snyder, Turtle Island.
1976—John Ashbery, Self-Portrait in a Convex Mirror.
1977—James Merrill, Divine Comedies.
1978—Howard Nemerov, Collected Poems.
1979—Robert Penn Warren, Now and Then: Poems 1976-1978.
1980—Donald Justice, Selected Poems.
1981—James Schuyler, The Morning of the Poem.
1982—Sylvia Plath, The Collected Poems.
1983—Galway Kinnell, Selected Poems.
1984—Mary Oliver, American Primitive.

General Non-Fiction

1962—Theodore H. White, The Making of the President 1960.
1963—Barbara W. Tuchman, The Guns of August.
1964—Richard Hofstadter, Anti-Intellectualism in American Life.
1965—Howard Mumford Jones, O Strange New World.
1966—Edwin Way Teale, Wandering Through Winter.
1967—David Brion Davis, The Problem of Slavery in Western Culture.
1968—Will and Ariel Durant, Rousseau and Revolution.
1969—Norman Mailer, The Armies of the Night; and Rene Jules Dubos, So Human an Animal: How We Are Shaped by Surroundings and Events.
1970—Eric H. Erikson, Gandhi's Truth.
1971—John Toland, The Rising Sun.
1972—Barbara W. Tuchman, Stilwell and the American Experience in China, 1911-1945.
1973—Frances FitzGerald, Fire in the Lake: The Vietnamese and the Americans in Vietnam; and Robert Coles, Children of Crisis, Volumes II and III.
1974—Ernest Becker, The Denial of Death.
1975—Annie Dillard, Pilgrim at Tinker Creek.
1976—Robert N. Butler, Why Survive? Being Old in America.
1977—William W. Warner, Beautiful Swimmers.
1978—Carl Sagan, The Dragons of Eden.
1979—Edward O. Wilson, On Human Nature.
1980—Douglas R. Hofstadter, Gödel, Escher, Bach: An Eternal Golden Braid.
1981—Carl E. Schorske, Fin-de-Siecle Vienna: Politics and Culture.
1982—Tracy Kidder, The Soul of a New Machine.
1983—Susan Sheehan, Is There No Place on Earth for Me?
1984—Paul Starr, Social Transformation of American Medicine.

Music

For composition by an American (before 1977, by a composer resident in the U.S.), in the larger forms of chamber, orchestra or choral music or for an operatic work including ballet. A special posthumous award was granted in 1976 to Scott Joplin.
1943—William Schuman, Secular Cantata No. 2, A Free Song.
1944—Howard Hanson, Symphony No. 4, Op. 34.
1945—Aaron Copland, Appalachian Spring.
1946—Leo Sowerby, The Canticle of the Sun.
1947—Charles E. Ives, Symphony No. 3.
1948—Walter Piston, Symphony No. 3.
1949—Virgil Thomson, Louisiana Story.
1950—Gian-Carlo Menotti, The Consul.
1951—Douglas Moore, Giants in the Earth.
1952—Gail Kubik, Symphony Concertante.
1954—Quincy Porter, Concerto for Two Pianos and Orchestra.
1955—Gian-Carlo Menotti, The Saint of Bleecker Street.
1956—Ernest Toch, Symphony No. 3.
1957—Norman Dello Joio, Meditations on Ecclesiastes.
1958—Samuel Barber, Vanessa.
1959—John La Montaine, Concerto for Piano and Orchestra.
1960—Elliott Carter, Second String Quartet.

1961—Walter Piston, Symphony No. 7.
1962—Robert Ward, The Crucible.
1963—Samuel Barber, Piano Concerto No. 1.
1966—Leslie Bassett, Variations for Orchestra.
1967—Leon Kirchner, Quartet No. 3.
1968—George Crumb, Echoes of Time and The River.
1969—Karel Husa, String Quartet No. 3.
1970—Charles W. Wuorinen, Time's Encomium.
1971—Mario Davidovsky, Synchronisms No. 6.
1972—Jacob Druckman, Windows.
1973—Elliott Carter, String Quartet No. 3.
1974—Donald Martino, Notturno. (Special citation) Roger Sessions.
1975—Dominick Argento, From the Diary of Virginia Woolf.
1976—Ned Rorem, Air Music.
1977—Richard Wernick, Visions of Terror and Wonder.
1978—Michael Colgrass, Deja Vu for Percussion and Orchestra.
1979—Joseph Schwantner, Aftertones of Infinity.
1980—David Del Tredici, In Memory of a Summer Day.
1982—Roger Sessions, Concerto For Orchestra. (Special Citation) Milton Babbitt.
1983—Ellen T. Zwilich, Three Movements for Orchestra.
1984—Bernard Rands, Canti del Sole.

Special Awards

Awarded in 1984 unless otherwise noted.

Books, Allied Arts

Academy of American Poets: fellowship, for distinguished achievement, $10,000: James Schuyler, Philip Booth: Lamont Selection: Sharon Olds, The Dead and the Living; Ivan Younger Poets Awards: Edward Hirsch, Brad Leithauser, Gjertrud Schnackenberg; Whitman Award, publication and $1,000: Eric Pankey, For the New Year.

American Academy and Institute of Arts and Letters: gold medal: George F. Kennan; new Institute members in literature: Russell Baker, E.L. Doctorow, William Gaddis, Paul Theroux, Lewis Thomas. Literature awards: Rome Fellowship: David St. John; Bynner Poetry Prize: Henry Taylor; Forster Award: Humphrey Carpenter; Kaufman First

Fiction Prize: Denis Johnson; Rosenthal Award: Danny Santiago; Stein Award: Andrea Lee; Vursell Memorial Award: W.M. Spackman; Zabel Award: Jamaica Kincaid.

Bancroft Prizes in History, by Columbia Univ., $4,000: Louis R. Harlan, Booker T. Washington; Paul Starr, The Social Transformation of American Medicine.

Caldecott Medal, by American Library Assn., for children's book illustration: The Glorious Flight, il. Alice and Martin Provensen.

Children's Science Book Awards, by N.Y. Academy of Sciences: Oak & Company, Richard Mabet, il. Clare Roberts; *Volcano Weather*, Henry Stommel, Elizabeth Stommel; Montroll special awards: *From Hand Ax to Laser*, John Purcell, il. Judy Skorpil.

Christopher Awards, for affirmation of human spirit: books for adults: *Alex*, Frank Deford; *Aunt Arie*, ed. Linda Garland Page, Eliot Wigginton; *A Bitter Fog*, Carol Van Strum; *Blue Highways*, William Least Heat Moon; *By Little and By Little*, Robert Ellsberg; *The Courting of Marcus Dupree*, Willie Morris; *Eleni*, Nicholas Gage; *Gracias!*, Henry J.M. Nouwen; *Marie*, Peter Maas; *Traits of a Healthy Family*, Dolores Curran.

Golden Kite Awards (1983), by Society of Children's Book Writers: fiction: Gloria Skurzynski; *The Tempering*; non-fiction: Helen Roney Sattler, *The Illustrated Dinosaur Dictionary*; picture book illustration: Trina Schart Hyman, *Little Red Riding Hood*.

Iowa School of Letters Award for Short Fiction, by Univ. of Iowa Writers' Workshop, $1,000: Ivy Goodman, *Heart Failure*.

National Book Critics Circle Awards: fiction: *Ironweed*, William Kennedy; criticism: *Hugging the Shore*, John Updike; nonfiction: *The Price of Power*, Seymour M. Hersh; biography: *Minor Characters*, Joyce Johnson; poetry: *The Changing Light at Sandover*, James Merrill.

National Medal for Literature, by Guinzburg Fund, for distinguished past and continuing contribution, $15,000: Mary McCarthy.

Nebula Awards, by Science Fiction Writers of America:

novel: *Star Tide Rising*, David Brin; novella: "Hardfought," Greg Bear; novelette: "Bloodmusic," Gardner Dozois.

Newbery Medal, by American Library Assn., for children's book: Beverly Cleary, *Dear Mr. Henshaw*.

Scott O'Dell Award, for children's historical fiction, $5,000: Elizabeth George Speare, *The Sign of the Beaver*.

PEN Awards: Hemingway Award for first fiction, $7,500: Joan Chase, *During the Reign of the Queen of Persia*; translation prize: $1,000: William Weaver, *The Name of the Rose* by Umberto Eco; Poggioli Translation Award, $3,000: Stephen Sartarelli, *Horrcynus Orca* by Stefano D'Arrigo; Algren Fiction Award for work in progress, $1,000: Chris Mazza, Martha Miyatake.

Present Tense Award, by American Jewish Committee, for books on Jewish themes, $1,000 each: fiction: Aharon Appelfeld, *Tzili*; social and political analysis: Peter Grose, *Israel in the Mind of America*; history: Salo Wittnayer Baron, *A Social and Religious History of the Jews, Vol. 18*; biography: Ruth Jordan, *Daughter of the Waves*; juvenile: Barbara Pomerantz, *Bubby Me and Memories*; religious thought: Rabbi Eliezer Berkovitz, *Not in Heaven*; translation: Grace Schulman, *At the Stone of Losses*; nonfiction: David Altshuler, *The Precious Legacy*.

Regina Medal, by Catholic Library Assn., for distinguished contribution: Madeleine L'Engle.

Delmore Schwartz Memorial Poetry Award, by N.Y.U.'s College of Arts and Sciences, $1,000: Ruth Stone.

Journalism Awards

Amer. Assn. for the Advancement of Science—Westinghouse Science Writing Awards, $3,000: John Noble Wilford, *New York Times*; Timothy Ferris, *New York Times Magazine*.

ASCAP/Deems Taylor Awards, for writing about music, $7,000: James Chute, *Cincinnati Post*; Robert Finn, *Cleveland Plain Dealer*; John Edward Hasse, Frank J. Gillis, Indiana Historical Society.

Worth Bingham Prizes, for political reporting or commentary, $1,000: Bill Hogan, Diane Kiesel, Alan Green, *New Republic*.

Heywood Broun Awards, for concern for the underdog (1983), $1,000: Stephen R. Morin, *Providence* (R.I.) *Journal-Bulletin*; Joel Brinkley, *Louisville Courier-Journal*; John Hurst, Ron Taylor, *Los Angeles Times*.

Raymond Clapper Award, for reporting on national govt. (1983), $1,000 each: Bruce Ingersoll, *Chicago Sun-Times*; Bill Prochnau, *Washington Post*.

Sidney Hillman Foundation Prizes, for humanitarian causes (1983), $750 each: Rita Ciolli, *Newsday*; Elizabeth Drew, *The New Yorker*; Jonathan Schell, *The Fate of the Earth*.

Robert F. Kennedy Awards, for problems of disadvantaged (1983), $7,000: *Philadelphia Inquirer*, Donald Drake; photography: Randi Eli Grothe, *Dallas Morning News*; cartoons: Don Wright, *Miami News*.

H.L. Mencken Prize, $2,500: Steve Knickmeyer, *Ada* (Okla.) *News*.

National Magazine Awards, by American Society of Magazine Editors: general excellence: *House & Garden*, *National Geographic*, *The American Lawyer*, *Outside*; public service: *The New Yorker*; fiction: *Seventeen*; reporting: *Vanity Fair*; essays, criticism: *The New Republic*; service to the individual: *New York Magazine*; single-topic issue: *Esquire*; design: *House & Garden*.

National Press Club Awards, for reporting for hometown readers, $1,000: George Antham, *Des Moines Register*; Stephen Engelberg, *Dallas Morning News*.

Pictures of the Year, by Canon U.S.A., Natl. Press Photographers Assn. & Univ. of Missouri, $12,000: newspaper photographer: Bill Frakes, *Miami Herald*; Bill Luster, *Louis-*

ville Courier-Journal; Chris Johns, *Seattle Times*; magazine photographer: Jim Brandenburg, *National Geographic*; Harry Benson, *Life*; Louie Psyihoys, *National Geographic*; editor: David M. Yarnold, *San Jose Mercury-News*; Bruce McElfresh, *National Geographic*; world understanding: Eli Reed, *San Francisco Examiner*.

Reuben Awards, by Natl. Cartoonists Society: cartoonist of the year: Bill Keane, "Family Circus"; editorial cartoons: Mike Peters, *Dayton Daily News*; humor: Brant Parker, "Wizard of Id"; sports: Karl Hubenthal, *L.A. Herald-Examiner*; story strip: Dick Moores, "Gasoline Alley"; syndicated panel: Jim Unger, "Herman"; magazine gags: Don Orehek, *Playboy*; animation: Bill Melendez, "Peanuts" specials; advertising: Arnold Roth, magazines & books; comic books: Bob Gustafson, "Beetle Bailey."

Science-in-Society Awards, by Natl. Assn. of Science Writers (1983), $1,000 each: Robert Zimmerman, Warren Froelich, *San Diego Union*; Thomas A. Preston, *Weekly—Seattle's Newsmagazine*.

Scripps-Howard Foundation Awards, $25,500: Charles M. Schulz Award, for promising cartoonist: Frank Pauer; Ernie Pyle Memorial Award, for human interest writing: Rheta Grimsley Johnson, (Memphis) *Commercial Appeal*; Edward J. Meeman Award, for conservation reporting: Maria Cone, Chuck Cook, *Orange County* (Cal.) *Register*; Jack Bowie, Peter Jensen, Rick Boyd, *Easton* (Md.) *Star-Democrat*. Walker Stone Award, for editorial writing: Jim Wooten, *Atlanta Journal*; Roy M. Howard Award, for public service, newspapers: Dan Biddle, *Philadelpha Inquirer*; E.W. Scripps Award, for service to first amendment: *Wilkes-Barre (Pa.) Times-Leader*.

Sigma Delta Chi Awards, by Society of Prof. Journalists (1983): public service: Gannett News Service; Loretta Tofani, *Washington Post*; Jackson (Miss.) *Clarion-Ledger*; editorials: David Rohn, *Indianapolis News*; Washington correspondence: Judith Bender, James M. Klurfeld, Earl B. Lane, Susan Page, *Newsday*; foreign correspondence: Robert Rivard, *Dallas Times Herald*; photography: Robert Fila, *Chicago Tribune*; others: *New Yorker*; *Mother Jones*; *Philadelphia*; Sally Bedell, Don Kowet, *TV Guide*; Robert W. Desmond, *Crisis in Conflict*.

Broadcasting and Theater Awards

Christopher Awards: special: "A Chorus Line"; Fred Rogers of "Mr. Rogers' Neighborhood"; the Library of America; TV specials: "Adam"; "Choices of the Heart"; "Frontline"; He Makes Me Feel Like Dancin' "; "The Life and Adventures of Nicholas Nickleby"; "Memorial Day"; "Mar-

vellous Machines, Expendable People"; "Paradise Lost"; "The Scarlet and the Black"; "Special Olympics"; "Who Will Love My Children?"; "The Woman Who Willed a Miracle."

Emmy Awards, by Acad. of Television Arts and Sciences, for nighttime programs (1982–83): dramatic series: *Hill Street Blues;* actor: Ed Flanders, *St. Elsewhere;* actress: Tyne Daly, *Cagney and Lacey;* supporting actor: James Coco, *St. Elsewhere;* supporting actress: Doris Roberts, *St. Elsewhere;* director: Jeff Bleckner, *Hill Street Blues;* writer: David Milch, *Hill Street Blues.* Comedy series: *Cheers;* actor: Judd Hirsch, *Taxi;* actress: Shelley Long, *Cheers;* director: James Burrows, *Cheers;* writer: Glen Charles, Les Charles, *Cheers.* Limited series: "...Nicholas Nickleby"; drama special: "Special Bulletin"; actor: Tommy Lee Jones, "The Executioner's Song"; actress: Barbara Stanwyck, "The Thorn Birds"; supporting actor: Richard Kiley, "The Thorn Birds"; supporting actress: Jean Simmons, "The Thorn Birds"; director: John Erman, "Who Will Love My Children?"; writer: Marshall Herskovitz, original story by Marshall Herskovitz, Edward Zwick, "Special Bulletin." Variety, music, or comedy program: "Motown 25"; performance: Leontyne Price, "Live from Lincoln Center"; director: Dwight Hemion, "Sheena Easton Act I"; writer: *SCTV Network.* Children's program: "Big Bird in China." Governors' award: Sylvester L. "Pat" Weaver.

George Jean Nathan Award, for theater criticism, $5,000: Herbert Blau.

Obie Awards, for Off-Broadway theater, $1,000: play: "Fool for Love"; musical: "Gospel at Colonus"; performances: Kathy Baker, Ed Harris, Will Patton, "Fool for Love"; F. Murray Abraham, "Uncle Vanya"; Shelia Dabney, "Saita"; Morgan Freeman, "Gospel at Colonus"; George Guidall, "Cinders"; Richard Jordan, "A Private View"; Ruth Maleczech, Frederick Neumann, "Through the Leaves"; Stephen McHattie, "Mensch Meier"; Dianne Wiest, "Serenading Louie" and "Other Places."

Peabody Awards, by Univ. of Georgia School of Journalism: *60 Minutes,* CBS News; "Vietnam," WGBH-TV, Central Independent TV, Antenne-2; Don McGannon, Westinghouse Broadcasting Corp.; *Grand Ole Opry,* WSM Radio,

Nashville, Tenn.; "Debbie Pielow: Waiting for a Heart," WCCO Radio, Minneapolis, Minn.; "Piano Jazz," So. Carolina Educational Radio Network; "The Jeffersonian World of Dumas Malone," WMAL Radio, Washington; "Times Beach," KMOX Radio, St. Louis; "New England Almanac," Thomas Looker, Montague Center, Mass.; "Victims," WRAL Radio, Raleigh, N.C.; "Asylum in the Streets," WNBC-TV, New York; "The Plane That Fell from the Sky," CBS News, New York; "I-Team," WCCO-TV, Minneapolis; "Motown 25," NBC and Motown Prod.; "Prisoner Without a Name, Cell Without a Number," Chrysalis-Yellen Prod. and NBC; "The Making of a Continent," WTTW, Chicago and BBC; "Portrait of America," WTBS-TV, Atlanta; "The Great Space Coaster," Sunbow Prod., New York; "Romeo and Juliet on Ice," CBS Enter. and Smith-Hemion Prod.; "The Woman Who Willed a Miracle," ABC and Dick Clark Prod.; "What Have We Learned, Charlie Brown?" CBS Enter., Mendelson-Melendez Prod.; "Studebaker," WBBM-TV, Chicago; "Give Me That Big-time Religion," WBRZ-TV, Baton Rouge, La.; "Climate of Death," KRON-TV, San Francisco; "Nova," WGBH-TV, Boston; "He Makes Me Feel Like Dancin'," NBC and Edgar J. Scherick Assoc.; "Diagnosis: AIDS," KCTS, Seattle.

Antoinette Perry Awards (Tonys), for Broadway theater: musical: "La Cage aux Folles"; director: Arthur Laurents, "La Cage aux Folles"; actor: George Hearn, "La Cage aux Folles"; actress: Chita Rivera, "The Rink"; supporting actor: Hinton Battle, "The Tap Dance Kid"; supporting actress: Lila Kedrova, "Zorba"; music: Jerry Herman, "La Cage aux Folles"; book: Harvey Fierstein, "La Cage aux Folles." Play: "The Real Thing"; actor: Jeremy Irons, "The Real Thing"; actress: Glenn Close, "The Real Thing"; supporting actor: Joe Mantegna, "Glengarry Glen Ross"; supporting actress: Christine Baranski, "The Real Thing."

Television Academy Hall of Fame: Milton Berle, Lucille Ball, Norman Lear, William S. Paley, Paddy Chayefsky, Edward R. Murrow, David Sarnoff.

Miscellaneous Awards

American Academy and Institute of Arts and Letters: gold medal: Gordon Bunshaft; distinguished service to the arts: Roger L. Stevens; award of merit in sculpture: Raoul Hague; new Academy members in art and music: Chaim Gross, Jacob Lawrence, Lukas Foss; new Institute members in art and music: Mary Frank, Al Held, Wolf Kahn, Ibram Lassaw, David Del Tredici. American honorary members: Frank Capra, Rouben Mamoulian, Billy Wilder, Merce Cunningham, Roman Vishnia. Awards in music and art: Berliawsky Award: Ross Bauer; Ives Scholarships: Richard Campanelli, Kenneth Fuchs, Laura Karpman, Bright Sheng, Larry Stukenholtz, Gregory Yontz; Ives Fellowship: Nicholas C.K. Thorne; Lieberson Fellowship: Primous Fountain III, Peter Lieberson; Waite Award: Herman Berlinski; Brunner Memorial Prize: Peter D. Eisenman; Rosenthal Foundation Award: James Brown.

Kennedy Center Honors, for lifetime achievement in the arts: Katharine Dunham; Elia Kazan; James Stewart; Virgil Thompson; Frank Sinatra.

Albert Lasker Medical Research and Public Service Awards (1983), $45,000: basic medical research: Eric R. Kandel, Vernon B. Mountcastle, Jr.; clinical medical research: F. Mason Sones, Jr.; public service: Saul Krugman, Maurice R. Hilleman.

Medal of Freedom, U.S. Government: Whittaker Chambers; James Cagney; Howard Baker; Tennessee Ernie Ford; Louis L'Amour; Rev. Norman Vincent Peale; Anwar Sadat; Jackie Robinson; Andrew Goodpaster; Dr. Denton Cooley; Eunice Kennedy Shriver; Lincoln Kirstein; Leo Cherne; Dr. Hector Garcia.

Pritzker Architecture Prize, $100,000: Richard Meier.

Samuel H. Scripps American Dance Festival Award, $25,000: Hanya Holm.

Motion Picture Academy Awards (Oscars)

1927-28
Actor: Emil Jannings, *The Way of All Flesh.*
Actress: Janet Gaynor, *Seventh Heaven.*
Director: Frank Borzage, *Seventh Heaven;* Lewis Milestone, *Two Arabian Knights.*
Picture: *Wings,* Paramount.

1928-29
Actor: Warner Baxter, *In Old Arizona.*
Actress: Mary Pickford, *Coquette.*
Director: Frank Lloyd, *The Divine Lady.*
Picture: *Broadway Melody,* MGM.

1929-30
Actor: George Arliss, *Disraeli.*
Actress: Norma Shearer, *The Divorcee.*
Director: Lewis Milestone, *All Quiet on the Western Front.*
Picture: *All Quiet on the Western Front,* Univ.

1930-31
Actor: Lionel Barrymore, *Free Soul.*

Actress: Marie Dressler, *Min and Bill.*
Director: Norman Taurog, *Skippy.*
Picture: *Cimarron,* RKO.

1931-32
Actor: Fredric March, *Dr. Jekyll and Mr. Hyde;* Wallace Beery, *The Champ* (tie).
Actress: Helen Hayes, *Sin of Madelon Claudet.*
Director: Frank Borzage, *Bad Girl.*
Picture: *Grand Hotel,* MGM.
Special: Walt Disney, *Mickey Mouse.*

1932-33
Actor: Charles Laughton, *Private Life of Henry VIII.*
Actress: Katharine Hepburn, *Morning Glory.*
Director: Frank Lloyd, *Cavalcade.*
Picture: *Cavalcade,* Fox.

1934
Actor: Clark Gable, *It Happened One Night.*
Actress: Claudette Colbert, same.

Director: Frank Capra, *It Happened One Night.*
Picture: *It Happened One Night,* Columbia.

1935
Actor: Victor McLaglen, *The Informer.*
Actress: Bette Davis, *Dangerous.*
Director: John Ford, *The Informer.*
Picture: *Mutiny on the Bounty,* MGM.

1936
Actor: Paul Muni, *Story of Louis Pasteur.*
Actress: Luise Rainer, *The Great Ziegfeld.*
Sup. Actor: Walter Brennan, *Come and Get It.*
Sup. Actress: Gale Sondergaard, *Anthony Adverse.*
Director: Frank Capra, *Mr. Deeds Goes to Town.*
Picture: *The Great Ziegfeld,* MGM.

1937
Actor: Spencer Tracy, *Captains Courageous.*
Actress: Luise Rainer, *The Good Earth.*
Sup. Actor: Joseph Schildkraut, *Life of Emile Zola.*
Sup. Actress: Alice Brady, *In Old Chicago.*
Director: Leo McCarey, *The Awful Truth.*
Picture: *Life of Emile Zola,* Warner.

1938
Actor: Spencer Tracy, *Boys Town.*
Actress: Bette Davis, *Jezebel.*
Sup. Actor: Walter Brennan, *Kentucky.*
Sup. Actress: Fay Bainter, *Jezebel.*
Director: Frank Capra, *You Can't Take It With You.*
Picture: *You Can't Take It With You,* Columbia.

1939
Actor: Robert Donat, *Goodbye Mr. Chips.*
Actress: Vivien Leigh, *Gone With the Wind.*
Sup. Actor: Thomas Mitchell, *Stage Coach.*
Sup. Actress: Hattie McDaniel, *Gone With the Wind.*
Director: Victor Fleming, *Gone With the Wind.*
Picture: *Gone With the Wind,* Selznick International.

1940
Actor: James Stewart, *The Philadelphia Story.*
Actress: Ginger Rogers, *Kitty Foyle.*
Sup. Actor: Walter Brennan, *The Westerner.*
Sup. Actress: Jane Darwell, *The Grapes of Wrath.*
Director: John Ford, *The Grapes of Wrath.*
Picture: *Rebecca,* Selznick International.

1941
Actor: Gary Cooper, *Sergeant York.*
Actress: Joan Fontaine, *Suspicion.*
Sup. Actor: Donald Crisp, *How Green Was My Valley.*
Sup. Actress: Mary Astor, *The Great Lie.*
Director: John Ford, *How Green Was My Valley.*
Picture: *How Green Was My Valley,* 20th Cent.-Fox.

1942
Actor: James Cagney, *Yankee Doodle Dandy.*
Actress: Greer Garson, *Mrs. Miniver.*
Sup. Actor: Van Heflin, *Johnny Eager.*
Sup. Actress: Teresa Wright, *Mrs. Miniver.*
Director: William Wyler, *Mrs. Miniver.*
Picture: *Mrs. Miniver,* MGM.

1943
Actor: Paul Lukas, *Watch on the Rhine.*
Actress: Jennifer Jones, *The Song of Bernadette.*
Sup. Actor: Charles Coburn, *The More the Merrier.*
Sup. Actress: Katina Paxinou, *For Whom the Bell Tolls.*
Director: Michael Curtiz, *Casablanca.*
Picture: *Casablanca,* Warner.

1944
Actor: Bing Crosby, *Going My Way.*
Actress: Ingrid Bergman, *Gaslight.*
Sup. Actor: Barry Fitzgerald, *Going My Way.*
Sup. Actress: Ethel Barrymore, *None But the Lonely Heart.*
Director: Leo McCarey, *Going My Way.*
Picture: *Going My Way,* Paramount.

1945
Actor: Ray Milland, *The Lost Weekend.*
Actress: Joan Crawford, *Mildred Pierce.*
Sup. Actor: James Dunn, *A Tree Grows in Brooklyn.*
Sup. Actress: Anne Revere, *National Velvet.*
Director: Billy Wilder, *The Lost Weekend.*
Picture: *The Lost Weekend,* Paramount.

1946
Actor: Fredric March, *Best Years of Our Lives.*
Actress: Olivia de Havilland, *To Each His Own.*
Sup. Actor: Harold Russell, *The Best Years of Our Lives.*
Sup. Actress: Anne Baxter, *The Razor's Edge.*
Director: William Wyler, *The Best Years of Our Lives.*
Picture: *The Best Years of Our Lives,* Goldwyn, RKO.

1947
Actor: Ronald Colman, *A Double Life.*
Actress: Loretta Young, *The Farmer's Daughter.*
Sup. Actor: Edmund Gwenn, *Miracle on 34th Street.*
Sup. Actress: Celeste Holm, *Gentleman's Agreement.*

Director: Elia Kazan, *Gentleman's Agreement.*
Picture: *Gentleman's Agreement,* 20th Cent.-Fox.

1948
Actor: Laurence Olivier, *Hamlet.*
Actress: Jane Wyman, *Johnny Belinda.*
Sup. Actor: Walter Huston, *Treasure of Sierra Madre.*
Sup. Actress: Claire Trevor, *Key Largo.*
Director: John Huston, *Treasure of Sierra Madre.*
Picture: *Hamlet,* Two Cities Film, Universal International.

1949
Actor: Broderick Crawford, *All the King's Men.*
Actress: Olivia de Havilland, *The Heiress.*
Sup. Actor: Dean Jagger, *Twelve O'Clock High.*
Sup. Actress: Mercedes McCambridge, *All the King's Men.*
Director: Joseph L. Mankiewicz, *Letter to Three Wives.*
Picture: *All the King's Men,* Columbia.

1950
Actor: Jose Ferrer, *Cyrano de Bergerac.*
Actress: Judy Holliday, *Born Yesterday.*
Sup. Actor: George Sanders, *All About Eve.*
Sup. Actress: Josephine Hull, *Harvey.*
Director: Joseph L. Mankiewicz, *All About Eve.*
Picture: *All About Eve,* 20th Century-Fox.

1951
Actor: Humphrey Bogart, *The African Queen.*
Actress: Vivien Leigh, *A Streetcar Named Desire.*
Sup. Actor: Karl Malden, *A Streetcar Named Desire.*
Sup. Actress: Kim Hunter, *A Streetcar Named Desire.*
Director: George Stevens, *A Place in the Sun.*
Picture: *An American in Paris,* MGM.

1952
Actor: Gary Cooper, *High Noon.*
Actress: Shirley Booth, *Come Back, Little Sheba.*
Sup. Actor: Anthony Quinn, *Viva Zapata!*
Sup. Actress: Gloria Grahame, *The Bad and the Beautiful.*
Director: John Ford, *The Quiet Man.*
Picture: *Greatest Show on Earth,* C.B. DeMille, Paramount.

1953
Actor: William Holden, *Stalag 17.*
Actress: Audrey Hepburn, *Roman Holiday.*
Sup. Actor: Frank Sinatra, *From Here to Eternity.*
Sup. Actress: Donna Reed, *From Here to Eternity.*
Director: Fred Zinnemann, *From Here to Eternity.*
Picture: *From Here to Eternity,* Columbia.

1954
Actor: Marlon Brando, *On the Waterfront.*
Actress: Grace Kelly, *The Country Girl.*
Sup. Actor: Edmond O'Brien, *The Barefoot Contessa.*
Sup. Actress: Eva Marie Saint, *On the Waterfront.*
Director: Elia Kazan, *On the Waterfront.*
Picture: *On the Waterfront,* Horizon-American, Colum.

1955
Actor: Ernest Borgnine, *Marty.*
Actress: Anna Magnani, *The Rose Tattoo.*
Sup. Actor: Jack Lemmon, *Mister Roberts.*
Sup. Actress: Jo Van Fleet, *East of Eden.*
Director: Delbert Mann, *Marty.*
Picture: *Marty,* Hecht and Lancaster's Steven Prods., U.A.

1956
Actor: Yul Brynner, *The King and I.*
Actress: Ingrid Bergman, *Anastasia.*
Sup. Actor: Anthony Quinn, *Lust for Life.*
Sup. Actress: Dorothy Malone, *Written on the Wind.*
Director: George Stevens, *Giant.*
Picture: *Around the World in 80 Days,* Michael Todd, U.A.

1957
Actor: Alec Guinness, *The Bridge on the River Kwai.*
Actress: Joanne Woodward, *The Three Faces of Eve.*
Sup. Actor: Red Buttons, *Sayonara.*
Sup. Actress: Miyoshi Umeki, *Sayonara.*
Director: David Lean, *The Bridge on the River Kwai.*
Picture: *The Bridge on the River Kwai,* Columbia.

1958
Actor: David Niven, *Separate Tables.*
Actress: Susan Hayward, *I Want to Live.*
Sup. Actor: Burl Ives, *The Big Country.*
Sup. Actress: Wendy Hiller, *Separate Tables.*
Director: Vincente Minnelli, *Gigi.*
Picture: *Gigi,* Arthur Freed Production, MGM.

1959
Actor: Charlton Heston, *Ben-Hur.*
Actress: Simone Signoret, *Room at the Top.*
Sup. Actor: Hugh Griffith, *Ben-Hur.*
Sup. Actress: Shelley Winters, *Diary of Anne Frank.*
Director: William Wyler, *Ben-Hur.*
Picture: *Ben-Hur,* MGM.

1960

Actor: Burt Lancaster, *Elmer Gantry.*
Actress: Elizabeth Taylor, *Butterfield 8.*
Sup. Actor: Peter Ustinov, *Spartacus.*
Sup. Actress: Shirley Jones, *Elmer Gantry.*
Director: Billy Wilder, *The Apartment.*
Picture: *The Apartment,* Mirisch Co., U.A.

1961

Actor: Maximilian Schell, *Judgment at Nuremberg.*
Actress: Sophia Loren, *Two Women.*
Sup. Actor: George Chakiris, *West Side Story.*
Sup. Actress: Rita Moreno, *West Side Story.*
Director: Jerome Robbins, Robert Wise, *West Side Story.*
Picture: *West Side Story,* United Artists.

1962

Actor: Gregory Peck, *To Kill a Mockingbird.*
Actress: Anne Bancroft, *The Miracle Worker.*
Sup. Actor: Ed Begley, *Sweet Bird of Youth.*
Sup. Actress: Patty Duke, *The Miracle Worker.*
Director: David Lean, *Lawrence of Arabia.*
Picture: *Lawrence of Arabia,* Columbia.

1963

Actor: Sidney Poitier, *Lilies of the Field.*
Actress: Patricia Neal, *Hud.*
Sup. Actor: Melvyn Douglas, *Hud.*
Sup. Actress: Margaret Rutherford, *The V.I.P.s.*
Director: Tony Richardson, *Tom Jones.*
Picture: *Tom Jones,* Woodfall Prod., UA-Lopert Pictures.

1964

Actor: Rex Harrison, *My Fair Lady.*
Actress: Julie Andrews, *Mary Poppins.*
Sup. Actor: Peter Ustinov, *Topkapi.*
Sup. Actress: Lila Kedrova, Zorba the Greek.
Director: George Cukor, *My Fair Lady.*
Picture: *My Fair Lady,* Warner Bros.

1965

Actor: Lee Marvin, *Cat Ballou.*
Actress: Julie Christie, *Darling.*
Sup. Actor: Martin Balsam, *A Thousand Clowns.*
Sup. Actress: Shelley Winters, *A Patch of Blue.*
Director: Robert Wise, *The Sound of Music.*
Picture: *The Sound of Music,* 20th Century-Fox.

1966

Actor: Paul Scofield, *A Man for All Seasons.*
Actress: Elizabeth Taylor, *Who's Afraid of Virginia Woolf?*
Sup. Actor: Walter Matthau, *The Fortune Cookie.*
Sup. Actress: Sandy Dennis, *Who's Afraid of Virginia Woolf?*
Director: Fred Zinnemann, *A Man for All Seasons.*
Picture: *A Man for All Seasons,* Columbia.

1967

Actor: Rod Steiger, *In the Heat of the Night.*
Actress: Katharine Hepburn, *Guess Who's Coming to Dinner.*
Sup. Actor: George Kennedy, *Cool Hand Luke.*
Sup. Actress: Estelle Parsons, *Bonnie and Clyde.*
Director: Mike Nichols, *The Graduate.*
Picture: *In the Heat of the Night.*

1968

Actor: Cliff Robertson, *Charly.*
Actress: Katharine Hepburn, *The Lion in Winter;* Barbra Streisand, *Funny Girl* (tie).
Sup. Actor: Jack Albertson, *The Subject Was Roses.*
Sup. Actress: Ruth Gordon, *Rosemary's Baby.*
Director: Sir Carol Reed, *Oliver!*
Picture: *Oliver!*

1969

Actor: John Wayne, *True Grit.*
Actress: Maggie Smith, *The Prime of Miss Jean Brodie.*
Sup. Actor: Gig Young, *They Shoot Horses, Don't They?*
Sup. Actress: Goldie Hawn, *Cactus Flower.*
Director: John Schlesinger, *Midnight Cowboy.*
Picture: *Midnight Cowboy.*

1970

Actor: George C. Scott, *Patton* (refused).
Actress: Glenda Jackson, *Women in Love.*
Sup. Actor: John Mills, *Ryan's Daughter.*
Sup. Actress: Helen Hayes, *Airport.*
Director: Franklin Schaffner, *Patton.*
Picture: *Patton.*

1971

Actor: Gene Hackman, *The French Connection.*
Actress: Jane Fonda, *Klute.*
Sup. Actor: Ben Johnson, *The Last Picture Show.*
Sup. Actress: Cloris Leachman, *The Last Picture Show.*
Director: William Friedkin, *The French Connection.*
Picture: *The French Connection.*

1972

Actor: Marlon Brando, *The Godfather* (refused).
Actress: Liza Minnelli, *Cabaret.*
Sup. Actor: Joel Grey, *Cabaret.*
Sup. Actress: Eileen Heckart, *Butterflies are Free.*
Director: Bob Fosse, *Cabaret.*
Picture: *The Godfather.*

1973

Actor: Jack Lemmon, *Save the Tiger.*
Actress: Glenda Jackson, *A Touch of Class.*
Sup. Actor: John Houseman, *The Paper Chase.*
Sup. Actress: Tatum O'Neal, *Paper Moon.*
Director: George Roy Hill, *The Sting.*
Picture: *The Sting.*

1974

Actor: Art Carney, *Harry and Tonto.*
Actress: Ellen Burstyn, *Alice Doesn't Live Here Anymore.*
Sup. Actor: Robert DeNiro, *The Godfather, Part II.*
Sup. Actress: Ingrid Bergman, *Murder on the Orient Express.*
Director: Francis Ford Coppola, *The Godfather, Part II.*
Picture: *The Godfather, Part II.*

1975

Actor: Jack Nicholson, *One Flew Over the Cuckoo's Nest.*
Actress: Louise Fletcher, same.
Sup. Actor: George Burns, *The Sunshine Boys.*
Sup. Actress: Lee Grant, *Shampoo.*
Director: Milos Forman, *One Flew Over the Cuckoo's Nest.*
Picture: *One Flew Over the Cuckoo's Nest.*

1976

Actor: Peter Finch, *Network.*
Actress: Faye Dunaway, same.
Sup. Actor: Jason Robards, *All the President's Men.*
Sup. Actress: Beatrice Straight, *Network.*
Director: John G. Avildsen, *Rocky.*
Picture: *Rocky.*

1977

Actor: Richard Dreyfuss, *The Goodbye Girl.*
Actress: Diane Keaton, *Annie Hall.*
Sup. Actor: Jason Robards, *Julia.*
Sup. Actress: Vanessa Redgrave, *Julia.*
Director: Woody Allen, *Annie Hall.*
Picture: *Annie Hall.*

1978

Actor: Jon Voight, *Coming Home.*
Actress: Jane Fonda, *Coming Home.*
Sup. Actor: Christopher Walken, *The Deer Hunter.*
Sup. Actress: Maggie Smith, *California Suite.*
Director: Michael Cimino, *The Deer Hunter.*
Picture: *The Deer Hunter.*

1979

Actor: Dustin Hoffman, *Kramer vs. Kramer.*
Actress: Sally Field, *Norma Rae.*
Sup. Actor: Melvyn Douglas, *Being There.*
Sup. Actress: Meryl Streep, *Kramer vs. Kramer.*
Director: Robert Benton, *Kramer vs. Kramer.*
Picture: *Kramer vs. Kramer.*

1980

Actor: Robert De Niro, *Raging Bull.*
Actress: Sissy Spacek, *Coal Miner's Daughter.*
Sup. Actor: Timothy Hutton, *Ordinary People.*
Sup. Actress: Mary Steenburgen, *Melvin & Howard.*
Director: Robert Redford, *Ordinary People* .
Picture: *Ordinary People.*

1981

Actor: Henry Fonda, *On Golden Pond.*
Actress: Katharine Hepburn, *On Golden Pond.*
Sup. Actor: John Gielgud, *Arthur.*
Sup. Actress: Maureen Stapleton, *Reds.*
Director: Warren Beatty, *Reds.*
Picture: *Chariots of Fire.*

1982

Actor: Ben Kingsley, *Gandhi.*
Actress: Meryl Streep, *Sophie's Choice.*
Sup. Actor: Louis Gossett, Jr., *An Officer and a Gentleman.*
Sup. Actress: Jessica Lange, *Tootsie.*
Director: Richard Attenborough, *Gandhi.*
Picture: *Gandhi.*
Foreign Film: *Volver A Empezar.*
Screenplay (original): John Briley, *Gandhi.*
(adapted): Costa-Gavras, Donald Stewart, *Missing.*
Editing: John Bloom, *Gandhi.*
Cinematography: Billy Williams, Ronnie Taylor, *Gandhi.*
Score (original): John Williams, *E.T.: The Extra-Terrestrial.*
Song: "Up Where We Belong," *An Officer and a Gentleman.*

Art Direction: Stuart Craig, Bob Lang, *Gandhi.*
Costumes: John Mollo, Bhanu Athaiya, *Gandhi.*
Sound: Buzz Knudson, Robert Glass, Con Digirolamo, Gene Cantamessa, *E.T.: The Extra-Terrestrial.*
Honorary Oscar: Mickey Rooney.

1983

Actor: Robert Duvall, *Tender Mercies.*
Actress: Shirley MacLaine, *Terms of Endearment.*
Supporting Actor: Jack Nicholson, *Terms of Endearment.*
Supporting Actress: Linda Hunt, *The Year of Living Dangerously.*
Director: James L. Brooks, *Terms of Endearment.*
Picture: *Terms of Endearment.*
Foreign Film: *Fanny and Alexander,* Sweden.
Original Song: *"Flashdance...What a Feeling," Flashdance.*
Original Screenplay: Horton Foote, *Tender Mercies.*

Screenplay Adaptation: James L. Brooks, *Terms of Endearment.*
Cinematography: Sven Nykvist, *Fanny and Alexander.*
Original Score: Bill Conti, *The Right Stuff.*
Original Song Score or Adaptation Score: Michel Legrand and Alan and Marilyn Bergman, *Yentl.*
Art Director: *Fanny and Alexander.*
Costume Design: *Fanny and Alexander.*
Documentary Feature: *He Makes Me Feel Like Dancin'.*
Documentary Short: *Flamenco at 5:15.*
Editing: *The Right Stuff.*
Animated Short: *Sundae in New York.*
Live Action Short: *Boys and Girls.*
Sound: *The Right Stuff.*
Sound Effects Editing: *The Right Stuff.*
Honorary: Hal Roach.
Jean Hersholt Humanitarian: M.J. Frankovich.

The Spingarn Medal

The Spingarn Medal has been awarded annually since 1914 by the National Association for the Advancement of Colored People for the highest achievement by a black American.

1946	Dr. Percy L. Julian	1958	Edward Kennedy (Duke) Ellington	1971	Gordon Parks
1947	Channing H. Tobias	1959	Langston Hughes	1972	Wilson C. Riles
1948	Ralph J. Bunche	1960	Kenneth B. Clark	1973	Damon Keith
1949	Charles Hamilton Houston	1961	Robert C. Weaver	1974	Henry (Hank) Aaron
1950	Mabel Keaton Staupers	1962	Medgar Wiley Evers	1975	Alvin Ailey
1951	Harry T. Moore	1963	Roy Wilkins	1976	Alex Haley
1952	Paul R. Williams	1964	Leontyne Price	1977	Andrew Young
1953	Theodore K. Lawless	1965	John H. Johnson	1978	Mrs. Rosa L. Parks
1954	Carl Murphy	1966	Edward W. Brooke	1979	Dr. Rayford W. Logan
1955	Jack Roosevelt Robinson	1967	Sammy Davis Jr.	1980	Coleman Young
1956	Martin Luther King Jr.	1968	Clarence M. Mitchell Jr.	1981	Dr. Benjamin Elijah Mays
1957	Mrs. Daisy Bates and the Little Rock Nine	1969	Jacob Lawrence	1982	Lena Horne
		1970	Leon Howard Sullivan		

Genie (Canadian Film) Awards
Source: Academy of Canadian Cinema

(To qualify, films must be Canadian-made; actors and actresses must be Canadian citizens or landed immigrants starring in a Canadian film. Awards apply to films released the previous year.)

1978
Actor: Richard Gabourie, Three Card Monte
Actress: Helen Shaver, In Praise of Older Women
Picture: The Silent Partner

1979
No awards

1980
Actor: Christopher Plummer, Murder By Decree
Actress: Kate Lynch, Meatballs
Picture: The Changeling

1981
Actor: Thomas Peacocke, The Hounds of Notre Dame
Actress: Marie Tifo, Les Bons Debarras

Picture: Les Bons Debarras

1982
Actor: Nick Mancuso, Ticket to Heaven
Actress: Margot Kidder, Heartaches
Picture: Ticket to Heaven

1983
Actor: Donald Sutherland, Threshold
Actress: Rae Dawn Chong, Quest For Fire
Picture: The Grey Fox

1984
Actor: Eric Fryer, The Terry Fox Story
Actress: Martha Henry, The Wars
Picture: The Terry Fox Story

The Governor General's Literary Awards

Canada's most prestigious literary awards, instituted in 1937 by the Canadian Authors Association with the agreement of then Governor General John Buchan (Lord Tweedsmuir), a novelist. The awards, now administered by the Canada Council, include a $5,000 cash prize.

English	French
1981	
Fiction: Home Truths, Mavis Gallant	La Province Lunaire, Denys Chabot
Non-fiction: Caribou and the Barren Lands, George Calef	L'Echappee des Discours de L'Oeil, Madeleine Ouellette-Michalska
Poetry: Collected Poems, R.F. Scott	Visages, Michele Beaulieu
Drama: Blood Relations and Other Plays, Sharon Pollock	C'Etait Avant A Guerre A L'anse A Gilles, Marie Laberge
1982	
Fiction: Man Descending, Guy Vanderhaeghe	Le Cercle des Arenes, Roger Fournier
Non-Fiction: Louis Bourg Portraits: Life in an Eighteenth-Century Garrison Town, Christopher Moore	Le marxisme des annees soixante; une saison dans l'histoire de la pensee critique, Maurice Lagueux
Poetry: The Vision Tree: Selected Poems, Phyllis Webb	Forages, Michel Savard
Drama: Billy Bishop Goes to War, John Gray	HA ha!..., Rejean Ducharme
1983	
Fiction: Shakespeare's Dog, Leon Rooke	Laura Laur, Suzanne Jacob
Non-fiction: Byng fo Vimy: General and Governor General, Jeffery Williams	Le contrôle social du crime, Maurice Cusson
Poetry: Settlements, David Donnell	Un goût de sel, Suzanne Paradis
Drama: Quiet in the Land, Anne Chislett	Syncope, René Gingras

ARTS AND MEDIA

Notable New York Theater Openings, 1983-84 Season

A...My Name is Alice, comedy revue that looks at today's women; songs and sketches by Anne Meara, Steve Tesich, others.

A Moon for the Misbegotten, revival of the Eugene O'Neill drama; with Kate Nelligan, Ian Bannen, and Jerome Kitty.

Amen Corner, musical by Gerry Sherman and Peter Udell based on the James Baldwin play; with Rhetta Hughes.

American Buffalo, revival of the David Mamet play; with Al Pacino.

Awake and Sing, revival of the Clifford Odets 1930s drama; with Harry Hamlin, Michael Lombard, Thomas G. Waites, and Nancy Marchand.

Baby, musical by David Shire and Richard Maltby; with Liz Callaway and Catherine Cox.

Balm in Gilead, revival of the 1964 Lanford Wilson drama; with Laurie Metcalf and Gary Sinise.

Beethoven's Tenth, comedy by Peter Ustinov; with Peter Ustinov and George Rose.

Brothers, drama by George Sibbald; with Carroll O'Connor and Frank Converse.

Cinders, play by Janusz Glowacki set in contemporary Poland; with Christopher Walken and Lucinda Jenney.

Death of a Salesman, revival of the Arthur Miller classic; with Dustin Hoffman, John Malkovich, and Kate Reid.

Design for Living, revival of the 1933 Noel Coward comedy; with Frank Langella, Jill Clayburgh, and Raul Julia.

Doonesbury, musical by Garry Trudeau and Elizabeth Swados based on Trudeau's comic strip; with Ralph Bruneau, Kate Burton, and Albert Macklin.

Edmund Kean, one-man play by Raymond FitzSimons about the 19th century actor and scoundrel; with Ben Kingsley.

Endgame, revival of the Samuel Beckett play; with Alvin Epstein and Peter Evans.

End of the World, comedy by Arthur Kopit; with John Shea, Barnard Hughes, and Linda Hunt.

Glengarry Glen Rose, play by David Mamet; with Robert Prosky, Mike Nussbaum, and Joe Mantegna.

Heartbreak House, revival of the Shaw classic; with Rex Harrison, Rosemary Harris, Amy Irving, and Philip Bosco.

Hurlyburly, play by David Rabe; with William Hurt, Christopher Walken, Harvey Keitel, and Sigourney Weaver.

La Cage aux Folles, musical by Jerry Herman based on the Jean Poiret play; with George Hearn and Gene Barry.

La Tragedie de Carmen, Peter Brook's production of the Bizet opera.

Mame, revival of the 1966 Jerry Herman musical; with Angela Lansbury, Jane Connell, and Anne Francine.

Noises Off, Michael Frayn's British farce; with Dorothy Loudon, Brian Murray, and Linda Thorson.

Old Times, revival of the 1971 Harold Pinter play; with Anthony Hopkins, Marsha Mason, and Jane Alexander.

Oliver, revival of the Lionel Bart musical which is based on Dicken's *Oliver Twist;* with Ron Moody, Patti LuPone, and Brandon Danner.

Open Admissions, drama by Shirley Lauro; with Marilyn Rockafellow and Calvin Levels.

Play Memory, drama by Joanna M. Glass; with Donald Moffat, Jo Henderson, and Valerie Mahaffey.

Rockaby, three plays by Samuel Beckett; with Billie Whitelaw.

Serenading Louie, play by Lanford Wilson; with Lindsay Crouse, Peter Weller, Jimmie Ray Weeks, and Dianne West.

Spookhouse, play by Harvey Fierstein; with Anne Meara and Tom Noonan.

. Sunday in the Park with George, musical by Stephen Sondheim; with Bernadette Peters and Mandy Patinkin.

Terra Nova, drama by Ted Tally about British explorer Robert Falcon Scott; with Robert Foxworth.

The Corn is Green, revival of the Emlyn Williams play about a Welsh school teacher; with Cicely Tyson, Peter Gallagher, and Mia Dillon.

The Glass Menagerie, revival of the Tennessee Williams play; with Jessica Tandy, Amanda Plummer, John Heard, and Bruce Davison.

The Golden Age, play by A.R. Gurney Jr.; with Irene Worth, Stockard Channing, and Jeff Daniels.

The Nest of the Wood Grouse, play by Soviet author Viktor Rozov; with Eli Wallach, Anne Jackson, Mary Beth Hurt, and Phoebe Cates.

The Real Thing, play by Tom Stoppard; with Jeremy Irons and Glenn Close.

The Rink, musical by John Kander and Fred Ebb; with Liza Minnelli and Chita Rivera.

The Tap Dance Kid, musical by Henry Krieger and Robert Lorick; with Hilton Battle, Alfonso Ribeiro, and Samuel E. Wright.

The Wiz, revival of Charlie Smalls 1975 musical based on *The Wizard of Oz;* with Stephanie Mills.

Zorba, musical by John Kander and Fred Ebb based on the novel and film *Zorba the Greek;* with Anthony Quinn and Lila Kedrova.

Record Long Run Broadway Plays

*Chorus Line 3,704	*42d Street 1,604	Cactus Flower 1,234
Grease 3,388	Ain't Misbehavin' 1,604	Sleuth 1,222
*Oh, Calcutta (revival). 3,349	Best Little Whorehouse in Texas . . 1,584	"1776" 1,217
Fiddler on the Roof 3,242	Mary, Mary 1,572	Equus 1,209
Life With Father 3,224	Evita 1,567	Sugar Babies 1,208
Tobacco Road 3,182	Voice of the Turtle 1,557	Guys and Dolls 1,200
Hello Dolly 2,844	Barefoot in the Park 1,530	Cabaret 1,165
My Fair Lady 2,717	Mame 1,508	Mister Roberts 1,157
Annie 2,377	Same Time, Next Year 1,453	Amadeus 1,155
Man of La Mancha 2,328	Arsenic and Old Lace 1,444	Annie Get Your Gun 1,147
Abie's Irish Rose 2,327	The Sound of Music 1,443	Seven Year Itch 1,141
Oklahoma! 2,212	How To Succeed in Business	Butterflies Are Free 1,128
Pippin 1,994	Without Really Trying 1,417	Pins and Needles 1,108
South Pacific 1,925	Hellzapoppin 1,404	Plaza Suite 1,097
Magic Show 1,920	The Music Man 1,375	They're Playing Our Song. 1,082
Deathtrap 1,792	Funny Girl 1,348	Kiss Me Kate 1,070
Gemini 1,788	Mumenschanz 1,326	Don't Bother Me, I Can't Cope . . . 1,065
Harvey 1,775	Oh! Calcutta! (original). 1,314	Pajama Game 1,065
Dancin' 1,774	Angel Street 1,295	*Dreamgirls 1,054
Hair 1,750	Lightnin' 1,291	Shenandoah 1,050
The Wiz 1,672	Promises, Promises 1,281	
Born Yesterday. 1,642	The King and I 1,246	

*Still Running July 2, 1984

Major Movies of the Year (Sept. 1983 to Aug. 1984)

Movie	Stars	Director
A Time to Die	Rex Harrison, Rod Taylor, Raf Vallone	Matt Cimber
Against All Odds	Rachel Ward, Jeff Bridges, James Woods	Taylor Hackford
All the Right Moves	Tom Cruise, Craig T. Nelson, Lea Thompson	Michael Chapman
And the Ship Sails On	Freddie Jones, Barbara Jefford	Federico Fellini
Angel	Cliff Gorman, Susan Tyrrell, Dick Shawn, Donna Wilkes	Robert Vincent O'Neil
Bachelor Party	Tom Hanks, Adrian Zmed	Neal Israel
Beyond the Limit	Michael Caine, Richard Gere, Bob Hoskins	John Mackenzie
Blame It on Rio	Michael Caine, Joseph Bologna, Valerie Harper	Stanley Donen
Brainstorm	Natalie Wood, Christopher Walken, Cliff Robertson, Louise Fletcher	Douglas Trumbull
Broadway Danny Rose	Woody Allen, Mia Farrow, Nick Apollo Forte	Woody Allen
Cannonball Run II	Burt Reynolds, Dean Martin, Shirley MacLaine, Sammy Davis Jr.	Hal Needham
Christine	Keith Gordon, Robert Prosky, Alexandra Paul	John Carpenter
Crackers	Donald Sutherland, Jack Warden, Sean Penn	Louis Malle
Cross Creek	Mary Steenburgen, Rip Torn, Peter Coyote	Martin Ritt
D.C. Cab	Mr. T., Irene Cara, Gary Busey, Max Gail	Joel Schumacher
Eddie and the Cruisers	Tom Berenger, Michael Pare	Martin Davidson
Educating Rita	Michael Caine, Julie Walters	Lewis Gilbert
Finders Keepers	Michael O'Keefe, Beverly D'Angelo, Louis Gossett Jr., David Wayne	Richard Lester
Footloose	Kevin Bacon, Lori Singer, John Lithgow	Herbert Ross
Ghostbusters	Bill Murray, Dan Aykroyd, Sigourney Weaver	Ivan Reitman
Gorky Park	William Hurt, Lee Marvin, Brian Dennehy, Joanna Pacula	Michael Apted
Grandview, U.S.A.	Jamie Lee Curtis, C. Thomas Howell, Patrick Swayze	Randal Kleiser
Gremlins	Zach Galligan, Phoebe Cates, Polly Holliday	Joe Dante
Greystoke: The Legend of Tarzan, Lord of the Apes	Ralph Richardson, Ian Holm, Christopher Lambert	Hugh Hudson
Hanna K	Jill Clayburgh, Jean Young	Constantine Costa-Gavras
Harry & Son	Paul Newman, Robby Benson	Paul Newman
Heart Like a Wheel	Bonnie Bedella, Beau Bridges	Jonathan Kaplan
Hot Dog	David Naughton, Patrick Houser, Shannon Tweed	Peter Markle
Ice Man	Timothy Hutton, Lindsay Crouse, John Lone	Fred Schepisi
Indiana Jones and the Temple of Doom	Harrison Ford, Kate Capshaw	Steven Spielberg
Lassiter	Tom Selleck, Jane Seymour, Lauren Hutton, Bob Hoskins	Roger Young
Lonely Guy	Steve Martin, Charles Grodin, Steve Lawrence	Arthur Hiller
Mr. Mom	Michael Keaton, Teri Garr, Martin Mull, Ann Jillian	Stan Dragoti
Moscow on the Hudson	Robin Williams, Alejandro Rey	Paul Mazursky
Never Cry Wolf	Charles Martin Smith, Brian Dennehy	Carroll Ballard
Never Say Goodbye Again	Sean Connery, Klaus Maria Brandauer	Irvin Kershner
Once Upon a Time in America	Robert DeNiro, James Woods, Elizabeth McGovern, Treat Williams	Sergio Leone
Over the Brooklyn Bridge	Elliott Gould, Margaux Hemingway, Shelley Winters, Burt Young	Menahem Golen
Police Academy	Steve Guttenberg, Kim Cattrall	Hugh Wilson
Racing with the Moon	Sean Penn, Elizabeth McGovern, Nicholas Cage	Richard Benjamin
Rhinestone	Sylvester Stallone, Dolly Parton, Ron Leibman	Bob Clark
Romancing the Stone	Michael Douglas, Kathleen Turner, Danny DeVito	Robert Zemekis
Romantic Comedy	Dudley Moore, Mary Steenbergen, Frances Sternhagen	Arthur Hiller
Rumble Fish	Matt Dillon, Diane Ladd, Michael O'Rourke	Francis Coppola
Scandalous	Robert Hays, John Gielgud, Pamela Stephenson	Rob Cohen
Scarface	Al Pacino	Brian De Palma
Silkwood	Meryl Streep, Kurt Russell, Cher	Mike Nichols
Spinal Tap	Michael McKean, Christopher Guest, Rob Reiner	Rob Reiner
Splash	Tom Hanks, Daryl Hannah, John Candy	Ron Howard
Star 80	Mariel Hemingway, Eric Roberts, Cliff Robertson, Carroll Baker	Bob Fosse
Star Trek III: The Search for Spock	William Shatner, DeForrest Kelley, George Takei	Leonard Nimoy
Sudden Impact	Clint Eastwood, Sondra Locke	Clint Eastwood
Swing Shift	Goldie Hawn, Kurt Russell	Jonathan Demme
Terms of Endearment	Shirley MacLaine, Debra Winger, Jack Nicholson	James L. Brooks
Testament	Jane Alexander, William Devane	Lynne Littman
The Big Chill	Tom Beranger, Glenn Close, Kevin Kline, Meg Tilly	Lawrence Kasdan
The Bostonians	Christopher Reeve, Vanessa Redgrave, Madeleine Potter	James Ivory
The Bounty	Mel Gibson, Anthony Hopkins	Bernard Williams
The Dead Zone	Christopher Walken, Martin Sheen, Brooke Adams, Colleen Dewhurst	David Croneberg
The Dresser	Albert Finney, Tom Courtenay	Peter Yates
The Karate Kid	Ralph Macchio, Pat Morita, Randee Heller	John Avildsen
The Last Starfighter	Lance Guest, Dan O'Herlihy, Robert Preston	Nick Castle
The Lonely Lady	Pia Zadora, Lloyd Bochner, Jared Martin	Peter Sasdy
The Man Who Loved Women	Burt Reynolds, Julie Andrews, Marilu Henner, Kim Basinger	Blake Edwards
The Muppets Take Manhattan	Linda Lavin, Art Carney, Joan Rivers, James Coco	Frank Oz
The Natural	Robert Redford, Robert Duvall, Glenn Close	Barry Levinson
The Osterman Weekend	John Hurt, Craig T. Nelson, Burt Lancaster	Sam Peckinpah
The Pope of Greenwich Village	Eric Roberts, Mickey Rourke, Daryl Hannah	Stuart Rosenberg
The Riddle of the Sands	Michael York, Jenny Agutter, Simon MacCorkindale	Tony Maylam
The Right Stuff	Sam Shepard, Scott Glenn, Ed Harris	Philip Kaufman
The Wicked Lady	Faye Dunaway, John Gielgud, Alan Bates	Michael Winner
To Be or Not To Be	Mel Brooks, Anne Bancroft	Alan Johnson
Top Secret	Val Lilmer, Lucy Gutteridge	several
Two of a Kind	John Travolta, Olivia Newton-John	John Herzfeld
Under the Volcano	Albert Finney, Jacqueline Bisset, Anthony Andrews	John Huston
Unfaithfully Yours	Dudley Moore, Nastassia Kinski, Armand Assante	Howard Zeiff
Yentl	Barbra Streisand, Mandy Patinkin, Amy Irving	Barbra Streisand

Best-Selling Books of 1983-84

Listed according to position and frequency of citation on best seller reports from June 1983 through May 1984.
Numbers in parentheses show rank on top ten list for calendar year 1983, according to Publishers Weekly.

Hardcover Fiction

1. The Name of the Rose, Umberto Eco (7)
2. Poland, James A. Michener (2)
3. Pet Sematary, Stephen King (3)
4. Who Killed the Robins Family? Bill Adler and Thomas Chastain
5. Return of the Jedi, Joan D. Vinge (1)
   (tie) The Acquitaine Progression, Robert Ludlum
6. The Little Drummer Girl, John le Carre (4)
7. Changes, Danielle Steele (6)
8. Heartburn, Nora Ephron
9. Christine, Stephen King (5)
10. The Butter Battle Book, Dr. Seuss
11. Hollywood Wives, Jackie Collins (9)
12. Almost Paradise, Susan Isaacs
    (tie) August, Judith Rossner
13. The Hag, Leon Uris
    (tie) The Summer of Katja, Trevanian
    (tie) The Berlin Game, Len Deighton
14. Heretics of Dune, Frank Herbert
    (tie) The Wicked Day, Mary Stewart
15. Godplayer, Robin Cook
16. Lord of the Dance, Andrew M. Greeley
    (tie) The Robots of Dawn, Isaac Asimov
17. The Seduction of Peter S., Lawrence Sanders
18. The Story of Henri Tod, William F. Buckley Jr.
19. White Gold Wielder, Stephen R. Donaldson
20. The Saga of Baby Divine, Bette Midler

Hardcover General Nonfiction

1. In Search of Excellence, Thomas J. Peters and Robert H. Waterman Jr. (1)
2. Motherhood: The Second Oldest Profession, Erma Bombeck (3)
3. Megatrends, John Naisbitt (2)
4. Tough Times Never Last, But Tough People Do, Robert H. Schuller
5. The Best of James Herriot, James Herriot (6)
6. Mayor, Edward I. Koch and William Rauch
7. The March of Folly, Barbara Tuchman
8. On Wings of Eagles, Ken Follett (8)
9. Lines and Shadows, Joseph Wambaugh
10. Blue Highways, William Least Heat Moon
11. The Discoverers, Daniel J. Boorstin
12. One Writer's Beginnings, Eudora Welty
13. Out on a Limb, Shirley MacLaine
14. The Price of Power, Seymour M. Hirsch
15. While Reagan Slept, Art Buchwald
16. Growing Up, Russell Baker
17. Vietnam: A History, Stanley Karnow
18. Tough-Minded Faith for Tender-Hearted People, Robert H. Schuller
19. Mafia Princess, Antoinette Giancana and Thomas C. Renner
    (tie) Past Imperfect, Joan Collins
20. Approaching Hoofbeats: The Four Horsemen of the Apocalypse, Billy Graham

Hardcover How-to, Advice and Others

1. The One Minute Manager, Kenneth Blanchard and Spencer Johnson (4)
2. Creating Wealth, Robert G. Allen (9)

3. Nothing Down, Robert G. Allen
4. Eat to Win, Robert Haas
   (tie) Jane Fonda's Workout Book, Jane Fonda (5)
5. The James Coco Diet, James Coco with Marion Paone
6. Putting the One Minute Manager to Work, Kenneth Blanchard and Robert Lorber
7. Weight Watchers Fast and Fabulous Cookbook, Weight Watchers
8. The Body Principal, Victoria Principal
9. Webster's New World Dictionary, 2nd College Edition
10. How to Live to Be 100—Or More, George Burns
    (tie) The Mary Kay Guide to Beauty, Mary Kay Cosmetics (7)
11. The Life Extension Companion, Durk Pearson and Sandy Shaw
12. Webster's Ninth Collegiate Dictionary
    (tie) The Human Body, Jonathan Miller
13. The Pritikin Promise, Nathan Pritikin
14. Grandmother Remembers, Judith Levy
    (tie) Working Out, Charles Hix
15. Totally Tasteless Jokes, Blanche Knott

Paperback Fiction

1. The Color Purple, Alice Walker
2. Master of the Game, Sidney Sheldon
3. Seeds of Yesterday, V.C. Andrews
4. Thurston House, Danielle Steele
5. 1984, George Orwell
6. Christine, Stephen King
7. Crossings, Danielle Steele
8. Space, James A. Michener
9. The Prodigal Daughter, Jeffrey Archer
   (tie) Different Seasons, Stephen King
10. Return of the Jedi, James Kahn
11. Lace, Shirley Conran
12. The Valley of Horses, Jean M. Auel
13. The Case of Lucy Bending, Lawrence Sanders
14. Foundation's Edge, Isaac Asimov
15. The Delta Star, Joseph Wambaugh
16. Cinnamon Skin, John D. MacDonald
17. The Man from St. Petersburg, Ken Follett
    (tie) Mistral's Daughter, Judith Krantz
18. Spellbinder, Harold Robbins
19. Eden Burning, Belva Plain
20. Acceptable Losses, Irwin Shaw

Paperback General Nonfiction

1. Living, Loving & Learning, Leo Buscaglia
2. Megatrends, John Naisbitt
3. Growing Up, Russell Baker
4. Blue Highways, William Least Heat Moon
5. In Search of Excellence, Thomas J. Peters and Robert H. Waterman Jr.
6. The Road Less Travelled, M. Scott Peck
7. And More By Andy Rooney, Andrew A. Rooney
8. The Michael Jackson Story, Nelson George
9. Out on a Limb, Shirley MacLaine
10. The Right Stuff, Tom Wolfe
11. The Shoemaker, Flora Rheta Schreiber
12. Michael! Mark Bego
13. The Magic of Michael Jackson
14. Charlie Company, Peter Goldman and Tony Fuller

15. Tough Times Never Last, But Tough People Do, Robert H. Schuller
16. The Love You Make, Peter Brown and Steve Gaines
17. Michael Jackson Thrills, Caroline Latham (tie) Washington, James Thomas Flexner
18. Return of the Jedi Portfolio, Ralph McQuarrie
19. Personhood, Leo F. Buscaglia
20. The Read-Aloud Handbook, Jim Trelease

Paperback How-to, Advice and Others

1. Color Me Beautiful, Carole Jackson
2. The One Minute Manager, Kenneth Blanchard and Spencer Johnson
3. J.K. Lasser's Your Income Tax, J.K. Lasser Tax Inst.

4. Truly Tasteless Jokes Three, Blanche Knott
5. Life Extension, Durk Pearson and Sandy Shaw
6. Jane Fonda's Workout Book, Jane Fonda
7. Truly Tasteless Jokes, Blanche Knott
8. Truly Tasteless Jokes Two, Blanche Knott (tie) Garfield Sits Around the House, Jim Davis
9. Garfield Tips the Scale, Jim Davis
10. Bloom County, Berke Breathed
11. Garfield Eats His Heart Out, Jim Davis
12. Rand McNally Road Atlas, Rand McNally
13. 'Toons for Our Times, Berke Breathed
14. The World Almanac and Book of Facts 1984
15. Thin Thighs in 30 Days, Wendy Stehling

Recordings

The Recording Industry Association of America, Inc. confers Gold Record Awards on single records that sell one million units, Platinum Awards to those selling two million, Gold Awards to albums and their tape equivalents that sell 500,000 units, Platinum Awards to those selling one million. Platinum Album Awards, Platinum and Gold Single Awards in 1983 follow:

Artists and Recording Titles

Albums, Platinum

Bryan Adams; *Cuts Like a Knife.*
Air Supply; *Now and Forever.*
Air Supply; *Air Supply Greatest Hits.*
Alabama; *The Closer You Get.*
Asia; *Alpha.*
Pat Benatar; *Get Nervous.*
Pat Benatar; *Live from Earth.*
David Bowie; *Let's Dance.*
The Clash; *Combat Rock.*
John Cougar Mellencamp; *Uh-Huh.*
Crosby, Stills & Nash; *Daylight Again.*
Culture Club; *Kissing to Be Clever.*
Culture Club; *Colour By Numbers.*
Def Leppard; *Pyromania.*
Def Leppard; *High 'N' Dry.*
Duran Duran; *Rio.*
Dan Fogelberg; *Greatest Hits.*
Jane Fonda; *Jane Fonda Workout.*
Genesis; *Genesis.*
Hall & Oates; *Rock 'N' Roll Soul, Part I.*
Michael Jackson; *Thriller.*
Billy Joel; *An Innocent Man.*
George Jones; *I Am What I Am.*
Journey; *Frontiers.*
Judas Priest; *Screaming for Vengeance.*
Led Zeppelin; *Coda.*
Loverboy; *Keep It Up.*
Men at Work; *Cargo.*
Midnight Star; *No Parking on the Dance Floor.*
Stevie Nicks; *The Wild Heart.*
Alan Parsons Project; *Eye in the Sky.*
Pink Floyd; *The Final Cut.*
Police; *Synchronicity.*
Elvis Presley; *Welcome to My World.*
Prince; *1999.*
Quiet Riot; *Metal Health.*
Lionel Richie; *Can't Slow Down.*
Kenny Rogers; *Eyes That See in the Dark.*
Kenny Rogers; *20 Greatest Hits.*
Linda Ronstadt; *What's New.*
Bob Seger/Silver Bullet Band; *The Distance.*
Soundtrack; *Flashdance.*
Soundtrack; *Stayin' Alive.*
Rick Springfield; *Living in Oz.*
Styx; *Kilroy Was Here.*
Thirty-Eight Special; *Special Forces.*
Bonnie Tyler; *Faster Than the Speed of Night.*
Luther Vandross; *Forever, For Always, For Love.*
ZZ Top; *Eliminator*

Singles, Platinum

Toni Basil; *Mickey.*
Kenny Rogers (with Dolly Parton); *Islands in the Stream.*

Singles, Gold

Air Supply; *Making Love Out of Nothing at All.*
John Anderson; *Swingin'.*
Patty Austin & James Ingram; *Baby Come to Me.*
David Bowie; *Let's Dance.*
Laura Branigan; *Gloria.*
Irene Cara; *Flashdance...What a Feeling.*
Eurythmics; *Sweet Dreams (Are Made of This).*
Eddy Grant; *Electric Avenue.*
Hall & Oates; *Maneater.*
Don Henley; *Dirty Laundry.*
Michael Jackson & Paul McCartney; *The Girl Is Mine.*
Michael Jackson; *Billie Jean.*
Michael Jackson; *Beat It.*
Paul McCartney & Michael Jackson; *Say Say Say.*
Men at Work; *Down Under.*
Mtume; *Juicy Fruit.*
Police; *Every Breath You Take.*
Elvis Presley; *I Got Stung.*
Elvis Presley; *Are You Lonesome Tonight.*
Elvis Presley; *Don't.*
Elvis Presley; *Return to Sender.*
Elvis Presley; *It's Now or Never.*
Elvis Presley; *A Fool Such As I.*
Elvis Presley; *Wear My Ring Around Your Neck.*
Quiet Riot; *Cum Feel the Noize.*
Lionel Richie; *All Night Long.*
Kenny Rogers (With Dolly Parton); *Islands in the Stream.*
Styx; *Mr. Roboto.*
Taco; *Puttin' on the Ritz.*
Bonnie Tyler; *Total Eclipse of the Heart.*
Various; *The Fox and the Hound.*
Various; *Peter Pan.*
Various; *Bambi.*
Various; *Cinderella.*
Various; *Lady and the Tramp.*
Various; *Snow White.*
Various; *Pinocchio.*
Various; *Dumbo.*
Various; *Mary Poppins.*
Various; *The Three Little Pigs.*
Various; *Sleeping Beauty.*
Various; *It's a Small World.*
Various; *E.T.—The Extra Terrestrial.*
Various; *Pete's Dragons.*
Various; *Winnie the Pooh and Tigger Too.*
Various; *Brer Rabbit & the Tar Baby.*
Various; *Return of the Jedi.*

Grammy Awards

Source: National Academy of Recording Arts & Sciences

1958
Record: Domenico Modugno, *Nel Blu Dipinto Di Blu (Volare)*.
Album: Henry Mancini, *The Music from Peter Gunn*.
Male vocalist: Perry Como, *Catch a Falling Star*.
Female vocalist: Ella Fitzgerald, *The Irving Berlin Song Book* (album).
Group: Louis Prima & Keely Smith, *That Old Black Magic*.
1959
Record: Bobby Darin, *Mack the Knife*.
Album: Frank Sinatra, *Come Dance With Me*.
Male vocalist: Frank Sinatra, *Come Dance With Me* (album).
Female vocalist: Ella Fitzgerald, *But Not For Me*.
Group: Mormon Tabernacle Choir, *Battle Hymn of the Republic*.
1960
Record: Percy Faith, *Theme From A Summer Place*.
Album: Bob Newhart, *Button Down Mind*.
Male vocalist (single): Ray Charles, *Georgia On My Mind*.
Female vocalist (single): Ella Fitzgerald, *Mack the Knife*.
Group: Steve Lawrence & Eydie Gorme, *We Got Us*.
1961
Record: Henry Mancini, *Moon River*.
Album: Judy Garland, *Judy At Carnegie Hall*.
Male vocalist: Jack Jones, *Lollipops and Roses*.
Female vocalist: Judy Garland, *Judy at Carnegie Hall* (album).
Group: Lambert, Hendricks and Ross, *High Flying*.
1962
Record: Tony Bennett, *I Left My Heart in San Francisco*.
Album: Vaughn Meader, *The First Family*.
Male vocalist: Tony Bennett, *I Left My Heart in San Francisco*.
Female vocalist: Ella Fitzgerald, *Ella Swings Brightly with Nelson Riddle* (album).
Group: Peter, Paul and Mary, *If I Had a Hammer*.
1963
Record: Henry Mancini, *The Days of Wine and Roses*.
Album: *The Barbra Streisand Album*.
Male vocalist: Jack Jones, *Wives and Lovers*.
Female vocalist: *The Barbra Streisand Album*.
Group: Peter, Paul and Mary, *Blowin' in the Wind*.
1964
Record: Stan Getz and Astrud Gilberto, *The Girl From Ipanema*.
Album: *Getz/Gilberto*.
Male vocalist: Louis Armstrong, *Hello, Dolly!*
Female vocalist: Barbra Streisand, *People*.
Group: The Beatles, *A Hard Day's Night*.
1965
Record: Herb Alpert, *A Taste Of Honey*.
Album: Frank Sinatra, *September of My Years*.
Male vocalist: Frank Sinatra, *It Was a Very Good Year*.
Female vocalist: Barbra Streisand, *My Name is Barbra* (album).
Group: Anita Kerr Singers, *We Dig Mancini* (album).
1966
Record: Frank Sinatra, *Strangers in the Night*.
Album: Frank Sinatra, *A Man and His Music*.
Male vocalist: Frank Sinatra, *Strangers in the Night*.
Female vocalist: Eydie Gorme, *If He Walked into My Life*.
Group: Anita Kerr Singers, *A Man and A Woman*.
1967
Record: 5th Dimension, *Up, Up and Away*.
Album: The Beatles, *Sgt. Pepper's Lonely Hearts Club Band*.
Male vocalist: Glen Campbell, *By the Time I Get to Phoenix*.
Female vocalist: Bobbie Gentry, *Ode to Billie Joe*.
Group: 5th Dimension, *Up, Up and Away*.
1968
Record: Simon & Garfunkel, *Mrs. Robinson*.
Album: Glen Campbell, *By the Time I Get to Phoenix*.
Male pop vocalist: Jose Feliciano, *Light My Fire*.
Female pop vocalist: Dionne Warwick, *Do You Know the Way to San Jose*.
Pop group: Simon & Garfunkel, *Mrs. Robinson*.
1969
Record: 5th Dimension, *Aquarius/Let the Sunshine In*.
Album: *Blood, Sweat and Tears*.
Male pop vocalist: Harry Nilsson, *Everybody's Talkin'*.
Female pop vocalist: Peggy Lee, *Is That All There Is*.
Pop group: 5th Dimension, *Aquarius/Let the Sunshine In*.
1970
Record: Simon & Garfunkel, *Bridge Over Troubled Waters*.
Album: *Bridge Over Troubled Waters*.
Male pop vocalist: Ray Stevens, *Everything is Beautiful*.
Female pop vocalist: Dionne Warwick, *I'll Never Fall in Love Again*.
Pop group: The Carpenters, *Close to You*.
1971
Record: Carole King, *It's Too Late*.
Album: Carole King, *Tapestry*.
Male pop vocalist: James Taylor, *You've Got a Friend*.

Female pop vocalist: Carole King, *Tapestry (album)*.
Pop group: The Carpenters *(album)*.
1972
Record: Roberta Flack, *The First Time Ever I Saw Your Face*.
Album: *The Concert For Bangla Desh*.
Male pop vocalist: Harry Nilsson, *Without You*.
Female pop vocalist: Helen Reddy, *I Am Woman*.
Pop group: Roberta Flack, Donny Hathaway, *Where is the Love*.
1973
Record: Roberta Flack, *Killing Me Softly with His Song*.
Album: Stevie Wonder, *Innervisions*.
Male pop vocalist: Stevie Wonder, *You Are the Sunshine of My Life*.
Female pop vocalist: Roberta Flack, *Killing Me Softly with His Song*.
Pop group: Gladys Knight & The Pips, *Neither One of Us (Wants to Be the First to Say Goodbye)*.
1974
Record: Olivia Newton-John, *I Honestly Love You*.
Album: Stevie Wonder, *Fulfillingness' First Finale*.
Male pop vocalist: Stevie Wonder, *Fulfillingness' First Finale* (album).
Female pop vocalist: Olivia Newton-John, *I Honestly Love You*.
Pop group: Paul McCartney & Wings, *Band on the Run*.
1975
Record: Captain & Tennille, *Love Will Keep Us Together*.
Album: Paul Simon, *Still Crazy After All These Years*.
Male pop vocalist: Paul Simon, *Still Crazy After All These Years* (album).
Female pop vocalist: Janis Ian, *At Seventeen*.
Pop group: Eagles, *Lyin' Eyes*.
1976
Record: George Benson, *This Masquerade*.
Album: Stevie Wonder, *Songs in the Key of Life*.
Male pop vocalist: Stevie Wonder, *Songs in the Key of Life* (album).
Female pop vocalist: Linda Ronstadt, *Hasten Down the Wind* (album).
Pop group: Chicago, *If You Leave Me Now*.
1977
Record: Eagles, *Hotel California*.
Album: Fleetwood Mac, *Rumours*.
Male pop vocalist: James Taylor, *Handy Man*.
Female pop vocalist: Barbra Streisand, *Evergreen*.
Pop group: Bee Gees, *How Deep is Your Love*.
1978
Record: Billy Joel, *Just the Way You Are*.
Album: Bee Gees, *Saturday Night Fever*.
Male pop vocalist: Barry Manilow, *Copacabana*.
Female pop vocalist: Anne Murray, *You Needed Me*.
Pop group: Bee Gees, *Saturday Night Fever* (album).
1979
Record: The Doobie Brothers, *What a Fool Believes*.
Album: Billy Joel, *52nd Street*.
Male pop vocalist: Billy Joel, *52nd Street* (album).
Female pop vocalist: Dionne Warwick, *I'll Never Love This Way Again*.
Pop group: The Doobie Brothers, *Minute by Minute* (album).
1980
Record: Christopher Cross, *Sailing*.
Album: Christopher Cross, *Christopher Cross*.
Male pop vocalist: Kenny Loggins, *This Is It*.
Female pop vocalist: Bette Midler, *The Rose*.
Pop group: Barbra Streisand & Barry Gibb, *Guilty* (album).
1981
Record: Kim Carnes, *Bette Davis Eyes*.
Album: John Lennon, Yoko Ono, *Double Fantasy*.
Male pop vocalist: Al Jarreau, *Breaking Away* (album).
Female pop vocalist: Lena Horne, *Lena Horne: The Lady and Her Music*, Live on Broadway (album).
Pop group: Manhattan Transfer, *Boy from New York City*.
1982
Record: Toto, *Rosanna*.
Album: Toto, *Toto IV*.
Male pop vocalist: Lionel Richie, *Truly*.
Female pop vocalist: Melissa Manchester, *You Should Se How She Talks About You*.
Pop Group: Joe Cocker & Jennifer Warnes, *Up Where We Belong*.
1983
Record: Michael Jackson, *Beat It*.
Album: Michael Jackson, *Thriller*.
Male pop vocalist: Michael Jackson, *Thriller*.
Female pop vocalist: Irene Cara, *Flashdance*.
Pop group: Police, *Every Breath You Take*.

Selected U.S. Daily Newspaper Circulation

Source: Audit Bureau of Circulations' FAS-FAX Report of average paid circulation for 60 months to Mar. 31, 1984.

For the 6 months up to Sept. 30, 1983, 1,701 English language dailies in the U.S. (446 morning, 1,284 evening, 29 all day) had an average audited circulation of 62,644,603; Sunday papers included 772 with audited average circulation of 56,747,436. (Totals used by permission from *Editor & Publisher 1984 International Yearbook*.)

Newspaper	Daily	Sunday	Newspaper	Daily	Sunday
Akron Beacon Journal (e)	167,310	233,230	New Haven Journal-Courier (m)	*39,189	
Albuquerque Journal (m)	†94,420	†133,566	New Orleans Times-Picayune/		
Albuquerque Tribune (e)	†46,103		States-Item (m&e)	*†249,076	†339,506
Allentown Call (m)	*128,756	166,476	New York News (m)	1,374,858	1,513,941
Asbury Park Press (e)	120,396	177,950	New York Post (m&e)	*963,069	961,044
Atlanta Constitution (m)	*226,232	567,993	New York Times (m)	*737,193	1,593,107
Atlanta Journal (e)	*185,278		Norfolk Ledger-Star (e)	†87,099	
Austin American-Statesman (m&e)	*154,039	182,960	Norfolk Virginian-Pilot (m)	†139,627	†216,422
Baltimore News-American (e)	*124,354	161,244	Oakland Tribune (e)	*†193,340	308,651
Baltimore Sun (m&e)	349,182	407,436	Omaha World-Herald (m&e)	225,705	284,980
Bergen Co. (N.J.) Record (e)	*†153,480	†223,782	Orange Co. (Cal.) Register (m&e)	*279,452	311,062
Birmingham News (e)	*144,638	211,543	Orlando Sentinel (m&e)	*233,124	287,137
Birmingham Post-Herald (m)	*62,807		Peoria Journal Star (m&e)	100,271	120,475
Boston Globe (m&e)	*510,261	793,151	Philadelphia Inquirer (m)	*536,065	1,008,225
Boston Herald (m)	*325,086	276,265	Philadelphia News (e)	*293,031	
Bristol Herald-Courier (m)	*41,051	33,666	Phoenix Gazette (e)	†121,058	
Bristol Virginia-Tennessean (e)	*7,188	39,794	Phoenix Republic (m)	†314,460	469,179
Buffalo News (m&e)	*320,028	375,276	Pittsburgh Post Gazette (m)	*178,284	
Camden (N.J.) Courier-Post (e)	*†114,146	†99,980	Pittsburgh Press (e)	*222,434	613,795
Charlotte News (e)	*41,904		Portland, Me. Press-Herald (m)	59,014	
Charlotte Observer (m)	184,586	255,459	Portland, Me. Express (e) & Maine		
Chicago Sun-Times (m)	*628,285	687,386	Sunday Telegram	87,736	127,826
Chicago Tribune (m&e)	*762,882	1,145,387	Portland Oregonian (m&e)	*288,724	410,519
Christian Science Monitor (m)	*148,683		Providence Bulletin (e)	*129,698	
Cincinnati Enquirer (m)	192,106	300,162	Providence Journal (m)	*84,336	252,225
Cincinnati Post (e)	134,098		Raleigh News & Observer (m)	†132,086	†172,426
Cleveland Plain Dealer (m)	*492,002	502,573	Raleigh Times (e)	†34,807	
Columbia, S.C. State (m)	107,968	139,432	Richmond News Leader (e)	113,369	
Columbia, S.C. Record (e)	31,689		Richmond Times Dispatch (m)	138,297	230,545
Columbus, Ga. Enquirer (m)	*33,975		Rochester Democrat-Chronicle (m)	*132,440	246,976
Columbus, Ga. Ledger (e)	*26,193	55,839	Rochester Times-Union (e)	*108,474	
Columbus, O. Citizen-Journal (m)	121,232		Sacramento Bee (m)	224,589	259,069
Columbus, O. Dispatch (e)	206,548	358,289	Sacramento Union (m)	99,366	98,418
Dallas News (m)	340,502	437,067	St. Louis Globe-Democrat (m)	*†251,250	
Dallas Times Herald (m&e)	282,933	381,318	St. Louis Post-Dispatch (e)	*†288,333	388,522
Dayton Journal-Herald (m)	101,840		St. Paul Dispatch (e)	*99,729	
Dayton News (e)	117,286	229,643	St. Paul Pioneer Press (m)	*105,802	247,196
Denver Post (m)	244,953	356,986	St. Petersburg Independent (e)	37,660	
Denver: Rocky Mountain News (m)	319,177	368,590	St. Petersburg Times (m)	282,653	357,089
Des Moines Register (m)	238,609	382,745	Salt Lake City Tribune (m)	109,157	128,971
Detroit Free Press (m)	*631,087	787,300	San Diego Union (m)	†220,301	†349,961
Detroit News (m&e)	*657,015	861,004	San Diego Tribune (e)	†121,670	
Flint Journal (e)	*109,438	117,245	San Francisco Examiner (e)	152,321	
Ft. Myers News-Press (m)	80,943	93,705	San Francisco Chronicle (m)	*539,450	706,150
Ft. Worth Star-Telegram (m&e)	248,947	280,751	San Jose Mercury/News (m)	*245,868	298,797
Fresno Bee (m)	†139,958	†161,197	Seattle Post-Intelligencer (m)	*192,494	473,155
Grand Rapids Press (e)	132,831	167,636	Seattle Times (e)	*226,038	
Hartford Courant (m)	218,830	306,767	South Bend Tribune (e)	102,277	123,631
Honolulu Advertiser (m)	87,799		Spokane Chronicle (e)	50,155	
Honolulu Star-Bulletin (e)	113,608	200,462	Spokane Spokesman-Review (m)	80,275	138,857
Indianapolis News (e)	†133,044		Springfield, Ill. State Journal-Register		
Indianapolis Star (m)	†228,819	†388,123	(m)	61,055	71,409
Jacksonville Journal (e)	*42,876		Springfield, Mass. Union (m)	71,789	
Jacksonville: Fla. Times Union (m)	*162,831	216,376	Springfield, Mass. News (e)	71,847	
Kansas City Star (e)	*240,142	402,206	Syracuse Herald-Journal (e)	103,899	
Kansas City Times (m)	288,635		Syracuse Post-Standard (m)	80,376	
Knoxville News-Sentinel (e)	98,020	162,825	Tacoma News Tribune (e)	106,375	115,925
Little Rock: Ark. Gazette (m)	129,040	158,056	Tampa Tribune (m&e)	216,864	282,331
Long Island, N.Y.: Newsday (e)	*533,384	608,640	Toledo Blade (e)	162,780	215,654
Los Angeles Herald-Examiner (m)	*236,660	219,900	Tucson Daily Star (m)	†81,082	†150,743
Los Angeles Times (m)	*1,057,536	1,321,244	Tulsa Tribune (e)	†78,003	
Louisville Courier-Journal (m)	177,289	329,998	Tulsa World (m)	†136,949	†227,325
Louisville Times (e)	135,869		Wall St. Journal (m) (total)	*2,888,627	
Madison, Wis. State Journal (m)	76,527	134,740	Washington, D.C. Post (m)	*768,288	1,042,821
Miami Herald (m)	451,206	545,356	West Palm Beach Post (m)	*108,922	174,760
Milwaukee Journal (e)	306,055	527,085	West Palm Beach Times (e)	*27,665	
Milwaukee Sentinel (m)	180,371		Wichita Eagle-Beacon (m)	123,777	188,028
Minneapolis Star Tribune (m)	*372,179	586,876	Winston-Salem Journal (m)	*74,323	97,613
Nashville Banner (e)	72,366		Winston-Salem Sentinel (e)	*32,566	
Nashville Tennessean (m)	124,966	241,717	Worcester Telegram (m)	†55,615	†122,631
Newark Star-Ledger (m)	*432,328	†654,446	Worcester Gazette (e)	†84,796	
New Haven Register (e)	92,284	142,242	Youngstown Vindicator (e)	†99,830	†152,081

(m) morning; (e) evening; *Mon.-Fri. average; † 3 months.

Circulation of Leading U.S. Magazines

Source: Audit Bureau of Circulations' FAS-FAX Report

General magazines, exclusive of groups and comics. Based on total average paid circulation during the 6 months prior to Dec. 31, 1983.

Magazine	Circulation	Magazine	Circulation	Magazine	Circulation
Reader's Digest	17,937,045	Changing Times	1,375,732	Gourmet	631,028
TV Guide	17,066,126	Money	1,374,101	Catholic Digest	623,479
National Geographic		Bon Appetit	1,300,103	Saturday Evening Post	609,470
Magazine	10,626,224	The American Hunter	1,294,642	Working Woman	605,902
Modern Maturity	9,296,187	The Dial	1,288,815	The Sporting News	603,398
AARP News Bulletin	8,760,153	Mademoiselle	1,265,081	Architectural Digest	602,397
Better Homes & Gardens	8,041,951	Discovery	1,173,305	Colonial Homes	601,397
Family Circle	7,193,079	Vogue	1,142,542	Flower & Garden	587,714
Woman's Day	7,025,290	Self	1,091,112	The Homeowner	583,846
McCall's	6,358,293	Hustler	1,083,744	GQ-Gentlemen's Quarterly	573,328
Good Housekeeping	5,393,087	US	1,083,320	Stereo Review	559,908
Ladies' Home Journal	5,252,444	New Woman	1,055,589	Science Digest	554,847
National Enquirer	4,706,165	Country Living	1,033,601	Sports Afield	544,740
Time	4,615,594	'Teen	1,022,552	Home	540,769
Playboy	4,209,324	Scouting	950,402	American Health	535,292
Redbook	4,019,611	Travel & Leisure	925,926	Computers & Electronics	523,299
The Star	3,689,337	Popular Photography	912,546	Tennis	512,516
Penthouse	3,500,275	National Examiner	912,462	The New Yorker	508,406
Newsweek	3,038,832	Mother Earth News	911,996	Food & Wine	505,083
Cosmopolitan	3,038,400	Discover	904,647	Gallery	490,509
People Weekly	2,781,542	Consumers Digest	903,034	Natural History	486,640
Prevention	2,769,560	Jet	871,595	Guns & Ammo	485,808
American Legion	2,507,338	Nation's Business	871,201	NRTA News Bulletin	485,615
Sports Illustrated	2,448,486	Health	870,123	Working Mother	484,656
Glamour	2,275,743	House Beautiful	864,459	Personal Computing	483,690
Southern Living	2,213,878	Workbench	853,071	Ms.	479,185
U.S. News & World Report	2,122,619	Weekly World News	836,641	Rotarian	477,929
Field & Stream	2,021,360	Car & Driver	815,989	National Lampoon	453,772
Smithsonian	1,954,273	Hot Rod	811,610	Inc.	450,622
V.F.W. Magazine	1,909,142	Young Miss	788,694	Forum	447,420
Globe	1,908,676	Weight Watchers		Shape	438,881
The Workbasket	1,856,805	Magazine	779,137	Skiing Magazine	435,945
Popular Science	1,838,906	Rolling Stone	777,153	New York Magazine	431,234
Parents	1,692,553	Cuisine	766,286	Ski	430,807
Seventeen	1,688,954	Soap Opera Digest	765,408	Cycle	420,801
Ebony	1,659,243	Esquire Magazine	764,321	Crafts	413,797
The Elks Magazine	1,633,234	Signature	746,549	Easyriders	408,784
Popular Mechanics	1,624,827	Metropolitan Home	722,846	Car Craft	397,484
Mechanix Illustrated	1,622,821	Harper's Bazaar	720,427	Westways	396,108
True Story	1,582,649	Forbes	719,908	Woman	395,579
Outdoor Life	1,530,118	Decorating & Craft Ideas	714,450	Bassmaster Magazine	393,434
Life	1,506,953	Science 83	710,031	World Tennis	386,526
Boy's Life	1,452,201	Essence	700,119	High Fidelity	379,744
Motorland	1,426,979	Fortune	692,314	Audubon	378,812
1001 Home Ideas	1,419,953	Modern Photography	681,751	Cycle World	375,642
Sunset	1,411,609	New Shelter	669,329	High Society	372,171
Organic Gardening	1,399,223	Games	652,492	Cheri	359,537
The American Rifleman	1,380,991	Playgirl	641,016		

Selected Canadian Daily Newspaper Circulation

Source: *Editor & Publisher 1984 International Yearbook*, report of average paid circulation for 6 months ending Sept. 30, 1983.

115 daily newspapers in Canada (26 morning: 92 evening), had an average audited circulation of 5,260,743; 34 Saturday-Sunday-weekend newspapers had an average circulation of 4,803,562.

Newspaper	Daily	Saturday	Newspaper	Daily	Saturday
Calgary Sun. (m)	*72,552	85,400	Regina Leader Post (e)	69,670	
Calgary Herald (e)	145,145	184,498	St. Catharines Standard (e)	41,678	
Edmonton Journal (e)	162,364	**136,188	St. John's Daily News (m)	8,245	7,430
Edmonton Sun (e)	*74,469	91,717	St. John's Telegram (e)	34,482	47,885
Halifax Chronicle-Herald (m)	76,888		Saint John Telegraph-Journal (m)	35,953	
Halifax Mail-Star (e)	56,937		Saint John Times Globe (e)	*31,637	
Hamilton Spectator (e)	143,572		Saskatoon Star-Phoenix (e)	56,618	
Kingston Whig-Standard (e)	34,745		Sudbury Star (e)	27,872	
Kitchener-Waterloo Record (e)	72,274		Sydney: Cape Breton Post (e)	31,119	
London Free Press (m)	124,881		Toronto Globe and Mail (m)	*310,689	
Montreal Gazette (m)	197,075	268,724	Toronto Star (m & e)	*497,909	799,038
Montreal: La Presse (m)	179,806	280,196	Toronto Sun (m)	*246,552	438,814
Montreal: Le Devoir (m)	33,707	36,383	Trois Rivieres Nouvelliste (e)	50,627	
Montreal: Le Journal de Montreal (m)	301,202	322,089	Vancouver Province (m)	*142,894	179,098
Ottawa Citizen (m & e)	*180,223	226,653	Vancouver Sun (e)	230,423	273,187
Ottawa: Le Droit (e)	40,397	45,578	Windsor Star (e)	85,418	
Quebec: Le Journal de Quebec (m)	101,399	99,351	Winnipeg Free Press (e)	172,335	241,793
Quebec: Le Soleil (e)	115,655	132,499			

(m) Morning; (e) Evening; * Based on Monday to Friday average; **Sunday.

Average Television Viewing Time

Source: A.C. Nielsen estimates, Nov. 1983 (hours: minutes, per week)

		Total	Mon.-Fri. 10am-4:30pm	Mon.-Fri. 4:30pm-7:30pm	Mon.-Sun. 8-11pm	Sat. 8am-1pm	Mon.-Fri. 11:30pm-1am
Avg. all persons		30:47	4:41	4:36	9:08	:53	1:05
Women	Total 18+	34:36	6:47	4:55	10:25	:34	1:17
	18-24	27:26	6:13	3:39	7:36	:38	1:02
	55+	41:13	8:19	6:44	11:59	:34	1:24
Men	Total 18+	30:13	2:56	4:07	9:34	:34	1:52
	18-24	24:52	3:13	3:04	7:04	:31	1:24
	55+	35:53	4:10	5:58	11:03	:32	1:23
Teens	Female	24:16	3:50	4:07	7:30	1:13	:32
	Male	25:17	2:46	4:24	8:04	1:23	:30
Children	2-5	27:09	6:00	5:05	4:37	2:17	:06
	6-11	24:50	2:34	5:22	6:14	2:17	:05

America's Favorite Television Programs

Source: A.C. Nielsen
(Percent of TV households and persons in TV households)

Network Programs (November 1983)

(Nielsen average audience estimates)

	TV Households	Women	Men	Teens	Children
ABC Sunday Night Movie	27.7	21.0	25.8	19.9	
Dallas	26.3	23.6	13.9		
60 Minutes	24.8	18.7	17.9		
A Team	24.6	16.1	19.3	21.0	25.0
Simon & Simon	24.3	19.4	15.6		
Falcon Crest	22.9	20.0			
Magnum, P.I.	22.8	18.6	15.8	12.6	
Dynasty	22.4	20.1	12.2		
Hotel	20.8	17.5			
AfterMash	20.7	16.2	12.2	13.8	
Knots Landing	20.0	18.0			
Newhart	19.6	15.7			
Fall Guy	19.4		12.3	14.5	
Love Boat	18.9	15.7			
CBS NFL Football Game 1	18.9		16.6		
NFL Monday Night Football			16.0		
NBC Monday Night Movies		15.6			
Scarecrow & Mrs. King		14.9			
Hill Street Blues			14.3		
NFL Football Game 2-NBC			14.2		
Hardcastle and McCormick			13.9	13.4	
CBS NFL Football-Game 2			13.9		
Facts Of Life				19.8	
Happy Days				18.0	
Just Our Luck				17.1	
Knight Rider				15.9	19.7
Family Ties				15.7	
Ripley's Believe It or Not				14.7	
Three's Company				14.7	
Movie of the Week-Friday				13.7	
That's Incredible				12.9	
Smurfs III				12.6	22.9
Dukes of Hazzard					27.2
Smurfs II					22.7

	TV Households	Women	Men	Teens	Children
Mr. T					22.2
Alvin & The Chipmunks					20.0
Diff'rent Strokes					17.9
Silver Spoons					16.8
Rubik, The Amazing Cube					16.7
Smurfs I					16.6
Dungeons & Dragons					15.4
Saturday Supercade					15.2
Gimme A Break					15.2
Littles					14.8

Syndicated Programs (Nov. 1983)*

(Average ratings for total U.S.)

	TV households	Women	Men	Teens	Children
Family Feud PM	12.3	10.7	7.4	5.5	6.4
Wheel of Fortune	12.1	10.6	7.2	6.2	6.3
M*A*S*H	11.2	7.7	7.5	7.2	5.1
Three's Company	10.3	6.7	5.4	11.8	10.0
PM Magazine	9.8	7.6	6.3	4.1	3.9
People's Court	9.1	7.2	5.5	3.6	2.8
Hee Haw	9.0	7.2	6.6	3.0	4.4
Entertainment Tonight	8.8	7.0	5.3	3.6	2.5
Jeffersons	8.3	6.0	4.3	8.1	6.9
Solid Gold	7.6	5.6	4.4	8.7	7.1
WKRP in Cincinnati	7.4	4.8	4.5	5.9	4.9
Dance Fever	7.3	5.8	4.1	5.5	5.4
Taxi	7.0	4.4	4.4	5.6	4.9
Barney Miller	6.6	4.7	4.3	2.9	2.4
Little House On-Prairie	6.5	4.4	2.2	6.2	8.5
Love Boat	6.5	4.5	2.5	5.7	4.6
Tic-Tac Dough	6.4	5.4	3.3	2.1	2.4
Alice	6.1	4.1	2.6	6.1	5.0
Happy Days	6.1	3.2	2.2	8.4	8.7
Phil Donahue	6.0	4.8	2.1	0.5	0.6

*Programs that cleared in 20+ markets.

Total TV Households — 83.3 million, 18+women — 86.35 million; 18+men — 77.77 million; teens 12-17 — 21.68 million; children 2-11 — 32.33 million.

Network TV Program Ratings

Source: A. C. Nielsen, November, 1983

	TV Households		Audience Composition (thousands)			
Program or type	Rating %	No. (000)	Men (18+)	Women (18+)	Teens 12-17	Children 2-11
Today (7:30-8:00)	4.0	3,350	1,690	2,320	80	190
Morning (7:30-8:00)	4.0	3,350	1,780	2,220	80	200
Good Morning Am.						
(7:30-8:00)	4.9	4,110	1,720	2,940	140	300
Daytime						
Drama (Soaps)	7.2	6,030	1,340	5,530	500	430
Quiz & Aud.						
Participation	4.8	4,020	1,190	3,190	210	400
All 10am-4:30pm	6.2	5,180	1,270	4,560	400	430
Evening						
Informational	12.4	10,360	6,450	7,980	780	890
General Drama	16.4	13,770	7,070	11,830	1,430	1,500
Susp. & Mystery	18.9	15,810	9,890	12,710	1,810	1,820
Sit. Comedy	15.8	13,280	7,080	10,760	2,380	3,450
Feature Film	17.8	14,930	9,540	12,510	2,230	1,610
All 7-11pm regular	16.9	14,170	8,610	11,190	2,090	2,460

All-time Top Television Programs

Source: A.C. Nielsen estimates

Program	Date	Network	Households	Program	Date	Network	Households
M*A*S*H Special	2/28/83	CBS	50,150,000	Super Bowl XII	1/15/78	CBS	34,410,000
Dallas	11/21/80	CBS	41,470,000	Winds of War	2/13/83	ABC	34,150,000
Super Bowl XVII	1/30/83	NBC	40,480,000	Gone With The Wind,			
Super Bowl XVI	1/24/82	CBS	40,020,000	Pt. 1	11/7/76	NBC	33,960,000
Super Bowl XVIII	1/22/84	CBS	38,800,000	Gone With The Wind,			
The Day After	11/20/83	ABC	38,550,000	Pt. 2	11/8/76	NBC	33,750,000
Roots	1/30/77	ABC	36,380,000	Winds of War	2/7/83	ABC	33,490,000
Thorn Birds	3/29/83	ABC	35,990,000	Thorn Birds	3/27/83	ABC	32,900,000
Thorn Birds	3/30/83	ABC	35,900,000	Roots	1/28/77	ABC	32,680,000
Thorn Birds	3/28/83	ABC	35,400,000	Winds of War	2/6/83	ABC	32,570,000
Super Bowl XIV	1/20/80	CBS	35,330,000	Roots	1/27/77	ABC	32,540,000
Super Bowl XIII	1/21/79	NBC	35,090,000	Winds of War	2/9/83	ABC	32,490,000
CBS NFC				Winds of War	2/8/83	ABC	32,240,000
Championship Game	1/10/82	CBS	34,960,000	Roots	1/25/77	ABC	31,900,000
Super Bowl XV	1/25/81	NBC	34,540,000	World Series Game 7	10/20/82	NBC	31,820,000

U.S. Television Sets and Stations Received

Set Ownership
(Nielsen est. as of Jan. 1, 1984)

Total TV homes	85,430,000	100%
(98% of U.S. homes own at least one TV set)		
Homes with:		
Color TV sets	75,810,000	90%
B&W only	7,990,000	10
2 or more sets	45,840,000	55
One set	37,960,000	45
Cable (Feb. 1984)	34,740,300	41.2

Number of Stations
(FCC, Jan. 1, 1984)

Commercial 831

Educational 283

Total 1,114

Stations Receivable
(Nielsen, Jan. 1984)
% of TV homes receiving:

1-4 stations	. . . .	5%
5	. . . .	5
6	. . . .	9
7	. . . .	9
8	. . . .	11
9	. . . .	10
10	. . . .	10
11+	. . . .	41%

Television Network Addresses

American Broadcasting Company (ABC)
1330 Avenue of Americas
New York, NY 10019

CBS, Inc.
51 W. 52nd St.
New York, NY 10019

National Broadcasting Company (NBC)
30 Rockefeller Plaza
New York, NY 10020

Westinghouse Broadcasting (Group W)
90 Park Ave.
New York, NY 10016

Metromedia
485 Lexington Ave.
New York, NY 10017

Public Broadcasting Service (PBS)
609 Fifth Ave.
New York, NY 10017

Canadian Broadcasting Corp. (CBC)
1500 Bronson Ave.
Ottawa, Ontario, Canada K1G 3J5

Symphony Orchestras of the U.S. and Canada

Source: American Symphony Orchestra League
(as of Mar. 22, 1984)
Classifications are based on annual incomes or budgets of orchestras.

Major Symphony Orchestras

		Conductor
Atlanta Symphony	1280 Peachtree St., NE, Atlanta, GA 30309	Robert Shaw
Baltimore Symphony	1212 Cathedral St., Baltimore, MD 21210	Sergiu Comissiona
Boston Symphony	301 Massachusetts Ave., Boston, MA 02115.	Seiji Ozawa
Buffalo Philharmonic	71 Symphony Circle, Buffalo, NY 14222	Julius Rudel
Chicago Symphony	220 S. Michigan Ave., Chicago, IL 60604	Sir Georg Solti
Cincinnati Symphony	1241 Elm St., Cincinnati, OH 45210	Michael Gielen
Cleveland Orchestra	11001 Euclid Ave., Cleveland, OH 44106.	Christoph von Dohnanyi
Dallas Symphony	P.O. Box 26207, Dallas, TX 75226.	Eduardo Mata
Denver Symphony	910 Fifteenth St., Denver, CO 80202	Gaetano Delogu
Detroit Symphony	Ford Auditorium, Detroit, MI 48226	Antal Dorati
Houston Symphony	615 Louisiana, Houston, TX 77002	Sergiu Comissiona
Indianapolis Symphony	P.O. Box 88207, Indianapolis, IN 46208	John Nelson
Los Angeles Philharmonic	135 North Grand, Los Angeles, CA 90012	Carlo Giulini
Milwaukee Symphony	212 W. Wisconsin Ave., Milwaukee, WI 53202	Lukas Foss
Minnesota Orchestra	1111 Nicollet Mall, Minneapolis, MN 55403.	Neville Marriner
Montreal Symphony	200 de Maisonneuve W., Montreal, Que. H2X 1Y9	Charles Dutoit
National Arts Centre Orchestra	P.O. Box 1534, Sta. B, Ottawa, ON K1P 5W1	Franco Mannino
National Symphony	JFK Center for the Performing Arts, Wash., DC 20566	Mstislav Rostropovich
New Orleans Philharmonic-Symphony	203 Carondelet St., New Orleans, LA 70130.	Philippe Entremont
New York Philharmonic.	Avery Fisher Hall, New York, NY 10023	Zubin Mehta
Oregon Symphony	813 SW Alder St., Portland, OR 97205	James DePreist
Philadelphia Orchestra	1420 Locust St., Philadelphia, PA 19102	Ricardo Muti
Pittsburgh Symphony	600 Penn Ave., Pittsburgh, PA 15222	Andre Previn
Rochester Philharmonic	108 East Ave., Rochester, NY 14604	David Zinman
St. Louis Symphony	718 N. Grand Blvd., St. Louis, MO 63103.	Leonard Slatkin
St. Paul Chamber Orchestra.	75 W. Fifth St., St. Paul, MN 55102	Pinchas Zukerman
San Antonio Symphony	109 Lexington Ave., San Antonio, TX 78205	Lawrence Leighton Smith
San Diego Symphony	P.O. Box 3175, San Diego, CA 92103	David Atherton
San Francisco Symphony	Davies Symphony Hall, San Fran., CA 94102	Edo de Waart
Seattle Symphony	305 Harrison St., Seattle, WA 98109	Gerard Schwarz
Syracuse Symphony	411 Montgomery St., Syracuse, NY 13202	Christopher Keene
Toronto Symphony	60 Simcoe St., Suite C-116, Toronto, ON M5J 2H5	Andrew Davis
Utah Symphony.	123 W. South Temple, Salt Lake City, UT 84101	Joseph Silverstein
Vancouver Symphony	400 E. Broadway, Vancouver, B.C. V5T 1X2	Kazuyoshi Akiyama

Regional Orchestras

Alabama Symphony	P.O. Box 2125, N., Birmingham, AL 35201	Amerigo Marino
American Symphony	161 W. 54th St., New York, NY 10019	Moshe Atzmon Guiseppe Patane
Austin Symphony	1101 Red River, Austin, TX 78701	Sung Kwak
Calgary Philharmonic.	200-505 Fifth St. SW, Calgary, Alta. T2P 3J2	Mario Bernardi
Charlotte Symphony	110 E. Seventh Street, Charlotte, NC 28202	Leo B. Driehuys
Colorado Springs Symphony	P.O. Box 1692, Colorado Springs, CO 80901	Charles A. Ansbacher
Columbus Symphony	101 E. Town St., Columbus, OH 43215	Christian Badea
Edmonton Symphony Society	11712-87th Ave., Edmonton, Alta. T6G 0Y3	Uri Mayer
Flint Symphony	1025 E. Kearsley St., Flint, MI 48503	Isaiah Jackson
Florida Orchestra	P.O. Box 24419, Tampa, FL 33624	Irwin Hoffman
Florida Symphony	P.O. Box 782, Orlando, FL 32802	Sidney Rothstein
Fort Worth Symphony	4401 Trail Lake Dr., Fort Worth, TX 76109	John Giordano
Grand Rapids Symphony.	415 Exhibitors Plaza, Grand Rapids, MI 49503	Semyon Bychkov
Hamilton Philharmonic	P.O. Box 2080, Sta. A, Hamilton, Ont. L8N 3Y7	Boris Brott
Hartford Symphony	609 Farmington, Hartford, CT 06105	Arthur Winograd
Honolulu Symphony	1000 Bishop St., Honolulu, HI 96813	Donald Johanos
Jacksonville Symphony	580 W. 8th St., Suite 9009, Jacksonville, FL 32209	William McNeiland
Kansas City Symphony.	1029 Central, Kansas City, Mo 64105.	Russell Patterson
Long Beach Symphony.	121 Linden Ave., Long Beach, CA 90802	Murry Sidlin
Los Angeles Chamber Orchestra	285 W. Green St., Pasadena, CA 91105	Gerard Schwarz
Louisville Orchestra.	609 W. Main St., Louisville, KY 40202.	Lawrence L. Smith
Memphis Symphony	3100 Walnut Grove Rd., Memphis, TN 38111	Vincent de Frank
Nashville Symphony	1805 West End Ave., Nashville, TN 37203	Kenneth Schermerhorn
New Jersey Symphony	213 Washington St., Newark, NJ 07101.	George Manahan
New Mexico Symphony	P.O. Box 769, Albuquerque, NM 87103	Yoshimi Takeda
North Carolina Symphony	P.O. Box 28026, Raleigh, NC 27611.	Gerhardt Zimmerman
Oakland Symphony.	Paramount Theatre, 2025 Broadway, Oakland, CA 94612	Richard Buckley
Oklahoma Symphony	512 Civic Center Music Hall, Oklahoma City, OK 73102	Luis Herrera de la Fuente
Omaha Symphony	310 Aquila Ct., Omaha, NE 68102.	Thomas Briccetti
Phoenix Symphony	6328 N. Seventh St., Phoenix, AZ 85014	Theo Alcantara
Puerto Rico Symphony	P.O. Box 41227, Minillas Sta., Santurce, PR 00940	John Barnett
Quebec Symphony	580 Grand-Allee est # 50, Quebec G1R 2B4	James DePreist
Richmond Symphony	211 W. Franklin St., Richmond, VA 23220	Jacques Houtmann
Sacramento Symphony	2848 Arden Way, # 210, Sacramento, CA 95825.	Carter Nice
San Jose Symphony	476 Park Ave., San Jose, CA 95113	George Cleve
Spokane Symphony	West 621 Mallon, Spokane, WA 99201	Donald Thulean
Springfield Symphony	56 Dwight St., Springfield, MA 01103	Robert Gutter
Toledo Symphony.	1 Stranahan Sq., Toledo, OH 43604.	Yuval Zaliouk
Tulsa Philharmonic	2210 South Main, Tulsa, OK 74114	Vacant
Victoria Symphony	631 Superior St., Victoria, B.C. V8V 1V1	Paul Freeman
Virginia Orchestra Group.	P.O. Box 26, Norfolk, VA 23501	Richard D. Williams
Wichita Symphony	225 W. Douglas, Wichita, KS 67202	Michael Palmer
Winnipeg Symphony	101-555 Main St., Winnipeg, Man. R3B 1C3	Kazuhiro Koizumi

U.S. and Canadian Opera Companies with Budgets of $500,000 or More

Source: Central Opera Service, New York, N.Y.; Apr. 1984

Anchorage Civic Opera; Michael More, adm. dir.

Arizona Opera Co. (Tucson); Glynn Ross, gen. dir.

Long Beach Civic Light Opera (Calif.); Harvey Waggoner, exec. dir.

Los Angeles Opera Theatre; Johanna Dordick, art. dir.

San Diego Civic Light Opera; Leon Drew, gen mgr.

San Diego Opera Assn.; Ian Campbell, gen. mgr.

San Francisco Opera; Terence McEwen, gen. dir.

San Francisco Opera Center; Steven Jordan, adm.

Western Opera Theater (San Francisco); Terence McEwen, gen. dir.

Central City Opera (Denver); Anne A. Randolph, gen. mgr.

Opera Colorado (Denver); Nathaniel Merrill, art. dir.

Connecticut Opera (Hartford); George Osborne, gen. dir.

Washington Opera (D.C.); Martin Feinstein, gen. dir.

Greater Miami Opera Assn.; Robert Herman, gen. mgr.

Palm Beach Opera; Anton Guadagno, art. dir.

Chicago Opera Theatre; Alan Stone, art. dir.

Lyric Opera of Chicago; Ardis Krainik, gen. mgr.

Indianapolis Opera Co.; Robert Driver, art. dir.

Music Theatre of Wichita; John Holly, prod. dir.

Kentucky Opera Assn. (Louisville); Thomson Smillie, gen. dir.

New Orleans Opera Assn.; Arthur Cosenza, gen. dir.

Baltimore Opera Co.; Jay Holbrook, gen. mgr.

Boston Lyric Opera; John Balme, gen. dir.

Opera Company of Boston; Sarah Caldwell, art. dir.

Michigan Opera Theatre (Detroit); David DiChiera, gen. dir.

Children's Theatre Co.; Sarah Lawless, exec. dir.

Minnesota Opera Co. (St. Paul); Edward Korn, gen. dir.

Lyric Opera of Kansas City (Missouri); Russell Patterson, gen. dir. & art. dir.

Opera Theatre of St. Louis (Missouri); Richard Gaddes, gen. dir.

St. Louis Municipal Theatre; Edward Greenberg, exec. prod.

New Jersey State Opera (Newark); Alfredo Silipigni, art. dir.

Washington Crossing State Park Summer Theatre (Titusville, N.J.); Jack M. Rees, mgr.

Santa Fe Opera (Calif.); John Crosby, gen. dir.

Lake George Opera Festival (Glens Falls, N.Y.); Paulette

Haupt-Nolen, gen. dir.

Artpark/Natural Heritage Trust (Lewiston, N.Y.); Joanne Allison, exec. dir.

Light Opera of Manhattan; Karen Schlotter, exec. sec.

Metropolitan Opera Assn. (New York City); Anthony A. Bliss, gen. mgr.

New York City Opera; Beverly Sills, gen. dir.

New York City Opera Natl. Co.; Nancy Kelly, adm.

Charlotte (No. Carolina) Opera Assn.; Bruce Chalmers, gen. dir.

Cincinnati Opera Assn.; James deBlasis, gen. mgr.

Cleveland Opera Company; David Bamberger, gen. mgr. & art. dir.

Lyric Theatre of Oklahoma (Oklahoma City); Jackie West, adm.

Tulsa Opera (Oklahoma); Edward Purrington, gen. dir.

Portland Opera Assn. (Oregon); Robert Bailey, exec. dir.

Opera Company of Philadelphia; Margaret Anne Everitt, mgr

Pittsburgh Opera Co.; Tito Capobiano, gen. dir.

Spoleto Festival USA (Charleston, So. Carolina); Philip Semark, gen. mgr.

Opera Memphis; vacant.

Dallas Opera; Plato Karayanis, gen. dir.

Fort Worth Opera; Dwight Bowes, gen. dir.

Houston Grand Opera Assn.; R. David Gockley, gen. dir.

Texas Opera Theater (Houston); M. Jane Weaver, gen. mgr.

Theatre Under the Stars (Houston); Ange Finn, gen. mgr.

Pioneer Memorial Theatre (Salt Lake City); Keith Engar exec. dir.

Utah Opera Company (Salt Lake City); Glade Peterson gen. dir.

Virginia Opera (Norfolk); Peter Mark, gen. dir.

Seattle Opera Assn.; Speight Jenkins, gen. dir.

Florentine Opera of Milwaukee; John Gage, gen. mgr.

Calgary Opera Assn.; Brian Hanson, gen. mgr.

Edmonton Opera Assn.; James Boyles, gen mgr.

Vancouver Opera; Valerie Beale, gen. mgr.

Manitoba Opera Assn.; Irving Guttman, art. dir.

Canadian Opera Co. (Toronto); Lotfi Mansouri, gen. dir.

L'Opera de Montreal; Jean-Paul Jeannotte, art. dir.

Miss America Winners

1921	Margaret Gorman, Washington, D.C.
1922-23	Mary Campbell, Columbus, Ohio
1924	Ruth Malcolmson, Philadelphia, Pennsylvania
1925	Fay Lamphier, Oakland, California
1926	Norma Smallwood, Tulsa, Oklahoma
1927	Lois Delaner, Joliet, Illinois
1933	Marion Bergeron, West Haven, Connecticut
1935	Henrietta Leaver, Pittsburgh, Pennsylvania
1936	Rose Coyle, Philadelphia, Pennsylvania
1937	Bette Cooper, Bertrand Island, New Jersey
1938	Marilyn Meseke, Marion, Ohio
1939	Patricia Donnelly, Detroit, Michigan
1940	Frances Marie Burke, Philadelphia, Pennsylvania
1941	Rosemary LaPlanche, Los Angeles, California
1942	Jo-Caroll Dennison, Tyler, Texas
1943	Jean Bartel, Los Angeles, California
1944	Venus Ramey, Washington, D.C.
1945	Bess Myerson, New York City, N.Y.
1946	Marilyn Buferd, Los Angeles, California
1947	Barbara Walker, Memphis, Tennessee
1948	BeBe Shopp, Hopkins, Minnesota
1949	Jacque Mercer, Litchfield, Arizona
1951	Yolande Betbeze, Mobile, Alabama
1952	Coleen Kay Hutchins, Salt Lake City, Utah
1953	Neva Jane Langley, Macon, Georgia
1954	Evelyn Margaret Ay, Ephrata, Pennsylvania
1955	Lee Meriwether, San Francisco, California
1956	Sharon Ritchie, Denver, Colorado
1957	Marian McKnight, Manning, South Carolina

1958	Marilyn Van Derbur, Denver, Colorado
1959	Mary Ann Mobley, Brandon, Mississippi
1960	Lynda Lee Mead, Natchez, Mississippi
1961	Nancy Fleming, Montague, Michigan
1962	Maria Fletcher, Asheville, North Carolina
1963	Jacquelyn Mayer, Sandusky, Ohio
1964	Donna Axum, El Dorado, Arkansas
1965	Vonda Kay Van Dyke, Phoenix, Arizona
1966	Deborah Irene Bryant, Overland Park, Kansas
1967	Jane Anne Jayroe, Laverne, Oklahoma
1968	Debra Dene Barnes, Moran, Kansas
1969	Judith Anne Ford, Belvidere, Illinois
1970	Pamela Anne Eldred, Birmingham, Michigan
1971	Phyllis Ann George, Denton, Texas
1972	Laurie Lea Schaefer, Columbus, Ohio
1973	Terry Anne Meeuwsen, DePere, Wisconsin
1974	Rebecca Ann King, Denver, Colorado
1975	Shirley Cothran, Fort Worth, Texas
1976	Tawney Elaine Godin, Yonkers, N.Y.
1977	Dorothy Kathleen Benham, Edina, Minnesota
1978	Susan Perkins, Columbus, Ohio
1979	Kylene Baker, Galax, Virginia
1980	Cheryl Prewitt, Ackerman, Mississippi
1981	Susan Powell, Elk City, Oklahoma
1982	Elizabeth Ward, Russellville, Arkansas
1983	Debra Maffett, Anaheim, California
1984	Vanessa Williams, Milwood, New York*
	Suzette Charles, Mays Landing, New Jersey

*Resigned July 23, 1984.

50 Leading U.S. Advertisers, 1982

Source: Advertising Age, Sept. 8, 1983; copyright © Crain Communications Inc. 1983.

Rank	Company	Ad Costs (000)	Sales (000)	Ads as % sales
	Appliances, TV, radio			
38	RCA Corp.	$160,000	$ 8,237,000	1.9
40	General Electric	159,000	26,500,000	0.6
	Automobiles			
3	General Motors Corp.	549,000	60,025,600	0.9
12	Ford Motor Corp.	313,500	37,067,200	0.9
35	Chrysler Corp.	173,000	10,044,900	1.7
	Chemicals			
47	American Cyanamid Co.	133,000	3,453,700	3.9
	Communications, Entertainment			
25	Warner Communications	232,200	3,990,000	5.8
41	CBS Inc.	159,000	4,122,800	3.9
49	Time Inc.	130,100	3,564,000	3.7
	Drugs			
50	Richardson-Vicks	129,300	1,115,600	11.6
	Food			
6	General Foods Corp.	429,100	8,256,400	5.2
9	Nabisco Brands Inc.	335,200	5,871,100	5.7
16	Beatrice Foods Co.	271,000	9,788,200	2.9
19	McDonald's Corp.	265,500	7,809,000	3.4
21	General Mills	244,400	5,550,800	4.4
23	H.J. Heinz Co.	235,700	3,738,500	6.3
27	Ralston Purina Co.	220,000	4,802,600	4.6
31	Dart & Kraft	199,200	9,974,000	2.0
32	Esmark Inc.	197,800	3,389,100	5.8
33	Norton Simon Inc.	191,200	2,994,300	6.4
34	Consolidated Foods Corp.	178,000	6,660,000	2.7
36	Pillsbury Co.	170,400	3,700,000	4.6
43	Kellogg Co.	154,200	2,370,000	6.5
	Retail Chains			
2	Sears, Roebuck & Co.	631,100	30,020,000	2.1
8	K mart Corp.	366,100	16,772,200	2.2
26	J.C. Penney Co.	230,000	11,414,000	2.0
	Soaps, Cleansers			
1	Procter & Gamble	726,100	12,452,000	5.8
14	Unilever U.S. Inc.	304,600	2,954,900	10.3
18	Colgate-Palmolive Co.	268,000	4,888,000	5.5
	Soft drinks			
13	PepsiCo Inc.	305,000	7,499,000	4.1
20	Coca-Cola Co.	255,300	6,249,700	4.1
	Telephone service, equipment			
7	American T & T	373,600	65,757,000	0.6
39	International T & T	159,100	21,921,000	0.7
	Tobacco			
4	R.J. Reynolds Industries	530,300	13,057,000	4.1
5	Philip Morris	501,700	11,716,100	4.3
24	B.A.T. Industries PLC	235,000	5,506,700	4.3
	Toiletries, Cosmetics			
10	American Home Products	325,400	4,580,000	7.1
15	Warner Lambert Co.	294,700	3,246,000	9.1
17	Bristol-Myers Co.	270,000	3,304,000	8.2
30	Johnson & Johnson	205,000	3,599,900	5.7
37	Gillette Co.	163,000	2,239,000	7.3
46	Chesebrough-Pond's	140,200	1,796,200	7.8
48	Sterling Drug	131,000	1,623,190	8.0
	Wine, Beer, Liquor			
22	Anheuser-Busch Cos.	243,400	5,185,700	4.7
44	Seagram Co. Ltd.	153,000	2,826,200	5.4
	Miscellaneous			
11	Mobil Corp.	320,000	64,137,000	0.5
28	Mattel Inc.	217,900	1,341,900	16.2
29	U.S. Government	205,500	NA	NA
42	Gulf & Western	155,000	6,423,000	2.4
45	Eastman Kodak Co.	142,800	10,815,000	1.3

30 Top U.S. Advertisers: Expenditures by Type of Media

Source: Advertising Age, Sept. 8, 1983; copyright © Crain Communications Inc., 1983.

Rank	Company	News-papers	Genl. mags.	Farm pub.	Spot TV	Net TV	Spot Radio	Net Radio	Out-door
				% of Total Dollars					
1	Procter & Gamble	1.4	4.9	—	29.4	64.1	—	0.2	—
2	Sears, Roebuck & Co.	—	27.2	0.1	54.5	9.3	5.9	3.0	—
3	General Motors	20.8	21.8	0.4	41.6	6.9	2.0	5.2	1.3
4	R.J. Reynolds Industries	29.4	26.5	—	13.6	11.4	—	0.7	18.4
5	Philip Morris Inc.	19.4	30.1	—	25.6	8.0	—	5.2	11.7
6	General Foods Corp.	1.3	8.5	—	66.5	20.3	2.0	1.4	—
7	AT&T Co.	13.1	15.5	—	36.1	24.9	2.8	7.1	0.5
8	K Mart Corp.	—	15.9	—	57.8	14.6	1.4	10.0	0.3
9	Nabisco Brands	5.4	10.2	—	57.8	17.4	7.8	1.0	0.4
10	American Home Products Corp.	1.0	6.1	0.2	74.1	16.9	0.8	0.9	—
11	Mobil Corp.	16.7	12.8	—	20.3	42.5	—	7.7	—
12	Ford Motor Co.	15.8	20.4	1.2	44.7	7.7	2.2	7.6	0.4
13	PepsiCo Inc.	1.5	4.8	—	38.6	44.7	1.4	8.4	0.6
14	Unilever U.S.	3.0	9.8	—	62.3	24.5	0.4	—	—
15	Warner-Lambert Co.	1.0	6.0	—	61.6	25.0	5.0	1.4	—
16	Beatrice Foods Co.	1.4	30.8	—	8.4	51.6	1.2	—	6.6
17	Johnson & Johnson	1.9	17.4	0.2	74.5	4.4	1.0	0.6	—
18	Colgate-Palmolive Co.	2.6	7.4	0.2	61.0	24.4	—	4.4	—
19	McDonald's Corp.	—	0.5	—	38.8	57.8	1.1	1.3	2.5
20	Coca-Cola Co.	2.5	3.3	—	50.1	34.1	0.1	8.1	1.8
21	General Mills	1.8	7.6	—	40.7	46.6	0.8	2.4	0.1
22	Anheuser-Busch Cos.	1.6	5.1	—	46.8	23.0	3.1	18.0	2.4
23	H.J. Heinz Co.	4.7	7.5	—	58.4	28.8	—	0.6	—
24	Batus Inc.	24.5	42.0	—	—	9.1	—	0.1	24.3
25	Warner Communications	12.7	16.8	—	50.8	18.3	0.8	0.6	—
26	J.C. Penney Co.	—	20.6	—	43.6	30.2	4.0	1.3	0.3
27	Ralston Purina Co.	2.1	7.2	0.7	66.4	18.9	—	4.6	0.1
28	Mattel Inc.	6.0	9.5	—	62.4	20.4	1.5	0.2	—
29	U.S. Government	6.6	31.3	—	26.7	17.9	9.1	7.2	0.9
30	Bristol-Myers Co.	1.3	16.5	0.1	69.1	8.2	1.1	3.6	0.1

UNITED STATES FACTS

Superlative U.S. Statistics

Source: National Geographic Society, Washington, D.C.

Area for 50 states	Total	3,623,420 sq. mi.
	Land 3,543,883 sq. mi.—Water 79,537 sq. mi.	
Largest state	Alaska	591,004 sq. mi.
Smallest state	Rhode Island	1,212 sq. mi.
Largest county	San Bernardino County, California	20,102 sq. mi.
Smallest county	New York, New York	34 sq. mi.
Northernmost city	Barrow, Alaska	71°17'N.
Northernmost point	Point Barrow, Alaska	71°23'N.
Southernmost city	Hilo, Island of Hawaii	19°43'N.
Southernmost town	Naalehu, Island of Hawaii	19°03'N.
Southernmost point	Ka Lae (South Cape), Island of Hawaii	18°56'N. (155°41'W.)
Easternmost city	Eastport, Maine	66°59'02"W.
Easternmost town	Lubec, Maine	66°58'49"W.
Easternmost point	West Quoddy Head, Maine	66°57'W.
Westernmost city	Lihue, Island of Kauai, Hawaii	159°22'W.
Westernmost town	Adak, Aleutians, Alaska	176°45'W.
Westernmost point	Cape Wrangell, Attu Island, Aleutians, Alaska	172°27'E.
Highest city	Leadville, Colorado	10,200 ft.
Lowest town	Calipatria, California	−184 ft.
Highest point on Atlantic coast	Cadillac Mountain, Mount Desert Is., Maine	1,530 ft.
Oldest national park	Yellowstone National Park (1872), Wyoming, Montana, Idaho	3,468 sq. mi.
Largest national park	Wrangell-St. Elias, Alaska	12,730 sq. mi.
Largest national monument	Death Valley, California, Nevada	3,231 sq. mi.
Highest waterfall	Yosemite Falls—Total in three sections	2,425 ft.
	Upper Yosemite Fall	1,430 ft.
	Cascades in middle section	675 ft.
	Lower Yosemite Fall	320 ft.
Longest river	Mississippi-Missouri	3,710 mi.
Highest mountain	Mount McKinley, Alaska	20,320 ft.
Lowest point	Death Valley, California	−282 ft.
Deepest lake	Crater Lake, Oregon	1,932 ft.
Rainiest spot	Mt. Waialeale, Hawaii	Annual aver. rainfall 460 inches
Largest gorge	Grand Canyon, Colorado River, Arizona	277 miles long, 600 ft to 18 miles wide, 1 mile deep
Deepest gorge	Hell's Canyon, Snake River, Idaho-Oregon	7,900 ft.
Strongest surface wind	Mount Washington, New Hampshire recorded 1934	231 mph
Biggest dam	New Cornelia Tailings, Ten Mile Wash, Arizona	274,026,000 cu. yds. material used
Tallest building	Sears Tower, Chicago, Illinois	1,454 ft
Largest building	Boeing 747 Manufacturing Plant, Everett, Washington	205,600,000 cu. ft.; covers 47 acres
Tallest structure	TV tower, Blanchard, North Dakota	2,063 ft
Longest bridge span	Verrazano-Narrows, New York	4,260 ft
Highest bridge	Royal Gorge, Colorado	1,053 ft. above water
Deepest well	Gas well, Washita County, Oklahoma	31,441 ft

The 49 States, Including Alaska

Area for 49 states	Total	3,616,949 sq. mi
	Land 3,537,458 sq. mi.—Water 79,491 sq. mi.	

The 48 Contiguous States

Area for 48 states	Total	3,025,945 sq. mi
	Land 2,966,625 sq. mi.—Water 59,320 sq. mi.	
Largest state	Texas	267,338 sq. mi
Northernmost town	Angle Inlet, Minnesota	49°22'N
Northernmost point	Northwest Angle, Minnesota	49°23'N
Southernmost city	Key West, Florida	24°33'N
Southernmost mainland city	Florida City, Florida	25°27'N
Southernmost point	Key West, Florida	24°33'N
Westernmost town	La Push, Washington	124°38'W
Westernmost point	Cape Alava, Washington	124°44'W
Highest mountain	Mount Whitney, California	14,494 ft

Note to users: The distinction between cities and towns varies from state to state. In this table the U.S. Bureau of the Census usage was followed.

Geodetic Datum Point of North America

The geodetic datum point of the U.S. is the National Ocean Service's triangulation station Meades Ranch in Osborn County, Kansas, at latitude 39° 13'26". 686 N and longitude 98° 32'30". 506 W. This geodetic datum point is a fundamental point from which all latitude and longitude computations originate for North America and Central America.

Statistical Information about the U.S.

In the *Statistical Abstract of the United States* the Bureau of the Census, U.S. Dept. of Commerce, annually publishes summary of social, political, and economic information. A book of more than 1,000 pages, it presents in 33 sections comprehensive data on population, housing, health, education, employment, income, prices, business, banking, energy, science, defense, trade, government finance, foreign country comparison, and other subjects. Special features include a section on Recent Trends and appendixes on statistical methodology and reliability and Standard Metropolitan Statistical Areas. The book prepared under the direction of Glenn W. King, Chief, Statistical Compendia Staff, Bureau of the Census. Supplements to the *Statistical Abstract* are *Pocket Data Book USA, 1979; County and City Data Book, 1983, Historical Statistics of the United States, Colonial Times to 1970;* and *State and Metropolitan Area Data Book, 1982* (1985, in production). Information concerning these and other publications may be obtained from the Supt. of Documents, Government Printing Office, Wash., D.C. 20402, or from the U.S. Bureau of the Census, Data User Services Division, Wash., D.C. 20233.

Highest and Lowest Altitudes in the U.S. and Territories

Source: Geological Survey, U.S. Interior Department. (Minus sign means below sea level; elevations are in feet.)

State	Highest Point Name	County	Elev.	Lowest Point Name	County	Elev.
Alabama	Cheaha Mountain	Cleburne	2,407	Gulf of Mexico		Sea level
Alaska	Mount McKinley		20,320	Pacific Ocean		Sea level
Arizona	Humphreys Peak	Coconino	12,633	Colorado R.	Yuma	70
Arkansas	Magazine Mountain	Logan	2,753	Ouachita R.	Ashley Union	55
California	Mount Whitney	Inyo-Tulare	14,494	Death Valley	Inyo	−282
Colorado	Mount Elbert	Lake	14,433	Arkansas R.	Prowers	3,350
Connecticut	Mount Frissell	Litchfield	2,380	L.I. Sound		Sea level
Delaware	On Ebright Road	New Castle	442	Atlantic Ocean		Sea level
Dist. of Col.	Tenleytown	N. W. part	410	Potomac R.		1
Florida	Sec. 30, T 6N, R 20W.	Walton	345	Atlantic Ocean		Sea level
Georgia	Brasstown Bald	Towns-Union	4,784	Atlantic Ocean		Sea level
Guam	Mount Lamlam	Agat District	1,329	Pacific Ocean		Sea level
Hawaii	Mauna Kea	Hawaii	13,796	Pacific Ocean		Sea level
Idaho	Borah Peak	Custer	12,662	Snake R.	Nez Perce	710
Illinois	Charles Mound	Jo Daviess	1,235	Mississippi R.	Alexander	279
Indiana	Franklin Township	Wayne	1,257	Ohio R.	Posey	320
Iowa	Sec. 29, T 100N, R 41W.	Osceola	1,670	Mississippi R.	Lee	480
Kansas	Mount Sunflower	Wallace	4,039	Verdigris R.	Montgomery	680
Kentucky	Black Mountain	Harlan	4,145	Mississippi R.	Fulton	257
Louisiana	Driskill Mountain	Bienville	535	New Orleans	Orleans	−5
Maine	Mount Katahdin	Piscataquis	5,268	Atlantic Ocean		Sea level
Maryland	Backbone Mountain	Garrett	3,360	Atlantic Ocean		Sea level
Massachusetts	Mount Greylock	Berkshire	3,491	Atlantic Ocean		Sea level
Michigan	Mount Arvon	Baraga	1,979	Lake Erie		572
Minnesota	Eagle Mountain	Cook	2,301	Lake Superior		602
Mississippi	Woodall Mountain	Tishomingo	806	Gulf of Mexico		Sea level
Missouri	Taum Sauk Mt.	Iron	1,772	St. Francis R.	Dunklin	230
Montana	Granite Peak	Park	12,799	Kootenai R.	Lincoln	1,800
Nebraska	Johnson Township	Kimball	5,426	S.E. cor. State	Richardson	840
Nevada	Boundary Peak	Esmeralda	13,143	Colorado R.	Clark	470
New Hamp.	Mt. Washington	Coos	6,288	Atlantic Ocean		Sea level
New Jersey	High Point	Sussex	1,803	Atlantic Ocean		Sea level
New Mexico	Wheeler Peak	Taos	13,161	Red Bluff Res.	Eddy	2,817
New York	Mount Marcy	Essex	5,344	Atlantic Ocean		Sea level
North Carolina	Mount Mitchell	Yancey	6,684	Atlantic Ocean		Sea level
North Dakota	White Butte	Slope	3,506	Red R.	Pembina	750
Ohio	Campbell Hill	Logan	1,550	Ohio R.	Hamilton	433
Oklahoma	Black Mesa	Cimarron	4,973	Little R.	McCurtain	287
Oregon	Mount Hood	Clackamas-Hood R.	11,239	Pacific Ocean		Sea level
Pennsylvania	Mt. Davis	Somerset	3,213	Delaware R.	Delaware	Sea level
Puerto Rico	Cerro de Punta	Ponce District	4,389	Atlantic Ocean		Sea level
Rhode Island	Jerimoth Hill	Providence	812	Atlantic Ocean		Sea level
Samoa	Lata Mountain	Tau Island	3,160	Pacific Ocean		Sea level
South Carolina	Sassafras Mountain	Pickens	3,560	Atlantic Ocean		Sea level
South Dakota	Harney Peak	Pennington	7,242	Big Stone Lake	Roberts	962
Tennessee	Clingmans Dome	Sevier	6,643	Mississippi R.	Shelby	182
Texas	Guadalupe Peak	Culberson	8,749	Gulf of Mexico		Sea level
Utah	Kings Peak	Duchesne	13,528	Beaverdam Cr.	Washington	2,000
Vermont	Mount Mansfield	Lamoille	4,393	Lake Champlain	Franklin	95
Virginia	Mount Rogers	Grayson-Smyth	5,729	Atlantic Ocean		Sea level
Virgin Islands	Crown Mountain	St. Thomas Island	1,556	Atlantic Ocean		Sea level
Washington	Mount Rainier	Pierce	14,410	Pacific Ocean		Sea level
West Virginia	Spruce Knob	Pendleton	4,863	Potomac R.	Jefferson	240
Wisconsin	Timms Hill	Price	1,952	Lake Michigan		581
Wyoming	Gannett Peak	Fremont	13,804	B. Fourche R.	Crook	3,100

U.S. Coastline by States

Source: NOAA, U.S. Commerce Department
(statute miles)

State	Coastline[1]	Shoreline[2]	State	Coastline[1]	Shoreline[2]
Atlantic coast	2,069	28,673	**Gulf coast**	1,631	17,141
Connecticut	0	618	Alabama	53	607
Delaware	28	381	Florida	770	5,095
Florida	580	3,331	Louisiana	397	7,721
Georgia	100	2,344	Mississippi	44	359
Maine	228	3,478	Texas	367	3,359
Maryland	31	3,190			
Massachusetts	192	1,519	**Pacific coast**	7,623	40,298
New Hampshire	13	131	Alaska	5,580	31,383
New Jersey	130	1,792	California	840	3,427
New York	127	1,850	Hawaii	750	1,052
North Carolina	301	3,375	Oregon	296	1,410
Pennsylvania	0	89	Washington	157	3,026
Rhode Island	40	384			
South Carolina	187	2,876	**Arctic coast, Alaska**	1,060	2,521
Virginia	112	3,315			
			United States	12,383	88,633

(1) Figures are lengths of general outline of seacoast. Measurements were made with a unit measure of 30 minutes of latitude on charts as near the scale of 1:1,200,000 as possible. Coastline of sounds and bays is included to a point where they narrow to width of unit measure, and includes the distance across at such point. (2) Figures obtained in 1939-40 with a recording instrument on the largest-scale charts and maps then available. Shoreline of outer coast, offshore islands, sounds, bays, rivers, and creeks is included to the head of tidewater or to a point where tidal waters narrow to a width of 100 feet.

States: Settled, Capitals, Entry into Union, Area, Rank

The original 13 states—The 13 colonies that seceded from Great Britain and fought the War of Independence (American Revolution) became the 13 original states. They were: Delaware, Pennsylvania, New Jersey, Georgia, Connecticut, Massachusetts, Maryland, South Carolina, New Hampshire, Virginia, New York, North Carolina, and Rhode Island. The order for the original 13 states is the order in which they ratified the Constitution.

State	Set-tled*	Capital	Entered Union Date	Order	Extent in miles Long (approx. mean)	Wide	Area in square miles Land	Inland water	Total	Rank in area
Ala. . .	1702	. . Montgomery . .	Dec. 14, 1819	22	330	190	50,708	901	51,609	29
Alas. .	1784	. . Juneau	Jan. 3, 1959	49	(a)1,480	810	569,600	20,157	589,757	1
Ariz. . .	1776	. . Phoenix.	Feb. 14, 1912	48	400	310	113,417	492	113,909	6
Ark. . .	1686	. . Little Rock . . .	June 15, 1836	25	260	240	51,945	1,159	53,104	27
Cal. . .	1769	. . Sacramento . .	Sept. 9, 1850	31	770	250	156,361	2,332	158,693	3
Col. . .	1858	. . Denver	Aug. 1, 1876	38	380	280	103,766	481	104,247	8
Conn. .	1634	. . Hartford.	Jan. 9, 1788	5	110	70	4,862	147	5,009	48
Del. . .	1638	. . Dover	Dec. 7, 1787	1	100	30	1,982	75	2,057	49
D.C. . .	. . . . .	. . Washington. . .			. . .	. . .	61	6	67	51
Fla. . .	1565	. . Tallahassee . .	Mar. 3, 1845	27	500	160	54,090	4,470	58,560	22
Ga. . .	1733	. . Atlanta	Jan. 2, 1788	4	300	230	58,073	803	58,876	21
Ha. . .	1820	. . Honolulu	Aug. 21, 1959	50	. . .	. . .	6,425	25	6,450	47
Ida. . .	1842	. . Boise	July 3, 1890	43	570	300	82,677	880	83,557	13
Ill. . .	1720	. . Springfield . . .	Dec. 3, 1818	21	390	210	55,748	652	56,400	24
Ind. . .	1733	. . Indianapolis. . .	Dec. 11, 1816	19	270	140	36,097	194	36,291	38
Ia. . . .	1788	. . Des Moines . .	Dec. 28, 1846	29	310	200	55,941	349	56,290	25
Kan. . .	1727	. . Topeka	Jan. 29, 1861	34	400	210	81,787	477	82,264	14
Ky. . .	1774	. . Frankfort	June 1, 1792	15	380	140	39,650	745	40,395	37
La. . . .	1699	. . Baton Rouge . .	Apr. 30, 1812	18	380	130	44,930	3,593	48,523	31
Me. . .	1624	. . Augusta.	Mar. 15, 1820	23	320	190	30,920	2,295	33,215	39
Md. . .	1634	. . Annapolis. . . .	Apr. 28, 1788	7	250	90	9,891	686	10,577	42
Mass. .	1620	. . Boston-.	Feb. 6, 1788	6	190	50	7,826	431	8,257	45
Mich. .	1668	. . Lansing	Jan. 26, 1837	26	490	240	56,817	1,399	58,216	23
Minn. .	1805	. . St. Paul	May 11, 1858	32	400	250	79,289	4,779	84,068	12
Miss. .	1699	. . Jackson.	Dec. 10, 1817	20	340	170	47,296	420	47,716	32
Mo. . .	1735	. . Jefferson City .	Aug. 10, 1821	24	300	240	68,995	691	69,686	19
Mon. .	1809	. . Helena	Nov. 8, 1889	41	630	280	145,587	1,551	147,138	4
Neb. . .	1823	. . Lincoln	Mar. 1, 1867	37	430	210	76,483	744	77,227	15
Nev. . .	1849	. . Carson City . .	Oct. 31, 1864	36	490	320	109,889	651	110,540	7
N.H. . .	1623	. . Concord	June 21, 1788	9	190	70	9,027	277	9,304	44
N.J. . .	1664	. . Trenton	Dec. 18, 1787	3	150	70	7,521	315	7,836	46
N.M. . .	1610	. . Santa Fe	Jan. 6, 1912	47	370	343	121,412	254	121,666	5
N.Y. . .	1614	. . Albany	July 26, 1788	11	330	283	47,831	1,745	49,576	30
N.C. . .	1660	. . Raleigh	Nov. 21, 1789	12	500	150	48,798	3,788	52,586	28
N.D. . .	1812	. . Bismarck	Nov. 2, 1889	39	340	211	69,273	1,392	70,665	17
Oh. . .	1788	. . Columbus . . .	Mar. 1, 1803	17	220	220	40,975	247	41,222	35
Okla. .	1889	. . Oklahoma City.	Nov. 16, 1907	46	400	220	68,782	1,137	69,919	18
Ore. . .	1811	. . Salem.	Feb. 14, 1859	33	360	261	96,184	797	96,981	10
Pa. . .	1682	. . Harrisburg . . .	Dec. 12, 1787	2	283	160	44,966	367	45,333	33
R.I. . .	1636	. . Providence . . .	May 29, 1790	13	40	30	1,049	165	1,214	50
S.C. . .	1670	. . Columbia	May 23, 1788	8	260	200	30,225	830	31,055	40
S.D. . .	1859	. . Pierre	Nov. 2, 1889	40	380	210	75,955	1,092	77,047	16
Tenn. .	1769	. . Nashville	June 1, 1796	16	440	120	41,328	916	42,244	34
Tex. . .	1682	. . Austin.	Dec. 29, 1845	28	790	660	262,134	5,204	267,338	2
Ut. . . .	1847	. . Salt Lake City .	Jan. 4, 1896	45	350	270	82,096	2,820	84,916	11
Vt. . . .	1724	. . Montpelier . . .	Mar. 4, 1791	14	160	80	9,267	342	9,609	43
Va. . .	1607	. . Richmond. . . .	June 25, 1788	10	430	200	39,780	1,037	40,817	36
Wash. .	1811	. . Olympia	Nov. 11, 1889	42	360	240	66,570	1,622	68,192	20
W.Va. .	1727	. . Charleston . . .	June 20, 1863	35	240	130	24,070	111	24,181	41
Wis. . .	1766	. . Madison	May 29, 1848	30	310	260	54,464	1,690	56,154	26
Wy. . .	1834	. . Cheyenne . . .	July 10, 1890	44	360	280	97,203	711	97,914	9

*First European permanent settlement. (a) Aleutian Islands and Alexander Archipelago are not considered in these lengths.

The Continental Divide

Source: Geological Survey, U.S. Interior Department

The Continental Divide: watershed, created by mountain ranges or table-lands of the Rocky Mountains, from which the drainage is easterly or westerly; the easterly flowing waters reaching the Atlantic Ocean chiefly through the Gulf of Mexico, and the westerly flowing waters reaching the Pacific Ocean through the Columbia River, or through the Colorado River, which flows into the Gulf of California.

The location and route of the Continental Divide across the United States may briefly be described as follows:

Beginning at point of crossing the United States-Mexican boundary, near long. 108°45'W., the Divide, in a northerly direction, crosses New Mexico along the western edge of the Rio Grande drainage basin, entering Colorado near long. 106°41'W.

Thence by a very irregular route northerly across Colorado along the western summits of the Rio Grande and of the Arkansas, the South Platte, and the North Platte River basins, and across Rocky Mountain National Park, entering Wyoming near long. 106°52'W.

Thence in a northwesterly direction, forming the western rims of the North Platte, Big Horn, and Yellowstone River basins, crossing the southwestern portion of Yellowstone National Park.

Thence in a westerly and then a northerly direction forming the common boundary of Idaho and Montana, to a point on said boundary near long. 114°00'W.

Thence northeasterly and northwesterly through Montana and the Glacier National Park, entering Canada near long. 114°04'W.

Chronological List of Territories

Source: National Archives and Records Service

Name of territory	Date of Organic Act	Organic Act effective	Admission as state	Yrs. terr.
Northwest Territory(a)	July 13, 1787	No fixed date	Mar. 1, 1803(b)	16
Territory southwest of River Ohio	May 26, 1790	No fixed date	June 1, 1796(c)	6
Mississippi	Apr. 7, 1798	When president acted	Dec. 10, 1817	19
Indiana	May 7, 1800	July 4, 1800	Dec. 11, 1816	16
Orleans	Mar. 26, 1804	Oct. 1, 1804	Apr. 30, 1812(d)	7
Michigan	Jan. 11, 1805	June 30, 1805	Jan. 26, 1837	31
Louisiana-Missouri(e)	Mar. 3, 1805	July 4, 1805	Aug. 10, 1821	16
Illinois	Feb. 3, 1809	Mar. 1, 1809	Dec. 3, 1818	9
Alabama	Mar. 3, 1817	When Miss. became a state	Dec. 14, 1819	2
Arkansas	Mar. 2, 1819	July 4, 1819	June 15, 1836	17
Florida	Mar. 30, 1822	No fixed date	Mar. 3, 1845	23
Wisconsin	Apr. 20, 1836	July 3, 1836	May 29, 1848	12
Iowa	June 12, 1838	July 3, 1838	Dec. 28, 1846	7
Oregon	Aug. 14, 1848	Date of act	Feb. 14, 1859	10
Minnesota	Mar. 3, 1849	Date of act	May 11, 1858	9
New Mexico	Sept. 9, 1850	On president's proclamation	Jan. 6, 1912	61
Utah	Sept. 9, 1850	Date of act	Jan. 4, 1896	44
Washington	Mar. 2, 1853	Date of act	Nov. 11, 1889	36
Nebraska	May 30, 1854	Date of act	Mar. 1, 1867	12
Kansas	May 30, 1854	Date of act	Jan. 29, 1861	6
Colorado	Feb. 28, 1861	Date of act	Aug. 1, 1876	15
Nevada	Mar. 2, 1861	Date of act	Oct. 31, 1864	3
Dakota	Mar. 2, 1861	Date of act	Nov. 2, 1889	28
Arizona	Feb. 24, 1863	Date of act	Feb. 14, 1912	49
Idaho	Mar. 3, 1863	Date of act	July 3, 1890	27
Montana	May 26, 1864	Date of act	Nov. 8, 1889	25
Wyoming	July 25, 1868	When officers were qualified	July 10, 1890	22
Alaska(f)	May 17, 1884	No fixed date	Jan. 3, 1959	75
Oklahoma	May 2, 1890	Date of act	Nov. 16, 1907	17
Hawaii	Apr. 30, 1900	June 14, 1900	Aug. 21, 1959	59

(a) Included Ohio, Indiana, Illinois, Michigan, Wisconsin, eastern Minnesota; (b) as the state of Ohio; (c) as the state of Tennessee; (d) as the state of Louisiana; (e) organic act for Missouri Territory of June 4, 1812, became effective Dec. 7, 1812; (f) Although the May 17, 1884 act actually constituted Alaska as a district, it was often referred to as a territory, and unofficially administered as such. The Territory of Alaska was legally and formally organized by an act of Aug. 24, 1912.

Geographic Centers, U.S. and Each State

Source: Geological Survey, U.S. Interior Department

United States, including Alaska and Hawaii — South Dakota; Butte County, W of Castle Rock, Approx. lat. 44°58'N. long. 103°46'W.

Contiguous U. S. (48 states) — Near Lebanon, Smith Co., Kansas, lat. 39°50'N. long. 98°35'W.

North American continent — The geographic center is in Pierce County, North Dakota, 6 miles W of Balta, latitude 48°10', longitude 100°10'W.

State—county, locality

Alabama—Chilton, 12 miles SW of Clanton.
Alaska—lat. 63°50'N. long. 152°W. Approx. 60 mi. NW of Mt. McKinley.
Arizona—Yavapai, 55 miles ESE of Prescott.
Arkansas—Pulaski, 12 miles NW of Little Rock.
California—Madera, 38 miles E of Madera.
Colorado—Park, 30 miles NW of Pikes Peak.
Connecticut—Hartford, at East Berlin.
Delaware—Kent, 11 miles S of Dover.
District of Columbia—Near 4th and L Sts., NW.
Florida—Hernando, 12 miles NNW of Brooksville.
Georgia—Twiggs, 18 miles SE of Macon.
Hawaii—Hawaii, 20°15'N, 156°20'W, off Maui Island.
Idaho—Custer, at Custer, SW of Challis.
Illinois—Logan, 28 miles NE of Springfield.
Indiana—Boone, 14 miles NNW of Indianapolis.
Iowa—Story, 5 miles NE of Ames.
Kansas—Barton, 15 miles NE of Great Bend.
Kentucky—Marion, 3 miles NNW of Lebanon.
Louisiana—Avoyelles, 3 miles SE of Marksville.
Maine—Piscataquis, 18 miles north of Dover.

Maryland—Prince Georges, 4.5 miles NW of Davidsonville.
Massachusetts—Worcester, north part of city.
Michigan—Wexford, 5 miles NNW of Cadillac.
Minnesota—Crow Wing, 10 miles SW of Brainerd.
Mississippi—Leake, 9 miles WNW of Carthage.
Missouri—Miller, 20 miles SW of Jefferson City.
Montana—Fergus, 12 miles west of Lewistown.
Nebraska—Custer, 10 miles NW of Broken Bow.
Nevada—Lander, 26 miles SE of Austin.
New Hampshire—Belknap, 3 miles E of Ashland.
New Jersey—Mercer, 5 miles SE of Trenton.
New Mexico—Torrance, 12 miles SSW of Willard.
New York—Madison, 12 miles S of Oneida and 26 miles SW of Utica.
North Carolina—Chatham, 10 miles NW of Sanford.
North Dakota—Sheridan, 5 miles SW of McClusky.
Ohio—Delaware, 25 miles NNE of Columbus.
Oklahoma—Oklahoma, 8 miles N of Oklahoma City.
Oregon—Crook, 25 miles SSE of Prineville.
Pennsylvania—Centre, 2.5 miles SW of Bellefonte.
Rhode Island—Kent, 1 mile SSW of Crompton.
South Carolina—Richland, 13 miles SE of Columbia.
South Dakota—Hughes, 8 miles NE of Pierre.
Tennessee—Rutherford, 5 mi. NE of Murfreesboro.
Texas—McCulloch, 15 miles NE of Brady.
Utah—Sanpete, 3 miles N of Manti.
Vermont—Washington, 3 miles E of Roxbury.
Virginia—Buckingham, 5 miles SW of Buckingham.
Washington—Chelan, 10 mi. WSW of Wenatchee.
West Virginia—Braxton, 4 miles E of Sutton.
Wisconsin—Wood, 9 miles SE of Marshfield.
Wyoming—Fremont, 58 miles ENE of Lander.

There is no generally accepted definition of geographic center, and no satisfactory method for determining it. The geographic center of an area may be defined as the center of gravity of the surface, or that point on which the surface of the area would balance if it were a plane of uniform thickness.

No marked or monumented point has been established by any government agency as the geographic center of either the 50 states, the contiguous United States, or the North American continent. A monument was erected in Lebanon, Kan., contiguous U.S. center, by a group of citizens.

International Boundary Lines of the U.S.

The length of the northern boundary of the contiguous U.S. — the U.S.-Canadian border, excluding Alaska — is 3,987 miles according to the U.S. Geological Survey, Dept. of the Interior. The length of the Alaskan-Canadian border is 1,538 miles. The length of the U.S.-Mexican border, from the Gulf of Mexico to the Pacific Ocean, is approximately 1,933 miles (1963 boundary agreement).

Origin of the Names of U.S. States

Source: State officials, the Smithsonian Institution, and the Topographic Division, U.S. Geological Survey.

Alabama—Indian for tribal town, later a tribe (Alabamas or Alibamons) of the Creek confederacy.

Alaska—Russian version of Aleutian (Eskimo) word, alakshak, for "peninsula," "great lands," or "land that is not an island."

Arizona—Spanish version of Pima Indian word for "little spring place," or Aztec arizuma, meaning "silver-bearing."

Arkansas—French variant of Kansas, a Sioux Indian name for "south wind people."

California—Bestowed by the Spanish conquistadors (possibly by Cortez). It was the name of an imaginary island, an earthly paradise, in "Las Serges de Esplandian," a Spanish romance written by Montalvo in 1510. Baja California (Lower California, in Mexico) was first visited by Spanish in 1533. The present U.S. state was called Alta (Upper) California.

Colorado—Spanish, red, first applied to Colorado River.

Connecticut—From Mohican and other Algonquin words meaning "long river place."

Delaware—Named for Lord De La Warr, early governor of Virginia; first applied to river, then to Indian tribe (Lenni-Lenape), and the state.

District of Columbia—For Columbus, 1791.

Florida—Named by Ponce de Leon on Pascua Florida, "Flowery Easter," on Easter Sunday, 1513.

Georgia—For King George II of England by James Oglethorpe, colonial administrator, 1732.

Hawaii—Possibly derived from native world for homeland, Hawaiki or Owhyhee.

Idaho—A coined name with an invented Indian meaning: "gem of the mountains;" originally suggested for the Pike's Peak mining territory (Colorado), then applied to the new mining territory of the Pacific Northwest. Another theory suggests Idaho may be a Kiowa Apache term for the Comanche.

Illinois—French for Illini or land of Illini, Algonquin word meaning men or warriors.

Indiana—Means "land of the Indians."

Iowa—Indian word variously translated as "one who puts to sleep" or "beautiful land."

Kansas—Sioux word for "south wind people."

Kentucky—Indian word variously translated as "dark and bloody ground," "meadow land" and "land of tomorrow."

Louisiana—Part of territory called Louisiana by Sieur de La Salle for French King Louis XIV.

Maine—From Maine, ancient French province. Also: descriptive, referring to the mainland as distinct from the many coastal islands.

Maryland—For Queen Henrietta Maria, wife of Charles I of England.

Massachusetts—From Indian tribe named after "large hill place" identified by Capt. John Smith as being near Milton, Mass.

Michigan—From Chippewa words mici gama meaning "great water," after the lake of the same name.

Minnesota—From Dakota Sioux word meaning "cloudy water" or "sky-tinted water" of the Minnesota River.

Mississippi—Probably Chippewa; mici zibi, "great river" or "gathering-in of all the waters." Also: Algonquin word, "Messipi."

Missouri—Algonquin Indian tribe named after Missouri River, meaning "muddy water."

Montana—Latin or Spanish for "mountainous."

Nebraska—From Omaha or Otos Indian word meaning "broad water" or "flat river," describing the Platte River.

Nevada—Spanish, meaning snow-clad.

New Hampshire—Named 1629 by Capt. John Mason of Plymouth Council for his home county in England.

New Jersey—The Duke of York, 1664, gave a patent to John Berkeley and Sir George Carteret to be called Nova Caesaria, or New Jersey, after England's Isle of Jersey.

New Mexico—Spaniards in Mexico applied term to land north and west of Rio Grande in the 16th century.

New York—For Duke of York and Albany who received patent to New Netherland from his brother Charles II and sent an expedition to capture it, 1664.

North Carolina—In 1619 Charles I gave a large patent to Sir Robert Heath to be called Province of Carolana, from Carolus, Latin name for Charles. A new patent was granted by Charles II to Earl of Clarendon and others. Divided into North and South Carolina, 1710.

North Dakota—Dakota is Sioux for friend or ally.

Ohio—Iroquois word for "fine or good river."

Oklahoma—Choctaw coined word meaning red man, proposed by Rev. Allen Wright, Choctaw-speaking Indian.

Oregon—Origin unknown. One theory holds that the name may have been derived from that of the Wisconsin River shown on a 1715 French map as "Ouaricon-sint."

Pennsylvania—William Penn, the Quaker, who was made full proprietor by King Charles II in 1681, suggested Sylvania, or woodland, for his tract. The king's government owed Penn's father, Admiral William Penn, £16,000, and the land was granted as partial settlement. Charles II added the Penn to Sylvania, against the desires of the modest proprietor, in honor of the admiral.

Puerto Rico—Spanish for Rich Port.

Rhode Island—Exact origin is unknown. One theory notes that Giovanni de Verrazano recorded an island about the size of Rhodes in the Mediterranean in 1524, but others believe the state was named Roode Eylandt by Adriaen Block, Dutch explorer, because of its red clay.

South Carolina—See North Carolina.

South Dakota—See North Dakota.

Tennessee—Tanasi was the name of Cherokee villages on the Little Tennessee River. From 1784 to 1788 this was the State of Franklin, or Frankland.

Texas—Variant of word used by Caddo and other Indians meaning friends or allies, and applied to them by the Spanish in eastern Texas. Also written texias, tejas, teysas.

Utah—From a Navajo word meaning upper, or higher up, as applied to a Shoshone tribe called Ute. Spanish form is Yutta, English Uta or Utah. Proposed name Deseret, "land of honeybees," from Book of Mormon, was rejected by Congress.

Vermont—From French words vert (green) and mont (mountain). The Green Mountains were said to have been named by Samuel de Champlain. The Green Mountain Boys were Gen. Stark's men in the Revolution. When the state was formed, 1777, Dr. Thomas Young suggested combining vert and mont into Vermont.

Virginia—Named by Sir Walter Raleigh, who fitted out the expedition of 1584, in honor of Queen Elizabeth, the Virgin Queen of England.

Washington—Named after George Washington. When the bill creating the Territory of Columbia was introduced in the 32d Congress, the name was changed to Washington because of the existence of the District of Columbia.

West Virginia—So named when western counties of Virginia refused to secede from the United States, 1863.

Wisconsin—An Indian name, spelled Ouisconsin and Mesconsing by early chroniclers. Believed to mean "grassy place" in Chippewa. Congress made it Wisconsin.

Wyoming—The word was taken from Wyoming Valley, Pa., which was the site of an Indian massacre and became widely known by Campbell's poem, "Gertrude of Wyoming." In Algonquin it means "large prairie place."

Accession of Territory by the U.S.

Source: Statistical Abstract of the United States

Division	Year	Sq. mi.[1]	Division	Year	Sq. mi.[1]	Division	Year	Sq. mi.[1]
Total U.S.	1970	3,630,854	Oregon	1846	285,580	American Samoa	1900	76
50 states & D.C.		3,618,467	Mexican Cession	1848	529,017	Corn Islands[4]	1914	4
Territory in 1790[2]		888,685	Gadsden Purchase	1853	29,640	Virgin Islands, U.S.	1917	133
Louisiana Purchase	1803	827,192	Alaska	1867	589,757	Trust Territory of		
By treaty with Spain:			Hawaii	1898	6,450	the Pacific Is.	1947	8,489
Florida	1819	58,560	The Philippines[3]	1898	115,600	All other[5]		42
Other areas	1819	13,443	Puerto Rico	1899	3,435			
Texas	1845	390,143	Guam	1899	212			

(1) Gross area (land and water). (2) Includes drainage basin of Red River on the north, south of 49th parallel, sometimes considered a part of the Louisiana Purchase. (3) Area not included in total; became Republic of the Philippines July 4, 1946. (4) Leased from Nicaragua for 99 years but returned Apr. 25, 1971; area not included in total. (5) See index for Outlying Areas, U.S.

Public Lands of the U. S.

Source: Bureau of Land Management, U.S. Interior Department

Acquisition of the Public Domain 1781-1867

Acquisition	Area* (acres) Land	Water	Total	Cost[1]
State Cessions (1781-1802)	233,415,680	3,409,920	236,825,600	*$6,200,000
Louisiana Purchase (1803)[2]	523,446,400	6,465,280	529,911,680	23,213,568
Red River Basin[4]	29,066,880	535,040	29,601,920	
Cession from Spain (1819)	43,342,720	2,801,920	46,144,640	6,674,057
Oregon Compromise (1846)	180,644,480	2,741,760	183,386,240	
Mexican Cession (1848)	334,479,360	4,201,600	338,680,960	16,295,149
Purchase from Texas (1850)	78,842,880	83,840	78,926,720	15,496,448
Gadsden Purchase (1853)	18,961,920	26,880	18,988,800	10,000,000
Alaska Purchase (1867)	362,516,480	12,787,200	375,303,680	7,200,000
Total	**1,804,716,800**	**33,053,440**	**1,837,770,240**	**$85,079,222**

*All areas except Alaska were computed in 1912, and have not been adjusted for the recomputation of the area of the United States which was made for the 1950 Decennial Census. (1) Cost data for all except "State Cessions" obtained from U.S. Geological Survey. (2) Paid by federal government for Georgia cession, 1802 (56,689,920 acres). (3) Excludes areas eliminated by Treaty of 1819 with Spain. (4) Basin of the Red River of the North, south of the 49th parallel.

Disposition of Public Lands 1781 to 1982

Disposition by methods not elsewhere classified[1]	Acres	Granted to states for:	Acres
	303,500,000	Support of common schools	77,630,000
Granted or sold to homesteaders	287,500,000	Reclamation of swampland	64,920,000
Granted to railroad corporations	94,400,000	Construction of railroads	37,130,000
Granted to veterans as military bounties.	61,000,000	Support of misc. institutions[6]	21,700,000
Confirmed as private land claims[2]	34,000,000	Purposes not elsewhere classified[7]	117,600,000
Sold under timber and stone law[3]	13,900,000	Canals and rivers	6,100,000
Granted or sold under timber culture law[4]	10,900,000	Construction of wagon roads	3,400,000
Sold under desert land law[5]	10,700,000	**Total granted to states**	**328,480,000**

(1) Chiefly public, private, and preemption sales, but includes mineral entries, script locations, sales of townsites and townlots. (2) The Government has confirmed title to lands claimed under valid grants made by foreign governments prior to the acquisition of the public domain by the United States. (3) The law provided for the sale of lands valuable for timber or stone and unfit for cultivation. (4) The law provided for the granting of public lands to settlers on condition that they plant and cultivate trees on the lands granted. (5) The law provided for the sale of arid agricultural public lands to settlers who irrigate them and bring them under cultivation. (6) Universities, hospitals, asylums, etc. (7) For construction of various public improvements (individual items not specified in the granting act) reclamation of desert lands, construction of water reservoirs, etc.

Public Lands Administered by Federal Agencies

Agency (Acres, March, 1, 1984)	Public domain	Acquired	Total
Bureau of Land Management	340,686,540.0	2,363,964.7	343,050,504.7
Forest Service	146,177,771.8	37,379,282.5	183,557,054.3
Fish and Wildlife Service	75,452,640.5	6,183,010.5	81,635,651.0
National Park Service	61,540,879.0	6,913,398.0	68,454,277.2
U.S. Army	5,983,176.0	4,637,086.0	10,620,262.0
U.S. Air Force	6,919,076.0	1,230,635.0	8,149,711.0
Corps of Engineers	661,400.9	7,563,554.4	8,224,955.3
U.S. Navy	1,785,608.6	998,593.9	2,784,202.5
Bureau of Reclamation	3,626,147.0	1,712,216.1	5,338,363.1
Bureau of Indian Affairs	2,945,506.0	383,370.2	3,328,876.2
Energy Research and Development Admin.	1,441,710.0	660,820.0	2,102,530.0
Other	768,472.0	1,506,758.4	2,275,230.4
Grand Total	**647,988,928.0**	**71,532,689.7**	**719,521,617.7**

National Parks, Other Areas Administered by Nat'l Park Service

Figures given are date area initially protected by Congress or presidential proclamation, date given current designation, and gross area in acres 12/31/83.

National Parks

Acadia, Me. (1916/1929) 39,625. Includes Mount Desert Island, half of Isle au Haut, Schoodic Point on mainland. Highest elevation on Eastern seaboard.

Arches, Ut. (1929/1978) 73,379. Contains giant red sandstone arches and other products of erosion.

Badlands, S.D. (1929/1978) 243,302; eroded prairie, bison, bighorn and antelope. Contains animal fossils of 40 million years ago.

Big Bend, Tex. (1935/1944) 741,118. Rio Grande, Chisos Mts.

Biscayne, Fla. (1968/1980) 172,845. Aquatic park encompasses chain of islands south of Miami.

Bryce Canyon, Ut. (1923/1928) 35,835. Spectacularly colorful and unusual display of erosion effects.

Canyonlands, Ut. (1964) 337,570. At junction of Colorado and Green rivers, extensive evidence of prehistoric Indians.

Capitol Reef, Ut. (1937/1971) 241,904. A 60-mile uplift of sandstone cliffs dissected by high-walled gorges.

Carlsbad Caverns, N.M. (1923/1930) 46,755. Largest known caverns; not yet fully explored.

Channel Islands, Cal. (1938/1980) 249,354. Seal lion breeding place, nesting sea birds, unique plants.

Crater Lake, Ore. (1902) 160,290. Extraordinary blue lake in crater of extinct volcano encircled by lava walls 500 to 2,000 feet high.

Denali, Alas. (1917/1980) 4,700,000. Name changed from Mt. McKinley NP. Contains highest mountain in U.S.; wildlife.

Everglades, Fla. (1934) 1,398,800. Largest remaining subtropical wilderness in continental U.S.

Gates of the Arctic, Alas. (1978/1980) 7,500,000. Vast wilderness in north central region.

Glacier, Mon. (1910) 1,013,595. Superb Rocky Mt. scenery, numerous glaciers and glacial lakes. Part of Waterton-Glacier Intl. Peace Park established by U.S. and Canada in 1932.

Glacier Bay, Alas. (1925/1980) 3,225,197. Great tidewater glaciers that move down mountain sides and break up into the sea; much wildlife.

Grand Canyon, Ariz. (1908/1919) 1,218,375. Most spectacular part of Colorado River's greatest canyon.

Grand Teton, Wy. (1929) 310,517. Most impressive part of the Teton Mountains, winter feeding ground of largest American elk herd.

Great Smoky Mountains, N.C.-Tenn. (1926) 520,269. Largest eastern mountain range, magnificent forests.

Guadalupe Mountains, Tex. (1966/1972) 76,293. Extensive Permian limestone fossil reef; tremendous earth fault.

Haleakala, Ha. (1916/1960) 28,655. Dormant volcano on Maui with large colorful craters.

Hawaii Volcanoes, Ha. (1916/1961) 229,177. Contains Kilauea and Mauna Loa, active volcanoes.

Hot Springs, Ark. (1832/1921) 5,824. Government supervised bath houses use waters of 45 of the 47 natural hot springs.

Isle Royale, Mich. (1931) 571,790. Largest island in Lake Superior, noted for its wilderness area and wildlife.

Katmai, Alas. (1918/1980) 3,716,000. Valley of Ten Thousand Smokes, scene of 1917 volcanic eruption.

Kenai Fjords, Alas. (1978/1980) 670,000. Abundant mountain goats, marine mammals, birdlife; the Harding Icefield, one of the major icecaps in U.S.

Kings Canyon, Cal. (1890/1940) 460,136. Mountain wilderness, dominated by Kings River Canyons and High Sierra; contains giant sequoias.

Kobuk Valley, Alas. (1978/1980) 1,750,000. Broad river is core of native culture.

Lake Clark, Alas. (1978/1980) 2,874,000. Across Cook Inlet from Anchorage. A scenic wilderness rich in fish and wildlife.

Lassen Volcanic, Cal. (1907/1916) 106,372. Contains Lassen Peak, recently active volcano, and other volcanic phenomena.

Mammoth Cave, Ky. (1926) 52,379. 144 miles of surveyed underground passages, beautiful natural formations, river 300 feet below surface.

Mesa Verde, Col. (1906) 52,085. Most notable and best preserved prehistoric cliff dwellings in the United States.

Mount Rainier, Wash. (1899) 235,404. Greatest single-peak glacial system in the lower 48 states.

North Cascades, Wash. (1968) 504,781. Spectacular mountainous region with many glaciers, lakes.

Olympic, Wash. (1909/1938) 914,579. Mountain wilderness containing finest remnant of Pacific Northwest rain forest, active glaciers, Pacific shoreline, rare elk.

Petrified Forest, Ariz. (1906/1962) 93,493. Extensive petrified wood and Indian artifacts. Contains part of Painted Desert.

Redwood, Cal. (1968) 110,131. Forty miles of Pacific coastline, groves of ancient redwoods and world's tallest trees.

Rocky Mountain, Col. (1915) 265,193. On the continental divide, includes 107 named peaks over 11,000 feet.

Sequoia, Cal. (1890) 402,488. Groves of giant sequoias, highest mountain in contiguous United States — Mount Whitney (14,494 feet). World's largest tree.

Shenandoah, Va. (1926/1935) 195,072. Portion of the Blue Ridge Mountains; overlooks Shenandoah Valley; Skyline Drive.

Theodore Roosevelt, N.D. (1947/1978) 70,416. Contains part of T.R.'s ranch and scenic badlands.

Virgin Islands, V.I. (1956) 14,696. Covers 75% of St. John Island, lush growth, lovely beaches, Indian relics, evidence of colonial Danes.

Voyageurs, Minn. (1971/1975) 217,892. Abundant lakes, forests, wildlife, canoeing, boating.

Wind Cave, S.D. (1903) 28,292. Limestone caverns in Black Hills. Extensive wildlife includes a herd of bison.

Wrangell-St. Elias, Alas. (1978/1980) 8,945,000. Largest area in park system, most peaks over 16,000 feet, abundant wildlife; day's drive east of Anchorage.

Yellowstone, Ida., Mon., Wy., (1872) 2,219,823. Oldest national park. World's greatest geyser area has about 3,000 geysers and hot springs; spectacular falls and impressive canyons of the Yellowstone River; grizzly bear, moose, and bison.

Yosemite, Cal. (1890) 760,917. Yosemite Valley, the nation's highest waterfall, 3 groves of sequoias, and mountainous.

Zion, Ut. (1909/1919) 146,551. Unusual shapes and landscapes have resulted from erosion and faulting; Zion Canyon, with sheer walls ranging up to 2,500 feet, is readily accessible.

National Historical Parks

Appomattox Court House, Va. (1930/1954) 1,325. Where Lee surrendered to Grant.

Boston, Mass. (1974) 41. Includes Faneuil Hall, Old North Church, Bunker Hill, Paul Revere House.

Chaco Culture, N.M. (1907/1980) 33,978. Ruins of pueblos built by prehistoric Indians.

Chesapeake and Ohio Canal, Md.-W.Va.-D.C. (1961/1971) 20,781. 185 mile historic canal; D.C. to Cumberland, Md.

Colonial, Va. (1930/1936) 9,315. Includes most of Jamestown Island, site of first successful English colony; Yorktown, site of Cornwallis' surrender to George Washington; and the Colonial Parkway.

Cumberland Gap, Ky.-Tenn.-Va. (1940) 20,351. Mountain pass of the Wilderness Road which carried the first great migration of pioneers into America's interior.

George Rogers Clark, Vincennes, Ind. (1966) 24. Commemorates American defeat of British in west during Revolution.

Harpers Ferry, Md., W. Va. (1944/1963) 2,238. At the confluence of the Shenandoah and Potomac rivers, the site of John Brown's 1859 raid on the Army arsenal.

Independence, Pa. (1948/1956) 45. Contains several properties in Philadelphia associated with the Revolutionary War and the founding of the U.S.

Jean Laffite (and preserve), La. (1939/1978) 20,0C0. Includes Chalmette, site of 1814 Battle of New Orleans; French Quarter.

Kalaupapa, Ha. (1980) 10,902. Molokai's former leper colony site and other historic areas.

Kaloko-Honokohau, Ha. (1978) 1,161. Culture center has 234 historic features and grave of first king, Kamehameha.

Klondike Gold Rush, Alas.-Wash. (1976) 13,272. Alaskan Trails in 1898 Gold Rush. Museum in Seattle.

Lowell, Mass. (1978) 137. Seven mills, canal, 19th C. structures, park to show planned city of Industrial Revolution.

Lyndon B. Johnson, Tex. (1969/1980) 1,478. President's birthplace, boyhood home, ranch.

Minute Man, Mass. (1959) 752. Where the colonial Minute Men battled the British, April 19, 1775. Also contains Nathaniel Hawthorne's home.

Morristown, N.J. (1933) 1,678. Sites of important military encampments during the Revolutionary War; Washington's headquarters 1777, 1779-80.

Nez Perce, Ida. (1965) 2,109. Illustrates the history and culture of the Nez Perce Indian country. 22 separate sites.

Pu'uhonua o Honaunau, Ha. (1955/1978) 182. Until 1819, a sanctuary for Hawaiians vanquished in battle, and those guilty of crimes or breaking taboos.

San Antonio Missions, Tex. (1978) 477. Four of finest Spanish missions in U.S., 18th C. irrigation system.

San Juan Island, Wash. (1966) 1,752. Commemorates peaceful relations of the U.S., Canada and Great Britain since the 1872 boundary disputes.

Saratoga, N.Y. (1938) 3,406. Scene of a major battle which became a turning point in the War of Independence.

Sitka, Alas. (1910/1972) 108. Scene of last major resistance of the Tlingit Indians to the Russians, 1804.

Valley Forge, Pa. (1976) 3,465. Continental Army campsite in 1777-78 winter.

War in the Pacific, Guam (1978) 1,926. Scenic park memorial for WWII combatants in Pacific.

Women's Rights, N.Y. (1980) 2.45. Seneca Falls site where Susan B. Anthony, Elizabeth Cady Stanton began rights movement in 1848.

National Battlefields

Antietam, Md. (1890) 3,246. Battle ended first Confederate invasion of North, Sept. 17, 1862.

Big Hole, Mon. (1910/1963) 656. Site of major battle with Nez Perce Indians.

Cowpens, S.C. (1929/1972) 841. Revolutionary War battlefield.

Fort Necessity, Pa. (1931/1961) 903. First battle of French and Indian War.

Monocacy, Md. (1934/1976) 1,659. Civil War battle in defense of Wash., D.C., July 9, 1864.

Moores Creek, N.C. (1926) 87. Pre-Revolutionary War battle.

Petersburg, Va. (1926/1962) 1,535. Scene of 10-month Union campaign 1864-65.

Stones River, Tenn. (1927/1960) 331. Civil War battle leading to Sherman's "March to the Sea."

Tupelo, Miss. (1929/1961) 1. Crucial battle over Sherman's supply line.

Wilson's Creek, Mo. (1960/1970) 1,750. Civil War battle for control of Missouri.

National Battlefield Parks

Kennesaw Mountain, Ga. (1917/1935) 2,884. Two major battles of Atlanta campaign in Civil War.

Manassas, Va. (1940) 4,513. Two battles of Bull Run in Civil War, 1861 and 1862.

Richmond, Va. (1936) 771. Site of battles defending Confederate capital.

National Battlefield Site

Brices Cross Roads, Miss. (1929) 1. Civil War battlefield.

National Military Parks

Chickamauga and Chattanooga, Ga.-Tenn. (1890) 8,103. Four Civil War battlefields.

Fort Donelson, Tenn. (1928) 537. Site of first major Union victory.

Fredericksburg and Spotsylvania County, Va. (1927) 5,909. Sites of several major Civil War battles and campaigns.

Gettysburg, Pa. (1895) 3,863. Site of decisive Confederate defeat in North. Gettysburg Address.

Guilford Courthouse, N.C. (1917) 220. Revolutionary War battle site.

Horseshoe Bend, Ala. (1956) 2,040. On Tallapoosa River, where Gen. Andrew Jackson broke the power of the Creek Indian Confederacy.

Kings Mountain, S.C. (1931) 3,945. Revolutionary War battle.

Pea Ridge, Ark. (1956) 4,300. Civil War battle.

Shiloh, Tenn. (1894) 3,838. Major Civil War battle; site includes some well-preserved Indian burial mounds.

Vicksburg, Miss. (1899) 1,741. Union victory gave North control of the Mississippi and split the Confederacy in two.

National Memorials

Arkansas Post, Ark. (1960) 389. First permanent French settlement in the lower Mississippi River valley.

Arlington House, the Robert E. Lee Memorial, Va. (1925/1972) 28. Lee's home overlooking the Potomac.

Chamizal, El Paso, Tex. (1964/1966) 55. Commemorates 1963 settlement of 99-year border dispute with Mexico.

Coronado, Ariz. (1941/1952) 4,977. Commemorates first European exploration of the Southwest.

DeSoto, Fla. (1948) 27. Commemorates 16th-century Spanish explorations.

Federal Hall, N.Y. (1939/1955) 0.45. First seat of U.S. government under the Constitution.

Fort Caroline, Fla. (1950) 138. On St. Johns River, overlooks site of second attempt by French Huguenots to colonize North America.

Fort Clatsop, Ore. (1958) 125. Lewis and Clark encampment 1805-06.

General Grant, N.Y. (1958) 0.76. Tombs of Pres. and wife.

Hamilton Grange, N.Y. (1962) 0.71. Home of Alexander Hamilton.

John F. Kennedy Center for the Performing Arts, D.C. (1958/1964) 18.

Johnstown Flood, Pa. (1964) 163. Commemorates tragic flood of 1889.

Lincoln Boyhood, Ind. (1962) 198. Lincoln grew up here.

Lincoln Memorial, D.C. (1911) 164.

Lyndon B. Johnson Grove on the Potomac, D.C. (1973) 17.

Mount Rushmore, S.D. (1925) 1,278. World famous sculpture of 4 presidents.

Roger Williams, R.I. (1965) 5. Memorial to founder of Rhode Island.

Thaddeus Kosciuszko, Pa. (1972) 0.02. Memorial to Polish hero of American Revolution.

Theodore Roosevelt Island, D.C. (1932) 89.

Thomas Jefferson Memorial, D.C. (1934) 18.

USS Arizona, Ha. (1980). Memorializes American losses at Pearl Harbor.

Washington Monument, D.C. (1848) 106.

Wright Brothers, N.C. (1927/1953) 431. Site of first powered flight.

Vietnam Veterans National Memorial, D.C. (1980) 2. Honors and recognizes the men and women of the armed forces who served in the Vietnam war.

National Historic Sites

Abraham Lincoln Birthplace, Hodgenville, Ky. (1916/1959) 117.

Adams, Quincy, Mass. (1946/1952) 12. Home of Presidents John Adams, John Quincy Adams, and celebrated descendants.

Allegheny Portage Railroad, Pa. (1964) 1,135. Part of the Pennsylvania Canal system.

Andersonville, Andersonville, Ga. (1970) 476. Noted Civil War prison.

Andrew Johnson, Greeneville, Tenn. (1935/1963) 17. Home of the President.

Bent's Old Fort, Col. (1960) 800. Old West fur-trading post.

Carl Sandburg Home, N.C. (1968/1972) 264. Poet's home.

Christiansted, St. Croix; V.I. (1952/1961) 27. Commemorates Danish colony.

Clara Barton, Md. (1974) 9. Home of founder of American Red Cross.

Edgar Allan Poe, Pa. (1978/1980) 1. Poet's home.

Edison, West Orange, N.J. (1955/1962) 21. Home and laboratory.

Eisenhower, Gettysburg, Pa. (1967/1969) 690. Home of 34th president.

Eleanor Roosevelt, Hyde Park, N.Y. (1977) 181.

Eugene O'Neill, Danville, Cal. (1976) 14. Playwright's home.

Ford's Theatre, Washington, D.C. (1866/1970) 0.29. Includes theater, now restored, where Lincoln was assassinated, house where he died, and Lincoln Museum.

Fort Bowie, Ariz. (1964/1972) 1,000. Focal point of operations against Geronimo and the Apaches.

Fort Davis, Tex. (1961) 460. Frontier outpost battled Comanches and Apaches.

Fort Laramie, Wy. (1938/1960) 832. Military post on Oregon Trail.

Fort Larned, Kan. (1964) 718. Military post on Santa Fe Trail.

Fort Point, San Francisco, Cal. (1970) 29. Largest West Coast fortification.

Fort Raleigh, N.C. (1941) 157. First English settlement.

Fort Scott, Kan. (1978) 17. Commemorates events of Civil War period.

Fort Smith, Ark. (1961) 73. Active post from 1817 to 1890.

Fort Union Trading Post, Mon., N.D. (1966) 436. Principal fur-trading post on upper Missouri, 1828-1867.

Fort Vancouver, Wash. (1948/1961) 209. Hdqts. for Hudson's Bay Company in 1825. Early military and political seat.

Frederick Law Olmsted, Mass. (1979) 2. Home of famous park planner (1822-1903).

Friendship Hill, Pa. (1978) 675. Home of Albert Gallatin, Jefferson's Sec'y of Treasury. Not open to public.

Georgia O'Keeffe, Abiquiu, N.M. (1980) 4. Artist's home.

Golden Spike, Utah (1957) 2,738. Commemorates completion of first transcontinental railroad in 1869.

Grant-Kohrs Ranch, Mon. (1972) 1,502. Ranch house and part of 19th century ranch.

Hampton, Md. (1948) 59. 18th-century Georgian mansion.

Harry S Truman, Mo. (1980/1982). 0.78. Home of Pres. Truman after 1919.

Herbert Hoover, West Branch, Ia. (1965) 187. Birthplace and boyhood home of 31st president.

Home of Franklin D. Roosevelt, Hyde Park, N.Y. (1944) 264. Birthplace, home and "Summer White House".

Hopewell Village, Pa. (1938) 848. 19th-century iron making village.

Hubbell Trading Post, Ariz. (1965) 160. Indian trading post.

James A. Garfield, Mentor, Oh. (1980) 8. President's home.

Jefferson National Expansion Memorial, St. Louis, Mo. (1935/1954) 91. Commemorates westward expansion.

John Fitzgerald Kennedy, Brookline, Mass. (1967) 0.09. Birthplace and childhood home of the President.

John Muir, Martinez, Cal. (1964) 9. Home of early conservationist and writer.

Knife River Indian Villages, N.D. (1974) 1,293. Remnants of 5 Hidatsa villages.

Lincoln Home, Springfield, Ill. (1971) 12. Lincoln's residence when he was elected President, 1860.

Longfellow, Cambridge, Mass. (1972) 2. Longfellow's home, 1837-82, and Washington's hq. during Boston Siege, 1775-76. No federal facilities.

Maggie L. Walker, Va. (1978) 1. Richmond home of black leader and 1903 founder of bank.

Martin Luther King, Jr., Atlanta, Ga. (1980) 23. Birthplace, grave.

Martin Van Buren, N.Y. (1974) 40. Lindenwald, home of 8th president, near Kinderhook.

Ninety Six, S.C. (1976) 989. Colonial trading village.

Palo Alto Battlefield, Tex. (1978) 50. One of 2 Mexican War battles fought in U.S.

Puukohola Heiau, Ha. (1972) 77. Ruins of temple built by King Kamehameha.

Sagamore Hill, Oyster Bay, N.Y. (1962) 78. Home of President Theodore Roosevelt from 1885 until his death in 1919.

Saint-Gaudens, Cornish, N.H. (1964/1977) 148. Home, studio and gardens of American sculptor Augustus Saint-Gaudens.

Salem Maritime, Mass. (1938) 9. Only port never seized from the patriots by the British. Major fishing and whaling port.

San Juan, P.R. (1949) 53. 16th-century Spanish fortifications.

Saugus Iron Works, Mass. (1968) 9. Reconstructed 17th-century colonial ironworks.

Sewall-Belmont House, D.C. (1974) 0.35. National Women's Party headquarters 1929-74.

Springfield Armory, Mass. (1974) 55. Small arms manufacturing center for nearly 200 years.

Theodore Roosevelt Birthplace, N.Y., N.Y. (1962) 0.11.

Theodore Roosevelt Inaugural, Buffalo, N.Y. (1966) 1. Wilcox House where he took oath of office, 1901.

Thomas Stone, Md. (1978) 328. Home of signer of Declaration, built in 1771. Not open to public.

Tuskegee Institute, Ala. (1974) 74. College founded by Booker T. Washington in 1881 for blacks, includes student-made brick buildings.

Vanderbilt Mansion, Hyde Park, N.Y. (1940) 212. Mansion of 19th-century financier.

Whitman Mission, Wash. (1936/1963) 98. Site where Dr. and Mrs. Marcus Whitman ministered to the Indians until slain by them in 1847.

William Howard Taft, Cincinnati, Oh. (1969) 4. Birthplace and early home of the 27th president.

National Monuments

Name	State	Year	Acreage
Agate Fossil Beds	Neb.	1965	3,055
Alibates Flint Quarries	N.M.-Tex.	1965	1,371
Aniakchak	Alas.	1978	139,500
Aztec Ruins	N.M.	1923	27
Bandelier	N.M.	1916	36,917
Black Canyon of the Gunnison	Col.	1933	13,672
Booker T. Washington	Va.	1956	224
Buck Island Reef	V.I.	1961	880
Cabrillo	Cal.	1913	144
Canyon de Chelly	Ariz.	1931	83,840
Cape Krusenstern	Alas.	1978	660,000

Name	State	Year	Acreage
Capulin Mountain	N.M.	1916	775
Casa Grande Ruins	Ariz.	1892	473
Castillo de San Marcos	Fla.	1924	20
Castle Clinton	N.Y.	1946	1
Cedar Breaks	Ut.	1933	6,155
Chiricahua	Ariz.	1924	11,135
Colorado	Col.	1911	20,454
Congaree Swamp	S.C.	1976	15,138
Craters of the Moon	Ida.	1924	53,545
Custer Battlefield	Mon.	1879	765
Death Valley	Cal.-Nev.	1933	2,067,628
Devils Postpile	Cal.	1911	798
Devils Tower	Wy.	1906	1,347
Dinosaur	Col.-Ut.	1915	211,272
Effigy Mounds	Ia.	1949	1,475
El Morro	N.M.	1906	1,279
Florissant Fossil Beds**	Col.	1969	5,998
Fort Frederica	Ga.	1936	214
Fort Jefferson	Fla.	1935	64,700
Fort Matanzas	Fla.	1924	299
Fort McHenry National Monument and Historic Shrine	Md.	1925	43
Fort Pulaski	Ga.	1924	5,623
Fort Stanwix	N.Y.	1935	16
Fort Sumter	S.C.	1948	67
Fort Union	N.M.	1954	721
Fossil Butte	Wy.	1972	8,198
G. Washington Birthplace	Va.	1930	538
George Washington Carver	Mo.	1943	210
Gila Cliff Dwellings	N.M.	1907	533
Grand Portage	Minn.	1951	710
Great Sand Dunes	Col.	1932	38,662
Hohokam Pima*	Ariz.	1972	1,690
Homestead Nat'l. Monument of America	Neb.	1936	195
Hovenweep	Col.-Ut.	1923	785
Jewel Cave	S.D.	1908	1,274
John Day Fossil Beds	Ore.	1974	14,012
Joshua Tree	Cal.	1936	559,960
Lava Beds	Cal.	1925	46,560
Lehman Caves	Nev.	1922	640
Montezuma Castle	Ariz.	1906	858
Mound City Group	Oh.	1923	218
Muir Woods	Cal.	1908	554
Natural Bridges	Ut.	1908	7,791
Navajo	Ariz.	1909	360
Ocmulgee	Ga.	1934	683
Oregon Caves	Ore.	1909	488
Organ Pipe Cactus	Ariz.	1937	330,689
Pecos	N.M.	1965	365
Pinnacles	Cal.	1908	16,222
Pipe Spring	Ariz.	1923	40
Pipestone	Minn.	1937	282
Rainbow Bridge	Ut.	1910	160
Russell Cave	Ala.	1961	310
Saguaro	Ariz.	1933	83,574
Saint Croix Island**	Me.	1949	35
Salinas	N.M.	1909	1,080
Scotts Bluff	Neb.	1919	2,997
Statue of Liberty	N.J.-N.Y.	1924	58
Sunset Crater	Ariz.	1930	3,040
Timpanogos Cave	Ut.	1922	250
Tonto	Ariz.	1907	1,120
Tumacacori	Ariz.	1908	17
Tuzigoot	Ariz.	1939	809
Walnut Canyon	Ariz.	1915	2,249
White Sands	N.M.	1933	144,458
Wupatki	Ariz.	1924	35,253
Yucca House*	Col.	1919	10

National Preserves

Name	State	Year	Acreage
Aniakchak	Alas.	1978	475,500
Bering Land Bridge	Alas.	1978	2,700,000
Big Cypress	Fla.	1974	570,000
Big Thicket	Tex.	1974	85,842
Denali	Alas.	1917	1,330,000
Gates of the Arctic	Alas.	1978	940,000
Glacier Bay	Alas.	1925	55,000
Katmai	Alas.	1918	374,000
Lake Clark	Alas.	1978	1,171,000
Noatak	Alas.	1978	6,560,000
Wrangell-St. Elias	Alas.	1978	4,255,000
Yukon-Charley Rivers	Alas.	1978	2,520,000

National Seashores

Name	State	Year	Acreage
Assateague Island	Md.-Va.	1965	39,631
Canaveral	Fla.	1975	57,627
Cape Cod	Mass.	1961	44,596
Cape Hatteras	N.C.	1937	30,319
Cape Lookout**	N.C.	1966	28,415
Cumberland Island	Ga.	1972	36,978
Fire Island	N.Y.	1964	19,579
Gulf Islands	Fla.-Miss.	1971	139,775
Padre Island	Tex.	1962	130,697
Point Reyes	Cal.	1962	71,000

National Parkways

Name	State	Year	Acreage
Blue Ridge	Va.-N.C.	1936	82,329
George Washington Memorial	Va.-Md.	1930	7,142
John D. Rockefeller Jr. Mem.	Wy.	1972	23,777
Natchez Trace	Ala.-Miss.-Tenn.	1938	50,189

National Lakeshores

Name	State	Year	Acreage
Apostle Islands	Wis.	1970	67,885
Indiana Dunes	Ind.	1966	12,535
Pictured Rocks	Mich.	1966	72,899
Sleeping Bear Dunes	Mich.	1970	70,983

National Rivers

Name	State	Year	Acreage
Alagnak Wild River	Alas.	1980	25,000
Big South Fork	Ky.-Tenn.	1976	122,960
Buffalo	Ark.	1972	94,146
New River Gorge	W.Va.	1978	62,024

National Scenic Rivers and Riverways

Name	State	Year	Acreage
Delaware	N.Y.-N.J.-Pa.	1978	1,973
Lower Saint Croix	Minn.-Wis.	1972	9,365
Obed Wild	Tenn.	1976	5,250
Ozark	Mo.	1964	80,698
Rio Grande	Tex.	1978	9,600
Saint Croix	Minn.-Wis.	1968	64,150
Upper Delaware	N.Y.-N.J.	1978	75,000

Parks (no other classification)

Name	State	Year	Acreage
Catoctin Mountain	Md.	1954	5,769
Fort Benton	Mon.	1976	
Fort Washington	Md.	1930	341
Frederick Douglass Home	D.C.	1962	8
Greenbelt	Md.	1950	1,176
Perry's Victory	Oh.	1936	25
Piscataway	Md.	1961	4,251
Prince William Forest	Va.	1948	18,572
Rock Creek	D.C.	1890	1,754
Wolf Trap Farm Park for the Performing Arts	Va.	1966	130

National Recreation Areas

Name	State	Year	Acreage
Amistad	Tex.	1965	57,272
Bighorn Canyon	Mon.-Wy.	1966	120,278
Chattahoochee R.	Ga.	1978	8,699
Chickasaw	Okla.	1902	9,500
Coulee Dam	Wash.	1946	100,059
Curecanti	Col.	1965	42,114
Cuyahoga Valley	Oh.	1974	32,460
Delaware Water Gap	N.J.-Pa.	1965	66,705
Gateway	N.Y.-N.J.	1972	26,172
Glen Canyon	Ariz.-Ut.	1958	1,236,880
Golden Gate	Cal.	1972	72,815
Lake Chelan	Wash.	1968	61,891
Lake Mead	Ariz.-Nev.	1936	1,496,601
Lake Meredith	Tex.	1965	44,978
Ross Lake	Wash.	1968	117,574
Santa Monica Mts.	Cal.	1978	150,000
Whiskeytown	Cal.	1965	42,503

National Mall

Name	State	Year	Acreage
	D.C.	1933	146

National Scenic Trail

Name	State	Year	Acreage
Appalachian	Me. to Ga.	1968	101,450

*Not open to the public **No federal facilities

National Recreation Areas Administered by Forest Service

Name	State	Year	Acreage	Name	State	Year	Acreage
Arapaho	Col.	1978	35,697	Rattlesnake	Mon.	1980	61,000
Flaming Gorge	Ut.-Wyo.	1968	96,413	Sawtooth	Ida.	1972	754,999
Hell's Canyon	Ida.-Ore.	1975	392,308	Whiskeytown Shasta-Trinity	Cal.	1965	203,587
Mount Rogers	Va.	1966	154,770	Spruce Knob-Seneca Rocks	W. Va.	1965	100,000
Oregon Dunes	Ore.	1972	32,348				

The Homestead Act; Sale of Public Land

On October 21, 1976 Congress repealed the Homestead Act of 1862 for all states except Alaska. The Homestead Act is scheduled to expire in Alaska in 1986.

The Homestead Act was repealed because there was no longer any land in the public domain suitable for cultivation. The law had been in effect for 114 years. During that time it had exerted a profound influence on the settlement of the west. Under the authority of the Homestead Act more than 1.6 million settlers claimed more than 270 million acres of public lands. The influx of settlers into the west made such states as Oklahoma, Kansas, Nebraska, and North and South Dakota a reality and brought substantial numbers of settlers into many other western states.

Federal Indian Reservations[1]

Source: Bureau of Indian Affairs, U.S. Interior Department (data as of 1983)

State	No. of reser.	Tribally-owned acreage[2]	Allotted acreage[2]	No. of tribes[3]	No. of persons[4]	Avg. (%) unemp. rate[5]	Major tribes and/or natives
Alaska	1[6]	86,759	361,523	6	64,970	52	Aleut, Eskimo, Athapascan[7], Haida, Tlingit, Tsimpshian
Arizona	20	19,555,035	252,474	13	154,818	46	Navajo, Apache, Papago, Hopi, Yavapai, Pima
California	78	500,285	68,556	— [8]	23,625	53	Hoopa, Paiute, Yurok, Karok, Mission Bands
Colorado.	2	752,461	3,623	1	2,661	57	Ute
Florida	3	79,014	—	1	1,921	29	Seminole, Miccosukee[9]
Idaho.	4	461,543	332,240		7,108	48	Shoshone, Bannock, Nez Perce
Iowa	1	4,164	—		662	67	Sac and Fox[10]
Kansas.	4	5,768	22,522		2,243	17	Potawatomi, Kickapoo, Iowa
Louisiana	2	416	—		717	23	Chitimacha, Coushatta
Maine	3	245,424	—		2,261	33	Passamaquoddy, Penobscot, Maliseet
Michigan.	5	12,085	9,186		5,829	52	Chippewa, Potawatomi, Ottawa
Minnesota	14	713,076	50,914		18,260	61	Chippewa, Sioux
Mississippi. . . .	1	17,635	19		4,487	20	Choctaw
Montana.	7	2,220,383	3,016,409		27,529	40	Blackfeet, Crow, Sioux, Assiniboine, Cheyenne
Nebraska	3	22,656	42,339		4,404	60	Omaha, Winnebago, Santee Sioux
Nevada	23	1,138,462	79,567		8,259	48	Paiute, Shoshone, Washoe
New Mexico. . .	24	6,483,483	675,986		105,973	34	Zuni, Apache, Navajo
New York	6	—	—		11,167	50	Seneca, Mohawk, Onondaga, Oneida[11]
North Carolina .	1	56,461	—		5,971	38	Cherokee
North Dakota . .	5	207,820	643,959		21,552	53	Sioux, Chippewa, Mandan, Arikara, Hidatsa
Oklahoma	— [12]	86,684	1,127,751		159,852	14	Cherokee, Creek, Choctaw, Chickasaw, Osage, Cheyenne, Arapahoe, Kiowa, Comanche
Oregon	5	617,797	139,045		4,301	38	Warm Springs, Wasco, Paiute, Umatilla, Siletz
S. Dakota	9	2,621,228	2,473,118		46,101	55	Sioux
Utah	6	2,251,749	33,647		7,140	39	Ute, Goshute, Southern Paiute
Washington . . .	26	2,014,238	481,545		39,726	55	Yakima, Lummi, Quinault
Wisconsin . . .	15	328,886	80,795		18,279	47	Chippewa, Oneida, Winnebago
Wyoming	1	1,792,166	94,536		5,385	61	Shoshone, Arapahoe

(1) As of 1983 the federal government recognized and acknowledged that it had a special relationship with, and a trust responsibility for, 487 Federally recognized Indian entities in the U.S., including Alaska. The term "Indian entities" encompasses Indian tribes, bands, villages, groups, pueblos, Eskimos, and Aleuts, eligible for federal services and classified in the following 3 categories: (a) Officially approved Indian organizations pursuant to federal statutory authority (Indian Reorganization Act; Oklahoma Indian Welfare Act and Alaska Native Act.) (b) Officially approved Indian organizations outside of specified federal statutory authority. (c) Traditional Indian organizations recognized without formal federal approval of organizational structure.

(2) The acreages refer only to Indian lands which are either owned by the tribes or individual Indians, and held in trust by the U.S. government.

(3) "Tribe" among the North American Indians originally meant a body of persons bound together by blood ties who were socially, politically, and religiously organized, and who lived together, occupying a definite territory and having a common language or dialect. With the relegation of Indians to reservations, the word "tribe" developed a number of different meanings. Today, it can be a distinct group within an Indian village or community, the entire community, a large number of communities, several different groups or villages speaking different languages but sharing a common government, or a widely scattered number of villages with a common language but no common government.

(4) Number of Indians living on or adjacent to federally recognized reservations comprising the BIA service population.

(5) Unemployment rate of Indian work force consisting of all those 16 years old and over who are able and actively seeking work.

(6) Alaskan Indian Affairs are carried out under the Alaska Native Claims Settlement Act (Dec. 18, 1971). The Act provided for the establishment of regional and village corporations to conduct business for profit and non-profit purposes. There are 13 such regional corporations, each one with organized village corporations. The Metlakatla Reservation remains the only federally recognized reservation in Alaska in the sense of specific reservation boundaries, trust lands, etc.

(7) Aleuts and Eskimos are racially and linguistically related. Athapascans are related to the Navaho and Apache Indians.

(8) Some 62 distinct tribes are known to have lived in or wandered through what is now California at some time in the past. Many of these were village groups and are historically associated with bands which settled near Spanish missions where much of the traditional culture was destroyed. Many of these bands, however, still retain some of their Indian language and customs. Excluding the 30 mission bands, who are primarily of the Cahuilla, Diegueno, or Luiseno, there are some 22 tribes represented on the California reservations.

(9) "Seminole" means "runaways" and these Indians from various tribes were originally refugees from whites in the Carolinas and Georgia. Later joined by runaway slaves, the Seminole were united by their hostility to the United States. Formal peace with the Seminoles in Florida was not achieved until 1934. The Miccosukee are a branch of the Seminole; they retain their Indian religion and have not made formal peace with the United States.

(10) Once two tribes, the Sac and Fox formed a political alliance in 1734.

(11) These 4 tribes along with the Cayuga and Tuscarora made up the Iroquois League, which ruled large portions of New York, New England and Pennsylvania and ranged into the Midwest and South. The Onondaga, who traditionally provide the president of the league, maintain that they are a foreign nation within New York and the United States.

(12) Indian land status in Oklahoma is unique and there are no reservations in the sense that the term is used elsewhere in the U.S. Likewise, many of the Oklahoma tribes are unique in their high degree of assimilation to the white culture.

Declaration of Independence

The Declaration of Independence was adopted by the Continental Congress in Philadelphia, on July 4, 1776. John Hancock was president of the Congress and Charles Thomson was secretary. A copy of the Declaration, engrossed on parchment, was signed by members of Congress on and after Aug. 2, 1776. On Jan. 18, 1777, Congress ordered that "an authenticated copy, with the names of the members of Congress subscribing the same, be sent to each of the United States, and that they be desired to have the same put upon record." Authenticated copies were printed in broadside form in Baltimore, where the Continental Congress was then in session. The following text is that of the original printed by John Dunlap at Philadelphia for the Continental Congress.

IN CONGRESS, July 4, 1776.

A DECLARATION

By the REPRESENTATIVES of the

UNITED STATES OF AMERICA,

In GENERAL CONGRESS assembled

When in the Course of human Events, it becomes necessary for one People to dissolve the Political Bands which have connected them with another, and to assume among the Powers of the Earth, the separate and equal Station to which the Laws of Nature and of Nature's God entitle them, a decent Respect to the Opinions of Mankind requires that they should declare the causes which impel them to the Separation.

We hold these Truths to be self-evident, that all Men are created equal, that they are endowed by their Creator with certain unalienable Rights, that among these are Life, Liberty, and the Pursuit of Happiness—That to secure these Rights, Governments are instituted among Men, deriving their just Powers from the Consent of the Governed, that whenever any Form of Government becomes destructive of these Ends, it is the Right of the People to alter or to abolish it, and to institute new Government, laying its Foundation on such Principles, and organizing its Powers in such Form, as to them shall seem most likely to effect their Safety and Happiness. Prudence, indeed, will dictate that Governments long established should not be changed for light and transient Causes; and accordingly all Experience hath shewn, that Mankind are more disposed to suffer, while Evils are sufferable, than to right themselves by abolishing the Forms to which they are accustomed. But when a long Train of Abuses and Usurpations, pursuing invariably the same Object, evinces a Design to reduce them under absolute Despotism, it is their Right, it is their Duty, to throw off such Government, and to provide new Guards for their future Security. Such has been the patient Sufferance of these Colonies; and such is now the Necessity which constrains them to alter their former Systems of Government. The History of the present King of Great-Britain is a History of repeated Injuries and Usurpations, all having in direct Object the Establishment of an absolute Tyranny over these States. To prove this, let Facts be submitted to a candid World.

He has refused his Assent to Laws, the most wholesome and necessary for the public Good.

He has forbidden his Governors to pass Laws of immediate and pressing Importance, unless suspended in their Operation till his Assent should be obtained; and when so suspended, he has utterly neglected to attend to them.

He has refused to pass other Laws for the Accommodation of large Districts of People, unless those People would relinquish the Right of Representation in the Legislature, a Right inestimable to them, and formidable to Tyrants only.

He has called together Legislative Bodies at Places unusual, uncomfortable, and distant from the Depository of their Public Records, for the sole Purpose of fatiguing them into Compliance with his Measures.

He has dissolved Representative Houses repeatedly, for opposing with manly Firmness his Invasions on the Rights of the People.

He has refused for a long Time, after such Dissolutions, to cause others to be elected; whereby the Legislative Powers, incapable of Annihilation, have returned to the People at large for their exercise; the State remaining in the mean time exposed to all the Dangers of Invasion from without, and Convulsions within.

He has endeavoured to prevent the Population of these States; for that Purpose obstructing the Laws for Naturalization of Foreigners; refusing to pass others to encourage their Migrations hither, and raising the Conditions of new Appropriations of Lands.

He has obstructed the Administration of Justice, by refusing his Assent to Laws for establishing Judiciary Powers.

He has made Judges dependent on his Will alone, for the Tenure of their Offices, and the Amount and payment of their Salaries.

He has erected a Multitude of new Offices, and sent hither Swarms of Officers to harrass our People, and eat out their Substance.

He has kept among us, in Times of Peace, Standing Armies, without the consent of our Legislatures.

He has affected to render the Military independent of, and superior to the Civil Power.

He has combined with others to subject us to a Jurisdiction foreign to our Constitution, and unacknowledged by our Laws; giving his Assent to their Acts of pretended Legislation:

For quartering large Bodies of Armed Troops among us:

For protecting them, by a mock Trial, from Punishment for any Murders which they should commit on the Inhabitants of these States:

For cutting off our Trade with all Parts of the World:

For imposing Taxes on us without our Consent:

For depriving us, in many Cases, of the Benefits of Trial by Jury:

For transporting us beyond Seas to be tried for pretended Offences:

For abolishing the free System of English Laws in a neighbouring Province, establishing therein an arbitrary Government, and enlarging its Boundaries, so as to render it at once an Example and fit Instrument for introducing the same absolute Rule into these Colonies:

For taking away our Charters, abolishing our most valuable Laws, and altering fundamentally the Forms of our Governments:

For suspending our own Legislatures, and declaring themselves invested with Power to legislate for us in all Cases whatsoever.

He has abdicated Government here, by declaring us out of his Protection and waging War against us.

He has plundered our Seas, ravaged our Coasts, burnt our towns, and destroyed the Lives of our People.

He is, at this Time, transporting large Armies of foreign Mercenaries to compleat the works of Death, Desolation, and Tyranny, already begun with circumstances of Cruelty and Perfidy, scarcely paralleled in the most barbarous Ages, and totally unworthy the Head of a civilized Nation.

He has constrained our fellow Citizens taken Captive on the high Seas to bear Arms against their Country, to become the Executioners of their Friends and Brethren, or to fall themselves by their Hands.

He has excited domestic Insurrections amongst us, and has endeavoured to bring on the Inhabitants of our Frontiers, the merciless Indian Savages, whose known Rule of Warfare, is an undistinguished Destruction, of all Ages, Sexes and Conditions.

In every stage of these Oppressions we have Petitioned for Redress in the most humble Terms: Our repeated Petitions have been answered only by repeated Injury. A Prince, whose Character is thus marked by every act which may define a Tyrant, is unfit to be the Ruler of a free People.

Nor have we been wanting in Attentions to our British Brethren. We have warned them from Time to Time of Attempts by their Legislature to extend an unwarrantable Jurisdiction over us. We have reminded them of the Circumstances of our Emigration and Settlement here. We have appealed to their native Justice and Magnanimity, and we have conjured them by the Ties of our common Kindred to disavow these Usurpations, which, would inevitably interrupt our Connections and Correspondence. They too have been deaf to the Voice of Justice and of Consanguinity. We must, therefore, acquiesce in the Necessity, which denounces our Separation, and hold them, as we hold the rest of Mankind, Enemies in War, in Peace, Friends.

We, therefore, the Representatives of the UNITED STATES OF AMERICA, in General Congress, Assembled, appealing to the Supreme Judge of the World for the Rectitude of our Intentions, do, in the Name, and by Authority of the good People of these Colonies, solemnly Publish and Declare, That these United Colonies are, and of Right ought to be, Free and Independent States; that they are absolved from all Allegiance to the British Crown, and that all political Connection between them and the State of Great-Britain, is and ought to be totally dissolved; and that as Free and Independent States, they have full Power to levy War, conclude Peace, contract Alliances, establish Commerce, and to do all other Acts and Things which Independent States may of right do. And for the support of this declaration, with a firm Reliance on the Protection of divine Providence, we mutually pledge to each other our lives, our Fortunes, and our sacred Honor.

JOHN HANCOCK, President

Attest.
CHARLES THOMSON, Secretary.

Signers of the Declaration of Independence

Delegate and state	Vocation	Birthplace	Born	Died
Adams, John (Mass.)	Lawyer	Braintree (Quincy), Mass.	Oct. 30, 1735	July 4, 1826
Adams, Samuel (Mass.)	Political leader	Boston, Mass.	Sept. 27, 1722	Oct. 2, 1803
Bartlett, Josiah (N.H.)	Physician, judge	Amesbury, Mass.	Nov. 21, 1729	May 19, 1795
Braxton, Carter (Va.)	Farmer	Newington Plantation, Va.	Sept. 10, 1736	Oct. 10, 1797
Carroll, Chas. of Carrollton (Md.)	Lawyer	Annapolis, Md.	Sept. 19, 1737	Nov. 14, 1832
Chase, Samuel (Md.)	Judge	Princess Anne, Md.	Apr. 17, 1741	June 19, 1811
Clark, Abraham (N.J.)	Surveyor	Roselle, N.J.	Feb. 15, 1726	Sept. 15, 1794
Clymer, George (Pa.)	Merchant	Philadelphia, Pa.	Mar. 16, 1739	Jan. 23, 1813
Ellery, William (R.I.)	Lawyer	Newport, R.I.	Dec. 22, 1727	Feb. 15, 1820
Floyd, William (N.Y.)	Soldier	Brookhaven, N.Y.	Dec. 17, 1734	Aug. 4, 1821
Franklin, Benjamin (Pa.)	Printer, publisher.	Boston, Mass.	Jan. 17, 1706	Apr. 17, 1790
Gerry, Elbridge (Mass.)	Merchant	Marblehead, Mass.	July 17, 1744	Nov. 23, 1814
Gwinnett, Button (Ga.)	Merchant	Down Hatherly, England.	c. 1735	May 19, 1777
Hall, Lyman (Ga.)	Physician	Wallingford, Conn.	Apr. 12, 1724	Oct. 19, 1790
Hancock, John (Mass.)	Merchant	Braintree (Quincy), Mass.	Jan. 12, 1737	Oct. 8, 1793
Harrison, Benjamin (Va.)	Farmer	Berkeley, Va.	Apr. 5, 1726	Apr. 24, 1791
Hart, John (N.J.)	Farmer	Stonington, Conn.	c. 1711	May 11, 1779
Hewes, Joseph (N.C.)	Merchant	Princeton, N.J.	Jan. 23, 1730	Nov. 10, 1779
Heyward, Thos. Jr. (S.C.)	Lawyer, farmer.	St. Luke's Parish, S.C.	July 28, 1746	Mar. 6, 1809
Hooper, William (N.C.)	Lawyer	Boston, Mass.	June 28, 1742	Oct. 14, 1790
Hopkins, Stephen (R.I.)	Judge, educator	Providence, R.I.	Mar. 7, 1707	July 13, 1785
Hopkinson, Francis (N.J.)	Judge, author.	Philadelphia, Pa.	Sept. 21, 1737	May 9, 1791
Huntington, Samuel (Conn.)	Judge	Windham County, Conn.	July 3, 1731	Jan. 5, 1796
Jefferson, Thomas (Va.)	Lawyer	Shadwell, Va.	Apr. 13, 1743	July 4, 1826
Lee, Francis Lightfoot (Va.)	Farmer	Westmoreland County, Va.	Oct. 14, 1734	Jan. 11, 1797
Lee, Richard Henry (Va.)	Farmer	Westmoreland County, Va.	Jan. 20, 1732	June 19, 1794
Lewis, Francis (N.Y.)	Merchant	Llandaff, Wales	Mar., 1713	Dec. 31, 1802
Livingston, Philip (N.Y.)	Merchant	Albany, N.Y.	Jan. 15, 1716	June 12, 1778
Lynch, Thomas Jr. (S.C.)	Farmer	Winyah, S.C.	Aug. 5, 1749	(at sea) 1779
McKean, Thomas (Del.)	Lawyer	New London, Pa.	Mar. 19, 1734	June 24, 1817
Middleton, Arthur (S.C.)	Farmer	Charleston, S.C.	June 26, 1742	Jan. 1, 1787
Morris, Lewis (N.Y.)	Farmer	Morrisania (Bronx County), N.Y.	Apr. 8, 1726	Jan. 22, 1798
Morris, Robert (Pa.)	Merchant	Liverpool, England	Jan. 20, 1734	May 9, 1806
Morton, John (Pa.)	Judge	Ridley, Pa.	1724	Apr., 1777
Nelson, Thos. Jr. (Va.)	Farmer	Yorktown, Va.	Dec. 26, 1738	Jan. 4, 1789
Paca, William (Md.)	Judge	Abingdon, Md.	Oct. 31, 1740	Oct. 23, 1799
Paine, Robert Treat (Mass.)	Judge	Boston, Mass.	Mar. 11, 1731	May 12, 1814
Penn, John (N.C.)	Lawyer	Near Port Royal, Va.	May 17, 1741	Sept. 14, 1788
Read, George (Del.)	Judge	Near North East, Md.	Sept. 18, 1733	Sept. 21, 1798
Rodney, Caesar (Del.)	Judge	Dover, Del.	Oct. 7, 1728	June 29, 1784
Ross, George (Pa.)	Judge	New Castle, Del.	May 10, 1730	July 14, 1779
Rush, Benjamin (Pa.)	Physician	Byberry, Pa. (Philadelphia)	Dec. 24, 1745	Apr. 19, 1813
Rutledge, Edward (S.C.)	Lawyer	Charleston, S.C.	Nov. 23, 1749	Jan. 23, 1800
Sherman, Roger (Conn.)	Lawyer	Newton, Mass.	Apr. 19, 1721	July 23, 1793
Smith, James (Pa.)	Lawyer	Dublin, Ireland	c. 1719	July 11, 1806
Stockton, Richard (N.J.)	Lawyer	Near Princeton, N.J.	Oct. 1, 1730	Feb. 28, 1781
Stone, Thomas (Md.)	Lawyer	Charles County, Md.	1743	Oct. 5, 1787
Taylor, George (Pa.)	Ironmaster	Ireland.	1716	Feb. 23, 1781
Thornton, Matthew (N.H.)	Physician	Ireland.	1714	June 24, 1803
Walton, George (Ga.)	Judge	Prince Edward County, Va.	1741	Feb. 2, 1804
Whipple, William (N.H.)	Merchant, judge.	Kittery, Me.	Jan. 14, 1730	Nov. 28, 1785
Williams, William (Conn.)	Merchant	Lebanon, Conn.	Apr. 23, 1731	Aug. 2, 1811
Wilson, James (Pa.)	Judge	Carskerdo, Scotland	Sept. 14, 1742	Aug. 28, 1798
Witherspoon, John (N.J.)	Educator	Gifford, Scotland	Feb. 5, 1723	Nov. 15, 1794
Wolcott, Oliver (Conn.)	Judge	Windsor, Conn.	Dec. 1, 1726	Dec. 1, 1797
Wythe, George (Va.)	Lawyer	Elizabeth City Co. (Hampton), Va.	1726	June 8, 1806

Constitution of the United States
The Original 7 Articles

PREAMBLE

We, the people of the United States, in order to form a more perfect Union, establish justice, insure domestic tranquility, provide for the common defense, promote the general welfare, and secure the blessings of liberty to ourselves and our posterity do ordain and establish this Constitution for the United States of America.

ARTICLE I.

Section 1—Legislative powers; in whom vested:

All legislative powers herein granted shall be vested in a Congress of the United States, which shall consist of a Senate and House of Representatives.

Section 2—House of Representatives, how and by whom chosen. Qualifications of a Representative. Representatives and direct taxes, how apportioned. Enumeration. Vacancies to be filled. Power of choosing officers, and of impeachment.

1. The House of Representatives shall be composed of members chosen every second year by the people of the several States, and the electors in each State shall have the qualifications requisite for electors of the most numerous branch of the State Legislature.

2. No person shall be a Representative who shall not have attained to the age of twenty-five years, and been seven years a citizen of the United States, and who shall not, when elected, be an inhabitant of that State in which he shall be chosen.

3. *(Representatives and direct taxes shall be apportioned among the several States which may be included within this Union, according to their respective numbers, which shall be determined by adding to the whole number of free persons, including those bound to service for a term of years, and excluding Indians not taxed, three-fifths of all other persons.) (The previous sentence was superseded by Amendment XIV, section 2.)* The actual enumeration shall be made within three years after the first meeting of the Congress of the United States, and within every subsequent term of ten years, in such manner as they shall by law direct. The number of Representatives shall not exceed one for every thirty thousand, but each State shall have at least one Representative; and until such enumeration shall be made, the State of New Hampshire shall be entitled to choose three, Massachusetts eight, Rhode Island and Providence Plantations one, Connecticut five, New York six, New Jersey four, Pennsylvania eight, Delaware one, Maryland six, Virginia ten, North Carolina five, South Carolina five, and Georgia three.

4. When vacancies happen in the representation from any State, the Executive Authority thereof shall issue writs of election to fill such vacancies.

5. The House of Representatives shall choose their Speaker and other officers; and shall have the sole power of impeachment.

Section 3—Senators, how and by whom chosen. How classified. Qualifications of a Senator. President of the Senate, his right to vote. President pro tem., and other officers of the Senate, how chosen. Power to try impeachments. When President is tried, Chief Justice to preside. Sentence.

1. The Senate of the United States shall be composed of two Senators from each State, *(chosen by the Legislature thereof), (The preceding five words were superseded by Amendment XVII, section 1.)* for six years; and each Senator shall have one vote.

2. Immediately after they shall be assembled in consequence of the first election, they shall be divided as equally as may be into three classes. The seats of the Senators of the first class shall be vacated at the expiration of the second year, of the second class at the expiration of the fourth year, and of the third class at the expiration of the sixth year, so that one-third may be chosen every second year; *(and if vacancies happen by resignation, or otherwise, during the recess of the Legislature of any State, the Executive thereof may make temporary appointments until the next meeting of the Legislature, which shall then fill such vacancies.) (The words*

in parentheses were superseded by Amendment XVII, section 2.)

3. No person shall be a Senator who shall not have attained to the age of thirty years, and been nine years a citizen of the United States, and who shall not, when elected, be an inhabitant of that State for which he shall be chosen.

4. The Vice President of the United States shall be President of the Senate, but shall have no vote, unless they be equally divided.

5. The Senate shall choose their other officers, and also a President pro tempore, in the absence of the Vice President, or when he shall exercise the office of President of the United States.

6. The Senate shall have the sole power to try all impeachments. When sitting for that purpose, they shall be on oath or affirmation. When the President of the United States is tried, the Chief Justice shall preside: and no person shall be convicted without the concurrence of two-thirds of the members present.

7. Judgment in cases of impeachment shall not extend further than to removal from office, and disqualification to hold and enjoy any office of honor, trust or profit under the United States: but the party convicted shall nevertheless be liable and subject to indictment, trial, judgment and punishment, according to law.

Section 4—Times, etc., of holding elections, how prescribed. One session each year.

1. The times, places and manner of holding elections for Senators and Representatives, shall be prescribed in each State by the Legislature thereof; but the Congress may at any time by law make or alter such regulations, except as to the places of choosing Senators.

2. The Congress shall assemble at least once in every year, and such meeting shall *(be on the first Monday in December,) (The words in parentheses were superseded by Amendment XX, section 2).* unless they shall by law appoint a different day.

Section 5—Membership, quorum, adjournments, rules. Power to punish or expel. Journal. Time of adjournments, how limited, etc.

1. Each House shall be the judge of the elections, returns and qualifications of its own members, and a majority of each shall constitute a quorum to do business; but a smaller number may adjourn from day to day, and may be authorized to compel the attendance of absent members, in such manner, and under such penalties as each House may provide.

2. Each House may determine the rules of its proceedings, punish its members for disorderly behavior, and, with the concurrence of two-thirds, expel a member.

3. Each House shall keep a journal of its proceedings, and from time to time publish the same, excepting such parts as may in their judgment require secrecy; and the yeas and nays of the members of either House on any question shall, at the desire of one-fifth of those present, be entered on the journal.

4. Neither House, during the session of Congress, shall, without the consent of the other, adjourn for more than three days, nor to any other place than that in which the two Houses shall be sitting.

Section 6—Compensation, privileges, disqualifications in certain cases.

1. The Senators and Representatives shall receive a compensation for their services, to be ascertained by law, and paid out of the Treasury of the United States. They shall in all cases, except treason, felony and breach of the peace, be privileged from arrest during their attendance at the session of their respective Houses, and in going to and returning from the same; and for any speech or debate in either House, they shall not be questioned in any other place.

2. No Senator or Representative shall, during the time for which he was elected, be appointed to any civil office under the authority of the United States, which shall have been created, or the emoluments whereof shall have been increased during such time; and no person holding any office under the United States, shall be a member of either House

during his continuance in office.

Section 7—House to originate all revenue bills. Veto. Bill may be passed by two-thirds of each House, notwithstanding, etc. Bill, not returned in ten days, to become a law. Provisions as to orders, concurrent resolutions, etc.

1. All bills for raising revenue shall originate in the House of Representatives; but the Senate may propose or concur with amendments as on other bills.

2. Every bill which shall have passed the House of Representatives and the Senate, shall, before it becomes a law, be presented to the President of the United States; if he approves he shall sign it, but if not he shall return it, with his objections to that House in which it shall have originated, who shall enter the objections at large on their journal, and proceed to reconsider it. If after such reconsideration two-thirds of that House shall agree to pass the bill, it shall be sent, together with the objections, to the other House, by which it shall likewise be reconsidered, and if approved by two-thirds of that House, it shall become a law. But in all such cases the votes of both Houses shall be determined by yeas and nays, and the names of the persons voting for and against the bill shall be entered on the journal of each House respectively. If any bill shall not be returned by the President within ten days (Sundays excepted) after it shall have been presented to him, the same shall be a law, in like manner as if he had signed it, unless the Congress by their adjournment prevent its return, in which case it shall not be a law.

3. Every order, resolution, or vote to which the concurrence of the Senate and House of Representatives may be necessary (except on a question of adjournment) shall be presented to the President of the United States; and before the same shall take effect, shall be approved by him, or being disapproved by him, shall be repassed by two-thirds of the Senate and House of Representatives, according to the rules and limitations prescribed in the case of a bill.

Section 8—Powers of Congress.

The Congress shall have power

1. To lay and collect taxes, duties, imposts and excises, to pay the debts and provide for the common defense and general welfare of the United States; but all duties, imposts and excises shall be uniform throughout the United States;

2. To borrow money on the credit of the United States;

3. To regulate commerce with foreign nations, and among the several States, and with the Indian tribes;

4. To establish a uniform rule of naturalization, and uniform laws on the subject of bankruptcies throughout the United States;

5. To coin money, regulate the value thereof, and of foreign coin, and fix the standard of weights and measures;

6. To provide for the punishment of counterfeiting the securities and current coin of the United States;

7. To establish post-offices and post-roads;

8. To promote the progress of science and useful arts, by securing for limited times to authors and inventors the exclusive right to their respective writings and discoveries;

9. To constitute tribunals inferior to the Supreme Court;

10. To define and punish piracies and felonies committed on the high seas, and offenses against the law of nations;

11. To declare war, grant letters of marque and reprisal, and make rules concerning captures on land and water;

12. To raise and support armies, but no appropriation of money to that use shall be for a longer term than two years;

13. To provide and maintain a navy;

14. To make rules for the government and regulation of the land and naval forces;

15. To provide for calling forth the militia to execute the laws of the Union, suppress insurrections and repel invasions;

16. To provide for organizing, arming, and disciplining the militia, and for governing such part of them as may be employed in the service of the United States, reserving to the States respectively, the appointment of the officers, and the authority of training the militia according to the discipline prescribed by Congress;

17. To exercise exclusive legislation in all cases whatsoever, over such district (not exceeding ten miles square) as

may, by cession of particular States, and the acceptance of Congress, become the seat of the Government of the United States, and to exercise like authority over all places purchased by the consent of the Legislature of the State in which the same shall be, for the erection of forts, magazines, arsenals, dockyards, and other needful buildings;—And

18. To make all laws which shall be necessary and proper for carrying into execution the foregoing powers, and all other powers vested by this Constitution in the Government of the United States, or in any department or officer thereof.

Section 9—Provision as to migration or importation of certain persons. Habeas corpus, bills of attainder, etc. Taxes, how apportioned. No export duty. No commercial preference. Money, how drawn from Treasury, etc. No titular nobility. Officers not to receive presents, etc.

1. The migration or importation of such persons as any of the States now existing shall think proper to admit, shall not be prohibited by the Congress prior to the year one thousand eight hundred and eight, but a tax or duty may be imposed on such importation, not exceeding ten dollars for each person.

2. The privilege of the writ of habeas corpus shall not be suspended, unless when in cases of rebellion or invasion the public safety may require it.

3. No bill of attainder or ex post facto law, shall be passed.

4. No capitation, or other direct, tax shall be laid, unless in proportion to the census or enumeration herein before directed to be taken. *(Modified by Amendment XVI.)*

5. No tax or duty shall be laid on articles exported from any State.

6. No preference shall be given by any regulation of commerce or revenue to the ports of one State over those of another: nor shall vessels bound to, or from, one State, be obliged to enter, clear, or pay duties in another.

7. No money shall be drawn from the Treasury, but in consequence of appropriations made by law; and a regular statement and account of the receipts and expenditures of all public money shall be published from time to time.

8. No title of nobility shall be granted by the United States: and no person holding any office of profit or trust under them, shall, without the consent of the Congress, accept of any present, emolument, office, or title, of any kind whatever, from any king, prince, or foreign state.

Section 10—States prohibited from the exercise of certain powers.

1. No State shall enter into any treaty, alliance, or confederation; grant letters of marque and reprisal; coin money; emit bills of credit; make anything but gold and silver coin a tender in payment of debts; pass any bill of attainder, ex post facto law, or law impairing the obligation of contracts, or grant any title of nobility.

2. No State shall, without the consent of the Congress, lay any imposts or duties on imports or exports, except what may be absolutely necessary for executing its inspection laws: and the net produce of all duties and imposts, laid by any State on imports or exports, shall be for the use of the Treasury of the United States; and all such laws shall be subject to the revision and control of the Congress.

3. No State shall, without the consent of Congress, lay any duty of tonnage, keep troops, or ships of war in time of peace, enter into any agreement or compact with another State, or with a foreign power, or engage in war, unless actually invaded, or in such imminent danger as will not admit of delay.

ARTICLE II.

Section 1—President: his term of office. Electors of President; number and how appointed. Electors to vote on same day. Qualification of President. On whom his duties devolve in case of his removal, death, etc. President's compensation. His oath of office.

1. The Executive power shall be vested in a President of the United States of America. He shall hold his office during the term of four years, and together with the Vice President, chosen for the same term, be elected as follows

2. Each State shall appoint, in such manner as the Legis-

lature thereof may direct, a number of electors, equal to the whole number of Senators and Representatives to which the State may be entitled in the Congress: but no Senator or Representative, or person holding an office of trust or profit under the United States, shall be appointed an elector.

(The electors shall meet in their respective States, and vote by ballot for two persons, of whom one at least shall not be an inhabitant of the same State with themselves. And they shall make a list of all the persons voted for, and of the number of votes for each; which list they shall sign and certify, and transmit sealed to the seat of the Government of the United States, directed to the President of the Senate. The President of the Senate shall, in the presence of the Senate and House of Representatives, open all the certificates, and the votes shall then be counted. The person having the greatest number of votes shall be the President, if such number be a majority of the whole number of electors appointed; and if there be more than one who have such majority, and have an equal number of votes, then the House of Representatives shall immediately choose by ballot one of them for President; and if no person have a majority, then from the five highest on the list the said House shall in like manner choose the President. But in choosing the President, the votes shall be taken by States, the representation from each State having one vote; a quorum for this purpose shall consist of a member or members from two-thirds of the States, and a majority of all the States shall be necessary to a choice. In every case, after the choice of the President, the person having the greatest number of votes of the electors shall be the Vice President. But if there should remain two or more who have equal votes, the Senate shall choose from them by ballot the Vice President.)

(This clause was superseded by Amendment XII.)

3. The Congress may determine the time of choosing the electors, and the day on which they shall give their votes; which day shall be the same throughout the United States.

4. No person except a natural born citizen, or a citizen of the United States, at the time of the adoption of this Constitution, shall be eligible to the office of President; neither shall any person be eligible to that office who shall not have attained to the age of thirty-five years, and been fourteen years a resident within the United States.

(For qualification of the Vice President, see Amendment XII.)

5. In case of the removal of the President from office, or of his death, resignation, or inability to discharge the powers and duties of the said office, the same shall devolve on the Vice President, and the Congress may by law provide for the case of removal, death, resignation or inability, both of the President and Vice President, declaring what officer shall then act as President, and such officer shall act accordingly, until the disability be removed, or a President shall be elected.

(This clause has been modified by Amendments XX and XXV.)

6. The President shall, at stated times, receive for his services, a compensation, which shall neither be increased nor diminished during the period for which he shall have been elected, and he shall not receive within that period any other emolument from the United States, or any of them.

7. Before he enter on the execution of his office, he shall take the following oath or affirmation:

"I do solemnly swear (or affirm) that I will faithfully execute the office of President of the United States, and will to the best of my ability, preserve, protect and defend the Constitution of the United States."

Section 2—President to be Commander-in-Chief. He may require opinions of cabinet officers, etc., may pardon. Treaty-making power. Nomination of certain officers. When President may fill vacancies.

1. The President shall be Commander-in-Chief of the Army and Navy of the United States, and of the militia of the several States, when called into the actual service of the United States; he may require the opinion, in writing, of the principal officer in each of the executive departments, upon any subject relating to the duties of their respective offices, and he shall have power to grant reprieves and pardons for offenses against the United States, except in cases of impeachment.

2. He shall have power, by and with the advice and consent of the Senate, to make treaties, provided two-thirds of the Senators present concur; and he shall nominate, and by and with the advice and consent of the Senate, shall appoint ambassadors, other public ministers and consuls, judges of the Supreme Court, and all other officers of the United States, whose appointments are not herein otherwise provided for, and which shall be established by law: but the Congress may by law vest the appointment of such inferior officers, as they think proper, in the President alone, in the courts of law, or in the heads of departments.

3. The President shall have power to fill up all vacancies that may happen during the recess of the Senate, by granting commissions, which shall expire at the end of their next session.

Section 3—President shall communicate to Congress. He may convene and adjourn Congress, in case of disagreement, etc. Shall receive ambassadors, execute laws, and commission officers.

He shall from time to time give to the Congress information of the state of the Union, and recommend to their consideration such measures as he shall judge necessary and expedient; he may, on extraordinary occasions, convene both Houses, or either of them, and in case of disagreement between them, with respect to the time of adjournment, he may adjourn them to such time as he shall think proper; he shall receive ambassadors and other public ministers; he shall take care that the laws be faithfully executed, and shall commission all the officers of the United States.

Section 4—All civil offices forfeited for certain crimes.

The President, Vice President, and all civil officers of the United States, shall be removed from office on impeachment for, and conviction of, treason, bribery, or other high crimes and misdemeanors.

ARTICLE III.

Section 1—Judicial powers, Tenure. Compensation.

The judicial power of the United States, shall be vested in one Supreme Court, and in such inferior courts as the Congress may from time to time ordain and establish. The judges, both of the Supreme and inferior courts, shall hold their offices during good behavior, and shall at stated times, receive for their services, a compensation, which shall not be diminished during their continuance in office.

Section 2—Judicial power; to what cases it extends. Original jurisdiction of Supreme Court; appellate jurisdiction. Trial by jury, etc. Trial, where.

1. The judicial power shall extend to all cases, in law and equity, arising under this Constitution, the laws of the United States, and treaties made, or which shall be made, under their authority; to all cases affecting ambassadors, other public ministers and consuls; to all cases of admiralty and maritime jurisdiction; to controversies to which the United States shall be a party; to controversies between two or more States; between a State and citizens of another State; between citizens of different States, between citizens of the same State claiming lands under grants of different States, and between a State, or the citizens thereof, and foreign states, citizens or subjects.

(This section is modified by Amendment XI.)

2. In all cases affecting ambassadors, other public ministers and consuls, and those in which a State shall be party, the Supreme Court shall have original jurisdiction. In all the other cases before mentioned, the Supreme Court shall have appellate jurisdiction, both as to law and fact, with such exceptions, and under such regulations as the Congress shall make.

3. The trial of all crimes, except in cases of impeachment, shall be by jury; and such trial shall be held in the State where the said crimes shall have been committed; but when not committed within any State, the trial shall be at such place or places as the Congress may by law have directed.

Section 3—Treason Defined, Proof of, Punishment of.

1. Treason against the United States, shall consist only in levying war against them, or in adhering to their enemies,

giving them aid and comfort. No person shall be convicted of treason unless on the testimony of two witnesses to the same overt act, or on confession in open court.

2. The Congress shall have power to declare the punishment of treason, but no attainder of treason shall work corruption of blood, or forfeiture except during the life of the person attainted.

ARTICLE IV.

Section 1—Each State to give credit to the public acts, etc., of every other State.

Full faith and credit shall be given in each State to the public acts, records, and judicial proceedings of every other State. And the Congress may by general laws prescribe the manner in which such acts, records and proceedings shall be proved, and the effect thereof.

Section 2—Privileges of citizens of each State. Fugitives from justice to be delivered up. Persons held to service having escaped, to be delivered up.

1. The citizens of each State shall be entitled to all privileges and immunities of citizens in the several States.

2. A person charged in any State with treason, felony, or other crime, who shall flee from justice, and be found in another State, shall on demand of the Executive authority of the State from which he fled, be delivered up, to be removed to the State having jurisdiction of the crime.

(3. No person held to service or labor in one State, under the laws thereof, escaping into another, shall in consequence of any law or regulation therein, be discharged from such service or labor, but shall be delivered up on claim of the party to whom such service or labor may be due.) (This clause was superseded by Amendment XIII.)

Section 3—Admission of new States. Power of Congress over territory and other property.

1. New States may be admitted by the Congress into this Union; but no new State shall be formed or erected within the jurisdiction of any other State; nor any State be formed by the junction of two or more States, or parts of States, without the consent of the Legislatures of the States concerned as well as of the Congress.

2. The Congress shall have power to dispose of and make all needful rules and regulations respecting the territory or other property belonging to the United States; and nothing in this Constitution shall be so construed as to prejudice any claims of the United States, or of any particular State.

Section 4—Republican form of government guaranteed. Each state to be protected.

The United States shall guarantee to every State in this Union a Republican form of government, and shall protect each of them against invasion; and on application of the Legislature, or of the Executive (when the Legislature cannot be convened) against domestic violence.

ARTICLE V.

Constitution: how amended; proviso.

The Congress, whenever two-thirds of both Houses shall deem it necessary, shall propose amendments to this Constitution, or, on the application of the Legislatures of two-thirds of the several States, shall call a convention for proposing amendments, which, in either case, shall be valid to all intents and purposes, as part of this Constitution, when ratified by the Legislatures of three-fourths of the several States, or by conventions in three-fourths thereof, as the one

or the other mode of ratification may be proposed by the Congress; provided that no amendment which may be made prior to the year one thousand eight hundred and eight shall in any manner affect the first and fourth clauses in the Ninth Section of the First Article; and that no State, without its consent, shall be deprived of its equal suffrage in the Senate.

ARTICLE VI.

Certain debts, etc., declared valid. Supremacy of Constitution, treaties, and laws of the United States. Oath to support Constitution, by whom taken. No religious test.

1. All debts contracted and engagements entered into, before the adoption of this Constitution, shall be as valid against the United States under this Constitution, as under the Confederation.

2. This Constitution, and the laws of the United States which shall be made in pursuance thereof; and all treaties made, or which shall be made, under the authority of the United States, shall be the supreme law of the land; and the judges in every State shall be bound thereby, any thing in the Constitution or laws of any State to the contrary notwithstanding.

3. The Senators and Representatives before mentioned, and the members of the several State Legislatures, and all executive and judicial officers, both of the United States and of the several States, shall be bound by oath or affirmation, to support this Constitution; but no religious test shall ever be required as a qualification to any office or public trust under the United States.

ARTICLE VII.

What ratification shall establish Constitution.

The ratification of the Conventions of nine States, shall be sufficient for the establishment of this Constitution between the States so ratifying the same.

Done in convention by the unanimous consent of the States present the Seventeenth day of September in the year of our Lord one thousand seven hundred and eighty seven, and of the independence of the United States of America the Twelfth. In witness whereof we have hereunto subscribed our names.

George Washington, President and deputy from Virginia.

New Hampshire—John Langdon, Nicholas Gilman.

Massachusetts—Nathaniel Gorham, Rufus King.

Connecticut—Wm. Saml. Johnson, Roger Sherman.

New York—Alexander Hamilton.

New Jersey—Wil: Livingston, David Brearley, Wm. Paterson, Jona: Dayton.

Pennsylvania—B. Franklin, Thomas Mifflin, Robt. Morris, Geo. Clymer, Thos. FitzSimons, Jared Ingersoll, James Wilson, Gouv. Morris.

Delaware—Geo: Read, Gunning Bedford Jun., John Dickinson, Richard Bassett, Jaco: Broom.

Maryland—James McHenry, Daniel of Saint Thomas' Jenifer, Danl. Carroll.

Virginia—John Blair, James Madison Jr.

North Carolina—Wm. Blount, Rich'd. Dobbs Spaight, Hugh Williamson.

South Carolina—J. Rutledge, Charles Cotesworth Pinckney, Charles Pinckney, Pierce Butler.

Georgia—William Few, Abr. Baldwin.

Attest: William Jackson, Secretary.

Ten Original Amendments: The Bill of Rights
In force Dec. 15, 1791

(The First Congress, at its first session in the City of New York, Sept. 25, 1789, submitted to the states 12 amendments to clarify certain individual and state rights not named in the Constitution. They are generally called the Bill of Rights.

(Influential in framing these amendments was the Declaration of Rights of Virginia, written by George Mason (1725-1792) in 1776. Mason, a Virginia delegate to the Constitutional Convention, did not sign the Constitution and opposed its ratification on the ground that it did not sufficiently oppose slavery or safeguard individual rights.

(In the preamble to the resolution offering the proposed amendments, Congress said: "The conventions of a number of the States having at the time of their adopting the Constitution, expressed a desire, in order to prevent misconstruction or abuse of its powers, that further declaratory and restrictive clauses should be added, and as extending the ground of public confidence in the government will best insure the beneficent ends of its institution, be it resolved," etc.

(Ten of these amendments now commonly known as one to 10 inclusive, but originally 3 to 12 inclusive, were ratified by the states as follows: New Jersey, Nov. 20, 1789; Maryland, Dec. 19, 1789; North Carolina, Dec. 22, 1789; South Carolina, Jan. 19, 1790; New Hampshire, Jan 25, 1790; Delaware, Jan 28, 1790; New York, Feb. 24, 1790; Pennsylvania, Mar. 10, 1790; Rhode

Island, June 7, 1790; Vermont, Nov 3, 1791; Virginia, Dec. 15, 1791; Massachusetts, Mar. 2, 1939; Georgia, Mar. 18, 1939; Connecticut, Apr. 19, 1939. These original 10 ratified amendments follow as Amendments I to X inclusive.

(Of the two original proposed amendments which were not ratified by the necessary number of states, the first related to apportionment of Representatives; the second, to compensation of members.)

AMENDMENT I.

Religious establishment prohibited. Freedom of speech, of the press, and right to petition.

Congress shall make no law respecting an establishment of religion, or prohibiting the free exercise thereof; or abridging the freedom of speech, or of the press; or the right of the people peaceably to assemble, and to petition the Government for a redress of grievances.

AMENDMENT II.

Right to keep and bear arms.

A well-regulated militia, being necessary to the security of a free State, the right of the people to keep and bear arms, shall not be infringed.

AMENDMENT III.

Conditions for quarters for soldiers.

No soldier shall, in time of peace be quartered in any house, without the consent of the owner, nor in time of war, but in a manner to be prescribed by law.

AMENDMENT IV.

Right of search and seizure regulated.

The right of the people to be secure in their persons, houses, papers, and effects, against unreasonable searches and seizures, shall not be violated, and no warrants shall issue, but upon probable cause, supported by oath or affirmation, and particularly describing the place to be searched, and the persons or things to be seized.

AMENDMENT V.

Provisions concerning prosecution. Trial and punishment—private property not to be taken for public use without compensation.

No person shall be held to answer for a capital, or otherwise infamous crime, unless on a presentment or indictment of a Grand Jury, except in cases arising in the land or naval forces, or in the militia, when in actual service in time of war or public danger; nor shall any person be subject for the same offense to be twice put in jeopardy of life or limb; nor shall be compelled in any criminal case to be a witness against himself, nor be deprived of life, liberty, or property, without due process of law; nor shall private property be taken for public use without just compensation.

AMENDMENT VI.

Right to speedy trial, witnesses, etc.

In all criminal prosecutions, the accused shall enjoy the right to a speedy and public trial, by an impartial jury of the State and district wherein the crime shall have been committed, which district shall have been previously ascertained by law, and to be informed of the nature and cause of the accusation; to be confronted with the witnesses against him; to have compulsory process for obtaining witnesses in his favor, and to have the assistance of counsel for his defense.

AMENDMENT VII.

Right of trial by jury.

In suits at common law, where the value in controversy shall exceed twenty dollars, the right of trial by jury shall be preserved, and no fact tried by a jury shall be otherwise re-examined in any court of the United States, than according to the rules of the common law.

AMENDMENT VIII.

Excessive bail or fines and cruel punishment prohibited.

Excessive bail shall not be required, nor excessive fines imposed, nor cruel and unusual punishments inflicted.

AMENDMENT IX.

Rule of construction of Constitution.

The enumeration in the Constitution, of certain rights, shall not be construed to deny or disparage others retained by the people.

AMENDMENT X.

Rights of States under Constitution.

The powers not delegated to the United States by the Constitution, nor prohibited by it to the States, are reserved to the States respectively, or to the people.

Amendments Since the Bill of Rights

AMENDMENT XI.

Judicial powers construed.

The judicial power of the United States shall not be construed to extend to any suit in law or equity, commenced or prosecuted against one of the United States by citizens of another State, or by citizens or subjects of any foreign state.

(This amendment was proposed to the Legislatures of the several States by the Third Congress on March 4, 1794, and was declared to have been ratified in a message from the President to Congress, dated Jan. 8, 1798.

(It was on Jan 5, 1798, that Secretary of State Pickering received from 12 of the States authenticated ratifications, and informed President John Adams of that fact.

(As a result of later research in the Department of State, it is now established that Amendment XI became part of the Constitution on Feb. 7, 1795, for on that date it had been ratified by 12 States as follows:

(1. New York, Mar. 27, 1794. 2. Rhode Island, Mar. 31, 1794. 3. Connecticut, May 8, 1794. 4. New Hampshire, June 16, 1794. 5. Massachusetts, June 26, 1794. 6. Vermont, between Oct 9, 1794, and Nov. 9, 1794. 7. Virginia, Nov. 18, 1794. 8. Georgia, Nov. 29, 1794. 9. Kentucky, Dec. 7, 1794. 10. Maryland, Dec. 26, 1794. 11. Delaware, Jan 23, 1795. 12. North Carolina, Feb. 7, 1795.

(On June 1, 1796, more than a year after Amendment XI had become a part of the Constitution (but before anyone was officially aware of this), Tennessee had been admitted as a State; but not until Oct. 16, 1797, was a certified copy of the resolution of Congress proposing the amendment sent to the Governor of Tennessee (John Sevier) by Secretary of State Pickering, whose office was then at Trenton, New Jersey, because of the epidemic of yellow fever at Philadelphia; it seems, however, that the Legislature of Tennessee took no action on Amendment XI, owing doubtless to the fact that public announcement of its adoption was made soon thereafter.*

(Besides the necessary 12 States, one other, South Carolina, ratified Amendment XI, but this action was not taken until Dec. 4, 1797; the two remaining States, New Jersey and Pennsylvania, failed to ratify.)

AMENDMENT XII.

Manner of choosing President and Vice-President.

(Proposed by Congress Dec. 9, 1803; ratification completed June 15, 1804.)

The Electors shall meet in their respective States and vote by ballot for President and Vice-President, one of whom, at least, shall not be an inhabitant of the same State with themselves; they shall name in their ballots the person voted for as President, and in distinct ballots the person voted for as Vice-President, and they shall make distinct lists of all persons voted for as President, and of all persons voted for as Vice-President, and of the number of votes for each, which lists they shall sign and certify, and transmit sealed to the seat of the Government of the United States, directed to the President of the Senate; the President of the Senate shall, in the presence of the Senate and House of Representatives, open all the certificates and the votes shall then be counted;—The person having the greatest number of votes for President, shall be the President, if such number be a majority of the whole number of Electors appointed; and if no person have such majority, then from the persons having the highest numbers not exceeding three on the list of those voted for as President, the House of Representatives shall choose immediately, by ballot, the President. But in choosing the President, the votes shall be taken by States, the representation from each State having one vote; a quorum for this purpose shall consist of a member or members from two-thirds of the States, and a majority of all the States shall be necessary to a choice. *(And if the House of Representatives shall not choose a President whenever the right of choice shall devolve upon them, before the fourth day of March next following, then the Vice-President shall act as President, as in the case of the death or other constitutional disability of the President.) (The words in parentheses were superseded by Amendment XX, section 3.)* The person having the greatest number of votes as Vice-President, shall be the Vice-President, if such number be a majority of the whole number of Electors appointed, and if no person have a majority, then from the two highest numbers on the list, the Senate shall choose the Vice-President; a quorum for the purpose shall consist of two-thirds of the whole number of Senators, and a majority of the whole number shall be necessary to a choice. But no person constitutionally ineligible to the office of President shall be eligible to that of Vice-President of the United States.

THE RECONSTRUCTION AMENDMENTS

(Amendments XIII, XIV, and XV are commonly known as the Reconstruction Amendments, inasmuch as they followed the Civil War, and were drafted by Republicans who were bent on imposing their own policy of reconstruction on the South. Post-bellum legislatures there—Mississippi, South Carolina, Georgia, for example—had set up laws which, it was charged, were contrived to perpetuate Negro slavery under other names.)

AMENDMENT XIII.

Slavery abolished.

(Proposed by Congress Jan. 31, 1865; ratification completed Dec. 18, 1865. The amendment, when first proposed by a resolution in Congress, was passed by the Senate, 38 to 6, on Apr. 8, 1864, but was defeated in the House, 95 to 66 on June 15, 1864. On reconsideration by the House, on Jan. 31, 1865, the resolution passed, 119 to 56. It was approved by President Lincoln on Feb. 1, 1865, although the Supreme Court had decided in 1798 that the President has nothing to do with the proposing of amendments to the Constitution, or their adoption.)

1. Neither slavery nor involuntary servitude, except as a punishment for crime whereof the party shall have been duly convicted, shall exist within the United States or any place subject to their jurisdiction.

2. Congress shall have power to enforce this article by appropriate legislation.

AMENDMENT XIV.

Citizenship rights not to be abridged.

(The following amendment was proposed to the Legislatures of the several states by the 39th Congress, June 13, 1866, and was declared to have been ratified in a proclamation by the Secretary of State, July 28, 1868.

(The 14th amendment was adopted only by virtue of ratification subsequent to earlier rejections. Newly constituted legislatures in both North Carolina and South Carolina (respectively July 4 and 9, 1868), ratified the proposed amendment, although earlier legislatures had rejected the proposal. The Secretary of State issued a proclamation, which, though doubtful as to the effect of attempted withdrawals by Ohio and New Jersey, entertained no doubt as to the validity of the ratification by North and South Carolina. The following day (July 21, 1868), Congress passed a resolution which declared the 14th Amendment to be a part of the Constitution and directed the Secretary of State so to promulgate it. The Secretary waited, however, until the newly constituted Legislature of Georgia had ratified the amendment, subsequent to an earlier rejection, before the promulgation of the ratification of the new amendment.)

1. All persons born or naturalized in the United States, and subject to the jurisdiction thereof, are citizens of the United States and of the State wherein they reside. No State shall make or enforce any law which shall abridge the privileges or immunities of citizens of the United States; nor shall any State deprive any person of life, liberty, or property, without due process of law; nor deny to any person within its jurisdiction the equal protection of the laws.

2. Representatives shall be apportioned among the several States according to their respective numbers, counting the whole number of persons in each State, excluding Indians not taxed. But when the right to vote at any election for the choice of Electors for President and Vice-President of the United States, Representatives in Congress, the executive and judicial officers of a State, or the members of the Legislature thereof, is denied to any of the male inhabitants of such State, being twenty-one years of age, and citizens of the United States, or in any way abridged, except for participation in rebellion, or other crime, the basis of representation therein shall be reduced in the proportion which the number of such male citizens shall bear to the whole number of male citizens twenty-one years of age in such State.

3. No person shall be a Senator or Representative in Congress, or Elector of President and Vice-President, or hold any office, civil or military, under the United States, or under any State, who, having previously taken an oath, as a member of Congress, or as an officer of the United States, or as a member of any State Legislature, or as an executive or judicial officer of any State, to support the Constitution of the United States, shall have engaged in insurrection or rebellion against the same, or given aid or comfort to the enemies thereof. But Congress may by a vote of two-thirds of each House, remove such disability.

4. The validity of the public debt of the United States, authorized by law, including debts incurred for payment of pensions and bounties for services in suppressing insurrection or rebellion, shall not be questioned. But neither the United States nor any State shall assume or pay any debt or obligation incurred in aid of insurrection or rebellion against the United States, or any claim for the loss or emancipation of any slave; but all such debts, obligations and claims, shall be held illegal and void.

5. The Congress shall have power to enforce, by appropriate legislation, the provisions of this article.

AMENDMENT XV.

Race no bar to voting rights.

(The following amendment was proposed to the legislatures of the several States by the 40th Congress, Feb. 26, 1869, and was declared to have been ratified in a proclamation by the Secretary of State, Mar. 30, 1870.)

1. The right of citizens of the United States to vote shall not be denied or abridged by the United States or by any State on account of race, color, or previous condition of servitude.

2. The Congress shall have power to enforce this article by appropriate legislation.

AMENDMENT XVI.

Income taxes authorized.

(Proposed by Congress July 12, 1909; ratification declared by the Secretary of State Feb. 25, 1913.)

The Congress shall have power to lay and collect taxes on incomes, from whatever source derived, without apportionment among the several States, and without regard to any census or enumeration.

AMENDMENT XVII.

United States Senators to be elected by direct popular vote.

(Proposed by Congress May 13, 1912; ratification declared by the Secretary of State May 31, 1913.)

1. The Senate of the United States shall be composed of two Senators from each State, elected by the people thereof, for six years; and each Senator shall have one vote. The electors in each State shall have the qualifications requisite for electors of the most numerous branch of the State Legislatures.

2. When vacancies happen in the representation of any State in the Senate, the executive authority of such State shall issue writs of election to fill such vacancies: Provided, That the Legislature of any State may empower the Executive thereof to make temporary appointments until the peo-

ple fill the vacancies by election as the Legislature may direct.

3. This amendment shall not be so construed as to affect the election or term of any Senator chosen before it becomes valid as part of the Constitution.

AMENDMENT XVIII.

Liquor prohibition amendment.

(Proposed by Congress Dec. 18, 1917; ratification completed Jan. 16, 1919. Repealed by Amendment XXI, effective Dec. 5, 1933.)

(1. After one year from the ratification of this article the manufacture, sale, or transportation of intoxicating liquors within, the importation thereof into, or the exportation thereof from the United States and all territory subject to the jurisdiction thereof for beverage purposes is hereby prohibited.

(2. The Congress and the several States shall have concurrent power to enforce this article by appropriate legislation.

(3. This article shall be inoperative unless it shall have been ratified as an amendment to the Constitution by the Legislatures of the several States, as provided in the Constitution, within seven years from the date of the submission hereof to the States by the Congress.)

(The total vote in the Senates of the various States was 1,310 for, 237 against—84.6% dry. In the lower houses of the States the vote was 3,782 for, 1,035 against—78.5% dry.

(The amendment ultimately was adopted by all the States except Connecticut and Rhode Island.)

AMENDMENT XIX.

Giving nationwide suffrage to women.

(Proposed by Congress June 4, 1919; ratification certified by Secretary of State Aug. 26, 1920.)

1. The right of citizens of the United States to vote shall not be denied or abridged by the United States or by any State on account of sex.

2. Congress shall have power to enforce this Article by appropriate legislation.

AMENDMENT XX.

Terms of President and Vice President to begin on Jan. 20; those of Senators, Representatives, Jan. 3.

(Proposed by Congress Mar. 2, 1932; ratification completed Jan. 23, 1933.)

1. The terms of the President and Vice President shall end at noon on the 20th day of January, and the terms of Senators and Representatives at noon on the 3rd day of January, of the years in which such terms would have ended if this article had not been ratified; and the terms of their successors shall then begin.

2. The Congress shall assemble at least once in every year, and such meeting shall begin at noon on the 3rd day of January, unless they shall by law appoint a different day.

3. If, at the time fixed for the beginning of the term of the President, the President elect shall have died, the Vice President elect shall become President. If a President shall not have been chosen before the time fixed for the beginning of his term, or if the President elect shall have failed to qualify, then the Vice President elect shall act as President until a President shall have qualified; and the Congress may by law provide for the case wherein neither a President elect nor a Vice President elect shall have qualified, declaring who shall then act as President, or the manner in which one who is to act shall be selected, and such person shall act accordingly until a President or Vice President shall have qualified.

4. The Congress may by law provide for the case of the death of any of the persons from whom the House of Representatives may choose a President whenever the right of choice shall have devolved upon them, and for the case of the death of any of the persons from whom the Senate may choose a Vice President whenever the right of choice shall have devolved upon them.

5. Sections 1 and 2 shall take effect on the 15th day of October following the ratification of this article (Oct., 1933).

6. This article shall be inoperative unless it shall have been ratified as an amendment to the Constitution by the Legislatures of three-fourths of the several States within seven years from the date of its submission.

AMENDMENT XXI.

Repeal of Amendment XVIII.

(Proposed by Congress Feb. 20, 1933; ratification completed Dec. 5, 1933.)

1. The eighteenth article of amendment to the Constitution of the United States is hereby repealed.

2. The transportation or importation into any State, Territory, or Possession of the United States for delivery or use therein of intoxicating liquors, in violation of the laws thereof, is hereby prohibited.

3. This article shall be inoperative unless it shall have been ratified as an amendment to the Constitution by conventions in the several States, as provided in the Constitution, within seven years from the date of the submission hereof to the States by the Congress.

AMENDMENT XXII.

Limiting Presidential terms of office.

(Proposed by Congress Mar. 24, 1947; ratification completed Feb. 27, 1951.)

1. No person shall be elected to the office of the President more than twice, and no person who has held the office of President, or acted as President, for more than two years of a term to which some other person was elected President shall be elected to the office of the President more than once. But this Article shall not apply to any person holding the office of President when this Article was proposed by the Congress, and shall not prevent any person who may be holding the office of President, or acting as President, during the term within which this Article becomes operative from holding the office of President or acting as President during the remainder of such term.

2. This article shall be inoperative unless it shall have been ratified as an amendment to the Constitution by the Legislatures of three-fourths of the several States within seven years from the date of its submission to the States by the Congress.

AMENDMENT XXIII.

Presidential vote for District of Columbia.

(Proposed by Congress June 16, 1960; ratification completed Mar. 29, 1961.)

1. The District constituting the seat of Government of the United States shall appoint in such manner as the Congress may direct:

A number of electors of President and Vice President equal to the whole number of Senators and Representatives in Congress to which the District would be entitled if it were a State, but in no event more than the least populous State; they shall be in addition to those appointed by the States, but they shall be considered, for the purposes of the election of President and Vice President, to be electors appointed by a State; and they shall meet in the District and perform such duties as provided by the twelfth article of amendment.

2. The Congress shall have power to enforce this article by appropriate legislation.

AMENDMENT XXIV.

Barring poll tax in federal elections.

(Proposed by Congress Aug. 27, 1962; ratification completed Jan. 23, 1964.)

1. The right of citizens of the United States to vote in any primary or other election for President or Vice President, for electors for President or Vice President, or for Senator or Representative in Congress, shall not be denied or abridged by the United States or any State by reason of failure to pay any poll tax or other tax.

2. The Congress shall have power to enforce this article by appropriate legislation.

AMENDMENT XXV.

Presidential disability and succession.

(Proposed by Congress July 6, 1965; ratification completed Feb. 10, 1967.)

1. In case of the removal of the President from office or of

his death or resignation, the Vice President shall become President.

2. Whenever there is a vacancy in the office of the Vice President, the President shall nominate a Vice President who shall take office upon confirmation by a majority vote of both houses of Congress.

3. Whenever the President transmits to the President pro tempore of the Senate and the Speaker of the House of Representatives his written declaration that he is unable to discharge the powers and duties of his office, and until he transmits to them a written declaration to the contrary, such powers and duties shall be discharged by the Vice President as Acting President.

4. Whenever the Vice President and a majority of either the principal officers of the executive departments or of such other body as Congress may by law provide, transmit to the President pro tempore of the Senate and the Speaker of the House of Representatives their written declaration that the President is unable to discharge the powers and duties of his office, the Vice President shall immediately assume the powers and duties of the office as Acting President.

Thereafter, when the President transmits to the President pro tempore of the Senate and the Speaker of the House of Representatives his written declaration that no inability exists, he shall resume the powers and duties of his office unless the Vice President and a majority of either the principal officers of the executive department or of such other body as Congress may by law provide, transmit within four days to the President pro tempore of the Senate and the Speaker of the House of Representatives their written declaration that the President is unable to discharge the powers and duties of his office. Thereupon Congress shall decide the issue, assembling within forty-eight hours for that purpose if not in session. If the Congress, within twenty-one days after receipt of the latter written declaration, or, if Congress is not in session, within twenty-one days after Congress is required to

assemble, determines by two-thirds vote of both houses that the President is unable to discharge the powers and duties of his office, the Vice President shall continue to discharge the same as Acting President; otherwise, the President shall resume the powers and duties of his office.

AMENDMENT XXVI.

Lowering voting age to 18 years.

(Proposed by Congress Mar. 8, 1971; ratification completed July 1, 1971.)

1. The right of citizens of the United States, who are 18 years of age or older, to vote shall not be denied or abridged by the United States or any state on account of age.

2. The Congress shall have the power to enforce this article by appropriate legislation.

PROPOSED D.C. REPRESENTATION AMENDMENT

(Proposed by Congress Aug. 22, 1978; ratified, as of March, 1984, by 13 states.)

1. For purposes of representation in the Congress, election of the President and Vice President, and article V of this Constitution, the District constituting the seat of government of the United States shall be treated as though it were a State.

2. The exercise of the rights and powers conferred under this article shall be by the people of the District constituting the seat of government, and as shall be provided by the Congress.

3. The twenty-third article of amendment to the Constitution of the United States is hereby repealed.

4. This article shall be inoperative, unless it shall have been ratified as an amendment to the Constitution by the legislatures of three-fourths of the several States within seven years from the date of its submission.

Origin of the Constitution

The War of Independence was conducted by delegates from the original 13 states, called the Congress of the United States of America and generally known as the Continental Congress. In 1777 the Congress submitted to the legislatures of the states the Articles of Confederation and Perpetual Union, which were ratified by New Hampshire, Massachusetts, Rhode Island, Connecticut, New York, New Jersey, Pennsylvania, Delaware, Virginia, North Carolina, South Carolina, and Georgia, and finally, in 1781, by Maryland.

The first article of the instrument read: "The stile of this confederacy shall be the United States of America." This did not signify a sovereign nation, because the states delegated only those powers they could not handle individually, such as power to wage war, establish a uniform currency, make treaties with foreign nations and contract debts for general expenses (such as paying the army). Taxes for the payment of such debts were levied by the individual states. The president under the Articles signed himself "President of the United States in Congress assembled," but here the United States were considered in the plural, a cooperating group. Canada was invited to join the union on equal terms but did not act.

When the war was won it became evident that a stronger federal union was needed to protect the mutual interests of the states. The Congress left the initiative to the legislatures. Virginia in Jan. 1786 appointed commissioners to meet with representatives of other states, with the result that delegates from Virginia, Delaware, New York, New Jersey, and Pennsylvania met at Annapolis. Alexander Hamilton prepared for their call to ask delegates from all states to meet in Philadelphia in May 1787 "to render the Constitution of the Federal government adequate to the exigencies of the union." Congress endorsed the plan Feb. 21, 1787. Delegates

were appointed by all states except Rhode Island.

The convention met May 14, 1787. George Washington was chosen president (presiding officer). The states certified 65 delegates, but 10 did not attend. The work was done by 55, not all of whom were present at all sessions. Of the 55 attending delegates, 16 failed to sign, and 39 actually signed Sept. 17, 1787, some with reservations. Some historians have said 74 delegates (9 more than the 65 actually certified) were named and 19 failed to attend. These 9 additional persons refused the appointment, were never delegates and never counted as absentees. Washington sent the Constitution to Congress with a covering letter and that body, Sept. 28, 1787, ordered it sent to the legislatures, "in order to be submitted to a convention of delegates chosen in each state by the people thereof."

The Constitution was ratified by votes of state conventions as follows: Delaware, Dec. 7, 1787, unanimous; Pennsylvania, Dec. 12, 1787, 43 to 23; New Jersey, Dec. 18, 1787, unanimous; Georgia, Jan 2, 1788, unanimous; Connecticut, Jan. 9, 1788, 128 to 40; Massachusetts, Feb. 6, 1788, 187 to 168; Maryland, Apr. 28, 1788, 63 to 11; South Carolina, May 23, 1788, 149 to 73; New Hampshire, June 21, 1788, 57 to 46; Virginia, June 26, 1788, 89 to 79; New York, July 26, 1788, 30 to 27. Nine states were needed to establish the operation of the Constitution "between the states so ratifying the same" and New Hampshire was the 9th state. The government did not declare the Constitution in effect until the first Wednesday in Mar. 1789 which was Mar. 4. After that North Carolina ratified it Nov. 21, 1789, 194 to 77; and Rhode Island, May 29, 1790, 34 to 32. Vermont in convention ratified it Jan. 10, 1791, and by act of Congress approved Feb. 18, 1791, was admitted into the Union as the 14th state, Mar. 4, 1791.

How the Declaration of Independence Was Adopted

On June 7, 1776, Richard Henry Lee, who had issued the first call for a congress of the colonies, introduced in the Continental Congress at Philadelphia a resolution declaring "that these United Colonies are, and of right ought to be, free and independent states, that they are absolved from all allegiance to the British Crown, and that all political connection between them and the state of Great Britain is, and ought to be, totally dissolved."

The resolution, seconded by John Adams on behalf of the Massachusetts delegation, came up again June 10 when a committee of 5, headed by Thomas Jefferson, was appointed to express the purpose of the resolution in a declaration of independence. The others on the committee were John Adams, Benjamin Franklin, Robert R. Livingston, and Roger Sherman.

Drafting the Declaration was assigned to Jefferson, who worked on a portable desk of his own construction in a room at Market and 7th Sts. The committee reported the result June 28, 1776. The members of the Congress suggested a number of changes, which Jefferson called "deplorable." They didn't approve Jefferson's arraignment of the British people and King George III for encouraging and fostering the slave trade, which Jefferson called "an execrable commerce." They made 86 changes, eliminating 480 words and leaving 1,337. In the final form capitalization was erratic. Jefferson had written that men were endowed with "inalienable" rights; in the final copy it came out as "unalienable" and has been thus ever since.

The Lee-Adams resolution of independence was adopted by 12 yeas July 2 — the actual date of the act of independence. The Declaration, which explains the act, was adopted July 4, in the evening.

After the Declaration was adopted, July 4, 1776, it was turned over to John Dunlap, printer, to be printed on broadsides. The original copy was lost and one of his broadsides was attached to a page in the journal of the Congress. It was read aloud July 8 in Philadelphia, Easton, Pa., and Trenton, N.J. On July 9 at 6 p.m. it was read by order of Gen. George Washington to the troops assembled on the Common in New York City (City Hall Park).

The Continental Congress of July 19, 1776, adopted the following resolution:

"Resolved, That the Declaration passed on the 4th, be fairly engrossed on parchment with the title and stile of 'The Unanimous Declaration of the thirteen United States of America' and that the same, when engrossed, be signed by every member of Congress."

Not all delegates who signed the engrossed Declaration were present on July 4. Robert Morris (Pa.), William Williams (Conn.) and Samuel Chase (Md.) signed on Aug. 2, Oliver Wolcott (Conn.), George Wythe (Va.), Richard Henry Lee (Va.) and Elbridge Gerry (Mass.) signed in August and September, Matthew Thornton (N. H.) joined the Congress Nov. 4 and signed later. Thomas McKean (Del.) rejoined Washington's Army before signing and said later that he signed in 1781.

Charles Carroll of Carrollton was appointed a delegate by Maryland on July 4, 1776, presented his credentials July 18, and signed the engrossed Declaration Aug. 2. Born Sept. 19, 1737, he was 95 years old and the last surviving signer when he died Nov. 14, 1832.

Two Pennsylvania delegates who did not support the Declaration on July 4 were replaced.

The 4 New York delegates did not have authority from their state to vote on July 4. On July 9 the New York state convention authorized its delegates to approve the Declaration and the Congress was so notified on July 15, 1776. The 4 signed the Declaration on Aug. 2.

The original engrossed Declaration is preserved in the National Archives Building in Washington.

The Liberty Bell: Its History and Significance

The Liberty Bell, in Independence Hall, Philadelphia, is an object of great reverence to Americans because of its association with the historic events of the War of Independence.

The original Province bell, ordered to commemorate the 50th anniversary of the Commonwealth of Pennsylvania, was cast by Thomas Lister, Whitechapel, London, and reached Philadelphia in Aug. 1752. It bore an inscription from Leviticus XXV, 10: "Proclaim liberty throughout all the land unto all the inhabitants thereof."

The bell was cracked by a stroke of its clapper in Sept. 1752 while it hung on a truss in the State House yard for testing. Pass & Stow, Philadelphia founders, recast the bell, adding 1 1/2 ounces of copper to a pound of the original metal to reduce brittleness. It was found that the bell contained too much copper, injuring its tone, so Pass & Stow recast it again, this time successfully.

In June 1753 the bell was hung in the wooden steeple of the State House, erected on top of the brick tower. In use while the Continental Congress was in session in the State House, it rang out in defiance of British tax and trade restrictions, and proclaimed the Boston Tea Party and the first public reading of the Declaration of Independence.

On Sept. 18, 1777, when the British Army was about to occupy Philadelphia, the bell was moved in a baggage train of the American Army to Allentown, Pa. where it was hidden in the Zion Reformed Church until June 27, 1778. It was moved back to Philadelphia after the British left.

In July 1781 the wooden steeple became insecure and had to be taken down. The bell was lowered into the brick section of the tower. Here it was hanging in July, 1835, when it cracked while tolling for the funeral of John Marshall, chief justice of the United States. Because of its association with the War of Independence it was not recast but remained mute in this location until 1846, the year of the Mexican War, when it was placed on exhibition in the Declaration Chamber of Independence Hall.

In 1876, when many thousands of Americans visited Philadelphia for the Centennial Exposition, it was placed in its old walnut frame in the tower hallway. In 1877 it was hung from the ceiling of the tower by a chain of 13 links. It was returned again to the Declaration Chamber and in 1896 taken back to the tower hall, where it occupied a glass case. In 1915 the case was removed so that the public might touch it. On Jan. 1, 1976, just after midnight to mark the opening of the Bicentennial Year, the bell was moved to a new glass and steel pavilion behind Independence Hall for easier viewing by the larger number of visitors expected during the year.

The measurements of the bell follow: circumference around the lip, 12 ft.; circumference around the crown, 7 ft. 6 in.; lip to the crown, 3 ft.; height over the crown, 2 ft. 3 in.; thickness at lip, 3 in.; thickness at crown, 1 1/4 in.; weight, 2080 lbs.; length of clapper, 3 ft. 2 in.; cost, £60 14s 5d.

Confederate States and Secession

The American Civil War, 1861-65, grew out of sectional disputes over the continued existence of slavery in the South and the contention of Southern legislators that the states retained many sovereign rights, including the right to secede from the Union.

The war was not fought by state against state but by one federal regime against another, the Confederate government in Richmond assuming control over the economic, political, and military life of the South, under protest from Georgia and South Carolina.

South Carolina voted an ordinance of secession from the Union, repealing its 1788 ratification of the U.S. Constitution on Dec. 20, 1860, to take effect Dec. 24. Other states seceded in 1861. Their votes in conventions were:

Mississippi, Jan. 9, 84-15; Florida, Jan. 10, 62-7; Alabama, Jan. 11, 61-39; Georgia, Jan. 19, 208-89; Louisiana, Jan. 26, 113-17; Texas, Feb. 1, 166-7, ratified by popular vote Feb. 23 (for 34,794, against 11,325); Virginia, Apr. 17, 88-55, ratified by popular vote May 23 (for 128,884; against 32,134); Arkansas, May 6, 69-1; Tennessee, May 7, ratified by popular vote June 8 (for 104,019, against 47,238); North Carolina, May 21.

Missouri Unionists stopped secession in conventions Feb. 28 and Mar. 9. The legislature condemned secession Mar. 7. Under the protection of Confederate troops, secessionist members of the legislature adopted a resolution of secession at Neosho, Oct. 31. The Confederate Congress seated the secessionists' representatives.

Kentucky did not secede and its government remained Unionist. In a part occupied by Confederate troops, Kentuckians approved secession and the Confederate Congress admitted their representatives.

The Maryland legislature voted against secession Apr. 27, 53-13. Delaware did not secede. Western Virginia held conventions at Wheeling, named a pro-Union governor June 11, 1861; admitted to Union as West Virginia June 30, 1863; its constitution provided for gradual abolition of slavery.

Confederate Government

Forty-two delegates from South Carolina, Georgia, Alabama, Mississippi, Louisiana, and Florida met in convention at Montgomery, Ala., Feb. 4, 1861. They adopted a provisional constitution of the Confederate States of America, and elected Jefferson Davis (Miss.) provisional president, and Alexander H. Stephens (Ga.) provisional vice president.

A permanent constitution was adopted Mar. 11; it abolished the African slave trade. The Congress moved to Richmond, Va. July 20. Davis was elected president in October, and was inaugurated Feb. 22, 1862.

The Congress adopted a flag, consisting of a red field with a white stripe, and a blue jack with a circle of white stars. Later the more popular flag was the red field with blue diagonal cross bars that held 13 white stars. The stars represented the 11 states actually in the Confederacy plus Kentucky and Missouri.

(See also Civil War, U.S., in Index)

Lincoln's Address at Gettysburg, 1863

Fourscore and seven years ago our fathers brought forth on this continent a new nation, conceived in liberty and dedicated to the proposition that all men are created equal.

Now we are engaged in a great civil war, testing whether that nation or any nation so conceived and so dedicated can long endure. We are met on a great battle field of that war. We have come to dedicate a portion of that field, as a final resting-place for those who here gave their lives that that nation might live. It is altogether fitting and proper that we should do this.

But, in a larger sense, we can not dedicate — we can not consecrate — we can not hallow — this ground. The brave men, living and dead, who struggled here, have consecrated it, far above our poor power to add or detract. The world will little note, nor long remember, what we say here, but it can never forget what they did here. It is for us the living, rather, to be dedicated here to the unfinished work which they who fought here have thus far so nobly advanced. It is rather for us to be here dedicated to the great task remaining before us — that from these honored dead we take increased devotion to that cause for which they gave the last full measure of devotion — that we here highly resolve that these dead shall not have died in vain — that this nation, under God, shall have a new birth of freedom — and that government of the people, by the people, for the people, shall not perish from the earth.

Origin of the United States National Motto

In God We Trust, designated as the U. S. National Motto by Congress in 1956, originated during the Civil War as an inscription for U. S. coins, although it was used by Francis Scott Key in a slightly different form when he wrote The Star Spangled Banner in 1814. On Nov. 13, 1861, when Union morale had been shaken by battlefield defeats, the Rev. M. R. Watkinson, of Ridleyville, Pa. wrote to Secy. of the Treasury Salmon P. Chase, "From my heart I have felt our national shame in disowning God as not the least of our present national disasters," the minister wrote, suggesting "recognition of the Almighty God in some form on our coins." Secy. Chase ordered designs prepared with the inscription *In God We Trust* and backed coinage legislation which authorized use of this slogan. It first appeared on some U. S. coins in 1864, disappeared and reappeared on various coins until 1955, when Congress ordered it placed on all paper money and all coins.

The National Anthem — The Star-Spangled Banner

The Star-Spangled Banner was ordered played by the military and naval services by President Woodrow Wilson in 1916. It was designated the National Anthem by Act of Congress, Mar. 3, 1931. It was written by Francis Scott Key, of Georgetown, D. C., during the bombardment of Fort McHenry, Baltimore, Md., Sept. 13-14, 1814. Key was a lawyer, a graduate of St. John's College, Annapolis, and a volunteer in a light artillery company. When a friend, Dr. Beanes, a physician of Upper Marlborough, Md., was taken aboard Admiral Cockburn's British squadron for interfering with ground troops, Key and J. S. Skinner, carrying a note from President Madison, went to the fleet under a flag of truce on a cartel ship to ask Beanes' release. Admiral Cockburn consented, but as the fleet was about to sail up the Patapsco to bombard Fort McHenry he detained them, first on H. M. S. Surprise, and then on a supply ship.

Key witnessed the bombardment from his own vessel. It began at 7 a.m., Sept. 13, 1814, and lasted, with intermissions, for 25 hours. The British fired over 1,500 shells, each weighing as much as 220 lbs. They were unable to approach closely because the Americans had sunk 22 vessels in the channel. Only four Americans were killed and 24 wounded. A British bomb-ship was disabled.

During the bombardment Key wrote a stanza on the back of an envelope. Next day at Indian Queen Inn, Baltimore, he wrote out the poem and gave it to his brother-in-law, Judge J. H. Nicholson. Nicholson suggested the tune, Anacreon in Heaven, and had the poem printed on broadsides, of which two survive. On Sept. 20 it appeared in the "Baltimore American." Later Key made 3 copies; one is in the Library of Congress and one in the Pennsylvania Historical Society.

The copy that Key wrote in his hotel Sept. 14, 1814, remained in the Nicholson family for 93 years. In 1907 it was sold to Henry Walters of Baltimore. In 1934 it was bought at auction in New York from the Walters estate by the Walters Art Gallery, Baltimore, for $26,400. The Walters Gallery in 1953 sold the manuscript to the Maryland Historical Society for the same price.

The flag that Key saw during the bombardment is preserved in the Smithsonian Institution, Washington. It is 30 by 42 ft., and has 15 alternate red and white stripes and 15 stars, for the original 13 states plus Kentucky and Vermont.

It was made by Mary Young Pickersgill. The Baltimore Flag House, a museum, occupies her premises, which were restored in 1953.

The Star-Spangled Banner

I

Oh, say can you see by the dawn's early light
　What so proudly we hailed at the twilight's last gleaming?
Whose broad stripes and bright stars thru the perilous fight,
　O'er the ramparts we watched were so gallantly streaming?
And the rocket's red glare, the bombs bursting in air,
　Gave proof through the night that our flag was still there.
Oh, say does that star-spangled banner yet wave
　O'er the land of the free and the home of the brave?

II

On the shore, dimly seen through the mists of the deep,
　Where the foe's haughty host in dread silence reposes,
What is that which the breeze, o'er the towering steep,
　As it fitfully blows, half conceals, half discloses?
Now it catches the gleam of the morning's first beam,
　In full glory reflected now shines in the stream:

'Tis the star-spangled banner! Oh long may it wave
　O'er the land of the free and the home of the brave!

III

And where is that band who so vauntingly swore
　That the havoc of war and the battle's confusion,
A home and a country should leave us no more!
　Their blood has washed out their foul footsteps' pollution.
No refuge could save the hireling and slave
　From the terror of flight, or the gloom of the grave:
And the star-spangled banner in triumph doth wave
　O'er the land of the free and the home of the brave!

IV

Oh! thus be it ever, when freemen shall stand
　Between their loved home and the war's desolation!
Blest with victory and peace, may the heav'n rescued land
　Praise the Power that hath made and preserved us a nation.
Then conquer we must, when our cause it is just,
　And this be our motto: "In God is our trust."
And the star-spangled banner in triumph shall wave
　O'er the land of the free and the home of the brave!

Statue of Liberty National Monument

Since 1886, the Statue of Liberty Enlightening the World has stood as a symbol of freedom in New York harbor. It also commemorates French-American friendship for it was given by the people of France, designed by Frederic Auguste Bartholdi (1834-1904). A $2.5 million building housing the American Museum of Immigration was opened by Pres. Nixon Sept. 26, 1972, at the base of the statue. It houses a permanent exhibition of photos, posters, and artifacts tracing the history of American immigration. The Monument is administered by the National Park Service.

Nearby Ellis Island, gateway to America for more than 12 million immigrants between 1892 and 1954, was proclaimed part of the National Monument in 1965 by Pres. Johnson.

Edouard de Laboulaye, French historian and admirer of American political institutions, suggested that the French present a monument to the United States, the latter to provide pedestal and site. Bartholdi visualized a colossal statue at the entrance of New York harbor, welcoming the peoples of the world with the torch of liberty.

On Washington's birthday, Feb. 22, 1877, Congress approved the use of a site on Bedloe's Island suggested by Bartholdi. This island of 12 acres had been owned in the 17th century by a Walloon named Isaac Bedloe. It was called Bedloe's until Aug. 3, 1956, when Pres. Eisenhower approved a resolution of Congress changing the name to Liberty Island.

The statue was finished May 21, 1884, and formally presented to U.S. Minister Morton July 4, 1884, by Ferdinand de Lesseps, head of the Franco-American Union, promoter of the Panama Canal, and builder of the Suez Canal.

On Aug. 5, 1884, the Americans laid the cornerstone for the pedestal. This was to be built on the foundations of Fort Wood, which had been erected by the Government in 1811. The American committee had raised $125,000, but this was found to be inadequate. Joseph Pulitzer, owner of the New York World, appealed on Mar. 16, 1885, for general donations. By Aug. 11, 1885, he had raised $100,000.

The statue arrived dismantled, in 214 packing cases, from Rouen, France, in June, 1885. The last rivet of the statue was driven Oct. 28, 1886, when Pres. Grover Cleveland dedicated the monument.

The statue weighs 450,000 lbs. or 225 tons. The copper sheeting weighs 200,000 lbs. There are 167 steps from the land level to the top of the pedestal, 168 steps inside the statue to the head, and 54 rungs on the ladder leading to the arm that holds the torch.

Two years of restoration work, to be completed by the statue's centennial celebration on July 4, 1986, were begun in 1984. Among other repairs, the $39 million project will include replacing the 1,600 wrought iron bands that hold its copper skin to its frame, replacing its torch, and installing an elevator.

Dimensions of the Statue	Ft.	In.
Height from base to torch (45.3 meters)	151	1
Foundation of pedestal to torch (91.5 meters)	305	1
Heel to top of head	111	1
Length of hand	16	5
Index finger	8	0
Circumference at second joint	3	6
Size of finger nail … 13x10 in.		
Head from chin to cranium	17	3
Head thickness from ear to ear	10	0
Distance across the eye	2	6
Length of nose	4	6
Right arm, length	42	0
Right arm, greatest thickness	12	0
Thickness of waist	35	0
Width of mouth	3	0
Tablet, length	23	7
Tablet, width	13	7
Tablet, thickness	2	0

Emma Lazarus' Famous Poem

A poem by Emma Lazarus is graven on a tablet within the pedestal on which the statue stands.

The New Colossus

Not like the brazen giant of Greek fame,
With conquering limbs astride from land to land;
Here at our sea-washed, sunset gates shall stand
A mighty woman with a torch, whose flame
Is the imprisoned lightning, and her name
Mother of Exiles. From her beacon-hand
Glows world-wide welcome; her mild eyes command
The air-bridged harbor that twin cities frame.
"Keep ancient lands, your storied pomp!" cries she
With silent lips. "Give me your tired, your poor,
Your huddled masses yearning to breathe free,
The wretched refuse of your teeming shore.
Send these, the homeless, tempest-tost to me,
I lift my lamp beside the golden door!"

Forms of Address for Persons of Rank and Public Office

In these examples John Smith is used as a representative American name. The salutation Dear Sir or Dear Madam is always permissible when addressing a person not known to the writer.

President of the United States

Address: The President, The White House, Washington, DC 20500. Also, The President and Mrs. ___.

Salutation: Dear Sir or Mr. President or Dear Mr. President. More intimately: My dear Mr. President. Also: Dear Mr. President and Mrs. ___

The vice president takes the same forms.

Cabinet Officers

Address: Mr. John Smith, Secretary of State, Washington, D.C. or The Hon. John Smith. Similar addresses for other members of the cabinet. Also: Secretary and Mrs. John Smith.

Salutation: Dear Sir, or Dear Mr. Secretary. Also: Dear Mr. and Mrs. Smith.

The Bench

Address: The Hon. John Smith, Chief Justice of the United States. The Hon. John Smith, Associate Justice of the Supreme Court of the United States. The Hon. John Smith, Associate Judge, U.S. District Court.

Salutation: Dear Sir, or Dear Mr. Chief Justice. Dear Mr. Justice. Dear Judge Smith.

Members of Congress

Address: The Hon. John Smith, United States Senate, Washington, DC 20510, or Sen. John Smith, etc. Also The Hon. John Smith, House of Representatives, Washington, DC 20515, or Rep. John Smith, etc.

Salutation: Dear Mr. Senator or Dear Mr. Smith; for Representative, Dear Mr. Smith.

Officers of Armed Forces

Address: Careful attention should be given to the precise rank, thus: General of the Army John Smith, Fleet Admiral John Smith. The rules for Air Force are same as Army.

Salutation: Dear Sir, or Dear General. All general officers, whatever rank, are entitled to be addressed as generals. Likewise a lieutenant colonel is addressed as colonel and first and second lieutenants are addressed as lieutenant.

Warrant officers and flight officers are addressed as Mister. Chaplains are addressed as Chaplain. A Catholic chaplain may be addressed as Father. Cadets of the United States Military Academy and Air Force Academy are addressed as Cadet. Noncommissioned officers are addressed by their titles. In the U. S. Navy all men from midshipman at Annapolis up to and including lieutenant commander are addressed as Mister.

Ambassador, Governor, Mayor

Address: The Hon. John Smith, followed by his or her title. They can be addressed either at their embassy, or at the Department of State, Washington, D.C. An ambassador from a foreign nation may be addressed as His or Her Excellency. An American is not to be so addressed.

Salutation: Dear Mr. or Madam Ambassador. An ambassador from a foreign nation may be called Your Excellency.

Governors and mayors are often addressed as The Hon. Jane Smith, Governor of _____, or The Hon. John Smith, Mayor of _____; also Governor John Smith, State House, Albany, N.Y., or Mayor Jane Smith, City Hall, Erie, Pa.

The Clergy

Address: His Holiness, the Pope, or His Holiness Pope (name), State of Vatican City, Italy.

Salutation: Your Holiness or Most Holy Father.

Also: His Eminence, John, Cardinal Smith; salutation: Your Eminence. An archbishop or a bishop is addressed The Most Reverend, and the salutation is Your Excellency. A monsignor who is a papal chamberlain is The Very Reverend Monsignor and the salutation is Dear Sir or Very Reverend Monsignor; a monsignor who is a domestic prelate is The Right Reverend Monsignor and salutation is Right Reverend Monsignor. A priest is addressed Reverend John Smith. A brother of an order is addressed Brother —. A sister takes the same form.

A bishop of the Protestant Episcopal Church is The Right Reverend John Smith; salutation is Right Reverend Sir, or Dear Bishop Smith. If a clergyman is a doctor of divinity, he is addressed: The Reverend John Smith, D.D., and the salutation is Reverend Sir, or Dear Dr. Smith. When a clergyman does not have the degree the salutation is Dear Mr. Smith.

A bishop of the Methodist Church is addressed Bishop John Smith with titles following.

Royalty and Nobility

An emperor is to be addressed in a letter as Sir, or Your Imperial Majesty.

A king or queen is addressed as His Majesty (Name), King of (Name), or Her Majesty (Name), Queen of (Name), Salutation: Sir, or Madam, or May it please Your Majesty.

Princes and princesses and other persons of royal blood are addressed as His (or Her) Royal Highness, and saluted with May it please Your Royal Highness.

A duke or marquis is My Lord Duke (or Marquis), a duke is His (or Your) Grace.

Code of Etiquette for Display and Use of the U.S. Flag

Although the Stars and Stripes originated in 1777, it was not until 146 years later that there was a serious attempt to establish a uniform code of etiquette for the U.S. flag. The War Department issued Feb. 15, 1923, a circular on the rules of flag usage. These were adopted almost in their entirety June 14, 1923, by a conference of 68 patriotic organizations in Washington. Finally, on June 22, 1942, a joint resolution of Congress, amended by Public Law 94-344 July 7, 1976, codified "existing rules and customs pertaining to the display and use of the flag. . ."

When to Display the Flag—The flag should be displayed on all days, especially on legal holidays and other special occasions, on official buildings when in use, in or near polling places on election days, and in or near schools when in session. A citizen may fly the flag at any time he wishes. It is customary to display the flag only from sunrise to sunset on buildings and on stationary flagstaffs in the open. However, it may be displayed at night on special occasions, preferably lighted. In Washington, the flag now flies over the White House both day and night. It flies over the Senate wing of the Capitol when the Senate is in session and over the House wing when that body is in session. It flies day and night over the east and west fronts of the Capitol, without floodlights at night but receiving light from the illuminated Capitol Dome. It flies 24 hours a day at several other places, including the Fort McHenry Nat'l Monument in Baltimore, where it inspired Francis Scott Key to write The Star Spangled Banner.

How to Fly the Flag—The flag should be hoisted briskly and lowered ceremoniously, and should never be allowed to touch the ground or the floor. When hung over a sidewalk from a rope extending from a building to a pole, the union should be away from the building. When hung over the center of a street it should have the union to the north in an east-west street and to the east in a north-south street. No other flag may be flown above or, if on the same level, to the right of the U.S. flag, except that at the United Nations Headquarters the UN flag may be placed above flags of all member nations and other national flags may be flown with equal prominence or honor with the flag of the U.S. At services by Navy chaplains at sea, the church pennant may be flown above the flag.

When two flags are placed against a wall with crossed staffs, the U.S. flag should be at right—its own right, and its staff should be in front of the staff of the other flag; when a number of flags are grouped and displayed from staffs, it should be at the center and highest point of the group.

Church and Platform Use—In an auditorium, the flag may be displayed flat, above and behind the speaker. When displayed from a staff in a church or public auditorium, the flag should hold the position of superior prominence, in advance of the audience, and in the position of honor at the clergyman's or speaker's right as he faces the audience. Any other flag so displayed should be placed on the left of the clergyman or speaker or to the right of the audience. When the flag is displayed horizontally or vertically against a wall, the stars should be uppermost and at the observer's left.

When to Salute the Flag—All persons present should face the flag, stand at attention and salute on the following occasions: (1) When the flag is passing in a parade or in a review, (2) During the ceremony of hoisting or lowering, (3) When the National Anthem is played, and (4) During the Pledge of Allegiance. Those present in uniform should render the military salute. When not in uniform, men should remove the hat with the right hand holding it at the left shoulder, the hand being over the heart. Men without hats should salute in the same manner. Aliens should stand at attention. Women should salute by placing the right hand over the heart.

On Memorial Day, the flag should fly at half-staff until noon, then be raised to the peak.

As provided by Presidential proclamation the flag should fly at half-staff for 30 days from the day of death of a president or former president; for 10 days from the day of death of a vice president, chief justice or retired chief justice of the U.S., or speaker of the House of Representatives; from day of death until burial of an associate justice of the Supreme Court, cabinet member, former vice president, or Senate president pro tempore, majority or minority Senate leader, or majority or minority House leader; for a U.S. senator, representative, territorial delegate, or the resident commissioner of Puerto Rico, on day of death and the following day within the metropolitan area of the District of Columbia and from day of death until burial within the decedent's state, congressional district, territory or commonwealth; and for the death of the governor of a state, territory, or possession of the U.S., from day of death until burial within that state, territory, or possession.

When used to cover a casket, the flag should be placed so that the union is at the head and over the left shoulder. It should not be lowered into the grave nor touch the ground.

Prohibited Uses of the Flag—The flag should not be dipped to any person or thing. (An exception—customarily, ships salute by dipping their colors.) It should never be displayed with the union down save as a distress signal. It should never be carried flat or horizontally, but always aloft and free.

It should not be displayed on a float, motor car or boat except from a staff.

It should never be used as a covering for a ceiling, nor have placed upon it any word, design, or drawing. It should never be used as a receptacle for carrying anything. It should not be used to cover a statue or a monument.

The flag should never be used for advertising purposes, nor be embroidered on such articles as cushions or hankerchiefs, printed or otherwise impressed on boxes or used as a costume or athletic uniform. Advertising signs should not be fastened to its staff or halyard.

The flag should never be used as drapery of any sort, never festooned, drawn back, nor up, in folds, but always allowed to fall free. Bunting of blue, white and red always arranged with the blue above and the white in the middle, should be used for covering a speaker's desk, draping the front of a platform, and for decoration in general.

An Act of Congress approved Feb. 8, 1917, provided certain penalties for the desecration, mutilation or improper use of the flag within the District of Columbia. A 1968 federal law provided penalties of up to a year's imprisonment or a $1,000 fine or both, for

publicly burning or otherwise desecrating any flag of the United States. In addition, many states have laws against flag desecration.

How to Dispose of Worn Flags—The flag, when it is in such condition that it is no longer a fitting emblem for display, should be destroyed in a dignified way, preferably by burning in private.

Pledge of Allegiance to the Flag

I pledge allegiance to the flag of the United States of America and to the republic for which it stands, one nation under God, indivisible, with liberty and justice for all.

This, the current official version of the Pledge of Allegiance, has developed from the original pledge, which was first published in the Sept. 8, 1892, issue of the Youth's Companion, a weekly magazine then published in Boston. The original pledge contained the phrase "my flag," which was changed more than 30 years later to "flag of the United States of America." An act of Congress in 1954 added the words "under God."

The authorship of the pledge had been in dispute for many years. The Youth's Companion stated in 1917 that the original draft was written by James B. Upham, an executive of the magazine who died in 1910. A leaflet circulated by the magazine later named Upham as the originator of the draft "afterwards condensed and perfected by him and his associates of the Companion force."

Francis Bellamy, a former member of the Youth's Companion editorial staff, publicly claimed authorship of the pledge in 1923. The United States Flag Assn., acting on the advice of a committee named to study the controversy, upheld in 1939 the claim of Bellamy, who had died 8 years earlier. The Library of Congress issued in 1957 a report attributing the authorship to Bellamy.

The Flag of the U.S.—The Stars and Stripes

The 50-star flag of the United States was raised for the first time officially at 12:01 a.m. on July 4, 1960, at Fort McHenry National Monument in Baltimore, Md. The 50th star had been added for Hawaii; a year earlier the 49th, for Alaska. Before that, no star had been added since 1912, when N.M. and Ariz. were admitted to the Union.

History of the Flag

The true history of the Stars and Stripes has become so cluttered by a volume of myth and tradition that the facts are difficult, and in some cases impossible, to establish. For example, it is not certain who designed the Stars and Stripes, who made the first such flag, or even whether it ever flew in any sea fight or land battle of the American Revolution.

One thing all agree on is that the Stars and Stripes originated as the result of a resolution offered by the Marine Committee of the Second Continental Congress at Philadelphia and adopted June 14, 1777. It read:

Resolved: that the flag of the United States be thirteen stripes, alternate red and white; that the union be thirteen stars, white in a blue field, representing a new constellation.

Congress gave no hint as to the designer of the flag, no instructions as to the arrangement of the stars, and no information on its appropriate uses. Historians have been unable to find the original flag law.

The resolution establishing the flag was not even published until Sept. 2, 1777. Despite repeated requests, Washington did not get the flags until 1783, after the Revolutionary War was over. And there is no certainty that they were the Stars and Stripes.

Early Flags

Although it was never officially adopted by the Continental Congress, many historians consider the first flag of the United States to have been the Grand Union (sometimes called Great Union) flag. This was a modification of the British Meteor flag, which had the red cross of St. George and the white cross of St. Andrew combined in the blue canton. For the Grand Union flag, 6 horizontal stripes were imposed on the red field, dividing it into 13 alternate red and white stripes. On Jan. 1, 1776, when the Continental Army came into formal existence, this flag was unfurled on Prospect Hill, Somerville, Mass. Washington wrote that "we hoisted the Union Flag in compliment to the United Colonies."

One of several flags about which controversy has raged for years is at Easton, Pa. Containing the devices of the national flag in reversed order, this has been in the public library at Easton for over 150 years. Some contend that this flag was actually the first Stars and Stripes, first displayed on July 8, 1776. This flag has 13 red and white stripes in the canton, 13 white stars centered in a blue field.

A flag was hastily improvised from garments by the defenders of Fort Schuyler at Rome, N.Y., Aug. 3-22, 1777. Historians believe it was the Grand Union Flag.

The Sons of Liberty had a flag of 9 red and white stripes, to signify 9 colonies, when they met in New York in 1765 to oppose the Stamp Tax. By 1775, the flag had grown to 13 red and white stripes, with a rattlesnake on it.

At Concord, Apr. 19, 1775, the minute men from Bedford, Mass., are said to have carried a flag having a silver arm with

sword on a red field.

At Cambridge, Mass., the Sons of Liberty used a plain red flag with a green pine tree on it.

In June 1775, Washington went from Philadelphia to Boston to take command of the army, escorted to New York by the Philadelphia Light Horse Troop. It carried a yellow flag which had an elaborate coat of arms — the shield charged with 13 knots, the motto "For These We Strive" — and a canton of 13 blue and silver stripes.

In Feb., 1776, Col. Christopher Gadsden, member of the Continental Congress, gave the South Carolina Provincial Congress a flag "such as is to be used by the commander-in-chief of the American Navy." It had a yellow field, with a rattlesnake about to strike and the words "Don't Tread on Me."

At the battle of Bennington, Aug. 16, 1777, patriots used a flag of 7 white and 6 red stripes with a blue canton extending down 9 stripes and showing an arch of 11 white stars over the figure 76 and a star in each of the upper corners. The stars are seven-pointed. This flag is preserved in the Historical Museum at Bennington, Vt.

At the Battle of Cowpens, Jan. 17, 1781, the 3d Maryland Regt. is said to have carried a flag of 13 red and white stripes, with a blue canton containing 12 stars in a circle around one star.

Legends about the Flag

Who Designed the Flag? No one knows for a certainty. Francis Hopkinson, designer of a naval flag, declared he also had designed the flag and in 1781 asked Congress to reimburse him for his services. Congress did not do so. Dumas Malone of Columbia Univ. wrote: "This talented man . . . designed the American flag."

Who Called the Flag Old Glory? — The flag is said to have been named Old Glory by William Driver, a sea captain of Salem, Mass. One legend has it that when he raised the flag on his brig, the Charles Doggett, in 1824, he said: "I name thee Old Glory." But his daughter, who presented the flag to the Smithsonian Institution, said he named it at his 21st birthday celebration Mar. 17, 1824, when his mother presented the homemade flag to him.

The Betsy Ross Legend — The widely publicized legend that Mrs. Betsy Ross made the first Stars and Stripes in June 1776, at the request of a committee composed of George Washington, Robert Morris, and George Ross, an uncle, was first made public in 1870, by a grandson of Mrs. Ross. Historians have been unable to find a historical record of such a meeting or committee.

Adding New Stars

The flag of 1777 was used until 1795. Then, on the admission of Vermont and Kentucky to the Union, Congress passed and Pres. Washington signed an act that after May 1, 1795, the flag should have 15 stripes, alternate red and white, and 15 white stars on a blue field in the union.

When new states were admitted it became evident that the flag would become burdened with stripes. Congress thereupon ordered that after July 4, 1818, the flag should have 13 stripes, symbolizing the 13 original states; that the union have 20 stars, and that whenever a new state was admitted a new star should be added on the July 4 following admission. No law designates the permanent arrangement of the stars. However, since 1912 when a new state has been admitted, the new design has been announced by executive order. No star is specifically identified with any state.

AFGHANISTAN

ALBANIA

ALGERIA

ANDORRA

ANGOLA

ANTIGUA & BARBUDA

ARGENTINA

ARUBA

AUSTRALIA

AUSTRIA

BAHAMAS

BAHRAIN

BANGLADESH

BARBADOS

BELAU

BELGIUM

BELIZE

BENIN

BERMUDA

BHUTAN

BOLIVIA

BONAIRE

BOTSWANA

BRAZIL

BRUNEI

BULGARIA

BURMA

BURUNDI

CAMBODIA
(PEOP. REP. KAMPUCHEA)

CAMEROON

CANADA

CAPE VERDE

CENTRAL AFRICAN REP.

CHAD

CHILE

CHINA (MAINLAND)

458

CHINA (TAIWAN)	COLOMBIA	COMOROS	CONGO
COSTA RICA	CUBA	CURAÇAO	CYPRUS
CZECHOSLOVAKIA	DENMARK	DJIBOUTI	DOMINICA
DOMINICAN REPUBLIC	ECUADOR	EGYPT	EL SALVADOR
EQUATORIAL GUINEA	ETHIOPIA	FIJI	FINLAND
FRANCE	GABON	GAMBIA	EAST GERMANY
WEST GERMANY	GHANA	GREECE	GREENLAND (FLAG OF DENMARK)
GRENADA	GUATEMALA	GUINEA	GUINEA-BISSAU
GUYANA	HAITI	HONDURAS	HUNGARY

ICELAND INDIA INDONESIA IRAN

IRAQ IRELAND ISRAEL ITALY

IVORY COAST JAMAICA JAPAN JORDAN

KENYA KIRIBATI NORTH KOREA SOUTH KOREA

KUWAIT LAOS LEBANON LESOTHO

LIBERIA LIBYA LIECHTENSTEIN LUXEMBOURG

MADAGASCAR MALAWI MALAYSIA MALDIVES

MALI MALTA MARSHALL ISLANDS MAURITANIA

MAURITIUS MEXICO MICRONESIA MONACO

MONGOLIA

MOROCCO

MOZAMBIQUE

NAMIBIA
(FLAG OF S. AFRICA)

NAURU

NEPAL

NETHERLANDS

NETHERLANDS ANTILLES

NEW ZEALAND

NICARAGUA

NIGER

NIGERIA

NORWAY

OMAN

PAKISTAN

PANAMA

PAPUA NEW GUINEA

PARAGUAY

PERU

PHILIPPINES

POLAND

PORTUGAL

QATAR

ROMANIA

RWANDA

ST. CHRISTOPHER AND NEVIS

ST. LUCIA

ST. VINCENT & GRENS.

SAN MARINO

SÃO TOMÉ E PRINCIPE

SAUDI ARABIA

SENEGAL

SEYCHELLES

SIERRA LEONE

SINGAPORE

SOLOMON ISLANDS

SOMALIA

SOUTH AFRICA

SPAIN

SRI LANKA (CEYLON)

SUDAN

SURINAME

SWAZILAND

SWEDEN

SWITZERLAND

SYRIA

TANZANIA

THAILAND

TOGO

TONGA

TRINIDAD AND TOBAGO

TUNISIA

TURKEY

TUVALU

UGANDA

U.S.S.R.

UNITED ARAB EMIRATES

UNITED KINGDOM

UNITED STATES

UPPER VOLTA
(BOURKINA FASSO)

URUGUAY

VANUATU

VATICAN CITY

VENEZUELA

VIETNAM

WESTERN SAMOA

YEMEN (PEOPLES REP.)

YEMEN ARAB REPUBLIC

YUGOSLAVIA

ZAIRE

ZAMBIA

ZIMBABWE

462

THE WORLD

MERCATOR PROJECTION

Capitals of Countries............ ●

Copyright by C.S. HAMMOND & Co., N.Y.

EUROPE

LAMBERT AZIMUTHAL EQUAL-AREA PROJECTION

SCALE OF MILES

0 100 200 300 400 500 600

SCALE OF KILOMETRES

0 100 200 300 400 500 600

Capitals of Countries ..... ●

International Boundaries .....
Internal Boundaries .....

Copyright by C.S.HAMMOND & CO., N.Y.

THE NEAR and MIDDLE EAST

CONIC PROJECTION

SCALE OF MILES

| 0 | 100 | 200 | 300 | 400 |

KILOMETERS

| 0 | 100 | 200 | 300 | 400 |

⊛ Capitals of Countries
International Boundaries
Other Boundaries

© Copyright HAMMOND INCORPORATED, Maplewood, N.J.

NORTH AMERICA

LAMBERT AZIMUTHAL EQUAL-AREA PROJECTION

SCALE OF MILES

0   100   200   400   600   800

SCALE OF KILOMETERS

0   200   400   600   800

Capitals of Countries........★

International Boundaries........

Other Boundaries........

Canals........

Copyright by C. S. HAMMOND & CO., N.Y.

PACIFIC OCEAN

LAMBERT AZIMUTHAL EQUAL-AREA PROJECTION

Capitals of Countries
Other Capitals

Copyright by C.S. HAMMOND & Co., N.Y.

HISTORY

Memorable Dates in U.S. History

1492
Christopher Columbus and crew sighted land **Oct. 12** in the present-day Bahamas.

1497
John Cabot explored northeast coast to Delaware.

1513
Juan Ponce de Leon explored Florida coast.

1524
Giovanni da Verrazano led French expedition along coast from Carolina north to Nova Scotia; entered New York harbor.

1539
Hernando de Soto landed in Florida **May 28;** crossed Mississippi River, **1541.**

1540
Francisco Vazquez de Coronado explored Southwest north of Rio Grande. Hernando de Alarcon reached Colorado River, Don Garcia Lopez de Cardenas reached Grand Canyon. Others explored California coast.

1565
St. Augustine, Fla. founded by Pedro Menendez. Razed by Francis Drake **1586.**

1579
Francis Drake claimed California for Britain. Metal plate, found **1936,** thought to be left by Drake, termed probable hoax **1979.**

1607
Capt. John Smith and 105 cavaliers in 3 ships landed on Virginia coast, started first permanent English settlement in New World at **Jamestown, May 13.**

1609
Henry Hudson, English explorer of Northwest Passage, employed by Dutch, sailed into New York harbor in **Sept.,** and up Hudson to Albany. The same year, **Samuel de Champlain** explored Lake Champlain just to the north. Spaniards settled **Santa Fe., N.M.**

1619
House of Burgesses, first representative assembly in New World, elected **July 30** at Jamestown, Va.
First black laborers — indentured servants — in English N. American colonies, landed by Dutch at Jamestown in **Aug.** Chattel slavery legally recognized, **1650.**

1620
Plymouth Pilgrims, Puritan separatists from Church of England, some living in Holland, left Plymouth, England **Sept. 15** on Mayflower. Original destination Virginia, they reached Cape Cod **Nov. 19,** explored coast; 103 passengers landed **Dec. 21** (Dec. 11 Old Style) at Plymouth. Mayflower Compact was agreement to form a government and abide by its laws. Half of colony died during harsh winter.

1624
Dutch left 8 men from ship New Netherland on **Manhattan Island** in **May.** Rest sailed to Albany.

1626
Peter Minuit bought Manhattan for Dutch from Man-a-hat-a Indians **May 6** for trinkets valued at $24.

1634
Maryland founded as Catholic colony with religious tolerance.

1636
Harvard College founded **Oct. 28,** now oldest in U.S. Grammar school, compulsory education established at Boston.
Roger Williams founded Providence, R.I., **June,** as a democratically ruled colony with separation of church and state. Charter was granted, **1644.**

1654
First Jews arrived in New Amsterdam.

1660
British Parliament passed **Navigation Act,** regulating colonial commerce to suit English needs.

1664
Three hundred **British troops Sept. 8 seized New Netherland** from Dutch, who yield peacefully. Charles II granted province of New Netherland and city of New Amsterdam to brother, Duke of York; both renamed New York. The Dutch recaptured the colony **Aug. 9, 1673,** but ceded it to Britain **Nov. 10, 1674.**

1676
Nathaniel Bacon led planters against autocratic British Gov. Berkeley, burned Jamestown, Va. Bacon died, 23 followers executed.
Bloody Indian war in New England ended **Aug. 12.** King Philip, Wampanoag chief, and many Narragansett Indians killed.

1682
Robert Cavelier, Sieur de La Salle, claimed lower Mississippi River country for France, called it Louisiana **Apr. 9.** Had French outposts built in Illinois and Texas, **1684.** Killed during mutiny **Mar. 19, 1687.**

1683
William Penn signed treaty with Delaware Indians and made payment for Pennsylvania lands.

1692
Witchcraft delusion at Salem (now Danvers) Mass. inspired by preaching; 19 persons executed.

1696
Capt. William Kidd, American hired by British to fight pirates and take booty, becomes pirate. Arrested and sent to England, where he was hanged **1701.**

1699
French settlements made in Mississippi, Louisiana.

1704
Indians attacked Deerfield, Mass. **Feb. 28-29,** killed 40, carried off 100.
Boston News Letter, first regular newspaper, started by John Campbell, postmaster. (*Publick Occurences* was suppressed after one issue **1690.**)

1709
British-Colonial troops captured French fort, Port Royal, Nova Scotia, in **Queen Anne's War 1701-13.** France yielded Nova Scotia by treaty **1713.**

1712
Slaves revolted in New York **Apr. 6.** Six committed suicide, 21 were executed. Second rising, **1741;** 13 slaves hanged, 13 burned, 71 deported.

1716
First theater in colonies opened in Williamsburg, Va.

1728
Pennsylvania Gazette founded by Samuel Keimer in Philadelphia. Benjamin Franklin bought interest **1729.**

1732
Benjamin Franklin published first *Poor Richard's Almanac;* published annually to 1757.

1735
Freedom of the press recognized in New York by acquittal of John Peter Zenger, editor of *Weekly Journal,* on charge of libeling British Gov. Cosby by criticizing his conduct in office.

1740-41
Capt. Vitus Bering, Dane employed by Russians, reached Alaska.

1744
King George's War pitted British and colonials vs. French. Colonials captured Louisburg, Cape Breton Is. **June 17, 1745.** Returned to France **1748** by Treaty of Aix-la-Chapelle.

1752
Benjamin Franklin, flying kite in thunderstorm, proved

lightning is electricity **June 15;** invented lightning rod.

1754

French and Indian War (in Europe called 7 Years War, started 1756) began when French occupied Ft. Duquesne (Pittsburgh). British moved Acadian French from Nova Scotia to Louisiana **Oct. 1755.** British captured Quebec **Sept. 18, 1759** in battles in which French Gen. Montcalm and British Gen. Wolfe were killed. Peace signed **Feb. 10 1763.** French lost Canada and American Midwest. British tightened colonial administration in North America.

1764

Sugar Act placed duties on lumber, foodstuffs, molasses and rum in colonies.

1765

Stamp Act required revenue stamps to help defray cost of royal troops. Nine colonies, led by New York and Massachusetts at Stamp Act Congress in New York **Oct. 7-25, 1765,** adopted Declaration of Rights opposing taxation without representation in Parliament and trial without jury by admiralty courts. Stamp Act **repealed Mar. 17, 1766.**

1767

Townshend Acts levied taxes on glass, painter's lead, paper, and tea. In 1770 all duties except on tea were repealed.

1770

British troops fired **Mar. 5** into Boston mob, killed 5 including **Crispus Attucks,** a black man, reportedly leader of group; later called **Boston Massacre.**

1773

East India Co. tea ships turned back at Boston, New York, Philadelphia in **May.** Cargo ship burned at Annapolis **Oct. 14,** cargo thrown overboard at **Boston Tea Party Dec. 16.**

1774

"Intolerable Acts" of Parliament curtailed Massachusetts self-rule; barred use of Boston harbor till tea was paid for.

First Continental Congress held in Philadelphia **Sept. 5-Oct. 26;** protested British measures, called for civil disobedience.

Rhode Island abolished slavery.

1775

Patrick Henry addressed Virginia convention, **Mar. 23** said "Give me liberty or give me death."

Paul Revere and William Dawes on night of **Apr. 18** rode to alert patriots that British were on way to Concord to destroy arms. At Lexington, Mass. **Apr. 19** Minutemen lost 8 killed. On return from Concord British took 273 casualties.

Col. Ethan Allen (joined by Col. Benedict Arnold) captured Ft. **Ticonderoga, N.Y. May 10;** also Crown Point. Colonials headed for **Bunker Hill,** fortified Breed's Hill, Charlestown, Mass., repulsed British under Gen. William Howe twice before retreating **June 17;** British casualties 1,000; called Battle of Bunker Hill. Continental Congress **June 15** named **George Washington** commander-in-chief.

1776

France and Spain each agreed **May 2** to provide one million livres in arms to Americans.

In Continental Congress **June 7,** Richard Henry Lee (Va.) moved "that these united colonies are and of right ought to be free and independent states." Resolution adopted July 2. **Declaration of Independence** approved **July 4.**

Col. Moultrie's batteries at **Charleston, S.C.** repulsed British sea attack **June 28.**

Washington, with 10,000 men lost **Battle of Long Island Aug. 27,** evacuated New York.

Nathan Hale executed as spy by British **Sept. 22.**

Brig. Gen. Arnold's **Lake Champlain** fleet was defeated at Valcour **Oct. 11,** but British returned to Canada. Howe failed to destroy Washington's army at **White Plains Oct. 28.** Hessians captured Ft. **Washington, Manhattan,** and 3,000 men **Nov. 16;** Ft. Lee, N.J. **Nov. 18.**

Washington in Pennsylvania, recrossed **Delaware River Dec. 25-26,** defeated 1,400 Hessians at Trenton, N.J. **Dec. 26.**

1777

Washington defeated Lord Cornwallis at **Princeton Jan.**

3. Continental Congress adopted Stars and Stripes. *See Flag article.*

Maj. Gen. John Burgoyne with 8,000 from Canada captured **Ft. Ticonderoga July 6.** Americans beat back Burgoyne at Bemis Heights **Oct. 7** and cut off British escape route. Burgoyne surrendered 5,000 men at **Saratoga N.Y. Oct. 17.**

Marquis de Lafayette, aged 20, made major general.

Articles of Confederation and Perpetual Union adopted by Continental Congress **Nov. 15**

France recognized independence of 13 colonies **Dec. 17.**

1778

France signed treaty of aid with U.S. **Feb. 6.** Sent fleet; British evacuated Philadelphia in consequence **June 18.**

1779

John Paul Jones on the *Bonhomme Richard* defeated *Serapis* in British North Sea waters **Sept. 23.**

1780

Charleston, S.C. fell to the British **May 12,** but a British force was defeated near **Kings Mountain, N.C. Oct. 7** by militiamen.

Benedict Arnold found to be a traitor **Sept. 23.** Arnold escaped, made brigadier general in British army.

1781

Bank of North America incorporated in Philadelphia **May 26.**

Cornwallis, harrassed by U.S. troops, retired to **Yorktown, Va.** Adm. De Grasse landed 3,000 French and stopped British fleet in Hampton Roads. Washington and Rochambeau joined forces, arrived near Williamsburg **Sept. 26.** When siege of Cornwallis began **Oct. 6,** British had 6,000, Americans 8,846, French 7,800. **Cornwallis surrendered Oct. 19.**

1782

New **British** cabinet agreed **in March** to recognize U.S. independence. Preliminary agreement signed in Paris **Nov. 30.**

1783

Massachusetts Supreme Court **outlawed slavery** in that state, noting the words in the state Bill of Rights "all men are born free and equal."

Britain, U.S. signed **peace treaty Sept. 3** (Congress ratified it **Jan. 14, 1784).**

Washington ordered **army disbanded Nov. 3,** bade farewell to his officers at Fraunces Tavern, N.Y. City **Dec. 4.**

Noah Webster published *American Spelling Book,* great bestseller.

1784

First successful daily newspaper, **Pennsylvania Packet & General Advertiser,** published **Sept. 21.**

1786

Delegates from 5 states at **Annapolis, Md. Sept. 11-14** asked Congress to call convention in Philadelphia to write practical constitution for 13 states.

1787

Shays's Rebellion, of debt-ridden farmers in Massachusetts, failed **Jan. 25.**

Northwest Ordinance adopted **July 13** by Continental Congress. Determined government of Northwest Territory north of Ohio River, west of New York; 60,000 inhabitants could get statehood. Guaranteed freedom of religion, support for schools, no slavery.

Constitutional convention opened at Philadelphia **May 25** with George Washington presiding. Constitution adopted by delegates **Sept. 17;** ratification by 9th state, New Hampshire, **June 21, 1788,** meant adoption; declared in effect **Mar. 4, 1789.**

1789

George Washington chosen president by all electors voting (73 eligible, 69 voting, 4 absent); John Adams, vice president, 34 votes. **Feb. 4.** First Congress met at Federal Hall, N.Y. City; regular sessions began **Apr. 6.** Washington inaugurated there **Apr. 30.** Supreme Court created by Federal Judiciary Act **Sept. 24.**

1790

Congress met in Philadelphia **Dec. 6,** new temporary Capital.

1791
Bill of Rights went into effect **Dec. 15.**

1792
Gen. **"Mad" Anthony Wayne** made commander in Ohio-Indiana area, trained "American Legion"; established string of forts. Routed Indians at Fallen Timbers on Maumee River Aug. 20, 1794, checked British at Fort Miami, Ohio.

1793
Eli Whitney invented **cotton gin**, reviving southern slavery.

1794
Whiskey Rebellion, west Pennsylvania farmers protesting liquor tax of **1791**, was suppressed by 15,000 militiamen **Sept. 1794.** Alexander Hamilton used incident to establish authority of the new federal government in enforcing its laws.

1795
U.S. bought peace from **Algiers and Tunis** by paying $800,000, supplying a frigate and annual tribute of $25,000 **Nov. 28.**
Gen. Wayne signed peace with Indians at Fort Greenville.
Univ. of North Carolina became first operating state university.

1796
Washington's Farewell Address as president delivered **Sept. 19.** Gave strong warnings against permanent alliances with foreign powers, big public debt, large military establishment and devices of "small, artful, enterprising minority" to control or change government.

1797
U.S. **frigate United States** launched at Philadelphia **July 10;** Constellation at Baltimore **Sept. 7;** Constitution (Old Ironsides) at Boston **Sept. 20.**

1798
War with France threatened over French raids on U.S. shipping and rejection of U.S. diplomats. Congress voided all treaties with France, ordered Navy to capture French armed ships. Navy (45 ships) and 365 privateers captured 84 French ships. USS Constellation took French warship Insurgente **1799.** Napoleon stopped French raids after becoming First Consul.

1801
Tripoli declared war June 10 against U.S., which refused added tribute to commerce-raiding Arab corsairs. Land and naval campaigns forced Tripoli to conclude **peace June 4, 1805.**

1803
Supreme Court, in **Marbury v. Madison** case, for the first time overturned a U.S. law **Feb. 24.**
Napoleon, who had recovered Louisiana from Spain by secret treaty, sold all of **Louisiana**, stretching to Canadian border, to U.S., for $11,250,000 in bonds, plus $3,750,000 indemnities to American citizens with claims against France. U.S. took title **Dec. 20.** Purchases doubled U.S. area.

1804
Lewis and Clark expedition ordered by Pres. Jefferson to explore what is now northwest U.S. Started from St. Louis **May 14;** ended **Sept. 23, 1806.** Sacajawea, an Indian woman, served as guide.
Vice Pres. **Aaron Burr**, after long political rivalry, **shot Alexander Hamilton** in a duel **July 11** in Weehawken, N.J.; Hamilton died the next day.

1807
Robert Fulton made first practical steamboat trip; left N.Y. City **Aug. 17**, reached Albany, 150 mi., in 32 hrs.

1808
Slave importation outlawed. Some 250,000 slaves were illegally imported **1808-1860.**

1811
William Henry Harrison, governor of Indiana, defeated Indians under the Prophet, in battle of Tippecanoe **Nov. 7.**
Cumberland Road begun at Cumberland, Md.; became important route to West.

1812
War of 1812 had 3 main causes: Britain seized U.S. ships trading with France; Britain seized 4,000 naturalized U.S. sailors by **1810;** Britain armed Indians who raided western border. U.S. stopped trade with Europe **1807** and **1809.** Trade with Britain only was stopped, **1810.**
Unaware that Britain had raised the blockade 2 days before, **Congress declared war June 18** by a small majority. The West favored war, New England opposed it. The British were handicapped by war with France.
U.S. naval victories in 1812 included: USS Essex captured Alert **Aug. 13;** USS Constitution destroyed Guerriere **Aug. 19;** USS Wasp took Frolic **Oct. 18;** USS United States defeated Macedonian off Azores **Oct. 25;** Constitution beat Java **Dec. 29.** British captured Detroit **Aug. 16.**

1813
Commodore **Oliver H. Perry** defeated British fleet at Battle of Lake Erie, **Sept. 10.** U.S. victory at Battle of the Thames, Ont., **Oct. 5,** broke Indian allies of Britain, and made Detroit frontier safe for U.S. But Americans failed in Canadian invasion attempts. York (Toronto) and Buffalo were burned.

1814
British landed in Maryland in August, defeated U.S. force **Aug. 24, burned Capitol** and White House. Maryland militia stopped British advance **Sept. 12.** Bombardment of Ft. McHenry, Baltimore, for 25 hours, **Sept. 13-14,** by British fleet failed; Francis Scott Key wrote words to **Star Spangled Banner.**
U.S. won naval Battle of **Lake Champlain Sept. 11.** Peace treaty signed at Ghent **Dec. 24.**

1815
Some 5,300 British, unaware of peace treaty, attacked U.S. entrenchments near **New Orleans, Jan. 1.** British had over 2,000 casualties, Americans lost 71.
U.S. flotilla finally ended piracy by **Algiers, Tunis, Tripoli** by **Aug. 6.**

1816
Second Bank of the U.S. chartered.

1817
Rush-Bagot treaty signed **Apr. 28-29;** limited U.S., British armaments on the Great Lakes.

1819
Spain cedes **Florida** to U.S. **Feb. 22.**
American steamship Savannah made first part steam-powered, part sail-powered crossing of Atlantic, Savannah, Ga. to Liverpool, Eng., 29 days.

1820
Henry Clay's **Missouri Compromise** bill passed by Congress **May 3.** Slavery was allowed in Missouri, but not elsewhere west of the Mississippi River north of 36° 30' latitude (the southern line of Missouri). Repealed **1854.**

1821
Emma Willard founded Troy Female Seminary, first U.S. women's college.

1823
Monroe Doctrine enunciated **Dec. 2,** opposing European intervention in the Americas.

1824
Pawtucket, R.I. **weavers strike** in first such action by women.

1825
Erie Canal opened; first boat left Buffalo **Oct. 26,** reached N.Y. City **Nov. 4.** Canal cost $7 million but cut travel time one-third, shipping costs nine-tenths; opened Great Lakes area, made N.Y. City chief Atlantic port.
John Stevens, of Hoboken, N.J., built and operated first experimental **steam locomotive** in U.S.

1828
South Carolina **Dec. 19** declared the right of state **nullification of federal laws**, opposing the "Tariff of Abominations."
Noah Webster published his *American Dictionary of the English Language.*
Baltimore & Ohio first U.S. passenger railroad, was be-

gun **July 4.**

1830

Mormon church organized by Joseph Smith in Fayette, N.Y. **Apr. 6.**

1831

Nat Turner, black slave in Virginia, led local slave rebellion, killed 57 whites in **Aug.** Troops called in, Turner captured, tried, and hanged.

1832

Black Hawk War (Ill.-Wis.) **Apr.-Sept.** pushed Sauk and Fox Indians west across Mississippi.

South Carolina convention passed **Ordinance of Nullification in Nov.** against permanent tariff, threatening to withdraw from the Union. Congress **Feb. 1833** passed a compromise tariff act, whereupon South Carolina repealed its act.

1833

Oberlin College, first in U.S. to adopt coeducation; refused to bar students on account of race, **1835.**

1835

Texas proclaimed right to secede from Mexico; Sam Houston put in command of Texas army, **Nov. 2-4.**

Gold discovered on **Cherokee land** in Georgia. Indians forced to cede lands **Dec. 20** and to cross Mississippi.

1836

Texans besieged in Alamo in San Antonio by Mexicans under Santa Anna **Feb. 23-Mar. 6;** entire garrison killed. Texas independence declared, **Mar. 2.** At San Jacinto **Apr. 21** Sam Houston and Texans defeated Mexicans.

Marcus Whitman, H.H. Spaulding and wives reached Fort Walla Walla on Columbia River, Oregon. **First white women to cross plains.**

Seminole Indians in Florida under Osceola began attacks **Nov. 1,** protesting forced removal. The unpopular 8-year war ended **Aug. 14, 1842;** Indians were sent to Oklahoma. War cost the U.S. 1,500 soldiers.

1841

First emigrant **wagon train for California,** 47 persons, left Independence, Mo. **May 1,** reached Cal. **Nov. 4.**

Brook Farm commune set up by New England transcendentalist intellectuals. Lasts to **1846.**

1842

Webster-Ashburton Treaty signed **Aug. 9,** fixing the U.S.-Canada border in Maine and Minnesota.

First use of **anesthetic** (sulphuric ether gas).

Settlement of Oregon begins via **Oregon Trail.**

1844

First message over first **telegraph line** sent **May 24** by inventor Samuel F.B. Morse from Washington to Baltimore: "What hath God wrought!"

1845

Texas Congress **voted for annexation** to U.S. **July 4.** U.S. Congress admits Texas to Union **Dec. 29.**

1846

Mexican War. Pres. James K. Polk ordered Gen. Zachary Taylor to seize disputed Texan land settled by Mexicans. After border clash, U.S. declared war **May 13;** Mexico **May 23.** Northern Whigs opposed war, southerners backed it.

Bear flag of Republic of California raised by American settlers at Sonoma **June 14.**

About 12,000 U.S. troops took Vera Cruz Mar. 27, 1847, Mexico City Sept. 14, 1847. By **treaty, Feb. 1848,** Mexico ceded claims to Texas, California, Arizona, New Mexico, Nevada, Utah, part of Colorado. U.S. assumed $3 million American claims and paid Mexico $15 million.

Treaty with Great Britain **June 15** set **boundary in Oregon** territory at 49th parallel (extension of existing line). Expansionists had used slogan "54° 40' or fight."

Mormons, after violent clashes with settlers over polygamy, left Nauvoo, Ill. for West under Brigham Young, settled **July 1847 at Salt Lake City, Utah.**

Elias Howe invented **sewing machine.**

1847

First **adhesive U.S. postage stamps** on sale **July 1;** Benjamin Franklin 5¢, Washington 10¢.

Ralph Waldo Emerson published first book of poems; **Henry Wadsworth Longfellow** published *Evangeline.*

1848

Gold discovered Jan. 24 in California; 80,000 prospectors emigrate in **1849.**

Lucretia Mott and Elizabeth Cady Stanton lead **Seneca Falls, N.Y. Women's Rights Convention July 19-20.**

1850

Sen. Henry Clay's **Compromise of 1850** admitted California as 31st state **Sept. 9,** slavery forbidden; made Utah and New Mexico territories without decision on slavery; made Fugitive Slave Law more harsh; ended District of Columbia slave trade.

1851

Herman Melville's *Moby Dick,* **Nathaniel Hawthorne's** *House of the Seven Gables* published.

1852

Uncle Tom's Cabin, by **Harriet Beecher Stowe,** published.

1853

Commodore Matthew C. Perry, U.S.N., received by Lord of Toda, Japan **July 14; negotiated treaty to open Japan** to U.S. ships.

1854

Republican party formed at Ripon, Wis. **Feb. 28.** Opposed Kansas-Nebraska Act (became law **May 30**) which left issue of slavery to vote of settlers.

Henry David Thoreau published *Walden.*

1855

Walt Whitman published *Leaves of Grass.*

First railroad train crossed Mississippi on the river's first bridge, Rock Island, Ill.-Davenport, Ia. **Apr. 21.**

1856

Republican party's first nominee for president, **John C. Fremont,** defeated. Abraham Lincoln made 50 speeches for him.

Lawrence, Kan. sacked **May 21** by slavery party; abolitionist **John Brown** led anti-slavery men against Missourians at Osawatomie, Kan. **Aug. 30**

1857

Dred Scott decision by U.S. Supreme Court **Mar. 6** held, 6-3, that a slave did not become free when taken into a free state, Congress could not bar slavery from a territory, and blacks could not be citizens.

1858

First **Atlantic cable** completed by Cyrus W. Field **Aug. 5;** cable failed **Sept. 1.**

Lincoln-Douglas debates in Illinois **Aug. 21-Oct. 15.**

1859

First commercially productive **oil well,** drilled near Titusville, Pa., by Edwin L. Drake **Aug. 27.**

Abolitionist **John Brown** with 21 men seized U.S. Armory at Harpers Ferry (then Va.) **Oct. 16.** U.S. Marines captured raiders, killing several. Brown was hanged for treason by Virginia **Dec. 2.**

1860

New England shoe-workers, 20,000, strike, win higher wages.

Abraham Lincoln, Republican, elected president in 4-way race.

First **Pony Express** between Sacramento, Cal. and St. Joseph, Mo. started **Apr. 3;** service ended **Oct. 24, 1861** when first transcontinental telegraph line was completed.

1861

Seven southern states set up **Confederate States of America Feb. 8,** with Jefferson Davis as president. Confederates fired on **Ft. Sumter** in Charleston, S.C. **Apr. 12,** captured it **Apr. 14.**

President **Lincoln called for 75,000 volunteers Apr. 15.** By **May,** 11 states had seceded. Lincoln blockaded southern ports **Apr. 19,** cutting off vital exports, aid.

Confederates repelled Union forces at first **Battle of Bull Run July 21.**

First **transcontinental telegraph** was put in operation.

1862

Homestead Act was approved **May 20;** it granted free

family farms to settlers.

Land Grant Act approved **July 7,** providing for public land sale to benefit agricultural education; eventually led to establishment of state university systems.

Union forces were victorious in western campaigns, took **New Orleans.** Battles in East were inconclusive.

1863

Lincoln issued **Emancipation Proclamation Jan. 1,** freeing "all slaves in areas still in rebellion."

The entire **Mississippi River** was in Union hands by **July 4.** Union forces won a major victory at **Gettysburg, Pa. July 1-July 4.** Lincoln read his **Gettysburg Address Nov. 19.**

Draft riots in N.Y. City killed about 1,000, including blacks who were hung by mobs **July 13-16.** Rioters protested provision allowing money payment in place of service. Such payments were ended 1864.

1864

Gen. Sherman marched through Georgia, taking Atlanta **Sept. 1,** Savannah **Dec. 22.**

Sand Creek massacre of Cheyenne and Arapaho Indians **Nov. 29** in a raid by 900 cavalrymen who killed 150-500 men, women, and children; 9 soldiers died. The tribes were awaiting surrender terms when attacked.

1865

Robert E. Lee surrendered 27,800 Confederate troops to Grant at Appomattox Court House, Va. **Apr. 9.** J.E. Johnston surrendered 31,200 to Sherman at Durham Station, N.C. **Apr. 18.** Last rebel troops surrendered **May 26.**

President **Lincoln was shot Apr. 14** by John Wilkes Booth in Ford's Theater, Washington; died the following morning. Booth was reported dead **Apr. 26.** Four co-conspirators were hung **July 7.**

Thirteenth Amendment, abolishing slavery, took effect **Dec. 18.**

1866

First post of the **Grand Army of the Republic** formed **Apr. 6;** was a major national political force for years. Last encampment, **Aug. 31, 1949,** attended by 6 of the 16 surviving veterans.

Ku Klux Klan formed secretly in South to terrorize blacks who voted. Disbanded **1869-71.** A second Klan was organized **1915.**

Congress took control of southern Reconstruction, backed freedmen's rights.

1867

Alaska sold to U.S. by Russia for $7.2 million **Mar. 30** through efforts of Sec. of State William H. Seward.

Horatio Alger published first book, *Ragged Dick.*

The **Grange** was organized **Dec 4,** to protect farmer interests.

1868

The World Almanac, a publication of the *New York World,* appeared for the first time.

Pres. **Andrew Johnson** tried to remove Edwin M. Stanton, secretary of war; was impeached by House **Feb. 24** for violation of Tenure of Office Act; acquitted by Senate **March-May.** Stanton resigned.

1869

Financial **"Black Friday"** in New York **Sept. 24;** caused by attempt to "corner" gold.

Transcontinental railroad completed; golden spike driven at Promontory, Utah **May 10** marking the junction of Central Pacific and Union Pacific.

Knights of Labor formed in Philadelphia. By **1886,** it had 700,000 members nationally.

Woman suffrage law passed in Territory of Wyoming **Dec. 10.**

1871

Great fire destroyed Chicago Oct. 8-11; loss est. at $196 million.

1872

Amnesty Act restored civil rights to citizens of the South **May 22** except for 500 Confederate leaders.

Congress founded first national park — **Yellowstone** in Wyoming.

1873

First U.S. **postal card issued May 1.**

Banks failed, panic began in **Sept.** Depression lasted 5 years.

"Boss" William Tweed of N.Y. City convicted of stealing public funds. He died in jail in **1878.**

Bellevue Hospital in N.Y. City started the first **school of nursing.**

1875

Congress passed **Civil Rights Act Mar. 1** giving equal rights to blacks in public accommodations and jury duty. Act invalidated in **1883** by Supreme Court.

First **Kentucky Derby** held **May 17** at Churchill Downs, Louisville, Ky.

1876

Samuel J. Tilden, Democrat, received majority of popular votes for president over **Rutherford B. Hayes,** Republican, but 22 electoral votes were in dispute; issue left to Congress. Hayes given presidency **in Feb., 1877** after Republicans agree to end Reconstruction of South.

Col. George A. Custer and 264 soldiers of the 7th Cavalry killed **June 25** in "last stand," Battle of the Little Big Horn, Mont., in Sioux Indian War.

Mark Twain published *Tom Sawyer.*

1877

Molly Maguires, Irish terrorist society in Scranton, Pa. mining areas, broken up by hanging of 11 leaders for murders of mine officials and police.

Pres. Hayes sent troops in violent national **railroad strike.**

1878

First commercial **telephone** exchange opened, New Haven, Conn. **Jan. 28.**

1879

F.W. **Woolworth** opened his first five-and-ten store in Utica, N.Y. **Feb. 22.**

Henry George published *Progress & Poverty,* advocating single tax on land.

1881

Pres. **James A. Garfield shot** in Washington, D.C. **July 2;** died **Sept. 19.**

Booker T. Washington founded Tuskegee Institute for blacks.

Helen Hunt Jackson published *A Century of Dishonor* about mistreatment of Indians.

1883

Pendleton Act, passed **Jan. 16,** reformed federal civil service.

Brooklyn Bridge opened **May 24.**

1886

Haymarket riot and bombing, evening of **May 4,** followed bitter labor battles for 8-hour day in Chicago; 7 police and 4 workers died, 66 wounded. Eight anarchists found guilty. Gov. John P. Altgeld denounced trial as unfair.

Geronimo, Apache Indian, finally surrendered **Sept. 4.**

American Federation of Labor (AFL) formed **Dec. 8** by 25 craft unions.

1888

Great blizzard in eastern U.S. **Mar. 11-14;** 400 deaths.

1889

Johnstown, Pa. flood May 31; 2,200 lives lost.

1890

First execution by **electrocution:** William Kemmler **Aug. 6** at Auburn Prison, Auburn, N.Y., for murder.

Battle of **Wounded Knee, S.D. Dec. 29,** the last major conflict between Indians and U.S. troops. About 200 Indian men, women, and children, and 29 soldiers were killed.

Castle Garden closed as N.Y. immigration depot; **Ellis Island** opened **Dec. 31,** closed **1954.**

Sherman Antitrust Act begins federal effort to curb monopolies.

Jacob Riis published *How the Other Half Lives,* about city slums.

1892

Homestead, Pa., strike at Carnegie steel mills; 7 guards and 11 strikers and spectators shot to death **July 6;** setback for unions.

1893
Financial panic began, led to 4-year depression.

1894
Thomas A. **Edison's kinetoscope** (motion pictures) (invented 1887) given first public showing **Apr. 14** in N.Y. City.

Jacob S. Coxey led 500 unemployed from the Midwest into Washington, D.C. **Apr. 29.** Coxey was arrested for trespassing on Capitol grounds.

1896
William Jennings Bryan delivered "Cross of Gold" speech at Democratic National Convention in Chicago **July 8.**

Supreme Court, in **Plessy v. Ferguson,** approved racial segregation under the "separate but equal" doctrine.

1898
U.S. **battleship Maine** blown up **Feb. 15** at Havana, 260 killed.

U.S. **blockaded Cuba Apr. 22** in aid of independence forces. Spain declared war **Apr. 24.** U.S. destroyed Spanish fleet in Philippines **May 1,** took Guam **June 20.**

Puerto Rico taken by U.S. **July 25-Aug. 12.** Spain agreed **Dec. 10** to cede Philippines, Puerto Rico, and Guam, and approved independence for Cuba.

U.S. annexed independent republic of **Hawaii.**

1899
Filipino insurgents, unable to get recognition of independence from U.S., started guerrilla war **Feb. 4.** Crushed with capture **May 23, 1901** of leader, Emilio Aguinaldo.

U.S. declared **Open Door Policy** to make China an open international market and to preserve its integrity as a nation.

John Dewey published *School and Society,* backing progressive education.

1900
Carry Nation, Kansas anti-saloon agitator, began raiding with hatchet.

U.S. helped suppress **"Boxers"** in Peking.

1901
Pres. William **McKinley was shot Sept. 6** by an anarchist, Leon Czolgosz; died **Sept. 14.**

1903
Treaty between U.S. and Colombia to have U.S. dig **Panama Canal** signed **Jan. 22,** rejected by Colombia. Panama declared independence with U.S. support **Nov. 3;** recognized by Pres. Theodore Roosevelt **Nov. 6.** U.S., Panama signed canal treaty **Nov. 18.**

Wisconsin set first **direct primary** voting system **May 23.**

First **automobile trip** across U.S. from San Francisco to New York **May 23-Aug. 1.**

First successful flight in heavier-than-air mechanically propelled airplane by **Orville Wright Dec. 17** near Kitty Hawk, N.C., 120 ft. in 12 seconds. Fourth flight same day by **Wilbur Wright,** 852 ft. in 59 seconds. Improved plane patented **May 22, 1906.**

Jack London published *Call of the Wild.*

Great Train Robbery, pioneering film, produced.

1904
Ida Tarbell published muckraking *History of Standard Oil.*

1905
First **Rotary Club** of local businessmen founded in Chicago.

1906
San Francisco earthquake and fire **Apr. 18-19** left 452 dead, $350 million damages.

Pure Food and Drug Act and Meat Inspection Act both passed **June 30.**

1907
Financial panic and depression started **Mar. 13.**

First round-world cruise of U.S. **"Great White Fleet";** 16 battleships, 12,000 men.

1909
Adm. Robert E. Peary reached **North Pole Apr. 6** on 6th attempt, accompanied by Matthew Henson, a black man, and 4 Eskimos.

National Conference on the Negro convened **May 30,** leading to founding of the National Association for the Advancement of Colored People.

1910
Boy Scouts of America founded **Feb. 8.**

1911
Supreme Court dissolved **Standard Oil Co.**

First **transcontinental airplane flight** (with numerous stops) by C.P. Rodgers, New York to Pasadena, **Sept. 17-Nov. 5;** time in air 82 hrs., 4 min.

1912
U.S. sent marines **Aug. 14** to **Nicaragua,** which was in default of loans to U.S. and Europe.

1913
N.Y. Armory Show introduced modern art to U.S. public **Feb. 17.**

U.S. blockaded Mexico in support of revolutionaries.

Charles Beard published his *Economic Interpretation of the Constitution.*

Federal Reserve System was authorized **Dec. 23,** in a major reform of U.S. banking and finance.

1914
Ford Motor Co. raised basic wage rates from $2.40 for 9-hr. day to $5 for 8-hr. day **Jan. 5.**

When U.S. sailors were arrested at Tampico **Apr. 9,** Atlantic fleet was sent to **Veracruz,** occupied city.

Pres. Wilson proclaimed **U.S. neutrality** in the European war **Aug. 4.**

The **Clayton Antitrust Act** was passed **Oct. 15,** strengthening federal anti-monopoly powers.

1915
First **telephone talk,** New York to San Francisco, **Jan. 25** by Alexander Graham Bell and Thomas A. Watson.

British ship **Lusitania** sunk **May 7** by German submarine; 128 American passengers lost (Germany had warned passengers in advance). As a result of U.S. campaign, Germany issued apology and promise of payments **Oct. 5.** Pres. Wilson asked for a military fund increase **Dec. 7.**

U.S. troops landed in **Haiti July 28.** Haiti became a virtual U.S. protectorate under **Sept. 16** treaty.

1916
Gen. John J. **Pershing entered Mexico** to pursue Francisco (Pancho) Villa, who had raided U.S. border areas. Forces withdrawn **Feb. 5, 1917.**

Rural Credits Act passed **July 17,** followed by Warehouse Act. **Aug. 11;** both provided financial aid to farmers.

Bomb exploded during **San Francisco** Preparedness Day parade **July 22,** killed 10. Thomas J. Mooney, labor organizer, and Warren K. Billings, shoe worker, were convicted; both pardoned in **1939.**

U.S. bought **Virgin Islands** from Denmark **Aug. 4.**

U.S. established military government in the **Dominican Republic Nov. 29.**

Trade and loans to **European Allies** soared during the year.

John Dewey published *Democracy in Education.*

Carl Sandburg published *Chicago Poems.*

1917
Germany, suffering from British blockade, declared almost unrestricted **submarine warfare Jan. 31.** U.S. cut diplomatic ties with Germany **Feb. 3,** and formally declared war **Apr. 6.**

Conscription law was passed **May 18.** First U.S. troops arrived in Europe **June 26.**

The 18th **(Prohibition)** Amendment to the Constitution was submitted to the states by Congress **Dec. 18.** On **Jan. 16, 1919,** the 36th state (Nebraska) ratified it. Franklin D Roosevelt, as 1932 presidential candidate, endorsed repeal; 21st Amendment repealed 18th; ratification completed **Dec. 5, 1933.**

1918
Over one million **American troops** were in Europe by July. War ended Nov. 11.
Influenza epidemic killed an estimated 20 million worldwide, 548,000 in U.S.

1919
First **transatlantic flight**, by U.S. Navy seaplane, left Rockaway, N.Y. **May 8**, stopped at Newfoundland, Azores, Lisbon **May 27**.
Boston police strike Sept. 9; National Guard breaks strike.
Sherwood Anderson published *Winesburg, Ohio.*
About 250 **alien radicals** were deported **Dec. 22.**

1920
In national **Red Scare**, some 2,700 Communists, anarchists, and other radicals were arrested **Jan.-May.**
Senate refused **Mar. 19** to ratify the **League of Nations** Covenant.
Nicola Sacco, 29, shoe factory employee and radical agitator, and **Bartolomeo Vanzetti**, 32, fish peddler and anarchist, accused of killing 2 men in Mass. payroll holdup **Apr. 15**. Found guilty **1921**. A 6-year worldwide campaign for release on grounds of want of conclusive evidence and prejudice failed. Both were executed **Aug. 23, 1927**. Vindicated July 19, 1977 by proclamation of Mass. Gov. Dukakis.
First regular licensed **radio** broadcasting begun **Aug. 20.**
Wall St., N.Y. City, **bomb** explosion killed 30, injured 100, did $2 million damage **Sept. 16.**
Sinclair Lewis' *Main Street*, F. Scott Fitzgerald's *This Side of Paradise* published.

1921
Congress sharply curbed **immigration**, set national quota system **May 19.**
Joint Congressional resolution declaring **peace with Germany, Austria, and Hungary** signed **July 2** by Pres. Harding; treaties were signed in **Aug.**
Limitation of Armaments Conference met in Washington **Nov. 12 to Feb. 6, 1922**. Major powers agreed to curtail naval construction, outlaw poison gas, restrict submarine attack on merchantmen, respect integrity of China. Ratified **Aug. 5, 1925.**
Ku Klux Klan began revival with violence against blacks in North, South, and Midwest.

1922
Violence during **coal-mine strike** at Herrin, Ill., **June 22-23** cost 36 lives, 21 of them non-union miners.
Reader's Digest founded.

1923
First **sound-on-film motion picture**, "Phonofilm" was shown by Lee de Forest at Rivoli Theater, N.Y. City, beginning in **April.**

1924
Law approved by Congress **June 15** making all **Indians citizens.**
Nellie Tayloe Ross elected governor of Wyoming **Nov. 9** after death of her husband **Oct. 2**; installed **Jan. 5, 1925**, first woman governor. **Miriam (Ma) Ferguson** was elected governor of Texas **Nov. 9**; installed **Jan. 20, 1925.**
George Gershwin wrote *Rhapsody in Blue.*

1925
John T. Scopes found guilty of having taught evolution in Dayton, Tenn. high school, fined $100 and costs **July 24.**

1926
Dr. Robert H. Goddard demonstrated practicality of **rockets Mar. 16** at Auburn, Mass. with first liquid fuel rocket; rocket traveled 184 ft. in 2.5 secs.
Air Commerce Act passed, providing federal aid for airlines and airports.

1927
About 1,000 **marines landed in China Mar. 5** to protect property in civil war. U.S. and British consulates looted by nationalists **Mar. 24.**
Capt. **Charles A. Lindbergh** left Roosevelt Field, N.Y. **May 20** alone in plane Spirit of St. Louis on first New York-Paris nonstop flight. Reached Le Bourget airfield **May 21**, 3,610 miles in 33 ½ hours.
The Jazz Singer, with Al Jolson, demonstrated part-talking pictures in N.Y. City **Oct. 6.**
Show Boat opened in New York **Dec. 27.**
O. E. Rolvaag published *Giants in the Earth.*

1929
"St. Valentine's Day massacre" in Chicago **Feb. 14**; gangsters killed 7 rivals.
Farm price stability aided by **Agricultural Marketing Act**, passed **June 15.**
Albert B. Fall, former sec. of the interior, was convicted of accepting a bribe of $100,000 in the leasing of the **Elk Hills (Teapot Dome)** naval oil reserve; sentenced **Nov. 1** to $100,000 fine and year in prison.
Stock Market crash Oct. 29 marked end of postwar prosperity as stock prices plummeted. Stock losses for 1929-31 estimated at $50 billion; worst American depression began.
Thomas Wolfe published *Look Homeward, Angel*. **William Faulkner** published *The Sound and the Fury.*

1930
London **Naval Reduction Treaty** signed by U.S., Britain, Italy, France, and Japan **Apr. 22**; in effect **Jan. 1, 1931**; expired **Dec. 31, 1936.**
Hawley-Smoot Tariff signed; rate hikes slash world trade.

1931
Empire State Building opened in N.Y. City **May 1.**
Pearl Buck published *The Good Earth.*

1932
Reconstruction Finance Corp. established **Jan. 22** to stimulate banking and business. Unemployment stood at 12 million.
Charles Lindbergh Jr. kidnaped Mar. 1, found dead **May 12.**
Bonus March on Washington **May 29** by World War I veterans demanding Congress pay their bonus in full. Army, under Gen. Douglas MacArthur, disbanded the marchers on Pres. Hoover's orders.

1933
All banks in the U.S. were ordered closed by Pres. Roosevelt **Mar. 6.**
In the "100 days" special session, **Mar. 9—June 16**, Congress passed **New Deal** social and economic measures.
Gold standard dropped by U.S.; announced by Pres. Roosevelt **Apr. 19**, ratified by Congress **June 5.**
Prohibition ended in the U.S. as 36th state ratified 21st Amendment **Dec. 5.**
U.S. foreswore armed intervention in **Western Hemisphere** nations **Dec. 26.**

1934
U.S. troops pull out of **Haiti Aug. 6.**

1935
Comedian **Will Rogers** and aviator Wiley Post **killed Aug. 15** in Alaska plane crash.
Social Security Act passed by Congress **Aug. 14.**
Huey Long, Senator from Louisiana and national political leader, was **assassinated Sept. 8.**
Porgy and Bess, George Gershwin opera on American theme, opened **Oct. 10** in N.Y. City.
Committee for Industrial Organization (CIO) formed to expand industrial unionism **Nov. 9.**

1936
Boulder Dam completed.
Margaret Mitchell published *Gone With the Wind.*

1937
Amelia Earhart Putnam, aviator, and co-pilot Fred Noonan lost **July 2** near Howland Is. in the Pacific.
Pres. Roosevelt asked for 6 additional Supreme Court justices; **"packing" plan** defeated.
Auto, steel labor unions won first big contracts.

1938
Naval Expansion Act passed **May 17.**
National minimum wage enacted **June 28.**
Orson Welles radio dramatization of *War of the Worlds* caused nationwide scare **Oct. 30.**

1939
Pres. Roosevelt asked **defense budget hike Jan. 5, 12.**

N.Y. World's Fair opened **Apr. 30,** closed **Oct. 31;** reopened **May 11, 1940,** and finally closed **Oct. 21.**

Einstein alerts FDR to **A-bomb** opportunity in **Aug. 2** letter.

U.S. declares its neutrality in European war **Sept. 5.**

Roosevelt proclaimed a limited **national emergency Sept. 8,** an unlimited emergency **May 27, 1941.** Both ended by Pres. Truman **Apr. 28, 1952.**

John Steinbeck published *Grapes of Wrath.*

1940
U.S. authorized sale of **surplus war material** to Britain **June 3;** announced transfer of 50 overaged destroyers **Sept. 3.**

First **peacetime draft** approved **Sept. 14.**

Richard Wright published *Native Son.*

1941
The **Four Freedoms** termed essential by Pres. Roosevelt in speech to Congress **Jan. 6;** freedom of speech and religion, freedom from want and fear.

Lend-Lease Act signed **Mar. 11,** providing $7 billion in military credits for Britain. Lend-Lease for USSR approved in **Nov.**

U.S. occupied **Iceland July 7.**

The **Atlantic Charter,** 8-point declaration of principles, issued by Roosevelt and Winston Churchill **Aug. 14.**

Japan attacked **Pearl Harbor,** Hawaii, 7:55 a.m. **Dec. 7,** 19 ships sunk or damaged, 2,300 dead. U.S. declared war on Japan **Dec. 8,** on Germany and Italy **Dec. 11** after those countries declared war.

1942
Federal government forcibly moved 110,000 **Japanese-Americans** (including 75,000 U.S. citizens) from West Coast to detention camps. Exclusion lasted 3 years.

Battle of **Midway June 3-6** was Japan's first major defeat.

Marines landed on **Guadalcanal Aug. 7;** last Japanese not expelled until **Feb. 9, 1943.**

U.S., Britain invaded North Africa **Nov. 8.**

First **nuclear chain reaction** (fission of uranium isotope U-235) produced at Univ. of Chicago, under physicists Arthur Compton, Enrico Fermi, others **Dec. 2.**

1943
All war contractors barred from **racial discrimination May 27.**

Pres. Roosevelt signed **June 10** the pay-as-you-go income tax bill. Starting **July 1** wage and salary earners were subject to a **paycheck withholding** tax.

Race riot in Detroit June 21; 34 dead, 700 injured. Riot in Harlem section of N.Y. City; 6 killed.

U.S. troops invaded Italy **Sept. 9.**

Marines advanced in **Gilbert Is. in Nov.**

1944
U.S., Allied forces invaded Europe at **Normandy June 6.**

G.I. Bill of Rights signed **June 22,** providing veterans benefits.

U.S. forces landed on **Leyte,** Philippines **Oct. 20.**

1945
Yalta Conference met in the Crimea, USSR, **Feb. 3-11.** Roosevelt, Churchill, and Stalin agreed Russia would enter war against Japan.

Marines landed on **Iwo Jima Feb. 19;** U.S. forces invaded **Okinawa Apr. 1.**

Pres. Roosevelt, 63, **died** of cerebral hemorrhage in Warm Springs, Ga. **Apr. 12.**

Germany surrendered May 7.

First **atomic bomb,** produced at Los Alamos, N.M., exploded at Alamogordo, N.M. **July 16.** Bomb dropped on **Hiroshima Aug. 6,** on **Nagasaki Aug. 9.** Japan surrendered **Aug. 15.**

U.S. forces entered **Korea** south of 38th parallel to displace Japanese **Sept. 8.**

Gen. Douglas MacArthur took over supervision of Japan **Sept. 9.**

1946
Strike by 400,000 **mine workers** began **Apr. 1;** other industries followed.

Philippines given independence by U.S. **July 4.**

1947
Truman Doctrine: Pres. Truman asked Congress to aid Greece and Turkey to combat Communist terrorism **Mar. 12.** Approved **May 15.**

United Nations Security Council voted unanimously **Apr. 2** to place under **U.S. trusteeship** the Pacific islands formerly mandated to Japan.

Jackie Robinson on Brooklyn Dodgers **Apr. 11,** broke the color barrier in major league baseball.

Taft-Hartley Labor Act curbing strikes was vetoed by Truman **June 20;** Congress overrode the veto.

Proposals later known as the **Marshall Plan,** under which the U.S. would extend aid to European countries, were made by Sec. of State George C. Marshall **June 5.** Congress authorized some $12 billion in next 4 years.

1948
USSR began a land **blockade of Berlin's** Allied sectors **Apr. 1.** This blockade and Western counter-blockade were lifted **Sept. 30, 1949,** after British and U.S. planes had lifted 2,343,315 tons of food and coal into the city.

Organization of American States founded **Apr. 30.**

Alger Hiss, former State Dept. official, indicted Dec. 15 for perjury, after denying he had passed secret documents to Whittaker Chambers for transmission to a communist spy ring. His second trial ended in conviction **Jan. 21, 1950,** and a sentence of 5 years in prison.

Kinsey Report on Sexuality in the Human Male published.

1949
U.S. troops withdrawn from **Korea June 29.**

North Atlantic Treaty Organization **(NATO)** established **Aug. 24** by U.S., Canada, and 10 West European nations, agreeing that "an armed attack against one or more of them in Europe and North America shall be considered an attack against all."

Mrs. I. Toguri D'Aquino **(Tokyo Rose** of Japanese wartime broadcasts) was sentenced **Oct. 7** to 10 years in prison for treason. Paroled **1956,** pardoned **1977.**

Eleven leaders of U.S. **Communist party** convicted **Oct. 14,** after 9-month trial in N.Y. City, of advocating violent overthrow of U.S. government. Ten defendants sentenced to 5 years in prison each and the 11th, to 3 years. Supreme Court upheld the convictions **June 4, 1951.**

1950
U.S. **Jan 14** recalled all consular officials from **China** after the latter seized the American consulate general in Peking.

Masked bandits robbed **Brink's Inc.,** Boston express office, **Jan. 17** of $2.8 million, of which $1.2 million was in cash. Case solved **1956,** 8 sentenced to life.

Pres. Truman authorized production of **H-bomb Jan. 31.**

United Nations asked for troops to restore Korea peace **June 25.**

Truman ordered Air Force and Navy to Korea **June 27** after North Korea invaded South. Truman approved ground forces, air strikes against North **June 30.**

U.S. sent 35 military advisers to **South Vietnam June 27,** and agreed to provide military and economic aid to anti-Communist government.

Army seized all railroads Aug. 27 on Truman's order to prevent a general strike; roads returned to owners in **1952.**

U.S. forces landed at Inchon Sept. 15; UN force took Pyongyang **Oct. 20,** reached China border **Nov. 20,** China sent troops across border **Nov. 26.**

Two members of a **Puerto Rican nationalist** movement tried to kill Pres. Truman **Nov. 1.** (see Assassinations)

U.S. **Dec. 8** banned shipments to **Communist China** and to Asiatic ports trading with it.

1951

Sen. **Estes Kefauver** led Senate investigation into organized crime. Preliminary report **Feb. 28** said gambling take was over $20 billion a year.

Julius Rosenberg, his wife, Ethel, and Morton Sobell, all U.S. citizens, were found guilty **Mar. 29** of conspiracy to commit wartime espionage. Rosenbergs sentenced to death, Sobell to 30 years. Rosenbergs **executed June 19, 1953.** Sobell released **Jan. 14, 1969.**

Gen. **Douglas MacArthur** was removed from his Korea command **Apr. 11** for making unauthorized policy statements.

Korea cease-fire talks began in July; lasted 2 years. **Fighting ended July 27, 1953.**

Tariff concessions by the U.S. to the Soviet Union, Communist China, and all communist-dominated lands were suspended **Aug. 1.**

The U.S., **Australia,** and **New Zealand** signed a mutual security pact **Sept. 1.**

Transcontinental television inaugurated **Sept. 4** with Pres. Truman's address at the Japanese Peace Treaty Conference in San Francisco.

Japanese Peace Treaty signed in San Francisco **Sept. 8** by U.S., Japan, and 47 other nations.

J.D. Salinger published *Catcher in the Rye.*

1952

U.S. **seizure of nation's steel mills** was ordered by Pres. Truman **Apr. 8** to avert a strike. Ruled illegal by Supreme Court **June 2.**

Peace contract between West Germany, U.S., Great Britain, and France was signed **May 26.**

The last racial and ethnic barriers to naturalization were removed, **June 26-27,** with the passage of the **Immigration and Naturalization Act of 1952.**

First **hydrogen device** explosion **Nov. 1** at Eniwetok Atoll in Pacific.

1953

Pres. Eisenhower announced **May 8** that U.S. had given France $60 million for **Indochina War.** More aid was announced in **Sept.** In **1954** it was reported that three fourths of the war's costs were met by U.S.

1954

Nautilus, first atomic-powered submarine, was launched at Groton, Conn. **Jan. 21.**

Five members of Congress were wounded in the House **Mar. 1** by 4 **Puerto Rican independence supporters** who fired at random from a spectators' gallery.

Sen. **Joseph McCarthy** led televised hearings **Apr. 22-June 17** into alleged Communist influence in the Army.

Racial segregation in public schools was unanimously ruled unconstitutional by the Supreme Court **May 17,** as a violation of the 14th Amendment clause guaranteeing equal protection of the laws.

Southeast Asia Treaty Organization **(SEATO)** formed by collective defense pact signed in Manila **Sept. 8** by the U.S., Britain, France, Australia, New Zealand, Philippines, Pakistan, and Thailand.

Condemnation of Sen. **Joseph R. McCarthy** (R., Wis.) voted by Senate, 67-22 **Dec. 2** for contempt of a Senate elections subcommittee, for abuse of its members, and for insults to the Senate during his Army investigation hearings.

1955

U.S. agreed **Feb. 12** to help train **South Vietnamese** army.

Supreme Court ordered **"all deliberate speed"** in integration of public schools **May 31.**

A **summit meeting** of leaders of U.S., Britain, France, and USSR took place **July 18-23** in Geneva, Switzerland.

Rosa Parks refused **Dec. 1** to give her seat to a white man on a bus in Montgomery, Ala. Bus segregation ordinance

declared unconstitutional by a federal court following boycott and NAACP protest.

Merger of America's 2 largest labor organizations was effected **Dec. 5** under the name American Federation of Labor and Congress of Industrial Organizations. The merged AFL-CIO had a membership estimated at 15 million.

1956

Massive resistance to Supreme Court desegregation rulings was called for **Mar. 12** by 101 Southern congressmen.

Federal-Aid **Highway Act** signed **June 29,** inaugurating interstate highway system.

First transatlantic **telephone cable** went into operation **Sept. 25.**

1957

Congress approved first **civil rights bill** for blacks since Reconstruction **Apr. 29,** to protect voting rights.

National Guardsmen, called out by Arkansas Gov. Orval Faubus **Sept. 4,** barred 9 black students from entering previously all-white Central High School in **Little Rock.** Faubus complied **Sept. 21** with a federal court order to remove the National Guardsmen. The blacks entered school **Sept. 23** but were ordered to withdraw by local authorities because of fear of mob violence. Pres. Eisenhower sent federal troops **Sept. 24** to enforce the court's order.

Jack Kerouac published *On the Road,* beatnik journal.

1958

First U.S. earth satellite to go into orbit, **Explorer I,** launched by Army **Jan. 31** at Cape Canaveral, Fla.; discovered Van Allen radiation belt.

Five thousand U.S. Marines sent to **Lebanon** to protect elected government from threatened overthrow **July-Oct.**

First domestic **jet airline** passenger service in U.S. opened by National Airlines **Dec. 10** between New York and Miami.

1959

Alaska admitted as 49th state **Jan. 3; Hawaii** admitted **Aug. 21.**

St. Lawrence Seaway opened **Apr. 25.**

The George Washington, first U.S. ballistic-missile submarine, launched at Groton, Conn. **June 9.**

N.S. Savannah, world's first atomic-powered merchant ship, launched **July 21** at Camden, N.J.

Soviet Premier **Khrushchev** paid unprecedented visit to U.S. **Sept. 15-27,** made transcontinental tour.

1960

A wave of **sit-ins** began **Feb. 1** when 4 black college students in Greensboro, N.C. refused to move from a Woolworth lunch counter when they were denied service. By **Sept. 1961** more than 70,000 students, whites and blacks, had participated in sit-ins.

U.S. launched first **weather satellite,** Tiros I, **Apr. 1.**

Congress approved a strong **voting rights act Apr. 21.**

A U-2 **reconnaisance plane** of the U.S. was shot down in the Soviet Union **May 1.** The incident led to cancellation of an imminent Paris summit conference.

Mobs attacked U.S. embassy in **Panama Sept. 17** in dispute over flying of U.S. and Panamanian flags.

U.S. announced **Dec. 15** it backed rightist group in **Laos,** which took power the next day.

1961

The U.S. severed diplomatic and consular relations with **Cuba Jan. 3,** after disputes over nationalizations of U.S. firms, U.S. military presence at Guantanamo base, etc.

Invasion of Cuba's **"Bay of Pigs" Apr. 17** by Cuban exiles trained, armed, and directed by the U.S., attempting to overthrow the regime of Premier Fidel Castro, was repulsed.

Commander Alan B. Shepard Jr. was rocketed from Cape Canaveral, Fla., 116.5 mi. above the earth in a Mercury capsule **May 5** in the first U.S. manned sub-orbital space flight.

1962

Lt. Col. **John H. Glenn Jr.** became the first American in orbit **Feb. 20** when he circled the earth 3 times in the Mercury capsule **Friendship 7.**

Pres. Kennedy said **Feb. 14** U.S. military advisers in Vietnam would fire if fired upon.

Supreme Court **Mar. 26** backed **one-man one-vote** apportionment of seats in state legislatures.

First U.S. **communications satellite** launched in **July.**

James Meredith became first black student at Univ. of Mississippi **Oct. 1** after 3,000 troops put down riots.

A Soviet **offensive missile buildup in Cuba** was revealed **Oct. 22** by Pres. Kennedy, who ordered a naval and air quarantine on shipment of offensive military equipment to the island. Kennedy and Soviet Premier Khrushchev reached agreement **Oct. 28** on a formula to end the crisis. Kennedy announced **Nov. 2** that Soviet missile bases in Cuba were being dismantled.

Rachel Carson's *Silent Spring* launched environmentalist movement.

1963
Supreme Court ruled **Mar. 18** that all **criminal defendants** must have counsel and that illegally acquired evidence was not admissible in state as well as federal courts.

Supreme Court ruled, 8-1, **June 17** that laws requiring **recitation of the Lord's Prayer** or Bible verses in public schools were unconstitutional.

A limited **nuclear test-ban treaty** was agreed upon **July 25** by the U.S., Soviet Union and Britain, barring all nuclear tests except underground.

Washington demonstration by 200,000 persons **Aug. 28** in support of **black demands** for equal rights. Highlight was speech in which Dr. Martin Luther King said: "I have a dream that this nation will rise up and live out the true meaning of its creed, 'We hold these truths to be self-evident: that all men are created equal.' "

South Vietnam Pres. **Ngo Dinh Diem assassinated Nov. 2;** U.S. had earlier withdrawn support.

Pres. John F. Kennedy was shot and fatally wounded by an assassin **Nov. 22** as he rode in a motorcade through downtown Dallas, Tex. Vice Pres. Lyndon B. Johnson was inaugurated president shortly after in Dallas. Lee Harvey Oswald was arrested and charged with the murder. Oswald was shot and fatally wounded **Nov. 24** by Jack Ruby, 52, a Dallas nightclub owner, who was convicted of murder **Mar. 14, 1964** and sentenced to death. Ruby died of natural causes **Jan. 3, 1967** while awaiting retrial.

U.S. troops in **Vietnam** totalled over 15,000 by year-end; aid to South Vietnam was over $500 million in **1963.**

1964
Panama suspended relations with U.S. **Jan. 9** after riots. U.S. offered **Dec. 18** to negotiate a new canal treaty.

Supreme Court ordered **Feb. 17** that **congressional districts** have equal populations.

U.S. reported **May 27** it was sending military planes to **Laos.**

Omnibus **civil rights bill** passed **June 29** banning discrimination in voting, jobs, public accommodations, etc.

Three **civil rights workers** were reported missing in Mississippi **June 22;** found buried **Aug. 4.** Twenty-one white men were arrested. On **Oct. 20, 1967,** an all-white federal jury convicted 7 of conspiracy in the slayings.

U.S. Congress **Aug. 7** passed **Tonkin Resolution,** authorizing presidential action in Vietnam, after North Vietnam boats reportedly attacked 2 U.S. destroyers **Aug. 2.**

Congress approved War on Poverty bill **Aug. 11.**

The **Warren Commission** released **Sept. 27** a report concluding that Lee Harvey Oswald was solely responsible for the Kennedy assassination.

1965
Pres. Johnson in **Feb.** ordered continuous **bombing of North Vietnam** below 20th parallel.

Some 14,000 U.S. troops sent to **Dominican Republic** during civil war **Apr. 28.** All troops withdrawn by following year.

New **Voting Rights Act** signed **Aug. 6.**

Los Angeles riot by blacks living in **Watts** area resulted in death of 35 persons and property damage est. at $200 mil-

lion **Aug. 11-16.**

Water Quality Act passed **Sept. 21** to meet pollution, shortage problems.

National origins quota system of **immigration** abolished **Oct. 3.**

Massive **electric power failure** blacked out most of northeastern U.S, parts of 2 Canadian provinces the night of **Nov. 9-10.**

U.S. forces in **South Vietnam** reached 184,300 by year-end.

1966
U.S. forces began firing into **Cambodia May 1.**

Bombing of Hanoi area of North Vietnam by U.S. planes began **June 29.** By **Dec. 31,** 385,300 U.S. troops were stationed in South Vietnam, plus 60,000 offshore and 33,000 in Thailand.

Medicare, government program to pay part of the medical expenses of citizens over 65, began **July 1.**

Edward Brooke (R, Mass.) elected **Nov. 8** as first black U.S. senator in 85 years.

1967
Black representative **Adam Clayton Powell** (D, N.Y.) was denied **Mar. 1** his seat in Congress because of charges he misused government funds. Reelected in 1968, he was seated, but fined $25,000 and stripped of his 22 years' seniority.

Pres. Johnson and Soviet Premier Aleksei Kosygin met **June 23 and 25** at **Glassboro State College** in N.J.; agreed not to let any crisis push them into war.

Black riots in **Newark, N.J. July 12-17** killed some 26, injured 1,500; over 1,000 arrested. In Detroit, Mich., **July 23-30** at least 40 died; 2,000 injured, and 5,000 left homeless by rioting, looting, burning in city's black ghetto. Quelled by 4,700 federal paratroopers and 8,000 National Guardsmen.

Thurgood Marshall sworn in **Oct. 2** as first black U.S. Supreme Court Justice. Carl B. Stokes (D, Cleveland) and Richard G. Hatcher (D, Gary, Ind.) were elected first black mayors of major U.S. cities **Nov. 7.**

By **December** 475,000 U.S. troops were in **South Vietnam,** all North Vietnam was subject to bombing. Protests against the war mounted in U.S. during year.

1968
USS Pueblo and 83-man crew seized in Sea of Japan **Jan. 23** by North Koreans; 82 men released **Dec. 22.**

"Tet offensive": Communist troops attacked Saigon, 30 province capitals **Jan. 30,** suffer heavy casualties.

Pres. Johnson **curbed bombing** of North Vietnam **Mar. 31.** Peace talks began in Paris **May 10.** All bombing of North is halted **Oct. 31.**

Martin Luther King Jr., 39, **assassinated Apr. 4** in Memphis, Tenn. James Earl Ray, an escaped convict, pleaded guilty to the slaying, was sentenced to 99 years.

Sen. Robert F. Kennedy (D, N.Y.) 42, **shot June 5** in Hotel Ambassador, Los Angeles, after celebrating presidential primary victories. Died **June 6.** Sirhan Bishara Sirhan, Jordanian, convicted of murder.

1969
Expanded four-party **Vietnam peace talks** began **Jan. 18.** U.S. force peaked at 543,400 in April. Withdrawal started **July 8.** Pres. Nixon set Vietnamization policy **Nov. 3.**

A car driven by **Sen. Edward M. Kennedy** (D, Mass.) plunged off a bridge into a tidal pool on Chappaquiddick Is., Martha's Vineyard, Mass. **July 18.** The body of Mary Jo Kopechne, a 28-year-old secretary, was found drowned in the car.

U.S. astronaut **Neil A. Armstrong,** 38, commander of the Apollo 11 mission, became the first man to **set foot on the moon July 20.** Air Force Col. Edwin E. Aldrin Jr. accompanied Armstrong.

Anti-Vietnam War **demonstrations reached peak** in U.S.; some 250,000 marched in Washington, D.C. **Nov. 15.**

Massacre of hundreds of civilians at **Mylai, South Vietnam** in 1968 incident was reported **Nov. 16.**

1970

United Mine Workers official **Joseph A. Yablonski,** his wife, and their daughter were found shot **Jan. 5** in their Clarksville, Pa. home. UMW chief W. A. (Tony) Boyle was later convicted of the killing.

A federal jury **Feb. 18** found the defendants in the **"Chicago 7"** trial innocent of conspiring to incite riots during the 1968 Democratic National Convention. However, 5 were convicted of crossing state lines with intent to incite riots.

Millions of Americans participated in anti-pollution demonstrations **Apr. 22** to mark the first **Earth Day.**

U.S. and South Vietnamese forces crossed **Cambodian** borders **Apr. 30** to get at enemy bases. Four students were killed **May 4** at **Kent St.** Univ. in Ohio by National Guardsmen during a protest against the war.

Two **women generals,** the first in U.S. history, were named by Pres. Nixon **May 15.**

A **postal reform** measure was signed **Aug. 12,** creating an independent U.S. Postal Service, thus relinquishing governmental control of the U.S. mails after almost 2 centuries.

1971

Charles Manson, 36, and 3 of his followers were found guilty **Jan. 26** of first-degree murder in the 1969 slaying of actress Sharon Tate and 6 others.

U.S. air and artillery forces aided a 44-day incursion by South Vietnam forces into **Laos** starting **Feb. 8.**

A Constitutional Amendment lowering the **voting age to 18** in all elections was approved in the Senate by a vote of 94-0 **Mar. 10.** The proposed 26th Amendment got House approval by a 400-19 vote **Mar. 23.** Thirty-eighth state ratified **June 30.**

A court-martial jury **Mar. 29,** convicted **Lt. William L. Calley Jr.** of premeditated murder of 22 South Vietnamese at Mylai on **Mar. 16, 1968.** He was sentenced to life imprisonment **Mar. 31.** Sentence was reduced to 20 years **Aug. 20.**

Publication of classified **Pentagon papers** on the U.S. involvement in Vietnam was begun **June 13** by the New York Times. In a 6-3 vote, the U.S. Supreme Court **June 30** upheld the right of the Times and the Washington Post to publish the documents under the protection of the First Amendment.

U.S. bombers struck massively in North Vietnam for 5 days starting **Dec. 26,** in retaliation for alleged violations of agreements reached prior to the 1968 bombing halt. U.S. forces at year-end were down to 140,000.

1972

Pres. Nixon arrived in **Peking Feb. 21** for an 8-day visit to China, which he called a "journey for peace." The unprecedented visit ended with a joint communique pledging that both powers would work for "a normalization of relations."

By a vote of 84 to 8, the Senate approved **Mar. 22** a Constitutional Amendment banning **discrimination against women** because of their sex and sent the measure to the states for ratification.

North Vietnamese forces launched the biggest attacks in 4 years across the demilitarized zone **Mar. 30.** The U.S. responded **Apr. 15** by resumption of bombing of Hanoi and Haiphong after a 4-year lull.

Nixon announced **May 8** the mining of **North Vietnam ports.** Last U.S. combat troops left **Aug. 11.**

Alabama Gov. George C. Wallace, campaigning at a Laurel, Md. shopping center **May 15, was shot** and seriously wounded as he greeted a large crowd. Arthur H. Bremer, 21, was sentenced Aug. 4 to 63 years for shooting Wallace and 3 bystanders.

In the first visit of a U.S. president to Moscow, Nixon arrived **May 22** for a week of summit talks with Kremlin leaders which culminated in a landmark **strategic arms pact.**

Five men were arrested **June 17** for breaking into the offices of the Democratic National Committee in the **Watergate** office complex in Washington, D.C.

The White House announced **July 8** that the U.S. would sell to the USSR at least $750 million of **American wheat,** corn, and other grains over a period of 3 years.

1973

Five of seven defendants in the **Watergate** break-in trial pleaded guilty **Jan. 11 and 15,** and the other 2 were convicted **Jan. 30.**

The Supreme Court ruled 7-2, **Jan. 22,** that a state may not prevent a woman from having an **abortion** during the **first 6 months of pregnancy,** invalidating abortion laws in Texas and Georgia, and, by implication, overturning restrictive abortion laws in 44 other states.

Four-party **Vietnam peace pacts** were signed in Paris **Jan. 27,** and North Vietnam released some 590 U.S. prisoners by **Apr. 1.** Last U.S. troops left **Mar. 29.**

The end of the **military draft** was announced **Jan. 27.**

China and the U.S. agreed **Feb. 22** to set up permanent liaison offices in each other's country.

Top **Nixon** aides H.R. Haldeman, John D. Ehrlichman, and John W. Dean, and Attorney General Richard Kleindienst **resigned Apr. 30** amid charges of White House efforts to obstruct justice in the Watergate case.

The Senate Armed Services Committee **July 16** began a probe into allegations that the U.S. Air Force had made 3,500 secret **B-52 raids into Cambodia** in 1969 and 1970.

John Dean, former Nixon counsel, told Senate hearings **June 25** that Nixon, his staff and campaign aides, and the Justice Department all had conspired to cover up Watergate facts. Nixon refused July 23 to release **tapes** of relevant White House conversations. Some tapes were turned over to the court **Nov. 26.**

The U.S. officially ceased bombing in **Cambodia** at midnight **Aug. 14** in accord with a June Congressional action.

Vice Pres. Spiro T. **Agnew Oct. 10 resigned** and pleaded "nolo contendere" (no contest) to charges of tax evasion on payments made to him by Maryland contractors when he was governor of that state. Gerald Rudolph Ford **Oct. 12** became first appointed vice president under the 25th Amendment; sworn in **Dec. 6.**

A total ban on **oil exports** to the U.S. was imposed by Arab oil-producing nations **Oct. 19-21** after the outbreak of an Arab-Israeli war. The ban was lifted **Mar. 18, 1974.**

Atty. Gen. Elliot Richardson resigned, and his deputy William D. Ruckelshaus and Watergate Special Prosecutor Archibald Cox were fired by Pres. Nixon **Oct. 20** when Cox threatened to secure a judicial ruling that Nixon was violating a court order to turn tapes over to Watergate case Judge John Sirica.

Leon Jaworski, conservative Texas Democrat, was named **Nov. 1** by the Nixon administration to be special prosecutor to succeed Archibald Cox.

Congress overrode **Nov. 7** Nixon's veto of the **war powers** bill which curbed the president's power to commit armed forces to hostilities abroad without Congressional approval.

1974

Impeachment hearings were opened **May 9** against Nixon by the House Judiciary Committee.

John D. Ehrlichman, and 3 **White House "plumbers"** were found guilty **July 12** of conspiring to violate the civil rights of Dr. Lewis Fielding, formerly psychiatrist to Pentagon Papers leaker Daniel Ellsberg, by breaking into his Beverly Hills, Cal. office.

The U.S. Supreme Court ruled, 8-0, **July 24** that Nixon had to turn over **64 tapes** of White House conversations sought by Watergate Special Prosecutor Leon Jaworski.

The House Judiciary Committee, in televised hearings **July 24-30,** recommended 3 **articles of impeachment** against Nixon. The first, voted 27-11 **July 27,** charged Nixon with taking part in a criminal conspiracy to obstruct justice in the Watergate cover-up. The second, voted 28-10 **July 29,** charged he "repeatedly" failed to carry out his constitutional oath in a series of alleged abuses of power. The third, voted 27-17 **July 30,** accused him of unconstitutional defiance of committee subpoenas. The House of Representatives voted without debate **Aug. 20,** by 412-3, to accept the committee report, which included the recommended impeachment articles.

Nixon resigned Aug. 9. His support began eroding Aug. 5 when he released 3 tapes, admitting he originated plans to have the FBI stop its probe of the Watergate break-in for political as well as national security reasons. **Vice President Gerald R. Ford** was sworn in as the 38th U.S. president on **Aug. 9.**

An **unconditional pardon** to ex-Pres. Nixon for all federal crimes that he "committed or may have committed" while president was issued by Pres. Gerald Ford **Sept. 8.**

1975

Found guilty of **Watergate** cover-up charges **Jan. 1** were ex-Atty. Gen. John N. Mitchell, ex-presidential advisers H.R. Haldeman and John D. Ehrlichman.

U.S. civilians were evacuated from **Saigon Apr. 29** as communist forces completed takeover of South Vietnam.

U.S. merchant ship **Mayaguez** and crew of 39 seized by Cambodian forces in Gulf of Siam **May 12.** In rescue operation, U.S. Marines attacked Tang Is., planes bombed air base; Cambodia surrendered ship and crew; U.S. losses were 15 killed in battle and 23 dead in a helicopter crash.

Congress voted $405 million for South **Vietnam refugees May 16;** 140,000 were flown to the U.S.

Illegal **CIA operations,** including records on 300,000 persons and groups, and infiltration of agents into black, anti-war and political movements, were described by a "blue-ribbon" panel headed by Vice Pres. Rockefeller **June 10.**

FBI agents captured **Patricia (Patty) Hearst,** kidnaped **Feb. 4, 1974,** in San Francisco **Sept. 18** with others. She was indicted for bank robbery; a San Francisco jury convicted her **Mar. 20, 1976.**

1976

Payments abroad of $22 million in bribes by Lockheed Aircraft Corp. to sell its planes were revealed **Feb. 4** by a Senate subcommittee. Lockheed admitted payments in Japan, Turkey, Italy, and Holland.

The U.S. celebrated its **Bicentennial July 4,** marking the 200th anniversary of its independence with festivals, parades, and N.Y. City's Operation Sail, a gathering of tall ships from around the world viewed by 6 million persons.

A mystery ailment **"legionnaire's disease"** killed 29 persons who attended an American Legion convention **July 21-24** in Philadelphia. The cause was found to be a bacterium, it was reported **June 18, 1977.**

The **Viking II** lander set down on **Mars'** Utopia Plains **Sept. 3,** following the successful landing by Viking I **July 20.**

1977

Pres. Jimmy Carter **Jan. 27** pardoned most Vietnam War **draft evaders,** who numbered some 10,000.

Convicted murderer **Gary Gilmore** was executed by a Utah firing squad **Jan. 17,** in the first exercise of capital punishment anywhere in the U.S. since **1967.** Gilmore had opposed all attempts to delay the execution.

Carter signed an act **Aug. 4** creating a new Cabinet-level **Energy Department.**

1978

Sen. Hubert H. Humphrey (D., Minn.), 66, lost a battle with cancer **Jan. 13,** after 32 years of public service, including 4 years as vice-president of the United States.

U.S. Senate voted **Apr. 18** to turn over the **Panama Canal** to Panama on Dec. 31, 1999, by a vote of 68-32, ending several months of heated debate; an earlier vote (**Mar. 16**) had given approval to a treaty guaranteeing the area's neutrality after the year 2000.

California voters **June 6** approved (by a 65% majority) the **Proposition 13** initiative to cut property taxes in the state by 57%, thus severely limiting government spending.

The U.S. Supreme Court **June 28** voted 5-4 not to allow a firm quota system in affirmative action plans; the Court did uphold programs that were more "flexible" in nature.

The **House Select Committee on Assassinations** opened hearings **Sept. 6** into assassinations of Pres. Kennedy and Martin Luther King Jr.; the committee recessed **Dec. 30** after concluding conspiracies likely in both cases, but with no further hard evidence for further prosecutions.

Congress passed the **Humphrey-Hawkins "full employment" Bill Oct. 15,** which set national goal of reducing unemployment to 4% by 1983, while reducing inflation to 3% in same period; Pres. Carter signed bill, **Oct. 27.**

1979

A major accident occurred, **Mar. 28,** at a nuclear reactor on **Three Mile Island** near Middletown, Pa. Radioactive gases escaped through the plant's venting system and a large hydrogen gas bubble formed in the top of the reactor containment vessel.

In the worst disaster in U.S. aviation history, an American Airlines **DC-10** jetliner lost its left engine and crashed shortly after takeoff in Chicago, **May 25,** killing 275 people.

Pope John Paul II, Oct. 1-6, visited the U.S. and reaffirmed traditional Roman Catholic teachings.

The federal government announced, **Nov. 1,** a $1.5 billion loan-guarantee plan to aid the nation's 3d largest automaker, **Chrysler Corp.,** which had reported a loss of $460.6 million for the 3d quarter of 1979.

Some 90 people, including 63 Americans, were taken hostage, **Nov. 3,** at the **American embassy in Teheran,** Iran, by militant student followers of Ayatollah Khomeini who demanded the return of former Shah Mohammad Reza Pahlavi, who was undergoing medical treatment in New York City.

1980

Citing "an extremely serious threat to peace," Pres. Carter announced, **Jan. 4,** a series of **punitive measures against the USSR,** most notably an embargo on the sale of grain and high technology, in retaliation for the Soviet invasion of Afghanistan. At Carter's request, the **U.S. Olympic Committee** voted, **Apr. 12,** not to attend the Moscow Summer Olympics.

Eight Americans were killed and 5 wounded, **Apr. 24,** in an ill-fated attempt to **rescue the hostages** held by Iranian **militants** at the U.S. Embassy in Teheran.

In Washington, **Mt. St. Helens erupted, May 18,** in a violent blast estimated to be 500 times as powerful as the Hiroshima atomic bomb. The blast, followed by others on **May 25** and **June 12,** left 25 confirmed dead, at least 40 missing, and economic losses estimated at nearly $3 billion.

In a sweeping victory, **Nov. 4, Ronald Wilson Reagan** was elected 40th President of the United States, defeating incumbent Jimmy Carter. The stunning GOP victory extended to the U.S. Congress where Republicans gained control of the Senate and wrested 33 House seats from the Democrats.

Former Beatle **John Lennon** was shot and killed, **Dec. 8,** outside his apartment building in New York City, by Mark David Chapman, a former psychiatric patient.

1981

Minutes after the **inauguration of Pres. Ronald Reagan, Jan. 20,** the **52 Americans** who had been held **hostage in Iran** for 444 days were flown to freedom following an agreement in which the U.S. agreed to return to Iran $8 billion in frozen assets.

President Reagan was **shot in the chest** by John W. Hinckley, Jr., a would-be assassin, **Mar. 30,** in Washington, D.C., as he walked to his limousine following an address at the Washington Hilton.

The world's first reusable spacecraft, the **Space Shuttle Columbia,** was sent into space, **Apr. 12,** and completed its successful mission 2 days later.

Both houses of Congress passed, **July 29,** President Reagan's **tax-cut legislation.** The bill, the largest tax cut in the nation's history, was expected to reduce taxes by $37.6 billion in fiscal year 1982, and would save taxpayers $750 billion over the next 5 years.

Federal air traffic controllers, Aug. 3, began an illegal nationwide strike after their union rejected the government's final offer for a new contract. Most of the 13,000 striking controllers defied the back-to-work order, and were dismissed by President Reagan on **Aug. 5.**

In a 99-0 vote, the Senate confirmed, **Sept. 21,** the appointment of **Sandra Day O'Connor** as an **associate justice of the U.S. Supreme Court.** She was the first woman appointed to that body.

President Reagan ordered a series of **sanctions against the new Polish military government, Dec. 23**, in response to the imposition of martial law that had occurred in that country. This was followed, **Dec. 29**, by reprisals against the **Soviet Union** for its alleged role in the crackdown.

1982

The 13-year-old lawsuit brought against **AT&T** by the **Justice Department** was settled on **Jan. 8.** AT&T agreed to give up the 22 **Bell System** companies but, in return, was allowed to expand its operations into previously prohibited areas such as data processing, telephone and computer equipment sales, and computer communication devices.

On **Mar. 2**, the Senate voted 57-37 in favor of a bill that virtually eliminated busing for the purposes of racial integration.

On **June 12**, in **New York's Central Park**, hundreds of thousands of demonstrators gathered to protest nuclear arms.

The Senate adopted a bill on **June 18** extending for an additional 25 years the section of the **Voting Rights Act** dealing with changes in election procedures.

The **Equal Rights Amendment was defeated** after a 10-year struggle for ratification.

Secretary of State **Alexander M. Haig resigned on June 25.** George P. Shultz, a former Secretary of the Treasury, was nominated and approved as Haig's replacement.

The **elections** on **Nov. 2** resulted in gains for the Democrats—the margin in the new House was 269-166. In the Senate elections, Democrats won 20 out of 33 seats, but were still the minority, 54-46.

The **highest unemployment rate since 1940**, 10.4%, was reported on **Nov. 5.** The rate for Nov. reached 10.8%, with over 11 million unemployed.

Leonid Brezhnev, 75, general secretary of the central committee of the Communist Party and the **Soviet Union**, died of a heart attack on **Nov. 10.** On **Nov. 12**, the central committee unanimously elected Yuri V. Andropov, 68, to succeed him. Andropov was a member of the ruling Politburo and a former head of the state security police.

Lech Walesa, former leader of **Solidarity**, the Polish labor union, was freed **Nov. 13**, after 11 months of internment following the imposition of martial law and the outlawing of Solidarity in Dec. 1981. The Polish government declared Walesa "no longer a threat to internal security." In response, Pres. Reagan lifted the **U.S. embargo on sales of oil and gas equipment to the Soviet Union.**

The **Space Shuttle Columbia** completed its first operational flight on **Nov. 16.**

The 8-week-old **National Football League players' strike** ended **Nov. 16.** It was estimated that the strike had cost players, owners, media, cities, and businesses nearly $450 million.

Sen Edward M. Kennedy (D., Mass.) announced on **Dec. 1** that he would not seek his party's **1984 nomination for the presidency.** Kennedy had been regarded as the leading contender.

A retired dentist, **Dr. Barney B. Clark**, 61, became the first recipient of a **permanent artificial heart** during a 7½ hour operation in Salt Lake City on **Dec. 2.** The heart was designed by **Dr. Robert Jarvik**, who also served on the surgical team.

On **Dec. 16**, Anne M. Gorsuch, administrator of the **Environmental Protection Agency**, became the first Cabinet level official to be cited for contempt by the House when she declined to submit certain documents requested by a House subcommittee.

1983

Four aspirants for the **1984 Democratic presidential nomination** declared their candidacy in **Feb.: Sen. Alan Cranston** (Cal.), the Senate Democratic whip; **Sen. Gary Hart** (Col.); former vice president **Walter Mondale**; and former two-term governor of Florida, **Reuben Askew.** Mondale was considered the front-runner.

Anne McGill (Gorsuch) Burford stepped down on **Mar. 9**

as administrator of the federal **Environmental Protection Agency**, as criticism of the agency continued to build.

On **Mar. 14**, for the first time in its 23-year-history, the **Organization of Petroleum Exporting Countries (OPEC)** agreed to cut the prices of its **crude oil.** The decision in London reflected falling worldwide demand for OPEC products.

In **Apr.**, Sen. **Ernest Hollings** (S.C.), **and Sen. John Glenn** (Ohio) announced their candidacies for the **1984 Democratic presidential nomination.**

On **Apr. 20**, Pres. Reagan signed into law a compromise and bipartisan bill designed to rescue the **Social Security System** from bankruptcy.

The **National Commission on Excellence in Education** issued its report on **Apr. 26.** The report labelled U.S. elementary and secondary education "mediocre," and recommended that: schools put more emphasis on English, math, social studies, and computer science; the school day be lengthened; teachers be rewarded for merit rather than seniority; and college admissions standards be raised.

In an 8-1 decision, **the U.S. Supreme Court** held, **May 24**, that the **Internal Revenue Service** could deny **tax exemptions** to private schools that practiced **racial discrimination.**

The **House, May 24**, and the **Senate, May 25**, voted to free $625 million for the **MX missile**, after Congress received assurances from **Pres. Reagan** that he would be more flexible in **arms talks** with the Soviet Union.

Sally Ride became the first American **woman** to travel in space, **June 18**, when the **space shuttle Challenger** was launched from Cape Canaveral, Fla.

The **Soviet Union** shot a **South Korean airliner** out of the sky on **Sept. 1**, killing all 269 people aboard. The attack occurred in Soviet air space, and the plane crashed onto the Sea of Japan. The USSR charged that the plane, which carried 240 passengers and a crew of 29, had been on a **spying mission.** Most of the noncommunist world, led by **Pres. Reagan**, responded with condemnation.

The **Big 3 auto companies** reported, **Oct. 4**, that sales had increased 16.7 percent during the 1983 model year. It was the biggest gain from the previous year since 1978.

Lech Walesa, the founder of **Solidarity**, the Polish labor union, was named winner of the 1983 **Nobel Peace Prize** on **Oct. 5.**

On **Oct. 23**, 241 U.S. **Marines and sailors**, members of the multinational **peacekeeping force** in Lebanon, were killed when a TNT-laden suicide **terrorist** blew up Marine headquarters at **Beirut Intl. Airport.** Almost simultaneously, a second truck bomb blew up a **French paratroop** barracks two miles away, killing more than 40.

U.S. Marines and Rangers and a small force from 6 **Caribbean** nations invaded the island of **Grenada** on **Oct. 25.** Pres. Reagan said the action was in response to an **Oct. 23** request from the **Organization of Eastern Caribbean States** to help restore order to Grenada, whose government had been overthrown the previous week, and also to protect the lives of the 1,000 U.S. citizens on the island. After a few days of intense fighting, Grenadian militia and Cuban "construction workers" were overcome, hundreds of U.S. citizens evacuated safely, and the hard-line Marxist regime deposed. Caches of Soviet-made arms were said to have been found, and 600 Cubans captured. A majority of members of the OAS, U.N. Security Council, and U.N. General Assembly voted for resolutions condemning the invasion. The U.S. Senate and the House approved resolutions applying the War Powers Resolution to the conflict, requiring U.S. troops to leave Grenada by **Dec. 24.** The Defense Dept. said, **Nov. 2**, that the hostilities had ended. Casualties were put at 45 Grenadians, 24 Cubans, and 18 Americans killed, with 115 Americans wounded in action. The last 190 U.S. combat troops left Grenada, **Dec. 15**, but some 300 noncombat troops remained.

For events of 1984 and late 1983,
see Chronology

WORLD HISTORY

by Barry Youngerman

Prehistory: Our Ancestors Take Over

Homo sapiens. The precise origins of *homo sapiens,* the species to which all humans belong, are subject to broad speculation based on a small number of fossils, genetic and anatomical studies, and the geological record. But nearly all scientists agree that we evolved from ape-like primate ancestors in a process that began millions of years ago.

Current theories say the first hominid (human-like primate) was *Ramapithecus,* who emerged 12 million years ago. Its remains have been found in Asia, Europe, and Africa. Further development was apparently limited to Africa, where 2 lines of hominids appeared some 5 or 6 million years ago. One was *Australopithecus,* a tool-maker and social animal, who lived from perhaps 4 to 3 million years ago, and then apparently became extinct.

The 2nd was a human line, *Homo habillus,* a large-brained specimen that walked upright and had a dextrous hand. *Homo habillus* lived in semi-permanent camps and had a food-gathering and sharing economy.

Homo erectus, our nearest ancestor, appeared in Africa perhaps 1.75 million years ago, and began spreading into Asia and Europe soon after. It had a fairly large brain and a skeletal structure similar to ours. *Homo erectus* learned to control fire, and probably had primitive language skills. The final brain development to *Homo sapiens* and then to our sub-species *Homo sapiens sapiens* occurred between 500,000 and 50,000 years ago, over a wide geographic area and in many different steps and recombinations. All humans of all races belong to this sub-species.

The spread of mankind into the remaining habitable continents próbably took place during the last ice age up to 100,000 years ago: to the Americas across a land bridge from Asia, and to Australia across the Timor Straits.

Earliest cultures. A variety of cultural modes — in tool-making, diet, shelter, and possibly social arrangements and spiritual expression, arose as early mankind adapted to different geographic and climatic zones.

Three basic tool-making traditions are recognized by archeologists as arising and often coexisting from one million years ago to the near past: the *chopper tradition,* found largely in E. Asia, with crude chopping tools and simple flake tools; the *flake tradition,* found in Africa and W. Europe, with a variety of small cutting and flaking tools, and the *biface tradition,* found in all of Africa, W. and S. Europe, and S. Asia, producing pointed hand axes chipped on both faces. Later biface sites yield more refined axes and a variety of other tools, weapons, and ornaments using bone, antler, and wood as well as stone.

Only sketchy evidence remains for the different stages in man's increasing control over the environment. Traces of 400,000-year-old covered wood shelters have been found at Nice, France. Scraping tools at Neanderthal sites (200,000-30,000 BC in Europe, N. Africa, the Middle East and Central Asia) suggest the treatment of skins for clothing. Sites from all parts of the world show seasonal migration patterns and exploitation of a wide range of plant and animal food sources.

Painting and decoration, for which there is evidence at the Nice site, flourished along with stone and ivory sculpture after 30,000 years ago; 60 caves in France and 30 in Spain show remarkable examples of wall painting. Other examples have been found in Africa. Proto-religious rites are suggested by these works, and by evidence of ritual cannibalism by Peking Man, 500,000 BC, and of ritual burial with medicinal plants and flowers by Neanderthals at Shanidar in Iraq.

The Neolithic Revolution. Sometime after 10,000 BC, among widely separated human communities, a series of dramatic technological and social changes occurred that are summed up as the Neolithic Revolution. The cultivation of previously wild plants encouraged the growth of permanent settlements. Animals were domesticated as a work force and food source. The manufacture of pottery and cloth began. These techniques permitted a huge increase in world population and in human control over the earth.

No region can safely claim priority as the "inventor" of these techniques. Dispersed sites in Cen. and S. America, S.E. Europe, and the Middle East show roughly contemporaneous (10-8,000 BC) evidence of one or another "neolithic" trait. Dates near 6-3,000 BC have been given for E. and S. Asian, W. European, and sub-Saharan African neolithic remains. The variety of crops — field grains, rice, maize, and roots, and the varying mix of other traits suggest that the revolution occurred independently in all these regions.

History Begins: 4000 - 1000 BC

Near Eastern cradle. If history began with writing, the first chapter opened in Mesopotamia, the Tigris-Euphrates river valley. Clay tablets with pictographs were used by the Sumerians to keep records after 4000 BC. A **cuneiform** (wedge shaped) script evolved by 3000 BC as a full syllabic alphabet. Neighboring peoples adapted the script to their own language.

Sumerian life centered, from 4000 BC, on large cities (Eridu, Ur, Uruk, Nippur, Kish, Lagash) organized around temples and priestly bureaucracies, with the surrounding plains watered by vast irrigation works and worked with traction plows. Sailboats, wheeled vehicles, potters wheels, and kilns were used. Copper was smelted and tempered in Sumeria from c4000 BC and bronze was produced not long after. Ores, as well as precious stones and metals were obtained through long-distance ship and caravan trade. Iron was used from c2000 BC. Improved ironworking, developed partly by the **Hittites,** became widespread by 1200 BC.

Sumerian political primacy passed among cities and their kingly dynasties. Semitic-speaking peoples, with cultures derived from the Sumerian, founded a succession of dynasties that ruled in Mesopotamia and neighboring areas for most of 1800 years; among them the **Akkadians** (first under Sargon c2350 BC), the Amorites (whose laws, codified by **Hammurabi,** c1792-1750 BC, have Biblical parallels), and the Assyrians, with interludes of rule by the Hittites, Kassites, and Mitanni, all possibly Indo-Europeans. The political and cultural center of gravity shifted northwest with each successive empire.

Mesopotamian learning, maintained by scribes and preserved by successive rulers in vast libraries, was not abstract or theoretical. Algebraic and geometric problems could be solved on a practical basis in construction, commerce, or administration. Systematic lists of astronomical phenomena, plants, animals and stones were kept; medical texts listed ailments and their herbal cures.

The Sumerians worshipped anthropomorphic gods representing natural forces — Anu, god of heaven; Enlil (Ea), god of water. Epic poetry related these and other gods in a hierarchy. Sacrifices were made at **ziggurats** — huge stepped temples. Gods were thought to control all events, which could be foretold using oracular materials. This religious pattern persisted into the first millenium BC.

The Syria-Palestine area, site of some of the earliest urban remains (Jericho, 7000 BC), and of the recently uncovered **Ebla** civilization (fl. 2500 BC), experienced Egyptian cultural and political influence along with Mesopotamian. The **Phoenician** coast was an active commercial center. A phonetic alphabet was invented here before 1600 BC. It became the ancestor of all European, Middle Eastern, Indian, S.E.

Timeline (left margin, top to bottom):

4500

Thai bronzes

3500 — Bronze Age begins

1st pyramids

Sumerian cities

Egypt unified

Indus Valley civilization

2500

Asian, Ethiopian, and Korean alphabets.

Regional commerce and diplomacy were aided by the use of Akkadian as a *lingua franca*, later replaced by Aramaic.

Egypt. Agricultural villages along the Nile were united by 3300 BC into two kingdoms, Upper and Lower Egypt, unified under the Pharaoh Menes c3100 BC; Nubia to the south was added 2600 BC. A national bureaucracy supervised construction of canals and monuments (**pyramids** starting 2700 BC). Brilliant First Dynasty achievements in architecture, sculpture and painting, set the standards and forms for all subsequent Egyptian civilization and are still admired. **Hieroglyphic writing** appeared by 3400 BC, recording a sophisticated literature including romantic and philosophical modes after 2300 BC.

An ordered hierarchy of gods, including totemistic animal elements, was served by a powerful priesthood in Memphis. The pharaoh was identified with the falcon god Horus. Later trends were the belief in an afterlife, and the quasi-monotheistic reforms of **Akhenaton** (c1379-1362 BC).

After a period of conquest by Semitic Hyksos from Asia (c1700-1500 BC), the New Kingdom established an empire in Syria. Egypt became increasingly embroiled in Asiatic wars and diplomacy. Eventually it was conquered by Persia in 525 BC, and it faded away as an independent culture.

India. An urban civilization with a so-far-undeciphered writing system stretched across the Indus Valley and along the Arabian Sea c3000-1500 BC. Major sites are Harappa and **Mohenjo-Daro** in Pakistan, well-planned geometric cities with underground sewers and vast granaries. The entire region (600,000 sq. mi.) may have been ruled as a single state. Bronze was used, and arts and crafts were highly developed. Religious life apparently took the form of fertility cults.

Indus civilization was probably in decline when it was destroyed by **Aryan invaders** from the northwest, speaking an Indo-European language from which all the languages of Pakistan, north India and Bangladesh descend. Led by a warrior aristocracy whose legendary deeds are recorded in the **Rig Veda**, the Aryans spread east and south, bringing their pantheon of sky gods, elaborate priestly (Brahmin) ritual, and the beginnings of the caste system; local customs and beliefs were assimilated by the conquerors.

Europe. On Crete, the bronze-age **Minoan civilization** emerged c2500 BC. A prosperous economy and richly decorative art (e.g. at Knossos palace) was supported by seaborne commerce. Mycenae and other cities in Greece and Asia Minor (e.g. **Troy**) preserved elements of the culture to c1100 BC. Cretan Linear A script, c2000-1700 BC, is undeciphered; Linear B, c1300-1200 BC, records a Greek dialect.

Possible connection between Minoan-Mycenaean monumental stonework, and the great megalithic monuments and tombs of W. Europe, Iberia, and Malta (c4000-1500 BC) is unclear.

China. Proto-Chinese neolithic cultures had long covered northern and southeastern China when the first large political state was organized in the north by the **Shang dynasty** c1500 BC. Shang kings called themselves Sons of Heaven, and presided over a cult of human and animal sacrifice to ancestors and nature gods. The Chou dynasty, starting c1100 BC, expanded the area of the Son of Heaven's dominion, but feudal states exercised most temporal power.

A writing system with 2,000 different characters was already in use under the Shang, with **pictographs** later supplemented by phonetic characters. The system, with modifications, is still in use, despite changes in spoken Chinese.

Technical advances allowed urban specialists to create fine ceramic and jade products, and bronze casting after 1500 BC was the most advanced in the world.

Bronze artifacts have recently been discovered in northern Thailand dating to 3600 BC, hundreds of years before similar Middle Eastern finds.

Americas. Olmecs settled on the Gulf coast of Mexico, 1500 BC, and soon developed the first civilization in the Western Hemisphere. Temple cities and huge stone sculpture date to 1200 BC. A rudimentary calendar and writing system existed. Olmec religion, centering on a jaguar god, and art forms influenced all later Meso-American cultures.

Neolithic ceremonial centers were built on the Peruvian desert coast, c2000 BC.

Classical Era of Old World Civilizations

Greece. After a period of decline during the Dorian Greek invasions (1200-1000 BC), Greece and the Aegean area developed a unique civilization. Drawing upon Mycenaean traditions, Mesopotamian learning (weights and measures, lunisolar calendar, astronomy, musical scales), the Phoenician alphabet (modified for Greek), and Egyptian art, the revived **Greek city-states** saw a rich elaboration of intellectual life. Long-range commerce was aided by metal coinage (introduced by the Lydians in Asia Minor before 700 BC); colonies were founded around the Mediterranean and Black Sea shores (Cumae in Italy 760 BC, Massalia in France c600 BC).

Philosophy, starting with Ionian speculation on the nature of matter and the universe (Thales c634-546), and including mathematical speculation (Pythagoras c580-c500), culminated in Athens in the rationalist idealism of **Plato** (c428-347) and **Socrates** (c470-399); the latter was executed for alleged impiety. Aristotle (384-322) united all fields of study in his system. The arts were highly valued. Architecture culminated in the **Parthenon** in Athens (438, sculpture by Phidias); poetry and drama (Aeschylus 525-456) thrived. Male beauty and strength, a chief artistic theme, were enhanced at the gymnasium and the national games at Olympia.

Ruled by local tyrants or oligarchies, the Greeks were never politically united, but managed to resist inclusion in the Persian Empire (Darius defeated at Marathon 490 BC, Xerxes at Salamis, Plataea 479 BC). Local warfare was common; the **Peloponnesian Wars**, 431-404 BC, ended in Sparta's victory over Athens. Greek political power waned, but classical Greek cultural forms spread throughout the ancient world from the Atlantic to India.

Hebrews. Nomadic Hebrew tribes entered Canaan before 1200 BC, settling among other Semitic peoples speaking the same language. They brought from the desert a **monotheistic faith** said to have been revealed to Abraham in Canaan c1800 BC and to Moses at Mt. Sinai c1250 BC, after the Hebrews' escape from bondage in Egypt. David (ruled 1000-961 BC) and Solomon (ruled 961-922 BC) united the Hebrews in a kingdom that briefly dominated the area. Phoenicians to the north established colonies

*Timeline (right margin):*

- 2500 BC
- Ebla civilization
- Bronze-age Minoan civilization emerges on Crete
- Egyptian literature begins
- Peruvian neolithic ceremonial centers
- Phonetic alphabet invented before 1600
- Hammurabi
- 1750
- Aryans invade India
- Mt. Sinai revelations to Moses
- Chinese Shang dynasty
- Mexican Olmec civilization established
- 1000 BC

Paleontology: The History of Life

All dates are approximate, and are subject to change based on new fossil finds or new dating techniques; but the sequence of events is generally accepted. Dates are in years before the present.

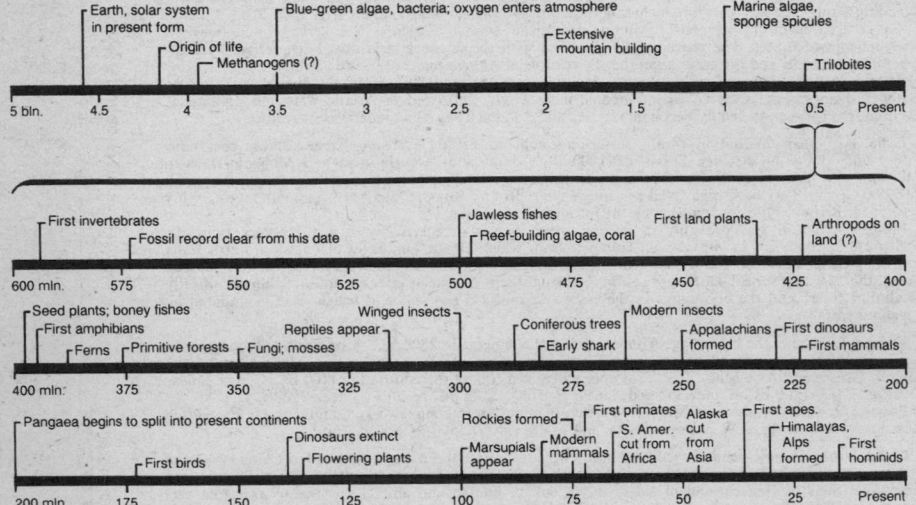

Ancient Near Eastern Civilizations
4000 B.C.-500 B.C.

around the E. and W. Mediterranean (**Carthage** c814 BC) and sailed into the Atlantic.

A temple in Jerusalem became the national religious center, with sacrifices performed by a hereditary priesthood. Polytheistic influences, especially of the fertility cult of Baal, were opposed by **prophets** (Elijah, Amos, Isaiah).

Divided into **two kingdoms** after Solomon, the Hebrews were unable to resist the revived Assyrian empire, which conquered Israel, the northern kingdom in 722 BC. Judah, the southern kingdom, was conquered in 586 BC by the Babylonians under Nebuchadnezzar II. But with the fixing of most of the Biblical canon by the mid-fourth century BC, and the emergence of rabbis, arbiters of law and custom, Judaism successfully survived the loss of Hebrew autonomy. A Jewish kingdom was revived under the Hasmoneans (168-42 BC).

China. During the **Eastern Chou** dynasty (770-256 BC), Chinese culture spread east to the sea and south to the Yangtze. Large feudal states on the periphery of the empire contended for pre-eminence, but continued to recognize the Son of Heaven (king), who retained a purely ritual role enriched with courtly music and dance. In the Age of Warring States (403-221 BC), when the first sections of the **Great Wall** were built, the Ch'in state in the West gained supremacy, and finally united all of China.

Iron tools entered China c500 BC, and casting techniques were advanced, aiding agriculture. Peasants owned their land, and owed civil and military service to nobles. Cities grew in number and size, though barter remained the chief trade medium.

Intellectual ferment among noble scribes and officials produced the Classical Age of Chinese literature and philosophy. **Confucius** (551-479 BC) urged a restoration of a supposedly harmonious social order of the past through proper conduct in accordance with one's station and through filial and ceremonial piety. The *Analects*, attributed to him, are revered throughout East Asia. **Mencius** (d. 289 BC) added the view that the Mandate of Heaven can be removed from an unjust dynasty. The Legalists sought to curb the supposed natural wickedness of people through new institutions and harsh laws; they aided the Ch'in rise to power. The Naturalists emphasized the balance of opposites — yin, yang — in the world. **Taoists** sought mystical knowledge through meditation and disengagement.

India. The political and cultural center of India shifted from the Indus to the Ganges River Valley. Buddhism, Jainism, and mystical revisions of orthodox Vedism all developed around 500-300 BC. The *Upanishads*, last part of the *Veda*, urged escape from the illusory physical world. Vedism remained the preserve of the priestly Brahmin caste. In contrast, **Buddhism**, founded by Siddarta Gautama (c563-c483 BC), appealed to merchants in the growing urban centers, and took hold at first (and most lastingly) on the geographic fringes of Indian civilization. The classic Indian epics were composed in this era: The *Ramayana* around 300 BC, the *Mahubharata* over a period starting 400 BC.

Northern India was divided into a large number of monarchies and aristocratic republics, probably derived from tribal groupings, when the Magadha kingdom was formed in Bihar c542 BC. It soon became the dominant power. The **Maurya dynasty**, founded by Chandragupta c321 BC, expanded the kingdom, uniting most of N. India in a centralized bureaucratic empire. The third Mauryan king, **Asoka** (ruled c274-236) conquered most of the subcontinent: he converted to Buddhism, and inscribed its tenets on pillars throughout India. He downplayed the caste system and tried to end expensive sacrificial rites.

Before its final decline in India, Buddhism developed the popular worship of heavenly Bodhisatvas (enlightened beings), and produced a refined architecture (stupa—shrine—at Sanchi 100 AD) and sculpture (Gandhara reliefs 1-400 AD).

Persia. Aryan peoples (Persians, Medes) dominated the area of present Iran by the beginning of the first millenium BC. The prophet **Zoroaster** (born c628 BC) introduced a dualistic religion in which the forces of good (Ahura Mazda, Lord of Wisdom) and evil (Ahiram) battle for dominance; individuals are judged by their actions and earn damnation or salvation. Zoroaster's hymns (*Gathas*) are included in the *Avesta*, the Zoroastrian scriptures. A version of this faith became the established religion of the Persian Empire, and probably influenced later monotheistic religions.

Africa. Nubia, periodically occupied by Egypt since the third millenium, ruled Egypt c750-661, and survived as an independent Egyptianized kingdom (**Kush;** capital Meroe) for 1,000 years.

The Iron Age Nok culture flourished c500 BC-200 AD on the Benue Plateau of **Nigeria.**

Americas. The Chavin culture controlled north Peru from 900-200 BC. Its ceremonial centers, featuring the jaguar god, survived long after. Chavin architecture, ceramics, and textiles influenced other Peruvian cultures.

Mayan civilization began to develop in Central America in the 5th century BC.

Great Empires Unite the Civilized World: 400 BC - 400 AD

Persia and Alexander. **Cyrus,** ruler of a small kingdom in Persia from 559 BC, united the Persians and Medes within 10 years, conquered Asia Minor and Babylonia in another 10. His son Cambyses and grandson **Darius** (ruled 522-486) added vast lands to the east and north as far as the Indus Valley and Central Asia, as well as Egypt and Thrace. The whole empire was ruled by an international bureaucracy and army, with Persians holding the chief positions. The resources and styles of all the subject civilizations were exploited to create a rich syncretic art.

The Hellenized kingdom of Macedon, which under Phillip II dominated Greece, passed to his son **Alexander** in 336 BC. Within 13 years, Alexander conquered all the Persian dominions. Imbued by his tutor Aristotle with Greek ideals, Alexander encouraged Greek colonization, and Greek-style cities were founded throughout the empire (e.g. Alexandria, Egypt). After his death in 323 BC, wars of succession divided the empire into three parts — **Macedon,** Egypt (ruled by the **Ptolemies**), and the **Seleucid** Empire.

In the ensuing 300 years (the **Hellenistic Era**), a cosmopolitan Greek-oriented culture permeated the ancient world from W. Europe to the borders of India, absorbing native elites everywhere.

Hellenistic philosophy stressed the private individual's search for happiness. The Cynics followed Diogenes (c372-287), who stressed satisfaction of animal needs and contempt for social convention. Zeno (c335-c263) and the Stoics exalted reason, identified it with virtue, and counseled an ascetic disregard for misfortune. The Epicureans tried to build lives of moderate pleasure without political or emotional

1000 BC — Chavin dynasty begins in Peru — Hebrew kingdom divided

Chou dynasty begins in China — Carthage established

800 — Nubia begins rule of Egypt — Metal coins in Asia Minor — Isaiah d.

Zoroaster b. — Pythagoras b.

600 — Indian Buddhism, Jainism begin — Confucius b. — Siddarta b. — Aeschylus b.

Socrates b. — Plato b. — Parthenon — Peloponnesian Wars

400 BC

The Rise of the Roman Empire

GERMANIA

SARMATIA

BELGICA

GAUL

RAETIA

ILLYRICUM

DACIA

THRACE

Constantinople

BITHYNIA

PONTUS

ARMENIA

MESOPOTAMIA

GALATIA

ASIA

ACHAEA

CILICIA

SYRIA

JUDEA

ARABIA

EGYPT

CYRENAICA

TRIPOLI

AFRICA

Carthage

ITALY

Rome

MAURETANIA

BAETICA

LUSITANIA

TARRACONENSIS

238 B.C.E.
133 B.C.E.
44 B.C.E.
A.D. 14
A.D. 117

involvement. Hellenistic arts imitated life realistically, especially in sculpture and literature (comedies of Menander, 342-292).

The sciences thrived, especially at Alexandria, where the Ptolemies financed a great library and museum. Fields of study included mathematics (**Euclid's** geometry, c300 BC; Menelaus' non-Euclidean geometry, c100 AD); astronomy (heliocentric theory of Aristarchus, 310-230 BC; Julian calendar 45 BC; Ptolemy's *Almagest*, c150 AD); geography (world map of Eratosthenes, 276-194 BC); hydraulics (**Archimedes**, 287-212 BC); medicine (Galen, 130-200 AD), and chemistry. Inventors refined uses for siphons, valves, gears, springs, screws, levers, cams, and pulleys.

A restored Persian empire under the **Parthians** (N. Iranian tribesmen) controlled the eastern Hellenistic world 250 BC-229 AD. The Parthians and the succeeding Sassanian dynasty (229-651) fought with Rome periodically. The **Sassanians** revived Zoroastrianism as a state religion, and patronized a nationalistic artistic and scholarly renaissance.

Rome. The city of Rome was founded, according to legend, by Romulus in 753 BC. Through military expansion and colonization, and by granting citizenship to conquered tribes, the city annexed all of Italy south of the Po in the 100-year period before 268 BC. The Latin and other Italic tribes were annexed first, followed by the Etruscans (a civilized people north of Rome) and the Greek colonies in the south. With a large standing army and reserve forces of several hundred thousand, Rome was able to defeat Carthage in the 3 **Punic Wars**, 264-241, 218-201, 149-146 (despite the invasion of Italy by Hannibal, 218), thus gaining Sicily and territory in Spain and North Africa.

New provinces were added in the East, as Rome exploited local disputes to conquer Greece and Asia Minor in the 2d century BC, and Egypt in the first (after the defeat and suicide of **Antony and Cleopatra**, 30 BC). All the Mediterranean civilized world up to the disputed Parthian border was now Roman, and remained so for 500 years. Less civilized regions were added to the Empire: Gaul (conquered by Julius Caesar, 56-49 BC), Britain (43 AD) and Dacia NE of the Danube (117 AD).

The original aristocratic republican government, with democratic features added in the fifth and fourth centuries BC, deteriorated under the pressures of empire and class conflict (**Gracchus** brothers, social reformers, murdered 133, 121; slave revolts 135, 73). After a series of civil wars (Marius vs. Sulla 88-82, Caesar vs. Pompey 49-45, triumvirate vs. Caesar's assassins 44-43, Antony vs. Octavian 32-30), the empire came under the rule of a deified monarch (first emperor, **Augustus**, 27 BC-14 AD). Provincials (nearly all granted citizenship by Caracalla, 212 AD) came to dominate the army and civil service. Traditional Roman law, systematized and interpreted by independent jurists, and local self-rule in provincial cities were supplanted by a vast tax-collecting bureaucracy in the 3d and 4th centuries. The legal rights of women, children, and slaves were strengthened.

Roman innovations in civil engineering included water mills, windmills, and rotary mills, and the use of cement that hardened under water. Monumental architecture (baths, theaters, apartment houses) relied on the arch and the dome. The network of roads (some still standing) stretched 53,000 miles, passing through mountain tunnels as long as 3.5 miles. Aqueducts brought water to cities, underground sewers removed waste.

Roman art and literature were derivative of Greek models. Innovations were made in sculpture (naturalistic busts and equestrian statues), decorative wall painting (as at Pompeii), satire (Juvenal, 60-127), history (Tacitus 56-120), prose romance (Petronius, d. 66 AD). Violence and torture dominated mass public amusements, which were supported by the state.

India. The Gupta monarchs reunited N. India c320 AD. Their peaceful and prosperous reign saw a revival of Hindu religious thought and Brahmin power. The old Vedic traditions were combined with devotion to a plethora of indigenous deities (who were seen as manifestations of Vedic gods). Caste lines were reinforced, and Buddhism gradually disappeared. The art (often erotic), architecture, and literature of the period, patronized by the Gupta court, are considered to be among India's finest achievements (Kalidasa, poet and dramatist, fl. c400). Mathematical innovations included the use of zero and decimal numbers. Invasions by White Huns from the NW destroyed the empire c550.

Rich cultures also developed in S. India in this era. Emotional Tamil religious poetry aided the Hindu revival. The Pallava kingdom controlled much of S. India c350-880, and helped spread Indian civilization to S.E. Asia.

China. The Ch'in ruler Shih Huang Ti (ruled 221 210 BC), known as the First Emperor, centralized political authority in China, standardized the written language, laws, weights, measures, and coinage, and conducted a census, but tried to destroy most philosophical texts. The **Han dynasty** (206 BC-220 AD) instituted the Mandarin bureaucracy, which lasted for 2,000 years. Local officials were selected by examination in the Confucian classics and trained at the imperial university and at provincial schools. The invention of **paper** facilitated this bureaucratic system. Agriculture was promoted, but the peasants bore most of the tax burden. Irrigation was improved; water clocks and sundials were used; astronomy and mathematics thrived; landscape painting was perfected.

With the expansion south and west (to nearly the present borders of today's China), trade was opened with India, S.E. Asia, and the Middle East, over sea and caravan routes. Indian missionaries brought Mahayana Buddhism to China by the first century AD, and spawned a variety of sects. Taoism was revived, and merged with popular superstitions. Taoist and Buddhist monasteries and convents multiplied in the turbulent centuries after the collapse of the Han dynasty.

The One God Triumphs: 1-750 AD

Christianity. Religions indigenous to particular Middle Eastern nations became international in the first 3 centuries of the Roman Empire. Roman citizens worshipped **Isis** of Egypt, **Mithras** of Persia, **Demeter** of Greece, and the great mother **Cybele** of Phrygia. Their cults centered on mysteries (secret ceremonies) and the promise of an afterlife, symbolized by the death and rebirth of the god. Judaism, which had begun as the national cult of Judea, also spread by emigration and conversion. It was the only ancient religion west of India to survive.

Christians, who emerged as a distinct sect in the second half of the 1st century AD, revered **Jesus**, a Jewish preacher said to have been killed by the Romans at the request of Jewish authorities in Jerusalem c30 AD. They considered him the Savior (Messiah, or Christ) who rose from the dead and could grant

Chinese Age of Warring States — 400 BC

Alexander becomes king

Aristotle b.

Mahabharata begun

Euclid's geometry

Great Wall of China begun

Hellenistic Era

200 BC

1st Roman slave revolt

Hannibal invades Italy

Julius Caesar b.

Punic Wars end

Antony, Cleopatra defeated

Julian calendar

Mayan civilization begins in Guatemala

Roman Empire

1 AD

Jesus d.

Nero's persecution

200 AD

200 AD

African Axum kingdom expands

1st Christian monastery

Constantinople founded

Japan united

350

Augustine b.

Ghana begins rule

W. Roman Empire ends

Gupta Empire in India

Huns in Europe

500

Clovis unites Franks

Patrick converts Ireland

Sui dynasty begins

Justinian code

Benedict founds monastery

Mohammed's life

Tang dynasty

Talmud completed

650 AD

eternal life to the faithful, despite their sinfulness. They believed he was an incarnation of the one god worshipped by the Jews, and that he would return soon to pass final judgment on the world. The missionary activities of such early leaders as **Paul of Tarsus** spread the faith, at first mostly among Jews or among quasi-Jews attracted by the Pauline rejection of such difficult Jewish laws as circumcision. Intermittent persecution, as in Rome under Nero in 64 AD, on grounds of suspected disloyalty, failed to disrupt the Christian communities. Each congregation, generally urban and of plebeian character, was tightly organized under a leader (bishop) elders (presbyters or priests), and assistants (deacons). Stories about Jesus (the Gospels) and the early church (Acts) were written down in the late first and early 2d centuries, and circulated along with letters of Paul. An authoritative canon of these writings was not fixed until the 4th century.

A school for priests was established at Alexandria in the second century. Its teachers (**Origen** c182-251) helped define Christian doctrine and promote the faith in Greek-style philosophical works. Pagan Neoplatonism was given Christian coloration in the works of Church Fathers such as Augustine (354-430). Christian hermits, often drawn from the lower classes, began to associate in monasteries, first in Egypt (St. Pachomius c290-345), then in other eastern lands, then in the West (**St. Benedict's rule,** 529). Popular adoration of saints, especially Mary, mother of Jesus, spread.

Under **Constantine** (ruled 306-337), Christianity became in effect the established religion of the Empire. Pagan temples were expropriated, state funds were used to build huge churches and support the hierarchy, and laws were adjusted in accordance with Christian notions. Pagan worship was banned by the end of the fourth century, and severe restrictions were placed on Judaism.

The newly established church was rocked by doctrinal disputes, often exacerbated by regional rivalries both within and outside the Empire. Chief heresies (as defined by church councils backed by imperial authority) were **Arianism,** which denied the divinity of Jesus; **Donatism,** which rejected the convergence of church and state and denied the validity of sacraments performed by sinful clergy; and the **Monophysite** position denying the dual nature of Christ.

Judaism. First century Judaism embraced several sects, including: the **Sadducees,** mostly drawn from the Temple priesthood, who were culturally Hellenized; the **Pharisees,** who upheld the full range of traditional customs and practices as of equal weight to literal scriptural law, and elaborated synagogue worship; and the **Essenes,** an ascetic, millenarian sect. Messianic fervor led to repeated, unsuccessful rebellions against Rome (66-70, 135). As a result, the Temple was destroyed, and the population decimated.

To avoid the dissolution of the faith, a program of codification of law was begun at the academy of Yavneh. The work continued for some 500 years in Palestine and Babylonia, ending in the final redaction of the **Talmud** (c600), a huge collection of legal and moral debates, rulings, liturgy, Biblical exegesis, and legendary materials.

Islam. The earliest Arab civilization emerged by the end of the 2d millenium BC in the watered highlands of Yemen. Seaborne and caravan trade in frankincense and myrrh connected the area with the Nile and Fertile Crescent. The Minaean, Sabean (Sheba), and Himyarite states successively held sway. By Mohammed's time (7th century AD), the region was a province of Sassanian Persia. In the North, the **Nabataean kingdom** at Petra and the kingdom of Palmyra were first Aramaicized and then Romanized, and finally absorbed like neighboring Judea into the Roman Empire. Nomads shared the central region with a few trading towns and oases. Wars between tribes and raids on settled communities were common, and were celebrated in a poetic tradition that by the 6th century helped establish a classic literary Arabic.

In 611 **Mohammed,** a wealthy 40-year-old Arab of Mecca, had a revelation from Allah, the one true god, calling on him to repudiate pagan idolatry. Drawing on elements of Judaism and Christianity, and eventually incorporating some Arab pagan traditions (such as reverence for the black stone at the kaaba shrine in Mecca), Mohammed's teachings, recorded in the **Koran,** forged a new religion, Islam (submission to Allah). Opposed by the leaders of Mecca, Mohammed made a *hejira* (migration) to Medina to the north in 622, the beginning of the Moslem lunar calendar. He and his followers defeated the Meccans in 624 in the first *jihad* (holy war), and by his death (632), nearly all the Arabian peninsula accepted his religious and secular leadership.

Under the first two **caliphs** (successors) Abu Bakr (632-34) and Oman (634-44), Moslem rule was confirmed over Arabia. Raiding parties into Byzantine and Persian border areas developed into campaigns of conquest against the two empires, which had been weakened by wars and by disaffection among subject peoples (including Coptic and Syriac Christians opposed to the Byzantine orthodox church). Syria, Palestine, Egypt, Iraq, and Persia all fell to the inspired Arab armies. The Arabs at first remained a distinct minority, using non-Moslems in the new administrative system, and tolerating Christians, Jews, and Zoroastrians as self-governing "Peoples of the Book," whose taxes supported the empire.

Disputes over the succession, and puritan reaction to the wealth and refinement that empire brought to the ruling strata, led to the growth of schismatic movements. The followers of Mohammed's son-in-law Ali (assassinated 661) and his descendants became the founders of the more mystical Shi'ite sect, still the largest non-orthodox Moslem sect. The Karijites, puritanical, militant, and egalitarian, persist as a minor sect to the present.

Under the **Ummayad** caliphs (661-750), the boundaries of Islam were extended across N. Africa and into Spain. Arab armies in the West were stopped at Tours in 732 by the Frank **Charles Martel.** Asia Minor, the Indus Valley, and Transoxiana were conquered in the East. The vast majority of the subject population gradually converted to Islam, encouraged by tax and career privileges. The Arab language supplanted the local tongues in the central and western areas, but Arab soldiers and rulers in the East eventually became assimilated to the indigenous languages.

New Peoples Enter History: 400-900

Barbarian invasions. Germanic tribes infiltrated S and E from their Baltic homeland during the 1st millenium BC, reaching S. Germany by 100 BC and the Black Sea by 214 AD. Organized into large federated tribes under elected kings, most resisted Roman domination and raided the empire in time of civil war (Goths took Dacia 214, raided Thrace 251-269). German troops and commanders came to dominate the Roman armies by the end of the 4th century. **Huns,** invaders from Asia, entered Europe 372, driving more Germans into the western empire. Emperor Valens allowed Visigoths to cross the Danube 376. Huns under Attila (d. 453) raided Gaul, Italy, Balkans. The western empire, weakened by overtaxation and social stagnation, was overrun in the 5th century. Gaul was effectively lost 406-7, Spain 409, Britain 410, Africa 429-39. Rome itself was sacked 410 by Visigoths under Alaric, 455 by Vandals. The last western emperor, Romulus Augustulus, was deposed 476 by the Germanic chief Odoacer.

Celts. Celtic cultures, which in pre-Roman times covered most of W. Europe, were confined almost entirely to the British Isles after the Germanic invasions. **St. Patrick** completed the conversion of Ireland (c457-92). A strong monastic tradition took hold. Irish monastic missionaries in Scotland, England, and the continent (Columba c521-597; Columban c543-615) helped restore Christianity after the Germanic invasions. The monasteries became renowned centers of classic and Christian learning, and presided over the recording of a Christianized Celtic mythology, elaborated by secular writers and bards. An intricate decorative art style developed, especially in book illumination (Lindisfarne Gospels, c700, Book of Kells, 8th century).

Successor states. The Visigoth kingdom in Spain (from 419) and much of France (to 507) saw a continuation of much Roman administration, language, and law (Breviary of Alaric 506), until its destruction by the Moslems, 711. The Vandal kingdom in Africa, from 429, was conquered by the Byzantines, 533. Italy was ruled in succession by an Ostrogothic kingdom under Byzantine suzerainty 489-554, direct Byzantine government, and the German Lombards (568-774). The latter divided the peninsula between the Byzantines and the papacy under the dynamic reformer Pope Gregory the Great (590-604) and his successors.

King Clovis (ruled 481-511) united the Franks on both sides of the Rhine, and after his conversion to orthodox Christianity, defeated the Arian Burgundians (after 500) and Visigoths (507) with the support of the native clergy and the papacy. Under the **Merovingian** kings a feudal system emerged: power was fragmented among hierarchies of military landowners. Social stratification, which in late Roman times had acquired legal, hereditary sanction, was reinforced. The Carolingians (747-987) expanded the kingdom and restored central power. **Charlemagne** (ruled 768-814) conquered nearly all the Germanic lands, including Lombard Italy, and was crowned Emperor by Pope Leo III in Rome in 800. A centuries-long decline in commerce and the arts was reversed under Charlemagne's patronage. He welcomed Jews to his kingdom, which became a center of Jewish learning (Rashi 1040-1105). He sponsored the "Carolingian Renaissance" of learning under the Anglo-Latin scholar Alcuin (c732-804), who reformed church liturgy.

Byzantine Empire. Under Diocletian (ruled 284-305) the empire had been divided into 2 parts to facilitate administration and defense. Constantine founded **Constantinople,** 330, (at old Byzantium) as a fully Christian city. Commerce and taxation financed a sumptuous, orientalized court, a class of hereditary bureaucratic families, and magnificent urban construction (Hagia Sophia, 532-37). The city's fortifications and naval innovations (Greek fire) repelled assaults by Goths, Huns, Slavs, Bulgars, Avars, Arabs, and Scandinavians. Greek replaced Latin as the official language by c700. Byzantine art, a solemn, sacral, and stylized variation of late classical styles (mosaics at S. Vitale, Ravenna, 526-48) was a starting point for medieval art in E. and W. Europe.

Justinian (ruled 527-65) reconquered parts of Spain, N. Africa, and Italy, codified Roman law (*codex Justinianus,* 529, was medieval Europe's chief legal text), closed the Platonic Academy at Athens and ordered all pagans to convert. Lombards in Italy, Arabs in Africa retook most of his conquests. The Isaurian dynasty from Anatolia (from 717) and the Macedonian dynasty (867-1054) restored military and commercial power. The Iconoclast controversy (726-843) over the permissibility of images, helped alienate the Eastern Church from the papacy.

Arab Empire. Baghdad, founded 762, became the seat of the **Abbasid** Caliphate (founded 750), while Ummayads continued to rule in Spain. A brilliant cosmopolitan civilization emerged, inaugurating an Arab-Moslem golden age. Arab lyric poetry revived; Greek, Syriac, Persian, and Sanskrit books were translated into Arabic, often by Syriac Christians and Jews, whose theology and Talmudic law, respectively, influenced Islam. The arts and music flourished at the court of **Harun al-Rashid** (786-809), celebrated in *The Arabian Nights.* The sciences, medicine, and mathematics were pursued at Baghdad, Cordova, and Cairo (founded 969). Science and Aristotelian philosophy culminated in the systems of Avicenna (980-1037), Averroes (1126-98), and Maimonides (1135-1204), a Jew; all influenced later Christian scholarship and theology. The Islamic ban on images encouraged a sinuous, geometric decorative tradition, applied to architecture and illumination. A gradual loss of Arab control in Persia (from 874) led to the capture of Baghdad by Persians, 945. By the next century, Spain and N. Africa were ruled by Berbers, while Turks prevailed in Asia Minor and the Levant. The loss of political power by the caliphs allowed for the growth of non-orthodox trends, especially the mystical **Sufi** tradition (theologian Ghazali, 1058-1111).

Africa. Immigrants from Saba in S. Arabia helped set up the **Axum** kingdom in Ethiopia in the 2d century (their language, Ge'ez, is preserved by the Ethiopian Church). In the 4th century, when the kingdom became Christianized, it defeated Kushite Meroe and expanded into Yemen. Axum was the center of a vast ivory trade; it controlled the Red Sea coast until c1100. Arab conquest in Egypt cut Axum's political and economic ties with Byzantium.

The Iron Age entered W. Africa by the end of the 1st millenium BC. **Ghana,** the first known sub-Saharan state, ruled in the upper Senegal-Niger region c400-1240, controlling the trade of gold from mines in the S to trans-Sahara caravan routes to the N. The **Bantu** peoples, probably of W. African origin, began to spread E and S perhaps 2000 years ago, displacing the Pygmies and Bushmen of central

Japan. The advanced Neolithic Yayoi period, when irrigation, rice farming, and iron and bronze casting techniques were introduced from China or Korea, persisted to c400 AD. The myriad Japanese states were then united by the **Yamato** clan, under an emperor who acted as the chief priest of the animistic **Shinto** cult. Japanese political and military intervention in Korea by the 6th century quickened a Chinese cultural invasion, bringing Buddhism, the Chinese language (which long remained a literary and governmental medium), Chinese ideographs and Buddhist styles in painting, sculpture, literature, and architecture (7th c. Horyu-ji temple at Nara). The Taika Reforms, 646, tried to centralize Japan according to Chinese bureaucratic and Buddhist philosophical values, but failed to curb traditional Japanese decentralization. A nativist reaction against the Buddhist **Nara period** (710-94) ushered in the

650 — Greek replaces Latin in Byzantium — Slav-Turk Bulgarian Empire begins

Chinese poet Li Po b.

Nara period begins, Japan — 750 — Baghdad founded

Charlemagne rules

Viking explorations, raids — 850 — Arab-Moslem golden age

Vietnam independent — 950

950

Otto I emperor
Cairo founded
Leif Eriksson b. reaches Amer.
Kiev Christian under Vladimir
Tales of Genji in Japan
Jewish scholar Rashi b.
Poland begins eastern conquest
Choir of St. Denis
E. W Church split
1050
Seljuk Turks take Baghdad
Christians capture Toledo
Sufi mystic Ghazali b.
Angkor Wat temple built
Univ. Bologna founded
Maimonides b.
German Frederick II born
Zen comes to Japan
Ghengis Khan b.
1150
Sultanate of Delhi founded
Crusades
Magna Carta
Aquinas b.
Dominicans, Franciscans founded
Mali replaces Ghana
1250

Heian period (794-1185) centered at the new capital, Kyoto. Japanese elegance and simplicity modified Chinese styles in architecture, scroll painting, and literature; the writing system was also simplified. The courtly novel *Tale of Genji* (1010-20) testifies to the enhanced role of women.

Southeast Asia. The historic peoples of southeast Asia began arriving some 2500 years ago from China and Tibet, displacing scattered aborigines. Their agriculture relied on rice and tubers (yams), which they may have introduced to Africa. Indian cultural influences were strongest; literacy and Hindu and Buddhist ideas followed the southern India-China trade route. From the southern tip of Indochina, the kingdom of **Funan** (1st-7th centuries) traded as far west as Persia. It was absorbed by Chenla, itself conquered by the **Khmer Empire** (600-1300). The Khmers, under Hindu god-kings (Suryavarman II, 1113-c1150), built the monumental Angkor Wat temple center for the royal phallic cult. The **Nam-Viet** kingdom in Annam, dominated by China and Chinese culture for 1,000 years, emerged in the 10th century, growing at the expense of the Khmers, who also lost ground in the NW to the new, highly-organized **Thai** kingdom. On Sumatra, the **Srivijaya** Empire at Palembang controlled vital sea lanes (7th to 10th centuries). A Buddhist dynasty, the Sailendras, ruled central **Java** (8th-9th centuries), building at Borobudur one of the largest stupas in the world.

China. The short-lived Sui dynasty (581-618) ushered in a period of commercial, artistic, and scientific achievement in China, continuing under the **T'ang** dynasty (618-906). Such inventions as the magnetic compass, gunpowder, the abacus, and printing were introduced or perfected. Medical innovations included cataract surgery. The state, from the cosmopolitan capital, Ch'ang-an, supervised foreign trade which exchanged Chinese silks, porcelains, and art works for spices, ivory, etc., over Central Asian caravan routes and sea routes reaching Africa. A golden age of poetry bequeathed tens of thousands of works to later generations (Tu Fu 712-70, Li Po 701-62). Landscape painting flourished. Commercial and industrial expansion continued under the **Northern Sung** dynasty (960-1126), facilitated by paper money and credit notes. But commerce never achieved respectability; government monopolies expropriated successful merchants. The population, long stable at 50 million, doubled in 200 years with the introduction of early-ripening rice and the double harvest. In art, native Chinese styles were revived.

Americas. An Indian empire stretched from the Valley of Mexico to Guatemala, 300-600, centering on the huge city **Teotihuacan** (founded 100 BC). To the S, in Guatemala, a high **Mayan** civilization developed, 150-900, around hundreds of rural ceremonial centers. The Mayans improved on Olmec writing and the calendar, and pursued astronomy and mathematics (using the idea of zero). In S. America, a widespread pre-Inca culture grew from **Tiahuanaco** near Lake Titicaca (Gateway of the Sun, c700).

Christian Europe Regroups and Expands: 900-1300

Scandinavians. Pagan Danish and Norse (**Viking**) adventurers, traders, and pirates raided the coasts of the British Isles (Dublin founded c831), France, and even the Mediterranean for over 200 years beginning in the late 8th century. Inland settlement in the W was limited to Great Britain (King Canute, 994-1035) and Normandy, settled under Rollo, 911, as a fief of France. Other Vikings reached Iceland (874), Greenland (c986), and probably N. America (Leif Eriksson c1000). Norse traders (**Varangians**) developed Russian river commerce from the 8th-11th centuries, and helped set up a state at Kiev in the late 9th century. Conversion to Christianity occurred during the 10th century, reaching Sweden 100 years later. Eleventh century Norman bands conquered S. Italy and Sicily. Duke **William of Normandy** conquered England, 1066, bringing continental feudalism and the French language, essential elements in later English civilization.

East Europe. Slavs inhabited areas of E. Central Europe in prehistoric times, and reached most of their present limits by c850. The first Slavic states were in the Balkans (Slav-Turk **Bulgarian Empire**, 680-1018) and Moravia (628). Missions of St. Cyril (whose Greek-based Cyrillic alphabet is still used by S. and E. Slavs) converted Moravia, 863. The Eastern Slavs, part-civilized under the overlordship of the Turkish-Jewish **Khazar** trading empire (7th-10th centuries), gravitated toward Constantinople by the 9th century. The **Kievan state** adopted Eastern Christianity under Prince Vladimir, 989. King Boleslav I (992-1025) began **Poland's** long history of eastern conquest. The Magyars (**Hungarians**) in Europe since 896, accepted Latin Christianity, 1001.

Germany. The German kingdom that emerged after the breakup of Charlemagne's Empire remained a confederation of largely autonomous states. The Saxon Otto I, king from 936, established the **Holy Roman Empire** of Germany and Italy in alliance with Pope John XII, who crowned him emperor, 962; he defeated the Magyars, 955. Imperial power was greatest under the **Hohenstaufens** (1138-1254), despite the growing opposition of the papacy, which ruled central Italy, and the Lombard League cities. Frederick II (1194-1250) improved administration, patronized the arts; after his death German influence was removed from Italy.

Christian Spain. From its northern mountain redoubts, Christian rule slowly migrated south through the 11th century, when Moslem unity collapsed. After the capture of **Toledo** (1085), the kingdoms of Portugal, Castile, and Aragon undertook repeated crusades of reconquest, finally completed in 1492. Elements of Islamic civilization persisted in recaptured areas, influencing all W. Europe.

Crusades. Pope Urban II called, 1095, for a crusade to restore Asia Minor to Byzantium and conquer the Holy Land from the Turks. Some 10 crusades (to 1291) succeeded only in founding 4 temporary Frankish states in the Levant. The 4th crusade sacked Constantinople, 1204. In Rhineland (1096), England (1290), France (1306), Jews were massacred or expelled, and wars were launched against Christian heretics (**Albigensian** crusade in France, 1229). Trade in eastern luxuries expanded, led by the Venetian naval empire.

Economy. The agricultural base of European life benefitted from improvements in **plow design** c1000, and by draining of lowlands and clearing of forests, leading to a rural population increase. Towns grew in N. Italy, Flanders, and N. Germany (Hanseatic League). Improvements in **loom design** permitted factory textile production. **Guilds** dominated urban trades from the 12th century. Banking (centered in Italy, 12th-15th century) facilitated long-distance trade.

The Church. The split between the Eastern and Western churches was formalized in 1054. W. and

Ancient Asian Empires

Caspian Sea

Sea of Japan

East China Sea

South China Sea

GOBI DESERT

Great Wall

Yellow R.

Lo-yang

Chang-an

Han Empire 100 B.C.

Yangtze R.

Mekong R.

Khmer Empire

Angkor

A.D. 1000

1250

ALTAI MTS.

TARIM BASIN

PAMIR MTS.

Tibet

HIMALAYA MTS.

Ganges R.

Pataliputra

Asoka's Empire 250 B.C.

Indus R.

Bay of Bengal

Arabian Sea

Approximate Borders

Central Europe was divided into 500 bishoprics under one united hierarchy, but conflicts between secular and church authorities were frequent (German **Investiture Controversy**, 1075-1122). Clerical power was first strengthened through the international monastic reform begun at Cluny, 910. Popular religious enthusiasm often expressed itself in heretical movements (Waldensians from 1173), but was channelled by the **Dominican** (1215) and **Franciscan** (1223) friars into the religious mainstream.

Arts. **Romanesque** architecture (11th-12th centuries) expanded on late Roman models, using the rounded arch and massed stone to support enlarged basilicas. Painting and sculpture followed Byzantine models. The literature of chivalry was exemplified by the epic (Chanson de Roland, c1100) and by courtly love poems of the troubadours of Provence and minnesingers of Germany. **Gothic architecture** emerged in France (choir of St. Denis, c1040) and spread as French cultural influence predominated in Europe. Rib vaulting and pointed arches were used to combine soaring heights with delicacy, and freed walls for display of stained glass. Exteriors were covered with painted relief sculpture and elaborate architectural detail.

Learning. Law, medicine, and philosophy were advanced at independent **universities** (Bologna, late 11th century), originally corporations of students and masters. Twelfth century translations of Greek classics, especially Aristotle, encouraged an analytic approach. Scholastic philosophy, from Anselm (1033-1109) to Aquinas (1225-74) attempted to reconcile reason and revelation.

Apogee of Central Asian Power; Islam Grows: 1250-1500

Turks. Turkic peoples, of Central Asian ancestry, were a military threat to the Byzantine and Persian Empires from the 6th century. After several waves of invasions, during which most of the Turks adopted Islam, the **Seljuk Turks** took Baghdad, 1055. They ruled Persia, Iraq, and, after 1071, Asia Minor, where massive numbers of Turks settled. The empire was divided in the 12th century into smaller states ruled by Seljuks, Kurds (**Saladin** c1137-93), and Mamelukes (a military caste of former Turk, Kurd, and Circassian slaves), which governed Egypt and the Middle East until the Ottoman era (c1290-1922).

Osman I (ruled c1290-1326) and succeeding sultans united Anatolian Turkish warriors in a militaristic state that waged holy war against Byzantium and Balkan Christians. Most of the Balkans had been subdued, and Anatolia united, when **Constantinople fell**, 1453. By the mid-16th century, Hungary, the Middle East, and North Africa had been conquered. The Turkish advance was stopped at Vienna, 1529, and at the naval battle of Lepanto, 1571, by Spain, Venice, and the papacy.

The **Ottoman state** was governed in accordance with orthodox Moslem law. Greek, Armenian, and Jewish communities were segregated, and ruled by religious leaders responsible for taxation; they dominated trade. State offices and most army ranks were filled by slaves through a system of child conscription among Christians.

India. Mahmud of Ghazni (971-1030) led repeated Turkish raids into N. India. Turkish power was consolidated in 1206 with the start of the **Sultanate at Delhi.** Centralization of state power under the early Delhi sultans went far beyond traditional Indian practice. Moslem rule of most of the subcontinent lasted until the British conquest some 600 years later.

Mongols. Genghis Khan (c1162-1227) first united the feuding Mongol tribes, and built their armies into an effective offensive force around a core of highly mobile cavalry. He and his immediate successors created the largest land empire in history; by 1279 it stretched from the east coast of Asia to the Danube, from the Siberian steppes to the Arabian Sea. East-West trade and contacts were facilitated (Marco Polo c1254-1324). The western Mongols were Islamized by 1295; successor states soon lost their Mongol character by assimilation. They were briefly reunited under the Turk Tamerlane (1336-1405).

Kublai Khan ruled China from his new capital Peking (founded 1264). Naval campaigns against Japan (1274, 1281) and Java (1293) were defeated, the latter by the Hindu-Buddhist maritime kingdom of Majapahit. The **Yuan** dynasty made use of Mongols and other foreigners (including Europeans) in official posts, and tolerated the return of Nestorian Christianity (suppressed 841-45) and the spread of Islam in the South and West. A native reaction expelled the Mongols, 1367-68.

Russia. The Kievan state in Russia, weakened by the decline of Byzantium and the rise of the Catholic Polish-Lithuanian state, was overrun by the Mongols, 1238-40. Only the northern trading republic of Novgorod remained independent. The grand dukes of Moscow emerged as leaders of a coalition of princes that eventually defeated the Mongols, by 1481. With the fall of Constantinople, the **Tsars** (Caesars) at Moscow (from Ivan III, ruled 1462-1505) set up an independent Russian Orthodox Church. Commerce failed to revive. The isolated Russian state remained agrarian, with the peasant class falling into serfdom.

Persia. A revival of Persian literature, using the Arab alphabet and literary forms, began in the 10th century (epic of Firdausi, 935-1020). An art revival, influenced by Chinese styles, began in the 12th. Persian cultural and political forms, and often the Persian language, were used for centuries by Turkish and Mongol elites from the Balkans to India. Persian mystics from Rumi (1207-73) to Jami (1414-92) promoted **Sufism** in their poetry.

Africa. Two Berber dynasties, imbued with Islamic militance, emerged from the Sahara to carve out empires from the Sahel to central Spain — the **Almoravids,** c1050-1140, and the fanatical **Almohads,** c1125-1269. The Ghanaian empire was replaced in the upper Niger by Mali, c1230-c1340, whose Moslem rulers imported Egyptians to help make **Timbuktu** a center of commerce (in gold, leather, slaves) and learning. The Songhay empire (to 1590) replaced Mali. To the S, forest kingdoms produced refined art works (Ife terra cotta, **Benin** bronzes). Other Moslem states in Nigeria (Hausas) and Chad originated in the 11th century, and continued in some form until the 19th century European conquest. Less developed Bantu kingdoms existed across central Africa.

Some 40 Moslem Arab-Persian trading colonies and city-states were established all along the E. African coast from the 10th century (Kilwa, Mogadishu). The interchange with Bantu peoples produced the **Swahili** language and culture. Gold, palm oil, and slaves were brought from the interior, stimulating the growth of the Monamatapa kingdom of the Zambezi (15th century). The Christian Ethiopian empire (from 13th century) continued the traditions of Axum.

Southeast Asia. Islam was introduced into Malaya and the Indonesian islands by Arab, Persian, and

Indian traders. Coastal Moslem cities and states (starting before 1300), enriched by trade, soon dominated the interior. Chief among these was the **Malacca** state, on the Malay peninsula, c1400-1511.

Arts and Statecraft Thrive in Europe: 1350-1600

Italian Renaissance & humanism. Distinctive Italian achievements in the arts in the late Middle Ages (Dante, 1265-1321, Giotto, 1276-1337) led to the vigorous new styles of the Renaissance (14th-16th centuries). Patronized by the rulers of the quarreling petty states of Italy (Medicis in Florence and the papacy, c1400-1737), the plastic arts perfected realistic techniques, including **perspective** (Masaccio, 1401-28, Leonardo 1452-1519). Classical motifs were used in architecture and increased talent and expense were put into secular buildings. The Florentine dialect was refined as a national literary language (Petrarch, 1304-74). Greek refugees from the E strengthened the respect of humanist scholars for the classic sources (Bruni 1370-1444). Soon an international movement aided by the spread of **printing** (Gutenberg c1400-1468), **humanism** was optimistic about the power of human reason (Erasmus of Rotterdam, 1466-1536, Thomas More's *Utopia*, 1516) and valued individual effort in the arts and in politics (Machiavelli, 1469-1527).

France. The French monarchy, strengthened in its repeated struggles with powerful nobles (Burgundy, Flanders, Aquitaine) by alliances with the growing commercial towns, consolidated bureaucratic control under Philip IV (ruled 1285-1314) and extended French influence into Germany and Italy (popes at Avignon, France, 1309-1417). The **Hundred Years War**, 1338-1453, ended English dynastic claims in France (battles of Crécy, 1346, Poitiers, 1356; Joan of Arc executed, 1431). A French Renaissance, dating from royal invasions of Italy, 1494, 1499, was encouraged at the court of Francis I (ruled 1515-47), who centralized taxation and law. French vernacular literature consciously asserted its independence (La Pleiade, 1549).

England. The evolution of England's unique political institutions began with the Magna Carta, 1215, by which King John guaranteed the privileges of nobles and church against the monarchy and assured jury trial. After the Wars of the Roses (1455-85), the **Tudor dynasty** reasserted royal prerogatives (Henry VIII, ruled 1509-47), but the trend toward independent departments and ministerial government also continued. English trade (wool exports from c1340) was protected by the nation's growing maritime power (**Spanish Armada** destroyed, 1588).

English replaced French and Latin in the late 14th century in law and literature (Chaucer, 1340-1400) and English translation of the Bible began (Wycliffe, 1380s). Elizabeth I (ruled 1558-1603) presided over a confident flowering of poetry (Spenser, 1552-99), drama (**Shakespeare**, 1564-1616), and music.

German Empire. From among a welter of minor feudal states, church lands, and independent cities, the **Hapsburgs** assembled a far-flung territorial domain, based in Austria from 1276. The family held the title Holy Roman Emperor from 1452 to the Empire's dissolution in 1806, but failed to centralize its domains, leaving Germany disunited for centuries. Resistance to Turkish expansion brought Hungary under Austrian control from the 16th century. The Netherlands, Luxembourg, and Burgundy were added in 1477, curbing French expansion.

The Flemish painting tradition of naturalism, technical proficiency, and bourgeois subject matter began in the 15th century (Jan Van Eyck, 1366-1440), the earliest northern manifestation of the Renaissance. **Durer** (1471-1528) typified the merging of late Gothic and Italian trends in 16th century German art. Imposing civic architecture flourished in the prosperous commercial cities.

Spain. Despite the unification of Castile and Aragon in 1479, the 2 countries retained separate governments, and the nobility, especially in Aragon and Catalonia, retained many privileges. Spanish lands in Italy (Naples, Sicily) and the Netherlands entangled the country in European wars through the mid-17th century, while explorers, traders, and conquerors built up a Spanish empire in the Americas and the Philippines.

From the late 15th century, a **golden age** of literature and art produced works of social satire (plays of Lope de Vega, 1562-1635; Cervantes, 1547-1616), as well as spiritual intensity (El Greco, 1541-1614; Velazquez, 1599-1660).

Black Death. The bubonic plague reached Europe from the E in 1348, killing as much as half the population by 1350. Labor scarcity forced a rise in wages and brought greater freedom to the peasantry, making possible **peasant uprisings** (Jacquerie in France, 1358, Wat Tyler's rebellion in England, 1381). In the *ciompi* revolt, 1378, Florentine wage earners demanded a say in economic and political power.

Explorations. Organized European maritime exploration began, seeking to evade the Venice-Ottoman monopoly of eastern trade and to promote Christianity. Expeditions from Portugal beginning 1418 explored the west coast of Africa, until **Vasco da Gama** rounded the Cape of Good Hope in 1497 and reached India. A Portuguese trading empire was consolidated by the seizure of Goa, 1510, and Malacca, 1551. Japan was reached in 1542. Spanish voyages (**Columbus**, 1492-1504) uncovered a new world, which Spain hastened to subdue. Navigation schools in Spain and Portugal, the development of large sailing ships (carracks), and the invention of the rifle, c1475, aided European penetration.

Mughals and Safavids. East of the Ottoman empire, two Moslem dynasties ruled unchallenged in the 16th and 17th centuries. The Mughal empire in India, founded by Persianized Turkish invaders from the NW under Babur, dates from their 1526 conquest of Delhi. The dynasty ruled most of India for over 200 years, surviving nominally until 1857. Akbar (ruled 1556-1605) consolidated administration at his glorious court, where Urdu (Persian-influenced Hindi) developed. Trade relations with Europe increased. Under Shah Jahan (1629-58), a secularized art fusing Hindu and Moslem elements flourished in miniature painting and architecture (**Taj Mahal**). Sikhism, founded c1519, combined elements of both faiths. Suppression of Hindus and Shi'ite Moslems in S India in the late 17th century weakened the empire.

Fanatical devotion to the Shi'ite sect characterized the Safavids of Persia, 1502-1736, and led to hostilities with the Sunni Ottomans for over a century. The prosperity and strength of the empire are evidenced by the mosques at its capital, **Isfahan**. The dynasty enhanced Iranian national consciousness.

China. The Ming emperors, 1368-1644, the last native dynasty in China, wielded unprecedented personal power, while the Confucian bureaucracy began to suffer from inertia. European trade (Portugese

Timeline:
1500 — Brazil discovered — Calvin b. — Watch invented — Persian Safavids rule — Vesalius b. — St. Theresa of Avila b. — Luther's 95 Theses — Cortes conquers Aztecs — Mughal empire starts — So. Ger. peasants rise — Pizarro conquers Incas — Jesuits founded — Council of Trent — 1550 — Dutch republic founded — Japan persecutes Christians — Civil War in France — Velazquez b. — Descartes b. — 1600

monopoly through **Macao** from 1557) was strictly controlled. Jesuit scholars and scientists (Matteo Ricci 1552-1610) introduced some Western science; their writings familiarized the West with China. Chinese technological inventiveness declined from this era, but the arts thrived, especially painting and ceramics.

Japan. After the decline of the first hereditary shogunate (chief generalship) at **Kamakura** (1185-1333), fragmentation of power accelerated, as did the consequent social mobility. Under Kamakura and the Ashikaga shogunate, 1338-1573, the daimyos (lords) and samurai (warriors) grew more powerful and promoted a martial ideology. Japanese pirates and traders plied the China coast. Popular Buddhist movements included the nationalist Nichiren sect (from c1250) and **Zen** (brought from China, 1191), which stressed meditation and a disciplined esthetic (tea ceremony, landscape gardening, judo, Noh drama).

Reformed Europe Expands Overseas: 1500-1700

Reformation begun. Theological debate and protests against real and perceived clerical corruption existed in the medieval Christian world, expressed by such dissenters as Wycliffe (c1320-84) and his followers, the Lollards, in England, and **Huss** (burned as a heretic, 1415) in Bohemia.

Luther (1483-1546) preached that only faith could lead to salvation, without the mediation of clergy or good works. He attacked the authority of the Pope, rejected priestly celibacy, and recommended individual study of the Bible (which he translated, c1525). His 95 Theses (1517) led to his excommunication (1520). **Calvin** (1509-64) said God's elect were predestined for salvation; good conduct and success were signs of election. Calvin in Geneva and Knox (1505-72) in Scotland erected theocratic states.

Henry VIII asserted English national authority and secular power by breaking away from the Catholic church, 1534. Monastic property was confiscated, and some Protestant doctrines given official sanction.

Religious wars. A century and a half of religious wars began with a South German peasant uprising, 1524, repressed with **Luther's** support. Radical sects—democratic, pacifist, milennarian—arose (Anabaptists ruled Muenster, 1534-35), and were suppressed violently. Civil war in France from 1562 between **Huguenots** (Protestant nobles and merchants) and Catholics ended with the 1598 Edict of Nantes tolerating Protestants (revoked 1685). Hapsburg attempts to restore Catholicism in Germany were resisted in 25 years of fighting; the 1555 Peace of Augsburg guarantee of religious independence to local princes and cities was confirmed only after the **Thirty Years War,** 1618-48, when much of Germany was devastated by local and foreign armies (Sweden, France).

A Catholic Reformation, or **counter-reformation,** met the Protestant challenge, clearly defining an official theology at the Council of Trent, 1545-63. The **Jesuit** order, founded 1534 by Loyola (1491-1556), helped reconvert large areas of Poland, Hungary, and S. Germany and sent missionaries to the New World, India, and China, while the Inquisition helped suppress heresy in Catholic countries. A revival of piety appeared in the devotional literature (Theresa of Avila, 1515-82) and the grandiose Baroque art (Bernini, 1598-1680) of Roman Catholic countries.

Scientific Revolution. The late nominalist thinkers (Ockham, c1300-49) of Paris and Oxford challenged Aristotelian orthodoxy, allowing for a freer scientific approach. But metaphysical values, such as the Neoplatonic faith in an orderly, mathematical cosmos, still motivated and directed subsequent inquiry. **Copernicus** (1473-1543) promoted the heliocentric theory, which was confirmed when Kepler (1571-1630) discovered the mathematical laws describing the orbits of the planets. The Christian-Aristotelian belief that heavens and earth were fundamentally different collapsed when **Galileo** (1564-1642) discovered moving sunspots, irregular moon topography, and moons around Jupiter. He and **Newton** (1642-1727) developed a mechanics that unified cosmic and earthly phenomena. To meet the needs of the new physics, Newton and Leibnitz (1646-1716) invented calculus, Descartes (1596-1650) invented analytic geometry.

An explosion of observational science included the discovery of blood circulation (Harvey, 1578-1657) and microscopic life (Leeuwenhoek, 1632-1723), and advances in anatomy (Vesalius, 1514-64, dissected corpses) and chemistry (Boyle, 1627-91). Scientific research institutes were founded: Florence, 1657, London (**Royal Society**), 1660, Paris, 1666. Inventions proliferated (Savery's steam engine, 1696).

Arts. Mannerist trends of the high Renaissance (**Michelangelo,** 1475-1564) exploited virtuosity, grace, novelty, and exotic subjects and poses. The notion of artistic genius was promoted, in contrast to the anonymous medieval artisan. Private connoisseurs entered the art market. These trends were elaborated in the 17th century **Baroque** era, on a grander scale. Dynamic movement in painting and sculpture was emphasized by sharp lighting effects, use of rich materials (colored marble, gilt), realistic details. Curved facades, broken lines, rich, deep-cut detail, and ceiling decoration characterized Baroque architecture, especially in Germany. Monarchs, princes, and prelates, usually Catholic, used Baroque art to enhance and embellish their authority, as in royal portraits by Velazquez (1599-1660) and Van Dyck (1599-1641).

National styles emerged. In France, a taste for rectilinear order and serenity (Poussin, 1594-1665), linked to the new rational philosophy, was expressed in classical forms. The influence of **classical values** in French literature (tragedies of Racine, 1639-99) gave rise to the "battle of the Ancients and Moderns." New forms included the essay (Montaigne, 1533-92) and novel (*Princesse de Cleves,* La Fayette, 1678).

Dutch painting of the 17th century was unique in its wide social distribution. The Flemish tradition of undemonstrative realism reached its peak in Rembrandt (1606-69) and Vermeer (1632-75).

Economy. European economic expansion was stimulated by the new trade with the East, New World gold and silver, and a doubling of population (50 mln. in 1450, 100 mln. in 1600). New business and financial techniques were developed and refined, such as joint-stock companies, insurance, and letters of credit and exchange. The Bank of Amsterdam, 1609, and the Bank of England, 1694, broke the old monopoly of private banking families. The rise of a business mentality was typified by the spread of clock towers in cities in the 14th century. By the mid-15th century, portable clocks were available; the first watch was invented in 1502.

By 1650, most governments had adopted the **mercantile system,** in which they sought to amass metallic wealth by protecting their merchants' foreign and colonial trade monopolies. The rise in prices and the new coin-based economy undermined the craft guild and feudal manorial systems. Expanding industries, such as clothweaving and mining, benefitted from technical advances. Coal replaced disappearing wood as the chief fuel; it was used to fuel new 16th century blast furnaces making cast iron.

New World. The **Aztecs** united much of the Mesoamerican culture area in a militarist empire by 1519, from their capital, Tenochtitlan (pop. 300,000), which was the center of a cult requiring enormous levels of ritual human sacrifice. Most of the civilized areas of S. America were ruled by the centralized **Inca Empire** (1476-1534), stretching 2,000 miles from Ecuador to N.W. Argentina. Lavish and sophisticated traditions in pottery, weaving, sculpture, and architecture were maintained in both regions.

These empires, beset by revolts, fell in 2 short campaigns to gold-seeking Spanish forces based in the Antilles and Panama. **Cortes** took Mexico, 1519-21; **Pizarro** Peru, 1531-35. From these centers, land and sea expeditions claimed most of N. and S. America for Spain. The Indian high cultures did not survive the impact of Christian missionaries and the new upper class of whites and mestizos. In turn, New World silver, and such Indian products as potatoes, tobacco, corn, peanuts, chocolate, and rubber exercised a major economic influence on Europe. While the Spanish administration intermittently concerned itself with the welfare of Indians, the population remained impoverished at most levels, despite the growth of a distinct South American civilization. European diseases reduced the native population.

Brazil, which the Portuguese discovered in 1500 and settled after 1530, and the Caribbean colonies of several European nations developed a plantation economy where sugar cane, tobacco, cotton, coffee, rice, indigo, and lumber were grown commercially by slaves. From the early 16th to the late 19th centuries, some 10 million Africans were transported to **slavery** in the New World.

Netherlands. The urban, Calvinist northern provinces of the Netherlands rebelled against Hapsburg Spain, 1568, and founded an oligarchic mercantile republic. Their strategic control of the Baltic grain market enabled them to exploit Mediterranean food shortages. Religious refugees — French and Belgian Protestants, Iberian Jews — added to the cosmopolitan commercial talent pool. After Spain absorbed Portugal in 1580, the Dutch seized Portuguese possessions and created a vast, though generally short-lived commercial empire in Brazil, the Antilles, Africa, India, Ceylon, Malacca, Indonesia, and Taiwan, and challenged or supplanted Portuguese traders in China and Japan.

England. Anglicanism became firmly established under Elizabeth I after a brief Catholic interlude under "Bloody Mary," 1553-58. But religious and political conflicts led to a rebellion by Parliament, 1642. Roundheads (Puritans) defeated Cavaliers (Royalists); Charles I was beheaded, 1649. The new **Commonwealth** was ruled as a military dictatorship by Cromwell, who also brutally crushed an Irish rebellion, 1649-51. Conflicts within the Puritan camp (democratic Levelers defeated 1649) aided the Stuart restoration, 1660, but Parliament was permanently strengthened and the peaceful **"Glorious Revolution"**, 1688, advanced political and religious liberties (writings of Locke, 1632-1704). British privateers (Drake, 1540-96) challenged Spanish control of the New World, and penetrated Asian trade routes (Madras taken, 1639). N. American colonies (Jamestown, 1607, Plymouth, 1620) provided an outlet for religious dissenters.

France. Emerging from the religious civil wars in 1628, France regained military and commercial great power status under the ministries of **Richelieu** (1624-42), Mazarin (1643-61), and Colbert (1662-83). Under Louis XIV (ruled 1643-1715) royal absolutism triumphed over nobles and local *parlements* (defeat of Fronde, 1648-53). Permanent colonies were founded in Canada (1608), the Caribbean (1626), and India (1674).

Sweden. Sweden seceded from the Scandinavian Union in 1523. The thinly-populated agrarian state (with copper, iron, and timber exports) was united by the Vasa kings, whose conquests by the mid-17th century made Sweden the dominant Baltic power. The empire collapsed in the Great Northern War (1700-21).

Poland. After the union with Lithuania in 1447, Poland ruled vast territories from the Baltic to the Black Sea, resisting German and Turkish incursions. Catholic nobles failed to gain the loyalty of the Orthodox Christian peasantry in the East; commerce and trades were practiced by German and Jewish immigrants. The bloody 1648-49 cossack uprising began the kingdom's dismemberment.

China. A new dynasty, the **Manchus**, invaded from the NE and seized power in 1644, and expanded Chinese control to its greatest extent in Central and Southeast Asia. Trade and diplomatic contact with Europe grew, carefully controlled by China. New crops (sweet potato, maize, peanut) allowed an economic and population growth (300 million pop. in 1800). Traditional arts and literature were pursued with increased sophistication (*Dream of the Red Chamber*, novel, mid-18th century).

Japan. Tokugawa Ieyasu, shogun from 1603, finally unified and pacified feudal Japan. Hereditary daimyos and samurai monopolized government office and the professions. An urban merchant class grew, literacy spread, and a cultural renaissance occurred (haiku of Basho, 1644-94). Fear of European domination led to persecution of Christian converts from 1597, and stringent isolation from outside contact from 1640.

Philosophy, Industry, and Revolution: 1700-1800

Science and Reason. Faith in human reason and science as the source of truth and a means to improve the physical and social environment, espoused since the Renaissance (Francis Bacon, 1561-1626), was bolstered by scientific discoveries in spite of theological opposition (**Galileo's forced retraction**, 1633). Descartes applied the logical method of mathematics to discover "self-evident" scientific and philosophical truths, while Newton emphasized induction from experimental observation.

The challenge of reason to traditional religious and political values and institutions began with **Spinoza** (1632-77), who interpreted the Bible historically and called for political and intellectual freedom.

French philosophes assumed leadership of the **"Enlightenment"** in the 18th century. Montesquieu (1689-1755) used British history to support his notions of limited government. Voltaire's (1694-1778) diaries and novels of exotic travel illustrated the intellectual trends toward secular ethics and relativism. Rousseau's (1712-1778) radical concepts of the **social contract** and of the inherent goodness of the common man gave impetus to anti-monarchical republicanism. The *Encyclopedia*, 1751-72, edited by Diderot and d'Alembert, designed as a monument to reason, was largely devoted to practical technology.

In England, ideals of political and religious liberty were connected with empiricist philosophy and science in the followers of Locke. But the extreme **empiricism of Hume** (1711-76) and Berkeley

Savery's steam engine

Racine d.

Glorious Revolution

Bank of England

Edict of Nantes revoked

1680

St. Petersburg founded

Locke d.

Great Northern War

Newcomen engine

Spectator!

Louis XIV d.

1715

Newton d.

Lettres philosophiques

Watteau d.

Maria Theresa rule

Frederick II,

Vico d.

Voltaire's

Montesquieu's *Spirit of Laws*

Poor Richard's Almanack

Hume's *Human Understanding*

1750

1750

1775

1800

Rosseau's Social Contract — Spinning jenny — Brit. rules Bengal — Encyclopedia — Watt's engine — Edinburgh plan — Austria serfs free — Kant's Critique of Pure Reason — American Revolution — China bans opium — Bastille stormed — Fr. Repub. declared — Adam Smith d. — Divisions of Poland — Burke d. — China pop. at 300 mln.

(1685-1753) posed limits to the identification of reason with absolute truth, as did the evolutionary approach to law and politics of Burke (1729-97) and the utilitarianism of Bentham (1748-1832). Adam Smith (1723-90) and other **physiocrats** called for a rationalization of economic activity by removing artificial barriers to a supposedly natural free exchange of goods.

Despite the political disunity and backwardness of most of Germany, German writers participated in the new philosophical trends popularized by Wolff (1679-1754). **Kant's** (1724-1804) **idealism,** unifying an empirical epistemology with *a priori* moral and logical concepts, directed German thought away from skepticism. Italian contributions included work on electricity by Galvani (1737-98) and Volta (1745-1827), the pioneer **historiography of Vico** (1668-1744), and writings on penal reform by Beccaria (1738-94). The American Franklin (1706-90) was celebrated in Europe for his varied achievements.

The growth of the **press** (*Spectator,* 1711-14) and the wide distribution of realistic but sentimental **novels** attested to the increase of a large bourgeois public.

Arts. Rococo art, characterized by extravagant decorative effects, asymmetries copied from organic models, and artificial pastoral subjects, was favored by the continental aristocracy for most of the century (Watteau, 1684-1721), and had musical analogies in the ornamentalized polyphony of late Baroque. The **Neoclassical** art after 1750, associated with the new scientific archeology, was more streamlined, and infused with the supposed moral and geometric rectitude of the Roman Republic (David, 1748-1825). In England, **town planning** on a grand scale began (Edinburgh, 1767).

Industrial Revolution in England. Agricultural improvements, such as the sowing drill (1701) and livestock breeding, were implemented on the large fields provided by enclosure of common lands by private owners. Profits from agriculture and from colonial and foreign trade (1800 volume, £ 54 million) were channelled through hundreds of banks and the **Stock Exchange** (founded 1773) into new industrial processes.

The Newcomen steam pump (1712) aided coal mining. Coal fueled the new efficient steam engines patented by Watt in 1769, and coke-smelting produced cheap, sturdy iron for machinery by the 1730s. The **flying shuttle** (1733) and **spinning jenny** (1764) were used in the large new cotton textile factories, where women and children were much of the work force. Goods were transported cheaply over **canals** (2,000 miles built 1760-1800).

Central and East Europe. The monarchs of the three states that dominated eastern Europe — Austria, Prussia, and Russia — accepted the advice and legitimation of philosophes in creating more modern, centralized institutions in their kingdoms, enlarged by the division of Poland (1772-95).

Under **Frederick II** (ruled 1740-86) Prussia, with its efficient modern army, doubled in size. State monopolies and tariff protection fostered industry, and some legal reforms were introduced. Austria's heterogeneous realms were legally unified under **Maria Theresa** (ruled 1740-80) and **Joseph II** (1780-90). Reforms in education, law, and religion were enacted, and the Austrian serfs were freed (1781). With its defeat in the Seven Years' War in 1763, Austria lost Silesia and ceased its active role in Germany, but was compensated by expansion to the E and S (Hungary, Slavonia, 1699, Galicia, 1772).

Russia, whose borders continued to expand in all directions, adopted some Western bureaucratic and economic policies under Peter I (ruled 1682-1725) and Catherine II (ruled 1762-96). Trade and cultural contacts with the West multiplied from the new Baltic Sea capital, **St. Petersburg** (founded 1703).

American Revolution. The British colonies in N. America attracted a mass immigration of religious dissenters and poor people throughout the 17th and 18th centuries, coming from all parts of the British Isles, Germany, the Netherlands, and other countries. The population reached 3 million whites and blacks by the 1770s. The small native population was decimated by European diseases and wars with and between the various colonies. British attempts to control colonial trade, and to tax the colonists to pay for the costs of colonial administration and defense clashed with traditions of local self government, and eventually provoked the colonies to rebellion. (*See American Revolution in Index.*)

French Revolution. The growing French middle class lacked political power, and resented aristocratic tax privileges, especially in light of liberal political ideals popularized by the American Revolution. Peasants lacked adequate land and were burdened with feudal obligations to nobles. Wars with Britain drained the treasury, finally forcing the king to call the **Estates-General** in 1789 (first time since 1614), in an atmosphere of food riots (poor crop in 1788).

Aristocratic resistance to absolutism was soon overshadowed by the reformist Third Estate (middle class), which proclaimed itself the **National Constituent Assembly** June 17 and took the "Tennis Court oath" on June 20 to secure a constitution. The storming of the **Bastille** July 14 by Parisian artisans was followed by looting and seizure of aristocratic property throughout France. Assembly reforms included abolition of class and regional privileges, a Declaration of Rights, suffrage by taxpayers (75% of males), and the **Civil Constitution of the Clergy** providing for election and loyalty oaths for priests. A republic was declared Sept. 22, 1792, in spite of royalist pressure from Austria and Prussia, which had declared war in April (joined by Britain the next year). Louis XVI was beheaded Jan. 21, 1793, Queen Marie Antoinette was beheaded Oct. 16, 1793.

Royalist uprisings in La Vendee and the S and military reverses led to a **reign of terror** in which tens of thousands of opponents of the Revolution and criminals were executed. Radical reforms in the **Convention** period (Sept. 1793-Oct. 1795) included the abolition of colonial slavery, economic measures to aid the poor, support of public education, and a short-lived de-Christianization.

Division among radicals (execution of Hebert, March 1794, Danton, April, and Robespierre, July) aided the ascendance of a moderate **Directory,** which consolidated military victories. **Napoleon Bonaparte** (1769-1821), a popular young general, exploited political divisions and participated in a coup Nov. 9, 1799, making himself first consul (dictator).

India. Sikh and Hindu rebels (Rajputs, Marathas) and Afghans destroyed the power of the Mughals during the 18th century. After France's defeat in the Seven Years War, 1763, Britain was the chief European trade power in India. Its control of inland **Bengal and Bihar** was recognized by the Mughal shah in 1765, who granted the **British East India Co.** (under Clive, 1727-74) the right to collect land revenue there. Despite objections from Parliament (1784 India Act) the company's involvement in local wars and politics led to repeated acquisitions of new territory. The company exported Indian textiles, sugar, and indigo.

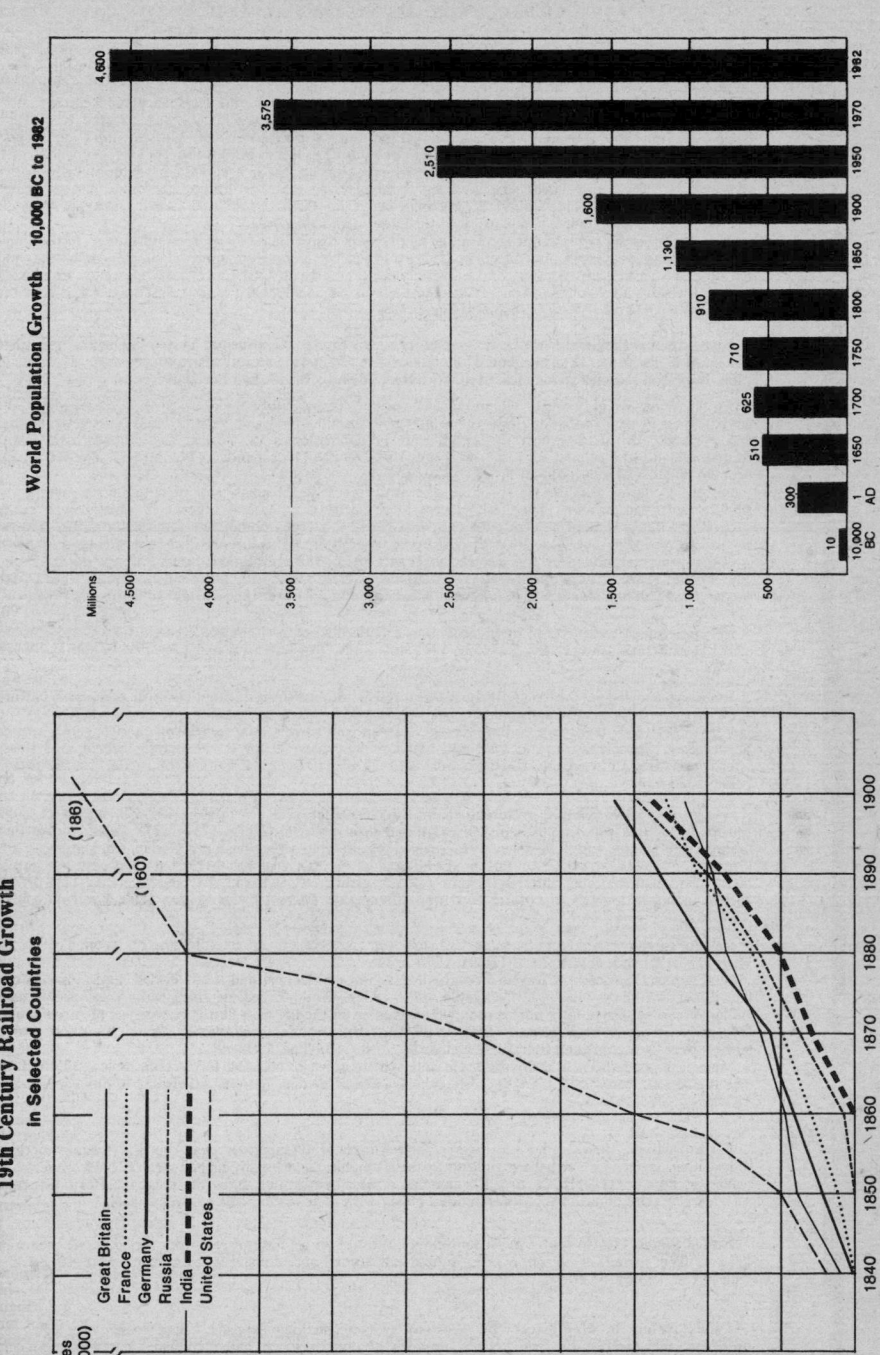

World Population Growth   10,000 BC to 1982

Millions

Year	Population
10,000 BC	10
1 AD	300
1650	510
1700	625
1750	710
1800	910
1850	1,130
1900	1,600
1950	2,510
1970	3,575
1982	4,600

19th Century Railroad Growth
In Selected Countries

Miles (1,000)

Great Britain
France
Germany
Russia
India
United States

(186)   (160)

Change Gathers Steam: 1800-1840

French ideals and empire spread. Inspired by the ideals of the French Revolution, and supported by the expanding French armies, new republican regimes arose near France: the **Batavian** Republic in the Netherlands (1795-1806), the **Helvetic** Republic in Switzerland (1798-1803), the **Cisalpine** Republic in N. Italy (1797-1805), the **Ligurian** Republic in Genoa (1797-1805), and the **Parthenopean** Republic in S. Italy (1799). A Roman Republic existed briefly in 1798 after Pope Pius VI was arrested by French troops. In Italy and Germany, new nationalist sentiments were stimulated both in imitation of and reaction to France (anti-French and anti-Jacobin peasant uprisings in Italy, 1796-9).

From 1804, when Napoleon declared himself emperor, to 1812, a succession of military victories (Austerlitz, 1805, Jena, 1806) extended his control over most of Europe, through puppet states (**Confederation of the Rhine** united W. German states for the first time and **Grand Duchy of Warsaw** revived Polish national hopes), expansion of the empire, and alliances.

Among the lasting reforms initiated under Napoleon's absolutist reign were: establishment of the Bank of France, centralization of tax collection, codification of law along Roman models (*Code Napoleon*), and reform and extension of secondary and university education. In an 1801 concordat, the papacy recognized the effective autonomy of the French Catholic Church. Some 400,000 French soldiers were killed in the Napoleonic Wars, along with 600,000 foreign troops.

Last gasp of old regime. France's coastal blockade of Europe (**Continental System**) failed to neutralize Britain. The disastrous 1812 invasion of Russia exposed Napoleon's overextension. After an 1814 exile at Elba, Napoleon's armies were defeated at **Waterloo**, 1815, by British and Prussian troops.

At the **Congress of Vienna**, the monarchs and princes of Europe redrew their boundaries, to the advantage of Prussia (in Saxony and the Ruhr), Austria (in Illyria and Venetia), and Russia (in Poland and Finland). British conquest of Dutch and French colonies (S. Africa, Ceylon, Mauritius) was recognized, and France, under the restored Bourbons, retained its expanded 1792 borders. The settlement brought 50 years of international peace to Europe.

But the Congress was unable to check the advance of liberal ideals and of nationalism among the smaller European nations. The 1825 **Decembrist uprising** by liberal officers in Russia was easily suppressed. But an independence movement in **Greece**, stirred by commercial prosperity and a cultural revival, succeeded in expelling Ottoman rule by 1831, with the aid of Britain, France, and Russia.

A constitutional monarchy was secured in France by an **1830 revolution**; Louis Philippe became king. The revolutionary contagion spread to **Belgium**, which gained its independence from the Dutch monarchy, 1830; to **Poland**, whose rebellion was defeated by Russia, 1830-31; and to Germany.

Romanticism. A new style in intellectual and artistic life began to replace Neo-classicism and Rococo after the mid-18th century. By the early 19th, this style, Romanticism, had prevailed in the European world.

Rousseau had begun the reaction against excessive rationalism and skepticism; in education (*Emile*, 1762) he stressed subjective spontaneity over regularized instruction. In Germany, Lessing (1729-81) and Herder (1744-1803) favorably compared the German folk song to classical forms, and began a cult of Shakespeare, whose passion and "natural" wisdom was a model for the Romantic *Sturm und Drang* (storm and stress) movement. **Goethe's** *Sorrows of Young Werther* (1774) set the model for the tragic, passionate genius.

A new interest in **Gothic architecture** in England after 1760 (Walpole, 1717-97) spread through Europe, associated with an aesthetic Christian and mystic revival (Blake, 1757-1827). Celtic, Norse, and German mythology and folk tales were revived or imitated (Macpherson's Ossian translation, 1762, Grimm's *Fairy Tales*, 1812-22). The medieval revival (Scott's *Ivanhoe*, 1819) led to a new interest in history, stressing national differences and organic growth (Carlyle, 1795-1881; Michelet, 1798-1874), corresponding to theories of natural evolution (Lamarck's *Philosophie zoologique*, 1809, Lyell's *Geology*, 1830-33).

Revolution and war fed an obsession with freedom and conflict, expressed by poets (**Byron**, 1788-1824, **Hugo**, 1802-85) and philosophers (**Hegel**, 1770-1831).

Wild gardens replaced the formal French variety, and painters favored rural, stormy, and mountainous landscapes (**Turner**, 1775-1851; **Constable**, 1776-1837). Clothing became freer, with wigs, hoops, and ruffles discarded. Originality and genius were expected in the life as well as the work of inspired artists (Murger's *Scenes from Bohemian Life*, 1847-49). Exotic locales and themes (as in "Gothic" horror stories) were used in art and literature (Delacroix, 1798-1863, **Poe**, 1809-49).

Music exhibited the new dramatic style and a breakdown of classical forms (Beethoven, 1770-1827). The use of folk melodies and modes aided the growth of distinct national traditions (Glinka in Russia, 1804-57).

Latin America. Haiti, under the former slave **Toussaint L'Ouverture**, was the first Latin American independent state, 1800. All the mainland Spanish colonies won their independence 1810-24, under such leaders as **Bolivar** (1783-1830). Brazil became an independent empire under the Portuguese prince regent, 1822. A new class of military officers divided power with large landholders and the church.

United States. Heavy immigration and exploitation of ample natural resources fueled rapid economic growth. The spread of the franchise, public education, and antislavery sentiment were signs of a widespread democratic ethic.

China. Failure to keep pace with Western arms technology exposed China to greater European influence, and hampered efforts to bar imports of opium, which had damaged Chinese society and drained wealth overseas. In the **Opium War**, 1839-42, Britain forced China to expand trade opportunities and to cede Hong Kong.

(Left margin timeline, top to bottom)

1800

Haiti indep.

Hugo b.
Dix b.

Mill b.

Lamarck's *Philosophie Zoologique*

Napoleon emperor

Congress of Vienna

Brazil indep.

1815

Scott's *Ivanhoe*

Grimm's *Fairy Tales*

Byron d.

Greek indep. movement

Decembrist uprising

S. Amer. colonies win indep.

Blake d.

1830

Volta d.

Beethoven d.

Belgian indep.

1st Eng. reform bill

1st Brit. Factory Act.

Brit. Emp. slavery banned

Opium War

Brook Farm, Mass.

Telegraph perfected by Morse

1845

Triumph of Progress: 1840-80

Idea of Progress. As a result of the cumulative scientific, economic, and political changes of the preceding eras, the idea took hold among literate people in the West that continuing growth and improvement was the usual state of human and natural life.

Darwin's statement of the **theory of evolution** and survival of the fittest (*Origin of Species*, 1859), defended by intellectuals and scientists against theological objections, was taken as confirmation that progress was the natural direction of life. The controversy helped define popular ideas of the dedicated scientist and ever-expanding human knowledge of and control over the world (Foucault's demonstration of earth's rotation, 1851, Pasteur's germ theory, 1861).

Liberals following Ricardo (1772-1823) in their faith that unrestrained competition would bring continuous economic expansion sought to adjust political life to the new social realities, and believed that unregulated competition of ideas would yield truth (Mill, 1806-73). In England, successive reform bills (1832, 1867, 1884) gave representation to the new industrial towns, and extended the franchise to the middle and lower classes and to Catholics, Dissenters, and Jews. On both sides of the Atlantic, reformists tried to improve conditions for the mentally ill (Dix, 1802-87), women (Anthony, 1820-1906), and prisoners. Slavery was barred in the British Empire, 1833; the United States, 1865; and Brazil, 1888.

Socialist theories based on ideas of human perfectibility or historical progress were widely disseminated. Utopian socialists like Saint-Simon (1760-1825) envisaged an orderly, just society directed by a technocratic elite. A model factory town, New Lanark, Scotland, was set up by utopian Robert Owen (1771-1858), and utopian communal experiments were tried in the U.S. (Brook Farm, Mass., 1841-7). Bakunin's (1814-76) anarchism represented the opposite utopian extreme of total freedom. Marx (1818-83) posited the inevitable triumph of socialism in the industrial countries through a historical process of class conflict.

Spread of industry. The technical processes and managerial innovations of the English industrial revolution spread to Europe (especially Germany) and the U.S., causing an explosion of industrial production, demand for raw materials, and competition for markets. Inventors, both trained and self-educated, provided the means for larger-scale production (Bessemer steel, 1856, sewing machine, 1846). Many inventions were shown at the 1851 London Great Exhibition at the Crystal Palace, whose theme was universal prosperity.

Local specialization and long-distance trade were aided by a revolution in transportation and communication. Railroads were first introduced in the 1820s in England and the U.S. Over 150,000 miles of track had been laid worldwide by 1880, with another 100,000 miles laid in the next decade. Steamships were improved (*Savannah* crossed Atlantic, 1819). The telegraph, perfected by 1844 (Morse), connected the Old and New Worlds by cable in 1866, and quickened the pace of international commerce and politics. The first commercial telephone exchange went into operation in the U.S. in 1878.

The new class of industrial workers, uprooted from their rural homes, lacked job security, and suffered from dangerous overcrowded conditions at work and at home. Many responded by organizing trade unions (legalized in England, 1824; France, 1884). The U.S. Knights of Labor had 700,000 members by 1886. The First International, 1864-76, tried to unite workers internationally around a Marxist program. The quasi-Socialist Paris Commune uprising, 1871, was violently suppressed. Factory Acts to reduce child labor and regulate conditions were passed (1833-50 in England). Social security measures were introduced by the Bismarck regime in Germany, 1883-89.

Revolutions of 1848. Among the causes of the continent-wide revolutions were an international collapse of credit and resulting unemployment, bad harvests in 1845-7, and a cholera epidemic. The new urban proletariat and expanding bourgeoisie demanded a greater political role. Republics were proclaimed in France, Rome, and Venice. Nationalist feelings reached fever pitch in the Hapsburg empire, as Hungary declared independence under Kossuth, a Slav Congress demanded equality, and Piedmont tried to drive Austria from Lombardy. A national liberal assembly at Frankfurt called for German unification.

But riots fueled bourgeois fears of socialism (Marx and Engels' 1848 *Communist Manifesto*) and peasants remained conservative. The old establishment — The Papacy, the Hapsburgs (using Croats and Romanians against Hungary), the Prussian army — was able to rout the revolutionaries by 1849. The French Republic succumbed to a renewed monarchy by 1852 (Emperor Napoleon III).

Great nations unified. Using the "blood and iron" tactics of Bismarck from 1862, Prussia controlled N. Germany by 1867 (war with Denmark, 1864, Austria, 1866). After defeating France in 1870 (loss of Alsace-Lorraine), it won the allegiance of S. German states. A new **German Empire** was proclaimed, 1871. **Italy**, inspired by Mazzini (1805-72) and Garibaldi (1807-82), was unified by the reformed Piedmont kingdom through uprisings, plebiscites, and war.

The U.S., its area expanded after the 1846-47 Mexican War, defeated a secession attempt by slave states, 1861-65. The Canadian provinces were united in an autonomous **Dominion of Canada,** 1867. Control in **India** was removed from the East India Co. and centralized under British administration after the 1857-58 Sepoy rebellion, laying the groundwork for the modern Indian State. Queen Victoria was named Empress of India, 1876.

Europe dominates Asia. The Ottoman Empire began to collapse in the face of Balkan nationalisms and European imperial incursions in N. Africa (Suez Canal, 1869). The Turks had lost control of most of both regions by 1882. Russia completed its expansion south by 1884 (despite the temporary setback of the Crimean War with Turkey, Britain, and France, 1853-56) taking Turkestan, all the Caucasus, and Chinese states in the East and sponsoring Balkan Slavs against the Turks. A succession of reformist and reactionary regimes presided over a slow modernization (serfs freed, 1861). Persian independence suffered as Russia and British India competed for influence.

China was forced to sign a series of unequal treaties with European powers and Japan. Overpopulation and an inefficient dynasty brought misery and caused rebellions (Taiping, Moslems) leaving tens of millions dead. Japan was forced by the U.S. (Commodore Perry's visits, 1853-54) and Europe to end its isolation. The Meiji restoration, 1868, gave power to a Westernizing oligarchy. Intensified empire-building gave Burma to Britain, 1824-86, and Indo-China to France, 1862-95. Christian missionary activity followed imperial and trade expansion in Asia.

Respectability. The fine arts were expected to reflect and encourage the progress of morals and —

1845

Communist Manifesto

Sewing machine
Mexican War begins

Perry in Japan

Freud b.

Bessemer steel

1860

Second Empire in France
U.S. Civil War

Sepoy rebellion

Overseas cable

Canada united
Marxist 1st International

1870

Paris commune
German empire founded

Mazzini d.

1st telephone

1880

Africa 1914

- {+.+} British
- [::::] French
- [ ] German
- [:::] Belgian
- [+ + +] Italian
- [XXXX] Portuguese
- [|||||] Spanish
- [::::] Independent

Tangier
Tunisia
Ifni
Morocco
Algeria
Libya
Rio De Oro
Egypt
French West Africa
Anglo Egyptian Sudan
Eritrea
Fr. Somaliland
Gambia
Port. Guinea
Sierra Leone
Gold Coast
Togo
Nigeria
Abyssinia
Somaliland Prot.
It. Somaliland
Liberia
Kamerun
Rio Muni
EQUATORIAL AFRICA
FRENCH
Uganda Prot.
East Africa Prot.
Belgian Congo
German East Africa
Angola
Nyasaland Prot.
Rhodesia
German South-west Africa
Bechuana-land Prot.
Mozambique
Madagascar
Union of South Africa
Swaziland
Basutoland

manners among the different classes. "Victorian" prudery, exaggerated delicacy, and familial piety were heralded by **Bowdler's** expurgated edition of Shakespeare (1818). Government-supported mass education inculcated a work ethic as a means to escape poverty (Horatio Alger, 1832-99).

The official **Beaux Arts** school in Paris set an international style of imposing public buildings (Paris Opera, 1861-74, Vienna Opera, 1861-69) and uplifting statues (Bartholdi's *Statue of Liberty*, 1885). Realist painting, influenced by photography (Daguerre, 1837), appealed to a new mass audience with social or historical narrative (Wilkie, 1785-1841, Poynter, 1836-1919) or with serious religious, moral, or social messages (pre-Raphaelites, Millet's Angelus, 1858) often drawn from ordinary life. The **Impressionists** (Pissarro, 1830-1903, Renoir, 1841-1919) rejected the central role of serious subject matter in favor of a colorful and sensual depiction of a moment, but their sunny, placid depictions of bourgeois scenes kept them within the respectable consensus.

Realistic **novelists** presented the full panorama of social classes and personalities, but retained sentimentality and moral judgment (Dickens, 1812-70, Eliot, 1819-80, Tolstoy, 1828-1910, Balzac, 1799-1850).

Veneer of Stability: 1880-1900

Imperialism triumphant. The vast **African** interior, visited by European explorers (Barth, 1821-65, Livingstone, 1813-73) was conquered by the European powers in rapid, competitive thrusts from their coastal bases after 1880, mostly for domestic political and international strategic reasons. W. African Moslem kingdoms (Fulani), Arab slave traders (Zanzibar), and Bantu military confederations (Zulu) were alike subdued. Only Christian Ethiopia (defeat of Italy, 1896) and Liberia resisted successfully. France (W. Africa) and Britain ("Cape to Cairo," Boer War, 1899-1902) were the major beneficiaries. The ideology of "the white man's burden" (Kipling, *Barrack Room Ballads*, 1892) or of a "civilizing mission" (France) justified the conquests.

West European foreign capital investments soared to nearly $40 billion by 1914, but most was in E. Europe (France, Germany) the Americas (Britain) and the white colonies. The foundation of the modern interdependent world economy was laid, with cartels dominating raw material trade.

An industrious world. Industrial and technological proficiency characterized the 2 new great powers — Germany and the U.S. Coal and iron deposits enabled Germany to reach second or third place status in iron, steel, and shipbuilding by the 1900s. German electrical and chemical industries were world leaders. The U.S. post-civil war boom (interrupted by "panics," 1884, 1893, 1896) was shaped by massive immigration from S. and E. Europe from 1880, government subsidy of railroads, and huge private monopolies (Standard Oil, 1870, U.S. Steel, 1901). The **Spanish-American War**, 1898 (Philippine rebellion, 1899-1901) and the Open Door policy in China (1899) made the U.S. a world power.

England led in **urbanization** (72% by 1890), with **London** the world capital of finance, insurance, and shipping. Electric subways (London, 1890), sewer systems (Paris, 1850s), parks, and bargain department stores helped improve living standards for most of the urban population of the industrial world.

Asians assimilate. Asian reaction to European economic, military, and religious incursions took the form of imitation of Western techniques and adoption of Western ideas of progress and freedom. The Chinese "self-strengthening" movement of the 1860s and 70s included rail, port, and arsenal improvements and metal and textile mills. Reformers like **K'ang Yu-wei** (1858-1927) won liberalizing reforms in 1898, right after the European and Japanese "scramble for concessions."

A universal education system in Japan and importation of foreign industrial, scientific, and military experts aided Japan's unprecedented rapid modernization after 1868, under the authoritarian Meiji regime. Japan's victory in the **Sino-Japanese War**, 1894-95, put Formosa and Korea in its power.

In India, the British alliance with the remaining princely states masked reform sentiment among the Westernized urban elite; higher education had been conducted largely in English for 50 years. The **Indian National Congress**, founded in 1885, demanded a larger government role for Indians.

"Fin-de-siecle" sophistication. Naturalist writers pushed realism to its extreme limits, adopting a quasi-scientific attitude and writing about formerly taboo subjects like sex, crime, extreme poverty, and corruption (Flaubert, 1821-80, Zola, 1840-1902, Hardy, 1840-1928). Unseen or repressed psychological motivations were explored in the clinical and theoretical works of Freud (1856-1939) and in the fiction of Dostoevsky (1821-81), James (1843-1916), Schnitzler (1862-1931) and others.

A contempt for bourgeois life or a desire to shock a complacent audience was shared by the French **symbolist** poets (Verlaine, 1844-96, Rimbaud, 1854-91), neo-pagan English writers (Swinburne, 1837-1909), continental dramatists (Ibsen, 1828-1906) and satirists (Wilde, 1854-1900). Nietzsche (1844-1900) was influential in his elitism and pessimism.

Post-impressionist art neglected long-cherished conventions of representation (Cezanne, 1839-1906) and showed a willingness to learn from primitive and non-European art (Gauguin, 1848-1903, Japanese prints).

Racism. Gobineau (1816-82) gave a pseudo-biological foundation to modern racist theories, which spread in the later 19th century along with **Social Darwinism**, the belief that societies are and should be organized as a struggle for survival of the fittest. The Medieval period was interpreted as an era of natural Germanic rule (Chamberlain, 1855-1927) and notions of superiority were associated with German national aspirations (Treitschke, 1834-96). **Anti-Semitism**, with a new racist rationale, became a significant political force in Germany (Anti-Semitic Petition, 1880), Austria (Lueger, 1844-1910), and France (Dreyfus case, 1894-1906).

Last Respite: 1900-1909

Alliances. While the peace of Europe (and its dependencies) continued to hold (1907 **Hague Conference** extended the rules of war and international arbitration procedures), imperial rivalries, protectionist trade practices (in Germany and France), and the escalating arms race (British *Dreadnought* battleship launched, Germany widens Kiel canal, 1906) exacerbated minor disputes (German-French Moroccan "crises", 1905, 1911).

Security was sought through alliances: **Triple Alliance** (Germany, Austria-Hungary, Italy) renewed

1880 — Dostoyevsky d.

— Marx d.

Indian Natl. Cong.

1885 — Brazil bans slavery

Kipling's *Barrack Room Ballads*
Europe conquers Africa

— radio
— Rimbaud d.
— Sino-Jap. War

Span.-Am. War 1895

Russ. Soc. Dem. Party

Dreyfus case
Gorky's *Lower Depths*

Boxer rebellion
Wilde d.

Ford Motor Co.
Panama Canal
Australia united

1904

Timeline labels (left margin, top to bottom):
1904
Pure Food & Drug Act
Rev. in Russia
Russo-Jap. War
Labour Party
Ibsen d.
Dreadnought launched
Hague Conf.
Young Turks rev.
Robie House
Mex. rev. starts
Portugal rev. starts
Futurist Manifesto
Japan annexes Korea
1910
2d Morocco crisis
Ottomans lose Europe
Diaz Mex. rule ends
Chinese repub.
Theory of Relativity
Maugham's "Of Human Bondage"
World War I
1916

1902, 1907; Anglo-Japanese Alliance, 1902; Franco-Russian Alliance, 1899; **Entente Cordiale** (Britain, France) 1904; Anglo-Russian Treaty, 1907; German-Ottoman friendship.

Ottomans decline. The inefficient, corrupt Ottoman government was unable to resist further loss of territory. Nearly all European lands were lost in 1912 to Serbia, Greece, Montenegro, and Bulgaria. Italy took Libya and the Dodecanese islands the same year, and Britain took Kuwait, 1899, and the Sinai, 1906. The **Young Turk** revolution in 1908 forced the sultan to restore a constitution, introduced some social reform, industrialization, and secularization.

British Empire. British trade and cultural influence remained dominant in the empire, but constitutional reforms presaged its eventual dissolution: the colonies of **Australia** were united in 1901 under a self-governing commonwealth. **New Zealand** acquired dominion status in 1907. The old Boer republics joined Cape Colony and Natal in the self-governing **Union of South Africa** in 1910.
The 1909 Indian Councils Act enhanced the role of elected province legislatures in **India.** The Moslem League, founded 1906, sought separate communal representation.

East Asia. Japan exploited its growing industrial power to expand its empire. Victory in the 1904-05 war against Russia (naval battle of Tsushima, 1905) assured Japan's domination of **Korea** (annexed 1910) and Manchuria (took Port Arthur 1905).
In China, central authority began to crumble (empress died, 1908). Reforms (Confucian exam system ended 1905, modernization of the army, building of railroads) were inadequate and secret societies of reformers and nationalists, inspired by the Westernized **Sun Yat-sen** (1866-1925) fomented periodic uprisings in the south.
Siam, whose independence had been guaranteed by Britain and France in 1896, was split into spheres of influence by those countries in 1907.

Russia. The population of the Russian Empire approached 150 million in 1900. Reforms in education, law, and local institutions (*zemstvos*), and an industrial boom starting in the 1880s (oil, railroads) created the beginnings of a modern state, despite the autocratic tsarist regime. Liberals (1903 Union of Liberation), Socialists (Social Democrats founded 1898, Bolsheviks split off 1903), and populists (Social Revolutionaries founded 1901) were periodically repressed, and national minorities persecuted (anti-Jewish pogroms, 1903, 1905-6).
An industrial crisis after 1900 and harvest failures aggravated poverty in the urban proletariat, and the 1904-05 defeat by Japan (which checked Russia's Asian expansion) sparked the revolution of 1905-06. A **Duma** (parliament) was created, and an agricultural reform (under Stolypin, prime minister 1906-11) created a large class of landowning peasants (kulaks).

The world shrinks. Developments in transportation and communication and mass population movements helped create an awareness of an interdependent world. Early **automobiles** (Daimler, Benz, 1885) were experimental, or designed as luxuries. Assembly-line mass production (Ford Motor Co., 1903) made the invention practicable, and by 1910 nearly 500,000 motor vehicles were registered in the U.S. alone. **Heavier-than-air flights** began in 1903 in the U.S. (Wright brothers), preceded by glider, balloon, and model plane advances in several countries. Trade was advanced by improvements in ship design (gyrocompass, 1907), speed (Lusitania crossed Atlantic in 5 days, 1907), and reach (Panama Canal begun, 1904).
The first transatlantic **radio** telegraphic transmission occurred in 1901, 6 years after Marconi discovered radio. Radio transmission of human speech had been made in 1900. Telegraphic transmission of photos was achieved in 1904, lending immediacy to news reports. **Phonographs,** popularized by Caruso's recordings (starting 1902) made for quick international spread of musical styles (ragtime). **Motion pictures,** perfected in the 1890s (Dickson, Lumiere brothers), became a popular and artistic medium after 1900; newsreels appeared in 1909.
Emigration from crowded European centers soared in the decade: 9 million migrated to the U.S., and millions more went to Siberia, Canada, Argentina, Australia, South Africa, and Algeria. Some 70 million Europeans emigrated in the century before 1914. Several million Chinese, Indians, and Japanese migrated to Southeast Asia, where their urban skills often enabled them to take a predominant economic role.

Social reform. The social and economic problems of the poor were kept in the public eye by realist fiction writers (Dreiser's *Sister Carrie,* 1900; Gorky's *Lower Depths,* 1902; Sinclair's *Jungle,* 1906), journalists (U.S. **muckrakers** — Steffens, Tarbell) and artists (Ashcan school). Frequent labor strikes and occasional assassinations by anarchists or radicals (Austrian Empress, 1898; King Umberto I of Italy, 1900; U.S. Pres. McKinley, 1901; Russian Interior Minister Plehve, 1904; Portugal's King Carlos, 1908) added to social tension and fear of revolution.
But democratic reformism prevailed. In Germany, Bernstein's (1850-1932) **revisionist Marxism,** downgrading revolution, was accepted by the powerful Social Democrats and trade unions. The British Fabian Society (the Webbs, Shaw) and the Labour Party (founded 1906) worked for reforms such as social security and union rights (1906), while women's suffragists grew more militant. U.S. **progressives** fought big business (Pure Food and Drug Act, 1906). In France, the 10-hour work day (1904) and separation of church and state (1905) were reform victories, as was universal suffrage in Austria (1907).

Arts. An unprecedented period of experimentation, centered in France, produced several new **painting** styles: fauvism exploited bold color areas (Matisse, *Woman with Hat,* 1905); expressionism reflected powerful inner emotions (the Brücke group, 1905); cubism combined several views of an object on one flat surface (Picasso's *Demoiselles,* 1906-07); futurism tried to depict speed and motion (Italian Futurist Manifesto, 1910). **Architects** explored new uses of steel structures, with facades either neo-classical (Adler and Sullivan in U.S.); curvilinear Art Nouveau (Gaudi's Casa Mila, 1905-10); or functionally streamlined (Wright's Robie House, 1909).
Music and **Dance** shared the experimental spirit. Ruth St. Denis (1877-1968) and Isadora Duncan (1878-1927) pioneered modern dance, while Diaghilev in Paris revitalized classic ballet from 1909. Composers explored atonal music (Debussy, 1862-1918) and dissonance (Schönberg, 1874-1951), or revolutionized classical forms (Stravinsky, 1882-71), often showing jazz or folk music influences.

War and Revolution: 1910-1919

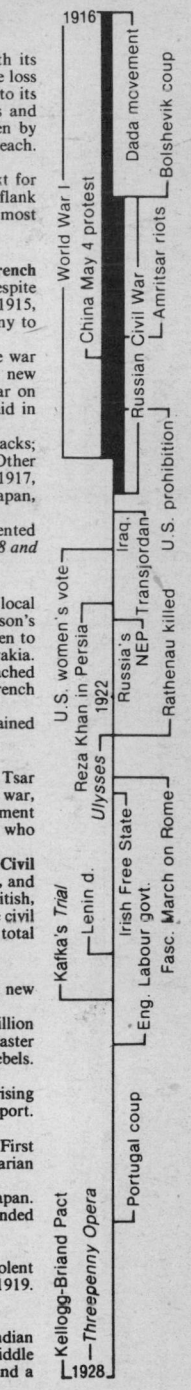

War threatens. Germany under Wilhelm II sought a political and imperial role consonant with its industrial strength, challenging Britain's world supremacy and threatening France, still resenting the loss of Alsace-Lorraine. Austria wanted to curb an expanded Serbia (after 1912) and the threat it posed to its own Slav lands. Russia feared Austrian and German political and economic aims in the Balkans and Turkey. An accelerated arms race resulted: the German standing army rose to over 2 million men by 1914. Russia and France had over a million each, Austria and the British Empire nearly a million each. Dozens of enormous battleships were built by the powers after 1906.

The **assassination of Austrian Archduke Ferdinand** by a Serbian, June 28, 1914, was the pretext for war. The system of alliances made the conflict Europe-wide; Germany's invasion of Belgium to outflank France forced Britain to enter the war. Patriotic fervor was nearly unanimous among all classes in most countries.

World War I. German forces were stopped in France in one month. The rival armies dug **trench networks.** Artillery and improved machine guns prevented either side from any lasting advance despite repeated assaults (600,000 dead at **Verdun,** Feb.-July 1916). Poison gas, used by Germany in 1915, proved ineffective. Over one million U.S. troops tipped the balance after mid-1917, forcing Germany to sue for peace.

In the East, the Russian armies were thrown back (battle of **Tannenberg,** Aug. 20, 1914) and the war grew unpopular. An allied attempt to relieve Russia through Turkey failed (**Gallipoli** 1916). The new Bolshevik regime signed the capitulatory Brest-Litovsk peace in March, 1918. Italy entered the war on the allied side, Apr. 1915, but was pushed back by Oct. 1917. A renewed offensive with Allied aid in Oct.-Nov. 1918 forced Austria to surrender.

The British Navy successfully blockaded Germany, which responded with submarine U-boat attacks; **unrestricted submarine warfare** against neutrals after Jan. 1917 helped bring the U.S. into the war. Other battlefields included Palestine and Mesopotamia, both of which Britain wrested from the Turks in 1917, and the African and Pacific colonies of Germany, most of which fell to Britain, France, Australia, Japan, and South Africa.

From 1916, the civilian population and economy of both sides were mobilized to an unprecedented degree. Over 10 million soldiers died (May 1917 French mutiny crushed). *For further details, see 1978 and earlier editions of The World Almanac.*

Settlement. At the **Versailles conference** (Jan.-June 1919) and in subsequent negotiations and local wars (Russian-Polish War 1920), the map of Europe was redrawn with a nod to U.S. Pres. Wilson's principle of self-determination. Austria and Hungary were separated and much of their land was given to Yugoslavia (formerly Serbia), Romania, Italy, and the newly independent Poland and Czechoslovakia. Germany lost territory in the West, North, and East, while Finland and the Baltic states were detached from Russia. Turkey lost nearly all its Arab lands to British-sponsored Arab states or to direct French and British rule.

A huge **reparations** burden and partial demilitarization were imposed on Germany. Wilson obtained approval for a League of Nations, but the U.S. Senate refused to allow the U.S. to join.

Russian revolution. Military defeats and high casualties caused a contagious lack of confidence in Tsar Nicholas, who was forced to abdicate, Mar. 1917. A liberal provisional government failed to end the war, and massive desertions, riots, and fighting between factions followed. A moderate socialist government under Kerensky was overthrown in a violent **coup by the Bolsheviks** in Petrograd under Lenin, who disbanded the elected Constituent Assembly, Nov. 1917.

The Bolsheviks brutally suppressed all opposition and ended the war with Germany, Mar. 1918. **Civil war** broke out in the summer between the Red Army, including the Bolsheviks and their supporters, and monarchists, anarchists, nationalities (Ukrainians, Georgians, Poles) and others. Small U.S., British, French and Japanese units also opposed the Bolsheviks, 1918-19 (Japan in Vladivostok to 1922). The civil war, anarchy, and pogroms devastated the country until the 1920 Red Army victory. The wartime total monopoly of political, economic, and police power by the Communist Party leadership was retained.

Other European revolutions. An unpopular monarchy in **Portugal** was overthrown in 1910. The new republic took severe anti-clerical measures, 1911.

After a century of Home Rule agitation, during which **Ireland** was devastated by famine (one million dead, 1846-47) and emigration, republican militants staged an unsuccessful uprising in Dublin, Easter 1916. The execution of the leaders and mass arrests by the British won popular support for the rebels. The Irish Free State, comprising all but the 6 northern counties, achieved dominion status in 1922.

In the aftermath of the world war, radical revolutions were attempted in Germany (**Spartacist** uprising Jan. 1919), **Hungary** (Kun regime 1919), and elsewhere. All were suppressed or failed for lack of support.

Chinese revolution. The Manchu Dynasty was overthrown and a republic proclaimed, Oct. 1911. First president Sun Yat-sen resigned in favor of strongman Yuan Shih-k'ai. Sun organized the parliamentarian **Kuomintang** party.

Students launched protests May 4, 1919 against League of Nations concessions in China to Japan. Nationalist, liberal, and socialist ideas and political groups spread. The **Communist Party** was founded 1921. A communist regime took power in Mongolia with Soviet support in 1921.

India restive. Indian objections to British rule erupted in nationalist riots as well as in the non-violent tactics of Gandhi (1869-1948). Nearly 400 unarmed demonstrators were shot at **Amritsar,** Apr. 1919. Britain approved limited self-rule that year.

Mexican revolution. Under the long Diaz dictatorship (1876-1911) the economy advanced, but Indian and mestizo lands were confiscated, and concessions to foreigners (mostly U.S.) damaged the middle class. A **revolution in 1910** led to civil wars and U.S. intervention (1914, 1916-17). Land reform and a more democratic constitution (1917) were achieved.

The Aftermath of War: 1920-29

U.S. Easy credit, technological ingenuity, and war-related industrial decline in Europe caused a long economic boom, in which ownership of the new products — autos, phones, radios — became democratized. Prosperity, an increase in women workers, women's suffrage (1920) and drastic change in fashion (flappers, mannish bob for women, clean-shaven men), created a wide perception of social change, despite prohibition of alcoholic beverages (1919-33). Union membership and strikes increased. Fear of radicals led to Palmer raids (1919-20) and Sacco/Vanzetti case (1921-27).

Europe sorts itself out. Germany's liberal **Weimar constitution** (1919) could not guarantee a stable government in the face of rightist violence (Rathenau assassinated 1922) and Communist refusal to cooperate with Socialists. Reparations and allied occupation of the Rhineland caused staggering inflation which destroyed middle class savings, but economic expansion resumed after mid-decade, aided by U.S. loans. A sophisticated, innovative culture developed in architecture and design (Bauhaus, 1919-28), film (Lang, *M*, 1931), painting (Grosz), music (Weill, *Threepenny Opera*, 1928), theater (Brecht, *A Man's a Man*, 1926), criticism (Benjamin), philosophy (Jung), and fashion. This culture was considered decadent and socially disruptive by rightists.

England elected its first labor governments (Jan. 1924, June 1929). A 10-day general strike in support of coal miners failed, May 1926. In **Italy**, strikes, political chaos and violence by small Fascist bands culminated in the Oct. 1922 Fascist March on Rome, which established Mussolini's dictatorship. Strikes were outlawed (1926), and Italian influence was pressed in the Balkans (Albania a protectorate 1926). A conservative dictatorship was also established in **Portugal** in a 1926 military coup.

Czechoslovakia, the only stable democracy to emerge from the war in Central or East Europe, faced opposition from Germans (in the Sudetenland), Ruthenians, and some Slovaks. As the industrial heartland of the old Hapsburg empire, it remained fairly prosperous. With French backing, it formed the Little Entente with Yugoslavia (1920) and **Romania** (1921) to block Austrian or Hungarian irredentism. **Hungary** remained dominated by the landholding classes and expansionist feeling. Croats and Slovenes in **Yugoslavia** demanded a federal state until King Alexander proclaimed a dictatorship (1929). Poland faced nationality problems as well (Germans, Ukrainians, Jews); Pilsudski ruled as dictator from 1926. The Baltic states were threatened by traditionally dominant ethnic Germans and by Soviet-supported communists.

An economic collapse and famine in **Russia**, 1921-22, claimed 5 million lives. The New Economic Policy (1921) allowed land ownership by peasants and some private commerce and industry. Stalin was absolute ruler within 4 years of Lenin's 1924 death. He inaugurated a brutal collectivization program 1929-32, and used foreign communist parties for Soviet state advantage.

Internationalism. Revulsion against World War I led to pacifist agitation, the Kellogg-Briand Pact renouncing aggressive war (1928), and **naval disarmament** pacts (Washington, 1922, London, 1930). But the League of Nations was able to arbitrate only minor disputes (Greece-Bulgaria, 1925).

Middle East. Mustafa Kemal (Ataturk) led **Turkish** nationalists in resisting Italian, French, and Greek military advances, 1919-23. The sultanate was abolished 1922, and elaborate reforms passed, including secularization of law and adoption of the Latin alphabet. Ethnic conflict led to persecution of **Armenians** (over 1 million dead in 1915, 1 million expelled), Greeks (forced Greek-Turk population exchange, 1923), and Kurds (1925 uprising).

With evacuation of the Turks from **Arab** lands, the puritanical Wahabi dynasty of eastern Arabia conquered present Saudi Arabia, 1919-25. British, French, and Arab dynastic and nationalist maneuvering resulted in the creation of two more Arab monarchies in 1921: Iraq and Transjordan (both under British control), and two French mandates: Syria and Lebanon. Jewish immigration into British-mandated **Palestine**, inspired by the Zionist movement, was resisted by Arabs, at times violently (1921, 1929 massacres).

Reza Khan ruled **Persia** after his 1921 coup (shah from 1925), centralized control, and created the trappings of a modern state.

China. The Kuomintang under **Chiang Kai-shek** (1887-1975) subdued the warlords by 1928. The Communists were brutally suppressed after their alliance with the Kuomintang was broken in 1927. Relative peace thereafter allowed for industrial and financial improvements, with some Russian, British, and U.S. cooperation.

Arts. Nearly all bounds of subject matter, style, and attitude were broken in the arts of the period. **Abstract** art first took inspiration from natural forms or narrative themes (Kandinsky from 1911), then worked free of any representational aims (Malevich's suprematism, 1915-19, Mondrian's geometric style from 1917). The **Dada** movement from 1916 mocked artistic pretension with absurd collages and constructions (Arp, Tzara, from 1916). Paradox, illusion, and psychological taboos were exploited by **surrealists** by the latter 1920s (Dali, Magritte). Architectural schools celebrated industrial values, whether vigorous abstract constructivism (Tatlin, *Monument to 3rd International*, 1919) or the machined, streamlined **Bauhaus** style, which was extended to many design fields (Helvetica type 1920s).

Prose writers explored revolutionary narrative modes related to dreams (Kafka's *Trial*, 1925), internal monologue (Joyce's *Ulysses*, 1922), and word play (Stein's *Making of Americans*, 1925). Poets and novelists wrote of modern alienation (Eliot's *Waste Land*, 1922) and aimlessness (Lost Generation).

Sciences. Scientific specialization prevailed by the 20th century. Advances in knowledge and technological aptitude increased with the geometric increase in the number of practitioners. Physicists challenged common-sense views of causality, observation, and a mechanistic universe, putting science further beyond popular grasp (Einstein's general theory of relativity, 1915; Bohr's quantum mechanics, 1913; Heisinger's uncertainty principle, 1927).

Timeline (left margin, top to bottom):

1928
— India salt march
— Stock market crash
— Smoot-Hawley Tariff
— Alfonso leaves Spain
— Japan seizes Manchuria
— Gandhi's fast
1933
— Hitler dictator
— International Style
— FDR in office
— Nuremberg Laws
— Hitler takes Rhineland
— Long March in China
— Fr. Popular Front
— Italy takes Ethiopia
— Japan invades China
— Civil War in Spain
1938

Rise of the Totalitarians: 1930-39

Depression. A worldwide financial panic and economic depression began with the Oct. 1929 U.S. stock market crash and the May 1931 failure of the Austrian Credit-Anstalt. A credit crunch caused international bankruptcies and **unemployment:** 12 million jobless by 1932 in the U.S., 5.6 million in Germany, 2.7 million in England. Governments responded with **tariff restrictions** (Smoot-Hawley Act 1930; Ottawa Imperial Conference, 1932) which dried up world trade. Government public works programs were vitiated by deflationary budget balancing.

Germany. Years of agitation by violent extremists was brought to a head by the Depression. Nazi leader **Hitler** was named chancellor by Pres. Hindenburg Jan. 1933, and given dictatorial power by the Reichstag in Mar. Opposition parties were disbanded, strikes banned, and all aspects of economic, cultural, and religious life brought under central government and Nazi party control and manipulated by sophisticated propaganda. Severe persecution of Jews began (**Nuremberg Laws** Sept. 1935). Many Jews, political opponents and others were sent to concentration camps (Dachau, 1933) where thousands died or were killed. Public works, renewed conscription (1935), arms production, and a 4-year plan (1936) ended unemployment.

Hitler's expansionism started with reincorporation of the Saar (1935), occupation of the **Rhineland** (Mar. 1936), and annexation of Austria (Mar. 1938). At **Munich,** Sept. 1938, an indecisive Britain and France sanctioned German dismemberment of Czechoslovakia.

Russia. Urbanization and education advanced. Rapid industrialization was achieved through successive **5-year-plans** starting 1928, using severe labor discipline and mass forced labor. Industry was financed by a decline in living standards and exploitation of agriculture, which was almost totally collectivized by the early 1930s (*kolkhoz,* collective farm; *sovkhoz,* state farm, often in newly-worked lands). Successive **purges** increased the role of professionals and management at the expense of workers. Millions perished in a series of man-made disasters: elimination of kulaks (peasant land-owners), 1929-34; severe famine, 1932-33; party purges (Great Purge, 1936-38); suppression of nationalities; and poor conditions in labor camps.

Spain. An industrial revolution during World War I created an urban proletariat, which was attracted to socialism and anarchism; Catalan nationalists challenged central authority. The 5 years after King Alfonso left Spain, Apr. 1931, were dominated by tension between intermittent leftist and anti-clerical governments and clericals, monarchists and other rightists. Anarchist and communist rebellions were crushed, but a July, 1936, extreme right rebellion led by Gen. Francisco Franco and aided by Nazi Germany and Fascist Italy succeeded, after a 3-year **civil war** (over 1 million dead in battles and atrocities). The war polarized international public opinion.

Italy. Despite propaganda for the ideal of the Corporate State, few domestic reforms were attempted. An entente with Hungary and Austria, Mar. 1934, a pact with Germany and Japan, Nov. 1937, and intervention by 50-75,000 troops in Spain, 1936-39, sealed Italy's identification with the fascist bloc (anti-Semitic laws after Mar. 1938). Ethiopia was conquered, 1935-37, and **Albania** annexed, Jan. 1939, in conscious imitation of ancient Rome.

East Europe. Repressive regimes fought for power against an active opposition (liberals, socialists, communists, peasants, Nazis). Minority groups and Jews were restricted within national boundaries that did not coincide with ethnic population patterns. In the destruction of **Czechoslovakia,** Hungary occupied southern Slovakia (Mar. 1938) and Ruthenia (Mar. 1939), and a pro-Nazi regime took power in the rest of Slovakia. Other boundary disputes (e.g. Poland-Lithuania, Yugoslavia-Bulgaria, Romania-Hungary) doomed attempts to build joint fronts against Germany or Russia. Economic depression was severe.

East Asia. After a period of liberalism in **Japan,** nativist militarists dominated the government with peasant support. Manchuria was seized, Sept. 1931-Feb. 1932, and a puppet state set up (Manchukuo). Adjacent Jehol (inner Mongolia) was occupied in 1933. China proper was invaded July 1937; large areas were conquered by Oct. 1938.

In **China** Communist forces left Kuomintang-besieged strongholds in the South in a Long March (1934-35) to the North. The Kuomintang-Communist civil war was suspended Jan. 1937 in the face of threatening Japan.

The democracies. The Roosevelt Administration, in office Mar. 1933, embarked on an extensive program of social reform and economic stimulation, including protection for labor unions (heavy industries organized), social security, public works, wages and hours laws, assistance to farmers. Isolationist sentiment (1937 Neutrality Act) prevented U.S. intervention in Europe, but military expenditures were increased in 1939.

French political instability and polarization prevented resolution of economic and international security questions. The **Popular Front** government under Blum (June 1936-Apr. 1938) passed social reforms (40-hour week) and raised arms spending. National coalition governments ruled Britain from Aug. 1931, brought some economic recovery, but failed to define a consistent foreign policy until Chamberlain's government (from May 1937), which practiced deliberate **appeasement** of Germany and Italy.

India. Twenty years of agitation for autonomy and then for independence (Gandhi's **salt march,** 1930) achieved some constitutional reform (extended provincial powers, 1935) despite Moslem-Hindu strife. Social issues assumed prominence with peasant uprisings (1921), strikes (1928), Gandhi's efforts for untouchables (1932 "fast unto death"), and social and agrarian reform by the provinces after 1937.

Arts. The streamlined, geometric design motifs of Art Deco (from 1925) prevailed through the 1930s. Abstract art flourished (Moore sculptures from 1931) alongside a new realism related to social and political concerns (**Socialist Realism** the official Soviet style from 1934; Mexican muralists Rivera, 1886-1957, and Orozco, 1883-1949), which was also expressed in fiction and poetry (Steinbeck's *Grapes of Wrath,* 1939; Sandburg's *The People, Yes,* 1936). Modern architecture (*International Style,* 1932) was unchallenged in its use of man-made materials (concrete, glass), lack of decoration, and monumentality (Rockefeller Center, 1929-40). U.S.-made films captured a world-wide audience with their larger-than-life fantasies (*Gone with the Wind,* 1939).

1938

Nazi-Soviet pact
Munich pact
Germany attacks Poland

Germans win Balkans
Russia seizes E. Poland
Axis in Russia
Russia takes Baltic
Dunkirk

World War II
Stranger
Stalingrad
Midway
Being & Nothingness
Abstract Expressionism starts
Allies in Germany
A-bombs on Japan
Germany surrenders

UN charter
Japan surrenders
Jap. constitution

Cominform
Truman Doctrine
Nuremberg convictions

1948

War, Hot and Cold: 1940-49

War in Europe. The Nazi-Soviet non-agression pact (Aug. '39) freed Germany to attack Poland (Sept.). Britain and France, who had guaranteed Polish independence, declared war on Germany. Russia seized East Poland (Sept.), attacked Finland (Nov.) and took the Baltic states (July '40). Mobile German forces staged "blitzkrieg" attacks Apr.-June, '40, conquering neutral Denmark, Norway, and the low countries and defeating France; 350,000 British and French troops were evacuated at Dunkirk (May). The Battle of Britain, June-Dec. '40, denied Germany air superiority. German-Italian campaigns won the Balkans by Apr. '41. Three million Axis troops **invaded Russia** June '41, marching through the Ukraine to the Caucasus, and through White Russia and the Baltic republics to Moscow and Leningrad. Russian winter counterthrusts, '41-'42 and '42-'43 stopped the German advance (Stalingrad Sept. '42-Feb. '43). With British and U.S. Lend-Lease aid and sustaining great casualties, the Russians drove the Axis from all E. Europe and the Balkans in the next 2 years. Invasions of N. Africa (Nov. '42), Italy (Sept. '43), and Normandy (June '44) brought U.S., British, Free French and allied troops to Germany by spring '45. Germany surrendered May 7, 1945.

War in Asia-Pacific. Japan occupied Indochina Sept. '40, dominated Thailand Dec. '41, attacked Hawaii, the Philippines, Hong Kong, Malaya Dec. 7, 1941. Indonesia was attacked Jan. '42, Burma conquered Mar. 42. Battle of **Midway** (June '42) turned back the Japanese advance. "Island-hopping" battles (Guadalcanal Aug. '42-Jan. '43, **Leyte Gulf** Oct. '44, Iwo Jima Feb.-Mar. '45, Okinawa Apr. '45) and massive bombing raids on Japan from June '44 wore out Japanese defenses. Two U.S. atom bombs, dropped Aug. 6 and 9, forced Japan to surrender Aug. 14, 1945. *For further details, see 1978 and earlier editions of The World Almanac.*

Atrocities. The war brought 20th-century cruelty to its peak. Nazi murder camps (Auschwitz) systematically killed 6 million Jews. Gypsies, political opponents, sick and retarded people, and others deemed undesirable were murdered by the Nazis, as were vast numbers of Slavs, especially leaders. German bombs killed 70,000 English civilians. Some 100,000 Chinese civilians were killed by Japanese forces in the capture of Nanking. Severe retaliation by the Soviet army, E. European partisans, Free French and others took a heavy toll. U.S. and British bombing of Germany killed hundreds of thousands, as did U.S. bombing of Japan (80-200,000 at Hiroshima alone). Some 45 million people lost their lives in the war.

Home front. All industries were reoriented to war production and support, and rationing was universal. Science was harnessed for the war effort, yielding such innovations as radar, jet planes, and synthetic materials. Unscathed U.S. industry, partly staffed by women, helped decide the war.

Settlement. The United Nations charter was signed in San Francisco June 26, 1945 by 50 nations. The International Tribunal at Nuremberg convicted 22 German leaders for war crimes Sept. '46, 23 Japanese leaders were convicted Nov. '48. Postwar border changes included large gains in territory for the USSR, losses for Germany, a shift westward in Polish borders, and minor losses for Italy. Communist regimes, supported by Soviet troops, took power in most of E. Europe, including Soviet-occupied Germany (GDR proclaimed Oct. '49). Japan lost all overseas lands.

Recovery. Basic political and social changes were imposed on Japan and W. Germany by the western allies (Japan constitution Nov. '46, W. German basic law May '49). U.S. Marshall Plan aid ($12 billion '47-'51) spurred W. European economic recovery after a period of severe inflation and strikes in Europe and the U.S. The British Labour Party introduced a national health service and nationalized basic industries in 1946.

Cold War. Western fears of further Soviet advances (Cominform formed Oct. '47, Czechoslovakia coup, Feb. '48, Berlin blockade Apr.'48-Sept. '49) led to formation of NATO. Civil War in Greece and Soviet pressure on Turkey led to U.S. aid under the Truman Doctrine (Mar. '47). Other anti-communist security pacts were the Org. of American States (Apr. '48) and Southeast Asia Treaty Org. (Sept. '54). A new wave of Soviet purges and repression intensified in the last years of Stalin's rule, extending to E. Europe (Slansky trial in Czechoslovakia, 1951). Only Yugoslavia resisted Soviet control (expelled by Cominform, June '48; U.S. aid, June '49).

China, Korea. Communist forces emerged from World War II strengthened by the Soviet takeover of industrial Manchuria. In 4 years of fighting, the Kuomintang was driven from the mainland; the People's Republic was proclaimed Oct. 1, 1949. Korea was divided by Russian and U.S. occupation forces. Separate republics were proclaimed in the 2 zones Aug.-Sept. '48.

India. India and Pakistan became independent dominions Aug. 15, 1947. Millions of Hindu and Moslem refugees were created by the partition; riots, 1946-47, took hundreds of thousands of lives; Gandhi himself was assassinated Jan. '48. Burma became completely independent Jan. '48; Ceylon took dominion status in Feb.

Middle East. The UN approved partition of Palestine into Jewish and Arab states. Israel was proclaimed May 14, 1948. Arabs rejected partition, but failed to defeat Israel in war, May '48-July '49. Immigration from Europe and the Middle East swelled Israel's Jewish population. British and French forces left Lebanon and Syria, 1946. Transjordan occupied most of Arab Palestine.

Southeast Asia. Communists and others fought against restoration of French rule in Indochina from 1946; a non-communist government was recognized by France Mar. '49, but fighting continued. Both Indonesia and the Philippines became independent, the former in 1949 after 4 years of war with Netherlands, the latter in 1946. Philippine economic and military ties with the U.S. remained strong; a communist-led peasant rising was checked in '48.

Arts. New York became the center of the world art market; abstract expressionism was the chief mode (Pollock from '43, de Kooning from '47). Literature and philosophy explored existentialism (Camus' *Stranger*, 1942, Sartre's *Being and Nothingness*, 1943). Non-western attempts to revive or create regional styles (Senghor's Negritude, Mishima's novels) only confirmed the emergence of a universal culture. Radio and phonograph records spread American popular music (swing, bebop) around the world.

1948

Israel indep.

China People's Rep.

Gandhi killed

Burma independent

Ger. Dem. Rep.

Lonely Crowd

Indonesia indep.

Indochina War

H-bomb

Egypt rev.

Korean War

Stalin d.

Ghana indep.

Sputnik

Suez War

McCarthy censured

Peron ousted

Hungary rev.

Bandung conf.

On the Road

SEATO founded

EEC Treaty

1958

The American Decade: 1950-59

Polite decolonization. The peaceful decline of European political and military power in Asia and Africa accelerated in the 1950s. Nearly all of N. Africa was freed by 1956, but France fought a bitter war to retain Algeria, with its large European minority, until 1962. **Ghana**, independent 1957, led a parade of new black African nations (over 2 dozen by 1962) which altered the political character of the UN. Ethnic disputes often exploded in the new nations after decolonization (UN troops in Cyprus 1964; **Nigeria** civil war 1967-70). Leaders of the new states, mostly sharing socialist ideologies, tried to create an Afro-Asian bloc (Bandung Conf. 1955), but Western economic influence and U.S. political ties remained strong (Baghdad Pact, 1955).

Trade. World trade volume soared, in an atmosphere of monetary stability assured by international accords (**Bretton Woods** 1944). In Europe, economic integration advanced (**European Economic Community** 1957, European Free Trade Association 1960). Comecon (1949) coordinated the economies of Soviet-bloc countries.

U.S. Economic growth produced an abundance of consumer goods (9.3 million motor vehicles sold, 1955). Suburban housing tracts changed life patterns for middle and working classes (Levittown 1946-51). **Eisenhower's** landslide election victories (1952, 1956) reflected consensus politics. Censure of McCarthy (Dec. '54) curbed the political abuse of anti-communism. A system of alliances and military bases bolstered U.S. influence on all continents. Trade and payments surpluses were balanced by overseas investments and foreign aid ($50 billion, 1950-59).

USSR. In the "thaw" after Stalin's death in 1953, relations with the West improved (evacuation of Vienna, Geneva summit conf., both 1955). Repression of scientific and cultural life eased, and many prisoners were freed or rehabilitated culminating in **de-Stalinization** (1956). Khrushchev's leadership aimed at consumer sector growth, but farm production lagged, despite the virgin lands program (from 1954). The 1956 Hungarian revolution, the 1960 U-2 spy plane episode, and other incidents renewed East-West tension and domestic curbs.

East Europe. Resentment of Russian domination and Stalinist repression combined with nationalist, economic and religious factors to produce periodic violence. East Berlin workers rioted in 1953, Polish workers rioted in Poznan, June 1956, and a broad-based revolution broke out in Hungary, Oct. 1956. All were suppressed by Soviet force or threats (at least 7,000 dead in Hungary). But Poland was allowed to restore private ownership of farms, and a degree of personal and economic freedom returned to Hungary. Yugoslavia experimented with worker self-management and a market economy.

Korea. The 1945 division of Korea left industry in the North, which was organized into a militant regime and armed by Russia. The South was politically disunited. Over 60,000 North Korean troops invaded the South June 25, 1950. The U.S., backed by the UN Security Council, sent troops. UN troops reached the Chinese border in Nov. Some 200,000 Chinese troops crossed the Yalu River and drove back UN forces. Cease-fire in July 1951 found the opposing forces near the original 38th parallel border. After 2 years of sporadic fighting, an armistice was signed July 27, 1953. U.S. troops remained in the South, and U.S. economic and military aid continued. The war stimulated rapid economic recovery in Japan. *For details, see 1978 and earlier editions of The World Almanac.*

China. Starting in 1952, industry, agriculture, and social institutions were forcibly collectivized. As many as several million people were executed as Kuomintang supporters or as class and political enemies. The Great Leap Forward, 1958-60, unsuccessfully tried to force the pace of development by substituting labor for investment.

Indochina. Ho's forces, aided by Russia and the new Chinese Communist government, fought French and pro-French Vietnamese forces to a standstill, and captured the strategic Dienbienphu camp in May, 1954. The Geneva Agreements divided Vietnam in half pending elections (never held), and recognized Laos and Cambodia as independent. The U.S. aided the anti-Communist Republic of Vietnam in the South.

Middle East. Arab revolutions placed leftist, militantly nationalist regimes in power in Egypt (1952) and Iraq (1958). But Arab unity attempts failed (United Arab Republic joined Egypt, Syria, Yemen 1958-61). Arab refusal to recognize Israel (Arab League economic blockade began Sept. 1951) led to a permanent state of war, with repeated incidents (Gaza, 1955). Israel occupied Sinai, Britain and France took the Suez Canal, Oct. 1956, but were replaced by the UN Emergency Force. The Mossadegh government in Iran nationalized the British-owned oil industry May 1951, but was overthrown in a U.S.-aided coup Aug. 1953.

Latin America. Dictator Juan Peron, in office 1946, enforced land reform, some nationalization, welfare state measures, and curbs on the Roman Catholic Church, but crushed opposition. A Sept. 1955 coup deposed Peron. The 1952 revolution in Bolivia brought land reform, nationalization of tin mines, and improvement in the status of Indians, who nevertheless remained poor. The Batista regime in Cuba was overthrown, Jan. 1959, by Fidel Castro, who imposed a communist dictatorship, aligned Cuba with Russia, improved education and health care. A U.S.-backed anti-Castro invasion (Bay of Pigs, Apr. 1961) was crushed. Self-government advanced in the British Caribbean.

Technology. Large outlays on research and development in the U.S. and USSR focussed on military applications (H-bomb in U.S. 1952, USSR 1953, Britain 1957, intercontinental missiles late 1950s). Soviet launching of the Sputnik satellite, Oct. 1957, spurred increases in U.S. science education funds (National Defense Education Act).

Literature and letters. Alienation from social and literary conventions reached an extreme in the theater of the absurd (Beckett's *Waiting for Godot* 1952), the "new novel" (Robbe-Grillet's *Voyeur* 1955), and avant-garde film (Antonioni's *L'Avventura* 1960). U.S. Beatniks (Kerouac's *On the Road* 1957) and others rejected the supposed conformism of Americans (Riesman's *Lonely Crowd* 1950).

1958

Castro in Cuba

Sino-Soviet split begins

Man in Space

Berlin Wall

Algeria indep.

Silent Spring

March on Wash.

Feminine Mystique

JFK killed

Diem deposed

Tonkin Gulf res.

Indonesia coup

Mideast War

U.S. in Vietnam

China Cult. Rev.

GATT

1968

1968

Sino-Soviet fighting

Woodstock festival

Men on moon

U.S. SST barred

Bangladesh indep.

Solzhenitsyn exiled

Chile coup

Portugal rev.

Turks in Cyprus

Nixon resigns

Greece junta quits

Worldwide recession

Indochina War ends

Gandhi loses vote

Mao d.

Lebanon civil war

Sadat in Jerusalem

1978

Rising Expectations: 1960-69

Economic boom. The longest sustained economic boom on record spanned almost the entire decade in the capitalist world; the closely-watched GNP figure doubled in the U.S. 1960-70, fueled by Vietnam War-related budget deficits. The **General Agreement on Tariffs and Trade**, 1967, stimulated West European prosperity, which spread to peripheral areas (Spain, Italy, E. Germany). Japan became a top economic power ($20 billion exports 1970). Foreign investment aided the industrialization of Brazil. Soviet 1965 economic reform attempts (decentralization, material incentives) were limited; but growth continued.

Reform and radicalization. A series of political and social reform movements took root in the U.S., later spreading to other countries with the help of ubiquitous U.S. film and television programs and heavy overseas travel (2.2 million U.S. passports issued 1970). Blacks agitated peaceably and with partial success against segregation and poverty (1963 March on Washington, 1964 **Civil Rights Act**); but some urban ghettos erupted in extensive riots (Watts, 1965; Detroit, 1967; King assassination, Apr. 4, 1968). New concern for the poor (Harrington's *Other America,* 1963) led to Pres. Johnson's **"Great Society"** programs (Medicare, Water Quality Act, Higher Education Act, all 1965). Concern with the **environment** surged (Carson's *Silent Spring,* 1962). **Feminism** revived as a cultural and political movement (Friedan's *Feminine Mystique,* 1963, National Organization for Women founded 1966) and a movement for homosexual rights emerged (Stonewall riot, in NYC, 1969).

Opposition to U.S. involvement in Vietnam, especially among university students (**Moratorium** protest Nov. '69) turned violent (Weatherman Chicago riots Oct. '69). New Left and Marxist theories became popular, and membership in radical groups swelled (Students for a Democratic Society, Black Panthers). Maoist groups, especially in Europe, called for total transformation of society. In France, students sparked a nationwide strike affecting 10 million workers May-June '68, but an electoral reaction barred revolutionary change.

Arts and styles. The boundary between fine and popular arts were blurred by Pop Art (Warhol) and rock musicals (Hair, 1968). Informality and exaggeration prevailed in fashion (beards, miniskirts). A non-political "counterculture" developed, rejecting traditional bourgeois life goals and personal habits, and use of marijuana and hallucinogens spread (Woodstock festival Aug. '68). Indian influence was felt in music (Beatles), religion (Ram Dass), and fashion.

Science. Achievements in space (men on moon July '69) and electronics (lasers, integrated circuits) encouraged a faith in scientific solutions to problems in agriculture ("green revolution"), medicine (heart transplants 1967) and other areas. The harmful effects of science, it was believed, could be controlled (1963 nuclear weapon test ban treaty, 1968 non-proliferation treaty).

China. Mao's revolutionary militance caused disputes with Russia under "revisionist" Khrushchev, starting 1960. The two powers exchanged fire in 1969 border disputes. China used force to capture areas disputed with India, 1962. The "Great Proletarian Cultural Revolution" tried to impose a utopian egalitarian program in China and spread revolution abroad; political struggle, often violent, convulsed China 1965-68.

Indochina. Communist-led guerrillas aided by N. Vietnam fought from 1960 against the S. Vietnam government of Ngo Dinh Diem (killed 1963). The U.S. military role increased after the 1964 Tonkin Gulf incident. U.S. forces peaked at 543,400, Apr. '69. Massive numbers of N. Viet troops also fought. Laotian and Cambodian neutrality were threatened by communist insurgencies, with N. Vietnamese aid, and U.S. intrigues. *For details, see 1978 and earlier editions of The World Almanac.*

Third World. A bloc of authoritarian leftist regimes among the newly independent nations emerged in political opposition to the U.S.-led Western alliance, and came to dominate the conference of nonaligned nations (Belgrade 1961, Cairo 1964, Lusaka 1970). Soviet political ties and military bases were established in Cuba, Egypt, Algeria, Guinea, and other countries, whose leaders were regarded as revolutionary heros by opposition groups in pro-Western or colonial countries. Some leaders were ousted in coups by pro-Western groups—Zaire's Lumumba (killed 1961), Ghana's Nkrumah (exiled 1966), and Indonesia's Sukarno (effectively ousted 1965 after a Communist coup failed).

Middle East. Arab-Israeli tension erupted into a brief war June 1967. Israel emerged as a major regional power. Military shipments before and after the war brought much of the Arab world into the Soviet political sphere. Most Arab states broke U.S. diplomatic ties, while Communist countries cut their ties to Israel. Intra-Arab disputes continued: Egypt and Saudi Arabia supported rival factions in a bloody Yemen civil war 1962-70; Lebanese troops fought Palestinian commandos in 1969.

East Europe. To stop the large-scale exodus of citizens, E. German authorities built a fortified wall across Berlin Aug. '61. Soviet sway in the Balkans was weakened by Albania's support of China (USSR broke ties Dec. '61) and Romania's assertion of industrial and foreign policy autonomy in 1964. Liberalization in Czechoslovakia, spring 1968, was crushed by troops of 5 Warsaw Pact countries. West German treaties with Russia and Poland, 1970, facilitated the transfer of German technology and confirmed post-war boundaries.

Disillusionment: 1970-79

U.S.: Caution and neoconservatism. A relatively sluggish economy, energy and resource shortages (natural gas crunch 1975, gasoline shortage 1979), and environmental problems contributed to a **"limits of growth"** philosophy that affected politics (Cal. Gov. Brown). Suspicion of science and technology killed or delayed major projects (supersonic transport dropped 1971, DNA recombination curbed 1976, Seabrook A-plant protests 1977-78) and was fed by the Three Mile Island nuclear reactor accident in Mar. '79.

Mistrust of big government weakened support for government reform plans among liberals. School busing and racial quotas were opposed (**Bakke decision** June '78); the Equal Rights Amendment for women languished; civil rights for homosexuals were opposed (Dade County referendum June '77).

U.S. defeat in **Indochina** (evacuation Apr. '75), revelations of Central Intelligence Agency misdeeds (Rockefeller Commission report June '75), and the **Watergate** scandals (Nixon quit Aug. '74) reduced faith in U.S. moral and material capacity to influence world affairs. Revelations of Soviet crimes (Solzhenitsyn's *Gulag Archipelago* from 1974) and Russian intervention in Africa aided a revival of anti-Communist sentiment.

Economy sluggish. The 1960s boom faltered in the 1970s; a severe recession in the U.S. and Europe 1974-75 followed a huge oil price hike Dec. '73. Monetary instability (U.S. cut ties to gold Aug. '71), the decline of the dollar, and **protectionist** moves by industrial countries (1977-78) threatened trade. Business investment and spending for research declined. Severe inflation plagued many countries (25% in Britain, 1975; 18% in U.S., 1979).

China picks up pieces. After the 1976 deaths of Mao and Chou, a power struggle for the leadership succession was won by pragmatists. A nationwide purge of orthodox Maoists was carried out, and the **"Gang of Four"**, led by Mao's widow Chiang Ching, was arrested.

The new leaders freed over 100,000 political prisoners, and reduced public adulation of Mao. Political and trade ties were expanded with Japan, Europe, and the U.S. in the late 1970's, as relations worsened with Russia, Cuba, and Vietnam (4-week invasion by China in 1979). Ideological guidelines in industry, science, education, and the armed forces, which the ruling faction said had caused chaos and decline, were reversed (bonuses to workers, Dec. '77; exams for college entrance, Oct. '77). Severe restrictions on cultural expression were eased (Beethoven ban lifted Mar. '77).

Europe. European unity moves (EEC-EFTA trade accord 1972) faltered as economic problems appeared (Britain floated pound 1972; France floated franc 1974). Germany and Switzerland curbed guest workers from S. Europe. Greece and Turkey quarreled over Cyprus (Turks intervened 1974) and Aegean oil rights.

All of non-Communist Europe was under democratic rule after free elections were held in **Spain** June '76, 7 months after the death of Franco. The conservative, colonialist regime in **Portugal** was overthrown Apr. '74. In **Greece**, the 7-year-old military dictatorship yielded power in 1974. Northern Europe, though ruled mostly by Socialists (**Swedish** Socialists unseated 1976, after 44 years in power), turned conservative. The **British** Labour government imposed wage curbs 1975, and suspended nationalization schemes. Terrorism in **Germany** (1972 Munich Olympics killings) led to laws curbing some civil liberties. **French** "new philosophers" rejected leftist ideologies, and the shaky Socialist-Communist coalition lost a 1978 election bid.

Religion back in politics. The improvement in Moslem countries' political fortunes by the 1950s (with the exception of Central Asia under Soviet and Chinese rule), and the growth of Arab oil wealth, was followed by a resurgence of traditional piety. **Libyan** dictator Qaddafi mixed strict Islamic laws with socialism in his militant ideology and called for an eventual Moslem return to Spain and Sicily. The illegal Moslem Brotherhood in **Egypt** was accused of violence, while extreme Moslem groups bombed theaters, 1977, to protest secular values.

In **Turkey**, the National Salvation Party was the first Islamic group to share power (1974) since secularization in the 1920s. Religious authorities, such as Ayatollah Ruholla Khomeini, led the **Iranian** revolution and religiously motivated Moslems took part in the insurrection in Saudi Arabia that briefly seized the Grand Mosque in Mecca in 1979. Moslem puritan opposition to **Pakistan** Pres. Bhutto helped lead to his overthrow July '77. However, Moslem solidarity could not prevent Pakistan's eastern province (**Bangladesh**) from declaring independence, Dec. '71, after a bloody civil war.

Moslem and Hindu resentment against coerced sterilization in **India** helped defeat the Gandhi government, which was replaced Mar. '77 by a coalition including religious Hindu parties and led by devout Hindu Desai. Moslems in the southern **Philippines**, aided by Libya, conducted a long rebellion against central rule from 1973.

Evangelical Protestant groups grew in numbers and prosperity in the U.S. ("**born again**" Pres. Carter elected 1976), and the Catholic charismatic movement obtained respectability. A revival of interest in Orthodox Christianity occurred among **Russian** intellectuals (Solzhenitsyn). The secularist **Israeli** Labor party, after decades of rule, was ousted in 1977 by conservatives led by Begin, an observant Jew; religious militants founded settlements on the disputed West Bank, part of Biblically-promised Israel. U.S. Reform Judaism revived many previously discarded traditional practices.

The Buddhist Soka Gakkai movement launched the Komeito party in Japan, 1964, which became a major opposition party in 1972 and 1976 elections.

Old-fashioned religious wars raged intermittently in **N. Ireland** (Catholic vs. Protestant, 1969-   ) and **Lebanon** (Christian vs. Moslem, 1975-   ), while religious militancy complicated the Israel-Arab dispute (1973 Israel-Arab war. In spite of a **1979 peace treaty between Egypt and Israel** which looked forward to a resolution of the Palestinian issue, increased religious militancy on the West Bank made such a resolution seem unlikely.

Latin America. Repressive conservative regimes strengthened their hold on most of the continent, with the violent coup against the elected Allende government in **Chile**, Sept. '73, the 1976 military coup in **Argentina**, and coups against reformist regimes in **Bolivia**, 1971 and 1979, and **Peru**, 1976. In Central America, increasing liberal and leftist militancy led to the ouster of the Somoza regime of Nicaragua in 1979 and civil conflict in El Salvador.

Indochina. Communist victory in Vietnam, Cambodia, and Laos by May '75 did not bring peace. Attempts at radical social reorganization left over one million dead in Cambodia during 1975-78 and caused hundreds of thousands of ethnic Chinese and others to flee Vietnam ("boat people," 1979). The Vietnamese invasion of Cambodia swelled the refugee population and contributed to widespread starvation in that devastated country.

Russian expansion. Soviet influence, checked in some countries (troops ousted by Egypt 1972) was projected further afield, often with the use of Cuban troops (Angola 1975-   , Ethiopia 1977-   ), and aided by a growing navy, merchant fleet, and international banking ability. Detente with the West — 1972 Berlin pact, 1970 strategic arms pact (**SALT**) — gave way to a more antagonistic relationship in the late 1970s, exacerbated by the Soviet invasion of Afghanistan in 1979.

Africa. The last remaining European colonies were granted independence (**Spanish Sahara** 1976, **Djibouti** 1977) and, after 10 years of civil war and many negotiation sessions, a black government took over Zimbabwe (Rhodesia) in 1979; white domination remained in S. Africa. Great power involvement in local wars (Russia in **Angola, Ethiopia;** France in **Chad, Zaire, Mauritania**) and the use of tens of thousands of Cuban troops was denounced by some African leaders as neocolonialism. Ethnic or tribal clashes made Africa the chief world locus of sustained warfare in the late 1970s.

Arts. Traditional modes in painting, architecture, and music, pursued in relative obscurity for much of the 20th century, returned to popular and critical attention in the 1970s. The pictorial emphasis in neorealist and photorealist painting, the return of many architects to detail, decoration, and traditional natural materials, and the concern with ordered structure in musical composition were, ironically, novel experiences for artistic consumers after the exhaustion of experimental possibilities. However, these more conservative styles coexisted with modernist works in an atmosphere of variety and tolerance.

100 Years Ago

In January of 1885, Grover Cleveland was inaugurated as the 22nd U.S. President. The "clean-government" candidate, Cleveland had been opposed by New York's Tammany Hall and favored by political reformers, including many Republicans—the "Mugwumps" who voted against their party.

On July 23rd, Ulysses S. Grant, former commander-in-chief of the Union army and the 18th president, died at age 63. Grant's body was laid to rest in a New York City tomb that would become a landmark. Scandals had obscured Grant's achievements during his two terms as president, and in his last years, money had been so scarce that he had sold his wartime swords and souvenirs. Dying of throat cancer, he had dictated his autobiography from his sickroom. Later published by his friend Mark Twain, the two-volume *Personal Memoirs* would be considered among the great military autobiographies and would bring Grant's family almost half a million dollars in royalties.

International

At the Berlin Conference on African Affairs, 14 countries, including the U.S., agreed to a treaty that made it necessary for imperial powers to formally announce acquisitions of territory and also to demonstrate that the territory actually was occupied. This introduced a new element of urgency in the partition of Africa. By a series of bilateral agreements conducted on the sidelines of the conference, King Leopold of Belgium emerged as sovereign of the Congo Free State, which was eighty times the size of Belgium. Leopold also continued his quest for rule or concessions in other parts of the world, from Mongolia to the Canary Islands and from Eritrea to Siberia. Even his chief agent, the explorer and journalist Henry Stanley, soon would complain of "the enormous voracity to swallow a million of square miles with a gullet that will not take a herring."

In the Battle of Khartoum, troops of the Messianic Sudanese leader Muhammed al-Mahdi destroyed the capital of the Sudan. General Charles George Gordon, the Egyptian governor general was killed. Many British held Prime Minister William Gladstone personally responsible, which contributed to Gladstone's resignation later in the year.

King Alfonso XII of Spain died. His wife, Queen Maria Cristina II, became regent, and began her rule by granting freedom of the press and amnesty to political prisoners.

Social Progress

The Knights of Labor won a strike against railroad executive Jay Gould. During the next decade, the union's membership would climb from 111,395 to 729,677.

Bishop Benjamin William Arnett of the African Methodist Episcopal Church was elected to the Lower House of the Ohio State Legislature. He was the first black legislator to represent a predominantly white constituency.

Stanford University, Georgia Tech, the University of Arizona, and McAlester College were founded.

Bryn Mawr College, a private institution of higher education for women, was founded in Bryn Mawr, Pa. by Dr. Joseph Taylor, a Quaker physician. Originally associated with the Society of Friends, but later nonsectarian, Bryn Mawr was the site of several firsts in its initial year: it was the first college to offer a general biology course; the first women's institution to offer graduate degrees; and the first history course in a women's college was taught there by Professor Woodrow Wilson.

Medicine

After three years of studying rabies, Louis Pasteur developed a vaccine to prevent the disease in dogs and to treat humans bitten by rabid dogs. This achievement spread Pasteur's fame worldwide, and funds came in to him for the creation of the Pasteur Institute.

The first successful appendectomy—removal of the appendix—was performed in Davenport, Iowa by Dr. William West Grant on 22-year-old Mary Gartside.

The first sanatorium to use modern methods of treating tuberculosis was opened by Dr. Edward Livingston Trudeau at Saranac Lake, New York.

Inventions and Practicalities

Carl Benz ran his first car in 1885. It was a three-wheeled vehicle with a steel frame in the shape of a horseshoe, and was powered by a two-cycle, one-cylinder engine. Benz circled a cinder track in the little machine, while his wife and his workmen ran beside. The vehicle made four circuits and stalled twice before it was stopped by a broken chain. Later in the year, Benz attempted a public showing of a slightly improved version, but forgot to steer and smashed it into a brick wall.

The first motor boat pleasure craft was produced by F.E. Ofeldt and manufactured by the Gas Engine and Power Company, New York City. The boat was 21 feet long, with a 64-inch beam and a draught of 22 inches. A two-horsepower engine propelled by naphtha developed a speed of five to seven knots.

The first watch movement to be electrically wound and synchronized was made by J. Chester Pond in Chicago.

The first commercial moving picture film was manufactured by Eastman Dry Plate & Film Company of Rochester, New York.

Morton's salt was introduced by the new Joy Morton & Co.

While studying heredity, Sir Francis Galton established that no two fingerprints were identical. A committee was appointed by the British government to consider the adoption of fingerprints to identify criminals.

Arts and Entertainment

Guy de Maupassant wrote the short story "Bel Ami," H. Rider Haggard the adventure novel *King Solomon's Mines*, Richard Burton *The Arabian Nights*, and Robert Louis Stevenson *A Child's Garden of Verses*. Henrik Ibsen's "The Wild Duck" was produced. The second volume of Karl Marx's *Das Kapital* was posthumously published. Cezanne painted "Mont Saint-Victoire."

"Good Housekeeping" magazine began publication.

The first Yiddish daily newspaper, the "Yiddishes Tageblatt," or "Jewish Daily News," was founded in New York City by Kasriel Hersch Sarasohn.

The Boston Pops was founded by the four-year-old Boston Symphony.

Sitting Bull, who led the Sioux Indians in defeating U.S. Army troops at "Custer's Last Stand," toured with Buffalo Bill's Wild West Show.

The first self-service restaurant opened. Located opposite the New York Stock Exchange, it was called the Exchange Buffet.

Inventor George Swinerton Parker, 18, started Parker Brothers, to manufacture his game, "Banking." "Monopoly" would be introduced in 1935.

Sports

The first important prize fight under the Marquis of Queensbury rules was held, pitting John S. Sullivan against Dominick F. McCaffery. Sullivan was declared the winner and world champion. He attributed his failure to knock out McCaffery partly to the restrictions of the new rules.

The Cuban Giants, the first black professional baseball team, was organized in New York City. The players received expenses and weekly salaries according to positions—pitchers and catchers, $18; infielders, $15; outfielders, $12.

The Scottish sport of golf took hold in America after John M. Fox introduced it to Foxburg, Pa.

Milestones

French novelist Victor Hugo died. British novelist D.H. Lawrence, American novelist Sinclair Lewis, and American poet Ezra Pound were born, as were Danish physicist Niels Bohr and Russian ballerina Anna Pavlova.

The first monument to George Washington was dedicated in the District of Columbia.

NATIONS OF THE WORLD

The nations of the world are listed in alphabetical order. Initials in the following articles include UN (United Nations), OAS (Org. of American States), NATO (North Atlantic Treaty Org.), EC (European Communities or Common Market), OAU (Org. of African Unity). **Sources:** U.S. Dept. of State; U.S. Census Bureau; International Monetary Fund; UN Statistical Yearbook; UN Demographic Yearbook; The Environmental Fund; International Iron and Steel Institute; The Statesman's Year-Book; Encyclopaedia Britannica. All embassy addresses are Wash., DC; area codes (202), unless otherwise noted.

See special color section for maps and flags of all nations.

Afghanistan

Democratic Republic of Afghanistan

People: Population (1983 est.): 14,177,000. **Pop. density:** 51.9 per sq. mi. **Ethnic groups:** Pashtoon 50%; Tajiks 25%; Uzbek 9%; Hazara 9%. **Languages:** Pashta (Iranian), Dari Persian (spoken by Tajiks, Hazaras), Uzbek (Turkic). **Religions:** Sunni Muslim (80%), Shi'a Muslim (20%).

Geography: Area: 251,773 sq. mi., about the size of Texas. **Location:** Between Soviet Central Asia and the Indian subcontinent. **Neighbors:** Pakistan on E, S, Iran on W, USSR on N; the NE tip touches China. **Topography:** The country is landlocked and mountainous, much of it over 4,000 ft. above sea level. The Hindu Kush Mts. tower 16,000 ft. above Kabul and reach a height of 25,000 ft. to the E. Trade with Pakistan flows through the 35-mile long Khyber Pass. The climate is dry, with extreme temperatures, and large desert regions, though mountain rivers produce intermittent fertile valleys. **Capital:** Kabul. **Cities** (1979 est.): Kabul 891,750; Kandahar 230,000; Herat 150,000; Baghlan 110,874; Kundus 108,000; Mazir-i-Sharif 100,000.

Government: Type: People's Republic. **Head of state, and President of the Revolutionary Council:** Pres. Babrak Karmal; b. 1929; in office: Dec. 27, 1979. **Head of Government:** Prime Min. Sultan Ali Keshtmand; in office: 1981. **Local divisions:** 24 provinces, each under a governor. **Armed forces:** regulars 90,000.

Economy: Industries: Textiles, carpets, cement. **Chief crops:** Cotton, wheat, fruits. **Minerals:** Copper, lead, gas, coal, zinc, iron. **Crude oil reserves** (1978): 284 mln. bbls. **Other resources:** Wool, hides, karacul pelts. **Per capita arable land:** 1.3 acres. **Meat prod.** (1980): beef: 67,000 metric tons; lamb: 125,000 metric tons. **Electricity prod.** (1981): 1 bln. kwh. **Labor force:** cannot be estimated due to war.

Finance: Currency: Afghani (Mar. 1984: 50.60 = $1 US). **Gross domestic product** (1978 est.): $3.76 bln. **Per capita income** (1978): $168. **Imports** (1981): $562 mln.; partners: USSR 53%, Jap. 21%, Iran 13%. **Exports** (1982): $707 mln.; partners: USSR 60%, Pak. 12%, UK 12%. **International reserves less gold** (Jan. 1984): $209.1 mln. **Gold:** 965,000 oz t. **Consumer prices** (change in 1981): 4.9%

Transport: Motor vehicles: in use (1980): 34,100 passenger cars, 29,000 comm. vehicles. **Civil aviation** (1981): 129 mln. passenger-km; 19.4 mln. net ton-km.

Communications: Radios: 1.2 mln. in use (1980). **Telephones in use** (1980): 32,000. **Daily newspaper circ.** (1982): 4 per 1,000 pop.

Health: Life expectancy at birth (1975): 39.9 male; 40.7 female. **Births** (per 1,000 pop. 1979): 52. **Deaths** (per 1,000 pop. 1979): 30. **Natural increase** (1979): 2.2%. **Hospital beds** (per 100,000 pop. 1977): 21. **Physicians** (per 100,000 pop. 1978): 27.

Education (1982): **Literacy:** 10%.

Embassy: 2341 Wyoming Ave. NW, 20008; 234-3770.

Afghanistan, occupying a favored invasion route since antiquity, has been variously known as Ariana or Bactria (in ancient times) and Khorasan (in the Middle Ages). Foreign empires alternated rule with local emirs and kings until the 18th century, when a unified kingdom was established. In 1973, a military coup ushered in a republic.

Pro-Soviet leftists took power in a bloody 1978 coup, and concluded an economic and military treaty with the USSR.

Late in Dec. 1979, the USSR began a massive military airlift into Kabul. The three-month old regime of Hafizullah Amin ended with a Soviet backed coup, Dec. 27th. He was replaced by Ba-

brak Karmal, considered a more pro-Soviet leader. Soviet troops, estimated at between 60,000-100,000, fanned out over Afghanistan, fighting rebels. Fighting continued during 1984 as the Soviets found themselves engaged in a long, protracted guerrilla war.

Albania

People's Socialist Republic of Albania

People: Population (1983 est.): 2,846,000. **Pop. density:** 236 per sq. mi. **Urban** (1980): 33%. **Ethnic groups:** Albanians (Gegs in N, Tosks in S) 95%, Greeks 2.5%. **Languages:** Albanian (Tosk is official dialect), Greek. **Religions:** officially atheist; (historically) mostly Moslems. All public worship and religious institutions were outlawed in 1967.

Geography: Area: 11,100 sq. mi., slightly larger than Maryland. **Location:** On SE coast of Adriatic Sea. **Neighbors:** Greece on S, Yugoslavia on N, E. **Topography:** Apart from a narrow coastal plain, Albania consists of hills and mountains covered with scrub forest, cut by small E-W rivers. **Capital:** Tirana. **Cities** (1980 est.): Tirana 198,000; Durres 80,000; Vlore 58,400.

Government: Type: Communist. **Head of state:** Pres. Ramiz Alia, in office: Nov. 22, 1982. **Head of government:** Premier Adil Carcani; in office: Jan. 18, 1982. **Head of Communist Party:** Enver Hoxha; b. Oct. 16, 1908; in office: Nov. 8, 1941. **Local divisions:** 26 administrative districts and one independent city. **Defense:** 13% of budget (1980).

Economy: Industries: Chem. fertilizers, textiles, electric cables. **Chief crops:** Grain, sugar beets, cotton, potatoes, tobacco, fruits. **Minerals:** Chromium, coal, copper, bitumen, iron, oil. **Other resources:** Forests. **Per capita arable land:** 0.5 acres. **Meat prod.** (1980): beef: 20,000 metric tons; pork: 12,000 metric tons; lamb: 24,000 metric tons. **Electricity prod.** (1980): 2.6 bln. kwh. **Labor force:** 60% agric; 40% industry and commerce.

Finance: Currency: Lek (Sept. 1983: 6.71 = $1 US). **Gross domestic product** (1976 est.) $1.3 bln. **Per capita income** (1976): $490. **Imports** (1976): $250 mln.; partners (1979): Czech., Yugoslavia, China. **Exports** (1976): $200 mln.; partners (1979): Czech., Yugoslavia, China, Italy.

Transport: Motor vehicles: in use (1971): 3,500 passenger cars, 11,200 comm. vehicles. **Chief ports:** Durres, Vlone.

Communications: Television sets: 10,000 in use (1981). **Radios:** 200,000 in use (1981). **Daily newspaper circ.** (1982): 52 per 1,000 pop.

Health: Life expectancy at birth (1979): 66.8 male; 71.4 female. **Births** (per 1,000 pop. 1980): 26.5. **Deaths** (per 1,000 pop. 1980): 6.4. **Natural increase** 2.01%. **Hospital beds** (per 1,000 pop. 1982): 70. **Physicians** (1982): 4,476 doctors & dentists. **Infant mortality** (per 1,000 live births 1971): 86.8.

Education (1978): **Literacy:** 75%. **Pop. 5-19:** in school: 64%, teachers per 1,000: 29.

Ancient Illyria was conquered by Romans, Slavs, and Turks (15th century); the latter Islamized the population. Independent Albania was proclaimed in 1912, republic was formed in 1920. Self-styled King Zog I ruled 1925-39, until Italy invaded.

Communist partisans took over in 1944, allied Albania with USSR, then broke with USSR in 1960 over de-Stalinization. Strong political alliance with China followed, leading to several billion dollars in aid, which was curtailed after 1974. China cut off aid in 1978 when Albania attacked its policies after the death of Chinese ruler Mao Tse-tung.

Industrialization, pressed in 1960s, slowed in 1970s. Large-scale purges of officials occurred 1973-76.

Algeria
Democratic and Popular Republic of Algeria

People: Population (1984 est.); 21,300,000. **Age distrib. (%):** 0–14: 47.9; 15–59: 46.3; 60+: 5.7. **Pop. density:** 21.45 per sq. mi. **Urban** (1983): 45%. **Ethnic groups:** Arabs 75%, Berbers 25%. **Languages:** Arabic (official), Berber (indigenous language), French. **Religions:** Sunni Moslem (state religion).

Geography: Area: 918,497 sq. mi., more than 3 times the size of Texas. **Location:** In NW Africa, from Mediterranean Sea into Sahara Desert. **Neighbors:** Morocco on W, Mauritania, Mali, Niger on S, Libya, Tunisia on E. **Topography:** The Tell, located on the coast, comprises fertile plains 50-100 miles wide, with a moderate climate and adequate rain. Two major chains of the Atlas Mts., running roughly E-W, and reaching 7,000 ft., enclose a dry plateau region. Below lies the Sahara, mostly desert with major mineral resources. **Capital:** Algiers. **Cities** (1981 est.): Algiers 2,200,000; Oran 633,000; Constantine 384,000; Annaba 284,000.

Government: Type: Republic. **Head of state:** Pres. Chadli Bendjedid; b. Apr. 14, 1929; in office: Feb. 9, 1979. **Head of government:** Premier Abdel Hamid Brahimi; in office: Jan. 22, 1984. **Local divisions:** 31 wilayaat (states). **Defense:** 2.4% of GDP (1980).

Economy: Industries: Oil, iron, steel, textiles, fertilizer, plastics. **Chief crops:** Grains, wine-grapes, potatoes, dates, tomatoes, oranges. **Minerals:** Mercury, oil, iron, zinc, lead, coal, copper, natural gas, phosphates. **Crude oil reserves** (1982): 8.3 bln. bbls. **Other resources:** Cork trees. **Arable land:** 13%. **Meat prod.** (1980): beef: 33,000 metric tons; lamb: 67,000 metric tons. **Electricity prod.** (1981): 7.1 bln. kwh. **Crude steel prod.** (1981): 550,000 metric tons. **Labor force:** 30% agric.; 40% ind. and commerce; 17% government; 10% services.

Finance: Currency: Dinar (Feb. 1984: 4.84 = $1 US). **Gross domestic product** (1982): $40 bln. **Per capita income** (1982): $1,951. **Imports** (1982): $10.7 bln.; partners: France 18%, W. Ger. 18%, It. 11%, Japan 9%. **Exports** (1982): $12.9 bln.; partners: U.S. 51%, W. Ger. 14%, France 11%, It. 7%. **National budget** (1983): $21.9 bln. **International reserves less gold** (Feb. 1984): $1.9 bln. **Gold:** 5.58 mln. oz t. **Consumer prices** (change in 1982): 6.7%

Transport: Railway traffic (1979): 1.8 bln. passenger-km; 2.5 bln. net ton-km. **Motor vehicles:** in use (1978): 396,800 passenger cars, 206,500 comm. vehicles; assembled (1977): 6,360 comm. vehicles. **Chief ports:** Algiers, Oran, Annaba.

Communications: Television sets: 975,000 in use (1980). **Radios:** 3.2 mln. in use (1980). **Telephones in use** (1981): 484,973. **Daily newspaper circ.** (1982): 29 per 1,000 pop.

Health: Life expectancy at birth (1975): 52.9 male; 55.0 female. **Births** (per 1,000 pop. 1979): 46. **Deaths** (per 1,000 pop. 1979): 14. **Natural increase** (1979): 3.2%. **Hospital beds** (1980): 45,160. **Physicians** (1980): 6,081. **Infant mortality** (per 1,000 live births 1982): 110

Education (1978): **Literacy:** 46%. **School:** Free and compulsory to age 13; Attendance: 86% primary, 31% secondary.

Embassy: 2118 Kalorama Rd. NW; 328-5300.

Earliest known inhabitants were ancestors of Berbers, followed by Phoenicians, Romans, Vandals, and, finally, Arabs; but 25% still speak Berber dialects. Turkey ruled 1518 to 1830, when France took control.

Large-scale European immigration and French cultural inroads did not prevent an Arab nationalist movement from launching guerilla war. Peace, and French withdrawal, was negotiated with French Pres. Charles de Gaulle. One million Europeans left.

Ahmed Ben Bella was the victor of infighting, and ruled 1962-65, when an army coup installed Col. Houari Boumedienne as leader. Ben Bella remained under house arrest until 1979.

In 1967, Algeria declared war with Israel, broke with U.S., and moved toward eventual military and political ties with the USSR. French oil interests were partly seized in 1971, but relations with the West have since improved.

Algeria, strongly backing Saharan guerillas' demands for a cease fire and self-determination, encouraged Mauritania to come to terms with the Polisario Front, 1979.

The one-party Socialist regime faces endemic mass unemployment and poverty, despite land reform and industrialization attempts.

Andorra
Principality of Andorra

People: Population (1983 est.): 42,000. **Age distrib. (%):** 0–14: 29.2; 14–59: 61.7; 60+: 9.1. **Pop. density:** 180.85 per sq. mi. **Ethnic groups:** Spanish over 60%, Andorran 30%, French 6%. **Languages:** Catalan (official), Spanish, French. **Religion:** Roman Catholic.

Geography: Area: 188 sq. mi., half the size of New York City. **Location:** In Pyrenees Mtns. **Neighbors:** Spain on S, France on N. **Topography:** High mountains and narrow valleys over the country. **Capital:** Andorra la Vella.

Government: Type: Co-Principality. **Head of state:** Co-princes are the president of France (François Mitterrand; in office: May 21, 1981) and the Roman Catholic bishop of Urgel in Spain. **Local divisions:** 7 parishes.

Economy: Industries: Tourism, tobacco products. **Labor force:** 20% agric.; 80% ind. and commerce; services; government.

Finance: Currency: French franc, Spanish peseta.

Communications: Television sets: 4,000 in use (1980). **Radios:** 7,000 in use (1980). **Telephones in use** (1981): 15,785.

Health: Births (per 1,000 pop. 1976): 16.5. **Deaths** (per 1,000 pop. 1976): 5.0. **Natural increase** (1976): 1.2%.

Education (1981): **Literacy:** 100%. School compulsory to age 16.

The present political status, with joint sovereignty by France and the bishop of Urgel, dates from 1278.

Tourism, especially skiing, is the economic mainstay. A free port, allowing for an active trading center, draws some 7 million tourists annually. The ensuing economic prosperity accompanied by Andorra's virtual law-free status, has given rise to calls for reform.

Angola
People's Republic of Angola

People: Population (1984 est.): 7,770,000. **Pop. density:** 14.70 per sq. mi. **Ethnic groups:** Ovimbundu 38%, Kimbundu 23%; Bakongo 13%, European 1%; Mesticos 2%. **Languages:** Portuguese (official), various Bantu languages. **Religions:** Roman Catholic 46%, Protestant 12%, animist 42%.

Geography: Area: 481,353 sq. mi., larger than Texas and California combined. **Location:** In SW Africa on Atlantic coast. **Neighbors:** Namibia (SW Africa) on S, Zambia on E, Zaire on N; Cabinda, an enclave separated from rest of country by short Atlantic coast of Zaire, borders Congo Republic. **Topography:** Most of Angola consists of a plateau elevated 3,000 to 5,000 feet above sea level, rising from a narrow coastal strip. There is also a temperate highland area in the west-central region, a desert in the S, and a tropical rain forest covering Cabinda. **Capital:** Luanda 475,300 (1979 est.).

Government: Type: People's Republic, one-party rule. **Head of state:** Pres. Jose Eduardo dos Santos b. Aug. 28, 1942; in office: Sept. 20, 1979. **Local divisions:** 18 provinces. **Armed forces:** regulars 31,500 (1980).

Economy: Industries: Alcohol, cotton goods, fishmeal, paper, palm oil, footwear. **Chief crops:** Coffee, bananas. **Minerals:** Iron, diamonds (over 2 mln. carats a year), copper, manganese, sulphur, phosphates, oil. **Crude oil reserves** (1980): 1.2 bln. bbls. **Arable land:** 2%. **Meat prod.** (1980): beef: 51,000 metric tons; pork: 13,000 metric tons. **Fish catch** (1981): 121,000 metric tons. **Electricity prod.** (1981): 1.5 bln.kwh. **Labor force:** 60% agric., 15% industry.

Finance: Currency: Kwanza (Sept. 1983: 30.2 = $1 US). **Gross domestic product** (1980): $1.82 bln. **Per capita income** (1976): $500. **Imports** (1982): $1.1 bln.; partners: U.S. 16%, Fra. 12%; USSR 8%. **Exports** (1982): $1.7 bln.; partners: Bahamas 18%, U.S. 38%.

Transport: Railway traffic (1974): 418 mln. passenger-km; 5.46 bln. net ton-km. Motor vehicles: in use (1980): 142,000 passenger cars, 43,000 comm. vehicles. Chief ports: Cabinda, Lobito, Luanda.
Communications: Radios: 125,000 in use (1980). Telephones in use (1980): 40,000. Daily newspaper circ. (1982): 16 per 1,000 pop.
Health: Life expectancy at birth (1975): 37.0 male; 40.1 female. Births (per 1,000 pop. 1979): 47.0. Deaths (per 1,000 pop. 1979): 23. Natural increase (1979): 1.3% Hospital beds (per 100,000 pop. 1977): 306. Physicians (per 100,000 pop 1977): 6. Infant mortality (per 1,000 live births 1979): 182.
Education (1980): Literacy: 20%. Pop. 5-19: in school: 28%, teachers per 1,000: 9.

From the early centuries AD to 1500, Bantu tribes penetrated most of the region. Portuguese came in 1583, allied with the Bakongo kingdom in the north, and developed the slave trade. Large-scale colonization did not begin until the 20th century, when 400,000 Portuguese immigrated.

A guerrilla war begun in 1961 lasted until 1974, when Portugal offered independence. Violence between the National Front, based in Zaire, the Soviet-backed Popular Movement, and the National Union, aided by the U.S. and S. Africa, killed thousands of blacks, drove most whites to emigrate, and completed economic ruin. Some 15,000 Cuban troops and massive Soviet aid helped the Popular Movement win most of the country after independence Nov. 11, 1975.

S. African troops crossed the southern Angolan border June 7, 1981, killing more than 300 civilians and occupying several towns. The S. Africans withdrew in Sept.

Russian influence, backed by 25,000 Cubans, East Germans, and Portuguese Communists, is strong in the Marxist regime.

Antigua and Barbuda

People: Population (1984 est.) 80,000. Urban: 34%. Language: English. Religion: Predominantly Church of England.
Geography: Area: 171 sq. mi. Location: Eastern Caribbean. Neighbors: approx. 30 mi. north of Guadeloupe. Capital: St. John's, (1979 est.) 25,000.
Government: Head of State: Queen Elizabeth II; represented by Sir Wilfred E. Jacobs. Head of Government: Prime Min. Vere Cornwall Bird; b. Dec. 7, 1910; in office Nov. 1, 1981.
Economy: Industries: manufacturing, tourism (96,084 visitors in 1981). Arable Land: 55%
Finance: Currency: East Caribbean dollar (Apr. 1984): 2.70 = $1 U.S. Consumer prices (change in 1982): 4.4%.
Embassy: 2000 N St. NW; 296-6310.

Antigua was discovered by Columbus in 1493. The British colonized it in 1632.

The British associated state of Antigua achieved independence as Antigua and Barbuda on Nov. 1, 1981. The government maintains close relations with the U.S., United Kingdom, and Venezuela.

Argentina
Argentine Republic

People: Population (1983 est.): 29,627,000. Age distrib. (%): 0–14: 28.5; 15–59: 59.6; 60+: 11.9. Pop. density: 25.46 per sq. mi. Urban (1980): 86.3%. Ethnic groups: Europeans 97% (Spanish, Italian), Indians, Mestizos, Arabs. Languages: Spanish (official), English, Italian, German, French. Religions: Roman Catholic 92%.
Geography: Area: 1,065,189 sq. mi., 4 times the size of Texas, second largest in S. America. Location: Occupies most of southern S. America. Neighbors: Chile on W, Bolivia, Paraguay on N, Brazil, Uruguay on NE. Topography: The mountains in W: the Andean, Central, Misiones, and Southern. Aconcagua is the highest peak in the Western hemisphere, alt. 22,834 ft. E of the Andes are heavily wooded plains, called the Gran Chaco in the N, and the fertile, treeless Pampas in the central region. Patagonia, in the S, is bleak and arid. Rio de la Plata, 170 by 140 mi., is mostly fresh water, from 2,485-mi. Parana and 1,000-mi. Uruguay rivers. Capital: Buenos Aires. Cities (1982

cen.): Buenos Aires 2,908,000; Cordoba 969,000; Rosario 750,455; Mendoza 597,000; San Miguel de Tucuman 497,000.
Government: Type: Federal Republic. Head of state: Pres. Raul Alfonsin; b. Mar. 3, 1926; in office Dec. 10, 1983. Local divisions: 22 provinces, 1 natl. terr. and 1 federal dist., under military governors. Armed forces: regulars 136,000; reserves 250,000.
Economy: Industries: Meat processing, flour milling, chemicals, textiles, machinery, autos. Chief crops: Grains, corn, grapes, linseed, sugar, tobacco, rice, soybeans, citrus fruits. Minerals: Oil, coal, lead, zinc, iron, sulphur, silver, copper, gold. Crude oil reserves (1980): 2.40 bln. bbls. Arable land: 11%. Meat prod. (1980): beef: 2.92 mln. metric tons; pork: 246,000 metric tons; lamb: 117,000 metric tons. Fish catch (1981): 359,600 metric tons. Electricity prod. (1982): 36.2 bln. kwh. Crude steel prod. (1982): 2.9 mln. metric tons. Labor force: 19% agric.; 36% ind. and man.; 20% services.
Finance: Currency: Peso (Mar. 1984: 23.3 = $1 US). Gross domestic product (1978 est.): $61.5 bln. Per capita income (1978 est.): $2,331. Imports (1982): $5.3 bln.; partners (1981): U.S. 22%, W. Ger. 10%, Braz. 9%, Jap. 10%. Exports (1982): $7.6 bln.; partners (1981): USSR 32%, Braz. 7%, Neth. 8%, U.S. 9%. Tourists (1977): 1,350,000; receipts: $213 mln. National budget (1980): $4.9 bln. revenues; $5.7 bln. expenditures. International reserves less gold (Jan. 1984): $1.5 bln. Gold: 4.37 mln. oz t. Consumer prices (change in 1983): 343.8%.
Transport: Railway traffic (1981): 10.1 bln. passenger-km; 11.4 bln. net ton-km. Motor vehicles: in use (1978): 2.8 mln. passenger cars, 1.2 mln. comm. vehicles. Civil aviation (1982) 5.1 mln. passenger-km; 175.9 mln. net ton-km. Chief ports: Buenos Aires, Bahia Blanca, La Plata.
Communications: Television sets: 5.6 mln. in use (1980), 219,000 manuf. (1978). Radios: 7.5 mln. in use (1980). Telephones in use (1981): 2.8 mln. Daily newspaper circ. (1982): 848 per 1,000 pop.
Health: Life expectancy at birth (1983): 66.8 male; 73.2 female. Births (per 1,000 pop. 1979): 26. Deaths (per 1,000 pop. 1979): 9. Natural increase (1979): 1.6%. Hospital beds (per 100,000 pop. 1977): 524. Physicians (per 100,000 pop. 1977): 192. Infant mortality (per 1,000 live births 1979): 40.8.
Education (1978): Literacy: 94%. School attendance 21.5% through secondary school.
Embassy: 1600 New Hampshire Ave. NW 20009; 387-0705.

Nomadic Indians roamed the Pampas when Spaniards arrived, 1515-1516, led by Juan Diaz de Solis. Nearly all the Indians were killed by the late 19th century. The colonists won independence, 1810-1819, and a long period of disorders ended in a strong centralized government.

Large-scale Italian, German, and Spanish immigration in the decades after 1880 spurred modernization, making Argentina the most prosperous, educated, and industrialized of the major Latin American nations. Social reforms were enacted in the 1920s, but military coups prevailed 1930-46, until the election of Gen. Juan Peron as president.

Peron, with his wife Eva Duarte effected labor reforms, but also suppressed speech and press freedoms, closed religious schools, and ran the country into debt. A 1955 coup exiled Peron, who was followed by a series of military and civilian regimes. Peron returned in 1973, and was once more elected president. He died 10 months later, succeeded by his wife, Isabel, who had been elected vice president, and who became the first woman head of state in the Western hemisphere.

A military junta ousted Mrs. Peron in 1976 amid charges of corruption. Under a continuing state of siege, the army battled guerrillas and leftists, killed 5,000 people, and jailed and tortured others. The government rejected a report of the Inter-American Human Rights Commission, 1980, which charged widespread killing, torture, and arbitrary detention.

A severe worsening in economic conditions placed extreme pressure on the military government. In 1983, inflation was over 300% and payments on foreign debt were suspended.

Argentine troops seized control of the British-held Falkland Islands on Apr. 2, 1982. Both countries had claimed sovereignty over the islands, located 250 miles off the Argentine coast, since 1833. The British dispatched a task force and declared a total air and sea blockade around the Falklands. Fighting began May 1;

several hundred lost their lives as the result of the destruction of a British destroyer and the sinking of an Argentine cruiser.

British troops landed in force on East Falkland Island May 21. By June 2, the British had surrounded Stanley, the capital city and Argentine stronghold. The Argentine troops surrendered, June 14; Argentine President Leopoldo Galtieri resigned June 17.

Democratic rule returned to Argentina in 1983 as Raul Alfonsin's Radical Civic Union gained an absolute majority in the presidential electoral college and Congress.

Australia

Commonwealth of Australia

People: Population (1983 est.): 15,265,000. **Age distrib. (%):** 0–14: 25; 15–44: 46.1; 45+: 28.9. **Pop. density:** 4.93 per sq. mi. **Urban** (1982): 85%. **Ethnic groups:** British 95%, other European 3%, aborigines (including mixed) 1.5%. **Languages:** English, aboriginal languages. **Religions:** Anglican 36%, other Protestant 25%, Roman Catholic 33%.

Geography: Area: 2,966,200 sq. mi., almost as large as the continental U.S. **Location:** SE of Asia, Indian O. is W and S, Pacific O. (Coral, Tasman seas) is E; they meet N of Australia in Timor and Arafura seas; Tasmania lies 150 mi. S of Victoria state, across Bass Strait. **Neighbors:** Nearest are Indonesia, Papua New Guinea on N, Solomons, Fiji, and New Zealand on E. **Topography:** An island continent. The Great Dividing Range along the E coast has Mt. Kosciusko, 7,310 ft. The W plateau rises to 2,000 ft., with arid areas in the Great Sandy and Great Victoria deserts. The NW part of Western Australia and Northern Terr. are arid and hot. The NE has heavy rainfall and Cape York Peninsula has jungles. The Murray R. rises in New South Wales and flows 1,600 mi. to the Indian O. **Capital:** Canberra. **Cities** (1981 est.): Sydney 3,280,900; Melbourne 2,803,600; Brisbane 1,086,500; Adelaide 952,700; Perth 918,000.

Government: Type: Democratic, federal state system. **Head of state:** Queen Elizabeth II, represented by Gov.-Gen. Ninian Martin Stephen; in office: July 29, 1982. **Head of government:** Prime Min. Robert James Lee Hawke; b. Dec. 9, 1929; in office: Mar. 11, 1983. **Local divisions:** 6 states, with elected governments and substantial powers; 2 territories. **Defense:** 2.6% of GNP (1981).

Economy: Industries: Iron, steel, textiles, electrical equip., chemicals, autos, aircraft, ships, machinery. **Chief crops:** Wheat (a leading export), barley, oats, corn, sugar, wine, fruit, vegetables. **Minerals:** Bauxite, coal, copper, iron, lead, nickel, silver, tin, tungsten, uranium, zinc. **Crude oil reserves** (1980): 2.13 bln. bbls. **Other resources:** Wool (30% of world output). **Per capita arable land:** 7.8 acres. **Meat prod.** (1983): beef: 1.55 mln. metric tons; pork: 237,000 metric tons; lamb: 517,000 metric tons. **Fish catch** (1978): 122,900 metric tons. **Electricity prod.** (1982): 106.1 bln. kwh. **Crude steel prod.** (1982): 6.3 mln. metric tons. **Labor force:** 7% agric.; 30% ind. and commerce; 32.6% service.

Finance: Currency: Dollar (Mar. 1984: .87 = $1 US). **Gross domestic product** (1980): $144.9 bln. **Per capita income** (1981): $9,914. **Imports** (1983): $21.4 bln; partners: U.S. 23%, Jap. 20%, UK 7%, W. Ger. 6%. **Exports** (1983): $20.7 bln.; partners: Jap. 27%, U.S. 11%, NZ 5%. **Tourists** (1981): 936,727. **National budget** (1980): $38.80 bln. revenues; $36.15 bln. expenditures. **International reserves less gold** (Mar. 1984): $8.3 bln. **Gold:** 7.93 mln. oz t. **Consumer prices** (change in 1983): 10.1%.

Transport: Railway traffic (1979): 39.8 bln. net ton-km. **Motor vehicles:** in use (1981): 6.9 mln. passenger cars, 399,000 comm. vehicles; manuf. (1982): 379,000 passenger cars; 37,000 comm. vehicles. **Civil aviation** (1981): 24.5 mln. passenger-km.; 608.7 mln. freight ton-km. **Chief ports:** Sydney, Melbourne, Newcastle, Port Kembla, Fremantle, Geelong.

Communications: Television sets: 5.5 mln. (1980). **Radios:** 15 mln. (1980), 68,000 manuf. (1977). **Telephones in use** (1980): 7.3 mln. **Daily newspaper circ.** (1982): 426 per 1,000 pop.

Health: Life expectancy at birth (1980): 70.0 male; 76.0 female. **Births** (per 1,000 pop. 1981): 15.8. **Deaths** (per 1,000 pop. 1981): 7.3. **Natural Increase** (1979): 1.2%. **Hospital beds** (per 100,000 pop. 1977): 1,244. **Physicians** (per 100,000 pop. 1977): 154. **Infant mortality** (per 1,000 live births 1981): 10.7.

Education (1983): **Literacy:** 99%. **School:** compulsory to age 15; attendance 94%.

Embassy: 1601 Massachusetts Ave NW 20036; 797-3000.

Capt. James Cook explored the E coast in 1770, when the continent was inhabited by a variety of different tribes. Within decades, Britain had claimed the entire continent, which became a penal colony until immigration increased in the 1850s. The commonwealth was proclaimed Jan. 1, 1901. Northern Terr. was granted limited self-rule July 1, 1978. Their capitals and 1981 pop.:

	Area (sq. mi.)	Population
New South Wales, Sydney	309,418	5,125,683
Victoria, Melbourne	87,854	3,948,555
Queensland, Brisbane	666,699	2,295,123
South Aust., Adelaide	379,824	1,285,033
Western Aust., Perth	974,843	1,299,100
Tasmania, Hobart	26,178	427,300
Aust. Capital Terr., Canberra	926	226,600
Northern Terr., Darwin	519,633	115,900

Australia's racially discriminatory immigration policies were abandoned in 1973, after 3 million Europeans (half British) had entered since 1945. The 50,000 aborigines and 150,000 part-aborigines are mostly detribalized, but there are several preserves in the Northern Territory. They remain economically disadvantaged.

Australia's agricultural success makes it among the top exporters of beef, lamb, wool, and wheat. Major mineral deposits have been developed as well, largely for exports. Industrialization has been completed.

Australia harbors many plant and animal species not found elsewhere, including the kangaroo, koala bear, platypus, dingo (wild dog), Tasmanian devil (racoon-like marsupial), wombat (bear-like marsupial), and barking and frilled lizards.

Australian External Territories

Norfolk Is., area 13½ sq. mi., pop. (1981) 1,800, was taken over, 1914. The soil is very fertile, suitable for citrus fruits, bananas, and coffee. Many of the inhabitants are descendants of the Bounty mutineers, moved to Norfolk 1856 from Pitcairn Is. Australia offered the island limited home rule, 1978.

Coral Sea Is. Territory, 1 sq. mi., is administered from Norfolk Is.

Territory of Ashmore and Cartier Is., area 2 sq. mi., in the Indian O. came under Australian authority 1934 and are administered as part of Northern Territory. **Heard and McDonald Is.** are administered by the Dept. of Science.

Cocos (Keeling) Is., 27 small coral islands in the Indian O. 1,750 mi. NW of Australia. Pop. (1981) 569, area: 5½ sq. mi. The residents voted to become part of Australia, Apr. 1984.

Christmas Is., 52 sq. mi., pop. 3,018 (1982), 230 mi. S of Java, was transferred by Britain in 1958. It has phosphate deposits.

Australian Antarctic Territory was claimed by Australia in 1933, including 2,472,000 sq. mi. of territory S of 60th parallel S Lat. and between 160th-45th meridians E Long.

Austria

Republic of Austria

People: Population (1983 est.): 7,574,000. **Age distrib. (%):** 0–14: 22.8; 15–59: 57.0; 60+: 20.2. **Pop. density:** 231.97 per sq. mi. **Urban** (1981): 55.1%. **Ethnic groups:** German 98%, Slovene, Croatian. **Languages:** German 95%, Slovene. **Religions:** Roman Catholic 85%.

Geography: Area: 32,374 sq. mi., slightly smaller than Maine. **Location:** In S Central Europe. **Neighbors:** Switzerland, Liechtenstein on W, W. Germany, Czechoslovakia on N, Hungary on E, Yugoslavia, Italy on S. **Topography:** Austria is primarily mountainous, with the Alps and foothills covering the western and southern provinces. The eastern provinces and Vienna are located in the Danube River Basin. **Capital:** Vienna. **Cities** (1981 cen.): Vienna 1,504,200.

Government: Type: Parliamentary democracy. **Head of state:** Pres. Rudolf Kirchschlaeger; b. Mar. 20, 1915; in office: July 8, 1974. **Head of government:** Chancellor Fred Sinowatz; b. Feb. 5, 1929; in office: May 24, 1983. **Local divisions:** 9

lander (states), each with a legislature. **Defense:** 0.6% of GNP (1983).

Economy: Industries: Steel, machinery, autos, electrical and optical equip., glassware, sport goods, paper, textiles, chemicals, cement. **Chief crops:** Grains, potatoes, beets, grapes. **Minerals:** Iron ore, oil, magnesite, aluminum, coal, lignite, copper. **Crude oil reserves** (1980): 140 mln. bbls. **Other resources:** Forests, hydro power. **Per capita arable land:** 0.5 acres. **Meat prod.** (1983): beef: 212,000 metric tons; pork: 470,000 metric tons. **Electricity prod.** (1982): 44.4 bln. kwh. **Crude steel prod.** (1982): 4.2 mln. metric tons. **Labor force:** 13.8% agric.; 60% ind. & comm.; 25.5% service.

Finance: Currency: Schilling (Mar. 1984: 18.25 = $1 US). **Gross domestic product** (1980): $76.34 bln. **Per capita income** (1980): $8,280. **Imports** (1983): $19.3 bln.; partners: W. Ger. 41%, It. 9%, Switz. 5%. **Exports** (1983): $15.4 bln.; partners: W. Ger. 29%, It. 9%, Switz. 7%. **Tourists** (1981): 14.2 mln.; receipts: $5.7 bln. **National budget** (1979): $14.19 bln. revenues; $16.55 bln. expenditures. **International reserves less gold** (Jan. 1984): $4.95 bln. **Gold:** 21.13 mln. oz t. **Consumer prices** (change in 1983): 3.3%.

Transport: Railway traffic (1981): 7.2 bln. passenger-km; 10.8 bln. net ton-km. **Motor vehicles:** in use (1981): 2.2 mln. passenger cars, 183,700 comm. **Civil aviation** (1982): 1.2 bln. passenger-km; 20.3 mln. freight ton-km.

Communications: Television sets: 2.2 mln. licensed (1980). **Radios:** 3.3 mln. licensed (1980). **Telephones in use** (1982): 2.3 mln. **Daily newspaper circ.** (1982): 780 per 1,000 pop.

Health: Life expectancy at birth (1981): 69.3 male; 76.4 female. **Births** (per 1,000 pop. 1982): 12.5. **Deaths** (per 1,000 pop. 1982): 12.0. **Natural increase** (1978): −.1%. **Hospital beds** (1981): 84,313. **Physicians** (1981): 19,157. **Infant mortality** (per 1,000 live births 1983): 16.

Education (1983): Literacy: 98%. School years compulsory 9; attendance 95%.

Embassy: 2343 Massachusetts Ave. NW 20008; 483-4474.

Rome conquered Austrian lands from Celtic tribes around 15 BC. In 788 the territory was incorporated into Charlemagne's empire. By 1300, the House of Hapsburg had gained control; they added vast territories in all parts of Europe to their realm in the next few hundred years.

Austrian dominance of Germany was undermined in the 18th century and ended by Prussia by 1866. But the Congress of Vienna, 1815, confirmed Austrian control of a large empire in southeast Europe consisting of Germans, Hungarians, Slavs, Italians, and others.

The dual Austro-Hungarian monarchy was established in 1867, giving autonomy to Hungary and almost 50 years of peace.

World War I, started after the June 28, 1914 assassination of Archduke Franz Ferdinand, the Hapsburg heir, by a Serbian nationalist, destroyed the empire. By 1918 Austria was reduced to a small republic, with the borders it has today.

Nazi Germany invaded Austria Mar. 13, 1938. The republic was reestablished in 1945, under Allied occupation. Full independence and neutrality were restored in a 1955.

Austria produces most of its food, as well as an array of industrial products. A large part of Austria's economy is controlled by state enterprises. Socialists have shared or alternated power with the conservative People's Party.

Economic agreements with the Common Market give Austria access to a free-trade area encompassing most of West Europe.

The Bahamas
Commonwealth of the Bahamas

People: Population (1983 est.): 223,000. **Age distrib.** (%): 0–14: 43.6; 15–59: 50.9; 60+: 5.5. **Pop. density:** 44.61 per sq. mi. **Urban** (1970): 57.9%. **Ethnic groups:** Negro 85%, Caucasian (British, Canadian, U.S.). **Languages:** English. **Religions:** Baptist 29%, Anglican 23%, Roman Catholic 22%.

Geography: Area: 5,380 sq. mi., about the size of Connecticut. **Location:** In Atlantic O., E of Florida. **Neighbors:** Nearest are U.S. on W, Cuba on S. **Topography:** Nearly 700 islands (30 inhabited) and over 2,000 islets in the western Atlantic extend 760 mi. NW to SE. **Capital:** Nassau. **Cities** (1979 est.) Nassau 138,500; Freeport 16,000.

Government: Type: Independent Commonwealth. **Head of state:** Queen Elizabeth II, represented by Gov.-Gen. Gerald C. Cash; b. May 28, 1917, in office: Sept. 29, 1979. **Head of government:** Prime Min. Lynden Oscar Pindling; b. Mar. 22, 1930; in office: Jan. 16, 1967. **Local divisions:** 18 districts.

Economy: Industries: Tourism (70% of GNP), intl. banking, rum, drugs. **Chief crops:** Fruits, vegetables. **Minerals:** Salt. **Other resources:** Lobsters. **Arable land:** 2%. **Electricity prod.** (1977): 650.00 mln. kwh. **Labor force:** 6% agric.; 25% tourism, 30% government.

Finance: Currency: Dollar (Mar. 1984: 1 = $1 US). **Gross domestic product** (1979): $1.08 bln. **Per capita income** (1979): $4,650. **Imports** (1981): $551 bln.; partners (1981): U.S. 74%, U.K. 13%. **Exports** (1981): $3.1 bln.; partners (1981): U.S. 41%, U.K. 7%. **Tourists** (1981): 1.7 mln.; receipts: $650 mln. **National budget** (1981): $278 mln. revenues; $278 mln. expenditures. **International reserves less gold** (Mar. 1984): $167.3 mln. **Consumer prices** (change in 1983): 4.1%.

Transport: Motor vehicles: in use (1980): 32,000 passenger cars, 12,000 comm. vehicles. **Chief ports:** Nassau, Freeport.

Communications: Radios: 110,000 in use (1980). **Television sets** (1980): 31,000. **Telephones in use** (1981): 71,883. **Daily newspaper circ.** (1982): 142 per 1,000 pop.

Health: Life expectancy at birth (1982): 64.0 male; 69 female. **Births** (per 1,000 pop. 1979): 25. **Deaths** (per 1,000 pop. 1978): 5. **Natural increase** (1979): 3.6%. **Infant mortality** (per 1,000 live births 1982): 32.4.

Education (1982): Literacy: 89%; School compulsory through age 14.

Embassy: 600 New Hampshire Ave. NW 20037; 338-3940.

Christopher Columbus first set foot in the New World on San Salvador (Watling I.) in 1492, when Arawak Indians inhabited the islands. British settlement began in 1647; the islands became a British colony in 1783. Internal self-government was granted in 1964; full independence within the Commonwealth was attained July 10, 1973.

International banking and investment management has become a major industry alongside tourism, despite controversy over financial irregularities.

Bahrain
State of Bahrain

People: Population (1983 est.): 393,000. **Age distrib.** (%): 0–14: 32.9; 15–59: 63.4; 60+: 3.7. **Pop. density:** 1,471.86 per sq. mi. **Urban** (1981): 80.7%. **Ethnic groups:** Arabs 73%, Iranians 9%, Indians, Pakistanis 5%. **Languages:** Arabic (official), Persian. **Religions:** Sunni Moslem 40%, Shi'ah Moslem 60%.

Geography: Area: 258 sq. mi., smaller than New York City. **Location:** In Persian Gulf. **Neighbors:** Nearest are Saudi Arabia on W. Qatar on E. **Topography:** Bahrain Island, and several adjacent, smaller islands, are flat, hot and humid, with little rain. **Capital:** Manama. **Cities** (1981 cen.): Manama 121,986.

Government: Type: Traditional emirate. **Head of state:** Amir Isa bin Sulman al-Khalifa; b. July 3, 1933; in office: Nov. 2, 1961. **Head of government:** Prime Min. Kahlifa ibn Sulman al-Khalifa; b. 1935; in office: Jan. 19, 1970. **Local divisions:** 6 towns and cities. **Armed forces:** regulars 2,500 (1982).

Economy: Industries: Oil products, aluminum smelting, shipping. **Chief crops:** Fruits, vegetables. **Minerals:** Oil, gas. **Crude oil reserves** (1980): 240 mln. bbls. **Per capita arable land:** 0.007 acres. **Electricity prod.** (1981): 1.8 bln. kwh. **Labor force:** 5% agric.; 85% ind. and commerce; 5% services; 3% gov.

Finance: Currency: Dinar (Mar. 1984: 0.38 = $1 US). **Gross domestic product** (1980 est.): $3.4 bln. **Per capita income** (1980 est.): $6,315. **Imports** (1980): $3.6 bln.; partners: Sau. Ar. 60%, UK 6%, U.S. 9%. **Exports** (1981): $4.22 bln.; partners: UAE 18%, Jap. 12%, Sing. 10%, U.S. 6%. **National Budget** (1980): $622 mln. revenues; $407 mln. expenditures. **International reserves less gold** (Mar. 1984): $1.3 bln. **Gold:** 150,000 oz t. **Consumer prices** (change in 1982): 8.9%.

Transport: Motor vehicles: in use (1977): 35,500 passenger cars, 13,200 comm. vehicles. **Chief ports:** Sitra.

Communications: Television sets: 31,000 in use (1976). **Radios:** 100,000 in use (1980). **Telephones in use** (1981): 84,593.

Health: Births (per 1,000 pop. 1978): 37. **Deaths** (per 1,000 pop. 1978): 8. **Natural Increase** (1978): 2.8. **Hospital beds** (per 100,000 pop. 1977): 303. **Physicians** (per 100,000 pop. 1977): 62.
Education (1982): **Literacy:** 40%. **Pop. 5–19:** in school: 58%, teachers per 1,000: 36.
Embassy: 3502 International Dr. NW 20008; 342-0741.

Long ruled by the Khalifa family, Bahrain was a British protectorate from 1861 to 1971, when it regained independence.

Pearls, shrimp, fruits, and vegetables were the mainstays of the economy until oil was discovered in 1932. By the 1970s, oil reserves were depleted; international banking thrived.

Bahrain took part in the 1973-74 Arab oil embargo against the U.S. and other nations. The government bought controlling interest in the oil industry in 1975.

Saudi Arabia is building a 15-mile causeway linking Bahrain with the Arab mainland.

Bangladesh

People's Republic of Bangladesh

People: Population (1983 est.): 96,539,000. **Age distrib.** (%): 0-14: 43.2; 15-59: 52.4; 60+: 4.4. **Pop. density:** 1,530 per sq. mi. **Urban** (1979): 10.1%. **Ethnic groups:** Bengali 98%, Bihari, tribesmen. **Languages:** Bengali (official), English. **Religions:** Moslems 86%, Hindu 13%.
Geography: Area: 55,598 sq. mi. slightly smaller than Wisconsin. **Location:** In S Asia, on N bend of Bay of Bengal. **Neighbors:** India nearly surrounds country on W, N, E; Burma on SE. **Topography:** The country is mostly a low plain cut by the Ganges and Brahmaputra rivers and their delta. The land is alluvial and marshy along the coast, with hills only in the extreme SE and NE. A tropical monsoon climate prevails, among the rainiest in the world. **Capital:** Dacca. **Cities** (1981 est.): Dacca (met.) 3.4 mln.; Chittagong (met.) 889,760; Khulna (met.) 437,304.
Government: Type: Republic. **Head of state:** Pres. Hossain Mohammad Ershad, b. Feb. 1, 1930, in office: Dec. 11, 1983. **Local divisions:** 20 districts. **Armed forces:** regulars 76,500; para-military 66,000.
Economy: Industries: Cement, jute, fertilizers, petroleum products. **Chief crops:** Jute (most of world output), rice. **Minerals:** Natural gas, offshore oil. **Per capita arable land:** 0.3 acres. **Fish catch** (1981): 687,000 metric tons. **Electricity prod.** (1981): 2.9 bln. kwh. **Labor force:** 74% agric.
Finance: Currency: Taka (Mar. 1984: 25.2 = $1 US). **Gross domestic product** (1980): $10.50 bln. **Per capita income** (1980) $105. **Imports** (1980): $2.42 bln.; partners: Jap. 13%, U.S. 8%. **Exports** (1980): $758 mln.; partners: U.S. 10%, Sing. 11%; Pak 5%. **International reserves less gold** (Mar. 1984): $593.1 mln. **Gold:** 56,000 oz t. **Consumer prices** (change in 1983): 8.0%.
Transport: Railway traffic (1981): 5.1 bln. passenger-km; 739 mln. net ton-km. **Motor vehicles:** in use (1979): 29,400 passenger cars, 11,000 comm. vehicles. **Chief ports:** Chittagong, Khulna.
Communications: Telephones in use (1981): 129,000. **Daily newspaper circ.** (1982) 6 per 1,000 pop.
Health: Life expectancy at birth (1974): 45.8 male; 46.6 female. **Births** (per 1,000 pop. 1979): 46. **Deaths** (per 1,000 pop. 1979): 19. **Natural increase** (1979): 2.8%. **Hospital beds** (1979): 17,494. **Physicians** (per 100,000 pop. 1977): 8.
Education (1981): **Literacy:** 25%. **Pop. 5–19:** in school: 35%.
Embassy: 3421 Massachusetts Ave. NW 20007; 337-6644.

Moslem invaders conquered the formerly Hindu area in the 12th century. British rule lasted from the 18th century to 1947, when East Bengal became part of Pakistan.

Charging West Pakistani domination, the Awami League, based in the East, won National Assembly control in 1971. Assembly sessions were postponed; riots broke out. Pakistani troops attacked Mar. 25; Bangladesh independence was proclaimed the next day. In the ensuing civil war, one million died amid charges of Pakistani atrocities. Ten million fled to India.

War between India and Pakistan broke out Dec. 3, 1971. Pakistan surrendered in the East Dec. 15. Sheik Mujibur Rahman became prime minister. The country moved into the Indian and Soviet orbits, in response to U.S. support of Pakistan, and much of the economy was nationalized.

In 1974, the government took emergency powers to curb widespread violence; Mujibur was assassinated and a series of coups followed.

Chronic destitution among the densely crowded population has been worsened by the decline of jute as a major world commodity.

A Ganges waterpact with India, signed 1977, was recommitted by the 2 nations, 1979. Martial law, in force since 1975, was lifted on Apr. 6, 1979, prior to the opening of the new parliament.

On May 30, 1981, Pres. Ziaur Rahman was shot and killed in an unsuccessful coup attempt by army rivals. Vice President Abdus Sattar assumed the presidency but was ousted in a coup led by army chief of staff Gen. H.M. Ershad, Mar. 1982. Ershad promised a return to democracy by 1984.

Barbados

People: Population (1983 est.): 251,000 **Age distrib.** (%): 0-14: 28.9%; 15–59: 57.7; 60+: 13.3. **Pop. density:** 1,506.02 per sq. mi. **Urban** (1970): 3.7%. **Ethnic groups:** African 80%, mixed 16%, Caucasian 4%. **Languages:** English. **Religions:** Anglican 70%, Methodist 9%, Roman Catholic 4%.
Geography: Area: 166 sq. mi. **Location:** In Atlantic, farthest E of W. Indies. **Neighbors:** Nearest are Trinidad, Grenada on SW. **Topography:** The island lies alone in the Atlantic almost completely surrounded by coral reefs. Highest point is Mt. Hillaby, 1,115 ft. **Capital:** Bridgetown. **Cities** (1980 est.): Bridgetown 7,600.
Government: Type: Independent sovereign state within the Commonwealth. **Head of state:** Queen Elizabeth II, represented by Gov.-Gen. Deighton L. Ward; b. May 16, 1909; in office: Nov. 17, 1976. **Head of government:** Prime Min. John M.G. Adams; b. Sept. 24, 1931; in office: Sept. 2, 1976. **Local divisions:** 11 parishes and Bridgetown.
Economy: Industries: Rum, molasses, tourism. **Chief crops:** Sugar, corn. **Minerals:** Lime. **Crude oil reserves** (1980): 1.5 mln. bbls. **Other resources:** Fish. **Arable land:** 60%. **Electricity prod.** (1978): 264.00 mln. kwh. **Labor force:** 9.8% agric.; 24.6% ind. and commerce; 65.6% services and government.
Finance: Currency: Dollar (Apr. 1984: 2.01 = $1 US). **Gross domestic product** (1979): $636.90 mln. **Per capita income** (1978): $3,040. **Imports** (1980): $524 mln.; partners: U.S. 35%, UK 12%, Trin./Tob. 12%, Can. 9%. **Exports** (1980): $226 mln.; partners: U.S. 37%, UK 7%, Trin./Tob. 15%. **Tourists** (1981): 352,555; receipts: $252 million. **National budget** (1980): $188 mln. revenues; $198 mln. expenditures. **International reserves less gold** (Mar. 1984): $120.80 mln. **Consumer prices** (change in 1983): 5.3%.
Transport: Motor vehicles: in use (1978): 22,000 passenger cars; 6,200 comm. vehicles. **Chief ports:** Bridgetown.
Communications: Television sets: 48,000 in use (1976). **Radios:** 130,000 in use (1976). **Telephones in use** (1981): 66,679. **Daily newspaper circ.** (1982): 410 per 1,000 pop.
Health: Life expectancy at birth (1981): 70.8. **Births** (per 1,000 pop. 1979): 16. **Deaths** (per 1,000 pop. 1979): 7. **Natural increase** (1976): 2.3%. **Hospital beds** (per 100,000 pop. 1977): 833. **Physicians** (per 100,000 pop. 1977): 76. **Infant mortality** (per 1,000 live births 1981): 28.3.
Education (1978): **Literacy:** 97%. **Pop. 5-19:** in school: 71%, teachers per 1,000: 36.
Embassy: 2144 Wyoming Ave. NW 20008; 387-7374.

Barbados was probably named by Portuguese sailors in reference to bearded fig trees. An English ship visited in 1605, and British settlers arrived on the uninhabited island in 1627. Slaves worked the sugar plantations, but were freed in 1834.

Self-rule came gradually, with full independence proclaimed Nov. 30, 1966. British traditions have remained.

Belgium

Kingdom of Belgium

People: Population (1983 est.): 9,865,000. **Age distrib.** (%): 0-14: 20.0; 15-59: 61.4; 60+: 18.6 **Pop. density:** 842.18 per sq. mi. **Urban** (1976): 94.6%. **Ethnic groups:** Flemings 58%, Walloons 41%. **Languages:** Flemish (Dutch) 57%, French 33%, legally bilingual 10%, German 1%. **Religions:** Roman Catholic 75%, Protestant.

Geography: Area: 11,779 sq. mi., slightly larger than Maryland. **Location:** In NW Europe, on N. Sea. **Neighbors:** France on W, S, Luxembourg on SE, W. Germany on E, Netherlands on N. **Topography:** Mostly flat, the country is trisected by the Scheldt and Meuse, major commercial rivers. The land becomes hilly and forested in the SE (Ardennes) region. **Capital:** Brussels. **Cities** (1982 est.): Brussels (Met.) 994,774; Ghent 237,687; Charleroi 219,579; Liege 211,528.

Government: Type: Parliamentary democracy under a constitutional monarch. **Head of state:** King Baudouin; b. Sept. 7, 1930; in office: July 17, 1951. **Head of government:** Premier Wilfried Martens; b. Apr. 19, 1936; in office: Dec. 17, 1981. **Local divisions:** 9 provinces; 589 communes. **Defense:** 5.8% of govt. budget (1983).

Economy: Industries: Steel, glassware, diamond cutting, textiles, chemicals. **Chief crops:** Grains, barley, potatoes, sugar beets. **Minerals:** Coal. **Other resources:** Forests. **Per capita arable land** (incl. Lux.): 0.2 acres. **Meat prod.** (1983): beef: 290,000 metric tons; pork: 650,000 metric tons. **Fish catch** (1981): 49,000 metric tons. **Electricity prod.** (1982): 50.6 bln. kwh. **Crude steel prod.** (1982): 9.9 mln. metric tons. **Labor force:** 3% agric.; 33% ind. & comm.; 36% services; 21% public service.

Finance: Currency: Franc (Mar. 1984: 53.08 = $1 US). **Gross national product** (1981): $97 bln. **Per capita income** (1981): $9,827. *Note:* the following trade and tourist data includes Luxembourg. **Imports** (1982): $57.9 bln.; partners: W. Ger. 20%, Neth. 18%, France 14%, UK 7%, U.S. 7%. **Exports** (1982): $52.3 bln.; partners: W. Ger. 20%, France 19%, Neth. 14%, UK 10%. **Tourists** (1981): receipts: $1.5 bln. **National budget** (1983): $31.20 bln. **International reserves less gold** (Mar. 1984): $4.60 bln. **Gold:** 34.18 mln. oz t. **Consumer prices** (change in 1983): 7.7%.

Transport: Railway traffic (1981): 6.8 bln. passenger-km; 6.7 bln. net ton-km. **Motor vehicles:** in use (1982): 3.2 mln. passenger cars, 267,700 comm. vehicles; assembled (1978): 1.01 mln. passenger cars; 18,744 comm. vehicles. **Civil aviation** (1982): 5.2 bln. passenger-km; 492 mln. freight ton-km. **Chief ports:** Antwerp, Zeebrugge, Ghent.

Communications: Television sets: 2.9 mln. licensed (1980). **Radios:** 4.5 mln. licensed (1980). **Telephones in use** (1981): 3.6 mln. **Daily newspaper circ.** (1982): 314 per 1,000 pop.

Health: Life expectancy at birth (1980): 68.6 male; 75.1 female. **Births** (per 1,000 pop. 1980): 12.7. **Deaths** (per 1,000 pop. 1980): 11.6. **Natural increase** (1978) .07%. **Hospital beds** (1981): 92,436. **Physicians:** 25,629. **Infant mortality** (per 1,000 live births 1980): 15.3.

Education (1983): Literacy: 98%. School compulsory to age 16.

Embassy: 3330 Garfield St. NW 20008; 333-6900

Belgium derives its name from the Belgae, the first recorded inhabitants, probably Celts. The land was conquered by Julius Caesar, and was ruled for 1800 years by conquerors, including Rome, the Franks, Burgundy, Spain, Austria, and France. After 1815, Belgium was made a part of the Netherlands, but it became an independent constitutional monarchy in 1830.

Belgian neutrality was violated by Germany in both world wars. King Leopold III surrendered to Germany, May 28, 1940. After the war, he was forced by political pressure to abdicate in favor of his son, King Baudouin.

The Flemings of northern Belgium speak Dutch while French is the language of the Walloons in the south. The language difference has been a perennial source of controversy. Antagonism between the 2 groups has continued.

Belgium lives by its foreign trade; about 50% of its entire production is sold abroad.

In 1982, the government attempted to deal with the nation's economic and financial problems by instituting wage and price controls and devaluing the franc.

Belize

People: Population (1983 est.): 154,000. **Age distrib.** (%): 0–14: 46.1; 15–64: 49.2; 65+: 4.7. **Pop. density:** 16.7 per sq. mi. **Languages:** English (official), Spanish, native Creole dialects. **Religions:** Roman Catholic 66%, Methodist 13%, Anglican 13%.

Geography: Area: 8,867 sq. mi. **Location:** eastern coast of Central America. **Neighbors:** Mexico on N., Guatemala on W. and S. **Capital:** Belmopan. **Cities:** (1980 cen.): Belize City 39,887.

Government: Type: Parliamentary. **Head of State:** Gov. Gen. Minita Gordon. **Head of government:** Prime Min. George Cadle Price; b. Jan. 15, 1919; in office: Sept. 21, 1981. **Local divisions:** 6 districts.

Economy: Sugar is the main export.

Finance: Currency: Belize dollar (Mar. 1984) 2 − $1 U.S. **Gross domestic product** (1981): $1,000. **Per capita income** (1981): $1,000. **Imports** (1982) $130 mln.; partners: U.S. 42%, UK 15%. **Exports:** (1982): 90 mln.; partners: U.S. 47%, UK 44%. **National Budget** (1981): $93.6 mln.

Health: life expectancy (1981) 60 yrs. **Births** (per 1,000 pop. 1981): 40.7. **Deaths** (per 1,000 pop. 1981): 4.8. **Infant mortality** (per 1,000 live births, 1981): 27.9.

Education: (1981) **Literacy:** 80%.; approximately 40,000 pupils attend primary schools.

Embassy: 1129-20th St. NW 20036; 347-4465.

Belize (formerly called British Honduras), Great Britain's last colony on the American mainland, achieved independence on Sept. 21, 1981. Guatemala claims territorial sovereignty over the country and has refused to recognize Belize's independence. There are 1,600 British troops in Belize to guarantee security.

Benin

People's Republic of Benin

People: Population (1983 est.): 3,792,000. **Age distrib.** (%): 0–14: 46.1; 15–59: 48.3; 60+: 5.6. **Pop. density:** 82.10 per sq. mi. **Urban** (1982): 15%. **Ethnic groups:** Fons, Adjas, Baribas, Yorubas. **Languages:** French (official), local dialects. **Religions:** Mainly animist with Christian, Muslim minorities.

Geography: Area: 43,475 sq. mi., slightly smaller than Pennsylvania. **Location:** In W Africa on Gulf of Guinea. **Neighbors:** Togo on W, Upper Volta, Niger on N, Nigeria on E. **Topography:** most of Benin is flat and covered with dense vegetation. The coast is hot, humid, and rainy. **Capital:** Porto-Novo. **Cities** (1982 est.): Cotonou 487,000; Porto-Novo 208,000.

Government: Type: Marxist-Leninist. **Head of state:** Pres. Ahmed Kerekou; b. Sept. 2, 1933; in office: Oct. 27, 1972. **Local divisions:** 6 provinces, 84 districts. **Defense:** 15% of govt. budget (1981).

Economy: Chief crops: Palm products, peanuts, cotton, kapok, coffee, tobacco. **Minerals:** Oil. **Arable land:** 11,%. **Fish catch** (1979): 25,500 metric tons. **Electricity prod.** (1977): 5.00 mln. kwh. **Labor force:** 60% agric; 30% serv. & comm.

Finance: Currency: CFA franc (Mar. 1984: 399.00 = $1 US). **Gross domestic product** (1980): $965 mln. **Per capita income** (1980): $230. **Imports** (1980): $410 mln.; partners: Fr. 27%, UK 13%, W. Ger. 6%, Neth. 6%. **Exports** (1980): $170 mln.; partners: Neth. 28%, Jap. 27%, Fr. 24%. **International reserves less gold** (Jan. 1984): $3.9 mln. **Gold:** 11,000 oz t.

Transport: Railway traffic (1978): 133.2 mln. passenger-km; 152 mln. net ton-km. **Motor vehicles:** in use (1979): 14,000 passenger cars, 9,500 comm. vehicles. **Chief ports:** Cotonou.

Communications: Radios: 65,000 in use (1981). **Daily newspaper circ.** (1980): 3 per 1,000 pop.

Health: Life expectancy at birth (1982): 41 yrs. **Births** (per 1,000 pop. 1978): 52. **Deaths** (per 1,000 pop. 1978): 25. **Natural increase** (1978): 2.7%. **Hospital beds** (per 100,000 pop. 1977): 137. **Physicians** (per 100,000 pop. 1977): 3. **Infant mortality** (per 1,000 live births 1982): 150.

Education (1982): **Literacy:** 20%. Years compulsory 6; attendance 43%.

Embassy: 2737 Cathedral Ave. NW 20008; 232-6656.

The Kingdom of Abomey, rising to power in wars with neighboring kingdoms in the 17th century, came under French domination in the late 19th century, and was incorporated into French West Africa by 1904.

Under the name Dahomey, the country became independent Aug. 1, 1960. The name was changed to Benin in 1975. In the fifth coup since independence Col. Ahmed Kerekou took power in 1972; two years later he declared a socialist state with a "Marxist-Leninist" philosophy. The economy relies on the development of agriculturally-based industries.

Bhutan

Kingdom of Bhutan

People: Population (1983 est.): 1,386,000. **Pop. density:** 67.34 per sq. mi. **Ethnic groups:** Bhotia (Tibetan) 60%. Nepalese 25%, Lepcha (indigenous), Indians. **Languages:** Dzongkha (official), Nepali. **Religions:** Buddhist 70%, Hindu 25%.

Geography: Area: 17,800 sq. mi., the size of Vermont and New Hampshire combined. **Location:** In eastern Himalayan Mts. **Neighbors:** India on W (Sikkim) and S, China on N. **Topography:** Bhutan is comprised of very high mountains in the N, fertile valleys in the center, and thick forests in the Duar Plain in the S. **Capital:** Thimphu. **City** (1982 est.): Thimphu 15,000.

Government: Type: Monarchy. **Head of state:** King Jigme Singye Wangchuk; b. Nov. 11, 1955; in office: July 21, 1972. **Local divisions:** 4 regions comprised of 17 districts.

Economy: Industries: Handicrafts. **Chief crops:** Rice, corn, wheat. **Other resources:** Timber. **Per capita arable land:** 0.5 acres. **Labor force:** 95% agric.

Finance: Currency: Ngultrum (Oct. 1983: 10.21 = 1 US) (Indian Rupee also used). **Gross national product** (1981): $113 mln. **Per capita income** (1981): $100. **Imports** (1981): $19 mln.; partners India 99%. **Exports** (1982): $12 mln.; partners India 99%.

Communications: Radios: 10,000 licensed (1976). **Telephones in use** (1978): 1,355.

Health: Life expectancy at birth (1975): 42.0 male; 40.5 female. **Births** (per 1,000 pop. 1978): 43. **Deaths** (per 1,000 pop. 1978): 20. **Natural increase** (1978): 2.3%. **Hospital beds** (1979): 536. **Physicians** (1979): 52.

Education (1983): **Literacy:** 5%.

The region came under Tibetan rule in the 16th century. British influence grew in the 19th century. A monarchy, set up in 1907, became a British protectorate by a 1910 treaty. The country became independent in 1949, with India guiding foreign relations and supplying aid.

Links to India have been strengthened by airline service and a road network. Most of the population engages in subsistence agriculture.

Bolivia

Republic of Bolivia

People: Population (1983 est.): 5,883,000. **Age distrib.** (%): 0–14: 41.9; 15–59: 52.0; 60+: 6.4. **Pop. density:** 13.20 per sq. mi. **Ethnic groups:** Quechua 30%, Aymara 25%, Mestizo (cholo) 25-30%, European 5-15%. **Languages:** Spanish (official), Quechua, Aymara. **Religions:** Roman Catholic 95%.

Geography: Area: 424,165 sq. mi., the size of Texas and California combined. **Location:** In central Andes Mtns. **Neighbors:** Peru, Chile on W, Argentina, Paraguay on S, Brazil on E and N. **Topography:** The great central plateau, at an altitude of 12,000 ft., over 500 mi. long, lies between two great cordilleras having 3 of the highest peaks in S. America. Lake Titicaca, on Peruvian border, is highest lake in world on which steamboats ply (12,506 ft.). The E central region has semitropical forests; the llanos, or Amazon-Chaco lowlands are in E. **Capitals:** Sucre, (legal), La Paz (de facto). **Cities** (1982 est.): La Paz 881,400; Santa Cruz 300,000; Cochabamba 216,000.

Government: Type: Republic. **Head of state:** Pres. Hernan Siles Zuazo; in office: Oct. 10, 1982. **Local divisions:** 9 departments, 94 provinces. **Armed forces:** regulars 21,500 (1980).

Economy: Industry: Textiles, food processing, chemicals, plastics. **Chief crops:** Potatoes, sugar, coffee, barley, cocoa, rice, corn, bananas, citrus. **Minerals:** Antimony, tin, tungsten, silver, zinc, oil, gas, iron. **Crude oil reserves** (1980): 150 mln. bbls. **Other resources:** rubber, cinchona bark. **Arable land:** 27%. **Electricity prod.** (1981): 1.6 bln. kwh. **Labor force:** 47% agric., 19% ind. & comm, 34% serv. & govt.

Finance: Currency: Peso (Mar. 1984: 500 = $1 US). **Gross domestic product** (1981): $7.5 bln. **Per capita income** (1982): $570. **Imports** (1982): $522 mln.; partners: U.S. 28%, Jap. 10%, Arg. 11%, Braz. 7%. **Exports** (1982): $832 mln.; partners: U.S. 27%, Arg. 36%. **National budget** (1980): $3.8 bln. revenues; $4.7 bln. expenditures. **International reserves less gold**

(Jan. 1984): $145 mln. **Gold:** 929,000 oz t. **Consumer prices** (change in 1983): 275%

Transport: Railway traffic (1980): 398 mln. passenger-km; 563 mln. net ton-miles. **Motor vehicles:** in use (1980): 48,000 passenger cars, 53,700 comm. vehicles. **Civil aviation** (1982): 780 mln. passenger-km.; 28.3 mln. freight ton-km.

Communications: Television sets: 300,000 (1980). **Radios:** 500,000 in use (1980). **Telephones in use** (1981): 135,000. **Daily newspaper circ.** (1982): 45 per 1,000 pop.

Health: Life expectancy at birth (1983): 49 yrs. **Births** (per 1,000 pop. 1978): 44. **Deaths** (per 1,000 pop. 1978): 19. **Natural increase** (1978): 2.4%. **Hospital beds** (per 100,000 pop. 1977): 228. **Physicians** (per 100,000 pop. 1977): 38. **Infant mortality** (per 1,000 live births 1983): 142.

Education (1983): **Literacy:** 75%. **Years compulsory:** ages 7-14; attendance 60%.

Embassy: 3014 Massachusetts Ave. NW 20008; 483-4410.

The Incas conquered the region from earlier Indian inhabitants in the 13th century. Spanish rule began in the 1530s, and lasted until Aug. 6, 1825. The country is named after Simon Bolivar, independence fighter.

In a series of wars, Bolivia lost its Pacific coast to Chile, the oilbearing Chaco to Paraguay, and rubber-growing areas to Brazil, 1879-1935.

Economic unrest, especially among the militant mine workers, has contributed to continuing political instability. A reformist government under Victor Paz Estenssoro, 1951-64, nationalized tin mines and attempted to improve conditions for the Indian majority, but was overthrown by a military junta. A series of coups and countercoups continued through 1981, until the military junta elected Gen. Villa as president.

In July 1982, the military junta assumed power amid a growing economic crisis and foreign debt difficulties. The junta resigned in October and allowed the Congress, elected democratically in 1980, to take power. The Congress elected Hernan Siles Zuazo to a 4-year term as president.

Botswana

Republic of Botswana

People: Population (1983 est.): 1,001,000. **Age distrib.** (%): 0–14: 46.1; 15–59: 43.1; 60+: 7.4. **Pop. density:** 3.73 per sq. mi. **Urban** (1981): 16%. **Ethnic groups:** Batswana, others. **Languages:** English (official), Setswana (national). **Religions:** indigenous beliefs (majority), Christian 15%.

Geography: Area: 231,804 sq. mi., slightly smaller than Texas. **Location:** In southern Africa. **Neighbors:** Namibia (S.W. Africa) on N and W, S. Africa on S, Zimbabwe on NE; Botswana claims border with Zambia on N. **Topography:** The Kalahari Desert, supporting nomadic Bushmen and wildlife, spreads over SW; there are swamplands and farming areas in N, and rolling plains in E where livestock are grazed. **Capital:** Gaborone. **Cities** (1983 est.): Gaborone 72,000.

Government: Type: Republic, parliamentary democracy. **Head of state:** Pres. Quett Masire; b. 1925; in office: July 13, 1980. **Local divisions:** 9 districts and 4 independent towns, all with local councils. **Defense:** 6% of govt. budget (1980).

Economy: Industries: Tourism. **Chief crops:** Corn, sorghum, peanuts. **Minerals:** Copper, coal, nickel, diamonds. **Other resources:** Big game. **Arable land:** 1%. **Electricity prod.** (1981): 540 mln. kwh. **Labor force:** 70% agric.

Finance: Currency: Pula (Mar. 1984: 0.86 = $1 US). **Gross domestic product** (1982): $620 mln. **Per capita income** (1978): $544. **Imports** (1981): $610 mln.; partners: S. Africa 88%. **Exports** (1981): $504 mln.; partners: Europe 67%, U.S. 17%, S. Africa 7%. **National budget** (1980): $221 mln. **International reserves less gold** (Mar. 1984): $413 mln. **Consumer prices** (change in 1982): 11.5%

Transport: Railway traffic (1978): 1.04 bln. net ton km. **Motor vehicles:** in use (1980): 8,000 passenger cars, 14,500 comm. vehicles.

Communications: Radios: 60,000 in use (1976). **Daily newspaper circ.** (1982): 20 per 1,000 pop.

Health: Life expectancy at birth (1975): 44.3 male; 47.5 female. **Births** (annual per 1,000 pop. 1978): 40 **Deaths** (per 1,000 pop. 1978): 13. **Natural increase** (1978): 2.8%. **Hospital**

beds (per 100,000 pop. 1980): 970. **Physicians** (per 100,000 pop. 1977): 14.
Education (1983): **Literacy:** 30%.
Embassy: 4301 Connecticut Ave. NW 20008; 244-4990.

First inhabited by bushmen, then by Bantus, the region became the British protectorate of Bechuanaland in 1886, halting encroachment by Boers and Germans from the south and southwest. The country became fully independent Sept. 30, 1966, changing its name to Botswana.

Cattle-raising and mining (diamonds, copper, nickel) have contributed to the country's economic growth.

Brazil

Federative Republic of Brazil

People: Population (1983 est.): 131,305,000. **Age distrib.** (%): 0–14: 39.1; 15–59: 55.0; 60+: 5.9. **Pop. density:** 37 per sq. mi. **Urban** (1981): 56%. **Ethnic groups:** Portuguese, Africans, and mulattoes make up the vast majority; Italians, Germans, Japanese, Indians, Jews, Arabs. **Languages:** Portuguese (official), English. **Religions:** Roman Catholic 89%.
Geography: Area: 3,286,470 sq. mi., larger than contiguous 48 U.S. states; largest country in S. America. **Location:** Occupies eastern half of S. America. **Neighbors:** French Guiana, Suriname, Guyana, Venezuela on N, Colombia, Peru, Bolivia, Paraguay, Argentina on W, Uruguay on S. **Topography:** Brazil's Atlantic coastline stretches 4,603 miles. In N is the heavily-wooded Amazon basin covering half the country. Its network of rivers navigable for 15,814 mi. The Amazon itself flows 2,093 miles in Brazil, all navigable. The NE region is semiarid scrubland, heavily settled and poor. The S central region, favored by climate and resources, has 45% of the population, produces 75% of farm goods and 80% of industrial output. The narrow coastal belt includes most of the major cities. Almost the entire country has a tropical or semitropical climate. **Capital:** Brasilia. **Cities** (1980 cen.): Sao Paulo 7 mln.; Rio de Janeiro 5 mln.; Belo Horizonte 1.4 mln.; Recife 1.1 mln.; Salvador 1.4 mln.; Porto Alegre 1.1 mln.
Government: Type: Federal Republic. **Head of state:** Pres. Joao Baptista de Oliveira Figueiredo; b. Jan. 15, 1918; in office: Mar. 15, 1979. **Local divisions:** 23 states, with individual constitutions and elected governments; 3 territories, federal district. **Defense:** 7% of govt. budget (1981).
Economy: Industries: Steel, autos, chemicals, ships, appliances, shoes, paper, petrochemicals, machinery. **Chief crops:** Coffee (largest grower), cotton, soybeans, sugar, cocoa, rice, corn, fruits. **Minerals:** Chromium, iron, manganese, tin, quartz crystals, beryl, sheet mica, columbium, titanium, diamonds, thorium, gold, nickel, gem stones, coal, tin, tungsten, bauxite, oil. **Crude oil reserves** (1980): 1.22 bln. bbls. **Arable land:** 17%. **Meat prod.** (1983): beef: 2.5 mln. metric tons; pork: 970 metric tons; lamb: 52,000 metric tons. **Fish catch** (1981): 900,000 metric tons. **Electricity prod.** (1981): 142.4 bln. kwh. **Crude steel prod.** (1982): 12.8 mln. metric tons. **Labor force:** 41% service, 36% agric.; 23% ind.
Finance: Currency: Cruzeiro (Mar. 1984: 1,335 = $1 US). **Gross domestic product** (1981): $289 bln. **Per capita income** (1978): $1,523. **Imports** (1983): $15.4 bln.; partners: U.S. 15%, Iraq 13%, Sau. Ar. 15%, Jap. 5%. **Exports** (1983): $21.8 bln.; partners: U.S. 20%, W. Ger. 6%, Neth. 6%, Japan 7%. **Tourists** (1980): 1.2 mln.; receipts: $182 mln. **National budget** (1979): $18.91 bln. revenues; $18.83 bln. expenditures. **International reserves less gold** (Dec. 1983): $4.35 bln. **Gold:** 73 mln. oz t. **Consumer prices** (change in 1983): 211%.
Transport: Railway traffic (1980): 11.3 bln. passenger-km; 73 bln. net ton-km. **Motor vehicles:** in use (1981): 9.5 mln. passenger cars, 954,000 mln. comm. vehicles; manuf. (1982): 659,000 passenger cars; 143,000 comm. vehicles. **Civil aviation** (1982): 16.3 bln. passenger-km: 670 mln. freight ton-km: **Chief ports:** Santos, Rio de Janeiro, Vitoria, Salvador, Rio Grande, Recife.
Communications: Television sets: 15 mln. in use (1980). **Radios:** 35 mln. in use (1980), 759,000 manuf. (1976). **Telephones in use** (1981): 7.4 mln. **Daily newspaper circ.** (1982): 44 per 1,000 pop.
Health: Life expectancy at birth (1980): 61.3 male; 65.5 female. **Births** (per 1,000 pop. 1980): 23.3. **Deaths** (per 1,000

pop. 1980): 6.8. **Natural increase** (1978): 2.3%. **Hospital beds** (1980): 488,323. **Physicians** (per 100,000 pop. 1980): 68.1. **Infant mortality** (per 1,000 live births 1981): 92.
Education (1980): **Literacy:** 68%. **Pop. 5-19:** in school: 52%, teachers per 1,000: 25.
Embassy: 3006 Massachusetts Ave. NW 20008; 797-0100.

Pedro Alvares Cabral, a Portuguese navigator, is generally credited as the first European to reach Brazil, in 1500. The country was thinly settled by various Indian tribes. Only a few have survived to the present, mostly in the Amazon basin.

In the next centuries, Portuguese colonists gradually pushed inland, bringing along large numbers of African slaves. Slavery was not abolished until 1888.

The King of Portugal, fleeing before Napoleon's army, moved the seat of government to Brazil in 1808. Brazil thereupon became a kingdom under Dom Joao VI. After his return to Portugal, his son Pedro proclaimed the independence of Brazil, Sept. 7, 1822, and was acclaimed emperor. The second emperor, Dom Pedro II, was deposed in 1889, and a republic proclaimed, called the United States of Brazil. In 1967 the country was renamed the Federative Republic of Brazil.

A military junta took control in 1930; dictatorial power was assumed by Getulio Vargas, who alternated with military coups until finally forced out by the military in 1954. A democratic regime prevailed 1956-64, during which time the capital was moved from Rio de Janeiro to Brasilia in the interior.

The next 5 presidents were all military leaders. Censorship was imposed, and much of the opposition was suppressed amid charges of torture. In 1974 elections, the official opposition party made gains in the chamber of deputies; some relaxation of censorship occurred, though church liberals, labor leaders, and intellectuals continued to report cases of arrest and torture.

Since 1930, successive governments have pursued industrial and agricultural growth and the development of interior areas. Exploiting vast mineral resources, fertile soil in several regions, and a huge labor force, Brazil became the leading industrial power of Latin America by the 1970s, while agricultural output soared. The 1979 government declared an amnesty and enacted democratic reforms.

However, income maldistribution, inflation and government land policies have all led to severe economic recession. Foreign debt reached $100 bln. in 1983, the largest in the world.

Brunei

People: Population (1083 est.): 209,000. **Ethnic groups:** Malay 62%, Chinese 20%, Indian 3%. **Language:** Malay (official), English. **Religion:** Muslim 64%, Buddhist 14%, Christian 10%.
Geography: Area: 2,226 sq. mi. **Location:** on the north coast of the island of Borneo; it is surrounded on its landward side by the Malaysian state of Sarawak. **Capital:** Bandar Seri Begawan. **Cities** (1982 est.): Bandar Seri Begawan 51,000.
Government: Type: Independent sultanate. **Head of Government:** Sultan Sir Muda Hassanal Bolkiah Mu'izzadin Waddaulah; in office: Jan. 1, 1984.
Economy: Industries: petroleum (about 90% of revenue is derived from oil exports). **Chief crops:** rice, bananas, cassava.
Finance: Currency: Brunei dollar (Oct 1983: 2.14 = $1).
Communications: Television sets: 32,000 (1981). **Radios:** 38,000 (1981). **Telephones:** 17,930 (1981).

The Sultanate of Brunei was a powerful state in the early 16th century with authority over all of the island of Borneo as well as parts of the Sulu Islands and the Philippines. In 1888, a treaty was signed which placed the state under the protection of Great Britain.

Brunei became a fully sovereign and independent state at the end of 1983.

Bulgaria

People's Republic of Bulgaria

People: Population (1983 est.): 8,944,000. **Age distrib. (%):** 0–14: 22.3; 15–59: 61.7; 60+: 16.0. **Pop. density:** 207 per sq. mi. **Urban** (1978): 60.5%. **Ethnic groups:** Bulgarians 85%,

Turks 8.5%. **Languages:** Bulgarian, Turkish, Greek. **Religions:** Orthodox 85%, Moslem 13%.

Geography: Area: 44,365 sq. mi., about the size of Ohio. **Location:** In eastern Balkan Peninsula on Black Sea. **Neighbors:** Romania on N, Yugoslavia on W, Greece, Turkey on S. **Topography:** The Stara Planina (Balkan) Mts. stretch E-W across the center of the country, with the Danubian plain on N, the Rhodope Mts. on SW, and Thracian Plain on SE. **Capital:** Sofia. **Cities** (1981 est.): Sofia 1,070,000; Plovdiv 307,414; Varna 257,731.

Government: Type: Communist. **Head of state:** Pres. Todor Zhivkov; b. Sept. 7, 1911; in office: July 7, 1971. **Head of government:** Premier Grisha Filipov; in office: June 16, 1981. **Head of Communist Party:** First Sec. Todor Zhivkov; b. 1911; in office: Jan. 1954. **Local divisions:** 27 provinces, one city. **Defense:** 5.9% of govt. budget.

Economy: Industries: Chemicals, machinery, metals, textiles, fur, leather goods, vehicles, wine, processed food. **Chief crops:** Grains, fruit, corn, potatoes, tobacco. **Minerals:** Lead, bauxite, coal, oil, zinc. **Per capita arable land:** 1.1 acres. **Meat prod.** (1983): beef: 130,000 metric tons; pork: 359,000 metric tons; lamb: 101,000 metric tons. **Fish catch** (1980): 140,000 metric tons. **Electricity prod.** (1982): 40.4 bln. kwh. **Crude steel prod.** (1982): 2.5 mln. metric tons. **Labor force:** 23% agric.; 42% ind. & comm.

Finance: Currency: Lev (Sept. 1983: .98 = $1 US). **National income** (1981): $23.3 bln. **Per capita income** (1980): $2,625. **Imports** (1982): $11.3 bln.; partners: USSR 54%, E. Ger. 6%, W. Ger. 5%. **Exports** (1982): $11.2 bln.; partners: USSR 48%, E. Ger. 6%. **Tourists** (1981): 6 mln: revenues $260 mln.

Transport: Railway traffic (1981): 7.1 bln. passenger-km; 18 bln. net ton-km. **Motor vehicles:** in use (1980) 815,549 passenger cars, 130,000 commercial; manuf. (1977): 15,000 passenger cars, 6,900 comm. vehicles. **Chief ports:** Burgas, Varna.

Communications: Television sets: 1.6 mln. licensed (1981). **Radios:** 2.1 mln. licensed (1981). **Telephones in use** (1981): 1.3 mln. **Daily newspaper circ.** (1982): 245 per 1,000 pop.

Health: Life expectancy at birth (1983): 69 male; 74 female. **Births** (per 1,000 pop. 1980): 15.5. **Deaths** (per 1,000 pop. 1980): 10.5. **Natural increase** (1978): .2%. **Hospital beds** (1977): 73,033. **Physicians** (1979): 21,249. **Infant mortality** (per 1,000 live births 1983): 20.2

Education (1983): **Literacy:** 95%. **Years compulsory:** 8. **Embassy:** 1621-22d St. NW 20008; 387-7969.

Bulgaria was settled by Slavs in the 6th century. Turkic Bulgars arrived in the 7th century, merged with the Slavs, became Christians by the 9th century, and set up powerful empires in the 10th and 12th centuries. The Ottomans prevailed in 1396 and remained for 500 years.

A revolt in 1876 led to an independent kingdom in 1908. Bulgaria expanded after the first Balkan War but lost its Aegean coastline in World War I, when it sided with Germany. Bulgaria joined the Axis in World War II, but withdrew in 1944. Communists took power with Soviet aid; the monarchy was abolished Sept. 8, 1946.

In 1983, the U.S. and Italy asserted that Bulgaria was involved in the May 1981 shooting of Pope John Paul II.

Burma

Socialist Republic of the Union of Burma

People: Population (1983 est.): 35,480,000. **Age distrib.** (%): 0–14: 40.5; 15–59: 53.5; 60+: 6.0. **Pop. density:** 123.04 per sq. mi. **Ethnic groups:** Burmans (related to Tibetans) 72%; Karen 7%, Shan 6%, Indians 6%, others. **Languages:** Burmese (official). **Religions:** Buddhist 85%; Hinduism, Islam, Christians.

Geography: Area: 261,288 sq. mi., nearly as large as Texas. **Location:** Between S. and S.E. Asia, on Bay of Bengal. **Neighbors:** Bangladesh, India on W, China, Laos, Thailand on E. **Topography:** Mountains surround Burma on W, N, and E, and dense forests cover much of the nation. N-S rivers provide habitable valleys and communications, especially the Irrawaddy, navigable for 900 miles. The country has a tropical monsoon climate. **Capital:** Rangoon. **Cities** (1980 est.): Rangoon 2,186,000; Mandalay 458,000; Karbe ('73 cen.): 253,600; Moulmein 188,000.

Government: Type: Socialist Rep. **Head of state:** Pres. U San Yu in office: Nov. 9, 1981. **Head of government:** Prime Min. U. Maung Maung Kha; b. Nov. 2, 1917; in office: Mar. 29,

1977. **Local divisions:** 7 states and 7 divisions. **Defense:** 5.9% of GDP (1981).

Economy: Chief crops: Rice, sugarcane, peanuts, beans. **Minerals:** Oil, lead, silver, tin, tungsten, precious stones. **Crude oil reserves** (1980): 25 mln. bbls. **Other resources:** Rubber, teakwood. **Per capita arable land:** 0.7 acres. **Meat prod.** (1980): beef: 94,000 metric tons; pork: 81,000 metric tons; lamb: 4,000 metric tons. **Fish catch** (1981): 624,000 metric tons. **Electricity prod.** (1980): 1.4 bln. kwh. **Labor force:** 67% agric; 9% ind.

Finance: Currency: Kyat (Mar. 1984: 8.05 = $1 US). **Gross domestic product** (1981): $5.62 bln. **Per capita income** (1981): $174. **Imports** (1980): $354 mln.; partners: Jap. 34%, U.S. 12%, UK 9%, W. Ger. 9%. **Exports** (1980): $472 mln.; partners: Switz. 12%, Sing. 10%. **National budget** (1982): $4.4 bln. revenues; $4.2 bln. expenditures. **International reserves less gold** (Mar. 1984): $91.5 mln. **Gold:** 251,000 oz t. **Consumer prices** (change in 1982): 5%.

Transport: Railway traffic (1979): 3.7 bln. passenger-km; 600 mln. net ton-km. **Motor vehicles:** in use (1980): 43,000 passenger cars, 44,000 comm. vehicles. **Civil aviation** (1981): 229 mln. passenger-km.; 1.5 mln. net ton-km. **Chief ports:** Rangoon, Sittwe, Bassein, Moulmein, Tavoy.

Communications: Radios: 700,000 licensed (1980). **Telephones in use** (1982): 49,000. **Daily newspaper circ.** (1982): 14 per 1,000 pop.

Health: Life expectancy at birth (1975): 48.6 male; 51.5 female. **Births** (per 1,000 pop. 1978): 39. **Deaths** (per 1,000 pop. 1978): 14. **Natural increase** (1978): 2.4%. **Hospital beds** (per 100,000 pop. 1977): 89. **Physicians** (per 100,000 pop. 1977): 19. **Infant mortality** (per 1,000 live births 1982): 100.

Education (1982): **Literacy:** 78%. **Pop. 5-19:** in school: 40%, teachers per 1,000: 8.

Embassy: 2300 S St. NW 20008; 332-9044.

The Burmese arrived from Tibet before the 9th century, displacing earlier cultures, and a Buddhist monarchy was established by the 11th. Burma was conquered by the Mongol dynasty of China in 1272, then ruled by Shans as a Chinese tributary, until the 16th century.

Britain subjugated Burma in 3 wars, 1824-84, and ruled the country as part of India until 1937, when it became self-governing. Independence outside the Commonwealth was achieved Jan. 4, 1948.

Gen. Ne Win dominated politics during the 1960s and 1970s. He led a Revolutionary Council set up in 1962, which drove Indians from the civil service and Chinese from commerce. Socialization of the economy was advanced, isolation from foreign countries enforced. Lagging production and export have begun to turn around, due to government incentives in the agriculture and petroleum sectors and receptivity to foreign investment in the economy.

A bomb killed 21 persons, including 4 S. Korean cabinet members, during a wreath-laying ceremony Oct. 9, 1983. Burma severed relations with N. Korea after 2 N. Korean officers confessed to the bombing.

Burundi

Republic of Burundi

People: Population (1983 est.): 4,561,000. **Age distrib.** (%): 0–14: 44.1; 15–59: 51.9; 60+: 4.1. **Pop. density:** 419.96 per sq. mi. **Urban** (1970): 2.2%. **Ethnic groups:** Hutu 85%, Tutsi 14%, Twa (pygmy) 1%. **Languages:** French, Kirundi (both official). **Religions:** Roman Catholic 62%, traditional African 32%.

Geography: Area: 10,759 sq. mi., the size of Maryland. **Location:** In central Africa. **Neighbors:** Rwanda on N, Zaire on W, Tanzania on E. **Topography:** Much of the country is grassy highland, with mountains reaching 8,900 ft. The southernmost source of the White Nile is located in Burundi. Lake Tanganyika is the second deepest lake in the world. **Capital:** Bujumbura. **Cities** (1983 est.): Bujumbura 141,000.

Government: Type: Republic. **Head of state and head of government:** Pres. Jean Baptiste Bagaza; b. Aug. 29, 1946; in office: Nov. 9, 1976 (govt: Oct. 1978). **Local divisions:** 15 provinces, 114 communes. **Defense** (1982): 19.3% of govt. budget.

Economy: Chief crops: Coffee (90% of exports), cotton, tea. **Minerals:** Nickel. **Arable land:** 61%. **Fish catch** (1979): 11,000

metric tons. **Electricity prod.** (1977): 27.00 mln. kwh. **Labor force:** 93% agric.
Finance: Currency: Franc (Apr. 1984: 1.16 = $1 US). **Gross domestic product** (1982): $1.2 bln. **Per capita income** (1982) $235. **Imports** (1980): $168 mln.; partners: Iran 14%, Belg.-Lux. 16%, Jap. 8%. **Exports** (1980): $65.1 mln.; partners: U.S. 32%, Belg. 10%. **National budget** (1982): $238 mln. **International reserves less gold** (Mar. 1984): $27.5 mln. **Gold:** 17,000 oz t. **Consumer prices** (change in 1982): 10%
Transport: Motor vehicles: in use (1979): 5,600 passenger cars, 2,800 comm. vehicles.
Communications: Radios: 105,000 in use (1976). **Telephones in use** (1979): 6,000.
Health: Life expectancy at birth (1983): 45.3 male; 48.6 female. **Births** (per 1,000 pop. 1978): 42. **Deaths** (per 1,000 pop. 1978): 17. **Natural increase** (1978): 2.5%. **Hospital beds** (per 100,000 pop. 1977): 118. **Physicians** (per 100,000 pop. 1977): 3. **Infant mortality** (per 1,000 live births 1983): 121.
Education (1983): **Literacy:** 25%.
Embassy: 2233 Wisconsin Ave. NW 20007; 342-2574.

The pygmy Twa were the first inhabitants, followed by Bantu Hutus, who were conquered in the 16th century by the tall Tutsi (Watusi), probably from Ethiopia. Under German control in 1899, the area fell to Belgium in 1916, which exercised successively a League of Nations mandate and UN trusteeship over Ruanda-Urundi (now 2 countries).
Independence came in 1962, and the monarchy was overthrown in 1966. An unsuccessful Hutu rebellion in 1972-73 left 10,000 Tutsi and 150,000 Hutu dead. Over 100,000 Hutu fled to Tanzania and Zaire. The present regime is pledged to ethnic reconciliation, but Burundi remains one of the poorest and most densely populated countries in Africa.

Cambodia (Kampuchea)

Cambodian People's Republic

People: Population (1983 est.): 5,996,000. **Pop. density:** 126.89 per sq. mi. **Ethnic groups:** Khmers 93%, Vietnamese 4%, Chinese 3%. **Languages:** Khmer (official), French. **Religions:** Theravada Buddhism, animism, atheism.
Geography: Area: 69,900 sq. mi., the size of Missouri. **Location:** In Indochina Peninsula. **Neighbors:** Thailand on W, N, Laos on NE, Vietnam on E. **Topography:** The central area, formed by the Mekong R. basin and Tonle Sap lake, is level. Hills and mountains are in SE, a long escarpment separates the country from Thailand on NW. 75% of the area is forested. **Capital:** Phnom Penh. **Cities** (1981 est.): Phnom Penh 500,000.
Government: Head of government: Pres., People's Revolutionary Council Heng Samrin; in office: Jan. 7, 1979. **Head of State:** Premier Chan Sy; in office: Feb. 9, 1982. **Local divisions:** 5 regions and a special capital region.
Economy: Industries: Textiles, paper, plywood, oil products. **Chief crops:** Rice, corn, pepper, tobacco, cotton, oil seeds, beans, palm sugar. **Minerals:** Iron, copper, manganese, gold. **Other resources:** Forests, rubber, kapok. **Per capita arable land:** 0.8 acres. **Meat prod.** (1980): beef: 17,000 metric tons; pork: 26,000 metric tons. **Fish catch** (1980): 84,700 metric tons. **Electricity prod.** (1977): 150.00 mln. kwh.
Finance: Currency: Riel (Jan. 1983: 4 = $1 US). **Per capita income** (1976): $90. **Imports** (1981): $103 mln. **Exports** (1981): $43 mln.
Transport: Railway traffic (1973): 33.53 mln. passenger-miles; 6.21 mln. net ton-miles. **Motor vehicles:** in use (1972): 27,200 passenger cars, (1973) 10,100 comm. vehicles. **Chief ports:** Kompong Som.
Communications: Television sets: 35,000 in use (1977). **Radios:** 171,000 in use (1978). **Telephones in use** (1977): 71,000.
Health: Life expectancy at birth (1975): 44.0 male; 46.9 female. **Births** (per 1,000 pop. 1975): 45.9. **Deaths** (per 1,000 pop. 1975): 16.9. **Natural increase** (1975): 2.9%. **Hospital beds** (per 100,000 pop. 1977): 106. **Physicians** (per 100,000 pop. 1977): 7.
Education (1978): **Literacy:** 48%. **Pop. 5-19:** (1975): in school: 40%, per teacher: 124.

Early kingdoms dating from that of Funan in the 1st century AD culminated in the great Khmer empire which flourished from

the 9th century to the 13th, encompassing present-day Thailand, Cambodia, Laos, and southern Vietnam. The peripheral areas were lost to invading Siamese and Vietnamese, and France established a protectorate in 1863. Independence came in 1953.
Prince Norodom Sihanouk, king 1941-1955 and head of state from 1960, tried to maintain neutrality. Relations with the U.S. were broken in 1965, after South Vietnam planes attacked Vietcong forces within Cambodia. Relations were restored in 1969, after Sihanouk charged Viet communists with arming Cambodian insurgents.
In 1970, pro-U.S. premier Lon Nol seized power, demanding removal of 40,000 North Viet troops; the monarchy was abolished. Sihanouk formed a government-in-exile in Peking, and open war began between the government and Khmer Rouge. The U.S. provided heavy military and economic aid. U.S. troops fought Vietcong forces within Cambodia for 2 months in 1970.
Khmer Rouge forces captured Phnom Penh April 17, 1975. Over 100,000 people had died in 5 years of fighting. The new government evacuated all cities and towns, and shuffled the rural population, sending virtually the entire population to clear jungle, forest, and scrub, which covered half the country. Over one million people were killed in executions and enforced hardships.
Severe border fighting broke out with Vietnam in 1978; developed into a full-fledged Vietnamese invasion. The Vietnamese-backed Kampuchean National United Front for National Salvation, a Cambodian rebel movement, announced, Jan. 8, 1979, the formation of a government one day after the Vietnamese capture of Phnom Pehn. Thousands of refugees flowed into Thailand. Widespread starvation was reported; by Sept., when the UN confirmed diplomatic recognition to the ousted Pol Pot government, international food assistance was allowed to aid the famine-stricken country. In July 1981, renewed efforts to bring about a Vietnamese troop withdrawal and institute supervised elections were pursued in a UN conference on Cambodia. But prospects for a diplomatic settlement were dimmed when Vietnam and the Soviet Union boycotted the proceedings.
On Jan. 10, 1983, Vietnam launched an offensive against anti-communist forces in the west. They overran a refugee camp, Jan. 31, driving 30,000 residents into Thailand. In March, Vietnam launched a major offensive against camps on the Cambodian-Thailand border, engaged Khmer Rouge guerrillas, and crossed the border instigating clashes with Thai troops.

Cameroon

United Republic of Cameroon

People: Population (1983 est.): 9,251,000. **Age distrib.** (%): 0–14: 43.4; 15–59: 50.8; 60+: 5.8. **Pop. density:** 44 per sq. mi. **Urban** (1976): 28.5%. **Ethnic groups:** Some 200 tribes; largest are Bamileke 30%, Fulani 7%. **Languages:** English, French (both official), Bantu, Sudanic. **Religions:** Roman Catholic 35%, animist 25%, Moslim 22%, Protestant 18%.
Geography: Area: 179,558 sq. mi., somewhat larger than California. **Location:** Between W and central Africa. **Neighbors:** Nigeria on NW, Chad, Central African Republic on E, Congo, Gabon, Equatorial Guinea on S. **Topography:** A low coastal plain with rain forests is in S; plateaus in center lead to forested mountains in W, including Mt. Cameroon, 13,000 ft.; grasslands in N lead to marshes around Lake Chad. **Capital:** Yaounde. **Cities** (1981 est.): Douala 637,000; Yaounde 435,000.
Government: Type: Independent Republic. **Head of state:** Pres. Paul Biya; b. Feb. 13, 1933; in office: Nov. 6, 1982. **Head of government:** Prime Minister Luc Ayang; in office: Aug. 22, 1983. **Local divisions:** 7 provinces with appointed governors. **Armed forces:** regulars 8,500 (1980).
Economy: Industries: Aluminum processing, palm products. **Chief crops:** Cocoa, coffee, peanuts, tea, bananas, cotton, tobacco. **Crude oil reserves** (1980): 140 mln. bbls. **Other resources:** Timber, rubber. **Arable land:** 4%. **Fish catch** (1980): 71,600 metric tons. **Electricity prod.** (1981): 1.6 bln. kwh. **Labor force:** 83% agric., 7% ind. and commerce.
Finance: Currency: CFA franc (Mar. 1984: 399 = $1 US). **Gross domestic product** (1979): $5.2 bln. **Per capita income** (1979): $628. **Imports** (1982): 1.2 bln.; partners (1981): Fr. 41%, W. Ger. 5%, Jap. 6%. **Exports** (1982): $1.6 bln.; partners (1981): Fr. 19%, Neth. 15%, U.S. 38%, It. 5%. **National budget** (1980): $928 mln. revenues; $928 mln. expenditures.

International reserves less gold (Oct. 1983): $62.3 mln. **Gold:** 30,000 oz t. **Consumer prices** (change in 1982): 12.3%.

Transport: Railway traffic (1981): 280 mln. passenger-km; 710 mln. net ton-km. **Motor vehicles:** in use (1980): 66,800 passenger cars, 47,100 comm. vehicles. **Chief ports:** Douala.

Communications: Radios: 240,000 in use (1980). **Telephones in use** (1979): 26,000. **Daily newspaper circ.** (1982): 6 per 1,000 pop.

Health: Life expectancy at birth (1975): 41.9 male; 45.1 female. **Births** (per 1,000 pop. 1978): 46. **Deaths** (per 1,000 pop. 1978): 20. **Natural increase** (1978): 2.6%. **Hospital beds** (per 100,000 pop. 1977): 269. **Physicians** (per 100,000 pop. 1977): 6.

Education (1978): **Literacy:** 34%. **Pop. 5-19:** in school: 52%, teachers per 1,000: 10.

Embassy: 2349 Massachusetts Ave. NW 20008; 265-8790.

Portuguese sailors were the first Europeans to reach Cameroon, in the 15th century. The European and American slave trade was very active in the area. German control lasted from 1884 to 1916, when France and Britain divided the territory, later receiving League of Nations mandates and UN trusteeships. French Cameroon became independent Jan. 1, 1960; one part of British Cameroon joined Nigeria in 1961, the other part joined Cameroon. Stability has allowed for development of roads, railways, agriculture, and petroleum production.

Canada

See also Canada in Index.

People: Population (1983 est.): 24,882,000. **Age distrib.** (%): 0–14: 22.5; 15–44: 48.6; 44+: 28.8. **Pop. density:** 6.10 per sq. mi. **Urban** (1976): 75.5%. **Cities** (met. 1982 est.): Montreal 2,850,000; Toronto 3,029,000; Vancouver 1,100,000; Ottawa 695,000; Winnipeg 570,000; Edmonton 529,000.

Government: Type: Confederation with parliamentary democracy. **Head of state:** Queen Elizabeth II, represented by Gov.-Gen. Edward R. Schreyer; b. Dec. 21, 1935; in office: Jan. 22, 1979. **Head of government:** (see *Chronology* and *Canada*). **Local divisions:** 10 provinces, 2 territories. **Defense:** 2% of GNP.

Economy: Minerals: Nickel, zinc, copper, gold, lead, molybdenum, potash, silver. **Crude oil reserves** (1980): 6.8 bln. bbls. **Per capita arable land:** 4.6 acres. **Meat prod.** (1983): beef: 1.2 mln. metric tons; pork 850,000 metric tons. **Fish catch** (1981): 1.3 mln. metric tons. **Electricity prod.** (1981): 377.6 bln. kwh. **Crude steel prod.** (1982): 11.9 mln. metric tons. **Labor force:** 5% agric.; 43.5% ind. & comm., 38% service.

Finance: Currency: Dollar (Mar. 1984: 1.27 = $1 US). **Gross domestic product** (1982): $272 bln. **Per capita income** (1982 est.) $10,193. **Imports** (1983): $65 bln.; partners (1982): U.S. 71%, Jap. 5%. **Exports** (1983): $76 bln.; partners (1982): U.S. 68%, Jap. 5%. **Tourists** (1981): 12.8 mln.; receipts: $2.5 bln. **National budget** (1983-84): 71.1 bln. **International reserves less gold** (Mar. 1984): $2.90 bln. **Gold:** 20.17 mln. oz t. **Consumer prices** (change in 1983): 5.8%.

Transport: Railway traffic (1980): 1.6 bln. passenger-km; 200.8 bln. net ton-km. **Motor vehicles:** in use (1981): 10.1 mln. passenger cars, 3.1 mln. comm. vehicles; manuf. (1982): 814,000 passenger cars; 470,000 comm. vehicles. **Civil aviation** (1981): 31.4 bln. passenger-km: 776.5 mln. net ton-km.

Communications: Television sets: 11 mln. in use (1979), 606,000 manuf. (1977). **Radios:** 26.1 mln. in use (1979), 837,000 manuf. (1976). **Telephones in use** (1982): 16.4 mln. **Daily newspaper circ.** (1982): 218 per 1,000 pop.

Health: Life expectancy at birth (1983): 69 male; 76 female. **Births** (per 1,000 pop. 1982): 15.1. **Deaths** (per 1,000 pop. 1982): 6.9. **Natural increase** (1977): .8%. **Hospital beds** (per 100,000 pop. 1977): 875. **Physicians** (per 100,000 pop. 1977): 178. **Infant mortality** (por 1,000 live births 1982): 15.

Education (1982): **Literacy:** 99%. **Pop. 5-19:** in school: 75%, teachers per 1,000: 40.

Embassy: 1746 Massachusetts Ave. NW 20036; 785-1400.

Cape Verde

Republic of Cape Verde

People: Population (1983 est.): 297,000. **Age distrib.** (%): 0–14: 46.9; 15–59: 44.9; 60+: 7.9. **Pop. density:** 199.10 per sq. mi. **Urban** (1980): 26.2%. **Ethnic groups:** Creole (mulatto) 70%, African 28%, European 1%. **Languages:** Portuguese (official), Crioulo. **Religions:** 65% Roman Catholic.

Geography: Area: 1,557 sq. mi., a bit larger than Rhode Island. **Location:** In Atlantic O., off western tip of Africa. **Neighbors:** Nearest are Mauritania, Senegal. **Topography:** Cape Verde Islands are 15 in number, volcanic in origin (active crater on Fogo). The landscape is eroded and stark, with vegetation mostly in interior valleys. **Capital:** Praia. **Cities** (1980 est.): Mindelo 40,000; Praia 36,600.

Government: Type: Republic. **Head of state:** Pres. Aristide Pereira; b. Nov. 17, 1923; in office: July 5, 1975. **Head of government:** Prime Min. Pedro Pires, b. Apr. 29, 1934; in office: July 5, 1975. **Local divisions:** 24 electoral districts.

Economy: Chief crops: Bananas, coffee, sugarcane, corn. **Minerals:** Salt. **Other resources:** Fish. **Per capita arable land:** 0.3 acres. **Electricity prod.** (1977): 7.00 mln. kwh.

Finance: Currency: Escudo (Sept. 1983: 72.67 = $1 US). **Gross domestic product** (1979 est.): $57 mln. **Per capita income** (1979): $200. **Imports** (1979): $40 mln.; partners: Port. 58%, Neth. 5%. **Exports** (1979): $4 mln.; partners: Port. 63%, Ang. 14%, UK 5%, Zaire 5%.

Transport: Motor vehicles: in use (1977): 3,100 passenger cars, 900 comm. vehicles. **Chief ports:** Mindelo, Praia.

Communications: Radios: 36,000 licensed (1976). **Telephones in use** (1978): 1,717.

Health: Life expectancy at birth (1975): 56.3 male; 60.0 female. **Births** (per 1,000 pop. 1978): 29. **Deaths** (per 1,000 pop. 1978): 8. **Natural increase** (1978): 2.1%. **Pop. per hospital bed** (1977): 516. **Pop. per physician** (1977): 7,750. **Infant mortality** (per 1,000 live births 1975): 104.9.

Education (1981): **Literacy:** 37%.

Embassy: 3415 Massachusetts Ave. NW 20007; 965-6820.

The uninhabited Cape Verdes were discovered by the Portuguese in 1456 or 1460. The first Portuguese colonists landed in 1462; African slaves were brought soon after, and most Cape Verdeans descend from both groups. Cape Verde independence came July 5, 1975. The islands have suffered from repeated extreme droughts and famines, especially 1978. Emphasis is placed on the development of agriculture and on fishing, which accounts for 70% of export earnings.

Central African Republic

People: Population (1983 est.): 2,512,000. **Pop. density:** 10.82 per sq. mi. **Ethnic groups:** Banda 27%, Baya 34%, Mandja 21%, Sara 10%. **Languages:** French (official), local dialects. **Religions:** Protestant 25%, Roman Catholic 25%, traditional 24%.

Geography: Area: 240,324 sq. mi., slightly smaller than Texas. **Location:** In central Africa. **Neighbors:** Chad on N, Cameroon on W, Congo, Zaire on S, Sudan on E. **Topography:** Mostly rolling plateau, average altitude 2,000 ft., with rivers draining S to the Congo and N to Lake Chad. Open, well-watered savanna covers most of the area, with an arid area in NE, and tropical rainforest in SW. **Capital:** Bangui. **Cities** (1983 est.): Bangui (met.) 375,000.

Government: Type: Republic. **Head of state:** Gen. Andre Kolingba; in office: Sept. 1, 1981. **Local divisions:** 16 prefectures. **Defense:** 14.2% of govt., budget.

Economy: Industries: Textiles, light manuf. **Chief crops:** Cotton, coffee, peanuts, corn, sorghum. **Minerals:** Diamonds (chief export), uranium, iron, copper. **Other resources:** Timber. **Arable land:** 15%. **Electricity prod.** (1981): 65 mln. kwh. **Labor force:** 88% agric.

Finance: Currency: CFA franc (Mar. 1984: 399 = $1 US). **Gross domestic product** (1982): $627 mln. **Per capita in-**

come (1982): $310. **Imports** (1981): $145 mln.; partners (1981): Fr. 58%. **Exports** (1981): $118 mln.; partners (1980): Fr. 52%, Bel.-Lux. 14%. **International reserves less gold** (Oct. 1983): $35.3 mln. **Gold:** 11,000 oz t. **Consumer prices** (change in 1982): 14%.

Transport: Motor vehicles: in use (1979): 10,000 passenger cars, 6,000 comm. vehicles.

Communications: Radios: 77,000 in use (1977).

Health: Life expectancy at birth (1983): 44 years. **Births** (per 1,000 pop. 1978): 47. **Deaths** (per 1,000 pop. 1978): 20%. **Natural increase** (1978): 2.7%. **Hospital beds** (per 100,000 pop. 1977): 138. **Physicians** (per 100,000 pop. 1977): 5. **Infant mortality** (per 1,000 live births 1983): 148.

Education (1983): **Literacy:** 20%. **Attendance:** primary school 64%; secondary school 11%.

Embassy: 1618 22d St. NW 20008; 483-7800.

Various Bantu tribes migrated through the region for centuries before French control was asserted in the late 19th century, when the region was named Ubangi-Shari. Complete independence was attained Aug. 13, 1960.

All political parties were dissolved in 1960, and the country became a center for Chinese political influence in Africa. Relations with China were severed after 1965. Elizabeth Domitien, premier 1975-76, was the first woman to hold that post in an African country. Pres. Jean-Bedel Bokassa, who seized power in a 1965 military coup, proclaimed himself constitutional emperor of the renamed Central African Empire Dec. 1976.

Emp. Bokassa's rule was characterized by virtually unchecked ruthless and cruel authority, and human rights violations. Bokassa was ousted in a bloodless coup aided by the French government, Sept. 20, 1979, and replaced by his cousin David Dacko, former president from 1960 to 1965. In 1981, the political situation deteriorated amid strikes and economic crisis. Gen. Kolingba replaced Dacko as head of state in a bloodless coup.

Chad
Republic of Chad

People: Population (1983 est.): 4,990,000. **Age distrib.** (%): 0–14: 40.7; 15–59: 54.9; 60+: 4.4. **Pop. density:** 8.69 per sq. mi. **Urban** (1978): 18.4%. **Ethnic groups:** Sudanese Arab 30%, Sudanic tribes 25%, Nilotic, Saharan tribes. **Languages:** French (official), Arabic, others. **Religions:** Moslems 44%, animist 23%, Christian 33%.

Geography: Area: 495,755 sq. mi., four-fifths the size of Alaska. **Location:** In central N. Africa. **Neighbors:** Libya on N, Niger, Nigeria, Cameroon on W, Central African Republic on S, Sudan on E. **Topography:** Southern wooded savanna, steppe, and desert, part of the Sahara, in the N. Southern rivers flow N to Lake Chad, surrounded by marshland. **Capital:** N'Djamena. **Cities** (1979 est.): N'Djamena (met.) 303,000.

Government: Head of state: Hissen Habre; b. 1942; in office: June 19, 1982. **Local divisions:** 14 prefectures with appointed governors. **Armed forces:** regulars 20,000.

Economy: Chief crops: Cotton. **Minerals:** Uranium. **Arable land:** 7%. **Fish catch** (1981): 115,000 metric tons. **Electricity prod.** (1978): 62.40 mln. kwh. **Labor force:** 85% agric.

Finance: Currency: CFA franc (Mar. 1984: 399 = $1 US). **Gross domestic product** (1976 est.): $540 mln. **Per capita income** (1976): $73. **Imports** (1979): $140 mln.; partners (1976): Fr. 47%, Nigeria 22%. **Exports** (1979): $58 mln.; partners (1976): Nigeria 19%, Fr. 13%, Jap. 13%. **Tourist receipts** (1977): $7 mln. **National budget** (1978): $64 mln. revenues; $64 mln. expenditures. **International reserves less gold** (Oct. 1983): $8.2 mln. **Gold:** 11,000 oz t.

Transport: Motor vehicles: in use (1979): 10,000 passenger cars, 10,000 comm. vehicles.

Communications: Radios: 70,000 in use (1981). **Telephones in use** (1978): 3,850.

Health: Life expectancy at birth (1964): 29 male; 35 female. **Births** (per 1,000 pop. 1978): 50. **Deaths** (per 1,000 pop. 1978): 26. **Natural increase** (1978): 2.4%. **Hospital beds** (per 100,000 pop. 1977): 82. **Physicians** (per 100,000 pop. 1977): 2. **Infant mortality** (per 1,000 live births 1975): 160.

Education (1978): **Literacy:** 15%. **Pop. 5-19:** in school: 18%, teachers per 1,000: 2.

Embassy: 2002 R St. NW 20009; 462-4009.

Chad was the site of paleolithic and neolithic cultures before the Sahara Desert formed. A succession of kingdoms and Arab slave traders dominated Chad until France took control around 1900. Independence came Aug. 11, 1960.

Northern Moslem rebels, have fought animist and Christian southern government and French troops from 1966, despite numerous cease-fires and peace pacts.

Libyan troops entered the country at the request of the Chad government, December 1980. On Jan. 6, 1981 Libya and Chad announced their intention to unite. France together with several African nations condemned the agreement as a menace to African security. The Libyan troops were withdrawn from Chad in November 1981.

Rebel forces, led by Hissen Habre, captured the capital and forced Pres. Oueddei to flee the country in June 1982.

In 1983, France sent some 3,000 troops to Chad to assist Habre in opposing Libyan-backed rebels.

Chile
Republic of Chile

People: Population (1983 est.): 11,486,000. **Age distrib.** (%): 0–14: 32.2; 15–59: 59.7; 60+: 8.1. **Pop. density:** 38.76 per sq. mi. **Urban** (1983): 82%. **Ethnic groups:** Mestizo 66%, Spanish 25%, Indian 5%. **Languages:** Spanish. **Religions:** Predominantly Roman Catholic.

Geography: Area: 292,135 sq. mi., larger than Texas. **Location:** Occupies western coast of southern S. America **Neighbors:** Peru on N, Bolivia on NE, Argentina on E. **Topography:** Andes Mtns. are on E border including some of the world's highest peaks; on W is 2,650-mile Pacific Coast. Width varies between 100 and 250 miles. In N is Atacama Desert, in center are agricultural regions, in S are forests and grazing lands. **Capital:** Santiago. **Cities** (1983 metro est.) Santiago 4,085,000.

Government: Head of state: Pres. Augusto Pinochet Ugarte; b. Nov. 25, 1915; in office: Sept. 11, 1973. **Local divisions:** 12 regions and Santiago region. **Defense:** 6.5% of GNP (1982).

Economy: Industries: Steel, textiles, wood products. **Chief crops:** Grain, onions, beans, potatoes, peas, fruits, grapes. **Minerals:** Copper (27% world resources), molybdenum, nitrates, iodine (half world output), iron, coal, oil, gas, gold, cobalt, zinc, manganese, borate, mica, mercury, salt, sulphur, marble, onyx. **Crude oil reserves** (1980): 400 mln. bbls. **Other resources:** Water, forests. **Arable land:** 6%. **Meat prod.** (1983): beef: 205,000 metric tons; pork: 61,000 metric tons; lamb: 21,000 metric tons. **Fish catch** (1981): 3.3 mln. metric tons. **Electricity prod.** (1982): 11.8 bln. kwh. **Crude steel prod.** (1982): 481,000 metric tons. **Labor force:** 9% agric.; 33% ind & comm., 31% serv.

Finance: Currency: Peso (Apr. 1984: 88 = $1 US). **Gross domestic product** (1982): $23.6 bln. **Per capita income** (1979): $1,950. **Imports** (1983): $2.7 bln.; partners: U.S. 26%, Braz. 7%. **Exports** (1983): $3.8 bln.; partners: W. Ger. 11%, Jap. 11%, U.S. 21%. **Tourists** (1980): 326,415. **National budget** (1982): $9.4 bln. **International reserves less gold** (Feb. 1984): $2.1 bln. **Gold:** 1.53 mln. oz. t. **Consumer prices** (change in 1983): 27.3%

Transport: Railway traffic (1982): 1.5 bln. passenger-km; 1.7 bln. net ton-km. **Motor vehicles:** in use (1981): 505,000 passenger cars, 210,000 comm. vehicles. **Civil aviation** (1982): 1.7 bln. passenger-km; 137 mln. net ton-km. **Chief ports:** Valparaiso, Arica, Antofagasta.

Communications: Television sets: 1.2 mln. in use (1980). **Radios:** 3.2 mln. in use (1980). **Telephones in use** (1981): 570,000.

Health: Life expectancy at birth (1983): 63.8 male; 70.4 female. **Births** (per 1,000 pop. 1980): 22. **Deaths** (per 1,000 pop. 1978): 7. **Natural increase** (1978): 1.5%. **Hospital beds** (per 100,000 pop. 1977): 359. **Physicians** (per 100,000 pop. 1977): 62. **Infant mortality** (per 1,000 live births 1981): 27.2.

Education (1983): **Literacy:** 90%. **Pop. 5–19:** in school: 71%, teachers per 1,000: 25.

Embassy: 1732 Massachusetts Ave. NW 20036; 785-1746.

Northern Chile was under Inca rule before the Spanish conquest, 1536-40. The southern Araucanian Indians resisted until the late 19th century. Independence was gained 1810-18, under Jose de San Martin and Bernardo O'Higgins; the latter, as supreme director 1817-23, sought social and economic reforms until deposed. Chile defeated Peru and Bolivia in 1836-39 and 1879-84, gaining mineral-rich northern land.

Eduardo Frei Montalva came into office in 1964, instituting social programs and gradual nationalization of foreign-owned mining companies. In 1970, Salvador Allende Gossens, a Marxist, became president with a third of the national vote.

The Allende government furthered nationalizations, and improved conditions for the poor. But illegal and violent actions by extremist supporters of the government, the regime's failure to attain majority support, and poorly planned socialist economic programs led to political and financial chaos.

A military junta seized power Sept. 11, 1973, and said Allende killed himself. The junta named a mostly military cabinet, and announced plans to "exterminate Marxism."

Repression continued during 1984 with no sign of any political liberalization.

Tierra del Fuego is the largest (18,800 sq. mi.) island in the archipelago of the same name at the southern tip of South America, an area of majestic mountains, tortuous channels, and high winds. It was discovered 1520 by Magellan and named the Land of Fire because of its many Indian bonfires. Part of the island is in Chile, part in Argentina. Punta Arenas, on a mainland peninsula, is a center of sheep-raising and the world's southernmost city (pop. 67,600); Puerto Williams, pop. 949, is the southernmost settlement.

China

People's Republic of China

People: Population (1983 est.): 1,022,054,000. **Pop. density:** 278.24 per sq. mi. **Ethnic groups:** Han Chinese 94%, Mongol, Korean, Manchu, others. **Languages:** Mandarin Chinese (official), Shanghai, Canton, Fukien, Hakka dialects; Tibetan, Vigus (Turkic). **Religions:** officially atheist; Confucianism, Buddhism, Taoism, are traditional.

Geography: Area: 3,691,521 sq. mi., slightly larger than the U.S. **Location:** Occupies most of the habitable mainland of E. Asia. **Neighbors:** Mongolia on N, USSR on NE and NW, Afghanistan, Pakistan on W, India, Nepal, Bhutan, Burma, Laos, Vietnam on S, N. Korea on NW. **Topography:** Two-thirds of the vast territory is mountainous or desert, and only one-tenth is cultivated. Rolling topography rises to high elevations in the N in the Daxinganlingshanmai separating Manchuria and Mongolia; the Tienshan in Xinjiang; the Himalayan and Kunlunshanmai in the SW and in Tibet. Length is 1,860 mi. from N to S, width E to W is more than 2,000 mi. The eastern half of China is one of the best-watered lands in the world. Three great river systems, the Changjiang, the Huanghe, and the Xijiang provide water for vast farmlands. **Capital:** Peking. **Cities** (1981 est.): Shanghai 12,000,000; Peking 8,500,000; Tianjin 7,200,000; Canton 5,200,000; Shenyang 4,800,000; Wuhan 4,400,000; Chendu 4,000,000.

Government: People's Republic. **Head of state:** Pres. Li Xiannian; in office: June 18, 1983. **Head of government:** Party Chairman Hu Yaobang, b. 1915; in office: June 29, 1981. **Effective head of government:** Premier Zhao Ziyang; b. 1919; in office: Sept. 1980. **Local divisions:** 21 provinces, 5 autonomous regions, and 3 cities. **Defense:** 8.5% of GNP (1982).

Economy: Industries: Iron and steel, plastics, agriculture implements, trucks. **Chief crops:** Grain, rice, cotton. **Minerals:** Tungsten, antimony, coal, iron, lead, manganese, mercury, molybdenum, phosphates, potash, tin. **Crude oil reserves** (1980): 20 bln. bbls. **Other resources:** Silk. **Arable land:** 11%. **Meat prod.** (1983): beef: 2.5 mln. metric tons; pork: 17 mln. metric tons; lamb: 793,000 metric tons. **Fish catch** (1981): 4.6 mln. metric tons. **Electricity prod.** (1982): 327 bln. kwh. **Crude steel prod.** (1982): 37.1 mln. metric tons. **Labor force:** 74% agric.; 15% ind. & comm.

Finance: Currency: Yuan (Mar. 1984): 2.05 = $1 US). **Gross national product** (1981): $301 bln. **Per capita income** (1980): $566. **Imports** (1983): $21.3 bln.; partners: Jap. 22%, U.S. 18%, Hong Kong 12%. **Exports** (1983): $22.1 bln.; partners: Hong Kong 24%, Jap. 23%, U.S. 10%. **National budget** (1982): $56.8 bln. revenues, $58.3 bln. expenditures. **International reserves less gold** (Dec. 1983): 14.8 bln. **Gold:** 12.7 mln. oz t.

Transport: Railway traffic (1982): 157 bln. net ton-km. **Motor vehicles:** in use (1980): 60,000 passenger cars, 870,000

comm. vehicles. **Civil aviation** (1982): 6 bln. passenger km, 200 mln. net ton-km. **Chief ports:** Shanghai, Tianjin, Luda.

Communications: Television sets: over 15 mln. in use (1983). **Radios:** 190 mln. in use (1983). **Telephones** (1983): 2.4 mln.; **Daily newspaper circ.** (1982): 74 per 1,000 pop.

Health: Life expectancy at birth (1984): 68 years. **Births** (per 1,000 pop. 1980): 21.3. **Deaths** (per 1,000 pop. 1980): 7.4. **Natural increase** (1978): 1.6%. **Hospital beds** (1980): 1.9 mln. **Physicians** (1980): 891,000 Western style, 262,000 Chinese medicine.

Education (1984): **Literacy:** 75%. Years compulsory 5; first grade enrollment 93%.

Embassy: 2300 Conn. Ave. NW 20008; 328-2520.

History. Remains of various man-like creatures who lived as early as several hundred thousand years ago have been found in many parts of China. Neolithic agricultural settlements dotted the Huanghe basin from about 5,000 BC. Their language, religion, and art were the sources of later Chinese civilization.

Bronze metallurgy reached a peak and Chinese pictographic writing, similar to today's, was in use in the more developed culture of the Shang Dynasty (c. 1500 BC-c. 1000 BC) which ruled much of North China.

A succession of dynasties and interdynastic warring kingdoms ruled China for the next 3,000 years. They expanded Chinese political and cultural domination to the south and west, and developed a brilliant technologically and culturally advanced society. Rule by foreigners (Mongols in the Yuan Dynasty, 1271-1368, and Manchus in the Ch'ing Dynasty, 1644-1911) did not alter the underlying culture.

A period of relative stagnation left China vulnerable to internal and external pressures in the 19th century. Rebellions left tens of millions dead, and Russia, Japan, Britain, and other powers exercised political and economic control in large parts of the country. China became a republic Jan. 1, 1912, following the Wuchang Uprising inspired by Dr. Sun Yat-sen.

For a period of 50 years, 1894-1945, China was involved in conflicts with Japan. In 1895, China ceded Korea, Taiwan, and other areas. On Sept. 18, 1931, Japan seized the Northeastern Provinces (Manchuria) and set up a puppet state called Manchukuo. The border province of Jehol was cut off as a buffer state in 1933. Japan invaded China proper July 7, 1937. After its defeat in World War II, Japan gave up all seized land.

Following World War II, internal disturbances arose involving the Kuomintang, communists, and other factions. China came under domination of communist armies, 1949-1950. The Kuomintang government moved to Taiwan, 90 mi. off the mainland, Dec. 8, 1949.

The People's Republic of China was proclaimed in Peking Sept. 21, 1949, by the Chinese People's Political Consultative Conference under Mao Tse-tung.

China and the USSR signed a 30-year treaty of "friendship, alliance and mutual assistance," Feb. 15, 1950.

The U.S. refused recognition of the new regime. On Nov. 26, 1950, the People's Republic sent armies into Korea against U.S. troops and forced a stalemate.

By the 1960s, relations with the USSR deteriorated, with disagreements on borders, idealogy and leadership of world communism. The USSR cancelled aid accords, and China, with Albania, launched anti-Soviet propaganda drives. High level talks were held with the USSR in 1982 and 1983 to seek improved trade and cultural contracts; little progress was reported.

On Oct. 25, 1971, the UN General Assembly ousted the Taiwan government from the UN and seated the People's Republic in its place. The U.S. had supported the mainland's admission but opposed Taiwan's expulsion.

U.S. Pres. Nixon visited China Feb. 21-28, 1972, on invitation from Premier Chou En-lai, ending years of antipathy between the 2 nations. China and the U.S. opened liaison offices in each other's capitals, May-June 1973. The U.S., Dec. 15, 1978, formally recognized the People's Republic of China as the sole legal government of China; diplomatic relations between the 2 nations were established, Jan. 1, 1979. President Ronald Reagan and Premier Zhao Ziyang exchanged visits in 1984.

In a continuing "reassessment" of the policies of Mao Zedong, Mao's widow, Jiang Quing, and other Gang of Four members were convicted of "committing crimes during the 'Cultural Revolution,' " Jan. 25, 1981. The ouster of Hua Guofeng, Jun. 29, 1981, the handpicked successor of Mao, was seen as another step in China's attempt to redefine Maoist policies.

Internal developments. After an initial period of consolidation, 1949-52, industry, agriculture, and social and economic institutions were forcibly molded according to Maoist ideals. However, frequent drastic changes in policy and violent factionalism interfered with economic development

In 1957, Mao Tse-tung admitted an estimated 800,000 people had been executed 1949-54; opponents claimed much higher figures.

The Great Leap Forward, 1958-60, tried to force the pace of economic development through intensive labor on huge new rural communes, and through emphasis on ideological purity and enthusiasm. The program caused resistance and was largely abandoned. Serious food shortages developed, and the government was forced to buy grain from the West.

The Great Proletarian Cultural Revolution, 1965, was an attempt to oppose pragmatism and bureaucratic power and instruct a new generation in revolutionary principles. Massive purges took place. A program of forcibly relocating millions of urban teenagers into the countryside was launched.

By 1968 the movement had run its course; many purged officials returned to office in subsequent years, and reforms in education and industry that had placed ideology above expertise were gradually weakened.

In the mid-1970s, factional and ideological fighting increased, and emerged into the open after the 1976 deaths of Mao and Premier Chou En-lai. Mao's widow and 3 other leading leftists were purged and placed under arrest, after reportedly trying to seize power. Their opponents said the "gang of four" had used severe repression and mass torture, had sparked local fighting and had disrupted production. The new ruling group modified Maoist policies in education, culture, and industry, and sought better ties with non-communist countries.

Relations with Vietnam deteriorated in 1978 as China charged persecution of ethnic Chinese. In retaliation for Vietnam's invasion of Cambodia, China attacked 4 Vietnamese border provinces Feb. 17, 1979; heavy border fighting ensued.

The first Chinese atomic bomb was exploded in 1964; the first hydrogen bomb in 1967. There is a growing stockpile of nuclear weapons and intermediate range missiles. Long range missiles have been tested. The Chinese navy has been built into one of the world's largest. The first orbiting space satellite was launched in 1970.

Sweeping reforms of the central bureaucracy were announced March 1982.

Manchuria. Home of the Manchus, rulers of China 1644-1911, Manchuria has accommodated millions of Chinese settlers in the 20th century. Under Japanese rule 1931-45, the area became industrialized. China no longer uses the name Manchuria for the region, which is divided into the 3 NE provinces of Heilongjiang, Jilin, and Liaoning.

Guandong is the southernmost part of Manchuria. Russia in 1898 forced China to lease it Guandong, and built Port Arthur (Lushun) and the port of Dairen (Luda). Japan seized Port Arthur in 1905. It was turned over to the USSR by the 1945 Yalta agreement, but finally returned to China in 1950.

Inner Mongolia was organized by the People's Republic in 1947. Its boundaries have undergone frequent changes, reaching its greatest extent (and restored in 1979) in 1956, with an area of 460,000 sq. mi., allegedly in order to dilute the minority Mongol population. Chinese settlers outnumber the Mongols more than 10 to 1. Total pop., 8.5 million. Capital: Hohhot.

Xinjiang Uygur Autonomous Region, in Central Asia, is 633,802 sq. mi., pop. 11 million (75% Uygurs, a Turkic Moslem group, with a heavy Chinese increase in recent years). Capital: Urumqi. It is China's richest region in strategic minerals. Some Uygurs have fled to the USSR, claiming national oppression.

Tibet, 470,000 sq. mi., is a thinly populated region of high plateaus and massive mountains, the Himalayas on the S, the Kunluns on the N. High passes connect with India and Nepal; roads lead into China proper. Capital: Lhasa. Average altitude is 15,000 ft. Jiachan, 15,870 ft., is believed to be the highest inhabited town on earth. Agriculture is primitive. Pop. 1.7 million (of whom 500,000 are Chinese). Another 4 million Tibetans form the majority of the population of vast adjacent areas that have long been incorporated into China.

China ruled all of Tibet from the 18th century, but independence came in 1911. China reasserted control in 1951, and a communist government was installed in 1953, revising the theocratic Lamaist Buddhist rule. Serfdom was abolished, but all land remained collectivized.

A Tibetan uprising within China in 1956 spread to Tibet in 1959. The rebellion was crushed with Chinese troops, and Buddhism was almost totally suppressed. The Dalai Lama and 100,000 Tibetans fled to India.

China (Taiwan)
Republic of China

People: Population (1983 est.): 18,786,000. **Pop. density:** 1,181 per sq. mi. **Ethnic groups:** Han Chinese 98% (18% from mainland), aborigines (of Indonesian origin) 2%. **Languages:** Mandarin Chinese (official), Taiwan, Hakka dialects. **Religions:** Buddhism, Taoism, Confucianism prevail.

Geography: Area: 13,814 sq. mi., the size of Maryland and Delaware combined. **Location:** Off SE coast of China, between E. and S. China Seas. **Neighbors:** Nearest is China. **Topography:** A mountain range forms the backbone of the island; the eastern half is very steep and craggy, the western slope is flat, fertile, and well-cultivated. **Capital:** Taipei. **Cities** (1982 est.): Taipei (met.) 2,298,000; Kaohsiung 1,200,000; Taichung 606,734; Tainan 582,199.

Government: Type: One-party system. **Head of state:** Chiang Ching-kuo; b. Mar. 18, 1910; in office: May 20, 1978. **Head of government:** Prime Min. Sun Yun-suan; b. Nov. 11, 1913; in office: May 30, 1978. **Local divisions:** Taiwan province, Taipei and Kaohsiung municipalities. **Defense:** 9% of GNP (1981).

Economy: Industries: Textiles, clothing, electronics, processed foods, chemicals, plastics. **Chief crops:** Rice, bananas, pineapples, sugarcane, sweet potatoes, peanuts. **Minerals:** Coal, limestone, marble. **Crude oil reserves** (1980): 10.2 mln. bbls. **Cultivated land:** 25%. **Meat prod.** (1977): beef: 15,798 metric tons; pork: 574,656 metric tons. **Fish catch** (1981): 911,678 metric tons. **Electricity prod.** (1981): 40.1 bln. kwh. **Crude steel prod.** (1982): 4.1 mln. metric tons. **Labor force:** 20% agric.; 41% ind. & comm.; 32% services.

Finance: Currency: New Taiwan dollar (Sept. 1983: 40.15 = $1 US). **Gross national product** (1981): $46.2 bln. **Per capita income** (1981): $2,570. **Imports** (1981): $21.1 bln.; partners: U.S. 24%, Jap. 25%, Kuw. 7%, Saudi Ar. 10%. **Exports** (1981): $22.6 bln.; partners: U.S. 39%, Jap. 11%, Hong Kong 7%. **Tourists** (1981): 1.1 mln.; receipts: $1 bln. **National budget** (1981): $23.2 bln. **International reserves less gold** (Mar. 1980): $1.51 bln. **Gold:** 2.49 mln. oz t. **Consumer prices** (change in 1979): 9.7%.

Transport: Motor vehicles: in use (1982): 592,000 passenger cars, 314,000 comm. vehicles. **Civil Aviation** (1982): 8.1 bln. passenger-km; 1.2 mln. net ton-km. **Chief ports:** Kaohsiung; Keelung, Hualien, Taichung.

Communications: Television sets: 3.9 mln. in use (1980). **Radios:** 1.4 mln. in use (1976). **Telephones in use** (1981): 2.8 mln. **Daily newspaper circ.** (1982): 163 per 1,000 pop.

Health: Life expectancy at birth (1983): 69.6 male; 74.5 female. **Births** (per 1,000 pop. 1981): 22.9. **Deaths** (per 1,000 pop. 1981): 4.8. **Natural increase** (1981): 1.81%. **Hospital beds** (per 100,000 pop. 1977): 143. **Physicians** (1981): 20,779 **Infant mortality** (per 1,000 live births 1983): 11.1.

Education (1983): **Literacy:** 89%. Years compulsory 9; attendance 99%.

Large-scale Chinese immigration began in the 17th century. The island came under mainland control after an interval of Dutch rule, 1620-62. Taiwan (also called Formosa) was ruled by Japan 1895-1945. Two million Kuomintang supporters fled to Taiwan in 1949. Both the Taipei and Peking governments consider Taiwan an integral part of China. Taiwan has rejected Peking's efforts at reunification.

The U.S. upon its recognition of the People's Republic of China, Dec. 15, 1978, severed diplomatic ties with Taiwan. It maintains the unofficial American Institute in Taiwan, while Taiwan has established the Coordination Council for North American Affairs in Washington, D.C.

Land reform, government planning, U.S. aid and investment, and free universal education have brought huge advances in industry, agriculture, and mass living standards.

The Penghu (Pescadores), 50 sq. mi., pop. 120,000, lie between Taiwan and the mainland. **Quemoy** and **Matsu,** pop. (1980) 61,000 lie just off the mainland.

Colombia

Republic of Colombia

People: Population (1983 est.): 27,663,000. **Age distrib.** (%): 0–14: 44.6; 15–59: 50.7; 60+: 4.7. **Pop. density:** 60.44 per sq. mi. **Urban** (1979): 69%. **Ethnic groups:** Mestizo 58%, Caucasian 20%, Mulatto 14%, Negro 4%, Indian 1%. **Languages:** Spanish. **Religions:** Roman Catholic 97%.

Geography: Area: 440,831 sq. mi., about the size of Texas and New Mexico combined. **Location:** At the NW corner of S. America. **Neighbors:** Panama on NW, Ecuador, Peru on S, Brazil, Venezuela on E. **Topography:** Three ranges of Andes, the Western, Central, and Eastern Cordilleras, run through the country from N to S. The eastern range consists mostly of high table lands, densely populated. The Magdalena R. rises in Andes, flows N to Carribean, through a rich alluvial plain. Sparsely-settled plains in E are drained by Orinoco and Amazon systems. **Capital:** Bogota. **Cities** (1981 est.): Bogota 4,486,200; (1973 cen.); Medellin 1,112,390; Cali 967,908; Barranquilla 690,471.

Government: Type: Republic. **Head of state:** Pres. Belisario Betancur Cuartas; in office: Aug. 7, 1982. **Local divisions:** 23 departments, 8 national territories, and special district of Bogota. **Defense:** 5.5% of govt. budget (1981).

Economy: Industries: Textiles, processed goods, hides, steel, cement, chemicals. **Chief crops:** Coffee (50% of exports), rice, tobacco, cotton, sugar, bananas. **Minerals:** Oil, gas, emeralds (90% world output), gold, copper, lead, coal, iron, nickel, salt. **Crude oil reserves** (1981): 3.2 bln. bbls. **Other resources:** Rubber, balsam, dye-woods, copaiba, hydro power. **Arable land:** 5%. **Meat prod.** (1983): beef: 542,000 metric tons; pork: 61,000 metric tons; lamb 13,000 metric tons. **Fish catch** (1978): 64,000 metric tons. **Electricity prod.** (1981): 23.6 bln. kwh. **Crude steel prod.** (1982): 215,000 metric tons. **Labor force:** 27% agric.; 21% man.; 18% services.

Finance: Currency: Peso (Mar. 1984: 94.4 = $1 US). **Gross national product** (1981): $33.9 bln. **Per capita income** (1981): $1,112. **Imports** (1983): $4.9 bln.; partners: U.S. 34%, Jap. 10%. **Exports** (1983): $3.0 bln.; partners: U.S. 23%, W. Ger. 20%, Venez. 12%. **Tourists** (1981): 1.2 mln.; receipts: $357 mln. **National budget** (1981): $4.8 bln. **International reserves less gold** (Mar. 1984): $1.2 bln. **Gold** 4.08 mln. oz t. **Consumer prices** (change in 1983): 19.8.

Transport: Railway traffic (1980): 312 mln. passenger-km; 888 mln. net ton-km. **Motor vehicles:** in use (1981): 672,385 passenger cars, 110,943 comm. vehicles; assembled (1976): 26,900 passenger cars; 9,500 comm. vehicles. **Civil aviation** (1982): 4.1 bln. passenger-km; 240 mln. net ton-km. **Chief ports:** Buena Ventura, Santa Marta, Barranquilla, Cartagena.

Communications: Television sets: 2.2 mln. in use (1981). **Radios:** 3 mln. in use (1981). **Telephones in use** (1981): 1.1 mln. **Daily newspaper circ.** (1982): 48 per 1,000 pop.

Health: Life expectancy at birth (1979): 65 male; 70 female. **Births** (per 1,000 pop. 1978): 31. **Deaths** (per 1,000 pop. 1978): 8. **Natural increase** (1978): 2.1%. **Hospital beds** (per 100,000 pop. 1977): 161. **Physicians** (per 100,000 pop. 1977): 51. **Infant mortality** (per 1,000 live births 1982): 65%.

Education (1978): **Literacy:** 82%. Only 28% finish primary school.

Embassy: 2118 Leroy Pl. NW, 20008; 387-8338.

Spain subdued the local Indian kingdoms (Funza, Tunja) by the 1530s, and ruled Colombia and neighboring areas as New Granada for 300 years. Independence was won by 1819. Venezuela and Ecuador broke away in 1829-30, and Panama withdrew in 1903.

One of the few functioning Latin American democracies, Colombia is nevertheless plagued by rural and urban violence, though scaled down from "La Violencia" of 1948-58, which claimed 200,000 lives. Attempts at land and social reform, and progress in industrialization have not yet succeeded in reducing massive social problems aggravated by a very high birth rate.

A national state of siege was declared, May 1, 1984, following the assassination of the justice minister.

Comoros

Federal Islamic Republic of the Comoros

People: Population (1983 est.): 442,000. **Age distrib.** (%): 0–14: 43.0; 15–59: 47.0; 60+: 8.0. **Pop. density:** 461.76 per sq. mi. **Ethnic groups:** Arabs, Africans, East Indians. **Languages:** Arabic, French (official), Comoran. **Religions:** Islam (official).

Geography: Area: 838 sq. mi., half the size of Delaware. **Location:** 3 islands (Grande Comore, Anjouan, and Moheli) in the Mozambique Channel between NW Madagascar and SE Africa. **Neighbors:** Nearest are Mozambique on W, Madagascar on E. **Topography:** The islands are of volcanic origin, with an active volcano on Grand Comoro. **Capital:** Moroni. **Cities** (1982 est.): Moroni (met.) 22,000.

Government: Type: Republic. **Head of state:** Pres. Ahmed Abdallah; b. 1919; in office: May 23, 1978. **Head of govt.:** Prime Min. Ali Mroudjae; in office: Feb. 8, 1982. **Local divisions:** each of the 3 main islands is a prefecture.

Economy: Industries: Perfume. **Chief crops:** Vanilla, copra, perfume plants, fruits. **Arable land:** 45%. **Electricity prod.** (1977): 3.0 mln. kwh. **Labor force:** 87% agric.

Finance: Currency: CFA franc (Sept. 1982: 353 = $1 US). **Gross national product** (1979 est.): $92.4 mln. **Per capita income** (1982): $240. **Imports** (1979): $24 mln.; partners: Fr. 41%, Madag. 20%, Pak. 8%, Ken. 5%. **Exports** (1979): $15 mln.; partners: Fr. 65%, U.S. 21%, Mad. 5%.

Transport: Chief ports: Dzaoudzi.

Communications: Radios: 36,000 in use (1976). **Telephones in use** (1979): 1,100.

Health: Life expectancy at birth (1975): 43.4 male; 46.6 female. **Births** (per 1,000 pop. 1978): 43. **Deaths** (per 1,000 pop. 1978): 18. **Natural increase** (1978): 2.5%. **Infant mortality** (per 1,000 live births 1975): 51.7.

Education (1982): **Literacy:** 15%; less than 20% attend secondary school.

The islands were controlled by Moslem sultans until the French acquired them 1841-1909. A 1974 referendum favored independence, with only the Christian island of Mayotte preferring association with France. The French National Assembly decided to allow each of the islands to decide its own fate. The Comoro Chamber of Deputies declared independence July 6, 1975. In a referendum in 1976, Mayotte voted to remain French. A leftist regime that seized power in 1975 was deposed in a pro-French 1978 coup.

Congo

People's Republic of the Congo

People: Population (1983 est.): 1,694,000. **Pop. density:** 11.66 per sq. mi. **Ethnic groups:** Bakongo 45%, Bateke 20%, others. **Languages:** French (official), Bantu dialects. **Religions:** Christians 50% (two-thirds Roman Catholic), animists 47%, Muslim 2%.

Geography: Area: 132,046 sq. mi., slightly smaller than Montana. **Location:** In western central Africa. **Neighbors:** Gabon, Cameroon on W, Central African Republic on N, Zaire on E, Angola (Cabinda) on SW. **Topography:** Much of the Congo is covered by thick forests. A coastal plain leads to the fertile Niari Valley. The center is a plateau; the Congo R. basin consists of flood plains in the lower and savanna in the upper portion. **Capital:** Brazzaville. **Cities** (1980 est.): Brazzaville (met.) 200,000; Pointe-Noire 135,000; Loubomo 34,000.

Government: Type: People's Republic. **Head of state:** Pres. Denis Sassou-Nguesso; b. 1943; in office: Feb. 8, 1979. **Head of government:** Prime Min. Louis Sylvain Ngoma; b. 1941; in office: Dec. 18, 1975. **Local divisions:** 9 regions and capital district. **Defense:** 17% of govt. budget (1978).

Economy: Chief crops: Palm oil and kernels, cocoa, coffee, tobacco. **Minerals:** Oil, potash, natural gas. **Crude oil reserves** (1980): 400 mln. bbls. **Arable land:** 2%. **Fish catch** (1978):

17,300 metric tons. **Electricity prod.** (1981): 165 mln. kwh. **Labor force:** 90% agric.
Finance: Currency: CFA franc (Mar. 1984: 399 = $1 US).
Gross domestic product (1978 est.): $89 mln. **Per capita income** (1978): $500. **Imports** (1978): $261 mln.; partners (1978): Fr. 50%, W. Ger. 5%. **Exports** (1977): $185 mln.; partners (1978): Ital. 31%, Fr. 24%, Sp. 8%. **Tourist receipts** (1977): $4 mln. **International reserves less gold** (Oct. 1983): $3.6 mln. **Gold:** 11,000 oz t. **Consumer prices** (change in 1983): 7.8%.
Transport: Railway traffic (1980): 286 mln. passenger-km; 470 mln. net ton-km. **Motor vehicles:** in use (1980): 20,000 passenger cars, 14,000 comm. vehicles. **Chief ports:** Pointe-Noire, Brazzaville.
Communications: Television sets: 3,500 in use (1980). **Radios:** 92,000 in use (1980). **Telephones in use** (1980): 14,000.
Health: Life expectancy at birth (1980): 46.9 male; 50.2 female. **Births** (per 1,000 pop. 1978): 45. **Deaths** (per 1,000 pop. 1978): 18. **Natural increase** (1978): 2.7%. **Hospital beds** (per 100,000 pop. 1977): 499. **Physicians** (per 100,000 pop. 1977): 14. **Infant mortality** (per 1,000 live births 1978): 200.
Education (1980): **Literacy:** 80%. Years compulsory 10; attendance 80%.
Embassy: 4891 Colorado Ave. NW 20011; 726-5500.

The Loango Kingdom flourished in the 15th century, as did the Anzico Kingdom of the Batekes; by the late 17th century they had become weakened. France established control by 1885. Independence came Aug. 15, 1960.
After a 1963 coup sparked by trade unions, the country adopted a Marxist-Leninist stance, with the USSR and China vying for influence. Tribal divisions remain strong. France remains a dominant trade partner and source of technical assistance, and French-owned private enterprise retained a major economic role. However, the government of Pres. Sassou-Nguesso favored a strengthening of relations with the USSR, a socialist constitution was adopted, 1979, and on May 13, 1981 a treaty of friendship and cooperation was signed with the Soviets.

Costa Rica
Republic of Costa Rica

People: Population (1983 est.): 2,624,000. **Age distrib.** (%): 0–14: 44.0; 15–59: 50.4; 60+: 5.6. **Pop. density:** 115.2 per sq. mi. **Urban** (1980): 43%. **Ethnic groups:** Spanish (with Mestizo minority). **Language:** Spanish (official). **Religions:** Roman Catholicism prevails.
Geography: Area: 19,653 sq. mi., smaller than W. Virginia. **Location:** In central America. **Neighbors:** Nicaragua on N, Panama on S. **Topography:** Lowlands by the Caribbean are tropical. The interior plateau, with an altitude of about 4,000 ft., is temperate. **Capital:** San Jose. **Cities** (1982 est.): San Jose 867,800; Alajuela (1979 est.) 40,000; Cartago (1979 est.) 40,000.
Government: Type: Democratic Republic. **Head of state:** Pres. Luis Alberto Monge Alvarez; b. Dec. 29, 1925; in office May 8, 1982. **Local divisions:** 7 provinces and 80 cantons. **Armed forces:** para-military 5,000.
Economy: Industries: Fiberglass, aluminum, textiles, fertilizers, roofing, cement. **Chief crops:** Coffee (chief export), bananas, sugar, cocoa, cotton, hemp. **Minerals:** Gold, salt, sulphur, iron. **Other resources:** Fish, forests. **Arable land:** 10%. **Meat prod.** (1980): beef: 81,000 metric tons; pork: 10,000 metric tons. **Fish catch** (1978): 14,500 metric tons. **Electricity prod.** (1981): 2.3 bln. kwh. **Labor force:** 33% agric.; 40% ind. & comm.; 25% service and government.
Finance: Currency: Colone (Mar. 1984: 43.40 = $1 US). **Gross domestic product** (1981): $4.9 bln. **Per capita income** (1981): $2,238. **Imports** (1980): $1.46 bln.; partners: U.S. 33%, Jap. 10%, Guat. 5%, W. Ger. 5%. **Exports** (1980): $1.0 bln.; partners: U.S. 33%, W. Ger. 11%. **Tourists** (1980): 345,000; receipts: $87 mln. **National budget** (1979): $217 mln. revenues; $332 mln. expenditures. **International reserves less gold** (Mar. 1984): $388.7 mln. **Gold:** 95,000 oz t. **Consumer prices** (change in 1983): 32.6%.
Transport: Railway traffic (1979): 81 mln. passenger-km; 14 mln. net ton-km. **Motor vehicles:** in use (1981): 48,188 passenger cars, 13,863 comm. vehicles. **Civil aviation** (1981): 530 mln.

passenger-km; 21 mln. net ton-km. **Chief ports:** Limon, Puntarenas.
Communications: Television sets: 162,000 in use (1981). **Radios:** 180,000 in use (1981). **Telephones in use** (1981): 236,000. **Daily newspaper circ.** (1982): 121 per 1,000 pop.
Health: Life expectancy at birth (1981): 67.5 male; 71.9 female. **Births** (per 1,000 pop. 1978): 31. **Deaths** (per 1,000 pop. 1978): 5. **Natural increase** (1978): 2.6%. **Hospital beds** (per 100,000 pop 1977): 345. **Physicians** (per 100,000 pop. 1977): 72. **Infant mortality** (per 1,000 live births 1982): 37.6.
Education (1982): **Literacy:** 90%. Years compulsory 6; attendance 99%.
Embassy: 2112 S St. NW, 20008; 234-2945.

Guaymi Indians inhabited the area when Spaniards arrived, 1502. Independence came in 1821. Costa Rica seceded from the Central American Federation in 1838. Since the civil war of 1948-49, there has been little violent social conflict, and free political institutions have been preserved.
Costa Rica, though still a largely agricultural country, has achieved a relatively high standard of living and social services, and land ownership is widespread.

Cuba
Republic of Cuba

People: Population (1983 est.): 9,889,000. **Age distrib.** (%): 0–29: 57.8; 30–59: 31.3; 60+: 10.9. **Pop. density:** 224 per sq. mi. **Urban** (1981): 67%. **Ethnic groups:** Spanish, African. **Languages:** Spanish. **Religions:** Roman Catholic 42%, none 49%.
Geography: Area: 44,218 sq. mi., nearly as large as Pennsylvania. **Location:** Westernmost of West Indies. **Neighbors:** Bahamas, U.S., on N, Mexico on W, Jamaica on S, Haiti on E. **Topography:** The coastline is about 2,500 miles. The N coast is steep and rocky, the S coast low and marshy. Low hills and fertile valleys cover more than half the country. Sierra Maestra, in the E is the highest of 3 mountain ranges. **Capital:** Havana. **Cities** (1981 cen.): Havana 1,924,886; Santiago de Cuba 563,455; Camaguey 480,620.
Government: Type: Communist state. **Head of state:** Pres. Fidel Castro Ruz; b. Aug. 13, 1926; in office: Dec. 3, 1976 (formerly Prime Min. since Feb. 16, 1959). **Local divisions:** 14 provinces, 169 municipal assemblies. **Armed forces:** regulars 189,000; reserves 90,000.
Economy: Industries: Texiles, wood products, cement, chemicals, cigars. **Chief crops:** Sugar (83% of exports), tobacco, coffee, pineapples, bananas, citrus fruit, coconuts. **Minerals:** Cobalt, nickel, iron, copper, manganese, salt. **Other resources:** Forests. **Arable land:** 40%. **Meat prod.** (1983): beef: 162,000 metric tons; pork: 73,000 metric tons. **Fish catch** (1978): 213,200 metric tons. **Electricity prod.** (1982): 10.7 bln. kwh. **Crude steel prod.** (1981): 300,000 metric tons. **Labor force:** 30% agric.; 45% ind. & comm.; 20% services.
Finance: Currency: Peso (Sept. 1983: .87 = $1 US). **Gross national product** (1979): $13.9 bln. **Per capita income** (1981): $840. **Imports** (1979): $5.1 bln.; partners (1980): USSR 62%, Jap. 8%, Canada 6%. **Exports** (1979): $5.3 bln.; partners (1980): USSR 64%.
Transport: Railway traffic (1981): 1.8 bln. passenger-km; 2.6 bln. net ton-km. **Motor vehicles:** in use (1979): 152,600 passenger cars, 40,000 comm. vehicles. **Civil aviation** (1981): 1.2 bln. passenger-km.; 14.5 mln. net ton-km. **Chief ports:** Havana, Matanzas, Cienfuegos, Santiago de Cuba.
Communications: Television sets: 1.2 mln. in use (1981). **Radios:** 2.9 mln. in use (1981). **Telephones in use** (1980): 390,000. **Daily newspaper circ.** (1982): 133 per 1,000 pop.
Health: Life expectancy at birth: (1980): 71.0 male; 74.0 female. **Births** (per 1,000 pop. 1982): 16.3. **Deaths** (per 1,000 pop. 1982): 5.8. **Natural increase** (1978): 1.2%. **Hospital beds** (per 100,000 pop. 1977): 413. **Physicians** (per 100,000 pop. 1977): 94. **Infant mortality** (per 1,000 live births 1983): 25.
Education (1983): **Literacy:** 96%. School is free & compulsory between ages 6–14.

Some 50,000 Indians lived in Cuba when it was discovered by Columbus in 1492. Its name derives from the Indian Cubanacan. Except for British occupation of Havana, 1762-63, Cuba remained Spanish until 1898. A slave-based sugar plantation economy developed from the 18th century, aided by early mechanization of milling. Sugar remains the chief product and chief export despite government attempts to diversify.

A ten-year uprising ended in 1878 with guarantees of rights by Spain, which Spain failed to carry out. A full-scale movement under Jose Marti began Feb. 24, 1895.

The U.S. declared war on Spain in April, 1898, after the sinking of the U.S.S. Maine in Havana harbor, and defeated it in the short Spanish-American War. Spain gave up all claims to Cuba. U.S. troops withdrew in 1902, but under 1903 and 1934 agreements, the U.S. leases a site at Guantanamo Bay in the SE as a naval base. U.S. and other foreign investments acquired a dominant role in the economy. In 1952, former president Fulgencio Batista seized control and established a dictatorship, which grew increasingly harsh and corrupt. Former student leader Fidel Castro assembled a rebel band in 1956; guerrilla fighting intensified in 1958. Batista fled Jan. 1, 1959, and in the resulting political vacuum Castro took power, becoming premier Feb. 16.

The government, quickly dominated by extreme leftists, began a program of sweeping economic and social changes, without restoring promised liberties. Opponents were imprisoned and some were executed. Some 700,000 Cubans emigrated in the years after the Castro takeover, mostly to the U.S.

Cattle and tobacco lands were nationalized, while a system of cooperatives was instituted. By the end of 1960 all banks and industrial companies had been nationalized, including over $1 billion worth of U.S.-owned properties, mostly without compensation.

Poor sugar crops resulted in collectivization of farms, stringent labor controls, and rationing, despite continued aid from the USSR and other Communist countries.

The U.S. cut back Cuba's sugar quota in 1960, and imposed a partial export embargo, which became total in 1962, severely damaging the economy. In 1961, some 1,400 Cubans, trained and backed by the U.S. Central Intelligence Agency, unsuccessfully tried to invade and overthrow the regime. It was revealed in 1975 that CIA agents had plotted to kill Castro in 1959 or 1960.

In the fall of 1962, the U.S. learned that the USSR had brought nuclear missiles to Cuba. After an Oct. 22 warning from Pres. Kennedy, the missiles were removed.

In 1973, Cuba and the U.S. signed an agreement providing for extradition or punishment of hijackers of planes or vessels, and for each nation to bar activity from its territory against the other. In 1977, the 2 countries signed agreements to exchange diplomats, without restoring full ties, and to regulate offshore fishing. In 1978, and again in 1980, the U.S. agreed to accept political prisoners released by Cuba some of whom, it was later discovered, were criminals and mental patients .

But relations are strained by ongoing Cuban military involvement abroad. In 1975-78, Cuba sent over 20,000 troops to aid one faction in the Angola Civil War. Some 25,000 Cuban troops or advisers are stationed in Africa, mainly in Angola and Ethiopia. This presence, along with Cuba's growing involvement in Central America and the Caribbean has contributed to worsening relations with the U.S.

In 1983, 24 Cubans died and over 700 were captured, later repatriated, as a result of the U.S. led invasion of Grenada.

Cyprus
Republic of Cyprus

People: Population (1983 est.): 653,000. **Age distrib.** (%): 0–14: 25.0; 15–59: 61.0; 60+: 14.0. **Pop. density:** 176.37 per sq. mi. **Urban** (1974): 42.2%. **Ethnic groups:** Greeks 80%, Turks 18.7%, Armenians, Maronites. **Languages:** Greek, Turkish. **Religions:** Orthodox 77%, Moslems 18%.

Geography: Area: 3,572 sq. mi., smaller than Connecticut. **Location:** In eastern Mediterranean Sea, off Turkish coast. **Neighbors:** Nearest are Turkey on N, Syria, Lebanon on E. **Topography:** Two mountain ranges run E-W, separated by a wide, fertile plain. **Capital:** Nicosia. **Cities** (1982 est.): Nicosia 121,500.

Government: Type: Republic. **Head of state:** Pres. Spyros Kyprianou; b. Oct. 28, 1932; in office: Aug. 3, 1977. **Local divisions:** 6 districts. **Defense:** 6.3% of govt. budget (1981). Greek: regulars 9,000; Turkish: 4,500 (1980).

Economy: Industries: Wine, clothing, construction. **Chief crops:** Grains, grapes, carobs, citrus fruits, potatoes, olives.

Minerals: Copper, iron, asbetos, gypsum, umber. **Per capita arable land:** 1.5 acres. **Meat prod.** (1980): pork: 15,000 metric tons; lamb: 10,000 metric tons. **Electricity prod.** (1982): 1.1 mln. kwh. **Labor force:** 20% agric.; 22% ind., 19% comm., 16% serv.

Finance: Currency: Pound (Mar. 1984: 0.46 = $1 US). **Gross domestic product** (1980): $2.12 bln. **Per capita income** (1981): $2,940. **Imports** (1980): $1.21 bln.; partners (1982): UK 13%, Gre. 7%. **Exports** (1980): $536 mln.; partners (1982): UK 20%, Leb. 12%, Sau. Ar. 9%. **Tourists** (1981): 429,000; receipts: $244 mln. **National budget** (1980): $331 mln. revenues; $244 mln. expenditures. **International reserves less gold** (Mar. 1984): $519.2 mln. **Gold:** 459,000 oz. t. **Consumer prices** (change in 1983): 5%.

Transport: Motor vehicles: in use (1981): 96,000 passenger cars, 26,000 comm. vehicles. **Civil aviation** (1982): 854 mln. passenger-km; 19.9 mln. net ton-km. **Chief ports:** Famagusta, Limassol.

Communications: Television sets: 150,000 licensed (1981). **Radios:** 313,000 licensed (1981). **Telephones in use** (1981): 113,400. **Daily newspaper circ.** (1981): 137 per 1,000 pop.

Health: Life expectancy at birth (1981): 69.5 male; 73.4 female. **Births** (per 1,000 pop. 1981): 20.6. **Deaths** (per 1,000 pop. 1981): 8.3. **Natural increase** (1978): .7%. **Hospital beds** (per 100,000 pop. 1981): 600. **Physicians** (per 100,000 pop. 1981): 100. **Infant mortality** (per 1,000 live births 1982): 16.

Education (1982): **Literacy:** 89%. **Pop. 15-19:** in school: 66%, teachers per 1,000: 22.

Embassy: 2211 R St. NW, 20008; 462-5772.

Agitation for enosis (union) with Greece increased after World War II, with the Turkish minority opposed, and broke into violence in 1955-56. In 1959, Britain, Greece, Turkey, and Cypriot leaders approved a plan for an independent republic, with constitutional guarantees for the Turkish minority and permanent division of offices on an ethnic basis. Greek and Turkish Communal Chambers dealt with religion, education, and other matters.

Archbishop Makarios, formerly the leader of the enosis movement, was elected president, and full independence became final Aug. 16, 1960. Makarios was re-elected in 1968 and 1973.

Further communal strife led the United Nations to send a peace-keeping force in 1964; its mandate has been repeatedly renewed.

The Cypriot National Guard, led by officers from the army of Greece, seized the government July 15, 1974, and named Nikos Sampson, an advocate of union with Greece, president. Makarios fled the country. On July 20, Turkey invaded the island; Greece mobilized its forces but did not intervene. A cease-fire was arranged July 22. On the 23d, Sampson turned over the presidency to Glafkos Clerides (on the same day, Greece's military junta resigned). A peace conference collapsed Aug. 14; fighting resumed. By Aug. 16 Turkish forces had occupied the NE 40% of the island, despite the presence of UN peace forces. Makarios resumed the presidency in Dec., until his death, 1977.

Turkish Cypriots voted overwhelmingly, June 8, 1975, to form a separate Turkish Cypriot federated state. A president and assembly were elected in 1976. Some 200,000 Greeks have been expelled from the Turkish-controlled area, replaced by thousands of Turks, some from the mainland.

A unilateral declaration of independence was announced by Turkish-Cypriot leader Rauf Denktash, Nov. 15, 1983. The new state, which was not recognized by other nations, was named the Turkish Rep. of Northern Cyprus.

Czechoslovakia
Czechoslovak Socialist Republic

People: Population (1983 est.): 15,420,000. **Age distrib.** (%): 0–14: 24.3; 15–59: 59.9; 60+: 15.7. **Pop. density:** 310.30 per sq. mi. **Urban** (1980): 65.5%. **Ethnic groups:** Czechs 65%, Slovaks 30%, Hungarians 4%, Germans, Poles, Ukrainians. **Languages:** Czech, Slovak (both official). **Religions:** Roman Catholics were majority, Lutherans, Orthodox.

Geography: Area: 49,365 sq. mi., the size of New York. **Location:** In E central Europe. **Neighbors:** Poland, E. Germany on N, W. Germany on W. Austria, Hungary on S, USSR on E. **Topography:** Bohemia, in W, is a plateau surrounded by mountains; Moravia is hilly. Slovakia, in E, has mountains (Carpathi-

ans) in N, fertile Danube plain in S. Vltava (Moldau) and Labe (Elbe) rivers flow N from Bohemia to G. **Capital:** Prague. **Cities** (1981 est.): Prague 1.1 mln.; Brno 369,000; Bratislava 368,000; Ostrava 322,000.
Government: Type: Communist. **Head of state:** Pres. Gustav Husak; b. Jan 10, 1913; in office: May 29, 1975; **Head of government:** Prime Min. Lubomir Strougal; b. Oct. 19, 1924; in office: Jan. 28, 1970. **Head of Communist Party:** First Sec. Gustav Husak; in office: Apr. 17, 1969. **Local divisions:** Czech and Slovak republics each have an assembly. **Defense:** 7.3% of govt. budget (1982).
Economy: Industries: Machinery, oil products, iron and steel, glass, chemicals, motor vehicles, cement. **Chief crops:** Wheat, sugar beets, potatoes, rye, corn, barley. **Minerals:** Mercury, coal, iron. Jachymor has Europe's greatest pitchblende (for uranium and radium) deposits. **Per capita arable land:** 0.8 acres. **Meat prod.** (1983): beef: 375,000 metric tons; pork: 770,000 metric tons; lamb 7,000 metric tons. **Electricity prod.** (1981): 74 bln. kwh. **Crude steel prod.** (1982): 14.9 mln. metric tons. **Labor force:** 12% agric.; 66% ind., comm.; 18% service, govt.
Finance: Currency: Koruna (Sept. 1983: 6.45 = $1 US). **Gross national product** (1980): $89 bln. **Per capita income** (1980): $5,800. **Imports** (1982): $15.6 bln.; partners (1982): USSR 43%, E. Ger. 9%, Pol. 6%, W. Ger. 5%. **Exports** (1982): $15.7 bln.; partners (1981): USSR 38%, E. Ger. 10%, Pol. 7%, Hung. 5%. **Tourists** (1978): 14.4 mln. **Consumer prices** (change in 1982): 8%.
Transport: Railway traffic (1980): 18.0 bln. passenger-km; 73.2 bln. net ton-km. **Motor vehicles:** in use (1980): 2.2 mln. passenger cars, 324,800 comm. vehicles; manuf. (1982): 173,000 passenger cars; 90,000 comm. vehicles. **Civil aviation** (1982): 1.5 bln. passenger-km; 17.1 mln. net ton-km.
Communications: Television sets: 4.2 mln. licensed (1982), 482,000 manuf. (1978). **Radios:** 4 mln. licensed (1982), 241,000 manuf. (1978). **Telephones in use** (1981): 3.2 mln. **Daily newspaper circ.** (1982): 283 per 1,000 pop.
Health: Life expectancy at birth (1980): 66.8 male; 74.0 female. **Births** (per 1,000 pop. 1982): 15.2 **Deaths** (per 1,000 pop. 1982): 11.7. **Natural increase** (1978): .7%. **Hospital beds** (per 100,000 pop. 1977): 1,229. **Physicians** (per 100,000 pop. 1977): 254. **Infant mortality** (per 1,000 live births 1981): 16.8.
Education (1981): **Literacy:** 99%. **Pop. 5–19:** in school: 60%, teachers per 1,000: 30.
Embassy: 3900 Linnean Ave. NW 20008; 263-6315.

Bohemia, Moravia and Slovakia were part of the Great Moravian Empire in the 9th century. Later, Slovakia was overrun by Magyars, while Bohemia and Moravia became part of the Holy Roman Empire. Under the kings of Bohemia, Prague in the 14th century was the cultural center of Central Europe. Bohemia and Hungary became part of Austria-Hungary.

In 1914-1918 Thomas G. Masaryk and Eduard Benes formed a provisional government with the support of Slovak leaders including Milan Stefanik. They proclaimed the Republic of Czechoslovakia Oct. 30, 1918.

By 1938 Nazi Germany had worked up disaffection among German-speaking citizens in Sudetenland and demanded its cession. Prime Min. Neville Chamberlain of Britain, with the acquiescense of France, signed with Hitler at Munich, Sept. 30, 1938, an agreement to the cession, with a guarantee of peace by Hitler and Mussolini. Germany occupied Sudetenland Oct. 1-2.

Hitler on Mar. 15, 1939, dissolved Czechoslovakia, made protectorates of Bohemia and Moravia, and supported the autonomy of Slovakia, which was proclaimed independent Mar. 14, 1939, with Josef Tiso president.

Soviet troops with some Czechoslovak contingents entered eastern Czechoslovakia in 1944 and reached Prague in May 1945; Benes returned as president. In May 1946 elections, the Communist Party won 38% of the votes, and Benes accepted Klement Gottwald, a Communist, as prime minister. Tiso was executed in 1947.

In February, 1948, the Communists seized power in advance of scheduled elections. In May 1948 a new constitution was approved. Benes refused to sign it. On May 30 the voters were offered a one-slate ballot and the Communists won full control. Benes resigned June 7. Gottwald became president and Benes died Sept. 3. A harsh Stalinist period followed, with complete and violent suppression of all opposition.

In Jan. 1968 a liberalization movement spread explosively through Czechoslovakia. Antonin Novotny, long the Stalinist

boss of the nation, was deposed as party leader and succeeded by Alexander Dubcek, a Slovak, who declared he intended to make communism democratic. On Mar. 22 Novotny resigned as president and was succeeded by Gen. Ludvik Svoboda. On Apr. 6, Premier Joseph Lenart resigned and was succeeded by Oldrich Cernik, whose new cabinet was pledged to carry out democratization and economic reforms.

In July 1968 the USSR and 4 Warsaw Pact nations demanded an end to liberalization. On Aug. 20, the Russian, Polish, East German, Hungarian, and Bulgarian armies invaded Czechoslovakia.

Despite demonstrations and riots by students and workers, press censorship was imposed, liberal leaders were ousted from office and promises of loyalty to Soviet policies were made by some old-line Communist Party leaders.

On Apr. 17, 1969, Dubcek resigned as leader of the Communist Party and was succeeded by Gustav Husak. In Jan. 1970, Premier Cernik was ousted. Censorship was tightened and the Communist Party expelled a third of its members. In 1972, more than 40 liberals were jailed on subversion charges. In 1973, amnesty was offered to some of the 40,000 who fled the country after the 1968 invasion, but repressive policies continue to remain in force.

More than 700 leading Czechoslovak intellectuals and former party leaders signed a human rights manifesto in 1977, called Charter 77, prompting a renewed crackdown by the regime.

Czechoslovakia has long been an industrial and technological leader of the eastern European countries, though its relative standing has declined in recent years because of the government's rejection of economic reforms.

Denmark
Kingdom of Denmark

People: Population (1983 est.): 5,115,000. **Age distrib. (%):** 0–14: 19.5 15–44: 44.2; 45+: 35.8. **Pop. density:** 308 per sq. mi. **Urban** (1979): 83.3%. **Ethnic groups:** Almost all Scandinavian. **Languages:** Danish. **Religions:** Predominantly Lutherans.
Geography: Area: 16,633 sq. mi., the size of Massachusetts and New Hampshire combined. **Location:** In northern Europe, separating the North and Baltic seas. **Neighbors:** W. Germany on S., Norway on NW, Sweden on NE. **Topography:** Denmark consists of the Jutland Peninsula and about 500 islands, 100 inhabited. The land is flat or gently rolling, and is almost all in productive use. **Capital:** Copenhagen. **Cities** (1982): Copenhagen 645,198; Arhus 246,679.
Government: Type: Constitutional Monarchy. **Head of state:** Queen Margrethe II; b. Apr. 16, 1940; in office: Jan. 14, 1972. **Head of government:** Prime Min. Poul Schluter; b. 1929; in office: Sept. 10, 1982. **Local divisions:** 14 counties and one city (Copenhagen). **Defense:** 2.2% of GNP (1981).
Economy: Industries: Machinery, textiles, furniture, electronics. **Chief crops:** Dairy products. **Crude oil reserves** (1980): 375 mln. bbls. **Per capita arable land:** 1.2 acres. **Meat prod.** (1983): beef: 375,000 metric tons; pork: 1 mln. metric tons. **Fish catch** (1981): 1.8 mln. metric tons. **Electricity prod.** (1982): 22.0 bln. kwh. **Crude steel prod.** (1982): 560,000 metric tons. **Labor force:** 8.2% agric.; 45% manuf.
Finance: Currency: Krone (Mar. 1984: 9.54 = $1 US). **Gross domestic product** (1980): $66.40 bln. **Per capita income** (1980): $12,956. **Imports** (1983): $16.2 bln.; partners (1982): W. Ger. 20%, Swed. 12%, UK 11%, Neth. 7%. **Exports** (1983): $16.0 bln.; partners (1982): W. Ger. 17%, UK 14%, Swed. 11%, Nor. 6%. **Tourists** (1980): 3.5 mln. visitors; receipts: 1.2 bln. **National budget** (1980): $15.4 bln. revenues; $16.9 bln. expenditures. **International reserves less gold** (Mar. 1984): $3.3 bln. **Gold:** 1.62 mln. oz t. **Consumer prices** (change in 1983): 6.9%.
Transport: Railway traffic (1980): 3.3 bln. passenger-km; 1.5 bln. net ton-km. **Motor vehicles:** in use (1981): 1.3 mln. passenger cars, 242,800 comm. vehicles. **Civil aviation** (1982): 2.9 bln. passenger-km; 128.6 mln. net ton-km. **Chief ports:** Copenhagen, Alborg, Arhus, Odense.
Communications: Television sets: 1.8 mln. licensed (1982). **Radios:** 1.9 mln. licensed (1982). **Telephones in use** (1981): 3.3 mln. **Daily newspaper circ.** (1982): 356 per 1,000 pop.
Health: Life expectancy at birth (1981): 71.3 male; 77.4 female. **Births** (per 1,000 pop. 1982): 10.3. **Deaths** (per 1,000

pop. 1982): 10.8. **Natural increase** (1978): .2%. **Hospital beds** (per 100,000 pop. 1977): 853. **Physicians** (per 100,000 pop. 1977): 204. **Infant mortality** (per 1,000 live births 1982): 7.9. **Education** (1981): **Literacy:** 99%. Years compulsory 9; attendance 100%. **Embassy:** 3200 Whitehaven St. NW 20008; 234-4300.

The origin of Copenhagen dates back to ancient times, when the fishing and trading place named Havn (port) grew up on a cluster of islets, but Bishop Absalon (1128-1201) is regarded as the actual founder of the city.

Danes formed a large component of the Viking raiders in the early Middle Ages. The Danish kingdom was a major north European power until the 17th century, when it lost its land in southern Sweden. Norway was separated in 1815, and Schleswig-Holstein in 1864. Northern Schleswig was returned in 1920. Severe economic difficulties plagued Denmark in 1982 as foreign debt grew to 25% of GNP.

The **Faeroe Islands** in the N. Atlantic, about 300 mi. NE of the Shetlands, and 850 mi. from Denmark proper, 18 inhabited, have an area of 540 sq. mi. and pop. (1982) of 45,000. They are self-governing in most matters.

Greenland
(Kalaallit Nunaat)

Greenland, a huge island between the N. Atlantic and the Polar Sea, is separated from the North American continent by Davis Strait and Baffin Bay. Its total area is 840,000 sq. mi., 84% of which is ice-capped. Most of the island is a lofty plateau 9,000 to 10,000 ft. in altitude. The average thickness of the cap is 1,000 ft. The population (1982 est.) is 51,000. Under the 1953 Danish constitution the colony became an integral part of the realm with representatives in the Folketing. The Danish parliament, 1978, approved home rule for Greenland, effective May 1, 1979. Accepting home rule the islanders elected a socialist-dominated legislature, Apr. 4th. With home rule, Greenlandic place names came into official use. The technically-correct name for Greenland is now Kalaallit Nunaat; its capital is Nuuk, rather than Gothab. Fish is the principal export.

Djibouti
Republic of Djibouti

People: Population (1983 est.): 316,000. **Pop. density:** 12.23 per sq. mi. **Ethnic groups:** Issa (Somali) 60%; Afar 35%; European, Arab. **Languages:** French (official); Somali, Saho-Afar, Arabic. **Religions:** Most are Moslems.
Geography: Area: 8,996 sq. mi., about the size of New Hampshire. **Location:** On E coast of Africa, separated from Arabian Peninsula by the strategically vital strait of Bab el-Mandeb. **Neighbors:** Ethiopia on N (Eritrea) and W, Somalia on S. **Topography:** The territory, divided into a low coastal plain, mountains behind, and an interior plateau, is arid, sandy, and desolate. The climate is generally hot and dry. **Capital:** Djibouti. **Cities** (1980): Djibouti (met.) 200,000.
Government: Type: Republic. **Head of state:** Pres. Hassan Gouled Aptidon b. 1916; in office: June 24, 1977; **Head of government:** Prem. Barkat Gourat Hamadou; in office: Sept. 30, 1978. **Local divisions:** 5 cercles (districts).
Economy: Minerals: Salt. **Electricity prod.** (1977): 62 mln. kwh.
Finance: Currency Franc (Sept. 1983: 177 = $1 US). **Gross domestic product:** $331 mln. **Per capita income** (1982): $400. **Imports** (1979): $140 mln.; partners (1979): Fr. 47%, Jap. 8%, UK 8%. **Exports** (1979): $20 mln.; partners (1979): Fr. 87%.
Transport: Motor vehicles: in use (1977): 11,800 passenger cars, 3,300 commercial vehicles. **Chief ports:** Djibouti.
Communications: Television sets: 10,000 in use (1979). **Radios:** 16,000 in use (1979). **Telephones in use** (1980): 4,000.
Health: Life expectancy at birth (1982): 50 years. **Births** (per 1,000 pop. 1978): 49. **Deaths** (per 1,000 pop. 1978): 23. **Natural increase** (1978): 9.2%.
Education (1981): **Literacy:** 20%.
Embassy: 866 United Nations Plaza, New York, NY 10017; (212) 753-3163.

France gained control of the territory in stages between 1862 and 1900.

Ethiopia and Somalia have renounced their claims to the area, but each has accused the other of trying to gain control. There were clashes between Afars (ethnically related to Ethiopians) and Issas (related to Somalis) in 1976. Immigrants from both countries continued to enter the country up to independence, which came June 27, 1977.

Unemployment is about 80%. There are few natural resources; trade is the main contributor to domestic product. French aid is the mainstay of the economy and some 5,000 French troops are present.

Dominica
Commonwealth of Dominica

People: Population (1983 est.): 74,000. **Pop. density:** 275.86 per sq. mi. **Ethnic groups:** nearly all African or mulatto, Caribs. **Languages:** English (official), French patois. **Religions:** mainly Roman Catholic.
Geography: Area: 290 sq. mi., about one-fourth the size of Rhode Island. **Location:** In Eastern Caribbean, most northerly Windward Is. **Neighbors:** Guadeloupe to N, Martinique to S. **Topography:** Mountainous, a central ridge running from N to S, terminating in cliffs; volcanic in origin, with numerous thermal springs; rich deep topsoil on leeward side, red tropical clay on windward coast. **Capital** (1981 est.) Roseau 20,000.
Government: Head of state: Pres. Aurelius Marie; in office: 1980. **Head of government:** Prime Min. Mary Eugenia Charles; b. 1919; in office: July 21, 1980. **Local divisions:** 25 village councils and 2 town councils.
Economy: Industries: Agriculture, tourism. **Chief crops:** Bananas, citrus fruits, coconuts. **Minerals:** Pumice. **Other resources:** Forests. **Per capita arable land:** 0.2 acres. **Electricity prod.** (1977): 16 mln. kwh.
Finance: Currency: East Caribbean dollar (Mar. 1984: 2.70 = $1 US). **Gross domestic product** (1977): $33.48 mln. **Per capita income** (1976): $460. **Imports** (1978): $28.4 mln.; partners (1978): UK 27%, U.S. 15%, Can. 5%. **Exports** (1978): $15.8 mln.; partners (1978): UK 67%. **Tourists** (1977): 31,000; receipts: $3 mln. **National budget** (1976): $6.29 mln. revenues; $7.51 mln. expenditures. **Consumer prices** (change in 1983): 4.1%.
Transport: Chief ports: Roseau.
Communications: Telephones in use (1982): 2,972.
Health: Life expectancy at birth (1962): 56.97 male; 59.18 female. **Births** (per 1,000 pop. 1978): 21.4. **Deaths** (per 1,000 pop. 1978): 5.3. **Natural increase** (1978): 1.6%. **Hospital beds** (1982): 237. **Physicians** (1982): 25. **Infant mortality** (per 1,000 live births 1978): 19.6.
Education: Pop. 5–19: in school (1975): 24,113.

A British colony since 1805, Dominica was granted self government in 1967. Independence was achieved Nov. 3, 1978.

Hurricane David struck, Aug. 30, 1979, devastating the island and destroying the banana plantations, Dominica's economic mainstay. Coups were attempted in 1980 and 1981.

Dominica took a leading role in the instigation of the October 1983 invasion of Grenada.

Dominican Republic

People: Population (1983 est.): 6,248,000. **Age distrib.** (%): 0–14: 47.5; 15–59: 47.5; 60 +: 4.9. **Pop. density:** 273.74 per sq. mi. **Urban** (1981): 52.0%. **Ethnic groups:** Caucasian 16%, mulatto 73%, Negro 11%. **Languages:** Spanish. **Religions:** Roman Catholic 98%.
Geography: Area: 18,704 sq. mi., the size of Vermont and New Hampshire combined. **Location:** In West Indies, sharing I. of Hispaniola with Haiti. **Neighbors:** Haiti on W. **Topography:** The Cordillera Central range crosses the center of the country, rising to over 10,000 ft., highest in the Caribbean. The Cibao valley to the N is major agricultural area. **Capital:** Santo Domingo. **Cities** (1981 est.): Santo Domingo 1,313,000; Santiago de Los Caballeros 326,000.
Government: Type: Representative Democracy. **Head of state:** Pres. Salvador Jorge Blanco; b. July 5, 1926, in office:

Aug. 16, 1982. **Local divisions:** 26 provinces and Santo Domingo. **Defense:** 1.4% of GDP. (1980).

Economy: Industries: Sugar refining, cement, textiles, pharmaceuticals. **Chief crops:** sugar, cocoa, coffee, tobacco, rice. **Minerals:** Nickel, gold, silver, bauxite. **Other resources:** Timber. **Arable land:** 25%. **Meat prod.** (1980): beef: 43,000 metric tons; pork: 12,000 metric tons. **Electricity prod.** (1981): 3.3 bln. kwh **Labor force:** 47% agric., 23% manuf.

Finance: Currency: Peso (Feb. 1984: 1 = $1 US). **Gross domestic product** (1980): $6.7 bln. **Per capita income** (1980): $1,221. **Imports** (1983): $1.4 bln.; partners (1982): U.S. 39%, Venez. 18%, Mex. 14%. **Exports** (1983): $780 mln.; partners (1982): U.S. 54%, Swit. 12%, USSR 8%, Neth. 5%. **Tourists** (1977): 265,000; receipts: $93 mln. **National budget** (1979): $745.6 mln. revenues; $973.9 mln. expenditures. **International reserves less gold** (Mar. 1984): $110.3 mln **Gold:** 18,000 oz t. **Consumer prices** (change in 1982): 7.6%

Transport: Motor vehicles: in use (1981): 102,100 passenger cars, 56,830 comm. vehicles. **Chief ports:** Santo Domingo, San Pedro de Macoris, Puerto Plata.

Communications: Television sets: 385,000 in use (1981). **Radios:** 220,000 in use (1981). **Telephones in use** (1981): 165,253. **Daily newspaper circ.** (1982): 52 per 1,000 pop.

Health: Life expectancy at birth (1961): 57.15 male; 58.59 female. **Births** (per 1,000 pop. 1978): 36. **Deaths** (per 1,000 pop. 1978): 9. **Natural increase** (1978): 2.5%. **Hospital beds** (per 100,000 pop. 1977): 233. **Physicians** (per 100,000 pop. 1977): 53. **Infant mortality** (per 1,000 live births 1981): 96.

Education (1981): **Literacy:** 62%. Years compulsory 8; attendance 60%

Embassy: 1715-22d St. NW 20008; 332-6280.

Carib and Arawak Indians inhabited the island of Hispaniola when Columbus landed in 1492. The city of Santo Domingo, founded 1496, is the oldest settlement by Europeans in the hemisphere and has the supposed ashes of Columbus in an elaborate tomb in its ancient cathedral.

The western third of the island was ceded to France in 1697. Santo Domingo itself was ceded to France in 1795. Haitian leader Toussaint L'Ouverture seized it, 1801. Spain returned intermittently 1803-21, as several native republics came and went. Haiti ruled again, 1822-44, and Spanish occupation occurred 1861-63.

The country was occupied by U.S. Marines from 1916 to 1924, when a constitutionally elected government was installed.

In 1930, Gen. Rafael Leonidas Trujillo Molina was elected president. Trujillo ruled brutally until his assassination in 1961. Pres. Joaquin Balaguer, appointed by Trujillo in 1960, resigned under pressure in 1962. Juan Bosch, elected president in the first free elections in 38 years, was overthrown in 1963.

On April 24, 1965, a revolt was launched by followers of Bosch and others, including a few communists. Four days later U.S. Marines intervened against the pro-Bosch forces. Token units were later sent by 5 So. American countries as a peace-keeping force.

A provisional government supervised a June 1966 election, in which Balaguer defeated Bosch by a 3-2 margin; there were some charges of election fraud.

The Inter-American Peace Force completed its departure Sept. 20, 1966. Balaguer was reelected, 1970 and 1974, the latter time without real opposition.

Continued depressed world prices have affected the main export commodity, sugar.

Ecuador
Republic of Ecuador

People: Population (1983 est.): 8,811,000. **Age distrib.** (%): 0–14: 44.5; 15–59: 49.6; 60+: 6.0. **Pop. density:** 79.00 per sq. mi. **Urban** (1978): 42.8% **Ethnic groups:** Indians 25%, Mestizos 55%, Spanish 10%, Negroes 10%. **Languages:** Spanish (official), Quechuan, Jivaroan. **Religions:** Predominantly Roman Catholic.

Geography: Area: 108,624 sq. mi., the size of Colorado. **Location:** In NW S. America, on Pacific coast, astride Equator. **Neighbors:** Colombia to N, Peru to E and S. **Topography:** Two ranges of Andes run N and S, splitting the country into 3 zones: hot, humid lowlands on the coast; temperate highlands between

the ranges, and rainy, tropical lowlands to the E. **Capital:** Quito. **Cities** (1983 est.): Guayaquil 1,278,900; Quito 918,900.

Government: Type: Republic. **Head of state:** Pres. Leon Febres-Cordero; b. Mar. 9, 1931; in office: Aug., 1984. **Local divisions:** 20 provinces. **Defense:** 9.3% of govt. budget (1981).

Economy: Industries: Food processing, wood prods. **Chief crops:** Bananas (largest exporter), coffee, rice, grains, fruits, cocoa, kapok. **Minerals:** Oil, copper, iron, lead, coal, sulphur. **Crude oil reserves** (1980): 1.1 bln. bbls. **Other resources:** Rubber, bark. **Arable land:** 10%. **Meat prod.** (1980): beef: 92,000 metric tons; pork: 63,000 metric tons; lamb: 10,000 metric tons. **Fish catch** (1981): 686,000 metric tons. **Electricity prod.** (1981): 2.9 bln. kwh. **Labor force:** 50% agric., 20% ind., 15% services.

Finance: Currency: Sucre (Feb. 1984: 58.6 = $1 US). **Gross domestic product** (1980): $11.3 bln. **Per capita income** (1980): $1,050. **Imports** (1983): $1.4 bln.; partners: U.S. 34%, Jap. 12%, W. Ger. 7%. **Exports** (1983): $2.2 bln.; partners: U.S. 39%, Jap. 12%. **National budget** (1981): $2.5 bln. **International reserves less gold** (Mar. 1984): $483 mln. **Gold:** 414,000 oz t. **Consumer prices** (change in 1983): 44.9%.

Transport: Railway traffic (1980) 65 mln. passenger-km; 34 mln. net ton-km. **Motor vehicles:** in use (1981): 232,600 passenger cars, 23,900 comm. vehicles. **Civil aviation** (1982): 862 mln. passenger-km; 39.4 mln. net ton-km. **Chief ports:** Guayaquil, Manta, Esmeraldas.

Communications: Television sets: 500,000 in use (1981). **Radios:** 2.6 mln. in use (1981). **Telephones in use** (1981): 272,000. **Daily newspaper circ.** (1982): 38 per 1,000 pop.

Health: Life expectancy at birth (1974): 54.89 male; 58.07 female. **Births** (per 1,000 pop. 1978): 42. **Deaths** (per 1,000 pop. 1978): 10. **Natural increase** (1983): 3.1%. **Hospital beds** (per 100,000 pop.1977): 204. **Physicians** (per 100,000 pop. 1977): 64. **Infant mortality** (per 1,000 live births 1978): 66.

Education (1982): **Literacy:** 84%. Attendance through 6th grade—76% urban, 33% rural. Teachers per 1,000: 20.

Embassy: 2535 15th St. NW 20009; 234-7200.

Spain conquered the region, which was the northern Inca empire, in 1633. Liberation forces defeated the Spanish May 24, 1822, near Quito. Ecuador became part of the Great Colombia Republic but seceded, May 13, 1830.

Ecuador had been ruled by civilian and military dictatorships since 1968. A peaceful transfer of power from the military junta to the democratic civilian government took place, 1979.

Since 1972, the economy has revolved around its petroleum exports, which declined in 1982 causing severe economic problems.

Ecuador and Peru have long disputed their Amazon Valley boundary.

The **Galapagos Islands,** 600 mi. to the W, are the home of hugh tortoises and other unusual animals.

Egypt
Arab Republic of Egypt

People: Population (1983 est.): 45,809,000. **Pop. density:** 115.60 per sq. mi. **Urban** (1977): 44.1%. **Ethnic groups:** Egyptians, Bedouins, Nubians. **Languages:** Arabic. **Religions:** 90% Sunni Moslem.

Geography: Area: 385,201 sq. mi, the size of Texas and Oregon combined. **Location:** NE corner of Africa. **Neighbors:** Libya on W, Sudan on S, Israel on E. **Topography:** Almost entirely desolate and barren, with hills and mountains in E and along Nile. The Nile Valley, where most of the people live, stretches 550 miles. **Capital:** Cairo. **Cities** (1976 cen.): Cairo 5,084,463; Alexandria 2,318,655; Giza 1,246,713; Subra-El Khema 393,700; El-Mahalla El-Kubra 292,853.

Government: Type: Republic. **Head of state:** Pres. Hosni Mubarak; b. 1929; in office: Oct. 14, 1981. **Head of Government:** Kamal Hassan Ali, act.; in office: June, 1984. **Local divisions:** 25 governorates. **Armed forces:** regulars 450,000 (1982).

Economy: Industries: Textiles, chemicals, petrochemicals, cement. **Chief crops:** Cotton (one of largest producers), grains, vegetables, sugar, corn. **Minerals:** Oil, phosphates, salt, iron, manganese, limestone. **Crude oil reserves** (1980): 3.1 bln. bbls. **Arable land:** 4%. **Meat prod.** (1983): beef: 278,000 metric tons; lamb: 48,000 metric tons. **Fish catch** (1978): 99,900 metric tons. **Electricity prod.** (1981): 18.5 bln. kwh. **Crude steel prod.** (1981 est.): 900,000 metric tons. **Labor force:** 50% agric.; 29% ind. & comm.; 21% services.

Finance: Currency: Pound (Mar. 1984: .74 = $1 US). **Gross domestic product** (1980): $26 bln. **Per capita income** (1982): $560. **Imports** (1982): $9 bln.; partners: U.S. 19%, W. Ger. 10%, It. 8%, France 8%. **Exports** (1982): $3.1 bln.; partners: It. 22%, Isr. 14%. **Tourists** (1977): 1,003,900; receipts: $658 mln. **International reserves less gold** (Jan. 1984): $779 mln. **Gold:** 2.43 mln. oz t. **Consumer prices** (change in 1983): 16.1%.

Transport: Railway traffic (1981): 10.9 bln. passenger-km; 2.4 bln. net ton-km. **Motor vehicles:** in use (1982): 461,300 passenger cars, 176,000 comm. vehicles. **Civil aviation** (1982): 3.6 bln. passenger-km, 56 mln. freight ton-km. **Chief ports:** Alexandria, Port Said, Suez.

Communications: Television sets: 1.4 mln. in use (1981). **Radios:** 6.4 mln. in use (1981). **Telephones in use** (1981): 534,021. **Daily newspaper circ.** (1982): 124 per 1,000 pop.

Health: Life expectancy at birth (1983): 55.9 male; 58.4 female. **Births** (per 1,000 pop. 1982): 36.9. **Deaths** (per 1,000 pop. 1982): 10.3. **Natural increase** (1978): 2.7%. **Hospital beds** (per 100,000 pop. 1977): 209. **Physicians** (per 100,000 pop. 1977): 92. **Infant mortality** (per 1,000 live births 1982): 110-120.

Education (1982): **Literacy:** 40%. Compulsory ages 6-12.; teachers per 1,000: 13.

Embassy: 2310 Decatur Pl. NW 20008; 232-5400.

Archeological records of ancient Egyptian civilization date back to 4000 BC. A unified kingdom arose around 3200 BC, and extended its way south into Nubia and north as far as Syria. A high culture of rulers and priests was built on an economic base of serfdom, fertile soil, and annual flooding of the Nile banks.

Imperial decline facilitated conquest by Asian invaders (Hyksos, Assyrians). The last native dynasty fell in 341 BC to the Persians, who were in turn replaced by Greeks (Alexander and the Ptolemies), Romans, Byzantines, and Arabs, who introduced Islam and the Arabic language. The ancient Egyptian language is preserved only in the liturgy of the Coptic Christians.

Egypt was ruled as part of larger Islamic empires for several centuries. The Mamluks, a military caste of Caucasian origin, ruled Egypt from 1250 until defeat by the Ottoman Turks in 1517. Under Turkish sultans the khedive as hereditary viceroy had wide authority. Britain intervened in 1882 and took control of administration, though nominal allegiance to the Ottoman Empire continued until 1914.

The country was a British protectorate from 1914 to 1922. A 1936 treaty strengthened Egyptian autonomy, but Britain retained bases in Egypt and a condominium over the Sudan. Britain fought German and Italian armies from Egypt, 1940-42, but Egypt did not declare war against Germany until 1945. In 1951 Egypt abrogated the 1936 treaty. The Sudan became independent in 1956.

The uprising of July 23, 1952, led by the Society of Free Officers, named Maj. Gen. Mohammed Naguib commander in chief and forced King Farouk to abdicate. When the republic was proclaimed June 18, 1953, Naguib became its first president and premier. Lt. Col. Gamal Abdel Nasser removed Naguib and became premier in 1954. In 1956, he was voted president. Nasser died in 1970 and was replaced by Vice Pres. Anwar Sadat.

A series of decrees in July, 1961, nationalized about 90% of industry. Economic liberalization was begun, 1974, with more emphasis on private domestic and foreign investment.

In July, 1956, the U. S. and UK withdrew support for loans to start the Aswan High Dam. Nasser obtained credits and technicians from the USSR to build the dam. The billion-dollar Aswan High Dam project, begun 1960, completed 1971, provided irrigation for more than a million acres of land and a potential of 10 billion kwh of electricity per year. Artesian wells, drilled in the Western Desert, reclaimed 43,000 acres, 1960-66.

When the state of Israel was proclaimed in 1948, Egypt joined other Arab nations invading Israel and was defeated.

After terrorist raids across its border, Israel invaded Egypt's Sinai Peninsula, Oct. 29, 1956. Egypt rejected a cease-fire demand by Britain and France; on Oct. 31 the 2 nations dropped bombs and on Nov. 5-6 landed forces. Egypt and Israel accepted a UN cease-fire; fighting ended Nov. 7.

A UN Emergency Force guarded the 117-mile long border between Egypt and Israel until May 19, 1967, when it was withdrawn at Nasser's demand. Egyptian troops entered the Gaza

Strip and the heights of Sharm el Sheikh and 3 days later closed the Strait of Tiran to all Israeli shipping. Full-scale war broke out June 5 and before it ended under a UN cease-fire June 10, Israel had captured Gaza and the Sinai Peninsula, controlled the east bank of the Suez Canal and reopened the gulf.

Sporadic fighting with Israel broke out late in 1968 and continued almost daily, 1969-70. Military and economic aid was received from the USSR. Israel and Egypt agreed, Aug. 7, 1970, to a cease-fire and peace negotiations proposed by the U.S. Negotiations failed to achieve results, but the cease-fire continued into 1973.

In July 1972 Sadat ordered most of the 20,000 Soviet military advisers and personnel to leave Egypt.

In a surprise attack Oct. 6, 1973, Egyptian forces crossed the Suez Canal into the Sinai. (At the same time, Syrian forces attacked Israelis on the Golan Heights.) Egypt was supplied by a USSR military airlift; the U.S. responded with an airlift to Israel. Israel counter-attacked, crossed the canal, surrounded Suez City. A UN cease-fire took effect Oct. 24.

A disengagement agreement was signed Jan. 18, 1974. Under it, Israeli forces withdrew from the canal's W bank; limited numbers of Egyptian forces occupied a strip along the E bank. A second accord was signed in 1975, with Israel yielding Sinai oil fields. Pres. Sadat's surprise visit to Jerusalem, Nov. 1977, opened the prospect of peace with Israel, but worsened relations with Libya (border clashes, July 1977). On Mar. 26, 1979, Egypt and Israel signed a formal peace treaty, ending 30 years of war, and establishing diplomatic relations. Israel returned control of the Sinai to Egypt in April 1982.

Tension between Muslim fundamentalists and Christians in 1981 caused street riots and culminated in a nationwide security crackdown in September. Pres Sadat was assassinated on Oct. 6.

The **Suez Canal**, 103 mi. long, links the Mediterranean and Red seas. It was built by a French corporation 1859-69, but Britain obtained controlling interest in 1875. The last British troops were removed June 13, 1956. On July 26, Egypt nationalized the canal. French and British stockholders eventually received some compensation.

Egypt had barred Israeli ships and cargoes destined for Israel since 1948, and closed the canal to all shipping after the 1967 Arab-Israeli War. The canal was reopened in 1975; Egypt agreed to allow passage to Israeli cargo in third party ships. A $1.3 billion expansion project will enable the canal to accommodate larger tankers.

El Salvador
Republic of El Salvador

People: Population (1983 est.): 4,685,000. **Age distrib.** (%): 0-14; 46.2; 15-59: 48.4; 60+: 5.4. **Pop. density:** 570 per sq. mi. **Urban** (1978): 40.1%. **Ethnic groups:** Mestizos 89%, Indians 10%, Caucasians 1%. **Languages:** Spanish, Nahuatl (among some Indians). **Religions:** Roman Catholicism prevails.

Geography: Area: 8,124 sq. mi., the size of Massachusetts. **Location:** In Central America. **Neighbors:** Guatemala on W, Honduras on N. **Topography:** A hot Pacific coastal plain in the south rises to a cooler plateau and valley region, densely populated. The N is mountainous, including many volcanoes. **Capital:** San Salvador. **Cities** (1982 est.): San Salvador 440,000.

Government: Type: Republic. **Head of state:** Pres., Jose Napoleon Duarte; b. Nov. 23, 1926; in office: June 1, 1984. **Local divisions:** 14 departments; pres. appoints governors. **Armed forces:** regulars 32,000; para-military 10,000.

Economy: Industries: Food and beverages, textiles, petroleum products. **Chief crops:** Coffee, cotton, corn, sugar. **Other resources:** Rubber, forests. **Arable land:** 32%. **Meat prod.** (1980): beef: 28,000 metric tons; pork: 16,000 metric tons. **Electricity prod.** (1981): 1.5 bln. kwh. **Labor force:** 47% agric.; 8% man.; 14% services.

Finance: Currency: Colon (Mar. 1984: 2.50 = $1 US). **Gross domestic product** (1980): $3.6 bln. **Per capita income** (1983): $470. **Imports** (1982): $883 mln.; partners (1981): U.S. 25%, Guat. 25%. **Exports** (1982): $704 mln.; partners (1981): U.S. 17%, W. Ger. 22%, Guat. 18%. **National budget** (1980): $412 mln. revenues; $569 mln. expenditures. **International reserves less gold** (Mar. 1984): $143.6 mln. **Gold:** 469,000 oz t. **Consumer prices** (change in 1983): 13.1%.

Transport: Railway traffic (1981): 14 mln. passenger-km; 31 mln. net ton-km. **Motor vehicles:** in use (1981): 77,300 passenger cars, 63,000 comm. vehicles. **Chief ports:** La Union, Acajutla.

Communications: Television sets: 300,000 in use (1981). **Radios:** 1.5 mln. in use (1981). **Telephones in use** (1981): 75,920. **Daily newspaper circ.** (1982): 71 per 1,000 pop.

Health: Life expectancy at birth (1980): 56.7 male; 59.7 female. **Births** (per 1,000 pop. 1980): 34.7. **Deaths** (per 1,000 pop. 1980): 7.9. **Natural increase** (1977): 3.4%. **Hospital beds** (per 100,000 pop. 1977): 161. **Physicians** (per 100,000 pop. 1977): 27. **Infant mortality** (per 1,000 live births 1979): 60.0.

Education (1978): **Literacy:** 50% (urban areas); 30% (rural areas). Years compulsory 10; attendance 65%.

Embassy: 2308 California St. NW 20008; 265-3480.

El Salvador became independent of Spain in 1821, and of the Central American Federation in 1839.

A fight with Honduras in 1969 over the presence of 300,000 Salvadorean workers left 2,000 dead. Clashes were renewed 1970 and 1974.

A military coup overthrew the Romero government, 1979, but the ruling military-civilian junta failed to quell the civil war which has resulted in some 50,000 deaths. Some 10,000 leftists insurgents, armed by Cuba and Nicaragua, control about 25% of the country, mostly in the east. Extreme right-wing death squads organized to eliminate suspected leftists were blamed for over 1,000 deaths in 1983. The Reagan administration has staunchly supported the government with military aid.

Voters turned out in large numbers in the May 1984 presidential election. Christian Democrat Jose Napoleon Duarte, a moderate, was victorious with 54% of the vote.

Leftist guerrillas continued their offensive in 1984; numerous clashes with government forces were reported.

Equatorial Guinea

Republic of Equatorial Guinea

People: Population (1983 est.): 268,000. **Age distrib.** (%): 0–14: 35.2; 15–59: 57.1; 60+: 7.7. **Pop. density:** 33.23 per sq. mi. **Ethnic groups:** Fangs 75%, several other groups. **Languages:** Spanish (official), Fang, English. **Religions:** Roman Catholics 60%, Protestants, others.

Geography: Area: 10,832 sq. mi., the size of Maryland. **Location:** Bioko Is. off W. Africa coast in Gulf of Guinea, and Rio Muni, mainland enclave. **Neighbors:** Gabon on S, Cameroon on E, N. **Topography:** Bioko Is. consists of 2 volcanic mountains and a connecting valley. Rio Muni, with over 90% of the area, has a coastal plain and low hills beyond. **Capital:** Malabo. **Cities** (1974 est.): Malabo 25,000.

Government: Head of state: Pres., Supreme Military Council Teodoro Obiang Nguema Mbasogo; b. June 5, 1942; in office: Oct. 10, 1979. **Local divisions:** 2 provinces.

Economy: Chief crops: Cocoa, coffee, bananas, sweet potatoes. **Other resources:** Timber. **Per capita arable land:** 0.9 acres. **Electricity prod.** (1977): 23 mln. kwh. **Labor force:** 95% agric.

Finance: Currency: Ekuele (Sept. 1983: 304 = $1 US). **Gross domestic product** (1976 est.): $112 mln. **Per capita income** (1975): $342. **Imports** (1980): $54 mln.; partners (1981): Spain 54%, China 17%. **Exports** (1980): $16 mln.; partners (1981): Sp. 40%, Neth. 28%, W. Ger. 23%.

Transport: Chief ports: Malabo, Bata.

Communications: Radios: 80,000 in use (1976).

Health: Life expectancy at birth (1975): 41.9 male; 45.1 female. **Births** (per 1,000 pop. 1978): 42. **Deaths** (per 1,000 pop. 1978): 19. **Natural increase** (1978): 2.3% **Hospital beds** (per 100,000 pop. 1977): 704. **Physicians** (per 100,000 pop. 1977): 2. **Infant mortality** (per 1,000 live births 1975): 53.2.

Education (1978): **Literacy:** 20%. **Pop. 5–19:** in school: 45%, teachers per 1,000: 9.

Embassy: 801 2d Ave., New York, NY 10017; (212) 599-1523.

Fernando Po (now Bioko) Island was discovered by Portugal in the late 15th century and ceded to Spain in 1778. Independence came Oct. 12, 1968. Riots occurred in 1969 over disputes between the island and the more backward Rio Muni province on the mainland. Masie Nguema Biyogo, himself from the mainland, became president for life in 1972.

Masie's 11-year reign was one of the most brutal in Africa, resulting in a bankrupted nation. Most of the nation's 7,000 Europeans emigrated. In 1976, 45,000 Nigerian workers were evacuated amid charges of a reign of terror. Masie was ousted in a military coup, Aug., 1979.

Ethiopia

Socialist Ethiopia

People: Population (1983 est.): 31,265,000. **Age distrib.** (%): 0–14: 43.1; 15–59: 52.5; 60+: 4.4. **Pop. density:** 71.31 per sq. mi. **Urban** (1979): 13.5%. **Ethnic groups:** Oromo 40%, Amhara 25%, Tigre 12%, Somali, Afar, Sidama. **Languages:** Amharic, Tigre (Semitic languages); Galla (Hamitic), Arabic, others. **Religions:** Orthodox Christian 40%, Moslem 40%.

Geography: Area: 472,400 sq. mi., four-fifths the size of Alaska. **Location:** In E. Africa. **Neighbors:** Sudan on W, Kenya on S. Somalia, Djibouti on E. **Topography:** A high central plateau, between 6,000 and 10,000 ft. high, rises to higher mountains near the Great Rift Valley, cutting in from the SW. The Blue Nile and other rivers cross the plateau, which descends to plains on both W and SE. **Capital:** Addis Ababa. **Cities** (1982 est.): Addis Ababa 1,408,000.

Government: Type: Provisional military govt. **Head of state and head of gov't.:** Chmn. of Provisional Military Administrative Council Mengistu Haile Mariam; b. 1937; in office: Feb. 11, 1977. **Local divisions:** 14 administrative regions. **Armed forces:** 250,000.

Economy: Industries: Food processing, cement, textiles. **Chief crops:** Coffee (61% export earnings), grains. **Minerals:** Coal, platinum, gold, copper, asbestos, potash. **Other resources:** Hydro power potential. **Arable land:** 12%. **Meat prod.** (1980): beef: 214,000 metric tons; lamb: 132,000 metric tons. **Fish catch** (1978): 26,800 metric tons. **Electricity prod.** (1981): 677 mln. kwh. **Labor force:** 80% agric.

Finance: Currency: Birr (Feb. 1984: 2.07 = $1 US). **Gross domestic product** (1980): $4.07 bln. **Per capita income** (1980): $117. **Imports** (1982): $786 mln.; partners (1981): USSR 20%, U.S. 8%, Jap. 7%, W.Ger. 9%. **Exports** (1982): $404 mln.; partners (1981): U.S. 21%, Italy 7%, Saud. Ar. 9%. **National budget** (1980): $985 mln. revenues; $1.8 bln. expenditures. **International reserves less gold** (Mar. 1984): $85.5 min. **Gold:** 209,000 oz t. **Consumer prices** (change in 1982): 5.9%.

Transport: Railway traffic (1981): 171 mln. passenger-km; 148 mln. net ton-km. **Motor vehicles:** in use (1981): 43,100 passenger cars, 13,000 comm. vehicles. **Civil aviation** (1982): 762 mln. passenger-km; 26.2 mln. net ton-km. **Chief ports:** Masewa, Aseb.

Communications: Television sets: 30,000 in use (1981), **Radios:** 250,000 in use (1981). **Telephones in use** (1981): 87,800. **Daily newspaper circ.** (1982): 1 per 1,000 pop.

Health: Life expectancy at birth (1975): 37.0 male; 40.1 female. **Births** (per 1,000 pop. 1978): 48. **Deaths** (per 1,000 pop. 1978): 23. **Natural increase** (1978): 2.4%. **Hospital beds** (per 100,000 pop. 1977): 29. **Physicians** (per 100,000 pop. 1977): 1. **Infant mortality** (per 1,000 live births 1981): 155.

Education (1981): **Literacy:** 8%. **Pop 5-19:** in school: 12%, teachers per 1,000: 3.

Embassy: 2134 Kalorama Rd. NW 20008; 234-2281.

Ethiopian culture was influenced by Egypt and Greece. The ancient monarchy was invaded by Italy in 1880, but maintained its independence until another Italian invasion in 1936. British forces freed the country in 1941.

The last emperor, Haile Selassie I, established a parliament and judiciary system in 1931, but barred all political parties.

A series of droughts since 1972 have killed hundreds of thousands. An army mutiny, strikes, and student demonstrations led to the dethronement of Selassie in 1974. The ruling junta pledged to form a one-party socialist state, and instituted a successful land reform; opposition was violently suppressed. The influence of the Coptic Church, embraced in 330 AD, was curbed, and the monarchy was abolished in 1975.

The regime, torn by bloody coups, faced uprisings by tribal and political groups in part aided by Sudan and Somalia. Ties with the U.S., once a major arms and aid source, deteriorated, while cooperation accords were signed with the USSR in 1977. In 1978, Soviet advisors and 20,000 Cuban troops helped defeat Somali rebels & Somalia forces.

Fiji
Dominion of Fiji

People: Population (1983 est.): 676,000. **Age distrib.** (%): 0–14: 41.1; 15–59: 54.7; 60+: 4.0. **Pop. density:** 87.87 per sq. mi. **Urban** (1976): 37.2%. **Ethnic groups:** Indian 50%, Fijian (Melanesian-Polynesian) 45%, Europeans 2%. **Languages:** English (official), Fijian, Hindustani. **Religions:** Christian 49%, Hindu 40%.

Geography: Area: 7,056 sq. mi., the size of Massachusetts. **Location:** In western S. Pacific O. **Neighbors:** Nearest are Solomons on NW, Tonga on E. **Topography:** 322 islands (106 inhabited), many mountainous, with tropical forests and large fertile areas. Viti Levu, the largest island, has over half the total land area. **Capital:** Suva. **Cities** (1983 est.): Suva 65,000.

Government: Type: Parliamentary Democracy. **Head of state:** Queen Elizabeth II, represented by Gov. Gen. George Cakobau; b. Nov. 6, 1912; in office: Jan. 13, 1973. **Head of government:** Prime Min. Kamisese Mara; b. May 13, 1920; in office: Oct. 10, 1970. **Local divisions:** 4 divisions. **Armed forces:** regulars 1,900 (1980).

Economy: Industries: Sugar refining, light industry, tourism. **Chief crops:** Sugar, bananas, ginger. **Minerals:** Gold. **Other resources:** Timber. **Per capita arable land:** 0.6 acres. **Electricity prod.** (1981): 311 mln. kwh. **Labor force:** 44% agric.

Finance: Currency: Dollar (Mar. 1984: 1.03 = $1 US). **Gross domestic product** (1982): $1.1 bln. **Per capita income** (1982): $1,852. **Imports** (1981): $562 mln.; partners (1981): Austral. 39%, Jap. 14%, N.Z. 16%. **Exports** (1981): $280 mln.; partners: UK 22%, N.Z. 10%, Aust. 11%. **Tourists** (1981): 206,000; receipts $143 mln. **National budget** (1980): $249 mln. revenues: $253 mln. expenditures. **International reserves less gold** (Mar. 1984): $106 mln. **Gold:** 11,000 oz t. **Consumer prices** (change in 1983): 6.7%.

Transport: Motor vehicles: in use (1982): 26,000 passenger cars, 16,700 comm. vehicles. **Civil aviation** (1982): 397 mln. passenger-km; 4.3 mln. net ton-km. **Chief ports:** Suva, Lautoka.

Communications: Radios: 300,000 in use (1981). **Telephones in use** (1981): 45,323. **Daily newspaper circ.** (1982): 106 per 1,000 pop.

Health: Life expectancy at birth (1975): 68.5 male; 71.7 female. **Births** (per 1,000 pop. 1978): 27 **Deaths** (per 1,000 pop. 1978): 4. **Natural increase** (1978): 1.8%. **Hospital beds** (per 100,000 pop. 1977): 264. **Physicians** (per 100,000 pop. 1977): 50. **Infant mortality** (per 1,000 live births 1983): 29.

Education (1978): **Literacy:** 75%. **Pop. 5-19:** in school: 73%, teachers per 1,000 27.

Embassy: 1140 19th St. NW 20036; 296-3928.

A British colony since 1874, Fiji became an independent parliamentary democracy Oct. 10, 1970.

Cultural differences between the majority Indian community, descendants of contract laborers brought to the islands in the 19th century, and the less modernized native Fijians, who by law own 83% of the land in communal villages, have led to political polarization.

The discovery of copper on Viti Levu, and favorable off-shore oil prospects, along with increased sugar production bode well for the economy.

Finland
Republic of Finland

People: Population (1983 est.): 4,850,000. **Age distrib.** (%): 0–14: 20.2; 15–59: 63.4; 60+: 16.5. **Pop. density:** 36.74 per sq. mi. **Urban** (1981): 59.9% **Ethnic groups:** Finns, Swedes. **Languages:** Finnish 93.5%, Swedish 6.5% (both official). **Religions:** Lutheran 97%.

Geography: Area: 130,119 sq. mi., slightly smaller than Montana. **Location:** In northern Baltic region of Europe. **Neighbors:** Norway on N, Sweden on W, USSR on E. **Topography:** South and central Finland are mostly flat areas with low hills and many lakes. The N has mountainous areas, 3,000-4,000 ft. **Capital:** Helsinki. **Cities** (1983 est.): Helsinki 483,051; Tampere 167,028; Turku 163,526.

Government: Type: Constitutional Republic. **Head of state:** Pres. Mauno Koivisto; b. Nov. 25, 1923; in office: Jan. 27, 1982.

Head of government: Prime Min. Kaleva Sorsa; b. 1930; in office: Feb. 25, 1982. **Local divisions:** 12 laanit (provinces). **Defense:** 1.39% of GNP (1980).

Economy: Industries: Machinery, metal, shipbuilding, textiles, clothing. **Chief crops:** Grains, potatoes, dairy prods. **Minerals:** Copper, iron, zinc. **Other resources:** Forests (40% of exports). **Arable land:** 7%. **Meat prod.** (1980): beef: 115,000 metric tons; pork: 176,000 metric tons. **Fish catch** (1981): 133,000 metric tons. **Electricity prod.** (1982): 39.3 bln. kwh. **Crude steel prod.** (1982): 2.4 mln. metric tons. **Labor force:** 11% agric.; 46% ind. & comm.; 24% services.

Finance: Currency: Markkaa (Mar. 1984: 5.57 = $1 US). **Gross domestic product** (1980): $50.1 bln. **Per capita income** (1980): $10,477. **Imports** (1983): $12.8 bln.; partners (1982): USSR 25%, Swed. 12%, W. Ger. 13%, UK 7%. **Exports** (1983): $12.5 bln.; partners (1982): USSR 27%, Swed. 12%, UK 11%, W. Ger. 9%. **Tourists** (1977): 259,000. **National budget** (1980): $11.67 bln. revenues; $12.03 bln. expenditures. **International reserves less gold** (Mar. 1984): $1.69 bln. **Gold** 1.2 mln. oz t. **Consumer prices** (change in 1983): 8.5%.

Transport: Railway traffic (1982): 3.3 bln. passenger-km; 8.0 bln. net ton-km. **Motor vehicles:** in use (1982): 1.3 mln. passenger cars, 161,700 comm. vehicles; manuf. (1976): 27,300 passenger cars. **Civil aviation** (1982): 2.5 bln. passenger-km; 66.8 mln. freight ton-km. **Chief ports:** Helsinki, Turku.

Communications: Television sets: 1.6 mln. licensed (1982). **Radios:** 2.4 mln. licensed (1981). **Telephones in use** (1981): 2.5 mln. **Daily newspaper circ.** (1982): 506 per 1,000 pop.

Health: Life expectancy at birth (1980): 69.2 male; 77.6 female. **Births** (per 1,000 pop. 1981): 13.2. **Deaths** (per 1,000 pop. 1981): 9.3. **Natural increase** (1978): .4%. **Hospital beds** (1980): 74,280. **Physicians** (1980): 9,016. **Infant mortality** (per 1,000 live births 1981): 7.6.

Education (1982): **Literacy:** 99%. Years compulsory 9; attendance 99%.

Embassy: 3216 New Mexico Ave. NW 20016; 363-2430

The early Finns probably migrated from the Ural area at about the beginning of the Christian era. Swedish settlers brought the country into Sweden, 1154 to 1809, when Finland became an autonomous grand duchy of the Russian Empire. Russian exactions created a strong national spirit; on Dec. 6, 1917, Finland declared its independence and in 1919 became a republic. On Nov. 30, 1939, the Soviet Union invaded, and the Finns were forced to cede 16,173 sq. mi., including the Karelian Isthmus, Viipuri, and an area on Lake Ladoga. After World War II, in which Finland tried to recover its lost territory, further cessions were exacted. In 1948, Finland signed a treaty of mutual assistance with the USSR. In 1956 Russia returned Porkkala, which had been ceded as a military base.

Finland is an integral member of the Nordic group of five countries and maintains good relations with the Soviet Union. The governing coalition usually includes the Communist Party.

Aland, constituting an autonomous department, is a group of small islands, 572 sq. mi., in the Gulf of Bothnia, 25 mi. from Sweden, 15 mi. from Finland. Mariehamn is the principal port.

France
French Republic

People: Population (1983 est.): 54,652,000. **Age distrib.** (%): 0–14: 22.0; 15–59: 60; 60+: 17.6. **Pop. density:** 252.19 per sq. mi. **Urban** (1975): 73.0%. **Ethnic groups:** A mixture of various European and Mediterranean groups. **Languages:** French; minorities speak Breton, Alsatian German, Flemish, Italian, Basque, Catalan. **Religions:** Mostly Roman Catholic.

Geography: Area: 210,040 sq. mi., four-fifths the size of Texas. **Location:** In western Europe, between Atlantic O. and Mediterranean Sea. **Neighbors:** Spain on S, Italy, Switzerland, W. Germany on E, Luxembourg, Belgium on N. **Topography:** A wide plain covers more than half of the country, in N and W, drained to W by Seine, Loire, Garonne rivers. The Massif Central is a mountainous plateau in center. In E are Alps (Mt. Blanc is tallest in W. Europe, 15,771 ft.), the lower Jura range, and the forested Vosges. The Rhone flows from Lake Geneva to Mediterranean. Pyrenees are in SW, on border with Spain. **Capital:** Paris. **Cities** (1975 cen.): Paris 2,296,945; Marseille 912,130;

Lyon 457,410; Toulouse 371,835; Nice 344,040; Nantes 255,700; Strasbourg 253,355; Bordeaux 223,845.

Government: Type: Republic. **Head of state:** Pres. François Mitterrand; b. Oct. 26, 1916; in office: May 21, 1981. **Head of government:** Prime Min. Pierre Mauroy; b. 1928; in office: May 21, 1981. **Local divisions:** 95 departments. **Defense:** 18% of govt. budget. (1984).

Economy: Industries: Steel, chemicals, autos, textiles, wine, perfume, aircraft, ships, electronic equipment. **Chief crops:** Grains, corn, rice, fruits, vegetables. France is largest food producer, exporter, in W. Eur. **Minerals:** Bauxite, iron, coal. **Crude oil reserves** (1980): 50 mln. bbls. **Other resources:** Forests. **Per capita arable land:** 0.8 acres. **Meat prod.** (1983): beef: 1.8 mln. metric tons; pork: 1.86 mln. metric tons; lamb: 185,000 metric tons. **Fish catch** (1981): 768,100 metric tons. **Electricity prod.** (1982): 262.8 bln. kwh. **Crude steel prod.** (1982): 18.4 mln. metric tons. **Labor force:** 9% agric., 45% ind. & comm.; 46% services.

Finance: Currency: Franc (Mar. 1984: 7.98 = $1 US). **Gross domestic product** (1983): $920 bln. **Per capita income** (1983): $7,179. **Imports** (1983): $105.4 bln.; partners: W. Ger. 17%, It. 10%, Belg. 8%, U.S. 8%. **Exports** (1983): $94.9 bln.; partners: W. Ger. 14%, It. 11%, Belg. 8%, UK 7%. **Tourists** (1981) 30 mln.; receipts: $7.1 bln. **National budget** (1980): $113.5 bln. revenues; $113.6 bln. expenditures. **International reserves less gold** (Feb. 1984): $19.3 bln. **Gold:** 81.85 mln. oz t. **Consumer prices** (change in 1983): 9.6%.

Transport: Railway traffic (1982): 56.8 bln. passenger-km; 61.1 bln. net ton-km. **Motor vehicles:** in use (1982): 20.3 mln. passenger cars, 2.6 mln. comm. vehicles; manuf. (1982): 3 mln. passenger cars; 466,000 comm. vehicles. **Civil aviation** (1982): 37.8 bln. passenger-km; 2.2 bln net ton-km. **Chief ports:** Marseille, LeHavre, Nantes, Bordeaux, Rouen.

Communications: Television sets: 19 mln. in use (1981). **Radios:** 22.2 mln. licensed (1979). **Telephones in use** (1980): 22.2 mln. **Daily newspaper circ.** (1982): 211 per 1,000 pop.

Health: Life expectancy at birth (1980): 70.2 male; 78.5 female. **Births** (per 1,000 pop. 1982): 12.8. **Deaths** (per 1,000 pop. 1982): 7.1. **Natural increase** (1977): .4%. **Hospital beds** (1981): 439,310. **Physicians** (1981): 104,073. **Infant mortality** (per 1,000 live births 1982): 9.3.

Education (1984): **Literacy:** 99%. Years compulsory 10; 17.7% of natl. budget.

Embassy: 2535 Belmont Rd. NW 20008; 328-2600.

Celtic Gaul was conquered by Julius Caesar 58-51 BC; Romans ruled for 500 years. Under Charlemagne, Frankish rule extended over much of Europe. After his death France emerged as one of the successor kingdoms.

The monarchy was overthrown by the French Revolution (1789-93) and succeeded by the First Republic; followed by the First Empire under Napoleon (1804-15), a monarchy (1814-48), the Second Republic (1848-52), the Second Empire (1852-70), the Third Republic (1871-1946), the Fourth Republic (1946-58), and the Fifth Republic (1958 to present).

France suffered severe losses in manpower and wealth in the first World War, 1914-18, when it was invaded by Germany. By the Treaty of Versailles, France exacted return of Alsace and Lorraine, French provinces seized by Germany in 1871. Germany invaded France again in May, 1940, and signed an armistice with a government based in Vichy. After France was liberated by the Allies Sept. 1944, Gen. Charles de Gaulle became head of the provisional government, serving until 1946.

De Gaulle again became premier in 1958, during a crisis over Algeria, and obtained voter approval for a new constitution, ushering in the Fifth Republic. Using strong executive powers, he promoted French economic and technological advances in the context of the European Economic Community, and guarded French foreign policy independence.

France had withdrawn from Indochina in 1954, and from Morocco and Tunisia in 1956. Most of its remaining African territories were freed 1958-62, but France retained strong economic and political ties.

France tested atomic bombs in the Sahara beginning in 1960. Land-based and submarine launched strategic missiles were also developed. In 1966, France withdrew all its troops from the integrated military command of NATO, though 60,000 remained stationed in Germany. France continued to attend political meetings of NATO.

In May 1968 rebellious students in Paris and other centers rioted, battled police, and were joined by workers who launched nationwide strikes. The government awarded pay increases to the strikers May 26. In elections to the Assembly in June, de Gaulle's backers won a landslide victory. Nevertheless, he resigned from office in April, 1969, after losing a nationwide referendum on constitutional reform. De Gaulle's policies were largely continued after his death in 1970.

On May 10, 1981, France elected François Mitterand, a Socialist candidate, president in a stunning victory over Valéry Giscard d'Estaing. In September, the government nationalized 5 major industries and most private banks.

France committed troops and military aid to the government of Chad, June 1983. On Oct. 23, 58 members of the French peacekeeping force in Lebanon were killed in a suicide terrorist attack.

The island of **Corsica,** in the Mediterranean W of Italy and N of Sardinia, is an official region of France comprising 2 departments. Area: 3,369 sq. mi.; pop. (1975 cen.): 289,842. The capital is Ajaccio, birthplace of Napoleon. A militant separatist movement led to violence after 1975.

Overseas Departments

French Guiana is on the NE coast of South America with Suriname on the W and Brazil on the E and S. Its area is 32,252 sq. mi.; pop. (1982 est.): 66,800. Guiana sends one senator and one deputy to the French Parliament. Guiana is administered by a prefect and has a Council General of 16 elected members; capital is Cayenne.

The famous penal colony, Devil's Island, was phased out between 1938 and 1951.

Immense forests of rich timber cover 90% of the land. Placer gold mining is the most important industry. Exports are shrimp, timber, and machinery.

Guadeloupe, in the West Indies' Leeward Islands, consists of 2 large islands, Basse-Terre and Grande-Terre, separated by the Salt River, plus Marie Galante and the Saintes group to the S and, to the N, Desirade, St. Barthelemy, and over half of St. Martin (the Netherlands portion is St. Maarten). A French possession since 1635, the department is represented in the French Parliament by 2 senators and 3 deputies; administration consists of a prefect (governor) and an elected General Council.

Area of the islands is 687 sq. mi.; pop. (1982 est.) 314,800, mainly descendants of slaves; capital is Basse-Terre on Basse-Terre Is. The land is fertile; sugar, rum, and bananas are exported; tourism is an important industry.

Martinique, one of the Windward Islands, in the West Indies, has been a possession since 1635, and a department since March, 1946. It is represented in the French Parliament by 2 senators and 3 deputies. The island was the birthplace of Napoleon's Empress Josephine.

It has an area of 425 sq. mi.; pop. (1982 est.) 307,700, mostly descendants of slaves. The capital is Fort-de-France. It is a popular tourist stop. The chief exports are rum, bananas, and petroleum products.

Mayotte, formerly part of Comoros, voted in 1976 to become an overseas department of France. An island NW of Madagascar, area is 144 sq. mi., pop. (1982 est.) 53,000.

Reunion is a volcanic island in the Indian O. about 420 mi. E of Madagascar, and has belonged to France since 1665. Area, 969 sq. mi.; pop. (1982 est.) 504,400, 30% of French extraction. Capital: Saint-Denis. The chief export is sugar. It elects 3 deputies, 2 senators to the French Parliament.

St. Pierre and Miquelon, formerly an Overseas Territory, made the transition to department status in 1976. It consists of 2 groups of rocky islands near the SW coast of Newfoundland, inhabited by fishermen. The exports are chiefly fish products. The St. Pierre group has an area of 10 sq. mi.; Miquelon, 83 sq. mi. Total pop. (1982 est.), 6,300. The capital is St. Pierre. A deputy and a senator are elected to the French Parliament.

Overseas Territories

French Polynesia Overseas Territory, comprises 130 islands widely scattered among 5 archipelagos in the South Pacific; administered by a governor. Territorial Assembly and a Council with headquarters at Papeete, Tahiti, one of the **Society Islands** (which include the **Windward** and **Leeward** islands). A deputy and a senator are elected to the French Parliament.

Other groups are the **Marquesas Islands,** the **Tuamotu Archipelago,** including the **Gambier Islands,** and the **Austral Islands.**

Total area of the islands administered from Tahiti is 1,544 sq. mi.; pop. (1981 est.), 160,000, more than half on Tahiti. Tahiti is picturesque and mountainous with a productive coastline bearing coconut, banana and orange trees, sugar cane and vanilla.

Tahiti was visited by Capt. James Cook in 1769 and by Capt. Bligh in the Bounty, 1788-89. Its beauty impressed Herman Melville, Paul Gauguin, and Charles Darwin.

French Southern and Antarctic Lands Overseas Territory, comprises **Adelie Land**, on Antarctica, and 4 island groups in the Indian O. Adelie, discovered 1840, has a research station, a coastline of 185 mi. and tapers 1,240 mi. inland to the South Pole. The U.S. does not recognize national claims in Antarctica. There are 2 huge glaciers, Ninnis, 22 mi. wide, 99 mi. long, and Mentz, 11 mi. wide, 140 mi. long. The Indian O. groups are:

Kerguelen Archipelago, discovered 1772, one large and 300 small islands. The chief is 87 mi. long, 74 mi. wide, and has Mt. Ross, 6,429 ft. tall. Principal research station is Port-aux-Francais. Seals often weigh 2 tons; there are blue whales, coal, peat, semi-precious stones. **Crozet Archipelago**, discovered 1772, covers 195 sq. mi. Eastern Island rises to 6,560 ft. **Saint Paul**, in southern Indian O., has warm springs with earth at places heating to 120° to 390° F. **Amsterdam** is nearby; both produce cod and rock lobster.

New Caledonia and its dependencies, an overseas territory, are a group of islands in the Pacific O. about 1,115 mi. E of Australia and approx. the same distance NW of New Zealand. Dependencies are the **Loyalty Islands**, the **Isle of Pines, Huon Islands** and the **Chesterfield Islands**.

New Caledonia, the largest, has 6,530 sq. mi. Total area of the territory is 8,548 sq. mi.; population (1981 est.) 142,500. The group was acquired by France in 1853.

The territory is administered by a governor and government council. There is a popularly elected Territorial Assembly. A deputy and a senator are elected to the French Parliament. Capital: Noumea.

Mining is the chief industry. New Caledonia is one of the world's largest nickel producers. Other minerals found are chrome, iron, cobalt, manganese, silver, gold, lead, and copper. Agricultural products include coffee, copra, cotton, manioc (cassava), corn, tobacco, bananas and pineapples.

Wallis and Futuna Islands, 2 archipelagos raised to status of overseas territory July 29, 1961, are in the SW Pacific S of the Equator between Fiji and Samoa. The islands have a total area of 106 sq. mi. and population (1982 est.) of 11,000. **Alofi**, attached to Futuna, is uninhabited. Capital: Mata-Utu. Chief products are copra, yams, taro roots, bananas. A senator and a deputy are elected to the French Parliament.

Gabon
Gabonese Republic

People: Population (1983 est.): 921,000. **Pop. density:** 5.72 per sq. mi. **Urban** (1970): 32.0%. **Ethnic groups:** Fangs 25%, Bapounon 10%, others. **Languages:** French (official), Bantu dialects. **Religions:** Tribal beliefs, Christian minority.

Geography: Area: 102,317 sq. mi., the size of Colorado. **Location:** On Atlantic coast of central Africa. **Neighbors:** Equatorial Guinea, Cameroon on N, Congo on E, S. **Topography:** Heavily forested, the country consists of coastal lowlands plateaus in N, E, and S, mountains in N, SE, and center. The Ogooue R. system covers most of Gabon. **Capital:** Libreville. **Cities** (1983 est.): Libreville 180,000.

Government: Type: Republic. **Head of state:** Pres. Omar Bongo; b. Dec. 30, 1935; in office: Dec. 2, 1967. **Head of government:** Prime Min. Leon Mebiame, b. Sept. 1, 1934; in office: Apr. 16, 1975. **Local divisions:** 9 provinces, 37 prefectures. **Defense:** 7.2% of govt. budget (1982).

Economy: Industries: Oil products. **Chief crops:** Cocoa, coffee, rice, peanuts, palm products, cassava, bananas. **Minerals:** Manganese, uranium, oil, iron, gas. **Crude oil reserves** (1980): 500 mln. bbls. **Other resources:** Timber. **Arable land:** 1%. **Electricity prod.** (1981): 450 mln. kwh. **Labor force:** 65% agric.; 30% ind. & comm.; 2.5% services.

Finance: Currency: CFA franc (Mar. 1984: 399 = $1 US). **Gross domestic product** (1981) $3.7 bln. **Per capita income** (1981): $2,974. **Imports** (1982): $724 mln.; partners: Fr. 53%, U.S. 14%. **Exports** (1982): $2.1 bln.; partners: Fr. 25%, U.S. 20%, Arg. 11%. **Tourists receipts** (1977): $17 mln. **National**

budget (1982): $545 mln. **International reserves less gold** (Oct. 1983): $235.1 mln. **Gold:** 13,000 oz t. **Consumer prices** (change in 1982): 16.7%.

Transport: Motor vehicles: in use (1982): 16,000 passenger cars, 10,000 comm. vehicles. **Civil aviation** (1982): 430 mln. passenger-km. **Chief ports** Libreville, Port-Gentil.

Communications: Television sets: 9,000 licensed (1981). **Radios:** 96,000 licensed (1981). **Telephones in use** (1981): 11,600.

Health: Life expectancy at birth (1961): 25 male; 45 female. **Births** (per 1,000 pop. 1978): 34. **Deaths** (per 1,000 pop. 1978): 22. **Natural increase** (1978): 1.2%. **Hospital beds** (per 100,000 pop. 1977): 736. **Physicians** (per 100,000 pop. 1977): 32. **Infant mortality** (per 1,000 live births 1983): 117.

Education (1983): **Literacy:** 65%. Compulsory to age 16; attendance: 84% primary, 14% secondary. **Embassy:** 2034 20th St NW 20009; 797-1000.

France established control over the region in the second half of the 19th century. Gabon became independent Aug. 17, 1960. It is one of the most prosperous black African countries, thanks to abundant natural resources, foreign private investment, and government development programs.

The Gambia
Republic of The Gambia

People: Population (1983 est.): 700,000. **Age distrib.** (%): 0–14: 45.9; 15–59: 54.4; 60+: 3.8. **Pop. density:** 149.89 per sq. mi. **Urban** (1982): 15.9%. **Ethnic groups:** Mandinka 37.7%, Fula 16.2%, Wolof 14%, others. **Languages:** English (official), Mandinka, Wolof. **Religions:** Moslems 85%, Christian 14%.

Geography: Area: 4,361 sq. mi., smaller than Connecticut. **Location:** On Atlantic coast near western tip of Africa. **Neighbors:** Surrounded on 3 sides by Senegal. **Topography:** A narrow strip of land on each side of the lower Gambia. **Capital:** Banjul. **Cities** (1982 est.): Banjul 40,000.

Government: Type: Republic. **Head of state:** Pres. Dawda Kairaba Jawara; b. May 16, 1924; in office: Apr. 24, 1970 (prime min. from June 12, 1962). **Local divisions:** 5 divisions and Banjul.

Economy: Industries: Tourism. **Chief crops:** Peanuts (main export), rice. **Arable land:** 50%. **Fish catch** (1981): 35,000 metric tons. **Electricity prod.** (1978): 31.40 mln. kwh. **Labor force:** 75% agric.; 18% ind. & comm.

Finance: Currency: Dalasi (Mar. 1984: 2.74 = $1 US). **Gross domestic product** (1981): $198 mln. **Per capita income** (1981): $330. **Imports** (1980): $164 mln.; partners (1979): UK 25%, China 13%, Fr. 9%, W. Ger. 8%. **Exports** (1980): $31.9 mln.; partners (1979): Neth. 22%, UK 14%, Swit. 13%. **Tourist receipts** (1977): $8 mln. **National budget** (1980): $35.1 mln. revenues; $33.3 mln. expenditures. **International reserves less gold** (Mar. 1984): $3.9 mln. **Consumer prices** (change in 1982): 10.6%.

Transport: Motor vehicles: in use (1979): 8,500 passenger cars, 2,500 comm. vehicles. **Chief ports:** Banjul.

Communications: Radios: 61,000 in use (1976). **Telephones in use** (1980): 3,500.

Health: Life expectancy at birth (1982): 32 male; 34 female. **Births** (per 1,000 pop. 1978): 49. **Deaths** (per 1,000 pop. 1978): 28. **Natural increase** (1978): 2.8%. **Hospital beds** (1980): 635. **Physicians** (1980): 65. **Infant mortality** (per 100,000 live births 1979): 217.

Education (1982): **Literacy:** 12%. **Pop. 5-19:** in school: 14.2%. **Embassy:** 1785 Massachusetts Ave. NW 20036; 265-3252.

The tribes of Gambia were at one time associated with the West African empires of Ghana, Mali, and Songhay. The area became Britain's first African possession in 1588.

Independence came Feb. 18, 1965; republic status within the Commonwealth was achieved in 1970. Gambia is one of the only functioning democracies in Africa. The country suffered from severe famine in 1977-78.

An unsuccessful coup was launched July 30, 1981, while Pres. Jawara was in the UK for the royal wedding. Gambia has a treaty with Senegal to form a confederation of the 2 countries under the name of Senegambia. However, each country will retain its sovereignty.

Germany

Now comprises 2 nations: **Federal Republic of Germany (West Germany)**, **German Democratic Republic (East Germany)**.

Germany, prior to World War II, was a central European nation composed of numerous states which had a common language and traditions and which had been united in one country since 1871; since World War II it has been split in 2 parts.

History and government. Germanic tribes were defeated by Julius Caesar, 55 and 53 BC, but Roman expansion N of the Rhine was stopped in 9 AD. Charlemagne, ruler of the Franks, consolidated Saxon, Bavarian, Rhenish, Frankish, and other lands; after him the eastern part became the German Empire. The Thirty Years' War, 1618-1648, split Germany into small principalities and kingdoms. After Napoleon, Austria contended with Prussia for dominance, but lost the Seven Weeks' War to Prussia, 1866. Otto von Bismarck, Prussian chancellor, formed the North German Confederation, 1867.

In 1870 Bismarck maneuvered Napoleon III into declaring war. After the quick defeat of France, Bismarck formed the **German Empire** and on Jan. 18, 1871, in Versailles, proclaimed King Wilhelm I of Prussia German emperor (Deutscher kaiser).

The German Empire reached its peak before World War I in 1914, with 208,780 sq. mi., plus a colonial empire. After that war Germany ceded Alsace-Lorraine to France; West Prussia and Posen (Poznan) province to Poland; part of Schleswig to Denmark; lost all of its colonies and the ports of Memel and Danzig.

Republic of Germany, 1919-1933, adopted the Weimar constitution; met reparation payments and elected Friedrich Ebert and Gen. Paul von Hindenburg presidents.

Third Reich, 1933-1945, Adolf Hitler led the National Socialist German Workers' (Nazi) party after World War I. In 1923 he attempted to unseat the Bavarian government and was imprisoned. Pres. von Hindenburg named Hitler chancellor Jan. 30, 1933; on Aug. 3, 1934, the day after Hindenburg's death, the cabinet joined the offices of president and chancellor and made Hitler fuehrer (leader). Hitler abolished freedom of speech and assembly, and began a long series of persecutions climaxed by the murder of millions of Jews and opponents.

Hitler repudiated the Versailles treaty and reparations agreements. He remilitarized the Rhineland 1936 and annexed Austria (Anschluss, 1938). At Munich he made an agreement with Neville Chamberlain, British prime minister, which permitted Hitler to annex part of Czechoslovakia. He signed a non-aggression treaty with the USSR, 1939. He declared war on Poland Sept. 1, 1939, precipitating World War II.

With total defeat near, Hitler committed suicide in Berlin Apr. 1945. The victorious Allies voided all acts and annexations of Hitler's Reich.

Postwar changes. The zones of occupation administered by the Allied Powers and later relinquished gave the USSR Saxony, Saxony-Anhalt, Thuringia, and Mecklenburg, and the former Prussian provinces of Saxony and Brandenburg.

The territory E of the Oder-Neisse line within 1937 boundaries comprising the provinces of Silesia, Pomerania, and the southern part of East Prussia, totaling about 41,220 sq. mi., was taken by Poland. Northern East Prussia was taken by the USSR.

The Western Allies ended the state of war with Germany in 1951. The USSR did so in 1955.

There was also created the area of Greater Berlin, within but not part of the Soviet zone, administered by the 4 occupying powers under the Allied Command. In 1948 the USSR withdrew, established its single command in East Berlin, and cut off supplies. The Allies utilized a gigantic airlift to bring food to West Berlin, 1948-1949. In Aug. 1961 the East Germans built a wall dividing Berlin, after over 3 million E. Germans had emigrated.

East Germany
German Democratic Republic

People: Population (1983 est.): 16,724,000. **Age distrib.** (%): 0–14: 20.6; 15–59: 58.7; 60+: 20.7. **Pop. density:** 413.32 per sq. mi. **Urban** (1981): 76.4%. **Ethnic groups:** German 99%. **Languages:** German. **Religions:** traditionally 80% Protestant. **Geography: Area:** 41,825 sq. mi., the size of Virginia. **Location:** In E. Central Europe. **Neighbors:** W. Germany on W, Czechoslovakia on S, Poland on E. **Topography:** E. Germany

lies mostly on the North German plains, with lakes in N, Harz Mtns., Elbe Valley, and sandy soil of Bradenburg in center, and highlands in S. **Capital:** East Berlin. **Cities** (1980 est.): East Berlin 1,145,743; Leipzig 563,388; Dresden 516,284

Government: Type: Communist. **Head of state:** Chmn. Erich Honecker; b. Aug. 25, 1912; in office: Oct. 29, 1976. **Head of government:** Prime Min. Willi Stoph; b. July 9, 1914; in office: Oct. 29, 1976. **Head of Communist Party:** Sec.-Gen. Erich Honecker; in office: May 3, 1971. **Local divisions:** 15 administrative districts. **Defense:** 8% of GNP.

Economy: Industries: Steel, chemicals, electrical prods., textiles, machinery. **Chief crops:** Grains, potatoes, sugar beets. **Minerals:** Potash, lignite, uranium, coal. **Per capita arable land:** 0.7 acres. **Meat prod.** (1983): beef: 370,000 metric tons; pork: 1.2 min. metric tons; lamb: 17,000 metric tons. **Fish catch** (1981): 241,300 metric tons. **Electricity prod.** (1981): 100.7 bln. kwh. **Crude steel prod.** (1982): 7.1 min metric tons. **Labor force:** 10% agric.; 42.5% manuf.

Finance: Currency: Mark (Sept. 1983: 2.67 = $1 US). **Gross national product** (1979): $89.1 bln. **Per capita income** (1979): $5,340. **Imports:** (1979): $16.21 bln.; partners (1981): USSR 38%, Czech. 7%, Pol. 5%, W. Ger. 8%. **Exports** (1979): $15.06 bln.; partners (1981): USSR 37%, Czech. 8%, Pol. 6%. **Tourists** (1977): 1,100,000.

Transport: Railway traffic (1982): 24.7 bln. passenger-km; 53.6 bln. net ton-km. **Motor vehicles:** in use (1981): 2.8 min. passenger cars, 237,311 comm. vehicles; manuf. (1982): 183,000 passenger cars; 39,000 comm. vehicles. **Civil aviation** (1980): 2 bln. passenger-km; 67 mln. freight ton-km. **Chief ports:** Rostack, Wismar, Stralsund.

Communications: Television sets: 5.7 mln. licensed (1981). **Radios:** 6.4 min. licensed (1981). **Telephones in use** (1981): 3.1 mln. **Daily newspaper circ.** (1982): 515 per 1,000 pop.

Health: Life expectancy at birth (1981): 68.8 male; 74.7 female. **Births** (per 1,000 pop. 1981): 14.2. **Deaths** (per 1,000 pop. 1981): 13.9. **Natural increase** (1978): 0.0%. **Hospital beds** (1980): 171,895. **Physicians** (1980): 33,894. **Infant mortality** (per 1,000 live births 1981): 13.1.

Education (1981): **Literacy:** 99%. **Pop. 5-19:** in school: 66%, teachers per 1,000: 43.

Embassy: 1717 Massachusetts Ave. NW 20036; 232-3134.

The German Democratic Republic was proclaimed in the Soviet sector of Berlin Oct. 7, 1949. It was proclaimed fully sovereign in 1954, but 400,000 Soviet troops remain on grounds of security and the 4-power Potsdam agreement.

Coincident with the entrance of W. Germany into the European Defense community in 1952, the East German government decreed a prohibited zone 3 miles deep along its 600-mile border with W. Germany and cut Berlin's telephone system in two. Berlin was further divided by erection of a fortified wall in 1961, but the exodus of refugees to the West continued, though on a smaller scale.

E. Germany suffered severe economic problems until the mid-1960s. A "new economic system" was introduced, easing the former central planning controls and allowing factories to make profits provided they were reinvested in operations or redistributed to workers as bonuses. By the early 1970s, the economy was highly industrialized. In May 1972 the few remaining private firms were ordered sold to the government. The nation was credited with the highest standard of living among communist countries. But growth slowed in the late 1970s, due to shortages of natural resources and labor, and a huge debt to lenders in the West. There were severe shortages of food items in 1982.

West Germany
Federal Republic of Germany

People: Population (1983 est.): 61,493,000. **Age distrib.** (%): 0–14: 16.8; 15–59: 61.5; 60+: 21.7. **Pop. density:** 642.49 per sq. mi. **Ethnic groups:** Primarily German. **Languages:** German. **Religions:** Protestant 44%, Roman Catholic 45%.

Geography: Area: 96,011 sq. mi., the size of Wyoming. **Location:** In central Europe. **Neighbors:** Denmark on N, Netherlands, Belgium, Luxembourg, France on W, Switzerland, Austria on S, Czechoslovakia, E. Germany on E. **Topography:** West Germany is flat in N, hilly in center and W, and mountainous in Bavaria. Chief rivers are Elbe, Weser, Ems, Rhine, and Main, all flowing toward North Sea, and Danube, flowing toward Black

Sea. **Capital:** Bonn. **Cities** (1982 est.): Berlin 2 mln.; Hamburg 2 mln.; Munich 1.3 mln.; Cologne 976,136; Essen 652,501; Frankfurt 628,203; Dortmund 609,954; Dusseldorf 594,770; Stuttgart 581,989.

Government: Type: Federal Republic. **Head of state:** Pres. Richard von Weizsacker; b. Apr. 15, 1920; in office: May 23, 1984. **Head of government:** Chan. Helmut Kohl; b. Apr. 3, 1930; in office: Oct. 1, 1982. **Local divisions:** West Berlin and 10 laender (states) with substantial powers: Schleswig-Holstein, Hamburg, Lower Saxony, Bremen, North Rhine-Westphalia, Hessen, Rhineland-Palatinate, Baden-Wurttemberg, Bavaria, Saarland. **Defense:** 3.4% of GNP.

Economy: Industries: Steel, ships, autos, machinery, coal, cement, chemicals. **Chief crops:** Grains, potatoes, sugar beets. **Minerals:** Coal, mercury, potash, lignite, iron, zinc, lead, copper, salt, oil. **Crude oil reserves** (1980): 480 mln. bbls. **Per capita arable land:** 0.3 acres. **Meat prod.** (1983): beef: 1.4 mln. metric tons; pork: 3.2 mln. metric tons; lamb: 27,000 metric tons. **Fish catch** (1982): 313,000 metric tons. **Electricity prod.** (1982): 365 bln. kwh. **Crude steel prod.** (1982): 36.3 mln. metric tons. **Labor force:** 6% agric.; 48% ind. & comm.; 25% service.

Finance: Currency: Mark (Mar. 1984: 2.59 = $1 US). **Gross domestic product** (1982): $658.8 bln. **Per capita income** (1982): $11,142. **Imports** (1983): $152.9 bln.; partners: Neth. 12%, Fr. 11%, It. 8%, Belg. 7%. **Exports** (1983): $169.4 bln.; partners: Fr. 14%, Neth. 8%, Belg. 7%, It. 8%. **Tourists** (1981): 9.3 mln.; receipts $6.2 bln. **National budget** (1982): $101.1. bln. **International reserves less gold** (Mar. 1984): $46.2 bln. **Gold:** 95.18 mln. oz t. **Consumer prices** (change in 1983): 3.0%.

Transport: Railway traffic (1982): 36 bln. passenger-km; 57 bln. net ton-km. **Motor vehicles:** in use (1982): 24 mln. passenger cars, 1.2 mln. comm. vehicles; manuf. (1982): 3.7 mln. passenger cars; 286,000 comm. vehicles. **Civil aviation** (1982): 21 bln. passenger-km; 1.6 bln. freight ton-km. **Chief ports:** Hamburg, Bremen, Lubeck.

Communications: Television sets: 19.4 mln. licensed (1979), 4.2 mln. manuf. (1978). **Radios:** 21.1 mln. licensed (1979), 4.6 mln. manuf. (1978). **Telephones in use** (1980): 22.6 mln. **Daily newspaper circ.** (1982): 584 per 1,000 pop.

Health: Life expectancy at birth (1982): 67.2 male; 73.4 female. **Births** (per 1,000 pop. 1980): 10.0. **Deaths** (per 1,000 pop. 1980): 11.5. **Natural increase** (1980): −.2%. **Hospital beds** (1980): 707,710. **Physicians** (1980): 120,000. **Infant mortality** (per 1,000 live births 1983): 13.5.

Education (1983): **Literacy:** 99%. **Years compulsory:** 10; attendance 100%.

Embassy: 4645 Reservoir Rd. NW 20007; 298-4000.

The Federal Republic of Germany was proclaimed May 23, 1949, in Bonn, after a constitution had been drawn up by a consultative assembly formed by representatives of the 11 laender (states) in the French, British, and American zones. Later reorganized into 9 units, the laender numbered 10 with the addition of the Saar, 1957. Berlin also was granted land (state) status, but the 1945 occupation agreements placed restrictions on it.

The occupying powers, the U.S., Britain, and France, restored the civil status, Sept. 21, 1949. The U. S. resumed diplomatic relations July 2, 1951. The powers lifted controls and the republic became fully independent May 5, 1955.

Dr. Konrad Adenauer, Christian Democrat, was made chancellor Sept. 15, 1949, re-elected 1953, 1957, 1961. Willy Brandt, heading a coalition of Social Democrats and Free Democrats, became chancellor Oct. 21, 1969.

In 1970 Brandt signed friendship treaties with the USSR and Poland. In 1971, the U.S., Britain, France, and the USSR signed an agreement on Western access to West Berlin. In 1972 the Bundestag approved the USSR and Polish treaties and East and West Germany signed their first formal treaty, implementing the agreement easing access to West Berlin. In 1973 a West Germany-Czechoslovakia pact normalized relations and nullified the 1938 "Munich Agreement."

In May 1974 Brandt resigned, saying he took full responsibility for "negligence" for allowing an East German spy to become a member of his staff. Helmut Schmidt, Brandt's finance minister, succeeded him.

West Germany has experienced tremendous economic growth since the 1950s. The country leads Europe in provisions for worker participation in the management of industry.

The international economic recession has affected W. Germany; unemployment reached a record 10.4% in March 1983. The NATO decision to deploy medium-range nuclear missiles in Western Europe sparked a demonstration by some 400,000 protesters in April.

Helgoland, an island of 130 acres in the North Sea, was taken from Denmark by a British Naval Force in 1807 and later ceded to Germany to become a part of Schleswig-Holstein province in return for rights in East Africa. The heavily fortified island was surrendered to UK, May 23, 1945, demilitarized in 1947, and returned to W. Germany, Mar 1, 1952. It is a free port.

Ghana
Republic of Ghana

People: Population (1983 est.): 13,367,000. **Age distrib.** (%): 0–14: 46.9; 15-59: 47.7; 60+: 5.3. **Pop. density:** 123 per sq. mi. **Urban** (1974): 31.4%. **Ethnic groups:** Akan 44%, Moshi-Dagomba 16%, Ewe 13%, Ga 8%, others. **Languages:** English (official), 50 tribal languages. **Religions:** Christian 43%, traditional beliefs 45%.

Geography: Area: 92,098 sq. mi., slightly smaller than Oregon. **Location:** On southern coast of W. Africa. **Neighbors:** Ivory Coast on W, Upper Volta on N, Togo on E. **Topography:** Most of Ghana consists of low fertile plains and scrubland, cut by rivers and by the artificial Lake Volta. **Capital:** Accra. **Cities** (1982 est.): Accra 1,045,000.

Government: Type: Authoritarian. **Head of government:** Pres. Jerry Rawlings; b. 1947; in office: Dec. 31, 1981. **Local divisions:** 10 regions.

Economy: Industries: Aluminum, light industry. **Chief crops:** Cocoa (70% of exports), coffee. **Minerals:** Gold, manganese, industrial diamonds, bauxite. **Crude oil reserves:** (1980): 7 mln. bbls. **Other resources:** Timber, rubber. **Arable land:** 70%. **Fish catch** (1981): 240,000 metric tons. **Electricity prod.** (1981): 5 bln. kwh. **Labor force:** 60% agric.; 10% ind.

Finance: Currency: Cedi (Mar. 1984: 3.00 = $1 US). **Gross domestic product** (1980): $13.7 bln. **Per capita income** (1980): $420. **Imports** (1982): $705 mln.; partners (1978): UK 18%, W. Ger. 12%, Nigeria 12%. **Exports** (1982): $873 mln.; partners (1978): UK 16%, U.S. 16%, Neth. 9%, W. Ger. 9%. **Tourists** (1977): 58,900; receipts $6 mln. **National budget** (1979): $1.2 bln. revenues; $1.0 bln. expenditures. **International reserves less gold** (Jan. 1984): 144.9 mln. **Gold:** 384,000 oz t. **Consumer prices** (change in 1982): 22.3%.

Transport: Railway traffic (1980): 521 mln. passenger-km; 312 mln. net ton-km. **Motor vehicles:** in use (1980): 66,000 passenger cars, 48,000 comm. vehicles. **Civil aviation** (1982): 291 mln. passenger-km; 4.8 mln. freight ton-km. **Chief ports:** Tema, Takoradi.

Communications: Television sets: 57,000 in use (1981). **Radios:** 1.9 mln. in use (1981). **Telephones in use** (1980): 68,850.

Health: Life expectancy at birth (1975): 41.9 male; 45.1 female. **Births** (per 1,000 pop. 1978): 46. **Deaths** (per 1,000 pop. 1978): 14. **Natural increase** (1978): 3.3%. **Physicians** (1980): 1,244. **Infant mortality** (per 1,000 live births 1975): 156.

Education (1983): **Literacy:** 30%.

Embassy: 2460 16th St. NW 20009; 462-0761.

Named for an African empire along the Niger River, 400-1240 AD, Ghana was ruled by Britain for 113 years as the Gold Coast. The UN in 1956 approved merger with the British Togoland trust territory. Independence came March 6, 1957. Republic status within the Commonwealth was attained in 1960.

Pres. Kwame Nkrumah built hospitals and schools, promoted development projects like the Volta R. hydroelectric and aluminum plants, but ran the country into debt, jailed opponents, and was accused of corruption. A 1964 referendum gave Nkrumah dictatorial powers and set up a one-party socialist state.

Nkrumah was overthrown in 1966 by a police-army coup, which expelled Chinese and East German teachers and technicians. Elections were held in 1969, but 4 further coups occurred in 1972, 1978, 1979, and 1981. The 1979 and 1981 coups were led by Flight Lieut. Jerry Rawlings. The stagnant economy has continued to deteriorate.

Greece
Hellenic Republic

People: Population (1983 est.): 9,898,000. **Age distrib.** (%): 0–14: 23.7; 15–59: 58.9; 60+: 17.5. **Pop. density:** 190.47 per sq. mi. **Urban** (1981): 58.1%. **Ethnic groups:** Greeks 98.5%. **Languages:** Greek, others. **Religions:** Greek Orthodox 97%. **Geography: Area:** 50,962 sq. mi., the size of New York State. **Location:** Occupies southern end of Balkan Peninsula in SE Europe. **Neighbors:** Albania, Yugoslavia, Bulgaria on N, Turkey on E. **Topography:** About 75% of Greece is non-arable, with mountains in all areas. Pindus Mts. run through the country N to S. The heavily indented coastline is 9,385 mi. long. Of over 2,000 islands, only 169 are inhabited, among them Crete, Rhodes, Milos, Kerkira (Corfu), Chios, Lesbos, Samos, Euboea, Delos, Mykonos. **Capital:** Athens. **Cities** (1981 est.): Athens (met.) 3,016,457; Thessaloniki (met.) 800,000; Patras 120,000.
Government: Type: Presidential Parliamentary Republic. **Head of state:** Pres. Constantine Karamanlis; b. Feb. 23, 1907; in office: May 15, 1980. **Head of government:** Prime Min. Andreas Papandreou; b. Feb. 5, 1919, in office: Oct. 21, 1981. **Local divisions:** 51 prefectures. **Defense:** 4.5% of GNP (1981).
Economy: Industries: Textiles, chemicals, metals, wine, food processng, cement. **Chief crops:** Grains, corn, rice, cotton, tobacco, olives, citrus fruits, raisins, figs. **Minerals:** Bauxite, lignite, oil, manganese. **Crude oil reserves** (1980): 150 mln. bbls. **Per capita arable land:** 0.8 acres. **Meat prod.** (1983): beef: 90,000 metric tons; pork: 155,000 metric tons; lamb: 120,000 metric tons. **Fish catch** (1978): 106,000 metric tons. **Electricity prod.** (1982): 21.0 bln. kwh. **Crude steel prod.** (1982): 910,000 metric tons. **Labor force:** 29% agric.; 30% manuf. 41% service.
Finance: Currency: Drachma (Mar. 1984: 103.34 = $1 US). **Gross domestic product** (1980): $43.8 bln. **Per capita income** (1980): $4,590. **Imports** (1983): $9.5 bln.; partners (1982): W. Ger. 17%, It. 9%, Fr. 7%. **Exports** (1983): $4.4 bln.; partners (1982): W. Ger. 19%, It. 9%, Fr. 7%, Saudi Ar. 6%. **Tourists** (1981): 5 mln.; receipts $1.8 bln. **National budget** (1980): $6.7 bln. revenues; $6.9 bln. expenditures. **International reserves less gold** (Mar. 1984): $807.4 mln. **Gold:** 3.95 mln. oz t. **Consumer prices** (change in 1983): 20.5%.
Transport: Railway traffic (1981): 1.5 bln. passenger-km; 700 mln. net ton-km. **Motor vehicles:** in use (1980): 877,900 passenger cars, 401,970 comm. vehicles. **Civil aviation** (1982): 4.9 bln. passenger-km; 69.4 mln. freight ton-km. **Chief ports:** Piraeus, Thessaloniki, Patrai.
Communications: Television sets: 1.5 mln. in use (1983). **Radios:** 3.3 mln. in use (1983). **Telephones in use** (1982): 2.9 mln. **Daily newspaper circ.** (1982): 88 per 1,000 pop.
Health: Life expectancy at birth (1980): 71 male; 75 female. **Births** (per 1,000 pop. 1979): 15.9. **Deaths** (per 1,000 pop. 1979): 8.7. **Natural increase** (1977): .7%. **Hospital beds** (per 100,000 pop. 1977): 638. **Physicians** (per 100,000 pop. 1977): 221. **Infant mortality** (per 1,000 live births 1978): 17.
Education (1978): Literacy: 95%. **Pop. 5–19:** in school: 70%, teachers per 1,000: 25.
Embassy: 2221 Massachusetts Ave. NW 20008; 667-3168.

The achievements of ancient Greece in art, architecture, science, mathematics, philosophy, drama, literature, and democracy became legacies for succeeding ages. Greece reached the height of its glory and power, particularly in the Athenian city-state, in the 5th century BC.

Greece fell under Roman rule in the 2d and 1st centuries BC. In the 4th century AD it became part of the Byzantine Empire and, after the fall of Constantinople to the Turks in 1453, part of the Ottoman Empire.

Greece won its war of independence from Turkey 1821-1829, and became a kingdom. A republic was established 1924; the monarchy was restored, 1935, and George II, King of the Hellenes, resumed the throne. In Oct., 1940, Greece rejected an ultimatum from Italy. Nazi support resulted in its defeat and occupation by Germans, Italians, and Bulgarians. By the end of 1944 the invaders withdrew. Communist resistance forces were defeated by Royalist and British troops. A plebiscite recalled King George II. He died Apr. 1, 1947, was succeeded by his brother, Paul I.

Communists waged guerrilla war 1947-49 against the government but were defeated with the aid of the U.S.

A period of reconstruction and rapid development followed, mainly with conservative governments under Premier Constantine Karamanlis. The Center Union led by George Papandreou won elections in 1963 and 1964. King Constantine, who acceded in 1964, forced Papandreou to resign. A period of political maneuvers ended in the military takeover of April 21, 1967, by Col. George Papadopoulos. King Constantine tried to reverse the consolidation of the harsh dictatorship Dec. 13, 1967, but failed and fled to Italy. Papadopoulos was ousted Nov. 25, 1973, in a coup led by rightist Brig. Demetrius Ioannides.

Greek army officers serving in the National Guard of Cyprus staged a coup on the island July 15, 1974. Turkey invaded Cyprus a week later, precipitating the collapse of the Greek junta, which was implicated in the Cyprus coup.

The military turned the government over to Karamanlis, who named a civilian cabinet, freed political prisoners, and sought to solve the Cyprus crisis. In Nov. 1974 elections his party won a large parliamentary majority, reduced by socialist gains in 1977. A Dec. 1974 referendum resulted in the proclamation of a republic.

Greece was reintegrated into the military wing of NATO in October 1980, and it became the 10th full member of the European Community on Jan. 1, 1981.

The 1981 victory of the Panhellenic Socialist Movement (Pasok) of Andreas Papandreou has brought about substantial changes in the internal and external policies that Greece has pursued for the past 5 decades.

Grenada
State of Grenada

People: Population (1983 est.): 111,000. **Pop. density:** 812.03 per sq. mi. **Ethnic groups:** Mostly African descent. **Languages:** English (official), French-African patois. **Religions:** Catholic 64%, Anglican 22%.
Geography: Area: 133 sq. mi., twice the size of Washington, D.C. **Location:** 90 mi. N. of Venezuela. **Topography:** Main island is mountainous; country includes Carriacon and Petit Martinique islands. **Capital:** St. George's. **Cities** (1980 est.): St. George's 7,500.
Government: Head of state: Queen Elizabeth II, represented by Gov.-Gen. Paul Scoon, b. July 4, 1935; in office: Sept. 30, 1978. **Head of government:** Chairman of Advisory Council: Nicholas Braithwaite; in office: Dec. 9, 1983. **Local divisions:** 6 parishes and one dependency.
Economy: Industries: Rum. **Chief crops:** Nutmegs, bananas, cocoa, mace. **Arable land:** 45%. **Electricity prod.** (1977): 28.00 mln. kwh. **Labor force:** 23% agric.; 24% ind.
Finance: Currency: East Caribbean dollar (Apr. 1984: 2.70 = $1 US). **Gross domestic product** (1982): $56 mln. **Per capita income** (1977): $500. **Imports** (1982): $56 mln.; partners (1981): UK 16%, Trin./Tob. 19%. **Exports** (1982): $17 mln.; partners (1981): UK 35%, W. Ger. 9%, Neth. 15%. **Tourists** (1981): 102,668. **National budget** (1980): $38.1 mln. revenues; $38.1 mln. expenditures. **International reserves less gold** (Jan. 1984): $12.3 mln.
Transport: Motor vehicles: in use (1971): 3,800 passenger cars, 100 comm. vehicles. **Chief ports:** Saint George's.
Communications: Radios: 63,500 in use (1978). **Telephones in use** (1978): 5,217.
Health: Life expectancy at birth (1984): 69 yrs. **Births** (per 1,000 pop. 1975): 27.4. **Deaths** (per 1,000 pop. 1975): 5.9. **Natural increase** (1975): 2.2%. **Infant mortality** (per 1,000 live births 1984): 16.7.
Education (1984): Literacy: 85%; **Years compulsory:** 6.
Embassy: 1701 New Hampshire Ave. NW 20009; 265-2561.

Columbus sighted the island 1498. First European settlers were French, 1650. The island was held alternately by France and England until final British occupation, 1784. Grenada became fully independent Feb. 7, 1974 during a general strike. It is the smallest independent nation in the Western Hemisphere. The U.S. has criticized the government for following Soviet and Cuban policies.

On Oct. 14, 1983, a military coup ousted Prime Minister Maurice Bishop, who was put under house arrest, later freed by supporters, rearrested, and, finally, on Oct. 19, executed. U.S. forces, with a token force from 6 area nations, invaded Grenada,

Oct. 25. Resistance from the Grenadian army and Cuban advisors was quickly overcome as most of the population welcomed the invading forces as liberators.

Guatemala
Republic of Guatemala

People: Population (1983 est.): 7,714,000. **Age distrib.** (%): 0–14: 45.1; 15–59: 50.6; 60+: 4.4. **Pop. density:** 172.68 per sq. mi. **Urban** (1975): 35.6%. **Ethnic groups:** Indians 54%, Mestizos 42%, whites 4%. **Languages:** Spanish, Indian dialects. **Religions:** Roman Catholics over 88%; Mayan religion practiced.
Geography: Area: 42,042 sq. mi., the size of Tennessee. **Location:** In Central America. **Neighbors:** Mexico N, W; El Salvador on S, Honduras, Belize on E. **Topography:** The central highland and mountain areas are bordered by the narrow Pacific coast and the lowlands and fertile river valleys on the Caribbean. There are numerous volcanoes in S, more than half a dozen over 11,000 ft. **Capital:** Guatemala City. **Cities** (1981 est.): Guatemala City 1,307,300.
Government: Head of state: Pres. Oscar Humberto Mejia Victores; b. 1930; in office: Aug. 8, 1983. **Local divisions:** Guatemala City and 22 departments. **Defense:** 1.2% of GNP (1981).
Economy: Industries: Prepared foods, tires, textiles. **Chief crops:** Coffee (one third of exports), sugar, bananas, cotton. **Minerals:** Oil, nickel. **Crude oil reserves** (1981): 120 mln. bbls. **Other resources:** Rare woods, fish, chicle. **Arable land:** 15%. **Meat prod.** (1980): beef; 79,000 metric tons; pork: 16,000 metric tons. **Electricity prod.** (1981): 1.9 bln. kwh. **Labor force:** 53% agric.; 17.2% manuf., 23.3% services.
Finance: Currency: Quetzal (Apr. 1984: 1.00 = $1 US). **Gross domestic product** (1980): $7.8 bln. **Per capita income** (1980): $1,083. **Imports** (1983): $1.1 bln.; partners: U.S. 34%, Jap. 8%, Venez. 7%. **Exports** (1983): $1.1 bln.; partners: U.S. 18%, W. Ger. 8%, El Salv. 18%. **National budget** (1980): $407 mln. revenues; $603 mln. expenditures. **International reserves less gold** (Mar. 1984): $238.7 mln. **Gold:** 522,000 oz t. **Consumer prices** (change in 1982): 0.4%.
Transport: Railway traffic (1976): 117 mln. net ton-km. **Motor vehicles:** in use (1980): 166,900 passenger cars, 81,500 comm. vehicles. **Civil aviation** (1982) 160 mln. passenger-km; 5.5 mln. freight ton-km. **Chief ports:** Puerto Barrios, San Jose.
Communications: Television sets: 175,000 in use (1981). **Radios:** 285,000 in use (1981). **Telephones in use** (1981): 81,622. **Daily newspaper circ.** (1982): 47 per 1,000 pop.
Health: Life expectancy at birth (1965): 48.29 male; 49.74 female. **Births** (per 1,000 pop. 1978): 42. **Deaths** (per 1,000 pop. 1978): 11. **Natural increase** (1978): 3.1% **Hospital beds** (per 100,000 pop. 1977): 187. **Physicians** (per 100,000 pop. 1977): 40. **Infant mortality** (per 1,000 live births 1981): 77.
Education (1981): **Literacy:** 47%. **Pop. 5-19:** in school: 31%, teachers per 1,000: 11.
Embassy: 2220 R St. NW 20008; 745-4952.

The old Mayan Indian empire flourished in what is today Guatemala for over 1,000 years before the Spanish.

Guatemala was a Spanish colony 1524-1821; briefly a part of Mexico and then of the U.S. of Central America, the republic was established in 1839.

Since 1945 when a liberal government was elected to replace the long-term dictatorship of Jorge Ubico, the country has seen a swing toward socialism, an armed revolt, renewed attempts at social reform and a military coup. Assassinations and political violence from left and right plagued the country. The Guerrilla Army of the Poor, an insurgent group founded 1975, has stepped up their military offensive by attacking army posts and has succeeded in incorporating segments of the large Indian population in its struggle against the government.

Dissident army officers seized power, Mar. 23, 1982, denouncing the Mar. 7 Presidential election as fraudulent and pledging to restore "authentic democracy" to the nation. Political violence has caused some 200,000 Guatemalans to seek refuge in Mexico. A second military coup occurred Oct. 8, 1983; a return to democracy was promised by 1985.

Guinea
Republic of Guinea

People: Population (1983 est.): 5,430,000. **Pop. density:** 55.83 per sq. mi. **Ethnic groups:** Foulah 40%, Malinké 25%, Soussous 10%, 15 other tribes. **Languages:** French (official), tribal languages. **Religions:** Muslims 75%, tribal 24%.
Geography: Area: 94,925 sq. mi., slightly smaller than Oregon. **Location:** On Atlantic coast of W. Africa. **Neighbors:** Guinea-Bissau, Senegal, Mali on N, Ivory Coast on E, Liberia on S. **Topography:** A narrow coastal belt leads to the mountainous middle region, the source of the Gambia, Senegal, and Niger rivers. Upper Guinea, farther inland, is a cooler upland. The SE is forested. **Capital:** Conakry. **Cities** (1980 est.): Conakry 575,000; Labe 419,000; N'Zerekore 291,000; Kankan 265,000.
Government: Type: Republic. **Head of state:** Pres. Col. Lansana Conte; b. 1944; in office: Apr. 5, 1984. **Head of government:** Prime Min. Louis Lansana Beavogui; b. 1923; in office: Apr. 26, 1972. **Local divisions:** 33 districts. **Defense:** 29% of govt. budget.
Economy: Chief crops: Bananas, pineapples, rice, corn, palm nuts, coffee, honey. **Minerals:** Bauxite, iron, diamonds. **Arable land:** 30%. **Meat prod.** (1980): beef 18,000 metric tons. **Electricity prod.** (1977) 500.00 mln. kwh. **Labor force:** 82% agric.; 11% ind. & comm.
Finance: Currency: Syli (Sept. 1982: 22.86 = $1 US). **Gross domestic product** (1981): $1.6 bln. **Per capita income** (1980): $293. **Imports** (1981): $375 mln.; partners (1979): Fr. 36% USSR 11%, U.S. 6% It. 6%. **Exports** (1981): $385 mln.; partners (1979): U.S. 18%, Fr. 13%, W. Ger. 12%, USSR 12%. **National budget** (1982): 140 mln. **Consumer prices** (change in 1981): 5.6%.
Transport: Motor vehicles: in use (1979): 10,000 passenger cars, 11,000 comm. vehicles. **Chief ports:** Conakry.
Communications: Radios: 121,000 in use (1979). **Daily newspaper circ.** (1982): 2 per 1,000 pop.
Health: Life expectancy at birth (1975): 39.4 male; 42.6 female. **Births** (per 1,000 pop. 1978): 47. **Deaths** (per 1,000 pop. 1978): 26. **Natural increase** (1978): 2.6%. **Hospital beds** (per 100,000 pop. 1977): 158. **Physicians** (per 100,000 pop. 1977): 6. **Infant mortality** (per 1,000 live births 1980): 172.
Education (1983): **Literacy:** 48%. **Years compulsory:** 12; attendance: 34% primary, 15% secondary.
Embassy: 2112 Leroy Pl. NW 20008; 438-9420.

Part of the ancient West African empires, Guinea fell under French control 1849-98. Under Sekou Toure, it opted for full independence in 1958, and France withdrew all aid.

Toure turned to communist nations for support, and set up a militant one-party state. Western firms, as well as the Soviet government, have invested in Guinea's vast bauxite mines.

Thousands of opponents were jailed in the 1970s, in the aftermath of an unsuccessful Portuguese invasion. Many were tortured and killed.

The military took control of the government in a bloodless coup after the March 1984 death of Toure.

Guinea-Bissau
Republic of Guinea-Bissau

People: Population (1983 est.): 827,000. **Pop. density:** 39.43 per sq. mi. **Ethnic groups:** Balanta 30%, Fula 20%, Mandyako 14%, Mandinga 13%. **Languages:** Portuguese (official) Criolo, tribal languages. **Religions:** Moslems 38%, Christians 5%, tribal 50%.
Geography: Area: 13,948 sq. mi. **Location:** On Atlantic coast of W. Africa. **Neighbors:** Senegal on N, Guinea on E, S. **Topography:** A swampy coastal plain covers most of the country; the east is a low savanna region. **Capital:** Bissau. **Cities** (1979) Bissau 109,500.
Government: Type: Republic. **Head of government:** Gen. Joao Bernardo Vieira; b. 1939; in office: Nov. 14,1980. **Local divisions:** 8 regions. **Defense:** 31% of govt. budget (1981).

Economy: Chief crops: Peanuts, cotton, rice. **Minerals:** Bauxite. **Arable land:** 8%. **Electricity prod.** (1977): 24.00 mln. kwh. **Labor force:** 90% agric.
Finance: Currency: Peso (Sept. 1983: 41.84 = $1 US). **Gross domestic product** (1979): $132 mln. **Per capita income** (1979): $170. **Imports** (1980): $60 mln.; partners: Port. 31%, Swed. 8%, USSR 7%, Fr. 11%. **Exports** (1980): $10 mln.; partners: Port. 27%, Sp. 25%.
Communications: Radios: 11,000 licensed (1976). **Daily newspaper circ.** (1982): 7 per 1,000 pop.
Health: Life expectancy at birth (1982): 35 years. **Births** (per 1,000 pop. 1978): 40. **Deaths** (per 1,000 pop. 1978): 23. **Natural increase** (1978): 1.7%. **Infant mortality** (per 1,000 live births 1982): 250.
Education (1982): Literacy 9%. **Years compulsory:** 4.
Embassy: 211 E 43d St., New York, NY 10017; (212) 661-3977.

Portuguese mariners explored the area in the mid-15th century; the slave trade flourished in the 17th and 18th centuries, and colonization began in the 19th.

Beginning in the 1960s, an independence movement waged a guerrilla war and formed a government in the interior that achieved international support. Full independence came Sept. 10, 1974, after the Portuguese regime was overthrown.

The November 1980 coup gave Joao Bernardo Vieira absolute power.

Guyana

Cooperative Republic of Guyana

People: Population (1983 est.): 833,000. **Age distrib.** (%): 0–14: 43.7; 5–59: 50.7; 60+: 5.6. **Pop. density:** 9.88 per sq. mi. **Urban** (1971): 29.6%. **Ethnic groups:** East Indians 51%, African 30%, mixed 10%. **Languages:** English (official), Hindi, Portuguese, Chinese, Negro patois. **Religions:** Christians 57%, Hindus 34%, Moslems 9%.
Geography: Area: 83,000 sq. mi., the size of Idaho. **Location:** On N coast of S. America. **Neighbors:** Venezuela on W, Brazil on S, Suriname on E. **Topography:** Dense tropical forests cover much of the land, although a flat coastal area up to 40 mi. wide, where 90% of the population lives, provides rich alluvial soil for agriculture. A grassy savanna divides the 2 zones. **Capital:** Georgetown. **Cities** (1982 est.): Georgetown 170,000.
Government: Type: Republic within the Commonwealth of Nations. **Head of state:** President Linden Forbes Burnham; b. Feb. 20, 1923; in office: Dec. 14, 1964. **Head of Government:** Prime Min. Ptolemy Reid. **Local divisions:** 10 regions. **Defense:** 7.4% of GDP (1982).
Economy: Industries: Cigarettes, rum, clothing, furniture, drugs. **Chief crops:** Sugar, rice, citrus and other fruits. **Minerals:** Bauxite, diamonds. **Other resources:** Timber, shrimp. **Arable land:** 2%. **Fish catch** (1978): 17,700 metric tons. **Electricity prod.** (1981): 440 bln. kwh. **Labor force:** 33% agric.; 45% ind. & comm.; 22% services.
Finance: Currency: Dollar (Mar. 1984: 3.75 = $1 US). **Gross national product** (1981): $507 mln. **Per capita income** (1981): $603. **Imports** (1982): $705 mln.; partners: U.S. 28%, Trin-Tob. 24%, UK 20%. **Exports** (1982): $873 mln.; partners: UK 28%, U.S. 18%, Trin-Tob. 7%. **National budget** (1981): $381 mln. **International reserves less gold** (Feb. 1984): $3.72 mln. **Consumer prices** (change in 1983): 56.8%.
Transport: Railway traffic (1974): 6 mln. passenger-km. **Motor vehicles:** in use (1980): 35,000 passenger cars, 18,000 comm. vehicles. **Chief ports:** Georgetown.
Communications: Radios: 275,000 in use (1976). **Telephones in use** (1978): 27,064. **Daily newspaper circ.** (1982): 195 per 1,000 pop.
Health: Life expectancy at birth (1982): 69.1 years. **Births** (per 1,000 pop. 1978): 28.3. **Deaths** (per 1,000 pop. 1978): 7.3. **Natural increase** (1978): 2.1% **Hospital beds** (per 100,000 pop. 1977): 485. **Physicians** (per 100,000 pop. 1977): 25. **Infant mortality** (per 1,000 live births 1982): 45.
Education (1982): **Literacy:** 85%. **Years compulsory:** ages 5-14.
Embassy: 2490 Tracy Pl. NW 20008; 265-6900.

Guyana became a Dutch possession in the 17th century, but sovereignty passed to Britain in 1815. Indentured servants from India soon outnumbered African slaves. Ethnic tension has affected political life.

Guyana became independent May 26, 1966. A Venezuelan claim to the western half of Guyana was suspended in 1970 but renewed in 1982. The Suriname border is also disputed. The government has nationalized most of the economy which has remained severely depressed.

The Port Kaituma ambush of U.S. Rep. Leo J. Ryan and others investigating mistreatment of American followers of the Rev. Jim Jones' People's Temple cult, triggered a mass suicide-execution of 911 cultists in the Guyana jungle, Nov. 18, 1978.

Haiti

Republic of Haiti

People: Population (1983 est.): 5,690,000. **Age distrib.** (%): 4–14: 41.5; 15–59: 51.8; 60+: 6.7. **Pop. density:** 535.75 per sq. mi. **Urban** (1981): 20.7%. **Ethnic groups:** African descent 95%. **Languages:** French (official), Creole (majority). **Religions:** Roman Catholics 80%, Protestants 10%; Voodoo widely practiced.
Geography: Area: 10,714 sq. mi., the size of Maryland. **Location:** In West Indies, occupies western third of I. of Hispaniola. **Neighbors:** Dominican Republic on E, Cuba on W. **Topography:** About two-thirds of Haiti is mountainous. Much of the rest is semiarid. Coastal areas are warm and moist. **Capital:** Port-au-Prince. **Cities** (1978 est.): Port-au-Prince 763,000.
Government: Type: Republic. **Head of state:** Pres. Jean-Claude Duvalier; b. July 3, 1951; in office: Apr. 22, 1971. **Local divisions:** 9 departments. **Armed forces:** regulars 6,550; paramilitary 14,900.
Economy: Industries: Rum, molasses, tourism. **Chief crops:** Coffee, sisal, cotton, sugar, bananas, cocoa, tobacco, rice. **Minerals:** Bauxite, copper, gold, silver, metric tons. **Other resources:** Timber. **Arable land:** 30%. **Meat prod.** (1980): beef: 24,000 metric tons; pork: 33,000 metric tons; lamb: 6,000 metric tons. **Electricity prod.** (1981): 325 mln. kwh. **Labor force:** 79% agric.; 7% man.; 14% services.
Finance: Currency: Gourde (Apr. 1984: 5.00 = $1 US). **Gross domestic product** (1978): $1.34 bln. **Per capita income** (1983): $300. **Imports** (1978): $221 mln.; partners: U.S. 45%, Neth. Ant. 10%, Jap. 9%. Can. 8%. **Exports** (1980): $185 mln.; partners (1978): U.S. 59%, Fr. 13%, It. 7%, Belg. 6%. **Tourists** (1977): 96,000; receipts $37 mln. **National budget** (1979): $94 mln. revenues; $94 mln. expenditures. **International reserves less gold** (Mar. 1984): $13.5 mln. **Gold:** 18,000 oz t. **Consumer prices** (change in 1982): 1.4%.
Transport: Motor vehicles: in use (1981): 17,400 passenger cars, 3,100 comm. vehicles. **Chief ports:** Port-au-Prince, Les Cayes.
Communications: Television sets: 25,000 in use (1980). **Radios:** 120,000 in use (1980). **Telephones in use** (1980): 34,900 **Daily newspaper circ.** (1982): 4 per 1,000 pop.
Health: Life expectancy at birth (1975): 47.1 male; 50.0 female. **Births** (per 1,000 pop. 1978): 42. **Deaths** (per 1,000 pop. 1978): 16. **Natural increase** (1978): 2.4%. **Hospital beds** (per 100,000 pop. 1977): 72. **Physicians** (per 100,000 pop. 1977): 7.
Education (1978): **Literacy:** 23% **Pop. 5-19:** in school: 33%, teachers per 1,000: 9.
Embassy: 2311 Massachusetts Ave. NW 20008; 332-4090.

Haiti, visited by Columbus, 1492, and a French colony from 1677, attained its independence, 1804, following the rebellion led by former slave Toussaint L'Ouverture. Following a period of political violence, the U.S. occupied the country 1915-34.

Dr. Francois Duvalier was voted president in 1957; in 1964 he was named president for life. Upon his death in 1971, he was succeeded by his son, Jean-Claude. Drought in 1975-77 brought famine, and Hurricane Allen in 1980 destroyed most of the rice, bean, and coffee crops.

Haiti is the poorest nation in the Western hemisphere with 77% of the population earning less than $150 per year. The U.S. has sent aid despite serious human rights abuses.

Honduras

Republic of Honduras

People: Population (1983 est.): 4,276,000. **Age distrib. (%):** 0–14: 48.1; 15–59: 47.5; 60+: 4.5. **Pop. density:** 85.26 per sq. mi. **Urban** (1974): 31.4%. **Ethnic groups:** Mestizo 90%, Europeans, Negroes, Indians. **Languages:** Spanish, Indian dialects. **Religions:** Roman Catholics, small Protestant minority. **Geography: Area:** 43,277 sq. mi., slightly larger than Tennessee. **Location:** In Central America. **Neighbors:** Guatemala on W, El Salvador, Nicaragua on S. **Topography:** The Caribbean coast is 500 mi. long. Pacific coast, on Gulf of Fonseca, is 40 mi. long. Honduras is mountainous, with wide fertile valleys and rich forests. **Capital:** Tegucigalpa. **Cities** (1981 est.) Tegucigalpa 502,500; San Pedro Sula 342,800.
Government: Type: Democratic. **Head of State:** Pres. Roberto Suazo Cordova; in office: Jan. 27, 1982. **Local divisions:** 18 departments. **Defense:** 9.3% of govt. budget (1980).
Economy: Industries: Clothing, textiles, cement, wood prods. **Chief crops:** Bananas (chief export), coffee, corn, beans. **Minerals:** Gold, silver, copper, lead, zinc, iron, antimony, coal. **Other resources:** Timber. **Arable land:** 10%. **Meat prod.** (1980): beef: 56,000 metric tons; pork: 9,000 metric tons. **Electricity prod.** (1981): 955 mln. kwh. **Labor force:** 59% agric.; 20% ind. & comm.; 15% service.
Finance: Currency: Lempira (Apr. 1984): 2.00 = $1 US). **Gross national product** (1980): $5.0 bln. **Per capita income** (1980): $822. **Imports** (1981): $900 mln.; partners: U.S. 41%, Jap. 7%, Guat. 6%. **Exports** (1981): $760 mln.; partners: U.S. 52%, W. Ger. 8%, Jap. 5%. **Tourists** (1980): 97,581. **National budget** (1980): $378 mln. revenues; $448 mln. expenditures. **International reserves less gold** (Feb. 1984): $106.1 mln. **Gold:** 16,000 oz t. **Consumer prices** (change in 1982): 3.1%.
Transport: Motor vehicles: in use (1982) 58,900 passenger cars, 18,200 comm. vehicles. **Civil aviation** (1982): 331 mln. passenger-km; 3.1 mln. freight ton-km. **Chief ports:** Puerto Cortes, La Ceiba.
Communications: Television sets: 49,000 in use (1981). **Radios:** 176,000 in use (1981). **Telephones in use** (1980): 27,400. **Daily newspaper circ.** (1982): 99 per 1,000 pop.
Health: Life expectancy at birth (1982): 53 yrs. **Births** (per 1,000 pop. 1980): 49.3. **Deaths** (per 1,000 pop. 1980): 12.4. **Natural increase** (1978): 3.5%. **Hospital beds** (1980): 5,230. **Physicians** (1980): 1,370. **Infant mortality** (per 1,000 live births 1982): 117.
Education (1982): **Literacy:** 47%. **Years compulsory:** 6; attendance: 70%.
Embassy: 4301 Connecticut Ave. NW 20008; 966-7700.

Mayan civilization flourished in Honduras in the 1st millenium AD. Columbus arrived in 1502. Honduras became independent after freeing itself from Spain, 1821 and from the Fed. of Central America, 1838.

Gen. Oswaldo Lopez Arellano, president for most of the period 1963-75 by virtue of one election and 2 coups, was ousted by the Army in 1975 over charges of pervasive bribery by United Brands Co. of the U.S.

The government has resumed land distribution, raised minimum wages, and started a literacy campaign. An elected civilian government took power in 1982, the country's first in 10 years.

The U.S. has provided military aid and advisors to help withstand pressures from Nicaragua and help block arms shipments from Nicaragua to rebel forces in El Salvador. The U.S. conducted large-scale joint military exercises with Honduras in 1983 and 1984.

Hungary

Hungarian People's Republic

People: Population (1983 est.): 10,691,000. **Age distrib. (%):** 0–14: 21.7; 15–59: 61.4; 60+: 16.9. **Pop. density:** 298 per sq. mi. **Urban** (1980): 54%. **Ethnic groups:** Magyar 92%, German 2.5%, Gypsy 3%. **Languages:** Hungarian (Magyar). **Religions:** Roman Catholics 67%, Protestant 25%.
Geography: Area: 35,919 sq. mi., slightly smaller than Indiana. **Location:** In East Central Europe. **Neighbors:** Czechoslovakia on N, Austria on W, Yugoslavia on S, Romania, USSR on

E. Topography: The Danube R. forms the Czech border in the NW, then swings S to bisect the country. The eastern half of Hungary is mainly a great fertile plain, the Alfold; the W and N are hilly. **Capital:** Budapest. **Cities** (1982 est.): Budapest 2,085,615; Miskolc 210,000; Debrecen 196,000.
Government: Type: Communist unitary state. **Head of state:** Pres. Pal Losonczi; b. Sept. 18, 1919; in office: Apr. 14, 1967. **Head of government:** Prem. Gyorgy Lazar; b. Sept. 15, 1924; in office: May 15, 1975. **Head of Communist Party:** Janos Kadar; b. May 26, 1912; in office: Oct. 25, 1956. **Local divisions:** 19 counties, 5 cities with county status. **Defense:** 3.9% of govt. budget (1983).
Economy: Industries: Iron and steel, machinery, pharmaceuticals, vehicles, communications equip., milling, distilling. **Chief crops:** Grains, vegetables, fruits, grapes. **Minerals:** Bauxite, natural gas. **Arable land:** 50.4%. **Meat prod.** (1983): beef: 133,000 metric tons; pork: 1.1 mln. metric tons. **Electricity prod.** (1982): 24.4 bln. kwh. **Crude steel prod.** (1982): 3.7 mln. metric tons. **Labor force:** 20% agric.; 42% ind. & comm.; 32% services.
Finance: Currency: Forint (Feb. 1984: 45.70 = $1 US). **Gross domestic product** (1981): $20.9 bln. **Per capita income** (1982): $4,180. **Imports** (1981): $9.2 bln.; partners: USSR 29%, W. Ger. 11%, E. Ger. 7%, Czech. 5%. **Exports** (1981): $8.7 bln.; partners: USSR 34%, E. Ger. 6%, W. Ger. 7%, Czech. 6%. **National budget** (1983): $13.4 bln. **Tourists** (1977): 7,194,000; receipts $320 mln. **Consumer prices** (change in 1983): 23%.
Transport: Railway traffic (1982): 11.8 bln. passenger-km; 22.7 bln. net ton-km. **Motor vehicles:** in use (1981): 1.1 mln. passenger cars, 129,800 comm. vehicles; manuf. (1982): 11,000 comm. vehicles. **Civil aviation** (1982): 1.2 bln. Passenger-km; 9.2 mln. net freight-km.
Communications: Television sets: 2.8 mln. licensed (1982). **Radios:** 2.7 mln. licensed (1981). **Telephones in use** (1981): 1.2 mln. **Daily newspaper circ.** (1982): 383 per 1,000 pop.
Health: Life expectancy at birth (1981): 66.0 male; 73.4 female. **Births** (per 1,000 pop. 1982): 12.5 **Deaths** (per 1,000 pop. 1982): 12.5. **Natural increase** (1980): .3%. **Hospital beds** (1980): 95,539. **Physicians** (1980): 30,836. **Infant mortality** (per 1,000 live births 1983): 20.6
Education (1983): **Literacy:** 98%. **Years compulsory:** to age 16; attendance 99%.
Embassy: 3910 Shoemaker St. NW 20008; 362-6730.

Earliest settlers, chiefly Slav and Germanic, were overrun by Magyars from the east. Stephen I (997-1038) was made king by Pope Sylvester II in 1000 AD. The country suffered repeated Turkish invasions in the 15th-17th centuries. After the defeats of the Turks, 1686-1697, Austria dominated, but Hungary obtained concessions until it regained internal independence in 1867, with the emperor of Austria as king of Hungary in a dual monarchy with a single diplomatic service. Defeated with the Central Powers in 1918, Hungary lost Transylvania to Romania, Croatia and Bacska to Yugoslavia, Slovakia and Carpatho-Ruthenia to Czechoslovakia, all of which had large Hungarian minorities. A republic under Michael Karolyi and a bolshevist revolt under Bela Kun were followed by a vote for a monarchy in 1920 under Admiral Nicholas Horthy as regent.

Hungary joined Germany in World War II, and was allowed to annex most of its lost territories. Russian troops captured the country, 1944-1945. By terms of an armistice with the Allied powers Hungary agreed to give up territory acquired by the 1938 dismemberment of Czechoslovakia and to return to its borders of 1937.

A republic was declared Feb. 1, 1946; Zoltan Tildy was elected president. In 1947 the communists forced Tildy out. Premier Imre Nagy, in office since mid-1953, was ousted for his moderate policy of favoring agriculture and consumer production, April 18, 1955.

In 1956, popular demands for the ousting of Erno Gero, Communist party secretary, and for formation of a government by Nagy, resulted in the latter's appointment Oct. 23; demonstrations against communist rule developed into open revolt. Gero called in Soviet forces. On Nov. 4 Soviet forces launched a massive attack against Budapest with 200,000 troops, 2,500 tanks and armored cars.

Estimates varied from 6,500 to 32,000 dead, and thousands deported. About 200,000 persons fled the country. In the spring of 1963 the regime freed many anti-communists and captives from the revolution in a sweeping amnesty. Nagy was executed by the Russians.

Some 60,000 Soviet troops are stationed in Hungary. Hungarian troops participated in the 1968 Warsaw Pact invasion of Czechoslovakia.

Major economic reforms were launched early in 1968, switching from a central planning system to one in which market forces and profit control much of production. Productivity and living standards have improved. Hungary leads the communist states in comparative tolerance for cultural freedoms and small private enterprise.

Iceland

Republic of Iceland

People: Population (1983 est.): 236,000. **Age distrib. (%):** 0–14: 26.7; 15–59: 59.5; 60+: 13.8. **Pop. density:** 5.79 per sq. mi. **Urban** (1982): 88.9% **Ethnic groups:** Homogeneous, descendants of Norwegians, Celts. **Language:** Icelandic. **Religion:** Evangelical Lutheran 97%.

Geography: Area: 39,769 sq. mi., the size of Virginia. **Location:** At N end of Atlantic O. **Neighbors:** Nearest is Greenland. **Topography:** Iceland is of recent volcanic origin. Three-quarters of the surface is wasteland: glaciers, lakes, a lava desert. There are geysers and hot springs, and the climate is moderated by the Gulf Stream. **Capital:** Reykjavik. **Cities** (1983 est.): Reykjavik 85,782.

Government: Type: Constitutional Republic. **Head of state:** Pres. Vigdis Finnbogadottir; b. Apr. 15, 1930; in office: Aug. 1, 1980. **Head of government:** Prime Min. Steingrimur Hermannsson; b. June 22, 1928; in office: May 26, 1983. **Local divisions:** 7 districts.

Economy: Industries: Fish products (some 80% of exports), aluminum. **Chief crops:** Potatoes, turnips, hay. **Arable land:** 0.5%. **Meat prod.** (1983): lamb: 14,000 metric tons. **Fish catch** (1982): 776,000 metric tons. **Electricity prod.** (1982): 3.2 bln. kwh. **Labor force:** 19% agric.; 43% ind. & comm.; 34% services & govt.

Finance: Currency: Kronur (Mar. 1984: 28.99 = $1 US). **Gross domestic product** (1980): $1.7 bln. **Per capita income** (1979): $9,000. **Imports** (1980): $1.00 bln.; partners: USSR 9%, W. Ger. 12%, UK 9%, Den. 10%. **Exports** (1980): $929 mln.; partners: U.S. 26%, UK 13%, Port. 12%. **Tourists** (1977): 72,700; receipts: $15 mln. **National budget** (1980): $455 mln. revenues; $451 mln. expenditures. **International reserves less gold** (Mar. 1984): $161.9 mln. **Gold:** 49,000 oz t. **Consumer prices** (change in 1983): 55.9%.

Transport: Motor vehicles: in use (1982): 91,457 passenger cars, 9,479 comm. vehicles. **Civil aviation** (1982): 1.4 bln. passenger-km; 23.7 mln. freight ton-km . **Chief ports:** Reykjavik.

Communications: Television sets: 62,500 in use (1982). **Radios:** 69,700 licensed (1982). **Telephones in use** (1982): 111,358. **Daily newspaper circ.** (1982): 557 per 1,000 pop.

Health: Life expectancy at birth (1981): 73.4 male; 79.3 female. **Births** (per 1,000 pop. 1978): 18.6. **Deaths** (per 1,000 pop. 1978): 6.5. **Natural increase** (1978): 1.2%. **Hospital beds** per 100,000 pop. 1977): 1,700. **Physicians** (per 100,000 pop. 977): 180. **Infant mortality** per (1,000 live births 1981): 9.6.

Education (1981): **Literacy:** 99.9%. **Pop. 5-19:** in school: 0%, teachers per 1,000: 46.

Embassy: 2022 Connecticut Ave. NW 20008; 265-6653.

Iceland was an independent republic from 930 to 1262, when joined with Norway. Its language has maintained its purity for ,000 years. Danish rule lasted from 1380-1918; the last ties ith the Danish crown were severed in 1941. The Althing, or assembly, is the world's oldest surviving parliament.

A four-year dispute with Britain ended in 1976 when the latter accepted Iceland's 200-mile territorial waters claim.

India

Republic of India

People: Population (1983 est.): 730,572,000. **Age distrib. %):** 0–14: 40.8; 15–59: 53.9; 60+: 5.3. **Pop. density:** 572 per q. mi. **Urban** (1981): 21.5%. **Ethnic groups:** Indo-Aryan groups 72%, Dravidians 25%, Mongoloids 3%. **Languages:** 16 languages, including Hindi (official) and English (associate official). **Religions:** Hindu 83%, Moslem 11%, Christian 3%, Sikh 2%.

Geography: Area: 1,269,420 sq. mi., one third the size of the U.S. **Location:** Occupies most of the Indian subcontinent in S. Asia. **Neighbors:** Pakistan on W, China, Nepal, Bhutan on N, Burma, Bangladesh on E. **Topography:** The Himalaya Mts., highest in world, stretch across India's northern borders. Below, the Ganges Plain is wide, fertile, and among the most densely populated regions of the world. The area below includes the Deccan Peninsula. Close to one quarter the area is forested. The climate varies from tropical heat in S to near-Arctic cold in N. Rajasthan Desert is in NW; NE Assam Hills get 400 in. of rain a year. **Capital:** New Delhi. **Cities** (1980 cen.): Calcutta 9.1 mln.; Bombay (met.) 8.2 mln.; Delhi 5.2 mln.; Madras 4.3 mln.; Bangalore 2.9 mln.; Hyderabad 1.5 mln.; Ahmedabad 2.5 mln.; Kanpur 1.7 mln.; Pune 1.7 mln.; Nagpur 1.3 mln.

Government: Type: Federal Republic. **Head of state:** Pres. Zail Singh; b. May 5, 1916; in office: July 12, 1982. **Head of government:** Prime Min. Indira Gandhi; b. Nov. 19, 1917; in office: Jan. 14, 1980. **Local divisions:** 22 states, 9 union territories. **Defense:** 3.1% of GNP (1980).

Economy: Industries: Textiles, steel, processed foods, cement, machinery, chemicals, fertilizers, consumer appliances, autos. **Chief crops:** Rice, grains, coffee, sugar cane, spices, tea, cashews, cotton, copra, coir, juta, linseed. **Minerals:** Chromium, coal, iron, manganese, mica salt, bauxite, gypsum, oil. **Crude oil reserves** (1980): 2.60 bln. bbls. **Other resources:** Rubber, timber. **Per capita arable land:** 0.6 acres. **Meat prod.** (1983): beef: 210,000 metric tons; pork: 80,000 metric tons; lamb: 420,000 metric tons. **Fish catch** (1981): 2.4 mln. metric tons. **Electricity prod.** (1981): 125 bln. kwh. **Crude steel prod.** (1982): 10.8 mln. metric tons. **Labor force:** 70% agric.; 19% ind. & comm.

Finance: Currency: Rupee (Mar. 1984: 10.70 = $1 US). **Gross domestic product** (1981): $167 bln. **Per capita income** (1977): $150. **Imports** (1982): $14.7 bln.; partners: U.S. 12%, USSR 8%, W. Ger. 6%, Iran 11%. **Exports** (1983): $9.3 bln.; partners: U.S. 11%, USSR 18%, UK 6%, Jap. 9%. **Tourists** (1977): 640,400; receipts: $350 mln. **National budget** (1980): $13.4 bln. revenues; $14.7 bln. expenditures. **International reserves less gold** (Jan. 1984): $4.9 bln. **Gold:** 8.59 mln. oz. t. **Consumer prices** (change in 1983): 16.5%.

Transport: Railway traffic (1982): 221 bln. passenger-km; 173 bln. net ton-km. **Motor vehicles:** in use (1979): 1.03 mln. passenger cars, 440,200 comm. vehicles; manuf. (1982): 63,000 passenger cars, 87,000 comm. vehicles. **Civil aviation** (1982): 13.2 bln. passenger-km; 446 mln. freight ton-km. **Chief ports:** Calcutta, Bombay, Madras, Cochin, Vishakhapatnam.

Communications: Television sets: 1.1 mln. licensed (1981). **Radios:** 30 mln. licensed (1981).**Telephones in use** (1981): 2.7 mln. **Daily newspaper circ.** (1981): 21 per. 1,000 pop.

Health: Life expectancy at birth (1981): 52 male; 50 female. **Births** (per 1,000 pop. 1980): 33.5. **Deaths** (per 1,000 pop. 1980): 12.5. **Natural increase** (1978): 1.9%. **Hospital beds** (per 100,000 pop. 1977): 75. **Physicians** (per 100,000 pop. 1977): 26. **Infant mortality** (per 1,000 live births 1978): 139.

Education (1981): **Literacy:** 36%. **Pop. 5-19:** in school: 42%, teachers per 1,000: 13.

Embassy: 2107 Massachusetts Ave. NW 20008; 265-5050.

India has one of the oldest civilizations in the world. Excavations trace the Indus Valley civilization back for at least 5,000 years. Paintings in the mountain caves of Ajanta, richly carved temples, the Taj Mahal in Agra, and the Kutab Minar in Delhi are among relics of the past.

Aryan tribes, speaking Sanskrit, invaded from the NW around 1500 BC, and merged with the earlier inhabitants to create classical Indian civilization.

Asoka ruled most of the Indian subcontinent in the 3d century BC, and established Buddhism. But Hinduism revived and eventually predominated. During the Gupta kingdom, 4th-6th century AD, science, literature, and the arts enjoyed a "golden age."

Arab invaders established a Moslem foothold in the W in the 8th century, and Turkish Moslems gained control of North India by 1200. The Mogul emperors ruled 1526-1857.

Vasco de Gama established Portuguese trading posts 1498-1503. The Dutch followed. The British East India Co. sent Capt. William Hawkins, 1609, to get concessions from the Mogul emperor for spices and textiles. Operating as the East India Co.

the British gained control of most of India. The British parliament assumed political direction; under Lord Bentinck, 1828-35, rule by rajahs was curbed. After the Sepoy troops mutinied, 1857-58, the British supported the native rulers.

Nationalism grew rapidly after World War I. The Indian National Congress and the Moslem League demanded constitutional reform. A leader emerged in Mohandas K. Gandhi (called Mahatma, or Great Soul), born Oct. 2, 1869, assassinated Jan. 30, 1948. He began advocating self-rule, non-violence, removal of untouchability in 1919. In 1930 he launched "civil disobedience," including boycott of British goods and rejection of taxes without representation.

In 1935 Britain gave India a constitution providing a bicameral federal congress. Mohammed Ali Jinnah, head of the Moslem League, sought creation of a Moslem nation, Pakistan.

The British government partitioned British India into the dominions of India and Pakistan. Aug. 15, 1947, was designated Indian Independence Day. India became a self-governing member of the Commonwealth and a member of the UN. It became a democratic republic, Jan. 26, 1950.

More than 12 million Hindu & Moslem refugees crossed the India-Pakistan borders in a mass transferral of some of the 2 peoples during 1947; about 200,000 were killed in communal fighting.

After Pakistan troops began attacks on Bengali separatists in East Pakistan, Mar. 25, 1971, some 10 million refugees fled into India. On Aug. 9, India and the USSR signed a 20-year friendship pact while U.S.-India relations soured. India and Pakistan went to war Dec. 3, 1971, on both the East and West fronts. Pakistan troops in the East surrendered Dec. 16; Pakistan agreed to a cease-fire in the West Dec. 17.

India and Pakistan signed a pact agreeing to withdraw troops from their borders and seek peaceful solutions, July 3, 1972. In Aug. 1973 India agreed to release 93,000 Pakistanis held prisoner since 1971; the return was completed in Apr. 1974. The 2 countries resumed full relations in 1976.

In 2 days of carnage, the Bengali population of the village of Mandai, Tripura State, 700 people, were massacred in a raid by indigenous tribal residents of the area, June 8-9, 1980. A similar year-long campaign against Bengali immigrants had been going on in Assam State.

Prime Min. Mrs. Indira Gandhi, named Jan. 19, 1966, was the 2d successor to Jawaharlal Nehru, India's prime minister from 1947 to his death, May 27, 1964.

Long the dominant power in India's politics, the Congress party lost some of its near monopoly by 1967. The party split into New and Old Congress parties in 1969. Mrs. Gandhi's New Congress party won control of the House.

Threatened with adverse court rulings in a voting law case, an opposition protest campaign and strikes, Gandhi invoked emergency provisions of the constitution June, 1975. Thousands of opponents were arrested and press censorship imposed. Measures to control prices, protect small farmers, and improve productivity were adopted.

The emergency, especially enforcement of coercive birth control measures in some areas, and the prominent extra-constitutional role of Indira Gandhi's son Sanjay, was widely resented. Opposition parties, united in the Janata coalition, scored massive victories in federal and state parliamentary elections in 1977, turning the New Congress Party from power.

Amid growing political tensions within the majority Janata party, and facing a censure vote in Parliament, Prime Min. Morarji R. Desai resigned, July 15, 1979. He was succeeded by a coalition government which only lasted 24 days.

With 350 candidates of her party winning seats to Parliament, Indira Gandhi became prime minister for the second time, Jan. 14, 1980.

India's 1st nuclear power plant was dedicated in 1970 near Bombay. In May, 1974, India exploded a nuclear device underground.

Sikkim, bordered by Tibet, Bhutan and Nepal, formerly British protected, became a protectorate of India in 1950. Area, 2,818 sq. mi.; pop. 1981 cen. 315,000; capital, Gangtok. In Sept. 1974 India's parliament voted to make Sikkim an associate Indian state, absorbing it into India. The monarchy was abolished in an April, 1975, referendum.

Kashmir, a predominantly Moslem region in the northwest, has been in dispute between India and Pakistan since 1947. A cease-fire was negotiated by the UN Jan. 1, 1949; it gave Pakistan control of one-third of the area, in the west and northwest, and India the remaining two-thirds, the Indian state of Jammu

and Kashmir, which enjoys internal autonomy. Repeated clashes broke out along the line.

There were also clashes in April 1965 along the Assam-East Pakistan border and in the Rann (swamp) of Kutch area along the West Pakistan-Gujarat border near the Arabian Sea. An international arbitration commission on Feb. 19, 1968, awarded 90% of the Rann to India, 10% to Pakistan.

France, 1952-54, peacefully yielded to India its 5 colonies, former French India, comprising Pondicherry, Karikal, Mahe, Yanaon (which became Pondicherry Union Territory, area 185 sq. mi., pop. 1981, 604,136) and Chandernagor (which was incorporated into the state of West Bengal).

Goa, 1,429 sq. mi., pop., 1981, 1 mln., which had been ruled by Portugal since 1505 AD, was taken by India by military action Dec. 18, 1961, together with 2 other Portuguese enclaves, Daman and Diu, located near Bombay.

Indonesia
Republic of Indonesia

People: Population (1983 est.): 165,787,000. **Age distrib.** (%): 0–14: 44.8; 15–59: 50.0; 60+: 5.1. **Pop. density:** 206.65 per sq. mi. **Urban** (1980): 22.3%. **Ethnic groups:** Malay, Chinese, Irianese. **Languages:** Bahasa Indonesian (Malay) (official), Javanese, other Austronesian languages. **Religions:** Muslims 90%.

Geography: Area: 741,101 sq. mi. **Location:** Archipelago SE of Asia along the Equator. **Neighbors:** Malaysia on N, Papua New Guinea on E. **Topography:** Indonesia comprises 13,500 islands, including Java (one of the most densely populated areas in the world with 1,500 persons to the sq. mi.), Sumatra, Kalimantan (most of Borneo), Sulawesi (Celebes), and West Irian (Irian Jaya, the W. half of New Guinea). Also: Bangka, Billiton, Madura, Bali, Timor. The mountains and plateaus on the major islands have a cooler climate than the tropical lowlands. **Capital:** Jakarta. **Cities** (1981 est.): Jakarta 5,500,000; Surabaja 2,000,000; Bandung 1,400,000; Medan 1,000,000.

Government: Type: Independent Republic. **Head of state:** Pres. Suharto; b. June 8, 1921; in office: Mar. 6, 1967. **Local divisions:** 27 provinces, 281 regencies. **Defense:** 3% of govt. budget (1982).

Economy: Industries: Food processing, textiles, light industry. **Chief crops:** Rice, coffee, sugar. **Minerals:** Nickel, tin, oil, bauxite, copper, natural gas. **Crude oil reserves** (1980): 9.6 bln. bbls. **Other resources:** Rubber. **Per capita arable land:** 0.3 acres. **Meat prod.** (1983): beef: 164,000 metric tons; pork: 94,000 metric tons, lamb: 61,000 metric tons. **Fish catch** (1981): 1.8 mln. metric tons. **Electricity prod.** (1981): 7.7 bln. kwh. **Crude steel prod.** (1981): 375,000 metric tons. **Labor force:** 66% agric.; 23% ind. & comm.; 10% services. **Finance: Currency:** Rupiah (Mar. 1984: 1,000 = $1 US). **Gross domestic product** (1981): $89 bln. **Per capita income** (1982): $560. **Imports** (1982): $16.8 bln.; partners: Jap. 30%, U.S. 14%, Sing. 9%. **Exports** (1982): $16.8 bln.; partners: Jap. 47%, U.S. 18%, Sing. 10%. **Tourists** (1980): 561,000; receipts: $39 mln. **National budget** (1982): $21 bln. **International reserves less gold** (Feb. 1984): $4.06 bln. **Gold:** 3.10 mln. oz t. **Consumer prices** (change in 1982): 9.5%.

Transport: Railway traffic (1982): 6.2 bln. passenger-km 890 mln. net ton-km. **Motor vehicles:** in use (1980): 639,500 passenger cars, 473,800 comm. **Civil aviation** (1982): 8.4 bln passenger-km; 190 mln. freight ton-km. **Chief ports:** Jakarta Surabaja, Medan, Palembang, Semarang.

Communications: Television sets: 1.4 mln. in use (1981) **Radios:** 6.2 mln. licensed (1981). **Telephones in use** (1981) 487,000.

Health: Life expectancy at birth (1981): 48 years. **Birth** (per 1,000 pop. 1978): 35. **Deaths** (per 1,000 pop. 1978): 15 **Natural increase** (1978) 2.1%. **Hospital beds** (per 100,000 pop. 1977): 60. **Physicians** (per 100,000 pop. 1977): 7. **Infant mortality** (per 1,000 live births 1983): 100.

Education (1981): **Literacy:** 64%. 86% attend primar school; 15% secondary school.

Embassy: 2020 Massachusetts Ave. NW 20036; 393-1745.

Hindu and Buddhist civilization from India reached the people of Indonesia nearly 2,000 years ago, taking root especially i Java. Islam spread along the maritime trade routes in the 15 century, and became predominant by the 16th century. Th

Dutch replaced the Portuguese as the most important European trade power in the area in the 17th century. They secured territorial control over Java by 1750. The outer islands were not finally subdued until the early 20th century, when the full area of present-day Indonesia was united under one rule for the first time in history.

Following Japanese occupation, 1942-45, nationalists led by Sukarno and Hatta proclaimed a republic. The Netherlands ceded sovereignty Dec. 27, 1949, after 4 years of fighting. West Irian, on New Guinea, remained under Dutch control.

After the Dutch in 1957 rejected proposals for new negotiations over West Irian, Indonesia stepped up the seizure of Dutch property. A U.S. mediator's plan was adopted in 1962. In 1963 the UN turned the area over to Indonesia, which promised a plebiscite. In 1969, voting by tribal chiefs favored staying with Indonesia, despite an uprising and widespread opposition.

Sukarno suspended Parliament in 1960, and was named president for life in 1963. Russian-armed Indonesian troops staged raids in 1964 and 1965 into Malaysia, whose formation Sukarno had opposed.

Indonesia's popular, pro-Peking Communist party tried to seize control in 1965; the army smashed the coup, later intimated that Sukarno had played a role in it. In parts of Java, Communists seized several districts before being defeated; over 300,000 Communists were executed.

Gen. Suharto, head of the army, was named president for 5 years in 1968, reelected 1973 and 1978. A coalition of his supporters won a strong majority in House elections in 1971, the first national vote in 16 years. Moslem opposition parties made gains in 1977 elections but lost ground in the 1982 elections. The military retains a predominant political role.

In 1966 Indonesia and Malaysia signed an agreement ending hostility. After ties with Peking were cut in 1967, there were riots against the economically important ethnic Chinese minority. Riots against Chinese and Japanese also occurred in 1974.

The former Portuguese Timor became Indonesia's 27th province in 1976 during a local civil war.

Oil export earnings, and political stability have made Indonesia's economy one of the most stable in the world.

Iran
Islamic Republic of Iran

People: Population (1983 est.): 42,490,000. **Age distrib.** (%): 0–14: 44.4; 15–59: 50.3; 60+: 5.2. **Pop. density:** 59.84 per sq. mi. **Urban** (1978): 48.8%. **Ethnic groups:** Persian 63%, Turkomans & Baluchis 19%, Kurds 3%, Arabs 4%. **Languages:** Farsi, Turk, Kurdish, Arabic, English, French. **Religions:** Shi'a Moslems 93%.

Geography: Area: 636,363 sq. mi. **Location:** Between the Middle East and S. Asia. **Neighbors:** Turkey, Iraq on W, USSR of N (Armenia, Azerbaijan, Turkmenistan), Afghanistan, Pakistan on E. **Topography:** Interior highlands and plains are surrounded by high mountains, up to 18,000 ft. Large salt deserts cover much of the area, but there are many oases and forest areas. Most of the population inhabits the N and NW. **Capital:** Teheran. **Cities** (1976 cen.): Teheran 4,496,159; Isfahan 671,825; Mashhad 670,180; Tabriz 598,576.

Government: Type: Islamic republic. **Religious head (Faghi):** Ayatollah Ruhollah Khomeini, b. 1901. **Head of state:** Prime Minister Mir Hussein Moussavi; b. 1937; in office: Oct. 29, 1981. **Local divisions:** 23 provinces, 9 governates. **Defense:** 15% of govt. budget (1982).

Economy: Industries: Steel, petrochemicals, cement, auto assembly, sugar refining, carpets. **Chief crops:** Grains, rice, fruits, sugar beets, cotton, grapes. **Minerals:** Chromium, oil, gas, copper, iron, lead, manganese, zinc, barite, sulphur, coal, emeralds, turquoise. **Crude oil reserves** (1980): 58.00 bln. bbls. **Other resources:** Gums, wool, silk, caviar. **Arable land:** 30%. **Meat prod.** (1983): beef: 199,000 metric tons; lamb: 278,000 metric tons. **Electricity prod.** (1981): 16.9 bln. kwh. **Crude steel prod.** (1982) 1.2 mln. metric tons. **Labor force:** 40% agric.; 33% ind. & comm; 27% services.

Finance: Currency: Rial (Mar. 1984: 86.85 = $1 US). **Gross domestic product** (1977): $76.37 bln. **Per capita income** (1977): $2,160. **Imports** (1982): $18.1 bln.; partners: W. Ger. 14%, Jap. 9%, UK 6%. **Exports** (1983): $19.4 bln.; partners: Jap. 13%, Bah. 7%, It. 14%. **National budget** (1983): $33.3 bln.

expenditures. **International reserves less gold** (Jun. 1980): $15.48 bln. **Gold:** 4.34 mln. oz t. **Consumer prices** (change in 1983) 20%.

Transport: Railway traffic (1978): 2.9 bln. passenger-km; 4.08 bln. net ton-km. **Motor vehicles:** in use (1980): 1.07 mln. passenger cars, 406,000 comm. vehicles. **Chief ports:** Khorramshahr, Bushehr, Bandar-e Shahpur, Bendar Abbas.

Communications: Television sets: 2.1 mln. in use (1980). **Radios:** 10 mln. in use (1980). **Telephones in use** (1981): 1.2 mln. **Daily newspaper circ.** (1982): 25 per 1,000 pop.

Health: Life expectancy at birth (1976): 57.63 male; 57.44 female. **Births** (per 1,000 pop. 1978): 41. **Deaths** (per 1,000 pop. 1978): 11. **Natural increase** (1978): 2.8%. **Hospital beds** (per 100,000 pop. 1977): 148. **Physicians** (per 100,000 pop. 1977): 39. **Infant mortality** (per 1,000 live births 1982): 14.

Education (1980): **Literacy:** 48%. **Pop. 5-19:** in school: 52%, teachers per 100,000: 20.

Iran is the official name of the country long known as Persia. The Iranians, who supplanted an earlier agricultural civilization, came from the E during the 2d millenium BC; they were an Indo-European group related to the Aryans of India.

In 549 BC Cyrus the Great united the Medes and Persians in the Persian Empire, conquered Babylonia in 538 BC, restored Jerusalem to the Jews. Alexander the Great conquered Persia in 333 BC, but Persians regained their independence in the next century under the Parthians, themselves succeeded by Sassanian Persians in 226 AD. Arabs brought Islam to Persia in the 7th century, replacing the indigenous Zoroastrian faith. After Persian political and cultural autonomy was reasserted in the 9th century, the arts and sciences flourished for several centuries.

Turks and Mongols ruled Persia in turn from the 11th century to 1502, when a native dynasty reasserted full independence. The British and Russian empires vied for influence in the 19th century, and Afghanistan was severed from Iran by Britain in 1857.

The previous dynasty was founded by Reza Khan, a military leader, in 1925. He abdicated as shah in 1941, and was succeeded by his son, Mohammad Reza Pahlavi.

British and Russian forces entered Iran Aug. 25, 1941, withdrawing later. Britain and the USSR signed an agreement Jan. 29, 1942, to respect Iranian integrity and give economic aid. In 1946 a Soviet attempt to take over the Azerbaijan region in the NW was defeated when a puppet regime was ousted by force.

Parliament, under Premier Mohammed Mossadegh, nationalized the oil industry in 1951, leading to a British blockade. Mossadegh was overthrown in 1953; the shah assumed control. Under his rule, Iran underwent economic and social change. However, political opposition was not tolerated. Thousands were arrested in the 1970s, while hundreds of purported terrorists were executed.

Conservative Moslem protests led to 1978 violence. Martial law in 12 cities was declared Sept. 8. A military government was appointed Nov. 6 to deal with striking oil workers. Continued clashes with demonstrators led to greater violence; oil production fell to a 27-year low, Dec. 27. In a 3d change of government in 5 months, Prime Min. Shahpur Bakhtiar was designated by the shah to head a regency council in his absence. The shah left Iran Jan. 16, 1979.

Violence continued throughout January. Exiled religious leader Ayatollah Ruhollah Khomeini named a provisional government council in preparation for his return to Iran, Jan. 31. Clashes between Khomeini's supporters and government troops culminated in a rout of Iran's elite Imperial Guard Feb. 11, leading to the fall of Bakhtiar's government. Ayatollah Khomeini's choice for prime minister, Mehdi Bazargan, headed an interim government pledged to establish an Islamic republic, but resigned Nov. 6, 1979, conceding power to the Islamic authority of Ayatollah Khomeini.

The Iranian revolution was marked by revolts among the ethnic minorities and by a continuing struggle between the clerical forces and westernized intellectuals and liberals. The Islamic Constitution, drafted under the domination of the clergy, established final authority to be vested in a Faghi, the Ayatollah Khomeini.

Iranian militants seized the U.S. embassy, Nov. 4, 1979, and took hostages including 62 Americans. The militants vowed to stay in the embassy until the deposed shah was returned to Iran. Despite international condemnations and U.S. efforts, including an abortive Apr., 1980, rescue attempt, the crisis continued. The

U.S. broke diplomatic relations with Iran, Apr. 7th. The shah died in Egypt, July 27th. The hostage drama finally ended Jan. 21, 1981 when an accord, involving the release of frozen Iranian assets, was reached.

On June 28, 1981, a bomb destroyed the Teheran headquarters of Iran's ruling Islamic Party, killing the party's leader, and 71 other persons.

Turmoil continued in Teheran however. The ruling Islamic Party, increasingly dissatisfied with President Abolhassan Bani-Sadr, declared him unfit for office. In the weeks following Bani-Sadr's dismissal, June 22, 1981, a new wave of executions began. Over 2,000 people, reportedly members of the Majahedeen-i-Khalq and smaller Marxist-Leninist/Maoist factions, had died before revolutionary firing squads by the end of 1981.

The political upheavals have brought Iran to virtual civil war and almost total isolation from other countries. In May, 1983, Iran's Communist Party was dissolved and 18 Soviet diplomats ordered to leave the country amid charges of treason and espionage.

A dispute over the Shatt al-Arab waterway that divides the two countries brought Iran and Iraq, Sept. 22, 1980, into open warfare. Iraqi planes attacked Iranian air fields including Teheran airport. Iranian planes bombed Iraqi bases. Iraqi troops occupied Iranian territory including the port city of Khorramshahr in October. Iranian troops recaptured the city and drove Iraqi troops back across the border, May 1982. Iran launched several offenses in 1983, but they were unable to break through Iraqi lines. At least 50,000 Iranians were killed in action. Iran's threat to close the Strait of Hormuz to maritime traffic brought a strong response from Western nations. Iraq, and later Iran, attacked several oil tankers in the Persian Gulf during 1984, prompting Lloyd's of London to increase insurance rates in the area. Saudi Arabian war planes shot down 2 Iranian jets, June 5, which they felt were threatening Saudi shipping (*See Chronology*).

Iraq
Republic of Iraq

People: Population (1983 est.): 14,509,000. **Age distrib.** (%): 0–14: 48.3; 15–59: 46.5; 60+: 5.3. **Pop. density:** 76.04 per sq. mi. **Urban** (1977): 65.9%. **Ethnic groups:** Arabs, 75% Kurds, 15% Turks. **Languages:** Arabic (official), Kurdish, others. **Religions:** Moslems 95% (Shiites 55%, Sunnis 40%), Christians 5%.

Geography: Area: 168,928 sq. mi., larger than California. **Location:** In the Middle East, occupying most of historic Mesopotamia. **Neighbors:** Jordan, Syria on W, Turkey on N, Iran on E, Kuwait, Saudi Arabia on S. **Topography:** Mostly an alluvial plain, including the Tigris and Euphrates rivers, descending from mountains in N to desert in SW. Persian Gulf region is marshland. **Capital:** Baghdad. **Cities** (1975 est.): Baghdad (met.) 3,205,645.

Government: Type: Ruling council. **Head of state:** Pres. Saddam Hussein At-Takriti, b. 1935 in office: July 16, 1979. **Local divisions:** 18 provinces. **Armed forces:** regulars 222,000; reserves 250,000.

Economy: Industries: Textiles, petrochemicals, oil refining, cement. **Chief crops:** Grains, rice, dates, cotton, tobacco. **Minerals:** Oil, gas. **Crude oil reserves** (1980): 31.00 bln. bbls. **Other resources:** Wool, hides. **Per capita arable land:** 1.0 acres. **Meat prod.** (1983): lamb: 60,000 metric tons. **Fish catch** (1978): 26,100 metric tons. **Electricity prod.** (1981): 6.2 bln. kwh. **Labor force:** 50% agric.

Finance: Currency: Dinar (Mar. 1984: 0.32 = $1 US). **Gross domestic product** (1979 est.): $31 bln. **Per capita income** (1979): $2,410. **Imports** (1982): $212 bln.; partners: W. Ger. 16%, Jap. 14%, Fr. 7%. **Exports** (1983): $9.7 bln.; partners: It. 13%, Tur. 11%, Braz. 22%, Jap. 6%. **International reserves less gold** (Dec. 1977): $6.82 bln. **Gold:** 4.14 mln. oz t. **Consumer prices** (change in 1981): 30%

Transport: Railway traffic (1978): 821 mln. passenger-km; 2.4 bln. net ton-km. **Motor vehicles:** in use (1982): 229,000 passenger cars, 118,700 comm. vehicles. **Civil aviation** (1982): 1.7 bln. passenger-km; 54.7 mln. freight ton-km. **Chief ports:** Basra.

Communications: Television sets: 650,000 in use (1981). **Radios:** 2 mln. in use (1981). **Telephones in use** (1978): 319,600. **Daily newspaper circ.** (1982): 19 per 1,000 pop.

Health: Life expectancy at birth (1982): 56.1 yrs. **Births** (per 1,000 pop. 1978): 47. **Deaths** (per 1,000 pop. 1978): 13.

Natural increase (1978): 3.4%. **Hospital beds** (per 100,000 pop. 1977): 199. **Physicians** (per 100,000 pop. 1977): 44. **Infant mortality** (per 1,000 live births 1982): 25. **Education** (1982): **Literacy:** 70%. Compulsory to age 10.

The Tigris-Euphrates valley, formerly called Mesopotamia, was the site of one of the earliest civilizations in the world. The Sumerian city-states of 3,000 BC originated the culture later developed by the Semitic Akkadians, Babylonians, and Assyrians.

Mesopotamia ceased to be a separate entity after the conquests of the Persians, Greeks, and Arabs. The latter founded Baghdad, from where the caliph ruled a vast empire in the 8th and 9th centuries. Mongol and Turkish conquests led to a decline in population, the economy, cultural life, and the irrigation system.

Britain secured a League of Nations mandate over Iraq after World War I. Independence under a king came in 1932. A leftist, pan-Arab revolution established a republic in 1958, which oriented foreign policy toward the USSR. Most industry has been nationalized, and large land holdings broken up.

A local faction of the international Baath Arab Socialist party has ruled by decree since 1968. Russia and Iraq signed an aid pact in 1972, and arms were sent along with several thousand advisers. The 1978 execution of 21 Communists and a shift of trade to the West signalled a more neutral policy, straining relations with the USSR. In the 1973 Arab-Israeli war Iraq sent forces to aid Syria. Relations with Syria were improving steadily to negotiations of uniting the 2 nations as a single political entity, but were halted by the Hussein government, July, 1979. Within a month of assuming power, Saddam Hussein instituted a bloody purge in the wake of a reported coup attempt against the new regime.

Years of battling with the Kurdish minority resulted in total defeat for the Kurds in 1975, when Iran withdrew support. Kurdish rebels continued their war, 1979; fighting led to Iraqi bombing of Kurdish villages in Iran, causing relations with Iran to deteriorate.

After skirmishing intermittently for 10 months over the sovereignty of the disputed Shatt al-Arab waterway that divides the two countries, Iraq and Iran, Sept. 22, 1980, entered into open warfare when Iraqi fighter-bombers attacked 10 Iranian airfields, including Teheran airport, and Iranian planes retaliated with strikes on 2 Iraqi bases. In the following days, there was heavy ground fighting around Abadan and the adjacent port of Khorramshahr as Iraq pressed its attack on Iran's oil-rich province of Khuzistan. In May 1982, Iraqi troops were driven back across the border. A fierce border war continued through 1984 with both sides suffering heavy casualties.

Israeli airplanes destroyed a nuclear reactor near Baghdad on June 7, 1981, claiming that it could be used to produce nuclear weapons.

Iraq and Iran expanded their war to the Persian Gulf in Apr. 1984. Several attacks on oil tankers were reported, prompting Lloyd's of London to increase insurance rates in the area. (*See Chronology*).

Ireland
Irish Republic

People: Population (1983 est.): 3,534,000. **Age distrib. (%):** 0–14: 31.2; 15–59: 53.5; 60+:15.3. **Pop. density:** 121.8 per sq. mi. **Urban** (1971): 52.2%. **Ethnic groups:** Irish, Anglo-Irish minority. **Languages:** English predominates, Irish (Gaelic) spoken by minority. **Religions:** Roman Catholics 94%, Anglican 4%.

Geography: Area: 27,137 sq. mi. **Location:** In the Atlantic O. just W of Great Britain. **Neighbors:** United Kingdom (Northern Ireland). **Topography:** Ireland consists of a central plateau surrounded by isolated groups of hills and mountains. The coastline is heavily indented by the Atlantic O. **Capital:** Dublin. **Cities** (1981 est.): Dublin 525,360; Cork (met.) 136,269.

Government: Type: Parliamentary Republic. **Head of State:** Pres. Patrick J. Hillery; b. May 2, 1923; in office: Dec. 3, 1976. **Head of government:** Prime Min. Garret FitzGerald; in office: Dec. 14, 1982. **Local divisions:** 26 counties. **Defense:** 2% of GNP (1982).

Economy: Industries: Food processing, auto assembly, metals, textiles, chemicals, brewing, electrical and non-electrical machinery, tourism. **Chief crops:** Potatoes, grain, sugar beets, fruits, vegetables. **Minerals:** Zinc, lead, silver, gas. **Arable land:** 17%. **Meat prod.** (1983): beef: 360,000 metric tons; pork:

154,000 metric tons; lamb: 42,000 metric tons. **Fish catch** (1981): 190,000 metric tons. **Electricity prod.** (1982): 10.9 bln. kwh. **Crude steel prod.** (1981): 32,000 metric tons. **Labor force:** 26% agric.; 19% manuf.; 15% comm.
Finance: Currency: Pound (Mar. 1984: 0.85 = $1 US). **Gross domestic product** (1980): $17.2 bln. **Per capita income** (1980): $5,000. **Imports** (1983): $9.1 bln.; partners: UK 48%, U.S. 13%, W. Ger. 8%, Fr. 5%. **Exports** (1983): $8.5 bln.; partners: UK 39%, Fr. 9%, W. Ger. 9%, U.S. 7%. **Tourists** (1981); 2.2 mln; receipts: $537 mln. **National budget** (1980): $6.70 bln. revenues; $9.35 bln. expenditures. **International reserves less gold** (Feb. 1984): $2.82 bln. **Gold:** 360,000 oz. t. **Consumer prices** (change in 1983): 10.5%.
Transport: Railway traffic (1982): 832 mln. passenger-km; 629 mln. net ton-km. **Motor vehicles:** in use (1981): 774,594 passenger cars, 73,000 comm. vehicles. **Civil aviation:** (1982): 2.3 bln. passenger-km; 79.4 mln. freight ton-km. **Chief ports:** Dublin, Cork.
Communications: Television sets: 785,300 licensed (1981). **Radios:** 1.5 mln. licensed (1981). **Telephones in use** (1981): 536,000. **Daily newspaper circ.** (1982): 224 per 1,000 pop.
Health: Life expectancy at birth (1982): 72 years. **Births** (per 1,000 pop. 1981): 21.01. **Deaths** (per 1,000 pop. 1981): 9.4. **Natural increase** (1977): 1.1%. **Hospital beds** (per 100,000 pop. 1977): 1,051. **Physicians** (per 100,000 pop. 1977): 116. **Infant mortality** (per 1,000 live births 1981): 12.4
Education (1982): **Literacy:** 99%. **Years compulsory:** 10; attendance 91%.
Embassy: 2234 Massachusetts Ave. NW 20008; 462-3939.

Celtic tribes invaded the islands about the 4th century BC; their Gaelic culture and literature flourished and spread to Scotland and elsewhere in the 5th century AD, the same century in which St. Patrick converted the Irish to Christianity. Invasions by Norsemen began in the 8th century, ended with defeat of the Danes by the Irish King Brian Boru in 1014. English invasions started in the 12th century; for over 700 years the Anglo-Irish struggle continued with bitter rebellions and savage repressions.
The Easter Monday Rebellion (1916) failed but was followed by guerrilla warfare and harsh reprisals by British troops, the "Black and Tans." The Dail Eireann, or Irish parliament, reaffirmed independence in Jan. 1919. The British offered dominion status to Ulster (6 counties) and southern Ireland (26 counties) Dec. 1921. The constitution of the Irish Free State, a British dominion, was adopted Dec. 11, 1922. Northern Ireland remained part of the United Kingdom.
A new constitution adopted by plebiscite came into operation Dec. 29, 1937. It declared the name of the state Eire in the Irish language (Ireland in the English) and declared it a sovereign democratic state.
On Dec. 21, 1948, an Irish law declared the country a republic rather than a dominion and withdrew it from the Commonwealth. The British Parliament recognized both actions, 1949, but reasserted its claim to incorporate the 6 northeastern counties in the United Kingdom. This claim has not been recognized by Ireland. *(See United Kingdom — Northern Ireland.)*
First president was William T. Cosgrave, 1922-32. Eamon de Valera, hero of the rebellion, was president 1932-37, 1959-66, 1966-73; prime minister 1937-48, 1951-54, 1957-59.
Irish governments have favored peaceful unification of all Ireland. Ireland cooperated with England against terrorist groups.

Israel
State of Israel

People: Population (1983 est.): 3,958,000. **Age distrib.** (%): 0–14: 33.2; 15–59: 63.0; 60+: 11.7. **Pop. density:** 448.96 per sq. mi. **Urban** (1977): 87.2%. **Ethnic groups:** Jews (half Ashkenazi, half Sephardi), Arabs, Druzes, Christians. **Languages:** Hebrew and Arabic (official), Yiddish, various European and West Asian languages. **Religions:** Jews 83%, Moslems, Christians, others.
Geography: Area: 8,219 sq. mi. (the size of Massachusetts), the "Green Line" border before the 1967 war; 2,986 sq. mi. occupied territory, excluding Sinai Peninsula, 23,622 sq. mi. **Location:** On eastern end of Mediterranean Sea. **Neighbors:** Lebanon on N, Syria, Jordan on E, Egypt on W. **Topography:** The Mediterranean coastal plain is fertile and well-watered. In the center is the Judean Plateau. A triangular-shaped semi-desert

region, the Negev, extends from south of Beersheba to an apex at the head of the Gulf of Aqaba. The eastern border drops sharply into the Jordan Rift Valley, including Lake Tiberias (Sea of Galilee) and the Dead Sea, which is 1,296 ft. below sea level, lowest point on the earth's surface. **Capital:** Jerusalem. **Cities** (1980 est.): Jerusalem 398,000; Tel Aviv-Yafo 336,300; Haifa 229,300.
Government: Type: Parliamentary democracy. **Head of state:** Pres. Chaim Herzog; b. Sept. 17, 1918; in office: May 5, 1983. **Head of government:** Prime Min. Yitzhak Shamir; b. 1915; in office: Oct. 20, 1983. **Local divisions:** 6 administrative districts. **Armed forces:** regulars 165,600; reserves 460,000.
Economy: Industries: Diamond cutting, textiles, electronics, machinery, plastics, tires, drugs, aircraft, munitions, wine. **Chief crops:** Citrus fruit, grains, olives, fruits, grapes, figs, cotton, vegetables. **Minerals:** Potash, limestone, gypsum, copper, iron, phosphates, magnesium, manganese, salt, sulphur. **Crude oil reserves** (1980): 1.0 mln. bbls. **Arable land:** 20%. **Meat prod.** (1980): beef: 21,000 metric tons; pork: 13,000 metric tons. **Fish catch** (1978): 25,900 metric tons. **Electricity prod.** (1982): 13.8 bln. kwh. **Crude steel prod.** (1981 est.): 114,000 metric tons. **Labor force:** 6.5% agric.; 25.3% manuf.
Finance: Currency: Shekel (Mar. 1984: 153.26 = $1 US). **Gross domestic product** (1980): $19.91 bln. **Per capita income** (1978): $3,332. **Imports** (1982): $9.6 bln.; partners: U.S. 19%, Switz. 6%, W. Ger. 11%, UK 8%. **Exports** (1983): $5.0 bln.; partners: U.S. 21%, W. Ger. 7%, UK 8%. **Tourists** (1981): 1.0 mln.; receipts $866 mln. **National budget** (1980): $20.8 bln. revenues; $959 bln. expenditures. **International reserves less gold** (Jan. 1984): $3.8 bln. **Gold:** 1.01 mln. oz t. **Consumer prices** (change in 1983): 145.6%.
Transport: Railway traffic (1981): 242 mln. passenger-km; 806 mln. net ton-km. **Motor vehicles:** in use (1981): 459,000 passenger cars, 96,000 comm. vehicles. **Civil aviation** (1982): 4.6 bln. passenger-km; 301 mln. freight ton-km. **Chief ports:** Haifa, Ashdod, Eilat.
Communications: Television sets: 581,000 in use (1981). **Radios:** 802,000 in use (1981). **Telephones in use** (1981): 1.3 mln. **Daily newspaper circ.** (1982): 416 per 1,000 pop.
Health: Life expectancy at birth (1978) Jewish pop. only 71.9 male; 75.6 female. **Births** (per 1,000 pop. 1981): 23.6. **Deaths** (per 1,000 pop. 1981): 6.6%. **Natural increase** (1977): 2.0%. **Hospital beds** (per 100,000 pop. 1977): 556. **Physicians** (per 100,000 pop. 1977): 277. **Infant mortality** (per 1,000 live births 1981): 14.6.
Education (1978): **Literacy:** 88%. **Pop. 5-19:** in school: 62%, teachers per 1,000: 50.
Embassy: 3541 International Dr. NW 20008; 364-5500.

Occupying the SW corner of the ancient Fertile Crescent, Israel contains some of the oldest known evidence of agriculture and of primitive town life. A more advanced civilization emerged in the 3d millenium BC. The Hebrews probably arrived early in the 2d millennium BC. Under King David and his successors (c.1000 BC-597 BC), Judaism was developed and secured. After conquest by Babylonians, Persians, and Greeks, an independent Jewish kingdom was revived, 168 BC, but Rome took effective control in the next century, suppressed Jewish revolts in 70 AD and 135 AD, and renamed Judea Palestine, after the earlier coastal inhabitants, the Philistines.
Arab invaders conquered Palestine in 636. The Arabic language and Islam prevailed within a few centuries, but a Jewish minority remained. The land was ruled from the 11th century as a part of non-Arab empires by Seljuks, Mamluks, and Ottomans (with a crusader interval, 1098-1291).
After 4 centuries of Ottoman rule, during which the population declined to a low of 350,000 (1785), the land was taken in 1917 by Britain, which in the Balfour Declaration that year pledged to support a Jewish national homeland there, as foreseen by the Zionists. In 1920 a British Palestine Mandate was recognized; in 1922 the land east of the Jordan was detached.
Jewish immigration, begun in the late 19th century, swelled in the 1930s with refugees from the Nazis; heavy Arab immigration from Syria and Lebanon also occurred. Arab opposition to Jewish immigration turned violent in 1920, 1921, 1929, and 1936. The UN General Assembly voted in 1947 to partition Palestine into an Arab and a Jewish state. Britain withdrew in May 1948.
Israel was declared an independent state May 14, 1948; the Arabs rejected partition. Egypt, Jordan, Syria, Lebanon, Iraq, and Saudi Arabia invaded, but failed to destroy the Jewish state, which gained territory. Separate armistices with the Arab nations

were signed in 1949; Jordan occupied the West Bank, Egypt occupied Gaza, but neither granted Palestinian autonomy. No peace settlement was obtained, and the Arab nations continued policies of economic boycott, blockade in the Suez Canal, and support of guerrillas. Several hundred thousand Arabs left the area of Jewish control; an equal number of Jews left the Arab countries for Israel 1949-53.

After persistent terrorist raids, Israel invaded Egypt's Sinai, Oct. 29, 1956, aided briefly by British and French forces. A UN cease-fire was arranged Nov. 6.

An uneasy truce between Israel and the Arab countries, supervised by a UN Emergency Force, prevailed until May 19, 1967, when the UN force withdrew at the demand of Egypt's Pres. Nasser. Egyptian forces reoccupied the Gaza Strip and closed the Gulf of Aqaba to Israeli shipping. In a 6-day war that started June 5, the Israelis took the Gaza Strip, occupied the Sinai Peninsula to the Suez Canal, and captured Old Jerusalem, Syria's Golan Heights, and Jordan's West Bank. The fighting was halted June 10 by UN-arranged cease-fire agreements.

Egypt and Syria attacked Israel, Oct. 6, 1973 (Yom Kippur, most solemn day on the Jewish calendar). Egypt and Syria were supplied by massive USSR military airlifts; the U.S. responded with an airlift to Israel. Israel counter-attacked, driving the Syrians back, and crossed the Suez Canal.

A cease fire took effect Oct. 24; a UN peace-keeping force went to the area. A disengagement agreement was signed Jan. 18, 1974, following negotiations by U.S. Secretary of State Henry Kissinger. Israel withdrew from the canal's W bank. A second withdrawal was completed in 1976; Israel returned the Sinai to Egypt in 1982.

Israel and Syria agreed to disengage June 1; Israel completed withdrawing from its salient (and a small part of the land taken in the 1967 war) June 25.

In the wake of the war, Golda Meir, long Israel's premier, resigned; severe inflation gripped the nation. Palestinian guerrillas staged massacres, killing scores of civilians 1974-75. Israel conducted preventive attacks in Lebanon through 1975. Israel aided Christian forces in the 1975-76 Lebanese civil war.

Israeli forces raided Entebbe, Uganda, July 3, 1976, and rescued 103 hostages seized by Arab and German terrorists.

In 1977, the conservative opposition, led by Menachem Begin, was voted into office for the first time. Egypt's Pres. Sadat visited Jerusalem Nov. 1977 and on Mar. 26, 1979. Egypt and Israel signed a formal peace treaty, ending 30 years of war, and establishing diplomatic relations.

Israel invaded S. Lebanon, March 1978, following a Lebanon-based terrorist attack in Israel. Israel withdrew in favor of a 6,000-man UN force, but continued to aid Christian militiamen.

A 5-day occupation of Israeli forces in southern Lebanon took place April 1980, in retaliation for the Palestinian raid on a kibbutz earlier that month. Violence on the Israeli-occupied West Bank rose in 1982 when Israel announced plans to build new Jewish settlements.

Israel affirmed the entire city of Jerusalem as its capital, July, 1980, encompassing the annexed Arab East Jerusalem.

Israel shot down, Apr. 28, 1981, two Syrian helicopters Israel claimed were attacking Lebanese Christian militia forces in the Beirut-Zahle area of Lebanon. Syria responded by installing Soviet-built surface-to-air missiles in Lebanon. Both the U.S. and Israel were unable to persuade Syria to withdraw the missiles, and Israel threatened to destroy them.

On June 7, 1981, Israeli jets destroyed an Iraqi atomic reactor near Baghdad that, Israel claimed, would have enabled Iraq to manufacture nuclear weapons. The attack came as a complete surprise to Israeli friends and foes alike, and brought widespread condemnation.

In a close election, June 30, 1981, Prime Min. Menachem Begin was able to assemble a narrow coalition, he survived a no confidence motion in the Knesset by one vote, May 1982. He retired and was replaced by Yitzhak Shamir, Oct. 1983.

Israeli jets bombed Palestine Liberation Organization (PLO) strongholds in Lebanon April, May 1982. In reaction to the wounding of the Israeli ambassador to Great Britain, Israeli forces in a coordinated land, sea, and air attack invaded Lebanon, June 6, to destroy PLO strongholds in that country. Israeli and Syrian forces engaged in the Bekka Valley, June 9, but quickly agreed to a truce. Israeli forces encircled Beirut June 14. Following massive Israeli bombing of West Beirut, the PLO agreed to evacuate the city. The Aug. 21 withdrawal was supervised by U.S., French and Italian troops.

Israeli troops entered West Beirut after newly-elected Lebanese president Bashir Gemayel was assassinated on Sept. 14. Israel received widespread condemnation when Lebanese Christian forces, Sept. 16, entered 2 West Beirut refugee camps and slaughtered hundreds of Palestinian refugees. Israeli Defense Minister Ariel Sharon resigned Feb. 11, 1983, after Israel's State Board of Inquiry cited him for neglect of duty during the massacre.

Lebanon and Israel accepted a plan for withdrawal of foreign troops, May 6; Syria rejected the accord.

Italy

Italian Republic

People: Population (1983 est.): 56,833,000. **Age distrib.** (%): 0–14: 23.7; 15–59: 58.8; 60+: 17.5. **Pop. density:** 490.44 per sq. mi. **Ethnic groups:** Italians, small minorities of Germans, Slovenes, Albanians, French, Ladins, Greeks. **Languages:** Italian. **Religions:** Predominantly Roman Catholic.

Geography: Area: 116,303 sq. mi., slightly larger than Arizona. **Location:** In S Europe, jutting into Mediterranean S. **Neighbors:** France on W, Switzerland, Austria on N, Yugoslavia on E. **Topography:** Occupies a long boot-shaped peninsula, extending SE from the Alps into the Mediterranean, with the islands of Sicily and Sardinia offshore. The alluvial Po Valley drains most of N. The rest of the country is rugged and mountainous, except for intermittent coastal plains, like the Campajna, S of Rome. Appenine Mts. run down through center of peninsula. **Capital:** Rome. **Cities** (1981 cen.): Rome 2.8 mln.; Milan 1.6 mln.; Naples 1.2 mln.; Turin 1.1 mln.

Government: Type: Republic. **Head of state:** Pres. Alessandro Pertini; b. Sept. 25, 1896; in office: July 9, 1978; **Head of government:** Prime Min. Bettino Craxi; b. Feb. 24, 1934; in office: Aug. 4, 1983. **Local divisions:** 20 regions with some autonomy, 94 provinces. **Defense:** 2.2% of GNP (1980).

Economy: Industries: Steel, machinery, autos, textiles, shoes, machine tools, chemicals. **Chief crops:** Grapes, olives, citrus fruits, vegetables, wheat, rice. **Minerals:** Mercury, potash, gas, marble, sulphur, coal. **Crude oil reserves** (1980): 645 mln. bbls. **Per capita arable land:** 0.4 acres. **Meat prod.** (1983): beef: 1.13 mln. metric tons; pork: 1.1 mln. metric tons; lamb: 69,000 metric tons. **Fish catch** (1981): 449,000 metric tons. **Electricity prod.** (1981): 181.7 bln. kwh. **Crude steel prod.** (1982): 23.9 mln. metric tons. **Labor force:** 15% agric.; 38% ind. and commerce; 46% services.

Finance: Currency: Lira (Mar. 1984: 1,618 = $1 US). **Gross domestic product** (1980): $394.0 bln. **Per capita income** (1980): $6,914. **Imports** (1983): $80.3 bln.; partners: W. Ger. 16%, Fr. 12%, U.S. 7%. **Exports** (1983): $72.7 bln.; partners: W. Ger. 16%, Fr. 15%, U.S. 7%, UK 6%. **Tourists** (1981): 16 mln.; receipts $7.5 bln. **National budget** (1980): $108.12 bln. revenues; $141.90 bln. expenditures. **International reserves less gold** (Apr. 1984): $18.9 bln. **Gold:** 66.67 mln. oz t. **Consumer prices** (change in 1983): 14.7%.

Transport: Railway traffic (1982): 40.5 bln. passenger-km; 16.4 bln. net ton-km. **Motor vehicles:** in use (1981): 18.6 mln. passenger cars, 1.4 mln. comm. vehicles; manuf. (1981): 1.2 mln. passenger cars, 175,000 comm. vehicles. **Civil aviation** (1982): 15.1 bln. passenger-km; 582 mln. freight ton-km. **Chief ports:** Genoa, Venice, Trieste, Taranto, Naples, La Spezia.

Communications: Television sets: 13.3 mln. licensed (1981). **Radios:** 13.7 mln. licensed (1981). **Telephones in use** (1981): 19,269,000. **Daily newspaper circ.** (1982): 132 per 1,000 pop.

Health: Life expectancy at birth (1980): 70.0 male; 76.1 female. **Births** (per 1,000 pop. 1982): 11.7. **Deaths** (per 1,000 pop. 1982): 9.5. **Natural increase** (1977): .4%. **Hospital beds** (per 100,000 pop. 1977): 1,036. **Physicians** (per 100,000 pop. 1977): 208. **Infant mortality** (per 1,000 live births 1982): 12.6.

Education (1982): **Literacy:** 98%. **Years compulsory:** 8, teachers per 1,000: 42.

Embassy: 1601 Fuller St. NW 20009; 328-5500.

Rome emerged as the major power in Italy after 500 BC, dominating the more civilized Etruscans to the N and Greeks to the S. Under the Empire, which lasted until the 5th century AD Rome ruled most of Western Europe, the Balkans, the Near East, and North Africa.

After the Germanic invasions, lasting several centuries, a high civilization arose in the city-states of the N, culminating in the Renaissance. But German, French, Spanish, and Austrian intervention prevented the unification of the country. In 1859 Lombardy came under the crown of King Victor Emmanuel II of Sardinia. By plebiscite in 1860, Parma, Modena, Romagna, and Tuscany joined, followed by Sicily and Naples, and by the Marches and Umbria. The first Italian parliament declared Victor Emmanuel king of Italy Mar. 17, 1861. Mantua and Venetia were added in 1866 as an outcome of the Austro-Prussian war. The Papal States were taken by Italian troops Sept. 20, 1870, on the withdrawal of the French garrison. The states were annexed to the kingdom by plebiscite. Italy recognized the State of Vatican City as independent Feb. 11, 1929.

Fascism appeared in Italy Mar. 23, 1919, led by Benito Mussolini, who took over the government at the invitation of the king Oct. 28, 1922. Mussolini acquired dictatorial powers. He made war on Ethiopia and proclaimed Victor Emmanuel III emperor, defied the sanctions of the League of Nations, joined the Berlin-Tokyo axis, sent troops to fight for Franco against the Republic of Spain and joined Germany in World War II.

After Fascism was overthrown in 1943, Italy declared war on Germany and Japan and contributed to the Allied victory. It surrendered conquered lands and lost its colonies. Mussolini was killed by partisans Apr. 28, 1945.

Victor Emmanuel III abdicated May 9, 1946; his son Humbert II was king until June 10, when Italy became a republic after a referendum, June 2-3.

Reorganization of the Fascist party is forbidden. The cabinet normally represents a coalition of the Christian Democrats, largest of Italy's many parties, and one or 2 other parties.

The Vatican agreed in 1976 to revise its 1929 concordat with the state, depriving Roman Catholicism of its status as state religion. In 1974 Italians voted by a 3-to-2 margin to retain a 3-year-old law permitting divorce, which was opposed by the church.

Italy has enjoyed an extraordinary growth in industry and living standards since World War II, in part due to membership in the Common Market. Italy joined the European Monetary System, 1980. But in 1973-74, a fourfold increase in international oil prices helped disrupt the economy. Taxes were boosted in 1974. Western aid helped ease the crisis in 1975, but inflation and decline in confidence continued through 1982. A wave of left-wing political violence worsened in 1977 with kidnappings and assassinations and continued through 1982. Christian Dem. leader and former Prime Min. Moro was murdered May 1978 by Red Brigade terrorists.

There were 5 political kidnappings by terrorists in 1981 including U.S. Brig. Gen. James Dozier, a senior NATO officer, who was later rescued by Italian police.

The Cabinet of Prime Min. Arnaldo Forlani resigned, May 26, 1981, in the wake-of revelations that numerous high-ranking officials were members of an illegally secret Masonic lodge. The June 1983 elections saw Bettino Craxi chosen the nation's first Socialist premier. Italy has accepted U.S. cruise missiles. Some 2,000 troops were contributed to the Lebanese peace-keeping force.

Sicily, 9,822 sq. mi., pop. (1980) 5,000,000, is an island 180 by 120 mi., seat of a region that embraces the island of **Pantelleria,** 32 sq. mi., and the **Lipari** group, 44 sq. mi., 63 14,000, including 2 active volcanoes: **Vulcano,** 1,637 ft. and **Stromboli,** 3,038 ft. From prehistoric times Sicily has been settled by various peoples; a Greek state had its capital at Syracuse. Rome took Sicily from Carthage 215 BC. **Mt. Etna,** 10,705 ft. active volcano, is tallest peak.

Sardinia, 9,262 sq. mi., pop. (1980) 1,610,000, lies in the Mediterranean, 115 mi. W of Italy and 7-½ mi. S of Corsica. It is 160 mi. long, 68 mi. wide, and mountainous, with mining of coal, zinc, lead, copper. In 1720 Sardinia was added to the possessions of the Dukes of Savoy in Piedmont and Savoy to form the Kingdom of Sardinia. Giuseppe Garibaldi is buried on the nearby isle of Caprera. **Elba,** 86 sq. mi., lies 6 mi. W of Tuscany. Napoleon I lived in exile on Elba 1814-1815.

Trieste. An agreement, signed Oct. 5, 1954, by Italy and Yugoslavia, confirmed, Nov. 10, 1975, gave Italy provisional administration over the northern section and the seaport of Trieste, and Yugoslavia the part of Istrian peninsula it has occupied.

Ivory Coast
Republic of Ivory Coast

People: Population (1983 est.): 8,890,000. **Age distrib. (%):** 0–14: 44.6; 15–59: 52.0; 60+: 3.4. **Pop. density:** 64.01 per sq. mi. **Urban** (1975): 32.4%. **Ethnic groups:** Baule 23%, Bete 18%, Senufo 15%, Malinke 11%, over 60 tribes. **Languages:** French (official), tribal languages. **Religions:** Moslems 15%, Christians 12%, indigenous 63%.

Geography: Area: 124,503 sq. mi., slightly larger than New Mexico. **Location:** On S. coast of W. Africa. **Neighbors:** Liberia, Guinea on W, Mali, Upper Volta on N, Ghana on E. **Topography:** Forests cover the W half of the country, and range from a coastal strip to halfway to the N on the E. A sparse inland plain leads to low mountains in NW. **Capital:** Abidjan. **Cities** (1981 est.): Abidjan 1,686,100 (met.).

Government: Type: Republic. **Head of state:** Pres. Felix Houphouet-Boigny; b. Oct. 18, 1905; in office: Aug. 7, 1960. **Local divisions:** 25 departments.

Economy: Chief crops: Coffee, cocoa. **Minerals:** Diamonds, manganese. **Other resources:** Timber, rubber. **Arable land:** 12%. **Meat prod.** (1980): beef: 41,000 metric tons; pork: 13,000 metric tons; lamb: 13,000 metric tons. **Fish catch** (1981): 80,000 metric tons. **Electricity prod.** (1981): 1.9 bln. kwh. **Labor force:** 75% agric.; 25% ind. and commerce.

Finance: Currency: CFA franc (Mar. 1984: 399 = $1 US). **Gross domestic product** (1981 est.): $9.8 bln. **Per capita income** (1981): $1,153. **Imports** (1982): $2.1 bln.; partners: Fr. 31%, Venoz. 8%, Jap. 5%, U.S. 5% **Exports** (1982): $2.2 bln.; partners: Fr. 19%, Neth. 13%, U.S. 11%, It. 8%. **Tourists** (1976): 122,200; receipts: $26 mln. **International reserves less gold** (Jan. 1984): $15.9 mln. **Gold:** 45,000 oz t. **Consumer prices** (changed in 1983): 5.9%.

Transport: Railway traffic (1980): 1.2 bln. passenger-km; 600 mln. net ton-km. **Motor vehicles:** in use (1982): 166,000 passenger cars, 69,500 comm. vehicles. **Chief ports:** Abidjan, Sassandra.

Communications: Television sets: 300,000 in use (1981). **Radios:** 1 mln. in use (1981). **Telephones in use** (1981): 88,000. **Daily newspaper circ.** (1982): 8 per 1.000 pop.

Health: Life expectancy at birth (1983): 46.9 male; 50.2 female. **Births** (per 1,000 pop. 1978): 47. **Deaths** (per 1,000 pop. 1978): 18. **Natural increase** (1978): 3.4%. **Hospital beds** (per 100,000 pop. 1977): 124. **Physicians** (per 100,000 pop. 1977): 4. **Infant mortality** (per 1,000 live births 1982): 127.

Education (1983): **Literacy:** 24%. **Years compulsory:** none; attendance 75%.

Embassy: 2424 Massachusetts Ave. NW 20008; 483-2400.

A French protectorate from 1842, Ivory Coast became independent in 1960. It is the most prosperous of tropical African nations, due to diversification of agriculture for export, close ties to France, and encouragement of foreign investment. About 20% of the population are workers from neighboring countries. Ivory Coast is a leader of the pro-Western bloc in Africa.

Jamaica

People: Population (1983 est.): 2,347,000. **Age distrib. (%):** 0–14: 36.7; 15–59: 52.8; 60+: 8.5. **Pop. density:** 501.89 per sq. mi. **Urban** (1970): 37.1%. **Ethnic groups:** African 76%, mixed 15%, Chinese, Caucasians, East Indians. **Languages:** English, Jamaican Creole. **Religions:** Anglicans and Baptists in majority.

Geography: Area: 4,244 sq. mi., slightly smaller than Connecticut. **Location:** In West Indies. **Neighbors:** Nearest are Cuba on N, Haiti on E. **Topography:** The country is four-fifths covered by mountains. **Capital:** Kingston. **Cities** (1982 est.): Kingston 684,000 (met.).

Government: Type: Constitutional monarchy. **Head of state:** Queen Elizabeth II, represented by Gov.-Gen. Florizel A. Glasspole; b. Sept. 25, 1909; in office: Mar. 2, 1973. **Head of government:** Prime Min. Edward Seaga; b. May 28, 1930; in office: Oct., 1980. **Local divisions:** 12 parishes; Kingston and St. Andrew corporate area. **Defense:** 0.8% of GDP (1981).

Economy: Industries: Rum, molasses, cement, paper, tourism. **Chief crops:** Sugar cane, coffee, bananas, coconuts, citrus fruits. **Minerals:** Bauxite, limestone, gypsum. **Arable land:** 30%. **Meat prod.** (1980): beef: 13,000 metric tons; pork: 9,000 metric tons. **Fish catch** (1978): 9,600 metric tons. **Electricity prod.** (1981): 2.3 bln. kwh. **Labor force:** 36.4% agric.; 32.7% services; 14.9% ind. & comm.

Finance: Currency: Dollar (Apr. 1984: 3.27 = $1 US). **Gross domestic product** (1981): $3.0 bln. **Per capita income** (1981): $1,340. **Imports** (1983): $1.4 bln.; partners: U.S. 35%, Venez. 14%, Neth. Ant. 13%, UK 8%. **Exports** (1983): $782 mln.; partners: U.S. 33%, UK 18%, Nor. 8%, Can. 12%. **Tourists** (1981): 406,000; receipts: $284 mln. **National budget** (1982): $825 mln. revenues. **International reserves less gold** (Feb. 1984): $62.7 mln. **Consumer prices** (change in 1982): 6.8%.

Transport: Railway traffic (1977): 83 mln. passenger-km; 186 mln. net ton-km. **Chief ports:** Kingston, Montego Bay.

Communications: Television sets: 115,000 in use (1979). **Radios:** 750,000 in use (1979). **Telephones in use** (1980): 118,000. **Daily newspaper circ.** (1982): 137 per 1,000 pop.

Health: Life expectancy at birth (1981): 65 years. **Births** (per 1,000 pop. 1978): 27. **Deaths** (per 1,000 pop. 1978): 6. **Natural increase** (1978): 1.2%. **Hospital beds** (1980): 6,229. **Physicians** (1980): 700. **Infant mortality** (per 1,000 live births 1981): 26.3.

Education (1981): **Literacy:** 82%. Compulsory to age 14. **Embassy:** 1850 K St. NW 20006; 452-0660.

Jamaica was visited by Columbus, 1494, and ruled by Spain (under whom Arawak Indians died out) until seized by Britain, 1655. Jamaica won independence Aug. 6, 1962.

In 1974 Jamaica sought an increase in taxes paid by U.S. and Canadian companies which mine bauxite on the island. The socialist government acquired 50% ownership of the companies' Jamaican interests in 1976, and was reelected that year. Rudimentary welfare state measures were passed, but unemployment increased. Relations with the U.S. improved greatly in 1981; Prime Minister Seaga was the first official visitor to Washington after Pres. Ronald Reagan's inauguration. Jamaica broke diplomatic relations with Cuba in December.

In 1982, Reagan became the first U.S. President to visit Jamaica and voiced strong support for the free-enterprise policies of the Seaga government. Jamaica took part in the October 1983 invasion of Grenada.

Japan

People: Population (1983 est.): 119,205,000. **Age distrib.** (%): 0–14: 23.5; 15–59: 63.6; 60+: 12.9. **Pop. density:** 810.97 per sq. mi. **Urban** (1980): 76.2%. **Language:** Japanese. **Ethnic groups:** Japanese 99.4%, Korean 0.5%. **Religions:** Buddhism, Shintoism shared by large majority.

Geography: Area: 147,470 sq. mi., slightly smaller than California. **Location:** Archipelago off E. coast of Asia. **Neighbors:** USSR on N, S. Korea on W. **Topography:** Japan consists of 4 main islands: Honshu ("mainland"), 87,805 sq. mi.; Hokkaido, 30,144 sq. mi.; Kyushu, 14,114 sq. mi.; and Shikoku, 7,049 sq. mi. The coast, deeply indented, measures 16,654 mi. The northern islands are a continuation of the Sakhalin Mts. The Kunlun range of China continues into southern islands, the ranges meeting in the Japanese Alps. In a vast transverse fissure crossing Honshu E-W rises a group of volcanoes, mostly extinct or inactive, including 12,388 ft. Fuji-San (Fujiyama) near Tokyo. **Capital:** Tokyo. **Cities** (1980 cen.): Tokyo 8.3 mln.; Osaka 2.6 mln.; Yokohama 2.7 mln.; Nagoya 2 mln.; Kyoto 1.4 mln.; Kobe 1.3 mln.; Sapporo 1.4 mln.; Kitakyushu 1 mln.; Kawasaki 1 mln.

Government: Type: Parliamentary democracy. **Head of state:** Emp. Hirohito; b. Apr. 29, 1901; in office: Dec. 25, 1926. **Head of government:** Prime Min. Yasuhiro Nakasone; in office: Nov. 26, 1982. **Local divisions:** 47 prefectures. **Defense:** Less than 1% of GNP (1983).

Economy: Industries: Electrical & electronic equip., autos, machinery, chemicals. **Chief crops:** Rice, grains, vegetables, fruits. **Minerals:** negligible. **Crude oil reserves** (1980): 55 mln. bbls. **Arable land:** 19%. **Meat prod.** (1983): beef: 490,000 metric tons; pork: 1.43 mln. metric tons. **Fish catch** (1981): 10.6 mln. metric tons. **Electricity prod.** (1981): 521.8 bln. kwh. **Crude steel prod.** (1983): 97.2 mln. metric tons. **Labor force:** 11% agric.; 34% manuf; 48% services.

Finance: Currency: Yen (Mar. 1984: 227.70 = $1 US). **Gross national product** (1982): $1.04 trl. **Per capita income** (1980): $8,460. **Imports** (1983): $126 bln.; partners: U.S. 18%, Saudi Ar. 16%, Austral. 5%, Indon. 9%. **Exports** (1983): $146 bln.; partners: U.S. 26%. **Tourists** (1980): 1,316,000. **National budget** (1980): $190.1 bln. revenues; $190.1 bln. expenditures. **International reserves less gold** (Mar. 1984): $25.2 bln. **Gold:** 24.23 mln. **Consumer prices** (change in 1983): 1.9%.

Transport: Railway traffic (1982): 314.9 bln. passenger-km; 31.3 bln. net ton-km. **Motor vehicles:** in use (1982): 21.5 mln. passenger cars, 15.3 mln. comm. vehicles; manuf. (1982): 6.8 mln. passenger cars; 3.8 mln. comm. vehicles. **Civil aviation** (1982): 55.7 bln. passenger-km; 2.3 bln. freight ton-km. **Chief ports:** Yokohama, Tokyo, Kobe, Osaka, Nagoya, Chiba, Kawasaki, Hakodate.

Communications: Television sets: 62.9 mln. in use (1981), 16.3 mln. manuf. (1980). **Radios:** 79 mln. in use (1981), 15.1 mln. manuf. (1981). **Telephones in use** (1982): 58.6 mln. **Daily newspaper circ.** (1982): 569 per 1,000 pop.

Health: Life expectancy at birth (1983): 73 male; 78 female. **Births** (per 1,000 pop. 1981): 13.0. **Deaths** (per 1,000 pop. 1981): 6.1. **Natural increase** (1977): 1.0%. **Hospital beds** (1981): 1.3 mln. **Physicians** (1981): 156,235. **Infant mortality** (per 1,000 live births 1981): 7.1.

Education (1983): **Literacy:** 99%. Most attend school for 12 years.

Embassy: 2520 Massachusetts Ave. NW 20008; 234-2266.

According to Japanese legend, the empire was founded by Emperor Jimmu, 660 BC, but earliest records of a unified Japan date from 1,000 years later. Chinese influence was strong in the formation of Japanese civilization. Buddhism was introduced before the 6th century.

A feudal system, with locally powerful noble families and their samurai warrior retainers, dominated from 1192. Central power was held by successive families of shoguns (military dictators), 1192-1867, until recovered by the Emperor Meiji, 1868. The Portuguese and Dutch had minor trade with Japan in the 16th and 17th centuries; U.S. Commodore Matthew C. Perry opened it to U.S. trade in a treaty ratified 1854. Japan fought China, 1894-95, gaining Taiwan. After war with Russia, 1904-05, Russia ceded S half of Sakhalin and gave concessions in China. Japan annexed Korea 1910. In World War I Japan ousted Germany from Shantung, took over German Pacific islands. Japan took Manchuria 1931, started war with China 1932. Japan launched war against the U.S. by attack on Pearl Harbor Dec. 7, 1941. Japan surrendered Aug. 14, 1945.

In a new constitution adopted May 3, 1947, Japan renounced the right to wage war; the emperor gave up claims to divinity; the Diet became the sole law-making authority.

The U.S. and 48 other non-communist nations signed a peace treaty and the U.S. a bilateral defense agreement with Japan, in San Francisco Sept. 8, 1951, restoring Japan's sovereignty as of April 28, 1952. Japan signed separate treaties with Nationalist China, 1952; India, 1952; a declaration with USSR ending a technical state of war, 1956. In Dec. 1965 Japan and South Korea agreed to resume diplomatic relations.

On June 26, 1968, the U.S. returned to Japanese control the Bonin Is., the Volcano Is. (including Iwo Jima) and Marcus Is. On May 15, 1972, Okinawa, the other Ryukyu Is. and the Daito Is. were returned to Japan by the U.S.; it was agreed the U.S. would continue to maintain military bases on Okinawa. Japan and the USSR have failed to resolve disputed claims of sovereignty over 4 of the Kurile Is. and over offshore fishing rights.

In 1972, Japan and China resumed diplomatic relations; Japan and Taiwan severed diplomatic relations.

Industrialization was begun in the late 19th century. After World War II, Japan emerged as one of the most powerful economies in the world, and as a leader in technology.

The U.S. and EC member nations have criticized Japan for its restrictive policy on imports which has given Japan a substantial trade surplus. In 1984, Japan, under the threat of sanctions, agreed to increase the import quotas on U.S. beef and citrus products.

Jordan

Hashemite Kingdom of Jordan

Population (1982 est.): 2,588,000. **Age distrib.** (%): 0–14: 51.8; 15–59: 44.0; 60+: 4.2. **Pop. density:** 85.53 per sq. mi. **Urban** (1979): 59.5%. **Ethnic groups:** Arabs, small minorities of Circassians, Armenians, Kurds. **Languages:** Arabic (official), English. **Religions:** Sunni Moslems 93.6%, Christians 5%.
Geography: Area: 37,297 sq. mi., slightly larger than Indiana. **Location:** In W Asia. **Neighbors:** Israel on W, Saudi Arabia on S, Iraq on E, Syria on N. **Topography:** About 88% of Jordan is arid. Fertile areas are in W. Only port is on short Aqaba Gulf coast. Country shares Dead Sea (1,296 ft. below sea level) with Israel. **Capital:** Amman. **Cities** (1980 est.): Amman 1,232,600; Irbid 634,200.
Government: Type: Constitutional monarchy. **Head of state:** King Hussein I; b. Nov. 14, 1935; in office: Aug. 11, 1952. **Head of government:** Prime Min. Ahmed Abdel Obeidat; b. 1934; in office: Jan. 10, 1984. **Local divisions:** 8 governorates. **Defense:** 13% of GNP (1981).
Economy: Industries: Textiles, cement, food processing. **Chief crops:** Grains, olives, vegetables, fruits. **Minerals:** Phosphate, potash. **Per capita arable land:** 1.0 acres. **Electricity prod.** (1981): 1.2 bln. kwh. **Labor force:** 30% agric.
Finance: Currency: Dinar (Mar. 1984: 0.37 = $1 US). **Gross domestic product** (1983): $3.8 bln. **Per capita income** (1976): $552. **Imports** (1982): $3.2 bln.; partners: Saudi Ar. 17%, W. Ger. 11%, Jap. 8%. **Exports** (1982): $752 mln.; partners: Saudi Ar. 12%, Syria 6%, Iraq. 38%. **Tourists** (1981): 1.5 mln.; receipts: $504 mln. **National budget** (1980): $751.59 mln. revenues; $1.68 bln. expenditures. **International reserves less gold** (Feb. 1984): $632.9 mln. **Gold:** 1.08 mln. oz t. **Consumer prices** (change in 1983): 5.0%.
Transport: Motor vehicles: in use (1982): 118,900 passenger cars, 43,600 comm. vehicles. **Civil aviation** (1982): 3.2 bln. passenger-km; 131 mln. freight ton-km. **Chief ports:** Aqaba.
Communications: Television sets: 171,000 licensed (1981). **Radios:** 536,000 in use (1981). **Telephones in use** (1983): 86,000. **Daily newspaper circ.** (1982): 73 per 1,000 pop.
Health: Life expectancy at birth (1963): 52.6 male; 52.0 female. **Births** (per 1,000 pop. 1978): 49. **Deaths** (per 1,000 pop. 1978): 11. **Natural increase** (1978): 3.9%. **Hospital beds** (1980): 2,743. **Physicians** (1980): 1,715. **Infant mortality** (per 1,000 live births 1976): 88.
Education (1978): **Literacy:** 58%. **Pop. 5-19:** in school: 56%, teachers per 1,000: 20.
Embassy: 2319 Wyoming Ave NW 20008; 265-1606.

From ancient times to 1922 the lands to the E of the Jordan were culturally and politically united with the lands to the W. Arabs conquered the area in the 7th century; the Ottomans took control in the 16th. Britain's 1920 Palestine Mandate covered both sides of the Jordan. In 1921, Abdullah, son of the ruler of Hejaz in Arabia, was installed by Britain as emir of an autonomous Transjordan, covering two-thirds of Palestine. An independent kingdom was proclaimed, 1946.

During the 1948 Arab-Israeli war the West Bank and old city of Jerusalem were added to the kingdom, which changed its name to Jordan. All these territories were lost to Israel in the 1967 war, which swelled the number of Arab refugees on the East Bank. A 1974 Arab summit conference designated the Palestine Liberation Organization as the sole representative of Arabs on the West Bank. Jordan accepted the move, and was granted an annual subsidy by Arab oil states. The U.S. has also provided substantial economic and military support.

King Hussein actively promoted rejection of the Egyptian-Israeli peace treaty; Jordan was the first Arab country to sever diplomatic relations with Egypt, Mar. 1979.

Kenya

Republic of Kenya

People: Population (1983 est.): 18,580,000. **Age distrib.** (%): 0–14: 48.4; 15–59: 46.3; 60+: 5.4. **Pop. density:** 72.90 per sq. mi. **Urban** (1981): 10%. **Ethnic groups:** Kikuyu 21%, Luo 13%, Luhya 14%, Kalenjin 11%, Kamba 11%, others, including

280,000 Asians, Arabs, Europeans. **Languages:** Swahili (official), English. **Religions:** Protestants 38%, Roman Catholics 28%, Moslems 6%, others.
Geography: Area: 224,081 sq. mi., slightly smaller than Texas. **Location:** On Indian O. coast of E. Africa. **Neighbors:** Uganda on W, Tanzania on S, Somalia on E, Ethopia, Sudan on N. **Topography:** The northern three-fifths of Kenya is arid. To the S, a low coastal area and a plateau varying from 3,000 to 10,000 ft. The Great Rift Valley enters the country N-S, flanked by high mountains. **Capital:** Nairobi. **Cities** (1978): Nairobi (met.) 959,000; Mombasa (met.) 401,000.
Government: Type: Republic. **Head of state:** Pres. Daniel arap Moi, b. Sept., 1924; in office: Aug. 22, 1978. **Local divisions:** Nairobi and 7 provinces. **Defense:** 5.4% of GDP (1982).
Economy: Industries: Tourism, light industry. **Chief crops:** Coffee, corn, tea, cereals, cotton, sisal. **Minerals:** Gold, limestone, diatomite, salt, barytes, magnesite, felspar, sapphires, fluospar, garnets. **Other resources:** Timber, hides. **Arable land:** 20%. **Meat prod.** (1980): beef: 193,000 metric tons; pork: 4,000 metric tons; lamb: 38,000 metric tons. **Fish catch** (1981): 60,000 metric tons. **Electricity prod.** (1981): 1.7 bln. kwh. **Labor force:** 17% agric.; 18% ind. and commerce; 13% services; 47% public sector.
Finance: Currency: Shilling (Mar. 1984: 13.61 = $1 US). **Gross domestic product** (1981): $3.2 bln. **Per capita income** (1981): $196. **Imports** (1982): $1.7 bln.; partners: UK 17%, W. Ger. 8%, Jap. 8, Saudi Ar. 19%. **Exports** (1982): $1.04 bln.; partners: W. Ger. 11%, UK 11%, Ugan. 9%. **Tourists** (1981): 373,500; receipts: $240 mln. **National budget** (1981): $1.4 bln. **International reserves less gold** (Mar. 1984): $396.9 mln. **Gold:** 80,000 oz t. **Consumer prices** (change in 1983): 11.5%.
Transport: Motor vehicles: in use (1980): 113,600 passenger cars, 23,600 comm. vehicles. **Chief ports:** Mombasa.
Communications: Television sets: 65,000 in use (1981). **Radios:** 540,000 in use (1981). **Telephones in use** (1981): 198,294. **Daily newspaper circ.** (1982): 13 per 1,000 pop.
Health: Life expectancy at birth (1983): 56.3 male; 60.0 female. **Births** (per 1,000 pop. 1978): 54. **Deaths** (per 1,000 pop. 1978): 14. **Natural increase** (1978): 4.0%. **Hospital beds** (per 100,000 pop. 1977): 128. **Physicians** (per 100,000 pop. 1977): 8. **Infant mortality** (per 1,000 live births 1982): 83.
Education (1978): **Literacy:** 40%. **Pop. 5-19:** in school: 62%, teachers per 1,000: 18.
Embassy: 2249 R St. NW 20008; 387-6101.

Arab colonies exported spices and slaves from the Kenya coast as early as the 8th century. Britain obtained control in the 19th century. Kenya won independence Dec. 12, 1963, 4 years after the end of the violent Mau Mau uprising.

Kenya has shown steady growth in industry and agriculture under a modified private enterprise system, and has had a relatively free political life. But stability was shaken in 1974-5, with opposition charges of corruption and oppression.

In 1968 ties with Somalia were restored after 4 years of skirmishes. Tanzania closed its Kenya border in 1977 in a dispute over the collapse of the East African Community. Kenya welcomed the overthrow of Idi Amin.

A military and economic aid accord giving the U.S. access to air and naval bases was concluded, Apr. 1980.

Kiribati

Republic of Kiribati

People: Population (1983 est.): 60,000. **Pop. density:** 227.27 per sq. mi. **Ethnic groups:** nearly all Micronesian, some Polynesians. **Languages:** Gilbertese and English (official). **Religions:** evenly divided between Protestant and Roman Catholic.
Geography: Area: 266 sq. mi., slightly smaller than New York City. **Location:** 33 Micronesian islands (the Gilbert, Line, and Phoenix groups) in the mid-Pacific scattered in a 2-mln. sq. mi. chain around the point where the International Date Line cuts the Equator. **Neighbors:** Nearest are Nauru to SW, Tuvalu and Tokelau Is. to S. **Topography:** except Banaba (Ocean) I., all are low-lying, with soil of coral sand and rock fragments, subject to erratic rainfall. **Capital** (1980): Tarawa 22,148.
Government: Head of state and of government: Pres. Ieremia Tabai, b. Dec. 16, 1950; in office: July 12, 1979.

Economy: Industries: Copra. **Chief crops:** Coconuts, breadfruit, pandanus, bananas, paw paw. **Other resources:** Fish. **Electricity prod.** (1978): 5 mln. kwh.
Finance: Currency: Australian dollar. **Imports** (1979): $15.0 mln.; partners: Austral. 57%, NZ 5%, UK 6%, Jap. 13%. **Exports** (1979): $20 mln.; partners: UK 89%. **National budget** (1978): $16.3 mln. revenues; $14 mln. expenditures.
Transport: Chief port: Tarawa.
Communications: Radios: 8,200 in use (1976). **Telephones in use** (1981): 1,724.
Health: Pop. per hospital bed (1977): 200.
Education: Pop. 5–19: in school (1977): 13,679.

A British protectorate since 1892, the Gilbert and Ellice Islands colony was completed with the inclusion of the Phoenix Islands, 1937. Self-rule was granted 1971; the Ellice Islands separated from the colony 1975 and became independent Tuvalu, 1978. Kiribati (pronounced *Kiribass*) independence was attained July 12, 1979. Under a Treaty of Friendship, pending ratification by the U.S. Senate, the U.S. relinquishes its claims to several of the Line and Phoenix islands, including Christmas, Canton, and Enderbury.

Tarawa Atoll was the scene of some of the bloodiest fighting in the Pacific during WW II.

North Korea
Democratic People's Republic of Korea

People: Population (Jan. 1983 est.): 19,185,000. **Pop. density:** 406.26 per sq. mi. **Ethnic groups:** Korean. **Languages:** Korean. **Religions:** activities discouraged; traditionally Buddhism, Confucianism, Chondokyo.
Geography: Area: 47,077 sq. mi., slightly smaller than Mississippi. **Location:** In northern E. Asia. **Neighbors:** China, USSR on N, S. Korea on S. **Topography:** Mountains and hills cover nearly all the country, with narrow valleys and small plains in between. The N and the E coast are the most rugged areas. **Capital:** Pyongyang. **Cities** (1981 est.): Pyongyang 1,283,000.
Government: Type: Communist state. **Head of state:** Pres. Kim Il-Sung; b. Apr. 15, 1912; in office: Dec. 28, 1972. **Head of government:** Premier Li Jong Ok; in office: Dec. 15, 1977. **Head of Communist Party:** Gen. Sec. Kim Il-Sung; in office: 1945. **Local divisions:** 9 provinces, 4 municipalities, 3 urban district. **Defense:** 25% of GNP.
Economy: Industries: Textiles, fertilizers, cement. **Chief crops:** Grain, rice. **Minerals:** Coal, lead tungsten, zinc, graphite, magnesite, iron, copper, gold, phosphate, salt, fluorspar. **Per capita arable land:** 0.3 acres. **Meat prod.** (1983): pork: 130,000 metric tons. **Fish catch** (1981): 3.5 mln. metric tons. **Crude steel prod.** (1982) 3.5 mln. metric tons. **Labor force:** 48% agric.
Finance: Currency: Won (Sept. 1983): .94 = $1 US). **Gross domestic product** (1978 est.): $10.4 bln. **Per capita income** (1978, in 1975 U.S. dollars): $570. **Imports** (1980): $2.1 bln.; partners: China 17%, USSR 22%, Jap. 18%. **Exports** (1980): $1.9 bln.; partners: USSR 26% China 17%, Saudi Ar. 9%, Jap. 9%.
Transport: Chief ports: Chonglin, Hamhung, Nampo.
Health: Life expectancy at birth (1980): 70 male; 76 female. **Births** (per 1,000 pop. 1978): 43. **Deaths** (per 1,000 pop. 1978): 11. **Natural increase** (1978): 3.2%. **Hospital beds** (per 100,000 pop. 1977): 59. **Physicians** (per 100,000 pop. 1977): 40.
Education (1978): **Literacy:** 85%. **Pop. 5–19:** in school: 61%, teachers per 1,000: 13.

The Democratic People's Republic of Korea was founded May 1, 1948, in the zone occupied by Russian troops after World War II. Its armies tried to conquer the south, 1950. After 3 years of fighting with Chinese and U.S. intervention, a cease-fire was proclaimed.

Industry, begun by the Japanese during their 1910-45 occupation, and nationalized in the 1940s, had grown substantially, using N. Korea's abundant mineral and hydroelectric resources.

Two N. Korean Army officers were sentenced to death by Burmese authorities after they confessed to the October 9, 1983 bombing which killed 17, including 4 S. Korean cabinet ministers, in Rangoon.

South Korea
Republic of Korea

People: Population (1983 est.): 41,366,000. **Age distrib. (%):** 0–14: 34; 15–59: 56.3; 60+: 6.1. **Pop. density:** 973.42 per sq. mi. **Urban** (1980): 57.3%. **Ethnic groups:** Korean. **Languages:** Korean. **Religions:** Buddhism, Confucianism, Christian.
Geography: Area: 38,211 sq. mi., slightly larger than Indiana. **Location:** In Northern E. Asia. **Neighbors:** N. Korea on N. **Topography:** The country is mountainous, with a rugged east coast. The western and southern coasts are deeply indented, with many islands and harbors. **Capital:** Seoul. **Cities** (1980 est.): Seoul 8,000,000; Pusan 3,000,000; Taegu 1,309,131.
Government: Type: Republic, with power centralized in a strong executive. **Head of state:** Pres. Chun Doo Hwan; b. Jan. 18, 1931; in office: Dec. 1979. **Head of government:** Prime Min. Chin Lee Chong; in office: Oct. 14, 1983. **Local divisions:** 9 provinces and Seoul, Pusan, Inchon, and Taegu. **Defense:** 6% of GNP (1983).
Economy: Industries: Electronics, ships, textiles, clothing, motor vehicles. **Chief crops:** Rice, barley, vegetables. **Minerals:** Tungsten, coal, graphite. **Arable land:** 22%. **Meat prod.** (1983): pork: 295,000 metric tons. **Fish catch:** (1981): 2.3 mln. metric tons. **Electricity prod.** (1982): 36 bln. kwh. **Crude steel prod.** (1981): 3.5 mln. metric tons. **Labor force:** 30% agric.; 22% manuf. & mining; 47% services.
Finance: Currency: Won (Mar. 1984: 791.80 = $1 US). **Gross national product** (1982): $65.9 bln. **Per capita income** (1978): $1,187. **Imports** (1983): $26.1 bln.; partners: Jap. 24%, U.S. 23%, Saudi Ar. 14%, Kuw. 6%. **Exports** (1983): $24.4 bln.; partners: U.S. 27%, Jap. 16%. **Tourists** (1981): 1 mln.; receipts: $448 mln. **National budget** (1983): 13.9 bln. expenditures. **International reserves less gold** (Mar. 1984): $1.9 bln. **Gold:** 305,000 oz t. **Consumer prices** (change in 1983): 3.4%.
Transport: Railway traffic (1981): 21.2 bln. passenger-km; 10.6 bln. net ton-km. **Motor vehicles:** in use (1982): 305,800 passenger cars, 263,900 comm. vehicles, assembled (1978): 92,328 passenger cars; 65,616 comm. vehicles. **Civil aviation** (1982): 12.1 bln. passenger-km; 1 bln. freight ton-km. **Chief ports:** Pusan, Inchon.
Communications: Television sets: 6.2 mln. in use (1981), 5.8 mln. manuf. (1979). **Radios:** 15 mln. in use (1981), 4.7 mln. manuf. (1979). **Telephones in use** (1981): 3.3 mln. **Daily newspaper circ.** (1982): 190 per 1,000 pop.
Health: Life expectancy at birth (1979): 68 years. **Births** (per 1,000 pop. 1981): 23.4. **Deaths** (per 1,000 pop. 1981): 6.6. **Natural increase** (1978): 1.6%. **Hospital beds** (per 100,000 pop. 1977): 68. **Physicians** (per 100,000 pop. 1977): 49. **Infant mortality** (per 1,000 live births 1983): 32.
Education (1983): **Literacy:** 92%. **Attendance:** High school 57%, college 14%.
Embassy: 2320 Massachusetts Ave. NW 20008; 483-6892.

Korea, once called the Hermit Kingdom, has a recorded history since the 1st century BC. It was united in a kingdom under the Silla Dynasty, 668 AD. It was at times associated with the Chinese empire; the treaty that concluded the Sino-Japanese war of 1894-95 recognized Korea's complete independence. In 1910 Japan forcibly annexed Korea as Chosun.

At the Potsdam conference, July, 1945, the 38th parallel was designated as the line dividing the Soviet and the American occupation. Russian troops entered Korea Aug. 10, 1945, U.S. troops entered Sept. 8, 1945. The Soviet military organized socialists and communists and blocked efforts to let the Koreans unite their country. *(See Index for Korean War.)*

The South Koreans formed the Republic of Korea in May 1948 with Seoul as the capital. Dr. Syngman Rhee was chosen president but a movement spearheaded by college students forced his resignation Apr. 26, 1960.

In an army coup May 16, 1961, Gen. Park Chung Hee became chairman of the ruling junta. He was elected president, 1963; a 1972 referendum allowed him to be reelected for 6 year terms unlimited times. Park was assassinated by the chief of the Korean CIA, Oct. 26, 1979. The calm of the new government was halted by the rise of Gen. Chon Too Hwan, head of the military intelligence, who reinstated martial law, and reverted South Korea to the police state it was under Park.

North Korean raids across the border tapered off in 1971, but incidents occurred in 1973 and 1974. In July 1972 South and North Korea agreed on a common goal of reunifying the 2 nations by peaceful means. But there has been no sign of a thaw in relations between the two regimes.

A Korean Air Lines passenger airliner was shot down by a Soviet jet fighter, Sept. 1, 1983, after it strayed into Soviet airspace; all 269 people aboard died.

During a 6-nation tour by Pres. Chun Doo Hwan, Oct. 9, a bomb exploded in Rangoon, Burma killing 17 S. Koreans, including 4 cabinet ministers. Two N. Korean Army officers confessed to the bombing.

Kuwait
State of Kuwait

People: Population (1983 est.): 1,652,000. **Age distrib.** (%): 0–14: 40.2; 15–59: 57.6; 60+: 2.3. **Pop. density:** 176.09 per sq. mi. **Ethnic groups:** Arabs 83%, Iranians, Indians, Pakistanis 13%. **Languages:** Arabic, others. **Religions:** Islam 95%.

Geography: Area: 6,532 sq. mi., slightly smaller than New Jersey. **Location:** In Middle East, at N end of Persian Gulf. **Neighbors:** Iraq on N, Saudi Arabia on S. **Topography:** The country is flat, very dry, and extremely hot. **Capital:** Kuwait. **Cities** (1980 cen.): Hawalli 152,300; Kuwait City 60,400.

Government: Type: Constitutional monarchy. **Head of state:** Emir Shaikh Jabir al-Ahmad al-Jabir as-Sabah; b. 1928; in office: Jan. 1, 1978. **Head of government:** Prime Min. Shaikh Saad Abdulla as-Salim as-Sabah; in office: Feb. 8, 1978. **Local divisions:** 4 governorates.

Economy: Industries: Oil products. **Minerals:** Oil, gas. **Crude oil reserves** (1981): 70 bln. bbls. **Cultivated land:** 1%. **Electricity prod.** (1982): 10.3 bln. kwh. **Labor force:** 2% agric.; 8%. manuf.; 53% services.

Finance: Currency: Dinar (Sept. 1983: 0.29 = $1 US). **Gross domestic product** (1981): $24.3 bln. **Per capita income** (1975): $11,431. **Imports** (1982): $9.0 bln.; partners: Jap. 21%, U.S. 14%, UK 9%, W. Ger. 9%. **Exports** (1983): $12.4 bln.; partners: Jap. 20%, U.S. 14%, UK 9%, It. 6%. **National budget** (1982): $11.1 bln. revenues; $10 bln. expenditures. **International reserves less gold** (Feb. 1984): $5.1 bln. **Gold:** 2.53 mln. oz t. **Consumer prices** (change in (1983): 4.7%.

Transport: Motor vehicles: in use (1981): 435,000 passenger cars, 146,000 comm. vehicles. **Civil aviation** (1982): 3.5 bln. passenger-km; 115.6 mln. freight ton-km. **Chief ports:** Mina al-Ahmadi.

Communications: Television sets: 250,000 in use (1980). **Radios:** 1 mln. in use (1980). **Telephones in use** (1980): 192,000. **Daily newspaper circ.** (1982): 267 per 1,000 pop.

Health: Life expectancy at birth (1980): 67.3 male; 71.6 female. **Births** (per 1,000 pop. 1981): 37.2. **Deaths** (per 1,000 pop. 1981): 3.6. **Natural increase** (1978): 5.9%. **Hospital beds** (per 100,000 pop. 1977): 388. **Physicians** (per. 100,000 pop. 1977): 124. **Infant mortality** (per 1,000 live births 1983): 33.9.

Education (1983): **Literacy:** 71%. **Years compulsory:** 8. **Embassy:** 2940 Tilden St. NW 20008; 966-0702.

Kuwait is ruled by the Al-Sabah dynasty, founded 1759. Britain ran foreign relations and defense from 1899 until independence in 1961. The majority of the population is non-Kuwaiti, with many Palestinians, and cannot vote.

Iraqi troops crossed the Kuwait border in 1973 but soon withdrew. Kuwait has ordered weapons from France and the U.S.

Oil, first exported in 1946, is the fiscal mainstay, providing most of Kuwait's income. Oil pays for free medical care, education, and social security. There are no taxes, except customs duties.

Two Kuwaiti oil tankers were attacked in the Persian Gulf by Iranian planes, May 1984.

Laos
Lao People's Democratic Republic

People: Population (1983 est.): 3,647,000. **Pop. density:** 40.69 per sq. mi. **Urban** (1973): 14.7%. **Ethnic groups:** Lao 50%, Thai 20%, Meo and Yao 15%, others. **Languages:** Lao (official), French, English. **Religions:** Buddhists 58%, tribal 34%.

Geography: Area: 91,428 sq. mi., slightly larger than Utah. **Location:** In Indochina Peninsula in SE Asia. **Neighbors:** Burma, China on N, Vietnam on E, Cambodia on S, Thailand on W. **Topography:** Landlocked, dominated by jungle. High mountains along the eastern border are the source of the E-W rivers slicing across the country to the Mekong R., which defines most of the western border. **Capital:** Vientiane. **Cities** (1978 est.); Vientiane 200,000.

Government: Type: Communist. **Head of state:** Pres. Souphanouvong; b. July 13, 1909; in office: Dec. 2, 1975. **Head of government:** Prime Min. Kaysone Phomvihan; b. Dec. 13, 1920; in office: Dec. 2, 1975. **Local divisions:** 13 provinces. **Armed forces:** regulars 54,550 (1980).

Economy: Industries: Wood products. **Chief crops:** Rice, corn, tobacco, cotton, opium, citrus fruits, coffee. **Minerals:** Tin. **Other resources:** Forests. **Per capita arable land:** 0.7 acres. **Meat prod.** (1980): beef: 12,000 metric tons; pork: 30,000 metric tons. **Fish catch** (1978): 20,000 metric tons. **Electricity prod.** (1981): 1.1 bln. kwh. **Labor force:** 76% agric.

Finance: Currency: New kip (Nov. 1983): 10 = $1 US). **Gross domestic product** (1978 est.): $220 mln. **Per capita income** (1976 est.): $85. **Imports** (1982): $150.1 mln.; partners (1974): Thai. 49%, Jap. 19%, Fr. 7%, W. Ger. 7%. **Exports** (1982): $14 mln.; partners (1974): Thai. 73%, Malaysia 11%, HK 10%.

Transport: Motor vehicles: in use (1974): 14,100 passenger cars, 2,500 comm. vehicles. **Civil Aviation** (1982): 8 mln. passenger km; 100,000 net ton-km.

Communications: Radios: 350,000 licensed (1981).

Health: Life expectancy at birth (1975): 39.1 male; 41.8 female. **Births** (per 1,000 pop. 1978): 44. **Deaths** (per 1,000 pop. 1978): 21. **Natural increase** (1978): 0.9%. **Hospital beds** (per 100,000 pop. 1977): 98. **Physicians** (per 100,000 pop. 1977): 6. **Education** (1978): **Literacy:** 28%. **Pop. 5-19:** in school: 40%, teachers per 1,000: 14.

Embassy: 2222 S St. NW 20008; 332-6416.

Laos became a French protectorate in 1893, but regained independence as a constitutional monarchy July 19, 1949.

Conflicts among neutralist, communist and conservative factions created a chaotic political situation. Armed conflict increased after 1960.

The 3 factions formed a coalition government in June 1962, with neutralist Prince Souvanna Phouma as premier. A 14-nation conference in Geneva signed agreements, 1962, guaranteeing neutrality and independence. By 1964 the Pathet Lao had withdrawn from the coalition, and, with aid from N. Vietnamese troops, renewed sporadic attacks. U.S. planes bombed the Ho Chi Minh trail, supply line from N. Vietnam to communist forces in Laos and S. Vietnam. An estimated 2.75 million tons of bombs were dropped on Laos during the fighting.

In 1970 the U.S. stepped up air support and military aid. There were an est. 67,000 N. Vietnamese troops in Laos, and some 15,000 Thais financed by the U.S.

After Pathet Lao military gains, Souvanna Phouma in May 1975 ordered government troops to cease fighting; the Pathet Lao took control. A Lao People's Democratic Republic was proclaimed Dec. 3, 1975; it is strongly influenced by Vietnam.

Lebanon
Republic of Lebanon

People: Population (1983 est.): 2,598,000. **Age distrib.** (%): 0–14: 42.6; 15–59: 49.6; 60+: 7.7. **Pop. density:** 787.05 per sq. mi. **Urban** (1982): 64%. **Ethnic groups:** Arabs 93%, Armenians 6%. **Languages:** Arabic (official), French, Armenian. **Religions:** Predominately Moslems and Christians; Druze minority.

Geography: Area: 3,950 sq. mi., smaller than Connecticut. **Location:** On Eastern end of Mediterranean Sea. **Neighbors:** Syria on E. Israel on S. **Topography:** There is a narrow coastal strip, and 2 mountain ranges running N-S enclosing the fertile Beqaa Valley. The Litani R. runs S through the valley, turning W to empty into the Mediterranean. **Capital:** Beirut. **Cities** (1982 est.): Beirut 1,100,000; Tripoli 240,000.

Government: Type: Parliamentary Republic. **Head of state:** Pres. Amin Gemayel; in office: Sept. 23, 1982; **Head of government:** Prime Min. Rashid Abdul Hamid Karami; b. Dec. 30, 1921; in office: Apr. 26, 1984. **Local divisions:** 5 provinces. **Defense:** 19% of govt. budget (1981).

Economy: Industries: Trade, food products, textiles, cement, oil products. **Chief crops:** Fruits, olives, tobacco, grapes, vegetables, grains. **Minerals:** Iron. **Arable land:** 38%. **Meat prod.** (1980): beef: 13,000 metric tons; lamb: 13,000 metric tons. **Electricity prod.** (1981): 1.8 bln. kwh. **Labor force:** 17% agric.; 75% ind., comm., services.

Finance: Currency: Pound (Jan. 1984: 5.85 = $1 US). **Gross domestic product** (1977 est.): $2.6 bln. **Per capita income** (1977): $884. **Imports** (1982): $3.3 bln.; partners: It. 15%, Fr. 10%, U.S. 9%, Saudi Ar. 6%. **Exports** (1982): $775 mln.; partners: Saudi Ar. 33%, Syria 8%, Jor. 6%, Kuw. 8%. **International reserves less gold** (Feb. 1984): $1.5 bln. **Gold:** 9.22 mln. oz t.

Transport: Railway traffic (1974): 2 mln. passenger-km; 42 mln. net ton-km. **Motor vehicles:** in use (1982): 460,000 passenger cars, 21,000 comm. vehicles. **Civil aviation** (1982): 968 mln. passenger-km; 465 mln. freight ton-km. **Chief ports:** Beirut, Tripoli, Sidon.

Communications: Television sets: 750,000 in use (1981). **Radios:** 2 mln. in use (1981). **Telephones:** in use (1978): 231,000. **Daily newspaper circ.** (1982): 49 per 1,000 pop.

Health: Life expectancy at birth (1975): 61.4 male; 65.1 female. **Births** (per 1,000 pop. 1978): 36. **Deaths** (per 1,000 pop. 1978): 11. **Natural increase** (1978): 2.5%. **Hospital beds** (per 100,000 pop. 1977): 384. **Physicians** (per 100,000 pop. 1977): 75. **Infant mortality** (per 1,000 live births 1982): 45.

Education: (1982): **Literacy:** 75%. **Years compulsory:** 5; attendance 93%.

Embassy: 2560 28th St. NW 20008; 462-8600.

Formed from 5 former Turkish Empire districts, Lebanon became an independent state Sept. 1, 1920, administered under French mandate 1920-41. French troops withdrew in 1946.

Under the 1943 National Covenant, all public positions were divided among the various religious communities, with Christians in the majority. By the 1970s, Moslems became the majority, and demanded a larger political and economic role.

U.S. Marines intervened, May-Oct. 1958, during a Syrian-aided revolt. Lebanon's efforts to restrain Palestinian commandos caused armed clashes in 1969. Continued raids against Israeli civilians, 1970-75, brought Israeli attacks against guerrilla camps and villages. Israeli troops occupied S. Lebanon, March 1978, but were replaced by a UN force, and again in Apr. 1980.

An estimated 60,000 were killed and billions of dollars in damage inflicted in a 1975-76 civil war. Palestinian units and leftist Moslems fought against the Maronite militia, the Phalange, and other Christians. Several Arab countries provided political and arms support to the various factions, while Israel aided Christian forces. Up to 15,000 Syrian troops intervened in 1976, and fought Palestinian groups. Arab League troops from several nations tried to impose a cease-fire.

Clashes between Syrian troops and Christian forces erupted, Apr. 1, 1981, near Zahle, Lebanon, bringing to an end the cease-fire that had been in place. By Apr. 22, fighting had broken out not only between Syrians and Christians, but also between two Moslem factions. Israeli commandos attacked Palestinian positions at Tyre and Tulin. In July, Israeli air raids on Beirut killed or wounded some 800 persons. A cease-fire between Israel and the Palestinians was concluded July 24, but hostilities continued.

Israeli forces invaded Lebanon June 6, 1982, in a coordinated land, sea, and air attack aimed at crushing strongholds of the Palestine Liberation Organization (PLO). Israeli and Syrian forces engaged in the Bekka Valley. By June 14, Israeli troops had encircled Beirut. On Aug. 21, the PLO evacuated West Beirut following massive Israeli bombings of the city. The withdrawal was supervised by U.S., French, and Italian troops.

Israeli troops entered West Beirut following the Sept. 14 assassination of newly-elected Lebanese Pres. Bashir Gemayel. On Sept. 16, Lebanese Christian troops entered 2 refugee camps and massacred hundreds of Palestinian refugees.

In 1983, terrorist bombings became a way of life in Beirut as some 50 people were killed in an explosion at the U.S. Embassy, Apr. 18; 241 U.S. servicemen and 58 French soldiers died in separate Muslim suicide attacks, Oct. 23.

PLO leader Yasir Arafat and PLO dissidents backed by Syria fought a 6-week battle in Tripoli until negotiations allowed Arafat and some 4,000 followers to evacuate the city.

On Apr. 26, 1984, pro-Syrian Rashid Karami was appointed premier. The appointment ended virtual civil war in Beirut between the Lebanese army, Christian forces, and Druse and Shiite Moslem militias. (*See Chronology*)

Lesotho
Kingdom of Lesotho

People: Population (1983 est.): 1,438,000. **Age distrib. (%):** 0–14: 39.5; 15–59: 53.9; 60+: 6.6. **Pop. density:** 114.37 per sq. mi. **Ethnic groups:** Sotho 85%, Nguni 15%. **Languages:** English, Southern Sotho (official). **Religions:** Roman Catholic 43%, Protestant 49%.

Geography: Area: 11,716 sq. mi., slightly larger than Maryland. **Location:** In Southern Africa. **Neighbors:** Completely surrounded by Republic of South Africa. **Topography:** Landlocked and mountainous, with altitudes ranging from 5,000 to 11,000 ft. **Capital:** Maseru. **Cities** (1981 est.): Maseru 75,000.

Government: Type: Constitutional monarchy. **Head of state:** King Moshoeshoe II, b. May 2, 1938; in office: Mar. 12, 1960. **Head of government:** Prime Min. Leabua Jonathan; b. Oct. 31, 1914; in office: Oct. 4, 1966. **Local divisions:** 10 districts.

Economy: Industries: Diamond polishing, food processing. **Chief crops:** Corn, grains, peas, beans. **Other resources:** Wool, mohair. **Arable land:** 13%. **Electricity prod.** (1967): 5.00 mln. kwh. **Labor force:** 87% agric.; 3% ind. and commerce.

Finance: Currency: Maloti (Mar. 1984: 1.18 = $1 US). **Gross domestic product** (1979 est.): $540 mln. **Per capita income** (1979): $355. **Imports** (1979): $170 mln.; partners: Mostly So. Afr. **Exports** (1979): $40 mln.; partners: Mostly So. Afr. **National budget** (1981): $204 mln. revenues; $265 mln. expenditures. **Consumer prices** (change in 1979): 19%.

Transport: Motor vehicles: in use (1979): 4,000 passenger cars, 8,000 comm. vehicles.

Communications: Radios: 80,000 licensed (1978). **Daily newspaper circ.** (1982): 32 per 1,000 pop.

Health: Life expectancy at birth (1975): 46.7 male; 48.9 female. **Births** (per 1,000 pop. 1978): 37. **Deaths** (per 1,000 pop. 1978): 14. **Natural increase** (1978): 2.3%. **Hospital beds** (per 100,000 pop. 1977): 205. **Physicians** (per 100,000 pop. 1977): 8. **Infant mortality** (per 1,000 live births 1981): 111.

Education (1978): **Literacy:** 55%. **Pop. 5-19:** in school: 58%, teachers per 1,000: 12.

Embassy: 1601 Connecticut Ave. NW 20009; 462-4190.

Lesotho (once called Basutoland) became a British protectorate in 1868 when Chief Moshesh sought protection against the Boers. Independence came Oct. 4, 1966. Elections were suspended in 1970. Over 50% of males work abroad in So. Africa. Livestock raising is the chief industry; diamonds are the chief export.

Liberia
Republic of Liberia

People: Population (1983 est.): 2,091,000. **Age distrib. (%):** 0–14: 40.9; 15–59: 53.1; 60+: 5.9. **Pop. density:** 43.26 per sq. mi. **Urban** (1971): 27.6%. **Ethnic groups:** Americo-Liberians 5%, 16 tribes 95% **Languages:** English (official), tribal dialects. **Religions:** Moslems 21%, Christians 35%, traditional 43%.

Geography: Area: 38,250 sq. mi., slightly smaller than Pennsylvania. **Location:** On SW coast of W. Africa. **Neighbors:** Sierra Leone on W, Guinea on N, Ivory Coast on E. **Topography:** Marshy Atlantic coastline rises to low mountains and plateaus in the forested interior; 6 major rivers flow in parallel courses to the ocean. **Capital:** Monrovia. **Cities** (1981 est.): Monrovia 306,000.

Government: Type: Military. **Head of state:** Pres. Samuel K. Doe; in office: Apr. 12, 1980. **Local divisions:** 9 counties and 6 territories. **Defense:** 2% of GDP (1981).

Economy: Industries: Food processing and other light industry. **Chief crops:** Rice, cassava, coffee, cocoa, sugar. **Minerals:** Iron, diamonds, gold. **Other resources:** Rubber, timber. **Per capita arable land:** 0.2 acres. **Fish catch** (1978): 18,800 metric tons. **Electricity prod.** (1981): 1.1 bln. kwh. **Labor force:** 70.5% agric.

Finance: Currency: Dollar (Apr. 1984: 1.00 = $1 US). **Gross domestic product** (1981): $372 mln. **Per capita income** (1976): $453. **Imports** (1981): $477 mln.; partners: U.S. 29%, W. Ger. 10%, Saudi Ar. 19%, Jap. 5%, Neth. 8%. **Exports** (1981): $601 mln.; partners: W. Ger. 25%, U.S. 23%, It. 13%, Fr. 10%. **National budget** (1980): $202.3 mln. revenues; $281 mln.

expenditures. **International reserves less gold** (Feb. 1984): $8.5 mln. **Consumer prices** (change in 1982): 6.0%.

Transport: Motor vehicles: in use (1980): 22,000 passenger cars, 20,000 comm. vehicles. **Chief ports:** Monrovia, Buchanan.

Communications: Television sets: 21,000 in use (1980). **Radios:** 320,000 in use (1981): **Telephones in use** (1980): 7,740. **Daily newspaper circ.** (1982): 6 per 1,000 pop.

Health: Life expectancy at birth (1971): 45.8 male; 44.0 female. **Births** (per 1,000 pop. 1978): 50. **Deaths** (per 1,000 pop. 1978): 20. **Natural increase** (1978): 3.1%. **Hospital beds** (1980): 3,000. **Physicians** (1980): 236. **Infant mortality** (per 1,000 live births 1981): 148.

Education (1982): **Literacy:** 24%. **School attendance:** primary 40%, secondary 16%.

Embassy: 5201 16th St. NW 20011; 723-0437.

Liberia was founded in 1822 by U.S. black freedmen who settled at Monrovia with the aid of colonization societies. It became a republic July 26, 1847, with a constitution modeled on that of the U.S. Descendants of freedmen dominated politics.

Charging rampant corruption, an Army Redemption Council of enlisted men staged a bloody predawn coup, April 12, 1980, in which Pres. Tolbert was killed and replaced as head of state by Sgt. Samuel Doe. Doe promised a return to civilian rule in 1985.

Libya

Socialist People's Libyan Arab Jamahiriya

People: Population: (1983 est.): 3,498,000. **Age distrib.** (%): 0–14: 51.4; 15–59: 42.6; 60+: 5.9. **Pop. density:** 5 per sq. mi. **Urban** (1983): 53%. **Ethnic groups:** Arab-Berber 97%, Italian 1.4%, others. **Languages:** Arabic. **Religions:** Predominantly Sunni Moslems.

Geography: Area: 679,536 sq. mi., larger than Alaska. **Location:** On Mediterranean coast of N. Africa. **Neighbors:** Tunisia, Algeria on W, Niger, Chad on S, Sudan, Egypt on E. **Topography:** Desert and semidesert regions cover 92% of the land, with low mountains in N, higher mountains in S, and a narrow coastal zone. **Capital:** Tripoli. **Cities** (1981 est.): Tripoli 858,500.

Government: Type: Centralized republic, under military control. **Head of state:** Col. Muammar al-Qaddafi; b. Sept. 1942; in office: Sept. 1969. **Head of government:** Secy. Gen. Jadallah Azzuz at-Talhi. **Local divisions:** 10 regions. **Armed forces:** regulars 49,000 (1980).

Economy: Industries: Carpets, textiles, shoes. **Chief crops:** Dates, olives, citrus and other fruits, grapes, tobacco. **Minerals:** Gypsum, oil, gas. **Crude oil reserves** (1980): 23.5 bln. bbls. **Per capita arable land:** 2.2 acres. **Meat prod.** (1980): beef: 33,000 metric tons; lamb: 53,000 metric tons. **Electricity prod.** (1981): 5.6 bln. kwh. **Labor force:** 20% agric.; 20% manuf.; 10% oil ind.

Finance: Currency: Dinar (Feb. 1984: 0.33 = $1 US). **Gross domestic product** (1982): $25 bln. **Per capita income** (1978): $6,335. **Imports** (1982): $8.3 bln.; partners: It. 30%, W. Ger. 11%, Fr. 6%, Jap. 8%. **Exports** (1983): $11.3 bln.; partners: U.S. 27%, It. 24%, W. Ger. 10%, Sp. 7%. **International reserves less gold** (Mar. 1984): $4.7 bln. **Gold:** 3.57 mln. oz t.

Transport: Motor vehicles: in use (1980): 367,400 passenger cars, 278,900 comm. vehicles. **Chief ports:** Tripoli, Benghazi.

Communications: Television sets: 165,000 licensed (1981). **Radios:** 135,000 (1981). **Daily newspaper circ.** (1980): 22 per 1,000 pop.

Health: Life expectancy at birth (1975): 51.4 male; 54.5 female. **Births** (per 1,000 pop. 1978): 48. **Deaths** (per 1,000 pop. 1978): 13. **Natural increase** (1978): 3.5%. **Hospital beds** (per 100,000 pop. 1977): 476. **Physicians** (per 100,000 pop. 1977): 106.

Education (1983): Literacy: 40%. **Pop. 5-19:** in school: 76%, teachers per 1,000: 40.

First settled by Berbers, Libya was ruled by Carthage, Rome, and Vandals, the Ottomans, Italy from 1912, and Britain and France after WW II. It became an independent constitutional monarchy Jan. 2, 1952. In 1969 a junta lead by Col. Muammar al-Qaddafi seized power.

In the mid-1970s, Libya helped arm violent revolutionary groups in Egypt and Sudan, and had aided terrorists of various nationalities. The USSR sold Libya advanced arms, and established close political ties.

Libya and Egypt fought several air and land battles along their border in July, 1977. Chad charged Libya with military occupation of its uranium-rich northern region in 1977. Libya's 1979 offensive into the Aouzou Strip was repulsed by Chadian forces. Libyan forces withdrew from Chad, Nov. 1981.

Widespread nationalization, arrests, imposition of currency regulations, wholesale conscription of civil servants into the army, and the fall in crude oil prices have hurt the economy.

On May 6, 1981, the U.S., citing "a wide range of Libyan provocations and misconduct," closed the Libyan mission in Wash. In August, 2 Libyan jets were shot down by U.S. Navy planes taking part in naval exercises in the Gulf of Sidra. Great Britain severed diplomatic relations with Libya April 22, 1984, following the death of a British policewoman and the wounding of 10 Libyan-exile demonstrators by machine-gun fire from within the Libyan embassy in London.

Liechtenstein

Principality of Liechtenstein

People: Population (1983 est.): 26,000. **Age distrib.** (%): 0–14: 27.9; 15–59: 60.2; 60+: 11.9. **Pop. density:** 416 per sq. mi. **Ethnic groups:** Alemannic. **Languages:** German (official), Alemannic dialect. **Religions:** Roman Catholic 82%, Protestants 7%.

Geography: Area: 62 sq. mi., the size of Washington, D.C. **Location:** In the Alps. **Neighbors:** Switzerland on W, Austria on E. **Topography:** The Rhine Valley occupies one-third of the country, the Alps cover the rest. **Capital:** Vaduz. **Cities** (1981 cen.): Vaduz 4,980.

Government: Type: Hereditary constitutional monarchy. **Head of state:** Prince Franz Josef II; b. Aug. 16, 1906; in office: Mar. 30, 1938. **Head of government:** Hans Brunhart; b. Mar. 28, 1945; in office: Apr. 26, 1978. **Local divisions:** 2 districts, 11 communities.

Economy: Industries: Machines, instruments, chemicals, furniture, ceramics. **Per capita arable land:** 0.3 acres. **Labor force:** 54.6% industry, trade and building; 41.5% services; 3.9% agric., fishing, forestry.

Finance: Currency: Swiss Franc (Nov. 1983): 2.16 = $1. **Tourists** (1981): 85,300.

Communications: Radios: 7,296 in use (1981). **Telephones in use** (1981): 10,600. **Daily newspaper circ.** (1982): 558 per 1,000 pop.

Health: Births (per 1,000 pop. 1977): 12.5. **Deaths** (per 1,000 pop. 1977): 6.0. **Natural increase** (1977): .7%. **Infant mortality** (per 1,000 live births 1983): 5.8.

Education: Literacy: 100%. **Years compulsory** 9; attendance 100%.

Liechtenstein became sovereign in 1866. Austria administered Liechtenstein's ports up to 1920; Switzerland has administered its postal services since 1921. Liechtenstein is united with Switzerland by a customs and monetary union. Taxes are low; many international corporations have headquarters there. Foreign workers comprise a third of the population.

Luxembourg

Grand Duchy of Luxembourg

People: Population: (1983 est.): 366,000. **Age distrib.** (%): 0–14: 19.0; 15–59: 63.5; 60+: 17.6. **Pop. density:** 360.36 per sq. mi. **Urban** (1974): 67.9%. **Ethnic groups:** Mixture of French and Germans predominate. **Languages:** French, German, Luxembourgian. **Religions:** Roman Catholic 94%.

Geography: Area: 1,034 sq. mi., smaller than Rhode Island. **Location:** In W. Europe. **Neighbors:** Belgium on W, France on S, W. Germany on E. **Topography:** Heavy forests (Ardennes) cover N, S is a low, open plateau. **Capital:** Luxembourg. **Cities** (1982 est.): Luxembourg 80,000.

Government: Type: Constitutional monarchy. **Head of state:** Grand Duke Jean; b. Jan. 5, 1921; in office: Nov. 12, 1964. **Head of government:** Prime Min. Pierre Werner, b. Dec. 29, 1913; in office: July 16, 1979. **Local divisions:** 3 districts, 12 cantons. **Defense:** 2.8% of govt. budget (1982).

Economy: Industries: Steel, chemicals, beer, tires, tobacco, metal products, cement. **Chief crops:** Corn, wine. **Minerals:** Iron. **Arable land:** 43.9%. **Electricity prod.** (1982): 972 mln. kwh. **Crude steel prod.** (1982): 3.5 min. metric tons. **Labor force:** 1% agric.; 42% ind. & comm.; 45% services.

Finance: Currency: Franc (Mar. 1984: 53.08 = $1 US). **Gross domestic product** (1981): $3.8 bln. **Per capita income** (1981): $10,444. **Note:** trade and tourist data included in Belgian statistics. **Consumer prices** (change in 1983): 8.7%.

Transport: Railway traffic (1982): 310 mln. passenger-km; 551 mln. net ton-km. **Motor vehicles:** in use (1982): 137,900 passenger cars, 10,800 comm. vehicles. **Civil aviation:** (1980): 55 mln. passenger-miles; 200,000 freight ton-miles.

Communications: Television sets: 140,000 in use (1981). **Radios:** 200,000 in use (1981). **Telephones in use** (1981): 214,964. **Daily newspaper circ.** (1982): 352 per 1,000 pop.

Health: Life expectancy at birth (1978): 68.0 male; 75 female. **Births** (per 1,000 pop. 1980): 11.4. **Deaths** (per 1,000 pop. 1980): 11.3. **Natural increase** (1978): −.04%. **Hospital beds:** 4,778. **Physicians** (1981): 563. **Infant mortality** (per 1,000 live births 1982): 12.

Education (1982): **Literacy:** 100%. **Years compulsory** 9; attendance 100%.

Embassy: 2200 Massachusetts Ave. NW 20008; 265-4171.

Luxembourg, founded about 963, was ruled by Burgundy, Spain, Austria, and France from 1448 to 1815. It left the Germanic Confederation in 1866. Overrun by Germany in 2 world wars, Luxembourg ended its neutrality in 1948, when a customs union with Belgium and Netherlands was adopted.

Madagascar
Democratic Republic of Madagascar

People: Population (1983 est.): 9,389,000. **Pop. density:** 38.56 per sq. mi. **Urban** (1975): 16.3%. **Ethnic groups:** 18 Malayan-Indonesian tribes (Merina 26%), with Arab and African presence. **Languages:** Malagasy (national), French. **Religions:** animists 54%, Christian 40%, Muslim 5%.

Geography: Area: 226,658 sq. mi., slightly smaller than Texas. **Location:** In the Indian O., off the SE coast of Africa. **Neighbors:** Comoro Is., Mozambique (across Mozambique Channel). **Topography:** Humid coastal strip in the E, fertile valleys in the mountainous center plateau region, and a wider coastal strip on the W. **Capital:** Antananarivo. **Cities** (1982 est.): Antananarivo 600,000.

Government: Type: Republic. **Head of state:** Pres. Didier Ratsiraka; b. Nov. 4, 1936; in office: June 15, 1975. **Head of government:** Prime Min. Desire Rakotoarijaona, b. June 19, 1934; in office. Aug. 4, 1977. **Local divisions:** 6 provinces. **Defense:** 13.1% of govt. budget.

Economy: Industries: Light industry. **Chief crops:** Coffee (over 50% of exports), cloves, vanilla, rice, sugar, sisal, tobacco, peanuts. **Minerals:** Chromium, graphite. **Arable land:** 5%. **Meat prod.** (1983): beef: 119,000 metric tons; pork: 28,000 metric tons; lamb: 6,000 metric tons. **Fish catch** (1981): 49,000 metric tons. **Electricity prod.** (1978): 300.00 mln. kwh. **Labor force:** 88% agric.; 1.5% ind. and commerce.

Finance: Currency: Franc (Mar. 1984: 492.16 = $1 US). **Gross domestic product** (1980): $3.3 bln. **Per capita income** (1980): $350. **Imports** (1980): $603 mln.; partners (1980): Fr. 41%, W. Ger. 10%. **Exports** (1980): $339 mln.; partners (1980): Fr. 20%, U.S. 19%. **National budget** (1982): $1.03 bln. **International reserves less gold** (Mar. 1984): $23.8 mln. **Consumer prices** (change in 1982): 31.4%.

Transport: Railway traffic (1980): 274 mln. passenger-km; 201 mln. net ton-km. **Motor vehicles:** in use (1980): 49,000 passenger cars, 49,000 comm. vehicles. **Civil aviation:** (1980): 310 mln. passenger-km; 20 mln. freight ton-km. **Chief ports:** Tamatave, Diego-Suarez, Majunga, Tulear.

Communications: Television sets: 45,000 in use (1981). **Radios:** 1.7 mln. in use (1981). **Telephones in use** (1980): 37,000.

Health: Life expectancy at birth (1982): 46 years. **Births** (per 1,000 pop. 1981): 45. **Deaths** (per 1,000 pop. 1981): 18. **Natural increase** (1978): 2.6%. **Hospital beds** (per 100,000 pop. 1977): 245. **Physicians** (per 100,000 pop. 1977): 10. **Infant mortality** (per 1,000 live births 1982): 177.

Education (1981): **Literacy:** 53%. **Years compulsory:** 5; attendance 83%.

Embassy: 2374 Massachusetts Ave. NW 20008; 265-5525.

Madagascar was settled 2,000 years ago by Malayan-Indonesian people, whose descendants still predominate. A unified kingdom ruled the 18th and 19th centuries. The island became a French protectorate, 1885, and a colony 1896. Independence came June 26, 1960.

Discontent with inflation and French domination led to a coup in 1972. The new regime nationalized French-owned financial interests, closed French bases and a U.S. space tracking station, and obtained Chinese aid. The government conducted a program of arrests, expulsion of foreigners, and repression of strikes, 1979.

Malawi
Republic of Malawi

People: Population (1983 est.): 6,612,000. **Age distrib.** (%): 0–14: 43.9; 15–59: 50.4; 60+: 5.6. **Pop. density:** 130.50 per sq. mi. **Urban** (1977): 8.3%. **Ethnic groups:** Chewa, 90%, Nyanja, Lomwe, other Bantu tribes. **Languages:** English, Chichewa (both official). **Religions:** Christian 75%, Muslim 20%.

Geography: Area: 45,747 sq. mi., the size of Pennsylvania. **Location:** In SE Africa. **Neighbors:** Zambia on W, Mozambique on SE, Tanzania on N. **Topography:** Malawi stretches 560 mi. N-S along Lake Malawi (Lake Nyasa), most of which belongs to Malawi. High plateaus and mountains line the Rift Valley the length of the nation. **Capital:** Lilongwe. **Cities** (1983 est.): Blantyre 250,000; Lilongwe 130,000.

Government: Type: Republic. **Head of state:** Pres. Hastings Kamuzu Banda, b. May 14, 1906; in office: July 6, 1966. **Local divisions:** 24 administrative districts. **Defense:** 8% of govt. budget (1983).

Economy: Industries: Textiles, sugar, farm implements. **Chief crops:** Tea, tobacco, peanuts, cotton, sugar, soybeans, coffee. **Other resources:** Rubber. **Arable land:** 34%. **Fish catch** (1978): 67.7 metric tons. **Electricity prod.** (1978): 276.00 mln. kwh. **Labor force:** 45% agric.; 17% ind. and comm.; 20% govt.; 18% services.

Finance: Currency: Kwacha (Mar. 1984: 1.31 = $1 US). **Gross national product** (1980): $1.23 bln. **Per capita income** (1979): $220. **Imports** (1981): $263 mln.; partners: So. Afr. 32%, UK 10%, Jap. 6%. **Exports** (1981): $230 mln.; partners: UK 17%, U.S. 28%, Neth. 5%. W. Ger. 7%. **National budget** (1983): $386.4 mln. **International reserves less gold** (Feb. 1984): $36.9 mln. **Gold:** 13,000 oz t. **Consumer prices** (change in 1983): 15%.

Transport: Railway traffic (1982): 95 mln. passenger-km; 187 mln. net ton-km. **Motor vehicles:** in use (1981): 14,100 passenger cars, 13,600 comm. vehicles. **Civil aviation** (1982) 96 mln. passenger-km; 1.5 freight ton-km.

Communications: Radios: 275,000 in use (1981). **Telephones in use** (1981): 15,130. **Daily newspaper circ.** (1982): 2 per 1,000 pop.

Health: Life expectancy at birth (1972): 40.9 male; 44.2 female. **Births** (per 1,000 pop. 1978): 53. **Deaths** (per 1,000 pop. 1978): 26. **Natural increase** (1978): 2.8%. **Hospital beds** (per 100,000 pop. 1977): 174. **Physicians** (per 100,000 pop. 1977): 2. **Infant mortality** (per 1,000 live births 1983): 14.

Education (1983): **Literacy:** 25%. About 45% attend school.

Embassy: 1400 20th St. NW 20036; 296-5530.

Bantus came in the 16th century, Arab slavers in the 19th. The area became the British protectorate Nyasaland, in 1891. It became independent July 6, 1964, and a republic in 1966. It has a pro-West foreign policy and cooperates economically with Zimbabwe and S. Africa.

Malaysia

People: Population (1983 est.): 14,995,000. **Age distrib.** (%): 0–14: 41.5; 15–59: 53.0; 60+: 5.4. **Pop. density:** 100.99 per sq. mi. **Urban** (1970): 20.6%. **Ethnic groups:** Malays 50%, Chinese 36%, Indians 10%, others. **Languages:** Malay (official),

English, Chinese, Indian languages. **Religions:** Moslem, Hindu, Buddhist, Confucian, Taoist, local religions.

Geography: Area: 127,316 sq. mi., slightly larger than New Mexico. **Location:** On the SE tip of Asia, plus the N. coast of the island of Borneo. **Neighbors:** Thailand on N, Indonesia on S. **Topography:** Most of W. Malaysia is covered by tropical jungle, including the central mountain range that runs N-S through the peninsula. The western coast is marshy, the eastern, sandy. E. Malaysia has a wide, swampy coastal plain, with interior jungles and mountains. **Capital:** Kuala Lumpur. **Cities** (1980 est.): Kuala Lumpur 1,081,000 (met.).

Government: Type: Federal parliamentary democracy with a constitutional monarch. **Head of state:** Paramount Ruler Mahmood Iskander; b. 1932; in office: Apr. 26, 1984. **Head of government:** Prime Min. Datuk Seri Mahathir bin Mohamad; b. Dec. 20, 1925; in office: July 16, 1981. **Local divisions:** 13 states and capital. **Defense:** 8.4% of GNP (1981).

Economy: Industries: Rubber goods, steel, electronics. **Chief crops:** Palm oil, copra, rice, pepper. **Minerals:** Tin (35% world output), iron. **Crude oil reserves** (1980): 2.80 bln. bbls. **Other resources:** Rubber (35% world output). **Per capita arable land:** 0.6 acres. **Meat prod.** (1980): beef: 17,000 metric tons; pork: 71,000 metric tons. **Fish catch** (1981): 796,000 metric tons. **Electricity prod.** (1981): 9.5 bln. kwh. **Crude steel prod.** (1981 est.): 210,000 metric tons. **Labor force:** 41% agric.; 24% ind. and comm.; 21% service & trade.

Finance: Currency: Ringgit (Mar. 1984: 2.29 = $1 US). **Gross national product** (1982): $28.9 bln. **Per capita income** (1975): $714. **Imports** (1982): $13.2 bln.; partners: Jap. 25%, U.S. 18%, Sing. 14%. **Exports** (1982): $12 bln.; partners: Jap. 20%, U.S. 12% Sing. 25%, Neth. 6%. **National budget** (1982): $14.2 bln. **International reserves less gold** (Jan. 1984): $4.36 bln. **Gold:** 2.33 mln. oz t. **Consumer prices** (change in 1983): 3.7%.

Transport: Railway traffic (incl. Singapore) (1981): 1.6 bln. passenger-km; 1.1 bln. net ton-km. **Motor vehicles:** in use (1979): 690,000 passenger cars, 154,000 comm. vehicles. **Civil aviation:** (1982): 5.4 bln. passenger-km; 148 mln. freight ton-km. **Chief ports:** George Town, Kelang, Melaka, Kuching.

Communications: Television sets: 1 mln. in use (1981). **Radios:** 2 mln. in use (1981). **Telephones in use** (1981): 597,000. **Daily newspaper circ.** (1982): 133 per 1,000 pop.

Health: Life expectancy at birth (1983): 64 years. **Births** (per 1,000 pop. 1978): 32. **Deaths** (per 1,000 pop. 1978): 8. **Natural increase** (1978): 2.5%. **Hospital beds** (per 100,000 pop. 1977): 308. **Physicians** (per 100,000 pop. 1977): 12. **Infant mortality** (per 1,000 live births 1983): 31.8.

Education (1983): **Literacy:** 75%; 94% attend primary school, 48% attend secondary.

Embassy: 2401 Massachusetts Ave. NW 20008; 328-2700.

European traders appeared in the 16th century; Britain established control in 1867. Malaysia was created Sept. 16, 1963. It included Malaya (which had become independent in 1957 after the suppression of Communist rebels), plus the formerly-British Singapore, Sabah (N Borneo), and Sarawak (NW Borneo). Singapore was separated in 1965, in order to end tensions between Chinese, the majority in Singapore, and Malays in control of the Malaysian government. Chinese have charged economical and political discrimination.

A monarch is elected by a council of hereditary rulers of the Malayan states every 5 years.

Abundant natural resources have assured prosperity, and foreign investment has aided industrialization.

Maldives
Republic of Maldives

People: Population (1983 est.): 168,000. **Age distrib.** (%): 0–14: 44.9; 15–59: 51.3; 60+: 3.8. **Pop. density:** 1,100 per sq. mi. **Urban** (1978): 20.7%. **Ethnic groups:** Sinhalese, Dravidian, Arab mixture. **Languages:** Divehi (Sinhalese dialect). **Religions:** Sunni Moslems.

Geography: Area: 115 sq. mi., twice the size of Washington, D.C. **Location:** In the Indian O. SW of India. **Neighbors:** Nearest is India on N. **Topography:** 19 atolls with 1,087 islands, about 200 inhabited. None of the islands are over 5 sq. mi. in area, and all are nearly flat. **Capital:** Male. **Cities** (1980 est.): Male 32,000.

Government: Type: Republic. **Head of state:** Pres. Maumoon Abdul Gayoom; b. Dec. 29, 1939; in office: Nov. 11, 1978. **Local divisions:** 19 atolls, each with an elected committee and a government-appointed chief.

Economy: Industries: Fish processing, tourism. **Chief crops:** Coconuts, fruit, millet. **Other resources:** Shells. **Fish catch** 1978): 25,800 metric tons. **Electricity prod.** (1977): 2.00 mln. kwh. **Labor force:** 80% fishing.

Finance: Currency: Rufiyaa (Sept. 1983: 7.05 = $1 US). **Gross domestic product** (1978 IMF est.): $22 mln. **Per capita income** (1978 IMF est.): $150. **Imports** (1979): $24 mln.; partners: Ind. 25%, Jap. 14%, Sri Lan 11°. **Exports** (1979): $5.8 mln.; partners: (1979) Jap. 44%, Sri Lan. 14%, Thai. **Tourists** (1981): 48,000.

Transport: Chief ports: Male Atoll.

Communications: Radios: 3,500 licensed (1976). **Telephones in use** (1978): 556.

Health: Births (per 1,000 pop. 1977): 40.5. **Deaths** (per 1,000 pop. 1977): 11.8. **Natural increase** (1977): 2.9%. **Pop. per hospital bed** (1977): 3,500. **Pop. per physician** (1977): 15,555. **Infant morality** (per 1,000 live births 1983): 119.

Education (1975): **Literacy:** 36%. **Pop. 5-19:** in school: 40%, per teacher: 80.

The islands had been a British protectorate since 1887. The country became independent July 26, 1965. Long a sultanate, the Maldives became a republic in 1968. Natural resources and tourism are being developed; however, it remains one of the world's poorest countries.

Mali
Republic of Mali

People: Population (1983 est.): 7,393,000. **Age distrib.** (%): 0–14: 47.9; 15–59: 49.1; 60+: 3.0. **Pop. density:** 14.86 per sq. mi. **Urban** (1983): 16.6%. **Ethnic groups:** Mande (Bambara, Malinke, Sarakolle) 50%, Peul 17%, Voltaic 12%, Songhai, Tuareg, Moors. **Languages:** French (official), Bambara. **Religions:** Moslem 90%.

Geography: Area: 478,841 sq. mi., larger than Texas and California combined. **Location:** In the interior of W. Africa. **Neighbors:** Mauritania, Senegal on W, Guinea, Ivory Coast, Upper Volta on S, Niger on E, Algeria on N. **Topography:** A landlocked grassy plain in the upper basins of the Senegal and Niger rivers, extending N into the Sahara. **Capital:** Bamako. **Cities** (1984 est.): Bamako (met.) 620,000.

Government: Type: Republic. **Head of state and head of govt.:** Pres. Moussa Traore; b. Sept. 25, 1936; in office: Dec. 6, 1968 (state); Sept. 19, 1969 (govt.). **Local divisions:** 7 regions and a capital district. **Defense:** 2.9% of GDP (1980).

Economy: Chief crops: Millet, rice, peanuts, cotton. **Other resources:** Bauxite, iron, gold. **Arable land:** 2%. **Meat prod.** (1983): lamb: 49,000 metric tons. **Fish catch** (1981): 100,000 metric tons. **Electricity prod.** (1977): 98 mln. kwh. **Labor force:** 73% agric.; 12% ind. & comm.; 16% services.

Finance: Currency: Franc (Mar. 1984: 798.00 = $1 US). **Gross domestic product** (1981): $1.1 bln. **Per capita income** (1981): $140. **Imports** (1980): $417 mln.; partners: Fr. 38% Ivory Coast 19%, Sen. 19%. **Exports** (1980): $176 mln.; partners: Fr. 29%, Ivory Coast 14%, China 12%. **Tourists** (1977): 19,500; receipts: $8 mln. **International reserves less gold** (Feb. 1984): $19 mln. **Gold:** 19,000 oz t.

Transport: Railway traffic (1977): 129 mln. passenger-km; 148 mln. net ton-km. **Motor vehicles:** in use (1979): 20,000 passenger cars, 5,000 comm. vehicles. **Civil aviation:** 97 mln. passenger-km (1977); 612,000 freight ton-km (1977).

Communications: Radios: 82,000 in use (1976).

Health: Life expectancy at birth (1975): 39.4 male; 42.5 female. **Births** (per 1,000 pop. 1978): 52. **Deaths** (per 1,000 pop. 1978): 24. **Natural increase** (1978): 2.9%. **Hospital beds** (1980): 3,200. **Physicians** (1980): 337. **Infant mortality** (per 1,000 live births 1984): 152.

Education (1984): **Literacy:** 10%. **Attendance:** 28% under 15 attend school.

Embassy: 2130 R St. NW 20008; 332-2250.

Until the 15th century the area was part of the great Mali Empire. Timbuktu was a center of Islamic study. French rule was secured, 1898. The Sudanese Rep. and Senegal became independent as the Mali Federation June 20, 1960, but Senegal withdrew, and the Sudanese Rep. was renamed Mali.

Mali signed economic agreements with France and, in 1963, with Senegal. In 1968, a coup ended the socialist regime. Famine struck in 1973-74, killing as many as 100,000 people. Drought conditions returned 1977-78. There has been continued unrest in the 1980s.

Malta

People: Population (1983 est.): 358,000. **Age distrib. (%):** 0–14: 24.6; 15–59: 63.2; 60+: 12.2. **Pop. density:** 2,555 per sq. mi. **Ethnic groups:** Italian, Arab, French. **Languages:** Maltese, English both official. **Religions:** Mainly Roman Catholics.

Geography: Area: 122 sq. mi., twice the size of Washington, D.C. **Location:** In center of Mediterranean Sea. **Neighbors:** Nearest is Italy on N. **Topography:** Island of Malta is 95 sq. mi.; other islands in the group: Gozo, 26 sq. mi., Comino, 1 sq. mi. The coastline is heavily indented. Low hills cover the interior. **Capital:** Valletta. **Cities** (1982 est.): Valletta 14,000; Sliema 20,000.

Government: Type: Republic. **Head of state:** Pres. Agatha Barbara; in office: Feb. 16, 1982. **Head of government:** Prime Min. Dominic Mintoff; b. Aug. 6, 1916; in office: June 17, 1971. **Armed forces:** regulars 1,000; para-military 1,400.

Economy: Industries: Textiles, tourism. **Chief crops:** Potatoes, onions, beans. **Per capita arable land:** 0.1 acres. **Electricity prod.** (1978): 456.00 mln. kwh. **Labor force:** 27.8% manuf.; 31.4% market services; 21.5% gov.

Finance: Currency: Pound (Mar. 1984: 0.42 = $1 US). **Gross domestic product** (1979): $979 mln. **Per capita income** (1978): $2,036. **Imports** (1979): $759 mln.; partners: UK 18%, It. 27%, W. Ger. 14%, U.S. 7%. **Exports** (1979): $425 mln.; partners: W. Ger. 31%, UK 20%, Libya 8%. **Tourists** (1981): 706,000; receipts: $265 mln. **National budget** (1981): $561 mln. revenues; $562 mln. expenditures. **International reserves less gold** (Mar. 1984): 1.1 bln. **Gold:** 471,000 oz t. **Consumer prices** (change in 1983): −0.9%.

Transport: Motor vehicles: in use (1982): 69,973 passenger cars, 17,288 comm. vehicles. **Civil aviation** (1982): 644 mln. passenger-km; 3.8 mln. freight ton-km. **Chief ports:** Valletta.

Communications: Television sets: 76,000 licensed (1981). **Radios:** 137,000 in use (1981). **Telephones in use** (1982): 90,997.

Health: Life expectancy at birth (1976): 68.27 male; 73.10 female. **Births** (per 1,000 pop. 1980: 15.4. **Deaths** (per 1,000 pop. 1980): 9.1. **Natural increase** (1978): .7%. **Hospital beds** (per 100,000 pop. 1977): 1,040. **Physicians** (per 100,000 pop. 1977): 127. **Infant mortality** (per 1,000 live births 1980): 15.

Education (1981): **Literacy:** 83%. **Compulsory:** until age 16. **Embassy:** 2017 Connecticut Ave. NW 20008; 462-3611.

Malta was ruled by Phoenicians, Romans, Arabs, Normans, the Knights of Malta, France, and Britain (since 1814). It became independent Sept. 21, 1964. Malta became a republic in 1974. The withdrawal of the last of its sailors, Apr. 1, 1979, ended 179 years of British military presence on the island. Malta is democratic but nonaligned.

Mauritania

Islamic Republic of Mauritania

People: Population (1983 est.): 1,591,000. **Age distrib. (%):** 0–14: 42.2; 15–59: 49.8; 60+: 13.4. **Pop. density:** 3.89 per sq. mi. **Urban** (1977): 22.8%. **Ethnic groups:** Arab-Berber 80%, Negroes 20%. **Languages:** French (official), Hassanya Arabic (national), Niger-Congo languages. **Religions:** Predominately Moslems.

Geography: Area: 398,000 sq. mi., the size of Texas and California combined. **Location:** In W. Africa. **Neighbors:** Morocco on N, Algeria, Mali on E, Senegal on S. **Topography:** The fertile Senegal R. valley in the S gives way to a wide central region of sandy plains and scrub trees. The N is arid and extends into the Sahara. **Capital:** Nouakchott. **Cities** (1981 est.): Nouakchott 250,000; Nouadhibou 22,000; Kaedi 21,000.

Government: Type: Military Republic. **Head of state:** Pres. Mohamed Khouna Ould Haidalla, b. 1940: in office: May 31,

1979. **Head of Government:** Premier Maaouya Ould Sidi Ahmed Taya; in office: Apr. 25, 1981. **Local divisions:** 8 regions, one district. **Defense:** 16% of GDP (1979).

Economy: Chief crops: Dates, grain. **Minerals:** Iron, ore, gypsum. **Per capita arable land:** 0.3 acres. **Meat prod.** (1980): beef: 17,000 metric tons; lamb: 12,000 metric tons. **Fish catch** (1978): 34,200 metric tons. **Electricity prod.** (1978): 96.00 mln. kwh. **Labor force:** 47% agric., 14% ind. & comm., 29% services.

Finance: Currency: Ouguiya (Mar. 1984: 57.98 = $1 US). **Gross domestic product** (1979): $618 mln. **Per capita income** (1980): $462. **Imports** (1979): $259 mln.; partners: Fr. 29%, Sp. 9%. **Exports** (1980): $194 mln.; partners: Fr. 21%, It. 26%, Jap. 20%. **International reserves less gold** (Feb. 1984): $105.2 mln. **Gold:** 11,000 oz t. **Consumer prices** (change in 1983): 1%.

Transport: Railway traffic (1974): 7.81 bln. net ton-km. **Motor vehicles:** in use (1972): 4,400 passenger cars, 5,000 comm. vehicles. **Chief ports:** Nouakchott, Nouadhibou.

Communications: Radios: 300,000 in use (1979).

Health: Life expectancy at birth (1980): 42 years. **Births** (per 1,000 pop. 1980): 50.2. **Deaths** (per 1,000 pop. 1980): 22.3. **Natural increase** (1978): 1.9%. **Hospital beds** (per 100,000 pop. 1977): 38. **Physicians** (per 100,000 pop. 1977): 7. **Infant mortality** (per 1,000 live births 1981): 169.

Education (1981): **Literacy:** 17%. **Attendance:** 24% in primary school, 4% in secondary school.

Embassy: 2129 Leroy Pl. NW 20008; 232-5700.

Mauritania became independent Nov. 28, 1960. It annexed the south of former Spanish Sahara in 1976. Saharan guerrillas stepped up attacks in 1977; 8,000 Moroccan troops and French bomber raids aided the government. Mauritania signed a peace treaty with the Polsario Front, 1980, resumed diplomatic relations with Algeria while breaking a defense treaty with Morocco, and renounced sovereignty over its share of former Spanish Sahara. Morocco annexed the territory.

Famine struck in the 1970s and again in 1982 and 1983.

Mauritius

People: Population (1983 est.): 1,002,000. **Age distrib. (%):** 0–14: 36.3; 15–59: 57.2; 60+: 6.4. **Pop. density:** 1,219.82 per sq. mi. **Urban** (1976): 43.6%. **Ethnic groups:** Indo-Mauritians 68%, Creoles 27%, others. **Languages:** English (official), French, Creole. **Religions:** Hindu 51%, Christian 30%, Moslem 16%.

Geography: Area: 787 sq. mi., smaller than Rhode Island. **Location:** In the Indian O., 500 mi. E of Madagascar. **Neighbors:** Nearest is Madagascar on W. **Topography:** A volcanic island nearly surrounded by coral reefs. A central plateau is encircled by mountain peaks. **Capital:** Port Louis. **Cities** (1982 est.): Port Louis 146,884.

Government: Type: Parliamentary democracy under a constitutional monarch. **Head of state:** Queen Elizabeth II, represented by Gov.-Gen. Dayendranath Burrenchobay; b. Mar. 24, 1919; in office: Mar. 23, 1978. **Head of government:** Prime Min. Aneerood Jugnauth; in office: June 12, 1982. **Local divisions:** 9 administrative divisions.

Economy: Industries: Tourism. **Chief crops:** Sugar cane, tea. **Arable land:** 55%. **Electricity prod.** (1978): 336.00 mln. kwh. **Labor force:** 29% agric. & fishing; 23% ind. and commerce; 28% govt. services.

Finance: Currency: Rupee (Mar. 1984: 12.59 = $1 US). **Gross national product** (1981): $938 mln. **Per capita income** (1981): $1,052. **Imports** (1982): $463 mln.; partners: UK 9%, Fr. 10%, So. Afr. 9%. **Exports** (1982): $365 mln.; partners: UK 53%, Fr. 22%, U.S. 8%. **Tourists** (1981): 122,000; receipts: $47 mln. **National budget** (1981): $450 mln. **International reserves less gold** (Feb. 1984): $28.7 mln. **Gold:** 38,000 oz t. **Consumer prices** (change in 1983): 6.0%.

Transport: Motor vehicles: in use (1981): 25,006 passenger cars, 12,585 comm. vehicles. **Chief ports:** Port Louis.

Communications: Television sets: 84,184 in use (1982). **Radios:** 114,580 in use (1982). **Telephones in use** (1982): 37,812. **Daily newspaper circ.** (1982): 69 per 1,000 pop.

Health: Life expectancy at birth (1982): 69 years. **Births** (per 1,000 pop. 1982): 22.8. **Deaths** (per 1,000 pop. 1982): 6.7. **Natural increase** (1978): 2.0%. **Hospital beds** (1981): 2,776.

Physicians (1981): 562. **Infant mortality** (per 1,000 live births 1982): 33.
Education (1982): **Literacy:** 61%. **Attendance:** primary school 78%.
Embassy: 4301 Connecticut Ave. NW 20008; 244-1491.

Mauritius was uninhabited when settled in 1638 by the Dutch, who introduced sugar cane. France took over in 1721, bringing African slaves. Britain ruled from 1810 to Mar. 12, 1968, bringing Indian workers for the sugar plantations.

The economy suffered in the 1980s because of low world sugar prices.

Mexico
United Mexican States

People: Population (1983 est.): 75,702,000. **Age distrib.** (%): 0–14: 42.9; 15–59: 52.3; 60+: 5.9. **Pop. density:** 94.49 per sq. mi. **Urban** (1978): 65.2%. **Ethnic groups:** Mestizo 55%, American Indian 29%, Caucasian 10%. **Languages:** Spanish. **Religions:** Roman Catholics 97%.

Geography: Area: 761,604 sq. mi., three times the size of Texas. **Location:** In southern N. America. **Neighbors:** U.S. on N, Guatemala, Belize on S. **Topography:** The Sierra Madre Occidental Mts. run NW-SE near the west coast; the Sierra Madre Oriental Mts., run near the Gulf of Mexico. They join S of Mexico City. Between the 2 ranges lies the dry central plateau, 5,000 to 8,000 ft. alt., rising toward the S, with temperate vegetation. Coastal lowlands are tropical. About 45% of land is arid. **Capital:** Mexico City. **Cities** (1980 est.): Mexico City (metro) 15 mln.; Guadalajara (metro) 2.4 mln.; Monterrey (metro) 2 mln.

Government: Type: Federal republic. **Head of state:** Pres. Miguel de la Madrid Hurtado; b. Dec. 12, 1934; in office: Dec. 1, 1982. **Local divisions:** Federal district and 31 states. **Armed forces:** regulars 107,000 (1980).

Economy: Industries: Steel, chemicals, electric goods, textiles, rubber, petroleum handicrafts, tourism. **Chief crops:** Cotton, coffee, sugar cane, vegetables, corn. **Minerals:** Silver, lead, zinc, gold, oil, natural gas. **Crude oil reserves** (1982): 72 bln. bbls. **Arable land:** 11.7%. **Meat prod.** (1983): beef: 609,000 metric tons; pork: 495,000 metric tons; lamb: 37,000 metric tons. **Fish catch** (1981): 1.5 mln. metric tons. **Electricity prod.** (1981): 73.0 bln. kwh. **Crude steel prod.** (1982): 6.9 mln. metric tons. **Labor force:** 41% agric.; 18% manuf.

Finance: Currency: Peso (Mar. 1984: 155.63 = $1 US). **Gross domestic product** (1982): $162 bln. **Per capita income** (1980): $1,800. **Imports** (1982): $14.5 bln.; partners: U.S. 64%, Jap. 5%, W. Ger. 5%. **Exports** (1982): $21.5 bln.; partners: U.S. 55% Spa. 10%. **Tourists** (1981): 4.0 mln.; receipts: $1.7 bln. **National budget** (1983): $93.3 bln. revenues: $93.3 bln. expenditures. **International reserves less gold** (Jan. 1984): $3.9 bln. **Gold:** 2.3 mln. oz t. **Consumer prices** (change in 1983): 101.9%.

Transport: Railway traffic (1981): 5.3 bln. passenger-km; 42.8 bln. net ton-km. **Motor vehicles:** in use (1982): 5.2 mln. passenger cars, 1.8 mln. comm. vehicles; manuf. (1981): 357,000 passenger cars, 171,000 comm. vehicles. **Civil aviation** (1982): 13.4 bln. passenger-km; 118 mln. freight ton-km. **Chief ports:** Veracruz, Tampico, Mazatlan, Coatzacoalcos.

Communications: Television sets: 7.5 mln. in use (1981), 964,000 manuf. (1981). **Radios:** 20 mln. in use (1981), 1.2 mln. manuf. (1980). **Telephones in use** (1981): 4.9 mln. **Daily newspaper circ.** (1982): 130 per 1,000 pop.

Health: Life expectancy at birth (1980): 62.0 male; 67.0 female. **Births** (per 1,000 pop. 1981): 33.6. **Deaths** (per 1,000 pop. 1981): 5.3. **Natural increase** (1975): 3.3%. **Hospital beds** (per 100,000 pop. 1977): 115. **Physicians** (per 100,000 pop. 1977): 57. **Infant mortality** (per 1,000 live births 1981): 38.5.
Education (1983): **Literacy:** 74%. **Years compulsory:** 10.
Embassy: 2829 16th St. NW 20009; 234-6000.

Mexico was the site of advanced Indian civilizations. The Mayas, an agricultural people, moved up from Yucatan, built immense stone pyramids, invented a calendar. The Toltecs were overcome by the Aztecs, who founded Tenochtitlan 1325 AD, now Mexico City. Hernando Cortes, Spanish conquistador, destroyed the Aztec empire, 1519-1521.

After 3 centuries of Spanish rule the people rose, under Fr. Miguel Hidalgo y Costilla, 1810, Fr. Morelos y Payon, 1812, and Gen. Agustin Iturbide, who made independence effective Sept. 27, 1821, but made himself emperor as Agustin I. A republic was declared in 1823.

Mexican territory extended into the present American Southwest and California until Texas revolted and established a republic in 1836; the Mexican legislature refused recognition but was unable to enforce its authority there. After numerous clashes, the U.S.-Mexican War, 1846-48, resulted in the loss by Mexico of the lands north of the Rio Grande.

French arms supported an Austrian archduke on the throne of Mexico as Maximilian I, 1864-67, but pressure from the U.S. forced France to withdraw. A dictatorial rule by Porfirio Diaz, president 1877-80, 1884-1911, led to fighting by rival forces until the new constitution of Feb. 5, 1917 provided social reform. Since then Mexico has developed large-scale programs of social security, labor protection, and school improvement. A constitutional provision requires management to share profits with labor.

The Institutional Revolutionary Party has been dominant in politics since 1929. Radical opposition, including some guerrilla activity, has been contained by strong measures.

The presidency of Luis Echeverria, 1970-76, was marked by a more leftist foreign policy and domestic rhetoric. Some land redistribution begun in 1976 was reversed under the succeeding administration.

Some gains in agriculture, industry, and social services have been achieved. The land is rich, but the rugged topography and lack of sufficient rainfall are major obstacles. Crops and farm prices are controlled, as are export and import. Economic prospects brightened with the discovery of vast oil reserves, perhaps the world's greatest. But half the work force is jobless or underemployed.

Inflation and the drop in world oil prices caused an economic crisis in 1982. The peso was devalued by 40% and private banks were nationalized to restore financial stability.

President de la Madrid visited Washington, May 1984, urging the U.S. to avoid the use of force to solve differences in Central America. Mexico has friendly relations with Cuba and Nicaragua.

Monaco
Principality of Monaco

People: Population (1983 est.): 28,000. **Age distrib.** (%): 0–14: 12.7; 15–59: 56.3 60+: 30.7. **Ethnic groups:** French 58%, Italian 17%, Monegasque 15%. **Languages:** French (official). **Religions:** Predominately Roman Catholic.

Geography: Area: 0.73 sq. mi. **Location:** On the NW Mediterranean coast. **Neighbors:** France to W, N, E. **Topography:** Monaco-Ville sits atop a high promontory, the rest of the principality rises from the port up the hillside. **Capital:** Monaco-Ville (1979 est.): 1,700.

Government: Type: Constitutional monarchy. **Head of state:** Prince Rainier III; b. May 31, 1923; in office: May 9, 1949. **Head of government:** Min. of State Jean Herly; in office: July, 1981.

Economy: Industries: Tourism, gambling, chemicals, precision instruments, plastics.

Finance: Currency: French franc or Monégasque franc. **Tourists** (1981): 209,000.

Transport: Chief ports: La Condamine.

Communications: Television sets: 16,000 in use (1976). **Radios:** 7,500 in use (1976). **Telephones in use** (1978): 32,000. **Daily newspaper circ.** (1977): 11,000; 420 per 1,000 pop.

Health: Births (per 1,000 pop. 1980): 20.6. **Deaths** (per 1,000 pop. 1980): 21.1. **Natural increase** (1977): —.3%. **Infant mortality** (per 1,000 live births 1970): 9.3.
Education: (1983): **Literacy:** 99%. **Years compulsory:** 10; attendance 99%.

An independent principality for over 300 years, Monaco has belonged to the House of Grimaldi since 1297 except during the French Revolution. It was placed under the protectorate of Sardinia in 1815, and under that of France, 1861. The Prince of Monaco was an absolute ruler until a 1911 constitution.

Monaco's fame as a tourist resort is widespread. It is noted for its mild climate and magnificent scenery. The area has been extended by land reclamation.

Mongolia
Mongolian People's Republic

People: Population (1983 est.): 1,809,000. **Pop. density:** 2.76 per sq. mi. **Urban** (1982): 45%. **Ethnic groups:** Khalkha Mongols 75%, other Mongols 8%, Kazakhs 5%. **Languages:** Khalkha Mongolian (official, written in Cyrillic letters since 1941), Russian, Chinese. **Religions:** Lama Buddhism prevailed, has been curbed.

Geography: Area: 604,247 sq. mi., more than twice the size of Texas. **Location:** In E Central Asia. **Neighbors:** USSR on N, China on S. **Topography:** Mostly a high plateau with mountains, salt lakes, and vast grasslands. Arid lands in the S are part of the Gobi Desert. **Capital:** Ulaanbaatar. **Cities** (1983 est.): Ulaanbaatar 435,400, Darhan 56,000.

Government: Type: Communist state. **Head of state:** Chmn. Yumzhagiyen Tsedenbal; b. Sept. 17, 1916; in office: June 11, 1974. **Head of government:** Premier Zhambyn Batmunkh; b. Mar. 10, 1926; in office: June 11, 1974. **Local divisions:** 18 provinces, 3 autonomous municipalities. **Defense:** 12% of GNP.

Economy: Industries: Food processing, textiles, chemicals, cement. **Chief crops:** Grain. **Minerals:** Coal, tungsten, copper, molybdenum, gold, tin. **Arable land:** 1%. **Meat prod.** (1983): beef: 70,000 metric tons; lamb: 129,000 metric tons. **Electricity prod.** (1982): 1.6 bln. kwh. **Labor force:** 52% agric.; 10% manuf.

Finance: Currency: Tugrik (Sept. 1983: 3.36 = $1 US). **Gross domestic product** (1976 est.): $1.20 bln. **Per capita income** (1976 est.): $750. **Imports** (1982): $1.4 bln.; partners: USSR 91%. **Exports** (1982): $550 mln.; partners: USSR 80%.

Transport: Railway traffic (1982): 297 mln. passenger-km; 3.4 bln. net ton-km.

Communications: Television sets: 52,900 in use (1980). **Radios:** 164,300 in use (1980). **Telephones in use** (1981): 39,800. **Daily newspaper circ.** (1982): 103 per 1,000 pop.

Health: Life expectancy at birth (1979): 63 years. **Births** (per 1,000 pop. 1978): 38. **Deaths** (per 1,000 pop. 1978): 9. **Natural increase** (1978): 2.6%. **Hospital beds** (per 10,000 pop. 1982): 107. **Physicians** (per 10,000 pop. 1982): 22. **Education** (1983): **Literacy:** 80%. **Years compulsory:** 7 in major population centers.

One of the world's oldest countries, Mongolia reached the zenith of its power in the 13th century when Genghis Khan and his successors conquered all of China and extended their influence as far W as Hungary and Poland. In later centuries, the empire dissolved and Mongolia came under the suzerainty of China.

With the advent of the 1911 Chinese revolution, Mongolia, with Russian backing, declared its independence. A Mongolian Communist regime was established July 11, 1921.

Mongolia has been changed from a nomadic culture to one of settled agriculture and growing industries with aid from the USSR and East European nations.

Mongolia has sided with the Russians in the Sino-Soviet dispute. A Mongolian-Soviet mutual assistance pact was signed Jan. 15, 1966, and thousands of Soviet troops are based in the country.

Morocco
Kingdom of Morocco

People: Population (1983 est.): 22,889,000. **Age distrib.** (%): 0–14: 46.4; 15–59: 49.2; 60+: 4.2. **Pop. density:** 109.97 per sq. mi. **Urban** (1981): 42%. **Ethnic groups:** Arab-Berber 99%. **Languages:** Arabic (official), with Berber, French, Spanish minorities. **Religions:** Sunni Moslems 99%.

Geography: Area: 171,117 sq. mi., larger than California. **Location:** on NW coast of Africa. **Neighbors:** W. Sahara on S, Algeria on E. **Topography:** Consists of 5 natural regions: mountain ranges (Riff in the N, Middle Atlas, Upper Atlas, and Anti-Atlas); rich plains in the W; alluvial plains in SW; well-cultivated plateaus in the center; a pre-Sahara arid zone extend-

ing from SE. **Capital:** Rabat. **Cities** (1978 est.): Casablanca 1,371,330; Rabat-Sale 435,510; Marrakech 330,400, Tangier.

Government: Type: Constitutional Monarchy. **Head of state:** King Hassan II; b. July 9, 1929; in office: Mar. 3, 1961. **Head of government:** Prime Min. Mohammad Karim Lamrani; in office: Nov. 30, 1983. **Local divisions:** 6 prefectures, 35 provinces. **Defense:** 40% of govt. budget (1981).

Economy: Industries: Carpets, clothing, leather goods, tourism. **Chief crops:** Grain, fruits, dates, grapes. **Minerals:** Antimony, cobalt, manganese, phosphates, lead, oil, coal. **Crude oil reserves** (1980): 100 mln. bbls. **Arable land:** 2%. **Meat prod.** (1980): beef: 77,000 metric tons; lamb: 58,000 metric tons. **Fish catch** (1981): 382,000 metric tons. **Electricity prod.** (1982): 5.4 bln. kwh. **Labor force:** 50% agric., 26% services.

Finance: Currency: Dirham (Mar. 1984: 8.26 = $1 US). **Gross domestic product** (1981): $16 bln. **Per capita income** (1981): $800. **Imports** (1982): $4.3 bln.; partners: Fr. 25%, Sp. 7%, Saudi Ar. 15%. **Exports** (1982): $2.06 bln.; partners: Fr. 22%, W. Ger. 7%, Sp. 7%, It. 5%. **Tourists** (1981): 1.5 mln.; receipts $440 mln. **National budget** (1981): $6 bln. revenues; $6.6 bln. expenditures. **International reserves less gold** (Jan. 1984): $41 mln. **Gold:** 704,000 oz t. **Consumer prices** (change in 1982): 10.5%.

Transport: Railway traffic (1980): 920 mln. passenger-km; 3.8 bln. net ton-km. **Motor vehicles:** in use (1982): 480,300 passenger cars, 200,000 comm. vehicles. **Civil aviation** (1982): 1.8 bln. passenger-km; 38.9 mln. freight ton-km. **Chief ports:** Tangier, Casablanca, Kenitra.

Communications: Television sets: 750,000 licensed (1981). **Radios:** 3 mln. licensed (1981). **Telephones in use** (1981): 231,000. **Daily newspaper circ.** (1982): 12 per 1,000 pop.

Health: Life expectancy at birth (1975): 51.4 male; 54.5 female. **Births** (per 1,000 pop. 1978): 43. **Deaths** (per 1,000 pop. 1978): 14. **Natural increase** (1978): 2.9%. **Hospital beds** (1981): 24,453. **Physicians** (1981): 1,153. **Infant mortality** (per 1,000 live births 1975): 149.

Education (1978): **Literacy:** 24%. **Pop. 5-19:** in school: 34%, teachers per 1,000: 9.

Embassy: 1601 21st St. NW 20009; 462-7979.

Berbers were the original inhabitants, followed by Carthaginians and Romans. Arabs conquered in 683. In the 11th and 12th centuries, a Berber empire ruled all NW Africa and most of Spain from Morocco.

Part of Morocco came under Spanish rule in the 19th century; France controlled the rest in the early 20th. Tribal uprisings lasted from 1911 to 1933. The country became independent Mar. 2, 1956. Tangier, an internationalized seaport, was turned over to Morocco, 1956. Ifni, a Spanish enclave, was ceded in 1969.

Morocco annexed over 70,000 sq. mi. of phosphate-rich land Apr. 14, 1976, two-thirds of former Spanish Sahara, with the remainder annexed by Mauritania. Spain had withdrawn in February. Polisario, a guerrilla movement, proclaimed the region independent Feb. 27, and launched attacks with Algerian support. Morocco accepted U.S. military and economic aid. When Mauritania signed a treaty with the Polisario Front, and gave up its portion of the former Spanish Sahara, Morocco occupied the area, 1980. Morocco accused Algeria of instigating Polisario attacks.

After years of bitter fighting, Morocco controls the main urban areas, but the Polisario Front's guerrillas move freely in the vast, sparsely populated deserts.

Mozambique
People's Republic of Mozambique

People: Population (1983 est.): 13,047,000. **Age distrib.** (%): 0–14: 45.3; 15–59: 50.6; 60+: 4.1. **Pop. density:** 33.1 per sq. mi. **Ethnic groups:** Bantu tribes. **Languages:** Portuguese (official), Bantu languages predominate. **Religions:** Traditional beliefs 60%, Christians 30%, Moslems 10%.

Geography: Area: 303,769 sq. mi., larger than California. **Location:** On SE coast of Africa. **Neighbors:** Tanzania on N, Malawi, Zambia, Zimbabwe on W, South Africa, Swaziland on S. **Topography:** Coastal lowlands comprise nearly half the country with plateaus rising in steps to the mountains along the western border. **Capital:** Maputo. **Cities:** (1982 est.): Maputo 785,000.

Government: Type: Marxist one-party state. **Head of state:** Pres. Samora Machel; b. Sept. 29, 1933; in office: June 25, 1975. **Local divisions:** 10 provinces. **Defense:** 29% of govt. budget (1982).

Economy: Industries: Cement, alcohol, textiles. **Chief crops:** Cashews, cotton, sugar, copra, tea. **Minerals:** Coal, bauxite. **Arable land:** 30%. **Meat prod.** (1980): beef: 36,000 metric tons; pork: 8,000 metric tons. **Fish catch** (1978): 23,000 metric tons. **Electricity prod.** (1981): 14 bln. kwh. **Labor force:** 85% agric., 9% ind. & comm., 2% services.

Finance: Currency: Metical (Sept. 1983: 40.93 = $1 US). **Gross domestic product** (1981): $2.7 bln. **Per capita income** (1980): $220. **Imports** (1981): $737 mln.; partners: So. Afr. 20%, W. Ger. 15%, Port. 10%. **Exports** (1981): $385 mln.; partners: U.S. 27%, Port. 16%, UK 7%, So. Afr. 7%. **National budget** (1982): $611 mln. **Consumer prices** (change in 1976): 4.5%.

Transport: Railway traffic (1980): 556 mln. passenger-km; 970 mln. net ton-km. **Motor vehicles:** in use (1980): 99,400 passenger cars, 24,700 comm. vehicles. **Chief ports:** Maputo, Beira, Nacala.

Communications: Television sets: 1,500 in use (1981). **Radios:** 255,000 licensed (1981). **Telephones in use** (1980): 51,600. **Daily newspaper circ.** (1982): 6 per 1,000 pop.

Health: Life expectancy at birth (1982): 47 years. **Births** (per 1,000 pop. 1978): 44. **Deaths** (per 1,000 pop. 1978): 19. **Natural increase** (1978): 3.1%. **Hospital beds** (per 100,000 pop. 1977): 129. **Physicians** (per 100,000 pop. 1977): 6. **Infant mortality** (per 1,000 live births 1982): 115.

Education (1982): **Literacy:** 14%.

The first Portuguese post on the Mozambique coast was established in 1505, on the trade route to the East. Mozambique became independent June 25, 1975, after a ten-year war against Portuguese colonial domination. The 1974 revolution in Portugal paved the way for the orderly transfer of power to Frelimo (Front for the Liberation of Mozambique). Frelimo took over local administration Sept. 20, 1974, over the opposition, in part violent, of some blacks and whites. The new government, led by Maoist Pres. Samora Machel, promised a gradual transition to a communist system. Private schools were closed, rural collective farms organized, and private homes nationalized. Economic problems included the emigration of most of the country's 160,000 whites, a politically untenable economic dependence on white-ruled South Africa, and a large external debt.

In 1983, severe drought caused Mozambique to appeal to the international community for aid.

Nauru
Republic of Nauru

People: Population (1983): 8,000. **Pop density:** 906.75 per sq. mi. **Ethnic groups:** Nauruans 57%, Pacific Islanders 26%, Chinese 8%, European 8%. **Languages:** Nauruan (official), English. **Religions:** Predominately Christian.

Geography: Area: 8 sq. mi. **Location:** In Western Pacific O. just S of Equator. **Neighbors:** Nearest are Solomon Is. **Topography:** Mostly a plateau bearing high grade phosphate deposits, surrounded by a coral cliff and a sandy shore in concentric rings. **Capital:** Yaren.

Government: Type: Republic. **Head of state:** Pres. Hammer DeRoburt, b. Sept. 25, 1922; in office: May 11, 1978. **Local divisions:** 14 districts.

Economy: Phosphate mining. **Electricity prod.** (1981): 26.00 mln. kwh.

Finance: Currency: Australian dollar. **Gross domestic product** (1981 est.): $155 mln. **Per capita income** (1981): $21,400. **Imports** (1979): $11 mln. **Exports** (1979): $75 mln. **National budget** (1979): $46 mln. revenues; $38 mln. expenditures.

Communications: Radios: 3,600 in use (1976). **Telephones in use** (1978): 1,500.

Health: Births (per 1,000 pop. 1976): 19.8. **Deaths** (per 1,000 pop. 1976): 4.5. **Natural increase** (1976): 1.5%. **Infant mortality** (per 1,000 live births 1976): 19.0.

Education: Literacy 99%; Compulsory ages 6-16.

The island was discovered in 1798 by the British but was formally annexed to the German Empire in 1886. After World War I, Nauru became a League of Nations mandate administered by Australia. During World War II the Japanese occupied the island

and shipped 1,200 Nauruans to the fortress island of Truk as slave laborers.

In 1947 Nauru was made a UN trust territory, administered by Australia. Nauru became an independent republic Jan. 31, 1968.

Phosphate exports provide one of the world's highest per capita revenues for the Nauru people. The deposits are expected to be nearly exhausted by 1990.

Nepal
Kingdom of Nepal

People: Population (1983 est.): 16,169,000. **Age distrib.** (%): 0–14: 40.5; 15–59: 53.9; 60+: 5.6. **Pop. density:** 270 per sq. mi. **Urban** (1971): 4.0%. **Ethnic groups:** The many tribes are descendants of Indian, Tibetan, and Central Asian migrants. **Languages:** Nepali (official) (an Indic language), 12 others. **Religions:** Hindus 90%, Buddhists 7%.

Geography: Area: 56,136 sq. mi., the size of North Carolina. **Location:** Astride the Himalaya Mts. **Neighbors:** China on N, India on S. **Topography:** The Himalayas stretch across the N, the hill country with its fertile valleys extends across the center, while the southern border region is part of the flat, subtropical Ganges Plain. **Capital:** Kathmandu. **Cities** (1982 est.): Kathmandu 125,000, Pokhara, Biratnagar, Birganj.

Government: Type: Constitutional monarchy. **Head of state:** King Birendra Bir Bikram Shah Dev; b. Dec. 28, 1945; in office: Jan. 31, 1972. **Head of government:** Prime Min. Lokendra Bahadur Chand; in office: July 12, 1983. **Local divisions:** 14 zones; 75 districts. **Defense:** 4% of govt. budget (1982).

Economy: Industries: Hides, drugs, tourism. **Chief crops:** Jute, rice, grain. **Minerals:** Quartz. **Other resources:** Forests. **Arable land:** 13%. **Meat prod.** (1980): beef: 23,000 metric tons; pork: 5,000 metric tons; lamb: 18,000 metric tons. **Electricity prod.** (1977): 180 mln. kwh. **Labor force:** 93% agric.

Finance: Currency: Rupee (Mar. 1984: 15.75 = $1 US). **Gross domestic product** (1980): $1.99 bln. **Per capita income** (1982): $140. **Imports** (1981): $369 mln.; partners: India 20%, Jap. 15%. **Exports** (1981): $134 mln.; partners: India 14%, W. Ger. 12%. **Tourists** (1981): 162,000; receipts: $52 mln. **National budget** (1982): $539 mln. **International reserves less gold** (Mar. 1984): $131.5 mln. **Gold:** 151,000 oz t. **Consumer prices** (change in 1982): 10.9%.

Communications: Radios: 150,000 in use (1976). **Telephones in use** (1978): 9,425. **Daily newspaper circ.** (1982): 8 per 1,000 pop.

Health: Life expectancy at birth (1975): 42.2 male; 45.0 female. **Births** (per 1,000 pop. 1978): 45. **Deaths** (per 1,000 pop. 1978): 20. **Natural increase** (1978): 2.5%. **Hospital beds** (1979): 2,586. **Physicians** (1979): 420.

Education (1981): **Literacy:** 20%. **Years compulsory:** 3; Attendance: 71% primary, 14% secondary.

Embassy: 2131 Leroy Pl. NW 20008; 667-4550.

Nepal was originally a group of petty principalities, the inhabitants of one of which, the Gurkhas, became dominant about 1769. In 1951 King Tribhubana Bir Bikram, member of the Shah family, ended the system of rule by hereditary premiers of the Ranas family, who had kept the kings virtual prisoners, and established a cabinet system of government.

Virtually closed to the outside world for centuries, Nepal is now linked to India and Pakistan by roads and air service and to Tibet by road. Polygamy, child marriage, and the caste system were officially abolished in 1963.

Students and political opponents were arrested in 1974 following violent protests. A new wave of protests, 1979, led to more arrests and executions, but a change in premiers.

Netherlands
Kingdom of the Netherlands

People: Population (1983 est.): 14,374,000. **Age distrib.** (%): 0–14: 21.5; 15–44: 46.9; 45+: 31.6. **Pop. density:** 1,002.62 per sq. mi. **Urban** (1976): 88.4%. **Ethnic groups:** Dutch. **Languages:** Dutch. **Religions:** Roman Catholics 40%, Dutch Reformed 23.5%.

Geography: Area: 16,464 sq. mi., the size of Mass., Conn., and R.I. combined. **Location:** In NW Europe on North Sea. **To-**

pography: The land is flat, an average alt. of 37 ft. above sea level, with much land below sea level reclaimed and protected by 1,500 miles of dikes. Since 1927 the government has been draining the IJsselmeer, formerly the Zuider Zee. By 1972, 410,000 of a planned 550,000 acres had been drained and reclaimed. **Capital:** Amsterdam. **Cities** (1982): Amsterdam 700,759; Rotterdam 568,167; Hague 456,886.

Government: Type: Parliamentary democracy under a constitutional monarch. **Head of state:** Queen Beatrix; b. Jan. 31, 1938; in office: Apr. 30, 1980. **Head of government:** Prime Min. Ruud Lubbers; in office: Nov. 4, 1982. **Seat of govt.:** The Hague. **Local divisions:** 11 provinces. **Defense:** 3.5% of GNP (1981).

Economy: Industries: Metals, machinery, chemicals, textiles, oil refinery, diamond cutting, pottery, electronics, tourism. **Chief crops:** Grains, potatoes, sugar beets, vegetables, fruits, flowers. **Minerals:** Natural gas, oil. **Crude oil reserves** (1980): 60 mln. bbls. **Per capita arable land:** 0.1 acres. **Meat prod.** (1983): beef: 440,000 metric tons; pork: 1.2 mln. metric tons; lamb: 11,000 metric tons. **Fish catch** (1981): 399,438 metric tons. **Electricity prod.** (1982): 60.3 bln. kwh. **Crude steel prod.** (1982): 4.3 mln. metric tons. **Labor force:** 6% agric.; 30% ind. and commerce, 20% services, 15% gov.

Finance: Currency: Guilder (Mar. 1984: 2.92 = $1 US). **Gross domestic product** (1981): $139 bln. **Per capita income** (1981): $9,749. **Imports** (1983): $62.5 bln.; partners: W. Ger. 22%, Belg. 11%, U.S. 9%, U.K. 9%. **Exports** (1983): $65.5 bln.; partners : W. Ger. 30%, Belg. 14%, Fr. 10%, UK 9%. **Tourists** (1981): 2.8 mln.; receipts: $1.6 bln. **National budget** (1980): $58.02 bln. revenues; $63.33 bln. expenditures. **International reserves less gold** (Feb. 1984): $10.9 bln. **Gold:** 43.94 mln. oz t. **Consumer prices** (change in 1983): 2.8%.

Transport: Railway traffic (1982): 9.3 bln. passenger-km; 2.8 bln. net ton-km. **Motor vehicles:** in use (1982): 4.6 mln. passenger cars, 317,000 comm. vehicles; manuf. (1978): 62,400 passenger cars; 11,520 comm. vehicles. **Civil aviation** (1982): 16.2 bln. passenger-km; 1 bln. freight ton-km. **Chief ports:** Rotterdam, Amsterdam, IJmuiden.

Communications: Television sets: 4.3 mln. licensed (1981). **Radios:** 4.3 mln. licensed (1981). **Telephones in use** (1982): 5.1 mln. **Daily newspaper circ.** (1982): 325 per 1,000 pop.

Health: Life expectancy at birth (1982): 72 male; 78 female. **Births** (per 1,000 pop. 1982): 12.0. **Deaths** (per 1,000 pop. 1982): 8.2. **Natural increase** (1978): .4%. **Hospital beds** (1982): 69,600. **Physicians** (1982): 28,037. **Infant mortality** (per 1,000 live births 1982): 9.

Education (1982): **Literacy:** 99%. **Years compulsory:** 10; attendance: 100%.

Embassy: 4200 Linnean Ave. NW 20008; 244-5300.

Julius Caesar conquered the region in 55 BC, when it was inhabited by Celtic and Germanic tribes.

After the empire of Charlemagne fell apart, the Netherlands (Holland, Belgium, Flanders) split among counts, dukes and bishops, passed to Burgundy and thence to Charles V of Spain. His son, Philip II, tried to check the Dutch drive toward political freedom and Protestantism (1568-1573). William the Silent, prince of Orange, led a confederation of the northern provinces, called Estates, in the Union of Utrecht, 1579. The Estates retained individual sovereignty, but were represented jointly in the States-General, a body that had control of foreign affairs and defense. In 1581 they repudiated allegiance to Spain. The rise of the Dutch republic to naval, economic, and artistic eminence came in the 17th century.

The United Dutch Republic ended 1795 when the French formed the Batavian Republic. Napoleon made his brother Louis king of Holland, 1806; Louis abdicated 1810 when Napoleon annexed Holland. In 1813 the French were expelled. In 1815 the Congress of Vienna formed a kingdom of the Netherlands, including Belgium, under William I. In 1830, the Belgians seceded and formed a separate kingdom.

The constitution, promulgated 1814, and subsequently revised, assures a hereditary constitutional monarchy.

The Netherlands maintained its neutrality in World War I, but was invaded and brutally occupied by Germany from 1940 to 1945. After the war, neutrality was abandoned, and the country joined NATO, the Western European Union, the Benelux Union, and, in 1957, became a charter member of the Common Market.

In 1949, after several years of fighting, the Netherlands granted independence to Indonesia, where it had ruled since the 17th century. In 1963, West New Guinea was turned over to In-

donesia, after five years of controversy and seizure of Dutch property in Indonesia.

Some 200,000 Indonesians emigrated to the Netherlands. Of them, 35,000 were from the South Moluccan islands. Terrorists demanding independence for South Molucca from Indonesia staged train hijackings and other incidents in the Netherlands in 1975 and 1977.

The independence of Suriname, 1975, instigated mass emigrations to the Netherlands, adding to problems of unemployment.

Though the Netherlands has been heavily industrialized, its productive small farms export large quantities of pork and dairy foods.

Rotterdam, located along the principal mouth of the Rhine, handles the most cargo of any ocean port in the world. Canals, of which there are 3,478 miles, are important in transportation.

Netherlands Antilles

The **Netherlands Antilles,** constitutionally on a level of equality with the Netherlands homeland within the kingdom, consist of 2 groups of islands in the West Indies. **Curacao, Aruba,** and **Bonaire** are near the South American coast; **St. Eustatius, Saba,** and the southern part of **St. Maarten** are SE of Puerto Rico. Northern two-thirds of St. Maarten belong to French Guadeloupe; the French call the island St. Martin. Total area of the 2 groups is 385 sq. mi., including: Aruba 75, Bonaire 111, Curacao 171, St. Eustatius 11, Saba 5, St. Maarten (Dutch part) 13.

Total pop. (est. 1981) was 253,300. Willemstad, on Curacao, is the capital. Chief products are corn, pulse, salt and phosphate; principal industry is the refining of crude oil from Venezuela. Tourism is an important industry, as are electronics and shipbuilding.

New Zealand

People: Population: (1983 est.): 3,203,000. **Age distrib. (%):** 0–14: 26.8; 15–59: 59.1; 60+: 14.1 **Pop. density:** 30.80 per sq. mi. **Urban** (1982): 83.0%. **Ethnic groups:** European (mostly British) 84%, Polynesian (mostly Maori) 8.5%. **Languages:** English (official), Maori. **Religions:** Anglican 29%, Presbyterian 18%, Roman Catholics 15%, others.

Geography: Area: 103,883 sq. mi., the size of Colorado. **Location:** In SW Pacific O. **Neighbors:** Nearest are Australia on W, Fiji, Tonga on N. **Topography:** Each of the 2 main islands (North and South Is.) is mainly hilly and mountainous. The east coasts consist of fertile plains, especially the broad Canterbury Plains on South Is. A volcanic plateau is in center of North Is. South Is. has glaciers and 15 peaks over 10,000 ft. **Capital:** Wellington. **Cities** (1981 cen.): Christchurch 321,000; Auckland 829,000; Wellington 342,000.

Government: Type: Parliamentary. **Head of state:** Queen Elizabeth II, represented by Gov.-Gen. David Stuart Beattie; in office: Nov. 6, 1980. **Head of government:** Prime Min. David Lange; elected: July 14, 1984. **Local divisions:** 96 counties, 132 boroughs, 3 towns, 4 districts. **Defense:** 1.2% of GNP (1980).

Economy: Industries: Food processing, textiles, paper, steel, aluminum, oil products. **Chief crops:** Grain. **Minerals:** Oil, gas, iron, coal. **Crude oil reserves** (1980): 110 mln. bbls. **Other resources:** Wool, timber. **Arable land:** 78%. **Meat prod.** (1983): beef: 530,000 metric tons; pork: 33,000 metric tons; lamb: 711,000 metric tons. **Fish catch** (1981): 108,000 metric tons. **Electricity prod.** (1982): 23.9 bln. kwh. **Crude steel prod.** (1981): 221,000 metric tons. **Labor force:** 10.3% agric.; 34% ind. and commerce, 55% services and gov.

Finance: Currency: Dollar (Mar. 1984: 1.38 = $1 US). **Gross domestic product** (1981): $23.4 bln. **Per capita income** (1981): $7,363. **Imports** (1981): $5.5 bln.; partners: Austral. 20%, U.S. 17%, Jap. 17%. **Exports** (1981): $5.9 bln.; partners: UK 14%, U.S. 13%, Jap. 13%, Austral. 15%. **Tourists** (1981): 478,000; receipts $252 mln. **National budget** (1980): $5.6 bln. revenues; $6.5 bln. expenditures. **International reserves less gold** (Feb. 1984): $818 mln. **Gold:** 22,000 oz t. **Consumer prices** (change in 1981): 16%.

Transport: Railway traffic (1981): 404 mln. passenger-km; 3.1 bln. net ton-km. **Motor vehicles:** in use (1982): 1.2 mln. passenger cars; 264,548 comm. vehicles; assembled (1978): 51,828 passenger cars; 11,088 comm. vehicles. **Civil aviation:** (1982): 5.8 bln. passenger-km, 229 mln. freight ton-km. **Chief ports:** Auckland, Wellington, Lyttleton, Tauranga.

Communications: Television sets: 913,837 mln. licensed (1982): 90,000 manuf. (1978). **Radios:** 2.7 mln. in use (1980): 143,000 manuf. (1978). **Telephones in use** (1982): 1.8 mln. **Daily newspaper circ.** (1982): 326 per 1,000 pop.

Health: Life expectancy at birth (1982): 69 male; 75.5 female. **Births** (per 1,000 pop. 1981): 16.0. **Deaths** (per 1,000 pop. 1981): 7.9 **Natural increase** (1977): .9%. **Hospital beds** (1981): 26,716. **Physicians** (1981): 8,327. **Infant mortality** (per 1,000 live births 1982): 14.2

Education (1982): **Literacy:** 99%. Compulsory ages 6-15; attendance: 100%.

Embassy: 37 Observatory Cir. NW 20008; 328-4800.

The Maoris, a Polynesian group from the eastern Pacific, reached New Zealand before and during the 14th century. The first European to sight New Zealand was Dutch navigator Abel Janszoon Tasman, but Maoris refused to allow him to land. British Capt. James Cook explored the coasts, 1769-1770.

British sovereignty was proclaimed in 1840, with organized settlement beginning in the same year. Representative institutions were granted in 1853. Maori Wars ended in 1870 with British victory. The colony became a dominion in 1907, and is an independent member of the Commonwealth.

New Zealand fought on the side of the Allies in both world wars, and signed the ANZUS Treaty of Mutual Security with the U.S. and Australia in 1951. New Zealand joined with Australia and Britain in a pact to defend Singapore and Malaysia; New Zealand units are stationed in those 2 countries.

A labor tradition in politics dates back to the 19th century. Private ownership is basic to the economy, but state ownership or regulation affects many industries. Transportation, broadcasting, mining, and forestry are largely state-owned.

The native Maoris number about 250,000. Four of 92 members of the House of Representatives are elected directly by the Maori people.

New Zealand comprises **North Island,** 44,035 sq. mi.; **South Island,** 58,304 sq. mi.; **Stewart Island,** 674 sq. mi.; **Chatham Islands,** 372 sq. mi.

In 1965, the **Cook Islands** (pop. 1983 est., 16,900; area 93 sq. mi.) became self-governing although New Zealand retains responsibility for defense and foreign affairs. **Niue** attained the same status in 1974; it lies 400 mi. to W (pop. 1981 est., 3,400; area 100 sq. mi.). **Tokelau Is.,** (pop. 1981 est., 1,600; area 4 sq. mi.) are 300 mi. N of Samoa.

Ross Dependency, administered by New Zealand since 1923, comprises 160,000 sq. mi. of Antarctic territory.

Nicaragua

Republic of Nicaragua

People: Population (1983 est.): 2,812,000. **Age distrib.** (%): 0–14: 48.1; 15–59: 47.2; 60+: 4.7. **Pop. density:** 40 per sq. mi. **Urban** (1982): 40%. **Ethnic groups:** Mestizo 69%, Caucasian 17%, Negro 9%, Indian 5%. **Languages:** Spanish, English (on Caribbean coast). **Religions:** Predominantly Roman Catholics.

Geography: Area: 57,000 sq. mi., about the size of Iowa. **Location:** In Central America. **Neighbors:** Honduras on N, Costa Rica on S. **Topography:** Both Atlantic and Pacific coasts are over 200 mi. long. The Cordillera Mtns., with many volcanic peaks, runs NW-SE through the middle of the country. Between this and a volcanic range to the E lie Lakes Managua and Nicaragua. **Capital:** Managua. **Cities** (1979 est.): Managua 552,900.

Government: 3-member junta; as of Mar. 5, 1981. Coordinator of the junta: Daniel Ortega Saavedra. **Local divisions:** 16 departments; one national district. **Defense:** 13.3% of govt. budget (1980).

Economy: Industries: Oil refining, chemicals, textiles. **Chief crops:** Bananas, cotton, fruit, yucca, coffee, sugar, corn, beans, cocoa, rice, sesame, tobacco, wheat. **Minerals:** Gold, silver, copper, tungsten. **Other resources:** Forests, shrimp. **Arable land:** 7%. **Meat prod.** (1980): beef: 69,000 metric tons; pork: 11,000 metric tons. **Fish catch:** (1981): 6,000 metric tons. **Electricity prod.** (1981): 1.1 bln. kwh. **Labor force:** 65% agric.

Finance: Currency: Cordoba (Apr. 1984: 10.05 = $1 US). **Gross domestic product** (1980): $2.3 bln. **Per capita income** (1980): $804. **Imports** (1981): $877 mln.; partners (1980): U.S. 27%, Venez. 18%, Costa Rica 13%, Guat. 12%. **Exports** (1981): $526 mln.; partners (1980): U.S. 39%, W. Ger. 14%, Costa Rica 8%. **National budget** (1980): $622 mln. expendi-

tures. **International reserves less gold** (June 1983): $233 mln. **Gold:** 18,000 oz t. **Consumer prices** (change in 1982): 248%.

Transport: Railway traffic (1981): 20 mln. passenger-miles; 14 mln. net ton-miles. **Motor vehicles:** in use (1981): 24,000 passenger cars, 7,900 comm. vehicles. **Civil aviation** (1982): 20 mln. passenger-km; 14 mln. freight ton-km. **Chief ports:** Corinto, Puerto Somoza, San Juan del Sur.

Communications: Television sets: 175,000 in use (1981). **Radios:** 700,000 in use (1981). **Telephones in use** (1980): 57,900 **Daily newspaper circ.** (1982): 63 per 1,000 pop.

Health: Life expectancy at birth (1975): 51.2 male; 54.6 female. **Births** (per 1,000 pop. 1978): 46. **Deaths** (per 1,000 pop. 1978): 16. **Natural increase** (1978): 0.7%. **Hospital beds** (per 100,000 pop. 1977): 207. **Physicians** (per 100,000 pop. 1977): 60. **Infant mortality** (per 1,000 live births 1982): 37.0.

Education (1982): **Literacy:** 87%. **Pop. 5-19:** in school: 48%, teachers per 1,000: 13.

Embassy: 1627 New Hampshire Ave. NW 20009; 387-4371.

Nicaragua, inhabited by various Indian tribes, was conquered by Spain in 1552. After gaining independence from Spain, 1821, Nicaragua was united for a short period with Mexico, then with the United Provinces of Central America, finally becoming an independent republic, 1838.

U.S. Marines occupied the country at times in the early 20th century, the last time from 1926 to 1933.

Gen. Anastasio Somoza-Debayle was elected president 1967. He resigned 1972, but was elected president again in 1974. Martial law was imposed in Dec. 1974, after officials were kidnapped by the Marxist Sandinista guerrillas. The country's Roman Catholic bishops charged in 1977 that the government had mistreated civilians in its anti-guerrilla campaign. Violent opposition spread to nearly all classes, 1978; a nationwide strike called against the government Aug. 25 touched off a state of civil war at Matagalpa.

Months of simmering civil war erupted when Sandinist guerrillas invaded Nicaragua May 29, 1979, touching off a 7-week-offensive that culminated in the resignation and exile of Somoza, July 17.

Relations with the U.S. have been strained due to Nicaragua's military aid to leftist guerrillas in El Salvador and the U.S. backing anti-Sandinista rebels.

In 1983, Nicaragua accused the U.S. of aiding anti-Sandinista rebels who were invading from Honduras. The charge sparked a debate in the U.S. Congress over funds for covert aid to the rebels. Relations worsened in May when the U.S. slashed Nicaragua's sugar imports by 90% for fiscal 1984, and in June, when Nicaragua expelled 3 U.S. diplomats amid charges that they were CIA agents plotting to poison the Nicaraguan defense minister.

Nicaragua accused the U.S. CIA of directing the mining of its ports, Apr. 6, 1984. It asked the International Court of Justice in The Hague to order the U.S. to halt the mining and cease aiding attacks on its territory. The Court ruled, May 10, that the U.S. should immediately halt any actions to blockade or mine Nicaragua's ports.

Niger

Republic of Niger

People: Population (1983 est.): 6,083,000. **Age distrib.** (%): 0–14: 43.0; 15–59: 52.2; 60+: 4.8. **Pop. density:** 10.2 per sq. mi. **Ethnic groups:** Hausa 56%, Djerma 22%, Fulani 8%, Tuareg 8%. **Languages:** French (official), Hausa, Djerma. **Religions:** Muslims 85%, animists 14%.

Geography: Area: 490,100 sq. mi., almost 3 times the size of California. **Location:** In the interior of N. Africa. **Neighbors:** Libya, Algeria on N, Mali, Upper Volta on W, Benin, Nigeria on S, Chad on E. **Topography:** Mostly arid desert and mountains. A narrow savanna in the S and the Niger R. basin in the SW contain most of the population. **Capital:** Niamey. **Cities** (1982 est.): Niamey 300,000.

Government: Type: Republic. **Head of state:** Pres. Seyni Kountche; b. 1931; in office: Apr. 15, 1974. **Head of government:** Premier Ahmid Algabid; in office: Nov. 11, 1983. **Local divisions:** 7 departments. **Defense:** 4.3% of govt. budget (1983).

Economy: Chief crops: Peanuts, cotton. **Minerals:** Uranium. **Arable land:** 3%. **Meat prod.** (1980): beef: 37,000 metric tons; lamb: 33,000 metric tons. **Electricity prod.** (1981): 60 mln. kwh. **Labor force:** 90% agric. **Finance: Currency:** CFA franc (Mar. 1984: 399 = $1 US). **Gross domestic product** (1982): $2.3 bln. **Per capita income** (1981) : $475. **Imports** (1980): $525 mln.; partners: Fr. 36%, Nig. 13%. **Exports** (1980): $458 mln.; partners: Fr. 36%, Nig. 17%. **National budget** (1983): $232 mln. **International reserves less gold** (Jan. 1984): $54.9 mln. **Gold:** 11,000 oz t. **Consumer prices** (change in 1982): 11.6%.

Transport: Motor vehicles: in use (1980): 25,800 passenger cars, 4,400 comm. vehicles.

Communications: Radios: 250,000 in use (1981). **Telephones in use** (1978): 8,000. **Daily newspaper cir.** (1982): 1 per 1,000 pop.

Health: Life expectancy at birth (1982): 42 years. **Births** (per 1,000 pop. 1978): 51. **Deaths** (per 1,000 pop. 1978): 23. **Natural increase** (1978): 2.9%. **Hospital beds** (per 100,000 pop 1977): 69. **Physicians** (per 100,000 pop. 1977): 2. **Infant mortality** (per 1,000 live births 1978): 162.

Education (1982): **Literacy:** 5%. **Years compulsory:** 6; attendance: 15%.

Embassy: 2204 R St. NW 20008; 483-4224.

Niger was part of ancient and medieval African empires. European explorers reached the area in the late 18th century. The French colony of Niger was established 1900-22, after the defeat of Tuareg fighters, who had invaded the area from the N a century before. The country became independent Aug. 3, 1960. The next year it signed a bilateral agreement with France retaining close economic and cultural ties, which have continued. Hamani Diori, Niger's first president, was ousted in a 1974 coup. Drought and famine struck in 1973-74, and again in 1975.

Nigeria
Federal Republic of Nigeria

People: Population (1983 est.): 85,219,000. **Pop. density:** 216.09 per sq. mi. **Ethnic groups:** Hausa 21%, Yoruba 20%, Ibo 17%, Fulani 9%, others. **Languages:** English (official), Hausa, Yoruba, Ibo. **Religions:** Moslems 47% (in N), Christians 34% (in S), others.

Geography: Area: 356,700 sq. mi., more than twice the size of California. **Location:** On the S coast of W. Africa. **Neighbors:** Benin on W, Niger on N, Chad, Cameroon on E. **Topography:** 4 E-W regions divide Nigeria: a coastal mangrove swamp 10-60 mi. wide, a tropical rain forest 50-100 mi. wide, a plateau of savanna and open woodland, and semidesert in the N. **Capital:** Lagos. **Cities** (1982 est.): Lagos 1,404,000; Ibadan 1,009,000.

Government: Type: Federal military. **Head of state:** Gen. Mohammed Buhari; in office: Dec. 31, 1983. **Local divisions:** 19 states plus federal capital territory. **Defense:** 10% of govt. budget (1982).

Economy: Industries: Crude oil (95% of export), food processing, assembly of vehicles and other equipment. **Chief crops:** Cocoa (main export crop), tobacco, palm products, peanuts, cotton, soybeans. **Minerals:** Oil, gas, coal, iron, limestone, columbium, tin. **Crude oil reserves** (1980): 17.4 bln. bbls. **Other resources:** Timber, rubber, hides. **Arable land:** 25%. **Meat prod.** (1983): beef: 235,000 metric tons; pork: 48,000 metric tons; lamb: 181,000 metric tons. **Fish catch** (1981): 496,000 metric tons. **Electricity prod.** (1981): 7.2 bln. kwh. **Labor force:** 56% agric., 17% ind., comm. and serv. **Finance: Currency:** Naira (Feb. 1984: .66 = $1 US). **Gross domestic product** (1980): $77 bln. **Per capita income** (1980): $750. **Imports** (1981): $20.9 bln.; partners (1981): UK 18%, W. Ger. 13%, U.S. 9%, Jap. 13%. **Exports** (1982): $16.6 bln.; partners (1981): U.S. 46%, W. Ger. 8%, Neth. 7%. **Tourist receipts** (1977): $60 mln. **National budget** (1982): $16.6 bln. **International reserves less gold** (Jan. 1984): $885 mln. **Gold:** 687,000 oz t. **Consumer prices** (change in 1982): 21%.

Transport: Railway traffic (1978): 1.4 bln. passenger-km; 1.6 bln. net ton-km. **Motor vehicles:** in use (1980): 215,000 passenger cars, 33,100 comm. vehicles. **Civil aviation** (1982): 2.3 bln. passenger-km; 26.9 mln. freight ton-km. **Chief ports:** Port Harcourt, Lagos.

Communications: Television sets: 450,000 licensed (1981). **Radios:** 5.6 mln. licensed (1981). **Telephones in use** (1980): 154,200. **Daily newspaper circ.** (1982): 15 per 1,000 pop.

Health: Life expectancy at birth (1983): 48.3 male; 51.7 female. **Births** (per 1,000 pop. 1978): 50. **Deaths** (per 1,000 pop. 1978): 19. **Natural increase** (1978): 3.2%. **Hospital beds** (per 100,000 pop. 1977): 80. **Physicians** (per 100,000 pop. 1977): 7.

Education (1982): **Literacy:** 25%. **Primary school attendance:** 42%.

Embassy: 2201 M St. NW 20037; 822-1500.

Early cultures in Nigeria date back to at least 700 BC. From the 12th to the 14th centuries, more advanced cultures developed in the Yoruba area, at Ife, and in the north, where Moslem influence prevailed.

Portuguese and British slavers appeared from the 15th-16th centuries. Britain seized Lagos, 1861, during an anti-slave trade campaign, and gradually extended control inland until 1900. Nigeria became independent Oct. 1, 1960, and a republic Oct. 1, 1963.

On May 30, 1967, the Eastern Region seceded, proclaiming itself the Republic of Biafra, plunging the country into civil war. Casualties in the war were est. at over 1 million, including many "Biafrans" (mostly Ibos) who died of starvation despite international efforts to provide relief. The secessionists, after steadily losing ground, capitulated Jan. 12, 1970. Within a few years, the Ibos were reintegrated into national life, but mistrust among the regions persists.

Oil revenues have made possible a massive economic development program, largely using private enterprise, but agriculture has lagged. Slumping oil revenues forced Nigeria to impose import restrictions in 1982 and 1983.

After 13 years of military rule, the nation experienced a peaceful return to civilian government, Oct., 1979.

Nigeria announced that it would expel 2 million illegal immigrants from Ghana, Niger, and other neighboring countries, Feb. 1983. Military rule returned to Nigeria, Dec. 31, as a coup ousted the democratically-elected government.

Norway
Kingdom of Norway

People: Population (1983 est.): 4,131,000. **Age distrib. (%):** 0-14: 23.5; 15-59: 57.2; 60+: 19.6. **Pop. density:** 34 per sq. mi. **Urban** (1977): 44.2%. **Ethnic groups:** Germanic (Nordic, Alpine, Baltic), minority Lapps. **Languages:** Norwegian (official), Lapp. **Religions:** Lutherans 97%.

Geography: Area: 125,057 sq. mi., slightly larger than New Mexico. **Location:** Occupies the W part of Scandinavian peninsula in NW Europe (extends farther north than any European land). **Neighbors:** Sweden, Finland, USSR on E. **Topography:** A highly indented coast is lined with tens of thousands of islands. Mountains and plateaus cover most of the country, which is only 25% forested. **Capital:** Oslo. **Cities** (1982): Oslo 450,386; Bergen 207,419.

Government: Type: Hereditary constitutional monarchy. **Head of state:** King Olav V, b. July 2, 1903; in office: Sept. 21, 1957. **Head of government:** Prime Min. Kare Isaachsen Willoch, b. Oct. 3, 1928; in office: Oct. 14, 1981. **Local divisions:** Oslo, Svalbard and 18 fylker (counties). **Defense:** 8.6% of GNP (1981).

Economy: Industries: Paper, shipbuilding, engineering, metals, chemicals, food processing oil, gas. **Chief crops:** Grains, potatoes, fruits. **Minerals:** Oil, copper, pyrites, nickel, iron, zinc, lead. **Crude oil reserves** (1980): 5.75 bln. bbls. **Other resources:** Timber. **Per capita arable land:** 0.5 acres. **Meat prod.** (1983): beef: 74,000 metric tons; pork: 83,000 metric tons; lamb: 23,000 metric tons. **Fish catch** (1981): 2.7 mln. metric tons. **Electricity prod.** (1982): 91.8 bln. kwh. **Crude steel prod.** (1982): 767,000 metric tons. **Labor force:** 4.7% agric.; 20.5% ind., 32% services, 29% govt. **Finance: Currency:** Kroner (Mar. 1984: 7.51 = $1 US). **Gross domestic product** (1980): $57.32 bln. **Per capita income** (1980): $12,432. **Imports** (1983): $13.4 bln.; partners: Swed. 17%, W. Ger. 16%, UK 12%, U.S. 9%. **Exports** (1983): $17.9 bln.; partners: UK 37%, W. Ger. 20%, Swed. 9%. **Tourists** (1977): 447,800; receipts: $478 mln. **National budget** (1981): $16.6 bln. revenues; $17.3 bln. expenditures. **International reserves less gold (Mar. 1984): $6.82 bln. Gold: 1.18 mln. oz t. Consumer prices (change in 1983): 8.4%.

Transport: Railway traffic (1982): 2.2 bln. passenger-km; 2.5 bln. net ton-km. Motor vehicles: in use (1982): 1.2 mln. passenger cars, 158,740 comm. vehicles. Civil aviation: (1982): 4.1 bln. passenger-km; 139 mln. net ton-km. Chief ports: Bergen, Stavanger, Oslo, Tonsberg.

Communications: Television sets: 1.2 mln. licensed (1982). Radios: 1.3 mln. licensed (1981) Telephones in use (1981): 1.9 mln. Daily newspaper circ. (1982): 479 per 1,000 pop.

Health: Life expectancy at birth (1981): 72.5 male; 79.2 female. Births (per 1,000 pop. 1980): 12.5. Deaths (per 1,000 pop. 1980): 10.0. Natural increase (1978): .3%. Hospital beds (1980): 64,909. Physicians (1980): 8,981. Infant mortality (per 1,000 live births 1981): 8.5.

Education (1978): Literacy: 99%. Pop. 5-19: in school: 70%, teachers per 1,000: 46.

Embassy: 2720 34th St. NW 20008; 333-6000.

The first supreme ruler of Norway was Harald the Fairhaired who came to power in 872 AD. Between 800 and 1000, Norway's Vikings raided and occupied widely dispersed parts of Europe.

The country was united with Denmark 1381-1814, and with Sweden, 1814-1905. In 1905, the country became independent with Prince Charles of Denmark as king.

Norway remained neutral during World War I. Germany attacked Norway Apr. 9, 1940, and held it until liberation May 8, 1945. The country abandoned its neutrality after the war, and joined the NATO alliance. Norway rejected membership in the Common Market in a 1972 referendum.

Abundant hydroelectric resources provided the base for Norway's industrialization, producing one of the highest living standards in the world.

Norway's merchant marine is one of the world's largest.

Norway and the Soviet Union have disputed their territorial waters boundary in the Barents Sea, north of the 2 countries' common border.

Petroleum output from oil and mineral deposits under the continental shelf has raised state revenues.

Svalbard is a group of mountainous islands in the Arctic O., c. 23,957 sq. mi., pop. varying seasonally from 1,500 to 3,600. The largest, Spitsbergen (formerly called West Spitsbergen), 15,060 sq. mi., seat of governor, is about 370 mi. N of Norway. By a treaty signed in Paris, 1920, major European powers recognized the sovereignty of Norway, which incorporated it in 1925. Both Norway and the USSR mine rich coal deposits. Mt. Newton (Spitsbergen) is 5,633 ft. tall.

Oman

Sultanate of Oman

People: Population (1983 est.): 978,000. Pop. density: 10.85 per sq. mi. Ethnic groups: Arab 88%, Baluchi 4%, Persian 3%, Indian 2%, African 2%. Languages: Arabic (official), English, Urdu, others. Religions: Ibadhi Moslems 75%, Sunni Moslems.

Geography: Area: 115,800 sq. mi., about the size of New Mexico. Location: On SE coast of Arabian peninsula. Neighbors: United Arab Emirates, Saudi Arabia, South Yemen on W. Topography: Oman has a narrow coastal plain up to 10 mi. wide, a range of barren mountains reaching 9,900 ft., and a wide, stony, mostly waterless plateau, avg. alt. 1,000 ft. Also the tip of the Ruus-al-Jebal peninsula controls access to the Persian Gulf. Capital: Muscat. Cities (1981 est.): Muscat 50,000.

Government: Type: Absolute monarchy. Head of state: Sultan Qabus ibn Said; b. Nov. 18, 1942; in office: July 23, 1970. Local divisions: 1 province, numerous districts. Defense: 25% of GNP.

Economy: Chief crops: Dates, fruits vegetables, wheat, bananas. Minerals: Oil (95% of exports). Crude oil reserves (1981): 2.5 bln. bbls. Per capita arable land: 0.05 acres. Fish catch (1979): 198,000 metric tons. Electricity prod. (1982): 965.00 mln. kwh. Labor force: 66% agric.

Finance: Currency: Rial Omani (Feb. 1984: .34 = $1 US). Gross national product (1981): $6.2 bln. Per capita income (1976): $2,400. Imports (1982): $2.7 bln.; partners: Jap. 21%, UAE 14%, UK 14%. Exports (1982): $4.4 bln.; partners: Jap. 52%, Europe 30%. National budget (1983): $4.8 bln. revenues;

$4.8 bln. expenditures. International reserves less gold (Nov. 1984): $1.4 bln. Gold: 288,000 oz t.

Transport: Chief ports: Matrah, Muscat.

Communications: Telephones in use (1978): 13,068.

Health: Hospital beds (per 100,000 pop. 1977): 173. Physicians (per 100,000 pop 1977): 49.

Education (1983): Literacy: 20%. Attendance: 60% primary, 10% secondary.

Embassy: 2342 Massachusetts Ave. NW 20008; 387-1980.

A long history of rule by other lands, including Portugal in the 16th century, ended with the ouster of the Persians in 1744. By the early 19th century, Muscat and Oman was one of the most important countries in the region, controlling much of the Persian and Pakistan coasts, and ruling far-away Zanzibar, which was separated in 1861 under British mediation.

British influence was confirmed in a 1951 treaty, and Britain helped suppress an uprising by traditionally rebellious interior tribes against control by Muscat in the 1950s. Enclaves on the Pakistan coast were sold to that country in 1958.

On July 23, 1970, Sultan Said bin Taimur was overthrown by his son. The new sultan changed the nation's name to Sultanate of Oman. He launched a domestic development program, and battled leftist rebels in the southern Dhofar area to their defeat, Dec. 1975.

Oil has been the major source of income. Economic and military aid accords with the U.S. gave U.S. forces access to air and naval bases around the Indian O., 1980.

Pakistan

Islamic Republic of Pakistan

People: Population (1983 est.): 94,140,000. Pop. density: 262 per sq. mi. Urban (1981): 28.2%. Ethnic groups: Punjabi 66%, Sindhi 13%, Pushtun (Iranian) 8.5%, Urdu 7.6%, Baluchi 2.5%, others. Languages: Urdu, English are both official. Religions: Muslim 97%.

Geography: Area: 307,374 sq. mi., larger than Texas. Location: In W part of South Asia. Neighbors: Iran on W, Afghanistan, China on N, India on E. Topography: The Indus R. rises in the Hindu Kush and Himalaya mtns. in the N (highest is K2, or Godwin Austen, 28,250 ft., 2d highest in world), then flows over 1,000 mi. through fertile valley and empties into Arabian Sea. Thar Desert, Eastern Plains flank Indus Valley. Capital: Islamabad. Cities (1981 cen.): Karachi 5.1 mln.; Lahore 2.9 mln.; Faisalabad 1 mln.; Hyderabad 795,000; Rawalpindi 928,000.

Government: Type: Martial law regime. Head of state and head of government: Pres. Mohammad Zia ul-Haq; b. 1924; in office: Sept. 16, 1978 (state), July 5, 1977 (govt.). Local divisions: Federal capital, 4 provinces, tribal areas. Armed forces: regulars 436,600 (1980).

Economy: Industries: Textiles, food processing, chemicals, tobacco, Chief crops: Rice, wheat. Minerals: Natural gas, iron ore. Crude oil reserves (1980): 200 mln. bbls. Other resources: Wool. Per capita arable land: 0.6 acres. Meat prod. (1983): beef: 357,000 metric tons; lamb: 399,000 metric tons. Fish catch (1981): 318,000 metric tons. Electricity prod. (1982): 18.0 bln. kwh. Labor force: 60% agric.; 16% ind.

Finance: Currency: Rupee (Mar. 1984: 13.40 = $1 US). Gross domestic product (1980): $23.22 bln. Per capita income (1980): $280. Imports (1982): $5.37 bln.; partners: Sau. Ar. 15%, Jap. 12%, U.S. 9%, Kuwait 10%. Exports (1982): $2.3 bln.; partners: China 6%, Jap. 8%, U.S. 7%. National budget (1981): $3.71 bln. revenues; $3.71 bln. expenditures. International reserves less gold (Mar. 1984): $1.8 bln. Gold: 1.86 mln. oz t. Consumer prices (change in 1983): 7.4%.

Transport: Railway traffic (1982): 17.0 bln. passenger-km; 7.2 bln. net ton-km. Motor vehicles: in use (1980): 135,700 passenger cars, 36,100 comm. vehicles. Civil aviation (1982): 6.2 bln. passenger-km; 230.4 mln. freight ton-km. Chief ports: Karachi.

Communications: Television sets: 800,000 in use (1981). Radios: 5.5 mln. in use (1981). Telephones in use (1981): 367,000. Daily newspaper circ. (1982): 24 per 1,000 pop.

Health: Life expectancy at birth (1983): 54.4 male; 54.2 female. Births (per 1,000 pop. 1978): 45. Deaths (per 1,000 pop. 1978): 17. Natural increase 1978): 2.9%. Hospital beds

(1980): 42,469. **Physicians** (1980): 23,000. **Infant mortality** (per 1,000 live births 1979): 142.
Education (1978): **Literacy:** 23%. **Pop. 5-19:** in school: 28%, teachers per 1,000: 9.
Embassy: 2315 Massachusetts Ave. NW 20008; 332-8330.

Present-day Pakistan shares the 5,000-year history of the India-Pakistan sub-continent. At present day Harappa and Mohenjo Daro, the Indus Valley Civilization, with large cities and elaborate irrigation systems, flourished c. 4,000-2,500 BC.

Aryan invaders from the NW conquered the region around 1,500 BC, forging a Hindu civilization that dominated Pakistan as well as India for 2,000 years.

Beginning with the Persians in the 6th century BC, and continuing with Alexander the Great and with the Sassanians, successive nations to the west ruled or influenced Pakistan, eventually separating the area from the Indian cultural sphere.

The first Arab invasion, 712 AD, introduced Islam. Under the Mogul empire (1526-1857), Moslems ruled most of India, yielding to British encroachment and resurgent Hindus.

After World War I the Moslems of British India began agitation for minority rights in elections. Mohammad Ali Jinnah (1876-1948) was the principal architect of Pakistan. A leader of the Moslem League from 1916, he worked for dominion status for India; from 1940 he advocated a separate Moslem state.

When the British withdrew Aug. 14, 1947, the Islamic majority areas of India acquired self-government as Pakistan, with dominion status in the Commonwealth. Pakistan was divided into 2 sections, West Pakistan and East Pakistan. The 2 areas were nearly 1,000 mi. apart on opposite sides of India.

Pakistan became a republic in 1956. Pakistan had a National Assembly (legislature) with equal membership from East and West Pakistan, and 2 Provincial Assemblies. In Oct. 1958, Gen. Mohammad Ayub Khan took power in a coup. He was elected president in 1960, reelected in 1965.

As a member of the Central Treaty Organization, Pakistan had been aligned with the West. Following clashes between India and China in 1962, Pakistan made commercial and aid agreements with China.

Ayub resigned Mar. 25, 1969, after several months of violent rioting and unrest, most of it in East Pakistan, which demanded autonomy. The government was turned over to Gen. Agha Mohammad Yahya Khan and martial law was declared.

The Awami League, which sought regional autonomy for East Pakistan, won a majority in Dec. 1970 elections to a National Assembly which was to write a new constitution. In March, 1971 Yahya postponed the Assembly. Rioting and strikes broke out in the East.

On Mar. 25, 1971, government troops launched attacks in the East. The Easterners, aided by India, proclaimed the independent nation of Bangladesh. In months of widespread fighting, countless thousands were killed. Some 10 million Easterners fled into India.

Full scale war between India and Pakistan had spread to both the East and West fronts by December 3. Pakistan troops in the East surrendered Dec. 16; Pakistan agreed to a cease-fire in the West Dec. 17. On July 3, 1972, Pakistan and India signed a pact agreeing to withdraw troops from their borders and seek peaceful solutions to all problems. Diplomatic relations were resumed in 1976.

Zulfikar Ali Bhutto, leader of the Pakistan People's party, which had won the most West Pakistan votes in the Dec. 1970 elections, became president Dec. 20.

Bhutto was overthrown in a military coup July, 1977. Convicted of complicity in a 1974 political murder, Bhutto was executed Apr.4, 1979.

Relations with the U.S. were strained, 1979, when the U.S. embassy in Islamabad was stormed and burned and 2 Americans were killed, Nov. 21, along with attacks on other U.S. installations. But by June 1981, the U.S., pressured by the Soviet threat in Afghanistan, agreed to a six-year economic and military aid program with Pakistan. There are some 2 million Afghan refugees now in Pakistan.

Panama

Republic of Panama

People: Population (1983 est.): 2,058,000. **Age distrib.** (%): 0–14: 31.6; 15–59: 57.2; 60+: 11.1. **Pop. density:** 66.20 per sq.

mi. **Urban** (1980): 49.3%. **Ethnic groups:** Mestizo 70%, West Indian 14%, Caucasian 10%, Indian 6%. **Languages:** Spanish (official), English. **Religions:** Roman Catholics 93%, Protestants.

Geography: Area: 29,762 sq. mi., slightly larger than West Virginia. **Location:** In Central America. **Neighbors:** Costa Rica on W., Colombia on E. **Topography:** 2 mountain ranges run the length of the isthmus. Tropical rain forests cover the Caribbean coast and eastern Panama. **Capital:** Panama. **Cities** (1981 est.): Panama 655,000; Colon 117,000.

Government: Type: Centralized republic. **Head of state and head of government:** Pres. Nicholas Ardito-Barletta; b. Aug. 21, 1938; in office: May 6, 1984. **Local divisions:** 9 provinces, 1 territory. **Defense:** 1.4% of GNP (1981).

Economy: Industries: Oil refining, international banking. **Chief crops:** Bananas, pineapples, cocoa, corn, coconuts, sugar. **Minerals:** Copper. **Other resources:** Forests (mahogany), shrimp. **Arable land:** 24%. **Meat prod.** (1980): beef: 52,000 metric tons; pork: 7,000 metric tons. **Fish catch** (1981): 132,000 metric tons. **Electricity prod.** (1981): 2.5 bln. kwh. **Labor force:** 29% agric., 29.4% ind. and commerce.

Finance: Currency: Balboa (Apr. 1984: 1.00 = $1 US). **Gross domestic product** (1980): $3.2 bln. **Per capita income** (1978): $1,116. **Imports** (1981): $1.5 bln.; partners: U.S. 35%, Saudi Ar. 8%. **Exports** (1981): $315 mln.; partners: U.S. 51%, W. Ger. 5%. **Tourists** (1980): 392,062. **National budget** (1982): $2.8 bln. **International reserves less gold** (Jan. 1984): $206 mln. **Consumer prices** (change in 1983): 2.1%.

Transport: Motor vehicles: in use (1979): 97,300 passenger cars, 25,800 comm. vehicles. **Civil aviation** (1982): 400 mln. passenger-km; 15 mln. net ton-km. **Chief ports:** Balboa, Cristobal, Puerto Armuelles.

Communications: Television sets: 220,000 in use (1981). **Radios:** 285,000 in use (1981). **Telephones in use** (1981): 191,913. **Daily newspaper circ.** (1982): 95 per 1,000 pop.

Health: Life expectancy at birth (1980): 68.0 male; 72.0 female. **Births** (per 1,000 pop. 1980): 26.8. **Deaths** (per 1,000 pop. 1980): 4.3. **Natural increase** (1975): 2.8%. **Hospital beds** (per 100,000 pop. 1977): 386. **Physicians** (per 100,000 pop. 1977): 78. **Infant mortality** (per 1,000 live births 1981): 29.

Education (1982): **Literacy:** 85%. **Primary school attendance:** 93%.

Embassy: 2862 McGill Terrace NW 20008; 483-1407.

The coast of Panama was sighted by Rodrigo de Bastidas, sailing with Columbus for Spain in 1501, and was visited by Columbus in 1502. Vasco Nunez de Balboa crossed the isthmus and "discovered" the Pacific O. Sept. 13, 1513. Spanish colonies were ravaged by Francis Drake, 1572-95, and Henry Morgan, 1668-71. Morgan destroyed the old city of Panama which had been founded in 1519. Freed from Spain, Panama joined Colombia in 1821.

Panama declared its independence from Colombia Nov. 3, 1903, with U.S. recognition. U.S. naval forces deterred action by Colombia. On Nov. 18, 1903, Panama granted use, occupation and control of the Canal Zone to the U.S. by treaty, ratified Feb. 26, 1904. *(See also Panama Canal.)*

Rioting began Jan. 9, 1964, in a dispute over the flying of the U.S. and Panamanian flags and terms of the 1903 treaty.

New treaties were proposed in 1967 and 1974. In 1977, the U.S. and Panama initialed two treaties that would provide for a gradual takeover by Panama of the canal, and withdrawal of U.S. troops, to be completed by 1999. U.S. payments would be substantially increased in the interim. The permanent neutrality of the canal would also be guaranteed. The treaties were ratified by the U.S. Senate in 1978.

Due to easy Panama ship regulations and strictures in the U.S., merchant tonnage registered in Panama since World War II ranks high in size. Similarly easy financial regulations have made Panama a center for international banking.

Papua New Guinea

People: Population (1983 est.): 3,259,000. **Age distrib.** (%): 0–14: 43.8; 15–59: 50.3; 60+: 11.4. **Pop. density:** 17.28 per sq. mi. **Urban** (1980): 13.1%. **Ethnic groups:** Papuans (in S and interior), Melanesian (N,E), pygmies, minorities of Chinese, Australians, Polynesians. **Languages:** Melanesian Pidgin, Police Motu, English, numerous local languages. **Religions:** Protestant 63%, Roman Catholic 31%, local religions.

Geography: Area: 178,704 sq. mi., slightly larger than California. **Location:** Occupies eastern half of island of New Guinea. **Neighbors:** Indonesia (West Irian) on W, Australia on S. **Topography:** Thickly forested mtns. cover much of the center of the country, with lowlands along the coasts. Included are some of the nearby islands of Bismarck and Solomon groups, including Admiralty Is., New Ireland, New Britain, and Bougainville. **Capital:** Port Moresby. **Cities** (1980 cen.): Port Moresby 123,624.

Government: Type: Parliamentary democracy. **Head of state:** Queen Elizabeth II, represented by Gov. Gen. Sir Kingsford Dibela; in office: Mar. 1, 1983. **Head of government:** Prime Min. Michael Somare; b. 1936; in office: Aug. 2, 1982. **Local divisions:** National capital and 20 provinces with elected legislatures. **Armed forces:** regulars 3,500.

Economy: Chief crops: Coffee, coconuts, cocoa. **Minerals:** Gold, copper, silver, gas. **Per capita arable land:** 0.01 acres. **Meat prod.** (1980): pork: 22,000 metric tons. **Fish catch** (1978): 74,200 metric tons. **Electricity prod.** (1981): 1.2 bln. kwh. **Labor force:** 53% agric., 17% ind. and commerce, 10% services.

Finance: Currency: Kina (Oct. 1983: .87 = $1 US). **Gross domestic product** (1979): $2.27 bln. **Per capita income** (1978): $480. **Imports** (1979): $939 mln.; partners: Austral. 41%, Jap. 18%, Sing. 15%. **Exports** (1980): $1.07 bln.; partners: Jap. 34%, W. Ger. 27%, Austral. 9%. **National budget** (1980): $917 mln. revenues; $916 mln. expenditures **International reserves less gold** (Mar. 1984): $487 mln. **Gold:** 63,000 oz t. **Consumer prices** (change in 1983): 7.9%.

Transport: Motor vehicles: in use (1981): 17,700 passenger cars, 24,400 comm. vehicles. **Chief ports:** Port Moresby, Lae.

Communications: Telephones in use (1981): 45,274. **Daily newspaper circ.** (1981) 9 per 1,000 pop.

Health: Life expectancy at birth (1975): 47.5 male; 47.0 female. **Births** (per 1,000 pop. 1978): 45. **Deaths** (per 1,000 pop. 1978): 15. **Natural increase** (1978): 2.7%. **Hospital beds** (per 100,000 pop. 1977): 469. **Physicians** (per 100,000 pop. 1977): 7.

Education (1978): **Literacy:** 32%. **Pop. 5-19:** in school: 29%, teachers per 1,000: 10.

Embassy: 1140 19th St. NW 20036; 659-0856.

Human remains have been found in the interior of New Guinea dating back at least 10,000 years and possibly much earlier. Successive waves of peoples probably entered the country from Asia through Indonesia. Europeans visited in the 15th century, but land claims did not begin until the 19th century, when the Dutch took control of the western half of the island.

The southern half of eastern New Guinea was first claimed by Britain in 1884, and transferred to Australia in 1905. The northern half was claimed by Germany in 1884, but captured in World War I by Australia, which was granted a League of Nations mandate and then a UN trusteeship over the area. The 2 territories were administered jointly after 1949, given self-government Dec. 1, 1973, and became independent Sept. 16, 1975. Australia promised financial aid, and pledged assistance in defense and foreign affairs.

The indigenous population consists of a huge number of tribes, many living in almost complete isolation with mutually unintelligible languages.

Paraguay

Republic of Paraguay

People: Population (1983 est.): 3,526,000. **Age distrib.** (%): 0–14: 41.0; 15–59: 52.0; 60+: 7.0. **Pop. density:** 18.4 per sq. mi. **Urban** (1982): 42.2%. **Ethnic groups:** Mestizos 95%, small Caucasian, Indian, Negro minorities. **Languages:** Spanish (official), Guarani (used by 90%). **Religions:** Roman Catholic (official) 97%.

Geography: Area: 157,047 sq. mi., the size of California. **Location:** One of the 2 landlocked countries of S. America. **Neighbors:** Bolivia on N, Argentina on S, Brazil on E. **Topography:** Paraguay R. bisects the country. To E are fertile plains, wooded slopes, grasslands. To W is the Chaco plain, with marshes and scrub trees. Extreme W is arid. **Capital:** Asunción. **Cities** (1982 cen.): Asunción 455,517.

Government: Type: Constitutional republic with powerful executive branch. **Head of state:** Pres. Alfredo Stroessner; b. Nov. 3, 1912; in office: Aug. 15, 1954. **Local divisions:** 19 departments. **Defense:** 15% of govt. budget (1980).

Economy: Industries: Food processing, wood products, textiles. **Chief crops:** Corn, wheat, cotton, beans, peanuts, tobacco, citrus fruits, yerba mate. **Minerals:** Iron, manganese, limestone. **Other resources:** Forests. **Arable land:** 2%. **Meat prod.** (1980): beef: 110,000 metric. tons; pork: 79,000 metric tons. **Electricity prod.** (1981): 1 bln. kwh. **Labor force:** 44% agric., 34% ind. and commerce, 18% services.

Finance: Currency: Guarani (Mar. 1984 126.00 = $1 US). **Gross domestic product** (1980): $4.5 bln. **Per capita income** 1979 est.): $1,038. **Imports** (1980): $615 mln.; partners: Braz. 27%, Arg. 19%, U.S. 8%. **Exports** (1980): $310 mln.; partners: Arg. 18%, W. Ger. 13%, Braz. 25%. **National budget** (1980): $432 mln. revenues; $424 mln. expenditures. **International reserves less gold** (Mar. 1984): $636 mln. **Gold:** 35,000 oz t. **Consumer prices** (change in 1983): 13.4%.

Transport: Railway traffic (1978): 23 mln. passenger-km; 17 mln. net ton-km. **Motor vehicles:** in use (1980): 25,200 passenger cars, 33,500 comm. vehicles. **Civil aviation** (1982): 479 mln. passenger-km; 2.9 mln. net ton-km. **Chief ports:** Asuncion.

Communications: Television sets: 60,000 in use (1981). **Radios:** 195,000 in use (1981). **Telephones in use** (1981): 58,713. **Daily newspaper circ.** (1982): 78 per 100,000 pop.

Health: Life expectancy at birth (1975): 60.3 male; 63.6 female. **Births** (per 1,000 pop. 1978): 34. **Deaths** (per 1,000 pop. 1978): 7. **Natural increase** (1978): 2.5%. **Hospital beds** (per 100,000 pop. 1977): 135. **Physicians** (per 100,000 pop. 1977): 77. **Infant mortality** (per 1,000 live births 1982): 64.

Education (1978): **Literacy:** 82%. **Pop. 5-19:** in school: 52%, teachers per 1,000: 24.

Embassy: 2400 Massachusetts Ave. NW 20008; 483-6960.

The Guarani Indians were settled farmers speaking a common language before the arrival of Europeans.

Visited by Sebastian Cabot in 1527 and settled as a Spanish possession in 1535, Paraguay gained its independence from Spain in 1811. It lost much of its territory to Brazil, Uruguay, and Argentina in the War of the Triple Alliance, 1865-1870. Large areas were won from Bolivia in the Chaco War, 1932-35.

Gen. Alfredo Stroessner has ruled since 1954. Suppression of the opposition and decimation of small Indian groups has been charged by international rights groups.

Peru

Republic of Peru

People: Population (1983 est.): 18,663,000. **Age distrib.** (%): 0–14: 41.4; 15–59: 54.4; 60+: 4.2. **Pop. density:** 35.83 per sq. mi. **Urban** (1981): 72.6%. **Ethnic groups:** Indians 45%, Mestizos 37%, Caucasians 15%, blacks, Asians. **Languages:** Spanish, Quechua both official, Aymara; 30% speak no Spanish. **Religions:** Roman Catholics over 90%.

Geography: Area: 496,222 sq. mi., five-sixths the size of Alaska. **Location:** On the Pacific coast of S. America. **Neighbors:** Ecuador, Colombia on N, Brazil, Bolivia on E, Chile on S. **Topography:** An arid coastal strip, 10 to 100 mi. wide, supports much of the population thanks to widespread irrigation. The Andes cover 27% of land area. The uplands are well-watered, as are the eastern slopes reaching the Amazon basin, which covers half the country with its forests and jungles. **Capital:** Lima. **Cities** (1979 cen.): Lima 3.1 mln.

Government: Type: Constitutional republic. **Head of state:** Pres. Fernando Belaunde Terry; b. Oct. 7, 1912; in office: July 28, 1980. **Head of government:** Prime Min. Sandro Mariategui; in office: Apr. 9, 1984. **Local divisions:** 24 departments, 1 province. **Defense:** 4% of GDP (1979).

Economy: Industries: Fish meal, steel. **Chief crops:** Cotton, sugar, coffee, rice, potatoes, beans, corn, barley, tobacco. **Minerals:** Copper, lead, molybdenum, silver, zinc, iron, oil. **Crude oil reserves** (1980): 655 mln. bbls. **Other resources:** Wool, sardines. **Arable land:** 3%. **Meat prod.** (1983): beef: 102,000 metric tons; pork: 74,000 metric tons; lamb: 31,000 metric tons. **Fish catch** (1981): 2.7 mln. metric tons. **Electricity prod.** (1981): 10.1 bln. kwh. **Crude steel prod.** (1981): 359,000 metric tons. **Labor force:** 40% agric.; 19% ind. and mining; 41% govt. and other services.

Finance: Currency: Sol (Mar. 1984: 2,685 = $1 US). **Gross domestic product** (1981): $20.1 bln. **Per capita income** (1979): $655. **Imports** (1983): $2.5 bln.; partners: U.S. 33%, W. Ger. 7%. **Exports** (1983): $3.0 bln.; partners: U.S. 33%, Jap.

15%. **Tourists** (1976): 264,000; receipts (1977): $113 mln. **National budget** (1982): $4.7 bln. **International reserves less gold** (Sept. 1983): $2 bln. **Gold:** 1.39 mln. oz t. **Consumer prices** (change in 1983): 111.2%.

Transport: Railway traffic (1978): 528 mln. passenger-km; 612 mln. net ton-km. **Motor vehicles:** in use (1980): 318,000 passenger cars, 169,000 comm. vehicles. **Civil aviation** (1982): 1.6 bln. passenger-km; 94.3 mln. net ton-km. **Chief ports:** Callao, Chimbate, Mollendo.

Communications: Television sets: 850,000 in use (1981). **Radios:** 2.7 mln. in use (1981). **Telephones in use** (1981): 475,500. **Daily newspaper circ.** (1982): 118 per 1,000 pop.

Health: Life expectancy at birth (1983): 56.7 male; 59.7 female. **Births** (per 1,000 pop. 1982): 35.4. **Deaths** (per 1,000 pop. 1982): 10.8. **Natural increase** (1978): 2.6%. **Hospital beds** (per 100,000 pop. 1977): 184. **Physicians** (per 100,000 pop. 1977): 64. **Infant mortality** (per 1,000 live births 1982): 80.

Education (1978): **Literacy:** 72%. **Years compulsory:** 10.

Embassy: 1700 Massachusetts Ave. NW 20036; 833-9860.

The powerful Inca empire had its seat at Cuzco in the Andes covering most of Peru, Bolivia, and Ecuador, as well as parts of Colombia, Chile, and Argentina. Building on the achievements of 800 years of Andean civilization, the Incas had a high level of skill in architecture, engineering, textiles, and social organization.

A civil war had weakened the empire when Francisco Pizarro, Spanish conquistador, began raiding Peru for its wealth, 1532. In 1533 he had the seized ruling Inca, Atahualpa, fill a room with gold as a ransom, then executed him and enslaved the natives.

Lima was the seat of Spanish viceroys until the Argentine liberator, Jose de San Martin, captured it in 1821; Spain was defeated by Simon Bolivar and Antonio J. de Sucre; recognized Peruvian independence, 1824. Chile defeated Peru and Bolivia, 1879-84, and took Tarapaca, Tacna, and Arica; returned Tacna, 1929.

On Oct. 3, 1968, a military coup ousted Pres. Fernando Belaunde Terry. In 1968-74, the military government put through sweeping agrarian changes, and nationalized oil, mining, fishmeal, and banking industries.

Food shortages, escalating foreign debt, and strikes led to another coup, Aug. 29, 1976, and to a slowdown of socialist programs.

After 12 years of military rule, Peru returned to democratic leadership under former Pres. Fernando Belaunde Terry, July 1980. The new government encouraged the return of private enterprise to stimulate the inflation-ridden economy.

Fighting again erupted, Jan. 28, 1981, in the ongoing border dispute between Peru and Ecuador. The border was reopened in April. There was a wave of terrorist bombings during 1981, including the U.S. embassy in August. Terrorist activity, mostly by Maoist groups, continued in 1983 and 1984.

In 1984, there were strikes by farmers, Mar. 1–3, and by the 4 major labor unions, Mar. 22, to protest the government's economic policies.

Philippines

Republic of the Philippines

People: Population (1983 est.): 54,252,000. **Age distrib.** (%): 0–14: 42.9; 15–59: 52.5; 60+: 4.6. **Pop. density:** 415 per sq. mi. **Urban** (1970): 31.8%. **Ethnic groups:** Malays the large majority, Chinese, Americans, Spanish are minorities. **Languages:** Pilipino (based on Tagalog), English both official; numerous others spoken. **Religions:** Roman Catholics 83%, Protestants 9%, Moslems 5%.

Geography: Area: 115,831 sq. mi., slightly larger than Nevada. **Location:** An archipelago off the SE coast of Asia. **Neighbors:** Nearest are Malaysia, Indonesia on S, Taiwan on N. **Topography:** The country consists of some 7,100 islands stretching 1,100 mi. N-S. About 95% of area and population are on 11 largest islands, which are mountainous, except for the heavily indented coastlines and for the central plain on Luzon. **Capital:** Quezon City (Manila is de facto capital). **Cities** (1980 est.): Manila 1.6 mln.; Quezon City 1.1 mln.; Davao 611,311.

Government: Type: Republic. **Head of state:** Pres. Ferdinand E. Marcos; b. Sept. 11, 1917; in office: Dec. 30, 1965 (pres.), Jan. 17, 1973 (premier). **Head of govt:** Prime Min. Cesar Virata; b. Dec. 12, 1930; in office: Apr. 8, 1981. **Local divi-**

sions: 13 regions, 73 provinces, 60 cities. **Defense:** 2.1% of GNP (1983).

Economy: Industries: Food processing, textiles, clothing, drugs, wood prods., appliances. **Chief crops:** Sugar, rice, corn, pineapple, coconut. **Minerals:** Cobalt, copper, gold, nickel, silver, iron, petroleum. **Crude oil reserves** (1980): 25 mln. bbls. **Other resources:** Forests (42% of area). **Per capita arable land:** 0.3 acres. **Meat prod.** (1983): beef: 127,000 metric tons; pork: 480,000 metric tons; lamb: 6,000 metric tons. **Fish catch** (1981): 1.7 mln. metric tons. **Electricity prod.** (1982): 17.6 bln. kwh. **Crude steel prod.** (1981 est.): 350,000 metric tons. **Labor force:** 47% agric., 20% ind. and comm., 13% services.

Finance: Currency: Peso (Mar. 1984: 14.00 = $1 US). **Gross national product** (1982): $39.2 bln. **Per capita income** (1982): $772. **Imports** (1983): $7.9 bln.; partners: U.S. 22%, Jap. 23%, Saudi Ar. 12%. **Exports** (1982): $4.9 bln.; partners: U.S. 31%, Jap. 23%. **Tourists** (1981): 939,000; receipts: $344 mln. **National budget** (1982): $72 bln. **International reserves less gold** (Mar. 1984): $686 mln. **Gold:** 368,000 oz t. **Consumer prices** (change in 1983): 10.9%.

Transport: Railway traffic (1982): 209 mln. passenger-km; 22 mln. net ton-km. **Motor vehicles:** in use (1980): 465,000 passenger cars, 294,800 comm. vehicles. **Civil aviation** (1982): 7.3 bln. passenger-km; 187 mln. freight ton-km. **Chief ports:** Cebu, Manila, Iloilo, Davao.

Communications: Television sets: 1 mln. in use (1981). **Radios:** 2.1 mln. in use (1981). **Telephones in use** (1981): 537,000. **Daily newspaper circ.** (1982): 52 per 1,000 pop.

Health: Life expectancy at birth (1975): 56.9 male; 60.0 female. **Births** (per 1,000 pop. 1978): 35. **Deaths** (per 1,000 pop. 1978): 10. **Natural increase** (1978): 2.4%. **Hospital beds** (1981): 88,070. **Physicians** (1981): 43,736. **Infant mortality** (per 1,000 live births 1982): 59.

Education (1983): **Literacy:** 88%. **Attendance:** 95% in elementary, 57% secondary.

Embassy: 1617 Massachusetts Ave. NW 20036; 483-1414

The Malay peoples of the Philippine islands, whose ancestors probably migrated from Southeast Asia, were mostly hunters, fishers, and unsettled cultivators when first visited by Europeans.

The archipelago was visited by Magellan, 1521. The Spanish founded Manila, 1571. The islands, named for King Philip II of Spain, were ceded by Spain to the U.S. for $20 million, 1898, following the Spanish-American War. U.S. troops suppressed a guerrilla uprising in a brutal 6-year war, 1899-1905.

Japan attacked the Philippines Dec. 8, 1941 (Far Eastern time). Japan occupied the islands during WW II.

On July 4, 1946, independence was proclaimed in accordance with an act passed by the U.S. Congress in 1934. A republic was established.

A rebellion by Communist-led Huk guerrillas was put down by 1954. But urban and rural political violence periodically reappears.

The Philippines and the U.S. have treaties for U.S. military and naval bases and a mutual defense treaty. Riots by radical youth groups and terrorism by leftist guerrillas and outlaws, increased from 1970. On Sept. 21, 1972, Marcos declared martial law. Ruling by decree, he ordered some land reform and stabilized prices. But opposition was suppressed, and a high population growth rate aggravated poverty and unemployment. Political corruption was believed to be widespread. On Jan. 17, 1973, Marcos proclaimed a new constitution with himself as president. His wife received wide powers in 1978 to supervise planning and development.

Martial law was lifted Jan. 17, 1981. Marcos turned over legislative power to the National Assembly, released political prisoners, and said he would no longer rule by decree. He was elected to a new 6-year term as president, June, with 88% of the vote.

The assassination of prominent opposition leader Benigno S. Aquino Jr, Aug. 21, 1983, sparked demonstrations calling for the resignation of Marcos. The May 1984 elections saw Marcos retain his majority in the National Assembly although opponents made a strong showing in key areas like Manila.

Government troops battled Moslem (Moro) secessionists, 1973-76, in southern Mindanao. Fighting resumed, 1977, after a Libyan-mediated agreement on autonomy was rejected by the region's mainly Christian voters.

The archipelago has a coastline of 10,850 mi. Manila Bay, with an area of 770 sq. mi., and a circumference of 120 mi., is the finest harbor in the Far East.

All natural resources of the Philippines belong to the state; their exploitation is limited to citizens of the Philippines or corporations of which 60% of the capital is owned by citizens.

Poland
Polish People's Republic

People: Population (1983 est.): 36,566,000. **Age distrib. (%):** 0–14: 23.9; 15–59: 62.7; 60+: 13.5. **Pop. density:** 295.61 per sq. mi. **Urban** (1978): 57.5%. **Ethnic groups:** Polish 98%, Germans, Ukrainians, Byelorussians. **Language:** Polish. **Religions:** Roman Catholic 95%.

Geography: Area: 120,727 sq. mi. **Location:** On the Baltic Sea in E Central Europe. **Neighbors:** E. Germany on W, Czechoslovakia on S, USSR (Lithuania, Byelorussia, Ukraine) on E. **Topography:** Mostly lowlands forming part of the Northern European Plain. The Carpathian Mts. along the southern border rise to 8,200 ft. **Capital:** Warsaw. **Cities** (1979): Warsaw 1.5 mln., Lodz 832,000, Cracow 705,000, Wroclaw 608,000, Poznan 544,000.

Government: Type: Communist. **Head of state:** Chairman, council of state: Henryk Jablonski, b. Dec. 27, 1909; in office: Mar. 28, 1972. **Head of government:** Premier Wojciech Jaruzelski; in office: Oct. 18, 1981. **Local divisions:** 49 provinces. **Defense:** 4.9% of govt. budget (1982).

Economy: Industries: Shipbuilding, chemicals, metals, autos, food processing. **Chief crops:** Grains, potatoes, sugar beets, tobacco, flax. **Minerals:** Coal, copper, silver, zinc, sulphur, natural gas. **Per capita arable land:** 1.0 acres. **Meat prod.** (1983): beef: 600,000 metric tons; pork: 1.4 mln. metric tons; lamb: 17,000 metric tons. **Fish catch** (1981): 630,000 metric tons. **Electricity prod.** (1982): 117 bln. kwh. **Crude steel prod.** (1982): 14.4 mln. metric tons. **Labor force:** 27% agric.; 41% manuf.

Finance: Currency: Zloty (Sept. 1983: 95.49 = $1 US). **Gross national product** (1982): $170 bln. **Per capita income** (1982): $4,670. **Imports** (1982): $4.6 bln.; partners: USSR 38%, E. Ger. 7% W. Ger. 7% Czech. 5%. **Exports** (1982): $4.9 bln.; partners: USSR 30%, E. Ger. 6%, Czech. 6%, W. Ger. 10%. **National budget** (1982): 19.1 bln. **Tourists** (1981): 2.1 mln. **Consumer prices** (change in 1982): 100%.

Transport: Railway traffic (1982): 48.9 bln. passenger-km; 112.6 bln. net ton-km. **Motor vehicles:** in use (1982): 2.8 mln. passenger cars, 615,000 comm. vehicles; manuf. (1982): 229,000 passenger cars; 47,000 comm. vehicles. **Civil aviation** (1982): 778 mln. passenger-km; 6.4 mln. freight ton-km. **Chief ports:** Gdansk, Gdynia, Szczecin.

Communications: Television sets: 8.1 mln. licensed (1981), 972,000 manuf. (1978). **Radios:** 8.7 mln. licensed (1981), 2.5 mln. manuf. (1978). **Telephones in use** (1981): 3.3 mln. **Daily newspaper circ.** (1982): 287 per 1,000 pop.

Health: Life expectancy at birth (1980): 66 male; 74.4 female. **Births** (per 1,000 pop. 1982): 19.4. **Deaths** (per 1,000 pop. 1982): 9.2. **Natural increase** (1978): 1.0%. **Hospital beds** (1981): 239,000. **Physicians** (1981): 65,012. **Infant mortality** (per 1,000 live births 1982): 20.2.

Education (1983): **Literacy:** 98%. **Years compulsory:** 8; attendance 98%.

Embassy: 2640 16th St. NW 20009; 234-3800.

Slavic tribes in the area were converted to Latin Christianity in the 10th century. Poland was a great power from the 14th to the 17th centuries. In 3 partitions (1772, 1793, 1795) it was apportioned among Prussia, Russia, and Austria. Overrun by the Austro-German armies in World War I, its independence, self-declared on Nov.11, 1918, was recognized by the Treaty of Versailles, June 28, 1919. Large territories to the east were taken in a war with Russia, 1921.

Nazi Germany and the USSR invaded Poland Sept. 1-27, 1939, and divided the country. During the war, some 6 million Polish citizens were killed by the Nazis, half of them Jews. With Germany's defeat, a Polish government-in-exile in London was recognized by the U.S., but the USSR pressed the claims of a rival group. The election of 1947 was completely dominated by the Communists.

In compensation for 69,860 sq. mi. ceded to the USSR, 1945, Poland received approx. 40,000 sq. mi. of German territory E of the Oder-Neisse line comprising Silesia, Pomerania, West Prussia, and part of East Prussia.

In 12 years of rule by Stalinists, large estates were abolished, industries nationalized, schools secularized, and Roman Catholic prelates jailed. Farm production fell off. Harsh working conditions caused a riot in Poznan June 28-29, 1956.

A new Politburo, committed to development of a more independent Polish Communism, was named Oct. 1956, with Wladyslaw Gomulka as first secretary of the Communist Party. Collectivization of farms was ended and many collectives were abolished.

In Dec. 1970 workers in port cities rioted because of price rises and new incentive wage rules. On Dec. 20 Gomulka resigned as party leader; he was succeeded by Edward Gierek; the incentive rules were dropped, price rises were revoked.

Poland was the first Communist state to get most-favored nation trade terms from the U.S.

A law promulgated Feb. 13, 1953, required government consent to high Roman Catholic church appointments. In 1956 Gomulka agreed to permit religious liberty and religious publications, provided the church kept out of politics. In 1961 religious studies in public schools were halted. Government relations with the Church improved in the 1970s. The number of priests and churches was greater in 1971 than in 1939.

After 2 months of labor turmoil had crippled the country, the Polish government, Aug. 30, 1980, met the demands of striking workers at the Lenin Shipyard, Gdansk. Among the 21 concessions granted were the right to form independent trade unions and the right to strike — unprecedented political developments in the Soviet bloc. By 1981, 9.5 mln. workers had joined the independent trade union (Solidarity). Farmers won official recognition for their independent trade union in May. Solidarity leaders proposed, Dec. 12, a nationwide referendum on establishing a non-Communist government if the government failed to agree to a series of demands which included access to the mass media and free and democratic elections to local councils in the provinces.

Spurred by the fear of Soviet intervention, the government, Dec. 13, imposed martial law. Public gatherings, demonstrations, and strikes were banned and an internal and external blackout was imposed. Solidarity leaders called for a nationwide strike, but there were only scattered work stoppages. Lech Walesa and other Solidarity leaders were arrested. The U.S. imposed economic sanctions which were lifted when martial law was suspended December 1982.

In 1983 there were demonstrations outside the Lenin Shipyards in March, and antigovernment protests in some 20 cities in May. Pope John Paul II visited his homeland in June.

A government directive ordering the removal of crucifixes from public schools and hospitals sparked student demonstrations in the Mietno region, March 1984.

Portugal
Republic of Portugal

People: Population (1983 est.): 10,008,000. **Age distrib. (%):** 0–14: 27.9; 15–59: 57.9; 60+: 14.3. **Pop. density:** 280.98 per sq. mi. **Ethnic groups:** Homogeneous Mediterranean stock with small African minority. **Languages:** Portuguese. **Religions:** Roman Catholics 97%.

Geography: Area: 36,390 sq. mi., slightly smaller than Indiana. **Location:** At SW extreme of Europe. **Neighbors:** Spain on N, E. **Topography:** Portugal N of Tajus R, which bisects the country NE-SW, is mountainous, cool and rainy. To the S there are drier, rolling plains, and a warm climate. **Capital:** Lisbon. **Cities** (1981 est.): Lisbon 812,400.

Government: Type: Parliamentary democracy. **Head of state:** Pres. Antonio dos Santos Ramalho Eanes; b. Jan. 25, 1935; in office: July 14, 1976. **Head of government:** Prime Min. Mario Soares; b. Dec. 7, 1924; in office: June 9, 1983. **Local divisions:** 18 districts, 2 autonomous regions, one dependency. **Defense:** 3% of GNP (1979).

Economy: Industries: Textiles, footwear, cork, chemicals, fish canning, wine, paper. **Chief crops:** Grains, potatoes, rice, grapes, olives, fruits. **Minerals:** Tungsten, uranium, iron. **Other resources:** Forests (world leader in cork production). **Per capita arable land:** 0.8 acres. **Meat prod.** (1983): beef: 117,000 metric tons; pork: 183,000 metric tons; lamb: 25,000 metric tons. **Fish catch** (1981): 255,000 metric tons. **Electricity prod.** (1982): 14.6 bln. kwh. **Crude steel prod.** (1982): 362,000 metric

tons. **Labor force:** 27% agric.; 36% ind. and comm.; 36% services and govt.
Finance: Currency: Escudo (Mar. 1984: 131.67 = $1 US).
Gross domestic product (1982): $23 bln. **Per capita income** (1982): $2,370. **Imports** (1983): $8.1 bln.; partners: W. Ger. 12%, U.S. 11%, UK 8%, Fr. 9%. **Exports** (1983): $4.5 bln.; partners: UK 15%, W. Ger. 13%, Fr. 13%, U.S. 6%. **Tourists** (1981): 3.0 min.; receipts: $1.0 bln. **National budget** (1982): $5.3 bln. expenditures. **International reserves less gold** (Jan. 1984): $277 mln. **Gold:** 20.43 mln. oz t. **Consumer prices** (change in 1983): 25.1%.
Transport: Railway traffic (1982): 5.4 bln. passenger-km; 1.0 bln. net ton-km. **Motor vehicles:** in use (1980): 1.2 mln. passenger cars, 186,100 comm. vehicles. **Civil aviation** (1982): 4.1 bln. passenger-km; 106.7 mln. freight ton-km. **Chief ports:** Lisbon, Setubal, Leixoes.
Communications: Television sets: 1.3 mln. licensed (1981). **Radios:** 1.5 licensed (1981). **Telephones in use** (1981): 1.3 mln. **Daily newspaper circ.** (1982): 74 per 1,000 pop.
Health: Life expectancy at birth (1980): 66 male; 74 female. **Births** (per 1,000 pop. 1978): 17.1. **Deaths** (per 1,000 pop. 1978): 9.8. **Natural increase** (1977): .9%. **Hospital beds** (per 100,000 pop. 1977): 528. **Physicians** (per 100,000 pop. 1977): 142. **Infant mortality** (per 1,000 live births 1983): 35.
Education (1983): **Literacy:** 80%, **Years compulsory:** 6; attendance 60%.
Embassy: 2125 Kalorama Rd. NW 20008; 265-1643.

Portugal, an independent state since the 12th century, was a kingdom until a revolution in 1910 drove out King Manoel II and a republic was proclaimed.

From 1932 a strong, repressive government was headed by Premier Antonio de Oliveira Salazar. Illness forced his retirement in Sept. 1968; he was succeeded by Marcello Caetano.

On Apr. 25, 1974, the government was seized by a military junta led by Gen. Antonio de Spinola, who was named president.

The new government reached agreements providing independence for Guinea-Bissau, Mozambique, Cape Verde Islands, Angola, and Sao Tome and Principe. Spinola resigned Sept. 30, 1974, in face of increasing pressure from leftist officers. Despite a 64% victory for democratic parties in April 1975, the Soviet-supported Communist party increased its influence. Banks, insurance companies, and other industries were nationalized. A countercoup in November halted this trend. After years of turmoil the economy and political life were in disarray, despite aid from the U.S. and West European countries.

Azores Islands, in the Atlantic, 740 mi. W. of Portugal, have an area of 888 sq. mi. and a pop. (1975) of 292,000. A 1951 agreement gave the U.S. the rights to use defense facilities in the Azores. The **Madeira Islands,** 350 mi. off the NW coast of Africa, have an area of 307 sq. mi. and a pop. (1976) of 270,000. Both groups were offered partial autonomy in 1976.

Macao, area of 6 sq. mi., is an enclave, a peninsula and 2 small islands, at the mouth of the Canton R. in China. Portugal granted broad autonomy in 1976. Pop. (1981 est.): 276,700.

Qatar

State of Qatar

People: Population (1983 est.): 267,000. **Pop. density:** 55.0 per sq. mi. **Ethnic groups:** Arabs 40%, Pakistani 18%, Indian 18%, Iranian 10%, others. **Languages:** Arabic (official), English. **Religions:** Moslems 95%.
Geography: Area: 4,247 sq. mi., smaller than Connecticut. **Location:** Occupies peninsula on W coast of Persian Gulf. **Neighbors:** Saudi Arabia on W, United Arab Emirates on S. **Topography:** Mostly a flat desert, with some limestone ridges, vegetation of any kind is scarce. **Capital:** Doha. **Cities** (1983 est.): Doha 190,000.
Government: Type: Traditional emirate. **Head of state and head of government:** Khalifah ibn Hamad ath-Thani; b. 1932; in office: Feb. 22, 1972 (amir), 1970 (prime min.) **Defense:** 18% of govt. budget (1981).
Economy: Crude oil reserves (1981): 4.76 mln. bbls. **Per capita arable land:** 0.02 acres. **Electricity prod.** (1981): 2.5 bln. kwh. **Crude steel prod.** (1981 est.): 469,000 metric tons. **Labor force:** 10% agric., 70% ind., services and commerce.
Finance: Currency: Riyal (Feb. 1984: 3.64 = $1 US). **Gross domestic product** (1981 est.): $6 bln. **Per capita income**

(1981): $29,000. **Imports** (1981): $1.5 bln.; partners: Jap. 20%, UK 16%, U.S. 11%. **Exports** (1981): $5.8 bln.; partners: Neth. 11%, Jap. 35%, Fr. 13%. **National budget** (1981): $4.2 bln. expenditures. **International reserves less gold** (Sept. 1983): $351.4 mln. **Gold:** 1.04 mln. oz. t.
Transport: Chief ports: Doha, Musayid.
Communications: Radios: 40,000 in use (1976). **Telephones in use** (1981): 53,324.
Health: Life expectancy at birth (1982): 57.5 years. **Hospital beds** (per 100,000 pop. 1977): 389. **Physicians** (per 100,000 pop. 1977): 105.
Education (1982): **Literacy:** 40%. **Pop. 6-16:** in school: 98%, teachers per 1,000: 48.
Embassy: 600 New Hampshire Ave. NW 20037; 338-0111.

Qatar was under Bahrain's control until the Ottoman Turks took power, 1872 to 1915. In a treaty signed 1916, Qatar gave Great Britain responsibility for its defense and foreign relations. After Britain announced it would remove its military forces from the Persian Gulf area by the end of 1971, Qatar sought a federation with other British protected States in the area; this failed and Qatar declared itself independent, Sept. 1 1971.

Oil revenues give Qatar a per capita income among the highest in the world, but lack of skilled labor hampers development plans.

Romania

Socialist Republic of Romania

People: Population (1983 est.): 22,579,000. **Age distrib.** (%): 0–14: 25.4; 15–59; 60.5; 60+: 14.2. **Pop. density:** 245.3 per sq. mi. **Urban** (1982): 49.6%. **Ethnic groups:** Romanians 88.1%, Hungarians 7.9%, Germans 1.6%. **Languages:** Romanian, Hungarian, German. **Religions:** Orthodox 80%, Roman Catholics 6%.
Geography: Area: 91,699 sq. mi., slightly smaller than New York and Pennsylvania combined. **Location:** In SE Europe on the Black Sea. **Neighbors:** USSR on E (Moldavia) and N (Ukraine), Hungary, Yugoslavia on W, Bulgaria on S. **Topography:** The Carpathian Mts. encase the north-central Transylvanian plateau. There are wide plains S and E of the mountains, through which flow the lower reaches of the rivers of the Danube system. **Capital:** Bucharest. **Cities** (1980 est.): Bucharest 1,861,007, Brasov 299,172, Timisoara 281,320, Constanta 279,308.
Government: Type: Communist. **Head of state:** Pres. Nicolae Ceausescu; b. Jan. 26, 1918; in office; Dec. 9, 1967. **Head of government:** Prime Min. Constantin Dascalescu; in office; May 21, 1982. **Head of Communist Party:** Pres. Nicolae Ceausescu; in office: Mar. 23, 1965. **Local divisions:** Bucharest and 40 counties. **Defense:** 11.7% of net national product (1982).
Economy: Industries: Steel, metals, machinery, oil products, chemicals, textiles, shoes, tourism. **Chief crops:** Corn, wheat, oilseeds, potatoes. **Minerals:** Oil, gas, coal. **Other resources:** Timber. **Arable land:** 41%. **Meat prod.** (1983): beef: 320,000 metric tons; pork: 1 mln. metric tons; lamb: 79,000 metric tons. **Fish catch** (1978): 137,700 metric tons. **Electricity prod.** (1981): 70.1 bln. kwh. **Crude steel prod.** (1982): 13.0 mln. metric tons. **Labor force:** 40% agric.; 25% ind. and commerce.
Finance: Currency: Leu (Mar. 1984: 4.47 = $1 US). **Gross domestic product** (1980): $116 bln. **Per capita income** (1980): $5,250. **Imports** (1982): $10.5 bln.; partners: USSR 18%, W. Ger. 6%, U.S. 8%, Iran 7%. **Exports** (1982): $11.5 bln.; partners: USSR 18%, W. Ger. 7%. **Tourists** (1977): 3,684,800; receipts (1976): $112 min. **National budget** (1979): $76 mln. revenues; $75 mln. expenditures. **International reserves less gold** (Oct. 1983): $504 mln. **Gold:** 3.58 mln. oz t.
Transport: Railway traffic (1981): 24.3 bln. passenger-km; 75.2 bln. net ton-km. **Motor vehicles:** in use (1980): 250,000 passenger cars; 130,000 comm. vehicles. **Civil aviation** (1982): 1.1 bln. passenger-km; 10 mln. freight ton-km. **Chief ports:** Constanta, Galati, Braila.
Communications: Television sets: 3.8 mln. licensed (1982). **Radios:** 3.2 mln. licensed (1982). **Telephones in use** (1981): 1.6 mln. **Daily newspaper circ.** (1982): 181 per 1,000 pop.
Health: Life expectancy at birth (1980): 68.0 male; 73.0 female. **Births** (per 1,000 pop. 1981): 17. **Deaths** (per 1,000 pop 1981): 10.4. **Natural increase** (1981): 7.0%. **Hospital beds**

(1980): 208,213. **Physicians** (1980): 39,791. **Infant mortality** (per 1,000 live births 1983): 31.
Education (1983): **Literacy:** 98%. **Years compulsory:** 10; attendance 98%.
Embassy: 1607 23d St. NW 20008; 232-4747.

Romania's earliest known people merged with invading Proto-Thracians, preceding by centuries the Dacians. The Dacian kingdom was occupied by Rome, 106 AD-271 AD; people and language were Romanized. The principalities of Wallachia and Moldavia, dominated by Turkey, were united in 1859, became Romania in 1861. In 1877 Romania proclaimed independence from Turkey, became an independent state by the Treaty of Berlin, 1878, a kingdom, 1881, under Carol I. In 1886 Romania became a constitutional monarchy with a bicameral legislature.
Romania helped Russia in its war with Turkey, 1877-78. After World War I it acquired Bessarabia, Bukovina, Transylvania, and Banat. In 1940 it ceded Bessarabia and Northern Bukovina to the USSR and part of Southern Dobrudja to Bulgaria.
Marshal Ion Antonescu, leader of a militarist movement, forced Romania to join Germany against the USSR in World War II in 1941. In 1944 Antonescu was overthrown by King Michael with Soviet help and Romania joined the Allies.
With occupation by Soviet troops the Communist-headed National Democratic Front displaced the National Peasant party. A People's Republic was proclaimed, Dec. 30, 1947; Michael was forced to abdicate. Land owners were dispossessed; most banks, factories and transportation units were nationalized.
On Aug. 22, 1965, a new constitution proclaimed Romania a Socialist, rather than a People's Republic. Since 1966, Romania has adopted an independent attitude toward the USSR. Since 1959, USSR troops have not been permitted to enter Romania.
Internal policies remain oppressive. Ethnic Hungarians have protested cultural and job discrimination.
Romania has become industrialized, but lags in consumer goods and in personal freedoms. All industry is state owned, and state farms and cooperatives own over 90% of arable land.
A major earthquake struck Bucharest in March, 1977, killing over 1,300 people and causing extensive damage to housing and industry.
In 1982, Romania asked Western creditors for a rescheduling of debt repayments which totaled some $3 billion.

Rwanda

Republic of Rwanda

People: Population (1983 est.): 5,644,000. **Age distrib.** (%): 0-14: 50.8; 15-59: 46.2; 60+: 3.0. **Pop. density:** 496.61 per sq. mi. **Urban** (1978): 4.3%. **Ethnic groups:** Hutu 85%, Tutsi 14%, Twa (pygmies) 1%. **Languages:** French, Kinyarwandu (both official), Swahili. **Religions:** Christian 65%, traditional 34%.
Geography: Area: 10,169 sq. mi., the size of Maryland. **Location:** In E central Africa. **Neighbors:** Uganda on N, Zaire on W, Burundi on S, Tanzania on E. **Topography:** Grassy uplands and hills cover most of the country, with a chain of volcanoes in the NW. The source of the Nile R. has been located in the headwaters of the Kagera (Akagera) R., SW of Kigali. **Capital:** Kigali. **Cities** (1983 est.): Kigali 150,000.
Government: Type: Republic. **Head of state:** Pres. Juvenal Habyarimana; b. Mar. 8, 1937; in office: July 5, 1973. **Local divisions:** 10 prefectures, 143 communes. **Defense:** 14% of govt. budget (1982).
Economy: Chief crops: Coffee, tea. **Minerals:** Tin, gold, wolframite. **Arable land:** 48%. **Electricity prod.** (1977): 149 mln. kwh. **Labor force:** 93% agric.
Finance: Currency: Franc (Apr. 1984: 96.65 = $1 US). **Gross domestic product** (1982): $1.4 bln. **Per capita income** (1982): $250. **Imports** (1982): $219 mln.; partners: Belg. 16%, Jap. 12%, W. Ger. 9%. **Exports** (1982): $116 mln.; partners: Tanz. 63%, Kenya 13%. **National budget** (1983): $174 mln. revenues; $193 mln. expenditures. **International reserves less gold** (Feb. 1984): $110 mln. **Consumer prices** (change in 1983): 6.8%.
Transport: Motor vehicles: in use (1975): 6,500 passenger cars, 4,800 comm. vehicles.
Communications: Radios: 80,000 in use (1979), 10,000 manuf. (1978). **Telephones in use** (1979): 6,000. **Daily newspaper circ.** (1977): 200; 0.1 per 1,000 pop.

Health: Life expectancy at birth (1983): 45.2 years. **Births** (per 1,000 pop. 1980): 19.5. **Deaths** (per 1,000 pop. 1980): 5.2. **Natural increase** (1978): 3.0%. **Hospital beds** (per 100,000 pop. 1977): 154. **Physicians** (per 100,000 pop. 1977): 13. **Infant mortality** (per 1,000 live births 1983): 137.
Education (1983): **Literacy:** 37%. **Years compulsory:** 8; attendance: 70%.
Embassy: 1714 New Hampshire Ave. NW 20009; 232-2882.

For centuries, the Tutsi (an extremely tall people) dominated the Hutus (90% of the population). A civil war broke out in 1959 and Tutsi power was ended. A referendum in 1961 abolished the monarchic system.
Rwanda, which had been part of the Belgian UN trusteeship of Rwanda-Urundi, became independent July 1, 1962. The government was overthrown in a 1973 military coup. Rwanda is one of the most densely populated countries in Africa. All available arable land is being used, and is being subject to erosion. The government has carried out economic and social improvement programs, using foreign aid and volunteer labor on public works projects.

St. Christopher (St. Kitts) and Nevis

People: Population (1983 est.): 44,500. **Ethnic groups:** black 95%. **Language:** English. **Religion:** Protestant 76%.
Geography: Area: 101 sq. mi. in the northern part of the Leeward group of the Lesser Antilles in the eastern Caribbean Sea. **Capital:** Basseterre. **Cities:** (1980 est.): 14,700.
Government: Head of State: Queen Elizabeth represented by Sir Clement Aurindell. **Head of Government:** Prime Minister Kennedy A. Simmonds; b. Apr. 12, 1936; in office: Sept. 19, 1983.
Economy: Sugar is the principal industry.
Finance: Currency: E. Caribbean Dollar (Mar. 1984): 2.70 = $1 U.S.
Communications: 3,290 telephones (1982).
Education: school compulsory ages 5-14.

St. Christopher (known by the natives as Liamuiga) and Nevis were discovered and named by Columbus in 1493. They were settled by Britain in 1623, but ownership was disputed with France until 1713. They were part of the Leeward Islands Federation, 1871-1956, and the Federation of the W. Indies, 1958-62. The colony achieved self-government as an Associated State of the UK in 1967, and became fully independent Sept. 19, 1983. Nevis, the smaller of the islands, has the right of secession.

Saint Lucia

People: Population (1983 est.): 119,000. **Age distrib.** (%): 0-20: 49.6; 21-64: 42.7; 65+: 7.7. **Pop. density:** 462.18 per sq. mi. **Ethnic groups:** Predominantly African descent. **Languages:** English (official), French patois. **Religions:** Roman Catholic 90%.
Geography: Area: 238 sq. mi., about one-fifth the size of Rhode Island. **Location:** In Eastern Caribbean, 2d largest of the Windward Is. **Neighbors:** Martinique to N, St. Vincent to SW. **Topography:** Mountainous, volcanic in origin; Soufriere, a volcanic crater, in the S. Wooded mountains run N-S to Mt. Gimie, 3,145 ft., with streams through fertile valleys. **Capital:** Castries. **City:** Castries (1981 est.): 45,000.
Government: Type: Parliamentary democracy. **Head of state:** Queen Elizabeth II, represented by Gov.-Gen. Sir Allen Lewis; **Head of government:** Prime Min. John Compton; in office: May 3, 1982. **Local divisions:** 16 parishes and Castries.
Economy: Industries: Agriculture, tourism, manufacturing. **Chief crops:** Bananas, coconuts, cocoa, citrus fruits. **Other resources:** Forests. **Arable land:** 50%. **Electricity prod.** (1977): 50.00 mln. kwh. **Labor force:** 43.4% agric., 17.7% ind. & commerce, 38.9% services.
Finance: Currency: East Caribbean dollar (Mar. 1984: 2.70 = $1 US). **Gross domestic product** (1979): $99.2 mln. **Per capita income** (1978): $698. **Imports** (1979): $72 mln.; partners: U.S. 36%, UK 12%, Trin./Tob. 11%. **Exports** (1979): $35 mln.; partners: U.S. 28%, UK 25%. **Tourists** (1981): 85,900; receipts: $34 mln. **National budget** (1977-78 est.): $18.4 mln. revenues; $17.2 mln. expenditures.

Transport: Motor vehicles: in use (1980): 5,500 passenger cars, 2,500 comm. vehicles. **Chief ports:** Castries, Vieux Fort. **Communications: Television sets:** 1,700 in use (1975). **Radios:** 82,000 in use (1976). **Telephones in use** (1980): 8,000. **Daily newspaper circ.** (1976): 4,000; 36 per 1,000 pop.

Health: Life expectancy at birth (1981): 65.3 male; 70.6 female. **Births** (per 1,000 pop. 1975): 35.0. **Deaths** (per 1,000 pop. 1975): 7.3. **Natural increase** (1975): 2.8%. **Pop. per hospital bed** (1975): 202. **Pop. per physician** (1975): 4,231. **Infant mortality** (per 1,000 live births 1979): 21.8.

Education: Literacy (1981) 78%; **Pop. 5–15:** in school: 80%.

St. Lucia was ceded to Britain by France at the Treaty of Paris, 1814. Self government was granted with the West Indies Act, 1967. Independence was attained Feb. 22, 1979.

St. Lucia has suffered economic stagnation in the 1980s.

Saint Vincent and the Grenadines

People: Population (1983 est.): 134,000. **Pop. density:** 800 per sq. mi. **Ethnic groups:** Mainly of African descent. **Languages:** English. **Religions:** Methodists, Anglicans, Roman Catholics.

Geography: Area: 150 sq. mi., about twice the size of Washington, D.C. **Location:** In the eastern Caribbean, St. Vincent (133 sq. mi.) and the northern islets of the Grenadines form a part of the Windward chain. **Neighbors:** St. Lucia to N, Barbados to E, Grenada to S. **Topography:** St. Vincent is volcanic, with a ridge of thickly-wooded mountains running its length; Soufriere, rising in the N, erupted in Apr. 1979. **Capital:** Kingstown. **Cities** (1979): Kingstown 23,200.

Government: Head of state: Queen Elizabeth II, represented by Gov.-Gen. Sir Sydney Douglas Gun-Munro; b. Nov. 29, 1916; in office: Jan. 1, 1977. **Head of government:** Robert Milton Cato; b. June 3, 1915; in office: Dec. 11, 1974.

Economy: Industries: Agriculture, tourism. **Chief crops:** Bananas (62% of exports), arrowroot, coconuts. **Per capita arable land:** 0.3 acres. **Electricity prod.** (1977): 20 mln. kwh. **Labor force:** 30% agric.

Finance: Currency: East Caribbean dollar (Mar. 1984: 2.70 = $1 US). **Per capita income** (1979): $250. **Imports** (1979): $36 mln.; partners: UK 23%, Trin./Tob. 14%, Can. 12%, U.S. 20%. **Exports** (1979): $15 mln.; partners: UK 49%, Trin./Tob. 22%. **Tourists** (1981): 83,283. **National budget** (1981): $17 mln. revenues; $20.3 mln. expenditures.

Transport: Motor vehicles: in use (1980): 3,500 passenger cars, 800 comm. vehicles. **Chief ports:** Kingstown.

Communications: Telephones in use (1980): 5,450.

Health: Life expectancy at birth (1961): 58.46 male; 59.67 female. **Births** (per 1,000 pop. 1977): 31. **Deaths** (per 1,000 pop. 1973): 10.0. **Natural increase** (1973): 2.2%. **Infant mortality** (per 1,000 pop. under 1 yr. 1977): 55.

Education (1979): **Literacy:** 95%. **Pop. 5–19:** in school (1975): 26,938; per teacher: 18.5.

Columbus landed on St. Vincent on Jan. 22, 1498 (St. Vincent's Day). Britain and France both laid claim to the island in the 17th and 18th centuries; the Treaty of Versailles, 1783, finally ceded it to Britain. Associated State status was granted 1969; independence was attained Oct. 27, 1979.

The entire economic life of St. Vincent is dependent upon agriculture and tourism.

San Marino

Most Serene Republic of San Marino

People: Population (1983 est.): 22,000. **Age distrib. (%):** 0–14: 24.4; 15–59: 60.3; 60+: 15.3. **Pop. density:** 897 per sq. mi. **Urban** (1970): 92.4%. **Ethnic groups:** Sanmarinese. **Languages:** Italian. **Religions:** Roman Catholics predominate.

Geography: Area: 24 sq. mi. **Location:** In N central Italy near Adriatic coast. **Neighbors:** Completely surrounded by Italy. **Topography:** The country lies on the slopes of Mt. Titano. **Capital:** San Marino. **City** (1981 est.): San Marino 3,000.

Government: Type: Independent republic. **Head of state:** Two co-regents appt. every 6 months. **Local divisions:** 11 districts, 9 sectors.

Economy: Industries: Postage stamps, tourism, woolen goods, paper, cement, ceramics. **Arable land:** 54%.

Finance: Currency: Italian lira. **Tourists** (1980): 3.5 mln.

Communications: Television sets: 4,000 licensed (1976). **Radios:** 6,000 licensed (1976). **Telephones in use** (1981): 7,685. **Daily newspaper circ.** (1976): 1,300; 65 per 1,000 pop.

Births (per 1,000 pop. 1977): 14.2. **Deaths** (per 1,000 pop. 1977): 6.9. **Natural increase** (1977): .8%. **Infant mortality** (per 1,000 live births 1981): 10.8.

San Marino claims to be the oldest state in Europe and to have been founded in the 4th century. A communist-led coalition ruled 1947-57; a similar coalition took power in 1978. It has had a treaty of friendship with Italy since 1862.

Sao Tome and Principe

Democratic Republic of Sao Tome and Principe

People: Population (1983 est.): 88,000. **Pop. density:** 269 per sq. mi. **Ethnic groups:** Portuguese-African mixture, African minority (Angola, Mozambique immigrants). **Languages:** Portuguese. **Religions:** Christian 80%.

Geography: Area: 372 sq. mi., slightly larger than New York City. **Location:** In the Gulf of Guinea about 125 miles off W Central Africa. **Neighbors:** Gabon, Equatorial Guinea on E. **Topography:** Sao Tome and Principe islands, part of an extinct volcano chain, are both covered by lush forests and croplands. **Capital:** Sao Tome. **Cities** (1981 est.): Sao Tome 20,000.

Government: Type: Republic. **Head of state and head of government:** Pres. Manuel Pinto da Costa, b. 1910; in office: July 12, 1975. **Local divisions:** 2 provinces, 12 counties.

Economy: Chief crops: Cocoa (82% of exports), coconut products, cinchona. **Per capita arable land:** 0.03 acres. **Electricity prod.** (1977): 8.00 mln. kwh.

Finance: Currency: Dobra (Sept. 1983): 39.38 = $1 US). **Gross domestic product** (1981 est.): $30 mln. **Per capita income** (1981): $300. **Imports** (1981): $20 mln.; partners: Port. 61%, Angola 13%. **Exports** (1981): $8 mln.; partners: Neth. 52%, Port. 33%, W. Ger. 8%.

Transport: Motor vehicles: in use (1979): 1,300 passenger cars, 1,900 comm. vehicles. **Chief ports:** Sao Tome, Santo Antonio.

Communications: Radios: 20,000 in use (1976).

Health: Births (per 1,000 pop. 1972): 45.0. **Deaths** (per 1,000 pop. 1972): 11.2. **Natural increase** (1972): 3.4%. **Pop. per hospital bed** (1976): 160. **Pop. per physician** (1973): 6,666. **Infant mortality** (per 1,000 live births 1972): 64.3.

Education (1983): **Literacy:** 50%.

The islands were uninhabited when discovered in 1471 by the Portuguese, who brought the first settlers — convicts and exiled Jews. Sugar planting was replaced by the slave trade as the chief economic activity until coffee and cocoa were introduced in the 19th century.

Portugal agreed, 1974, to turn the colony over to the Gabon-based Movement for the Liberation of Sao Tome and Principe, which proclaimed as first president its East German-trained leader Manuel Pinto da Costa. Independence came July 12, 1975.

Agriculture and fishing are the mainstays of the economy.

Saudi Arabia

Kingdom of Saudi Arabia

People: Population (1983 est.): 10,443,000. **Pop. density:** 9.01 per sq. mi. **Ethnic groups:** Arab tribes, immigrants from other Arab and Muslim countries. **Languages:** Arabic. **Religions:** Muslims 99%.

Geography: Area: 830,000 sq. mi., one-third the size of the U.S. **Location:** Occupies most of Arabian Peninsula in Middle East. **Neighbors:** Kuwait, Iraq, Jordan on N, Yemen, South Yemen, Oman on S, United Arab Emirates, Qatar on E. **Topography:** The highlands on W, up to 9,000 ft., slope as an arid, barren desert to the Persian Gulf. **Capital:** Riyadh. **Cities** (1983 est.): Riyadh 1,793,000; Jidda 983,000; Mecca 463,000.

Government: Type: Monarchy with council of ministers. **Head of state and head of government:** King Fahd; b. 1922; in office: June 13, 1982. **Local divisions:** 14 provinces. **Defense:** 29.6% of govt. budget (1983).

Economy: Industries: Oil products. **Chief crops:** Dates, wheat, barley,'fruit. **Minerals:** Oil, gas, gold, silver, iron. **Crude oil reserves** (1981): 178 bln bbls. **Arable land:** 2%. **Meat prod.** (1980): beef: 19,000 metric tons, lamb: 29,000 metric tons. **Electricity prod.** (1982): 25 bln. kwh. **Labor force:** 28% agric.; 4% ind; 44% serv., comm., & govt.; 21% construction.

Finance: Currency: Riyal (Mar. 1984: 3.51 = $1 US). **Gross domestic product** (1982): $165.1 bln. **Per capita income** (1979): $11,500. **Imports** (1982): $40.6 bln.; partners: US 21%, Jap. 18%, W. Ger. 10%. **Exports** (1983): $46.9 bln.; partners: US 13%, Jap., 17%, Fr. 10%. **Tourist receipts** (1981): $1.5 bln. **International reserves less gold** (Mar. 1984): $25.1 bln. **Gold:** 4.59 mln. oz t. **Consumer prices** (change in 1982): 1.1%.

Transport: Railway traffic (1981): 95 mln. passenger-km; 272 mln. net ton-km. **Motor vehicles:** in use (1981): 757,000 passenger cars, 587,000 comm. vehicles. **Civil aviation** (1982): 12.2 bln. passenger-km. 373 mln. net ton-km. **Chief ports:** Jidda, Ad-Dammam, Ras Tannurah.

Communications: Television sets: 1.7 mln. in use (1982). **Radios:** 2.7 mln. in use (1982). **Telephones in use** (1981): 442,514. **Daily newspaper circ.** (1981): 29 per 1,000 pop.

Health: Life expectancy at birth (1982): 54 years. **Births** (per 1,000 pop. 1978): 49. **Deaths** (per 1,000 pop. 1978): 18. **Natural increase** (1978): 5.6%. **Hospital beds** (per 100,000 pop. 1977): 155. **Physicians** (per 100,000 pop. 1982): 118.

Education (1978): **Literacy:** 15%. **Pop. 5-19:** in school: 36%, teachers per 1,000: 22.

Embassy: 1520 18th Street NW 20036; 483-2100.

Arabia was united for the first time by Mohammed, in the early 7th century. His successors conquered the entire Near East and North Africa, bringing Islam and the Arabic language. But Arabia itself soon returned to its former status as political and cultural backwater.

Nejd, long an independent state and center of the Wahhabi sect, fell under Turkish rule in the 18th century, but in 1913 Ibn Saud, founder of the Saudi dynasty, overthrew the Turks and captured the Turkish province of Hasa; took the Hejaz in 1925 and by 1926, most of Asir. The discovery of oil by a U.S. oil company in the 1930s transformed the new country.

Crown Prince Khalid was proclaimed king on Mar. 25, 1975, after the assassination of King Faisal. Fahd became king on June 13, 1982 following Khalid's death. There is no constitution and no parliament. The king exercises authority together with a Council of Ministers. The Islamic religious code is the law of the land. Alcohol and public entertainments are restricted, and women have an inferior legal status.

Saudi units fought against Israel in the 1948 and 1973 Arab-Israeli wars. Many billions of dollars of advanced arms have been purchased from Britain, France, and the U.S., including jet fighters, missiles, and, in 1981, 5 airborne warning and control system (AWACS) aircraft from the U.S., despite strong opposition from Israel. Beginning with the 1967 Arab-Israeli war, Saudi Arabia provided large annual financial gifts to Egypt; aid was later extended to Syria, Jordan, and Palestinian guerrilla groups, as well as to other Moslem countries. The country has aided anti-radical forces in Yemen and Oman.

Faisal played a leading role in the 1973-74 Arab oil embargo against the U.S. and other nations in an attempt to force them to adopt an anti-Israel policy. Saudi Arabia joined most other Arab states, 1979, in condemning Egypt's peace treaty with Israel.

Between 1973 and 1976, Saudi Arabia acquired full ownership of Aramco (Arabian American Oil Co.). In the 1980s, Saudi Arabia's moderate position on crude oil prices has often prevailed at OPEC meetings. Saudi Arabia announced, 1979, it will build a $1 billion causeway linking the island state Bahrain to the Arab mainland.

The Hejaz contains the holy cities of Islam — Medina where the Mosque of the Prophet enshrines the tomb of Mohammed, who died in the city June 7, 632, and Mecca, his birthplace. More than 600,000 Moslems from 60 nations pilgrimage to Mecca annually. The regime faced its first serious opposition when Moslem fundamentalists seized the Grand Mosque in Mecca, Nov. 20, 1979.

Two Saudi oil tankers were attacked May 1984, as Iran and Iraq began air attacks against shipping in the Persian Gulf. On May 29, the U.S., citing grave concern over the growing escala-

tion of the Iran-Iraq war in the Persian Gulf, authorized the sale of 400 Stinger antiaircraft missiles to the Saudis. Saudi warplanes shot down 2 Iranian jets, June 5.

Senegal
Republic of Senegal

People: Population (1983 est.): 6,335,000. **Age distrib. (%):** 0–14: 44.2; 15–59: 50.5; 60+: 5.3. **Pop. density:** 74.35 per sq. mi. **Urban** (1981): 30%. **Ethnic groups:** Wolof 37%, Serer 17%, Peulh 17%, Diola 9%, Mandingo 9%. **Languages:** French (official), tribal languages. **Religions:** Muslims 91%, Christians 6%.

Geography: Area: 75,995 sq. mi., the size of South Dakota. **Location:** At western extreme of Africa. **Neighbors:** Mauritania on N, Mali on E, Guinea, Guinea-Bissau on S, Gambia surrounded on three sides. **Topography:** Low rolling plains cover most of Senegal, rising somewhat in the SE. Swamp and jungles are in SW. **Capital:** Dakar. **Cities** (1979): Dakar 978,553; Thies 126,889; Kaolack 115,679.

Government: Type: Republic. **Head of state:** Pres. Abdou Diouf; b. Sept. 7, 1935; in office: Jan. 1, 1981. **Local divisions:** 8 regions. **Armed forces:** regulars 9,010 (1980).

Economy: Industries: Food processing, fishing. **Chief crops:** Peanuts are chief export; millet, rice. **Minerals:** Phosphates. **Arable land:** 15%. **Meat prod.** (1980): beef: 40,000 metric tons; pork: 8,000 metric tons; lamb: 11,000 metric tons. **Fish catch** (1981): 359,200 metric tons. **Electricity prod.** (1978): 456.00 mln. kwh. **Labor force:** 70% agric.

Finance: Currency: CFA franc (Mar. 1984: 399.00 = $1 US). **Gross domestic product** (1980): $2.2 bln. **Per capita income** (1975): $342. **Imports** (1979): $713 mln.; partners Fr. 37%, U.S. 6%. **Exports** (1979): $426 mln.; partners Fr. 25%, UK 6%. **Tourists** (1979): 198,433. **International reserves less gold** (Jan. 1984): $9.2 mln. **Gold:** 29,000 oz t. **Consumer prices** (change in 1983): 11.7%.

Transport: Railway traffic (1976): 180 mln. passenger-km; 164 mln. net ton-km. **Motor vehicles:** in use (1979): 65,000 passenger cars, 10,000 comm. vehicles. **Chief ports:** Dakar, Saint-Louis.

Communications: Television sets: 40,000 in use (1979). **Radios:** 300,000 in use (1979). **Telephones in use** (1979): 40,000. **Daily newspaper circ.** (1982): 13 per 1,000 pop.

Health: Life expectancy at birth (1975): 39.4 male; 42.5 female. **Births** (per 1,000 pop. 1978): 47. **Deaths** (per 1,000 pop. 1978): 20. **Natural increase** (1978): 2.7%. **Hospital beds** (per 100,000 pop. 1977): 111. **Physicians** (per 100,000 pop. 1977): 2. **Infant mortality** (per 1,000 live births 1981): 158.

Education (1981): **Literacy:** 10%. **Attendance:** 53% primary, 11% secondary.

Embassy: 2112 Wyoming Ave. NW 20008; 234-0540.

Portuguese settlers arrived in the 15th century, but French control grew from the 17th century. The last independent Moslem state was subdued in 1893. Dakar became the capital of French West Africa.

Independence as part, along with the Sudanese Rep., of the Mali Federation, came June 20, 1960. Senegal withdrew Aug. 20 that year. French political and economic influence is strong.

A long drought brought famine, 1972-73, and again in 1978.

Senegal is recognized as the most democratic of the French-speaking West African nations. Opposition parties were allowed to form in 1976, 1979, and 1981.

Senegal, Dec. 17, 1981, signed an agreement with The Gambia for confederation of the 2 countries under the name of Senegambia. The confederation began Feb. 1, 1982. The 2 nations retained their individual sovereignty but adopted joint defense and monetary policies.

Seychelles
Republic of Seychelles

People: Population (1983 est.): 65,000. **Age distrib. (%):** 0–14: 39.7; 15–59: 51.1; 60+: 9.1. **Pop. density:** 409.36 per sq. mi. **Urban** (1977): 37.1% **Ethnic groups:** Creoles (mixture of Asians, Africans, and French) predominate. **Languages:** English and French (both official), Creole. **Religions:** Roman Catholics 90%, Protestants 8%, Hindus, Muslems.

Geography: Area: 171 sq. mi. **Location:** In the Indian O. 700 miles NE of Madagascar. **Neighbors:** Nearest are Madagascar on SW, Somalia on NW. **Topography:** A group of 86 islands, about half of them composed of coral, the other half granite, the latter predominantly mountainous. **Capital:** Victoria. **Cities** (1980): Port Victoria 23,000.

Government: Type: Single party republic. **Head of state:** Pres. France-Albert Rene, b. Nov. 16, 1935; in office: June 5, 1977. **Defense:** 11.7% of govt. budget (1983).

Economy: Industries: Food processing. **Chief crops:** Coconut products, cinnamon, vanilla, patchouli. **Other resources:** Guano, shark fins, tortoise shells, fish. **Electricity prod.** (1981): 50.7 mln. kwh. **Labor force:** 18.5% agric.; 19.4% ind. & comm.; 13.5% serv.; 49% govt.

Finance: Currency: Rupee (Mar. 1984: 6.78 = $1 US). **Gross domestic product** (1980): $1,030. **Imports** (1981): $88.5 mln.; partners: UK 25%, So. Afr. 10%, Bah. 24%. **Exports** (1981): $13 mln.; partners: Pak. 45%. **National Budget** (1983): $65 mln. **Tourists** (1981): 60,425; receipts: $41 mln. **International reserves less gold** (Mar. 1984): $6.97 mln. **Consumer prices** (change in 1983): 6.1%.

Transport: Motor vehicles: in use (1979): 5,000 passenger cars, 900 comm. vehicles. **Port:** Victoria.

Communications: Radios: 17,000 in use (1976). **Telephones in use** (1981): 7,105. **Daily newspaper circ.** (1982): 63 per 1,000 pop.

Health: Life expectancy at birth (1983): 66 years. **Births** (per 1,000 pop. 1982: 24.0. **Deaths** (per 1,000 pop. 1982): 7.5. **Natural increase** (1977): 1.8%. **Hospital beds** (1981): 315. **Physicians** (1981): 45. **Infant mortality** (per 1,000 live births 1982): 19.4.

Education (1983): **Literacy:** 60%. **Years compulsory** 9; attendance 95%.

Embassy: 820 2d Ave., New York, NY 10017; (212) 687-9766.

The islands were occupied by France in 1768, and seized by Britain in 1794. Ruled as part of Mauritius from 1814, the Seychelles became a separate colony in 1903. The ruling party had opposed independence as impractical, but pressure from the OAU and the UN became irresistible, and independence was declared June 29, 1976. The first president was ousted in a coup a year later by a socialist leader.

A new Constitution, announced Mar. 1979, turned the country into a one-party state.

Sierra Leone
Republic of Sierra Leone

People: Population (1983 est.): 3,705,000. **Age distrib. (%):** 0–14: 40.6; 15–59: 51.5; 60+: 7.8. **Pop. density:** 124.26 per sq. mi. **Ethnic groups:** Temne 30%, Mende 30%, others. **Languages:** English (official), tribal languages. **Religions:** animist 30%, Muslims 60%.

Geography: Area: 27,699 sq. mi., slightly smaller than South Carolina. **Location:** On W coast of W. Africa. **Neighbors:** Guinea on N, E, Liberia on S. **Topography:** The heavily-indented, 210-mi. coastline has mangrove swamps. Behind are wooded hills, rising to a plateau and mountains in the E. **Capital:** Freetown. **Cities** (1982 est.): Freetown 375,000; Bo, Kenema, Makeni.

Government: Type: Republic. **Head of state and head of government:** Pres. Siaka P. Stevens; b. Aug. 24, 1905; in office: Apr. 21, 1971 (state), June 14, 1978 (gov't.). **Local divisions:** 3 provinces and one region including Freetown.

Economy: Industries: Mining, tourism. **Chief crops:** Cocoa, coffee, palm kernels, rice, ginger. **Minerals:** Diamonds, bauxite. **Arable land:** 8%. **Fish catch** (1981): 49,000 metric tons. **Electricity prod.** (1981): 235 mln. kwh. **Labor force:** 75% agric.; 15% ind. & serv.

Finance: Currency: Leone (Sept. 1983: 2.50 = $1 US). **Gross national product** (1981): $1.1 bln. **Per capita income** (1980): $176. **Imports** (1982): $323 mln.; partners: UK 22%, Fr. 11%. **Exports** (1982): $80 mln.; partners: UK 40%, U.S. 27%. **National budget** (1981): $185 mln. revenues; $161 mln. ex-

penditures. **International reserves less gold** (Mar. 1984): $10.8 mln. **Consumer prices** (change in 1982): 33%.

Transport: Motor Vehicles: in use (1979): 70,000 passenger cars, 33,000 comm. vehicles. **Chief ports:** Freetown, Bonthe.

Communications: Television sets: 20,000 in use (1981). **Radios:** 500,000 in use (1981). **Telephones in use** (1981): 220,000. **Daily newspaper circ.** (1982): 3 per 1,000 pop.

Health: Life expectancy at birth (1984): 46 yrs. **Births** (per 1,000 pop. 1978): 45. **Deaths** (per 1,000 pop. 1978): 27. **Natural increase** (1978): 1.9%. **Hospital beds** (per 100,000 pop. 1977): 99. **Physicians** (per 100,000 pop. 1979): 7.

Education (1984): **Literacy:** 15%.

Embassy: 1701 19th St. NW 20009; 939-9261.

Freetown was founded in 1787 by the British government as a haven for freed slaves. Their descendants, known as Creoles, number more than 60,000.

Successive steps toward independence followed the 1951 constitution. Full independence arrived Apr. 27, 1961. Sierra Leone became a republic Apr. 19, 1971. A one-party state approved by referendum 1978, brought political stability, but the economy has been plagued by inflation, corruption, and dependence upon the International Monetary Fund and creditors.

Singapore
Republic of Singapore

People: Population (1983 est.): 2,501,000. **Age distrib. (%):** 0–14: 27; 15–59: 65.8; 60+: 7.2. **Pop. density:** 10,700 per sq. mi. **Ethnic groups:** Chinese 77%, Malays 15%, Indians 6%. **Languages:** Chinese, Malay, Tamil, English all official. **Religions:** Buddhism, Taoism, Islam, Hinduism, Christianity.

Geography: Area: 239 sq. mi., smaller than New York City. **Location:** Off tip of Malayan Peninsula in S.E. Asia. **Neighbors:** Nearest are Malaysia on N, Indonesia on S. **Topography:** Singapore is a flat, formerly swampy island. The nation includes 40 nearby islets. **Capital:** Singapore. **Cities** (1978 est.): Singapore 2,334,400.

Government: Type: Parliamentary democracy. **Head of state:** Pres. Chengara Veetil Devan Nair; in office: Oct. 21, 1981. **Head of government:** Prime Min. Lee Kuan Yew; b. Sept. 16, 1923; in office: June 5, 1959. **Defense:** 15% of govt. budget (1981).

Economy: Industries: Shipbuilding, oil refining, electronics, banking, textiles, food, rubber, lumber processing, tourism. **Meat prod.** (1980): pork: 43,000 metric tons. **Fish catch** (1981): 16,111 metric tons. **Electricity prod.** (1982): 7.8 bln. kwh. **Crude steel prod.** (1981): 350,000 metric tons. **Labor force:** 2% agric.; 52% ind. & comm.; 33% services.

Finance: Currency: Dollar (Mar. 1984: 2.08 = $1 US). **Gross domestic product** (1980): $9.01 bln. **Per capita income** (1980): $4,100. **Imports** (1983): $28.1 bln.; partners: Jap. 18%, Malay. 13%, U.S. 13%, Sau. Ar. 16%. **Exports** (1983): $21.8 bln., partners: U.S. 13%, Malay. 18%, Jap. 11%, HK 8%. **Tourists** (1981): 2.8 mln.; receipts $1 bln. **National budget** (1984): $5.1 bln. revenues; $8.1 bln. expenditures. **International reserves** (Nov. 1983): $9.2 bln. **Consumer prices** (change in 1983): 1.2%.

Transport: Motor vehicles: in use (1982): 194,400 passenger cars, 96,900 comm. vehicles. **Civil aviation:** (1982) 18.1 bln. passenger-km; 758 mln. freight ton-km.

Communications: Television sets: 424,100 licensed (1983). **Radios:** 608,000 licensed (1983). **Telephones in use** (1983): 852,000. **Daily newspaper circ.** (1982): 264 per 1,000 pop.

Health: Life expectancy at birth (1982): 67.5 years. **Births** (per 1,000 pop. 1981: 17.0. **Deaths** (per 1,000 pop. 1981): 5.3. **Natural increase** (1978): 1.2%. **Hospital beds** (1981): 8,365. **Physicians** (1981): 2,091. **Infant mortality** (per 1,000 live births 1982): 11.7.

Education (1982): **Literacy:** 84%. **Years compulsory:** none; attendance 66%.

Embassy: 1824 R St. NW 20009; 667-7555.

Founded in 1819 by Sir Thomas Stamford Raffles, Singapore was a British colony until 1959 when it became autonomous within the Commonwealth. On Sept. 16, 1963, it joined with Malaya, Sarawak and Sabah to form the Federation of Malaysia.

Tensions between Malayans, dominant in the federation, and ethnic Chinese, dominant in Singapore, led to an agreement under which Singapore became a separate nation, Aug. 9, 1965. Singapore is one of the world's largest ports. Standards in health, education, and housing are high. International banking has grown.

Solomon Islands

People: Population (1983 est.): 254,000. **Age distrib. (%):** 0–14: 49; 15–59: 47.5; 60+: 3.5. **Pop. density:** 18.26 per sq. mi. **Urban** (1976): 9.1%. **Ethnic groups:** A variety of Melanesian groups and mixtures, some Polynesians. **Languages:** English (official), Pidgin, local languages. **Religions:** Anglican 34%, Roman Catholic 19%, Evangelical 24%, traditional religions. **Geography: Area:** 10,640 sq. mi., slightly larger than Maryland. **Location:** Melanesian archipelago in the western Pacific O. **Neighbors:** Nearest is Papua New Guinea on W. **Topography:** 10 large volcanic and rugged islands and 4 groups of smaller ones. **Capital:** Honiara. **Cities:** (1981): Honiara 19,200.

Government: Type: Parliamentary democracy within the Commonwealth of Nations. **Head of state:** Queen Elizabeth II, represented by Gov.-Gen. Baddeley Devesi; b. Oct. 16, 1941; in office: July 7, 1978. **Head of government:** Prime Min. Solomon Mamaloni; in office: Aug. 31, 1981. **Local divisions:** 7 provinces and Honiara.

Economy: Industries: Fish canning. **Chief crops:** Coconuts, rice, bananas, yams. **Other resources:** Forests, marine shell. **Per capita arable land:** 0.6 acres. **Fish catch** (1980): 21,578 metric tons. **Electricity prod.** (1977): 18.00 mln. kwh. **Labor force:** 32% agric., 32% services, 18% ind. & comm.

Finance: Currency: Dollar (Sept. 1983: 1.19 = $1 US). **Gross domestic product** (1978): $93.9 mln. **Per capita income** (1978): $440. **Imports** (1979): $57 mln.; partners: Austral. 29%, Jap. 14%, UK 7%, Sing. 23%. **Exports** (1979): $67 mln.; partners: Jap. 37%, U.S. 22%, UK 12%, Neth. 12%.

Communications: Radios: 11,000 in use (1976). **Telephones in use** (1981): 2,474.

Health: Births (per 1,000 pop. 1978): 44. **Deaths** (per 1,000 pop. 1978): 9. **Natural increase** (1978): 3.5%. **Infant mortality** (per 1,000 live births 1981): 52.

The Solomon Islands were sighted in 1568 by an expedition from Peru. Britain established a protectorate in the 1890s over most of the group, inhabited by Melanesians. The islands saw major World War II battles. Self-government came Jan. 2, 1976, and independence was formally attained July 7, 1978.

Somalia
Somali Democratic Republic

People: Population (1983 est.): 6,248,000. **Pop. density:** 14.83 per sq. mi. **Ethnic groups:** mainly Hamitic, others. **Languages:** Somali, Arabic (both official). **Religions:** Sunni Muslims 99%. **Geography: Area:** 246,300 sq. mi., slightly smaller than Texas. **Location:** Occupies the eastern horn of Africa. **Neighbors:** Djibouti, Ethiopia, Kenya on W. **Topography:** The coastline extends for 1,700 mi. Hills cover the N; the center and S are flat. **Capital:** Mogadishu. **Cities** (1981 est.): Mogadishu 400,000.

Government: Head of state: Pres. Mohammed Siad Barrah; b. 1919; in office: Oct. 21, 1969. **Local divisions:** 17 regions. **Armed forces:** regulars 61,000 (1980).

Economy: Chief crops: Incense, sugar, bananas, sorghum, corn, gum. **Minerals:** Iron, tin, gypsum, bauxite, uranium. **Arable land:** 2%. **Meat prod.** (1980): beef: 45,000 metric tons; lamb: 66,000 metric tons. **Fish catch** (1978): 32,600 metric tons. **Electricity prod.** (1981): 75 mln. kwh. **Labor force:** 60% agric.

Finance: Currency: Shilling (Mar. 1984: 15.26 = $1 US). **Gross domestic product** (1978 est.): $407 mln. **Per capita income** (1978): $105. **Imports** (1979): $287 mln.; partners: It. 35%, UK 8%, U.S. 9%. **Exports** (1979): $111 mln.; partners: Saudi Ar. 66%, It. 12%. **International reserves less gold** (Sept. 1983): $3.2 mln. **Gold:** 19,000 oz t. **Consumer prices** (change in 1982): 23.6%.

Transport: Motor vehicles: in use (1980): 17,200 passenger cars, 8,050 comm. vehicles. **Chief ports:** Mogadishu, Berbera.

Communications: Radios: 87,000 in use (1981). **Daily newspaper circ.** (1970): 4,500; 2 per 1,000 pop.

Health: Life expectancy at birth (1975): 39.4 male; 42.6 female. **Births** (per 1,000 pop. 1978): 48. **Deaths** (per 1,000 pop. 1978): 22. **Natural increase** (1978): 2.6%. **Hospital beds** (per 100,000 pop. 1977): 179. **Physicians** (per 100,000 pop. 1977): 3.

Education (1978): Literacy: 5%. **Pop. 5-19:** in school: 19%, teachers per 1,000: 7.

Embassy: 600 New Hampshire Ave. NW 20037; 342-1575.

Arab trading posts developed into sultanates. The Italian Protectorate of Somalia, acquired from 1885 to 1927, extended along the Indian O. from the Gulf of Aden to the Juba R. The UN in 1949 approved eventual creation of Somalia as a sovereign state and in 1950 Italy took over the trusteeship held by Great Britain since World War II.

British Somaliland was formed in the 19th century in the NW. Britain gave it independence June 26, 1960; on July 1 it joined with the former Italian part to create the independent Somali Republic.

On Oct. 21, 1969, a Supreme Revolutionary Council seized power in a bloodless coup, named a Council of Secretaries of State, and abolished the Assembly. In May, 1970, several foreign companies were nationalized.

A severe drought in 1975 killed tens of thousands, and spurred efforts to resettle nomads on collective farms.

Somalia has laid claim to Ogaden, the huge eastern region of Ethiopia, peopled mostly by Somalis. Ethiopia battled Somali rebels and accused Somalia of sending troops and heavy arms in 1977. Russian forces were expelled in 1977 in retaliation for Soviet support of Ethiopia. Some 11,000 Cuban troops with Soviet arms defeated Somali army troops and ethnic Somali rebels in Ethiopia, 1978. As many as 1.5 mln. refugees entered Somalia. Guerrilla fighting in Ogaden has continued, although the Somali government no longer officially supports the Ogaden secessionists.

South Africa
Republic of South Africa

People: Population (1983 est.): 30,938,000. **Age distrib. (%):** 0–14: 41.5; 15–59: 54.5; 60+: 3.8. **Pop. density:** 62.08 per sq. mi. **Urban** (1972): 47.9%. **Ethnic groups:** Afrikaner, English, Zulu, Asian, Xhosa. **Religions:** Mainly Christian. **Languages:** Afrikaans, English (both official), Bantu languages predominate.

Geography: Area: 435,868 sq. mi., four-fifths the size of Alaska. **Location:** At the southern extreme of Africa. **Neighbors:** Namibia (SW Africa), Botswana, Zimbabwe on N, Mozambique, Swaziland on E; surrounds Lesotho. **Topography:** The large interior plateau reaches close to the country's 2,700-mi. coastline. There are few major rivers or lakes; rainfall is sparse in W, more plentiful in E. **Capitals:** Cape Town (legislative), Pretoria (administrative), and Bloemfontein (judicial). **Cities** (1980): Durban 505,963; Cape Town 213,830; Johannesburg 1,536,457; Pretoria 528,407.

Government: Type: Parliamentary (limited to white adults). **Head of state:** Pres. Marais Viljoen, b. Dec. 2, 1915, in office: June 19, 1979. **Head of government:** Prime Min. Pieter Willem Botha; b. Jan. 12, 1916; in office: Sept. 28, 1978. **Local divisions:** 4 provinces. **Defense:** 15% of govt. budget (1984).

Economy: Industries: Steel, tires, motors, textiles, plastics. **Chief crops:** Corn, wool, dairy products, grain, tobacco, sugar, fruit, peanuts, grapes. **Minerals:** Gold (largest producer), chromium, antimony, coal, iron, manganese, nickel, phosphates, tin, uranium, gem diamonds, platinum, copper, vanadium. **Other resources:** Wool. **Arable land:** 10%. **Meat prod.** (1983): beef: 538,000 metric tons; pork: 91,000 metric tons; lamb: 164,000 metric tons. **Fish catch** (1981): 611,000 metric tons. **Electricity prod.** (1982): 119.8 bln. kwh. **Crude steel prod.** (1982): 8.2 mln. metric tons. **Labor force:** 30% agric.; 29% ind. and commerce; 34% serv.; 7% mining.

Finance: Currency: Rand (Mar. 1984: 1.20 = $1 US). **Gross domestic product** (1981): $81.9 bln. **Per capita income** (1978): $1,296. **Imports** (1983): $15.7 bln.; partners (1981): W. Ger. 15%, U.S. 15%, UK 12%, Jap. 10%. **Exports** (1983): $18.6 bln.; partners: U.S. 8%, UK 7%, Jap. 8%. **Tourist receipts** (1977): $321 mln. **National budget** (1984): $20.7 bln.

International reserves less gold (Mar. 1984): $618 mln. **Gold:** 7.66 mln. oz t. **Consumer prices** (change in 1983): 12.3%.

Transport: Railway traffic (1981): 96.7 bln. net ton-km. **Motor vehicles:** in use (1982): 2.5 mln. passenger cars, 912,000 comm. vehicles. **Civil aviation:** (1982): 9.2 bln. passenger-km: 338.8 mln. freight ton-km. **Chief ports:** Durban, Cape Town, East London, Port Elizabeth.

Communications: Television sets (1980): 1.4 mln.; **Radios:** 8 mln. in use (1981). **Telephones in use** (1981): 2.6 mln. **Daily newspaper circ.** (1982): 70 per 1,000 pop.

Health: Life expectancy at birth (1982): White: 70 years; Asians: 65 years; Africans: 59 years. **Births** (per 1,000 pop. 1978): 36. **Deaths** (per 1,000 pop. 1978): 13. **Natural increase** (1978): 2.1%. **Hospital beds** (per 100,000 pop. 1977): 614. **Physicians** (per 100,000 pop. 1977): 6. **Infant mortality** (per 1,000 live births 1982): Africans 94, Asians 25.3, whites 14.9

Education (1982): **Literacy:** 98% (whites), 85% (Asians), 75% (Coloureds), 50% (Africans).

Embassy: 3051 Massachusetts Ave. NW 20008; 232-4400.

Bushmen and Hottentots were the original inhabitants. Bantus, including Zulu, Xhosa, Swazi, and Sotho, had occupied the area from Transvaal to south of Transkei before the 17th century.

The Cape of Good Hope area was settled by Dutch, beginning in the 17th century. Britain seized the Cape in 1806. Many Dutch trekked north and founded 2 republics, the Transvaal and the Orange Free State. Diamonds were discovered, 1867, and gold, 1886. The Dutch (Boers) resented encroachments by the British and others; the Anglo-Boer War followed, 1899-1902. Britain won and, effective May 31, 1910, created the Union of South Africa, incorporating the British colonies of the Cape and Natal, the Transvaal and the Orange Free State. After a referendum, the Union became the Republic of South Africa, May 31, 1961, and withdrew from the Commonwealth.

With the election victory of Daniel Malan's National party in 1948, the policy of separate development of the races, or apartheid, already existing unofficially, became official. This called for separate development, separate residential areas, and ultimate political independence for the whites, Bantus, Asians, and Coloreds. In 1959 the government passed acts providing the eventual creation of several Bantu nations or Bantustans on 13% of the country's land area, though most black leaders have opposed the plan.

Under apartheid, blacks are severely restricted to certain occupations, and are paid far lower wages than are whites for similar work. Only whites may vote or run for public office, and militant white opposition has been curbed. There is an advisory Indian Council, partly elected, partly appointed. In 1969, a Colored People's Representative Council was created. Minor liberalization measures were allowed in the 1970s.

At least 600 persons, mostly Bantus, were killed in 1976 riots protesting apartheid. Black protests continued through 1984. A new constitution was approved by referendum, Nov. 1983, which extended the parliamentary franchise to the Coloured and Asian minorities.

In 1963, the Transkei, an area in the SE, became the first of these partially self-governing territories or "Homelands." Transkei became independent on Oct. 26, 1976, Bophuthatswana on Dec. 6, 1977, and Venda on Sept. 13, 1979; none received international recognition.

In 1981, So. Africa launched military operations in Angola and Mozambique to combat terrorists groups; So. African troops attacked the South West African People's Organization (SWAPO) guerrillas in Angola, March, 1982.

A car bomb exploded outside air force headquarters in Pretoria, May 20, 1983, killing or injuring hundreds of people. The African National Congress (ANC), a black nationalist group, claimed responsibility. South African fighter planes attacked ANC guerrilla bases in Maputo, Mozambique, May 23, in retaliation for the Pretoria bombing.

Bophuthatswana: Population (1983 est.): 1,502,000. **Area:** 15,571 sq. mi., 6 discontinuous geographic units. **Capital:** Mmabatho. **Cities:** (1980 est.): Ga-Rankawa 48,300. **Head of state:** Pres. Kgosi Lucas Manyane Mangope, b. Dec. 27, 1923; in office: Dec. 6, 1977.

Ciskei: Population (1983 est.): 1,664,000. **Area:** 3,200 sq. mi. **Capitol:** Bisho. **Head of State:** Pres. Lennox Sebe.

Transkei: Population (1983 est.): 2,765,000. **Area:** 15,831 sq. mi., 3 discontinuous geographic units. **Capital:** Umtata (1978 est.): 30,000. **Head of state:** Pres. Kaiser Matanzima; in office:

Feb. 20, 1979. Head of government: Prime Min. George Matanzima; in office: Feb. 20, 1979.

Venda: Population (1983 est.): 390,000. **Area:** 2,448 sq. mi., 2 discontinuous geographic units. **Capital:** Thohoyandou. **City:** Makearela (1976 est.): 1,972. **Head of state:** Patrick Mphephu; in office: Sept. 13, 1979.

Namibia (South-West Africa)

South-West Africa is a sparsely populated land twice the size of California. Made a German protectorate in 1884, it was surrendered to South Africa in 1915 and was administered by that country under a League of Nations mandate. S. Africa refused to accept UN authority under the trusteeship system.

Other African nations charged S. Africa imposed apartheid, built military bases, and exploited S-W Africa. The UN General Assembly, May 1968, created an 11-nation council to take over administration of S-W Africa and lead it to independence. The council charged that S. Africa had blocked its efforts to visit S-W Africa.

In 1968 the UN General Assembly gave the area the name Namibia. In Jan. 1970 the UN Security Council condemned S. Africa for "illegal" control of the area. In an advisory opinion, June 1971, the International Court of Justice declared S. Africa was occupying the area illegally.

In a 1977 referendum, white voters backed a plan for a multiracial interim government to lead to independence. The Marxist South-West Africa People's Organization (SWAPO) rejected the plan, and launched a guerrilla war. Both S. Africa and Namibian rebels agreed to a UN plan for independence by the end of 1978. S. Africa rejected the plan, Sept. 20, 1978, and held elections, without UN supervision, for Namibia's constituent assembly, Dec., that were ignored by the major black opposition parties.

The UN peace plan, proposed 1980, called for a cease-fire and a demilitarized zone 31 miles deep on each side of S-W Africa's borders with Angola and Zambia that would be patrolled by UN peacekeeping forces against guerrilla actions. Impartial elections would follow. In 1982, So. African and SWAPO agreed in principal on a cease-fire and the holding of UN-supervised elections. So. Africa, however, insisted on the withdrawal of Cuban forces from Angola as a precondition to Namibian independence. On Jan. 18, 1983, South Africa dissolved the Namibian National Assembly and resumed direct control of the territory.

Most of Namibia is a plateau, 3,600 ft. high, with plains in the N, Kalahari Desert to the E, Orange R. on the S, Atlantic O. on the W. Area is 318,827 sq. mi.; pop. (1982 est.) 1,038,000; capital, Windhoek.

Products include cattle, sheep, diamonds, copper, lead, zinc, fish. People include Namas (Hottentots), Ovambos (Bantus), Bushmen, and others.

Walvis Bay, the only deepwater port in the country, was turned over to South African administration in 1922. S. Africa said in 1978 it would discuss sovereignty only after Namibian independence.

Spain
Spanish State

People: Population (1984 est.): 38,234,000 **Age distrib. (%):** 0-14: 27.6; 15-59: 58.0; 60+: 14.4. **Pop. density:** 193 per sq. mi. **Ethnic groups:** Spanish (Castilian, Valencian, Andalusian, Asturian) 72.8%, Catalan 16.4%, Galician 8.2%, Basque 2.3%. **Languages:** Spanish (official), Catalan, Galician, Basque. **Religions:** Roman Catholic.

Geography: Area: 195,988 sq. mi., the size of Arizona and Utah combined. **Location:** In SW Europe. **Neighbors:** Portugal on W. France on N. **Topography:** The interior is a high, arid plateau broken by mountain ranges and river valleys. The NW is heavily watered, the south has lowlands and a Mediterranean climate. **Capital:** Madrid. **Cities** (1981 cen.): Madrid 3,188,297; Barcelona 1,754,900; Valencia 751,734; Seville 653,833; Zaragoza 590,750.

Government: Type: Constitutional monarchy. **Head of state:** King Juan Carlos I de Borbon y Borbon, b. Jan. 5, 1938; in office: Nov. 22, 1975. **Head of government:** Prime Min. Felipe Gonzalez Marquez; in office: Dec. 2, 1982. **Local divisions:** 50 provinces, 2 territories, 3 islands. **Defense:** 11.4% of govt. budget (1982).

Economy: Industries: Machinery, steel, textiles, shoes, autos, ships. **Chief crops:** Grains, olives, grapes, citrus fruits, vegetables, olives. **Minerals:** Mercury, potash, uranium, lead, iron, copper, zinc, coal. **Crude oil reserves** (1980): 150 mln. bbls. **Other resources:** Forests (cork). **Per capita arable land:** 1.1 acres. **Meat prod.** (1983): beef: 410,000 metric tons; pork: 1.2 mln. metric tons; lamb: 140,000 metric tons. **Fish catch** (1981): 1.2 mln. tons. **Electricity prod.** (1982): 113.7 bln. kwh. **Crude steel prod.** (1982): 12.7 mln. metric tons. **Labor force:** 18% agric.; 35% ind. and comm.; 47% serv.

Finance: Currency: Peseta (Mar. 1984: 148.75 = $1 US). **Gross domestic product** (1981): $185.5 bln. **Per capita income** (1979): $5,500. **Imports** (1983): $29.1 bln.; partners: U.S. 14%, W. Ger. 9%, Fr. 8%, Saudi Ar. 9%. **Exports** (1983): $19.7 bln.; partners: Fr. 16%, W. Ger. 8%, U.S. 6%, UK 7%. **Tourists** (1981): 40.1 mln.; receipts: $6.9 bln. **National budget** (1981): $25.8 bln. revenues; $32.1 bln. expenditures. **International reserves less gold** (Jan. 1984): $8.09 bln. **Gold:** 14.61 min. oz t. **Consumer prices** (change in 1983): 12.1%.

Transport: Railway traffic (1981): 14.1 bln. passenger-km; 10.4 bln. net ton-km. **Motor vehicles:** in use (1982): 8.3 mln. passenger cars, 1.4 mln. comm. vehicles; manuf. (1982): 915,000 passenger cars; 111,000 comm. vehicles. **Civil aviation:** (1982): 16.4 bln. passenger-km; 482 mln. freight ton-km. **Chief ports:** Barcelona, Bilbao, Valencia, Cartagena, Gijon. **Communications: Television sets:** 9.4 mln. in use (1980). **Radios:** 9.6 mln. in use (1981). **Telephones in use** (1981): 12.3 mln. **Daily newspaper circ.** (1980): 116 per 1,000 pop.

Health: Life expectancy at birth (1980): 70.0 male; 76.0 female. **Births** (per 1,000 pop. 1981): 14.1. **Deaths** (per 1,000 pop. 1981): 7.6. **Natural increase** (1977): 1.0%. **Hospital beds** (per 100,000 pop. 1977): 543. **Physicians** (per 100,000 pop. 1977): 176. **Infant mortality** (per 1,000 live births 1981): 10.3.

Education (1983): Literacy: 97%. **School compulsory:** to age 14.

Embassy: 2700 15th St. NW 2009; 265-0190.

Spain was settled by Iberians, Basques, and Celts, partly overrun by Carthaginians, conquered by Rome c.200 BC. The Visigoths, in power by the 5th century AD, adopted Christianity but by 711 AD lost to the Islamic invasion from Africa. Christian reconquest from the N led to a Spanish nationalism. In 1469 the kingdoms of Aragon and Castile were united by the marriage of Ferdinand II and Isabella I, and the last Moorish power was broken by the fall of the kingdom of Granada, 1492. Spain became a bulwark of Roman Catholicism.

Spain obtained a colonial empire with the discovery of America by Columbus, 1492, the conquest of Mexico by Cortes, and Peru by Pizarro. It also controlled the Netherlands and parts of Italy and Germany. Spain lost its American colonies in the early 19th century. It lost Cuba, the Philippines, and Puerto Rico during the Spanish-American War, 1898.

Primo de Rivera became dictator in 1923. King Alfonso XIII revoked the dictatorship, 1930, but was forced to leave the country 1931. A republic was proclaimed which disestablished the church, curtailed its privileges, and secularized education. A conservative reaction occurred 1933 but was followed by a Popular Front (1936-1939) composed of socialists, communists, republicans, and anarchists.

Army officers under Francisco Franco revolted against the government, 1936. In a destructive 3-year war, in which some one million died, Franco received massive help and troops from Italy and Germany, while the USSR, France, and Mexico supported the republic. War ended Mar. 28, 1939. Franco was named caudillo, leader of the nation. Spain was neutral in World War II but its relations with fascist countries caused its exclusion from the UN until 1955.

In July 1969, Franco and the Cortes designated Prince Juan Carlos as the future king and chief of state. After Franco's death, Nov. 20, 1975, Juan Carlos was sworn in as king. He presided over the formal dissolution of the institutions of the Franco regime. In free elections June 1976, moderates and democratic socialists emerged as the largest parties.

In an unsuccessful attempt at a military coup, Feb. 23, 1981, rightist Civil Guards seized the lower house of Parliament and took most of the country's leaders hostage. The plot collapsed the next day when the army remained loyal to King Juan Carlos.

Catalonia and the Basque country were granted autonomy, Jan. 1980, following overwhelming approval in home-rule refer-

endums. Basque extremists, however, have continued their campaign for independence.

The **Balearic Islands** in the western Mediterranean, 1,935 sq. mi., are a province of Spain; they include **Majorca** (Mallorca), with the capital, Palma; **Minorca, Cabrera, Ibiza** and **Formentera.** The **Canary Islands,** 2,807 sq. mi., in the Atlantic W of Morocco, form 2 provinces, including the islands of **Tenerife, Palma, Gomera, Hierro, Grand Canary, Fuerteventura,** and **Lanzarote** with Las Palmas and Santa Cruz thriving ports. **Ceuta** and **Melilla,** small enclaves on Morocco's Mediterranean coast, are part of Metropolitan Spain.

Spain has sought the return of Gibraltar, in British hands since 1704.

Sri Lanka

Democratic Socialist Republic of Sri Lanka

People: Population (1983 est.): 15,300,000. **Age distrib.** (%): 0-14: 35.3; 15-59: 58.1; 60+: 6.6. **Pop. density:** 581.87 per sq. mi. **Urban** (1981): 21.5%. **Ethnic groups:** Sinhalese 74%, Tamils 18%, Moors 7%. **Languages:** Sinhala (official), Tamil, English. **Religions:** Buddhists 69%, Hindus 15%, Christians 7%, Muslims 7%.

Geography: Area: 25,332 sq. mi. **Location:** In Indian O. off SE coast of India. **Neighbors:** India on NW. **Topography:** The coastal area and the northern half are flat; the S-central area is hilly and mountainous. **Capital:** Colombo. **Cities** (1983): Colombo 1,262,000.

Government: Type: Republic. **Head of state:** Pres. Junius Richard Jayawardene; b. Sept. 17, 1906; in office: Feb. 4, 1978. **Head of government:** Ranasinghe Premadasa, b. June 23, 1924, in office: Feb. 6, 1978. **Local divisions:** 24 districts. **Defense:** 3.2% of govt. budget (1982).

Economy: Industries: Plywood, paper, milling, chemicals, textiles. **Chief crops:** Tea, coconuts, rice. **Minerals:** Graphite, limestone, gems, phosphate. **Other resources:** Forests, rubber **Arable land:** 59%. **Meat prod.** (1000). beef: 18,000 metric tons. **Fish catch** (1981): 207,000 metric tons. **Electricity prod.** (1982): 2 bln. kwh. **Labor force:** 46% agric.; 29% ind. and comm.; 19% serv.

Finance: Currency: Rupee (Mar. 1984: 25.12 = $1 US). **Gross domestic product** (1981): $4 bln. **Per capita income** (1981): $266. **Imports** (1983): $1.8 bln.; partners: Jap. 15%, Saudi Ar. 12%, UK 7%. **Exports** (1983): $1.06 bln.; partners: U.S. 14%, UK 7%. **Tourists** (1977): 153,700; receipts: $40 mln. **National budget** (1982): $873 mln. revenues; $1.8 bln. expenditures. **International reserves less gold** (Mar. 1984): $330 mln. **Gold:** 63,000 oz t. **Consumer prices** (change in 1983): 14.0%

Transport: Railway traffic (1982): 3.1 bln. passenger-km; 218 mln. net ton-km. **Motor vehicles:** in use (1981): 126,000 passenger cars, 67,200 comm. vehicles. **Civil aviation** (1982): 1.9 bln. passenger-km; 43 mln. freight ton-km. **Chief ports:** Colombo, Trincomalee, Galle.

Communications: Radios: 1.5 mln. in use (1981). **Telephones in use** (1981): 63,500.

Health: Life expectancy at birth (1983): 68 years. **Births** (per 1,000 pop. 1981): 28.0. **Deaths** (per 1,000 pop. 1981): 6.0. **Natural increase** (1978): 1.7%. **Hospital beds** (1981): 44,029. **Physicians** (1981): 2,889. **Infant mortality** (per 1,000 live births 1983): 37.

Education (1983): Literacy: 84%. **Years compulsory:** To age 12; attendance 84%.

Embassy: 2148 Wyoming Ave. NW 20008; 483-4025.

The island was known to the ancient world as Taprobane (Greek for copper-colored) and later as Serendip (from Arabic). Colonists from northern India subdued the indigenous Veddahs about 543 BC; their descendants, the Buddhist Sinhalese, still form most of the population. Hindu descendants of Tamil immigrants from southern India account for one-fifth of the population; separatism has grown. Parts were occupied by the Portuguese in 1505 and by the Dutch in 1658. The British seized the island in 1796. As Ceylon it became an independent member of the Commonwealth in 1948. On May 22, 1972, Ceylon became the Republic of Sri Lanka.

Prime Min. W. R. D. Bandaranaike was assassinated Sept. 25, 1959. In new elections, the Freedom Party was victorious under Mrs. Sirimavo Bandaranaike, widow of the former prime minister.

In Apr., 1962, the government expropriated British and U.S. oil companies. In Mar. 1965 elections, the conservative United National Party won; the new government agreed to pay compensation for the seized oil companies.

After May 1970 elections, Mrs. Bandaranaike became prime minister again. In 1971 the nation suffered economic problems and terrorist activities by ultra-leftists, thousands of whom were executed. Massive land reform and nationalization of foreign-owned plantations was undertaken in the mid-1970s. Mrs. Bandaranaike was ousted in 1977 elections by the United Nationals. A presidential form of government was installed in 1978 to restore stability.

Racial tension between the Sinhalese and Tamil communities erupted into violence in 1983.

Sudan
Democratic Republic of the Sudan

People: Population (1983 est.): 20,539,000. **Pop. density:** 19.32 per sq. mi. **Urban** (1976): 20.4%. **Ethnic groups:** North: Arabs, Nubians; South; Nilotic; Sudanic, Negro tribes. **Languages:** Arabic (official), various tribal languages. **Religions:** Muslims 73%, animist 18%, Christians 9%.

Geography: Area: 966,757 sq. mi., the largest country in Africa, over one-fourth the size of the U.S. **Location:** At the E end of Sahara desert zone. **Neighbors:** Egypt on N, Libya, Chad, Central African Republic on W, Zaire, Uganda, Kenya on S, Ethiopia on E. **Topography:** The N consists of the Libyan Desert in the W, and the mountainous Nubia desert in E, with narrow Nile valley between. The center contains large, fertile, rainy areas with fields, pasture, and forest. The S has rich soil, heavy rain. **Capital:** Khartoum. **Cities** (1973 cen.): Khartoum 333,921; Omdurman 299,401; North Khartoum 150,991; Port Sudan 132,631.

Government: Type: Republic, single party. **Head of state and head of government:** Pres., Prime Min. Gaafar Mohammed Nimeiri; b. Jan. 1, 1930; in office: May 25, 1969 (P.M.: Sept. 10, 1977). **Local divisions:** 15 provinces; the southern 3 have a regional government. **Defense:** 24% of GNP (1982).

Economy: Industries: Textiles, food processing. **Chief crops:** Gum arabic (principal world source), durra (sorghum), cotton (main export), sesame, peanuts, rice, coffee, sugar cane, tobacco, wheat, dates. **Minerals:** Chrome, gold, copper, white mica, vermiculite, asbestos. **Other resources:** Mahogany. **Arable land:** 12%. **Meat prod.** (1983): beef: 239,000 metric tons; lamb: 137,000 metric tons. **Electricity prod.** (1981): 1 bln. kwh. **Labor force:** 78% agric.; 9% ind., commerce, serv.

Finance: Currency: Pound (Mar. 1984: 1.30 = $1 US). **Gross domestic product** (1981 est.): $8.8 bln. **Per capita income** (1982 est.): $370. **Imports** (1982): $1.8 bln.; partners: US 13%, W. Ger. 8%, Saudi Ar. 11%. **Exports** (1982): $650 mln.; partners: China 6%, It. 9%, Saudi Ar. 21%. **National Budget** (1983): $1.5 bln. expenditures. **International reserves less gold** (Mar. 1984): $19.1 mln. **Consumer prices** (change in 1982): 25.7%.

Transport: Railway traffic (1980): 1.1 bln. net ton-km. **Motor vehicles:** in use (1980): 34,600 passenger cars, 38,000 comm. vehicles. **Civil aviation:** (1982): 657 mln. passenger-km; 6.3 mln. freight ton-km. **Chief ports:** Port Sudan.

Communications: Television sets: 105,000 in use (1979). **Radios:** 1.3 mln. licensed (1979). **Telephones in use** (1980): 63,400. **Daily newspaper circ.** (1982): 8 per 1,000 pop.

Health: Life expectancy at birth (1975): 43.0 male; 45.0 female. **Births** (per 1,000 pop. 1978): 49. **Deaths** (per 1,000 pop. 1978): 18 **Natural increase** (1978): 3.7%. **Hospital beds** (per 100,000 pop. 1977): 100. **Physicians** (per 100,000 pop. 1977): 50. **Infant mortality** (per 1,000 live births 1979): 141.

Education (1982): Literacy: 20%. **Years compulsory:** 9; attendance 50%.

Embassy: 2210 Massachusetts Ave. NW 20008; 338-8565.

Northern Sudan, ancient Nubia, was settled by Egyptians in antiquity, and was converted to Coptic Christianity in the 6th century. Arab conquests brought Islam in the 15th century.

In the 1820s Egypt took over the Sudan, defeating the last of earlier empires, including the Fung. In the 1880s a revolution

was led by Mohammed Ahmed who called himself the Mahdi (leader of the faithful) and his followers, the dervishes.

In 1898 an Anglo-Egyptian force crushed the Mahdi's successors. In 1951 the Egyptian Parliament abrogated its 1899 and 1936 treaties with Great Britain, and amended its constitution, to provide for a separate Sudanese constitution.

Sudan voted for complete independence as a parliamentary government effective Jan. 1, 1956. Gen. Ibrahim Abboud took power 1958, but resigned under pressure, 1964.

In 1969, in a second military coup, a Revolutionary Council took power, but a civilian premier and cabinet were appointed; the government announced it would create a socialist state. The northern 12 provinces are predominantly Arab-Moslem and have been dominant in the central government. The 3 southern provinces are Negro and predominantly pagan. A 1972 peace agreement gave the South regional autonomy.

The government nationalized a number of businesses in May 1970.

Sudan charged Libya with aiding an unsuccessful coup in Sudan in 1976. Sudan claimed that Libyan planes bombed several border towns, Sept. 1981, and the city of Omdurman, 1984.

Economic problems plagued the nation in the 1980s, aggravated by a hugh influx of refugees from Chad.

Suriname

People: Population (1983 est.): 363,000. **Pop. density:** 5.85 per sq. mi. **Ethnic groups** Hindustanis 37%, Creole 31%, Javanese 15%. **Languages:** Dutch (official), Sranan (Creole), English, others. **Religions:** Muslim, Hindu, Christian.

Geography: Area: 63,037 sq. mi., slightly larger than Georgia. **Location:** On N shore of S. America. **Neighbors:** Guyana on W, Brazil on S, French Guiana on E. **Topography:** A flat Atlantic coast, where dikes permit agriculture. Inland is a forest belt; to the S, largely unexplored hills cover 75% of the country. **Capital:** Paramaribo. **Cities** (1980): Paramaribo 67,700.

Government: Type: Military-civilian executive. **Head of Military Council:** Col. Desire Bouterse; in office: Feb. 5, 1982. **Head of state:** Prime Min. Wim Ebenhout; in office: Feb. 3, 1984. **Local divisions:** 9 districts.

Economy: Industries: Aluminum. **Chief crops:** Rice, sugar, fruits. **Minerals:** Bauxite. **Other resources:** Forests, shrimp. **Arable land:** 1%. **Electricity prod.** (1981): 1.6 bln. kwh. **Labor force:** 29% agric.; 15% ind. and commerce; 40% govt.

Finance: Currency: Guilder (Mar. 1984: 1.78 = $1 US). **Gross national product** (1981): $924 mln. **Per capita income** (1981): $2,600. **Imports** (1980): $504 mln.; partners: U.S. 31%, Neth. 19%, Trin./Tob. 15%, Jap. 7%. **Exports** (1980): $514 mln.; partners: U.S. 36%, Neth. 17%, Nor. 13%. **Tourists** (1976): 54,700; receipts: $10 mln. **National budget** (1981): $413 expenditures. **International reserves less gold** (Mar. 1984): $136 mln. **Gold:** 54,000 oz t. **Consumer prices** (change in 1983): 4.4%.

Transport: Motor vehicles: in use (1980): 26,400 passenger cars, 8,500 comm. vehicles. **Chief ports:** Paramaribo, Nieuw-Nickerie.

Communications: Television sets: 40,000 in use (1981). **Radios:** 189,000 in use (1981). **Telephones in use** (1980): 21,300. **Daily newspaper circ.** (1981): 107 per 1,000 pop.

Health: Life expectancy at birth (1980): 64.8 male; 69.8 female. **Births** (per 1,000 pop. 1978): 29. **Deaths** (per 1,000 pop. 1978): 7. **Natural increase** (1978): 2.8%. **Pop. per hospital bed** (1975): 184. **Pop. per physician** (1974): 2,030. **Infant mortality** (per 1,000 live births 1982): 30.

Education (1982): Literacy: 80%; compulsory ages 6–12.

Embassy: 2600 Virginia Ave. NW 20037; 338-6980.

The Netherlands acquired Suriname in 1667 from Britain, in exchange for New Netherlands (New York). The 1954 Dutch constitution raised the colony to a level of equality with the Netherlands and the Netherlands Antilles. In the 1970s the Dutch government pressured for Suriname independence, which came Nov. 25, 1975, despite objections from East Indians and some Bush Negroes. Some 40% of the population (mostly East Indians) emigrated to the Netherlands in the months before independence. The Netherlands promised $1.5 billion in aid for the first decade of independence.

The National Military Council took over control of the government, Feb. 1982. The Netherlands has suspended aid.

Swaziland
Kingdom of Swaziland

People: Population (1983 est.): 632,000. **Age distrib.** (%): 0–14: 47.7; 15–59: 46.8; 60+: 5.4. **Pop. density:** 82.03 per sq. mi. **Urban** (1976): 15.2%. **Ethnic groups:** Swazi 90%, Zulu 2.3%, European 2.1%, other African, non-African groups. **Languages:** siSwati, English, (both official). **Religions:** Christians 77%, animist 23%.

Geography: Area: 6,704 sq. mi., slightly smaller than New Jersey. **Location:** In southern Africa, near Indian O. coast. **Neighbors:** South Africa on N, W, S, Mozambique on E. **Topography:** The country descends from W-E in broad belts, becoming more arid in the lowveld region, then rising to a plateau in the E. **Capital:** Mbabane. **Cities** (1982 est.): Mbabane 33,000.

Government: Type: Monarchy. **Head of state:** Queen Ntombi; as of: Aug. 10, 1983. **Head of government:** Prime Min. Prince Bhekimpi Dlamini; in office: Mar. 25, 1983. **Local divisions:** 4 districts, 2 municipalities, 40 regions.

Economy: Industries: Wood pulp. **Chief crops:** Corn, cotton, rice, pineapples, sugar, citrus fruits. **Minerals:** Asbestos, iron, coal. **Other resources:** Forests. **Arable land:** 19%. **Meat prod.** (1980): beef: 14,000 metric tons. **Electricity prod.** (1981): 310 mln. kwh. **Labor force:** 53% agric.; 9% ind. and commerce; 9% serv.

Finance: Currency: Lilangeni (Mar. 1984: 1.20 = $1 US). **Gross domestic product** (1981): $425 mln. **Per capita income** (1981 est.): $840. **Imports** (1981): $635 mln.; partners (1982): So. Afr., 96%. **Exports** (1981): $353 mln.; partners (1977): UK 33%, So. Afr. 20%. **National budget** (1982): $182 mln. **International reserves less gold** (Feb. 1984): $74.2 mln. **Consumer prices** (change in 1983): 11.6%.

Transport: Motor vehicles: in use (1979): 10,000 passenger cars, 8,000 comm. vehicles.

Communications: Radios: 70,000 in use (1977). **Telephones in use** (1981): 12,300. **Daily newspaper circ.** (1982): 17 per 1,000 pop.

Health: Life expectancy at birth (1983): 46.8 male; 50.0 female. **Births** (per 1,000 pop. 1978): 47. **Deaths** (per 1,000 pop. 1978): 19. **Natural increase** (1978): 2.7%. **Hospital beds** (1980): 1,560. **Physicians** (1981): 80. **Infant mortality rate** (per 1,000 live births 1982): 156.

Education (1983): **Literacy:** 65%. Almost all attend primary school.

Embassy: 4301 Connecticut Ave. NW 20008; 362-6683.

The royal house of Swaziland traces back 400 years, and is one of Africa's last ruling dynasties. The Swazis, a Bantu people, were driven to Swaziland from lands to the N by the Zulus in 1820. Their autonomy was later guaranteed by Britain and Transvaal, with Britain assuming control after 1903. Independence came Sept. 6, 1968. In 1973 the king repealed the constitution and assumed full powers.

A new Parliament was opened, 1979. Under the new constitution political parties were forbidden; Parliament's role in government was limited to debate and advice.

Sweden
Kingdom of Sweden

People: Population (1983 est.): 8,331,000. **Age distrib.** (%): 0–14: 19.4; 15–59: 57.5; 60+: 22.1. **Pop. density:** 47.85 per sq. mi. **Urban** (1975): 82.7%. **Ethnic groups:** Swedish 93%, Finnish 3%, Lapps, European immigrants. **Languages:** Swedish, Finnish. **Religions:** Lutherans (official) 95%, other Protestants 5%.

Geography: Area: 179,896 sq. mi., larger than California. **Location:** On Scandinavian Peninsula in N. Europe. **Neighbors:** Norway on W, Denmark on S (across Kattegat), Finland on E. **Topography:** Mountains along NW border cover 25% of Sweden, flat or rolling terrain covers the central and southern areas, which includes several large lakes. **Capital:** Stockholm. **Cities**

(1980 est.): Stockholm 1,386,980; Goteborg 693,483; Malmo 453,337.

Government: Type: Constitutional monarchy. **Head of state:** King Carl XVI Gustaf; b. Apr. 30, 1946; in office: Sept. 19, 1973. **Head of government:** Olof Palmo; b. Jan. 27, 1927; in office: Oct. 7, 1982. **Local divisions:** 24 lan (counties). **Defense:** 9.2% of govt. budget.

Economy: Industries: Steel, machinery, instruments, autos, shipbuilding, shipping, paper. **Chief crops:** Grains, potatoes, sugar beets. **Minerals:** Zinc, iron, lead, copper, gold, silver. **Other resources:** Forests (half the country); yield one fourth exports. **Per capita arable land:** 0.9 acres. **Meat prod.** (1983): beef: 160,000 metric tons; pork: 313,000 metric tons; lamb: 5,000 metric tons. **Fish catch** (1981): 253,000 metric tons. **Electricity prod.** (1982): 96.5 bln. kwh. **Crude steel prod.** (1982): 3.8 mln. metric tons. **Labor force:** 5% agric.; 39% ind. and commerce, 20% serv, 35% govt.

Finance: Currency: Krona (Mar. 1984: 7.71 = $1 US). **Gross national product** (1980): $123 bln. **Per capita income** (1980): $14,821. **Imports** (1983): $25.9 bln.; partners: W. Ger. 17%, UK 12%, U.S. 9%, Fin. 7%. **Exports** (1983): $27.4 bln.; partners: UK 10%, W. Ger. 10%, Nor. 11%, Den. 8%. **National budget** (1982): $28.9 bln. revenues; $42.9 bln. expenditures. **International reserves less gold** (Mar. 1984): $4.32 bln. **Gold:** 6.06 mln. oz t. **Consumer prices** (change in 1983): 8.9%.

Transport: Railway traffic (1982): 6.3 bln. passenger-km; 13.6 bln. net ton-km. **Motor vehicles:** in use (1981): 2.8 mln. passenger cars, 199,325 comm. vehicles; manuf. (1982): 269,000 passenger cars. **Civil aviation** (1982): 5.5 bln. passenger-km: 189 mln. freight ton-km. **Chief ports:** Goteborg, Stockholm, Malmo.

Communications: Television sets: 3.2 mln. licensed (1982). **Radios:** 8.3 mln. (1977). **Telephones in use** (1981): 6.4 mln. **Daily newspaper circ.** (1982): 578 per 1,000 pop.

Health: Life expectancy at birth (1981): 73.1 male; 79.1 female. **Births** (per 1,000 pop. 1982): 11.1. **Deaths** (per 1,000 pop. 1982): 10.9. **Natural increase** (1976): 0.4%. **Hospital beds** (per 100,000 pop. 1977): 1,496. **Physicians** (per 100,000 pop. 1977): 178. **Infant mortality** (per 1,000 live births 1982): 6.8.

Education (1982): **Literacy:** 99%. **Years compulsory:** 9; attendance 100%.

Embassy: 600 New Hampshire Ave. NW 20037; 298-3500.

The Swedes have lived in present-day Sweden for at least 5,000 years, longer than nearly any other European people. Gothic tribes from Sweden played a major role in the disintegration of the Roman Empire. Other Swedes helped create the first Russian state in the 9th century.

The Swedes were Christianized from the 11th century, and a strong centralized monarchy developed. A parliament, the Riksdag, was first called in 1435, the earliest parliament on the European continent, with all classes of society represented.

Swedish independence from rule by Danish kings (dating from 1397) was secured by Gustavus I in a revolt, 1521-23; he built up the government and military and established the Lutheran Church. In the 17th century Sweden was a major European power, gaining most of the Baltic seacoast, but its international position subsequently declined.

The Napoleonic wars, in which Sweden acquired Norway (it became independent 1905), were the last in which Sweden participated. Armed neutrality was maintained in both world wars.

Over 4 decades of Social Democratic rule was ended in 1976 parliamentary elections but the party was returned to power in the 1982 elections. Although 90% of the economy is in private hands, the government holds a large interest in water power production and the railroads are operated by a public agency.

Consumer cooperatives are in extensive operation and also are important in agriculture and housing. Per capita GNP is among the highest in the world.

A labor crisis of strikes locking out more than 800,000 workers; May 1980, brought the country to an industrial standstill and shattered its image of labor tranquillity.

A Soviet submarine went aground inside Swedish territorial waters near the Karlskrona Naval Base, Oct. 27, 1981. Sweden claimed the submarine was armed with nuclear weapons and the incident a "flagrant violation" of Swedish neutrality. The submarine was towed back to international waters Nov. 6. Sweden claimed in 1983 that Soviet submarines have repeatedly violated its territorial waters.

Switzerland
Swiss Confederation

People: Population (1983 est.): 6,463,000. **Age distrib. (%):** 0–14: 19.8; 15–59: 62.1; 60+: 17.2. **Pop. density:** 397.72 per sq. mi. **Urban** (1980): 50.9%. **Ethnic groups:** Mixed European stock. **Languages:** German 65%, French 18%, Italian 9%, Romansh 1%. (all official). **Religions:** Roman Catholic 48%, Protestant 44%.

Geography: Area: 15,941 sq. mi., as large as Mass., Conn., and R.I., combined. **Location:** In the Alps Mts. in Central Europe. **Neighbors:** France on W, Italy on S, Austria on E, W. Germany on N. **Topography:** The Alps cover 60% of the land area, the Jura, near France, 10%. Running between, from NE to SW, are midlands, 30%. **Capital:** Bern. **Cities** (1982 est.): Zurich 375,000; Basel 183,200; Geneva 157,000; Bern 145,000.

Government: Type: Federal State. **Head of government:** Pres. Leon Schlumpf; in office: Jan. 1, 1984. **Local divisions:** 20 full cantons, 6 half cantons. **Defense:** 2% of GNP (1982).

Economy: Industries: Machinery, machine tools, steel, instruments, watches, textiles, foodstuffs (cheese, chocolate), chemicals, drugs, banking, tourism. **Chief crops:** Grains, potatoes, sugar beets, vegetables, tobacco. **Minerals:** Salt. **Other resources:** Hydro power potential. **Arable land:** 45%. **Meat prod.** (1983): beef: 154,000 metric tons; pork: 290,000 metric tons. **Electricity prod.** (1982): 50.7 bln. kwh. **Crude steel Prod.** (1981): 900,000 metric tons. **Labor force:** 39% ind. and commerce, 7% agric., 50% serv.

Finance: Currency: Franc (Mar. 1984: 2.15 = $1 US). **Gross domestic product** (1981): $100.5 bln. **Per capita income** (1981): $15,698. **Imports** (1983): $29.1 bln.; partners: W. Ger. 30%, Fr. 11%, It. 10%, U.K. 5%. **Exports** (1983): $25.5 bln.; partners: W. Ger. 18%, Fr. 9%, It. 8%, U.S. 8%. **Tourists** (1981): 11.2 mln.; receipts: $3.0 bln. **National budget** (1982): $9.8 bln. expenditures. **International reserves less gold** (Mar. 1984): $13.47 bln. **Gold:** 83.28 mln. oz t. **Consumer prices** (change in 1983): 3.0%.

Transport: Railway traffic (1982): 9.0 bln. passenger-km; 6.5 bln. net ton-km. **Motor vehicles:** in use (1982): 2.3 mln. passenger cars, 169,400 comm. vehicles. **Civil aviation:** (1982): 11.7 bln. passenger-km; 500.7 mln. freight ton-km.

Communications: Television sets: 2 mln. licensed (1981). **Radios:** 2.2 mln. licensed (1981). **Telephones in use** (1981): 4.7 mln. **Daily newspaper circ.** (1982): 593 per 1,000 pop.

Health: Life expectancy at birth (1982): 70.3 male; 76.2 female. **Births** (per 1,000 pop. 1980): 11.9. **Deaths** (per 1,000 pop. 1980): 9.2. **Natural increase** (1978): .2%. **Hospital beds** (per 100,000 pop. 1977): 1,141. **Physicians** (per 100,000 pop. 1977): 201. **Infant mortality** (per 1,000 live births 1982): 9. **Education** (1982): **Literacy:** 99%. **Years compulsory:** 9; attendance 100%.

Embassy: 2900 Cathedral Ave. NW 20008; 745-7900.

Switzerland, the Roman province of Helvetia, is a federation of 23 cantons (20 full cantons and 6 half cantons), 3 of which in 1291 created a defensive league and later were joined by other districts. Voters in the French-speaking part of Canton Bern voted for self-government, 1978; Canton Jura was created Jan. 1, 1979.

In 1648 the Swiss Confederation obtained its independence from the Holy Roman Empire. The cantons were joined under a federal constitution in 1848, with large powers of local control retained by each canton.

Switzerland has maintained an armed neutrality since 1815, and has not been involved in a foreign war since 1515. It is not a member of NATO or the UN. However, the Cabinet took steps, Mar. 28, 1979, to recommend Swiss membership in the UN. Switzerland is a member of several UN agencies and of the European Free Trade Assoc. and has ties with the EC. It is also the seat of many UN and other international agencies.

Switzerland is a leading world banking center; stability of the currency brings funds from many quarters. In 1984, voters rejected a proposal that would have opened bank records to authorities investigating domestic and foreign tax evasion. Some 20% of all workers are foreign residents.

Syria
Syrian Arab Republic

People: Population (1982 est.): 9,700,000. **Age distrib. (%):** 0–14: 47.9; 15–59: 47.6; 60+: 4.5. **Pop. density:** 125.60 per sq. mi. **Urban** (1981): 47.9%. **Ethnic groups:** Arabs 90%, Kurds, Armenians, Turks, Circassians, Assyrians. **Languages:** Arabic (official), Kurdish, Armenian, French, English. **Religions:** Sunni Muslim 70%, Christian 13%.

Geography: Area: 71,498 sq. mi., the size of North Dakota. **Location:** At eastern end of Mediterranean Sea. **Neighbors:** Lebanon, Israel on W, Jordan on S, Iraq on E, Turkey on N. **Topography:** Syria has a short Mediterranean coastline, then stretches E and S with fertile lowlands and plains, alternating with mountains and large desert areas. **Capital:** Damascus. **Cities** (1978 est.): Damascus 1,142,000; Aleppo 878,000; Homs 306,000.

Government: Type: Socialist. **Head of state:** Pres. Hafez al-Assad; b. Mar. 1930; in office: Feb. 22, 1971. **Head of government:** Prime Min. Abdul Rauf al-Kassem; in office: Jan. 16, 1980. **Local divisions:** Damascus and 13 provinces. **Defense:** 29% of govt. budget (1982).

Economy: Industries: Oil products, textiles, cement, tobacco, glassware, sugar, brassware. **Chief crops:** Cotton, grain, olives, fruits, vegetables. **Minerals:** Oil, phosphate, gypsum. **Crude oil reserves** (1980): 2.00 bln. bbls. **Other resources:** Wool. **Arable land:** 48%. **Meat prod.** (1983): beef: 26,000 metric tons; lamb: 99,000 metric tons. **Electricity prod.** (1982): 5.4 bln. kwh. **Labor force:** 32% agric.; 29% ind. & comm.; 39% services.

Finance: Currency: Pound (Mar. 1984: 3.92 = $1 US). **Gross domestic product** (1980): $12.6 bln. **Per capita income** (1975): $702. **Imports** (1982): $4.0 bln.; partners: Iraq 19%, It. 10%, W. Ger. 7%, Fr. 5%. **Exports** (1983): $2.0 bln.; partners: It. 42%, Rom. 10%. **Tourists** (1977): 681,100; receipts: $110 mln. **International reserves less gold** (June 1982): $115 mln. **Gold** (June 1982): 833,000 oz t. **Consumer prices** (change in 1982): 14.3%.

Transport: Railway traffic (1981): 443 mln. passenger-km; 704 mln. net ton-km. **Motor vehicles:** in use (1980): 65,000 passenger cars, 69,000 comm. vehicles **Civil aviation** (1982): 947 mln. passenger-km; 12.9 mln. net ton-km. **Chief ports:** Latakia, Tartus.

Communications: Television sets: 385,000 in use (1981). **Radios:** 2 mln. in use (1981). **Telephones in use** (1982): 355,000. **Daily newspaper circ.** (1982): 7 per 1,000 pop.

Health: Life expectancy at birth (1970): 54.49 male; 58.73 female. **Births** (per 1,000 pop. 1978): 43. **Deaths** (per 1,000 1978): 9. **Natural increase** (1978): 3.4%. **Hospital beds** (per 100,000 pop. 1977): 104. **Physicians** (per 100,000 pop. 1977): 39. **Infant mortality** (per 1,000 live births 1976): 15.3.

Education (1981): **Literacy:** 65%. **Years compulsory:** 6; attendance: 90%.

Embassy: 2215 Wyoming Ave. NW 20008; 232-6313.

Syria contains some of the most ancient remains of civilization. It was the center of the Seleucid empire, but later became absorbed in the Roman and Arab empires. Ottoman rule prevailed for 4 centuries, until the end of World War I.

The state of Syria was formed from former Turkish districts, made a separate entity by the Treaty of Sevres 1920 and divided into the states of Syria and Greater Lebanon. Both were administered under a French League of Nations mandate 1920-1941.

Syria was proclaimed a republic by the occupying French Sept. 16, 1941, and exercised full independence effective Jan. 1, 1944. French troops left in 1946. Syria joined in the Arab invasion of Israel in 1948.

Syria joined with Egypt in Feb. 1958 in the United Arab Republic but seceded Sept. 30, 1961. The Socialist Baath party and military leaders seized power in Mar. 1963. The Baath, a pan-Arab organization, became the only legal party. The government has been dominated by members of the minority Alawite sect.

In the Arab-Israeli war of June 1967, Israel seized and occupied the Golan Heights area inside Syria, from which Israeli settlements had for years been shelled by Syria.

Syria aided Palestinian guerrillas fighting Jordanian forces in Sept. 1970 and, after a renewal of that fighting in July 1971, broke off relations with Jordan. But by 1975 the 2 countries had entered a military coordination pact.

On Oct. 6, 1973, Syria joined Egypt in an attack on Israel. Arab oil states agreed in 1974 to give Syria $1 billion a year to aid anti-Israel moves. Military supplies used or lost in the 1973 war were replaced by the USSR in 1974. Some 30,000 Syrian troops entered Lebanon in 1976 to mediate in a civil war, and fought Palestinian guerrillas and, later, fought Christian militiamen. Syrian troops again battled Christian forces in Lebanon, Apr. 1981, ending a ceasefire that had been in place.

Following the June 6, 1982 Israeli invasion of Lebanon, Israeli planes destroyed 17 Syrian antiaircraft missile batteries in the Bekka Valley, June 9. Some 25 Syrian planes were downed during the engagement. Syrian and Israeli troops exchanged fire in central Lebanon. Israel and Syria agreed to a cease fire June 11. Syria has rejected a peace settlement in Lebanon until Israel withdraws its forces from Lebanon and the Golan Heights. In 1983, Syria backed the PLO rebels who ousted Yasir Arafat's forces from Tripoli.

In Feb. 1982, an uprising by antigovernment Muslim brotherhood militants brought heavy fighting and caused some 5,000 deaths.

Tanzania

United Republic of Tanzania

People: Population (1983 est.) 20,524,000. **Pop. density:** 47.96 per sq. mi. **Urban** (1984): 20%. **Ethnic groups:** African. **Languages:** Swahili, English are official. **Religions:** Moslems 35%, Christians 35%, traditional beliefs 30%.

Geography: Area: 364,886 sq. mi., more than twice the size of California. **Location:** On coast of E. Africa. **Neighbors:** Kenya, Uganda on N, Rwanda, Burundi, Zaire on W, Zambia, Malawi, Mozambique on S. **Topography:** Hot, arid central plateau, surrounded by the lake region in the W, temperate highlands in N and S, the coastal plains. Mt. Kilimanjaro, 19,340 ft., is highest in Africa. **Capital:** Dar-es-Salaam. **Cities** (1984): Dar-es-Salaam 1.4 mln.

Government: Type: Republic. **Head of state:** Pres. Julius Kambarage Nyerere; b. Mar. 1922; in office: Apr. 26, 1964. **Head of government:** Salim Ahmed Salim; b. 1942; in office: Apr. 24, 1984. **Local divisions:** 25 regions (20 on mainland). **Defense:** 10.4% of GDP (1982).

Economy: Industries: Food processing, clothing. **Chief crops:** Sisal, cotton, coffee, tea, tobacco. **Minerals:** Diamonds, gold, nickel. **Other resources:** Hides. **Arable land:** 15%. **Meat prod.** (1980): beef: 139,000 metric tons; lamb: 34,000 metric tons. **Fish catch** (1981): 226,000 metric tons. **Electricity prod.** (1981): 710 mln. kwh. **Labor force:** 83% agric., 17% ind. & comm.

Finance: Currency: Shilling (Mar. 1984: 12.36 = $1 US). **Gross domestic product** (1982): $4.56 bln. **Per capita income** (1982): $240. **Imports** (1982): $899 mln.; partners: UK 14%, Jap. 12%, W. Ger. 10%. **Exports** (1982): $373 mln.; partners: W. Ger. 15%, UK 13%. **Tourists** (1981): 91,600; receipts: $9 mln. **National budget** (1980): $973 mln. revenues; $933 mln. expenditures. **International reserves less gold** (Jan. 1984): $20.7 mln. **Consumer prices** (change in 1981): 25.6%.

Transport: Motor vehicles: in use (1981): 43,000 passenger cars, 22,500 comm. vehicles. **Chief ports:** Dar-es-Salaam, Mtwara, Tanga.

Communications: Radios: 500,000 in use (1981). **Telephones in use** (1981): 93,238. **Daily newspaper circ.** (1981): 3 per 1,000 pop.

Health: Life expectancy at birth (1984): 52 yrs. **Births** (per 1,000 pop. 1978): 47. **Deaths** (per 1,000 pop. 1978): 17. **Natural increase** (1978): 2.9%. **Hospital beds** (1981): 21,352. **Physicians** (1981): 599. **Infant mortality** (per 1,000 live births 1984): 103.

Education (1984): Literacy: 66%. **Attendance:** 87%.

Embassy: 2139 R. St. NW 20008; 939-6125.

The Republic of Tanganyika in E. Africa and the island Republic of Zanzibar, off the coast of Tanganyika, joined into a single nation, the United Republic of Tanzania, Apr. 26, 1964. Zanzibar retains internal self-government.

Tanganyika: Arab colonization and slaving began in the 8th century AD; Portuguese sailors explored the coast by about 1500. Other Europeans followed.

In 1885 Germany established German East Africa of which Tanganyika formed the bulk. It became a League of Nations mandate and, after 1946, a UN trust territory, both under Britain. It became independent Dec. 9, 1961, and a republic within the Commonwealth a year later.

In 1967 the government set on a socialist course; it nationalized all banks and many industries. The government also ordered that Swahili, not English, be used in all official business. Nine million people have been moved into cooperative villages. Tanzania exchanged invasion attacks with Uganda, 1978-79. Tanzanian forces drove Idi Amin from Uganda, Mar., 1979.

Zanzibar, the Isle of Cloves, lies 23 mi. off the coast of Tanganyika; its area is 640 sq. mi. The island of **Pemba,** 25 mi. to the NE, area 380 sq. mi., is included in the administration. The total population (1978 cen.) is 475,655.

Chief industry is the production of cloves and clove oil of which Zanzibar and Pemba produce the bulk of the world's supply.

Zanzibar was for centuries the center for Arab slave-traders. Portugal ruled for 2 centuries until ousted by Arabs around 1700. Zanzibar became a British Protectorate in 1890; independence came Dec. 10, 1963. Revolutionary forces overthrew the Sultan Jan. 12, 1964. The new government ousted American and British diplomats and newsmen, slaughtered thousands of Arabs, and nationalized farms. Union with Tanganyika followed, 1964. The ruling parties of Tanganyika and Zanzibar were united in 1977, as political tension eased.

Thailand

Kingdom of Thailand

People: Population (1983 est.): 50,731,000. **Age distrib. (%):** 0–14: 38.5; 15–59: 54.9; 60+: 6.6. **Pop. density:** 227.26 per sq. mi. **Urban** (1982): 15%. **Ethnic groups:** Thais 75%, Chinese 14%, others 11%. **Languages:** Thai, Chinese. **Religions:** Buddhists 95%, Moslems 4%.

Geography: Area: 198,500 sq. mi., about the size of Texas. **Location:** On Indochinese and Malayan Peninsulas in S.E. Asia. **Neighbors:** Burma on W, Laos on N, Cambodia on E, Malaysia on S. **Topography:** A plateau dominates the NE third of Thailand, dropping to the fertile alluvial valley of the Chao Phraya R. in the center. Forested mountains are in N, with narrow fertile valleys. The southern peninsula region is covered by rain forests. **Capital:** Bangkok. **Cities** (1980 est.): Bangkok (met.): 4.7 mln.

Government: Type: Constitutional monarchy. **Head of state:** King Bhumibol Adulyadej; b. Dec. 5, 1927; in office: June 9, 1946. **Head of government:** Prime Min. Prem Tinsulanond; b. 1920; in office: Mar. 3, 1980. **Local divisions:** 73 provinces. **Defense:** 4.2% of GNP (1982).

Economy: Industries: Auto assembly, drugs, textiles, electrical goods. **Chief crops:** Rice (a major export), corn tapioca, jute, sugar, coconuts, tobacco, pepper, peanuts, beans, cotton. **Minerals:** Antimony, tin (5th largest producer), tungsten, iron, manganese, gas. **Crude oil reserves** (1979): 200 bbls. **Other resources:** Forests (teak is exported), rubber. **Arable land:** 24%. **Meat prod.** (1983): beef: 220,000 metric tons; pork: 250,000 metric tons. **Fish catch** (1981): 1.6 mln. metric tons. **Electricity prod.** (1981): 450,000 metric tons. **Labor force:** 76% agric.; 9% ind. & comm.; 9% serv.; 6% govt.

Finance: Currency: Baht (Mar. 1984: 23.00 = $1 US). **Gross domestic product** (1981): $36 bln. **Per capita income** (1981): $758. **Imports** (1983): $10.0 bln.; partners: Jap. 24%, U.S. 13%, Saudi Ar. 13%. **Exports** (1981): $7.03 bln.; partners: Jap. 14%, U.S. 13%, Sing. 14%. **Tourists** (1981): 2 mln. receipts: $983 mln. **National budget** (1982): $7 bln. **International reserves less gold** (Mar. 1984): $1.9 bln. **Gold:** 2.48 mln. oz t. **Consumer prices** (change in 1983): 3.7%.

Transport: Railway traffic (1981): 8.8 bln. passenger-km; 2.8 bln. net ton-km. **Motor vehicles:** in use (1981): 451,000 passenger cars, 471,000 comm. vehicles. **Civil aviation** (1982): 8.6 bln. passenger-km; 320 mln. freight ton-km. **Chief ports:** Bangkok, Sattahip.

Communication: Television sets: 810,000 in use (1981). **Radios:** 5.9 mln. in use (1981). **Telephones in use** (1981): 496,558. **Daily newspaper circ.** (1982): 53 per 1,000 pop.

Health: Life expectancy at birth (1983): 59.5 male; 65.1 female. **Births** (per 1,000 pop. 1979): 25. **Deaths** (per 1,000 pop. 1978): 8. **Natural increase** (1978): 2.3%. **Hospital beds** (per 100,000 pop. 1977): 121. **Physicians** (per 100,000 pop. 1977): 12. **Infant mortality** (per 1,000 live births 1982): 68.
Education (1983): **Literacy:** 84%. **Years compulsory:** 7; attendance 83%.
Embassy: 2300 Kalorama Rd. NW 20008; 667-1446.

Thais began migrating from southern China in the 11th century. Thailand is the only country in SE Asia never taken over by a European power, thanks to King Mongkut and his son King Chulalongkorn who ruled from 1851 to 1910, modernized the country, and signed trade treaties with both Britain and France. A bloodless revolution in 1932 limited the monarchy.
Japan occupied the country in 1941. After the war, Thailand followed a pro-West foreign policy. Some 11,000 Thai troops fought in S. Vietnam, but were withdrawn by 1972.
The military took over the government in a bloody 1976 coup. Kriangsak Chomanan, prime minister since a 1977 military coup, resigned, Feb. 1980, under opposition over soaring inflation, oil price increases, labor unrest and growing crime.
Vietnamese troops crossed the border but were repulsed by Thai forces, Apr. 1983.

Togo

Republic of Togo

People: Population (1983 est.): 2,838,000. **Age distrib. (%):** 0-14: 49.8; 15-59: 44.6; 60+:5.6.**Pop. density:** 93 per sq. mi. **Urban** (1974): 15.2%. **Ethnic groups:** Ewe 20%, Mina 6%, Kabye 14%. **Languages:** French (official), others. **Religions:** Animist 60%, Christian 20%.
Geography: Area: 21,853 sq. mi., slightly smaller than West Virginia. **Location:** On S coast of W. Africa. **Neighbors:** Ghana on W, Upper Volta on N, Benin on E. **Topography:** A range of hills running SW-NE splits Togo into 2 savanna plains regions. **Capital:** Lomé. **Cities** (1980 est.): Lomé 283,000.
Government: Type: Republic. **Head of state:** Pres. Gnassingbe Eyadema; b. Dec. 26, 1937; in office: Apr. 14, 1967. **Local divisions:** 22 circumscriptions. **Armed forces:** regulars 3,000 (1980).
Economy: Industries: Textiles, shoes. **Chief crops:** Coffee, cocoa, yams, manioc, millet, rice. **Minerals:** Phosphates. **Arable land:** 15%. **Electricity prod.** (1980): 75 mln. kwh. **Labor force:** 78% agric.; 22% industry.
Finance: Currency: CFA franc (Mar. 1984: 399.00 = $1 US). **Gross domestic product** (1978): $765.5 mln. **Per capita income** (1978): $319. **Imports** (1979): $518 mln.; partners (1980): Fr. 25%, Nig. 16%, U.K 8%, W. Ger. 6%. **Exports** (1979): $219 mln.; partners (1980): Neth. 20%, Fr. 15%, W. Ger. 7%, Nig. 10%. **International reserves less gold** (Jan. 1984): $178.1 mln. **Gold:** 13,000 oz t. **Consumer prices** (change in 1982): 10.7%.
Transport: Railway traffic (1976): 91.2 mln. passenger-km; 37.7 mln. net ton-km. **Motor vehicles:** in use (1979): 20,000 passenger cars, 12,000 comm. vehicles. **Chief ports:** Lome.
Communications: Radios: 125,000 in use (1981). **Telephones in use** (1981): 7,870. **Daily newspaper circ.** (1982): 5 per 1,000 pop.
Health: Life expectancy at birth (1961): 31.6 male; 38.5 female. **Births** (per 1,000 pop. 1978): 45. **Deaths** (per 1,000 pop. 1978): 17. **Natural increase** (1978): 2.9%. **Hospital beds** (per 100,000 pop. 1977): 143. **Physicians** (per 100,000 pop. 1977): 6. **Infant mortality** (per 1,000 live births 1975): 127.
Education (1981): **Literacy:** 10%.
Embassy: 2208 Massachusetts Ave. NW 20008; 234-4212.

The Ewe arrived in southern Togo several centuries ago. The country later became a major source of slaves. Germany took control from 1884 on. France and Britain administered Togoland as UN trusteeships. The French sector became the republic of Togo Apr. 27, 1960.
The population is divided between Bantus in the S and Hamitic tribes in the N. Togo has actively promoted regional integration, as a means of stimulating the backward economy.

Tonga

Kingdom of Tonga

People: Population (1983 est.): 104,000. **Age distrib. (%):** 0-14: 44.4; 15-59; 50.5; 60+:5.1. **Pop. density:** 370.37 per sq. mi. **Ethnic groups:** Tongans 98%, other Polynesian, European. **Languages:** Tongan, English. **Religions:** Free Wesleyan 47%, Roman Catholics 14%, Free Church of Tonga 14%, Mormons 9%, Church of Tonga 9%.
Geography: Area: 270 sq. mi., smaller than New York City. **Location:** In western S. Pacific O. **Neighbors:** Nearest is Fiji, on W, New Zealand, on S. **Topography:** Tonga comprises 169 volcanic and coral islands, 45 inhabited. **Capital:** Nuku'alofa. **Cities** (1980 est.): Nuku'alofa (met.) 19,900.
Government: Type: Monarchy. **Head of state:** King Taufa'ahau Tupou IV; b. July 4, 1918; in office: Dec. 16, 1965. **Head of government:** Prime Min. Fatafehi Tu'ipelehake; b. Jan. 7, 1922; in office: Dec. 16, 1965. **Local divisions:** 3 island districts.
Economy: Industries: Tourism. **Chief crops:** Coconut products, bananas are exported. **Other resources:** Fish. **Per capita arable land:** 0.4 acres. **Electricity prod.** (1977): 7.00 mln. kwh. **Labor force:** 75% agric.
Finance: Currency: Pa'anga (Sept. 1982: 1.04 = $1 US). **Gross domestic product** (1976 est.): $40 mln. **Per capita income** (1976): $430. **Imports** (1979): $29 mln.; partners: N Z 37%, Austral. 23%, Jap. 6%, Fiji 7%. **Exports** (1979): $7 mln.; partners: Aust. 40%, N Z 38%.
Transport: Motor vehicles: in use (1974): 1,000 passenger cars, 400 comm. vehicles. **Chief ports:** Nuku'alofa.
Communications: Radios: 15,000 in use (1976). **Telephones in use** (1981): 2,196.
Health: Births (per 1,000 pop. 1976): 13.0. **Deaths** (per 1,000 pop. 1976): 1.9. **Natural increase** (1976): 1.1%. **Pop. per hospital bed** (1976): 300. **Pop. per physician** (1976): 3,000. **Infant mortality** (per 1,000 live births 1976): 20.5.

The islands were first visited by the Dutch in the early 17th century. A series of civil wars ended in 1845 with establishment of the Tupou dynasty. In 1900 Tonga became a British protectorate. On June 4, 1970, Tonga became completely independent and a member of the Commonwealth.

Trinidad and Tobago

Republic of Trinidad and Tobago

People: Population (1983 est.): 1,149,000. **Age distrib. (%):** 0-14: 38.0; 15-59: 55.4; 60+: 6.6. **Pop. density:** 570.71 per sq. mi. **Urban** (1970): 49.4%. **Ethnic groups:** Negroes 43%, East Indians 40%, mixed 14%. **Languages:** English (official), Hindi, French, Spanish. **Religions:** Roman Catholics 36%, Protestants 13%, Hindus 23%, Muslims 6%.
Geography: Area: 1,970 sq. mi., the size of Delaware. **Location:** Off eastern coast of Venezuela. **Neighbors:** Nearest is Venezuela on SW. **Topography:** Three low mountain ranges cross Trinidad E-W, with a well-watered plain between N and Central Ranges. Parts of E and W coasts are swamps. Tobago, 116 sq. mi., lies 20 mi. NE. **Capital:** Port-of-Spain. **Cities** (1981 est.): Port-of-Spain (met.) 250,000; San Fernando 50,000.
Government: Type: Parliamentary democracy. **Head of state:** Pres. Ellis E. I. Clarke; b. Dec. 28, 1917; in office: July 31, 1976. **Head of government:** Prime Min. George Chambers; b. Oct. 4, 1928; in office: Mar. 30, 1981. **Local divisions:** 8 counties, Tobago, 4 cities.
Economy: Industries: Oil products, rum, cement, tourism. **Chief crops:** Sugar, cocoa, coffee, citrus fruits, bananas. **Minerals:** Asphalt, oil, **Crude oil reserves** (1980): 700 mln. bbls. **Arable land:** 25%. **Electricity prod.** (1982): 2 bln. kwh. **Labor force:** 10% agric., 66% construction, mining, commerce.
Finance: Currency: Dollar (Feb. 1984: 2.40 = $1 US). **Gross domestic product** (1980): $5.03 bln. **Per capita income** (1980): $4,800. **Imports** (1983): $2.5 bln.; partners: Saudi Ar. 26%, U.S. 26%, UK 9%. **Exports** (1983): $2.3 bln.; partners: U.S. 59%, Neth. 5%. **National budget** (1980): $2.5 bln. revenues; $2.6 bln. expenditures. **International reserves less gold**

(Mar. 1984): $1.8 bln. **Gold:** 54,000 oz t. **Consumer prices** (change in 1983): 17.3%.

Transport: Motor vehicles: in use (1982): 180,000 passenger cars, 45,000 comm. vehicles. **Civil aviation:** (1982): 1.5 bln. passenger-km; 5.5 mln. freight ton-km. **Chief ports:** Port-of-Spain.

Communications: Television sets: 150,000 in use (1981). **Radios:** 300,000 licensed (1981). **Telephones in use** (1980): 77,800. **Daily newspaper circ.** (1982): 143 per 1,000 pop.

Health: Life expectancy at birth (1980): 66 male; 72 female. **Births** (per 1,000 pop. 1979): 23.8. **Deaths** (per 1,000 pop. 1979): 6.6. **Natural increase** (1978): 1.9%. **Hospital beds** (per 100,000 pop. 1977): 445. **Physicians** (per 100,000 pop 1977): 54. **Infant mortality** (per 1,000 pop. 1978): 286.

Education (1978): **Literacy:** 92%. **Pop. 5-19:** in school: 48%, teachers per 1,000: 22.

Embassy: 1708 Massachusetts Ave. NW 20036; 467-6490.

Columbus sighted Trinidad in 1498. A British possession since 1802, Trinidad and Tobago won independence Aug. 31, 1962. It became a republic in 1976. The People's National Movement party has held control of the government since 1956.

The nation is one of the most prosperous in the Caribbean, but unemployment usually averages 13%. Oil production has increased with offshore finds. Middle Eastern oil is refined and exported, mostly to the U.S.

Tunisia
Republic of Tunisia

People: Population (1983 est.): 7,020,000. **Age distrib. (%)** 0–14: 43.3 15–59: 50.9; 60+: 5.8. **Pop. density:** 100.35 per sq. mi. **Ethnic groups:** Arab 98%. **Languages:** Arabic (official), French. **Religions:** Mainly Muslim, Christian and Jewish minorities.

Geography: Area: 63,378 sq. mi., about the size of Missouri. **Location:** On N coast of Africa. **Neighbors:** Algeria on W, Libya on E. **Topography:** The N is wooded and fertile. The central coastal plains are given to grazing and orchards. The S is arid, approaching Sahara Desert. **Capital:** Tunis. **Cities** (1982 est.) Tunis 1,000,000, Sfax 475,000.

Government: Type: Republic. **Head of state:** Pres. Habib Bourguiba; b. Aug. 3, 1903; in office: July 25, 1957. **Head of government:** Prime Min. Mohammed Mzali; b. Dec. 23, 1925; in office: Apr. 23, 1980. **Local divisions:** 21 governorates. **Defense:** less than 2% of GDP (1982).

Economy: Industries: Food processing, textiles, oil products, construction materials, tourism. **Chief crops:** Grains, dates, olives, citrus fruits, figs, vegetables, grapes. **Minerals:** Phosphates, iron, oil, lead, zinc. **Crude oil reserves** (1980): 2.25 bln. bbls. **Arable land:** 30%. **Meat prod.** (1980): beef: 26,000 metric tons; lamb: 27,000 metric tons. **Fish catch** (1981): 57,500 metric tons. **Electricity prod.** (1982): 3.0 bln. kwh. **Crude steel prod.** (1982): 106,000 metric tons. **Labor force:** 35% agric.; 22% industry; 11% serv.

Finance: Currency: Dinar (Mar. 1984: .71 = $1 US). **Gross domestic product** (1982): $8.4 bln. **Per capita income** (1981) $1,200. **Imports** (1983): $3.1 bln.; partners: Fr. 26%, W. Ger. 11%, It. 15%. **Exports** (1983): $1.8 bln.; partners: It. 17%, Fr. 19%, W. Ger. 10%, U.S. 23%. **Tourists** (1981): 2.1 mln.; receipts: $581 mln. **National budget** (1980): $1.54 bln. revenues; $1.50 bln. expenditures. **International reserves less gold** (Mar. 1984): $437.2 mln. **Gold:** 187,000 oz t. **Consumer prices** (change in 1983): 9.0%.

Transport: Railway traffic (1982): 930 mln. passenger-km; 1.5 bln. net ton-km. **Motor vehicles:** in use (1982): 141,000 passenger cars, 141,000 comm. vehicles; **Civil aviation:** (1982): 1.5 bln. passenger-km; 17.3 mln. freight ton-km. **Chief ports:** Tunis, Sfax, Bizerte.

Communications: Television sets: 300,000 in use (1981). Radios: 1 mln. in use (1982). **Telephones in use** (1981): 188,000. **Daily newspaper circ.** (1982): 49 per 1,000 pop.

Health: Life expectancy at birth (1975): 54.0 male; 56.0 female. **Births** (per 1,000 pop. 1978): 34.1. **Deaths** (per 1,000 pop. 1975): 12.5. **Natural increase** (1975): 2.4%. **Hospital beds** (per 100,000 pop. 1977): 229. **Physicians** (per 100,000 pop. 1977): 4. **Infant mortality** (per 1,000 pop. under 1 yr. 1982): 90.

Education (1982): **Literacy:** 62%. **Years compulsory:** 8; attendance 85%.

Embassy: 2408 Massachusetts Ave. NW 20008; 234-6644.

Site of ancient Carthage, and a former Barbary state under the suzerainty of Turkey, Tunisia became a protectorate of France under a treaty signed May 12, 1881. The nation became independent Mar. 20, 1956, and ended the monarchy the following year. Habib Bourguiba has headed the country since independence.

Although Tunisia is a member of the Arab League, Bourguiba in the 1960s urged negotiations to end Arab-Israeli disputes and was denounced by other members. In 1966 he broke relations with Egypt but resumed them after the 1967 Arab-Israeli war.

Tunisia survived a Libyan-engineered raid against the southern mining center of Gafsa, Jan. 1980. A liberal-minded government undertook steps to ease the blocked political situation. Some 1,000 rioters were arrested following an announced 125% increase in the price of bread.

Turkey
Republic of Turkey

People: Population (1983 est.): 49,155,000. **Age distrib. (%):** 0–14: 38.5; 15–59: 54.9; 60+: 6.6. **Pop. density:** 150.50 per sq. mi. **Urban** (1977): 44.6%. **Ethnic groups:** Turks 85%, Kurds 12%. **Languages:** Turkish (official), Kurdish, Arabic. **Religions:** Muslims 98%, Christians, Jews.

Geography: Area: 300,948 sq. mi., twice the size of California. **Location:** Occupies Asia Minor, between Mediterranean and Black Seas. **Neighbors:** Bulgaria, Greece on W, USSR (Georgia, Armenia) on N, Iran on E, Iraq, Syria on S. **Topography:** Central Turkey has wide plateaus, with hot, dry summers and cold winters. High mountains ring the interior on all but W, with more than 20 peaks over 10,000 ft. Rolling plains are in W; mild, fertile coastal plains are in S, W. **Capital:** Ankara. **Cities** (1980 cen.): Istanbul 2,772,708; Ankara 1,877,755; Izmir 757,854; Adana 574,515.

Government: Type: Republic. **Head of state:** Pres. Kenan Evren; b. 1918; in office: Oct. 27, 1980. **Head of government:** Prime Min. Turgut Ozal; in office: Dec. 13, 1983. **Local divisions:** 67 provinces, with appointed governors. **Defense:** 4.8% of GNP (1981).

Economy: Industries: Silk, textiles, steel, shoes, furniture, cement, paper, glassware, appliances. **Chief crops:** Tobacco (6th largest producer), cereals, cotton, olives, figs, nuts, sugar, opium gums. **Minerals:** Antimony, chromium, mercury, borate, copper, molybdenum, magnesite, asbestos. **Crude oil reserves** (1980): 125 mln. bbls. **Other resources:** Wool, silk, forests. **Arable land:** 35%. **Meat prod.** (1983): beef: 240,000 metric tons; lamb: 433,000 metric tons. **Fish catch** (1981): 470,000 metric tons. **Electricity prod.** (1982): 26.4 bln. kwh. **Crude steel prod.** (1982): 2.1 mln. metric tons. **Labor force:** 61% agric.; 12% ind. and comm.; 27% serv.

Finance: Currency: Lira (Mar. 1984: 322.69 = $1 US). **Gross domestic product** (1981): $59.7 bln. **Per capita income** (1981): $1,300. **Imports** (1983): $9.2 bln.; partners: Iraq 16%, W. Ger. 11%, Libya 10%, U.S. 9%. **Exports** (1983): $5.7 bln.; partners: W. Ger. 12%, Iraq 10%, Iran 14%. **Tourists** (1981): 1.4 mln.; receipts: $327 mln. **National budget** (1983): $12 bln. expenditures. **International reserves less gold** (Feb. 1984): $1.16 bln. **Gold:** 3.77 mln. oz t. **Consumer prices** (change in 1983): 28.9%.

Transport: Railway traffic (1981): 6.1 bln. passenger-km; 5.9 bln. net ton-km. **Motor vehicles:** in use (1981): 714,000 passenger cars, 341,000 comm. vehicles. **Civil aviation** (1982): 1.1 bln. passenger-km; 20 mln. freight ton-km. **Chief ports:** Istanbul, Izmir, Mersin, Samsun.

Communications: Television sets: 4.5 mln. in use (1982). **Radios:** 4.2 mln. licensed (1982). **Telephones in use** (1982): 1.2 mln.

Health: Life expectancy at birth (1983): 57 years. **Births** (per 1,000 pop. 1978): 35. **Deaths** (per 1,000 pop. 1978): 12. **Natural increase** (1978): 2.4%. **Hospital beds** (1980): 99,177. **Physicians** (1980): 27,241. **Infant mortality** (per 1,000 live births 1983): 15.3.

Education (1983): **Literacy:** 70%. **Years compulsory:** 6; attendance 95%.

Embassy: 1606 23d St. NW 20008; 667-6400.

Ancient inhabitants of Turkey were among the worlds first agriculturalists. Such civilizations as the Hittite, Phrygian, and Lydian flourished in Asiatic Turkey (Asia Minor), as did much of Greek civilization. After the fall of Rome in the 5th century, Constantinople was the capital of the Byzantine Empire for 1,000 years. It fell in 1453 to Ottoman Turks, who ruled a vast empire for over 400 years.

Just before World War I, Turkey, or the Ottoman Empire, ruled what is now Syria, Lebanon, Iraq, Jordan, Israel, Saudi Arabia, Yemen, and islands in the Aegean Sea.

Turkey joined Germany and Austria in World War I and its defeat resulted in loss of much territory and fall of the sultanate. A republic was declared Oct. 29, 1923. The Caliphate (spiritual leadership of Islam) was renounced 1924.

Long embroiled with Greece over Cyprus, off Turkey's south coast, Turkey invaded the island July 20, 1974, after Greek officers seized the Cypriot government as a step toward unification with Greece. Turkey sought a new government for Cyprus, with Greek Cypriot and Turkish Cypriot zones. In reaction to Turkey's moves, the U.S. cut off military aid in 1975. Turkey, in turn, suspended the use of most U.S. bases. Aid was restored in 1978. There was a military takeover, Sept. 12, 1980.

Religious and ethnic tensions and active left and right extremists have caused endemic violence. Martial law, imposed since 1978, was lifted in 1984. The military formally transferred power to an elected parliament in 1983.

Tuvalu

People: Population (1983 est.): 8,000. **Pop. density:** 700 per sq. mi. **Ethnic group:** Polynesian. **Languages:** Tuvaluan, English. **Religions:** mainly Protestant.

Geography: Area: 10 sq. mi., less than one-half the size of Manhattan. **Location:** 9 islands forming a NW-SE chain 360 mi. long in the SW Pacific O. **Neighbors:** Nearest are Samoa on SE, Fiji on S. **Topography:** The islands are all low-lying atolls, nowhere rising more than 15 ft. above sea level, composed of coral reefs. **Capital:** Funafuti (pop. 1979): 2,200.

Government: Head of state: Queen Elizabeth II, represented by Gov.-Gen. Penitala Fiatau Teo, b. July 23, 1911; in office: Oct. 1, 1978. **Head of government:** Prime Min. Tomasi Puapua; in office: Sept. 8, 1981. **Local divisions:** 8 island councils on the permanently inhabited islands.

Economy: Industries: Copra. **Chief crops:** Coconuts. **Labor force:** Approx. 1,500 Tuvaluans work overseas in the Gilberts' phosphate industry, or as overseas seamen.

Finance: Currency: Australian dollar. **Imports** (1979): $1.83 mln. **Exports** (1979): $276,047; partners: UK, Australia.

Transport: Chief port: Funafuti.

Health: (including former Gilbert Is.) **Life expectancy at birth** (1962): 56.9 male; 59.0 female. **Births** (per 1,000 pop. 1971): 22.3. **Deaths** (per 1,000 pop. 1971): 6.5. **Natural increase** (1971): 1.6%. **Infant mortality** (per 1,000 pop. under 1 yr. 1971): 48.9.

Education (1978): Pop. 5–19: in school (1976): 1,794.

The Ellice Islands separated from the British Gilbert and Ellice Islands colony, 1975, and became independent Tuvalu Oct. 1, 1978.

Britain is committed to providing extensive economic aid. Australian funding has provided for a marine training school and a deep-sea wharf.

Uganda
Republic of Uganda

People: Population (1983 est.): 13,819,000. **Age distrib.** (%): 0–14: 46.1; 15–59: 47.9; 60+: 5.8. **Pop. density:** 140.23 per sq. mi. **Urban** (1980): 8.1%. **Ethnic groups:** Bantu, Nilotic, Nilo-Hamitic, Sudanic tribes. **Languages:** English (official), Luganda, Swahili. **Religions:** Christians 63%, Moslems 6%, traditional beliefs.

Geography: Area: 91,104 sq. mi., slightly smaller than Oregon. **Location:** In E. Central Africa. **Neighbors:** Sudan on N, Zaire on W, Rwanda, Tanzania on S, Kenya on E. **Topography:** Most of Uganda is a high plateau 3,000–6,000 ft. high, with high Ruwenzori range in W (Mt. Margherita 16,750 ft.), volcanoes in

SW, NE is arid, W and SW rainy. Lakes Victoria, Edward, Albert form much of borders. **Capital:** Kampala. **Cities** (1980): Kampala 458,000.

Government: Type: Republic. **Head of state:** Pres. Milton Obote; b. 1925; assumed full control Sept. 17, 1980; elections held Dec. 1980. **Head of government:** Prime Min. Erifasi Otema Allimadi; in office: Dec. 1980. **Local divisions:** 10 provinces, 34 districts. **Armed forces:** regulars 21,000 (1980).

Economy: Chief Crops: Coffee, cotton, tea, corn, peanuts, bananas, sugar. **Minerals:** Copper, cobalt. **Arable land:** 25%. **Meat prod.** (1980): beef: 92,000 metric tons; lamb: 13,000 metric tons. **Fish catch** (1981): 167,000 metric tons. **Electricity prod.** (1981): 657 mln. kwh. **Labor force:** 90% agric.

Finance: Currency: Shilling (Mar. 1984: 292.04 = $1 US). **Gross domestic product** (1978): $8.36 bln. **Per capita income** (1976): $240. **Imports** (1978): $255 mln.; partners: (1979): Kenya 28%, UK 17%, W. Ger. 13%, Jap. 8%, It. 7%. **Exports** (1979): $426 mln.; partners (1978): U.S. 21%, UK 16%, Fr. 10%, Jap. 9%. **National budget** (1981): $641 mln. revenues; $871 mln. expenditures. **International reserves less gold** (Apr. 1981): $45.3 mln. **Consumer prices** (change in 1978): 36.5%.

Transport: Motor vehicles: in use (1979): 26,000 passenger cars, 5,400 comm. vehicles.

Communications: Television sets: 72,000 in use (1981). **Radios:** 275,000 in use (1981). **Telephones in use** (1981): 47,000. **Daily newspaper circ.** (1982): 2 per 1,000 pop.

Health: Life expectancy at birth (1975): 48.3 male; 51.7 female. **Births** (per 1,000 pop. 1978): 48. **Deaths** (per 1,000 pop. 1978): 17. **Natural increase** (1978): 3.2%. **Hospital beds** (per 100,000 pop. 1977): 157. **Physicians** (per 100,000 pop. 1977): 20. **Infant mortality** (per 1,000 live births (1981): 120.

Education (1978): **Literacy:** 25%. **Pop. 5-19:** in school: 27%, teachers per 1,000: 8.

Embassy: 5909 16th St. NW 20011; 726-7100.

Britain obtained a protectorate over Uganda in 1894. The country became independent Oct. 9, 1962, and a republic within the Commonwealth a year later. In 1967, the traditional kingdoms, including the powerful Buganda state, were abolished and the central government strengthened.

Gen. Idi Amin seized power from Prime Min. Milton Obote in 1971. As many as 300,000 of his opponents were reported killed in subsequent years. Amin was named president for life in 1976.

In 1972 Amin expelled nearly all of Uganda's 45,000 Asians. In 1973 the U.S., Canada, and Norway ended economic aid programs; the U.S. withdrew all diplomatic personnel.

A June 1977 Commonwealth conference condemned the Amin government for its "disregard for the sanctity of human life."

Amid worsening economic and domestic crises, Uganda's troops exchanged invasion attacks with long-standing foe Tanzania, 1978 to 1979. Tanzanian forces, coupled with Ugandan exiles and rebels, ended the dictatorial rule of Amin, Apr. 11, 1979.

The U.S. reopened its embassy, reinstated economic aid, and ended its trade embargo in 1979.

Four governments have been in power since Amin fled. The country remains in economic and social chaos.

Union of Soviet Socialist Republics

People: Population (1983 est.): 272,500,000. **Age distrib.** (%): 0–19: 36.7; 20-59: 50.5; 60+: 12.7. **Pop. density:** 31 per sq. mi. **Urban** (1979): 62%. **Ethnic groups:** Russians 52% Ukrainians 16%, Uzbeks 5%, Byelorussians 4%, many others. **Languages:** Slavic (Russian, Ukrainian, Byelorussian, Polish), Altaic (Turkish, etc.), other Indo-European, Uralian, Caucasian. **Religions:** Russian Orthodox 18%, Moslems 9%, other Orthodox, Protestants, Jews, Buddhists.

Geography: Area: 8,649,490 sq. mi., the largest country in the world, nearly 2½ times the size of the U.S. **Location:** Stretches from E. Europe across N Asia to the Pacific O. **Neighbors:** Finland, Poland, Czechoslovakia, Hungary, Romania on W, Turkey, Iran, Afghanistan, China, Mongolia, N. Korea on S. **Topography:** Covering one-sixth of the earth's land area, the USSR contains every type of climate except the distinctly tropical, and has a varied topography.

The European portion is a low plain, grassy in S, wooded in N with Ural Mtns. on the E. Caucasus Mts. on the S. Urals stretch N-S for 2,500 mi. The Asiatic portion is also a vast plain, with mountains on the S and in the E; tundra covers extreme N, with forest belt below; plains, marshes are in W, desert in SW. **Capital:** Moscow. **Cities** (1981 est.): Moscow 8.2 mln.; Leningrad 4.6 mln.; Kiev 2.2 mln.; Tashkent 1.8 mln.; Kharkov 1.4 mln.; Gorky 1.3 mln.; Novosibirsk 1.3 mln.; Minsk 1.3 mln.; Kuibyshev 1.2 mln.; Sverdlovsk 1.2 mln.

Government: Type: Federal Union. **Head of state:** Pres. Konstantin U. Chernenko; b. Sept. 24, 1911; in office: Apr. 11, 1984. **Head of government:** Premier Nikolai A. Tikhonov; b. May 1, 1905; in office: Oct. 23, 1980. **Head of Communist Party:** Gen. Sec. Konstantin U. Chernenko; in office Feb. 13, 1984. **Local divisions:** 15 union republics, within which are 20 autonomous republics, 6 krays (territories), 120 oblasts (regions), 8 autonomous oblasts, 10 national areas. **Defense:** 12%-14% of GNP (1980).

Economy: Industries: Steel, machinery, machine tools, vehicles, chemicals, cement, textiles, appliances, paper. **Chief crops:** Grain, cotton, sugar beets, potatoes, vegetables, sunflowers. **Minerals:** Iron, manganese, mercury, potash, antimony, bauxite, cobalt, chromium, copper, coal, gold, lead, molybdenum, nickel, phosphates, silver, tin, tungsten, zinc, oil (59%), potassium salts. **Crude oil reserves** (1980): 67.00 bln. bbls. **Other resources:** Forests (25% of world reserves). **Per capita arable land:** 2.1 acres. **Meat prod.** (1980): beef: 6.7 mln. metric tons; pork; 5.0 mln. metric tons; lamb: 853,000 metric tons. **Fish catch** (1982): 9.5 mln. metric tons. **Electricity prod.** (1982): 1,366 bln. kwh. **Crude steel prod.** (1982): 147 mln. metric tons. **Labor force:** 20% agric.; 29% industry, 21% services.

Finance: Currency: Ruble (Sept. 1983: .77 = $1 US). **Gross national product** (1980): $1.5 tln. **Per capita income** (1976): $2,600. **Imports** (1980): $59.19 bln.; partners: E. Ger. 10%, Pol. 7%, Czech. 8%, Bulg. 8%. **Exports** (1980): $66.29 bln.; partners: E. Ger. 10%, Pol. 8%, Bulg. 8%, Czech. 8%. **National budget** (1981): $381 bln. revenues; $381 bln. expenditures. **Tourists** (1977): 4,399,800. **Consumer prices** (change in 1979): 0.7%.

Transport: Railway traffic (1981): 344.6 bln. passenger-km; 3,581 bln. net ton-km. **Motor vehicles:** in use (1980): 9.2 mln. passenger cars, 7.9 mln. comm. vehicles; manuf. (1982): 1.3 mln. passenger cars; 874,000 comm. vehicles. **Civil aviation** (1982): 172 bln. passenger-km; 3 bln. freight ton-km. **Chief ports:** Leningrad, Odessa, Murmansk, Kaliningrad, Archangelsk, Riga, Vladivostok.

Communications: Television sets: 80 mln. in use (1979). **Radios:** 130 mln. in use (1981). **Telephones in use** (1981): 23.7 mln. **Daily newspaper circ.** (1982): 312 per 1,000 pop.

Health: Life expectancy at birth (1972): 64 male; 74 female. **Births** (per 1,000 pop. 1980): 18.3. **Deaths** (per 1,000 pop. 1980): 9.3. **Natural increase** (1976): .9%. **Hospital beds** (per 100,000 pop. 1977): 1,213. **Physicians** (per 100,000 pop. 1977): 346. **Infant mortality** (per 1,000 live births 1981): 44.

Education (1981): **Literacy:** 99%. Most receive 10 years of schooling.

Embassy: 1125 16th St. NW 20036; 628-7551.

The USSR is nominally a federation consisting of 15 union republics, the largest being the Russian Soviet Federated Socialist Republic. Important positions in the republics are filled by centrally chosen appointees, often ethnic Russians.

Beginning in 1939 the USSR by means of military action and negotiation overran contiguous territory and independent republics, including all or part of Lithuania, Latvia, Estonia, Poland, Czechoslovakia, Romania, Germany, Finland, Tannu Tuva, and Japan. The union republics are:

Republic	Area sq. mi.	Pop. (cen. 1979)
Russian SFSR	6,593,391	137,552,000
Ukrainian SSR	232,046	49,757,000
Uzbek SSR	158,069	15,391,000
Kazakh SSR	1,064,092	14,685,000

Republic	Area sq. mi.	Pop. (cen. 1979)
Byelorussian SSR	80,154	9,559,000
Azerbaijan SSR	33,436	6,028,000
Georgian SSR	26,911	5,016,000
Moldavian SSR	13,012	3,948,000
Tadzhik SSR	54,019	3,801,000
Kirghiz SSR	76,642	3,529,000
Lithuanian SSR	26,173	3,399,000
Armenian SSR	11,306	3,031,000
Turkmen SSR	188,417	2,759,000
Latvian SSR	24,695	2,521,000
Estonian SSR	17,413	1,466,000

The **Russian Soviet Federated Socialist Republic** contains over 50% of the population of the USSR and includes 76% of its territory. It extends from the old Estonian, Latvian, and Finnish borders and the Byelorussian and Ukrainian lines on the W, to the shores of the Pacific, and from the Arctic on the N to the Black and Caspian seas and the borders of Kazakh SSR, Mongolia, and Manchuria on the S. Siberia encompasses a large part of the RSFSR area. Capital: Moscow.

Parts of eastern and western Siberia have been transformed by steel mills, huge dams, oil and gas industries, electric railroads, and highways.

The **Ukraine**, the most densely populated of the republics, borders on the Black Sea, with Poland, Czechoslovakia, Hungary, and Romania on the W and SW. Capital: Kiev.

The Ukraine contains the arable black soil belt, the chief wheat-producing section of the Soviet Union. Sugar beets, potatoes, and livestock are important.

The Donets Basin has large deposits of coal, iron and other metals. There are chemical and machine industries and salt mines.

Byelorussia (White Russia). Capital: Minsk. Chief industries include machinery, tools, appliances, tractors, clocks, cameras, steel, cement, textiles, paper, leather, glass. Main crops are grain, flax, potatoes, sugar beets.

Azerbaijan boasts near Baku, the capital, important oil fields. Its natural wealth includes deposits of iron ore, cobalt, etc. A high-yield winter wheat is grown, as are fruits. It produces iron, steel, cement, fertilizers, synthetic rubber, electrical and chemical equipment. It borders on Iran and Turkey.

Georgia, in the western part of Transcaucasia, contains the largest manganese mines in the world. There are rich timber resources and coal mines. Basic industries are food, textiles, iron, steel. Grain, tea, tobacco, fruits, grapes are grown. Capital: Tbilisi (Tiflis). Despite massive party and government purges since 1972, illegal private enterprise and Georgian nationalist feelings persist; attempts to repress them have led to violence.

Armenia is mountainous, sub-tropical, extensively irrigated. Copper, zinc, aluminum, molybdenum, and marble are mined. Instrument making is important. Capital: Erevan.

Uzbekistan, most important economically of the Central Asia republics, produces 67% of USSR cotton, 50% of rice, 33% of silk, 34% of astrakhan, 85% of hemp. Industries include iron, steel, cars, tractors, TV and radio sets, textiles, food. Mineral wealth includes coal, sulphur, copper, and oil. Capital: Tashkent.

Turkmenistan in Central Asia, produces cotton, maize, carpets, chemicals. Minerals: oil, coal, sulphur, barite, lime, salt, gypsum. The Kara Kum desert occupies 80% of the area. Capital: Ashkhabad.

Tadzhikistan borders on China and Afghanistan. Over half the population are Tadzhiks, mostly Moslems, speaking an Iranian dialect. Chief occupations are farming and cattle breeding. Cotton, grain, rice, and a variety of fruits are grown. Heavy industry, based on rich mineral deposits, coal and hydroelectric power, has replaced handicrafts. Capital: Dushanbe.

Kazakhstan extends from the lower reaches of the Volga in Europe to the Altai Mtns. on the Chinese border. It has vast deposits of coal, oil, iron, tin, copper, lead, zinc, etc. Fish for its canning industry are caught in Lake Balkhash and the Caspian and Aral seas. The capital is Alma-Ata. About 50% of the population is Russian or Ukrainian, working in the virgin-grain lands opened up after 1954, and in the growing industries. Capital: Alma-Ata.

Kirghizia is the eastern part of Soviet Central Asia, on the frontier of Xinjiang, China. The people breed cattle and horses and grow tobacco, cotton, rice, sugar beets. Industries include machine and instrument making, chemicals. Capital: Frunze.

Moldavia, in the SW part of the USSR, is a fertile black earth plain bordering Romania and includes Bessarabia. It is an agricultural region that grows grains, fruits, vegetables, and tobacco. Textiles, wine, food and electrical equipment industries have been developed. Capital: Kishinev. The region was taken from Romania in 1940; the people speak Romanian.

Lithuania, on the Baltic, produces cattle, hogs, electric motors, and appliances. The capital is Vilnius (Vilna). **Latvia** on the Baltic and the Gulf of Riga, has timber and peat resources est. at 3 bln. tons. In addition to agricultural products it produces rubber goods, dyes, fertilizers, glassware, telephone apparatus, TV and radio sets, railroad cars. Capital: Riga.

Estonia, also on the Baltic, has textiles, shipbuilding, timber, roadmaking and mining equipment industries and a shale oil refining industry. Capital: Tallinn. The 3 Baltic states were provinces of imperial Russia before World War I, were independent nations between World Wars I and II, but were conquered by Russia in 1940. The U.S. has never formally recognized the takeover.

Economy. Almost all legal economic enterprises are state-owned. There were 29,600 collective farms in 1976, along with 18,064 larger state farms. A huge illegal black market plays an important role in distribution; illegal private production and service firms are periodically exposed.

The USSR is incalculably rich in natural resources; distant Siberian reserves are being exploited with Japanese assistance. Its heavy industry is 2d only to the U.S. It leads the world in oil and steel production. Consumer industries have lagged comparatively. Agricultural output has expanded, but in poor crop years the USSR has been forced to make huge grain purchases from the West. Shortages and rationing of basic food products periodically occur.

Exports include petroleum and its products, iron and steel, rolled non-ferrous metals, industrial plant equipment, arms, lumber, cotton, asbestos, gold, manganese, and others.

Industrial growth has dropped, due to short falls in oil, coal, and steel industries, as well as poor grain harvests since 1979.

History. Slavic tribes began migrating into Russia from the W in the 5th century AD. The first Russian state, founded by Scandinavian chieftains, was established in the 9th century, centering in Novgorod and Kiev.

In the 13th century the Mongols overran the country. It recovered under the grand dukes and princes of Muscovy, or Moscow, and by 1480 freed itself from the Mongols. Ivan the Terrible was the first to be formally proclaimed Tsar (1547). Peter the Great (1682-1725), extended the domain and in 1721, founded the Russian Empire.

Western ideas and the beginnings of modernization spread through the huge Russian empire in the 19th and early 20th centuries. But political evolution failed to keep pace.

Military reverses in the 1905 war with Japan and in World War I led to the breakdown of the Tsarist regime. The 1917 Revolution began in March with a series of sporadic strikes for higher wages by factory workers. A provisional democratic government under Prince Georgi Lvov was established but was quickly followed in May by the second provisional government, led by Alexander Kerensky. The Kerensky government and the freely-elected Constituent Assembly were overthrown in a Communist coup led by Vladimir Ilyich Lenin Nov. 7.

Lenin's death Jan. 21, 1924, resulted in an internal power struggle from which Joseph Stalin eventually emerged the absolute ruler of Russia. Stalin secured his position at first by exiling opponents, but from the 1930s to 1953, he resorted to a series of "purge" trials, mass executions, and mass exiles to work camps. These measures resulted in millions of deaths, according to most estimates.

Germany and the USSR signed a non-aggression pact Aug. 1939; Nazi forces launched a massive invasion of the Soviet Union, June 1941. Notable heroic episode was the "900 days" siege of Leningrad, lasting to Jan. 1944, and causing 1,000,000 deaths; the city was never taken. Russian winter counterthrusts, 1941 to '42 and 1942 to '43, stopped the German advance. Turning point was the failure of German troops to take and hold Stalingrad, Sept. 1942 to Feb. 1943. With British and U.S. Lend-Lease aid and sustaining great casualties, the Russians drove the Axis from eastern Europe and the Balkans in the next 2 years.

After Stalin died, Mar. 5, 1953, Nikita Khrushchev was elected first secretary of the Central Committee. In 1956 he condemned Stalin. "De-Stalinization" of the country on all levels was effected after Stalin's body was removed from the Lenin-Stalin tomb in Moscow.

Under Khrushchev the open antagonism of Poles and Hungarians toward domination by Moscow was brutally suppressed in 1956. He advocated peaceful co-existence with the capitalist countries, but continued arming the USSR with nuclear weapons. He aided the Cuban revolution under Fidel Castro but withdrew Soviet missiles from Cuba during confrontation by U.S. Pres. Kennedy, Sept.-Oct. 1962.

The USSR, the U.S., and Great Britain initialed a joint treaty July 25, 1963, banning above-ground nuclear tests.

Khrushchev was suddenly deposed, Oct. 1964, and replaced as party first secretary by Leonid I. Brezhnev, and as premier by Aleksei N. Kosygin.

In Aug. 1968 Russian, Polish, East German, Hungarian, and Bulgarian military forces invaded Czechoslovakia to put a curb on liberalization policies of the Czech government.

The USSR in 1971 continued heavy arms shipments to Egypt. In July 1972 Egypt ordered most of the 20,000 Soviet military personnel in that country to leave. When Egypt and Syria attacked Israel in Oct. 1973, the USSR launched huge arms airlifts to the 2 Arab nations. In 1974, the Soviet replenished the arms used or lost by the Syrians in the 1973 war, and continued some shipments to Egypt.

Massive Soviet military aid to North Vietnam in the late 1960s and early 1970s helped assure Communist victories throughout Indo-China. Soviet arms aid and advisers were sent to several African countries in the 1970s, including Algeria, Angola, Somalia, and Ethiopia.

In 1972, the U.S. and USSR reached temporary agreements to freeze intercontinental missiles at their current levels, to limit defensive missiles to 200 each and to cooperate on health, environment, space, trade, and science.

More than 130,000 Jews and over 40,000 ethnic Germans were allowed to emigrate from the USSR in the 1970s, following pressure from the West. Many leading figures in the arts also left the country.

A limitation on grain sales, imposed by Pres. Carter, Jan. 4, 1980, in response to the Soviet invasion of Afghanistan, was lifted, Apr. 24, 1981, by the Reagan administration. Nevertheless, there were serious food shortages reported, and a new agricultural program, covering 1982-90, was announced in May amid Soviet fears of becoming dependent on foreign, especially U.S., grain imports. The Afghan invasion continued to go badly in 1984 with no end in sight.

The USSR drew international condemnation on Sept. 1, 1983 when it shot down a Korean 747 commercial airliner, killing 269. The airliner had strayed off course. Relations with the Reagan administration have been strained. The Soviets have been unable to prevent U.S. Pershing II and cruise missiles from being deployed in Western Europe. The Soviets led the Eastern bloc boycott of the 1984 Los Angeles Olympics.

Government. The Communist Party leadership dominates all areas of national life. A Politburo of 14 full members and 8 candidate members makes all major political, economic, and foreign policy decisions. Party membership in 1978 was reported to be over 16,000,000.

United Arab Emirates

People: Population (1983 est.): 1,374,000. **Pop. density:** 28.13 per sq. mi. **Ethnic groups:** Arab, Iranian, Pakistani and Indian. **Languages:** Arabic (official), Farsi, English, Hindi, Urdu. **Religions:** Moslems 90%, Christian, Hindu.

Geography: Area: 32,000 sq. mi., the size of Maine. **Location:** On the S shore of the Persian Gulf. **Neighbors:** Qatar on N, Saudi Ar. on W, S, Oman on E. **Topography:** A barren, flat coastal plain gives way to uninhabited sand dunes on the S. Hajar Mtns. are on E. **Capital:** Abu Dhabi. **Cities** (1980 cen.): Abu Dhabi 449,000; Dubai 278,000.

Government: Type: Federation of emirates. **Head of state:** Pres. Zaid ibn Sultan an-Nahayan b. 1923; in office: Dec. 2, 1971. **Head of government:** Prime Min. Rashid ibn Said al-Maktum; in office: June 25, 1979. **Local divisions:** 7 autonomous emirates: Abu Dhabi, Ajman, Dubai, Fujaira, Ras al-Khaimah, Sharjah, Umm al-Qaiwain. **Defense:** 35% of govt. budget (1982).

Economy: Chief crops: Vegetables, dates, limes. **Minerals:** Oil. **Crude oil reserves** (1980): 29.4 bln. bbls. **Per capita arable land:** 0.02 acres. **Electricity prod.** (1982): 6 bln. kwh. **Labor force:** 5% agric. 85% ind. and commerce; 5% serv.; 5% gvt.

Finance: Currency: Dirham (Apr. 1984: 3.67 = $1 US). **Gross domestic product** (1981): $27 bln. **Per capita income** (1981 est.) $24,000. **Imports** (1981): $9.6 bln.; partners: Jap. 18%, UK 11%, W. Ger. 6%. **Exports** (1982): $16.9 bln.; partners: Jap. 36%, U.S. 7%, Fr. 10%. **International reserves less gold** (Feb. 1984): $1.9 bln. **Gold:** 817,000 oz t.

Transport: Chief ports: Dubai, Abu Dhabi.
Communications: Radios: 55,000 in use (1975). **Telephones in use** (1978): 96,847. **Daily newspaper circ.,** (1977): 2,000, 8 per 1,000 pop.
Health: Life Expectancy at Birth (1982):62.4 years. **Hospital beds** (1980): 2,972. **Physicians** (1980): 1,202.
Education (1982): **Literacy:** 53%. **Years Compulsory:** ages 6-12.
Embassy: 600 New Hampshire Ave. NW 20037; 338-6500.

The 7 "Trucial Sheikdoms" gave Britain control of defense and foreign relations in the 19th century. They merged to become an independent state Dec. 2, 1971.
The Abu Dhabi Petroleum Co. was fully nationalized in 1975. Oil revenues have given the UAE one of the highest per capita GNPs in the world. International banking has grown in recent years.

United Kingdom of Great Britain and Northern Ireland

People: Population (1983 est.): 56,009,000. **Age distrib. (%):** 0–4: 21.1; 15–59: 59.0; 60+: 19.9. **Pop. density:** 589 per sq. mi. **Urban** (1981): Eng. & Wales: 76.9%, N. Ire.: 54.7%, Scot. (1974): 70.0%. **Ethnic groups:** English 81.5%, Scottish 9.6%, Irish 2.4, Welsh 1.9%, Ulster 1.8%; West Indian, Indian, Pakistani over 2%; others. **Languages:** English, Welsh spoken in western Wales; Gaelic. **Religions:** Mainly Church of England with Roman Catholic, Muslim, and Jewish minorities.
Geography: Area: 94,222 sq. mi., slightly smaller than Oregon. **Location:** Off the NW coast of Europe, across English Channel, Strait of Dover, and North Sea. **Neighbors:** Ireland to W, France to SE. **Topography:** England is mostly rolling land, rising to Uplands of southern Scotland; Lowlands are in center of Scotland, granite Highlands are in N. Coast is heavily indented, especially on W. British Isles have milder climate than N Europe, due to the Gulf Stream, and ample rainfall. Severn, 220 mi., and Thames, 215 mi., are longest rivers. **Capital:** London. **Cities** (1981 cen.): London 6,696,008; Birmingham 1,058,800; Glasgow 832,097; Leeds 744,500; Sheffield 588,000; Liverpool 539,700; Manchester 490,000; Edinburgh 463,923; Bradford 458,900; Bristol 416,300; Belfast 357,600.
Government: Type: Constitutional monarchy. **Head of state:** Queen Elizabeth II; b. Apr. 21, 1926; in office: Feb. 6, 1952. **Head of government:** Prime Min. Margaret Thatcher; b. Oct. 13, 1925; in office: May 4, 1979. **Local divisions:** England and Wales: 47 non-metro counties, 6 metro counties, Greater London; Scotland: 9 regions, 3 island areas; N. Ireland: 26 districts. **Defense:** 6.2% of GDP (1982).
Economy: Industries: Steel, metals, vehicles, shipbuilding, shipping, banking, insurance, textiles, chemicals, electronics, aircraft, machinery, distilling. **Chief crops:** Grains, sugar beets, fruits, vegetables. **Minerals:** Coal, tin, oil, gas, limestone, iron, salt, clay, chalk, gypsum, lead, silica. **Crude oil reserves** (1980): 15.4 bln. bbls. **Arable land:** 30%. **Meat prod.** (1983): beef: 1.03 mln. metric tons; pork: 1 mln. metric tons; lamb: 275,000 metric tons. **Fish catch** (1981): 848,000 metric tons. **Electricity prod.** (1982): 272 bln. kwh. **Crude steel prod.** (1982): 13.6 mln. metric tons. **Labor force:** 1.5% agric.; 30% manuf. & eng., 59% services.
Finance: Currency: Pound (Mar. 1984: .66 = $1 US). **Gross domestic product** (1982): $353 bln. **Per capita income** (1979): $7,216. **Imports** (1983): $101.1 bln.; partners: W. Ger. 13%, U.S. 12%, Fr. 7%, Neth. 8%. **Exports** (1983): $91.6 bln.; partners: U.S. 13%, W. Ger. 10%, Fr. 8%, Neth. 8%. **Tourists** (1981): 11.4 mln.; **National budget** (1983) $182 bln. **International reserves less gold** (Mar. 1984): $11.4 bln. **Gold:** 19.01 mln. oz t. **Consumer prices** (change in 1983): 4.6%.
Transport: Railway traffic (1982): 27.7 bln. passenger-km; 15.8 bln. net ton-km. **Motor vehicles:** in use (1981): 15.7 mln. passenger cars, 1.7 mln. comm. vehicles; manuf. (1982): 888,000 passenger cars; 269,000 comm. vehicles. **Civil aviation** (1982): 43.9 bln. passenger-km: 1.2 bln. freight ton-km. **Chief ports:** London, Liverpool, Glasgow, Southampton, Cardiff, Belfast.
Communications: Television sets: 22.6 mln. licensed (1981). **Radios:** 53 mln. licensed (1981). **Telephones in use** (1981): 27.7 mln. **Daily newspaper circ.** (1982): 419 per 1,000 pop.

Health: Life expectancy at birth: (1983): 70.2 male; 76.2 female. **Births:** (per 1,000 pop. 1981): 13.1. **Deaths:** (per 1,000 pop. 1981): 11.8. **Natural increase:** (1977): .01%. **Hospital beds** (per 100,000 pop. 1977): 894. **Physicians** (per 100,000 pop. 1977): 153. **Infant mortality:** (per 1,000 live births 1984): 13.3.
Education (1981): **Literacy:** 99%. **Years compulsory:** 12; attendance 99%.
Embassy: 3100 Massachusetts Ave. NW 20008; 462-1340.

The United Kingdom of Great Britain and Northern Ireland comprises England, Wales, Scotland, and Northern Ireland.
Queen and Royal Family. The ruling sovereign is Elizabeth II of the House of Windsor, born Apr. 21, 1926, elder daughter of King George VI. She succeeded to the throne Feb. 6, 1952, and was crowned June 2, 1953. She was married Nov. 20, 1947, to Lt. Philip Mountbatten, born June 10, 1921, former Prince of Greece. He was created Duke of Edinburgh, Earl of Merioneth, and Baron Greenwich, and given the style H.R.H., Nov. 19, 1947; he was given the title Prince of the United Kingdom and Northern Ireland Feb. 22, 1957. Prince Charles Philip Arthur George, born Nov. 14, 1948, is the Prince of Wales and heir apparent. His son, William Philip Arthur Louis, born June 21, 1982, is second in line to the throne.
Parliament is the legislative governing body for the United Kingdom, with certain powers over dependent units. It consists of 2 houses: The **House of Lords** includes 763 hereditary and 314 life peers and peeresses, certain judges, 2 archbishops and 24 bishops of the Church of England. Total membership is over 1,000. The **House of Commons** has 635 members, who are elected by direct ballot and divided as follows: England 516; Wales 36; Scotland 71; Northern Ireland 12.
Resources and Industries. Great Britain's major occupations are manufacturing and trade. Metals and metal-using industries contribute more than 50% of the exports. Of about 60 million acres of land in England, Wales and Scotland, 46 million are farmed, of which 17 million are arable, the rest pastures.
Large oil and gas fields have been found in the North Sea. Commercial oil production began in 1975. There are large deposits of coal.
The railroads, nationalized since 1948, have been reduced in total length, with a basic network, Dec. 1978, of 11,123 mi. The merchant marine totaled 126,000 gross registered tons in 1982.
The world's first power station using atomic energy to create electricity for civilian use began operation Oct. 17, 1956, at Calder Hall in Cumbria.
Britain imports all of its cotton, rubber, sulphur, 80% of its wool, half of its food and iron ore, also certain amounts of paper, tobacco, chemicals. Manufactured goods made from these basic materials have been exported since the industrial age began. Main exports are machinery, chemicals, woolen and synthetic textiles, clothing, autos and trucks, iron and steel, locomotives, ships, jet aircraft, farm machinery, drugs, radio, TV, radar and navigation equipment, scientific instruments, arms, whisky.
Religion and Education. The Church of England is Protestant Episcopal. The queen is its temporal head, with rights of appointments to archbishoprics, bishoprics, and other offices. There are 2 provinces, Canterbury and York, each headed by an archbishop. About 48% of the population is baptized into the Church, less than 10% is confirmed. Most famous church is Westminster Abbey (1050-1760), site of coronations, tombs of Elizabeth I, Mary of Scots, kings, poets, and of the Unknown Warrior.
The most celebrated British universities are Oxford and Cambridge, each dating to the 13th century. There are about 40 other universities.
History. Britain was part of the continent of Europe until about 6,000 BC, but migration of peoples across the English Channel continued long afterward. Celts arrived 2,500 to 3,000 years ago. Their language survives in Welsh, Cornish, and Gaelic enclaves.
England was added to the Roman Empire in 43 AD. After the withdrawal of Roman legions in 410, waves of Jutes, Angles, and Saxons arrived from German lands. They contended with Danish raiders for control from the 8th through 11th centuries.
The last successful invasion was by French speaking Normans in 1066, who united the country with their dominions in France.
Opposition by nobles to royal authority forced King John to sign the Magna Carta in 1215, a guarantee of rights and the rule

of law In the ensuing decades, the foundations of the parliamentary system were laid.

English dynastic claims to large parts of France led to the Hundred Years War, 1338-1453, and the defeat of England. A long civil war, the War of the Roses, lasted 1455-85, and ended with the establishment of the powerful Tudor monarchy. A distinct English civilization flourished. The economy prospered over long periods of domestic peace unmatched in continental Europe. Religious independence was secured when the Church of England was separated from the authority of the Pope in 1534.

Under Queen Elizabeth I, England became a major naval power, leading to the founding of colonies in the new world and the expansion of trade with Europe and the Orient. Scotland was united with England when James VI of Scotland was crowned James I of England in 1603.

A struggle between Parliament and the Stuart kings led to a bloody civil war, 1642-49, and the establishment of a republic under the Puritan Oliver Cromwell. The monarchy was restored in 1660, but the "Glorious Revolution" of 1688 confirmed the sovereignty of Parliament: a Bill of Rights was granted 1689.

In the 18th century, parliamentary rule was strengthened. Technological and entrepreneurial innovations led to the Industrial Revolution. The 13 North American colonies were lost, but replaced by growing empires in Canada and India. Britain's role in the defeat of Napoleon, 1815, strengthened its position as the leading world power.

The extension of the franchise in 1832 and 1867, the formation of trade unions, and the development of universal public education were among the drastic social changes which accompanied the spread of industrialization and urbanization in the 19th century. Large parts of Africa and Asia were added to the empire during the reign of Queen Victoria, 1837-1901.

Though victorious in World War I, Britain suffered huge casualties and economic dislocation. Ireland became independent in 1921, and independence movements became active in India and other colonies.

The country suffered major bombing damage in World War II, but held out against Germany singlehandedly for a year after the fall of France in 1940.

Industrial growth continued in the postwar period, but Britain lost its leadership position to other powers. Labor governments passed socialist programs nationalizing some basic industries and expanding social security. The 1983 re-election of Thatcher's Conservative Party, however, indicated an increased role for private enterprise.

Britain broke diplomatic relations with Libya, Apr. 22, 1984, 5 days after a policewoman was killed and 10 Libyan exile demonstrators wounded by machine-gun fire from within the Libyan embassy in London. The embassy occupants, including the killer, left Britain, Apr. 27.

Britain joined the NATO alliance and, in 1973, the European Communities (Common Market).

Wales

The Principality of Wales in western Britain has an area of 8,016 sq. mi. and a population (1981 cen.) of 2,790,000. Cardiff is the capital, pop. (1981 est.) 273,856.

England and Wales are administered as a unit. Less than 20% of the population of Wales speak both English and Welsh; about 32,000 speak Welsh solely. Welsh nationalism is advocated by a segment. A 1979 referendum rejected, 4-1, the creation of an elected Welsh Assembly.

Early Anglo-Saxon invaders drove Celtic peoples into the mountains of Wales, terming them Waelise (Welsh, or foreign). There they developed a distinct nationality. Members of the ruling house of Gwynedd in the 13th century fought England but were crushed, 1283. Edward of Caernarvon, son of Edward I of England, was created Prince of Wales, 1301.

Scotland

Scotland, a kingdom now united with England and Wales in Great Britain, occupies the northern 37% of the main British island, and the Hebrides, Orkney, Shetland and smaller islands. Length, 275 mi., breadth approx. 150 mi., area, 30,405 sq. mi., population (1981 cen.) 5,117,146.

The Lowlands, a belt of land approximately 60 mi. wide from the Firth of Clyde to the Firth of Forth, divide the farming region of the Southern Uplands from the granite Highlands of the North, contain 75% of the population and most of the industry. The

Highlands, famous for hunting and fishing, have been opened to industry by many hydroelectric power stations.

Edinburgh, pop. (1981 cen.) 419,187, is the capital. Glasgow, pop. (1981 cen.) 762,288, is Britain's greatest industrial center. It is a shipbuilding complex on the Clyde and an ocean port. Aberdeen, pop. (1981 cen.) 190,200, NE of Edinburgh, is a major port, center of granite industry, fish processing, and North Sea oil exploitation. Dundee, pop. (1981 cen.) 174,746, NE of Edinburgh, is an industrial and fish processing center. About 90,000 persons speak Gaelic as well as English.

History. Scotland was called Caledonia by the Romans who battled early Pict and Celtic tribes and occupied southern areas from the 1st to the 4th centuries. Missionaries from Britain introduced Christianity in the 4th century; St. Columba, an Irish monk, converted most of Scotland in the 6th century.

The Kingdom of Scotland was founded in 1018. William Wallace and Robert Bruce both defeated English armies 1297 and 1314, respectively.

In 1603 James VI of Scotland, son of Mary, Queen of Scots, succeeded to the throne of England as James I, and effected the Union of the Crowns. In 1707 Scotland received representation in the British Parliament, resulting from the union of former separate Parliaments. Its executive in the British cabinet is the Secretary of State for Scotland. The growing Scottish National Party urges independence. A 1979 referendum on the creation of an elected Scotland Assembly was defeated.

There are 8 universities. Memorials of Robert Burns, Sir Walter Scott, John Knox, Mary, Queen of Scots draw many tourists, as do the beauties of the Trossachs, Loch Katrine, Loch Lomond and abbey ruins.

Industries. Engineering products are the most important industry, with growing emphasis on office machinery, autos, electronics and other consumer goods. Oil has been discovered offshore in the North Sea, stimulating on-shore support industries.

Scotland produces fine woolens, worsteds, tweeds, silks, fine linens and jute. It is known for its special breeds of cattle and sheep. Fisheries have large hauls of herring, cod, whiting. Whisky is the biggest export.

The Hebrides are a group of c. 500 islands, 100 inhabited, off the W coast. The Inner Hebrides include Skye, Mull, and Iona, the last famous for the arrival of St. Columba, 563 AD. The Outer Hebrides include Lewis and Harris. Industries include sheep raising and weaving. The Orkney Islands, c. 90, are to the NE. The capital is Kirkwall, on Pomona Is. Fish curing, sheep raising and weaving are occupations. NE of the Orkneys are the 200 Shetland Islands, 24 inhabited, home of Shetland pony. The Orkneys and Shetlands have become centers for the North Sea oil industry.

Northern Ireland

Six of the 9 counties of Ulster, the NE corner of Ireland, constitute Northern Ireland, with the parliamentary boroughs of Belfast and Londonderry. Area 5,463 sq. mi., 1981 cen. pop. 1,490,228, capital and chief industrial center, Belfast, (1981 cen.) 297,862.

Industries. Shipbuilding, including large tankers, has long been an important industry, centered in Belfast, the largest port. Linen manufacture is also important, along with apparel, rope, and twine. Growing diversification has added engineering products, synthetic fibers, and electronics. They are large numbers of cattle, hogs, and sheep, potatoes, poultry, and dairy foods are also produced.

Government. An act of the British Parliament, 1920, divided Northern from Southern Ireland, each with a parliament and government. When Ireland became a dominion, 1921, and later a republic, Northern Ireland chose to remain a part of the United Kingdom. It elects 12 members to the British House of Commons.

During 1968-69, large demonstrations were conducted by Roman Catholics who charged they were discriminated against in voting rights, housing, and employment. The Catholics, a minority comprising about a third of the population, demanded abolition of property qualifications for voting in local elections. Violence and terrorism intensified, involving branches of the Irish Republican Army (outlawed in the Irish Republic), Protestant groups, police, and up to 15,000 British troops.

A succession of Northern Ireland prime ministers pressed reform programs but failed to satisfy extremists on both sides. Over 2,000 were killed in over 13 years of bombings and shootings through 1984, many in England itself. Britain suspended the Northern Ireland parliament Mar. 30, 1972, and imposed direct British rule. A coalition government was formed in 1973 when moderates won election to a new one-house Assembly. But a Protestant general strike overthrew the government in 1974 and direct rule was resumed.

The turmoil and agony of Northern Ireland was dramatized in 1981 by the deaths of 10 imprisoned Irish nationalist hunger strikers in Maze Prison near Belfast. The inmates had starved themselves to death in an attempt to achieve status as political prisoners, but the British government refused to yield to their demands.

Education and Religion. Northern Ireland is 2/3 Protestant, 1/3 Roman Catholic. Education is compulsory through age 15. There are 2 universities and 24 technical colleges.

Channel Islands

The Channel Islands, area 75 sq. mi., cen. pop. 1980 130,000, off the NW coast of France, the only parts of the one-time Dukedom of Normandy belonging to England, are **Jersey, Guernsey** and the dependencies of Guernsey — **Alderney, Brechou, Great Sark, Little Sark, Herm, Jethou and Lihou.** Jersey and Guernsey have separate legal existences and lieutenant governors named by the Crown. The islands were the only British soil occupied by German troops in World War II.

Isle of Man

The Isle of Man, area 227 sq. mi., 1982 est. pop. 61,000, is in the Irish Sea, 20 mi. from Scotland, 30 mi. from Cumberland. It is rich in lead and iron. The island has its own laws and a lieutenant governor appointed by the Crown. The Tynwald (legislature) consists of the Legislative Council, partly elected, and House of Keys, elected. Capital: Douglas. Farming, tourism (413,000 visitors in 1982), fishing (kippers, scallops) are chief occupations. Man is famous for the Manx tailless cat.

Gibraltar

Gibraltar, a dependency on the southern coast of Spain, guards the entrance to the Mediterranean. The Rock has been in British possession since 1704. The Rock is 2.75 mi. long, 3/4 of a mi. wide and 1,396 ft. in height; a narrow isthmus connects it with the mainland. Est. pop. 1982, 30,000.

In 1966 Spain called on Britain to give "substantial sovereignty" of Gibraltar to Spain and imposed a partial blockade. In 1967, residents voted 12,138 for remaining under Britain, 44 for returning to Spain. A new constitution, May 30, 1969, gave an elected House of Assembly more control in domestic affairs. A UN General Assembly resolution requested Britain to end Gibraltar's colonial status by Oct. 1, 1969. No settlement has been reached.

British West Indies

Swinging in a vast arc from the coast of Venezuela NE, then N and NW toward Puerto Rico are the Leeward Islands, forming a coral and volcanic barrier sheltering the Caribbean from the open Atlantic. Many of the islands are self-governing British possessions. Universal suffrage was instituted 1951-54; ministerial systems were set up 1956-1960.

The **Leeward Islands,** are **Montserrat** (1980 pop. 11,600, area 32 sq. mi., capital Plymouth), and **St. Kitts (St. Christopher)-Nevis,** 2 islands (1980 pop. 44,400, area 104 sq. mi., capital Basseterre on St. Kitts). Nearby are the small **British Virgin Islands.**

Britain granted self-government to 5 of these islands (exception, Montserrat) and island groups in 1967-1969; each became an Associated State, with Britain controlling foreign affairs and defense.

Anguilla gained its independence from St. Kitts Dec. 19, 1980. A 1976 constitution provides for an autonomous elected government. Area 35 sq. mi., pop. (1982 est.) 7,000.

The three **Cayman Islands,** a dependency, lie S of Cuba, NW of Jamaica. Pop. 18,000 (1981), most of it on Grand Cayman. It is a free port; in the 1970s Grand Cayman became a tax-free refuge for foreign funds and branches of many Western banks were opened there. Total area 102 sq. mi., capital Georgetown.

The **Turks and Caicos Islands,** at the SE end of the Bahama Islands, are a separate possession. There are about 30 islands, only 6 inhabited, 1980 pop. est. 7,000, area 193 sq. mi., capital Grand Turk. Salt, crayfish and conch shells are the main exports.

Bermuda

Bermuda is a British dependency governed by a royal governor and an Assembly, dating from 1620, the oldest legislative body among British dependencies. Capital is Hamilton.

It is a group of 360 small islands of coral formation, 20 inhabited, comprising 21 sq. mi. in the western Atlantic, 580 mi. E of North Carolina. Pop., 1980 cen., was 54,893 (about 61% of African descent). Density is high.

The U.S. has air and naval bases under long-term lease, and a NASA tracking station.

Bermuda boasts many resort hotels, serving 429,000 visitors in 1981. The government raises most revenue from import duties. Exports: petroleum products, drugs.

South Atlantic

Falkland Islands and Dependencies, a British dependency, lies 300 mi. E of the Strait of Magellan at the southern end of South America.

The Falklands or Islas Malvinas include about 200 islands, area 4,700 sq. mi., pop. (1980 est.) 1,800. Sheep-grazing is the main industry; wool is the principal export. There are indications of large oil and gas deposits. The islands are also claimed by Argentina though 97% of inhabitants are of British origin. Argentina invaded the islands Apr. 2, 1982. The British responded by sending a task force to the area, landing their main force on the Falklands, May 21, and forcing an Argentine surrender at Port Stanley, June 14. **South Georgia,** area 1,450 sq. mi., and the uninhabited **South Sandwich Is.** are dependencies of the Falklands.

British Antarctic Territory, south of 60° S lat., was made a separate colony in 1962 and comprises mainly the **South Shetland Islands,** the **South Orkneys** and **Graham's Land.** A chain of meteorological stations is maintained.

St. Helena, an island 1,200 mi. off the W coast of Africa and 1,800 E of South America, has 47 sq. mi. and est. pop., 1981 of 5,300. Flax, lace and rope making are the chief industries. After Napoleon Bonaparte was defeated at Waterloo the Allies exiled him to St. Helena, where he lived from Oct. 16, 1815, to his death, May 5, 1821. Capital is Jamestown.

Tristan da Cunha is the principal of a group of islands of volcanic origin, total area 40 sq. mi., half way between the Cape of Good Hope and South America. A volcanic peak 6,760 ft. high erupted in 1961. The 262 inhabitants were removed to England, but most returned in 1963. The islands are dependencies of St. Helena.

Ascension is an island of volcanic origin, 34 sq. mi. in area, 700 mi. NW of St. Helena, through which it is administered. It is a communications relay center for Britain, and has a U.S. satellite tracking center. Est. pop., 1976, was 1,179, half of them communications workers. The island is noted for sea turtles.

Asia and Indian Ocean

Hong Kong is a Crown Colony at the mouth of the Canton R. in China, 90 mi. S of Canton. Its nucleus is Hong Kong Is., 35$\frac{1}{2}$ sq. mi., acquired from China 1841, on which is located Victoria, the capital. Opposite is Kowloon Peninsula, 3 sq. mi. and Stonecutters Is., $\frac{1}{4}$ sq. mi., added, 1860. An additional 355 sq. mi. known as the New Territories, a mainland area and islands, were leased from China, 1898, for 99 years. China has indicated its intention to reclaim sovereignty over Hong Kong when the lease expires in 1997. Total area of the colony is 409 sq. mi., with a population, 1983 est., of 5,287,000 including fewer than 20,000 British. From 1949 to 1962 Hong Kong absorbed more than a million refugees from the mainland.

Hong Kong harbor was long an important British naval station and one of the world's great trans-shipment ports.

Principal industries are textiles and apparel (25% of exports); also tourism, 2.5 mln. visitors, $1.5 bln. expenditures (1981), shipbuilding, iron and steel, fishing, cement, and small manufactures.

Spinning mills, among the best in the world, and low wages compete with textiles elsewhere and have resulted in the protective measures in some countries. Hong Kong also has a booming electronics industry.

British Indian Ocean Territory was formed Nov. 1965, embracing islands formerly dependencies of Mauritius or Seychelles: the Chagos Archipelago (including Diego Garcia), Aldabra, Farquhar and Des Roches. The latter 3 were transferred to Seychelles, which became independent in 1976. Area 22 sq mi. No civilian population remains.

Pacific Ocean

Pitcairn Island is in the Pacific, halfway between South America and Australia. The island was discovered in 1767 by Carteret but was not inhabited until 23 years later when the mutineers of the Bounty landed there. The area is 18 sq. mi. and pop. 1983, was 61. It is a British colony and is administered by a British Representative in New Zealand and a local Council. The uninhabited islands of **Henderson, Ducie** and **Oeno** are in the Pitcairn group.

United States of America

People: Population (1983 est.): 234,249,000. **Age distrib.**(%): 0–14: 22.6; 15–59: 61.7; 60+: 15.7. **Pop. density:** 64.0 per sq. mi. **Urban** (1980): 79.2%.
Armed forces: regulars 2,022,000; reserves 797,000.
Economy: Minerals: Coal, copper, lead, molybdenum, phosphates, uranium, bauxite, gold, iron, mercury, nickel, potash, silver, tungsten, zinc. **Crude oil reserves** (1980): 26.50 bln. bbls. **Per capita arable land:** 2.1 acres. **Meat prod.** (1983): beef: 10 mln. metric tons; pork: 6.8 mln. metric tons; lamb: 172,000 metric tons. **Fish catch** (1981): 3.7 mln. metric tons. **Electricity prod.** (1982): 2,241 bln. kwh. **Crude steel prod.** (1982): 66.6 mln. metric tons.
Finance: Gross domestic product (1981): $2,626.1 bln. **Per capita income** (1983): $11,675. **Imports** (1983): $269 bln.; partners: Can. 18%, Jap. 16%, Mex. 6%. **Exports** (1983): $200 bln.; partners: Can. 16%, Jap. 10%, Mex. 6%, UK 5%. **Tourists** (1981): 23.1 mln.; receipts $12 bln. **National budget** (1983): $659.7 bln. revenues; $848.5 bln. expenditures and lending. **International reserves less gold** (Mar. 1984): $23.8 bln. **Gold:** 263.1 mln. oz t. **Consumer prices** (change in 1983): 3.2%.
Transport: Railway traffic (1980): 17.9 bln. passenger-km; 1.3 bln. net ton-km. **Motor vehicles:** in use (1981): 123 mln. passenger cars, 34 mln. comm. vehicles; manuf. (1982): 5.0 mln. passenger cars; 1.9 mln. comm. vehicles. **Civil aviation** (1982): 408 bln. passenger-km; 9.8 bln. freight ton-km.
Communications: Television sets: 142 mln. in use (1981). **Radios:** 478 mln. in use (1981). **Telephones in use** (1981): 191 mln. **Daily newspaper circ.** (1982): 279 per 1,000 pop.
Health: Life expectancy at birth (1982): 70.8 male; 78.2 female. **Births** (per 1,000 pop. 1982): 16.0. **Deaths** (per 1,000 pop. 1982): 8.6. **Natural increase** (1977): .7%. **Hospital beds** (1980): 1.3 mln. **Physicians** (per 100,000 pop. 1977): 176. **Infant mortality** (per 1,000 live births 1982): 11.2.
Education (1980): **Literacy:** 99%.

Upper Volta (Bourkina Fasso)

Republic of Upper Volta

People: Population (1983 est.): 6,569,000. **Pop. density:** 65.27 per sq. mi. **Ethnic groups:** Voltaic groups (Mossi, Bobo), Mande. **Languages:** French (official), More, Sudanic tribal languages. **Religions:** animist 50%, Moslems 16%, Roman Catholics 8%, others.
Geography: Area: 105,869 sq. mi., the size of Colorado. **Location:** In W. Africa, S of the Sahara. **Neighbors:** Mali on NW, Niger on NE, Benin, Togo, Ghana, Ivory Coast on S. **Topography:** Landlocked Upper Volta is in the savannah region of W. Africa. The N is arid, hot, and thinly populated. **Capital:** Ouagadougou. **Cities** (1981 est.): Ouagadougou 200,000; Bobo-Dioulasso 150,000.
Government: Type: Republic. **Head of state:** Pres. Thomas Sankara; b. 1948; in office: Aug. 4, 1983. **Local divisions:** 10 departments. **Defense:** 18.6% of govt. budget. (1980).
Economy: Chief crops: Millet, sorghum, rice, peanuts, grain. **Minerals:** Manganese, gold, diamonds. **Arable land:** 10%. **Meat prod.** (1980): beef: 29,000 metric tons; lamb: 8,000 metric tons. **Electricity prod.** (1980): 140 mln. kwh. **Labor force:** 83% agric.; 12% industry.
Finance: Currency: CFA franc (Mar. 1984: 399.00 = $1 US). **Gross domestic product** (1979 est.): $969 mln. **Per capita income** (1978): $160. **Imports** (1979): $300 mln.; partners: Fr. 33%, Ivory Coast 22%, U.S. 11%. **Exports** (1979): $76 mln.; partners: Ivory Coast 31%, Fr. 12%. **International reserves less gold** (Jan. 1984): $84.6 mln. **Gold:** 11,000 oz t. **Consumer prices** (change in 1982): 12.0%.

Transport: Motor vehicles: in use (1979): 11,000 passenger cars, 12,000 comm. vehicles.
Communications: Television sets: 5,500 in use (1981). **Radios:** 90,000 in use (1981). **Telephones in use** (1980): 4,000. **Daily newspaper circ.** (1982): 2 per 1,000 pop.
Health: Life expectancy at birth (1961): 32.1 male; 31.1 female. **Births** (per 1,000 pop. 1978): 50. **Deaths** (per 1,000 pop. 1978): 27. **Natural increase** (1978): 2.3%. **Hospital beds** (per 100,000 pop. 1977): 57. **Physicians** (per 100,000 pop. 1977): 3. **Infant mortality** (per 1,000 live births 1981): 260.
Education (1980): **Literacy:** 7%.
Embassy: 2340 Massachusetts Ave. NW 20008; 332-5577.

The Mossi tribe entered the area in the 11th to 13th centuries. Their kingdoms ruled until defeated by the Mali and Songhai empires.

French control came by 1896, but Upper Volta was not finally established as a separate territory until 1947. Full independence came Aug. 5, 1960, and a pro-French government was elected. A 1982 coup established the current regime.

Several hundred thousand farm workers migrate each year to Ivory Coast and Ghana. Droughts brought famine in the 1970s. Upper Volta is heavily dependent on foreign aid.

On Aug. 4, 1984, Upper Volta changed its name to Bourkina Fasso.

Uruguay

Oriental Republic of Uruguay

People: Population (1983 est.): 2,916,000. **Age distrib.** (%): 0–14: 27.0; 15–59: 58.7; 60+: 14.3. **Pop. density:** 41.72 per sq. mi. **Urban** (1975): 83.0%. **Ethnic groups:** Caucasians (Iberians, Italians) 89%, mestizos 10%, mulatto and Negro. **Languages:** Spanish. **Religions:** 60% Roman Catholic.
Geography: Area: 68,037 sq. mi., the size of Washington State. **Location:** In southern S. America, on the Atlantic O. **Neighbors:** Argentina on W, Brazil on N. **Topography:** Uruguay is composed of rolling, grassy plains and hills, well-watered by rivers flowing W to Uruguay R. **Capital:** Montevideo. **Cities** (1983 est.): Montevideo 1,255,600.
Government: Type: Republic. **Head of state:** Pres. Gregorio Conrado Alvarez Armelino; b. Nov. 26, 1925; in office: Sept. 1, 1981. **Local divisions:** 19 departments. **Defense:** 3.2% of GDP.
Economy: Industries: Meat-packing, metals, textiles, wine, cement, oil products. **Chief crops:** Corn, wheat, citrus fruits, rice, oats, linseed. **Arable land:** 12%. **Meat prod.** (1983): beef: 418,000 metric tons; pork: 15,000 metric tons; lamb: 41,000 metric tons. **Fish catch** (1981): 145,000 metric tons. **Electricity prod.** (1981): 3.6 bln. kwh. **Labor force** 16% agric.; 31% ind. and commerce; 12% serv.; 19% govt.
Finance: Currency: New Peso (Mar. 1984: 55.25 = $1 US). **Gross domestic product** (1980): $9.4 bln. **Per capita income** (1980): $2,780. **Imports** (1983): $706 mln.; partners: Braz. 12%, Arg. 8%, U.S. 12%. **Exports** (1983): $1.0 bln.; partners: Braz. 14%, U.S. 7%, W. Ger. 9%, Arg. 11%. **Tourists** (1979): 1.1 mln.; receipts: $268 mln. **National budget** (1979): $1.30 bln. revenues; $1.24 bln. expeditures. **International reserves less gold** (Jan. 1984): $196 mln. **Gold:** 2.60 mln. oz t. **Consumer prices** (change in 1983): 49.2%.
Transport: Railway traffic (1981): 339 mln. passenger-km; 221 mln. net ton-km. **Motor vehicles:** in use (1981): 281,000 passenger cars, 43,000 comm. vehicles. **Civil aviation** (1982): 293 mln. passenger-km; 1.1 mln. freight ton-km. **Chief ports:** Montevideo.
Communications: Television sets: 440,000 in use (1981). **Radios:** 1 mln. in use (1981). **Telephones in use** (1981): 287,140. **Daily newspaper circ.** (1982): 337 per 1,000 pop.
Health: Life expectancy at birth (1983): 67.1 male; 73.7 female. **Births** (per 1,000 pop. 1981): 18.3. **Deaths** (per 1,000 pop. 1981): 9.0. **Natural increase** (1978): 0.6%. **Hospital beds** (1981): 23,000. **Physicians** (1981): 5,600. **Infant mortality** (per 1,000 live births 1981): 34.1.
Education (1978): **Literacy:** 94%.
Embassy: 1918 F St. NW 20006; 331-1313.

Spanish settlers did not begin replacing the indigenous Charrua Indians until 1624. Portuguese from Brazil arrived later, but Uruguay was attached to the Spanish Viceroyalty of Rio de la Plata in the 18th century. Rebels fought against Spain beginning in 1810. An independent republic was declared Aug. 25, 1825.

Liberal governments adopted socialist measures as far back as 1911. More than a third of the workers are employed by the state, which owns the power, telephone, railroad, cement, oil-refining and other industries. Social welfare programs are among the most advanced in the world.

Uruguay's standard of living was one of the highest in South America, and political and labor conditions among the freest. Economic stagnation, inflation, plus floods, drought in 1967 and a general strike in 1968 brought attempts by the government to strengthen the economy through a series of devaluations of the peso and wage and price controls. But inflation continued in the 1980s and the country was forced to ask international creditors to restructure $2.7 billion in debt in 1983.

Tupamaros, leftist guerrillas drawn from the upper classes, increased terrorist actions in 1970. Violence continued and in Feb. 1973 Pres. Juan Maria Bordaberry agreed to military control of his administration. In June he abolished Congress and set up a Council of State in its place. By 1974 the military had apparently defeated the Tupamaros, using severe repressive measures. Bordaberry was removed by the military in a 1976 coup. Elections were promised for November 1984.

Vanuatu
Republic of Vanuatu

People: Population (1983 est.): 127,000. **Population density:** 19.58 per sq. mi. **Ethnic groups:** Mainly Melanesian, some European, Polynesian, Micronesian. **Languages:** Bislama (national), French and English both official. **Religions:** Presbyterian 40%, Anglican 14%, Roman Catholic 16%, animist 15%.

Geography: Area: 4,707 sq. mi. **Location:** SW Pacific, 1,200 mi NE of Brisbane, Australia. **Topography:** dense forest with narrow coastal strips of cultivated land. **Capital:** Vila. **Cities:** Vila (1979): 15,100.

Government: Type: Republic. **Head of state:** Pres. George Sokomanu; in office: July 30, 1980. **Head of gov't:** Prime Min. Rev. Walter Lini; in office: July 30, 1980.

Economy: Industries: Fish-freezing, meat canneries, tourism. **Chief crops:** Copra (38% of export), cocoa, coffee. **Minerals:** Manganese. **Other resources:** Forests, cattle. **Fish catch** (1981): 2.7 metric tons.

Finance: Currency: Australian dollar and Vanuatu franc (Sept. 1983: 101 vatu = $1 US). **Imports** (1980): $51 mln.; partners: Aus. 39%, Fr. 10%, Japan 13%. **Exports** (1981): $28 mln.; partners: Fr. 27%, Belg.-Lux. 34%.

Education: Education not compulsory, but 85-90% of children of primary school age attend primary schools.

The Anglo-French condominium of the New Hebrides, administered jointly by France and Great Britain since 1906, became the independent Republic of Vanuatu on July 30, 1980.

Vatican
State of Vatican City

People: Population (1983 est.): 1,000. **Ethnic groups:** Italians, Swiss. **Languages:** Italian, Latin. **Religion:** Roman Catholicism.

Geography: Area: 108.7 acres. **Location:** In Rome, Italy. **Neighbors:** Completely surrounded by Italy. **Currency:** Lira.

The popes for many centuries, with brief interruptions, held temporal sovereignty over mid-Italy (the so-called Papal States), comprising an area of some 16,000 sq. mi., with a population in the 19th century of more than 3 million. This territory was incorporated in the new Kingdom of Italy, the sovereignty of the pope being confined to the palaces of the Vatican and the Lateran in Rome and the villa of Castel Gandolfo, by an Italian law, May 13, 1871. This law also guaranteed to the pope and his successors a yearly indemnity of over $620,000. The allowance, however, remained unclaimed.

A Treaty of Conciliation, a concordat and a financial convention were signed Feb. 11, 1929, by Cardinal Gasparri and Premier Mussolini. The documents established the independent state of Vatican City, and gave the Catholic religion special status in Italy. The treaty (Lateran Agreement) was made part of the Constitution of Italy (Article 7) in 1947. Italy and the Vatican

reached preliminary agreement in 1976 on revisions of the concordat, that would eliminate Roman Catholicism as the state religion and end required religious education in Italian schools.

Vatican City includes St. Peter's, the Vatican Palace and Museum covering over 13 acres, the Vatican gardens, and neighboring buildings between Viale Vaticano and the Church. Thirteen buildings in Rome, outside the boundaries, enjoy extraterritorial rights; these buildings house congregations or officers necessary for the administration of the Holy See.

The legal system is based on the code of canon law, the apostolic constitutions and the laws especially promulgated for the Vatican City by the pope. The Secretariat of State represents the Holy See in its diplomatic relations. By the Treaty of Conciliation the pope is pledged to a perpetual neutrality unless his mediation is specifically requested. This, however, does not prevent the defense of the Church whenever it is persecuted.

The present sovereign of the State of Vatican City is the Supreme Pontiff John Paul II, Karol Wojtyla, born in Wadowice, Poland, May 18, 1920, elected Oct. 16, 1978 (the first non-Italian to be elected Pope in 456 years).

The U.S. restored formal relations in 1984 after the U.S. Congress repealed an 1867 ban on diplomatic relations with the Vatican.

Venezuela
Republic of Venezuela

People: Population (1983 est.): 17,993,000. **Age distrib. (%):** 0–14: 42.8; 15–59: 52.4; 60+: 4.8. **Pop. density:** 37.26 per sq. mi. **Urban** (1981): 75.5%. **Ethnic groups:** Mestizo 69%, white (Spanish, Portuguese, Italian) 20%, Negro 9%, Indian 2%. **Languages:** Spanish (official), Indian languages 2%. **Religions:** Predominantly Roman Catholic.

Geography: Area: 352,143 sq. mi., more than twice the size of California. **Location:** On the Caribbean coast of S. America. **Neighbors:** Colombia on W, Brazil on S, Guyana on E. **Topography:** Flat coastal plain and Orinoco Delta are bordered by Andes Mtns. and hills. Plains, called llanos, extend between mountains and Orinoco. Guyana Highlands and plains are S of Orinoco, which stretches 1,600 mi. and drains 80% of Venezuela. **Capital:** Caracas. **Cities** (1981 est.): Caracas 2,700,000; Maracaibo 845,000; Barquisimeto 459,000; Valencia 471,000.

Government: Type: Federal republic. **Head of state:** Pres. Jaime Lusinchi; in office: Feb., 1984. **Local divisions:** 20 states, 2 federal territories, federal district, federal dependency. **Defense:** 6.4% of govt. budget (1981).

Economy: Industries: Steel, oil products, textiles, containers, paper, shoes. **Chief crops:** Coffee, rice, fruits, sugar. **Minerals:** Oil (5th largest producer), iron (extensive reserves and production), gold. **Crude oil reserves** (1980): 17.87 bln. bbls. **Arable land:** 5%. **Meat prod.** (1983): beef: 359,000 metric tons; pork: 96,000 metric tons; lamb: 41,000 metric tons. **Fish catch** (1981): 181,000 metric tons. **Electricity prod.** (1981): 37.5 bln. kwh. **Crude steel prod.** (1982): 2.0 mln. metric tons. **Labor force:** 15% agric.; 42% ind. and commerce; 41% services.

Finance: Currency: Bolivar (Apr. 1984: 4.30 = $1 US). **Gross domestic product** (1980): $59.9 bln. **Per capita income** (1980): $3,639. **Imports** (1983): $10.2 bln.; partners: U.S. 48%, W. Ger. 6%, Jap. 8%. **Exports** (1982): $16.4 bln.; partners: U.S. 25%, Neth Ant. 21%, Can. 9%. **Tourists** (1977): 652,400; receipts: $261 mln. **National budget** (1981): $17.8 bln. expenditures. **International reserves less gold** (Mar. 1984): $7.5 bln. **Gold:** 11.46 mln. oz t. **Consumer prices** (change in 1983): 6.2%.

Transport: Railway traffic (1979): 25 mln. passenger-km; 18 mln. net ton-km. **Motor vehicles:** in use (1981): 1.5 mln. passenger cars, 763,000 comm. vehicles. **Civil aviation** (1982): 5.0 bln. passenger-km; 144.6 mln. freight ton-km. **Chief ports:** Maracaibo, La Guaira, Puerto Cabello.

Communications: Television sets: 1.7 mln. in use (1981). **Radios:** 5.3 mln. in use (1981). **Telephones in use** (1980): 1.1 mln. **Daily newspaper circ.** (1982): 120 per 1,000 pop.

Health: Life expectancy at birth (1980): 64.0 male; 69.0 female. **Births** (per 1,000 pop. 1980): 35.6 **Deaths** (per 1,000 pop. 1980): 5.5. **Natural increase** (1978): 3.3%. **Hospital beds** (per 100,000 pop. 1977): 292. **Physicians** (per 100,000 pop. 1977): 107. **Infant mortality** (per 1,000 live births 1981): 31.

Education (1981): Literacy: 85.6%. **Years compulsory:** 9; attendance 82%.

Embassy: 2445 Massachusetts Ave. NW 20008; 797-3800

Columbus first set foot on the South American continent on the peninsula of Paria, Aug. 1498. Alonso de Ojeda, 1499, found Lake Maracaibo, called the land Venezuela, or Little Venice, because natives had houses on stilts. Venezuela was under Spanish domination until 1821. The republic was formed after secession from the Colombian Federation in 1830.

Military strongmen ruled Venezuela for most of the 20th century. They promoted the oil industry; some social reforms were implemented. Since 1959, the country has enjoyed progressive, democratically-elected governments.

Venezuela helped found the Organization of Petroleum Exporting States (OPEC). The government, Jan. 1, 1976, nationalized the oil industry with compensation. Development has begun of the Orinoco tar belt, believed to contain the world's largest oil reserves. Oil accounts for 95% of total export earnings and the economy suffered a severe cash crisis in 1983 as the result of falling oil revenues.

Oil profits help finance a new $150 billion national development plan for 1981-85. The funds are to be spent for housing, education, and industrial expansion.

A dispute with Guyana over the Essequibo border region was renewed in 1982.

Vietnam

Socialist Republic of Vietnam

People: Population (1983 est.): 57,612,000. **Pop. density:** 413.65 per sq. mi. **Ethnic groups:** Vietnamese 84%, Chinese 2%, remainder Muong, Thai, Meo, Khmer, Man, Cham. **Languages:** Vietnamese (official), French, English. **Religions:** Buddhists, Confucians, and Taoists most numerous, Roman Catholics, animists, Muslims, Protestants.

Geography: Area: 127,207 sq. mi., the size of New Mexico. **Location:** On the E coast of the Indochinese Peninsula in SE Asia. **Neighbors:** China on N, Laos, Cambodia on W. **Topography:** Vietnam is long and narrow, with a 1,400-mi. coast. About 24% of country is readily arable, including the densely settled Red R. valley in the N, narrow coastal plains in center, and the wide, often marshy Mekong R. Delta in the S. The rest consists of semi-arid plateaus and barren mountains, with some stretches of tropical rain forest. **Capital:** Hanoi. **Cities** (1981): Ho Chi Minh City 3.5 mln.; Hanoi 2 mln.

Government: Type: Communist people's republic. **Head of state:** Pres. Truong Chinh; in office: July 4, 1981. **Head of government:** Prime Min. Pham Van Dong; b. 1906; in office: Sept. 20, 1955. **Head of Communist Party:** First Sec. Le Duan; b. 1907; in office: Sept. 10, 1960. **Local divisions:** 39 provinces. **Defense:** 50% of govt. budget (1980 est.)

Economy: Industries: Food processing, textiles, machine building, mining, cement, chemical fertilizers, glass, tires. **Chief crops:** Rice, rubber, fruits and vegetables, corn, manioc, sugarcane, fish. **Minerals:** Phosphates, coal, iron, manganese, bauxite, apatite, chromate. **Other resources:** Forests. **Arable land:** 14%. **Meat prod.** (1981): beef: 102,000 metric tons; pork: 424,000 metric tons. **Fish catch** (1981): 1 mln. metric tons. **Electricity prod.** (1981): 4.0 bln. kwh. **Labor force:** 70% agric.; 8% ind. and commerce.

Finance: Currency: Dong (Sept. 1983: 9.90 = $1 US). **Gross domestic product** (1978): $7.6 mln. **Per capita income** (1978): $150. **Imports** (1982): $1.9 bln.; partners: USSR 58%, Jap. 6%. **Exports** (1982): $550 mln.; partners: USSR 52%, Jap. 6%.

Transport: Motor vehicles: in use (1976): 100,000 passenger cars, 200,000 comm. vehicles. **Chief ports:** Ho Chi Minh City, Haiphong, Da Nang.

Communications: Television sets (1981) 2 mln. **Radios:** 5 mln. in use (1981). **Daily newspaper circ.** (1982): 9 per 1,000 pop.

Health: Life expectancy at birth (1981): 52 years. **Births** (per 1,000 pop. 1978): 41. **Deaths** (per 1,000 pop. 1978): 20. **Natural increase** 1978): 2.2%. **Hospital beds** (per 100,000 pop. 1977): 343. **Physicians** (per 100,000 pop. 1977): 18.

Education (1978): **Literacy:** 78%. **Pop. 5-19:** in school: 63%, teachers per 1,000: 24.

Vietnam's recorded history began in Tonkin before the Christian era. Settled by Viets from central China, Vietnam was held

by China, 111 BC-939 AD, and was a vassal state during subsequent periods. Vietnam defeated the armies of Kublai Khan, 1288. Conquest by France began in 1858 and ended in 1884 with the protectorates of Tonkin and Annam in the N. and the colony of Cochin-China in the S.

In 1940 Vietnam was occupied by Japan; nationalist aims gathered force. A number of groups formed the Vietminh (Independence) League, headed by Ho Chi Minh, communist guerrilla leader. In Aug. 1945 the Vietminh forced out Bao Dai, former emperor of Annam, head of a Japan-sponsored regime. France, seeking to reestablish colonial control, battled communist and nationalist forces, 1946-1954, and was finally defeated at Dienbienphu, May 8, 1954. Meanwhile, on July 1, 1949, Bao Dai had formed a State of Vietnam, with himself as chief of state, with French approval. Communist China backed Ho Chi Minh.

A cease-fire accord signed in Geneva July 21, 1954, divided Vietnam along the Ben Hai R. It provided for a buffer zone, withdrawal of French troops from the North and elections to determine the country's future. Under the agreement the communists gained control of territory north of the 17th parallel, 22 provinces with area of 62,000 sq. mi. and 13 million pop., with its capital at Hanoi and Ho Chi Minh as president. South Vietnam came to comprise the 39 southern provinces with approx. area of 65,000 sq. mi. and pop. of 12 million. Some 900,000 North Vietnamese fled to South Vietnam. Neither South Vietnam nor the U.S. signed the agreement.

On Oct. 26, 1955, Ngo Dinh Diem, premier of the interim government of South Vietnam, proclaimed the Republic of Vietnam and became its first president.

The Democratic Republic of Vietnam, established in the North, adopted a constitution Dec. 31, 1959, based on communist principles and calling for reunification of all Vietnam. North Vietnam sought to take over South Vietnam beginning in 1954. Fighting persisted from 1956, with the communist Vietcong, aided by North Vietnam, pressing war in the South and South Vietnam receiving U.S. aid. Northern aid to Vietcong guerrillas was intensified in 1959, and large-scale troop infiltration began in 1964, with Soviet and Chinese arms assistance. Large Northern forces were stationed in border areas of Laos and Cambodia.

A serious political conflict arose in the South in 1963 when Buddhists denounced authoritarianism and brutality. This paved the way for a military coup Nov. 1-2, 1963, which overthrew Diem. Several military coups followed. In elections Sept. 3, 1967, Chief of State Nguyen Van Thieu was chosen president.

In 1964, the U.S. began air strikes against North Vietnam. Beginning in 1965, the raids were stepped up and U.S. troops became combatants. U.S. troop strength in Vietnam, which reached a high of 543,400 in Apr. 1969, was ordered reduced by President Nixon in a series of withdrawals, beginning in June 1969. U.S. bombings were resumed in 1972-73.

A ceasefire agreement was signed in Paris Jan. 27, 1973 by the U.S., North and South Vietnam, and the Vietcong. It was never implemented. U.S. aid was curbed in 1974 by the U.S. Congress. Heavy fighting continued for two years throughout Indochina.

North Vietnamese forces launched attacks against remaining government outposts in the Central Highlands in the first months of 1975. Government retreats turned into a rout, and the Saigon regime surrendered April 30. A Provisional Revolutionary Government assumed control, aided by officials and technicians from Hanoi, and first steps were taken to transform society along communist lines. All businesses and farms were collectivized.

The U.S. accepted over 165,000 Vietnamese refugees, while scores of thousands more sought refuge in other countries.

The war's toll included — Combat deaths: U.S. 47,752; South Vietnam over 200,000; other allied forces 5,225. Civilian casualties were over a million. Displaced war refugees in South Vietnam totaled over 6.5 million.

After the fighting ended, 8 Northern divisions remained stationed in the South. Over 1 million urban residents and 260,000 Montagnards were resettled in the countryside by 1978, the first of 10 million scheduled for forced resettlement. Many were sent to long-term re-education camps, including thousands of adherents of the Hoa Hao sect.

The first National Assembly of both parts of the country met and the country was officially reunited July 2, 1976. The Northern capital, flag, anthem, emblem, and currency were applied to the new state. Nearly all major government posts went to officials of the former Northern government.

Heavy fighting with Cambodia took place, 1977-80, amid mutual charges of aggression and atrocities against civilians. Increasing numbers of Vietnamese civilians, ethnic Chinese, escaped the country, via the sea, or the overland route across Cambodia. Vietnam launched an offensive against Cambodian refugee strongholds along the Thai-Cambodian border in 1983; they also engaged Thai troops.

Relations with China soured as 140,000 ethnic Chinese left Vietnam charging discrimination; China cut off economic aid. Reacting to Vietnam's invasion of Cambodia, China attacked 4 Vietnamese border provinces, Feb., 1979, instigating heavy fighting. Several border clashes were reported with China in 1984.

Western Samoa

Independent State of Western Samoa

People: Population (1983 est.): 160,000. **Age distrib.** (%): 0–14: 50.4; 15–59: 45.4; 60+: 4.3. **Pop. density:** 141.22 per sq. mi. **Urban** (1979): 21.5%. **Ethnic groups:** Samoan (Polynesian) 88%, Euronesian (mixed) 10%, European, other Pacific Islanders. **Languages:** Samoan, English both official. **Religions:** Protestants 70%, Roman Catholics 20%.

Geography: Area: 1,133 sq. mi., the size of Rhode Island. **Location:** In the S. Pacific O. **Neighbors:** Nearest are Fiji on W, Tonga on S. **Topography:** Main islands, Savai'i (670 sq. mi.) and Upolu (429 sq. mi.), both ruggedly mountainous, and small islands Manono and Apolima. **Capital:** Apia. **Cities** (1983 est.): Apia 35,000.

Government: Type: Parliamentary democracy. **Head of state:** King Malietoa Tanumafili II; b. Jan. 4, 1913; in office: Jan. 1, 1962. **Head of government:** Prime Min. Tupuola Efi; b. Mar. 1, 1938; in office: Sept. 18, 1982. **Local divisions:** 24 districts.

Economy: Chief crops: Cocoa, copra, bananas. **Other resources:** Hardwoods, fish. **Per capita arable land:** 0.9 acres. **Electricity prod.** (1977): 25.00 mln. kwh. **Labor force:** 67% agric.

Finance: Currency: Tala (Mar. 1984: 1.40 = $1 US). **Gross domestic product** (1978): $65 mln. **Per capita income** (1978): $400. **Imports** (1982): $38 mln.; partners: NZ 24% Austral. 16%, Jap. 9%, U.S. 23%. **Exports** (1982): $9 mln.; partners: NZ 33%, W. Ger. 13%, Neth. 13%. **Tourists** (1977): 22,000; receipts (1976): $3 mln. **International reserves less gold** (Mar. 1984): $4.8 mln. **Consumer prices** (change in 1981): 20.5%.

Transport: Motor vehicles: in use (1979): 1,573 passenger cars, 2,203 comm. vehicles. **Chief ports:** Apia, Asau.

Communications: Radios: 50,000 in use (1975). **Telephones in use** (1978): 3,810.

Health: Life expectancy at birth (1983): 63 years. **Births** (per 1,000 pop. 1978): 20.0. **Deaths** (per 1,000 pop. 1978): 2.8. **Natural increase** (1978): 1.7%. **Pop. per hospital bed** (1977): 214. **Pop. per physician** (1977): 2,884. **Infant mortality** (per 1,000 live births 1983): 36.

Education (1983): **Literacy:** 90%. 95% attend elementary school.

Western Samoa was a German colony, 1899 to 1914, when New Zealand landed troops and took over. It became a New Zealand mandate under the League of Nations and, in 1945, a New Zealand UN Trusteeship.

An elected local government took office in Oct. 1959 and the country became fully independent Jan. 1, 1962. New Zealand has continued economic aid and educational assistance.

North Yemen

Yemen Arab Republic

People: Population (1982 est.): 5,744,000. **Pop. density:** 78.76 per sq. mi. **Ethnic groups:** Arabs, some Negroids. **Languages:** Arabic. **Religions:** Sunni Moslems 50%, Shiite Moslems 50%.

Geography: Area: 77,200 sq. mi., slightly smaller than South Dakota. **Location:** On the southern Red Sea coast of the Arabian Peninsula. **Neighbors:** Saudi Arabia on NE, South Yemen on S. **Topography:** A sandy coastal strip leads to well-watered fertile mountains in interior. **Capital:** Sanaa. **Cities** (1981 est.): Sanaa 277,800.

Government: Type: Republic. **Head of state:** Pres. Ali Abdullah Saleh, b. 1942; in office: July 17, 1978. **Head of govern-**

ment: Prime Min. Abdul Aziz Abdel Ghani; in office: Nov. 13, 1983. **Local divisions:** 11 governorates. **Armed forces:** regulars 31,800 (1980).

Economy: Industries: Textiles, cement. **Chief crops:** Wheat, sorghum, qat, fruits, coffee, cotton. **Minerals:** Salt. **Crude oil reserves** (1978): 370 mln. bbls. **Per capita arable land:** 0.7 acres. **Meat prod.** (1980): beef: 14,000 metric tons; lamb: 54,000 metric tons. **Fish catch** (1978): 19,300 metric tons. **Electricity prod.** (1977): 65.00 mln. kwh. **Labor force:** 55% agric.; 4% ind. and commerce; 16% serv.

Finance: Currency: Rial (Apr. 1984: 4.98 = $1 US). **Gross domestic product** (1977-78): $2.7 bln. **Per capita income** (1977-78): $475. **Imports** (1981): $1.7 bln.; partners: Saudi Ar. 20%, Fr. 8%, Jap. 16%. **Exports** (1981): $47 mln.; partners: S. Yemen 23%, Saudi Ar. 8%, Pak. 19%. **International reserves less gold** (Feb. 1984): $352.9 mln. **Gold:** 9,000 oz t. **Consumer prices** (change in 1982): 2.7%.

Transport: Chief ports: Al-Hudaydah, Al-Mukha.

Communications: Radios: 90,000 in use (1976). **Telephones in use** (1981): 90,350.

Health: Life expectancy at birth (1975): 37.3 male; 38.7 female. **Births** (per 1,000 pop. 1978): 48. **Deaths** (per 1,000 pop. 1978): 25. **Natural increase** (1978): 2.3%. **Hospital beds** (per 100,000 pop. 1977): 58. **Physicians** (per 100,000 pop. 1977): 8.

Education (1982): **Literacy:** 12%. **Primary school attendance:** 29%.

Embassy: 600 New Hampshire Ave. NW 20037; 965-4760.

Yemen's territory once was part of the ancient kindgom of Sheba, or Saba, a prosperous link in trade between Africa and India. A Biblical reference speaks of its gold, spices and precious stones as gifts borne by the Queen of Sheba to King Solomon.

Yemen became independent in 1918, after years of Ottoman Turkish rule, but remained politically and economically backward. Imam Ahmed ruled 1948-1962. The king was reported assassinated Sept. 26, 1962, and a revolutionary group headed by Brig. Gen. Abdullah al-Salal declared the country to be the Yemen Arab Republic.

The Imam Ahmed's heir, the Imam Mohamad al-Badr, fled to the mountains where tribesmen joined royalist forces; internal warfare between them and the republican forces continued. Egypt sent troops and Saudi Arabia military aid to the royalists. About 150,000 people died in the fighting.

After its defeat in the June 1967 Arab-Israeli war, Egypt announced it would withdraw its troops from Yemen.

There was a bloodless coup Nov. 5, 1967.

In April 1970 hostilities ended with an agreement between Yemen and Saudi Arabia and appointment of several royalists to the Yemen government. There were border skirmishes with forces of the People's Democratic Republic of Yemen in 1972-73.

On June 13, 1974, an Army group, led by Col. Ibrahim al-Hamidi, seized the government. Hamidi pursued close Saudi and U.S. ties; he was assassinated in 1977.

The People's Democratic Republic of Yemen went to war with Yemen on Feb. 24, 1979. Swift Arab mediation led to a cease-fire and a mutual withdrawal of forces, Mar. 19. An Arab League-sponsored agreement between North and South Yemen on unification of the 2 countries was signed Mar. 29th.

The remittances from 400,000 Yemenis living in Arab oil countries provide most of foreign earnings.

South Yemen

People's Democratic Republic of Yemen

People: Population (1983 est.): 2,086,000. **Age distrib.** (%): 0–14: 49.4; 15–59: 45.5; 60+: 5.5. **Pop. density:** 16.67 per sq. mi. **Urban** (1973): 33.3%. **Ethnic groups:** Arabs, 75%, Indians 11%, Somalis 8%, others. **Languages:** Arabic. **Religions:** Muslims (Sunni) 91%, Christians 4%, Hindus 3.5%.

Geography: Area: 130,541 sq. mi., the size of Nevada. **Location:** On the southern coast of the Arabian Peninsula. **Neighbors:** Yemen on W, Saudi Arabia on N, Oman on E. **Topography:** The entire country is very hot and very dry. A sandy coast rises to mountains which give way to desert sands. **Capital:** Aden. **Cities** (1981 est.): Aden 365,000.

Government: Type: Republic. **Head of state:** Pres. Ali Nasir Muhammad Husani; b. 1938; in office: Apr. 21, 1980. **Head of Communist Party:** Sec. Gen. Ali Nasir Muhammad Husani; in office: April 21, 1980. **Local divisions:** 6 governorates. **Armed forces:** regulars 23,750 (1980).

Economy: Industries: Transshipment. **Chief crops:** Cotton (main export), grains. **Per capita arable land:** 0.3 acres. **Meat prod.** (1980) lamb: 11,000 metric tons. **Fish catch** (1981): 175,000 metric tons. **Electricity prod.** (1981) 260 mln. kwh. **Labor force:** 43.8% agric.; 28% ind. and commerce; 28% serv.

Finance: Currency: Dinar (Mar. 1984: .35 = $1 US). **Gross domestic product** (1977 est.): $550 mln. **Per capita income** (1977): $310. **Imports** (1979) $480 mln.; partners: UAE 28%, Kuw. 9%, Jap. 6%. **Exports** (1979): $250 mln.; partners: It. 11%, UAE 22%. **National budget** (1977): $101 mln. revenues; $137 mln. expenditures. **International reserves less gold** (Jan. 1984): $288.8 mln. **Gold:** 42,000 oz t. **Consumer prices** (change in 1980): 10.0%.

Transport: Motor vehicles: in use (1980): 12,200 passenger cars, 15,300 comm. vehicles. **Chief ports:** Aden.

Communications: Television sets: 32,000 in use (1976). **Radios:** 100,000 in use (1976). **Daily newspaper circ.** (1982): 6 per 1,000 pop.

Health: Life expectancy at birth (1975): 40.6 male; 42.4 female. **Births** (per 1,000 pop. 1978): 47. **Deaths** (per 1,000 pop. 1978): 21. **Natural increase** (1978): 1.8%. **Hospital beds** (per 100,000 pop. 1977): 154. **Physicians** (per 100,000 pop. 1977): 11. **Infant mortality rate** (per 1,000 live births in 1980): 114.

Education (1978): **Literacy:** 25%. About 90% attend primary school.

Aden, mentioned in the Bible, has been a port for trade in incense, spice and silk between the East and West for 2,000 years. British rule began in 1839. Aden provided Britain with a controlling position at the southern entrance to the Red Sea.

A war for independence began in 1963. The National Liberation Front (NLF) and the Egypt-supported Front for the Liberation of Occupied South Yemen, waged a guerrilla war against the British and local dynastic rulers. The 2 groups vied with each other for control. The NLF won out. Independence came Nov. 30, 1967. In 1969, the left wing of the NLF seized power and inaugurated a thorough nationalization of the economy and regimentation of daily life.

The new government broke off relations with the U.S. and nationalized some foreign firms. Aid has been furnished by the USSR and China.

In 1972-73 there were border skirmishes with forces of the Yemen Arab Republic. South Yemen aided leftist guerrillas in neighboring Oman. Relations with Saudi Arabia later improved. S. Yemen troops fought in Ethiopia against Eritrean rebels in 1978.

Pres. Salem Robaye Ali, who had tried to improve relations with Yemen, Saudi Arabia, Oman, and the U.S., was executed after a bloody coup June 1978. The new ruling faction was accused by N. Yemen of the murder of N. Yemen's president 2 days earlier. N. Yemen, Egypt, and Saudi Arabia froze ties with S. Yemen in July.

The People's Democratic Republic of Yemen went to war with Yemen on Feb. 24, 1979. Swift Arab mediation led to a ceasefire and a mutual withdrawal of forces, Mar. 19th. An Arab League-sponsored agreement between North and South Yemen on unification of the 2 countries was signed Mar. 29th.

The Port of Aden is the country's most valuable resource.

Socotra, the largest island in the Arabian Sea, Kamaran, an island in the Red Sea near the coast of North Yemen, and Perim, an island in the strait between the Gulf of Aden and the Red Sea, are controlled by South Yemen.

Yugoslavia

Socialist Federal Republic of Yugoslavia

People: Population (1983 est.): 22,826,000. **Age distrib.** (%): 0–14: 24.7; 15-59: 63.7; 60+: 12.6. **Pop. density:** 226.19 per sq. mi. **Urban** (1971): 38.6%. **Ethnic groups:** Serbs 36%, Croats 20%, Bosnian Muslims 9%, Slovenes 8%, Macedonians 6%, Albanians 8%, Montenegrin Serbs 3%, Hungarians 2%. **Languages:** Serbo-Croatian, Macedonian, Slovenian (all official), Albanian. **Religions:** Orthodox 50%, Roman Catholics 30%, Moslems 10%, Protestants 1%.

Geography: Area: 98,766 sq. mi., the size of Wyoming. **Location:** On the Adriatic coast of the Balkan Peninsula in SE Europe. **Neighbors:** Italy on W, Austria, Hungary on N, Romania, Bulgaria on E, Greece, Albania on S. **Topography:** The Dinaric

Alps run parallel to the Adriatic coast, which is lined by offshore islands. Plains stretch across N and E river basins. S and NW are mountainous. **Capital:** Belgrade. **Cities** (1980 est.): Belgrade 1,300,000; Zagreb 700,000; Skopje 440,000; Sarajevo 400,000; Ljubljana 300,000.

Government: Type: Federal republic. **Head of state:** Pres. Veselin Djuranovic; in office: May 15, 1984. **Head of government:** Prime Min. Milka Planinc; b. 1924; in office: May 16, 1982; **Head of Communist Party:** Mitja Ribicic; in office: June 29, 1982. **Local divisions:** 6 republics, 2 autonomous provinces. **Defense:** 5.2% of GNP (1983).

Economy: Industries: Steel, wood products, cement, textiles, tourism. **Chief crops:** Corn, grains, tobacco, sugar beets. **Minerals:** Antimony, bauxite, lead, mercury, coal, iron, copper, chrome, zinc, salt. **Crude oil reserves** (1980): 275 mln. bbls. **Arable land:** 69%. **Meat prod.** (1983): beef: 343,000 metric tons; pork: 755,000 metric tons; lamb: 60,000 metric tons. **Fish catch:** (1978): 63,000 metric tons. **Electricity prod.** (1982): 60.3 bln. kwh. **Crude steel prod.** (1982): 2.8 mln. metric tons. **Labor force:** 30% agric.; 70% ind.

Finance: Currency: Dinar (Mar. 1984: 124.75 = $1 US). **Gross national product** (1981): $51.5 bln. **Per capita income:** $3,109. **Imports** (1982): $13.3 bln.; partners: W. Ger. 15%, USSR 19%, It. 8%, U.S. 6%. **Exports** (1982): $10.2 bln.; partners: USSR 33%, It. 9%, W. Ger. 8%, Czech. 5%. **Tourists** (1981): 6.6 mln.; receipts: 1.1 bln. **National budget** (1980): $3.5 bln. revenues; $3.5 bln. expenditures. **International reserves less gold** (Feb. 1984): $937 mln. **Gold:** 1.86 mln. oz t. **Consumer prices** change in 1983): 40%.

Transport: Railway traffic (1982): 10.8 bln. passenger-km; 25.8 bln. net ton-km. **Motor vehicles:** in use (1981): 2.5 mln. passenger cars, 227,689 comm. vehicles; manuf. (1981): 175,000 passenger cars; 73,000 comm. vehicles. **Civil aviation** (1982): 2.8 bln. passenger-km; 59.7 mln. freight ton-km. **Chief ports:** Rijeka, Split, Dubrovnik.

Communications: Television sets: 4.8 mln. licensed (1980), 599,000 manuf. (1979). **Radios:** 4.8 mln. licensed (1980), 172,000 manuf. (1979). **Telephones in use** (1981): 1.6 mln. **Daily newspaper circ.** (1982): 97 per 1,000 pop.

Health: Life expectancy at birth (1983): 68 male; 73 female. **Births** (per 1,000 pop. 1980): 17.0. **Deaths** (per 1,000 pop. 1980): 9.0. **Natural increase** (1978): .9%. **Hospital beds** (1980): 133,399. **Physicians** (1980): 32,850. **Infant mortality** (per 1,000 live births 1981): 32.8.

Education (1983): **Literacy:** 85%. Almost all attend primary school.

Embassy: 2410 California St. NW 20008; 462-6566.

Serbia, which had since 1389 been a vassal principality of Turkey, was established as an independent kingdom by the Treaty of Berlin, 1878. Montenegro, independent since 1389, also obtained international recognition in 1878. After the Balkan wars Serbia's boundaries were enlarged by the annexation of Old Serbia and Macedonia, 1913.

When the Austro-Hungarian empire collapsed after World War I, the Kingdom of the Serbs, Croats, and Slovenes was formed from the former provinces of Croatia, Dalmatia, Bosnia, Herzegovina, Slovenia, Voyvodina and the independent state of Montenegro. The name was later changed to Yugoslavia.

Nazi Germany invaded in 1941. Many Yugoslav partisan troops continued to operate. Among these were the Chetniks led by Draja Mikhailovich, who fought other partisans led by Josip Broz, known as Marshal Tito. Tito, backed by the USSR and Britain from 1943, was in control by the time the Germans had been driven from Yugoslavia in 1945. Mikhailovich was executed July 17, 1946, by the Tito regime.

A constituent assembly proclaimed Yugoslavia a republic Nov. 29, 1945. It became a federated republic Jan. 31, 1946, and Marshal Tito, a communist, became head of the government.

The Stalin policy of dictating to all communist nations was rejected by Tito. He accepted economic aid and military equipment from the U.S. and received aid in foreign trade also from France and Great Britain. Tito also supported the liberal government of Czechoslovakia in 1968 before the Russian invasion.

A separatist movement among Croatians, 2d to the Serbs in numbers, brought arrests and a change of leaders in the Croatian Republic in Jan. 1972. Violence by extreme Croatian nationalists and fears of Soviet political intervention have led to restrictions on political and intellectual dissent, which had previously been freer than in other East European countries. Serbians, Montenegrins, and Macedonians use Cyrillic, Croatians and Slovenians use Latin letters. Croatia and Slovenia have been the most prosperous republics.

Most industry is socialized and private enterprise is restricted to small-scale production. Since 1952 workers are guaranteed a basic wage and a share in cooperative profits. Management of industrial enterprises is handled by workers' councils. Farmland is 85% privately owned but farms are restricted to 25 acres.

Beginning in 1965, reforms designed to decentralize the administration of economic development and to force industries to produce more efficiently in competition with foreign producers were introduced.

Yugoslavia has developed considerable trade with Western Europe as well as with Eastern Europe. Money earned by Yugoslavs working temporarily in Western Europe helps pay for imports.

Pres. Tito died May 4, 1980; with his death, the post as head of the Collective Presidency and also that as head of the League of Communists became a rotating system of succession among the members representing each republic and autonomous province.

Zaire

Republic of Zaire

People: Population (1983 est.): 31,250,000. **Pop. density:** 30 per sq. mi. **Urban** (1981): 30.3%. **Ethnic groups:** Bantu tribes 80%, over 200 other tribes. **Languages:** French (official), Bantu dialects. **Religions:** Christian 70%, Muslim 10%.

Geography: Area: 905,063 sq. mi., one-fourth the size of the U.S. **Location:** In central Africa. **Neighbors:** Congo on W, Central African Republic, Sudan on N, Uganda, Rwanda, Burundi, Tanzania on E, Zambia, Angola on S. **Topography:** Zaire includes the bulk of the Zaire (Congo) R. Basin. The vast central region is a low-lying plateau covered by rain forest. Mountainous terraces in the W, savannas in the S and SE, grasslands toward the N, and the high Ruwenzori Mtns. on the E surround the central region. A short strip of territory borders the Atlantic O. The Zaire R. is 2,718 mi. long. **Capital:** Kinshasa. **Cities** (1983 est.): Kinshasa 3,000,000; Kananga 601,239.

Government: Type: Republic with strong presidential authority. **Head of state:** Pres. Mobutu Sese Seko; b. Oct. 14, 1930; in office: Nov. 25, 1965. **Local divisions:** 9 regions, Kinshasa. **Armed forces:** regulars 21,000 (1980).

Economy: Chief crops: Coffee, cotton, rice, sugar cane, bananas, plantains, coconuts, manioc, mangoes, tea, cacao, palm oil. **Minerals:** Cobalt (60% of world reserves), copper, cadmium, gold, silver, tin, germanium, zinc, iron, manganese, uranium, radium. **Crude oil reserves** (1980): 135 mln. bbls. **Other resources:** Forests, rubber, ivory. **Arable land:** 50%. **Meat prod.** (1980): beef: 22,000 metric tons; pork: 29,000 metric tons; lamb: 9,000 metric tons. **Fish catch** (1981): 102,000 metric tons. **Electricity prod.** (1981): 4.5 bln. kwh. **Labor force:** 75% agric..

Finance: Currency: Zaire (Mar. 1984: 32.88 = $1 US). **Gross domestic product** (1982): $9.9 bln. **Per capita income** (1975): $127. **Imports** (1982): $480 mln.; partners: Belg. 22%, U.S. 10%, W. Ger. 10%, Fra. 13%. **Exports** (1982): $569 mln.; partners: Belg.-Lux. 31%, U.S. 36%. **Tourists** (1977): 24,500; receipts (1976): $11 mln. **National budget** (1978): $886 mln. revenues; $1.8 bln. expenditures. **International reserves less gold** (Oct. 1983): $279.5 mln. **Gold:** 431,000 oz t. **Consumer prices** (change in 1982): 37.2%.

Transport: Railway traffic (1979): 554 mln. passenger-km; 1.5 bln. net ton-km. **Motor vehicles:** in use (1980): 94,000 passenger cars, 84,900 comm. vehicles. **Civil aviation** (1982): 683 mln. passenger-km. 31.5 mln. freight ton-km. **Chief ports:** Matadi, Boma.

Communications: Television sets: 8,000 in use (1981). **Radios:** 150,000 mln. in use (1981). **Telephones in use** (1980): 30,300. **Daily newspaper circ.** (1982): 1 per 1,000 pop.

Health: Life expectancy at birth (1983): 46 male; 49 female. **Births** (per 1,000 pop. 1978): 46. **Deaths** (per 1,000 pop. 1978): 18. **Natural increase** (1978): 3.5%. **Hospital beds** (per 100,000 pop. 1977): 291. **Physicians** (per 100,000 pop. 1977): 2. **Infant mortality** (per 1,000 live births 1983): 117.

Education (1980): **Literacy:** males 40%, females 15%. **Pop. 5-19 in school:** 43%; teachers per 1,000: 11.

Embassy: 1800 New Hampshire Ave. NW 20009; 234-7690.

The earliest inhabitants of Zaire may have been the pygmies, followed by Bantus from the E and Nilotic tribes from the N. The large Bantu Bakongo kingdom ruled much of Zaire and Angola when Portuguese explorers visited in the 15th century.

Leopold II, king of the Belgians, formed an international group to exploit the Congo in 1876. In 1877 Henry M. Stanley explored the Congo and in 1878 the king's group sent him back to organize the region and win over the native chiefs. The Conference of Berlin, 1884-85, organized the Congo Free State with Leopold as king and chief owner. Exploitation of native laborers on the rubber plantations caused international criticism and led to granting of a colonial charter, 1908.

Belgian and Congolese leaders agreed Jan. 27, 1960, that the Congo would become independent June 30. In the first general elections, May 31, the National Congolese movement of Patrice Lumumba won 35 of 137 seats in the National Assembly. He was appointed premier June 21, and formed a coalition cabinet.

Widespread violence caused Europeans and others to flee. The UN Security Council Aug. 9, 1960, called on Belgium to withdraw its troops and sent a UN contingent. President Kasavubu removed Lumumba as premier. Lumumba fought for control backed by Ghana, Guinea and India; he was murdered in 1961.

The last UN troops left the Congo June 30, 1964, and Moise Tshombe became president.

On Sept. 7, 1964, leftist rebels set up a "People's Republic" in Stanleyville. Tshombe hired foreign mercenaries and sought to rebuild the Congolese Army. In Nov. and Dec. 1964 rebels slew scores of white hostages and thousands of Congolese; Belgian paratroops, dropped from U.S. transport planes, rescued hundreds. By July 1965 the rebels had lost their effectiveness.

In 1965 Gen. Joseph D. Mobutu was named president. He later changed his name to Mobutu Sese Seko. The country changed its name to Republic of Zaire on Oct. 27, 1971; in 1972 Zairians with Christian names were ordered to change them to African names.

In 1969-74, political stability under Mobutu was reflected in improved economic conditions. In 1974 most foreign-owned businesses were ordered sold to Zaire citizens, but in 1977 the government asked the original owners to return.

In 1977, a force of Zairians invaded Shaba province (Katanga) from Angola. Zaire repelled the attack, with the aid of Egyptian pilots and Moroccan troops flown in by France. But many European mining experts failed to return after a 2d unsuccessful invasion from Angola in May 1978.

Serious economic difficulties, amid charges of corruption by government officials, plagued Zaire in 1983; the nation was unable to service its foreign debt.

Zambia

Republic of Zambia

People: Population (1983 est.): 6,346,000. **Age distrib.** (%): 0-14: 46.5; 15-59: 49.3; 60+: 4.1. **Pop. density:** 18.82 per sq. mi. **Urban** (1980): 43.0%. **Ethnic groups:** Mostly Bantu tribes. **Languages:** English (official), Bantu dialects. **Religions:** Predominantly animists, Roman Catholics 21%, Protestant, Hindu, Muslim minorities.

Geography: Area: 290,586 sq. mi., larger than Texas. **Location:** In southern central Africa. **Neighbors:** Zaire on N, Tanzania, Malawi, Mozambique on E, Zimbabwe, Namibia on S, Angola on W. **Topography:** Zambia is mostly high plateau country covered with thick forests, and drained by several important rivers, including the Zambezi. **Capital:** Lusaka. **Cities** (1982 est.): Lusaka 538,000; Kitwe 314,794; Ndola 282,439.

Government: Type: Republic. **Head of state:** Pres. Kenneth David Kaunda; b. Apr. 28, 1924; in office: Oct. 24, 1964. **Head of government:** Prime Min. Nalumino Mundia; in office: Feb. 18, 1981. **Local divisions:** 9 provinces. **Defense:** 20% of GDP (1982 est)

Economy: Chief crops: Corn, tobacco, peanuts, cotton, sugar. **Minerals:** Cobalt, copper, zinc, gold, lead, vanadium, manganese, coal. **Other resources:** Rubber, ivory. **Per capita arable land:** 2.3 acres. **Meat prod.** (1980): beef: 24,000 metric tons; pork: 7,000 metric tons. **Fish catch** (1978): 47,600 metric tons. **Electricity prod.** (1981): 9.7 bln. kwh. **Labor force:** 65% agric.; 35% ind. and commerce.

Finance: Currency: Kwacha (Mar. 1984: 1.40 = $1 US). **Gross domestic product** (1979): $3.24 bln. **Per capita income** (1978): $414. **Imports** (1982): $1.0 bln.; partners: UK 26%, Saudi Ar. 18%, W. Ger. 18%, U.S. 9%. **Exports** (1982):

$1.0 bln.; partners: Jap. 19%, Fr. 15%, UK 13%, U.S. 10%, W. Ger. 9%. **National budget** (1979): $753 mln. revenues; $973 mln. expenditures. **International reserves less gold** (Jan. 1984): $54.5 mln. **Gold:** 217,000 oz t. **Consumer prices** (change in 1982): 12.5%.

Transport: Motor vehicles: in use (1980): 103,500 passenger cars, 66,300 comm. vehicles. **Civil aviation** (1982): 55.7 mln. passenger-km; 23.5 mln. freight ton-km.

Communications: Television sets: 60,000 in use (1980). **Radios:** 135,000 in use (1981). **Telephones in use** (1981): 61,000. **Daily newspaper circ.** (1982): 20 per 1,000 pop.

Health: Life expectancy at birth (1975): 44.3 male; 47.5 female. **Births** (per 1,000 pop. 1978): 49. **Deaths** (per 1,000 pop. 1978): 17. **Natural increase** (1978): 3.2%. **Hospital beds** (per 100,000 pop. 1977): 366. **Physicians** (per 100,000 pop. 1977): 5. **Infant mortality** (per 1,000 live births 1982): 140.

Education (1982): **Literacy:** 54%. **Attendance:** less than 50% in grades 1–7.

Embassy: 2419 Massachusetts Ave. NW 20008; 265-9717.

As Northern Rhodesia, the country was under the administration of the South Africa Company, 1889 until 1924, when the office of governor was established, and, subsequently, a legislature. The country became an independent republic within the Commonwealth Oct. 24, 1964.

After the white government of Rhodesia declared its independence from Britain Nov. 11, 1965, relations between Zambia and Rhodesia became strained and use of their jointly owned railroad was disputed.

Britain gave Zambia an extra $12 million aid in 1966 after imposing an oil embargo on Rhodesia, and Zambia set up a temporary airlift to carry copper out from its mines and gasoline in. In Aug. 1968 a 1,058-mi. pipeline was completed, bringing oil from Tanzania. In 1973 a truck road to carry copper to Tanzania's port of Dar es Salaam was completed with U.S. aid. A railroad, built with Chinese aid across Tanzania, reached the Zambian border in 1974.

As part of a program of government participation in major industries, a government corporation in 1970 took over 51% of the ownership of 2 foreign-owned copper mining companies. Privately-held land and other enterprises were nationalized in 1975, as were all newspapers. Decline in copper prices has hurt the economy in the early 1980's.

Severe drought has devastated the area in 1982 and 1983.

Zimbabwe

People: Population (1983 est.): 8,077,000. **Age distrib. (%):** 0–14: 49.2; 15–59: 47.8; 60+: 3.0. **Pop. density:** 48.96 per sq. mi. **Urban** (1979): 19.6%. **Ethnic groups:** Shona 77%, Ndebele 19%, white 3%. **Languages:** English (official), Shona, Sindebele. **Religions:** Predominantly traditional tribal beliefs, Christian minority.

Geography: Area: 150,873 sq. mi., nearly as large as California. **Location:** In southern Africa. **Neighbors:** On N, Botswana on W, S. Africa on S, Mozambique on E. **Topography:** Rhodesia is high plateau country, rising to mountains on eastern border, sloping down on the other borders. **Capital:** Harare. **Cities** (1981 est.): Harare (met.) 686,000; Bulawayo (met.) 400,000.

Government: Type: Parliamentary democracy. **Head of state:** Pres. Rev. Cannan Banana, b. Mar. 5, 1936; in office: Apr. 18, 1980. **Head of government:** Prime Min. Robert G. Mugabe, b. Apr. 14, 1928; in office: Apr. 18, 1980. **Local divisions:** 8 provinces. **Defense:** 15.3% of govt. budget (1982).

Economy: Industries: Clothing, chemicals, light industries.

Chief crops: Tobacco, sugar, cotton, corn, wheat. **Minerals:** Chromium, gold, nickel, asbestos, copper, iron, coal. **Per capita arable land:** 0.9 acres. **Meat prod.** (1980): beef: 125,000 metric tons; pork: 9,000 metric tons; lamb: 7,000 metric tons. **Electricity prod.** (1982): 4.1 bln. kwh. **Crude steel prod.** (1981): 691,000 metric tons. **Labor force:** 35% agric.; 30% ind. and commerce; 20% serv.; 15% gvt.

Finance: Currency: Dollar (Mar. 1984: 1.10 = $1 US). **Gross domestic product** (1981): $5.7 bln. **Per capita income** (1981): White $13,480, African $314-655. **Imports** (1981): $1.3 bln.; partners: UK 10%, So. Afr. 27%, U.S. 7%, W. Ger. 7%. **Exports** (1981): $937 mln.; partners: UK 7%, So. Afr. 22%, W. Ger. 8%. **Consumer prices** (change in 1983): 10.6%.

Transport: Railway traffic (1982): 6.2 bln. net ton-km. **Motor vehicles:** in use (1982): 224,000 passenger cars, 17,000 comm. vehicles.

Communications: Television sets: 75,200 in use (1981). **Radios:** 224,960 in use (1981). **Telephones in use** (1982): 224,500. **Daily newspaper circ.** (1982): 20 per 1,000 pop.

Health: Life expectancy at birth (1975): 49.8 male; 53.3 female. **Births** (per 1,000 pop. 1978): 49. **Deaths** (per 1,000 pop. 1978): 16. **Natural increase** (1978): 2.2%. **Hospital beds** (per 100,000 pop. 1977): 258. **Physicians** (per 100,000 pop. 1977): 9. **Infant mortality** (per 1,000 live births 1975): 122.

Education (1982): **Literacy:** 45%. **Attendance:** 90% primary, 15% secondary for Africans; higher for whites, Asians.

Embassy: 2852 McGill Terrace NW 20008; 332-7100.

Britain took over the area as Southern Rhodesia in 1923 from the British South Africa Co. (which, under Cecil Rhodes, had conquered the area by 1897) and granted internal self-government. Under a 1961 constitution, voting was restricted to maintain whites in power. On Nov. 11, 1965, Prime Min. Ian D. Smith announced his country's unilateral declaration of independence. Britain termed the act illegal, and demanded Rhodesia broaden voting rights to provide for eventual rule by the majority Africans.

Urged by Britain, the UN imposed sanctions, including embargoes on oil shipments to Rhodesia. Some oil and gasoline reached Rhodesia, however, from South Africa and Mozambique, before the latter became independent in 1975. In May 1968, the UN Security Council ordered a trade embargo.

A new constitution came into effect, Mar. 2, 1970, providing for a republic with a president and prime minister. The election law effectively prevented full black representation through income tax requirements.

A proposed British-Rhodesian settlement was dropped in May 1972 when a British commission reported most Rhodesian blacks opposed it. Intermittent negotiations between the government and various black nationalist groups failed to prevent increasing skirmishes. By mid-1978, over 6,000 soldiers and civilians had been killed. Rhodesian troops battled guerrillas within Mozambique and Zambia. An "internal settlement" signed Mar. 1978 in which Smith and 3 popular black leaders share control until transfer of power to the black majority was rejected by guerrilla leaders.

In the country's first universal-franchise election, Apr. 21, 1979, Bishop Abel Muzorewa's United African National Council gained a bare majority control of the black-dominated parliament. Britain's Thatcher government, 1979, began efforts to normalize its relationship with Zimbabwe. A British cease-fire was accepted by all parties, Dec. 5th. Independence was finally achieved Apr. 18, 1980.

Decline in Growth Rate for World Population

For the first time in modern history, the growth rate of the world's population declined, according to the *State of World Population 1984*, a report released by the United Nations Fund for Population Activities.

The report states that the annual population growth rate declined from 2 percent to 1.7 percent in the last decade. Some 80 to 90 million each year were added to the 4.76 billion people in the world. The report projects a continuing

decline in population growth rates, but a rise in world population to 6.1 billion in the year 2000 and 10.5 billion in 2095 when, it is hoped, the growth rate will go down to zero and the population stabilize.

In the first 4 decades of the next century, India, with a growth rate of 2 percent, will replace China as the world's most populous country. China's growth rate is 1.3 percent.

Population of the World's Largest Cities

The table below represents one attempt at comparing the world's largest cities. The figures are for the city proper unless otherwise indicated. City proper is defined as a large locality with legally fixed boundaries and an administratively recognized urban status which is usually characterized by some form of local government.

City	Population	City	Population
Ahmedabad, India, metro (1981 census)	2,515,195	Los Angeles, Cal. (1980 census)	2,966,850
Baghdad, Iraq (1977 census)	3,205,645	Madras, India, metro (1981 census)	4,276,635
Bangalore, India, metro (1981 census)	2,913,537	Madrid, Spain (1981 estimate)	3,267,500
Bangkok, Thailand, metro (1979 census)	4,870,509	Manchester, England, greater (1981 census)	2,594,000
Berlin (1980 estimate)	3,039,200	Melbourne, Australia (1980 census)	2,759,700
East	1,140,300	Mexico City, Mexico (1978 estimate)	8,988,230
West	1,898,900	Moscow, USSR (1981 estimate)	8,203,000
Bogota, Colombia (1978 estimate)	3,800,000	Nanjing, China (1977 estimate)	3,000,000
Bombay, India, metro (1981 census)	8,202,759	New York City (1980 census)	7,071,039
Buenos Aires, Argentina (1980 estimate)	2,908,000	Osaka, Japan (1980 census)	2,648,000
Cairo, Egypt (1979 estimate)	5,399,000	Paris, France (1975 census)	2,317,227
Calcutta, India (1981 estimate)	9,165,650	Peking, China, metro (1980 estimate)	9,029,000
Canton, China (1977 estimate)	5,000,000	Pusan, South Korea (1980 census)	3,160,000
Chicago, Ill. (1980 census)	3,005,072	Rio de Janeiro, Brazil (1980 census)	5,093,232
Chongquig, China (1977 estimate)	6,000,000	Rome, Italy (1980 census)	2,916,414
Dacca, Bangladesh (1981 estimate)	3,000,000	Santiago, Chile, metro (1983 estimate)	4,085,300
Delhi, India, metro (1981 census)	5,277,730	Sao Paulo, Brazil (1980 census)	7,033,529
Ho Chi Minh City, Vietnam (1981 estimate)	3,500,000	Seoul, South Korea (1980 census)	8,367,000
Hong Kong (1981 census)	5,021,066	Shanghai, metro (1979 estimate)	11,000,000
Hyderabad, India, metro (1981 census)	2,565,536	Shenyang, China (1977 estimate)	4,400,000
Istambul, Turkey (1980 census)	2,772,708	Sydney, Australia (1980 estimate)	3,231,700
Jakarta, Indonesia (1980 estimate)	6,503,400	Teheran, Iran (1976 census)	4,496,159
Karachi, Pakistan, metro (1980 estimate)	5,005,000	Tianjin, China, metro (1980 estimate)	7,390,000
Leningrad, USSR (1981 estimate)	4,676,000	Tokyo, Japan (1980 census)	8,349,000
Lima, Peru (1979 census)	3,158,417	Wuhan, China (1977 census)	3,500,000
London, England, greater (1981 census)	6,696,000	Yokohama, Japan (1980 census)	2,774,000

World Population Changes

Source: U.S. Commerce Department (at least 5 million people)

Fastest Growing Nations

	1983 Population (million)	Annual Growth Rate		1983 Population (million)	Annual Growth Rate		1983 Population (million)	Annual Growth Rate
Kenya	18.5	4.1%	Zimbabwe	8.4	3.2%	Iran	42.5	3.1%
Saudi Arabia	10.4	3.4%	Ghana	13.4	3.2%	Uganda	13.8	3.0%
Syria	9.7	3.4%	Ivory Coast	8.9	3.2%	Zaire	31.3	2.9%
Nigeria	85.2	3.4%	Niger	6.1	3.2%	Morocco	22.9	2.9%
Iraq	14.5	3.3%	Senegal	6.3	3.2%	Egypt	45.9	2.8%
Rwanda	5.6	3.3%	Algeria	20.7	3.1%	Sudan	20.5	2.8%
Malawi	6.6	3.2%	Ecuador	8.8	3.1%	Pakistan	94.8	2.8%
Tanzania	20.5	3.2%	Venezuela	18.0	3.1%	**World Average**		**1.7%**
Zambia	6.3	3.2%	Bangladesh	96.5	3.1%			

Slowest Growing Nations

	1983 Population (million)	Annual Growth Rate		1983 Population (million)	Annual Growth Rate		1983 Population (million)	Annual Growth Rate
Afghanistan	14.2	−0.2%	Belgium	9.9	0.1%	Japan	119.2	0.6%
West Germany	61.5	−0.2%	Italy	56.3	0.1%	Romania	22.6	0.7%
Denmark	5.1	−0.1%	Switzerland	6.5	0.2%	Soviet Union	272.3	0.8%
Hungary	10.7	−0.1%	Czechoslovakia	15.4	0.3%	Yugoslavia	22.8	0.8%
East Germany	16.7	0.0%	Netherlands	14.4	0.4%	Greece	9.9	0.9%
Sweden	8.3	0.0%	Portugal	10.0	0.4%	Poland	36.6	0.9%
Britain	56.0	0.0%	France	54.6	0.5%	United States	234.2	0.9%
Austria	7.6	0.0%	Spain	38.2	0.6%	Canada	24.9	1.0%

World Population Characteristics and Projections

Source: U.S. Bureau of the Census

Item	1975	1980	1983	1985	1990	1995	2000
World total (millions)	4,107	4,478	4,722	4,889	5,326	5,786	6,246
Population per sq. mi.	78	85	90	93	102	110	119
Males (millions)	2,059	2,247	2,370	2,455	2,677	2,910	3,142
Females (millions)	2,048	2,231	2,352	2,434	2,648	2,876	3,104
Under 5 years old (%)	13.3	12.3	12.1	12.0	11.7	11.2	10.8
5 to 14 years (%)	23.3	22.8	22.1	21.7	20.7	20.4	19.9
15 to 64 years old (%)	57.7	59.1	60.0	60.5	61.6	62.1	62.7
65 years and over (%)	5.7	5.8	5.8	5.8	6.0	6.3	6.6
Median age	21.9	22.6	23.1	23.5	24.3	25.2	26.1
More developed regions (millions)	1,095	1,136	1,158	1,172	1,204	1,232	1,255
Less developed regions (millions)	3,011	3,343	3,564	3,717	4,122	4,554	4,991

U.S. Aid to Foreign Nations

Source: Bureau of Economic Analysis, U.S. Commerce Department

Figures are in millions of dollars. (*Less than $500,000.) Data exclude military supplies and services furnished under the Foreign Assistance Act and direct Defense Department appropriations, and include credits extended to private entities.

Net grants and credits take into account all known returns to the U.S., including reverse grants, returns of grants, and payments of principal. A minus sign (−) indicates that the total of these returns is greater than the total of grants or credits.

Other assistance represents the transfer of U.S. farm products in exchange for foreign currencies, less the government's disbursements of the currencies as grants, credits, or for purchases.

Amounts do not include investments in the following: Asian Development Bank, $56 mln.; Inter-American Development Bank, $235 mln.; International Development Assn., $1 bln.; International Bank for Reconstruction and Development, $34 mln.; African Development Bank, $18 mln.; African Development Fund, $23 mln.

	Total	Net grants	Net credits	Net other		Total	Net grants	Net credits	Net other
Total	9,988	6,421	3,570	−3	Burundi	6	6	—	—
Military grants	1,295	1,295	—	—	Cameroon	3	12	−9	(*)
Other grants, credits, ass't.	8,693	5,126	3,570	−3	Cape Verde	10	10	—	—
Western Europe	−111	49	−161	2	Cen. African Rep.	6	2	4	—
Belgium-Luxembourg	−17	—	−17	—	Chad	9	9	—	—
Denmark	−13	—	−13	—	Congo	2	2	—	—
Finland	19	—	19	(*)	Djibouti	2	2	—	—
France	6	—	6	—	Ethiopia	2	5	−3	(*)
Germany, West	−6	—	−6	—	Gabon	−2	1	−3	—
Ireland	−7	—	−7	—	Gambia	6	6	—	—
Italy	−25	15	−40	—	Ghana	5	10	−6	1
Liechtenstein	−2	—	−2	—	Guinea	2	2	(*)	−1
Netherlands	−20	—	−20	—	Guinea-Bissau	3	3	—	—
Norway	−12	—	−12	—	Ivory Coast	−3	(*)	−3	(*)
Portugal	23	24	−1	(*)	Kenya	73	56	18	(*)
Spain	81	9	71	1	Lesotho	25	25	—	—
Sweden	−5	—	−5	—	Liberia	62	40	22	—
Switzerland	−14	—	−14	—	Madagascar	10	2	8	(*)
United Kingdom	−119	—	−119	—	Malawi	6	6	(*)	—
Yugoslavia	19	(*)	19	1	Mali	16	16	(*)	(*)
Atomic EC	−5	—	−5	—	Mauritania	20	20	—	—
Other & unspecified	−15	2	−17	(*)	Mauritius	3	1	3	(*)
Eastern Europe	113	33	−19	−1	Morocco	85	25	61	−1
Czechoslovakia	−2	—	−2	—	Mozambique	11	13	−2	—
Hungary	−2	—	−2	—	Niger	16	17	(*)	—
Poland	33	33	1	−1	Nigeria	80	(*)	79	—
Romania	5	—	5	—	Rwanda	9	10	(*)	(*)
Soviet Union	−21	—	−21	—	Senegal	48	41	7	(*)
Near East & South Asia	5,153	2,623	2,516	13	Seychelles	3	3	—	—
Afghanistan	−2	(*)	−2	(*)	Sierra Leone	10	5	5	—
Bangladesh	218	169	49	(*)	Somalia	83	37	46	(*)
Bhutan	1	1	—	—	Sudan	161	112	48	(*)
Egypt	1,780	674	1,104	2	Swaziland	11	8	3	—
Greece	8	(*)	8	−1	Tanzania	19	14	6	—
India	47	125	−82	4	Togo	7	8	(*)	—
Iran	−306	—	−306	—	Tunisia	118	8	110	(*)
Iraq	30	—	30	—	Uganda	4	5	(*)	—
Israel	2,322	1,319	1,002	(*)	Upper Volta (Bourkina Fasso)	25	25	(*)	(*)
Jordan	61	10	52	(*)	Zaire	39	13	26	−1
Lebanon	56	29	27	—	Zambia	25	11	14	—
Nepal	25	26	(*)	−1	Zimbabwe	62	56	6	—
Oman	3	1	3	—	Other & unspecified	43	44	−2	(*)
Pakistan	342	69	265	8	Western Hemisphere	558	497	90	1
Saudi Arabia	−2	—	−2	—	Argentina	26	(*)	26	—
Sri Lanka (Ceylon)	59	14	45	(*)	Barbados	8	(*)	8	—
Syria	25	4	21	(*)	Belize	6	1	5	—
Turkey	368	75	293	(*)	Bolivia	44	32	12	(*)
Yemen (Sana)	35	23	11	—	Brazil	35	2	33	(*)
Other & unspecified	84	85	−1	—	Canada	97	—	97	—
East Asia & Pacific	1,139	354	805	−19	Cayman Islands	4	—	4	—
Australia	75	—	75	—	Chile	−55	2	−58	1
Burma	3	21	−1	−16	Colombia	82	1	81	(*)
China-mainland	9	—	9	—	Costa Rica	119	47	152	—
China-Taiwan	−43	(*)	−45	1	Dominican Republic	36	9	27	—
Fiji	1	2	−1	—	Ecuador	8	8	(*)	—
Hong Kong	−9	(*)	−9	—	El Salvador	264	151	112	—
Indonesia	251	38	213	(*)	Guatemala	27	12	15	—
Japan	−15	(*)	−15	—	Guyana	2	2	(*)	—
Kampuchea (Cambodia)	2	2	(*)	—	Haiti	38	27	11	—
Korea (So.)	448	—	448	(*)	Honduras	75	31	44	—
Malaysia	60	1	60	—	Jamaica	110	8	103	—
Nauru	−4	—	−4	—	Mexico	−610	10	−620	—
New Zealand	−15	—	−15	—	Netherlands Antilles	1	—	1	—
Philippines	215	120	100	−4	Nicaragua	3	3	(*)	—
Singapore	−34	—	−34	—	Panama	12	7	5	—
Thailand	45	20	24	—	Paraguay	3	3	(*)	(*)
Trust Terr. Pacific	130	130	—	—	Peru	50	35	15	(*)
Other & unspecified	20	20	(*)	—	Trinidad-Tobago	−19	(*)	−19	—
Africa	1,053	708	343	2	Uruguay	−5	(*)	−5	—
Algeria	−83	—	−83	—	Venezuela	8	—	8	—
Angola	−9	1	−10	—	Other & unspecified	139	105	34	—
Benin	2	2	(*)	—	Intl. orgs. & unspecified	858	862	−3	—
Botswana	16	16	(*)	—					

Ambassadors and Envoys

As of mid-1984.

The address of U.S. embassies abroad is the appropriate foreign capital. The U.S. does not have diplomatic relations with the following countries: Albania,[1] Angola,[2] Cambodia,[3] Rep. of China (Taiwan),[4] Cuba,[5] Iran,[6] Iraq,[7] Libya,[8] Vietnam,[3] S. Yemen.[3]

Countries	Envoys from United States	Envoys to United States
Afghanistan	Vacant	M. Haider Refq, Chargé
Algeria	Michael H. Newlin, Amb.	Layachi Yaker, Amb.
Antigua & Barbuda	Milan D. Bish, Amb.	Edmund H. Lake, Amb.
Argentina	Frank V. Ortiz Jr., Amb.	Lucio Garcia Del Solar, Amb.
Australia	Robert D. Nesen, Amb.	Robert Cotton, Amb.
Austria	Helene A. von Damm, Amb.	Thomas Klestil, Amb.
Bahamas	Lev Dobriansky, Amb.	Reginald L. Wood, Amb.
Bahrain	Donald C. Leidel, Amb.	Ahmed Mahdi Al-Haddad, Chargé
Bangladesh	Howard B. Schaffer, Amb.	Humayin Rasheed Choudhury, Amb.
Barbados	Milan D. Bish, Amb.	Peter D. Laurie, Amb.
Belgium	Geoffrey Swaebe, Amb.	J. Raoul Schoumaker, Amb.
Belize	Malcolm R. Barnebey, Chargé	Henry E. C. Cain, Amb.
Benin	George E. Moose	Guy L. Hazoume, Amb.
Bolivia	Edwin G. Corr, Amb.	Mariano Baptista Gumucio, Amb.
Botswana	Theodore C. Maino, Amb.	Mashite K. Motsepe, Chargé
Bourkina Fasso (Upper Volta)	Julius W. Walker Jr., Amb.	Doulaye Corentin Ki, Amb.
Brazil	Diego C. Asencio, Amb.	Sergeo C. da Costa, Amb.
Bulgaria	Robert L. Barry, Amb.	Stoyan I. Zhulev, Amb.
Burma	Daniel A. O'Donohue, Amb.	U Kyee Myint, Amb.
Burundi	James R. Bullington, Amb.	Simon Sabimbona, Amb.
Cameroon	Miles R. Frechette, Amb.	Paul Pondi, Amb.
Canada	Paul H. Robinson Jr., Amb.	Allan Gotlieb, Amb.
Cape Verde	John M. Yates, Amb.	Jose Luis Fernandes Lopes, Amb.
Central African Rep.	Ernest T. Dejarnette, Amb.	Christian Lingama-Toleque, Amb.
Chad	Jay P. Moffat	Mahamat Ali Adoum, Amb.
Chile	James D. Theberge	Octavio Errazuriz, Chargé
China	Arthur W. Hummel Jr., Amb.	Zhang Wenjin, Amb.
Colombia	Lewis A. Tambs, Amb.	Alvaro Gomez, Amb.
Comoros	Fernando E. Rondon, Amb.	Ali Mlahaili, Amb.
Congo	Kenneth L. Brown, Amh	Nicolas Mondjo, Amb.
Costa Rica	Curtin Winsor Jr., Amb.	Luis Guardia, Chargé
Cyprus	Raymond C. Ewing, Amb.	Andrew J. Jacovides, Amb.
Czechoslovakia	William H. Luers, Amb.	Stanislav Suja, Amb.
Denmark	Terence A. Todman, Amb	Eigil Jorgensen, Amb.
Djibouti	Alvin P. Adams Jr.	Salah Hadji Farah Dirir, Amb.
Dominica	Milan D. Bish, Amb.	Franklin Baron, Amb.
Dominican Republic	Robert Anderson, Amb.	Carlos Despradel, Amb.
Ecuador	Samuel F. Hart, Amb.	Rafael Garcia-Velasco, Amb.
Egypt	Nicholas A. Veliotes, Amb.	Ashraf A. Ghorbal, Amb.
El Salvador	Thomas R. Pickering, Amb.	Ernesto Rivas-Gallont, Amb.
Equatorial Guinea	Alan M. Hardy, Amb.	Florencio Maye Ela, Amb.
Estonia[s]		Ernst Jaakson, Consul General
Ethiopia	David A. Korn, Chargé	Tesfaye Demeke, Chargé
Fiji	Fred J. Eckert, Amb.	Ratu Radrodro, Amb.
Finland	Keith F. Nyborg, Amb.	Richard Muller, Amb.
France	Evan G. Galbraith, Amb.	Bernard Vernier-Palliez, Amb.
Gabon	Francis T. McNamara, Amb.	Mocktar Abdoulaye-Mbingt, Amb.
Gambia, The	Alan Logan, Chargé	Lamin A. Mbye, Amb.
Germany, East	Rozanne L. Ridgway, Amb.	Gerhard Herder, Amb.
Germany, West	Arthur F. Burns, Amb.	Peter Hermes, Amb.
Ghana	Robert E. Fritts, Amb.	Eric K. Otoo, Amb.
Greece	Monteagle Stearns, Amb.	George D. Papaulias, Amb
Grenada	Milan D. Bish	Vacant
Guatemala	Frederic L. Chapin, Amb.	Federico Fahsen, Amb.
Guinea	James D. Rosenthal, Amb.	Thierno H. Diallo, Amb.
Guinea-Bissau	Wesley W. Egan Jr., Amb.	Inacio Semedo Jr., Amb.
Guyana	David R. Beall, Chargé	Cedric H. Grant, Amb.
Haiti	Clayton E. McManaway Jr., Amb.	Fritz N. Cineas, Amb.
Honduras	John D. Negroponte, Amb.	Juan Agurcia Ewing, Amb.
Hungary	Nicholas M. Salgo, Amb.	Vencel Hazi, Amb.
Iceland	Marshall Brement, Amb.	Hans G. Andersen, Amb.
India	Harry G. Barnes, Amb.	P. L. Sinai, Amb.
Indonesia	John H. Holdridge, Amb.	A. Hasnan Habib, Amb.
Ireland	Vacant	Tadhg F. O'Sullivan, Amb.
Israel	Samuel W. Lewis, Amb.	Meir Rosenne, Amb.
Italy	Maxwell M. Rabb, Amb.	Rinaldo Petrignani, Amb.
Ivory Coast	Robert H. Miller, Amb.	Rene Amany, Amb.
Jamaica	William A. Hewitt, Amb.	Keith Johnson, Amb.
Japan	Michael J. Mansfield, Amb.	Yoshio Okawara, Amb.
Jordan	Richard N. Viets, Amb.	Ibrahim Izziddin, Amb.
Kenya	Gerald E. Thomas, Amb.	Wafula Wabuge, Amb.
Kiribati	William Bodde Jr., Min.	Atanradi Baiteke, Amb.
Korea, South	Richard L. Walker, Amb.	Byong H. Lew, Amb.
Kuwait	Philip J. Griffin, Chargé	Shaikh S. N. Al-Sabah, Amb.
Laos	Vacant	Bounkeut Sangsomsak, Chargé
Latvia[s]		Anatol Dinbergs, Chargé
Lebanon	Reginald Bartholomew, Amb.	Adballah Bouhabib, Amb.
Lesotho	Vacant	'M'alineo N. Tau, Amb.
Liberia	William Swing, Amb.	G. Toe Washington, Amb.
Lithuania[s]		Stasys A. Backis, Chargé
Luxembourg	John E. Dolibois, Amb.	Paul Peters, Amb.
Madagascar	Robert B. Keating, Amb.	Leon M. Rajaobelina, Amb.

Countries	Envoys from United States	Envoys to United States
Malawi	John A. Burroughs Jr., Amb.	Nelson T. Mizere, Amb.
Malaysia	Thomas P. Shoesmith, Amb.	Dato Lew Sip Hon, Amb.
Maldives	John H. Reed, Amb.	*Vacant*
Mali	Robert J. Ryan, Amb.	Lassana Keita, Amb.
Malta	James M. Rentschier, Amb.	Leslie Agius, Amb.
Mauritania	Edward L. Peck, Amb.	Abdellah Ould Daddah, Amb.
Mauritius	George R. Andrews, Amb.	Chitmansing Jesseramsing, Amb.
Mexico	John A. Gavin, Amb.	J. Espinosa de los Reyes, Amb.
Morocco	Joseph V. Reed, Amb.	Ali Bengelloun, Amb.
Mozambique	Peter Jon de Vos, Amb.	Valeriano Ferrao, Amb.
Nauru	Robert D. Nesen, Amb.	T.W. Star, Amb.
Nepal	Carleton S. Coon, Amb.	Bhekh B. Thapa, Amb.
Netherlands	L. Paul Bremer 3d, Amb.	Jan Hendrik Lubbers, Amb.
New Zealand	H. Monroe Browne, Amb.	L. R. Adams-Schneider, Amb.
Nicaragua	Harry E. Bergold Jr., Amb.	Carlos Tunnerman Bernheim, Amb.
Niger	William R. Casey Jr., Amb.	Joseph Diatta, Amb.
Nigeria	Peter Jon de Vos, Amb.	M. W. Lamino, Chargé
Norway	Mark E. Austad, Amb.	Knut Hedemann, Amb.
Oman	John R. Countryman, Amb.	Ali Salim Bader Al-Hanai, Amb.
Pakistan	Deane R. Hinton, Amb.	Ejaz Azim, Amb.
Panama	Everett E. Briggs, Amb.	Aquilino E. Boyd, Amb.
Papua New Guinea	Paul F. Gardner, Amb.	John Balagetuna, Chargé
Paraguay	Arthur H. Davis, Amb.	Marcos Martinez Mendieta, Amb.
Peru	*Vacant*	Alan Wagner, Chargé
Philippines	Michael H. Armacost, Amb.	Benjamin T. Romualdez, Amb.
Poland	*Vacant*	Zdzislaw Ludwiczak, Chargé
Portugal	H. Allen Holmes, Amb.	Leonardo Mathias, Amb.
Qatar	Charles F. Dunbar, Amb.	Abdelkader B. Al-Ameri, Amb.
Romania	David B. Funderburk, Amb.	Mircea Malitza, Amb.
Rwanda	John Blane, Amb.	Simon Insonere, Amb.
St. Lucia	Milan D. Bish, Amb.	Donatus St. Aimee, Chargé
St. Vincent and The Grenadines	Milan D. Bish, Amb.	Hudson K. Tannis, Amb.
Samoa, Western	Anne C. Martindell, Amb.	Maiava I. Toma, Amb.
Sao Tome and Principe	Francis T. McNamera, Amb.	*Vacant*
Saudi Arabia	*Vacant*	Bandar Bin Sultan, Amb.
Senegal	Charles W. Bray, Amb.	Abdourahmane Dia, Amb.
Seychelles	David J. Fischer, Amb.	Giovinella Gonthier, Amb.
Sierra Leone	Arthur W. Lewis, Amb.	Dauda S. Kamara, Amb.
Singapore	Harry E. T. Thayer, Amb.	Punch Coomaraswamy, Amb.
Solomon Islands	Paul F. Gardner, Amb.	*Vacant*
Somalia	Robert B. Oakley, Amb.	Mohamud Haji Nur, Amb.
South Africa	Herman W. Nickel, Amb.	Bernardus G. Fourie, Amb.
Spain	Thomas O. Enders, Amb.	Gabriel Manueco, Amb.
Sri Lanka	John H. Reed, Amb.	Ernest Corea, Amb.
Sudan	Hume A. Horan, Amb.	Omer Salih Eissa, Amb.
Suriname	Robert W. Duemling, Amb.	Henricus A. F. Heidweiller, Amb.
Swaziland	Robert H. Phinny, Amb.	Peter H. Mtetwa, Amb.
Sweden	Franklin S. Forsberg, Amb.	Wilhelm Wachtmeister, Amb.
Switzerland	John D. Lodge, Amb.	Anton Hegner, Amb.
Syria	Robert P. Paganelli, Amb.	Rafic Jouejati, Amb.
Tanzania	David C. Miller, Amb.	Benjamin Mkapa, Amb.
Thailand	John G. Dean, Amb.	Kasem S. Kasemsri, Amb.
Togo	Howard K. Walker, Amb.	Ellom-Kodjo Schuppius, Amb.
Tonga	Fred J. Eckert, Amb.	*Vacant*
Trinidad and Tobago	Melvin H. Evans, Amb.	James O'Neil-Lewis, Amb.
Tunisia	Walter L. Cutler, Amb.	Habib B. Yahia, Amb.
Turkey	Robert Strausz-Hope, Amb.	Sukru Elekdag, Amb.
Tuvalu	Fred J. Eckert, Amb.	Ionatana Ionatana, Amb.
Uganda	Allen C. Davis, Amb.	John Wycliffe Lwamafa, Amb.
USSR	Arthur A. Hartman, Amb.	Anatoliy F. Dobrynin, Amb.
United Arab Emirates	G. Quincy Lumsden Jr., Amb.	A.S. Al-Mokarrab, Amb.
United Kingdom	Charles S. Price 2d, Amb.	Oliver Wright, Amb.
Uruguay	Thomas Aranda Jr., Amb.	Italo L. Sordo Alonso, Chargé
Vatican	William Wilson, Amb.	Pio Laghi, Amb.
Venezuela	George W. Landau, Amb.	Marcial Perez-Chiriboga, Amb.
Yemen Arab Rep.	David E. Zweifel, Amb.	Mohammad Al-Eryani, Amb.
Yugoslavia	David Anderson, Amb.	Mico Rakic, Amb.
Zaire	Peter Constable, Amb.	Kasongo Mutuale, Amb.
Zambia	Nicholas Platt, Amb.	Putteho M. Ngonda, Amb.
Zimbabwe	Robert V. Keeley, Amb.	Edmund O.Z. Chipamaunga, Amb.

Ambassadors at Large: Vernon Walters, Daniel J. Terra, Richard T. Kennedy, Howard E. Douglas, Harry W. Shlaudeman, Richard Fairbanks.

Special Missions

U.S. Mission to North Atlantic Treaty Organization, Brussels—David M. Abshire
U.S. Mission to the European Communities, Brussels—George S. Vest
U.S. Mission to the International Atomic Energy Agency, Vienna—Richard T. Kennedy
U.S. Mission to the United Nations, New York—Jeane J. Kirkpatrick
U.S. Mission to the European Office of the UN, Geneva—Vacant
U.S. Mission to the Organization for Economic Cooperation and Development, Paris—Abraham Katz
U.S. Mission to the Organization of American States, Washington—J. William Middendorf, Amb.
U.S. Mission to United Nations Educational, Scientific, and Cultural Organization, Paris—Jean B. Gerard
U.S. Mission to International Civic Aviation Organization, Montreal—Edmond P. Stohr

(1) Relations severed in 1939. (2) Post closed in 1975. (3) U.S. embassy closed in 1975. (4) U.S. severed relations in 1978; unofficial relations are maintained. (5) Relations severed in 1961; limited ties restored in 1977. (6) U.S. severed relations on Apr. 7, 1980. (7) Relations severed in 1967, limited staff returned in 1972; Belgium protects U.S. interest. (8) U.S. does not officially recognize 1940 annexation by USSR. (9) Embassy closed, May 2, 1980. U.S. closed the Libyan mission in Wash., DC, May 6, 1981.

Major International Organizations

Association of Southeast Asian Nations (ASEAN),was formed in 1967 to promote political and economic cooperation among the non-communist states of the region. Members in 1984 are Brunei, Indonesia, Malaysia, Philippines, Singapore, Thailand. Annual ministerial meetings set policy; a central Secretariat in Jakarta and 9 permanent committees work in trade, transportation, communications, agriculture, science, finance, and culture.

Commonwealth of Nations originally called the British Commonwealth of Nations, is an association of nations and dependencies loosely joined by a common interest based on having been parts of the old British Empire. The British monarch is the symbolic head of the Commonwealth.

There are 48 self-governing independent nations in the Commonwealth, plus various colonies and protectorates. As of Jan. 1984, the members were the United Kingdom of Great Britain and Northern Ireland and 17 other nations recognizing the British monarch, represented by a governor-general, as their head of state: Antigua and Barbuda, Australia, Bahamas, Barbados, Belize, Canada, Fiji, Grenada, Jamaica, Mauritius, New Zealand, Papua New Guinea, St. Kitts-Nevis, St. Lucia, St. Vincent and the Grenadines (a special member), Solomon Islands, and Tuvalu (a special member); and 28 countries with their own heads of state: Bangladesh, Botswana, Cyprus, Dominica, The Gambia, Ghana, Guyana, India, Kenya, Kiribati, Lesotho, Malawi, Malaysia, The Maldives (a special member), Malta, Nauru (a special member), Nigeria, Samoa, Seychelles, Sierra Leone, Singapore, Sri Lanka, Swaziland, Tanzania, Tonga, Trinidad and Tobago, Uganda, Vanuatu, Zambia, and Zimbabwe. In addition various Caribbean dependencies take part in certain Commonwealth activities.

The Commonwealth facilitates consultation among member states through meetings of prime ministers and finance ministers, and through a permanent Secretariat. Members consult on economic, scientific, educational, financial, legal, and military matters, and try to coordinate policies.

European Communities (EC, the Common Market) is the collective designation of three organizations with common membership: the European Economic Community (Common Market), the European Coal and Steel Community, and the European Atomic Energy Community. The 10 full members are: Belgium, Denmark, France, West Germany, Greece, Ireland, Italy, Luxembourg, Netherlands, United Kingdom. Some 50 nations in Africa, the Caribbean, and the Pacific are affiliated under the Lomé Convention.

A merger of the 3 communities executives went into effect July 1, 1967, though the component organizations date back to 1951 and 1958. A Council of Ministers, a Commission, a European Parliament, and a Court of Justice comprise the permanent structure. The communities aim to integrate their economies, coordinate social developments, and bring about political union of the democratic states of Europe.

European Free Trade Association (EFTA), consisting of Austria, Iceland, Norway, Portugal, Sweden, Switzerland and associated member Finland, was created Jan. 4, 1960, to gradually reduce customs duties and quantitative restrictions between members on industrial products. By Dec. 31, 1966, all tariffs and quotas had been eliminated. The United Kingdom and Denmark withdrew to become members of EC Jan. 1, 1973 at which time EFTA members entered into free trade agreements with the EC. All industrial customs barriers between the two blocs were removed July 1, 1976.

League of Arab States (The Arab League) was created Mar. 22, 1945, by Egypt, Iraq, Jordan, Lebanon, Saudi Arabia, Syria, and Yemen. Joining later were Algeria, Bahrain, Djibouti, Kuwait, Libya, Mauritania, Morocco, Oman, Qatar, Somalia, Sudan, Tunisia, United Arab Emirates and South Yemen. The Palestine Liberation Org. has been admitted as a full member. The League fosters cultural, economic, and communication ties and mediates disputes among the Arab states; it represents Arab states in certain international negotiations, and coordinates a military, economic, and diplomatic offensive against Israel. As a result of

Egypt signing a peace treaty with Israel, the League, Mar. 1979, suspended Egypt's membership and transferred the League's headquarters from Cairo to Tunis.

North Atlantic Treaty Org. (NATO) was created by treaty (signed Apr. 4, 1949; in effect Aug. 24, 1949) among Belgium, Canada, Denmark, France, Iceland, Italy, Luxembourg, Netherlands, Norway, Portugal, United Kingdom, and the U.S. Greece, Turkey, West Germany, and Spain have joined since. The members agreed to settle disputes by peaceful means; to develop their individual and collective capacity to resist armed attack; to regard an attack on one as an attack on all, and to take necessary action to repel an attack under Article 51 of the United Nations Charter.

The NATO structure consists of a Council and a Military Committee of 3 commands (Allied Command Europe, Allied Command Atlantic, Allied Command Channel) and the Canada-U.S. Regional Planning Group.

Following announcement in 1966 of nearly total French withdrawal from the military affairs of NATO, organization hq. moved, 1967, from Paris to Brussels. In August, 1974, Greece announced a total withdrawal of armed forces from NATO, in response to Turkish intervention in Cyprus. Greece rejoined NATO's military wing, Oct. 20, 1980.

Organization of African Unity (OAU), formed May 25, 1963, by 30 African countries (50 in 1984) to coordinate cultural, political, scientific and economic policies; to end colonialism in Africa; and to promote a common defense of members' independence. It holds annual conferences of heads of state. Hq. is in Addis Ababa, Ethiopia.

Organization of American States (OAS) was formed in Bogota, Colombia, in 1948. Hq. is in Washington, D.C. It has a Permanent Council, Inter-American Economic and Social Council, and Inter-American Council for Education, Science and Culture, a Juridical Committee and a Commission on Human Rights. The Permanent Council can call meetings of foreign ministers to deal with urgent security matters. A General Assembly meets annually. A secretary general and assistant are elected for 5-year terms. There are 31 members, each with one vote in the various organizations: Antigua, Argentina, Bahamas, Barbados, Bolivia, Brazil, Chile, Colombia, Costa Rica, Cuba, Dominica, Dominican Republic, Ecuador, El Salvador, Grenada, Guatemala, Haiti, Honduras, Jamaica, Mexico, Nicaragua, Panama, Paraguay, Peru, St. Kitts-Nevis, St. Lucia, Suriname, Trinidad & Tobago, U.S., Uruguay, Venezuela. In 1962, the OAS excluded Cuba from OAS activities but not from membership.

Organization for Economic Cooperation and Development (OECD) was established Sept. 30, 1961 to promote economic and social welfare in member countries, and to stimulate and harmonize efforts on behalf of developing nations. Nearly all the industrialized "free market" countries belong, with Yugoslavia as an associate member. OECD collects and disseminates economic and environmental information. Members in 1984 were: Australia, Austria, Belgium, Canada, Denmark, Finland, France, West Germany, Greece, Iceland, Ireland, Italy, Japan, Luxembourg, Netherlands, New Zealand, Norway, Portugal, Spain, Sweden, Switzerland, Turkey, United Kingdom, United States, Yugoslavia (special member). Hq. is in Paris.

Organization of Petroleum Exporting Countries (OPEC) was created Nov. 14, 1960 at Venezuelan initiative. The group has often been successful in determining world oil prices, and in advancing members' interests in trade and development dealings with industrialized oil-consuming nations. Members in 1984 were Algeria, Ecuador, Gabon, Indonesia, Iran, Iraq, Kuwait, Libya, Nigeria, Qatar, Saudi Arabia, United Arab Emirates, Venezuela.

Warsaw Pact was created May 14, 1955, as a mutual defense alliance. Members in 1984 were Bulgaria, Czechoslovakia, East Germany, Hungary, Poland, Romania, and the USSR. Hq. is in Moscow. It provides for a unified military command; if one member is attacked, the others will aid it with all necessary steps including armed force; joint maneuvers are held.

United Nations

The 39th regular session of the United Nations General Assembly was scheduled to open in September, 1984. See *Chronology for developments at UN sessions during 1984.*

UN headquarters are in New York, N.Y., between First Ave. and Roosevelt Drive and E. 42d St. and E. 48th St. The General Assembly Bldg., Secretariat, Conference and Library bldgs. are interconnected. A new UN office building-hotel was opened in New York in 1976.

A European office at Geneva includes Secretariat and agency staff members. Other offices of UN bodies and related organizations are scattered throughout the world.

The UN has a post office originating its own stamps.

Proposals to establish an organization of nations for maintenance of world peace led to the United Nations Conference on International Organization at San Francisco, Apr. 25-June 26, 1945, where the charter of the United Nations was drawn up. It was signed June 26 by 50 nations, and by Poland, one of the original 51, on Oct. 15, 1945. The charter came into effect Oct. 24, 1945, upon ratification by the permanent members of the Security Council and a majority of other signatories.

Roster of the United Nations

(As of mid-1984)

The 159 members of the United Nations, with the years in which they became members.

Member	Year	Member	Year	Member	Year	Member	Year
Afghanistan	1946	Ecuador	1945	Lesotho	1966	Samoa (Western)	1976
Albania	1955	Egypt[2]	1945	Liberia	1945	Sao Tome e Principe	1975
Algeria	1962	El Salvador	1945	Libya	1955	Saudi Arabia	1945
Angola	1976	Equatorial Guinea	1968	Luxembourg	1945	Senegal	1960
Antigua and Barbuda	1981	Ethiopia	1945			Seychelles	1976
Argentina	1945					Sierra Leone	1961
Australia	1945	Fiji	1970	Madagascar (Malagasy)	1960	Singapore[1]	1965
Austria	1955	Finland	1955	Malawi	1964	Solomon Islands	1978
		France	1945	Malaysia[1]	1957	Somalia	1960
				Maldives	1965	South Africa[5]	1945
Bahamas	1973			Mali	1960	Spain	1955
Bahrain	1971	Gabon	1960	Malta	1964	Sri Lanka	1955
Bangladesh	1974	Gambia	1965	Mauritania	1961	Sudan	1956
Barbados	1966	Germany, East	1973	Mauritius	1968	Suriname	1975
Belgium	1945	Germany, West	1973	Mexico	1945	Swaziland	1968
Belize	1981	Ghana	1957	Mongolia	1961	Sweden	1946
Benin	1960	Greece	1945	Morocco	1956	Syria[2]	1945
Bhutan	1971	Grenada	1974	Mozambique	1975		
Bolivia	1945	Guatemala	1945			Tanzania[3]	1961
Botswana	1966	Guinea	1958	Nepal	1955	Thailand	1946
Brazil	1945	Guinea-Bissau	1974	Netherlands	1945	Togo	1960
Brunei	1984	Guyana	1966	New Zealand	1945	Trinidad & Tobago	1962
Bulgaria	1955			Nicaragua	1945	Tunisia	1956
Burma	1948	Haiti	1945	Niger	1960	Turkey	1945
Burundi	1962	Honduras	1945	Nigeria	1960		
Byelorussia	1945	Hungary	1955	Norway	1945	Uganda	1962
						Ukraine	1945
Cambodia (Kampuchea)	1955	Iceland	1946	Oman	1971	USSR	1945
Cameroon	1960	India	1945			United Arab Emirates	1971
Canada	1945	Indonesia[6]	1950	Pakistan	1947	United Kingdom	1945
Cape Verde	1975	Iran	1945	Panama	1945	United States	1945
Central Afr. Rep.	1960	Iraq	1945	Papua New Guinea	1975	Upper Volta	
Chad	1960	Ireland	1955	Paraguay	1945	(Bourkina Fasso)	1960
Chile	1945	Israel	1949	Peru	1945	Uruguay	1945
China[4]	1945	Italy	1955	Philippines	1945		
Colombia	1945	Ivory Coast	1960	Poland	1945		
Comoros	1975			Portugal	1955	Vanuatu	1981
Congo	1960					Venezuela	1945
Costa Rica	1945	Jamaica	1962	Qatar	1971	Vietnam	1977
Cuba	1945	Japan	1956				
Cyprus	1960	Jordan	1955	Romania	1955	Yemen	1947
Czechoslovakia	1945			Rwanda	1962	Yemen, South	1967
		Kenya	1963			Yugoslavia	1945
		Kuwait	1963	Saint Christopher			
Denmark	1945			& Nevis	1983		
Djibouti	1977			Saint Lucia	1979	Zaire	1960
Dominica	1978	Laos	1955	Saint Vincent and the		Zambia	1964
Dominican Rep.	1945	Lebanon	1945	Grenadines	1980	Zimbabwe	1980

(1) Malaya joined the UN in 1957. In 1963, its name was changed to Malaysia following the accession of Singapore, Sabah, and Sarawak. Singapore became an independent UN member in 1965. (2) Egypt and Syria were original members of the UN. In 1958, the United Arab Republic was established by a union of Egypt and Syria and continued as a single member of the UN. In 1961, Syria resumed its separate membership. (3) Tanganyika was a member of the United Nations from 1961 and Zanzibar was a member from 1963. Following the ratification in 1964 of Articles of Union between Tanganyika and Zanzibar, the United Republic of Tanganyika and Zanzibar continued as a single member of the United Nations, later changing its name to United Republic of Tanzania. (4) The General Assembly voted in 1971 to expel the Chinese government on Taiwan and admit the Peking government in its place. (5) The General Assembly rejected the credentials of the South African delegates in 1974, and suspended the country from the Assembly. (6) Indonesia withdrew from the UN in 1965 and rejoined in 1966.

Organization

The text of the UN Charter, and further information, may be obtained from the Office of Public Information, United Nations, N.Y.

General Assembly. The General Assembly is composed of representatives of all the member nations. Each nation is entitled to one vote.

The General Assembly meets in regular annual sessions and in special session when necessary. Special sessions are convoked by the Secretary General at the request of the Security Council or of a majority of the members of the UN.

On important questions a two-thirds majority of members present and voting is required; on other questions a simple majority is sufficient.

The General Assembly must approve the budget and apportion expenses among members. A member in arrears will have no vote if the amount of arrears equals or exceeds the amount of the contributions due for the preceeding two full years.

Security Council. The Security Council consists of 15 members, 5 with permanent seats. The remaining 10 are elected for 2-year terms by the General Assembly; they are not eligible for immediate reelection.

Permanent members of the Council: China, France, USSR, United Kingdom, United States.

Non-permanent members are Egypt, India, Peru, Ukraine, and Upper Volta (until Dec. 31, 1985); Malta, The Netherlands, Nicaragua, Pakistan, and Zimbabwe (until Dec. 31, 1984).

The Security Council has the primary responsiblity within the UN for maintaining international peace and security. The Council may investigate any dispute that threatens international peace and security.

Any member of the UN at UN headquarters may participate in its discussions and a nation not a member of UN may appear if it is a party to a dispute.

Decisions on procedural questions are made by an affirmative vote of 9 members. On all other matters the affirmative vote of 9 members must include the concurring votes of all permanent members; it is this clause which gives rise to the so-called "veto." A party to a dispute must refrain from voting.

The Security Council directs the various truce supervisory forces deployed in the Middle East, India-Pakistan, and Cyprus.

Economic and Social Council. The Economic and Social Council consists of 54 members elected by the General Assembly for 3-year terms of office. The council is responsible under the General Assembly for carrying out the functions of the United Nations with regard to international economic, social, cultural, educational, health and related matters. The council meets usually twice a year.

Trusteeship Council. The administration of trust territories is under UN supervision. The only remaining trust territory is the Pacific Islands, administered by the U.S.

Secretariat. The Secretary General is the chief administrative officer of the UN. He may bring to the attention of the Security Council any matter that threatens international peace. He reports to the General Assembly.

Javier Perez de Cuellar (Peru), secretary general, was elected to a 5-year term beginning Jan. 1, 1982.

The 1984-85 budget is $1.5 billion, exclusive of trust funds, special contributions, and expenses for the Specialized or the Related Organizations.

The U.S. contributes 25% of the regular budget, the Soviet Union 11.33%, Japan 8.66%, W. Germany 7.74%, and France, China, and Britain about 5% each.

International Court of Justice. The International Court of Justice is the principal judicial organ of the United Nations. All members are *ipso facto* parties to the statute of the Court, as are three nonmembers — Liechtenstein, San Marino, and Switzerland. Other states may become parties to the Court's statute.

The jurisdiction of the Court comprises cases which the parties submit to it and matters especially provided for in the charter or in treaties. The Court gives advisory opinions and renders judgments. Its decisions are only binding between the parties concerned and in respect to a particular dispute. If any party to a case fails to heed a judgment, the other party may have recourse to the Security Council.

The 15 judges are elected for 9-year terms by the General Assembly and the Security Council. Retiring judges are eligible for re-election. The Court remains permanently in session, except during vacations. All questions are decided by majority. The Court sits in The Hague, Netherlands.

Judges: 9-year term in office ending 1991: Nagendra Singh, India. Jose Maria Ruda, Argentina. Robert Y. Jennings, United Kingdom. Guy Ladreit de Lacharriere, France. Keba Mbaye, Senegal. **9-year term in office ending 1988:** Robert Ago, Italy. Stephen M. Schwebel, U.S. Abdullah Ali, Egypt. Platon D. Morozov, USSR. Jose Sette Camara, Brazil. **9-year term in office ending 1985:** Taslim Olawala Elias, Nigeria. Hermann Mosier, W. Germany. Shigeru Oda, Japan. Abdullah Fikri Al-Khani, Syria. Manfred Lachs, Poland.

Specialized and Related Agencies

These agencies are autonomous, with their own memberships and organs which have a functional relationship or working agreement with the UN. (Headquarters.)

International Labor Org. (ILO) aims to promote productive employment; improve labor conditions and living standards. (4 route de Morillons, CH-1211, Geneva 22, Switzerland.)

Food & Agriculture Org. (FAO) aims to increase production from farms, forests, and fisheries; improve distribution, marketing, and nutrition; better conditions for rural people. (Viale delle Terme di Caracalla, 00100 Rome, Italy.)

United Nations Educational, Scientific, & Cultural Org. (UNESCO) aims to promote collaboration among nations through education, science, and culture. The U.S. has announced its intention to withdraw from this organization at the end of 1984 because of UNESCO's lack of response to Western concerns. (9 Place de Fontenoy, 75700 Paris, France.)

World Health Org. (WHO) aims to aid the attainment of the highest possible level of health. (20 Ave. Appia, 1211 Geneva, Switzerland.)

International Monetary Fund (IMF) aims to promote international monetary co-operation and currency stabilization; expansion of international trade. (700 19th St., NW, Washington, DC, 20431.)

International Civil Aviation Org. (ICAO) promotes international civil aviation standards and regulations. (1000 Sherbrooke St. W., Montreal, Quebec, Canada H3A 2R2.)

Universal Postal Union (UPU) aims to perfect postal services and promote international collaboration. (Weltpoststrasse 4, 3000 Berne, 15 Switzerland.)

International Telecommunication Union (ITU) sets up international regulations of radio, telegraph, telephone and space radio-communications. Allocates radio frequencies. (Place des Nations, 1211 Geneva 20, Switzerland.)

World Meteorological Org. (WMO) aims to co-ordinate and improve world meteorological work. (Case Postale 5, CH-1211, Geneva, Switzerland.)

International Fund for Agricultural Development (IFAD) aims to mobilize funds for agricultural and rural projects in developing countries. (107 Via del Serafico, 00142 Rome, Italy.)

International Maritime Org. (IMO) aims to promote co-operation on technical matters affecting international shipping. (4 Albert Embankment, London, SE1 7SR, England.)

World Intellectual Property Organization (WIPO) seeks to protect, through international cooperation, literary, industrial, scientific, and artistic works, i.e. "intellectual property." (34, Chemin des Colom Bettes, 1211 Geneva, Switzerland.)

International Atomic Energy Agency (IAEA) aims to promote the safe, peaceful uses of atomic energy. (Vienna International Centre, PO Box 100, A-1400, Vienna, Austria.)

General Agreement on Tariffs and Trade (GATT) is the only treaty setting rules for world trade. Provides a forum for settling trade disputes and negotiating trade liberalization. (Centre William Rappard, 154 rue de Lausanne, 1211

Geneva 21, Switzerland.)

International Bank for Reconstruction and Development (IBRD) (World Bank) provides loans and technical assistance for economic development projects in developing member countries; encourages cofinancing for projects from other public and private sources. **International Development Association (IDA)**, an affiliate of the Bank, provides funds for development projects on concessionary terms to the poorer developing member countries. (both 1818 H St., NW, Washington, DC 20433.) **International Finance Corporation (IFC)** an affiliate of the Bank, promotes the growth of the private sector in developing member countries; encourages the development of local capital markets; stimulates the international flow of private capital. (1818 H St., NW, Washington, DC 20433.)

The World's Refugees in 1983

Source: United States Committee for Refugees

Country of Asylum	From	Number
Total Africa		**1,921,000**
Algeria	Mostly Western Sahara	54,000
Angola	Namibia, Zaire	93,000
Botswana	Angola, Namibia, South Africa	1,300
Burundi	Rwanda	55,000
Cameroon	Chad	1,000
Central African Rep.	Chad	5,600
Djibouti	Ethiopia	31,500
Egypt	various	1,200
Ethiopia	Sudan	5,400
Kenya	Ethiopia, Rwanda, various	3,800
Lesotho	South Africa, various	1,000
Niger	Chad	5,500
Nigeria	Chad	400
Rwanda	Mostly Uganda	60,000
Senegal	various	5,200
Somalia	Ethiopia	500,000
Sudan	Ethiopia, Uganda, Chad, Zaire	513,000
Swaziland	South Africa	6,300
Tanzania	Burundi, Zaire	155,000
Uganda	Rwanda, Zaire	102,900
Zaire	Angola, Uganda, Zambia	270,000
Zambia	Angola, Namibia, Zaire	49,800
Total East Asia/Pacific		**921,200**
Australia	various	317,000
Burma	China, Malaysia	1,000
China	Indochina	266,500
Hong Kong	Vietnam	12,000
Indonesia	Vietnam	12,800
Japan	Vietnam	1,800
Laos	Cambodia	3,500
Macau	Vietnam	1,000
Malaysia	Vietnam, others	78,400
New Zealand	various	10,600
Philippines	Vietnam	14,900
Singapore	Vietnam	500
Thailand*	Vietnam, Laos, Cambodia	169,000
Vietnam	Cambodia	30,000
*Not including border camps		
Total Europe		**568,600**
Austria	Poland, other eastern Europe	47,700
Belgium	various	22,000
Denmark	various	1,800
France	various	150,000
W. Germany	various	100,000

Country of Asylum	From	Number
Greece	Iraq, Iran	7,400
Italy	various	20,000
Netherlands	various	13,000
Norway	various	6,000
Portugal	various	7,600
Romania	various	1,000
Spain	various	21,900
Sweden	various	20,000
Turkey	various	300
United Kingdom	various	146,000
Yugoslavia	Eastern Europe	3,900
Total Latin America/Caribbean		**314,500**
Argentina	Europe, Latin America, SE Asia	12,300
Belize	El Salvador	5,000
Brazil	Europe, Latin America	5,400
Chile	Europe	1,500
Costa Rica	El Salvador, Latin America	15,000
Cuba	Latin America	2,000
Dominican Rep.	Haiti	5,000
Guatemala	El Salvador	70,000
Honduras	El Salvador, Nicaragua, others	33,300
Mexico	El Salvador, Guatemala	140,000
Nicaragua	El Salvador	22,500
Panama	El Salvador	1,500
Peru	Europe, Latin America	500
Venezuela	Europe, Latin America	600
Total North America		**1,356,000**
Canada	various	353,000
United States	various	1,003,000
Total Middle East/South Asia		**5,295,600**
India	Afghanistan, Iran	4,700
Iran	Afghanistan, Iraq	560,000
Lebanon	various	3,100
Pakistan	Afghanistan	2,800,800
Others		40,000
Palestinians		
Gaza Strip		377,000
Jordan		749,000
Lebanon		239,000
Syria		221,000
West Bank		341,000
Total Refugees		**10,376,900**

Sources of Largest Refugee Groups

Afghanistan	3,304,000	El Salvador	241,000
Palestinians	1,927,000	Angola	237,000
Ethiopia	883,000	Uganda	230,000
Indochina	256,000		

Customs Exemptions and Advice to Travelers

U.S. residents returning after a stay abroad of at least 48 hours are usually granted customs exemptions of $400 each. The duty-free articles must accompany the traveler at the time of his return, be for personal or household use, have

been acquired as an incident of his trip, and be properly declared to Customs. Not more than one liter of alcoholic beverages may be included in the $400 exemption.

If a U.S. resident arrives directly or indirectly from American Samoa, Guam, or the U.S. Virgin Islands, the purchase may be valued up to $800 fair retail value, but not more than $400 of the exemption may be applied to the value of articles acquired elsewhere than in such insular possessions, and 5 liters of alcoholic beverages may be included in the exemption, but not more than 1 liter of such beverages may have been acquired elsewhere than in the designated islands.

The exemption for alcoholic beverages is accorded only when the returning resident has attained 21 years of age at the time of his arrival. One hundred cigars and 200 cigarettes may be included in either exemption. Cuban cigars may be included if obtained in Cuba and all articles acquired there do not exceed $100 in retail value.

The $400 or $800 exemption may be granted only if the exemption, or any part of it, has not been used within the preceding 30-day period and the stay abroad was for at least 48 hours. The 48-hour absence requirement does not apply if you return from Mexico or the U.S. Virgin Islands.

Gifts costing no more than $50 fair retail value or $100 from American Samoa, Guam, or the Virgin Islands, may be mailed duty-free.

Most items—including alcoholic beverages, cigars, cigarettes and perfume—made in designated Caribbean and Central American countries may enter the U.S. duty-free under the Caribbean Basin Economic Recovery Act. Countries currently designated for such duty-free treatment are: Antigua and Barbuda, Barbados, Belize, British Virgin Islands, Costa Rica, Dominica, Dominican Republic, El Salvador, Grenada, Guatemala, Haiti, Honduras, Jamaica, Montserrat, Netherlands Antilles, Panama, Saint Christopher-Nevis, Saint Lucia, Saint Vincent and the Grenadines, and Trinidad and Tobago. Exceptions are: most textiles (incl. clothing), footwear, handbags, luggage, flat goods, work gloves and leather wearing apparel, and certain watches and watch parts. Alcoholic beverages and perfumes, remain subject to IRS tax.

U.S. Passport, Visa, and Health Requirements

Source: Passport Services, U.S. State Department as of May, 1984

Passports are issued by the United States Department of State to citizens and nationals of the United States for the purpose of documenting them for foreign travel and identifying them as Americans.

How to Obtain a Passport

An applicant for a passport who has never been previously issued a passport in his own name, must execute an application in person before (1) a passport agent; (2) a clerk of any federal court or state court of record or a judge or clerk of any probate court, accepting applications; (3) a postal employee designated by the postmaster at a Post Office which has been selected to accept passport applications; or (4) a diplomatic or consular officer of the U.S. abroad. It is no longer possible to include family members of any age in a U.S. passport. All persons are required to obtain individual passports in their own name.

A passport previously issued to the applicant, or one in which he was included, will be accepted as proof of citizenship in lieu of the following documents. A person born in the United States shall present his birth certificate. To be acceptable, the certificate must show the given name and surname, the date and place of birth and that the birth record was filed shortly after birth. A delayed birth certificate (a record filed more than one year after the date of birth) is acceptable provided that it shows that the report of birth was supported by acceptable secondary evidence of birth.

If such primary evidence is not obtainable, a notice from the registrar shall be submitted stating that no birth record exists. The notice shall be accompanied by the best obtainable secondary evidence such as a baptismal certificate, a certificate of circumcision, or a hospital birth record.

A person who has been issued a passport in his own name within the last eight years may obtain a new passport by filling out, signing and mailing a passport by mail application together with his previous passport, two recent identical signed photographs and $35.00 to the nearest Passport Agency or to the Passport Services in Wash., D.C. Those persons applying for a passport for the first time, or whose prior passport was issued before their 18th birthday, must execute a passport application in person.

A naturalized citizen should present his naturalization certificate. A person born abroad claiming citizenship through either a native-born or naturalized citizen must submit a certificate of citizenship issued by the Immigration and Naturalization Service; or a Consular Report of Birth or Certification of Birth issued by the Dept. of State. If one of the above documents has not been obtained, he must submit evidence of citizenship of the parent(s) through whom citizenship is claimed and evidence which would establish the parent/child relationship. Additionally, if through birth to citizen parent(s), parents' marriage certificate plus an affidavit from parent(s) showing periods and places of residence or physical presence in the U.S. and abroad, specifying periods spent abroad in the employment of the U.S. government, including the armed forces, or with certain international organizations; if through naturalization of parents, evidence of admission to the U.S. for permanent residence.

Under certain conditions, married women must present evidence of marriage. Special laws govern women married prior to Mar. 3, 1931.

Aliens — An alien leaving the U.S. must request passport facilities from his home government. He must have a permit from his local Collector of Internal Revenue, and if he wishes to return he should request a re-entry permit from the Immigration and Naturalization Service if it is required.

Contract Employees — Persons traveling because of a contract with the Government must submit with their applications letters from their employer stating position, destination and purpose of travel, armed forces contract number, and expiration date of contract when pertinent.

Photographs and Fees

Photographs — Two identical photographs which are sufficiently recent (normally not more than 6 months old) to be a good likeness of and satisfactorily identify the applicant. Photographs should be 2 × 2 inches in size. The image size measured from the bottom of the chin to the top of the head (including hair) should be not less than one inch nor more than 1 3/8 inches. Photographs must be signed in the center on the reverse. Photographs should be portrait-type prints. They must be clear, front view, full face, with a plain light (white or off-white) background. Photographs which depict the applicant as relaxed and smiling are encouraged.

Fees — As of Jan. 1, 1983, the passport fee is $20.00 for passports issued to persons under 18 years of age and the passports are valid for 5 years from the date of issue. The passport fee is $35.00 for passports issued to persons 18 years old and older and the passports are valid for 10 years from the date of issuance except where limited by the Secretary of State to a shorter period. A fee of $7.00 shall be charged for the execution of the application. No execution fee is payable when using DSP-82, "Application For Passport By Mail." Applicants eligible to use this procedure will pay only the $35.00 passport fee.

The loss or theft of a valid passport is a serious matter and should be reported in writing immediately to Passport Services, Dept. of State, Wash., D.C. 20524, or to the nearest passport agency, or to the nearest consular office of the U.S. when abroad.

Foreign Regulations

A visa, usually rubber stamped in a passport by a representative of the country to be visited, certifies that the bearer of the passport is permitted to enter that country for a certain purpose and length of time. Visa information can be obtained by writing directly to foreign consular officials.

U.S. Immigration Law

Source: Immigration and Naturalization Service, U.S. Justice Department

The Immigration and Nationality Act, as amended, provides for the numerical limitation of most immigration. Not subject to any numerical limitations are immigrants classified as immediate relatives who are spouses or children of U.S. citizens, or parents of citizens who are 21 years of age or older; returning residents; certain former U.S. citizens; ministers of religion; and certain long-term U.S. government employees.

The Refugee Act of 1980 (P.L. 96-212) became effective on April 1, 1980. Congress stated that the objectives of the Refugee Act are to provide a permanent and systematic procedure for the admission of refugees who are of special humanitarian concern to the United States, and to provide uniform provisions for the effective settlement and absorption of those refugees. The number of refugees who may be admitted is determined by the President, after consultation with the Committees on the Judiciary of the Senate and of the House of Representatives. For fiscal year 1984, the ceiling was set at 72,000 authorized refugee admissions.

Numerical Limitation of Immigrants

Immigration to the U.S. is numerically limited to 270,000 per year. Within this quota there is an annual limitation of 20,000 for each country. The colonies and dependencies of foreign states are limited to 600 per year, chargeable to the country limitation of the mother country.

Visa Categories

Of those immigrants subject to numerical limitations, applicants for immigration are classified as either preference or nonpreference. The preference visa categories are based on certain relationships to persons in the U.S., i.e., unmarried sons and daughters over 21 of U.S. citizens, spouses and unmarried sons and daughters of resident aliens, married sons and daughters of U.S. citizens, brothers and sisters of U.S. citizens 21 or over (first, 2d, 4th, and 5th preference, respectively); members of the professions or persons of exceptional ability in the sciences and arts whose services are sought by U.S. employers (3d preference); and skilled and unskilled workers in short supply (6th preference). Spouses and children of preference applicants are entitled to the same preference if accompanying or following to join such persons.

Preference status is based upon approved petitions, filed with the Immigration and Naturalization Service, by the appropriate relative or employer (or in the 3d preference by the alien himself).

Other immigrants not within one of the above-mentioned preference groups may qualify as nonpreference applicants and receive only those visa numbers not needed by preference applicants. The nonpreference category has not been available since 1978 due to 6 preferences using the allocation.

Labor Certification

The Act of October 3, 1965, established new controls to protect the American labor market from an influx of skilled and unskilled foreign labor. Prior to the issuance of a visa, the potential 3d, 6th, and nonpreference immigrant must obtain the Secretary of Labor's certification, establishing that there are not sufficient workers in the U.S. at the alien's destination who are able, willing, and qualified to perform the job; and that the employment of the alien will not adversely affect the wages and working conditions of workers in the U.S. similarly employed; or that there is satisfactory evidence that the provisions of that section do not apply to the alien's case.

Immigrants Admitted from All Countries

Fiscal Year Ends June 30 through 1976, Sept. 30 thereafter

Year	Number	Year	Number	Year	Number	Year	Number
1820	8,385	1871-1880	2,812,191	1931-1940	528,431	1976 July-Sept.	103,676
1821-1830	143,439	1881-1890	5,246,613	1941-1950	1,035,039	1977	462,315
1831-1840	599,125	1891-1900	3,687,564	1951-1960	2,515,479	1978	601,442
1841-1850	1,713,251	1901-1910	8,795,386	1961-1970	3,321,677	1979	460,348
1851-1860	2,598,214	1911-1920	5,735,811	1971-1975	1,936,282	1980	530,639
1861-1870	2,314,824	1921-1930	4,107,209	1976	398,613	1981	596,600
						1820-1981	50,252,552

Naturalization: How to Become an American Citizen

Source: The Federal Statutes

A person who desires to be naturalized as a citizen of the United States may obtain the necessary application form as well as detailed information from the nearest office of the Immigration and Naturalization Service or from the clerk of a court handling naturalization cases.

An applicant must be at least 18 years old. He must have been a lawful resident of the United States continuously for 5 years. For husbands and wives of U.S. citizens the period is 3 years in most instances. Special provisions apply to certain veterans of the Armed Forces.

An applicant must have been physically present in this country for at least half of the required 5 years' residence.

Every applicant for naturalization must:

(1) demonstrate an understanding of the English language, including an ability to read, write, and speak words in ordinary usage in the English language (persons physically unable to do so, and persons who, on the date of their examinations, are over 50 years of age and have been lawful permanent residents of the United States for 20 years or more are exempt).

(2) have been a person of good moral character, attached to the principles of the Constitution, and well disposed to the good order and happiness of the United States for five years just before filing the petition or for whatever other period of residence is required in his case and continue to be such a person until admitted to citizenship; and

(3) demonstrate a knowledge and understanding of the fundamentals of the history, and the principles and form of government, of the U.S.

The petitioner also is obliged to have two credible citizen witnesses. These witnesses must have personal knowledge of the applicant.

When the applicant files his petition he pays the court clerk $25. At the preliminary hearing he may be represented by a lawyer or social service agency. There is a 30-day wait. If action is favorable, there is a final hearing before a judge, who administers the following oath of allegiance:

I hereby declare, on oath, that I absolutely and entirely renounce and abjure all allegiance and fidelity to any foreign prince, potentate, state or sovereignty, to whom or which I have heretofore been a subject or citizen; that I will support and defend the Constitution and laws of the United States of America against all enemies, foreign and domestic; that I will bear true faith and allegiance to the same; that I will bear arms on behalf of the United States when required by the law; that I will perform noncombatant service in the armed forces of the United States when required by the law; that I will perform work of national importance under civilian direction when required by the law; and that I take this obligation freely without any mental reservation or purpose of evasion; so help me God.

HISTORICAL FIGURES

Ancient Greeks and Latins

Greeks

Aeschines, orator, 389-314BC.
Aeschylus, dramatist, 525-456BC.
Aesop, fableist, c620-c560BC.
Alcibiades, politician, 450-404BC.
Anacreon, poet, c582-c485BC.
Anaxagoras, philosopher, c500-428BC.
Anaximander, philosopher, 611-546BC.
Antiphon, speechwriter, c480-411BC.
Apollonius, mathematician, c265-170BC.
Archimedes, math. c287-212BC.
Aristophanes, dramatist, c448-380BC.
Aristotle, philosopher, 384-322BC.
Athenaeus, scholar, fl.c200.
Callicrates, architect, fl.5th cent.BC.
Callimachus, poet, c305-240BC.
Cratinus, comic dramatist, 520-421BC.
Democritus, philosopher, c460-370BC.
Demosthenes, orator, 384-322BC.
Diodorus, historian, fl.20BC.
Diogenes, philosopher, c372-c287BC.

Dionysius, historian, d.c7BC.
Empedocles, philosopher, c490-430BC.
Epicharmus, dramatist, c530-440BC.
Epictetus, philosopher, c55-c135.
Epicurus, philosopher, 341-270BC.
Eratosthenes, scientist, c276-194BC.
Euclid, mathematician, fl.c300BC.
Euripides, dramatist, c484-406BC.
Galen, physician, c129-199.
Heraclitus, philosopher, c535-c475BC.
Herodotus, historian, c484-420BC.
Hesiod, poet, 8th cent. BC.
Hippocrates, physician, c460-377BC.
Homer, poet, believed lived c850BC.
Isocrates, orator, 436-338BC.
Menander, dramatist, 342-292BC.
Phidias, sculptor, c500-435BC.
Pindar, poet, c518-c438BC.
Plato, philosopher, c428-c347BC.
Plutarch, biographer, c46-120.

Polybius, historian, c200-c118BC.
Praxiteles, sculptor, 400-330BC.
Pythagoras, phil., math., c580-c500BC.
Sappho, poet, c610-c580BC.
Simonides, poet, 556-c468BC.
Socrates, philosopher, c470-399BC.
Solon, statesman, 640-560BC.
Sophocles, dramatist, C496-406BC.
Strabo, geographer, c63BC-AD24.
Thales, philosopher, c634-c546BC.
Themistocles, politician, c524-c460BC.
Theocritus, poet, c310-250BC.
Theophrastus, phil. c372-c287BC.
Thucydides, historian, fl.5th cent.BC.
Timon, philosopher, c320-c230BC.
Xenophon, historian, c434-c355BC.
Zeno, philosopher, c495-c430BC.

Latins

Ammianus, historian, c330-395.
Apuleius, satirist, c124-c170.
Boethius, scholar, c480-524
Caesar, Julius, general, 100-44BC.
Catilina, politician, c108-62BC.
Carus, poet, c98-55BC.
Cato(Elder), statesman, 234-149BC.
Catullus, poet, c84-54BC.
Cicero, orator, 106-43BC.
Claudian, poet, c370-c404.
Ennius, poet, 239-170BC.
Gellius, author, c130-c165.

Horace, poet, 65-8BC.
Juvenal, satirist, c60-c127.
Livy, historian, 59BC-AD17.
Lucan, poet, 39-65.
Lucilius, poet, c180-c102BC.
Lucretius, poet, c99-c55BC.
Martial, epigrammatist, c38-c103.
Nepos, historian, c100-c25BC.
Ovid,poet, 43BC-AD17.
Persius, satirist, 34-62.
Plautus, dramatist, c254-c184BC.
Pliny, scholar, 23-79.

Pliny(Younger), author, 62-113.
Quintilian, rhetorician, c35-c97.
Sallust, historian, 86-34BC.
Seneca, philosopher, 4BC-AD65.
Silius, poet, c25-101.
Statius, poet, c45-c96.
Suetonius, biographer, c69-c122.
Tacitus, historian, c56-c120.
Terence, dramatist, 185-c159BC.
Tibullus, poet, c55-c19BC.
Virgil, poet, 70-19BC.
Vitruvius, architect, fl.1st cent.BC.

Rulers of England and Great Britain

Name	England	Began	Died	Age	Rgd
	Saxons and Danes				
Egbert	King of Wessex, won allegiance of all English	829	839	—	10
Ethelwulf	Son, King of Wessex, Sussex, Kent, Essex	839	858	—	19
Ethelbald	Son of Ethelwulf, displaced father in Wessex	858	860	—	2
Ethelbert	2d son of Ethelwulf, united Kent and Wessex	860	866	—	6
Ethelred I	3d son, King of Wessex, fought Danes	866	871	—	5
Alfred	The Great, 4th son, defeated Danes, fortified London	871	899	52	28
Edward	The Elder, Alfred's son, united English, claimed Scotland	899	924	55	25
Athelstan	The Glorious, Edward's son, King of Mercia, Wessex	924	940	45	16
Edmund I	3d son of Edward, King of Wessex, Mercia	940	946	25	6
Edred	4th son of Edward	946	955	32	9
Edwy	The Fair, eldest son of Edmund, King of Wessex	955	959	18	3
Edgar	The Peaceful, 2d son of Edmund, ruled all English	959	975	32	17
Edward	Tho Martyr, eldest son of Edgar, murdered by stepmother	975	978	17	4
Ethelred II	The Unready, 2d son of Edgar, married Emma of Normandy	978	1016	48	37
Edmund II	Ironside, son of Ethelred II, King of London	1016	1016	27	0
Canute	The Dane, gave Wessex to Edmund, married Emma	1016	1035	40	19
Harold I	Harefoot, natural son of Canute	1035	1040	—	5
Hardecanute	Son of Canute by Emma, Danish King	1040	1042	24	2
Edward	The Confessor, son of Ethelred II (Canonized 1161)	1042	1066	62	24
Harold II	Edward's brother-in-law, last Saxon King	1066	1066	44	0
	House of Normandy				
William I	The Conqueror, defeated Harold at Hastings	1066	1087	60	21
William II	Rufus, 3d son of William I, killed by arrow	1087	1100	43	13
Henry I	Beauclerc, youngest son of William I	1100	1135	67	35
	House of Blois				
Stephen	Son of Adela, daughter of William I, and Count of Blois	1135	1154	50	19
	House of Plantagenet				
Henry II	Son of Geoffrey Plantagenet (Angevin) by Matilda, dau. of Henry I	1154	1189	56	35
Richard I	Coeur de Lion, son of Henry II, crusader	1189	1199	42	10
John	Lackland, son of Henry II, signed Magna Carta, 1215	1199	1216	50	17
Henry III	Son of John, acceded at 9, under regency until 1227	1216	1272	65	56
Edward I	Longshanks, son of Henry III	1272	1307	68	35
Edward II	Son of Edward I, deposed by Parliament, 1327	1307	1327	43	20
Edward III	Of Windsor, son of Edward II	1327	1377	65	50
Richard II	Grandson of Edw. III, minor until 1389, deposed 1399	1377	1400	34	22
	House of Lancaster				
Henry IV	Son of John of Gaunt, Duke of Lancaster, son of Edw. III	1399	1413	47	13
Henry V	Son of Henry IV, victor of Agincourt	1413	1422	34	9
Henry VI	Son of Henry V, deposed 1461, died in Tower	1422	1471	49	39

House of York

Edward IV	Great-great-grandson of Edward III, son of Duke of York	1461	1483	41	22
Edward V	Son of Edward IV, murdered in Tower of London	1483	1483	13	0
Richard III	Crookback, bro. of Edward IV, fell at Bosworth Field	1483	1485	35	2

House of Tudor

Henry VII	Son of Edmund Tudor, Earl of Richmond, whose father had married the widow of Henry V; descended from Edward III through his mother, Margaret Beaufort via John of Gaunt. By marriage with dau. of Edward IV he united Lancaster and York	1485	1509	53	24
Henry VIII	Son of Henry VII by Elizabeth, dau. of Edward IV.	1509	1547	56	38
Edward VI	Son of Henry VIII, by Jane Seymour, his 3d queen. Ruled under regents. Was forced to name Lady Jane Grey his successor. Council of State proclaimed her queen July 10, 1553. Mary Tudor won Council, was proclaimed queen July 19, 1553. Mary had Lady Jane Grey beheaded for treason, Feb., 1554	1547	1553	16	6
Mary I	Daughter of Henry VIII, by Catherine of Aragon	1553	1558	43	5
Elizabeth I	Daughter of Henry VIII, by Anne Boleyn	1558	1603	69	44

Great Britain
House of Stuart

James I	James VI of Scotland, son of Mary, Queen of Scots. *First to call himself King of Great Britain. This became official with the Act of Union, 1707*	1603	1625	59	22
Charles I	Only surviving son of James I; beheaded Jan. 30, 1649	1625	1649	48	24

Commonwealth, 1649-1660
Council of State, 1649; Protectorate, 1653

The Cromwells	Oliver Cromwell, Lord Protector	1653	1658	59	—
	Richard Cromwell, son, Lord Protector, resigned May 25, 1659	1658	1712	86	—

House of Stuart (Restored)

Charles II	Eldest son of Charles I, died without issue	1660	1685	55	25
James II	2d son of Charles I. Deposed 1688. Interregnum Dec. 11, 1688, to Feb. 13, 1689	1685	1701	68	3
William III	Son of William, Prince of Orange, by Mary, dau. of Charles I	1689	1702	51	13
and Mary II	Eldest daughter of James II and wife of William III		1694	33	6
Anne	2d daughter of James II	1702	1714	49	12

House of Hanover

George I	Son of Elector of Hanover, by Sophia, grand-dau. of James I	1714	1727	67	13
George II	Only son of George I, married Caroline of Brandenburg	1727	1760	77	33
George III	Grandson of George II, married Charlotte of Mecklenburg	1760	1820	81	59
George IV	Eldest son of George III, Prince Regent, from Feb., 1811	1820	1830	67	10
William IV	3d son of George III, married Adelaide of Saxe-Meiningen	1830	1837	71	7
Victoria	Dau. of Edward, 4th son of George III; married (1840) Prince Albert of Saxe-Coburg and Gotha, who became Prince Consort	1837	1901	81	63

House of Saxe-Coburg and Gotha

Edward VII	Eldest son of Victoria, married Alexandra, Princess of Denmark	1901	1910	68	9

House of Windsor
Name Adopted July 17, 1917

George V	2d son of Edward VII, married Princess Mary of Teck	1910	1936	70	25
Edward VIII	Eldest son of George V; acceded Jan. 20, 1936, abdicated Dec. 11	1936	1972	77	1
George VI	2d son of George V; married Lady Elizabeth Bowes-Lyon	1936	1952	56	15
Elizabeth II	Elder daughter of George VI, acceded Feb. 6, 1952	1952	—	—	—

Rulers of Scotland

Kenneth I MacAlpin was the first Scot to rule both Scots and Picts, 846 AD.

Duncan I was the first general ruler, 1034. Macbeth seized the kingdom 1040, was slain by Duncan's son, Malcolm III MacDuncan (Canmore), 1057.

Malcolm married Margaret, Saxon princess who had fled from the Normans. Queen Margaret introduced English language and English monastic customs. She was canonized, 1250. Her son Edgar, 1097, moved the court to Edinburgh. His brothers Alexander I and David I succeeded. Malcolm IV, the Maiden, 1153, grandson of David I, was followed by his brother, William the Lion, 1165, whose son was Alexander II, 1214. The latter's son, Alexander III, 1249, defeated the Norse and regained the Hebrides. When he died, 1286, his granddaughter, Margaret, child of Eric of Norway and grandniece of Edward I of England, known as the Maid of Norway, was chosen ruler, but died 1290, aged 8.

John Baliol, 1292-1296. (Interregnum, 10 years).

Robert Bruce (The Bruce), 1306-1329, victor at Bannockburn, 1314.

David II, only son of Robert Bruce, ruled 1329-1371.

Robert II, 1371-1390, grandson of Robert Bruce, son of Walter, the Steward of Scotland, was called The Steward, first of the so-called Stuart line.

Robert III, son of Robert II, 1390-1406.

James I, son of Robert III, 1406-1437.

James II, son of James I, 1437-1460.

James III, eldest son of James II, 1460-1488.

James IV, eldest son of James III, 1488-1513.

James V, eldest son of James IV, 1513-1542.

Mary, daughter of James V, born 1542, became queen when one week old; was crowned 1543. Married, 1558, Francis, son of Henry II of France, who became king 1559, died 1560. Mary ruled Scots 1561 until abdication, 1567. She also married (2) Henry Stewart, Lord Darnley, and (3) James, Earl of Bothwell. Imprisoned by Elizabeth I, Mary was beheaded 1587.

James VI, 1566-1625, son of Mary and Lord Darnley, became King of England on death of Elizabeth in 1603. Although the thrones were thus united, the legislative union of Scotland and England was not effected until the Act of Union, May 1, 1707.

Rulers of France: Kings, Queens, Presidents

Caesar to Charlemagne

Julius Caesar subdued the Gauls, native tribes of Gaul (France) 57 to 52 BC. The Romans ruled 500 years. The Franks, a Teutonic tribe, reached the Somme from the East ca. 250 AD. By the 5th century the Merovingian Franks ousted the Romans. In 451 AD, with the help of Visigoths, Burgundians and others, they defeated Attila and the Huns at Chalons-sur-Marne.

Childeric I became leader of the Merovingians 458 AD. His son Clovis I (Chlodwig, Ludwig, Louis), crowned 481, founded the dynasty. After defeating the Alemanni (Germans) 496, he was baptized a Christian and made Paris his capital. His line ruled until Childeric III was deposed, 751.

The West Merovingians were called Neustrians, the eastern

Austrasians. Pepin of Herstal (687-714) major domus, or head of the palace, of Austrasia, took over Neustria as dux (leader) of the Franks. Pepin's son, Charles, called Martel (the Hammer) defeated the Saracens at Tours-Poitiers, 732; was succeeded by his son, Pepin the Short, 741, who deposed Childeric III and ruled as king until 768.

His son, Charlemagne, or Charles the Great (742-814) became king of the Franks, 768, with his brother Carloman, who died 771. He ruled France, Germany, parts of Italy, Spain, Austria, and enforced Christianity. Crowned Emperor of the Romans by Pope Leo III in St. Peter's, Rome, Dec. 25, 800 AD. Succeeded by son, Louis I the Pious, 814. At death, 840, Louis left empire to sons, Lothair (Roman emperor); Pepin I (king of Aquitaine); Louis II (of Germany); Charles the Bald (France). They quarreled and by the peace of Verdun, 843, divided the empire.

The Carolingians

AD	Name, year of accession
843	Charles I (the Bald), Roman Emperor, 875
877	Louis II (the Stammerer), son
879	Louis III (died 882) and Carloman, brothers
885	Charles II (the Fat), Roman Emperor, 881
888	Eudes (Odo) elected by nobles
898	Charles III (the Simple), son of Louis II, defeated by
922	Robert, brother of Eudes, killed in war
923	Rudolph (Raoul) Duke of Burgundy
936	Louis IV, son of Charles III
954	Lothair, son, aged 13, defeated by Capet
986	Louis V (the Sluggard), left no heirs

The Capets

987	Hugh Capet, son of Hugh the Great
996	Robert II (the Wise), his son
1031	Henry I, his son, last Norman
1060	Philip I (the Fair), son
1108	Louis VI (the Fat), son
1137	Louis VII (the Younger), son
1180	Philip II (Augustus), son, crowned at Reims
1223	Louis VIII (the Lion), son
1226	Louis IX, son, crusader; Louis IX (1214-1270) reigned 44 years, arbitrated disputes with English King Henry III; led crusades, 1248 (captured in Egypt 1250) and 1270, when he died of plague in Tunis. Canonized 1297 as St. Louis.
1270	Philip III (the Hardy), son
1285	Philip IV (the Fair), son, king at 17
1314	Louis X (the Headstrong), son. His posthumous son, John I, lived only 7 days
1316	Philip V (the Tall), brother of Louis X
1322	Charles IV (the Fair), brother of Louis X

House of Valois

1328	Philip VI (of Valois), grandson of Philip III
1350	John II (the Good), his son, retired to England
1364	Charles V (the Wise), son
1380	Charles VI (the Beloved), son
1422	Charles VII (the Victorious), son. In 1429 Joan of Arc (Jeanne d'Arc) promised Charles to oust the English, who occupied northern France. Joan won at Orleans and Patay and had Charles crowned at Reims July 17, 1429. Joan was captured May 24, 1430, and executed May 30, 1431, at Rouen for heresy. Charles ordered her rehabilitation, effected 1455.
1461	Louis XI (the Cruel), son, civil reformer
1483	Charles VIII (the Affable), son
1498	Louis XII, great-grandson of Charles V
1515	Francis I, of Angouleme, nephew, son-in-law. Francis I (1494-1547) reigned 32 years, fought 4 big wars, was patron of the arts, aided Cellini, del Sarto, Leonardo da Vinci, Rabelais, embellished Fontainebleau.
1547	Henry II, son, killed at a joust in a tournament. He was the husband of Catherine de Medicis (1519-1589) and the lover of Diane de Poitiers (1499-1566). Catherine was born in Florence, daughter of Lorenzo de Medicis. By her marriage to Henry II she became the mother of Francis II, Charles IX, Henry III and Queen Margaret (Reine Margot) wife of Henry IV. She persuaded Charles IX to order the massacre of Huguenots on the Feast of St. Bartholomew, Aug. 24, 1572, the day her daughter was married to Henry of Navarre.
1559	Francis II, son. In 1548, Mary, Queen of Scots since infancy, was betrothed when 6 to Francis, aged 4. They were married 1558. Francis died 1560, aged 16; Mary ruled Scotland, abdicated 1567.
1560	Charles IX, brother

1574	Henry III, brother, assassinated

House of Bourbon

1589	Henry IV, of Navarre, assassinated. Henry IV made enemies when he gave tolerance to Protestants by Edict of Nantes, 1598. He was grandson of Queen Margaret of Navarre, literary patron. He married Margaret of Valois, daughter of Henry II and Catherine de Medicis; was divorced; in 1600 married Marie de Medicis, who became Regent of France, 1610-17 for her son, Louis XIII, but was exiled by Richelieu, 1631.
1610	Louis XIII (the Just), son. Louis XIII (1601-1643) married Anne of Austria. His ministers were Cardinals Richelieu and Mazarin.
1643	Louis XIV (The Grand Monarch), son. Louis XIV was king 72 years. He exhausted a prosperous country in wars for thrones and territory. By revoking the Edict of Nantes (1685) he caused the emigration of the Huguenots. He said: "I am the state."
1715	Louis XV, great-grandson. Louis XV married a Polish princess; lost Canada to the English. His favorites, Mme. Pompadour and Mme. Du Barry, influenced policies. Noted for saying "After me, the deluge".
1774	Louis XVI, grandson; married Marie Antoinette, daughter of Empress Maria Therese of Austria. King and queen beheaded by Revolution, 1793. Their son, called Louis XVII, died in prison, never ruled.

First Republic

1792	National Convention of the French Revolution
1795	Directory, under Barras and others
1799	Consulate, Napoleon Bonaparte, first consul. Elected consul for life, 1802.

First Empire

1804	Napoleon I, emperor. Josephine (de Beauharnais) empress, 1804-09; Marie Louise, empress, 1810-1814. Her son, Francois (1811-1832), titular King of Rome, later Duke de Reichstadt and "Napoleon II," never ruled. Napoleon abdicated 1814, died 1821.

Bourbons Restored

1814	Louis XVIII king; brother of Louis XVI.
1824	Charles X, brother; reactionary; deposed by the July Revolution, 1830.

House of Orleans

1830	Louis-Philippe, the "citizen king."

Second Republic

1848	Louis Napoleon Bonaparte, president, nephew of Napoleon I. He became:

Second Empire

1852	Napoleon III, emperor; Eugenie (de Montijo) empress: Lost Franco-Prussian war, deposed 1870. Son, Prince Imperial (1856-79), died in Zulu War. Eugenie died 1920.

Third Republic—Presidents

1871	Thiers, Louis Adolphe (1797-1877)
1873	MacMahon, Marshal Patrice M. de (1808-1893)
1879	Grevy, Paul J. (1807-1891)
1887	Sadi-Carnot, M. (1837-1894), assassinated
1894	Casimir-Perier, Jean P. P. (1847-1907)
1895	Faure, Francois Felix (1841-1899)
1899	Loubet, Emile (1838-1929)
1906	Fallieres, C. Armand (1841-1931)
1913	Poincare, Raymond (1860-1934)
1920	Deschanel, Paul (1856-1922)
1920	Millerand, Alexandre (1859-1943)
1924	Doumergue, Gaston (1863-1937)
1931	Doumer, Paul (1857-1932), assassinated
1932	Lebrun, Albert (1871-1950), resigned 1940
1940	Vichy govt. under German armistice: Henri Philippe Petain (1856-1951) Chief of State, 1940-1944. **Provisional govt.** after liberation: Charles de Gaulle (1890-1970) Oct. 1944-Jan. 21, 1946; Felix Gouin (1884-1977) Jan. 23, 1946; Georges Bidault (1899-) June 24, 1946.

Fourth Republic—Presidents

1947	Auriol, Vincent (1884-1966)
1954	Coty, Rene (1882-1962)

Fifth Republic—Presidents

1959	de Gaulle, Charles Andre J. M. (1890-1970)
1969	Pompidou, Georges (1911-1974)
1974	Giscard d'Estaing, Valery (1926-)
1981	Mitterrand, Francois (1916-)

Rulers of Middle Europe; Rise and Fall of Dynasties

Carolingian Dynasty

Charles the Great, or Charlemagne, ruled France, Italy, and Middle Europe; established Ostmark (later Austria); crowned Roman emperor by pope in Rome, 800 AD; died 814.
Louis I (Ludwig) the Pious, son; crowned by Charlemagné 814,

d. 840.

Louis II, the German, son; succeeded to East Francia (Germany) 843-876.

Charles the Fat, son; inherited East Francia and West Francia (France) 876, reunited empire, crowned emperor by pope, 881, deposed 887.

Arnulf, nephew, 887-899. Partition of empire.

Louis the Child, 899-911, last direct descendant of Charlemagne.

Conrad I, duke of Franconia, first elected German king, 911-918, founded House of Franconia.

Saxon Dynasty; First Reich

Henry I, the Fowler, duke of Saxony, 919-936.

Otto I, the Great, 936-973, son; crowned Holy Roman Emperor by pope, 962.

Otto II, 973-983, son; failed to oust Greeks and Arabs from Sicily.

Otto III, 983-1002, son; crowned emperor at 16.

Henry II, the Saint, duke of Bavaria, 1002-1024, greatgrandson of Otto the Great.

House of Franconia

Conrad II, 1024-1039, elected king of Germany.

Henry III, the Black, 1039-1056, son; deposed 3 popes; annexed Burgundy.

Henry IV, 1056-1106, son; regency by his mother, Agnes of Poitou. Banned by Pope Gregory VII, he did penance at Canossa.

Henry V, 1106-1125, son; last of Salic House.

Lothair, duke of Saxony, 1125-1137. Crowned emperor in Rome, 1134.

House of Hohenstaufen

Conrad III, duke of Swabia, 1138-1152. In 2d Crusade.

Frederick I, Barbarossa, 1152-1190; Conrad's nephew.

Henry VI, 1190-1196, took lower Italy from Normans. Son became king of Sicily.

Philip of Swabia, 1197-1208, brother.

Otto IV, of House of Welf, 1198-1215; deposed.

Frederick II, 1215-1250, son of Henry VI; king of Sicily; crowned king of Jerusalem; in 5th Crusade.

Conrad IV, 1250-1254, son; lost lower Italy to Charles of Anjou.

Conradin (1252-1268) son, king of Jerusalem and Sicily, beheaded. Last Hohenstaufen.

Interregnum, 1254-1273, Rise of the Electors.

Transition

Rudolph I of Hapsburg, 1273-1291, defeated King Ottocar II of Bohemia. Bequeathed duchy of Austria to eldest son, Albert.

Adolph of Nassau, 1292-1298, killed in war with Albert of Austria.

Albert I, king of Germany, 1298-1308, son of Rudolph.

Henry VII, of Luxemburg, 1308-1313, crowned emperor in Rome. Seized Bohemia, 1310.

Louis IV of Bavaria (Wittelsbach), 1314-1347. Also elected was Frederick of Austria, 1314-1330 (Hapsburg). Abolition of papal sanction for election of Holy Roman Emperor.

Charles IV, of Luxemburg, 1347-1378, grandson of Henry VII, German emperor and king of Bohemia, Lombardy, Burgundy; took Mark of Brandenburg.

Wenceslaus, 1378-1400, deposed.

Rupert, Duke of Palatine, 1400-1410.

Hungary

Stephen I, house of Arpad, 997-1038. Crowned king 1000; converted Magyars; canonized 1083. After several centuries of feuds Charles Robert of Anjou became Charles I, 1308-1342.

Louis I, the Great, son, 1342-1382; joint ruler of Poland with Casimir III, 1370. Defeated Turks.

Mary, daughter, 1382-1395, ruled with husband. Sigismund of Luxemburg, 1387-1437, also king of Bohemia. As bro. of Wenceslaus he succeeded Rupert as king of Holy Roman Emperor, 1410.

Albert II, 1438-1439, son-in-law of Sigismund; also Roman emperor. (see under Hapsburg.)

Ulaszlo I of Poland, 1440-1444.

Ladislaus V, posthumous son of Albert II, 1444-1457. John Hunyadi (Hunyadi Janos) governor (1446-1452), fought Turks, Czechs; died 1456.

Matthias I (Corvinus) son of Hunyadi, 1458-1490. Shared rule of Bohemia, captured Vienna, 1485, annexed Austria, Styria, Carinthia.

House of Piasts

Miesko I, 962?-992; Poland Christianized 966. Expansion under 3 Boleslavs: I, 992-1025, son, crowned king 1024; II, 1058-1079, great-grandson, exiled after killing bishop Stanislav who became chief patron saint of Poland: III, 1106-1138, nephew, divided Poland among 4 sons eldest suzerain.

1138-1306, feudal division. 1226 founding in Prussia of military

Ladislas II (king of Bohemia), 1490-1516.

Louis II, son, aged 10, 1516-1526. Wars with Suleiman, Turk. In 1527 Hungary was split between Ferdinand I, Archduke of Austria, bro.-in-law of Louis II, and John Zapolya of Transylvania. After Turkish invasion, 1547, Hungary was split between Ferdinand, Prince John Sigismund (Transylvania) and the Turks.

House of Hapsburg

Albert V of Austria, Hapsburg, crowned king of Hungary, Jan. 1438, Roman emperor, March, 1438, as Albert II; died 1439.

Frederick III, cousin, 1440-1493. Fought Turks.

Maximilian I, son, 1493-1519. Assumed title of Holy Roman Emperor (German), 1493.

Charles V, grandson, 1519-1556. King of Spain with mother co-regent; crowned Roman emperor at Aix, 1520. Confronted Luther at Worms; attempted church reform and religious conciliation; abdicated 1556.

Ferdinand I, king of Bohemia, 1526, of Hungary, 1527; disputed. German king, 1531. Crowned Roman emperor on abdication of brother Charles V, 1556.

Maximilian II, son, 1564-1576.

Rudolph II, son, 1576-1612.

Matthias, brother, 1612-1619, king of Bohemia and Hungary.

Ferdinand II of Styria, king of Bohemia, 1617, of Hungary, 1618, Roman emperor, 1619. Bohemian Protestants deposed him, elected Frederick V of Palatine, starting Thirty Years War.

Ferdinand III, son, king of Hungary, 1625, Bohemia, 1627, Roman emperor, 1637. Peace of Westphalia, 1648, ended war. Leopold I, 1658-1705; Joseph I, 1705-1711; Charles VI, 1711-1740.

Maria Theresa, daughter, 1740-1780, Archduchess of Austria, queen of Hungary; ousted pretender, Charles VII, crowned 1742; in 1745 obtained election of her husband Francis I as Roman emperor and co-regent (d. 1765). Fought Seven Years' War with Frederick II (the Great) of Prussia. Mother of Marie Antoinette, Queen of France.

Joseph II, son 1765-1790, Roman emperor, reformer; powers restricted by Empress Maria Theresa until her death, 1780. First partition of Poland. Leopold II, 1790-1792.

Francis II, son, 1792-1835. Fought Napoleon. Proclaimed first hereditary emperor of Austria, 1804. Forced to abdicate as Roman emperor, 1806; last use of title. Ferdinand I, son, 1835-1848, abdicated during revolution.

Austro-Hungarian Monarchy

Francis Joseph I, nephew, 1848-1916, emperor of Austria, king of Hungary. Dual monarchy of Austria-Hungary formed, 1867. After assassination of heir, Archduke Francis Ferdinand, June 28, 1914, Austrian diplomacy precipitated World War I.

Charles I, grand-nephew, 1916-1918, last emperor of Austria and king of Hungary. Abdicated Nov. 11-13, 1918, died 1922.

Rulers of Prussia

Nucleus of Prussia was the Mark of Brandenburg. First margrave was Albert the Bear (Albrecht), 1134-1170. First Hohenzollern margrave was Frederick, burgrave of Nuremberg, 1417-1440.

Frederick William, 1640-1688, the Great Elector. Son, Frederick III, 1688-1713, was crowned King Frederick of Prussia, 1701.

Frederick William I, son, 1713-1740.

Frederick II, the Great, son, 1740-1786, annexed Silesia part of Austria.

Frederick William II, nephew, 1786-1797.

Frederick William III, son, 1797-1840. Napoleonic wars.

Frederick William IV, son, 1840-1861. Uprising of 1848 and first parliament and constitution.

Second and Third Reich

William I, 1861-1888, brother. Annexation of Schleswig and Hanover; Franco-Prussian war, 1870-71, proclamation of German Reich, Jan. 18, 1871, at Versailles; William, German emperor (Deutscher Kaiser), Bismarck, chancellor.

Frederick III, son, 1888.

William II, son, 1888-1918. Led Germany in World War I, abdicated as German emperor and king of Prussia, Nov. 9, 1918. Died in exile in Netherlands June 4, 1941. Minor rulers of Bavaria, Saxony, Wurttemberg also abdicated.

Germany proclaimed a republic at Weimar, July 1, 1919. Presidents: Frederick Ebert, 1919-1925, Paul von Hindenburg-Beneckendorff, 1925, reelected 1932, d. Aug. 2, 1934. Adolf Hitler, chancellor, chosen successor as Leader-Chancellor (Fuehrer & Reichskanzler) of Third Reich. Annexed Austria, March, 1938. Precipitated World War II, 1939-1945. Committed suicide April 30, 1945.

Rulers of Poland

order Teutonic Knights. 1226 invasion by Tartars/Mongols.

Vladislav I, 1306-1333, reunited most Polish territories, crowned king 1320. Casimir III the Great, 1333-1370, son, developed economic, cultural life, foreign policy.

House of Anjou

Louis I, 1370-1382, nephew/identical with Louis I of Hungary.

Jadwiga, 1384-1399, daughter, married 1386 Jagiello, Grand Duke of Lituania.

House of Jagelloneans

Vladislav II, 1386-1434, Christianized Lituania, founded personal union between Poland & Lituania. Defeated 1410 Teutonic Knights at Grunwald.

Vladislav III, 1434-1444, son, simultaneously king of Hungary. Fought Turks, killed 1444 in battle of Varna.

Casimir IV, 1446-1492, brother, competed with Hapsburgs, put son Vladislav on throne of Bohemia, later also of Hungary.

Sigismund I, 1506-1548, brother, patronized science & arts, his & son's reign "Golden Age."

Sigismund II, 1548-1572, son, established 1569 real union of Poland and Lituania (lasted until 1795).

Elective kings

Polish nobles proclaimed 1572 Poland a Republic headed by king to be elected by whole nobility.

Stephen Batory, 1576-1586, duke of Transylvania, married Ann, sister of Sigismund II August. Fought Russians.

Sigismund III Vasa, 1587-1632, nephew of Sigismund II. 1592-1598 also king of Sweden. His generals fought Russians, Turks.

Vladislav II Vasa, 1632-1648, son. Fought Russians.

John II Casimir Vasa, 1648-1668, brother. Fought Cossacks, Swedes, Russians, Turks, Tartars (the "Deluge"). Abdicated 1668.

John III Sobieski, 1674-1696. Won Vienna from Turks, 1683.

Stanislav II, 1764-1795, last king. Encouraged reforms; 1791 1st modern Constitution in Europe. 1772, 1793, 1795 Poland partitioned among Russia, Prussia, Austria. Unsuccessful insurrection against foreign invasion 1794 under Kosciuszko, Amer-Polish gen.

1795-1918 Poland under foreign rule

1807-1815 Grand Duchy of Warsaw created by Napoleon I, Frederick August of Saxony grand duke.

1815 Congress of Vienna proclaimed part of Poland "Kingdom" in personal union with Russia.

Polish uprisings: 1830 against Russia, 1846, 1848 against Austria, 1863 against Russia—all repressed.

1918-1939 Second Republic

1918-1922 Head of State Jozef Pilsudski. Presidents: Gabriel Narutowicz 1933, assassinated. Stanislav Wojsiechowski 1922-1926, had to abdicate after Pilsudski's coup d'état. Ignacy Mosciecki, 1926-1939, ruled with Pilsudski as (until 1935) virtual dictator.

1939-1945 Poland under foreign occupation

Nazi aggression Sept. 1939. Polish govt.-in-exile, first in France, then in England. Vladislav Raczkiewicz pres., Gen. Vladislav Sikorski, then Stanislav Mikolajczyk, prime ministers. Polish Committee of Natl. Liberation proclaimed at Lublin July 1944, transformed into govt. Jan. 1, 1945.

Rulers of Denmark, Sweden, Norway

Denmark

Earliest rulers invaded Britain; King Canute, who ruled in London 1016-1035, was most famous. The Valdemars furnished kings until the 15th century. In 1282 the Danes won the first national assembly, Danehof, from King Erik V.

Most redoubtable medieval character was Margaret, daughter of Valdemar IV, born 1353, married at 10 to King Haakon VI of Norway. In 1376 she had her first infant son Olaf made king of Denmark. After his death, 1387, she was regent of Denmark and Norway. In 1388 Sweden accepted her as sovereign. In 1389 she made her grand-nephew, Duke Erik of Pomerania, titular king of Denmark, Sweden, and Norway, with herself as regent. In 1397 she effected the Union of Kalmar of the three kingdoms and had Erik VII crowned. In 1439 the three kingdoms deposed him and elected, 1440, Christopher of Bavaria king (Christopher III). On his death, 1448, the union broke up.

Succeeding rulers were unable to enforce their claims as rulers of Sweden until 1520, when Christian II conquered Sweden. He was thrown out 1522, and in 1523 Gustavus Vasa united Sweden. Denmark continued to dominate Norway until the Napoleonic wars, when Frederick VI, 1808-1839, joined the Napoleonic cause after Britain had destroyed the Danish fleet, 1807. In 1814 he was forced to cede Norway to Sweden and Helgoland to Britain, receiving Lauenburg. Successors Christian VIII, 1839; Frederick VII, 1848; Christian IX, 1863; Frederick VIII, 1906; Christian X, 1912; Frederick IX, 1947; Margrethe II, 1972.

Sweden

Early kings ruled at Uppsala, but did not dominate the country. Sverker, c1130-c1156, united the Swedes and Goths. In 1435 Sweden obtained the Riksdag, or parliament. After the Union of Kalmar, 1397, the Danes either ruled or harried the country until Christian II of Denmark conquered it anew, 1520. This led to a

rising under Gustavus Vasa, who ruled Sweden 1523-1560, and established an independent kingdom. Charles IX, 1599-1611, crowned 1604, conquered Moscow. Gustavus II Adolphus, 1611-1632, was called the Lion of the North. Later rulers: Christina, 1632; Charles X, Gustavus 1654; Charles XI, 1660; Charles XII (invader of Russia and Poland, defeated at Poltava, June 28, 1709), 1697; Ulrika Eleanora, sister, elected queen 1718; Frederick I (of Hesse), her husband, 1720; Adolphus Frederick, 1751; Gustavus III, 1771; Gustavus IV Adolphus, 1792; Charles XIII, 1809. (Union with Norway began 1814.) Charles XIV John, 1818. He was Jean Bernadotte, Napoleon's Prince of Ponte Corvo, elected 1810 to succeed Charles XIII. He founded the present dynasty: Oscar I, 1844, Charles XV, 1859; Oscar II, 1872; Gustavus V, 1907; Gustav VI Adolf, 1950; Carl XVI Gustaf, 1973.

Norway

Overcoming many rivals, Harald Haarfager, 872-930, conquered Norway, Orkneys, and Shetlands; Olaf I, great-grandson, 995-1000, brought Christianity into Norway, Iceland, and Greenland. In 1035 Magnus the Good also became king of Denmark. Haakon V, 1299-1319, had married his daughter to Erik of Sweden. Their son, Magnus, became ruler of Norway and Sweden at 6. His son, Haakon VI, married Margaret of Denmark; their son Olaf IV became king of Norway and Denmark, followed by Margaret's regency and the Union of Kalmar, 1397.

In 1450 Norway became subservient to Denmark. Christian IV, 1588-1648, founded Christiania, now Oslo. After Napoleonic wars, when Denmark ceded Norway to Sweden, a strong nationalist movement forced recognition of Norway as an independent kingdom united with Sweden under the Swedish kings, 1814-1905. In 1905 the union was dissolved and Prince Carl of Denmark became Haakon VII. He died Sept 21, 1957, aged 85; succeeded by son, Olav V, b. July 2, 1903.

Rulers of the Netherlands and Belgium

The Netherlands (Holland)

William Frederick, Prince of Orange, led a revolt against French rule, 1813, and was crowned King of the Netherlands, 1815. Belgium seceded Oct. 4, 1830, after a revolt, and formed a separate government. The change was ratified by the two kingdoms by treaty Apr. 19, 1839.

Succession: William II, son, 1840; William III, son, 1849; Wilhelmina, daughter of William III and his 2d wife Princess Emma of Waldeck, 1890; Wilhelmina abdicated, Sept. 4, 1948, in favor of daughter, Juliana. Juliana abdicated Apr. 30, 1980, in favor of daughter, Beatrix.

Belgium

A national congress elected Prince Leopold of Saxe-Coburg King; he took the throne July 21, 1831, as Leopold I. Succession: Leopold II, son 1865; Albert I, nephew of Leopold II, 1909; Leopold III, son of Albert, 1934; Prince Charles, Regent 1944; Leopold returned 1950, yielded powers to son Baudouin, Prince Royal, Aug. 6, 1950, abdicated July 16, 1951. Baudouin I took throne July 17, 1951.

For political history prior to 1830 see articles on the Netherlands and Belgium.

Roman Rulers

From Romulus to the end of the Empire in the West. Rulers of the Roman Empire in the East sat in Constantinople and for a brief period in Nicaea, until the capture of Constantinople by the Turks in 1453, when Byzantium was succeeded by the Ottoman Empire.

BC	Name	BC	Name	AD	Name
	The Kingdom	534	L. Tarquinius Superbus	435	Censorship instituted
			The Republic	366	Praetorship established
753	Romulus (Quirinus)	509	Consulate established	366	Curule Aedileship created
716	Numa Pompilius	509	Quaestorship instituted	362	Military Tribunate elected
673	Tullus Hostilius	498	Dictatorship introduced	326	Proconsulate introduced
640	Ancus Marcius	494	Plebeian Tribunate created	311	Naval Duumvirate elected
616	L. Tarquinius Priscus	494	Plebeian Aedileship created	217	Dictatorship of Fabius Maximus
578	Servius Tullius	444	Consular Tribunate organized	133	Tribunate of Tiberius Gracchus

123 Tribunate of Gaius Gracchus	238 Gordianus I and Gordianus II;
82 Dictatorship of Sulla	Pupienus and Balbinus
60 First Triumvirate formed	238 Gordianus III
(Caesar, Pompeius, Crassus)	244 Philippus (the Arabian)
46 Dictatorship of Caesar	249 Decius
43 Second Triumvirate formed	251 Gallus and Volusianus
(Octavianus, Antonius, Lepidus)	253 Aemilianus
The Empire	253 Valerianus and Gallienus
27 Augustus (Gaius Julius	258 Gallienus (alone)
Caesar Octavianus)	268 Claudius II (the Goth)
AD	270 Quintillus
	270 Aurelianus
14 Tiberius I	275 Tacitus
37 Gaius Caesar (Caligula)	276 Florianus
41 Claudius I	276 Probus
54 Nero	282 Carus
68 Galba	283 Carinus and Numerianus
69 Galba; Otho, Vitellius	284 Diocletianus
69 Vespasianus	286 Diocletianus and Maximianus
79 Titus	305 Galerius and Constantius I
81 Domitianus	306 Galerius, Maximinus II, Severus I
96 Nerva	307 Galerius, Maximinus
98 Trajanus	II, Constantinus I, Licinius,
117 Hadrianus	Maxentius
138 Antoninus Pius	311 Maximinus II, Constantinus I,
161 Marcus Aurelius and Lucius Verus	Licinius, Maxentius
169 Marcus Aurelius (alone)	314 Maximinus II, Constantinus I,
180 Commodus	Licinius
193 Pertinax; Julianus I	314 Constantinus I and Licinius
193 Septimius Severus	324 Constantinus I (the Great)
211 Caracalla and Geta	337 Constantinus II, Constans I,
212 Caracalla (alone)	Constantius II
217 Macrinus	340 Constantius II and Constans I
218 Elagabalus (Heliogabalus)	350 Constantius II
222 Alexander Severus	361 Julianus II (the Apostate)
235 Maximinus I (the Thracian)	363 Jovianus

West (Rome) and East (Constantinople)

364 Valentinianus I (West) and Valens (East)
367 Valentinianus I with Gratianus (West) and Valens (East)
375 Gratianus with Valentinianus II (West) and Valens (East)
378 Gratianus with Valentinianus II (West) Theodosius I (East)
383 Valentinianus II (West) and Theodosius I (East)
394 Theodosius I (the Great)
395 Honorius (West) and Arcadius (East)
408 Honorius (West) and Theodosius II (East)
423 Valentinianus III (West) and Theodosius II (East)
450 Valentinianus III (West) and Marcianus (East)
455 Maximus (West); Avitus (West); Marcianus (East)
456 Avitus (West), Marcianus (East)
457 Majorianus (West), Leo I (East)
461 Severus II (West), Leo I (East)
467 Anthemius (West), Leo I (East)
472 Olybrius (West), Leo I (East)
473 Glycerius (West), Leo I (East)
474 Julius Nepos (West), Leo II (East)
475 Romulus Augustulus (West) and Zeno (East)
476 End of Empire in West; Odovacar, King, drops title of Emperor; murdered by King Theodoric of Ostrogoths 493 AD

Rulers of Modern Italy

After the fall of Napoleon in 1814, the Congress of Vienna, 1815, restored Italy as a political patchwork, comprising the Kingdom of Naples and Sicily, the Papal States, and smaller units. Piedmont and Genoa were awarded to Sardinia, ruled by King Victor Emmanuel I of Savoy.

United Italy emerged under the leadership of Camillo, Count di Cavour (1810-1861), Sardinian prime minister. Agitation was led by Giuseppe Mazzini (1805-1872) and Giuseppe Garibaldi (1807-1882), soldier, Victor Emmanuel I abdicated 1821. After a brief regency for a brother, Charles Albert was King 1831-1849, abdicating when defeated by the Austrians at Novara. Succeeded by Victor Emmanuel II, 1849-1861.

In 1859 France forced Austria to cede Lombardy to Sardinia, which gave rights to Savoy and Nice to France. In 1860 Garibaldi led 1,000 volunteers in a spectacular campaign, took Sicily and expelled the King of Naples. In 1860 the House of Savoy annexed Tuscany, Parma, Modena, Romagna, the Two Sicilies, the Marches, and Umbria. Victor Emmanuel assumed the title of King

of Italy at Turin Mar. 17, 1861. In 1866 he allied with Prussia in the Austro-Prussian War, with Prussia's victory received Venetia. On Sept. 20, 1870, his troops under Gen. Raffaele Cadorna entered Rome and took over the Papal States, ending the temporal power of the Roman Catholic Church.

Succession: Umberto I; 1878, assassinated 1900; Victor Emmanuel III, 1900, abdicated 1946, died 1947; Umberto II, 1946, ruled a month. In 1921 Benito Mussolini (1883-1945) formed the Fascist party and became prime minister Oct. 31, 1922. He made the King Emperor of Ethiopia, 1937; entered World War II as ally of Hitler. He was deposed July 25, 1943.

At a plebiscite June 2, 1946, Italy voted for a republic; Premier Alcide de Gasperi became chief of state June 13, 1946. On June 28, 1946, the Constituent Assembly elected Enrico de Nicola, Liberal, provisional president. Successive presidents: Luigi Einaudi, elected May 11, 1948, Giovanni Gronchi, Apr. 29, 1955; Antonio Segni, May 6, 1962; Giuseppe Saragat, Dec. 29, 1964; Giovanni Leone, Dec. 29, 1971; Alessandro Pertini, July 9, 1978.

Rulers of Spain

From 8th to 11th centuries Spain was dominated by the Moors (Arabs and Berbers). The Christian reconquest established small competing kingdoms of the Asturias, Aragon, Castile, Catalonia, Leon, Navarre, and Valencia. In 1474 Isabella (Isabel), b. 1451, became Queen of Castile & Leon. Her husband, Ferdinand, b. 1452, inherited Aragon 1479, with Catalonia, Valencia, and the Balearic Islands, became Ferdinand V of Castile. By Isabella's request Pope Sixtus IV established the Inquisition, 1478. Last Moorish kingdom, Granada, fell 1492. Columbus opened New World of colonies, 1492. Isabella died 1504, succeeded by her daughter, Juana "the Mad," but Ferdinand ruled until his death 1516.

Charles I, b. 1500, son of Juana and grandson of Ferdinand and Isabella, and of Maximilian I of Hapsburg; succeeded later as Holy Roman Emperor, Charles V, 1520; abdicated 1556. Philip II, son, 1556-1598, inherited only Spanish throne; conquered Portugal, fought Turks, persecuted non-Catholics, sent Armada against England. Was briefly married to Mary I of England, 1554-1558. Succession: Philip III, 1598-1621; Philip IV, 1621-1665; Charles II, 1665-1700, left Spain to Philip of Anjou, grandson of Louis XIV, who as Philip V, 1700-1746, founded Bourbon dynasty. Ferdinand VI, 1746-1759; Charles III, 1759-1788; Charles IV, 1788-1808, abdicated.

Napoleon now dominated politics and made his brother Joseph King of Spain 1808, but the Spanish ousted him finally in 1813. Ferdinand VII, 1808, 1814-1833, lost American colonies; succeeded by daughter Isabella II, aged 3, with wife Maria Christina of Na-

ples until regent until 1843. Isabella deposed by revolution 1868. Elected king by the Cortes, Amadeo of Savoy, 1870; abdicated 1873. First republic, 1873-1874. Alphonso XII, son of Isabella, 1875-1885. His posthumous son was Alphonso XIII, with his mother, Queen Maria Christina regent; Spanish-American war, Spain lost Cuba, gave up Puerto Rico, Philippines, Sulu Is., Marianas. Alphonso took throne 1902, aged 16, married British Princess Victoria Eugenia of Battenberg. The dictatorship of Primo de Rivera, 1923-30, precipitated the revolution of 1931. Alphonso agreed to leave without formal abdication. The monarchy was abolished and the second republic established, with strong socialist backing. Presidents were Niceto Alcala Zamora, to 1936, when Manuel Azaña was chosen.

In July, 1936, the army in Morocco revolted against the government and General Francisco Franco led the troops into Spain. The revolution succeeded by Feb., 1939, when Azaña resigned. Franco became chief of state, with provisions that if he was incapacitated the Regency Council by two-thirds vote may propose a king to the Cortes, which must have a two-thirds majority to elect him.

Alphonso XIII died in Rome Feb. 28, 1941, aged 54. His property and citizenship had been restored.

A succession law restoring the monarchy was approved in a 1947 referendum. Prince Juan Carlos, son of the pretender to the throne, was designated by Franco and the Cortes in 1969 as the future king and chief of state. Upon Franco's death, Nov. 20, 1975, Juan Carlos was proclaimed king, Nov. 22, 1975.

Leaders in the South American Wars of Liberation

Simon Bolivar (1783-1830), Jose Francisco de San Martin (1778-1850), and Francisco Antonio Gabriel Miranda (1750-1816), are among the heroes of the early 19th century struggles of South American nations to free themselves from Spain. All three, and their contemporaries, operated in periods of intense factional strife, during which soldiers and civilians suffered.

Miranda, a Venezuelan, who had served with the French in the American Revolution and commanded parts of the French Revolutionary armies in the Netherlands, attempted to start a revolt in Venezuela in 1806 and failed. In 1810, with British and American backing, he returned and was briefly a dictator, until the British withdrew their support. In 1812 he was overcome by the royalists in Venezuela and taken prisoner, dying in a Spanish prison in 1816.

San Martin was born in Argentina and during 1789-1811 served in campaigns of the Spanish armies in Europe and Africa. He first joined the independence movement in Argentina in 1812 and then in 1817 invaded Chile with 4,000 men over the high mountain passes. Here he and General Bernardo O'Higgins (1778-1842) defeated the Spaniards at Chacabuco, 1817, and O'Higgins was named Liberator and became first director of Chile, 1817-1823. In 1821 San Martin occupied Lima and Callao, Peru, and became protector of Peru.

Bolivar, the greatest leader of South American liberation from Spain, was born in Venezuela, the son of an aristocratic family. His organizing and administrative abilities were superior and he foresaw many of the political difficulties of the future. He first served under Miranda in 1812 and in 1813 captured Caracas, where he was named Liberator. Forced out next year by civil strife, he led a campaign that captured Bogota in 1814. In 1817 he was again in control of Venezuela and was named dictator. He organized Nueva Granada with the help of General Francisco de Paula Santander (1792-1840). By joining Nueva Granada, Venezuela, and the present terrain of Panama and Ecuador, the republic of Colombia was formed with Bolivar president. After numerous setbacks he decisively defeated the Spaniards in the second battle of Carabobo, Venezuela, June 24, 1821.

In May, 1822, Gen. Antonio Jose de Sucre, Bolivar's trusted lieutenant, took Quito. Bolivar went to Guayaquil to confer with San Martin, who resigned as protector of Peru and withdrew from politics. With a new army of Colombians and Peruvians Bolivar defeated the Spaniards in a saber battle at Junín in 1824 and cleared Peru.

De Sucre organized Charcas (Upper Peru) as Republica Bolivar (now Bolivia) and acted as president in place of Bolivar, who wrote its constitution. De Sucre defeated the Spanish faction of Peru at Ayacucho, Dec. 19, 1824.

Continued civil strife finally caused the Colombian federation to break apart. Santander turned against Bolivar, but the latter defeated him and banished him. In 1828 Bolivar gave up the presidency he had held precariously for 14 years. He became ill from tuberculosis and died Dec. 17, 1830. He was honored as the great liberator and is buried in the national pantheon in Caracas.

Rulers of Russia; Premiers of the USSR

First ruler to consolidate Slavic tribes was Rurik, leader of the Russians who established himself at Novgorod, 862 A.D. He and his immediate successors had Scandinavian affiliations. They moved to Kiev after 972 AD and ruled as Dukes of Kiev. In 988 Vladimir was converted and adopted the Byzantine Greek Orthodox service, later modified by Slav influences. Important as organizer and lawgiver was Yaroslav, 1019-1054, whose daughters married kings of Norway, Hungary, and France. His grandson, Vladimir II (Monomakh), 1113-1125, was progenitor of several rulers, but in 1169 Andrew Bogolubski overthrew Kiev and began the line known as Grand Dukes of Vladimir.

Of the Grand Dukes of Vladimir, Alexander Nevsky, 1246-1263, had a son, Daniel, first to be called Duke of Muscovy (Moscow) who ruled 1294-1303. His successors became Grand Dukes of Muscovy. After Dmitri III Donskoi defeated the Tartars in 1380, they also became Grand Dukes of all Russia. Independence of the Tartars and considerable territorial expansion were achieved under Ivan III, 1462-1505.

Tsars of Muscovy—Ivan III was referred to in church ritual as Tsar. He married Sofia, niece of the last Byzantine emperor. His successor, Basil III, died in 1533 when Basil's son Ivan was only 3. He became Ivan IV, "the Terrible"; crowned 1547 as Tsar of all the Russias, ruled till 1584. Under the weak rule of his son, Feodor I, 1584-1598, Boris Godunov had control. The dynasty died, and after years of tribal strife and intervention by Polish and Swedish armies, the Russians united under 17-year-old Michael Romanov, distantly related to the first wife of Ivan IV. He ruled 1613-1645 and established the Romanov line. Fourth ruler after Michael was Peter I.

Tsars, or Emperors of Russia (Romanov)—Peter I, 1682-1725, known as Peter the Great, took title of Emperor in 1721. His successors and dates of accession were: Catherine, his widow, 1725; Peter II, his grandson, 1727-1730; Anne, Duchess of Courland, 1730, daughter of Peter the Great's brother, Tsar Ivan V; Ivan VI, 1740-1741, great-grandson of Ivan V, child, kept in prison and murdered 1764; Elizabeth, daughter of Peter I, 1741; Peter III, grandson of Peter I, 1761, deposed 1762 for his consort, Catherine II, former princess of Anhalt Zerbst (Germany) who is known as Catherine the Great, 1762-1796; Paul I, her son, 1796, killed 1801; Alexander I, son of Paul, 1801-1825, defeated Napoleon; Nicholas I, his brother, 1825; Alexander II, son of Nicholas, 1855, assassinated 1881 by terrorists; Alexander III, son, 1881-1894.

Nicholas II, son, 1894-1917, last Tsar of Russia, was forced to abdicate by the Revolution that followed losses to Germany in WWI. The Tsar, the Empress, the Tsesarevich (Crown Prince) and the Tsar's 4 daughters were murdered by the Bolsheviks in Ekaterinburg, July 16, 1918.

Provisional Government—Prince Georgi Lvov and Alexander Kerensky, premiers, 1917.

Union of Soviet Socialist Republics

Bolshevik Revolution, Nov. 7, 1917, displaced Kerensky; council of People's Commissars formed, Lenin (Vladimir Ilyich Ulyanov), premier. Lenin died Jan. 21, 1924. Aleksei Rykov (executed 1938) and V. M. Molotov held the office, but actual ruler was Joseph Stalin (Joseph Vissarionovich Djugashvili), general secretary of the Central Committee of the Communist Party. Stalin became president of the Council of Ministers (premier) May 7, 1941, died Mar. 5, 1953. Succeeded by Georgi M. Malenkov, as head of the Council and premier and Nikita S. Khrushchev, first secretary of the Central Committee. Malenkov resigned Feb. 8, 1955, became deputy premier, was dropped July 3, 1957. Marshal Nikolai A. Bulganin became premier Feb. 8, 1955; was demoted and Khrushchev became premier Mar. 27 1958. Khrushchev was ousted Oct. 14-15, 1964, replaced by Leonid I. Brezhnev as first secretary of the party and by Aleksei N. Kosygin as premier. On June 16, 1977, Brezhnev took office as president. Brezhnev died Nov. 10, 1982; 2 days later the Central Committee unanimously elected former KGB head Yuri V. Andropov president. Andropov died Feb. 9, 1984; on Feb. 13, Konstantin U. Chernenko was chosen by Central Committee to succeed Andropov as its general secretary.

Governments of China

(Until 221 BC and frequently thereafter, China was not a unified state. Where dynastic dates overlap, the rulers or events referred to appeared in different areas of China.)

Hsia	c1994BC	-	c1523BC	ture; capital: Sian)	618	-	906
Shang	c1523	-	c1028	Five Dynasties (Yellow River basin)	902	-	960
Western Chou	c1027	-	770	Ten Kingdoms (southern China)	907	-	979
Eastern Chou	770	-	256	Liao (Khitan Mongols; capital: Peking)	947	-	1125
Warring States	403	-	222			
Ch'in (first unified empire)	221	-	206	Sung	960	-	1279
Han	202BC	-	220AD	Northern Sung (reunified central and southern China)	960	-	1126
Western Han (expanded Chinese state beyond the Yellow and Yangtze River valleys)	202BC	-	9AD	Western Hsai (non-Chinese rulers in northwest)	990	-	1227
Hsin (Wang Mang, usurper)	9AD	-	23AD	Chin (Tartars; drove Sung out of central China)	1115	-	1234
Eastern Han (expanded Chinese state into Indo-China and Turkestan)	25	-	220	Yuan (Mongols; Kublai Khan made Peking his capital in 1267)	1271	-	1368
Three Kingdoms (Wei, Shu, Wu)	220	-	265	Ming (China reunified under Chinese rule; capital: Nanking, then Peking in 1420)	1368	-	1644
Chin (western)	265	-	317			
(eastern)	317	-	420	Ch'ing (Manchus, descendents of Tartars)	1644	-	1911
Northern Dynasties (followed several short-lived governments by Turks, Mongols, etc.)	386	-	581	Republic (disunity; provincial rulers, warlords)	1912	-	1949
Southern Dynasties (capital: Nanking)	420	-	589	People's Republic of China (Nationalist China established on Taiwan)	1949	-	—
Sui (reunified China)	581	-	618			
Tang (a golden age of Chinese cul-						

Chronological List of Popes

Source: Annuario Pontificio. Table lists year of accession of each Pope.

The Roman Catholic Church names the Apostle Peter as founder of the Church in Rome. He arrived there c. 42, was martyred there c. 67, and raised to sainthood.

The Pope's temporal title is: Sovereign of the State of Vatican City.

The Pope's spiritual titles are: Bishop of Rome, Vicar of Jesus Christ, Successor of St. Peter, Prince of the Apostles, Supreme Pontiff of the Universal Church, Patriarch of the West, Primate of Italy, Archbishop and Metropolitan of the Roman Province.

Anti-Popes are in *Italics*. Anti-Popes were illegitimate claimants of or pretenders to the papal throne.

Year	Name of Pope	Year	Name of Pope	Year	Name of Pope	Year	Name of Pope
See above.	St. Peter	615	St. Deusdedit	974	Benedict VII	1305	Clement V
67	St. Linus		or Adeodatus	983	John XIV	1316	John XXII
76	St. Anacletus	619	Boniface V	985	John XV	*1328*	*Nicholas V*
	or Cletus	625	Honorius I	996	Gregory V	1334	Benedict XII
88	St. Clement I	640	Severinus	*997*	*John XVI*	1342	Clement VI
97	St. Evaristus	640	John IV	999	Sylvester II	1352	Innocent VI
105	St. Alexander I	642	Theodore I	1003	John XVII	1362	Bl. Urban V
115	St. Sixtus I	649	St. Martin I, Martyr	1004	John XVIII	1370	Gregory XI
125	St. Telesphorus	654	St. Eugene I	1009	Sergius IV	1378	Urban VI
136	St. Hyginus	657	St. Vitalian	1012	Benedict VIII	*1378*	*Clement VII*
140	St. Pius I	672	Adeodatus II	*1012*	*Gregory*	1389	Boniface IX
155	St. Anicetus	676	Donus	1024	John XIX	*1394*	*Benedict XIII*
166	St. Soter	678	St. Agatho	1032	Benedict IX	1404	Innocent VII
175	St. Eleutherius	682	St. Leo II	1045	Sylvester III	1406	Gregory XII
189	St. Victor I	684	St. Benedict II	1045	Benedict IX	*1409*	*Alexander V*
199	St. Zephyrinus	685	John V	1045	Gregory VI	*1410*	*John XXIII*
217	St. Callistus I	686	Conon	1046	Clement II	1417	Martin V
217	*St. Hippolytus*	*687*	*Theodore*	1047	Benedict IX	1431	Eugene IV
222	St. Urban I	*687*	*Paschal*	1048	Damasus II	*1439*	*Felix V*
230	St. Pontian	687	St. Sergius I	1049	St. Leo IX	1447	Nicholas V
235	St. Anterus	701	John VI	1055	Victor II	1455	Callistus III
236	St. Fabian	705	John VII	1057	Stephen IX (X)	1458	Pius II
251	St. Cornelius	708	Sisinnius	*1058*	*Benedict X*	1464	Paul II
251	*Novatian*	708	Constantine	1059	Nicholas II	1471	Sixtus IV
253	St. Lucius I	715	St. Gregory II	1061	Alexander II	1484	Innocent VIII
254	St. Stephen I	731	St. Gregory III	*1061*	*Honorius II*	1492	Alexander VI
257	St. Sixtus II	741	St. Zachary	1073	St. Gregory VII	1503	Pius III
259	St. Dionysius	752	Stephen II (III)	*1080*	*Clement III*	1503	Julius II
269	St. Felix I	757	St. Paul I	1086	Bl. Victor III	1513	Leo X
275	St. Eutychian	*767*	*Constantine*	1088	Bl. Urban II	1522	Adrian VI
283	St. Caius	*768*	*Philip*	1099	Paschal II	1523	Clement VII
296	St. Marcellinus	768	Stephen III (IV)	*1100*	*Theodoric*	1534	Paul III
308	St. Marcellus I	772	Adrian I	*1102*	*Albert*	1550	Julius III
309	St. Eusebius	795	St. Leo III	*1105*	*Sylvester IV*	1555	Marcellus II
311	St. Melchiades	816	Stephen IV (V)	1118	Gelasius II	1555	Paul IV
314	St. Sylvester I	817	St. Paschal I	*1118*	*Gregory VIII*	1559	Pius IV
336	St. Marcus	824	Eugene II	1119	Callistus II	1566	St. Pius V
337	St. Julius I	827	Valentine	1124	Honorius II	1572	Gregory XIII
352	Liberius	827	Gregory IV	*1124*	*Celestine II*	1585	Sixtus V
355	*Felix II*	*844*	*John*	1130	Innocent II	1590	Urban VII
366	St. Damasus I	844	Sergius II	*1130*	*Anacletus II*	1590	Gregory XIV
366	*Ursinus*	847	St. Leo IV	*1138*	*Victor IV*	1591	Innocent IX
384	St. Siricius	855	Benedict III	1143	Celestine II	1592	Clement VIII
399	St. Anastasius I	*855*	*Anastasius*	1144	Lucius II	1605	Leo XI
401	St. Innocent I	858	St. Nicholas I	1145	Bl. Eugene III	1605	Paul V
417	St. Zosimus	867	Adrian II	1153	Anastasius IV	1621	Gregory XV
418	St. Boniface I	872	John VIII	1154	Adrian IV	1623	Urban VIII
418	*Eulalius*	882	Marinus I	1159	Alexander III	1644	Innocent X
422	St. Celestine I	884	St. Adrian III	*1159*	*Victor IV*	1655	Alexander VII
432	St. Sixtus III	885	Stephen V (VI)	*1164*	*Paschal III*	1667	Clement IX
440	St. Leo I	891	Formosus	*1168*	*Callistus III*	1670	Clement X
461	St. Hilary	896	Boniface VI	*1179*	*Innocent III*	1676	Bl. Innocent XI
468	St. Simplicius	896	Stephen VI (VII)	1181	Lucius III	1689	Alexander VIII
483	St. Felix III (II)	897	Romanus	1185	Urban III	1691	Innocent XII
492	St. Gelasius I	897	Theodore II	1187	Gregory VIII	1700	Clement XI
496	Anastasius II	898	John IX	1187	Clement III	1721	Innocent XIII
498	St. Symmachus	900	Benedict IV	1191	Celestine III	1724	Benedict XIII
498	*Lawrence*	903	Leo V	1198	Innocent III	1730	Clement XII
	(501-505)	*903*	*Christopher*	1216	Honorius III	1740	Benedict XIV
514	St. Hormisdas	904	Sergius III	1227	Gregory IX	1758	Clement XIII
523	St. John I, Martyr	911	Anastasius III	1241	Celestine IV	1769	Clement XIV
526	St. Felix IV (III)	913	Landus	1243	Innocent IV	1775	Pius VI
530	Boniface II	914	John X	1254	Alexander IV	1800	Pius VII
530	*Dioscorus*	928	Leo VI	1261	Urban IV	1823	Leo XII
533	John II	928	Stephen VII (VIII)	1265	Clement IV	1829	Pius VIII
535	St. Agapitus I	931	John XI	1271	Bl. Gregory X	1831	Gregory XVI
536	St. Silverius, Martyr	936	Leo VII	1276	Bl. Innocent V	1846	Pius IX
537	Vigilius	939	Stephen VIII (IX)	1276	Adrian V	1878	Leo XIII
556	Pelagius I	942	Marinus II	1276	John XXI	1903	St. Pius X
561	John III	946	Agapitus II	1277	Nicholas III	1914	Benedict XV
575	Benedict I	955	John XII	1281	Martin IV	1922	Pius XI
579	Pelagius II	963	Leo VIII	1285	Honorius IV	1939	Pius XII
590	St. Gregory I	964	Benedict V	1288	Nicholas IV	1958	John XXIII
604	Sabinian	965	John XIII	1294	St. Celestine V	1963	Paul VI
607	Boniface III	973	Benedict VI	1294	Boniface VIII	1978	John Paul I
608	St. Boniface IV	*974*	*Boniface VII*	1303	Bl. Benedict XI	1978	John Paul II

WORLD FACTS
Early Explorers of the Western Hemisphere

The first men to discover the New World or Western Hemisphere are believed to have walked across a "land bridge" from Siberia to Alaska, an isthmus since broken by the Bering Strait. From Alaska, these ancestors of the Indians spread through North, Central, and South America. Anthropologists have placed these crossings at between 18,000 and 14,000 B.C.; but evidence found in 1967 near Puebla, Mex., indicates mankind reached there as early as 35,000-40,000 years ago.

At first, these people were hunters using flint weapons and tools. In Mexico, about 7000-6000 B.C., they founded farming cultures, developing corn, squash, etc. Eventually, they created complex civilizations — Olmec, Toltec, Aztec, and Maya and, in South America, Inca. Carbon-14 tests show men lived about 8000 B.C. near what are now Front Royal, Va., Kanawha, W. Va., and Dutchess Quarry, N.Y. The Hopewell Culture, based on farming, flourished about 1000 B.C.; remains of it are seen today in large mounds in Ohio and other states.

Norsemen (Norwegian Vikings sailing out of Iceland and Greenland) are credited by most scholars with being the first Europeans to discover America, with at least 5 voyages around 1000 A.D. to areas they called Helluland, Markland, Vinland—possibly Labrador, Nova Scotia or Newfoundland, and New England.

Christopher Columbus, most famous of the explorers, was born at Genoa, Italy, but made his discoveries sailing for the Spanish rulers Ferdinand and Isabella. Dates of his voyages, places he discovered, and other information follow:

1492—First voyage. Left Palos, Spain, Aug. 3 with 88 men (est.). Discovered San Salvador (Guanahani or Watling Is., Bahamas) Oct. 12. Also Cuba, Hispaniola (Haiti-Dominican Republic); built Fort La Navidad on latter.

1493—Second voyage, first part, Sept. 25, with 17 ships, 1,500 men. Dominica (Lesser Antilles) Nov. 3; Guadeloupe, Montserrat, Antigua, San Martin, Santa Cruz, Puerto Rico, Virgin Islands. Settled Isabela on Hispaniola. **Second part** (Columbus having remained in Western Hemisphere), Jamaica, Isle of Pines, La Mona Is.

1498—Third voyage. Left Spain May 30, 1498, 6 ships. Discovered Trinidad. Saw South American continent Aug. 1, 1498, but called it Isla Sancta (Holy Island). Entered Gulf of Paria and landed, first time on continental soil. At mouth of Orinoco Aug. 14 he decided this was the mainland.

1502—Fourth voyage, 4 caravels, 150 men. St. Lucia, Guanaja off Honduras; Cape Gracias a Dios, Honduras; San Juan River, Costa Rica; Almirante, Portobelo, and Laguna de Chiriqui, Panama.

Year	Explorer	Nationality and employer	Discovery or exploration
1497	John Cabot	Italian-English	Newfoundland or Nova Scotia
1498	John and Sebastian Cabot	Italian-English	Labrador to Hatteras
1499	Alonso de Ojeda	Spanish	South American coast, Venezuela
1500, Feb.	Vicente y Pinzon	Spanish	South American coast, Amazon River
1500, Apr.	Pedro Alvarez Cabral	Portuguese	Brazil (for Portugal)
1500-02	Gaspar Corte-Real	Portuguese	Labrador
1501	Rodrigo de Bastidas	Spanish	Central America
1513	Vasco Nunez de Balboa	Spanish	Pacific Ocean
1513	Juan Ponce de Leon	Spanish	Florida
1515	Juan de Solis	Spanish	Rio de la Plata
1519	Alonso de Pineda	Spanish	Mouth of Mississippi River
1519	Hernando Cortes	Spanish	Mexico
1520	Ferdinand Magellan	Portuguese-Spanish	Straits of Magellan, Tierra del Fuego
1524	Giovanni da Verrazano	Italian-French	Atlantic coast-New York harbor
1532	Francisco Pizarro	Spanish	Peru
1534	Jacques Cartier	French	Canada, Gulf of St. Lawrence
1536	Pedro de Mendoza	Spanish	Buenos Aires
1536	A.N. Cabeza de Vaca	Spanish	Texas coast and interior
1539	Francisco de Ulloa	Spanish	California coast
1539-41	Hernando de Soto	Spanish	Mississippi River near Memphis
1539	Marcos de Niza	Italian-Spanish	Southwest (now U.S.)
1540	Francisco V. de Coronado	Spanish	Southwest (now U.S.)
1540	Hernando Alarcon	Spanish	Colorado River
1540	Garcia de L. Cardenas	Spanish	Grand Canyon of the Colorado
1541	Francisco de Orellana	Spanish	Amazon River
1542	Juan Rodriguez Cabrillo	Portuguese-Spanish	San Diego harbor
1565	Pedro Menendez de Aviles	Spanish	St. Augustine
1576	Martin Frobisher	English	Frobisher's Bay, Canada
1577-80	Francis Drake	English	California coast
1582	Antonio de Espejo	Spanish	Southwest (named New Mexico)
1584	Amadas & Barlow (for Raleigh)	English	Virginia
1585-87	Sir Walter Raleigh's men	English	Roanoke Is., N.C.
1595	Sir Walter Raleigh	English	Orinoco River
1603-09	Samuel de Champlain	French	Canadian interior, Lake Champlain
1607	Capt. John Smith	English	Atlantic coast
1609-10	Henry Hudson	English-Dutch	Hudson River, Hudson Bay
1634	Jean Nicolet	French	Lake Michigan; Wisconsin
1673	Jacques Marquette, Louis Jolliet	French	Mississippi S to Arkansas
1682	Sieur de La Salle	French	Mississippi S to Gulf of Mexico
1789	Alexander Mackenzie	Canadian	Canadian Northwest

Arctic Exploration

Early Explorers

1587 — John Davis (England). Davis Strait to Sanderson's Hope, 72° 12′ N.

1596 — Willem Barents and Jacob van Heemskerck (Holland). Discovered Bear Island, touched northwest tip of Spitsbergen, 79° 49′ N, rounded Novaya Zemlya, wintered at Ice Haven.

1607 — Henry Hudson (England). North along Greenland's east coast to Cape Hold-with-Hope, 73° 30′, then north of Spitsbergen to 80° 23′. Returning he discovered Hudson's Touches (Jan Mayen).

1616 — William Baffin and Robert Bylot (England). Baffin Bay to Smith Sound.

1728 — Vitus Bering (Russia). Proved Asia and America were separated by sailing through strait.

1733-40 — Great Northern Expedition (Russia). Surveyed Siberian Arctic coast.

1741 — Vitus Bering (Russia). Sighted Alaska from sea, named Mount St. Elias. His lieutenant, Chirikof, discovered coast.

1771 — Samuel Hearne (Hudson's Bay Co.). Overland from Prince of Wales Fort (Churchill) on Hudson Bay to mouth of Coppermine River.

1778 — James Cook (Britain). Through Bering Strait to Icy Cape, Alaska, and North Cape, Siberia.

1789 — Alexander Mackenzie (North West Co., Britain). Montreal to mouth of Mackenzie River.

1806 — William Scoresby (Britain). N. of Spitsbergen to 81° 30'.

1820-3 — Ferdinand von Wrangel (Russia). Completed a survey of Siberian Arctic coast. His exploration joined that of James Cook at North Cape, confirming separation of the continents.

1845 — Sir John Franklin (Britain) was one of many to seek the Northwest Passage—an ocean route connecting the Atlantic and Pacific via the Arctic. His 2 ships (the Erebus and Terror) were last seen entering Lancaster Sound July 26.

1888 — Fridtjof Nansen (Norway) crossed Greenland's icecap, 1893-96 — Nansen in Fram drifted from New Siberian Is. to Spitsbergen; tried polar dash in 1895, reached Franz Josef Land.

1896 — Salomon A. Andree (Sweden). In June, made first attempt to reach North Pole by balloon; failed and returned in August. On July 11, 1897, Andree and 2 others started in balloon from Danes, Is., Spitsbergen, to drift across pole to America, and disappeared. Over 33 years later, Aug. 6, 1930, their frozen bodies were found on White Is., 82° 57' N 29° 52' E.

1903-06 — Roald Amundsen (Norway) first sailed Northwest Passage.

Discovery of North Pole

Robert E. Peary explored Greenland's coast 1891-92, tried for North Pole 1893. In 1900 he reached northern limit of Greenland and 83° 50' N; in 1902 he reached 84° 06' N; in 1906 he went from Ellesmere Is. to 87° 06' N. He sailed in the Roosevelt, July, 1908, to winter off Cape Sheridan, Grant Land. The dash for the North Pole began Mar. 1 from Cape Columbia, Ellesmere Land. Peary reached the pole, 90° N, Apr. 6, 1909.

Peary had several supporting groups carrying supplies until the last group turned back at 87° 47' N. Peary, Matthew Henson, and 4 eskimos proceeded with dog teams and sleds. They crossed the pole several times, finally built an igloo at 90°, remained 36 hours. Started south Apr. 7 at 4 p.m. for Cape Columbia. Eskimos were Coqueeh, Ootah, Eginwah, and Seegloo.

1914 — Donald Macmillan (U.S.). Northwest, 200 miles, from Axel Heiberg Island to seek Peary's Crocker Land.

1915-17 — Vihjalmur Stefansson (Canada) discovered Borden, Brock, Meighen, and Lougheed Islands.

1918-20 — Roald Amundsen sailed Northeast Passage.

1925 — Amundsen and Lincoln Ellsworth (U.S.) reached 87° 44' N in attempt to fly to North Pole from Spitsbergen.

1926 — Richard E. Byrd and Floyd Bennett (U.S.) first over North Pole by air, May 9.

1926 — Amundsen, Ellsworth, and Umberto Nobile (Italy) flew from Spitsbergen over North Pole May 12, to Teller, Alaska, in dirigible Norge.

1928 — Nobile crossed North Pole in airship May 24, crashed May 25. Amundsen lost while trying to effect rescue by plane.

North Pole Exploration Records

On Aug. 3, 1958, the Nautilus, under Comdr. William R. Anderson, became the first ship to cross the North Pole beneath the Arctic ice.

The nuclear-powered U.S. submarine Seadragon, Comdr. George P. Steele 2d, made the first east-west underwater transit through the Northwest Passage during August, 1960. It sailed from Portsmouth N.H., headed between Greenland and Labrador through Baffin Bay, then west through Lancaster Sound and McClure Strait to the Beaufort Sea. Traveling submerged for the most part, the submarine made 850 miles from Baffin Bay to the Beaufort Sea in 6 days.

On Aug. 16, 1977, the Soviet nuclear icebreaker Arktika reached the North Pole and became the first surface ship to break through the Arctic ice pack to the top of the world.

On April 30, 1978, Naomi Uemura, a Japanese explorer, became the first man to reach the North Pole alone by dog sled. During the 54-day, 600-mile trek over the frozen Arctic, Uemura survived attacks by a marauding polar bear.

In April, 1982, Sir Ranulph Fiennes and Charles Burton, British explorers, reached the North Pole and became the first to circle the earth from pole to pole. They had reached the South Pole 16 months earlier. The 52,000-mile trek took 3 years, involved 23 people, and cost an estimated $18 million. The expedition was also the first to travel down the Scott Glacier and the first to journey up the Yukon and through the Northwest Passage in a single season.

Antarctic Exploration

Early History

Antarctica has been approached since 1773-75, when Capt. James Cook (Britain) reached 71° 10' S. Many sea and landmarks bear names of early explorers. Bellingshausen (Russia) discovered Peter I and Alexander I Islands, 1819-21. Nathaniel Palmer (U.S.) discovered Palmer Peninsula, 60° W, 1820, without realizing that this was a continent. James Weddell (Britain) found Weddell Sea, 74° 15' S, 1823.

First to announce existence of the continent of Antarctica was Charles Wilkes (U.S.), who followed the coast for 1,500 mi., 1840. Adelie Coast, 140° E, was found by Dumont d'Urville (France), 1840. Ross Ice Shelf was found by James Clark Ross (Britain), 1841-42.

1895 — Leonard Kristensen (Norway) landed a party on the coast of Victoria Land. They were the first ashore on the main continental mass. C.E. Borchgrevink, a member of that party, returned in 1899 with a British expedition, first to winter on Antarctica.

1902-04 — Robert F. Scott (Britain) discovered Edward VII Peninsula. He reached 82° 17' S, 146° 33' E from McMurdo Sound.

1908-09 — Ernest Shackleton (Britain) introduced the use of Manchurian ponies in Antarctic sledging. He reached 88° 23' S, discovering a route on to the plateau by way of the Beardmore Glacier and pioneering the way to the pole.

Discovery of South Pole

1911 — Roald Amundsen (Norway) with 4 men and dog teams reached the pole Dec. 14.

1912 — Capt. Scott reached the pole from Ross Island Jan. 18, with 4 companions. They found Amundsen's tent. None of Scott's party survived. They were found Nov. 12.

1928 — First man to use an airplane over Antarctica was Hubert Wilkins (Britain).

1929 — Richard E. Byrd (U.S.) established Little America on Bay of Whales. On 1,600-mi. airplane flight begun Nov. 28 he crossed South Pole Nov. 29 with 3 others.

1934-35 — Byrd led 2d expedition to Little America, explored 450,000 sq. mi., wintered alone at weather station, 80° 08' S.

1934-37 — John Rymill led British Graham Land expedition; discovered that Palmer Peninsula is part of Antarctic mainland.

1935 — Lincoln Ellsworth (U.S.) flew south along Palmer Peninsula's east coast, then crossed continent to Little America, making 4 landings on unprepared terrain in bad weather.

1939-41 — U.S. Antarctic Service built West Base on Ross Ice Shelf under Paul Siple, and East Base on Palmer Peninsula under Richard Black. U.S. Navy plane flights discovered about 150,000 sq. miles of new land.

1940 — Byrd charted most of coast between Ross Sea and Palmer Peninsula.

1946-47 — U.S. Navy undertook Operation High-jump under Byrd. Expedition included 13 ships and 4,000 men. Airplanes photomapped coastline and penetrated beyond pole.

1946-48 — Ronne Antarctic Research Expedition, Comdr. Finn Ronne, USNR, determined the Antarctic to be only one continent with no strait between Weddell Sea and Ross Sea; discovered 250,000 sq. miles of land by flights to 79° S Lat., and made 14,000 aerial photographs over 450,000 sq. miles of land. Mrs. Ronne and Mrs. H. Darlington were the first women to winter on Antarctica.

1955-57 — U.S. Navy's Operation Deep Freeze led by Adm. Byrd. Supporting U.S. scientific efforts for the International Geophysical Year, the operation was commanded by Rear Adm. George Dufek. It established 5 coastal stations fronting the Indian, Pacific, and Atlantic oceans and also 3 interior stations; explored more than 1,000,000 sq. miles in Wilkes Land.

1957-58 — During the International Geophysical year, July, 1957, through Dec. 1958, scientists from 12 countries conducted ambitious programs of Antarctic research. A network of some 60 stations on the continent and sub-Arctic islands studied oceanography, glaciology, meteorology, seismology, geomagnetism, the ionosphere, cosmic rays, aurora, and airglow.

Dr. V.E. Fuchs led a 12-man Trans-Antarctic Expedition on the first land crossing of Antarctica. Starting from the Weddell Sea, they reached Scott Station Mar. 2, 1958, after traveling 2,158 miles in 98 days.

1958 — A group of 5 U.S. scientists led by Edward C. Thiel, seismologist, moving by tractor from Ellsworth Station on Weddell Sea, identified a huge mountain range, 5,000 ft. above the ice sheet and 9,000 ft. above sea level. The range, originally seen by a Navy plane, was named the Dufek Massif, for Rear Adm. George Dufek.

1959 — Twelve nations — Argentina, Australia, Belgium, Chile, France, Japan, New Zealand, Norway, South Africa, the Soviet Union, the United Kingdom, and the U.S. — signed a treaty suspending any territorial claims for 30 years and reserving the continent for research.

1961-62 — Scientists discovered a trough, the Bentley Trench, running from Ross Ice Shelf, Pacific, into Marie Byrd Land, around the end of the Ellsworth Mtns., toward the Weddell Sea.

1962 — First nuclear power plant began operation at McMurdo Sound.

1963 — On Feb. 22 a U.S. plane made the longest nonstop flight ever made in the S. Pole area, covering 3,600 miles in 10 hours. The flight was from McMurdo Station south past the geographical S. Pole to Shackleton Mtns., southeast to the "Area of Inaccessibility" and back to McMurdo Station.

1964 — A British survey team was landed by helicopter on Cook Island, the first recorded visit since its discovery in 1775.

1964 — New Zealanders completed one of the last and most important surveys when they mapped the mountain area from Cape Adare west some 400 miles to Pennell Glacier.

Notable Active Volcanoes of the World

More than 75 per cent of the world's 850 active volcanoes lie within the "Ring of Fire," a zone running along the west coast of the Americas from Chile to Alaska and down the east coast of Asia from Siberia to New Zealand. Twenty per cent of these volcanoes are located in Indonesia. Other prominent groupings are located in Japan, the Aleutian Islands, and Central America. Almost all active regions are found at the boundaries of the large moving plates which comprise the earth's surface. The "Ring of Fire" marks the boundary between the plates underlying the Pacific Ocean and those underlying the surrounding continents. Other active regions, such as the Mediterranean Sea and Iceland, are located on plate boundaries.

Major Historical Eruptions

Approximately 7,000 years ago, Mazama, a 9,900-feet-high volcano in southern Oregon, erupted violently, ejecting ash and lava. The ash spread over the entire northwestern United States and as far away as Saskatchewan, Canada. During the eruption, the top of the mountain collapsed, leaving a caldera 6 miles across and about a half mile deep, which filled with rain water to form what is now called Crater Lake.

In 79 A.D., Vesuvio, or Vesuvius, a 4,190 feet volcano overlooking Naples Bay became active after several centuries of quiescence. On Aug. 24 of that year, a heated mud and ash flow swept down the mountain engulfing the cities of Pompeii, Herculaneum, and Stabiae with debris over 60 feet deep. About 10 percent of the population of the 3 towns was killed.

The largest eruptions in recent centuries have been in Indonesia. In 1883, an eruption similar to the Mazama eruption occurred on the island of Krakatau. On August 27, the 2,640-feet-high peak of the volcano collapsed to 1,000 feet below sea level, leaving only a small portion of the island standing above the sea. Ash from the eruption colored sunsets around the world for 2 years. A tsunami ("tidal wave") generated by the collapse killed 36,000 people in nearby Java and Sumatra and eventually reached England. A similar, but even more powerful, eruption had taken place 68 years earlier at Tambora volcano on the Indonesian island of Sumbawa.

Name, latest activity	Location	Feet	Name, latest activity	Location	Feet
Africa			Alaid (1972)	Kuril Is.	7,662
			Ulawun (1983)	New Britain	7,532
Cameroon (1982)	Cameroons	13,354	Ngauruhoe (1975)	New Zealand	7,515
Nyirangongo (1977)	Zaire	11,400	Chokai (1974)	Japan	7,300
Nyamuragira (1984)	Zaire	10,028	Galunggung (1982)	Java	7,113
Karthala (1977)	Comoro Is.	8,000	Amburombu (1969)	Indonesia	7,051
Piton de la Fournaise (1983)	Reunion Is.	5,981	Azuma (1978)	Japan	6,700
Erta-Ale (1973)	Ethiopia	1,650	Tangkuban Prahu (1967)	Java	6,637
			Sangeang Api (1966)	Indonesia	6,351
			Nasu (1977)	Japan	6,210
Antarctica			Tiatia (1973)	Kuril Islands	6,013
			Manam (1984)	Papua New	
Erebus (1984)	Ross Island	12,450		Guinea	6,000
Big Ben (1960)	Heard Island	9,007	Soputan (1982)	Indonesia	5,994
Deception Island (1970)	South Shetland		Siau (1976)	Indonesia	5,853
	Islands	1,890	Kelud (1967)	Java	5,679
			Batur (1968)	Bali	5,636
			Ternate (1963)	Indonesia	5,627
			Kirisima (1982)	Japan	5,577
Asia-Oceania			Keli Mutu (1968)	Indonesia	5,460
Klyuchevskaya (1974)	USSR	15,584	Akita Komaga take (1970)	Japan	5,449
Kerintji (1968)	Sumatra	12,467	Gamkonora (1981)	Indonesia	5,364
Rindjani (1966)	Indonesia	12,224	Aso (1981)	Japan	5,223
Semeru (1981)	Java	12,060	Lewotobi Laki-Laki (1968)	Indonesia	5,217
Slamet (1967)	Java	11,247	Lokon-Empung (1970)	Celebes	5,187
Raung (1982)	Java	10,932	Bulusan (1983)	Philippines	5,115
Shiveluch (1964)	USSR	10,771	Sarycheva (1976)	Kuril Islands	4,960
Agung (1964)	Bali	10,308	Me-akan (1966)	Japan	4,931
On-Take (1980)	Japan	10,049	Karkar (1981)	Papua New	
Mayon (1978)	Philippines	9,991		Guinea	4,920
Merapi (1982)	Java	9,551	Karymskaya (1976)	USSR	4,869
Bezymianny (1983)	USSR	9,514	Lopevi (1982)	New Hebrides	4,755
Marapi (1982)	Sumatra	9,485	Ambrym (1979)	New Hebrides	4,376
Ruapehu (1982)	New Zealand	9,175	Awu (1968)	Indonesia	4,350
Asama (1983)	Japan	8,300	Sakurazima (1984)	Japan	3,668
Niigata Yakeyama (1983)	Japan	8,111	Langila (1984)	New Britain	3,586
Yake Dake (1963)	Japan	8,064	Dukono (1971)	Indonesia	3,566

Name, latest activity	Location	Feet
Suwanosezima (1982)	Japan	2,640
O-Sima (1977)	Japan	2,550
Usu (1978)	Japan	2,400
White Island (1984)	New Zealand	1,075
Taal (1977)	Philippines	984

Central America—Caribbean

Name, latest activity	Location	Feet
Acatenango (1972)	Guatemala	12,992
Fuego (1980)	Guatemala	12,582
Santiaguito (Santa Maria) (1983)	Guatemala	12,362
Irazu (1967)	Costa Rica	11,260
Poas (1982)	Costa Rica	8,930
Pacaya (1983)	Guatemala	8,346
Izalco (1966)	El Salvador	7,749
San Miguel (1976)	El Salvador	6,994
Rincon de la Vieja (1968)	Costa Rica	6,234
El Viejo (San Cristobal) (1981)	Nicaragua	5,840
Ometepe (Concepcion) (1982)	Nicaragua	5,106
Arenal (1984)	Costa Rica	5,092
Momotombo (1982)	Nicaragua	4,199
Soufriere (1979)	St. Vincent	4,048
Telica (1982)	Nicaragua	3,409

South America

Name, latest activity	Location	Feet
Lascar (1968)	Chile	19,652
Cotopaxi (1975)	Ecuador	19,347
Tupungatito (1980)	Chile	18,504
Sangay (1976)	Ecuador	17,159
Guagua Pichincha (1982)	Ecuador	15,696
Purace (1977)	Colombia	15,604
Llaima (1979)	Chile	10,239
Villarica (1983)	Chile	9,318
Hudson (1973)	Chile	8,580
Alcedo (1970)	Galapagos Is.	3,599

Mid-Pacific

Name, latest activity	Location	Feet
Mauna Loa (1984)	Hawaii	13,680
Kilauea (1984)	Hawaii	4,077

Mid-Atlantic Ridge

Name, latest activity	Location	Feet
Beerenberg (1970)	Jan Mayen Is.	7,470
Hekla (1981)	Iceland	4,892
Leirhnukur (1975)	Iceland	2,145
Krafla (1981)	Iceland	2,145
Surtsey (1967)	Iceland	568

Europe

Name, latest activity	Location	Feet
Etna (1984)	Italy	11,053
Stromboli (1975)	Italy	3,038

North America

Name, latest activity	Location	Feet
Colima (1983)	Mexico	14,003
Redoubt (1966)	Alaska	10,197
Iliamna (1978)	Alaska	10,092
Mt. St. Helens (1984)	Washington	9,677
Shishaldin (1981)	Aleutian Is.	9,387
Pavlof (1984)	Aleutian Is.	8,215
El Chichon (1983)	Mexico	7,300
Makushin (1980)	Aleutian Is.	6,680
Pogromni (1964)	Aleutian Is.	6,568
Trident 1963)	Alaska	6,010
Great Sitkin (1974)	Aleutian Is.	5,710
Gareloi (1982)	Aleutian Is.	5,334
Akutan (1980)	Aleutian Is.	4,275
Kiska (1969)	Aleutian Is.	4,275
Augustine (1976)	Alaska	3,927
Seguam (1977)	Alaska	3,458

Record Oil Spills

Name, place	Date	Cause	Tons
Ixtoc I oil well, southern Gulf of Mexico	June 3, 1979	Blowout	600,000
Nowruz oil field, Persian Gulf	Feb., 1983	Blowout	600,000(est.)
Atlantic Empress & Aegean Captain, off Trinidad & Tobago	July 19, 1979	Collision	300,000
Castillo de Bellver, off Cape Town, South Africa	Aug. 6, 1983	Fire	250,000
Amoco Cadiz, near Portsall, France	March 16, 1978	Grounding	223,000
Torrey Canyon, off Land's End, England	March 18, 1967	Grounding	119,000
Sea Star, Gulf of Oman	Dec. 19, 1972	Collision	115,000
Urquiola, La Coruna, Spain	May 12, 1976	Grounding	100,000
Hawaiian Patriot, northern Pacific	Feb. 25, 1977	Fire	99,000
Othello, Tralhavet Bay, Sweden	March 20, 1970	Collision	60,000-100,000
Jacob Maersk, Porto do Leixoes, Portugal	Jan. 29, 1975	Grounding	84,000
Wafra, Cape Agulhas, South Africa	Feb. 27, 1971	Grounding	63,000
Epic Colacotroni, Caribbean	May, 1975	Grounding	57,000

Other Notable Oil Spills

Name, place	Date	Cause	Gallons
World Glory, off South Africa	June 13, 1968	Hull failure	13,524,000
Keo, off Massachusetts	Nov. 5, 1969	Hull failure	8,820,000
Storage tank, Sewaren, N.J.	Nov. 4, 1969	Tank rupture	8,400,000
Ekofisk oil field, North Sea	Apr. 22, 1977	Well blowout	8,200,000
Argo Merchant, Nantucket, Mass.	Dec. 15, 1976	Grounding	7,700,000
Pipeline, West Delta, La.	Oct. 15, 1967	Dragging anchor	6,720,000
Tanker off Japan	Nov. 30, 1971	Ship broke in half	6,258,000

Highest and Lowest Continental Altitudes

Source: National Geographic Society, Washington, D.C.

Continent	Highest point	Feet elevation	Lowest point	Feet below sea level
Asia	Mount Everest, Nepal-Tibet	29,028	Dead Sea, Israel-Jordan	1,312
South America . .	Mount Aconcagua, Argentina	22,834	Valdes Peninsula, Argentina	131
North America . .	Mount McKinley, Alaska	20,320	Death Valley, California	282
Africa	Kilimanjaro, Tanzania	19,340	Lake Assal, Djibouti	512
Europe	Mount El'brus, USSR	18,510	Caspian Sea, USSR	92
Antarctica	Vinson Massif	16,864	Unknown	. . . .
Australia.	Mount Kosciusko, New South Wales	7,310	Lake Eyre, South Australia	52

Height of Mount Everest

Mt. Everest was considered to be 29,002 ft. tall when Edmund Hillary and Tenzing Norgay scaled it in 1953. This triangulation figure had been accepted since 1850. In 1954 the Surveyor General of the Republic of India set the height at 29,028 ft., plus or minus 10 ft. because of snow. The National Geographic Society accepts the new figure, but many mountaineering groups still use 29,002 ft.

High Peaks in United States, Canada, Mexico

Name	Place	Feet	Name	Place	Feet	Name	Place	Feet
McKinley	Alas . . .	20,320	Crestone	Col	14,294	Columbia	Col	14,073
Logan	Can	19,850	Lincoln	Col	14,286	Augusta	Alas-Can .	14,070
Citlaltepec (Orizaba)	Mexico. . .	18,700	Grays	Col	14,270	Missouri	Col	14,067
St. Elias	Alas-Can .	18,008	Antero	Col	14,269	Humboldt	Col	14,064
Popocatepetl	Mexico. . .	17,887	Torreys	Col	14,267	Bierstadt	Col	14,060
Foraker	Alas . . .	17,400	Castle	Col	14,265	Sunlight	Col	14,059
Iztaccihuatl	Mexico. . .	17,343	Quandary	Col	14,265	Split	Cal	14,058
Lucania	Can	17,147	Evans	Col	14,264	Nauhcampatepetl		
King	Can	16,971	Longs	Col	14,256	(Cofre de Perote) . .	Mexico. . .	14,049
Steele	Can	16,644	McArthur	Can	14,253	Handies	Col	14,048
Bona.	Alas . . .	16,550	Wilson	Col	14,246	Culebra	Col	14,047
Blackburn	Alas . . .	16,390	White	Cal	14,246	Langley	Cal	14,042
Kennedy	Alas . . .	16,286	North Palisade	Cal	14,242	Lindsey	Col	14,042
Sanford	Alas . . .	16,237	Shavano	Col	14,229	Middle Palisade . .	Cal	14,040
South Buttress	Alas . . .	15,885	Belford	Col	14,197	Little Bear.	Col	14,037
Wood	Can	15,885	Princeton	Col	14,197	Sherman	Col	14,036
Vancouver	Alas-Can .	15,700	Crestone Needle. . .	Col	14,197	Redcloud	Col	14,034
Churchill	Alas . . .	15,638	Yale	Col	14,196	Tyndall	Cal	14,018
Fairweather.	Alas-Can .	15,300	Bross	Col	14,172	Pyramid	Col	14,018
Zinantecatl (Toluca) .	Mexico. . .	15,016	Kit Carson	Col	14,165	Wilson Peak	Col	14,017
Hubbard	Alas-Can .	15,015	Wrangell	Alas . . .	14,163	Muir	Cal	14,015
Bear.	Alas . . .	14,831	Shasta	Cal	14,162	Wetterhorn	Col	14,015
Walsh	Can	14,780	Sill	Cal	14,162	North Maroon	Col	14,014
East Buttress	Alas . . .	14,730	El Diente	Col	14,159	San Luis	Col	14,014
Matlalcueyetl	Mexico. . .	14,636	Maroon	Col	14,156	Huron	Col	14,005
Hunter.	Alas . . .	14,573	Tabeguache	Col	14,155	Holy Cross	Col	14,005
Alverstone	Alas-Can .	14,565	Oxford	Col	14,153	Colima	Mexico. . .	14,003
Browne Tower	Alas . . .	14,530	Sneffels	Col	14,150	Sunshine	Col	14,001
Whitney	Cal . . .	14,494	Point Success	Wash . . .	14,150	Grizzly.	Col	14,000
Elbert	Col	14,433	Democrat	Col	14,148	Barnard	Cal	13,990
Massive	Col	14,421	Capitol	Col	14,130	Stewart	Col	13,980
Harvard	Col	14,420	Liberty Cap	Wash . . .	14,112	Keith.	Cal	13,977
Rainier	Wash . . .	14,410	Pikes Peak	Col	14,110	Ouray	Col	13,971
Williamson	Cal	14,375	Snowmass	Col	14,092	Le Conte	Cal	13,960
Blanca.	Col	14,345	Windom	Col	14,087	Meeker	Col	13,911
La Plata.	Col	14,336	Russell	Cal	14,086	Kennedy	Can	13,905
Uncompahgre	Col	14,309	Eolus	Col	14,084			

South America

Peak, Country	Feet	Peak, Country	Feet	Peak, Country	Feet
Aconcagua, Argentina	22,834	Laudo, Argentina	20,997	Polleras, Argentina	20,456
Ojos del Salado, Arg.-Chile . .	22,572	Ancohuma, Bolivia	20,958	Pular, Chile	20,423
Bonete, Argentina	22,546	Ausangate, Peru	20,945	Chani, Argentina	20,341
Tupungato, Argentina-Chile . .	22,310	Toro, Argentina-Chile	20,932	Aucanquilcha, Chile.	20,295
Pissis, Argentina.	22,241	Illampu, Bolivia	20,873	Juncal, Argentina-Chile.	20,276
Mercedario, Argentina	22,211	Tres Cruces, Argentina-Chile .	20,853	Negro, Argentina	20,184
Huascaran, Peru	22,205	Huandoy, Peru	20,852	Quela, Argentina	20,128
Llullaillaco, Argentina-Chile . .	22,057	Parinacota, Bolivia-Chile	20,768	Condoriri, Bolivia	20,095
El Libertador, Argentina	22,047	Tortolas, Argentina-Chile. . . .	20,745	Palermo, Argentina	20,079
Cachi, Argentina.	22,047	Ampato, Peru	20,702	Solimana, Peru	20,068
Yerupaja, Peru	21,709	Condor, Argentina.	20,669	San Juan, Argentina-Chile . . .	20,049
Galan, Argentina	21,654	Salcantay, Peru.	20,574	Sierra Nevada, Arg.-Chile . . .	20,023
El Muerto, Argentina-Chile . .	21,457	Chimborazo, Ecuador	20,561	Antofalla, Argentina.	20,013
Sajama, Bolivia	21,391	Huancarhuas, Peru	20,531	Marmolejo, Argentina-Chile . .	20,013
Nacimiento, Argentina	21,302	Famatina, Argentina	20,505	Chachani, Peru	19,931
Illimani, Bolivia.	21,201	Pumasillo, Peru	20,492	Licancabur, Argentina-Chile . .	19,425
Coropuna, Peru	21,083	Solo, Argentina	20,492		

The highest point in the West Indies is in the Dominican Republic, Pico Duarte (10,417 ft.)

Africa, Australia, and Oceania

Peak, country	Feet	Peak, country	Feet	Peak, country	Feet
Kilimanjaro, Tanzania	19,340	Meru, Tanzania	14,979	Toubkal, Morocco	13,665
Kenya, Kenya	17,058	Wilhelm, New Guinea	14,793	Kinabalu, Malaysia	13,455
Margherita Pk., Uganda-Zaire	16,763	Karisimbi, Zaire-Rwanda	14,787	Kerinci, Sumatra	12,467
Jaja, New Guinea	16,500	Elgon, Kenya-Uganda	14,178	Cook, New Zealand	12,349
Trikora, New Guinea	15,585	Batu, Ethiopia	14,131	Teide, Canary Islands	12,198
Mandala, New Guinea	15,420	Guna, Ethiopia	13,881	Semeru, Java	12,060
Ras Dashan, Ethiopia	15,158	Gughe, Ethiopia	13,780	Kosciusko, Australia	7,310

Europe

Peak, country	Feet	Peak, county	Feet	Peak, country	Feet
Alps		Breithorn, It., Switz.	13,665	Eiger, Switz.	13,025
		Bishorn, Switz.	13,645	Jagerhorn, Switz.	13,024
Mont Blanc, Fr. It.	15,771	Jungfrau, Switz.	13,642	Rottalhorn, Switz.	13,022
Monte Rosa (highest peak of group), Switz.	15,203	Ecrins, Fr.	13,461		
Dom, Switz.	14,911	Monch, Switz.	13,448		
Liskamm, It., Switz.	14,852	Pollux, Switz.	13,422	**Pyrenees**	
Weisshom, Switz.	14,780	Schreckhorn, Switz.	13,379		
Taschhorn, Switz.	14,733	Ober Gabelhorn, Switz.	13,330	Aneto, Sp.	11,168
Matterhorn, It., Switz.	14,690	Gran Paradiso, It.	13,323	Posets, Sp.	11,073
Dent Blanche, Switz.	14,293	Bernina, It., Switz.	13,284	Perdido, Sp.	11,007
Nadelhorn, Switz.	14,196	Fiescherhorn, Switz.	13,283	Vignemale, Fr., Sp.	10,820
Grand Combin, Switz.	14,154	Grunhorn, Switz.	13,266	Long, Sp.	10,479
Lenzpitze, Switz.	14,088	Lauteraarhorn, Switz.	13,261	Estats, Sp.	10,304
Finsteraarhorn, Switz.	14,022	Durrenhorn, Switz.	13,238	Montcalm, Sp.	10,105
Castor, Switz.	13,865	Allalinhorn, Switz.	13,213		
Zinalrothorn, Switz.	13,849	Weissmies, Switz.	13,199	**Caucasus (Europe-Asia)**	
Hohberghorn, Switz.	13,842	Lagginhorn, Switz.	13,156		
Alphubel, Switz.	13,799	Zupo, Switz.	13,120	El'brus, USSR	18,510
Rimpfischhorn, Switz.	13,776	Fletschhorn, Switz.	13,110	Shkara, USSR	17,064
Aletschorn, Switz.	13,763	Adlerhorn, Switz.	13,081	Dykh Tau, USSR	17,054
Strahlhorn, Switz.	13,747	Gletscherhorn, Switz.	13,068	Kashtan Tau, USSR	16,877
Dent D'Herens, Switz.	13,686	Schalihorn, Switz.	13,040	Dzhangi Tau, USSR	16,565
		Scerscen, Switz.	13,028	Kazbek, USSR	16,558

Asia

Peak	Country	Feet	Peak	Country	Feet	Peak	Country	Feet
Everest	Nepal-Tibet.	29,028	Kungur	Sinkiang	25,325	Badrinath	India	23,420
K2 (Godwin Austen)	Kashmir	28,250	Tirich Mir	Pakistan	25,230	Nunkun	Kashmir	23,410
Kanchenjunga	India-Nepal	28,208	Makalu II	Nepal-Tibet.	25,120	Lenina Peak	USSR	23,405
Lhotse I (Everest)	Nepal-Tibet.	27,923	Minya Konka	China	24,900	Pyramid	India-Nepal	23,400
Makalu I	Nepal-Tibet.	27,824	Kula Gangri	Bhutan-Tibet	24,784	Api	Nepal	23,399
Lhotse II (Everest)	Nepal-Tibet.	27,560	Changtzu (Everest)	Nepal-Tibet.	24,780	Pauhunri	India-Tibet	23,385
Dhaulagiri	Nepal	26,810	Muz Tagh Ata.	Sinkiang.	24,757	Trisul	India	23,360
Manaslu I	Nepal	26,760	Skyang Kangri	Kashmir	24,750	Kangto	India-Tibet	23,260
Cho Oyu	Nepal-Tibet.	26,750	Communism Peak	USSR	24,590	Nyenchhen Thanglha	Tibet.	23,255
Nanga Parbat.	Kashmir	26,660	Jongsang Peak	India-Nepal	24,472	Trisuli	India	23,210
Annapurna I	Nepal	26,504	Pobedy Peak	Sinkiang-USSR	24,406	Pumori	Nepal-Tibet.	23,190
Gasherbrum	Kashmir	26,470				Dunagiri	India	23,184
Broad	Kashmir	26,400	Sia Kangri	Kashmir	24,350	Lombo Kangra	Tibet.	23,165
Gosainthan	Tibet.	26,287	Haramosh Peak	Pakistan	24,270	Saipal	Nepal	23,100
Annapurna II	Nepal	26,041	Istoro Nal	Pakistan	24,240	Macha Pucchare	Nepal	22,958
Gyachung Kang	Nepal-Tibet.	25,910	Tent Peak	India-Nepal	24,165	Numbar	Nepal	22,817
Disteghil Sar	Kashmir	25,868	Chomo Lhari	Bhutan-Tibet	24,040	Kanjiroba	Nepal	22,580
Himalchuli	Nepal	25,801	Chamlang	Nepal	24,012	Ama Dablam	Nepal	22,350
Nuptse (Everest)	Nepal-Tibet.	25,726	Kabru	India-Nepal	24,002	Cho Polu	Nepal	22,093
Masherbrum	Kashmir	25,660	Alung Gangri	Tibet.	24,000	Lingtren	Nepal-Tibet.	21,972
Nanda Devi	India	25,645	Baltoro Kangri	Kashmir	23,990	Khumbutse	Nepal-Tibet.	21,785
Rakaposhi.	Kashmir	25,550	Mussu Shan.	Sinkiang.	23,890	Hlako Gangri	Tibet.	21,266
Karnet	India-Tibet	25,447	Mana	India	23,860	Mt. Grosvenor	China	21,190
Namcha Barwa	Tibet.	25,445	Baruntse	Nepal	23,688	Thagchhab Gangri	Tibet.	20,970
Gurla Mandhata	Tibet.	25,355	Nepal Peak	India-Nepal	23,500	Damavand	Iran	18,606
Ulugh Muz Tagh	Sinkiang-Tibet.	25,340	Amne Machin	China	23,490	Ararat	Turkey	16,804
			Gauri Sankar	Nepal-Tibet.	23,440			

Antarctica

Peak	Feet	Peak	Feet	Peak	Feet	Peak	Feet
Vinson Massif	16,864	Andrew Jackson	13,750	Shear	13,100	Campbell	12,434
Tyree.	16,290	Sidley	13,720	Odishaw	13,008	Don Pedro Christophersen	12,355
Shinn.	15,750	Ostenso	13,710	Donaldson	12,894	Lysaght	12,326
Gardner	15,375	Minto.	13,668	Ray	12,808	Huggins	12,247
Epperly	15,100	Miller.	13,650	Sellery	12,779	Sabine	12,247
Kirkpatrick	14,855	Long Gables	13,620	Waterman	12,730	Astor	12,175
Elizabeth.	14,698	Dickerson	13,517	Anne	12,703	Mohl	12,172
Markham	14,290	Giovinetto	13,412	Press	12,566	Frankes	12,064
Bell.	14,117	Wade	13,400	Falla.	12,549	Jones.	12,040
Mackellar	14,098	Fisher	13,386	Rucker	12,520	Gjelsvik	12,008
Anderson	13,957	Fridtjof Nansen	13,350	Goldthwait	12,510	Coman	12,000
Bentley.	13,934	Wexler	13,202	Morris	12,500		
Kaplan	13,878	Lister.	13,200	Erebus	12,450		

How Deep Is the Ocean?

Principal ocean depths. **Source:** Defense Mapping Agency Hydrographic/Topographic Center

Name of area	Location		Meters	Depth Fathoms	Feet
Pacific Ocean					
Mariana Trench	11°20'N	142°12'E	10,915	5,968	35,810
Tonga Trench	23°16'S	174°44'W	10,800	5,906	35,433
Philippine Trench	10°38'N	126°36'E	10,057	5,499	32,995
Kermadec Trench	31°53'S	177°21'W	10,047	5,494	32,963
Bonin Trench	24°30'N	143°24'E	9,994	5,007	30,040
Kuril Trench	44°15'N	150°34'E	9,750	5,331	31,988
Izu Trench	31°05'N	142°10'E	9,695	5,301	31,808
New Britain Trench	06°19'S	153°45'E	8,940	4,888	29,331
Yap Trench	08°33'N	138°02'E	8,527	4,663	27,976
Japan Trench	36°08'N	142°43'E	8,412	4,600	27,599
Peru-Chile Trench	23°18'S	71°14'W	8,064	4,409	26,457
Palau Trench	07°52'N	134°56'E	8,054	4,404	26,424
Aleutian Trench	50°51'N	177°11'E	7,679	4,199	25,194
New Hebrides Trench	20°36'S	168°37'E	7,570	4,139	24,836
North Ryukyu Trench	24°00'N	126°48'E	7,181	3,927	23,560
Mid. America Trench	14°02'N	93°39'W	6,662	3,643	21,857
Atlantic Ocean					
Puerto Rico Trench	19°55'N	65°27'W	8,605	4,705	28,232
So. Sandwich Trench	55°42'S	25°56'E	8,325	4,552	27,313
Romanche Gap	0°13'S	18°26'W	7,728	4,226	25,354
Cayman Trench	19°12'N	80°00'W	7,535	4,120	24,721
Brazil Basin	09°10'S	23°02'W	6,119	3,346	20,076
Indian Ocean					
Java Trench	10°19'S	109°58'E	7,125	3,896	23,376
Ob' Trench	09°45'S	67°18'E	6,874	3,759	22,553
Diamantina Trench	35°50'S	105°14'E	6,602	3,610	21,660
Vema Trench	09°08'S	67°15'E	6,402	3,501	21,004
Agulhas Basin	45°20'S	26°50'E	6,195	3,387	20,325
Arctic Ocean					
Eurasia Basin	82°23'N	19°31'E	5,450	2,980	17,881
Mediterranean Sea					
Ionian Basin	36°32'N	21°06'E	5,150	2,816	16,896

Ocean Areas and Average Depths

Four major bodies of water are recognized by geographers and mapmakers. They are: the Pacific, Atlantic, Indian, and Arctic oceans. The Atlantic and Pacific oceans are considered divided at the equator into the No. and So. Atlantic; the No. and So. Pacific. The Arctic Ocean is the name for waters north of the continental land masses in the region of the Arctic Circle.

	Sq. miles	Avg. depth in feet		Sq. miles	Avg. depth in feet
Pacific Ocean	64,186,300	12,925	Hudson Bay	281,900	305
Atlantic Ocean	33,420,000	11,730	East China Sea	256,600	620
Indian Ocean	28,350,500	12,598	Andaman Sea	218,100	3,667
Arctic Ocean	5,105,700	3,407	Black Sea	196,100	3,906
South China Sea	1,148,500	4,802	Red Sea	174,900	1,764
Caribbean Sea	971,400	8,448	North Sea	164,900	308
Mediterranean Sea	969,100	4,926	Baltic Sea	147,500	180
Bering Sea	873,000	4,893	Yellow Sea	113,500	121
Gulf of Mexico	582,100	5,297	Persian Gulf	88,800	328
Sea of Okhotsk	537,500	3,192	Gulf of California	59,100	2,375
Sea of Japan	391,100	5,468			

The Malayan Sea is not considered a geographical entity but a term used for convenience for waters between the South Pacific and the Indian Ocean.

Continental Statistics

Source: National Geographic Society, Washington, D.C.

Continents	Area (sq. mi.)	% of Earth	Population (est.)	% of World total	Highest point (in feet)	Lowest point
Asia	16,999,000	29.7	2,850,567,000	59.9	Everest, 29,028	Dead Sea, −1,312
Africa	11,688,000	20.4	531,000,000	11.2	Kilimanjaro, 19,340	Lake Assal, −512
North America	9,366,000	16.3	395,000,000	8.3	McKinley, 20,320	Death Valley, −282
South America	6,881,000	12.0	264,000,000	5.5	Aconcagua, 22,834	Valdes Penin., −131
Europe	4,017,000	7.0	696,433,000	14.6	El'brus, 18,510	Caspian Sea, −92
Australia	2,966,000	5.2	15,500,000	0.3	Kosciusko, 7,310	Lake Eyre, −52
Antarctica	5,100,000	8.9			Vinson Massif, 16,864	Not Known
Est. World Population			4,762,000,000			

Important Islands and Their Areas

Source: National Geographic Society, Washington, D.C.

Figure in parentheses shows rank among the world's 10 largest islands; some islands have not been surveyed accurately; in such cases estimated areas are shown.

Location-Ownership
Area in square miles

Arctic Ocean

Canadian

Axel Heiberg	16,671
Baffin (5)	195,928
Banks	27,038
Bathurst	6,194
Devon	21,331
Ellesmere (10)	75,767
Melville	16,274
Prince of Wales	12,872
Somerset	9,570
Southampton	15,913
Victoria (9)	83,896

USSR

Franz Josef Land	8,000
Novaya Zemlya (two is.)	35,000
Wrangel	2,800

Norwegian

Svalbard	23,940
Nordaustlandet	5,410
Spitsbergen	15,060

Atlantic Ocean

Anticosti, Canada	3,066
Ascension, UK	34
Azores, Portugal	902
Faial	67
Sao Miguel	291
Bahamas	5,353
Bermuda Is., UK	20
Block, Rhode Island	10
Canary Is., Spain	2,808
Fuerteventura	668
Gran Canaria	592
Tenerife	795
Cape Breton, Canada	3,981
Cape Verde Is.	1,750
Faeroe Is., Denmark	540
Falkland Is., UK	4,700
Fernando de Noronha Archipelago, Brazil	7
Greenland, Denmark (1)	840,000
Iceland	39,769
Long Island, N. Y.	1,396
Bioko Is.	
Equatorial Guinea	785
Madeira Is., Portugal	307
Marajo, Brazil	15,528
Martha's Vineyard, Mass.	91
Mount Desert, Me.	108
Nantucket, Mass.	46
Newfoundland, Canada	42,030
Prince Edward, Canada	2,184
St. Helena, UK	47
South Georgia, UK	1,450
Tierra del Fuego, Chile and Argentina	18,800
Tristan da Cunha, UK	40

British Isles

Great Britain, mainland (8)	84,200
Channel Islands	75
Guernsey	24
Jersey	45
Sark	2
Hebrides	2,744
Ireland	32,599
Irish Republic	27,136
Northern Ireland	5,463
Man	227

Orkney Is.	390
Scilly Is.	6
Shetland Is.	567
Skye	670
Wight	147

Baltic Sea

Aland Is., Finland	581
Bornholm, Denmark	227
Gotland, Sweden	1,164

Caribbean Sea

Antigua	108
Aruba, Netherlands	75
Barbados	166
Cuba	44,218
Isle of Youth	1,182
Curacao, Netherlands	171
Dominica	290
Guadeloupe, France	687
Hispaniola, Haiti and Dominican Republic	29,530
Jamaica	4,244
Martinique, France	425
Puerto Rico, U.S.	3,515
Tobago	116
Trinidad	1,864
Virgin Is., UK	59
Virgin Is., U.S.	132

Indian Ocean

Andaman Is., India	2,500
Madagascar (4)	226,658
Mauritius	720
Pemba, Tanzania	380
Reunion, France	969
Seychelles	171
Sri Lanka	25,332
Zanzibar, Tanzania	640

Persian Gulf

Bahrain	258

Mediterranean Sea

Balearic Is., Spain	1,936
Corfu, Greece	229
Corsica, France	3,365
Crete, Greece	3,186
Cyprus	3,572
Elba, Italy	86
Euboea, Greece	1,409
Malta	122
Rhodes, Greece	542
Sardinia, Italy	9,262
Sicily, Italy	9,822

Pacific Ocean

Aleutian Is., U.S.	6,821
Adak	289
Amchitka	121
Attu	388
Kanaga	135
Kiska	110
Tanaga	209
Umnak	675
Unalaska	1,064
Unimak	1,600
Canton, Kiribati*	4
Caroline Is., U.S. trust terr.	472
Christmas, Kiribati*	94

Diomede, Big, USSR	11
Diomede, Little, U.S.	2
Easter, Chile	69
Fiji	7,056
Vanua Levu	2,242
Viti Levu	4,109
Funafuti, Tuvalu*	2
Galapagos Is., Ecuador	3,043
Guadalcanal, UK	2,500
Guam	209
Hainan, China	13,000
Hawaiian Is., U.S.	6,450
Hawaii	4,037
Oahu	593
Hong Kong, UK	29
Japan	145,809
Hokkaido	30,144
Honshu (7)	87,805
Iwo Jima	8
Kyushu	14,114
Okinawa	459
Shikoku	7,049
Kodiak, U.S.	3,670
Marquesas Is., France	492
Marshall Is., U.S. trust terr.	70
Bikini*	2
Nauru	8
New Caledonia, France	6,530
New Guinea (2)	306,000
New Zealand	103,883
Chatham	372
North	44,035
South	58,305
Stewart	674
Northern Mariana Is.	184
Philippines	115,831
Leyte	2,787
Luzon	40,880
Mindanao	36,775
Mindoro	3,790
Negros	4,907
Palawan	4,554
Panay	4,446
Samar	5,050
Quemoy	56
Sakhalin, USSR	29,500
Samoa Is.	1,177
American Samoa	77
Tutuila	52
Samoa (Western)	1,101
Savaii	670
Upolu	429
Santa Catalina, U.S.	72
Tahiti, France	402
Taiwan	13,823
Tasmania, Australia	26,178
Tonga Is.	270
Vancouver, Canada	12,079
Vanuatu	5,700

East Indies

Bali, Indonesia	2,147
Borneo, Indonesia-Malaysia, UK (3)	280,100
Celebes, Indonesia	69,000
Java, Indonesia	48,900
Madura, Indonesia	2,113
Moluccas, Indonesia	28,766
New Britain, Papua New Guinea	14,093
New Ireland, Papua New Guinea	3,707
Sumatra, Indonesia (6)	165,000
Timor	11,570

*Atolls: Bikini (lagoon area, 230 sq. mi., land area 2 sq. mi.), U.S. Trust Territory of the Pacific Islands; Canton (lagoon 20 sq. mi., land 4 sq. mi.), Kiribati; Christmas (lagoon 140 sq. mi., land 94 sq. mi.), Kiribati; Funafuti (lagoon 84 sq. mi., land 2 sq. mi.), Tuvalu.
Australia, often called an island, is a continent. Its mainland area is 2,939,975 sq. mi.
Islands in minor waters: Manhattan (22 sq. mi.) Staten (59 sq. mi.) and Governors (173 acres), all in New York Harbor, U.S.; Isle Royale (209 sq. mi.), Lake Superior. U.S.; Manitoulin (1,068 sq. mi.), Lake Huron, Canada; Pinang (110 sq. mi.), Strait of Malacca, Malaysia; Singapore (239 sq. mi.), Singapore Strait, Singapore.

Major Rivers in North America

Source: U.S. Geological Survey

River	Source or Upper Limit of Length	Outflow	Miles
Alabama	Gilmer County, Ga.	Mobile River	735
Albany	Lake St. Joseph, Ont., Can.	James Bay	610
Allegheny	Potter County, Pa.	Ohio River	325
Altamaha-Ocmulgee	Junction of Yellow and South Rivers, Newton County, Ga.	Atlantic Ocean	392
Apalachicola-Chattahoochee	Towns County, Ga.	Gulf of Mexico, Fla.	524
Arkansas	Lake County, Col.	Mississippi River, Ark.	1,459
Assiniboine	Eastern Saskatchewan	Red River	450
Attawapiskat	Attawapiskat, Ont., Can.	James Bay	465
Big Black (Miss.)	Webster County, Miss.	Mississippi River	330
Black (N.W.T.)	Contwoyto Lake	Chantrey Inlet	600
Brazos	Junction of Salt and Double Mountain Forks, Stonewall County, Tex.	Gulf of Mexico	870
Canadian	Las Animas County, Col.	Arkansas River, Okla.	906
Cedar (Iowa)	Dodge County, Minn.	Iowa River, Ia.	329
Cheyenne	Junction of Antelope Creek and Dry Fork, Converse County, Wyo.	Missouri River	290
Churchill	Methy Lake	Hudson Bay	1,000
Cimarron	Colfax County, N.M.	Arkansas River, Okla.	600
Clark Fork-Pend Oreille	Silver Bow County, Mon.	Columbia River, B.C.	505
Colorado (Ariz.)	Rocky Mountain National Park, Col. (90 miles in Mexico)	Gulf of Cal., Mexico	1,450
Colorado (Texas)	West Texas	Matagorda Bay	840
Columbia	Columbia Lake, British Columbia	Pacific Ocean, bet. Ore. and Wash.	1,243
Columbia, Upper	Columbia Lake, British Columbia	To mouth of Snake River	890
Connecticut	Third Connecticut Lake, N.H.	L.I. Sound, Conn.	407
Coppermine (N.W.T.)	Lac de Gras	Coronation Gulf (Atlantic Ocean)	525
Cumberland	Letcher County, Ky.	Ohio River	720
Delaware	Schoharie County, N.Y.	Liston Point, Delaware Bay	390
Fraser	Near Mount Robson (on Continental Divide)	Strait of Georgia	850
Gila	Catron County, N.M.	Colorado River, Ariz.	630
Green (Ut.-Wyo.)	Junction of Wells and Trail Creeks, Sublette County, Wyo.	Colorado River, Ut.	730
Hamilton (Lab.)	Lake Ashuanipi	Atlantic Ocean	600
Hudson	Henderson Lake, Essex County, N.Y.	Upper N.Y. Bay, N.Y.,-N.J.	306
Illinois	St. Joseph County, Ind.	Mississippi River	420
James (N.D.-S.D.)	Wells County, N.D.	Missouri River, S.D.	710
James (Va.)	Junction of Jackson and Cowpasture Rivers, Botetourt County, Va.	Hampton Roads	340
Kanawha-New	Junction of North and South Forks of New River, N.C.	Ohio River	352
Kentucky	Junction of North and Middle Forks, Lee County, Ky.	Ohio River	259
Klamath	Lake Ewauna, Klamath Falls, Ore.	Pacific Ocean	250
Koyukuk	Endicott Mountains, Alaska	Yukon River	470
Kuskokwim	Alaska Range	Kuskokwim Bay	680
Liard	Southern Yukon, Alaska	Mackenzie River	693
Little Missouri	Crook County, Wyo.	Missouri River	560
Mackenzie	Great Slave Lake	Arctic Ocean	900
Milk	Junction of North and South Forks, Alberta Province	Missouri River, Mon.	625
Minnesota	Big Stone Lake, Minn.	Mississippi River, St. Paul, Minn.	332
Mississippi	Lake Itasca, Minn.	Mouth of Southwest Pass	2,348
Mississippi, Upper	Lake Itasca, Minn.	To mouth of Missouri R.	1,171
Mississippi-Missouri-Red Rock	Source of Red Rock, Beaverhead Co., Mon.	Mouth of Southwest Pass	3,710
Missouri	Junction of Jefferson, Madison, and Gallatin Rivers, Madison County, Mon.	Mississippi River	2,315
Missouri-Red Rock	Source of Red Rock, Beaverhead Co., Mon.	Mississippi River	2,533
Mobile-Alabama-Coosa	Gilmer County, Ga.	Mobile Bay	780
Nelson (Manitoba)	Lake Winnipeg	Hudson Bay	410
Neosho	Morris County, Kan.	Arkansas River, Okla.	460
Niobrara	Niobrara County, Wyo.	Missouri River, Neb.	431
North Canadian	Union County, N.M.	Canadian River, Okla.	760
North Platte	Junction of Grizzly and Little Grizzly Creeks, Jackson County, Col.	Platte River, Neb.	618
Ohio	Junction of Allegheny and Monongahela Rivers, Pittsburgh, Pa.	Mississippi River, Ill.-Ky.	981
Ohio-Allegheny	Potter County, Pa.	Mississippi River	1,306
Osage	East-central Kansas	Missouri River, Mo.	500
Ottawa	Lake Capimitchigama	St. Lawrence	790
Ouachita	Polk County, Ark.	Red River, La.	605
Peace	Stikine Mountains, B.C.	Slave River	1,195
Pearl	Neshoba County, Miss.	Gulf of Mexico, Miss.-La.	411
Pecos	Mora County, N.M.	Rio Grande, Tex.	735
Pee Dee-Yadkin	Watauga County, N.C.	Winyah Bay, S.C.	435
Pend Oreille	Near Butte, Mon.	Columbia River	490
Platte	Junction of North and South Platte Rivers, Neb.	Missouri River, Neb.	310
Porcupine	Ogilvie Mountains, Alaska	Yukon River, Alaska	460
Potomac	Garrett County, Md.	Chesapeake Bay	383
Powder	Junction of South and Middle Forks, Wyo.	Yellowstone River, Mon.	375
Red (Okla.-Tex.-La.)	Curry County, N.M.	Mississippi River	1,270
Red River of the North	Junction of Otter Tail and Bois de Sioux Rivers, Wilkin County, Minn.	Lake Winnipeg, Manitoba	545

River	Source or Upper Limit of Length	Outflow	Miles
Republican	Junction of North Fork and Arikaree River, Neb.	Kansas River, Kan.	445
Rio Grande	San Juan County, Col.	Gulf of Mexico	1,885
Roanoke	Junction of North and South Forks, Montgomery County, Va.	Albemarle Sound, N.C.	380
Rock (Ill.-Wis.)	Dodge County, Wis.	Mississippi River, Ill.	300
Sabine	Junction of South and Caddo Forks, Hunt County, Tex.	Sabine Lake, Tex.-La.	380
Sacramento	Siskiyou County, Cal.	Suisun Bay	377
St. Francis	Iron County, Mo.	Mississippi River, Ark.	425
St. Lawrence	Lake Ontario	Gulf of St. Lawrence (Atlantic Ocean)	800
Salmon (Idaho)	Custer County, Ida.	Snake River, Ida.	420
San Joaquin	Junction of South and Middle Forks, Madera County, Cal.	Suisun Bay	350
San Juan	Silver Lake, Archuleta County, Col.	Colorado River, Ut.	360
Santee-Wateree-Catawba	McDowell County, N.C.	Atlantic Ocean, S.C.	538
Saskatchewan, North	Rocky Mountains	Lake Winnipeg	1,100
Saskatchewan, South	Rocky Mountains	Lake Winnipeg	1,205
Savannah	Junction of Seneca and Tugaloo Rivers, Anderson County, S.C.	Atlantic Ocean, Ga.-S.C.	314
Severn (Ontario)	Sandy Lake	Hudson Bay	610
Smoky Hill	Cheyenne County, Col.	Kansas River, Kan.	540
Snake	Teton County, Wyo.	Columbia River, Wash.	1,038
South Platte	Junction of South and Middle Forks, Park County, Col.	Platte River, Neb.	424
Susitna	Alaska Range	Cook Inlet	300
Susquehanna	Otsego Lake, Otsego County, N.Y.	Chesapeake Bay, Md.	444
Tallahatchie	Tippah County, Miss.	Yazoo River, Miss.	301
Tanana	Wrangell Mountains	Yukon River, Alaska	620
Tennessee	Junction of French Broad and Holston Rivers	Ohio River, Ky.	652
Tennessee-French Broad	Bland County, Va.	Ohio River	900
Tombigbee	Prentiss County, Miss.	Mobile River, Ala.	525
Trinity	North of Dallas, Tex.	Galveston Bay, Tex.	360
Wabash	Darke County, Oh.	Ohio River, Ill.-Ind.	529
Washita	Hemphill County, Tex.	Red River, Okla.	500
White (Ark.-Mo.)	Madison County, Ark.	Mississippi River	720
Willamette	Douglas County, Ore.	Columbia River	270
Wind-Bighorn	Junction of Wind and Little Wind Rivers, Fremont Co., Wyo. (Source of Wind R. is Togwotee Pass, Teton Co., Wyo.)	Yellowstone R., Mon.	336
Wisconsin	LeVieux Desert, Vilas County, Wis.	Mississippi River	430
Yellowstone	Park County, Wyo.	Missouri River, N.D.	671
Yukon	Coast Mountains of British Columbia	Bering Sea, Alaska	1,900

Flows of Largest U.S. Rivers

Source: U.S. Geological Survey (average discharges for the period 1941-70). Ranked according to average discharge in cubic feet per second (cfs) at mouth.

Rank	River	Average discharge	Length[a] (miles)	Drainage area	Most distant source	Maximum discharge at gauging station farthest downstream	Date
1	Mississippi	[b]640,000	[c]3,710	[d]1,247,300	Beaverhead Co., Mont.	2,080,000	2-17-37
2	Columbia	262,000	1,243	258,000	Columbia Lake, B.C.	1,240,000	June 1894
3	Ohio	258,000	1,306	203,900	Potter Co., Pa.	1,850,000	2-1-37
4	St. Lawrence	[e]243,000	—	[e]302,000	—	[f]350,000	July 1973
5	Yukon	[g]240,000	1,900	327,600	Coast Mountains, B.C.	1,030,000	6-22-64
6	[h]Atchafalaya	183,000	135	95,105	Curry Co., N. Mex.	—	—
7	Missouri	76,300	2,533	529,400	Beaverhead Co., Mont.	892,000	June 1844
8	Tennessee	[m]64,000	900	40,910	Bland Co., Va.	500,000	2-17-48
9	Red	[i]62,300	1,270	93,244	Curry Co., N. Mex.	233,000	4-17-45
10	Kuskokwim	62,000	680	49,000	Alaska Range, Alas.	392,000	6-5-64
11	Mobile	61,400	780	43,800	Gilmer, Co., Ga.	—	—
12	Snake	50,000	1,038	109,000	Teton Co., Wyo.	409,000	June 1894
13	Arkansas	45,100	1,459	160,600	Lake Co., Col.	536,000	5-27-43
14	Copper	[j]43,000	280	24,000	Alaska Range, Alas.	265,000	7-15-71
15	Tanana	[k]41,000	620	44,000	Wrangell Mtn., Alas.	186,000	8-18-67
16	Susitna	[j]40,000	300	20,000	Alaska Range, Alas.	230,000	7-29-80
17	Susquehanna	37,190	444	27,570	Otsego Co., N.Y.	1,080,000	6-23-72
18	Willamette	35,660	270	11,200	Douglas Co., Ore.	500,000	12-4-1861
19	Alabama	32,400	735	22,600	Gilmer Co., Ga.	267,000	3-7-61
20	White	32,100	720	28,000	Madison Co., Ark.	343,000	4-17-45
21	Wabash	30,400	529	33,150	Darke Co., Oh.	428,000	3-30-13
22	Pend Oreille	29,900	490	25,820	Near Butte, Mont.	200,000	June 1894
23	Tombigbee	27,300	525	20,100	Prentiss Co., Miss.	290,000	4-22-79
24	Cumberland	[m]26,900	720	18,080	Letcher Co., Ky.	209,000	3-16-75
25	Stikine	[n]26,000	310	20,000	Stikine Range, B.C.	223,900	7-22-79
26	Sacramento	—	377	27,100	Siskiyou Co., Cal.	[o]322,000	12-25-64
27	Apalachicola	24,700	524	19,600	Towns Co., Ga.	293,000	3-20-29
28	Illinois	22,800	420	27,900	St. Joseph Co., Ind.	123,000	May 1943
29	Koyukuk	[p]22,000	470	32,400	Endicott Mtns., Alas.	266,000	6-6-64
30	Porcupine	[q]20,000	460	45,000	Ogilvie Mtns., Alas.	299,000	5-24-73

(a) Because river lengths and methods of measurement may change from time to time, the length figures given are subject to revision; (b) about 25 percent of flow occurs in the Atchafalaya River; (c) the length from mouth to source of the Mississippi River in Minnesota is 2,348 miles; (d) at Baptiste Collete Bayou, Louisiana; (e) at international boundary lat. 45°; (f) maximum monthly discharge; (g) period 1957-70; (h) continuation of Red River; (i) flow of Ouachita River added; (j) period 1956-69; (k) period 1962-69; (l) based on records of Chulitna, Talkeetna, and Yetna rivers; (m) period 1931-60; (n) period 1954-63; summer records only; (o) discharge of American River not included (p) period 1960-69; (q) period 1964-69; (r) at Liston Point on Delaware Bay.

Principal World Rivers

Source: National Geographic Society, Washington, D.C. (length in miles)

River	Outflow	Lgth	River	Outflow	Lgth	River	Outflow	Lgth
Albany	James Bay	610	Indus	Arabian Sea	1,800	Red River of N.	Lake Winnipeg	545
Amazon	Atlantic Ocean	4,000	Irrawaddy	Bay of Bengal	1,337	Rhine	North Sea	820
Amu	Aral Sea	1,578	Japura	Amazon River	1,750	Rhone	Gulf of Lions	505
Amur	Tatar Strait	2,744	Jordan	Dead Sea	200	Rio de la Plata	Atlantic Ocean	150
Angara	Yenisey River	1,151	Kootenay	Columbia River	485	Rio Grande	Gulf of Mexico	1,885
Arkansas	Mississippi	1,459	Lena	Laptev Sea	2,734	Rio Roosevelt	Aripuana	400
Back	Arctic Ocean	605	Loire	Bay of Biscay	634	Saguenay	St. Lawrence R.	434
Brahmaputra	Bay of Bengal	1,800	Mackenzie	Arctic Ocean	2,635	St. John	Bay of Fundy	418
Bug, Southern	Dnieper River	532	Madeira	Amazon River	2,013	St. Lawrence	Gulf of St. Law.	800
Bug, Western	Wisla River	481	Magdalena	Caribbean Sea	956	Salween	Andaman Sea	1,500
Canadian	Arkansas River	906	Marne	Seine River	326	Sao Francisco	Atlantic Ocean	1,988
Chang Jiang	E. China Sea	3,964	Mekong	S. China Sea	2,600	Saskatchewan	Lake Winnipeg	1,205
Churchill, Man.	Hudson Bay	1,000	Meuse	North Sea	580	Seine	English Chan.	496
Churchill, Que.	Atlantic Ocean	532	Mississippi	Gulf of Mexico	2,348	Shannon	Atlantic Ocean	230
Colorado	Gulf of Calif.	1,450	Missouri	Mississippi	2,533	Snake	Columbia River	1,038
Columbia	Pacific Ocean	1,243	Murray-Darling	Indian Ocean	2,310	Sungari	Amur River	1,150
Congo	Atlantic Ocean	2,900	Negro	Amazon	1,400	Syr	Aral Sea	1,370
Danube	Black Sea	1,776	Nelson	Hudson Bay	1,600	Tajo, Tagus	Atlantic Ocean	626
Dnieper	Black Sea	1,420	Niger	Gulf of Guinea	2,590	Tennessee	Ohio River	652
Dniester	Black Sea	877	Nile	Mediterranean	4,145	Thames	North Sea	236
Don	Sea of Azov	1,224	Ob-Irtysh	Gulf of Ob	3,362	Tiber	Tyrrhenian Sea	252
Drava	Danube River	447	Oder	Baltic Sea	567	Tigris	Shatt al-Arab	1,180
Dvina, North	White Sea	824	Ohio	Mississippi	975	Tisza	Danube River	600
Dvina, West	Gulf of Riga	634	Orange	Atlantic Ocean	1,300	Tocantins	Para River	1,677
Ebro	Mediterranean	565	Orinoco	Atlantic Ocean	1,600	Ural	Caspian Sea	1,575
Elbe	North Sea	724	Ottawa	St. Lawrence R.	790	Uruguay	Rio de la Plata	1,000
Euphrates	Shatt al-Arab	1,700	Paraguay	Parana River	1,584	Volga	Caspian Sea	2,194
Fraser	Str. of Georgia	850	Parana	Rio de la Plata	2,485	Weser	North Sea	454
Gambia	Atlantic Ocean	700	Peace	Slave River	1,195	Wisla	Bay of Danzig	675
Ganges	Bay of Bengal	1,560	Pilcomayo	Paraguay River	1,000	Yellow (See Huang)		
Garonne	Bay of Biscay	357	Po	Adriatic Sea	405	Yenisey	Kara Sea	2,543
Hsi	S. China Sea	1,200	Purus	Amazon River	2,100	Yukon	Bering Sea	1,979
Huang	Yellow Sea	2,903	Red	Mississippi	1,270	Zambezi	Indian Ocean	1,700

Large Rivers in Canada

Source: "Inland Waters Directorate," Environment Canada

(Ranked according to average discharge in cubic feet per second (cfs). Figures indicate discharge and drainage to river mouths, unless otherwise indicated.)

Rank	River	Average discharge	Length (miles)	Drainage area (sq. mi.)
1	St. Lawrence (to Nicolet)	355,000	1,900	396,000[1]
2	Mackenzie (to head of Finlay)	350,000	2,635	690,000
3	Fraser	128,000	850	89,900[2]
4	Columbia (International Boundary to head of Columbia Lake)	102,000	498	59,700[3]
5	Nelson (to head of Bow)	100,000	1,600	437,000[4]
6	Kokosak (to head of Caniapiscau)	85,500	543	51,500
7	Yukon (International Boundary to head of Nisutlin)	83,000	714	115,000[5]
8	Ottawa	70,500	790	56,500
9	Saguenay (to head of Peribonea)	62,200	434	34,000
10	Skeena	62,100	300	21,200

(1) Including 195,000 sq. mi. in U.S. (2) Including diversion. (3) Including 20,000 sq. mi. in U.S. (4) Including 69,500 sq. mi. in U.S. (5) Including 9,000 sq. mi. in U.S.

Famous Waterfalls

Source: National Geographic Society, Washington, D.C.

The earth has thousands of waterfalls, some of considerable magnitude. Their importance is determined not only by height but volume of flow, steadiness of flow, crest width, whether the water drops sheerly or over a sloping surface, and in one leap or a succession of leaps. A series of low falls flowing over a considerable distance is known as a cascade.

Sete Quedas or Guaira is the world's greatest waterfall when its mean annual flow (estimated at 470,000 cusecs, cubic feet per second) is combined with height. A greater volume of water passes over Boyoma Falls (Stanley Falls), though not one of its seven cataracts, spread over nearly 60 miles of the Congo River, exceeds 10 feet.

Estimated mean annual flow, in cusecs, of other major waterfalls are: Niagara, 212,200; Paulo Afonso, 100,000; Urubupunga, 97,000; Iguazu, 61,000; Patos-Maribondo, 53,000; Victoria, 35,400; and Kaieteur, 23,400.

Height = total drop in feet in one or more leaps. † = falls of more than one leap; * = falls that diminish greatly seasonally; ** = falls that reduce to a trickle or are dry for part of each year. If river names not shown, they are same as the falls. R. = river; L. = lake; (C) = cascade type.

Name and location	Ht.	Name and location	Ht.	Name and location	Ht.
Africa		Tesissat, Blue Nile R.	140	**Tanzania-Zambia**	
		Lesotho		*Kalambo	726
Angola		*Maletsunyane	630	**Uganda**	
Duque de Braganca,		**Zimbabwe-Zambia**		Kabalega (Murchison) Victoria	
Lucala R.	344	*Victoria, Zambezi R.	343	Nile R.	130
Ruacana, Cuene R.	406	**South Africa**			
Ethiopia		*Augrabies, Orange R.	480	**Asia**	
Dal Verme,		Howick, Umgeni R.	364		
Dorya R.	98	† Tugela	2,014	India—*Cauvery	330
Fincha	508	Highest fall	597	*Gokak, Ghataprabha R.	170
				*Jog (Gersoppa), Sharavathi R.	830

Name and location	Ht.
Japan	
*Kegon, Daiya R.	330
Laos	
Khon Cataracts,	
Mekong R. (C)	70

Australasia

Name and location	Ht.
Australia	
New South Wales	
† Wentworth	614
Highest fall	360
Wollomombi	1,100
Queensland	
Coomera	210
Tully	885
† Wallaman, Stony Cr.	1,137
Highest fall	937
New Zealand	
Bowen	540
Helena	890
Stirling	505
† Sutherland, Arthur R.	1,904
Highest fall	815

Europe

Name and location	Ht.
Austria—† Gastein	492
Highest fall	280
† *Golling, Schwarzbach R.	250
† Krimml	1,312
France—*Gavarnie	1,385
Great Britain—Scotland	
Glomach	370
Wales	
Cain	150
Rhaiadr	240
Iceland—Detti	144
† Gull, Hvita R.	105
Italy—Frua, Toce R. (C).	470
Norway	
Mardalsfossen (Northern)	1,535
† Mardalsfossen (Southern)	2,149
† **Skjeggedal, Nybuai R.	1,378
**Skykje	984
Vetti, Morka-Koldedola R.	900
Voring, Bjoreio R.	597
Sweden	
† Handol	427
† Tannforsen, Are R.	120
Switzerland	
† Diesbach	394
Giessbach (C)	984

Name and location	Ht.
Handegg, Aare R.	150
Iffigen	120
Pissevache, Salanfe R.	213
† Reichenbach	656
Rhine	79
† Simmen	459
Staubbach	984
† Trummelbach	1,312

North America

Name and location	Ht.
Canada	
Alberta	
Panther, Nigel Cr.	600
British Columbia	
† Della	1,443
† Takakkaw, Daly Glacier	1,200
Northwest Territories	
Virginia, S. Nahanni R.	294
Quebec	
Montmorency	274
Canada—United States	
Niagara: American	182
Horseshoe	173
United States	
California	
*Feather, Fall R.	640
Yosemite National Park	
*Bridalveil	620
*Illilouette	370
*Nevada, Merced R.	594
**Ribbon	1,612
**Silver Strand, Meadow Br.	1,170
*Vernal, Merced R.	317
† **Yosemite	2,425
Yosemite (upper)	1,430
Yosemite (lower)	320
Yosemite (middle) (C)	675
Colorado	
† Seven, South Cheyenne Cr.	300
Hawaii	
Akaka, Kolekole Str.	442
Idaho	
**Shoshone, Snake R.	212
Twin, Snake R.	120
Kentucky	
Cumberland	68
Maryland	
*Great, Potomac R. (C)	71
Minnesota	
**Minnehaha	53

Name and location	Ht.
New Jersey	
Passaic	70
New York	
*Taughannock	215
Oregon	
† Multnomah	620
Highest fall	542
Tennessee	
Fall Creek	256
Washington	
Mt. Rainier Natl. Park	
Narada, Paradise R.	168
Sluiskin, Paradise R.	300
Palouse	197
**Snoqualmie	268
Wisconsin	
*Big Manitou, Black R. (C).	165
Wyoming	
Yellowstone Natl. Pk. Tower	132
*Yellowstone (upper)	109
*Yellowstone (lower)	308
Mexico	
El Salto	218
**Juanacatlan, Santiago R.	72

South America

Name and location	Ht.
Argentina-Brazil	
Iguazu	230
Brazil	
Glass	1,325
Patos-Maribondo, Grande R.	115
Paulo Afonso, Sao Francisco R.	275
Urubupunga, Parana R.	40
Brazil-Paraguay	
Sete Quedas	
Parana R.	130
Colombia	
Catarata de Candelas,	
Cusiana R.	984
*Tequendama, Bogota R.	427
Ecuador	
*Agoyan, Pastaza R.	200
Guyana	
Kaieteur, Potaro R.	741
Great, Kamarang R.	1,600
† Marina, Ipobe R.	500
Highest fall	300
Venezuela—	
† *Angel	3,212
Highest fall	2,648
Cuquenan	2,000

Notable Deserts of the World

Arabian (Eastern), 70,000 sq. mi. in Egypt between the Nile river and Red Sea, extending southward into Sudan.

Atacama, 600 mi. long area rich in nitrate and copper deposits in N. Chile.

Black Rock, 600 sq. mi. barren plain in NW Nev.

Death Valley, 3,300 sq. mi. in E. Cal. and SW Nev. Contains lowest point below sea level (282 ft.) in Western Hemisphere.

Gibson, 120,000 sq. mi. in the interior of W. Australia.

Gobi, 500,000 sq. mi. in Mongolia and China.

Great Sandy, 150,000 sq. mi. in W. Australia.

Great Victoria, 150,000 sq. mi. in W. and S. Australia.

Kalahari, 225,000 sq. mi. in southern Africa.

Kara-Kum, 120,000 sq. mi. in Turkmen SSR.

Kavir (Dasht-e Kavir), great salt waste in central Iran some 400 mi. long.

Kyzyl Kum, 100,000 sq. mi. in Kazakh and Uzbek SSRs.

Libyan, 450,000 sq. mi. in the Sahara extending from Lybia through SW Egypt into Sudan.

Lut (Dasht-e Lut), 20,000 sq. mi. in E. Iran.

Mojave, 15,000 sq. mi. in S. Cal.

Nafud (An Nafud), 40,000 sq. mi. near Jawf in Saudi Arabia.

Namib, long narrow area extending 800 miles along SW coast of Africa.

Nubian, 100,000 sq. mi. in the Sahara in NE Sudan.

Painted Desert, section of high plateau in N. Ariz. extending 150 mi.

Rub al Khali (Empty Quarter), 250,000 sq. mi. in the south Arabian Peninsula.

Sahara, 3,500,000 sq. mi. in N. Africa extending westward to the Atlantic. Largest desert in the world.

Simpson, 40,000 sq. mi. in central Australia.

Sonoran, 70,000 sq. mi. in SW Ariz. and SE Cal. extending into Mexico.

Syrian, 100,000 sq. mi. arid wasteland extending over much of N. Saudi Arabia, E. Jordan, S. Syria, and W. Iraq.

Taklimakan, 140,000 sq. mi. in Sinkiang Province, China.

Thar (Great Indian), 100,000 sq. mi. arid area extending 400 mi. along India-Pakistan border.

The Great Lakes

Source: National Ocean Service, U.S. Commerce Department

The Great Lakes form the largest body of fresh water in the world and with their connecting waterways are the largest inland water transportation unit. Draining the great North Central basin of the U.S., they enable shipping to reach the Atlantic via their outlet, the St. Lawrence R., and also the Gulf of Mexico via the Illinois Waterway, from Lake Michigan to the Mississippi R. A third outlet connects with the Hudson R. and thence the Atlantic via the N. Y. State Barge Canal System. Traffic on the Illinois Waterway and the N.Y. State Barge Canal System is limited to recre-

ational boating and small shipping vessels.

Only one of the lakes, Lake Michigan, is wholly in the United States; the others are shared with Canada. Ships carrying grain, lumber and iron ore move from the shores of Lake Superior to Whitefish Bay at the east end of the lake, thence through the Soo (Sault Ste. Marie) locks, through the St. Mary's River and into Lake Huron. To reach the steel mills at Gary, and Port of Indiana and South Chicago, Ill., ore ships move west from Lake Huron to Lake Michigan through the Straits of Mackinac.

Lake Huron discharges its waters into Lake Erie through a narrow waterway, the St. Clair R., Lake St. Clair (both included in the drainage basin figures) and the Detroit R. Lake St. Clair, a marshy basin, is 26 miles long and 24 miles wide at its maximum. A ship channel has been dredged through the lake.

Lake Superior is 600 feet above mean water level at Point-au-Pere, Quebec, on the International Great Lakes Datum (1955). From Duluth, Minn., to the eastern end of Lake Ontario is 1,156 mi.

	Superior	Michigan	Huron	Erie	Ontario
Length in miles	350	307	206	241	193
Breadth in miles	160	118	183	57	53
Deepest soundings in feet	1,330	923	750	210	802
Volume of water in cubic miles	2,900	1,180	850	116	393
Area (sq. miles) water surface—U.S.	20,600	22,300	9,100	4,980	3,560
Canada	11,100	.....	13,900	4,930	3,990
Area (sq. miles) entire drainage basin—U.S.	16,900	45,600	16,200	18,000	15,200
Canada	32,400	.....	35,500	4,720	12,100
Total Area (sq. miles) U.S. and Canada	**81,000**	**67,900**	**74,700**	**32,630**	**34,850**
Mean surface above mean water level at Point-au-Pere, Quebec, aver. level in feet (1900-1983)	600.59	578.25	578.25	570.42	244.71
Latitude, North	46° 25'	41° 37'	43° 00'	41° 23'	43° 11'
	49° 00'	46° 06'	46° 17'	42° 52'	44° 15'
Longitude, West	84° 22'	84° 45'	79° 43'	78° 51'	76° 03'
	92° 06'	88° 02'	84° 45'	83° 29'	79° 53'
National boundary line in miles	282.8	None	260.8	251.5	174.6
United States shore line (mainland only) miles	863	1,400	580	431	300

Largest Lake in Each Province and Territory of Canada
Source: "Inland Waters Directorate," Environment Canada.

Province	Lake	Origin	Area (sq. miles)	Ft. above sea level
Alberta	Athabasca	Natural	3,066[1]	700
British Columbia	Williston	Manmade	640	2,180
Manitoba	Winnipeg	Natural	9,417	713
Newfoundland	Smallwood Reservoir	Manmade	2,520	S.L.
New Brunswick	Grand	Natural	70	4
Northwest Territories	Great Bear	Natural	12,096	512
Nova Scotia	Bras d'Or	Natural	424	Tidal
Ontario	Huron*	Natural	23,000[2]	580
Prince Edward Island	Forest Hill Pond	Manmade	.7	50
Quebec	Mistassini	Natural	902	1,230
Saskatchewan	Athabasca	Natural	3,066[3]	700
Yukon Territory	Kluane	Natural	158	2,563

(1) Shared with Saskatchewan. (2) Includes 9,100 sq. mi. in U.S. (3) Shared with Alberta. (*) Lake Superior is larger than Lake Huron but has less water area in Canada; 11,100 sq. mi. Can., 20,600 sq. mi. U.S.

Lakes of the World
Source: National Geographic Society, Washington, D.C.

A lake is a body of water surrounded by land. Although some lakes are called seas, they are lakes by definition. The Caspian Sea is bounded by the Soviet Union and Iran and is fed by eight rivers.

Name	Continent	Area sq. mi.	Length mi.	Depth feet	Elev. feet
Caspian Sea	Asia-Europe	143,244	760	3,363	−92
Superior	North America	31,700	350	1,333	600
Victoria	Africa	26,828	250	270	3,720
Aral Sea	Asia	24,904	280	220	174
Huron	North America	23,000	206	750	579
Michigan	North America	22,300	307	923	579
Tanganyika	Africa	12,700	420	4,823	2,534
Baykal	Asia	12,162	395	5,315	1,493
Great Bear	North America	12,096	192	1,463	512
Malawi	Africa	11,150	360	2,280	1,550
Great Slave	North America	11,031	298	2,015	513
Erie	North America	9,910	241	210	570
Winnipeg	North America	9,417	266	60	713
Ontario	North America	7,550	193	802	245
Balkhash	Asia	7,115	376	85	1,115
Ladoga	Europe	6,835	124	738	13
Chad	Africa	6,300	175	24	787
Maracaibo	South America	5,217	133	115	Sea level
Onega	Europe	3,710	145	328	108
Eyre	Australia	3,600	90	4	−52
Volta	Africa	3,276	250	....	....
Titicaca	South America	3,200	122	922	12,500
Nicaragua	North America	3,100	102	230	102
Athabasca	North America	3,064	208	407	700
Reindeer	North America	2,568	143	720	1,106
Turkana	Africa	2,473	154	240	1,230
Issyk Kul	Asia	2,355	115	2,303	5,279
Torrens	Australia	2,230	130	....	92
Vanern	Europe	2,156	91	328	144
Nettilling	North America	2,140	67	....	95
Winnipegosis	North America	2,075	141	38	830
Albert	Africa	2,075	100	168	2,030
Kariba	Africa	2,050	175	390	1,590
Nipigon	North America	1,872	72	540	1,050
Gairdner	Australia	1,840	90	....	112
Urmia	Asia	1,815	90	49	4,180
Manitoba	North America	1,799	140	12	813

STATES AND OTHER AREAS OF THE U.S.

Sources: Population: Commerce Dept., Bureau of the Census (July, 1983 provisional estimates, inc. armed forces personnel in each state but excluding such personnel stationed overseas); area: Bureau of the Census, Geography Division; forested land: Agriculture Dept., Forest Service; lumber production: Bureau of the Census, Industry Division; mineral production: Interior Dept., Bureau of Mines; commercial fishing: Commerce Dept., Natl. Marine Fisheries Service; value of construction: McGraw-Hill Information Systems Co., F.W. Dodge Division; per capita income (estimate): Commerce Dept., Bureau of Economic Analysis; unemployment: Labor Dept., Bureau of Labor Statistics; finance: Federal Deposit Insurance Corp., Federal Home Loan Bank Bd.; federal employees: Labor Dept., Office of Personnel Management; energy: Energy Dept., Energy Information Administration; education: Education Dept., Natl. Center for Education Statistics, National Education Assn. Other information from sources in individual states, usually Commerce Dept.

Alabama

Heart of Dixie, Cotton State

People. Population (1983): 3,959,000; **rank:** 22. **Pop. density:** 78.1 per sq. mi. **Urban** (1980): 60%. **Racial distrib.** (1980): 73.7% White; 26.3% Black; Hispanic 33,100. **Net migration** (1970-80): +151,880.

Geography. Total area: 51,609 sq. mi.; **rank:** 29. **Land area:** 50,708 sq. mi. **Acres forested land:** 21,361,100. **Location:** in the east south central U.S., extending N-S from Tenn. to the Gulf of Mexico; east of the Mississippi River. **Climate:** long, hot summers; mild winters; generally abundant rainfall. **Topography:** coastal plains inc. Prairie Black Belt give way to hills, broken terrain; highest elevation, 2,407 ft. **Capital:** Montgomery.

Economy. Principal industries: pulp and paper, chemicals, electronics, apparel, textiles, primary metals, lumber and wood, food processing, fabricated metals, automotive tires. **Principal manufactured goods:** electronics, cast iron and plastic pipe, ships, paper products, chemicals, steel, mobile homes, fabrics, poultry processing. **Agriculture: Chief crops:** soybeans, cotton, peanuts, corn, hay, wheat, pecans, peaches, potatoes, tomatoes. **Livestock** (1982): 1.9 mln. cattle; 480,000 hogs/pigs; 17.4 mln. poultry. **Timber/lumber** (1982): pine, hardwoods; 875 mln. bd. ft. **Minerals** (1983): $349.2 mostly cement, crushed stone, lime, clays, sand & gravel. **Commercial fishing** (1982): $47.4 mln. **Chief ports:** Mobile. **Value of construction** (1983): $2.8 bln. **Employment distribution:** 25.4% manuf.; 20.4% trade; 16.4% serv. **Per capita income** (1983): $9,235. **Unemployment** (1983): 13.7%. **Tourism** (1982): tourists spent $2.7 bln. **Finance. No. banks** (1983): 273; **No. savings assns.** (1982): 38.

Federal government. No. federal civilian employees (Mar. 1983): 49,633. **Avg. salary:** $24,048. **Notable federal facilities:** George C. Marshall NASA Space Center, Huntsville; Maxwell AFB, Montgomery; Ft. Rucker, Ozark; Ft. McClellan, Anniston; Natl. Fertilizer Development Center, Muscle Shoals.

Energy. Electricity production (1983, mwh, by source): Hydroelectric: 11.1 mln. Mineral: 39.9 mln. Nuclear: 25.2 mln.

Education. No. schools (1981): 1,650 elem. and second.; 57 higher ed. **Avg. salary, public school teachers:** $18,164.

State data. Motto: We dare defend our rights. **Flower:** Camellia. **Bird:** Yellowhammer. **Tree:** Southern pine. **Song:** Alabama. **Entered union** Dec. 14, 1819; rank, 22d. **State fair at:** Birmingham; Oct. 6-15.

History. First Europeans were Spanish explorers in the early 1500s. The French made the first permanent settlement, on Mobile Bay, 1701-02; later, English settled in the northern areas. France ceded the entire region to England at the end of the French and Indian War, 1763, but Spanish Florida claimed the Mobile Bay area until U. S. troops took it, 1813. Gen. Andrew Jackson broke the power of the Creek Indians, 1814, and they were removed to Oklahoma. The Confederate States were organized Feb. 4, 1861, at Montgomery, the first capital.

Tourist attractions. Jefferson Davis' "first White House" of the Confederacy; Ivy Green, Helen Keller's birthplace at Tuscumbia; statue of Vulcan in Birmingham; George Washington Carver Museum at Tuskegee Institute; Alabama Space and Rocket Center at Huntsville. At Russell Cave National Monument, near Bridgeport, may be seen a detailed record of occupancy by humans from about 10,000 BC to 1650 AD.

Famous Alabamians include Hank Aaron, Tallulah Bankhead, Hugo L. Black, Paul "Bear" Bryant, George Washington Carver, Nat King Cole, William C. Handy, Helen Keller, Harper Lee, Joe Louis, John Hunt Morgan, Jesse Owens, Booker T. Washington, Hank Williams.

Chamber of Commerce: 468 S. Perry St., P.O. Box 76, Montgomery, AL 36195.

Alaska

No official nickname

People. Population (1983): 479,000; **rank:** 50. **Pop. density:** 0.84 per sq. mi., **Urban** (1980): 64.3%. **Net migration** (1970-82): +60,130.

Geography. Total area: 586,412 sq. mi.; **rank:** 1. **Land area:** 569,600 sq. mi. **Acres forested land:** 119,114,900. **Location:** NW corner of North America, bordered on east by Canada. **Climate:** SE, SW, and central regions, moist and mild; far north extremely dry. Extended summer days, winter nights, throughout. **Topography:** includes Pacific and Arctic mountain systems, central plateau, and Arctic slope. Mt. McKinley, 20,320 ft., is the highest point in North America. **Capital:** Juneau.

Economy. Principal industries: oil, gas, tourism, commercial fishing. **Principal manufactured goods:** fish products, lumber and pulp, furs. **Agriculture: Chief crops:** barley, hay, silage, potatoes, lettuce, milk, eggs. **Livestock:** 9,600 cattle; 3,200 hogs/pigs; 3,100 sheep. 78,000 poultry; 25,000 reindeer. **Timber/lumber:** spruce. yellow cedar, hemlock. **Minerals** (1983): $156 mln.; sand & gravel, crushed stone, gold. **Commercial fishing** (1982): $575.6 mln. **Chief ports:** Anchorage, Dutch Harbor, Seward, Skagway, Juneau, Sitka, Valdez, Wrangell. **International airports at:** Anchorage, Fairbanks, Ketchikan, Juneau. **Value of construction** (1983): $2.0 bln. **Employment distribution:** 29.3% gvt.; 19.7% trade. 18.3% serv.; 8.7% transp. **Per capita income** (1983): $16,820. **Unemployment** (1983): 10.3%. **Tourism** (1983): out-of-state visitors spent $535 mln.

Finance. No. banks: (1983): 15; **No. savings assns.** (1982): 5.

Federal government. No. federal civilian employees (Mar. 1983): 8,954. **Avg. salary:** $27,872.

Energy. Electricity production (1983, mwh, by source): Hydroelectric: 593,000. Mineral: 3.4 mln.

Education. No. schools (1981): 477 elem. and second.; 15 higher ed. **Avg. salary, public school teachers:** $34,510.

State data. Motto: North to the future. **Flower:** Forget-me-not. **Bird:** Willow ptarmigan. **Tree:** Sitka spruce. **Song:** Alaska's Flag. **Entered union:** Jan. 3, 1959; rank 49th. **State fair at:** Palmer; late Aug.—early Sept.

History. Vitus Bering, a Danish explorer working for Russia, was the first European to land in Alaska, 1741. Alexander Baranov, first governor of Russian America, set up headquarters at Archangel, near present Sitka, in 1799. Secretary of State William H. Seward in 1867 bought Alaska from Russia for $7.2 million, a bargain some called "Seward's Folly." In 1896 gold was discovered and the famed Gold Rush was on.

Tourist attractions: Glacier Bay National Park, Katmai National Park & Preserve, Denali National Park, one of North America's great wildlife sanctuaries, Pribilof Islands fur seal rookeries, restored St. Michael's Russian Orthodox Cathedral, Sitka.

Famous Alaskans include Carl Eielson, Ernest Gruening, Joe Juneau, Sydney Laurence, James Wickersham.

Chamber of Commerce: 310 Second St., Juneau, AK 99801.

Arizona
Grand Canyon State

People. Population (1983): 2,963,000; **rank:** 28. **Pop. density:** 26.1 per sq. mi. **Urban** (1980): 83.8% **Racial distrib. (1980):** 82.4% White; 2.7% Black; 14.8% Other (includes American Indians); Hispanic 440,915. **Net migration** (1970-79): +464,000.

Geography. Total area: 113,909 sq. mi.; **rank:** 6. **Land area:** 113,417 sq. mi. **Acres forested land:** 18,493,900. **Location:** in the southwestern U.S. **Climate:** clear and dry in the southern regions and northern plateau; high central areas have heavy winter snows. **Topography:** Colorado plateau in the N, containing the Grand Canyon; Mexican Highlands running diagonally NW to SE; Sonoran Desert in the SW. **Capital:** Phoenix.

Economy. Principal industries: manufacturing, tourism, mining, agriculture. **Principal manufactured goods:** electronics, printing and publishing, foods, primary and fabricated metals, aircraft and missiles, apparel. **Agriculture: Chief crops:** cotton, sorghum, barley, corn, wheat, sugar beets, citrus fruits. **Livestock:** 1.14 mln. cattle; 99,000 hogs/pigs; 490,000 sheep; 565,000 poultry. **Timber/lumber** (1982): pine, fir, spruce; 229 mln. bd. ft. **Minerals** (1983): $1.6 bln.; copper, molybdenum, gold, silver. **International airports at:** Phoenix, Tucson, Yuma. **Value of construction** (1983): $5.3 bln. **Employment distribution** (1981): 24% trade, 19% gvt., 21% serv., 16% manuf. **Per capita income** (1983): $10,719. **Unemployment** (1983): 9.1% **Tourism** (1980): tourists spent $4.0 bln.

Finance. No. banks: (1983): 48; **No. savings assns.** (1982): 10.

Federal government: No. federal civilian employees (Mar. 1983): 26,144. **Avg. salary:** $22,181. **Notable federal facilities:** Williams, Luke, Davis-Monthan AF bases; Ft. Huachuca Army Base; Yuma Proving Grounds.

Energy. Electricity production (1983, mwh, by source): Hydroelectric: 14.5 mln.; Mineral: 26.9.

Education. No. schools (1981): 1,081 elem. and second.; 28 higher ed. **Avg. salary, public school teachers:** $22,000.

State data. Motto: Ditat Deus (God enriches). **Flower:** Blossom of the Seguaro cactus. **Bird:** Cactus wren. **Tree:** Paloverde. **Song:** Arizona. **Entered union** Feb. 14, 1912; rank, 48th. **State fair at:** Phoenix; late Oct.–early Nov.

History. Marcos de Niza, a Franciscan, and Estevan, a black slave, explored the area, 1539. Eusebio Francisco Kino, Jesuit missionary, taught Indians Christianity and farming, 1690-1711, left a chain of missions. Spain ceded Arizona to Mexico, 1821. The U.S. took over at the end of the Mexican War, 1848. The area below the Gila River was obtained from Mexico in the Gadsden Purchase, 1854. Long Apache wars did not end until 1886, with Geronimo's surrender.

Tourist attractions. The Grand Canyon of the Colorado, an immense, vari-colored fissure 217 mi. long, 4 to 13 mi. wide at the brim, 4,000 to 5,500 ft. deep; the Painted Desert, extending for 30 mi. along U.S. 66; the Petrified Forest; Canyon Diablo, 225 ft. deep and 500 ft.

wide; Meteor Crater, 4,150 ft. across, 570 ft. deep, made by a prehistoric meteor. Also, London Bridge at Lake Havasu City.

Famous Arizonans include Cochise, Geronimo, Barry Goldwater, Zane Grey, George W. P. Hunt, Helen Jacobs, Percival Lowell, William H. Pickering, Morris Udall, Stewart Udall, Frank Lloyd Wright.

Chamber of Commerce: 2701 E. Camelback Rd. Phoenix, AZ 85016.

Arkansas
Land of Opportunity

People. Population (1983): 2,328,000; **rank:** 33. **Pop. density:** 44.8 per sq. mi. **Urban** (1980): 51.5%. **Racial distrib.** (1980): 66.1% White; 16.3% Black; Hispanic 17,873. **Net migration** (1970-80): +14,616.

Geography. Total area: 53,104 sq. mi.; **rank:** 27. **Land area:** 51,945 sq. mi. **Acres forested land:** 18,281,500. **Location:** in the west south-central U.S. **Climate:** long, hot summers, mild winters; generally abundant rainfall. **Topography:** eastern delta and prairie, southern lowland forests, and the northwestern highlands, which include the Ozark Plateaus. **Capital:** Little Rock.

Economy. Principal industries: manufacturing, agriculture, tourism. **Principal manufactured goods:** poultry products, forestry products, aluminum, electric motors, transformers, garments, shoes, bricks, fertilizer, petroleum products. **Agriculture: Chief crops:** soybeans, rice, cotton, hay, wheat, sorghum, tomatoes, strawberries. **Livestock:** 2.05 mln. cattle; 720,000 hogs/pigs; 6.35 mln. poultry. **Timber/lumber** (1982): oak, hickory, gum, cypress, pine; 948 mln. bd. ft. **Minerals** (1983): $252.3; abrasives, bauxite, bromine, stone, sand & gravel. **Commercial fishing** (1982): $7.4 mln. **Chief ports:** Little Rock, Pine Bluff, Osceola, Helena, Fort Smith, Van Buren, Camden. **Value of construction** (1983): $1.5 bln. **Employment distribution:** 14.0% manuf.; 13.9% trade; 6.8% agric. **Per capita income** (1983): $9,040. **Unemployment** (1983): 10.1% **Tourism** (1983): travelers spent $1.6 bln.

Finance. No. banks (1983): 262; **No. savings assns.** (1982): 48.

Federal government. No. federal civilian employees (Mar. 1983): 11,938. **Avg. salary:** $21,487. **Notable federal facilities:** Nat'l. Center for Toxicological Research, Jefferson; Pine Bluff Arsenal.

Energy. Electricity production (1983, mwh, by source): Hydroelectric: 3.3 mln.; Mineral: 21.5 mln.; Nuclear: 7.7 mln.

Education. No. schools (1981): 1,294 elem. and second.; 35 higher ed. **Avg. salary, public school teachers:** $15,549.

State data. Motto: Regnat Populus (The people rule). **Flower:** Apple Blossom. **Bird:** Mockingbird. **Tree:** Pine. **Song:** Arkansas. **Entered union:** June 15, 1836; rank, 25th. **State fair at:** Little Rock; late Sept.- early Oct.

History. First European explorers were de Soto, 1541, Jolliet, 1673; La Salle, 1682. First settlement was by the French under Henri de Tonty, 1686, at Arkansas Post. In 1762 the area was ceded by France to Spain, then back again in 1800, and was part of the Louisiana Purchase by the U.S. in 1803. Arkansas seceded from the Union in 1861, only after the Civil War began, and more than 10,000 Arkansans fought on the Union side.

Tourist attractions. Hot Springs National Park, water ranging from 95° to 147°F; Blanchard Caverns, near Mountain View, are among the nation's largest; Crater of Diamonds, near Murfreesboro, only U.S. diamond mine; Buffalo Natl. River.

Famous Arkansans include Hattie Caraway, "Dizzy" Dean, Orval Faubus, James W. Fulbright, Douglas MacArthur, John L. McClellan, James S. McDonnel, Winthrop Rockefeller, Edward Durell Stone, Archibald Yell.

Chamber of Commerce: One Spring Bldg., Little Rock, AR 72201.

California

Golden State

People. Population (1983): 25,174,000; **rank:** 1. **Pop. density:** 161.0 per sq. mi. **Urban** (1980): 91.3%. **Racial distrib.** (1980): 76.1% White; 7.6% Black; 16.1% Other (includes American Indians, Asian Americans, and Pacific Islanders); Hispanic 4,543,770. **Net migration** (1982): +233,460.

Geography. Total area 158,693 sq. mi.; **rank:** 3. **Land area:** 156,361 sq. mi. **Acres forested land:** 40,152,100. **Location:** on western coast of the U.S. **Climate:** moderate temperatures and rainfall along the coast; extremes in the interior. **Topography:** long mountainous coastline; central valley; Sierra Nevada on the east; desert basins of the southern interior; rugged mountains of the north. **Capital:** Sacramento.

Economy. Principal industries: agriculture, aerospace, manufacturing, construction, recreation. **Principal manufactured goods:** foods, primary and fabricated metals, machinery, electric and electronic equipment, chemicals and allied products. **Agriculture: Chief crops:** dairy products, grapes, cotton, nursery products, hay, tomatoes, lettuce, eggs, oranges, almonds, wheat, strawberries, rice. **Livestock** (1982): 1.9 mln. cattle; 1.8 mln. hogs/pigs; 1.4 mln. sheep; 209.5 mln. poultry. **Timber/lumber** (1982): fir, pine, redwood, oak; 3.0 bln. bd. ft. **Minerals:** (1983): leading state in U.S. in nonfuel minerals prod. with value of $1.8 bln.; mostly cement, boron minerals, sand & gravel, crushed stone. **Commercial fishing** (1982): $241.2 mln. **Chief ports:** Long Beach, San Diego, Oakland, San Francisco, Sacramento, Stockton. **International airports at:** Los Angeles, San Francisco. **Value of construction** (1983): $22.3 bln. **Employment distribution** (1983): 23.6% serv.; 23.6% trade; 19.4% mfg; 17.2% gvt. **Per capita income** (1983): $13,239. **Unemployment** (1983): 9.7% **Tourism** (1982): out-of-state visitors spent $24.7 bln.

Finance. No. banks (1983): 441; **No. savings assns.** (1982): 171.

Federal government. No. federal civilian employees (Mar. 1983): 206,486. **Avg. salary:** $23,441. **Notable federal facilities:** Vandenberg, Beale, Travis, McClellan AF bases, San Francisco Mint.

Energy. Electricity production (1983, mwh, by source): Hydroelectric: 56.8 mln.; Mineral: 21.5 mln.; Nuclear: 3.9 mln.

Education. No. schools (1981): 9,021 elem. and second.; 268 higher ed. **Avg. salary, public school teachers:** $27,553.

State Data. Motto: Eureka (I have found it). **Flower:** Golden poppy. **Bird:** California valley quail. **Tree:** California redwood. **Song:** I Love You, California. **Entered Union** Sept. 9, 1850; rank, 31st. **State fair** at: Sacramento; late Aug.—early Sept.

History. First European explorers were Cabrillo, 1542, and Drake, 1579. First settlement was the Spanish Alta California mission at San Diego, 1769, first in a string founded by Franciscan Father Junipero Serra. U. S. traders and settlers arrived in the 19th century and staged the abortive Bear Flag Revolt, 1846; the Mexican War began later in 1846 and U.S. forces occupied California; Mexico ceded the province to the U.S., 1848, the same year the Gold Rush began.

Tourist attractions. Scenic regions are Yosemite Valley; Lassen and Sequoia-Kings Canyon national parks; Lake Tahoe; the Mojave and Colorado deserts; San Francisco Bay; and Monterey Peninsula. Oldest living things on earth are believed to be a stand of Bristlecone pines in the Inyo National Forest, est. to be 4,600 years old. The world's tallest tree, the Howard Libbey redwood, 362 ft. with a girth of 44 ft., stands on Redwood Creek, Humboldt County.

Also, Palomar Observatory; Disneyland; J. Paul Getty Museum, Malibu; Tournament of Roses and Rose Bowl.

Famous Californians include Luther Burbank, John C. Fremont, Bret Harte, Wm. R. Hearst, Jack London, Aimee Semple McPherson, John Muir, William Saroyan, Junipero Serra, Leland Stanford, John Steinbeck, Earl Warren.

Chamber of Commerce: 455 Capitol Mall, Sacramento, CA 95814.

Colorado

Centennial State

People. Population (1983): 3,139,000; **rank:** 26. **Pop. density:** 30.3 per sq. mi. **Urban** (1980): 80.6%. **Racial distrib.** (1980): 88.9% White; 3.5% Black; Hispanic 339,300. **Net migration** (1970-80): +668,811.

Geography. Total area: 104,247 sq. mi.; **rank:** 8. **Land area:** 103,766 sq. mi. **Acres forested land:** 22,271,000. **Location:** in west central U.S. **Climate:** low relative humidity, abundant sunshine, wide daily, seasonal temperatures ranges; alpine conditions in the high mountains. **Topography:** eastern dry high plains; hilly to mountainous central plateau; western Rocky Mountains of high ranges alternating with broad valleys and deep, narrow canyons. **Capital:** Denver.

Economy. Principal industries: manufacturing, government, mining, tourism, agriculture, aerospace, electronics equipment. **Principal manufactured goods:** computer equipment, instruments, foods, machinery, aerospace products, rubber, steel. **Agriculture: Chief crops:** corn, wheat, hay, sugar beets, barley, potatoes, apples, peaches, pears, soy beans. **Livestock** (1982): 3.0 mln. cattle; 330,000 hogs/pigs; 710,000 sheep; (1981) 7.4 mln. poultry. **Timber/lumber** (1982): oak, ponderosa pine, Douglas fir; 128 mln. bd. ft. **Minerals** (1983): $349.8; cement, sand & gravel, molybdenum. **International airports at:** Denver. **Value of construction** (1983): $4.7 bln. **Employment distribution** (1983): 21.8% trade; 19.1% serv.; 15.9% gvt.; 12.0% manuf. **Per capita income** (1983): $12,580. **Unemployment** (1983): 6.6%. **Tourism** (1983): $4.0 bln.

Finance. No. banks (1983): 551; **No. savings assns.** (1982): 43.

Federal government. No. federal civilian employees (Mar. 1983): 34,787. **Avg. salary:** $24,485. **Notable federal facilities:** U.S. Air Force Academy; U.S. Mint; Ft. Carson, Lowry AFB; Solar Energy Research Institute; U.S. Rail Transport. Test Center; N. Amer. Aerospace Defense Command; Consolidated Space Operations Center; U.S. Documents Center.

Energy. Electricity production (1983, mwh, by source): Hydroelectric: 1.9 mln.; Mineral: 23.0 mln.; Nuclear: 748,000.

Education. No. schools (1981): 1,466 elem. and second.; 44 higher ed. **Avg. salary, public school teachers:** $22,291.

State data. Motto: Nil Sine Numine (Nothing without Providence). **Flower:** Rocky Mountain columbine. **Bird:** Lark bunting. **Tree:** Colorado blue spruce. **Song:** Where the Columbines Grow. **Entered union** Aug. 1, 1876; rank 38th. **State fair** at: Pueblo; last week in Aug.

History. Early civilization centered around Mesa Verde 2,000 years ago. The U.S. acquired eastern Colorado in the Louisiana Purchase, 1803; Lt. Zebulon M. Pike explored the area, 1806, discovering the peak that bears his name. After the Mexican War, 1846-48, U.S. immigrants settled in the east, former Mexicans in the south.

Tourist attractions. Rocky Mountain National Park; Garden of the Gods; Great Sand Dunes, Dinosaur, Black Canyon of the Gannison, and Colorado national monuments; Pikes Peak (pre-historic cliff dwellings); 35 major ski areas. The Grand Mesa tableland comprises Grand Mesa Forest, 659,584 acres, with 200 lakes stocked with trout.

Famous Coloradans include Frederick Bonfils, William N. Byers, M. Scott Carpenter, Jack Dempsey, Mamie Eisenhower, Douglas Fairbanks, Scott Hamilton, Lowell Thomas, Byron R. White, Paul Whiteman.

Tourist information: Dept. of Local Affairs, 1313 Sherman St., Denver, CO 80203.

Connecticut

Constitution State, Nutmeg State

People. Population (1983): 3,138,000; **rank:** 27. **Pop. density:** 645.4 per sq. mi. **Urban** (1980): 78.8% **Racial distrib.** (1980): 90.0% White; 6.9% Black; Hispanic 124,499. **Net migration** (1970-80): +75,576.

Geography. Total area: 5,009 sq. mi.; **rank:** 48. **Land area:** 4,862 sq. mi. **Acres forested land:** 1,860,800. **Location:** New England state in the northeastern corner of the U.S. **Climate:** moderate; winters avg. slightly below freezing, warm, humid summers. **Topography:** western upland, the Berkshires, in the NW, highest elevations; narrow central lowland N-S; hilly eastern upland drained by rivers. **Capital:** Hartford.

Economy. Principal industries: manufacturing, retail trade, government, services. **Principal manufactured goods:** aircraft engines and parts, submarines, copper wire and tubing, helicopters, bearings, instruments, electrical equipment, machine tools. **Agriculture: Chief crops:** tobacco, hay, apples, potatoes, nursery stock. **Livestock:** 106,000 cattle; 8,000 hogs/pigs; 6,000 sheep; 5.9 mln. poultry. **Timber/lumber** (1980): oak, birch, beech, maple; 73 mln. bd. ft. **Minerals** (1983): $59 mln; sand & gravel; crushed stone. **Commercial fishing** (1982): $9.6 mln. **Chief ports:** New Haven, Bridgeport, New London. **International airports at:** Windsor Locks. **Value of construction** (1983): $2.3 bln. **Employment distribution:** 28% manuf.; 22% serv. **Per capita income** (1983): $14,826. **Unemployment** (1983): 6.0%. **Tourism** (1983): out-of-state visitors spent $2.2 bln.

Finance. No. banks (1983): 108; **No. savings assns.** (1982): 38.

Federal Government. No. federal civilian employees (Mar. 1983): 9,157. **Avg. salary:** $24,340. **Notable federal facilities:** U.S. Coast Guard Academy; U.S. Navy Submarine Base.

Energy. Electricity production (1982, mwh, by source): Hydroelectric: 372,000; Mineral: 12.3 mln.; Nuclear: 11.6 mln.

Education. No. schools (1981): 1,317 elem. and second.; 47 higher ed. **Avg. salary, public school teachers:** $21,728.

State data. Motto: Qui Transtulit Sustinet (He who transplanted still sustains). **Flower:** Mountain laurel. **Bird:** American robin. **Tree:** White oak. **Song:** Yankee Doodle Dandy. **Fifth** of the 13 original states to ratify the Constitution, Jan. 9, 1788.

History. Adriaen Block, Dutch explorer, was the first European visitor, 1614. By 1634, settlers from Plymouth Bay started colonies along the Connecticut River and in 1637 defeated the Pequot Indians. In the Revolution, Connecticut men fought in most major campaigns and turned back British raids on Danbury and other towns, while Connecticut privateers captured British merchant ships.

Tourist attractions. Mark Twain House, Hartford; Yale University's Art Gallery, Peabody Museum, all in New Haven; Mystic Seaport, Mystic, a recreated 19th century seaport village; P.T. Barnum Museum, Bridgeport.

Famous "Nutmeggers" include Ethan Allen, Phineas Barnum, Samuel Colt, Jonathan Edwards, Nathan Hale, Katharine Hepburn, Isaac Hull, J. Pierpont Morgan, Israel Putnam, Harriet Beecher Stowe, Mark Twain, Noah Webster, Eli Whitney.

Tourist information: State Dept. of Economic Development, 210 Washington St., Hartford, CT 06106.

Delaware

First State, Diamond State

People. Population (1983): 606,000; **rank:** 47. **Pop. density:** 305.8 per sq. mi. **Urban** (1980): 70.6%. **Racial distrib.** (1980): 82.0% White; 16.1% Black; Hispanic 9,671. **Net migration** (1970-80): +8,000.

Geography. Total area: 2,057 sq. mi.; **rank:** 49. **Land area:** 1,982 sq. mi. **Acres forested land:** 391,800. **Location:** occupies the Delmarva Peninsula on the Atlantic coastal plain. **Climate:** moderate. **Topography:** Piedmont plateau to the N, sloping to a near sea-level plain. **Capital:** Dover.

Economy. Principal industries: chemistry, agriculture, poultry, shellfish, tourism, auto assembly, food processing, transportation equipment. **Principal manufactured goods:** nylon, apparel, luggage, foods, autos, processed meats and vegetables, railroad and aircraft equipment. **Agriculture: Chief crops:** soybeans, potatoes, corn, mushrooms, lima beans, green peas, barley, cucumbers, snap beans, watermelons, apples. **Livestock:** 36,000 cattle; 1.78 mln. poultry. **Timber/Lumber:** (1982) forest products $1.8 mln. **Minerals** (1983): $3.2 mln; sand & gravel, magnesium compounds. **Commercial fishing** (1982): $2.3 mln. **Chief ports:** Wilmington. **International airports at:** Philadelphia/Wilmington. **Value of construction** (1983): $473 mln. **Employment distribution:** 76% non-manufacturing; 24% manuf. **Per capita income** (1983): $12,442. **Unemployment** (1983): 8.1%. **Tourism** (1981): out-of-state visitors spent $460.9 mln.

Finance. No. banks (1983): 34; **No. savings assns.** (1982): 5.

Federal government. No. federal civilian employees (Mar. 1983): 3,060. **Avg. salary:** $22,754. **Notable federal facilities:** Dover Air Force Base, Federal Wildlife Refuge, Bombay Hook.

Energy. Electricity production (1982, mwh, by source): Mineral: 9.5 mln.

Education. No. schools (1981): 242 elem. and second.; 10 higher ed. **Avg. salary, public school teachers:** $21,348.

State data. Motto: Liberty and independence. **Flower:** Peach blossom. **Bird:** Blue hen chicken. **Tree:** American holly. **Song:** Our Delaware. **First** of original 13 states to ratify the Constitution, Dec. 7, 1787. **State fair** at: Harrington; end of July.

History. The Dutch first settled in Delaware near present Lewes, 1631, but were wiped out by Indians. Swedes settled at present Wilmington, 1638; Dutch settled anew, 1651, near New Castle and seized the Swedish settlement, 1655, only to lose all Delaware and New Netherland to the British, 1664.

Tourist attractions. Ft. Christina Monument, the site of founding of New Sweden; John Dickinson "Penman of the Revolution" home, Dover; Henry Francis du Pont Winterthur Museum; Hagley Museum, Wilmington; Old Swedes (Trinity Parish) Church, erected 1698, is the oldest Protestant church in the U.S. still in use.

Famous Delawareans include Thomas F. Bayard, Henry Seidel Canby, E. I. du Pont, John P. Marquand, Howard Pyle, Caesar Rodney.

Chamber of Commerce: One Commerce Center, Wilmington, DE 19801.

Florida

Sunshine State

People. Population (1983): 10,680,000; **rank:** 7. **Pop. density:** 197.3 per sq. mi. **Urban** (1980): 84.3%. **Racial distrib.** (1980): 83.9% White; 13.7% Black; Hispanic 858,158. **Net migration** (1970-81): +3,281,954.

Geography: Total area: 58,560 sq. mi.; **rank:** 22. **Land area:** 54,136 sq. mi. **Acres forested land:** 17,932,900. **Location:** peninsula jutting southward 500 mi. bet. the Atlantic and the Gulf of Mexico. **Climate:** subtropical N of Bradenton-Lake Okeechobee-Vero Beach line; tropical S of line. **Topography:** land is flat or rolling; highest point is 345 ft. in the NW. **Capital:** Tallahassee.

Economy. Principal industries: services, trade, gvt., manufacturing, tourism. **Principal manufactured goods:** electric & electronic equip., transp. equipment; food; printing & publishing; apparel & textile. **Agriculture: Chief crops:** citrus fruits, vegetables, corn soybean, avocados, sugarcane, peanuts, hay crops, tobacco, strawberries, watermelon. **Livestock** (1981): 2.8 mln. cattle; 370,000 hogs/pigs; 4,500 sheep; 12 mln. poultry. **Timber/lumber** (1980): pine, cypress, cedar; 468 mln. bd. ft. **Minerals** (1983): $1.3 bln.; mostly crushed stone, cement, and phosphate rock. **Commercial fishing** (1983): $168.0 mln. **Chief ports:** Tampa, Jacksonville, Miami, Pensacola. **International airports at:** Miami, Tampa, Jacksonville, Orlando, Ft. Lauderdale, W. Palm Beach. **Value of construction** (1983): $14.4 bln. **Per capita income** (1983): $11,592. **Unemployment** (1983): 8.6% **Tourism** (1982): out-of-state visitors spent $20 bln.

Finance. No. banks (1983): 472; **No. savings assns.** (1982): 115.

Federal government. No. federal civilian employees (Mar. 1983): 53,079. **Avg. salary:** $23,663. **Notable federal facilities:** John F. Kennedy Space Center, Cape Canaveral; Eglin Air Force Base.

Energy. Electricity production (1982, mwh, by source): Hydroelectric: 220,000; Mineral: 76.5 mln.; Nuclear: 14.8 mln.

Education. No. schools (1981): 2,680 elem. and second.; 79 higher ed. **Avg. salary, public school teachers:** $19,605.

State data. Motto: In God we trust. **Flower:** Orange blossom. **Bird:** Mockingbird. **Tree:** Sabal palmetto palm. **Song:** Swanee River. **Entered union** Mar. 3, 1845; rank, 27th. **State fair at:** Tampa; Feb. 8-19.

History. First European to see Florida was Ponce de Leon, 1513. France established a colony, Fort Caroline, on the St. Johns River, 1564; Spain settled St. Augustine, 1565, and Spanish troops massacred most of the French. Britain's Francis Drake burned St. Augustine, 1586. Britain held the area briefly, 1763-83, returning it to Spain. After Andrew Jackson led a U.S. invasion, 1818, Spain ceded Florida to the U.S., 1819. The Seminole War, 1835-42, resulted in removal of most Indians to Oklahoma. Florida seceded from the Union, 1861, was readmitted, 1868.

Tourist attractions. Miami, with the nation's greatest concentration of luxury hotels at Miami Beach; St. Augustine, oldest city in U.S.; Walt Disney World and EPCOT; Kennedy Space Center, Cape Canaveral.

Everglades National Park, 3d largest of U.S. national parks, preserves the beauty of the vast Everglades swamp. Castillo de San Marcos, St. Augustine, is a national monument. Also, the Ringling Museum of Art, and the Ringling Museum of the Circus, both in Sarasota; Sea World, and Circus World, Orlando; Busch Gardens, Tampa.

Famous Floridians include Henry M. Flagler, James Weldon Johnson, MacKinlay Kantor, Henry B. Plant, Marjorie Kinnan Rawlings, Joseph W. Stilwell, Charles P. Summerall.

Chamber of Commerce: P.O. Box 5497, Tallahassee, FL 32301.

Georgia

Empire State of the South, Peach State

People. Population (1983): 5,732,000; **rank:** 12. **Pop. density:** 98.7 per sq. mi. **Urban** (1980): 62.4%. **Racial distrib.** (1980): 72.2% White; 26.8% Black; Hispanic 61,261. **Net migration** (1970-80): +441,658.

Geography. Total area: 58,876 sq. mi.; **rank:** 21. **Land area:** 58,073 sq. mi. **Acres forested land:** 25,256,100. **Location:** South Atlantic state. **Climate:** maritime tropical

air masses dominate in summer; continental polar air masses in winter; east central area drier. **Topography:** most southerly of the Blue Ridge Mtns. cover NE and N central; central Piedmont extends to the fall line of rivers; coastal plain levels to the coast flatlands. **Capital:** Atlanta.

Economy. Principal industries: manufacturing, forestry, agriculture, chemicals. **Principal manufactured goods:** textiles, transportation equipment, foods, clothing, paper and wood products, chemical products. **Agriculture: Chief crops:** peanuts, corn, soybeans, tobacco, oats and wheat, cotton and cottonseed. **Livestock** (1982): 1.95 mln. cattle; 1.4 mln. hogs/pigs; 3,200 sheep; 64.8 mln. poultry. **Timber/lumber** (1982): pine, hardwood; 1.4 bln. bd. ft. **Minerals** (1983): $809.2 mln.; clays, crushed stone. **Commercial fishing** (1982): $22.3 mln. **Chief ports:** Savannah, Brunswick. **International airports at:** Atlanta. **Value of construction** (1983): $5.9 bln. **Employment distribution:** 30% trade; 23% mfg.; 19% gvt.; 17% serv. **Per capita income** (1983): $10,283. **Unemployment** (1983): 7.5% **Tourism** (1982): tourists spent $6.38 bln.

Finance. No. banks (1983): 394. **No. savings assns.** (1982): 69.

Federal government. No. federal civilian employees (Mar. 1983): 60,270. **Avg. salary:** $23,165. **Notable federal facilities:** Dobbins AFB; Fts. Benning, Gordon, McPherson; Nat'l. Law Enforcement Training Ctr., Glynco.

Energy. Electricity production (1983, mwh, by source): Hydroelectric: 4.1 mln.; Mineral: 54.7 mln.; Nuclear: 7.8 mln.

Education. No. schools (1981): 2,092 elem. and second.; 76 higher ed. **Avg. salary, public school teachers:** $18,282.

State data. Motto: Wisdom, justice and moderation. **Flower:** Cherokee rose. **Bird:** Brown thrasher. **Tree:** Live oak. **Song:** Georgia On My Mind. **Fourth** of the 13 original states to ratify the Constitution, Jan. 2, 1788.

History. Gen. James Oglethorpe established the first settlements, 1733, for poor and religiously-persecuted Englishmen. Oglethorpe defeated a Spanish army from Florida at Bloody Marsh, 1742. In the Revolution, Georgians seized the Savannah armory, 1775, and sent the munitions to the Continental Army; they fought seesaw campaigns with Cornwallis' British troops, twice liberating Augusta and forcing final evacuation by the British from Savannah, 1782.

Tourist attractions. The Little White House in Warm Springs where Pres. Franklin D. Roosevelt died Apr. 12, 1945, 2,500-acre Callaway Gardens, Jekyll Island State Park, the restored 1850s farming community of Westville; Alpine Helen, tiny mountain town converted to Alpine Village. Dahlonega, site of America's first gold rush; Stone Mountain, and Six Flags Over Georgia.

Okefenokee in the SE is one of the largest swamps in the U.S., a wetland wilderness and peat bog covering 660 sq. mi. A large part of it is a National Wildlife Refuge, a home for wild birds, alligators, bear, deer.

Famous Georgians include Hank Aaron, James Bowie, Erskine Caldwell, Jimmy Carter, Lucius D. Clay, Ty Cobb, John C. Fremont, Joel Chandler Harris, Martin Luther King Jr., Sidney Lanier, Margaret Mitchell, Jackie Robinson, Joseph Wheeler.

Chamber of Commerce: 1200 Commerce Bldg., Atlanta, GA 30303.

Hawaii

The Aloha State

People. Population (1983): 1,023,000; **rank:** 39. **Pop. density:** 159.2 per sq. mi. **Urban** (1980): 86.5%. **Racial distrib.** (1980): 33.0% White; 1.7% Black; 65.1% Other (includes Asian Americans and Pacific Islanders); Hispanic 71,479. **Net migration** (1970-83): +15,000.

Geography. Total area: 6,450 sq. mi.; **rank:** 47. **Land area:** 6,425 sq. mi. **Acres forested land:** 1,986,000. **Location:** Hawaiian Islands lie in the North Pacific, 2,397 mi. SW from San Francisco. **Climate:** temperate, mountainous regions cooler; Waialeale, on Kauai, wettest spot in the

U.S. annual rainfall 451 in. **Topography:** islands are tops of a chain of submerged volcanic mountains; active volcanoes: Mauna Loa, Kilauea. **Capital:** Honolulu.

Economy. Principal industries: tourism, defense and other government, sugar refining, agriculture, aquaculture, fishing, motion pictures, manufacturing. **Principal manufactured goods:** sugar, canned pineapple, clothing, foods, printing and publishing. **Agriculture: Chief crops:** sugar, pineapples, macadamia nuts, fruits, coffee, vegetables, melons, and floriculture. **Livestock:** 230,000 cattle; 49,000 hogs/pigs; 1.15 mln. poultry. **Minerals** (1983): $41 mln.; cement, crushed stone. **Commercial fishing** (1982): $14.4 mln. **Chief ports:** Honolulu, Nawiliwili, Barber's Point, Kahului, Hilo. **International airports at:** Honolulu. **Value of construction** (1983): $711.6 mln. **Employment distribution:** 22.8% serv.; 20.4% gvt.; 23.9% trade. **Per capita income** (1983): $12,101. **Tourism** (1982): visitors spent $3.7 bln.

Finance. No. banks (1983): 18; **No. savings assns.** (1982): 6.

Federal government. No. federal civilian employees (Mar. 1983): 23,331. **Avg. salary:** $24,247. **Notable federal facilities:** Pearl Harbor Naval Shipyard; Hickam AFB; Schofield Barracks.

Energy. Electricity production (1983, mwh, by source): Hydroelectric: 17,000; Mineral: 6.5 mln.

Education. No. schools (1981): 339 elem. and second.; 12 higher ed. **Avg. salary, public school teachers:** $25,423.

State data. Motto: The life of the land is perpetuated in righteousness. **Flower:** Hibiscus. **Bird:** Hawaiian goose. **Tree:** Candlenut. **Song:** Hawaii Ponoi. **Entered union** Aug. 21, 1959; rank, 50th. **State fair** at: Honolulu; late May through mid-June.

History. Polynesians from islands 2,000 mi. to the south settled the Hawaiian Islands, probably about 700 A.D. First European visitor was British Capt. James Cook, 1778. Missionaries arrived, 1820, taught religion, reading and writing. King Kamehameha III and his chiefs created the first Constitution and a Legislature which set up a public school system. Sugar production began in 1835 and it became the dominant industry. In 1893, Queen Liliuokalani was deposed, followed, 1894, by a republic headed by Sanford B. Dole. Annexation by the U.S. came in 1898.

Tourist attractions. Natl. Memorial Cemetery of the Pacific, USS Arizona Memorial, Pearl Harbor; Hawaii Volcanoes, Haleakala National Parks; Polynesian Cultural Center, Diamond Head, Waikiki Beach, Nuuanu Pali, Oahu.

Famous Islanders include John A. Burns, Father Joseph Damien, Sanford B. Dole, Wallace R. Farrington, Hiram L. Fong, Daniel K. Inouye, Duke Kahanamoku, King Kamehameha the Great, Queen Kaahumanu, Queen Liliuokalani, Bernice Pauahi Bishop.

Chamber of Commerce: Dillingham Bldg., 735 Bishop St., Honolulu, HI 96813.

Idaho

Gem State

People. Population (1983): 989,000; **rank:** 40. **Pop. density:** 12.0 per sq. mi. **Urban** (1980): 54.0%. **Racial distrib.** (1980): 95.5% White; 0.3% Black; Hispanic 36,615. **Net migration** (1970-83): +130,000.

Geography. Total area: 83,557 sq. mi.; **rank:** 13. **Land area:** 82,677 sq. mi. **Acres forested land:** 21,726,600. **Location:** Pacific Northwest-Mountain state bordering on British Columbia. **Climate:** tempered by Pacific westerly winds; drier, colder, continental clime in SE; altitude an important factor. **Topography:** Snake R. plains in the S; central region of mountains, canyons, gorges (Hells Canyon, 7,000 ft., deepest in N.A.); subalpine northern region. **Capital:** Boise.

Economy. Principal industries: agriculture, manufacturing, tourism, lumber, mining, electronics. **Principal manufactured goods:** processed foods, lumber and wood products, chemical products, primary metals, fabricated metal products, machinery, electronic components.

Agriculture: Chief crops: potatoes, peas, sugar beets, alfalfa seed, wheat, hops, barley, plums and prunes, mint, onions, corn, cherries, apples, hay. **Livestock:** 1.99 mln. cattle; 175,000 hogs/pigs; 512,000 sheep; 1.023 mln. poultry. **Timber/lumber** (1982): yellow, white pine; Douglas fir; white spruce; 704 mln. bd. ft. **Minerals** (1983): $434 mln.; crushed stone, phosphate rock. **Commercial fishing** (1982): $28,000. **Chief ports:** Lewiston. **Value of construction** (1983): $559 mln. **Employment distribution:** 21% trade; 15% serv., 12% manuf.; 17% agric. **Per capita income** (1983): $9,342. **Unemployment** (1983): 9.8%. **Tourism** (1982): travellers spent $1.1 bln.

Finance. No. banks (1983): 26; **No. savings assns.** (1982): 9.

Federal government. No. federal civilian employees (Mar. 1983): 7,108. **Avg. salary:** $23,696. **Notable federal facilities:** Ida. Nat'l. Engineering Lab, Idaho Falls; Nat'l. Reactor Testing Sta., Upper Snake River Plains.

Energy. Electricity production (1982, mwh, by source): Hydroelectric: 12.8 mln..

Education: No. schools (1981): 609 elem. and second.; 9 higher ed. **Avg. salary, public school teachers:** $18,270.

State data. Motto: Esto Perpetua (It is perpetual). **Flower:** Syringa. **Bird:** Mountain bluebird. **Tree:** White pine. **Song:** Here We Have Idaho. **Entered union** July 3, 1890; rank, 43d. **State fair** at: Boise, late Aug.; and Blackfoot, early Sept.

History. Exploration of the Idaho area began with Lewis and Clark, 1805-06. Next came fur traders, setting up posts, 1809-34, and missionaries, establishing missions, 1830s-1850s. Mormons made their first permanent settlement at Franklin, 1860. Idaho's Gold Rush began that same year, and brought thousands of permanent settlers. Strangest of the Indian Wars was the 1,300-mi. trek in 1877 of Chief Joseph and the Nez Perce tribe, pursued by troops that caught them a few miles short of the Canadian border. In 1890, Idaho adopted a progressive Constitution and became a state.

Tourist attractions. Hells Canyon, deepest gorge in N.A.; Craters of the Moon; Sun Valley, year-round resort in the Sawtooth Mtns.; Crystal Falls Cave; Shoshone Falls; Lava Hot Springs; Lake Pend Oreille; Lake Coeur d'Alene; Sawtooth Natl. Recreation Area.

Famous Idahoans include William E. Borah, Fred T. Dubois, Chief Joseph, Sacagawea.

Chamber of Commerce: P.O. Box 2368, Boise, ID 83701.

Illinois

The Inland Empire

People. Population (1983): 11,486,000; **rank:** 5. **Pop. density:** 206.0 per sq. mi. **Urban** (1980): 83.3%. **Racial distrib.** (1980): 80.7% White; 14.6% Black; Hispanic 635,525. **Net migration** (1970-80): −686,300.

Geography. Total area: 56,400 sq. mi.; **rank:** 24. **Land area:** 55,748 sq. mi. **Acres forested land:** 3,810,400. **Location:** east-north central state; western, southern, and eastern boundaries formed by Mississippi, Ohio, and Wabash Rivers, respectively. **Climate:** temperate; typically cold, snowy winters, hot summers. **Topography:** prairie and fertile plains throughout; open hills in the southern region. **Capital:** Springfield.

Economy. Principal industries: manufacturing, wholesale and retail trade, finance, insurance, real estate, agriculture, services. **Principal manufactured goods:** machinery, electric and electronic equipment, foods, primary and fabricated metals, chemical products, printing and publishing. **Agriculture: Chief crops:** corn, soybeans, wheat, oats, hay. **Livestock** (1982): 2.8 mln. cattle; 5.6 mln. hogs/pigs; 140,000 sheep; 4.81 mln. poultry. **Timber/lumber** (1982): oak, hickory, maple, cottonwood. **Minerals** (1983): $423.7 mln.; mostly crushed stone, cement, sand & gravel. **Commercial fishing** (1982): $1.4 mln. **Chief ports:** Chicago. **International airports at:** Chicago. **Value of construction** (1983): $6.0 bln. **Employment distribution:** 23% manuf.; 24% trade; 21%

serv.; 1% agric. **Per capita income** (1983): $12,626. **Unemployment** (1983) 11.4%. **Tourism** (1983): out-of-state visitors spent $6.8 bln.

Finance. No. banks (1983): 1,297; **No. savings assns.** (1982): 295.

Federal government. No. federal civilian employees (Mar. 1983): 53,733. **Avg. salary:** $23,831. **Notable federal facilities:** Fermi Nat'l. Accelerator Lab; Argonne Nat'l. Lab; Ft. Sheridan; Rock Island; Great Lakes, Rantoul, Scott Field.

Energy. Electricity production (1983, mwh, by source): Hydroelectric: 117,000; Mineral: 42.3 mln.; Nuclear: 28.0 mln.

Education. No. schools (1981): 5,220 elem. and second.; 157 higher ed. **Avg. salary, public school teachers:** $23,089.

State data. Motto: State sovereignty—national union. **Flower:** Native violet. **Bird:** Cardinal. **Tree:** White oak. **Song:** Illinois. **Entered union** Dec. 3, 1818; rank, 21st. **State fair** at: Springfield; early Aug.

History: Fur traders were the first Europeans in Illinois, followed shortly, 1673, by Jolliet and Marquette, and, 1680, La Salle, who built a fort near present Peoria. First settlements were French, at Fort St. Louis on the Illinois River, 1692, and Kaskaskia, 1700. France ceded the area to Britain, 1763; Amer. Gen. George Rogers Clark, 1778, took Kaskaskia from the British without a shot. Defeat of Indian tribes in Black Hawk War, 1832, and railroads in 1850s, inspired immigration.

Tourist attractions: Lincoln shrines at Springfield, New Salem, Sangamon; Cahokia Mounds, E. St. Louis; Starved Rock State Park; Crab Orchard Wildlife Refuge; Mormon settlement at Nauvoo; Fts. Kaskaskia, Chartres, Massac (parks).

Famous Illinoisans include Jane Addams, Ray Bradbury, St. Francis Xavier Cabrini, William Jennings Bryan, Stephen A. Douglas, James T. Farrell, Ernest Hemingway, Edgar Lee Masters, Carl Sandburg, Adlai Stevenson, Frank Lloyd Wright.

Tourist Information: Illinois Dept. of Commerce and Community Affairs, 222 South College, Springfield, IL 62706.

Indiana

Hoosier State

People. Population (1983): 5,479,000; **rank:** 14. **Pop. density:** 151.8 per sq. mi. **Urban** (1980): 64.2%. **Racial distrib.** (1980): 91.1 White; 7.5% Black; Hispanic 87,020. **Net migration** (1970-80): −82,807.

Geography. Total area: 36,291 sq. mi.; **rank:** 38. **Land area:** 36,097 sq. mi. **Acres forested land:** 3,942,900. **Location:** east north-central state; Lake Michigan on northern border. **Climate:** 4 distinct seasons with a temperate climate. **Topography:** hilly southern region; fertile rolling plains of central region; flat, heavily glaciated north; dunes along Lake Michigan shore. **Capital:** Indianapolis.

Economy. Principal industries: manufacturing, wholesale and retail trade, agriculture, government, services. **Principal manufactured goods:** primary and fabricated metals, transportation equipment, electrical and electronic equipment, non-electrical machinery, chemical products, foods. **Agriculture: Chief crops** (1983): corn, soybeans, wheat, hay. **Livestock** (1983): 1.7 mln. cattle; 4.4 mln. hogs/pigs; 118,000 sheep; 23.5 mln. poultry. **Timber/lumber:** oak, tulip, beech, sycamore. **Minerals** (1983): $252.3 mln.; mostly crushed stone, abrasives, cement, gypsum, lime, sand & gravel. **Commercial fishing** (1982): $53,000. **Chief ports:** Lake Michigan facility, east of Gary, Southwind Maritime Centre at Mt. Vernon. **International airports at:** Indianapolis. **Value of construction** (1983): $3.1 bln. **Employment distribution** (1983): 29.0% manuf.; 22.6% trade; 17.6% serv. **Per capita income** (1983): $10,567 **Unemployment** (1983): 11.1%. **Tourism** (1983): tourists spent $2.3 bln.

Finance. No. banks (1983): 396; **No. savings assns.** (1982): 128.

Federal government. No. federal civilian employees (Mar. 1983): 24,427. **Avg. salary:** $21,791. **Notable federal facilities:** Naval Avionics Ctr.; Ft. Benjamin Harrison; Grissom AFB; Navy Weapons Support Ctr., Crane.

Energy. Electricity production (1983 mwh, by source): Hydroelectric: 418,000; Mineral: 67.4 mln.

Education. No. schools (1981): 2,552 elem. and second.; 74 higher ed. **Avg. salary, public school teachers:** $20,949.

State data. Motto: Crossroads of America. **Flower:** Peony. **Bird:** Cardinal. **Tree:** Tulip poplar. **Song:** On the Banks of the Wabash, Far Away. **Entered union** Dec. 11, 1816; rank, 19th. **State fair** at: Indianapolis; mid-Aug.

History: Pre-historic Indian Mound Builders of 1,000 years ago were the earliest known inhabitants. A French trading post was built, 1731-32, at Vincennes and La Salle visited the present South Bend area, 1679 and 1681. France ceded the area to Britain, 1763. During the Revolution, American Gen. George Rogers Clark captured Vincennes, 1778, and defeated British forces 1779; at war's end Britain ceded the area to the U.S. Miami Indians defeated U.S. troops twice, 1790, but were beaten, 1794, at Fallen Timbers by Gen. Anthony Wayne. At Tippecanoe, 1811, Gen. William H. Harrison defeated Tecumseh's Indian confederation.

Tourist attractions. Lincoln, George Rogers Clark memorials; Wyandotte Cave; Vincennes, Tippecanoe sites; Indiana Dunes; Hoosier Nat'l. Forest; Benjamin Harrison Home.

Famous "Hoosiers" include Ambrose Burnside, Hoagy Carmichael, Eugene V. Debs, Theodore Dreiser, Paul Dresser, Cole Porter, Gene Stratton Porter, Ernie Pyle, James Whitcomb Riley, Booth Tarkington, Lew Wallace, Wendell L. Willkie, Wilbur Wright.

Chamber of Commerce: One North Capital, Indianapolis, IN 46204.

Iowa

Hawkeye State

People. Population (1983): 2,905,000; **rank:** 29. **Pop. density:** 51.9 per sq. mi. **Urban** (1980): 58.6%. **Racial distrib.** (1980): 97.4% White; 1.4% Black; Hispanic 15,852. **Net migration** (1970-80): −60,491.

Geography. Total area: 56,290 sq. mi.; **rank:** 25. **Land area:** 55,941 sq. mi. **Acres forested land:** 1,561,300. **Location:** Midwest state bordered by Mississippi R. on the E and Missouri R. on the W. **Climate:** humid, continental. **Topography:** Watershed from NW to SE; soil especially rich and land level in the N central counties. **Capital:** Des Moines.

Economy. Principal industries: manufacturing, agriculture. **Principal manufactured goods:** tires, farm machinery, electronic products, appliances, office furniture, chemicals, fertilizers, auto accessories. **Agriculture: Chief crops** (1983): silage and grain corn, soybeans, oats, hay. **Livestock** (1983): 2.5 mln. cattle; 22.8 mln. hogs/pigs; 370,000 sheep; 8.2 mln. poultry. **Timber/lumber:** red cedar. **Minerals** (1983): $261.4 mln.; mostly crushed stone cement, sand & gravel. **Commercial fishing** (1982): 1.3 mln. **Value of construction** (1983): 1.5 bln. **Employment distribution:** 25.6% trade; 20.3% serv; 20.2% manuf. 19.6% gvt. **Per capita income** (1983): $11,048. **Unemployment** (1983): 8.1%. **Tourism** (1981): tourists spent $1.6 bln.

Finance. No. banks (1983): 642; **No. savings assns** (1982): 58.

Federal government. No. federal civilian employees (Mar. 1983): 7,646. **Avg. salary:** $22,879.

Energy. Electricity production (1983, mwh, by source): Hydroelectric: 918,000; Mineral: 19.0 mln.; Nuclear: 2.3 mln.

Education. No. schools (1981): 2,055 elem. and second.; 61 higher ed. **Avg. salary, public school teachers:** $19,954.

State data. Motto: Our liberties we prize and our right we will maintain. **Flower:** Wild rose. **Bird:** Eastern gold finch. **Tree:** Oak. **Song:** The Song of Iowa. **Entered union** Dec. 28, 1846; rank, 29th. **State fair** at: Des Moines; mid-to-late Aug.

History. A thousand years ago several groups of prehistoric Indian Mound Builders dwelt on Iowa's fertile plains. Marquette and Jolliet gave France its claim to the area, 1673. It became U.S. territory through the 1803 Louisiana Purchase. Indian tribes were moved into the area from states further east, but by mid-19th century were forced to move on to Kansas. Before and during the Civil War, Iowans strongly supported Abraham Lincoln and became traditional Republicans.

Tourist attractions. Herbert Hoover birthplace and library, West Branch; Effigy Mounds Nat'l. Monument, Marquette, a pre-historic Indian burial site; Davenport Municipal Art Gallery's collection of Grant Wood's paintings and memorabilia.

Famous Iowans include James A. Van Allen, Marquis Childs, Buffalo Bill Cody, Susan Glaspell, James Norman Hall, Harry Hansen, Billy Sunday, Carl Van Vechten, Henry Wallace, Meredith Willson, Grant Wood.

Tourist information: Visitors' Group, Iowa Development Commission, 600 E. Court, Suite A, Des Moines, IA 50309.

Kansas

Sunflower State

People. Population (1983): 2,425,000; **rank:** 32. **Pop. density:** 29.7 per sq. mi. **Urban** (1980): 66.7%. **Racial distrib.** (1980): 91.7% White; 5.3% Black; Hispanic 63,333. **Net migration** (1970-80): -20,334.

Geography. Total area: 82,264 sq. mi.; **rank:** 14. **Land area:** 81,787 sq. mi. **Acres forested land:** 1,344,400. **Location:** West North Central state, with Missouri R. on E. **Climate:** temperate but continental, with great extremes bet. summer and winter. **Topography:** hilly Osage Plains in the E; central region level prairie and hills; high plains in the W. **Capital:** Topeka.

Economy. Principal industries: agriculture, machinery, mining, aerospace. **Principal manufactured goods:** processed foods, aircraft, petroleum products, farm machinery. **Value added by manufacture** (1980): $7.5 bln. **Agriculture: Chief crops:** wheat, sorghum, corn, hay. **Livestock:** 6.0 mln. cattle; 1.77 mln. hogs/pigs; 200,000 sheep; 2.23 mln. poultry. **Timber/lumber:** oak, walnut. **Minerals** (1983): $283.4 mln.; cement, salt, crushed stone. **Commercial fishing** (1982): $55,000 **Chief ports:** Kansas City. **International airports at:** Wichita. **Value of construction** (1983): $1.9 bln. **Employment distribution** (1983): 24.5% trade; 18.0% manuf.; 20.3% gvt.; 18.9% serv. **Per capita income** (1983): $12,285. **Unemployment** (1983): 6.1%. **Tourism** (1981): out-of-state visitors spent $1.5 bln.

Finance. No. banks (1983): 624; **No. savings assns.** (1982): 71.

Federal government. No. federal civilian employees (Mar. 1983): 13,616. **Avg. salary:** $22,341. **Notable federal facilities:** McConnell AFB; Fts. Riley, Leavenworth.

Energy. Electricity production (1983, mwh, by source): Hydroelectric: 6,000; Mineral: 23.8 mln.

Education. No. schools (1981): 1,709 elem. and second.; 57 higher ed. **Avg. salary, public school teachers:** $19,169.

State data. Motto: Ad Astra per Aspera (To the stars through difficulties). **Flower:** Native sunflower. **Bird:** Western meadowlark. **Tree:** Cottonwood. **Song:** Home on the Range. **Entered union** Jan. 29, 1861; rank, 34th. **State fair** at: Hutchinson; 2d week of Sept.

History. Coronado marched through the Kansas area, 541; French explorers came next. The U.S. took over in the Louisiana Purchase, 1803. In the pre-war North-South struggle over slavery, so much violence swept the area it was called Bleeding Kansas. Railroad construction after the war made Abilene and Dodge City terminals of large cattle drives from Texas.

Tourist attractions. Eisenhower Center and "Place of Meditation," Abilene; Agricultural Hall of Fame and National Ctr., Bonner Springs, displays farm equipment; Dodge City; Ft. Scott; Kansas Cosmosphere and Space Discovery Center, Hutchinson.

Famous Kansans include Thomas Hart Benton, John Brown, Walter P. Chrysler, Amelia Earhart, Cyrus Holliday, William Inge, Walter Johnson, Alf Landon, Carry Nation, Gordon Parks, William Allen White.

Chamber of Commerce: 500 First National Tower, One Townsite Plaza, Topeka, KS 66603.

Kentucky

Bluegrass State

People. Population (1983): 3,714,000 **rank:** 23. **Pop. density:** 93.7 per sq. mi. **Urban** (1980): 50.9% **Racial Distrib.** (1980): 92.3% White; 7.1% Black; Hispanic (1980): 27,406. **Net migration** (1970-80): +204,747.

Geography. Total area: 40,409 sq. mi.; **rank:** 37. **Land area:** 39,650 sq. mi. **Acres forested land:** 12,160,800. **Location:** east south central state, bordered on N by Illinois, Indiana, Ohio; on E by West Virginia and Virginia; in S by Tennessee; on W by Missouri. **Climate:** moderate, with plentiful rainfall. **Topography:** mountainous in E; rounded hills of the Knobs in the N; Bluegrass, heart of state; wooded rocky hillsides of the Pennyroyal; Western Coal Field; the fertile Purchase the SW. **Capital:** Frankfort.

Economy. Principal industries: manufacturing, coal mining, construction, agriculture. **Principal manufactured goods:** nonelectrical machinery, electric equipment, apparel, food products, primary metals. **Agriculture: Chief crops:** tobacco, soybeans, corn, wheat, hay, fruit. **Livestock:** 2.7 mln. cattle; 920,000 hogs/pigs; 23,000 sheep; 2.1 mln. chickens. **Timber/lumber** (1982): hardwoods, pines; 166 mln. bd. ft. **Minerals** (1983): $241.5 mln.; crushed stone, ball clay, lime, primary aluminum. **Commercial fishing** (1978): $923,000. **Chief ports:** Paducah, Louisville, Covington, Owensboro, Ashland. **International airports at:** Covington. **Value of construction** (1983): $2.7 bln. **Employment distribution:** mfg. 20.9%; trade 23.0%; gvt. 19.1%; serv. 19.4%. **Per capita income** (1983): $9,162. **Unemployment** (1983): 11.7%. **Tourism** (1982): tourists spent $2.1 bln.

Finance. No. banks (1983): 338; **No. savings assns.** (1982): 79.

Federal government. No. federal civilian employees (Mar. 1983): 26,387. **Avg. salary:** $21,360. **Notable federal facilities:** U.S. Gold Bullion Depository; Ft. Knox; Addiction Research Center and Federal Correction Institution, Lexington.

Energy. Electricity production (1983, mwh, by source): Hydroelectric: 3.2 mln.; Mineral: 54.4 mln.

Education. No. schools (1981): 1,627 elem. and second.; 57 higher ed. **Avg. salary, public school teachers:** $19,247.

State data. Motto: United we stand, divided we fall. **Flower:** Goldenrod. **Bird:** Cardinal. **Tree:** Kentucky coffee tree. **Song:** My Old Kentucky Home. **Entered union** June 1, 1792; rank, 15th. **State fair** at: Louisville.

History. Kentucky was the first area west of the Alleghenies settled by American pioneers; first permanent settlement, Harrodsburg, 1774. Daniel Boone blazed the Wilderness Trail through the Cumberland Gap and founded Fort Boonesborough, 1775. Indian attacks, spurred by the British, were unceasing until, during the Revolution, Gen. George Rogers Clark captured British forts in Indiana and Illinois, 1778. In 1792, after Virginia dropped its claims to the region, Kentucky became the 15th state.

Tourist attractions. Kentucky Derby and accompanying festivities, Louisville; Land Between the Lakes Nat'l. Recreation Area encompassing Kentucky Lake and Lake Barkley; Mammoth Cave with 300 mi. of explored passageways, 200-ft. high rooms, blind fish, and Echo River, 360 ft. below ground; Old Ft. Harrod State Park; Lincoln birthplace, Hodgenville; My Old Kentucky Home, Bardstown.

. **Famous Kentuckians** include Muhammad Ali, Alben Barkley, Daniel Boone, Louis D. Brandeis, Kit Carson, Albert B. "Happy" Chandler, Henry Clay, Jefferson Davis, John Fox Jr., Thomas Hunt Morgan, Elizabeth Madox Roberts, Col. Harland Sanders, Robert Penn Warren.

Chamber of Commerce: Versailles Rd., P.O. Box 817, Frankfort, KY 40601.

Louisiana
Pelican State

People. Population (1983): 4,438,000; **rank:** 18. **Pop. density:** 98.8 per sq. mi. **Urban** (1980): 68.7%. **Racial distrib.** (1980): 69.2% White; 29.4% Black; Hispanic 99,105. **Net migration** (1980-83): +77,292.

Geography. Total area: 48,523 sq. mi.; **rank:** 31. **Land area:** 44,930 sq. mi. **Acres forested land:** 14,558,100. **Location:** south central Gulf Coast state. **Climate:** subtropical, affected by continental weather patterns. **Topography:** lowlands of marshes and Mississippi R. flood plain; Red R. Valley lowlands; upland hills in the Florida Parishes; average elevation, 100 ft. **Capital:** Baton Rouge.

Economy. Principal industries: wholesale and retail trade, government, manufacturing, construction, transportation, mining. **Principal manufactured goods:** chemical products, foods, transportation equipment, electronic equipment, apparel, petroleum products. **Agriculture: Chief crops:** soybean, sugarcane, rice, corn, cotton, sweet potatoes, melons, pecans. **Livestock:** 1.3 mln. cattle; 240,000 hogs/pigs; 21,000 sheep; 3.2 mln. poultry. **Timber/lumber** (1982): pines, hardwoods, oak; 504 mln. bd. ft. **Minerals** (1982): Led U.S. in salt, second in Frasch sulfur prod. Total nonfuel minerals $426 mln., mostly salt, sulfur, cement, sand & gravel, stone. **Commercial fishing** (1982): $239.9 mln. **Chief ports:** New Orleans, Baton Rouge, Lake Charles, S. Louisiana Port Commission at La Place. **International airports at:** New Orleans. **Value of construction** (1983): $4.4 bln. **Employment distribution:** 28% trade; 23% gvt.; 22% serv.; 15% manuf.; 12% constr. **Per capita income** (1983): $10,406. **Unemployment** (1983): 11.8%. **Tourism** (1981): out-of-state visitors spent $3.3 bln.

Finance. No. banks (1983): 286; **No. savings assn.** (1982): 118.

Federal government. No. federal civilian employees (Mar. 1983): 19,787. **Avg. salary:** $22,031. **Notable federal facilities:** Barksdale, England, Ft. Polk military bases; Strategic Petroleum Reserve, New Orleans; Michoud Assembly Plant, New Orleans; U.S. Public Service Hospital, Carville.

Energy. Electricity production (1983, mwh, by source): Mineral: 37.0 mln. .

Education. No. schools (1981): 1,854 elem. and second.; 22 higher ed. **Avg. salary, public school teachers:** $19,700.

State data. Motto: Union, justice and confidence. **Flower:** Magnolia. **Bird:** Eastern brown pelican. **Tree:** Cypress. **Song:** Give Me Louisiana. **Entered union** Apr. 30, 1812; rank, 18th. **State fair at:** Shreveport; Oct.

History. The area was first visited, 1530, by Cabeza de Vaca and Panfilo de Narvaez. The region was claimed for France by LaSalle, 1682. First permanent settlement was by French at Biloxi, now in Mississippi, 1699. France ceded the region to Spain, 1762, took it back, 1800, and sold it to the U.S., 1803, in the Louisiana Purchase. During the Revolution, Spanish Louisiana aided the Americans. Admitted to statehood, 1812, Louisiana was the scene of the Battle of New Orleans, 1815.

Louisiana Creoles are descendants of early French and/or Spanish settlers. About 4,000 Acadians, French settlers in Nova Scotia, Canada, were forcibly transported by the British to Louisiana in 1755 (an event commemorated in Longfellow's *Evangeline*) and settled near Bayou Teche; their descendants became known as Cajuns. Another group, the Islenos, were descendants of Canary Islanders brought to Louisiana by a Spanish governor in 1770. Traces of Spanish and French survive in local dialects.

Tourist attractions. Mardi Gras, French Quarter, Superdome, Dixieland jazz, all New Orleans; Battle of New Orleans site; Longfellow-Evangeline Memorial Park; Kent House Museum, Alexandria; Hodges Gardens, Natchiloches.

Famous Louisianians include Louis Armstrong, Pierre Beauregard, Judah P. Benjamin, Braxton Bragg, Grace King, Huey Long, Leonidas K. Polk, Henry Miller Shreve, Edward D. White Jr.

Chamber of Commerce: P.O. Box 3988, Baton Rouge, LA 70821.

Maine
Pine Tree State

People. Population (1983): 1,146,000; **rank:** 38. **Pop. density:** 37.1 per sq. mi. **Urban** (1980): 47.5% **Racial distrib.** (1980): 98.3% White; 0.3% Black; Hispanic: 5,005. **Net migration** (1970-82): +72,884.

Geography. Total area: 33,215 sq. mi.; **rank:** 39. **Land area:** 30,920 sq. mi. **Acres forested land:** 17,718,300. **Location:** New England state at northeastern tip of U.S. **Climate:** Southern interior and coastal, influenced by air masses from the S and W; northern clime harsher, avg. +100 in. snow in winter. **Topography:** Appalachian Mtns. extend through state; western borders have rugged terrain; long sand beaches on southern coast; northern coast mainly rocky promontories, peninsulas, fjords. **Capital:** Augusta.

Economy. Principal industries: manufacturing, services, trade, government, agriculture, fisheries, forestry. **Principal manufactured goods:** paper and wood products, textiles, leather, processed foods. **Agriculture: Chief crops:** potatoes, apples, blueberries, sweet corn, peas, beans. **Livestock:** 141,000 cattle; 9,000 hogs/pigs; 17,000 sheep; 17.2 mln. poultry. **Timber/lumber** (1982): pine, spruce, fir; more than 1 bln. bd ft. **Minerals** (1983): $291.1 mln.; sand & gravel, crushed stone. **Commercial fishing** (1982): $100.9 mln. **Chief ports:** Searsport, Portland. **International airports at:** Portland, Bangor. **Value of construction** (1983): $625 mln. **Employment distribution** (1982): 25.7% manuf.; 22.2% trade; 19.6% gvt.; 19.8% serv. **Per capita income** (1983): $9,619. **Unemployment** (1983): 9.0% **Tourism** (1983): $650 mln.

Finance. No. banks (1983): 52; **No. savings assns.** (1982): 17.

Federal government. No. federal civilian employees (Mar. 1983): 4,718. **Avg. salary:** $21,981. **Notable federal facilities:** Kittery Naval Shipyard; Brunswick Naval Air Station; Loring Air Force Base.

Energy. Electricity production (1983, mwh, by source): Hydroelectric: 1.94 mln.; Mineral: 2.1 mln.; Nu clear: 5.7 mln.

Education. No. schools (1981): 832 elem. and sec ond.; 28 higher ed. **Avg. salary, public school teachers** $16,771.

State data. Motto: Dirigo (I direct). **Flower:** White pine cone and tassel. **Bird:** Chickadee. **Tree:** Eastern white pine. **Song:** State of Maine Song. **Entered union:** Mar 15, 1820; rank, 23d.

History. Maine's rocky coast was explored by the Ca bots, 1498-99. French settlers arrived, 1604, at the St Croix River; English, 1607, on the Kennebec. In 1691 Maine was made part of Massachusetts. In the Revolu tion, a Maine regiment fought at Bunker Hill; a British flee destroyed Falmouth (now Portland), 1775, but the British ship Margaretta was captured near Machiasport. In 1820 Maine broke off from Massachusetts, became a separat state.

Tourist attractions. Acadia Nat'l. Park, Bar Harbor, o Mt. Desert Is.; Bath Iron Works and Marine Museun Boothbay (Harbor) Railway Museum; Portland Art Mu seum; Sugarloaf/USA Ski Area; Ogunquit, Portland, Yor

Famous "Down Easters" include James G. Blain Cyrus H.K. Curtis, Hannibal Hamlin, Longfellow, Sir Hirai

and Hudson Maxim, Edna St. Vincent Millay, Kate Douglas Wiggin, Ben Ames Williams.
Chamber of Commerce: 1 Canal Plaza, Portland, ME 04112.

Maryland

Old Line State, Free State

People. Population (1983): 4,304,000; **rank:** 19. **Pop. density:** 435.1 per sq. mi. **Urban** (1980): 80.3% **Racial distrib.** (1980): 74.9% White; 22.7% Black; Hispanic 64,740. **Net migration** (1970-80): +48,000.

Geography. Total area: 10,577 sq. mi.; **rank:** 42. **Land area:** 9,891 sq. mi. **Acres forested land:** 2,653,200. **Location:** Middle Atlantic state stretching from the Ocean to the Allegheny Mtns. **Climate:** continental in the west; humid subtropical in the east. **Topography:** Eastern Shore of coastal plain and Maryland Main of coastal plain, piedmont plateau, and the Blue Ridge, separated by the Chesapeake Bay. **Capital:** Annapolis.

Economy. Principal industries: food, manufacturing, tourism. **Principal manufactured goods:** food and kindred products, primary metals, electric and electronic equipment. **Agriculture: Chief crops:** tobacco, corn, soybeans. **Livestock:** 405,000 cattle; 200,000 hogs/pigs; 19,000 sheep; 4.4 mln. poultry. **Timber/lumber** (1981): hardwoods; 5.2 mln. bd. ft. **Minerals** (1982): $178.4 mln.; crushed stone, sand & gravel. **Commercial fishing** (1982): $51.4 mln. **Chief ports:** Baltimore. **International airports at:** Baltimore. **Value of construction** (1983): 4.3 bln. **Employment distribution:** 24% government; 23.8% wholesale and retail trade; 19.9% services and mining. **Per capita income** (1983): $12,994. **Unemployment** (1983): 6.9%. **Tourism** (1980): tourists spent $3 bln.

Finance. No. banks (1983): 92; **No. savings assns.** (1982): 57.

Federal government. No. federal civilian employees (Mar. 1983): 105,244. **Avg. salary:** $26,529. **Notable federal facilities:** U.S. Naval Academy, Annapolis; Natl. Agric. Research Cen.; Ft. George C. Meade, Aberdeen Proving Ground.

Energy. Electricity production (1983, mwh, by source): Hydroelectric: 1.7 mln.; Mineral: 19.4 mln.; Nuclear: 11.7 mln.

Education. No. schools (1981): 1,611 elem. and second.; 57 higher ed. **Avg. salary, public school teachers:** $23,773.

State data. Motto. Fatti Maschii, Parole Femine (Manly deeds, womanly words). **Flower:** Black-eyed susan. **Bird:** Baltimore oriole. **Tree:** White oak. **Song:** Maryland, My Maryland. **Seventh** of the original 13 states to ratify Constitution, Apr. 28, 1788. **State fair** at: Timonium; end-Aug. to Sept. 7.

History. Capt. John Smith first explored Maryland, 1608. William Claiborne set up a trading post on Kent Is. in Chesapeake Bay, 1631. Britain granted land to Cecilius Calvert, Lord Baltimore, 1632; his brother led 200 settlers to St. Marys River, 1634. The bravery of Maryland troops in the Revolution, as at the Battle of Long Island, won the state its nickname, The Old Line State. In the War of 1812, when a British fleet tried to take Fort McHenry, Marylander Francis Scott Key, 1814, wrote *The Star-Spangled Banner.*

Tourist Attractions. Racing events include the Preakness, at Pimlico track, Baltimore; the International at Laurel Race Course; the John B. Campbell Handicap at Bowie. Also Annapolis yacht races; Ocean City summer resort; restored Ft. McHenry, Baltimore, near which Francis Scott Key wrote *The Star-Spangled Banner;* Antietam Battlefield, 1862, near Hagerstown; South Mountain Battlefield, 1862; Edgar Allan Poe house, Baltimore; The State House, Annapolis, 1772, the oldest still in use in the U.S.

Famous Marylanders include Benjamin Banneker, Francis Scott Key, H.L. Mencken, William Pinkney, Upton Sinclair, Roger B. Taney, Charles Willson Peale.

Chamber of Commerce: 60 West St., Suite 405, Annapolis, MD 21401.

Massachusetts

Bay State, Old Colony

People. Population (1983): 5,767,000; **rank:** 11. **Pop. density:** 736.9 per sq. mi. **Urban** (1980): 83.8% **Racial distrib.** (1980): 93.4% White; 3.8% Black; Hispanic 141,043. **Net migration** (1970-79): −145,225.

Geography. Total area: 8,257 sq. mi.; **rank:** 45. **Land area:** 7,826 sq. mi. **Acres forested land:** 2,952,300. **Location:** New England state along Atlantic seaboard. **Climate:** temperate, with colder and drier clime in western region. **Topography:** jagged indented coast from Rhode Island around Cape Cod; flat land yields to stony upland pastures near central region and gentle hilly country in west; except in west, land is rocky, sandy, and not fertile. **Capital:** Boston.

Economy. Principal industries: manufacturing, services, trade, construction. **Principal manufactured goods** (1981): electronics, machinery, instruments, fabricated metals, printing and publishing. **Agriculture: Chief crops:** cranberries, greenhouse, nursery, vegetables. **Livestock** (1983): 120,000 cattle; 50,000 hogs/pigs; 8,000 sheep; 125,000 horses, ponies; 3.6 mln. poultry. **Timber/lumber** (1983): white pine, oak, other hard woods; 240 mln. bd. ft. **Minerals** (1983): $88.4; mostly sand & gravel, crushed stone, lime. **Commercial fishing** (1982): $204.2 mln. **Chief ports:** Boston, Fall River, Salem, Gloucester. **International airport at:** Boston. **Value of construction** (1983): $3.8 bln. **Employment distribution** (1981): 25.6% manuf.; 23.7% serv.; 22.3% trade. **Per capita income** (1983): $13,089. **Unemployment** (1983): 6.9%. **Tourism** (1983): out-of-state visitors spent $3.0 bln.

Finance. No. banks (1983): 286; **No. savings assns.** (1982): 63.

Federal government. No. federal civilian employees (Mar. 1983): 30,592. **Avg. salary:** $23,840. **Notable federal facilities:** Ft. Devens; U.S. Customs House, Boston; Q.M. Laboratory, Natick.

Energy. Electricity production (1983, mwh, by source): Hydroelectric: 252,000; Mineral: 28.5 mln.; Nuclear: 6.1 mln.

Education. No. schools (1981): 2,583 elem. and second.; 116 higher ed. **Avg. salary, public school teachers:** $23,000.

State data. Motto: Ense Petit Placidam Sub Libertate Quietem (By the sword we seek peace, but peace only under liberty). **Flower:** Mayflower. **Bird:** Chickadee. **Tree:** American elm. **Song:** All Hail to Massachusetts. **Sixth** of the original 13 states to ratify Constitution, Feb. 6, 1788.

History. The Pilgrims, seeking religious freedom, made their first settlement at Plymouth, 1620; the following year they gave thanks for their survival with the first Thanksgiving Day. Indian opposition reached a high point in King Philip's War, 1675-76, won by the colonists. Demonstrations against British restrictions set off the "Boston Massacre," 1770, and Boston "tea party," 1773. First bloodshed of the Revolution was at Lexington, 1775.

Tourist attractions. Cape Cod with Provincetown artists' colony; Freedom Trail; Berkshire Music Festival, Tanglewood; Boston "Pops" concerts; Museum of Fine Arts, Arnold Arboretum, all Boston; Jacob's Pillow Dance Festival, West Becket; historical Shaker Village, Old Sturbridge, Lexington, Concord, Salem, Plymouth Rock.

Famous "Bay Staters" include Samuel Adams, Louisa May Alcott, Horatio Alger, Clara Barton, Emily Dickinson, Emerson, Hancock, Hawthorne, Oliver W. Holmes, Winslow Homer, Elias Howe, Samuel F.B. Morse, Poe, Revere, Sargent, Thoreau, Whistler, Whittier.

Tourist information: Massachusetts Dept. of Commerce, 100 Cambridge St., Boston, MA 02202.

Michigan

Great Lake State, Wolverine State

People. Population (1983): 9,069,000; **rank:** 8. **Pop. density:** 159.6 per sq. mi. **Urban** (1980): 70.7%. **Racial distrib.** (1980): 84.9% White; 12.9% Black; Hispanic 162,388. **Net migration** (1970-80): +299,974.

Geography. Total area: 58,216 sq. mi.; **rank:** 23. **Land area:** 56,817 sq. mi. **Acres forested land:** 19,270,400. **Location:** east north central state bordering on 4 of the 5 Great Lakes, divided into an Upper and Lower Peninsula by the Straits of Mackinac, which link lakes Michigan and Huron. **Climate:** well-defined seasons tempered by the Great Lakes. **Topography:** low rolling hills give way to northern tableland of hilly belts in Lower Peninsula; Upper Peninsula is level in the east, with swampy areas; western region is higher and more rugged. **Capital:** Lansing.

Economy. Principal industries: manufacturing, mining, agriculture, food processing, tourism, fishing. **Principal manufactured goods:** automobiles, machine tools, chemicals, foods, primary metals and metal products, plastics. **Agriculture: Chief crops:** corn, winter wheat, soybeans, dry beans, oats, hay, sugar beets, honey, asparagus, sweet corn, apples, cherries, grapes, peaches, blueberries, flowers. **Livestock:** 1.45 mln. cattle; 690,000 mln. hogs/pigs; 130,000 sheep; 8.7 mln. poultry. **Timber/lumber:** hickory, ash, oak, hemlock. **Minerals** (1983): $1.1 bln.; mostly cement, salt, crushed stone, sand & gravel. **Commercial fishing** (1982): $8.1 mln. **Chief ports:** Detroit, Muskegon, Sault Ste. Marie. **International airports at:** Detroit. **Value of construction** (1983): $3.5 bln. **Employment distribution:** 30% manuf.; 22% serv.; **Per capita income** (1983): $11,574. **Unemployment** (1983): 14.2%. **Tourism** (1983): out-of-state visitors spent $4.7 bln.

Finance. No. banks (1983): 374; **No. savings assns.** (1982): 53.

Federal government. No. federal civilian employees (Mar. 1983): 26,843. **Avg. salary:** $23,736. **Notable federal facilities:** Isle Royal, Sleeping Bear Dunes national parks.

Energy. Electricity production (1983, mwh, by source): Hydroelectric: 1.1 mln; Mineral: 53.4 mln.; Nuclear: 16.4 mln.

Education. No. schools (1981): 4,544 elem. and second.; 93 higher ed. **Avg. salary, public school teachers:** $27,933.

State data. Motto: Si Quaeris Peninsulam Amoenam Circumspice (If you seek a pleasant peninsula, look about you). **Flower:** Apple blossom. **Bird:** Robin. **Tree:** White pine. **Song:** Michigan, My Michigan. **Entered union** Jan. 26, 1837; rank, 26th. **State fair** at: Detroit, Aug. 27–Sept. 6; Upper Peninsula (Escanaba) Aug. 26–Sept. 5.

History. French fur traders and missionaries visited the region, 1616, set up a mission at Sault Ste. Marie, 1641, and a settlement there, 1668. The whole region went to Britain, 1763. During the Revolution, the British led attacks from the area on American settlements to the south until Anthony Wayne defeated their Indian allies at Fallen Timbers, Ohio, 1794. The British returned, 1812, seized Ft. Mackinac and Detroit. Oliver H. Perry's Lake Erie victory and William H. Harrison's troops, who carried the war to the Thames River in Canada, 1813, freed Michigan once more.

Tourist attractions. Henry Ford Museum, Greenfield Village, reconstruction of a typical 19th cent. American village, both in Dearborn; Michigan Space Ctr.; Jackson; Tahquamenon *(Hiawatha)* Falls; DeZwaan windmill and Tulip Festival, Holland; "Soo Locks," St. Marys Falls Ship Canal, Sault Ste. Marie.

Famous Michiganders include George Custer, Paul de Kruif, Thomas Dewey, Edna Ferber, Henry Ford, Edgar Guest, Betty Hutton, Robert Ingersoll, Will Kellogg, Danny Thomas, Stewart Edward White.

Chamber of Commerce: 200 N. Washington Sq., Suite 400, Lansing, MI 48933.

Minnesota

North Star State, Gopher State

People. Population (1983): 4,144,000; **rank:** 21. **Pop. density:** 52.3 per sq. mi. **Urban** (1980): 66.9%. **Racial distrib.** (1980): 96.5% White; 1.3% Black; Hispanic 32,124. **Net migration** (1980-82): −12,800 est.

Geography. Total area: 84,068 sq. mi.; **rank:** 12. **Land area:** 79,289 sq. mi. **Acres forested land:** 16,709,200. **Location:** north central state bounded on the E by Wisconsin and Lake Superior, on the N by Canada, on the W by the Dakotas, and on the S by Iowa. **Climate:** northern part of state lies in the moist Great Lakes storm belt; the western border lies at the edge of the semi-arid Great Plains. **Topography:** central hill and lake region covering approx. half the state; to the NE, rocky ridges and deep lakes; to the NW, flat plain; to the S, rolling plains and deep river valleys. **Capital:** St. Paul.

Economy. Principal industries: agri business, forest products, mining, manufacturing, tourism. **Principal manufactured goods:** food processing, non-electrical machinery, chemicals, paper, electric and electronic equipment, printing and publishing, instruments, fabricated metal products. **Value added by manufacture** (1978): $10.9 bln. **Agriculture: Chief crops:** corn, soybeans, wheat, sugar beets, sunflowers, barley. **Livestock** (1983): 3.9 mln. cattle; 4.3 mln. hogs/pigs; 255,000 sheep; 40.9 mln. poultry. **Timber/lumber:** needle-leaves and hardwoods. **Minerals** (1983): 725.3 mln.; mostly lead, cement, crushed stone. **Commercial fishing** (1982): $2.8 mln. **Chief ports:** Duluth, St. Paul, Minneapolis. **International airports at:** Minneapolis-St. Paul. **Value of construction** (1983): $4.2 bln. **Employment distribution** (1982): 25.2% trade; 20.3% manuf.; 22.3% serv.; 16.9% gvt. **Per capita income** (1983): $11,666. **Unemployment** (1983): 8.2%. **Tourism** (1982): out-of-state visitors spent $1.4 bln.

Finance. No. banks (1983): 754; **No. savings assns.** (1982): 40.

Federal government. No. federal civilian employees (Mar. 1983): 13,067. **Avg. salary:** $24,032.

Energy. Electricity production (1983, mwh, by source): Hydroelectric: 925,000; Mineral: 17.1 mln.; Nuclear: 11.8 mln.

Education. No. schools (1981): 2,137 elem. and second.; 70 higher ed. **Avg. salary, public school teachers:** $23,742.

State data. Motto: L'Etoile du Nord (The star of the north). **Flower:** Pink and white lady's-slipper. **Bird:** Common loon. **Tree:** Red pine. **Song:** Hail! Minnesota. **Entered union** May 11, 1858; rank, 32d. **State fair** at: Saint Paul; end-Aug. to early Sept.

History. Fur traders and missionaries from French Canada opened the region in the 17th century. Britain took the area east of the Mississippi, 1763. The U.S. took over that portion after the Revolution and in 1803 bought the western area as part of the Louisiana Purchase. The U.S. built present Ft. Snelling, 1820, bought lands from the Indians, 1837. Sioux Indians staged a bloody uprising, 1862, and were driven from the state.

Tourist attractions. Minnehaha Falls, Minneapolis, inspiration for Longfellow's *Hiawatha;* Voyageurs Nat'l. Park, a water wilderness along the Canadian border; Mayo Clinic, Rochester; St. Paul Winter Carnival; the "land of 10,000 lakes" actually has 12,034 lakes over 10 acres in size; many water and winter sports and activities throughout the state.

Famous Minnesotans include F. Scott Fitzgerald, Cass Gilbert, Hubert Humphrey, Sister Elizabeth Kenny, Sinclair Lewis, Paul Manship, E. G. Marshall, William and Charles Mayo, Walter F. Mondale, Charles Schulz, Harold Stassen, Thorstein Veblen.

Tourist Information: Minnesota Tourism Division, 419 N. Robert St., 240 Bremer Bldg., St. Paul, MN 55101.

Mississippi

Magnolia State

People. Population (1983): 2,587,000; **rank:** 31. **Pop. density:** 54.7 per sq. mi. **Urban** (1980): 47.3%. **Racial distrib.** (1980): 64.1% White; 35.2% Black; Hispanic (1970): 8,182. **Net migration** (1970-80): +84,879.

Geography. Total area: 47,716 sq. mi.; **rank:** 32. **Land area:** 47,296 sq. mi. **Acres forested land:** 16,715,600. **Location:** south central state bordered on the W by the Mississippi R. and on the S by the Gulf of Mexico. **Climate:** semi-tropical, with abundant rainfall, long growing season, and extreme temperatures unusual. **Topography:** low, fertile delta bet. the Yazoo and Mississippi rivers; loess bluffs stretching around delta border; sandy Gulf coastal terraces followed by piney woods and prairie; rugged, high sandy hills in extreme NE followed by black prairie belt. Pontotoc Ridge, and flatwoods into the north central highlands. **Capital:** Jackson.

Economy. Principal industries: manufacturing, food processing, seafood, government, wholesale and retail trade, agriculture. **Principal manufactured goods:** apparel, transportation equipment, lumber and wood products, foods, electrical machinery and equipment. **Agriculture: Chief crops:** soybeans, cotton, rice. **Livestock:** 1.80 mln. cattle; 410,000 hogs/pigs; 4,500 sheep; 10.18 mln. poultry. **Timber/lumber** (1982): pine, oak, hardwoods; 1.1 bln. bd. ft. **Minerals** (1982): $79.5 mln., mostly sand & gravel, clays. **Commercial fishing** (1982): $39.9 mln. **Chief ports:** Pascagoula, Vicksburg, Gulfport, Natchez, Greenville. **Value of construction** (1983): $1.6 bln. **Employment distribution:** 21.7% manuf.; 19.4% gvt.; 17.6% trade; 13.4% serv. **Per capita income** (1982): $8,072. **Unemployment** (1983): 12.6%. **Tourism** (1982): out-of-state visitors spent $1.2 bln.

Finance. No. banks (1983): 162; **No. savings assns.** (1982): 51.

Federal government. No. federal civilian employees (Mar. 1983): 18,145. **Avg. salary:** $22,411. **Notable federal facilities:** Columbus, Keesler AF bases; Meridian Naval Air Station, NASA/NOAA International Earth Sciences Center.

Energy. Electricity production (1983, mwh, by source): Mineral 13.4 mln.

Education. No. schools (1981): 1,041 elem. and second.; 42 higher ed. **Avg. salary, public school teachers:** $14,821.

State data. Motto: Virtute et Armis (By valor and arms). **Flower:** Magnolia. **Bird:** Mockingbird. **Tree:** Magnolia. **Song:** Go, Mississippi! **Entered union** Dec. 10, 1817; rank, 20th. **State fair** at: Jackson; Fall.

History. De Soto explored the area, 1540, discovered the Mississippi River, 1541. La Salle traced the river from Illinois to its mouth and claimed the entire valley for France, 1682. First settlement was the French Ft. Maurepas, near Ocean Springs, 1699. The area was ceded to Britain, 1763; American settlers followed. During the Revolution, Spain seized part of the area and refused to leave even after the U.S. acquired title at the end of the Revolution, finally moving out, 1798. Mississippi seceded 1861. Union forces captured Corinth and Vicksburg and destroyed Jackson and much of Meridian.

Tourist attractions. Vicksburg National Military Park and Cemetery, other Civil War sites; Natchez Trace; Indian mounds; estate pilgrimage at Natchez; Mardi Gras and blessing of the shrimp fleet, Aug., both in Biloxi.

Famous Mississippians include Dana Andrews, William Faulkner, Lucius O.C. Lamar, Elvis Presley, Leontyne Price, Charlie Pride, Eudora Welty.

Chamber of Commerce: P.O. Box 1849, Jackson, MS 39205.

Missouri

Show Me State

People. Population (1983): 4,970,000; **rank:** 15. **Pop. density:** 72.0 per sq. mi. **Urban** (1980): 68.1%. **Racial distrib.** (1980): 88.3% White; 10.4% Black; Hispanic 51,667. **Net migration** (1970-80): +10,726.

Geography. Total area: 69,686 sq. mi.; **rank:** 19. **Land area:** 68,995 sq. mi. **Acres forested land:** 12,876,000. **Location:** West North central state near the geographic center of the conterminous U.S.; bordered on the E by the Mississippi R., on the NW by the Missouri R. **Climate:** continental, susceptible to cold Canadian air, moist, warm Gulf air, and drier SW air. **Topography:** Rolling hills, open, fertile plains, and well-watered prairie N of the Missouri R.; south of the river land is rough and hilly with deep, narrow valleys; alluvial plain in the SE; low elevation in the west. **Capital:** Jefferson City.

Economy. Principal industries: agriculture, manufacturing, aerospace, tourism. **Principal manufactured goods:** transportation equipment, food and related products, electrical and electronic equipment, chemicals. **Agriculture: Chief crops:** soybeans, corn, wheat, cotton. **Livestock** (1982): 5.5 mln. cattle; 3.5 mln. hogs/pigs; 116,000 sheep; 19.7 mln. poultry. **Timber/lumber:** oak, hickory. **Minerals** (1983): $725.3 mln., mostly lead, cement, zinc. **Commercial fishing** (1982) $310,000. **Chief ports:** St. Louis, Kansas City. **International airports at:** St. Louis, Kansas City. **Value of construction** (1983): $3.3 bln. **Employment distribution:** 23% trade; 21% serv.; 21% manuf.; 17% gvt.; 7% transp. **Per capita income** (1983): $10,790. **Unemployment** (1983): 9.9%. **Tourism** (1983): total travelers spent $4.5 bln.

Finance. No. banks (1983): 739; **No. savings assns.** (1982): 96.

Federal government. No. federal civilian employees (Mar. 1983): 43,903. **Avg. salary:** $23,000. **Notable federal facilities:** Federal Reserve banks, St. Louis, Kansas City; Ft. Leonard Wood, Rolla.

Energy. Electricity production (1983 mwh, by source): Hydroelectric: 1.7 mln.; Mineral: 51.0 mln.

Education. No. schools (1981): 2,594 elem. and second.; 86 higher ed. **Avg. salary, public school teachers:** $18,239.

State data. Motto: Salus Populi Suprema Lex Esto (The welfare of the people shall be the supreme law). **Flower:** Hawthorn. **Bird:** Bluebird. **Tree:** Dogwood. **Song:** Missouri Waltz. **Entered union** Aug. 10, 1821; rank, 24th. **State fair** at: Sedalia; 3d week in Aug.

History. DeSoto visited the area, 1541. French hunters and lead miners made the first settlement, c. 1735, at Ste. Genevieve. The U.S. acquired Missouri as part of the Louisiana Purchase, 1803. The fur trade and the Santa Fe Trail provided prosperity; St. Louis became the "jump-off" point for pioneers on their way West. Pro- and anti-slavery forces battled each other there during the Civil War.

Tourist attractions. Mark Twain Area, Hannibal; Pony Express Museum, St. Joseph; Harry S. Truman Library, Independence; Gateway Arch, St. Louis; Silver Dollar City, Branson Worlds of Fun, Kansas City; Lake of the Ozarks, Churchill Memorial, Fulton.

Famous Missourians include Thomas Hart Benton, George Caleb Bingham, Gen. Omar Bradley, George Washington Carver, Walter Cronkite, Dale Carnegie, Walt Disney, Jesse James, J. C. Penney; John J. Pershing, Joseph Pulitzer, Mark Twain.

Chamber of Commerce: 400 E. High St., P.O. Box 149, Jefferson City, MO 65101.

Montana

Treasure State

People. Population (1983): 817,000; **rank:** 44. **Pop. density:** 5.61 per sq. mi. **Urban** (1980): 52.9%. **Racial distrib.** (1980): 94.0% White; 0.2% Black; 5.6% Other (includes American Indians); Hispanic 9,974. **Net migration** (1970-82): +34,000.

Geography. Total area: 147,138 sq. mi.; **rank:** 4. **Land area:** 145,587 sq. mi. **Acres forested land:** 22,559,300. **Location:** Mountain state bounded on the E by the Dakotas, on the S by Wyoming, on the S/SW by Idaho, and on the N by Canada. **Climate:** colder, continental climate with low humidity. **Topography:** Rocky Mtns. in western third of the state; eastern two-thirds gently rolling northern Great Plains. **Capital:** Helena.

Economy. Principal industries: manufacturing, agriculture, mining, tourism. **Principal manufactured goods:** lumber and wood products, petroleum products, primary metals and minerals, farm machinery, processed foods. **Agriculture: Chief crops:** wheat, barley, sugar beets, hay, flax, oats. **Livestock** (1983): 3.15 mln. cattle; 180,000 hogs/pigs; 509,000 sheep; 940,200 poultry. **Timber/lumber** (1983): Douglas fir, pines, larch; 704 mln. bd. ft. **Minerals** (1983): $240 mln. mostly metallics. **International airports at:** Great Falls, Billings. **Value of construction** (1983): 650 mln. **Employment distribution** (1983): 23% trade; 19% gvt.; 22% serv.; 11% agric; 7% manuf. **Per capita income** (1983): $9,999. **Unemployment** (1983): 8.8%. **Tourism** (1980): out-of-state visitors spent $600 mln.

Finance. No. banks (1983): 169; **No. savings assns.** (1982): 12.

Federal government. No. federal civilian employees (Mar. 1983): 8,404. **Avg. salary:** $23,445. **Notable federal facilities:** Malmstrom AFB; Ft. Peck, Hungry Horse, Libby, Yellowtail dams.

Energy. Electricity production (1983, mwh, by source): Hydroelectric: 11.6 mln; Mineral: 3.5 mln.

Education. No. schools (1981): 864 elem. and second.; 16 higher ed. **Avg. salary, public school teachers:** $20,176.

State data. Motto: Oro y Plata (Gold and silver). **Flower:** Bitterroot. **Bird:** Western meadowlark. **Tree:** Ponderosa pine. **Song:** Montana. **Entered union** Nov. 8, 1889; rank, 41st. **State fair** at: Great Falls; end July to early Aug.

History. French explorers visited the region, 1742. The U.S. acquired the area partly through the Louisiana Purchase, 1803, and partly through the explorations of Lewis and Clark, 1805-06. Fur traders and missionaries established posts in the early 19th century. Indian uprisings reached their peak with the Battle of the Little Big Horn, 1876. The coming of the Northern Pacific Railway, 1883, brought population growth.

Tourist attractions. Glacier National Park, on the Continental Divide, is a scenic and recreational wonderland, with 60 glaciers, 200 lakes, and many trout streams.

Also, Museum of the Plains Indian, Blackfeet Reservation near Browning; Custer Battlefield National Cemetery; Flathead Lake, in the NW, Lewis and Clark Cavern, Morrison Cave State Park, near Whitehall.

There are 7 Indian reservations, covering over 5 million acres; tribes are Blackfeet, Crow, Confederated Salish & Kootenai, Assiniboine, Gros Ventre, Sioux, Northern Cheyenne, Chippewa, Cree. Population of the reservations is approximately 25,500.

Famous Montanans include Gary Cooper, Marcus Daly, Chet Huntley, Will James, Myrna Loy, Mike Mansfield, Jeannette Rankin, Charles M. Russell, Brent Musberger.

Chamber of Commerce: 110 Neil Ave., P.O. Box 1730, Helena, MT 59601.

Nebraska

Cornhusker State

People. Population (1983): 1,597,000; **rank:** 36. **Pop. density:** 20.9 per sq. mi. **Urban** (1980): 62.9%. **Racial distrib.** (1980): 94.9% White; 3.1% Black; Hispanic 28,020. **Net migration** (1980-82): −13,000.

Geography. Total area: 77,227 sq. mi.; **rank:** 15. **Land area:** 76,483 sq. mi. **Acres forested land:** 1,029,100. **Location:** West North Central state with the Missouri R. for a N/NE border. **Climate:** continental semi-arid. **Topography:** till plains of the central lowland in the eastern third rising to the Great Plains and hill country of the north central and NW. **Capital:** Lincoln.

Economy. Principal industries: agriculture, food processing, manufacturing. **Principal manufactured goods:** foods, machinery, electric and electronic equipment, primary and fabricated metal products, chemicals. **Agriculture: Chief crops:** corn, wheat, sorghum, soy beans, hay, beans, popcorn, oats, potatoes, sugar beets. **Livestock:** 6.9 mln. cattle; 3.9 mln. hogs/pigs; 195,000 sheep; 3.85 mln. poultry. **Minerals** (1983): $92.9 mln.; mostly cement, sand & gravel. **Commercial fishing** (1982): $39,000. **Chief ports:** Omaha, Sioux City, Brownville, Blair, Plattsmouth, Nebraska City. **Value of construction** (1983): $1.0 bln. **Employment distribution:** 21.0% trade; 16.9% gvt.; 15.6% serv.; 12.2% manuf. **Per capita income** (1983): $10,940. **Unemployment** (1983): 5.7%. **Tourism** (1980): traveler expenditures $1.1 bln.

Finance. No. banks (1982): 482; **No. savings assns.** (1982): 26.

Federal government. No. federal civilian employees (Mar. 1983): 8,524. **Avg. salary:** $23,478. **Notable federal facilities:** Strategic Air Command Base, Omaha.

Energy. Electricity production (1983, mwh, by source): Hydroelectric: 1.4 mln.; Mineral: 9.6 mln.; Nuclear: 6.1 mln.

Education. No. schools (1981): 1,959 elem. and second.; 30 higher ed. **Avg. salary, public school teachers:** $18,488.

State data. Motto: Equality before the law. **Flower:** Goldenrod. **Bird:** Western meadowlark. **Tree:** Cottonwood. **Song:** Beautiful Nebraska. **Entered union** Mar. 1, 1867; rank, 37th. **State fair** at: Lincoln; Aug. 30-Sept. 8.

History. Spanish and French explorers and fur traders visited the area prior to the Louisiana Purchase, 1803. Lewis and Clark passed through, 1804-06. First permanent settlement was Bellevue, near Omaha, 1823. Many Civil War veterans settled under free land terms of the 1862 Homestead Act; struggles followed between homesteaders and ranchers.

Tourist attractions. Boys Town, founded by Fr. Flanagan, west of Omaha, is a self-contained community of under-privileged and homeless boys. Arbor Lodge State Park, Nebraska City, is a memorial to J. Sterling Morton, founder of Arbor Day. Buffalo Bill Ranch State Historical Park, North Platte, contains Cody's home and memorabilia of his Wild West Show.

Also, Pioneer Village, Minden; Oregon Trail, landmarks, Scotts Bluff National Monument and Chimney Rock Historic Site.

Famous Nebraskans include Fred Astaire, Charles W. and William Jennings Bryan, Willa Cather, Michael and Edward A. Cudahy, Loren Eiseley, Rev. Edward J. Flanagan, Henry Fonda, Rollin Kirby, Harold Lloyd, Wright Morris, Mari Sandoz, Malcolm X, Roscoe Pound.

Chamber of Commerce: Room 1008, 941 O St., Lincoln, NE 68508.

Nevada

Sagebrush State, Battle Born State, Silver State

People. Population (1983): 891,000; **rank:** 43. **Pop. density:** 8.1 per sq. mi. **Urban** (1980): 85.3%. **Racial distrib.** (1980): 87.5% White; 6.3% Black; Hispanic 53,786. **Net migration** (1970-82): +374,000.

Geography. Total area: 110,540 sq. mi.; **rank:** 7. **Land area:** 109,889 sq. mi. **Acres forested land:** 7,683,300. **Location:** Mountain state bordered on N by Oregon and Idaho, on E by Utah and Arizona, on SE by Arizona, and on SW/W by California. **Climate:** semi-arid. **Topography:** rugged N-S mountain ranges; southern area is within the Mojave Desert; lowest elevation, Colorado R. Canyon, 470 ft. **Capital:** Carson City.

Economy. Principal industries: gaming, tourism, mining, manufacturing, government, agriculture, warehousing, trucking. **Principal manufactured goods:** gaming devices, electronics, chemicals, stone-clay-glass products. **Agriculture: Chief crops:** alfalfa, barley, wheat, oats, cotton. **Livestock:** 700,000 cattle; 13,000 hogs/pigs; 129,000 sheep; 13,000 poultry. **Timber/lumber:** pine, fir, spruce. **Minerals** (1983): $502 mln.; mostly barite, gold, mercury. **International airports at** Las Vegas, Reno. **Value of construction** (1983): $1.4 bln. **Employment distribution** (1983): 45% serv.; 20% trade; 14% gvt. **Per capita income** (1983): $12,516. **Unemployment** (1983): 9.8% **Tourism** (1981): out-of-state visitors spent $2.6 bln.

Finance. No. banks (1983): 15; **No. savings assns.** (1982): 7.

Federal government. No. federal civilian employees (Mar. 1983): 6,134. **Avg. salary:** $24,591. **Notable federal facilities:** Nevada Test Site.

Energy. Electricity production (1983, mwh, by source): Hydroelectric: 4.1 mln.; Mineral: 13.3 mln.

Education. No. schools (1981): 306 elem. and second.; 7 higher ed. **Avg. salary, public school teachers:** $23,120.

State data. Motto: All for our country. **Flower:** Sagebrush. **Bird:** Mountain bluebird. **Tree:** Single-leaf pinon. **Song:** Home Means Nevada. **Entered union** Oct. 31, 1864; rank, 36th. **State fair** at Reno; early Sept.

History. Nevada was first explored by Spaniards in 1776. Hudson's Bay Co. trappers explored the north and central region, 1825; trader Jedediah Smith crossed the state, 1826 and 1827. The area was acquired by the U.S., in 1848, at the end of the Mexican War. First settlement, Mormon Station, now Genoa, was est. 1849. In the early 20th century, Nevada adopted progressive measures such as the initiative, referendum, recall, and woman suffrago.

Tourist attractions. Legalized gambling provided the impetus for the development of resort areas Lake Tahoe, Reno, and Las Vegas. Ghost towns, rodeos, trout fishing, water sports and hunting important.

Notable are Helldorado Week in May, Las Vegas; Basque Festival, Elko; Reno Rodeo, 4th of July; Valley of Fire State Park, Overton; Death Valley, on the California border; Lehman Caves National Monument.

Famous Nevadans include Walter Van Tilburg Clark, Sarah Winnemucca Hopkins, John William MacKay, Pat McCarran, William Morris Stewart.

Tourist Information: Department of Economic Development, 1100 E. William St., Carson City, NV 89710.

New Hampshire

Granite State

People. Population (1983): 959,000; **rank:** 41. **Pop. density:** 106.2 per sq. mi. **Urban** (1980): 52.2%. **Racial distrib.** (1980): 98.8% White; 0.4% Black; Hispanic 5,587. **Net migration** (1970-79): +101,000.

Geography. Total area: 9,304 sq. mi.; **rank:** 44. **Land area:** 9,027 sq. mi. **Acres forested land:** 5,013,500. **Location:** New England state bounded on S by Massachusetts, on W by Vermont, on N/NW by Canada, on E by Maine and the Atlantic O. **Climate:** highly varied, due to its nearness to high mountains and ocean. **Topography:** low, rolling coast followed by countless hills and mountains rising out of a central plateau. **Capital:** Concord.

Economy. Principal industries: manufacturing, tourism, agriculture, trade, mining. **Principal manufactured goods:** machinery, computers, electrical & electronic equipment, pulp & paper, lumber & furniture, leather prod. **Agriculture: Chief crops:** dairy products, nursery and greenhouse products, hay, vegetables, apples, maple syrup & sugar prods. **Livestock:** 45,000 cattle; 6,400 hogs/pigs; 8,000 sheep; 850,000 poultry. **Timber/lumber:** white pine, hemlock, oak, birch. **Minerals** (1983): $23.7 mln.; mostly sand & gravel. **Commercial fishing** (1982): $3.8 mln. **Chief ports:** Portsmouth. **Value of construction** (1983): ·$789 mln. **Employment distribution:** 28.9% manuf.; 22% trade; 19.1% serv; 15.1 gvt. **Per capita income** (1983): $11,620. **Unemployment** (1983): 5.4%. **Tourism** (1983): out-of-state visitors spent $1.2 bln.

Finance. No. banks (1983): 88; ·**No. savings assns.** (1982): 13.

Federal government. No. federal civilian employees (Mar. 1983): 12,298. **Avg. salary:** $21,868. **Notable federal facilities:** Pease Air Base, Newington.

Energy. Electricity production (1983, mwh, by source): Hydroelectric: 1.2 mln.; Mineral: 4.1 mln.

Education. No. schools (1981): 527 elem. and second.; 25 higher ed. **Avg. salary, public school teachers:** $17,172.

State data. Motto: Live free or die. **Flower:** Purple lilac. **Bird:** Purple finch. **Tree:** White birch. **Song:** Old New Hampshire. **Ninth** of the original 13 states to ratify the Constitution, June 21, 1788.

History. First explorers to visit the New Hampshire area were England's Martin Pring, 1603, and Champlain, 1605. First settlement was Little Harbor, near Rye, 1623. Indian raids were halted, 1759, by Robert Rogers' Rangers. Before the Revolution, New Hampshire men seized a British fort at Portsmouth, 1774, and drove the royal governor out, 1775. Three regiments served in the Continental Army and scores of privateers raided British shipping.

Tourist attractions. Mt. Washington, highest peak in Northeast, hub of network of trails; Lake Winnipesaukee; White Mt. Natl. Forest; Crawford, Franconia, Pinkham notches in White Mt. region—Franconia famous for the Old Man of the Mountains, described by Hawthorne as the Great Stone Face; the Flume, a spectacular gorge; the aerial tramway on Cannon Mt; Strawberry Bank, Portsmouth; Shaker Village, Canterbury.

Famous New Hampshirites include Salmon P. Chase, Ralph Adams Cram, Mary Baker Eddy, Daniel Chester French, Robert Frost, Horace Greeley, Sarah Buell Hale, Augustus Saint-Gaudens, Daniel Webster.

Tourist Information: Department of Resources and Economic Development, Office of Vacation Travel, P.O. Box 856, Concord, NH 03301.

New Jersey

Garden State

People. Population (1983): 7,468,000; **rank:** 9. **Pop. density:** 993.0 per sq. mi. **Urban** (1980): 89.0%. **Racial distrib.** (1980): 83.2% White; 12.5% Black; Hispanic 491,867. **Net migration** (1980-82): +8,000.

Geography. Total area: 7,836 sq. mi.; **rank:** 46. **Land area:** 7,521 sq. mi. **Acres forested land:** 1,928,400. **Location:** Middle Atlantic state bounded on the N and E by New York and the Atlantic O., on the S and W by Delaware and Pennsylvania. **Climate:** moderate, with marked difference bet. NW and SE extremities. **Topography:** Appalachian Valley in the NW also has highest elevation, High Pt., 1,801 ft.; Appalachian Highlands, flat-topped NE-SW mountain ranges; Piedmont Plateau, low plains broken by high ridges (Palisades) rising 400-500 ft.; Coastal Plain, covering three-fifths of state in SE, gradually rises from sea level to gentle slopes. **Capital:** Trenton.

Economy. Principal industries: manufacturing, trade, services. **Principal manufactured goods:** chemicals, electronic and electrical equipment, non-electrical machinery, fabricated metals. **Value added by manufacture** (1978): $40.5 bln. **Agriculture: Chief crops:** hay, corn, soybeans, tomatoes, blueberries, peaches, cranberries. **Livestock:** 95,000 cattle; 53,800 hogs/pigs; 11,900 sheep; 966,800 poultry. **Timber/lumber:** pine, cedar, mixed hardwoods. **Minerals** (1983): $149.1 mln.; mostly stone, sand & gravel. **Commercial fishing** (1982): $45.0 mln. **Chief ports:** Newark, Elizabeth, Hoboken, Ameri-Port (Delaware R.). **International airports at:** Newark. **Value of construction** (1983): $5.5 bln. **Employment distribution** (1982): 23.6% manuf., 22.6% trade, 21.4% serv., 17.0% gvt. **Per capita income** (1983): $14,057. **Unemployment** (1983): 7.8%. **Tourism** (1982): tourists spent $8 bln.

Finance. No. banks (1983): 152; **No. savings assns.** (1982): 141.

Federal government. No. federal civilian employees (Mar. 1983): 39,694. **Avg. salary:** $24,265. **Notable federal facilities:** McGuire AFB Fort Dix; Fort Monmouth; Picatinny Arsenal; Lakewood Naval Air Station, Lakehurst Naval Air Engineering Center.

Energy. Electricity production (1983, mwh, by source): Mineral: 21.2 mln.; Nuclear: 6.3 mln.

Education. No. schools (1981): 3,015 elem. and second.; 62 higher ed. **Avg. salary, public school teachers:** $22,571.

State Data. Motto: Liberty and prosperity. **Flower:** Purple violet. **Bird:** Eastern goldfinch. **Tree:** Red oak. **Third** of the original 13 states to ratify the Constitution, Dec. 18, 1787. **State fair:** 2d week of Sept.

History. The Lenni Lenape (Delaware) Indians had mostly peaceful relations with European colonists who arrived after the explorers Verrazano, 1524, and Hudson, 1609. The Dutch were first; when the British took New Netherland, 1664, the area between the Delaware and Hudson Rivers was given to Lord John Berkeley and Sir George Carteret. New Jersey was the scene of nearly 100 battles, large and small, during the Revolution, including Trenton, 1776, Princeton, 1777, Monmouth, 1778.

Tourist attractions. Grover Cleveland birthplace, Caldwell; 127 miles of beaches; Miss America Pageant and hotel-casinos, Atlantic City; Cape May Historic District; Edison Labs, W. Orange; Great Adventure amusement park; Liberty State Park; Meadowlands Sports Complex; Pine Barrens wilderness area; Princeton University; numerous Revolutionary War historical sites.

Famous New Jerseyites include Count Basie, Aaron Burr, James Fenimore Cooper, Stephen Crane, Thomas Edison, Albert Einstein, Alexander Hamilton, Joyce Kilmer, Gen. George McClellan, Thomas Paine, Molly Pitcher, Paul Robeson, Walter Schirra, Walt Whitman.

Chamber of Commerce: 5 Commerce St., Newark, NJ 07102.

New Mexico

Land of Enchantment

People. Population (1983): 1,399,000; **rank:** 37. **Pop. density:** 11.5 per sq. mi. **Urban** (1980): 72.1%. **Racial distrib.** (1980): 75.1% White; 1.8% Black; 15.3% Other (includes American Indians); Hispanic 476,089. **Major ethnic groups:** Spanish, Indian, English. **Net migration** (1970-82): +284,000.

Geography. Total area: 121,666 sq. mi.; **rank:** 5. **Land area:** 121,412 sq. mi. **Acres forested land:** 18,059,800. **Location:** southwestern state bounded by Colorado on the N, Oklahoma, Texas, and Mexico on the E and S, and Arizona on the W. **Climate:** dry, with temperatures rising or falling 5°F with every 1,000 ft. elevation. **Topography:** eastern third, Great Plains; central third Rocky Mtns. (85% of the state is over 4,000 ft. elevation); western third high plateau. **Capital:** Santa Fe.

Economy. Principal industries: extractive industries, tourism, agriculture. **Principal manufactured goods:** foods, electrical machinery, apparel, lumber, printing,

transportation equipment. **Agriculture: Chief crops:** wheat, hay, sorghum, grain, onions, cotton, corn. **Livestock:** 1.72 mln. cattle; 72,000 hogs/pigs; 578,000 sheep; 1.21 mln. poultry. **Timber/lumber** (1982): Ponderosa pine, Douglas fir; 154 mln. bd. ft. **Minerals** (1983): $507 mln.; mostly potash, copper. **International airports at:** Albuquerque. **Value of construction** (1983): $2.1 bln. **Employment distribution:** 23.0% serv.; 18.0% agric.; 10% manuf.; 8.9% gvt. **Per capita income** (1983): $9,560. **Unemployment** (1983): 10.1%. **Tourism** (1982): out-of-state visitors spent $1.32 bln.

Finance. No. banks (1983): 94; **No. savings assns.** (1982): 28.

Federal government. No. federal civilian employees (Mar. 1983): 21,967. **Avg. salary:** $22,866. **Notable federal facilities:** Kirtland, Cannon, Holloman AF bases; Los Alamos Scientific Laboratory; White Sands Missile Range.

Energy. Electricity production (1983, mwh, by source): Hydroelectric: 89,000; Mineral: 27.1 mln.

Education. No. schools (1981): 712 elem. and second.; 19 higher ed. **Avg. salary, public school teachers:** $21,030.

State data. Motto: Crescit Eundo (It grows as it goes). **Flower:** Yucca. **Bird:** Roadrunner. **Tree:** Pinon. **Song:** O, Fair New Mexico, Asi Es Nuevo Mexico. **Entered union** Jan. 6, 1912; rank, 47th. **State fair** at: Albuquerque; mid-Sept.

History. Franciscan Marcos de Niza and a black slave Estevan explored the area, 1539, seeking gold. First settlements were at San Juan Pueblo, 1598, and Santa Fe, 1610. Settlers alternately traded and fought with the Apaches, Comanches, and Navajos. Trade on the Santa Fe Trail to Missouri started 1821. The Mexican War was declared May, 1846, Gen. Stephen Kearny took Santa Fe, August. In the 1870s, cattlemen staged the famed Lincoln County War in which Billy (the Kid) Bonney played a leading role. Pancho Villa raided Columbus, 1916.

Tourist Attractions. Carlsbad Caverns, a national park, has caverns on 3 levels and the largest natural cave "room" in the world, 1,500 by 300 ft., 300 ft. high; White Sands Natl. Monument, the largest gypsum deposit in the world.

Pueblo ruins from 100 AD, Chaco Canyon; Acoma, the "sky city," built atop a 357-ft. mesa; 19 Pueblo, 4 Navajo, and 2 Apache reservations. Also, ghost towns, dude ranches, skiing, hunting, and fishing.

Famous New Mexicans include Billy (the Kid) Bonney, Kit Carson, Peter Hurd, Archbishop Jean Baptiste Lamy, Bill Mauldin, Georgia O'Keeffe, Kim Stanley, Lew Wallace.

Tourist information: New Mexico Travel Division, Bataan Bldg., Santa Fe, N.M. 87503.

New York

Empire State

People. Population (1983): 17,667,000; **rank:** 2. **Pop. density:** 369.4 per sq. mi. **Urban** (1980): 84.6%. **Racial distrib.** (1980): 79.5% White; 13.68% Black; Hispanic (1980): 1,659,245. **Net migration** (1980-83): −136,000.

Geography. Total area: 49,576 sq. mi.; **rank:** 30. **Land area:** 47,831 sq. mi. **Acres forested land:** 17,218,400. **Location:** Middle Atlantic state, bordered by the New England states, Atlantic Ocean, New Jersey and Pennsylvania, Lakes Ontario and Erie, and Canada. **Climate:** variable; the SE region moderated by the ocean. **Topography:** highest and most rugged mountains in the NE Adirondack upland; St. Lawrence-Champlain lowlands extend from Lake Ontario NE along the Canadian border; Hudson-Mohawk lowland follows the flows of the rivers N and W, 10-30 mi. wide; Atlantic coastal plain in the SE; Appalachian Highlands, covering half the state westward from the Hudson Valley, include the Catskill Mtns., Finger Lakes; plateau of Erie-Ontario lowlands. **Capital:** Albany.

Economy. Principal industries: manufacturing, finance, communications, tourism, transportation, services. **Principal manufactured goods:** books and periodicals, clothing and apparel, pharmaceuticals, machinery, instruments, toys and sporting goods, electronic equipment, automotive and aircraft components. **Agriculture: Chief crops:** apples, cabbage, cauliflower, celery, cherries, grapes, corn, peas, snap beans, sweet corn. **Products:** milk, cheese, maple syrup. **Livestock:** 2.03 mln. cattle; 100,000 hogs/pigs; 63,000 sheep; 14.2 mln. poultry **Timber/lumber** (1981): saw log production; 630 mln. bd. ft. **Minerals** (1983): $508.8 mln.; mostly stone, salt, cement. **Commercial fishing** (1982): $45.4 mln. **Chief ports:** New York, Buffalo, Albany. **International airports at:** New York, Buffalo, Syracuse, Massena, Ogdensburg, Watertown, Monroe and Sullivan counties. **Value of construction** (1983): $8.3 bln. **Employment distribution:** 1.3% agric.; 21% manuf.; 33% serv.; 19% trade. **Per capita income** (1983): $13,146. **Unemployment** (1983): 8.6%. **Tourism** (1982): tourists spent $11.4 bln.

Finance. No. banks (1983): 451; **No. savings assns.** (1982): 89.

Federal government. No. federal civilian employees (Mar. 1983): 70,224. **Avg. salary:** $23,073. **Notable federal facilities:** West Point Military Academy; Merchant Marine Academy; Ft. Drum; Griffiss, Plattsburgh AF bases; Watervliet Arsenal.

Energy. Electricity production (1983, mwh, by source): Hydroelectric: 26.9 mln.; Mineral: 73.0 mln.; Nuclear: 16.4 mln.

Education: No. schools (1981): 5,823 elem. and second.; 293 higher ed. **Avg. salary, public school teachers:** $25,600.

State data. Motto: Excelsior (Ever upward). **Flower:** Rose. **Bird:** Bluebird. **Tree:** Sugar maple. **Eleventh** of the original 13 states to ratify the Constitution, July 26, 1788. **State fair** at: Syracuse, Aug. 24 to Sept. 3.

History. In 1609 Henry Hudson discovered the river that bears his name and Champlain explored the lake, far upstate, which was named for him. Dutch built posts near Albany 1614 and 1624; in 1626 they settled Manhattan. A British fleet seized New Netherland, 1664. Ninety-two of the 300 or more engagements of the Revolution were fought in New York, including the Battle of Bemis Heights-Saratoga, a turning point of the war.

Tourist attractions. New York City; Adirondack and Catskill mtns.; Finger Lakes, Great Lakes; Thousand Islands; Niagara Falls; Saratoga Springs racing and spas; Philipsburg Manor, Sunnyside, the restored home of Washington Irving, The Dutch Church of Sleepy Hollow, all in North Tarrytown; Corning Glass Center and Steuben factory, Corning; Fenimore House, National Baseball Hall of Fame and Museum, both in Cooperstown; Ft. Ticonderoga overlooking lakes George and Champlain.

The Franklin D. Roosevelt National Historic Site, Hyde Park, includes the graves of Pres. and Mrs. Roosevelt, the family home since 1867, the Roosevelt Library. Sagamore Hill, Oyster Bay, the Theodore Roosevelt estate, includes his home.

Famous New Yorkers include Peter Cooper, George Eastman, Julia Ward Howe, Charles Evans Hughes, Henry and William James, Herman Melville, Alfred E. Smith, Elizabeth Cady Stanton, Walt Whitman.

Tourist information: N.Y. State Dept. of Commerce, 1 Commerce Plaza, Albany, NY 12245.

hills; southern Appalachian Mtns. contains the Blue Ridge and Great Smoky mtns. **Capital:** Raleigh.

Economy. Principal industries: manufacturing, agriculture, tobacco, tourism. **Principal manufactured goods:** textiles, tobacco products, electrical/electronic equip., chemicals, furniture, food products, non-electrical machinery. **Agriculture: Chief crops:** tobacco, soybeans, corn, peanuts, small sweet potatoes, grains, vegetables, fruits. **Livestock:** 1.10 mln. cattle; 2.15 mln. hogs/pigs; 7,000 sheep; 19.2 mln. chickens. **Timber/lumber** (1982): yellow pine, oak, hickory, poplar, maple. 783 mln. bd. ft. **Minerals** (1983): Total $335.2 mln., mostly crushed stone, sand & gravel, feldspar. **Commercial fishing** (1982): $63.8 mln. **Chief ports:** Morehead City, Wilmington. **Value of construction** (1983): $4.9 bln. **Employment distribution:** 34.5% manuf.; 19.8% trade; 17.2% gvt.; 14.3% serv. **Per capita income** (1983): $9,656. **Unemployment** (1983): 8.9%. **Tourism** (1983): out-of-state visitors spent $3.4 bln.

Finance. No. banks (1983): 71; **No. savings assns.** (1982): 124.

Federal government. No. federal civilian employees (Mar. 1983): 27,315. **Avg. salary:** $21,742. **Notable federal facilities:** Ft. Bragg; Camp LeJeune Marine Base; U.S. EPA Research and Development Labs, Cherry Point Marine Corps Air Station.

Energy. Electricity production (1983, mwh, by source): Hydroelectric: 6.1 mln.; Mineral: 56.2 mln.; Nuclear: 12.4 mln.

Education. No. schools (1981): 2,284 elem. and second.; 126 higher ed. **Avg. salary, public school teachers:** $18,071.

State data. Motto: Esse Quam Videri (To be rather than to seem). **Flower:** Dogwood. **Bird:** Cardinal. **Tree:** Pine. **Song:** The Old North State. **Twelfth** of the original 13 states to ratify the Constitution, Nov. 21, 1789. **State fair** at: Raleigh; mid-Oct.

History. The first English colony in America was the first of 2 established by Sir Walter Raleigh on Roanoke Is., 1585 and 1587. The first group returned to England; the second, the "Lost Colony," disappeared without trace. Permanent settlers came from Virginia, c. 1660. Roused by British repressions, the colonists drove out the royal governor, 1775; the province's congress was the first to vote for independence; ten regiments were furnished to the Continental Army. Cornwallis' forces were defeated at Kings Mountain, 1780, and forced out after Guilford Courthouse, 1781.

Tourist attractions. Cape Hatteras and Cape Lookout national seashores; Great Smoky Mtns. (half in Tennessee); Guilford Courthouse and Moore's Creek parks, Revolutionary battle sites; Bennett Place, NW of Durham, where Gen. Joseph Johnston surrendered the last Confederate army to Gen. Wm. Sherman; Ft. Raleigh, Roanoke Is., where Virginia Dare, first child of English parents in the New World, was born Aug. 18, 1587; Wright Brothers National Memorial, Kitty Hawk.

Famous North Carolinians include Richard J. Gatling, Billy Graham, Wm. Rufus King, Dolley Madison, Edward R. Murrow, Enos Slaughter, Moses Waddel.

Tourist information: Division of Travel & Tourism Development, P.O. Box 25249, Raleigh, NC 27611.

North Carolina

Tar Heel State, Old North State

People. Population (1983): 6,082,000; **rank:** 10. **Pop. density:** 124.6 per sq. mi. **Urban** (1980): 42.9%. **Racial distrib.** (1980): 75.8% White; 22.4% Black; Hispanic (1980): 56,607. **Net migration** (1970-80): +393,369.

Geography. Total area: 52,586 sq. mi.; **rank:** 28. **Land area:** 48,798 sq. mi. **Acres forested land:** 20,043,300. **Location:** South Atlantic state bounded by Virginia, South Carolina, Georgia, Tennessee, and the Atlantic O. **Climate:** sub-tropical in SE, medium-continental in mountain region; tempered by the Gulf Stream and the mountains in W. **Topography:** coastal plain and tidewater, two-fifths of state, extending to the fall line of the rivers; piedmont plateau, another two-fifths, 200 mi. wide of gentle to rugged

North Dakota

Peace Garden State

People. Population (1983): 680,000; **rank:** 46. **Pop. density:** 9.8 per sq. mi. **Urban** (1980): 48.8%. **Racial distrib.** (1980): 95.8% White; 0.39% Black; Hispanic (1980): 3,903. **Net migration** (1980-84): −6,800.

Geography. Total area: 70,665 sq. mi.; **rank:** 17. **Land area:** 69.273 sq. mi. **Acres forested land:** 421,800. **Location:** West North Central state, situated exactly in the middle of North America, bounded on the N by Canada, on the E by Minnesota, on the S by South Dakota, on the W by Montana. **Climate:** continental, with a wide range of temperature and moderate rainfall. **Topography:** Central

Lowland in the E comprises the flat Red River Valley and the Rolling Drift Prairie; Missouri Plateau of the Great Plains on the W. **Capital:** Bismarck.

Economy. Principal industries: agriculture, mining, tourism, manufacturing. **Principal manufactured goods:** farm equipment, processed foods. **Agriculture: Chief crops:** spring wheat, durum, barley, rye, flaxseed, oats, potatoes, dried edible beans, honey, soybeans, sugarbeets, sunflowers, hay. **Livestock:** 2.1 mln. cattle; 210,000 hogs/pigs; 220,000 sheep; 1.5 mln. poultry. **Minerals** (1982): $13 mln. mostly sand & gravel. **Commercial fishing** (1982): $157,000. **International airports at:** Fargo, Grand Forks, Bismarck, Minot. **Value of construction** (1983): $581 mln. **Employment distribution:** 21.9% trade; 20.4% gvt.; 18.6% serv.; 17.2% agric. **Per capita income** (1983): $11,350. **Unemployment** (1983): 5.6%. **Tourism** (1983): out-of-state visitors spent $11.6 mln.

Finance No. banks (1983): 181; **No. savings assns.** (1982): 7.

Federal government. No. federal civilian employees (Mar. 1983): 4,668. **Avg. salary:** $22,442. **Notable federal facilities:** Strategic Air Command bases at Minot, Grand Forks; Northern Prairie Wildlife Research Center; Garrison Dam; Theodore Roosevelt Natl. Park; Grand Forks Energy Research Center; Ft. Union Natl. Historic Site.

Energy. Electricity production (1983, mwh, by source): Hydroelectric: 2.4 mln.; Mineral: 17.3 mln.

Education. No. schools (1981): 760 elem. and second.; 16 higher ed. **Avg. salary, public school teachers:** $18,830.

State data. Motto: Liberty and union, now and forever, one and inseparable. **Flower:** Wild prairie rose. **Bird:** Western Meadowlark. **Tree:** American elm. **Song:** North Dakota Hymn. **Entered union** Nov. 2, 1889; rank, 39th. **State fair** at: Minot; 3d week in July.

History. Pierre La Verendrye was the first French fur trader in the area, 1738, followed later by the English. The U.S. acquired half the territory in the Louisiana Purchase, 1803. Lewis and Clark built Ft. Mandan, spent the winter of 1804-05 there. In 1818, American ownership of the other half was confirmed by agreement with Britain. First permanent settlement was at Pembina, 1812. Missouri River steamboats reached the area, 1832; the first railroad, 1873, bringing many homesteaders. The state was first to hold a presidential primary, 1912.

Tourist attractions. International Peace Garden, a 2,200-acre tract extending across the border into Manitoba, commemorates the friendly relations between the U.S. and Canada; 65,000-acre Theodore Roosevelt National Park, Badlands, contains the president's Elkhorn Ranch; Ft. Abraham Lincoln State Park and Museum, S of Mandan.

Famous North Dakotans include Maxwell Anderson, Angie Dickinson, John Bernard Flannagan; Louis L'Amour, Peggy Lee, Eric Sevareid, Vilhjalmur Stefansson, Lawrence Welk.

Chamber of Commerce: P.O. Box 2467, Fargo, ND 58108.

Economy. Principal industries: manufacturing, tourism, government, trade. **Principal manufactured goods:** transportation equipment, machinery, primary and fabricated metal products. **Agriculture: Chief crops:** corn, hay, winter wheat, oats, soybeans. **Livestock** (1983): 1.9 mln. cattle; 2.1 mln. hogs/pigs; 265,000 sheep; 16.3 mln. poultry. **Timber/lumber** (1980): oak, ash, maple, walnut, beech; 420 mln. bd. ft. **Minerals** (1983): $506 mln.; mostly crushed stone, sand & gravel, salt, lime, clays, cement. **Commercial fishing** (1982): $2.7 mln. **Chief ports:** Cleveland, Toledo, Cincinnati, Ashtabula. **International airports at:** Cleveland, Cincinnati, Columbus, Dayton. **Value of construction** (1983): $5.9 bln. **Employment distribution:** 23.8% manuf.; 20.6% trade; 19.5% serv.; 14.7% gvt. **Per capita income** (1983): $11,254. **Unemployment** (1983): 12.2%. **Tourism** (1981): travelers spent nearly $5.6 bln.

Finance. No. banks (1983): 344; **No. savings assns.** (1982): 270.

Federal government. No. federal civilian employees (Mar. 1983): 53,218. **Avg. salary:** $25,123. **Notable federal facilities:** Wright Patterson, Rickenbacker AF bases; Defense Construction Supply Center; Lewis Research Ctr.; Portsmouth Gaseous Diffusion Plant; Mound Laboratory.

Energy. Electricity production (1983, mwh, by source): Hydroelectric: 135,000; Mineral: 100.8 mln.; Nuclear: 4.9 mln.

Education. No. schools (1981): 4,826 elem. and second.; 135 higher ed. **Avg. salary, public school teachers:** $20,730.

State data. Motto: With God, all things are possible. **Flower:** Scarlet carnation. **Bird:** Cardinal. **Tree:** Buckeye. **Song:** Beautiful Ohio. **Entered union** Mar. 1, 1803; rank, 17th. **State fair** at: Columbus; mid-Aug.

History. LaSalle visited the Ohio area, 1669. American fur-traders arrived, beginning 1685; the French and Indians sought to drive them out. During the Revolution, Virginians defeated the Indians, 1774, but hostilities were renewed, 1777. The region became U.S. territory after the Revolution. First organized settlement was at Marietta, 1788. Indian warfare ended with Anthony Wayne's victory at Fallen Timbers, 1794. In the War of 1812, Oliver H. Perry's victory on Lake Erie and William H. Harrison's invasion of Canada, 1813, ended British incursions.

Tourist attractions. Memorial City Group National Monuments, a group of 24 prehistoric Indian burial mounds; Neil Armstrong Air and Space Museum, Wapakoneta; Air Force Museum, Dayton; Pro Football Hall of Fame, Canton; birthplaces, homes, and memorials to Ohio's 6 U.S. presidents: Wm. Henry Harrison, U.S. Grant, Garfield, Hayes, McKinley, Harding.

Famous Ohioans include Sherwood Anderson, Neil Armstrong, George Bellows, Ambrose Bierce, Paul Laurence Dunbar, Thomas Edison, John Glenn, Bob Hope, Eddie Rickenbacker, John D. Rockefeller Sr. and Jr., Gen. Wm. Sherman, Charles Taft, Robert A. Taft, William H. Taft, Orville Wright.

Chamber of Commerce: 17 S. High St., 8th Fl., Columbus, OH 43215.

Ohio
Buckeye State

People. Population (1983): 10,746,000; **rank:** 6. **Pop. density:** 262.3 per sq. mi. **Urban** (1980): 73.3%. **Racial distrib.** (1980): 88.8% White; 9.9% Black; Hispanic (1980): 119,880. **Net migration** (1970-80): −575,853.

Geography. Total area: 41,222 sq. mi.; **rank:** 35. **Land area:** 40,975 sq. mi. **Acres forested land:** 6,146,600. **Location:** East North Central state bounded on the N by Michigan and Lake Erie; on the E and S by Pennsylvania, West Virginia; and Kentucky; on the W by Indiana. **Climate:** temperate but variable; weather subject to much precipitation. **Topography:** generally rolling plain; Allegheny plateau in E; Lake [Erie] plains extend southward; central plains in the W. **Capital:** Columbus.

Oklahoma
Sooner State

People. Population (1983): 3,298,000; **rank:** 24. **Pop. density:** 48.0 per sq. mi. **Urban** (1980): 67.3%. **Racial distrib.** (1980): 85.8% White; 6.76% Black; 5.6% Amer. Ind. **Net migration** (1970-80): +292,164.

Geography. Total area: 69,919 sq. mi.; **rank:** 18. **Land area:** 68,782 sq. mi. **Acres forested land:** 8,513,300. **Location:** West South Central state bounded on the N by Colorado and Kansas; on the E by Missouri and Arkansas; on the S and W by Texas and New Mexico. **Climate:** temperate; southern humid belt merging with colder northern continental; humid eastern and dry western zones. **Topography:** high plains predominate the W, hills and small mountains in the E; the east central region is dominated by the Arkansas R. Basin, and the Red R. Plains, in the S. **Capital:** Oklahoma City.

Economy. Principal industries: mineral and energy exploration and production, manufacturing, agriculture **Principal manufactured goods:** oil field machinery and equipment; non-electrical machinery, food and kindred products, fabricated metal products. **Agriculture: Chief crops:** wheat, cotton lint, sorghum grain, peanuts, hay, soybeans, cotton seed, barley, oats, pecans. **Livestock:** 5.4 mln. cattle; 180,000 hogs/pigs; 117,000 sheep; 56 mln. poultry. **Timber/lumber** (1981): pine, oaks, hickory; 438 mln. bd. ft. **Minerals** (1983): $257.4 mln.; mostly cement, crushed stone, sand & gravel, gypsum, lime, clay, salt. **Commercial fishing** (1979): $2.8 mln. **Chief ports:** Catoosa, Muskogee. **International airports at:** Oklahoma City, Tulsa. **Value of construction** (1983): $4.2 bln. **Employment distribution** (1981): 24.2% trade; 18.1% gvt.; 18.1% serv.; 16.4% manuf. **Per capita income** (1983): $11,187. **Unemployment** (1983): 9.0%. **Tourism** (1982): tourists spent $3.2 bln.

Finance. No. banks (1983): 533; **No. savings assns.** (1982): 53.

Federal government. No. federal civilian employees (Mar. 1983): 36,273. **Avg. salary:** $22,268. **Notable federal facilities:** Federal Aviation Agency and Tinker AFB, both Oklahoma City; Ft. Sill, Lawton; Altus AFB, Altus; Vance AFB, Enid.

Energy. Electricity production (1983, mwh, by source): Hydroelectric: 2.5 mln.; Mineral: 43.2 mln.

Education. No. schools (1981): 1,937 elem. and second.; 45 higher ed. **Avg. salary, public school teachers:** $18,900.

State data. Motto: Labor Omnia Vincit (Labor conquers all things). **Flower:** Mistletoe. **Bird:** Scissortailed flycatcher. **Tree:** Redbud. **Song:** Oklahoma! **Entered union** Nov. 16, 1907; rank, 46th. **State fair** at: Oklahoma City; last week of Sept.

History. Part of the Louisiana Purchase, 1803, Oklahoma was known as Indian Territory (but was not given territorial government) after it became the home of the "Five Civilized Tribes"—Cherokee, Choctaw, Chickasaw, Creek, and Seminole—1828-1846. The land was also used by Comanche, Osage, and other Plains Indians. As white settlers pressed west, land was opened for homesteading by runs and lottery, the first run taking place Apr. 22, 1889. The most famous run was to the Cherokee Outlet, 1893.

Tourist attraction. Will Rogers Memorial, Claremore; National Cowboy Hall of Fame, Oklahoma City; restored Ft. Gibson Stockade, near Muskogee, the Army's largest outpost in Indian lands; Indian pow-wows; rodeos; fishing; hunting; Ouachita National Forest; Enterprise Square, museum devoted to American economic system.

Famous Oklahomans include Carl Albert, Woody Guthrie, Gen. Patrick J. Hurley, Karl Jansky, Mickey Mantle, Wiley Post, Oral Roberts, Will Rogers, Maria Tallchief, Jim Thorpe.

Chamber of Commerce: 4020 N. Lincoln Blvd., Oklahoma City, OK 73105.

Oregon

Beaver State

People. Population (1983): 2,662,000; **rank:** 30. **Pop. density:** 27.7 per sq. mi. **Urban** (1980): 67.9%. **Racial distrib.** (1980): 94.5% White; 1.4% Black; Hispanic (1980): 65,883. **Net migration** (1970-83): +543,467.

Geography. Total area: 96,981 sq. mi.; **rank:** 10. **Land area:** 96,184 sq. mi. **Acres forested land:** 29,810,000. **Location:** Pacific state, bounded on N by Washington; on E by Idaho; on S by Nevada and California; on W by the Pacific. **Climate:** coastal mild and humid climate; continental dryness and extreme temperatures in the interior. **Topography:** Coast Range of rugged mountains; fertile Willamette R. Valley to E and S; Cascade Mtn. Range of volcanic peaks E of the valley; plateau E of Cascades, remaining two-thirds of state. **Capital:** Salem.

Economy. Principal industries: manufacturing, agriculture, forestry, tourism. **Principal manufactured goods:** lumber & wood products, foods, machinery, fabricated metals, paper, printing & publishing, primary metals.

Agriculture: Chief crops: wheat, hay, potatoes, pears, barley, onions, strawberries, sweet corn, cherries, hops. **Livestock:** 1,710,000 cattle; 85,000 hogs/pigs; 495,000 sheep; 20 mln. poultry. **Timber/lumber** (1982): Douglas fir, hemlock, ponderosa pine; 4.9 bln. bd. ft. **Minerals** (1982): $108 mln.; mostly sand & gravel, stone, cement. **Commercial fishing** (1982): $57.5 mln. **Chief ports:** Portland, Astoria, Newport, Coos Bay. **International airports at:** Portland. **Value of construction** (1983): $1.4 bln. **Employment distribution:** 25% trade; 19.7% manuf.; 20% govt.; 19% serv. **Per capita income** (1983): $10,920. **Unemployment** (1983): 10.8%. **Tourism** (1982): out-of-state visitors spent $1.3 bln.

Finance: No. banks (1983): 91; **No. savings assns.** (1982): 21.

Federal government. No. federal civilian employees (Mar. 1983): 18,839. **Avg. salary:** $23,963. **Notable federal facilities:** Bonneville Power Administration.

Energy: Electricity production (1983, mwh, by source): Hydroelectric: 45.1 mln.; Mineral: 446,000; Nuclear: 3.7 mln.

Education. No. schools (1981): 1,471 elem. and second.; 45 higher ed. **Avg. salary, public school teachers:** $22,763.

State data. Motto: The union. **Flower:** Oregon grape. **Bird:** Western meadowlark. **Tree:** Douglas fir. **Song:** Oregon, My Oregon. **Entered union** Feb. 14, 1859; rank, 33d. **State fair** at: Salem; end-Aug. to early Sept.

History. American Capt. Robert Gray discovered and sailed into the Columbia River, 1792; Lewis and Clark, traveling overland, wintered at its mouth 1805-06; fur traders followed. Settlers arrived in the Willamette Valley, 1834. In 1843 the first large wave of settlers arrived via the Oregon Trail. Early in the 20th century, the "Oregon System," reforms which included the initiative, referendum, recall, direct primary, and woman suffrage, was adopted.

Tourist attractions. John Day Fossil Beds National Monument; Columbia River Gorge; Mt. Hood & Timberline Lodge; Crater Lake National Park; Oregon Dunes National Recreation Area; Ft. Clatsop National Memorial; Oregon Caves National Monument; Shakespearean Festival, Ashland; High Desert Museum, Bend. Also, skiing, fishing; Annual Albany Timber Carnival, Pendelton Round-Up, Portland Rose Festival.

Famous Oregonians include Ernest Bloch, Ernest Haycox, Chief Joseph, Edwin Markham, Tom McCall, Dr. John McLoughlin, Joaquin Miller, Linus Pauling, John Reed, Alberto Salazar, Mary Decker, William Simon U'Ren.

Chamber of Commerce: 220 Cottage St., N.E., Salem, OR 97301.

Pennsylvania

Keystone State

People. Population (1983): 11,895,000; **rank:** 4. **Pop. density:** 264.5 per sq. mi. **Urban** (1980): 69.3%. **Racial distrib.** (1980): 89.7% White; 8.8% Black; Hispanic (1980): 154,004. **Net migration** (1970-79): −478,000.

Geography. Total area: 45,333 sq. mi.; **rank:** 33. **Land area:** 44,966 sq. mi. **Acres forested land:** 16,825,900. **Location:** Middle Atlantic state, bordered on the E by the Delaware R., on the S by the Mason-Dixon Line; on the W by West Virginia and Ohio; on the N/NE by Lake Erie and New York. **Climate:** continental with wide fluctuations in seasonal temperatures. **Topography:** Allegheny Mtns. run SW to NE, with Piedmont and Coast Plain in the SE triangle; Allegheny Front a diagonal spine across the state's center; N and W rugged plateau falls to Lake Erie Lowland. **Capital:** Harrisburg.

Economy. Principal industries: steel, travel, health, apparel, machinery, food & agriculture. **Principal manufactured goods:** primary metals, foods, fabricated metal products, non-electrical machinery, electrical machinery. **Agriculture: Chief crops:** corn, hay, mushrooms, apples, potatoes, winter wheat, oats, vegetables, tobacco, grapes. **Livestock:** 2.0 mln. cattle; 830,000 hogs/pigs; 98,000 sheep; 22.5 mln. poultry. **Timber/lumber** (1982): pine, oak, maple; 644.1 mln. bd. ft. **Minerals** (1983): $623.5 mln.; mostly cement, crushed stone, lime, sand & gravel. **Commercial fishing** (1982): $79,000. **Chief ports:** Philadelphia, Pittsburgh, Erie. **International airports at:** Philadelphia, Pittsburgh, Erie, Harrisburg. **Value of construction** (1983): $4.8 bln. **Employment distribution:** 27.9% manuf.; 20.8% trades; 20.4% serv.; 15.3% gvt. **Per capita income** (1983): $11,510. **Unemployment** (1983): 11.8%. **Tourism** (1982): out-of-state visitors spent $7.0 bln.

Finance. No. banks (1983): 355; **No. savings and loan assns.** (1982): 230.

Federal government. No. federal civilian employees (Mar. 1983): 85,472. **Avg. salary:** $22,091. **Notable federal facilities:** Army War College, Carlisle; Ships Control Ctr., Mechanicsburg; New Cumberland Army Depot; Philadelphia Navy Yard, Philadelphia.

Energy. Electricity production (1983, mwh, by source): Hydroelectric: 1.2 mln.; Mineral: 107.7 mln. Nuclear: 14.7 mln.

Education. No. schools (1981): 5,095 elem. and second.; 200 higher ed. **Avg. salary, public school teachers:** $21,799.

State data. Motto: Virtue, liberty and independence. **Flower:** Mountain laurel. **Bird:** Ruffed grouse. **Tree:** Hemlock. **Second** of the original 13 states to ratify the Constitution, Dec. 12, 1787. **State fair** at: Harrisburg; 2d week in Jan.

History. First settlers were Swedish, 1643, on Tinicum Is. In 1655 the Dutch seized the settlement but lost it to the British, 1664. The region was given by Charles II to William Penn, 1681, Philadelphia (brotherly love) was the capital of the colonies during most of the Revolution, and of the U.S., 1790-1800. Philadelphia was taken by the British, 1777; Washington's troops encamped at Valley Forge in the bitter winter of 1777-78. The Declaration of Independence, 1776, and the Constitution, 1787, were signed in Philadelphia.

Tourist attractions. Independence Hall, Liberty Bell, Carpenters Hall, all in Philadelphia; Valley Forge; Gettysburg battlefield; Amish festivals, Lancaster Cty., Hershey Chocolate World; Pocono Mtns.; Delaware Water Gap; Longwood Gardens, near Kennett Square; Pine Creek Gorge; hunting, fishing, winter sports.

Famous Pennsylvanians include Marian Anderson, Maxwell Anderson, Andrew Carnegie, Stephen Foster, Benjamin Franklin, George C. Marshall, Andrew W. Mellon, Robert E. Peary, Mary Roberts Rinehart, Betsy Ross.

Chamber of Commerce: 222 N. 3d St., Harrisburg, PA 17101.

Rhode Island

Little Rhody, Ocean State

People. Population (1983): 955,000; **rank:** 42. **Pop. density:** 910.4 per sq. mi. **Urban** (1980): 87.0% **Racial distrib.** (1980): 94.6% White; 2.9% Black; Hispanic (1980): 19,707. **Net migration** (1970-80): −33,000.

Geography. Total area: 1,214 sq. mi.; **rank:** 50. **Land area:** 1,049 sq. mi. **Acres forested land:** 404,200. **Location:** New England state. **Climate:** invigorating and changeable. **Topography:** eastern lowlands of Narragansett Basin; western uplands of flat and rolling hills. **Capital:** Providence.

Economy. Principal industries: manufacturing, services. **Principal manufactured goods:** costume jewelry, machinery, textiles, electronics, silverware. **Agriculture: Chief crops:** potatoes, apples, corn. **Livestock:** 10,000 cattle; 8,700 hogs/pigs; 2,100 sheep; 260,000 poultry. **Timber/lumber:** oak, chestnut. **Minerals** (1983): $3.5 mln.; entirely sand & gravel. **Commercial fishing** (1982): $55.4 mln. **Chief ports:** Providence, Newport, Tiverton. **Value of construction** (1983): $513 mln. **Employment**

distribution (1983): 29.3% manuf.; 23.6% serv.; 21.0% trade. **Per capita income** (1983): $11,504. **Unemployment** (1983): 8.3%. **Tourism** (1983): out-of-state visitors spent $500 mln.

Finance. No. banks (1983): 24; **No. savings assns.** (1982): 4.

Federal government. No. federal civilian employees (Mar. 1983): 5,663. **Avg. salary:** $23,842. **Notable federal facilities:** Naval War College.

Energy. Electricity production (1983, mwh, by source): Hydroelectric: 3,000; Mineral: 581,000.

Education. No. schools (1981): 409 elem. and second.; 13 higher ed. **Avg. salary, public school teachers:** $23,600.

State data. Motto: Hope. **Flower:** Violet. **Bird:** Rhode Island red. **Tree:** Red maple. **Song:** Rhode Island. **Thirteenth** of original 13 states to ratify the Constitution, May 29, 1790. **State fair** at: E. Greenwich; mid-Aug.

History. Rhode Island is distinguished for its battle for freedom of conscience and action, begun by Roger Williams, founder of Providence, who was exiled from Massachusetts Bay Colony in 1636, and Anne Hutchinson, exiled in 1638. Rhode Island gave protection to Quakers in 1657 and to Jews from Holland in 1658.

The colonists broke the power of the Narragansett Indians in the Great Swamp Fight, 1675, the decisive battle in King Philip's War. British trade restrictions angered the colonists and they burned the British revenue cutter Gaspee, 1772. The colony declared its independence May 4, 1776. Gen. John Sullivan and Lafayette won a partial victory, 1778, but failed to oust the British.

Tourist attractions. Newport mansions; summer resorts and water sports; various yachting races inc. Newport to Bermuda. Touro Synagogue, Newport, 1763; first Baptist Church in America, Providence, 1638; Gilbert Stuart birthplace, Saunderstown; Narragansett Indian Fall Festival.

Famous Rhode Islanders include Ambrose Burnside, George M. Cohan, Nelson Eddy, Jabez Gorham, Nathanael Greene, Christopher and Oliver La Farge, Matthew C. and Oliver Perry, Gilbert Stuart.

Chamber of Commerce: 206 Smith St., Providence, RI 02908.

South Carolina

Palmetto State

People. Population (1983): 3,264,000; **rank:** 25. **Pop. density:** 108.1 per sq. mi. **Urban** (1980): 54.1%. **Racial distrib.** (1980): 68.8% White; 30.4% Black; Hispanic (1980): 33,414. **Net migration** (1980-82): +32,000.

Geography. Total area: 31,055 sq. mi.; **rank:** 40. **Land area:** 30,203.37 sq. mi. **Acres forested land:** 12,249,400. **Location:** south Atlantic coast state, bordering North Carolina on the N; Georgia on the SW and W; the Atlantic O. on the E, SE and S. **Climate:** humid sub-tropical. **Topography:** Blue Ridge province in NW has highest peaks; piedmont lies between the mountains and the fall line; coastal plain covers two-thirds of the state. **Capital:** Columbia.

Economy: Principal industries: tourism, textiles, apparel, chemical, agriculture, manufacturing. **Principal manufactured goods:** textiles, chemicals and allied products, machinery & fabricated metal products, apparel and related products. **Agriculture: Chief crops:** tobacco, soybeans, corn, cotton, peaches, hay. **Livestock** (1982): 700,000 cattle; 440,000 hogs/pigs; 8.55 mln. poultry. **Timber/lumber** (1983): pine, oak; 711 mln. **Minerals** (1983): $235.5 mln.; mostly cement, clay, sand & gravel, stone. **Commercial fishing** (1982): $23.7 mln. **Chief ports:** Charleston, Georgetown, Port Royal. **International airports at:** Charleston. **Value of construction** (1983): $2.6 bln. **Employment distribution** (1982): 31.2% manuf.; 19.7% gvt.; 14.6% serv. **Per capita income** (1983): $8,954. **Unemployment** (1983): 10.0%. **Tourism** (1982): out-of-state visitors spent $2.5 bln.

Finance. No. banks (1983): 72; **No. savings assns.** (1982): 44.

Federal government: No. federal civilian employees (Mar. 1983): 25,311. **Avg. Salary:** $21,592. **Notable federal facilities:** Polaris Submarine Base; Barnwell Nuclear Power Plant; Ft. Jackson.

Energy. Electricity production (1983, mwh, by source): Hydroelectric: 3.1 mln.; Mineral: 17.3 mln.; Nuclear: 25.6 mln.

Education. No. schools (1981): 1,320 elem. and second.; 61 higher ed. **Avg. salary, public school teachers** (1983): $17,330.

State data. Motto: Dum Spiro Spero (While I breathe, I hope). **Flower:** Carolina jessamine. **Bird:** Carolina wren. **Tree:** Palmetto. **Song:** Carolina. **Eighth** of the original 13 states to ratify the Constitution, May 23, 1788. **State fair** at: Columbia; Oct.

History. The first English colonists settled, 1670, on the Ashley River, moved to the site of Charleston, 1680. The colonists seized the government, 1775, and the royal governor fled. The British took Charleston, 1780, but were defeated at Kings Mountain that year, and at Cowpens and Eutaw Springs, 1781. In the 1830s, South Carolinians, angered by federal protective tariffs, adopted the Nullification Doctrine, holding a state can void an act of Congress. The state was the first to secede and, in 1861, Confederate troops fired on and forced the surrender of U. S. troops at Ft. Sumter, in Charleston Harbor, launching the Civil War.

Tourist attractions. Restored historic Charleston harbor area and Charleston gardens: Middleton Place, Magnolia, Cypress; other gardens at Brookgreen, Edisto, Glencairn; state parks; coastal islands; shore resorts such as Myrtle Beach and Hilton Head Island; fishing and quail hunting; Ft. Sumter National Monument, in Charleston Harbor; Charleston Museum, est. 1773, is the oldest museum in the U.S.

Famous South Carolinians include James F. Byrnes, John C. Calhoun, DuBose Heyward, Ernest F. Hollings, James Longstreet, Francis Marion, Charles Pinckney, John Rutledge, Thomas Sumter, Strom Thurmond.

Chamber of Commerce: 1301 Gervais St., Suite 520, Bankers Trust Tower, Columbia, SC 29201.

eral facilities: Bureau of Indian Affairs, Ellsworth AFB, Corp of Engineers, Nat'l Park Service.

Energy. Electricity production (1983, mwh, by source): Hydroelectric: 5.5 mln.; Mineral: 2.3 mln.

Education. No. schools (1981): 818 elem. and second.; 20 higher ed. **Avg. salary, public school teachers** (1983): $16,493.

State data. Motto: Under God, the people rule. **Flower:** Pasque flower. **Bird:** Ringnecked pheasant. **Tree:** Black Hills spruce. **Song:** Hail, South Dakota. **Entered union** Nov. 2, 1889; rank, 40th. **State fair** at: Huron; late Aug.-early Sept.

History. Les Verendryes explored the region, 1742-43. Lewis and Clark passed through the area, 1804 and 1806. First white American settlement was at Fort Pierre, 1817. Gold was discovered, 1874, on the Sioux Reservation; miners rushed in. The U.S. first tried to stop them, then relaxed its opposition. Custer's defeat by the Sioux followed; the Sioux relinquished the land, 1877 and the "great Dakota Boom" began, 1879. A new Indian uprising came in 1890, climaxed by the massacre of Indian families at Wounded Knee.

Tourist attractions. Needles Highway through the Black Hills; Badlands National Park "moonscape"; Custer State Park's bison and burro herds; Ft. Sisseton, a restored army frontier post of 1864; the "Great Lakes of South Dakota," reservoirs created behind Oahe, Big Bend, Ft. Randall, and Gavins Point dams on the Missouri R.

Mount Rushmore, in the Black Hills, has an altitude of 6,200 ft. Sculptured on its granite face are the heads of Washington, Jefferson, Lincoln, and Theodore Roosevelt. These busts by Gutzon Borglum are proportionate to men 465 ft. tall. Rushmore is visited by about 2 million persons annually.

Famous South Dakotans include Tom Brokaw, "Calamity Jane," Crazy Horse, Alvin H. Hansen, Dr. Ernest O. Lawrence, Sacagawea, Sitting Bull, Laura Ingalls Wilder.

Chamber of Commerce: P.O. Box 190, Pierre, SD 57501.

South Dakota
Coyote State, Sunshine State

People. Population (1983): 700,000; **rank:** 45. **Pop. density:** 9.2 per sq. mi. **Urban** (1980): 46.4%. **Racial distrib.** (1980): 92.6% White; 0.31% Black; 7.1% Other (includes American Indians); Hispanic (1980): 4,028. **Net migration** (1970-82): −26,384.

Geography. Total area: 77,047 sq. mi.; **rank:** 16. **Land area:** 75,955 sq. mi. **Acres forested land:** 1,702,000. **Location:** West North Central state bounded on the N by North Dakota; on the E by Minnesota and Iowa; on the S by Nebraska; on the W by Wyoming and Montana. **Climate:** characterized by extremes of temperature, persistent winds, low precipitation and humidity. **Topography:** Prairie Plains in the E; rolling hills of the Great Plains in the W; the Black Hills, rising 3,500 ft. in the SW corner. **Capital:** Pierre.

Economy. Principal industries: agriculture, tourism, manufacturing. **Principal manufactured goods:** apparel, machinery, fabricated metals and stone, clay and glass products. **Agriculture. Chief crops:** wheat, corn, oats, hay, rye, sorghum, barley, soybeans, flaxseed, sunflowers. **Livestock** (1983): 4.2 mln. cattle; 1.65 mln. hogs/ pigs; 730,000 sheep; 3.65 mln. poultry. **Timber/lumber:** ponderosa pine. **Minerals** (1983): $210.1 mln.; mostly gold, cement, stone. **Commercial fishing** (1983): $478,000. **Value of construction** (1983): $433 mln. **Employment distribution:** 28.8% serv.; 16.1% agric.; 9.6% manuf. **Per capita income** (1983): $9,704. **Unemployment** (1983): 5.4%. **Tourism** (1982): out-of-state visitors spent $450 mln.

Finance. No. banks (1983): 146; **No. savings assns.** (1982): 16.

Federal government. No. federal civilian employees (Mar. 1983): 6,529. **Avg. salary:** $21,780. **Notable fed-**

Tennessee
Volunteer State

People. Population (1983): 4,685,000; **rank:** 17. **Pop. density:** 113.4 per sq. mi. **Urban** (1980): 60.4%. **Racial distrib.** (1980): 83.5% White; 15.8% Black; Hispanic (1980): 34,081. **Major ethnic groups:** German, English, Italian. **Net migration** (1970-80): +231,925.

Geography. Total area: 42,244 sq. mi.; **rank:** 34. **Land area:** 41,328 sq. mi. **Acres forested land:** 13,160,500. **Location:** East South Central state bounded on the N by Kentucky and Virginia; on the E by North Carolina; on the S by Georgia, Alabama, and Mississippi; on the W by Arkansas and Missouri. **Climate:** humid continental to the N; humid sub-tropical to the S. **Topography:** rugged country in the E; the Great Smoky Mtns. of the Unakas; low ridges of the Appalachian Valley; the flat Cumberland Plateau; slightly rolling terrain and knobs of the Interior Low Plateau, the largest region; Eastern Gulf Coastal Plain to the W, is laced with meandering streams; Mississippi Alluvial Plain, a narrow strip of swamp and flood plain in the extreme W. **Capital:** Nashville.

Economy. Principal industries: trade, services, construction; transp., commun., public utilities; finance, ins., real estate. **Principal manufactured goods:** chemicals & allied prods.; food & kindred prods.; nonelectrical machinery; electric/electronic equip.; apparel; fabr. metal prods.; transp. equip.; rubber/misc. plastic prods.; paper & allied prods. **Agriculture. Chief crops:** soybeans, tobacco, wheat, cotton, corn. **Livestock:** 2.4 mln. cattle; 1.1 mln. hogs/pigs; 11,000 sheep; 5.7 mln. poultry. **Timber/lumber** (1982): red oak, white oak, yellow poplar, hickory; 331 mln. bd. ft. **Minerals** (1983): $410.8 mln.; mostly crushed stone, zinc. **Chief ports:** Memphis, Nashville, Chattanooga, Knoxville. **International airports at:** Memphis. **Value of construction** (1983): $3.6 bln. **Employment distribution** (1983): 27.3% manuf.; 22.7% trade;

18.7% serv.; 13.7% gvt. **Per capita income** (1983): $9,362. **Unemployment** (1983): 11.5%. **Tourism** (1982): out-of-state visitors spent $2.1 bln.

Finance. No. banks (1983): 336; **No. savings assns.** (1982): 81.

Federal government. No. federal civilian employees (Mar. 1983): 44,962. **Avg. salary:** $23,936. **Notable federal facilities:** Tennessee Valley Authority; Oak Ridge Nat'l. Laboratories.

Energy. Electricity production (1983, mwh, by source): Hydroelectric: 10.0 mln.; Mineral: 45.4 mln.; Nuclear: 14.1 mln.

Education. No. schools (1981): 1,961 elem. and second.; 77 higher ed. **Avg. salary, public school teachers** (1983): $17,700.

State data. Motto: Agriculture and commerce. **Flower:** Iris. **Bird:** Mockingbird. **Tree:** Tulip poplar. **Song:** The Tennessee Waltz. **Entered union** June 1, 1796; rank, 16th. **State fair** at: Nashville; 3d week of Sept.

History. Spanish explorers first visited the area, 1541. English traders crossed the Great Smokies from the east while France's Marquette and Jolliet sailed down the Mississippi on the west, 1673. First permanent settlement was by Virginians on the Watauga River, 1769. During the Revolution, the colonists helped win the Battle of Kings Mountain, N.C., 1780, and joined other eastern campaigns. The state seceded from the Union 1861, and saw many engagements of the Civil War, but 30,000 soldiers fought for the Union.

Tourist attractions. Natural wonders include Reelfoot Lake, the reservoir basin of the Mississippi R. formed by the 1811 earthquake; Lookout Mountain, Chattanooga; Fall Creek Falls, 256 ft. high; Great Smoky Mountains National Park.

Also, the Hermitage, 13 mi. E of Nashville, home of Andrew Jackson; the homes of presidents Polk and Andrew Johnson; the Parthenon, Nashville, a replica of the Parthenon of Athens; the Grand Old Opry, Nashville.

Famous Tennesseans include Davy Crockett, David Farragut, William C. Handy, Sam Houston, Cordell Hull, Grace Moore, Dinah Shore, Alvin York.

Tourist Information: Tourist Development Office, 601 Broadway, Nashville, TN 37202.

Dallas/Ft. Worth, San Antonio. **Value of construction** (1983) $21.9 bln. **Employment distribution:** 16% manuf.; 19% serv.; 6% transp. **Per capita income** (1983): $11,702. **Unemployment** (1983): 8.0%. **Tourism** (1982): out-of-state visitors spent $12.5 mln.

Finance. No. banks (1983) 1,733; **No. savings assns.** (1982): 288.

Federal government. No. federal civilian employees (Mar. 1983): 108,252. **Avg. salary:** $22,280. **Notable federal facilities:** Fort Hood (Killeen).

Energy. Electricity production (1982, mwh, by source): Hydroelectric: 1.1 mln.; Mineral: 205.0 mln.

Education. No. schools (1982): 5,978 elem. and second.; 153 higher ed. **Avg. salary, public school teachers** (1983): $20,334.

State data. Motto: Friendship. **Flower:** Bluebonnet. **Bird:** Mockingbird. **Tree:** Pecan. **Song:** Texas, Our Texas. **Entered union** Dec. 29, 1845; rank, 28th. **State fair** at: Dallas; mid-Oct.

History. Pineda sailed along the Texas coast, 1519; Cabeza de Vaca and Coronado visited the interior, 1541. Spaniards made the first settlement at Ysleta, near El Paso, 1682. Americans moved into the land early in the 19th century. Mexico, of which Texas was a part, won independence from Spain, 1821; Santa Anna became dictator, 1835. Texans rebelled; Santa Anna wiped out defenders of the Alamo, 1836. Sam Houston's Texans defeated Santa Anna at San Jacinto and independence was proclaimed the same year. In 1845, Texas was admitted to the Union.

Tourist attractions. Padre Island National Seashore; Big Bend, Guadalupe Mtns. national parks; The Alamo; Ft. Davis; Six Flags Amusement Park. Named for Pres. Lyndon B. Johnson are a state park, a natl. historic site marking his birthplace, boyhood home, and ranch, all near Johnson City, and a library in Austin.

Famous Texans include Stephen Austin, James Bowie, Carol Burnett, J. Frank Dobie, Sam Houston, Howard Hughes, Mary Martin, Chester Nimitz, Katharine Ann Porter, Sam Rayburn.

Chamber of Commerce: 1012 Perry-Brooks Bldg., Austin, TX 78701.

Texas

Lone Star State

People. Population (1983): 15,724,000; **rank:** 3. **Pop. density:** 60.0 per sq. mi. **Urban** (1980): 79.6%. **Racial distrib.** (1980): 78.6% White; 12.0% Black; Hispanic (1980): 2,985,643. **Major ethnic groups:** Mexican, German, peanuts. **Net migration** (1970-79): +1,045,000.

Geography: Total area: 267,338 sq. mi.; **rank:** 2. **Land area:** 262,134 sq. mi.; **Acres forested land:** 23,279,300. **Location:** Southwestern state, bounded on the SE by the Gulf of Mexico; on the SW by Mexico, separated by the Rio Grande; surrounding states are Louisiana, Arkansas, Oklahoma, New Mexico. **Climate:** extremely varied; driest region is the Trans-Pecos; wettest is the NE. **Topography:** Gulf Coast Plain in the S and SE; North Central Plains slope upward with some hills; the Great Plains extend over the Panhandle, are broken by low mountains; the Trans-Pecos is the southern extension of the Rockies. **Capital:** Austin.

Economy. Principal industries: petroleum, manufacturing, construction. **Principal manufactured goods:** machinery, transportation equipment, foods, refined petroleum, apparel. **Agriculture. Chief crops:** cotton, grain sorghum, grains, vegetables, citrus and other fruits, pecans, peanuts. **Livestock:** 15.0 mln. cattle; 550,000 hogs/pigs; 2.25 mln. sheep; 17.2 mln. poultry. **Timber/lumber** (1982): pine, cypress; 686 mln. bd. ft. **Minerals** (1983): $1.7 bln.; mostly cement, magnesium chloride, sand & gravel, crushed stone, Frasch sulfur, talc. **Commercial fishing** (1982): $186.2 mln. **Chief ports:** Houston, Galveston, Brownsville, Beaumont, Port Arthur, Corpus Christi. **Major international airports at:** Houston,

Utah

Beehive State

People. Population (1983): 1,619,000; **rank:** 35. **Pop. density:** 19.7 per sq. mi. **Urban** (1980): 84.4%. **Racial distrib.** (1980): 92.6% White; 4.1% Hispanic. **Net migration** (1970-80): +149,000.

Geography. Total area: 84,916 sq. mi.; **rank:** 11. **Land area:** 82,096 sq. mi. **Acres forested land:** 15,557,400. **Location:** Middle Rocky Mountain state; its southeastern corner touches Colorado, New Mexico, and Arizona, and is the only spot in the U.S. where 4 states join. **Climate:** arid; ranging from warm desert in SW to alpine in NE. **Topography:** high Colorado plateau is cut by brilliantly-colored canyons of the SE; broad, flat, desert-like Great Basin of the W; the Great Salt Lake and Bonneville Salt Flats to the NW; Middle Rockies in the NE run E-W; valleys and plateaus of the Wasatch Front. **Capital:** Salt Lake City.

Economy. Principal industries: manufacturing, tourism, trade, services, mining, transportation. **Principal manufactured goods:** guided missiles and parts, electronic components, food products, primary metals, electrical and transportation equipment. **Agriculture. Chief crops:** wheat, hay, apples, barley, alfalfa seed, corn, potatoes, cherries, onions. **Livestock:** 850,000 cattle; 40,000 hogs/pigs; 650,000 sheep; 3.8 mln. poultry. **Timber/lumber:** aspen, spruce, pine. **Minerals** (1983): $659.6 mln.; mostly gem stones, gypsum. **International airports at:** Salt Lake City. **Value of construction** (1983): $3.8 bln. **Employment distribution:** (1983) 23.6% trade; 22.8% govt., 19.7% serv.; 15.1% manuf. **Per capita income** (1983): $9,031. **Unemployment**

(1983): 9.2%. **Tourism** (1982): out-of-state visitors spent $500 mln.

Finance. No. banks (1983): 63; **No. savings assns.** (1982): 15.

Federal government. No. federal civilian employees (Mar. 1983): 31,829. **Avg. salary:** $21,983. **Notable federal facilities:** Hill AFB; Tooele Army Depot, IRS Western Service Center.

Energy. Electricity production (1982, mwh, by source): Hydroelectric: 1.4 mln.; Mineral: 11.0 mln.

Education. No. schools (1982): 645 elem. and second.; 14 higher ed. **Avg. salary, public school teachers** (1983): $22,768.

State data. Motto: Industry. **Flower:** Sego lily. **Bird:** Seagull. **Tree:** Blue spruce. **Song:** Utah, We Love Thee. **Entered union** Jan. 4, 1896; rank, 45th. **State fair** at: Salt Lake City; Sept.

History. Spanish Franciscans visited the area, 1776, the first white men to do so. American fur traders followed. Permanent settlement began with the arrival of the Mormons, 1847. They made the arid land bloom and created a prosperous economy, organized the State of Deseret, 1849, and asked admission to the Union. This was not achieved until 1896, after a long period of controversy over the Mormon Church's doctrine of polygamy, which it discontinued in 1890.

Tourist attractions. Temple Square, Mormon Church hdqtrs., Salt Lake City; Great Salt Lake; fishing streams; lakes and reservoirs, numerous winter sports; campgrounds. Natural wonders may be seen at Zion, Canyonlands, Bryce Canyon, Arches, and Capitol Reef national parks; Dinosaur, Rainbow Bridge, Timpanogas Cave, and Natural Bridges national monuments. Also Lake Powell and Flaming Gorge Dam.

Famous Utahans include Maude Adams, Ezra Taft Benson, John Moses Browning, Philo Farnsworth, Osmond Family, Merlin Olsen, Ivy Baker Priest, George Romney, Brigham Young, Loretta Young.

Tourist information: Division of Travel Development, Council Hall, Salt Lake City, UT 84114.

Vermont

Green Mountain State

People. Population (1983): 525,000; **rank:** 48. **Pop. density:** 56.7 per sq. mi. **Urban** (1980): 33.8%. **Racial distrib.** (1980): 99.0% White; 0.22% Black; Hispanic (1980): 3,304. **Net migration** (1970-82): +38,000.

Geography. Total area: 9,609 sq. mi.; **rank:** 43. **Land area:** 9,267 sq. mi. **Acres forested land:** 4,511,700. **Location:** northern New England state. **Climate:** temperate, with considerable temperature extremes; heavy snowfall in mountains. **Topography:** Green Mtns. N-S backbone 20-36 mi. wide; avg. altitude 1,000 ft. **Capital:** Montpelier.

Economy. Principal industries: manufacturing, tourism, agriculture, mining, government. **Principal manufactured goods:** machine tools, furniture, scales, books, computer components, skis, fishing rods. **Agriculture:** **Chief crops:** apples, maple syrup, silage corn, hay; also, dairy products. **Livestock:** 339,000 cattle; 8,000 hogs/pigs; 9,200 sheep; 435,000 poultry. **Timber/lumber:** pine, spruce, fir, hemlock. **Minerals** (1983): $51.8 mln.; mostly asbestos, dimension stone, talc. **International airports at:** Burlington. **Value of construction** (1983): $376 mln. **Employment distribution:** 22% manuf.; 19% serv.; 15% retail trade. **Per capita income** (1983): $10,036. **Unemployment** (1983): 6.9%. **Tourism** (1983): out-of-state visitors spent $1.2 bln.

Finance. No. banks (1983): 33; **No. savings assns.** (1982): 5.

Federal government. No. federal civilian employees (Mar. 1983): 2,225. **Avg. salary:** $22,846.

Energy. Electricity production (1983, mwh, by source): Hydroelectric: 936,000; Mineral: 60,000; Nuclear: 2.9 mln.

Education. No. schools (1981): 428 elem. and second.; 21 higher ed. **Avg. salary, public school teachers** (1983): $15,776.

State data. Motto: Freedom and unity. **Flower:** Red clover. **Bird:** Hermit thrush. **Tree:** Sugar maple. **Song:** Hail, Vermont. **Entered union** Mar. 4, 1791; rank, 14th. **State fair** at: Rutland; early Sept.

History. Champlain explored the lake that bears his name, 1609. First American settlement was Ft. Dummer, 1724, near Brattleboro. Ethan Allen and the Green Mountain Boys captured Ft. Ticonderoga, 1775; John Stark defeated part of Burgoyne's forces near Bennington, 1777. In the War of 1812, Thomas MacDonough defeated a British fleet on Champlain off Plattsburgh, 1814.

Tourist attractions. Year-round outdoor sports, esp. hiking, camping and skiing; there are over 56 ski areas in the state. Popular are the Shelburne Museum; Rock of Ages Tourist Center, Graniteville; Vermont Marble Exhibit, Proctor; Bennington Battleground; Pres. Coolidge homestead, Plymouth; Maple Grove Maple Museum, St. Johnsbury.

Famous Vermonters include Ethan Allen, Adm. George Dewey, John Dewey, Stephen A. Douglas, Dorothy Canfield Fisher, James Fisk.

Chamber of Commerce: P.O. Box 37, Montpelier, VT 05602.

Virginia

Old Dominion

People. Population (1983): 5,550,000; **rank:** 13. **Pop. density:** 139.5 per sq. mi. **Urban** (1980): 66.0% **Racial distrib.** (1980): 79.1% White; 18.9% Black; Hispanic (1980): 79,873. **Net migration** (1980-82): +48,800.

Geography. Total area: 40,817 sq. mi.; **rank:** 36. **Land area:** 39,780 sq. mi. **Acres forested land:** 16,417,400. **Location:** South Atlantic state bounded by the Atlantic O. on the E and surrounded by North Carolina, Tennessee, Kentucky, West Virginia, and Maryland. **Climate:** mild and equable. **Topography:** mountain and valley region in the W, including the Blue Ridge Mtns.; rolling piedmont plateau; tidewater, or coastal plain, including the eastern shore. **Capital:** Richmond.

Economy. Principal industries: government, trade, manufacturing, tourism, agriculture. **Principal manufactured goods:** textiles, food processing, apparel, transportation equipment, chemicals. **Agriculture: Chief crops:** tobacco, soybeans, peanuts, corn. **Livestock:** 1.85 mln. cattle; 640,000 hogs/pigs; 170,000 sheep; 1.34 mln. poultry. **Timber/lumber** (1982): pine and hardwoods; 1.1 bln. bd. ft. **Minerals** (1983): $283.2 mln.; mostly crushed stone, sand & gravel, lime. **Commercial fishing** (1982): $68.8 mln. **Chief ports:** Hampton Roads. **International airports at:** Norfolk, Dulles, Richmond, Newport News. **Value of construction** (1983): $5.1 bln. **Employment distribution:** 19% manuf.; 21% trade; 20% serv.; 23% gvt. **Per capita income** (1983): $11,835. **Unemployment** (1983): 6.1%. **Tourism** (1978): out-of-state visitors spent $3.0 bln.

Finance. No. banks (1983): 191; **No. savings assns.** (1982): 75.

Federal government. No. federal civilian employees (Mar. 1983): 130,587. **Avg. salary:** $25,013. **Notable federal facilities:** Pentagon; Naval Sta., Norfolk; Naval Air Sta., Norfolk, Virginia Beach; Naval Shipyard, Portsmouth; Marine Corps Base, Quantico; Langley AFB; NASA at Langley.

Energy. Electricity production (1983, mwh, by source): Hydroelectric: 1.2 mln.; Mineral: 17.9 mln.; Nuclear: 25.6 mln.

Education. No. schools (1981): 2,062 elem. and second.; 69 higher ed. **Avg. salary, public school teachers** (1983): $19,292.

State data. Motto: Sic Semper Tyrannis (Thus always to tyrants). **Flower:** Dogwood. **Bird:** Cardinal. **Tree:** Dogwood. **Song:** Carry Me Back to Old Virginia. **Tenth of** the original 13 states to ratify the Constitution, June 26, 1788. **State fair** at: Richmond; late Sept.-early Oct.

History. English settlers founded Jamestown, 1607. Virginians took over much of the government from royal Gov. Dunmore in 1775, forcing him to flee. Virginians under

George Rogers Clark freed the Ohio-Indiana-Illinois area of British forces. Benedict Arnold burned Richmond and Petersburg for the British, 1781. That same year, Britain's Cornwallis was trapped at Yorktown and surrendered. **Tourist attractions.** Colonial Williamsburg; Busch Gardens; Wolf Trap Farm, near Falls Church; Arlington National Cemetery; Mt. Vernon, home of George Washington; Jamestown Festival Park; Yorktown; Jefferson's Monticello, Charlottesville; Robert E. Lee's birthplace, Stratford Hall, and grave, at Lexington; Appomattox; Shenandoah National Park; Blue Ridge Parkway; Virginia Beach.

Famous Virginians include Richard E. Byrd, James B. Cabell, Patrick Henry, Joseph E. Johnston, Robert E. Lee, Meriwether Lewis and William Clark, John Marshall, Edgar Allan Poe, Walter Reed, Booker T. Washington.

Chamber of Commerce: 611 E. Franklin St., Richmond, VA 23219.

Washington

Evergreen State

People. Population (1983): 4,300,000; **rank:** 20. **Pop. density:** 64.6 per sq. mi. **Urban** (1980): 73.5%. **Racial distrib.** (1980): 91.4% White; 2.5% Black; Hispanic (1980): 119,986. **Net migration** (1970-83): +514,600.

Geography. Total area: 68,192 sq. mi.; **rank:** 20. **Land area:** 66,570 sq. mi. **Acres forested land:** 23,181,000. **Location:** northwestern coastal state bordered by Canada on the N; Idaho on the E; Oregon on the S; and the Pacific O. on the W. **Climate:** mild, dominated by the Pacific O. and protected by the Rockies. **Topography:** Olympic Mtns. on NW peninsula; open land along coast to Columbia R.; flat terrain of Puget Sound Lowland; Cascade Mtns. region's high peaks to the E; Columbia Basin in central portion; highlands to the NE; mountains to the SE. **Capital:** Olympia.

Economy. Principal industries: aerospace, forest products, food products, petroleum refining, primary metals, agriculture. **Principal manufactured goods:** aircraft, pulp and paper, lumber and plywood, aluminum, processed fruits and vegetables. **Agriculture: Chief crops:** wheat, apples, hay, potatoes, barley, nursery/greenhouse products, hops, corn, pears. **Livestock** (1983): 1.65 mln. cattle; 53,000 hogs/pigs; 62,000 sheep; 6.13 mln. poultry. **Timber/lumber** (1982): Douglas fir, hemlock, cedar, pine; 2.7 bln. bd. ft. **Minerals** (1983): $211 mln.; mostly cement, sand & gravel, stone. **Commercial fishing** (1982): $90.1 mln. **Chief ports:** Seattle, Tacoma, Vancouver, Kelso-Longview. **International airports at:** Seattle/Tacoma, Spokane, Boeing Field. **Value of construction** (1983): $3.7 bln. **Employment distribution:** 25% trade; 21% serv.; 18% mfg.; 14% gvt. **Per capita income** (1983): $12,051. **Unemployment** (1983): 11.2%. **Tourism** (1983): $3.6 bln.

Finance. No. banks (1983): 123; **No. savings assns.** (1982): 45.

Federal government. No. federal civilian employees (Mar. 1983): 47,835. **Avg. salary:** $23,857. **Notable federal facilities:** Bonneville Power Admin.; Ft. Lewis; McChord AFB; Hanford Nuclear Reservation; Bremerton Naval Shipyards.

Energy. Electricity production (1983, mwh, by source): Hydroelectric: 85.5 mln.; Mineral: 6.1 mln.; Nuclear: 3.5 mln.

Education. No. schools (1981): 2,041 elem. and second.; 49 higher ed. **Avg. salary, public school teachers** (1983): $24,519.

State data. Motto. Alki (By and by). **Flower:** Western rhododendron. **Bird:** Willow goldfinch. **Tree:** Western hemlock. **Song:** Washington, My Home. **Entered union** Nov. 11, 1889; **rank,** 42d.

History. Spain's Bruno Hezeta sailed the coast, 1775. American Capt. Robert Gray sailed up the Columbia River, 1792. Canadian fur traders set up Spokane House, 1810; Americans under John Jacob Astor established a post at Fort Okanogan, 1811. Missionary Marcus Whitman settled near Walla Walla, 1836. Final agreement on the border of Washington and Canada was made with Britain, 1846, and gold was discovered in the state's northeast, 1855, bringing new settlers.

Tourist attractions. Mt. Rainier, Olympic and North Cascades National Parks; Mt. St. Helens; Pacific beaches; Puget Sound; wineries; Indian cultures; year-round outdoor sports.

Famous Washingtonians include Bing Crosby, William O. Douglas, Henry M. Jackson, Mary McCarthy, Edward R. Murrow, Theodore Roethke, Marcus Whitman, Minoru Yamasaki.

Local Chambers of Commerce: P.O. Box 658, Olympia, WA 98507.

West Virginia

Mountain State

People. Population (1983): 1,965,000. **rank:** 34. **Pop. density:** 81.6 per sq. mi. **Urban** (1980): 36.2. **Racial distrib.** (1980): 96.1% White; 3.3% Black; Hispanic (1980): 12,707. **Net migration** (1975-80): +5,289.

Geography. Total area: 24,181 sq. mi.; **rank:** 41. **Land area:** 24,070 sq. mi. **Acres forested land:** 11,668,600. **Location:** South Atlantic state bounded on the N by Ohio, Pennsylvania, Maryland; on the S and W by Virginia, Kentucky, Ohio; on the E by Maryland and Virginia. **Climate:** humid continental climate except for marine modification in the lower panhandle. **Topography:** ranging from hilly to mountainous; Allegheny Plateau in the W, covers two-thirds of the state; mountains here are the highest in the state, over 4,000 ft. **Capital:** Charleston.

Economy. Principal industries: mining, mineral and chemical production, primary metals and stone, clay, and glass prods., timber, tourism. **Principal manufactured goods:** machinery, plastic and hardwood prods., fabricated metals, basic organic and inorganic chemicals, aluminum, steel. **Agriculture: Chief crops:** apples, peaches, hay, tobacco, corn, wheat, oats, barley. **Chief products:** milk, eggs, honey. **Livestock** (1983): 590,000 cattle; 38,000 hogs/pigs; 91,000 sheep; 870,000 chickens. **Timber/lumber:** oak, yellow poplar, hickory, walnut, cherry. **Minerals** (1983): $92.7 mln.; mostly crushed stone, sand & gravel, salt, cement, dimension stone. **Commercial fishing** (1982): $21,000. **Chief port:** Huntington. **Value of construction** (1983): $871 mln. **Per capita income** (1983): $8,937. **Unemployment** (1983): 18.0%. **Tourism** (1981): out-of-state visitors spent $1.2 bln.

Finance. No. banks (1983): 231; **No. savings assns.** (1982): 25.

Federal government. No. federal civilian employees (Mar. 1983): 9,451. **Avg. salary:** $22,898. **Notable federal facilities:** National Radio Astronomy Observatory, Green Bank; Bureau of Public Debt. Bldg., Parkersburg; Natl. Park, Harper's Ferry; Correctional Institution for Women, Alderson.

Energy. Electricity production (1983, mwh, by source): Hydroelectric: 419,000; Mineral: 72.1 mln.

Education. No. schools (1981): 1,194 elem. and second.; 28 higher ed. **Avg. salary, public school teachers** (1983): $18,054.

State Data. Motto: Montani Semper Liberi (Mountaineers are always free) **Flower:** Big rhododendron. **Bird:** Cardinal. **Tree:** Sugar maple. **Songs:** The West Virginia Hills; This Is My West Virginia; West Virginia, My Home, Sweet Home. **Entered union** June 20, 1863; rank, 35th. **State fair** at: Lewisburg (Fairlea), Aug. 17-25.

History. Early explorers included George Washington, 1753, and Daniel Boone. The area became part of Virginia and often objected to rule by the eastern part of the state. When Virginia seceded, 1861, the Wheeling Conventions repudiated the act and created a new state, Kanawha, subsequently changed to West Virginia. It was admitted to the Union as such, 1863.

Tourist attractions. Harpers Ferry National Historic Park has been restored to its condition in 1859, when John Brown seized the U.S. Armory.

Also Science and Cultural Center, Charleston; White Sulphur and Berkeley Springs mineral water spas; Monongahela Natl. Forest; state parks and forests; trout fishing; turkey, deer, and bear hunting.

Famous West Virginians include Newton D. Baker, Pearl Buck, John W. Davis, Thomas "Stonewall" Jackson, Don Knotts, Dwight Whitney Morrow, Michael Owens, Cyrus Vance, Col. Charles "Chuck" Yeager.

Tourist information: Governor's Office of Economic & Community Development, State Capitol, Charleston WV 25305.

lakes for water sports, ice boating and fishing; skiing and hunting.

Famous Wisconsinites include Edna Ferber, King Camp Gillette, Harry Houdini, Robert LaFollette, Alfred Lunt, Joseph R. McCarthy, Spencer Tracy, Thorstein Veblen, Orson Welles, Thornton Wilder, Frank Lloyd Wright.

Tourist information: Wisconsin Dept. of Development, Division of Tourism, 123 W. Washington Ave., Madison, WI 53702.

Wisconsin

Badger State

People. Population (1983): 4,751,000; **rank:** 16. **Pop. density:** 87.2 per sq. mi. **Urban** (1980): 64.2%. **Racial distrib.** (1980): 94.4% White; 3.8% Black; Hispanic (1980): 62,981. **Net migration** (1970-80): +9,000.

Geography. Total area: 56,154 sq. mi.; **rank:** 26. **Land area:** 54,464 sq. mi. **Acres forested land:** 14,907,700. **Location:** North central state, bounded on the N by Lake Superior and Upper Michigan; on the E by Lake Michigan; on the S by Illinois; on the W by the St. Croix and Mississippi rivers. **Climate:** long, cold winters and short, warm summers tempered by the Great Lakes. **Topography:** narrow Lake Superior Lowland plain met by Northern Highland which slopes gently to the sandy crescent Central Plain; Western Upland in the SW; 3 broad parallel limestone ridges running N-S are separated by wide and shallow lowlands in the SE. **Capital:** Madison.

Economy. Principal industries: manufacturing, trade, services, government, transportation, communications, agriculture, tourism. **Principal manufactured goods:** machinery, foods, fabricated metals, transportation equipment, paper and wood products. **Agriculture: Chief crops:** corn, beans, beets, peas, hay, oats, cabbage, cranberries. **Chief products:** milk, butter, cheese. **Livestock:** 4.4 mln. cattle, 1.2 mln. hogs/pigs; 99,000 sheep; 10.9 mln. poultry. **Timber/lumber:** maple, birch, oak, evergreens. **Minerals** (1983): $111.5 mln.; mostly crushed stone, sand & gravel, lime. (mainly nonmetallic minerals). **Commercial fishing** (1982): $3,129 mln. **Chief ports:** Superior, Ashland, Milwaukee, Green Bay, Kewaunee, Pt. Washington, Manitowoc, Sheboygan, Marinette, Kenosha. **International airports at:** Milwaukee. **Value of construction** (1983): $2.6 bln. **Employment distribution** (1983): 26.6% manuf.; 22.5% trade; 20.6% serv.; 16.9% gvt. **Per capita income** (1983): $11,132. **Unemployment** (1983): 10.4%. **Tourism** (1982): out-of-state visitors spent $6.4 bln.

Finance. No. banks (1983): 611; **No. savings assns.** (1982): 87.

Federal government. No. federal civilian employees (Mar. 1983): 12,014. **Avg. salary:** $22,618. **Notable federal facilities:** Ft. McCoy.

Energy. Electricity production (1983, mwh, by source): Hydroelectric: 2.3 mln.; Mineral: 27.7 mln.; Nuclear: 9.3 mln.

Education. No. schools (1981): 2,989 elem and second.; 65 higher ed. **Avg. salary, public school teachers** (1983): $22,100.

State data. Motto: Forward. **Flower:** Wood violet. **Bird:** Robin. **Tree:** Sugar maple. **Song:** On, Wisconsin! **Entered union** May 29, 1848; rank, 30th. **State fair** at: West Allis; mid-Aug.

History. Jean Nicolet was the first European to see the Wisconsin area, arriving in Green Bay, 1634; French missionaries and fur traders followed. The British took over, 1763. The U.S. won the land after the Revolution but the British were not ousted until after the War of 1812. Lead miners came next, then farmers. Railroads were started in 1851, serving growing wheat harvests and iron mines.

Tourist attractions. Old Wade House and Carriage Museum, Greenbush; Villa Louis, Prairie du Chien; Circus World Museum, Baraboo; Wisconsin Dells; Old World Wisconsin, Eagle; Door County peninsula; Chequamegon and Nicolet national forests; Lake Winnebago; numerous

Wyoming

Equality State

People. Population (1983) 514,000; **rank:** 49. **Pop. density:** 5.3 per sq. mi. **Urban** (1980): 62.7%. **Racial distrib.** (1980): 95.0% White; 0.71% Black; Hispanic (1980): 24,499. **Major ethnic groups:** German, English, Russian. **Net migration** (1970-82): +103,000.

Geography. Total area: 97,914 sq. mi.; **rank:** 9. **Land area:** 97,203 sq. mi. **Acres forested land:** 9.8 mln. **Location:** Mountain state lying in the high western plateaus of the Great Plains. **Climate:** semi-desert conditions throughout; true desert in the Big Horn and Great Divide basins. **Topography:** the eastern Great Plains rise to the foothills of the Rocky Mtns.; the Continental Divide crossed the state from the NW to the SE. **Capital:** Cheyenne.

Economy. Principal industries: mineral extraction, tourism and recreation, agriculture. **Principal manufactured goods:** refined petroleum products, foods, wood products, stone, clay and glass products. **Agriculture: Chief crops:** wheat, beans, barley, oats, sugar beets, hay. **Livestock:** 1.39 mln. cattle; 33,000 hogs/pigs; 1.13 mln. sheep. **Timber/lumber** (1982): aspen, yellow pine; 134 mln. bd. ft. **Minerals** (1983): $610 mln.; mostly clays, stone, sand & gravel. **International airports at:** Casper. **Value of construction** (1983): $879 mln. **Employment distribution:** 27% serv.; 15% mining; 18% trade. **Per capita income** (1983): $11,969. **Unemployment** (1983): 8.4%. **Tourism** (1982): out-of-state visitors spent $750 mln.

Finance. No. banks (1983): 112; **No. savings and loan assns.** (1982): 12.

Federal government. No. federal civilian employees (Mar. 1983): 4,673. **Avg. salary:** $23,381. **Notable federal facilities:** Warren AFB.

Energy. Electricity production (1983, mwh, by source): Hydroelectric: 1.2 mln. Mineral: 25.1 mln.

Education. No. schools (1981): 404 elem. and second.; 9 higher ed. **Avg. salary, public school teachers** (1983): $23,820.

State data. Motto: Equal Rights. **Flower:** Indian paintbrush. **Bird:** Meadowlark. **Tree:** Cottonwood. **Song:** Wyoming. **Entered union** July 10, 1890; rank, 44th. **State fair** at: Douglas; end of Aug.

History. Francés Francois and Louis Verendrye were the first Europeans, 1743. John Colter, American, was first to traverse Yellowstone Park, 1807-08. Trappers and fur traders followed in the 1820s. Forts Laramie and Bridger became important stops on the pioneer trail to the West Coast. Indian wars followed massacres of army detachments in 1854 and 1866. Population grew after the Union Pacific crossed the state, 1869. Women won the vote, for the first time in the U.S., from the Territorial Legislature, 1869.

Tourist attractions. Yellowstone National Park, 3,472 sq. mi. in the NW corner of Wyoming and the adjoining edges of Montana and Idaho, the oldest U.S. national park, est. 1872, has some 10,000 geysers, hot springs, mud volcanoes, fossil forests, a volcanic glass (obsidian) mountain, the 1,000-ft.-deep canyon and 308-ft.-high waterfall of the Yellowstone River, and a wide variety of animals living free in their natural habitat.

Also, Grand Teton National Park, with mountains 13,000 ft. high; National Elk Refuge, covering 25,000 acres; Devils Tower, a columnar rock of igneous origin 865 ft. high; Fort Laramie and surrounding areas of pioneer trails; Buffalo Bill Museum, Cody; Cheyenne Frontier Days Celebration, last full week in July, the state's largest rodeo, and world's largest purse.

Famous Wyomingites include James Bridger, Buffalo Bill Cody, Nellie Tayloe Ross.

Tourist information: Travel Commission, Etchepare Circle, Cheyenne, WY 82002.

District of Columbia

Area: 67 sq. mi. **Population:** (1983): 623,000. **Motto:** Justitia omnibus, Justice for all. **Flower:** American beauty rose. **Tree:** Scarlet oak. **Bird:** Wood thrush. The city of Washington is coextensive with the District of Columbia.

The District of Columbia is the seat of the federal government of the United States. It lies on the west central edge of Maryland on the Potomac River, opposite Virginia. Its area was originally 100 sq. mi. taken from the sovereignty of Maryland and Virginia. Virginia's portion south of the Potomac was given back to that state in 1846.

The 23d Amendment, ratified in 1961, granted residents the right to vote for president and vice president for the first time and gave them 3 members in the Electoral College. The first such votes were cast in Nov. 1964.

Congress, which has legislative authority over the District under the Constitution, established in 1878 a government of 3 commissioners appointed by the president. The Reorganization Plan of 1967 substituted a single commissioner (also called mayor), assistant, and 9-member City Council. Funds were still appropriated by Congress; residents had no vote in local government, except to elect school board members.

In Sept. 1970, Congress approved legislation giving the District one delegate to the House of Representatives. The delegate could vote in committee but not on the House floor. The first was elected 1971.

In May 1974 voters approved a charter giving them the right to elect their own mayor and a 13-member city council; the first took office Jan. 2, 1975. The district won the right to levy its own taxes but Congress retained power to veto council actions, and approve the city's annual budget.

Proposals for a "federal town" for the deliberations of the Continental Congress were made in 1783, 4 years before the adoption of the Constitution that gave the Confederation a national government. Rivalry between northern and southern delegates over the site appeared in the First Congress, 1789. John Adams, presiding officer of the Senate, cast the deciding vote of that body for Germantown, Pa. In 1790 Congress compromised by making Philadelphia the temporary capital for 10 years. The Virginia members of the House wanted a capital on the eastern bank of the Potomac; they were defeated by the Northerners, while the Southerners defeated the Northern attempt to have the nation assume the war debts of the 13 original states, the Assumption Bill fathered by Alexander Hamilton. Hamilton and Jefferson arranged a compromise: the Virginia men voted for the Assumption Bill, and the Northerners conceded the capital to the Potomac. President Washington chose the site in Oct. 1790 and persuaded landowners to sell their holdings to the government at £25, then about $66, an acre. The capital was named Washington.

Washington appointed Pierre Charles L'Enfant, a French engineer who had come over with Lafayette, to plan the capital on an area not over 10 mi. square. The L'Enfant plan, for streets 100 to 110 feet wide and one avenue 400 feet wide and a mile long, seemed grandiose and foolhardy. But Washington endorsed it. When L'Enfant ordered a wealthy landowner to remove his new manor house because it obstructed a vista, and demolished it when the owner refused, Washington stepped in and dismissed the architect. The official map and design of the city was completed by Benjamin Banneker, a distinguished black architect and astronomer, and Andrew Ellicott.

On Sept. 18, 1793, Pres. Washington laid the cornerstone of the north wing of the Capitol. On June 3, 1800, Pres. John Adams moved to Washington and on June 10,

Philadelphia ceased to be the temporary capital. The City of Washington was incorporated in 1802; the District of Columbia was created as a municipal corporation in 1871, embracing Washington, Georgetown, and Washington County.

Outlying U.S. Areas

Commonwealth of Puerto Rico

(Estado Libre Asociado de Puerto Rico)

People. Population (1980): 3,196,520. **Pop. density:** 931 per sq. mi. **Urban** (1975): 61.8%. **Racial distribution:** 99% Hispanic. **Net migration** (1982): −33,297.

Geography. Total area: 3,435 sq. mi. **Land area:** 3,421 sq. mi. **Location:** island lying between the Atlantic to the N and the Caribbean to the S; it is easternmost of the West Indies group called the Greater Antilles, of which Cuba, Hispaniola, and Jamaica are the larger units. **Climate:** mild, with a mean temperature of 76°. **Topography:** mountainous throughout three-fourths of its rectangular area, surrounded by a broken coastal plain; highest peak is Cerro de Punta, 4,389 ft. **Capital:** San Juan.

Economy. Principal industries: manufacturing. **Principal manufactured goods:** pharmaceuticals; petrochemicals; food products, apparel. **Agriculture: Chief crops:** sugar; coffee; plantains; bananas; yams; taniers; pineapples; pidgeon peas; peppers; pumpkins; coriander; lettuce; tobacco. **Livestock** (1983): 585,088 cattle; 205,597 pigs; 6.1 mln. poultry. **Minerals** (1983): cement, crushed stone, sand and gravel, lime. Total value mineral production, $88.8 mln. **Commercial fishing** (1983): $9.1 mln. **Chief ports/river shipping:** San Juan, Ponce, Mayaguez, Guayanillá, Guánica, Yabucoa, Aguirre. **International airports at:** San Juan. **Value of construction** (1982): $1.2 bln. **Employment distribution:** 24% gvt.; 19% manuf.; 19% trade; 19% serv. **Per capita income** (1982): $3,865. **Unemployment** (1983): 23.4%. **Tourism** (1983): No. out-of-area visitors: 1.5 mln.; $690.9 mln. spent.

Finance. No. banks (1983): 24; No. savings and loan assns. (1983): 12; Other: 4 retirement fund systems; over 100 credit unions.

Federal government. No. federal civilian employees (1981): 11,097. **Federal payroll** (1981): $211.0 mln. **Notable federal facilities:** U.S. Naval Station at Roosevelt Roads; U.S. Army Salinas Training Area and Ft. Allen; Sabana SECA Communications Center (U.S. Navy); Ft. Buchanan.

Energy Production (1983): Hydroelectric: 12,067 mln. kwh.

Education. No. schools: 1,786 public, 770 private elem. and second.; 43 higher ed. **Avg. salary, public school teachers** (1981): $5,400.

Misc. Data. Motto. Joannes Est Nomen Eius (John is his name). **Flower:** Maga. **Bird:** Reinita. **Tree:** Ceiba. **Song:** La Borinqueña.

History: Puerto Rico (or Borinquen, after the original Arawak Indian name Boriquen), was discovered by Columbus, Nov. 19, 1493. Ponce de Leon conquered it for Spain, 1509, and established the first settlement at Caparra, across the bay from San Juan.

Sugar cane was introduced, 1515, and slaves were imported 3 years later. Gold mining petered out, 1570. Spaniards fought off a series of British and Dutch attacks; slavery was abolished, 1873. Under the treaty of Paris, Puerto Rico was ceded to the U.S. after the Spanish-American War, 1898.

General tourist attractions: Ponce Museum of Art; forts El Morro and San Cristobal; Old Walled City of San Juan; Arecibo Observatory; Cordillera Central and state parks; El Yunque Rain Forest; San Juan Cathedral; Porta Coeli Chapel and Museum of Religious Art, San Germán; Condado Convention Center; Casa Blanca, Ponce de León family home, Puerto Rican Family Museum of 16th and 17 centuries and the Fine Arts Center in San Juan.

Cultural facilities, festivals, etc.: Festival Casals classical music concerts, mid-June; Puerto Rico Symphony Orchestra at Music Conservatory; Botanical Garden and Museum of Anthropology, Art, and History at the University of Puerto Rico; Institute of Puerto Rican Culture, at the Dominican Convent.

The Commonwealth of Puerto Rico is a self-governing part of the U.S. with a primary Hispanic culture. Puerto Ricans are U.S. citizens and about 1.5 million now live in the continental U.S., although since 1974, there has also been a reverse migration flow.

The current commonwealth political status of Puerto Rico gives the island's citizens virtually the same control over their internal affairs as the fifty states of the U.S. However, they do not vote in national elections, although they do vote in national primary elections.

Puerto Rico is represented in Congress solely by a resident commissioner who has a voice but no vote, except in committees.

No federal income tax is collected from residents on income earned from local sources in Puerto Rico.

Puerto Rico's famous "Operation Bootstrap," begun in the late 1940s, succeeded in changing the island from "The Poorhouse of the Caribbean" to an area with the highest per capita income in Latin America. This pioneering program encouraged manufacturing and the development of the tourist trade by selective tax exemption, low-interest loans, and other incentives. Despite the marked success of Puerto Rico's development efforts over an extended period of time, per capita income in Puerto Rico is low in comparison to that of the U.S. In calendar year 1983, the transfer payments from the U.S. government to individuals and governments in Puerto Rico totalled $3,219.3 mln., or 25% of the Gross Domestic Product of $12,907.7 mln.

Famous Puerto Ricans include: Pablo Casals, Orlando Cepeda, Roberto Clemente, José Feliciano, Luis A. Ferré, José Ferrer, Doña Felisa Rincón de Gautier, Commodore Diégo E. Hernández, Rafael Hernández (El Jibarito), Luis Muñoz Marín, René Marqués, Concha Meléndez, Rita Moreno, Adm. Horacio Rivero.

Chamber of Commerce: 100 Tetuán P.O.Box. S-3789, San Juan, PR 00904; Ponce & South: El Señorial Bldg., Ponce, PR 00731.

Guam

Where America's Day Begins

People. Population (1980): 106,000. **Pop. density:** 521.5 per sq. mi. **Urban** (1970): 25.5%. Native Guamanians, ethnically called chamorros, are basically of Indonesian stock, with a mixture of Spanish and Filipino. In addition to the offical language, they speak the native Chamorro.

Geography. Total area: 209 sq. mi. land, 30 mi. long and 4 to 8.5 mi. wide. **Location:** largest and southernmost of the Mariana Islands in the West Pacific, 3,700 mi. W of Hawaii. **Climate:** tropical, with temperatures from 70° to 90°F; avg. annual rainfall, about 70 in. **Topography:** coralline limestone plateau in the N; southern chain of low volcanic mountains sloping gently to the W, more steeply to coastal cliffs on the E; general elevation, 500 ft.; highest pt., Mt. Lamlam, 1,334 ft. **Capital:** Agana.

Economy. Principal industries: construction, light manufacturing, tourism, petroleum refining, banking. **Principal manufactured goods:** textiles, foods, petroleum products. **Value added by manufacture:** $187.5 million/yr. **Agriculture: Chief crops:** cabbages, eggplants, cucumber, long beans, tomatoes, bananas, coconuts, watermelon, yams, canteloupe, papayas, maize, sweet potatoes. **Livestock:** 1,011 cattle; 9,842 hogs/pigs; 108,862 poultry. **Commercial fishing:** $187,000. **Chief ports:** Apra Harbor. **International airports at:** Tamuning. **Value of construction** (1980): $80.61 mln. **Employment distribution:** 45% gvt.; 13% construct.; 3% manufacturing; 12% services; 18% trade. **Per capita income** (1979): $4,769. **Unemployment** (1980): 10%. **Tourism** (1980): No. out-of-area visitors: 300,000.

Finance. Notable industries: insurance, real estate, finance. **No. banks:** 13; **No. savings and loan assns.:** 2.

Federal government. No. federal employees (1980): 6,600. **Notable federal facilities:** Andersen AFB; other naval and air bases.

Education. No. public schools: 27 elementary; 9 secondary; 1 higher education. **Avg. salary, public school teachers** (1979): $12,684.

Misc. Data. Flower: Puti Tai Nobio (Bougainvillea). **Bird:** Toto (Fruit dove). **Tree:** Ifit (Intsiabijuga). **Song:** Stand Ye Guamanians.

History. Magellan arrived in the Marianas Mar. 6, 1521, and called them the Ladrones (thieves). They were colonized in 1668 by Spanish missionaries who renamed them the Mariana Islands in honor of Maria Anna, queen of Spain. When Spain ceded Guam to the U.S., it sold the other Marianas to Germany. Japan obtained a League of Nations mandate over the German islands in 1919; in Dec. 1941 it seized Guam; the island was retaken by the U.S. in July 1944.

Guam is under the jurisdiction of the Interior Department. It is administered under the Organic Act of 1950, which provides for a governor and a 21-member unicameral legislature, elected biennially by the residents who are American citizens but do not vote for president.

Beginning in Nov., 1970, Guamanians elected their own governor, previously appointed by the U.S. president. He took office in Jan. 1971. In 1972 a U.S. law gave Guam one delegate to the U.S. House of Representatives; the delegate may vote in committee but not on the House floor.

General tourist attractions. annual mid-Aug. Merizo Water Festival; Tarzan Falls; beaches; water sports, duty-free port shopping.

Virgin Islands

St. John, St. Croix, St. Thomas

People. Population (1980): 95,000. **Pop. density:** 757.6 per sq. mi. **Urban** (1970): 25%. **Racial distribution:** 15% White; 85% Black. **Major ethnic groups:** West Indian, Chachas. **Net migration** (1977): +9,000.

Geography. Total area: 133 sq. mi.; **Land area:** 132 sq. mi. **Location:** 3 larger and 50 smaller islands and cays in the S and W of the V.I. group (British V.I. colony to the N and E) which is situated 70 mi. E of Puerto Rico, located W of the Anegada Passage, a major channel connecting the Atlantic O. and the Caribbean Sea. **Climate:** subtropical; the sun tempered by gentle trade winds; humidity is low; average temperature, 78° F. **Topography:** St. Thomas is mainly a ridge of hills running E and W, and has little tillable land; St. Croix rises abruptly in the N but slopes to the S to flatlands and lagoons; St. John has steep, lofty hills and valleys with little level tillable land. **Capital:** Charlotte Amalie, St. Thomas.

Economy. Principal industries: tourism, rum, petroleum refining, bauxite processing, watch assembly, textiles. **Principal manufactured goods:** rum, textiles, pharmaceuticals, perfumes. **Gross Domestic Product** (1977): $500 million. **Agriculture: Chief crops:** truck garden produce. **Minerals:** sand, gravel. **Chief ports:** Cruz Bay, St. John; Frederiksted and Christiansted, St. Croix; Charlotte Amalie, St. Thomas. **International airports on:** St. Thomas, St. Croix. **Value of construction** (1976): $42,303,000. **Per capita income** (1980 est.): $5,500. **Unemployment** (Dec. 1981): 7.0%. **Tourism** (1980): No. out-of-area visitors: 1,172,113; $355 mln. spent. **No. banks** (1979): 6.

Education. No. public schools: 33 elem. and second.; 1 higher education. **Avg. salary, public school teachers** (1980): $13,575.

Misc. data. Flower: Yellow elder or yellow cedar. **Bird:** Yellow breast. **Song:** Virgin Islands March.

History. The islands were discovered by Columbus in 1493, who named them for the virgins of St. Ursula, the sailor's patron saint. Spanish forces, 1555, defeated the Caribes and claimed the territory; by 1596 the native population was annihilated. First permanent settlement in the

U.S. territory, 1672, by the Danes; U.S. purchased the islands, 1917, for defense purposes.

The inhabitants have been citizens of the U.S. since 1927. Legislation originates in a unicameral house of 15 senators, elected for 2 years. The governor, formerly appointed by the U.S. president, was popularly elected for the first time in Nov. 1970. In 1972 a U.S. law gave the Virgin Islands one delegate to the U.S. House of Representatives; the delegate may vote in committee but not in the House.

General tourist attractions. Megen Bay, St. Thomas; duty-free shopping; Virgin Islands National Park, 14,488 acres on St. John of lush growth, beaches, Indian relics, and evidence of colonial Danes.

Chamber of Commerce: for St. Thomas and St. John: P.O. Box 324, St. Thomas, VI 00802; for St. Croix: 17 Church St., Christiansted, St. Croix, VI 00820.

American Samoa

Capital: Fagatogo, Island of Tutuila. **Area:** 76 sq. mi. **Population:** (1978 est.) 31,171. **Motto:** Samoa Muamua ie Atua (In Samoa, God Is First). **Song:** Amerika Samoa. **Flower:** Paogo (Ula-fala). **Plant:** Ava.

Blessed with spectacular scenery and delightful South Seas climate, American Samoa is the most southerly of all lands under U. S. ownership. It is an unincorporated territory consisting of 6 small islands of the Samoan group: **Tutuila, Aunu'u, Manu'a Group (Ta'u, Olosega and Ofu),** and **Rose.** Also administered as part of American Samoa is **Swain's Island,** 210 mi. to the NW, acquired by the U.S. in 1925. The islands are 2,600 mi. SW of Honolulu.

American Samoa became U. S. territory by a treaty with the United Kingdom and Germany in 1899. The islands were ceded by local chiefs in 1900 and 1904.

Samoa (Western), comprising the larger islands of the Samoan group, was a New Zealand mandate and UN Trusteeship until it became an independent nation Jan. 1, 1962 *(see Index.)*

Tutuila and Annu'u have an area of 52 sq. mi. Ta'u has an area of 17 sq. mi., and the islets of Ofu and Olosega, 5 sq. mi. with a population of a few thousand. Swain's Island has nearly 2 sq. mi. and a population of about 100.

About 70% of the land is bush. Chief products and exports are fish products, copra, and handicrafts. Taro, bread-fruit, yams, coconuts, pineapples, oranges, and bananas are also produced.

Formerly under jurisdiction of the Navy, since July 1, 1951, it has been under the Interior Dept. On Jan. 3, 1978, the first popularly elected Samoan governor and lieutenant governor were inaugurated. Previously, the governor was appointed by the Secretary of the Interior. American Samoa has a bicameral legislature and an elected delegate to appear before U.S. agencies in Washington. In 1980 the Territory will elect a non-voting delegate to Congress.

The American Samoans are of Polynesian origin. They are nationals of the U.S.; there are more than 15,000 in Hawaii and 90,000 on the U.S. west coast.

Minor Caribbean Islands

Quita Sueño Bank, Roncador and Serrana, lie in the Caribbean between Nicaragua and Jamaica. They are uninhabited. U.S. claim to the islands was relinquished in a treaty with Colombia, which entered into force on Sept. 17, 1981.

Navassa lies between Jamaica and Haiti, covers about 2 sq. mi., is reserved by the U.S. for a lighthouse and is uninhabited.

Wake, Midway, Other Islands

Wake Island, and its sister islands, **Wilkes** and **Peale,** lie in the Pacific Ocean on the direct route from Hawaii to Hong Kong, about 2,000 mi. W of Hawaii and 1,290 mi. E of Guam. The group is 4.5 mi. long, 1.5 mi. wide, and totals less than 3 sq. mi.

The U.S. flag was hoisted over Wake Island, July 4, 1898, formal possession taken Jan. 17, 1899; Wake has been administered by the U.S. Air Force since 1972. Population (1980) was 300.

The **Midway Islands,** acquired in 1867, consist of 2, **Sand** and **Eastern,** in the North Pacific 1,150 mi. NW of Hawaii, with area of about 2 sq. mi., administered by the Navy Dept. Population (1975 est.) was 2,256.

Johnston Atoll, SW of Hawaii, area 1 sq. mi., pop. 300 (1978), is operated by Nuclear Defense Agency, and **Kingman Reef,** S of Hawaii, is under Navy control.

Howland, Jarvis, and **Baker Islands** south of the Hawaiian group, uninhabited since World War II, are under the Interior Dept.

Palmyra is an atoll SW of Hawaii, 4 sq. mi. Privately owned, it is under the Interior Dept.

Islands Under Trusteeship

The U. S. Trust Territory of the Pacific Islands, also called Micronesia, includes 3 major archipelagoes: the **Caroline Islands, Marshall Islands,** and **Mariana Islands** (except Guam: see above). There are 2,141 islands, 98 of them inhabited. Total land area is 715.8 sq. mi., but the islands are scattered over 3 million sq. mi. in the western Pacific N of the equator and E of the Philippines. Population (1980 est.): 116,662.

The Marianas

In process of becoming a U.S. commonwealth are the Northern Mariana Islands, which since 1947 have been part of the Trust Territory of the Pacific Islands, assigned to U.S. administration by the United Nations. The Northern Marianas comprise all the Marianas except Guam, stretching N-S in a 500-mi. arc of tropical islands east of the Philippines and southeast of Japan.

Residents of the islands on June 17, 1975, voted 78% in favor of becoming a commonwealth of the U.S. rather than continuing with the Carolines and Marshalls in the U.S.-UN Trusteeship. On Mar. 24, 1976, U.S. Pres. Ford signed a congressionally-approved commonwealth covenant giving the Marianas control of domestic affairs and giving the U.S. control of foreign relations and defense, and the right to maintain military bases on the islands. The full force of commonwealth status will come into effect at the termination of the trusteeship.

Pres. Carter, on Oct. 24, 1977, approved the Constitution of the Northern Mariana Islands with the effective date of Jan. 9, 1978. In December 1977, the voters of the Northern Marianas elected a governor, lieutenant governor, and members of a bicameral legislature for the new government.

Ferdinand Magellan was the first European to visit the Marianas, 1521. Spain, Germany, and Japan held the islands in turn until World War II when the U.S. seized them in bitter battles on 2 of the main islands, Saipan and Tinian.

Population in 1980 was estimated at 16,600, mostly on Saipan. English is the official language, Roman Catholicism the major religion. The people are descendants of the early Chamorros, Spanish, Japanese, Filipinos, and Mexicans. Land area is 181.9 sq. mi.

Tourism is an important industry; visitors are mostly from Japan. Crops include coconuts, breadfruit, melons and tomatoes.

The Carolines and Marshalls

In 1885, many of the Carolines, Marshalls, and Marianas were claimed by Germany. Others, held by Spain, were sold to Germany at the time of the Spanish-American War, 1898. After the outbreak of World War I, Japan took over the 3 archipelagoes; following that war, League of Nations mandates over them were awarded to Japan.

After World War II, the United Nations assigned them, 1947, as a Trust Territory to be administered by the U.S. They were placed, 1951, under administration of the U.S. Interior Dept.

There is a high commissioner, appointed by the U.S. president. Saipan is the headquarters of the administration. The Congress of Micronesia, an elected legislature with limited powers, held its first meeting, 1965.

In 1969, a commission of the Congress of Micronesia recommended that Micronesia be given internal self-government in free association with the U.S. All the Micronesian entities now have their own locally-elected governments, including legislatures, which have preempted the Congress of Micronesia.

A U.S. offer of commonwealth status was rejected by Micronesian leaders in 1970.

The U.S. and three Trust Territory negotiating commissions representing, respectively, the Marshall Islands, Palau, and the Federated States of Micronesia, comprised of Truk, Yap, Ponape and Kosrae, are negotiating a free association arrangement: the three Micronesian areas would enjoy full self-government; the U.S. would retain responsibility for defense. The Compacts of Free Association, initialled in late 1980, must be approved by the people locally and by the U.S. Congress. If the new status is approved, the U.N. will take action to terminate the trusteeship agreement.

Among the noted islands are the former Japanese strongholds of **Belau, Peleliu, Truk,** and **Yap** in the Carolines; **Bikini** and **Enewetak,** where U.S. nuclear tests were staged, and **Kwajalein,** another World War II battle scene, all in the Marshalls.

Many of the islands are volcanic with luxuriant vegetation; others are of coral formation. Only a few are self-sustaining. Principal exports are copra, trochus shells, fish products, handicrafts, and vegetables.

Disputed Pacific Islands

In the central Pacific, S and SW of Hawaii lie 25 islands that were claimed by the U.S.; 18 of them were also claimed by the United Kingdom and 7 by New Zealand. **Kiribati** achieved its independence from the U.K. in July, 1979.

The **Tuvalu (Ellice) Islands,** including Funafuti, Nukufetau, Nukulailai, and Nurakita, became independent of the UK, Oct. 1, 1978.

The **Cook Islands,** including Danger, Manahiki, Rakahanga, and Penrhyn (Tongareva), are self-governing in free association with New Zealand. **Tokelau** is a New Zealand territory.

The U.S. signed a treaty with Kiribati on Sept. 20, 1979; with Tuvalu on Feb. 7, 1979; and with the Cook Islands and New Zealand for Tokelau on Dec. 2, 1980. These treaties, which relinquished U.S. claim to the disputed islands, were ratified in August, 1983.

U.S. Ancestral Origins

Listed by greatest population in each state.

Source: U.S. Bureau of the Census (1980)

☐ English   ⠿ Irish   ⫶ Mexican   ▤ French

▨ German   ▨ African   ⣿ Japanese

NORTH AMERICAN CITIES

Sources: Bureau of the Census: population (1980); population growth (1970-1980); population over 65 and under 35 (1980). Geography Division. Bureau of the Census: population density (1980); area (1980). Bureau of Labor Statistics: employment (Jan. 1984). Bureau of Economic Analysis: per capita income (MSA, 1982). For Canadian cities: Statistics Canada. All other information was gathered from sources in the individual cities.

Akron, Ohio

Population: 237,177; **Pop. density:** 4,312 per sq. mi.; **Pop. growth:** −13.9%; **Pop. over 65:** 13.5%; **Pop. under 35:** 57.1%. **Area:** 55 sq. mi. **Employment:** 88,740 employed, 13.4% unemployed; **Per capita income:** $10,557.

Transportation: Akron-Canton airport served by 2 major carriers; Greyhound, Continental Trailways bus lines; Conrail; metro transit system. **Communications:** 1 TV, and 7 radio stations; 2 public broadcast outlets. **Medical facilities:** 4 major hospitals; specialized children's treatment center. **Educational facilities:** Univ. of Arkon and School of Law; 68 public schools. **Further information:** Akron Regional Development Board or Akron-Summit Convention and Visitors Bureau, both One Cascade Plaza, Akron, OH 44308.

Albuquerque, New Mexico

Population: 331,767; **Pop. density:** 3,492 per sq. mi.; **Pop. growth:** 35.7%; **Pop. over 65:** 8.4%; **Pop. under 35:** 61.6%. **Area:** 95 sq. mi. **Employment:** 160,586 employed, 7.8% unemployed; **Per capita income:** $10,626.

Transportation: 1 international airport; 2 railroads; 2 bus lines. **Communications:** 5 TV, 21 radio stations; 3 cable TV systems. **Medical facilities:** 9 major hospitals. **Educational facilities:** 2 universities. **Further information:** Chamber of Commerce, 401 2d NW, Albuquerque, NM 87102.

Anaheim, California

Population: 219,311; **Pop. density:** 5,349 per sq. mi.; **Pop. growth:** 31.6%; **Pop. over 65:** 7.7%; **Pop. under 35:** 60.7%. **Area:** 41 sq. mi. **Employment:** 136,375 employed, 6.2% unemployed; **Per capita income:** $13,927.

Transportation: John Wayne, Fullerton, and Long Beach Municipal airports; 4 railroads; Greyhound buses. **Communications:** 12 TV channels, one CATV; 4 radio stations. **Medical facilities:** 7 general hospitals with 1,311 beds. **Educational facilities:** 3 colleges, 5 junior colleges; 62 elementary, 8 junior high, 17 high schools. **Further information:** Chamber of Commerce, P.O. Box 969, Anaheim, CA 92805.

Anchorage, Alaska

Population: 174,431; **Pop. density:** 100 per sq. mi.; **Pop. growth:** 259.5%; **Pop. over 65:** 2.0%; **Pop. under 35:** 70.2%. **Area:** 1,732 sq. mi. **Employment:** 95,018 employed, 8.8% unemployed; **Per capita income:** $18,429.

Transportation: Anchorage International Airport, 5 other airports. **Communications:** 4 TV, 11 radio stations. **Medical facilities:** 3 hospitals. **Educational facilities:** Univ. of Alaska, Alaska Pacific Univ. **Further information:** Chamber of Commerce, 415 F St., Anchorage, AK 99501.

Atlanta, Georgia

Population: 425,022; **Pop. density:** 3,244 per sq. mi.; **Pop. growth:** −14.1%; **Pop. over 65:** 11.5%; **Pop. under 35:** 60.7%. **Area:** 131 sq. mi. **Employment:** 206,122 employed, 7.6% unemployed; **Per capita income:** $11,590.

Transportation: 1 international airport; 7 railroad lines, 2 systems; bus terminal; rapid rail under construction; 6 legs of 3 interstate highways intersecting downtown interchange. **Communications:** 8 TV, 41 radio stations; 8 cable TV companies. **Medical facilities:** 56 hospitals; VA hospital; Natl. Centers for Disease Control; Natl. Cancer Center. **Educational facilities:** 28 colleges, universities,

seminaries, junior colleges. **Further information:** Chamber of Commerce, 1300 N. Omni Intl., Atlanta, GA 30302.

Austin, Texas

Population: 345,496; **Pop. density:** 2,978 per sq. mi.; **Pop. growth:** 36.3%; **Pop. over 65:** 7.5%; **Pop. under 35:** 69%. **Area:** 116 sq. mi. **Employment:** 208,197 employed, 4.2% unemployed; **Per capita income:** $11,249.

Transportation: 1 international airport; 4 railroads. **Communications:** 4 TV, 18 radio stations. **Medical facilities:** 9 hospitals. **Educational facilities:** 10 universities and colleges. **Further information:** Austin Chamber of Commerce, 901 W. Riverside Dr., Austin, TX 78701.

Baltimore, Maryland

Population: 786,775; **Pop. density:** 9,835 per sq. mi.; **Pop. growth:** −13.1%; **Pop. over 65:** 12.8%; **Pop. under 35%:** 56.9%. **Area:** 80 sq. mi. **Employment:** 360,839 employed, 8.8% unemployed; **Per capita income:** $11,560.

Transportation: 1 major airport; 3 railroads, bus system; subway under construction; 1 underwater tunnel. **Communications:** 5 TV stations; 33 radio stations. **Medical facilities:** 33 hospitals; 2 major medical centers. **Educational facilities:** 42 universities and colleges; major public library system. **Further information:** Promotion Council, 1102 St. Paul Street, Baltimore, MD 21202.

Baton Rouge, Louisiana

Population: 219,419; **Pop. density:** 3,597 per sq. mi.; **Pop. growth:** 32.2%; **Pop. over 65:** 8.7%; **Pop. under 35:** 64.0%. **Area:** 61 sq. mi. **Employment:** 162,806 employed; 7.1% unemployed; **Per capita income:** $11,024.

Transportation: 1 airport with 5 airlines; 2 bus lines; 4 railroad trunk lines; Port of Baton Rouge is one of largest in U.S. **Communications:** 5 TV, 13 radio stations. **Educational facilities:** Louisiana St. Univ., center of 8-campus system; Southern Univ. **Further information:** Chamber of Commerce, P.O. Box 1868, Baton Rouge, LA 70821.

Birmingham, Alabama

Population: 284,413; **Pop. density:** 2,872 per sq. mi.; **Pop. growth:** −5.5%; **Pop. over 65%:** 13.9%; **Pop. under 35:** 57.5%. **Area:** 99 sq. mi. **Employment:** 114,563 employed, 15.5% unemployed; **Per capita income:** $9,941.

Transportation: 1 airport; 5 major rail freight lines, Amtrak; 2 bus lines; 75 truck line terminals; 3 interstate highways. **Communications:** 3 TV, 16 radio stations; 1 educational TV, 1 educational radio station. **Medical facilities:** Univ. of Alabama in Birmingham Medical Center; VA hospital with organ transplant program; 15 other hospitals. **Educational facilities:** 1 university, 3 colleges, 2 junior colleges. **Further information:** Chamber of Commerce, 2027 First Ave. N., Birmingham, AL 35202.

Boston, Massachusetts

Population: 562,994; **Pop. density:** 11,979 per sq. mi.; **Pop. growth:** −12.2%; **Pop. over 65:** 12.7%; **Pop. under 35:** 60.4%. **Area:** 47 sq. mi. **Employment:** 264,064 employed, 8.2% unemployed; **Per capita income:** $13,087.

Transportation: 1 major airport; 2 railroads; city rail and subway system; 2 underwater tunnels. **Communications:** 8 TV stations; 33 radio stations. **Medical facilities:** numerous hospitals; 3 major medical research centers. **Educational facilities:** 16 universities and colleges (plus 47 in metro area); major public library system. **Further information:** Chamber of Commerce, 125 High Street, Boston, MA 02110.

Buffalo, New York

Population: 357,870; **Pop. density:** 8,520 per sq. mi.; **Pop. growth:** −22.7%; **Pop. over 65:** 15.0%; **Pop. under 35:** 55.3%. **Area:** 42 sq. mi.. **Employment:** 117,045 employed, 15.6% unemployed; **Per capita income:** $11,160.
Transportation: 1 international airport; 6 major railroads, 22 freight terminals; 350 motor carriers; direct highway & rail to all of Canada; water service to Great Lakes-St. Lawrence seaways system, overseas, and Atlantic seaboard. **Communications:** 5 TV, 23 AM & FM radio stations, 3 cable systems. **Medical facilities:** 21 hospitals; 1 psychiatric hospital, 1 alcoholism clinic. **Educational facilities:** 2 universities; 9 colleges. **Further information:** Chamber of Commerce, 107 Delaware, Buffalo, NY 14202.

Calgary, Alberta

Population: 619,814 (1984); **Pop. density:** 3,157 per sq. mi.; **Pop. growth:** 47.0% (1971-81); **Pop. over 65:** 6.1%; **Pop. under 35:** 66.2%. **Area:** 196.3 sq. mi. **Employment:** 317,000 employed, 13.1% unemployed (Apr. 1984).
Transportation: International Airport served by 10 airlines; railway passenger service on VIA Rail, freight service on CN and CP Rail. **Communications:** 15 radio and 3 TV stations plus cable. **Medical facilities:** 7 major hospitals with 2,900 beds, 5 auxiliary hospitals with 1,276 beds for extended care. **Educational facilities:** 296 public and separate schools, 5 private schools, Univ. of Calgary, Mount Royal College, Southern Alberta Institute of Technology, Alberta Vocational Centre. **Further information:** Calgary Economic Development Authority, P.O. Box 2100, Postal Station "M", Calgary, AB, T2P, 2M5.

Charlotte, North Carolina

Population: 314,447; **Pop. density:** 2,278 per sq. mi.; **Pop. growth:** 30.2%; **Pop. over 65:** 8.6%; **Pop. under 35:** 60.4%. **Area:** 138 sq. mi. **Employment:** 174,892 employed, 5.9% unemployed; **Per capita income:** $10,323.
Transportation: Douglas-Municipal Airport; 2 major railway lines; 3 bus lines; 120 trucking firms. **Communications:** 6 TV, 12 radio stations. **Medical facilities:** 7 hospitals, 1 medical center. **Educational facilities:** 2 universities, 5 colleges. **Further information:** Chamber of Commerce, P.O. Box 32785, Charlotte, NC 28232.

Chicago, Illinois

Population: 3,005,072; **Pop. density:** 13,180 per sq. mi.; **Pop. growth:** −10.8%; **Pop. over 65:** 11.4%; **Pop. under 35:** 58.5%. **Area:** 228 sq. mi. **Employment:** 1,304,310 employed, 10.2% unemployed; **Per capita income:** $13,069.
Transportation: 3 airports; major railroad system; major trucking industry; 12 major highways. **Communications:** 9 TV stations; 31 radio stations. **Medical facilities:** over 123 hospitals. **Educational facilities:** 95 institutions of higher learning; major public library system. **Further information:** Visitors Bureau and Information Center, Association of Commerce and Industry, 130 S. Michigan Avenue, Chicago, IL 60603.

Cincinnati, Ohio

Population: 385,457; **Pop. density:** 4,941 per sq. mi.; **Pop. growth:** −15.0%; **Pop. over 65:** 14.5%; **Pop. under 35:** 58.5%. **Area:** 78 sq. mi. **Employment:** 159,783 employed, 11.0% unemployed; **Per capita income:** $11,224.
Transportation: 1 international airport; 7 railroads; 1 bus system. **Communications:** 6 TV, 12 AM & 25 FM radio stations. **Medical facilities:** 30 hospitals; Children's Hospital Medical Center; burn institute; VA hospital. **Educational facilities:** 3 universities; 6 4-year colleges, 8 technical & 2-year colleges. **Further information:** Chamber of Commerce, 120 W. 5th St., Cincinnati, OH 45202.

Cleveland, Ohio

Population: 573,822; **Pop. density:** 7,264 per sq. mi.; **Pop. growth:** −23.6%; **Pop. over 65:** 13.0%; **Pop. under 35:** 56.7%. **Area:** 79 sq. mi. **Employment:** 208,974 employed, 13.8% unemployed; **Per capita income:** $12,757.
Transportation: 2 airports; rail service; major port; rapid transit system. **Communications:** 7 TV stations; 53 radio stations. **Medical facilities:** numerous hospitals; major medical research center. **Educational facilities:** 8 universities and colleges; major public library system. **Further information:** Convention Visitor's Bureau, 1301 E. 6th Street, Cleveland, OH 44114.

Colorado Springs, Colorado

Population: 215,150; **Pop. density:** 2,088 per sq. mi.; **Pop. growth:** 58.8%; **Pop. over 65:** 8.3%; **Pop. under 35:** 62.3%. **Area:** 103 sq. mi. **Employment:** 107,729 employed, 5.8% unemployed; **Per capita income:** $10,493.
Transportation: Municipal airport served by 6 air lines; Denver & Rio Grande, Santa Fe, Burlington railroads; Greyhound, Continental Trailways buses. **Communications:** 13 TV, 15 radio stations. **Medical facilities:** 9 hospitals, 1,418 beds. **Educational facilities:** Univ. of Colorado at Colo. Springs, U.S. Air Force Acad., Pikes Peak Comm. College. **Further information:** Chamber of Commerce, P.O. Drawer B, Colorado Springs, CO 80901.

Columbus, Ohio

Population: 564,871; **Pop. density:** 3,121 per sq. mi.; **Pop. growth:** 4.6%; **Pop. over 65:** 8.9%; **Pop. under 35:** 64.4%. **Area:** 181 sq. mi.. **Employment:** 269,646 employed, 8.5% unemployed; **Per capita income:** $10,629.
Transportation: 2 airports; 3 railroads; 4 intercity bus lines; major highway system. **Communications:** 5 TV stations; 19 radio stations. **Medical facilities:** 12 hospitals. **Educational facilities:** 8 universities and colleges; major public library system. **Further information:** Chamber of Commerce, P.O. Box 1527, Columbus, OH 43216.

Corpus Christi, Texas

Population: 231,999; **Pop. density:** 2,230 per sq. mi.; **Pop. growth:** 13.4%; **Pop. over 65:** 8.2%; **Pop. under 35:** 63.2%. **Area:** 104 sq. mi. **Employment:** 106,525 employed, 9.6% unemployed; **Per capita income:** $10,439.
Transportation: 5 airlines, 2 bus lines, 3 freight railroads. **Communications:** 5 TV stations (one public service, one Spanish), CATV. **Medical facilities:** 10 hospitals including a children's center. **Educational facilities:** Del Mar Coll., Corpus Christi State Univ. **Further information:** Chamber of Commerce, PO Box 640, Corpus Christi, TX 78403.

Dallas, Texas

Population: 904,078; **Pop. density:** 2,715 per sq. mi.; **Pop. growth:** 7%; **Pop. over 65:** 9.5%; **Pop. under 35:** 61.1%. **Area:** 333 sq. mi. **Employment:** 524,738 employed, 5.1% unemployed; **Per capita income:** $13,846.

Transportation: 2 airports; 8 railroads; 2 transcontinental bus lines; major transit system. **Communications:** 26 TV stations; 37 radio stations. **Medical facilities:** 42 hospitals; major medical center. **Educational facilities:** 33 universities and colleges; major public library system. **Further information:** Chamber of Commerce, Fidelity Union Tower, Dallas, TX 75201.

Dayton, Ohio

Population: 203,371; **Pop. density:** 4,236 per sq. mi.; **Pop. growth:** −16.3%; **Pop. over 65:** 11.8%; **Pop. under 35:** 59.8%. **Area:** 48 sq. mi. **Employment:** 73,333 employed, 12.4% unemployed; **Per capita income:** $10,797.

Transportation: 2 airports, 9 airlines, 2 trunk rail systems; 4 bus lines; countywide Dayton Regional Transit Authority. **Communications:** 5 TV, 8 radio stations. **Medical facilities:** 14 hospitals including VA facility. **Educational facilities:** Univ. of Dayton, Wright St. Univ.; Sinclair, Miami Jacobs jr. colleges. **Further information:** Chamber of Commerce, Suite 1980, Kettering Tower, Dayton Oh 45423.

Denver, Colorado

Population: 492,365; **Pop. density:** 4,435 per sq. mi.; **Pop. growth:** −4.3%; **Pop. over 65:** 12.6%; **Pop. under 35:** 58.9%. **Area:** 111 sq. mi.. **Employment:** 286,272 employed, 5.3% unemployed; **Per capita income:** $13,964.

Transportation: 1 international airport; 5 major rail freight lines, Amtrak; 2 bus lines; 3 interstate highways intersect city. **Communications:** 7 TV, 35 radio stations. **Medical facilities:** 34 hospitals. **Educational facilities:** 2 universities; 3 colleges. **Further information:** Denver Chamber of Commerce, 1301 Welton St., Denver 80204.

Des Moines, Iowa

Population: 191,003; **Pop. density:** 2,890 per sq. mi.; **Pop. growth:** −5.2%; **Pop. over 65:** 12.5; **Pop. under 35:** 58.4%. **Area:** 66 sq. mi. **Employment:** 96,616 employed, 7.8% unemployed; **Per capita income:** $12,365.

Transportation: 6 major airlines; 4 bus lines; 4 railroads; 69 truck lines; highways 80 and 35. **Communications:** 4 TV, 13 radio stations; CATV. **Medical facilities:** 9 hospitals with 2,700 beds. **Educational facilities:** Drake Univ.; 2 Bible colleges. **Further information:** Chamber of Commerce, 8th & High Sts., Des Moines, IA 50309.

Detroit, Michigan

Population: 1,203,339; **Pop. density:** 8,848 per sq. mi.; **Pop. growth:** −20.5%; **Pop. over 65:** 11.7%; **Pop. under 35:** 59.5%. **Area:** 136 sq. mi. **Employment:** 414,400 employed, 15.5% unemployed (Mar. 1984); **Per capita income:** $12,092.

Transportation: 1 major airport; 10 railroads; major international port; public transit system. **Communications:** 9 TV stations, 37 radio stations. **Medical facilities:** 28 hospitals, major medical center. **Educational facilities:** 13 universities and colleges; major public library system. **Further information:** Chamber of Commerce, 150 Michigan Avenue, Detroit, MI 48226.

Edmonton, Alberta

Population: 560,085 (1983); **Pop. density:** 2,135 per sq. mi.; **Pop. growth:** 27% (1973-83); **Pop. over 65:** 7.0%; **Pop. under 35:** 63%. **Area:** 263 sq. mi.. **Employment:** 360,000 (metro) employed, 12.1% unemployed (1983).

Transportation: crossroads of Yellowhead, Alaska, and Mackenzie highways; Canadian National (VIA), Canadian Pacific; 2 airports with 9 airlines; Light Rail Transit System. **Communications:** 18 (including 1 French) radio stations, 4 (including 1 French) TV stations. **Medical facilities:** 8 active treatment hospitals with 3,876 beds plus the W.W. Cross Cancer Institute and the Walter C. MacKenzie Health Sciences Centre. **Educational facilities:** 2 universities and 4 colleges. **Further information:** Chamber of Commerce, 600 Sun Life Place, 10123–99 St., Edmonton, T5J 3G9; Edmonton Convention and Tourism Authority, 104, 9797-Jasper Ave., Edmonton T5J 1N9; Edmonton Economic Development Authority, 2410 Oxford Tower, 10235-101 St., Edmonton T5J 3G1.

El Paso, Texas

Population: 425,259; **Pop. density:** 1,779 per sq. mi.. **Pop. growth:** 32.0%; **Pop. over 65:** 6.9%; **Pop. under 35:** 65%. **Area:** 239 sq. mi. **Employment:** 159,702 employed, 11.0% unemployed; **Per capita income:** $7,832.

Transportation: International airport; 5 major rail lines; 8 bus lines; 9 major highways; gateway to Mexico. **Communications:** 6 TV, 23 radio stations. **Medical facilities:** 16 hospitals; 1 medical school; 1 nursing school; 1 cancer treatment center. **Educational facilities:** 2 colleges and universities. **Further information:** Convention and Visitors Bureau, 5 Civic Center Plaza, El Paso, TX 79901.

Fort Wayne, Indiana

Population: 172,196; **Pop. density:** 3,311 per sq. mi.; **Pop. growth:** −3.4%; **Pop. over 65:** 11.9%; **Pop. under 35:** 60.1%. **Area:** 52 sq. mi. **Employment:** 71,320 employed, 13.1% unemployed; **Per capita income:** $10,422.

Transportation: Baer Field airport, 2 rail freight lines; Amtrak; I-69 connects city with Indianapolis, U.S. 30 dual lane to Chicago. **Communications:** 5 TV, 10 radio stations; 2 cable stations. **Medical facilities:** 4 hospitals including VA facility. **Educational facilities:** St. Francis Coll., Ft. Wayne Bible Coll., Indiana Inst. of Technology. **Further information:** Chamber of Commerce, 826 Ewing St., Ft. Wayne, IN 46802.

Fort Worth, Texas

Population: 385,164; **Pop. density:** 1,604 per sq. mi.; **Pop. growth:** −21.1%; **Pop. over 65:** 11.8%; **Pop. under 35:** 58.5%. **Area:** 240 sq. mi. **Employment:** 212,841 employed, 6.4% unemployed; **Per capita income:** $11,923.

Transportation: Dallas/Fort Worth airport; 8 major railroads, Amtrak; 41 motor carriers; local bus service; 2 transcontinental, 2 intrastate bus lines. **Communications:** 9 TV, 37 radio stations. **Medical facilities:** 35 hospitals; 2 children's hospitals; 4 government hospitals. **Educational facilities:** 8 colleges & universities. **Further information:** Chamber of Commerce, 700 Throckmorton, Fort Worth, TX 76102.

Fresno, California

Population: 218,202; **Pop. density:** 3,356 per sq. mi.; **Pop. growth:** 31.7%; **Pop. over 65:** 10.9%; **Pop. under 35:** 62.5%. **Area:** 65 sq. mi. **Employment:** 106,681 employed, 13.5% unemployed; **Per capita income:** $10,731.

Transportation: 7 airlines; Amtrak; freeways connect to all major areas in state; U.S. port of entry. **Communications:** one public, 6 commercial TV stations, 5 CATV services; 18 commercial, 2 public radio stations. **Medical facilities:** 6 general hospitals including a VA facility. **Educational facilities:** Cal. State-Fresno, Pacific Coll., Frenso City Coll. (oldest jr. coll. in Cal.). **Further information:** Chamber of Commerce, P.O. Box 1469, Fresno, CA 93721.

Hamilton, Ontario

Population: 306,434 (1981); **Pop. density:** 6,456 per sq. mi.; **Pop. growth:** −1.0% (1971-81); **Pop. over 65:** 11.9%; **Pop. under 35:** 55.0%. **Area:** 47.4 sq. mi. **Employment:** 144,320 employed, 6.5% unemployed (1981, city).

Transportation: airport served by Nordair flights to Ottawa and Montreal; VIA passenger rail service, GO Transit links to nearby municipalities. **Communications:** 1 local TV station plus cable; 4 radio stations. **Medical facilities:** 7 general hospitals including McMaster Hospital and Hamilton Psychiatric Hospital. **Educational facilities:** 177 public and separate schools plus 7 vocational and 5 for the trainable retarded; McMaster University, Mohawk College of Applied Arts and Technology; 2 private business colleges. **Further information:** Hamilton & District Chamber of Commerce, 100 King St. West, Suite 830, Hamilton, Ont. L8P 1A2; Economic Development Dept., Regional Municipality of Hamilton-Wentworth, 119 King St. West, Hamilton, Ont. L8P 4T7.

Honolulu Co., Hawaii

Population: 762,874; **Pop. density:** 1,280 per sq. mi.; **Pop. growth:** 20.9%; **Pop. over 65:** 7.4%; **Pop. under 35:** 62.4%. **Area:** 596 sq. mi. **Employment:** 340,478 employed, 5.1% unemployed; **Per capita income:** $12,130. **Transportation:** 1 major airport; large, active port for passengers and cargo. **Communications:** 5 TV stations; 23 radio stations. **Medical facilities:** 43 hospitals. **Educational facilities:** 230 public schools (state); 146 private schools (state); 1 university (9 campus centers); major public library system. **Further information:** Visitors Bureau, 2270 Kalakaua Avenue, Honolulu, HI 96815.

Houston, Texas

Population: 1,595,138; **Pop. density:** 2,869 per sq. mi.; **Pop. growth:** 29.3%; **Pop. over 65:** 6.9%; **Pop. under 35:** 64.4%. **Area:** 556 sq. mi. **Employment:** 899,577 employed; 8.6% unemployed; **Per capita income:** $14,128. **Transportation:** 2 airports; 5 railroads; major bus transit system; major international port. **Communications:** 8 TV stations; 40 radio stations. **Medical facilities:** 59 hospitals; major medical center. **Educational facilities:** 29 universities and colleges; 7th largest U.S. public school system; major public library system. **Further information:** Chamber of Commerce, 1100 Milam, Houston, TX 77002.

Huntington Beach, California

Population: 170,505; **Pop. density:** 6,315 per sq. mi.; **Pop. growth:** 47%. **Area:** 27 sq. mi. **Employment:** 107,957 employed, 5.4% unemployed; **Per capita income:** $9,782 (1979). **Transportation:** Southern Pacific railroad, Amtrak; John Wayne, Long Beach, L.A. intl. airports; Orange Co. transit dist. with linkages to Los Angeles metro area. **Communications:** TV, radio stations. **Medical facilities:** 2 hospitals, 250 beds. **Educational facilities:** Cal St. Univ., Long Beach; Cal St. Univ., Fullerton; Univ. of Cal., Irvine; Golden West Comm. **Further information:** Chamber of Commerce, Seacliff Village, 2213 Main #32, Huntington Beach, CA 92648.

Indianapolis, Indiana

Population: 700,807; **Pop. density:** 1,991 per sq. mi.; **Pop. growth:** −4.9%; **Pop. over 65;** 10.3%; **Pop. under 35:** 59.4%. **Area:** 352 sq. mi.. **Employment:** 356,511 employed, 10.5% unemployed; **Per capita income:** $11,236. **Transportation:** 1 major airport; 6 railroads; 3 interstate bus lines. **Communications:** 6 TV stations; 27 radio stations. **Medical facilities:** 20 hospitals; major medical center. **Educational facilities:** 6 universities and colleges; major public library system. **Further information:** Chamber of Commerce, 320 N. Meridan Street, Indianapolis, IN 46204.

Jackson, Mississippi

Population: 202,895; **Pop. density:** 1,914 per sq. mi.; **Pop. growth:** 31.8%; **Pop. over 65:** 9.9%; **Pop. under 35:** 59.3%. **Area:** 106.2 sq. mi. **Employment:** 91,181 employed, 6.8% unemployed; **Per capita income:** $9,821.

Transportation: American, Delta, Royale, and Sunbelt airlines; Greyhound, Trailways buses; Ill. Central Gulf railroad. **Communications:** 4 TV, 18 radio stations. **Medical facilities:** 11 hospitals including a VA facility. **Educational facilities:** Jackson St. Univ.; Belhaven, Millsaps, Mississippi, Tougaloo, and Wesley colleges. **Further information:** Chamber of Commerce, P.O. Box 22548, Jackson, MS 39205.

Jacksonville, Florida

Population: 540,920; **Pop. density:** 712 per sq. mi.; **Pop. growth:** 7.3%; **Pop. over 65:** 9.6%; **Pop. under 35:** 60.0%. **Area:** 760 sq. mi.. **Employment:** 249,709 employed, 7.1% unemployed; **Per capita income:** $10,483. **Transportation:** 1 major airport; 3 railroads; 2 interstate bus lines. **Communications:** 6 TV stations; 21 radio stations. **Medical facilities:** 14 hospitals. **Educational facilities:** 5 universities and colleges; major public library system. **Further information:** Chamber of Commerce, 3 Independent Drive, P.O. Drawer 329, Jacksonville, FL 32201.

Kansas City, Missouri

Population: 448,159; **Pop. density:** 1,418 per sq. mi.; **Pop. growth:** −11.7%; **Pop. over 65:** 12.3%; **Pop. under 35:** 57.1%. **Area:** 316 sq. mi. **Employment:** 208,718 employed, 10.1% unemployed; **Per capita income:** $10,994. **Transportation:** 1 international airport; a major rail center; 191 trunk lines; several barge companies. **Communications:** 6 TV, 14 AM, 18 FM radio stations. **Medical facilities:** 41 hospitals; 18 clinics. **Educational facilities:** 13 colleges & universities. **Further information:** The Chamber of Commerce of Greater Kansas City, 600 Charterbank Center, 920 Main St., Kansas City, MO 64105.

Knoxville, Tennessee

Population: 175,030; **Pop. density:** 2,273 per sq. mi.; **Pop. growth:** 2.5%; **Pop. over 65:** 13.8%; **Pop. under 35:** 57.8%. **Area:** 77 sq. mi.. **Employment:** 74,300 employed, 11.5% unemployed; **Per capita income:** $9,448. **Transportation:** 5 airlines, 2 bus lines, 44 motor freight carriers; L&N and Southern railroads; interstate I-40 and I-75 intersect city. **Educational facilities:** Univ. of Tennessee, Knoxville College. **Further information:** Chamber of Commerce, P.O. Box 2229, Knoxville, TN 37901.

Laval, Quebec

Population: 268,335 (1981); **Pop. density:** 2,834 per sq. mi.; **Pop. growth:** 18.0% (1971-1981); **Pop. over 65:** 5.7%; **Pop. under 35:** 59.4%. **Area:** 94.7 sq. mi.. **Employment:** 126,040 employed, 7.6% unemployed (1981, city). **Transportation:** (see City of Montreal). **Communications:** 2 radio stations; see also City of Montreal. **Medical facilities:** 4 hospitals; see also City of Montreal. **Educational facilities:** 116 public schools. **Further information:** La Chambre de Commerce de Laval, 1435 St-Martin Ouest, Suite 600, Laval, Que. H7S 2C6.

Lexington–Fayette, Kentucky

Population: 204,165; **Pop. density:** 719 per sq. mi.; **Pop. growth:** 88.8%; **Pop. over 65:** 8.6%; **Pop. under 35:** 63.3%. **Area:** 284 sq. mi. **Employment:** 114,833 employed, 5.3% unemployed; **Per capita income:** $10,918. **Transportation:** 5 airlines, 4 railroads; city buses. **Communications:** 4 TV stations, CATV; 7 radio stations. **Medical facilities:** 4 general, 5 specialized hospitals. **Educational facilities:** Univ. of Kentucky, Transylvania Univ., Lexington Baptist College. **Further information:** Chamber of Commerce, 421 North Broadway, Lexington, KY 40508.

Lincoln, Nebraska

Population: 171,932; **Pop. density:** 2,866 per sq. mi.; **Pop. growth:** 15.0%; **Pop. over 65:** 10.3%; **Pop. under 35:** 63.9%. **Area:** 60 sq. mi.. **Employment:** 91,871 employed, 4.2% unemployed; **Per capita income:** $10,898. **Transportation:** 5 airlines serve Lincoln Municipal Airport; Greyhound, Trailways buses; Amtrak. **Communications:** 5 TV, 13 radio stations; CATV. **Medical facilities:** 4 hospitals including a VA facility. **Educational facilities:** 4 4-year colleges with 26,946 enrollment; 8 business, professional, or technical schools. **Further information:** Chamber of Commerce, 1221 N St., Lincoln, NE 68508.

London, Ontario

Population: 266,319 (1982); **Pop. density:** 4,254 per sq. mi.; **Pop. growth:** 14% (1971-81); **Pop. over 65:** 10.2%; **Pop. under 35:** 58.5%. **Area:** 62.6 sq. mi.. **Employment:** 128,055 employed, 7.7% unemployed (1984, city).
Transportation: London International Airport served by Air Canada and Air Ontario; passenger train service on VIA Rail and Amtrak; 3 inter-city bus lines. **Communications:** 1 television station; 7 radio stations. **Medical facilities:** 3 general hospitals, London Psychiatric Hospital, and Shute Institute for Clinical and Laboratory Medicine. **Educational facilities:** Univ. of Western Ontario, Fanshawe College. **Further information:** Visitors & Convention Services, 300 Dufferin Ave., P.O. Box 5035, London, Ont. N6A 4L9.

Long Beach, California

Population: 361,334; **Pop. density:** 7,226 per sq. mi.; **Pop. growth:** 0.7%; **Pop. over 65:** 14.0%; **Pop. under 35:** 56.6%. **Area:** 49.8 sq. mi. **Employment:** 162,734 employed, 8.1% unemployed; **Per capita income:** $13,080. **Transportation:** 1 airport; 3 railroads. **Communications:** 1 cable TV station; 2 AM, 6 FM radio stations. **Medical facilities:** 10 hospitals. **Educational facilities:** 1 university; 1 college. **Further information:** Long Beach Chamber of Commerce, 50 Oceangate Plaza, Long Beach, CA 90802.

Los Angeles, California

Population: 2,966,850; **Pop. density:** 6,380 per sq. mi.; **Pop. growth:** +0.5%; **Pop. over 65:** 10.6%; **Pop. under 35:** 58.1%. **Area:** 465 sq. mi.. **Employment:** 1,394,146 employed, 9.4% unemployed; **Per capita income:** $13,080.
Transportation: 1 major airport; 4 railroads; major bus carrier service; major freeway system. **Communications:** 19 TV stations; 71 radio stations. **Medical facilities:** 822 hospitals and clinics; 409 nursing homes. **Educational facilities:** 11 universities and colleges; 1,642 public schools; 800 private schools; 61 public libraries. **Further information:** Chamber of Commerce, P.O. Box 3696, Terminal Annex, Los Angeles, CA 90051.

Louisville, Kentucky

Population: 298,451; **Pop. density:** 4,974 per sq. mi.; **Pop. growth:** −17.5%; **Pop. over 65:** 15.3%; **Pop. under 35:** 54.1%. **Area:** 60 sq. mi. **Employment:** 128,396 employed, 9.8% unemployed; **Per capita income:** $10,579.
Transportation: 2 municipal airports; 1 terminal, 6 trunk-line railroads; 3 bus lines; 125 inter-city truck lines; 5 barge lines. **Communications:** 4 TV, 20 radio stations, 2 educational, 3 cable. **Medical facilities:** 21 hospitals. **Educational facilities:** 10 colleges & universities, 3 business colleges & technical schools. **Further information:** Louisville Area Chamber of Commerce, 300 W. Liberty, Louisville, KY 40202.

Lubbock, Texas

Population: 173,979; **Pop. density:** 1,933 per sq. mi.; **Pop. growth:** 16.7%; **Pop. over 65:** 7.8%; **Pop. under 35:** 66.9%. **Area:** 90 sq. mi. **Employment:** 87,972 employed, 7.3% unemployed; **Per capita income:** $10,544.
Transportation: Lubbock International Airport with 5 major airlines; 2 railroads, bus line; 6 major highways. **Communications:** 5 TV, 16 radio stations. **Medical facilities:** 7 hospitals, Lubbock State School for Mentally Retarded; Texas Tech Medical School. **Educational facilities:** Texas Tech Univ., Lubbock Christian College. **Further information:** Chamber of Commerce, P.O. Box 561, Lubbock, TX 79408.

Madison, Wisconsin

Population: 170,616; **Pop. density:** 3,219 per sq. mi.; **Pop. growth:** −0.7%; **Pop. over 65:** 8.7%; **Pop. under 35:** 66.5%. **Area:** 53 sq. mi. **Employment:** 96,342 employed, 6.4% unemployed; **Per capita income:** $11,989.
Transportation: Dane County Regional Airport with 5 airlines; 4 bus lines; highways I-90, I-94. **Communications:** 3 commercial, 1 public, 2 cable TV stations; 17 radio stations. **Medical facilities:** 5 hospitals including Univ. of Wis. and a VA facility; 21 clinics. **Educational facilities:** Univ. of Wisconsin; Madison Area Technical colleges. **Further information:** Chamber of Commerce, 625 W. Washington Ave., Madison, WI 53701.

Memphis, Tennessee

Population: 646,356; **Pop. density:** 2,448 per sq. mi.; **Pop. growth:** 3.6%; **Pop. over 65:** 10.4%; **Pop. under 35:** 60.5%. **Area:** 264 sq. mi.. **Employment:** 280,972 employed, 9.9% unemployed; **Per capita income:** $9,968.
Transportation: 1 major airport; 6 railroads; 6 barge lines. **Communications:** 5 TV stations; 24 radio stations. **Medical facilities:** 15 hospitals. **Educational facilities:** 4 universities and colleges; 160 public schools; 100 private schools; 22 public libraries. **Further information:** Chamber of Commerce, 555 Beale Street, Memphis TN 38103.

Miami, Florida

Population: 346,865; **Pop. density:** 8,671 per sq. mi.; **Pop. growth:** 3.6%; **Pop. over 65:** 17.0%; **Pop. under 35:** 46.5%. **Area:** 34 sq. mi.. **Employment:** 168,127 employed; 10.6% unemployed; **Per capita income:** $11,717.
Transportation: 1 international airport; 2 passenger railroads, 1 all-freight; 2 bus lines; 65 truck lines. **Communications:** 6 commercial, 5 educational TV stations; 31 radio stations. **Medical facilities:** 41 hospitals, 39 nursing homes; VA Hospital. **Educational facilities:** 6 colleges & universities. **Further information:** Metro-Dade Department of Tourism, 234 W. Flagler St., Miami, FL 33130.

Milwaukee, Wisconsin

Population: 636,212; **Pop. density:** 6,627 per sq. mi.; **Pop. growth:** −11.3%; **Pop. over 65:** 12.5%; **Pop. under 35:** 59.8%. **Area:** 96 sq. mi.. **Employment:** 282,412 employed, 10.1% unemployed; **Per capita income:** $12,597.
Transportation: 1 major airport; 4 railroads; major port; 4 bus lines. **Communications:** 7 TV stations; 23 radio stations. **Medical facilities:** 28 hospitals; major medical center. **Educational facilities:** 11 universities and colleges; major public school and library system. **Further information:** Association of Commerce, 756 N. Milwaukee Street, Milwaukee, WI 53202.

Minneapolis, Minnesota

Population: 370,951; **Pop. density:** 6,744 per sq. mi.; **Pop. growth:** −14.6%; **Pop. over 65:** 15.4%; **Pop. under 35:** 59.4%. **Area:** 55 sq. mi.. **Employment:** 200,804 employed; 4.9% unemployed; **Per capita income:** $12,811.
Transportation: 1 international airport; 5 trunk railroads; 150 trucking firms; 5 major barge lines. **Communications:** 6 TV, 39 radio stations. **Medical facilities:** 21

hospitals, including leading heart hospital at Univ. of Minnesota. **Educational facilities:** 13 colleges and universities; 6 2-year institutions; 6 professional schools. **Further information:** Greater Minneapolis Chamber of Commerce, 15 S. 5th St., Minneapolis, MN 55402.

Mississauga, Ontario

Population: 340,000 (1983); **Pop. density:** 3,217 per sq. mi.; **Pop. growth:** 69.8% (1973-83); **Pop. over 65:** 4.9%; **Pop. under 35:** 63.0%. **Area:** 105.7 sq. mi.. **Employment:** 175,720 labor force, 169,585 employed, 3.5% unemployed (1981, city).
Transportation: Pearson International Airport is within Mississauga; GO Transit connects with Toronto and other municipalities; bus connections to Metro Toronto subway system. **Communications:** 1 local radio station; see also City of Toronto. **Medical facilities:** Mississauga General Hospital; Credit Valley Hospital. **Educational facilities:** Erindale Campus of the University of Toronto, Sheridan College; 132 public and separate schools, 2 schools for trainable mentally retarded. **Further information:** Public Relations Office, Mississauga City Hall, One City Centre Drive, Mississauga, Ont. L5B 1M2.

Mobile, Alabama

Population: 200,452; **Pop. density:** 1,630 per sq. mi.; **Pop. growth:** 5.5%; **Pop. over 65:** 11.1%; **Pop. under 35:** 59.3%. **Area:** 123 sq. mi.. **Employment:** 75,317 employed, 16.2% unemployed; **Per capita income:** $6,871.

Transportation: 4 railroads, 4 major airlines, 55 truck lines; leading river system. **Communications:** 3 TV, 15 radio stations; CATV. **Medical facilities:** Univ. of South Alabama Medical Center, cancer research center, 6 hospitals. **Educational facilities:** Univ. of South Alabama; Spring Hill, Mobile colleges. **Further information:** Chamber of Commerce, P.O. Box 2187, Mobile, AL 36652.

Montgomery, Alabama

Population: 177,857; **Pop. density:** 1,389 per sq. mi.; **Pop. growth:** 33.3%; **Pop. over 65:** 10.1%; **Pop. under 35:** 60.7%. **Area:** 128 sq. mi.. **Employment:** 74,717 employed, 11.2% unemployed; **Per capita income:** $9,581.

Transportation: 3 airlines, 5 railroads, 2 bus lines; city bus line; Interstate 65 and 85 intersect in city; Alabama River is navigable to Gulf of Mexico. **Communications:** 4 TV, 14 radio stations; CATV. **Medical facilities:** 5 general hospitals; VA and mental health facilities. **Educational facilities:** 5 colleges and universities. **Further information:** Chamber of Commerce, P.O. Box 79, Montgomery, AL 36192.

Montreal, Quebec

Population: 1,020,720 (1982); **Pop. density:** 15,077 per sq. mi.; **Pop. growth:** −19% (1971-81); **Pop. over 65:** 13.1%; **Pop. under 35:** 51.6%. **Area:** 67.7 sq. mi.. **Employment:** 1,240,000 (metro) employed, 12.8% unemployed (May 1984).
Transportation: served by 2 major airports at Dorval and Mirabel; headquarters of Canadian National (VIA) and Canadian Pacific railways; major port on St. Lawrence Seaway; subway system (Metro) 51 miles long. **Communications:** 5 TV stations, 22 radio stations. **Medical facilities:** over 80 hospitals with 26,000 beds, including the renowned Montreal Neurological Institute and the Montreal Children's Hospital. **Educational facilities:** Concordia University, McGill University, Universite de Montreal, Universite de Quebec. **Further information:** Convention and Tourism Bureau of Greater Montreal, Salle F49 Frontenac, Box 889, Place Bonaventure, Montreal, Quebec H5A 1E6.

Nashville-Davidson, Tennessee

Population: 455,651; **Pop. density:** 949 per sq. mi.; **Pop. growth:** 7.0%; **Pop. over 65:** 11.0%; **Pop. under 35:** 58.7%. **Area:** 480 sq. mi.. **Employment:** 240,400 employed, 6.0% unemployed; **Per capita income:** $10,229.
Transportation: 1 airport; 2 railroads; more than 100 motor freight lines; 9 U.S. highways, 6 branches of interstate system. **Communications:** 5 TV, 30 radio stations. **Medical facilities:** 17 hospitals; 2 medical schools; VA Hospital, speech-hearing center. **Educational facilities:** 16 colleges & universities. **Further information:** Chamber of Commerce, 161 4th Ave., Nashville, TN 37219.

Newark, New Jersey

Population: 329,248; **Pop. density:** 13,718 per sq. mi.; **Pop. growth:** −13.8%; **Pop. over 65:** 8.8%; **Pop. under 35:** 61.6%. **Area:** 24 sq. mi.. **Employment:** 125,204 employed, 13.1% unemployed; **Per capita income:** $13,671.
Transportation: 1 international airport; 2 railroads; 2 subways. **Communications:** 2 TV, 2 radio stations. **Medical facilities:** 6 hospitals. **Educational facilities:** 6 universities and colleges. **Further information:** Greater Newark Chamber of Commerce, 50 Park Pl., Newark, NJ 07102.

New Orleans, Louisiana

Population: 557,515; **Pop. density:** 2,802 per sq. mi.; **Pop. growth:** −6%; **Pop. over 65:** 11.7%; **Pop. under 35:** 60.1%. **Area:** 199 sq. mi.. **Employment:** 226,572 employed, 8.4% unemployed; **Per capita income:** $11,680.
Transportation: 2 airports; major railroad center; major international port. **Communications:** 5 TV stations; 20 radio stations. **Medical facilities:** numerous hospitals; major medical research center. **Educational facilities:** 7 universities and colleges; major public library system. **Further information:** Chamber of Commerce, 301 Camp Street, New Orleans, LA 70130.

New York City, New York

Population: 7,071,639; **Pop. density:** 23,494 per sq. mi.; **Pop. growth:** −10.4%; **Pop. over 65:** 13.5%; **Pop. under 35:** 53.7%. **Area:** 301 sq. mi. **Employment:** 2,761,000 employed, 8.1% unemployed; **Per capita income:** $12,874.
Transportation: 2 airports; 4 heliports; 2 railroads; 2 rail terminals; 34 bus carriers; major subway network; ferry system; 4 underwater tunnels. **Communications:** 15 TV stations, 39 radio stations. **Medical facilities:** over 100 hospitals; 5 medical research centers. **Educational facilities:** 29 universities and colleges; 1,000 public schools, 879 private schools; 201 public libraries. **Further information:** Convention and Visitors Bureau, 2 Columbus Circle, New York, NY 10019.

Norfolk, Virginia

Population: 266,979; **Pop. density:** 5,037 per sq. mi.; **Pop. growth:** −13.3%; **Pop. over 65:** 9.2%; **Pop. under 35:** 68.6%. **Area:** 53 sq. mi.. **Employment:** 100,399 employed, 4.8% unemployed; **Per capita income:** $10,491.
Transportation: 1 international airport; 4 major railroad systems in area. **Communications:** 5 TV, 18 radio stations. **Medical facilities:** 9 hospitals, 1 medical school. **Educational facilities:** 2 universities, 1 college. **Further information:** Norfolk Chamber of Commerce, 480 Bank St., Norfolk, VA 23510.

North York, Ontario

Population (1983): 553,867; **Pop. density:** 8,109 per sq. mi.; **Pop. growth:** 5.9% (1973-83); **Pop. over 65:** 10.8%; **Pop. under 35:** 53.2%. **Area:** 68.3 sq. mi.. **Employment:** 300,110 employed, 4.2% unemployed (1981, city).

Transportation: (see City of Toronto). Communications: (see City of Toronto). Medical facilities: 10 hospitals; see also City of Toronto. Educational facilities: York University, Seneca College; 274 public and private elementary, intermediate and secondary schools. Further information: Public Information Office, 5100 Yonge St., North York, Ont. M2N 5V7.

Oakland, California

Population: 339,337; Pop. density: 6,284 per sq. mi.; Pop. growth: −6.2%; Pop. over 65: 13.2%; Pop. under 35: 57%. Area: 54 sq. mi.. Employment: 154,001 employed, 11.1% unemployed; Per capita income: $13,671. Transportation: 1 international airport; western terminus for 3 railroads; underground, underwater 75-mile subway. Communications: 1 TV, 3 radio stations. Medical facilities: 9 hospitals, including Children's Hospital Medical Center, VA hospital. Educational facilities: 1 university; 6 colleges. Further information: Chamber of Commerce, 1320 Webster St., Oakland, CA 94612.

Oklahoma City, Oklahoma

Population: 403,213; Pop. density: 667 per sq. mi.; Pop. growth: 9.5%; Pop. over 65: 11.3%; Pop. under 35: 58.2%. Area: 604 sq. mi.. Employment: 214,864 employed, 6.7% unemployed; Per capita income: $12,776. Transportation: 1 international airport; 3 railroads; 5 major bus lines; 4 interstate highways, 6 federal highways. Communications: 7 TV, 24 radio stations; cable TV. Medical facilities: 18 hospitals; 9 community health clinics; Oklahoma Health Center, including Univ. of Oklahoma Medical Schools, VA hospital; medical research foundation; eye institute. Further information: Oklahoma City Chamber of Commerce, One Santa Fe Plaza, Oklahoma City, OK 73102.

Omaha, Nebraska

Population: 314,255; Pop. density: 3,453 per sq. mi.; Pop. growth: −9.5%; Pop. over 65: 12.2%; Pop. under 35: 41.9%. Area: 91 sq. mi.. Employment: 146,419 employed, 6.5% unemployed; Per capita income: $11,397. Transportation: 8 major airlines; major rail center, with 6 major railroads; 98 truck lines; 2 interstate highways; 2 intercity bus lines; 5 barge lines. Communications: 6 TV, 19 radio stations; cable TV. Medical facilities: 16 hospitals; 2 medical, 1 dental, 7 nursing schools; institute for cancer research. Educational facilities: 3 universities, 6 colleges. Further information: Greater Omaha Chamber of Commerce, 1606 Douglas, Omaha, NE 68102.

Ottawa, Ontario

Population: 295,163 (1981); Pop. density: 6,945 per sq. mi.; Pop. growth: −2.4% (1971-81); Pop. over 65: 12.5%; Pop. under 35: 54.0%. Area: 42.5 sq. mi.. Employment: 154,690 employed, 6.3% unemployed (1981, city).
Transportation: Ottawa International Airport, served by 8 airlines, more than 100 flights daily; surface transport by VIA Rail and intercity bus service. Communications: 6 TV and 14 radio stations. Medical facilities: 11 hospitals with more than 4,000 beds. Educational facilities: Carleton Univ., the bi-lingual Univ. of Ottawa, Algonquin Community College. Further information: Canada's Capital Visitors Bureau, 7th Floor, 222 Queen St., Ottawa, Ont. K1P 5V9.

Philadelphia, Pennsylvania

Population: 1,688,210; Pop. density: 12,413 per sq. mi.; Pop. growth: −13.4%; Pop. over 65: 14.1%; Pop. under 35: 54.4%. Area: 136 sq. mi.. Employment: 740,085 employed, 7.9% unemployed; Per capita income: $11,946.
Transportation: 1 major airport; 3 railroads; biggest freshwater port in world; subway, el, rail commuter, bus,

and streetcar system. Communications: 6 TV stations; 53 radio stations. Medical facilities: 124 hospitals. Educational facilities: 88 degree-granting institutions; major public library system. Further information: Office of City Representative, 1660 Municipal Services Bldg., Philadelphia, PA 19107.

Phoenix, Arizona

Population: 789,704; Pop. density: 2,438 per sq. mi.; Pop. growth: 35.1%; Pop. over 65: 9.3%; Pop. under 35: 60.4%. Area: 324 sq. mi.. Employment: 463,539 employed, 5.0% unemployed; Per capita income: $11,086.
Transportation: 1 major airport; 2 railroads; 2 transcontinental bus lines; public transit system. Communications: 8 TV stations; 38 radio stations. Medical facilities: 33 hospitals, 1 medical research center. Educational facilities: 8 universities and colleges; 6 community colleges; major public library system. Further information: Chamber of Commerce, 34 W. Monroe, Suite 900, Phoenix, AZ 85003.

Pittsburgh, Pennsylvania

Population: 423,938; Pop. density: 7,707 per sq. mi.; Pop. growth: −18%; Pop. over 65: 16.0%; Pop. under 35: 52.9%. Area: 55 sq. mi.. Employment: 163,399 employed, 10.6% unemployed; Per capita income: $11,762.
Transportation: 1 international airport; 20 railroads; 2 bus lines; more than 400 common carriers; 5 trolley lines, 1 incline; 9 major highways; another busway, and light rail trolley system, including downtown subway. Communications: 6 TV, 25 radio stations. Medical facilities: 32 hospitals; VA installation. Educational facilities: 3 universities; 6 colleges. Further information: Chamber of Commerce, 411 Seventh Ave., Pittsburgh, PA 15219.

Portland, Oregon

Population: 366,383; Pop. density: 3,557 per sq. mi.; Pop. growth: −3.6%; Pop. over 65: 10.9%; Pop. under 35: 58.9%. Area: 103 sq. mi.. Employment: 172,970 employed, 11.4% unemployed; Per capita income: $11,793.
Transportation: 1 international airport; 3 major rail freight lines, Amtrak; 2 bus lines; 27-mi. frontage freshwater port; mass transit system. Communications: 5 TV, 27 radio stations. Medical facilities: 32 hospitals; Oregon Health Sciences University Hospital; VA hospital. Educational facilities: 9 universities; 4 community colleges; 2 Bible colleges. Further information: Chamber of Commerce, 824 SW 5th, Portland, OR 97204.

Quebec, Quebec

Population: 166,474 (1981); Pop. density: 4,839 per sq. mi.; Pop. growth: −10.5% (1971-81); Pop. over 65: 13%; Pop. under 35: 53.2%. Area: 34.4 sq. mi.. Employment: 69,935 employed, 12.9% unemployed (1981, city).
Transportation: airport served by Air Canada, Quebecair, Nordair; VIA Rail passenger train service; major port; bus centre. Communications: 3 TV stations (2 French, one English), 10 radio stations. Medical facilities: 5 large general hospitals. Educational facilities: Laval University, the first in North America; 4 colleges. Further information: Quebec City Hall, Communications Service, 2 Rue des Jardins, Quebec, Que. J1R 4L5.

Regina, Saskatchewan

Population: 169,120 (1983); Pop. density: 3,989 per sq. mi.; Pop. growth: 17.0% (1971-81); Pop. over 65: 9.2%; Pop. under 35: 62.4%. Area: 42.8 sq. mi.. Employment: 89,000 employed, 8% unemployed (1983, city).
Transportation: 2 rail lines, 4 airlines, 3 bus lines; main Trans-Canada Highway bisects. Communications: 3 TV

and 9 radio stations plus cable television. **Medical facilities:** 4 major hospitals with 1,453 beds. **Educational facilities:** Regina University; 14 collegiates; 98 elementary, 7 specialized schools, Wascana Institute of Applied Arts and Sciences. **Further information:** Regina Chamber of Commerce, 2145 Albert St., Regina, Sask. S4P 2V1.

Richmond, Virginia

Population: 219,214; **Pop. density:** 3,650 per sq. mi.; **Pop. growth:** −12.1%; **Pop. over 65:** 14.1%; **Pop. under 35:** 56.9%. **Area:** 60 sq. mi.. **Employment:** 115,135 employed, 5.5% unemployed; **Per capita income:** $11,968.

Transportation: 4 commercial, 3 commuter air lines; 4 railroads, 5 intercity bus lines; deepwater terminal accessible to ocean-going ships. **Communications:** 6 TV, 25 radio stations; 2 CATV stations. **Medical facilities:** Medical Coll. of Virginia renowned for heart and kidney transplants; 17 other hospitals including VA facility. **Educational facilities:** Va. Commonwealth, Univ. of Richmond, Va. Union, Randolph-Macon College. **Further information:** Chamber of Commerce, 201 E. Franklin St., Richmond, VA 23219.

Riverside, California

Population: 170,876; **Pop. density:** 2,406 per sq. mi.; **Pop. growth:** 22.0%; **Pop. over 65:** 8.8%; **Pop. under 35:** 62.8%. **Area:** 71 sq. mi.. **Employment:** 73,893 employed, 10.1% unemployed; **Per capita income:** $10,092. **Communications:** 11 TV, 13 radio stations. **Educational facilities:** Univ. of Cal.- Riverside, Cal. Baptist. **Further information:** Chamber of Commerce, 4261 Main St., Riverside, CA 92501.

Rochester, New York

Population: 241,741; **Pop. density:** 7,068 per sq. mi.; **Pop. growth:** −18.1%; **Pop. over 65:** 14.0%; **Pop. under 35:** 60.0%. **Area:** 34 sq. mi.. **Employment:** 95,825 employed, 10.8% unemployed; **Per capita income:** $12,463.

Transportation: Amtrak; Greyhound, Trailways, Blue Bird bus lines; Monroe Co. airport with 8 major airlines; Rochester Transit Service; Port of Rochester; some 75 motor freight firms. **Communications:** 5 TV, 18 radio stations. **Medical facilities:** 8 general hospitals including Strong Memorial. **Educational facilities:** 8 private and 2 public 4-year colleges; 3 community colleges. **Further information:** Chamber of Commerce, 55 St. Paul St., Rochester, NY 14604.

Sacramento, California

Population: 275,741; **Pop. density:** 2,872 per sq. mi.; **Pop. growth:** 10.7%; **Pop. over 65:** 9.6%; **Pop. under 35:** 59%. **Area:** 96 sq. mi.. **Employment:** 123,794 employed, 11.3% unemployed; **Per capita income:** $11,176. **Transportation:** metropolitan airport; Port of Sacramento with direct link to Pacific; 2 mainline transcontinental rail carriers; junction 4 major highways. **Communications:** 6 TV, 23 radio stations. **Medical facilities:** 14 hospitals. **Educational facilities:** 2 universities, 4 community colleges, 1 college of law. **Further information:** Sacramento Metropolitan Chamber of Commerce, 917 7th St., P.O. Box 1017, Sacramento, CA 95805.

St. Louis, Missouri

Population: 453,085; **Pop. density:** 7,427 per sq. mi.; **Pop. growth:** −27.2%; **Pop. over 65:** 17.6%; **Pop. under 35:** 54%. **Area:** 61 sq. mi.. **Employment:** 193,431 employed, 11.9% unemployed; **Per capita income:** $12,338.

Transportation: 1 airport; 2d largest rail center in U.S.; 17 trunk line railroads; largest inland port in U.S.; 9 major

highways; 14 bus lines; 350 motor freight lines, 14 barge lines. **Communications:** 6 TV, 35 radio stations. **Medical facilities:** 65 hospitals. **Educational facilities:** 4 universities, 26 colleges and seminaries. **Further information:** Convention and Visitors Bureau, 500 N. Broadway, St. Louis, MO 63101.

St. Paul, Minnesota

Population: 270,230; **Pop. density:** 5,196 per sq. mi.; **Pop. growth:** −12.8%; **Pop. over 65:** 15.0%; **Pop. under 35:** 41.5%. **Area:** 52 sq. mi.. **Employment:** 146,282 employed, 5.7% unemployed; **Per capita income:** $12,811.

Transportation: 1 metropolitan airport, downtown airport; 5 major, 2 regional rail lines, Amtrak; 21 intercity truck firms; 3 interstate bus lines; 60 barge firms. **Communications:** 6 TV, 29 radio stations. **Medical facilities:** 12 private hospitals; community hospital and research center. **Educational facilities:** 1 university; 5 colleges; 1 college of law; 1 institute of agriculture. **Further information:** St. Paul Area Chamber of Commerce, 701 N. Central Tower, 445 Minnesota St., St. Paul, MN 55101.

St. Petersburg, Florida

Population: 238,647; **Pop. density:** 4,186 per sq. mi.; **Pop. growth:** 10.4%; **Pop. over 65:** 25.8%; **Pop. under 35:** 43.7%. **Area:** 57 sq. mi.. **Employment:** 105,075 employed, 6.7% unemployed; **Per capita income:** $10,675. **Transportation:** Tampa Intl. Airport; Amtrak, Seaboard Coast Line railroads; Greyhound and Trailways buses; U.S. 19, 41, 98 link city to rest of gulf-coast Florida; Interstate 175, 75, 4 link city with Tampa, Orlando, and east coast. **Communications:** 8 TV, 46 radio stations. **Medical facilities:** 18 hospitals with 4,687 beds. **Educational facilities:** Univ. of South Florida's downtown Bayboro campus, Stetson Coll. of Law, Eckerd College. **Further information:** St. Petersburg Chamber of Commerce, 225 4th St. S., St. Petersburg, FL 33701.

San Antonio, Texas

Population: 785,880; **Pop. density:** 2,988 per sq. mi.; **Pop. growth:** 20%; **Pop. over 65:** 9.5%; **Pop. under 35:** 62.1%. **Area:** 263 sq. mi.. **Employment:** 354,625 employed, 6.4% unemployed; **Per capita income:** $10,131. **Transportation:** 1 major airport; 4 railroads; 6 bus lines; major freeway system. **Communications:** 5 TV, 20 radio stations. **Medical facilities:** 16 hospitals; major medical center. **Educational facilities:** 7 universities and colleges; major public library system. **Further information:** Chamber of Commerce, 602 E. Commerce, P.O. Box 1628, San Antonio, TX 78296.

San Diego, California

Population: 875,538; **Pop. density:** 2,736 per sq. mi.; **Pop. growth:** 25.5%; **Pop. over 65:** 9.7%; **Pop. under 35:** 62.1%. **Area:** 320 sq. mi.. **Employment:** 379,040 employed, 7.6% unemployed; **Per capita income:** $11,638. **Transportation:** 1 major airport; 1 railroad; major freeway system; bus system. **Communications:** 8 TV, 33 radio stations. **Medical facilities:** 18 hospitals; 2 major medical research centers. **Educational facilities:** 8 universities and colleges; major public library system. **Further information:** Chamber of Commerce, 110 West "C," Suite 1600, San Diego, CA 92101.

San Francisco, California

Population: 678,974; **Pop. density:** 14,760 per sq. mi.; **Pop. growth:** −5.1%; **Pop. over 65:** 15.4%; **Pop. under 35:** 51.7%. **Area:** 46 sq. mi.. **Employment:** 341,211 employed, 8.2% unemployed; **Per capita income:** $17,131. **Transportation:** 1 major airport; intra-city railway system; 2 railway transit systems; bus and railroad service;

ferry system; 1 underwater tunnel. **Communications:** 7 TV stations; 45 radio stations. **Medical facilities:** 29 hospitals; 1 major medical center. **Educational facilities:** 4 universities and colleges; major public library system. **Further information:** Chamber of Commerce, 465 California Street, San Francisco, CA 94104.

San Jose, California

Population: 629,442; **Pop. density:** 3,984 per sq. mi.; **Pop. growth:** 36.9%; **Pop. over 65:** 6.2%; **Pop. under 35:** 64.7%. **Area:** 158 sq. mi.. **Employment:** 375,326 employed, 7.4% unemployed; **Per capita income:** $14,998.
Transportation: 1 major airport; 2 railroads; major highway system; bus system. **Communications:** 4 TV stations; 15 radio stations. **Medical facilities:** 5 hospitals. **Educational facilities:** 3 universities and colleges; major public library system. **Further information:** Chamber of Commerce, One Paseo de San Antonio, San Jose, CA 95113.

Santa Ana, California

Population: 203,713; **Pop. density:** 7,544 per sq. mi.; **Pop. growth:** 30.8%; **Pop. over 65:** 7.4%; **Pop. under 35:** 66.9%. **Area:** 27 sq. mi.. **Employment:** 114,761 employed, 7.1% unemployed (county); **Per capita income:** $13,927.
Transportation: John Wayne airport; 8 major freeways including main Los Angeles-San Diego artery; Amtrak. **Communications:** $27 mln. installation of CATV system. **Medical facilities:** 4 hospitals with 561 beds. **Educational facilities:** 1 university, 1 community college, 1 law school. **Further information:** Chamber of Commerce, 1616 E. 4th St., P.O. Box 205, Santa Ana, CA 92702.

Seattle, Washington

Population: 493,846; **Pop. density:** 5,879 per sq. mi.; **Pop. growth:** −7.0%; **Pop. over 65:** 15.4%; **Pop. under 35:** 54.9%. **Area:** 84 sq. mi.. **Employment:** 256,025 employed, 9.8% unemployed; **Per capita income:** $13,239.
Transportation: 1 international airport; 3 railroads; ferries serve Puget Sound, Alaska, Canada. **Communications:** 7 TV, 23 AM & 19 FM radio stations. **Medical facilities:** 27 hospitals. **Educational facilities:** 4 colleges; 11 community colleges. **Further information:** Chamber of Commerce, 215 Columbia St., Seattle, WA 98104.

Shreveport, Louisiana

Population: 205,820; **Pop. density:** 2,572 per sq. mi.; **Pop. growth:** 13%; **Pop. over 65:** 11.7%; **Pop. under 35:** 59.4%. **Area:** 80 sq. mi.. **Employment:** 83,307 employed, 9.2% unemployed; **Per capita income:** $11,006.
Transportation: 6 air lines service Shreveport Regional airport; Continental Trailways buses. **Communications:** 4 TV, 17 radio stations; CATV. **Medical facilities:** 11 hospitals with over 3,000 beds. **Educational facilities:** La. Tech., Northwestern St., and Grambling univs.; Centenary Coll., Bossier Parish Comm. College. **Further information:** Chamber of Commerce, P.O. Box 20074, Shreveport, LA 71120.

Spokane, Washington

Population: 171,300; **Pop. density:** 3,358 per sq. mi.; **Pop. growth:** 0.5%; **Pop. over 65:** 15.3%; **Pop. under 35:** 56.7%. **Area:** 54 sq. mi.. **Employment:** 70,916 employed, 10.9% unemployed; **Per capita income:** $9,839.
Transportation: international airport served by 5 major airlines, 2 commuter lines; Amtrak. **Communications:** public cable TV; 21 radio stations. **Medical facilities:** 6 major, 7 specialized hospitals. **Educational facilities:** 2 universities, 1 college, 2 community colleges. **Further information:** Chamber of Commerce, P.O. Box 2147, Spokane, WA 99210.

Syracuse, New York

Population: 170,105; **Pop. density:** 7,395 per sq. mi.; **Pop. growth:** −13.7%; **Pop. over 65:** 10.7%; **Pop. under 35:** 58.8%. **Area:** 23 sq. mi.. **Employment:** 67,870 employed, 8.3% unemployed; **Per capita income:** $10,755.
Transportation: 2 rail freight lines, Amtrak; 3 bus lines; 10 airlines. **Communications:** 4 TV, 16 radio stations. **Medical facilities:** 4 major hospital complexes. **Educational facilities:** Syracuse Univ., State Univ. Coll. of Environmental Science and Forestry. **Further information:** Chamber of Commerce, One MONY Plaza, Syracuse, NY 13202.

Tampa, Florida

Population: 271,523; **Pop. density:** 3,232 per sq. mi.; **Pop. growth:** −2.2%; **Pop. over 65:** 14.8%; **Pop. under 35:** 54%. **Area:** 84 sq. mi.. **Employment:** 137,918 employed, 7.8% unemployed; **Per capita income:** $10,675.
Transportation: 1 international airport; Port of Tampa, 140 steamship lines; 2 railroads; 5 bus lines; 46 trucking lines; junction of 2 highways. **Communications:** 7 TV, 27 radio stations in Bay area. **Medical facilities:** 7 major hospitals. **Educational facilities:** 2 universities, 2 colleges, 1 community college. **Further information:** Greater Tampa Chamber of Commerce, 801 E. Kennedy Blvd., Tampa, FL 33602.

Toledo, Ohio

Population: 354,635; **Pop. density:** 4,221 per sq. mi.; **Pop. growth:** −7.4%; **Pop. over 65:** 12.5%; **Pop. under 35:** 58.5%. **Area:** 84 sq. mi.. **Employment:** 143,976 employed, 10.6% unemployed; **Per capita income:** $10,892.
Transportation: 9 major airlines; 7 railroads; 100 motor freight lines; 2 interstate bus lines; 13 major highways. **Communications:** 4 TV, 13 radio stations; 1 cablevision company. **Medical facilities:** 10 major hospital complexes. **Educational facilities:** 2 universities; 3 colleges. **Further information:** Convention and Visitors Bureau, 218 Huron, Toledo, OH 43604.

Toronto, Ontario

Population: 599,217 (1981); **Pop. density:** 15,979 per sq. mi.; **Pop. growth:** −16.0% (1971-81); **Pop. over 65:** 12.4% **Pop. under 35:** 54.5%. **Area:** 37.5 sq. mi.. **Employment:** 327,610 employed, 4.7% unemployed (1981, city).
Transportation: 792 miles of bus routes, 34 miles of subway; Pearson International Airport served by 22 major airlines and 27 charter companies; Toronto Island Airport handles small aircraft; major Great Lakes port; passenger and freight train service. **Communications:** 7 TV stations including educational and French-language channels; 18 radio stations. **Medical facilities:** 40 active treatment hospitals (metro) including Hospital for Sick Children; special treatment centers: Clarke Institute of Psychiatry, Addiction Research Foundation, Ontario Crippled Children's Centre, Ontario Centre for the Deaf. **Educational facilities:** Univ. of Toronto, Ryerson Polytechnical Institute, George Brown College (plus York Univ. and 3 more community colleges within metro), Ontario College of Art, Royal Conservatory of Music, Osgoode Hall Law School (at York Univ.). **Further information:** Convention and Visitors Association, Toronto Eaton Centre, Toronto, Ontario M5B 2H1.

Tucson, Arizona

Population: 330,537; **Pop. density:** 3,330 per sq. mi.; **Pop. growth:** 25.7%; **Pop. over 65:** 11.7%; **Pop. under 35:** 60.7%. **Area:** 99 sq. mi.. **Employment:** 158,469 employed, 5.9% unemployed; **Per capita income:** $9,969.
Transportation: 1 international airport, 3 smaller airports; 1 railroad; 2 national, 1 local bus line. **Communica-**

tions: 5 TV, 18 radio stations. **Medical facilities:** 9 hospitals. **Educational facilities:** 1 university, 1 college. **Further information:** Tucson Metro. Chamber of Commerce, P.O. Box 991, Tucson, AZ 85702.

Tulsa, Oklahoma

Population: 360,919; **Pop. density:** 1,940 per sq. mi.; **Pop. growth:** 9.3%; **Pop. over 65:** 10.8%; **Pop. under 35:** 58.1%. **Area:** 185.6 sq. mi.. **Employment:** 179,161 employed, 8.9% unemployed; **Per capita income:** $12,750.
Transportation: 14 airlines; 4 rail lines; 2 regional bus lines, 2 national bus lines; 30 truck lines; nation's most inland port. **Communications:** 5 TV, 14 radio stations. **Medical facilities:** 5 hospitals; City of Faith medical center, osteopathic college, medical school. **Educational facilities:** 4 colleges and universities. **Further information:** Metropolitan Tulsa Chamber of Commerce, 616 S. Boston Ave., Tulsa, OK 74119.

Vancouver, British Columbia

Population: 414,281 (1981); **Pop. density:** 9,480 per sq. mi.; **Pop. growth:** −2.8%; **Pop. over 65:** 15.3%; **Pop. under 35:** 51.3%. **Area:** 43.7 sq. mi.. **Employment:** 217,000 employed, 6.0% unemployed (1981, city).
Transportation: International Airport served by 8 major airlines; western terminus of Canada's 2 national railways, Canadian National (VIA passenger service) and Canadian Pacific; provincially operated British Columbia linked to U.S. by Amtrak; 3 long-distance bus carriers (Trailways, Greyhound, Pacific Coach Lines); Canada's busiest port. **Communications:** 19 radio stations, 4 local TV stations. **Medical facilities:** General and St. Paul's are largest hospitals; also Shaughnessy and New Children's in Vancouver, Royal Columbian in New Westminster, Burnaby General, Lion's Gate in North Vancouver, and Riverview Psychiatric Hospital. **Educational facilities:** Univ. of British Columbia and Simon Fraser Univ.; 5 institutes of technology, 4 community colleges, Trinity Western (private) Univ., Open Learning Institute. **Further information:** Greater Vancouver Convention & Visitors Bureau, P.O. Box 11142-1055 West Georgia Street, Vancouver B.C., V6E 4C8.

Virginia Beach, Virginia

Population: 262,199; **Pop. density:** 1,028 per sq. mi.; **Pop. growth:** 52.3%; **Pop. over 65:** 4.5%; **Pop. under 35:** 66.0%. **Area:** 255 sq. mi.. **Employment:** 110,300 employed, 4.2% unemployed; **Per capita income:** $10,491.
Transportation: 10 airlines serve Norfolk/Virginia Beach Airport; Greyhound, Trailways buses. **Communications:** 6 TV, 30 radio stations. **Medical facilities:** Bayside and Virginia Beach General hospitals with over 500 beds. **Educational facilities:** Norfolk State Univ., Old Dominion Univ.; Tidewater Comm., Commonwealth, Va. Wesleyan colleges. **Further information:** Chamber of Commerce, 4512 Virginia Beach Blvd., Virginia Beach, VA 23462.

Washington, District of Columbia

Population: 637,651; **Pop. density:** 10,121 per sq. mi.; **Pop. growth:** −15.7%; **Pop. over 65:** 11.6%; **Pop. under 35:** 56.9%. **Area:** 63 sq. mi.. **Employment:** 282,000 employed, 12.1% unemployed; **Per capita income:** $14,960.
Transportation: 2 airports; rail transit system; extensive local bus service; long distance rail and bus service. **Communications:** 8 TV stations; 40 radio stations. **Medical facilities:** 43 hospitals; major medical research center. **Educational facilities:** 6 universities and colleges; 24

public libraries. **Further information:** Convention and Visitors Association, 1575 I Street NW, Suite 250, Washington, DC 20005.

Wichita, Kansas

Population: 279,272; **Pop. density:** 2,765 per sq. mi.; **Pop. growth:** 1.0%; **Pop. over 65:** 10.6%; **Pop. under 35:** 59.9%. **Area:** 101.4 sq. mi.. **Employment:** 141,587 employed, 6.2% unemployed; **Per capita income:** $12,433.
Transportation: 2 airports; 4 major rail freight lines; 1 bus line; 72 truck lines; 9 major highways. **Communications:** 4 TV, 7 AM, 6 FM radio stations; cable TV. **Medical facilities:** 6 hospital complexes, including a VA; world's largest speech & hearing rehabilitation center. **Educational facilities:** 3 universities, 1 college. **Further information:** Chamber of Commerce, 350 W. Douglas, Wichita, KS 67202.

Windsor, Ontario

Population: 192,546 (1984); **Pop. density:** 4,158 per sq. mi.; **Pop. growth:** −5.5% (1971-81); **Pop. over 65:** 12.1%; **Pop. under 35:** 55.6%. **Area:** 46.2 sq. mi.. **Employment:** 80,170 employed, 12.2% unemployed (1981, city).
Transportation: VIA Rail passenger service; Windsor International Airport served by Air Canada; linked to Detroit by vehicular tunnel and suspension bridge. **Communications:** 8 radio stations; 1 TV station. **Medical facilities:** 4 major hospitals, regional children's center; handicapped children's rehabilitation center. **Educational facilities:** Univ. of Windsor, St. Clair College of Applied Arts & Technology. **Further information:** Chamber of Commerce, 500 Riverside Drive West, Windsor, Ont. N9A 5K6; Tourist Information, 80 Chatham St. East.

Winnipeg, Manitoba

Population: 564,473; **Pop. density:** 2,559 per sq. mi.; **Pop. growth:** 129.0% (1971-81); **Pop. over 65:** 11.6%; **Pop. under 35:** 57.2%. **Area:** 220.6 sq. mi.. **Employment:** 283,780 employed, 5.2% unemployed (1981, city).
Transportation: International Airport served by 10 airlines; 2 national railways, VIA Rail passenger service; one rail line to U.S.; 5 national and regional bus lines; trucking hub. **Communications:** 4 TV and 11 radio stations. **Medical facilities:** 13 active treatment hospitals, including 2 major teaching centres plus the Univ. of Manitoba Rh Institute. **Educational facilities:** Univ. of Manitoba with 4 affiliated colleges; Univ. of Winnipeg, Red River Community College. **Further information:** Winnipeg Chamber of Commerce, 500-167 Lombard Ave., Winnipeg, Man. R3B 3E5; Winnipeg Visitor and Convention Bureau, 226 - 375 York Ave.

Yonkers, New York

Population: 195,351; **Pop. density:** 10,852 per sq. mi.; **Pop. growth:** −4%. **Area:** 18 sq. mi.. **Employment:** 95,367 employed, 6.6% unemployed; **Per capita income:** $8,339 (1979).
Transportation: intracity bus system; rail service. **Medical facilities:** St. Joseph's Medical Center, St. John's Riverside Hospital, Yonkers General Hospital. **Educational facilities:** Elizabeth Seton, Mercy, Sarah Lawrence colleges. **Further information:** Chamber of Commerce, 101 N. Broadway, Yonkers, NY 10701.

Washington, Capital of the U.S.

Arlington National Cemetery

Arlington National Cemetery, on the former Custis estate in Virginia, is the site of the **Tomb of the Unknown Soldier** and the final resting place of John Fitzgerald Kennedy, president of the United States, who was buried there Nov. 25, 1963. A torch burns day and night over his grave. The remains of his brother Sen. Robert F. Kennedy (N.Y.) were interred on June 8, 1968, in an area adjacent. Many other famous Americans are also buried at Arlington, as well as American soldiers from every major war.

Arlington House, The Robert E. Lee Memorial

On a hilltop above the cemetery, stands Arlington House, the Robert E. Lee Memorial, which from 1955 to 1972 was officially called the Custis-Lee Mansion.

U.S. Marine Corps War Memorial

North of the National Cemetery, approximately 350 yards, stands the bronze statue of the raising of the United States flag on Iwo Jima, executed by Felix de Weldon from the photograph by Joe Rosenthal, and presented to the nation by members and friends of the U.S. Marine Corps.

Vietnam War Memorial

On November 13, 1982, a memorial was dedicated to the American soldiers killed or missing during the Vietnam War. It is located near the Lincoln Memorial and the Washington Monument.

The Capitol

The United States Capitol was originally designed by Dr. William Thornton, an amateur architect, who submitted a plan in the spring of 1793 that won him $500 and a city lot.

The south, or House wing, was completed in 1807 under the direction of Benjamin H. Latrobe.

The present Senate and House wings and the iron dome were designed and constructed by Thomas U. Walter, the 4th architect of the Capitol, between 1851-1863.

The present cast iron dome at its greatest exterior measures 135 ft. 5 in., and it is topped by the bronze Statue of Freedom that stands 19½ ft. and weighs 14,985 pounds. On its base are the words "E Pluribus Unum (Out of Many One).

The Capitol is normally open from 9 a.m. to 4:30 p.m. daily, closed Christmas, New Year's Day, and Thanksgiving Day.

Tours through the Capitol, including the House and Senate Galleries, are conducted from 9 a.m. to 4 p.m. without charge.

Folger Shakespeare Library

The **Folger Shakespeare Library** on Capitol Hill, Washington, D. C., is a research institution devoted to the advancement of learning in the background of Anglo-American civilization in the 16th and 17th centuries and in most aspects of the continental Renaissance. It has the largest collection of Shakespeareana in the world with 79 copies of the First Folio.

Library of Congress

Established by and for Congress in 1800, the Library of Congress has extended its services over the years to other Government agencies and other libraries, to scholars, and to the general public, and it now serves as the national library.

The library's exhibit halls are open to the public. Guided tours are given every hour from 9 a.m. through 4 p.m. Monday through Friday. Arrangements for groups should be made in advance with the Tour Coordinator.

Thomas Jefferson Memorial

The **Thomas Jefferson Memorial** stands on the south shore of the Tidal Basin in West Potomac park. It is a circular stone structure, with Vermont marble on the exterior and Georgia white marble inside and combines architectural elements of the dome of the Pantheon in Rome and the rotunda designed by Jefferson for the University of Virginia.

The memorial is open daily from 8 a.m. to midnight, except Christmas Day. An elevator and curb ramps for the handicapped are in service.

Lincoln Memorial

The **Lincoln Memorial** in West Potomac Park, on the axis of the Capitol and the Washington Monument, consists of a large marble hall enclosing a heroic statue of Abraham Lincoln in meditation sitting on a large armchair. It was dedicated on Memorial Day, May 30, 1922. The Memorial was designed by Henry Bacon. The statue was made by Daniel Chester French. Murals and ornamentation on the bronze ceiling beams are by Jules Guerin.

The memorial is open daily from 8 a.m. to midnight, except Christmas Day. A new elevator for the handicapped is in service.

John F. Kennedy Center

John F. Kennedy Center for the Performing Arts, designated by Congress as the National Cultural Center and the official memorial in Washington to President Kennedy, opened September 8, 1971. Tours are available daily, free of charge, between 10:00 a.m. and 1:15 p.m.

Mount Vernon

Mount Vernon on the south bank of the Potomac, 16 miles below Washington, D. C., is part of a large tract of land in northern Virginia which was originally included in a royal grant made to Lord Culpepper, who in 1674 granted 5,000 acres to Nicholas Spencer and John Washington.

The present house is an enlargement of one apparently built on the site of an earlier one by John's grandson, Augustine Washington, who lived there 1735-1738. His son Lawrence came there in 1743, when he renamed the plantation Mount Vernon in honor of Admiral Vernon under whom he had served in the West Indies. Lawrence Washington died in 1752 and was succeeded as proprietor of Mount Vernon by his half-brother, George Washington.

National Arboretum

The **National Arboretum**, one of Washington's great showplaces, occupies 444 acres in the northeastern section of the city. The National Herb Garden and National Bonsai Collection are special attractions in the nation's only federally-supported gardens.

The Arboretum is open every day of the year except Christmas.

National Archives

The Declaration of Independence, the Constitution of the United States, and the Bill of Rights are on permanent display in the National Archives Exhibition Hall. They are sealed in glass-and-bronze cases. The National Archives also holds the permanently valuable federal records of the United States government.

National Gallery of Art

The **National Gallery of Art**, situated in an area bounded by Constitution Avenue and the Mall, between Third and Seventh Streets, was established by Joint Resolution of Congress Mar. 24, 1937, and opened Mar. 17, 1941.

Open daily except Christmas and New Year's, from 10 a.m. to 5 p.m. Monday through Saturday and noon to 9 p.m. Sunday. Summer, 10 a.m. to 9 p.m., noon to 9 p.m. on Sunday.

The Pentagon

The **Pentagon**, headquarters of the Department of Defense, is the world's largest office building, with 3 times the floor space of the Empire State Building in New York. Situated in Arlington, Va., it houses more than 23,000 employees in offices that occupy 3,707,745 square feet.

Tours are available Monday through Friday (excluding federal holidays), from 9 a.m. to 3:30 p.m.

Smithsonian Institution

The **Smithsonian Institution** is one of the world's great historical, scientific, educational, and cultural establishments. It comprises numerous facilities, mostly in Wash., D.C.

Washington Monument

The **Washington Monument** is a tapering shaft or obelisk of white marble, 555 ft. 5-⅛ inches in height and 55 ft., 1-½ inches square at base. Eight small windows, 2 on each side, are located at the 500-ft. level, where Washington points of interest are indicated.

The Monument is open 7 days a week, 9 a.m. to 5 p.m., 8 a.m. to 12 midnight in the summer. It is closed Christmas Day.

The White House

The **White House**, the president's residence, stands on 18 acres on the south side of Pennsylvania Avenue, between the Treasury and the Executive Office Building.

The walls are of sandstone, quarried at Aquia Creek, Va. The exterior walls were painted, causing the building to be termed the "White House." On Aug. 24, 1814, during Madison's administration, the house was burned by the British. James Hoban rebuilt it by Oct. 1817, for President Monroe to move in.

The White House is open from 10 a.m. to 12 noon, Tuesday through Friday, except on Thanksgiving, Christmas, and New Year. Also Saturdays, 10 a.m. to 2 p.m. Jun. 1 through Labor Day, and 10 a.m. to noon Labor Day through May 31. Only the public rooms on the ground floor and state floor may be visited.

Notable Tall Buildings in North American Cities

Height from sidewalk to roof, including penthouse and tower if enclosed as integral part of structure; actual number of stories beginning at street level. Asterisks (*) denote buildings still under construction Jan. 1985.

City	Hgt. ft.	Stories
Akron, Oh.		
First National Tower	330	28
Ohio Edison Bldg.	321	24
Albany, N.Y.		
Erastus Corning II Tower	589	44
State Office Building	388	34
Agency (4 bldgs.), So. Mall	310	23
Atlanta, Ga.		
Western Peachtree Plaza	723	71
Georgia Pacific Tower	697	51
Southern Bell Telephone	677	47
First National Bank, 2 Peachtree	556	44
*Marriott Marquis	554	52
Equitable Building, 100 Peachtree	453	34
101 Marietta Tower, 101 Marietta St.	446	36
Peachtree Summit No. 1	406	31
North Avenue Tower, 310 North Ave.	403	26
Tower Place, 3361 Piedmont Road	401	29
National Bank of Georgia	390	32
Richard B. Russell, Federal Bldg.	383	26
Atlanta Hilton Hotel	383	32
Peachtree Center Harris Bldg.	382	31
AT&T Long Line Bldg.	380	...
*Marquis One	378	30
Trust Company Bank	377	28
Coastal States Insurance	377	27
Peachtree Center Cain Building	376	30
Peachtree Center Building	374	31
Life of Georgia Tower	371	29
Georgia Power Tower, 333 Piedmont	349	24
Peachtree Center South	332	27
Gas Light Tower, 235 Peachtree	331	27
Hyatt Regency Hotel, 265 Peachtree	330	23
100 Colony Square, 1175 Peachtree	328	25
Austin, Tex.		
Austin National Bank	328	26
American Bank	313	21
State Capitol	309	...
Univ. of Texas Admin. Bldg.	307	29
Baltimore, Md.		
U.S. Fidelity & Guaranty Co.	529	40
Maryland National Bank Bldg.	509	34
World Trade Center Bldg.	405	32
Saint-Paul Apartments Bldg.	385	37
Arlington Federal S & L Bldg.	370	28
Blaustein Bldg.	370	30
Charles Plaza Apts. So.	350	31
Charles Center South	330	26
Tower Bldg.	330	16
Baltinore Arts Tower	319	15
First National Bank of Maryland	315	22
Lord Baltimore Hotel	315	24
Mercantile-Safe Deposit and Trust Co.	315	21
Charles Plaza Apts. No.	315	28
Baton Rouge, La.		
State Capitol	460	34
American Bank Bldg.	315	24
Birmingham, Ala.		
First Natl. Southern Natural Bldg.	390	30
South Central Bell Hdqts. Bldg.	390	30
City Federal Bldg.	325	27
Boston, Mass.		
John Hancock Tower	790	60
Prudential Tower	750	52
Boston Co. Bldg., Court St.	605	41
Federal Reserve Bldg.	604	32
First National Bank of Boston	591	37
One Financial Center	590	46
Shawmut Bank Bldg.	520	38
Exchange Place, 53 State St.	510	39
Sixty State St.	509	38
One Post Office Sq.	507	40
One Beacon St.	507	40
New England Merch. Bank Bldg.	500	40
U.S. Custom House	496	32
John Hancock Bldg.	495	26
State St. Bank Bldg.	477	34
One Hundred Summer St.	450	33
McCormack Bldg.	401	22

City	Hgt. ft.	Stories
Keystone Custodian Funds	400	32
Saltonstall Office Bldg.	396	22
Devonshire, 250 Wash. St.	396	40
Harbor Towers (2 bldgs.)	396	40
Westin Hotel, Copley Place	395	36
John F. Kennedy Bldg.	387	24
Marriott Hotel, Copley Place	383	39
Longfellow Towers (2 bldgs.)	380	38
Federal Bldg. & Post Office	345	22
Suffolk County Courthouse	330	19
Jamaicaway Towers	320	30
Sheraton-Boston Hotel	310	29
Buffalo, N.Y.		
Marine Midland Center	529	40
City Hall	378	32
Rand Bldg., not incl. 40-ft. beacon	351	29
Main Place Tower	350	26
One M&T Plaza	317	21
Liberty Bank	305	23
Calgary, Alta.		
Petro-Canada Tower #2	689	52
Calgary Tower	626	...
First Canadian Centre	547	44
Scotia Centre	504	38
Nova Bldg., 801 7th Ave. SW	500	37
Petro-Canada Tower #1	469	33
Two Bow Valley Square	468	39
Fifth & Fifth Bldg.	460	35
Oxford Square North	463	34
Shell Tower	460	34
Oxford Square South	449	33
Four Bow Valley Square	441	37
Esso Plaza (twin towers)	435	34
Cascade 300	432	31
T.D. Square	421	33
Family Life Bldg.	410	33
Pan Canadian Bldg., 150 9th Ave. SW	410	28
Norcen Tower	408	33
Sun Oil Bldg.	397	34
Western Centre	385	40
Three Bow Valley Square	382	33
Sun Life Bldg. (twin towers)	374	28
Mobil Tower	369	29
A.G.T. Tower, 411 1st St. SE.	366	28
Amgoy Bldg.	358	31
One Palliser Square	350	28
Royal Bank Bldg.	345	30
Mount Royal House	330	34
Standard Life Bldg.	327	25
Place Concorde (twin towers)	321	36
Bow Valley Inn	320	25
Charlotte, N.C.		
NCNB Plaza	503	40
First Union Plaza	433	32
Wachovia Center	420	32
Charlotte Plaza	388	27
Southern National Center	300	22
Chicago, Ill.		
Sears Tower (world's tallest)	1,454	110
Standard Oil (Indiana)	1,136	80
John Hancock Center	1,127	100
Water Tower Place (a)	859	74
First Natl. Bank	850	60
Three First National Plaza	775	57
One Magnificent Mile	770	58
Olympia Centre	727	63
Huron Apts.	723	56
IBM Bldg.	695	52
Neiman-Marcus Tower	690	65
Daley Center	662	31
Lake Point Tower	645	70
Board of Trade, incl. 81 ft. statue	605	44
Prudential Bldg., 130 E. Randolph	601	41
Antenna tower, 311 ft., makes total	912	
1000 Lake Shore Plaza Apts.	590	55
Marina City Apts., 2 buildings	588	61
Mid Continental Plaza, 55 E. Monroe	580	50
Pittsfield, 55 E. Washington St.	557	38
Kemper Insurance Bldg.	555	45
Newberry Plaza, State & Oak	553	56
One South Wacker Dr.	550	40

City	Hgt. ft.	Stories
Harbor Point	550	54
LaSalle Natl. Bank, 135 S. LaSalle St.	535	44
One LaSalle Street	530	49
111 E. Chestnut St.	529	56
River Plaza, Rush & Hubbard	524	56
Pure Oil, 35 E. Wacker Drive	523	40
United Ins. Bldg., 1 E. Wacker Dr.	522	41
Lincoln Tower, 75 E. Wacker Dr.	519	42
Carbide & Carbon, 230 N. Mich.	503	37
Walton Colonnade	500	44
LaSalle-Wacker, 221 N. LaSalle St.	491	41
Amer. Nat'l. Bank, 33 N. LaSalle St.	479	40
Bankers, 105 W. Adams St.	476	41
Brunswick Bldg.	475	37
Continental Companies	475	45
American Furniture Mart	474	24
333 Wacker Dr.	472	36
Sheraton Hotel, 505 N. Mich. Ave.	471	42
Playboy Bldg., 919 N. Mich. Ave.	468	37
188 Randolph Tower	465	45
Tribune Tower, 435 N. Mich. Ave.	462	36
Chicago Marriott, Mich. & Ohio Sts.	460	45
(a) World's tallest reinforced concrete bldg.		

Cincinnati, Oh.

City	Hgt. ft.	Stories
Carew Tower	568	49
Central Trust Tower	504	33
Dubois Tower, 5th & Walnut	423	32
Netherland Plaza	372	31
Central Trust Center	355	27
First Natl. Bank Center	351	26
Clarion North Tower	350	33
Kroger Bldg.	320	25
Federated Bldg.	317	21

Cleveland, Oh.

City	Hgt. ft.	Stories
Terminal Tower	708	52
Sohio Tower	650	46
Erieview Plaza Tower	529	40
One Cleveland Center	450	31
Justice Center, 1250 Ontario	420	26
Federal Bldg.	419	32
National City Complex	410	35
Cleveland Trust Tower No. 1	383	29
Eaton Center	360	28
Ohio-Bell Hqs.	360	22
Cleveland State Univ. Tower	319	21
Central Natl. Bank Bldg.	305	21

Columbus, Oh.

City	Hgt. ft.	Stories
James A. Rhodes (State Office Tower)	624	41
LeVeque Tower, 50 W. Broad	555	47
One Nationwide Plaza	485	40
Borden Bldg., 180 E. Broad	438	34
Columbus Center, 100 E. Broad	357	24
Ohio Bell Bldg., 150 E. Gay St.	346	26
88 E. Broad St.	324	20
BancOhio Plaza, 155 E. Broad	317	25

Dallas, Tex.

City	Hgt. ft.	Stories
Main Centre, 901 Main St.	939	73
First International Bldg.	710	56
LTV Center	686	50
Arco Tower, 1601 Bryan St.	660	49
Thanksgiving Tower, 1600 Pacific Ave.	645	50
Two Dallas Centre	635	50
First National Bank	625	52
Republic Bank Tower	598	50
First City Center, 1700 Pacific Ave.	595	49
SW Bell Admin. Tower	580	37
One Lincoln Plaza	579	45
Olympia York, 1999 Bryan St.	562	37
Reunion Tower	560	50
Southland Life Tower	550	42
Diamond Shamrock, 717 N. Harwood St.	550	34
2001 Bryan St.	512	40
San Jacinto Tower	456	33
Republic Bank Bldg., not incl. 150-ft. ornamental tower	452	36
Wyndham Hotel	451	29
One Main Place	445	34
LTV Tower	434	31
Mercantile Natl. Bank Bldg., not incl. 115-ft. weather beacon	430	31
Mobil Bldg.	430	31
Mart Hotel	400	29

City	Hgt. ft.	Stories
Fidelity Union Tower	400	33
One Dallas Centre	386	30
Southwestern Bell Toll Bldg.	372	22
Court House & Fedl. Office Bldg.	362	16
Mercantile Dallas Bldg.	360	22
Sheraton Hotel	352	38
Plaza of The America's (E. Tower)	344	26
Hyatt Hotel, 303 Reunion Blvd.	343	30
Elm Place, 1005-09 Elm St.	341	22
Main Tower	336	26
Dallas Galleria Tower	333	26
Plaza of the America's (N. & S. Tower)	332	25

Dayton, Oh.

City	Hgt. ft.	Stories
Kettering Tower	405	30
Mead Tower, 10 W. 2d St.	365	28
Centre City Office Bldg.	297	21
Hulman Bldg.	295	23
Miami Valley Tower	290	22

Denver, Col.

City	Hgt. ft.	Stories
Republic Plaza	714	56
City Center Four	706	54
United Bank of Denver	697	52
*1999 Broadway	544	43
Arco Tower	527	41
Anaconda Tower	507	40
One Denver Place	467	35
Amoco Bldg., 17th Ave. & Broadway	450	36
17th Street Plaza	438	34
Brooks Towers, 1020 15th St.	420	42
First of Denver Plaza	415	32
Stellar Plaza	410	32
*Tabor Center, #1	405	32
Energy Center 1	404	29
Colorado Nat'l. Bank, 17th & Curtis	389	26
First National Bank	385	28
Security Life Bldg.	384	33
Centennial Plaza	374	31
Dominion Plaza	368	30
Lincoln Center	366	30
Denver Natl. Bank Plaza	363	29
Western Fed. Savings	357	27
Colorado State Bank	352	26
Executive Tower	350	30
Larimer Place	335	32
410 Building	335	24
Mountain Bell, 17th & Curtis	330	21
D&F Tower	330	20
Great West Plaza (twin towers)	325	29
Prudential Tower Plaza	322	25

Des Moines, Ia.

City	Hgt. ft.	Stories
Ruan Center	457	36
Financial Center, 7th & Walnut	345	25
Marriott Hotel, 700 Grand Ave.	340	33
Equitable Bldg.	318	19

Detroit, Mich.

City	Hgt. ft.	Stories
Detroit Plaza Hotel	720	71
Penobscot Bldg.	557	47
15000 Town Center Dr.	554	40
Guardian	485	40
Renaissance Center (4 bldgs.)	479	39
Book Tower	472	35
Prudential Town Center	448	32
13000 Town Center Dr.	443	32
Cadillac Tower	437	40
David Stott	436	38
Mich. Cons. Gas Co. Bldg.	430	32
Fisher	420	28
J. L. Hudson Bldg.	397	28
McNamara Federal Office Bldg.	393	27
Detroit Bank & Trust Bldg., 6438 Woodward	374	27
American Center	374	27
Top of Troy Bldg.	374	27
Detroit Bank & Trust Bldg., 211 N. Fort	370	28
Edison Plaza	365	25
Woodward Tower at the Park	358	34
Amer. Center Bldg. #2	350	25
Buhl, 535 Griswold	350	26
Ford Bldg.	346	25
Michigan Bell Telephone	340	19
1st Federal of Michigan	338	23
Pontchartrain Motor Hotel	336	23
Troy Center Tower	332	24
1st Natl. Bldg.	330	25

City	Hgt. ft.	Stories
Commonwealth Bldg.	325	25
1300 Lafayette East.	325	30

Edmonton, Alta.

Manulife Place, 10170-101 St.	479	39
Royal Trust Tower.	476	30
AGT Tower, 10020-100 St.	441	34
CCB Tower, 10124-103 Ave.	410	34
Principal Plaza, 10303 Jasper Ave.	370	30
Scotia Place, 10060 Jasper Ave.	366	30
CN Tower, 1004-104 Ave.	365	26
Phipps McKinnon	359	21
Toronto Dominion Tower	325	27
Oxford Tower	325	29
Sun Life Bldg.	320	25

Fort Wayne, Ind.

One Summit Square, 911 S. Calhoun.	442	27
Ft. Wayne Natl. Bank	339	26
Lincoln Bank Tower	312	23

Fort Worth, Tex.

Center Tower II	546	38
1st United Tower	536	40
Continental Plaza	525	40
1st City Bank Tower.	475	33
Texas American Bank.	454	37
Continental Natl. Bank Bldg.	380	30
Continental Life	307	24
First National Bank, 500 W. 7th	300	21
One Tandy Center	300	20
Two Tandy Center.	300	20

Hamilton, Ont.

Century Twenty One	418	43
Stelco Tower.	339	25
The Olympia	321	33

Harrisburg, Pa.

State Office Tower #2	334	21
333 Market St. (incl. tower).	327	19

Hartford, Conn.

City Place	535	38
Travelers Ins. Co. Bldg.	527	34
Hartford Plaza	420	22
Hartford Natl. Bank & Trust	360	26
One Commercial Plaza	349	27
One Financial Plaza, 755 Main.	335	26

Honolulu, Ha.

Ala Moana Hotel.	390	38
Pacific Trade Center	360	30
Ala Nanala Apt.	350	41
Honolulu Tower	350	40
Lakeside Development	350	40
Discovery Bay	350	42
Hyatt Regency Waikiki	350	39
Hemmeter Center	350	39
Mehelani Waikiki Lodge.	350	43
Regency Tower, 2525 Date St.	350	42
Regency Tower #2.	350	43
Yacht Harbor Towers	350	40
Canterbury Place	350	40
Iolani Towers.	350	38
Diamond Head Tower.	350	38
Ala Wai Sunset	350	44
Century Center	350	41
Pacific Beach Hotel	350	43
Waikiki Ala Wai Waterfront	350	43
Waikiki Lodge II	350	43

Houston, Tex.

Texas Commerce Tower	1,002	75
Allied Bank Plaza, 1000 Louisiana.	985	71
Transco Tower.	899	64
RepublicBank Center	780	56
Interfirst Plaza	744	55
1600 Smith St.	729	54
Gulf Tower, 1301 McKinney	725	52
One Shell Plaza		
(not incl. 285 ft. TV tower)	714	50
Four Allen Center	692	50
Capital Natl. Bank Plaza	685	50
One Houston Center	678	47
First City Tower	662	47
1100 Milam Bldg.	651	47
*San Felipe Plaza	620	45

City	Hgt. ft.	Stories
Exxon Bldg.	606	44
The America Tower	577	42
Marathon Oil Tower	572	41
Two Houston Center	570	40
Dresser Tower.	550	40
1415 Louisiana Tower.	550	44
Pennzoil, 700 Milam (2 bldgs.).	523	36
Two Allen Center	521	36
Entex Bldg.	518	35
Huntington	506	34
Tenneco Bldg.	502	33
Conoco Tower.	465	32
One Allen Center	452	34
Summit Tower West	441	31
Coastal Tower.	441	31
Four Leafs Towers (2 bldgs.).	439	40
*Phoenix Tower.	434	34
Gulf Bldg.	428	37
The Spires	426	41
Central Tower (4 Oaks Place)	420	30
First City Natl. Bank.	410	32
Houston Lighting & Power	410	27
Neils Esperson Bldg.	409	31
Hyatt Regency Houston	401	34

Hull, Que.

Les Terrasses De La Chaudiere.	383	30
Place Du Portage, Phase 1.	333	24

Indianapolis, Ind.

American United Life Ins. Co.	533	38
Indiana Natl. Bank Tower.	504	37
City-County Bldg.	377	26
Merchants Plaza/Hyatt Regency Hotel.	328	26
Indiana Bell Telephone	320	20
Blue Cross-Blue Shield Bldg.	302	18

Jacksonville, Fla.

Independent Life & Accident Ins. Co.	535	37
Gulf Life Ins. Co. Bldg.	432	28
Prudential Ins. Co. of America	295	22

Kansas City, Mo.

Kansas City Power and Light Bldg.	476	32
City Hall	443	29
Federal Office Bldg.	413	35
Commerce Tower.	402	32
Southwest Bell Telephone Bldg.	394	27
Pershing Road Associates	352	28
A. T. & T. Long Line Bldg.	331	20
Bryant Bldg.	319	26
Federal Reserve Bldg.	311	21
City Center Square, 1100 Main	302	30
Holiday Inn	300	28

Las Vegas, Nev.

Sundance Hotel	400	33
Landmark Hotel	356	31
Las Vegas Hilton	345	30

Little Rock, Ark.

First National Bank	454	30
Worthen Bank & Trust	375	23
Tower Bldg.	350	18
Union National Bank.	331	21

Los Angeles, Cal.

First Interstate Bank.	858	62
Crocker Center, North	750	53
Security Pacific Natl. Bank.	735	55
Atlantic Richfield Plaza (2 bldgs.)	699	52
Wells Fargo Bank	625	48
Crocker-Citizen Plaza.	620	42
Century Plaza Towers (2 bldgs.).	571	44
Union Bank Square	516	41
City Hall	454	28
Equitable Life Bldg.	454	34
Transamerica Center	452	32
Mutual Benefit Life Ins. Bldg.	435	31
Broadway Plaza	414	33
1900 Ave. of Stars	398	27
1 Wilshire Bldg.	395	28
The Evian, 10490 Wilshire Blvd.	390	31
Bonaventure Hotel, 404 S. Figueroa	367	35
Beaudry Center	365	26
400 S. Hope St.	375	26
Cal. Fed. Savings & Loan Bldg.	363	28
Century City Office Bldg.	363	26
Bunker Hill Towers	349	32
International Industries Plaza.	347	24

City	Hgt. ft.	Stories
Louisville, Ky.		
First Natl. Bank	512	40
Citizen's Plaza	420	30
Meindinger Tower	338	26
Brown & Williamson Tower	338	26
Galt House	325	25
United Kentucky Bldg.	312	24
Memphis, Tenn.		
100 N. Main Bldg.	430	37
Commerce Square	396	31
Sterick Bldg.	365	31
Clark, 5100 Poplar	365	32
First Natl. Bank Bldg.	332	25
Hyatt Regency	329	28
Miami, Fla.		
One Biscayne Corp.	456	40
First Federal Savings & Loan	375	32
Dade County Court House	357	28
New World Center	340	30
Plaza Venetia	332	33
Flagler Center Bldg.	318	25
Milwaukee, Wis.		
First Wis. Center & Office Tower	625	42
City Hall	350	9
Wisconsin Telephone Co.	313	19
Minneapolis, Minn.		
IDS Center	775	57
Multifoods Tower	715	52
*Piper Tower	579	44
Pillsbury Bldg., 200 S. 6th St.	552	40
Foshay Tower, not including 163-ft.		
antenna tower	447	32
Amfac Hotel	440	32
North Western Bell Telephone	416	26
Hennepin County Government Center	403	24
First Natl. Bank Bldg.	366	28
Municipal Building	355	14
100 Washington Square	340	22
Cedar-Riverside	337	39
Dain Tower	311	26
Montreal, Que.		
Place Victoria	624	47
Place Ville Marie	616	42
Canadian Imperial Bank		
of Commerce	604	43
Le Complexe Desjardins		
La Tour du Sud	498	40
La Tour du L'Est.	428	32
La Tour du Nord	355	27
La Tour Laurier	425	36
C.I.L. House	429	32
Chateau Champlain Hotel	420	38
Port Royal Apts.	400	33
Royal Bank Tower	397	22
Sun Life Bldg.	390	26
Banque Canadienne National	390	32
Place du Canada	372	33
Hydro Quebec	360	27
Alexis Nihon Plaza	331	33
Nashville, Tenn.		
Natl. Life & Acc. Ins. Co.	452	31
Nashville Life & Casualty Tower	409	30
James K. Polk State Office Bldg.	392	32
First American N.A. Bank	354	28
Hyatt Regency	300	28
Newark, N.J.		
Midlantic Natl. Bank	465	36
Raymond-Commerce	448	36
Park Plaza Bldg.	400	26
Prudential Plaza	370	24
Public Service Elec. & Gas	360	26
Prudential Ins. Co., 753 Broad St.	360	26
Western Electric Bldg.	359	31
Gateway 1	355	30
American Insurance Company	326	21
New Orleans, La.		
One Shell Square	697	51
Plaza Tower	531	45
Marriott Hotel	450	42
Canal Place One	439	32
Bank of New Orleans	438	31
Int'l. Trade Mart Bldg.	407	33

City	Hgt. ft.	Stories
225 Baronne St.	362	28
Hyatt-Regency Hotel, Poydras Plaza	360	25
Hibernia Bank Bldg.	355	23
1250 Poydras Plaza	341	24
New Orleans Hilton, Intl. River Center	340	29
American Bank Bldg.	330	23
Pan American Life Bldg.	323	27
New York, N.Y.		
World Trade Center (2 towers)	1,350	110
Empire State, 34th St. & 5th Ave.	1,250	102
TV tower, 222 ft., makes total	1,472	...
Chrysler, Lexington Ave. & 43d St.	1,046	77
American International Bldg., 70 Pine St.	950	67
40 Wall Tower	927	71
Citicorp Center	914	46
RCA Bldg., Rockefeller Center	850	70
1 Chase Manhattan Plaza	813	60
Pan Am Bldg., 200 Park Ave.	808	59
Woolworth, 233 Broadway	792	60
1 Penn Plaza	764	57
Exxon, 1251 Ave. of Americas	750	54
1 Liberty Plaza	743	50
Citibank	741	57
One Astor Plaza	730	54
Union Carbide Bldg., 270 Park Ave.	707	52
General Motors Bldg.	705	50
Metropolitan Life, 1 Madison Ave.	700	50
500 5th Ave.	697	60
9 W. 57th St.	688	50
Chem. Bank, N.Y. Trust Bldg.	687	50
55 Water St.	687	53
Chanin, Lexington Ave. & 42d St.	680	56
Gulf & Western Bldg.	679	44
Marine Midland Bldg., 140 Bway.	677	52
McGraw Hill, 1221 Ave. of Am.	674	51
Lincoln, 60 E. 42d Street	673	53
1633 Broadway	670	48
Trump Tower, 725 5th Ave.	664	68
Museum Tower Apts.	650	58
American Brands, 245 Park Ave.	648	47
A. T. & T. Tower, 570 Madison Ave.	648	37
General Electric, 570 Lexington	640	50
Irving Trust, 1 Wall St.	640	50
345 Park Ave.	634	44
Grace Plaza, 1114 Ave. of Am.	630	50
1 New York Plaza	630	50
Home Insurance Co. Bldg.	630	44
N.Y. Telephone, 1095 Ave. of Am.	630	40
888 7th Ave.	628	42
1 Hammarskjold Plaza	628	50
Waldorf-Astoria, 301 Park Ave.	625	47
Burlington House, 1345 Ave. of Am.	625	50
Olympic Tower, 645 5th Ave.	620	51
10 E. 40th St.	620	48
101 Park Ave.	618	50
New York Life, 51 Madison Ave.	615	40
Penney Bldg., 1301 Ave. of Am.	609	46
IBM, 590 Madison Ave.	603	41
780 3rd Ave.	600	50
560 Lexington Ave.	600	22
Celanese Bldg., 1211 Ave. of Am.	592	45
U.S. Court House, 505 Pearl St.	590	37
Federal Bldg., Foley Square	587	41
Time & Life, 1271 Ave. of Am.	587	47
Cooper Bregstein Bldg., 1250 Bway.	580	40
1185 Ave. of Americas	580	42
Municipal, Park Row & Centre St.	580	34
1 Madison Square Plaza	576	42
Westvaco Bldg. 299 Park Ave.	574	42
Socony Mobil Bldg., East 42d St.	572	45
Sperry Rand Bldg., 1290 Ave. of Am.	570	43
600 3d Ave.	570	42
Helmsley Bldg., 230 Park Ave.	565	35
1 Bankers Trust Plaza	565	40
Palace Hotel, Madison & 51st St.	563	51
30 Broad St.	562	48
Sherry-Netherland, 5th Ave. & 59th St.	560	40
Continental Can, 633 3d Ave.	557	39
Sperry & Hutchinson, 330 Madison	555	39
Galleria, 117 E. 57th St.	552	57
Interchem Bldg., 1133 Ave. of Am.	552	45
151 E. 44th St.	550	44
N.Y. Telephone, 323 Bway.	550	45
919 3d Ave.	550	47
Burroughs Bldg., 605 3d Ave.	550	44
Bankers Trust, 33 E. 48 St.	547	41
Transportation Bldg., 225 Bway.	546	45
Equitable, 120 Broadway	545	42

City	Hgt. ft.	Stories
1 Brooklyn Bridge Plaza	540	42
Equitable Life, 1285 Ave. of Am.	540	42
Ritz Tower, Park Ave. & 57th St.	540	41
Bankers Trust, 6 Wall St.	540	39
1166 Ave. of Americas	540	44
1700 Broadway	533	41
Downtown Athletic Club, 19 West St.	530	45
Nelson Towers, 7th Ave. & 34th St.	525	45
767 3d Ave.	525	39
Hotel Pierre, 5th Ave. & 61st St.	525	44
House of Seagram, 375 Park Ave.	525	38
7 World Trade Center.	525	44
Random House, 825 3d Ave.	522	40
3 Park Ave.	522	42
North American Plywood, 800 3d Ave.	520	41
Du Mont Bldg., 515 Madison Ave.	520	42
26 Broadway.	520	31
Newsweek Bldg., 444 Madison Ave.	518	43
Sterling Drug Bldg., 90 Park Ave.	515	41
First National City Bank.	515	41
Bank of New York, 48 Wall St.	513	32
Navarre, 512 7th Ave.	513	43
Williamsburgh Savings Bank, Bklyn.	512	42
ITT—American, 437 Madison Ave.	512	40
International, Rockefeller Center	512	41
1407 Broadway Realty Corp.	512	44
United Nations, 405 E. 42 St.	505	39

Oakland, Cal.

City	Hgt. ft.	Stories
Ordway Bldg., 2150 Valdez St.	404	28
Kaiser Bldg.	390	28
Raymond Kaiser Engineer Bldg.	336	25
Clorox Bldg.	330	24
Tribune Tower	305	21

Oklahoma City, Okla.

City	Hgt. ft.	Stories
Liberty Tower	500	36
First National Bank	493	33
City National Bank Tower.	440	32
First Oklahoma Tower	425	31
Kerr-McGee Center	393	30
Mid America Plaza	362	19
Penn Bank Tower	321	21
Fidelity Plaza.	310	15
Southwestern Bell Telephone	303	15

Omaha, Neb.

City	Hgt. ft.	Stories
Woodmen Tower	469	30
Northwestern Bell Telephone Hdqrs.	334	16
Masonic Manor	320	22

Ottawa, Ont.

City	Hgt. ft.	Stories
Place de Ville, Tower C.	368	29
R.H. Coats Bldg.	326	27
Place Bell Canada.	318	26
DBS Tower.	308	26
Holiday Inn	308	28
Parliament Bldgs., Peace Tower	303	

Philadelphia, Pa.

City	Hgt. ft.	Stories
City Hall Tower, incl. 37-ft.		
statue of Wm. Penn.	548	7
1818 Market St.	500	40
Provident Mutual Life	491	40
Fidelity Mutual Life Ins. Bldg.	490	38
Phila. Saving Fund Society	490	39
Central Penn Natl. Bank	490	36
Centre Square (2 towers)	490/416	38/32
Industrial Valley Bank Bldg.	482	32
Philadelphia National Bank.	475	25
Two Girard Plaza	450	30
2000 Market St. Bldg.	435	29
One Reading Center	417	32
Fidelity Bank Bldg.	405	30
Lewis Tower, 15th & Locust	400	33
1500 Locust St.	390	44
Academy House, 1420 Locust St.	390	37
Philadelphia Electric Co.	384	27
INA Annex, 1600 Arch St.	383	27
Penn Mutual Life.	375	20
The Drake, 15th & Spruce	375	33
Medical Tower, 255 So. 17th.	364	33
State Bldg., 1400 Spring Garden	351	18
One Logan Square	350	30
United Engineers, 17th & Ludlow	344	20
Land Title, Broad & Chestnut	344	22
Packard, 15th & Chestnut	340	25
Inquirer Building	340	18

Phoenix, Ariz.

City	Hgt. ft.	Stories
Valley National Bank	483	40
Arizona Bank Downtown	407	31
First Interstate Bank Plaza	372	27
United Bank Plaza.	356	28
First Federal Savings Bldg.	341	26
Hyatt Regency.	317	20

Pittsburgh, Pa.

City	Hgt. ft.	Stories
U.S. Steel Bldg.	841	64
One Mellon Bank Center	725	54
One PPG Place	635	40
One Oxford Centre	615	46
Gulf, 7th Ave. and Grant St.	582	44
University of Pittsburgh	535	42
Mellon Bank Bldg.	520	41
1 Oliver Plaza	511	39
Grant, Grant St. at 3rd Ave.	485	40
Koppers, 7th Ave. and Grant	475	34
Equibank Bldg.	445	34
Pittsburgh National Bldg.	424	30
Alcoa Bldg., 425 Sixth Ave.	410	30
Liberty Tower	358	29
Westinghouse Bldg.	355	23
Oliver, 535 Smithfield St.	347	25
Gateway Bldg. No. 3	344	24
Centre City Tower.	341	26
Federal Bldg., 1000 Liberty Ave.	340	23
Bell Telephone, 416 7th Ave.	339	21
Hilton Hotel.	333	22
Frick, 437 Grant St.	330	20

Portland, Ore.

City	Hgt. ft.	Stories
First Natl. Bank of Oregon	546	41
U.S. Bancorp Tower.	536	39
Georgia Pacific Bldg.	367	27

Providence, R.I.

City	Hgt. ft.	Stories
Industrial National Bank.	420	26
Rhode Island Hospital Trust Tower	410	30
40 Westminster Bldg.	301	24

Richmond, Va.

City	Hgt. ft.	Stories
James Monroe Bldg.	450	29
City Hall (incl. penthouse)	425	17
United Virginia Bank Bldg.	400	24
Federal Reserve Bank	393	26
First & Merchants Natl. Bank.	333	25
One James River Plaza.	305	22

Rochester, N.Y.

City	Hgt. ft.	Stories
Xerox Tower.	443	30
Lincoln First Tower	390	26
Eastman Kodak Bldg.	360	19
First Federal Bank Plaza	305	22

St. Louis, Mo.

City	Hgt. ft.	Stories
Gateway Arch	630	
S.W. Bell Telephone Bldg.	560	44
Mercantile Trust Bldg.	550	37
Centerre Bldg.	433	31
Laclede Gas. Bldg., 8th & Olive	400	30
S.W. Bell Telephone Bldg.	398	31
Civil Courts.	387	13
Queeny Tower.	321	24
Counsel House Plaza	320	30
Park Plaza Hotel.	310	30
Pierre Laclede Tower.	308	23

St. Paul, Minn.

City	Hgt. ft.	Stories
First Natl. Bank Bldg., incl.		
100-ft. sign.	517	32
Osborn Bldg., 320 Wabasha	368	20
Kellogg Square Apts.	366	32
Northwestern Bell Telephone (2 bldgs.)	340	16
American National Bank Bldg.	335	25
North Central Tower, 445 Minn.	328	27
Amhoist/Park Tower	324	26
Minn. Mutual Life Center	315	21
St. Paul Cathedral.	307	
Conwed Tower	305	25

Salt Lake City, Ut.

City	Hgt. ft.	Stories
L.D.S. Church Office Bldg.	420	30
Beneficial Life Tower	351	21
Amer. Towers (2 bldgs.)	324	27

San Antonio, Tex.

City	Hgt. ft.	Stories
Tower of the Americas	622	
Tower Life	404	30
Nix Professional Bldg.	375	23

	Ft.	Stories
Natl. Bank of Commerce	310	24
First Natl. Bank Tower	302	20
Frost Bank Tower	300	21

San Diego, Cal.

	Ft.	Stories
California First Bank	388	27
Columbia Centre	379	27
Imperial Bank	355	24
Wells Fargo Bldg.	348	20
Wickes Bldg.	340	25
Financial Square	339	24
Central Federal	320	22
Union Bank	320	22

San Francisco, Cal.

	Ft.	Stories
Transamerica Pyramid	853	48
Bank of America	778	52
101 California St.	600	48
5 Fremont Center	600	43
Embarcadero Center, No. 4	570	45
Security Pacific Bank	569	45
One Market Plaza, Spear St.	565	43
Wells Fargo Bldg.	561	43
Standard Oil, 575 Market St.	551	39
One Sansome-Citicorp	550	39
Shaklee Bldg., 444 Market	537	38
Aetna Life	529	38
First & Market Bldg.	529	38
Metropolitan Life	524	38
Crocker National Bank	500	38
Hilton Hotel	493	46
Pacific Gas & Electric	492	34
Union Bank	487	37
Pacific Insurance	476	34
Bechtel Bldg., Fremont St.	475	33
333 Market Bldg.	474	33
Hartford Bldg.	465	33
Mutual Benefit Life	438	32
Russ Bldg.	435	31
Pacific Telephone Bldg.	435	26
Pacific Gateway	416	30
Embarcadero Center, No. 3	412	31
Embarcadero Center, No. 2	412	31
595 Market Bldg.	410	31
101 Montgomery St.	405	28
Cal. State Automobile Assn.	399	29
Alcoa Bldg.	398	27
St. Francis Hotel	395	32
Shell Bldg.	386	29
Del Monte	378	28
Pacific 3-Apparel Mart	376	30
Meridien Hotel	374	34
Union Square Hyatt House Hotel	355	35

Seattle, Wash.

	Ft.	Stories
Columbia Center	954	76
Seattle-1st Natl. Bank Bldg.	609	50
Space Needle	605	...
First Interstate Center	574	48
Seafirst 5th Ave. Plaza	543	42
Bank of Cal., 900 4th Ave.	536	42
Rainer Bank Tower, 4th & Univ.	514	42
Smith Tower	500	42
Federal Office Bldg.	487	37
Pacific Northwest Bell	466	33
One Union Square	456	38
1111 3d Ave. Bldg.	454	35
Washington Plaza Second Tower	448	44
Westin Bldg., 2001 6th Ave.	409	34
Washington Plaza	397	40
Financial Center	389	30
Daon Bldg., 840 Olive Way	381	19
Sheraton Seattle Hotel	371	34
Fourth & Blanchard Bldg.	360	24
Park Hilton Hotel	352	33
First Hill Plaza	344	33
Safeco Plaza	325	22

Tampa, Fla.

	Ft.	Stories
Tampa City Center	537	39
First Financial Tower	458	36

Toledo, Oh.

	Ft.	Stories
Owens-Illinois Corp. Headquarters	411	32
Owens-Corning Fiberglas Tower	400	30
Ohio Citizens Bank Bldg.	368	27
Toledo Govt. Center	327	22
City-County State Office Bldg.	300	22

Toronto, Ont.

	Ft.	Stories
CN Tower, World's tallest self-supporting structure	1,821	...
First Canadian Place	952	72
*Scotia Square	886	68
Bank of Nova Scotia	838	66
Commerce Court West	784	57
Toronto-Dominion Tower (TD Centre)	758	56
Royal Trust Tower (TD Centre)	600	46
Royal Bank Plaza—South Tower	589	41
Manulife Centre	545	53
*TD Centre	493	36
Two Bloor West	486	34
Exchange Tower	480	36
Commerce Court North	476	34
Simpson Tower	473	33
Cadillac-Fairview Bldg., 10 Queen St.	465	36
Palace Pier	452	46
Continental Bank Bldg.	450	35
Sheraton Centre	443	43
Hudson's Bay Centre	442	35
Leaside Towers (2 bldgs.)	423	44
Commercial Union Tower (TD Centre)	420	32
Maple Leaf Mills Tower	419	30
Plaza 2 Hotel	415	41
Sun Life Bldg., 150 King St.	410	28
Royal York Hotel	399	27
390 Bay St.	394	31
Royal Bank Plaza—North Tower	387	26
Eaton Tower	385	29
Maclean-Hunter Bldg.	380	30
Harborside Apts.	380	39
Harbour Castle Hilton, East	374	35
Travellers Tower	369	27
360 Sun Life, 200 King St.	360	24
York Centre	360	27
*Standard Life Bldg.	360	26
3 Massey Square	354	38
Harbour Castle Hilton, West	353	35
Mowat Block	349	24
Toronto Professional Tower	346	26
L'Apartel at Harbour Square	344	36
Sutton Place Hotel	340	32
Richmond-Adelaide Centre	340	27
50 Cordova Ave.	340	36

Tulsa, Okla.

	Ft.	Stories
Bank of Oklahoma Tower	667	52
City of Faith Clinic Tower	640	60
Mid-Continent Tower	530	36
1st National Tower	516	41
4th Natl. Bank of Tulsa	412	33
320 South Boston Bldg.	400	24
Cities Service Bldg.	388	28
Univ. Club Tower	377	32
Philtower	343	24

Vancouver, B.C.

	Ft.	Stories
Harbour Centre (incl. 100 ft. pylon)	581	32
Royal Bank Tower	468	37
Canada Trust Tower, 1055 Melville	454	35
Scotiabank Tower	451	36
Vancouver Centre	450	36
Park Place	450	35
Bentall IV	443	34
T-D Bank Tower	410	31
200 Granville Square	403	30
Bentall III, 595 Burrand	399	31
Sheraton-Landmark Hotel	394	41
Hyatt Regency Vancouver	357	36
Hotel Vancouver	352	22
Oceanic Plaza	342	26
Board of Trade Tower	342	26

Winnipeg, Man.

	Ft.	Stories
Richardson Bldg., 375 Main	406	32
Commodity Exchange Tower	393	32

Winston-Salem, N.C.

	Ft.	Stories
Wachovia Bldg.	410	30
Reynolds Bldg.	315	21

Other Notable Tall Buildings

Cape Canaveral, Fla., Vehicle Assembly Bldg., 40 (552); Allentown, Pa., Power & Light Bldg., 23 (320); Amarillo, Tex., American Natl. Bank, 33 (374); Bethlehem, Pa., Martin Tower, 21 (332); Charleston, W. Va., Kanawha Valley Bldg., 20 (384); Frankfort, Ky., Capital Plaza Office Tower, 28 (338); Galveston, Tex., American National Ins., 20 (358); Knoxville, Tenn., United American Bank, 30 (400); Lansing, Mich., Michigan Natl. Tower, 25 (300, not including antenna tower); Lexington, Ky., Kinkaid Tower, 22 (333); Lincoln, Neb., State Capitol (432); Mobile, Ala., First Natl. Bank, 33 (420); New Haven, Conn., Knights of Columbus Hqs. (319); Niagara Falls, Ont., Skylon, (520); Springfield, Mass., Valley Bank Tower, 29 (370); Tallahassee, Fla., State Capitol Tower, 22 (345).

Notable Bridges in North America

Source: State Highway Engineers: Canadian Civil Engineering — ASCE

Asterisk (*) designates railroad bridge. Span of a bridge is distance (in feet) between its supports.

Suspension

Year	Bridge	Location	Longest span
1964	Verrazano-Narrows	New York, N.Y.	4,260
1937	Golden Gate	San Fran. Bay, Cal.	4,200
1957	Mackinac	Sts. of Mackinac	3,800
1931	Geo. Washington	Hudson River	3,500
1950	Tacoma Narrows	Washington	2,800
1936	¹Transbay	San Fran. Bay, Cal.	2,310
1939	Bronx-Whitestone	East R., N.Y.C.	2,300
1970	Pierre Laporte	Quebec	2,190
1951	Del. Memorial	Wilmington, Del.	2,150
1968	Del. Mem. (new)	Wilmington, Del.	2,150
1957	Walt Whitman	Phila., Pa.	2,000
1929	Ambassador	Detroit-Canada	1,850
1961	Throgs Neck	Long Is. Sound	1,800
1926	Benjamin Franklin	Philadelphia	1,750
1924	Bear Mt., N.Y.	Hudson River	1,632
1952	²Wm. Preston Lane Mem.	Sandy Point, Md.	1,600
1903	Williamsburg	East R., N.Y.C.	1,600
1969	Newport	Narragansett Bay, R.I.	1,600
1883	Brooklyn	East R., N.Y.C.	1,595
1939	Lion's Gate	Burrard Inlet, B.C.	1,550
1930	Mid-Hudson, N.Y.	Poughkeepsie	1,500
1964	Vincent Thomas	Los Angeles Harbor	1,500
1909	Manhattan	East R., N.Y.C.	1,470
1936	Triboro	East R., N.Y.C.	1,380
1931	St. Johns	Portland, Ore.	1,207
1929	Mount Hope	Rhode Island	1,200
1960	Ogdensburg, N.Y.	St. Lawrence R.	1,150
1939	Deer Isle	Maine	1,080
1931	Maysville (Ky.)	Ohio River	1,060
1867	Cincinnati	Ohio River	1,057
1971	Dent.	Clearwater Co., Ida.	1,050
1900	Miampimi	Mexico	1,030
1849	Wheeling, W. Va.	Ohio River	1,010

Cantilever

Year	Bridge	Location	Longest span
1917	Quebec	Quebec	1,800
1974	Commodore Barry	Chester, Pa.	1,644
1958	New Orleans, La.	Mississippi R.	1,575
1936	Transbay	San Fran. Bay	1,400
1968	Baton Rouge, La.	Mississippi R.	1,235
1955	Tappan Zee	Hudson River	1,212
1930	Longview, Wash.	Columbia River	1,200
1909	Queensboro	East R., N.Y.C.	1,182
1927	Carquinez Strait	California	1,100
1958	Parallel Span	"	1,100
1930	Jacques Cartier	Montreal, P.Q.	1,097
1968	Isaiah D. Hart	Jacksonville, Fla.	1,088
1957	³Richmond	San Fran. Bay, Cal.	1,070
1929	Grace Memorial	Charleston, S.C.	1,050
1963	Newburgh-Beacon	Hudson, R., N.Y.	1,000
1975	Caruthersville, Mo.	Mississippi R.	920
1977	Saint Marys	Saint Marys, W. Va.	900
1969	Silver Memorial	Pt. Pleasant, W. Va.	900
1940	Natchez	Mississippi R.	875
1938	Blue Water	Pt. Huron, Mich.	871
1972	Vicksburg	Mississippi River	870
1954	Sunshine Skyway	St. Petersburg, Fla.	864
1972	N. Fork American R.	Auburn, Cal.	862
1940	*Baton Rouge	Mississippi R.	848
1899	*Cornwall	St. Lawrence R.	843
1940	Greenville	Mississippi R.	840
1961	Helena, Ark.	Mississippi R.	840
1963	Brent Spence	Covington, Ky.	831
1963	Cincinnati, Oh.	Ohio River	830
1963	Sunshine, Don'ville	Mississippi, La.	825
1930	*Vicksburg	Mississippi R.	825
1929	Louisville	Ohio River	820
1961	Campbellton-Cross Point	New Brunswick-Quebec	815
1950	Maurice J. Tobin	Boston, Mass.	800
1935	Rip Van Winkle	Catskill, N.Y.	800
1938	Cairo	Ohio River, Ill.-Ky.	800
1940	Ludlow Ferry	Potomac R.	800
1932	Washington Mem.	Seattle, Wash.	800
1936	McCullough	Coos Bay, Ore.	793
1935	⁴Huey P Long	New Orleans	790
1916	*Memphis (Harahan)	Mississippi R.	790
1892	*Memphis	Mississippi R.	790
1949	Memphis-Arkansas	Mississippi R.	790

Year	Bridge	Location	Longest span
1904	*Mingo Jct., W. Va.	Ohio River	769
1910	*Beaver, Pa.	Ohio River	767
1966	⁵S.N. Pearman	Charleston, S.C.	760
1940	Owensboro	Ohio River	750
1911	Sewickley, Pa.	Ohio River	750
1928	Outerbridge, N.Y.-N.J.	Arthur Kill	750

Simple Truss

Year	Bridge	Location	Longest span
1977	Chester	Chester, W. Va.	746
1917	*Metropolis	Ohio River	720
1929	Irvin S. Cobb	Ohio River-Ill.-Ky.	716
1922	*Tanana River	Nenana, Alaska	700
1933	*Henderson	Ohio River-Ind.-Ky.	665
1967	I-77, Ohio River	Marietta, Oh.	650
1917	⁴MacArthur, Ill.-Mo.	St. Louis	647
1919	Louisville	Ohio River	644
1933	Atchafalaya	Morgan City, La.	608
1924	*Castleton	Hudson River	598
1889	*Cincinnati	Ohio River	542
1951	Allegheny River	Allegheny Co., Pa.	533
1914	Pittsburgh	Allegheny R.	531
1930	*Martinez	California	528
1967	Tanana River	Alaska	500

Steel Truss

Year	Bridge	Location	Longest span
1940	Gov. Nice Mem.	Potomac River, Md.	800
1973	Atchafalaya R.	Krotz Springs, La.	780
1975	I-24	Tenn R., Ky.	720
1938	US-62, Ky.	Green River	700
1952	US-62, Ky.	Cumberland River.	700
1940	Jamestown	Jamestown, R.I.	640
1940	Greenville	Mississippi R., Ark.	640
1949	Memphis	Mississippi R., Ark.	621
1938	US-22	Delaware River, N.J.	540
1910	⁴McKinley, St. Louis	Mississippi River.	517
1972	Mississippi River	Muscatine, Ia.	512
1942	Wax Lake Outlet	Louisiana	511
1896	Newport	Ohio River, Ky.	511
1931	US-60	Cumberland R., Ky.	500
1958	Lake Oahe	Mobridge, S.D.	500
1958	Lake Oahe	Gettysburg, S.D.	500
1963	Millard E. Tydings	Susquehanna R., Md.	490
1955	Four Bears	Missouri R., N.D.	475
1930	Lake Champlain	Lake Champlain, N.Y.	434

Continuous Truss

Year	Bridge	Location	Longest span
1966	Astoria, Ore.	Columbia R.	1,232
1977	Francis Scott Key	Baltimore, Md.	1,200
1966	⁹Marquam	Willamette R., Ore.	1,044
1943	Dubuque, Ia.	Mississippi R.	845
1956	⁸Earl C. Clements	Ohio R., Ill-Ky.	825
1953	John E. Mathews	Jacksonville, Fla.	810
1957	Kingston-Rhinecliff	Hudson R., N.Y.	800
1918	*Sciotoville	Ohio River	775
1974	Betsy Ross	Philadelphia, Pa.	729
1929	Madison-Milton	Ohio River	727
1966	⁶Matthew E. Welsh	Mauckport	707
1962	Champlain	Montreal, P.Q.	707
1975	Girard Point	Philadelphia, Pa.	700
1938	Port Arthur-Orange	Texas	680
1929	*Cincinnati	Ohio River	675
1928	Cape Girardeau, Mo.	Mississippi R.	672
1946	Chester, Ill.	Mississippi R.	670
1930	Quincy, Ill.	Mississippi R.	628
1959	US 181, over harbor	Corpus Christi, Tex.	620
1934	Bourne	Cape Cod Canal	616
1935	Sagamore	Cape Cod Canal	616
1965	Clarion River	Clarion Co., Pa.	612
1957	Blatnik	Duluth, Minn.	600
1965	Rio Grande Gorge	Taos, N.M.	600
1941	Columbia River	Kettle Falls, Wash.	600
1954	Columbia River	Umatilla, Ore.	600
1954	Columbia River	The Dalles, Ore.	576
1962	W. Br. Feather River	Oroville, Cal.	576
1936	Meredosia	Illinois River	567
1936	Mark Twain Mem.	Hannibal. Mo.	562
1957	Mackinac	Mackinac Straits, Mich.	560
1937	Homestead	Pittsburgh	553
1961	Ship Canal	Seattle, Wash.	552
1932	Pulaski Skyway	Passaic R., N.J.	550
1973	I-95, Thames River	New London, Conn.	540
1927	Ross Island	Portland, Ore.	535

Continuous Box and Plate Girder

Year	Bridge	Location	Longest span
1983	Luling-Destrehan	Luling, La.	1,222
1982	Houston Ship Chan	Texas.	750
1967	San Mateo-Hayward No. 2.	San Fran. Bay, Cal.	750
1963	Gunnison River	Gunnison, Col.	720
1969	San Diego-Coronado	San Diego Bay, Cal.	660
1973	Ship Channel	Houston, Tex.	630
1981	Douglas.	Juneau, Alaska	620
1967	Poplar St.	St. Louis, Mo.	600
1982	Illinois R.	Perkin, Ill.	550
1982	I-440	Arkansas R.	540
1977	US-64, Tennessee R.	Savannah, Tenn.	525
1965	McDonald-Cartier	Ottawa, Ont.	520
1971	Lake Koocanusa	Lincoln Co., Mon.	500
1972	Sitka Harbor	Sitka, Alaska	450
1970	I-205	Willamette R., Ore.	430
1974	I-430	Arkansas R.	430
1985	I-435	Missouri R., Ks.-Mo.	425
1984	US-36.	Missouri R., Ks.-Mo.	425
1972	I-635, Kansas City	Missouri R., Kan.-Mo.	425
1967	I-24, Tennessee R.	Marion Co., Tenn.	420
1978	Snake River	Clarkston, Wash.	420
1979	Arkansas R.	Clarksville, Ark.	410
1975	Yukon River	Alaska	410
1972	I-75, Tennessee River.	Loudon Co., Tenn.	400
1941	Susquehanna	Susquehanna R., Md.	400
1963	Lake Charles B'Pass	Louisiana.	399
1957	Conn. Turnpike	Quinnipiac R.	387
1960	Route 34	New Haven, Conn.	379
1971	US-165	Pendleton, Ark.	377
1960	I-24, Tennessee R.	Chattanooga, Tenn.	375
1966	I-80, LeClaire, Ia.	Mississippi	370
1971	Sacramento R.	Bryte, Cal.	370
1963	I-40, Tennessee River.	Benton Co., Tenn.	365
1950	US-62, Kentucky Dam.	Tennessee R., Ky.	350
1972	Franklin Falls.	Snoq'lmie Pass, Wash.	350
1971	Don Pedro Reserv	Tuolumne Co., Cal.	350

Continuous Plate

Year	Bridge	Location	Longest span
1971	W. Atchafalaya	Henderson, La.	573
1981	Illinois 23	Illinois R., Ill.	510
1968	Trinity R.	Dallas, Tex.	480
1975	I-129	Missouri R., Ia.	450
1967	Mississippi River	LaCrescent, Minn.	450
1966	I-480	Missouri R., Ia.-Neb.	425
1970	I-435	Missouri R., Mo.	425
1972	I-80	Missouri R., Ia.-Neb.	425
1971	St. Croix River	Hudson, Wisc.	390
1968	Lafayette St.	St. Paul, Minn.	362
1967	San Mateo Creek	Hillsborough, Cal.	360
1969	Fort Smith	Arkansas River	353
1961	Whiskey Creek	Shasta Co., Cal.	350
1964	Lexington Ave.	St. Paul, Minn.	340

I-Beam Girder

Year	Bridge	Location	Longest span
1980	Shreveport Int.	Louisiana.	438
1941	US-31E.	Rolling Fork R., Ky.	340
1948	US-27.	Licking River, Ky.	316
1947	US-31E.	Green River, Ky.	316
1941	US-62.	Rolling Fork, Ky.	240
1942	Licking River.	Owingsville, Ky.	240
1954	Fuller Warren	Jacksonville, Fla.	224

Steel Arch

Year	Bridge	Location	Longest span
1977	New River Gorge	Fayetteville, W. Va.	1,700
1931	Bayonne, N.J.	Kill Van Kull	1,652
1973	Fremont	Portland, Ore.	1,255
1964	Port Mann	British Columbia.	1,200
1916	Hell Gate	East R., N.Y.C.	1,038
1959	Glen Canyon	Colorado River	1,028
1967	Trois-Rivieres	St. Lawrence R., P.Q.	1,100
1962	Lewiston-Queenston	Niagara River, Ont.	1,000
1976	Perrine	Twin Falls, Ida.	993
1941	Rainbow	Niagara Falls	984
1984	I-255	Mississippi R., Mo.	909
1972	I-40, Mississippi R.	Memphis, Tenn.	900
1970	Lake Quinsigamond	Worcester, Mass.	849
1966	Charles Braga	Somerset, Mass.	840
1936	Henry Hudson	Harlem River, N.Y.C.	840
1967	Lincoln Trail	Ohio R., Ind.-Ky.	825
1978	I-57, Cairo, Ill.	Mississippi R.	821
1961	Sherman Minton	Louisville, Ky.	800
1936	French King	Conn. R. (Rt. 2, Mass.)	782
1931	West End.	Pittsburgh	778
1972	Piscataqua R.	I-95, N.H.-Me.	756
1979	SR 156, Tennessee R.	So. Pittsburgh, Tenn.	750
1973	I-24, Paducah, Ky.	Ohio River	730

Concrete Arch

Year	Bridge	Location	Longest span
1971	Selah Creek (twin)	Selah, Wash.	549
1968	Cowlitz River.	Mossyrock, Wash.	520
1931	Westinghouse	Pittsburgh	425
1923	Cappelen.	Minneapolis	400
1930	Jack's Run	Pittsburgh	400
1973	Elwha River	Port Angeles, Wash.	380
1931	Bixby Creek	Monterey Coast, Cal.	330
1953	Arroyo Seco	Pasadena, Cal.	320

Twin Concrete Trestle

Year	Bridge	Location	Longest span
1963	Slidell, La.	L. Pontchartrain	28,547

Concrete Slab Dam

Year	Bridge	Location	Longest span
1927	Conowingo Dam.	Maryland.	4,611
1952	John H. Kerr Dam.	Roanoke River, Va.	2,785
1936	Hoover Dam.	Boulder City, Nev.	1,324

Drawbridges

Vertical Lift

Year	Bridge	Location	Longest span
1937	Marine Parkway	Jamaica Bay, N.Y.C.	590
1959	Arthur Kill	N.Y.-N.J.	558
1935	Cape Cod Canal	Massachusetts	544
1960	Delair, N.J.	Delaware River	542
1931	Burlington, N.J.	Delaware R.	534
1968	Second Narrows	Vancouver, B.C.	493
1912	A-S-B Fratt	Kansas City	428
1945	Harry S. Truman	Kansas City	427
1955	Roosevelt Island	East River, N.Y.C.	418
1979	James River	Newport News, Va.	415
1932	M-K-T R.R.	Missouri R.	414
1969	Wilm'gtn Mem.	Wilmington, N.C.	408
1930	Aerial	Duluth, Minn.	386
1941	Main St.	Jacksonville, Fla.	386
1962	Burlington	Ontario	370
1941	Acosta	St. Johns R., Fla.	365
1922	Cincinnati	Ohio River	365
1967	Benj. Harrison Mem.	James River, Va.	363
1936	Tribo	Harlem River, N.Y.C.	344
1961	Corpus Christi Harbor	Corpus Christi, Tex.	344
1941	U.S. 1&9, Passaic R.	Newark, N.J.	332
1929	Carlton	Bath-Woolwich, Me.	328
1930	Martinez	California.	328
1960	St. Andrews Bay.	Panama City, Fla.	327
1929	Penn-Lehigh	Newark Bay	322
1920	Chattanooga	Tennessee R.	310
1936	Hardin	Illinois River	309
1960	Sacramento River	Rio Vista, Cal.	306
1957	Claiborne Ave.	New Orleans	305
1927	Cochrane.	Mobile, Ala.	300
1929	Dumbarton	California.	300
1926	Missouri Pacific.	Kragen, Ark.	300

Bascule

Year	Bridge	Location	Longest span
1969	Pearl River.	Slidell, La.	482
1917	SR-8, Tennessee River.	Chattanooga, Tenn.	306
1940	Lorain, Ohio	Black River	300
1958	Morrison	Portland, Ore.	285
1969	Elizabeth River.	Chesapeake, Va.	281
1954	Fuller Warren	St. Johns R., Fla.	267
1977	Curtis Creek	Baltimore, Md.	251
1957	Craig Memorial	I-280, Toledo, Oh.	245

Swing Bridges

Year	Bridge	Location	Longest span
1926	Fort Madison	Mississippi R.	525
1930	Rigolets Pass	New Orleans, La.	400
1950	Douglass Memorial	Wash. D.C.	386
1916	Keokuk Municipal	Mississippi R., Ia.	377
1945	Lord Delaware	Mattaponi River, Va.	252
1957	Eltham	Pamunkey River, Va.	237
1939	Chickahominy River	Route 5, Va.	222
1930	Nansemond River	Route 125, Va.	200

Swing Span

Year	Bridge	Location	Longest span
1908	Willamette R.	Portland, Ore.	521
1903	East Omaha	Missouri R.	519
1952	Yorktown	York River, Va.	500
1897	Duluth, Minn.	St. Louis Bay	486
1899	C.M.&N.R.R.	Chicago	474
1914	Coos Bay	Oregon	458

Floating Pontoon

Year	Bridge	Location	Longest span
1963	Evergreen Pt.	Seattle, Wash.	7,518
1940	Lacey V. Murrow	Seattle	6,561
1961	Hood Canal	Pt. Gamble, Wash.	6,471

(1) The Transbay Bridge has 2 spans of 2,310 ft. each. (2) A second bridge in parallel was completed in 1973. (3) The Richmond Bridge has twin spans 1,070 ft. each. (4) Railroad and vehicular bridge. (5) Two spans each 760 ft. (6) Two spans each 707 ft. (7) Two spans each 660 ft. (8) Two spans each 825 ft. (9) Total length of bridge. (10) Two spans each 900 ft.

Underwater Vehicular Tunnels in North America

(3,000 feet in length or more)

Name	Location	Waterway	Lgth. Ft.
Bart Trans-Bay Tubes (Rapid Transit)	San Francisco, Cal.	S.F. Bay	3.6 miles
Brooklyn-Battery	New York, N.Y.	East River	9,117
Holland Tunnel	New York, N.Y.	Hudson River	8,557
Lincoln Tunnel	New York, N.Y.	Hudson River	8,216
Baltimore Harbor Tunnel	Baltimore, Md.	Patapsco River	7,650
Hampton Roads	Norfolk, Va.	Hampton Roads	7,479
Queens Midtown	New York, N.Y.	East River	6,414
Thimble Shoal Channel	Cape Henry, Va.	Chesapeake Bay	5,738
Sumner Tunnel	Boston, Mass.	Boston Harbor	5,650
Chesapeake Channel	Cape Charles, Va.	Chesapeake Bay	5,450
Louis-Hippolyte Lafontaine Tunnel	Montreal, Que.	St. Lawrence River	5,280
Detroit-Windsor	Detroit, Mich.	Detroit River	5,135
Callahan Tunnel	Boston, Mass.	Boston Harbor	5,046
Midtown Tunnel	Norfolk, Va.	Elizabeth River	4,194
Baytown Tunnel	Baytown, Tex.	Houston Ship Channel	4,111
Posey Tube	Oakland, Cal.	Oakland Estuary	3,500
Downtown Tunnel	Norfolk, Va.	Elizabeth River	3,350
Webster St.	Alameda, Cal.	Oakland Estuary	3,350
Bankhead Tunnel	Mobile, Ala.	Mobile River	3,109
I-10 Twin Tunnel	Mobile, Ala.	Mobile River	3,000

Land Vehicular Tunnels in U.S.

(over 1,450 feet in length.)

Name	Location	Lgth. Ft.	Name	Location	Lgth. Ft.
E. Johnson Memorial	I-70, Col.	8,959	Ft. Cronkhite	Sausalito, Cal.	2,690
Eisenhower Memorial	I-70, Col.	8,941	Cross-Town	178 St. N.Y.C.	2,414
Allegheny (twin)	Penna. Turnpike	6,070	F.D. Roosevelt Dr.	81-89 Sts. N.Y.C.	2,400
Liberty Tubes	Pittsburgh, Pa.	5,920	Dewey Sq.	Boston, Mass.	2,400
Zion Natl. Park	Rte. 9, Utah.	5,766	Battery Park	N.Y.C.	2,300
East River Mt. (twin)	Interstate 77, W. Va.-Va.	5,661	Battery St.	Seattle, Wash.	2,140
Tuscarora (twin)	Penna. Turnpike	5,326	Big Oak Flat	Yosemite Natl. Park	2,083
Kittatinny (twin)	Penna. Turnpike	4,727	Prudential	Boston, Mass.	1,980
Lehigh	Penna. Turnpike	4,379	Internatl. Underpass	Los Angeles, Cal.	1,910
Blue Mountain (twin)	Penna. Turnpike	4,339	Collier	Crescent City, Cal.	1,886
Wawona	Yosemite Natl. Park	4,233	Broadway (twin)	San Francisco, Cal.	1,850
Squirrel Hill	Pittsburgh, Pa.	4,225	Street-Car	Providence, R.I.	1,793
Big Walker Mt.	Route I-77, Va.	4,200	Second Street	Los Angeles, Cal.	1,734
Fort Pitt	Pittsburgh, Pa.	3,560	Broadway	San Francisco, Cal.	1,616
Mall Tunnel	Dist. of Columbia.	3,400	9th Street Expy.	Washington, D.C.	1,610
Caldecott	Oakland, Cal.	3,371	F.D. Roosevelt Dr.	42-48 Sts. N.Y.C.	1,600
Cody No. 1	U.S. 14, 16, 20, Wyo.	3,224	Lowry Hill	Minneapolis.	1,496
Kalihi	Honolulu, Ha.	2,780	Wheeling	Interstate 70, W. Va.	1,490
Memorial	W. Va. Tpke. (I-77)	2,669	Mt. Baker Ridge (3)	Seattle, Wash.	1,466

World's Longest Railway Tunnels

Source: Railway Directory & Year Book 1980. Tunnels over 4.9 miles in length.

Tunnel	Date	Miles	Yds	Operating railway	Country
Dai-shimizu	1979	13	1,384	Japanese National	Japan
Simplon No. 1 and 2	1906, 1922	12	546	Swiss Fed. & Italian St.	Switz.-Italy
Kanmon	1975	11	1,093	Japanese National	Japan
Apennine	1934	11	881	Italian State	Italy
Rokko	1972	10	158	Japanese National	Japan
Gotthard	1882	9	552	Swiss Federal	Switzerland
Lotschberg	1913	9	130	Bern-Lotschberg-Simplon	Switzerland
Hokuriku	1962	8	1,079	Japanese National	Japan
Mont Cenis (Frejus)	1871	8	847	Italian State	France-Italy
Shin-Shimizu	1961	8	675	Japanese National	Japan
Aki	1975	8	161	Japanese National	Japan
Cascade	1929	7	1,388	Burlington Northern	U.S.
Flathead	1970	7	1,319	Great Northern	U.S.
Keijo	1970	7	88	Japanese National	Japan
Lierasen	1973	6	1,135	Norwegian State	Norway
Santa Lucia	1977	6	656	Italian State	Italy
Arlberg	1884	6	643	Austrian Federal	Austria
Moffat	1928	6	366	Denver & Rio Grande Western	U.S.
Shimizu	1931	6	44	Japanese National	Japan
Kvineshei	1943	5	1,107	Norwegian State	Norway
Bigo	1975	5	927	Japanese National	Japan
Rimutaka	1955	5	816	New Zealand Gov.	New Zealand
Ricken	1910	5	603	Swiss Federal	Switzerland
Kaimai	1978	5	873	New Zealand Gov.	New Zealand
Grenchenberg	1915	5	575	Swiss Federal	Switzerland
Otira	1923	5	559	New Zealand Gov.	New Zealand
Tauern	1909	5	546	Austrian Federal	Austria
Haegebostad	1943	5	462	Norwegian State	Norway
Ronco	1889	5	272	Italian State	Italy
Hauenstein (Lower)	1916	5	90	Swiss Federal	Switzerland
Connaught	1916	5	34	Canadian Pacific	Canada
Karawanken	1906	4	1,677	Austrian Federal	Austria-Yugo.
Kobe	1972	4	1,671	Japanese National	Japan
New Tanna	1964	4	1,658	Japanese National	Japan

Notable International Bridges

Angostura, suspension type, span 2,336 feet, 1967 at Ciudad Bolivar, Venezuela. Total length, 5,507.

Bendorf Bridge on the Rhine River, 5 mi. n. of Coblenz, completed 1965, is a 3-span cement girder bridge, 3,378 ft. overall length, 101 ft. wide, with the main span 682 ft.

Gladesville Bridge at Sydney, Australia, has the longest concrete arch in the world (1,000 ft. span).

Humber Bridge, with a suspension span of 4,626 ft., the longest in the world, crosses the Humber estuary 5 miles west of the city of Kingston upon Hull, England. Unique in a large suspension bridge are the towers of reinforced concrete instead of steel.

Second Narrow's Bridge, Canada's longest railway lift span connecting Vancouver and North Vancouver over Burrard Inlet.

Oland Island Bridge in Sweden was completed in 1972. It is 19,882 feet long, Europe's longest.

Oosterscheldebrug, opened Dec. 15, 1965, is a 3.125-mile causeway for automobiles over a sea arm in Zeeland, the Netherlands. It completes a direct connection between Flushing and Rotterdam.

Rio-Niteroi, Guanabara Bay, Brazil, completed in 1972, is world's longest continuous box and plate girder bridge, 8 miles, 3,363 feet long, with a center span of 984 feet and a span on each side of 656 feet.

Tagus River Bridge near Lisbon, Portugal, longest suspension bridge outside the United States, has a 3,323-ft. main span. Opened Aug. 6, 1966, it was named Salazar Bridge for the former premier.

Zoo Bridge across the Rhine at Cologne, with steel box girders, has a main span of 850 ft.

Scientific Achievements and Discoveries of 1984
As of Mid-1984

Global Extinctions

The preliminary results of a six-year review of global extinctions of marine organisms, made by J. John Sepkoski and David M. Raup of the Univ. of Chicago, revealed a curious pattern to the mass extinctions of life on earth. Based on an analysis of fossils, it now appears that over the last 250 million years, life forms have vanished in staggering numbers at regular intervals roughly every 26 million years. The idea of a cyclical pattern to mass extinctions calls into question some assumptions about the slow, steady workings of nature and elevates the importance of rare, catastrophic events in setting the course of life. As the most recent widespread extinctions occurred 11 million years ago, the next mass extinction is not due for 15 million years.

In a related finding, five geological studies conducted by U.S., Dutch and Danish Scientists indicated that several species of plants and animals became extinct at about the same time 65 million years ago. These new studies add support to the growing theory that an asteroid comet smashing into the earth was responsible for the abrupt extinction of dinosaurs and many other creatures.

Matter Created in Lab

An unusually dense form of matter, believed to exist only at the core of collapsed stars such as pulsars, neutron stars and supernovas, was observed for the first time in the world's most powerful accelerator of atomic nuclei at the Lawrence-Berkeley Laboratory. The finding will help astrophysicists better understand how matter behaves under the tremendous pressures and temperatures found during the birth of the universe and the death throes of stars.

Neurons and Brain Functions

A more detailed picture of the neuron, the nerve cell that is the basic functional unit of the brain, is emerging from a new set of discoveries concerning brain chemicals. Ten years ago, less than six nerve signal chemicals, called neurotransmitters, were known. Beginning with the discovery of two new brain chemicals, called the enkeplalins, in 1975, more than thirty substances that act in the brain have been discovered. Even with 10 billion neurons of the human brain, it was once difficult to imagine the chemical basis of memory, of rational thought, and such complex subtleties as joy, sadness, and love of music or visual beauty. The newly appreciated complexity of brain chemistry seems more compatible with the nature of the human mind.

Medicine

An important link between a cancer gene and a natural substance that promotes cell growth within the body has been discovered by a team of scientists in Israel, Britain and the U.S. The links between cancer genes and the action of normal growth-promoting substances are considered critical because cancer is known to be a process in which cell growth gets out of control and cannot be turned off.

Scientists from the Univ. of Maryland, Univ. of Roches-

ter, and the National Institutes of Health reported the development of a new vaccine, given by nose drops, that promises longer and substantially better immunity to influenza, and may reduce the likelihood of major flu epidemics. In addition to preventing influenza, the vaccine, made from live viruses, caused a noted reduction in the amount of disease-causing flu viruses released into the air.

A chicken pox vaccine was produced by Merck Sharp & Dohme Research Labs, of West Point, Pa., under the direction of Dr. Edward M. Scolnick, which has proved highly effective in protecting healthy children against the potentially dangerous disease. The vaccine was produced by using a virus first isolated more than 10 years ago by scientists in Japan. Although more testing is required, the vaccine could be available for widespread use in about 18 months.

The first experimental vaccine for humans produced through gene-splicing (prepared by recombinant DNA technology) has given healthy adults immunity to hepatitis B virus, a major cause of liver disease throughout the world. This vaccine, also produced undder Dr. Scolnick's direction, could be available in 2 to 3 years.

The largest and most complex protein ever created artificially in the laboratory, a substance vital to the normal clotting of blood, was produced by Genentech, Inc., a biotechnology company in South San Francisco. While production of the protein was probably years in the future, the feat is considered a major step toward artificial commercial production of the human blood substance, which is crucial to the lives and health of about 20,000 American hemophiliacs.

A 5½ pound infant girl was the world's first baby produced from a frozen embryo. The birth, in Australia, resulted after an ovum from the mother was fertilized in a laboratory with the husband's sperm. The embryo was then frozen, reportedly for two months, before being implanted in the woman's uterus, where it developed normally.

Patents

Among the many patents issued in 1984 were: a Containerized Hospital Emergency Mobile, which provides a 34-bed emergency hospital, with an operating room, and can be airlifted by helicopter or put aboard a large aircraft for transportation to a disaster site; a voice warning device to alert occupants of a motor vehicle to abnormal conditions; a nuclear waste storage system which permanently prevents radioactive particles from seeping into the environment; a system for detecting physical flaws in U.S. currency by sending light and electrical signals through a bill; a public-access telephone network that would allow a call to be made from suitably equipped booths by housing a standard credit card instead of coins; and an electronic Bible, described as a hand-held calculator for enhancing the learning and appreciation of messages from the Bible.

A projection of the total patents to be issued for fiscal year 1984 is 71,830, an increase of more than 12,000 over FY of 1983. Patent applications filed in FY 1983 totaled 105,704. For FY 1984, the excepted total is 114,500. Foreign residents received about 41 percent of the patents in FY 1983. Trademark applications totaled 51,014 in FY 1983.

Invention	Date	Inventor	Nation.
Adding machine	1642	Pascal	French
Adding machine	1885	Burroughs	U.S.
Addressograph	1892	Duncan	U.S.
Aerosol spray	1941	Goodhue	U.S.
Air brake	1868	Westinghouse	U.S.
Air conditioning	1911	Carrier	U.S.
Air pump	1650	Guericke	German
Airplane, automatic pilot	1929	Green	U.S.
Airplane, experimental	1896	Langley	U.S.
Airplane jet engine	1939	Ohain	German
Airplane with motor	1903	Wright bros.	U.S.
Airplane, hydro	1911	Curtiss	U.S.
Airship	1852	Giffard	French
Airship, rigid dirigible	1900	Zeppelin	German
Arc tube	1923	Alexanderson	U.S.
Autogyro	1920	de la Cierva	Spanish
Automobile, differential gear	1885	Benz	German
Automobile, electric	1892	Morrison	U.S.
Automobile, exp'mtl	1875	Marcus	Austrian
Automobile, gasoline	1887	Daimler	German
Automobile, gasoline	1892	Duryea	U.S.
Automobile magneto	1897	Bosch	German
Automobile muffler	...	Maxim, H.P.	U.S.
Automobile self-starter	1911	Kettering	U.S.
Automobile, steam	1889	Roper	U.S.
Babbitt metal	1839	Babbitt	U.S.
Bakelite	1907	Baekeland	Belg., U.S.
Balloon	1783	Montgolfier	French
Barometer	1643	Torricelli	Italian
Bicycle, modern	1884	Starley	English
Bifocal lens	1780	Franklin	U.S.
Block signals, railway	1867	Hall	U.S.
Bomb, depth	1916	Tait	U.S.
Bottle machine	1903	Owens	U.S.
Braille printing	1829	Braille	French
Burner, gas	1855	Bunsen	German
Calculating machine	1823	Babbage	English
Camera—see also Photography			
Camera, Kodak	1888	Eastman, Walker	U.S.
Camera, Polaroid Land	1948	Land	U.S.
Car coupler	1873	Janney	U.S.
Carburetor, gasoline	1876	Daimler	German
Card time recorder	1894	Cooper	U.S.
Carding machine	1797	Whittemore	U.S.
Carpet sweeper	1876	Bissell	U.S.
Cash register	1879	Ritty	U.S.
Cathode ray tube	1878	Crookes	English
Cellophane	1911	Brandenberger	Swiss
Celluloid	1870	Hyatt	U.S.
Cement, Portland	1845	Aspdin	English
Chronometer	1735	Harrison	English
Circuit breaker	1925	Hilliard	U.S.
Clock, pendulum	1657	Huygens	Dutch
Coaxial cable system	1929	Affel, Espensched	U.S.
Coke oven	1893	Hoffman	Austrian
Compressed air rock drill	1871	Ingersoll	U.S.
Comptometer	1887	Felt	U.S.
Computer, automatic sequence	1939	Aiken et al.	U.S.
Condenser microphone (telephone)	1920	Wente	U.S.
Corn, hybrid	1917	Jones	U.S.
Cotton gin	1793	Whitney	U.S.
Cream separator	1880	DeLaval	Swedish
Cultivator, disc	1878	Mallon	U.S.
Cystoscope	1877	Nitze	German
Dental plate, rubber	1855	Goodyear	U.S.
Diesel engine	1895	Diesel	German
Dynamite	1866	Nobel	Swedish
Dynamo, continuous current	1860	Picinotti	Italian
Dynamo, hydrogen cooled	1915	Schuler	U.S.
Electric battery	1800	Volta	Italian
Electric fan	1882	Wheeler	U.S.
Electrocardiograph	1903	Einthoven	Dutch
Electroencephalograph	1929	Berger	German
Electromagnet	1824	Sturgeon	English

Invention	Date	Inventor	Nation.
Electron spectrometer	1944	Deutsch, Elliott, Evans	U.S.
Electron tube multigrid	1913	Langmuir	U.S.
Electroplating	1805	Brugnatelli	Italian
Electrostatic generator	1929	Van de Graaff	U.S.
Elevator brake	1852	Otis	U.S.
Elevator, push button	1922	Larson	U.S.
Engine, automobile	1879	Benz	German
Engine, coal-gas 4-cyclo	1877	Otto	German
Engine, compression ignition	1883	Daimler	German
Engine, electric ignition	1880	Benz	German
Engine, gas, compound	1926	Eickemeyer	U.S.
Engine, gasoline	1872	Brayton, Geo.	U.S.
Engine, gasoline	1886	Daimler	German
Engine, steam, piston	1705	Newcomen	English
Engine, steam, piston	1769	Watt	Scottish
Engraving, half-tone	1893	Ives	U.S.
Filament, tungsten	1915	Langmuir	U.S.
Flanged rail	1831	Stevens	U.S.
Flatiron, electric	1882	Seeley	U.S.
Furnace (for steel)	1861	Siemens	German
Galvanometer	1820	Sweigger	German
Gas discharge tube	1922	Hull	U.S.
Gas lighting	1792	Murdoch	Scottish
Gas mantle	1885	Welsbach	Austrian
Gasoline (lead ethyl)	1922	Midgley	U.S.
Gasoline, cracked	1913	Burton	U.S.
Gasoline, high octane	1930	Ipatieff	Russian
Geiger counter	1913	Geiger	German
Glass, laminated safety	1909	Benedictus	French
Glider	1853	Cayloy	English
Gun, breechloader	1811	Thornton	U.S.
Gun, Browning	1916	Browning	U.S.
Gun, magazine	1875	Hotchkiss	U.S.
Gun, silencer	1909	Maxim, H.P.	U.S.
Guncotton	1846	Schoenbein	German
Gyrocompass	1911	Sperry	U.S.
Gyroscope	1852	Foucault	French
Harvester-thresher	1888	Matteson	U.S.
Helicopter	1939	Sikorsky	U.S.
Hydrometer	1768	Baume	French
Ice-making machine	1851	Gorrie	U.S.
Iron lung	1928	Drinker, Slaw.	U.S.
Kaleidoscope	1817	Brewster	Scottish
Kinetoscope	1887	Edison	U.S.
Lacquer, nitrocellulose	1921	Flaherty	U.S.
Lamp, arc	1879	Brush	U.S.
Lamp, incandescent	1879	Edison	U.S.
Lamp, incand., frosted	1924	Pipkin	U.S.
Lamp, incand., gas	1916	Langmuir	U.S.
Lamp, Klieg	1911	Kliegl, A.&J.	U.S.
Lamp, mercury vapor	1912	Hewitt	U.S.
Lamp, miner's safety	1816	Davy	English
Lamp, neon	1915	Claude	French
Lathe, turret	1845	Fitch	U.S.
Launderette	1934	Cantrell	U.S.
Lens, achromatic	1758	Dollond	English
Lens, fused bifocal	1908	Borsch	U.S.
Leydenjar (condenser)	1745	von Kleist	German
Lightning rod	1752	Franklin	U.S.
Linoleum	1860	Walton	English
Linotype	1885	Mergenthaler	U.S.
Lock, cylinder	1865	Yale	U.S.
Locomotive, electric	1851	Vail	U.S.
Locomotive, exp'mtl	1801	Trevithick	English
Locomotive, exp'mtl	1812	Fenton et al.	English
Locomotive, exp'mtl	1813	Hedley	English
Locomotive, exp'mtl	1814	Stephenson	English
Locomotive practical	1829	Stephenson	English
Locomotive, 1st U.S.	1830	Cooper, P.	U.S.
Loom, power	1785	Cartwright	English
Loudspeaker, dynamic	1924	Rice, Kellogg	U.S.
Machine gun	1861	Gatling	U.S.
Machine gun, improved	1872	Hotchkiss	U.S.
Machine gun (Maxim)	1883	Maxim, H.S.	U.S., Eng.
Magnet, electro	1828	Henry	U.S.
Mantle, gas	1885	Welsbach	Austrian
Mason jar	1858	Mason, J.	U.S.

Invention	Date	Inventor	Nation.
Match, friction	1827	John Walker	English
Mercerized textiles	1843	Mercer, J.	English
Meter, induction	1888	Shallenberger	U.S.
Metronome	1816	Maizel	Austrian
Micrometer	1636	Gascoigne	English
Microphone	1877	Berliner	U.S.
Microscope, compound	1590	Janssen	Dutch
Microscope, electronic	1931	Knoll, Ruska	German
Microscope, field ion.	1951	Mueller	Germany
Monitor, warship	1861	Ericsson	U.S.
Monotype	1887	Lanston	U.S.
Motor, AC	1892	Tesla	U.S.
Motor, induction	1887	Tesla	U.S.
Motorcycle	1885	Daimler	German
Movie machine	1894	Jenkins	U.S.
Movie, panoramic	1952	Waller	U.S.
Movie, talking	1927	Warner Bros.	U.S.
Mower, lawn	1868	Hills	U.S.
Mowing machine	1831	Manning	U.S.
Neoprene	1930	Carothers	U.S.
Nylon synthetic	1930	Carothers	U.S.
Nylon	1937	Du Pont lab.	U.S.
Oil cracking furnace	1891	Gavrilov	Russian
Oil filled power cable	1921	Emanueli	Italian
Oleomargarine	1868	Mege-Mouries	French
Ophthalmoscope	1851	Helmholtz	German
Paper machine	1809	Dickinson	U.S.
Parachute	1785	Blanchard	French
Pen, ballpoint	1888	Loud	U.S.
Pen, fountain	1884	Waterman	U.S.
Pen, steel	1780	Harrison	English
Pendulum	1581	Galileo	Italian
Percussion cap	1814	Shaw	U.S.
Phonograph	1877	Edison	U.S.
Photo, color	1892	Ives	U.S.
Photo film, celluloid	1887	Goodwin	U.S.
Photo film, transparent	1878	Eastman, Goodwin	U.S.
Photoelectric cell	1895	Elster	German
Photographic paper	1898	Baekeland	U.S.
Photography	1835	Talbot	English
Photography	1837	Daguerre	French
Photography	1839	Niepce	French
Photophone	1880	Bell	U.S.-Scot.
Phototelegraphy	1925	Bell Labs	U.S.
Piano	1709	Cristofori	Italian
Piano, player	1863	Fourneaux	French
Pin, safety	1849	Hunt	U.S.
Pistol (revolver)	1835	Colt	U.S.
Plow, cast iron	1797	Newbold	U.S.
Plow, disc.	1896	Hardy	U.S.
Pneumatic hammer	1890	King	U.S.
Powder, smokeless	1863	Schultze	German
Printing press, rotary	1846	Hoe	U.S.
Printing press, web	1865	Bullock	U.S.
Propeller, screw	1804	Stevens	U.S.
Propeller, screw	1837	Ericsson	Swedish
Punch card accounting	1884	Hollerith	U.S.
Radar	1922	Taylor, Young	U.S.
Radio amplifier	1907	De Forest	U.S.
Radio beacon	1928	Donovan	U.S.
Radio crystal oscillator	1918	Nicolson	U.S.
Radio receiver, cascade tuning	1913	Alexanderson	U.S.
Radio receiver, heterodyne	1913	Fessenden	U.S.
Radio transmitter triode modulation	1914	Alexanderson	U.S.
Radio tube-diode	1905	Fleming	English
Radio tube oscillator	1915	De Forest	U.S.
Radio tube triode	1907	De Forest	U.S.
Radio, signals	1895	Marconi	Italian
Radio, magnetic detector	1902	Marconi	Italian
Radio FM 2-path	1929	Armstrong	U.S.
Rayon	1883	Swan	English
Razor, electric	1931	Schick	U.S.
Razor, safety	1895	Gillette	U.S.
Reaper	1834	McCormick	U.S.
Record, cylinder	1887	Bell, Tainter	U.S.
Record, disc	1887	Berliner	U.S.
Record, long playing	1948	Goldmark	U.S.
Record, wax cylinder	1888	Edison	U.S.
Refrigerants, low-boiling fluorine compound	1930	Midgely and co-workers	U.S.
Refrigerator car	1868	David	U.S.
Resin, synthetic	1931	Hill	English
Rifle, repeating	1860	Spencer	U.S.
Rocket engine	1929	Goddard	U.S.
Rubber, vulcanized	1839	Goodyear	U.S.
Saw, band	1808	Newberry	English
Saw, circular	1777	Miller	English
Searchlight, arc	1915	Sperry	U.S.
Sewing machine	1846	Howe	U.S.
Shoe-sewing machine	1860	McKay	U.S.
Shrapnel shell	1784	Shrapnel	English
Shuttle, flying	1733	Kay	English
Sleeping-car	1858	Pullman	U.S.
Slide rule	1620	Oughtred	English
Soap, hardwater	1928	Bertsch	German
Spectroscope	1859	Kirchoff, Bunsen	German
Spectroscope (mass)	1918	Dempster	U.S.
Spinning jenny	1767	Hargreaves	English
Spinning mule	1779	Crompton	English
Steamboat, exp'mtl	1783	Jouffroy	French
Steamboat, exp'mtl	1785	Fitch	U.S.
Steamboat, exp'mtl	1787	Rumsey	U.S.
Steamboat, exp'mtl	1788	Miller	Scottish
Steamboat, exp'mtl	1803	Fulton	U.S.
Steamboat, exp'mtl	1804	Stevens	U.S.
Steamboat, practical	1802	Symington	Scottish
Steamboat, practical	1807	Fulton	U.S.
Steam car	1770	Cugnot	French
Steam turbine	1884	Parsons	English
Steel	1856	Bessemer	English
Steel alloy	1891	Harvey	U.S.
Steel alloy, high-speed	1901	Taylor, White	U.S.
Steel, electric	1900	Heroult	French
Steel, manganese	1884	Hadfield	English
Steel, stainless	1916	Brearley	English
Stereoscope	1838	Wheatstone	English
Stethoscope	1819	Laennec	French
Stethoscope, binaural	1840	Cammann	U.S.
Stock ticker	1870	Edison	U.S.
Storage battery, recharge-able	1859	Plante	French
Stove, electric	1896	Hadaway	U.S.
Submarine	1891	Holland	U.S.
Submarine, even keel	1894	Lake	U.S.
Submarine, torpedo	1776	Bushnell	U.S.
Tank, military	1914	Swinton	English
Tape recorder, magnetic	1899	Poulsen	Danish
Telegraph, magnetic	1837	Morse	U.S.
Telegraph, quadruplex	1874	Edison	U.S.
Telegraph, railroad	1887	Woods	U.S.
Telegraph, wireless high frequency	1896	Marconi	Italian
Telephone	1876	Bell	U.S.-Scot
Telephone amplifier	1912	De Forest	U.S.
Telephone, automatic	1891	Stowger	U.S.
Telephone, radio	1902	Poulsen, Fessenden	U.S.
Telephone, radio	1906	De Forest	U.S.
Telephone, radio, l. d	1915	AT&T	U.S.
Telephone, recording	1898	Poulseon	Danish
Telephone, wireless	1899	Collins	U.S.
Telescope	1608	Lippershey	Neth.
Telescope	1609	Galileo	Italian
Telescope, astronomical	1611	Kepler	German
Teletype	1928	Morkrum, Kleinschmidt	U.S.
Television, iconoscope	1923	Zworykin	U.S.
Television, electronic	1927	Farnsworth	U.S.
Television, (mech. scanner)	1926	Baird	Scottish
Thermometer	1593	Galileo	Italian
Thermometer	1710	Reaumur	French
Thermometer, mercury	1714	Fahrenheit	German
Time recorder	1890	Bundy	U.S.
Time, self-regulator	1918	Bryce	U.S.
Tire, double-tube	1845	Thomson	Scottish
Tire, pneumatic	1888	Dunlop	Scottish
Toaster, automatic	1918	Strite	U.S.
Tool, pneumatic	1865	Law	English
Torpedo, marine	1804	Fulton	U.S.
Tractor, crawler	1900	Holt	U.S.
Transformer A.C.	1885	Stanley	U.S.
Transistor	1947	Shockley, Brattain, Bardeen	U.S.
Trolley car, electric	1884 -87	Van DePoele, Sprague	U.S.

Invention	Date	Inventor	Nation.
Tungsten, ductile	1912	Coolidge	U.S.
Turbine, gas	1899	Curtis, C.G.	U.S.
Turbine, hydraulic	1849	Francis	U.S.
Turbine, steam	1896	Curtis, C.G.	U.S.
Type, movable	1450	Gutenberg	German
Typewriter	1868	Soule, Glidden	U.S.
Vacuum cleaner, electric	1907	Spangler	U.S.
Washer, electric	1907	Hurley Co.	U.S.

Invention	Date	Inventor	Nation.
Welding, atomic hydrogen	1924	Langmuir, Palmer	U.S.
Welding, electric	1877	Thomson	U.S.
Wind tunnel	1923	Munk	U.S.
Wire, barbed	1874	Glidden	U.S.
Wire, barbed	1875	Haisn	U.S.
Wrench, double-acting	1913	Owen	U.S.
X-ray tube	1913	Coolidge	U.S.
Zipper	1891	Judson	U.S.

Discoveries and Innovations: Chemistry, Physics, Biology, Medicine

	Date	Discoverer	Nation.
Acetylene gas	1892	Wilson	U.S.
ACTH	1949	Armour & Co.	U.S.
Adrenalin	1901	Takamine	Japanese
Aluminum, electrolytic process	1886	Hall	U.S.
Aluminum, isolated	1825	Oersted	Danish
Analine dye	1856	Perkin	English
Anesthesia, ether	1842	Long	U.S.
Anesthesia, local	1885	Koller	Austrian
Anesthesia, spinal	1898	Bier	German
Anti-rabies	1885	Pasteur	French
Antiseptic surgery	1867	Lister	English
Antitoxin, diphtheria	1891	Von Behring	German
Argyrol	1901	Barnes	U.S.
Arsphenamine	1910	Ehrlich	German
Aspirin	1889	Dresser	German
Atabrine	. . .	Mietzsch, et al.	German
Atomic numbers	1913	Moseley	English
Atomic theory	1803	Dalton	English
Atomic time clock	1947	Libby	U.S.
Atom-smashing theory	1919	Rutherford	English
Aureomycin	1948	Duggar	U.S.
Bacitracin	1945	Johnson, et al.	U.S.
Bacteria (described)	1676	Leeuwenhoek	Dutch
Barbital	1903	Fischer	German
Bleaching powder	1798	Tennant	English
Blood, circulation	1628	Harvey	English
Bordeaux mixture	1885	Millardet	French
Bromine from sea	1924	Edgar Kramer	U.S.
Calcium carbide	1888	Wilson	U.S.
Calculus	1670	Newton	English
Camphor synthetic	1896	Haller	French
Canning (food)	1804	Appert	French
Carbomycin	1952	Tanner	U.S.
Carbon oxides	1925	Fisher	German
Chlorine	1810	Davy	English
Chloroform	1831	Guthrie, S.	U.S.
Chloromycetin	1947	Burkholder	U.S.
Classification of plants and animals	1735	Linnaeus	Swedish
Cocaine	1860	Niermann	German
Combustion explained	1777	Lavoisier	French
Conditioned reflex	1914	Pavlov	Russian
Conteben	1950	Belmisch, Mietzsch, Domagk	German
Cortisone	1936	Kendall	U.S.
Cortisone, synthesis	1946	Sarett	U.S.
Cosmic rays	1910	Gockel	Swiss
Cyanimide	1905	Frank, Caro	German
Cyclotron	1930	Lawrence	U.S.
DDT	1874	Zeidler	German
(not applied as insecticide until 1939)			
Deuterium	1932	Urey, Brickwedde, Murphy	U.S.
DNA (structure)	1951	Crick	English
		Watson	U.S.
		Wilkins	English
Electric resistance (law)	1827	Ohm	German
Electric waves	1888	Hertz	German
Electrolysis	1852	Faraday	English
Electromagnetism	1819	Oersted	Danish
Electron	1897	Thomson, J.	English
Electron diffraction	1936	Thomson, G.	English
		Davisson	U.S.
Electroshock treatment	1938	Cerletti, Bini	Italian

	Date	Discoverer	Nation.
Erythromycin	1952	McGuire	U.S.
Evolution, natural selection	1858	Darwin	English
Falling bodies, law	1590	Galileo	Italian
Gases, law of combining volumes	1808	Gay-Lussac	French
Geometry, analytic	1619	Descartes	French
Gold (cyanide process for extraction)	1887	MacArthur, Forest	British
Gravitation, law	1687	Newton	English
Holograph	1948	Gabor	British
Human heart transplant	1967	Barnard	S. African
Indigo, synthesis of	1880	Baeyer	German
Induction, electric	1830	Henry	U.S.
Insulin	1922	Banting, Best, Macleod	Canadian, Scottish
Intelligence testing	1905	Binet, Simon	French
Isinazid	1952	Hoffman-La-Roche	U.S.
		Domagk	German
Isotopes, theory	1912	Soddy	English
Laser (light amplification by stimulated emission of radiation)	1958	Townes, Schawlow	U.S.
Light, velocity	1675	Roemer	Danish
Light, wave theory	1690	Huygens	Dutch
Lithography	1796	Senefelder	Bohemian
Lobotomy	1935	Egas Moniz	Portuguese
LSD-25	1943	Hoffman	Swiss
Mendelian laws	1866	Mendel	Austrian
Mercator projection (map)	1568	Mercator (Kremer)	Flemish
Methanol	1925	Patard	French
Milk condensation	1853	Borden	U.S.
Molecular hypothesis	1811	Avogadro	Italian
Motion, laws of	1687	Newton	English
Neomycin	1949	Waksman, Lechevalier	U.S.
Neutron	1932	Chadwick	English
Nitric acid	1648	Glauber	German
Nitric oxide	1772	Priestley	English
Nitroglycerin	1846	Sobrero	Italian
Oil cracking process	1891	Dewar	U.S.
Oxygen	1774	Priestley	English
Ozone	1840	Schonbein	German
Paper, sulfite process	1867	Tilghman	U.S.
Paper, wood pulp, sulfate process	1884	Dahl	German
Penicillin	1929	Fleming	Scottish
practical use	1941	Florey, Chain	English
Periodic law and table of elements	1869	Mendeleyev	Russian
Planetary motion, laws	1609	Kepler	German
Plutonium fission	1940	Kennedy, Wahl, Seaborg, Segre	U.S.
Polymixin	1947	Ainsworth	English
Positron	1932	Anderson	U.S.
Proton	1919	Rutherford	N. Zealand
Psychoanalysis	1900	Freud	Austrian
Quantum theory	1900	Planck	German
Quasars	1963	Matthews, Sandage	U.S.

	Date	Discoverer	Nation.
Quinine synthetic	1918	Rabe	German
Radioactivity	1896	Becquerel	French
Radium	1898	Curie, Pierre	French
		Curie, Marie	Pol.-Fr.
Relativity theory	1905	Einstein	German
Reserpine	1949	Jal Vaikl	Indian
Salvarsan (606)	1910	Ehrlich	German
Schick test	1913	Schick	U.S.
Silicon	1823	Berzelius	Swedish
Streptomycin	1945	Waksman	U.S.
Sulfadiazine	1940	Roblin	U.S.
Sulfanilamide	1934	Domagk	German
Sulfanilamide theory	1908	Gelmo	German
Sulfapyridine	1938	Ewins, Phelps	English
Sulfathiazole	. . .	Fosbinder, Walter	U.S.
Sulfuric acid	1831	Phillips	English
Sulfuric acid, lead	1746	Roebuck	English
Terramycin	1950	Finlay, et al.	U.S.
Tuberculin	1890	Koch	German

	Date	Discoverer	Nation.
Uranium fission (theory)	1939	Hahn, Meitner, Strassmann	German
		Bohr	Danish
		Fermi	Italian
		Einstein, Pegram, Wheeler	U.S.
Uranium fission, atomic reactor	1942	Fermi, Szilard	U.S.
Vaccine, measles	1954	Enders, Peebles	U.S.
Vaccine, polio	1953	Salk	U.S.
Vaccine, polio, oral	1955	Sabin	U.S.
Vaccine, rabies	1885	Pasteur	French
Vaccine, smallpox	1796	Jenner	English
Vaccine, typhus	1909	Nicolle	French
Van Allen belts, radiation	1958	Van Allen	U.S.
Vitamin A	1913	McCollum, Davis.	U.S.
Vitamin B	1916	McCollum.	U.S.
Vitamin C	1912	Holst, Froelich	Norwegian
Vitamin D	1922	McCollum.	U.S.
Wassermann test	1906	Wassermann	German
Xerography	1938	Carlson	U.S.
X-ray	1895	Roentgen	German

Chemical Elements, Discoverers, Atomic Weights

Atomic weights, based on the exact number 12 as the assigned atomic mass of the principal isotope of carbon, carbon 12, are provided through the courtesy of the International Union of Pure and Applied Chemistry and Butterworth Scientific Publications.

For the radioactive elements, with the exception of uranium and thorium, the mass number of either the isotope of longest half-life (*) or the better known isotope (**) is given.

Chemical element	Symbol	Atomic number	Atomic weight	Year discov.	Discoverer
Actinium	Ac	89	227*	1899	Debierne
Aluminum	Al	13	26.9815	1825	Oersted
Americium	Am	95	243*	1944	Seaborg, et al.
Antimony	Sb	51	121.75	1450	Valentine
Argon	Ar	18	39.948	1894	Rayleigh, Ramsay
Arsenic	As	33	74.9216	13th c.	Albertus Magnus
Astatine	At	85	210*	1940	Corson, et al.
Barium	Ba	56	137.34	1808	Davy
Berkelium	Bk	97	249**	1949	Thompson, Ghiorso, Seaborg
Beryllium	Be	4	9.0122	1798	Vauquelin
Bismuth	Bi	83	208.980	15th c.	Valentine
Boron	B	5	10.811a	1808	Gay-Lussac, Thenard
Bromine	Br	35	79.904b	1826	Balard
Cadmium	Cd	48	112.40	1817	Stromeyer
Calcium	Ca	20	40.08	1808	Davy
Californium	Cf	98	251*	1950	Thompson, et al.
Carbon	C	6	12.01115a	B.C.	
Cerium	Ce	58	140.12	1803	Klaproth
Cesium	Cs	55	132.905	1860	Bunsen, Kirchhoff
Chlorine	Cl	17	35.453b	1774	Scheele
Chromium	Cr	24	51.996b	1797	Vauquelin
Cobalt	Co	27	58.9332	1735	Brandt
Copper	Cu	29	63.546b	B.C.	
Curium	Cm	96	247*	1944	Seaborg, James, Ghiorso
Dysprosium	Dy	66	162.50	1886	Boisbaudran
Einsteinium	Es	99	254*	1952	Ghiorso, et al.
Erbium	Er	68	167.26	1843	Mosander
Europium	Eu	63	151.96	1901	Demarcay
Fermium	Fm	100	257*	1953	Ghiorso, et al.
Fluorine	F	9	18.9984	1771	Scheele
Francium	Fr	87	223*	1939	Perey
Gadolinium	Gd	64	157.25	1886	Marignac
Gallium	Ga	31	69.72	1875	Boisbaudran
Germanium	Ge	32	72.59	1886	Winkler
Gold	Au	79	196.967	B.C.	
Hafnium	Hf	72	178.49	1923	Coster, Hevesy
Hahnium	Ha	105	262*	1970	Ghiorso, et al.
Helium	He	2	4.0026	1868	Janssen, Lockyer
Holmium	Ho	67	164.930	1878	Soret, Delafontaine
Hydrogen	H	1	1.00797a	1766	Cavendish
Indium	In	49	114.82	1863	Reich, Richter
Iodine	I	53	126.9044	1811	Courtois
Iridium	Ir	77	192.2	1804	Tennant
Iron	Fe	26	55.847b	B.C.	
Krypton	Kr	36	83.80	1898	Ramsay, Travers
Lanthanum	La	57	138.91	1839	Mosander
Lawrencium	Lr	103	260*	1961	Ghiorso, T. Sikkeland, A.E. Larsh, and R.M. Latimer
Lead	Pb	82	207.19	B.C.	
Lithium	Li	3	6.939	1817	Arfvedson
Lutetium	Lu	71	174.97	1907	Welsbach, Urbain
Magnesium	Mg	12	24.312	1829	Bussy

Chemical element	Symbol	Atomic number	Atomic weight	Year discov.	Discoverer
Manganese	Mn	25	54.9380	1774	Gahn
Mendelevium	Md	101	258*	1955	Ghiorso, et al.
Mercury	Hg	80	200.59	B.C.	
Molybdenum	Mo	42	95.94	1782	Hjelm
Neodymium	Nd	60	144.24	1885	Welsbach
Neon	Ne	10	20.183	1898	Ramsay, Travers
Neptunium	Np	93	237*	1940	McMillan, Abelson
Nickel	Ni	28	58.71	1751	Cronstedt
Niobium¹	Nb	41	92.906	1801	Hatchett
Nitrogen	N	7	14.0067	1772	Rutherford
Nobelium	No	102	258*	1958	Ghiorso, et al.
Osmium	Os	76	190.2	1804	Tennant
Oxygen	O	8	15.9994a	1774	Priestley, Scheele
Palladium	Pd	46	106.4	1803	Wollaston
Phosphorus	P	15	30.9738	1669	Brand
Platinum	Pt	78	195.09	1735	Ulloa
Plutonium	Pu	94	242**	1940	Seaborg, et al.
Polonium	Po	84	210**	1898	P. and M. Curie
Potassium	K	19	39.102	1807	Davy
Praseodymium	Pr	59	140.907	1885	Welsbach
Promethium	Pm	61	147**	1945	Glendenin, Marinsky, Coryell
Protactinium	Pa	91	231*	1917	Hahn, Meitner
Radium	Ra	88	226*	1898	P. & M. Curie, Bemont
Radon	Rn	86	222*	1900	Dorn
Rhenium	Re	75	186.2	1925	Noddack, Tacke, Berg
Rhodium	Rh	45	102.905	1803	Wollaston
Rubidium	Rb	37	85.47	1861	Bunsen, Kirchhoff
Ruthenium	Ru	44	101.07	1845	Klaus
Rutherfordium	Rf	104	261*	1969	Ghiorso, et al.
Samarium	Sm	62	150.35	1879	Boisbaudran
Scandium	Sc	21	44.956	1879	Nilson
Selenium	Se	34	78.96	1817	Berzelius
Silicon	Si	14	28.086a	1823	Berzellus
Silver	Ag	47	107.868b	B.C.	
Sodium	Na	11	22.9898	1807	Davy
Strontium	Sr	38	87.62	1790	Crawford
Sulfur	S	16	32.064a	B.C.	
Tantalum	Ta	73	180.948	1802	Ekeberg
Technetium	Tc	43	99**	1937	Perrier and Segre
Tellurium	Te	52	127.60	1782	Von Reichenstein
Terbium	Tb	65	158.924	1843	Mosander
Thallium	Tl	81	204.37	1861	Crookes
Thorium	Th	90	232.038	1828	Berzelius
Thulium	Tm	69	168.934	1879	Cleve
Tin	Sn	50	118.69	B.C.	
Titanium	Ti	22	47.90	1791	Gregor
Tungsten (Wolfram)	W	74	183.85	1783	d'Elhujar
Uranium	U	92	238.03	1789	Klaproth
Vanadium	V	23	50.942	1830	Sefstrom
Xenon	Xe	54	131.30	1898	Ramsay, Travers
Ytterbium	Yb	70	173.04	1878	Marignac
Yttrium	Y	39	88.905	1794	Gadolin
Zinc	Zn	30	65.37	B.C.	
Zirconium	Zr	40	91.22	1789	Klaproth

(1) Formerly Columbium. (a) Atomic weights so designated are known to be variable because of natural variations in isotopic composition. The observed ranges are: hydrogen±0.0001; boron±0.003; carbon±0.005; oxygen±0.0001; silicon±0.001; sulfur±0.003. (b) Atomic weights so designated are believed to have the following experimental uncertainties: chlorine±0.001; chromium±0.001; iron±0.003; bromine ± 0.001; silver±0.001; copper±0.001.

Copyright Law of The United States

Source: Copyright Office, Library of Congress

Original works of authorship in any tangible medium of expression are entitled to protection under the copyright law (Title 17 of the United States Code). The law came into effect on January 1, 1978 (Public Law 94-553, 90 Stat. 2541); it superseded the Copyright Act of 1909, as amended. Before the 1976 Act, there had been only three general revisions of the original copyright law of 1790, namely those of 1831, 1870, and 1909.

Categories of Works

Copyright protection under the new law extends to original works of authorship fixed in any tangible medium of expression, now known or later developed, from which they can be perceived, reproduced, or otherwise communicated, either directly or with the aid of a machine or device. Works of authorship include books, periodicals, computer programs and other literary works, musical compositions with accompanying lyrics, dramas and dramatico-musical compositions, pantomimes and choreographic works, motion pictures and other audiovisual works, and sound recordings.

The owner of a copyright is given the exclusive right to reproduce the copyrighted work in copies or phonorecords and distribute them to the public by sale, rental, lease, or lending. The owner of a copyright also enjoys the exclusive right to make derivative works based upon the copyrighted work, to perform the work publicly if it be a literary, musical, dramatic, or choreographic work, a pantomime, motion picture, or other audiovisual work, and in the case of literary, musical, dramatic, and choreographic works, pantomimes, and pictorial, graphic, or sculptural works, including the individual images of a motion picture or other audiovisual work, to display the copyrighted work publicly. All of these rights are subject to certain specified exceptions, including the so-called judicial doctrine of "fair use," which is included in the law for the first time.

The act also provides special provisions permitting compulsory licensing for the recording and distribution of phonorecords of nondramatic musical compositions, noncommercial transmissions by public broadcasters of published musical, pictorial, sculptural, and graphic works, performances of copyrighted nondramatic music by means of jukeboxes, and the secondary transmission of copyrighted works on cable television systems.

Single National System

The law establishes a single national system of statutory protection for all copyrightable works fixed in tangible form, whether published or unpublished. Before Jan. 1, 1978 unpublished works were entitled to protection under the common law of the various states while published works came under the Federal statute.

Registration of a claim to copyright in any work, whether published or unpublished, may be made voluntarily at any time during the copyright term by the owner of the copyright or of any exclusive right in the work. Registration is not a condition of copyright protection, but is a prerequisite to an infringement suit. Subject to certain exceptions, the remedies of statutory damages and attorney's fees are not available for those infringements occurring before registration. Even if registration is not made, copies or phonorecords of works published in the U.S. with notice of copyright are required to be deposited for the collections of the Library of Congress. This deposit requirement is not a condition of protection, but does render the copyright owner subject to penalties for failure to deposit after a demand by the Register of Copyrights.

Duration of Copyright

For works created on or after Jan. 1, 1978, copyright subsists from their creation for a term consisting of the life of the author and 50 years after the author's death. For works made for hire, and for anonymous and pseudonymous works (unless the author's identity is revealed in Copyright Office records), the term is 100 years from creation or 75 years from first publication, whichever is shorter.

The law retains for works that were under statutory protection on January 1, 1978, the 28 year term of copyright from first publication (or from registration in some cases), renewable by certain persons for a second term of protection of 47 years. Copyrights in their first 28-year term on Jan. 1, 1978, have to be renewed in order to be protected for the full maximum term of 75 years. Copyrights in their second term on Jan. 1, 1978 were automatically extended to last for a total term of 75 years.

For works that had been created before the law came into effect but had neither been published nor registered for copyright before Jan. 1, 1978, the term of copyright is generally computed in the same way as for new works: the life-plus-50 or 75/100-year terms will apply. However, all works in this category are guaranteed at least 25 years of statutory protection. The law specifies that copyright in a work of this kind will not expire before Dec. 31, 2002, and if the work is published before that date the term is extended by another 25 years, through the end of the year 2027.

Notice of Copyright

Under the 1909 copyright law the copyright notice was the most important requirement for obtaining copyright protection for a published work. For published works, all copies had to bear the prescribed notice from the time of first publication. If a work was published before Jan. 1, 1978 without the required notice, copyright protection was lost permanently and cannot be regained.

The present copyright law requires a notice on copies or phonorecords of sound recordings that are distributed to the public. Errors and omissions, however, do not immediately result in forfeiture of the copyright and can be corrected within prescribed time limits. Innocent infringers misled by an omission or error in the notice generally are shielded from liability.

The notice of copyright required on all visually perceptible copies published in the U.S. or elsewhere under the 1976 Act consists of the symbol © (the letter C in a circle), the word "Copyright," or the abbreviation "Copr.," and the year of first publication, and the name of the owner of copyright in the work. Example: © 1981 JOHN DOE

The notice must be affixed in such manner and location as to give reasonable notice of the claim of copyright.

The notice of copyright prescribed for all published phonorecords of sound recordings consists of the symbol ℗ (the letter P in a circle), the year of first publication of the sound recording, and the name of the owner of copyright in the sound recording, placed on the surface of the phonorecord, or on the phonorecord label or container in such manner and location as to give reasonable notice of the claim of copyright. Example: ℗ 1981 DOE RECORDS, INC.

Manufacturing Requirements

The requirement in the copyright law, known as the manufacturing clause, mandating that certain textual literary works be manufactured in the U.S. was preserved in the copyright law until July 1, 1986, after Congress elected to override a veto of the extension by President Ronald Reagan. The manufacturing clause, section 601 of the 1976 Copyright Act, requires that works consisting preponderantly of nondramatic literary material (textual material) be manufactured in the United States or Canada to receive full copyright protection. The clause, which was due to expire in July 1982, was extended by Congress for another 4 years.

The manufacturing clause applies only to published works in the English language; as an exception to its provisions, the statute prescribes that, when manufacture has taken place outside the United States or Canada, a maximum of 2,000 copies of the foreign edition may be imported into the United States without affecting the copyright owners' rights. For this purpose, the copyright Office will issue an Import Statement (Form IS) upon request and payment of a fee of $3 at the time of registration or at any later time.

International Protection

The U.S. has copyright relations with more than 70 countries, under which works of American authors are protected in those countries, and the works of their authors are protected in the U.S. The basic feature of this protection is "national treatment," under which the alien author is treated by a country in the same manner that it treats its own authors. Relations exist by virtue of bilateral agreements or through the Buenos Aires Convention or the Universal Copyright Convention. U.S. legislation implementing the latter convention, which became effective Sept. 16, 1955, gives the works of foreign authors the benefit of exemptions from the manufacturing requirements of the U.S. copyright law, provided the works are first published abroad with a copyright notice including the symbol © , the name of the copyright owner and the year date of first publication, and that the work either is by an "author" who is a citizen or subject of a foreign country which belongs to the Convention or is first published in a foreign member country. Conversely, works of U.S. authors are exempt from certain burdensome requirements in particular foreign member countries.

Works published on or after Jan. 1, 1978, are subject to protection under the copyright statute if, on the date of first publication, one or more of the authors is a national or domiciliary of the U.S., or is a national, domiciliary, or sovereign authority of a foreign nation that is a party to a copyright treaty to which the United States is also a party, or is a stateless person, regardless of domicile, or if the work is first published either in the U.S. or in a foreign nation that, on the date of first publication is a party to the Universal Copyright Convention. All unpublished works are protected here regardless of the citizenship or domicile of the author.

A U.S. author may obtain copyright protection in all countries that are members of the Universal Copyright Convention (UCC). In member countries, where no formalities are required, the works of U.S. authors are protected automatically. Member countries whose laws impose formalities protect U.S. works if all published copies bear a convention notice which consists of the symbol ©, together with the name of the copyright owner and the year date of publication. Example: © JOHN DOE 1981.

Further information and application forms may be obtained free of charge by writing to the Information and Publications Section LM-455, Copyright Office, The Library of Congress, Washington, D.C. 20559.

Copyright registration application forms may be ordered on a 24-hour basis by calling (202) 287-9100.

DISASTERS
Some Notable Marine Disasters Since 1850
(Figures indicate estimated lives lost)

1854, Mar.—City of Glasgow; British steamer missing in North Atlantic; 480.

1854, Sept. 27—Arctic; U.S. (Collins Line) steamer sunk in collision with French steamer Vesta near Cape Race; 285-351.

1856, Jan. 23—Pacific; U.S. (Collins Line) steamer missing in North Atlantic; 186-286.

1858, Sept. 23—Austria; German steamer destroyed by fire in North Atlantic; 471.

1863, Apr. 27—Anglo-Saxon; British steamer wrecked at Cape Race; 238.

1865, Apr. 27—Sultana; a Mississippi River steamer blew up near Memphis, Tenn; 1,400.

1869, Oct. 27—Stonewall; steamer burned on Mississippi River below Cairo, Ill.; 200.

1870, Jan. 25—City of Boston; British (Inman Line) steamer vanished between New York and Liverpool; 177.

1870, Oct 19—Cambria; British steamer wrecked off northern Ireland; 196.

1872, Nov. 7—Mary Celeste; U.S. half-brig sailed from New York for Genoa; found abandoned in Atlantic 4 weeks later in mystery of sea; crew never heard from; loss of life unknown.

1873, Jan. 22—Northfleet; British steamer foundered off Dungeness, England; 300.

1873, Apr. 1—Atlantic; British (White Star) steamer wrecked off Nova Scotia; 585.

1873, Nov. 23—Ville du Havre; French steamer, sunk after collision with British sailing ship Loch Earn; 226.

1875, May 7—Schiller; German steamer wrecked off Scilly Isles; 312.

1875, Nov. 4—Pacific; U.S. steamer sunk after collision off Cape Flattery; 236.

1878, Sept. 3—Princess Alice; British steamer sank after collision in Thames; 700.

1878, Dec. 18—Byzantin; French steamer sank after Dardanelles collision; 210.

1881, May 24—Victoria; steamer capsized in Thames River, Canada; 200.

1883, Jan. 19—Cimbria; German steamer sunk in collision with British steamer Sultan in North Sea; 389.

1887, Nov. 15—Wah Yeung; British steamer burned at sea; 400.

1890, Feb. 17—Duburg; British steamer wrecked, China Sea; 400.

1890, Sept. 19—Ertogrul; Turkish frigate foundered off Japan; 540.

1891, Mar. 17—Utopia; British steamer sank in collision with British ironclad Anson off Gibraltar; 562.

1895, Jan. 30—Elbe; German steamer sank in collision with British steamer Craithie in North Sea; 332.

1895, Mar. 11—Reina Regenta; Spanish cruiser foundered near Gibraltar; 400.

1898, Feb. 15—Maine; U.S. battleship blown up in Havana Harbor; 266.

1898, July 4—La Bourgogne; French steamer sunk in collision with British sailing ship Cromartyshire off Nova Scotia; 549.

1904, June 15—General Slocum; excursion steamer burned in East River, New York City; 1,030.

1904, June 28—Norge; Danish steamer wrecked on Rockall Island, Scotland; 620.

1906, Aug. 4—Sirio; Italian steamer wrecked off Cape Palos, Spain; 350.

1908, Mar. 23—Matsu Maru; Japanese steamer sank in collision near Hakodate, Japan; 300.

1909, Aug. 1—Waratah; British steamer, Sydney to London, vanished; 300.

1910, Feb. 9—General Chanzy; French steamer wrecked off Minorca, Spain; 200.

1911, Sept. 25—Liberté; French battleship exploded at Toulon; 285.

1912, Apr. 14-15—Titanic; British (White Star) steamer hit iceberg in North Atlantic; 1,503.

1912, Sept. 28—Kichemaru; Japanese steamer sank off Japanese coast; 1,000.

1914, May 29—Empress of Ireland; British (Canadian Pacific) steamer sunk in collision with Norwegian collier in St. Lawrence River; 1,014.

1915, May 7—Lusitania; British (Cunard Line) steamer torpedoed and sunk by German submarine U. 20 off Ireland; 1,198.

1915, July 24—Eastland; excursion steamer capsized in Chicago River; 812.

1916, Feb. 26—Provence; French cruiser sank in Mediterranean; 3,100.

1916, Mar. 3—Principe de Asturias; Spanish steamer wrecked near Santos, Brazil; 558.

1916, Aug. 29—Hsin Yu; Chinese steamer sank off Chinese coast; 1,000.

1917, Dec. 6—Mont Blanc, Imo; French ammunition ship and Belgian steamer collided in Halifax Harbor; 1,600.

1918, Apr. 25—Kiang-Kwan Chinese steamer sank in collision off Hankow; 500.

1918, July 12—Kawachi; Japanese battleship blew up in Tokayama Bay; 500.

1918, Oct. 25—Princess Sophia; Canadian steamer sank off Alaskan coast; 398.

1919, Jan. 17—Chaonia; French steamer lost in Straits of Messina, Italy; 460.

1919, Sept. 9—Valbanera; Spanish steamer lost off Florida coast; 500.

1921, Mar. 18—Hong Kong; steamer wrecked in South China Sea; 1,000.

1922, Aug. 26—Niitaka; Japanese cruiser sank in storm off Kamchatka, USSR; 300.

1927, Oct. 25—Principessa Mafalda; Italian steamer blew up, sank off Porto Seguro, Brazil; 314.

1934, Sept. 8—Morro Castle; U.S. steamer, Havana to New York, burned off Asbury Park, N.J.; 125.

1939, May 23—Squalus; U.S. submarine sank off Portsmouth, N.H.; 26.

1939, June 1—Thetis; British submarine, sank in Liverpool Bay; 99.

1942, Feb. 18—Truxton and Pollux; U.S. destroyer and cargo ship ran aground, sank off Newfoundland; 204.

1942, Oct. 2—Curacao; British cruiser sank after collision with liner Queen Mary; 335.

1947, Jan. 19—Himera; Greek steamer hit a mine off Athens; 392.

1947, Apr. 16—Grandcamp; French freighter exploded in Texas City, Tex., Harbor, starting fires; 510.

1952, Apr. 26—Hobson and Wasp; U.S. destroyer and aircraft carrier collided in Atlantic; 176.

1953, Jan. 31—Princess Victoria; British ferry foundered off northern Irish coast; 134.

1954, Sept. 26—Toya Maru; Japanese ferry sank in Tsugaru Strait, Japan; 1,172.

1956, July 26—Andrea Doria and Stockholm; Italian liner and Swedish liner collided off Nantucket; 51.

1957, July 14—Eshghabad; Soviet ship ran aground in Caspian Sea; 270.

1961, Apr. 8—Dara; British liner burned in Persian Gulf; 212.

1961, Apr. 8—Save; Portuguese ship ran aground off Mozambique; 259.

1963, Apr. 10—Thresher; U.S. Navy atomic submarine sank in North Atlantic; 129.

1964, Feb. 10—Voyager, Melbourne; Australian destroyer sank after collision with Australian aircraft carrier Melbourne off New South Wales; 82.

1968, Jan. 25—Dakar; Israeli submarine vanished in Mediterranean; 69.

1968, Jan. 27—Minerve; French submarine vanished in Mediterranean; 52.

1968, May 21—Scorpion; U.S. nuclear submarine sank in Atlantic near Azores; 99.

1969, June 2—Evans; U.S. destroyer cut in half by Australian carrier Melbourne, S. China Sea; 74.

1970, Mar. 4—Eurydice; French submarine sank in Mediterranean near Toulon; 57.

1970, Dec. 15—Namyong-Ho; South Korean ferry sank in Korea Strait; 308.

1974, May 1— Motor launch capsized off Bangladesh; 250.

1974, Sept. 26— Soviet destroyer burned and sank in Black Sea; est. 200.

1976, Oct. 20—George Prince and Frosta; ferryboat and Norwegian tanker collided on Mississippi R. at Luling, La.; 77.

1976, Dec. 25—Patria; Egyptian liner caught fire and sank in the Red Sea; c. 100.

1977, Jan. 11—Grand Zenith; Panamanian-registered tanker sank off Cape Cod, Mass.; 38.

**1977, Jan. 17—Spanish freighter collided with launch in Barcelona, Spain harbor; 46.

**1979, Aug. 14—23 yachts competing in Fastnet yacht race sunk or abandoned during storm in S. Irish Sea; 18.

1981, Jan. 27—Tamponas II; Indonesian passenger ship caught fire and sank in Java Sea; 580.

1981, May 26—Nimitz; U.S. Marine combat jet crashed on deck of U.S. aircraft carrier; 14.

1983, Feb. 12—Marine Electric; coal freighter sank during storm off Chincoteague, Va.; 33.

Major Earthquakes

Magnitude of earthquakes (Mag.), distinct from deaths or damage caused, is measured on the Richter scale, on which each higher number represents a tenfold increase in energy measured in ground motion. Adopted in 1935, the scale has been applied in the following table to earthquakes as far back as reliable seismograms are available.

Date		Place	Deaths	Mag.	Date		Place	Deaths	Mag.
526	May 20	Syria, Antioch.	250,000	N.A.	1956	June 10-17	N. Afghanistan	2,000	7.7
856	....	Greece, Corinth	45,000	"	1957	July 2	Northern Iran	2,500	7.4
1057	....	China, Chihli	25,000	"	1957	Dec. 13	Western Iran	2,000	7.1
1268	....	Asia Minor, Cilicia	60,000	"	1960	Feb. 29	Morocco, Agadir	12,000	5.8
1290	Sept. 27	China, Chihli	100,000	"	1960	May 21-30	Southern-Chile	5,000	8.3
1293	May 20	Japan, Kamakura	30,000	"	1962	Sept. 1	Northwestern Iran	12,230	7.1
1531	Jan. 26	Portugal, Lisbon	30,000	"	1963	July 26	Yugoslavia, Skopje	1,100	6.0
1556	Jan. 24	China, Shaanxi	830,000	"	1964	Mar. 27	Alaska	114	8.5
1667	Nov.	Caucasia, Shemaka	80,000	"	1966	Aug. 19	Eastern Turkey	2,520	6.9
1693	Jan. 11	Italy, Catania	60,000	"	1968	Aug. 31	Northeastern Iran	12,000	7.4
1730	Dec. 30	Japan, Hokkaido	137,000	"	1970	Mar. 28	Western Turkey	1,086	7.4
1737	Oct. 11	India, Calcutta	300,000	"	1970	May 31	Northern Peru	66,794	7.7
1755	June 7	Northern Persia	40,000	"	1971	Feb. 9	Cal., San Fernando Val-		
1755	Nov. 1	Portugal, Lisbon	60,000	8.75*			ley.	65	6.5
1783	Feb. 4	Italy, Calabria.	30,000	N.A.	1972	Apr. 10	Southern Iran	5,057	6.9
1797	Feb. 4	Ecuador, Quito	41,000	N.A.	1972	Dec. 23	Nicaragua.	5,000	6.2
1822	Sept. 5	Asia Minor, Aleppo.	22,000	N.A.	1974	Dec. 28	Pakistan (9 towns).	5,200	6.3
1828	Dec. 28	Japan, Echigo	30,000	"	1975	Sept. 6	Turkey (Lice, etc.)	2,312	6.8
1868	Aug. 13-15	Peru and Ecuador	40,000	"	1976	Feb. 4	Guatemala	22,778	7.5
1875	May 16	Venezuela, Colombia	16,000	"	1976	May 6	Northeast Italy	946	6.5
1896	June 15	Japan, sea wave	27,120	"	1976	June 26	New Guinea, Irian Jaya	443	7.1
1906	Apr. 18-19	Cal., San Francisco	452	8.3	1976	July 28	China, Tangshan	800,000	8.2
1906	Aug. 16	Chile, Valparaiso	20,000	8.6	1976	Aug. 17	Philippines, Mindanao	8,000	7.8
1908	Dec. 28	Italy, Messina.	83,000	7.5	1976	Nov. 24	Eastern Turkey.	4,000	7.9
1915	Jan. 13	Italy, Avezzano	29,980	7.5	1977	Mar. 4	Romania, Bucharest, etc.	1,541	7.5
1920	Dec. 16	China, Gansu	100,000	8.6	1977	Aug. 19	Indonesia	200	8.0
1923	Sept. 1	Japan, Tokyo.	99,330	8.3	1977	Nov. 23	Northwestern Argentina	100	8.2
1927	May 22	China, Nan-Shan.	200,000	8.3	1978	June 12	Japan, Sendai	21	7.5
1932	Dec. 26	China, Gansu	70,000	7.6	1978	Sept. 16	Northeast Iran	25,000	7.7
1933	Mar. 2	Japan	2,990	8.9	1979	Sept. 12	Indonesia	100	8.1
1934	Jan. 15	India, Bihar-Nepal	10,700	8.4	1979	Dec. 12	Colombia, Ecuador	800	7.9
1935	May 31	India, Quetta	30,000	7.5	1980	Oct. 10	Northwestern Algeria	4,500	7.3
1939	Jan. 24	Chile, Chillan	28,000	8.3	1980	Nov. 23	Southern Italy	4,800	7.2
1939	Dec. 26	Turkey, Erzincan	30,000	7.9	1982	Dec. 13	North Yemen	2,800	6.0
1946	Dec. 21	Japan, Honshu	2,000	8.4	1983	Mar. 31	Southern Colombia	250	5.5
1948	June 28	Japan, Fukui	5,131	7.3	1983	May 26	N. Honshu, Japan	81	7.7
1949	Aug. 5	Ecuador, Pelileo	6,000	6.8	1983	Oct. 30	Eastern Turkey.	1,300	7.1
1950	Aug. 15	India, Assam	1,530	8.7					
1953	Mar. 18	NW Turkey	1,200	7.2	(*) estimated from earthquake intensity. (N.A.) not available.				

Some Recent Earthquakes

Source: Scientific Event Alert Network, Smithsonian Institution

Attached is a list of recent earthquakes. Magnitude of earthquakes is measured on the Richter scale, on which each higher number represents a tenfold increase in energy measured in ground motion.

Date	Place	Magnitude	Date	Place	Magnitude
May 30, 1984	Papua New Guinea	6.7	Dec. 21	New Britain	6.4
May 26	W. Indian Ocean	6.7	Dec. 2	Guatemala	7.1
May 11	Central Italy	5.3	Nov. 30	Central Indian Ocean	7.6
May 7	Central Italy	5.8	Nov. 24	Banda Sea	6.8
Apr. 29	Central Italy	5.1	Nov. 16	Hawaii	6.6
Apr. 24	Nr. San Jose, California, U.S.	6.1	Oct. 30	E. Turkey	7.1
Apr. 23	Lancaster County, Pa., U.S.	4.1	Oct. 28	Custer Co:, Idaho	6.9
Mar. 27	Papua New Guinea	6.5	Oct. 22	S. Sandwich Islands	7.0
Mar. 24	Kuril Islands	7.0	Oct. 15	Solomon Islands	6.7
Mar. 19	Turkmen, SSR	7.0	Oct. 7	Adirondak Mts., N.Y.	5.2
Mar. 6	Nr. Honshu, Japan	6.5	Oct. 4	N. Chile	7.3
Mar. 5	Mindanao, Philippines	6.7	Sept. 7	S. Alaska	6.3
Feb. 17	NE Afghanistan	5.8	Aug. 17	Luzon, Philippines	6.7
Feb. 7	Solomon Islands	7.5	Aug. 6	N. Aegean Sea	7.1
Feb. 1	NE Afghanistan	5.7	July 21	Central California	5.9
Jan. 8	Indonesia	6.6	July 12	S. Alaska	6.3
Jan. 1	Nr. Honshu, Japan	6.5	June 24	NW Vietnam	6.6
Dec. 31, 1983	Off Hokkaido, Japan	7.0	June 24	Off Taiwan	6.5
Dec. 30	NE Afghanistan	7.0	June 21	Sea of Japan	6.9
Dec. 22	W. Africa	6.3	June 11	Central California	5.4
Dec. 22	New Britain	6.5			

Some Major Tornadoes In U.S. Since 1925

Source: National Climatic Center, NOAA, U.S. Commerce Department

Date			Place	Deaths	Date			Place	Deaths
1925	Mar.	18	Mo., Ill. Ind.	689	1942	Mar.	16	Central to NE Miss.	75
1927	Apr.	12	Rock Springs, Tex.	74	1942	Apr.	27	Rogers & Mayes Co., Okla.	52
1927	May	9	Arkansas, Poplar Bluff, Mo.	92	1944	June	23	Oh., Pa., W. Va., Md.	150
1930	May	6	Hill & Ellis Co., Tex.	41	1945	Apr.	12	Okla.-Ark.	102
1932	Mar.	21	Ala. (series of tornadoes)	268	1947	Apr.	9	Tex., Okla. & Kan.	169
1936	Apr.	5	Tupelo, Miss.	216	1948	Mar.	19	Bunker Hill & Gillespie, Ill.	33
1936	Apr.	6	Gainesville, Ga.	203	1949	Jan.	3	La. & Ark.	58
1938	Sept.	29	Charleston, S.C.	32	1952	Mar.	21	Ark., Mo., Tenn. (series)	208

Date		Place	Deaths	Date		Place	Deaths
1953	May 11	Waco, Tex.	114	1969	Jan. 23	Mississippi.	32
1953	June 8	Flint to Lakeport, Mich.	116	1971	Feb. 21	Mississippi delta	110
1953	June 9	Worcester and vicinity, Mass.	90	1973	May 26-7	South, Midwest (series)	47
1953	Dec. 5	Vicksburg, Miss.	38	1974	Apr. 3-4	Ala., Ga., Tenn., Ky., Oh.	350
1955	May 25	Udall, Kan.	80	1977	Apr. 1	Southeast Bangladesh	600
1957	May 20	Kan., Mo.	48	1977	Apr. 4	Ala., Miss., Ga.	22
1958	June 4	Northwestern Wisconsin	30	1978	Apr. 16	Orissa, India	500
1959	Feb. 10	St. Louis, Mo.	21	1979	Apr. 10	Tex., Okla.	60
1960	May 5, 6	SE Oklahoma, Arkansas	30	1980	June 3	Grand Island, Neb. (series)	4
1965	Apr. 11	Ind., Ill., Oh., Mich., Wis.	271	1982	Mar. 2-4	South, Midwest (series)	17
1966	Mar. 3	Jackson, Miss.	57	1982	May 29	So. Ill.	10
1966	Mar. 3	Mississippi, Alabama	61	1983	May 18-22	Tex.	12
1967	Apr. 21	Illinois	33	1984	Mar. 29	N. Carolina; S. Carolina	67
1968	May 15	Arkansas	34	1984	Apr. 21-22	Mississippi	15

Hurricanes, Typhoons, Blizzards, Other Storms

Names of hurricanes and typhoons in italics—H.—hurricane; T.—typhoon

Date	Location	Deaths	Date	Location	Deaths
1888 Mar. 11-14	Blizzard, Eastern U.S.	400	1965 Sept. 7-10	H.*Betsy*, Fla., Miss., La.	74
1900 Sept. 8	H., Galveston, Tex.	6,000	1965 Dec. 15	Windstorm, Bangladesh	10,000
1926 Sept. 16-22	H., Fla., Ala.	372	1966 June 4-10	H.*Alma*, Honduras, SE U.S.	51
1926 Oct. 20	H., Cuba	600	1966 Sept. 24-30	H.*Inez*, Carib., Fla., Mex.	293
1928 Sept. 12-17	H., W. Indies, Fla.	4,000	1967 July 9	T.*Billie*, Japan	347
1930 Sept. 3	H., San Domingo	2,000	1967 Sept. 5-23	H.*Beulah*, Carib., Mex., Tex.	54
1938 Sept. 21	H., New England	600	1967 Dec. 12-20	Blizzard, Southwest, U.S.	51
1942 Oct. 15-16	H., Bengal, India	11,000	1968 Nov. 18-28	T.*Nina*, Philippines	63
1944 Sept. 12-16	H., N.C. to New Eng.	389	1969 Aug. 17-18	H.*Camille*, Miss., La.	256
1953 Sept. 25-27	T., Vietnam, Japan	1,300	1970 July 30-		
1954 Aug. 30	H. *Carol*, Northeast U.S.	68	Aug. 5	H.*Celia*, Cuba, Fla., Tex.	31
1954 Oct. 12-13	H.*Hazel*, Eastern, U.S., Haiti	347	1970 Aug. 20-21	H.*Dorothy*, Martinique	42
1955 Aug. 12-13	H. *Connie*, Carolinas, Va., Md.	43	1970 Sept. 15	T.*Georgia*, Philippines	300
1955 Aug. 18-19	H.*Diane*, Eastern U.S.	400	1970 Oct. 14	T.*Sening*, Philippines	583
1955 Sept. 19	H.*Hilda*, Mexico	200	1970 Oct. 15	T.*Titang*, Philippines	526
1955 Sept. 22-28	H.*Janet*, Caribbean	500	1970 Nov. 13	Cyclone, Bangladesh	300,000
1956 Feb. 1-29	Blizzard, Western Europe	1,000	1971 Aug. 1	T.*Rose*, Hong Kong	130
1957 June 27-30	H.*Audrey*, La., Tex.	430	1972 June 19-29	H.*Agnes*, Fla. to N.Y.	118
1958 Feb. 15-16	Blizzard, NE U.S.	171	1972 Dec. 3	T.*Theresa*, Philippines	169
1959 Sept. 17-19	T.*Sarah*, Far East	2,000	1973 June-Aug.	Monsoon rains in India	1,217
1959 Sept. 26-27	T.*Vera*, Honshu, Japan.	4,466	1974 June 11	Storm*Dinah*, Luzon Is., Philip.	71
1960 Sept. 4-12	H.*Donna*, Caribbean, E. U.S.	148	1974 July 11	T.*Gilda*, Japan, S. Korea	108
1961 Oct. 31	H.*Hattie*, Br. Honduras	400	1974 Sept. 19-20	H.*Fifi*, Honduras	2,000
1962 Feb. 17	Flooding, German Coast	343	1974 Dec. 25	Cyclone leveled Darwin, Aus.	50
1962 Sept. 27	Flooding, Barcelona, Spain	445	1975 Sept. 13-27	H.*Eloise*, Caribbean, NE U.S.	71
1963 May 28-29	Windstorm, Bangladesh	22,000	1976 May 20	T.*Olga*, floods, Philippines	215
1963 Oct. 4-8	H.*Flora*, Cuba, Haiti	6,000	1977 July 25, 31	T.*Thelma*, T. *Vera*, Taiwan	39
1964 Oct. 4-7	H.*Hilda*, La., Miss., Ga.	38	1978 Oct. 27	T. *Rita*, Philippines	c. 400
1964 June 30	T.*Winnie*, N. Philippines	107	1979 Aug. 30-		
1964 Sept. 5	T.*Ruby*, Hong Kong and China	735	Sept. 7	H.*David*, Caribbean, E U.S.	1,100
1964 Sept. 14	Flooding, central S. Korea	563	1980 Aug. 4-11	H.*Allen*, Caribbean, Texas	272
1964 Nov. 12	Flooding, S. Vietnam	7,000	1981 Nov. 25	T.*Irma*, Luzon Is., Philip.	176
1965 May 11-12	Windstorm, Bangladesh	17,000	1983 June	Monsoon rains in India	900
1965 June 1-2	Windstorm, Bangladesh	30,000	1983 Aug. 18	H.*Alicia*, Southern Texas	17

Floods, Tidal Waves

Date		Location	Deaths	Date		Location	Deaths
1887	....	Huang He River, China	900,000	1969	Aug. 25	Western Virginia	189
1889	May 31	Johnstown, Pa.	2,200	1969	Sept. 15	South Korea	250
1900	Sept. 8	Galveston, Tex.	5,000	1969	Oct. 1-8	Tunisia	500
1903	June 15	Heppner, Ore.	325	1970	May 20	Central Romania	160
1911	....	Chang Jiang River, China.	100,000	1970	July 22	Himalayas, India	500
1913	Mar. 25-27	Ohio, Indiana	732	1971	Feb. 26	Rio de Janeiro, Brazil	130
1915	Aug. 17	Galveston, Tex.	275	1972	Feb. 26	Buffalo Creek, W. Va.	118
1928	Mar. 13	Collapse of St. Francis		1972	June 9	Rapid City, S.D.	236
		Dam, Santa Paula, Cal.	450	1972	Aug. 7	Luzon Is., Philippines	454
1928	Sept. 13	Lake Okeechobee, Fla.	2,000	1974	Mar. 29	Tubaro, Brazil	1,000
1931	Aug.	Huang He River, China	3,700,000	1974	Aug. 12	Monty-Long, Bangladesh	2,500
1937	Jan. 22	Ohio, Miss. Valleys	250	1975	Jan. 11	Southern Thailand	131
1939	....	Northern China	200,000	1976	June 5	Teton Dam collapse, Ida.	11
1947	....	Honshu Island, Japan.	1,900	1976	July 31	Big Thompson Canyon, Col.	130
1951	Aug.	Manchuria	1,800	1976	Nov. 17	East Java, Indonesia	136
1953	Jan. 31	Western Europe	2,000	1977	July 19-20	Johnstown, Pa.	68
1954	Aug. 17	Farahzad, Iran	2,000	1978	June-Sept.	Northern India	1,200
1955	Oct. 7-12	India, Pakistan	1,700	1979	Jan.-Feb.	Brazil	204
1959	Nov. 1	Western Mexico	2,000	1979	July	Lomblem Is., Indonesia	539
1959	Dec. 2	Frejus, France	412	1979	Aug. 11	Morvi, India	5,000-15,000
1960	Oct. 10	Bangladesh	6,000	1980	Feb. 13-22	So. Cal., Ariz.	26
1960	Oct. 31	Bangladesh	4,000	1981	Apr.	Northern China	550
1962	Feb. 17	German North Sea coast	343	1981	July	Sichuan, Hubei Prov., China	1,300
1962	Sept. 27	Barcelona, Spain	445	1982	Jan. 23	Nr. Lima, Peru	600
1963	Oct. 9	Dam collapse, Vaiont, Italy	1,800	1982	May 12	Guangdong, China	430
1966	Nov. 4-6	Florence, Venice, Italy	113	1982	June 6	So. Conn.	12
1967	Jan. 18-24	Eastern Brazil	894	1982	Sept. 17-21	El Salvador, Guatemala	1,300+
1967	Mar. 19	Rio de Janeiro, Brazil	436	1982	Dec. 2-9	Ill., Mo., Ark.	22
1968	Aug. 7-14	Gujarat State, India	1,000	1983	Feb.-Mar.	Cal. coast	13
1968	Oct. 7	Northeastern India	780	1983	Apr. 6-12	Ala., Miss., Tenn.	15
1969	Mar. 17	Mundau Valley, Alagoas, Brazil	218				

Explosions

Date			Location	Deaths	Date			Location	Deaths
1910	Oct.	1	Los Angeles Times Bldg.	21	1963	Jan.	2	Packing plant, Terre Haute, Ind.	16
1913	Mar.	7	Dynamite, Baltimore harbor	55	1963	Mar.	9	Dynamite plant, S. Africa	45
1915	Sept.	27	Gasoline tank car, Ardmore, Okla.	47	1963	Aug.	13	Explosives dump, Gauhiti, India	32
1917	Apr.	10	Munitions plant, Eddystone, Pa.	133	1963	Oct.	31	State Fair Coliseum, Indianapolis	73
1917	Dec.	6	Halifax Harbor, Canada	1,654	1964	July	23	Bone, Algeria, harbor munitions	100
1918	May	18	Chemical plant, Oakdale, Pa.	193	1965	Mar.	4	Gas pipeline, Natchitoches, La.	17
1918	July	2	Explosives, Split Rock, N.Y.	50	1965	Aug.	9	Missile silo, Searcy, Ark.	53
1918	Oct.	4	Shell plant, Morgan Station, N.J.	64	1965	Oct.	21	Bridge, Tila Bund, Pakistan	80
1919	May	22	Food plant, Cedar Rapids, Ia.	44	1965	Oct.	30	Cartagena, Colombia	48
1920	Sept.	16	Wall Street, New York, bomb	30	1965	Nov.	24	Armory, Keokuk, Ia.	20
1924	Jan.	3	Food plant, Pekin, Ill.	42	1966	Oct.	13	Chemical plant, La Salle, Que.	11
1928	April	13	Dance hall, West Plains, Mo.	40	1967	Feb.	17	Chemical plant, Hawthorne, N.J.	11
1937	Mar.	18	New London, Tex., school	294	1967	Dec.	25	Apartment bldg., Moscow	20
1940	Sept.	11	Hercules Powder, Kenvil, N.J.	51	1968	Apr.	6	Sports store, Richmond, Ind.	43
1942	June	5	Ordnance plant, Elwood, Ill.	49	1970	Apr.	8	Subway construction, Osaka, Japan	73
1944	Apr.	14	Bombay, India, harbor	700	1971	June	24	Tunnel, Sylmar, Cal.	17
1944	July	17	Port Chicago, Cal., pier	322	1971	June	28	School, fireworks, Pueblo, Mex.	13
1944	Oct.	21	Liquid gas tank, Cleveland	135	1971	Oct.	21	Shopping center, Glasgow, Scot.	20
1947	Apr.	16	Texas City, Tex., pier	561	1973	Feb.	10	Liquified gas tank, Staten Is., N.Y.	40
1948	July	28	Farben works, Ludwigshafen, Ger.	184	1975	Dec.	27	Chasnala, India, mine	431
1950	May	19	Munitions barges, S. Amboy, N.J.	30	1976	Apr.	13	Lapua, Finland, munitions works	45
1956	Aug.	7	Dynamite trucks, Cali, Colombia	1,100	1977	Nov.	11	Freight train, Iri, S. Korea	57
1958	Apr.	18	Sunken munitions ship, Okinawa	40	1977	Dec.	22	Grain elevator, Westwego, La.	35
1958	May	22	Nike missiles, Leonardo, N.J.	10	1978	Feb.	24	Derailed tank car, Waverly, Tenn.	12
1959	Apr.	10	World War II bomb, Philippines	38	1978	July	11	Propylene tank truck, Spanish	
1959	June	28	Rail tank cars, Meldrin, Ga.	25				coastal campsite	150
1959	Aug.	7	Dynamite truck, Roseburg, Ore.	13	1980	Oct.	23	School, Ortuella, Spain	64
1959	Nov.	2	Jamuri Bazar, India, explosives	46	1981	Feb.	13	Sewer system, Louisville, Ky.	0
1959	Dec.	13	Dortmund, Ger., 2 apt. bldgs.	26	1982	Apr.	7	Tanker truck, tunnel, Oakland, Gal.	7
1960	Mar.	4	Belgian munitions ship, Havana	100	1982	Apr.	25	Antiques exhibition, Todi, Italy.	33
1960	Oct.	25	Gas, Windsor, Ont., store	11	1982	Nov.	2	Salang Tunnel, Afghanistan	1,000-3,000
1962	Jan.	16	Gas pipeline, Edson, Alberta, Canada	8	1984	Feb.	25	Oil pipeline, Cubatao, Brazil	508
1962	Oct.	3	Telephone Co. office, N.Y. City	23					

Fires

Date			Location	Deaths	Date			Location	Deaths
1845	May		Theater, Canton, China	1,670	1960	Nov.	13	Movie theater, Amude, Syria	152
1871	Oct.	8	Chicago, $196 million loss	250	1961	Jan.	6	Thomas Hotel, San Francisco	20
1871	Oct.	8	Peshtigo, Wis., forest fire	1,182	1961	Dec.	8	Hospital, Hartford, Conn.	16
1876	Dec.	5	Brooklyn (N.Y.), theater	295	1961	Dec.	17	Circus, Niteroi, Brazil	323
1877	June	20	St. John, N.B., Canada	100	1963	May	4	Theater, Diourbel, Senegal	64
1881	Dec.	8	Ring Theater, Vienna	850	1963	Nov.	18	Surfside Hotel, Atlantic City, N.J.	25
1887	May	25	Opera Comique, Paris	200	1963	Nov.	23	Rest home, Fitchville, Oh.	63
1887	Sept.	4	Exeter, England, theater	200	1963	Dec.	29	Roosevelt Hotel, Jacksonville, Fla.	22
1894	Sept.	1	Hinckley, Minn., forest fire	413	1964	May	8	Apartment building, Manila	30
1897	May	4	Charity bazaar, Paris	150	1964	Dec.	18	Nursing home, Fountaintown, Ind.	20
1900	June	30	Hoboken, N.J., docks	326	1965	Mar.	1	Apartment, LaSalle, Canada	28
1902	Sept.	20	Church, Birmingham, Ala.	115	1966	Mar.	11	Numata, Japan, 2 ski resorts	31
1903	Dec.	30	Iroquois Theater, Chicago	602	1966	Aug.	13	Melbourne, Australia, hotel	29
1908	Jan.	13	Rhoads Theater, Boyertown, Pa.	170	1966	Sept.	12	Anchorage, Alaska, hotel	14
1908	Mar.	4	School, Collinwood, Oh.	176	1966	Oct.	17	N.Y. City bldg. (firemen)	12
1911	Mar.	25	Triangle factory, N.Y. City	145	1966	Dec.	7	Erzurum, Turkey, barracks	68
1913	Oct.	14	Colliery, Mid Glamorgan, Wales	439	1967	Feb.	7	Restaurant, Montgomery, Ala.	25
1918	Apr.	13	Norman Okla., state hospital	38	1967	May	22	Store, Brussels, Belgium	322
1918	Oct.	12	Cloquet, Minn., forest fire	400	1967	July	16	State prison, Jay, Fla.	37
1919	June	20	Mayaguez Theater, San Juan.	150	1968	Feb.	26	Shrewsbury, England, hospital	22
1923	May	17	School, Camden, S.C.	76	1968	May	11	Vijayawada, India, wedding hall	58
1924	Dec.	24	School, Hobart, Okla.	35	1968	Nov.	18	Glasgow, Scotland, factory	24
1929	May	15	Clinic, Cleveland, Oh.	125	1969	Jan.	26	Victoria Hotel, Dunnville, Ont.	13
1930	Apr.	21	Penitentiary, Columbus, Oh.	320	1969	Dec.	2	Nursing home, Notre Dame, Can.	54
1931	July	24	Pittsburgh, Pa., home for aged	48	1970	Jan.	9	Nursing home, Marietta, Oh.	27
1934	Dec.	11	Hotel Kerns, Lansing, Mich.	34	1970	Mar.	20	Hotel, Seattle, Wash.	19
1938	May	16	Atlanta, Ga., Terminal Hotel	35	1970	Nov.	1	Dance hall, Grenoble, France	145
1940	Apr.	23	Dance hall, Natchez, Miss.	198	1970	Dec.	20	Hotel, Tucson, Arizona	28
1942	Nov.	28	Cocoanut Grove, Boston	491	1971	Mar.	6	Psychiatric clinic, Burghoezli,	
1942			Hostel, St. John's, Newfoundland	100				Switzerland	28
1943	Sept.	7	Gulf Hotel, Houston	55	1971	Apr.	20	Hotel, Bangkok, Thailand	24
1944	July	6	Ringling Circus, Hartford	168	1971	Oct.	19	Nursing home, Honesdale, Pa.	15
1946	June	5	LaSalle Hotel, Chicago	61	1971	Dec.	25	Hotel, Seoul, So. Korea	162
1946	Dec.	7	Winecoff Hotel, Atlanta	119	1972	May	13	Osaka, Japan, nightclub	116
1946	Dec.	12	New York, ice plant, tenement	37	1972	July	5	Sherborne, England, hospital	30
1949	Apr.	5	Hospital, Effingham, Ill.	77	1973	Feb.	6	Paris, France, school	21
1950	Jan.	7	Davenport, Ia., Mercy Hospital	41	1973	Nov.	6	Fukui, Japan, train	28
1953	Mar.	29	Largo, Fla., nursing home	35	1973	Nov.	29	Kumamoto, Japan, department	
1953	Apr.	16	Chicago, metalworking plant	35				store.	107
1957	Feb.	17	Home for aged, Warrenton, Mo.	72	1973	Dec.	2	Seoul, Korea, theater	50
1958	Mar.	19	New York City loft building	24	1974	Feb.	1	Sao Paulo, Brazil, bank building	189
1958	Dec.	1	Parochial school, Chicago	95	1974	June	30	Port Chester, N.Y., discotheque	24
1958	Dec.	16	Store, Bogota, Colombia	83	1974	Nov.	3	Seoul, So. Korea, hotel discotheque	88
1959	June	23	Resort hotel, Stalheim, Norway	34	1975	Dec.	12	Mina, Saudi Arabia, tent city	138
1960	Mar.	12	Pusan, Korea, chemical plant	68	1976	Oct.	24	Bronx, N.Y., social club	25
1960	July	14	Mental hospital, Guatemala City	225	1977	Feb.	25	Rossiya Hotel, Moscow	45

Date			Location	Deaths	Date			Location	Deaths
1977	May	28	Southgate, Ky., nightclub	164	1980	Dec.	4	Stouffer Inn, Harrison, N.Y.	26
1977	June	9	Abidjan, Ivory Coast nightclub	41	1981	Jan.	9	Keansburg, N.J., boarding home	30
1977	June	26	Columbia, Tenn., jail	42	1981	Feb.	10	Las Vegas Hilton	8
1977	Nov.	14	Manila, Pl, hotel.	47	1981	Feb.	14	Dublin, Ireland, discotheque	44
1978	Jan.	28	Kansas City, Coates House Hotel	16	1982	Sept.	4	Los Angeles, apartment house	24
1979	Dec.	31	Chapais, Quebec, social club	42	1982	Nov.	8	Biloxi, Miss., county jail	29
1980	May	20	Kingston, Jamaica, nursing home.	157	1983	Feb.	13	Turin, Italy, movie theater	64
1980	Nov.	21	MGM Grand Hotel, Las Vegas	84	1983	Dec.	17	Madrid, Spain, discotheque	83

Major U.S. Railroad Wrecks

Date			Location	Deaths	Date			Location	Deaths
1876	Dec.	29	Ashtabula, Oh.	92	1925	June	16	Hackettstown, N. J.	50
1880	Aug.	11	Mays Landing, N. J.	40	1925	Oct.	27	Victoria, Miss.	21
1887	Aug.	10	Chatsworth, Ill.	81	1926	Sept.	5	Waco, Col.	30
1888	Oct.	10	Mud Run, Pa.	55	1928	Aug.	24	I.R.T. subway, Times Sq., N. Y.	18
1896	July	30	Atlantic City, N. J.	60	1938	June	19	Saugus, Mont.	47
1903	Dec.	23	Laurel Run, Pa.	53	1939	Aug.	12	Harney, Nev.	24
1904	Aug.	7	Eden, Col.	96	1940	Apr.	19	Little Falls, N. Y.	31
1904	Sept.	24	New Market Tenn.	56	1940	July	31	Cuyahoga Falls, Oh.	43
1906	Mar.	16	Florence, Col.	35	1943	Aug.	29	Wayland, N. Y.	27
1906	Oct.	28	Atlantic City, N. J.	40	1943	Sept.	6	Frankford Junction, Philadelphia, Pa.	79
1906	Dec.	30	Washington, D. C.	53	1943	Dec.	16	Between Rennert and Buie, N. C.	72
1907	Jan.	2	Volland, Kan.	33	1944	July	6	High Bluff, Tenn.	35
1907	Jan.	19	Fowler, Ind.	29	1944	Aug.	4	Near Stockton, Ga.	47
1907	Feb.	16	New York, N.Y.	22	1944	Sept.	14	Dewey, Ind.	29
1907	Feb.	23	Colton, Cal.	26	1944	Dec.	31	Bagley, Utah	50
1907	July	20	Salem, Mich.	33	1945	Aug.	9	Michigan, N. D.	34
1910	Mar.	1	Wellington, Wash.	96	1946	Apr.	25	Naperville, Ill.	45
1910	Mar.	21	Green Mountain, Ia.	55	1947	Feb.	18	Gallitzin, Pa.	24
1911	Aug.	25	Manchester, N. Y.	29	1950	Feb.	17	Rockville Centre, N. Y.	31
1912	July	4	East Corning, N. Y.	39	1950	Sept.	11	Coshocton, Oh.	33
1912	July	5	Ligonier, Pa.	23	1950	Nov.	22	Richmond Hill, N. Y.	79
1914	Aug.	5	Tipton Ford, Mo.	43	1951	Feb.	6	Woodbridge, N. J.	84
1914	Sept.	15	Lebanon, Mo.	28	1951	Nov.	12	Wyuta, Wyo.	17
1916	Mar.	29	Amherst, Oh.	27	1951	Nov.	25	Woodstock, Ala.	17
1917	Sept.	28	Kellyville, Okla.	23	1953	Mar.	27	Conneaut, Oh.	21
1917	Dec.	20	Shepherdsville, Ky.	46	1956	Jan.	22	Los Angeles, Cal.	30
1918	June	22	Ivanhoe, Ind.	68	1956	Feb.	28	Swampscott, Mass.	13
1918	July	9	Nashville, Tenn.	101	1956	Sept.	5	Springer, N. M.	20
1918	Nov.	2	Brooklyn, N. Y., Malbone St. Tunnel	97	1957	June	11	Vroman, Col.	12
1919	Jan.	12	South Byron, N. Y.	22	1958	Sept.	15	Elizabethport, N. J.	48
1919	July	1	Dunkirk, N. Y.	12	1960	Mar.	14	Bakersfield, Cal.	14
1919	Dec.	20	Onawa, Maine	23	1962	July	28	Steelton, Pa.	19
1921	Feb.	27	Porter, Ind.	37	1966	Dec.	28	Everett, Mass.	13
1921	Dec.	5	Woodmont, Pa.	27	1971	June	10	Salem, Ill.	11
1922	Aug.	5	Sulphur Spring, Mo.	34	1972	Oct.	30	Chicago, Ill.	45
1922	Dec.	13	Humble, Tex.	22	1977	Feb.	4	Chicago, Ill., elevated train	11

World's worst train wreck occurred Dec. 12, 1917, Modane, France, passenger train derailed, 543 killed.

Some Notable Aircraft Disasters Since 1937

Date			Aircraft	Site of accident	Deaths
1937	May	6	German zeppelin Hindenburg	Burned at mooring, Lakehurst, N.J.	36
1944	Aug.	23	U.S. Air Force B-24	Hit school, Freckelton, England.	76[1]
1945	July	28	U.S. Army B-25.	Hit Empire State bldg., N.Y.C.	14[1]
1947	May	30	Eastern Air Lines DC-4	Crashed near Port Deposit, Md.	53
1952	Dec.	20	U.S. Air Force C-124	Fell, burned, Moses Lake, Wash.	87
1953	Mar.	3	Canadian Pacific Comet Jet	Karachi, Pakistan	11[2]
1953	June	18	U.S. Air Force C-124	Crashed, burned near Tokyo	129
1955	Nov.	1	United Air Lines DC-6B	Exploded, crashed near Longmont, Col.	44[3]
1956	June	20	Venezuelan Super-Constellation	Crashed in Atlantic off Asbury Park, N.J.	74
1956	June	30	TWA Super-Const., United DC-7.	Collided over Grand Canyon, Arizona	128
1960	Dec.	16	United DC-8 jet, TWA Super-Const.	Collided over N.Y. City.	134[4]
1962	Mar.	4	Br. Caledonian Airlines DC-7C	Crashed near Douala, Cameroon.	111
1962	Mar.	16	Flying Tiger Super-Const.	Vanished in Western Pacific.	107
1962	June	3	Air France Boeing 707 jet	Crashed on takeoff from Paris	130
1962	June	22	Air France Boeing 707 jet.	Crashed in storm, Guadeloupe, W.I.	113
1963	June	3	Chartered Northw. Airlines DC-7	Crashed in Pacific off British Columbia.	101
1963	Nov.	29	Trans-Canada Airlines DC-8F	Crashed after takeoff from Montreal	118
1965	May	20	Pakistani Boeing 720-B	Crashed at Cairo, Egypt, airport	121
1966	Jan.	24	Air India Boeing 707 jetliner	Crashed on Mont Blanc, France-Italy.	117
1966	Feb.	4	All-Nippon Boeing 727.	Plunged into Tokyo Bay.	133
1966	Mar.	5	BOAC Boeing 707 jetliner.	Crashed on Mount Fuji, Japan	124
1966	Dec.	24	U.S. military-chartered CL-44.	Crashed into village in So. Vietnam.	129[1]
1967	Apr.	20	Swiss Britannia turboprop.	Crashed at Nicosia, Cyprus	126
1967	July	19	Piedmont Boeing 727, Cessna 310.	Collided in air, Hendersonville, N.C.	82
1968	Apr.	20	S. African Airways Boeing 707	Crashed on takeoff, Windhoek, SW Africa.	122
1968	May	3	Braniff International Electra.	Crashed in storm near Dawson, Tex.	85
1969	Mar.	16	Venezuelan DC-9.	Crashed after takeoff from Maracaibo, Venezuela	155[5]
1969	Mar.	20	United Arab Ilyushin-18.	Crashed at Aswan airport, Egypt.	87
1969	June	4	Mexican Boeing 727.	Rammed into mountain near Monterrey, Mexico	79
1969	Dec.	8	Olympia Airways DC-6B.	Crashed near Athens in storm	93
1970	Feb.	15	Dominican DC-9.	Crashed into sea on takeoff from Santo Domingo	102
1970	July	3	British chartered jetliner.	Crashed near Barcelona, Spain.	112

Date		Aircraft	Site of accident	Deaths
1970	July	5	Air Canada DC-8	Crashed near Toronto International Airport	108
1970	Aug.	9	Peruvian turbojet	Crashed after takeoff from Cuzco, Peru	101[1]
1970	Nov.	14	Southern Airways DC-9	Crashed in mountains near Huntington, W. Va.	75[5]
1971	July	30	All-Nippon Boeing 727 and Japanese Air Force F-86	Collided over Morioka, Japan	162[7]
1971	Aug.	11	Soviet Aeroflot Tupolev-104	Crashed at Irkutsk airport, USSR	97
1971	Sept.	4	Alaska Airlines Boeing 727	Crashed into mountain near Juneau, Alaska	111
1972	Aug.	14	E. German Ilyushin-62	Crashed on take-off East Berlin	156
1972	Oct.	13	Aeroflot Ilyushin-62	E. German airline crashed near Moscow	176
1972	Dec.	3	Chartered Spanish airliner	Crashed on take-off, Canary Islands	155
1972	Dec.	29	Eastern Airlines Lockheed Tristar	Crashed on approach to Miami Int'l. Airport	101
1973	Jan.	22	Chartered Boeing 707	Burst into flames during landing, Kano Airport, Nigeria	176
1973	Apr.	10	British Vanguard turboprop	Crashed during snowstorm at Basel, Switzerland	104
1973	June	3	Soviet Supersonic TU-144	Exploded in air near Goussainville, France	14[8]
1973	July	11	Brazilian Boeing 707	Crashed on approach to Orly Airport, Paris	122
1973	July	31	Delta Airlines jetliner	Crashed, landing in fog at Logan Airport, Boston	89
1973	Dec.	23	French Caravelle jet	Crashed in Morocco	106
1974	Jan.	31	Pan American Boeing 707 jet	Crashed in Pago Pago, American Samoa	96
1974	Mar.	3	Turkish DC-10 jet	Crashed at Ermenonville near Paris	346
1974	Apr.	23	Pan American 707 jet	Crashed in Bali, Indonesia	107
1974	Sept.	8	TWA 707 jet	Crashed in Ionian Sea off Greece, after bomb explosion	80
1974	Dec.	1	TWA-727	Crashed in storm, Upperville, Va.	92
1974	Dec.	4	Dutch-chartered DC-8	Crashed in storm near Colombo, Sri Lanka	191
1975	Apr.	4	Air Force Galaxy C-5B	Crashed near Saigon, So. Vietnam, after takeoff with load of orphans	172
1975	June	24	Eastern Airlines 727 jet	Crashed in storm, JFK Airport, N.Y. City	113
1975	Aug.	3	Chartered 707	Hit mountainside, Agadir, Morocco	168
1976	Sept.	10	British Airways Trident, Yugoslav DC-9	Collided near Zagreb, Yugoslavia	176
1976	Sept.	19	Turkish 727	Hit mountain, southern Turkey	155
1976	Oct.	6	Cuban DC-8	Crashed near Barbados after bomb explosion	73
1976	Oct.	12	Indian Caravelle jet	Crashed after takeoff, Bombay airport	95
1976	Oct.	13	Bolivian 707 cargo jet	Crashed in Santa Cruz, Bolivia	100[9]
1976	Dec.	28	Aeroflot TU-104	Crashed at Moscow's Sheremetyevo airport	72
1977	Jan.	13	Aeroflot TU-104	Exploded and crashed at Alma-Ata, Central Asia	90
1977	Mar.	27	KLM 747, Pan American 747	Collided on runway, Tenerife, Canary Islands	581
1977	Nov.	19	TAP Boeing 727	Crashed on Madeira	130
1977	Dec.	4	Malaysian Boeing 737	Hijacked, then exploded in mid-air over Straits of Johore	100
1977	Dec.	13	U.S. DC-3	Crashed after takeoff at Evansville, Ind.	29[10]
1978	Jan.	1	Air India 747	Exploded, crashed into sea off Bombay	213
1978	Mar.	16	Bulgarian TU-134	Crashed at Vratsa, Bulgaria	73
1978	Sept.	25	Boeing 727, Cessna 172	Collided in air, San Diego, Cal.	150
1978	Nov.	15	Chartered DC-8	Crashed near Colombo, Sri Lanka	183
1979	May	25	American Airlines DC-10	Crashed after takeoff at O'Hare Intl. Airport, Chicago	275[11]
1979	Aug.	17	Two Soviet Aeroflot jetliners	Collided over Ukraine	173
1979	Oct.	31	Western Airlines DC-10	Mexico City Airport	74
1979	Nov.	26	Pakistani Boeing 707	Crashed near Jidda, Saudi Arabia	156
1979	Nov.	28	New Zealand DC-10	Crashed into mountain in Antarctica	257
1980	Mar.	14	Polish Ilyushin 62	Crashed making emergency landing, Warsaw	87[12]
1980	Aug.	19	Saudi Arabian Tristar	Burned after emergency landing, Riyadh	301
1981	Dec.	1	Yugoslavian DC-9	Crashed into mountain in Corsica	174
1982	Jan.	13	Air Florida Boeing 737	Crashed into Potomac River after takeoff	78
1982	July	9	Pan-Am Boeing 727	Crashed after takeoff in Kenner, La.	153[13]
1982	Sept.	11	U.S. Army CH-47 Chinook helicopter	Crashed during air show in Mannheim, W. Germany	46
1983	Sept.	1	S. Korean Boeing 747	Shot down after violating Soviet airspace	269
1983	Nov.	27	Colombian Boeing 747	Crashed near Barajas Airport, Madrid	183

(1) Including those on the ground and in buildings. (2) First fatal crash of commercial jet plane. (3) Caused by bomb planted by John G. Graham in insurance plot to kill his mother, a passenger. (4) Including all 128 aboard the planes and 6 on ground. (5) Killed 84 on plane and 71 on ground. (6) Including 43 Marshall U. football players and coaches. (7) Airliner-fighter crash, pilot of fighter parachuted to safety, was arrested for negligence. (8) First supersonic plane crash killed 6 crewmen and 8 on the ground; there were no passengers. (9) Crew of 3 killed; 97, mostly children, killed on ground. (10) Including U. of Evansville basketball team. (11) Highest death toll in U.S. aviation history. (12) Including 22 members of U.S. boxing team. (13) Including 8 on ground.

Principal U.S. Mine Disasters

Source: Bureau of Mines, U.S. Interior Department

Note: Prior to 1968, only disasters with losses of 60 or more lives are listed; since 1968, all disasters in which 5 or more people were killed are listed. Only fatalities to mining company employees are included. All Bituminous-coal mines unless otherwise noted.

Date	Location	Deaths	Date	Location	Deaths
1867 Apr. 3	Winterpock, Va.	69	1910 May 5	Palos, Ala.	90
1869[1] Sept. 6	Plymouth, Pa.	110	1910 Nov. 8	Delagua, Col.	79
1883 Feb. 16	Braidwood, Ill.	69	1911 Apr. 7	Throop, Pa.	72
1884 Mar. 13	Pocahontas, Va.	112	1911 Apr. 8	Littleton, Ala.	128
1891 Jan. 27	Mount Pleasant, Pa.	109	1911 Dec. 9	Briceville, Tenn.	84
1892 Jan. 7	Krebs, Okla.	100	1912 Mar. 20	McCurtain, Okla.	73
1895 Mar. 20	Red Canyon, Wy.	60	1912 Mar. 26	Jed, W. Va.	83
1900 Jan. 1	Scofield, Ut.	200	1913 Apr. 23	Finleyville, Pa.	96
1902 May 19	Coal Creek, Tenn.	184	1913 Oct. 22	Dawson, N.M.	263
1902 July 10	Johnstown, Pa.	112	1914 Apr. 28	Eccles, W. Va.	181
1903 June 30	Hanna, Wy.	169	1915 Mar. 2	Layland, W. Va.	112
1904 Jan. 25	Cheswick, Pa.	179	1917 Apr. 27	Hastings, Col.	121
1905 Feb. 20	Virginia City, Ala.	112	1917[2] June 8	Butte, Mon.	163
1907 Jan. 29	Stuart W. Va.	84	1917 Aug. 4	Clay, Ky.	62
1907 Dec. 6	Monongah, W. Va.	361	1919[1] June 5	Wilkes-Barre, Pa.	92
1907 Dec. 19	Jacobs Creek, Pa.	239	1922 Nov. 6	Spangler, Pa.	77
1908 Nov. 28	Marianna, Pa.	154	1922 Nov. 22	Dolomite, Ala.	90
1909 Jan. 12	Switchback, W. Va.	67	1923 Feb. 8	Dawson, N.M.	120
1909 Nov. 13	Cherry, Ill.	259	1923 Aug. 14	Kemmerer, Wy.	99
1910 Jan. 31	Primero, Col.	75	1924 Mar. 8	Castle Gate, Ut.	171

Date	Location	Deaths	Date	Location	Deaths
1924 Apr. 28	Benwood, W. Va.	119	1951 Dec. 21	West Frankfort, Ill.	119
1926 Jan. 13	Wilburton, Okla.	91	1968[3]Mar. 6	Calumet, La.	21
1926[2]Nov. 3	Ishpeming, Mich.	51	1968 Nov. 20	Farmington, W. Va.	78
1927 Apr. 30	Everettville, W. Va.	97	1970 Dec. 30	Hyden, Ky.	38
1928 May 19	Mather, Pa.	195	1972[2]May 2	Kellogg, Ida	91
1929 Dec. 17	McAlester, Okla	61	1976 Mar. 9, 11	Oven Fork, Ky.	26
1930 Nov. 5	Millfield, Oh.	79	1977 Mar. 1	Tower City, Pa.	9
1940 Jan. 10	Bartley, W. Va.	91	1981 Apr. 15	Redstone, Col.	15
1940 Mar. 16	St. Clairsville, Oh.	72	1981 Dec. 7	Topmost, Ky.	8
1940 July 15	Portage, Pa.	63	1981 Dec. 8	nr. Chattanooga, Tenn.	13
1943 Feb. 27	Washoe, Mon.	74	1982 Jan. 20	Floyd County, Ky.	7
1944 July 5	Belmont, Oh.	66	1983 June 21	McClure, Va	7
1947 Mar. 25	Centralia, Ill.	111			

(1) Anthracite mine. (2) Metal mine. (3) Nonmetal mine.
World's worst mine disaster killed 1,549 workers in Honkeiko Colliery in Manchuria Apr. 25, 1942.

Historic Assassinations Since 1865

1865—Apr. 14. U. S. Pres. Abraham Lincoln, shot in Washington, D. C.; died Apr. 15.
1881—Mar. 13. Alexander II. of Russia—July 2. U. S. Pres. James A. Garfield, Washington; died Sept. 19.
1900—July 29. Umberto I. king of Italy.
1901—Sept. 6. U. S. Pres. William McKinley in Buffalo, N. Y., died Sept. 14. Leon Czolgosz executed for the crime Oct. 29.
1913—Feb. 23. Mexican Pres. Francisco, I. Madero and Vice Pres. Jose Pino Suarez.—Mar. 18. George, king of Greece.
1914—June 28. Archduke Francis Ferdinand of Austria-Hungary and his wife in Sarajevo, Bosnia (later part of Yugoslavia), by Gavrilo Princip.
1916—Dec. 30. Grigori Rasputin, politically powerful Russian monk.
1918—July 12. Grand Duke Michael of Russia, at Perm.—July 16. Nicholas II, abdicated as czar of Russia; his wife, the Czarina Alexandra, their son, Czarevitch Alexis, and their daughters, Grand Duchesses Olga, Tatiana, Marie, Anastasia, and 4 members of their household were executed by Bolsheviks at Ekaterinburg.
1920—May 20. Mexican Pres. Gen. Venustiano Carranza in Tlaxcalantongo.
1922—Aug. 22. Michael Collins, Irish revolutionary.
1923—July 20. Gen. Francisco "Pancho" Villa, ex-rebel leader, in Parral, Mexico.
1928—July 17. Gen. Alvaro Obregon, president-elect of Mexico, in San Angel, Mexico.
1933—Feb. 15. In Miami, Fla. Joseph Zangara, anarchist, shot at Pres.-elect Franklin D. Roosevelt, but a woman seized his arm, and the bullet fatally wounded Mayor Anton J. Cermak, of Chicago, who died Mar. 6. Zangara was electrocuted on Mar. 20, 1933.
1934—July 25. In Vienna, Austrian Chancellor Engelbert Dollfuss by Nazis.
1935—Sept. 8. U. S. Sen. Huey P. Long, shot in Baton Rouge, La., by Dr. Carl Austin Weiss, who was slain by Long's bodyguards.
1940—Aug. 20. Leon Trotsky (Lev Bronstein), 63, exiled Russian war minister, near Mexico City. Killer identified as Ramon Mercador del Rio, a Spaniard, served 20 years in Mexican prison.
1948—Jan. 30. Mohandas K. Gandhi, 78, shot in New Delhi, India, by Nathuran Vinayak Godse.—Sept. 17. Count Folke Bernadotte, UN mediator for Palestine, ambushed in Jerusalem.
1951—July 20. King Abdullah ibn Hussein of Jordan.
1956—Sept. 21. Pres. Anastasio Somoza of Nicaragua, in Leon; died Sept. 29.
1957—July 26. Pres. Carlos .Castillo Armas of Guatemala, in Guatemala City by one of his own guards.
1958—July 14. King Faisal of Iraq; his uncle, Crown Prince Abdul Illah, and July 15. Premier Nuri as-Said, by rebels in Baghdad.
1959—Sept. 25. Prime Minister Solomon Bandaranaike of Ceylon, by Buddhist monk in Colombo.
1961—Jan. 17. Ex-Premier Patrice Lumumba of the Congo, in Katanga Province—May 30. Dominican dictator Rafael Leonidas Trujillo Molina shot to death by assassins near Ciudad Trujillo.
1963—June 12. Medgar W. Evers, NAACP's Mississippi field secretary, in Jackson, Miss.—Nov. 2. Pres. Ngo Dinh Diem of the Republic of Vietnam and his brother, Ngo Dinh Nhu, in a military coup.—Nov. 22. U. S. Pres. John F. Kennedy fatally shot in Dallas, Tex.; accused Lee Harvey Oswald murdered while awaiting trial.
1965—Jan. 21. Iranian premier Hassan Ali Mansour fatally wounded by assassin in Teheran; 4 executed.—Feb. 21. Malcolm X, black nationalist, fatally shot in N. Y. City; 3 sentenced to life.
1966—Sept. 6. Prime Minister Hendrik F. Verwoerd of South Africa stabbed to death in parliament at Capetown.
1968—Apr. 4. Rev. Dr. Martin Luther King Jr. fatally shot in Memphis, Tenn.; James Earl Ray sentenced to 99 years.—June 5. Sen. Robert F. Kennedy (D-N. Y.) fatally shot in Los Angeles; Sirhan Sirhan, resident alien, convicted of murder.
1971—Nov. 28. Jordan Prime Minister Wasfi Tal, in Cairo, by Palestinian guerrillas.
1973—Mar. 2. U. S. Ambassador Cleo A. Noel Jr. U. S. Charge d'Affaires George C. Moore and Belgian Charge d'Affaires Guy Eid killed by Palestinian guerrillas in Khartoum, Sudan.
1974—Aug. 15. Mrs. Park Chung Hee, wife of president of So. Korea, hit by bullet meant for her husband.—Aug. 19. U. S. Ambassador to Cyprus, Rodger P. Davies, killed by sniper's bullet in Nicosia.
1975—Feb. 11. Pres. Richard Ratsimandrava, of Madagascar, shot in Tananarive.—Mar. 25. King Faisal of Saudi Arabia shot by nephew Prince Musad Abdel Aziz, in royal palace, Riyadh.—Aug. 15. Bangladesh Pres. Sheik Mujibur Rahman killed in coup.
1976—Feb. 13. Nigerian head of state, Gen. Murtala Ramat Mohammed, slain by self-styled "young revolutionaries."
1977—Mar. 16. Kamal Jumblat, Lebanese Druse chieftain, was shot near Beirut.—Mar. 18. Congo Pres. Marien Ngouabi shot in Brazzaville.
1978—July 9. Former Iraqi Premier Abdul Razak Al-Naif shot in London.
1979—Feb. 14. U.S. Ambassador Adolph Dubs shot and killed by Afghan Moslem extremists in Kabul.—Mar. 30. British Tory MP Airey Neave killed when bomb in his car exploded. IRA claimed responsibility.—Aug. 27. Lord Mountbatten, WW2 hero, and 2 others were killed when a bomb exploded on his fishing boat off the coast of Co. Sligo, Ire. The IRA claimed responsibility.—Oct. 26. So. Korean President Park Chung Hee and 6 bodyguards fatally shot by Kim Jae Kyu, head of Korean CIA, and 5 aides in Seoul.
1980—Apr. 12. Liberian President William R. Tolbert slain in military coup.—Sept. 17. Former Nicaraguan President Anastasio Somoza Debayle and 2 others shot in Paraguay.
1981—Aug. 30. Iranian President Mohammed Ali Raji and Premier Mohammed Jad Bahonar killed by bomb in Teheran.—Oct. 6. Egyptian President Anwar El-Sadat fatally shot by a band of commandos while reviewing a military parade in Cairo.
1982—Sept. 14. Lebanese President-elect Bishir Gemayel killed by bomb in east Beirut.
1983—Apr. 10. PLO representative Dr. Issam Sartawi was fatally shot by an unknown gunman in Albufeira, Portugal. A PLO splinter group claimed responsibility.—Aug. 21. Philippine opposition political leader Benigno Aquino Jr. fatally shot by a gunman at Manila International Airport.—Oct. 9. Four S. Korea cabinet ministers and 17 others killed by bomb blast in Rangoon, Burma.

Assassination Attempts

1910—Aug. 6. N. Y. City Mayor William J. Gaynor shot and seriously wounded by discharged city employee.
1912—Oct. 14. Former U. S. President Theodore Roosevelt shot and seriously wounded by demented man in Milwaukee.
1950—Nov. 1. In an attempt to assassinate President Truman, 2 members of a Puerto Rican nationalist movement—Griselio Torresola and Oscar Collazo—tried to shoot their way into Blair House. Torresola was killed, and a guard, Pvt. Leslie Coffelt was fatally shot. Collazo was convicted Mar. 7, 1951 for the murder of Coffelt.
1970—Nov. 27. Pope Paul VI unharmed by knife-wielding assailant who attempted to attack him in Manila airport.
1972—May 15. Alabama Gov. George Wallace shot in Laurel, Md. by Arthur Bremer; seriously crippled.
1972—Dec. 7. Mrs. Ferdinand E. Marcos, wife of the Philippine president, was stabbed and seriously injured in Pasay City, Philippines.
1975—Sept. 5. Pres. Gerald R. Ford was unharmed when a Secret Service agent grabbed a pistol aimed at him by Lynette (Squeaky) Fromme, a Charles Manson follower, in Sacramento.
1975—Sept. 22. Pres. Gerald R. Ford escaped unharmed when Sara Jane Moore, a political activist, fired a revolver at him.

1980—Apr. 14. Indian Prime Minister Indira Gandhi was unharmed when a man threw a knife at her in New Delhi.

1981—Jan. 16. Irish political activist Bernadette Devlin McAliskey and her husband were shot and seriously wounded by 3 members of a protestant paramilitary group in Co. Tyrone, Ire.

1981—Mar. 30. Pres. Ronald Reagan, Press Secy. James Brady, Secret Service agent Timothy J. McCarthy, and Washington, D.C. policeman Thomas Delahanty were shot and seriously wounded by John W. Hinckley Jr. in Washington, D.C.

1981—May 13. Pope John Paul II and 2 bystanders were shot and wounded by Mehmet Ali Agca, an escaped Turkish murderer, in St. Peter's Square, Rome.

1982—May 12. Pope John Paul II was unharmed when a man with a knife was overpowered by security guards, in Fatima, Portugal.

1982—June 3. Israel's ambassador to Britain Shlomo Argov was shot and seriously wounded by Arab terrorists in London.

Major Kidnapings

Edward A. Cudahy Jr., 16, in Omaha, Neb., **Dec. 18, 1900.** Returned Dec. 20 after $25,000 paid. Pat Crowe confessed.

Robert Franks, 13, in Chicago, **May 22, 1924,** by 2 youths, Richard Loeb and Nathan Leopold, who killed boy. Demand for $10,000 ignored. Loeb died in prison, Leopold paroled 1958.

Charles A. Lindbergh Jr., 20 mos. old, in Hopewell, N.J., **Mar. 1, 1932;** found dead May 12. Ransom of $50,000 was paid to man identified as Bruno Richard Hauptmann, 35, paroled German convict who entered U.S. illegally. Hauptmann passed ransom bill and $14,000 marked money was found in his garage. He was convicted after spectacular trial at Flemington, and electrocuted in Trenton, N.J., prison, Apr. 3, 1936.

William A. Hamm Jr., 39, in St. Paul, **June 15, 1933.** $100,000 paid. Alvin Karpis given life, paroled in 1969.

Charles F. Urschel, in Oklahoma City, **July 22, 1933.** Released July 31 after $200,000 paid. George (Machine Gun) Kelly and 5 others given life.

Brooke L. Hart, 22, in San Jose, Cal. Thomas Thurmond and John Holmes arrested after demanding $40,000 ransom. When Hart's body was found in San Francisco Bay, Nov. 26, 1933, a mob attacked the jail at San Jose and lynched the 2 kidnapers.

George Weyerhaeuser, 9, in Tacoma, Wash., **May 24, 1935.** Returned home June 1 after $200,000 paid. Kidnappers given 20 to 60 years.

Charles Mattson, 10, in Tacoma, Wash., **Dec. 27, 1936.** Found dead Jan. 11, 1937. Kidnaper asked $28,000, failed to contact.

Arthur Fried, in White Plains, N.Y., **Dec. 4, 1937.** Body not found. Two kidnapers executed.

Robert C. Greenlease, 6, taken from school Sept. 28, 1953, and held for $600,000. Body found Oct. 7. Mrs. Bonnie Brown Heady and Carl A. Hall pleaded guilty and were executed.

Peter Weinberger, 32 days old, Westbury, N.Y., **July 4, 1956,** for $2,000 ransom, not paid. Child found dead. Angelo John LaMarca, 31, convicted, executed.

Cynthia Ruotolo, 6 wks old, taken from carriage in front of Hamden, Conn. store **Sept. 1, 1956.** Body found in lake.

Lee Crary, 8 in Everett, Wash., **Sept. 22, 1957,** $10,000 ransom, not paid. He escaped after 3 days, led police to George E. Collins, who was convicted.

Eric Peugeot, 4, taken from playground at St. Cloud golf course, Paris, **Apr. 12, 1960.** Released unharmed 3 days later after payment of undisclosed sum. Two sentenced to prison.

Frank Sinatra Jr., 19, from hotel room in Lake Tahoe, Cal., **Dec. 8, 1963.** Released **Dec. 11** after his father paid $240,000 ransom. Three men sentenced to prison; most of ransom recovered.

Barbara Jane Mackle, 20, abducted **Dec. 17, 1968,** from Atlanta, Ga., motel, was found unharmed 3 days later, buried in a coffin-like wooden box 18 inches underground, after her father had paid $500,000 ransom; Gary Steven Krist sentenced to life; Ruth Eisenmann-Schier to 7 years; most of ransom recovered.

Anne Katherine Jenkins, 22, abducted **May 10, 1969,** from her Baltimore apartment, freed 3 days later after her father paid $10,000 ransom.

Mrs. Roy Fuchs, 35, and 3 children held hostage 2 hours, **May 14, 1969,** in Long Island, N.Y., released after her husband, a bank manager, paid kidnapers $129,000 in bank funds; 4 men arrested, ransom recovered.

C. Burke Elbrick, U.S. ambassador to Brazil, kidnaped by revolutionaries in Rio de Janeiro **Sept. 4, 1969;** released 3 days later after Brazil yielded to kidnaper's demands to publish manifesto and release 15 political prisoners.

Patrick Dolan, 18, found shot to death near Sao Paulo, Brazil, Nov. 5, 1969, after he was kidnaped and $12,500 paid.

Sean M. Holly, U.S. diplomat, in Guatemala **Mar. 6, 1970;** freed 2 days later upon release of 3 terrorists from prison.

Lt. Col. Donald J. Crowley, U.S. air attache, in Dominican Republic **Mar. 24, 1970;** released after government allowed 20 prisoners to leave the country.

Count Karl von Spreti, W. German ambassador to Guatemala, **Mar. 31, 1970;** slain after Guatemala refused demands for $700,000 and release of 22 prisoners.

Pedro Eugenio Aramburu, former Argentine president, by terrorists **May 29, 1970;** body found July 17.

Ehrenfried von Holleben, W. German ambassador to Brazil, by terrorists **June 11, 1970;** freed after release of 40 prisoners.

Daniel A. Mitrione, U.S. diplomat, **July 31, 1970,** by terrorists in Montevideo, Uruguay; body found Aug. 10 after government rejected demands for release of all political prisoners.

James R. Cross, British trade commissioner, **Oct. 5, 1970,** by French Canadian separatists in Quebec; freed Dec. 3 after 3 kidnapers and relatives flown to Cuba by government.

Pierre Laporte, Quebec Labor Minister, by separatists **Oct. 10, 1970;** body found Oct. 18.

Giovanni E. Bucher, Swiss ambassador **Dec. 7, 1970,** by revolutionaries in Rio de Janeiro; freed Jan. 16, 1971, after Brazil released 70 political prisoners.

Geoffrey Jackson, British ambassador, in Montevideo, **Jan. 8, 1971,** by Tupamaro terrorists. Held as ransom for release of imprisoned terrorists, he was released Sept. 9, after the prisoners escaped.

Ephraim Elrom, Israel consul general in Istanbul, **May 17, 1971.** Held as ransom for imprisoned terrorists, he was found dead May 23.

Mrs. Virginia Piper, 49 abducted July 27, 1972, from her home in suburban Minneapolis; found unharmed near Duluth 2 days later after her husband paid $1 million ransom to the kidnapers.

Victor E. Samuelson, Exxon executive, **Dec. 6, 1973,** in Campana, Argentina, by Marxist guerrillas, freed Apr. 29, 1974, after payment of record $14.2 million ransom.

J. Paul Getty 3d, 17, grandson of the U.S. oil mogul, released **Dec. 15, 1973,** in southern Italy after $2.8 million ransom paid.

Patricia (Patty) Hearst, 19, taken from her Berkeley, Cal., apartment **Feb. 4, 1974.** Symbionese Liberation Army demanded her father, Randolph A. Hearst, publisher, give millions to poor. Hearst offered $2 million in food; the Hearst Corp. offered $4 million worth. Kidnapers objected to way food was distributed. Patricia, in message, said she had joined SLA; she was identified by FBI as taking part in a San Francisco bank holdup, **Apr. 15;** she claimed, in message, she had been coerced. Again identified by FBI in a store holdup, **May 16,** she was classified by FBI as "an armed, dangerous fugitive." FBI, **Sept. 18, 1975,** captured Patricia and others in San Francisco; they were indicted on various charges. Patricia for bank robbery. A San Francisco jury convicted her, **Mar. 20, 1976.** She was released from prison under executive clemency, Feb. 1, 1979. In 1978, William and Emily Harris were sentenced to 10 years to life for the Hearst kidnaping.

J. Reginald Murphy, 40, an editor of *Atlanta* (Ga.) *Constitution,* kidnaped **Feb. 20, 1974,** freed Feb. 22 after payment of $700,000 ransom by the newspaper. Police arrested William A. H. Williams, a contractor; most of the money was recovered.

J. Guadalupe Zuno Hernandez, 83, father-in-law of Mexican President Luis Echeverria Alvarez, seized by 4 terrorists **Aug. 28, 1974;** government refused to negotiate; he was released **Sept. 8.**

E. B. Reville, Hepzibah, Ga., banker, and wife Jean, kidnaped **Sept. 30, 1974.** Ransom of $30,000 paid. He was found alive; Mrs. Reville was found dead of carbon monoxide fumes in car trunk Oct. 2.

Jack Teich, Kings Point, N.Y., steel executive, seized **Nov. 12, 1974;** released Nov. 19 after payment of $750,000.

Samuel Bronfman, 21, heir to Seagram liquor fortune, allegedly abducted **Aug. 9, 1975,** in Purchase, N.Y.; $2.3 million ransom paid. FBI and N.Y.C. police found Samuel **Aug. 17** in Brooklyn, N.Y., apartment, recovered ransom, and arrested Mel Patrick Lynch and Dominic Byrne. Two found not guilty of kidnap, but convicted of extortion after they claimed Sam masterminded ransom plot.

Hanns-Martin Schleyer, a West German industrialist, was kidnaped in Cologne, **Sept. 5, 1977** by armed terrorists. Schleyer was found dead, Oct. 19, in an abandoned car shortly after 3 jailed terrorist leaders of the Baader-Meinhof gang were found dead in their prison cells near Stuttgart, West Germany.

Aldo Moro, former Italian premier, kidnaped in Rome, **Mar. 16, 1978,** by left-wing terrorists. Five of his bodyguards killed during abduction. Moro's bullet-ridden body was found in a parked car, May 9, in Rome. Six members of the Red Brigades arrested, charged, June 5, with complicity in the kidnaping.

James L. Dozier, a U.S. Army general, kidnapped from his apartment in Verona, Italy, **Dec. 17, 1981,** by members of the Red Brigades terrorist organization. He was rescued, **Jan. 28, 1982,** by Italian police.

Dr. Hector Zevalloses, owner of an abortion clinic, and his wife were kidnapped in Edwardsville, Ill., Aug. 13, 1982, by the Army of God, an anti-abortion group. The Zevalloses were released unharmed, Aug. 20.

CANADA

See Index for Calgary, Edmonton, Hamilton, Laval, London, Mississauga, Montreal, North York, Ottawa, Quebec, Regina, Toronto, Vancouver, Windsor, Winnipeg.

Capital: Ottawa. Area: 3,849,670 sq. mi. Population (est., Jan. 1984): 25,015,800. Monetary unit: Canadian dollar.

The Land

The world's second largest country in land size, Canada stretches 3,223 miles from east to west and extends southward from the North Pole to the U.S. border. Its seacoast includes 36,356 miles of mainland and 115,133 miles of islands, including the Arctic islands almost from Greenland to near the Alaskan border.

Canada's continental climate, while generally temperate, varies from freezing winter cold to blistering summer heat - a range beyond 100 degrees Fahrenheit.

Major cities, industrial centres, agricultural regions, and the vast majority of the population are situated along a thin, southern fringe bordering the United States. To the north lie vast expanses of varied, virgin land. The remote north, due to extreme cold, is virtually uninhabitable.

Fragmented by history, geography, and economic factors, the country is as diverse as it is large. Regionally, Canada's 10 provinces can be put into 5 groups: the industrially-poor Atlantic Provinces of New Brunswick, Newfoundland, Nova Scotia, and Prince Edward Island; predominantly French-speaking Quebec; Ontario, financial and governmental heartland of the nation; the Prairies, including Manitoba, Saskatchewan, and oil-rich Alberta; and British Columbia, separated from the rest of the country by the Rocky Mountains.

Despite continuing problems of regional disparity in political, economic, and cultural outlook, Canada has survived as a nation by accepting the need to recognize and tolerate differences. Unlike the U.S., Canada has never been a melting pot, nor has it strived to become one.

History

French explorer Jacques Cartier, who discovered the Gulf of St. Lawrence in 1534, is generally regarded as the founder of Canada. But English seaman John Cabot sighted Newfoundland 37 years earlier, in 1497, and Vikings are believed to have reached the Atlantic coast centuries before either explorer.

Canadian settlement was pioneered by the French who established Quebec City (1608) and Montreal (1642) and declared New France a colony in 1663.

Britain, as part of its American expansion, acquired Acadia (later Nova Scotia) in 1717 and, through military victory over French forces in Canada (an extension of a European conflict between the 2 powers), captured Quebec (1759) and obtained control of the rest of New France in 1763. The French, through the Quebec Act of 1774, retained the rights to their own language, religion, and civil law.

The British presence in Canada increased during the American Revolution when many colonials, proudly calling themselves United Empire Loyalists, moved north to Canada.

Fur traders and explorers led Canadians westward across the continent. Sir Alexander Mackenzie reached the Pacific in 1793 and scrawled on a rock by the ocean, "from Canada by land."

In Upper and Lower Canada (later called Ontario and Quebec) and in the Maritimes, legislative assemblies appeared in the 18th century and reformers called for responsible government. But the War of 1812 intervened. The war, a conflict between Great Britain and the United States fought mainly in Upper Canada, ended in a stalemate in 1814.

In 1837 political agitation for more democratic government culminated in rebellions in Upper and Lower Canada. Britain sent Lord Durham to investigate and, in a famous report (1839), he recommended union of the 2 parts into one colony called Canada. The union lasted until Confederation, July 1, 1867, when proclamation of the British North America (BNA) Act launched the Dominion of Canada, consisting of Ontario, Quebec, and the former colonies of Nova Scotia and New Brunswick.

Since 1840 the Canadian colonies had held the right to internal self-government. The BNA act, which became the country's written constitution, established a federal system of government on the model of a British parliament and cabinet structure under the crown. Canada was proclaimed a self-governing Dominion within the British Empire in 1931. Empire has given way to Commonwealth, of which Canada is an independent member.

In 1982 Canada severed its last formal legislative link with Britain by obtaining the right to amend its constitution (the British North America Act of 1867). The new Constitution Act, 1982 includes a formula allowing the federal Parliament to make constitutional changes with the support of 7 provinces representing at least 50% of the Canadian population.

The Government

Canada is a constitutional monarchy with a parliamentary system of government. It is also a federal state. Official head of state remains England's Queen Elizabeth, represented by a resident governor-general. But in practice the nation is governed by the Prime Minister, leader of the party able to command the support of a majority of members of the House of Commons, dominant chamber of Canada's bicameral Parliament.

The Commons' 282 members are elected at least every 5 years - sooner if the Prime Minister so chooses or if the government is defeated in Parliament. This can occur either through passage of a motion of nonconfidence in the government or by defeat of a major piece of government legislation.

The upper house of Canada's Parliament is the Senate, comprised of 104 members traditionally appointed by party patronage and serving to age 75.

Legislation becomes law by receiving 3 "readings" in the Commons, passing in the Senate and obtaining assent from the governor-general. The latter 2 steps are, in practice, mere formality.

The Prime Minister heads the executive branch of government composed of the cabinet and governor-general. The cabinet is chosen by the Prime Minister, almost always from among members of his party holding seats in the House of Commons.

Provincial governments follow a modified version of the Ottawa pattern, with a unicameral legislature and an executive head usually referred to as the Premier.

Politics

The Progesssive Conservative Party won a landslide victory in Canada's Sept. 1984 federal election, ending 2 decades of almost continuous Liberal government. Under leader Brian Mulroney the Conservatives won 50% of the popular vote and 211 of 282 seats in the House of Commons. The Liberal Party, with only 28% of the vote and 40 seats, suffered its worst defeat ever. The New Democratic Party maintained strong 3d party support with 19% of the vote and 30 seats.

The massive Conservative victory represented a strong desire for change in government but not necessarily a major shift in political ideology. Mulroney said his priorities as Canada's 18th prime minister would be to create jobs, improve the economy, and unify the nation.

The Liberals were led in the election by John Turner, chosen party leader in June 1984 following the resignation of Pierre Trudeau who stepped down after 16 years as Liberal leader and prime minister. Following the 1984 defeat, Turner, who served as prime minister for less than 3 months after succeeding Trudeau, said he intended to remain as Liberal leader and work towards rebuilding the party.

Underscoring the Conservative victory was the party's ability to obtain strong support in all areas of the country. Federal elections in 1979 and 1980 had been marked by regional political fragmentation, with voting split along geographic and linguistic lines. Mulroney, the first Conservative leader from Quebec in 90 years, captured 58 of 75 seats in the predominantly french-speaking province, traditionally a Liberal stronghold. In 1980 the Conservatives had held only one seat in Quebec while the Liberals won 74 seats there but only 2 in western Canada.

Federal-provincial conflicts have been less pronounced in recent years following the Nov. 1981 constitutional agreement reached between Ottawa and 9 (all except Quebec) of the 10 provinces. But the constitutional accord further isolated Quebec's separatist Parti Quebecois (PQ) government which viewed it as a challenge to the province's legislative autonomy, particularly regarding minority language rights— an area in which the new constitution's Charter of Rights is in conflict with Quebec's own language legislation. The PQ was re-elected by a wide margin in April 1981, when it chose not to make separation from Canada a major issue. But the party, which has until early 1986 to call the next provincial election, has said it will base its next campaign on separation.

The Economy

The Canadian economy continued its moderate recovery throughout 1983 and early 1984. Real (after inflation) growth in the Gross Domestic Product (the value of all goods and services produced in the country and considered the best measure of economic performance) was 3.3% in 1983 and maintained the same pace with a .8% gain during the first 3 months of 1984. This was a major improvement over 1982 when the GNP fell 4.4%, the worst decline since the Depression.

The rate of inflation, as measured by the Consumer Price Index, fell to 5.8% in 1983, almost half of the 1982 level. During mid 1984, inflation was running at 4.8% amid concern that it might be pushed upward by the declining value of Canadian currency relative to the U.S. dollar. The Canadian dollar hit an all-time low of less than .75 U.S. in July, 1984, meaning increased Canadian costs for imported American products; more than 2/3 of all Canadian imports are from the U.S. The devalued dollar also puts pressure on the federal government to try to protect the value of Canadian currency by allowing interest rates to rise.

Unemployment improved only slightly during the first half of 1984. It stood at 11.2% in June, down from an annual average of 11.9% in 1983 and a post-Depression high of 12.8% in Dec. 1982.

Principal Canadian industries are motor vehicle manufacturing, petroleum refining, pulp and paper production, slaughtering and meat processing, iron and steel production, the manufacture of miscellaneous machinery and equipment, saw and planing mill industries, and smelting and refining.

In Canada, an historical tradition of state aid necessitated by a harsh climate and sparse population has fostered development of a mixed economic system in which publicly-owned corporations exist alongside—and sometimes compete with—private enterprise. Most hydroelectric and many transportation and communication enterprises are government-owned. Air Canada and the Canadian National Railways, both large federal Crown corporations, compete with the privately-owned Canadian Pacific Ltd, whose 1982 operating revenue was the 2d largest of any company in Canada.

Foreign Policy

Canada's chief foreign ally and trading partner remains the United States with whom she shares a broad range of mutually beneficial ties. More than two thirds of all 1983 Canadian exports went to the U.S.; the U.S., in turn, sells almost twice as much to Canada as to its next largest single trading partner, Japan. The 2 nations have, since 1958, provided for joint air defense of the continent through the North American Aerospace Defence Command (NORAD) and are founding members of the North Atlantic Treaty Organization (NATO). Canada's NATO commitment is based on the premise that by contributing to the direct defense of Europe, Canada is also contributing to its own defense.

Canada has continued to be a strong advocate of joint East-West nuclear arms reductions. In late 1983, then Prime Minister Pierre Trudeau began a major peace initiative, meeting with the leaders of more than 50 countries, including the 5 nuclear powers, to promote renewed arms control discussions. Said Trudeau: "We cannot wait until the United States and the Soviet Union. . .are ready to reach agreement. We must demonstrate our stake in their deliberations and force their attention to the threat to which they subject the rest of mankind."

At the same time, Canada has supported NATO's policy of matching the Soviet arms buildup in Europe if reductions can't be negotiated. In July 1983, Canada gave the U.S. permission to test unarmed cruise missiles over northern Alberta, British Columbia and the Northwest Territories, beginning early in 1984.

Despite co-operation on international issues, current Canadian-U.S. relations have been clouded by disagreement over such bilateral issues as foreign investment policies, environmental pollution and fishing rights. Through its National Energy Program of 1980 and its Foreign Investment Review Agency, Canada aims to reduce foreign dominance of its economy, especially its energy industry; U.S. officials claim these policies discriminate against American firms in Canada. "Acid rain" pollution of Canadian lakes from U.S. industrial emissions has been a long-standing cause of friction between the 2 nations; Canadian officials have blamed the U.S. for lack of action to resolve the problem. Other prolonged U.S.-Canada disputes over maritime boundaries and fish catch quotas had still not been settled by mid 1984.

Canada has promoted a North-South dialogue to reduce the economic gap between the developed nations of the northern hemisphere and the under-developed ones below the Equator in the interests of justice and world security.

Canada's Middle East policy calls for Israeli withdrawal from territories occupied after the 1967 war.

On Latin America and the Caribbean, Canadian policy is to encourage peaceful solutions instead of armed confrontations and widespread violations of human rights. Canada has spoken out against human rights violations, especially in Poland, El Salvador, Guatemala, South Africa and Afghanistan.

Canada's Native Peoples

Canada's native population consists of 3 groups, the Indian, Inuit (Eskimo), and Métis. The Indian and Inuit are thought to have crossed from Asia via the Bering Sea several thousand years before the arrival of Europeans in North America. Metis are of mixed native Indian and non-Indian ancestry.

There are approximately 332,178 "status" Indians - those registered under the federal Indian Act - most of whom belong to one of 576 Indian bands. About 70% live on one of the 2,250 federal reserves or on other government lands set aside for their use. Only Newfoundland had no registered Indians. The majority (83%) live in Ontario and the 4 western provinces. In addition, there are an estimated one million non-registered Indians and Metis.

The number of Inuit (meaning "the people" in their language, Inuktitut; Eskimo is an Indian word adopted by European settlers) in Canada is approximately 28,000. More than 75% live in the Northwest Territories, the remainder in Arctic Quebec and northern Labrador.

Due to the remoteness of their settlements close to the northern coasts where sea mammals provided the chief source of food, fuel and clothing, the Inuit lifestyle was affected later and less directly than that of the Indian by the encroachment of western civilization. Many Inuit still live by their traditional skills of hunting, trapping and fishing as well as through the production and sale of artwork. But increasing numbers now find work outside their communities, particularly since the search for oil, gas and minerals has brought more jobs to the north.

Both Inuit and status Indians are entitled to a broad range of government benefits administered through the federal Dept. of Indian Affairs and Northern Development as well as through provincial and territorial governments. Indian people living on reserves are eligible for direct federal assistance in such areas as education, housing, social services, and community development.

In addition, approximately half the registered Indians in Canada (mainly those living in Ontario and the 3 Prairie provinces) are in areas covered by treaties that granted reserves of land to their ancestors during the late 19th and early 20th centuries. In remote and less-settled areas, however, no such claims were made, and now Indian and Inuit groups are negotiating land claims in British Columbia, the Yukon and Northwest Territories, Quebec and Labrador.

In 1982 the federal government re-affirmed a 1973 commitment to settle both comprehensive (based on aboriginal rights) and specific (based on treaties or the Indian Act) claims. A 1975 agreement settled the claims of the Inuit and Cree of northern Quebec; in 1978 this settlement was extended to include the Naskapis of Schefferville. In June 1984, the government signed a final agreement with the Committee for Original Peoples' Entitlement, representing the Inuit of the western Arctic (the Inuvialuit). In 1984 an agreement in principle was also reached with the Council for Yukon Indians.

Inuit cultural and legal interests are represented by district Inuit associations and nationally by the Inuit Tapirisat, founded in 1971. The interests of status Indians are represented by provincial Indian associations and, at the national level, by the Assembly of First Nations. The Métis and non-status Indians are represented by the Native Council of Canada.

Provinces of Canada

Alberta

People. Population (Jan. 1984): 2,345,100; **rank:** 4. **Pop. density:** 9.4 per sq. mi. **Urban** (1981) 77%. **Ethnic distrib.** (1981): English 81%; German 4.1%; Ukrainian 3%; French 2.8%. **Net interprovincial migration** (1981-82): +32,060.

Geography: Total area: 255,290 sq. mi.; **rank:** 4. **Land area:** 248,800 sq. mi. **Forested land:** 134,714 sq. mi. **Location:** Canada's 2d most westerly province, bounded to the W by British Columbia, to the E by Saskatchewan, to the N by the Northwest Territories, and to the S by Montana. **Climate:** great variance in temperatures between regions and seasons; summer highs can range between 16°C and 32°C; winter temperatures can drop as low as −45°C; mean Jan. temperature in Edmonton is −14°C. **Topography:** ranges from the Rocky Mountains in the SW to flat prairie in the SE; the far north is a wilderness of forest and muskeg.

Economy. Principal industries: mining, oil production, agriculture, manufacturing, construction. **Principal manufactured goods:** foods and beverages, wood products, fabricated metal, transportation equipment, refined petroleum. **GDP, manufacturing** (1981): $3.4 billion. **Gross Domestic Product** (1982): $53.1 billion. **Agriculture. Chief crops:** wheat, barley, rapeseed, sugar beets, flaxseed. **Livestock** (1983): 3,485,000 cattle; 1,185,000 pigs; 134,000 sheep. **GDP, forestry** (1981): $53.8 million. **Mineral production** (1982): total value, $20.9 billion; fuels, $20 billion (87% of national production of petroleum, 94% of natural gas); structural materials, $318 million. **GDP, fishing** (1981): $.5 million. **GDP, construction** (1981): $4.5 billion. **Employment distribution** (1983): 31% services; 18% trade; 8% construction; 8% manufacturing; 7% agriculture; 7% public administration. **Per capita income** (1982): $14,025. **Unemployment** (1983): 10.8%.

Finance. No. banks: 812; **No. credit unions, caisses populaires:** 282.

International airports: Edmonton, Calgary.

Federal government: No. federal employees (Dec. 1983): 31,007; **Federal payroll** (1983): $760.3 million.

Energy. Electricity production, by mwh, (1983): mineral, 24,307,242; hydroelectric, 1,479,902.

Education. No. schools: 1,449 elementary; 177 secondary; 23 higher education. **Avg. salary, public school teachers** (1982-83): N.A.

Provincial data. Motto: none. **Flower:** The Wild Rose. **Bird:** Great horned owl. **Date entered Confederation:** 1905. **Capital:** Edmonton. **Politics. Premier:** Peter Lougheed (Progressive Conservative). **Leaders, opposition parties:** Grant Notley (New Democratic). **Composition of legislature** (June, 1984): PC 75; NDP 2; 2 independent. **Date of last general election:** Nov. 2, 1982.

Tourist attractions: Banff, Jasper, and Waterton Lakes, Elk Island and Wood Buffalo national parks; resorts at Banff, Jasper and Lake Louise; spectacular skiing, hiking, trail riding and camping in the Canadian Rockies; Dinosaur Park in Drumheller.

British Columbia

People. Population (Jan. 1984): 2,851,700; **rank:** 3. **Pop. density:** 7.9 per sq. mi. **Urban** (1981) 78%. **Ethnic distrib.** (1981): English 82%; German 3.4%; Chinese 2.8%; French 1.7%. **Net interprovincial migration** (1981-82): +6,129.

Geography. Total area: 365,950 sq. mi.; **rank:** 3. **Land area:** 358,970 sq. mi. **Forested land:** 244,338 sq. mi. **Location:** bounded to the N by the Yukon and Northwest Territories, to the NW by the Alaskan panhandle, to the W by the Pacific Ocean, to the E by Alberta, and to the S by Washington, Idaho and Montana. **Climate:** maritime with mild termperatures and abundant rainfall in the coastal areas; continental climate with temperature extremes in the interior and northeast. **Topography:** mostly mountainous except for the NE corner which is an extension of the Great Plains.

Economy. Principal industries: forestry, mining, tourism, agriculture, fishing, manufacturing. **Principal manufactured goods:** wood products, paper and allied products, food and beverages, petroleum and coal products, primary metals, transportation equipment. **GDP, manufacturing** (1981): $5.7 billion. **Gross Domestic Product** (1982): $44.7 billion (including GDP for Yukon and NWT). **Agriculture: Chief crops:** fruits and vegetables, barley, oats. **Livestock** (1983): 658,000 cattle; 250,000 pigs; 40,000 sheep. **GDP, forestry** (1981): $970 million. **Mineral production** (1982): $2.8 billion; fuels, $1.4 billion; metals, $1.1 billion; structural materials, $178 million. **GDP, fishing** (1981): $165.5 million. **GDP, construction** (1981): $3 billion. **Employment distribution** (1983): 33% services; 18% trade; 13% manufacturing; 7% public administration; 6% construction; 2.8% agriculture. **Per capita income** (1983): $13,811. **Unemployment** (1983): 13.8%.

Finance: No. banks: 851; **No. credit unions, caisses populaires:** 312.

International airports: Vancouver, Victoria.

Federal government: No. federal employees (Dec. 1983): 44,238. **Federal payroll** (1983): $1.1 billion.

Energy. Electricity production, by mwh, (1983): hydroelectric, 35,710,463.

Education. No schools: 1,567 elementary; 335 secondary; 27 higher education. **Avg. salary, public school teachers** (1982-83): $32,596.

Provincial data. Motto: Splendor Sine Occasu (Spendor Without Diminishment). **Flower:** Dogwood. **Bird:** None. **Date entered Confederation:** 1871. **Capital:** Victoria.

Politics. Premier: William R. Bennett (Social Credit). **Leaders, opposition parties:** Bob Skelly (New Democratic), Arthur Lee (Liberal), James McNeil (Progressive Conservative). **Composition of legislature** (June, 1984): SC 34; NDP 21; 2 vacant. **Date of last general election:** May 5, 1983.

Tourist attractions. Victoria: Butchart Gardens, Crystal Garden, Provincial Museum; Vancouver: Stanley Park Zoo, Capilano Canyon, Gastown, Public Aquarium, Grouse Mountain, Planetarium; also National Parks, the Gulf Islands, Okanagan Valley, Totem Triangle Tour, fishing, skiing.

Manitoba

People. Population (Jan. 1984): 1,051,500; **rank:** 5. **Pop. density:** 5 per sq. mi. **Urban** (1981) 71.2%. **Ethnic distrib.** (1981): English 71.7%; German 7.3%; Ukrainian 5.7%; French 5.1%; Native Indians 2.5%. **Net interprovincial migration** (1981-82): −2,201.

Geography. Total area: 250,950 sq. mi.; **rank:** 6. **Land area:** 211,720 sq. mi. **Forested land:** 134,714 sq. mi. **Location:** bounded to the N by the Northwest Territories, to the S by Minnesota and North Dakota, to the E by Ontario and Hudson Bay, to the W by Saskatchewan. **Climate:** continental, with seasonal extremes: Winnipeg avg. Jan. low −23°C, avg. July high 26°C. **Topography:** the land rises gradually S and W from Hudson Bay; most of the province is between 500 and 1,000 feet above sea level.

Economy. Principal industries: manufacturing, agriculture, slaughtering and meat processing, mining. **Principal manufactured goods:** agricultural implements, processed food, machinery, transportation equipment, clothing. **GDP, manufacturing** (1981): $1.8 billion. **Gross Domestic Product** (1982): $13.9 billion. **Agriculture: Chief crops:** cereal grains, mustard seed, sunflower seeds, rape, flax. **Livestock** (1983): 955,000 cattle; 900,000 pigs; 24,500 sheep; **GDP, forestry** (1981): $16.5 million. **Mineral production** (1982): total value, $530 million; metals, $353 million; structural materials, $71 million; petroleum, $89 million. **GDP, fishing:** (1981): $12.7 million. **GDP, construction** (1981): $474.5 million. **Employment distribution** (1983): 31% services; 18% trade; 13% manufacturing; 9% agriculture; 8% public administration; 4% construction. **Per capita income** (1982): $11,987. **Unemployment** (1983): 9.4%.

Finance: No. banks: 345; **No. credit unions, caisses populaires:** 193.

International airports: Winnipeg.

Federal Government: No. federal employees (Dec. 1983): 20,019. **Federal payroll** (1983): $507.1 million.

Energy. Electricity production, by mwh, (1983): mineral, 86,513; hydroelectric, 21,893,196.

Education. No. schools: 723 elementary; 113 secondary; 12 higher education. **Avg. salary, public school teachers** (1982-83): $29,714.

Provincial data. Motto: None. **Flower:** Prairie crocus. **Bird:** none. **Date entered Confederation:** July 15, 1870. **Capital:** Winnipeg.

Politics. Premier: Howard Pawley (New Democratic). **Leaders, opposition parties:** Gary Filmon (Progressive Conservative). **Composition of legislature:** (June, 1984): NDP 32; PC 23; 2 independent. **Date of last general election:** Nov. 17, 1981.

Tourist attractions. Museum of Man and Nature (Winnipeg), Lower Fort Garry (near Lockport), Red River cruises, Riding Mountain National Park, canoeing, fishing and camping on northern lakes.

New Brunswick

People. Population (Jan. 1984): 710,500; **rank:** 8. **Pop. density:** 25.5 per sq. mi. **Urban** (1981) 51.1%. **Ethnic distrib.** (1981): English 65%; French 33.6%. **Net interprovincial migration** (1981-82): −900.

Geography. Total area: 28,360 sq. mi.; **rank:** 8. **Land area:** 27,840 sq. mi. **Forested land:** 25,090 sq. mi. **Location:** bounded by Quebec to the N, Nova Scotia and the Bay of Fundy to the S, the Gulf of St. Lawrence and Northumberland Strait to the E, and Maine to the W. **Climate:** humid continental climate except along the shores where there is a marked maritime effect; avg. Jan. low in Fredericton is −14°C, avg. July high 22°C. **Topography:** upland, lowland and plateau regions throughout the province.

Economy. Principal industries: manufacturing, mining, forestry, pulp and paper. **Principal manufactured goods:** paper and allied products, wood products, fish products, semi-processed mineral products. **GDP, manufacturing** (1981): $884.6 million. **Gross Domestic Product** (1982): $6.7 billion. **Agriculture: Chief crops:** potatoes, apples, blueberries, oats. **Livestock** (1983): 102,000 cattle; 125,000 pigs; 8,300 sheep. **GDP, forestry** (1981): $126.6 million. **Mineral production** (1982): total value, $498 million; metals, $410 million; structural materials, $43 million; coal, $25 million. **GDP, fishing** (1981): $38.5 million. **GDP, construction** (1981): $339.4 million. **Employment distribution** (1983): 32% services; 19% trade; 13% manufacturing; 9% public administration; 6% construction; 2.8% agriculture. **Per capita income** (1982): $9,229. **Unemployment** (1983): 14.8%.

Finance: No. banks: 179; **No. credit unions, caisses populaires:** 128.

International airports: none.

Federal Government: No. federal employees (Dec. 1983): 14,383. **Federal payroll** (1983): $358.5 million.

Energy. Electricity production, by mwh, (1983): mineral, 3,263,526; hydroelectric, 3,030,458; nuclear, 4,759,403.

Education. No. schools: 409 elementary; 66 secondary; 13 higher education. **Avg. salary, public school teachers** (1982-83): $26,499.

Provincial Data. Motto: Spem Reduxit (Hope Restored). **Flower:** Purple violet. **Bird:** none. **Date entered Confederation:** 1867. **Capital:** Fredericton.

Politics. Premier: Richard Hatfield (Progressive Conservative). **Leaders, opposition parties:** Raymond Frenette (Liberal). **Composition of legislature** (June, 1984): P.C. 39; Lib. 18; NDP 1. **Date of last general election:** Oct. 12, 1982.

Tourist attractions: Roosevelt-Campobello International Memorial Park; the tidal bore (Moncton); Magnetic Hill (Moncton); sport salmon fishing in the Miramichi River; world's longest covered bridge at Hartland; Fundy and Kouchibouguac national parks.

Newfoundland

People. Population (Jan. 1984): 579,400; **rank:** 9. **Pop. density:** 4 per sq. mi. **Urban** (1981) 58.6%. **Ethnic distrib.** (1981): English 98.7%. **Net interprovincial migration** (1981-82): —4,046.

Geography. Total area: 156,650 sq. mi.; **rank:** 7. **Land area:** 143,510 sq. mi. **Forested land:** 54,812 sq. mi. **Location:** 2 parts: a 43,010 sq. mi. Atlantic island and 100,500 sq. mi. mainland Labrador, bordered to the W by northern Quebec and to the E by the Atlantic Ocean. **Climate:** ranges from subarctic in Labrador and northern tip of island to humid continental with cool summers and heavy precipitation. **Topography:** highlands of the Long Range (max. elev. 2,673 ft.) along the western coast; central plateau contains uplands descending to lowlands towards the northeast; interior barren and rocky with many lakes and bogs; Labrador is part of the Canadian Shield.

Economy. Principal industries: mining, manufacturing, fishing, pulp and paper, electricity production. **Principal manufactured goods:** fish products, paper products. **GDP, manufacturing** (1981): $463.6 million. **Gross Domestic Product** (1982): $4.7 billion. **Agriculture: GDP, forestry** (1981): $54 million. **Livestock** (1983) 6,400 cattle; 23,000 pigs; 4,000 sheep. **Mineral production** (1982): total value, $647 million; metals, $613 million; asbestos, $9 million; structural materials, $18 million. **GDP, fishing:** (1981) $117.1 million. **GDP, construction** (1981): $280.1 million. **Employment distribution** (1983): 30% services; 18% trade; 13% manufacturing; 10% public administration; 6% construction. **Per capita income** (1982): $8,580. **Unemployment** (1983): 18.8%.

Finance: No. banks: 140; **no. credit unions, caisses populaires:** 15.

International airports: Gander.

Federal Government: No. federal employees (Dec. 1983): 9,478. **Federal payroll** (1983): $234.1 million.

Energy. Electricity production, by mwh, (1983): mineral, 574,170; hydroelectric, 38,984,417.

Education. No. schools: 509 elementary; 135 secondary; 7 higher education. **Avg. salary, public school teachers** (1982-83): $26,725.

Provincial data. Motto: Quaerite prime regnum Dei (Seek ye first the kingdom of God). **Flower:** Pitcher plant. **Bird:** none. **Date entered Confederation:** 1949. **Capital:** St. John's.

Politics. Premier: Brian Peckford (Progressive Conservative). **Leaders, opposition parties:** Steve Neary, (Liberal) Peter Fenwick, (New Democratic). **Composition of legislature** (June, 1984): PC 44; Lib. 8. **Date of last general election:** April 6, 1982.

Tourist attractions: numerous picturesque "outport" fishing villages; Signal Hill National Historical Park (St. John's); the Aviation Museum at Gander International Airport; Witless Bay Island Seabird Sanctuary.

Nova Scotia

People. Population (Jan. 1984): 866,100; **rank:** 7. **Pop. density:** 42.5 per sq. mi. **Urban** (1981) 55.19. **Ethnic distrib.** (1981): English 93.6%; French 4.3%. **Net interprovincial migration** (1981-82): —466.

Geography. Total area: 21,420 sq. mi.; **rank:** 9. **Land area:** 20,400 sq. mi. **Forested land:** 15,826 sq. mi. **Location:** connected to New Brunswick by a 17-mi. isthmus, otherwise surrounded by water - the Gulf of St. Lawrence, Atlantic Ocean and Bay of Fundy. **Climate:** humid continental, with some moderating effects due to the province's maritime location; avg. July temperature high in Halifax is 23°C, avg. Jan. low —10°C. **Topography:** the Atlantic Uplands in the southern half of the province descend to lowlands in the northern portion; 6,479 mi. of coastline, 3,000 lakes, hundreds of rivers.

Economy. Principal industries: manufacturing, fishing, mining, tourism, agriculture, petroleum refining. **Principal manufactured goods:** paper and allied products, petroleum and coal products, fish products. **GDP, manufacturing** (1981): $1.1 billion. **Gross Domestic Product** (1982); $6.3 billion. **Agriculture: Chief crops:** apples, blueberr-

ies, strawberries, oats, potatoes. **Livestock** (1983): 133,000 cattle; 140,000 pigs; 29,000 sheep. **GDP, Forestry** (1981): $30 million. **Mineral production** (1982): total value, $281 million; coal, $166 million; structural materials, $44 million; gypsum, $30 million. **GDP, fishing** (1981): $184.6 million. **GDP, construction** (1981): $421.7 million. **Employment distribution** (1983): 33% services; 18% trade; 13% manufacturing; 10% public administration; 6% construction; 1.9% agriculture. **Per capita income** (1982): $10,090. **Unemployment** (1983): 13.2%.

Finance: No. banks: 243; **No. credit unions, caisses populaires:** 117.

International airports: Halifax.

Federal Government: No. federal employees (Dec. 1983): 35,568. **Federal payroll** (1983): $867.7 million.

Energy. Electricity production, by mwh, (1983): mineral, 4,866,583; hydroelectric, 958,161.

Education. No. schools: 524 elementary; 78 secondary; 23 higher education. **Avg. salary, public school teachers** (1982-83): $29,234.

Provincial Data. Motto: Munit Haec et Altera Vincit (One Defends and the Other Conquers). **Flower:** Trailing arbutus. **Bird:** None. **Date entered Confederation:** 1867. **Capital:** Halifax.

Politics. Premier: John M. Buchanan (Progressive conservative). **Leaders, opposition parties:** A.M. "Sandy" Cameron (Liberal); Alexa McDonough (New Democratic). **Composition of legislature** (June, 1984): P.C. 38; Lib. 12; NDP 1; 1 Cape Breton Labor Party. **Date of last general election:** Oct. 6, 1981.

Tourist attractions: Cabot Trail around Cape Breton Island; Fortress Louisbourg; Peggy's Cove; Alexander Graham Bell Museum (Baddeck); the Miners' Museum (Glace Bay); Nova Scotia Museum (Halifax); Citadel Hill (Halifax).

Ontario

People. Population (Jan. 1984); 8,887,000; **rank:** 1. **Pop. density:** 25.8 per sq. mi. **Urban** (1981) 81.7% **Ethnic distrib.** (1981): English 77.4%; French 5.5%; Italian 3.9%; German 2%; Portuguese 1.3%. **Net interprovincial migration** (1981-82): —8,853.

Geography. Total area: 412,580 sq. mi.; **rank:** 2. **Land area:** 344,090 sq. mi. **Forested land:** 311,502 sq. mi. **Location:** Canada's most centrally-situated province, with Quebec on the E and Manitoba to the W; extends N to shores of James and Hudson Bays; southern boundary with New York, Michigan, Minnesota, and 4 Great Lakes. **Climate:** ranges from humid continental in southern regions to subarctic in the far north, westerly winds bring winter storms; the Great Lakes moderate winter temperatures. **Topography:** 2/3 of province is Precambrian rock of the Canadian Shield; lowland areas lie along the shores of Hudson Bay, the St. Lawrence River and the southern Great Lakes region.

Economy. Principal industries: manufacturing, construction, tourism, agriculture, mining, forestry, fisheries and wildlife. **Principal manufactured goods:** motor vehicles, iron and steel, motor vehicle parts and accessories, foods and beverages, paper and allied products. **GDP, manufacturing** (1981): $31.3 billion. **Gross Domestic Product** (1982): $137.2 billion. **Agriculture: Chief crops:** corn, wheat, oats, barley, soybeans, tobacco, tree fruits. **Livestock** (1983): 2,730,000 cattle; 3,400,000 pigs; 175,000 sheep. **GDP, forestry** (1981): $355.1 million. **Mineral production** (1982): total value, $3.1 billion; metals, $2.3 billion; structural materials, $603 million. **GDP, fishing** (1981): $22.2 million. **GDP, construction** (1981): $4.7 billion. **Employment distribution** (1983): 31% services; 23% manufacturing; 17% trade; 7% public administration; 5% construction; 3.3% agriculture. **Per capita income:** (1982): $13,842. **Unemployment** (1983): 10.4%.

Finance: No. banks: 2,770; **No credit unions, caisses populaires:** 1,100

International airports: Pearson (at Toronto), Ottawa.

Federal Government: No. federal employees (Dec. 1983): 173,617. **Federal payroll** (1983): $4.7 billion.

Energy. Electricity production, by mwh, (1983): mineral, 35,835,973; hydroelectric, 38,559,965; nuclear, 39,472,300.

Education. No. schools: 4,684 elementary; 847 secondary; 52 higher education. **Avg. salary, public school teachers** (1982-83): $31,294.

Provincial data. Motto: Ut Incepit Fidelis Sic Permanet (Loyal she began, loyal she remains). **Flower:** White trillium. **Bird:** none. **Date entered Confederation:** 1867. **Capital:** Toronto.

Politics. Premier: William (Bill) Davis (Progressive Conservative), **Leaders, opposition parties:** David Peterson (Liberal); Bob Rae (New Democratic). **Composition of legislature** (June, 1984): PC 71; Lib. 32; NDP 22. **Date of last general election:** March 19, 1981.

Tourist attractions. Toronto C.N. Tower, Ontario Science Centre, Ontario Place, Metro Toronto Zoo, McLaughlin Planetarium, Black Creek Pioneer Village, Canadian Nation Exhibition (mid Aug. to Labor Day); Ottawa's Parliament buildings; Niagara Falls; Polar Bear Express and Agawa Canyon train rides into northern Ontario.

Prince Edward Island

People. Population (Jan. 1984): 124,600; **rank:** 10. **Pop. density:** 57.2 per sq. mi. **Urban** (1981) 36.3% **Ethnic distrib.** (1981): English 93.9%; French 5%. **Net interprovincial migration** (1981-82): −629.

Geography. Total area: 2,180 sq. mi.; **rank:** 10. **Land area:** 2,180 sq. mi. **Forested land:** 1,158 sq. mi. **Location:** an island 140 mi. long, between 40 and 140 mi. wide, situated in the Gulf of St. Lawrence approx. 10 mi. from the coasts of Nova Scotia and New Brunswick. **Climate:** humid continental with temperatures moderated by maritime location; avg. Jan. low in Charlottetown is −11°C, avg. July high 23°C. **Topography:** gently rolling hills; sharply indented coastline; many streams but only small rivers and lakes.

Economy. Principal industries: agriculture, tourism, fisheries, light manufacturing. **Principal manufactured goods:** paint, farm vehicles, metal products, electronic equipment. **GDP, manufacturing** (1981): $63 million. **Gross Domestic Product** (1982): $990 million. **Agriculture. Chief crops:** potatoes, mixed grains, oats, barley. **Livestock** (1983): 99,000 cattle; 109,000 pigs; 5,000 sheep. **Mineral production** (1982): total value, $1.8 million, all from sand and gravel. **GDP, fishing:** (1981): $22.4 million. **GDP, construction** (1981): $46.4 million. **Employment distribution** (1983): 33% services; 17% trade; 10% agriculture; 8% manufacturing; 10% public administration. **Per capita income** (1982): $8,894. **Unemployment** (1983): 12.2%.

Finance: No. banks: 30; **No. credit unions, caisses populaires:** 12.

International airports: none.

Federal Government: No. federal employees (Dec. 1983): 3,227. **Federal payroll:** (1983): $80.3 million.

Energy. Electricity production, hy mwh, (1983): mineral, 10,824.

Education. No. schools: 59 elementary; 13 secondary; 3 higher education. **Avg. salary, public school teachers** (1982-83): $28,166.

Provincial Data. Motto: Parva Sub Ingenti (The small under the protection of the large). **Flower:** Lady's slipper. **Bird:** Blue jay. **Date entered Confederation:** 1873. **Capital:** Charlottetown.

Politics. Premier: James M. Lee (Progressive Conservative). **Leaders, opposition parties:** Joe Ghiz (Liberal), Jim Mayne (New Democratic). **Composition of legislature** (June, 1984): P.C. 21; Lib. 11. **Date of last general election:** Sept. 27, 1982.

Tourist attractions: P.E.I. National Park; beaches all along the coastline; 9 golf courses; 70 campgrounds; Summerside Lobster Carnival, 3d wk. in July; Charlottetown Old Home Week, 3d wk. in Aug.; Charlottetown Confederation Centre; Woodleigh Replicas (Burlington).

Quebec

People. Population (Jan. 1984): 6,529,300; **rank:** 2. **Pop. density:** 12.5 per sq. mi. **Urban** (1981) 77.6%. **Ethnic distrib.** (1981): French 82.4%; English 11%; Italian 2%. **Net interprovincial migration** (1980-81): −23,291. **Geography. Total area:** 594,860 sq. mi.; **rank:** 1. **Land area:** 523,860 sq. mi. **Forested land:** 362,840 sq. mi. **Location:** borders Ontario on the W and Labrador and New Brunswick on the E; extends N to Hudson Strait and NW to James and Hudson Bays; the southern border touches New York, Vermont, New Hampshire and Maine. **Climate:** varies from subarctic in the northern half of the province to continental in the southern populated regions; avg. Jan. low in Montreal is −14°C, avg. Jan. High 26°C. **Topography:** half a million sq. mi. of Quebec consists of the Laurentian Uplands, part of the Canadian Shield; Appalachian Highlands are in southeastern Quebec; lowlands form a small area along the shore of the St. Lawrence River.

Economy. Principal industries: manufacturing, agriculture, electrical production, mining, meat processing, petroleum refining. **Principal manufactured goods:** foods and beverages, clothing, textiles, paper and paper products, furniture. **GDP, manufacturing** (1981): $17.2 billion. **Gross Domestic Product** (1982): $83.2 billion. **Agriculture. Chief crops:** oats, corn grains, potatoes, mixed grains, tame hay, apples. **Livestock** (1983): 1,500,000 cattle; 3,260,000 pigs; 88,000 sheep. **GDP, forestry** (1981): $389.7 million. **Mineral production** (1982): total value, $2.1 billion; metals, $1.2 billion; asbestos, $298 million; structural materials, $362 million. **GDP, fishing** (1981): $33.5 million. **GDP, construction** (1981): $3.3 billion. **Employment distribution** (1983): 32% services; 20% manufacturing; 17% trade; 7% public administration; 4% construction; 3% agriculture. **Per capita income** (1982): $12,021. **Unemployment** (1983): 13.9%.

Finance: No. banks: 1,270; **no. credit unions, caisses populaires:** 1,670.

International airports: Dorval, Mirabel (both near Montreal).

Federal Government: No. federal employees (Dec. 1983): 82,908. **Federal payroll** (1983): $2.1 billion.

Energy. Electricity production, by mwh, (1983): hydroelectric, 90,129,732; nuclear 1,989,621.

Education. No. schools: 1,921 elementary; 700 secondary; 91 higher education. **Avg. salary, public school teachers** (1982-83): N.A.

Provincial Data. Motto Je me souviens (I remember). **Flower:** Fleur de Lys. **Birds:** Alouette (lark). **Date entered Confederation:** 1867. **Capital:** Quebec City.

Politics. Premier: Rene Levesque (Parti Quebecois). **Leaders, opposition parties:** vacant (Liberal). **Composition of legislature** (June, 1984): PQ 71; Lib. 48; 2 independent. **Date of last general election:** April 13, 1981.

Tourist attractions: Quebec City, often described as North America's "most European city", and sophisticated Montreal each offer numerous attractions; the north shore of the St. Lawrence River and the Gaspé Peninsula are picturesque.

Saskatchewan

People. Population (Jan. 1984): 1,000,000; **rank:** 6. **Pop. density:** 4.5 per sq. mi. **Urban** (1981) 58.2% **Ethnic distrib.** (1981): English 79.6%; German 5.2%; Ukrainian 4.6%; French 2.6%; Native Indian 2.4%. **Net interprovincial migration** (1981-82): +2,088.

Geography. Total area: 251,870 sq. mi.; **rank:** 5. **Land area:** 220,350 sq. mi. **Forested land:** 66,708 sq. mi. **Location:** borders on the Northwest Territories to the N, Manitoba to the E, Alberta to the W, and Montana and North Dakota to the S. **Climate:** continental, with cold winters (Jan. avg. low in Regina is −23°C) and hot summers (July avg. high in Regina is 26°C). **Topography:** southern 2/3ds of province is plains and grassland; northern 3d is Canadian Shield.

Economy. Principal industries: agriculture, mining of

potash and uranium, meat processing, electricity production, petroleum refining. **Principal manufactured goods:** foods and beverages, agricultural implements, fabricated metals, non-metallic mineral products. **GDP, manufacturing** (1981): $679.1 million. **Gross domestic product** (1982): $15.7 billion. **Agriculture: Chief crops:** wheat (57% of national total), barley, oats, mustard seed, rapeseed, flax. **Livestock** (1983): 1,930,000 cattle; 530,000 pigs; 46,000 sheep. **GDP, forestry** (1981): $34.4 million. **Mineral production** (1982): total value, $2.3 billion; potash, $631 million; petroleum, $1.2 billion; metals, $269 million. **GDP, fishing** (1981): $2.2 million. **GDP, construction** (1981): $820.9 million. **Employment distribution** (1983): 29% services; 20% agriculture; 17% trade; 8% public administration; 6% construction; 6% manufacturing. **Per capita income** (1982): $12,372. **Unemployment** (1983): 7.4%.

Finance: No. banks: 395; **No. credit unions, caisses populaires:** 357.

International airports: none.

Federal Government: No. Federal employees (Dec. 1983): 12,585. **Federal payroll** (1983): $323.2 million.

Energy. Electricity production, by mwh. (1983): mineral, 7,776,124; hydroelectric, 2,177,271.

Education. No. schools: 927 elementary; 143 secondary; 7 higher education. **Avg. salary, public school teachers** (1982-83): $28,872.

Provincial Data. Motto: none. **Flower:** Western red lily. **Bird:** Prairie sharp-tailed grouse. **Date entered Confederation:** 1905. **Capital:** Regina.

Politics. Premier: Grant Devine (Progressive Conservative). **Leader, opposition party:** Allan Blakeney (New Democratic). **Composition of legislature** (June, 1984): PC 55; NDP 8; Lib. 1. **Date of last general election:** Apr. 26, 1982.

Tourist attractions. Regina: RCMP Museum, Museum of Natural History, Wascana Centre; Western Development Museums located at Saskatoon, Yorkton, North Battleford, Moose Jaw.

Territories of Canada

In addition to its 10 provinces, Canada contains the Yukon and Northwest Territories making up more than a third of the nation's land area but less than .3% of its population. A resident commissioner in each territory is appointed by the federal government which retains control over natural resources excluding wildlife. An elected legislative assembly in each territory exercises jurisdiction over such matters as education, housing, social services and renewable resources. The Commissioner of the Northwest Territories serves as chairman of and acts on the advice of a 9-member executive council, 8 of them appointed from a 24-member elected assembly. The Yukon commissioner acts on the advice of a 6-member executive council, all of whom are appointed on the recommendation of the leader of the majority party in the legislature.

The NWT elects 2 members to the federal parliament, Yukon one member. Each territory has one Senate representative. There is strong support in both territories for increased autonomy or provincial status.

Yukon

*Data apply to both territories.

People. Population (Jan. 1984): 21,600; **Pop. density:** 0.1 per sq. mi. **Urban** (1981) 64%. **Ethnic distrib. by mother tongue** (1981): English 87.4%; Native Indian 3.6%; French 2.5%; German 2.1%. (Using other criteria Native Indians make up 19% of the population). **Net migration** (1981-82): +199.

Geography. Total area: 186,660 sq. mi. **Land area:** 184,930 sq. mi. **Forested land:** 93,412 sq. mi. **Location:** extreme northwestern area of mainland Canada; bounded on the N by the Beaufort Sea, on the S by British Columbia, on the E by the Mackenzie District of the Northwest Territories, and on the W by Alaska. **Climate:** great variance in temperatures; warm summers, very cold winters; low precipitation. **Topography:** main feature is the Yukon plateau with 21 peaks exceeding 10,000 ft.; open tundra in the far north.

Economy. Principal industries: mining, tourism. **Principal manufactured goods:** small amounts of cement, explosives, forest products, canoes, native Indian products. **GDP, manufacturing** (1981): $6 million.* **Gross domestic product** (1982): $1.2 billion.* **Agriculture:** hay, oats, vegetable gardens for local use. **Mineral production** (1982): total value, $169 million—all from metals. **GDP, fishing** (1981): $1.5 million.* **GDP, construction** (1981): $279.2 million.* **Per capita income** (1982): $13,014.* **No. of banks:** 12.

Federal Government: No. federal employees (Dec. 1983): 1,290. **Federal payroll** (1983): $35.6 million.

Energy. Electricity production, by mwh. (1983): hydroelectric, 221,022.

Education. No. schools: 23 elementary; 2 secondary; 0 higher education. **Avg. salary, public school teachers** (1982-83): $37,360.

Territorial Data. Flower: Fireweed. **Date established:** June 13, 1898. **Capital:** Whitehorse. **Commissioner:** Doug Bell. **Government Leader:** Chris Pearson (Progressive Conservative). **Other party leaders:** Ron Veale (Liberal), Tony Penikett (New Democratic). **Composition of assembly** (June, 1984): P.C. 9; NDP 6; 1 independent. **Date of last general election:** June 7, 1982.

Tourist attractions. Historic sites from the Gold Rush period in Whitehorse and Dawson City; Miles Canyon; Kluane National Park; Takhini Hot Springs.

The Northwest Territories

People. Population (Jan. 1984): 49,000; **Pop. density:** 0.04 per sq. mi. **Urban** (1981) 48%. **Ethnic distrib. by mother tongue** (1981): English 54.1%; Inuit 28.9%; Native Indian 10.7%; French 2.7%. (Using other criteria the Inuit make up 34% of the population, Native Indians 18%.) **Net migration** (1981-82): −90.

Geography. Total area: 1,322,900 sq. mi. **Land area:** 1,271,440 sq. mi. **Forested land:** 237,390 sq. mi. **Location:** all land north of the 60th parallel between the Yukon Territory and Hudson Bay and all northern islands east to Greenland; land area bounded by the Yukon Territory to the W, Hudson Bay to the E, the Beaufort Sea to the N and B.C., Alta., Sask. and Man. to S. **Climate:** extreme temperatures and low precipitation; Arctic and sub-Arctic.

Topography: mostly tundra plains formed on the rocks of the Canadian Shield; the Mackenzie Lowland is a continuation of the Great Plains; the Mackenzie River Valley is forested.

Economy. Principal industries: mining, mineral and hydrocarbon exploration; oil refining. **GDP, manufacturing** (1981): see Yukon. **Gross domestic product** (1982): see Yukon. **Agriculture:** scattered market gardening in the southern Mackenzie area only. **Mineral production** (1982): total value, $503 million; metals, $383 million; fuels, $56 million. **GDP, fishing:** (1981): see Yukon. **GDP, construction** (1981): see Yukon. **Per capita income** (1982): see Yukon. **No. of banks** 16.

Federal Government: No. federal employees (Dec. 1983): 2,575. **Federal payroll** (1983): $67.7 million.

Energy. Electricity production, by mwh. (1983): hydroelectric, 235,446.

Education. No. schools: 67 elementary; 5 secondary; 1 higher education. **Avg. salary, public school teachers** (1982-83): $36,956.

Territorial Data. Flower: Mountain avens. **Date Established:** June 22, 1869. **Capital:** Yellowknife. **Commissioner:** John H. Parker. **Council:** 24 independent elected representatives.

Tourist attractions: Wood Buffalo, Auyuittuq, and Nahanni National Parks; Mackenzie River and Delta; annual Midnight Golf Tournament in Yellowknife June 21.

Head of State and Cabinet

Canada's official head of state, Queen Elizabeth of England, who succeeded to the throne in 1952, is represented by Governor-General Jeanne Sauvé, appointed in 1984. Titles: Minister unless otherwise stated or *Minister of State.

(Sept. 17, 1984)

Prime Minister — Brian Mulroney
Veterans Affairs — George Hees
Senate Government Leader — Duff Roblin
External Affairs — Joe Clark
Employment and Immigration — Flora MacDonald
Deputy Prime Minister and President of Privy Council — Erik Neilsen
Justice, Attorney-General — John Crosbie
Public Works — Roch LaSalle
Transport —·Donald Mazankowski
Solicitor-General — Elmer MacKay
Health and Welfare — Jake Epp
Fisheries and Oceans — John Fraser
Regional Industrial Expansion — Sinclair Stevens
Agriculture — John Wise
Government House Leader — Raymon Hnatyshyn
Indian Affairs and Northern Development — David Crombie
President of the Treasury Board — Robert René de Contret
National Revenue — Perrin Beatty
Finance — Michael Wilson

Defense — Robert Coates
*Multiculturalism — Jack Murta
Supply and Services — Harvie Andre
*Fitness and Amateur Sport — Otto Jelinek
*Science and Technology — Thomas Siddon
*Wheat Board — Charles Mayer
*Labor — William McKnight
*Secretary of State — Walter McLean
*Tourism — Thomas McMillan
Energy, Mines and Resources — Pat Carney
*Small Business — André Bissonnette
Environment — Suzanne Blais-Grenier
*Transport — Benoit Bouchard
*Youth — Andrée Champagne
Consumer and Corporate Affairs — Michael Coté
*International Trade — James Kelleher
Mines —Robert Layton
*Finance — Barbara McDougall
*Forestry — Gerald Merrithew
External Relations — Monique Vézina

Governors-General of Canada Since Confederation, 1867

Name	Term	Name	Term
The Viscount Monck of Ballytrammon	1867-1868	General The Baron Byng of Vimy	1921-1926
The Baron Lisgar of Lisgar and Bailieborough	1869-1872	The Viscount Willingdon of Ratton	1926-1931
		The Earl of Bessborough	1931-1935
The Earl of Dufferin	1872-1878	The Baron Tweedsmuir of Elsfield	1935-1940
The Marquis of Lorne	1878-1883	Major General The Earl of Athlone	1940-1946
The Marquis of Lansdowne	1883-1888	Field Marshal The Viscount Alexander of Tunis	1946-1952
The Baron Stanley of Preston	1888-1893		
The Earl of Aberdeen	1893-1898	The Right Hon. Vincent Massey	1952-1959
The Earl of Minto	1898-1904	General The Right Hon. Georges P. Vanier	1959-1967
The Earl Grey	1904-1911	The Right Hon. Roland Michener	1967-1974
Field Marshal H.R.H. The Duke of Connaught	1911-1916	The Right Hon. Jules Leger	1974-1979
		The Right Hon. Edward Schreyer	1979-1984
The Duke of Devonshire	1916-1921	The Right Hon. Jeanne Sauvé	1984-

Fathers of Confederation

Union of the British North American colonies into the Dominion of Canada was discussed and its terms negotiated at 3 confederation conferences held at Charlottetown (C), Sept. 1, 1864; Quebec (Q), Oct. 10, 1864; and London (L), Dec. 4, 1866. The names of delegates are followed by the provinces they represented. Canada refers to what are now the provinces of Ontario and Quebec.

Adams G. Archibald, N.S.	(C,Q,L)	Hector L. Langevin, Canada	(C,Q,L)
George Brown, Canada	(C,Q)	Jonathan McCully, N.S.	(C,Q,L)
Alexander Campbell, Canada	(C,Q)	A.A. Macdonald, P.E.I.	(C,Q)
Frederick B.T. Carter, Nfld.	(Q)	John A. Macdonald, Canada	(C,Q,L)
George-Etienne Cartier, Canada	(C,Q,L)	William McDougall, Canada	(C,Q,L)
Edward B. Chandler, N.B.	(C,Q)	Thomas D'Arcy McGee, Canada	(C,Q)
Jean-Charles Chapais, Canada	(Q)	Peter Mitchell, N.B.	(Q,L)
James Cockburn, Canada	(Q)	Oliver Mowat, Canada	(Q)
George H. Coles, P.E.I.	(C,Q)	Edward Palmer, P.E.I.	(C,Q)
Robert B. Dickey, N.S.	(Q)	William H. Pope, P.E.I.	(C,Q)
Charles Fisher, N.B.	(Q,L)	John W. Ritchie, N.S.	(L)
Alexander T. Galt, Canada	(C,Q,L)	J. Ambrose Shea, Nfld.	(Q)
John Hamilton Gray, N.B.	(C,Q)	William H. Steeves, N.B.	(C,Q)
John Hamilton Gray, P.E.I.	(C,Q)	Sir Etienne-Paschal Tache, Canada	(Q)
Thomas Heath Haviland, P.E.I.	(Q)	Samuel Leonard Tilley, N.B.	(C,Q,L)
William A. Henry, N.S.	(C,Q,L)	Charles Tupper, N.S.	(C,Q,L)
William P. Howland, Canada	(L)	Edward Whelan, P.E.I.	(Q)
John M. Johnson, N.B.	(C,Q,L)	R.D. Wilmot, N.B.	(L)

The Political Parties

Canadian parties, from whatever point in the political spectrum they begin, gravitate towards the middle of the road where most of the votes lie. Despite variations in outlook and policy, all 3 official parties tend to adopt a practical rather than dogmatic line on most issues.

Progressive Conservatives — Canada's oldest party and

theoretically the furthest to the right, the Conservatives have nevertheless endorsed an extension of social welfare. Though their support is based in western Canada, the Conservatives received strong support in all provinces in 1984. Until the '84 victory the party had held office only 9 months during the preceeding 21 years, mainly due to a failure to gain support in Quebec. **Leader:** Brian Mulroney.

Liberals — Though politically situated between the Conservatives to the right and the New Democrats on the left, the Liberals are flexible enough to lean in either direction depending on specific issues and political situations. In 1975 they belatedly adopted a Conservative proposal for wage and price controls; in 1979 they sided with the NDP to oppose Conservative plans to return some government-owned corporations to the private sector. Most of their traditional electoral support comes from middle and upper class urban residents, from ethnic voters, and among French-speaking Canadians. **Leader:** John Turner.

New Democratic Party — Successor to the Cooperative Commonwealth Federation, which combined the agrarian protest movement in western Canada with a democratic socialism of the British Labor Party variety, the NDP was founded in 1961. It now attempts to attract the vote of middle-class Canadians and fuse it with the party's labor support. **Leader:** Ed Broadbent.

Political power in Canada has been dominated by the Conservative and Liberal parties. Of 33 federal elections since Confederation, the Conservatives have won 14, holding power for 47 years; the Liberals have gained office 19 times, governing for 70 years.

Despite the dominance of the Liberals and Conservatives, third parties have played an important role under Canada's parliamentary system in which a governing party holding less than half the seats in the House of Commons can remain in office and pass legislation only with the support of a minor party. A minority Conservative Government lost power in 1979 when none of the opposition parties supported its proposed budget.

The NDP has been the most influential of the third parties, consistently winning between 15% and 20% of the popular vote—though its proportion of elected members is always less. NDP pressure from the left has influenced policy decisions by both major parties. The Social Credit Party, once a strong political force with federal support in Quebec and the western provinces, has declined in stature over the past 2 decades and has failed to elect any members to Parliament in the past two elections.

Prime Ministers of Canada

Name	Party	Term	Name	Party	Term
Sir John A. MacDonald	Conservative	1867-1873			1926-1930
		1878-1891			1935-1948
Alexander Mackenzie	Liberal	1873-1878	R. B. Bennett.	Conservative	1930-1935
Sir John J. C. Abbott	Conservative	1891-1892	Louis St. Laurent	Liberal	1948-1957
Sir John S. D. Thompson . . .	Conservative	1892-1894	John G. Diefenbaker.	Prog. Cons.	1957-1963
Sir Mackenzie Bowell	Conservative	1894-1896	Lester B. Pearson	Liberal	1963-1968
Sir Charles Tupper	Conservative	1896	Pierre Elliott Trudeau	Liberal	1968-1979
Sir Wilfrid Laurier	Liberal	1896-1911	Joe Clark	Prog. Cons.	1979-1980
Sir Robert L. Borden	Conservative	1911-1920	Pierre Elliott Trudeau	Liberal	1980-1984
	Unionist		John Turner	Liberal	1984-1984
Arthur Meighen	Cons. Union.	1920-1921	Brian Mulroney	Prog. Cons.	1984-
W. L. Mackenzie King	Liberal	1921-1926			

(1) King's term was interrupted from June 26-Sept. 25, 1926, when Arthur Meighen again served as prime minister.

Canadian Political Party Leaders
Progressive Conservative Party[1]

Leader	Term				
John A.		Robert Borden	2/6/1901-7/10/1920	George Drew	10/2/1948-12/14/1956
MacDonald	1854-6/6/1891	Arthur Meighen	7/10/1920-10/11/1926	John G.	
J.C. Abbott	6/16/1891-12/5/1892	Hugh Guthrie	10/11/1926-10/12/1927	Diefenbaker	12/14/1956-9/9/1967
John Thompson	12/5/1892-12/12/1894	R.B. Bennett	11/12/1927-7/7/1938	Robert	
Mackenzie		R.J. Manion	7/7/1938-5/13/1940	Stanfield	9/9/1967-2/22/1976
Bowell	12/21/1894-4/27/1896	R.B. Hanson	5/13/1940-1/27/1943	Joe Clark	2/22/1976-6/13/1983
Charles Tupper	5/1/1896-2/5/1901	Arthur Meighen	11/12/1941-12/11/1942	Brian Mulroney	6/13/1983-
		John Bracken	12/11/1942-10/2/1948		

Liberal Party

Leader	Term				
Alexander		W.L. Mackenzie		Lester B.	
Mackenzie	3/6/1873-4/27/1880	King	8/7/1919-8/7/1948	Pearson	1/16/1958-4/2/1968
Edward Blake	5/4/1880-6/2/1887	Louis St.		Pierre Elliott	
Wilfrid Laurier	June/1887-2/17/1919	Laurent	8/7/1948-1/16/1958	Trudeau	4/6/1968-6/16/1984
				John Turner	6/16/1984-

New Democratic Party[2]

Leader	Term				
James S.		Hazen Argue	Aug./1960-Aug./1961	Ed Broadbent	Jul./1975-present
Woodsworth	Aug./1932-Jul./1942	Tommy			
M.J. Coldwell	Jul./1942-Aug./1960	Douglas	Aug./1961-Apr./1971		
		David Lewis	Apr./1971-Jul./1975		

(1) Changed name from Conservative to Progressive Conservative Dec., 1942. (2) Prior to August 1961 was called the Co-operative Commonwealth Federation.

Election Results by Province and Party, September 4, 1984

Province	Total Valid Votes	Liberal	Conservative	New Dem.	Other
Alberta	1,020,364	129,702	700,191	143,221	47,250
British Columbia.	1,431,151	234,581	661,177	498,897	31,496
Manitoba.	516,046	112,123	221,946	139,999	40,937
New Brunswick	379,813	120,363	202,044	53,364	4,042
Newfoundland	242,217	87,706	138,828	13,996	1,687
Nova Scotia	461,575	154,839	233,192	69,587	3,957
Ontario	4,457,402	1,325,636	2,111,354	912,107	108,305
Prince Edward Island	73,801	30,075	38,160	4,737	829
Quebec	3,485,611	1,219,377	1,728,567	301,446	234,609
Saskatchewan	524,090	95,134	217,887	200,871	10,198
N.W. Territories	19,659	5,271	8,095	5,528	763
Yukon	11,704	2,535	6,648	1,884	637
TOTAL	12,621,778	3,518,342	6,273,089	2,345,637	484,710
Percent.	100	27.88	49.70	18.58	3.84
Seats	282	40	211	30	1

Party Representation by Regions, 1953-1984

Canada	1953	1957	1958	1962	1963	1965	1968	1972	1974	1979	1980	1984
Liberal	171	105	48	100	129	131	155	109	141	114	147	40
Conservative	51	112	208	116	95	97	72	107	95	136	103	211
New Democratic	23	25	8	19	17	21	22	31	16	26	32	30
Social Credit	15	19	—	30	24	14	14	15	11	6	0	—
Other	5	4	1	—	—	2	1	2	1	0	0	1
Ontario												
Liberal	51	21	14	44	52	51	64	36	55	32	52	14
Conservative	33	61	67	35	27	25	17	40	25	57	38	67
New Democratic	1	3	3	6	6	9	6	11	8	6	5	13
Quebec												
Liberal	66	62	25	35	47	56	56	56	60	67	74	17
Conservative	4	9	50	14	8	8	4	2	3	2	1	58
Social Credit	—	—	—	26	20	9	14	15	11	6	—	—
Atlantic												
Liberal	27	12	8	14	20	15	7	10	13	12	19	7
Conservative	5	21	25	18	13	18	25	22	17	18	13	25
New Democratic	1	—	—	1	—	—	—	—	1	2	—	—
Western[2]												
Liberal	27	10	1	7	10	9	28	7	13	3	2	2
Conservative	9	21	66	49	47	46	26	43	50	59	51	61
New Democratic	21	22	5	12	11	12	16	20	7	18	27	17
Social Credit	15	19	—	4	4	5	—	—	—	—	—	—

(1) Prior to 1962 election was known as the Cooperative Commonwealth Federation.
(2) Includes the Yukon and Northwest Territories.

Canadian Armed Forces

Canada has an all-volunteer Armed Forces which, since 1968, has been a single body composed of what had been a separate army, navy, and air force. Canada's defense budget for 1983-84 (ending Mar. 31) was $7,868,398,000. The projected 1984-85 budget is $8,752,743,000.

Chief of the Defense Staff: Gen. Gerard C.E. Theriault
Vice Chief of the Defense Staff: Vice-Admiral Daniel N. Mainguy

Maritime Command — Vice Admiral J.C. Wood
Mobile Command — Lieut. Gen. C. H. Belzile
Air Command — Lieut. Gen. P.D. Manson

Communications Command — Brig. Gen. G. D. Simpson
Canadian Forces Europe — Maj. Gen. D.P. Wightman

Regular Forces Strength

(as of March 31)

Year	Navy	Army	Air Force	Total	Year	Total	Year	Total	Year	Total
1945	92,529	494,258	174,254	761,041	1970	91,433	1979	78,974	1982	82,858
1955	19,207	49,409	49,461	118,077	1975	78,448	1980	78,909	1983	82,905
1965	19,756	46,264	48,144	114,164	1978	79,656	1981	79,549	1984	81,675

Canadian Military Participation in Major Conflicts

Northwest Rebellion (1885)[1]
Participants—3,323
Killed—38
Last veteran died at the age of 104 in 1971.
South African War (1899-1902)
Participants—7,368[2]
Killed—89
Living Veterans—1
First World War (1914-1918)
Participants—626,636[3]

Killed—61,332[4]
Living Veterans—22,500[5]
Second World War (1939-1945)
Participants—1,086,343 (inc. 45,423 women)
Killed—32,714 (inc. 8 women)
Living Veterans—649,200[6]
Korean War (1950-1953)
Participants—25,583
Killed—314
Living Veterans—24,800[6]

(1) First battle in history to be fought entirely by Canadian troops. (2) Includes Canadians in the South African constabulary and 8 nursing sisters. (3) Includes 2,854 nursing sisters. (4) Includes 21 nursing sisters and 1,563 airmen serving with the British air forces. (5) 1984 est. based on mortality rates applied to 1971 census data. (6) Includes 4,000 who also served in WWII.

Canadian Peacekeeping Operations

Canada has played a major role in the United Nations' efforts to preserve peace and promote international security, participating in almost all UN peacekeeping operations to date - in Egypt, Israel, Syria, Lebanon, Cyprus, Korea, India, Pakistan, West New Guinea, the Congo, Yemen and Nigeria.

Nearly 900 Canadian soldiers served in the Gaza Strip following the Israeli-Egyptian crisis of 1956 until the peacekeeping force there was disbanded in 1967. Another 850 Canadians served with the United Nations Emergency Force in the Middle East from 1973 until it was disbanded in Nov., 1979.

In the Congo, a 300-man signals unit provided communications for the UN force from 1960 to 1964.

Canadian participation in the International Commission for Control and Supervision in Vietnam and Laos began in 1954, and, at its height following U.S. military withdrawal from Vietnam in 1973, involved 245 Canadian Forces personnel. The Canadian Vietnam supervisory contingent was withdrawn in July 1973, the Laos mission in 1974.

Canadian peacekeeping operations in 1984:
—some 515 Canadians in the UN Peacekeeping Force in Cyprus where Canadian participation began in 1964 and was augmented in 1974.
—250 Canadians, mostly logistics troops, with the UN Disengagement Observer Force in the Middle East.
—20 Canadian combat arms officers with the UN Truce Supervisory Organization, Israel.

Area of Canada by Provinces

Source: Energy. Mines. and Resources Canada

Province, territory	Capital	Area in square miles			Area in square kilometers		
		Land	Fresh water	Total	Land	Fresh water	Total
Newfoundland	St. John's	143,510	13,140	156,650	371,690	34,030	405,720
Prince Edward Island	Charlottetown	2,180	...	2,180	5,660	...	5,660
Nova Scotia	Halifax	20,400	1,020	21,420	52,840	2,650	55,490
New Brunswick	Fredericton	27,840	520	28,360	72,090	1,350	73,440
Quebec	Quebec	523,860	71,000	594,860	1,356,790	183,890	1,540,680
Ontario	Toronto	344,090	68,490	412,580	891,190	177,390	1,068,580
Manitoba	Winnipeg	211,720	39,230	250,950	548,360	101,590	649,950
Saskatchewan	Regina	220,350	31,520	251,870	570,700	81,630	652,330
Alberta	Edmonton	248,800	6,490	255,290	644,390	16,800	661,190
British Columbia	Victoria	358,970	6,980	365,950	929,730	18,070	947,800
Yukon Territory	Whitehorse	184,930	1,730	186,660	478,970	4,480	483,450
Northwest Territories	Yellowknife	1,271,440	51,460	1,322,900	3,293,020	133,300	3,426,320
Total		**3,558,090**	**291,580**	**3,849,670**	**9,215,430**	**755,180**	**9,970,610**

Population of Canada by Province, 1871 - 1981

Source: Statistics Canada

Province, territory	1871 census	1901 census	1941 census	1951 census	1961 census	1971 census	1976 census	1981 census
Newfoundland	—	—	—	361,416	457,853	522,104	557,725	567,681
Prince Edward Island	94,021	103,259	95,047	98,429	104,629	111,641	118,229	122,506
Nova Scotia	387,800	459,574	577,942	642,584	737,007	788,960	828,571	847,442
New Brunswick	285,594	331,120	457,401	515,697	597,936	634,557	677,250	691,403
Quebec	1,191,516	1,648,898	3,331,882	4,055,681	5,259,211	6,027,764	6,234,445	6,438,403
Ontario	1,620,851	2,182,947	3,787,655	4,597,542	6,236,092	7,703,106	8,264,465	8,625,107
Manitoba	25,228	255,211	729,744	776,541	921,686	988,247	1,021,506	1,026,241
Saskatchewan	—	91,279	895,992	831,728	925,181	926,242	921,323	968,313
Alberta	—	73,022	796,169	939,501	1,331,944	1,627,874	1,838,037	2,237,724
British Columbia	36,247	178,657	817,861	1,165,210	1,629,082	2,184,621	2,466,608	2,744,467
Yukon	—	27,219	4,914	9,096	14,628	18,388	21,836	23,153
Northwest Territories	48,000	20,129	12,028	16,004	22,998	34,807	42,609	45,741
Total	**3,689,257**	**5,371,315**	**11,506,655**	**14,009,429**	**18,238,247**	**21,568,311**	**22,992,604**	**24,343,181**

Population of Major Canadian Cities and Metropolitan Areas

Source: Statistics Canada. from 1981 Census.

	City	Metro Area[1]		City	Metro Area[1]
Montreal, Quebec	980,354	2,828,349	Regina, Saskatchewan	162,613	164,313
Toronto, Ontario	599,217	2,998,947[2]	Saskatoon, Saskatchewan	154,210	154,210
Calgary, Alberta	592,743	592,743	Brampton, Ontario	149,030	—
Winnipeg, Manitoba	564,473	584,842	Kitchener, Ontario	139,734	287,801
North York, Ontario	559,521	—	Longueuil, Quebec	124,320	—
Edmonton, Alberta	532,246	657,057	St. Catharines, Ontario	124,018	304,353
Vancouver, British Columbia	414,281	1,268,183	Oshawa, Ontario	117,519	154,217
Mississauga, Ontario	315,056	—	Burlington, Ontario	114,853	—
Hamilton, Ontario	306,434	542,095	Halifax, Nova Scotia	114,594	277,727
Ottawa, Ontario	295,163	717,578[3]	Thunder Bay, Ontario	112,486	121,379
Laval, Quebec	268,335	—	Sudbury, Ontario	91,829	149,923
London, Ontario	254,280	283,668	St. John's, Newfoundland	83,770	154,820
Windsor, Ontario	192,083	246,110	Saint John, New Brunswick	80,521	112,974
Quebec, Quebec	166,474	576,075	Victoria, British Columbia	64,379	233,481

(1) Figures are for Census Metro Areas which. in some cases. include municipalities outside of metro political boundaries. (2) Census area includes Mississauga; actual metro political area (pop. 2.137.395) is composed of the cities of North York. Scarborough. Etobicoke. York and the borough of East York. (3) Includes Hull. Que.

Superlative Canadian Statistics

Source: Statistics Canada; Energy. Mines and Resources Canada

Area	Total: Land 3,558,090 sq. mi.; Water 291,580 sq. mi.	3,849,670 sq. mi.
Largest city in area	Timmins, Ont.	1,160 sq. mi.
Smallest city in area (east)	Vanier, Ont.	1.1 sq. mi.
Smallest city in area (west)	Chilliwack, B.C.	1.6 sq. mi.
Northernmost point	Cape Columbia, Ellesmere Island, N.W.T.	83°07'30"N, 70°32'07"W.
Southernmost point	Middle Island (Lake Erie), Ont.	41°41'N, 82°40'47"W.
Easternmost point	Cape Spear, Nfld.	47°31'12"N, 52°37'28"W.
Westernmost point	Mount St. Elias, Yukon (at Alaskan border)	60°18'24"N, 141°W.
Highest city	Rossland, B.C. at R.R. Stn. (49°05'N,117°47'W)	3,465 ft.
Highest town	Lake Louise, Alta.	5,051 ft.
Highest waterfall	Takakkaw Falls (Daly Glacier), B.C. (51°30'N,116°29'W)	1,650 ft.
Longest river	Mackenzie (from head of Finlay R.)	2,635 mi.
Highest mountain	Mt. Logan (Yukon)	19,524 ft.
Rainiest spot	Henderson Lake, Vancouver Is. yrly. avg. rainfall	262 inches
Highest lake	Chilco Lake (51°20'N,124°05'W) 75.1 sq. mi.	3,842 ft.

Immigration to Canada by Country of Last Permanent Residence

Source: Canadian Statistical Review, April 1984

Year	Total	UK and Ireland	France	Germany	Netherlands	Greece	Italy
1979	112,096	13,406	1,900	1,323	1,479	1,247	1,996
1980	143,117	18,924	1,900	1,643	1,866	1,093	1,740
1981	128,618	21,964	2,089	2,188	1,797	958	2,043
1982	121,147	17,075	2,393	4,425	1,827	885	1,506
1983	88,846	5,991	1,643	2,513	670	601	819

Year	Portugal	Other Europe	Asia	Australasia	United States	West Indies	All Other
1979	3,723	7,784	50,540	1,395	9,617	6,262	11,424
1980	4,228	9,774	71,602	1,555	9,926	7,254	11,612
1981	1,866	13,374	48,831	1,318	10,559	8,566	13,045
1982	1,388	16,657	41,686	938	9,360	8,630	14,377
1983	813	11,094	36,734	474	7,325	7,123	13,046

Canadian Population by Mother Tongue, 1981

Source: Statistics Canada: 1981 Census

Province	English	French	Italian	German	Ukrainian	Indian, Inuit	Chinese	Portuguese	Other
Newfoundland	560,460	2,655	90	445	50	1,600	725	205	1,450
Prince Edward Island	115,045	6,080	20	175	35	90	115	20	925
Nova Scotia	793,165	36,030	1,055	1,865	640	3,055	1,305	235	1,440
New Brunswick	453,310	234,030	525	1,220	195	2,115	730	165	4,115
Quebec	706,115	5,307,010	133,710	24,060	10,765	28,080	15,270	25,495	187,895
Ontario	6,678,770	475,605	338,980	174,545	81,595	22,255	89,355	114,275	649,725
Manitoba	735,920	52,560	6,170	75,180	58,855	27,185	6,075	6,840	57,455
Saskatchewan	770,815	25,535	1,280	59,625	44,660	24,265	5,000	335	36,795
Alberta	1,810,545	62,145	16,175	91,480	68,130	27,565	28,910	5,560	127,215
British Columbia	2,249,310	45,615	30,595	93,380	26,950	11,445	76,270	12,340	198,560
Yukon	20,245	580	45	495	170	835	125	5	655
Northwest Territories	24,755	1,240	130	385	210	18,090	145	25	765
Total	**14,918,445**	**6,249,095**	**528,775**	**522,855**	**292,265**	**166,575**	**224,030**	**165,510**	**1,275,630**

Population by Religious Denomination

Source: Statistics Canada

Denomination	1971	1981	Denomination	1971	1981
Adventist	28,590	41,605	Jewish	276,025	296,425
Anglican	2,543,180	2,436,375	Latter Day Saints (Mormons)	66,635	89,865
Baptist	667,245	696,850	Lutheran	715,740	702,905
Buddhist	16,175	51,955	Mennonite	168,150	189,370
Chr. & Miss'nary Alliance	23,630	33,895	Pentecostal	220,390	338,790
Christian Reformed	83,390	77,370	Presbyterian	872,335	812,110
Ch. of Christ, Disciples	16,405	15,350	Roman Catholic	9,974,895	11,210,385
Doukhobors	9,170	6,700	Salvation Army	119,665	125,085
Free Methodist	19,125	12,270	Sikh	(1)	67,710
Greek Orthodox	316,605	314,870	Ukrainian Catholic	227,730	190,585
Hindu	(1)	69,500	Unitarian	20,995	14,500
Hutterite	13,650	16,530	United Church	3,768,800	3,758,015
Islam	(1)	98,165	Other	293,240	476,225
Jehovah's Witnesses	174,810	143,485	No religion	929,575	1,788,995

(1) Not included in census data prior to 1981.

Births and Deaths in Canada by Province

Source: Statistics Canada

Province	Births 1982	Births 1983[1]	Deaths 1982	Deaths 1983[1]	Province	Births 1982	Births 1983[1]	Deaths 1982	Deaths 1983[1]
Newfoundland	9,173	9,630	3,385	3,140	Saskatchewan	17,722	16,300	8,202	7,410
Prince Edward Island	1,924	1,960	980	1,000	Alberta	45,036	45,400	12,968	12,130
Nova Scotia	12,325	12,090	6,941	6,930	British Columbia	42,747	43,040	20,707	20,160
New Brunswick	10,489	10,590	5,197	5,280	Yukon	525	530	118	120
Quebec	90,800	90,140	43,497	44,430	Northwest Territories	1,362	1,250	232	240
Ontario	124,856	125,490	63,696	66,440					
Manitoba	16,123	16,500	8,490	8,480	**Total**	**373,082**	**372,920**	**174,413**	**175,760**

(1) Preliminary estimates.

Marriages, Divorces in Canada

Source: Statistics Canada
(Rates per 1,000 population)

Year	Marriages No.	Marriages Rate	Divorces No.	Divorces Rate	Year	Marriages No.	Marriages Rate	Divorces No.	Divorces Rate
1940	125,709	10.8	2,416	0.21	1975	197,585	8.7	50,611	2.22
1950	125,083	9.1	5,386	0.39	1980	191,069	8.0	62,019	2.59
1960	130,338	7.3	6,980	0.39	1981	190,082	7.8	67,671	2.78
1970	188,428	8.8	29,775	1.39	1982	188,360	7.6	70,436	2.86

Canadian Legal or Public Holidays, 1985

Legal public holidays in all provinces are: New Year's Day, Good Friday, Easter Monday, Victoria Day, Canada Day, Labor Day, Remembrance Day and Christmas Day. Additional holidays may be proclaimed provincially by the Lieutenant-Governor or in the municipalities by an order of the local council. For some holidays, government and business closing practices vary. In most provinces the provincial Ministry or Department of Labor can provide details of holiday closings.

Chief Legal or Public Holidays

Jan. 1 (Tuesday) - New Year's Day. All provinces.

Apr. 7 - Good Friday. All provinces.

Apr. 10 - Easter Monday. Que. (businesses remain open in other provinces)

May 20 (the Monday preceding May 25) - Victoria Day. All provinces.

July 1 (Monday) - Canada Day. All provinces.

Aug. 5 (1st Monday in Aug.) - Civic Holiday. Alb., B.C., Man., N.B., NWT, Ont., Sask.

Sept. 2 (1st Monday in Sept.) - Labor Day. All provinces.

Oct. 14 (2d Monday in Oct.) - Thanksgiving. All provinces.

Nov. 11 (Monday) - Remembrance Day. Observed in all provinces but most businesses remain open.

Dec. 25 (Wednesday) - Christmas Day. All provinces.

Dec. 26 (Thursday) - Boxing Day. All provinces except Que.

Other Legal or Public Holidays

Jan. 11 (Friday) - Sir John A. MacDonald's Birthday. Schools closed in some provinces.

March 18 (Monday nearest March 17) - St. Patrick's Day. Nfld.

April 23 (Tuesday) - St. George's Day. Nfld.

June 24 (Monday) - St. John the Baptist's Day. Que.

June 24 (Monday nearest June 24) - Discovery Day. Nfld.

July 15 (Monday nearest July 12) - Orangemen's Day. Nfld.

Aug. 19 (3d Monday in Aug.) - Discovery Day. Yukon.

Widely Known Canadians of the Present

Statesmen, authors, performers, artists, industrialists, and other prominent persons. (Canadians widely known in the North American entertainment industry are found on pages 392-402; some sports personalities can be found in sports section.)

Barbara Amiel, b. Watford, Eng., 12/4/40, columnist, author, editor of Toronto Sun.

Doris Anderson, b. Calgary, Alta., 11/20/25, women's rights activist, journalist and author.

Margaret Atwood, b. Ottawa, Ont., 11/18/39, poet and author; *Lady Oracle* (1976), *Bodily Harm* (1981).

Harold Ballard, b. Toronto, Ont., 7/30/03, majority owner of Toronto Maple Leafs, Hamilton Tiger-Cats, Maple Leaf Gardens.

Carling Bassett, b. Toronto, Ont., 10/9/67, Canadian women's tennis champion.

Alex Baumann, b. Prague, Czechoslovakia, 4/21/64, winner of 2 gold medals for swimming at the 1984 Summer Olympics.

William Bennett, b. Kelowna, B.C., 4/14/32, leader of British Columbia Social Credit Party since 1973, B.C. premier (1975-   ).

Pierre Berton, b. Whitehorse, Yukon, 7/12/20, author; *The National Dream* (1970), *The Last Spike* (1971), *Flames Across the Border* (1981).

Conrad Black, b. Montreal, Que., 8/25/44, businessman, including chairman of the board of Argus Corp. Ltd.

Gaetan Boucher, b. Charlesbourg, Que., 5/10/58, speed skater, winner of 2 gold and 1 bronze medal in the 1984 Olympics, a silver in 1980 Olympics.

Gerald Bouey, b. Axford, Sask., 4/2/20, governor of the Bank of Canada (1973-   ).

Ed Broadbent, b. Oshawa, Ont., 3/21/36, national leader of New Democratic Party (1975-   ).

Charles Bronfman, b. Montreal, Que., 6/27/31, deputy chairman of the Seagram Co. Ltd.; Chairman of the Montreal Expos.

John M. Buchanan, b. Sydney, N.S., 4/22/31, leader of Nova Scotia Progressive Conservative Party since 1971; Nova Scotia premier (1978-   ).

Iona Campagnolo, b. Vancouver, B.C. 10/18/32, national president of Liberal Party (1982-   ).

Jean Chrétien, b. Shawinigan, Que., 1/11/34, minister of energy, mines and resources (1982-1984), justice minister (1980-1982); finished 2d in 1984 Liberal leadership contest.

Joe Clark, b. High River, Alta., 6/5/39, former prime minister (May 1979-Feb. 1980), former leader of Progressive Conservative Party (1976-1983).

Leonard Cohen, b. Montreal, Que., 9/21/34, poet, novelist, songwriter.

Alex Colville, b. Toronto, Ont., 8/24/20, artist.

David Crombie, b. Toronto, Ont. 4/24/36, candidate for Progressive Conservative leadership 1983, minister of national health and welfare (1979), mayor of Toronto 1972-78.

John Crosbie, b. St. John's, Nfld., 1/30/31, former finance minister (1979), finished 3d in 1983 Progressive Conservative leadership contest.

Ken Danby, b. Sault Ste. Marie, Ont., 3/16/40, artist.

Robertson Davies, b. Thamesville, Ont., 8/28/13, educator, author of *The Rebel Angels* (1981).

Bill Davis, b. Brampton, Ont., 7/30/29, Ontario premier (1971-   ).

Paul Desmarais, b. Sudbury, Ont., 1/4/27, industrial executive, including chairman of Power Corp. of Canada.

Grant Devine, b. Regina, Sask., 7/5/44, leader Saskatchewan Progressive Conservative Party since 1979, Saskatchewan premier (1982-   ).

Brian Dickson, b. Yorkton, Sask., 5/25/16, chief justice, Supreme Court of Canada (1984-   ).

Jean Drapeau, b. Montreal, Que., 2/18/16, mayor of Montreal (1954-57 and 1960-   ).

Alan Eagleson, b. St. Catharines, Ont., 4/24/33, executive director of National Hockey League Players' Assn.; arranges international hockey competition.

Maureen Forrester, b. Montreal, Que., 7/25/30, contralto.

Barbara Frum, b. Niagara Falls, Ont., 9/8/38, broadcaster.

Northrop Frye, b. Sherbrooke, Que., 7/14/12, educator, literary critic and author *The Great Code* (1982).

Peter Gzowski, b. Toronto, Ont., 7/13/34, radio host and author of *The Game of Our Lives* (1981).

Don Harron, b. Toronto, Ont., 9/19/24, comedian and actor, best known for alter-ego Charlie Farquharson.

Richard Hatfield, b. Hartland, N.B., 4/9/31, New Brunswick premier (1970-   ).

Mel Hurtig, b. Edmonton, Alta., 6/24/32, book publisher, proponent of Canadian nationalism.

Donald Johnston, b. Ottawa, Ont., 6/26/36, finished 3d in 1984 Liberal leadership contest.

Karen Kain, b. Hamilton, Ont., 3/28/51, principal dancer of the National Ballet of Canada.

Yousuf Karsh, b. Armenia-in-Turkey, 12/23/08, portrait photographer.

Margaret (Trudeau) Kemper, b. Vancouver, B.C., 9/10/48, author of autobiographies *Beyond Reason* and *Consequences,* television host.

Margaret Laurence, b. Neapawa, Man., 7/18/26, novelist; *The Stone Angel* (1964), *The Diviners* (1974).

Irving Layton, b. Neamtz, Romania, 3/12/12, poet.

René Lévesque, b. New Carlisle, Que., 8/24/22, leader of Quebec separatist Parti Quebecois since 1968, Quebec premier (1976-   ).

James Lee, b. Charlottetown, P.E.I., 3/26/37, leader P.E.I. Progressive Conservative Party and premier (1981-   ).

Peter Lougheed, b. Calgary, Alta., 7/26/28, Alberta Progressive Conservative leader since 1965, Alberta premier (1971-   ).

Flora Macdonald, b. North Sydney, N.S., 6/3/26, secretary of state for external affairs in 1979; candidate for Progressive Conservative Party leadership in 1976.

Allan MacEachen, b. Inverness, N.S., 7/6/21, federal Cabinet minister (1963-   ), including deputy prime minister (1980-84).

Dennis McDermott, b. Portsmouth, Eng., 11/3/22, president of Canadian Labour Congress (1978-   ).

W.O. Mitchell, b. Weyburn, Sask., 3/13/14, author; *Who Has Seen the Wind* (1947), *How I Spent My Summer Holidays* (1981).

Farlay Mowat, b. Belleville, Ont., 5/12/21, author, known for books on the North.

Brian Mulroney, b. Baie Comeau, Que., 3/20/39, Canada's 18th prime minister, elected 9/4/84; leader of Progressive Conservative Party since June 1983, finished 3d for P.C. leadership 1976, former pres. of Iron Ore Co. of Canada, labor lawyer.

Mila Mulroney, b. Sarajevo, Yugoslavia, 7/13/53, wife of Prime Minister Brian Mulroney, campaigned actively in 1984 elections.

Knowlton Nash, b. Toronto, Ont., 11/18/27, broadcaster, announcer for CBC national news.

Peter C. Newman, b. Vienna, Austria, 5/10/29, author, editor of Maclean's magazine (1971-82); *The Canadian Establishment* (1975), *Bronfman Dynasty* (1978), *The Acquisitors* (1981).

Howard Pawley, b. Brampton, Ont., 11/21/34, leader of Manitoba New Democratic Party since 1979, Manitoba premier (1981-   ).

Brian Peckford, b. Whitehorse, Nfld., 8/27/42, leader of Newfoundland Progressive Conservative Party and premier since 1979.

Peter Pocklington, b. Regina, Sask., 11/18/41, entrepreneur, owner of Edmonton Oilers and other sports franchises.

Steve Podborski, b. Toronto, Ont., 7/25/57, 1982 men's downhill World Cup skiing champion.

Christopher Pratt, b. St. John's, Nfld., 12/9/35, artist, has developed style known as "conceptual realism."

Mordecai Richler, b. Montreal, Que., 1/27/31, author; *The Apprenticeship of Duddy Kravitz* (1959), *Joshua Then and Now* (1980).

Jeanne Sauvé, b. Howell, Sask., 4/26/22, governorgeneral of Canada (1984-   ), speaker of the House of Commons (1980-83).

Edward Schreyer, b. Beausejour, Man., 12/21/35, premier of Manitoba (1969-77); governor-general of Canada, (1979-1984).

Joey Smallwood, b. Gambo, Nfld., 12/24/00, led Newfoundland into Canada and served as province's first premier (1949-72).

David Suzuki, b. Vancouver, B.C., 3/24/36, scientist, educator, television personality.

E.P. (Edward Plunket) **Taylor,** b. Ottawa, Ont., 1/29/01, industrialist, financier; now lives in the Bahamas.

Ken Taylor, b. Calgary, Alta., 10/5/34, diplomat, engineered escape of 6 U.S. embassy staff members from Iran (1980); Canadian counsul general in New York (1981-1984).

Ken Thomson, b. Toronto, Ont., 9/1/23, chairman of the board of Thomson Newspapers Ltd.

Pierre Elliott Trudeau, b. Montreal, Que., 10/18/19, Canadian prime minister (1968-79) and (1980-1984); leader federal Liberal Party (1968-1984).

Geills (Jill) Turner, b. Winnipeg, Man., 12/23/37, wife of Prime Minister John Turner.

John Turner, b. Richmond, Eng., 6/7/29, leader of Liberal Party since June 1984; Canada's 17th prime minister (6/84-9/84); practiced corporate law (1975-84); cabinet minister (1965-75).

Galen Weston, b. England, 10/26/40, chairman and president of George Weston Ltd.

Noted Canadians of the Past

William Aberhart, 1878-1943, b. Hibbard twp., Ont., spellbinding orator, founded Social Credit Party in Canada, premier of Alberta (1935-43).

Frederick G. Banting, 1891-1941, b. Alliston, Ont., codiscoverer of insulin, demonstrated its beneficial effects on diabetes (1922), awarded Nobel prize (1923).

W. "Max" Aitken (Baron Beaverbrook), 1879-1964, b. Maple, Ont., best known in Canada as publisher and philanthropist, held several positions in British Cabinet up to 1945.

Charles H. Best, 1899-1978, b. West Pembroke, Me., co-discoverer of insulin.

Norman Bethune, 1890-1939, b. Gravenhurst, Ont., died in northern China as a surgeon with the Chinese revolutionary army.

Billy Bishop, 1894-1956, b. Owen Sound, Ont., WWI flying ace, shot down 72 enemy aircraft, including 25 in a 10-day period in 1918.

Samuel Bronfman, 1891-1971, b. Brandon, Man., industrialist, established Distiller's Corporation—Seagram's Limited.

Emily Carr, 1871-1945, b. Victoria, B.C., painter, best known for sketches of Indian life.

George Etienne Cartier, 1814-1873, b. St. Antoine, Upper Canada; leading French-Canadian Father of Confederation, joint premier of United Canada (1857-62).

John Diefenbaker, 1895-1979, b. Grey Co., Ont., leader of Progressive Conservative Party (1956-67) and prime minister of Canada (1957-63).

Terry Fox, 1958-1981, b. Winnipeg, Man., in 1980, with an artificial leg, began "Marathon of Hope" run across Canada to raise funds for cancer research; run halted by recurring cancer but succeeded in raising more than $20 million.

Glenn Gould, 1932-1982, b. Toronto, Ont., classical pianist and composer.

Joseph Howe, 1804-1873, b. Halifax, N.S., politician, orator and writer, at first fought Nova Scotia entry into Canadian union but later accepted post in federal cabinet.

A.Y. Jackson, 1882-1974, b. Montreal Que., best known of "Group of Seven" Canadian painters.

Pauline Johnson, 1862-1913, b. Six Nations Indian Reserve, Ont., poet.

Cornelius Krieghoff, 1815-1872, b. Amsterdam, Holland, painter, did finest work after moving to Canada in 1846.

W.L. Mackenzie King, 1874-1950, b. Kitchener, Ont., prime minister of Canada a record 22 years (1921-26, 1926-30, 1935-48).

Wilfrid Laurier, 1841-1919, b. Saint Lin, Lower Canada, leader of Canadian Liberal Party (1887-1919) and prime minister (1896-1911).

Stephen Leacock, 1869-1944, b. Swanmoor, Hants, Eng., humorist, author, *Sunshine Sketches of a Little Town.*

John A. Macdonald, 1815-1891, b. Glasgow, Scotland, chief architect of Confederation and Canada's first prime minister (1867-1873 and 1878-1891).

William Lyon Mackenzie, 1795-1861, b. Scotland; politician and rebel, chief organizer of 1837 rebellion for political reform in Upper Canada, first mayor of Toronto (1835).

Vincent Massey, 1887-1967, b. Toronto, Ont., first native-born governor-general of Canada (1952-1959).

Thomas D'Arcy McGee, 1825-1868, b. Carlingford, Ireland, eloquent advocate of confederation; assassinated Apr. 7, 1868.

Marshall McLuhan, 1911-1980, b. Edmonton, Alta., author and educator best known for theories on communication. *The Medium is the Massage* (1967).

Nellie McClung, 1873-1951, b. Chatsworth, Ont., author and feminist.

John McCrae, 1872-1918, b. Guelph, Ont., poet, best known for *In Flanders Fields.*

Lucy Maud Montgomery, 1874-1942, b. Clifton, P.E.I., author, *Anne of Green Gables* (1908)

Susanna Moodie, 1803-1885, b. Suffolk, Eng., author, best known for *Roughing It In the Bush* (1852).

William Osler, 1849-1919, b. Bond Head, Upper Canada, physician and author.

Louis Joseph Papineau, 1786-1871, b. Montreal, Lower Canada, led movement for political reform in Lower Canada.

Lester B. Pearson, 1897-1972, b. Toronto, Ont., Canadian prime minister (1963-68); awarded Nobel peace prize (1957) for organizing United Nations intervention in 1956 Suez Canal crisis.

Edwin J. Pratt, 1883-1964, b. Western Bay, Nfld., poet.

Louis Riel, 1844-1885, b. St. Boniface, Man., led Metis of Western Canada in North West rebellions of 1870 and 1885, hung for treason in Regina.

Hans Selye, 1907-1982, b. Vienna, Austria, discovered evidence (1936) that mental stress affects the body's physical state.

Robert W. Service, 1874-1958, b. Preston, Eng., poet, *Songs of a Sourdough* (1907).

Roy Thomson (Lord Thomson of Fleet), 1894-1976, b. Toronto, Ont., newspaper publisher.

Tom Thomson, 1877-1917, b. Claremont, Ont., painter, influenced "Group of Seven" Canadian artists.

W. Garfield Weston, 1898-1978, b. Toronto, Ont., industrialist.

James S. Woodsworth, 1874-1942, b. Etobicoke, Ont., a founder of the Co-operative Commonwealth Federation, forerunner of the New Democratic Party.

Canadian Government Budget
Source: Canadian Statistical Review
(millions of Canadian dollars)

Expenditures

Fiscal Year	National defense	Health and welfare	Agriculture	Post Office	Public works	Transport	Veterans affairs	Payments to provinces	Total expenditures
1977-78..	3,771	11,635	959	1,237	1,431	1,478	841	3,003	42,902
1978-79..	4,108	13,024	768	1,275	1,657	1,725	890	3,028	46,923
1979-80..	4,389	14,038	782	1,412	1,615	1,726	933	3,522	52,297
1980-81..	5,078	15,792	881	1,597	1,883	2,640	1,006	3,788	58,813
1981-82..	6,028	17,818	1,125	639	2,188	2,279	1,140	4,535	67,440
1982-83..	6,993	19,588	1,009	290	2,669	2,906	1,282	5,390	79,466

Revenues[1]

Fiscal year	Personal income tax	Corporation income tax	Sales tax	Other excise tax	Excise duties	Customs duties	Estate taxes	Post Office	Total budgetary revenues
1977-78..	13,439	5,828	5,026	904	882	2,312	66	773	32,866
1978-79..	14,048	6,262	5,245	827	878	2,747	77	903	35,216
1979-80..	16,327	7,537	5,119	1,252	895	3,000	96	1,118	40,159
1980-81..	19,837	8,133	5,882	1,602	1,042	3,188	99	1,109	46,731
1981-82..	24,046	9,136	6,621	2,079	1,175	3,439	595	—	54,068
1982-83..	26,329	8,137	6,302	2,341	1,274	2,831	132	—	55,126

(1) This statement includes only receipts relating to revenue. Excluded are non-budgetary revenues such as Old Age Security Fund taxes, Prairie Farm Assistance Act levies, employer and employee contributions to government-held funds.

Canadian Income Tax Rates
Source: Revenue Canada

1983 Rates of Federal Income Tax

Taxable income		Tax	
$ 1,238 or less	—		
1,239	$ 74	+ 16% on next	$ 1,238
2,476	272	+ 17% on next	2,476
4,952	693	+ 18% on next	2,476
7,428	1,139	+ 19% on next	4,952
12,380	2,080	+ 20% on next	4,952
17,332	3,070	+ 23% on next	4,952
22,284	4,209	+ 25% on next	12,380
34,664	7,304	+ 30% on next	24,760
59,424	14,732	+ 34% on remainder	

1984 Rates of Provincial Income Tax

	Tax Rate[1]
Newfoundland	60%
Prince Edward Island	52.5%
Nova Scotia	56.5%
New Brunswick	58%
Quebec	not applicable
Ontario	48%[2]
Manitoba	54%[3]
Saskatchewan	51%[4]
Alberta	43.5%
British Columbia	44%
N.W.T. and Yukon	45%

(1) Rates are applied to basic federal tax payable. (2) Plus surtax of 5% of basic provincial tax over $110.80. (3) Plus surtax of 20% of basic provincial tax over $2,639.52. (4) Plus surtax of 12% of basic provincial tax over $4,000; basic provincial tax may be reduced by Saskatchewan general reduction of $160 plus $50 for each dependent child under 18 years (max. $300), less 30% of your Saskatchewan income tax; if taxable income is $2,722 or less, no provincial tax is payable.

Canada: Taxable Returns by Income, 1981
Source: Revenue Canada Taxation Statistics

Total income in dollars	Number of tax returns	Percent of tax returns	Total income (millions)	Percent of total income	Taxed income (millions)	Federal tax (millions)	Percent of Fed. tax	Fed. Tax rate on total income
$1-2,500	1,306,249	8.60	1,545.3	.50	6.0	—	—	—
2,500-5,000	1,429,698	9.42	5,339.0	2.28	377.0	.5	—	.01
5,000-7,500	1,444,392	9.52	8,997.9	3.84	2,476.6	81.1	.33	.9
7,500-10,000	1,363,468	8.98	11,919.7	5.10	4,890.4	404.2	1.62	3.4
10,000-15,000	2,473,420	16.30	30,773.1	13.15	16,737.7	2,077.1	8.33	6.7
15,000-20,000	1,987,640	13.09	34,550.7	14.76	21,595.4	3,216.8	12.91	9.3
20,000-25,000	1,550,697	10.22	34,685.8	14.83	23,316.5	3,787.3	15.19	10.9
25,000-30,000	1,054,431	6.94	28,805.9	12.31	20,192.4	3,460.7	13.88	12.0
30,000-40,000	1,018,274	6.71	34,743.4	14.85	25,308.6	4,465.7	18.64	13.4
40,000-50,000	344,347	2.27	15,186.4	6.49	11,491.3	2,282.4	9.15	15.0
50,000-100,000	284,864	1.88	18,417.1	7.87	14,600.2	3,081.9	12.37	16.7
100,000-200,000	45,244	.29	5,900.6	2.52	4,801.8	1,163.2	4.66	19.7
200,000 and over	9,903	.07	3,515.6	1.50	2,499.9	727.1	2.92	20.7

Average Canadian Income and Taxes by Occupation, 1981

Source: Revenue Canada Taxation Statistics

Occupation	Number[1]	Average income[2]	Average federal tax	Occupation	Number[1]	Average income[2]	Average federal tax
Self-employed doctors and surgeons	30,542	$66,722	$13,969	Investors	1,179,343	18,568	1,698
Self-employed dentists	7,892	60,139	12,302	Business employees	7,403,747	16,827	1,887
Self-employed lawyers and notaries	16,124	53,123	10,032	Property owners	105,940	16,326	1,863
Self-employed engineers	4,041	40,001	6,953	Farmers	277,470	16,159	1,209
Self-employed accountants	10,733	38,406	5,923	Self-employed salesmen	33,001	15,484	1,655
Teachers and professors	321,241	27,665	3,528	Employees of institutions	857,682	15,413	1,500
Federal government employees	364,116	22,041	2,653	Business proprietors	493,234	12,800	1,192
Provincial government employees	515,258	21,019	2,461	Fishermen	34,391	12,691	1,045
Armed Forces	80,628	20,348	2,289	Self-employed entertainers and artists	19,287	9,795	727
Other self-employed professionals	39,981	20,181	2,568	Unclassified employees	399,712	9,383	712
Municipal government employees	533,777	18,786	2,077	Pensioners	951,866	9,432	437
				Unclassified	1,499,135	2,495	133
				Total	15,179,141	15,415	1,642

(1) Based on number of tax returns (2) Average total income after business expense deductions but before personal deductions.

Average Income in Selected Canadian Cities, 1981

Source: Revenue Canada Taxation Statistics

City	Average income[1]	Rank	No. of tax returns	City	Average income[1]	Rank	No. of tax returns
Markham, Ont.	$21,411	1	59,994	Whitby, Ont.	17,163	20	23,774
Oakville, Ont.	19,982	2	48,468	Medicine Hat, Alta.	17,038	21	26,644
Calgary, Alta.	19,932	3	417,185	Lethbridge, Alta.	16,931	22	36,828
Dollard des Ormeaux, Que.	19,381	4	21,697	Regina, Sask.	16,930	23	106,765
North Vancouver, B.C.	19,153	5	68,186	Prince George, B.C.	16,889	24	48,438
Burlington, Ont.	18,548	6	71,613	Pierrefonds, Que.	16,839	25	22,164
Etobicoke, Ont.	18,399	7	110,785	Victoria, B.C.	16,740	27	149,687
North York, Ont.	18,348	8	275,837	Toronto, Ont.	16,677	29	728,810
Ottawa, Ont.	18,075	9	255,346	Saskatoon, Sask.	16,123	36	101,297
Edmonton, Alta.	18,031	10	368,460	Scarborough, Ont.	16,082	37	279,894
Mississauga, Ont.	17,789	11	202,093	London, Ont.	15,345	44	168,781
Nepean, Ont.	17,757	12	32,881	Halifax, N.S.	15,332	45	75,081
Richmond Hill, Ont.	17,750	13	24,218	Quebec, Que.	14,568	61	111,472
Vancouver, B.C.	17,423	14	315,954	Montreal, Que.	14,385	65	651,885
Sarnia, Ont.	17,388	15	44,192	Hamilton, Ont.	14,363	66	201,670
Pickering, Ont.	17,369	16	25,541	St. John's, Nfld.	14,210	70	56,873
Brossard, Que.	17,264	17	30,357	Winnipeg, Man.	14,136	74	412,994
Port Coquitlam, B.C.	17,235	18	21,663	Fredericton, N.B.	14,110	75	36,109
Red Deer, Alta.	17,166	19	32,881	Chicoutimi, Que.	11,214	100	35,474

(1) Average total income after business deductions but before personal deductions.

Canadian Labor Force

Source: Statistics Canada; 1983 annual averages (thousands of persons)

	Can.	Nfld.	P.E.I.	N.S.	N.B.	Que.	Ont.	Man.	Sask.	Alta.	B.C.
Labor force	12,183	214	55	369	290	3,069	4,570	508	470	1,249	1,389
Employed	10,734	174	48	320	247	2,642	4,096	460	436	1,115	1,197
Unemployed	1,448	40	7	49	43	427	474	48	35	134	192
Percent unemployed	11.9	18.8	12.2	13.2	14.8	13.9	10.4	9.4	7.4	10.8	13.8

Canadian Labor Force Characteristics

Source: Statistics Canada (thousands of workers)

Year	Labor force	Employed	Unemployed	Agriculture	Manufacturing	Private sector	Govt. business(1)	Govt. admin.
1975	9,974	9,284	690	497	2,020	6,546	456	1,373
1978	10,895	9,987	908	494	2,125	7,018	501	1,435
1979	11,231	10,395	836	505	2,222	7,463	466	1,391
1980	11,573	10,708	865	500	2,292	7,750	482	1,419
1981	11,904	11,006	898	508	2,303	7,983	500	1,449
1982	11,958	10,644	1,314	493	2,228	7,603	514	1,459
1983	12,183	10,734	1,448	513	2,167	7,609	517	1,497

(1) Employees of Crown corporations and govt. institutions involved in financial transactions.

Average Weekly Canadian Wages and Salaries, by Province

Source: Statistics Canada (Canadian dollars)

Year & month	Canada[1]	Nfld.	P.E.I.	N.S.	N.B.	Que.	Ont.	Man.	Sask.	Alta.	B.C.
1970	126.82	117.70	83.82	104.21	104.01	122.38	131.52	115.88	114.87	128.15	137.97
1975	203.34	196.50	149.84	172.40	182.40	199.22	204.86	186.01	188.31	207.39	229.97
1979	288.32	271.64	209.77	245.23	261.98	284.18	285.57	259.00	275.79	306.79	327.14
1980	317.39	288.90	230.03	265.95	284.36	315.36	311.45	283.20	303.71	341.93	363.51
1981	355.28	328.08	250.13	296.35	313.37	351.57	347.92	314.26	336.78	390.40	407.03
1982	390.79	361.82	278.53	329.06	342.14	386.11	381.88	346.49	373.80	435.47	445.43
1983 (Jan.) . . .	402.63	375.14	290.55	338.67	366.71	400.73	392.83	358.60	385.15	446.57	455.09

(1) Includes Yukon and Northwest Territories.

Canadian Minimum Wages

(hourly rate for experienced adult workers)

Source: Labour Canada

	Fed.[1]	Newf.	P.E.I.	N.S.	N.B.	Que.	Ont.	Man.	Sask.	Alb.	B.C.	Yukon	N.W.T.
1984	$3.50	$3.75	$3.75	$3.75	$3.80	$4.00	$4.00	$4.00	$4.25	3.80	$3.65	$3.60	$4.25
1983	3.50	3.75	3.75	3.75	3.80	4.00	3.50	4.00	4.25	3.80	3.65	3.60	4.25
1982	3.50	3.75	3.75	3.75	3.80	4.00	3.50	4.00	4.25	3.80	3.65	3.60	4.25
1981	3.50	3.45	3.30	3.30	3.35	4.00	3.50	3.55	4.00	3.80	3.65	3.60	3.50
1980	3.25	3.15	3.00	3.00	3.05	3.65	3.00	3.15	3.65	3.50	3.65	3.35	3.50
1975	2.60	2.20	2.30	2.25	2.30	2.80	2.40	2.60	2.50	2.50	2.75	2.70	2.50
1970	1.65	1.25(M)	1.25(M)	1.25(M)	1.15	1.40	1.50	1.50	1.25	1.55	1.50	1.50	1.50
		1.00(F)	.95(F)	1.00(F)									
1965	1.25	.70(M)	1.00	1.05(M)	.80	.85	1.00	.85	$38/wk	1.00	1.00	. . . .	. . . .
		.50(F)		.80(F)									

M = male; F = female

(1) Applies to work under federal govt. jurisdiction as defined by the Constitution Act, 1867, Sections 91 and 92. (2) Minimum wage rates (1984) for other categories of workers are as follows: **Federal:** under 17, $3.25; **Newf.:** domestics, $2.25; **P.E.I.:** under 18, $3.00; **N.S.:** 14-18 yrs., $3.40; **Que.:** under 18, $3.54; receiving gratuities, $3.28 (18 and over) or $2.95 (under 18); live-in domestics, $134/wk.; other domestics and agricultural workers, $4.00 (18 and over) or $3.54 (under 18); **Ont.:** students under 18 (working up to 28 hrs./wk.), $3.15; serving alcohol, $3.50; construction workers, $4.25; domestics (working more than 24 hrs./wk.), $3.50; **Man.:** under 18, $3.55; serving alcohol, $4.00; **Alb.:** under 18 not attending school, $3.65; under 18 attending school, $3.30; salespersons, $125/wk.; **B.C.:** under 18 $3.00; domestics, farm workers, $29.20 per day or part day; **N.W.T.:** under 17, $3.75.

Canadian Unemployment Insurance Commission

Source: Canadian Statistical Review, April, 1984
(Canadian dollars)

	Claims data				Benefits paid				
Year	Benefi-ciaries[1][2] (000)	Claims received (000)	Weeks paid	Total paid (thousands of dollars)	Regular	Sickness	Maternity	Retirement	Fishing
1978 . .	803	2,809	41,355	4,536,910	4,006,868	157,405	195,297	14,831	63,434
1979 . .	713	2,602	36,896	4,008,002	3,431,216	145,183	207,649	15,055	70,897
1980 . .	703	2,762	36,333	4,393,307	3,748,551	154,671	234,746	15,950	82,570
1981 . .	720	2,895	37,013	4,828,273	4,115,888	164,262	273,054	17,582	92,444
1982 . .	1,138	3,921	60,440	8,575,445	7,646,023	174,415	315,973	18,166	111,856
1983 . .	1,247	3,434	66,584	10,169,064	9,069,503	179,476	344,170	18,515	141,836

(1) Refer to the number of persons receiving $1.00 or more in unemployment insurance benefits during a specific week each month.
(2) Annual figures are average of 12 months.

Canadian Provincial Unemployment Rates

Source: Statistics Canada

Year	Can.	Nfld.	P.E.I.	N.S.	N.B.	Que.	Ont.	Man.	Sask.	Alta.	B.C.
1978 . .	8.4	16.4	9.9	10.6	12.6	10.9	7.2	6.5	4.9	4.7	8.3
1979 . .	7.5	15.4	11.3	10.2	11.1	9.6	6.5	5.4	4.2	3.9	7.7
1980 . .	7.5	13.5	10.8	9.8	11.1	9.9	6.9	5.5	4.4	3.7	6.8
1981 . .	7.6	14.1	11.4	10.2	11.7	10.4	6.6	6.0	4.6	3.8	6.7
1982 . .	11.0	16.8	12.9	13.2	14.0	13.8	9.8	8.5	6.2	7.7	12.1
1983 . .	11.9	18.8	12.2	13.2	14.8	13.9	10.4	9.4	7.4	10.8	13.8

Canadian Consumer Price Index

Source: Statistics Canada
(All items: 1971 = 100)

Year	Avg.	Year	Avg.	Year	Avg.	Year	Avg.
1965	80.5	1972	104.7	1976	148.9	1980	210.6
1969	94.1	1973	112.7	1977	160.8	1981	236.9
1970	97.2	1974	125.0	1978	175.2	1982	262.5
1971	100.0	1975	138.5	1979	191.2	1983	277.6

Price Indexes By Item

Source: Canadian Statistical Review. April. 1984 (1971 = 100)

Year and month	All items	Food	Shelter	Clothing	Trans-portation	Health, personal	Recreation, education	Tobacco, alcohol	Total services
1978	175.2	208.0	170.8	146.4	162.2	166.2	148.2	155.5	174.3
1980	210.6	260.6	192.4	178.7	200.7	199.3	173.5	185.3	201.8
1981	236.9	290.4	213.2	191.4	237.6	221.0	191.0	209.2	225.0
1982	262.5	311.3	239.2	202.1	271.1	244.4	207.6	241.6	254.0
1983	277.6	322.9	255.4	210.2	284.6	261.2	221.2	272.0	270.5
1984 (Jan.). .	284.8	332.8	261.6	208.6	295.1	265.9	222.3	286.8	275.9

Personal Expenditure on Consumer Goods and Services in Current Dollars

Source: Statistics Canada   (millions of dollars)

	1970	1975	1977	1978	1979	1980	1981	1982
Food and non-alcoholic beverages . .\	7,923	15,206	17,871	20,014	22,475	24,945	28,267	30,618
Alcoholic beverages	1,898	3,501	4,133	4,464	4,867	5,576	6,400	7,241
Tobacco products	1,396	2,050	2,469	2,689	2,973	3,302	3,863	4,423
Clothing and footwear	4,034	7,155	8,773	9,507	10,632	11,613	12,987	13,227
Gross rent, fuel and power.	9,861	16,445	22,939	25,613	28,824	33,010	38,188	44,824
Furniture, appliances, and other household furnishing & services	4,785	9,884	11,990	13,006	14,333	15,509	17,079	17,247
Medical care and health services	1,758	2,896	3,822	4,346	4,791	5,455	6,324	7,192
New and used cars	2,337	5,132	5,942	6,546	7,527	7,787	8,424	7,494
Car repairs and parts.	1,038	1,980	2,548	2,755	3,139	3,370	3,834	3,881
Gasoline, oil and grease	1,383	2,948	3,769	4,100	4,640	5,578	7,297	8,136
Recreation and reading.	3,065	7,249	6,713	7,245	8,148	8,903	10,047	10,549
Educational and cultural services	1,402	2,723	6,136	6,780	7,462	8,414	9,531	10,463
Personal goods and services	7,133	15,062	19,348	21,679	24,285	27,683	31,249	33,007
Total, consumer goods and services . . .	**50,327**	**96,995**	**123,565**	**136,532**	**152,088**	**170,236**	**193,477**	**209,801**

Canada's Largest Corporations

Source: The Financial Post 500: Toronto. Canada: June. 1984

Company (Home office)	Sales or operating revenue C$000	Assets	Foreign owner-ship %	Major Shareholders
General Motors of Canada Ltd. (Oshawa, Ont.)	13,805,450	3,027,638	100	General Motors Corp., Detroit
Canadian Pacific Ltd. (Montreal, Que.)	12,759,297	17,601,949		Power Corp. of Canada 12%.
Imperial Oil Ltd. (Toronto, Ont.)	8,919,000	8,049,000	70	Exxon Corp., New York
Bell Canada Enterprises Inc. (Montreal, Que.)	8,874,700	14,940,400		Wide distribution
Ford Motor Co. of Canada (Oakville, Ont.)	8,580,600	2,256,600	90	Ford Motor Co., Dearborn, Mich.
George Weston Ltd. (Toronto, Ont.)	7,799,600	2,167,600		Weston family 57%
Alcan Aluminium Ltd. (Montreal, Que.)	6,418,339	8,213,040		Wide distribution
Texaco Canada Inc. (Toronto, Ont.)	5,652,000	3,288,000	90	Texaco Inc. 68%; Texaco International 22%
Canadian Wheat Board (Winnipeg, Man.)	5,469,000	4,297,000		Federal govt. 100%
Shell Canada Ltd. (Toronto, Ont.)	5,300,000	5,240,000	79	Shell Investments Ltd., Neth./Brit.
Gulf Canada Ltd. (Toronto, Ont.)	5,078,000	5,112,000	60	Gulf Oil Corp., Pittsburgh
Canadian National Railways (Montreal, Que.)	4,625,000	6,789,765		Federal govt. 100%
Hudson's Bay Co. (Winnipeg, Man.)	4,370,528	3,675,863		Woodbridge Co. (Thomson family) 73%
Chrysler Canada Ltd. (Windsor, Ont.)	4,325,500	980,300	100	Chrysler Corp., Detroit
PetroCanada (Calgary, Alta.)	4,123,817	8,239,025		Federal govt. 100%
Provigo Inc. (Montreal, Que.)	3,891,151	660,806		Caisse de depot 27%; Sobey Stores Ltd. 15%
Canada Development Corp. (Vancouver, B.C.)	3,834,700	7,558,600		Federal govt. 48%
Nova Corp. (Calgary, Alta.)	3,823,005	6,796,056		Wide distribution
Ontario Hydro (Toronto, Ont.)	3,805,131	23,193,894		Ontario govt. 100%
Hydro-Quebec (Montreal, Que.)	3,656,000	25,199,000		Quebec govt. 100%.

(1) Converted from U.S. S.

Work Stoppages (Strikes and Lockouts) in Canada

Source: Labour Canada

Year	Number of stoppages	Workers involved	Person days idle	% of working time	Year	Number of stoppages	Workers involved	Person days idle	% of working time
1964	343	100,535	1,580,550	.11	1974	1,218	580,912	9,221,890	.46
1965	501	171,870	2,349,870	.17	1975	1,171	506,443	10,908,810	.53
1966	617	411,459	5,178,170	.34	1976	1,039	1,570,940	11,609,890	.55
1967	522	252,018	3,974,760	.25	1977	803	217,557	3,307,880	.15
1968	582	223,562	5,082,732	.32	1978	1,058	401,688	7,392,820	.34
1969	595	306,799	7,751,880	.46	1979	1,050	462,504	7,834,230	.34
1970	542	261,706	6,539,560	.39	1980	1,028	441,025	8,975,390	.38
1971	569	239,631	2,866,590	.16	1981	1,048	338,548	8,878,490	.37
1972	598	706,474	7,753,530	.43	1982	677	444,302	5,795,420	.25
1973	724	348,470	5,776,080	.30	1983	645	329,309	4,443,960	.19

Canadian Economic Indicators

Source: Statistics Canada; Dept. of Finance

Year	Per capita personal income	Unemploy-ment rate	Inflation rate(1)	Federal budget surplus or deficit(2) (millions of $)	Per capita national debt(3)(4)	Gross national product(5) (millions of $)	GNP real growth(6)
1950	$ 1,040	3.6%	2.9%	+ 650	$ 834	33,762	7.6%
1955	1,355	4.4%	.1%	+ 202	722	43,891	9.4%
1960	1,656	7.0%	1.4%	− 229	781	53,231	2.9%
1965	2,091	3.9%	2.4%	+ 544	840	69,981	6.7%
1970	3,129	5.7%	3.3%	+ 266	865	88,390	2.5%
1975	6,001	6.9%	10.8%	− 3,805	1,237	113,005	1.2%
1979	9,069	7.4%	9.2%	− 9,131	2,858	130,362	3.2%
1980	10,178	7.5%	10.2%	− 10,393	3,346	131,675	1.0%
1981	11,853	7.5%	12.5%	− 7,366	3,859	136,114	3.4%
1982	12,887	11.0%	10.8%	− 18,904	4,810	130,069	−4.4%
1983	13,542	11.9%	5.8%	− 24,100	6,011	134,353	3.3%

(1) As measured by % change in the Consumer Price Index from previous year. (2) Difference between federal govt. revenues and expenditures. (3) For fiscal year ending March 31 of the following calendar year. (4) Federal govt. debt measured by accumulated budgetary deficits since 1867, divided by Canadian population. (5) Gross National Product is a measure of all goods and services produced in the country; in constant dollars. (6) Real (after inflation) change in Gross National Product over the previous year.

Canadian Direct Investment Abroad

Source: Statistics Canada
(millions of Canadian dollars)

Location	1977	%	1978	%	1979	%	1980	%	1981	%
North America and Caribbean	8,019	59.4	10,147	61.8	13,633	68.1	18,311	71.6	23,715	72.5
United States	7,116	52.7	8,965	54.6	12,104	60.4	16,395	63.5	21,633	66.2
Europe	2,671	19.4	2,904	17.7	3,729	18.7	4,338	16.8	5,164	15.8
United Kingdom	1,423	10.5	1,524	9.3	2,082	10.4	2,405	9.3	2,928	9.0
South and Central America	1,603	11.9	1,980	12.0	979	4.9	1,034	4.0	1,147	3.5
Asia	544	4.0	621	3.8	783	3.9	1,083	4.2	1,271	3.9
Australasia	482	3.6	509	3.1	643	3.2	745	2.9	1,023	3.1
Africa	190	1.4	261	1.6	260	1.3	289	1.1	381	1.2
Total	13,509		16,422		20,027		25,800		32,701	

Canadian Foreign Trade with Leading Countries

Source: Statistics Canada

(millions of dollars)

Exports from Canada to the following areas and countries and imports into Canada from those areas and countries:

	Imports			Exports		
	1981	1982	1983	1981	1982	1983
Total	79,482	67,926	75,694	81,337	81,829	88,426
United States.	54,538	47,917	54,203	53,900	55,840	64,461
Western Europe . . . . , ...	8,027	7,026	7,519	10,140	8,506	7,547
United Kingdom	2,386	1,904	1,811	3,306	2,668	2,446
West Germany.	1,610	1,384	1,576	1,287	1,233	1,156
France	879	877	841	981	705	627
Italy	703	725	798	917	692	546
Netherlands	296	267	351	1,196	1,042	953
Belgium and Luxembourg	297	264	296	830	773	696
Asia . . . . •	6,899	6,191	7,830	7,473	8,084	8,630
Japan	4,057	3,536	4,410	4,498	4,573	4,734
Taiwan	729	661	926	233	293	341
Hong Kong	675	669	821	184	243	221
South Korea	608	586	791	445	488	555
China, People's Republic of	220	204	246	1,018	1,229	1,605
India.	107	91	101	364	293	261
South America	3,250	2,700	2,056	1,897	1,504	1,318
Venezuela	2,385	1,810	1,014	545	438	232
Brazil	431	483	499	678	527	598
Middle East	2,848	967	867	1,514	1,821	1,412
Saudi Arabia	2,393	731	96	456	442	365
Central America and Antilles	1,892	1,629	1,766	1,874	1,469	1,412
Mexico	1,049	999	1,079	715	446	375
Cuba	193	95	56	453	324	361
Jamaica	98	125	110	81	68	64
Africa	1,017	658	677	1,233	1,153	934
Oceania	660	595	522	941	839	576
Australia	498	446	358	777	651	438
New Zealand.	146	140	157	140	157	122
Eastern Europe	350	241	252	2,341	2,578	2,109
USSR.	78	43	35	1,866	2,069	1,762

Canadian Imports and Exports of Leading Commodities

Source: Statistics Canada

(millions of dollars)

Commodity	Imports			Exports		
	1981	1982	1983	1981	1982	1983
Total	79,482	67,926	75,694	81,337	81,829	88,426
Live animals	201	142	132	229	326	340
Food, beverages, tobacco	5,033	4,804	4,872	9,913	9,899	10,076
Meat.	329	326	356	628	779	701
Fish	360	352	418	1,483	1,583	1,546
Fruits and vegetables	1,802	1,873	1,880	383	400	395
Wheat	...	...	...	3,728	4,287	4,648
Crude petroleum	8,004	4,985	3,274	2,505	2,729	3,457
Natural gas.	...	...	...	4,370	4,755	3,958
Coal	834	932	• 840	1,147	1,269	1,313
Sulphur	...	...	...	810	720	571
Wood and paper.	1,173	873	1,199	12,629	11,670	12,835
Textiles	1,426	1,193	1,480	267	244	227
Chemicals	3,814	3,586	4,393	4,614	4,073	4,345
Iron and steel	2,275	1,238	1,176	2,315	1,969	1,634
Aluminum, including alloys	445	367	• 439	1,467	1,428	1,744
General and industrial machinery	7,297	5,657	5,304	2,739	2,485	2,366
Agricultural machinery	2,386	1,688	1,513	885	651	551
Transportation equipment	19,713	17,526	22,598	15,847	19,460	23,732
Cars and chassis.	5,066	4,044	6,212	5,500	7,335	9,637
Trucks, tractors, chassis	1,386	935	1,167	2,927	3,949	4,204
Motor vehicle parts, except engines	7,537	7,976	9,384	3,635	3,922	5,749
Motor vehicle engines	1,244	1,275	1,403	640	926	1,549
Other equipment and tools	9,947	9,692	11,328	2,307	2,465	2,761

Canadian Sea Fish Catch and Exports

Source: Fisheries and Oceans Canada

Year	Total Value	Landings of Sea Fish							Exports to[1]		
		Total	Nfld.	P.E.I.	N.S.	N.B.	Que.	B.C.	Total	U.S.	Other
		(in metric tons)							(in metric tons)		
1976 . . .	364,754,000	1,063,071	340,241	17,123	368,456	117,937	41,948	177,366	296,154	193,777	102,377
1977 . . .	456,130,000	1,211,408	394,148	19,801	407,368	131,937	54,292	203,862	376,758	204,436	172,322
1978 . . .	668,191,000	1,352,027	463,959	25,660	444,869	151,393	67,350	198,796	422,390	224,077	198,177
1979 . . .	840,267,000	1,393,295	569,107	31,059	421,154	137,217	79,165	155,593	425,746	233,421	192,325
1980 . . .	692,356,000	1,286,014	499,199	33,463	436,822	105,356	81,248	129,926	430,917	220,494	210,106
1981 . . .	804,323,000	1,377,694	498,721	38,515	467,473	102,257	87,591	183,137	531,866	276,308	255,558
1982 . . .	829,184,000	1,355,475	504,458	36,788	460,792	109,001	86,593	157,843	550,078	294,106	255,972

Marketed Value of Canadian Fish Catches

Source: Fisheries and Oceans Canada (thousands of Canadian dollars)

Province	1981[1]	1982[1]	Province	1981[1]	1982[1]
Newfoundland	457,791	504,453	Manitoba.	31,035	31,941
Prince Edward Island	55,354	58,153	Saskatchewan	7,277	6,988
Nova Scotia	484,182	523,191	Alberta	1,873	1,748
New Brunswick	240,265	289,167	British Columbia.	526,935	466,899
Quebec	85,946	104,543	Yukon & NWT	2,725	2,948
Ontario	63,534	73,576	Total[2]	1,912,809	2,022,051

(1) Value after processing, both sea and freshwater fisheries; includes marine plants, aquatic mammals etc. (2) The sum of the provincial totals differs from the Canada total due to removal of inter-provincial shipments.

Canadian Balance of International Payments

Source: Statistics Canada (millions of Canadian dollars)

Year	Total current receipts	Total current payments	Current account balance	Goods and Services			Merchandise trade			Service transactions		
				Receipts	Payments	Balance	Exports	Imports	Balance	Receipts	Payments	Balance
1930	1,297	1,634	−337	1,272	1,579	−307	880	973	−93	392	606	−214
1935	1,152	1,027	+125	1,129	1,000	+129	732	526	+206	397	474	−77
1940	1,799	1,648	+151	1,749	1,606	+143	1,202	1006	+196	547	600	−53
1945	4,486	3,797	+689	4,402	2,889	1,513	3,474	1,442	2,032	928	1,447	−519
1950	4,284	4,603	−319	4,158	4,492	−334	3,139	3,132	+7	1,019	1,360	−341
1955	5,926	6,613	−687	5,737	6,390	−653	4,332	4,543	−211	1,405	1,847	−442
1960	7,215	8,448	−1,233	6,982	8,089	−1,107	5,392	5,540	−148	1,590	2,549	959
1965	11,648	12,778	−1,130	11,182	12,341	−1,159	8,745	8,627	+118	2,437	3,714	−1,277
1970	21,932	20,826	+1,106	21,167	20,214	+953	16,921	13,869	+3,052	4,246	6,345	−2,099
1975	41,840	46,597	−4,757	40,452	45,589	−5,137	33,511	33,962	−451	6,941	11,627	−4,686
1979	79,088	83,982	−4,894	77,087	82,671	−5,584	65,275	61,125	+4,150	11,812	21,546	−9,734
1980	92,921	94,825	−1,904	90,258	93,443	−3,185	76,170	68,360	+7,810	14,088	25,083	−10,995
1981	102,543	107,889	−5,346	99,468	106,375	−6,907	84,221	76,870	7,351	15,247	29,505	−14,258
1982	104,617	101,600	+3,017	101,438	99,863	+1,575	84,577	66,239	+18,338	16,861	33,624	−16,763
1983	110,966	109,389	+1,577	108,181	107,488	+693	91,268	73,227	+18,041	16,913	34,261	−17,348

Canadian Farm Cash Receipts by Province

Source: Statistics Canada
(millions of Canadian dollars)

Province	1976	1977	1978	1979	1980	1981	1982	1983
Newfoundland	20.5	21.9	23.4	26.4	28.1	32.4	35.2	36.3
Prince Edward Island	105.6	89.7	100.4	123.1	138.8	188.7	162.4	175.8
Nova Scotia	126.0	134.6	157.7	180.6	197.1	226.6	235.8	239.3
New Brunswick	115.2	110.7	122.7	141.7	151.0	201.4	199.4	195.1
Quebec	1,382.7	1,449.0	1,694.2	1,982.9	2,279.8	2,709.0	2,794.3	2,750.5
Ontario	2,785.7	2,859.1	3,422.7	4,021.9	4,393.5	4,976.5	4,878.3	4,958.0
Manitoba	892.4	893.6	1,141.0	1,326.9	1,480.5	1,662.4	1,697.3	1,743.4
Saskatchewan	2,311.5	2,160.9	2,507.9	3,021.8	3,302.4	4,009.1	4,021.0	3,960.1
Alberta	1,908.7	1,961.9	2,283.9	2,829.9	3,143.0	3,879.1	3,808.6	3,704.8
British Columbia	475.1	508.7	578.8	669.5	768.7	888.9	942.4	901.6
Total	**10,123.5**	**10,190.2**	**12,032.7**	**14,324.7**	**15,882.9**	**18,774.1**	**18,774.7**	**18,664.9**

Harvested Acreage of Principal Canadian Crops

Source: Statistics Canada (thousands of acres)

Province	1980	1981	1982	1983	Province	1980	1981	1982	1983
Prince Edward Island	372	373	376	371	Saskatchewan	26,610	28,390	28,698	29,397
Nova Scotia	226	231	232	233	Alberta	19,242	20,097	20,597	20,947
New Brunswick	294	290	294	295	British Columbia	1,296	1,235	1,360	1,402
Quebec	3,933	3,940	4,053	4,172	Total	70,087[1]	73,641[1]	74,756[1]	76,109[1]
Ontario	8,368	8,456	8,396	8,399					
Manitoba	9,745	10,629	10,749	10,892					

Crops included are winter wheat, spring wheat, oats, barley, fall rye, flaxseed, mixed grains, corn for grain, buckwheat, peas, dry beans, soybeans, rapeseed, potatoes, mustard seed, sunflower seed, tame hay, fodder corn, and sugar beets. (1) Totals include Newfoundland potatoes (1980) 880 acres; (1981) 840 acres; (1982) 800 acres; (1983) 700 acres.

Production of Principal Field Crops in Canada

Source: Statistics Canada

1983	Wheats 1,000 bushels	Oats 1,000 bushels	Barley 1,000 bushels	Ryes 1,000 bushels	Flaxseed 1,000 bushels
Canada[1]	988,915	179,817	487,562	32,695	18,300
Prince Edward Island	270	1,736	2,250	—	—
Nova Scotia	230	1,117	563	168	—
New Brunswick	369	1,950	720	—	—
Quebec	3,013	19,453	15,386	177	—
Ontario	29,533	15,200	24,143	3,060	—
Manitoba	125,300	26,000	73,000	6,420	11,700
Saskatchewan	574,000	42,000	120,000	13,300	5,500
Alberta	250,000	68,000	243,000	8,800	1,100
British Columbia	6,200	4,361	8,500	770	—

	Mixed grains 1,000 bushels	Corn grains 1,000 bushels	Soybeans 1,000 bushels	Rapeseed 1,000 bushels	Potatoes 1,000 c.w.t.
Canada(1)	60,709	231,256	26,500	118,200	55,557
Prince Edward Island	4,316	—	—	—	17,500
Nova Scotia	318	—	—	—	800
New Brunswick	150	—	—	—	11,176
Quebec	6,369	38,384	—	—	6,504
Ontario	33,786	182,622	26,500	—	6,460
Manitoba	4,800	9,000	—	18,000	5,616
Saskatchewan	2,800	—	—	48,000	408
Alberta	7,600	1,250	—	49,000	4,400
British Columbia	570	—	—	3,200	2,002

	Mustard seed 1,000 pounds	Sunflower seed 1,000 pounds	Tame hay 1,000 tons	Fodder corn 1,000 tons	Sugar beets 1,000 tons
Canada(1)	200,500	112,000	27,393	11,050	1,290
Prince Edward Island	—	—	282	65	—
Nova Scotia	—	—	493	111	—
New Brunswick	—	—	327	54	—
Quebec	—	—	4,409	2,756	276
Ontario	—	—	7,402	6,836	—
Manitoba	25,500	100,000	2,400	340	386
Saskatchewan	120,000	12,000	2,900	—	—
Alberta	55,000	—	7,200	420	628
British Columbia	—	—	1,980	468	—

(1) Excluding Newfoundland.

Off-Beat News Stories of 1984

Don't leave home without it — Carlo M. Mastrototaro was once described by a U.S. judge as "the mainspring of organized crime in central Massachusetts." He had been allowed 21 days to put his affairs in order before going to federal prison for conspiracy to commit mail fraud when he was arrested and convicted of shoplifting in a Natick, Mass. shopping mall. Among the items Mastrototaro stole to make life in prison more pleasant were a radio, hand fan, shaving case, cheese slicer, shower sandals, corkscrews, oyster openers, espresso coffeepot, and two copies of *The World Almanac.*

Eat your heart out, Carl Lewis — The U.S. Army awarded 8,612 medals as a result of the brief 1983 Grenada campaign even though it never had more than 7,000 officers and enlisted soldiers on the island. Army officials explained that many medals were given to staff and rear area support troops at several bases in the U.S. The Army defended its awards system as a "valuable and effective leadership tool to build morale and esprit."

Another day, another dollar — In order to improve attendance, officials at the Richmond (Ind.) High School offered $100 to any student who came to school every day. The officials found themselves owing $20,000 since 200 students had a perfect attendance record. Only 37 students had perfect attendance the previous year. The school planned to offer only non-monetary awards in the future.

Justice of the pizza — John Clark and Gary Kumpa spent a weekend in jail for eating a pizza. The two 18-year-olds were cited for violating an anti-litter ordinance after they walked out of a pizza parlor with their pizza slices in the Fire Island, N.Y. village of Ocean Beach. They planned to plead guilty with an explanation, but when told that the fine would be $25, they changed their plea to not guilty. Warrants were issued for their arrest when they misunderstood and failed to appear for a trial before the village justice. After they were released on bond, Clark explained that the pair had walked out of the pizza parlor because it was too crowded to eat inside.

War and peace? — The 640 year-round residents of Block Island, an ocean resort 15 miles off the Rhode Island coast, voted to proceed with a formal study on seceding from Rhode Island. The secession movement was sparked by the state legislature's refusal to permit the island to regulate motor scooters. Islanders complained that the 500 mopeds tourists rented every summer were traffic hazards which caused countless accidents, jeopardized the island's fragile marine environment, and upset the serenity of the community. Residents indicated that they would consider joining either Connecticut or Massachusetts.

Meanwhile, St. Peter and St. Paul ended their 127-year-old feud. When St. Paul Mayor George Latimer addressed a meeting of the St. Peter Chamber of Commerce, it was the first official visit between the cities since 1857. At that time, a St. Paul man stole the only copy of a territorial legislature bill that would have moved the Minnesota capital from St. Paul to St. Peter. Minnesota became a state the following year and since the legislature couldn't act on the measure without the official document, St. Paul remained the capital.

Cab-gab — The Greek government issued a decree prohibiting the nation's 35,000 taxi drivers from talking with their passengers about "subjects unrelated to their services." Political discussions had led to at least three jail sentences for drivers who allegedly insulted Socialist Premier Andreas Papandreou. A union spokesman for the taxi drivers called the decree "a ridiculous attempt to tell us how to go about our job." He also claimed that "passengers expect to be entertained during their journey by a talkative driver."

Don't talk to strangers — Greg Wandel, a Westbury, N.Y. cab driver, was held up by a gunman. As the robber fled with $50, three other men jumped into his cab. As Wandel told them about the robbery, they demanded the rest of his money. They escaped with $108.

Marital/missile crisis — Spec 4 Liam Fowler is a U.S. soldier assigned to the Army base outside Schwaebisch-Gmuend, the first West German base to receive Pershing 2 missiles. The base had been a target of West German anti-

missile protestors. After being absent for several hours, Fowler called his wife, Nikki, to say that he had been kidnapped by protesters. The next day, Fowler was found in a barn 100 miles from his army garrison. Questioned by German police, Fowler admitted that he had faked the abduction because he was afraid his wife would be angry with him for failing to pick her up from work.

Jimmy, who? — Ursula Stadt, maitre d'hotel at the Cafe Plaza restaurant in the Copley Plaza Hotel in Boston, refused to let a man in a cardigan sweater into the restaurant because he was not properly dressed. The Secret Service agent accompanying the man informed Ms. Stadt that she was turning away former president Jimmy Carter. She replied, "All the more reason he should wear a jacket."

Down the drain — NASA officials have much of which to be proud, but in one area they admit failure—plumbing. After five years and $12 million of intensive research they have yet to come up with a system that works away from Earth. As of May, 1984, the toilets have failed on 10 of the 11 shuttle flights.

Outhouses are "in" — State Senator Joseph Strohl found himself in a fight when he introduced a proposal to ban outhouses in Wisconsin. Residents united as the People's Organization for Outhouse Preservation rallied against the proposal. Among their arguments: outhouses keep flies away from the house, provide Halloween entertainment, and keep people in better physical shape from running to and fro.

Instant replay — At a news conference following a team handball match between West Germany and the U.S., a reporter, speaking German, asked U.S. coach Javier Garcia Cuesta how long his team had trained and how hard. Cuesta replied in English, "We've been together since January, training 5 days a week, 4 or 5 hours a day." He then turned the microphone over to the translator, who said, "We've been together since January, training 5 days a week, 4 to 5 hours a day." This also in perfect English.

Bubble, bubble, toil and trouble —Elizabeth, a self-proclaimed witch, started a charcoal fire behind second base in Cleveland Stadium on Friday the 13th, burned incense and herbs, and called on a "supreme goddess" to remove the curse put on the Cleveland Indians. Legend had it, that in 1958, on the night he was fired as manager, Bobby Bragan invoked a curse against the team, so that it would never again win an American League pennant. Elizabeth asked that the Indians be given the "intelligence, strength, and virtue to win their games." After the invocation, she declared, "The curse is gone." In mid August, the Indians were in last place.

But who will pay for college —A California judge awarded a childless couple joint custody of their dog in accordance with that state's child custody laws. The husband had offered his wife $20,000 for her "share" of the 2-year-old mongrel bitch, but his wife spurned the offer. The judge ruled that the dog was a child substitute and should be jointly owned and shared on a monthly basis by the pair, and that neither owner would be allowed to take the dog out of the state without written permission of the other.

Hydrophilia — A city judge ordered the utility company to install a restrictive-flow water meter at the home of a Richmond, Cal. woman ending more than a year of round-the-clock lawn watering. The woman, whose last monthly bill was $465, was using as much as 21,433 gallons of water a day, drenching the neighborhood, undermining the foundation of nearby homes, and turning the neighborhood into a quagmire.

But Garfield prefers lasagna — Cat fanciers and railroad workers joined together to oppose the Metro-North commuter rail line's plan to capture stray cats in the tunnels under Grand Central Terminal in New York City. Metro North said that they had to conduct the roundup of the flea-ridden cats because the fleas forced them to evacuate an underground repair shop. An official of the Transport Workers Union said that his members preferred to keep the cats since the cats kept away the rats. The official explained "we're not just talking about your usual rat. These things were as big as dogs. Since the cats have been down here, we haven't had the rats."

ASTRONOMY AND CALENDAR

Edited by Dr. Kenneth L. Franklin, Astronomer
American Museum-Hayden Planetarium

Celestial Events Highlights, 1985

(All times are Greenwich Mean Time)

No nighttime this year will pass without some planets to watch. Venus will grace our evening skies until spring, then the morning heavens will find Saturn and Jupiter taking over. They will gradually be visible earlier each night and be the major features of the summer nights. In May, Venus will dominate the morning sky and be prominent there until fall. Jupiter will still be seen in our evening twilight to year's end. Then, if you search diligently, you may be able to find Mars brightening in dawn's glow as it gets ready for a fine opposition next year.

This is a poor year for occultations of bright objects by the moon: Mars and Mercury are hidden twice, and Venus once. No bright stars are obscured either.

But perhaps the year will be spent in anticipation of the reappearance of Halley's comet. It was recovered by the professionals using sophisticated electronic light amplifiers and the 200-inch telescope on Palomar Mountain in October, 1982. It has been observed frequently ever since. There are reports that the body of it is apparently red while still beyond the orbit of Jupiter, and it seems to vary in light as if it were rotating. But observers in different observatories do not seem to agree on the speed of rotation. Those of us without telescopes may be able to find it with binoculars, maybe as early as November in the western evening sky. It is expected to brighten to naked eye visibility in December and, probably into January, but it will begin to set earlier. This means it will move into the evening twilight where the sky glow may be too much competition for it. Thus it will fade from our sight even though it may actually be getting brighter.

It will pass closest to the sun on February 9 of next year, but the sun will be between the earth and the comet. The view from Venus will be great, however, and the National Aeronautical and Space Administration expects to train its Venus-orbiting Pioneer satellite on the very active comet. P/Halley, as astronomers know it, will leave the sun to approach the earth, as near as 39 million miles on April 9. By this time, however, it will have relaxed considerably from its exciting sun passage, most spectacle being left far behind it. And a further insult to northerners, it will be so far south in our sky as to be virtually unseeable from the United States. Our only recourse is to travel to the Caribbean, or beyond. Unfortunately, this apparition has been labeled the worst geometrical arrangement for viewing in the comet's 2,000-year history. Whether this statement is true, P/Halley this time will be a disappointment.

January, 1985

Mercury is a "morning star" all month, and is possibly visible in the predawn eastern sky in the first week, when it is 23° west of the sun; it will look like a 0 magnitude star, and pass brighter Jupiter on the 31st.

Venus is the prominent "evening star" in the western sky all month, reaching its greatest eastern spread from the sun (47°) on the 22nd (the evening of the 21st in the U.S.).

Mars is another "evening star," but not nearly as prominent as nearby Venus, resembling a reddish star fainter than 1st magnitude, but still brighter than the surrounding stars as it moves from Aquarius into Pisces.

Jupiter is in conjunction with the sun on the 14th, thus invisible to us all month, with the possible exception of the 31st, when it will be near Mercury in the dawn twilight.

Saturn, a little brighter than the 1st magnitude, is found in the morning sky, in Libra, rising 2 or 3 hours before Mercury in mid-month.

Moon is at perigee on the 12th, passes Saturn on the 16th, Uranus on the 17th, Neptune on the 18th, Mercury on the 19th, Venus and Mars on the 25th, and is at apogee on the 27th.

Jan. 3—Mercury at greatest elongation, 23° west of the sun; Earth at perihelion, 91.4 million miles from the sun; the Quadrantid meteor shower should not suffer too much from the waxing gibbous moon which moon set fairly early.

Jan. 13—Mercury is 0°.7 S of Neptune.

Jan. 14—Jupiter in conjunction with sun.

Jan. 19—Sun enters Capricorn.

Jan. 22—Venus greatest elongation, 47° E of sun.

Jan. 31—Mercury close to Jupiter.

February

Mercury, passing superior conjunction with the sun on the 19th, is lost in the sun's glare all month.

Venus remains prominent all month, passing close to Mars on the 8th, and attaining maximum brilliance on the 26th.

Mars, in Pisces, continues to fade all month, resembling a star of about 1.5 magnitude as it comes close to the dazzling Venus on the 8th.

Jupiter may show itself with increasing ease in the dawn twilight by the end of the month.

Saturn, in Libra, gradually increases in brightness as it puts more distance between it and the sun, rising earlier each day.

Moon is at perigee on the 8th, passes Saturn on the 12th, Uranus on the 14th, Neptune on the 15th, Jupiter on the 17th, Venus and Mars on the 23rd, and is at apogee on the 24th.

Feb. 8—Venus close to Mars.

Feb. 11—Pluto stationary, begins its retrograde motion.

Feb. 16—Sun enters Aquarius.

Feb. 19—Mercury in superior conjunction with the sun.

Feb. 26—Venus at greatest brilliancy.

March

Mercury is technically an evening object all month, but almost impossible to see in the western evening twilight, reaching an elongation of only 18° east of the sun on the 17th, and beginning its retrograde motion on the 24th.

Venus is also an evening object all month, but as the month passes, Venus will become invisible to us.

Mars continues its gradual fade into the evening twilight, but still seems to be the brightest star in the region as it moves from Pisces into Aries.

Jupiter, in Capricornus, dominates the morning sky, rising more than 2 hours before the sun.

Saturn, in Libra, begins its retrograde (western) motion on the 7th, and slowly brightens.

Moon is at perigee on the 8th, passes Saturn on the 11th, Uranus on the 13th, Neptune on the 14th, Jupiter on the 17th, Mercury and Venus on the 22nd, is at apogee on the 23rd, and passes Mars on the 24th.

Mar. 7—Saturn stationary, begins retrograde motion.

Mar. 11—Sun enters Pisces.

Mar. 12—Venus stationary, beginning its retrograde motion.

Mar. 17—Mercury at greatest elongation, 18° east of the sun.

Mar. 20—Sun at Vernal Equinox; spring begins in the northern hemisphere at 4:14 pm GMT (11:14 am EST).

Mar. 22—Uranus stationary, begins retrograde motion.

Mar. 24—Mercury stationary, beginning its retrograde motion.

April

Mercury is at inferior conjunction, between the earth and

717

the sun, on the 3rd, stationary on the 16th, thus resuming its direct (easterly) motion among the background stars.

Venus is in inferior conjunction on the 3rd, 10 hours after Mercury, and is stationary on the 22nd, resuming its direct motion over the sky.

Mars continues to fade slowly as it moves from Aries into Taurus, ending the month just a few degrees south of the Pleiades low in the evening twilight.

Jupiter, rising about 1 am, is by far the brightest object in Capricornus.

Saturn, in retrograde motion, remains in Libra all month.

Moon is at perigee on the 5th, passes Saturn on the 8th, Uranus on the 9th, Neptune on the 10th, Jupiter on the 13th, Venus on the 17th, Mercury on the 18th, is at apogee on the 19th, and occults Mars on the 22nd.

Apr. 3—Mercury and Venus in inferior conjunctions with the sun.

Apr. 5—Neptune stationary, begins retrograde motion.

Apr. 16—Mercury stationary, resumes direct motion.

Apr. 18—Sun enters Aries.

Apr. 22—Venus stationary, resumes direct motion; Lyrid meteor shower undisturbed by the moon.

Apr. 23—Pluto in opposition to the sun in Virgo.

May

Mercury, at greatest elongation on the 1st, 27° west of the sun, is nevertheless not in the best place for morning observation, being too far south of the sun.

Venus is very prominent in the dawn sky, reaching its greatest brilliancy on the 9th.

Mars, as a nearly 2nd magnitude star, persists in its slide to the east through Taurus, almost totally unnoticed in the evening twilight, even as it passes Aldebaran on the 11th.

Jupiter plays second fiddle to Venus as the brighter object in the morning sky, but the giant planet has Capricornus all to itself, and the sky, too, for about 3 or 4 hours, before Venus rises to take the dazzle honors.

Saturn is in the sky all night long as it stands just opposite to the sun on the 15th, achieving nearly 0 magnitude at that time.

Moon is at perigee and in total eclipse on the 4th, passes Saturn on the 5th, Uranus on the 7th, Neptune on the 8th, Jupiter on the 11th, passes Venus on the 15th, is at apogee on the 17th, passes Mercury on the 18th, and Mars on the 21st.

May 1—Mercury at greatest elongation, 27° west of sun.

May 4—Moon in total eclipse, but not at the right time to allow a good observation of the Eta Aquarid meteor shower (possibly related to Halley's comet).

May 9—Venus at greatest brilliancy.

May 13—Sun enters Taurus.

May 11—Mars passes 6° north of Aldebaran.

May 15—Saturn at opposition to the sun.

June

Mercury is in superior conjunction with the sun on the 7th, thus being invisible to us, except for possibly the very end of the month.

Venus is a fine bright object in the eastern dawn sky all month, attaining its greatest elongation on the 12th, 46° west of the sun.

Mars is lost to view in the evening twilight.

Jupiter begins its retrograde motion in Capricornus, being stationary on the 5th.

Saturn, past opposition, continues its retrograde motion in Libra all month.

Moon is at perigee and passes Saturn on the 1st, Uranus on the 3rd, Neptune on the 4th, Jupiter on the 7th, is at apogee on the 13th, passes Venus on the 14th, passes Saturn again and is at perigee the second time this month on the 29th, and passes Uranus again on the 30th.

June 5—Jupiter stationary, beginning its retrograde motion.

June 6—Uranus at opposition to the sun.

June 7—Mercury in superior conjunction.

June 12—Venus at greatest elongation, 46° west of the sun.

June 20—Sun enters Gemini.

June 21—Sun at Summer Solstice, summer begins in the northern hemisphere at 10:44 a.m. GMT (5:44 am EST).

June 23—Neptune at opposition.

July

Mercury may be at its best for observation in the evening sky, for it is at greatest elongation on the 14th, 27° east of the sun; look in the twilight glow above the horizon and to the left of where the sun actually set for a star brighter than 1st magnitude; it is stationary on the 27th, beginning its retrograde motion.

Venus is the brightest star-like object in the morning twilight, in Taurus all month, passing 3° north of Aldebaran on the 15th.

Mars is in conjunction with the sun on the 18th, and is completely invisible to us.

Jupiter is the bright object visible all night long among the faint stars of Capricornus.

Saturn resumes its direct motion in Libra when it is stationary on the 26th.

Moon passes Neptune on the 1st, Jupiter on the 4th, is at apogee on the 11th, passes Venus on the 14th, Mercury on the 19th, is at perigee on the 25th, passes Saturn on the 26th, Uranus on the 28th, and Neptune for the second time this month on the 29th.

July 5—Earth at aphelion, 94.4 million miles from the sun.

July 14—Mercury at greatest elongation, 27° east of sun.

July 15—Venus passes 3° north of Aldebaran.

July 18—Mars in conjunction with the sun; Pluto stationary, resumes direct motion.

July 20—Sun enters Cancer.

July 26—Saturn stationary, resuming its direct motion.

July 27—Mercury stationary, beginning its retrograde motion.

August

Mercury is in inferior conjunction, between the earth and the sun, on the 10th, and will not be favorably placed for observation even at its greatest elongation on the 28th, only 18° west of the sun.

Venus is still the object to watch in the dawn sky, although it is getting into the morning twilight in Gemini.

Mars, on the western side of the sun, is still too close to the morning twilight to be seen this month.

Jupiter is at its brightest early this month, at −2.4 magnitude, the most obvious star-like body in the night sky as it stands at opposition to the sun on the 4th.

Saturn, still in Libra, is fading as the earth actually pull farther away from the ringed beauty.

Moon passes Jupiter on the 1st, is at apogee on the 4th, passes Venus on the 13th, is at perigee on the 20th, passes Saturn on the 22nd, Uranus on the 24th, Neptune on the 25th, and Jupiter on the 28th.

Aug. 4—Jupiter at opposition.

Aug. 10—Mercury in inferior conjunction; sun enters Leo.

Aug. 11, 12—The Perseid meteor shower should not be severely disturbed by the waning crescent moon.

Aug. 20—Mercury stationary, resuming direct motion.

Aug. 23—Venus passes 7° south of Pollux; Uranus stationary, resumes direct motion.

Aug. 28—Mercury at greatest elongation, 18° west of the sun.

September

Mercury and Mars are a good telescopic treat on the 4th: they pass 0°.01 from each other—Mercury to the south—about 9 pm, GMT (4 pm EST); they should be observed from North America before dawn on the mornings of the 4th and 5th; Mercury also passes 1° north of Regulus on the 6th.

Venus, still visible in the dawn sky, passes through Cancer into Leo this month, passing 0°.4 from Regulus on the 21st.

Mars passes Regulus within a degree on the 9th, but its real show comes with Mercury (q.v.) on the 4th.

Jupiter is still in retrograde motion, the dominant object in Capricornus.

Saturn sets from 3 to 5 hours after sunset in Libra, but does nothing spectacular this month.

Moon is at apogee on the 4th, passes Venus on the 12th, Mars on the 13th, is at perigee on the 16th, passes Saturn on the 19th, Uranus on the 20th, Neptune on the 21st, and Jupiter on the 24th.

Sept. 4—Mercury passes 0°.01 south of Mars.
Sept. 6—Mercury passes 1° north of Regulus.
Sept. 9—Mars passes 0°.8 north of Regulus.
Sept. 12—Neptune stationary, resumes its direct motion.
Sept. 16—Sun enters Virgo.
Sept. 21—Venus passes 0°.4 north of Regulus.
Sept. 22—Mercury in superior conjunction.
Sept. 23—Sun at Autumnal Equinox; fall begins in northern hemisphere at 2:08 am GMT (9:08 pm EST on the 22nd).

October

Mercury is east of the sun all month, being occulted by the moon on the 15th, but not favorably placed for viewing until perhaps the very end of October, when it passes 4° from Saturn on the 30th.

Venus is entering the morning twilight as Mars is leaving, so they pass each other at 0°.1 on the 4th, perhaps best seen in a telescope; watch the mornings of the 4th and the 5th.

Mars passes very near Venus (q.v.) on the 4th, but is no brighter than a 2nd magnitude star in the morning twilight.

Jupiter is stationary on the 3rd, resuming its direct motion, still a nice object in our evening sky.

Saturn, resembling a 1st magnitude star among the faint ones in Libra, is becoming lost in the evening twilight by month's end, although it misses Mercury by 4° on the 30th.

Moon is at apogee on the 2nd, passes Mars and Venus on the 12th, is at perigee and occults Mercury on the 15th, passes Saturn on the 16th, Uranus on the 17th, Neptune on the 18th, Jupiter on the 21st, is totally eclipsed on the 28th, and is at apogee on the 29th.

Oct. 3—Jupiter stationary, resuming its direct motion.
Oct. 4—Venus passes 0°.1 north of Mars.
Oct. 21—Orionid meteor shower (may be related to Halley's comet) may not be too disturbed by the 1st quarter moon.
Oct. 28—Pluto in conjunction with the sun; total lunar eclipse.
Oct. 30—Mercury passes 4° south of Saturn; sun enters Libra.

November

Mercury may be favorably placed for viewing in the evening early in the month, as it is at greatest elongation on the 8th, 23° east of the sun; look in the southeast a while after sunset.

Venus is getting very difficult to see in the morning dawn twilight, but it passes 4° north of Spica on the 3rd.

Mars, although not much brighter than a 2nd magnitude star, is emerging from the morning twilight, and will become increasing easy to see in Virgo as the year ends.

Jupiter is no problem in the evening twilight, lending a beautiful bright spot to the sunset glow.

Saturn is lost to view as it is in conjunction with the sun on the 23rd.

Moon passes Mars on the 9th, occults Venus on the 11th, totally eclipses the sun on the 12th, occults Mercury and passes Uranus on the 14th, Neptune on the 15th, Jupiter on the 18th, and is at apogee on the 25th.

Nov. 3—Venus passes 4° north of Spica.
Nov. 8—Mercury at greatest elongation, 23° east of the sun, and passes 1°.8 north of Antares.
Nov. 12—Total solar eclipse.
Nov. 18—Mercury stationary, beginning its retrograde motion; Leonid meteor shower should not be hurt by the 1st quarter moon, which sets about midnight.
Nov. 22—Sun enters Scorpius.
Nov. 23—Saturn in conjunction with the sun.
Nov. 28—Mercury in inferior conjunction.
Nov. 29—Sun enters Ophiuchus.

December

Mercury may be visible in the morning sky, for it is 21° west of the sun at its greatest elongation on the 17th, but Venus may help find it on the 4th when they pass 1°.6 from each other, and brighter Mercury may help find Saturn when they pass less than 1° from each other on the 16th.

Venus is lost to view in the morning twilight as it heads for superior conjunction early next month; see Mercury, above, for a close approach of these two; see Saturn for another near-miss.

Mars is becoming brighter in Virgo, heading for a very good opposition by mid-1986.

Jupiter continues its decoration of the western sky after sunset.

Saturn emerges from the dawn glow by month's end, but it is not well placed for sighting even then, although Venus may point it out on the 5th, and Mercury, less than a degree away, may help on the 16th.

Moon occults on the 8th, passes Mercury and Saturn on the 10th, is at perigee on the 11th, passes Jupiter on the 15th, and is at apogee on the 23rd.

Dec. 2—Mars passes 3° north of Spica.
Dec. 4—Mercury passes 0°.6 south of Venus.
Dec. 5—Venus passes 1°.1 south of Saturn.
Dec. 8—Mercury stationary, beginning its retrograde motion.
Dec. 10—Uranus in conjunction with the sun.
Dec. 13—Geminid meteor shower, famous for fireballs, is not disturbed by the moon this month.
Dec. 16—Mercury passes 0°.5 north of Saturn; sun enters Sagittarius.
Dec. 17—Mercury at greatest elongation, 21° west of the sun.
Dec. 21—Mercury passes 6° north of Antares; sun enters Winter Solstice, winter begins in the northern Hemisphere at 10:08 pm GMT (5:08 pm EST).
Dec. 25—Neptune in conjunction with the sun.

Planets and the Sun

The planets of the solar system, in order of their mean distance from the sun, are Mercury, Venus, Earth, Mars, Jupiter, Saturn, Uranus, Neptune and Pluto. Both Uranus and Neptune are visible through good field glasses, but Pluto is so distant and so small that only large telescopes or long exposure photographs can make it visible.

Since Mercury and Venus are nearer to the sun than is the earth, their motions about the sun are seen from the earth as wide swings first to one side of the sun and then to the other, although they are both passing continuously around the sun in orbits that are almost circular. When their passage takes them either between the earth and the sun, or beyond the sun as seen from the earth, they are invisible to us. Because of the laws which govern the motions of planets about the sun, both Mercury and Venus require much less time to pass between the earth and the sun than around the far side of the sun, so their periods of visibility and invisibility are unequal.

The planets that lie farther from the sun than does the earth may be seen for longer periods of time and are invisible only when they are so located in our sky that they rise and set about the same time as the sun when, of course, they are overwhelmed by the sun's great brilliance. None of the planets has any light of its own but each shines only by reflecting sunlight from its surface. Mercury and Venus, because they are between the earth and the sun, show phases very much as the moon does. The planets farther from the sun are always seen as full, although Mars does occasionally present a slightly gibbous phase — like the moon when not quite full.

The planets move rapidly among the stars because they are very much nearer to us. The stars are also in motion, some of them at tremendous speeds, but they are so far away that their motion does not change their apparent positions in the heavens sufficiently for anyone to perceive that change in a single lifetime. The very nearest star is about 7,000 times as far away as the most distant planet.

Planets of the Solar System

Mercury, Venus, Mars, Jupiter and Saturn

Mercury

Mercury, nearest planet to the sun, is the second smallest of the nine planets known to be orbiting the sun. Its diameter is 3,100 miles and its mean distance from the sun is 36,000,000 miles.

Mercury moves with great speed in its journey about the sun, averaging about 30 miles a second to complete its circuit in 88 of our days. Mercury rotates upon its axis over a period of nearly 59 days, thus exposing all of its surface periodically to the sun. It is believed that the surface passing before the sun may have a temperature of about 800° F., while the temperature on the side turned temporarily away from the sun does not fall as low as might be expected. This night temperature has been described by Russian astronomers as "room temperature" — possibly about 70°. This would contradict the former belief that Mercury did not possess an atmosphere, for some sort of atmosphere would be needed to retain the fierce solar radiation that strikes Mercury. A shallow but dense layer of carbon dioxide would produce the "greenhouse" effect, in which heat accumulated during exposure to the sun would not completely escape at night. The actual presence of a carbon dioxide atmosphere is in dispute. Other research, however, has indicated a nighttime temperature approaching −300°.

This uncertainty about conditions upon Mercury and its motion arise from its shorter angular distance from the sun as seen from the earth, for Mercury is always too much in line with the sun to be observed against a dark sky, but is always seen during either morning or evening twilight.

Mariner 10 made 3 passes by Mercury in 1974 and 1975. A large fraction of the surface was photographed from varying distances, revealing a degree of cratering similar to that of the moon. An atmosphere of hydrogen and helium may be made up of gases of the solar wind temporarily concentrated by the presence of Mercury. The discovery of a weak but permanent magnetic field was a surprise. It has been held that both a fluid core and rapid rotation were necessary for the generation of a planetary magnetic field. Mercury may demonstrate these conditions to be unnecessary, or the field may reveal something about the history of Mercury.

Venus

Venus, slightly smaller than the earth, moves about the sun at a mean distance of 67,000,000 miles in 225 of our days. Its synodical revolution — its return to the same relationship with the earth and the sun, which is a result of the combination of its own motion and that of the earth — is 584 days. Every 19 months, then, Venus will be nearer to the earth than any other planet of the solar system. The planet is covered with a dense, white, cloudy atmosphere that conceals whatever is below it. This same cloud reflects sunlight efficiently so that when Venus is favorably situated, it is the third brightest object in the sky, exceeded only by the sun and the moon.

Spectral analysis of sunlight reflected from Venus' cloud tops has shown features that can best be explained by identifying the material of the clouds as sulphuric acid (oil of vitriol). Infrared spectroscopy from a balloon-borne telescope nearly 20 miles above the earth's surface gave indications of a small amount of water vapor present in the same region of the atmosphere of Venus. In 1956, radio astronomers at the Naval Research Laboratories in Washington, D. C., found a temperature for Venus of about 600° F., in marked contrast to minus 125° F., previously found at the cloud tops. Subsequent radio work confirmed a high temperature and produced evidence for this temperature to be associated with the solid body of Venus. With this peculiarity in mind, space scientists devised experiments for the U.S. space probe Mariner 2 to perform when it flew by in 1962. Mariner 2 confirmed the high temperature and the fact that it pertained to the ground rather than to some special activity of the atmo-

sphere. In addition, Mariner 2 was unable to detect any radiation belts similar to the earth's so-called Van Allen belts. Nor was it able to detect the existence of a magnetic field even as weak as 1/100,000 of that of the earth.

In 1967, a Russian space probe, Venera 4, and the American Mariner 5 arrived at Venus within a few hours of each other. Venera 4 was designed to allow an instrument package to land gently on the planet's surface via parachute. It ceased transmission of information in about 75 minutes when the temperature it read went above 500° F. After considerable controversy, it was agreed that it still had 20 miles to go to reach the surface. The U.S. probe, Mariner 5, went around the dark side of Venus at a distance of about 6,000 miles. Again, it detected no significant magnetic field but its radio signals passed to earth through Venus' atmosphere twice — once on the night side and once on the day side. The results are startling. Venus' atmosphere is nearly all carbon dioxide and must exert a pressure at the planet's surface of up to 100 times the earth's normal sea-level pressure of one atmosphere. Since the earth and Venus are about the same size, and were presumably formed at the same time by the same general process from the same mixture of chemical elements, one is faced with the question: which is the planet with the unusual history — earth or Venus?

Radar astronomers using powerful transmitters as well as sensitive receivers and computers have succeeded in determining the rotation period of Venus. It turns out to be 243 days clockwise — in other words, contrary to the spin of most of the other planets and to its own motion around the sun. If it were exactly 243.16 days, Venus would always present the same face toward the earth at every inferior conjunction. This rate and sense of rotation allows a "day" on Venus of 117.4 earth days. Any part of Venus will receive sunlight on its clouds for over 58 days and will be in darkness for 58 days. Recent radar observations have shown surface features below the clouds. Large craters, continent-sized highlands, and extensive, dry "ocean" basins have been identified.

Mariner 10 passed Venus before traveling on to Mercury in 1974. The carbon dioxide molecule found in such abundance in the atmosphere is rather opaque to certain ultraviolet wavelengths, enabling sensitive television cameras to take pictures of the Venusian cloud cover. Photos radioed to earth show a spiral pattern in the clouds from equator to the poles.

In December, 1978, two U. S. Pioneer probes arrived at Venus. One went into orbit about Venus, the other split into 5 separate probes targeted for widely-spaced entry points to sample different conditions. The instrumentation ensemble was selected on the basis of previous missions that had shown the range of conditions to be studied. The probes confirmed expected high surface temperatures and high winds aloft. Winds of about 200 miles per hour, there, may account for the transfer of heat into the night side in spite of the low rotation speed of the planet. Surface winds were light at the time, however. Atmosphere and cloud chemistries were examined in detail, providing much data for continued analysis. The probes detected 4 layers of clouds and more light on the surface than expected solely from sunlight. This light allowed Russian scientists to obtain at least two photos showing rocks on the surface. Sulphur seems to play a large role in the chemistry of Venus, and reactions involving sulphur may be responsible for the glow. To learn more about the weather and atmospheric circulation on Venus, the orbiter takes daily photos of the daylight side cloud cover. It confirms the cloud pattern and its circulation shown by Mariner 10. The ionosphere shows large variability. The orbiter's radar operates in 2 modes: one, for ground elevation variability, and the second for ground reflectivity in 2 dimensions, thus "imaging" the surface. Radar maps of the entire planet that show the features mentioned above have been produced.

Mars

Mars is the first planet beyond the earth, away from the sun. Mars' diameter is about 4,200 miles, although a determination of the radius and mass of Mars by the space-probe, Mariner 4, which flew by Mars on July 14, 1965 at a distance of less than 6,000 miles, indicated that these dimensions were slightly larger than had been previously estimated. While Mars' orbit is also nearly circular, it is somewhat more eccentric than the orbits of many of the other planets, and Mars is more than 30 million miles farther from the sun in some parts of its year than it is at others. Mars takes 687 of our days to make one circuit of the sun, traveling at about 15 miles a second. Mars rotates upon its axis in almost the same period of time that the earth does — 24 hours and 37 minutes. Mars' mean distance from the sun is 141 million miles, so that the temperature on Mars would be lower than that on the earth even if Mars' atmosphere were about the same as ours. The atmosphere is not, however, for Mariner 4 reported that atmospheric pressure on Mars is between 1% and 2% of the earth's atmospheric pressure. This thin atmosphere appears to be largely carbon dioxide. No evidence of free water was found.

There appears to be no magnetic field about Mars. This would eliminate the previous conception of a dangerous radiation belt around Mars. The same lack of a magnetic field would expose the surface of Mars to an influx of cosmic radiation about 100 times as intense as that on earth.

Deductions from years of telescopic observation indicate that 5/8ths of the surface of Mars is a desert of reddish rock, sand, and soil. The rest of Mars is covered by irregular patches that appear generally green in hues that change through the Martian year. These were formerly held to be some sort of primitive vegetation, but with the findings of Mariner 4 of a complete lack of water and oxygen, such growth does not appear possible. The nature of the green areas is now unknown. They may be regions covered with volcanic salts whose color changes with changing temperatures and atmospheric conditions, or they may be gray, rather than green. When large gray areas are placed beside large red areas, the gray areas will appear green to the eye.

Mars' axis of rotation is inclined from a vertical to the plane of its orbit about the sun by about 25° and therefore Mars has seasons as does the earth, except that the Martian seasons are longer because Mars' year is longer. White caps form about the winter pole of Mars, growing through the winter and shrinking in summer. These polar caps are now believed to be both water ice and carbon dioxide ice. It is the carbon dioxide that is seen to come and go with the seasons. The water ice is apparently in many layers with dust between them, indicating climatic cycles.

The canals of Mars have become more of a mystery than they were before the voyage of Mariner 4. Markings forming a network of fine lines crossing much of the surface of Mars have been seen there by men who have devoted much time to the study of the planet, but no canals have shown clearly enough in previous photographs to be universally accepted. A few of the 21 photographs sent back to earth by Mariner 4 covered areas crossed by canals. The pictures show faint, ill-defined, broad, dark markings, but no positive identification of the nature of the markings.

Mariners 6 & 7 in 1969 sent back many more photographs of higher quality than those of the pioneering Mariner 4. These pictures showed cratering similar to the earlier views, but in addition showed 2 other types of terrain. Some regions seemed featureless for many square miles, but others were chaotic, showing high relief without apparent organization into mountain chains or craters.

Mariner 9, the first artificial body to be placed in an orbit about Mars, has transmitted over 10,000 photographs covering 100% of the planet's surface. Preliminary study of these photos and other data shows that Mars resembles no other planet we know. Using terrestrial terms, however, scientists describe features that seem to be clearly of volcanic origin. One of these features is Nix Olympica, (now called Olympus Mons), apparently a shield volcano whose caldera is over 50 miles wide, and whose outer slopes are over 300 miles in diameter, and which stands about 90,000 feet above the surrounding plain. Some features may have been produced by cracking (faulting) of the surface and the sliding of one region over or past another. Many craters seem to have been produced by impacting bodies such as may have come from the nearby asteroid belt. Features near the south pole may have been produced by glaciers that are no longer present. Flowing water, non-existent on Mars at the present time, probably carved canyons, one 10 times longer and 3 times deeper than the Grand Canyon.

Although the Russians landed a probe on the Martian surface, it transmitted for only 20 seconds. In 1976, the U.S. landed 2 Viking spacecraft on the Martian surface. The landers had devices aboard to perform chemical analyses of the soil in search of evidence of life. The results have been inconclusive. The 2 Viking orbiters have returned the best pictures yet of Martian topographic features. Many features can be explained only if Mars once had large quantities of flowing water.

Mars' position in its orbit and its speed around that orbit in relation to the earth's position and speed bring Mars fairly close to the earth on occasions about two years apart and then move Mars and the earth too far apart for accurate observation and photography. Every 15-17 years, the close approaches are especially favorable to close observation.

Mars has 2 satellites, discovered in 1877 by Asaph Hall. The outer satellite, Deimos, revolves around Mars in about 31 hours. The inner satellite, Phobos, whips around Mars in a little more than 7 hours, making 3 trips around the planet each Martian day. Mariner and Viking photos show these bodies to be irregularly shaped and pitted with numerous craters. Phobos also shows a system of linear grooves, each about 1/3-mile across and roughly parallel. Phobos measures about 8 by 12 miles and Deimos about 5 by 7.5 miles in size.

Jupiter

Jupiter is the largest of the planets. Its equatorial diameter is 88,000 miles, 11 times the diameter of the earth. Its polar diameter is about 6,000 miles shorter. This is an equilibrium condition resulting from the liquidity of the planet and its extremely rapid rate of rotation: a Jupiter day is only 10 earth hours long. For a planet this size, this rotational speed is amazing, and it moves a point on Jupiter's equator at a speed of 22,000 miles an hour, as compared with 1,000 miles an hour for a point on the earth's equator. Jupiter is at an average distance of 480 million miles from the sun and takes almost 12 of our years to make one complete circuit of the sun.

The only directly observable chemical constituents of Jupiter's atmosphere are methane (CH_4) and ammonia (NH_3), but it is reasonable to assume the same mixture of elements available to make Jupiter as to make the sun. This would mean a large fraction of hydrogen and helium must be present also, as well as water (H_2O). The temperature at the tops of the clouds may be about minus 260° F. The clouds are probably ammonia ice crystals, becoming ammonia droplets lower down. There may be a space before water ice crystals show up as clouds: in turn, these become water droplets near the bottom of the entire cloud layer. The total atmosphere may be only a few hundred miles in depth, pulled down by the surface gravity (= 2.64 times earth's) to a relatively thin layer. Of course, the gases become denser with depth until they may turn into a slush or a slurry. Perhaps there is no surface — no real interface between the gaseous atmosphere and the body of Jupiter. Pioneers 10 and 11 provided evidence for considering Jupiter to be almost entirely liquid hydrogen. Long before a rocky core about the size of the earth is reached, hydrogen mixed with helium becomes a liquid metal at very high temperature. Jupiter's cloudy atmosphere is a fairly good reflector of sunlight and makes it appear far brighter than any of the stars.

Fourteen of Jupiter's 17 or more satellites have been found through earth-based observations. Four of the moons are large and bright, rivaling our own moon and the planet Mercury in diameter, and may be seen through a field glass. They move rapidly around Jupiter and their change of position from night to night is extremely interesting to watch. The other satellites are much smaller and in all but one instance much farther from Jupiter and cannot be seen except through powerful telescopes. The 4 outermost satellites are revolving around Jupiter clockwise as seen from the north, contrary to the motions of the great majority of the satellites in the solar system and to the direction of revolution of the planets around the sun. The reason for this retrograde motion is not known, but one theory is that Jupiter's tremendous gravitational power may have captured 4 of the minor planets or asteroids that move about the sun between Mars and Jupiter, and that these would necessarily revolve backward. At the great distance of these bodies from Jupiter — some 14 million miles — direct motion would result in decay of the orbits, while retrograde orbits would be stable. Jupiter's mass is more than twice the mass of all the other planets put together, and accounts for Jupiter's tremendous gravitational field and so, probably, for its numerous satellites and its dense atmosphere.

In December, 1973, Pioneer 10 passed about 80,000 miles from the equator of Jupiter and was whipped into a path taking it out of our solar system in about 50 years, and beyond the system of planets, on June 13, 1983. In December, 1974, Pioneer 11 passed within 30,000 miles of Jupiter, moving roughly from south to north, over the poles.

Photographs from both encounters were useful at the time but were far surpassed by those of Voyagers I and II. Thousands of high resolution multi-color pictures show rapid variations of features both large and small. The Great Red Spot exhibits internal counterclockwise rotation. Much turbulence is seen in adjacent material passing north or south of it. The satellites Amalthea, Io, Europa, Ganymede, and Callisto were photographed, some in great detail. Each is individual and unique, with no similarities to other known planets or satellites. Io has active volcanoes that probably have ejected material into a doughnut-shaped ring enveloping its orbit about Jupiter. This is not to be confused with the thin flat disk-like ring closer to Jupiter's surface. Now that such a ring has been seen by the Voyagers, older uncertain observations from Earth can be reinterpreted as early sightings of this structure.

Saturn

Saturn, last of the planets visible to the unaided eye, is almost twice as far from the sun as Jupiter, almost 900 million miles. It is second in size to Jupiter but its mass is much smaller. Saturn's specific gravity is less than that of water. Its diameter is about 71,000 miles at the equator; its rotational speed spins it completely around in a little more than 10 hours, and its atmosphere is much like that of Jupiter, except that its temperature at the top of its cloud layer is at least 100° lower. At about 300° F. below zero, the ammonia would be frozen out of Saturn's clouds. The theoretical construction of Saturn resembles that of Jupiter; it is either all gas, or it has a small dense center surrounded by a layer of liquid and a deep atmosphere.

Until Pioneer 11 passed Saturn in September 1979 only 10 satellites of Saturn were known. Since that time, the situation is quite confused. Added to data interpretations from the fly-by are earth-based observations using new techniques while the rings were edge-on and virtually invisible. It was hoped that the Voyager I and II fly-bys would help sort out the system. It is now believed that Saturn has at least 22 satellites, some sharing orbits. The Saturn satellite system is still confused.

Saturn's ring system begins about 7,000 miles above the visible disk of Saturn, lying above its equator and extending about 35,000 miles into space. The diameter of the ring system visible from Earth is about 170,000 miles; the rings are estimated to be no thicker than 10 miles in. In 1973, radar observation showed the ring particles to be large chunks of material averaging a meter on a side.

Voyager I and II observations showed the rings to be considerably more complex than had been believed, so much so that interpretation will take much time. To the untrained eye, the Voyager photographs could be mistaken for pictures of a colorful phonograph record.

Uranus

Voyager II, after passing Saturn in August 1981, heads for a rendezvous with Uranus in 1986. Uranus, discovered by Sir William Herschel on Mar. 13, 1781, lies at a distance of 1.8 billion miles from the sun, taking 84 years to make its circuit around our star. Uranus has a diameter of about 32,000 miles and spins once in some 15.5 hours. One of the most fascinating features of Uranus is how far it is tipped over. Its north pole lies 98° from being directly up and down

to its orbit plane. Thus, its seasons are extreme. If the sun rises at the north pole, it will stay up for 42 years; then it will set and the north pole will be in darkness (and winter) for 42 years.

Uranus has 5 satellites (known to date) whose orbits lie in the plane of the planet's equator. In that plane there are also 9 rings, discovered in 1978. Virtually invisible from Earth, the rings were found by observers watching Uranus pass before a star. As they waited, they saw their photoelectric equipment register a short eclipse of the star, then another, and another. Then the planet occulted the star as expected. After the star came out from behind Uranus, the star winked out several more times. Subsequent observations and analyses indicate 9 narrow, nearly opaque, rings circling Uranus.

The structure of Uranus is subject to some debate. Basically, however, it may have a rocky core surrounded by a thick icy mantle on top of which is a crust of hydrogen and helium that gradually becomes an atmosphere. Perhaps Voyager II will shed some light on this problem.

Neptune

Neptune, currently the most distant planet from the sun (until 1999), lies at an average distance of 2.8 billion miles. Having a diameter of about 31,000 miles and a rotation period of 18.2 hours, it is a virtual twin of Uranus. It is significantly more dense than Uranus, however, and this increases the debate over its internal structure. Neptune circles the sun in 164 years in a nearly circular orbit.

Neptune has 3 satellites, the third being found in 1981. The largest, Triton, is in a retrograde orbit suggesting that it was captured rather than being co-eval with Neptune. Triton is sufficiently large to raise significant tides on Neptune which will one day, say 100 million years from now, cause Triton to come close enough to Neptune for it to be torn apart. Nereid was found in 1949, and is in a long looping orbit suggesting it, too, was captured. The orbit of the third body is under analysis at this writing. Observations made in 1968 but not interpreted until 1982 suggest that Neptune, too, has a ring system.

As with the other giant planets, Neptune is emitting more energy than it receives from the sun. These excesses are thought to be cooling from internal heat sources and from the heat of the formation of the planets.

Little is known of Neptune beyond its distance, but Voyager II, if all continues to operate, will send us pictures and observations in 1989.

Pluto

Although Pluto on the average stays about 3.6 billion miles from the sun, its orbit is so eccentric that it is now approaching its minimum distance of 2.7 billion miles, less than the current distance of Neptune. Thus Pluto, until 1999, is temporarily planet number 8 from the sun. At its mean distance, Pluto takes 247.7 years to circumnavigate the sun. Until recently that was about all that was known of Pluto.

About a century ago, a hypothetical planet was believed to lie beyond Neptune and Uranus. Little more than a guess, a mass of one Earth was assigned to the mysterious body and mathematical searches were begun. Amid some controversy about the validity of the predictive process, Pluto was found nearly where it was predicted to be. It was found by Clyde Tombaugh at the Lowell Observatory in Flagstaff, Ariz., in 1930.

At the U.S. Naval Observatory, also in Flagstaff, on July 2, 1978, James Christy obtained a photograph of Pluto that was distinctly elongated. Repeated observations of this shape and its variation were convincing evidence of the discovery of a satellite of Pluto. Now named Charon, it may be 500 miles across, at a distance of over 10,000 miles, and taking 6.4 days to move around Pluto, the same length of time Pluto takes to rotate once. Gravitational laws allow these interactions to give us the mass of Pluto as 0.0017 of the Earth and a diameter of 1,500 miles. This makes the density about the same as that of water.

It is now clear that Pluto, the body found by Tombaugh, could not have influenced Neptune and Uranus to go astray. Theorists are again at work looking for a new planet X.

Greenwich Sidereal Time for 0ʰ GMT, 1985

(Add 12 hours to obtain Right Ascension of Mean Sun)

Date		h	m	Date		h	m	Date		h	m	Date		h	m
Jan.	1	06	42.4	Apr.	1	12	37.2	July	10	19	11.5	Oct.	8	01	05.8
	11	07	36.5		11	13	16.6		20	19	50.9		18	01	45.2
	21	08	02.0		21	13	56.0		30	20	30.3		28	02	24.6
	31	08	40.6	May	1	14	35.5	Aug.	9	21	09.7	Nov.	7	03	04.6
Feb.	10	09	33.8		11	15	14.9		19	21	49.2		17	03	43.6
	20	09	59.5		21	15	54.3		29	22	28.6		27	04	23.4
Mar.	2	10	38.9		31	16	33.8	Sept.	8	23	08.0	Dec.	7	05	02.8
	12	11	18.4	June	10	17	13.2		18	23	47.4		17	05	42.3
	22	11	57.8		20	17	52.6		28	00	26.9		27	06	21.7
					30	18	32.0								

Astronomical Signs and Symbols

☉	The Sun	⊕	The Earth	♅	Uranus	□	Quadrature
☽	The Moon	♂	Mars	♆	Neptune	☍	Opposition
☿	Mercury	♃	Jupiter	♇	Pluto	☊	Ascending Node
♀	Venus	♄	Saturn	☌	Conjunction	☋	Descending Node

Two heavenly bodies are in "conjunction" (☌) when they are due north and south of each other, either in Right Ascension (with respect to the north celestial pole) or in Celestial Longitude (with respect to the north ecliptic pole). If the bodies are seen near each other, they will rise and set at nearly the same time. They are in "opposition" (☍) when their Right Ascensions differ by exactly 12 hours, or their Celestial Longitudes differ by 180°. One of the two objects in opposition will rise while the other is setting. "Quadrature" (□) refers to the arrangement when the coordinates of two bodies differ by exactly 90°. These terms may refer to the relative positions of any two bodies as seen from the earth, but one of the bodies is so frequently the sun that mention of the sun is omitted; otherwise both bodies are named. The geocentric angular separation between sun and object is termed "elongation." Elongation is limited only for Mercury and Venus; the "greatest elongation" for each of these bodies is noted in the appropriate tables and is approximately the time for longest observation. When a planet is in its "ascending" (☊) or "descending" (☋) node, it is passing northward or southward, respectively, through the plane of the earth's orbit, across the celestial circle called the ecliptic. The term "perihelion" means nearest to the sun, and "aphelion," farthest from the sun. An "occultation" of a planet or star is an eclipse of it by some other body, usually the moon.

Planetary Configurations, 1985

Greenwich Mean Time (0 designates midnight; 12 designates noon)

Mo.	D.	h.	m.		
Jan.	3	15	-	☿	Gr Elong W (23°)
	3	20	-	⊕	at perihelion.
	13	05	-	☌ ☿ ♆	☿ 0°.7 S
	14	22	-	☌ ♃ ☉	
	16	08	-	☌ ♃ ☽	♃ 2° N
	19	13	-	☌ ☿ ☽	☿ 3° N
	22	02	-	♀	Gr Elong E (47°)
	25	00	-	☌ ♀ ☽	♀ 5° N
	25	04	-	☌ ♂ ☽	♂ 4° N
	31	05	-	☌ ♃ ☿	☿ 1°.3 S
Feb.	8	02	-	☌ ♀ ☿	♀ 3° N
	12	16	-	☌ ♄ ☽	♄ 3° N
	15	19	-	☌ ♀ ☿	♀ 4° N
	17	10	-	☌ ♃ ☽	♃ 4° N
	19	08	-	☌ ☿ ☉	Superior
	23	06	-	☌ ♀ ☽	♀ 8° N
	23	08	-	☌ ♂ ☽	♂ 3° N
	26	18	-	♀	Gr Brilliancy
Mar.	7	23	-	♄	stationary
	11	23	-	☌ ♄ ☽	♄ 3° N
	12	08	-	♀	stationary
	17	02	-	☌ ♃ ☽	♃ 5° N
	17	07	-	☿	Gr Elong E (18°)
	20	16 14	-		Vernal Equinox; Spring Begins, N. Hemisphere
	22	18	-	☌ ☿ ☽	☿ 6° N
	22	19	-	☌ ♀ ☽	♀ 12° N
	23	02	-	☌ ☿ ☽	☿ 5° S
	24	12	-	☌ ♂ ☽	♂ 1°.4 N
	24	13	-	☿	stationary
Apr.	3	14	-	☌ ☿ ☉	Inferior
	3	22	-	☌ ♀ ☉	Inferior
	8	07	-	☌ ♄ ☽	♄ 3° N
	13	17	-	☌ ♃ ☽	♃ 5° N
	16	00	-	☿	stationary
	17	23	-	☌ ♀ ☽	♀ 10° N
	18	04	-	☌ ☿ ☽	☿ 3° N
	22	11	-	♀	stationary
	22	13	-	☌ ♂ ☽	♂ 0°.4 S; Occultation

Mo.	D.	h.	m.		
May	1	15	-	☿	Gr Elong W (27°)
	4	20	-	☍ ☽ ☉	Total Eclipse
	5	15	-	☌ ♄ ☽	♄ 3° N
	9	13	-	♀	Gr Brilliancy
	11	05	-	☌ ♃ ☽	♃ 5° N
	11	13	-	☌ ♀ *	♂ 6° N of Aldebaran
	15	18	-	☍ ♃ ☉	
	15	23	-	☌ ♀ ☽	♀ 3° N
	18	01	-	☌ ☿ ☽	☿ 1°.5 S
	19	22	-	☌ ☽ ☉	Partial Eclipse
	21	10	-	☌ ♂ ☽	♂ 1°.9 S
June	1	22	-	☌ ♄ ☽	♄ 3° N
	5	08	-	♃	stationary
	7	14	-	☌ ☿ ☉	Superior
	7	16	-	☌ ♃ ☽	♃ 5° N
	12	22	-	♀	Gr Elong W (46°)
	14	11	-	☌ ♀ ☽	♀ 1°.9 S
	21	10 44	-		Summer Solstice; Summer begins; N. Hemisphere
	26	02	-	☌ ☿ *	☿ 5° S at Pollux
	29	05	-	☌ ♄ ☽	♄ 3° N
July	4	23	-	☌ ♃ ☽	♃ 5° N
	5	10	-	⊕	at Aphelion
	14	01	-	☿	Gr Elong E (27°)
	14	09	-	☌ ♀ ☽	♀ 5° S
	15	13	-	☌ ♀ *	♂ 3° N at Aldebaran
	18	03	-	☌ ♂ ☉	
	19	21	-	☌ ♀ ☽	♀ 7° S
	26	10	-	☌ ♄ ☽	♄ 3° N
	26	12	-	♄	stationary
	27	03	-	☿	stationary
Aug.	1	02	-	☌ ♃ ☽	♃ 4° N
	4	12	-	☽ ♃ ☉	
	10	22	-	☌ ☿ ☉	Inferior
	13	08	-	☌ ♀ ☽	♀ 5° S
	20	06	-	☿	stationary
	22	16	-	☌ ♄ ☽	♄ 3° N
	23	08	-	☌ ♀ *	♀ 7° S at Pollux
	28	04	-	☌ ♃ ☽	♃ 4° N

Mo. D. h. m.

28 12 -	☿ Gr Elong W (18°)
Sept 4 21 - ☌ ☿ ☐	☿ 0°.01 S
6 10 - ☌ ☿ *	☿ 1°.0 N of Regulus
9 01 - ☌ ♂ *	♂ 0°.8 N of Regulus
12 08 - ☌ ♀ ☽	♀ 5° S
13 08 - ☌ ♂ ☽	♂ 4° S
19 02 - ☌ ♄ ☽	♄ 3° N
21 17 - ☌ ♀ *	♀ 0°.4 N at Regulus
22 20 - ☌ ☿ ☉	Superior
23 02 08	Autumnal Equinox; Autumn begins; N. Hemisphere
24 06 - ☌ ♃ ☽	♃ 4° N
Oct. 3 10 -	♃ stationary
4 23 - ☌ ♀ ♂	♀ 0°.1 N
12 01 - ☌ ♂ ☽	♂ 3° S
12 09 - ☌ ♀ ☽	♀ 3° S
15 05 - ☌ ☿ ☽	☿ 1°.3 S; Occultation
16 15 - ☌ ♄ ☽	♄ 4° N
21 13 - ☌ ♃ ☽	♃ 5° N
28 18 - ☍ ☽ ☉	Total Eclipse
30 21 - ☌ ☿ ♄	☿ 4° S
Nov. 3 10 ☌ ♀ *	♀ 4° N of Spica

Mo. D. h. m.

8 09 -	☿ Gr Elong E (23°)
8 19 - ☌ ☿ *	☿ 1°.8 N of Antares
11 11 - ☌ ♀ ☽	♀ 0°.8 N; Occultation
12 14 - ☌ ☽ ☉	Total Eclipse
14 04 - ☌ ♀ ☽	♀ 0°.5 N; Occultation
18 01 - ☌ ♃ ☽	♃ 5° N
18 19 -	☿ stationary
23 02 - ☌ ♄ ☉	
28 22 - ☌ ☿ ☉	Inferior
Dec. 2 11 - ☌ ♂ *	♂ 3° N of Spica
4 04 - ☌ ☿ ♀	☿ 1°.6 N
5 11 - ☌ ♀ ♄	♀ 1°.1 S
8 10 - ☌ ♂ ☽	♂ 0°.01 S; Occultation
8 11 -	☿ stationary
10 18 - ☌ ☿ ☽	☿ 5° N
10 23 - ☌ ♄ ☽	♄ 4° N
15 18 - ☌ ♃ ☽	♃ 5° N
16 17 - ☌ ☿ ♄	☿ 0°.5 N
17 05 -	☿ Gr Elong W (21°)
21 10 - ☌ ☿ *	☿ 6° N of Antares
21 22 08	Winter Solstice; Winter begins; N. Hemisphere

Planetary Configurations, 1986

Mo. D. h. m.

Jan. 2 05 -	⊕ at perihelion
6 01 - ☌ ♂ ☽	♂ 1°.7 N
7 14 - ☌ ♄ ☽	♄ 4° N
12 14 - ☌ ♃ ☽	♃ 4°N
19 - ☌ ♀ ☉	Superior
Feb 1 01 - ☌ ☿ ☉	Superior
3 12 - ☌ ♂ ☽	☽ 3° N
4 01 - ☌ ♃ ☽	♃ 5° N
10 03 - ☌ ♄ *	♄ 7° N of Antares
17 06 - ☌ ♂ *	♂ 5° N of Antares
18 00 - ☌ ♂ ♄	♂ 1°.3 S
18 10 - ☌ ♃ ☉	

Mo. D. h. m.

28 16 -	☿ Gr Elong E (18°)
Mar 3 08 - ☌ ♄ ☽	♄ 5° N
3 20 - ☌ ♂ ☽	☽ 4° N
6 23 -	☿ stationary
8 13 - ☌ ☿ ☽	☿ 5° N
11 15 - ☌ ♀ ☽	♀ 1°.3 N
16 20 - ☌ ☿ ☉	Inferior
19 14 -	♄ stationary
20 22 03 *	Vernal Equinox; Spring begins; in N. Hemisphere
29 06 -	☿ stationary
30 15 - ☌ ♄ ☽	♄ 5° N

Rising and Setting of Planets, 1985

Greenwich Mean Time (0 designates midnight)

1985	20° N. Latitude Rise	Set	30° N. Latitude Rise	Set	40° N. Latitude Rise	Set	50° N. Latitude Rise	Set	60° N. Latitude Rise	Set
					Venus, 1985					
Jan 5	9:32	20:55	9:43	20:44	9:56	20:31	10:14	20:13	10:43	19:44
15	9:25	21:03	9:32	20:56	9:40	20:48	9:51	20:37	10:08	20:20
25	9:16	21:08	9:18	21:05	9:21	21:02	9:25	20:58	9:31	20:52
Feb 4	9:05	21:12	9:04	21:13	9:01	21:16	8:58	21:19	8:54	21:23
14	8:48	21:07	8:42	21:13	8:35	21:20	8:26	21:30	8:11	21:44
24	8:25	20:57	8:16	21:06	8:04	21:17	7:49	21:33	7:24	21:57
Mar 6	7:54	20:36	7:42	20:48	7:27	21:03	7:07	21:24	6:34	21:56
16	7:14	20:00	7:00	20:14	6:43	20:31	6:19	20:54	5:41	21:32
26	6:22	19:07	6:09	19:21	5:52	19:37	5:29	20:00	4:53	20:36
Apr 5	5:26	18:03	5:15	18:13	5:02	18:27	4:44	18:45	4:15	19:13
15	4:36	17:01	4:29	17:08	4:20	17:17	4:07	17:30	3:48	17:49
25	3:58	16:14	3:53	16:19	3:47	16:25	3:39	16:33	3:27	16:45
May 5	3:31	15:44	3:27	15:48	3:23	15:52	3:16	15:58	3:07	16:08
15	3:12	15:26	3:08	15:30	3:03	15:35	2:56	15:42	2:45	15:52
25	2:58	15:17	2:52	15:22	2:46	15:29	2:37	15:38	2:23	15:52
June 4	2:48	15:13	2:40	15:21	2:31	15:30	2:18	15:42	1:59	16:02
14	2:40	15:14	2:30	15:24	2:18	15:36	2:01	15:53	1:35	16:19
24	2:36	15:18	2:23	15:31	2:08	15:46	1:46	16:07	1:13	16:41
July 5	2:34	15:25	2:19	15:40	2:00	15:59	1:34	16:24	0:52	17:07
14	2:35	15:34	2:18	15:51	1:57	16:12	1:27	16:42	0:36	17:33
24	2:40	15:44	2:21	16:03	1:57	16:26	1:24	17:00	0:27	17:57
Aug 3	2:48	15:54	2:28	16:14	2:03	16:39	1:28	17:14	0:26	18:15
13	2:58	16:04	2:38	16:24	2:13	16:49	1:38	17:24	0:37	18:25
23	3:10	16:13	2:51	16:32	2:28	16:56	1:55	17:29	0:58	18:25
Sept 2	3:24	16:20	3:07	16:37	2:46	16:58	2:17	17:27	1:28	18:16
12	3:37	16:25	3:23	16:39	3:06	16:56	2:42	17:20	2:03	17:59
22	3:47	16:23	3:36	16:34	3:23	16:47	3:05	17:05	2:36	17:33
Oct 2	4:00	16:24	3:53	16:31	3:45	16:39	3:33	16:51	3:15	17:09
12	4:13	16:23	4:10	16:26	4:07	16:30	4:02	16:35	3:54	16:43
22	4:27	16:23	4:28	16:22	4:29	16:20	4:31	16:18	4:34	16:15
Nov 1	4:40	16:22	4:45	16:17	4:52	16:10	5:01	16:01	5:14	15:48
11	4:54	16:23	5:04	16:13	5:15	16:02	5:31	15:46	5:56	15:21
21	5:10	16:25	5:23	16:12	5:40	15:55	6:02	15:33	6:38	14:56
Dec 1	5:26	16:30	5:43	16:13	6:04	15:52	6:33	15:23	7:21	14:35
11	5:44	16:38	6:03	16:19	6:28	15:54	7:02	15:20	8:02	14:20
21	6:01	16:50	6:22	16:28	6:49	16:01	7:28	15:23	8:36	14:15
31	6:17	17:04	6:39	16:42	7:07	16:14	7:46	15:35	8:58	14:23

		20° N. Latitude		30° N. Latitude		40° N. Latitude		50° N. Latitude		60° N. Latitude	
		Rise	Set	Rise	Set	Rise	Set	Rise	Set	Rise	Set
Mars, 1985											
Jan	5	9:55	21:28	10:03	21:20	10:13	21:10	10:26	20:57	10:47	20:36
	15	9:38	21:19	9:43	21:14	9:49	21:08	9:58	20:59	10:12	20:45
	25	9:23	21:14	9:26	21:12	9:29	21:08	9:33	21:04	9:40	20:57
Feb	4	9:10	21:10	9:10	21:10	9:09	21:10	9:09	21:10	9:09	21:10
	14	8:53	21:02	8:50	21:05	8:47	21:08	8:42	21:13	8:36	21:20
	24	8:36	20:54	8:31	21:00	8:25	21:06	8:16	21:15	8:02	21:29
Mar	6	8:20	20:47	8:12	20:55	8:03	21:04	7:49	21:17	7:29	21:38
	16	8:04	20:39	7:54	20:49	7:41	21:02	7:24	21:19	6:56	21:47
	26	7:49	20:31	7:36	20:44	7:20	21:00	6:59	21:21	6:25	21:55
Apr	5	7:34	20:24	7:19	20:39	7:00	20:57	6:35	21:22	5:54	22:04
	15	7:19	20:16	7:03	20:33	6:42	20:54	6:12	21:23	5:24	22:12
	25	7:06	20:08	6:47	20:27	6:24	20:50	5:51	21:23	4:56	22:18
May	5	6:53	20:01	6:33	20:21	6:08	20:46	5:32	21:22	4:30	22:24
	15	6:41	19:52	6:20	20:14	5:53	20:40	5:15	21:19	4:07	22:26
	25	6:30	19:44	6:08	20:06	5:40	20:34	5:00	21:14	3:48	22:26
June	4	6:19	19:34	5:57	19:57	5:28	20:25	4:47	21:06	3:32	22:21
	14	6:09	19:24	5:46	19:47	5:18	20:16	4:37	20:57	3:21	22:16
	24	5:59	19:14	5:37	19:36	5:08	20:04	4:28	20:44	3:14	21:58
July	4	5:49	19:02	5:28	19:23	5:00	19:51	4:21	20:30	3:11	21:40
	14	5:39	18:49	5:19	19:09	4:53	19:35	4:16	20:12	3:11	21:17
	24	5:29	18:35	5:10	18:54	4:46	19:19	4:11	19:53	3:12	20:52
Aug	3	5:19	18:20	5:01	18:38	4:39	19:00	4:08	19:32	3:15	20:24
	13	5:09	18:04	4:53	18:20	4:32	18:40	4:04	19:08	3:18	19:55
	23	4:58	17:47	4:44	18:01	4:26	18:19	4:01	18:44	3:21	19:24
Sept	2	4:47	17:29	4:34	17:42	4:19	17:57	3:58	18:19	3:24	18:53
	12	4:35	17:11	4:25	17:21	4:12	17:34	3:54	17:52	3:26	18:20
	22	4:21	16:50	4:13	16:58	4:02	17:09	3:48	17:23	3:26	17:45
Oct	2	4:09	16:30	4:02	16:37	3:55	16:45	3:44	16:55	3:28	17:11
	12	3:56	16:11	3:52	16:15	3:47	16:20	3:40	16:27	3:29	16:38
	22	3:44	15:51	3:42	15:53	3:39	15:55	3:36	15:59	3:30	16:04
Nov	1	3:31	15:31	3:31	15:31	3:31	15:31	3:31	15:31	3:31	15:30
	11	3:18	15:11	3:20	15:09	3:23	15:06	3:27	15:02	3:32	14:57
	21	3:05	14:51	3:10	14:47	3:15	14:41	3:22	14:34	3:33	14:23
Dec	1	2:53	14:31	2:59	14:25	3:07	14:17	3:17	14:06	3:34	13:50
	11	2:40	14:11	2:48	14:03	2:59	13:53	3:13	13:39	3:34	13:17
	21	2:27	13:52	2:38	13:42	2:50	13:29	3:08	13:12	3:35	12:45
	31	2:15	13:33	2:27	13:21	2:42	13:06	3:03	12:46	3:36	12:13
Jupiter, 1985											
Jan	5	7:13	18:06	7:33	17:46	7:58	17:21	8:33	16:45	9:35	15:44
	15	6:43	17:37	7:02	17:17	7:27	16:53	8:01	16:18	9:01	15:19
	25	6:12	17:08	6:31	16:49	6:55	16:25	7:29	15:51	8:27	14:54
Feb	4	5:42	16:39	6:00	16:21	6:24	15:57	6:57	15:24	7:52	14:29
	14	5:11	16:10	5:29	15:52	5:52	15:29	6:24	14:57	7:18	14:04
	24	4:40	15:41	4:58	15:23	5:20	15:01	5:51	14:30	6:42	13:38
Mar	6	4:09	15:11	4:26	14:54	4:47	14:32	5:17	14:02	6:07	13:13
	16	3:37	14:41	3:53	14:24	4:14	14:03	4:43	13:34	5:31	12:46
	26	3:04	14:10	3:20	13:53	3:41	13:33	4:09	13:05	4:55	12:19
Apr	5	2:31	13:38	2:47	13:22	3:06	13:02	3:34	12:35	4:18	11:51
	15	1:57	13:05	2:13	12:50	2:32	12:31	2:58	12:04	3:42	11:21
	25	1:23	12:32	1:38	12:17	1:56	11:58	2:22	11:32	3:04	10:50
May	5	0:43	11:52	0:58	11:37	1:17	11:18	1:43	10:53	2:25	10:10
	15	0:10	11:21	0:25	11:07	0:43	10:48	1:08	10:23	1:49	9:43
	25	23:33	10:44	23:47	10:29	0:05	10:11	0:30	9:47	1:10	9:06
June	4	22:54	10:05	23:09	9:51	23:27	9:33	23:51	9:08	0:32	8:28
	14	22:14	9:25	22:29	9:11	22:47	8:53	23:12	8:28	23:52	7:47
	24	21:34	8:44	21:48	8:29	22:07	8:11	22:32	7:46	23:13	7:05
July	4	20:51	8:01	21:07	7:46	21:25	7:28	21:51	7:02	22:33	6:20
	14	20:09	7:17	20:24	7:02	20:43	6:43	21:09	6:17	21:52	5:34
	24	19:25	6:33	19:41	6:17	20:00	5:58	20:27	5:31	21:12	4:47
Aug	3	18:42	5:48	18:57	5:32	19:17	5:12	19:45	4:44	20:31	3:58
	13	17:57	5:02	18:14	4:46	18:34	4:26	19:03	3:57	19:49	3:10
	23	17:14	4:17	17:30	4:01	17:51	3:40	18:20	3:11	19:08	2:23
Sept	2	16:30	3:33	16:47	3:16	17:09	2:55	17:38	2:26	18:27	1:36
	12	15:48	2:50	16:05	2:33	16:27	2:11	16:57	1:42	17:47	0:52
	22	15:07	2:08	15:24	1:51	15:46	1:29	16:16	0:59	17:06	0:09
Oct	2	14:26	1:28	14:44	1:11	15:06	0:49	15:36	0:19	16:26	23:28
	12	13:47	0:49	14:05	0:32	14:26	0:10	14:57	23:40	15:47	22:49
	22	13:09	0:11	13:27	23:54	13:48	23:33	14:18	23:03	15:08	22:13
Nov	1	12:33	23:35	12:50	23:18	13:11	22:57	13:40	22:28	14:30	21:38
	11	11:57	23:01	12:14	22:44	12:34	22:23	13:04	21:54	13:52	21:06
	21	11:22	22:27	11:39	22:11	11:59	21:50	12:27	21:22	13:14	20:35
Dec	1	10:48	21:54	11:04	21:38	11:24	21:19	11:51	20:51	12:37	20:06
	11	10:15	21:23	10:30	21:07	10:50	20:48	11:16	20:22	12:00	19:38
	21	9:42	20:52	9:57	20:37	10:16	20:19	10:41	19:53	11:23	19:11
	31	9:10	20:22	9:24	20:07	9:42	19:50	10:06	19:25	10:46	18:46
Saturn, 1985											
Jan	5	3:01	14:10	3:17	13:55	3:35	13:36	4:02	13:10	4:44	12:27
	15	2:26	13:34	2:41	13:19	3:00	12:59	3:27	12:33	4:10	11:50
	25	1:50	12:57	2:05	12:42	2:24	12:22	2:51	11:56	3:35	11:12
Feb	4	1:13	12:20	1:28	12:05	1:48	11:45	2:15	11:18	2:59	10:34
	14	0:35	11:42	0:51	11:27	1:11	11:07	1:38	10:40	2:22	9:56
	24	23:57	11:04	0:13	10:48	0:32	10:29	0:59	10:02	1:44	9:17

		20° N. Latitude		30° N. Latitude		40° N. Latitude		50° N. Latitude		60° N. Latitude	
		Rise	Set	Rise	Set	Rise	Set	Rise	Set	Rise	Set
Mar	6	23:18	10:25	23:34	10:10	23:54	9:50	0:21	9:23	1:05	8:38
	16	22:39	9:46	22:54	9:30	23:14	9:11	23:41	8:44	0:25	7:59
	26	21:58	9:06	22:14	8:50	22:33	8:31	23:00	8:04	23:44	7:20
Apr	5	21:17	8:25	21:32	8:09	21:52	7:50	22:18	7:23	23:02	6:40
	15	20:35	7:43	20:51	7:28	21:10	7:09	21:36	6:43	22:19	5:59
	25	19:53	7:02	20:08	6:47	20:27	6:28	20:53	6:01	21:36	5:19
May	5	19:11	6:20	19:26	6:05	19:44	5:46	20:10	5:20	20:52	4:38
	15	18:28	5:38	18:43	5:23	19:01	5:04	19:27	4:39	20:08	3:57
	25	17:45	4:55	18:00	4:41	18:18	4:22	18:43	3:57	19:24	3:16
June	4	17:03	4:13	17:17	3:59	17:35	3:41	18:00	3:16	18:41	2:35
	14	16:20	3:31	16:35	3:17	16:53	2:59	17:17	2:34	17:57	1:54
	24	15:38	2:50	15:53	2:36	16:11	2:18	16:35	1:53	17:15	1:14
July	4	14:57	2:09	15:12	1:55	15:29	1:37	15:54	1:13	16:33	0:33
	14	14:17	1:28	14:31	1:14	14:49	0:57	15:13	0:32	15:52	23:53
	24	13:37	0:49	13:51	0:34	14:09	0:17	14:33	23:52	15:13	23:13
Aug	3	12:58	0:09	13:12	23:55	13:30	23:37	13:54	23:13	14:34	22:33
	13	12:19	23:30	12:34	23:16	12:51	22:58	13:16	22:34	13:56	21:54
	23	11:41	22:52	11:56	22:38	12:14	22:20	12:39	21:55	13:19	21:14
Sept	2	11:04	22:15	11:19	22:00	11:37	21:42	12:03	21:17	12:43	20:36
	12	10:28	21:38	10:43	21:23	11:01	21:04	11:27	20:39	12:08	19:57
	22	9:52	21:01	10:07	20:46	10:26	20:27	10:51	20:01	11:34	19:18
Oct	2	9:16	20:24	9:32	20:09	9:51	19:50	10:17	19:24	11:00	18:40
	12	8:41	19:49	8:57	19:33	9:16	19:14	9:43	18:47	10:27	18:03
	22	8:06	19:13	8:22	18:57	8:42	18:37	9:09	18:10	9:54	17:25
Nov	1	7:32	18:38	7:48	18:22	8:08	18:02	8:36	17:34	9:22	16:48
	11	6:58	18:03	7:14	17:46	7:35	17:26	8:03	16:58	8:50	16:11
	21	6:24	17:28	6:40	17:11	7:01	16:50	7:30	16:21	8:18	15:34
Dec	1	5:50	16:53	6:06	16:36	6:27	16:15	6:57	15:46	7:45	14:57
	11	5:15	16:18	5:32	16:01	5:54	15:39	6:24	15:10	7:13	14:20
	21	4:41	15:43	4:58	15:26	5:20	15:04	5:50	14:34	6:40	13:43
	31	4:07	15:08	4:24	14:50	4:46	14:28	5:16	13:58	6:07	13:07

Moonset Tonight

The idea of estimating the time of moonset tonight may have scared you off in the past because you assumed that it involved a difficult and mysterious series of calculations. The actual process is quite easy to do, however, especially with the little pocket calculators that seem ubiquitous today. The first major step involves finding three numbers for your city obtained from the latitude and longitude figures listed on page 734 to 735. If your city is not here, find the information from a map, atlas or other source. These answers are permanent and never need to be determined for that city again. You can write these numbers down and use them every year you stay in that city. The second step involves taking the correct four figures from the tables of moonrise and moonset for the date you want. The third major step involves adjusting this answer to standard time.

Let us determine the time of moonset on May 4 at Paducah, Kentucky.

First we must find the 3 numbers for Paducah:

I. Latitude: 37° 05′ 13″ N; Longitude: 88° 35′ 56″ W.
A. Convert the Lat. and Long. to decimal numbers:
13″ ÷ 60 = 0.′22
5′ + 0.′22 = 5.′22
5.′22 ÷ 60 = 0.°09
37° + 0.°09 = 37.°09
56″ ÷ 60 = 0.′93
35′ + 0.′93 = 35.′93
35.′93 ÷ 60 = 0.°60
88° + 0.°60 = 88.°60
B. Fraction between 40° and 30° that Paducah's latitude lies:
40° − 30° = 10°
37.09° − 30° = 7.09°
7.09 ÷ 10 = 0.709
C. Fraction of earth that Paducah lies west of Greenwich:
88.°60 ÷ 360 = 0.246
D. Local to standard time correction:
(Standard time meridian for Paducah (EST): 90°)
90° − 88.°60 = 1.°4 west (or later than at 90°)
@ 4 minutes of time per degree of longitude difference:
4 × 1.4 = 5.6 minutes (round to 6).
E. These 3 numbers are permanent for Paducah, Ky.
II. Find time of moonset at GMT meridian for Paducah's latitude:
A. From the calendar page 740 for May:

	30°	40°
May 4	18:32	18:50
May 5	19:45	20:10

B. What we want lies 0.709 (answer IB) times the difference between the values at 30 and 40, added to 30.
For the 4th:
18:50 − 18:32 = :18
18 × 0.709 = 12.8 (call it 13 minutes)
18:32 + :13 = 18:45 on the 4th.
For the 5th:
20:10 − 19:45 = :25
25 × 0.709 = 17.7 (call it 18 minutes)
19.45 + 18 = 20:03 on the 5th.
Thus for Paducah's latitude of 37.°09:
May 4   18:45
May 5   20:03
C. How much time elapsed between the two moonsets at Greenwich?
20:03 − 18:45 = 78 minutes
D. How much of this interval was used before the moon set in Paducah? (Use answer from IC.)
78 × .246 = 19 minutes
18:45 + :19 = 19:04, local time at Paducah.
III. What was the standard time? (Since the moonset happened at Paducah after it happened at 90° meridian, it is later, thus the correction from ID is added.)
19:04 + :06 = 18:58, or 6:58 p.m., EST.

Astronomical Constants; Speed of Light

The following astronomical constants were adopted in 1968, in accordance with the resolutions and recommendations of the International Astronomical Union (Hamburg 1964): Velocity of light, 299,792.5 kilometers per second, or about 186,282.3976 statute miles per second: solar parallax, 8″.794: constant of nutation, 9″.210; and constant of aberration, 20″.496.

Star Tables

These tables include stars of visual magnitude 2.5 and brighter. Co-ordinates are for mid-1985. Where no parallax figures are given, the trigonometric parallax figure is smaller than the margin for error and the distance given is obtained by indirect methods. Stars of variable magnitude designated by v.

To find the time when the star is on meridian, subtract R.A.M.S. of the sun table on page 723 from the star's right ascension, first adding 24h to the latter, if necessary. Mark this result P.M., if less than 12h; but if greater than 12, subtract 12h and mark the remainder A.M.

Star	Magnitude	Parallax "	Light yrs.	Right ascen. h. m.	Declination ° '
α Andromedae (Alpheratz)	2.06	0.02	90	0 07.6	+29 01
β Cassiopeiae	2.26v	0.07	45	0 08.4	+59 04
α Phoenicis	2.39	0.04	93	0 25.6	−42 23
α Cassiopeiae (Schedir)	2.22	0.01	150	0 39.7	+56 27
β Ceti	2.02	0.06	57	0 42.9	−18 04
γ Cassiopeiae	2.13v	0.03	96	0 55.8	+60 38
β Andromedae	2.02	0.04	76	1 08.9	+35 33
α Eridani (Achernar)	0.51	0.02	118	1 37.2	−57 19
γ Andromedae	2.14		260	2 03.0	+42 16
α Arietis	2.00	0.04	76	2 06.4	+23 24
α Ursae Min. (Pole Star)	1.99v		680	2 16.9	+89 12
o Ceti	2.00v	0.01	103	2 18.6	−3 03
β Persei (Algol)	2.06v	0.03	105	3 07.2	+40 54
α Persei	1.80	0.03	570	3 23.3	+49 49
α Tauri (Aldebaran)	0.86v	0.05	68	4 35.1	+16 29
β Orionis (Rigel)	0.14v		900	5 13.8	−8 13
α Aurigae (Capella)	0.05	0.07	45	5 15.6	+45 59
γ Orionis (Bellatrix)	1.64	0.03	470	5 24.4	+6 20
β Tauri (El Nath)	1.65v	0.02	300	5 25.4	+28 36
δ Orionis	2.20v		1500	5 31.3	−0 18
ε Orionis	1.70		1600	5 35.5	−1 13
ζ Orionis	1.79	0.02	1600	5 40.0	−1 57
κ Orionis	2.06	0.01	2100	5 47.1	−9 40
α Orionis (Betelgeuse)	0.41v		520	5 54.4	+7 24
β Aurigae	1.86	0.04	88	5 58.5	+44 57
β Canis Majoris	1.96	0.01	750	6 22.1	−17 57
α Carinae (Canopus)	−0.72	0.02	98	6 23.6	−52 41
γ Geminorum	1.93	0.03	105	6 36.9	+16 25
α Canis Majoris (Sirius)	−1.47	0.38	8.7	6 44.5	−16 42
ε Canis Majoris	1.48		680	6 58.1	−28 57
δ Canis Majoris	1.85		2100	7 07.8	−26 22
η Canis Majoris	2.46		2700	7 23.5	−29 16
α Geminorum (Castor)	1.97	0.07	45	7 33.7	+31 55
α Canis Minoris (Procyon)	0.37	0.29	11.3	7 38.5	+5 16
β Geminorum (Pollux)	1.16	0.09	35	7 44.4	+28 04
ζ Puppis	2.23		2400	8 03.1	−39 58
γ Velorum	1.88		520	8 09.1	−47 18
ε Carinae	1.90		340	8 22.2	−59 28
δ Velorum	1.95	0.04	76	8 44.3	−54 39
λ Velorum	2.24	0.02	750	9 07.5	−43 22
β Carinae	1.67	0.04	86	9 13.0	−69 39
ι Carinae	2.25		750	9 16.7	−59 13
κ Velorum	2.49	0.01	470	9 21.7	−54 57
α Hydrae	1.98	0.02	94	9 26.9	−8 36
α Leonis (Regulus)	1.36	0.04	84	10 07.6	+12 02
γ Leonis	1.99	0.02	90	10 19.2	+19 55
β Ursae Majoris (Merak)	2.37	0.04	78	11 01.0	+56 28
α Ursae Majoris (Dubhe)	1.81	0.03	105	11 02.8	+61 50
β Leonis (Denebola)	2.14	0.08	43	11 48.3	+14 40
γ Ursae Majoris (Phecda)	2.44	0.02	90	11 53.1	+53 47
α Crucis	1.39		370	12 25.6	−63 01
γ Crucis	1.69		220	12 30.4	−57 02
γ Centauri	2.17		160	12 40.7	−48 53
β Crucis	1.28v		490	12 46.8	−59 37
ε Ursae Majoris (Alioth)	1.79v	0.01	68	12 53.4	+56 02
ζ Ursae Majoris (Mizar)	2.26	0.04	88	13 23.3	+55 00
α Virginis (Spica)	0.91v	0.02	220	13 24.4	−11 05
ε Centauri	2.33v		570	13 39.0	−53 24
η Ursae Majoris (Alkaid)	1.87		210	13 47.0	+49 23
β Centauri	0.63v	0.02	490	14 02.8	−60 18
θ Centauri	2.04	0.06	55	14 05.8	−36 18
α Boötis (Arcturus)	−0.06	0.09	36	14 15.0	+19 15
η Centauri	2.39v		390	14 34.6	−42 06
α Centauri	0.01	0.75	4.3	14 38.6	−60 47
α Lupi	2.32v		430	14 41.0	−47 20
ε Boötis	2.37	0.01	103	14 44.4	+27 08
β Ursae Minoris	2.07	0.03	105	14 50.7	+74 13
α Coronae Borealis	2.23v	0.04	76	15 34.1	+26 46
δ Scorpii	2.34		590	15 59.5	−22 35
α Scorpii (Antares)	0.92v	0.02	520	16 28.5	−26 25
α Trianguli Australis	1.93	0.02	82	16 47.1	−69 00
ε Scorpii	2.28	0.05	66	16 49.2	−34 16
η Ophiuchi	2.43	0.05	69	17 09.5	−15 42
λ Scorpii	1.60v		310	17 32.6	−37 06
α Ophiuchi	2.09	0.06	58	17 34.3	+12 34
θ Scorpii	1.86	0.02	650	17 36.3	−42 59
κ Scorpii	2.39v		470	17 41.5	−39 01
γ Draconis	2.21	0.02	108	17 56.3	+51 29
ε Sagittarii	1.81	0.02	124	18 23.2	−34 24
α Lyrae (Vega)	0.04	0.12	26.5	18 36.4	+38 46
σ Sagittarii	2.12		300	18 54.4	−26 19
α Aquilae (Altair)	0.77	0.20	16.5	19 50.1	+8 50
γ Cygni	2.22		750	20 21.7	+40 13
α Pavonis	1.95		310	20 24.5	−56 47
α Cygni (Deneb)	1.26		1600	20 40.9	+45 14
ε Cygni	2.46	0.04	74	20 45.6	+33 55
α Cephei	2.44	0.06	52	21 18.2	+62 31
ε Pegasi	2.38		780	21 43.5	+9 48
α Gruis	1.76	0.05	64	22 07.3	−47 02
β Gruis	2.17v		280	22 41.8	−46 58
α Piscis Austrinis (Fomalhaut)	1.15	0.14	22.6	22 56.9	−29 42
β Pegasi	2.50v	0.02	210	23 03.1	+28 00
α Pegasi	2.50	0.03	109	23 04.0	+15 08

Aurora Borealis and Aurora Australis

The Aurora Borealis, also called the Northern Lights, is a broad display of rather faint light in the northern skies at night. The Aurora Australis, a similar phenomenon, appears at the same time in southern skies. The aurora appears in a wide variety of forms. Sometimes it is seen as a quiet glow, almost foglike in character; sometimes as vertical streamers in which there may be considerable motion; sometimes as a series of luminous expanding arcs. There are many colors, with white, yellow, and red predominating.

The auroras are most vivid and most frequently seen at about 20 degrees from the magnetic poles, along the northern coast of the North American continent and the eastern part of the northern coast of Europe. They have been seen as far south as Key West and as far north as Australia and New Zealand, but rarely.

While the cause of the auroras is not known beyond question, there does seem to be a definite correlation between auroral displays and sun-spot activity. It is thought that atomic particles ex-

pelled from the sun by the forces that cause solar flares speed through space at velocities of 400 to 600 miles per second. These particles are entrapped by the earth's magnetic field, forming what are termed the Van Allen belts. The encounter of these clouds of the solar wind with the earth's magnetic field weakens the field so that previously trapped particles are allowed to impact the upper atmosphere. The collisions between solar and terrestrial atoms result in the glow in the upper atmosphere called the aurora. The glow may be vivid where the lines of magnetic force converge near the magnetic poles.

The auroral displays appear at heights ranging from 50 to about 600 miles and have given us a means of estimating the extent of the earth's atmosphere.

The auroras are often accompanied by magnetic storms whose forces, also guided by the lines of force of the earth's magnetic field, disrupt electrical communication.

The Planets and the Solar System

Planet	Mean daily motion	Orbital velocity miles per sec.	Sidereal revolution days	Synodical revolution days	Dist. from sun in millions of mi. Max.	Min.	Dist. from Earth in millions of mi. Max.	Min.	Light at[1] peri- helion	aphe- lion
Mercury ..	14732	29.75	88.0	115.9	43.4	28.6	136	50	10.58	4.59
Venus ...	5768	21.76	224.7	583.9	67.7	66.8	161	25	1.94	1.89
Earth...	3548	18.51	365.3	—	94.6	91.4	—	—	1.03	0.97
Mars....	1887	14.99	687.0	779.9	155.0	128.5	248	35	0.524	0.360
Jupiter ..	299	8.12	4332.1	398.9	507.0	460.6	600	368	0.0408	0.0336
Saturn ...	120	5.99	10825.9	378.1	937.5	838.4	1031	745	0.01230	0.00984
Uranus ..	42	4.23	30676.1	369.7	1859.7	1669.3	1953	1606	0.00300	0.00250
Neptune ..	21	3.38	59911.1	367.5	2821.7	2760.4	2915	2667	0.00114	0.00109
Pluto	14	2.95	90824.2	366.7	4551.4	2756.4	4644	2663	0.00114	0.00042

1. Light at perihelion and aphelion is solar illumination in units of mean illumination at Earth.

Planet	Mean longitude of:[*] ascending node	perihelion	Inclination[*] of orbit to ecliptic	Mean[*] distance[**]	Eccentricity[*] of orbit	Mean longitude at the epoch[*]
Mercury....	48 09 04	77 13 19	7 00 17	0.387098	0.205636	242 06 54
Venus.....	76 32 42	131 29 24	3 23 40	0.723330	0.006759	298 45 24
Earth	— — —	102 42 22	— — —	0.999994	0.016755	35 32 32
Mars	49 26 35	335 43 16	1 50 59	1.523712	0.093348	329 44 05
Jupiter ...	100 20 20	15 23 56	1 18 19	5.20270	0.048061	293 28 58
Saturn....	113 32 20	93 29 13	2 29 08	9.57542	0.050822	224 21 44
Uranus ...	73 59 17	177 07 23	0 46 27	19.2998	0.047552	248 05 03
Neptune ...	131 37 34	354 40 12	1 46 15	30.2813	0.006608	271 32 56
Pluto	110 12 58	224 15 00	17 07 56	39.7138	0.253364	216 55 28

*Consistent for the standard Epoch: 1984 Oct. 27.0 Ephemeris Time **Astronomical units

Sun and planets	Semi-diameter at unit dis- tance	at mean least dist.	in miles mean s.d.	Volume ⊕=1.	Mass. ⊕=1.	Den- sity ⊕=1.	Sidereal period of rotation d. h. m. s.				Gravi- ty at sur- face ⊕=1.	Re- flect- ing power Pct.	Prob- able tem- per- ature °F.
Sun......	959.62	___	432560	1303730	332830	0.26	24	16	48		27.9		+ 10,000
Mercury ...	3.37	5.5	1515	0.0559	0.0553	0.99	58	21	58		0.37	0.06	+ 620
Venus	8.34	30.1	3760	0.8541	0.8150	0.95	243	R			0.88	0.72	+ 900
Earth			3963	1.000	1.000	1.00		23	56	4.1	1.00	0.39	+ 72
Moon	2.40	932.4	1080	0.020	0.0123	0.62	27	7	43		0.17	0.07	— 10
Mars	4.69	8.95	2108.4	0.1506	0.1074	0.71		24	37	23	0.38	0.16	— 10
Jupiter ...	98.35	23.4	44362	1403	317.83	0.23		9	3	30	2.64	0.70	— 240
Saturn	82.83	9.7	37280	832	95.16	0.11		10	30		1.15	0.75	— 300
Uranus ...	35.4	1.9	15800	63	14.50	0.23		15	36	R	1.15	0.90	— 340
Neptune ...	33.4	1.2	15100	55	17.20	0.31		18	26		1.12	0.82	— 370
Pluto*....	1.9	0.05	930	0.01	0.0025	0.25	6	9	17		0.04	0.14	?	?

*Much of this information is too new to be verified, but observers at the U.S. Naval Observatory have derived values similar to these after having discovered that Pluto has a satellite. It apparently revolves about Pluto in a period equal to Pluto's rotation period. (R) retrograde of Venus and Uranus.

Eclipses, 1985

(E.S.T.)

There are four eclipses, two of the sun and two of the moon.

1. *Total eclipse of the moon.* May 4: the beginning of the umbral phase in Antarctica. eastern Europe. Africa except the western part. Asia. the U.S.S.R. except the extreme northeastern part. Australia, New Zealand, and the Indian Ocean; the end visible in eastern South America, Europe, Asia except the eastern part. western Australia, Antarctica. the South Atlantic Ocean. the Indian Ocean. and western U.S.S.R.

		EST EST d h		m +5ᵇ	GMT
Moon enters penumbra	May	4 12	19.8	17ᵇ	
Moon enters umbra		4 13	16.6	18	
Total eclipse begins		4 14	22.1	19	
Middle of the eclipse		4 14	56.4	19	
Total eclipse ends		4 15	30.7	20	
Moon leaves umbra		4 16	36.2	21	
Moon leaves penumbra		4 17	33.0	22	

Magnitude of the eclipse 1.243

2. *Partial eclipse of the sun.* May 19: visible only in the Arctic regions.

		d h	m	GMT
Eclipse begins	May	19 14	14.8	19ᵇ
Greatest eclipse		19 16	28.7	21
Eclipse ends		19 18	42.3	23

Magnitude of greatest eclipse 0.841

3. *Total eclipse of the moon.* October 28: the beginning of the umbral phase visible in eastern Europe. Asia. the U.S.S.R.. Alaska. the Arctic regions. Arctic Ocean. northern Greenland. and Wilkes Land part of Antarctica: the end visible in Greenland. Iceland. Europe. Africa. Asia. the U.S.S.R.. Australia. the Arctic regions. the Indian Ocean. and Antarctica between Queen Maud Land and Wilkes Land.

		d	h	m	GMT
Moon enters penumbra	Oct.	28	09	38.0	14ᵇ
Moon enters umbra		28	10	54.6	15
Total eclipse begins		28	12	19.8	17
Middle of the eclipse		28	12	42.4	17
Total eclipse ends		28	13	05.0	18
Moon leaves umbra		28	14	30.2	19
Moon leaves penumbra		28	15	46.7	20

Magnitude of the eclipse 1.078

4. *Total eclipse of the sun:* November 12: visible in and near Antarctica; totality. less than 2 minutes.

		d	h	m	GMT
Eclipse begins	Nov.	12	07	08.7	12ᵇ
Central eclipse begins		12	08	50.9	13
Cent ecl. at local app. noon		12	09	10.5	14
Central eclipse ends		12	09	29.7	14
Eclipse ends		12	11	12.1	16

Largest Telescopes Are in Northern Hemisphere

Most of the world's major astronomical installations are in the northern hemisphere, while many of astronomy's major problems are found in the southern sky. This imbalance has long been recognized and is being remedied.

In the northern hemisphere the largest reflector is the 236-inch mirror at the Special Astrophysical Observatory in the Caucasus in the Soviet Union. The largest reflectors in the U.S. include 3 in California: at Palomar Mtn., 200 inches; at Lick Observatory, Mt. Hamilton, 120 inches; and at Mt. Wilson Observatory, 100 inches. Also in the U.S. are a 158 inch reflector at Kitt Peak, Arizona, dedicated in June 1973, and a 107-inch telescope at the McDonald Observatory on Mt. Locke in Texas. A telescope at the Crimean Astrophysical Observatory in the Soviet Union has a 104-inch mirror.

Placed in service in 1975 were three large reflectors for the southern hemisphere. Associated Universities for Research in Astronomy (AURA), the operating organization of Kitt Peak National Observatory, dedicated the 158-inch reflector (twin of the telescope on Kitt Peak) at Cerro Tololo International Observatory, Chile; the European Southern Observatory has a 141-inch reflector at La Silla, Chile; and the Anglo-Australian telescope, 152 inches in diameter, is at Siding Spring Observatory in Australia.

Optical Telescopes

Optical astronomical telescopes are of two kinds, refracting and reflecting. In the first, light passes through a lens which brings the light rays into focus, where the image may be examined after being magnified by a second lens, the eyepiece, or directly photographed.

The reflector consists of a concave parabolic mirror, generally of Pyrex or now of a relatively heat insensitive material, cervit, coated with silver or aluminum, which reflects the light rays back toward the upper end of the telescope, where they are either magnified and observed by the eyepiece or, as in the case of the refractors, photographed. In most reflecting telescopes, the light is reflected again by a secondary mirror and comes to a focus after passing through a hole in the side of the telescope, where the eye-piece or camera is located, or after passing through a hole in the center of the primary mirror.

World's Largest Refractors

Location and diameter in inches

Yerkes Obs., Williams Bay, Wis.	40
Lick Obs., Mt. Hamilton, Cal.	36
Astrophys. Obs., Potsdam, E. Germany	32
Paris Observatory, Meudon, France	32
Allegheny Obs., Pittsburgh, Pa.	30
Univ. of Paris, Nice, France	30
Royal Greenwich Obs., Herstmonceux, England	28

Union Obs., Johannesburg, South Africa	26.5
Universitats-Sternwarte, Vienna, Austria	26.5
Leander McCormick Obs., Univ. of Virginia, Charlottesville, Va.	26
Obs., Academy of Sciences, Pulkova, USSR	26
Astronomical Obs., Belgrade, Yugoslavia	26
Obs. Mitaka, Tokyo-to, Japan	26
US Naval Obs., Washington, D.C.	26
Mt. Stromlo Obs., Canberra, Australia	26

World's Largest Reflectors

Special Astrophysical Obs., Zelenchukskaya, USSR	236
Palomar Obs., Palomar Mtn., Cal.	200
Whipple Obs. (SAO), Mt. Hopkins, Ariz.	176*, 60
Kitt Peak National Obs., Tucson, Ariz.	158, 84, 60
Cerro Tololo, Chile	158, 60
Siding Spring, Australia	153
Mauna Kea Obs., Univ. of Hawaii, Ha.	150, 142, 120, 88
La Silla, Chile	141, 60
Lick Obs., Mt. Hamilton, Cal.	120
McDonald Obs., Fort Davis, Tex.	107, 82
Crimean Astrophys. Obs., Nauchny, USSR	104
Byurakan Obs., Armenia S.S.R.	102
Mt. Wilson Obs., Pasadena, Cal.	100, 60
Royal Greenwich Obs., Herstmonceux, England	98
Steward Obs., Tucson, Ariz.	90
Shemakha Astroph. Obs., Azerbaijan S.S.R.	79
Saint Michel l'Observatoire, Haute Provence, France	76, 60, 47
Tokyo Obs., Japan	74
Mt. Stromlo, Australia	74
David Dunlap Obs., Ont., Canada	74
Helwan Obs., Helwan, Egypt	74
Astrophys. Obs., Kamogata, Okayama-ken, Japan	74
Sutherland, South Africa	74
Dominion Astrophys. Obs., Victoria, B.C.	73
Perkins Obs., Flagstaff, Ariz.	72
Obs., Padua Univ., Asiago, Italy	72
Agassiz Station Harvard Obs., Cambridge, Mass.	61
National Obs., Bosque Alegre Sta., Argentina	61
U.S. Naval Obs., Flagstaff, Ariz.	61
Catalina Mtn., Ariz.	61
Arizona Univ. Obs., Tucson, Ariz.	60
Boyden Obs., Bloemfontein, South Africa	60
Mt. Haleakala, Ha.	60
Figl Astroph. Obs., Vienna, Austria	60

*Multiple mirror telescope, equivalent aperture.

Major U.S. Planetariums

Academy Planetarium, U.S. Air Force Academy
Adler Planetarium, Chicago, Ill.
American Museum-Hayden Planetarium, N.Y.C.
Buhl Planetarium, Pittsburgh, Pa.
Charles Hayden Planetarium, Boston, Mass.
Einstein Spacearium, Washington, D.C.
Fels Planetarium, Philadelphia, Pa.
Fernbank Science Center Planetarium, Altanta, Ga.

Griffith Planetarium, Los Angeles, Cal.
La. Arts and Science Planetarium, Baton Rouge, La.
McDonnell Planetarium, St. Louis, Mo.
Morehead Planetarium, Chapel Hill, N.C.
Morrison Planetarium, San Francisco, Cal.
Robert T. Longway Planetarium, Flint, Mich.
Strassenburgh Planetarium, Rochester, N.Y.

The Sun

The sun. the controlling body of our solar system. is a star whose dimensions cause it to be classified among stars as average in size. temperature. and brightness. Its proximity to the earth makes it appear to us as tremendously large and bright. A series of thermo-nuclear reactions involving the atoms of the elements of which it is composed produces the heat and light that make life possible on earth.

The sun has a diameter of 864.000 miles and is distant. on the average. 92.900.000 miles from the earth. It is 1.41 times as dense as water. The light of the sun reaches the earth in 499.012 seconds or slightly more than 8 minutes. The average solar surface temperature has been measured by several indirect methods which agree closely on a value of 6.000° Kelvin or about 10.000° F. The interior temperature of the sun is about 35.000.000 F.°.

When sunlight is analyzed with a spectroscope, it is found to consist of a continuous spectrum composed of all the colors of the rainbow in order, crossed by many dark lines. The "absorption lines" are produced by gaseous materials in the atmosphere of the sun. More than 60 of the natural terrestrial elements have been identified in the sun. all in gaseous form because of the intense heat of the sun.

Spheres and Corona

The radiating surface of the sun is called the **photosphere**, and just above it is the **chromosphere.** The chromosphere is visible to the naked eye only at times of total solar eclipses. appearing then to be a pinkish-violet layer with occasional great prominences projecting above its general level. With proper instruments the chromosphere can be seen or photographed whenever the sun is visible without waiting for a total eclipse. Above the chromosphere is the **corona,** also visible to the naked eye only at times of total eclipse. Instruments also permit the brighter portions of the corona to be studied whenever conditions are favorable. The pearly light of the corona surges millions of miles from the sun. Iron, nickel. and calcium are believed to be principal contributors to the composition of the corona. all in a state of extreme attenuation and high ionization that indicates temperatures on the order of a million degrees Fahrenheit.

Sunspots

There is an intimate connection between sunspots and the corona. At times of low sunspot activity. the fine streamers of the corona will be much longer above the sun's equator than over the polar regions of the sun. while during high sunspot activity. the corona extends fairly evenly outward from all regions of the sun. but to a much greater distance in space. Sunspots are dark. irregularly-shaped regions whose diameters may reach tens of thousands of miles. The average life of a sunspot group is from two to three weeks. but there have been groups that have lasted for more than a year. being carried repeatedly around as the sun rotated upon its axis. The record for the duration of a sunspot is 18 months. Sunspots reach a low point every 11.3 years. with a peak of activity occurring irregularly between two successive minima.

The sun is 400.000 times as bright as the full moon and gives the earth 6 million times as much light as do all the other stars put together. Actually, most of the stars that can be easily seen on any clear night are brighter than the sun.

The Zodiac

The sun's apparent yearly path among the stars is known as the **ecliptic.** The zone 16° wide. 8° on each side of the ecliptic. is known as the **zodiac.** Inside of this zone are the apparent paths of the sun. moon. earth. and major planets. Beginning at the point on the ecliptic which marks the position of the sun at the vernal equinox. and thence proceeding eastward. the zodiac is divided into twelve signs of 30° each. as shown herewith.

These signs are named from the twelve constellations of the zodiac with which the signs coincided in the time of the astronomer Hipparchus. about 2,000 years ago. Owing to the precession of the equinoxes. that is to say, to the retrograde motion of the equinoxes along the ecliptic. each sign in the zodiac has. in the course of 2,000 years. moved backward 30° into the constellation west of it; so that the sign Aries is now in the constellation Pisces. and so on. The vernal equinox will move from Pisces into Aquarius about the middle of the 26th century. The signs of the zodiac with their Latin and English names are as follows:

Spring	1.	♈ Aries.	The Ram.
	2.	♉ Taurus.	The Bull.
	3.	♊ Gemini.	The Twins.
Summer	4.	♋ Cancer.	The Crab.
	5.	♌ Leo.	The Lion.
	6.	♍ Virgo.	The Virgin.
Autumn	7.	♎ Libra.	The Balance.
	8.	♏ Scorpio.	The Scorpion.
	9.	♐ Sagittarius.	The Archer.
Winter	10.	♑ Capricorn.	The Goat.
	11.	♒ Aquarius.	The Water Bearer.
	12.	♓ Pisces.	The Fishes.

Moon's Perigee and Apogee, 1985

Perigee						Apogee					
Day	GMT	EST	Day	GMT	EST	Day	GMT	EST	Day	GMT	EST
Jan 12 . . .	03	22*	July 25 . . .	18	13	Jan 27 . . .	10	05	July 11 . . .	08	03
Feb 8 . . .	04	23*	Aug 20 . . .	04	23*	Feb 24 . . .	04	23*	Aug 8 . . .	02	21*
Mar 8 . . .	08	03	Sep 16 . . .	19	14	Mar 23 . . .	15	10	Sep 4 . . .	21	16
Apr 5	18	13	Oct 15 . . .	01	20*	Apr 19 . . .	17	12	Oct 29 . . .	22	17
May 4	05	00	Nov 12 . . .	13	08	May 17 . . .	00	19*	Nov 25 . . .	22	17
June 1 . . .	13	08	Dec 11 . . .	01	20*	June 13 . . .	14	09	Dec 23 . . .	07	02
June 29 . . .	09	04									

*Previous day

The Moon

The moon completes a circuit around the earth in a period whose mean or average duration is 27 days 7 hours 43.2 minutes. This is the moon's sidereal period. Because of the motion of the moon in common with the earth around the sun, the mean duration of the lunar month — the period from one new moon to the next new moon — is 29 days 12 hours 44.05 minutes. This is the moon's synodical period.

The mean distance of the moon from the earth according to the American Ephemeris is 238,857 miles. Because the orbit of the moon about the earth is not circular but elliptical, however, the maximum distance from the earth that the moon may reach is 252,710 miles and the least distance is 221,463 miles. All distances are from the center of one object to the center of the other.

The moon's diameter is 2,160 miles. If we deduct the radius of the moon, 1,080 miles, and the radius of the earth, 3,963 miles from the minimum distance or perigee, given above, we shall have for the nearest approach of the bodies' surfaces 216,420 miles.

The moon rotates on its axis in a period of time exactly equal to its sidereal revolution about the earth — 27.321666 days. The moon's revolution about the earth is irregular because of its elliptical orbit. The moon's rotation, however, is regular and this, together with the irregular revolution, produces what is called "libration in longitude" which permits us to see first farther around the east side and then farther around the west side of the moon. The moon's variation north or south of the ecliptic permits us to see farther over first one pole and then the other of the moon and this is "libration in latitude." These two libration effects permit us to see a total of about 60% of the moon's surface over a period of time. The hidden side of the moon was photographed in 1959 by the Soviet space vehicle Lunik III. Since then many excellent pictures of nearly all of the moon's surface have been transmitted to earth by Lunar Orbiters launched by the U.S.

The tides are caused mainly by the moon, because of its proximity to the earth. The ratio of the tide-raising power of the moon to that of the sun is 11 to 5.

Harvest Moon and Hunter's Moon

The Harvest Moon, the full moon nearest the Autumnal Equinox, ushers in a period of several successive days when the moon rises soon after sunset. This phenomenon gives farmers in temperate latitudes extra hours of light in which to harvest their crops before frost and winter come. The 1985 Harvest Moon falls on Sept. 29 GMT. Harvest moon in the south temperate latitudes falls on Apr. 5.

The next full moon after Harvest Moon is called the Hunter's Moon, accompanied by a similar phenomenon but less marked; — Oct. 28, northern hemisphere; May 4, southern hemisphere.

The Earth: Size, Computation of Time, Seasons

Size and Dimensions

The earth is the fifth largest planet and the third from the sun. Its mass is 6 sextillion, 588 quintillion short tons. Using the parameters of an ellipsoid adopted by the International Astronomical Union in 1964 and recognized by the International Union of Geodesy and Geophysics in 1967, the length of the equator is 24,901.55 miles, the length of a meridian is 24,859.82 miles, the equatorial diameter is 7,926.41 miles, and the area of this reference ellipsoid is approximately 196,938,800 square miles.

The earth is considered a solid, rigid mass with a dense core of magnetic, probably metallic material. The outer part of the core is probably liquid. Around the core is a thick shell or mantle of heavy crystalline rock which in turn is covered by a thin crust forming the solid granite and basalt base of the continents and ocean basins. Over broad areas of the earth's surface the crust has a thin cover of sedimentary rock such as sandstone, shale, and limestone formed by weathering of the earth's surface and deposition of sands, clays, and plant and animal remains.

The temperature in the earth increases about 1°F. with every 100 to 200 feet in depth, in the upper 100 kilometers of the earth, and the temperature near the core is believed to be near the melting point of the core materials under the conditions at that depth. The heat of the earth is believed to be derived from radioactivity in the rocks, pressures developed within the earth, and original heat (if the earth in fact was formed at high temperatures).

Atmosphere of the Earth

The earth's atmosphere is a blanket composed of nitrogen, oxygen, and argon, in amounts of about 78, 21, and 1% by volume. Also present in minute quantities are carbon dioxide, hydrogen, neon, helium, krypton, and xenon.

Water vapor displaces other gases and varies from nearly zero to about 4% by volume. The height of the ozone layer varies from approximately 12 to 21 miles above the earth. Traces exist as low as 6 miles and as high as 35 miles. Traces of methane have been found.

The atmosphere rests on the earth's surface with the weight equivalent to a layer of water 34 ft. deep. For about 300,000 ft. upward the gases remain in the proportions stated. Gravity holds the gases to the earth. The weight of the air compresses it at the bottom, so that the greatest density is at the earth's surface. Pressure, as well as density, decreases as height increases because the weight pressing upon any layer is always less than that pressing upon the layers below.

The temperature of the air drops with increased height until the **tropopause** is reached. This may vary from 25,000 to 60,000 ft. The atmosphere below the tropopause is the **troposphere**; the atmosphere for about twenty miles above the tropopause is the **stratosphere**, where the temperature generally increases with height except at high latitudes in winter. A temperature maximum near the 30-mile level is called the **stratopause**. Above this boundary is the **mesosphere** where the temperature decreases with height to a minimum, the **mesopause**, at a height of 50 miles. Extending above the mesosphere to the outer fringes of the atmosphere is the **thermosphere**, a region where temperature increases with height to a value measured in thousands of degrees Fahrenheit. The lower portion of this region, extending from 50 to about 400 miles in altitude, is characterized by a high ion density, and is thus called the **ionosphere**. The outer region is called **exosphere**; this is the region where gas molecules traveling at high speed may escape into outer space, above 600 miles.

Latitude, Longitude

Position on the globe is measured by means of meridians and parallels. Meridians, which are imaginary lines drawn around the earth through the poles, determine **longitude**. The meridian running through Greenwich, England, is the **prime meridian of longitude**, and all others are either east or west. Parallels, which are imaginary circles parallel with the equator, determine **latitude**. The length of a degree of longitude varies as the cosine of the latitude. At the equator a degree is 69.171 statute miles; this is gradually reduced toward the poles. Value of a longitude degree at the poles is zero.

Latitude is reckoned by the number of degrees north or south of the equator, an imaginary circle on the earth's surface everywhere equidistant between the two poles. According to the IAU Ellipsoid of 1964, the length of a degree of latitude is 68.708 statute miles at the equator and varies slightly north and south because of the oblate form of the globe; at the poles it is 69.403 statute miles.

Computation of Time

The earth rotates on its axis and follows an elliptical orbit around the sun. The rotation makes the sun appear to move across the sky from East to West. It determines day and night and the complete rotation, in relation to the sun, is called the **apparent** or **true solar day**. This varies but an average determines the **mean solar day** of 24 hours.

The mean solar day is in universal use for civil purposes. It may be obtained from apparent solar time by correcting observations of the sun for the equation of time, but when high precision is required, the mean solar time is calculated from its relation to sidereal time. These relations are extremely complicated, but for most practical uses, they may be considered as follows:

Sidereal time is the measure of time defined by the diurnal motion of the vernal equinox, and is determined from observation of the meridian transits of stars. One complete rotation of the earth relative to the equinox is called the **sidereal day**. The **mean sidereal day** is 23 hours, 56 minutes, 4.091 seconds of mean solar time.

The **Calendar Year** begins at 12 o'clock midnight precisely local clock time, on the night of Dec. 31-Jan. 1. The day and the calendar month also begin at midnight by the clock. The interval required for the earth to make one absolute revolution around the sun is a **sidereal year;** it consisted of 365 days, 6 hours, 9 minutes, and 9.5 seconds of mean solar time (approximately 24 hours per day) in 1900, and is increasing at the rate of 0.0001-second annually.

The **Tropical Year,** on which the return of the seasons depends, is the interval between two consecutive returns of the sun to the vernal equinox. The tropical year consists of 365 days, 5 hours, 48 minutes, and 46 seconds in 1900. It is decreasing at the rate of 0.530 seconds per century.

In 1956 the unit of time interval was defined to be identical with the second of **Ephemeris Time,** $1/31,556,925.9747$ of the tropical year for 1900 January 0d 12th hour E.T. A physical definition of the second based on a quantum transition of cesium (atomic second) was adopted in 1964. The atomic second is equal to $9,192,631,770$ cycles of the emitted radiation. In 1967 this atomic second was adopted as the unit of time interval for the Intern'l System of Units.

The Zones and Seasons

The five zones of the earth's surface are Torrid, lying between the Tropics of Cancer and Capricorn; North Temperate, between Cancer and the Arctic Circle; South Temperate, between Capricorn and the Antarctic Circle; The Frigid Zones, between the polar Circles and the Poles.

The inclination or tilt of the earth's axis with respect to the sun determines the seasons. These are commonly marked in the North Temperate Zone, where spring begins at the vernal equinox, summer at the summer solstice, autumn at the autumnal equinox and winter at the winter solstice.

In the South Temperate Zone, the seasons are reversed. Spring begins at the autumnal equinox, summer at the winter solstice, etc.

If the earth's axis were perpendicular to the plane of the earth's orbit around the sun there would be no change of seasons. Day and night would be of nearly constant length and there would be equable conditions of temperature. But the axis is tilted 23° 27' away from a perpendicular to the orbit and only in March and September is the axis at right angles to the sun.

The points at which the sun crosses the equator are the equinoxes, when day and night are most nearly equal. The points at which the sun is at a maximum distance from the equator are the solstices. Days and nights are then most unequal.

In June the North Pole is tilted 23° 27' toward the sun and the days in the northern hemisphere are longer than the nights, while the days in the southern hemisphere are shorter than the nights. In December the North Pole is tilted 23° 27' away from the sun and the situation is reversed.

The Seasons in 1985

In 1985 the 4 seasons will begin as follows: add one hour to EST for Atlantic Time; subtract one hour for Central, two hours for Mountain, 3 hours for Pacific, 4 hours for Yukon, 5 hours for Alaska-Hawaii and six hours for Bering Time. Also shown in Greenwich Mean Time.

		Date	GMT	EST
Vernal Equinox	Spring	Mar. 20	16:14	11.14
Summer Solstice	Summer	June 21	10:44	05:44
Autumnal Equinox	Autumn	Sept. 23	02:08	21:08
Winter Solstice	Winter	Dec. 21	22:08	17:08

Poles of The Earth

The geographic (rotation) poles, or points where the earth's axis of rotation cuts the surface, are not absolutely fixed in the body of the earth. The pole of rotation describes an irregular curve about its mean position.

Two periods have been detected in this motion: (1) an annual period due to seasonal changes in barometric pressure, load of ice and snow on the surface and to other phenomena of seasonal character; (2) a period of about 14 months due to the shape and constitution of the earth.

In addition there are small but as yet unpredictable irregularities. The whole motion is so small that the actual pole at any time remains within a circle of 30 or 40 feet in radius centered at the mean position of the pole.

The pole of rotation for the time being is of course the pole having a latitude of 90° and an indeterminate longitude.

Magnetic Poles

The **north magnetic pole** of the earth is that region where the magnetic force is vertically downward and the **south magnetic pole** that region where the magnetic force is vertically upward. A compass placed at the magnetic poles experiences no directive force.

There are slow changes in the distribution of the earth's magnetic field. These changes were at one time attributed in part to a periodic movement of the magnetic poles around the geographical poles, but later evidence refutes this theory and points, rather, to a slow migration of "disturbance" foci over the earth.

There appear shifts in position of the magnetic poles due to the changes in the earth's magnetic field. The center of the area designated as the north magnetic pole was estimated to be in about latitude 70.5° N and longitude 96° W in 1905; from recent nearby measurements and studies of the secular changes, the position in 1970 is estimated as latitude 76.2° N and longitude 101° W. Improved data rather than actual motion account for at least part of the change.

The position of the south magnetic pole in 1912 was near 71° S and longitude 150° E; the position in 1970 is estimated at latitude 66° S and longitude 139.1° E.

The direction of the horizontal components of the magnetic field at any point is known as magnetic north at that point, and the angle by which it deviates east or west of true north is known as the magnetic declination, or in the mariner's terminology, the **variation of the compass.**

A compass without error points in the direction of magnetic north. (In general this is *not* the direction of the magnetic north pole.) If one follows the direction indicated by the north end of the compass, he will travel along a rather irregular curve which eventually reaches the north magnetic pole (though not usually by a great-circle route). However, the action of the compass should not be thought of as due to any influence of the distant pole, but simply as an indication of the distribution of the earth's magnetism at the place of observation.

Rotation of The Earth

The **speed of** rotation of the earth about its axis has been found to be slightly variable. The variations may be classified as:

(A) **Secular.** Tidal friction acts as a brake on the rotation and causes a slow secular increase in the length of the day, about 1 millisecond per century.

(B) **Irregular.** The speed of rotation may increase for a number of years, about 5 to 10, and then start decreasing. The maximum difference from the mean in the length of the day during a century is about 5 milliseconds. The accumulated difference in time has amounted to approximately 44 seconds since 1900. The cause is probably motion in the interior of the earth.

(C) **Periodic.** Seasonal variations exist with periods of one year and six months. The cumulative effect is such that each year the earth is late about 30 milliseconds near June 1 and is ahead about 30 milliseconds near Oct. 1. The maximum seasonal variation in the length of the day is about 0.5 millisecond. It is believed that the principal cause of the annual variation is the seasonal change in the wind patterns of the Northern and Southern Hemispheres. The semiannual variation is due chiefly to tidal action of the sun, which distorts the shape of the earth slightly.

The secular and irregular variations were discovered by comparing time based on the rotation of the earth with time based on the orbital motion of the moon about the earth and of the planets about the sun. The periodic variation was determined largely with the aid of quartz-crystal clocks. The introduction of the cesium-beam atomic clock in 1955 made it possible to determine in greater detail than before the nature of the irregular and periodic variations.

Morning and Evening Stars 1985

GMT

	Morning	Evening		Morning	Evening
Jan.	Mercury	Venus	July	Venus	Mercury
	Jupiter (from 14)	Mars		Mars (from 18)	Mars (to 18)
	Saturn	Jupiter (to 14)		Jupiter	Saturn
Feb.	Mercury (to 19)	Mercury (from 19)	Aug.	Mercury (from 10)	Mercury (to 10)
	Jupiter	Venus		Venus	Jupiter (from 4)
	Saturn	Mars		Mars	Saturn
Mar.	Jupiter	Mercury		Jupiter (to 4)	
	Saturn	Venus	Sept.	Mercury (to 22)	Mercury (from 22)
		Mars		Venus	Jupiter
April	Mercury (from Apr. 3)	Mercury (to Apr. 3)		Mars	Saturn
	Venus (from 3)	Venus (to 3)	Oct.	Venus	Mercury
	Jupiter			Mars	Jupiter
	Saturn	Mars			Saturn
May	Mercury	Mars	Nov.	Mercury (from 28)	Mercury (to 28)
	Venus	Saturn (from 15)		Venus	Jupiter
	Jupiter			Mars	Saturn (to 23)
	Saturn (to 15)			Saturn (from 23)	
June	Mercury (to 7)	Mercury (from 7)	Dec.	Mercury	Jupiter
	Venus	Mars		Venus	
	Jupiter	Saturn		Mars	
				Saturn	

Astronomical Twilight—Meridian of Greenwich

Date 1985		20° Begin	End	30° Begin	End	40° Begin	End	50° Begin	End	60° Begin	End
		h m	h m	h m	h m	h m	h m	h m	h m	h m	h m
Jan.	1	5 16	6 50	5 30	6 35	5 45	6 21	6 00	6 07	6 18	5 49
	11	5 19	6 56	5 33	6 43	5 46	6 30	6 00	6 17	6 15	6 01
	21	5 21	7 01	5 32	6 51	5 43	6 40	5 55	6 30	6 06	6 18
Feb.	1	5 21	7 07	5 29	6 58	5 38	6 51	5 45	6 44	5 51	6 38
	11	5 18	7 11	5 24	7 05	5 29	7 01	5 32	6 59	5 32	7 01
	21	5 13	7 16	5 17	7 12	5 17	7 12	5 16	7 14	5 09	7 23
Mar.	1	5 08	7 18	5 08	7 19	5 06	7 21	4 59	7 29	4 44	7 45
	11	5 00	7 21	4 58	7 24	4 50	7 32	4 38	7 46	4 12	8 12
	21	4 52	7 24	4 45	7 32	4 33	7 44	4 14	8 04	3 37	8 43
Apr.	1	4 42	7 28	4 31	7 39	4 14	7 57	3 47	8 25	2 53	9 21
	11	4 32	7 32	4 18	7 47	3 56	8 09	3 20	8 47	2 03	10 10
	21	4 23	7 36	4 04	7 54	3 37	8 23	2 52	9 11	0 37	11 47
May	1	4 14	7 41	3 52	8 04	3 19	8 37	2 22	9 39		
	11	4 08	7 46	3 41	8 13	3 03	8 53	1 49	10 09		
	21	4 02	7 52	3 32	8 22	2 48	9 07	1 13	10 46		
June	1	3 58	7 58	3 26	8 30	2 36	9 20	0 21	11 52		
	11	3 56	8 03	3 22	8 36	2 29	9 30				
	21	3 57	8 06	3 22	8 40	2 28	9 35				
July	1	3 59	8 07	3 25	8 41	2 30	9 35				
	11	4 03	8 06	3 30	8 39	2 40	9 30				
	21	4 08	8 03	3 39	8 33	2 52	9 18	1 12	11 23		
Aug.	1	4 15	7 56	3 48	8 23	3 09	9 01	1 49	10 20		
	11	4 20	7 50	3 56	8 13	3 22	8 46	2 21	9 46		
	21	4 24	7 41	4 05	8 01	3 34	8 27	2 47	9 15		
Sept.	1	4 29	7 31	4 14	7 46	3 51	8 08	3 13	8 43	1 40	10 02
	11	4 32	7 20	4 20	7 33	4 02	7 50	3 33	8 16	2 36	9 12
	21	4 35	7 11	4 26	7 19	4 14	7 31	3 52	7 52	3 11	8 31
Oct.	1	4 38	7 02	4 33	7 05	4 25	7 13	4 10	7 28	3 41	7 54
	11	4 40	6 53	4 40	6 53	4 35	6 58	4 26	7 05	4 07	7 23
	21	4 43	6 47	4 45	6 44	4 45	6 43	4 41	6 46	4 32	6 55
Nov.	1	4 46	6 41	4 52	6 34	4 56	6 30	4 58	6 27	4 56	6 27
	11	4 50	6 38	4 59	6 28	5 06	6 21	5 13	6 14	5 17	6 08
	21	4 55	6 36	5 06	6 25	5 16	6 15	5 26	6 04	5 37	5 52
Dec.	1	5 00	6 37	5 13	6 24	5 25	6 11	5 38	5 58	5 53	5 42
	11	5 06	6 40	5 20	6 26	5 34	6 12	5 48	5 57	6 06	5 38
	21	5 11	6 45	5 25	6 30	5 39	6 16	5 55	6 00	6 15	5 40
	31	5 15	6 50	5 30	6 35	5 44	6 21	6 00	6 06	6 18	5 48

Latitude, Longitude, and Altitude of North American Cities

Source: National Oceanic and Atmospheric Administration. U.S. Commerce Department for geographic positions.
Source for Canadian cities: Geodetic Survey of Canada, Dept. of Energy, Mines, and Resources.
Altitudes U.S. Geological Survey and various sources. *Approx. altitude at downtown business area U.S.; in Canada at city hall except where (a) is at tower of major airport.

City	Lat. N °	′	″	Long. W °	′	″	Alt.* feet
Abilene, Tex.	32	27	05	99	43	51	1710
Akron, Oh.	41	05	00	81	30	44	874
Albany, N.Y.	42	39	01	73	45	01	20
Albuquerque, N.M.	35	05	01	106	39	05	4,945
Allentown, Pa.	40	36	11	75	28	06	255
Alert, N.W.T.	82	29	50	62	21	15	95
Altoona, Pa.	40	30	55	78	24	03	1,180
Amarillo, Tex.	35	12	27	101	50	04	3,685
Anchorage, Alas.	61	10	00	149	59	00	118
Ann Arbor, Mich.	42	16	59	83	44	52	880
Asheville, N.C.	35	35	42	82	33	26	1,985
Ashland, Ky.	38	28	36	82	38	23	536
Atlanta, Ga.	33	45	10	84	23	37	1,050
Atlantic City, N.J.	39	21	32	74	25	53	10
Augusta, Ga.	33	28	20	81	58	00	143
Augusta, Me.	44	18	53	69	46	29	45
Austin, Tex.	30	16	09	97	44	37	505
Bakersfield, Cal.	35	22	31	119	01	18	400
Baltimore, Md.	39	17	26	76	36	45	20
Bangor, Me.	44	48	13	68	46	18	20
Baton Rouge, La.	30	26	58	91	11	00	57
Battle Creek, Mich.	42	18	58	85	10	48	820
Bay City, Mich.	43	36	04	83	53	15	595
Beaumont, Tex.	30	05	20	94	06	09	20
Belleville, Ont.	44	09	42	77	23	11	257
Bellingham, Wash.	48	45	34	122	28	36	60
Berkeley, Cal.	37	52	10	122	16	17	40
Bethlehem, Pa.	40	37	16	75	22	34	235
Billings, Mon.	45	47	00	108	30	04	3,120
Biloxi, Miss.	30	23	48	88	53	00	20
Binghamton, N.Y.	42	06	03	75	54	47	865
Birmingham, Ala.	33	31	01	86	48	36	600
Bismarck, N.D.	46	48	23	100	47	17	1,674
Bloomington, Ill.	40	28	58	88	59	36	800
Boise, Ida.	43	37	07	116	11	58	2,704
Boston, Mass.	42	21	24	71	03	25	21
Bowling Green, Ky.	36	59	41	86	26	33	510
Brandon, Man.	49	51	00	99	57	00	1,265(a)
Brantford, Ont.	43	08	34	80	15	39	705(a)
Brattleboro, Vt.	42	51	06	72	33	48	300
Bridgeport, Conn.	41	10	49	73	11	22	10
Brockton, Mass.	42	05	02	71	01	25	130
Brownsville, Tex.	25	54	07	97	29	58	35
Buffalo, N.Y.	42	52	52	78	52	21	585
Burlington, Ont.	43	19	33	79	47	57	284
Burlington, Vt.	44	28	34	73	12	46	110
Butte, Mon.	46	01	06	112	32	11	5,765
Calgary, Alta.	51	02	46	114	03	24	3,427
Cambridge, Mass.	42	22	01	71	06	22	20
Camden, N.J.	39	56	41	75	07	14	30
Canton, Oh.	40	47	50	81	22	37	1,030
Carson City, Nev.	39	10	00	119	46	00	4,680
Cedar Rapids, Ia.	41	58	01	91	39	53	730
Central Islip, N.Y.	40	47	24	73	12	00	80
Champaign, Ill.	40	07	05	88	14	48	740
Charleston, S.C.	32	46	35	79	55	53	9
Charleston, W.Va.	38	21	01	81	37	52	601
Charlotte, N.C.	35	13	44	80	50	45	720
Charlottetown, P.E.I.	46	14	07	63	07	49	31
Chattanooga, Tenn.	35	02	41	85	18	32	675
Cheyenne, Wy.	41	08	09	104	49	07	6,100
Chicago, Ill.	41	52	28	87	38	22	595
Churchill, Man.	58	45	15	94	10	00	94(a)
Cincinnati, Oh.	39	06	07	84	30	35	550
Cleveland, Oh.	41	29	51	81	41	50	660
Colorado Springs	38	50	07	104	49	16	5,980
Columbia, Mo.	38	57	03	92	19	46	730
Columbia, S.C.	34	00	02	81	02	00	190
Columbus, Ga.	32	28	07	84	59	24	265
Columbus, Oh.	39	57	47	83	00	17	780
Concord, N.H.	43	12	22	71	32	25	290
Corpus Christi, Tex.	27	47	51	97	23	45	35
Dallas, Tex.	32	47	09	96	47	37	435
Dartmouth, N.S.	44	39	50	63	34	08	24
Davenport, Ia.	41	31	19	90	34	33	590
Dawson, Yukon	64	03	30	139	26	00	1,211(a)
Dayton, Oh.	39	45	32	84	11	43	574
Daytona Beach, Fla.	29	12	44	81	01	10	7
Decatur, Ill.	39	50	42	88	56	47	682
Denver, Col.	39	44	58	104	59	22	5,280
Des Moines, Ia.	41	35	14	93	37	00	805
Detroit, Mich.	42	19	48	83	02	57	585
Dodge City, Kan.	37	45	17	100	01	09	2,480
Dubuque, Ia.	42	29	55	90	40	08	620
Duluth, Minn.	46	46	56	92	06	24	610
Durham, N.C.	36	00	00	78	54	45	405
Eau Claire, Wis.	44	48	31	91	29	49	790
Edmonton, Alta.	53	32	43	113	29	21	2,186
El Paso, Tex.	31	45	36	106	29	11	3,695
Elizabeth, N.J.	40	39	43	74	12	59	21
Enid, Okla.	36	23	40	97	52	35	1,240
Erie, Pa.	42	07	15	80	04	57	685
Eugene, Ore.	44	03	16	123	05	30	422
Eureka, Cal.	40	48	08	124	09	46	45
Evansville, Ind.	37	58	20	87	34	21	385
Fairbanks, Alas.	64	48	00	147	51	00	448
Fall River, Mass.	41	42	06	71	09	18	40
Fargo, N.D.	46	52	30	96	47	18	900
Flagstaff, Ariz.	35	11	36	111	39	06	6,900
Flint, Mich.	43	00	50	83	41	33	750
Ft. Smith, Ark.	35	23	10	94	25	36	440
Fort Wayne, Ind.	41	04	21	85	08	26	790
Fort Worth, Tex.	32	44	55	97	19	44	670
Fredericton, N.B.	45	57	47	66	38	38	29
Fresno, Cal.	36	44	12	119	47	11	285
Gadsden, Ala.	34	00	57	86	00	41	555
Gainesville, Fla.	29	38	56	82	19	19	175
Gallup, N.M.	35	31	30	108	44	30	6,540
Galveston, Tex.	29	18	10	94	47	43	5
Gary, Ind.	41	36	12	87	20	19	590
Grand Junction, Col.	39	04	06	108	33	54	4,590
Grand Rapids, Mich.	42	58	03	85	40	13	610
Great Falls, Mon.	47	29	33	111	18	23	3,340
Green Bay, Wis.	44	30	48	88	00	50	590
Greensboro, N.C.	36	04	17	79	47	25	839
Greenville, S.C.	34	50	50	82	24	01	966
Guelph, Ont.	43	32	35	80	14	54	1,065
Gulfport, Miss.	30	22	04	89	05	36	20
Halifax, N.S.	44	38	54	63	34	30	60
Hamilton, Ont.	43	15	20	79	52	30	329
Hamilton, Oh.	39	23	59	84	33	47	600
Harrisburg, Pa.	40	15	43	76	52	59	365
Hartford, Conn.	41	46	12	72	40	49	40
Helena, Mon.	46	35	33	112	02	24	4,155
Hilo, Hawaii	19	43	30	155	05	24	40
Holyoke Mass.	42	12	29	72	36	36	115
Honolulu, Ha.	21	18	22	157	51	35	21
Houston, Tex.	29	45	26	95	21	37	40
Hull, Que.	45	25	42	75	42	41	185
Huntington, W.Va.	38	25	12	82	26	33	565
Huntsville, Ala.	34	44	18	86	35	19	640
Indianapolis, Ind.	39	46	07	86	09	46	710
Iowa City, Ia.	41	39	37	91	31	53	685
Jackson, Mich.	42	14	43	84	24	22	940
Jackson, Miss.	32	17	56	90	11	06	298
Jacksonville, Fla.	30	19	44	81	39	42	20
Jersey City, N.J.	40	43	50	74	03	56	20
Johnstown, Pa.	40	19	35	78	55	03	1,185
Joplin, Mo.	37	05	26	94	30	00	990
Juneau, Alas.	58	18	12	134	24	30	50
Kalamazoo, Mich.	42	17	29	85	35	14	755
Kansas City, Kan.	39	07	04	94	38	24	750
Kansas City, Mo.	39	04	56	94	35	20	750
Kenosha, Wis.	42	35	43	87	50	11	610
Key West, Fla.	24	33	30	81	48	12	5
Kingston, Ont.	44	13	53	76	28	48	264
Kitchener, Ont.	43	26	58	80	29	12	1,100
Knoxville, Tenn.	35	57	39	83	55	07	890
Lafayette, Ind.	40	25	11	86	53	39	550
Lancaster, Pa.	40	02	25	76	18	29	350
Lansing, Mich.	42	44	01	84	33	15	830
Laredo, Tex.	27	30	22	99	30	30	440
La Salle, Que.	45	25	30	73	39	30	110
Las Vegas, Nev.	36	10	20	115	08	37	2,030
Laval, Que.	45	33	05	73	44	42	142
Lawrence, Mass.	42	42	16	71	10	08	65
Lethbridge, Alta.	49	41	38	112	49	58	2,985
Lexington, Ky.	38	02	50	84	29	46	955
Lihue, Ha.	21	58	48	159	22	30	210
Lima, Oh.	40	44	35	84	06	20	865
Lincoln, Neb.	40	48	59	96	42	15	1,150
Little Rock, Ark.	34	44	42	92	16	37	286
London, Ont.	42	59	17	81	14	03	822
Long Beach, Cal.	33	46	14	118	11	18	35
Lorain, Oh.	41	28	05	82	10	49	610
Los Angeles, Cal.	34	03	15	118	14	28	340
Louisville, Ky.	38	14	47	85	45	49	450
Lowell, Mass.	42	38	25	71	19	14	100
Lubbock, Tex.	33	35	05	101	50	33	3,195

City	Lat. N °	′	″	Long. W °	′	″	Alt.* Feet
Macon, Ga.	32	50	12	83	37	36	335
Madison, Wis.	43	04	23	89	22	55	860
Manchester, N.H.	42	59	28	71	27	41	175
Marshall, Tex	32	33	00	94	23	00	410
Memphis, Tenn.	35	08	46	90	03	13	275
Meriden, Conn.	41	32	06	72	47	30	190
Mexico City, Mexico	19	25	45	99	07	00	7,347
Miami, Fla.	25	46	37	80	11	32	10
Milwaukee, Wis.	43	02	19	87	54	15	635
Minneapolis, Minn.	44	58	57	93	15	43	815
Minot, N.D.	48	14	09	101	17	38	1,550
Mississauga, Ont.	43	33	00	79	35	00	260(a)
Mobile, Ala.	30	41	36	88	02	33	5
Moline, Ill.	41	30	31	90	30	49	585
Moncton, N.B.	46	05	18	64	46	41	38
Montgomery, Ala.	32	22	33	86	18	31	160
Montpelier, Vt.	44	15	36	72	34	41	485
Montreal, Que.	45	30	33	73	33	14	90
Moose Jaw, Sask.	50	23	34	105	32	04	1,784
Muncie, Ind.	40	11	28	85	23	16	950
Nashville, Tenn.	36	09	33	86	46	55	450
Natchez, Miss.	31	33	48	91	23	30	210
Newark, N.J.	40	44	14	74	10	19	55
New Bedford, Mass.	41	38	13	70	55	41	15
New Britain, Conn.	41	40	08	72	46	59	200
New Haven, Conn.	41	18	25	72	55	30	40
New Orleans, La.	29	56	53	90	04	10	5
New York, N.Y.	40	45	06	73	59	39	55
Niagara Falls, N.Y.	43	05	34	79	03	26	570
Niagara Falls, Ont.	43	06	22	79	03	51	590
Nome, Alas.	64	30	00	165	25	00	25
Norfolk, Va.	36	51	10	76	17	21	10
North Bay, Ont.	46	18	35	79	27	45	670
Oakland, Cal.	37	48	03	122	15	54	25
Ogden, Ut.	41	13	31	111	58	21	4,295
Oklahoma City.	35	28	26	97	31	04	1,195
Omaha, Neb.	41	15	42	95	56	14	1,040
Orlando, Fla.	28	32	42	81	22	38	70
Oshawa, Ont.	43	53	46	78	51	57	350
Ottawa, Ont.	45	26	24	75	41	42	185
Paducah, Ky.	37	05	13	88	35	56	345
Pasadena, Cal.	34	08	44	118	08	41	830
Paterson, N.J.	40	55	01	74	10	21	100
Pensacola, Fla.	30	24	51	87	12	56	15
Peoria, Ill.	40	41	42	89	35	33	470
Peterborough, Ont.	44	18	32	78	19	13	673
Philadelphia, Pa.	39	56	58	75	09	21	100
Phoenix, Ariz.	33	27	12	112	04	28	1,090
Pierre, S.D.	44	22	18	100	20	54	1,480
Pittsburgh, Pa.	40	26	19	80	00	00	745
Pittsfield, Mass.	42	26	53	73	15	14	1,015
Pocatello, Ida.	42	51	38	112	27	01	4,460
Port Arthur, Tex.	29	52	30	93	56	15	10
Portland, Me.	43	39	33	70	15	19	25
Portland, Ore.	45	31	06	122	40	35	77
Portsmouth, N.H.	43	04	30	70	45	24	20
Portsmouth, Va.	36	50	07	76	18	14	10
Prince Rupert, B.C.	54	19	00	130	19	00	125(a)
Providence, R.I.	41	49	32	71	24	41	80
Provo, Ut.	40	14	06	111	39	24	4,550
Pueblo, Col.	38	16	17	104	36	33	4,690
Quebec City, Que.	46	48	51	71	12	30	163
Racine, Wis.	42	43	49	87	47	12	630
Rapid City, S.D.	44	04	52	103	13	11	3,230
Raleigh, N.C.	35	46	38	78	38	21	365
Reading, Pa.	40	20	09	75	55	40	265
Regina, Sask.	50	26	55	104	36	50	1,894(a)
Reno, Nev.	39	31	27	119	48	40	4,490
Richmond, Va.	37	32	15	77	26	09	160
Roanoke, Va.	37	16	13	79	56	44	905
Rochester, Minn.	44	01	21	92	28	03	990
Rochester, N.Y.	43	09	41	77	36	21	515
Rockford, Ill.	42	16	07	89	05	48	715
Sacramento, Cal.	38	34	57	121	29	41	30
Saginaw, Mich.	43	25	52	83	56	05	595
St. Catharines, Ont.	43	09	33	79	14	50	362(a)
St. Cloud, Minn.	45	34	00	94	10	24	1,040
Saint John, N.B.	45	16	22	66	03	48	27
St. John's, Nfld.	47	33	42	52	42	48	200(a)
St. Joseph, Mo.	39	45	57	94	51	02	850
St. Louis, Mo.	38	37	45	90	12	22	455
St. Paul, Minn.	44	57	19	93	06	07	780
St. Petersburg, Fla.	27	46	18	82	38	19	20
Salem, Ore.	44	56	24	123	01	59	155
Salina, Kan.	38	50	36	97	36	46	1,229
Salt Lake City, Ut.	40	45	23	111	53	26	4,390
San Angelo, Tex.	31	27	39	100	26	03	1,845
San Antonio, Tex.	29	25	37	98	29	06	650
San Bernardino, Cal.	34	06	30	117	17	28	1,080
San Diego, Cal.	32	42	53	117	09	21	20
San Francisco, Cal.	37	46	39	122	24	40	65
San Jose, Cal.	37	20	16	121	53	24	90
San Juan, P.R.	18	27	00	66	04	15	35
Santa Barbara, Cal.	34	25	18	119	41	55	100
Santa Cruz, Cal.	36	58	18	122	01	18	20
Santa Fe, N.M.	35	41	11	105	56	10	6,950
Sarasota, Fla.	27	20	05	82	32	30	20
Saskatoon, Sask.	52	07	49	106	39	35	1,587
Sault Ste. Marie, Ont.	46	30	24	84	20	04	589
Savannah, Ga.	32	04	42	81	05	37	20
Schenectady, N.Y.	42	48	42	73	55	42	245
Scranton, Pa.	41	24	32	75	39	46	725
Seattle, Wash.	47	36	32	122	20	12	10
Sheboygan, Wis.	43	45	03	87	42	52	630
Sherbrooke, Que.	45	24	27	71	51	07	535(a)
Sheridan, Wy.	44	47	55	106	57	10	3,740
Shreveport, La.	32	30	46	93	44	58	204
Sioux City, Ia.	42	29	46	96	24	30	1,110
Sioux Falls, S.D.	43	32	35	96	43	35	1,395
Somerville, Mass.	42	23	15	71	06	07	13
South Bend, Ind.	41	40	33	86	15	01	710
Spartanburg, S.C.	34	57	03	81	56	06	875
Spokane, Wash.	47	39	32	117	25	33	1,890
Springfield, Ill.	39	47	58	89	38	51	610
Springfield, Mass.	42	06	21	72	35	32	85
Springfield, Mo.	37	13	03	93	17	32	1,300
Springfield, Oh.	39	55	38	83	48	29	980
Stamford, Conn.	41	03	09	73	32	24	35
Steubenville, Oh.	40	21	42	80	36	53	660
Stockton, Cal.	37	57	30	121	17	16	20
Sudbury, Ont.	46	29	24	80	59	24	850(a)
Superior, Wis.	46	43	14	92	06	07	630
Sydney, N.S.	46	08	15	60	11	48	15
Syracuse, N.Y.	43	03	04	76	09	14	400
Tacoma, Wash.	47	14	59	122	26	15	110
Tallahassee, Fla.	30	26	30	84	16	56	150
Tampa, Fla.	27	56	58	82	27	25	15
Terre Haute, Ind.	39	28	03	87	24	26	496
Texarkana, Tex.	33	25	48	94	02	30	324
Thunder Bay, Ont.	48	22	54	89	14	42	616
Toledo, Oh.	41	39	14	83	32	39	585
Topeka, Kan.	39	03	16	95	40	23	930
Toronto, Ont.	43	39	10	79	23	00	300
Trenton, N.J.	40	13	14	74	46	13	35
Trois-Rivieres, Que.	46	20	36	72	32	37	115(a)
Troy, N.Y.	42	43	45	73	40	58	35
Tucson, Ariz.	32	13	15	110	58	08	2,390
Tulsa, Okla.	36	09	12	95	59	34	804
Urbana, Ill.	40	06	42	88	12	06	725
Utica, N.Y.	43	06	12	75	13	33	415
Vancouver, B.C.	49	18	56	123	04	44	141
Victoria, B.C.	48	25	43	123	21	49	57
Waco, Tex.	31	33	12	97	08	00	405
Walla Walla, Wash.	46	04	08	118	20	24	936
Washington, D.C.	38	53	51	77	00	33	25
Waterbury, Conn.	41	33	13	73	02	31	260
Waterloo, Ia.	42	29	40	92	20	20	850
West Palm Beach, Fla.	26	42	36	80	03	07	15
Wheeling, W. Va.	40	04	03	80	43	20	650
Whitehorse, Yukon	60	43	17	135	03	03	2,305(a)
White Plains, N.Y.	41	02	00	73	45	48	220
Wichita, Kan.	37	41	30	97	20	16	1,290
Wichita Falls, Tex.	33	54	34	98	29	28	945
Wilkes-Barre, Pa.	41	14	32	75	53	17	640
Wilmington, Del.	39	44	46	75	32	51	135
Wilmington, N.C.	34	14	14	77	56	58	35
Windsor, Ont.	42	18	56	83	02	10	603
Winnipeg, Man.	49	53	56	97	08	23	762
Winston-Salem, N.C.	36	05	52	80	14	42	860
Worcester, Mass.	42	15	37	71	48	17	475
Yakima, Wash.	46	36	09	120	30	39	1,060
Yellowknife, N.W.T.	62	27	16	114	22	33	674(a)
Yonkers, N.Y.	40	55	55	73	53	54	10
York, Pa.	39	57	35	76	43	36	370
Youngstown, Oh.	41	05	57	80	39	02	840
Yuma, Ariz.	32	42	54	114	37	24	160
Zanesville, Oh.	39	56	18	82	00	30	720

World Cities

City	Lat. N °	′	″	Long. W °	′	″	Alt.* Feet
London, UK (Greenwich)	51	30	00N	0	0	0	245
Paris, France.	48	50	14N	2	20	14E	300
Berlin, Germany	52	32	00N	13	25	00E	110
Rome, Italy.	41	53	00N	12	30	00E	95
Warsaw, Poland	52	15	00N	21	00	00E	360
Moscow, USSR	55	45	00N	37	42	00E	394
Athens, Greece	37	58	00N	23	44	00E	300
Jerusalem, Israel	31	47	00N	35	13	00E	2,500
Johannesburg, So. Afr.	26	10	00S	28	02	00E	5,740
New Delhi, India	28	38	00N	77	12	00E	770
Peking, China	39	54	00N	116	28	00E	600
Rio de Janeiro, Brazil	22	53	43S	43	13	22W	30
Tokyo, Japan	35	45	00N	139	45	00E	30
Sydney, Australia	33	52	00S	151	12	00E	25

1st Month   January, 1985   31 days

Greenwich Mean Time

NOTE: Light figures indicate Sun. **Dark** figures indicate **Moon.** *Degrees are North Latitude.*

CAUTION: Must be converted to local time. For instruction see page 726.

Day of month / week / year	Sun on Meridian / Moon Phase / h m s	Sun's Declination ° '	20° Rise Sun/Moon h m	20° Set Sun/Moon h m	30° Rise Sun/Moon h m	30° Set Sun/Moon h m	40° Rise Sun/Moon h m	40° Set Sun/Moon h m	50° Rise Sun/Moon h m	50° Set Sun/Moon h m	60° Rise Sun/Moon h m	60° Set Sun/Moon h m
1 Tu / 1	12 03 24	− 23 02	6 36	17 32	6 56	17 11	7 22	16 45	7 59	16 09	9 02	15 06
			13 17	1 27	13 06	1 36	12 53	1 46	12 36	2 01	12 09	2 23
2 We / 2	12 03 52	− 22 57	6 36	17 33	6 56	17 12	7 22	16 46	7 59	16 10	9 02	15 07
			13 52	2 18	13 37	2 31	13 19	2 47	12 53	3 10	12 13	3 47
3 Th / 3	12 04 20	− 22 51	6 36	17 33	6 56	17 13	7 22	16 47	7 49	16 11	9 01	15 08
			14 32	3 10	14 13	3 28	13 49	3 50	13 15	4 22	12 19	5 15
4 Fr / 4	12 04 48	− 22 45	6 36	17 34	6 56	17 14	7 22	16 48	7 48	16 12	9 00	15 10
			15 18	4 06	14 55	4 27	14 26	4 55	13 45	5 34	12 31	6 45
5 Sa / 5	12 05 15	− 22 39	6 37	17 34	6 57	17 14	7 22	16 49	7 48	16 13	9 00	15 12
			16 09	5 03	15 43	5 28	15 11	6 00	14 24	6 46	12 55	8 14
6 Su / 6	12 05 41	− 22 32	6 37	17 35	6 57	17 15	7 22	16 50	7 58	16 14	8 59	15 13
			17 05	6 02	16 39	6 28	16 06	7 02	15 17	7 50	14 56	9 27
7 Mo / 7	12 06 08 2 16 ○	− 22 24	6 37	17 36	6 57	17 16	7 22	16 51	7 58	16 16	8 58	15 15
			18 07	7 00	17 42	7 40	17 10	7 58	16 25	8 44	14 56	10 14
8 Tu / 8	12 06 33	− 22 17	6 37	17 36	6 57	17 16	7 22	16 52	7 57	16 17	8 57	15 17
			19 10	7 54	18 48	8 17	18 21	8 46	17 42	9 26	16 33	10 38
9 We / 9	12 06 59	− 22 08	06 37	17 37	6 57	17 17	7 22	16 53	7 56	16 18	8 56	15 19
			20 13	9 03	19 56	9 14	19 35	9 26	19 05	9 58	18 16	10 51
10 Th / 10	12 07 23	− 22 00	6 37	17 38	6 57	17 18	7 22	16 54	7 56	16 20	8 55	15 21
			21 14	9 29	21 03	9 43	20 49	10 00	20 29	10 23	19 58	10 58
11 Fr / 11	12 07 47	− 21 51	6 37	17 39	6 57	17 19	7 22	16 55	7 55	16 21	8 54	15 23
			22 14	10 11	22 08	10 19	22 01	10.29	21 52	10 42	21 38	11 03
12 Sa / 12	12 08 11	− 21 41	6 38	17 40	6 57	17 20	7 22	16 56	7 55	16 22	8 52	15 25
			23 12	10 51	23 13	10 53	23 13	10 56	23 14	11 00	23 15	11 06
13 Su / 13	12 08 34 23 27 ☾	− 21 31	6 38	17 40	6 57	17 21	7 21	16 57	7 54	16 24	8 50	15 27
				11 29		11 26		11 22		11 17		11 09
14 Mo / 14	12 08 56	− 21 21	6 38	17 41	6 57	17 22	7 21	16 58	7 54	16 25	8 49	15 29
			0 11	12 08	0 17	12 00	0 25	11 49	0 35	11 34	0 52	11 12
15 Tu / 15	12 09 18	− 21 10	6 38	17 41	6 57	17 23	7 21	16 59	7 53	16 26	8 48	15 32
			1 10	12 50	1 22	12 36	1 37	12 18	1 57	11 54	2 31	11 16
16 We / 16	12 09 39	− 20 59	6 38	17 42	6 56	17 23	7 20	17 00	7 52	16 28	8 46	15 34
			2 10	13 35	2 28	13 16	2 50	12 52	3 20	12 18	4 12	11 23
17 Th / 17	12 09 59	− 20 48	6 38	17 42	6 56	17 24	7 20	17 01	7 51	16 30	8 44	15 36
			3 13	14 24	3 34	14 01	4 02	13 32	4 42	12 50	4 12	11 35
18 Fr / 18	12 10 19	− 20 36	6 38	17 43	6 56	17 25	7 19	17 02	7 50	16 31	8 43	15 39
			4 15	15 18	4 40	14 53	5 12	14 20	5 59	13 32	7 30	12 00
19 Sa / 19	12 10 38	− 20 24	6 38	17 44	6 56	17 26	7 19	17 03	7 49	16 32	8 41	15 41
			5 15	16 16	5 42	15 50	6 15	15 16	7 05	14 27	8 44	12 57
20 Su / 20	12 10 57	− 20 11	6 38	17 44	6 55	17 27	7 18	17 04	7 48	16 34	8 40	15 44
			6 12	17 15	6 38	16 50	7 10	16 19	7 57	15 33	9 28	14 03
21 Mo / 21	12 11 14 2 28 ●	− 19 58	6 38	17 45	6 55	17 28	7 18	17 05	7 47	16 36	8 38	15 46
			7 03	18 14	7 26	17 52	7 55	17 25	8 36	16 45	9 50	15 34
22 Tu / 22	12 11 31	− 19 44	6 38	17 46	6 55	17 29	7 17	17 07	7 46	16 37	8 36	15 48
			7 49	19 10	8 08	18 53	8 32	18 31	9 05	18 00	10 01	17 07
23 We / 23	12 11 47	− 19 30	6 38	17 46	6 55	17 30	7 16	17 08	7 45	16 39	8 34	15 50
			8 29	20 04	8 44	19 51	9 02	19 35	9 27	19 13	10 07	18 37
24 Th / 24	12 12 02	− 19 16	6 37	17 47	6 54	17 30	7 16	17 10	7 44	16 40	8 32	15 53
			9 05	20 55	9 15	20 47	9 28	20 37	9 44	20 33	10 10	20 02
25 Fr / 25	12 12 17	− 19 02	6 37	17 47	6 54	17 31	7 15	17 11	7 43	16 42	8 30	15 56
			9 38	21 44	9 44	21 41	9 50	21 37	9 59	21 32	10 12	21 23
26 Sa / 26	12 12 30	− 18 47	6 37	17 48	6 54	17 32	7 14	17 12	7 42	16 44	8 28	15 58
			10 10	22 31	10 11	22 33	10 12	22 35	10 13	22 39	10 14	22 43
27 Su / 27	12 12 43	− 18 32	6 37	17 49	6 53	17 33	7 13	17 13	7 41	16 46	8 26	16 01
			10 42	23 19	10 38	23 26	10 33	23 34	10 26	23 45	10 16	
28 Mo / 28	12 12 55	− 18 16	6 36	17 49	6 53	17 33	7 12	17 14	7 40	16 48	8 24	16 04
			11 14		11 05		10 54		10 40		10 18	0 03
29 Tu / 29	12 13 06 3 29 ☾	− 18 00	6 36	17 50	6 52	17 34	7 12	17 16	7 38	16 49	8 21	16 06
			11 48	0 08	11 35	0 20	11 18	0 34	10 56	0 53	10 21	1 25
30 We / 30	12 13 17	− 17 44	6 36	17 51	6 52	17 35	7 11	17 17	7 37	16 51	8 19	16 09
			12 26	0 59	12 08	1 15	11 46	1 35	11 15	2 03	10 26	2 50
31 Th / 31	12 13 26	− 17 27	6 36	17 51	6 51	17 36	7 10	17 18	7 36	16 53	8 16	16 12
			13 08	1 52	12 46	2 13	12 19	2 38	11 41	3 14	10 34	4 18

2nd Month   February, 1985   28 Days

Greenwich Mean Time

NOTE: Light figures indicate Sun. **Dark** figures indicate **Moon.** *Degrees are North Latitude.*

CAUTION: Must be converted to local time. For instruction see page 726.

Day of month / week / year	Sun on meridian / Moon phase	Sun's Declination	20° Rise Sun/Moon	20° Set Sun/Moon	30° Rise Sun/Moon	30° Set Sun/Moon	40° Rise Sun/Moon	40° Set Sun/Moon	50° Rise Sun/Moon	50° Set Sun/Moon	60° Rise Sun/Moon	60° Set Sun/Moon
	h m s	° ′	h m	h m	h m	h m	h m	h m	h m	h m	h m	h m
1 Fr	12 13 35	−17 11	6 36	17 52	6 51	17 37	7 09	17 19	7 34	16 54	8 14	16 14
32			13 55	2 48	13 31	3 12	13 00	3 42	12 15	4 26	10 51	5 48
2 Sa	12 13 43	−16 53	6 35	17 52	6 50	17 38	7 08	17 20	7 32	16 56	8 12	16 16
33			14 49	3 46	14 23	4 12	13 50	4 45	13 01	5 33	11 25	7 09
3 Su	12 13 50	−16 36	6 35	17 53	6 49	17 39	7 07	17 21	7 31	16 58	8 09	16 19
34			15 49	4 45	15 23	5 11	14 50	5 44	14 02	6 33	12 27	8 08
4 Mo	12 13 56	−16 18	6 34	17 53	6 48	17 40	7 06	17 22	7 30	17 00	8 06	16 22
35			16 52	5 41	16 29	6 05	15 59	6 36	15 17	7 20	13 58	8 41
5 Tu	12 14 01	−16 00	6 34	17 54	6 48	17 40	7 05	17 24	7 28	17 01	8 04	16 24
36	15 19 ○		17 57	6 34	17 38	6 54	17 14	7 20	16 40	7 56	15 42	8 58
6 We	12 14 06	−15 42	6 33	17 54	6 47	17 41	7 04	17 25	7 26	17 02	8 02	16 27
37			19 01	7 22	18 47	7 38	18 30	7 57	18 07	8 24	17 28	9 07
7 Th	12 14 09	−15 23	6 33	17 55	6 46	17 42	7 03	17 26	7 25	17 04	7 59	16 30
38			20 03	8 06	19 55	8 17	19 46	8 29	19 33	8 46	19 13	9 12
8 Fr	12 14 12	−15 05	6 32	17 55	6 45	17 43	7 02	17 27	7 23	17 06	7 56	16 32
39			21 04	8 48	21 02	8 52	21 00	8 58	20 58	9 05	20 54	9 16
9 Sa	12 14 15	−14 46	6 32	17 56	6 44	17 44	7 00	17 28	7 22	17 08	7 54	16 35
40			22 04	9 28	22 04	9 26	22 14	9 24	22 22	9 22	22 34	9 18
10 Su	12 14 16	−14 26	6 31	17 56	6 44	17 45	6 59	17 30	7 20	17 09	7 52	16 38
41			23 04	10 08	23 15	10 00	23 28	9 51	23 46	9 39		9 21
11 Mo	12 14 17	−14 07	6 31	17 57	6 43	17 46	6 58	17 31	7 18	17 11	7 49	16 40
42				10 49		10 36		10 20		9 59	0 15	9 25
12 Tu	12 14 16	−13 47	6 30	17 57	6 42	17 47	6 57	17 32	7 16	17 13	7 46	16 43
43	7 57 ☾		0 05	11 33	0 21	11 15	0 41	10 53	1 09	10 21	1 57	9 30
13 We	12 14 16	−13 27	6 30	17 58	6 42	17 47	6 56	17 34	7 14	17 14	7 44	16 46
44			1 07	12 21	1 28	11 58	1 54	11 30	2 32	10 51	3 39	9 40
14 Th	12 14 14	−13 07	6 29	17 58	6 41	17 48	6 54	17 35	7 13	17 16	7 41	16 48
45			2 09	13 13	2 33	12 48	3 04	12 15	3 50	11 29	5 17	10 00
15 Fr	12 14 12	−12 46	6 29	17 59	6 40	17 49	6 53	17 36	7 11	17 18	7 38	16 51
46			3 09	14 09	3 35	13 42	4 09	13 08	4 59	12 19	6 39	10 38
16 Sa	12 14 09	−12 25	6 28	17 59	6 39	17 50	6 52	17 38	7 09	17 20	7 35	16 54
47			4 06	15 07	4 32	14 41	5 05	14 08	5 54	13 20	7 31	11 45
17 Su	12 14 05	−12 05	6 28	18 00	6 38	17 50	6 50	17 38	7 07	17 22	7 32	16 56
48			4 58	16 05	5 22	15 42	5 53	15 12	6 36	14 30	7 57	13 12
18 Mo	12 14 01	−11 44	6 27	18 00	6 37	17 51	6 49	17 39	7 05	17 23	7 30	16 58
49			5 45	17 01	6 05	16 42	6 31	16 18	7 08	15 44	8 10	14 44
19 Tu	12 13 55	−11 22	6 27	18 01	6 36	17 52	6 48	17 40	7 03	17 25	7 27	17 01
50	18 43 ●		6 26	17 56	6 43	17 41	7 03	17 23	7 31	16 57	8 17	16 15
20 We	12 13 50	−11 01	6 26	18 01	6 35	17 53	6 46	17 41	7 01	17 27	7 24	17 04
51			7 03	18 47	7 15	18 37	7 30	18 25	7 50	18 09	8 21	17 42
21 Th	12 13 43	−10 39	6 26	18 02	6 34	17 54	6 45	17 42	7 00	17 28	7 22	17 06
52			7 37	19 37	7 45	19 32	7 53	19 26	8 05	19 18	8 23	19 05
22 Fr	12 13 36	−10 18	6 25	18 02	6 33	17 54	6 44	17 44	6 58	17 30	7 19	17 09
53			8 10	20 25	8 12	10 25	8 15	20 25	8 19	20 25	8 24	20 26
23 Sa	12 13 28	−09 56	6 24	18 03	6 32	17 55	6 42	17 45	6 56	17 32	7 16	17 12
54			8 41	21 13	8 39	21 18	8 36	21 24	8 32	21 32	8 26	21 45
24 Su	12 13 20	−09 34	6 23	18 03	6 31	17 56	6 41	17 46	6 54	17 34	7 13	17 14
55			9 13	22 01	9 06	22 11	8 51	22 23	8 45	22 40	8 27	23 06
25 Mo	12 13 11	−09 11	6 23	18 03	6 30	17 57	6 40	17 47	6 52	17 36	7 10	17 17
56			9 46	22 51	9 34	23 05	9 19	23 23	9 00	23 48	8 29	
26 Tu	12 13 02	−08 49	6 22	18 04	6 29	17 57	6 38	17 48	6 50	17 37	7 08	17 20
57			10 21	23 42	10 05		9 45		9 17		8 33	0 30
27 We	12 12 51	−08 27	6 21	18 04	6 28	17 58	6 37	17 49	6 48	17 39	7 05	17 22
58	23 41 ☽		11 01		10 40	0 01	10 15	0 25	9 39	0 59	8 39	1 56
28 Th	12 12 41	−08 04	6 20	18 04	6 27	17 58	6 36	17 50	6 46	17 40	7 02	17 24
59			11 45	0 36	11 21	0 59	10 51	1 28	10 09	2 09	8 51	3 25

3rd Month   March, 1985   31 Days

Greenwich Mean Time

NOTE: Light figures indicate Sun. **Dark** figures indicate **Moon**. *Degrees are North Latitude.*

CAUTION: Must be converted to local time. For instruction see page 726.

Day of month week year	Sun on meridian Moon phase h m s	Sun's Declination °	20° Rise Sun/Moon h m	20° Set Sun/Moon h m	30° Rise Sun/Moon h m	30° Set Sun/Moon h m	40° Rise Sun/Moon h m	40° Set Sun/Moon h m	50° Rise Sun/Moon h m	50° Set Sun/Moon h m	60° Rise Sun/Moon h m	60° Set Sun/Moon h m
1 Fr / 60	12 12 29	− 07 41	6 20	18 05	6 26	17 59	6 34	17 52	6 44	17 42	6 59	17 27
			12 35	1 32	12 09	1 58	11 36	2 30	10 48	3 17	9 14	4 50
2 Sa / 61	12 12 18	− 07 18	6 19	18 05	6 25	17 59	6 32	17 53	6 42	17 44	6 52	17 30
			13 31	2 29	13 04	2 56	12 31	3 30	11 41	4 19	10 01	5 59
3 Su / 62	12 12 05	− 06 55	6 18	18 06	6 24	18 00	6 31	17 54	6 40	17 45	6 53	17 32
			14 31	3 26	14 06	3 51	13 35	4 24	12 48	5 11	11 19	6 42
4 Mo / 63	12 11 53	− 06 32	6 17	18 06	6 23	18 01	6 30	17 55	6 38	17 47	6 50	17 34
			15 35	4 19	15 14	4 42	14 46	5 11	14 08	5 52	12 58	7 04
5 Tu / 64	12 11 39	− 06 09	6 16	18 06	6 22	18 02	6 28	17 56	6 36	17 48	6 47	17 37
			16 39	5 09	16 23	5 28	16 02	5 51	15 33	6 23	14 45	7 15
6 We / 65	12 11 26	− 05 46	6 16	18 07	6 20	18 02	6 26	17 57	6 33	17 50	6 44	17 40
			17 44	5 56	17 33	6 09	17 20	6 25	17 01	6 47	16 32	7 21
7 Th / 66	2 13 ○	− 05 23	6 15	18 07	6 19	18 03	6 25	17 58	6 31	17 52	6 41	17 42
	12 11 11		18 47	6 39	18 42	6 47	18 37	6 55	18 29	7 07	18 18	7 25
8 Fr / 67	12 10 57	− 05 00	6 14	18 07	6 18	18 04	6 23	17 59	6 29	17 54	6 38	17 44
			19 49	7 21	19 51	7 22	19 54	7 23	19 57	7 25	20 02	7 28
9 Sa / 68	12 10 42	− 04 36	6 14	18 08	6 17	18 05	6 22	18 00	6 27	17 55	6 35	17 47
			20 52	8 02	21 00	7 57	21 10	7 51	21 24	7 43	21 47	7 30
10 Su / 69	12 10 27	− 04 13	6 13	18 08	6 16	18 05	6 20	18 02	6 25	17 56	6 32	17 50
			21 55	8 44	22 09	8 33	22 27	8 20	22 52	8 01	23 33	7 33
11 Mo / 70	12 10 11	− 03 49	6 12	18 08	6 15	18 06	6 18	18 03	6 23	17 58	6 29	17 52
			22 58	9 28	23 18	9 12	23 43	8 51		8 23		7 38
12 Tu / 71	12 09 55	− 03 26	6 11	18 08	6 14	18 06	6 16	18 04	6 21	18 00	6 26	17 54
				10 16		9 55		9 28	0 18	8 51	1 20	7 46
13 We / 72	17 34 ☾	− 03 02	6 10	18 09	6 12	18 07	6 15	18 05	6 18	18 02	6 23	17 57
	12 09 39		0 12	11 08	0 26	10 43	0 56	10 12	1 40	9 26	3 04	8 01
14 Th / 73	12 09 23	− 02 38	6 10	18 09	6 11	18 08	6 14	18 06	6 16	18 03	6 20	18 00
			1 04	12 04	1 30	11 37	2 04	11 03	2 54	10 13	4 34	8 32
15 Fr / 74	12 09 06	− 02 15	6 09	18 10	6 10	18 08	6 12	18 07	6 14	18 05	6 17	18 02
			2 03	13 02	2 29	12 35	3 03	12 01	3 53	11 12	5 35	9 31
16 Sa / 75	12 08 49	− 01 51	6 08	18 10	6 09	18 09	6 10	18 08	6 12	18 06	6 14	18 04
			2 56	13 59	3 21	13 35	3 53	13 05	4 39	12 20	6 06	10 54
17 Su / 76	12 08 32	− 01 27	6 07	18 10	6 08	18 10	6 08	18 09	6 10	18 08	6 11	18 07
			3 44	14 56	4 06	14 35	4 33	14 09	5 13	13 32	6 21	12 26
18 Mo / 77	12 08 15	− 01 04	6 06	18 11	6 06	18 10	6 07	18 10	6 07	18 10	6 08	18 10
			4 26	15 50	4 44	15 34	5 06	15 14	5 37	14 45	6 29	13 57
19 Tu / 78	12 07 57	− 00 40	6 05	18 11	6 05	18 11	6 05	18 11	6 05	18 11	6 05	18 12
			5 04	16 42	5 17	16 31	5 34	16 17	5 57	15 57	6 32	15 25
20 We / 79	12 07 40	− 00 16	6 04	18 11	6 04	18 11	6 04	18 11	6 04	18 12	6 02	18 14
			5 38	17 32	5 47	17 26	5 58	17 18	6 12	17 06	6 35	16 49
21 Th / 80	11 59 ●	+ 00 08	6 04	18 11	6 02	18 12	6 02	18 13	6 01	18 14	5 59	18 17
	12 07 22		6 11	18 21	6 15	18 19	6 20	18 17	6 26	18 14	6 36	18 10
22 Fr / 81	12 07 04	+ 00 31	6 03	18 12	6 01	18 12	6 00	18 14	6 00	18 16	5 56	18 20
			6 42	19 08	6 41	19 12	6 40	19 16	6 39	19 22	6 37	19 30
23 Sa / 82	12 06 46	+ 00 55	6 02	18 12	6 00	18 13	5 59	18 15	5 57	18 18	5 53	18 22
			7 14	19 57	7 08	20 05	7 01	20 15	6 52	20 29	6 38	20 51
24 Su / 83	12 06 28	+ 01 19	6 01	18 12	5 59	18 14	5 57	18 16	5 55	18 20	5 50	18 24
			7 46	20 46	7 36	20 59	7 52	21 15	7 06	21 37	6 39	22 14
25 Mo / 84	12 06 10	+ 01 42	6 00	18 12	5 58	18 15	5 56	18 17	5 52	18 21	5 47	18 26
			8 20	21 36	8 05	21 54	7 47	22 16	7 22	22 47	6 42	22 14
26 Tu / 85	12 05 52	+ 02 06	5 59	18 13	5 57	18 15	5 54	18 18	5 50	18 22	5 44	18 29
			8 58	22 29	8 39	22 51	8 15	23 18	7 42	23 57	6 46	
27 We / 86	12 05 34	+ 02 29	5 58	18 13	5 56	18 16	5 52	18 19	5 48	18 24	5 41	18 31
			9 40	23 24	9 17	23 48	8 48		8 07		6 55	1 07
28 Th / 87	12 05 15	+ 02 53	5 57	18 13	5 55	18 16	5 50	18 20	5 46	18 26	5 38	18 34
			10 27		10 01		9 29	0 20	8 42	1 06	7 12	2 34
29 Fr / 88	16 11)	+ 03 16	5 56	18 13	5 54	18 17	5 49	18 21	5 44	18 27	5 35	18 36
	12 04 57		11 19	0 19	10 52	0 46	10 18	1 20	9 28	2 09	7 46	3 50
30 Sa / 89	12 04 39	+ 03 40	5 56	18 14	5 52	18 17	5 48	18 22	5 41	18 28	5 32	18 38
			12 16	1 14	11 50	1 41	11 16	2 15	10 28	3 04	8 50	4 43
31 Su / 90	12 04 21	+ 04 03	5 55	18 14	5 51	18 18	5 46	18 23	5 39	18 30	5 29	18 41
			13 16	2 08	12 53	2 32	12 23	3 03	11 40	3 48	10 19	5 10

4th Month   April, 1985   30 Days

Greenwich Mean Time

NOTE: Light figures indicate Sun. **Dark** figures indicate **Moon.** *Degrees are North Latitude.*

CAUTION: Must be converted to local time. For instruction see page 726.

Day of month / week / year	Sun on meridian Moon phase h m s	Sun's Declination ° '	20° Rise Sun/Moon h m	20° Set Sun/Moon h m	30° Rise Sun/Moon h m	30° Set Sun/Moon h m	40° Rise Sun/Moon h m	40° Set Sun/Moon h m	50° Rise Sun/Moon h m	50° Set Sun/Moon h m	60° Rise Sun/Moon h m	60° Set Sun/Moon h m
1 Mo	12 04 03	+04 26	5 54	18 14	5 50	18 18	5 44	18 24	5 37	18 32	5 26	18 44
91			14 19	2 58	14 00	3 19	13 35	3 45	13 01	4 22	12 02	5 24
2 Tu	12 03 45	+04 49	5 53	18 14	5 48	18 19	5 43	18 25	5 35	18 33	5 23	18 46
92			15 22	3 45	15 08	4 01	14 51	4 21	14 27	4 48	13 47	5 32
3 We	12 03 27	+05 12	5 52	18 15	5 47	18 19	5 42	18 26	5 33	18 34	5 20	18 48
93			16 25	4 28	16 17	4 39	16 07	4 52	15 54	5 09	15 33	5 36
4 Th	12 03 09	+05 35	5 51	18 15	5 46	18 20	5 40	18 27	5 31	18 36	5 17	18 51
94			17 27	5 10	17 26	5 15	17 24	5 20	17 22	5 27	17 18	5 38
5 Fr	12 02 52	+05 58	5 50	18 15	5 45	18 21	5 38	18 28	5 29	18 38	5 14	18 54
95	11 32 ○		18 31	5 52	18 36	5 50	18 42	5 48	18 51	5 45	19 04	5 41
6 Sa	12 02 34	+06 21	5 50	18 15	5 44	18 22	5 36	18 29	5 26	18 40	5 11	18 56
96			19 35	6 34	19 47	6 26	20 01	6 16	20 21	6 03	20 53	5 43
7 Su	12 02 17	+06 44	5 49	18 16	5 42	18 22	5 35	18 30	5 24	18 41	5 08	18 58
97			20 41	7 18	20 58	7 04	21 20	6 47	21 51	6 23	22 44	5 46
8 Mo	12 02 00	+07 06	5 48	18 16	5 41	18 23	5 33	18 31	5 22	18 43	5 05	19 01
98			21 48	8 06	22 10	7 47	22 39	7 22	23 20	6 48		5 52
9 Tu	12 01 44	+07 28	5 47	18 16	5 40	18 23	5 32	18 32	5 20	18 44	5 02	19 04
99			22 53	8 59	23 19	8 35	23 52	8 04		7 21	0 36	6 03
10 We	12 01 27	+07 51	5 46	18 16	5 39	18 24	5 30	18 33	5 18	18 46	4 59	19 06
100			23 55	9 55		9 28		8 55	0 41	8 05	2 18	6 26
11 Th	12 01 11	+08 13	5 46	18 17	5 38	18 24	5 28	18 34	5 16	18 48	4 56	19 08
101				10 54	0 22	10 27	0 57	9 52	1 48	9 01	3 34	7 16
12 Fr	12 00 55	+08 35	5 45	18 17	5 37	18 25	5 27	18 35	5 14	18 49	4 53	19 11
102	04 41 ☽		0 52	11 53	1 18	11 28	1 51	10 56	2 40	10 08	4 14	8 35
13 Sa	12 00 40	+08 57	5 44	18 17	5 36	18 26	5 26	18 36	5 12	18 50	4 50	19 13
103			1 42	12 51	2 06	12 16	2 35	12 01	3 17	11 21	4 32	10 05
14 Su	12 00 24	+09 19	5 43	18 18	5 34	18 26	5 24	18 37	5 10	18 52	4 47	19 16
104			2 26	13 46	2 46	13 29	3 10	13 06	3 44	12 35	4 41	11 41
15 Mo	12 00 09	+09 40	5 42	18 18	5 33	18 27	5 22	18 38	5 07	18 54	4 44	19 18
105			3 05	14 39	3 21	14 26	3 39	14 10	4 05	13 47	4 45	13 10
16 Tu	11 59 55	+10 02	5 41	18 19	5 32	18 28	51 21	18 39	5 05	18 55	4 41	19 20
106			3 41	15 29	3 51	15 21	4 04	15 11	4 21	14 57	4 47	14 35
17 We	11 59 41	+10 23	5 40	18 19	5 31	18 28	5 20	18 40	5 03	18 56	4 38	19 22
107			4 13	16 18	4 19	16 14	4 26	16 10	4 35	16 05	4 49	15 56
18 Th	11 59 27	+10 44	5 40	18 19	5 30	18 29	5 18	18 41	5 01	18 58	4 35	19 25
108			4 45	17 05	4 45	17 07	4 46	17 09	4 48	17 12	4 49	17 17
19 Fr	11 59 14	+11 05	5 39	18 20	5 29	18 29	5 16	18 42	4 59	18 59	4 32	19 28
109			5 16	17 53	5 12	18 00	5 07	18 08	5 00	18 19	4 50	18 37
20 Sa	11 59 01	+11 25	5 38	18 20	5 28	18 30	5 15	18 43	4 57	19 01	4 29	19 30
110	05 22 ●		5 48	18 42	5 39	18 53	5 28	19 08	5 13	19 27	4 51	19 59
21 Su	11 58 48	+11 46	5 37	18 20	5 27	18 31	5 14	18 44	4 55	19 03	4 26	19 32
111			6 21	19 32	6 08	19 48	5 51	20 09	5 29	20 37	4 53	21 24
22 Mo	11 58 36	+12 06	5 36	18 20	5 26	18 31	5 12	18 45	4 54	19 04	4 24	19 35
112			6 58	20 25	6 40	20 45	6 18	21 11	5 47	21 47	4 56	22 52
23 Tu	11 58 25	+12 26	5 36	18 21	5 25	18 32	5 11	18 46	4 52	19 06	4 21	19 38
113			7 38	21 19	7 16	21 42	6 49	22 13	6 10	22 57	5 03	
24 We	11 58 13	+12 46	5 35	18 21	5 24	18 33	5 10	18 47	4 50	19 08	4 18	19 40
114			8 23	22 40	7 58	22 55	7 27	23 13	6 41		5 16	0 21
25 Th	11 58 03	+13 06	5 34	18 21	5 23	18 33	5 08	18 48	4 48	19 10	4 15	19 42
115			9 13	23 08	8 46	23 35	8 12		7 23	0 03	5 42	1 42
26 Fr	11 57 52	+13 26	5 33	18 21	5 22	18 34	5 07	18 49	4 46	19 11	4 12	19 45
116			10 08		9 41		9 07	0 09	8 17	1 00	6 34	2 43
27 Sa	11 57 43	+13 45	5 33	18 22	5 21	18 34	5 06	18 50	4 44	19 12	4 10	19 48
117			11 05	0 01	10 41	0 27	10 09	0 59	9 23	1 46	7 54	3 17
28 Su	11 57 33	+14 04	5 33	18 22	5 20	18 35	5 04	18 51	4 42	19 14	4 07	19 50
118	04 25 ☾		12 05	0 51	11 44	1 14	11 17	1 42	10 39	2 23	9 31	3 34
29 Mo	11 57 24	+14 23	5 32	18 22	5 19	18 36	5 03	18 52	4 40	19 16	4 04	19 52
119			13 06	1 38	12 50	1 56	12 29	2 19	12 00	2 50	11 12	3 42
30 Tu	11 57 16	+14 41	5 32	18 23	5 18	18 36	5 02	18 54	4 38	19 17	4 02	19 55
120			14 07	2 21	13 56	2 34	13 43	2 50	13 24	3 12	12 54	3 47

5th Month   May, 1985   31 days

Greenwich Mean Time

NOTE: Light figures indicate Sun. **Dark** figures indicate **Moon.** *Degrees are North Latitude.*

CAUTION: Must be converted to local time. For instruction see page 726.

Day of month / week / year	Sun on meridian / Moon phase (h m s)	Sun's Declination (° ')	20° Rise Sun/Moon (h m)	20° Set Sun/Moon (h m)	30° Rise Sun/Moon (h m)	30° Set Sun/Moon (h m)	40° Rise Sun/Moon (h m)	40° Set Sun/Moon (h m)	50° Rise Sun/Moon (h m)	50° Set Sun/Moon (h m)	60° Rise Sun/Moon (h m)	60° Set Sun/Moon (h m)
1 We 121	11 57 08	+ 15 00	5 31	18 24	5 17	18 37	5 00	18 55	4 37	19 18	3 59	19 58
			15 08	3 02	15 03	3 10	14 57	3 19	14 49	3 31	14 37	3 50
2 Th 122	11 57 01	+ 15 18	5 30	18 24	5 16	18 38	4 59	18 56	4 35	19 20	3 56	20 00
			16 09	3 42	16 11	3 44	16 13	3 46	16 15	3 48	16 20	3 52
3 Fr 123	11 56 54	+ 15 36	5 30	18 24	5 15	18 38	4 58	18 57	4 33	19 22	3 53	20 02
			17 12	4 23	17 20	4 18	17 30	4 13	17 44	4 05	18 06	3 53
4 Sa 124	11 56 48 19 53 ○	+ 15 53	5 29	18 24	5 14	18 39	4 58	18 58	4 32	19 23	3 50	20 05
			18 17	5 06	18 32	4 55	18 50	4 42	19 15	4 24	19 56	3 56
5 Su 125	11 56 42	+ 16 11	5 28	18 25	5 14	18 39	4 55	18 59	4 30	19 24	3 48	20 08
			19 25	5 52	19 45	5 35	20 10	5 14	20 47	4 46	21 51	4 00
6 Mo 126	11 56 37	+ 16 28	5 28	18 25	5 13	18 40	4 54	19 00	4 28	19 26	3 45	20 10
			20 33	6 43	20 57	6 21	21 29	5 54	22 15	5 15	23 43	4 07
7 Tu 127	11 56 33	+ 16 44	5 27	18 25	5 12	18 41	4 53	19 01	4 26	19 28	3 42	20 12
			21 39	7 39	22 06	7 14	22 41	6 41	23 32	5 54		4 24
8 We 128	11 56 29	+ 17 01	5 27	18 26	5 12	18 41	4 53	19 02	4 25	19 29	3 40	20 15
			22 41	8 39	23 08	8 12	23 42	7 37		6 40	1 17	5 00
9 Th 129	11 56 25	+ 17 17	5 26	18 26	5 11	18 42	4 51	19 02	4 24	19 30	3 38	20 18
			23 36	9 41		9 15		8 41	0 32	7 51	2 15	6 10
10 Fr 130	11 56 23	+ 17 33	5 26	18 27	5 10	18 43	4 50	19 03	4 22	19 32	3 35	20 20
				10 42	0 00	10 18	0 32	9 48	1 17	9 05	2 40	7 43
11 Sa 131	11 56 20 17 34 ☾	+ 17 49	5 25	18 27	5 09	18 44	4 49	19 04	4 20	19 34	3 32	20 22
			0 23	11 39	0 45	11 20	1 11	10 55	1 48	10 21	2 52	9 20
12 Su 132	11 56 19	+ 18 04	5 25	18 27	5 08	18 44	4 48	19 05	4 19	19 35	3 30	20 24
			1 05	12 34	1 22	12 19	1 42	12 01	2 11	11 35	2 57	10 52
13 Mo 133	11 56 18	+ 18 19	5 24	18 28	5 08	18 45	4 47	19 06	4 18	19 36	3 28	20 27
			1 42	13 25	1 54	13 15	2 09	13 03	2 29	12 46	3 00	12 19
14 Tu 134	11 56 17	+ 18 34	5 24	18 28	5 07	18 46	4 46	19 07	4 16	19 38	3 25	20 29
			2 15	14 14	2 23	14 09	2 31	14 03	2 43	13 55	3 01	13 42
15 We 135	11 56 17	+ 18 48	5 24	18 28	5 06	18 46	4 45	19 08	4 14	19 39	3 23	20 32
			2 47	15 02	2 49	15 02	2 52	15 02	2 56	15 02	3 02	15 03
16 Th 136	11 56 18	+ 19 02	5 24	18 29	5 06	18 47	4 44	19 09	4 13	19 40	3 20	20 34
			3 18	15 50	3 16	15 55	3 13	16 01	3 09	16 09	3 03	16 23
17 Fr 137	11 56 19	+ 19 16	5 23	18 29	5 05	18 47	4 43	19 10	4 12	19 42	3 18	20 36
			3 49	16 38	3 42	16 48	3 33	17 00	3 21	17 17	3 03	17 44
18 Sa 138	11 56 21	+ 19 29	5 23	18 30	5 05	18 48	4 42	19 11	4 10	19 43	3 16	20 39
			4 22	17 28	4 10	17 43	3 56	18 01	3 36	18 26	3 05	19 08
19 Su 139	11 56 24 21 41 ●	+ 19 43	5 23	18 30	5 04	18 49	4 41	19 12	4 09	19 44	3 14	20 41
			4 58	18 20	4 41	18 39	4 21	19 03	3 53	19 37	3 08	20 36
20 Mo 140	11 56 27	+ 19 55	5 23	18 31	5 04	18 49	4 40	19 13	4 08	19 46	3 12	20 44
			5 37	19 14	5 17	19 37	4 51	20 06	4 15	20 48	3 13	22 05
21 Tu 141	11 56 30	+ 20 08	5 22	18 31	5 03	18 50	4 39	19 14	4 06	19 48	3 09	20 46
			6 21	20 09	5 57	20 35	5 27	21 07	4 43	21 55	3 23	23 31
22 We 142	11 56 34	+ 20 20	5 22	18 32	5 03	18 51	4 39	19 15	4 05	19 49	3 07	20 48
			7 10	21 04	6 43	21 31	6 10	22 05	5 21	22 56	3 45	
23 Th 143	11 56 39	+ 20 32	5 22	18 32	5 02	18 51	4 38	19 16	4 04	19 50	3 05	20 50
			8 03	21 58	7 36	22 24	7 02	22 57	6 11	23 46	4 28	0 39
24 Fr 144	11 56 44	+ 20 43	5 22	18 32	5 02	18 52	4 38	19 18	4 03	19 52	3 03	20 52
			9 00	22 48	8 34	23 12	8 02	23 42	7 14		5 40	1 21
25 Sa 145	11 56 50	+ 20 54	5 21	18 33	5 02	18 52	4 37	19 17	4 02	19 53	3 01	20 54
			9 59	23 35	9 36	23 55	9 08		8 27	0 25	7 12	1 42
26 Su 146	11 56 56	+ 21 05	5 21	18 33	5 01	18 53	4 36	19 18	4 01	19 54	2 59	20 56
			10 58		10 40		10 17	0 20	9 45	0 54	8 50	1 52
27 Mo 147	11 57 02 12 56 ☽	+ 21 15	5 21	18 34	5 01	18 53	4 36	19 19	4 00	19 55	2 57	20 58
			11 57	0 18	11 44	0 33	11 28	0 52	11 06	1 17	10 30	1 58
28 Tu 148	11 57 09	+ 21 25	5 21	18 34	5 01	18 54	4 35	19 20	3 59	19 56	2 56	21 00
			12 56	0 59	12 48	1 09	12 39	1 20	12 27	1 36	12 08	2 01
29 We 149	11 57 17	+ 21 35	5 20	18 35	5 00	18 54	4 34	19 20	3 58	19 57	2 54	21 02
			13 54	1 38	13 53	1 42	13 52	1 47	13 50	1 53	13 47	2 03
30 Th 150	11 57 25	+ 21 44	5 20	18 35	5 00	18 55	4 34	19 21	3 57	19 58	2 52	21 04
			14 54	2 16	14 59	2 15	15 06	2 12	15 14	2 09	15 28	2 05
31 Fr 151	11 57 33	+ 21 53	5 20	18 35	5 00	18 55	4 33	19 22	3 56	19 59	2 51	21 06
			15 57	2 57	16 08	2 49	16 22	2 39	16 42	2 26	17 13	2 06

6th Month   **June, 1985**   **30 days**

Greenwich Mean Time

NOTE: Light figures indicate Sun. **Dark** figures indicate **Moon**. *Degrees are North Latitude.*

CAUTION: Must be converted to local time. For instruction see page 726.

Day of month / week / year	Sun on meridian Moon phase h m s	Sun's Declination °	20° Rise Sun / Moon h m	20° Set Sun / Moon h m	30° Rise Sun / Moon h m	30° Set Sun / Moon h m	40° Rise Sun / Moon h m	40° Set Sun / Moon h m	50° Rise Sun / Moon h m	50° Set Sun / Moon h m	60° Rise Sun / Moon h m	60° Set Sun / Moon h m
1 Sa	11 57 42	+ 22 01	05 20	18 35	05 00	18 56	04 33	19 22	03 56	20 00	02 50	21 08
152			**17 02**	**03 40**	**17 19**	**03 26**	**17 41**	**03 09**	**18 11**	**02 46**	**19 03**	**02 09**
2 Su	11 57 51	+ 22 09	05 20	18 36	04 59	18 56	04 32	19 23	03 55	20 01	02 48	21 09
153			**18 09**	**04 28**	**18 32**	**04 08**	**19 00**	**03 44**	**19 41**	**03 11**	**20 57**	**02 15**
3 Mo	11 58 00 / **3 50 ○**	+ 22 17	05 20	18 36	04 59	18 57	04 32	19 24	03 55	20 02	02 47	21 11
154			**19 17**	**05 21**	**19 43**	**04 57**	**20 17**	**04 27**	**21 06**	**03 44**	**22 44**	**02 26**
4 Tu	11 58 10	+ 22 24	05 20	18 36	04 59	18 57	04 32	19 25	03 54	20 03	02 46	21 12
155			**20 23**	**06 20**	**20 50**	**05 54**	**21 25**	**05 20**	**22 16**	**04 30**		**02 50**
5 We	11 58 20	+ 22 31	05 20	18 37	04 59	18 58	04 31	19 26	03 54	20 04	02 44	21 16
156			**21 22**	**07 23**	**21 48**	**06 56**	**22 21**	**06 21**	**23 09**	**05 30**	**00 02**	**03 44**
6 Th	11 58 31	+ 22 38	05 20	18 37	04 58	18 58	04 31	19 26	03 53	20 05	02 43	21 16
157			**22 15**	**08 26**	**22 38**	**08 01**	**23 06**	**07 29**	**23 47**	**06 42**	**00 42**	**05 11**
7 Fr	11 58 42	+ 22 44	05 20	18 38	04 58	18 59	04 31	19 27	03 52	20 06	02 42	21 17
158			**23 00**	**09 27**	**23 19**	**09 05**	**23 42**	**08 38**		**08 00**	**00 59**	**06 50**
8 Sa	11 58 53	+ 22 49	05 20	18 38	04 58	18 59	04 31	19 28	03 52	20 07	02 41	21 18
159			**23 40**	**10 24**	**23 54**	**10 07**		**09 47**	**00 14**	**09 17**	**01 07**	**08 28**
9 Su	11 59 04	┊ 22 55	05 20		04 58	19 00	04 31	19 28	03 52	20 08	02 40	21 20
160				**11 18**		**11 06**	**00 11**	**10 52**	**00 34**	**10 31**	**01 11**	**09 59**
10 Mo	11 59 16 / **08 19 ☾**	+ 23 00	05 20	18 39	04 58	19 00	04 31	19 29	03 51	20 08	02 39	21 21
161			**00 15**	**12 09**	**00 24**	**12 02**	**00 35**	**11 54**	**00 50**	**11 42**	**01 12**	**11 24**
11 Tu	11 59 28	+ 23 04	05 20	18 39	04 58	19 01	04 31	19 29	03 51	20 09	02 38	21 22
162			**00 48**	**12 57**	**00 52**	**12 56**	**00 57**	**12 54**	**01 03**	**12 51**	**01 14**	**12 46**
12 We	11 59 40	+ 23 08	05 20	18 40	04 58	19 01	04 31	19 29	03 51	20 10	02 38	21 23
163			**01 19**	**13 45**	**01 18**	**13 48**	**01 17**	**13 52**	**01 16**	**13 58**	**01 14**	**14 07**
13 Th	11 59 52	+ 23 12	05 20	18 40	04 58	19 01	04 30	19 30	03 50	20 10	02 37	21 24
164			**01 50**	**14 33**	**01 45**	**14 41**	**01 38**	**14 51**	**01 29**	**15 05**	**01 15**	**15 27**
14 Fr	12 00 05	+ 23 15	05 20	18 41	04 58	19 02	04 30	19 30	03 50	20 11	02 36	21 24
165			**02 23**	**15 22**	**02 12**	**15 35**	**02 00**	**15 52**	**01 43**	**16 14**	**01 16**	**16 50**
15 Sa	12 00 18	+ 23 18	05 20	18 41	04 58	19 02	04 30	19 30	03 50	20 11	02 36	21 25
166			**02 57**	**16 14**	**02 42**	**16 31**	**02 24**	**16 53**	**01 59**	**17 24**	**01 19**	**18 17**
16 Su	12 00 31	+ 23 20	05 20	18 41	04 58	19 03	04 30	19 30	03 50	20 11	02 36	21 26
167			**03 35**	**17 07**	**03 16**	**17 29**	**02 52**	**17 56**	**02 19**	**18 35**	**01 23**	**19 46**
17 Mo	12 00 44	+ 23 22	05 21	18 41	04 58	19 03	04 30	19 31	03 50	20 12	02 36	21 26
168			**04 17**	**18 02**	**03 55**	**18 27**	**03 26**	**18 59**	**02 45**	**19 45**	**01 31**	**21 14**
18 Tu	12 00 57 / **11 58 ●**	+ 23 24	05 21	18 42	04 59	19 03	04 31	19 31	03 50	20 12	02 35	21 27
169			**05 05**	**18 58**	**04 39**	**19 25**	**04 07**	**19 59**	**03 19**	**20 49**	**01 49**	**22 31**
19 We	12 01 10	+ 23 25	05 21	18 42	04 59	19 04	04 31	19 32	03 50	20 12	02 35	21 27
170			**05 58**	**19 53**	**05 31**	**20 20**	**04 57**	**20 53**	**04 06**	**21 43**	**02 24**	**23 22**
20 Th	12 01 23	+ 23 26	05 21	18 42	04 59	19 04	04 31	19 32	03 50	20 12	02 35	21 27
171			**06 54**	**20 45**	**06 28**	**21 10**	**05 55**	**21 41**	**05 06**	**22 26**	**03 28**	**23 48**
21 Fr	12 01 36	+ 23 27	05 22	18 42	04 59	19 04	04 31	19 32	03 50	20 12	02 36	21 28
172			**07 53**	**21 34**	**07 30**	**21 55**	**07 00**	**22 21**	**06 17**	**22 58**	**04 56**	
22 Sa	12 01 49	+ 23 27	05 22	18 42	05 00	19 04	04 32	19 33	03 51	20 13	02 36	21 28
173			**08 53**	**22 18**	**08 33**	**22 35**	**08 09**	**22 55**	**07 34**	**23 23**	**06 34**	**00 01**
23 Su	12 02 02	+ 23 26	05 22	18 42	05 00	19 04	04 32	19 33	03 51	20 13	02 36	21 28
174			**09 52**	**22 59**	**09 37**	**23 10**	**09 19**	**23 24**	**08 54**	**23 43**	**08 13**	**00 08**
24 Mo	12 02 15	+ 23 25	05 22	18 42	05 00	19 04	04 32	19 33	03 51	20 13	02 36	21 28
175			**10 50**	**23 38**	**10 41**	**23 43**	**10 30**		**10 15**		**09 51**	**00 12**
25 Tu	12 02 28 / **18 53 ☽**	+ 23 24	05 23	18 42	05 00	19 04	04 32	19 33	03 52	20 13	02 37	21 28
176			**11 47**		**11 44**		**11 41**		**11 36**	**00 00**	**11 28**	**00 14**
26 We	12 02 41	+ 23 22	05 23	18 43	05 01	19 05	04 33	19 33	03 52	20 13	02 38	21 27
177			**12 45**	**00 15**	**12 48**	**00 15**	**12 52**	**00 15**	**12 57**	**00 15**	**13 05**	**00 16**
27 Th	12 02 53	+ 23 20	05 23	18 43	05 01	19 05	04 33	19 33	03 53	20 13	02 38	21 27
178			**13 45**	**00 54**	**13 54**	**00 48**	**14 05**	**00 41**	**14 20**	**00 31**	**14 45**	**00 17**
28 Fr	12 03 06	+ 23 18	05 23	18 43	05 01	19 05	04 33	19 33	03 54	20 13	02 39	21 27
179			**14 46**	**01 34**	**15 01**	**01 23**	**15 20**	**01 08**	**15 46**	**00 49**	**16 29**	**00 19**
29 Sa	12 03 18	+ 23 15	05 24	18 43	05 01	19 05	04 33	19 33	03 54	20 12	02 40	21 26
180			**15 51**	**02 18**	**16 11**	**02 01**	**16 37**	**01 40**	**17 14**	**01 11**	**18 19**	**00 23**
30 Su	12 03 30	+ 23 11	05 24	18 43	05 02	19 05	04 34	19 33	03 55	20 12	02 41	21 26
181			**16 58**	**03 08**	**17 22**	**02 46**	**17 53**	**02 18**	**18 39**	**01 39**	**20 08**	**00 31**

7th Month

July, 1985

31 Days

Greenwich Mean Time

NOTE: Light figures indicate Sun. **Dark** figures indicate **Moon.** *Degrees are North Latitude.*

CAUTION: Must be converted to local time. For instruction see page 726.

Day of month / week / year	Sun on meridian Moon phase h m s	Sun's Declination ° '	20° Rise Sun/Moon h m	20° Set Sun/Moon h m	30° Rise Sun/Moon h m	30° Set Sun/Moon h m	40° Rise Sun/Moon h m	40° Set Sun/Moon h m	50° Rise Sun/Moon h m	50° Set Sun/Moon h m	60° Rise Sun/Moon h m	60° Set Sun/Moon h m
1 Mo	12 03 42	+23 08	5 24	18 43	5 02	19 05	4 35	19 33	3 55	20 12	2 42	21 25
182			18 04	4 04	18 30	3 38	19 05	3 05	19 56	2 18	21 41	0 48
2 Tu	12 03 53	+23 04	5 24	18 43	5 02	19 05	4 35	19 33	3 56	20 12	2 43	21 24
183	12 08 ○		19 06	5 04	19 33	4 37	20 07	4 02	20 57	3 11	22 38	1 26
3 We	12 04 04	+22 59	5 24	18 44	5 03	19 05	4 36	19 32	3 56	20 12	2 44	21 23
184			20 02	6 07	20 27	5 41	20 57	5 08	21 42	4 18	23 03	2 39
4 Th	12 04 15	+22 54	5 25	18 44	5 03	19 05	4 36	19 32	3 57	20 11	2 46	21 22
185			20 51	7 10	21 12	6 47	21 38	6 18	22 13	5 35	23 15	4 16
5 Fr	12 04 26	+22 49	5 25	18 44	5 04	19 05	4 37	19 32	3 58	20 11	2 47	21 21
186			21 34	8 10	21 50	7 52	22 10	7 28	22 37	6 54	23 20	5 56
6 Sa	12 04 36	+22 43	5 26	18 44	5 04	19 05	4 37	19 32	3 59	20 11	2 48	21 20
187			22 12	9 07	22 23	8 53	22 36	8 36	22 54	8 12	23 23	7 32
7 Su	12 04 46	+22 37	5 26	18 44	5 05	19 04	4 38	19 32	4 00	20 10	2 50	21 19
188			22 46	10 00	22 52	9 51	22 59	9 40	23 09	9 25	23 24	9 02
8 Mo	12 04 56	+22 31	5 27	18 43	5 05	19 04	4 38	19 31	4 00	20 10	2 52	21 18
189			23 18	10 50	23 19	10 46	23 21	10 42	23 22	10 36	23 25	10 26
9 Tu	12 05 05	+22 24	5 27	18 43	5 06	19 04	4 39	19 31	4 01	20 09	2 53	21 17
190			23 50	11 38	23 46	11 40	23 41	11 42	23 35	11 44	23 25	11 48
10 We	12 05 14	+22 16	5 27	18 43	5 06	19 04	4 40	19 30	4 02	20 08	2 54	21 16
191	00 49 ◖			12 27		12 33		12 41	23 48	12 52	23 26	13 09
11 Th	12 05 22	+22 09	5 28	18 43	5 07	19 04	4 40	19 30	4 03	20 08	2 56	21 14
192			0 22	13 15	0 13	13 27	0 02	13 41		14 00	23 28	14 31
12 Fr	12 05 30	+22 01	5 28	18 43	5 07	19 03	4 41	19 30	4 04	20 07	2 58	21 12
193			0 55	14 06	0 42	14 22	0 26	14 42	0 03	15 10	23 32	15 56
13 Sa	12 05 38	+21 52	5 28	18 43	5 08	19 03	4 42	19 29	4 05	20 06	2 59	21 11
194			1 32	14 58	1 14	15 18	0 52	15 44	0 22	16 20	23 38	17 24
14 Su	12 05 45	+21 43	5 29	18 43	5 08	19 03	4 43	19 29	4 06	20 05	3 01	21 09
195			2 12	15 53	1 51	16 16	1 23	16 47	0 45	17 31	23 51	18 54
15 Mo	12 05 51	+21 34	5 29	18 43	5 09	19 03	4 44	19 28	4 08	20 04	3 03	21 08
196			2 58	16 49	2 33	17 15	2 02	17 48	1 16	18 37		20 16
16 Tu	12 05 57	+21 25	5 30	18 42	5 09	19 02	4 44	19 28	4 09	20 03	3 05	21 06
197			3 49	17 45	3 22	18 11	2 48	18 46	1 59	19 36	0 19	21 18
17 We	12 06 03	+21 15	5 30	18 42	5 10	19 02	4 45	19 27	4 10	20 02	3 07	21 04
198	23 56 ●		4 45	18 39	4 18	19 04	3 44	19 36	2 54	20 23	1 13	21 52
18 Th	12 06 08	+21 05	5 30	18 42	5 10	19 02	4 46	19 26	4 11	20 01	3 09	21 02
199			5 44	19 29	5 20	19 52	4 48	20 20	4 03	20 59	2 35	22 09
19 Fr	12 06 13	+20 54	5 31	18 42	5 11	19 01	4 46	19 25	4 12	20 00	3 11	21 00
200			6 45	20 16	6 24	20 34	5 58	20 56	5 20	21 27	4 13	22 17
20 Sa	12 06 17	+20 43	5 31	18 41	5 11	19 01	4 47	19 25	4 13	19 59	3 13	20 58
201			7 45	20 58	7 29	21 11	7 09	21 27	6 41	21 48	5 55	22 22
21 Su	12 06 20	+20 32	5 32	18 41	5 12	19 00	4 48	19 24	4 14	19 58	3 15	20 56
202			8 45	21 38	8 34	21 45	8 21	21 54	8 03	22 06	7 35	22 24
22 Mo	12 06 23	+20 20	5 32	18 41	5 13	19 00	4 49	19 23	4 15	19 57	3 17	20 54
203			9 43	22 16	9 38	22 18	9 32	22 20	9 25	22 22	9 12	22 26
23 Tu	12 06 25	+20 08	5 32	18 41	5 13	18 59	4 50	19 22	4 16	19 56	3 20	20 52
204			10 40	22 54	10 42	22 50	10 43	22 45	10 46	22 38	10 49	22 28
24 We	12 06 27	+19 56	5 33	18 40	5 14	18 59	4 51	19 22	4 18	19 54	3 22	20 49
205 *	23 39 ☽		11 39	23 33	11 46	23 23	11 55	23 11	12 08	22 55	12 27	22 29
25 Th	12 06 28	+19 43	5 33	18 40	5 15	18 58	4 52	19 21	4 19	19 53	3 24	20 47
206			12 39		12 52		13 08	23 41	13 31	23 14	14 09	22 33
26 Fr	12 06 29	+19 30	5 33	18 40	5 15	18 57	4 53	19 20	4 20	19 52	3 26	20 45
207			13 41	0 15	14 00	0 00	14 23		14 57	23 39	15 54	22 38
27 Sa	12 06 29	+19 17	5 34	18 39	5 16	18 57	4 54	19 19	4 22	19 50	3 28	20 42
208			14 45	1 02	15 09	0 41	15 38	0 16	16 21		17 42	22 50
28 Su	12 06 28	+19 03	5 34	18 39	5 16	18 56	4 54	19 18	4 24	19 48	3 31	20 40
209			15 50	1 54	16 16	1 29	16 50	0 58	17 40	0 13	19 21	23 17
29 Mo	12 06 26	+18 49	5 34	18 38	5 17	18 55	4 55	19 17	4 25	19 47	3 33	20 38
210			16 53	2 51	17 20	2 24	17 54	1 50	18 46	0 59	20 32	
30 Tu	12 06 24	+18 35	5 34	18 38	5 17	18 55	4 56	19 16	4 26	19 46	3 36	20 36
211			17 51	3 52	18 16	3 25	18 49	2 51	19 36	2 00	21 07	0 15
31 We	12 06 22	+18 20	5 35	18 38	5 18	18 54	4 57	19 15	4 28	19 44	3 38	20 33
212	21 41 ○		18 42	4 55	19 05	4 30	19 33	3 59	20 12	3 13	21 22	1 44

8th Month   August, 1985   31 Days

Greenwich Mean Time

NOTE: Light figures indicate Sun. **Dark** figures indicate **Moon.** *Degrees are North Latitude.*

CAUTION: Must be converted to local time. For instruction see page 726.

Day of month / week / year	Sun on meridian Moon phase h m s	Sun's Decli-nation °	20° Rise Sun/Moon h m	20° Set Sun/Moon h m	30° Rise h m	30° Set h m	40° Rise h m	40° Set h m	50° Rise h m	50° Set h m	60° Rise h m	60° Set h m
1 Th	12 06 19	+18 05	5 36	18 37	5 18	18 54	4 58	19 14	4 29	19 42	3 40	20 30
213			19 28	5 56	19 45	5 35	20 08	5 09	20 38	4 31	21 29	3 25
2 Fr	12 06 15	+17 50	5 36	18 37	5 19	18 53	4 59	19 13	4 30	19 41	3 43	20 28
214			20 07	6 54	20 20	6 38	20 36	6 18	20 58	5 50	21 32	5 03
3 Sa	12 06 10	+17 35	5 36	18 36	5 20	18 52	5 00	19 12	4 32	19 40	3 45	20 26
215			20 43	7 49	20 51	7 38	21 01	7 25	21 14	7 06	21 34	9 36
4 Su	12 06 05	+17 19	5 36	18 36	5 20	18 51	5 01	19 11	4 33	19 38	3 48	20 23
216			21 16	8 41	21 19	8 35	21 23	8 28	21 28	8 19	21 35	8 04
5 Mo	12 06 00	+17 03	5 37	18 35	5 21	18 50	5 02	19 09	4 34	19 36	3 50	20 20
217			21 48	9 30	21 46	9 30	21 44	9 29	21 40	9 29	21 36	9 27
6 Tu	12 05 54	+16 47	5 37	18 34	5 22	18 49	5 03	19 08	4 36	19 35	3 52	20 18
218			22 20	10 19	22 13	10 24	22 05	10 29	21 53	10 37	21 36	10 49
7 We	12 05 47	+16 30	5 37	18 34	5 22	18 48	5 04	19 07	4 38	19 33	3 54	20 15
219			22 53	11 08	22 41	11 17	22 27	11 29	22 08	11 45	21 37	12 11
8 Th	12 05 39 18 29 ☾	+16 13	5 37	18 33	5 23	18 48	5 05	19 06	4 39	19 32	3 57	20 12
220			23 28	11 57	23 12	12 12	22 52	12 29	22 24	12 54	21 40	13 35
9 Fr	12 05 32	+15 56	5 38	18 32	5 23	18 47	5 06	19 04	4 40	19 30	4 00	20 10
221				12 49	23 46	13 07	23 21	13 31	22 45	14 06	21 45	15 02
10 Sa	12 05 23	+15 39	5 38	18 32	5 24	18 46	5 07	19 03	4 42	19 28	4 02	20 07
222			0 07	13 42		14 05	23 21	14 33	22 45	15 15	21 45	16 31
11 Su	12 05 14	+15 21	5 38	18 31	5 25	18 45	5 08	19 02	4 44	19 26	4 04	20 04
223			0 50	14 37	0 26	15 03		15 35	23 50	16 23	22 14	17 58
12 Mo	12 05 04	+15 03	5 39	18 30	5 26	18 44	5 08	19 01	4 45	19 24	4 06	20 02
224			1 38	15 33	1 12	16 00	0 38	16 34		17 25	22 55	19 09
13 Tu	12 04 54	+14 45	5 39	18 30	5 26	18 43	5 09	18 59	4 46	19 22	4 09	19 59
225			2 32	16 28	2 05	16 54	1 30	17 28	0 40	18 17		19 54
14 We	12 04 44	+14 27	5 40	18 29	5 27	18 42	5 10	18 58	4 48	19 20	4 11	19 56
226			3 30	17 20	3 04	17 44	2 32	18 14	1 43	18 57	0 08	20 16
15 Th	12 04 32	+14 08	5 40	18 29	5 28	18 41	5 11	18 57	4 50	19 18	4 14	19 53
227			4 31	18 09	4 09	18 29	3 40	18 54	2 58	19 28	1 42	20 26
16 Fr	12 04 21 10 06 ●	+13 50	5 40	18 28	5 28	18 40	5 12	18 56	4 51	19 16	4 16	19 50
228			5 33	18 54	5 15	19 09	4 52	19 27	4 20	19 52	3 25	20 32
17 Sa	12 04 08	+13 31	5 41	18 28	5 29	18 39	5 13	18 54	4 52	19 15	4 18	19 48
229			6 34	19 35	6 21	19 45	6 06	19 56	5 44	20 11	5 09	20 35
18 Su	12 03 56	+13 11	5 41	18 27	5 29	18 38	5 14	18 53	4 54	19 13	4 21	19 45
230			7 34	20 15	7 27	20 18	7 19	20 22	7 08	20 28	6 50	20 36
19 Mo	12 03 42	+12 52	5 41	18 26	5 30	18 37	5 15	18 52	4 56	19 11	4 24	19 42
231			8 33	20 53	8 33	20 51	8 32	20 48	8 31	20 44	8 30	20 38
20 Tu	12 03 28	+12 32	5 41	18 26	5 30	18 36	5 16	18 50	4 57	19 09	4 26	19 39
232			9 33	21 33	9 38	21 24	9 45	21 14	9 55	21 00	10 10	20 39
21 We	12 03 14	+12 13	5 42	18 25	5 31	18 35	5 17	18 48	4 58	19 07	4 28	19 36
233			10 33	22 14	10 45	22 00	10 59	21 43	11 19	21 19	11 52	20 42
22 Th	12 02 59	+11 53	5 42	18 24	5 31	18 34	5 18	18 47	5 00	19 05	4 31	19 33
234			11 35	22 59	11 52	22 40	12 14	22 16	12 45	21 42	13 38	20 46
23 Fr	12 02 44 04 36 ☽	+11 32	5 42	18 23	5 32	18 33	5 19	18 46	5 02	19 03	4 33	19 30
235			12 39	23 49	13 01	23 26	13 29	22 56	14 10	22 13	15 25	20 55
24 Sa	12 02 28	+11 12	5 42	18 22	5 32	18 32	5 20	18 44	5 03	19 01	4 36	19 28
236			13 43		14 09		14 42	23 44	15 30	22 54	17 08	21 15
25 Su	12 02 12	+10 51	5 43	18 21	5 33	18 31	5 21	18 42	5 04	18 59	4 38	19 25
237			14 45	0 44	15 12	0 18	15 47		16 39	23 49	18 28	22 00
26 Mo	12 01 56	+10 31	5 43	18 20	5 34	18 30	5 22	18 41	5 06	18 57	4 40	19 22
238			15 44	1 43	16 10	1 16	16 44	0 41	17 33		19 12	23 20
27 Tu	12 01 39	+10 10	5 43	18 19	5 34	18 29	5 23	18 40	5 08	18 55	4 42	19 19
239			16 36	2 44	17 00	2 19	17 30	1 46	18 13	0 57	19 31	
28 We	12 01 21	+09 49	5 43	18 18	5 35	18 28	5 24	18 38	5 09	18 52	4 45	19 16
240			17 23	3 45	17 43	3 23	18 07	2 54	18 42	2 13	19 39	0 58
29 Th	12 01 03	+09 27	5 44	18 18	5 35	18 26	5 25	18 36	5 10	18 50	4 48	19 13
241			18 04	4 44	18 19	4 26	18 38	4 03	19 03	3 32	19 43	2 37
30 Fr	12 00 45 09 27 ○	+09 06	5 44	18 17	5 36	18 25	5 26	18 35	5 12	18 48	4 50	19 10
242			18 41	5 39	18 51	5 26	19 03	5 10	19 20	4 48	19 45	4 12
31 Sa	12 00 27	+08 45	5 44	18 16	5 36	18 24	5 27	18 34	5 14	18 46	4 52	19 07
243			19 15	6 32	19 20	6 24	19 26	6 15	19 34	6 02	19 46	5 41

9th Month September, 1985 30 Days

Greenwich Mean Time

NOTE: Light figures indicate Sun. **Dark** figures indicate **Moon**. *Degrees are North Latitude.*

CAUTION: Must be converted to local time. For instruction see page 726.

Day of month week year	Sun on meridian Moon phase h m s	Sun's Declination ° '	20° Rise Sun/Moon h m	20° Set Sun/Moon h m	30° Rise Sun/Moon h m	30° Set Sun/Moon h m	40° Rise Sun/Moon h m	40° Set Sun/Moon h m	50° Rise Sun/Moon h m	50° Set Sun/Moon h m	60° Rise Sun/Moon h m	60° Set Sun/Moon h m
1 Su 244	12 00 08	+ 08 23	5 44	18 16	5 37	18 22	5 28	18 32	5 15	18 44	4 54	19 04
			19 47	7 22	19 47	7 20	19 47	7 17	19 47	7 13	19 46	7 07
2 Mo 245	11 59 49	+ 08 01	5 45	18 15	5 37	18 21	5 28	18 30	5 16	18 42	4 57	19 01
			20 19	8 12	20 14	8 14	20 08	8 18	19 59	8 22	19 47	8 29
3 Tu 246	11 59 30	+ 07 39	5 45	18 14	5 38	18 20	5 29	18 29	5 18	18 40	4 59	18 58
			20 15	9 00	20 41	9 08	20 29	9 18	20 13	9 31	19 47	9 52
4 We 247	11 59 10	+ 07 17	5 45	18 13	5 38	18 19	5 30	18 27	5 20	18 38	5 02	18 55
			21 25	9 50	21 11	10 02	20 53	10 18	20 28	10 40	19 49	11 15
5 Th 248	11 58 50	+ 06 55	5 45	18 12	5 39	18 18	5 31	18 26	5 21	18 36	5 04	18 52
			22 02	10 40	21 43	10 58	21 19	11 19	20 47	11 50	19 52	12 41
6 Fr 249	11 58 30	+ 06 33	5 46	18 11	5 39	18 16	5 32	18 24	5 22	18 33	5 06	18 49
			22 43	11 32	22 20	11 54	21 51	12 21	21 11	13 00	19 58	14 10
7 Sa 250	11 58 10	+ 06 10	5 46	18 10	5 40	18 15	5 33	18 22	5 24	18 31	5 09	18 46
	12 16 ((		23 28	12 26	23 03	12 51	22 30	13 23	21 43	14 09	20 12	15 38
8 Su 251	11 57 49	+ 05 48	5 46	18 09	5 40	18 14	5 34	18 20	5 26	18 29	5 11	18 43
				13 21	23 52	13 48	23 17	14 22	22 26	15 13	20 41	16 58
9 Mo 252	11 57 29	+ 05 25	5 46	18 08	5 41	18 13	5 35	18 19	5 27	18 27	5 14	18 40
			0 19	14 16		14 43		15 18	23 23	16 09	21 39	17 53
10 Tu 253	11 57 08	+ 05 03	5 46	18 07	5 41	18 12	5 36	18 18	5 28	18 25	5 16	18 37
			1 15	15 09	0 48	15 34	0 14	16 06		16 53	23 06	18 22
11 We 254	11 56 47	+ 04 40	5 46	18 06	5 42	18 11	5 37	18 16	5 30	18 23	5 18	18 34
			2 14	15 59	1 50	16 21	1 18	16 48	0 33	17 27		18 36
12 Th 255	11 56 26	+ 04 17	5 46	18 05	5 42	18 10	5 38	18 14	5 32	18 21	5 20	18 31
			3 15	16 45	2 55	17 02	2 29	17 24	1 52	17 54	0 47	18 42
13 Fr 256	11 56 05	+ 03 54	5 47	18 04	5 43	18 08	5 39	18 12	5 33	18 18	5 22	8 28
			4 17	17 28	4 02	17 40	3 42	17 55	3 16	18 15	2 31	18 46
14 Sa 257	11 55 44 19 20 ●	+ 03 31	5 47	18 04	5 43	18 07	5 40	18 11	5 34	18 16	5 25	18 25
			5 18	18 09	5 09	18 15	4 57	18 22	4 41	18 32	4 15	18 47
15 Su 258	11 55 23	+ 03 08	5 47	18 03	5 44	18 06	5 41	18 09	5 36	18 14	5 27	18 22
			6 19	18 48	6 16	18 48	6 12	18 49	6 07	18 49	5 58	18 49
16 Mo 259	11 55 01	+ 02 45	5 47	18 02	5 45	18 05	5 42	18 07	5 38	18 12	5 30	18 19
			7 20	19 28	7 23	19 22	7 27	19 15	7 33	19 05	7 41	18 50
17 Tu 260	11 54 40	+ 02 22	5 47	18 01	5 45	18 04	5 42	18 06	5 39	18 10	5 32	18 16
			8 22	20 10	8 32	19 58	8 43	19 43	9 00	19 23	9 26	18 51
18 We 261	11 54 19	+ 01 59	5 48	18 00	5 46	18 02	5 63	18 04	5 40	18 07	5 34	18 12
			9 25	20 55	9 41	20 37	10 01	20 15	10 28	19 45	11 14	18 55
19 Th 262	11 53 57	+ 01 35	5 48	17 59	5 47	18 01	5 44	18 02	5 42	18 05	5 37	18 09
			10 30	21 45	10 52	21 22	11 18	20 53	11 57	20 13	13 05	19 01
20 Fr 263	11 53 36	+ 01 12	5 48	17 58	5 48	18 00	5 45	18 00	5 44	18 03	5 39	18 06
			11 36	22 39	12 01	22 13	12 33	21 40	13 21	20 51	14 54	19 16
21 Sa 264	11 53 15 11 03))	+ 00 49	5 48	17 57	5 48	17 58	5 46	17 59	5 45	18 00	5 42	18 03
			12 40	23 38	13 07	23 10	13 42	22 35	14 34	21 42	16 25	19 51
22 Su 265	11 52 54	+ 00 25	5 49	17 56	5 49	17 57	5 47	17 58	5 46	17 58	5 44	18 00
			13 40		14 07		14 42	23 37	15 33	22 47	17 19	21 02
23 Mo 266	11 52 32	+ 00 02	5 49	17 55	5 49	17 56	5 48	17 56	5 48	17 56	5 46	17 57
			14 34	0 38	14 59	0 12	15 30		16 16		17 42	22 37
24 Tu 267	11 52 11	− 00 21	5 49	17 54	5 50	17 55	5 49	17 54	5 50	17 54	5 48	17 51
			15 22	1 39	15 43	1 15	16 09	0 45	16 47	0 01	17 51	
25 We 268	11 51 51	− 00 45	5 49	17 54	5 50	17 54	5 50	17 52	5 51	17 52	5 51	17 51
			16 04	2 37	16 20	2 18	16 41	1 53	17 09	1 18	17 55	0 17
26 Th 269	11 51 30	− 01 08	5 50	17 53	5 51	17 52	5 51	17 51	5 52	17 49	5 54	17 48
			16 41	3 33	16 53	3 18	17 07	3 00	17 27	2 34	17 57	1 52
27 Fr 270	11 51 09	− 09 31	5 50	17 52	5 51	17 51	5 52	17 49	5 54	17 47	5 56	17 45
			17 15	4 26	17 22	4 17	17 30	4 05	17 41	3 48	17 58	3 22
28 Sa 271	11 50 49	− 01 55	5 50	17 51	5 52	17 50	5 53	17 48	5 56	17 45	5 58	17 42
			17 48	5 17	17 49	5 12	17 51	5 07	17 54	5 00	17 58	4 48
29 Su 272	11 50 29 00 08 ○	− 02 18	5 50	17 50	5 52	17 48	5 54	17 46	5 57	17 43	6 00	17 39
			18 19	6 06	18 16	6 07	18 12	6 08	18 06	6 09	17 58	6 12
30 Mo 273	11 50 09	− 02 41	5 51	17 49	5 53	17 47	5 55	17 44	5 58	17 41	6 03	17 36
			18 51	6 55	18 43	7 01	18 33	7 08	18 19	7 18	17 58	7 34

10th Month | October, 1985 | 31 Days

Greenwich Mean Time

NOTE: Light figures indicate Sun. **Dark** figures indicate **Moon**. *Degrees are North Latitude.*

CAUTION: Must be converted to local time. For instruction see page 726.

Day of month week year	Sun on meridian Moon phase h m s	Sun's Decli- nation ° '	20° Rise Sun/Moon h m	20° Set Sun/Moon h m	30° Rise Sun/Moon h m	30° Set Sun/Moon h m	40° Rise Sun/Moon h m	40° Set Sun/Moon h m	50° Rise Sun/Moon h m	50° Set Sun/Moon h m	60° Rise Sun/Moon h m	60° Set Sun/Moon h m
1 Tu 274	11 49 49	− 03 05	5 51	17 48	5 53	17 46	5 56	17 43	6 00	17 39	6 05	17 33
			19 24	7 44	19 11	7 55	18 55	8 08	18 34	8 27	17 59	8 57
2 We 275	11 49 30	− 03 28	5 51	17 47	5 54	17 45	5 57	17 41	6 02	17 37	6 08	17 30
			20 00	8 34	19 42	8 49	19 21	9 09	18 51	9 37	18 01	10 23
3 Th 276	11 49 11	− 03 51	5 51	17 46	5 54	17 44	5 58	17 40	6 03	17 34	6 10	17 17
			20 39	9 25	20 17	9 45	19 50	10 11	19 12	10 47	18 06	11 51
4 Fr 277	11 48 52	− 04 14	5 52	17 46	5 55	17 42	5 59	17 38	6 04	17 32	6 12	17 24
			21 22	10 18	20 57	10 42	20 26	11 13	19 40	11 57	18 15	13 20
5 Sa 278	11 48 34	− 04 38	5 52	17 45	5 56	17 41	6 00	17 36	6 06	17 30	6 15	17 21
			22 10	11 12	21 43	11 39	21 09	12 13	20 18	13 02	18 36	14 44
6 Su 279	11 48 16	− 05 01	5 52	17 44	5 56	17 40	6 01	17 34	6 08	17 28	6 17	17 18
			23 03	12 06	22 36	12 34	22 01	13 09	21 09	14 01	19 20	15 50
7 Mo 280	11 47 58 05 04 ◑	− 05 24	5 52	17 43	5 57	17 38	6 02	17 33	6 09	17 26	6 20	17 15
			23 59	12 59	23 34	13 25	23 00	13 59	22 12	14 49	20 35	16 27
8 Tu 281	11 47 41	− 05 47	5 53	17 42	5 57	17 37	6 03	17 32	6 10	17 24	6 22	17 12
				13 49		14 13		14 43	23 26	15 26	22 09	16 45
9 Wo 282	11 47 24	− 06 09	5 53	17 41	5 58	17 36	6 04	17 30	6 12	17 22	6 24	17 09
			0 58	14 35	0 36	14 55	0 07	15 20		15 55	23 51	16 53
10 Th 283	11 47 08	− 06 32	5 53	17 40	5 58	17 35	6 05	17 28	6 14	17 20	6 26	17 06
			1 58	15 19	1 40	15 34	1 18	15 52	0 46	16 17		16 57
11 Fr 284	11 46 52	− 06 55	5 53	17 40	5 59	17 34	6 06	17 27	6 15	17 18	6 29	17 03
			2 59	16 00	2 46	16 09	2 31	16 21	2 09	16 36	1 34	16 59
12 Sa 285	11 46 37	− 07 18	5 54	17 39	5 59	17 33	6 07	17 26	6 16	17 15	6 32	17 00
			3 59	16 40	3 53	16 43	3 45	16 47	3 34	16 52	3 16	17 00
13 Su 286	11 46 22	− 07 40	5 54	17 38	6 00	17 32	6 08	17 24	6 18	17 13	6 34	16 57
			5 00	17 20	5 00	17 17	5 00	17 13	5 00	17 08	5 00	17 01
14 Mo 287	11 46 08 04 33 ●	− 08 03	5 54	17 37	6 01	17 31	6 09	17 22	6 20	17 11	6 36	16 54
			6 03	18 01	6 09	17 52	6 17	17 41	6 28	17 25	6 45	17 02
15 Tu 288	11 45 54	− 08 25	5 54	17 36	6 02	17 30	6 10	17 21	6 22	17 09	6 39	16 52
			7 07	18 46	7 20	18 30	7 36	18 11	7 58	17 45	8 35	17 04
16 We 289	11 45 41	− 08 47	5 55	17 36	6 02	.17 28	6 11	17 20	6 23	17 07	6 41	16 49
			8 14	19 35	8 33	19 44	8 57	18 48	9 31	18 11	10 30	17 08
17 Th 290	11 45 28	− 09 09	5 55	17 35	6 03	17 27	6 12	17 18	6 25	17 05	6 44	16 46
			9 22	20 29	9 46	20 04	10 16	19 32	11 01	18 46	12 26	17 19
18 Fr 291	11 45 16	− 09 31	5 56	17 34	6 04	17 26	6 13	17 16	6 26	17 03	6 46	16 43
			10 29	21 29	10 56	21 01	11 31	20 26	12 22	19 34	14 11	17 45
19 Sa 292	11 45 05	− 09 53	5 56	17 34	6 04	17 25	6 14	17 15	6 28	17 01	6 49	16 40
			11 33	22 30	12 00	22 03	12 36	21 28	13 29	20 36	15 21	18 44
20 Su 293	11 44 54 20 13 ☽	− 10 14	5 57	17 33	6 05	17 24	6 16	17 14	6 30	16 59	6 52	16 37
			12 30	23 32	12 56	23 07	13 29	22 36	14 17	21 49	15 51	20 17
21 Mo 294	11 44 44	− 10 36	5 57	17 32	6 06	17 23	6 17	17 12	6 31	16 57	6 54	16 34
			13 20		13 43		14 11	23 45	14 52	23 06	16 03	21 58
22 Tu 295	11 44 34	− 10 57	5 57	17 32	6 07	17 22	6 18	17 11	6 33	16 55	6 56	16 31
			14 04	0 32	14 22	0 11	14 45		15 16		16 08	23 35
23 We 296	11 44 25	− 11 18	5 58	17 31	6 08	17 21	6 19	17 10	6 34	16 54	6 59	16 28
			14 43	1 29	14 56	1 13	15 13	0 52	15 35	0 23	16 10	
24 Th 297	11 44 17	− 11 39	5 58	17 31	6 08	17 20	6 20	17 08	6 36	16 52	7 02	16 26
			15 18	2 22	15 26	2 11	15 36	1 57	15 50	1 38	16 11	1 07
25 Fr 298	11 44 09	− 12 00	5 58	17 30	6 09	17 19	6 21	17 07	6 38	16 50	7 04	16 23
			15 50	3 13	15 53	3 07	15 57	3 00	16 03	2 49	16 11	2 33
26 Sa 299	11 44 03	− 12 21	5 59	17 29	6 10	17 18	6 22	17 06	6 40	16 48	7 06	16 20
			16 21	4 02	16 20	4 01	16 18	4 00	16 15	3 59	16 11	3 57
27 Su 300	11 43 56	− 12 41	5 59	17 28	6 10	17 18	6 23	17 04	6 41	16 46	7 09	16 11
			16 53	4 51	16 46	4 55	16 38	5 00	16 27	5 07	16 11	5 19
28 Mo 301	11 43 51 17 38 ○	− 13 02	6 00	17 28	6 11	17 17	6 24	17 02	6 42	16 44	7 12	16 15
			17 25	5 39	17 14	5 49	17 00	6 00	16 41	6 16	16 11	6 41
29 Tu 302	11 43 46	− 13 22	6 00	17 27	6 11	17 16	6 25	17 01	6 44	16 42	7 14	16 12
			18 00	6 29	17 44	6 43	17 24	7 01	16 57	7 25	16 13	8 06
30 We 303	11 43 42	− 13 41	6 00	17 27	6 12	17 15	6 26	17 00	6 45	16 40	7 16	16 10
			18 38	7 20	18 17	7 39	17 52	8 02	17 16	8 36	16 16	9 33
31 Th 304	11 43 39	− 14 01	6 01	17 26	6 13	17 14	6 28	16 59	6 46	16 38	7 19	16 07
			19 19	8 13	18 55	8 35	18 25	9 04	17 42	9 46	16 23	11 03

11th Month　　　　　November, 1985　　　　　30 Days

Greenwich Mean Time

NOTE: Light figures indicate Sun. **Dark** figures indicate **Moon.** *Degrees are North Latitude.*

CAUTION: Must be converted to local time. For instruction see page 726.

Day of month week year	Sun on meridian Moon phase h m s	Sun's Decli- nation ° '	20° Rise Sun / Moon h m	20° Set Sun / Moon h m	30° Rise Sun / Moon h m	30° Set Sun / Moon h m	40° Rise Sun / Moon h m	40° Set Sun / Moon h m	50° Rise Sun / Moon h m	50° Set Sun / Moon h m	60° Rise Sun / Moon h m	60° Set Sun / Moon h m
1 Fr 305	11 43 37	−14 20	6 01	17 26	6 14	17 13	6 29	16 58	6 46	16 37	7 22	16 04
			20 06	9 06	19 39	9 32	19 05	10 05	18 16	10 53	16 38	12 30
2 Sa 306	11 43 35	−14 40	6 02	17 25	6 15	17 12	6 30	16 57	6 51	16 35	7 24	16 02
			20 56	10 00	20 29	10 28	19 54	11 03	19 02	11 54	17 12	13 44
3 Su 307	11 43 35	−14 59	6 02	17 25	6 16	17 11	6 31	16 56	6 50	16 34	7 27	16 00
			21 51	10 53	21 24	11 20	20 50	11 55	19 59	12 46	18 15	14 30
4 Mo 308	11 43 35	−15 17	6 03	17 24	6 17	17 10	6 32	16 54	6 52	16 32	7 30	15 57
			22 47	11 43	22 23	12 08	21 52	12 40	21 08	13 26	19 43	14 53
5 Tu 309	11 43 36 / 20 07 ☾	−15 36	6 03	17 23	6 17	17 10	6 34	16 53	6 55	16 30	7 32	15 54
			23 45	12 29	23 25	12 51	23 00	13 18	22 23	13 57	21 20	15 03
6 We 310	11 43 38	−15 54	6 04	17 23	6 18	17 09	6 35	16 52	6 58	16 29	7 35	15 52
				13 12		13 30		13 51	23 43	14 20	22 59	15 08
7 Th 311	11 44 40	−16 12	6 04	17 23	6 19	17 08	6 36	16 51	7 00	16 28	7 38	15 50
			0 43	13 53	0 28	14 05	0 09	14 20		14 40		15 10
8 Fr 312	11 43 44	−16 29	6 05	17 22	6 20	17 08	6 37	16 50	7 01	16 26	7 40	15 47
			1 42	14 32	1 32	14 38	1 20	14 46	1 04	14 56	0 38	15 12
9 Sa 313	11 43 48	−16 47	6 05	17 22	6 20	17 07	6 38	16 49	7 02	16 24	7 42	15 44
			2 41	15 10	2 37	15 11	2 33	15 11	2 27	15 12	2 18	15 12
10 Su 314	11 43 53	−17 04	6 06	17 22	6 21	17 07	6 39	16 48	7 04	16 23	7 45	15 42
			3 41	15 50	3 44	15 44	3 47	15 37	3 52	15 28	4 00	15 13
11 Mo 315	11 43 59	−17 21	6 06	17 22	6 22	17 06	6 40	16 47	7 06	16 22	7 48	15 40
			4 43	16 33	4 53	16 21	5 04	16 06	5 20	15 46	5 46	15 14
12 Tu 316	11 44 06 / 14 20 ●	−17 37	6 07	17 21	6 22	17 06	6 42	16 46	7 08	16 20	7 50	15 38
			5 49	17 20	6 05	17 02	6 25	16 39	6 52	16 08	7 39	15 17
13 We 317	11 44 14	−17 53	6 07	17 21	6 23	17 05	6 43	16 46	7 09	16 18	7 52	15 35
			6 58	18 13	7 20	17 49	7 47	17 20	8 26	16 38	9 37	15 24
14 Th 318	11 44 23	−18 09	6 08	17 21	6 24	17 04	6 44	16 45	7 11	16 17	7 55	15 33
			8 08	19 12	8 34	18 45	9 07	18 11	9 56	17 21	11 34	15 41
15 Fr 319	11 44 42	−18 25	6 09	17 21	6 25	17 04	6 45	16 44	7 12	16 16	7 58	15 31
			9 16	20 15	9 44	19 47	10 20	19 12	11 13	18 18	13 07	16 24
16 Sa 320	11 44 43	−18 40	6 10	17 21	6 26	17 04	6 46	16 44	7 14	16 14	8 00	15 28
			10 19	21 20	10 46	20 54	11 21	20 20	12 11	19 30	13 54	17 49
17 Su 321	11 44 54	−18 55	6 10	17 20	6 26	17 03	6 47	16 43	7 16	16 13	8 02	15 26
			11 14	22 23	11 38	22 00	12 09	21 31	12 42	20 50	14 12	19 32
18 Mo 322	11 45 06	−19 10	6 11	17 20	6 27	17 03	6 48	16 42	7 17	16 12	8 05	15 24
			12 02	23 22	12 22	23 04	12 46	22 41	13 21	22 09	14 19	21 15
19 Tu 323	11 45 18 / 09 04 ☽	−19 24	6 11	17 20	6 28	17 02	6 49	16 41	7 19	16 11	8 08	15 22
			12 43		12 58		13 16	23 49	13 42	23 26	14 22	22 50
20 We 324	11 45 32	−19 38	6 12	17 20	6 29	17 02	6 50	16 40	7 20	16 10	8 10	15 20
			13 19	0 18	13 29	0 05	13 41		13 58		14 23	
21 Th 325	11 45 46	−19 51	6 12	17 19	6 30	17 02	6 52	16 40	7 22	16 09	8 12	15 19
			13 52	1 10	13 57	1 02	14 03	0 52	14 11	0 39	14 24	0 19
22 Fr 326	11 46 02	−20 04	6 13	17 19	6 31	17 01	6 53	16 39	7 24	16 08	8 15	15 17
			14 24	1 59	14 24	1 57	14 24	1 54	14 24	1 49	14 23	1 43
23 Sa 327	11 46 08	−20 17	6 13	17 19	6 32	17 01	6 54	16 38	7 26	16 07	8 17	15 15
			14 55	2 48	14 50	2 50	14 44	2 53	14 36	2 58	14 23	3 05
24 Su 328	11 46 34	−20 30	6 14	17 19	6 32	17 01	6 55	16 38	7 27	16 06	8 20	15 14
			15 27	3 36	15 17	3 43	15 05	3 53	14 49	4 06	14 24	4 26
25 Mo 329	11 46 52	−20 42	6 14	17 19	6 33	17 00	6 56	16 38	7 28	16 06	8 22	15 12
			16 01	4 27	15 46	4 37	15 28	4 53	15 04	5 15	14 25	5 50
26 Tu 330	11 47 10	−20 53	6 15	17 19	6 34	17 00	6 57	16 37	7 30	16 05	8 24	15 10
			16 37	5 15	16 18	5 33	15 55	5 54	15 22	6 25	14 27	7 16
27 We 331	11 47 29 / 12 42 ○	−21 05	6 16	17 19	6 35	17 00	6 58	16 37	7 31	16 04	8 26	15 08
			17 18	6 08	16 55	6 29	16 26	6 56	15 45	7 35	14 33	8 46
28 Th 332	11 47 49	−21 15	6 16	17 19	6 36	17 00	6 59	16 36	7 32	16 04	8 28	15 07
			18 03	7 01	17 37	7 26	17 04	7 58	16 17	8 44	14 45	10 15
29 Fr 333	11 48 09	−21 26	6 17	17 19	6 36	17 00	7 00	16 36	7 34	16 03	8 31	15 06
			18 52	7 56	18 25	8 23	17 50	8 57	16 59	9 48	15 12	11 34
30 Sa 334	11 48 30	−21 36	6 18	17 19	6 37	17 00	7 01	16 35	7 35	16 02	8 33	15 04
			19 46	8 49	19 19	9 16	18 44	9 51	17 53	10 43	16 06	12 30

12th Month   December, 1985   31 days

Greenwich Mean Time

NOTE: Light figures indicate Sun. **Dark** figures indicate **Moon**. *Degrees are North Latitude.*

CAUTION: Must be converted to local time. For instruction see page 726.

Day of month week year	Sun on meridian Moon phase h m s	Sun's Decli-nation °'	20° Rise Sun Moon h m	20° Set Sun Moon h m	30° Rise Sun Moon h m	30° Set Sun Moon h m	40° Rise Sun Moon h m	40° Set Sun Moon h m	50° Rise Sun Moon h m	50° Set Sun Moon h m	60° Rise Sun Moon h m	60° Set Sun Moon h m
1 Su	11 48 52	−21 46	6 18	17 19	6 38	17 00	7 02	16 35	7 36	16 02	8 35	15 03
335			20 42	9 40	20 17	10 05	19 45	10 38	18 58	11 26	17 27	12 59
2 Mo	11 49 14	−21 55	6 19	17 20	6 38	17 00	7 03	16 35	7 38	16 01	8 37	15 02
336			21 39	10 27	21 17	10 50	20 50	11 18	20 11	11 59	19 01	13 12
3 Tu	11 49 37	−22 04	6 19	17 20	6 39	17 00	7 04	16 35	7 39	16 00	8 39	15 00
337			22 35	11 10	22 18	11 29	21 57	11 52	21 28	12 25	20 37	13 18
4 We	11 50 01	−22 12	6 20	17 20	6 40	17 00	7 05	16 35	7 40	16 00	8 41	14 59
338			23 32	11 50	23 20	12 04	23 06	12 21	22 46	12 45	22 14	13 21
5 Th	11 50 25	−22 20	6 21	17 20	6 41	17 00	7 06	16 35	7 41	16 00	8 43	14 58
339	09 01 ☾			12 28		12 37		12 47		13 01	23 49	13 23
6 Fr	11 50 50	−22 28	6 22	17 20	6 42	17 00	7 07	16 35	7 42	15 59	8 44	14 58
340			0 28	13 05	0 22	13 08	0 15	13 12	0 05	13 16		13 23
7 Sa	11 51 16	−22 35	6 22	17 21	6 42	17 00	7 08	16 35	7 44	15 58	8 46	14 57
341			1 25	13 43	1 25	13 40	1 25	13 36	1 25	13 31	1 25	13 24
8 Su	11 51 42	−22 41	6 23	17 21	6 43	17 00	7 09	16 35	7 45	15 58	8 48	14 56
342			2 24	14 22	2 30	14 13	2 38	14 02	2 49	13 48	3 05	13 25
9 Mo	11 52 08	−22 48	6 23	17 21	6 44	17 00	7 10	16 35	7 46	15 58	8 50	14 56
343			3 26	15 06	3 39	14 51	3 54	14 32	4 16	14 07	4 51	13 27
10 Tu	11 52 35	−22 53	6 24	17 22	6 44	17 00	7 10	16 35	7 47	15 58	8 51	14 55
344			4 32	15 55	4 51	15 34	5 14	15 08	5 47	14 32	6 44	13 31
11 We	11 53 03	−22 59	6 25	17 22	6 45	17 01	7 11	16 35	7 48	15 58	8 52	14 55
345			5 41	16 50	6 05	16 25	6 35	15 53	7 19	15 08	8 42	13 42
12 Th	11 53 30	−23 04	6 25	17 22	6 46	17 01	7 12	16 35	7 49	15 58	8 54	14 54
346	00 54 ●		6 51	17 52	7 18	17 25	7 53	16 50	8 45	15 57	10 32	14 09
13 Fr	11 53 59	−23 08	6 26	17 22	6 47	17 01	7 13	16 35	7 50	15 58	8 55	14 54
347			7 59	18 59	8 26	18 31	9 02	17 56	9 54	17 04	11 45	15 14
14 Sa	11 54 27	−23 12	6 26	17 23	6 48	17 01	7 14	16 36	7 51	15 58	8 56	14 54
348			9 00	20 05	9 25	19 40	9 58	19 09	10 45	18 23	12 16	16 55
15 Su	11 54 56	−23 15	6 27	17 23	6 48	17 02	7 14	16 36	7 52	15 59	8 57	14 53
349			9 52	21 08	10 14	20 48	10 42	20 23	11 20	19 46	12 27	18 43
16 Mo	11 55 25	−23 18	6 28	17 24	6 49	17 02	7 15	16 36	7 53	15 59	8 57	14 53
350			10 38	22 07	10 55	21 52	11 16	21 34	11 45	21 07	12 32	20 24
17 Tu	11 55 54	−23 21	6 28	17 24	6 50	17 02	7 16	16 36	7 54	15 59	8 59	14 53
351			11 17	23 02	11 29	22 52	11 43	22 41	12 03	22 24	12 34	21 58
18 We	11 56 23	−23 23	6 29	17 24	6 50	17 03	7 16	16 36	7 54	16 00	9 00	14 54
352			11 52	23 53	11 59	23 49	12 07	23 44	12 18	23 37	12 35	23 25
19 Th	11 56 53	−23 25	6 29	17 25	6 51	17 03	7 17	16 37	7 55	16 00	9 00	14 54
353	01 58 ☽		12 25		12 26		12 28		12 31		12 35	
20 Fr	11 57 23	−23 26	6 30	17 25	6 51	17 04	7 18	16 37	7 55	16 00	9 01	14 54
354			12 56	0 43	12 53	0 44	12 49	0 45	12 43	0 46	12 35	0 49
21 Sa	11 57 52	−23 26	6 30	17 25	6 52	17 04	7 18	16 38	7 56	16 00	9 02	14 54
355			13 28	1 31	13 19	1 37	13 09	1 45	12 56	1 55	12 35	2 11
22 Su	11 58 22	−23 27	6 31	17 26	6 52	17 05	7 19	16 38	7 56	16 01	9 02	14 55
356			14 01	2 20	13 48	2 31	13 32	2 45	13 10	3 04	12 36	3 34
23 Mo	11 58 52	−23 26	6 31	17 26	6 53	17 06	7 20	16 39	7 57	16 01	9 03	14 56
357			14 36	3 10	14 19	3 26	13 57	3 46	13 27	4 13	12 38	4 59
24 Tu	11 59 22	−23 26	6 32	17 27	6 53	17 06	7 20	16 40	7 57	16 02	9 03	14 56
358			15 16	4 02	14 54	4 22	14 27	4 47	13 49	5 23	12 42	6 27
25 We	11 59 52	−23 24	6 32	17 28	6 54	17 07	7 20	16 40	7 57	16 03	9 03	14 57
359			15 59	4 55	15 34	5 19	15 03	5 49	14 17	6 33	12 52	7 57
26 Th	12 00 21	−23 23	6 33	17 28	6 54	17 07	7 20	16 41	7 58	16 04	9 04	14 58
360			16 48	5 49	16 21	6 16	15 46	6 50	14 56	7 39	13 13	9 21
27 Fr	12 00 51	−23 21	6 33	17 29	6 55	17 08	7 21	16 41	7 58	16 04	9 04	15 00
361	07 30 ○		17 40	6 44	17 13	7 11	16 38	7 46	15 47	8 38	13 58	10 26
28 Sa	12 01 20	−23 18	6 34	17 30	6 55	17 09	7 21	16 42	7 58	16 05	9 04	15 00
362			18 36	7 36	18 11	8 02	17 38	8 36	16 49	9 25	15 13	11 03
29 Su	12 01 50	−23 15	6 34	17 30	6 55	17 09	7 21	16 43	7 58	16 06	9 04	15 01
363			19 34	8 25	19 11	8 48	18 42	9 19	18 01	10 02	16 45	11 20
30 Mo	12 02 19	−23 11	6 35	17 31	6 56	17 10	7 22	16 44	7 58	16 07	9 03	15 02
364			20 31	9 09	20 13	9 29	19 50	9 54	19 17	10 29	18 22	11 28
31 Tu	12 02 48	−23 07	6 35	17 32	6 56	17 10	7 22	16 44	7 59	16 08	9 03	15 04
365			21 27	9 51	21 14	10 06	20 58	10 25	20 35	10 50	19 58	11 31

Perpetual Calendar

The number shown for each year indicates which Gregorian calendar to use. For 1583-1802, or for Julian calendar, see page 750. For years 1803-1820, use numbers for 1983-2000, respectively.

1821....2	1847....6	1873....4	1899....1	1925....5	1951....2	1977....7	2003....4	2029....2	2055....6
1822....3	1848....14	1874....5	1900....2	1926....6	1952....10	1978....1	2004....12	2030....3	2056....14
1823....4	1849....2	1875....6	1901....3	1927....7	1953....5	1979....2	2005....7	2031....4	2057....2
1824....12	1850....3	1876....14	1902....4	1928....8	1954....6	1980....10	2006....1	2032....12	2058....3
1825....7	1851....4	1877....2	1903....5	1929....3	1955....7	1981....5	2007....2	2033....7	2059....4
1826....1	1852....12	1878....3	1904....13	1930....4	1956....8	1982....6	2008....10	2034....1	2060....12
1827....2	1853....7	1879....4	1905....1	1931....5	1957....3	1983....7	2009....5	2035....2	2061....7
1828....10	1854....1	1880....12	1906....2	1932....13	1958....4	1984....8	2010....6	2036....10	2062....1
1829....5	1855....2	1881....7	1907....3	1933....1	1959....5	1985....3	2011....7	2037....5	2063....2
1830....6	1856....10	1882....1	1908....11	1934....2	1960....13	1986....4	2012....8	2038....6	2064....10
1831....7	1857....5	1883....2	1909....6	1935....3	1961....1	1987....5	2013....3	2039....7	2065....5
1832....8	1858....6	1884....10	1910....7	1936....11	1962....2	1988....13	2014....4	2040....8	2066....6
1833....3	1859....7	1885....5	1911....1	1937....6	1963....3	1989....1	2015....5	2041....3	2067....7
1834....4	1860....8	1886....6	1912....9	1938....7	1964....11	1990....2	2016....13	2042....4	2068....8
1835....5	1861....3	1887....7	1913....4	1939....1	1965....6	1991....3	2017....1	2043....5	2069....3
1836....13	1862....4	1888....8	1914....5	1940....9	1966....7	1992....11	2018....2	2044....13	2070....4
1837....1	1863....5	1889....3	1915....6	1941....4	1967....1	1993....6	2019....3	2045....1	2071....5
1838....2	1864....13	1890....4	1916....14	1942....5	1968....9	1994....7	2020....11	2046....2	2072....13
1839....3	1865....1	1891....5	1917....2	1943....6	1969....4	1995....1	2021....6	2047....3	2073....1
1840....11	1866....2	1892....13	1918....3	1944....14	1970....5	1996....9	2022....7	2048....11	2074....2
1841....6	1867....3	1893....1	1919....4	1945....2	1971....6	1997....4	2023....1	2049....6	2075....3
1842....7	1868....11	1894....2	1920....12	1946....3	1972....14	1998....5	2024....9	2050....7	2076....11
1843....1	1869....6	1895....3	1921....7	1947....4	1973....2	1999....6	2025....4	2051....1	2077....6
1844....9	1870....7	1896....11	1922....1	1948....12	1974....3	2000....14	2026....5	2052....9	2078....7
1845....4	1871....1	1897....6	1923....2	1949....7	1975....4	2001....2	2027....6	2053....4	2079....1
1846....5	1872....9	1898....7	1924....10	1950....1	1976....12	2002....3	2028....14	2054....5	2080....9

Perpetual calendar grids numbered 1 through 14, each showing the twelve months (January–December) with day-of-week columns S M T W T F S, including example year labels 1985, 1986, and others.

Julian and Gregorian Calendars; Leap Year

Calendars based on the movements of sun and moon have been used since ancient times, but none has been perfect. The Julian calendar, under which western nations measured time until 1582 A.D., was authorized by Julius Caesar in 46 B.C., the year 709 of Rome. His expert was a Greek, Sosigenes. The Julian calendar, on the assumption that the true year was 365 1/4 days long, gave every fourth year 366 days. The Venerable Bede, an Anglo-Saxon monk, announced in 730 A.D. that the 365 1/4-day Julian year was 11 min., 14 sec. too long, making a cumulative error of about a day every 128 years, but nothing was done about it for over 800 years.

By 1582 the accumulated error was estimated to have amounted to 10 days. In that year Pope Gregory XIII decreed that the day following Oct. 4, 1582, should be called Oct. 15, thus dropping 10 days.

However, with common years 365 days and a 366-day leap year every fourth year, the error in the length of the year would have recurred at the rate of a little more than 3 days every 400 years. So 3 of every 4 centesimal years (ending in 00) were made common years, not leap years. Thus 1600 was a leap year, 1700, 1800 and 1900 were not, but 2000 will be. Leap years are those divisible by 4 except centesimal years, which are common unless divisible by 400.

The Gregorian calendar was adopted at once by France, Italy, Spain, Portugal and Luxembourg. Within 2 years most German Catholic states, Belgium and parts of Switzerland and the Netherlands were brought under the new calendar, and Hungary followed in 1587. The rest of the Netherlands, along with Denmark and the German Protestant states made the change in 1699-1700 (German Protestants retained the old reckoning of Easter until 1776).

The British Government imposed the Gregorian calendar on all its possessions, including the American colonies, in 1752. The British decreed that the day following Sept. 2, 1752, should be called Sept. 14, a loss of 11 days. All dates preceding were marked O.S., for Old Style. In addition New Year's Day was moved to Jan. 1 from Mar. 25. (e.g., under the old reckoning, Mar. 24, 1700 had been followed by Mar. 25, 1701.) George Washington's birth date, which was Feb. 11, 1731, O.S., became Feb. 22, 1732, N.S. In 1753 Sweden too went Gregorian, retaining the old Easter rules until 1844.

In 1793 the French Revolutionary Government adopted a calendar of 12 months of 30 days each with 5 extra days in September of each common year and a 6th extra day every 4th year. Napoleon reinstated the Gregorian calendar in 1806.

The Gregorian system later spread to non-European regions, first in the European colonies, then in the independent countries, replacing traditional calendars at least for official purposes. Japan in 1873, Egypt in 1875, China in 1912 and Turkey in 1917 made the change, usually in conjunction with political upheavals. In China, the republican government began reckoning years from its 1911 founding — e.g., 1948 was designated the year 37. After 1949, the Communists adopted the Common, or Christian Era year count, even for the traditional lunar calendar.

In 1918 the revolutionary government in Russia decreed that the day after Jan. 31, 1918, Old Style, would become Feb. 14, 1918, New Style. Greece followed in 1923. (In Russia the Orthodox Church has retained the Julian calendar, as have various Middle Eastern Christian sects.) For the first time in history, all major cultures have one calendar.

To change from the Julian to the Gregorian calendar, add 10 days to dates Oct. 5, 1582, through Feb. 28, 1700; after that date add 11 days through Feb. 28, 1800; 12 days through Feb. 28, 1900; and 13 days through Feb. 28, 2100.

A century consists of 100 consecutive calendar years. The 1st century consisted of the years 1 through 100. The 20th century consists of the years 1901 through 2000 and will end Dec. 31, 2000. The 21st century will begin Jan. 1, 2001.

Julian Calendar

To find which of the 14 calendars printed on pages 748-749 applies to any year, starting Jan. 1, under the Julian system, find the century for the desired year in the three left-hand columns below; read across. Then find the year in the four top rows; read down. The number in the intersection is the calendar designation for that year.

Year (last two figures of desired year)																											
01	02	03	04	05	06	07	08	09	10	11	12	13	14	15	16	17	18	19	20	21	22	23	24	25	26	27	28
29	30	31	32	33	34	35	36	37	38	39	40	41	42	43	44	45	46	47	48	49	50	51	52	53	54	55	56
57	58	59	60	61	62	63	64	65	66	67	68	69	70	71	72	73	74	75	76	77	78	79	80	81	82	83	84
Century	00	85	86	87	88	89	90	91	92	93	94	95	96	97	98	99											

Century			00																									
0	700	1400	12	7	1	2	10	5	6	7	8	3	4	5	13	1	2	3	11	6	7	1	9	4	5	6	14	2	3	4	12
100	800	1500	11	6	7	1	9	4	5	6	14	2	3	4	12	7	1	2	10	5	6	7	8	3	4	5	13	1	2	3	11
200	900	1600	10	5	6	7	8	3	4	5	13	1	2	3	11	6	7	1	9	4	5	6	14	2	3	4	12	7	1	2	10
300	1000	1700	9	4	5	6	14	2	3	4	12	7	1	2	10	5	6	7	8	3	4	5	13	1	2	3	11	6	7	1	9
400	1100	1800	8	3	4	5	13	1	2	3	11	6	7	1	9	4	5	6	14	2	3	4	12	7	1	2	10	5	6	7	8
500	1200	1900	14	2	3	4	12	7	1	2	10	5	6	7	8	3	4	5	13	1	2	3	11	6	7	1	9	4	5	6	14
600	1300	2000	13	1	2	3	11	6	7	1	9	4	5	6	14	2	3	4	12	7	1	2	10	5	6	7	8	3	4	5	13

Gregorian Calendar

Pick desired year from table below or on page 748 (for years 1800 to 2059). The number shown with each year shows which calendar to use for that year, as shown on pages 748-749 (The Gregorian calendar was inaugurated Oct. 15, 1582. From that date to Dec. 31, 1582, use calendar 6.)

1583-1802

1583 . . 7	1603 . . 4	1623 . . 1	1643 . . 5	1663 . . 2	1683 . . 6	1703 . . 2	1723 . . 6	1743 . . 3	1763 . . 7	1783 . . 4
1584 . . 8	1604 . 12	1624 . . 9	1644 . 13	1664 . 10	1684 . 14	1704 . 10	1724 . 14	1744 . 11	1764 . . 8	1784 . 12
1585 . . 3	1605 . . 7	1625 . . 4	1645 . . 1	1665 . . 5	1685 . . 2	1705 . . 5	1725 . . 2	1745 . . 6	1765 . . 3	1785 . . 7
1586 . . 4	1606 . . 1	1626 . . 5	1646 . . 2	1666 . . 6	1686 . . 3	1706 . . 6	1726 . . 3	1746 . . 7	1766 . . 4	1786 . . 1
1587 . . 5	1607 . . 2	1627 . . 6	1647 . . 3	1667 . . 7	1687 . . 4	1707 . . 7	1727 . . 4	1747 . . 1	1767 . . 5	1787 . . 2
1588 . 13	1608 . 10	1628 . 14	1648 . 11	1668 . . 8	1688 . 12	1708 . . 8	1728 . 12	1748 . . 9	1768 . 13	1788 . 10
1589 . . 1	1609 . . 5	1629 . . 2	1649 . . 6	1669 . . 3	1689 . . 7	1709 . . 3	1729 . . 7	1749 . . 4	1769 . . 1	1789 . . 5
1590 . . 2	1610 . . 6	1630 . . 3	1650 . . 7	1670 . . 4	1690 . . 1	1710 . . 4	1730 . . 1	1750 . . 5	1770 . . 2	1790 . . 6
1591 . . 3	1611 . . 7	1631 . . 4	1651 . . 1	1671 . . 5	1691 . . 2	1711 . . 5	1731 . . 2	1751 . . 6	1771 . . 3	1791 . . 7
1592 . 11	1612 . . 8	1632 . 12	1652 . . 9	1672 . 13	1692 . 10	1712 . 13	1732 . 10	1752 . 14	1772 . 11	1792 . . 8
1593 . . 6	1613 . . 3	1633 . . 7	1653 . . 4	1673 . . 1	1693 . . 5	1713 . . 1	1733 . . 5	1753 . . 2	1773 . . 6	1793 . . 3
1594 . . 7	1614 . . 4	1634 . . 1	1654 . . 5	1674 . . 2	1694 . . 6	1714 . . 2	1734 . . 6	1754 . . 3	1774 . . 7	1794 . . 4
1595 . . 1	1615 . . 5	1635 . . 2	1655 . . 6	1675 . . 3	1695 . . 7	1715 . . 3	1735 . . 7	1755 . . 4	1775 . . 1	1795 . . 5
1596 . . 9	1616 . 13	1636 . 10	1656 . 14	1676 . 11	1696 . . 8	1716 . 11	1736 . . 8	1756 . 12	1776 . . 9	1796 . 13
1597 . . 4	1617 . . 1	1637 . . 5	1657 . . 2	1677 . . 6	1697 . . 3	1717 . . 6	1737 . . 3	1757 . . 7	1777 . . 4	1797 . . 1
1598 . . 5	1618 . . 2	1638 . . 6	1658 . . 3	1678 . . 7	1698 . . 4	1718 . . 7	1738 . . 4	1758 . . 1	1778 . . 5	1798 . . 2
1599 . . 6	1619 . . 3	1639 . . 7	1659 . . 4	1679 . . 1	1699 . . 5	1719 . . 1	1739 . . 5	1759 . . 2	1779 . . 6	1799 . . 3
1600 . 14	1620 . 11	1640 . . 8	1660 . 12	1680 . . 9	1700 . . 6	1720 . . 9	1740 . 13	1760 . 10	1780 . 14	1800 . . 4
1601 . . 2	1621 . . 6	1641 . . 3	1661 . . 7	1681 . . 4	1701 . . 1	1721 . . 4	1741 . . 1	1761 . . 5	1781 . . 2	1801 . . 5
1602 . . 3	1622 . . 7	1642 . . 4	1662 . . 1	1682 . . 5	1702 . . 2	1722 . . 5	1742 . . 2	1762 . . 6	1782 . . 3	1802 . . 6

The Julian Period

How many days have you lived? To determine this, you must multiply your age by 365, add the number of days since your last birthday until today, and account for all leap years. Chances are your answer would be wrong. Astronomers, however, find it convenient to express dates and long time intervals in days rather than in years, months and days. This is done by placing events within the Julian period.

The Julian period was devised in 1582 by Joseph Scaliger and named after his father Julius (not after the Julian calendar). Scaliger had Julian Day (JD) #1 begin at noon, Jan. 1, 4713 B. C., the most recent time that three major chronological cycles began on the same day — 1) the 28-year solar cycle, after which dates in the Julian calendar (e.g., Feb. 11)

return to the same days of the week (e.g., Monday); 2) the 19-year lunar cycle, after which the phases of the moon return to the same dates of the year; and 3) the 15-year indiction cycle, used in ancient Rome to regulate taxes. It will take 7980 years to complete the period, the product of 28, 19, and 15.

Noon of Dec. 31, 1984, marks the beginning of JD 2,446,065; that many days will have passed since the start of the Julian period. The JD at noon of any date in 1984 may be found by adding to this figure the day of the year for that date, which is given in the left hand column in the chart below. Simple JD conversion tables are used by astronomers.

Days Between Two Dates

Table covers period of two ordinary years. Example—Days between Feb. 10, 1984 and Dec. 15, 1985; subtract 41 from 714; answer is 673 days. For leap year, such as 1984, one day must be added: final answer is 674.

Date	Jan	Feb	Mar	April	May	June	July	Aug	Sept	Oct	Nov	Dec	Date	Jan	Feb	Mar	April	May	June	July	Aug	Sept	Oct	Nov	Dec
1	1	32	60	91	121	152	182	213	244	274	305	335	1	366	397	425	456	486	517	547	578	609	639	670	700
2	2	33	61	92	122	153	183	214	245	275	306	336	2	367	398	426	457	487	518	548	579	610	640	671	701
3	3	34	62	93	123	154	184	215	246	276	307	337	3	368	399	427	458	488	519	549	580	611	641	672	702
4	4	35	63	94	124	155	185	216	247	277	308	338	4	369	400	428	459	489	520	550	581	612	642	673	703
5	5	36	64	95	125	156	186	217	248	278	309	339	5	370	401	429	460	490	521	551	582	613	643	674	704
6	6	37	65	96	126	157	187	218	249	279	310	340	6	371	402	430	461	491	522	552	583	614	644	675	705
7	7	38	66	97	127	158	188	219	250	280	311	341	7	372	403	431	462	492	523	553	584	615	645	676	706
8	8	39	67	98	128	159	189	220	251	281	312	342	8	373	404	432	463	493	524	554	585	616	646	677	707
9	9	40	68	99	129	160	190	221	252	282	313	343	9	374	405	433	464	494	525	555	586	617	647	678	708
10	10	41	69	100	130	161	191	222	253	283	314	344	10	375	406	434	465	495	526	556	587	618	648	679	709
11	11	42	70	101	131	162	192	223	254	284	315	345	11	376	407	435	466	496	527	557	588	619	649	680	710
12	12	43	71	102	132	163	193	224	255	285	316	346	12	377	408	436	467	497	528	558	589	620	650	681	711
13	13	44	72	103	133	164	194	225	256	286	317	347	13	378	409	437	468	498	529	559	590	621	651	682	712
14	14	45	73	104	134	165	195	226	257	287	318	348	14	379	410	438	469	499	530	560	591	622	652	683	713
15	15	46	74	105	135	166	196	227	258	288	319	349	15	380	411	439	470	500	531	561	592	623	653	684	714
16	16	47	75	106	136	167	197	228	259	289	320	350	16	381	412	440	471	501	532	562	593	624	654	685	715
17	17	48	76	107	137	168	198	229	260	290	321	351	17	382	413	441	472	502	533	563	594	625	655	686	716
18	18	49	77	108	138	169	199	230	261	291	322	352	18	383	414	442	473	503	534	564	595	626	656	687	717
19	19	50	78	109	139	170	200	231	262	292	323	353	19	384	415	443	474	504	535	565	596	627	657	688	718
20	20	51	79	110	140	171	201	232	263	293	324	354	20	385	416	444	475	505	536	566	597	628	658	689	719
21	21	52	80	111	141	172	202	233	264	294	325	355	21	386	417	445	476	506	537	567	598	629	659	690	720
22	22	53	81	112	142	173	203	234	265	295	326	356	22	387	418	446	477	507	538	568	599	630	660	691	721
23	23	54	82	113	143	174	204	235	266	296	327	357	23	388	419	447	478	508	539	569	600	631	661	692	722
24	24	55	83	114	144	175	205	236	267	297	328	358	24	389	420	448	479	509	540	570	601	632	662	693	723
25	25	56	84	115	145	176	206	237	268	298	329	359	25	390	421	449	480	510	541	571	602	633	663	694	724
26	26	57	85	116	146	177	207	238	269	299	330	360	26	391	422	450	481	511	542	572	603	634	664	695	725
27	27	58	86	117	147	178	208	239	270	300	331	361	27	392	423	451	482	512	543	573	604	635	665	696	726
28	28	59	87	118	148	179	209	240	271	301	332	362	28	393	424	452	483	513	544	574	605	636	666	697	727
29	29	—	88	119	149	180	210	241	272	302	333	363	29	394	—	453	484	514	545	575	606	637	667	698	728
30	30	—	89	120	150	181	211	242	273	303	334	364	30	395	—	454	485	515	546	576	607	638	668	699	729
31	31	—	90	—	151	—	212	243	—	304	—	365	31	396	—	455	—	516	—	577	608	—	669	—	730

Lunar Calendar, Chinese New Year, Vietnamese Tet

The ancient Chinese lunar calendar is divided into 12 months of either 29 or 30 days (compensating for the fact that the mean duration of the lunar month is 29 days, 12 hours, 44.05 minutes). The calendar is synchronized with the solar year by the addition of extra months at fixed intervals.

The Chinese calendar runs on a sexagenary cycle, i.e., 60 years. The cycles 1876-1935 and 1936-1995, with the years grouped under their twelve animal designations, are printed below. The Year 1985 is found in the second column, under Ox, and is known as a "Year of the Ox." Readers can find the animal name for the year of their birth, marriage, etc., in the same chart. (Note: the first 3-7 weeks of each of the western years belong to the previous Chinese year and animal designation.)

Both the western (Gregorian) and traditional lunar calendars are used publicly in China, and two New Year's celebrations are held. On Taiwan, in overseas Chinese communities, and in Vietnam, the lunar calendar has been used only to set the dates for traditional festivals, with the Gregorian system in general use.

The four-day Chinese New Year, Hsin Nien, and the three-day Vietnamese New Year festival, Tet, begin at the first new moon after the sun enters Aquarius. The day may fall, therefore, between Jan. 21 and Feb. 19 of the Gregorian calendar. Feb. 20, 1985 marks the start of the new Chinese year. The date is fixed according to the date of the new moon in the Far East. Since this is west of the International Date Line the date may be one day later than that of the new moon in the United States.

Rat	Ox	Tiger	Hare (Rabbit)	Dragon	Snake	Horse	Sheep (Goat)	Monkey	Rooster	Dog	Pig
1876	1877	1878	1879	1880	1881	1882	1883	1884	1885	1886	1887
1888	1889	1890	1891	1892	1893	1894	1895	1896	1897	1898	1899
1900	1901	1902	1903	1904	1905	1906	1907	1908	1909	1910	1911
1912	1913	1914	1915	1916	1917	1918	1919	1920	1921	1922	1923
1924	1925	1926	1927	1928	1929	1930	1931	1932	1933	1934	1935
1936	1937	1938	1939	1940	1941	1942	1943	1944	1945	1946	1947
1948	1949	1950	1951	1952	1953	1954	1955	1956	1957	1958	1959
1960	1961	1962	1963	1964	1965	1966	1967	1968	1969	1970	1971
1972	1973	1974	1975	1976	1977	1978	1979	1980	1981	1982	1983
1984	1985	1986	1987	1988	1989	1990	1991	1992	1993	1994	1995

Chronological Eras, 1985

The year 1984 of the Christian Era comprises the latter part of the 208th and the beginning of the 209th year of the independence of the United States of America.

Era	Year	Begins in 1985		Era	Year	Begins in 1984	
Byzantine	7494	Sept.	14	Grecian	2297	Sept.	14
Jewish	5746	Sept.	14	(Seleucidae)		or Oct.	14
		(sunset)		Diocletian	1702	Sept.	11
Roman (Ab Urbe Condita)	2738	Jan.	14	Indian (Saka)	1907	Mar.	22
Nabonassar (Babylonian)	2734	Apr.	27	Mohammedan (Hegira)	1406	Sept.	14
Japanese	2645	Jan.	1			(sunset)	

Chronological Cycles, 1984

Dominical Letter	F	Golden Number (Lunar Cycle)	X	Roman Indiction	8
Epact	8	Solar Cycle	6	Julian Period (year of)	6698

Standard Time Differences — North American Cities

At 12 o'clock noon, Eastern Standard Time, the standard time in N.A. cities is as follows:

City	Time		City	Time		City	Time	
Akron, Oh.	12.00	Noon	Frankfort, Ky.	12.00	Noon	Pierre, S.D.	11.00	A.M.
Albuquerque, N.M.	10.00	A.M.	Galveston, Tex.	11.00	A.M.	Pittsburgh, Pa.	12.00	Noon
Atlanta, Ga.	12.00	Noon	Grand Rapids, Mich.	12.00	Noon	Portland, Me.	12.00	Noon
Austin, Tex.	11.00	A.M.	Halifax, N.S.	1.00	P.M.	Portland, Ore.	9.00	A.M.
Baltimore, Md.	12.00	Noon	Hartford, Conn.	12.00	Noon	Providence, R.I.	12.00	Noon
Birmingham, Ala.	11.00	A.M.	Helena, Mon.	10.00	A.M.	*Regina, Sask.	11.00	A.M.
Bismarck, N.D.	11.00	A.M.	*Honolulu, Ha.	7.00	A.M.	Reno, Nev.	9.00	A.M.
Boise, Ida.	10.00	A.M.	Houston, Tex.	11.00	A.M.	Richmond, Va.	12.00	Noon
Boston, Mass.	12.00	Noon	*Indianapolis, Ind.	12.00	Noon	Rochester, N.Y.	12.00	Noon
Buffalo, N.Y.	12.00	Noon	Jacksonville, Fla.	12.00	Noon	Sacramento, Cal.	9.00	A.M.
Butte, Mon.	10.00	A.M.	Juneau, Alas.	9.00	A.M.	St. John's, Nfld.	1.30	P.M.
Calgary, Alta.	10.00	A.M.	Kansas City, Mo.	11.00	A.M.	St. Louis, Mo.	11.00	A.M.
Charleston, S.C.	12.00	Noon	Knoxville, Tenn.	12.00	Noon	St. Paul, Minn.	11.00	A.M.
Charleston, W.Va.	12.00	Noon	Lexington, Ky.	12.00	Noon	Salt Lake City, Ut.	10.00	A.M.
Charlotte, N.C.	12.00	Noon	Lincoln, Neb.	11.00	A.M.	San Antonio, Tex.	11.00	A.M.
Charlottetown, P.E.I.	1.00	P.M.	Little Rock, Ark.	11.00	A.M.	San Diego, Cal.	9.00	A.M.
Chattanooga, Tenn.	12.00	Noon	Los Angeles, Cal.	9.00	A.M.	San Francisco, Cal.	9.00	A.M.
Cheyenne, Wy.	10.00	A.M.	Louisville, Ky.	12.00	Noon	Santa Fe, N.M.	10.00	A.M.
Chicago, Ill.	11.00	A.M.	*Mexico City	11.00	A.M.	Savannah, Ga.	12.00	Noon
Cleveland, Oh.	12.00	Noon	Memphis, Tenn.	11.00	A.M.	Seattle, Wash.	9.00	A.M.
Colorado Spr., Col.	10.00	A.M.	Miami, Fla.	12.00	Noon	Shreveport, La.	11.00	A.M.
Columbus, Oh.	12.00	Noon	Milwaukee, Wis.	11.00	A.M.	Sioux Falls, S.D.	11.00	A.M.
Dallas, Tex.	11.00	A.M.	Minneapolis, Minn.	11.00	A.M.	Spokane, Wash.	9.00	A.M.
*Dawson, Yuk.	9.00	A.M.	Mobile, Ala.	11.00	A.M.	Tampa, Fla.	12.00	Noon
Dayton, Oh.	12.00	Noon	Montreal, Que.	12.00	Noon	Toledo, Oh.	12.00	Noon
Denver, Col.	10.00	A.M.	Nashville, Tenn.	11.00	A.M.	Topeka, Kan.	11.00	A.M.
Des Moines, Ia.	11.00	A.M.	New Haven, Conn.	12.00	Noon	Toronto, Ont.	12.00	Noon
Detroit, Mich.	12.00	Noon	New Orleans, La.	11.00	A.M.	*Tucson, Ariz.	10.00	A.M.
Duluth, Minn.	11.00	A.M.	New York, N.Y.	12.00	Noon	Tulsa, Okla.	11.00	A.M.
El Paso, Tex.	10.00	A.M.	Nome, Alas.	6.00	A.M.	Vancouver, B.C.	9.00	A.M.
Erie, Pa.	12.00	Noon	Norfolk, Va.	12.00	Noon	Washington, D.C.	12.00	Noon
Evansville, Ind.	11.00	A.M.	Okla. City, Okla.	11.00	A.M.	Wichita, Kan.	11.00	A.M.
Fairbanks, Alas.	7.00	A.M.	Omaha, Neb.	11.00	A.M.	Wilmington, Del.	12.00	Noon
Flint, Mich.	12.00	Noon	Peoria, Ill.	11.00	A.M.	Winnipeg, Man.	11.00	A.M.
*Fort Wayne, Ind.	12.00	Noon	Philadelphia, Pa.	12.00	Noon			
Fort Worth, Tex.	11.00	A.M.	*Phoenix, Ariz.	10.00	A.M.			

*Cities with an asterisk do not observe daylight savings time. During much of the year, it is necessary to add one hour to the cities which do observe daylight savings time to get the proper time relation.

Standard Time Differences—World Cities

The time indicated in the table is fixed by law and is called the legal time, or, more generally, Standard Time. Use of Daylight Saving Time varies widely. *Indicates morning of the following day. At 12:00 noon, Eastern Standard Time, the standard time (in 24-hour time) in foreign cities is as follows:

City	Time		City	Time		City	Time
Alexandria	19 00	Copenhagen	18 00	Lima	12 00	Santiago (Chile)	13 00
Amsterdam	18 00	Dacca	23 00	Lisbon	18 00	Seoul	2 00*
Athens	19 00	Delhi	22 30	Liverpool	17 00	Shanghai	1 00*
Auckland	5 00*			London	17 00	Singapore	00 30*
Baghdad	20 00	Dublin	17 00	Madrid	18 00	Stockholm	18 00
Bangkok	0 00	Gdansk	18 00	Manila	1 00*	Sydney (Australia)	3 00*
Belfast	17 00	Geneva	18 00	Melbourne	3 00*	Tashkent	23 00
Berlin	18 00	Havana	12 00	Montevideo	14 00	Teheran	20 30
Bogota	12 00	Helsinki	19 00	Moscow	20 00	Tel Aviv	19 00
Bombay	22 30	Ho Chi Minh City	1 00*	Nagasaki	2 00*	Tokyo	2 00*
Bremen	18 00	Hong Kong	1 00*				
Brussels	18 00	Istanbul	19 00	Oslo	18 00	Valparaiso	13 00
Bucharest	19 00	Jakarta	0 00	Paris	18 00		
Budapest	18 00	Jerusalem	19 00			Vladivostok	3 00*
Buenos Aires	14 00	Johannesburg	19 00	Peking	1 00*	Vienna	18 00
Calcutta	22 30	Karachi	22 00	Prague	18 00	Warsaw	18 00
Cape Town	19 00	Le Havre	18 00	Rangoon	23 30	Wellington (N.Z.)	5 00*
Caracas	13 00	Leningrad	20 00	Rio De Janeiro	14 00	Yokohama	2 00*
				Rome	18 00	Zurich	18 00

Standard Time, Daylight Saving Time, and Others

Source: Defense Mapping Agency Hydrographic Center; Department of Transportation; National Bureau of Standards; U.S. Naval Observatory

Standard Time

Standard time is reckoned from Greenwich, England, recognized as the Prime Meridian of Longitude. The world is divided into 24 zones, each 15° of arc, or one hour in time apart. The Greenwich meridian (0°) extends through the center of the initial zone, and the zones to the east are numbered from 1 to 12 with the prefix "minus" indicating the number of hours to be subtracted to obtain Greenwich Time.

Westward zones are similarly numbered, but prefixed "plus" showing the number of hours that must be added to get Greenwich Time. While these zones apply generally to sea areas, it should be noted that the Standard Time maintained in many countries does not coincide with zone time. A graphical representation of the zones is shown on the Standard Time Zone Chart of the World published by the Defense Mapping Agency Hydrographic Center, Washington, DC 20390.

The United States and possessions are divided into eight Standard Time zones, as set forth by the Uniform Time Act of 1966, which also provides for the use of Daylight Saving Time therein. Each zone is approximately 15° of longitude in width. All places in each zone use, instead of their own local time, the time counted from the transit of the "mean sun" across the Standard Time meridian which passes near the middle of that zone.

These time zones are designated as Atlantic, Eastern, Central, Mountain, Pacific, Yukon, Alaska-Hawaii, and Bering, and the time in these zones is basically reckoned from the 60th, 75th, 90th, 105th, 120th, 135th, 150th, 165th meridians west of Greenwich. The line wanders to conform to local geographical regions. The time in the various zones is earlier than Greenwich Time by 4, 5, 6, 7, 8, 9, 10, and 11 hours respectively.

24-Hour Time

24-hour time is widely used in scientific work throughout the world. In the United States it is used also in operations of the Armed Forces. In Europe it is used in preference to the 12-hour a.m. and p.m. system. With the 24-hour system the day begins at midnight and hours are numbered 0 through 23.

International Date Line

The Date Line is a zig-zag line that approximately coincides with the 180th meridian, and it is where each calendar day begins. The date must be advanced one day when crossing in a westerly direction and set back one day when crossing in an easterly direction.

The line is deflected between north latitude 48° and 75°, so that all Asia lies to the west of it.

Daylight Saving Time

Daylight Saving Time is achieved by advancing the clock one hour. Under the Uniform Time Act, which became effective in 1967, all states, the District of Columbia, and U.S. possessions were to observe Daylight Saving Time beginning at 2 a.m. on the last Sunday in April and ending at 2 a.m. on the last Sunday in October. Any state could, by law, exempt itself; a 1972 amendment to the act authorized states split by time zones to take that into consideration in exempting themselves. Arizona, Hawaii, Puerto Rico, the Virgin Islands, American Samoa, and part of Indiana are now exempt. Some local zone boundaries in Kansas, Texas, Florida, Michigan, and Alaska have been modified in the last several years by the Dept. of Transportation, which oversees the act. To conserve energy Congress put most of the nation on year-round Daylight Saving Time for two years effective Jan. 6, 1974 through Oct. 26, 1975; but a further bill, signed in October, 1974, restored Standard Time from the last Sunday in that month to the last Sunday in February, 1975. At the end of 1975, Congress failed to renew this temporary legislation and the nation returned to the older end-of April to end-of October DST system.

Legal or Public Holidays, 1985

Technically there are no national holidays in the United States; each state has jurisdiction over its holidays, which are designated by legislative enactment or executive proclamation. In practice, however, most states observe the federal legal public holidays, even though the President and Congress can legally designate holidays only for the District of Columbia and for federal employees.

Federal legal public holidays are: New Year's Day, Washington's Birthday, Memorial Day, Independence Day, Labor Day, Columbus Day, Veterans Day, Thanksgiving, and Christmas.

Chief Legal or Public Holidays

When a holiday falls on a Sunday or a Saturday it is usually observed on the following Monday or preceding Friday. For some holidays, government and business closing practices vary. In most states, the office of the Secretary of State can provide details of holiday closings. In most states, the following will be legal or public holidays in 1985:

Jan. 1 (Tuesday) — New Year's Day.
Feb. 12 (Tuesday) — Lincoln's Birthday.
Feb. 18 (3d Monday in Feb.) — Washington's Birthday, or Presidents' Day, or Washington-Lincoln Day.
May 27 (last Mon. in May) — Memorial Day.
July 4 (Thurs.) — Independence Day.
Sept. 2 (1st Mon. in Sept.) — Labor Day.
Oct. 14 (2d Mon. in Oct.) — Columbus Day, or Discoverers' Day, or Pioneers' Day.
Nov. 11 (Monday) — Veterans' Day.

Nov. 28 (4th Thurs. in Nov.) — Thanksgiving Day.
Dec. 25 (Wednesday) — Christmas Day.

In some states, the following will be legal or public holidays in 1985:

Jan. 15 (Tuesday) — Martin Luther King Day. In some states, combined with Robert E. Lee Day.
Apr. 5 (Friday) — Good Friday. In some states, observed for half or part of day.
Nov. 5 (Tuesday) — Election Day.

Other Legal or Public Holidays

Dates are for 1985 observance, when known.

Jan. 13 — Volunteer Fireman Day (2d Sunday in Jan.). In New Jersey.

Jan. 19 — Robert E. Lee's birthday observed in several southern states.

Jan. 22 (or 26 or 29) — Confederate Heroes' Day observed in various southern states.

Jan. 30 — Franklin D. Roosevelt Day. In Kentucky.

Feb. 14 — Admission Day. In Oregon.

Mar. 5 — Town Meeting Day (1st Tuesday in Mar.). In Vermont.

Mar. 25 — Greek Independence Day. In North Carolina.

Mar. 26 — Prince Jonah Kuhio Kalanianaole Day. In Hawaii.

Apr. 12 — Anniversary of signing of Halifax Resolves. In North Carolina.

Apr. 12 — Florida Day. In that state.

Apr. 15 — Patriot's Day. In Maine.

May 4 — Independence Day. In Rhode Island.

May 8 — Harry Truman's Birthday. In Missouri.

May 27 — Grandparents Day. In New Jersey.

June 3 — Jefferson Davis's Birthday. In Alabama, Florida, Mississippi.

June 11 — King Kameha I Day. In Hawaii.

June 14 — Flag Day.

June 17 — Bunker Hill Day. In Boston and Suffolk County, Massachusetts.

June 20 — W. Virginia Day. In that state.

June 25 — Pioneer Day. In Utah.

Aug. 5 — Colorado Day (1st Monday in Aug.). In that state.

Aug. 13 — Victory Day (2d Monday in Aug.). In Arkansas.

Aug. 16 — Bennington Battle Day. In Vermont.

Aug. 16 — Admission Day (3d Friday in Aug.). In Hawaii.

Sept. 12 — Defenders' Day. In Maryland.

Oct. 14 — Pioneer Day (2d Monday in Oct.). In South Dakota.

Oct. 31 — Nevada Day. In that state.

Nov. 1 — All Saints' Day. In Louisiana.

Days Usually Observed

American Family Day (Aug. 4 in 1985). Observed first Sunday in Aug. in Arizona.

Arbor Day. Tree-planting day. First observed April 10, 1872, in Nebraska. Now observed in most states, usually on the last Friday in Apr. (Apr. 26 in 1985).

Armed Forces Day (May 18 in 1985). Always third Saturday of May, by presidential proclamation. Replaced Army, Navy, and Air Force Days.

Bill of Rights Day, Dec. 15. By Act of Congress. Bill of Rights took effect Dec. 15, 1791.

Bird Day. Often observed with Arbor Day.

Child Health Day (Oct. 7 in 1985). Always first Monday in Oct., by presidential proclamation.

Citizenship Day, Sept. 17. President Truman, Feb. 29, 1952, signed bill designating Sept. 17 as annual Citizenship Day. It replaced I Am An American Day, formerly 3d Sunday in May, and Constitution Day, formerly Sept. 17.

Easter Sunday (Apr. 7 in 1985).

Easter Monday (Apr. 8 in 1985). A statutory day in Canada.

Elizabeth Cady Stanton Day, Nov. 12. Birthday of pioneer leader for equal rights for women.

Father's Day (June 16 in 1985). Always third Sunday in June.

Forefathers' Day, Dec. 21. Landing on Plymouth Rock, in 1620. Is celebrated with dinners by New England societies, especially "Down East."

Gen. Pulaski Memorial Day, Oct. 11. Native of Poland and Revolutionary War hero; died (Oct. 11, 1779) from wounds received at the siege of Savannah, Ga.

Georgia Day, Feb. 12. Observed in that state. Commemorates landing of first colonists in 1733.

Grandparents' Day (Sept. 7 in 1985). Always first Sunday after Labor Day. Legislated in 1979.

Groundhog Day, Feb. 2. A popular belief is that if the groundhog sees his shadow on this day, he returns to his burrow and winter continues 6 weeks longer.

Halloween, Oct. 31. The evening before All Saints or All-Hallows Day. Informally observed in the U.S. with masquerading and pumpkin decorating. Traditionally an occasion for children to play pranks.

Loyalty Day, May 1. By Act of Congress.

May Day. Name popularly given to May 1st. Celebrated as Labor Day in most of the world, and by some groups in the U.S. Observed in many schools as a Spring Festival.

Mother's Day (May 12 in 1985). Always second Sunday in that month. First celebrated in Philadelphia in 1908, Mother's Day has become an international holiday.

National Day of Prayer. By presidential proclamation each year on a day other than a Sunday.

National Freedom Day, Feb. 1. To commemorate the signing of the Thirteenth Amendment, abolishing slavery, Feb. 1, 1865. By presidential proclamation.

National Maritime Day, May 22. First proclaimed 1935 in commemoration of the departure of the SS Savannah, from Savannah, Georgia, on May 22, 1819, on the first successful transatlantic voyage under steam propulsion. By presidential proclamation.

Pan American Day, Apr. 14. In 1890 the First Intl. Conference of American States, meeting in Washington, was held on that date. A resolution was adopted which resulted in the creation of the organization known today as the Pan American Union. By presidential proclamation.

Primary Election Day. Observed usually only when presidential or general elections are held.

Reformation Day, Oct. 31. Observed by Protestant groups.

Sadie Hawkins Day (Nov. 16 in 1985). First Saturday after November 11.

St. Patrick's Day, Mar. 17. Observed by Irish societies, especially with parades.

St. Valentine's Day, Feb. 14. Festival of a martyr beheaded at Rome under Emperor Claudius. Association of this day with lovers has no connection with the saint and probably had its origin in an old belief that on this day birds begin to choose their mates.

Susan B. Anthony Day, Feb. 15. Birthday of a pioneer crusader for equal rights for women.

United Nations Day, Oct. 24. By presidential proclamation, to commemorate founding of United Nations.

Verrazano Day, Apr. 7. Observed by New York State, to commemorate the probable discovery of New York harbor by Giovanni da Verrazano in April, 1524.

Victoria Day (May 20 in 1985). Birthday of Queen Victoria, a statutory day in Canada, celebrated the first Monday before May 25.

World Poetry Day, Oct. 15.

Wright Brothers Day, Dec. 17. By presidential designation, to commemorate first successful flight by Orville and Wilbur Wright, Dec. 17, 1903.

Other Holidays, Anniversaries — 1985

Jan. 1, 1935	— Orange Bowl, Sugar Bowl held for first time.
Feb. 1, 1960	— U.S. blacks start to "sit-in" to desegregate Greensboro, N.C. lunch counters.
Feb. 11 (Mon.)	— National Inventors' Day; birthday of Thomas Edison.
Feb. 13, 1960	— France explodes her first atomic bomb, joining "atomic club" of U.S., USSR, Britain.
Feb. 20	— Ash Wednesday.
Mar. 11 (Mon.)	— Johnny Appleseed Day.
Mar. 12 (Tues.)	— Girl Scout Day.
Apr. 1 (Mon.)	— April Fool's Day.
Apr. 6 (Sat.)	— Passover begins.
Apr. 13 (Sat.)	— Birthday of Thomas Jefferson.
May 6, 1935	— Works Progress Administration (WPA) created by FDR.
May 14, 1935	— First major league night baseball game played.
May 30, 1910	— First Indianapolis 500 car race.
June 24 (Mon.)	— San Juan Day in Puerto Rico; St. Jean Day in Quebec.
July 1 (Mon.)	— Canada Day.

July 5, 1935	— Congress passes Wagner-Connery Act, creating Natl. Labor Relations Bd., reasserting right of collective bargaining.
Aug. 1, 1960	— Echo I, world's first communications satellite, launched by U.S.
Aug. 12 (Mon.)	— Ponce De Leon Day in Puerto Rico.
Aug. 14, 1935	— Social Security Act passed by Congress.
Sept. 8, 1910	— N.Y.'s Penn Station opens to trains.
Sept. 14, 1960	— OPEC meets for first time, with 5 charter members—Saudi Arabia, Iran, Iraq, Kuwait, Qatar.
Sept. 16 (Mon.)	— Rosh Hashanah.
Sept. 25 (Wed.)	— Yom Kippur.
Nov. 8, 1960	— Mass. sen. John F. Kennedy, 43, defeats vice president Richard M. Nixon to become youngest man and first Roman Catholic elected U.S. president.
Dec. 8 (Sun.)	— Channukah.
Dec. 14, 1910	— 5 Norwegians and 17 huskies, headed by Roald Amundsen, are first to reach South Pole.

Wind Chill Table

Source: National Weather Service, NOAA, U.S. Commerce Department

Both temperature and wind cause heat loss from body surfaces. A combination of cold and wind makes a body feel colder than the actual temperature. The table shows, for example, that a temperature of 20 degrees Fahrenheit, plus a wind of 20 miles per hour, causes a body heat loss equal to that in minus 10 degrees with no wind. In other words, the wind makes 20 degrees feel like minus 10.

Top line of figures shows actual temperatures in degrees Fahrenheit. Column at left shows wind speeds.

MPH	35	30	25	20	15	10	5	0	−5	−10	−15	−20	−25	−30	−35	−40	−45
5	33	27	21	16	12	7	0	−5	−10	−15	−21	−26	−31	−36	−42	−47	−52
10	22	16	10	3	−3	−9	−15	−22	−27	−34	−40	−46	−52	−58	−64	−71	−77
15	16	9	2	−5	−11	−18	−25	−31	−38	−45	−51	−58	−65	−72	−78	−85	−92
20	12	4	−3	−10	−17	−24	−31	−39	−46	−53	−60	−67	−74	−81	−88	−95	−103
25	8	1	−7	−15	−22	−29	−36	−44	−51	−59	−66	−74	−81	−88	−96	−103	−110
30	6	−2	−10	−18	−25	−33	−41	−49	−56	−64	−71	−79	−86	−93	−101	−109	−116
35	4	−4	−12	−20	−27	−35	−43	−52	−58	−67	−74	−82	−89	−97	−105	−113	−120
40	3	−5	−13	−21	−29	−37	−45	−53	−60	−69	−76	−84	−92	−100	−107	−115	−123
45	2	−6	−14	−22	−30	−38	−46	−54	−62	−70	−78	−85	−93	−102	−109	−117	−125

(Wind speeds greater than 45 mph have little additional chilling effect.)

Heat Index

The index is a measure of the contribution that high humidity makes with abnormally high temperatures in reducing the body's ability to cool itself. For example, the index shows that for an actual air temperature of 100 degrees Fahrenheit and a relative humidity of 50 percent, the effect on the human body would be same as 120 degrees. Sunstroke and heat exhaustion are likely when the heat index reaches 105. This index is a measure of what hot weather "feels like" to the average person for various temperatures and relative humidities.

Relative Humidity	Air Temperature* Apparent Temperature*										
	70	75	80	85	90	95	100	105	110	115	120
0%	64	69	73	78	83	87	91	95	99	103	107
10%	65	70	75	80	85	90	95	100	105	111	116
20%	66	72	77	82	87	93	99	105	112	120	130
30%	67	73	78	84	90	96	104	113	123	135	148
40%	68	74	79	86	93	101	110	123	137	151	
50%	69	75	81	88	96	107	120	135	150		
60%	70	76	82	90	100	114	132	149			
70%	70	77	85	93	106	124	144				
80%	71	78	86	97	113	136					
90%	71	79	88	102	122						
100%	72	80	91	108							

*Degrees Fahrenheit.

Tides and Their Causes

Source: NOAA, National Ocean Service, U.S. Department of Commerce

The tides are a natural phenomenon involving the alternating rise and fall in the large fluid bodies of the earth caused by the combined gravitational attraction of the sun and moon. The combination of these two variable force influences produce the complex recurrent cycle of the tides. Tides may occur in both oceans and seas, to a limited extent in large lakes, the atmosphere, and, to a very minute degree, in the earth itself. The period between succeeding tides varies as the result of many factors and force influences.

The tide-generating force represents the difference between (1) the centrifugal force produced by the revolution of the earth around the common center-of-gravity of the earth-moon system and (2) the gravitational attraction of the moon acting upon the earth's overlying waters. Since, on the average, the moon is only 238,852 miles from the earth compared with the sun's much greater distance of 92,956,000 miles, this closer distance outranks the much smaller mass of the moon compared with that of the sun, and the moon's tide-raising force is, accordingly, 2½ times that of the sun.

The effect of the tide-generating forces of the moon and sun acting tangentially to the earth's surface (the so-called "tractive force") tends to cause a maximum accumulation of the waters of the oceans at two diametrically opposite positions on the surface of the earth and to withdraw compensating amounts of water from all points 90° removed from the positions of these tidal bulges. As the earth rotates beneath the maxima and minima of these tide-generating forces, a sequence of two high tides, separated by two low tides, ideally is produced each day.

Twice in each lunar month, when the sun, moon, and earth are directly aligned, with the moon between the earth and the sun (at new moon) or on the opposite side of the

earth from the sun (at full moon), the sun and the moon exert their gravitational force in a mutual or additive fashion. Higher high tides and lower low tides are produced. These are called *spring* tides. At two positions 90° in between, the gravitational forces of the moon and sun — imposed at right angles—tend to counteract each other to the greatest extent, and the range between high and low tides is reduced. These are called *neap* tides. This semi-monthly variation between the spring and neap tides is called the *phase inequality*.

The inclination of the moon's orbit to the equator also produces a difference in the height of succeeding high tides and in the extent of depression of succeeding low tides which is known as the *diurnal inequality*. In extreme cases, this phenomenon can result in only one high tide and one low tide each day.

The actual range of tide in the waters of the open ocean may amount to only one or two feet. However, as this tide approaches shoal waters and its effects are augmented the tidal range may be greatly increased. In Nova Scotia along the narrow channel of the Bay of Fundy, the range of tides or difference between high and low waters, may reach 43 1/2 feet or more (under spring tide conditions) due to resonant amplification.

At New Orleans, the periodic rise and fall of the tide varies with the state of the Mississippi, being about 10 inches at low stage and zero at high. The Canadian Tide Tables for 1972 gave a maximum range of nearly 50 feet at Leaf Basin, Ungava Bay, Quebec.

In every case, actual high or low tide can vary considerably from the average due to weather conditions such as strong winds, abrupt barometric pressure changes, or prolonged periods of extreme high or low pressure.

The Average Rise and Fall of Tides

Places	Ft.	In.	Places	Ft.	In.	Places	Ft.	In.
Baltimore, Md.	1	1	Mobile, Ala.	1	6	San Diego, Cal.	5	9[1]
Boston, Mass.	9	6	New London, Conn.	2	7	Sandy Hook, N.J.	4	8
Charleston, S.C.	5	3	Newport, R.I.	3	6	San Francisco, Cal.	5	10[1]
Colon, Panama	1	1	New York, N.Y.	4	7	Savannah, Ga.	7	5
Eastport, Me.	18	4	Old Pt. Comfort, Va.	2	6	Seattle, Wash.	11	4[1]
Galveston, Tex.	1	5[1]	Philadelphia, Pa.	6	2	Tampa, Fla.	2	10[1]
Halifax, N.S.	4	5	Portland, Me.	9	1	Vancouver, B.C.	10	6[1]
Key West, Fla.	1	10[1]	St. John's, Nfld.	2	7	Washington, D.C.	2	9

(1) Diurnal range.

Speed of Winds in the U.S.

Source: National Oceanic and Atmospheric Administration, U.S. Department of Commerce
Miles per hour — average through 1982. High through 1982. Wind velocities in true values.

Station	Avg.	High	Station	Avg.	High	Station	Avg.	High
Albuquerque, N.M.	9.0	90	Helena, Mont.	7.8	73	New York, N.Y.(c)	9.4	70
Anchorage, Alas.	6.8	61	Honolulu, Ha.	11.7	67	Omaha, Neb.	10.6	109
Atlanta, Ga.	9.1	46	Jacksonville, Fla.	8.2	82	Pensacola, Fla.	8.4	53
Bismarck, N.D.	10.3	72	Key West, Fla.	11.3	58	Philadelphia, Pa.	9.6	73
Boston, Mass.	12.5	61	Knoxville, Tenn.	7.1	36	Pittsburgh, Pa.	9.2	58
Buffalo, N.Y.	12.1	91	Little Rock, Ark.	8.0	65	Portland, Ore.	7.9	88
Cape Hatteras, N.C.	11.4	(b)110	Louisville, Ky.	8.4	61	Rochester, N.Y.	9.8	73
Chattanooga, Tenn.	6.2	37	Memphis, Tenn.	9.0	46	St. Louis, Mo.	9.6	60
Chicago, Ill.	10.3	58	Miami, Fla.	9.2	(a)74	Salt Lake City, Ut.	8.8	71
Cincinnati, Oh.	7.1	49	Minneapolis, Minn.	10.5	92	San Diego, Cal.	6.8	56
Cleveland, Oh.	10.8	74	Mobile, Ala.	9.0	(b)63	San Francisco, Cal.	8.7	47
Denver, Col.	8.9	56	Montgomery, Ala.	6.7	72	Savannah, Ga.	8.0	66
Detroit, Mich.	10.1	46	Mt. Washington, N.H.	35.1	231	Spokane, Wash.	8.7	59
Fort Smith, Ark.	7.6	60	Nashville, Tenn.	8.0	35	Toledo, Oh.	9.4	72
Galveston, Tex.	11.0	(d)100	New Orleans, La.	8.2	(b)98	Washington, D.C.	9.3	78

(a) Highest velocity ever recorded in Miami area was 132 mph, at former station in Miami Beach in September, 1926.
(b) Previous location. (c) Data for Central Park, Battery Place data through 1960, avg. 14.5, high 113. (d) Recorded before anemometer blew away. Estimated high 120.

The Meaning of "One Inch of Rain"

An acre of ground contains 43,560 square feet. Consequently, a rainfall of 1 inch over 1 acre of ground would mean a total of 6,272,640 cubic inches of water. This is equivalent to 3,630 cubic feet.

As a cubic foot of pure water weighs about 62.4 pounds, the exact amount varying with the density, it follows that the weight of a uniform coating of 1 inch of rain over 1 acre of surface would be 226,512 pounds, or about 113 short tons. The weight of 1 U.S. gallon of pure water is about 8.345 pounds. Consequently a rainfall of 1 inch over 1 acre of ground would mean 27,143 gallons of water.

National Weather Service Watches and Warnings

Source: National Weather Service, NOAA, U.S. Commerce Department; Glossary of Meteorology, American Meteorological Society

National Weather Service forecasters issue a Tornado Watch for a specific area where tornadoes are most likely to occur during the valid time of the watch. A Watch is to alert people to watch for threatening weather, make plans for action, and listen for a Tornado Warning. A Tornado Warning means that a tornado has been sighted or indicated by radar, and that safety precautions should be taken at once. A Hurricane Watch means that an existing hurricane poses a threat to coastal and inland communities in the area specified by the Watch. A Hurricane Warning means hurricane force winds and/or dangerously high water and exceptionally high waves are expected in a specified coastal area within 24 hours.

Tornado—A violent rotating column of air in contact with the ground and pendant from a thundercloud, usually recognized as a funnel-shaped vortex accompanied by a loud roar. With rotating winds est. up to 300 mph., on a local scale, it is the most destructive storm. Tornado paths have varied in length from a few feet to nearly 300 miles (avg. 5 mi.); diameter from a few feet to over a mile (average 220 yards); average forward speed, 30 mph.

Cyclone—An atmospheric circulation of winds rotating counterclockwise in the northern hemisphere and clockwise in the southern hemisphere. Tornadoes, hurricanes, and the lows shown on weather maps are all examples of cyclones having various sizes and intensities. Cyclones are usually accompanied by precipitation or stormy weather.

Hurricane—A severe cyclone originating over tropical ocean waters and having winds 74 miles an hour or higher. (In the western Pacific, such storms are known as typhoons.) The area of strong winds takes the form of a circle or an oval, sometimes as much as 500 miles in diameter. In the lower latitudes hurricanes usually move toward the west or northwest at 10 to 15 mph. When the center approaches 25° to 30° North Latitude, direction of motion often changes to northeast, with increased forward speed.

Blizzard—A severe weather condition characterized by strong winds bearing a great amount of snow. The National Weather Service specifies, for blizzard, a wind of 35 miles an hour or higher, and sufficient falling and/or blowing snow to reduce visibility to less than 1/4 of a mile.

Monsoon—A name for seasonal winds (derived from Arabic "mausim," a season). It was first applied to the winds over the Arabian Sea, which blow for six months from northeast and six months from southwest, but it has been extended to similar winds in other parts of the world. The monsoons are strongest on the southern and eastern sides of Asia.

Flood—The condition that occurs when water overflows the natural or artificial confines of a stream or other body of water, or accumulates by drainage over low-lying areas.

National Weather Service Marine Warnings and Advisories

Small Craft Advisory: A Small Craft Advisory alerts mariners to sustained (exceeding two hours) weather and/or sea conditions either present or forecast, potentially hazardous to small boats. Hazardous conditions may include winds of 18 to 33 knots and/or dangerous wave or inlet conditions. It is the responsibility of the mariner, based on his experience and size or type of boat, to determine if the conditions are hazardous. When a mariner becomes aware of a Small Craft Advisory, he should immediately obtain the latest marine forecast to determine the reason for the Advisory.

Gale Warning indicates that winds within the range 34 to 47 knots are forecast for the area.

Storm Warning indicates that winds 48 knots and above, no matter how high the speed, are forecast for the area.

However, if the winds are associated with a tropical cyclone (hurricane), the storm warning indicates that winds within the range 48 to 63 knots are forecast.

Hurricane Warning indicates that winds 64 knots and above are forecast for the area.

Primary sources of dissemination are commercial radio, TV, U.S. Coast Guard Radio stations, and NOAA VHF-FM broadcasts. These broadcasts on 162.40 to 162.55 MHz can usually be received 20-40 miles from the transmitting antenna site, depending on terrain and quality of the receiver used. Where transmitting antennas are on high ground, the range is somewhat greater, reaching 60 miles or more.

Hurricane Names in 1985

U.S. government agencies responsible for weather and related communications have used girls' names to identify major tropical storms since 1953. A U.S. proposal that both male and female names be adopted for hurricanes, starting in 1979, was accepted by a committee of the World Meteorological Organization.

Names assigned to Atlantic hurricanes, 1985 — Ana, Bob, Claudette, Danny, Elena, Fabian, Gloria, Henri, Isabel, Juan, Kate, Larry, Mindy, Nicholas, Odette, Peter, Rose, Sam, Teresa, Victor, Wanda.

Names assigned to Eastern Pacific hurricanes, 1985 — Andres, Blanca, Carlos, Dolores, Enrique, Fefa, Guillermo, Hilda, Ignacio, Jimena, Kevin, Linda, Marty, Nora, Olaf, Pauline, Rick, Sandra, Terry, Vivian, Waldo.

Explanation of Normal Temperatures

Normal temperatures listed in the tables on pages 758 and 760 are based on records of the National Weather Service for the 30-year period from 1941-1970 inclusive. To obtain the average maximum or minimum temperature for any month, the daily temperatures are added; the total is then divided by the number of days in that month.

The normal maximum temperature for January, for example, is obtained by adding the average maximums for Jan., 1941, Jan., 1942, etc., through Jan., 1970. The total is then divided by 30. The normal minimum temperature is obtained in a similar manner by adding the average minimums for each January in the 30-year period and dividing by 30. The normal temperature for January is one half of the sum for the normal maximum and minimum temperatures for that month. The mean temperature for any one day is one-half the total of the maximum and minimum temperatures for that day.

Monthly Normal Temperature and Precipitation

Source: NOAA, U.S. Department of Commerce

These normals are based on records for the 30-year period 1941 to 1970 inclusive. See explanation on page 757. For stations that did not have continuous records from the same instrument site for the entire 30 years, the means have been adjusted to the record at the present site.

Airport station; *city office stations. T, temperature in Fahrenheit; P, precipitation in inches; L, less than .05 inch.

Station	Jan. T	Jan. P	Feb. T	Feb. P	Mar. T	Mar. P	Apr. T	Apr. P	May T	May P	June T	June P	July T	July P	Aug. T	Aug. P	Sept. T	Sept. P	Oct. T	Oct. P	Nov. T	Nov. P	Dec. T	Dec. P
Albany, N.Y.	22	2.2	24	2.1	33	2.6	47	2.7	58	3.3	68	3.0	72	3.1	70	2.9	62	3.1	51	2.6	40	2.8	26	2.9
Albuquerque, N.M.	35	0.3	40	0.4	46	0.5	56	0.5	65	0.5	75	0.5	79	1.4	77	1.3	70	0.8	58	0.8	45	0.3	36	0.5
Anchorage, Alas.	12	0.8	18	0.8	24	0.6	35	0.6	46	0.6	55	1.1	58	2.1	56	2.3	48	2.4	35	1.4	21	1.0	13	1.1
Asheville, N.C.	38	3.4	39	3.6	46	4.7	56	3.5	64	3.3	71	4.0	74	4.9	73	4.5	67	3.6	57	3.3	46	2.9	39	3.6
Atlanta, Ga.	42	4.3	44	4.4	51	5.8	61	4.6	69	3.7	76	3.7	78	4.9	78	3.5	72	3.2	62	2.5	51	3.4	44	4.2
Baltimore, Md.	33	2.9	35	2.8	43	3.7	54	3.1	64	3.6	72	3.8	77	4.1	75	4.2	69	3.1	57	2.8	46	3.1	35	3.3
Barrow, Alas.	-15	0.2	-19	0.2	-15	0.2	-1	0.2	19	0.2	33	0.4	39	0.9	38	1.0	30	0.6	15	0.6	-1	0.3	-12	0.2
Birmingham, Ala.	44	4.8	47	5.3	53	6.2	63	4.6	71	3.6	77	4.0	80	5.2	79	4.3	74	3.6	63	2.6	52	3.7	45	5.2
Bismarck, N.D.	8	0.5	14	0.4	25	0.7	43	1.4	54	2.2	64	3.6	71	2.2	69	2.0	58	1.3	47	0.8	29	0.6	16	0.5
Boise, Ida.	29	1.5	36	1.2	41	1.0	49	1.1	57	1.3	65	1.1	75	0.2	72	0.3	63	0.4	52	0.8	40	1.3	32	1.4
Boston, Mass.	29	3.7	30	3.5	38	4.0	49	3.5	59	3.5	68	3.2	73	2.7	71	3.5	65	3.2	55	3.0	45	4.5	33	4.2
Buffalo, N.Y.	24	2.9	24	2.6	32	2.9	45	3.2	55	3.0	66	2.2	70	2.9	68	3.5	62	3.3	52	3.0	40	3.7	28	3.0
Burlington, Vt.	17	1.7	19	1.7	29	1.9	43	2.6	55	3.0	65	3.5	70	3.5	67	3.7	59	3.1	49	2.7	37	2.9	23	2.2
Caribou, Me.	11	2.0	13	2.1	24	2.2	37	2.4	50	3.0	60	3.4	65	4.0	62	3.8	54	3.5	44	3.3	31	3.5	16	2.6
Charleston, S.C.	49	2.9	51	3.3	57	4.8	65	3.0	72	3.8	78	6.3	80	8.2	80	6.4	75	5.2	66	3.1	56	2.1	49	3.1
Chicago, Ill.	24	1.9	27	1.6	37	2.7	50	3.8	60	3.4	71	4.0	75	4.1	74	3.1	66	3.0	55	2.6	40	2.2	29	2.1
Cincinnati, Oh.*	32	3.4	34	3.0	43	4.1	55	3.9	64	4.0	73	3.9	76	4.0	75	3.0	68	2.7	58	2.2	45	3.1	34	2.9
Cleveland, Oh.	27	2.6	28	2.2	36	3.1	48	3.5	58	3.5	68	3.3	71	3.5	70	3.0	64	2.8	54	2.6	42	2.8	30	2.4
Columbus, Oh.	28	2.9	30	2.3	39	3.4	51	3.7	61	4.1	70	4.1	74	4.2	72	2.9	65	2.4	54	1.9	42	2.7	31	2.4
Dallas-Ft. Worth, Tex.	45	1.8	49	2.4	55	2.5	65	4.3	73	4.5	81	3.1	85	1.8	85	2.3	78	3.2	68	2.7	56	2.0	48	1.8
Denver, Col.	30	0.6	33	0.7	37	1.2	48	1.9	57	2.6	66	1.9	73	1.8	72	1.3	63	1.1	52	1.1	39	0.8	33	0.4
Des Moines, Ia.	19	1.1	24	1.1	34	2.3	50	2.9	61	4.2	71	4.9	75	3.3	73	3.3	64	3.1	54	2.1	38	1.4	25	1.1
Detroit, Mich.	26	1.9	27	1.8	35	2.3	48	3.1	58	3.4	69	3.0	73	3.0	72	3.0	65	2.3	54	2.5	41	2.3	30	2.2
Dodge City, Kan.	31	0.5	35	0.6	41	1.1	54	1.7	64	3.1	74	3.3	79	3.1	78	2.6	69	1.7	58	1.7	43	0.6	33	0.5
Duluth, Minn.	9	1.2	12	0.9	24	1.8	39	2.6	49	3.4	59	4.4	66	3.7	64	3.8	54	3.1	45	2.3	28	1.7	14	1.4
Eureka, Cal.*	47	7.4	48	5.2	48	4.8	50	3.0	53	2.1	55	0.7	56	0.1	57	0.3	57	0.7	54	3.2	52	5.8	49	6.6
Fairbanks, Alas.	-12	0.6	-3	0.5	10	0.5	30	0.3	47	0.7	59	1.4	61	1.9	55	2.2	44	1.1	25	0.7	3	0.7	-10	0.7
Fresno, Cal.	45	1.8	50	1.7	54	1.6	60	1.2	67	0.3	74	0.1	81	L	78	L	74	0.1	64	0.4	54	1.2	46	1.7
Galveston, Tex.*	54	3.0	56	2.7	61	2.6	69	2.6	76	3.2	81	4.1	83	4.4	83	4.4	80	5.6	73	2.8	64	3.2	57	3.7
Grand Junction, Col.	27	0.6	34	0.6	41	0.8	52	0.8	62	0.6	71	0.6	79	0.5	75	1.1	67	0.8	55	0.9	40	0.6	30	0.6
Gr. Rapids, Mich.	23	1.9	25	1.5	33	2.5	47	3.4	57	3.2	67	3.4	72	3.1	70	2.5	62	3.3	52	2.6	39	2.8	27	2.2
Hartford, Conn.	25	3.3	27	3.2	36	3.8	48	3.8	58	3.5	68	3.5	73	3.4	70	3.9	63	3.6	53	3.0	41	4.3	28	4.1
Helena, Mon.	18	0.6	25	0.4	31	0.7	43	0.9	52	1.8	59	2.4	68	1.0	66	1.0	56	1.0	45	0.6	32	0.6	23	0.6
Honolulu, Ha.	72	4.4	72	2.5	73	3.2	75	1.4	77	1.0	79	0.3	80	0.6	81	0.8	80	0.7	79	1.5	77	3.0	74	3.7
Houston, Tex.	52	3.6	55	3.5	61	2.7	69	3.5	76	5.1	81	4.5	83	4.1	83	4.4	79	4.7	71	4.1	61	4.0	55	4.0
Huron, S.D.	13	0.4	18	0.8	29	1.1	46	2.0	57	2.8	67	3.8	74	2.2	72	2.0	61	1.8	50	1.5	32	0.7	19	0.5
Indianapolis, Ind.	28	2.9	31	2.4	40	3.8	52	3.9	62	4.1	72	4.2	75	3.7	73	2.8	66	2.9	56	2.5	42	3.1	31	2.7
Jackson, Miss.	47	4.5	50	4.6	56	5.6	66	4.7	73	4.4	79	3.4	82	4.3	81	3.6	76	3.0	66	2.2	55	3.9	49	5.0
Jacksonville, Fla.	55	2.8	56	3.6	61	3.6	68	3.1	74	3.2	79	6.3	81	7.4	81	7.9	78	7.8	71	4.5	61	1.8	55	2.6
Juneau, Alas.	24	3.9	28	3.4	32	3.6	39	3.0	47	3.3	53	2.9	56	4.7	54	5.0	49	6.9	42	7.9	33	5.5	27	4.5
Kansas City, Mo.	27	1.3	32	1.3	41	2.6	54	3.5	64	4.3	73	5.6	78	4.4	77	3.8	68	4.2	58	3.2	42	1.5	31	1.5
Knoxville, Tenn.	41	4.7	43	4.7	50	4.9	60	3.5	68	3.4	76	3.6	78	4.7	77	3.2	72	2.8	61	2.7	49	3.6	42	4.5
Lander, Wyo.	20	0.5	26	0.7	31	1.2	43	2.4	53	2.6	61	1.9	71	0.6	69	0.4	58	1.1	47	1.2	32	0.9	23	0.5
Little Rock, Ark.	40	4.2	43	4.4	50	4.9	62	5.3	70	5.3	78	3.5	81	3.4	81	3.0	73	3.6	62	3.0	50	3.9	42	4.1
Los Angeles, Cal.*	57	3.0	58	2.8	59	2.2	62	1.3	65	0.1	68	L	73	L	74	L	73	0.2	68	0.3	63	2.0	58	2.2
Louisville, Ky.	33	3.5	36	3.5	44	5.1	56	4.1	65	4.2	73	4.1	77	3.8	76	3.0	69	2.9	58	2.4	45	3.3	36	3.3
Marquette, Mich.*	18	1.5	20	1.5	27	1.9	40	2.6	50	2.9	60	3.4	66	3.1	66	3.0	57	3.5	49	2.4	34	3.0	24	2.9
Memphis, Tenn.	41	4.9	44	4.7	51	5.1	63	5.4	71	4.4	79	3.5	82	3.5	80	3.3	74	3.0	63	2.6	51	3.9	43	4.7
Miami, Fla.	67	2.2	68	2.0	71	2.1	75	3.6	78	6.1	81	9.0	82	6.9	83	6.7	82	8.7	78	8.2	72	2.7	68	1.6
Milwaukee, Wis.	19	1.6	23	1.1	31	2.2	45	2.8	54	2.9	65	3.6	70	3.4	69	2.7	61	3.0	51	2.0	37	2.0	24	1.8
Minneapolis, Minn.	12	0.7	17	0.8	28	1.7	45	2.0	57	3.4	67	3.9	72	3.7	70	3.1	60	2.7	50	1.8	32	1.2	19	0.9
Mobile, Ala.	51	4.7	54	4.8	59	7.0	68	5.6	75	4.5	80	6.1	82	8.9	82	6.9	78	6.6	69	2.6	59	3.4	53	5.9
Moline, Ill.	22	1.7	26	1.3	36	2.6	51	3.8	61	3.9	71	4.4	75	4.6	73	3.4	65	3.8	54	2.7	39	1.9	27	1.8
Nashville, Tenn.	38	4.8	41	4.4	49	5.0	60	4.1	69	4.1	77	3.4	80	3.8	79	3.2	72	3.1	61	2.2	48	3.5	40	4.5
Newark, N.J.	31	2.9	33	3.0	41	3.9	52	3.4	62	3.6	71	3.0	76	4.0	75	4.3	68	3.4	58	2.8	46	3.6	35	3.5
New Orleans, La.	53	4.5	56	4.8	61	5.5	69	4.2	75	4.2	80	4.7	82	6.7	82	5.3	78	5.6	70	2.3	60	3.9	55	5.1
New York, N.Y.*	32	2.7	33	2.9	41	3.7	52	3.3	62	3.5	72	3.0	77	3.7	75	4.0	68	3.3	59	2.9	47	3.8	36	3.5
Nome, Alas.	6	0.9	5	0.8	7	0.9	10	0.7	35	0.7	46	1.0	50	2.4	49	3.6	42	2.4	29	1.4	16	1.0	4	0.7
Norfolk, Va.	41	3.4	41	3.3	48	3.4	58	2.7	67	3.3	75	3.6	78	5.7	77	5.9	72	4.2	62	3.1	52	2.9	42	3.1
Okla. City, Okla.	37	1.1	41	1.3	48	2.1	60	3.5	68	5.2	77	4.2	82	2.7	81	2.6	73	3.6	62	2.6	49	1.4	40	1.3
Omaha, Neb.	23	0.8	28	1.0	37	1.6	52	3.0	63	4.1	72	4.9	77	3.7	76	4.0	66	3.3	56	1.9	40	1.1	28	0.8
Parkersburg, W.Va.*	33	3.1	35	2.8	43	3.8	55	3.5	64	3.6	72	4.0	75	4.3	74	3.3	67	2.8	57	2.1	45	2.5	35	2.8
Philadelphia, Pa.	32	2.8	34	2.6	42	3.7	53	3.3	63	3.4	72	3.7	77	4.1	75	4.1	68	3.0	57	2.6	46	3.4	35	3.3
Phoenix, Ariz.	51	0.7	55	0.6	60	0.8	68	0.3	76	0.1	85	0.1	91	0.8	89	1.2	84	0.7	72	0.5	60	0.5	53	0.8
Pittsburgh, Pa.	28	2.8	29	2.4	38	3.6	50	3.4	60	3.5	69	3.5	72	3.8	70	3.2	64	2.5	53	2.5	41	2.5	31	2.5
Portland, Me.	22	3.4	23	3.5	32	4.1	43	3.8	53	3.2	62	3.1	68	2.6	66	2.6	59	3.1	49	3.3	39	4.9	26	4.1
Portland, Ore.	38	5.9	43	4.1	46	3.6	51	2.2	57	2.1	62	1.6	67	0.5	67	0.8	62	1.6	54	3.6	45	5.6	41	6.0
Providence, R.I.	28	3.5	29	3.5	37	4.0	47	3.7	57	3.5	66	2.7	72	2.9	70	3.9	63	3.4	53	3.3	43	4.5	32	4.1
Raleigh, N.C.	41	3.2	42	3.3	49	3.4	60	3.1	67	3.3	74	3.7	78	5.1	77	4.9	71	3.8	60	2.8	50	3.2	42	3.1
Rapid City, S.D.	22	0.5	26	0.6	31	1.0	45	2.1	55	2.8	64	3.7	73	2.1	72	1.5	61	1.2	50	0.9	35	0.5	27	0.4
Reno, Nev.	32	1.2	37	0.9	40	0.7	47	0.5	55	0.7	62	0.4	69	0.3	67	0.2	60	0.2	50	0.5	40	0.7	33	1.1
Richmond, Va.	38	2.9	39	3.0	47	3.4	58	2.8	67	3.4	74	3.5	78	5.6	76	5.1	70	3.9	60	3.0	51	3.0	39	3.2
St. Louis, Mo.	31	1.9	35	2.1	43	3.0	57	3.9	66	3.9	75	4.4	79	3.7	77	2.9	70	2.9	58	2.6	43	2.5	33	2.0
Salt Lake City, Ut.	28	1.3	33	1.2	40	1.6	49	2.1	58	1.5	66	1.3	77	0.7	75	0.9	65	0.7	52	1.2	39	1.3	30	1.4
San Antonio, Tex.	51	1.7	55	2.1	61	1.5	70	2.5	76	3.1	82	2.8	85	1.7	85	2.4	79	3.7	71	2.8	60	1.8	53	1.5
San Diego, Cal.	55	1.9	57	1.5	58	1.6	61	0.8	63	0.2	66	0.1	70	L	71	0.1	70	0.3	66	0.3	61	1.3	57	1.7
San Francisco, Cal.	48	4.4	51	3.0	53	2.5	55	1.6	58	0.4	62	0.1	63	L	63	L	64	0.2	61	1.0	55	2.3	50	4.0
San Juan, P.R.	75	3.7	75	2.5	76	2.0	78	4.0	79	6.5	81	5.6	81	6.4	81	7.0	81	6.1	81	5.6	79	5.5	77	4.7
Sault Ste. Marie, Mich.*	14	1.9	15	1.5	24	1.7	38	2.2	49	3.0	59	3.3	64	2.6	63	3.1	55	3.9	46	2.9	33	3.2	20	2.4
Savannah, Ga.	50	2.9	52	2.9	58	4.4	66	3.8	74	3.6	79	5.6	81	7.9	81	6.5	76	5.6	67	2.8	57	1.9	50	3.3
Seattle, Wash.	38	5.8	42	4.2	44	3.6	49	2.5	55	1.7	60	1.5	65	0.7	64	1.1	60	2.0	52	3.9	45	5.9	41	5.9
Spokane, Wash.	25	2.5	32	1.7	38	1.5	46	1.1	55	1.5	62	1.4	70	0.4	68	0.6	60	0.8	48	1.4	34	2.2	28	2.4
Springfield, Mo.	33	1.7	37	2.2	44	3.0	57	4.3	65	4.9	74	4.7	78	3.6	77	2.9	69	4.1	59	3.4	46	2.3	36	2.5
Syracuse, N.Y.	24	2.7	25	2.8	33	2.9	47	3.1	57	3.0	67	3.1	72	3.1	70	3.5	63	3.1	53	3.1	41	3.3	28	3.1
Tampa, Fla.	60	2.3	62	2.9	66	3.9	72	2.1	77	2.4	81	6.5	82	8.4	82	8.0	81	6.4	75	2.5	67	1.8	62	2.2
Trenton, N.J.*	32	2.8	33	2.7	41	3.8	52	3.2	62	3.4	71	3.2	76	4.7	74	4.2	67	3.2	57	2.5	46	3.5	35	3.3
Washington, D.C.	36	2.6	37	2.5	45	3.3	56	2.9	66	3.7	75	3.5	79	4.1	77	4.7	71	3.1	60	2.7	48	2.9	37	3.0
Wilmington, Del.	32	2.9	34	2.8	42	3.7	52	3.2	62	3.4	71	3.2	76	4.3	74	4.0	68	3.4	57	2.6	46	3.5	35	3.3

Annual Climatological Data

Source: NOAA, U.S. Department of Commerce

1982

Station	Elev. ft	Temperature °F Highest	Date	Lowest	Date	Precip. Total (in.)	Greatest in 24 hrs.	Date	Sleet or snow Total (in.)	Greatest in 24 hours	Date	Fastest Wind MPH	Date	No. of days Clear*	Cloudy*	Prec. .01 in. or more	Snow, sleet 1 in. or more
Albany, N.Y.	275	96	7/18	-11	1/18	32.07	1.75	6/5	70.7	17.5	4/6	40	1/5	68	179	120	14
Albuquerque, N.M.	5311	100	7/21	8	12/29	7.41	0.55	9/17	9.7	2.9	12/30	46	4/30	135	110	65	3
Anchorage, Alas.	114	76	6/26	-20	1/7	17.68	1.48	9/12	63.3	9.3	11/29	58	2/11	62	237	111	16
Asheville, N.C.	2140	92	7/3	-6	1/17	50.82	3.47	2/2	20.2	8.1	2/26	35	4/6	77	177	135	6
Atlanta, Ga.	1010	94	7/13	-5	1/11	56.21	3.46	10/12	7.7	5.8	1/12	41	1/4	85	181	134	3
Baltimore, Md.	148	96	7/26	-7	1/17	36.17	1.88	10/25	30.3	6.7	12/12	45	4/6	109	158	124	8
Barrow, Alas.	31	66	8/24	-45	2/17	4.72	0.34	10/18	30.9	2.8	10/18	52	2/4	59	180	94	8
Birmingham, Ala.	620	96	5/30	-1	1/11	57.85	—	—	6.6	—	—	—	—	—	—	128	2
Bismarck, N.D.	1647	98	9/10	-39	2/5	18.07	1.81	5/23	77.8	12.7	3/19	46	7/5	87	171	111	25
Boise, Ida.	2838	98	7/30	-10	1/6	13.83	0.68	10/29	27.1	4.7	1/22	49	8/11	99	190	103	10
Boston, Mass.	15	98	7/17	-2	1/18	44.61	3.23	6/4	49.7	13.2	4/6	50	4/1	94	171	119	16
Buffalo, N.Y.	705	93	7/16	-16	1/17	41.11	2.57	1/10	114.5	25.3	1/10	50	3/31	50	215	158	28
Burlington, Vt.	332	96	7/18	-17	1/12	32.34	1.60	7/31	50.6	9.1	3/7	46	8/25	55	217	148	15
Charleston, S.C.	40	96	7/4	10	1/11	47.02	4.33	6/17	T	T	1/14	35	7/5	75	193	120	0
Charleston, W. Va.	1016	93	7/16	-13	1/17	43.18	3.31	5/29	29.8	6.5	3/7	35	7/22	76	196	156	10
Chicago, Ill.	658	95	8/3	-26	1/10	44.68	4.53	12/2	53.3	9.4	4/5	40	12/28	73	192	130	13
Cincinnati, Oh.	869	93	7/17	-19	1/17	45.14	2.89	1/22	13.0	3.1	2/8	46	4/3	60	206	133	6
Cleveland, Oh.	777	93	7/18	-17	1/17	36.93	2.10	9/26	75.0	11.6	4/5	46	1/4	54	213	136	21
Columbus, Oh.	812	91	7/26	-16	1/17	39.32	2.12	5/29	24.9	4.3	4/8	52	5/29	59	206	144	10
Concord, N.H.	342	95	7/18	-25	1/26	34.74	2.45	6/1	61.9	13.9	4/6	40	12/26	75	169	128	16
Dallas, Tex.	551	103	8/6	7	1/11	40.75	4.30	5/12	0.8	0.8	1/31	44	4/28	99	132	90	0
Denver, Co.	5282	99	7/23	-15	2/5	14.45	2.00	12/24	40.8	23.6	12/24	44	1/24	98	141	98	8
Des Moines, Ia.	938	98	8/3	-22	1/10	44.80	2.41	8/4	53.3	7.1	1/2	51	4/3	95	185	136	16
Detroit, Mich.	633	91	7/17	-15	1/17	34.24	2.61	7/19	59.1	10.0	1/31	44	4/4	79	194	133	16
Dodge City, Kan.	2582	104	8/30	-13	2/5	19.52	2.89	7/8	23.2	5.0	11/27	54	4/2	114	133	81	8
Duluth, Minn.	1428	90	7/5	-38	1/17	34.23	2.46	10/5	104.5	14.7	1/22	51	3/13	75	202	145	26
Fairbanks, Alas.	436	87	7/7	-43	1/7	12.93	0.69	7/16	91.6	10.1	10/18	32	4/7	76	223	133	28
Fresno, Cal.	328	106	7/31	27	1/9	16.08	1.40	12/21	0.0	0.0	—	29	3/31	168	123	59	0
Galveston, Tex.	7	93	9/3	20	1/11	34.26	2.82	12/25	T	T	1/13	39	6/26	—	—	80	0
Grand Rapids, Mich.	784	92	8/3	-9	1/16	36.96	2.79	12/2	74.6	7.5	1/23	41	3/13	51	213	155	24
Hartford, Conn.	169	99	7/18	-9	1/19	48.01	6.14	6/5	49.0	14.1	4/6	38	4/1	87	173	117	12
Helena, Mont.	3828	94	8/1	-21	1/6	13.98	1.55	6/26	64.4	8.2	1/14	45	8/20	73	170	109	21
Honolulu, Ha.	7	92	9/7	56	12/8	34.92	3.60	1/20	0.0	0.0	—	46	11/23	51	136	124	0
Houston, Tex.	96	99	7/11	12	1/11	42.87	3.63	10/11	T	T	1/13	37	9/3	85	162	98	0
Huron, S.D.	1291	100	7/4	-25	2/5	25.04	1.83	7/25	53.4	12.3	1/22	49	7/20	92	169	97	15
Indianapolis, Ind.	792	92	8/4	-21	2/10	41.98	1.89	1/30	42.7	8.1	1/30	37	4/3	67	198	138	10
Jackson, Miss.	291	98	6/8	3	1/11	75.63	6.71	12/3	6.3	6.0	1/13	44	7/22	101	167	110	1
Jacksonville, Fla.	26	99	6/9	17	1/12	51.52	3.13	9/8	T	T	1/12	38	8/9	79	138	136	0
Juneau, Alas.	12	85	6/25	-7	1/18	41.12	2.03	10/11	121.5	15.3	1/12	—	—	—	—	194	29
Kansas City, Mo.	973	101	8/3	-19	2/6	47.21	6.19	8/12	25.2	5.2	2/4	50	6/7	101	173	115	7
Lander, Wyo.	5563	91	7/21	-21	2/5	13.26	1.98	9/13	107.9	16.9	9/13	52	12/19	105	152	75	26
Little Rock, Ark.	257	99	7/20	3	1/11	61.29	—	—	11.3	—	—	—	—	—	—	126	3
Los Angeles, Cal.	97	92	9/24	35	1/8	13.68	1.51	11/9	T	T	1/20	60	11/30	133	117	47	0
Louisville, Ky.	477	94	8/4	-11	1/10	45.38	2.78	1/22	7.3	2.5	1/12	42	4/3	69	186	130	3
Marquette, Mich.	1415	86	7/6	-25	1/17	37.06	2.39	7/10	171.4	12.7	1/22	44	4/3	—	—	179	45
Memphis, Tenn.	258	97	7/22	0	1/17	68.81	4.21	12/3	6.4	4.5	1/12	35	7/22	95	171	121	2
Miami, Fla.	7	96	8/2	33	1/12	67.41	7.25	4/24	0.0	0.0	—	30	8/3	91	92	149	0
Milford, Ut.	5028	98	7/31	-19	2/6	13.62	1.53	9/26	37.5	4.6	12/7	50	5/18	122	121	81	17
Milwaukee, Wis.	672	93	8/3	-26	1/17	36.56	2.24	12/2	60.4	8.7	4/5	54	1/23	67	194	135	17
Minneapolis, Minn.	834	100	7/5	-26	1/10	30.23	2.47	12/24	93.8	18.5	1/22	39	6/28	85	176	122	19
Mobile, Ala.	211	95	8/29	7	1/11	74.44	3.68	7/16	T	T	1/14	26	12/4	91	155	128	0
Moline, Ill.	582	96	8/3	-23	1/10	44.02	3.55	7/6	38.2	7.8	4/5	46	12/28	89	186	132	12
Nashville, Tenn.	590	93	7/16	-11	1/17	49.43	2.24	12/25	9.9	4.8	1/12	35	4/5	87	175	143	2
Newark, N.J.	7	100	7/18	-7	1/18	40.58	2.99	1/3	30.3	12.8	4/6	41	4/7	101	172	117	6
New Orleans, La.	4	96	8/26	15	1/11	65.62	5.71	12/3	T	T	1/14	32	6/16	71	170	123	0
New York, N.Y.	132	98	7/18	0	1/18	41.40	2.73	1/4	25.5	9.6	4/6	39	4/7	107	159	107	5
Nome, Alas.	13	80	6/25	-24	3/24	19.25	0.83	9/23	84.7	5.3	11/11	36	2/14	96	203	153	32
Norfolk, Va.	24	93	8/25	7	1/11	49.15	2.42	10/24	4.7	2.8	1/13	48	10/25	83	186	127	1
Oklahoma City, Okla.	1285	104	8/27	0	1/11	36.19	3.10	1/29	7.4	2.0	2/9	46	5/12	95	156	79	5
Omaha, Neb.	1309	98	8/3	-22	1/10	34.26	2.04	3/18	24.8	5.0	12/27	—	—	90	170	115	9
Philadelphia, Pa.	5	94	7/26	-7	1/17	40.43	2.33	5/28	29.4	6.8	12/11	43	4/1	100	148	122	7
Phoenix, Ariz.	1110	113	7/14	34	1/3	9.94	1.03	12/9	0.0	0.0	—	60	11/30	189	83	54	0
Pittsburgh, Pa.	1137	89	9/13	-18	1/17	32.01	1.73	5/22	41.9	6.7	3/2	40	1/4	58	197	149	10
Portland, Me.	43	95	7/18	-16	1/26	39.68	2.22	6/1	67.6	15.9	4/6	38	4/7	81	170	133	16
Portland, Ore.	21	100	6/18	14	1/6	43.04	2.38	9/19	2.1	1.1	1/3	43	12/16	75	213	157	2
Providence, R.I.	51	98	7/18	-9	1/18	49.26	3.14	6/4	38.3	7.6	4/6	37	4/1	89	171	126	13
Raleigh, N.C.	434	94	7/27	4	1/11	44.35	2.82	6/10	6.6	5.0	1/14	32	4/3	77	178	126	2
Rapid City, S.D.	3162	96	7/22	-26	1/16	25.97	2.60	8/4	34.8	4.6	3/17	57	3/30	95	152	117	12
Reno, Nev.	4404	101	8/22	0	1/7	11.10	0.91	9/15	34.8	4.3	1/20	52	12/21	130	129	78	14
Richmond, Va.	164	94	7/19	4	1/17	46.48	2.79	7/12	27.2	6.5	2/27	—	—	77	186	123	6
Rochester, N.Y.	547	95	7/7	-15	1/12	31.83	1.59	11/3	94.4	11.4	1/10	56	2/1	67	209	161	29
St. Louis, Mo.	535	98	8/5	-15	1/10	54.97	4.03	12/2	28.7	13.9	1/30	49	4/16	76	177	117	7
Salt Lake City, Ut.	4221	100	7/22	0	2/9	22.86	2.30	9/26	60.8	7.6	12/1	45	5/18	94	159	112	20
San Antonio, Tex.	788	102	8/17	13	1/11	22.96	3.54	5/5	0.5	0.5	1/13	32	6/30	88	160	87	0
San Diego, Cal.	13	91	9/3	40	1/8	12.96	2.15	3/17	0.0	0.0	—	—	—	116	143	56	0
San Francisco, Cal.	8	93	8/6	33	12/30	34.81	5.71	1/4	T	T	3/29	47	4/11	151	120	78	0
Sault Ste Marie. Mich.	718	86	7/6	-36	1/10	37.53	1.89	9/1	159.6	11.3	1/31	46	1/10	64	230	174	45
Savannah, Ga.	46	98	7/4	12	1/11	52.26	3.02	4/25	0.0	0.0	—	29	12/12	86	186	130	0
Seattle, Wash.	400	94	6/18	14	1/6	39.32	1.88	12/2	9.0	2.2	1/2	49	12/21	63	234	145	5
Sioux City, Ia.	1095	98	7/14	-22	1/10	30.50	1.90	10/8	61.9	17.4	1/22	57	4/3	84	182	116	16
Spokane, Wash.	2357	98	7/29	-15	1/6	17.25	1.01	4/10	56.4	7.9	1/22	50	8/9	63	192	124	16
Springfield, Mo.	1268	101	8/5	-11	1/10	47.67	4.50	12/2	21.5	6.1	1/7	42	12/27	81	175	107	5
Syracuse, N.Y.	410	93	7/18	-25	1/12	35.14	2.01	9/22	100.0	10.9	-1/9	47	7/7	59	203	164	28
Tampa, Fla.	19	94	6/7	24	1/12	55.81	3.96	9/25	0.0	0.0	—	35	4/11	107	114	106	0
Washington, D.C.	10	97	7/18	-5	1/17	35.77	1.86	6/12	27.4	6.6	12/12	42	4/6	88	181	106	6
Wilmington, Del.	74	95	7/19	-10	1/17	41.07	2.45	6/12	27.9	5.3	1/13	39	4/4	101	154	119	9

*To get partly cloudy days deduct the total of clear and cloudy days from 365 (1 yr.). T—trace. (1) Date shown is the starting date of the storm (in some cases it lasted more than one day).

Normal Temperatures, Highs, Lows, Precipitation

Source: National Oceanic and Atmospheric Administration, U.S. Commerce Department

These normals are based on records for the thirty-year period 1941-1970. (See explanation on page 757.) The extreme temperatures (through 1981) are listed for the stations shown and may not agree with the states records shown on page 761.

Airport stations; * designates city office stations. The minus (−) sign indicates temperatures below zero. Fahrenheit thermometer registration.

State	Station	Normal temperature				Extreme temperature		Normal annual precipitation (inches)
		January		July				
		Max.	Min.	Max.	Min.	Highest	Lowest	
Alabama	Mobile	61	41	91	73	104	7	66.98
Alabama	Montgomery	58	37	91	72	105	5	49.86
Alaska	Juneau	29	18	64	48	90	−22	54.67
Arizona	Phoenix	65	38	105	78	118	17	7.05
Arkansas	Little Rock	50	29	93	70	109	−5	48.52
California	Los Angeles*	67	47	83	64	110	28	14.05
California	San Francisco	55	41	71	54	106	20	19.53
Colorado	Denver	44	16	87	59	104	−30	15.51
Connecticut	Hartford	33	16	84	61	102	−26	43.37
Delaware	Wilmington	40	24	86	66	102	−6	40.25
Dist. of Col.	Washington	44	28	88	69	103	1	38.89
Florida	Jacksonville	65	45	90	72	105	12	54.47
Florida	Key West	76	66	89	80	95	41	39.99
Florida	Miami	76	59	89	76	98	31	59.80
Georgia	Atlanta	51	33	87	69	105	−3	48.34
Hawaii	Honolulu	79	65	87	73	93	53	22.90
Idaho	Boise	37	21	91	59	111	−23	11.50
Illinois	Chicago-Midway	32	17	84	65	102	−20	34.44
Indiana	Indianapolis	36	20	85	65	104	−20	38.74
Iowa	Des Moines	28	11	85	65	105	−24	30.85
Iowa	Dubuque	26	9	82	61	99	−28	40.27
Kansas	Wichita	41	21	92	70	113	−12	30.58
Kentucky	Louisville	42	25	87	66	105	−20	43.11
Louisiana	New Orleans	62	44	90	73	102	14	56.77
Maine	Portland	31	12	79	57	103	−39	40.80
Maryland	Baltimore	42	25	87	67	102	−7	40.46
Massachusetts	Boston	36	23	81	65	102	−12	42.52
Michigan	Detroit-City	32	19	83	63	105	−16	30.96
Michigan	Sault Ste. Marie*	22	6	75	53	98	−35	31.70
Minnesota	Minn.-St. Paul	21	3	82	61	104	−34	25.94
Mississippi	Jackson	58	36	93	71	106	6	49.19
Missouri	St. Louis	40	23	88	69	107	−14	35.89
Montana	Helena	28	8	84	52	105	−42	11.38
Nebraska	Omaha	33	12	89	66	114	−22	30.18
Nevada	Winnemucca	41	16	91	51	106	−34	8.47
New Hampshire	Concord	31	10	83	57	102	−37	36.17
New Jersey	Atlantic City	41	24	85	65	106	−11	45.46
New Mexico	Albuquerque	47	24	92	65	105	−17	7.77
New Mexico	Roswell	55	21	95	64	109	−9	10.61
New York	Albany	30	13	84	60	100	−28	33.36
New York	New York-La Guardia	38	26	84	69	107	−2	41.61
No. Carolina	Charlotte	52	32	88	69	104	−3	42.72
No. Carolina	Raleigh	51	30	88	67	105	−1	42.54
No. Dakota	Bismarck	19	−3	84	57	109	−44	16.16
Ohio	Cincinnati-Abbe	40	24	87	66	109	−17	40.03
Ohio	Cleveland	33	20	82	61	103	−19	34.99
Oklahoma	Oklahoma City	48	26	93	70	110	−4	31.37
Oregon	Portland	44	33	79	55	107	−3	37.61
Pennsylvania	Harrisburg	38	23	87	65	107	−8	36.47
Pennsylvania	Philadelphia	40	24	87	67	104	−5	39.93
Rhode Island	Block Island	37	25	76	63	92	−4	40.51
So. Carolina	Charleston	60	37	89	71	103	8	52.12
So. Dakota	Huron	23	2	87	61	112	−39	19.44
So. Dakota	Rapid City	34	10	86	59	110	−27	17.12
Tennessee	Nashville	48	29	90	69	107	−15	46.00
Texas	Amarillo	49	23	91	66	108	−14	20.28
Texas	Galveston*	59	48	87	79	101	8	42.20
Texas	Houston	63	42	94	73	107	17	48.19
Utah	Salt Lake City	37	19	93	61	107	−30	15.17
Vermont	Burlington	26	8	81	59	101	−30	32.54
Virginia	Norfolk	49	32	87	70	104	5	44.68
Washington	Seattle-Tacoma	43	33	75	54	99	0	38.79
Washington	Spokane	31	20	84	55	108	−25	17.42
West Virginia	Parkersburg*	41	24	86	65	106	−27	38.44
Wisconsin	Madison	25	8	81	59	104	−37	30.25
Wisconsin	Milwaukee	27	11	80	59	101	−24	29.07
Wyoming	Cheyenne	38	15	84	55	100	−34	14.65
Puerto Rico	San Juan	82	69	87	75	98	60	59.15

Mean Annual Snowfall (inches) based on record through 1980: Boston, Mass. 42; Sault Ste. Marie, Mich., 113; Albany, N.Y. 65.2; Rochester, N.Y. 89.2; Burlington, Vt., 78.6; Cheyenne, Wyo., 53.3; Juneau, Alas. 105.8.

Wettest Spot: Mount Waialeale, Ha., on the island of Kauai, is the rainiest place in the world, according to the National Geographic Society, with an average annual rainfall of 460 inches.

Highest Temperature: A temperature of 136° F. observed at Azizia, Tripolitania in Northern Africa on Sept. 13, 1922, is generally accepted as the world's highest temperature recorded under standard conditions.

The record high in the United States was 134° in Death Valley, Cal., July 10, 1913.

Lowest Temperature: A record low temperature of −128.6° F. was recorded at the Soviet Antarctica station Vostok on July 21, 1983.

The record low in the United States was −80° at Prospect Creek, Alas., Jan. 23, 1971.

The lowest official temperature on the North American continent was recorded at 81 degrees below zero in February, 1947, at a lonely airport in the Yukon called Snag.

These are the meteorological champions—the official temperature extremes—but there are plenty of other claimants to thermometer fame. However, sun readings are unofficial records, since meteorological data to qualify officially must be taken on instruments in a sheltered and ventilated location.

Record Temperatures by States Through 1982

Source: National Oceanic and Atmospheric Administration, U.S. Commerce Department

State	Lowest °F	Highest	Latest date	Station	Approximate elevation in feet
Alabama	−27		Jan. 30, 1966	New Market	725
		112	Sept. 5, 1925	Centerville	345
Alaska	−79.8		Jan. 23, 1971	Prospect Creek Camp	1,100
		100	June 27, 1915	Fort Yukon	419
Arizona	−40		Jan. 7, 1971	Hawley Lake	8,180
		127	July 7, 1905	Parker	345
Arkansas	−29		Feb. 13, 1905	Pond	1,250
		120	Aug. 10, 1936	Ozark	396
California	−45		Jan. 20, 1937	Boca	5,532
		134	July 10, 1913	Greenland Ranch	−178
Colorado	−60		Feb. 1, 1951	Taylor Park	9,206
		118	July 11, 1888	Bennett	5,484
Connecticut	−32		Feb. 16, 1943	Falls Village	585
		105	July 22, 1926	Waterbury	409
Delaware	−17		Jan. 17, 1893	Millsboro	20
		110	July 21, 1930	Millsboro	20
Dist. of Col.	−15		Feb. 11, 1899	Washington	112
		106	July 20, 1930	Washington	112
Florida	−2		Feb. 13, 1899	Tallahassee	193
		109	June 29, 1931	Monticello	207
Georgia	−17		Jan. 27, 1940	CCC Camp F-16	1,000
		113	May 27, 1978	Greenville	860
Hawaii	12		May 17, 1979	Mauna Kea Obs	13,770
		100	Apr. 27, 1931	Pahala	850
Idaho	−60		Jan. 16, 1943	Island Park Dam	6,285
		118	July 28, 1934	Orofino	1,027
Illinois	−35		Jan. 22, 1930	Mount Carroll	817
		117	July 14, 1954	E. St. Louis	410
Indiana	−35		Feb. 2, 1951	Greensburg	954
		116	July 14, 1936	Collegeville	672
Iowa	−47		Jan. 12, 1912	Washta	1,157
		118	July 20, 1934	Keokuk	614
Kansas	−40		Feb. 13, 1905	Lebanon	1,812
		121	July 24, 1936	Alton (near)	1,651
Kentucky	−34		Jan. 28, 1963	Cynthiana	719
		114	July 28, 1930	Greensburg	581
Louisiana	−16		Feb. 13, 1899	Minden	194
		114	Aug. 10, 1936	Plain Dealing	268
Maine	−48		Jan. 19, 1925	Van Buren	510
		105	July 10, 1911	North Bridgton	450
Maryland	−40		Jan. 13, 1912	Oakland	2,461
		109	July 10, 1936	Cumberland and Frederick	623-325
Massachusetts	−35		Jan. 12, 1981	Chester	640
		107	Aug. 2, 1975	Chester and New Bedford	120-640
Michigan	−51		Feb. 9, 1934	Vanderbilt	785
		112	July 13, 1936	Mio	963
Minnesota	−59		Feb. 16, 1903	Pokegama Dam	1,280
		114	July 6, 1936	Moorhead	904
Mississippi	−19		Jan. 30, 1966	Corinth	420
		115	July 29, 1930	Holly Springs	600
Missouri	−40		Feb. 13, 1905	Warsaw	700
		118	July 14, 1954	Warsaw and Union	687-560
Montana	−70		Jan. 20, 1954	Rogers Pass	5,470
		117	July 5, 1937	Medicine Lake	1,950
Nebraska	−47		Feb. 12, 1899	Camp Clarke	3,700
		118	July 24, 1936	Minden	2,169
Nevada	−50		Jan. 8, 1937	San Jacinto	5,200
		122	June 23, 1954	Overton	1,240
New Hampshire	−47		Jan. 1934	Mt. Washington	6,262
		106	July 4, 1911	Nashua	125
New Jersey	−34		Jan. 5, 1904	River Vale	70
		110	July 10, 1936	Runyon	18
New Mexico	−50		Feb. 1, 1951	Gavilan	7,350
		116	July 14, 1934	Orogrande	4,171
New York	−52		Feb. 9, 1934	Stillwater Reservoir	1,670
		108	July 22, 1926	Troy	35
North Carolina	−29		Jan. 30, 1966	Mt. Mitchell	6,525
		109	Sept. 7, 1954	Weldon	81
North Dakota	−60		Feb. 15, 1936	Parshall	1,929
		121	July 6, 1936	Steele	1,857
Ohio	−39		Feb. 10, 1899	Milligan	800
		113	July 21, 1934	Gallipolis (near)	673
Oklahoma	−27		Jan. 18, 1930	Watts	958
		120	July 26, 1943	Tishmoningo	670
Oregon	−54		Feb. 10, 1933	Seneca	4,700
		119	Aug. 10, 1938	Pendleton	1,074
Pennsylvania	−42		Jan. 5, 1904	Smethport	1,469
		111	July 10, 1936	Phoenixville	100
Rhode Island	−23		Jan. 11, 1942	Kingston	100
		104	Aug. 2, 1975	Providence	51
South Carolina	−20		Jan. 18, 1977	Caesar's Head	3,100
		111	June 28, 1954	Camden	170
South Dakota	−58		Feb. 17, 1936	McIntosh	2,277
		120	July 5, 1936	Gannvalley	1,750

State	Lowest °F	Highest	Latest date	Station	Approximate elevation in feet
Tennessee	−32		Dec. 30, 1917	Mountain City	2,471
		113	Aug. 9, 1930	Perryville	377
Texas	−23		Feb. 8, 1933	Seminole	3,275
		120	Aug. 12, 1936	Seymour	1,291
Utah	−50		Jan. 5, 1913	Strawberry Tunnel	7,650
		116	June 28, 1892	Saint George	2,880
Vermont	−50		Dec. 30, 1933	Bloomfield	915
		105	July 4, 1911	Vernon	310
Virginia	−29		Feb. 10, 1899	Monterey	3,008
		110	July 15, 1954	Balcony Falls	725
Washington	−48		Dec. 30, 1968	Mazama	2,120
	−48		Dec. 30, 1968	Winthrop	1,755
		118	Aug. 5, 1961	Ice Harbor Dam	475
West Virginia	−37		Dec. 30, 1917	Lewisburg	2,200
		112	July 10, 1936	Martinsburg	435
Wisconsin	−54		Jan. 24, 1922	Danbury	908
		114	July 13, 1936	Wisconsin Dells	900
Wyoming	−63		Feb. 9, 1933	Moran	6,770
		114	July 12, 1900	Basin	3,500

Canadian Normal Temperatures, Highs, Lows, Precipitation

Source: Atmospheric Environment Service, Environment Canada

These normals are based on varying periods of record over the thirty-year period 1951 to 1980 inclusive. Extreme temperatures are based on varying periods of record for each station through 1983. Airport station; * designates city office stations. The minus (−) sign indicates temperatures below zero. Celsius thermometer registration.

Province	Station	Normal January Max.	Normal January Min.	Normal July Max.	Normal July Min.	Extreme Highest	Extreme Lowest	Precipitation normal annual (millimeters)
Alberta	Calgary	−6	−18	23	9	36	−45	424
Alberta	Edmonton (Industrial Airport)	−11	−19	23	12	34	−48	466
British Columbia	Prince George	−8	−17	22	13	34	−50	628
British Columbia	Victoria	6	1	20	10	36	−16	647
British Columbia	Vancouver	5	0	22	13	33	−18	1113
Manitoba	Churchill	−27	−31	17	7	34	−45	402
Manitoba	Winnipeg	−14	−24	26	13	41	−45	526
Newfoundland	Gander	−2	−10	22	11	36	−31	1130
Newfoundland	St. John's	0	−7	21	11	30	−23	1514
New Brunswick	Fredericton	−4	−15	26	13	37	−37	1109
New Brunswick	Moncton	−3	−13	25	13	37	−38	1095
New Brunswick	Saint John	−3	−11	21	12	35	−38	1337
Nova Scotia	Halifax	−2	−10	23	13	35	−26	1491
Nova Scotia	Sydney	−1	−9	23	12	35	−27	1400
Ontario	Ottawa	−6	−15	26	15	38	−36	879
Ontario	Sudbury	−9	−19	24	13	38	−38	861
Ontario	Toronto	−1	−8	27	17	41	−33	801
Ontario	Windsor	−1	−9	28	17	38	−26	849
Prince Edward Island	Charlottetown	−3	−11	23	14	34	−28	1077
Quebec	Montreal	−6	−15	26	16	38	−38	946
Quebec	Quebec City	−8	−17	25	13	36	−36	1174
Quebec	Val-d'Or	−11	−23	23	11	36	−44	920
Saskatchewan	Prince Albert	−16	−27	24	11	38	−50	398
Saskatchewan	Regina	−13	−23	26	12	43	−50	384
Northwest Territories	Alert*	−28	−36	6	1	20	−50	154
Northwest Territories	Yellowknife	−25	−33	21	12	32	−51	267
Yukon Territory	Dawson*	−27	−34	22	9	36	−56	306
Yukon Territory	Whitehorse*	−16	−25	20	8	34	−52	261

Canadian Low and High Temperature Records Through 1983

Source: Atmospheric Environment Service, Environment Canada

Province	Lowest °C	Highest	Latest date	Station	Approximate elevation in meters
Alberta	−61		Jan. 11, 1911	Fort Vermillion	278
		42	July 12, 1886	Medicine Hat	721
British Columbia	−59		Jan. 31, 1947	Smith River	673
		44	July 17, 1941	Chinock Cove	404
		44	July 17, 1941	Lillooet	290
		44	July 17, 1941	Lytton	183
Manitoba	−53		Jan. 9, 1899	Norway House	219
		44	July 12, 1936	Emerson	241
Newfoundland	−49		Mar. 7, 1968	Twin Falls	457
		42	Aug. 11, 1914	Northwest River	61
New Brunswick	−47		Feb. 1, 1955	Sisson Dam	278
		39	Aug. 19, 1935	Rexton	6
Nova Scotia	−41		Jan. 31, 1920	Upper Stewiacke	23
		38	Aug. 19, 1935	Collegeville	76
Ontario	−58		Jan. 23, 1935	Iroquois Falls	244
		42	July 13, 1936	Fort Frances	354
Prince Edward Island	−37		Jan. 26, 1884	Kilmahumaig	6
		37	Aug. 19, 1935	Charlottetown	22
Quebec	−54		Feb. 5, 1923	Doucet	376
		40	Aug. 15, 1928	Bark Lake	365
Saskatchewan	−57		Feb. 1, 1893	Prince Albert	436
		45	July 5, 1937	Midale	582
		45	July 5, 1937	Yellow Grass	579
North West Territories	−57		Dec. 26, 1917	Fort Smith	202
		39	July 18, 1941	Fort Smith	207
Yukon Territory	−63		Feb. 3, 1947	Snag	586
		35	June 18, 1950	Mayo	495

Canadian Normal Temperature and Precipitation

Source: Atmospheric Environment Service, Environment Canada

Normal refers to the mean daily temperature and total monthly precipitation based on varying periods of record over the thirty-year period 1951 to 1980 inclusive. Airport station unless * designates city office station. T, temperature in Celsius; P, precipitation in millimeters.

Station	Jan. T	Jan. P	Feb. T	Feb. P	Mar. T	Mar. P	Apr. T	Apr. P	May T	May P	June T	June P	July T	July P	Aug. T	Aug. P	Sept. T	Sept. P	Oct. T	Oct. P	Nov. T	Nov. P	Dec. T	Dec. P
Calgary, Alta.	-12	16	-7	16	-4	16	3	33	9	49	14	89	16	65	15	55	11	38	6	18	-3	13	-8	16
Charlottetown, P.E.I.	-7	117	-8	97	-3	95	2	82	9	84	15	80	18	84	18	88	14	86	8	106	3	121	-4	129
Churchill, Man.	-28	15	-26	13	-20	18	-11	23	-2	32	6	44	12	46	11	58	5	51	-2	43	-12	39	-22	21
Dawson, Yukon*	-31	17	-24	16	-15	10	-2	10	8	21	14	39	16	47	13	44	7	28	-4	29	-17	22	-26	25
Edmonton, Alta.	-15	24	-10	18	-5	16	4	20	11	42	15	77	17	92	16	78	11	46	6	15	-4	17	-10	22
Fredericton, N.B.	-9	103	-8	90	-2	85	4	80	11	83	16	85	19	89	18	87	13	87	8	97	1	106	-7	118
Frobisher Bay, N.W.T.	-26	26	-26	23	-23	23	-14	26	-3	25	3	39	8	63	7	60	2	46	-5	44	-13	34	-22	22
Halifax, N.S.	-6	153	-6	134	-2	125	3	109	9	109	15	90	18	94	18	101	14	96	9	136	3	167	-3	163
Hamilton, Ont.	-6	63	-6	53	-1	71	6	79	13	66	18	65	21	71	20	75	16	74	9	61	3	68	-3	78
Kitchener, Ont.*	-7	60	-6	57	-1	72	6	75	13	77	18	86	21	84	20	89	16	72	10	69	3	80	-4	76
London, Ont.	-7	75	-6	61	-1	75	6	81	12	67	18	74	20	72	20	80	15	79	9	73	3	85	-4	88
Moncton, N.B.	-8	125	-8	99	-3	112	3	90	9	84	15	90	19	95	18	79	13	76	8	99	2	110	-5	121
Montreal, Que.	-10	72	-9	65	-3	74	6	74	13	66	18	82	21	90	20	92	15	88	9	76	2	81	-7	87
Ottawa, Ont.	-11	61	-10	60	-3	68	6	69	13	68	18	73	21	86	19	88	14	79	8	68	1	78	-8	80
Quebec City, Que.	-12	90	-11	78	-5	82	3	73	11	87	16	110	19	117	18	117	13	119	7	91	0	97	-9	114
Regina, Sask.	-18	17	-14	16	-8	18	3	24	11	64	16	80	19	53	18	45	12	37	5	19	-5	14	-13	17
Saint John, N.B.	-8	149	-8	116	-3	114	3	107	9	108	14	94	17	103	17	102	13	112	8	128	2	146	-5	166
St. John's, Nfld.	-4	156	-5	140	-2	132	1	116	5	102	11	86	16	75	15	122	12	117	7	146	3	163	-2	161
Saskatoon, Sask.	-19	16	-15	16	-9	18	3	21	11	40	16	59	19	54	17	38	11	31	5	17	-6	15	-14	20
Sault Ste. Marie, Ont.	-10	74	-10	68	-5	60	3	64	9	84	15	74	17	56	17	83	13	95	8	74	1	86	-7	80
Toronto, Ont.*	-5	61	-4	52	-1	70	8	73	14	66	19	64	22	74	21	73	17	66	11	61	5	68	-2	73
Vancouver, B.C.	3	154	5	115	6	101	9	60	12	52	15	45	17	32	17	41	14	67	10	114	6	150	4	182
Victoria, B.C.	3	154	5	99	6	72	8	39	12	29	14	29	16	18	16	27	14	40	10	78	6	131	4	157
Whitehorse, Yukon	-21	18	-13	13	-8	14	0	10	7	13	12	31	14	34	13	38	8	30	1	22	-9	20	-17	20
Windsor, Ont.	-5	55	-4	50	1	72	8	83	14	70	20	89	22	83	21	84	17	67	11	57	4	65	-2	73
Winnipeg, Man.	-19	21	-16	18	-8	23	3	39	11	66	17	80	20	76	18	75	12	53	6	31	-5	25	-14	19
Yellowknife, N.W.T.	-29	13	-25	11	-19	12	-7	10	5	17	13	17	16	34	14	44	7	31	-2	35	-14	25	-24	18

Canadian Annual Climatological Data

Source: Atmospheric Environment Service, Environment Canada

Station 1983	Elev. meters	Temperature (Celsius) Highest	Date D/Mo.	Lowest	Date D/Mo.	Precipitation Total (mm)	Greatest in 24 hrs.	Date D/Mo.	Snowfall Total (cm)	Greatest in 24 hrs.	Date D/Mo.	Fastest wind Km/h	Date D/Mo.	No. of days Precip., measurable	Snow, measurable
Calgary, Alta.	1084	34.5	5/8	-36.5	23/12	294.6	32.4	18/8	112.0	7.4	25/4	93	sev.	120	63
Charlottetown, P.E.I.	55	30.1	5/7	-20.4	26/12	1166.8	42.8	22/7	220.5	21.3	24/2	113	26/11	200	73
Churchill, Man.	29	31.3	11/8	-40.2	17/1	618.4	62.3	3/9	266.7	24.3	27/4	107	24/11	170	99
Dawson, Yukon	369	34.7	31/5	-51.4	10/1	384.1	14.3	10/8	164.5	14.2	24/9	65	2/6	127	59
Edmonton, Alta.	671	33.5	10/8	-35.1	24/12	427.5	42.5	25/6	87.9	9.2	27/10	76	26/7	126	60
Fredericton, N.B.	20	34.0	22/6	-24.0	20/12	1192.6	58.9	25/11	179.2	25.7	16/1	85	7/12	162	42
Frobisher Bay, N.W.T.	34	20.9	16/7	-44.0	25/2	396.0	19.8	11/7	259.9	18.2	12/5	100	10/2	164	127
Halifax, N.S.	145	33.0	23/6	-18.7	4/1	1557.4	90.7	7/8	155.1	26.0	12/2	104	7/12	161	31
Hamilton, Ont.	237	34.4	16/7	-19.4	30/12	1086.1	49.0	29/7	146.4	16.0	28/12	96	13/10	149	51
Moncton, N.B.	71	33.8	22/6	-24.7	20/12	1150.2	79.4	sev.	222.4	29.3	sev.	107	25/11	179	52
Montreal, Que.	36	33.1	4/7	-27.0	20/12	1123.2	31.0	21/9	254.2	21.3	16/11	72	22/12	168	63
Ottawa, Ont.	114	33.3	sev.	-28.7	20/12	1021.6	55.5	4/10	255.1	25.6	4/11	93	28/10	166	65
Quebec, Que.	73	34.8	4/7	-29.6	20/12	1365.6	53.4	3/2	362.2	26.8	22/12	100	7/6	176	74
Regina, Sask.	577	38.0	31/8	-42.2	23/12	448.6	73.6	9/7	106.4	21.2	sev.	85	9/7	116	58
St. John, N.B.	109	32.0	22/6	-24.0	20/12	1469.0	59.6	20/5	191.2	21.2	12/2	96	sev.	161	39
St. John's, Nfld.	140	31.5	6/7	-20.3	1	1679.3	55.8	sev.	206.9	41.0	sev.	130	25/12	236	63
Saskatoon, Sask.	501	37.6	6/8	-41.1	23/12	423.9	96.6	24/6	119.2	14.4	10/5	98	24/6	116	81
Sault Ste. Marie, Ont.	192	32.9	14/7	-29.0	19/12	846.2	30.9	31/7	219.5	25.7	19/3	100	26/6	158	73
Thunder Bay, Ont.	199	40.3	7/8	-33.3	19/12	758.9	38.9	10/8	208.8	21.8	sev.	78	24/12	137	60
Toronto, Ont.	111	35.7	15/7	-22.0	25/12	795.7	29.6	8/8	88.3	16.3	28/12	109	2/5	136	39
Vancouver, B.C.	2	30.4	29/5	-13.2	23/12	1489.5	46.6	24/11	12.5	4.2	7/12	72	8/1	182	8
Victoria, B.C.	69	31.5	28/5	-8.1	23/12	1029.1	45.2	1/9	17.1	9.0	7/12	67	24/12	164	4
Waterloo/Wellington, Ont.	314	34.1	15/7	-21.1	20/12	969.6	38.0	11/8	136.2	14.6	6/12	100	4/7	151	50
Whitehorse, Yukon	703	34.1	30/5	-45.0	10/1	232.0	24.6	4/9	90.0	9.8	11/1	80	30/6	104	50
Windsor, Ont.	190	34.6	15/7	-23.4	30/12	1067.1	82.0	29/7	79.2	12.4	6/12	83	19/7	133	35
Winnipeg, Man.	239	38.8	2/9	-33.0	19/12	479.4	47.2	20/8	89.7	14.9	2/3	78	9/5	124	62
Yellowknife, N.W.T.	205	28.0	sev.	-43.3	4/2	260.1	17.6	26/5	149.5	14.4	27/9	78	26/12	120	82

Speed of Winds in Canada

Source: Atmospheric Environment Service, Environment Canada

Kilometers-per-hour average is for the period of record 1951 to 1980. High is for gust wind speed based on varying periods of record, depending on the origin of the station, through 1983.

Station	Avg.	High	Station	Avg.	High	Station	Avg.	High
Calgary, Alta.	16.2	127	London, Ont.	16.0	128	Sault Ste. Marie, Ont.	15.1	119
Charlottetown, P.E.I.	19.3	177	Moncton, N.B.	18.1	161	Thunder Bay, Ont.	13.4	122
Churchill, Man.	22.7	151	Montreal, Que.	15.6	161	Toronto, Ont.	18.0	124
Dawson, Yukon	3.7	57	Ottawa, Ont.	14.6	135	Vancouver, B.C.	12.0	129
Edmonton, Alta.	14.1	117	Quebec City, Que.	16.0	177	Victoria, B.C.	17.7	145
Fredericton, N.B.	13.8	132	Regina, Sask.	20.8	153	Whitehorse, Yukon	14.1	106
Frobisher Bay, N.W.T.	16.7	156	Saint John, N.B.	18.5	146	Windsor, Ont.	17.0	148
Halifax, N.S.	18.2	132	Saint John's, Nfld.	24.3	193	Winnipeg, Man.	18.6	129
Hamilton, Ont.	17.7	133	Saskatoon, Sask.	17.5	151	Yellowknife, N.W.T.	15.5	105

WEIGHTS AND MEASURES

Source: National Bureau of Standards, U.S. Commerce Department

U.S. Moving, Inch by 25.4 mm, to Metric System

On July 2, 1971, following the report of a metric conversion study committee, Commerce Secy. Maurice H. Stans recommended a gradual U.S. changeover during a 10-year period at the end of which the U.S. would be predominantly, but not exclusively, on the metric system. The Metric Conversion Act of 1975, signed Dec. 23, 1975, declared a national policy of coordinating voluntary increasing use of the Metric System and established a U. S. Metric Board to coordinate the change over. That Board terminated its operations on Sept. 30, 1982 and transferred its functions to the Office of Metric Programs, U.S. Department of Commerce.

Currently conversion to metric for the most part is confined to the following industries: automotive, construction and farm equipment, computer, and bottling. In addition, with encouragement of the U.S. Office of Education, our school systems are emphasizing teaching of the metric system.

The International System of Units

Two systems of weights and measures exist side by side in the United States today, with roughly equal but separate legislative sanction: the U.S. Customary System and the International (Metric) System. Throughout U.S. history, the Customary System (inherited from, but now different from, the British Imperial System) has been, as its name implies, customarily used; a plethora of federal and state legislation has given it, through implication, standing as our primary weights and measures system. However, the Metric System (incorporated in the scientists' new SI or Systeme International d'Unites) is the only system that has ever received specific legislative sanction by Congress. The "Law of 1866" reads:

It shall be lawful throughout the United States of America to employ the weights and measures of the metric system; and no contract or dealing, or pleading in any court, shall be deemed invalid or liable to objection because the weights or measures expressed or referred to therein are weights or measures of the metric system.

Over the last 100 years, the Metric System has seen slow, steadily increasing use in the United States and, today, is of importance nearly equal to the Customary System.

On Feb. 10, 1964, the National Bureau of Standards issued the following bulletin:

Henceforth it shall be the policy of the National Bureau of Standards to use the units of the International System (SI), as adopted by the 11th General Conference on Weights and Measures (October 1960), except when the use of these units would obviously impair communication or reduce the usefulness of a report.

What had been the Metric System became the International System (SI), a more complete scientific system.

Seven units have been adopted to serve as the base for the International System as follows: length—meter; mass—kilogram; time—second; electric current—ampere; thermodynamic temperature—kelvin; amount of substance—mole; and luminous intensity—candela.

Prefixes

The following prefixes, in combination with the basic unit names, provide the multiples and submultiples in the International System. For example, the unit name "meter," with the prefix "kilo" added, produces "kilometer," meaning "1,000 meters."

Prefix	Symbol	Multiples	Equivalent	Prefix	Symbol	Submultiples	Equivalent
exa	E	10^{18}	quintillionfold	deci	d	10^{-1}	tenth part
peta	P	10^{15}	quadrillionfold	centi	c	10^{-2}	hundredth part
tera	T	10^{12}	trillionfold	milli	m	10^{-3}	thousandth part
giga	G	10^{9}	billionfold	micro	μ	10^{-6}	millionth part
mega	M	10^{6}	millionfold	nano	n	10^{-9}	billionth part
kilo	k	10^{3}	thousandfold	pico	p	10^{-12}	trillionth part
hecto	h	10^{2}	hundredfold	femto	f	10^{-15}	quadrillionth part
deka	da	10	tenfold	atto	a	10^{-18}	quintillionth part

Tables of Metric Weights and Measures

Linear Measure

10 millimeters (mm)	= 1 centimeter (cm)
10 centimeters	= 1 decimeter (dm) = 100 millimeters
10 decimeters	= 1 meter (m) = 1,000 millimeters
10 meters	= 1 dekameter (dam)
10 dekameters	= 1 hectometer (hm) = 100 meters
10 hectometers	= 1 kilometer (km) = 1,000 meters

Area Measure

100 square millimeters (mm²)	= 1 square centimeter (cm²)
10,000 square centimeters	= 1 square meter (m²) = 1,000,000 square millimeters
100 square meters	= 1 are (a)
100 ares	= 1 hectare (ha) = 10,000 square meters
100 hectares	= 1 square kilometer (km²) = 1,000,000 square meters

Fluid Volume Measure

10 milliliters (mL)	= 1 centiliter (cL)
10 centiliters	= 1 deciliter (dL) = 100 milliliters
10 deciliters	= 1 liter (L) = 1,000 milliliters
10 liters	= 1 dekaliter (daL)
10 dekaliters	= 1 hectoliter (hL) = 100 liters
10 hectoliters	= 1 kiloliter (kL) = 1,000 liters

Cubic Measure

1,000 cubic millimeters (mm³)	= 1 cubic centimeter (cm³)
1,000 cubic centimeters	= 1 cubic decimeter (dm³) = 1,000,000 cubic millimeters
1,000 cubic decimeters	= 1 cubic meter (m³) = 1 stere = 1,000,000 cubic centimeters = 1,000,000,000 cubic millimeters

Weight

10 milligrams (mg)	= 1 centigram (cg)
10 centigrams	= 1 decigram (dg) = 100 milligrams
10 decigrams	= 1 gram (g) = 1,000 milligrams
10 grams	= 1 dekagram (dag)
10 dekagrams	= 1 hectogram (hg) = 100 grams
10 hectograms	= 1 kilogram (kg) = 1,000 grams
1,000 kilograms	= 1 metric ton (t)

Table of U.S. Customary Weights and Measures

Linear Measure

12 inches (in)	= 1 foot (ft)
3 feet	= 1 yard (yd)
5 ½ yards	= 1 rod (rd), pole, or perch (16 ½ feet)
40 rods	= 1 furlong (fur) = 220 yards = 660 feet
8 furlongs	= 1 statute mile (mi) = 1,760 yards = 5,280 feet
3 miles	= 1 league = 5,280 yards = 15,840 feet
6076.11549 feet	= 1 International Nautical Mile

Liquid Measure

When necessary to distinguish the liquid pint or quart from the dry pint or quart, the word "liquid" or the abbreviation "liq" should be used in combination with the name or abbreviation of the liquid unit.

4 gills	= 1 pint (pt) = 28.875 cubic inches
2 pints	= 1 quart (qt) = 57.75 cubic inches
4 quarts	= 1 gallon (gal) = 231 cubic inches = 8 pints = 32 gills

Area Measure

Squares and cubes of units are sometimes abbreviated by using "superior" figures. For example, ft² means square foot, and ft³ means cubic foot.

144 square inches	= 1 square foot (ft²)
9 square feet	= 1 square yard (yd²) = 1,296 square inches
30 1/4 square yards	= 1 square rod (rd²) = 272 1/4 square feet
160 square rods	= 1 acre = 4,840 square yards = 43,560 square feet
640 acres	= 1 square mile (mi²)
1 mile square	= 1 section (of land)
6 miles square	= 1 township = 36 sections = 36 square miles

Cubic Measure

1 cubic foot (ft³)	= 1,728 cubic inches (in³)
27 cubic feet	= 1 cubic yard (yd³)

Gunter's or Surveyors' Chain Measure

7.92 inches (in)	= 1 link
100 links	= 1 chain (ch) = 4 rods = 66 feet
80 chains	= 1 survey mile (mi) = 320 rods = 5,280 feet

Troy Weight

24 grains	= 1 pennyweight (dwt)
20 pennyweights	= 1 ounce troy (oz t) = 480 grains
12 ounces troy	= 1 pound troy (lb t) = 240 pennyweights = 5,760 grains

Dry Measure

When necessary to distinguish the dry pint or quart from the liquid pint or quart, the word "dry" should be used in combination with the name or abbreviation of the dry unit.

2 pints (pt)	= 1 quart (qt) = 67.2006 cubic inches
8 quarts	= 1 peck (pk) = 537.605 cubic inches = 16 pints
4 pecks	= 1 bushel (bu) = 2,150.42 cubic inches = 32 quarts

Avoirdupois Weight

When necessary to distinguish the avoirdupois ounce or pound from the troy ounce or pound, the word "avoirdupois" or the abbreviation "avdp" should be used in combination with the name or abbreviation of the avoirdupois unit.

(The "grain" is the same in avoirdupois and troy weight.)

27 11/32 grains	= 1 dram (dr)
16 drams	= 1 ounce (oz) = 437 1/2 grains
16 ounces	= 1 pound (lb) = 256 drams = 7,000 grains
100 pounds	= 1 hundredweight (cwt)°
20 hundredweights	= 1 ton = 2,000 pounds°

In "gross" or "long" measure, the following values are recognized.

112 pounds	= 1 gross or long hundredweight°
20 gross or long hundredweights	= 1 gross or long ton = 2,240 pounds°

°When the terms "hundredweight" and "ton" are used unmodified, they are commonly understood to mean the 100-pound hundredweight and the 2,000-pound ton, respectively; these units may be designated "net" or "short" when necessary to distinguish them from the corresponding units in gross or long measure.

Tables of Equivalents

In this table it is necessary to distinguish between the "international" and the "survey" foot. The international foot, defined in 1959 as exactly equal to 0.3048 meter, is shorter than the old survey foot by exactly 2 parts in one million. The survey foot is still used in data expressed in feet in geodetic surveys within the U.S. In this table the survey foot is italicized.

When the name of a unit is enclosed in brackets thus, [1 hand], this indicates (1) that the unit is not in general current use in the United States, or (2) that the unit is believed to be based on "custom and usage" rather than on formal definition.

Equivalents involving decimals are, in most instances, rounded off to the third decimal place except where they are exact, in which cases these exact equivalents are so designated.

Lengths

1 angstrom (A)	{ 0.1 nanometer (exactly) / 0.000 1 micrometer (exactly) / 0.000 000 1 millimeter (exactly) / 0.000 000 004 inch }
1 cable's length	{ 120 fathoms (exactly) / 720 feet (exactly) / 219 meters }
1 centimeter (cm)	0.3937 inch
1 chain (ch) (Gunter's or surveyors)	{ 66 feet (exactly) / 20.1168 meters }
1 chain (engineers)	{ 100 feet / 30.48 meters (exactly) }
1 decimeter (dm)	3.937 inches
1 degree (geographical)	{ 364,566.929 feet / 69.047 miles (avg.) / 111.123 kilometers (avg.) }
-of latitude	{ 68.078 miles at equator / 69.043 miles at poles }
-of longitude	69.171 miles
1 dekameter (dam)	32.808 feet
1 fathom	{ 6 feet (exactly) / 1.8288 meters (exactly) }
1 foot (ft)	0.3048 meter (exactly)
1 furlong (fur)	{ 10 chains (surveyors) (exactly) / 660 feet (exactly) / 1/8 survey mile (exactly) / 201.168 meters }
[1 hand] (height measure for horses from ground to top of shoulders)	4 inches
1 inch (in)	2.54 centimeters (exactly)
1 kilometer (km)	{ 0.621 mile / 3,281.5 feet }

1 league (land)	{ 3 survey miles (exactly) / 4.828 kilometers }
1 link (Gunter's or surveyors)	{ 7.92 inches (exactly) / 0.201 meter }
1 link engineers	{ 1 foot / 0.305 meter }
1 meter (m)	{ 39.37 inches / 1.094 yards }
1 micrometer (μm) [the Greek letter mu]	{ 0.001 millimeter (exactly) / 0.000 039 37 inch }
1 mil	{ 0.001 inch (exactly) / 0.025 4 millimeter (exactly) }
1 mile (mi) (statute or land)	{ 5,280 feet (exactly) / 1.609 kilometers }
1 international nautical mile (nmi)	{ 1.852 kilometers (exactly) / 1.150779 survey miles / 6,076.11549 feet }
1 millimeter (mm)	0.039 37 inch
1 nanometer (nm)	{ 0.001 micrometer (exactly) / 0.000 000 039 37 inch }
1 pica (typography)	12 points
1 point (typography)	{ 0.013 837 inch (exactly) / 0.351 millimeter }
1 rod (rd), pole, or perch	{ 16 1/2 feet (exactly) / 5.029 meters }
1 yard (yd)	0.9144 meter (exactly)

Areas or Surfaces

1 acre	{ 43,560 square feet (exactly) / 4,840 square yards / 0.405 hectare }
1 are (a)	{ 119.599 square yards / 0.025 acre }

(*continued*)

1 bolt (cloth measure):

length	100 yards (on modern looms)
width	{ 42 inches (usually, for cotton) / 60 inches (usually, for wool)

1 hectare (ha) . . . . 2.471 acres
[1 square (building)] . . . . 100 square feet
1 square centimeter (cm²) . . . . 0.155 square inch
1 square decimeter (dm²). . . . . 15.500 square inches
1 square foot (ft²) . . . . 929.030 square centimeters
1 square inch (in²) . . . . 6.4516 square centimeters (exactly)

1 square kilometer (km²) . . . { 247.104 acres / 0.386 square mile

1 square meter (m²) . . . . . { 1.196 square yards / 10.764 square feet

1 square mile (mi²) . . . . 258.999 hectares
1 square millimeter (mm²). . . . . 0.002 square inch
1 square rod (rd²) sq. pole, or
sq. perch . . . . 25.293 square meters
1 square yard (yd²) . . . . 0.836 square meter

Capacities or Volumes

1 barrel (bbl) liquid . . . . 31 to 42 gallons°
°There are a variety of "barrels," established by law or usage. For example: federal taxes on fermented liquors are based on a barrel of 31 gallons: many state laws fix the "barrel for liquids" as 31 ½ gallons; one state fixes a 36-gallon barrel for cistern measurement; federal law recognizes a 40-gallon barrel for "proof spirits"; by custom, 42 gallons comprise a barrel of crude oil or petroleum products for statistical purposes, and this equivalent is recognized "for liquids" by 4 states.

1 barrel (bbl), standard, for fruits, vegetables, and other dry commodities except dry cranberries	{ 7,056 cubic inches / 105 dry quarts / 3.281 bushels, struck measure
1 barrel (bbl), standard, cranberry	{ 5,826 cubic inches / 86⁴⁵/₆₄ dry quarts / 2.709 bushels, struck measure
1 board foot (lumber measure) . .	a foot-square board 1 inch thick
1 bushel (bu) (U.S.) (struck measure)	{ 2,150.42 cubic inches (exactly) / 35.239 liters
[1 bushel, heaped (U.S.)]	{ 2,747.715 cubic inches / 1.278 bushels, struck measure°

°Frequently recognized as 1¼ bushels, struck measure.

[1 bushel (bu) (British Imperial) (struck measure)]	{ 1.032 U.S. bushels struck measure / 2,219.36 cubic inches
1 cord (cd) firewood	128 cubic feet (exactly)
1 cubic centimeter (cm³).	0.061 cubic inch
1 cubic decimeter (dm³)	61.024 cubic inches
1 cubic inch (in³)	{ 0.554 fluid ounce / 4.433 fluid drams / 16.387 cubic centimeters
1 cubic foot (ft³).	{ 7.481 gallons / 28.317 cubic decimeters
1 cubic meter (m³)	1.308 cubic yards
1 cubic yard (yd³)	0.765 cubic meter
1 cup, measuring	{ 8 fluid ounces (exactly) / ½ liquid pint (exactly)
[1 dram, fluid (fl dr) (British)]	{ 0.961 U.S. fluid dram / 0.217 cubic inch / 3.552 milliliters
1 dekaliter (daL)	{ 2.642 gallons / 1.135 pecks
1 gallon (gal) (U.S.)	{ 231 cubic inches (exactly) / 3.785 liters / 0.833 British gallon / 128 U.S. fluid ounces (exactly)
[1 gallon (gal) British Imperial]	{ 277.42 cubic inches / 1.201 U.S. gallons / 4.546 liters / 160 British fluid ounces (exactly)
1 gill (gi).	{ 7.219 cubic inches / 4 fluid ounces (exactly) / 0.118 liter
1 hectoliter (hL)	{ 26.418 gallons / 2.838 bushels
1 liter (L) (1 cubic decimeter exactly)	{ 1.057 liquid quarts / 0.908 dry quart / 61.025 cubic inches

1 milliliter (mL) (1 cu cm exactly)	{ 0.271 fluid dram / 16.231 minims / 0.061 cubic inch
1 ounce, liquid (U.S.)	{ 1.805 cubic inches / 29.573 milliliters / 1.041 British fluid ounces
[1 ounce, fluid (fl oz) (British)]	{ 0.961 U.S. fluid ounce / 1.734 cubic inches / 28.412 milliliters
1 peck (pk).	8.810 liters
1 pint (pt), dry	{ 33.600 cubic inches / 0.551 liter
1 pint (pt), liquid	{ 28.875 cubic inches (exactly) / 0.473 liter
1 quart (qt) dry (U.S.)	{ 67.201 cubic inches / 1.101 liters / 0.969 British quart
1 quart (qt) liquid (U.S.) . . .	{ 57.75 cubic in (exactly) / 0.946 liter / 0.833 British quart
[1 quart (qt) (British)]	{ 69.354 cubic inches / 1.032 U.S. dry quarts / 1.201 U.S. liquid quarts
1 tablespoon.	{ 3 teaspoons°(exactly) / 4 fluid drams / ½ fluid ounce (exactly)
1 teaspoon	{ ⅓ tablespoon°(exactly) / 1⅓ fluid drams°

°The equivalent "1 teaspoon—1⅓ fluid drams" has been found by the bureau to correspond more closely with the actual capacities of "measuring" and silver teaspoons than the equivalent "1 teaspoon—1 fluid dram" which is given by many dictionaries.

Weights or Masses

1 assay ton⁰⁰ (AT) . . . . 29.167 grams
⁰⁰Used in assaying. The assay ton bears the same relation to the milligram that a ton of 2,000 pounds avoirdupois bears to the ounce troy; hence the weight in milligrams of precious metal obtained from one assay ton of ore gives directly the number of troy ounces to the net ton.

1 bale (cotton measure). . . .	{ 500 pounds in U.S. / 750 pounds in Egypt
1 carat (c)	{ 200 milligrams (exactly) / 3.086 grains
1 dram avoirdupois (dr avdp) gamma, see microgram	{ 27¹¹/₃₂ (=27.344) grains / 1.772 grams
1 grain	64.799 milligrams
1 gram.	{ 15.432 grains / 0.035 ounce, avoirdupois
1 hundredweight, gross or long⁰⁰⁰ (gross cwt)	{ 112 pounds (exactly) / 50.802 kilograms
1 hundredweight, net or short (cwt. or net cwt.).	{ 100 pounds (exactly) / 45.359 kilograms
1 kilogram (kg)	2.205 pounds
1 microgram (μg [The Greek letter mu in combination with the letter g]) . .	0.000001 gram (exactly)
1 milligram (mg)	0.015 grain
1 ounce, avoirdupois (oz avdp)	{ 437.5 grains (exactly) / 0.911 troy ounce / 28.350 grams
1 ounce, troy (oz t)	{ 480 grains (exactly) / 1.097 avoirdupois ounces / 31.103 grams
1 pennyweight (dwt)	1.555 grams
1 pound, avoirdupois (lb avdp)	{ 7,000 grains (exactly) / 1.215 troy pounds / 453.592 37 grams (exactly)
1 pound, troy (lb t)	{ 5,760 grains (exactly) / 0.823 avoirdupois pound / 373.242 grams
1 ton, gross or long⁰⁰⁰ (gross ton)	{ 2,240 pounds (exactly) / 1.12 net tons (exactly) / 1.016 metric tons

⁰⁰⁰The gross or long ton and hundredweight are used commercially in the United States to only a limited extent, usually in restricted industrial fields. These units are the same as British "ton" and "hundredweight."

1 ton, metric (t)	{ 2,204.623 pounds / 0.984 gross ton / 1.102 net tons
1 ton, net or short (sh ton) . .	{ 2,000 pounds (exactly) / 0.893 gross ton / 0.907 metric ton

Tables of Interrelation of Units of Measurement

Units of length and area of the international and survey measures are included in the following tables. Units unique to the survey measure are italicized. See pg 809, Tables of Equivalents, 1st para.

1 international foot = 0.999 998 survey foot (exactly)
1 survey foot − 1200/3937 motor (exactly)
1 international foot = 12 × 0.0254 meter (exactly)

Bold face type indicates exact values

Units of Length

Units	Inches	*Links*	Feet	Yards	*Rods*	*Chains*	Miles	cm	Meters
1 inch=	1	0.126 263	0.083 333	0.027 778	0.005 051	0.001 263	**0.000 016**	2.54	0.025 4
1 *link*=	7.92	1	0.66	0.22	0.04	0.01	**0.000 125**	20.117	0.201 168
1 foot=	12	1.515 152	1	0.333 333	0.060 606	0.015 152	**0.000 189**	30.48	0.304 8
1 yard=	36	4.545 45	3	1	0.181 818	0.045 455	**0.000 568**	91.44	0.914 4
1 *rod*=	198	25	16.5	5.5	1	0.25	**0.003 125**	502.92	5.029 2
1 *chain*=	792	100	66	22	4	1	**0.012 5**	2011.68	20.116 8
1 mile=	63 360	8000	5280	1760	320	80	1	160 934.4	1609.344
1 cm=	0.3937	0.049 710	0.032 808	0.010 936	0.001 988	**0.000 497**	**0.000 006**	1	0.01
1 meter=	39.37	4.970 960	3.280 840	1.093 613	0.198 838	0.049 710	**0.000 621**	100	1

Units of Area

Units	Sq. inches	*Sq. links*	Sq. feet	Sq. yards	*Sq. rods*	*Sq. chains*
1 sq. inch=	1	.015 942 3	0.006 944	0.000 771 605	0.000 025 5	0.000 001 594
1 sq. *link*=	62.726 4	1	0.435 6	0.0484	0.0016	0.000 1
1 sq. foot=	144	2.295 684	1	0.111 111 1	0.003 673 09	0.000 229 568
1 sq. yard=	1296	20.661 16	9	1	0.033 057 85	0.002 066 12
1 sq. *rod*=	39 204	625	272.25	30.25	1	0.062 5
1 sq. *chain*=	627 264	10 000	4 356	484	16	1
1 *acre*=	6 272 640	100 000	43 560	4 840	160	10
1 sq. mile=	4 014 489 600	64 000 000	27 878 400	3 097 600	102 400	6400
1 sq. cm=	0.155 000 3	0.002 471 05	0.001 076	0.000 119 599	0.000 003 954	0.000 000 247
1 sq. meter=	1550.003	24.710 44	10.763 91	1.195 990	0.039 536 70	0.002 471 044
1 *hectare*=	15 500 031	247 104	107 639.1	11 959.90	395.367 0	24.710 44

Units	*Acres*	Sq. miles	Sq. cm	Sq. meters	*Hectares*
1 sq. inch=	0.000 000 159 423	0.000 000 000 249 10	6.451 6	**0.000 645 16**	0.000 000 065
1 sq. *link*=	**0.000 01**	0.000 000 015 625	404.685 642 24	0.040 468 56	0.000 004 047
1 sq. foot=	0.000 022 956 84	0.000 000 035 870 06	929.034 1	0.092 903 41	0.000 009 290
1 sq. yard=	0.000 206 611 6	0.000 000 322 830 6	8 361.273 6	**0.836 127 36**	0.000 083 613
1 sq. *rod*=	**0.006 25**	0.000 000 009 765 625	252 929.5	25.292 95	0.002 529 295
1 sq. *chain*=	**0.1**	0.000 156 25	4 046 873	404.687 3	0.040 468 73
1 *acre*=	1	0.001 562 5	40 468 73	4 046.873	0.404 687 3
1 sq. mile=	640	1	25 899 881 103	2 589 988.11	258.998 811 034
1 sq. cm=	0.000 000 024 711	0.000 000 000 038 610	1	**0.000 1**	**0.000 000 01**
1 sq. meter=	0.000 247 104 4	0.000 000 386 102 2	10 000	1	**0.0001**
1 *hectare*=	2.471 044	0.003 861 006	100 000 000	10 000	1

Units of Mass Not Greater than Pounds and Kilograms

Units	Grains	Pennyweights	Avdp drams	Avdp ounces
1 grain=	1	0.041 666 67	0.036 571 43	0.002 285 71
1 pennyweight=	24	1	0.877 714 3	0.054 857 14
1 dram avdp=	27.343 75	1.139 323	1	**0.062 5**
1 ounce avdp=	437.5	18.229 17	16	1
1 ounce troy=	480	20	17.554 29	1.097 143
1 pound troy=	5760	240	210.651 4	13.165 71
1 pound avdp=	7000	291.666 7	256	16
1 milligram=	0.015 432	0.000 643 015	0.000 564 383	0.000 035 274
1 gram=	15.432 36	0.643 014 9	0.564 383 4	0.035 273 96
1 kilogram=	15 432.36	643.014 9	564.383 4	35.273 96

Units	Troy ounces	Troy pounds	Avdp pounds	Milligrams	Grams	Kilograms
1 grain=	0.002 083 33	0.000 173 611	0.000 142 857	64.798 91	**0.064 798 91**	0.000 064 799
1 pennyw't.=	0.05	0.004 166 667	0.003 428 571	1555.173 84	1.555 173 84	0.001 555 174
1 dram avdp=	0.056 966 15	0.004 747 179	0.003 906 25	1771.845 195	1.771 845 195	0.001 771 845
1 oz avdp=	0.911 458 3	0.075 954 86	**0.062 5**	28 349.523 125	28.349 523 125	0.028 349 52
1 oz troy=	1	0.083 333 333	0.068 571 43	31 103.476 8	31.103 476 8	0.031 103 48
1 lb troy=	12	1	0.822 857 1	373 241.721 6	373.241 721 6	0.373 241 722
1 lb avdp=	14.583 33	1.215 278	1	453 592.37	453.592 37	**0.453 592 37**
1 milligram=	0.000 032 151	0.000 002 679	0.000 002 205	1	0.001	**0.000 001**
1 gram=	0.032 150 75	0.002 679 229	0.002 204 623	1000	1	0.001
1 kilogram=	32.150 75	2.679 229	2.204 623	1 000 000	1000	1

Units of Mass Not Less than Avoirdupois Ounces

Units	Avdp oz	Avdp lb	Short cwt	Short tons	Long tons	Kilograms	Metric tons
1 oz av=	1	**0.0625**	**0.000 625**	0.000 031 25	0.000 027 902	0.028 349 523	0.000 028 350
1 lb av=	16	1	**0.01**	**0.000 5**	0.000 446 429	**0.453 592 37**	0.000 453 592
1 sh cwt=	1 600	100	1	**0.05**	0.044 642 86	45.359 237	0.045 359 237
1 sh ton=	32 000	2000	22.4	1	0.892 857 1	907.184 74	0.907 184 74
1 long ton=	35 840	2240	22.4	1.12	1	1016.046 908 8	1.016 046 909
1 kg=	35.273 96	2.204 623	0.022 046 23	0.001 102 311	0.000 984 207	1	0.001
1 metric ton=	35 273.96	2 204.623	22.046 23	1.102 311	0.984 206 5	1000	1

(continued)

Units of Volume

Units	Cubic inches	Cubic feet	Cubic yards	Cubic cm	Cubic dm	Cubic meters
1 cubic inch=	1	0.000 578 704	0.000 021 433	16.387 064	0.016 387	0.000 016 387
1 cubic foot=	1728	1	0.037 037 04	28 316.846 592	28.316 847	0.028 316 847
1 cubic yard=	46 656	27	1	764 554.857 984	764.554 858	0.764 554 858
1 cubic cm=	0.061 023 74	0.000 035 315	0.000 001 308	1	0.001	0.000 001
1 cubic dm=	61.023 74	0.035 314 67	0.001 307 951	1 000	1	0.001
1 cubic meter	61 023.74	35.314 67	1.307 951	1 000 000	1000	1

Units of Capacity (Liquid Measure)

Units	Minims	Fluid drams	Fluid ounces	Gills	Liquid pt
1 minim=	1	0.016 666 7	0.002 083 33	0.000 520 833	0.000 130 208
1 fluid dram=	60	1	0.125	0.031 25	0.007 812 5
1 fluid ounce=	480	8	1	0.25	0.062 5
1 gill=	1920	32	4	1	0.25
1 liquid pint=	7680	128	16	4	1
1 liquid quart=	15 360	256	32	8	2
1 gallon=	61 440	1024	128	32	8
1 cubic inch=	265.974	4.432 900	0.554 112 6	0.138 528 1	0.034 632 03
1 cubic foot=	459 603.1	7 660.052	957.506 5	239.376 6	59.844 16
1 milliliter=	16.230 73	0.270 512 18	0.033 814 02	0.008 453 506	.002 113 376
1 liter=	16 230.73	270.512 18	33.814 02	8.453 506	2.113 376

Units	Liquid quarts	Gallons	Cubic inches	Cubic feet	Liters
1 minim=	0.000 065 104 17	0.000 016 276 04	0.003 759 766	0.000 002 175 790	0.000 061 611 52
1 flu. dram=	0.003 906 25	0.000 976 562 5	0.225 585 9	0.000 130 547 4	0.003 696 691
1 fluid oz=	0.031 25	0.007 812 5	1.804 687 5	0.001 044 379	0.029 573 53
1 gill=	0.125	0.031 25	7.218 75	0.004 177 517	0.118 294 118
1 liquid pt=	0.5	0.125	28.875	0.016 710 07	0.473 176 473
1 liquid qt=	1	0.25	57.75	0.033 420 14	0.946 352 946
1 gallon=	4	1	231	0.133 680 6	3.785 411 784
1 cubic in.=	0.017 316 02	0.004 329 004	1	0.000 578 703 7	0.016 387 064
1 cubic foot=	29.922 08	7.480 519	1728	1	28.316 846 592
1 liter=	1.056 688	0.264 172 05	61.023 74	0.035 314 67	1

Units of Capacity (Dry Measure)

Units	Dry pints	Dry quarts	Pecks	Bushels	Cubic in.	Liters
1 dry pint=	1	0.5	0.062 5	0.015 625	33.600 312 5	0.550 610 47
1 dry quart=	2	1	0.125	0.031 25	67.200 625	1.101 220 9
1 peck=	16	8	1	0.25	537.605	8.809 767 5
1 bushel=	64	32	4	1	2150.42	35.239 07
1 cubic inch=	0.029 761 6	0.014 880 8	0.001 860 10	0.000 465 025	1	0.016 387 06
1 liter=	1.816 166	0.908 083	0.113 510 37	0.028 377 59	61.023 74	1

Miscellaneous Measures

Caliber—the diameter of a gun bore. In the U.S., caliber is traditionally expressed in hundredths of inches, eg. .22 or .30. In Britain, caliber is often expressed in thousandths of inches, eg. .270 or .465. Now, it is commonly expressed in millimeters, eg. the 7.62 mm. M14 rifle and the 5.56 mm. M16 rifle. Heavier weapons' caliber has long been expressed in millimeters, eg. the 81 mm. mortar, the 105 mm. howitzer (light), the 155 mm. howitzer (medium or heavy).

Naval guns' caliber refers to the barrel length as a multiple of the bore diameter. A 5-inch, 50-caliber naval gun has a 5-inch bore and a barrel length of 250 inches.

Carat, karat—a measure of the amount of alloy per 24 parts in gold. Thus 24-carat gold is pure; 18-carat gold is one-fourth alloy.

Decibel (dB)—a measure of the relative loudness or intensity of sound. A 20-decibel sound is 10 times louder than a 10-decibel sound; 30 decibels is 100 times louder; 40 decibels is 1,000 times louder, etc. One decibel is the smallest difference between sounds detectable by the human ear. A 140-decibel sound is painful.

10 decibels	– a light whisper
20	– quiet conversation
30	– normal conversation
40	– light traffic
50	– typewriter, loud conversation
60	– noisy office
70	– normal traffic, quiet train
80	– rock music, subway
90	– heavy traffic, thunder
100	– jet plane at takeoff

Em—a printer's measure designating the square width of any given type size. Thus, an em of 10-point type is 10 points. An en is half an em.

Gauge—a measure of shotgun bore diameter. Gauge numbers originally referred to the number of lead balls of the gun barrel diameter in a pound. Thus, a 16 gauge shotgun's bore was smaller than a 12-gauge shotgun's. Today, an international agreement assigns millimeter measures to each gauge, eg:

Gauge	Bore diameter in mm
6	23.34
10	19.67
12	18.52
14	17.60
16	16.81
20	15.90

Horsepower—the power needed to lift 550 pounds one foot in one second, or to lift 33,000 pounds one foot in one minute. Equivalent to 746 watts or 2,546.0756 Btu/h.

Quire—25 sheets of paper

Ream—500 sheets of paper

Electrical Units

The **watt** is the unit of power (electrical, mechanical, thermal, etc.). Electrical power is given by the product of the voltage and the current.

Energy is sold by the **joule**, but in common practice the billing of electrical energy is expressed in terms of the **kilowatt-hour**, which is 3,600,000 joules or 3.6 megajoules.

The **horsepower** is a non-metric unit sometimes used in mechanics. It is equal to 746 watts.

The **ohm** is the unit of electrical resistance and represents the physical property of a conductor which offers a resistance to the flow of electricity, permitting just 1 ampere to flow at 1 volt of pressure.

Compound Interest

Compounded Annually

Principal	Period	4%	5%	6%	7%	8%	9%	10%	12%	14%	16%
$100	1 day	0.011	0.014	0.016	0.019	0.022	0.025	0.027	0.033	0.038	0.044
	1 week	0.077	0.096	0.115	0.134	0.153	0.173	0.192	0.230	0.268	0.307
	6 mos.	2.00	2.50	3.00	3.50	4.00	4.50	5.00	6.00	7.00	8.00
	1 year	4.00	5.00	6.00	7.00	8.00	9.00	10.00	12.00	14.00	16.00
	2 years	8.16	10.25	12.36	14.49	16.64	18.81	21.00	25.44	29.96	34.56
	3 years	12.49	15.76	19.10	22.50	25.97	29.50	33.10	40.49	48.15	56.09
	4 years	16.99	21.55	26.25	31.08	36.05	41.16	46.41	57.35	68.90	81.06
	5 years	21.67	27.63	33.82	40.26	46.93	53.86	61.05	76.23	92.54	110.03
	6 years	26.53	34.01	41.85	50.07	58.69	67.71	77.16	97.38	119.50	143.64
	7 years	31.59	40.71	50.36	60.58	71.38	82.80	94.87	121.07	150.23	182.62
	8 years	36.86	47.75	59.38	71.82	85.09	99.26	114.36	147.60	185.26	227.84
	9 years	42.33	55.13	68.95	83.85	99.90	117.19	135.79	177.31	225.19	280.30
	10 years	48.02	62.89	79.08	96.72	115.89	136.74	159.37	210.58	270.72	341.14
	12 years	60.10	79.59	101.22	125.22	151.82	181.27	213.84	289.60	381.79	493.60
	15 years	80.09	107.89	139.66	175.90	217.22	264.25	317.72	447.36	613.79	826.55
	20 years	119.11	165.33	220.71	286.97	366.10	460.44	572.75	864.63	1,274.35	1,846.08

Ancient Measures

Biblical
Cubit   = 21.8 inches
Omer   = 0.45 peck
        3.964 liters
Ephah = 10 omers
Shekel = 0.497 ounce
        14.1 grams

Greek
Cubit   = 18.3 inches
Stadion = 607.2 or 622 feet
Obolos = 715.38 milligrams
Drachma = 4.2923 grams
Mina   = 0.9463 pounds
Talent = 60 mina

Roman
Cubit   = 17.5 inches
Stadium = 202 yards
As, libra, = 325.971 grams,
pondus   .71864 pounds

Weight of Water

1	cubic inch	.0360 pound	1	imperial gallon	10.0 pounds
12	cubic inches	.433 pound	11.2	imperial gallons	112.0 pounds
1	cubic foot	62.4 pounds	224	imperial gallons	2240.0 pounds
1	cubic foot	7.48052 U.S. gal	1	U.S. gallon	8.33 pounds
1.8	cubic feet	112.0 pounds	13.45	U.S. gallons	112.0 pounds
35.96	cubic feet	2240.0 pounds	269.0	U.S. gallons	2240.0 pounds

Density of Gases and Vapors

at 0°C and 760 mmHg
Source: National Bureau of Standards (kilograms per cubic meter)

Gas	Wgt.	Gas	Wgt.	Gas	Wgt.
Acetylene	1.171	Ethylene	1.260	Methyl fluoride	1.545
Air	1.293	Fluorine	1.696	Mono methylamine	1.38
Ammonia	.759	Helium	.178	Neon	.900
Argon	1.784	Hydrogen	.090	Nitric oxide	1.341
Arsene	3.48	Hydrogen bromide	3.50	Nitrogen	1.250
Butane-iso.	2.60	Hydrogen chloride	1.639	Nitrosyl chloride	2.99
Butane-n	2.519	Hydrogen iodide	5.724	Nitrous oxide	1.997
Carbon dioxide	1.977	Hydrogen selenide	3.66	Oxygen	1.429
Carbon monoxide	1.250	Hydrogen sulfide	1.539	Phosphine	1.48
Carbon oxysulfide	2.72	Krypton	3.745	Propane	2.020
Chlorine	3.214	Methane	.717	Silicon tetrafluoride	4.67
Chlorine monoxide	3.89	Methyl chloride	2.25	Sulfur dioxide	2.927
Ethane	1.356	Methyl ether	2.091	Xenon	5.897

Temperature Conversion Table

The numbers in **bold face type** refer to the temperature either in degrees Celsius or Fahrenheit which are to be converted. If converting from degrees Fahrenheit to Celsius, the equivalent will be found in the column on the left, while if converting from degrees Celsius to Fahrenheit the answer will be found in the column on the right.

For temperatures not shown. To convert Fahrenheit to Celsius subtract 32 degrees and multiply by 5, divide by 9; to convert Celsius to Fahrenheit, multiply by 9, divide by 5 and add 32 degrees.

Celsius		Fahrenheit	Celsius		Fahrenheit	Celsius		Fahrenheit
− 273.2	− 459.7		− 17.8	0	32	35.0	95	203
− 184	− 300		− 12.2	10	50	36.7	98	208.4
− 169	− 273	− 459.4	− 6.67	20	68	37.8	100	212
− 157	− 250	− 418	− 1.11	30	86	43	110	230
− 129	− 200	− 328	4.44	40	104	49	120	248
− 101	− 150	− 238	10.0	50	122	54	130	266
− 73.3	− 100	− 148	15.6	60	140	60	140	284
− 45.6	− 50	− 58	21.1	70	158	66	150	302
− 40.0	− 40	− 40	23.9	75	167	93	200	392
− 34.4	− 30	− 22	26.7	80	176	121	250	482
− 28.9	− 20	− 4	29.4	85	185	149	300	572
− 23.3	− 10	14	32.2	90	194			

Water boils at 212°F at sea level. For every 550 feet above sea level, boiling point of water is lower by about 1°F. Methyl alcohol boils at 148°F. Average human oral temperature, 98.6°F. Water freezes at 32°F. Although "Centigrade" is still frequently used, the International Committee on Weights and Measures and the National Bureau of Standards have recommended since 1948 that this scale be called "Celsius."

Breaking the Sound Barrier; Speed of Sound

The prefix Mach is used to describe supersonic speed. It derives from Ernst Mach, a Czech-born German physicist, who contributed to the study of sound. When a plane moves at the speed of sound it is Mach 1. When twice the speed of sound it is Mach 2. When it is near but below the speed of sound its speed can be designated at less than Mach 1, for example, Mach .90. Mach is defined as "in jet propulsion, the ratio of the velocity of a rocket or a jet to the velocity of sound in the medium being considered."

When a plane passes the sound barrier—flying faster than sound travels—listeners in the area hear thunderclaps, but pilots do not hear them.

Sound is produced by vibrations of an object and is transmitted by alternate increase and decrease in pressures that radiate outward through a material media of molecules —somewhat like waves spreading out on a pond after a rock has been tossed into it.

The frequency of sound is determined by the number of times the vibrating waves undulate per second, and is measured in cycles per second. The slower the cycle of waves, the lower the sound. As frequencies increase, the sound is higher.

Sound is audible to human beings only if the frequency falls within a certain range. The human ear is usually not sensitive to frequencies of less than 20 vibrations per second, or more than about 20,000 vibrations per second—although this range varies among individuals. Anything at a pitch higher than the human ear can hear is termed ultrasonic.

Intensity or loudness is the strength of the pressure of these radiating waves, and is measured in decibels. The human ear responds to intensity in a range from zero to 120 decibels. Any sound with pressure over 120 decibels is painful.

The speed of sound is generally placed at 1,088 ft. per second at sea level at 32°F. It varies in other temperatures and in different media. Sound travels faster in water than in air, and even faster in iron and steel. If in air it travels a mile in 5 seconds, it does a mile under water in 1 second, and through iron in $\frac{1}{3}$ of a second. It travels through ice cold vapor at approximately 4,708 ft. per sec., ice-cold water, 4,938; granite, 12,960; hardwood, 12,620; brick, 11,960; glass, 16,410 to 19,690; silver, 8,658; gold, 5,717.

Colors of the Spectrum

Color, an electromagnetic wave phenomenon, is a sensation produced through the excitation of the retina of the eye by rays of light. The colors of the spectrum may be produced by viewing a light beam refracted by passage through a prism, which breaks the light into its wave lenghts.

Customarily, the primary colors of the spectrum are thought of as those 6 monochromatic colors which occupy relatively large areas of the spectrum: red, orange, yellow, green, blue, and violet. However, Sir Isaac Newton named a 7th, indigo, situated between blue and violet on the spectrum. Aubert estimated (1865) the solar spectrum to contain approximately 1,000 distinguishable hues of which according to Rood (1881) 2 million tints and shades can be distinguished; Luckiesh stated (1915) that 55 distinctly different hues have been seen in a single spectrum.

By many physicists only 3 primary colors are recognized: red, yellow, and blue (Mayer, 1775); red, green, and violet (Thomas Young, 1801); red, green, and blue (Clerk Maxwell, 1860).

The color sensation of black is due to complete lack of stimulation of the retina, that of white to complete stimulation. The infra-red and ultra-violet rays, below the red (long) end of the spectrum and above the violet (short) end respectively, are invisible to the naked eye. Heat is the principal effect of the infra-red rays and chemical action that of the ultra-violet rays.

Common Fractions Reduced to Decimals

8ths	16ths	32ds	64ths		8ths	16ths	32ds	64ths		8ths	16ths	32ds	64ths	
			1	.015625				23	.359375				45	.703125
		1	2	.03125	3	6	12	24	.375			23	46	.71875
			3	.046875				25	.390625				47	.734375
	1	2	4	.0625			13	26	.40625	6	12	24	48	.75
			5	.078125				27	.421875				49	.765625
		3	6	.09375		7	14	28	.4375			25	50	.78125
			7	.109375				29	.453125				51	.796875
1	2	4	8	.125			15	30	.46875		13	26	52	.8125
			9	.140625				31	.484375				53	.828125
		5	10	.15625	4	8	16	32	.5			27	54	.84375
			11	.171875				33	.515625				55	.859375
	3	6	12	.1875			17	34	.53125	7	14	28	56	.875
			13	.203125				35	.546875				57	.890625
		7	14	.21875		9	18	36	.5625			29	58	.90625
			15	.234375				37	.578125				59	.921875
2	4	8	16	.25			19	38	.59375		15	30	60	.9375
			17	.265625				39	.609375				61	.953125
		9	18	.28125	5	10	20	40	.625			31	62	.96875
			19	.296875				41	.640625				63	.984375
	5	10	20	.3125			21	42	.65625	8	16	32	64	1.
			21	.328125				43	.671875					
		11	22	.34375	11		22	44	.6875					

Spirits Measures

Pony	0.5 jigger
Shot	{ 0.666 jigger
	{ 1.0 ounce
Jigger	1.5 shot
Pint	{ 16 shots
	{ 0.625 fifth
Fifth	{ 25.6 shots
	{ 1.6 pints
	{ 0.8 quart
	{ 0.75706 liter

Quart	{ 32 shots
	{ 1.25 fifth
Magnum	{ 2 quarts
	{ 2.49797 bottles (wine)

For champagne and brandy only:

Jeroboam	{ 6.4 pints
	{ 1.6 magnum
	{ 0.8 gallon

For champagne only:

Rehoboam	3 magnums
Methuselah	4 magnums
Salmanazar	6 magnums
Balthazar	8 magnums
Nebuchadnezzar .	10 magnums

Wine bottle (standard):

. . . .	{ 0.800633 quart
	{ 0.7576778 liter

Mathematical Formulas

To find the CIRCUMFERENCE of a:

Circle — Multiply the diameter by 3.14159265 (usually 3.1416).

To find the AREA of a:

Circle — Multiply the square of the diameter by .785398 (usually .7854).

Rectangle — Multiply the length of the base by the height.

Sphere (surface) — Multiply the square of the radius by 3.1416 and multiply by 4.

Square — Square the length of one side.

Trapezoid — Add the two parallel sides, multiply by the height and divide by 2.

Triangle — Multiply the base by the height and divide by 2.

To find the VOLUME of a:

Cone — Multiply the square of the radius of the base by 3.1416, multiply by the height, and divide by 3.

Cube — Cube the length of one edge.

Cylinder — Multiply the square of the radius of the base by 3.1416 and multiply by the height.

Pyramid — Multiply the area of the base by the height and divide by 3.

Rectangular Prism — Multiply the length by the width by the height.

Sphere — Multiply the cube of the radius by 3.1416, multiply by 4 and divide by 3.

Playing Cards and Dice Chances

Poker Hands

Hand	Number possible	Odds against
Royal flush	4	649,739 to 1
Other straight flush	36	72,192 to 1
Four of a kind	624	4,164 to 1
Full house	3,744	693 to 1
Flush	5,108	508 to 1
Straight	10,200	254 to 1
Three of a kind	54,912	46 to 1
Two pairs	123,552	20 to 1
One pair	1,098,240	4 to 3 (1.37 to 1)
Nothing	1,302,540	1 to 1
Total	**2,598,960**	

Dice
(probabilities on 2 dice)

Total	Odds against (Single toss)	Total	Odds against (Single toss)
2	35 to 1	8	31 to 5
3	17 to 1	9	8 to 1
4	11 to 1	10	11 to 1
5	8 to 1	11	17 to 1
6	31 to 5	12	35 to 1
7	5 to 1		

Dice
(Probabilities of consecutive winning plays)

No. consecutive wins	By 7, 11 or point	No. consecutive wins	By 7, 11 or point
1	244 in 495	6	1 in 70
2	6 in 25	7	1 in 141
3	3 in 25	8	1 in 287
4	1 in 17	9	1 in 582
5	1 in 34		

Pinochle Auction
(Odds against finding in "widow" of 3 cards)

Open places	Odds against	Open places	Odds against
1	5 to 1	4	3 to 2 for
2	2 to 1	5	2 to 1 for
3	Even		

Bridge
The odds—against suit distribution in a hand of 4-4-3-2 are about 4 to 1, against 5-4-2-2 about 8 to 1, against 6-4-2-1 about 20 to 1, against 7-4-1-1 about 254 to 1, against 8-4-1-0 about 2,211 to 1, and against 13-0-0-0 about 158,753,389,899 to 1.

Measures of Force and Pressure

Dyne = force necessary to accelerate a 1-gram mass 1 centimeter per second squared = 0.000072 poundal

Poundal = force necessary to accelerate a 1-pound mass 1 foot per second squared = 13,825.5 dynes = 0.138255 newtons

Newton = force needed to accelerate a 1-kilogram mass 1 meter per second squared

Pascal (pressure) = 1 newton per square meter = 0.020885 pound per square foot

Atmosphere (air pressure at sea level) = 2,116.102 pounds per square foot = 14.6952 pounds per square inch = 1.0332 kilograms per square centimeter = 101,323 newtons per square meter.

Large Numbers

U.S.	Number of zeros	French British, German	U.S.	Number of zeros	French British, German
million	6	million	sextillion	21	1,000 trillion
billion	9	milliard	septillion	24	quadrillion
trillion	12	billion	octillion	27	1,000 quadrillion
quadrillion	15	1,000 billion	nonillion	30	quintillion
quintillion	18	trillion	decillion	33	1,000 quintillion

Roman Numerals

I	–	1	VI	–	6	XI	–	11	L	–	50	CD	–	400	$\overline{X}$	–	10,000
II	–	2	VII	–	7	XIX	–	19	LX	–	60	D	–	500	$\overline{L}$	–	50,000
III	–	3	VIII	–	8	XX	–	20	XC	–	90	CM	–	900	$\overline{C}$	–	100,000
IV	–	4	IX	–	9	XXX	–	30	C	–	100	M	–	1,000	$\overline{D}$	–	500,000
V	–	5	X	–	10	XL	–	40	CC	–	200	$\overline{V}$	–	5,000	$\overline{M}$	–	1,000,000

POSTAL INFORMATION

U.S. Postal Service

The Postal Reorganization Act, creating a government-owned postal service under the executive branch and replacing the old Post Office Department, was signed into law by President Nixon on Aug. 12, 1970. The service officially came into being on July 1, 1971.

The new U.S. Postal Service is governed by an 11-man Board of Governors. Nine members are appointed to 9-year terms by the president with Senate approval. These 9, in turn, choose a postmaster general, who is no longer a member of the president's cabinet. The board and the new post-master general choose the 11th member, who serves as deputy postmaster general. An independent Postal Rate Commission of 5 members, appointed by the president, recommends postal rates to the governors for their approval.

The first postmaster general under the new system was Winton M. Blount. He resigned Oct. 29, 1971, and was replaced by his deputy, E. T. Klassen, Dec. 7, 1971. Benjamin F. Bailar succeeded him Feb. 16, 1975, and was succeeded by William F. Bolger on March 15, 1978.

As of Oct. 1, 1983, there was a total of 29,990 post offices throughout the U.S. and possessions.

U.S. Domestic Rates

(In effect Nov. 1, 1981; for rate changes proposed Sept. 7, 1984 by Postal Rate Commission, See Addenda)

Domestic includes the U.S., territories and possessions, APO and FPO.

First Class

Letters written, and matter sealed against inspection, 20¢ for 1st oz. or fraction, 17¢ for each additional oz. or fraction.
U.S. Postal cards; single 13¢; double 26¢; private postcards, same.

First class includes written matter, namely letters, postal cards, postcards (private mailing cards) and all other matter wholly or partly in writing, whether sealed or unsealed, except manuscripts for books, periodical articles and music, manuscript copy accompanying proofsheets or corrected proofsheets of the same and the writing authorized by law on matter of other classes. Also matter sealed or closed against inspection, bills and statements of accounts.

Greeting Cards

May be sent first class or single piece third class.

Express Mail

Express Mail Service is available for any mailable article up to 70 pounds, and guarantees delivery between major U.S. cities or your money back. Articles received by the acceptance time authorized by the postmaster at a postal facility offering Express Mail will be delivered by 3 p.m. the next day or, if you prefer, your shipment can be picked up as early as 10 a.m. the next business day. Rates include insurance, Shipment Receipt, and Record of Delivery at the destination post office.

Consult Postmaster for other Express Mail Services and rates. (The Postal Service will refund, upon application to originating office, the postage for any Express Mail shipments not meeting the service standard except for those delayed by strike or work stoppage.)

Second Class

Single copy mailings by general public 19¢ for first ounce, 35¢ for over 1 to 2 ozs., 45¢ for over 2 to 3 ozs. and 10¢ for each additional ounce up to 8 ozs. Each additional 2 ozs. over 8 ozs., add 10¢.

Third Class

Third class (limit up to but not including 16 ounces): Mailable matter not in 1st and 2d classes.

Single mailing: Greeting cards (sealed or unsealed), small parcels, printed matter, booklets and catalogs, 20¢ the first ounce, 37¢ for over 1 to 2 ozs., 54¢ for over 2 to 3 ozs., 71¢ for over 3 to 4 ozs., 85¢ for over 4 to 6 ozs., 95¢ for over 6 to 8 ozs., $1.05 for over 8 to 10 ozs., $1.15 for over 10 to 12 ozs., $1.25 for over 12 to 14 ozs., $1.35 for over 14 but less than 16 ozs.

Bulk material: books, catalogs of 24 pages or more, seeds, cuttings, bulbs, roots, scions, and plants. 45¢ per pound, 10.9¢ minimum per piece.

Other matter: newsletters, shopper's guides, advertising circulars, 45¢ per pound, 10.9¢ minimum per piece. Separate rates for some nonprofit organizations. Bulk mailing fee, $40 per calendar year. Apply to postmaster for permit. One-time fee for permit imprint, $40.

Parcel Post—Fourth Class

Fourth class or parcel post (16 ounces and over): merchandise, printed matter, etc., may be sealed, subject to inspection.

On parcels weighing less than 15 lbs. and measuring more than 84 inches, but not more than 100 inches in length and girth combined, the minimum postal charge shall be the zone charge applicable to a 15-pound parcel.

Priority Mail

First class mail of more than 12 ounces can be sent "Priority Mail (Heavy Pieces)" service. The most expeditious handling and transportation available will be used for fastest delivery.

Forwarding Addresses

The mailer, in order to obtain a forwarding address, must endorse the envelope or cover "Address Correction Requested." The destination post office then will determine whether a forwarding address has been left on file and provide it for a fee of 25¢.

Priority Mail

Packages weighing up to 70 pounds and exceeding 100 inches in length and girth combined, including written and other material of the first class, whether sealed or unsealed, fractions of a pound being charged as a full pound, except in the 1 to 5 pound weight category where half-pound weight increments apply.

Rates according to zone apply between the U.S. and Puerto Rico and Virgin Islands.

Parcels weighing less than 15 pounds, measuring over 84 inches but not exceeding 100 inches in length and girth combined are chargeable with a minimum rate equal to that for a 15 pound parcel for the zone to which addressed.

Zones	To 1 lb.	1½	2	2½	3	3½	4	4½	5*
1, 2, 3	$2.24	$2.30	$2.54	$2.78	$3.01	$3.25	$3.49	3.73	$3.97
4	2.24	2.42	2.70	2.98	3.25	3.53	3.81	4.09	4.37
5	2.24	2.56	2.88	3.21	3.53	3.85	4.18	4.50	4.83
6	2.34	2.72	3.09	3.47	3.85	4.22	4.60	4.97	5.35
7	2.45	2.87	3.30	3.73	4.16	4.59	5.02	5.45	5.88
8	2.58	3.07	3.57	4.06	4.56	5.05	5.55	6.05	6.54

*Consult postmaster for parcels over 5 lbs.

Special Handling

Third and fourth class parcels will be handled and delivered as expeditiously as practicable (but not special delivery) upon payment, in addition to the regular postage: up to 10 lbs., 75¢; over 10 lbs., $1.30. Such parcels must be endorsed, Special Handling.

Special Delivery

First class mail up to 2 lbs. $2.10, over 2 lbs. and up to 10 lbs., $2.35; over 10 lbs. $3.00. All other classes up to 2 lbs. $2.35, over 2 and up to 10 lbs., $3.00, over 10 lbs. $3.40.

Bound Printed Matter Rates
(Fourth class single piece zone rate)

Weight lbs.	Local	1&2	Zones 3	4	5	6	7	8
1.5	$0.69	$0.92	$0.94	$0.97	$1.02	$1.08	$1.16	$1.19
2	.69	.93	.95	.99	1.06	1.14	1.25	1.28
2.5	.69	.93	.96	1.01	1.10	1.20	1.33	1.38
3	.69	.94	.97	1.03	1.14	1.25	1.41	1.47
3.5	.69	.94	.98	1.05	1.17	1.31	1.50	1.56
4	.69	.95	.99	1.07	1.21	1.37	1.58	1.66
4.5	.69	.95	1.00	1.09	1.25	1.42	1.67	1.75
5	.70	.96	1.02	1.12	1.29	1.48	1.75	1.85
6	.70	.96	1.04	1.16	1.36	1.59	1.92	2.03
7	.70	.97	1.06	1.20	1.44	1.71	2.09	2.22
8	.70	.98	1.08	1.24	1.51	1.82	2.25	2.41
9	.70	.99	1.10	1.28	1.59	1.94	2.42	2.59
10	.70	1.00	1.12	1.32	1.66	2.05	2.59	2.78

Zone Mileage

1.. Up to 50   3.. 150-300   5... 600-1,000   7. 1,400-1,800
2... 50-150   4.. 300-600   6.. 1,000-1,400   8. over 1,800

Domestic Mail Special Services

Registry — all mailable matter prepaid with postage at the first-class rate may be registered. The mailer is required to declare the value of mail presented for registration.

Registered Mail

	Insured	Uninsured
$0.00 to $100.	$3.30	$3.25
$100.01 to $500	3.60	3.55
$500.01 to $1,000 . .	3.90	3.85
$1,000.01 to $2,000 . .	4.20	4.10
$2,000.01 to $3,000 . .	4.50	4.35
$3,000.01 to $4,000 . .	4.80	4.60
$4,000.01 to $5,000 . .	5.10	4.85
$5,000.01 to $6,000 . .	5.40	5.10
$6,000.01 to $7,000 . .	5.70	5.35
$7,000.01 to $8,000 . .	6.00	5.60
$8,000.01 to $9,000 . .	6.30	5.85
$9,000.01 to $10,000 . .	6.60	6.10

Consult postmaster for registry rates above $10,000.

C.O.D.: Unregistered — is applicable to 3d and 4th class matter and sealed domestic mail of any class bearing postage at the 1st class rate. Such mail must be based on bona fide orders or be in conformity with agreements between senders and addressees. **Registered** — for details consult postmaster.

Insurance — is applicable to 3d and 4th class matter. Matter for sale addressed to prospective purchasers who have not ordered it or authorized its sending will not be insured.

Insured Mail

$0.01 to $20	$0.45
20.01 to 50	0.85
50.01 to 100.	1.25
100.01 to 150.	1.70
150.01 to 200.	2.05
200.01 to 300	3.45
300.01 to 400	4.70

Liability for insured mail is limited to $400.

Certified mail — service is available for any matter having no intrinsic value on which 1st class or air mail postage is paid. Receipt is furnished at time of mailing and evidence of delivery obtained. The fee is 75¢ ($1.00 restricted delivery) in addition to postage. Return receipt, restricted delivery, and special delivery are available upon payment of additional fees. No indemnity.

Special Fourth Class Rate
(limit 70 lbs.)

First pound or fraction, 63¢ (46¢ if 500 pieces or more of special rate matter are presorted to 5 digit ZIP code or 58¢ if 500 pieces or more are presorted to Bulk Mail Cntrs.); each additional pound or fraction through 7 pounds, 23¢; each additional pound, 14¢. Only following specific articles: books 24 pages or more, at least 22 of which are printed consisting wholly of reading matter or scholarly bibliography containing no advertisement other than incidental announcements of books; 16 millimeter films in final form (except when mailed to or from commercial theaters); printed music in bound or sheet form; printed objective test materials; sound recordings, playscripts, and manuscripts for books, periodicals, and music; printed educational reference charts; loose-leaf pages and binders therefor consisting of medical information for distribution to doctors, hospitals, medical schools, and medical students. Package must be marked "Special 4th Class Rate" stating item contained.

Library Rate (limit 70 lbs.)

First pound 32¢, each additional pound through 7 pounds, 11¢; each additional pound, 7¢. Books when loaned or exchanged between schools, colleges, public libraries, and certain non-profit organizations; books, printed music, bound academic theses, periodicals, sound recordings, other library materials, museum materials (specimens, collections), scientific or mathematical kits, instruments or other devices; also catalogs, guides or scripts for some of these materials. Must be marked "Library Rate".

Postal Union Mail Special Services

Registration — available to practically all countries. Fee $3.25. The maximum indemnity payable — generally only in case of complete loss (of both contents and wrapper) — is $25.20. To Canada only the fee is $3.55 providing indemnity for loss up to $200.

Parcel Post Rate Schedule

1 lb., not exceeding	Local	1 & 2	Zones 3	4	5	6	7	8
2	1.52	1.55	1.61	1.70	1.83	1.99	2.15	2.48
3	1.58	1.63	1.73	1.86	2.06	2.30	2.55	3.05
4	1.65	1.71	1.84	2.02	2.29	2.61	2.94	3.60
5	1.71	1.79	1.96	2.18	2.52	2.92	3.32	4.07
6	1.78	1.87	2.07	2.33	2.74	3.14	3.64	4.54
7	1.84	1.95	2.18	2.49	2.89	3.38	3.95	5.02
8	1.91	2.03	2.30	2.64	3.06	3.63	4.27	5.55
9	1.97	2.11	2.41	2.75	3.25	3.93	4.63	6.08
10	2.04	2.19	2.52	2.87	3.46	4.22	5.00	6.62
11	2.10	2.28	2.60	3.00	3.68	4.51	5.38	7.15
12	2.17	2.36	2.66	3.10	3.89	4.80	5.75	7.69
13	2.21	2.41	2.72	3.19	4.02	4.96	5.95	7.97
14	2.26	2.46	2.78	3.28	4.13	5.12	6.14	8.24
15	2.31	2.51	2.83	3.36	4.25	5.26	6.32	8.48
16	2.35	2.56	2.89	3.44	4.35	5.40	6.49	8.72
17	2.40	2.59	2.94	3.51	4.45	5.53	6.65	8.94
18	2.44	2.64	2.99	3.59	4.55	5.65	6.80	9.15
19	2.48	2.68	3.04	3.66	4.64	5.77	6.94	9.35
20	2.52	2.72	3.10	3.73	4.73	5.89	7.09	9.55

Consult postmaster for parcels over 20 pounds or measuring more than 84 inches, length and girth.

Return receipt —showing to whom and date deliv'd, 60¢.

Special delivery — Available to most countries. Consult post office. Fees: for post cards, letter mail, and airmail "other articles," $2.10 up to 2 pounds; over 2 to 10 pounds, $2.35; over 10 pounds, $3.00. For surface "other articles," $2.35, $3.00, and $3.40, respectively.

Marking — an article intended for special delivery service must have affixed to the cover near the name of the country of destination "EXPRESS" (special delivery) label, obtainable at the post office, or it may be marked on the cover boldly in red "EXPRESS" (special delivery).

Special handling — entitles AO surface packages to prior-ity handling between mailing point and U.S. point of dispatch. Fees: 75¢ for packages to 10 pounds, and $1.30 for packages over 10 pounds.

Airmail — there is daily air service to practically all countries.

Prepayment of replies from other countries — a mailer who wishes to prepay a reply by letter from another country may do so by sending his correspondent one or more international reply coupons, which may be purchased at United States post offices. One coupon should be accepted in any country in exchange for stamps to prepay a surface letter of the first unit of weight to the U.S.

Post Office-Authorized 2-Letter State Abbreviations

The abbreviations below are approved by the U.S. Postal Service for use in addresses only. They do not replace the traditional abbreviations in other contexts. The official list follows, including the District of Columbia, Guam, Puerto Rico, the Canal Zone, and the Virgin Islands (all capital letters are used):

Alabama	AL	Hawaii	HI	Missouri	MO	Puerto Rico	PR
Alaska	AK	Idaho	ID	Montana	MT	Rhode Island	RI
American Samoa	AS	Illinois	IL	Nebraska	NE	South Carolina	SC
Arizona	AZ	Indiana	IN	Nevada	NV	South Dakota	SD
Arkansas	AR	Iowa	IA	New Hampshire	NH	Tennessee	TN
California	CA	Kansas	KS	New Jersey	NJ	Texas	TX
Canal Zone	CZ	Kentucky	KY	New Mexico	NM	Trust Territories	TT
Colorado	CO	Louisiana	LA	New York	NY	Utah	UT
Connecticut	CT	Maine	ME	North Carolina	NC	Vermont	VT
Delaware	DE	Maryland	MD	North Dakota	ND	Virginia	VA
Dist. of Col.	DC	Massachusetts	MA	Northern Mariana Is.	CM	Virgin Islands	VI
Florida	FL	Michigan	MI	Ohio	OH	Washington	WA
Georgia	GA	Minnesota	MN	Oklahoma	OK	West Virginia	WV
Guam	GU	Mississippi	MS	Oregon	OR	Wisconsin	WI
				Pennsylvania	PA	Wyoming	WY

Also approved for use in addressing mail are the following abbreviations:

Alley	Aly	Courts	Cts	Heights	Hts	Rural	R
Arcade	Arc	Crescent	Cres	Highway	Hwy	Square	Sq
Boulevard	Blvd	Drive	Dr	Lane	Ln	Street	St
Branch	Br	Expressway	Expy	Manor	Mnr	Terrace	Ter
Bypass	Byp	Extended	Ext	Place	Pl	Trail	Trl
Causeway	Cswy	Extension	Ext	Plaza	Plz	Turnpike	Tpke
Center	Ctr	Freeway	Fwy	Point	Pt	Viaduct	Via
Circle	Cir	Gardens	Gdns	Road	Rd	Vista	Vis
Court	Ct	Grove	Grv				

Size Standards for Domestic Mail

Minimum Size

Pieces which do not meet the following requirements are prohibited from the mails:

  a. All pieces must be at least .007 of an inch thick, and

  b. All pieces (except keys and identification devices) which are ¼ inch or less thick must be:

    (1) Rectangular in shape,

    (2) At least 3½ inches high, and

    (3) At least 5 inches long.

Note: Pieces greater than ¼ inch thick can be mailed even if they measure less than 3½ by 5 inches.

Nonstandard Mail

All First-Class Mail weighing one ounce or less and all single-piece rate Third-Class mail weighing one ounce or less is nonstandard (and subject to a 9¢ surcharge in addition to the applicable postage and fees) if:

  1. Any of the following dimensions are exceeded:
    Length—11½ inches,
    Height—6⅛ inches,
    Thickness—¼ inch, or

  2. The piece has a height to length (aspect) ratio which does not fall between 1 to 1.3 and 1 to 2.5 inclusive. (The aspect ratio is found by dividing the length by the height. If the answer is between 1.3 and 2.5 inclusive, the piece has a standard aspect ratio.)

Stamps, Envelopes and Postal Cards

Form	Denomination and prices
Single or sheet	1,2,3,4,5,6,10,11,12,13,14,15,16,17,18,20,25,28,30,45 & 50 cents, $1 and $5.
Book	20 at 20¢ = $4.00
Coil of 100	20 cents. (Dispenser to hold coils of 100 stamps may be purchased for 10¢ additional.)
Coils of 500	1,2,3,5,6,9,10,12,13,15,16, & 20 cents and $1.
Coils of 3,000	1,2,3,5,6,9,10,15,16,20 and 25 cents.

Postal Receipts at Large Cities

Fiscal year	Boston	Chicago	L.A.	New York	Phila.	St. Louis	Wash., D.C.
1975	$136,453,079	$365,378,795	$193,229,077	$453,905,277	$134,571,376	$85,591,774	$115,489,343
1979	211,082,724	506,395,438	273,563,824	627,445,984	211,571,818	126,031,314	175,467,893
1980	224,428,760	528,233,991	271,136,828	666,377,778	221,161,624	127,427,555	187,334,312
1981	256,524,082	551,988,015	301,159,594	741,286,845	235,116,018	142,548,957	201,191,995
1982	292,971,572	597,246,568	338,798,409	848,507,590	265,242,959	160,596,946	215,772,861
1983	294,932,399	589,476,264	330,734,928	856,569,717	273,210,529	165,000,437	212,117,368

Other cities for fiscal year 1983: Atlanta, $284,108,138; Baltimore, $154,341,995; Cleveland, $158,066,356; Dallas, $300,309,779; Denver, $161,137,848; Houston, $203,050,544; Miami, $146,897,223; Minneapolis, $206,852,485; San Francisco, $203,050,544; St. Louis, $165,000,437.

Air Mail, Parcel Post International Rates

Aerogrammes — 30¢ each to all countries.
Air mail postcards (single) - 28¢ to all countries except Canada and Mexico (13¢)

Country	Rate group	Air parcel post rates First 4 oz.	Each add'l. 4 oz. or fraction up to first 5 lbs.	Country	Rate group	Air parcel post rates First 4 oz.	Each add'l. 4 oz. or fraction up to first 5 lbs.
Afghanistan	D	5.40	1.10	Guyana	B	3.80	.70
Albania	C	4.60	.90	Haiti	A	3.00	.50
Algeria	D	5.40	1.10	Honduras	B	3.80	.70
Andorra	B	3.80	.70	Hong Kong	C	4.60	.90
Angola	E	6.20	1.30	Hungary	C	4.60	.90
Argentina	D	5.40	1.10	Iceland	D	5.40	1.10
Ascension	(4)	—	—	India	D	5.40	1.10
Australia	D	5.40	1.10	Indonesia	E	6.20	1.30
Austria	B	3.80	.70	Iran	D	5.40	1.10
Azores	C	4.60	.90	Iraq	D	5.40	1.10
Bahamas	A	3.00	.50	Ireland (Eire)	C	4.60	.90
Bahrain	D	5.40	1.10	Israel	C	4.60	.90
Bangladesh	E	6.20	1.30	Italy	C	4.60	.90
Barbados	B	3.80	.70	Ivory Coast	D	5.40	1.10
Belgium	E	6.20	1.30	Jamaica	A	3.00	.50
Belize	A	3.00	.50	Japan	E	6.20	1.30
Benin	D	5.40	1.10	Jordan	C	4.60	.90
Bermuda	A	3.00	.50	Kampuchea	(5)	—	—
Bhutan	(5)	—	—	Kenya	D	5.40	1.10
Bolivia	B	3.80	.70	Kiribati	B	3.80	.70
Botswana	E	6.20	1.30	Korea, Democratic People's			
Brazil	E	6.20	1.30	Rep. (North)[1]	(5)	—	—
Brunei	D	5.40	1.10	Korea, Rep. of (South)	D	5.40	1.10
Bulgaria	D	5.40	1.10	Kuwait	C	4.60	.90
Burma	D	5.40	1.10	Lao	E	6.20	1.30
Burundi	E	6.20	1.30	Latvia	E	6.20	1.30
Cameroon	C	4.60	.90	Lebanon	C	4.60	.90
Canada[3,6]	(4)	—	—	Leeward Islands	A	3.00	.50
Cape Verde	D	5.40	1.10	Lesotho	E	6.20	1.30
Cayman Islands	A	3.00	.50	Liberia	B	3.80	.70
Central African Rep.	E	6.20	1.30	Libya	C	4.60	.90
Chad	D	5.40	1.10	Lithuania	E	6.20	1.30
Chile	D	5.40	1.10	Luxembourg	B	3.80	.70
China (People's Republic of)[7]	D	5.40	1.10	Macao	C	4.60	.90
				Madagascar	C	4.60	.90
Colombia	B	3.80	.70	Madeira Islands	B	3.80	.70
Comoros	E	6.20	1.30	Malawi	D	5.40	1.10
Congo	D	5.40	1.10	Malaysia	D	5.40	1.10
Corsica	E	6.20	1.30	Maldives	D	5.40	1.10
Costa Rica	A	3.00	.50	Mali	C	4.60	.90
Cuba	(5)	—	—	Malta	C	4.60	.90
Cyprus	D	5.40	1.10	Martinique	A	3.00	.50
Czechoslovakia	C	4.60	.90	Mauritania	D	5.40	1.10
Denmark	B	3.80	.70	Mauritius	E	6.20	1.30
Djibouti	E	6.20	1.30	Mexico	A	3.00	.50
Dominica	A	3.00	.50	Mongolia	(5)	—	—
Dominican Republic	A	3.00	.50	Morocco	C	4.60	.90
East Timor	(5)	—	—	Mozambique	E	6.20	1.30
Ecuador	B	3.80	.70	Nauru	C	4.60	.90
Egypt	C	4.60	.90	Nepal	D	5.40	1.10
El Salvador	A	3.00	.50	Netherlands	C	4.60	.90
Equatorial Guinea	D	5.40	1.10	Nertherlands Antilles	A	3.00	.50
Estonia	E	6.20	1.30	New Caledonia	D	5.40	1.10
Ethiopia	D	5.40	1.10	New Zealand	D	5.40	1.10
Faeroe Islands	C	4.60	.90	Nicaragua	B	3.80	.70
Falkland Islands	D	5.40	1.10	Niger	D	5.40	1.10
Fiji	B	3.80	.70	Nigeria	C	4.60	.90
Finland	D	5.40	1.10	Norway	D	5.40	1.10
France				Oman	D	5.40	1.10
(Including Monaco)	E	6.20	1.30	Pakistan	D	5.40	1.10
French Guiana	C	4.60	.90	Panama	A	3.00	.50
French Polynesia	D	5.40	1.10	Papua New Guinea	D	5.40	1.10
Gabon	D	5.40	1.10	Paraguay	C	4.60	.90
Gambia	B	3.80	.70	Peru	B	3.80	.70
German Democratic				Philippines	D	5.40	1.10
Republic (East Germany)	C	4.60	.90	Pitcairn Islands	B	3.80	.70
Germany, Federal Rep.				Poland	C	4.60	.90
of (West Germany)	C	4.60	.90	Portugal	B	3.80	.70
Ghana	D	5.40	1.10	Qatar	C	4.60	.90
Gibraltar	D	5.40	1.10	Reunion	E	6.20	1.30
Great Britain	C	4.60	.90	Romania	C	4.60	.90
Greece	C	4.60	.90	Rwanda	D	5.40	1.10
Greenland	D	5.40	1.10	St. Helena	B	3.80	.70
Grenada	B	3.80	.70	St. Lucia	A	3.00	.50
Guadeloupe	A	3.00	.50	St. Pierre & Miquelon	A	3.00	.50
Guatemala	A	3.00	.50	St. Thomas & Principe	D	5.40	1.10
Guinea	B	3.80	.70	St. Vincent & The Grenadines	A	3.00	.50
Guinea-Bissau	B	3.80	.70				

Country	Rate group	Air parcel post rates First 4 oz.	Each add'l. 4 oz. or fraction up to First 5 lbs.
Santa Cruz Islands	B	3.80	.70
Saudi Arabia	C	4.60	.90
Senegal	D	5.40	1.10
Seychelles	D	5.40	1.10
Sierre Leone	C	4.60	.90
Singapore	D	5.40	1.10
Solomon Islands	C	4.60	.90
Somalia (Southern Region)	D	5.40	1.10
Somalia (Northern Region)	(4)	—	—
South Africa	E	6.20	1.30
Spain	C	4.60	.90
Sri Lanka	D	5.40	1.10
Sudan	D	5.40	1.10
Suriname	B	3.80	.70
Swaziland	D	5.40	1.10
Sweden	D	5.40	1.10
Switzerland	B	3.80	.70
Syria	C	4.60	.90
Taiwan	C	4.60	.90
Tanzania	E	6.20	1.30
Thailand	D	5.40	1.10
Togo	D	5.40	1.10

Country	Rate group	Air parcel post rates First 4 oz.	Each add'l. 4 oz. or fraction up to First 5 lbs.
Tonga	B	3.80	.70
Trinidad & Tobago	B	3.80	.70
Tristan da Cunha	B	3.80	.70
Tunisia	C	4.60	.90
Turkey	C	4.60	.90
Turks & Caicos Islands	A	3.00	.50
Tuvalu (Ellice Islands)	B	3.80	.70
Uganda	D	5.40	1.10
USSR[3]	E	6.20	1.30
United Arab Emirates	D	5.40	1.10
Upper Volta	C	4.60	.90
Uruguay	B	3.80	.70
Vanuatu	B	3.80	.70
Vatican City State	C	4.60	.90
Venezuela	B	3.80	.70
Vietnam[1]	(5)	—	—
Western Samoa	B	3.80	.70
Yemen Arab Republic	D	5.40	1.10
Yemen, Peoples Democratic Republic of	D	5.40	1.10
Yugoslavia	C	4.60	.90
Zaire	D	5.40	1.10
Zambia	E	6.20	1.30
Zimbabwe	E	6.20	1.30

Miscellaneous International Rates

Letters and Letter Pkgs (Surface)

Over Lbs.	Over Ozs.	Through Lbs.	Through Ozs.	Canada	Mexico	All other countries
0	0	0	1	$0.20	$0.20	$0.30
0	1	0	2	.37	.37	.47
0	2	0	3	.54	.57	.64
0	3	0	4	.71	.71	.81
0	4	0	5	.88	.88	.98
0	5	0	6	1.05	1.05	1.15
0	6	0	7	1.22	1.22	1.32
0	7	0	8	1.39	1.39	1.49
0	8	0	9	1.56	1.56	2.76
0	9	0	10	1.73	1.73	2.76
0	10	0	11	1.90	1.90	2.76
0	11	0	12	2.07	2.07	2.76
0	12	1	0	2.58	2.58	2.76
1	0	1	8	3.07	3.07	3.78
1	8	2	0	3.57	3.57	4.80
2	0	2	8	4.06	4.06	5.55
2	8	3	0	4.56	4.56	6.30
3	0	3	8	5.05	5.05	7.05
3	8	4	0	5.55	5.55	7.80
4	0	4	8	6.05	...	...
4	8	5	0	6.54	...	...

Maximum limit: 60 pounds to Canada, 4 pounds to Mexico and all other countries.

Letters and Letter Pkgs (Air)

Canada and Mexico: Refer to rates listed under Letter and Letter Pkgs. (Surface). Mail paid at this rate receives First-Class service in the United States and air service in Canada and Mexico.

Colombia, Venezuela, Central America, the Caribbean Islands, Bahamas, Bermuda, St. Pierre & Miquelon: 35 cents per half ounce up to and including 2 ounces; 30 cents each additional half ounce up to and including 32 ounces; 30 cents per additional ounce over 32 ounces.

All Other Countries: 40 cents per half ounce up to and including 2 ounces; 35 cents each additional half ounce up to and including 32 ounces; 35 cents per additional ounce over 32 ounces.

Parcel Post (Surface)

Canada, Mexico, Central America, The Caribbean Islands, Bahamas, Bermuda, St. Pierre and Miquelon; $3.10 for the first 2 pounds and $1.00 each additional pound or fraction.

All Other Countries: $3.25 for the first 2 pounds and $1.05 for each additional pound or fraction.

For Parcel Post air rates, see tables, pages 973-974.

(1) Restrictions apply; consult post office. (2) To facilitate distribution and delivery, include "Union of Soviet Socialist Republics" or "USSR" as part of the address. (3) Small packets weight limit one pound to Canada. (4) No air parcel post service. (5) No parcel post service. (6) No airmail AO or parcel post to Canada; prepare and prepay all airmail packages as letter mail. (7) The continental China postal authorities will not deliver articles unless addressed to show name of the country as "People's Republic of China"; also, only acceptable spelling of capital is "Beijing."

International Mails

Weight and Dimensional Limits and Surface Rates

For air rates and parcel post see pages 775-776, and Addenda

Letters and letter packages: all written matter or correspondence must be sent as letter mail. Weight limit: 4 lbs. to all countries except Canada, which is 60 lbs. **Surface rates:** Canada and Mexico, 20¢ first ounce; 17¢ each additional oz. or fraction through 12 ozs.; eighth-zone priority rates for heavier weights. Countries other than Canada and Mexico, 1 oz., 30¢; over 1 to 2 ozs., 47¢; over 2 to 3 ozs., 64¢; over 3 to 4 ozs., 81¢; over 4 to 5 ozs., 98¢; over 5 to 6 ozs., $1.15; over 6 to 7 ozs., $1.32; over 7 to 8 ozs., $1.49; over 8 ozs. to 1 pound, $2.76; over 1 lb. to 1 lb., 8 ozs., $3.78; over 1 lb., 8 ozs. to 2 lbs., $4.80; over 2 lbs. to 2 lbs., 8 ozs., $5.55; over 2 lbs., 8 ozs. to 3 lbs., $6.30; over 3 lbs. to 3 lbs., 8 ozs., $7.05; over 3 lbs., 8 ozs. to 4 lbs. $7.80. **Air rates:** Canada and Mexico, 20¢ first ounce; 17¢ each additional ounce or fraction to 1 pound. Central America, Colombia, Venezuela, the Caribbean Islands, Bahamas, Bermuda, and St. Pierre and Miquelon, 35¢ per half ounce up to and including 2 ounces; 30¢ each additional half ounce or fraction. All other countries, 40¢ per half ounce up to and including 2 ounces; 35¢ each additional half ounce or fraction. Aerogrammes, which can be folded into the form of an envelope and sent by air to all countries, are available at post offices for 30¢ each.

Note. Mail to Canada and Mexico bearing postage paid at the surface letter rate will receive first class service in the U.S. and airmail service in Canada and Mexico during the Postal Service First Class Mail Service Improvement Program.

Postcards. Surface rates to Canada and Mexico, 13¢; to all other countries, 19¢. By air, Canada and Mexico, 13¢; to all other countries, 28¢. Maximum size permitted, 6 x 4¼ in.; minimum, 5½ x 3½.

Printed matter. To Canada, Mexico and all other countries: 20¢ (Canada and Mexico) and 23¢ (all other countries) the first ounce, 37¢ for 1 to 2 ozs., 54¢ for 2 to 3 ozs., 71¢ for 3 to 4 ozs., 85¢ for 4 to 6 ozs., 95¢ for 6 to 8 ozs., $1.14 for 8 to 10 ozs., $1.36 for 10 to 12 ozs., $1.58 for 12 to 14 ozs., $1.81 for 14 to 18 ozs., $1.94 for 18 to 20 ozs., $2.07 for 20 to 22 ozs., $2.21 for 22 to 24 ozs., $2.35 for 24 to 26 ozs., $2.49 for 26 to 28 ozs., $2.62 for 28 to 30 ozs., $2.76 for 30 to 32 ozs., $3.31 for 2 lbs. to 3 lbs., $3.86 for 3 lbs. to 4 lbs. and 96¢ for each add'l 1 lb. (Consult post office for rates and conditions applying to certain publications mailed by the publishers or by registered news agents.) Consult post office for book rates.

Exceptional weight limits for printed matter. Printed matter may weigh up to 22 lbs. to Argentina, Bolivia, Brazil, Chile, Colombia, Costa Rica, Cuba, Dominican Republic,

Ecuador, El Salvador, Guatemala, Haiti, Honduras, Mexico, Nicaragua, Panama, Paraguay, Peru, Spain (including Balearic Islands, and Canary Islands) Surinam, Uruguay, and Venezuela. For other countries, limit for books is 11 lbs., all other prints, 4 lbs.

Matter for the blind. Surface rate free; air service to Canada for matter prepared as letters/letter packages is at the letter rate. (For all other countries, consult postmaster.) Weight limit 15 lbs.

Small packets. Postage rates for small items of merchandise and samples; consult post office for weight limits and requirements for customs declarations. Rates: Canada, Mexico 20¢, all other countries 23¢ for the first ounce; 37¢ for 1 to 2 ozs.; 54¢ for 2 to 3 ozs.; 71¢ for 3 to 4 ozs.; 85¢ for 4 to 6 ozs.; 95¢ for 6 to 8 ozs.; $1.14 for 8 to 10 ozs.; $1.36 for 10 to 12 ozs.; $1.58 for 12 to 14 ozs.; $1.81 for 14 to 16 ozs. (Consult post office for rates for heavier packets.) For other rates, see schedule "Air Service Other Articles" under heading of International Rates for Air Mail and Surface Parcel Post, pages 973-974.

INTELPOST-A USPS International Service Offering

The U.S. Postal Service, in conjunction with several foreign countries is making available to the public a new service offering called INTELPOST. INTELPOST is an acronym for International Electronic Post.

The INTELPOST system is a very high speed digital facsimile network between the United States and participating countries. INTELPOST utilizes existing international postal acceptance and delivery mechanisms for the acceptance and distribution of the INTELPOST original and facsimile documents. The INTELPOST original document and a transmittal form are scanned by a facsimile reader operated by USPS personnel at the INTELPOST transmitting facility and sent via international satellite communications to its destination.

A black and white image of the original document is printed by a facsimile printer operated by foreign postal personnel and is inserted into an INTELPOST envelope for delivery by participating postal administration personnel according to the service offerings available in the particular country.

The cost of an INTELPOST transmission is $5.00 per page including First Class (normal) delivery in the destinating foreign country. If an optional express type delivery service is available and is selected, the cost of such service will be added to the price of the message. Service is currently available to Canada, the United Kingdom and the Netherlands. Several additional countries are in the process of building INTELPOST Centers.

International Parcel Post

For rates see pages 775-776, and Addenda

General dimensional limits — greatest length, 3½ feet; greatest length and girth combined, 6 feet.

Prohibited articles. Before sending goods abroad the mailer should consult the post office that they will not be confiscated or returned because their importation is prohibited or restricted by the country of address.

Packing. Parcels for transmission overseas should be even more carefully packed than those intended for delivery within the continental U.S. Containers should be used which will be strong enough to protect the contents from the weight of other mail, from pressure and friction, climatic

changes, and repeated handlings.

Sealing. Registered or insured parcels must be sealed. To some countries the sealing of ordinary (unregistered and uninsured) parcels is optional, and to others compulsory. Consult post office.

Customs declarations and other forms. At least one customs declaration is required for parcel post packages (surface or air) mailed to another country. In addition, to some countries, a dispatch note is required. The forms may be obtained at post offices.

First Class Postal Rates in Brief

U.S. Domestic

(In effect Nov. 1, 1981; for rate changes proposed Sept. 7, 1984 by the Postal Rate Commisssion, See Addenda)

Letters—20¢ first ounce, 17¢ each additional ounce.
Postal cards—13¢ each (up to 4½ × 6 in.). Double cards, 26¢. Private cards, 13¢; double 26¢.

U.S. International (in effect Nov. 1, 1981)

Letters—(1) Canada (max. weight 60 lbs.) and Mexico (max. weight 4 lbs.), 20¢ first ounce, 17¢ each addl. ounce to 12 ounces; over 12 ounces to 1 pound, $2.58; over 1 pound to 1½ pounds, $3.07; over 1½ to 2 pounds, $3.57; over 2 to 2½ pounds, $4.06; over 2½ to 3 pounds, $4.56; over 3 to 3½ pounds, $5.05; over 3½ to 4 pounds, $5.55; over 4 to 4½ pounds, $6.05; over 4½ to 5 pounds, $6.54. (2) Countries other than Canada and Mexico, 1 ounce, 30¢; over 1 to 2 ounces, 47¢; over 2 to 3 ounces, 64¢; over 3 to 4 ounces, 81¢; over 4 to 5 ounces, 98¢; over 5 to 6 ounces, $1.15; over 6 to 7 ounces $1.32; and over 7 to 8 ounces, $1.49.
Air mail letters—(1) Canada, and Mexico, same as domestic surface rates. (2) Cen. America, Colombia, Venezuela, the Caribbean Is., Bahamas, Bermuda, and St. Pierre and Miquelon, 35¢ per half ounce through 2 ounces; 30¢ each addl. ½ oz. through 32 ounces. (3) All other countries, 40¢ per half ounce through 2 ounces; 35¢ each addl. ½ oz. through 32 ounces.
Aerogrammes—to all countries, 30¢ each.
Postal cards—to Canada and Mexico 13¢ each. To all other countries, 19¢ each.
Air mail postcards—to Canada and Mexico 13¢ each, to other countries 28¢ each.

Canada (in effect July 1, 1982)

Letter mail and postcards—Up to 30g 30¢, 31-50g 45¢, 51-100g 60¢, 101-150g 80¢, 151-200g $1, 201-250g $1.20, 251-300g $1.40, 301-350g $1.60, 351-400g $1.80, 401-450g $2.00, 451-500g $2.20.
To U.S.A. territories and possessions—(1) Airmail letters and postcards, up to and including 30g 35¢, 30-50g 50¢ plus 25¢ for each additional 50g up to 500g. Over 500g up to and including 1kg $6.00 with increases up to $52.40 for a maximum of 30kg. (2) **Surface parcel post.** Up to and including 1kg $4.00 plus 60¢ for each additional 500g up to a maximum of 16g.

VITAL STATISTICS

Source: National Center for Health Statistics, U.S. Department of Health and Human Services

January-April 1984 (Provisional Data)

Births

During the first 4 months of 1984 there were 1,197,000 live births, 2 percent more than the first 4 months of 1983. The birth rate was 15.4, and the fertility rate was 65.0.

Marriages

For the first 4 months of 1984 a total of 623,000 marriages was reported, yielding a marriage rate of 8.0 per 1,000 population. The marriage rate was 1 percent lower than the corresponding figure for the first 4 months of 1983.

Divorces

In the 4 months from January through April, a cumulative total of 360,000 divorces was reported, and the divorce rate for the period was 4.6 per 1,000 population. This was a decrease of 8% over the level recorded in the first 4 months of 1983.

Deaths

The provisional count of deaths for April 1984 totaled 174,000 resulting in a rate of 9.0 deaths per 1,000 population. This rate was the same as the rate for April 1983.

Among the 174,000 deaths for April 1984 were 3,200 deaths at ages under 1 year, yielding an infant mortality rate of 10.6 deaths per 1,000 live births. This rate was 7 percent lower than the rate of 11.4 for April 1983.

The provisional death rate for the 12 months ending with March 1984 was 8.6 deaths per 1,000 population. This was the same as the rate for the 12 months ending with March 1983.

Provisional Statistics
12 months ending with April

	Number		Rate*	
	1984	1983	1984	1983
Live births	3,635,000	3,703,000	15.5	15.9
Deaths	2,020,000	2,005,000	8.6	8.6
Natural increase.	1,615,000	1,698,000	6.9	7.3
Marriages	2,445,000	2,486,000	10.4	10.7
Divorces	1,160,000	1,180,000	4.9	5.1
Infant deaths. . .	39,100	41,000	10.8	11.1
Population base (in millions) 234.5 232.3				

*Per 1,000 population
Note: Rates are based on the 1980 Census of Population.

Annual Report for the Year 1983 (Provisional Statistics)

Births

During 1983 an estimated 3,614,000 babies were born in the United States, nearly 2% fewer than in 1982. The birth rate was 15.5 per 1,000 population (16.0 in 1982) and the fertility rate was 65.4 per 1,000 women aged 15-44 years, 4% lower than the rate in 1982 (67.8).

The small decrease in the number of births in 1983 is evidently the decline in the number of women 15-24 years, who typically account for nearly half of all births, and the decline in the fertility rate.

As a result of natural increase, the number of births over deaths, an estimated 1,604,000 persons were added to the population in 1983. The rate of increase was 6.9 per 1,000 population, 7% below that of 1982 (7.4). This decrease was due to the decline in birth rate.

Deaths

The provisional count of deaths in the United States during 1983 totaled 2,010,000, a rate of 8.6 deaths per 1,000 population. This rate was the same as in 1982. Among these

deaths were 39,400 at ages under 1 year, resulting in an infant mortality rate of 10.9 per 1,000 live births. This rate was 3% lower than the provisional infant mortality rate of 11.2 for 1982.

Marriages and Divorces

The number of marriages declined for the first time since 1975. In 1983, 2,444,000 marriages were performed, a decrease of 2% from 1982 (2,495,000), but still higher than the total in 1981 (2,438,000).

The marriage rate was 10.5 per 1,000 population. This rate was 3% below that of 1982. The rate in 1982 (10.8) was higher than it had been since 1973. An estimated 183,000 couples were married in December 1983, with a resulting rate of 9.2 per 1,000 population.

Provisional data indicate that 1,179,000 couples were divorced during 1983, 1,000 fewer than in 1982.

The divorce rate declined from 5.1 per 1,000 population in 1982 to 5.0 in 1983. The divorce rate peaked in 1979 and 1981 (5.3) and has fluctuated since then.

Births and Deaths in the U.S.

Refers only to events occurring within the U.S., including Alaska and Hawaii beginning in 1960. Excludes fetal deaths. Rates per 1,000 population enumerated as of April 1 for 1960, and 1970; estimated as of July 1 for all other years. (p) provisional. (NA) not available. Beginning 1970 excludes births and deaths occurring to nonresidents of the U.S.

	Births				Deaths			
Year	Males	Females	Total number	Rate	Males	Females	Total number	Rate
1955	2,073,719	1,973,576	4,097,000	25.0	872,638	656,079	1,528,717	9.3
1960	2,179,708	2,078,142	4,257,850	23.7	975,648	736,334	1,711,982	9.5
1965	1,927,054	1,833,304	3,760,358	19.4	1,035,200	792,936	1,828,136	9.4
1970	1,915,378	1,816,008	3,731,386	18.4	1,078,478	842,553	1,921,031	9.5
1975	1,613,135	1,531,063	3,144,198	14.6	1,050,819	842,060	1,892,879	8.8
1980	1,852,616	1,759,642	3,612,258	15.9	NA	NA	1,986,000	8.7
1981	NA	NA	3,646,000	15.9	NA	NA	1,987,000	8.7
1982	NA	NA	3,614,000	16.0	NA	NA	1,975,550	8.6
1983	NA	NA	3,614,000	15.5	NA	NA	2,010,000	8.6

Births and Deaths by States

Source: National Center for Health Statistics, U.S. Department of Health and Human Services

State	Births 1983p	1982	Deaths 1983p	1982	State	Births 1983p	1982	Deaths 1983p	1982
Alabama	57,685	61,040	34,885	35,101	Nebraska	26,816	26,849	14,819	14,681
Alaska	11,500	11,068	1,921	1,770	Nevada	14,251	13,023	6,948	6,769
Arizona	52,659	52,565	23,183	22,613	New Hampshire	13,973	13,849	7,771	7,416
Arkansas	33,630	34,166	23,093	21,995	New Jersey	90,627	96,401	65,620	66,025
California	413,915	435,019	187,938	192,171	New Mexico	30,186	23,711	9,927	8,260
Colorado	55,159	55,116	19,978	20,184	New York	249,618	240,171	170,464	166,761
Connecticut	34,978	40,125	25,273	25,573	North Carolina	84,655	86,692	50,602	48,968
Delaware	9,538	9,510	5,071	5,131	North Dakota	13,200	13,608	5,880	5,685
Dist. of Col.	18,592	18,638	8,349	8,462	Ohio	160,330	163,767	98,234	93,647
Florida	148,695	144,246	114,443	109,792	Oklahoma	54,085	55,494	28,414	28,533
Georgia	91,090	91,924	45,988	44,610	Oregon	41,045	42,129	21,579	21,648
Hawaii	19,005	18,807	5,712	5,490	Pennsylvania	159,210	162,884	121,592	118,932
Idaho	18,541	19,351	6,951	6,611	Rhode Island	13,061	13,003	9,407	9,089
Illinois	175,679	180,423	99,964	97,121	South Carolina	48,513	49,418	25,300	24,578
Indiana	82,169	83,453	48,268	46,843	South Dakota	12,409	12,665	6,545	6,515
Iowa	43,783	45,631	27,169	26,792	Tennessee	67,739	71,744	42,148	43,251
Kansas	39,498	40,244	21,365	21,310	Texas	287,044	315,147	115,128	115,859
Kentucky	55,252	57,055	33,590	32,797	Utah	40,752	43,188	8,834	8,997
Louisiana	80,610	85,100	35,755	36,071	Vermont	7,671	7,772	4,908	4,472
Maine	16,323	16,425	11,242	10,045	Virginia	77,448	77,783	43,226	41,291
Maryland	57,436	57,063	33,981	33,313	Washington	63,729	66,327	31,039	33,474
Massachusetts	78,670	75,908	54,275	56,629	West Virginia	26,911	28,203	19,210	19,137
Michigan	131,873	135,585	74,302	74,537	Wisconsin	72,611	76,973	41,124	41,700
Minnesota	64,698	66,645	34,099	33,349	Wyoming	9,515	10,050	2,990	3,018
Mississippi	44,025	45,597	23,122	22,964					
Missouri	76,739	78,843	50,419	48,925	Total	4,140,129	4,266,970	2,256,981	2,240,345
Montana	13,794	14,222	6,697	6,545	(p) provisional				

Marriages and Divorces by States

Source: National Center for Health Statistics, U.S. Department of Health and Human Services

1983 provisional figures; divorces include reported annulments.

State	Marriages	Divorces	State	Marriages	Divorces	State	Marriages	Divorces
Alabama	48,923	25,739	Louisiana	45,710	NA	Oklahoma	44,043	23,752
Alaska	6,852	3,878	Maine	12,584	5,920	Oregon	23,337	16,548
Arizona	30,322	20,891	Maryland	47,182	15,957	Pennsylvania	91,438	40,369
Arkansas	30,393	15,786	Massachusetts	43,587	17,670	Rhode Island	8,040	3,532
California	224,891	129,131	Michigan	70,735	39,733	South Carolina	53,572	13,685
Colorado	36,031	19,738	Minnesota	36,432	14,501	South Dakota	7,970	2,550
Connecticut	25,998	9,868	Mississippi	26,416	14,020	Tennessee	56,827	30,740
Delaware	5,555	3,060	Missouri	53,487	26,749	Texas	194,962	96,988
Dist. of Col.	5,436	2,731	Montana	8,061	4,650	Utah	18,346	8,467
Florida	119,532	71,295	Nebraska	13,512	6,323	Vermont	5,513	2,529
Georgia	71,552	32,448	Nevada	NA	11,404	Virginia	61,784	25,519
Hawaii	14,121	4,574	New Hampshire	11,084	4,634	Washington	46,247	27,268
Idaho	13,390	6,240	New Jersey	60,316	26,593	West Virginia	15,988	10,125
Illinois	103,519	50,514	New Mexico	16,728	9,063	Wisconsin	40,795	17,123
Indiana	53,455	NA	New York	156,440	64,480	Wyoming	6,200	3,983
Iowa	26,747	10,653	North Carolina	51,991	30,285			
Kansas	25,836	12,431	North Dakota	5,966	2,326	Total	2,444,000	1,107,606
Kentucky	39,713	17,144	Ohio	99,991	53,999	NA — Not Available		

Marriages, Divorces, and Rates in the U.S.

Source: National Center for Health Statistics, Public Health Service

Data refer only to events occurring within the United States, including Alaska and Hawaii beginning with 1960. Rates per ,000 population.

Year	Marriages[1] No.	Rate	Divorces[2] No.	Rate	Year	Marriages[1] No.	Rate	Divorces[2] No.	Rate
1890	570,000	9.0	33,461	0.5	1945	1,612,992	12.2	485,000	[3]3.5
1895	620,000	8.9	40,387	0.6	1950	1,667,231	11.1	385,144	2.6
1900	709,000	9.3	55,751	0.7	1955	1,531,000	9.3	377,000	2.3
1905	842,000	10.0	67,976	0.8	1960	1,523,000	8.5	393,000	2.2
1910	948,166	10.3	83,045	0.9	1965	1,800,000	9.3	479,000	2.5
1915	1,007,595	10.0	104,298	1.0	1970	2,158,802	10.6	708,000	3.5
1920	1,274,476	12.0	170,505	1.6	1975	2,152,662	10.0	1,036,000	4.8
1925	1,188,334	10.3	175,449	1.5	1980	2,413,000	10.6	1,182,000	5.2
1930	1,126,856	9.2	195,961	1.6	1981	2,438,000	10.6	1,219,000	5.3
1935	1,327,000	10.4	218,000	1.7	1982	2,495,000	10.8	1,180,000	5.1
1940	1,595,879	12.1	264,000	2.0	1983(p)	2,444,000	10.5	1,179,000	5.0

(1) Includes estimates and marriage licenses for some states for all years. (2) Includes reported annulments. (3) Divorce ates for 1945 based on population including armed forces overseas.

Deaths and Death Rates for Selected Causes

Source: National Center for Health Statistics. U.S. Department of Health and Human Services

1983 Cause of death (est.)	Number	Rate[1]	1983 Cause of death (est.)	Number	Rate[1]
All causes	183,259	858.2	Influenza and pneumonia	4,888	22.9
Viral hepatitis	76	0.4	Influenza	133	0.6
Tuberculosis, all forms	174	0.8	Pneumonia	4,755	22.3
Septicemia	1,221	5.7	Chronic obstructive pulmonary diseases	6,039	28.3
Syphilis and its sequelae	10	0.0	Chronic and unspecified bronchitis	318	1.5
All other infective and parasitic diseases	419	2.0	Emphysema	1,216	5.7
Malignant neoplasms, including			Asthma	303	1.4
neoplasms of lymphatic and			Ulcer of stomach and duodenum	568	2.7
hematopoietic tissues	40,319	188.8	Hernia and intestinal obstruction	478	2.2
Diabetes mellitus	3,235	15.1	Cirrhosis of liver	2,516	11.8
Meningitis	122	0.6	Cholelithiasis, cholecystitis, and cholangitis	270	1.3
Major cardiovascular diseases	88,746	415.6	Nephritis, nephrosis and nephrotic syn.	1,719	8.1
Diseases of heart	69,576	325.8	Infections of kidney	170	0.8
Rheumatic fever and			Hyperplasia of prostate	49	0.2
rheumatic heart disease	621	2.9	Congenital anomalies	1,170	5.5
Hypertensive heart disease	1,923	9.0	Certain causes of mortality in early infancy	1,765	8.3
Ischemic heart disease	49,749	233.0	Symptoms and ill-defined conditions	3,486	16.3
Acute myocardial infarction	25,750	120.6	All other diseases	11,610	54.4
All other forms of heart disease	16,337	76.5	Accidents	8,256	38.7
Hypertension	699	3.3	Motor vehicle accidents	3,902	18.3
Cerebrovascular diseases	14,229	66.6	Suicide	2,564	12.0
Artherosclerosis	2,363	11.1	Homicide	1,753	8.2
Other diseases of arteries,			All other external causes	266	1.2
arterioles, and capillaries	1,879	8.8			
Acute bronchitis and bronchiolitis	49	0.2			

Due to rounding estimates of death, figures may not add to total. Data based on a 10% sampling of all death certificates for an 11-month (Jan.-Nov.) period. (1) Rates per 100,000 population.

Principal Types of Accidental Deaths

Source: National Safety Council

Year	Motor vehicle	Falls	Fires, Burns	Drown- ing	Fire- arms	Injest of Food, Object	Poison gases	Other poisons
1965	49,163	19,984	7,347	5,485	2,344	1,973	1,526	2,110
1970	54,633	16,926	6,718	6,391	2,406	2,877	1,620	3,679
1975	45,853	14,896	6,071	6,640	2,380	3,106	1,577	4,694
1980	52,600	12,300	5,500	7,000	1,800	3,249	1,500	2,800
1981	50,800	11,700	4,900	6,000	1,900	3,200	1,700	2,600
1982	46,000	11,600	5,000	6,200	1,900	3,200	1,400	3,000
1983	44,600	11,700	4,600	6,600	1,900	3,200	1,300	3,000
Death rates per 100,000 population								
1965	25.4	10.3	3.8	2.8	1.2	1.1	0.8	1.1
1970	26.9	8.3	3.3	3.1	1.2	1.4	0.8	1.8
1975	21.5	7.0	2.8	3.1	1.1	1.1	0.7	2.2
1980	23.2	5.4	2.4	3.1	0.8	1.4	0.7	1.2
1981	22.2	5.1	2.1	2.6	0.8	1.4	0.8	1.1
1982	19.9	5.0	2.2	2.7	0.8	1.4	0.6	1.3
1983	19.1	5.0	2.0	2.8	0.8	1.4	0.6	1.3

U.S. Civil Aviation Accidents

Source: National Safety Council

1983[3]	Accidents Total	Accidents Fatal	Deaths[1]	Per 100,000 Aircraft-Hours Total	Per 100,000 Aircraft-Hours Fatal	Per million Aircraft-Miles Total	Per million Aircraft-Miles Fatal
Large airlines	18	3	14	0.275	0.046	0.007	0.001
Commuter airlines	17	2	11	1.23	0.15	0.07	0.01
On-demand air taxis	141	28	60	4.55	0.90	—	—
General aviation[2]	3,091	548	1,049	9.4	1.67	—	—

(1) Includes passengers, crew members and others. (2) Suicide and sabotage included in accident and fatality totals but excluded from rates. (3) Preliminary.

Transportation Accident Passenger Death Rates, 1982

Source: National Safety Council

Kind of transportation	Passenger miles (billions)	Passenger deaths	Rate per 100,000,000 pass. miles	1980-1982 aver. death rate
Passenger automobiles and taxis[1]	2,154.4	22,859	1.06	1.20
Buses	88.8	32	0.04	0.04
Intercity buses[2]	26.9	5	0.02	—
Railroad passenger trains	10.9	9	0.08	0.05
Scheduled air transport planes (domestic)	213.6	218	0.10	0.04

(1) Drivers of passenger automobiles are considered passengers. (2) Class 1 only, representing 65 per cent of total intercity bus passenger mileage.

Motor Vehicle Traffic Deaths by State
Source: National Safety Council

Place of accidents	Number 1983	Number 1982	Mileage Rate[b] 1983	Mileage Rate[b] 1982	Place of accidents	Number 1983	Number 1982	Mileage Rate[b] 1983	Mileage Rate[b] 1982
Total U.S.[a]	44,600	46,000	2.7	2.9					
Alabama	940	845	3.2	3.1	Montana	286	254	4.0	3.6
Alaska	150	107	3.9	3.6	Nebraska	255	261	2.1	2.2
Arizona	675	724	2.6	3.8	Nevada	252	280	3.8	4.2
Arkansas	554	550	3.2	3.2	New Hampshire	181	173	2.6	2.6
California	4,571	4,609	2.6	2.8	New Jersey	932	1,061	1.7	2.0
Colorado	644	664	2.6	2.9	New Mexico	535	575	4.3	4.9
Connecticut	445	521	2.1	1.7	New York	2,077	2,147	2.5	2.7
Delaware	112	123	2.3	2.7	North Carolina	1,240	1,320	2.8	3.1
Dist. of Col	65	36	1.8	1.1	North Dakota	116	148	2.1	2.7
Florida	2,703	2,711	3.3	3.5	Ohio	1,585	1,618	2.1	2.2
Georgia	1,296	1,227	3.1	2.7	Oklahoma	853	1,064	2.7	3.6
Hawaii	139	161	2.2	2.7	Oregon	548	518	2.7	2.6
Idaho	263	255	3.2	3.6	Pennsylvania	1,751	1,848	2.4	2.5
Illinois	1,553	1,671	2.3	2.5	Rhode Island	100	109	1.6	1.9
Indiana	1,016	964	2.5	2.4	South Carolina	845	730	3.4	3.1
Iowa	509	474	2.5	2.4	South Dakota	174	148	2.6	2.4
Kansas	411	498	2.2	283	Tennessee	1,046	1,074	2.9	3.1
Kentucky	790	836	3.0	3.3	Texas	3,823	4,271	3.0	3.5
Louisiana	942	1,093	4.3	4.3	Utah	283	296	2.5	2.7
Maine	224	163	2.8	2.1	Vermont	94	106	2.3	2.7
Maryland	663	660	2.1	2.3	Virginia	900	881	2.1	2.3
Massachusetts	643	655	1.7	1.8	Washington	705	757	2.2	2.5
Michigan	1,325	1,417	2.1	2.3	West Virginia	427	452	4.4	4.3
Minnesota	558	581	1.8	2.0	Wisconsin	735	775	2.2	2.3
Mississippi	716	728	4.1	4.2	Wyoming	173	201	3.2	3.8
Missouri	921	908	2.5	2.5					

(a) Includes both traffic and nontraffic motor-vehicle deaths. (b) The mileage death rate is deaths per 100,000,000 vehicle miles. 1983 mileage death rates are National Safety Council estimates.

Accidental Deaths and Injuries by Severity of Injury
Source: National Safety Council

In 1983 accidental deaths were estimated to number 91,000, a reduction of 3,000 or 3 percent below the 1982 total. This was the third consecutive annual decrease. The death rate per 100,000 populaton was 38.9, down 4 percent from 1982 and the lowest death rate on record.

1983 Severity of injury	Total[*]	Motor vehicle	Work	Home	Public[1]
Deaths[*]	91,000	44,600	11,300	20,000	19,500
Disabling injuries[*]	8,800,000	1,600,000	1,900,000	3,000,000	2,500,000
Permanent impairments	350,000	150,000	90,000	80,000	60,000
Temporary total disabilities	8,400,000	1,450,000	1,800,000	2,900,000	2,400,000

Certain Costs of Accidental Deaths or Injuries, 1983 ($ billions)					
Total[*]	$92.7	$43.3	$33.4	$10.0	$7.6
Wage loss	24.3	12.6	5.4	3.5	4.1
Medical expense	12.7	3.8	3.8	3.0	2.4
Insurance administration	16.6	10.0	6.4	0.1	0.1

[*]Duplication between motor vehicle, work, and home are eliminated in the total column. (1) Excludes motor vehicle and work accidents in public places.

Home Accident Deaths
Source: National Safety Council

Year	Total home	Falls	Fires, burns[2]	Suffo., ingested object	Suffo., mech-anical	Poison (solid, liquid)	Poison by gas	Fire-arms	Other
1950	29,000	14,800	5,000	(1)	1,600	1,300	1,250	950	4,100
1955	28,500	14,100	5,400	(1)	1,250	1,150	900	1,100	4,600
1960	28,000	12,300	6,350	1,850	1,500	1,350	900	1,200	2,550
1965	28,500	11,700	6,100	1,300[*]	1,200	1,700	1,100	1,300	4,100
1970	27,000	9,700	5,600	1,800	1,100	3,000	1,100	1,400	3,300
1975	25,000	8,000	5,000	1,800	800	3,700	1,000	1,300	3,400
1980	23,000	6,600	4,400	1,700	500	2,300	700	1,000	5,800[3]
1983	20,000	6,300	3,900	2,000	600	2,400	800	1,100	2,900

[*]Data for this year and subsequent years not comparable with previous years due to classification changes. (1) Included in Other. (2) Includes deaths resulting from conflagration, regardless of nature of injury. (3) Includes 1,000 excessive deaths due to summer heat wave.

Pedalcycle Accidents
Source: National Safety Council

Year	Pedalcycles (millions)	Deaths	Death Rate[a]	Percent of Deaths by Age 0-14	15-24	25 & over
1940	7.8	750	9.59	48	39	13
1950	13.8	440	3.18	82	9	9
1960	28.2	460	1.63	78	9	13
1970	56.5	780	1.38	66	15	19
1980	100.0	1,200	1.20	35	36	29
1983	105.5	1,100	1.04	42	31	27

(a) Deaths per 100,000 pedalcycles.

Average Lifetime in the U.S.

Source: National Center for Health Statistics, U.S. Department of Health and Human Services

1981 Age interval	Number living[1]	Avg. life expect.[2]	1981p Age interval	Number living[1]	Avg. life expect.[2]
0-1	100,000	74.2	40-45	95,097	37.0
1-5	98,806	74.1	45-50	93,820	32.5
5-10	98,570	70.2	50-55	91,767	28.1
10-15	98,426	65.3	55-60	88,606	24.0
15-20	98,280	60.4	60-65	83,989	20.2
20-25	97,833	55.7	65-70	77,468	16.7
25-30	97,235	51.0	70-75	68,631	13.5
30-35	96,611	46.3	75-80	57,322	10.7
35-40	95,956	41.6	80-85	43,936	8.1
			85 and over	28,778	6.1

(1) Of 100,000 born alive, number living at beginning of age interval. (2) Average number of years of life remaining at beginning of age interval.

Years of Life Expected at Birth

Year	Total pop.	White, male	White, female	Black, male	Black, female
1981	74.2	71.1	78.5	64.4	73.0
1980	73.7	70.7	78.1	63.7	72.3
1969-1971	70.8	67.9	75.5	60.0	68.3
1959-61	69.9	67.6	74.2	—	—
1900-1902[1]	49.2	48.2	51.1	32.5	35.0

[1] Based on data for death-registration states only.

Ownership of Life Insurance in the U.S. and Assets of U.S. Life Insurance Companies

Source: American Council of Life Insurance

Legal Reserve Life Insurance Companies (millions of dollars)

Year	Purchases of life insurance				Insurance in force					
	Ordinary	Group	Industrial	Total	Ordinary	Group	Industrial	Credit	Total	Assets
1940	7,022	747	3,318	11,087	79,346	14,938	20,866	380	115,530	30,802
1950	18,260	6,237	5,492	29,989	149,116	47,793	33,415	3,844	234,168	64,020
1960	56,183	15,328	6,906	78,417	341,881	175,903	39,563	29,101	586,448	119,576
1965	89,643	52,867*	7,302	149,812*	499,638	308,078	39,818	53,020	900,554	158,884
1970	134,802	65,381*	6,612	206,795*	734,730	551,357	38,644	77,392	1,402,123	207,254
1975	207,052	102,659*	6,741	316,452*	1,083,421	904,695	39,423	112,032	2,139,571	289,304
1979	329,571	157,906	5,335	492,812	1,585,878	1,419,418	37,794	179,250	3,222,340	432,282
1980	385,575	183,418	3,609	572,602	1,760,474	1,579,355	35,994	165,215	3,541,038	479,210
1981	463,843	346,351*	2,097	812,291*	1,978,080	1,888,612	34,547	162,356	4,063,595	525,803
1982R	585,444	250,532	1,898	837,874	2,216,388	2,066,361	32,766	161,144	4,476,659	588,163
1983	753,444	271,609	1,388	1,026,441	2,544,275	2,219,573	31,354	170,659	4,965,861	654,948

*Includes Servicemen's Group Life Insurance $27.4 billion in 1965, $16.8 billion in 1970, and $1.7 billion in 1975, and $45.6 billion in 1981, as well as $84.4 billion of Federal Employees' Group Life Insurance in 1981. R = Revised.

Accidental Deaths by Month and Type, 1980 and 1983

Month	1983 totals	1980 details by type								
		All types‡	Motor vehicle	Falls	Drowning†	Fires, burns*	Ingest. of food, object	Firearms	Poison (solid, liquid)	Poison by gas
All months	91,000	105,718	53,172	13,294	7,257	5,822	3,249	1,955	3,089	1,242
January	7,150	7,827	3,623	1,217	210	702	280	194	279	158
February	6,100	7,502	3,444	1,152	237	688	291	120	230	139
March	6,850	7,833	3,815	1,143	320	651	276	121	256	113
April	6,800	7,785	3,909	1,064	530	477	252	134	237	84
May	7,850	8,818	4,641	978	880	343	256	129	263	58
June	7,750	9,902	5,130	1,071	1,250	315	245	127	247	68
July	9,300	11,643	5,059	1,129	1,580	297	251	152	278	57
August	8,500	10,174	5,537	1,098	1,060	256	258	141	285	51
September	7,700	8,566	4,701	1,023	540	310	242	166	236	55
October	7,600	8,414	4,554	1,118	280	379	287	183	242	119
November	7,400	8,387	4,401	1,107	190	590	286	272	249	124
December	8,000	8,867	4,358	1,194	180	814	325	216	287	216
Average	7,580	8,810	4,431	1,108	605	485	271	163	257	104

‡ Includes some deaths not shown separately. † Includes drowning in water transport accidents. Some totals partly estimated. * Includes deaths resulting from conflagration regardless of nature of injury.

Average Height and Weight for Children

Source: Physicians Handbook, 1983.

		Boys						Girls			
Age Years	ft	Height in	cm	Weight lb	kg	Age Years	ft	Height in	cm	Weight lb	kg
(Birth)	1	8	45.7	7½	3.4	(Birth)	1	8	50.8	7½	3.4
½	2	2	66.0	17	7.7	½	2	2	66.0	16	7.2
1	2	5	73.6	21	9.5	1	2	5	73.6	20	9.1
2	2	9	83.8	26	11.8	2	2	9	83.8	25	11.3
3	3	0	91.4	31	14.0	3	3	0	91.4	30	13.6
4	3	3	99.0	34	15.4	4	3	3	99.0	33	15.0
5	3	6	106.6	39	17.7	5	3	5	104.1	38	17.2
6	3	9	114.2	46	20.9	6	3	8	111.7	45	20.4
7	3	11	119.3	51	23.1	7	3	11	119.3	49	22.2
8	4	2	127.0	57	25.9	8	4	2	127.0	56	25.4
9	4	4	132.0	63	28.6	9	4	4	132.0	62	28.1
10	4	6	137.1	69	31.3	10	4	6	137.1	69	31.3
11	4	8	142.2	77	34.9	11	4	8	142.2	77	34.9
12	4	10	147.3	83	37.7	12	4	10	147.3	86	39.0
13	5	0	152.4	92	41.7	13	5	0	152.4	98	45.5
14	5	2	157.5	107	48.5	14	5	2	157.5	107	48.5

This table gives a general picture of American children at specific ages. When used as a standard, the individual variation in children's growth should not be overlooked. In most cases the height-weight relationship is probably a more valid index of weight status than a weight-for-age assessment.

Average Weight of Americans by Height and Age

Source: Society of Actuaries; from the *1979 Build and Blood Pressure Study*
The figures represent weights in ordinary indoor clothing and shoes, and heights with shoes.

	Men							Women					
Height	20-24	25-29	30-39	40-49	50-59	60-69	Height	20-24	25-29	30-39	40-49	50-59	60-69
5'2"	130	134	138	140	141	140	4'10"	105	110	113	118	121	123
5'3"	136	140	143	144	145	144	4'11"	110	112	115	121	125	127
5'4"	139	143	147	149	150	149	5'0"	112	114	118	123	127	130
5'5"	143	147	151	154	155	153	5'1"	116	119	121	127	131	133
5'6"	148	152	156	158	159	158	5'2"	120	121	124	129	133	136
5'7"	153	156	160	163	164	163	5'3"	124	125	128	133	137	140
5'8"	157	161	165	167	168	167	5'4"	127	128	131	136	141	143
5'9"	163	166	170	172	173	172	5'5"	130	132	134	139	144	147
5'10"	167	171	174	176	177	176	5'6"	133	134	137	143	147	150
5'11"	171	175	179	181	182	181	5'7"	137	138	141	147	152	155
6'0"	176	181	184	186	187	186	5'8"	141	142	145	150	156	158
6'1"	182	186	190	192	193	191	5'9"	146	148	150	155	159	161
6'2"	187	191	195	197	198	196	5'10"	149	150	153	158	162	163
6'3"	193	197	201	203	204	200	5'11"	155	156	159	162	166	167
6'4"	198	202	206	208	209	207	6'0"	157	159	164	168	171	172

"Ideal" Weight by Height

Source: Metropolitan Insurance Companies, 1983

The figures represent weights at age 25-29 based on lowest mortality; weight is in pounds according to frame, in indoor clothing weighing 5 lbs.; heights include shoes with one-inch heels.

		Men					Women		
Height		Small Frame	Medium Frame	Large Frame	Height		Small Frame	Medium Frame	Large Frame
5'	2" ...	128-134	131-141	138-150	4'	10" ...	102-111	109-121	118-131
5'	3" ...	130-136	133-143	140-153	4'	11" ...	103-113	111-123	120-134
5'	4" ...	132-138	135-145	142-156	5'	0" ...	104-115	113-126	122-137
5'	5" ...	134-140	137-148	144-160	5'	1" ...	106-118	115-129	125-140
5'	6" ...	136-142	139-151	146-164	5'	2" ...	108-121	118-132	128-143
5'	7" ...	138-145	142-154	149-168	5'	3" ...	111-124	121-135	131-147
5'	8" ...	140-148	145-157	152-172	5'	4" ...	114-127	124-138	134-151
5'	9" ...	142-151	148-160	155-176	5'	5" ...	117-130	127-141	137-155
5'	10" ...	144-154	151-163	158-180	5'	6" ...	120-133	130-144	140-159
5'	11" ...	146-157	154-166	161-184	5'	7" ...	123-136	133-147	143-163
6'	0" ...	149-160	157-170	164-188	5'	8" ...	126-139	136-150	146-167
6'	1" ...	152-164	160-174	168-192	5'	9" ...	129-142	139-153	149-170
6'	2" ...	155-168	164-178	172-197	5'	10" ...	132-145	142-156	152-173
6'	3" ...	158-172	167-182	176-202	5'	11" ...	135-148	145-159	155-176
6'	4" ...	162-176	171-187	181-207	6'	0" ...	138-151	148-162	158-179

U.S. Deaths and Death Rates, 1981
By Region, Division, State; Race and Sex

Source: National Center for Health Statistics

Race, Sex, Area	Total Deaths Number	Rate¹	Infant Deaths (under 1 year) Number	Rate²	Race, Sex, Area	Total Deaths Number	Rate¹	Infant Deaths (under 1 year) Number	Rate²
United States...	1,977,981	862.4	43,305	11.9	Nebraska....	14,616	926.8	270	9.9
Male	1,063,772	954.5	24,452	13.1	Kansas.....	21,701	909.9	470	11.4
Female.....	914,209	775.4	18,853	10.7	**South**				
White........	1,731,233	880.3	30,478	10.5	South Atlantic ..	335,949	891.3	7,501	13.6
Male	925,490	965.1	17,411	11.7	Delaware....	5,073	849.7	123	13.4
Female.....	805,743	799.6	13,067	9.2	Maryland....	33,949	797.1	771	12.6
All other......	246,748	755.0	12,827	17.8	District of				
Male	138,282	889.4	7,041	19.2	Columbia ..	6,954	1,098.6	231	25.1
Female.....	108,466	633.0	5,786	16.3	Virginia.....	42,237	778.6	991	12.5
Black	228,560	841.7	11,757	20.0	West Virginia..	19,053	-979.1	363	13.0
Male	127,296	991.6	6,451	21.7	North Carolina.	49,236	827.2	1,101	13.1
Female.....	101,264	707.3	5,306	18.3	South Carolina.	25,428	802.1	837	16.1
Regions					Georgia.....	44,892	806.7	1,238	13.8
Northeast......	466,887	946.2	7,678	11.6	Florida......	109,127	1,075.5	1,846	13.3
North Central...	518,871	880.1	11,407	12.2	East South Central	132,664	899.7	3,054	13.2
South	666,174	866.8	16,019	13.0	Kentucky....	33,283	908.1	697	12.2
West........	326,049	737.8	8,201	10.4	Tennessee...	40,509	876.1	847	12.6
Northeast					Alabama....	35,412	903.4	799	13.0
New England ...	111,334	894.4	1,721	10.5	Mississippi ...	23,460	925.1	711	15.4
Maine......	10,387	918.4	180	10.9	West South Central	197,561	809.1	5,464	12.1
New Hampshire	7,701	821.9	131	9.7	Arkansas....	22,372	975.7	425	11.9
Vermont	4,322	839.2	61	7.7	Louisiana....	36,024	838.7	1,130	13.7
Massachusetts.	52,982	917.6	720	9.7	Oklahoma ...	28,617	921.9	637	11.9
Rhode Island..	9,174	960.6	147	11.8	Texas......	110,548	750.8	3,272	11.6
Connecticut ..	26,768	853.6	482	12.1	**West**				
Middle Atlantic ..	355,553	963.7	5,957	11.9	Mountain	80,474	687.5	2,398	10.4
New York ...	168,184	955.7	3,006	12.4	Montana	6,729	846.4	153	10.7
New Jersey ..	67,280	906.6	1,038	10.7	Idaho	6,929	723.3	181	9.2
Pennsylvania..	120,089	1,011.3	1,913	11.9	Wyoming....	3,165	645.9	115	10.6
North Central					Colorado....	19,388	651.5	519	10.0
East North Central	362,017	868.6	8,243	12.6	New Mexico ..	8,678	651.0	261	9.8
Ohio.......	96,487	894.0	2,059	12.3	Arizona.....	21,358	765.2	606	11.8
Indiana.....	47,309	-862.5	993	11.7	Utah.......	8,343	550.3	405	9.8
Illinois......	101,819	889.7	2,573	13.9	Nevada.....	5,884	695.5	158	11.2
Michigan	75,842	823.0	1,845	13.1	Pacific.......	245,575	755.8	5,803	10.3
Wisconsin ...	40,560	855.7	773	10.4	Washington ..	32,031	759.0	733	10.5
West North Central	156,854	907.8	3,164	11.1	Oregon.....	21,843	820.2	467	10.9
Minnesota ...	32,837	798.4	706	10.3	California....	184,987	764.0	4,297	10.2
Iowa.......	26,949	924.8	459	10.0	Alaska.....	1,723	414.2	128	12.7
Missouri	48,848	988.8	973	12.6	Hawaii	4,991	509.8	178	9.8
North Dakota .	5,452	826.1	139	11.2					
South Dakota .	6,451	934.9	147	11.5					

(1) Per 100,000 population in each race-sex group and area. (2) Per 1,000 live births in each race-sex group and area.

Leading Causes of Death, by Sex and Race

Source: National Center for Health Statistics

Rank (1981)	Cause of Death	Ratio of Male to Female	Ratio of Black to White	Rank (1981)	Cause of Death	Ratio of Male to Female	Ratio of Black to White
	All causes.................	1.79	1.47	6	Pneumonia and influenza	1.80	1.52
1	Diseases of heart	2.00	1.28	7	Diabetes mellitus.............	1.04	2.21
2	Malignant neoplasms, including neoplasms of lymphatic and hematopoietic tissues	1.50	1.33	8	Chronic liver disease and cirrhosis..	2.16	1.82
				9	Atherosclerosis..............	1.30	1.09
3	Cerebrovascular diseases	1.17	1.80	10	Suicide	3.15	0.52
4	Accidents and adverse effects	2.95	1.16	11	Homicide and legal intervention ...	3.88	5.89
	Motor vehicle accidents........	2.89	0.81	12	Certain conditions originating in the perinatal period	1.25	2.26
	All other accidents and adverse effects	3.02	1.64	13	Nephritis, nephrotic syndrome, and nephrosis................	1.55	2.92
5	Chronic obstructive pulmonary diseases and allied conditions.....	2.75	0.75	14	Congenital anomalies	1.09	0.98
				15	Septicemia	1.41	2.72

Leading Causes of Infant Deaths

Source: National Center for Health Statistics

Rank (1981)	Cause of Death	Number	Rate	Rank (1981)	Cause of Death	Number	Rate
	All causes...............	43,305	1,193.2	6	Intrauterine hypoxia and birth asphyxia	1,405	38.7
1	Congenital anomalies	8,914	245.6	7	Accidents and adverse effects.....	981	27.0
2	Sudden infant death syndrome.....	5,295	145.9	8	Newborn affected by complications of placenta, cord, and membranes....	977	26.9
3	Respiratory distress syndrome.....	4,319	119.0				
4	Disorders relating to short gestation and unspecified low birthweight....	3,658	100.8	9	Birth trauma	918	25.3
				10	Neonatal hemorrhage..........	909	25.0
5	Newborn affected by maternal complications of pregnancy	1,458	40.2		All other causes	14,471	398.7

Patients' Expenditures in Mental Hospitals

Source: National Institute of Mental Health

Based on reports of 280 state and county hospitals on the Jan., 1981, Inventory of Mental Health Facilities.

State	No. patients	Tot. expend. ($000)	State	No. patients	Tot. expend. ($000)	State	No. patients	Tot. expend. ($000)	State	No. patients	Tot. expend. ($000)
U.S...	132,164	4,085,765	Ida. . .	208	6,040	Mo. . .	3,053	115,125	Pa. . .	10,308	344,821
Ala. . .	2,024	49,533	Ill. . . .	4,090	171,387	Mon. .	316	10,981	R.I. . .	723	28,345
Alas. .	143	8,056	Ind . . .	2,766	71,441	Neb.. .	600	21,260	S.C. . .	3,233	65,615
Ariz.. .	328	17,733	Ia. . . .	1,139	32,726	Nev.. .	116	6,921	S.D . .	437	9,748
Ark. . .	258	12,836	Kan.. .	1,155	37,900	N.H.. .	456	22,894	Tenn..	2,614	69,247
Cal. . .	6,508	252,607	Ky. . .	554	33,544	N.J.. .	5,294	160,107	Tex...	5,709	152,891
Col. . .	1,138	40,092	La. . .	2,271	54,925	N.M.. .	227	9,701	Ut.. . .	281	8,298
Conn..	2,360	71,062	Me. . .	654	18,104	N.Y.. .	24,713	740,061	Vt.. . .	244	9,812
Del. . .	630	17,010	Md. . .	3,334	98,629	N.C.. .	3,303	100,045	Va. . .	4,982	88,092
D.C.. .	2,090	110,530	Mass..	2,648	79,180	N.D.. .	573	14,141	Wash..	1,225	33,730
Fla. . .	5,385	113,415	Mich..	4,464	218,469	Oh. . .	5,915	183,984	W.Va..	1,746	20,094
Ga. . .	4,241	138,997	Minn..	2,325	62,616	Okla..	1,240	42,202	Wis.. .	856	41,169
Ha. . .	239	7,746	Miss. .	1,767	28,300	Ore...	1,011	25,882	Wy.. .	261	7,721

Patient Care Episodes in Mental Health Facilities

Source: National Institute of Mental Health

Year	Total all facilities[1]	State & county mental hospitals	Private mental[2] hospitals	Inpatient services Gen. hosp. psychiatric service (non-VA)	VA psychiatric inpatient services[3]	Federally assisted comm. men. health cen.	Outpatient services Federally assisted comm. men. health cen.	Other
1979	[4] 6,403,915	[4] 518,695	184,919	[4] 571,725	[4] 217,507	[4] 298,897	1,949,602	[4] 2,652,570
1977	6,392,979	574,226	184,189	571,725	217,507	266,966	1,741,729	2,834,637
1975	6,409,477	598,993	165,327	565,696	214,264	246,891	1,584,968	3,033,308
1969	3,572,822	767,115	123,850	535,493	186,913	65,000	291,148	1,603,303
1965	2,636,525	804,926	125,428	519,328	115,843	—	—	1,071,000
1955	1,675,352	818,832	123,231	265,934	88,355	—	—	379,000

(1) In order to present trends on the same set of facilities over this interval, it has been necessary to exclude from this table the following: private psychiatric office practice; psychiatric service modes of all types in hospitals or outpatient clinics of federal agencies other than the VA (e.g., Public Health Service, Indian Health Service, Department of Defense Bureau of Prisons, etc.); inpatient service modes of multiservice facilities not shown in this table; all partial care episodes, and outpatient episodes of VA hospitals. (2) Includes estimates of episodes of care in residential treatment centers for emotionally disturbed children. (3) Includes Veterans Administration neuropsychiatric hospitals and Veterans Administration general hospitals with separate psychiatric inpatient settings. (4) Since 1979 data are *not* available for Veterans Administration neuropsychiatric hospital inpatient units, general hospital inpatient psychiatric units (V.A. and non-Federal), and federally funded community mental health center (CMHCs) inpatient and outpatient services, data are shown for 1978 for CMHCs and for 1977 for V.A. psychiatric inpatient settings and for separate psychiatric inpatient and outpatient services of non-Federal general hospitals.

Legal Abortions in the U.S.

Source: Centers for Disease Control, U.S. Department of Health and Human Services

Legal abortions, according to selected characteristics of the patient.

	1974	1975	1976	1978	1979	1980	1981
Number	763,476	854,853	988,267	1,157,776	1,251,921	1,297,606	1,300,760
Age Characteristic				Percent distribution			
Under 20 years.	32.7	33.1	32.1	30.0	30.0	29.2	28.0
20-24 years.	31.8	31.9	33.3	35.0	35.4	35.5	35.3
25 years and over	35.6	35.0	34.6	34.9	34.6	35.3	36.7
Marital status							
Married	27.4	26.1	24.6	26.4	24.7	23.1	22.1
Unmarried.	72.6	73.9	75.4	73.6	75.3	76.9	77.9
Number of living children							
0	47.8	47.1	47.7	56.6	58.1	58.4	58.3
1	19.6	20.2	20.7	19.2	19.1	19.5	19.7
2	14.8	15.5	15.4	14.1	13.8	13.7	13.7
3	8.7	8.7	8.3	5.9	5.5	5.3	5.3
4	4.5	4.4	4.1	4.2*	3.5	3.2	3.0
5 or more	4.5	4.2	3.7	—	—	—	—
Location of abortion facility							
In state of residence	86.6	89.2	90.0	93.8	90.1	92.6	92.5
Out of state of residence	13.4	10.8	10.0	6.2	9.9	7.4	7.5
Period of gestation							
Under 8 weeks	42.6	44.6	47.0	53.2	52.1	51.7	51.2
9-10 weeks	28.7	28.4	28.0	26.9	27.0	26.2	26.8
11-12 weeks	15.4	14.9	14.4	12.3	12.5	12.2	12.1
13-15 weeks	5.5	5.0	4.5	4.0	4.2	5.2	5.2
16-20 weeks	6.5	6.1	5.1	3.7	3.4	3.9	3.7
21 weeks and over	1.2	1.0	0.9	0.9	0.9	0.9	1.0

*Beginning with 1978, 4 or more.

Handicapped Persons in the United States

Source: National Center for Health Statistics

Rate per 1,000 adults, 1979 Sex and Age Both Sexes	Needs Help in 1 or more Basic Activities	Walking	Going Outside	Bathing	Dressing	Using the Toilet	Getting In or Out of Bed or Chair	Eating
Total	22.5	16.1	13.7	9.1	7.1	5.5	4.9	2.0
18-44	5.1	3.6	2.6	1.7	1.8	1.4	1.3	0.6
45-64	20.6	13.7	10.2	7.3	7.2	4.3	4.8	1.8
45-54	13.3	8.9	6.6	4.0	5.8	2.8	3.7	*1.0
55-64	28.6	19.0	14.1	11.1	8.8	6.0	6.0	2.8
65-74	52.6	39.2	34.2	20.4	14.4	11.6	9.0	3.9
75 Years and Over	157.0	115.9	109.3	73.1	48.3	42.3	34.5	13.8
75-84	114.0	83.6	73.5	50.7	32.9	28.4	25.8	8.4
85 Years and Over	348.4	259.7	269.8	172.9	116.6	104.9	72.5	37.6
Male								
Total	19.5	14.5	10.1	7.9	6.3	4.5	3.9	2.0
18-44	5.7	4.3	2.3	1.9	1.8	1.5	1.1	*0.6
45-64	20.4	15.4	9.3	7.0	7.0	4.4	4.7	2.3
45-54	13.6	10.7	6.8	3.8	5.5	*2.9	3.4	*0.3
55-64	28.0	20.5	12.2	10.5	8.7	6.0	6.1	4.0
65-74	49.4	37.7	28.0	22.8	14.3	12.0	8.0	*5.2
75 Years and Over	136.1	96.1	82.3	63.4	45.2	30.7	27.5	11.9
75-84	101.7	73.5	52.6	45.6	31.3	22.0	20.1	*7.3
85 Years and Over	301.7	204.8	225.3	149.0	111.7	72.6	*63.3	*33.5
Female								
Total	25.1	17.6	16.9	10.1	7.8	6.3	5.7	2.0
18-44	4.6	3.0	2.8	1.6	1.8	1.3	1.5	*0.6
45-64	20.8	12.2	11.0	7.7	7.4	4.3	5.0	*1.4
45-54	12.9	7.2	6.5	4.0	6.0	*2.7	4.1	*1.1
55-64	29.3	17.6	15.9	11.6	9.0	6.0	5.9	*1.6
65-74	55.0	40.2	38.8	18.6	14.5	11.3	9.8	*2.8
75 Years and Over	169.2	127.8	125.3	78.8	50.1	49.1	38.6	14.9
75-84	121.4	89.7	86.2	53.7	34.1	32.0	29.2	9.1
85 Years and Over	372.0	289.7	292.7	185.5	118.1	122.0	78.4	39.7

*Figure does not meet standards of reliability or precision.

Surgery in Short-Stay Hospitals 1971-1981

Source: National Center For Health Statistics

Sex and Type of Operation	Number of Operations (mil.)						Rate Per 1,000 Population					
	1971	1975	1978	1979	1980	1981	1971	1975	1978	1979	1980	1981
Total	15.77	20.04	20.75	23.86	24.49	25.62	77.0	93.7	94.1	107.0	108.6	112.6
Male	6.16	7.37	7.83	8.18	8.50	8.77	62.4	71.4	73.6	76.0	78.1	79.8
Operations on the musculoskeletal system	1.07	1.34	1.47	1.53	1.54	1.56	10.8	13.0	13.8	14.2	14.2	14.1
Operations on the cardiovascular system	.30	.52	.71	.70	.80	.89	3.0	5.1	6.7	6.5	7.4	8.1
Biopsy	.24	.35	.45	.51	.55	.55	2.4	3.4	4.2	4.7	5.0	5.0
Repair of inguinal hernia	.44	.48	.45	.45	.48	.46	4.9	4.7	4.2	4.2	4.4	4.2
Operations on the eye	.25	.33	.37	.40	.45	.51	2.6	3.2	3.5	3.7	4.1	4.6
Prostatectomy	.21	.27	.30	.29	.34	.35	2.1	2.6	2.8	2.7	3.1	3.2
Tonsillectomy with or without adenoidectomy	.45	.30	.23	.22	.20	.19	4.5	2.9	2.2	2.0	1.8	1.7
Cardiac catheterization	.06	.13	.21	.20	.23	.27	.6	1.2	2.0	1.8	2.1	2.5
Appendectomy	.16	.16	.15	.16	.15	.17	1.7	1.5	1.4	1.5	1.3	1.6
Female	9.59	12.66	12.92	15.68	15.99	16.85	90.4	114.6	113.3	136.0	137.1	143.1
Operations on the female genital organs	2.79	3.89	3.82	4.23	4.26	4.22	26.3	35.2	33.5	36.7	36.5	35.8
Diagnostic dilation and curettage of uterus	.77	.98	.97	.94	.92	.83	7.3	8.8	8.5	8.1	7.9	7.1
Hysterectomy	.57	.73	.64	.64	.65	.67	5.4	6.6.	5.6	5.5	5.6	5.7
Bilateral destruction or occlusion of Fallopian tubes	.21	.37	.55	.61	.64	.65	2.0	3.3	4.9	5.3	5.5	5.5
Obstetrical procedures	.97	1.25	1.47	3.47	3.80	3.93	9.2	11.3	12.9	30.1	30.9	33.4
Cesarean section	.19	.33	.51	.60	.62	.70	1.8	3.0	4.5	5.2	5.3	6.0
Operations on the musculoskeletal system	.88	1.26	1.36	1.38	1.49	1.63	8.3	11.4	11.9	12.0	12.7	13.8
Biopsy	.52	.75	.73	.82	.80	.86	4.9	6.8	6.4	7.1	6.9	7.3
Operations on the eye	.31	.42	.51	.55	.60	.73	2.9	3.8	4.5	4.7	5.1	6.2
Cholecystectomy	.29	.34	.32	.33	.34	.35	2.7	3.1	2.8	2.8	2.9	3.0
Appendectomy	.15	.16	.15	.15	.15	.14	1.4	1.4	1.3	1.3	1.2	1.2
Tonsillectomy with or without adenoidectomy	.52	.39	.32	.29	.27	.27	4.9	3.5	2.8	2.5	2.3	2.3

Hospitals, Units, and Beds

Source: Hospital Statistics, 1983 © 1982 by American Hospital Association

General Medical and Surgical

Area	Hospitals Reporting	Adult Hospitals Number	Adult Beds	Adult Units Number	Adult Beds	Pediatric Hospitals Number	Pediatric Beds	Pediatric Units Number	Pediatric Beds	Burn Care Units	Burn Care Beds
United States. . . .	6,221	5,420	708,910	199	12,117	49	5,349	2,833	51,855	136	1,386
New England. . .	332	245	36,832	26	1,400	3	393	173	3,133	7	62
Connecticut. . .	59	38	8,006	5	158	1	64	32	688	1	10
Maine	46	42	3,171	3	256	0	0	26	304	3	8
Massachusetts .	155	104	18,802	14	773	2	329	78	1,571	3	44
New Hampshire	34	29	2,503	2	27	0	0	16	212	0	0
Rhode Island . .	20	15	2,861	2	186	0	0	11	239	0	0
Vermont.	18	17	1,489	0	0	0	0	10	119	0	0
Middle Atlantic. .	716	573	115,272	37	3,063	4	500	412	9,379	22	197
New Jersey. . .	122	94	21,397	7	399	1	16	79	2,042	2	22
New York. . . .	305	253	53,369	19	2,100	0	0	177	4,632	12	96
Pennsylvania . .	289	228	40,506	11	584	3	484	156	2,705	8	79
South Atlantic . .	890	760	118,807	28	2,137	7	549	395	8,258	15	152
Delaware	14	9	1,796	0	0	0	0	8	212	0	0
District of Columbia	17	12	4,341	1	82	1	81	5	173	1	10
Florida.	219	197	35,241	6	423	3	226	82	2,006	4	38
Georgia	153	135	17,119	3	126	2	160	62	1,046	3	44
Maryland	75	56	11,736	4	662	0	0	37	931	1	10
North Carolina .	150	132	17,641	8	600	0	0	62	1,259	3	32
South Carolina .	71	58	6,958	2	37	0	0	33	573	0	0
Virginia	122	96	18,084	3	182	1	82	60	1,211	3	18
West Virginia . .	69	65	7,891	1	25	0	0	46	847	0	0
East North Central	995	875	134,748	25	1,432	7	1,276	577	11,632	28	282
Illinois	263	238	41,390	5	257	1	203	162	3,918	7	59
Indiana	121	108	16,848	5	294	0	0	67	1,545	3	23
Michigan	224	196	26,584	10	650	1	198	152	2,392	8	83
Ohio	226	194	35,781	4	176	4	751	118	2,462	8	97
Wisconsin	161	139	14,143	1	55	1	124	78	1,215	2	20
East South Central	508	480	55,057	9	415	4	396	174	3,134	7	48
Alabama	132	120	14,364	2	66	1	119	48	722	2	9
Kentucky	106	98	11,442	0	0	0	0	47	954	2	12
Mississippi . . .	117	112	10,277	2	113	0	0	31	592	1	16
Tennessee . . .	153	130	18,974	5	236	3	277	48	866	2	11
West North Central	824	765	65,053	20	564	7	624	330	4,380	13	124
Iowa	125	117	9,829	4	122	0	0	55	882	2	16
Kansas	135	128	9,421	4	74	0	0	34	623	2	20
Minnesota. . . .	172	161	13,219	3	72	2	126	77	944	3	43
Missouri	165	146	20,164	6	188	3	390	65	947	5	33
Nebraska	100	92	6,622	2	55	2	108	33	357	1	12
North Dakota . .	59	56	2,805	0	0	0	0	35	334	0	0
South Dakota. .	68	65	2,993	1	53	0	0	31	293	0	0
West South Central	788	704	79,350	20	1,868	6	689	227	4,419	16	213
Arkansas	81	77	8,521	1	82	1	103	20	279	1	9
Louisiana	121	108	13,294	2	417	0	0	40	896	4	31
Oklahoma. . . .	123	113	9,913	5	154	0	0	37	692	3	55
Texas	464	406	47,622	12	1,215	5	586	130	2,552	8	118
Mountain	430	361	28,798	11	355	3	173	222	2,519	7	76
Arizona	76	69	7,247	1	28	0	0	44	678	2	29
Colorado	95	81	8,215	6	205	1	70	40	635	2	13
Idaho	49	45	2,210	0	0	0	0	17	143	0	0
Montana.	64	63	2,267	0	0	1	20	40	291	0	0
Nevada	23	20	1,777	1	40	0	0	12	140	1	9
New Mexico . .	56	50	3,020	1	25	0	0	35	367	1	13
Utah	36	34	2,745	0	0	1	83	19	234	1	12
Wyoming	31	29	1,317	2	57	0	0	15	131	0	0
Pacific.	737	647	72,995	23	883	8	749	323	5,012	21	211
Alaska.	25	24	896	0	0	0	0	14	146	2	11
California	505	438	54,703	19	750	6	574	224	3,838	15	142
Hawaii.	21	16	1,681	1	68	0	0	7	154	0	0
Oregon	77	70	6,861	1	11	0	0	29	299	1	12
Washington. . .	109	99	8,854	2	54	2	175	49	575	3	46

Selected Statistics on State and County Mental Hospitals

Source: National Institute of Mental Health

Year	Total admitted	Net releases	Deaths in hospital	Residents end of year	Expense per patient[1]
1955	178,033	NA	44,384	558,922	$1,116.59
1960	234,791	NA	49,748	535,540	1,702.41
1970	393,174	394,627	30,804	338,592	5,435.38
1975	376,156	391,345	13,401	193,436	13,634.53
1977	414,703	408,667*	9,716	159,523	NA
1978	406,407	NA	9,080	153,544	NA
1979	383,323	NA	7,830	140,423	NA
1980	370,344	NA	6,800	132,164	NA

*Includes estimates. NA-not available. (p)-provisional data. (1) Per average daily resident patient population.

Vital Statistics — Doctors; Expenditures; Accidental Deaths

Active Federal and Non-Federal Doctors (M.D.s) by State

Source: AMA Physician Masterfile, 1981. Special Tabulations, Division of Survey and Data Resources, American Medical Association, Chicago, 1983 (Dec. 31, 1981).

	Total	Fed.	Non-fed.		Total	Fed.	Non-fed.		Total	Fed.	Non-fed.
Total physicians..	485,123	19,862	465,261	Kentucky . . .	5,445	163	5,282	Oregon	5,465	130	5,335
Alabama . . .	5,469	240	5,229	Louisiana . . .	7,292	252	7,040	Pennsylvania .	24,864	417	24,447
Alaska	669	156	513	Maine	2,013	73	1,940	Puerto Rico. .	4,331	145	4,216
Arizona . . .	6,199	353	5,846	Maryland . . .	13,898	1,810	12,088	Rhode Island .	2,197	59	2,138
Arkansas . . .	3,195	135	3,060	Mass.	17,310	353	16,957	South Carolina	4,809	282	4,527
California. . .	63,163	2,530	60,633	Michigan . . .	16,000	242	15,758	South Dakota	925	72	853
Canal Zone. .	27	17	10	Minnesota . .	8,529	157	8,372	Tennessee . .	7,955	263	7,692
Colorado . . .	6,563	399	6,164	Mississippi . .	3,127	234	2,893	Texas	25,298	1,632	23,666
Connecticut .	8,602	169	8,433	Missouri. . . .	8,842	229	8,613	Utah.	2,704	82	2,622
Delaware. . .	1,110	50	1,060	Montana . . .	1,203	60	1,143	Vermont . . .	1,278	37	1,241
Wash., D.C. .	4,171	612	3,559	Nebraska. . .	2,563	72	2,491	Virginia	10,896	875	10,021
Florida	22,258	833	21,425	Nevada	1,357	65	1,292	Virgin Islands .	96	3	93
Georgia. . . .	8,976	581	8,395	N.H.	1,826	58	1,768	Washington. .	8,813	557	8,256
Hawaii	2,396	258	2,138	New Jersey .	15,732	302	15,430	West Virginia .	2,987	126	2,861
Idaho	1,198	48	1,150	New Mexico .	2,427	178	2,249	Wisconsin. . .	8,276	154	8,122
Illinois	22,997	557	22,440	New York. . .	51,590	956	50,634	Wyoming . . .	661	43	618
Indiana	7,726	125	7,601	North Carolina	10,117	455	9,662	Pacific Islands	88	2	86
Iowa.	4,039	82	3,957	North Dakota.	1,009	51	958	Outside U.S. Address			
Kansas	4,156	175	3,981	Ohio.	19,469	493	18,976	unknown . . .	5,213	80	5,133
				Oklahoma . .	4,402	208	4,194				

U.S. Health Expenditures

Source: Health Care Financing Administration, U.S. Department of Health and Human Services

	1960	1965	1970	1975	1979	1980	1981	1982
Total (billions)	$26.9	$41.7	$74.7	$132,7	$215.0	$249.0	$286.6	$322.4
Type of expenditure								
Health services and supplies.	25.2	38.2	69.3	124.3	204.5	237.1	273.5	308.3
Hospital care.	9.1	13.9	27.8	52.1	86.1	100.4	118.0	135.5
Physician services.	5.7	8.5	14.3	24.9	40.2	46.8	54.8	61.8
Dentist services	2.0	2.8	4.7	8.2	13.3	15.4	17.3	19.5
Nursing home care	.5	2.1	4.7	10.1	17.6	20.6	24.2	27.3
Other professional services	.9	1.0	1.6	2.6	4.7	5.6	6.4	7.1
Drugs and drug sundries	3.7	5.2	8.0	11.9	17.2	19.3	21.3	22.4
Eyeglasses and appliances.	.8	1.2	1.9	3.2	4.6	5.1	5.7	5.7
Expenses for prepayment and administration	1.1	1.7	2.7	4.4	9.3	10.7	11.1	12.7
Gov't public health activities	.4	.8	1.4	3.2	6.2	7.0	7.7	8.6
Other health services	1.1	1.1	2.1	3.7	5.1	6.0	6.9	7.6
Research and medical facilities construction	1.7	3.5	5.4	8.4	10.5	11.8	13.1	14.1
Research.	.7	1.5	2.0	3.3	4.8	5.3	5.7	5.9
Construction.	1.0	2.0	3.4	5.1	5.7	6.5	7.5	8.2

Accidental Deaths by Age, Sex, and Type, 1980

Source: National Safety Council

	All types[a]	Motor vehicle	Falls	Drowning[b]	Fires, burns[c]	Ingest. of food, object	Fire-arms	Poison (solid, liquid)	Poison by gas	% Male all types
All ages	105,718	53,172	13,294	7,257	5,822	3,249	1,955	3,089	1,242	70%
Under 5.	4,479	1,426	155	803	846	407	45	73	32	59%
5 to 14.	5,224	2,747	89	856	478	58	271	33	19	68%
15 to 24.	26,206	19,040	515	2,278	564	127	702	522	320	79%
25 to 44.	26,772	16,133	1,066	1,858	1,017	340	604	1,372	417	79%
45 to 64.	18,140	8,022	2,116	902	1,245	726	233	650	275	72%
65 to 74.	8,997	2,991	1,840	307	749	594	61	218	83	62%
75 & over.	15,950	2,813	7,513	253	923	997	39	221	96	46%
Male.	74,180	38,861	7,036	6,121	3,565	1,889	1,686	1,953	937	
Female	31,538	14,311	6,258	1,136	2,257	1,360	269	1,136	305	
Percent male	70%	73%	53%	84%	61%	58%	86%	63%	75%	

(a) Includes some deaths not shown separately. (b) Includes drowning in water transport accidents. (c) Includes deaths resulting from conflagration regardless of nature of injury.

Canadian Motor Vehicle Traffic Deaths

Source: Statistics Canada

Province	1981	1982[1]	Province	1981	1982[1]
Newfoundland.	59	57	Saskatchewan	262	240
Prince Edward Island	21	16	Alberta	700	502
Nova Scotia	165	170	British Columbia.	859	601
New Brunswick	188	204	Yukon	14	3
Quebec	1,464	1,082	Northwest Territories	8	5
Ontario.	1,445	1,138	Total.	5,383	4,169
Manitoba.	198	151			

(1) Preliminary.

Federal Bureau of Investigation

The Federal Bureau of Investigation (FBI) is the investigative arm of the Department of Justice, and is located at 9th Street and Pennsylvania Avenue, Northwest, Washington, D.C. 20535. It investigates all violations of Federal law except those specifically assigned to some other agency by legislative action, such violations including counterfeiting, and internal revenue, postal, and customs violations. It also investigates espionage, sabotage, treason, and other matters affecting internal security, as well as kidnaping, transportation of stolen goods across state lines, and violations of the Federal bank and atomic energy laws.

The FBI's Identification Division houses the largest fingerprint repository in the world, with over 175 million fingerprint cards on file. The file is utilized by law enforcement and other governmental authorities throughout the nation to identify persons having arrest records. The file is also available for humanitarian purposes, such as the identification of persons suffering from amnesia and the victims of major disasters.

The FBI has 59 field divisions in the principal cities of the country. (Consult telephone directories for locations and phone numbers.)

An applicant for the position of Special Agent of the FBI must be a citizen of the U.S., at least 23 and under 35 years old, and a graduate of an accredited law school or of an accredited college or university with a major in accounting. In addition, applicants with a four-year degree from an accredited college or university with a major in other academic areas may qualify with three additional years of full-time work experience. Specialized need areas include languages, science, and financial analysis. Those appointed to the Special Agent position must complete an initial training period of 15 weeks at the FBI Academy, Quantico, Virginia.

William H. Webster, a Federal Appeals Court judge from St. Louis, was sworn in as FBI Director for a ten-year term on February 23, 1978. He replaced Clarence M. Kelley.

U.S. Crime Reports

Source: Federal Bureau of Investigation

Offense	Number 1983	% Change over[1] 1982	1974
Murder	19,310	−8.8	−15.3
Forcible Rape	78,920	−1.2	+28.6
Robbery	500,220	−9.4	+2.2
Aggravated Assault	639,530	−3.4	+26.6
Burglary	3,120,800	−10.2	−7.2
Larceny-theft	6,707,000	−7.0	+15.1
Motor Vehicle theft	1,004,400	−6.1	−7.1

[1] Percent by which the rate of crime per 100,000 population changed in 1983 as compared with 1982 and 1974.

Households Touched by Crime

Source: Bureau of Justice Statistics

	1983 Number of households	1983 Percent	1982 Number of households	1982 Percent	Change 1982-83[2]
Households touched by					
All crimes	23,621,000	27.4	24,989,000	29.3	−7
Violent crime	4,400,000	5.1	4,776,000	5.6	−9
Rape	128,000	0.1	136,000	0.2	−6
Robbery	981,000	1.1	1,196,000	1.4	−19
Assault	3,620,000	4.2	3,835,000	4.5	−7
Aggravated	1,301,000	1.5	1,415,000	1.7	−9
Simple	2,568,000	3.0	2,712,000	3.2	−6
Larceny	16,983,000	19.7	17,835,000	20.9	−6
Personal	11,230,000	13.0	11,821,000	13.9	−6
With contact	533,000	0.6	574,000	0.7	−7
Without contact	10,836,000	12.6	11,381,000	13.4	−6
Household	7,706,000	8.9	8,181,000	9.6	−7
Burglary	5,268,000	6.1	5,865,000	6.9	−11
Motor vehicle theft	1,193,000	1.4	1,358,000	1.6	−13
Crimes of high concern[1]	7,681,000	8.9	8,521,000	10.0	−11
Total	**86,146,000**	**100.0%**	**85,178,000**	**100.0%**	**—**

(1) Rape, robbery, assault by strangers, burglary

Percent of Households Touched by Crime, by Selected Characteristics

Source: Bureau of Justice Statistics

Crime	Race of Head White 26.9%	Race of Head Black 31.8%	Annual Family Income Low Under $7,500 24.7%	Annual Family Income Medium $7,500—$14,999 25.9%	Annual Family Income Medium $15,000—$24,999 27.9%	Annual Family Income High $25,000 or more 32.4%	Urban 32.5%	Residence Suburban 28.4%	Rural 21.6%
Violent crime	4.9	6.5	5.9	4.9	4.9	5.3	6.5	5.2	3.7
Rape	0.1	0.2	0.3	0.1	0.1	0.1	0.2	0.1	0.2
Robbery	1.0	2.3	1.6	1.2	1.1	0.9	2.1	0.9	0.5
Assault	4.1	4.7	4.5	4.0	4.0	4.6	4.8	4.5	3.3
Aggravated	1.4	2.5	1.8	1.6	1.4	1.4	2.0	1.5	1.1
Simple	3.0	2.5	3.1	2.7	2.9	3.5	3.2	3.3	2.4
Property crime									
Personal larceny	13.0	13.1	9.1	10.9	13.7	18.3	14.8	14.3	9.9
Burglary	5.8	8.5	8.2	6.0	5.4	5.6	8.0	5.8	4.7
Household larceny	8.8	10.1	8.7	9.4	9.2	9.3	10.9	8.8	7.4
Motor vehicle theft	1.3	2.1	1.1	1.3	1.6	1.6	2.1	1.4	0.7
Serious violent crime[1]	2.4	4.6	3.4	2.7	2.5	2.3	4.0	2.4	1.7
Crimes of high concern[2]	8.6	11.7	10.7	8.6	8.2	8.9	11.9	8.8	6.3
Total larceny[3]	19.6	20.4	15.7	18.3	20.6	24.9	22.3	20.9	16.0

(1) Rape, robbery, aggravated assault (2) Rape, robbery, assault by stranger, burglary (3) Personal larceny, household larceny.

U.S. Crime Rate Down in 1983

The number of serious crimes reported to the police in the U.S. fell 7 percent in 1983, according to the F.B.I. Uniform Crime Reports. There were drops in all 7 major crimes, in every region, and in communities of all sizes. There had been a 3 percent decline in 1982—the first significant decrease since 1977. The 1981-1983 drop was the first significant two-year decline since 1960.

According to the Bureau of Justice Statistics, the proportion of U.S. households touched by a crime of violence or theft fell in 1983 to 27% from the 1982 level of 29%. This was the lowest level in the 9-year period for which data were available. The percent of households touched by crime had been declining slowly since 1975, but the 1982-83 drop was the largest year-to-year decline to date. The percentage of households victimized fell substantially in 1983 for virtually every type of crime.

Still, a substantial proportion of Americans felt the impact of serious crime in 1983. One household in five was the victim of personal or household larceny, and one in 10 either suffered a burglary or had a member who was the victim of a violent crime committed by a stranger.

Changes in Victimization, 1982–83

Source: Bureau of Justice Statistics

Personal sector	1982	1983ᴾ	% change	1982	1983	% change
Crimes of violence	6,459	5,891	−8.8	34.3	30.9	−9.8
Rape	153	162	5.9	0.8	0.9	4.9
Completed rape	46	68	47.8	0.3	0.4	48.0
Attempted rape	106	97	−8.5	0.6	0.5	−8.9
Robbery	1,334	1,092	−18.1	7.1	5.7	19.1
Robbery with injury	414	395	−4.6	2.2	2.1	−5.9
From serious assault	213	193	−9.4	1.1	1.0	−10.6
From minor assault	202	203	0.5	1.1	1.1	−0.9
Robbery without injury	919	701	−23.7	4.9	3.7	−24.4
Assault	4,973	4,648	−6.5	26.4	24.4	−7.6
Aggravated assault	1,754	1,577	−10.1	9.3	8.3	−11.1
With injury	587	575	−2.0	3.1	3.0	−3.2
Attempted with weapon	1,167	1,003	−14.1	6.2	5.3	−15.0
Simple assault	3,219	3,070	−4.6	17.1	16.1	−5.7
With injury	859	805	−6.3	4.6	4.2	−7.2
Attempted without weapon	2,360	2,265	−4.0	12.5	11.9	−5.0
Crimes of theft	15,553	14,450	−7.1	82.5	75.8	−8.1
Personal larceny with contact	577	515	−10.7	3.1	2.7	−11.8
Purse snatching	177	143	−19.2	1.0	0.8	−20.0
Completed purse snatching	131	93	−29.0	0.7	0.5	−30.0
Attempted purse snatching	46	53	15.2	0.3	0.3	12.0
Pocket picking	399	372	−6.8	2.1	2.0	−8.0
Personal larceny without contact	14,976	13,937	−6.9	79.5	73.1	−8.0
Total population 12 and over	**188,497**	**190,586**	**1.1**			
Household sector						
Household burglary	6,663	6,137	−7.9	78.2	71.2	−8.9
Forcible entry	2,104	1,892	−10.1	24.7	22.0	−11.1
Unlawful entry without force	2,932	2,667	−9.0	34.4	31.0	−10.1
Attempted forcible entry	1,627	1,580	−2.9	19.1	18.3	−4.0
Household larceny	9,705	9,187	−5.3	113.9	106.6	−6.4
Less than $50	4,614	4,442	−3.7	54.1	51.5	−4.8
$50 or more	3,964	3,714	−6.3	46.5	43.1	−7.4
Amount not available	444	399	−10.1	5.2	4.6	−11.1
Attempted larceny	683	632	−7.5	8.0	7.3	−8.5
Motor vehicle theft	1,377	1,215	−11.8	16.2	14.1	−12.8
Completed theft	947	819	−13.5	11.1	9.5	−14.4
Attempted theft	430	394	−8.4	5.1	4.6	−9.5
Total households	**85,211**	**86,179**	**1.1**			

P= Preliminary. Rates based on number of victimizations per 1,000 persons aged 12 and over (personal sector) or per 1,000 households (household sector).

Violent Victimizations Not Reported to Police

Source: Bureau of Justice Statistics

Reasons for nonreporting	Related Offenders	Unrelated Offenders	Reasons for nonreporting	Related Offenders	Unrelated Offenders
Private or personal matter	59%	23%	Not important enough	7%	28%
Fear of reprisal	13	5	Reported to someone else	5	15
Nothing could be done, lack of proof	8	19	Did not want to get involved	1	3
Police would not want to be bothered	8	8	Too inconvenient or time-consuming	1	3
			Other reasons	18	21

Note: Because some respondents gave more than one answer, the totals are greater than 100%.

Economic Loss to Crime Victims

Source: Bureau of Justice Statistics

Type of Crime	Total loss (in millions) 1981 Current dollars	Constant dollars	Median loss	Type of Crime	Total loss (in millions) 1981 Current dollars	Constant dollars	Median loss
Personal sector				1981 (538,700)	64	64	50
1981 (16,371,000)	$2,782	$2,782	$45	1980 (479,400)	43	47	39
1980 (15,270,000)	2,362	2,608	40	1975 (460,900)	34	57	30
1975 (16,378,500)	1,531	2,587	22	Personal larceny without			
Crimes of violence				contact			
1981 (1,742,500)	651	651	80	1981 (14,089,700)	2,066	2,066	40
1980 (1,493,400)	507	560	77	1980 (13,297,200)	1,812	2,000	40
1975 (1,409,300)	329	556	43	1975 (14,508,300)	1,168	1,974	20
Rape				**Household sector**			
1981 (56,100)	20	20	145	1981 (15,431,300)	8,129	8,129	65
1980 (50,600)	23	25	50	1980 (15,139,700)	7,724	8,525	60
1975 (53,700)	15	25	30	1975 (14,328,900)	4,037	6,822	40
Robbery				Burglary			
1981 (954,600)	421	421	85	1981 (5,309,000)	4,127	4,127	160
1980 (757,600)	283	312	85	1980 (4,958,300)	3,561	3,930	150
1975 (758,400)	184	311	43	1975 (4,831,000)	1,624	2,745	85
Assault				Household larceny			
1981 (731,900)	210	210	64	1981 (9,039,900)	1,249	1,249	40
1980 (685,200)	200	221	65	1980 (9,150,700)	1,310	1,446	40
1975 (597,100)	130	220	43	1975 (8,397,300)	608	1,028	20
Crimes of theft				Motor vehicle theft			
1981 (14,628,400)	2,130	2,130	40	1981 (1,082,500)	2,754	2,754	1,500
1980 (13,776,600)	1,855	2,047	40	1980 (1,030,700)	2,854	3,150	1,300
1975 (14,969,200)	1,202	2,031	20	1975 (1,100,500)	1,806	3,052	830
Personal larceny with contact							

NOTE: Because medical expenses, damage losses, and cash and theft losses can all result from a single victimization, the estimate of the number of victimizations in parentheses does not equal the sum of the entries from the tables that follow. When more than one form of loss occurred during a single victimization, the loss was summed.

Victimization Rates, 1973-83

Source: Bureau of Justice Statistics

Sector, Type of Crime	1973	1974	1975	1976	1977	1978	1979	1980	1981	1982	1983ᵖ
Personal sector											
Crimes of violence	32.6	33.0	32.8	32.6	33.9	33.7	34.5	33.3	35.3	34.3	30.9
Rape	1.0	1.0	0.9	0.8	0.9	1.0	1.1	0.9	1.0	0.8	0.9
Robbery	6.7	7.2	6.8	6.5	6.2	5.9	6.3	6.6	7.4	7.1	5.7
Assault	24.9	24.8	25.2	25.3	26.8	26.9	27.2	25.8	27.0	26.4	24.4
Aggravated	10.1	10.4	9.6	9.9	10.0	9.7	9.9	9.3	9.6	9.3	8.3
Simple	14.8	14.4	15.6	15.4	16.8	17.2	17.3	16.5	17.3	17.1	16.1
Crimes of theft	91.1	95.1	96.0	96.1	97.3	96.8	91.9	83.0	85.1	82.5	75.8
Personal larceny with contact	3.1	3.1	3.1	2.9	2.7	3.1	2.9	3.0	3.3	3.1	2.7
Personal larceny without contact	88.0	92.0	92.9	93.2	94.6	93.6	89.0	80.0	81.9	79.5	73.1
Household sector											
Household burglary	91.7	93.1	91.7	88.9	88.5	86.0	84.1	84.3	87.9	78.2	71.2
Household larceny	107.0	123.8	125.4	124.1	123.3	119.9	133.7	126.5	121.0	113.9	106.6
Motor vehicle theft	19.1	18.8	19.5	16.5	17.0	17.5	17.5	16.7	17.1	16.2	14.1

P = Preliminary.

Family Violence

The National Crime Survey (NCS), sponsored by the Bureau of Justice Statistics, collects information on criminal victimization, whether or not the event was reported to the police. Therefore, the survey provides statistical information about various aspects of family violence—but only for those events that a victim is willing to report to a crime survey. Survey findings indicate that family violence may be significantly under-reported. The figures below are estimates of the amount of family violence that people considered to be criminal and that victims chose to and were able to relate to survey interviewers. A relative of the victim was identified as the offender in 7 percent of all violent victimizations measured by the NCS during 1973-81; this represented 4.1 million violent victimizations by relatives during the 9-year period.

Reported Family Violence

Relationship	1973-81 Total	Yearly Average
Total by all relatives	4,108,000	456,000
Spouses or ex-spouses	2,333,000	259,000
Parents	263,000	29,000
Children	173,000	19,000
Brothers or sisters	351,000	39,000
Other relatives	988,000	110,000

All estimates rounded to nearest thousand.

Weapons Used in Family Violence

Type of Weapon	All Family Violence	Spousal Violence
Weapon	31%	26%
Gun	11	9
Knife	9	8
Other	10	8
Not known	3	2
No weapon or don't know	**69**	**74**

State and Federal Prison Population; Death Penalty

As of Jan. 1984

Source: Bureau of Justice Statistics, U.S. Justice Department

	Prisoners	More than a year	Sentenced per 100,000 population	Death penalty — Under sentence of death	Executions	Death penalty
Total	438,830	419,820	179	1,202	5	37
Federal institutions . . .	31,926	26,331	11	0	0	Yes
State institutions	406,904	393,489	167	1,202	0	...
Male	419,811	402,391	352	1,189	0	...
Female	19,019	17,429	14	13	0	...
Alabama	9,856	9,641	243	49	1	Yes
Alaska	1,634	1,075	219	0	0	No
Arizona	6,889	6,693	223	51	0	Yes
Arkansas	4,183	4,167	179	22	0	Yes
California	39,360	38,025	150	149	0	Yes
Colorado	3,450	3,450	109	1	0	Yes
Connecticut	5,474	3,577	114	0	0	Yes
Delaware	2,190	1,659	273	6	0	Yes
Dist. of Columbia	4,344	3,465	558	0	0	No
Florida	26,334	25,385	235	193	1	Yes
Georgia	15,347	14,929	259	102	1	Yes
Hawaii	1,731	1,065	103	0	0	No
Idaho	1,206	1,205	121	7	0	Yes
Illinois	15,595	15,522	135	64	0	Yes
Indiana	9,360	8,973	164	21	0	Yes
Iowa	2,814	2,676	92	0	0	No
Kansas	3,705	3,705	152	0	0	No
Kentucky	4,738	4,738	127	19	0	Yes
Louisiana	12,976	12,976	290	24	1	Yes
Maine	1,049	858	75	0	0	No
Maryland	12,606	11,968	277	11	0	Yes
Massachusetts	4,559	4,559	79	0	0	No
Michigan	14,382	14,382	159	0	0	No
Minnesota	2,156	2,156	52	0	0	No
Mississippi	5,586	5,481	211	37	1	Yes
Missouri	8,053	8,053	162	23	0	Yes
Montana	850	850	104	4	0	Yes
Nebraska	1,677	1,452	91	10	0	Yes
Nevada	3,200	3,200	354	23	0	Yes
New Hampshire	479	479	50	0	0	Yes
New Jersey	10,209	10,159	136	3	0	Yes
New Mexico	2,013	2,013	142	6	0	Yes
New York	30,489	30,489	172	1	0	Yes
North Carolina	15,395	14,257	233	33	0	Yes
North Dakota	410	350	51	0	0	No
Ohio	17,766	16,686	155	18	0	Yes
Oklahoma	7,487	7,096	212	39	0	Yes
Oregon	4,181	4,181	157	0	0	No
Pennsylvania	11,767	11,699	98	33	0	Yes
Rhode Island	1,157	878	92	0	0	No
South Carolina	9,583	9,076	276	28	0	Yes
South Dakota	824	807	115	0	0	Yes
Tennessee	8,768	8,768	187	31	0	Yes
Texas	35,259	35,259	221	163	0	Yes
Utah	1,275	1,262	77	4	0	Yes
Vermont	497	378	72	0	0	Yes
Virginia	10,093	9,855	177	20	0	Yes
Washington	6,701	6,701	155	0	0	Yes
West Virginia	1,628	1,628	83	0	0	No
Wisconsin	4,898	4,862	102	0	0	No
Wyoming	721	721	138	3	0	Yes

NA-figure not available

Greatest Prison Population Increases, by State

Source: Bureau of Justice Statistics

States with increases of 20% or more since 1982		States with increases of 1,000 or more since 1982		Incarceration rates of 200 or more per 100,000 U.S. population		Incarceration rates of 200 or more per 100,000 U.S. population	
North Dakota	27.3	California	4,720	Nevada	354	Florida	235
Alaska	25.1	New York	2,538	Louisiana	290	North Carolina	233
New Jersey[1]	24.6	Louisiana	2,041	Maryland	277	Arizona	223
Hawaii	20.5	New Jersey[1]	2,018	South Carolina	276	Texas	221
Kansas	20.4	Maryland	1,594	Delaware	273	Alaska	219
		Illinois	1,302	Georgia	259	Oklahoma	212
		Pennsylvania	1,245	Alabama	243	Mississippi	211

(1) New Jersey's increase affected by 1983 inclusion of inmates held in local jails because of overcrowding; these excluded from 1982 count.

Suicide Rates

Source: National Center for Health Statistics, U.S. Department of Health and Human Services

(Rates per 100,000 population)

Rates by Age Group, 1979-81				By Sex and Race, 1981		
Age Group	1981	1980	1979		Number	Rate
Total	12.0	11.9	12.1	Total	27,596	12.0
5-14 years	0.5	0.4	0.4	Male	20,809	18.7
12-24 years	12.3	12.3	12.4	Female	6,787	5.8
25-34 years	16.3	16.0	16.3	White	25,452	12.9
35-44 years	15.9	15.4	15.4	White male	19,166	20.0
45-54 years	16.1	15.9	16.5	White female	6,286	6.2
55-64 years	16.4	15.9	16.6	Black	1,658	6.1
65-74 years	16.2	16.9	17.8	Black male	1,315	10.2
75-84 years	18.6	19.1	20.8	Black female	343	2.4
85 years and over	17.7	19.2	17.9			

U.S. Fires

Source: National Fire Protection Assn.

Fires attended by the public fire service (1982 estimates)

Civilian Fire Deaths and Injuries	Deaths	Deaths	Injuries	Injuries	Structure Fires by Property Use	No. of fires	Property loss
Residential (total)	4,820	81.4	21,450	68.6	Public assembly	24,500	$354,000,000
One-and Two-Family					Educational.	11,500	103,000,000
Dwellings[1]	3,825	64.6	16,450	52.6	Institutional	23,000	14,000,000
Apartment	845	14.2	4,300	13.8	Residential	641,500	3,306,000,000
Hotels and Motels	80	1.4	450	1.4	One-/2-family dwellings[5].	523,500	2,792,000,000
Other Residential.	70	1.2	250	.8	Apartments	102,000	413,000,000
Non Residential					Hotels, motels.	9,000	64,000,000
Structures[2]	270	4.6	4,700	15.0	Other residential	7,000	37,000,000
Highway Vehicles	670	11.3	3,400	10.9	Stores and offices.	50,500	686,000,000
Other Vehicles[3]	55	.9	400	1.3	Industry, utility, defense[6] . . .	36,000	763,000,000
All Other[4]	105	1.8	1,325	4.2	Storage in structures[6].	48,000	473,000,000
					Special structures.	33,500	127,000,000
Total	5,920		31,275		Total[6].	868,500	$5,826,000,000

(1) Includes mobile homes. (2) Includes public assembly, educational, institutional, stores and offices, industry, utility, storage, and special structure properties. (3) Includes trains, boats, ships, aircraft, farm vehicles and construction vehicles. (4) Includes properties outside with value, brush, rubbish, and other. (5) Includes mobile homes. (6) The results represent only those fires reported to the NFPA.

Fire Fighters: Deaths and Injuries

Source: National Fire Protection Assn.

1982

Year	In line of duty Deaths	Injuries	% of Deaths by Cause		% of Deaths by Nature of Injury		% of Injuries by Cause		% of Injuries by Nature of Injury	
1977	134	112,540	Stress	44.4%	Heart Attack	46.1%	Exposure to		Strain, sprain	24.4%
1978	162	101,100	Falls, struck		Fracture	23.9	fire products	27.1%	Wound, cut	
1979	113	95,780	by object,		Smoke inhalation	10.2	Fell, slipped	20.5	bleeding,	
1980	134	98,070	contact with		Wound, cut,		Stepped on,		bruise	24.2
1981	123	103,340	object	24.8	bleeding	6.8	contact with		Smoke or gas	
1982	117	98,150	Structural		Electrocution	2.6	object	14.0	inhalation	17.7
1983	106	103,550	collapse	13.7	Burns & smoke		Struck by object	11.3	Other	10.9
			Exposure to		inhalation	2.6	Overexertion	10.7	Eye irritation	10.0
			fire products	8.5	Burns	2.6	Other	10.6	Burns (fire	
			Caught or		Internal injury	2.6	Exposure to		or chemical)	9.9
			trapped	7.7	Drowning	1.7	chemicals,		Dislocation,	
			Exposure to		Inhalation of		radiation	4.5	fracture	2.6
			chemicals	0.9	non-fire gases	0.9	Caught or trapped	1.3		

Police Roster
Source: Uniform Crime Reports

Police officers and civilian employees in large cities as of Oct. 31, 1982

City	Officer	Civilian	City	Officer	Civilian	City	Officer	Civilian
Anchorage, Alas. . .	263	83	Indianapolis, Ind. . .	937	315	Phoenix, Ariz.	1,621	694
Atlanta, Ga.	1,340	283	Jacksonville, Fla. . .	903	664	Pittsburgh, Pa. . . .	1,278	130
Baltimore, Md. . . .	3,056	525	Kansas City, Mo. . .	1,145	527	Portland, Ore.	699	190
Birmingham, Ala. . .	659	138	Little Rock, Ark. . . .	301	77	Rochester, N.Y. . . .	603	127
Boston, Mass.	1,737	392	Los Angeles, Cal. . .	6,861	2,441	Sacramento, Cal. . .	504	199
Bridgeport, Conn. . .	349	18	Louisville, Ky.	682	188	St. Louis, Mo.	1,808	543
Buffalo, N.Y.	1,034	112	Memphis, Tenn. . . .	1,200	298	St. Petersburg, Fla. .	401	208
Chicago, Ill.	12,562	2,463	Miami, Fla.	979	346	San Antonio, Tex. . .	1,132	258
Cincinnati, Oh. . . .	991	154	Milwaukee, Wis. . . .	2,087	305	San Diego, Cal. . . .	1,395	491
Cleveland, Oh. . . .	1,947	331	Minneapolis, Minn. .	690	92	San Francisco, Cal.	1,971	508
Columbus, Oh. . . .	1,216	337	Newark, N.J.	1,166	246	San Jose, Cal. . . .	891	206
Dallas, Tex.	1,996	573	New Orleans, La. . .	1,355	503	Santa Ana, Cal. . . .	310	157
Denver, Col. . . . . ⤳	1,388	303	New York, N.Y. . . .	22,855	5,876	Seattle, Wash. . . .	1,007	371
Detroit, Mich.	4,092	613	Norfolk, Va.	590	73	Stockton, Cal.	239	115
Ft. Worth, Tex. . . .	719	233	Oakland, Cal.	625	278	Tampa, Fla.	660	194
Fresno, Cal.	354	159	Oklahoma City, Ok.	767	216	Toledo, Oh.	655	40
Hartford, Conn. . . .	439	109	Omaha, Neb.	572	159	Tucson, Ariz.	557	182
Honolulu, Ha.	1,549	346	Pasadena, Cal. . . .	182	112	Washington, D.C. . .	3,861	524
Houston, Tex.	3,345	1,074	Philadelphia, Pa. . .	7,377	904	Wichita, Kan.	446	152

Law Enforcement Officers
Source: F.B.I. Uniform Crime Reports

As of Oct. 31, 1982, there was an average of 2 full-time law enforcement officers for every 1,000 inhabitants in the U.S. A total of 11,776 city, county, and state police agencies reported employing 448,927 officers; including full-time civilian employees, the total law enforcement employee force was 581,262—a rate of 2.6 per 1,000 inhabitants.

City law enforcement employee averages in 1982 ranged from 2 per 1,000 inhabitants in those cities with populations from 25,000 to 49,999 to 3.3 for those with populations of 250,000 or more. The suburban areas averaged 2.3 full-time law enforcement employees per 1,000 inhabitants; the average rate for sheriffs' or county police departments was 2.0.

Geographically, the highest law enforcement employee rate per 1,000 inhabitants was in the South Atlantic Division, with 3.1. The fewest number of employees per 1,000 population was in the West South Central Division, with an average of 2.1.

Nationwide, 94 percent of law enforcement personnel, excluding civilians, were males. Civilians represented 19 percent of all city law enforcement personnel, 23 percent in suburban areas, 27 percent in rural counties. Nationally, the percentage was 22.

During 1982, 92 law enforcement officers were killed in the line of duty; assaults on officers numbered 55,775—17.5 per 100 officers; 5.4 of every 100 officers suffered personal injuries as a result.

Canada: Criminal Offenses and Crime Rate
Source: Statistics Canada; Canadian Centre for Justice Statistics

	1982		1983[1]		Percent Change in Rate
	Actual Offenses	Rate[2]	Actual Offenses	Rate[2]	
Total Criminal Code	2,203,668	8,945.5	2,143,256	8,610.9	−3.7
Total Homicide	670	2.7	682	2.7	0.0
Murder, 1st degree	284	1.1	292	1.1	0.0
Murder, 2nd degree.	340	1.3	333	1.3	0.0
Manslaughter	42	0.1	51	0.2	100.0
Infanticide	4	0.0	6	0.0	0.0
Attempted Murder	943	3.8	879	3.5	−7.9
Total Sexual Offenses[4]	13,864	56.2	139,656[5]	561.0	N/A
Rape	2,528	10.2	2,937[6]	11.8	N/A
Indecent Assault—Female	7,024	28.5	282[7]	1.1	N/A
Indecent Assault—Male	1,438	5.8	419[8]	1.6	N/A
Other Sexual Offenses	2,874	11.6	1,570[9]	6.3	N/A
Total Property Crimes.	1,466,923	5,954.8	1,419,653	5,703.7	−4.2
Assaults (Not Indecent)[4]	125,912	511.1	—	—	—
Robbery	27,257	110.6	24,199	97.2	−12.1
Total crimes of violence	168,646	684.6	170,624	685.5	0.1
Breaking and entering	369,882	1,501.4	361,516	1,452.4	−3.3
Theft Motor Vehicle.	86,997	353.1	75,759	304.3	−13.8
Theft Over $200.	295,261	1,198.5	292,423	1,174.8	−2.0
Theft $200 and Under	570,556	2,316.1	547,176	2,198.3	−5.1
Have Stolen Goods.	25,830	104.8	24,705	99.2	−5.3
Fraud.	118,397	480.6	118,074	474.3	−1.3
Total other Criminal Code	568,099	2,306.1	552,979	2,221.7	−3.7
Prostitution	700	2.8	935	3.7	32.1
Gaming and Betting.	2,420	9.8	2,232	8.9	−9.2
Offensive Weapons.	17,660	71.6	16,390	65.8	−8.1
Other Criminal Code	547,319	2,221.7	533,422	2,143.1	−3.5
Federal Statute Drugs	64,636	262.2	54,791	220.1	−16.1
Other Federal Statutes[3]	48,229	195.7	45,760	183.8	−6.1
Provincial Statutes[3]	434,351	1,763.2	408,818	1,642.5	−6.8
Municipal By-Laws[3]	87,956	357.0	90,367	363.0	1.7
Total all offenses.	2,838,840	11,523.9	2,742,991	11,020.5	−4.3

(1) Preliminary data, subject to revision. (2) Rate per 100,000 population. (3) Excluding traffic. (4) The final year these specific offenses occur due to legislative change. (5) Assault Total. (6) Other Sexual Offenses - Total. (7) Abduction of Person Under 16 - Total. (8) Abduction W/WO Custody Order - Total. (9) Other Violent Crimes - Total.

SPORTS OF 1984

Winter Olympic Games Champions, 1924-1984

Sites and Unofficial Winners of Games

1924 Chamonix, France (Norway)
1928 St. Moritz, Switzerland (Norway)
1932 Lake Placid, N.Y. (U.S.)
1936 Garmisch-Partenkirchen (Norway)
1948 St. Moritz (Sweden)

1952 Oslo, Norway (Norway)
1956 Cortina d'Ampezzo, Italy (USSR)
1960 Squaw Valley, Cal. (USSR)
1964 Innsbruck, Austria (USSR)
1968 Grenoble, France (Norway)

1972 Sapporo, Japan (USSR)
1976 Innsbruck, Austria (USSR)
1980 Lake Placid, N.Y. (E. Germany)
1984 Sarajevo, Yugoslavia (USSR)
1988 Calgary, Alberta (scheduled)

Biathlon

10 Kilometers

		Time
1980	Frank Ulrich, E. Germany	32:10.69
1984	Eirik Kvalfoss, Norway	30:53.8

20 Kilometers

		Time
1960	Klas Lestander, Sweden	1:33:21.6
1964	Vladimir Melanin, USSR	1:20:26.8
1968	Magnar Solberg, Norway	1:13:45.9
1972	Magnar Solberg, Norway	1:15:55.50
1976	Nikolai Kruglov, USSR	1:14:12.26
1980	Anatoly Alabyev, USSR	1:08:16.31
1984	Peter Angerer, W. Germany	1:11:52.7

40-Kilometer Relay

		Time
1968	USSR, Norway, Sweden	2:13:02
1972	USSR, Finland, E. Germany	1:51:44
1976	USSR, Finland, E. Germany	1:57:55.64
1980	USSR, E. Germany, W. Germany (30 km.)	1:34:03.27
1984	USSR, Norway, W. Germany	1:38:51.70

Bobsledding

4-Man Bob

	(Driver in parentheses)	Time
1924	Switzerland (Edward Scherrer)	5:45.54
1928	United States (William Fiske) (5-man)	3:20.50
1932	United States (William Fiske)	7:53.68
1936	Switzerland (Pierre Musy)	5:19.85
1948	United States (Edward Rimkus)	5:20.10
1952	Germany (Andreas Ostler)	5:07.84
1956	Switzerland (Frank Kapus)	5:10.44
1964	Canada (Victor Emery)	4:14.46
1968	Italy (Eugenio Monti) (2 races)	2:17.39
1972	Switzerland (Jean Wicki)	4:43.07
1976	E. Germany (Meinhard Nehmer)	3:40.43
1980	E. Germany (Meinhard Nehmer)	3:59.92
1984	E. Germany (Wolfgang Hoppe)	3:20.22

2-Man Bob

		Time
1932	United States (Hubert Stevens)	8:14.74
1936	United States (Ivan Brown)	5:29.29
1948	Switzerland (F. Endrich)	5:29.20
1952	Germany (Andreas Ostler)	5:24.54
1956	Italy (Dalla Costa)	5:30.14
1964	Great Britain (Antony Nash)	4:21.90
1968	Italy (Eugenio Monti)	4:41.54
1972	W. Germany (Wolfgang Zimmerer)	4:47.07
1976	E. Germany (Meinhard Nehmer)	3:40.43
1980	Switzerland (Erich Schaerer)	4:09.36
1984	E.Germany (Wolfgang Hoppe)	3:25.56

Figure Skating

Men's Singles

1908 Ulrich Sachow, Sweden
1920 Gillis Grafstrom, Sweden
1924 Gillis Grafstrom, Sweden
1928 Gillis Grafstrom, Sweden
1932 Karl Schaefer, Austria
1936 Karl Schaefer, Austria
1948 Richard Button, U.S.
1952 Richard Button, U.S.
1956 Hayes Alan Jenkins, U.S.
1960 David W. Jenkins, U.S.
1964 Manfred Schnelldorfer, Germany
1968 Wolfgang Schwartz, Austria
1972 Ondrej Nepela, Czechoslovakia
1976 John Curry, Great Britain
1980 Robin Cousins, Great Britain
1984 Scott Hamilton, U.S.

Women's Singles

1908 Madge Syers, Great Britain
1920 Magda Julin-Mauroy, Sweden
1924 Heima von Szabo-Planck, Austria
1928 Sonja Henie, Norway
1932 Sonja Henie, Norway
1936 Sonja Henie, Norway
1948 Barbara Ann Scott, Canada
1952 Jeanette Altwegg, Great Britain
1956 Tenley Albright, U.S.
1960 Carol Heiss, U.S.
1964 Sjoukje Dijkstra, Netherlands
1968 Peggy Fleming, U.S.
1972 Beatrix Schuba, Austria
1976 Dorothy Hamill, U.S.
1980 Anett Poetzsch, E. Germany
1984 Katarina Witt, E. Germany

Pairs

1908 Anna Hubler & Heinrich Burger, Germany
1920 Ludovika & Walter Jakobsson, Finland
1924 Helene Engelman & Alfred Berger, Austria
1928 Andree Joly & Pierre Brunet, France
1932 Andree Joly & Pierre Brunet, France
1936 Maxie Herber & Ernest Baier, Germany
1948 Micheline Lannoy & Pierre Baugniet, Belgium
1952 Ria and Paul Falk, Germany
1956 Elisabeth Schwarz & Kurt Oppelt, Austria
1960 Barbara Wagner & Robert Paul, Canada
1964 Ludmila Beloussova & Oleg Protopopov, USSR
1968 Ludmila Beloussova & Oleg Protopopov, USSR
1972 Irina Rodnina & Alexei Ulanov, USSR
1976 Irina Rodnina & Aleksandr Zaitzev, USSR
1980 Irina Rodnina & Aleksandr Zaitzev, USSR
1984 Elena Valova & Oleg Vassiliev, USSR

Ice Dancing

1976 Ludmila Pakhomova & Aleksandr Gorschkov, USSR
1980 Natalya Linichuk & Gennadi Karponosov, USSR
1984 Jayne Torvill & Christopher Dean, Great Britain

Alpine Skiing

Men's Downhill

		Time
1948	Henri Oreiller, France	2:55.0
1952	Zeno Colo, Italy	2:30.8
1956	Anton Sailer, Austria	2:52.2
1960	Jean Vuarnet, France	2:06.0
1964	Egon Zimmermann, Austria	2:18.16
1968	Jean Claude Killy, France	1:59.85
1972	Bernhard Russi, Switzerland	1:51.43
1976	Franz Klammer, Austria	1:45.73
1980	Leonhard Stock, Austria	1:45.50
1984	Bill Johnson, U.S.	1:45:59

Men's Giant Slalom

		Time
1952	Stein Eriksen, Norway	2:25.0
1956	Anton Sailer, Austria	3:00.1
1960	Roger Staub, Switzerland	1:48.3
1964	Francois Bonlieu, France	1:46.71
1968	Jean Claude Killy, France	3:29.28
1972	Gustavo Thoeni, Italy	3:09.62
1976	Heini Hemmi, Switzerland	3:26.97
1980	Ingemar Stenmark, Sweden	2:40.74
1984	Max Julen, Switzerland	2:41.18

Men's Slalom

		Time
1948	Edi Reinalter, Switzerland	2:10.3
1952	Othmar Schneider, Austria	2:00.0
1956	Anton Sailer, Austria	194.7 pts.
1960	Ernst Hinterseer, Austria	2:08.9
1964	Josef Stiegler, Austria	2:11.13

1968	Jean Claude Killy, France	1:39.73
1972	Francesco Fernandez Ochoa, Spain	1:49.27
1976	Piero Gros, Italy	2:03.29
1980	Ingemar Stenmark, Sweden	1:44.26
1984	Phil Mahre, U.S.	1:39.41

Women's Downhill

		Time
1948	Heidi Schlunegger, Switzerland	2:28.3
1952	Trude Jochum-Beiser, Austria	1:47.1
1956	Madeline Berthod, Switzerland	1:40.7
1960	Heidi Biebl, Germany	1:37.6
1964	Christi Haas, Austria	1:55.39
1968	Olga Pall, Austria	1:40.87
1972	Marie Therese Nadig, Switzerland	1:36.68
1976	Rosi Mittermaier, W. Germany	1:46.16
1980	Annemarie Proell Moser, Austria	1:37.52
1984	Michela Figini, Switzerland	1:13.36

Women's Giant Slalom

		Time
1952	Andrea Mead Lawrence, U.S.	2:06.8
1956	Ossi Reichert, Germany	1:56.5
1960	Yvonne Ruegg, Switzerland	1:39.9
1964	Marielle Goitschel, France	1:52.24
1968	Nancy Greene, Canada	1:51.97
1972	Marie Therese Nadig, Switzerland	1:29.90
1976	Kathy Kreiner, Canada	1:29.13
1980	Hanni Wenzel, Liechtenstein (2 runs)	2:41.66
1984	Debbie Armstrong, U.S.	2:20.98

Women's Slalom

		Time
1948	Gretchen Fraser, U.S.	1:57.2
1952	Andrea Mead Lawrence, U.S.	2:10.6
1956	Renee Colliard, Switzerland	112.3 pts.
1960	Anne Heggtveigt, Canada	1:49.6
1964	Christine Goitschel, France	1:29.86
1968	Marielle Goitschel, France	1:25.86
1972	Barbara Cochran, U.S.	1:31.24
1976	Rosi Mittermaier, W. Germany	1:30.54
1980	Hanni Wenzel, Liechtenstein	1:25.09
1984	Paoletta Magoni, Italy	1:36.47

Ice Hockey

1920	Canada, U.S., Czechoslovakia
1924	Canada, U.S., Great Britain
1928	Canada, Sweden, Switzerland
1932	Canada, U.S., Germany
1936	Great Britain, Canada, U.S.
1948	Canada, Czechoslovakia, Switzerland
1952	Canada, U.S., Sweden
1956	USSR, U.S., Canada
1960	U.S., Canada, USSR
1964	USSR, Sweden, Czechoslovakia
1968	USSR, Czechoslovakia, Canada
1972	USSR, U.S., Czechoslovakia
1976	USSR, Czechoslovakia, W. Germany
1980	U.S., USSR, Sweden
1984	USSR, Czechoslovakia, Sweden

Nordic Skiing

Men's Cross-Country Events
15 kilometers (9.3 miles)

		Time
1924	Thorleif Haug, Norway	1:14:31
1928	Johan Grottumsbraaten, Norway	1:37:01
1932	Sven Utterstrom, Sweden	1:23:07
1936	Erik-August Larsson, Sweden	1:14:38
1948	Martin Lundstrom, Sweden	1:13:50
1952	Hallgeir Brenden, Norway	1:01:34
1956	Hallgeir Brenden, Norway	49:39.0
1960	Haakon Brusveen, Norway	51:55.0
1964	Eero Maentyranta, Finland	50:54.1
1968	Harald Groenningen, Norway	47:54.2
1972	Sven-Ake Lundback, Sweden	45:28.24
1976	Nikolai Bajukov, USSR	43:58.47
1980	Thomas Wassberg, Sweden	41:57.63
1984	Gunde Svan, Sweden	41:25.6

(Note: approx. 18-km. course 1924-1952)

30 kilometers (18.6 miles)

		Time
1956	Veikko Hakulinen, Finland	1:44:06.0
1960	Sixten Jernberg, Sweden	1:51:03.9
1964	Eero Maentyranta, Finland	1:30:50.7
1968	Franco Nones, Italy	1:35:39.2
1972	Vyacheslav Vedenin, USSR	1:36:31.15
1976	Sergei Savaliev, USSR	1:30:29.38
1980	Nikolai Zimyatov, USSR	1:27:02.80
1984	Nikolai Zimyatov, USSR	1:28:56.3

50 kilometers (31.2 miles)

		Time
1924	Thorleif Haug, Norway	3:44:32.0
1928	Per Erik Hedlund, Sweden	4:52:03.0
1932	Veli Saarinen, Finland	4:28:00.0
1936	Elis Viklund, Sweden	3:30:11.0
1948	Nils Karlsson, Sweden	3:47:48.0
1952	Veikko Hakulinen, Finland	3:33:33.0
1956	Sixten Jernberg, Sweden	2:50:27.0
1960	Kalevi Hamalainen, Finland	2:59:06.3
1964	Sixten Jernberg, Sweden	2:43:52.6
1968	Ole Ellefsaeter, Norway	2:28:45.8
1972	Paal Tyldum, Norway	2:43:14.75
1976	Ivar Formo, Norway	2:37:30.05
1980	Nikolai Zimyatov, USSR	2:27:24.60
1984	Thomas Wassberg, Sweden	2:15:55.8

40-km. Cross-Country Relay

		Time
1936	Finland, Norway, Sweden	2:41:33.0
1948	Sweden, Finland, Norway	2:32:08.0
1952	Finland, Norway, Sweden	2:20:16.0
1956	USSR, Finland, Sweden	2:15:30.0
1960	Finland, Norway, USSR	2:18:45.6
1964	Sweden, Finland, USSR	2:18:34.6
1968	Norway, Sweden, Finland	2:08:33.5
1972	USSR, Norway, Switzerland	2:04:47.94
1976	Finland, Norway, USSR	2:07:59.72
1980	USSR, Norway, Finland	1:57:03.46
1984	Sweden, USSR, Finland	1:55:06.30

Combined Cross-Country & Jumping

		Points
1924	Thorleif Haug, Norway	453.800
1928	Johan Grottumsbraaten, Norway	427.800
1932	Johan Grottumsbraaten, Norway	446.200
1936	Oddbjorn Hagen, Norway	430.300
1948	Heikki Hasu, Finland	448.800
1952	Simon Slattvik, Norway	451.621
1956	Sverre Stenersen, Norway	455.000
1960	Georg Thoma, Germany	457.952
1964	Tormod Knutsen, Norway	469.280
1968	Franz Keller, W. Germany	449.040
1972	Ulrich Wehling, E. Germany	413.340
1976	Ulrich Wehling, E. Germany	423.390
1980	Ulrich Wehling, E. Germany	432.200
1984	Tom Sandberg, Norway	422.595

Ski Jumping (90 meters)

		Points
1924	Jacob Thams, Norway	227.5
1928	Alfred Andersen, Norway	230.5
1932	Birger Ruud, Norway	228.0
1936	Birger Ruud, Norway	232.0
1948	Petter Hugsted, Norway	228.1
1952	Anders Bergmann, Norway	226.0
1956	Antti Hyvarinen, Finland	227.0
1960	Helmut Recknagel, Germany	227.2
1964	Toralf Engan, Norway	230.7
1968	Vladimir Beloussov, USSR	231.3
1972	Wojiech Fortuna, Poland	219.9
1976	Karl Schnabl, Austria	234.8
1980	Jouko Tormanen, Finland	231.5
1984	Matti Nykaenen, Finland	231.2

Ski Jumping (70 meters)

		Points
1964	Veikko Kankkonen, Finland	229.9
1968	Jiri Raska, Czechoslovakia	216.5
1972	Yukio Kasaya, Japan	244.2
1976	Hans Aschenbach, E. Germany	252.0
1980	Anton Innauer, Austria	266.3
1984	Jens Weissflog, E. Germany	215.2

Women's Events
5 kilometers (approx. 3.1 miles)

		Time
1964	Claudia Boyarskikh, USSR	17:50.5
1968	Toini Gustafsson, Sweden	16:45.2
1972	Galina Koulacova, USSR	17:00.50
1976	Helena Takalo, Finland	15:48.69
1980	Raisa Smetanina, USSR	15:06.92
1984	Marja-Liisa Haemaelainen, Finland	17:04.0

10 kilometers

		Time
1952	Lydia Wideman, Finland	41:40.0
1956	Lyubov Kosyreva, USSR	38:11.0
1960	Maria Gusakova, USSR	39:46.6
1964	Claudia Boyarskikh, USSR	40:24.3
1968	Toini Gustafsson, Sweden	36:46.5
1972	Galina Koulacova, USSR	34:17.82
1976	Raisa Smetanina, USSR	30:13.41
1980	Barbara Petzold, E. Germany	30:31.54
1984	Marja-Liisa Haemaelainen, Finland	31:44.2

20 kilometers

	Time
1984 Marja-Liisa Haemaelainen, Finland	1:01:45.0

20-km. Cross-Country Relay

	Time
1956 Finland, USSR, Sweden (15 km.)	1:09:01.0
1960 Sweden, USSR, Finland (15 km.)	1:04:21.4
1964 USSR, Sweden, Finland (15 km.)	59:20.2
1968 Norway, Sweden, USSR (15 km.)	57:30.0
1972 USSR, Finland, Norway (15 km.)......	48:46.1
1976 USSR, Finland, E. Germany	1:07:49.75
1980 E. Germany, USSR, Norway	1:02:11.10
1984 Norway, Czechoslovakia, Finland	1:06:49.70

Luge

Men's Singles

	Time
1964 Thomas Keohler, Germany	3:26.77
1968 Manfred Schmid, Austria	2:52.48
1972 Wolfgang Scheidel, E. Germany	3:27.58
1976 Detlef Guenther, E. Germany	3:27.688
1980 Bernhard Glass, E. Germany	2:54.796
1984 Paul Hildgartner, Italy	3:04.258

Men's Doubles

	Time
1964 Austria..................	1:41.62
1968 E. Germany...............	1:35.85
1972 Italy, E. Germany (tie)	1:28.35
1976 E. Germany...............	1:25.604
1980 E. Germany...............	1:19.331
1984 W. Germany...............	1:23.620

Women's Singles

	Time
1964 Ortun Enderlein, Germany	3:24.67
1968 Erica Lechner, Italy	2:28.66
1972 Anna M. Muller, E. Germany	2:59.18
1976 Margit Schumann, E. Germany	2:50.621
1980 Vera Zozulya, USSR............	2:36.537
1984 Steffi Martin, E. Germany	2:46.570

Speed Skating

Men's 500 meters

	Time
1924 Charles Jewtraw, U.S............	0:44.0
1928 Thunberg, Finland & Evensen, Norway (tie)	0:43.4
1932 John A. Shea, U.S.............	0:43.4
1936 Ivar Ballangrud, Norway.........	0:43.4
1948 Finn Helgesen, Norway	0:43.1
1952 Kenneth Henry, U.S............	0:43.2
1956 Evgeniy Grishin, USSR	0:40.2
1960 Evgeniy Grishin, USSR	0:40.2
1964 Terry McDermott, U.S.	0:40.1
1968 Erhard Keller, W. Germany	0:40.3
1972 Erhard Keller, W. Germany	0:39.44
1976 Evgeny Kulikov, USSR	0:39.17
1980 Eric Heiden, U.S..............	0:38.03
1984 Sergei Fokichev, USSR..........	0:38.19

Men's 1,000 meters

	Time
1976 Peter Mueller, U.S.............	1:19.32
1980 Eric Heiden, U.S..............	1:15.18
1984 Gaetan Boucher, Canada.........	1:15.80

Men's 1,500 meters

	Time
1924 Clas Thunberg, Finland	2:20.8
1928 Clas Thunberg, Finland	2:21.1
1932 John A. Shea, U.S.............	2:57.2
1936 Charles Mathiesen, Norway	2:19.2
1948 Sverre Farstad, Norway..........	2:17.6
1952 Hjalmar Andersen, Norway	2:20.4
1956 Grishin, & Mikhailov, both USSR (tie)	2:08.6
1960 Aas, Norway & Grishin, USSR (tie)	2:10.4

1964 Ants Anston, USSR	2:10.3
1968 Cornetis Verkerk, Netherlands	2:03.4
1972 Ard Schenk, Netherlands..........	2:02.96
1976 Jan Egil Storholt, Norway..........	1:59.38
1980 Eric Heiden, U.S..............	1:55.44
1984 Gaetan Boucher, Canada..........	1:58.36

Men's 5,000 meters

	Time
1924 Clas Thunberg, Finland	8:39.0
1928 Ivar Ballangrud, Norway..........	8:50.5
1932 Irving Jaffee, U.S..............	9:40.8
1936 Ivar Ballangrud, Norway..........	8:19.6
1948 Reidar Liaklev, Norway	8:29.4
1952 Hjalmar Andersen, Norway........	8:10.6
1956 Boris Shilkov, USSR............	7:48.7
1960 Viktor Kosichkin, USSR..........	7:51.3
1964 Knut Johannesen, Norway	7:38.4
1968 F. Anton Maier, Norway	7:22.4
1972 Ard Schenk, Netherlands..........	7:23.61
1976 Sten Stensen, Norway...........	7:24.48
1980 Eric Heiden, U.S..............	7:02.29
1984 Sven Tomas Gustafson, Sweden.	7:12:28

Men's 10,000 meters

	Time
1924 Julius Skutnabb, Finland.	18:04.8
1928 Event not held, thawing of ice	
1932 Irving Jaffee, U.S.	19:13.6
1936 Ivar Ballangrud, Norway..........	17:24.3
1948 Ake Seyffarth, Sweden	17:26.3
1952 Hjalmar Andersen, Norway	16:45.8
1956 Sigvard Ericsson, Sweden	16:35.9
1960 Knut Johannesen, Norway	15:46.6
1964 Jonny Nilsson, Sweden	15:50.1
1968 Jonny Hoeglin, Sweden	15:23.6
1972 Ard Schenk, Netherlands..........	15:01.3
1976 Piet Kleine, Netherlands	14:50.59
1980 Eric Heiden, U.S..............	14:28.13
1984 Igor Malkov, USSR	14:39.90

Women's 500 meters

	Time
1960 Helga Haase, Germany	0:45.9
1964 Lydia Skoblikova, USSR..........	0:45.0
1968 Ludmila Titova, USSR	0:46.1
1972 Anne Henning, U.S.............	0:43.44
1976 Sheila Young, U.S..............	0:42.76
1980 Karin Enke, E. Germany	0:41.78
1984 Christa Rothenburger, E. Germany	0:41.02

Women's 1,000 meters

	Time
1960 Klara Guseva, USSR	1:34.1
1964 Lydia Skoblikova, USSR..........	1:33.2
1968 Caroline Geijssen, Netherlands.......	1:32.6
1972 Monika Pflug, W. Germany	1:31.40
1976 Tatiana Averina, USSR	1:28.43
1980 Natalya Petruseva, USSR.	1:24.10
1984 Karin Enke, E. Germany.	1:21.61

Women's 1,500 meters

	Time
1960 Lydia Skoblikova, USSR..........	2:52.2
1964 Lydia Skoblikova, USSR..........	2:22.6
1968 Kaija Mustonen, Finland..........	2:22.4
1972 Dianne Holum, U.S.	2:20.85
1976 Galina Stepanskaya, USSR.	2:16.58
1980 Anne Borckink, Netherlands	2:10.95
1984 Karin Enke, E. Germany.	2:03.42

Women's 3,000 meters

	Time
1960 Lydia Skoblikova, USSR..........	5:14.3
1964 Lydia Skoblikova, USSR..........	5:14.9
1968 Johanna Schut, Netherlands	4:56.2
1972 Stien Baas-Kaiser, Netherlands	4:52.14
1976 Tatiana Averina, USSR	4:45.19
1980 Bjoerg Eva Jensen, Norway	4:32.13
1984 Andrea Schoene, E. Germany	4:24.79

Winter Olympic Medal Winners in 1984

Sarajevo, Yugoslavia, Feb. 7-18, 1984

	Gold	Silver	Bronze	Total
Austria	0	0	1	1
Canada	2	1	1	4
Czechoslovakia	0	2	4	6
Finland	4	3	6	13
France	0	1	2	3
Germany, East.......	9	9	6	24
Germany, West	2	1	1	4
Great Britain	1	0	0	1
Italy	2	0	0	2

	Gold	Silver	Bronze	Total
Japan	0	1	0	1
Liechtenstein	0	0	2	2
Norway	3	2	4	9
Sweden	4	2	2	8
Switzerland.........	2	2	1	5
USSR	6	10	9	25
United States	4	4	0	8
Yugoslavia	0	1	0	1

Individual Medals

Alpine Skiing

Men's Downhill—1. Bill Johnson, U.S.; 2. Peter Mueller, Switzerland; 3. Anton Steiner, Austria.

Men's Giant Slalom—1. Max Julen, Switzerland; 2. Jure Franko, Yugoslavia; 3. Andreas Wenzel, Liechtenstein.

Men's Slalom—1. Phil Mahre, U.S; 2. Steve Mahre, U.S.; 3. Didier Bouvet, France.

Women's Downhill—1. Michela Figini, Switzerland; 2. Maria Walliser, Switzerland; 3. Olga Charvatova, Czechoslovakia.

Women's Giant Slalom—1. Debbie Armstrong, U.S.; 2. Christin Cooper, U.S.; 3. Perrine Pelen, France.

Women's Slalom—1. Paoletta Magoni, Italy; 2. Perrine Pelen, France; 3. Ursula Konzett, Liechtenstein.

Nordic Skiing

Men's 15 km.—1. Gunde Svan, Sweden; 2. Aki Karvonen, Finland; 3. Harri Kirvesniemi, Finland.

Men's 30 km.—1. Nikolai Zimyatov, USSR; 2. Alexandre Zavialov, USSR; 3. Gunde Svan, Sweden.

Men's 50 km.—1. Thomas Wassberg, Sweden; 2. Gunde Svan, Sweden; 3. Aki Karvonen, Finland.

Men's Combined—1. Tom Sandberg, Norway; 2. Jouko Karjalainen, Finland; 3. Jukka Ylipulli, Finland.

Women's 5 km.—1. Marja-Liisa Haemaelainen, Finland; 2. Berit Aunli, Norway; 3. Kvetoslava Jeriova, Czechoslovakia.

Women's 10 km.—1. Marja-Liisa Haemaelainen, Finland; 2. Raisa Smetanina, USSR; 3. Brit Pettersen, Norway.

Women's 20 km.—1. Marja-Liisa Haemaelainen, Finland; 2. Raisa Smetanina, USSR; 3. Anne Jahren, Norway.

Figure Skating

Men's Singles—1. Scott Hamilton, U.S.; 2. Brian Orser, Canada; 3. Josef Sabovcik, Czechoslovakia.

Women's Singles—1. Katarina Witt, E. Germany; 2. Rosalynn Sumners, USSR; 3. Kira Ivanova, USSR.

Pairs—1. Elena Valova & Oleg Vassiliev, USSR; 2. Kitty Carruthers & Peter Carruthers, U.S.; 3. Larissa Selezneva & Oleg Makarov, USSR.

Ice Dancing

Ice Dancing—1. Jayne Torvill & Christopher Dean, Great Britain; 2. Natalia Bestemianova & Andrei Bukin, USSR; 3. Marina Klimova & Sergei Ponomarenko, USSR.

Speed Skating

Men's 500 Meters—1. Sergei Fokitchev, USSR; 2. Yoshihiro Katazawa, Japan; 3. Gaetan Boucher, Canada.

1,000 Meters—1. Gaetan Boucher, Canada; 2. Sergei Khlebnikov, USSR; 3. Kai Arne Engelstad, Norway.

1,500 Meters—1. Gaetan Boucher, Canada; 2. Sergei Khlebnikov, USSR; 3. Oleg Bogiev, USSR.

5,000 Meters—1. Sven Tomas Gustafson, Sweden; 2. Igor Malkov, USSR; 3. Rene Schoefisch, E. Germany.

Men's 10,000 Meters—1. Igor Malkov, USSR; 2. Sven Tomas Gustafson, Sweden; 3. Rene Schoefisch, E. Germany.

Women's 500 Meters—1. Christa Rothenburger, E. Germany; 2. Karin Enke, E. Germany; 3. Natalya Chive, USSR.

Women's 1,000 Meters—1. Karin Enke, E. Germany; 2. Andrea Schoene, E. Germany; 3. Natalya Petruseva, USSR.

Women's 3,000 Meters—1. Andrea Schoene, E. Germany; 2. Karin Enke, E. Germany; 3. Gabie Schoenbrunn, E. Germany.

Ski Jumping

70-Meters—1. Jens Weissflog, E. Germany; 2. Matti Nykaenen, Finland; 3. Jari Puikkonen, Finland.

90-Meters—1. Matti Nykaenen, Finland; 2. Jens Weissflog, E. Germany; 3. Pavel Ploc, Czechoslovakia.

Luge

Men's Singles—1. Paul Hildgartner, Italy; 2. Sergei Danilin, USSR; 3. Valery Doydin, USSR.

Women's Singles—1. Steffi Martin, E. Germany; 2. Bettina Schmidt, E. Germany; 3. Ute Weiss, E. Germany.

Biathlon

10 km.—1. Eirik Kvalfoss, Norway; 2. Peter Angerer, W. Germany; 3. Matthias Jacob, E. Germany.

20 km.—1. Peter Angerer, W. Germany; 2. Frank-Peter Roetsch, E. Germany; 3. Eirik Kvalfoss, Norway.

Figure Skating Champions

U.S. Champions

World Champions

Men	Women	Year	Men	Women
Richard Button	Tenley Albright	1952	Richard Button, U.S.	Jacqueline du Bief, France
Hayes Jenkins	Tenley Albright	1953	Hayes Jenkins, U.S.	Tenley Albright, U.S.
Hayes Jenkins	Tenley Albright	1954	Hayes Jenkins, U.S.	Gundi Busch, W. Germany
Hayes Jenkins	Tenley Albright	1955	Hayes Jenkins, U.S.	Tenley Albright, U.S.
Hayes Jenkins	Tenley Albright	1956	Hayes Jenkins, U.S.	Carol Heiss, U.S.
Dave Jenkins	Carol Heiss	1957	Dave Jenkins, U.S.	Carol Heiss, U.S.
Dave Jenkins	Carol Heiss	1958	Dave Jenkins, U.S.	Carol Heiss, U.S.
Dave Jenkins	Carol Heiss	1959	Dave Jenkins, U.S.	Carol Heiss, U.S.
Dave Jenkins	Carol Heiss	1960	Alain Giletti, France	Carol Heiss, U.S.
Bradley Lord	Laurence Owen	1961	none	none
Monty Hoyt	Barbara Roles Pursley	1962	Don Jackson, Canada	Sjoukje Dijkstra, Neth.
Tommy Litz	Lorraine Hanlon	1963	Don McPherson, Canada	Sjoukje Dijkstra, Neth.
Scott Allen	Peggy Fleming	1964	Manfred Schnelldorfer, W. Germany	Sjoukje Dijkstra, Neth.
Gary Visconti	Peggy Fleming	1965	Alain Calmat, France	Petra Burka, Canada
Scott Allen	Peggy Fleming	1966	Emmerich Danzer, Austria	Peggy Fleming, U.S.
Gary Visconti	Peggy Fleming	1967	Emmerich Danzer, Austria	Peggy Fleming, U.S.
Tim Wood	Peggy Fleming	1968	Emmerich Danzer, Austria	Peggy Fleming, U.S.
Tim Wood	Janet Lynn	1969	Tim Wood, U.S.	Gabriele Seyfert, E. Germany
Tim Wood	Janet Lynn	1970	Tim Wood, U.S.	Gabriele Seyfert, E. Germany
John Misha Petkevich	Janet Lynn	1971	Ondrej Nepela, Czech.	Beatrix Schuba, Austria
Ken Shelley	Janet Lynn	1972	Ondrej Nepela, Czech.	Beatrix Schuba, Austria
Gordon McKellen Jr.	Janet Lynn	1973	Ondrej Nepela, Czech.	Karen Magnussen, Canada
Gordon McKellen Jr.	Dorothy Hamill	1974	Jan Hoffmann, E. Germany	Christine Errath, E. Germany
Gordon McKellen Jr.	Dorothy Hamill	1975	Sergei Volkov, USSR	Dianne de Leeuw, Neth.-U.S.
Terry Kubicka	Dorothy Hamill	1976	John Curry, Gt. Britain	Dorothy Hamill, U.S.
Charles Tickner	Linda Fratianne	1977	Vladimir Kovalev, USSR	Linda Fratianne, U.S.
Charles Tickner	Linda Fratianne	1978	Charles Tickner, U.S.	Anett Potzsch, E. Germany
Charles Tickner	Linda Fratianne	1979	Vladimir Kovalev, USSR	Linda Fratianne, U.S.
Charles Tickner	Linda Fratianne	1980	Jan Hoffmann, E. Germany	Anett Potzsch, E. Germany
Scott Hamilton	Elaine Zayak	1981	Scott Hamilton, U.S.	Denise Biellmann, Switzerland
Scott Hamilton	Rosalynn Sumners	1982	Scott Hamilton, U.S.	Elaine Zayak, U.S.
Scott Hamilton	Rosalynn Sumners	1983	Scott Hamilton, U.S.	Rosalynn Sumners, U.S.
Scott Hamilton	Rosalynn Sumners	1984	Scott Hamilton, U.S.	Katarina Witt, E. Germany

U.S. Pairs and Dancing Champions in 1984

Kitty Carruthers and Peter Carruthers of Boston, Mass. won the 1984 U.S. pairs figure skating championship in Salt Lake City, Ut. Judy Blumberg of Tarzana, Cal. and Michael Seibert of Washington, Pa. triumphed in ice dancing.

National Hockey League, 1983-84

Final Standings

Wales Conference

Adams Division

	W	L	T	Pts	GF	GA
Boston	49	25	6	104	336	261
Buffalo	48	25	7	103	315	257
Quebec	42	28	10	94	360	278
Montreal	35	40	5	75	286	295
Hartford	28	42	10	66	288	320

Patrick Division

	W	L	T	Pts	GF	GA
N.Y. Islanders	50	26	4	104	357	269
Washington	48	27	5	101	308	226
Philadelphia	44	26	10	98	350	290
N.Y. Rangers	42	29	9	93	314	304
New Jersey	17	56	7	41	231	350
Pittsburgh	16	58	6	38	254	390

Campbell Conference

Norris Division

	W	L	T	Pts	GF	GA
Minnesota	39	31	10	88	345	344
St. Louis	32	41	7	71	293	316
Detroit	31	42	7	69	298	323
Chicago	30	42	8	68	277	311
Toronto	26	45	9	61	303	387

Smythe Division

	W	L	T	Pts	GF	GA
Edmonton	57	18	5	119	446	314
Calgary	34	32	14	82	311	314
Vancouver	32	39	9	73	306	328
Winnipeg	31	38	11	73	340	374
Los Angeles	23	44	13	59	309	376

Stanley Cup Playoff Results

Wales Conference

Washington defeated Philadelphia 3 games to 0.
Montreal defeated Boston 3 games to 0.
Quebec defeated Buffalo 3 games to 0.
N.Y. Islanders defeated N.Y. Rangers 3 games to 2.
Montreal defeated Quebec 4 games to 2.
N.Y. Islanders defeated Washington 4 games to 1.
N.Y. Islanders defeated Montreal 4 games to 2.

Campbell Conference

St. Louis defeated Detroit 3 games to 1.
Edmonton defeated Winnipeg 3 games to 0.
Calgary defeated Vancouver 3 games to 1.
Minnesota defeated Chicago 3 games to 2.
Edmonton defeated Calgary 4 games to 3.
Minnesota defeated St. Louis 4 games to 3.
Edmonton defeated Minnesota 4 games to 0.

Finals

Edmonton defeated N.Y. Islanders 4 games to 1.

Stanley Cup Champions Since 1928

Year	Champion	Coach	Final opponent	Year	Champion	Coach	Final opponent
1928	New York	Lester Patrick	Montreal	1957	Montreal	Toe Blake	Boston
1929	Boston	Cy Denneny	N.Y. Rangers	1958	Montreal	Toe Blake	Boston
1930	Montreal	Cecil Hart	Boston	1959	Montreal	Toe Blake	Toronto
1931	Montreal	Cecil Hart	Chicago	1960	Montreal	Toe Blake	Toronto
1932	Toronto	Dick Irvin	N.Y. Rangers	1961	Chicago	Rudy Pilous	Detroit
1933	New York	Lester Patrick	Toronto	1962	Toronto	Punch Imlach	Chicago
1934	Chicago	Tommy Gorman	Detroit	1963	Toronto	Punch Imlach	Detroit
1935	Montreal Maroons	Tommy Gorman	Toronto	1964	Toronto	Punch Imlach	Detroit
1936	Detroit	Jack Adams	Toronto	1965	Montreal	Toe Blake	Chicago
1937	Detroit	Jack Adams	N.Y. Rangers	1966	Montreal	Toe Blake	Detroit
1938	Chicago	Bill Stewart	Toronto	1967	Toronto	Punch Imlach	Montreal
1939	Boston	Art Ross	Toronto	1968	Montreal	Toe Blake	St. Louis
1940	N.Y. Rangers	Frank Boucher	Toronto	1969	Montreal	Claude Ruel	St. Louis
1941	Boston	Cooney Weiland	Detroit	1970	Boston	Harry Sinden	St. Louis
1942	Toronto	Hap Day	Detroit	1971	Montreal	Al MacNeil	Chicago
1943	Detroit	Jack Adams	Boston	1972	Boston	Tom Johnson	N.Y. Rangers
1944	Montreal	Dick Irvin	Chicago	1973	Montreal	Scotty Bowman	Chicago
1945	Toronto	Hap Day	Detroit	1974	Philadelphia	Fred Shero	Boston
1946	Montreal	Dick Irvin	Boston	1975	Philadelphia	Fred Shero	Buffalo
1947	Toronto	Hap Day	Montreal	1976	Montreal	Scotty Bowman	Philadelphia
1948	Toronto	Hap Day	Detroit	1977	Montreal	Scotty Bowman	Boston
1949	Toronto	Hap Day	Detroit	1978	Montreal	Scotty Bowman	Boston
1950	Detroit	Tommy Ivan	N.Y. Rangers	1979	Montreal	Scotty Bowman	N.Y. Rangers
1951	Toronto	Joe Primeau	Montreal	1980	N.Y. Islanders	Al Arbour	Philadelphia
1952	Detroit	Tommy Ivan	Montreal	1981	N.Y. Islanders	Al Arbour	Minnesota
1953	Montreal	Dick Irvin	Boston	1982	N.Y. Islanders	Al Arbour	Vancouver
1954	Detroit	Tommy Ivan	Montreal	1983	N.Y. Islanders	Al Arbour	Edmonton
1955	Detroit	Jimmy Skinner	Montreal	1984	Edmonton	Glen Sather	N.Y. Islanders
1956	Montreal	Toe Blake	Detroit				

Conn Smythe Trophy (MVP in Playoffs)

1965	Jean Beliveau, Montreal	1972	Bobby Orr, Boston	1979	Bob Gainey, Montreal
1966	Roger Crozier, Detroit	1973	Yvan Cournoyer, Montreal	1980	Bryan Trottier, N.Y. Islanders
1967	Dave Keon, Toronto	1974	Bernie Parent, Philadelphia	1981	Butch Goring, N.Y. Islanders
1968	Glenn Hall, St. Louis	1975	Bernie Parent, Philadelphia	1982	Mike Bossy, N.Y. Islanders
1969	Serge Savard, Montreal	1976	Reg Leach, Philadelphia	1983	Billy Smith, N.Y. Islanders
1970	Bobby Orr, Boston	1977	Guy Lafleur, Montreal	1984	Mark Messier, Edmonton
1971	Ken Dryden, Montreal	1978	Larry Robinson, Montreal		

Individual Leaders

Points

Gretzky, Edmonton, 205; Coffey, Edmonton, 126; Goulet, Quebec, 121; P. Stastny, Quebec, 119; Bossy, N.Y. Islanders, 118.

Goals

Gretzky, Edmonton, 87; Goulet, Quebec, 56; Anderson, Edmonton, 54; Kerr, Philadelphia, 54; Kurri, Edmonton, 52; Vaive, Toronto, 52.

Assists

Gretzky, Edmonton, 118; Coffey, Edmonton, 86; Pederson, Boston, 77; P. Stastny, Quebec, 73; Trottier, N.Y. Islanders, 71.

Power-play goals

Gretzky, Edmonton, 20; Larouche, N.Y. Rangers, 19; Ogrodnick, Detroit, 19; Tanti, Vancouver, 19; Turgeon, Hartford, 18.

Shorthanded goals

Gretzky, Edmonton, 12; Nilsson, Calgary, 9; Carbonneau, Montreal, 7; Bellows, Minnesota, Bourne, Goring, N.Y. Islanders, Kurri, Edmonton, 5.

Game-winning goals

Goulet, Quebec, 16; Gretzky, Anderson, Edmonton, Bossy, N.Y. Islanders, 11.

Shooting percentage
(minimum 80 shots)

Gretzky, Edmonton, 26.9; Kurri, Edmonton, 26.8; Gilbert, N.Y. Islanders, 26.3; Tonelli, N.Y. Islanders, 25.7; MacLean, Winnipeg, 25.3.

Goaltenders
Goals-against average
(minimum 25 games)

Riggins, Washington, 2.66; Barrasso, Buffalo, 2.84; Jensen, Washington, 2.91; Keans, Boston, 3.10; Froese, Philadelphia, 3.14.

Wins

Fuhr, Edmonton, 30; Peeters, Boston, Bouchard, Quebec, 29; Hanlon, N.Y. Rangers, Froese, Philadelphia, 28.

Save percentage

Melanson, N.Y. Islanders, .902; Smith, N.Y. Islanders, .896; Barrasso, Buffalo, .893; Lemenin, Calgary, .893; Hanlon, N.Y. Rangers, .890.

Shutouts

Riggins, Jensen, Washington, 4 each; Liut, St. Louis, 3.

Individual Scoring
(40 or more games played)

Boston Bruins

	GP	G	A	Pts	+/−	PIM
Barry Pederson	80	39	77	116	27	64
Rick Middleton	80	47	58	105	26	14
Ray Bourque	78	31	65	96	51	57
Tom Fergus	69	25	36	61	8	12
Mike O'Connell	75	18	42	60	18	42
Keith Crowder	63	24	28	52	12	128
Mike Krushelnyski	66	25	20	45	9	55
Craig MacTavish	70	20	23	43	9	35
Gord Kluzak	80	10	27	37	9	135
Nevin Markwart	70	14	16	30	2	121
Terry O'Reilly	58	12	18	30	9	124
Jim Nill	78	12	8	20	12 —	159
Bruce Crowder	74	6	14	20	1	44
Mike Milbury	74	2	17	19	2	159
Guy Lapointe	45	2	16	18	3 —	34
Mike Gillis	50	6	11	17	7 —	35
Randy Hillier	69	3	12	15	5 —	125
Luc Dufour	41	6	4	10	2	47

Buffalo Sabres

	GP	G	A	Pts	+/−	PIM
Gilbert Perreault	73	31	59	90	19	32
Dave Andreychuk	78	38	42	80	20	42
Phil Housley	75	31	46	77	4	33
Mike Foligno	70	32	31	63	32	151
Real Cloutier	77	24	36	60	1 —	25
Lindy Ruff	58	14	31	45	15	101
Gilles Hamel	75	21	23	44	4	37
Paul Cyr	71	16	27	43	3 —	52
Hannu Virta	70	6	30	36	14	12
Ric Seiling	78	13	22	35	10	42
Mike Ramsey	72	9	22	31	26	82
Sean McKenna	78	20	10	30	0	45
Bill Hajt	79	3	24	27	26	32
Craig Ramsay	76	9	17	26	3	17
Brent Peterson	70	9	12	21	3	52
Jim Wiemer	64	5	15	20	1	48
Mike Moller	59	5	11	16	2	27
Larry Playfair	76	5	11	16	4	209
Jerry Korab	48	2	9	11	4	82

Calgary Flames

	GP	G	A	Pts	+/−	PIM
Kent Nilsson	67	31	49	80	24 —	22
Ed Beers	73	36	39	75	7	88
Lanny McDonald	65	33	33	66	15 —	64
Hakan Loob	77	30	25	55	11	22
Dan Quinn	54	19	33	52	1 —	20

	GP	G	A	Pts	+/−	PIM
Doug Risebrough	77	23	28	51	11	161
Mike Eaves	61	14	36	50	9	20
Allan MacInnis	51	11	34	45	1	42
Kari Eloranta	78	5	34	39	12	44
Jim Peplinski	74	11	22	33	21 —	114
Jamie Macoun	72	9	23	32	3	97
Colin Patterson	56	13	14	27	17	15
Paul Baxter	74	7	20	27	1 —	182
Steve Tambellini	73	15	10	25	8 —	16
Richard Kromm	53	11	12	23	14	27
Steve Bozek	46	10	10	20	16 —	16
Jim Jackson	49	6	14	20	1	13
Steve Konroyd	80	1	13	14	8 —	94
Tim Hunter	43	4	4	8	0	130

Chicago Black Hawks

	GP	G	A	Pts	+/−	PIM
Denis Savard	75	37	57	94	13 —	71
Steve Larmer	80	35	40	75	1 —	34
Doug Wilson	66	13	45	58	11 —	64
Bill Gardner	79	27	21	48	1	12
Bob Murray	78	11	37	48	1	78
Tom Lysiak	54	17	30	47	13 —	35
Jeff Larmer	76	15	26	41	14 —	28
Darryl Sutter	59	20	20	40	18 —	44
Keith Brown	74	10	25	35	18 —	94
Behn Wilson	59	10	22	32	5 —	143
Troy Murray	61	15	15	30	10	45
Steve Ludzik	80	9	20	29	5 —	73
Rich Preston	75	10	18	28	21 —	50
Denis Cyr	46	12	13	25	0	19
Jack O'Callahan	70	4	13	17	6 —	67
Rick Paterson	72	7	6	13	13 —	41
Dave Feamster	46	6	7	13	8 —	42
Ken Yaremchuk	47	6	7	13	7 —	19
Peter Marsh	43	4	6	10	11 —	44

Detroit Red Wings

	GP	G	A	Pts	+/−	PIM
Steve Yzerman	80	39	48	87	17 —	33
Ivan Boldirev	75	35	48	83	3	20
Ron Duguay	80	33	47	80	26 —	34
John Ogrodnick	64	42	36	78	16 —	14
Reed Larson	78	23	39	62	10 —	122
Kelly Kisio	70	23	37	60	16	34
Brad Park	80	5	53	58	29 —	85

	GP	G	A	Pts	+/−	PIM
Lane Lambert	73	20	15	35	5−	115
Rick MacLeish	54	10	22	32	0	8
Blake Dunlop	74	7	24	31	14−	24
Danny Gare	63	13	13	26	3	147
Ed Johnstone	46	12	11	23	3	54
Greg Smith	75	3	20	23	6	108
Bob Manno	62	9	13	22	1−	60
Dwight Foster	52	9	12	21	4−	50
Randy Ladouceur	71	3	17	20	12−	58
John Barrett	78	2	8	10	0	78
Colin Campbell	68	3	4	7	0	108
Joe Paterson	41	2	5	7	0	148
Paul Woods	57	2	5	7	16−	18

Edmonton Oilers

	GP	G	A	Pts	+/−	PIM
Wayne Gretzky	74	87	118	205	76	39
Paul Coffey	80	40	86	126	52	104
Jari Kurri	64	52	61	113	38	14
Mark Messier	73	37	64	101	40	165
Glenn Anderson	80	54	45	99	41	65
Ken Linseman	72	18	49	67	30	119
Pat Hughes	77	27	28	55	18	61
Dave Hunter	80	22	26	48	25	90
Kevin Lowe	80	4	42	46	37	59
Charlie Huddy	75	8	34	42	50	43
Randy Gregg	80	13	27	40	40	56
Willy Lindstrom	73	22	16	38	17	38
Kevin McClelland	76	10	24	34	2	189
Jaroslav Pouzar	67	13	19	32	17	44
Dave Lumley	56	6	15	21	14	68
Lee Fogolin	80	5	16	21	33	125
Don Jackson	64	8	12	20	28	120
Dave Semenko	52	6	11	17	9	118
Pat Conacher	45	2	8	10	2−	31

Hartford Whalers

	GP	G	A	Pts	+/−	PIM
Mark Johnson	79	35	52	87	14−	27
Ron Francis	72	23	60	83	10−	45
Sylvain Turgeon	76	40	32	72	11−	55
Ray Neufeld	80	27	42	69	18−	97
Bob Crawford	80	36	25	61	1−	32
Greg Malone	78	17	37	54	10−	56
Risto Siltanen	75	15	38	53	21−	34
Tony Currie	50	15	19	34	3−	6
Mike Zuke	75	6	23	29	18−	36
Richie Dunn	63	5	20	25	20−	30
Norm Dupont	40	7	15	22	16−	12
Torrie Robertson	66	7	14	21	9−	198
Doug Sulliman	67	6	12	18	11−	20
Chris Kotsopoulos	72	5	13	18	2−	118
Joel Quenneville	80	5	8	13	11−	95
Jack Brownschilde	64	3	9	12	26−	29
Marty Howe	69	0	11	11	1	34
Ed Hospodar	59	0	9	9	17−	163
Mike Crombeen	56	1	4	5	13−	25

Los Angeles Kings

	GP	G	A	Pts	+/−	PIM
Bernie Nicholls	78	41	54	95	21−	83
Charlie Simmer	79	44	48	92	7	78
Marcel Dionne	66	39	53	92	8	28
Jim Fox	80	30	42	72	12−	26
Dave Taylor	63	20	49	69	3−	91
Brian MacLellan	72	25	29	54	21−	45
Mark Hardy	79	8	41	49	30−	122
Doug Smith	72	16	20	36	33−	28
Mike McEwen	62	10	26	36	17−	20
Anders Hakansson	80	15	17	32	7−	41
Terry Ruskowski	77	7	25	32	24−	92
Brian Engblom	80	2	28	30	13−	67
Billy Harris	71	9	14	23	23−	20
Wes Jarvis	61	9	13	22	7−	36
J. P. Kelly	72	7	14	21	34−	73
Jay Wells	69	3	13	21	10−	141
Russ Anderson	70	5	12	17	30−	126
Steve Christoff	58	8	7	15	19−	13
Marc Chorney	75	3	10	13	28−	66

Minnesota North Stars

	GP	G	A	Pts	+/−	PIM
Neal Broten	76	28	61	89	16	43
Brian Bellows	78	41	42	83	2−	66

	GP	G	A	Pts	+/−	PIM
Brad Maxwell	78	19	54	73	7−	225
Dino Ciccarelli	79	38	33	71	1	58
Tom McCarthy	66	39	31	70	17	49
Keith Acton	71	20	45	65	3−	64
Dennis Maruk	71	17	43	60	17−	42
Steve Payne	78	28	31	69	2	49
Gordie Roberts	77	8	45	53	14	132
Mark Napier	63	16	30	46	2	17
Willi Plett	73	15	23	38	6−	316
Al MacAdam	80	22	13	35	5−	23
Brian Lawton	58	10	21	31	0	33
Paul Holmgren	63	11	18	29	1−	151
Curt Giles	70	6	22	28	2	59
Lars Lindgren	66	3	16	19	3−	37
Brent Ashton	68	7	10	17	13−	54
George Ferguson	63	6	10	16	6−	19
Dave Richter	42	2	3	5	8−	132

Montreal Canadiens

	GP	G	A	Pts	+/−	PIM
Bobby Smith	80	29	43	72	8−	71
Guy Lafleur	80	30	40	70	14−	19
Mats Naslund	77	29	35	64	5	4
Guy Carbonneau	78	24	30	54	5	75
Ryan Walter	73	20	29	49	11−	83
John Chabot	56	18	25	43	2−	13
Larry Robinson	74	9	34	43	4	39
Bob Gainey	77	17	22	39	10	41
Mario Tremblay	67	14	25	39	2	112
Pierre Mondou	52	15	22	37	9	8
Steve Shutt	63	14	23	37	18−	29
Perry Turnbull	72	20	15	35	14	140
Chris Nilan	76	16	10	26	4−	338
Craig Ludwig	80	7	18	25	10−	52
Bill Root	72	4	13	17	26	45
Jean Hamel	79	1	12	13	7	92
Kent Carlson	65	3	7	10	15−	73

New Jersey Devils

	GP	G	A	Pts	+/−	PIM
Mel Bridgman	79	23	38	61	27−	121
Jan Ludvig	74	22	32	54	18−	70
Pat Verbeek	79	20	27	47	19−	158
Joe Cirella	79	11	33	44	43−	137
Bob MacMillan	71	17	23	40	21−	23
Aaron Broten	80	13	23	36	28−	36
Tim Higgins	69	19	14	33	3−	48
Don Lever	70	14	19	33	21−	44
Paul Gagne	66	14	18	32	22−	33
Phil Russell	76	9	22	31	27−	96
Rick Meagher	52	14	14	28	9−	16
Gary McAdam	62	10	11	21	7−	27
Dave Cameron	67	9	12	21	11−	85
Murray Brumwell	42	7	13	20	5−	14
Bob Hoffmeyer	58	4	12	16	20−	61
Bob Lorimer	72	2	10	12	28−	62
Yvon Vautour	42	3	4	7	18−	78
Dave Lewis	66	2	5	7	19−	63
Mike Kitchen	43	1	4	5	15−	24

N.Y. Islanders

	GP	G	A	Pts	+/−	PIM
Mike Bossy	67	51	67	118	66	8
Bryan Trottier	68	40	71	111	70	59
Denis Potvin	78	22	63	85	55	87
John Tonelli	73	27	40	67	21	66
Greg Gilbert	79	31	35	66	51	59
Bob Bourne	78	22	34	56	12	75
Brent Sutter	69	34	15	49	4	69
Tomas Jonsson	72	11	36	47	12	54
Butch Goring	71	22	24	46	8	8
Bob Nystrom	74	15	29	44	9	80
Duane Sutter	78	17	23	40	2	94
Stefan Persson	75	9	24	33	30	65
Clark Gillies	76	12	16	28	5	65
Anders Kallur	65	9	14	23	0	24
Dave Langevin	69	3	16	19	26	53
Ken Morrow	63	3	11	14	26	45
Gord Dineen	43	1	11	12	10	32
Mats Hallin	40	2	5	7	2−	27

N.Y. Rangers

	GP	G	A	Pts	+/-	PIM
Mark Pavelich	77	29	53	82	11	96
Pierre Larouche	77	48	33	81	15-	22
Anders Hedberg	79	32	35	67	18	16
Don Maloney	79	24	42	66	5-	62
Mike Rogers	78	23	38	61	24-	45
Reijo Ruotsalainen	74	20	39	59	17	26
Ron Greschner	77	12	44	56	5	117
Mark Osborne	73	23	28	51	1	88
Blaine Stoughton	68	28	16	44	25-	8
Peter Sundstrom	77	22	22	44	3	24
Barry Beck	72	9	27	36	12	132
Dave Maloney	68	7	26	33	11	168
Jan Erixon	75	5	25	30	14	16
Willie Huber	42	9	14	23	14-	60
Mike Allison	45	8	12	20	5	64
K.E. Andersson	63	5	15	20	5	8
Tom Laidlaw	79	3	15	18	10-	62
Rob McClanahan	41	6	8	14	0	21
Nick Fotiu	40	7	6	13	8	115

Philadelphia Flyers

	GP	G	A	Pts	+/-	PIM
Tim Kerr	79	54	39	93	30	29
Brian Propp	79	39	53	92	49	37
Dave Poulin	73	31	45	76	31	47
Darryl Sittler	76	27	36	63	13	38
Bobby Clarke	73	17	43	60	23	70
Bill Barber	63	22	32	54	4	36
Mark Howe	71	19	34	53	30	44
Ron Sutter	79	19	32	51	4	101
Ilkka Sinisalo	73	29	17	46	22	29
Thomas Eriksson	68	11	33	44	28	37
Doug Crossman	78	7	28	35	23	63
Miroslav Dvorak	66	4	27	31	19	27
Rich Sutter	75	16	12	28	8	93
Brad McCrimmon	71	0	24	42	19	76
Glen Cochrane	67	7	16	23	16	225
Brad Marsh	77	3	14	17	24	83

Pittsburgh Penguins

	GP	G	A	Pts	+/-	PIM
Mike Bullard	76	51	41	92	33-	57
Doug Shedden	67	22	35	57	38-	20
Mark Taylor	60	24	31	55	20-	24
Ron Flockhart	76	27	21	48	18-	44
Rick Kehoe	57	18	27	45	20-	8
Tom Roulston	77	16	24	40	31-	24
Pat Boutette	73	14	26	40	58-	142
Andy Brickley	50	18	20	38	7-	9
Kevin McCarthy	78	6	30	36	40-	113
Greg Hotham	76	5	25	30	25-	59
Bob Errey	65	9	13	22	20-	29
Bryan Maxwell	48	3	15	18	3	111
Gary Rissling	47	4	13	17	9-	297
Tom O'Regan	51	4	10	14	22-	8
Greg Fox	73	2	10	12	42-	97
Marty McSorley	72	2	7	9	39-	224
Rod Buskas	47	2	4	6	18-	60

Quebec Nordiques

	GP	G	A	Pts	+/-	PIM
Michel Goulet	75	56	65	121	62	76
Peter Stastny	80	46	73	119	22	73
Dale Hunter	77	24	55	79	35	232
Wilf Paiement	80	39	37	76	28	121
Anton Stastny	69	25	37	62	12	14
Marian Stastny	68	20	32	52	1	26
Tony McKegney	75	24	27	51	4	23
Mario Marois	80	13	36	49	51	151
Andre Savard	60	20	24	44	17	38
Alain Cote	77	19	24	43	21	41
Bo Bergland	75	16	27	43	6	20
Louis Sleigher	44	15	19	34	23	32
Andre Dore	80	4	28	32	4	83
Pat Price	72	3	25	28	20	188
Normand Rochefort	75	2	22	24	41	47
Randy Moller	74	4	14	18	26	147
Paul Gillis	57	8	9	17	10	59
Blake Wesley	46	2	8	10	14	75

St. Louis Blues

	GP	G	A	Pts	+/-	PIM
Bernie Federko	79	41	66	107	3-	43
Joe Mullen	80	41	44	85	8-	19
Brian Sutter	76	32	51	83	6-	162
Jorgen Pettersson	77	28	34	62	2-	29
Rob Ramage	80	15	45	60	11-	121
Doug Gilmour	80	25	28	53	6	57
Guy Chouinard	64	12	34	46	15-	10
Wayne Babych	70	13	29	42	1	52
Doug Wickenheiser	73	12	26	38	11	25
Mark Reeds	65	11	14	25	3-	23
Pat Hickey	67	9	11	20	3-	24
Dave Pichette	46	2	18	20	3-	18
Greg Paslawski	60	9	10	19	1-	21
Rik Wilson	48	7	11	18	4	53
Tim Bothwell	62	2	13	15	22	65
Jack Carlson	58	6	8	14	9	95
Dwight Schofield	70	4	10	14	3-	219
Gilbert Delorme	71	2	12	14	11-	49
Perry Anderson	50	7	5	12	13-	195
Terry Johnson	65	2	6	8	5	141

Toronto Maple Leafs

	GP	G	A	Pts	+/-	PIM
Rick Vaive	76	52	41	93	14-	114
Dan Daoust	78	18	56	74	16-	88
John Anderson	73	37	31	68	12-	22
Bill Derlago	79	40	20	60	7-	50
Jim Benning	79	12	39	51	4-	66
Dale McCourt	77	20	27	47	18-	10
Borje Salming	68	5	38	43	34-	92
Greg Terrion	79	15	24	39	6-	36
Stewart Gavin	80	10	22	32	6-	90
Gaston Gingras	59	7	20	27	30-	16
Jim Korn	65	12	14	26	33-	257
Miroslav Frycer	47	10	16	26	23-	55
Terry Martin	63	15	10	25	8-	51
Peter Ihnacak	47	10	13	23	21-	24
Dave Farrish	59	4	19	23	13-	57
Bill Stewart	56	2	17	19	1-	116
Gary Nylund	47	2	14	16	27-	103
Gary Leeman	52	4	8	12	14-	31
Pat Graham	41	4	4	8	8-	65
Dave Hutchison	47	0	3	3	5	137

Vancouver Canucks

	GP	G	A	Pts	+/-	PIM
Patrik Sundstrom	78	38	53	91	11-	37
Tony Tanti	79	45	41	86	12-	50
Thomas Gradin	75	21	57	78	2-	32
Stan Smyl	80	24	43	67	21-	136
Rick Lanz	79	18	39	57	3-	45
Darcy Rota	59	28	20	48	12-	73
Gary Lupul	69	17	27	44	16-	51
Jiri Bubla	62	6	33	39	10-	43
Peter McNab	65	15	22	37	5	20
Cam Neely	56	16	15	31	0	57
Tiger Williams	67	15	16	31	11-	294
Moe Lemay	56	12	18	30	4	38
Doug Halward	54	7	16	23	1	35
Neil Belland	44	7	13	20	8-	24
Harold Snepsts	79	4	16	20	19-	152
Michel Petit	44	6	9	15	6-	53
Lars Molin	42	6	7	13	9-	4
Andy Schliebener	51	2	10	12	9-	48
Ron Delorme	64	2	2	4	2-	68

Washington Capitals

	GP	G	A	Pts	+/-	PIM
Mike Gartner	80	40	54	85	22	90
Dave Christian	80	29	52	81	26	28
Bengt Gustafsson	69	32	43	75	29	16
Bob Carpenter	80	28	40	68	0	51
Alan Haworth	75	24	31	55	14	52
Craig Laughlin	80	20	32	52	4	69
Larry Murphy	78	13	36	49	8	50
Scott Stevens	78	13	32	45	26	201
Doug Jarvis	80	13	29	42	7	12
Bobby Gould	78	21	19	40	2-	74
Gaetan Duchesne	79	17	19	36	15	29
Glen Currie	80	12	24	36	9	20
Rod Langway	80	9	24	33	14	61
Bryan Erickson	45	12	17	29	10	16
Darren Veitch	46	6	18	24	0	17
Timo Blomqvist	65	1	19	20	17	84
Dave Shand	72	4	15	19	23	124
Peter Andersson	42	3	7	10	12	20
Greg Adams	57	2	6	8	1	133

Winnipeg Jets

	GP	G	A	Pts	+/−	PIM		GP	G	A	Pts	+/−	PIM
Dale Hawerchuk	80	37	65	102	14−	73	Doug Smail	66	20	17	37	5−	62
Lucien DeBlois	80	34	45	79	14−	50	Tim Young	44	15	19	34	11−	25
Laurie Boschman	61	28	46	74	4−	234	Andrew McBain	78	11	19	30	6−	37
Paul MacLean	76	40	31	71	15−	155	Randy Carlyle	55	3	26	29	23−	84
Thomas Steen	78	20	45	65	5−	69	Robert Picard	69	6	18	24	8	34
Brian Mullen	75	21	41	62	11−	28	Tim Watters	74	3	20	23	7	169
Dave Babych	66	18	39	57	31−	62	Wade Campbell	79	7	14	21	2−	147
Scott Arniel	80	21	35	56	10−	68	Bengt Lundholm	57	5	14	19	7−	20
Morris Lukowich	80	00	25	55	10	71	Ron Wilson	51	3	12	15	3−	12
Moe Mantha	72	16	38	54	14−	67	Jim Kyte	58	1	2	3	7−	73

NHL Trophy Winners

	Ross Trophy Leading scorer		Norris Trophy Best defenseman		Calder Trophy Best rookie
1984	Wayne Gretzky, Edmonton	1984	Rod Langway, Washington	1984	Tom Barrasso, Buffalo
1983	Wayne Gretzky, Edmonton	1983	Rod Langway, Washington	1983	Steve Larmer, Chicago
1982	Wayne Gretzky, Edmonton	1982	Doug Wilson, Chicago	1982	Dale Hawerchuk, Winnipeg
1981	Wayne Gretzky, Edmonton	1981	Randy Carlyle, Pittsburgh	1981	Peter Stastny, Quebec
1980	Marcel Dionne, Los Angeles	1980	Larry Robinson, Montreal	1980	Ray Bourque, Boston
1979	Bryan Trottier, N.Y. Islanders	1979	Denis Potvin, N.Y. Islanders	1979	Bob Smith, Minnesota
1978	Guy Lafleur, Montreal	1978	Denis Potvin, N.Y. Islanders	1978	Mike Bossy, N.Y. Islanders
1977	Guy Lafleur, Montreal	1977	Larry Robinson, Montreal	1977	Willi Plett, Atlanta
1976	Guy Lafleur, Montreal	1976	Denis Potvin, N.Y. Islanders	1976	Bryan Trottier N.Y. Islanders
1975	Bobby Orr, Boston	1975	Bobby Orr, Boston	1975	Eric Vail, Atlanta
1974	Phil Esposito, Boston	1974	Bobby Orr, Boston	1974	Denis Potvin, N.Y. Islanders
1973	Phil Esposito, Boston	1973	Bobby Orr, Boston	1973	Steve Vickers, N.Y. Rangers
1972	Phil Esposito, Boston	1972	Bobby Orr, Boston	1972	Ken Dryden, Montreal
1971	Phil Esposito, Boston	1971	Bobby Orr, Boston	1971	Gil Perreault, Buffalo
1970	Bobby Orr, Boston	1970	Bobby Orr, Boston	1970	Tony Esposito, Chicago
1969	Phil Esposito, Boston	1969	Bobby Orr, Boston	1969	Danny Grant, Minnesota
1968	Stan Mikita, Chicago	1968	Bobby Orr, Boston	1968	Derek Sanderson, Boston
1967	Stan Mikita, Chicago	1967	Harry Howell, N.Y. Rangers	1967	Bobby Orr, Boston
1966	Bobby Hull, Chicago	1966	Jacques Laperriere, Montreal	1966	Brit Selby, Toronto
1965	Stan Mikita, Chicago	1965	Pierre Pilote, Chicago	1965	Roger Crozier, Detroit

	Hart Trophy MVP		Vezina Trophy Leading goalie(1)		Lady Byng Trophy Sportsmanship
1984	Wayne Gretzky, Edmonton	1984	Tom Barrasso, Buffalo	1984	Mike Bossy, N.Y. Islanders
1983	Wayne Gretzky, Edmonton	1983	Pete Peeters, Boston	1983	Mike Bossy, N.Y. Islanders
1982	Wayne Gretzky, Edmonton	1982	Billy Smith, N.Y. Islanders	1982	Rick Middleton, Boston
1981	Wayne Gretzky, Edmonton	1981	Sevigny, Herron, Larocque, Montreal	1981	Rick Kehoe, Pittsburgh
1980	Wayne Gretzky, Edmonton	1980	Edwards, Sauve, Buffalo	1980	Wayne Gretzky, Edmonton
1979	Bryan Trottier, N.Y. Islanders	1979	Dryden, Larocque, Montreal	1979	Bob MacMillan, Atlanta
1978	Guy Lafleur, Montreal	1978	Dryden, Larocque, Montreal	1978	Butch Goring, Los Angeles
1977	Guy Lafleur, Montreal	1977	Dryden, Larocque, Montreal	1977	Marcel Dionne, Los Angeles
1976	Bobby Clarke, Philadelphia	1976	Ken Dryden, Montreal	1976	Jean Ratelle, Boston
1975	Bobby Clarke, Philadelphia	1975	Bernie Parent, Philadelphia	1975	Marcel Dionne, Detroit
1974	Phil Esposito, Boston	1974	Tony Esposito, Chicago	1974	John Bucyk, Boston
1973	Bobby Clarke, Philadelphia		Bernie Parent, Philadelphia	1973	Gilbert Perreault, Buffalo
1972	Bobby Orr, Boston	1973	Ken Dryden, Montreal	1972	Jean Ratelle, N.Y. Rangers
1971	Bobby Orr, Boston	1972	Esposito, Smith, Chicago	1971	John Bucyk, Boston
1970	Bobby Orr, Boston	1971	Giacomin, Villemure,	1970	Phil Goyette, St. Louis
1969	Phil Esposito, Boston		N.Y. Rangers	1969	Alex Devecchio, Detroit
1968	Stan Mikita, Chicago	1970	Tony Esposito, Chicago	1968	Stan Mikita, Chicago
1967	Stan Mikita, Chicago	1969	Hall, Plante, St. Louis	1967	Stan Mikita, Chicago
1966	Bobby Hull, Chicago	1968	Worsley, Vachon, Montreal	1966	Alex Devecchio, Detroit
1965	Bobby Hull, Chicago	1967	Hall, De Jordy, Chicago	1965	Bobby Hull, Chicago
		1966	Hodge, Worsley, Montreal		
		1965	Sawchuck, Bower, Toronto		

Frank Selke Trophy (best defensive forward)—1978-81, Bob Gainey, Montreal; 1982, Steve Kasper, Boston; 1983, Bobby Clarke, Philadelphia; 1984, Doug Jarvis, Washington.
(1) Most valuable goalie beginning in 1982.

NHL All Star Team, 1984

First team	Position	Second team
Tom Barrasso, Buffalo	Goalie	Pat Riggin, Washington
Ray Bourque, Boston	Defense	Paul Coffey, Edmonton
Rod Langway, Washington	Defense	Denis Potvin, N.Y. Islanders
Wayne Gretzky, Edmonton	Center	Bryan Trottier, N.Y. Islanders
Mike Bossy, N.Y. Islanders	Right Wing	Jari Kurri, Edmonton
Michel Goulet, Quebec	Left Wing	Mark Messier, Edmonton

NCAA Hockey Champions

1948	Michigan	1958	Denver	1967	Cornell	1976	Minnesota
1949	Boston College	1959	North Dakota	1968	Denver	1977	Wisconsin
1950	Colorado College	1960	Denver	1969	Denver	1978	Boston Univ.
1951	Michigan	1961	Denver	1970	Cornell	1979	Minnesota
1952	Michigan	1962	Michigan Tech	1971	Boston Univ.	1980	North Dakota
1953	Michigan	1963	North Dakota	1972	Boston Univ	1981	Wisconsin
1954	Rensselaer Poly	1964	Michigan	1973	Wisconsin	1982	North Dakota
1955	Michigan	1965	Michigan Tech	1974	Minnesota	1983	Wisconsin
1956	Michigan	1966	Michigan State	1975	Michigan Tech	1984	Bowling Green
1957	Colorado College						

World Record Fish Caught by Rod and Reel

Source: International Game Fish Association.

Records confirmed to June, 1984

Saltwater Fish

Species	Weight	Where caught	Date	Angler
Albacore	88 lbs. 2 oz.	Pt. Mogan, Canary Islands	Nov. 19, 1977	Siegried Dickemann
Amberjack, greater	155 lbs. 10 oz.	Bermuda	June 24, 1981	Joseph Dawson
Barracuda, great	83 lbs.	Lagos, Nigeria	Jan. 13, 1952	K.J.W. Hackett
Bass, black sea	9 lbs.	Montauk, N.Y.	Oct. 10, 1983	Salvatore Vicari
Bass, European	11 lbs. 15 oz.	Pont Lorois Belz, France	July 25, 1983	Bernard Peron
Bass, giant sea	563 lbs. 8 oz.	Anacaba Island, Cal.	Aug. 20, 1968	James D. McAdam Jr.
Bass, striped	78 lbs. 8 oz.	Atlantic City, N.J.	Sept. 21, 1982	Albert McReynolds
Bluefish	31 lbs. 12 oz.	Hatteras Inlet, N.C.	Jan. 30, 1972	James M. Hussey
Bonefish	19 lbs.	Zululand, S. Africa	May 26, 1962	Brian W. Batchelor
Bonito, Atlantic	16 lbs. 12 oz.	Canary Islands	Dec. 6, 1980	Rolf Fredderies
		Madeira Islands	Dec. 6, 1982	Wilfried Hobelmann
Bonito, Pacific	23 lbs. 8 oz.	Victoria, Mahe Seychelles	Feb. 19, 1975	Anne Cochain
Cobia	110 lbs. 5 oz.	Mombasa, Kenya	Sept. 8, 1964	Eric Tinworth
Cod, Atlantic	98 lbs. 12 oz.	Isle of Shoals, N.H.	June 8, 1969	Alphonse Bielevich
Cod, Pacific	9 lbs. 8 oz.	Adak, Alaska	May 14, 1983	Gordon Votuba
Conger	102 lbs. 8 oz.	Devon, England	July 18, 1983	Raymond E. Street
Dolphin	87 lbs.	Papagallo Gulf, Costa Rica	Sept. 25, 1976	Manual Salazar
Drum, black	113 lbs. 1 oz.	Lewes, Del.	Sept. 15, 1975	Gerald Townsend
Drum, red	90 lbs.	Rodanthe, N.C.	Nov. 7, 1973	Elvin Hooper
Flounder, summer	22 lbs. 7 oz.	Montauk, N.Y.	Sept. 15, 1975	Charles Nappi
Halibut, Atlantic	250 lbs.	Gloucester, Mass.	July 3, 1981	Louis Sirard
Halibut, California	45 lbs.	Santa Cruz Is., Cal.	June 19, 1982	Jack Meserve
Halibut, Pacific	350 lbs.	Homer, Alaska	June 30, 1982	Vern S. Foster
Jack, crevalle	54 lbs. 7oz.	Pt. Michel, Gabon	Jan. 15, 1982	Thomas Gibson Jr.
Jack, horse-eye	24 lbs. 8 oz.	Miami, Fla.	Dec. 20, 1982	Tito Schnau
Jack, Pacific crevalle	22 lbs. 15 oz.	Salinas, Ecuador	Nov. 19, 1983	Emilio Kronfle
Jewfish	680 lbs.	Fernandina Beach, Fla.	May 20, 1961	Lynn Joyner
Kawakawa	26 lbs.	Merimbula, Australia	Jan. 26, 1980	Wally Elfring
Lingcod	46 lbs.	Hakai Pass, B.C. Canada	Aug. 31, 1983	Betty Moore
Mackerel, king	90 lbs.	Key West, Fla.	Feb. 16, 1976	Norton Thomton
Mackeral, Spanish	10 lbs. 15 oz.	Oak Bluffs, Mass.	Sept. 18, 1983	Heather Wadsworth
Marlin, Atlantic blue	1,282 lbs.	St. Thomas, Virgin Islands	Aug. 6, 1977	Larry Martin
Marlin, black	1,560 lbs.	Cabo Blanco, Peru	Aug. 4, 1953	A. C. Glassell Jr.
Marlin, Pacific blue	1,376 lbs.	Kaaiwa Pt., Hawaii	May. 31, 1982	J.W. deBeaubien
Marlin, striped	455 lbs. 4 oz.	Mayor Island, New Zealand	Mar. 8, 1982	Bruce Jenkinson
Marlin, white	181 lbs. 14 oz.	Vitoria, Brazil	Dec. 8, 1979	Evandro Luiz Caser
Permit	51 lbs. 8 oz.	Lake Worth, Fla.	Apr. 28, 1978	William M. Kenney
Pollack	26 lbs.	Ile de Ouessant, France	Aug. 30, 1981	Loik La Chat
Pollock	46 lbs. 7 oz.	Brielle, N.J.	May 26, 1975	John Tomes Holton
Pompano, African	41 lbs. 8 oz.	Ft. Lauderdale, Fla.	Feb. 15, 1979	Wayne Sommers
Roosterfish	114 lbs.	La Paz, Mexico	June 1, 1960	Abe Sackheim
Runner, rainbow	33 lbs. 10 oz.	Clarion Is., Mexico	Mar. 14, 1976	Ralph A. Mikkelsen
Sailfish, Atlantic	128 lbs. 1 oz.	Luanda, Angola	Mar. 27, 1974	Harm Steyn
Sailfish, Pacific	221 lbs.	Santa Cruz Is., Ecuador	Feb. 12, 1947	C. W. Stewart
Seabass, white	83 lbs. 12 oz.	San Felipe, Mexico	Mar. 31, 1953	L.C. Baumgardner
Seatrout, spotted	16 lbs.	Mason's Beach, Va.	May 28, 1977	William Katko
Shark, blue	437 lbs.	Catherine Bay, N.S.W. Australia	Oct. 2, 1976	Peter Hyde
Shark, hammerhead	991 lbs.	Sarasota, Fla.	May 30, 1982	Allen Ogle
Shark, man-eater or white	2,664 lbs.	Ceduna, Australia	Apr. 21, 1959	Alfred Dean
Shark, mako	1,080 lbs.	Montauk, N.Y.	Aug. 26, 1979	James Melanson
Shark, porbeagle	465 lbs.	Cornwall, England	July 23, 1976	Jorge Potier
Shark, thresher	802 lbs.	Tutukaka, New Zealand	Feb. 8, 1981	Dianne North
Shark, tiger	1,780 lbs.	Cherry Grove, S.C.	June 14, 1964	Walter Maxwell
Skipjack, black	20 lbs. 5 oz.	Baja, Mexico	Oct. 14, 1983	Roger Torriero
Snapper, cubera	121 lbs. 8 oz.	Cameron, La.	July 5, 1982	Mike Hebert
Snook	53 lbs. 10 oz.	Costa Rica	Oct. 18, 1978	Gilbert Ponzi
Spearfish	90 lbs. 13 oz.	Madeira Island, Portugal	June 2, 1980	Joseph Larkin
Swordfish	1,182 lbs.	Iquique, Chile	May 7, 1953	L. Marron
Tanguigue	99 lbs.	Natal, So. Africa	Mar. 14, 1982	Michael J. Wilkinson
Tarpon	283 lbs.	Lake Maracaibo, Venezuela	Mar. 19, 1956	M. Salazar
Tautog	21 lbs. 6 oz.	Cape May, N.J.	June 12, 1954	R.N. Sheafer
Tope	71 lbs. 10 oz.	Knysna, So. Africa	July 10, 1982	William DeWit
Trevally, bigeye	9 lbs. 12 oz.	Pinas Bay, Panama	May 13, 1983	John McCulloch
Trevally, giant	137 lbs. 9 oz.	McKenzie St. Park, Hawaii	July 13, 1983	Roy Gushiken
Tuna, Atlantic bigeye	375 lbs. 8 oz.	Ocean City, Md.	Aug. 26, 1977	Cecil Browne
Tuna, blackfin	42 lbs.	Bermuda	June 2, 1978	Alan J. Card
Tuna, bluefin	1,496 lbs.	Aulds Cove, Nova Scotia	Oct. 26, 1979	Ken Fraser
Tuna, dog tooth	288 lbs. 12 oz.	Cheju-do, Korea	Oct. 6, 1982	Boo-Sl Oh
Tuna, longtail	79 lbs. 2 oz.	Montague Is., N.S.W., Australia	Apr. 12, 1982	Tim Simpson
Tuna, Pacific bigeye	435 lbs.	Cabo Blanco, Peru	Apr. 17, 1957	Dr. Russel Lee
Tuna, skipjack	41 lbs. 12 oz.	Mauritius	Mar. 13, 1982	Bruno de Ravel
Tuna, southern bluefin	348 lbs. 5 oz.	Whakatane, New Zealand	Jan. 16, 1981	Rex Wood
Tuna, yellowfin	388 lbs. 12 oz.	San Benedicto Island, Mexico	Apr. 1, 1977	Curt Wiesenhutter
Tunny, little	27 lbs.	Key Largo, Fla.	Apr. 20, 1976	William E. Allison
Wahoo	149 lbs.	Cay Cay, Bahamas	June 15, 1962	John Pirovano
Weakfish	19 lbs.	Chesapeake Bay, Va.	May 19, 1983	Philip Halstead
Yellowtail, California	71 lbs. 15 oz.	Alijos Rocks, Mexico	June 24, 1979	Michael Carpenter
Yellowtail, southern	111 lbs.	Bay of Islands, New Zealand	June 11, 1961	A.F. Plim

Freshwater Fish

Species	Weight	Where Caught	Date	Angler
Barramundi	59 lbs. 12 oz.	Pt. Stuart, Australia	Apr. 7, 1983	Andrew Davern
Bass, largemouth	22 lbs. 4 oz.	Montgomery Lake, Ga.	June 2, 1932	George W. Perry
Bass, peacock	26 lbs. 8 oz.	Matevini R., Colombia	Jan. 26, 1982	Rod Neubert
Bass, redeye	8 lbs. 3 oz.	Flint River, Ga.	Oct. 23, 1977	David A. Hubbard
Bass rock	3 lbs.	York River, Ont.	Aug. 1, 1974	Peter Gulgin
Bass, smallmouth	11 lbs. 15 oz.	Dale Hollow Lake, Ky.	July 9, 1955	David L. Hayes
Bass, spotted	8 lbs. 15 oz.	Lewis Smith Lake, Ala.	Mar. 18, 1978	Philip Terry Jr.
Bass, striped	59 lbs. 12 oz.	Colorado River, Ariz.	May 26, 1977	Frank Smith
Bass, white	5 lbs. 9 oz.	Colorado River, Tex.	Mar. 31, 1977	David Cordill
Bass, whiterock	20 lbs. 6 oz.	Savannah River, Ga.	May 28, 1978	Dan Wood
Bass, yellow	2 lbs. 4 oz.	Lake Monroe, Ind.	Mar. 27, 1977	Donald L. Stalker
Bluegill	4 lbs. 12 oz.	Ketona Lake, Ala.	Apr. 9, 1950	T.S. Hudson
Bowfin	21 lbs. 8 oz.	Florence, S.C.	Jan. 29, 1980	Robert Harmon
Buffalo, bigmouth	70 lbs. 5 oz.	Bastrop, La.	Apr. 21, 1980	Delbert Sisk
Buffalo, smallmouth	51 lbs.	Lawrence, Kan.	May 2, 1979	Scott Butler
Bullhead, black	8 lbs.	Lake Waccabuc, N.Y.	Aug. 1, 1951	Kani Evans
Bullhead, brown	5 lbs. 8 oz.	Veal Pond, Ga.	May 22, 1975	Jimmy Andrews
Bullhead, yellow	3 lbs.	Nelson Lake, Wis.	May 8, 1977	Mark Nessman
Burbot	18 lbs. 4 oz.	Pickford, Mich.	Jan. 31, 1980	Thomas Courtemanche
Carp	57 lbs. 13 oz.	Potomac R., Wash., D.C.	June 19, 1983	David Nikolow
Catfish, blue	97 lbs.	Missouri River, S.D.	Sept. 16, 1959	E.B. Elliott
Catfish, channel	58 lbs.	Santee-Cooper Res., S.C.	July 7, 1964	W.B. Whaley
Catfish, flathead	91 lbs. 4 oz.	Lake Lewisville, Tex.	Mar. 28, 1982	Mike Rogers
Catfish, white	17 lbs. 7 oz.	Success L., Tulare, Cal.	Nov. 15, 1981	Chuck Idell
Char, Arctic	29 lbs. 11 oz.	Arctic River, N.W.T., Canada	Aug. 21, 1968	Jeanne P. Branson
Crappie, black	6 lbs.	Westwago, La.	Nov. 28, 1969	Lettie T. Robertson
Crappie, white	5 lbs. 3 oz.	Enid Dam, Miss.	July 31, 1957	Fred L. Bright
Dolly Varden	4 lbs. 13 oz.	Nushagak R., Alaska	June 30, 1983	James F. Pfeifer
Dorado	48 lbs. 11 oz.	Corrientes, Argentina	Sept. 12, 1982	Sindo Farina
Drum, freshwater	54 lbs. 8 oz.	Nickajack Lake, Tenn.	Apr. 20, 1972	Benny E. Hull
Gar, alligator	279 lbs.	Rio Grande River, Tex.	Dec. 2, 1951	Bill Valverde
Gar, Florida	21 lbs. 3 oz.	Boca Raton, Fla.	June 3, 1981	Jeff Sabol
Gar, longnose	50 lbs. 5 oz.	Trinity River, Tex.	July 30, 1954	Townsend Miller
Gar, shortnose	3 lbs. 5 oz.	Lake Francis Case, S.D.	June 9, 1977	J. Pawlowski
Grayling, Arctic	5 lbs. 15 oz.	Katseyedie River, N.W.T.	Aug. 16, 1967	Jeanne P. Branson
Huchen	70 lbs. 12 oz.	Carinthia, Austria	Jan. 1, 1980	Martin Esterl
Inconnu	38 lbs. 2 oz.	Kobuk R., Alaska	Sept. 12, 1982	Mark Feldman
Kokanee	6 lbs. 9 oz.	Priest Lake, Ida.	June 9, 1975	Jerry Verge
Muskellunge	69 lbs. 15 oz.	St. Lawrence River, N.Y.	Sept. 22, 1957	Arthur Lawton
Muskellunge, tiger	51 lbs. 3 oz.	Lac Vieux-Desert, Wis., Mich.	July 16, 1919	John Knobla
Perch, white	4 lbs. 12 oz.	Messalonskee Lake, Me.	June 4, 1949	Mrs. Earl Small
Perch, yellow	4 lbs. 3 oz.	Bordentown, N.J.	May, 1865	Dr. C.C. Abbot
Pickerel, chain	9 lbs. 6 oz.	Homerville, Ga.	Feb. 17, 1961	Baxley McQuaig Jr.
Pike, northern	46 lbs. 2 oz.	Sacandaga Reservoir, N.Y.	Sept. 15, 1940	Peter Dubuc
Redhorse, northern	3 lbs. 11 oz.	Missouri River, S.D.	May 26, 1977	Philip Laumeyer
Redhorse, silver	9 lbs. 11 oz.	Winnipeg R., Manitoba, Canada	May 22, 1982	John Richards
Salmon, Atlantic	79 lbs. 2 oz.	Tana River, Norway	1928	Henrik Henriksen
Salmon, chinook	93 lbs.	Kelp Bay, Alas.	June 24, 1977	Howard C. Rider
Salmon, chum	27 lbs. 3 oz.	Raymond Cove, Alas.	June 11, 1977	Robert A. Jahnke
Salmon, coho	31 lbs.	Cowichan Bay, B.C.	Oct. 11, 1947	Mrs. Lee Hallberg
Salmon, pink	12 lbs. 9 oz.	Morse, Kenai rivers, Alas.	Aug. 17, 1974	Steven A. Lee
Salmon, sockeye	12 lbs. 8 oz.	Situk R., Alaska	June 23, 1983	Mike Boswell
Sauger	8 lbs. 12 oz.	Lake Sakakawea, N.D.	Oct. 6, 1971	Mike Fischer
Shad, American	9 lbs. 4 oz.	Delaware River, Pa.	Apr. 26, 1979	J. Edward Whitman
	9 lbs. 4 oz.	Connecticut R., Wilson, Conn.	Apr. 20, 1981	Edward W. Cypus
Splake	16 lbs. 12 oz.	Island Lake, Col.	Sept. 14, 1973	Del Canty
Sturgeon	468 lbs.	Benicia, Cal.	July 9, 1983	Joey Pallotta 3d
Sunfish, green	2 lbs. 2 oz.	Stockton Lake, Mo.	June 18, 1971	Paul M. Dilley
Sunfish, redbreast	1 lb. 8 oz.	Suwannee River, Fla.	Apr. 30, 1977	Tommy D. Cason Jr.
Sunfish, redear	4 lbs. 8 oz.	Chase City, Va.	June 19, 1970	Maurice E. Ball
Tigerfish	46 lbs. 4 oz.	L. Tanganyika, Zambia	Oct. 10, 1981	Giorgio Cuturi
Trout, brook	14 lbs. 8 oz.	Nipigon River, Ont.	July 1916	Dr. W.J. Cook
Trout, brown	35 lbs. 15 oz.	Nahuel Huapi, Argentina	Dec. 16, 1952	Eugenio Cavaglia
Trout, bull	32 lbs.	L. Pend Oreille, Ida.	Oct. 27, 1949	N.L. Higgins
Trout, cutthroat	41 lbs.	Pyramid Lake, Nev.	Dec. 1925	J. Skimmerhorn
Trout, golden	11 lbs.	Cook's Lake, Wyo.	Aug. 5, 1948	Charles S. Reed
Trout, lake	65 lbs.	Great Bear Lake, N.W.T.	Aug. 8, 1970	Larry Daunis
Trout, rainbow	42 lbs. 2 oz.	Bell Island, Alas.	June 22, 1970	David Robert White
Trout, tiger	20 lbs. 13 oz.	Lake Michigan, Wis.	Aug. 12, 1978	Pete Friedland
Walleye	25 lbs.	Old Hickory Lake, Tenn.	Aug. 1, 1960	Mabry Harper
Warmouth	2 lbs. 2 oz.	Douglas Swamp, S.C.	May 19, 1973	Willie Singletary
Whitefish, lake	13 lbs. 15 oz.	Meaford, Ont.	Apr. 19, 1981	Wayne Caswell
Whitefish, mountain	5 lbs. 2 oz.	Columbia R., Wash.	Nov. 30, 1983	Steven Becken
Whitefish, round	3 lbs. 4 oz.	Leland Harbor, Mich.	Nov. 2, 1977	Vernon Bauer

NCAA Wrestling Champions

Year	Champion	Year	Champion	Year	Champion	Year	Champion	Year	Champion
1963	Oklahoma	1968	Oklahoma State	1973	Iowa State	1977	Iowa State	1981	Iowa
1964	Oklahoma State	1969	Iowa State	1974	Oklahoma	1978	Iowa	1982	Iowa
1965	Iowa State	1970	Iowa State	1975	Iowa	1979	Iowa	1983	Iowa
1966	Oklahoma State	1971	Oklahoma State	1976	Iowa	1980	Iowa	1984	Iowa
1967	Michigan State	1972	Iowa State						

College Basketball
Final Regular Season Conference Standings, 1983–84

Atlantic Coast

	Conference W	L	All Games W	L
North Carolina	14	0	27	2
Maryland*	9	5	23	7
Wake Forest	7	7	21	8
Duke	7	7	24	9
Virginia	6	8	17	11
Georgia Tech.	6	8	18	10
N. C. State	4	10	19	13
Clemson	3	11	14	14

Atlantic 10

	Conference W	L	All Games W	L
Temple	18	0	25	4
St. Joseph's	13	5	20	8
George Washington	11	7	17	12
Rutgers	9	9	16	12
West Virginia*	9	9	19	11
St. Bonaventure	8	10	19	13
Duquesne	8	10	10	18
Massachusetts	6	12	12	17
Rhode Island	5	13	6	22
Penn State	3	15	6	22

Big East

	Conference W	L	All Games W	L
Georgetown*	14	2	29	3
Syracuse	12	4	22	8
Villanova	12	4	18	10
Boston College	8	8	17	11
St. John's	8	8	18	11
Pitt.	6	10	16	12
Providence	5	11	15	14
Connecticut	5	11	13	15
Seton Hall	2	14	9	19

Big Eight

	Conference W	L	All Games W	L
Oklahoma	13	1	29	4
Kansas*	9	5	21	9
Nebraska	7	7	17	11
Iowa State	6	8	16	12
Colorado	6	8	16	13
Missouri	5	9	16	14
Kansas State	5	9	14	15
Oklahoma State	5	9	13	15

Big Sky

	Conference W	L	All Games W	L
Weber State	12	2	22	7
Montana	9	5	23	7
Nevada-Reno*	7	7	17	13
Montana State	7	7	14	15
Boise State	6	8	15	13
Idaho State	6	8	12	20
Northern Arizona	5	9	12	15
Idaho	4	10	9	19

Big Ten

	Conference W	L	All Games W	L
Illinois	15	3	24	4
Purdue	15	3	22	7
Indiana	13	5	20	8
Michigan	10	8	18	10
Ohio State	8	10	15	13
Michigan State	8	10	15	13
Minnesota	6	12	15	13
Iowa	6	12	13	15
Northwestern	5	13	12	16
Wisconsin	4	14	8	20

East Coast

	Conference W	L	All Games W	L
Bucknell	14	2	26	6
Rider*	11	5	23	10
Drexel	10	6	17	12
Hofstra	9	7	14	14
Lafayette	9	7	12	17
Delaware	6	10	11	16
Towson State	5	11	9	19
American Univ.	5	11	6	22
Lehigh	3	13	4	23

ECAC North Atlantic

	Conference W	L	All Games W	L
Northeastern*	14	2	26	4
Canisius	9	5	19	11
Boston Univ.	9	5	16	13
Maine	7	7	17	10
New Hampshire	8	6	15	13
Niagara	3	9	10	18
Vermont	3	11	7	21
Colgate	1	13	5	22

ECAC South

	Conference W	L	All Games W	L
Richmond*	7	3	20	9
William & Mary	6	4	13	13
Navy	6	4	24	8
George Mason	5	5	21	7
James Madison	5	5	15	14
East Carolina	1	9	4	24

ECAC Metro

	Conference W	L	All Games W	L
LIU	11	5	20	10
Robert Morris	11	5	17	13
Fairleigh Dickinson	10	6	17	12
Marist (N.Y.)	8	8	14	15
St. Francis (Pa.)	8	8	13	16
Loyola (Md.)	10	6	16	12
Siena	8	8	15	13
Wagner	5	11	8	20
St. Francis (N.Y.)	1	15	2	24

Ivy League

	Conference W	L	All Games W	L
Princeton	10	4	17	9
Cornell	9	5	16	10
Harvard	9	5	15	11
Penn	7	7	10	16
Dartmouth	6	8	11	15
Brown	6	8	11	15
Columbia	5	9	8	18
Yale	4	10	7	19

Metro

	Conference W	L	All Games W	L
Memphis State	11	3	24	6
Louisville	11	3	22	10
Florida State	9	5	18	10
Virginia Tech.	8	6	18	12
Tulane	7	7	17	11
South Carolina	5	9	12	16
Southern Mississippi	4	10	13	15
Cincinnati	0	14	3	25

Metro Atlantic Athletic

	Conference W	L	All Games W	L
Iona*	11	3	23	7
St. Peter's	11	3	23	5
La Salle	11	3	20	10
Fordham	7	7	19	14
Fairfield	5	9	10	18
Holy Cross	5	9	12	18
Army	4	10	11	17
Manhattan	2	12	9	19

Mid-American

	Conference W	L	All Games W	L
Miami*	16	2	24	5
Ohio University	14	4	20	8
Bowling Green	11	7	19	10
Toledo	11	7	18	11
Kent State	8	10	15	14
Eastern Michigan	8	10	11	17
Northern Illinois	9	9	12	15
Central Michigan	6	12	11	16
Ball State	5	13	8	19
Western Michigan	2	16	4	22

Mid-Continent

	Conference W	L	All Games W	L
Illinois-Chicago	11	2	21	7
Northern Iowa	10	3	18	9
SW Missouri State	8	5	17	10
Eastern Illinois	6	7	15	13
Western Illinois	6	7	17	12
Wis.-Green Bay	5	9	9	19
Cleveland State	4	9	14	15
Valparaiso	3	11	9	19

Midwestern City

	Conference W	L	All Games W	L
Oral Roberts*	11	3	21	9
Loyola (Ill.)	10	4	20	9
Xavier	9	5	20	10
Butler	7	7	13	15
Evansville	7	7	15	14
St. Louis Univ.	5	9	12	16
Detroit	4	10	8	20
Oklahoma City	3	11	8	19

Mid-Eastern Athletic

	Conference W	L	All Games W	L
N.C. A&T*	9	1	22	6
Howard University	7	3	15	14
S.C. State	6	4	14	16
Delaware St.	3	7	12	16
Md.-Eastern Shore	3	7	7	21
Bethune-Cookman	2	8	6	22
Florida A&M			7	19

Missouri Valley

	Conference W	L	All Games W	L
Tulsa*	13	3	27	3
Illinois State	13	3	22	7
Wichita St.	11	5	18	10
Creighton	8	8	17	13
Southern Illinois	7	9	15	13
Bradley	7	9	15	13
Indiana State	6	10	14	13
Drake	4	12	8	20
West Texas State	3	13	8	19

Ohio Valley

	Conference W	L	All Games W	L
Morehead St.*	12	2	24	5
Tennessee Tech.	11	3	18	10
Youngstown State	9	5	18	10
Murray State	7	7	15	13
Eastern Kentucky	5	9	11	16
Austin Peay State	5	9	14	16
Middle Tenn. State	4	10	11	16
Akron	3	11	8	19

Pacific-10

	Conference W	L	All Games W	L
Washington	15	3	22	6
Oregon State	15	3	22	6
Oregon	11	7	16	12
UCLA	10	8	17	11
Stanford	8	10	19	12
Arizona	8	10	11	17
Arizona State	8	10	13	15
Southern Cal.	6	12	11	20
California	5	13	12	16
Washington State	4	14	10	18

PCAA

	Conference W	L	All Games W	L
Nevada-Las Vegas	16	2	27	5
Cal-Irvine	14	4	19	10
Fresno State*	13	5	25	7
Utah State	12	6	19	10
New Mexico State	9	9	13	15
Fullerton State	8	10	17	13
San Jose State	7	12	10	18
Long Beach State	6	12	9	19
Cal-Santa Barbara	5	13	10	17
Pacific	1	17	3	27

Southeastern

	Conference W	L	All Games W	L
Kentucky*	14	4	26	4
Auburn	12	6	20	10
Florida	11	7	16	12
Louisiana State	11	7	18	11
Alabama	10	8	18	11
Tennessee	9	9	19	13
Vanderbilt	8	10	14	15
Georgia	8	10	17	12
Mississippi State	4	14	9	19
Mississippi	3	15	8	21

Southern

	Conference W	L	All Games W	L
Marshall*	13	3	25	5
UT-Chattanooga	12	4	23	6
Western Carolina	9	7	15	13
The Citadel	8	8	14	14
Appalachian State	8	8	13	15
Furman	7	9	12	17
East Tenn. State	6	10	9	19
Davidson	5	11	9	19
VMI	4	12	8	19

Southwestern Athletic

	Conference W	L	All Games W	L
Alabama State	11	3	22	6
Alcorn State*	11	3	20	9
Southern (La.)	10	4	18	11
Grambling State	7	7	17	12
Miss. Valley State	6	8	14	14
Texas Southern	6	8	9	17
Jackson State	5	9	10	18
Prairie View A&M	0	14	2	26

	Confer-ence W L		All Games W L	
Southland				
Lamar	11	1	25	4
NE Louisiana	9	3	17	12
Louisiana Tech.*	8	4	25	6
McNeese State	6	6	15	15
Arkansas State	4	8	13	15
North Texas	3	9	9	19
Texas-Arlington	1	11	2	23
Southwest				
Houston*	15	1	28	4
Arkansas	14	2	25	6
SMU	12	4	24	7
Texas Tech	10	6	17	12
Texas A&M	7	9	16	14
Rice	6	10	13	17
TCU	4	12	11	17
Texas	3	13	7	21
Baylor	1	15	5	23
Sun Belt				
Va. Commonwealth	11	3	21	5
South Alabama	9	5	21	6
South Florida	9	5	16	10
Old Dominion	9	5	17	10
Ala.-Birmingham	8	6	20	10
Western Kentucky	5	9	11	16
Jacksonville	3	11	12	15
UNC Charlotte	2	12	9	18

	Confer-ence W L		All Games W L	
Trans America Athletic				
Houston Baptist*	11	3	24	6
Samford (Ala.)	10	4	22	8
Georgia Southern	8	6	16	13
Centenary	7	7	12	16
Ark.-Little Rock	7	7	15	15
Mercer	6	8	13	14
Hardin-Simmons	5	9	9	21
NW Louisiana State	2	12	6	22
Nicholls State			19	7
Georgia State			6	22
West Coast Athletic				
San Diego	9	3	18	9
Santa Clara	7	5	20	9
St. Mary's	7	5	12	16
Gonzaga	6	6	17	11
Pepperdine	6	6	15	13
Loyola Marymount	5	7	12	15
Portland	2	10	11	17
Western Athletic				
UTEP	13	3	27	3
Brigham Young	12	4	19	10
New Mexico	10	6	24	10
Wyoming	9	7	17	13
Colorado State	9	7	16	13
San Diego State	6	10	15	13
Hawaii	6	10	12	16
Utah	4	12	11	19
Air Force	3	13	8	19

Major Independents	W	L
DePaul	26	2
Southwestern Louisiana	20	8
Texas-San Antonio	20	8
Stetson (Fla.)	19	9
Dayton	18	10
Notre Dame	17	11
Marquette	16	12
Baptist (S.C.)	15	13
Pan American (Tex.)	14	12
New Orleans	13	15
Tennessee State	12	15
Southeastern Louisiana	11	16
North Carolina-Wilmington	11	17
Utica (N.Y.)	11	15
Campbell (N.C.)	10	18
Brooklyn (N.Y.)	8	20
Monmouth (N.J.)	6	19
Eastern Washington	4	22
U.S. International (Cal.)	2	25

*won postseason tournament

NCAA Basketball Championships in 1984

East
Preliminary—Richmond 89, Rider 65; Northeastern 90, LIU 87.

First round—Temple 65, St. John's 63; Richmond 72, Auburn 71; VCU 70, Northeastern 69; Virginia 58, Iona 57.

Second round—North Carolina 77, Temple 66; Indiana 75, Richmond 67; Syracuse 78, VCU 63; Virginia 53, Arkansas 51.

Semifinals—Indiana 72, North Carolina 68; Virginia 63, Syracuse 55.

Championship—Virginia 50, Indiana 48.

Mideast
Preliminary—Morehead St. 70, No. Carolina A&T 69.

First round—Brigham Young 84, Ala.-Birmingham 68; Louisville 72, Morehead St. 59; West Virginia 64, Oregon St. 62; Villanova 84, Marshall 72.

Second round—Kentucky 93, Brigham Young 68; Louisville 69, Tulsa 67; Maryland 102, West Virginia 77; Illinois 64, Villanova 56.

Semifinals—Kentucky 72, Louisville 67; Illinois 72, Maryland 70.

Championship—Kentucky 54, Illinois 51.

Midwest
Preliminary—Alcorn St. 79, Houston Baptist 60.

First round—Illinois St. 49, Alabama 48; Kansas 57, Alcorn St. 56; Memphis St. 92, Oral Roberts 83; Louisiana Tech 66, Fresno St. 56.

Second round—DePaul 75, Illinois St. 61; Wake Forest 69, Kansas 59; Memphis St. 66, Purdue 48; Houston 77, Louisiana Tech 69.

Semifinals—Wake Forest 73, DePaul 71; Houston 78, Memphis St. 71.

Championship—Houston 68, Wake Forest 63.

West
Preliminary—Princeton 65, San Diego 56.

First round—SMU 83, Miami, Ohio 69; Nevada-Las Vegas 68, Princeton 56; Washington 64, Nevada-Reno 54; Dayton 74, LSU 66.

Second round—Georgetown 37, SMU 36; Nevada-Las Vegas 73, Texas-El Paso 60; Washington, 80, Duke 78; Dayton 89, Oklahoma 85.

Semifinals—Georgetown 62, Nevada-Las Vegas 48; Dayton 64, Washington 58.

Championship—Georgetown 61, Dayton 49.

National Semifinals
Georgetown 53, Kentucky 40; Houston 49, Virginia 47.

Championship
Georgetown 84, Houston 75.

National Invitation Tournament Champions

Year	Champion	Year	Champion	Year	Champion	Year	Champion
1938	Temple	1950	CCNY	1962	Dayton	1974	Purdue
1939	Long Island Univ.	1951	Brigham Young	1963	Providence	1975	Princeton
1940	Colorado	1952	LaSalle	1964	Bradley	1976	Kentucky
1941	Long Island Univ.	1953	Seton Hall	1965	St. John's	1977	St. Bonaventure
1942	West Virginia	1954	Holy Cross	1966	Brigham Young	1978	Texas
1943	St. John's	1955	Duquesne	1967	Southern Illinois	1979	Indiana
1944	St. John's	1956	Louisville	1968	Dayton	1980	Virginia
1945	De Paul	1957	Bradley	1969	Temple	1981	Tulsa
1946	Kentucky	1958	Xavier (Ohio)	1970	Marquette	1982	Bradley
1947	Utah	1959	St. John's	1971	North Carolina	1983	Fresno State
1948	St. Louis	1960	Bradley	1972	Maryland	1984	Michigan
1949	San Francisco	1961	Providence	1973	Virginia Tech		

NCAA Division I Women's Champions

Year	Champion	Coach	Final opponent	Year	Champion	Coach	Final opponent
1982	Louisiana Tech	Sonja Hogg	Cheyney	1984	USC	Linda Sharp	Tennessee
1983	USC	Linda Sharp	Louisiana Tech				

NCAA Division I Champions

Year	Champion	Coach	Final opponent	Year	Champion	Coach	Final opponent
1939	Oregon	Howard Hobson	Ohio St.	1963	Loyola (Ill.)	George Ireland	Cincinnati
1940	Indiana	Branch McCracken	Kansas	1964	UCLA	John Wooden	Duke
1941	Wisconsin	Harold Foster	Washington St.	1965	UCLA	John Wooden	Michigan
1942	Stanford	Everett Dean	Dartmouth	1966	Texas-El Paso	Don Haskins	Kentucky
1943	Wyoming	Everett Shelton	Georgetown	1967	UCLA	John Wooden	Dayton
1944	Utah	Vadal Peterson	Dartmouth	1968	UCLA	John Wooden	N. Carolina
1945	Oklahoma St.	Henry Iba	NYU	1969	UCLA	John Wooden	Purdue
1946	Oklahoma St.	Henry Iba	North Carolina	1970	UCLA	John Wooden	Jacksonville
1947	Holy Cross	Alvin Julian	Oklahoma	1971	UCLA	John Wooden	Villanova*
1948	Kentucky	Adolph Rupp	Baylor	1972	UCLA	John Wooden	Florida St.
1949	Kentucky	Adolph Rupp	Oklahoma St.	1973	UCLA	John Wooden	Memphis St.
1950	CCNY	Nat Holman	Bradley	1974	N. Carolina St.	Norm Sloan	Marquette
1951	Kentucky	Adolph Rupp	Kansas St.	1975	UCLA	John Wooden	Kentucky
1952	Kansas	Forrest Allen	St. John's	1976	Indiana	Bob Knight	Michigan
1953	Indiana	Branch McCracken	Kansas	1977	Marquette	Al McGuire	N. Carolina
1954	La Salle	Kenneth Loeffler	Bradley	1978	Kentucky	Joe Hall	Duke
1955	San Francisco	Phil Woolpert	LaSalle	1979	Michigan St.	Jud Heathcote	Indiana St.
1956	San Francisco	Phil Woolpert	Iowa	1980	Louisville	Denny Crum	UCLA
1957	N. Carolina	Frank McGuire	Kansas	1981	Indiana	Bob Knight	N. Carolina
1958	Kentucky	Adolph Rupp	Seattle	1982	N. Carolina	Dean Smith	Georgetown
1959	California	Pete Newell	W. Virginia	1983	N. Carolina St.	Jim Valvano	Houston
1960	Ohio St.	Fred Taylor	California	1984	Georgetown	John Thompson	Houston
1961	Cincinnati	Edwin Jucker	Ohio St.				
1962	Cincinnati	Edwin Jucker	Ohio St.				

*Declared ineligible subsequent to the tournament.

NCAA Division II Champions

Year	Champion	Year	Champion	Year	Champion	Year	Champion
1966	Kentucky Wesleyan	1971	Evansville	1976	Puget Sound	1981	Florida Southern
1967	Winston-Salem	1972	Roanoke	1977	Tennessee-Chattanooga	1982	Univ. of D.C.
1968	Kentucky Wesleyan	1973	Kentucky Wesleyan	1978	Cheyney State	1983	Wright State
1969	Kentucky Wesleyan	1974	Morgan State	1979	North Alabama	1984	Central Missouri St.
1970	Philadelphia Textile	1975	Old Dominion	1980	Virginia Union		

James E. Sullivan Memorial Trophy Winners

The James E. Sullivan Memorial Trophy, named after the former president of the AAU and inaugurated in 1930, is awarded annually by the AAU to the athlete who "by his or her performance, example and influence as an amateur, has done the most during the year to advance the cause of sportsmanship."

Year	Winner	Sport	Year	Winner	Sport	Year	Winner	Sport
1930	Bobby Jones	Golf	1948	Robert Mathias	Track	1966	Jim Ryun	Track
1931	Barney Berlinger	Track	1949	Dick Button	Skating	1967	Randy Matson	Track
1932	Jim Bausch	Track	1950	Fred Wilt	Track	1968	Debbie Meyer	Swimming
1933	Glen Cunningham	Track	1951	Rev. Robert Richards	Track	1969	Bill Toomey	Track
1934	Bill Bonthron	Track	1952	Horace Ashenfelter	Track	1970	John Kinsella	Swimming
1935	Lawson Little	Golf	1953	Dr. Sammy Lee	Diving	1971	Mark Spitz	Swimming
1936	Glenn Morris	Track	1954	Mal Whitfield	Track	1972	Frank Shorter	Track
1937	Don Budge	Tennis	1955	Harrison Dillard	Track	1973	Bill Walton	Basketball
1938	Don Lash	Track	1956	Patricia McCormick	Diving	1974	Rick Wohlhuter	Track
1939	Joe Burk	Rowing	1957	Bobby Joe Morrow	Track	1975	Tim Shaw	Swimming
1940	Greg Rice	Track	1958	Glenn Davis	Track	1976	Bruce Jenner	Track
1941	Leslie MacMitchell	Track	1959	Parry O'Brien	Track	1977	John Naber	Swimming
1942	Cornelius Warmerdam	Track	1960	Rafer Johnson	Track	1978	Tracy Caulkins	Swimming
1943	Gilbert Dodds	Track	1961	Wilma Rudolph Ward	Track	1979	Kurt Thomas	Gymnastics
1944	Ann Curtis	Swimming	1962	James Beatty	Track	1980	Eric Heiden	Speed Skating
1945	Doc Blanchard	Football	1963	John Pennel	Track	1981	Carl Lewis	Track
1946	Arnold Tucker	Football	1964	Don Schollander	Swimming	1982	Mary Decker	Track
1947	John Kelly Jr.	Rowing	1965	Bill Bradley	Basketball	1983	Edwin Moses	Track

Westminster Kennel Club

Year	Best-in-show	Breed	Owner
1972	Ch. Chinoe's Adamant James	English springer spaniel	Dr. Milton Prickett
1973	Ch. Acadia Command Performance	Poodle	Mrs. Jo Ann Sering & Edward B. Jenner
1974	Ch. Gretchenhof Columbia River	German pointer	Dr. Richard Smith
1975	Ch. Sir Lancelot of Barvan	Old English sheepdog	Mr. & Mrs. Ronald Vanword
1976	Ch. Jo-Ni's Red Baron of Crofton	Lakeland terrier	Virginia Dickson
1977	Ch. Dersade Bobby's Girl	Sealyham	Dorothy Wymer
1978	Ch. Cede Higgens	Yorkshire terrier	Barbara & Charles Switzer
1979	Ch. Oak Tree's Irishtocrat	Irish water spaniel	Anne E. Snelling
1980	Ch. Sierra Cinnar	Siberian husky	Kathleen Kanzler
1981	Ch. Dhandy Favorite Woodchuck	Pug	Robert Houslohner
1982	Ch. St. Aubrey Dragonora of Elsdon	Pekingese	Anne Snelling
1983	Ch. Kabik's The Challenger	Afghan	Chris & Marguerite Terrell
1984	Ch. Seaward's Blackbeard	Newfoundland	Elinor Ayers

National Basketball Association, 1983-84

Final Standings

Eastern Conference

Atlantic Division

Club	W	L	Pct	GB
Boston	62	20	.756	.....
Philadelphia	52	30	.634	10
New York	47	35	.573	15
New Jersey	45	37	.549	17
Washington	35	47	.427	27

Central Division

Club	W	L	Pct	GB
Milwaukee	50	32	.610	.....
Detroit	49	33	.598	1
Atlanta	40	42	.488	10
Cleveland	28	54	.341	22
Chicago	27	55	.329	23
Indiana	26	56	.317	24

Western Conference

Midwest Division

Club	W	L	Pct	GB
Utah	45	37	.549	.....
Dallas	43	39	.524	2
Denver	38	44	.463	7
Kansas City	38	44	.463	7
San Antonio	37	45	.451	8
Houston	29	53	.354	16

Pacific Division

Club	W	L	Pct	GB
Los Angeles	54	28	.659	.....
Portland	48	34	.585	6
Seattle	42	40	.512	12
Phoenix	41	41	.500	13
Golden State	37	45	.451	17
San Diego	30	52	.366	24

NBA Playoff Results

Eastern Division

Boston defeated Washington 3 games to 1.
Milwaukee defeated Chicago 3 games to 2.
New Jersey defeated Philadelphia 3 games to 2.
New York defeated Detroit 3 games to 2.
Milwaukee defeated New Jersey 4 games to 2.
Boston defeated New York 4 games to 3.
Boston defeated Milwaukee 4 games to 1.

Western Division

Los Angeles defeated Kansas City 3 games to 0.
Utah defeated Denver 3 games to 2.
Phoenix defeated Portland 3 games to 2.
Dallas defeated Seattle 3 games to 2.
Los Angeles defeated Dallas 4 games to 1.
Phoenix defeated Utah 4 games to 2.
Los Angeles defeated Phoenix 4 games to 1.

Championship

Boston defeated Los Angeles 4 games to 3.

NBA Champions 1947-1984

Year	Regular season Eastern Conference	Western Conference	Playoffs Winner	Runner-up
1947	Washington	Chicago	Philadelphia	Chicago
1948	Philadelphia	St. Louis	Baltimore	Philadelphia
1949	Washington	Rochester	Minneapolis	Washington
1950	Syracuse	Minneapolis	Minneapolis	Syracuse
1951	Philadelphia	Minneapolis	Rochester	New York
1952	Syracuse	Rochester	Minneapolis	New York
1953	New York	Minneapolis	Minneapolis	New York
1954	New York	Minneapolis	Minneapolis	Syracuse
1955	Syracuse	Ft. Wayne	Syracuse	Ft. Wayne
1956	Philadelphia	Ft. Wayne	Philadelphia	Ft. Wayne
1957	Boston	St. Louis	Boston	St. Louis
1958	Boston	St. Louis	St. Louis	Boston
1959	Boston	St. Louis	Boston	Minneapolis
1960	Boston	St. Louis	Boston	St. Louis
1961	Boston	St. Louis	Boston	St. Louis
1962	Boston	Los Angeles	Boston	Los Angeles
1963	Boston	Los Angeles	Boston	Los Angeles
1964	Boston	San Francisco	Boston	San Francisco
1965	Boston	Los Angeles	Boston	Los Angeles
1966	Philadelphia	Los Angeles	Boston	Los Angeles
1967	Philadelphia	San Francisco	Philadelphia	San Francisco
1968	Philadelphia	St. Louis	Boston	Los Angeles
1969	Baltimore	Los Angeles	Boston	Los Angeles
1970	New York	Atlanta	New York	Los Angeles

Year	Atlantic	Central	Midwest	Pacific	Winner	Runner-up
1971	New York	Baltimore	Milwaukee	Los Angeles	Milwaukee	Baltimore
1972	Boston	Baltimore	Milwaukee	Los Angeles	Los Angeles	New York
1973	Boston	Baltimore	Milwaukee	Los Angeles	New York	Los Angeles
1974	Boston	Capital	Milwaukee	Los Angeles	Boston	Milwaukee
1975	Boston	Washington	Chicago	Golden State	Golden State	Washington
1976	Boston	Cleveland	Milwaukee	Golden State	Boston	Phoenix
1977	Philadelphia	Houston	Denver	Los Angeles	Portland	Philadelphia
1978	Philadelphia	San Antonio	Denver	Portland	Washington	Seattle
1979	Washington	San Antonio	Kansas City	Seattle	Seattle	Washington
1980	Boston	Atlanta	Milwaukee	Los Angeles	Los Angeles	Philadelphia
1981	Boston	Milwaukee	San Antonio	Phoenix	Boston	Houston
1982	Boston	Milwaukee	San Antonio	Los Angeles	Los Angeles	Philadelphia
1983	Philadelphia	Milwaukee	San Antonio	Los Angeles	Philadelphia	Los Angeles
1984	Boston	Milwaukee	Utah	Los Angeles	Boston	Los Angeles

Final Statistics

Individual Scoring Leaders

(Minimum: 70 games played or 1400 points)

	G	Pts	Avg
Dantley, Utah	79	2418	30.6
Aguirre, Dallas	79	2330	29.5
Vandeweghe, Denver	78	2295	29.4
English, Denver	82	2167	26.4
King, New York	77	2027	26.3
Gervin, San Antonio	76	1967	25.9
Bird, Boston	79	1908	24.2
Mitchell, San Antonio	79	1839	23.3
Cummings, San Diego	81	1854	22.9
Short, Golden State	79	1803	22.8
Malone, Philadelphia	71	1609	22.7
Erving, Philadelphia	77	1727	22.4
Blackman, Dallas	81	1815	22.4
Free, Cleveland	75	1669	22.3
Ruland, Washington	75	1665	22.2
E. Johnson, Kansas City	82	1794	21.9
Wilkins, Atlanta	81	1750	21.6
Abdul-Jabbar, Los Angeles	80	1717	21.5
Thomas, Detroit	82	1748	21.3
Tripucka, Detroit	76	1618	21.3

Field Goal Percentage Leaders

(Minimum: 300 FG made)

	FG	FGA	Pct
Gilmore, San Antonio	351	556	.631
Donaldson, San Diego	360	604	.596
McGee, Los Angeles	347	584	.594
Dawkins, New Jersey	507	855	.593
Natt, Portland	500	857	.583
Ruland, Washington	599	1035	.579
Abdul-Jabbar, Los Angeles	716	1238	.578
Nance, Phoenix	601	1044	.576
Lanier, Milwaukee	392	685	.572
King, New York	759	1391	.572

Free Throw Percentage Leaders

(Minimum: 125 FT made)

	FT	FTA	Pct
Bird, Boston	374	421	.888
Long, Detroit	243	275	.884
Laimbeer, Detroit	316	365	.866
Davis, Phoenix	233	270	.863
Pierce, San Diego	149	173	.861
Dantley, Utah	813	946	.859
Knight, Kansas City	243	283	.859
Sikma, Seattle	411	480	.856
Vandeweghe, Denver	494	580	.852
Johnson, Boston	281	330	.852

3-Pt. Field Goal Leaders

(Minimum: 25 made)

	FG	FGA	Pct
Griffith, Utah	91	252	.361
Evans, Denver	32	89	.360
Moore, San Antonio	28	87	.322
Cooper, Los Angeles	38	121	.314
Williams, New York	25	81	.309
Sobers, Washington	29	111	.261

Assist Leaders

(Minimum: 70 games or 400 assists)

	G	No	Avg
Johnson, Los Angeles	67	875	13.1
Nixon, San Diego	82	914	11.1
Thomas, Detroit	82	914	11.1
Lucas, San Antonio	63	673	10.7
Moore, San Antonio	59	566	9.6
Green, Utah	81	748	9.2
Williams, Seattle	80	675	8.4
Whatley, Chicago	80	662	8.3
Drew, Kansas City	73	558	7.6
Davis, Dallas	81	561	6.9

Rebound Leaders

(Minimum: 70 games or 800 rebounds)

	G	Tot	Avg
Malone, Philadelphia	71	950	13.4
Williams, New Jersey	81	1000	12.3
Ruland, Washington	75	922	12.3
Laimbeer, Detroit	82	1003	12.2
Sampson, Houston	82	913	11.1
Sikma, Seattle	82	911	11.1
Parish, Boston	80	857	10.7
Robinson, Cleveland	73	753	10.3
Greenwood, Chicago	78	786	10.1
Bird, Boston	79	796	10.1

Steals Leaders

(Minimum: 70 games or 125 steals)

	G	No	Avg
Green, Utah	81	215	2.65
Thomas, Detroit	82	204	2.49
Williams, Seattle	80	189	2.36
Cheeks, Philadelphia	75	171	2.28
Johnson, Los Angeles	67	150	2.24
Dunn, Denver	80	173	2.16
Williams, New York	76	162	2.13
Cook, New Jersey	82	164	2.00
Conner, Golden State	82	162	1.98
Erving, Philadelphia	77	141	1.83

Blocked Shots Leaders

(Minimum: 70 games or 100 blocked shots)

	G	No	Avg
Eaton, Utah	82	351	4.28
Rollins, Atlanta	77	277	3.60
Sampson, Houston	82	197	2.40
Nance, Phoenix	82	173	2.11
Gilmore, San Antonio	64	132	2.06
Hinson, Cleveland	80	145	1.81
Thompson, Kansas City	80	145	1.81
Erving, Philadelphia	77	139	1.81
Abdul-Jabbar, Los Angeles	80	143	1.79
Carroll, Golden State	80	142	1.78

NBA All League Team in 1984

First team	Position	Second team
Larry Bird, Boston	Forward	Julius Erving, Philadelphia
Bernard King, New York	Forward	Adrian Dantley, Utah
Kareem Abdul-Jabbar, Los Angeles	Center	Moses Malone, Philadelphia
Magic Johnson, Los Angeles	Guard	Jim Paxson, Portland
Isiah Thomas, Detroit	Guard	Sidney Moncrief, Milwaukee

NBA All-Defensive Team in 1984

First team	Position	Second team
Bobby Jones, Philadelphia	Forward	Larry Bird, Boston
Michael Cooper, Los Angeles	Forward	Dan Roundfield, Atlanta
Tree Rollins, Atlanta	Center	Kareem Abdul-Jabbar, Los Angeles
Sidney Moncrief, Milwaukee	Guard	Dennis Johnson, Boston
Maurice Cheeks, Philadelphia	Guard	T.R. Dunn, Denver

NBA Scoring Leaders

Year	Scoring champion	Pts	Avg	Year	Scoring champion	Pts	Avg
1947	Joe Fulks, Philadelphia	1,389	23.2	1967	Rick Barry, San Francisco	2,775	35.6
1948	Max Zaslofsky, Chicago	1,007	21.0	1968	Dave Bing, Detroit	2,142	27.1
1949	George Mikan, Minneapolis	1,698	28.3	1969	Elvin Hayes, San Diego	2,327	28.4
1950	George Mikan, Minneapolis	1,865	27.4	1970	Jerry West, Los Angeles	2,309	31.2
1951	George Mikan, Minneapolis	1,932	28.4	1971	Lew Alcindor, Milwaukee	2,596	31.7
1952	Paul Arizin, Philadelphia	1,674	25.4	1972	Kareem Abdul-Jabar (Alcindor),		
1953	Neil Johnston, Philadelphia	1,564	22.3		Milwaukee	2,822	34.8
1954	Neil Johnston, Philadelphia	1,759	24.4	1973	Nate Archibald, Kansas City-Omaha	2,719	34.0
1955	Neil Johnston, Philadelphia	1,631	22.7	1974	Bob McAdoo, Buffalo	2,261	30.6
1956	Bob Pettit, St. Louis	1,849	25.7	1975	Bob McAdoo, Buffalo	2,831	34.5
1957	Paul Arizin, Philadelphia	1,817	25.6	1976	Bob McAdoo, Buffalo	2,427	31.1
1958	George Yardley, Detroit	2,001	27.8	1977	Pete Maravich, New Orleans	2,273	31.1
1959	Bob Pettit, St. Louis	2,105	29.2	1978	George Gervin, San Antonio	2,232	27.2
1960	Wilt Chamberlain, Philadelphia	2,707	37.9	1979	George Gervin, San Antonio	2,365	29.6
1961	Wilt Chamberlain, Philadelphia	3,033	38.4	1980	George Gervin, San Antonio	2,585	33.1
1962	Wilt Chamberlain, Philadelphia	4,029	50.4	1981	Adrian Dantley, Utah	2,452	30.7
1963	Wilt Chamberlain, San Francisco	3,586	44.8	1982	George Gervin, San Antonio	2,551	32.3
1964	Wilt Chamberlain, San Francisco	2,948	36.5	1983	Alex English, Denver	2,326	28.4
1965	Wilt Chamberlain, San Fran., Phila.	2,534	34.7	1984	Adrian Dantley, Utah	2,418	30.6
1966	Wilt Chamberlain, Philadelphia	2,649	33.5				

NBA Most Valuable Player

Year	Player	Year	Player
1956	Bob Pettit, St. Louis	1971	Lew Alcindor, Milwaukee
1957	Bob Cousy, Boston	1972	Kareem Abdul-Jabbar (Alcindor), Milwaukee
1958	Bill Russell, Boston	1973	Dave Cowens, Boston
1959	Bob Pettit, St. Louis	1974	Kareem Abdul-Jabbar, Milwaukee
1960	Wilt Chamberlain, Philadelphia	1975	Bob McAdoo, Buffalo
1961	Bill Russell, Boston	1976	Kareem Abdul-Jabbar, Los Angeles
1962	Bill Russell, Boston	1977	Kareem Abdul-Jabbar, Los Angeles
1963	Bill Russell, Boston	1978	Bill Walton, Portland
1904	Oscar Robertson, Cincinnati	1979	Moses Malone, Houston
1965	Bill Russell, Boston	1980	Kareem Abdul-Jabbar, Los Angeles
1966	Wilt Chamberlain, Philadelphia	1981	Julius Erving, Philadelphia
1967	Wilt Chamberlain, Philadelphia	1982	Moses Malone, Houston
1968	Wilt Chamberlain, Philadelphia	1983	Moses Malone, Philadelphia
1969	Wes Unseld, Baltimore	1984	Larry Bird, Boston
1970	Willis Reed, New York		

NBA Rookie of the Year

Year	Player	Year	Player	Year	Player
1954	Don Meineke, Ft. Wayne	1965	Willis Reed, New York	1975	Keith Wilkes, Golden State
1955	Ray Felix, Baltimore	1966	Rick Barry, San Francisco	1976	Alvan Adams, Phoenix
1956	Maurice Stokes, Rochester	1967	Dave Bing, Detroit	1977	Adrian Dantley, Buffalo
1957	Tom Heinsohn, Boston	1968	Earl Monroe, Baltimore	1978	Walter Davis, Phoenix
1958	Woody Sauldsberry, Philadelphia	1969	Wes Unseld, Baltimore	1979	Phil Ford, Kansas City
1959	Elgin Baylor, Minnesota	1970	Lew Alcindor, Milwaukee	1980	Larry Bird, Boston
1960	Wilt Chamberlain, Philadelphia	1971	Dave Cowens, Boston;	1981	Darrell Griffith, Utah
1961	Oscar Robertson, Cincinnati		Geoff Petrie, Portland (tie)	1982	Buck Williams, New Jersey
1962	Walt Bellamy, Chicago	1972	Sidney Wicks, Portland	1983	Terry Cummings, San Diego
1963	Terry Dischinger, Chicago	1973	Bob McAdoo, Buffalo	1984	Ralph Sampson, Houston
1964	Jerry Lucas, Cincinnati	1974	Ernie DiGregorio, Buffalo		

1984 NBA Player Draft

The following are the first round picks of the National Basketball Assn.

Houston—Akeem Olajuwon, Houston
Portland—Sam Bowie, Kentucky
Chicago—Michael Jordan, North Carolina
Dallas—Sam Perkins, North Carolina
Philadelphia—Charles Barkley, Auburn
Washington—Melvin Turpin, Kentucky
San Antonio—Alvin Robertson, Arkansas
San Diego—Lancaster Gordon, Louisville
Kansas City—Otis Thorpe, Providence
Philadelphia—Leon Wood, Fullerton State
Atlanta—Kevin Willis, Michigan State
Cleveland—Tim McCormick, Michigan

Phoenix—Jay Humphries, Colorado
San Diego—Michael Cage, San Diego State
Dallas—Terence Stansbury, Temple
Utah—John Stockton, Gonzaga
Nets—Jeff Turner, Vanderbilt
Indiana—Vern Fleming, Georgia
Portland—Bernard Thompson, Fresno State
Detroit—Tony Campbell, Ohio State
Milwaukee—Kenny Fields, UCLA
Philadelphia—Tom Sewell, Lamar
Los Angeles—Earl Jones, Dist. of Columbia
Boston—Michael Young, Houston

American Basketball Association Champions, 1968-1976

	Regular season		Playoffs	
Year	Eastern division	Western division	Winner	Runner-up
1968	Pittsburgh	New Orleans	Pittsburgh	New Orleans
1969	Indiana	Oakland	Oakland	Indiana
1970	Indiana	Denver	Indiana	Los Angeles
1971	Virginia	Indiana	Utah	Kentucky
1972	Kentucky	Utah	Indiana	New York
1973	Carolina	Utah	Indiana	Kentucky
1974	New York	Utah	New York	Utah
1975	Kentucky	Denver	Kentucky	Indiana
1976		Denver	New York	Denver

Individual Statistics
(Over 500 Minutes Played)

Atlanta Hawks

	Min	FG%	FT%	RBs	Ast	Pts	Avg
Wilkins	2961	.479	.770	582	126	1750	21.6
Roundfield	2610	.485	.770	721	184	1380	18.9
Johnson	1893	.442	.770	146	374	886	13.2
Davis	2079	.443	.848	139	326	925	12.3
Rivers	1938	.462	.785	220	314	757	9.3
Rollins	2351	.518	.621	593	62	666	8.6
Glenn	1503	.563	.800	104	171	681	8.4
Wittman	1071	.503	.609	71	71	350	4.5
Hastings	1135	.468	.788	270	46	305	4.5
Brown	785	.468	.738	181	29	236	3.5

Boston Celtics

	Min	FG%	FT%	RBs	Ast	Pts	Avg
Bird	3028	.492	.888	796	520	1908	24.2
Parish	2867	.546	.745	857	139	1520	19.0
McHale	2577	.556	.765	610	104	1511	18.4
Johnson	2665	.437	.852	280	338	1053	13.2
Maxwell	2502	.532	.753	461	205	955	11.9
Henderson	2088	.524	.768	147	300	908	11.6
Ainge	1154	.460	.821	116	162	384	5.4
Wedman	916	.444	.829	139	67	327	4.8
Buckner	1249	.427	.649	137	214	324	4.1
Carr	585	.409	.875	75	49	185	3.1

Chicago Bulls

	Min	FG%	FT%	RBs	Ast	Pts	Avg
Woolridge	2544	.525	.715	369	136	1444	19.3
Dailey	2449	.474	.811	235	254	1491	18.2
Wiggins	2123	.448	.742	328	187	1018	12.4
Corzine	2674	.467	.840	575	202	1004	12.2
Greenwood	2718	.490	.737	786	139	951	12.2
Johnson	1487	.559	.575	418	81	769	9.5
Theus	601	.388	.778	46	142	271	8.7
Whatley	2159	.469	.730	197	662	668	8.4
Higgins	1577	.447	.724	206	116	500	6.4
Lester	687	.415	.862	46	168	232	5.4
Green	667	.439	.714	174	25	255	5.2
Oldham	870	.505	.591	233	33	259	4.0

Cleveland Cavaliers

	Min	FG%	FT%	RBs	Ast	Pts	Avg
Free	2375	.445	.784	217	226	1669	22.3
Robinson	2402	.450	.701	753	185	1301	17.8
Hubbard	1799	.511	.739	380	86	863	10.8
Shelton	2101	.476	.764	381	179	850	10.8
Huston	2041	.498	.714	96	413	808	10.5
Thompson	1731	.467	.772	312	122	742	9.0
Bagley	1712	.423	.793	156	333	673	8.9
Cook	1950	.486	.723	484	123	471	5.8
Hinson	1858	.496	.590	499	69	437	5.5
Granger	738	.429	.757	55	134	251	4.5
Poquette	858	.439	.791	182	49	185	3.6

Dallas Mavericks

	Min	FG%	FT%	RBs	Ast	Pts	Avg
Aguirre	2900	.524	.749	469	358	2330	29.5
Blackman	3025	.546	.812	373	288	1815	22.4
Cummings	2492	.494	.742	658	158	1045	13.1
Davis	2665	.530	.836	187	561	896	11.1
Vincent	1421	.435	.781	247	114	672	11.0
Ellis	1059	.456	.719	250	56	549	8.2
Nimphius	2284	.520	.623	513	176	646	7.9
Harper	1712	.443	.673	172	239	469	5.7
Garnett	1529	.472	.733	331	128	411	5.1
Turner	536	.360	.824	93	59	137	2.9

Denver Nuggets

	Min	FG%	FT%	RBs	Ast	Pts	Avg
Vandeweghe	2734	.558	.852	373	238	2295	29.4
English	2870	.529	.824	464	406	2167	26.4
Issel	2076	.493	.850	513	173	1506	19.8
Williams	1924	.461	.818	194	464	804	10.2
Anderson	1380	.426	.773	406	193	663	8.5
Evans	1687	.431	.847	138	288	629	8.1
Edmonson	622	.492	.746	88	34	410	7.5
Schayes	1420	.493	.790	433	91	581	7.1
Carter	688	.459	.770	86	71	342	6.2
Dunn	2705	.470	.731	574	228	454	5.7
Hanzlik	1469	.431	.807	205	252	434	5.4

Detroit Pistons

	Min	FG%	FT%	RBs	Ast	Pts	Avg
Thomas	3007	.462	.733	327	914	1748	21.3
Tripucka	2493	.459	.815	306	228	1618	21.3
Laimbeer	2864	.530	.866	1003	149	1422	17.3
Long	2514	.472	.884	289	205	1334	16.3
Johnson	1909	.473	.753	237	271	1063	13.0
Tyler	1602	.453	.712	285	76	722	8.8
Levingston	1746	.525	.672	545	109	583	7.3
Benson	1734	.550	.822	409	130	579	7.1
Cureton	907	.458	.525	287	36	193	2.6

Golden State Warriors

	Min	FG%	FT%	RBs	Ast	Pts	Avg
Short	2945	.473	.793	438	246	1803	22.8
Carroll	2962	.477	.723	636	198	1639	20.5
Floyd	2555	.463	.816	271	269	1291	16.8
Johnson	2122	.421	.785	518	219	1062	13.6
Conner	2573	.493	.718	305	401	907	11.1
Smith	2091	.560	.560	672	72	582	7.8
Collins	957	.483	.730	129	67	440	7.2
Bratz	1428	.409	.876	143	252	561	6.8
Tillis	730	.425	.651	184	24	257	3.6

Houston Rockets

	Min	FG%	FT%	RBs	Ast	Pts	Avg
Sampson	2693	.523	.661	913	163	1720	21.0
Lloyd	2578	.516	.789	295	321	1458	17.8
Reid	1936	.474	.659	341	217	895	14.0
Leavell	2009	.477	.832	117	459	947	11.5
McCray	2081	.499	.731	450	176	853	10.8
C. Jones	2506	.502	.837	582	156	801	9.9
Bailey	1174	.491	.719	294	79	646	8.8
Ford	2020	.502	.838	137	410	572	7.1
Teagle	616	.470	.841	78	63	340	5.0
Hayes	994	.406	.652	260	71	402	5.0
Walker	612	.490	.333	92	55	244	4.2

Indiana Pacers

	Min	FG%	FT%	RBs	Ast	Pts	Avg
Kellogg	2676	.519	.768	719	234	1506	19.1
Williams	2279	.478	.702	554	215	1029	14.9
Carter	2045	.479	.764	153	206	977	13.4
Johnson	2073	.465	.826	460	195	1056	13.0
Stipanovich	2426	.480	.753	562	170	970	12.0
Sichting	2497	.532	.867	171	457	917	11.5
Steppe	857	.471	.832	122	79	430	7.0
McKenna	923	.410	.816	95	114	387	6.3
Thomas	1219	.464	.727	149	130	455	6.3
Lowe	1238	.413	.777	122	269	324	4.2
Waiters	1040	.517	.608	227	60	277	3.6

Kansas City Kings

	Min	FG%	FT%	RBs	Ast	Pts	Avg
E. Johnson	2920	.485	.810	455	296	1794	21.9
Drew	2363	.462	.776	146	558	1194	16.4
Woodson	1838	.477	.818	175	175	1027	14.5
Knight	1885	.491	.859	255	160	963	12.8
Theus	1498	.419	.762	129	352	745	12.2
Thompson	1915	.523	.717	709	86	826	10.3
S. Johnson	893	.553	.571	252	63	479	9.6
Olberding	2160	.494	.821	445	192	759	9.4
Meriweather	1501	.532	.764	353	51	480	6.6
Buse	1327	.426	.788	116	303	381	5.0
Nealy	960	.500	.800	222	50	174	2.5

Los Angeles Lakers

	Min	FG%	FT%	RBs	Ast	Pts	Avg
Abdul-Jabbar	2622	.578	.723	587	211	1717	21.5
Johnson	2567	.565	.810	491	875	1178	17.6
Wilkes	2507	.514	.743	340	214	1294	17.3
Worthy	2415	.556	.759	515	207	1185	14.5
McAdoo	1456	.471	.803	289	74	916	13.1
Scott	1637	.484	.806	164	177	788	10.6
McGee	1425	.594	.540	193	81	757	9.8
Cooper	2387	.497	.838	262	482	739	9.0
Nater	829	.490	.692	264	27	311	4.5
Rambis	743	.558	.636	266	34	168	3.6

Milwaukee Bucks

	Min	FG%	FT%	RBs	Ast	Pts	Avg
Moncrief	3075	.498	.848	528	358	1654	20.9
Johnson	2715	.502	.709	480	315	1535	20.7
Bridgeman	2431	.465	.807	332	265	1220	15.1
Lanier	2007	.572	.708	455	186	978	13.6
Pressey	1730	.523	.600	282	252	674	8.3
Lister	1955	.500	.626	603	110	626	7.6
Archibald	1038	.487	.634	76	160	340	7.4
Grevey	923	.451	.893	81	75	446	7.0
Romar	1022	.459	.713	93	193	393	5.8
Mokeski	838	.479	.694	166	44	255	3.8
Catchings	1156	.399	.524	271	43	144	2.1

New Jersey Nets

	Min	FG%	FT%	RBs	Ast	Pts	Avg
Birdsong	2168	.508	.608	170	266	1365	19.8
Dawkins	2417	.593	.735	541	123	1357	16.8
Williams	3003	.535	.570	1000	130	1274	15.7
King	2103	.492	.786	388	203	1165	14.7
Richardson	1285	.460	.704	172	214	576	12.0
Ransey	1937	.434	.792	127	483	760	9.5
Cook	1870	.443	.754	156	356	714	8.7
Gminski	1655	.513	.799	433	92	621	7.6
O'Koren	1191	.483	.609	175	95	430	5.9
Johnson	818	.496	.730	138	40	346	4.8
Willoughby	936	.481	.873	193	56	303	4.5

New York Knickerbockers

	Min	FG%	FT%	RBs	Ast	Pts	Avg
King	2667	.572	.779	394	164	2027	26.3
Cartwright	2487	.561	.805	649	107	1310	17.0
Williams	2230	.445	.827	267	449	1124	14.8
Robinson	2135	.489	.646	545	94	701	10.8
Sparrow	2436	.474	.824	189	539	818	10.4
Orr	1640	.458	.820	228	61	697	8.9
Walker	1324	.417	.791	167	284	644	7.9
Tucker	1228	.500	.758	130	138	481	7.6
Grunfeld	1119	.459	.771	121	108	398	5.2
Webster	1290	.469	.564	366	53	290	3.8
Elmore	832	.408	.711	165	30	155	2.4

Philadelphia 76ers

	Min	FG%	FT%	RBs	Ast	Pts	Avg
Malone	2613	.483	.750	950	96	1609	22.7
Erving	2683	.512	.754	532	309	1727	22.4
Toney	2556	.527	.839	193	373	1588	20.4
Cheeks	2494	.550	.733	205	478	950	12.7
B. Jones	1761	.523	.784	323	187	619	8.3
Richardson	1571	.467	.767	165	155	521	7.6
Williams	1434	.473	.657	339	62	500	6.5
Johnson	1721	.468	.611	398	55	455	5.7
Iavaroni	1532	.463	.740	310	95	395	5.1
Edwards	654	.380	.708	59	90	202	3.4

Phoenix Suns

	Min	FG%	FT%	RBs	Ast	Pts	Avg
Davis	2546	.512	.863	202	429	1557	20.0
Nance	2899	.576	.707	678	214	1451	17.7
Lucas	2309	.497	.765	725	203	1195	15.9
Edwards	1897	.536	.720	348	184	1059	14.7
Macy	2402	.501	.833	186	353	832	10.1
Adams	1452	.462	.825	319	219	670	9.6
Foster	1424	.448	.787	120	172	664	8.3
Westphal	865	.460	.824	43	148	412	7.0
Robey	856	.545	.693	198	65	342	5.6
Pittman	989	.603	.683	214	70	321	4.7
Sanders	586	.478	.690	103	44	223	4.5
Scott	735	.444	.778	100	48	167	2.6
High	512	.346	.345	66	51	46	1.6

Portland Trail Blazers

	Min	FG%	FT%	RBs	Ast	Pts	Avg
Paxson	2686	.514	.841	173	251	1722	21.3
Natt	2638	.583	.797	476	179	1277	16.2
Thompson	2648	.524	.667	688	308	1240	15.7
Carr	2455	.561	.673	642	157	1283	15.6
Valentine	1893	.447	.789	127	395	696	10.2
Cooper	1662	.459	.804	476	76	793	9.8
Lever	2010	.447	.743	218	372	788	9.7
Drexler	1408	.451	.728	235	153	628	7.7
Lamp	660	.490	.896	63	51	318	5.0
Norris	1157	.504	.698	257	76	352	4.5

San Antonio Spurs

	Min	FG%	FT%	RBs	Ast	Pts	Avg
Gervin	2584	.490	.842	313	220	1967	25.9
Mitchell	2853	.488	.779	570	93	1839	23.3
Gilmore	2034	.631	.718	662	70	982	15.3
Banks	2600	.568	.741	582	254	1049	13.1
Lucas	1807	.462	.764	180	673	689	10.9
Jones	1770	.500	.727	449	85	826	10.2
Moore	1650	.446	.755	178	566	595	10.1
Edmonson	521	.493	.752	70	27	346	8.7
Brewer	992	.444	.776	63	50	413	7.8
Roberts	1531	.536	.837	304	98	573	7.3
McNamara	1037	.621	.471	317	31	388	5.5

San Diego Clippers

	Min	FG%	FT%	RBs	Ast	Pts	Avg
Cummings	2907	.494	.720	777	139	1854	22.9
Nixon	3053	.462	.760	203	914	1391	17.0
Walton	1476	.556	.597	477	183	668	12.1
Donaldson	2525	.596	.761	649	90	969	11.8
Brooks	1405	.479	.689	342	88	530	11.3
Kelser	1783	.519	.702	391	91	878	11.0
Pierce	1280	.470	.861	135	60	685	9.9
Smith	1297	.546	.755	170	82	600	9.8
Hodges	1571	.450	.750	86	116	592	7.8
Whitehead	921	.490	.822	245	19	376	5.4
McKinney	843	.446	.848	54	161	311	3.9
McDowell	611	.431	.679	155	37	208	3.6

Seattle Supersonics

	Min	FG%	FT%	RBs	Ast	Pts	Avg
Sikma	2993	.499	.856	911	327	1563	19.1
Williams	2818	.458	.750	204	675	1497	18.7
Chambers	2570	.499	.800	532	133	1483	18.1
Wood	2236	.494	.823	275	166	1160	14.3
Brown	1129	.510	.895	62	194	602	8.5
Vranes	2174	.521	.648	395	132	669	8.4
King	2086	.520	.660	470	179	602	7.8
Sundvold	1284	.445	.889	91	239	507	6.9
Hawes	1153	.481	.782	220	99	290	3.7
McCray	520	.388	.700	115	44	129	2.7

Utah Jazz

	Min	FG%	FT%	RBs	Ast	Pts	Avg
Dantley	2984	.558	.859	448	310	2418	30.6
Griffith	2650	.490	.696	338	283	1636	20.0
Drew	1797	.479	.778	338	135	1430	17.7
Green	2768	.486	.821	230	748	1072	13.2
Bailey	2009	.512	.752	464	129	692	8.5
Wilkins	1734	.479	.736	455	73	632	7.8
Eaton	2139	.466	.593	595	113	461	5.6
Kelley	1674	.500	.765	490	157	388	5.2
Eaves	1034	.451	.697	85	200	356	4.5

Washington Bullets

	Min	FG%	FT%	RBs	Ast	Pts	Avg
Ruland	3082	.579	.733	922	296	1665	22.2
Sobers	2624	.456	.837	179	377	1266	15.6
Ballard	2701	.481	.798	488	290	1188	14.5
Malone	1976	.444	.826	155	151	982	12.1
Johnson	2686	.467	.742	184	567	982	12.0
McMillen	1294	.497	.814	199	73	572	9.2
Mahorn	2701	.507	.651	738	131	739	9.0
Daye	1174	.441	.714	188	176	455	6.1
Kopicki	678	.485	.813	166	46	220	3.7

MVP in Playoffs

1969	Jerry West, Los Angeles
1970	Willis Reed, New York
1971	Lew Alcindor, Milwaukee
1972	Wilt Chamberlain, Los Angeles
1973	Willis Reed, New York
1974	John Havlicek, Boston
1975	Rick Barry, Golden State
1976	Jo Jo White, Boston
1977	Bill Walton, Portland
1978	Wes Unseld, Washington
1979	Dennis Johnson, Seattle
1980	Magic Johnson, Los Angeles
1981	Cedric Maxwell, Boston
1982	Magic Johnson, Los Angeles
1983	Moses Malone, Philadelphia
1984	Larry Bird, Boston

Individuals in The Basketball Hall of Fame

Springfield, Mass.

Players
Arizin, Paul
Baylor, Elgin
Beckman, John
Borgmann, Bennie
Bradley, Bill
Brennan, Joseph
Barlow, Thomas
Chamberlain, Wilt
Cooper, Charles
Cousy, Bob
Davies, Bob
DeBernardi, Forrest
DeBusschere, Dave
Dehnert, Dutch
Endacott, Paul
Foster, Bud
Friedman, Max
Fulks, Joe
Gale, Lauren
Gola, Tom
Greer, Hal
Gruenig, Ace
Hagan, Cliff
Hanson, Victor
Havlicek, John
Holman, Nat
Hyatt, Chuck
Johnson, William
Jones, Sam

Krause, Moose
Kurland, Bob
Lapchick, Joe
Lucas, Jerry
Luisetti, Hank
Martin, Slater
McCracken, Branch
McCracken, Jack
Macauley, Ed
Mikan, George
Murphy, Stretch
Page, Pat
Pettit, Bob
Phillip, Andy
Pollard, Jim
Ramsey, Frank
Reed, Willis
Robertson, Oscar
Roosma, John S.
Russell, Honey
Russell, Bill
Schayes, Adolph
Schmidt, Ernest
Schommer, John
Sedran, Barney
Sharman, Bill
Steinmetz, Christian
Thompson, Cat
Twyman, Jack
Vandivier, Fuzzy

Wachter, Edward
West, Jerry
Wooden, John

Coaches
Auerbach, Red
Barry, Sam
Blood, Ernest
Cann, Howard
Carlson, Dr. H. C.
Carnevale, Ben
Case, Everett
Dean, Everett
Diddle, Edgar
Drake, Bruce
Gaines, Clarence
Gardner, Jack
Gill, Slats
Hickey, Edgar
Hobson, Howard
Iba, Hank
Julian, Alvin
Keaney, Frank
Keogan, George
Lambert, Ward
Litwack, Harry
Loeffler, Kenneth
Lonborg, Dutch
McCutchan, Arad
McGuire, Frank

McLendon, John
Meyer, Ray
Meanwell, Dr. W.E.
Newell, Pete
Rupp, Adolph
Sachs, Leonard
Shelton, Everett
Smith, Dean
Wooden, John

Referees
Enright, James
Hepbron, George
Hoyt, George
Kennedy, Matthew
Leith, Lloyd
Nucatola, John
Quigley, Ernest
Shirley, J. Dallas
Tobey, David
Walsh, David

Contributors
Allen, Phog
Bee, Clair
Brown, Walter
Bunn, John
Douglas, Bob
Duer, Al O.
Fagan, Cliff
Fisher, Harry

Gottlieb, Edward
Gulick, Dr. L. H.
Harrison, Lester
Hepp, Dr. Ferenc
Hickox, Edward
Hinkle, Tony
Irish, Ned
Jones, R. W.
Kennedy, Walter
Liston, Emil
Mokray, Bill
Morgan, Ralph
Morgenweck, Frank
Naismith, Dr. James
O'Brien, John
Olsen, Harold
Podoloff, Maurice
Porter, H. V.
Reis, William
Ripley, Elmer
St. John, Lynn
Saperstein, Abe
Schabinger, Arthur
Stagg, Amos Alonzo
Steitz, Edward
Taylor, Chuck
Tower, Oswald
Trester, Arthur
Wells, Clifford
Wilke, Lou

Professional Sports Arenas

The seating capacity of sports arenas can vary depending on the event being presented. The figures below are the normal seating capacity for basketball. (*) indicates hockey seating capacity.

Name, location	Capacity
Arena, The, St. Louis, Mo.	20,000-*17,968
Arizona Veteran's Memorial Coliseum, Phoenix	14,660
Baltimore Civic Center	13,043-*10,200
Boston Garden	15,320-*14,673
Buffalo Memorial Auditorium	17,900-*16,433(a)
Byrne Meadowlands Arena, E. Rutherford, N.J.	20,149-*19,023
Capital Centre, Landover, Md.	19,105-*18,130
Chicago Stadium	17,374-*17,263
Cincinnati Gardens	11,650-*10,606
Cobo Hall, Detroit	11,147
The Coliseum, Richfield Township, Oh.	19,548
Convention Center, San Antonio	10,146
Cow Palace, San Francisco	14,500-*12,195
Freedom Hall, Louisville, Ky.	16,613
Greensboro Coliseum	15,500-*13,280
Halifax Metro Centre	*9,549
Hartford Civic Center	*14,800
HemisFair Arena, San Antonio	15,800
Jefferson County Coliseum, Birmingham, Ala.	*16,753
Joe Louis Sports Arena, Detroit	*19,275
Kemper Arena, Kansas City	16,668
Kingdome, Seattle	40,192
Los Angeles Forum	17,505-*16,005
Los Angeles Sports Arena	15,333-*11,325
Louisiana Superdome	47,284
Madison Square Garden, New York	19,591-*17,500

Name, location	Capacity
Maple Leaf Gardens, Toronto	*16,382(a)
Market Square Arena, Indianapolis	17,092-*15,861
McNichols Arena, Denver	17,251-*16,399
Met. Sports Center, Bloomington, Minn.	*15,184
Milwaukee Arena	11,052
Montreal Forum	*16,074
Nassau Veterans Memorial Coliseum, Uniondale, N.Y.	*15,837
Northlands Coliseum, Edmonton	*17,300-17,490(a)
Oakland Coliseum Arena	13,335
Olympia Stadium, Detroit	*16,673
Olympic Saddledome, Calgary, Alta.	*16,700
The Omni, Atlanta	15,700-*15,191
Pacific Coliseum, Vancouver, B.C.	*15,753
Pittsburgh Civic Arena	*16,033
Portland Memorial Coliseum	12,666
Quebec Coliseum	*15,264
Reunion Arena, Dallas	17,007
Riverfront Coliseum, Cincinnati	*15,794
Salt Palace, Salt Lake City	12,143-*10,640
San Diego Sports Arena	13,753-*13,039
Seattle Center Coliseum	14,098
Silverdome, Pontiac, Mich.	22,366
Spectrum, Philadelphia	18,482-*17,159
The Summit, Houston	15,816-*15,256
Thomas and Mack Center, Las Vegas	18,500
Winnipeg Arena	*15,250

(a) includes standees

Major Indoor Soccer League in 1984

Final Standings

Eastern Division

	W	L	Pct	GB	GF	GA
Baltimore	34	14	.708	—	280	203
Pittsburgh	32	16	.667	2	245	204
Cleveland	31	17	.646	3	269	229
New York	20	28	.417	14	232	280
Memphis	18	30	.375	16	216	284
Buffalo	15	33	.313	19	226	279

Western Division

	W	L	Pct	GB	GF	GA
St. Louis	26	22	.542	—	220	202
Witchita	25	23	.521	1	237	228
Los Angeles	24	24	.500	2	223	239
Kansas City	23	25	.479	3	232	246
Tacoma	22	26	.458	4	226	232
Phoenix	18	30	.375	8	221	249

Playoff Champion—Baltimore

Kentucky Derby

Churchill Downs, Louisville, Ky.; inaugurated 1875; distance 1-1/4 miles; 1-1/2 miles until 1896. 3-year olds.
Times—seconds in fifths.

Year	Winner	Jockey	Trainer	Wt.	Second	Winner's share	Time
1910	Donau	F. Herbert	G. Ham	117	Joe Morris	$4,850	2:06.2
1911	Meridian	G. Archibald	A. Ewing	117	Governor Gray	4,850	2:05.
1912	Worth	C. H. Shilling	F. M. Taylor	117	Duval	4,850	2:09.2
1913	Donerail	R. Goose	T. P. Hayes	117	Ten Point	5,475	2:04.4
1914	Old Rosebud	J. McCabe	F. D. Weir	114	Hodge	9,125	2:03.2
1915	Regret*	J. Notter	J. Rowe Sr.	112	Pebbles	11,450	2:05.2
1916	George Smith	J. Loftus	H. Hughes	117	Star Hawk	16,600	2:04.3
1917	Omar Khayyam	C. Borel	C. T. Patterson	117	Ticket	9,750	2:04.
1918	Exterminator	W. Knapp	H. McDaniel	114	Escoba	14,700	2:10.4
1919	Sir Barton	J. Loftus	H. G. Bedwell	112	Billy Kelly	20,825	2:09.4
1920	Paul Jones	T. Rice	W. Garth	126	Upset	30,375	2:09.
1921	Behave Yourself	C. Thompson	H. J. Thompson	126	Black Servant	38,450	2:04.1
1922	Morvich	A. Johnson	F. Burlew	126	Bet Mosie	46,775	2:04.3
1923	Zev	E. Sande	D. J. Leary	126	Martingale	53,600	2:05.2
1924	Black Gold	J. D. Mooney	H. Webb	126	Chilhowee	52,775	2:05.1
1925	Flying Ebony	E. Sande	W. B. Duke	126	Captain Hal	52,950	2:07.3
1926	Bubbling Over	A. Johnson	H. J. Thompson	126	Bagenbaggage	50,075	2:03.4
1927	Whiskery	L. McAtee	F. Hopkins	126	Osmand	51,000	2:06.
1928	Reigh Count	C. Lang	B. S. Michell	126	Misstep	55,375	2:10.2
1929	Clyde Van Dusen	L. McAtee	C. Van Dusen	126	Naishapur	53,950	2:10.4
1930	Gallant Fox	E. Sande	J. Fitzsimmons	126	Gallant Knight	50,725	2:07.3
1931	Twenty Grand	C. Kurtsinger	J. Rowe Jr.	126	Sweep All	48,725	2:01.4
1932	Burgoo King	E. James	H. J. Thompson	126	Economic	52,350	2:05.1
1933	Brokers Tip	D. Meade	H. J. Thompson	126	Head Play	48,925	2:06.4
1934	Cavalcade	M. Garner	R. A. Smith	126	Discovery	28,175	2:04.
1935	Omaha	W. Saunders	J. Fitzsimmons	126	Roman Soldier	39,525	2:05.
1936	Bold Venture	I. Hanford	M. Hirsch	126	Brevity	37,725	2:03.3
1937	War Admiral	C. Kurtsinger	G. Conway	126	Pompoon	52,050	2:03.1
1938	Lawrin	E. Arcaro	B. A. Jones	126	Dauber	47,050	2:04.4
1939	Johnstown	J. Stout	J. Fitzsimmons	126	Challedon	46,350	2:03.2
1940	Gallahadion	C. Bierman	R. Waldron	126	Bimelech	60,150	2:05.
1941	Whirlaway	E. Arcaro	B. A. Jones	126	Staretor	61,275	2:01.2
1942	Shut Out	W. D. Wright	J. M. Gaver	126	Alsab	64,225	2:04.2
1943	Count Fleet	J. Longden	G. D. Cameron	126	Blue Swords	60,275	2:04.
1944	Pensive	C. McCreary	B. A. Jones	126	Broadcloth	64,675	2:04.1
1945	Hoop, Jr.	E. Arcaro	I. H. Parke	126	Pot o'Luck	64,850	2:07.
1946	Assault	W. Mehrtens	M. Hirsch	126	Spy Song	96,400	2:06.3
1947	Jet Pilot	E. Guerin	T. Smith	126	Phalanx	92,160	2:06.3
1948	Citation	E. Arcaro	B. A. Jones	126	Coaltown	83,400	2:05.2
1949	Ponder	S. Brooks	B. A. Jones	126	Capot	91,600	2:04.1
1950	Middleground	W. Boland	M. Hirsch	126	Hill Prince	92,650	2:01.3
1951	Count Turf	C. McCreary	S. Rutchick	126	Royal Mustang	98,050	2:02.3
1952	Hill Gail	E. Arcaro	B. A. Jones	126	Sub Fleet	96,300	2:01.3
1953	Dark Star	H. Moreno	E. Hayward	126	Native Dancer	90,050	2:02.
1954	Determine	R. York	W. Molter	126	Hasty Road	102,050	2:03.
1955	Swaps	W. Shoemaker	M. A. Tenney	126	Nashua	108,400	2:01.4
1956	Needles	D. Erb	H. L. Fontaine	126	Fabius	123,450	2:03.2
1957	Iron Liege	W. Hartack	H. A. Jones	126	Gallant Man	107,950	2:02.1
1958	Tim Tam	I. Valenzuela	H. A. Jones	126	Lincoln Road	116,400	2:05.
1959	Tomy Lee	W. Shoemaker	F. Childs	126	Sword Dancer	119,650	2:02.1
1960	Venetian Way	W. Hartack	V. Sovinski	126	Bally Ache	114,850	2:02.2
1961	Carry Back	J. Sellers	J. A. Price	126	Crozier	120,500	2:04.
1962	Decidedly	W. Hartack	H. Luro	126	Roman Line	119,650	2:00.2
1963	Chateaugay	B. Baeza	J. Conway	126	Never Bend	108,900	2:01.4
1964	Northern Dancer	W. Hartack	H. Luro	126	Hill Rise	114,300	2:00.
1965	Lucky Debonair	W. Shoemaker	F. Catrone	126	Dapper Dan	112,000	2:01.1
1966	Kauai King	D. Brumfield	H. Forrest	126	Advocator	120,500	2:02.
1967	Proud Clarion	R. Ussery	L. Gentry	126	Barbs Delight	119,700	2:00.3
1968	Dancer's Image (a)	R. Ussery	H. Forrest	126	Forward Pass	122,600	2:02.1
1969	Majestic Prince	W. Hartack	J. Longden	126	Arts and Letters	113,200	2:01.4
1970	Dust Commander	M. Manganello	D. Combs	126	My Dad George	127,800	2:03.2
1971	Canonero II	G. Avila	J. Arias	126	Jim French	145,500	2:03.1
1972	Riva Ridge	R. Turcotte	L. Laurin	126	No Le Hace	140,300	2:01.4
1973	Secretariat	R. Turcotte	L. Laurin	126	Sham	155,050	1:59.2
1974	Cannonade	A. Cordero	W. Stephens	126	Hudson County	274,000	2:04.
1975	Foolish Pleasure	J. Vasquez	L. Jolley	126	Avatar	209,611	2:02.
1976	Bold Forbes	A. Cordero	L. Barrera	126	Honest Pleasure	165,200	2:01.3
1977	Seattle Slew	J. Cruguet	W. H. Turner Jr.	126	Run Dusty Run	214,700	2:02.1
1978	Affirmed	S. Cauthen	L. Barrera	126	Alydar	186,900	2:01.1
1979	Spectacular Bid	R. Franklin	G. Delp	126	General Assembly	228,650	2:02.2
1980	Genuine Risk*	J. Vasquez	L. Jolley	121	Rumbo	250,550	2:02
1981	Pleasant Colony	J. Velasquez	J. Campo	126	Woodchopper	317,200	2:02
1982	Gato del Sol	E. Delahoussaye	E. Gregson	126	Laser Light	428,850	2:02.2
1983	Sunny's Halo	E. Delahoussaye	D. Cross	126	Desert Wine	426,000	2:02.1
1984	Swale	L. Pincay	W. Stephens	126	Coax Me Chad	537,000	2:02.2

(a) Dancer's Image was disqualified from purse money after tests disclosed that he had run with a pain-killing drug, phenylbutazone, in his system. All wagers were paid on Dancer's Image. Forward Pass was awarded first place money.

The Kentucky Derby has been won five times by two jockeys, Eddie Arcaro, 1938, 1941, 1945, 1948 and 1952; and Bill Hartack, 1957, 1960, 1962, 1964 and 1969; and three times by each of three jockeys, Isaac Murphy, 1884, 1890, and 1891; Earle Sande, 1923, 1925 and 1930, and Willie Shoemaker, 1955, 1959, 1965. *Regret and Genuine Risk are the only fillies to win the Derby.

Preakness

Pimlico, Baltimore, Md.; inaugurated 1873; 1 3-16 miles, 3 yr. olds. Time—seconds in fifths.

Year	Winner	Jockey	Trainer	Wt.	Second	Winner's share	Time
1946	Assault	W. Mehrtens	M. Hirsch	126	Lord Boswell	$96,620	2:01.2
1947	Faultless	D. Dodson	H.A. Jones	126	On Trust	98,005	1:59
1948	Citation	E. Arcaro	H.A. Jones	126	Vulcan's Forge	91,870	2:02.2
1949	Capot	T. Atkinson	J.M. Gaver	126	Palestinian	79,985	1:56
1950	Hill Prince	E. Arcaro	J.H. Hayes	126	Middleground	56,115	1:59.1
1951	Bold	E. Arcaro	P.M. Burch	126	Counterpoint	83,110	1:56.2
1952	Blue Man	C. McCreary	W.C. Stephens	126	Jampol	86,135	1:57.2
1953	Native Dancer	E. Guerin	W.C. Winfrey	126	Jamie K	65,200	1:57.4
1954	Hasty Road	J. Adams	H. Trotsek	126	Correlation	91,600	1:57.2
1955	Nashua	E. Arcaro	J. Fitzsimmons	126	Saratoga	67,550	1:54.3
1956	Fabius	W. Hartack	H.A. Jones	126	Needles	84,250	1:58.2
1957	Bold Ruler	E. Arcaro	J. Fitzsimmons	126	Iron Liege	65,250	1:56.1
1958	Tim Tam	I. Valenzuela	H.A. Jones	126	Lincoln Road	97,900	1:57.1
1959	Royal Orbit	W. Harmatz	R. Cornell	126	Sword Dancer	136,200	1:57
1960	Bally Ache	R. Ussery	H.J. Pitt	126	Victoria Park	121,000	1:57.3
1961	Carry Back	J. Sellers	J.A. Price	126	Globemaster	126,200	1:57.3
1962	Greek Money	J.L. Rotz	V.W. Raines	126	Ridan	135,800	1:56.1
1963	Candy Spots	W. Shoemaker	M.A. Tenney	126	Chateaugay	127,500	1:56.1
1964	Northern Dancer	W. Hartack	H. Luro	126	The Scoundrel	124,200	1:56.4
1965	Tom Rolfe	R. Turcotte	F.Y. Whiteley Jr.	126	Dapper Dan	128,100	1:56.1
1966	Kauai King	D. Brumfield	H. Forrest	126	Stupendous	129,000	1:55.2
1967	Damascus	W. Shoemaker	F.Y. Whiteley Jr.	126	In Reality	141,500	1:55.1
1968	Forward Pass	I. Valenzuela	H. Forrest	126	Out of the Way	142,700	1:56.4
1969	Majestic Prince	W. Hartack	J. Longden	126	Arts and Letters	129,500	1:55.3
1970	Personality	E. Belmonte	J.W. Jacobs	126	My Dad George	151,300	1:56.1
1971	Canonero II	G. Avila	J. Arias	126	Eastern Fleet	137,400	1:54
1972	Bee Bee Bee	E. Nelson	D.W. Carroll	126	No Le Hace	135,300	1:55.3
1973	Secretariat	R. Turcotte	L. Laurin	126	Sham	129,900	1:54.2
1974	Little Current	M. Rivera	L. Rondinello	126	Neopolitan Way	156,000	1:54.3
1975	Master Derby	D. McHargue	W.E. Adams	126	Foolish Pleasure	158,100	1:56.2
1976	Elocutionist	J. Lively	P.T. Adwell	126	Play The Red	129,700	1:55
1977	Seattle Slew	J. Cruguet	W.H. Turner Jr.	126	Iron Constitution	138,600	1:54.2
1978	Affirmed	S. Cauthen	L. Barrera	126	Alydar	136,200	1:54.2
1979	Spectacular Bid	R. Franklin	G. Delp	126	Golden Act	165,300	1:54.1
1980	Codex	A. Cordero	D.W. Lucas	126	Genuine Risk	180,600	1:54.1
1981	Pleasant Colony	J. Velasquez	J. Campo	126	Bold Ego	270,800	1:54.3
1982	Aloma's Ruler	J. Kaenel	J. Lenzini	126	Linkage	209,990	1:55.2
1983	Deputed Testamony	D. Miller	J.W. Boniface	126	Desert Wine	251,200	1:55.2
1984	Gate Dancer	A. Cordero	J. Van Berg	126	Play On	243,600	1:53.3

Belmont Stakes

Elmont, N.Y.; inaugurated 1867; 1 ½ miles, 3 year olds. Time—seconds in fifths.

Year	Winner	Jockey	Trainer	Wt.	Second	Winner's share	Time
1946	Assault	W. Mehrtens	M. Hirsch	126	Natchez	$75,400	2:30.4
1947	Phalanx	R. Donoso	S. Veitch	126	Tide Rips	78,900	2:29.2
1948	Citation	E. Arcaro	H.A. Jones	126	Better Self	77,700	2:28.1
1949	Capot	T. Atkinson	J.M. Gaver	126	Ponder	60,900	2:30.1
1950	Middleground	W. Boland	M. Hirsch	126	Lights Up	61,350	2:28.3
1951	Counterpoint	D. Gorman	S. Veitch	125	Battlefield	82,000	2:29
1952	One Count	E. Arcaro	O. White	126	Blue Man	82,400	2:30.1
1953	Native Dancer	E. Guerin	W.C. Winfrey	126	Jamie K	82,500	2:28.3
1954	High Gun	E. Guerin	M. Hirsch	126	Fisherman	89,000	2:30.4
1955	Nashua	E. Arcaro	J. Fitzsimmons	126	Blazing Count	83,700	2:29
1956	Needles	D. Erb	H. Fontaine	126	Career Boy	83,600	2:29.4
1957	Gallant Man	W. Shoemaker	J. Nerud	126	Inside Tract	77,300	2:26.3
1958	Cavan	P. Anderson	T.J. Barry	126	Tim Tam	73,440	2:30.1
1959	Sword Dancer	W. Shoemaker	J.E. Burch	126	Bagdad	93,525	2:28.2
1960	Celtic Ash	W. Hartack	T.J. Barry	126	Venetian Way	96,785	2:29.3
1961	Sherluck	B. Baeza	H. Young	126	Globemaster	104,900	2:29.1
1962	Jaipur	W. Shoemaker	W.F. Mulholland	126	Admiral's Voyage	109,550	2:28.4
1963	Chateaugay	B. Baeza	J.P. Conway	126	Candy Spots	101,700	2:30.1
1964	Quadrangle	M. Ycaza	J.E. Burch	126	Roman Brother	110,850	2:28.2
1965	Hail to All	J. Sellers	E. Yowell	126	Tom Rolfe	104,150	2:28.2
1966	Amberoid	W. Boland	L. Laurin	126	Buffle	117,700	2:29.3
1967	Damascus	W. Shoemaker	F.Y. Whiteley Jr.	126	Cool Reception	104,950	2:28.4
1968	Stage Door Johnny	H. Gustines	J.M. Gaver	126	Forward Pass	117,700	2:27.1
1969	Arts and Letters	B. Baeza	J.E. Burch	126	Majestic Prince	104,050	2:28.4
1970	High Echelon	J.L. Rotz	J.W. Jacobs	126	Needles N Pens	115,000	2:34
1971	Pass Catcher	W. Blum	E. Yowell	126	Jim French	97,710	2:30.2
1972	Riva Ridge	R. Turcotte	L. Laurin	126	Ruritania	93,950	2:28
1973	Secretariat	R. Turcotte	L. Laurin	126	Twice A Prince	90,120	2:24
1974	Little Current	M. Rivera	L. Rondinello	126	Jolly Johu	101,970	2:29.1
1975	Avatar	W. Shoemaker	A.T. Doyle	126	Foolish Pleasure	116,160	2:28.1
1976	Bold Forbes	A. Cordero	Laz Barrera	126	McKenzie Bridge	116,850	2:29
1977	Seattle Slew	J. Cruguet	W.H. Turner Jr.	126	Run Dusty Run	109,080	2:29.3
1978	Affirmed	S. Cauthen	Laz Barrera	126	Alydar	110,580	2:26.4
1979	Coastal	R. Hernandez	D.A. Whiteley	126	Golden Act	161,400	2:28.3
1980	Temperence Hill	E. Maple	J. Cantey	126	Genuine Risk	176,220	2:29.4
1981	Summing	G. Martens	Luis Barrera	126	Highland Blade	170,580	2:29
1982	Conquistador Cielo	L. Pincay	W. Stephens	126	Gato Del Sol	159,720	2:28.1
1983	Caveat	L. Pincay	W. Stephens	126	Slew o'Gold	215,100	2:27.4
1984	Swale	L. Pincay	W. Stephens	126	Pine Circle	310,020	2:27.1

Triple Crown Turf Winners, Jockeys, and Trainers

(Kentucky Derby, Preakness, and Belmont Stakes)

Year	Horse	Jockey	Trainer	Year	Horse	Jockey	Trainer
1919	Sir Barton	J. Loftus	H. G. Bedwell	1946	Assault	Mehrtens	M. Hirsch
1930	Gallant Fox	E. Sande	J. Fitzsimmons	1948	Citation	E. Arcaro	H.A. Jones
1935	Omaha	W. Sanders	J. Fitzsimmons	1973	Secretariat	R. Turcotte	L. Laurin
1937	War Admiral	C. Kurtsinger	G. Conway	1977	Seattle Slew	J. Cruguet	W.H. Turner Jr.
1941	Whirlaway	E. Arcaro	B.A. Jones	1978	Affirmed	S. Cauthen	L.S. Barrera
1943	Count Fleet	J. Longden	G.D. Cameron				

Annual Leading Money-Winning Horses

Year	Horse	Dollars	Year	Horse	Dollars	Year	Horse	Dollars
1944	Pavot	179,040	1958	Round Table	662,780	1971	Riva Ridge	503,263
1945	Busher	273,735	1959	Sword Dancer	537,004	1972	Droll Roll	471,633
1946	Assault	424,195	1960	Bally Ache	455,045	1973	Secretariat	860,404
1947	Armed	376,325	1961	Carry Back	565,349	1974	Chris Evert	551,063
1948	Citation	709,470	1962	Never Bend	402,969	1975	Foolish Pleasure	716,278
1949	Ponder	321,825	1963	Candy Spots	604,481	1976	Forego	491,701
1950	Noor	346,940	1964	Gun Bow	580,100	1977	Seattle Slew	641,370
1951	Counterpoint	250,525	1965	Buckpasser	568,096	1978	Affirmed	901,541
1952	Crafty Admiral	277,255	1966	Buckpasser	669,078	1979	Spectacular Bid	1,279,334
1953	Native Dancer	513,425	1967	Damascus	817,941	1980	Temperance Hill	1,130,452
1954	Determine	328,700	1968	Forward Pass	546,674	1981	John Henry	1,148,800
1955	Nashua	752,550	1969	Arts and Letters	555,604	1982	Perrault	1,197,400
1956	Needles	440,850	1970	Personality	444,049	1983	All Along	2,138,963
1957	Round Table	600,383						

Annual Leading Jockey—Money Won

Year	Jockey	Dollars	Year	Jockey	Dollars	Year	Jockey	Dollars
1951	Willie Shoemaker	1,329,890	1962	Willie Shoemaker	2,916,844	1973	Laffit Pincay Jr.	4,093,492
1952	Eddie Arcaro	1,859,591	1963	Willie Shoemaker	2,526,925	1974	Laffit Pincay Jr.	4,251,060
1953	Willie Shoemaker	1,784,187	1964	Willie Shoemaker	2,649,553	1975	Braulio Baeza	3,695,198
1954	Willie Shoemaker	1,876,760	1965	Braulio Baeza	2,582,702	1976	Angel Cordero Jr.	4,709,500
1955	Eddie Arcaro	1,864,796	1966	Braulio Baeza	2,951,022	1977	Steve Cauthen	6,151,750
1956	Bill Hartack	2,343,955	1967	Braulio Baeza	3,088,888	1978	Darrel McHargue	6,029,885
1957	Bill Hartack	3,060,501	1968	Braulio Baeza	2,835,108	1979	Laffit Pincay Jr.	8,193,535
1958	Willie Shoemaker	2,961,693	1969	Jorge Velasquez	2,542,315	1980	Chris McCarron	7,663,300
1959	Willie Shoemaker	2,843,133	1970	Laffit Pincay Jr.	2,626,526	1981	Chris McCarron	8,397,604
1960	Willie Shoemaker	2,123,961	1971	Laffit Pincay Jr.	3,784,377	1982	Angel Cordero Jr.	9,483,590
1961	Willie Shoemaker	2,690,819	1972	Laffit Pincay Jr.	3,225,827	1983	Angel Cordero Jr.	10,116,697

Leading Money-Winning Horses

As of June, 1984

Horse	Sts.	1st	Dollars	Horse	Sts.	1st	Dollars	Horse	Sts.	1st	Dollars
John Henry	70	32	3,706,197	Excellor	33	15	1,654,002	Nashua	30	22	1,288,565
Spectacular Bid	30	26	2,781,607	Swale	14	9	1,583,661	Althea	14	8	1,275,255
Trinycarol	25	18	2,644,516	Temperence Hill	31	11	1,567,650	Ancient Title	57	24	1,252,791
All Along	17	9	2,439,299	Dahlia	48	15	1,543,139	Susan's Girl	63	29	1,251,667
Affirmed	29	22	2,393,818	Perrault	25	9	1,489,942	Carry Back	61	21	1,241,165
Kelso	63	39	1,977,896	Buckpasser	31	25	1,462,014	Foolish Pleasure	26	16	1,216,705
Forego	57	34	1,938,957	Allez France	21	13	1,386,146	Seattle Slew	17	14	1,208,726
Round Table	66	43	1,749,869	Secretariat	21	16	1,316,808				

Eclipse Awards in 1983

Sponsored by the Thoroughbred Racing Assn., Daily Racing Form, and the National Turf Writers Assn.

Horse of the Year—All Along
Best 2-year-old colt—Devil's Bag
Best 2-year-old filly—Althea
Best 3-year-old colt—Slew O' Gold
Best 3-year-old filly—Heartlight No. One
Best colt, horse, or gelding (4-year-olds & up)—Bates Motel
Best filly or mare (4-year-olds & up)—Ambassador of Luck
Best male turf horse—John Henry

Best turf filly or mare—All Along
Best sprinter—Chinook Pass
Best steeplechase horse—Flatterer
Best trainer—Woody Stephens
Best jockey—Angel Cordero Jr.
Best apprentice jockey—Declan Murphy
Best owner—John Franks

North American Squash in 1984

Jahangir Khan of Pakistan won the 1984 North American Open Squash championship by defeating Mark Talbott of Boston, Mass. in the final 12-15, 15-9, 15-4, 15-1. Khan received $10,000 for his victory.

American Bowling Congress Championships in 1984

81st Tournament, Reno, Nev.

Regular Division

Individual

1. (tie) Bob Antczak, Chicago, Ill. 208, 298, 258 — 764.
Neal Young, Louisville, Ky. 196, 289, 279 — 764.
3. (tie) Gary Mage, Tacoma, Wash. 243, 258, 259 — 760.
Bob Goike, Detroit, Mich. 266, 259, 235 — 760.

All Events

1. Bob Goike, Detroit, Mich. 672, 710, 760 — 2,142
2. Rod Toft, St. Paul, Minn. 683, 684, 679 — 2,046.
3. Jeff Nimke, Oshkosh, Wis. 655, 664, 704 — 2,023.

Doubles

1. Chris Cobus, 232, 222, 289 — 734 & John Megna, both Milwaukee, Wis. 218, 177, 245 — 640; aggregate 1,383.
2. Ron Wheeler, 227, 238, 233 — 698 & Mark Kuglitsch, both Milwaukee, Wis. 165, 213, 277 — 655; aggregate 1,353.

Team

1. Minnesota Loons No. 1, St. Paul, Minn. — Rod Toft 266, 222, 195 — 683; Terry Schacht 181, 244, 174 — 599; Denny Schacht 179, 207, 188 — 574; Todd Savoy 269, 208, 207 — 684; George Peterson 226, 214, 248 — 688; aggregate 3,228.
2. West Orange Pharmacy, Orange, Tex. — Russell Hebert 211, 180, 259 — 650; Pete Chiasson 203, 199, 195 — 597; Paul Vaughan 186, 232, 192 — 610; Marty Luginbuhl 204, 189, 222 — 615; Skipper Arsenault 210, 259, 181 — 650; aggregate 3,122.

Booster Division

Team

1. J&D Lawn Service, Lincoln, Neb. — Donald Neujahr Sr. 165, 148, 165 — 478; Ron Swenson 164, 182, 181 — 527; Doug Gruber 180, 168, 181 — 529; Donald Neujahr Jr. 220, 193, 165 — 578; Dennis Gage 257, 193, 258 — 708; aggregate 2,820.
2. Ray's Stupervisors, Las Vegas, Nev. — Ron Endley 184, 182, 200 — 566; Victor Everett 196, 127, 198 — 521; Sam Hayes 158, 187, 202 — 547; Jim Douglas 195, 257, 204 — 656; Ray Smith 191, 165, 155 — 511; aggregate 2,801.

Other Bowling Championships in 1984

U.S. Open, Men, Oak Lawn, Ill., March 12-17; Mark Roth, Spring Lake Heights, N.J., average 211, prize $38,000. Women, Chesterfield, Mo., Apr. 29-May 5; Karen Ellingsworth, Des Plaines, Ill., average 204, prize $10,000.

National Intercollegiate Championships, Men — Reno, Nev., May 11, doubles: Jack Jurek, West Texas St., and Mike Shequin, Chemeketa (Ore.) Comm. Coll., 1,167; singles: Gary Brobson, Akron, 673; all events: Jurek, 2,966 (14 games).

Women — Niagara Falls, N.Y., Apr. 9, doubles: Jan Schmidt, Indiana St. and Suzette Mitchell, Virginia Tech, 1,152; singles: Michelle Elkienbaum, Florida, 624; all events: Suzette Mitchell, 1,680 (9 games).

National Collegiate Team Championship — San Jose, Cal., May 4-6; Men: Buffalo State (N.Y.) Univ.; Women: Indiana State Univ.

Bowlers with 10 or More Sanctioned 300 Games

Elvin Mesger, Sullivan, Mo.	27	Robert Hart, Bay City, Mich.	13	Mike Berlin, Muscatine, Ia.	11
Dave Soutar, Kansas City, Mo.	19	Ron Woolet, Louisville, Ky.	13	George Pappas, Charlotte, N.C.	11
Dick Weber Sr., St. Louis, Mo.	18	James Ewald Jr., Louisville, Ky.	12	Dan Baudoin, Belmont, Cal.	10
George Billick, Old Forge, Pa.	17	Casey Jones, Plymouth, Wis.	12	Dick Beattie, Detroit, Mich.	10
Dave Williams, Westbury, N.Y.	16	Butch Soper, Santa Ana, Cal.	12	Larry Brott, Denver, Col.	10
John Wilcox Jr., Shavertown, Pa.	16	Walter Ward, Cleveland, Oh.	12	Mike Durbin, Chagrin Falls, Oh.	10
Ronnie Graham, Louisville, Ky.	15	Ted Long, Windgap, Pa.	12	Ken Ernske, Spring Valley, N.Y.	10
Don Johnson, Las Vegas, Nev.	15	Edward Lubanski, Oak Park, Mich.	12	Roger Fink, Lodi, Cal.	10
Teata Semiz, Fairfield, N.J.	15	Pat Patterson, St. Louis, Mo.	12	Al Fuscarino, Garfield, N.J.	10
Tony Torrice, Wolcott, Conn.	15	Ernie Schlegal, Vancouver, Wash.	12	Bob Handley, Pompano Beach, Fla.	10
Dennis Barnes, Oakland, Cal.	14	Frank Clause, Old Forge, Pa.	11	Mickey Higham, Kansas City, Mo.	10
Al Faragalli, Wayne, N.J.	14	Dave Davis, Tinton Falls, N.J.	11	Skip Pavone, San Jose, Cal.	10
Manny Salazar, San Jose, Cal.	14	Larry Laub, San Francisco, Cal.	11	Jim Stefanich, Joliet, Ill.	10
Dave Forcier, Providence, R.I.	14	*Hank Marino, Milwaukee, Wis.	11	Roy Buckley, New Albany, Oh.	10
Ray Bluth, St. Louis, Mo.	13	Norm Meyers, St. Louis, Mo.	11	Skee Foremsky, Conroe, Tex.	10
Don Carter, Miami, Fla.	13	Jim Rashleger, San Carlos, Cal.	11	Larry Gray, Torrance, Cal.	10
Fred McClain, Detroit, Mich.	13	Earl Anthony, Dublin, Cal.	11	Thomas Suchan, Akron, Oh.	10
Keith Orton, Brigham City, Ut.	13	Russell Fields, San Jose, Cal.	11	Alfie Cohn, Chicago, Ill.	10
Steve Carson, Oklahoma City, Okla.	13	Gus Lampo, Endicott, N.Y.	11	Joe Vito Buenrostro, San Antonio, Tex.	10

* Bowled two 300 games in official 3 game series.

Official Records of Annual ABC Tournaments

Type of record	Holder of record	Year	Score
High team total	Ace Mitchell Shur-Hooks, Akron	1966	3,357
High team game	Falstaff Beer, San Antonio	1958	1,226
High doubles score	John Klares-Steve Nagy, Cleveland	1952	1,453
High doubles game	Tommy Hudson, Akron, Ohio-Les Zikes, Chicago	1976	558
High singles total	Mickey Higham, Kansas City, Mo.	1977	801
High all events score	Jim Godman, Lorain, Oh.	1974	2,184
High team all events	Cook County Tobacco, Chicago, Ill.	1981	9,695
High life-time pin total	Bill Doehrman, Ft. Wayne	1908-1981	109,398

Record Averages for Consecutive Tournaments

No. in row	Holder of record	Span	Games	Average
Two	Rich Wonders, Racine, Wis.	1981-82	18	229.94
Three	Jim Godman, Lorain, Oh.	1974-76	27	223.96
Four	Jim Godman, Lorain, Oh.	1974-77	36	219.44
Five	Jim Godman, Lorain, Oh.	1973-77	45	216.33
Ten	Bob Strampe, Detroit	1961-70	111	211.10

All-Time Records for League and Tournament Play

Type of record	Holder of record	Year	Score	Competition
High team total	Budweiser Beer, St. Louis	1958	3,858	League
High team game	Edwards Concrete, Moscow, Pa.	1982	1,365	League
High doubles total	Nelson Burton Jr., Billy Walden, St. Louis	1970	1,614	Tournament
High doubles game	John Cotta and Steve Larson, Manteca, Cal.	1981	600	Tournament
High individual total	Albert Brandt, Lockport, N.Y.	1939	886	League
High all events score	Paul Andrews, East Moline, Ill.	1981	2,415	Tournament

Masters Bowling Tournament Champions

Year	Winner	Runner-up	W-L	Avg
1973	Dave Soutar, Gilroy, Cal.	Dick Ritger, Hartford, Wis.	7-0	218
1974	Paul Colwell, Tucson	Steve Neff, Sarasota, Fla.	7-0	234
1975	Ed Ressler Jr., Allentown, Pa.	Sam Flanagan, Parkersburg, W. Va.	9-1	213
1976	Nelson Burton Jr., St. Louis	Steve Carson, Oklahoma City	7-0	220
1977	Earl Anthony, Tacoma, Wash.	Jim Godman, Lorain, Oh.	7-0	218
1978	Frank Ellenburg, Mesa, Ariz.	Earl Anthony, Tacoma, Wash.	8-1	200
1979	Doug Myers, El Toro, Cal.	Bill Spigner, Hamden, Conn.	7-1	202
1980	Neil Burton, St. Louis, Mo.	Mark Roth, North Arlington, N.J.	7-1	206
1981	Randy Lightfoot, St. Charles, Mo.	Skip Tucker, Merritt Island, Fla.	7-1	218
1982	Joe Berardi, Brooklyn, N.Y.	Ted Hannahs, Zanesville, Oh.	7-0	205
1983	Mike Lastowski, Havre de Grace, Md.	Pete Weber, St. Louis, Mo.	7-1	212
1984	Earl Anthony, Dublin, Cal.	Gil Sliker, Washington, N.J.	7-0	212

Leading PBA Averages in 1983

(400 or more games in PBA tournaments)

Name	Games	Average	Name	Games	Average
Earl Anthony	668	216.645	Ted Hannahs	1,075	211.003
Marshall Holman	1,064	213.946	Joe Berardi	906	210.989
Tom Baker	894	212.345	Henry Gonzalez	653	210.914
Tom Milton	988	212.124	Mike Durbin	909	210.781
Mark Roth	681	211.950	Stever Fehr	844	210.626
Dave Husted	1,022	211.438	Brian Voss	866	210.532
Gil Sliker	827	211.243	Frank Ellenburg	718	210.433

Leading PBA Averages by Year

Year	Bowler	Tour-naments	Average	Year	Bowler	Tour-naments	Average
1962	Don Carter, St. Louis, Mo.	25	212.844	1974	Earl Anthony, Tacoma, Wash.	28	219.394
1963	Billy Hardwick, Louisville, Ky.	26	210.346	1975	Earl Anthony, Tacoma, Wash.	30	219.060
1964	Ray Bluth, St. Louis, Mo.	27	210.512	1976	Mark Roth, New York, N.Y.	28	215.970
1965	Dick Weber, St. Louis, Mo.	19	211.895	1977	Mark Roth, New York, N.Y.	28	218.174
1966	Wayne Zahn, Atlanta, Ga.	27	208.663	1978	Mark Roth, North Arlington, N.J.	25	219.834
1967	Wayne Zahn, Atlanta, Ga.	29	212.342	1979	Mark Roth, North Arlington, N.J.	26	221.662
1968	Jim Stefanich, Joliet, Ill.	33	211.895	1980	Earl Anthony, Dublin, Cal.	18	218.535
1969	Bill Hardwick, Louisville, Ky.	33	212.957	1981	Mark Roth, Spring Lake Hts., N.J.	25	216.699
1970	Nelson Burton Jr., St. Louis, Mo.	32	214.908	1982	Marshall Holman, Jacksonville, Ore.	25	212.844
1971	Don Johnson, Akron, Oh.	31	213.977				
1972	Don Johnson, Akron, Oh.	30	215.290	1983	Earl Anthony, Dublin, Cal.	20	216.645
1973	Earl Anthony, Tacoma, Wash.	29	215.799				

PBA Leading Money Winners

Total winnings are from PBA, ABC Masters, and BPAA All-Star tournaments only, and do not include numerous other tournaments or earnings from special television shows and matches.

Year	Bowler	Dollars	Year	Bowler	Dollars	Year	Bowler	Dollars
1960	Don Carter	22,525	1968	Jim Stefanich	67,377	1976	Earl Anthony	110,833
1961	Dick Weber	26,280	1969	Billy Hardwick	64,160	1977	Mark Roth	105,583
1962	Don Carter	49,972	1970	Mike Durbin	52,049	1978	Mark Roth	134,500
1963	Dick Weber	46,333	1971	Johnny Petraglia	85,065	1979	Mark Roth	124,517
1964	Bob Strampe	33,592	1972	Don Johnson	56,648	1980	Wayne Webb	116,700
1965	Dick Weber	47,674	1973	Don McCune	69,000	1981	Earl Anthony	164,735
1966	Wayne Zahn	54,720	1974	Earl Anthony	99,585	1982	Earl Anthony	134,760
1967	Dave Davis	54,165	1975	Earl Anthony	107,585	1983	Earl Anthony	135,605

Firestone Tournament of Champions

This is professional bowling's richest tournament and has been held each year since its inception in 1965, in Akron, Oh., the home of the Professional Bowlers Association.

Year	Winner	Year	Winner	Year	Winner	Year	Winner
1965	Billy Hardwick	1970	Don Johnson	1975	Dave Davis	1980	Wayne Webb
1966	Wayne Zahn	1971	Johnny Petraglia	1976	Marshall Holman	1981	Steve Cook
1967	Jim Stefanich	1972	Mike McGrath	1977	Mike Berlin	1982	Mike Durbin
1968	Dave Davis	1973	Jim Godman	1978	Earl Anthony	1983	Joe Berardi
1969	Jim Godman	1974	Earl Anthony	1979	George Pappas	1984	Mike Durbin

PBA Hall of Fame

Performance

			Meritorius service	
Bill Allen	Mike Durbin	Harry Smith	Eddie Elias	Steve Nagy
Glenn Allison	Buzz Fazio	Dave Soutar	Frank Esposito	Chuck Pezzano
Earl Anthony	Billy Hardwick	Jim Stefanich	E. A. "Bud" Fisher	Joe Richards
Ray Bluth	Don Johnson	Dick Weber	Lou Frantz	Chris Schenkel
Nelson Burton, Jr.	Johnny Petraglia	Billy Welu	Harry Golden	Lorraine Stitzlein
Don Carter	Dick Ritger	Wayne Zahn		
Dave Davis	Carmen Salvino			

Women's International Bowling Congress Champions

Individual	All events	Year	2-woman teams	5-woman teams

Mae Bolt,
  Berwyn, Ill. 709
	Annese Kelly,
	  New York, N.Y. 1,896
		1978	Barbara Shelton-
			  Annese Kelly,
			  New York, N.Y. 1,211
				Cook County Vending,
				  Chicago, Ill. 2,956

Betty Morris,
  Stockton, Cal. . . . 699
	Betty Morris,
	  Stockton, Cal. 1,945
		1979	Mary Ann Deptula-
			  Geri Beattie, Warren,
			  Dearborn Hts., Mich. . 1,314
				Alpine Lanes,
				  Euless, Tex. 3,096

Betty Morris,
  Stockton, Cal. . . . 674
	Cheryl Robinson,
	  Van Nuys, Cal. 1,848
		1980	Carol Lee-Dawn
			  Raddatz, Hempstead, E.
			  Northport, N.Y. 1,247
				All Japan,
				  Tokyo, Japan 3,014

Virginia Norton,
  So. Gate, Cal. . . . 672
	Virginia Norton,
	  So. Gate, Cal. 1,905
		1981	Nikki Gianulias-Donna
			  Adamek, Vallejo, Duarte,
			  Cal. 1,305
				Earl Anthony's
				  Dublin Bowl, Dublin
				  Cal. 2,963

Gracie Freeman,
  Alexandria, Va. . . 652
	Aleta Rzepecki,
	  Detroit, Mich. 1,905
		1982	Shirley Hintz-Lisa Rathgeber,
			  Merritt Island, Palmetto, Fla.;
			  Pat Costello-Donna
			  Adamek, Fremont, Durate,
			  Cal. (tie) 1,264
				Zavakos Realtors,
				  Dayton, Oh. 2,961

Aleta Sill,
  Detroit Mich. 726
	Virginia Norton,
	  So. Gate, Cal. 1,922
		1983	Jeanne Maiden-Sue Robb,
			  Solon, Euclid, Oh. . . . 1,312
				Teletronic Systems,
				  Philippines 2,868

Freida Gates,
  N. Syracuse, N.Y. . 712
	Shinobu Saito,
	  Tokyo, Japan 1,921
		1984	Bea Hoffmann-Sue Reese,
			  Novato, Cal. 1,292
				All Japan,
				  Tokyo. 3,019

Most Sanctioned 300 Games

Jeanne Maiden, Solon, Oh. 8	Pam Buckner, Reno, Nev.. 4	Ruby Thomas, Abilene, Tex. 3
Donna Adamek, Duarte, Cal. 6	Judith Seckel, Florissant, Mo. 4	Carolyn Trump, Akron, Oh. 3
Letitia Johnson, Napa, Cal. 6	Pat Adams, Santa Cruz, Cal. 3	Vesma Grinfelds, San Francisco, Cal. . 3
Betty Morris, Lodi, Cal. 5	Debbie Bennett, Akron, Oh. 3	Linda Kelly, Union, Oh. 3
Toni Gilliard, Beverly, Oh. 5	Kathy Lecroy, Fort Worth, Tex. 3	Rose Kotnik, Brook Park, Oh. 3
Regi Jonak, St. Louis, Mo. 5	Sylvia Martin, Philadelphia, Penn. . . . 3	Vickie Myers, El Segundo, Cal.. 3
Beverly Ortner, Tucson, Ariz.. 4	Cindy Mason, Sunnyvale, Cal. 3	Debbie Timberlake, Blue Springs, Mo.. 3

U.S. National Alpine Championships in 1984

Copper Mountain, Col., Feb. 23-26

Men		Women	
Downhill—Bill Johnson.	Giant Slalom—Steve Mahre.	Downhill—Lisa Wilcox.	Giant Slalom—Christin Cooper.
Slalom—Steve Mahre.	Combined—Andy Chambers.	Slalom—Tamara McKinney.	Combined—Eva Twardokens.

World Cup Alpine Champions

Men

1967	Jean Claude Killy, France	1973	Gustavo Thoeni, Italy	1979	Peter Luescher, Switzerland
1968	Jean Claude Killy, France	1974	Piero Gros, Italy	1980	Andreas Wenzel, Liechtenstein
1969	Karl Schranz, Austria	1975	Gustavo Thoeni, Italy	1981	Phil Mahre, U.S.
1970	Karl Schranz, Austria	1976	Ingemar Stenmark, Sweden	1982	Phil Mahre, U.S.
1971	Gustavo Thoeni, Italy	1977	Ingemar Stenmark, Sweden	1983	Phil Mahre, U.S.
1972	Gustavo Thoeni, Italy	1978	Ingemar Stenmark, Sweden	1984	Pirmin Zurbriggen, Switzerland

Women

1967	Nancy Greene, Canada	1973	Annemarie Proell, Austria	1979	Annemarie Proell Moser, Austria
1968	Nancy Greene, Canada	1974	Annemarie Proell, Austria	1980	Hanni Wenzel, Liechtenstein
1969	Gertrud Gabl, Austria	1975	Annemarie Proell, Austria	1981	Marie-Theres Nadig, Switzerland
1970	Michele Jacot, France	1976	Rose Mittermaier, W. Germany	1982	Erika Hess, Switzerland
1971	Annemarie Proell, Austria	1977	Lise-Marie Morerod, Austria	1983	Tamara McKinney, U.S.
1972	Annemarie Proell, Austria	1978	Hanni Wenzel, Liechtenstein	1984	Erika Hess, Switzerland

Canadian Interuniversity Athletic Union Champions

Men

	Basketball	Football	Hockey	Soccer	Swimming, Diving	Volleyball	Wrestling
1978	St. Mary's	Queen's	Alberta	Manitoba	Waterloo	Manitoba	O.U.A.A.
1979	St. Mary's	Acadia	Alberta	Alberta	Waterloo	Saskatchewan	O.U.A.A.
1980	Victoria	Alberta	Alberta	New Brunswick	Toronto	Manitoba	Lakehead
1981	Victoria	Acadia	Moncton	McGill	Toronto	Alberta	Guelph
1982	Victoria	British Columbia	Moncton	McGill	Calgary	Calgary	Guelph
1983	Victoria	Calgary	Saskatchewan	Laurentian	Calgary	British Columbia	Guelph
1984	Victoria	—	Toronto		Calgary	Manitoba	Concordia

Women

	Basketball	Field Hockey	Swimming, Diving	Volleyball	Gymnastics	Track & Field
1978	Laurentian	British Columbia	Acadia	British Columbia	—	—
1979	Laurentian	Toronto	Toronto	Saskatchewan	Alberta	—
1980	Victoria	York	Toronto	Saskatchewan	York	—
1981	Victoria	Toronto	Toronto	Saskatchewan	McMaster	Western Ont.
1982	Victoria	British Columbia	Toronto	Dalhousie	Manitoba	Western Ont.
1983	Bishop's	British Columbia	Toronto	Winnipeg	British Columbia	Western Ont.
1984	Bishop's	—	Toronto	Winnipeg	York	York

Professional Sports Directory

Baseball

Commissioner's Office
350 Park Ave.
New York, NY 10022

National League

National League Office
350 Park Ave.
New York, NY 10022

Atlanta Braves
PO Box 4064
Atlanta, GA 30302

Chicago Cubs
Wrigley Field
Chicago, IL 60613

Cincinnati Reds
100 Riverfront Stadium
Cincinnati, OH 45202

Houston Astros
Astrodome
Houston, TX 77001

Los Angeles Dodgers
Dodger Stadium
Los Angeles, CA 90012

Montreal Expos
PO Box 500, Station M
Montreal, Que. H1V 3P2

New York Mets
Shea Stadium
Flushing, NY 11368

Philadelphia Phillies
PO Box 7575
Philadelphia, PA 19101

Pittsburgh Pirates
P.O. Box 7000
Pittsburgh, PA 15212

St. Louis Cardinals
Busch Memorial Stadium
St. Louis, MO 63102

San Diego Padres
PO Box 2000
San Diego, CA 92108

San Francisco Giants
Candlestick Park
San Francisco, CA 94124

American League

American League Office
350 Park Ave.
New York, NY 10022

Baltimore Orioles
Memorial Stadium
Baltimore, MD 21218

Boston Red Sox
24 Yawkey Way
Boston, MA 02215

California Angels
Anaheim Stadium
Anaheim, CA 92806

Chicago White Sox
324 W. 35th St.
Chicago, IL 60616

Cleveland Indians
Boudreau Blvd.
Cleveland, OH 44114

Detroit Tigers
Tiger Stadium
Detroit, MI 48216

Kansas City Royals
Harry S. Truman Sports Complex
Kansas City, MO 64141

Milwaukee Brewers
Milwaukee County Stadium
Milwaukee, WI 53214

Minnesota Twins
501 Chicago Ave. South
Minneapolis, MN 55415

New York Yankees
Yankee Stadium
Bronx, NY 10451

Oakland A's
Oakland Coliseum
Oakland, CA 94621

Seattle Mariners
100 S. King St.
Seattle, WA 98104

Texas Rangers
P.O. Box 1111
Arlington, TX 76010

Toronto Blue Jays
Box 7777
Adelaide St. PO
Toronto, Ont. M5C 2K7

National Football League

League Office
410 Park Avenue
New York, NY 10022

Atlanta Falcons
Suwanee Road
Suwanee, GA 30174

Buffalo Bills
1 Bills Drive
Orchard Park, NY 14127

Chicago Bears
250 N. Washington
Lake Forest, IL 60045

Cincinnati Bengals
200 Riverfront Stadium
Cincinnati, OH 45202

Cleveland Browns
Cleveland Stadium
Cleveland, OH 44114

Dallas Cowboys
6116 North Central Expressway
Dallas, TX 75206

Denver Broncos
5700 Logan St.
Denver, CO 80216

Detroit Lions
1200 Featherstone Rd.
Pontiac, MI 48057

Green Bay Packers
1265 Lombardi Ave.
Green Bay, WI 54303

Houston Oilers
P.O. Box 1516
Houston, TX 77251

Indianapolis Colts
P.O. Box 20000
Indianapolis, IN 46220

Kansas City Chiefs
1 Arrowhead Drive
Kansas City, MO 64129

Los Angeles Raiders
3540 S. Figueroa St.
Los Angeles, CA 90007

Los Angeles Rams
2327 W. Lincoln Ave.
Anaheim, CA 92801

Miami Dolphins
4770 Biscayne Blvd.
Miami, FL 33137

Minnesota Vikings
9520 Viking Dr.
Eden Prairie, MN 55344

New England Patriots
Sullivan Stadium
Foxboro, MA 02035

New Orleans Saints
1500 Poydras St.
New Orleans, LA 70112

New York Giants
Giants Stadium
E. Rutherford, NJ 07073

New York Jets
598 Madison Ave.
New York, NY 10022

Philadelphia Eagles
Veterans Stadium
Philadelphia, PA 19148

Pittsburgh Steelers
Three Rivers Stadium
Pittsburgh, PA 15212

St. Louis Cardinals
Busch Stadium
St. Louis, MO 63102

San Diego Chargers
P.O. Box 20666
San Diego, CA 92108

San Francisco 49ers
711 Nevada St.
Redwood City, CA 94061

Seattle Seahawks
5305 Lake Washington Blvd.
Kirkland, WA 98033

Tampa Bay Buccaneers
1 Buccaneer Place
Tampa, FL 33607

Washington Redskins
PO Box 17247
Dulles Intl. Airport
Washington, DC 20041

Major Indoor Soccer League

League Office
One Bala Plaza
Bala Cynwyd, PA 19004

Baltimore Blast
201 W. Baltimore St.
Baltimore, MD 21201

Cleveland Force
34555 Chagrin Blvd.
Moreland Hills, OH 44022

Dallas Sidekicks
777 Sports St.
Dallas, TX 75207

Kansas City Comets
1800 Genesse St.
Kansas City, MO 64102

Los Angeles Lazers
P.O. Box 10
Inglewood, CA 90306

Memphis Americans
2771 Clarke Road
Memphis, TN 38115

New York Arrows
1101 Stewart Ave.
Garden City, NY 11530

Pittsburgh Spirit
Civic Center
Pittsburgh, PA 15219

St. Louis Steamers
212 N. Kirkwood
St. Louis, MO 63122

Tacoma Stars
P.O. Box 11367
Tacoma, WA 98411

Wichita Wings
114 S. Broadway
Wichita, KS 67202

National Basketball Association

League Office
645 5th Ave.
New York, NY 10022

Atlanta Hawks
100 Techwood Drive NW
Atlanta, GA 30303

Boston Celtics
Boston Garden
Boston, MA 02114

Chicago Bulls
333 North Michigan Ave.
Chicago, IL 60601

Cleveland Cavaliers
2923 Statesboro Rd.
Richfield, OH 44286

Dallas Mavericks
777 Sports St.
Dallas, TX 75207

Denver Nuggets
1635 Clay St.
Denver, CO 80204

Detroit Pistons
1200 Featherstone
Pontiac, MI 48057

Golden State Warriors
Oakland Coliseum
Oakland, CA 94621

Houston Rockets
The Summit
Houston, TX 77046

Indiana Pacers
920 Circle Tower Bldg.
Indianapolis, IN 46204

Kansas City Kings
1800 Genessee
Kansas City, MO 64102

Los Angeles Clippers
3939 Figueroa
Los Angeles, CA 90037

Los Angeles Lakers
PO Box 10
Inglewood, CA 90306

Milwaukee Bucks
901 North 4th St.
Milwaukee, WI 53203

New Jersey Nets
Byrne Meadowlands Arena
E. Rutherford, NJ 07073

New York Knickerbockers
4 Pennsylvania Plaza
New York, NY 10001

Philadelphia 76ers
PO Box 25040
Philadelphia, PA 19147

Phoenix Suns
2910 N. Central
Phoenix, AZ 85012

Portland Trail Blazers
700 NE Multnomah St.
Portland, OR 97232

San Antonio Spurs
P.O. Box 530
San Antonio, TX 78292

Seattle SuperSonics
419 Occidental South
Seattle, WA 98114

Utah Jazz
100 SW Temple
Salt Lake City, UT 84101

Washington Bullets
Capital Centre
Landover, MD 20785

National Hockey League

League Headquarters
960 Sun Life Bldg.
Montreal, Quebec H3B 2W2

Boston Bruins
150 Causeway St.
Boston, MA 02114

Buffalo Sabres
Memorial Auditorium
Buffalo, NY 14202

Calgary Flames
P.O. Box 1540
Calgary, Alta. T2P 3B9

Chicago Black Hawks
1800 W. Madison St.
Chicago, IL 60612

Detroit Red Wings
600 Civic Center Drive
Detroit, MI 48226

Edmonton Oilers
Northlands Coliseum
Edmonton, Alta. T5B 4M9

Hartford Whalers
One Civic Center Plaza
Hartford, CT 06103

Los Angeles Kings
PO Box 10
Inglewood, CA 90306

Minnesota North Stars
7901 Cedar Ave. S.
Bloomington, MN 55420

Montreal Canadiens
2313 St. Catherine St., West
Montreal, Quebec H3H 1N2

New Jersey Devils
Byrne Meadowlands Arena
E. Rutherford, NJ 07073

New York Islanders
Nassau Coliseum
Uniondale, NY 11553

New York Rangers
4 Pennsylvania Plaza
New York, NY 10001

Philadelphia Flyers
Pattison Place
Philadelphia, PA 19148

Pittsburgh Penguins
Civic Arena
Pittsburgh, PA 15219

Quebec Nordiques
2205 Ave. du Colisee
Charlesbourg, Que. G1L 4W7

St. Louis Blues
5700 Oakland Ave.
St. Louis, MO 63110

Toronto Maple Leafs
60 Carlton St.
Toronto, Ont. M5B 1L1

Vancouver Canucks
100 North Renfrew St.
Vancouver, B.C. V5K 3N7

Washington Capitals
Capital Centre
Landover, MD 20785

Winnipeg Jets
15-1430 Maroons Road
Winnipeg, Man. R3G 0L5

United States Football League

League Office
52 Vanderbilt Ave.
New York, NY 10017

Arizona Wranglers
515 N. 48th St.
Phoenix, AZ 85008

Birmingham Stallions
1919 Morris Ave.
Birmingham, AL 35203

Chicago Blitz
9511 Harrison St.
Des Plaines, IL 60016

Denver Gold
8702 Rosemary St.
Commerce City, CO 80022

Houston Gamblers
4828 Loop Central Dr.
Houston, TX 77081

Jacksonville Bulls
600 Wharfside Way
Jacksonville, FL 32207

Los Angeles Express
1501 Redondo Ave.
Manhattan Beach, CA 90266

Memphis Showboats
3767 New Getwell Rd.
Memphis, TN 38118

Michigan Panthers
575 Woodward St.
Rochester, MI 48063

New Jersey Generals
3 Empire Blvd.
S. Hackensack, NJ 07606

New Orleans Breakers
3501 Chateau Blvd.
Kenner, LA 70062

Oakland Invaders
7850 Edgewater Drive
Oakland, CA 94621

Oklahoma Outlaws
1751 E. 71st St.
Tulsa, OK 74136

Philadelphia Stars
Broad Street & Pattison Ave.
Philadelphia, PA 19148

Pittsburgh Maulers
Three Rivers Stadium
Pittsburgh, PA 15212

San Antonio Gunslingers
P.O. Box 12363
San Antonio, TX 78212

Tampa Bay Bandits
4221 North Himes, #201
Tampa, FL 33607

Washington Federals
1660 L Street, N.W. #915
Washington, DC 20036

North American Soccer League

League Office
1133 Ave. of the Americas
New York, NY 10036

Chicago Sting
Suite 1525
333 N. Michigan Ave.
Chicago, IL 60601

Golden Bay Earthquakes
800 Charcot Ave.
San Jose, CA 95131

Minnesota Strikers
8100 Cedar Ave. S.
Bloomington, MN 55420

New York Cosmos
44 E. 50th St.
New York, NY 10022

San Diego Sockers
9449 Friars Road
San Diego, CA 92108

Tampa Bay Rowdies
2225 N. Westshore Blvd.
Tampa, FL 33607

Toronto Blizzard
720 Spadina Ave.
Toronto, Ont. M5S 2T9

Tulsa Roughnecks
6511 E. 44th St.
Tulsa, OK 74145

Vancouver Whitecaps
Lougheed Hwy.
Burnaby, B.C. V5C 6A8

Canadian Football League

League Office
11 King St. W.
Suite 1800
Toronto, Ont. M5H 1A3

B.C. Lions
10605-135th St.
Surrey, B.C. V3T 4C8

Calgary Stampeders
McMahon Stadium
1817 Chowchild Trail N.W.
Calgary, Alta. T2M 4R6

Edmonton Eskimos
9023-111 Ave.
Edmonton, Alta T5B 0C3

Hamilton Tiger-Cats
75 Balsam Ave. N.
P.O. Box 172
Hamilton, Ont. L8N 3A2

Montreal Concordes
Olympic Stadium
P.O. Box 100, Station M
Montreal, Que. E1V 3L6

Ottawa Rough Riders
Lansdowne Park
Ottawa, Ont. K1S 2W7

Saskatchewan Roughriders
2940-10th Ave.
P.O. Box 1277
Regina, Sask. S4P 3B8

Toronto Argonauts
Exhibition Stadium
Exhibition Place
Toronto, Ont. M6K 3C3

Winnipeg Blue Bombers
1465 Maroons Rd.
Winnipeg, Man. R3G 0L6

Sports on Television

Source: Sports 1983, A.C. Nielsen Co.

	Household rating %	% Viewing audience			
		Men	Women	Teens	Children
Football					
NFL Superbowl	46.4	49	35	7	10
ABC-NFL (Monday evening)	18.1	62	29	5	4
CBS-NFL	16.7	55	29	8	8
NBC-NFL	12.6	58	29	7	6
College bowl games	11.2	56	34	5	5
College all-star games	6.4	55	33	9	4
NCAA regular season	10.1	58	28	7	7
Baseball					
World Series	23.3	52	38	5	5
All-star game	21.5	52	34	8	6
Regular season	7.1	54	34	5	6
Horse racing					
Average all	8.2	43	46	6	5
Basketball					
NBA average	7.6	58	27	8	6
NCAA average	6.7	55	29	8	8
Bowling					
Pro tour	7.3				
Auto racing	6.5	46	31	10	13
Golf	5.0	50	39	5	6
Tennis					
Wimbledon	4.1	40	44	8	8
Tournament average	3.7	41	42	8	9
Multi-sports series					
ABC Wide World of Sports	7.8	51	31	9	9
CBS Sports Sunday	6.4	52	34	6	8
Sportsworld	5.7	52	32	8	8

Curling Champions
Source: North American Curling News

World Champions

Year	Country, skip	Year	Country, skip	Year	Country, skip
1967	Scotland, Chuck Hay	1973	Sweden, Kjell Oscarius	1979	Norway, Kristian Soerum
1968	Canada, Ron Northcott	1974	United States, Bud Somerville	1980	Canada, Rich Folk
1969	Canada, Ron Northcott	1975	Switzerland, Otto Danieli	1981	Switzerland, Jurg Tanner
1970	Canada, Don Duguid	1976	United States, Bruce Roberts	1982	Canada, Al Hackner
1971	Canada, Don Duguid	1977	Sweden, Ragnar Kamp	1983	Canada, Ed Werenich
1972	Canada, Crest Melesnuk	1978	United States, Bob Nichols	1984	Norway, Eigil Ramsfjell

U.S. Men's Champions

Year	State, skip	Year	State, skip	Year	State, skip
1967	Washington, Bruce Roberts	1973	Massachusetts, Barry Blanchard	1979	Minnesota, Scotty Baird
1968	Wisconsin, Bud Somerville	1974	Wisconsin, Bud Somerville	1980	Minnesota, Paul Pustover
1969	Wisconsin, Bud Somerville	1975	Washington, Ed Risling	1981	Wisconsin, Somerville-Nichols
1970	North Dakota, Art Tallackson	1976	Minnesota, Bruce Roberts	1982	Wisconsin, Steve Brown
1971	North Dakota, Dale Dalziel	1977	Minnesota, Bruce Roberts	1983	Colorado, Don Cooper
1972	North Dakota, Bob LaBonte	1978	Wisconsin, Bob Nichols	1984	North Dakota, Bruce Roberts

U.S. Ladies Champions

Year	State, skip	Year	State, skip	Year	State, skip
1978	Wisconsin, Sandy Robarge	1981	Washington, Nancy Langley	1983	Washington, Nancy Langley
1979	Washington, Nancy Langley	1982	Illinois, Ruth Schwenker	1984	Minnesota, Amy Hatten
1980	Washington, Sharon Kozai				

Annual Results of Major Bowl Games

(Note: Dates indicate the year that the game was played).

Rose Bowl, Pasadena

1902 Michigan 49, Stanford 0
1916 Wash. State 14, Brown 0
1917 Oregon 14, Pennsylvania 0
1918-19 Service teams
1920 Harvard 7, Oregon 6
1921 California 28, Ohio State 0
1922 Wash. & Jeff. 0, California 0
1923 So. California 14, Penn State 3
1924 Navy 14, Washington 14
1925 Notre Dame 27, Stanford 10
1926 Alabama 20, Washington 19
1927 Alabama 7, Stanford 7
1928 Stanford 7, Pittsburgh 6
1929 Georgia Tech 8, California 7
1930 So. California 47, Pittsburgh 14
1931 Alabama 24, Wash. State 0
1932 So. California 21, Tulane 12
1933 So. California 35, Pittsburgh 0
1934 Columbia 7, Stanford 0
1935 Alabama 29, Stanford 13
1936 Stanford 7, So. Methodist 0
1937 Pittsburgh 21, Washington 0
1938 California 13, Alabama 0
1939 So. California 7, Duke 3

1940 So. California 14, Tennessee 0
1941 Stanford 21, Nebraska 13
1942 Oregon St. 20, Duke 16
    (at Durham)
1943 Georgia 9, UCLA 0
1944 So. California 29, Washington 0
1945 So. California 25, Tennessee 0
1946 Alabama 34, So. California 14
1947 Illinois 45, UCLA 14
1948 Michigan 49, So. California 0
1949 Northwestern 20, California 14
1950 Ohio State 17, California 14
1951 Michigan 14, California 6
1952 Illinois 40, Stanford 7
1953 So. California 7, Wisconsin 0
1954 Mich. State 28, UCLA 20
1955 Ohio State 20, So. California 7
1956 Mich. State 17, UCLA 14
1957 Iowa 35, Oregon St. 19
1958 Ohio State 10, Oregon 7
1959 Iowa 38, California 12
1960 Washington 44, Wisconsin 8
1961 Washington 17, Minnesota 7
1962 Minnesota 21, UCLA 3

1963 So. California 42, Wisconsin 37
1964 Illinois 17, Washington 7
1965 Michigan 34, Oregon St. 7
1966 UCLA 14, Mich. State 12
1967 Purdue 14, So. California 13
1968 Southern Cal. 14, Indiana 3
1969 Ohio State 27, Southern Cal 16
1970 Southern Cal 10, Michigan 3
1971 Stanford 27, Ohio State 17
1972 Stanford 13, Michigan 12
1973 So. California 42, Ohio State 17
1974 Ohio State 42, So. California 21
1975 So. California 18, Ohio State 16
1976 UCLA 23, Ohio State 10
1977 So. California 14, Michigan 6
1978 Washington 27, Michigan 20
1979 So. California 17, Michigan 10
1980 So. California 17, Ohio State 16
1981 Michigan 23, Washington 6
1982 Washington 28, Iowa 0
1983 UCLA 24, Michigan 14
1984 UCLA 45, Illinois 9

Orange Bowl, Miami

1935 Bucknell 26, Miami (Fla.) 0
1936 Catholic U. 20, Mississippi 19
1937 Duquesne 13, Miss. State 12
1938 Auburn 6, Mich. State 0
1939 Tennessee 17, Oklahoma 0
1940 Georgia Tech 21, Missouri 7
1941 Miss. State 14, Georgetown 7
1942 Georgia 40, TCU 26
1943 Alabama 37, Boston Col. 21
1944 LSU 19, Texas A&M 14
1945 Tulsa 26, Georgia Tech 12
1946 Miami (Fla.) 13, Holy Cross 6
1947 Rice 8, Tennessee 0
1948 Georgia Tech 20, Kansas 14
1949 Texas 41, Georgia 28
1950 Santa Clara 21, Kentucky 13
1951 Clemson 15, Miami (Fla.) 14

1952 Georgia Tech 17, Baylor 14
1953 Alabama 61, Syracuse 6
1954 Oklahoma 7, Maryland 0
1955 Duke 34, Nebraska 7
1956 Oklahoma 20, Maryland 6
1957 Colorado 27, Clemson 21
1958 Oklahoma 48, Duke 21
1959 Oklahoma 21, Syracuse 6
1960 Georgia 14, Missouri 0
1961 Missouri 21, Navy 14
1962 LSU 25, Colorado 7
1963 Alabama 17, Oklahoma 0
1964 Nebraska 13, Auburn 7
1965 Texas 21, Alabama 17
1966 Alabama 39, Nebraska 28
1967 Florida 27, Georgia Tech 12
1968 Oklahoma 26, Tennessee 24

1969 Penn State 15, Kansas 14
1970 Penn State 10, Missouri 3
1971 Nebraska 17, Louisiana St. 12
1972 Nebraska 38, Alabama 6
1973 Nebraska 40, Notre Dame 6
1974 Penn State 16, Louisiana St. 9
1975 Notre Dame 13, Alabama 11
1976 Oklahoma 14, Michigan 6
1977 Ohio State 27, Colorado 10
1978 Arkansas 31, Oklahoma 6
1979 Oklahoma 31, Nebraska 24
1980 Oklahoma 24, Florida St. 7
1981 Oklahoma 18, Florida St. 17
1982 Clemson 22, Nebraska 15
1983 Nebraska 21, Louisiana St. 20
1984 Miami (Fla.) 31, Nebraska 30

Sugar Bowl, New Orleans

1935 Tulane 20, Temple 14
1936 TCU 3, LSU 2
1937 Santa Clara 21, LSU 14
1938 Santa Clara 6, LSU 0
1939 TCU 15, Carnegie Tech 7
1940 Texas A&M 14, Tulane 13
1941 Boston Col. 19, Tennessee 13
1942 Fordham 2, Missouri 0
1943 Tennessee 14, Tulsa 7
1944 Georgia Tech 20, Tulsa 18
1945 Duke 29, Alabama 26
1946 Oklahoma A&M 33, St. Mary's 13
1947 Georgia 20, No. Carolina 10
1948 Texas 27, Alabama 7
1949 Oklahoma 14, No. Carolina 6
1950 Oklahoma 35, LSU 0
1951 Kentucky 13, Oklahoma 7

1952 Maryland 28, Tennessee 13
1953 Georgia Tech. 24, Mississippi 7
1954 Georgia Tech 42, West Virginia 19
1955 Navy 21, Mississippi 0
1956 Georgia Tech 7, Pittsburgh 0
1957 Baylor 13, Tennessee 7
1958 Mississippi 39, Texas 7
1959 LSU 7, Clemson 0
1960 Mississippi 21, LSU 0
1961 Mississippi 14, Rice 6
1962 Alabama 10, Arkansas 3
1963 Mississippi 17, Arkansas 13
1964 Alabama 12, Mississippi 7
1965 LSU 13, Syracuse 10
1966 Missouri 20, Florida 18
1967 Alabama 34, Nebraska 7
1968 LSU 20, Wyoming 13

1969 Arkansas 16, Georgia 2
1970 Mississippi 27, Arkansas 22
1971 Tennessee 34, Air Force 13
1972 Oklahoma 40, Auburn 22
*1972 (Dec.) Oklahoma 14, Penn State 0
1973 Notre Dame 24, Alabama 23
1974 Nebraska 13, Florida 10
1975 Alabama 13, Penn State 6
1977 (Jan.) Pittsburgh 27, Georgia 3
1978 Alabama 35, Ohio State 6
1979 Alabama 14, Penn State 7
1980 Alabama 24, Arkansas 9
1981 Georgia 17, Notre Dame 10
1982 Pittsburgh 24, Georgia 20
1983 Penn State 27, Georgia 23
1984 Auburn 9, Michigan 7
*Penn St. awarded game by forfeit

Cotton Bowl, Dallas

1937 TCU 16, Marquette 6
1938 Rice 28, Colorado 14
1939 St. Mary's 20, Texas Tech 13
1940 Clemson 6, Boston Col. 3
1941 Texas A&M 13, Fordham 12
1942 Alabama 29, Texas A&M 21
1943 Texas 14, Georgia Tech 7
1944 Randolph Field 7, Texas 7
1945 Oklahoma A&M 34, TCU 0
1946 Texas 40, Missouri 27
1947 Arkansas 0, LSU 0
1948 So. Methodist 13, Penn State 13
1949 So. Methodist 21, Oregon 13
1950 Rice 27, No. Carolina 13
1951 Tennessee 20, Texas 14
1952 Kentucky 20, TCU 7

1953 Texas 16, Tennessee 0
1954 Rice 28, Alabama 6
1955 Georgia Tech 14, Arkansas 6
1956 Mississippi 14, TCU 13
1957 TCU 28, Syracuse 27
1958 Navy 20, Rice 7
1959 TCU 0, Air Force 0
1960 Syracuse 23, Texas 14
1961 Duke 7, Arkansas 6
1962 Texas 12, Mississippi 7
1963 LSU 13, Texas 0
1964 Texas 28, Navy 6
1965 Arkansas 10, Nebraska 7
1966 LSU 14, Arkansas 7
1967 Georgia 24, So. Methodist 9
1968 Texas A&M 20, Alabama 16

1969 Texas 36, Tennessee 13
1970 Texas 21, Notre Dame 17
1971 Notre Dame 24, Texas 11
1972 Penn State 30, Texas 6
1973 Texas 17, Alabama 13
1974 Nebraska 19, Texas 3
1975 Penn State 41, Baylor 20
1976 Arkansas 31, Georgia 10
1977 Houston 30, Maryland 21
1978 Notre Dame 38, Texas 10
1979 Notre Dame 35, Houston 34
1980 Houston 17, Nebraska 14
1981 Alabama 30, Baylor 2
1982 Texas 14, Alabama 12
1983 SMU 7, Pittsburgh 3
1984 Georgia 10, Texas 9

Sun Bowl, El Paso

1936 Hardin Simmons 14, New Mex. St. 14
1937 Hardin-Simmons 34, Texas Mines 6
1938 West Virginia 7, Texas Tech 6
1939 Utah 26, New Mexico 0
1940 Catholic U. 0, Arizona St. 0
1941 Western Reserve 26, Arizona St. 13
1942 Tulsa 6, Texas Tech 0
1943 2d Air Force 13, Hardin-Simmons 7
1944 Southwestern (Tex.) 7, New Mexico 0
1945 Southwestern (Tex.) 35, U. of Mex. 0
1946 New Mexico 34, Denver 24
1947 Cincinnati 38, Virginia Tech 6
1948 Miami (O.) 13, Texas Tech 12
1949 West Virginia 21, Texas Mines 12
1950 Texas Western 33, Georgetown 20

1951 West Texas St. 14, Cincinnati 13
1952 Texas Tech 25, Col. Pacific 14
1953 Col. Pacific 26, Miss. Southern 7
1954 Texas Western 37, Miss. Southern 14
1955 Texas Western 47, Florida St. 20
1956 Wyoming 21, Texas Tech 14
1957 Geo. Washington 13, Tex. Western 0
1958 Louisville 34, Drake 20
1959 Wyoming 14, Hardin-Simmons 6
1960 New Mexico St. 28, No. Texas St. 8
1961 New Mexico St. 20, Utah State 13
1962 Villanova 17, Wichita 9
1963 West Texas St. 15, Ohio U. 14
1964 Oregon 21, So. Methodist 14
1965 Georgia 7, Texas Tech 0
1966 Texas Western 13, TCU 12

1967 Wyoming 28, Florida St. 20
1968 UTex El Paso 14, Mississippi 7
1969 Auburn 34, Arizona 10
1969 (Dec.) Nebraska 45, Georgia 6
1970 Georgia Tech. 17, Texas Tech. 9
1971 LSU 33, Iowa State 15
1972 North Carolina 32, Texas Tech 28
1973 Missouri 34, Auburn 17
1974 Mississippi St. 26, No. Carolina 24
1975 Pittsburgh 33, Kansas 19
1977 (Jan.) Texas A&M 37, Florida 14
1977 (Dec.) Stanford 24, Louisiana St. 14
1978 Texas 42, Maryland 0
1979 Washington 14, Texas 7
1980 Nebraska 31, Mississippi St. 17
1981 Oklahoma 40, Houston 14
1982 North Carolina 26, Texas 10
1983 Alabama 28, SMU 7

Gator Bowl, Jacksonville

1946 Wake Forest 26, So. Carolina 14
1947 Oklahoma 34, N.C. State 13
1948 Maryland 20, Georgia 20
1949 Clemson 24, Missouri 23
1950 Maryland 20, Missouri 7
1951 Wyoming 20, Wash. & Lee 7
1952 Miami (Fla.) 14, Clemson 0
1953 Florida 14, Tulsa 13
1954 Texas Tech 35, Auburn 13
1955 Auburn 33, Baylor 13
1956 Vanderbilt 25, Auburn 13
1957 Georgia Tech 21, Pittsburgh 14
1958 Tennessee 3, Texas A&M 0

1959 Mississippi 7, Florida 3
1960 Arkansas 14, Georgia Tech 7
1961 Florida 13, Baylor 12
1962 Penn State 30, Georgia Tech 15
1963 Florida 17, Penn State 7
1964 No. Carolina 35, Air Force 0
1965 Florida St. 36, Oklahoma 19
1966 Georgia Tech 31, Texas Tech 21
1967 Tennessee 18, Syracuse 12
1968 Penn State 17, Florida St. 17
1969 Missouri 35, Alabama 10
1969 (Dec.) Florida 14, Tenn. 13
1971 (Jan.) Auburn 35, Mississippi 28

1972 Georgia 7, N. Carolina 3
1973 Auburn 24, Colorado 3
1973 (Dec.) Tex. Tech. 28, Tenn. 19
1974 Auburn 27, Texas 3
1975 Maryland 13, Florida 0
1976 Notre Dame 20, Penn State 9
1977 Pittsburgh 34, Clemson 3
1978 Clemson 17, Ohio State 15
1979 No. Carolina 17, Michigan 15
1980 Pittsburgh 37, So. Carolina 9
1981 No. Carolina 31, Arkansas 27
1982 Florida St. 31, West Va. 12
1983 Florida 14, Iowa 6

Bluebonnet Bowl, Houston

1968 SMU 28, Oklahoma 27
1969 Houston 36, Auburn 7
1970 Oklahoma 24, Alabama 24
1971 Colorado 29, Houston 17
1972 Tennessee 24, Louisiana St. 17
1973 Houston 47, Tulane 7
1974 N. Carolina St. 31, Houston 31
1975 Texas 38, Colorado 21

1976 Nebraska 27, Texas Tech 24
1977 USC 47, Texas A&M 28
1978 Stanford 25, Georgia 22
1979 Purdue 27, Tennessee 22
1980 No. Carolina 16, Texas 7
1981 Michigan 33, UCLA 14
1982 Arkansas 28, Florida 24
1983 Oklahoma St. 24, Baylor 14

Peach Bowl, Atlanta

1974 Vanderbilt 6, Texas Tech. 6
1975 W. Virginia 13, No. Carolina St. 10
1976 Kentucky 21, North Carolina 0
1977 N. Carolina St. 24, Iowa St. 14
1978 Purdue 41, Georgia Tech. 21

1979 Baylor 24, Clemson 18
1981 (Jan.) Miami 20, Virginia Tech. 10
1981 (Dec.) West Virginia 26, Florida 6
1982 Iowa 28, Tennessee 22
1983 Florida St. 28, North Carolina 3

Fiesta Bowl, Tempe

1976 Oklahoma 41, Wyoming 7
1977 Penn St. 42, Arizona St. 30
1978 UCLA 10, Arkansas 10
1979 Pittsburgh 16, Arizona 10

1980 Penn St. 31, Ohio St. 19
1981 Penn St. 26, USC 10
1983 (Jan.) Arizona St. 32, Oklahoma 21
1984 Ohio State 28, Pittsburgh 23

Liberty Bowl, Memphis

1968 Mississippi 34, Va. Tech 17
1969 Colorado 47, Alabama 33
1970 Tulane 17, Colorado 3
1971 Tennessee 14, Arkansas 13
1972 Georgia Tech 31, Iowa State 30
1973 No. Carolina St. 31, Kansas 18
1974 Tennessee 7, Maryland 3
1975 USC 20, Texas A&M 0

1976 Alabama 36, UCLA 6
1977 Nebraska 27, N. Carolina 17
1978 Missouri 20, Louisiana St. 15
1979 Penn St. 9, Tulane 6
1980 Purdue 28, Missouri 25
1981 Ohio State 31, Navy 28
1982 Alabama 21, Illinois 15
1983 Notre Dame 19, Boston Coll. 18

Hall of Fame Classic, Birmingham

1980 Arkansas 34, Tulane 15
1981 Mississippi 10, Kansas 0

1982 Air Force 36, Vanderbilt 28
1983 W. Virginia 20, Kentucky 16

Independence Bowl, Shreveport

1979 Syracuse 31, McNeese St. 7
1980 So. Miss. 16, McNeese St. 14
1981 Texas A&M 33, Oklahoma St. 16

1982 Wisconsin 14, Kansas St. 3
1983 Air Force 9, Mississippi 3

1959 Clemson 23, TCU 7
1960 Texas 3, Alabama 3
1961 Kansas 33, Rice 7
1962 Missouri 14, Georgia Tech 10
1963 Baylor 14, LSU 7
1964 Tulsa 14, Mississippi 7
1965 Tennessee 27, Tulsa 6
1966 Texas 19, Mississippi 0
1967 Colorado 31, Miami (Fla.) 21

1968 LSU 31, Florida St. 27
1969 West Virginia 14, S. Carolina 3
1970 Arizona St. 48, N. Carolina 26
1971 Mississippi 41, Georgia Tech. 18
1972 N. Carolina St. 49, W. Va. 13
1973 Georgia 17, Maryland 16

1971 Arizona St. 45, Florida St. 38
1972 Arizona St. 49, Missouri 35
1973 Arizona St. 28, Pittsburgh 7
1974 Okla. St. 16, Brigham Young 6
1975 Arizona St. 17, Nebraska 14

1959 Penn State 7, Alabama 0
1960 Penn State 41, Oregon 12
1961 Syracuse 15, Miami 14
1962 Oregon State 6, Villanova 0
1963 Miss. State 16, N.C. State 12
1964 Utah 32, West Virginia 6
1965 Mississippi 13, Auburn 7
1966 Miami (Fla.) 14, Va. Tech 7
1967 N.C. State 14, Georgia 7

1977 Maryland 17, Minnesota 7
1978 Texas A&M 28, Iowa St. 12
1979 Missouri 24, So. Carolina 14

1976 McNeese St. 20, Tulsa 16
1977 Louisiana Tech 24, Louisville 14
1978 E. Carolina 35, La. Tech 13

Other Bowl Games in 1983

Aloha Bowl (Honolulu)—Penn State 13, Washington 10.
California Bowl (Fresno)—No. Ill. 20, Cal. St.-Fullerton 13.

Florida Citrus (Orlando)—Tennessee 30, Maryland 23.
Holiday Bowl (San Diego)—BYU 21, Missouri 17.

College Football Teams

Division I Teams

Team	Nickname	Team colors	Conference	Coach	1983 record (W-L-T)
Air Force	Falcons	Blue & silver	Western Athletic	Fisher De Berry	10-2-0
Akron	Zips	Blue & Gold	Ohio Valley	Jim Dennison	8-3-0
Alabama	Crimson Tide	Crimson & white	Southeastern	Ray Perkins	8-4-0
Alabama State	Hornets	Black & gold	Southwestern	Jim Parker	2-9-0
Alcorn State	Braves	Purple & gold	Southwestern	Marino Casem	7-3-0
Appalachian State	Mountaineers	Black & gold	Southern	Sparky Woods	6-5-0
Arizona	Wildcats	Red & blue	Pacific Ten	Larry Smith	7-3-1
Arizona State	Sun Devils	Maroon & gold	Pacific Ten	Darryl Rogers	6-4-1
Arkansas	Razorbacks	Cardinal & white	Southwest	Ken Hatfield	6-5-0
Arkansas State	Indians	Scarlet & black	Southland	Lawrence Lacewell	5-5-1
Army	Cadets	Black, gold, gray	1-A Eastern Ind.	Jim Young	2-9-0
Auburn	Tigers	Orange & blue	Southeastern	Pat Dye	11-1-0
Austin Peay State	Governors	Red & white	Ohio Valley	Emory Hale	6-5-0
Ball State	Cardinals	Cardinal & white	Mid-American	Dwight Wallace	6-5-0
Baylor	Bears	Green & gold	Southwest	Grant Teaff	7-4-1
Bethune-Cookman	Wildcats	Maroon & gold	Mid-Eastern	Larry Little	4-4-1
Boise State	Broncos	Orange & Blue	Big Sky	Lyle Setencich	6-5-0
Boston College	Eagles	Maroon & gold	1-A Eastern Ind.	Jack Bicknell	9-3-0
Boston Univ.	Terriers	Scarlet & white	Yankee	Rick Taylor	9-4-0
Bowling Green St.	Falcons	Orange & brown	Mid-American	Denny Stolz	8-3-0
Brigham Young	Cougars	Royal blue & white	Western Athletic	LaVell Edwards	11-1-0
Brown	Bruins, Bears	Brown, cardinal, white	Ivy	John Rosenberg	4-5-1
Bucknell	Bisons	Orange & blue	1-AA Eastern Ind.	Bob Curtis	4-5-1
California	Golden Bears	Blue & gold	Pacific Ten	Joe Kapp	5-5-1
Central Michigan	Chippewas	Maroon & gold	Mid-American	Herb Deromedi	8-3-0
Cincinnati	Bearcats	Red & black	Independent	Dave Currey	4-6-1
Citadel	Bulldogs	Blue & white	Southern	Tom Moore	3-8-0
Clemson	Tigers	Purple & orange	Atlantic Coast	Danny Ford	9-1-1
Colgate	Red Raiders	Maroon	1-AA Eastern Ind.	Fred Dunlap	8-4-0
Colorado State	Rams	Green & gold	Western Athletic	Leon Fuller	5-7-0
Colorado	Buffaloes	Silver, gold & blue	Big Eight	Bill McCartney	4-7-0
Columbia	Lions	Blue & white	Ivy	Bob Naso	1-7-2
Connecticut	Huskies	Blue & white	Yankee	Tom Jackson	5-6-0
Cornell	Big Red	Carnelian & white	ivy	Maxie Baughan	3-6-1
Dartmouth	Big Green	Dartmouth green & white	Ivy	Joe Yukica	4-5-1
Davidson	Wildcats	Red & black	Southern	Ed Farrell	2-8-0
Delaware	Fightin' Blue Hens	Blue & gold	1-A Eastern Ind.	Harold Raymond	4-7-0
Delaware State	Hornets	Red & blue	Mid-Eastern	Joe Purzycki	7-3-1
Drake	Bulldogs	Blue & white	Missouri Valley	Chuck Shelton	1-10-0
Duke	Blue Devils	Royal blue & white	Atlantic Coast	Steve Sloan	3-8-0
East Carolina	Pirates	Purple & gold	1-A Southern Ind.	Ed Emory	8-3-0
East Tennessee St.	Buccaneers	Blue & gold	Southern	Buddy Sasser	3-8-0
Eastern Illinois	Panthers	Blue & Gray	Mid-Continent	Al Molde	9-3-0
Eastern Kentucky	Colonels	Maroon & white	Ohio Valley	Roy Kidd	7-3-1
Eastern Michigan	Hurons	Green & white	Mid-American	Jim Harkema	1-10-0
Florida	Gators	Orange & blue	Southeastern	Charley Pell	9-2-1
Florida A&M	Rattlers	Orange & green	Mid-Eastern	Rudy Hubbard	7-4-0
Florida State	Seminoles	Garnet & gold	1-A Southern Ind.	Bobby Bowden	7-5-0
Fresno State	Bulldogs	Cardinal, white, blue	Pacific Coast	Jim Sweeney	6-5-0
Fullerton, Cal. State	Titans	Blue, orange, white	Pacific Coast	Gene Murphy	7-5-0
Furman	Paladins	Purple & white	Southern	Dick Sheridan	10-2-1
Georgia	Bulldogs	Red & black	Southeastern	Vince Dooley	10-1-1
Georgia Southern	Eagles	Blue & white	Independent	Erskine Russell	none
Georgia Tech	Yellow Jackets	Old gold & white	Atlantic Coast	Bill Curry	3-8-0
Grambling State	Tigers	Black & gold	Southwestern	Eddie Robinson	8-1-2
Harvard	Crimson	Crimson	Ivy	Joe Restic	6-2-2
Hawaii	Rainbow Warriors	Green & white	Western Athletic	Dick Tomey	5-5-1
Holy Cross	Crusaders	Royal purple	1-AA Eastern Ind.	Rick Carter	9-2-1
Houston	Cougars	Scarlet & white	Southwest	Bill Yeoman	4-7-0
Howard	Bison	Blue & white	Mid-Eastern	Willie Jeffries	1-9-0
Idaho	Vandals	Silver & gold	Big Sky	Dennis Erickson	8-3-0
Idaho State	Bengals	Orange & black	Big Sky	Jim Koetter	8-4-0
Illinois	Fighting Illini	Orange & blue	Big Ten	Mike White	10-2-0
Illinois State	Redbirds	Red & white	Missouri Valley	Bob Otolski	6-4-1
Indiana	Fightin' Hoosiers	Cream & crimson	Big Ten	Bill Mallory	3-8-0
Indiana State	Sycamores	Blue & white	Missouri Valley	Dennis Raetz	9-4-0
Iowa	Hawkeyes	Old gold & black	Big Ten	Hayden Fry	9-3-0
Iowa State	Cyclones	Cardinal & gold	Big Eight	Jim Criner	4-7-0
Jackson State	Tigers	Blue & white	Southwestern	W.C. Gorden	8-3-0
James Madison	Dukes	Purple & gold	1-AA Southern Ind.	Challace McMillin	3-8-0
Kansas	Jayhawks	Crimson & blue	Big Eight	Mike Gottfried	4-6-1
Kansas State	Wildcats	Purple & white	Big Eight	Jim Dickey	3-8-0
Kent State	Golden Flashes	Blue & gold	Mid-American	Dick Scesniak	1-10-0
Kentucky	Wildcats	Blue & white	Southeastern	Jerry Clairborne	6-5-1
Lafayette	Leopards	Maroon & white	1-AA Eastern Ind.	Bill Russo	6-5-0
Lamar	Cardinals	Red & white	Southland	Ken Stephens	2-9-0
Lehigh	Engineers	Brown & white	1-AA Eastern Ind.	John Whitehead	8-3-0
Long Beach, Cal. State	Forty-Niners	Brown & gold	Pacific Coast	Mike Sheppard	8-4-0
Louisiana State	Fignting Tigers	Purple & gold	Southeastern	Bill Arnsparger	4-7-0
Louisiana Tech	Bulldogs	Red & blue	Southland	A.L. Williams	4-7-0
Louisville	Cardinals	Red, black, white	1-A Southern Ind.	Bob Weber	3-8-0

Team	Nickname	Team colors	Conference	Coach	1983 record (W-L-T)
Maine	Black Bears	Blue & white	Yankee	Ron Rogerson	4-6-0
Marshall	Thundering Herd	Green & white	Southern	Stan Parrish	4-7-0
Maryland	Terps	Red, white, black & gold	Atlantic Coast	Bobby Ross	8-4-0
Massachusetts	Minutemen	Maroon & white	Yankee	Bob Stull	3-8-0
McNeese State	Cowboys	Blue & gold	Southland	John McCann	6-5-0
Memphis State	Tigers	Blue & gray	1-A Southern Ind.	Rey Dempsey	6-4-1
Miami (Fla.)	Hurricanes	Orange, green, white	1-A Southern Ind.	Jimmy Johnson	11-1-0
Miami (Ohio)	Redskins	Red & white	Mid-American	Tim Rose	4-7-0
Michigan	Wolverines	Maize & blue	Big Ten	Bo Schembechler	9-3-0
Michigan State	Spartans	Green & white	Big Ten	George Perles	4-6-1
Middle Tennessee St.	Blue Raiders	Blue & white	Ohio Valley	Boots Donnelly	8-2-0
Minnesota	Golden Gophers	Maroon & gold	Big Ten	Lou Holtz	1-10-0
Mississippi	Rebels	Red & blue	Southeastern	Billy Brewer	6-6-0
Mississippi State	Bulldogs	Maroon & white	Southeastern	Emory Bellard	3-8-0
Miss. Valley State	Delta Devils	Green & white	Southwestern	Archie Cooley	7-2-1
Missouri	Tigers	Old gold & black	Big Eight	Warren Powers	7-5-0
Montana	Grizzlies	Copper, silver, gold	Big Sky	Larry Donovan	4-6-0
Montana State	Bobcats	Blue & gold	Big Sky	Dave Arnold	1-10-0
Morehead State	Eagles	Blue & gold	Ohio Valley	Bill Baldridge	2-9-0
Murray State	Racers	Blue & gold	Ohio Valley	Frank Beamer	7-4-0
Navy	Midshipmen	Navy blue & gold	1-A Eastern Ind.	Gary Tranquill	3-8-0
Nebraska	Cornhuskers	Scarlet & cream	Big Eight	Tom Osborne	12-1-0
Nevada-Las Vegas	Rebels	Scarlet & gray	Pacific Coast	Harvey Hyde	7-4-0
Nevada-Reno	Wolf Pack	Silver & blue	Big Sky	Chris Ault	9-5-0
New Hampshire	Wildcats	Blue & white	Yankee	Bill Bowes	7-3-0
New Mexico	Lobos	Cherry & silver	Western Athletic	John Lee Dunn	6-6-0
New Mexico State	Aggies	Crimson & white	Pacific Coast	Fred Zechman	5-6-0
Nicholls St.	Colonels	Red & grey	Gulf Star	William Jackson	5-6-0
North Carolina	Tar Heels	Blue & white	Atlantic Coast	Dick Crum	8-4-0
North Carolina A & T	Aggies	Blue & gold	Mid-Eastern	Maurice Forte	3-7-1
North Carolina State	Wolfpack	Red & white	Atlantic Coast	Tom Reed	3-8-0
North Texas State	Mean Green, Eagles	Green & white	Southland	Corky Nelson	8-4-0
Northeast Louisiana	Indians	Maroon & gold	Southland	Pat Collins	8-3-0
Northeastern	Huskies	Red & black	1-AA Eastern Ind.	Pat Pawlak	6-4-1
Northern Arizona	Lumberjacks	Blue & gold	Big Sky	Joe Harper	4-7-0
Northern Illinois	Huskies	Cardinal & black	Mid-American	Lee Corso	10-2-0
Northern Iowa	Panthers	Purple & Old Gold	Mid-Continent	Darrell Mudra	6-5-0
Northwestern	Wildcats	Purple & white	Big Ten	Dennis Green	2-9-0
Northwestern State	Demons	Burnt orange, purple, white	Gulf Star	Sam Goodwin	4-7-0
Notre Dame	Fighting Irish	Gold & blue	Independent	Gerry Faust	7-5-0
Ohio State	Buckeyes	Scarlet & gray	Big Ten	Earle Bruce	9-3-0
Ohio Univ	Bobcats	Green & white	Mid-American	Brian Burke	4-7-0
Oklahoma	Sooners	Crimson & cream	Big Eight	Barry Switzer	8-4-0
Oklahoma State	Cowboys	Orange & black	Big Eight	Pat Jones	8-4-0
Oregon	Ducks	Green & yellow	Pacific Ten	Rich Brooks	4-6-1
Oregon State	Beavers	Orange & black	Pacific Ten	Joe Avezzano	2-8-1
Pacific	Tigers	Orange & black	Pacific Coast	Bob Cope	3-9-0
Penn State	Nittany Lions	Blue & white	1-AA Eastern Ind.	Joe Paterno	8-4-1
Pennsylvania	Red & Blue, Quakers	Red & blue	Ivy	Jerry Berndt	6-3-1
Pittsburgh	Panthers	Gold & blue	1-A Eastern Ind.	Serafino Fazio	8-3-1
Prairie View A & M	Panthers	Purple & gold	Southwestern	Conway Hayman	0-11-0
Princeton	Tigers	Orange & black	Ivy	Frank Navarro	4-6-0
Purdue	Boilermakers	Old gold & black	Big Ten	Leon Bertnett	3-7-1
Rhode Island	Rams	Blue & white	Yankee	Bob Griffin	6-4-0
Rice	Owls	Blue & gray	Southwest	Watson Brown	1-10-0
Richmond	Spiders	Red & blue	Yankee	Dal Shealy	3-8-0
Rutgers	Scarlet Knights	Scarlet	1-A Eastern Ind.	Dick Anderson	3-8-0
San Diego State	Aztecs	Scarlet & black	Western Athletic	Doug Scovil	2-9-1
San Jose State	Spartans	Blue, gold & white	Pacific Coast	Claude Gilbert	5-6-0
South Carolina	Fighting Gamecocks	Garnet & black	1-A Southern Ind.	Joe Morrison	5-6-0
South Carolina State	Bulldogs	Garnet & blue	Mid-Eastern	Bill Davis	7-3-0
Southeastern La.	Lions	Green & gold	Gulf Star	Oscar Lofton	6-5-0
Southern	Jaguars	Blue & gold	Southwestern	Otis Washington	7-4-0
Southern California	Trojans	Cardinal & gold	Pacific Ten	Ted Tollner	4-6-1
Southern Illinois	Salukis	Maroon & white	Missouri Valley	Ray Dorr	13-1-0
Southern Methodist	Mustangs	Red & blue	Southwest	Bobby Collins	10-2-0
Southern Mississippi	Golden Eagles	Black & gold	1-A Southern Ind.	Jim Carmody	7-4-0
SW Missouri St	Bears	Maroon & white	Mid-Continent	Rich Johanningmeier	6-5-0
Southwestern La.	Ragin' Cajuns	Vermillion & white	Independent	Sam Robertson	4-6-0
Stanford	Cardinals	Cardinal & white	Pacific Ten	Jack Elway	1-10-0
Syracuse	Orangemen	Orange	1-A Eastern Ind.	Dick MacPherson	6-5-0
Temple	Owls	Cherry & white	1-A Eastern Ind.	Bruce Arians	4-7-0
Tennessee	Volunteers	Orange & white	Southeastern	John Majors	9-3-0
Tenn.-Chattanooga	Moccasins	Navy blue & gold	Southern	Buddy Nix	7-4-0
Tennessee State	Tigers	Blue & white	1-AA Southern Ind.	Wilson Thomas	8-2-1
Tennessee Tech	Golden Eagles	Purple & gold	Ohio Valley	Gary Darnell	2-8-0
Texas	Longhorns	Orange & white	Southwest	Fred Akers	11-1-0
Texas-Arlington	Mavericks	Royal blue & white	Southland	Chuck Curtis	5-6-0
Texas-El Paso	Miners	Orange, white, blue	Western Athletic	Bill Yung	2-10-0
Texas A & M	Aggies	Maroon & white	Southwest	Jackie Sherrill	5-5-1
Texas Christian	Horned Frogs	Purple & white	Southwest	Jim Wacker	1-8-2
Texas Southern	Tigers	Maroon & gray	Southwestern	Lionel Taylor	4-6-0
Texas Tech	Red Raiders	Scarlet & black	Southwest	Jerry Moore	3-7-1
Toledo	Rockets	Blue & gold	Mid-American	Dan Simrell	9-2-0

Team	Nickname	Team colors	Conference	Coach	1983 record (W-L-T)
Tulane	Green Wave	Olive green & sky blue	1-A Southern Ind.	Wally English	4-7-0
Tulsa	Golden Hurricane	Blue & gold	Missouri Valley	John Cooper	8-3-0
UCLA	Bruins	Navy blue & gold	Pacific Ten	Terry Donahue	7-4-1
Utah State	Aggies	Navy blue & white	Pacific Coast	Chris Pella	5-6-0
Utah	Utes	Crimson & white	Western Athletic	Chuck Stobart	5-6-0
Vanderbilt	Commodores	Black & gold	Southeastern	George MacIntyre	2-9-0
Virginia	Cavaliers	Orange & blue	Atlantic Coast	George Welsh	6-5-0
VMI	Keydets	Red, white & yellow	Southern	Bob Thalman	2-9-0
Virginia Tech	Gobblers, Hokies	Orange & maroon	1-A Southern Ind.	Bill Dooley	9-2-0
Wake Forest	Demon Deacons	Old gold & black	Atlantic Coast	Al Groh	4-7-0
Washington	Huskies	Purple & gold	Pacific Ten	Don James	8-4-0
Washington State	Cougars	Crimson & gray	Pacific Ten	Jim Walden	7-4-0
Weber State	Wildcats	Purple & white	Big Sky	Mike Price	6-5-0
West Texas State	Buffaloes	Maroon & white	Missouri Valley	Don Davis	0-10-1
West Virginia	Mountaineers	Old gold & blue	1-A Eastern Ind.	Don Nehlen	9-3-0
Western Carolina	Catamounts	Purple & gold	Southern	Bob Waters	11-3-1
Western Illinois	Leathernecks	Purple & Gold	Mid-Continent	Bruce Craddock	3-8-0
Western Kentucky	Hilltoppers	Red & white	1-AA Southern Ind.	Dave Roberts	2-8-1
Western Michigan	Broncos	Brown & gold	Mid-American	Jack Harbaugh	6-5-0
Wichita State	Shockers	Yellow & black	Missouri Valley	Ron Chisnar	3-8-0
William & Mary	Indians	Green, gold, silver	1-AA Southern Ind.	Jimmye Laycock	6-5-0
Wisconsin	Badgers	Cardinal & white	Big Ten	Dave McClain	7-4-0
Wyoming	Cowboys	Brown & yellow	Western Athletic	Al Kincaid	7-5-0
Yale	Bulldogs, Elis	Yale blue & white	Ivy	Carmen Cozza	1-9-0
Youngstown St.	Penguins	Scarlet & white	Ohio Valley	Bill Narduzzi	4-7-0

All-Time Division 1-A Percentage Leaders

(Classified as Division 1 for last 10 years; including bowl games; ties computed as half won and half lost.)

	Years	Won	Lost	Tied	Pct	Bowl Games W	L	T
Notre Dame	95	634	181	40	.765	8	3	0
Michigan	104	649	216	31	.742	6	9	0
Alabama	89	601	207	42	.732	20	14	3
Texas	91	625	223	30	.729	15	13	2
Oklahoma	89	570	215	49	.713	16	7	1
Southern Cal	91	556	210	49	.712	20	7	0
Ohio State	94	580	230	48	.704	9	9	0
Penn State	97	587	260	40	.684	14	6	2
Tennessee	87	551	247	46	.680	13	13	0
Nebraska	94	581	269	39	.676	12	10	0
Miami (Oh.)	95	498	251	36	.657	5	1	0
Army	94	524	279	49	.644	1	0	0
Arizona State	71	380	209	21	.640	7	4	1
Louisiana State	90	508	278	43	.639	10	12	1
Georgia	90	515	292	50	.630	11	11	1
Minnesota	100	504	294	40	.625	1	2	0
Washington	94	477	279	47	.623	6	6	1
Michigan State	87	457	278	40	.616	2	2	0
Tulsa	79	421	261	26	.613	3	6	0
San Diego St.	61	345	214	26	.612	3	1	0
Pittsburgh	94	517	325	37	.609	7	9	0
Bowling Green	65	323	201	47	.607	0	2	0
Colorado	94	482	308	32	.606	4	6	0
Stanford	77	425	272	45	.603	7	5	1
Auburn	91	473	306	42	.602	8	7	1
Georgia Tech	91	493	320	39	.606	14	8	0
Southern Mississippi	67	357	236	25	.598	1	5	0

Longest Division 1-A Winning Streaks

Wins	Team	Years	Ended by	Score
47	Oklahoma	1953-57	Notre Dame	7-0
39	Washington	1908-14	Oregon State	0-0
37	Yale	1890-93	Princeton	6-0
37	Yale	1887-89	Princeton	10-0
35	Toledo	1969-71	Tampa	21-0
34	Pennsylvania	1894-96	Lafayette	6-4
31	Oklahoma	1948-50	Kentucky	13-7
31	Pittsburgh	1914-18	Cleveland Naval Reserve	10-9
31	Pennsylvania	1896-98	Harvard	10-0
30	Texas	1968-70	Notre Dame	24-11
29	Michigan	1901-03	Minnesota	6-6
28	Alabama	1978-80	Mississippi State	6-3
28	Oklahoma	1973-75	Kansas	23-3
28	Michigan State	1950-53	Purdue	6-0
27	Nebraska	1901-04	Colorado	6-0
26	Cornell	1921-24	Williams	14-7
26	Michigan	1903-05	Chicago	2-0
25	Michigan	1946-49	Army	21-7
25	Army	1944-46	Notre Dame	0-0
25	Southern Cal	1931-33	Oregon State	0-0

College Football Conference Champions

	Atlantic Coast		Ivy League		Big Eight		Big Ten
1970	Wake Forest	1970	Dartmouth	1970	Nebraska	1970	Ohio State
1971	North Carolina	1971	Dartmouth, Cornell	1971	Nebraska	1971	Michigan
1972	North Carolina	1972	Dartmouth	1972	Nebraska	1972	Ohio State, Michigan
1973	No. Carolina St.	1973	Dartmouth	1973	Oklahoma	1973	Ohio State, Michigan
1974	Maryland	1974	Yale, Harvard	1974	Oklahoma	1974	Ohio State, Michigan
1975	Maryland	1975	Harvard	1975	Oklahoma, Nebraska	1975	Ohio State
1976	Maryland	1976	Yale, Brown	1976	Oklahoma, Colorado,	1976	Michigan, Ohio State
1977	North Carolina	1977	Yale		Oklahoma State	1977	Michigan, Ohio State
1978	Clemson	1978	Dartmouth	1977	Oklahoma	1978	Michigan St., Michigan
1979	No. Carolina St.	1979	Yales	1978	Nebraska, Oklahoma	1979	Ohio State
1980	North Carolina	1980	Yale	1979	Oklahoma	1980	Michigan
1981	Clemson	1981	Yale, Dartmouth	1980	Oklahoma	1981	Iowa, Ohio State
1982	Clemson	1982	Harvard, Dartmouth	1981	Nebraska	1982	Michigan
1983	Maryland		Pennsylvania	1982	Nebraska	1983	Illinois
		1983	Harvard, Pennsylvania	1983	Nebraska		

	Mid-America		Missouri Valley		Southeastern		Southwest
1970	Toledo	1970	Louisville	1970	Louisiana State	1970	Texas
1971	Toledo	1971	Memphis State	1971	Alabama	1971	Texas
1972	Kent State	1972	Louisville, W. Texas,	1972	Alabama	1972	Texas
1973	Miami		Drake	1973	Alabama	1973	Texas
1974	Miami	1973	No. Texas St., Tulsa	1974	Alabama	1974	Baylor
1975	Miami	1974	Tulsa	1975	Alabama	1975	Texas A&M, Texas,
1976	Ball State	1975	Tulsa	1976	Georgia		Arkansas
1977	Miami	1976	Tulsa, N. Mexico St.	1977	Alabama	1976	Houston
1978	Ball State	1977	W. Texas St.	1978	Alabama	1977	Houston
1979	Central Michigan	1978	N. Mexico St.	1979	Alabama	1978	Houston
1980	Central Michigan	1979	W. Texas St.	1980	Georgia	1979	Houston, Arkansas
1981	Toledo	1980	Tulsa, Wichita St.	1981	Georgia, Alabama	1980	Baylor
1982	Bowling Green	1981	Drake, Tulsa	1982	Georgia	1981	SMU
1983	Northern Illinois	1982	Tulsa	1983	Auburn	1982	SMU
		1983	Tulsa			1983	Texas

	Pacific Ten		Southern		Western Athletic		Pacific Coast
1970	Stanford	1970	William & Mary	1970	Arizona State	1970	Long Beach State
1971	Stanford	1971	Richmond	1971	Arizona State	1972	San Diego State
1972	USC	1972	East Carolina	1972	Arizona State	1973	San Diego State
1973	USC	1973	East Carolina	1973	Arizona State, Arizona	1974	San Diego State
1974	USC	1974	VMI	1974	Brigham Young	1975	San Jose State
1975	UCLA, Cal.	1975	Richmond	1975	Arizona State	1976	San Diego State
1976	USC	1976	East Carolina	1976	Wyoming, Brigham Young	1977	Fresno State
1977	Washington	1977	Tenn.-Chattanooga	1977	Brigham Young, Arizona St.	1978	Utah St., San Jose St.
1978	USC	1978	Tenn.-Chattanooga,	1978	Brigham Young	1979	San Jose St.
1979	USC		Furman	1979	Brigham Young	1980	Long Beach State
1980	Washington	1979	Tenn.-Chattanooga	1980	Brigham Young	1981	San Jose State
1981	Washington	1980	Furman	1981	Brigham Young	1982	Fresno State
1982	UCLA	1981	Furman	1982	Brigham Young	1983	Cal State-Fullerton
1983	UCLA	1982	Furman	1983	Brigham Young		
		1983	Furman				

National College Football Champions

The NCAA recognizes as unofficial national champion the team selected each year by the AP (poll of writers) and the UPI (poll of coaches). When the polls disagree both teams are listed. The AP poll originated in 1936 and the UPI poll in 1950.

1936	Minnesota	1948	Michigan	1960	Minnesota	1972	Southern Cal.
1937	Pittsburgh	1949	Notre Dame	1961	Alabama	1973	Notre Dame, Alabama
1938	Texas Christian	1950	Oklahoma	1962	Southern Cal.	1974	Oklahoma, So. Cal.
1939	Texas A&M	1951	Tennessee	1963	Texas	1975	Oklahoma
1940	Minnesota	1952	Michigan State	1964	Alabama	1976	Pittsburgh
1941	Minnesota	1953	Maryland	1965	Alabama, Mich. State	1977	Notre Dame
1942	Ohio State	1954	Ohio State, UCLA	1966	Notre Dame	1978	Alabama, So. Cal.
1943	Notre Dame	1955	Oklahoma	1967	Southern Cal.	1979	Alabama
1944	Army	1956	Oklahoma	1968	Ohio State	1980	Georgia
1945	Army	1957	Auburn, Ohio State	1969	Texas	1981	Clemson
1946	Notre Dame	1958	Louisiana State	1970	Nebraska, Texas	1982	Penn State
1947	Notre Dame	1959	Syracuse	1971	Nebraska,	1983	Miami (Fla.)

Outland Awards

Honoring the outstanding interior lineman selected by the Football Writers' Association of America.

1946	George Connor, Notre Dame, T	1959	Mike McGee, Duke, T	1972	Rich Glover, Nebraska, MG
1947	Joe Steffy, Army, G	1960	Tom Brown, Minnesota, G	1973	John Hicks, Ohio State, G
1948	Bill Fischer, Notre Dame, G	1961	Merlin Olsen, Utah State, T	1974	Randy White, Maryland, DE
1949	Ed Bagdon, Michigan St., G	1962	Bobby Bell, Minnesota, T	1975	Leroy Selmon, Oklahoma, DT
1950	Bob Gain, Kentucky, T	1963	Scott Appleton, Texas, T	1976	Ross Browner, Notre Dame, DE
1951	Jim Weatherall, Oklahoma, T	1964	Steve Delong, Tennessee, T	1977	Brad Shearer, Texas, DT
1952	Dick Modzelewski, Maryland, T	1965	Tommy Nobis, Texas, G	1978	Greg Roberts, Oklahoma, G
1953	J. D. Roberts, Oklahoma, G	1966	Loyd Phillips, Arkansas, T	1979	Jim Ritcher, No. Carolina St., C
1954	Bill Brooks, Arkansas, G	1967	Ron Yary, Southern Cal, T	1980	Mark May, Pittsburgh, OT
1955	Calvin Jones, Iowa, G	1968	Bill Stanfill, Georgia, T	1981	Dave Rimington, Nebraska, C
1956	Jim Parker, Ohio State, G	1969	Mike Reid, Penn State, DT	1982	Dave Rimington, Nebraska, C
1957	Alex Karras, Iowa, T	1970	Jim Stillwagon, Ohio State, LB	1983	Dean Steinkuhler, Nebraska, G
1958	Zeke Smith, Auburn, G	1971	Larry Jacobson, Nebraska, DT		

College Football Stadiums

School	Capacity	School	Capacity
Alabama, Univ. of (Bryant-Denny Stad.), University	59,000	Northern Illinois Univ. (Huskie Stad.), DeKalb	30,437
Arizona State Univ. (Sun Devil), Tempe	70,021	Northwestern Univ. (Dyche Stad.), Evanston, Ill.	49,256
Arizona, Univ. of (Arizona Stad.), Tucson	52,000	Notre Dame Stad., South Bend, Ind.	59,075
Arkansas, Univ. of (Razorback Stad.) Fayetteville	42,100	Ohio State Univ. (Ohio Stad.), Columbus	85,290
Auburn Univ. (Jordan Hare Stad.), Auburn, Ala.	72,169	Oklahoma State (Lewis Stad.), Stillwater	50,817
Baylor Univ. Stad., Waco, Tex.	48,500	Oklahoma, Univ. of (Owen Field), Norman	75,008
Boston Coll. (Alumni Stad.), Boston, Mass.	32,000	Oregon St. Univ. (Parker Stad.), Corvallis	40,593
Bowling Green State Univ. (Doyt Perry Field), Oh.	30,000	Oregon, Univ. of (Autzen Stad.), Eugene	41,009
Brigham Young Univ. Stad., Provo, Ut.	66,000	Penn. State Univ. (Beaver Stad.), University Park	83,770
Cal., Univ. of (Memorial Stad.), Berkeley	76,780	Penn., Univ. of (Franklin Field), Phila.	60,546
Clemson Univ. (Memorial Stad.), S.C.	73,195	Pittsburgh, Univ. of (Pitt. Stad.), Pa.	56,500
Colorado, Univ. of (Folsom Field), Boulder	51,805	Princeton, (Palmer Stad.), Princeton, N.J.	45,725
Duke Univ., (Wade Stad.), Durham, N.C.	33,941	Purdue, (Ross-Ade Stad.), Lafayette, Ind.	69,250
E. Carolina Univ. (Ficklen Stad.), Greenville, N.C.	35,000	Rice Stad., Houston, Texas	70,000
Florida State, (Campbell Stad.), Tallahassee	55,246	So. Carolina, Univ. of (Williams-Brice), Columbia	72,400
Florida, Univ. of (Florida Field), Gainesville	72,000	So. Miss., Univ. of (Roberts Stad.), Hattiesburg	33,000
Georgia Tech. (Grant Field), Atlanta	58,121	Stanford Stad., Stanford, Cal.	84,892
Georgia, Univ. of (Sanford Stad.), Athens	82,122	Syracuse Univ., (Carrier Dome), N.Y.	50,000
Harvard Stad., Boston, Mass.	37,289	Tenn., Univ. of (Neyland Stad.), Knoxville	91,246
Hawaii, Univ. of (Aloha Stad.), Honolulu	50,000	Texas A. & M. Univ. (Kyle Field), College Station	72,300
Illinois, Univ. of (Memorial Stad.), Champaign	70,906	Texas Christian Univ. (TCU-Amon Carter Stad.)	
Indiana Univ. (Memorial Stad.), Bloomington	52,354	Ft. Worth	46,000
Iowa State Stad., Ames	50,000	Texas-El Paso (Sun Bowl)	52,000
Iowa, Univ. of (Kinnick Stad.), Iowa City	66,000	Texas Tech. Univ. (Jones Stad.), Lubbock	47,000
Kansas State Univ. Stad., Manhattan	42,000	Texas, Univ. of (Memorial Stad.), Austin	80,000
Kansas, Univ. of (Memorial Stad.), Lawrence	51,500	Tulsa, Univ. of (Skelly Stad.), Okla.	40,235
Kent State Univ. (Dix Stad.), Kent, Oh.	30,400	U.S. Air Force Acad. (Falcon Stad.), Col.	46,668
Kentucky, Univ. of (Commonwealth), Lexington	58,000	U.S. Military Academy (Michie Stad.), West Point, N.Y.	39,480
La. State Univ. (Tiger Stad.), Baton Rouge	75,672	U.S. Naval Academy (Navy-Marine Corps Mem. Stad.)	
Louisville, Univ. of (Cardinal Stad.), Ky.	35,500	Annapolis, Md.	30,000
Maryland, Univ. of (Byrd), College Park	45,000	Utah State Univ. (Romney Stad.), Logan	30,257
Memphis State (Liberty Bowl), Tenn.	50,180	Utah, Univ. of (Robert Rice Stad.), Salt Lake City	35,000
Michigan State Univ. (Spartan Stad.), E. Lansing	76,000	Vanderbilt Stad., Nashville	41,000
Michigan, Univ. of (Mich. Stad.), Ann Arbor	101,701	Virginia Tech. (Lane Stad.), Blacksburg	52,500
Mississippi St. Univ. (Scott Field)	32,000	Virginia, Univ. of (Scott Stad.), Charlottesville	42,000
Mississippi, Univ. of (Vaught-Hemingway Stad.), Univ.	41,500	Wake Forest (Groves Stad.), Winston-Salem, N.C.	30,500
Missouri, Univ. of (Faurot Field), Columbia	62,000	Wash. State Univ. (Clarence D. Martin), Pullman	40,000
Nebraska, Univ. of (Memorial Stad.), Lincoln	73,650	Washington, Univ. of (Husky Stad.), Seattle	59,800
Nevada-Las Vegas, Univ. of (Silver Bowl)	32,000	West Va. Univ. (Mountaineer Field), Morgantown	50,512
New Mexico State Univ. (Memorial Stad.), Las Cruces	30,343	Wichita State Univ. (Cessna Stad.), Kan.	31,500
New Mexico, Univ. Stad., Albuquerque	30,646	Wisconsin, Univ. of (Camp Randall), Madison	77,280
North Carolina St. U. (Carter-Finley Stad.), Raleigh	45,600	Wyoming, Univ. of (Memorial), Laramie	33,500
North Carolina, Univ. of (Kenan Stad.), Chapel Hill	49,500	Yale Bowl, New Haven, Conn.	70,896

College Football Coach of the Year

(Selected by the American Football Coaches Assn. & the Football Writers Assn. of America)

	AFCA		FWAA	AFCA
1935	Lynn Waldorf, Northwestern	1957	Woody Hayes, Ohio St.	Woody Hayes, Ohio St.
1936	Dick Harlow, Harvard	1958	Paul Dietzel, LSU	Paul Dietzel, LSU
1937	Edward Mylin, Lafayette	1959	Ben Schwartzwalder, Syracuse	Ben Schwartzwalder, Syracuse
1938	Bill Kern, Carnegie Tech	1960	Murray Warmath, Minnesota	Murray Warmath, Minnesota
1939	Eddie Anderson, Iowa	1961	Darrell Royal, Texas	Paul "Bear" Bryant, Alabama
1940	Clark Shaughnessy, Stanford	1962	John McKay, USC	John McKay, USC
1941	Frank Leahy, Notre Dame	1963	Darrell Royal, Texas	Darrell Royal, Texas
1942	Bill Alexander, Georgia Tech	1964	Ara Parseghian, Notre Dame	Frank Broyles, Arkansas; Ara Parseghian, Notre Dame
1943	Amos Alonzo Stagg, Pacific	1965	Duffy Daugherty, Michigan St.	Tommy Prothro, UCLA
1944	Carroll Widdoes, Ohio St.	1966	Tom Cahill, Army	Tom Cahill, Army
1945	Bo McMillin, Indiana	1967	John Pont, Indiana	John Pont, Indiana
1946	Earl "Red" Blaik, Army	1968	Woody Hayes, Ohio St.	Joe Paterno, Penn St.
1947	Fritz Crisler, Michigan	1969	Bo Schembechler, Michigan	Bo Schembechler, Michigan
1948	Bennie Oosterbaan, Michigan	1970	Alex Agase, Northwestern	Charles McClendon, LSU; Darrell Royal, Texas
1949	Bud Wilkinson, Oklahoma	1971	Bob Devaney, Nebraska	Paul "Bear" Bryant, Alabama
1950	Charlie Caldwell, Princeton	1972	John McKay, USC	John McKay, USC
1951	Chuck Taylor, Stanford	1973	Johnny Majors, Pittsburgh	Paul "Bear" Bryant, Alabama
1952	Biggie Munn, Michigan St.	1974	Grant Teaff, Baylor	Grant Teaff, Baylor
1953	Jim Tatum, Maryland	1975	Woody Hayes, Ohio St.	Frank Kush, Arizona St.
1954	Henry "Red" Sanders, UCLA	1976	Johnny Majors, Pittsburgh	Johnny Majors, Pittsburgh
1955	Duffy Daugherty, Michigan St.	1977	Lou Holtz, Arkansas	Don James, Washington
1956	Bowden Wyatt, Tennessee	1978	Joe Paterno, Penn St.	Joe Paterno, Penn St.
		1979	Earle Bruce, Ohio St.	Earle Bruce, Ohio St.
		1980	Vince Dooley, Georgia	Vince Dooley, Georgia
		1981	Danny Ford, Clemson	Danny Ford, Clemson
		1982	Joe Paterno, Penn St.	Joe Paterno, Penn St.
		1983	Howard Schnellenberger, Miami (Fla.)	Ken Hatfield, Air Force

All-Time Division 1-A Coaching Victories

Paul "Bear" Bryant	323	Eddie Anderson	201	John Vaught	190	Bo Schembechler	180
Amos Alonzo Stagg	314	Dana Bible	198	John Heisman	185	Ben Schwartzwalder	178
Glenn "Pop" Warner	313	Dan McGugin	197	Darrell Royal	184	Ralph Jordan	176
Woody Hayes	238	Fielding Yost	196	Carl Snavely	180	Frank Kush	176
Jess Neely	207	Howard Jones	194	Gil Dobie	180	Bob Neyland	173
Warren Woodson	207						

Heisman Trophy Winners

Awarded annually to the nation's outstanding college football player.

1935	Jay Berwanger, Chicago, HB	1952	Billy Vessels, Oklahoma, HB	1969	Steve Owens, Oklahoma, RB
1936	Larry Kelley, Yale, E	1953	John Lattner, Notre Dame, HB	1970	Jim Plunkett, Stanford, QB
1937	Clinton Frank, Yale, QB	1954	Alan Ameche, Wisconsin, FB	1971	Pat Sullivan, Auburn, QB
1938	David O'Brien, Tex. Christian, QB	1955	Howard Cassady, Ohio St., HB	1972	Johnny Rodgers, Nebraska, RB-R
1939	Nile Kinnick, Iowa, QB	1956	Paul Hornung, Notre Dame, QB	1973	John Cappelletti, Penn State, RB
1940	Tom Harmon, Michigan, HB	1957	John Crow, Texas A & M, HB	1974	Archie Griffin, Ohio State, RB
1941	Bruce Smith, Minnesota, HB	1958	Pete Dawkins, Army, HB	1975	Archie Griffin, Ohio State, RB
1942	Frank Sinkwich, Georgia, HB	1959	Billy Cannon, La. State, HB	1976	Tony Dorsett, Pittsburgh, RB
1943	Angelo Bertelli, Notre Dame, QB	1960	Joe Bellino, Navy, HB	1977	Earl Campbell, Texas, RB
1944	Leslie Horvath, Ohio State, QB	1961	Ernest Davis, Syracuse, HB	1978	Billy Sims, Oklahoma, RB
1945	Felix Blanchard, Army, FB	1962	Terry Baker, Oregon State, QB	1979	Charles White, USC, RB
1946	Glenn Davis, Army, HB	1963	Roger Staubach, Navy, QB	1980	George Rogers, So. Carolina, RB
1947	John Lujack, Notre Dame, QB	1964	John Huarte, Notre Dame, QB	1981	Marcus Allen, USC, RB
1948	Doak Walker, SMU, HB	1965	Mike Garrett, USC, HB	1982	Herschel Walker, Georgia, RB
1949	Leon Hart, Notre Dame, E	1966	Steve Spurrier, Florida, QB	1983	Mike Rozier, Nebraska, RB
1950	Vic Janowicz, Ohio State, HB	1967	Gary Beban, UCLA, QB		
1951	Richard Kazmaier, Princeton, HB	1968	O. J. Simpson, USC, RB		

Lacrosse Champions in 1984

NCAA Division I Championship—Newark, Del., May 26: Johns Hopkins 13, Syracuse 10. **Semi-finals**—Johns Hopkins 14, North Carolina 9; Syracuse 11, Army 9.

NCAA Division III Championship—Geneva, N.Y., May 19: Hobart 12, Washington 5.

All-Star College Game—Baltimore, Md., June 9: South 11, North 8.

National Junior College Championship—Farmingdale, N.Y., May 12: Nassau C.C. 18, Arundel C.C. 9.

U.S. Club Lacrosse Association Championship—Baltimore, Md., June 8: Maryland L.C. 15, Long Island-Hofstra L.C. 10.

Women NCAA Lacrosse Championship—Boston, Mass., May 20: Temple 6, Maryland 4.

USILA Division I All America Team

Attack: Tim Nelson, Syracuse; Kevin Cook, Cornell; Peter Scott, Johns Hopkins.

Midfield: Del Dressel, Johns Hopkins; Brad Kotz, Syracuse; Josh Hall, Pennsylvania; Joey Seivold, North Carolina.
Defense: Tom Haus, North Carolina; Mike Riccardi, Army; John DeTommaso, Johns Hopkins.
Goal: Larry Quinn, Johns Hopkins.
Note: 4 midfielders selected for the 3 midfield positions.

USILA Division III All America Team

Attack: Tom Grimaldi, Hobart; Mike Perkins, Cortland; Bill Bjorness, Rochester Tech.
Midfield: Patrick O'Hara, Hobart; James Holihan, Hobart; Jim Huelskamp, Salisbury.
Defense: Steve Beville, Washington; Charles Santry, St. Lawrence; Doug MacKenzie, Roanoke.
Goal: Greg Baker, Washington.

USILA Coach of the Year

Division I—Tony Seaman, Univ. of Pennsylvania
Division III—Hank Janczyk, Salisbury (Md.) State College

NCAA Divisions I Champions

1971	Cornell	1974	Johns Hopkins	1977	Cornell	1980	Johns Hopkins	1983	Syracuse
1972	Virginia	1975	Maryland	1978	Johns Hopkins	1981	North Carolina	1984	Johns Hopkins
1973	Maryland	1976	Cornell	1979	Johns Hopkins	1982	North Carolina		

Pro Rodeo Championship Standings in 1983

Event	Winner	Money won	Event	Winner	Money won
All Around	Roy Cooper, Durant, Okla.	$153,391	Steer Wrestling	Joel Edmondson, Columbus, Kan.	$68,747
Saddle Bronc	Brad Gjermundson, Marshall, N.D.	97,457	Team Roping	Leo Camarillo, Lockeford, Cal.	53,161
Bareback	Bruce Ford, Kersey, Col.	84,126	Steer Roping	Roy Cooper, Durant, Okla.	30,530
Bull Riding	Cody Snyder, Redcliff, Alberta	73,772	Women's Barrel Racing	Marlene Eddleman, Ordway, Col.	51,840
Calf Roping	Roy Cooper, Durant, Okla.	122,455			

Pro Rodeo Cowboy All Around Champions

Year	Winner	Money won	Year	Winner	Money won
1965	Dean Oliver, Boise, Ida.	$33,163	1975	Leo Camarillo, Oakdale, Cal.	$50,300
1966	Larry Mahan, Brooks, Ore.	40,358		Tom Ferguson, Miami, Okla.	50,300
1967	Larry Mahan, Brooks, Ore.	51,996	1976	Tom Ferguson, Miami, Okla.	87,908
1968	Larry Mahan, Salem, Ore.	49,129	1977	Tom Ferguson, Miami, Okla.	76,730
1969	Larry Mahan, Brooks, Ore.	57,726	1978	Tom Ferguson, Miami, Okla.	103,734
1970	Larry Mahan, Brooks, Ore.	41,493	1979	Tom Ferguson, Miami, Okla.	96,272
1971	Phil Lyne, George West, Tex.	49,245	1980	Paul Tierney, Rapid City, S.D.	105,568
1972	Phil Lyne, George West, Tex.	60,852	1981	Jimmie Cooper, Monument, N.M.	105,862
1973	Larry Mahan, Dallas, Tex.	64,447	1982	Chris Lybbert, Coyote, Cal.	123,709
1974	Tom Ferguson, Miami, Okla.	66,929	1983	Roy Cooper, Durant, Okla.	153,391

Tour de France in 1984

Laurent Fignon of France won the Tour de France, the world's most prestigious bicycle endurance race, for the second successive year on July 22, 1984. His time for the more-than-4,000-kilometer race, which began June 29, was 112 hours 3 minutes 40 seconds. Bernard Hinault of France, who has won the race four times, finished second. Greg Lemond of the United States finished third.

Canadian Football League

Final 1983 Standings

Eastern Division	W	L	T	PF	PA	Pts
Toronto	12	4	0	452	328	24
Ottawa	8	8	0	384	424	16
Hamilton	5	10	1	389	498	11
Montreal	5	10	1	367	447	11

Western Division	W	L	T	PF	PA	Pts
B.C.	11	5	0	477	326	22
Winnipeg	9	7	0	412	402	18
Edmonton	8	8	0	450	377	16
Calgary	8	8	0	425	378	16
Saskatchewan	5	11	0	360	536	10

East semifinal—Hamilton 33, Ottawa 31
West semifinal—Winnipeg 49, Edmonton 22
East final—Toronto 41, Hamilton 36

West final—B.C. 39, Winnipeg 21
Championship (Grey Cup)—Toronto 18, B.C. 17

Canadian Football League (Grey Cup)

Winners of Eastern and Western divisions meet in championship game for Grey Cup (donated by Governor-General Earl Grey in 1909). Canadian football features 3 downs, 110-yard field, and each team can have 12 players on field at one time.

1956	Edmonton Eskimos 50, Montreal Alouettes 27
1957	Hamilton Tiger-Cats 32, Winnipeg Blue Bombers 7
1958	Winnipeg Blue Bombers 35, Hamilton Tiger-Cats 28
1959	Winnipeg Blue Bombers 21, Hamilton Tiger-Cats 7
1960	Ottawa Rough Riders 16, Edmonton Eskimos 6
1961	Winnipeg Blue Bombers 21, Hamilton Tiger-Cats 14
1962	Winnipeg Blue Bombers 28, Hamilton Tiger-Cats 27
1963	Hamilton Tiger-Cats 21, British Columbia Lions 10
1964	British Columbia Lions 34, Hamilton Tiger-Cats 24
1965	Hamilton Tiger-Cats 22, Winnipeg Blue Bombers 16
1966	Saskatchewan Roughriders 29, Ottawa Rough Riders 14
1967	Hamilton Tiger-Cats 24, Saskatchewan Roughriders 1
1968	Ottawa Rough Riders 24, Calgary Stampeders 21
1969	Ottawa Rough Riders 29, Saskatchewan Roughriders 11
1970	Montreal Alouettes 23, Calgary Stampeders 10
1971	Calgary Stampeders 14, Toronto Argonauts 11
1972	Hamilton Tiger-Cats 13, Saskatchewan Roughriders 10
1973	Ottawa Rough Riders 22, Edmonton Eskimos 18
1974	Montreal Alouettes 20, Edmonton Eskimos 7
1975	Edmonton Eskimos 9, Montreal Alouettes 8
1976	Ottawa Rough Riders 23, Saskatchewan Roughriders 20
1977	Montreal Alouettes 41, Edmonton Eskimos 6
1978	Edmonton Eskimos 20, Montreal Alouettes 13
1979	Edmonton Eskimos 17, Montreal Alouettes 9
1980	Edmonton Eskimos 48, Hamilton Tiger-Cats 10
1981	Edmonton Eskimos 26, Ottawa Rough Riders 23
1982	Edmonton Eskimos 32, Toronto Argonauts 16
1983	Toronto Argonauts 18, B.C. Lions 17

1983 CFL Individual Leaders

Passing

	Comp	Pct Comp	Yards	TD
Moon, Edmonton	380	57.2	5648	31
Dewalt, B.C.	275	62.2	3637	22
Holloway, Toronto	210	56.4	3184	18
Brock, Winn.-Ham.	229	54.5	3133	18
Watts, Ottawa	175	48.8	3089	18
Quarles, Calgary	179	55.4	2841	17
Clements, Ham.-Winn.	220	57.4	2840	21
Hufnagel, Sask.-Winn.	169	52.0	2605	15
Barnes, Toronto	149	55.0	2274	11
Evans, Montreal	139	57.6	1864	9

Rushing

	Att	Yds	Avg	TD
Walker, Ottawa	238	1431	6.0	10
Shepherd, Hamilton	197	1069	5.4	1
Reaves, Winnipeg	164	898	5.5	9
L. Brown, Montreal	148	792	5.3	6
Crouse, Calgary	124	703	5.7	9
Washington, Sask.	155	639	4.1	1
Ferdinand, Montreal	102	603	5.9	5
Minter, Toronto	107	599	5.6	5
Watts, Ottawa	76	552	7.3	5
Moon, Edmonton	85	527	6.2	1

Pass-Receiving

	No	Yds	Avg	TD
Greer, Toronto	113	2003	17.7	8
Kelly, Edmonton	104	1812	17.4	11
Scott, Edmonton	80	1234	15.4	9
Fernandez, B.C.	78	1284	16.5	10
Greene, B.C.	75	755	10.1	5
Robinson, Sask.-Mont.	73	1379	18.9	14
DeFrance, Sask.	71	1165	16.4	9
Tolbert, Toronto	70	1225	17.5	11
Baker, Hamilton	66	911	13.8	10
Pankratz, B.C.	63	961	15.2	7

Scoring

	TD	Con	FG	S	Pts
Passaglia, B.C.	0	45	40	17	191
Kennerd, Winnipeg	0	34	40	12	166
Ruoff, Hamilton	0	35	31	21	149
Ilesic, Toronto	0	40	26	30	148
Cutler, Edmonton	0	44	27	18	143
Organ, Ottawa	0	34	30	15	139
Sweet, Montreal	0	36	31	8	137
Hay, Calgary	0	41	27	12	134
Ridgway, Sask.	0	31	22	14	111
R. Robinson, Sask.-Mont.	14	0	0	0	84

American Power Boat Assn. Gold Cup Champions

Year	Boat	Driver	Year	Boat	Driver
1971	Miss Madison	Jim McCormick	1978	Atlas Van Lines	Bill Muncey
1972	Atlas Van Lines	Bill Muncey	1979	Atlas Van Lines	Bill Muncey
1973	Miss Budweiser	Dean Chenoweth	1980	Miss Budweiser	Dean Chenoweth
1974	Pay'N Pak	George Henley	1981	Miss Budweiser	Dean Chenoweth
1975	Pay 'N Pak	George Henley	1982	Atlas Van Lines	Chip Hanauer
1976	Miss U.S.	Tom D'Eath	1983	Atlas Van Lines	Chip Hanauer
1977	Atlas Van Lines	Bill Muncey	1984	Atlas Van Lines	Chip Hanauer

U.S. National Table Tennis Closed Championship

Las Vegas, Nev., Dec. 14-18, 1983

Men's Singles — Dan Seemiller, Pittsburgh, Pa.
Women's Singles — In Sook Bhushan, Aurora, Col.
Men's Doubles — Dan & Rick Seemiller, Pittsburgh, Pa.
Women's Doubles — In Sook Bhushan & Diana Gee.

Mixed Doubles — Dan Seemiller & In Sook Bhushan.
Boys Under 21 — Eric Boggan, Merrick, N.Y.
Boys Under 17 — Sean O'Neill, Va.
Girls Under 17 — Diana Gee, Cal.

Olympic Games Records

The modern Olympic Games, first held in Athens, Greece, in 1896, were the result of efforts by Baron Pierre de Coubertin, a French educator, to promote interest in education and culture, also to foster better international understanding through the universal medium of youth's love of athletics.

His source of inspiration for the Olympic Games was the ancient Greek Olympic Games, most notable of the four Panhellenic celebrations. The games were combined patriotic, religious, and athletic festivals held every four years. The first such recorded festival was that held in 776 B.C., the date from which the Greeks began to keep their calendar by "Olympiads," or four-year spans between the games.

The first Olympiad is said to have consisted merely of a 200-yard foot race near the small city of Olympia, but the games gained in scope and became demonstrations of national pride. Only Greek citizens — amateurs — were permitted to participate. Winners received laurel, wild olive, and palm wreaths and were accorded many special privileges. Under the Roman emperors, the games deteriorated into professional carnivals and circuses. Emperor Theodosius banned them in 394 A.D.

Baron de Coubertin enlisted 9 nations to send athletes to the first modern Olympics in 1896; now more than 100 nations compete. Winter Olympic Games were started in 1924.

Sites and Unofficial Winners of Games

1896 Athens (U.S.)	**1920** Antwerp (U.S.)	**1952** Helsinki (U.S.)	**1972** Munich (USSR)
1900 Paris (U.S.)	**1924** Paris (U.S.)	**1956** Melbourne (USSR)	**1976** Montreal (USSR)
1904 St. Louis (U.S.)	**1928** Amsterdam (U.S.)	**1960** Rome (USSR)	**1980** Moscow (USSR)
1906 Athens (U.S.)*	**1932** Los Angeles (U.S.)	**1964** Tokyo (U.S.)	**1984** Los Angeles (U.S.)
1908 London (U.S.)	**1936** Berlin (Germany)	**1968** Mexico City (U.S.)	**1988** Seoul, S. Korea (scheduled)
1912 Stockholm (U.S.)	**1948** London (U.S.)		

*Games not recognized by International Olympic Committee. Games 6 (1916), 12 (1940), and 13 (1944) were not celebrated. The 1980 games were boycotted by 62 nations, including the U.S. The 1984 games were boycotted by the USSR and most eastern bloc nations. East and West Germany began competing separately in 1968.

Olympic Games Champions, 1896—1984

(*Indicates Olympic Records)

Track and Field — Men

100-Meter Run

1896	Thomas Burke, United States	12s
1900	Francis W. Jarvis, United States	10.8s
1904	Archie Hahn, United States	11s
1908	Reginald Walker, South Africa	10.8s
1912	Ralph Craig, United States	10.8s
1920	Charles Paddock, United States	10.8s
1924	Harold Abrahams, Great Britain	10.6s
1928	Percy Williams, Canada	10.8s
1932	Eddie Tolan, United States	10.3s
1936	Jesse Owens, United States	10.3s
1948	Harrison Dillard, United States	10.3s
1952	Lindy Remigino, United States	10.4s
1956	Bobby Morrow, United States	10.5s
1960	Armin Hary, Germany	10.2s
1964	Bob Hayes, United States	10.0s
1968	Jim Hines, United States	9.9s*
1972	Valeri Borzov, USSR	10.14s
1976	Hasely Crawford, Trinidad	10.06s
1980	Allan Wells, Great Britain	10.25s
1984	Carl Lewis, United States	9.99s

200-Meter Run

1900	Walter Tewksbury, United States	22.2s
1904	Archie Hahn, United States	21.6s
1908	Robert Kerr, Canada	22.4s
1912	Ralph Craig, United States	21.7s
1920	Allan Woodring, United States	22s
1924	Jackson Scholz, United States	21.6s
1928	Percy Williams, Canada	21.8s
1932	Eddie Tolan, United States	21.2s
1936	Jesse Owens, United States	20.7s
1948	Mel Patton, United States	21.1s
1952	Andrew Stanfield, United States	20.7s
1956	Bobby Morrow, United States	20.6s
1960	Livio Berruti, Italy	20.5s
1964	Henry Carr, United States	20.3s
1968	Tommie Smith, United States	19.83s
1972	Valeri Borzov, USSR	20.00s
1976	Donald Quarrie, Jamaica	20.23s
1980	Pietro Mennea, Italy	20.19s
1984	Carl Lewis, United States	19.80s*

400-Meter Run

1896	Thomas Burke, United States	54.2s
1900	Maxey Long, United States	49.4s
1904	Harry Hillman, United States	49.2s
1908	Wyndham Halswelle, Great Britain, walkover	50s
1912	Charles Reidpath, United States	48.2s
1920	Bevil Rudd, South Africa	49.6s
1924	Eric Liddell, Great Britain	47.6s
1928	Ray Barbuti, United States	47.8s
1932	William Carr, United States	46.2s
1936	Archie Williams, United States	46.5s
1948	Arthur Wint, Jamaica, B W I	46.2s
1952	George Rhoden, Jamaica, B W I	45.9s
1956	Charles Jenkins, United States	46.7s
1960	Otis Davis, United States	44.9s
1964	Michael Larrabee, United States	45.1s
1968	Lee Evans, United States	43.8s*
1972	Vincent Matthews, United States	44.66s
1976	Alberto Juantorena, Cuba	44.26s
1980	Viktor Markin, USSR	44.60s
1984	Alonzo Babers, United States	44.27s

800-Meter Run

1896	Edwin Flack, Great Britain	2m. 11s
1900	Alfred Tysoe, Great Britain	2m. 1.4s
1904	James Lightbody, United States	1m. 56s
1908	Mel Sheppard, United States	1m. 52.8s
1912	James Meredith, United States	1m. 51.9s
1920	Albert Hill, Great Britain	1m. 53.4s
1924	Douglas Lowe, Great Britain	1m. 52.4s
1928	Douglas Lowe, Great Britain	1m. 51.8s
1932	Thomas Hampson, Great Britain	1m. 49.8s
1936	John Woodruff, United States	1m. 52.9s
1948	Mal Whitfield, United States	1m. 49.2s
1952	Mal Whitfield, United States	1m. 49.2s
1956	Thomas Courtney, United States	1m. 47.7s
1960	Peter Snell, New Zealand	1m. 46.3s
1964	Peter Snell, New Zealand	1m. 45.1s
1968	Ralph Doubell, Australia	1m. 44.3s
1972	Dave Wottle, United States	1m. 45.9s
1976	Alberto Juantorena, Cuba	1m. 43.50s
1980	Steve Ovett, Great Britain	1m. 45.40s
1984	Joaquim Cruz, Brazil	1m. 43.00*

1,500-Meter Run

1896	Edwin Flack, Great Britain	4m. 33.2s
1900	Charles Bennett, Great Britain	4m. 6s
1904	James Lightbody, United States	4m. 5.4s
1908	Mel Sheppard, United States	4m. 3.4s
1912	Arnold Jackson, Great Britain	3m. 56.8s
1920	Albert Hill, Great Britain	4m. 1.8s
1924	Paavo Nurmi, Finland	3m. 53.6s

1928	Harry Larva, Finland	3m. 53.2s
1932	Luigi Beccali, Italy	3m. 51.2s
1936	Jack Lovelock, New Zealand	3m. 47.8s
1948	Henri Eriksson, Sweden	3m. 49.8s
1952	Joseph Barthel, Luxemburg	3m. 45.2s
1956	Ron Delany, Ireland	3m. 41.2s
1960	Herb Elliott, Australia	3m. 35.6s
1964	Peter Snell, New Zealand	3m. 38.1s
1968	Kipchoge Keino, Kenya	3m. 34.9s
1972	Pekka Vasala, Finland	3m. 36.3s
1976	John Walker, New Zealand	3m. 39.17s
1980	Sebastian Coe, Great Britain	3m. 38.4s
1984	Sebastian Coe, Great Britain	3m. 32.53*

3,000-Meter Steeplechase

1920	Percy Hodge, Great Britain	10m. 0.4s
1924	Willie Ritola, Finland	9m. 33.6s
1928	Toivo Loukola, Finland	9m. 21.8s
1932	Volmari Iso-Hollo, Finland	10m. 33.4s
	(About 3,450 mtrs. extra lap by error)	
1936	Volmari Iso-Hollo, Finland	9m. 3.8s
1948	Thure Sjoestrand, Sweden	9m. 4.6s
1952	Horace Ashenfelter, United States	8m. 45.4s
1956	Chris Brasher, Great Britain	8m. 41.2s
1960	Zdzislaw Krzyszkowiak, Poland	8m. 34.2s
1964	Gaston Roelants, Belgium	8m. 30.8s
1968	Amos Biwott, Kenya	8m. 51s
1972	Kipchoge Keino, Kenya	8m. 23.6s
1976	Anders Garderud, Sweden	8m. 08.2s*
1980	Bronislaw Malinowski, Poland	8m. 09.7s
1984	Julius Korir, Kenya	8m. 11.8s

5,000-Meter Run

1912	Hannes Kolehmainen, Finland	14m. 36.6s
1920	Joseph Guillemot, France	14m. 55.6s
1924	Paavo Nurmi, Finland	14m. 31.2s
1928	Willie Ritola, Finland	14m. 38s
1932	Lauri Lehtinen, Finland	14m. 30s
1936	Gunnar Hockert, Finland	14m. 22.2s
1948	Gaston Reiff, Belgium	14m. 17.6s
1952	Emil Zatopek, Czechoslovakia	14m. 6.6s
1956	Vladimir Kuts, USSR	13m. 39.6s
1960	Murray Halberg, New Zealand	13m. 43.4s
1964	Bob Schul, United States	13m. 48.8s
1968	Mohamed Gammoudi, Tunisia	14m. 05.0s
1972	Lasse Viren, Finland	13m. 26.4s
1976	Lasse Viren, Finland	13m. 24.76s
1980	Miruts Yifter, Ethiopia	13m. 21.0s
1984	Said Aouita, Morocco	13m. 05.59s*

10,000-Meter Run

1912	Hannes Kolehmainen, Finland	31m. 20.8s
1920	Paavo Nurmi, Finland	31m. 45.8s
1924	Willie Ritola, Finland	30m. 23.2s
1928	Paavo Nurmi, Finland	30m. 18.8s
1932	Janusz Kusocinski, Poland	30m. 11.4s
1936	Ilmari Salminen, Finland	30m. 15.4s
1948	Emil Zatopek, Czechoslovakia	29m. 59.6s
1952	Emil Zatopek, Czechoslovakia	29m. 17.0s
1956	Vladimir Kuts, USSR	28m. 45.6s
1960	Pytor Bolotnikov, USSR	28m. 32.2s
1964	Billy Mills, United States	28m. 24.4s
1968	Naftali Temu, Kenya	29m. 27.4s
1972	Lasse Viren, Finland	27m. 38.4s*
1976	Lasse Viren, Finland	27m. 40.38s
1980	Miruts Yifter, Ethiopia	27m. 42.7s
1984	Alberto Cova, Italy	27m. 47.54

Marathon

1896	Spiridon Loues, Greece	2h. 58m. 50s
1900	Michel Teato, France	2h. 59m. 45s
1904	Thomas Hicks, United States	3h. 28m. 53s
1908	John J. Hayes, United States	2h. 55m. 18.4s
1912	Kenneth McArthur, South Africa	2h. 36m. 54.8s
1920	Hannes Kolehmainen, Finland	2h. 32m. 35.8s
1924	Albin Stenroos, Finland	2h. 41m. 22.6s
1928	A.B. El Ouafi, France	2h. 32m. 57s
1932	Juan Zabala, Argentina	2h. 31m. 36s
1936	Kitei Son, Japan	2h. 29m. 19.2s
1948	Delfo Cabrera, Argentina	2h. 34m. 51.6s
1952	Emil Zatopek, Czechoslovakia	2h. 23m. 03.2s
1956	Alain Mimoun, France	2h. 25m.
1960	Abebe Bikila, Ethiopia	2h. 15m. 16.2s
1964	Abebe Bikila, Ethiopia	2h. 12m. 11.2s
1968	Mamo Wolde, Ethiopia	2h. 20m. 26.4s
1972	Frank Shorter, United States	2h. 12m. 19.8s
1976	Waldemar Cierpinski, E. Germany	2h. 09m. 55s
1980	Waldemar Cierpinski, E. Germany	2h. 11m. 03s
1984	Carlos Lopes, Portugal	2h. 09m. 21 s*

10,000-Meter Cross-Country

1920	Paavo Nurmi, Finland	27m. 15s*
1924	Paavo Nurmi, Finland	32m. 54.8s

20-Kilometer Walk

1956	Leonid Spirine, USSR	1h. 31m. 27.4s
1960	Vladimir Golubnichy, USSR	1h. 34m. 7.2s
1964	Kenneth Mathews, Great Britain	1h. 29m. 34.0s
1968	Vladimir Golubnichy, USSR	1h. 35m. 58.4s
1972	Peter Frenkel, E. Germany	1h. 26m. 42.4s
1976	Daniel Bautista, Mexico	1h. 24m. 40.6s
1980	Maurizio Damilano, Italy	1h. 23m. 35.5s
1984	Ernesto Canto, Mexico	1h. 23m. 13.2s*

50-Kilometer Walk

1932	Thomas W. Green, Great Britain	4h. 50m. 10s
1936	Harold Whitlock, Great Britain	4h. 30m. 41.4s
1948	John Ljunggren, Sweden	4h. 41m. 52s
1952	Giuseppe Dordoni, Italy	4h. 28m. 07.8s
1956	Norman Read, New Zealand	4h. 30m. 42.8s
1960	Donald Thompson, Great Britain	4h. 25m. 30s
1964	Abdon Pamich, Italy	4h. 11m. 11.4s
1968	Christoph Hohne, E. Germany	4h. 20m. 13.6s
1972	Bern Kannenberg, W. Germany	3h. 56m. 11.6s
1980	Hartwig Gauter, E. Germany	3h. 49m. 24.0s
1984	Raul Gonzalez, Mexico	3h. 47m. 26.05*

110-Meter Hurdles

1896	Thomas Curtis, United States	17.6s
1900	Alvin Kraenzlein, United States	15.4s
1904	Frederick Schule, United States	16s
1908	Forrest Smithson, United States	15s
1912	Frederick Kelly, United States	15.1s
1920	Earl Thomson, Canada	14.8s
1924	Daniel Kinsey, United States	15s
1928	Sydney Atkinson, South Africa	14.8s
1932	George Saling, United States	14.6s
1936	Forrest Towns, United States	14.2s
1948	William Porter, United States	13.9s
1952	Harrison Dillard, United States	13.7s
1956	Lee Calhoun, United States	13.5s
1960	Lee Calhoun, United States	13.8s
1964	Hayes Jones, United States	13.6s
1968	Willie Davenport, United States	13.3s
1972	Rod Milburn, United States	13.24s
1976	Guy Drut, France	13.30s
1980	Thomas Munkelt, E. Germany	13. 39s
1984	Roger Kingdom, United States	13.20s*

400-Meter Hurdles

1900	J.W.B. Tewksbury, United States	57.6s
1904	Harry Hillman, United States	53s
1908	Charles Bacon, United States	55s
1920	Frank Loomis, United States	54s
1924	F. Morgan Taylor, United States	52.6s
1928	Lord Burghley, Great Britain	53.4s
1932	Robert Tisdall, Ireland	51.8s
1936	Glenn Hardin, United States	52.4s
1948	Roy Cochran, United States	51.1s
1952	Charles Moore, United States	50.8s
1956	Glenn Davis, United States	50.1s
1960	Glenn Davis, United States	49.3s
1964	Rex Cawley, United States	49.6s
1968	Dave Hemery, Great Britain	48.1s
1972	John Akii-Bua, Uganda	47.82s
1976	Edwin Moses, United States	47.64s*
1980	Volker Beck, E. Germany	48.70s
1984	Edwin Moses, United States	47.75s

High Jump

1896	Ellery Clark, United States	5ft. 11 1-4 in.
1900	Irving Baxter, United States	6ft. 2 4-5 in.
1904	Samuel Jones, United States	5ft. 11 in.
1908	Harry Porter, United States	6ft. 3 in.
1912	Alma Richards, United States	6ft. 4 in.
1920	Richard Landon, United States	6ft. 4 1-4 in.
1924	Harold Osborn, United States	6ft. 6 in.
1928	Robert W. King, United States	6ft. 4 3-8 in.
1932	Duncan McNaughton, Canada	6ft. 5 5-8 in.
1936	Cornelius Johnson, United States	6ft. 7 15-16 in.
1948	John L. Winter, Australia	6ft. 6 in.
1952	Walter Davis, United States	6ft. 8.32 in.
1956	Charles Dumas, United States	6ft. 11 1-4 in.
1960	Robert Shavlakadze, USSR	7ft. 1 in.

1964	Valery Brumel, USSR.	7ft. 1 3-4 in.
1968	Dick Fosbury, United States	7ft. 4 1-4 in.
1972	Yuri Tarmak, USSR.	7ft. 3 3-4 in.
1976	Jacek Wszola, Poland	7ft. 4 1-2 in.
1980	Gerd Wessig, E. Germany	7ft. 8 3-4 in.*
1984	Dietmar Mogenburg, W. Germany	7 ft. 8 1-2 in.

Long Jump

1896	Ellery Clark, United States	20ft. 9 3-4 in.
1900	Alvin Kraenzlein, United States	23ft. 6 7-8 in.
1904	Myer Prinstein, United States	24ft. 1 in.
1908	Frank Irons, United States	24ft. 6 1-2 in.
1912	Albert Gutterson, United States.	24ft. 11 1-4 in.
1920	William Petterssen, Sweden	23ft. 5 1-2 in.
1924	DeHart Hubbard, United States	24ft. 5 1-8 in.
1928	Edward B. Hamm, United States	25ft. 4 3-4 in.
1932	Edward Gordon, United States	25ft. 3-4 in.
1936	Jesse Owens, United States	26ft. 5 5-16 in.
1948	William Steele, United States	25ft. 8 in.
1952	Jerome Biffle, United States	24ft. 10 in.
1956	Gregory Bell, United States	25ft. 8 1-4 in.
1960	Ralph Boston, United States	26ft. 7 3-4 in.
1964	Lynn Davies, Great Britain	26ft. 5 3-4 in.
1968	Bob Beamon, United States	29ft. 2 1-2 in.*
1972	Randy Williams, United States	27ft. 1-2 in.
1976	Arnie Robinson, United States	27ft. 4 1-2 in.
1980	Lutz Dombrowski, E. Germany	28ft. 1-4 in.
1984	Carl Lewis, United States	28ft. 1-4 in.

400-Meter Relay

1912	Great Britain	42.4s
1920	United States	42.2s
1924	United States	41s
1928	United States	41s
1932	United States	40s
1936	United States	39.8s
1948	United States	40.6s
1952	United States	40.1s
1956	United States	39.5s
1960	Germany (U.S. disqualified)	39.5s
1964	United States	39.0s
1968	United States	38.2s
1972	United States	38.19s
1976	United States	38.33s
1980	USSR	38.26s
1984	United States	37.83s*

1,600-Meter Relay

1908	United States.	3m. 27.2s
1912	United States	3m. 16.6s
1920	Great Britain	3m. 22.2s
1924	United States	3m. 16s
1928	United States	3m. 14.2s
1932	United States	3m. 8.2s
1936	Great Britain	3m. 9s
1948	United States	3m. 10.4s
1952	Jamaica, B.W.I.	3m. 03.9s
1956	United States	3m. 04.8s
1960	United States	3m. 02.2s
1964	United States	3m. 00.7s
1968	United States	2m. 56.1s*
1972	Kenya	2m. 59.8s
1976	United States	2m. 59.52s
1980	USSR	3m. 01.1s
1984	United States	2m.57.91 s

Pole Vault

1896	William Hoyt, United States.	10ft. 9 3-4 in.
1900	Irving Baxter, United States.	10ft. 9 7-8 in.
1904	Charles Dvorak, United States	11ft. 6 in.
1908	A. C. Gilbert, United States	
	Edward Cook Jr., United States	12ft. 2 in.
1912	Harry Babcock, United States	12ft. 11 1-2 in.
1920	Frank Foss, United States.	13ft. 5 in.
1924	Lee Barnes, United States	12ft. 11 1-2 in.
1928	Sabin W. Carr, United States	13ft. 9 3-8 in.
1932	William Miller, United States	14ft. 1 7-8 in.
1936	Earle Meadows, United States	14ft. 3 1-4 in.
1948	Guinn Smith, United States	14ft. 1 1-4 in.
1952	Robert Richards, United States.	14ft. 11 1-8 in.
1956	Robert Richards, United States.	14ft. 11 1-2 in.
1960	Don Bragg, United States	15ft. 5 1-8 in.
1964	Fred Hansen, United States	16ft. 8 3-4 in.
1968	Bob Seagren, United States	17ft. 8 1-2 in.
1972	Wolfgang Nordwig, E. Germany	18ft. 1-2 in.
1976	Tadeusz Slusarski, Poland	18ft. 1-2 in.
1980	Wladyslaw Kozakiewicz, Poland	18ft. 11 1-2 in.*
1984	Pierre Quinon, France	18ft. 10 1-4 in.

Hammer Throw

1900	John Flanagan, United States	167ft. 4 in.
1904	John Flanagan, United States	168ft. 1 in.
1908	John Flanagan, United States.	170ft. 4 1-4 in.
1912	Matt McGrath, United States	179ft. 7 1-8 in.
1920	Pat Ryan, United States	173ft. 5 5-8 in.
1924	Fred Tootell, United States	174ft. 10 1-8 in.
1928	Patrick O'Callaghan, Ireland	168ft. 7 1-2 in.
1932	Patrick O'Callaghan, Ireland.	176ft. 11 1-8 in.
1936	Karl Hein, Germany.	185ft. 4 in.
1948	Imre Nemeth, Hungary	183ft. 11 1-2 in.
1952	Jozsef Csermak, Hungary	197ft. 11 9-16 in.
1956	Harold Connolly, United States.	207ft. 3 1-2 in.
1960	Vasily Rudenkov, USSR.	220ft. 1 5-8 in.
1964	Romuald Klim, USSR	228ft. 9 1-2 in.
1968	Gyula Zsivotsky, Hungary	240ft. 8 in.
1972	Anatoli Bondarchuk, USSR	248ft. 8 in.
1976	Yuri Syedykh, USSR	254ft. 4 in.
1980	Yuri Syedykh, USSR	268ft. 4 1-2 in.*
1984	Juha Tiainen, Finland	256ft. 2 in.

Discus Throw

1896	Robert Garrett, United States	95ft. 7 1-2 in.
1900	Rudolf Bauer, Hungary	118ft. 2.9-10 in.
1904	Martin Sheridan, United States	128ft. 10 1-2 in.
1908	Martin Sheridan, United States	134ft. 2 in.
1912	Armas Taipale, Finland.	148ft. 4 in.
	Both hands—Armas Taipale, Finland.	271ft. 10 1-4 in.
1920	Elmer Niklander, Finland	146ft. 7 1-4 in.
1924	Clarence Houser, United States	151ft. 5 1-8 in.
1928	Clarence Houser, United States	155ft. 3 in.
1932	John Anderson, United States	162ft. 4 7-8 in.
1936	Ken Carpenter, United States.	165ft. 7 3-8 in.
1948	Adolfo Consolini, Italy	173ft. 2 in.
1952	Sim Iness, United States	180ft. 6.85 in.
1956	Al Oerter, United States	184ft. 10 1-2 in.
1960	Al Oerter, United States	194ft. 2 in.
1964	Al Oerter, United States.	200ft. 1.1-2 in.
1968	Al Oerter, United States	212ft. 6 1-2 in.
1972	Ludvik Danek, Czechoslovakia	211ft. 3 in.
1976	Mac Wilkins, United States	221ft. 5.4 in.*
1980	Viktor Rashchupkin, USSR	218ft. 8 in.
1984	Rolf Dannenberg, W. Germany	218ft. 6 in.

Triple Jump

1896	James Connolly, United States.	45ft.
1900	Myer Prinstein, United States	47ft. 4 1-4 in.
1904	Myer Prinstein, United States	47 ft.
1908	Timothy Aheame, Great Britain	48ft. 11 1-4 in.
1912	Gustaf Lindblom, Sweden.	48ft. 5 1-8 in.
1920	Vilho Tuulos, Finland	47ft. 6 7-8 in.
1924	Archie Winter, Australia	50ft. 11 1-4 in.
1928	Mikio Oda, Japan	49ft. 11 in.
1932	Chuhoi Nambu, Japan.	51ft. 7 in.
1936	Naoto Tajima, Japan	52ft. 5 7-8 in.
1948	Arne Ahman, Sweden	50ft. 6 1-4 in.
1952	Adhemar de Silva, Brazil	53ft. 2 9-16 in.
1956	Adhemar de Silva, Brazil	53ft. 7 1-2 in.
1960	Jozef Schmidt, Poland	55ft. 1 3-4 in.
1964	Jozef Schmidt, Poland	55ft. 3 1-4 in.
1968	Viktor Saneev, USSR	57ft. 3-4 in.
1972	Viktor Saneev, USSR	56ft. 11 in.
1976	Viktor Saneev, USSR	56ft. 8 3-4 in.
1980	Jaak Uudmae, USSR	56ft. 11 1-8 in.
1984	Al Joyner, United States.	56ft. 7 1-2 in.*

16-lb. Shot Put

1896	Robert Garrett, United States	36ft. 9 3-4 in.
1900	Robert Sheldon, United States	46ft. 3 1-8 in.
1904	Ralph Rose, United States	48ft. 7 in.
1908	Ralph Rose, United States	46ft. 7 1-2 in.
1912	Pat McDonald, United States	50ft. 4 in.
	Both hands—Ralph Rose,	
	United States.	90ft. 5 1-2 in.
1920	Ville Porhola, Finland	48ft. 7 1-8 in.
1924	Clarence Houser, United States	49ft. 2 1-2 in.
1928	John Kuck, United States	52ft. 3-4 in.
1932	Leo Sexton, United States	52ft. 6 3-16 in.
1936	Hans Woellke, Germany	53ft. 1 3-4 in.
1948	Wilbur Thompson, United States	56ft. 2 in.
1952	Parry O'Brien, United States	57ft. 1 7-16 in.
1956	Parry O'Brien, United States	60ft. 11 in.
1960	William Nieder, United States	64ft. 6 3-4 in.
1964	Dallas Long, United States	66ft. 8 1-4 in.
1968	Randy Matson, United States	67ft. 4 3-4 in.
1972	Wladyslaw Komar, Poland	69ft. 6 in.
1976	Udo Beyer, E. Germany	69ft. 3-4 in.
1980	Vladimir Kiselyov, USSR.	70ft. 1-2 in.*
1984	Alessandro Andrei, Italy.	69ft. 9 in.

Javelin

1908	Erik Lemming, Sweden	178ft. 7 1-2 in.
	Held in middle—Erik Lemming,	
	Sweden	179ft. 10 1-2 in.
1912	Erik Lemming, Sweden.............	198ft. 11 1-4 in.
	Both hands, Julius Saaristo,	
	Finland....................	358ft. 11 7-8 in.
1920	Jonni Myrra, Finland	215ft. 9 3-4 in.
1924	Jonni Myrra, Finland	206ft. 6 3-4 in.
1928	Eric Lundquist, Sweden	218ft. 6 1-8 in.
1932	Matti Jarvinen, Finland	238ft. 7 in.
1936	Gerhard Stoeck, Germany..........	235ft. 8 5-16 in.
1948	Kaj Rautavaara, Finland	228ft. 10 1-2 in.
1952	Cy Young, United States	242ft. 0.79 in.
1956	Egil Danielsen, Norway	281ft. 2 1-4 in.
1960	Viktor Tsibulenko, USSR	277ft. 8 3-8 in.
1964	Pauli Nevala, Finland.............	271ft. 2 1-2 in.
1968	Janis Lusis, USSR	295ft. 7 1-4 in.
1972	Klaus Wolfermann, W. Germany......	296ft. 10 in.
1976	Miklos Nemeth, Hungary...........	310ft. 4 in.*
1980	Dainis Kula, USSR	299ft. 2 3-8 in.
1984	Arto Haerkoenen, Finland..........	284ft. 8 in.

Decathlon

1912	Hugo Wieslander, Sweden	7,724.49 pts.(a)
1920	Helge Lovland, Norway...........	6,804.35 pts.
1924	Harold Osborn, United States	7,710.77 pts.
1928	Paavo Yrjola, Finland	8,053.29 pts.
1932	James Bausch, United States	8,462.23 pts.
1936	Glenn Morris, United States	7,900 pts.
1948	Robert Mathias, United States.....	7,139 pts.
1952	Robert Mathias, United States	7,887 pts.
1956	Milton Campbell, United States	7,937 pts.
1960	Rafer Johnson, United States	8,392 pts.
1964	Willi Holdorf, Germany	7,887 pts.
1968	Bill Toomey, United States	8,193 pts.
1972	Nikola Avilov, USSR............	8,454 pts.
1976	Bruce Jenner, United States	8,618 pts.
1980	Daley Thompson, Great Britain ...	8,495pts.
1984	Daley Thompson, Great Britain ...	8,797 pts.*
	Former point systems used prior to 1964.	

(a) Jim Thorpe of the U.S. won the 1912 Decathlon with
8,413 pts. but was disqualified and had to return his medals
because he had played professional baseball prior to the
Olympic games. The medals were restored posthumously in
1982.

Track and Field—Women

100-Meter Run

1928	Elizabeth Robinson, United States	12.2s
1932	Stella Walsh, Poland	11.9s
1936	Helen Stephens, United States	11.5s
1948	Francina Blankers-Koen, Netherlands	11.9s
1952	Marjorie Jackson, Australia	11.5s
1956	Betty Cuthbert, Australia...............	11.5s
1960	Wilma Rudolph, United States	11.0s
1964	Wyomia Tyus, United States	11.4s
1968	Wyomia Tyus, United States	11.0s
1972	Renate Stecher, E. Germany............	11.07s
1976	Annegret Richter, W. Germany	11.08s
1980	Ludmila Kondratyeva, USSR	11.6s
1984	Evelyn Ashford, United States	10.97s*

200-Meter Run

1948	Francina Blankers-Koen, Netherlands	24.4s
1952	Marjorie Jackson, Australia	23.7s
1956	Betty Cuthbert, Australia...............	23.4s
1960	Wilma Rudolph, United States	24.0s
1964	Edith McGuire, United States	23.0s
1968	Irena Szewinska, Poland...............	22.5s
1972	Renate Stecher, E. Germany............	22.40s
1976	Barbel Eckert, E. Germany..............	22.37s
1980	Barbel Wockel, E. Germany.............	22.03
1984	Valerie Brisco-Hooks, United States.......	21.81s*

400-Meter Run

1964	Betty Cuthbert, Australia...............	52s
1968	Colette Besson, France	52s
1972	Monika Zehrt, E. Germany	51.08s
1976	Irena Szewinska, Poland	49.29s
1980	Marita Koch, E. Germany	48.88s
1984	Valerie Brisco-Hooks, United States	48.83s*

800-Meter Run

1928	Lina Radke, Germany.................	2m. 16.8s
1960	Ludmila Shevcova, USSR	2m. 4.3s
1964	Ann Packer, Great Britain	2m. 1.1s
1968	Madeline Manning, United States	2m. 0.9s
1972	Hildegard Flack, W. Germany	1m. 58.6s
1976	Tatyana Kazankina, USSR	1m. 54.94s
1980	Nadezhda Olizaryenko, USSR	1m. 53.5s*
1984	Doina Melinte, Romania.	1m. 57.6s

1,500-Meter Run

1972	Ludmila Bragina, USSR.	4m. 01.4s
1976	Tatyana Kazankina, USSR.	4m. 05.48s
1980	Tatyana Kazankina, USSR.	3m. 56.6s*
1984	Gabriella Dorio, Italy.	4m. 03.26s

3,000-Meter Run

1984	Maricica Puica, Romania.	8:35.96*

400-Meter Relay

1928	Canada	48.4s
1932	United States	47.0s
1936	United States	46.9s
1948	Netherlands	47.5s
1952	United States	45.9s
1956	Australia	44.5s
1960	United States	44.5s
1964	Poland	43.6s
1968	United States	42.8s

1972	West Germany	42.81s
1976	East Germany	42.55s
1980	East Germany	41.60s*
1984	United States	41.65s

1,600-Meter Relay

1972	East Germany	3m. 23s
1976	East Germany	3m. 19.23s
1980	USSR	3m. 20.02s
1984	United States	3m. 18.29s*

80-Meter Hurdles

1932	Mildred Didrikson, United States	11.7s
1936	Trebisonda Villa, Italy	11.7s
1948	Francina Blankers-Koen, Netherlands	11.2s
1952	Shirley Strickland de la Hunty, Australia.....	10.9s
1956	Shirley Strickland de la Hunty, Australia.....	10.7s
1960	Irina Press, USSR...................	10.8s
1964	Karen Balzer, Germany	10.5s
1968	Maureen Caird, Australia..............	10.3s*

100-Meter Hurdles

1972	Annelie Ehrhardt, E. Germany	12.59s
1976	Johanna Schaller, E. Germany	12.77s
1980	Vera Komisova, USSR	12.56s*
1984	Benita Brown-Fitzgerald, United States.....	12.84s

400-Meter Hurdles

1984	Nawal el Moutawakii, Morocco.	54.61s*

Heptathlon

1984	Glynis Nunn, Australia.	6,390 pts.*

High Jump

1928	Ethel Catherwood, Canada.	5ft. 3 in
1932	Jean Shiley, United States.............	5ft. 5 1-4 in
1936	Ibolya Csak, Hungary.................	5ft. 3 in
1948	Alice Coachman, United States	5ft. 6 1-8 in
1952	Esther Brand, South Africa.	5ft. 5 3-4 in
1956	Mildred L. McDaniel, United States	5ft. 9 1-4 in
1960	Iolanda Balas, Romania...............	6ft. 3-4 in
1964	Iolanda Balas, Romania...............	6ft. 2 3-4 in
1968	Miloslava Reskova, Czechoslovakia.	5ft. 11 3-4 in
1972	Ulrike Meyfarth, W. Germany	6ft. 3 1-4 in
1976	Rosemarie Ackermann, E. Germany	6ft. 3 3-4 in
1980	Sara Simeoni, Italy	6ft. 5 1-2 in
1984	Ulrike Meyfarth, W. Germany	6ft. 7 1-2 in.*

Discus Throw

1928	Helena Konopacka, Poland	129ff. 11 7-8 in
1932	Lillian Copeland, United States	133ft. 2 in
1936	Gisela Mauermayer, Germany	156ft. 3 3-16 in
1948	Micheline Ostermeyer, France	137ft. 6 1-2 in
1952	Nina Romaschkova, USSR	168ft. 8 1-2 in
1956	Olga Fikotova, Czechoslovakia......	176ft. 1 1-2 in
1960	Nina Ponomareva, USSR	180ft. 8 1-4 in
1964	Tamara Press, USSR	187ft. 10 1-2 in
1968	Lia Manoliu, Romania	191ft. 2 1-2 in
1972	Faina Melnik, USSR	218ft. 7 in
1976	Evelin Schlaak, E. Germany	226ft. 4 1-2 in
1980	Evelin Jahl, E. Germany	229ft. 6 1-4 in.*
1984	Ria Stalman, Netherlands	214ft. 5 in

Javelin Throw

1932	Mildred Didrikson, United States	143ft. 4 in

1936	Tilly Fleischer, Germany	148ft. 2 3-4 in.
1948	Herma Bauma, Austria	149ft. 6 in.
1952	Dana Zatopkova, Czechoslovakia	165ft. 7 in.
1956	Inessa Janzeme, USSR	176ft. 8 in.
1960	Elvira Ozolina, USSR	183ft. 8 in.
1964	Mihaela Penes, Romania	198ft. 7 1-2 in.
1968	Angela Nemeth, Hungary	198ft. 1-2 in.
1972	Ruth Fuchs, E. Germany	209ft. 7 in.
1976	Ruth Fuchs, E. Germany	216ft. 4 in.
1980	Maria Colon, Cuba	224ft. 5 in.
1984	Tessa Sanderson, Great Britain	228ft. 2 in.*

Shot Put (8lb., 13oz.)

1948	Micheline Ostermeyer, France	45ft. 1 1-2 in.
1952	Galina Zybina, USSR	50ft. 1 1-2 in.
1956	Tamara Tishkyevich, USSR	54ft. 5 in.
1960	Tamara Press, USSR	56ft. 9 7-8 in.
1964	Tamara Press, USSR	59ft. 6 1-4 in.
1968	Margitta Gummel, E. Germany	64ft. 4 in.
1972	Nadezhda Chizova, USSR	69ft.
1976	Ivanka Christova, Bulgaria	69ft. 5 in.
1980	Ilona Slupianek, E. Germany	73ft. 6 1-4 in.*
1984	Claudia Losch, W. Germany	67ft. 2 1-4 in.

Long Jump

1948	Olga Gyarmati, Hungary	18ft. 8 1-4 in.
1952	Yvette Williams, New Zealand	20ft. 5 3-4 in.
1956	Elzbieta Krzeskinska, Poland	20ft. 9 3-4 in.
1960	Vyera Krepkina, USSR	20ft. 10 3-4 in.
1964	Mary Rand, Great Britain	22ft. 2 1-4 in.
1968	Viorica Viscopoleanu, Romania	22ft. 4 1-2 in.
1972	Heidemarie Rosendahl, W. Germany	22ft. 3 in.
1976	Angela Voigt, E. Germany	22ft. 2 1-2 in.
1980	Tatyana Kolpakova, USSR	23ft. 2 in.*
1984	Anisoara Stanciu, Romania	22ft. 10 in.

Pentathlon

1964	Irina Press, USSR	5,246 pts.
1968	Ingrid Becker, W. Germany	5,098 pts.
1972	Mary Peters, England	4,801 pts.
1976	Sigrun Siegl, E. Germany	4,745 pts.
1980	Nadyezhda Tkachenko, USSR	5,083pts.*
	Former point system, 1964–1968	

Marathon

1984	Joan Benoit, United States	2h. 24m. 52s*

Swimming—Men

100-Meter Freestyle

1896	Alfred Hajos, Hungary	1:22.2
1904	Zoltan de Halmay, Hungary (100 yards)	1:02.8
1908	Charles Daniels, U.S.	1:05.6
1912	Duke P. Kahanamoku, U.S.	1:03.4
1920	Duke P. Kahanamoku, U.S.	1:01.4
1924	John Weissmuller, U.S.	59.0
1928	John Weissmuller, U.S.	58.6
1932	Yasuji Miyazaki, Japan	58.2
1936	Ferenc Csik, Hungary	57.6
1948	Wally Ris, U.S.	57.3
1952	Clark Scholes, U.S.	57.4
1956	Jon Henricks, Australia	55.4
1960	John Devitt, Australia	55.2
1964	Don Schollander, U.S.	53.4
1968	Mike Wenden, Australia	52.2
1972	Mark Spitz, U.S.	51.22
1976	Jim Montgomery, U.S.	49.99
1980	Jorg Woithe, E. Germany	50.40
1984	Rowdy Gaines, U.S.	49.80*

200-Meter Freestyle

1968	Mike Wenden, Australia	1:55.2
1972	Mark Spitz, U.S.	1:52.78
1976	Bruce Furniss, U.S.	1:50.29
1980	Sergei Kopliakov, USSR	1:49.81
1984	Michael Gross, W. Germany	1:47.44*

400-Meter Freestyle

1904	C. M. Daniels, U.S. (440 yards)	6:16.2
1908	Henry Taylor, Great Britain	5:36.8
1912	George Hodgson, Canada	5:24.4
1920	Norman Ross, U.S.	5:26.8
1924	John Weissmuller, U.S.	5:04.2
1928	Albert Zorilla, Argentina	5:01.6
1932	Clarence Crabbe, U.S.	4:48.4
1936	Jack Medica, U.S.	4:44.5
1948	William Smith, U.S.	4:41.0
1952	Jean Boiteux, France	4:30.7
1956	Murray Rose, Australia	4:27.3
1960	Murray Rose, Australia	4:18.3
1964	Don Schollander, U.S.	4:12.2
1968	Mike Burton, U.S.	4:09.0
1972	Brad Cooper, Australia	4:00.27
1976	Brian Goodell, U.S.	3:51.93
1980	Vladimir Salnikov, USSR	3:51.31
1984	George DiCarlo, U.S.	3:51.23*

1,500-Meter Freestyle

1908	Henry Taylor, Great Britain	22:48.4
1912	George Hodgson, Canada	22:00.0
1920	Norman Ross, U.S.	22:23.2
1924	Andrew Charlton, Australia	20:06.6
1928	Arne Borg, Sweden	19:51.8
1932	Kusuo Kitamura, Japan	19:12.4
1936	Noboru Terada, Japan	19:13.7
1948	James McLane, U.S.	19:18.5
1952	Ford Konno, U.S.	18:30.0
1956	Murray Rose, Australia	17:58.9
1960	Jon Konrads, Australia	17:19.6
1964	Robert Windle, Australia	17:01.7
1968	Mike Burton, U.S.	16:38.9
1972	Mike Burton, U.S.	15:52.58
1976	Brian Goodell, U.S.	15:02.40
1980	Vladimir Salnikov, USSR	14:58.27*
1984	Michael O'Brien, U.S.	15:05.20

400-Meter Medley Relay

1960	United States	4:05.4
1964	United States	3:58.4
1968	United States	3:54.9
1972	United States	3:48.16
1976	United States	3:42.22
1980	Australia	3:45.70
1984	United States	3:39.30*

400-Meter Freestyle Relay

1964	United States	3:33.2
1968	United States	3:31.7
1972	United States	3:26.42
1984	United States	3:19.03*

800-Meter Freestyle Relay

1908	Great Britain	10:55.6
1912	Australia	10:11.6
1920	United States	10:04.4
1924	United States	9:53.4
1928	United States	9:36.2
1932	Japan	8:58.4
1936	Japan	8:51.5
1948	United States	8:46.0
1952	United States	8:31.1
1956	Australia	8:23.6
1960	United States	8:10.2
1964	United States	7:52.1
1968	United States	7:52.3
1972	United States	7:35.78
1976	United States	7:23.22
1980	USSR	7:23.50
1984	United States	7:15.69*

100-Meter Backstroke

1904	Walter Brack, Germany (100 yds.)	1:16.8
1908	Arno Bieberstein, Germany	1:24.6
1912	Harry Hebner, U.S.	1:21.2
1920	Warren Kealoha, U.S.	1:15.2
1924	Warren Kealoha, U.S.	1:13.2
1928	George Kojac, U.S.	1:08.2
1932	Masaji Kiyokawa, Japan	1:08.6
1936	Adolph Kiefer, U.S.	1:05.9
1948	Allen Stack, U.S.	1:06.4
1952	Yoshi Oyakawa, U.S.	1:05.4
1956	David Thiele, Australia	1:02.2
1960	David Thiele, Australia	1:01.9
1968	Roland Matthes, E. Germany	58.7
1972	Roland Matthes, E. Germany	56.58
1976	John Naber, U.S.	55.49*
1980	Bengt Baron, Sweden	56.53
1984	Rick Carey, U.S.	55.79

200-Meter Backstroke

1964	Jed Graef, U.S.	2:10.3
1968	Roland Matthes, E. Germany	2:09.6
1972	Roland Matthes, E. Germany	2:02.82
1976	John Naber, U.S.	1:59.19*
1980	Sandor Wladar, Hungary	2:01.93
1984	Rick Carey, U.S.	2:00.23

100-Meter Breaststroke

1968	Don McKenzie, U.S.	1:07.7
1972	Nobutaka Taguchi, Japan	1:04.94
1976	John Hencken, U.S.	1:03.11
1980	Duncan Goodhew, Great Britain	1:03.34
1984	Steve Lundquist, U.S.	1:01.65*

200-Meter Breaststroke

1908	Frederick Holman, Great Britain	3:09.2
1912	Walter Bathe, Germany	3:01.8
1920	Haken Malmroth, Sweden	3:04.4
1924	Robert Skelton, U.S.	2:56.6
1928	Yoshiyuki Tsuruta, Japan	2:48.8
1932	Yoshiyuki Tsuruta, Japan	2:45.4
1936	Tetsuo Hamuro, Japan	2:42.5
1948	Joseph Verdeur, U.S.	2:39.3
1952	John Davies, Australia	2:34.4
1956	Masura Furukawa, Japan	2:34.7
1960	William Mulliken, U.S.	2:37.4
1964	Ian O'Brien, Australia	2:27.8
1968	Felipe Munoz, Mexico	2:28.7
1972	John Hencken, U.S.	2:21.55
1976	David Wilkie, Great Britain	2:15.11
1980	Robertas Zulpa, USSR	2:15.85
1984	Victor Davis, Canada	2:13.34*

100-Meter Butterfly

1968	Doug Russell, U.S.	55.9
1972	Mark Spitz, U.S.	54.27
1976	Matt Vogel, U.S.	54.35
1980	Par Arvidsson, Sweden	54.92
1984	Michael Gross, W. Germany	53.08*

200-Meter Butterfly

1956	William Yorzyk, U.S.	2:19.3
1960	Michael Troy, U.S.	2:12.8
1964	Kevin J. Berry, Australia	2:06.6
1968	Carl Robie, U.S.	2:08.7
1972	Mark Spitz, U.S.	2:00.70
1976	Mike Bruner, U.S.	1:59.23
1980	Sergei Fesenko, USSR	1:59.76
1984	Jon Sieben, Australia	1:57.04*

200-Meter Individual Medley

1968	Charles Hickcox, U.S.	2:12.0
1972	Gunnar Larsson, Sweden	2:07.17
1984	Alex Baumann, Canada	2:10.42*

400-Meter Individual Medley

1964	Dick Roth, U.S.	4:45.4
1968	Charles Hickcox, U.S.	4:48.4
1972	Gunnar Larsson, Sweden	4:31.98
1976	Rod Strachan, U.S.	4:23.68
1980	Aleksandr Sidorenko, USSR	4:22.89
1984	Alex Baumann, Canada	4:17.41*

Springboard Diving

		Points
1908	Albert Zurner, Germany	85.5
1912	Paul Guenther, Germany	79.23
1920	Louis Kuehn, U.S.	675.00
1924	Albert White, U.S.	696.40
1928	Pete Desjardins, U.S.	185.04
1932	Michael Galitzen, U.S.	161.38
1936	Richard Degener, U.S.	161.57
1948	Bruce Harlan, U.S.	163.64
1952	David Browning, U.S.	205.29
1956	Robert Clotworthy, U.S.	159.56
1960	Gary Tobian, U.S.	170.00
1964	Kenneth Sitzberger, U.S.	159.90
1968	Bernie Wrightson, U.S.	170.15
1972	Vladimir Vasin, USSR	594.09
1976	Phil Boggs, U.S.	619.52
1980	Aleksandr Portnov, USSR	905.02
1984	Greg Louganis, U.S.	754.41

Platform Diving

		Points
1904	Dr. G.E. Sheldon, U.S.	12.75
1908	Hjalmar Johansson, Sweden	83.75
1912	Erik Adlerz, Sweden	73.94
1920	Clarence Pinkston, U.S.	100.67
1924	Albert White, U.S.	487.30
1928	Pete Desjardins, U.S.	98.74
1932	Harold Smith, U.S.	124.80
1936	Marshall Wayne, U.S.	113.58
1948	Sammy Lee, U.S.	130.05
1952	Sammy Lee, U.S.	156.28
1956	Joaquin Capilla, Mexico	152.44
1960	Robert Webster, U.S.	165.56
1964	Robert Webster, U.S.	148.58
1968	Klaus Dibiasi, Italy.	164.18
1972	Klaus Dibiasi, Italy.	504.12
1976	Klaus Dibiasi, Italy.	600.51
1980	Falk Hoffmann, E. Germany	835.65
1984	Greg Louganis, U.S.	710.91

Swimming—Women

100-Meter Freestyle

1912	Fanny Durack, Australia	1:22.2
1920	Ethelda Bleibtrey, U.S.	1:13.6
1924	Ethel Lackie, U.S.	1:12.4
1928	Albina Osipowich, U.S.	1:11.0
1932	Helene Madison, U.S.	1:06.8
1936	Hendrika Mastenbroek, Holland	1:05.9
1948	Greta Anderson, Denmark	1:06.3
1952	Katalin Szoke, Hungary	1:06.3
1956	Dawn Fraser, Australia	1:02.0
1960	Dawn Fraser, Australia	1:01.2
1964	Dawn Fraser, Australia	59.5
1968	Jan Henne, U.S.	1:00.0
1972	Sandra Neilson, U.S.	58.59
1976	Kornelia Ender, E. Germany	55.65
1980	Barbara Krause, E. Germany	54.79*
1984	(tie) Carrie Steinseifer, U.S.	55.92
	Nancy Hogshead, U.S.	55.92

200-Meter Freestyle

1968	Debbie Meyer, U.S.	2:10.5
1972	Shane Gould, Australia	2:03.56
1976	Kornelia Ender, E. Germany.	1:59.26
1980	Barbara Krause, E. Germany	1:58.33*
1984	Mary Wayte, U.S.	1:59.23

400-Meter Freestyle

1924	Martha Norelius, U.S.	6:02.2
1928	Martha Norelius, U.S.	5:42.8
1932	Helene Madison, U.S.	5:28.5
1936	Hendrika Mastenbroek, Netherlands	5:26.4
1948	Ann Curtis, U.S.	5:17.8
1952	Valerie Gyenge, Hungary	5:12.1
1956	Lorraine Crapp, Australia	4:54.6
1960	Susan Chris von Saltza, U.S.	4:50.6
1964	Virginia Duenkel, U.S.	4:43.3
1968	Debbie Meyer, U.S.	4:31.8
1972	Shane Gould, Australia	4:19.04
1976	Petra Thuemer E. Germany	4:09.89
1980	Ines Diers, E. Germany	4:08.76
1984	Tiffany Cohen, U.S.	4:07.10*

800-Meter Freestyle

1968	Debbie Meyer, U.S.	9:24.0
1972	Keena Rothhammer, U.S.	8:53.68
1976	Petra Thuemer, E. Germany	8:37.14
1980	Michelle Ford, Australia	8:28.90
1984	Tiffany Cohen, U.S.	8:24.95*

100-Meter Backstroke

1924	Sybil Bauer, U.S.	1:23.3
1928	Marie Braun, Netherlands.	1:22.0
1932	Eleanor Holm, U.S.	1:19.4
1936	Dina Senff, Netherlands.	1:18.9
1948	Karen Harup, Denmark	1:14.4
1952	Joan Harrison, South Africa	1:14.3
1956	Judy Grinham, Great Britain	1:12.9
1960	Lynn Burke, U.S.	1:09.3
1964	Cathy Ferguson, U.S.	1:07.7
1968	Kaye Hall, U.S.	1:06.2
1972	Melissa Belote, U.S.	1:05.78
1976	Ulrike Richter, E. Germany	1:01.83
1980	Rica Reinisch, E. Germany.	1:00.86*
1984	Theresa Andrews, U.S.	1:02.55

200-Meter Backstroke

1968	Pokey Watson, U.S.	2:24.8
1972	Melissa Belote, U.S.	2:19.19
1976	Ulrike Richter, E. Germany	2:13.43
1980	Rica Reinisch, E. Germany.	2:11.77*
1984	Jolanda De Rover, Netherlands	2:13.38

100-Meter Breaststroke

1968	Djurdjica Bjedov, Yugoslavia	1:15.8
1972	Cathy Carr, U.S.	1:13.58
1976	Hannelore Anke, E. Germany	1:11.16
1980	Ute Geweniger, E. Germany	1:10.22
1984	Petra Van Staveren, Netherlands	1:09.88*

200-Meter Breaststroke

1924	Lucy Morton, Great Britain	3:32.2
1928	Hilde Schrader, Germany	3:12.6
1932	Clare Dennis, Australia	3:06.3
1936	Hideko Maehata, Japan	3:03.6
1948	Nelly Van Vliet, Netherlands	2:57.2
1952	Eva Szekely, Hungary	2:51.7
1956	Ursula Happe, Germany	2:53.1
1960	Anita Lonsbrough, Great Britain	2:49.5
1964	Galina Prozumenschikova, USSR	2:46.4
1968	Sharon Wichman, U.S.	2:44.4
1972	Beverly Whitfield, Australia	2:41.71
1976	Marina Koshevaia, USSR	2:33.35
1980	Lina Kachushite, USSR	2:29.54*
1984	Anne Ottenbrite, Canada	2:30.38

200-Meter Individual Medley

1968	Claudia Kolb, U.S.	2:24.7
1972	Shane Gould, Australia	2:23.07
1984	Tracy Caulkins, U.S.	2:12.64*

400-Meter Individual Medley

1964	Donna de Varona, U.S.	5:18.7
1968	Claudia Kolb, U.S.	5:08.5
1972	Gail Neall, Australia	5:02.97
1976	Ulrike Tauber, E. Germany	4:42.77
1980	Petra Schneider, E. Germany	4:36.29*
1984	Tracy Caulkins, U.S.	4:39.24

100-Meter Butterfly

1956	Shelley Mann, U.S.	1:11.0
1960	Carolyn Schuler, U.S.	1:09.5
1964	Sharon Stouder, U.S.	1:04.7
1968	Lynn McClements, Australia	1:05.5
1972	Mayumi Aoki, Japan	1:03.34
1976	Kornelia Ender, E. Germany	1:00.13
1980	Caren Metschuck, E. Germany	1:00.42
1984	Mary T. Meagher, U.S.	59.26*

200-Meter Butterfly

1968	Ada Kok, Netherlands	2:24.7
1972	Karen Moe, U.S.	2:15.57
1976	Andrea Pollack, E. Germany	2:11.41
1980	Ines Geissler, E. Germany	2:10.44
1984	Mary T. Meagher, U.S.	2:06.90*

400-Meter Medley Relay

1960	United States	4:41.1
1960	United States	4:33.9
1968	United States	4:28.3

1972	United States	4:20.75
1976	East Germany	4.07.95
1980	East Germany	4:06.67*
1984	United States	4:08.34

400-Meter Freestyle Relay

1912	Great Britain	5:52.8
1920	United States	5:11.6
1924	United States	4:58.8
1928	United States	4:47.6
1932	United States	4:38.0
1936	Netherlands	4:36.0
1948	United States	4:29.2
1952	Hungary	4:24.4
1956	Australia	4:17.1
1960	United States	4:08.9
1964	United States	4:03.8
1968	United States	4:02.5
1972	United States	3:55.19
1976	United States	3:44.82
1980	East Germany	3:42.71*
1976	United States	3:43.43

Springboard Diving

		Points
1920	Aileen Riggin, U.S.	539.90
1924	Elizabeth Becker, U.S.	474.50
1928	Helen Meany, U.S.	78.62
1932	Georgia Coleman U.S.	87.52
1936	Marjorie Gestring, U.S.	89.27
1948	Victoria M. Draves, U.S.	108.74
1952	Patricia McCormick, U.S.	147.30
1956	Patricia McCormick, U.S.	142.36
1960	Ingrid Kramer, Germany	155.81
1964	Ingrid Engel-Kramer, Germany	145.00
1968	Sue Gossick, U.S.	150.77
1972	Micki King, U.S.	450.03
1976	Jenni Chandler, U.S.	506.19
1980	Irina Kalinina, USSR	725.91
1984	Sylvie Bernier, Canada	530.70

Platform Diving

		Points
1912	Greta Johansson, Sweden	39.90
1920	Stefani Fryland-Clausen, Denmark	34.60
1924	Caroline Smith, U.S.	166.00
1928	Elizabeth B. Pinkston, U.S.	31.60
1932	Dorothy Poynton, U.S.	40.26
1936	Dorothy Poynton Hill, U.S.	33.93
1948	Victoria M. Draves, U.S.	68.87
1952	Patricia McCormick, U.S.	79.37
1956	Patricia McCormick, U.S.	84.85
1960	Ingrid Kramer, Germany	91.28
1964	Lesley Bush, U.S.	99.80
1968	Milena Duchkova, Czech.	109.59
1972	Ulrika Knape, Sweden	390.00
1976	Elena Vaytsekhouskaya, USSR	406.59
1980	Martina Jaschke, E. Germany	596.25
1984	Zhou Jihong, China	435.51

Summer Olympic Medal Winners in 1984

Archery

Men—1. Darrell Pace, U.S.; 2. Richard McKinney, U.S.; 3. Hiroshi Yamamoto, Japan.
Women—1. Hyang-Soun Seo, S. Korea; 2. Li Lingjuan, China; 3. Jin Ho Kim, S. Korea.

Basketball

Men—1. U.S.; 2. Spain; 3. Yugoslavia.
Women—1. U.S.; 2. S. Korea; 3. China.

Boxing

106 lbs.—1. Paul Gonzales, U.S.; 2. Salvatore Todisco, Italy; 3. Keith Mwila, Zambia & Jose Bolivar, Venezuela.
112 lbs.—1. Steve McCrory, U.S.; 2. Redzep Redzepovski, Yugoslavia; 3. Eyup Can, Turkey & Ibrahim Bilali, Kenya.
119 lbs.—1. Maurizio Stecca, Italy; 2. Hector Lopez, Mexico; 3. Dale Walters, Canada & Pedro Nolasco, Dom. Republic.
126 lbs.—1. Meldrick Taylor, U.S.; 2. Peter Konyegwachie, Nigeria; 3. Omar Peraza, Venezuela & Turgut Aykac, Turkey.
132 lbs.—1. Pernell Whitaker, U.S.; 2. Luis Ortiz, Puerto Rico; 3. Martin Ndongo Ebanga, Cameroon & Chil-Sung Chung, S.

Korea.
139 lbs.—1. Jerry Page, U.S.; 2. Dhawee Umponmaha, Thailand; 3. Mirk Puzovic, Yugoslavia & Mircea Fulger, Romania.
147 lbs.—1. Mark Breland, U.S.; 2. Young-Su An, S. Korea; 3. Joni Nyman, Finland & Luciano Bruno, Italy.
157 lbs.—1. Frank Tate, U.S.; 2. Shawn O'Sullivan, Canada; 3. Manfred Zielonka, W. Germany & Christophe Tiozzo, France.
165 lbs.—1. Joun-Sup Shin, S. Korea; 2. Virgil Hill, U.S.; 3. Mohamed Zaoui, Algeria & Aristides Gonzalez, Puerto Rico.
178 lbs.—1. Anton Josipovic, Yugoslavia; 2. Kevin Barry, New Zealand; 3. Mustapha Moussa, Algeria & Evander Holyfield, U.S.
201 lbs.—1. Henry Tillman, U.S.; 2. Willie DeWitt, Canada; 3. Arnold Vanderlijde, Netherlands & Angelo Musone, Italy.
Over 201 lbs.—1. Tyrell Biggs, U.S.; 2. Francesco Damiani, Italy; 3. Robert Wells, Great Britain & Salihu Azis, Yugoslavia.

Canoeing—Men

500m One-Man Canoe—1. Larry Cain, Canada; 2. Henning Jakobssen, Denmark; 3. Costica Olaru, Romania.
500m Two-Man Canoe—1. Yugoslavia; 2. Romania; 3. Spain.
500m One-Man Kayak—1. Ian Ferguson, New Zealand; 2. Lars Erik Moberg, Sweden; 3. Bernard Bregeon, France.
500m Two-Man Kayak—1. New Zealand; 2. Sweden; 3. Canada.

1,000m One-Man Kayak—1. Alan Thompson, New Zealand; 2. Milan Jania, Yugoslavia; 3. Greg Barton, U.S.
1,000m Two-Man Kayak—1. Canada; 2. France; 3. Australia.
1,000m Four-Man Kayak—1. New Zealand; 2. Sweden; 3. France.
1,000m One-Man Canoe—1. Ulrich Eiche, W. Germany; 2. Larry Cain, Canada; 3. Henning Jakobssen, Denmark.
1,000m Two-Man Canoe—1. Romania; 2. Yugoslavia; 3. France.

Canoeing—Women

500m One-Woman Kayak—1. Agneta Andersson, Sweden; 2. Barbara Schuttpelz, W. Germany; 3. Annemiek Derckx, Netherlands.
500m Two-Woman Kayak—1. Sweden; 2. Canada; 3. W. Germany.
500m Four-Woman Kayak—1. Romania; 2. Sweden; 3. Canada.

Cycling

4,000 Individual Pursuit—1. Steve Hegg, U.S.; 2. Rolf Golz, W. Germany; 3. Leonard Harvey Nitz, U.S.
Individual Road Race—1. Alexi Grewal, U.S.; 2. Steve Bauer, Canada; 3. Dag Otto Lauritzen, Norway.
1,000m Time Trials—1. Fredy Schmidtke, W. Germany; 2. Curtis Harnett, Canada; 3. Fabrice Colas, France.
4,000m Team Pursuit—1. Australia; 2. U.S.; 3. W. Germany.
Sprint—1. Mark Gorski, U.S.; 2. Nelson Vails, U.S.; 3. Tsutomu Sakamoto, Japan.
Points Race—1. Roger Ilegems, Belgium; 2. Uwe Messerschmidt, W. Germany; 3. Jose Manuel Youshimatz, Mexico.
100km Road Team Trials—1. Italy; 2. Switzerland; 3. U.S.
Women's Individual Road Race—1. Connie Carpenter, U.S.; 2. Rebecca Twigg, U.S.; 3. Sandra Schumacher, W. Germany.

Diving

Men's Springboard—1. Greg Louganis, U.S.; 2. Tan Liangde, China; 3. Ron Merriott, U.S.
Men's Platform—1. Greg Louganis, U.S.; 2. Bruce Kimball, U.S.; 3. Li Kongzheng, China.
Women's Springboard—1. Sylvie Bernier, Canada; 2. Kelly McCormick, U.S.; 3. Christina Seufert, U.S.
Women's Platform—1. Zhou Jihong, China; 2. Michelle Mitchell, U.S.; 3. Wendy Wyland, U.S.

Equestrian

Individual 3-Day Event—1. Mark Todd, New Zealand; 2. Karen Stives, U.S.; 3. Virginia Holgate, Great Britain.
Team 3-Day Event—1. U.S.; 2. Great Britain; 3. W. Germany.
Team Jumping—1. U.S.; 2. Great Britain; 3. W. Germany.
Team Dressage—1. W. Germany; 2. Switzerland; 3. Sweden.
Individual Dressage—1. Reiner Klimke, W. Germany; 2. Anne Grethe Jensen, Denmark; 3. Otto Hofer, Switzerland.
Individual Jumping—1. Jose Fargis, U.S.; 2. Conrad Homfeld, U.S.; 3. Heidi Robbiani, Switzerland.

Fencing—Men

Individual Epee—1. Phillippe Boisse, France; 2. Bjorne Vaggo, Sweden; 3. Philippe Riboud, France.
Individual Foil—1. Mauro Numa, Italy; 2. Matthias Behr, W. Germany; 3. Stefano Cerioni, Italy.
Individual Sabre—1. Jean Francois Lamour, France; 2. Marco Marin, Italy; 3. Peter Westbrook, U.S.
Team Foil—1. Italy; 2. W. Germany; 3. France.
Team Epee—1. W. Germany; 2. France; 3. Italy.
Team Sabre—1. Italy; 2. France; 3. Romania.

Fencing—Women

Individual Foil—1. Luan Jujie, China; 2. Cornelia Hanisch, W. Germany; Dorina Vaccaroni, Italy.
Team Foil—1. W. Germany; 2. Romania; 3. France.

Field Hockey

Men.—1. Pakistan; 2. W. Germany; 3. Great Britain.
Women.—1. Netherlands; 2. W. Germany; 3. U.S.

Gymnastics—Men

All Around—1. Koji Gushiken, Japan; 2. Peter Vidmar, U.S.; 3. Li Ning, China.
Team—1. U.S.; 2. China; 3. Japan.
Floor Exercise—1. Li Ning, China; 2. Lou Yun, China; 3. Koji Sotomura, Japan & Philippe Vatuone, France.

Horizontal Bar—1. Shinji Morisue, Japan; 2. Tong Fei, China; 3. Koji Gushiken, Japan.
Parallel Bars—1. Bart Connor, U.S.; 2. Nobuyuki Kajitani, Japan; 3. Mitch Gaylord, U.S.
Pommel Horse—1. Li Ning, China & Peter Vidmar, U.S. (tie); 3. Tim Daggett, U.S.
Rings—1. Koji Gushiken, Japan & Li Ning, China (tie); 3. Mitch Gaylord, U.S.
Vault—1. Lou Yung, China; 2. Koji Gushiken, Japan, Shinji Morisue, Japan, Li Ning, China, & Mitch Gaylord, U.S. (tie).

Gymnastics—Women

Floor Exercise—1. Ecaterina Szabo, Romania; 2. Julianne McNamara, U.S.; 3. Mary Lou Retton, U.S.
Balance Beam—1. Simona Pauca & Ecaterina Szabo, both Romania (tie); 3. Kathy Johnson, U.S.
Vault—Ecaterina Szabo, Romania; 2. Mary Lou Retton, U.S.; 3. Lavinia Agache, Romania.
Uneven Parallel Bars—1. Ma Yanhonjg, China & Julianne McNamara, U.S. (tie); 3. Mary Lou Retton, U.S.
All-Around—1. Mary Lou Retton, U.S.; 2. Ecaterina Szabo, Romania; 3. Simona Pauca, Romania.
Team—1. Romania; 2. U.S.; 3. China.
Rhythmic—1. Lori Fung, Canada; 2. Doina Staiculescu, Romania; 3. Regina Weber, W. Germany.

Team Handball

Men—1. Yugoslavia; 2. W. Germany; 3. Romania.
Women—1. Yugoslavia; 2. S. Korea; 3. China.

Judo

Lightweight—1. Byeong-Keun Ahn, S. Korea; 2. Ezio Gamba, Italy; 3. Kerrith Brown, Great Britain & Louis Onmura, Brazil.
Extra Lightweight—1. Shinji Hosokawa, Japan; 2. Jae-Yup Kim, S. Korea; 3. Eddie Liddie, U.S. & Neil Eckersley, Great Britain.
Half Lightweight—1. Yoshiyuki Matsuoka, Japan; 2. Jung-Oh Hwang, S. Korea; 3. Marc Alexandre, France & Josef Reiter, Austria.
Half Middleweight—1. Frank Wieneke, W. Germany; 2. Neil Adams, Great Britain; 3. Michel Nowak, France & Mircea Fratica, Romania.
Middleweight—1. Peter Seisenbacher, Austria; 2. Robert Berland, U.S.; 3. Seiki Nose, Japan & Walter Carmna, Brazil.
Half Heavyweight—1. Hyong-Zoo Ha, S. Korea; 2. Douglas Vieira, Brazil; 3. Gunter Neureuther, W. Germany & Bjarni Fridriksson, Iceland.
Heavyweight—1. Hitoshi Saito, Japan; 2. Angelo Parisi, France; 3. Yong-Chul Cho, S. Korea & Mark Berger, Canada.
Open—1. Yasuhiro Yamashita, Japan; 2. Mohamed Rashwan, Egypt; 3. Mihac Cloc, Romania & Arthur Schanel, W. Germany.

Modern Pentathlon

Individual—1. Daniele Masala, Italy; 2. Svante Rasmuson, Sweden; 3. Carlos Massullo, Italy.
Team—1. Italy; 2. U.S.; 3. France.

Rowing

Single Sculls—1. Pertti Karppinen, Finland; 2. Peter-Michael Kolbe, W. Germany; 3. Robert Mills, Canada.
Double Sculls—1. U.S.; 2. Belgium; 3. Yugoslavia.
Quadruple Sculls—1. W. Germany; 2. Australia; 3. Canada.
Pair Oars With Coxswain—1. Italy; 2. Romania; 3. U.S.
Pair Oars Without Coxswain—1. Romania; 2. Spain; 3. Norway.
Four Oars With Coxswain—1. Great Britain; 2. U.S.; 3. New Zealand.
Four Oars Without Coxswain—1. New Zealand; 2. U.S.; 3. Denmark.
Eight Oars With Coxswain—1. Canada; 2. U.S.; 3. Australia.

Rowing—Women

Single Sculls—1. Valarie Racila, Romania; 2. Charlotte Geer, U.S.; 3. Ann Haesebrouck, Belgium.
Double Sculls—1. Romania; 2. Netherlands; 3. Canada.
Quadruple Sculls with Coxswain—1. Romania; 2. U.S.; 3. Denmark.
Pair Oars Without Coxswain—1. Romania; 2. Canada; 3. W. Germany.
Four Oars Without Coxswain—1. Romania; 2. Canada; 3. Australia.
Eight Oars—1. U.S.; 2. Romania; 3. Netherlands.

Shooting—Men

Air Rifle—1. Philippe Heberle, France; 2. Andreas Kronthaler, Austria; 3. Barry Dagger, Great Britain.
Clay Target Trap—1. Luciano Giovanetti, Italy; 2. Francisco Boza, Peru; 3. Dan Carlisle, U.S.
English Small Bore Rifle—1. Ed Etzel, U.S.; 2. Michel Bury, France; 3. Michael Sullivan, Great Britain.
Free Pistol—1. Xu Haifeng, China; 2. Ragnar Skanaker, Sweden; 3. Wang Yifu, China.
Rapid-Fire Pistol—1. Takeo Kamachi, Japan; 2. Corneliu Ion, Romania; 3. Rauno Bies, Finland.
Running Game Targets—1. Li Yuwei, China; 2. Helmut Bellingrodt, Colombia; 3. Huang Shiping, China.
Small Bore Rifle, 3 Positions—1. Malcolm Cooper, Great Britain; 2. Daniel Nipkow, Switzerland; 3. Alistair Allan, Great Britain.
Clay Target Skeet—1. Matthew Dryke, U.S.; 2. Ole Riber Rasmussen, Denmark; 3. Luca Scribani Rossi, Italy.

Shooting—Women

Air Rifle—1. Pat Spurgin, U.S.; 2. Edith Gufler, Italy; 3. Wu Xiaoxuan, China.
Small Bore Rifle, 3 Positions—1. Wu Xiaoxuan, China; 2. Ulkrie Holmer, W. Germany; 3. Wanda Jewell, U.S.
Sport Pistol—1. Linda Thom, Canada; 2. Ruby Fox, U.S.; 3. Patricia Dench, Australia.

Soccer

Championship—1. France; 2. Brazil; 3. Yugoslavia.

Swimming—Men

100-Meter Breaststroke—1. Steve Lundquist, U.S.; 2. Victor Davis, Canada; 3. Peter Evans, Australia.
100-Meter Butterfly—1. Michael Gross, W. Germany; 2. Pablo Morales, U.S.; 3. Glenn Buchanan, Australia.
100-Meter Freestyle—1. Rowdy Gaines, U.S.; 2. Mark Stockwell, Australia; 3. Per Johansson, Sweden.
100-Meter Backstroke—1. Rick Carey, U.S.; 2. David Wilson, U.S.; 3. Mike West, Canada.
200-Meter Butterfly—1. Jon Sieben, Australia; 2. Michael Gross, W. Germany; 3. Rafael Vidal Castro, Venezuela.
200-Meter Backstroke—1. Rick Carey, U.S.; 2. Frederic Delcourt, France; 3. Cameron Henning, Canada.
200-Meter Freestyle—1. Michael Gross, W. Germany; 2. Mike Heath, U.S.; 3. Thomas Fahrner, W. Germany.
200-Meter Breaststroke—1. Victor Davis, Canada; 2. Glenn Beringen, Australia; 3. Etienne Dagon, Switzerland.
200-Meter Individual Medley—1. Alex Baumann, Canada; 2. Pablo Morales, U.S.; 3. Neil Cochran, Great Britain.
400-Meter Freestyle—1. George DiCarlo, U.S.; 2. John Mykkanen, U.S.; 3. Justin Lemberg, Australia.
400-Meter Individual Medley—1. Alex Baumann, Canada; 2. Ricardo Prado, Brazil; 3. Robert Woodhouse, Australia.
1,500-Meter Freestyle—1. Mike O'Brien, U.S.; 2. George DiCarlo, U.S.; 3. Stefan Pfeiffer, W. Germany.
400-Meter Medley Relay—1. U.S.; 2. Canada; 3. Australia.
400-Meter Freestyle Relay—1. U.S.; 2. Australia; 3. Sweden.
800-Meter Freestyle Relay—1. U.S.; 2. W. Germany; 3. Great Britain.

Swimming—Women

100-Meter Freestyle—1. (tie) Carrie Steinselfer & Nancy Hogshead, both U.S.; 3. Annemarie Verstappen, Netherlands.
100-Meter Backstroke—1. Theresa Andrews, U.S.; 2. Betsy Mitchell, U.S.; 3. Jolanda De Rover, Netherlands.
100-Meter Butterfly—1. Mary T. Meagher, U.S.; 2. Jenna Johnson, U.S.; 3. Karin Seick, W. Germany.
100-Meter Breaststroke—1. Petra Van Staveren, Netherlands; 2. Anne Ottenbrite, Canada; 3. Catherine Poirot, France.
200-Meter Freestyle—1. Mary Wayte, U.S.; 2. Cynthia Woodhead, U.S.; 3. Annemarie Vestappen, Netherlands.
200-Meter Breaststroke—1. Anne Ottenbrite, Canada; 2. Susan Rapp, U.S.; 3. Ingrid Lempereur, Belgium.
200-Meter Individual Medley—1. Tracy Caulkins, U.S.; 2. Nancy Hogshead, U.S.; 3. Michele Pearson, Australia.
200-Meter Butterfly—1. Mary T. Meagher, U.S.; 2. Karen Phillips, Australia; 3. Ina Bayerman, W. Germany.
200-Meter Backstroke—1. Jolanda De Rover, Netherlands; 2. Amy White, U.S.; 3. Aneta Patrascoiu, Romania.
400-Meter Freestyle—1. Tiffany Cohen, U.S.; 2. Sarah Hardcastle, Great Britain; 3. June Croft, Great Britain.
400-Meter Individual Medley—1. Tracy Caulkins, U.S.; 2. Suzanne Landells, Australia; 3. Petra Zindler, W. Germany.

800-Meter Freestyle—1. Tiffany Cohen, U.S.; 2. Michele Richardson, U.S.; 3. Sarah Hardcastle, Great Britain.
400-Meter Medley Relay—1. U.S.; 2. Germany; 3. Canada.
400-Meter Freestyle Relay—1. U.S.; 2. Netherlands; 3. W. Germany.

Synchronized Swimming

Solo—1. Tracie Ruiz, U.S.; 2. Carolyn Waldo, Canada; 3. Miwako Motoyoshi, Japan.
Duet—1. U.S.; 2. Canada; 3. Japan.

Track and Field—Men

100-Meters—1. Carl Lewis, U.S.; 2. Sam Graddy, U.S.; 3. Ben Johnson, Canada.
110-Meter Hurdles—1. Roger Kingdom, U.S.; 2. Greg Foster, U.S.; 3. Arto Bryggare, Finland.
200-Meters—1. Carl Lewis, U.S.; 2. Kirk Baptiste, U.S.; 3. Thomas Jefferson, U.S.
400-Meters—1. Alonzo Babers, U.S.; 2. Gabriel Tiacoh, Ivory Coast; 3. Antonio McKay, U.S.
400-Meter Hurdles—1. Edwin Moses, U.S.; 2. Danny Harris, U.S.; 3. Harald Schmid, W. Germany.
400-Meter Relay—1. U.S.; 2. Jamaica; 3. Canada.
800-Meters—1. Joaquim Cruz, Brazil; 2. Sebastian Coe, Great Britain; 3. Earl Jones, U.S.
1,500 Meters—1. Sebastian Coe, Great Britain; 2. Steve Cram, Great Britain; 3. Jose Abascal, Spain.
1,600-Meter Relay—1. U.S.; 2. Great Britain; 3. Nigeria.
3,000-Meter Steeplechase—1. Julius Korir, Kenya; 2. Joseph Mahmoud, France; 3. Brian Diemer, U.S.
5,000-Meters—1. Said Aouita, Morocco; 2. Markus Ryffel, Switzerland; 3. Antonio Leitao, Portugal.
10,000-Meters—1. Alberto Cova, Italy; 2. Michael McLeod, Great Britain; 3. Mike Musyoki, Kenya.
Marathon—1. Carlos Lopes, Portugal; 2. John Treacy, Ireland; 3. Charles Spedding, Great Britain.
20-Kilometer Walk—1. Ernesto Canto, Mexico; 2. Raul Gonzalez, Mexico; 3. Maurizio Damilano, Italy.
50-Kilometer Walk—1. Raul Gonzalez, Mexico; 2. Bo Gustafsson, Sweden; 3. Sandro Bellucci, Italy.
Decathlon—1. Daley Thompson, Great Britain; 2. Juergen Hingsen, W. Germany; 3. Siegfried Wentz, W. Germany.
Discus—1. Rolf Danneberg, W. Germany; 2. Mac Wilkins, U.S.; 3. John Powell, U.S.
Hammer Throw—1. Juha Tiainen, Finland; 2. Karl-Hans Riehm, W. Germany; 3. Klaus Ploghaus, W. Germany.
High Jump—1. Dietmar Mogenburg, W. Germany; 2. Patrik Sjoberg, Sweden; 3. Zhu Jianhua, China.
Javelin—1. Arto Haerkoenen, Finland; 2. David Ottley, Great Britain; 3. Kenth Eldebrink, Sweden.
Long Jump—1. Carl Lewis, U.S.; 2. Gary Honey, Australia; 3. Giovanni Evangelisti, Italy.
Pole Vault—1. Pierre Quinon, France; 2. Mike Tully, U.S.; 3. Thierry Vigneron, France and Earl Bell, U.S. (tie).
Shot Put—1. Alessandro Andrei, Italy; 2. Michael Carter, U.S.; 3. Dave Laut, U.S.
Triple Jump—1. Al Joyner, U.S.; 2. Mike Conley, U.S.; 3. Keith Conner, Great Britain.

Track and Field—Women

100-Meters—1. Evelyn Ashford, U.S.; 2. Alice Brown, U.S.; 3. Merlene Ottey-Page, Jamaica.
100-Meter Hurdles—1. Benita Brown-Fitzgerald, U.S.; 2. Shirley Strong, Great Britain; 3. Kim Turner, U.S.
200-Meters—1. Valerie Brisco-Hooks, U.S.; 2. Florence Griffith, U.S.; 3. Merlene Ottey-Page, Jamaica.
400-Meters—1. Valerie Brisco-Hooks, U.S.; 2. Chandra Cheeseborough, U.S.; 3. Kathryn Cook, Great Britain.
400-Meter Hurdles—1. Nawal el Moutawakel, Morocco; 2. Judi Brown, U.S.; 3. Cristina Cojocaru, Romania.
400-Meter Relay—1. U.S.; 2. Canada; 3. Great Britain.
800-Meters—1. Doina Melinte, Romania; 2. Kim Gallagher, U.S.; 3. Fita Lovin, Romania.
1,500-Meters—1. Gabriella Dorio, Italy; 2. Doina Melinte, Romania; 3. Maricica Puica, Romania.
1,600-Meter Relay—1. U.S.; 2. Canada; 3. W. Germany.
3,000 Meters—1. Maricica Puica, Romania; 2. Wendy Sly, Great Britain, 3. Lynn Williams, Canada.
Marathon—1. Joan Benoit, U.S.; 2. Grete Waitz, Norway; 3. Rosa Mota, Portugal.
Heptathlon—1. Glynis Nunn, Australia; 2. Jackie Joyner, U.S.; 3. Sabine Everts, W. Germany.
Discus—1. Ria Stalman, Netherlands; 2. Leslie Deniz, U.S.; 3. Florenta Craciunescu, Romania.
High Jump—1. Ulrike Meyfarth, W. Germany; 2. Sara Simeoni, Italy; 3. Joni Huntley, U.S.

Javelin—1. Tessa Sanderson, Great Britain; 2. Tiina Lillak, Finland; 3. Fatima Whitbread, Great Britain.
Long Jump—1. Anisoara Stanciu, Romania; 2. Vali Ionescu, Romania; 3. Susan Hearnshaw, Great Britain.
Shot Put—1. Claudia Loch, W. Germany; 2. Mihaela Loghin, Romania; 3. Gael Martin, Australia.

Volleyball

Men—1. U.S.; 2. Brazil; 3. Italy.
Women—1. China; 2. U.S.; 3. Japan.

Water Polo

Championship—1. Yugoslavia; 2. U.S.; 3. W. Germany.

Weight Lifting

Bantamweight—1. Wu Shude, China; 2. Lai Rumming, China; 3. Masahiro Kotaka, Japan.
Flyweight—1. Zeng Guoqiang, China; 2. Zhou Pelshun, China; 3. Kazushito Manabe, Japan.
Featherweights—1. Chen Weiquiang, China; 2. Gelu Radu, Romania; 3. Wen Yee Tsai, Chinese Taipei.
Lightweights—1. Yao Jingyuang, China; 2. Andrei Socaci, Romania; 3. Jouni Gronman, Finland.
Middleweights—1. Karl-Heinz Radschinsky, W. Germany; 2. Jacques Demers, Canada; 3. Dragomir Cioroslan, Romania.
Light Heavyweights—1. Petre Becheru, Romania; 2. Robert Kabbas, Australia; 3. Ryoji Isaoka, Japan.
Middle Heavyweights—1. Niku Vlad, Romania; 2. Petre Dumitru, Romania; 3. David Mercer, Great Britain.
100 Kilograms—1. Rolf Milser, W. Germany; 2. Vasile Gropa, Romania; 3. Pekka Niemi, Finland.
110 Kilograms—1. Norberto Oberburger, Italy; 2. Stefan Tasnadi, Romania; 3. Guy Carlton, U.S.
Super Heavyweights—1. Dinko Lukim, Australia; 2. Mario Martinez, U.S.; 3. Manfred Nerlinger, W. Germany.

Wrestling—Freestyle

106 Pounds—1. Robert Weaver, U.S.; 2. Takashi Irie, Japan; 3. Kab Do Sohn, S. Korea.
115 Pounds—1. Saban Trstena, Yugoslavia; 2. Jong Kyu Kim, S. Korea; 3. Yuji Takada, Japan.
126 Pounds—1. Hideaki Tomiyama, Japan; 2. Barry Davis, U.S.; 3. Eui Kon Kim, S. Korea.

137 Pounds—1. Randy Lewis, U.S.; 2. Kosei Akaishi, Japan; 3. Jung Keun Lee, S. Korea.
150 Pounds—1. In Tak Yoo, S. Korea; 2. Andrew Rein, U.S.; 3. Jukka Rauhala, Finland.
163 Pounds—1. Dave Schultz, U.S.; 2. Martin Knosp, W. Germany; 3. Saban Sejdi, Yugoslavia.
181 Pounds—1. Mark Schultz, U.S.; 2. Hideyuki Nagashima, Japan; 3. Chris Rinke, Canada.
198 Pounds—1. Ed Banach, U.S.; 2. Akira Ohta, Japan; 3. Neil Loban, Great Britain.
220 Pounds—1. Lou Banach, U.S.; 2. Joseph Atiyeh, Syria; 3. Vasile Puscasu, Romania.
Over 220 Pounds—1. Bruce Baumgartner, U.S.; 2. Bob Molle, Canada; 3. Ayhan Taskin, Turkey.

Wrestling—Greco-Roman

106 Pounds—1. Vicenzo Maenza, Italy; 2. Markus Scherer, W. Germany; 3. Ikuzo Saito, Japan.
115 Pounds—1. Atsuji Miyahara, Japan; 2. Daniel Aceves, Mexico; 3. Dae Du Bang, S. Korea.
126 Pounds—1. Pasquale Passarelli, W. Germany; 2. Masaki Eto, Japan; 3. Haralambos Holidis, Greece.
137 Pounds—1. Weon Kee Kim, S. Korea; 2. Kentolle Johansson, Sweden; 3. Hugo Dietsche, Switzerland.
150 Pounds—1. Vlado Lisjak, Yugoslavia; 2. Tapio Sipila, Finland; 3. James Martinez, U.S.
163 Pounds—1. Jouko Salomaki, Finland; 2. Roger Tallroth, Sweden; 3. Stefan Rusu, Romania.
181 Pounds—1. Ion Draica, Romania; 2. Dimitrios Thanopoulos, Greece; 3. Soren Claeson, Sweden.
198 Pounds—1. Steven Fraser, U.S.; 2. Ilie Matfei, Romania; 3. Frank Andersson, Sweden.
202 Pounds—1. Vasile Andrei, Romania; 2. Greg Gibson; U.S.; Josef Tertelji, Yugoslavia;
Over 202 Pounds—1. Jeff Blatnick, U.S.; 2. Refik Memisevic, Yugoslavia; 3. Victor Dolipschi, Romania.

Yachting

Windglider Class—1. Stephen Van Den Berg, Netherlands; 2. Scott Steele, U.S.; 3. Bruce Kendall, New Zealand.
Soling Class—1. U.S.; 2. Brazil; 3. Canada.
Flying Dutchman Class—1. U.S.; 2. Canada; 3. Great Britain.
Star Class—1. U.S.; 2. W. Germany; 3. Italy.
Finn Class—1. Russell Coutts, New Zealand; 2. John Bertrand, U.S.; 3. Terry Neilson, Canada.
Tornado Class—1. New Zealand; 2. U.S.; 3. Australia.
470 Class—1. Spain; 2. U.S.; 3. France.

23d Summer Olympics

Los Angeles, Cal., July 29-Aug. 12, 1984

Final Medal Standings

(nations in alphabetical order)

	Gold	Silver	Bronze	Total		Gold	Silver	Bronze	Total
Algeria	0	0	2	2	Korea, South	6	6	7	19
Australia	4	8	12	24	Mexico	2	3	1	6
Austria	1	1	1	3	Morocco	2	0	0	2
Belgium	1	1	2	4	Netherlands	5	2	6	13
Brazil	1	5	2	8	New Zealand	8	1	2	11
Cameroon	0	0	1	1	Nigeria	0	1	1	2
Canada	10	18	16	44	Norway	0	1	2	3
China	15	8	9	32	Pakistan	1	0	0	1
Columbia	0	1	0	1	Peru	0	1	0	1
Denmark	0	3	3	6	Portugal	1	0	2	3
Dom. Republic	0	0	1	1	Puerto Rico	0	1	1	2
Egypt	0	1	0	1	Romania	20	16	17	53
Finland	4	3	6	13	Spain	1	2	2	5
France	5	7	15	27	Sweden	2	11	6	19
Germany, West	17	19	23	59	Switzerland	0	4	4	8
Great Britain	5	10	22	37	Syria	0	1	0	1
Greece	0	1	1	2	Taipei	0	0	1	1
Iceland	0	0	1	1	Thailand	0	1	0	1
Ireland	1	1	0	1	Turkey	0	0	3	3
Italy	14	6	12	32	United States	83	61	30	174
Ivory Coast	0	1	0	1	Venezuela	0	0	3	3
Jamaica	0	1	2	3	Yugoslavia	7	4	7	18
Japan	10	8	14	32	Zambia	0	0	1	1
Kenya	1	0	1	2	Duplicate medals awarded in some events			

Olympic Information

Symbol: Five rings or circles, linked together to represent the sporting friendship of all peoples. The rings also symbolize the 5 continents—Europe, Asia, Africa, Australia, and America. Each ring is a different color—blue, yellow, black, green, and red.

Flag: The symbol of the 5 rings on a plain white background.

Motto: "Citius, Altius, Fortius." Latin meaning "faster, higher, braver," or the modern interpretation "swifter, higher, stronger". The motto was coined by Father Didon, a French educator, in 1895.

Creed: "The most important thing in the Olympic Games is not to win but to take part, just as the most important thing in life is not the triumph but the struggle. The essential thing is not to have conquered but to have fought well."

Oath: An athlete of the host country recites the following at the opening ceremony. "In the name of all competitors I promise that we will take part in these Olympic Games, respecting and abiding by the rules which govern them, in the true spirit of sportsmanship for the glory of sport and the honor of our teams." Both the oath and the creed were composed by Pierre de Coubertin, the founder of the modern Games.

Flame: Symbolizes the continuity between the ancient and modern Games. The modern version of the flame was adopted in 1936. The torch used to kindle the flame is first lit by the sun's rays at Olympia, Greece, and then carried to the site of the Games by relays of runners. Ships and planes are used when necessary.

Chess

Chess dates back to antiquity. Its exact origin is unknown. The strongest players of their time, and therefore regarded by later generations as world champions, were Francois Philidor, France; Alexandre Deschappelles, France; Louis de la Bourdonnais, France; Howard Staunton, England; Adolph Anderssen, Germany and Paul Morphy, United States. In 1866 Wilhelm Steinitz of Czechoslovakia defeated Adolph Anderssen and claimed the title of world champion. The official world champions since the title was first used follow:

1866-1894 Wilhelm Steinitz, Austria	**1937-1946** Dr. Alexander A. Alekhine, France	**1961-1963** Mikhail Botvinnik, USSR
1894-1921 Dr. Emanuel Lasker, Germany	**1948-1957** Mikhail Botvinnik, USSR	**1963-1969** Tigran Petrosian, USSR
1921-1927 Jose R. Capablanca, Cuba	**1957-1958** Vassily Smyslov, USSR	**1969-1972** Boris Spassky, USSR
1927-1935 Dr. Alexander A. Alekhine, France	**1958-1959** Mikhail Botvinnik, USSR	**1972-1975** Bobby Fischer, U.S. (a)
1935-1937 Dr. Max Euwe, Netherlands	**1960-1961** Mikhail Tal, USSR	**1975** Anatoly Karpov, USSR

(a) Defaulted championship after refusal to accept International Chess Federation rules for a championship match, April 1975.

United States Champions

Unofficial champions		**1894-1895** Albert Hodges	**1957-1961** Bobby Fischer	**1980-1981** (tie) Larry Evans,
1857-1871 Paul Morphy		**1895-1897** Jackson Showalter	**1961-1962** Larry Evans	Larry Christiansen,
1871-1876 George Mackenzie		**1897-1906** Harry Pillsbury	**1962-1968** Bobby Fischer	Walter Browne
1876-1880 James Mason		**1906-1909** vacant	**1968-1969** Larry Evans	**1981-1983** (tie) Walter Browne,
1880-1889 George Mackenzie		**1909-1936** Frank Marshall	**1969-1972** Samuel Reshevsky	Yasser Seirawan
1889-1890 S. Lipschutz		**1936-1944** Samuel Reshevsky	**1972-1973** Robert Byrne	**1983** (tie) Walter Browne
1890 Jackson Showalter		**1944-1946** Arnold Denker	**1973-1974** Lubomir Kavalek,	Larry Christiansen
1890-1891 Max Judd		**1946-1948** Samuel Reshevsky	John Grefe	Roman
Official champions		**1948-1951** Herman Steiner	**1974-1977** Walter Browne	Dzindzichashvili
1891-1892 Jackson Showalter		**1951-1954** Larry Evans	**1978-1980** Lubomir Kavalek	
1892-1894 S. Lipschutz		**1954-1957** Arthur Bisguier		
1894 Jackson Showalter				

National Shuffleboard Championships in 1984

Lakeside, Oh. July 23-28, 1984

Men's Open — Tyler Brown, Lakeside, Oh.
Men's Closed — Jim Springer, Coldwater, Mich.
Women's Open — Ellie Bone, Mt. Dora, Fla.
Women's Closed — Esther DeBoer, New York, N.Y.

Men's Doubles — Bud Personette, Cicero, Ind. & Wilbur Estes, Sea Breeze, Fla.
Women's Doubles — Winnie McDonald, Ontario, Canada & Thelma Springer, Coldwater, Mich.

Football Stadiums

See index for major league baseball stadium seating capacity, and college football stadiums.

Name, location	Capacity	Name, location	Capacity
Anaheim Stadium, Anaheim, Cal.	69,000	Liberty Bowl, Memphis, Tenn.	50,180
Arrowhead Stadium, Kansas City, Mo.	78,067	Los Angeles Memorial Coliseum	92,516
Atlanta-Fulton County Stadium	60,748	Louisiana Superdome, New Orleans.	71,330
Astrodome, Houston, Tex.	50,496	Mile High Stadium, Denver, Col.	75,123
Baltimore Memorial Stadium	60,714	Milwaukee County Stadium.	55,958
Buffalo War Memorial Stadium.	46,206	Mississippi Memorial Stadium, Jackson.	61,000
Busch Memorial Stadium, St. Louis	51,392	Oakland-Alameda County Coliseum.	54,615
Candlestick Park, San Francisco, Cal.	61,185	Orange Bowl, Miami, Fla.	75,459
Cleveland Municipal Stadium.	80,322	Pontiac Silverdome, Mich..	80,638
Cotton Bowl, Dallas, Tex.	72,000	Rich Stadium, Buffalo, N.Y.	80,020
Franklin Field, Philadelphia, Pa.	60,546	Riverfront Stadium, Cincinnati, Oh..	59,754
Gator Bowl, Jacksonville, Fla.	70,000	Rose Bowl, Pasadena, Cal..	106,721
Giants Stadium, E. Rutherford, N.J.	76,891	San Diego Jack Murphy Stadium, San Diego.	52,675
Hoosier Stadium, Indianapolis, Ind.	61,000	Sullivan Stadium, Foxboro, Mass.	61,297
Hubert H. Humphrey Metrodome, Minneapolis	62,212	Shea Stadium, New York, N.Y.	60,372
John F. Kennedy Stadium, Philadelphia, Pa.	105,000	Soldier Field, Chicago, Ill.	65,077
Robert F. Kennedy Memorial Stadium, Wash., D.C.	55,031	Sugar Bowl, New Orleans, La.	80,982
Kezar Stadium, San Francisco, Cal.	59,636	Tampa Stadium, Tampa, Fla.	72,126
Kingdome, Seattle, Wash.	64,752	Texas Stadium, Dallas, Tex.	65,101
Ladd Memorial Stadium, Mobile, Ala.	40,605	Three Rivers Stadium, Pittsburgh, Pa.	50,350
Lambeau Field, Green Bay, Wis.	56,189	Veterans Stadium, Philadelphia, Pa.	72,204
Legion Field, Birmingham, Ala.	75,412		

National Football League

Final 1983 Standings

National Conference

Eastern Division

	W	L	T	Pct	Pts	Opp
Washington	14	2	0	.875	541	332
Dallas	12	4	0	.750	479	360
St. Louis	8	7	1	.531	374	428
Philadelphia	5	11	0	.313	233	322
N.Y. Giants	3	12	1	.219	267	347

Central Division

	W	L	T	Pct	Pts	Opp
Detroit	9	7	0	.562	347	286
Green Bay	8	8	0	.500	429	439
Chicago	8	8	0	.500	311	301
Minnesota	8	8	0	.500	316	348
Tampa Bay	2	14	0	.125	241	380

Western Division

	W	L	T	Pct	Pts	Opp
San Francisco	10	6	0	.625	432	293
L.A. Rams	9	7	0	.562	361	344
New Orleans	8	8	0	.500	319	337
Atlanta	7	9	0	.438	370	389

American Conference

Eastern Division

	W	L	T	Pct	Pts	Opp
Miami	12	4	0	.750	389	250
New England	8	8	0	.500	274	289
Buffalo	8	8	0	.500	283	351
Baltimore	7	9	0	.438	264	354
N.Y. Jets	7	9	0	.438	313	331

Central Division

	W	L	T	Pct	Pts	Opp
Pittsburgh	10	6	0	.625	355	303
Cleveland	9	7	0	.562	356	342
Cincinnati	7	9	0	.438	346	302
Houston	2	14	0	.125	288	460

Western Division

	W	L	T	Pct	Pts	Opp
L.A. Raiders	12	4	0	.750	442	338
Seattle	9	7	0	.562	403	397
Denver	9	7	0	.562	302	327
San Diego	6	10	0	.375	358	462
Kansas City	6	10	0	.375	386	367

NFC playoffs—L.A. Rams 24, Dallas, 17; Washington 51, L.A. Rams 7; San Francisco 24, Detroit 23; Wash. 24, San Francisco 21.
AFC playoffs—Seattle 31, Denver 7; Seattle 27, Miami 20; L.A. Raiders 38, Pittsburgh 10; L.A. Raiders 30, Seattle 14.
Championship game—L.A. Raiders 38, Washington 9.

Raiders defeat Redskins in Super Bowl

The Los Angeles Raiders won their third Super Bowl championship by demolishing the defending champion Washington Redskins 38-9 at Tampa Stadium in Tampa, Fla. Marcus Allen of the Raiders, who rushed for a Super Bowl record 191 yards and scored two touchdowns, was chosen the game's most valuable player.

Score by Periods

Washington	0	3	6	0— 9
Los Angeles	7	14	14	3—38

Scoring

L.A.—Jensen blocks punt and recovers ball in end zone (Bahr, kick).
L.A.—Branch 12 yd. pass from Plunkett (Bahr, kick).
Wash.—Moseley 24 yd. field goal.
L.A.—Squirek 5 yd. interception (Bahr, kick).
Wash.—Riggins 1 yd. run.
L.A.—Allen 5 yd. run (Bahr, kick).
L.A.—Allen 74 yd. run (Bahr, kick).
L.A.—Bahr 21 yd. field goal.

Individual Statistics

Rushing — Washington—Riggins 26-64, Theismann 3-18, J. Washington 3-8. Los Angeles—Allen 20-191, King 3-12, Hawkins 3-6, Pruitt 5-17, Plunkett 1-minus 2, Willis 1-7.

Passing — Washington—Theismann 16-35-2-243. Los Angeles—Plunkett 16-25-0-172.

Receiving — Washington—Didier 5-65, J. Washington 3-20, Garrett 1-17, Brown 3-93, Giaquinto 2-21, Monk 1-26, Riggins 1-1. Los Angeles—Allen 2-8, King 2-8, Christensen 4-32, Branch 6-94, Hawkins 2-20.

Team Statistics

	Wash.	L.A.
First downs	19	18
Rushes-yards	32-90	33-231
Passing yards	243	172
Sacks by-yards	2-18	6-50
Return yards	167	30
Passes	16-35-2	16-25-0
Punts	8-32.4	7-42.7
Fumbles-lost	1-1	3-2
Penalties-yards	4-62	7-56
Time of possession	30:38	29:22

Super Bowl

Year	Winner	Loser	Site
1967	Green Bay Packers, 35	Kansas City Chiefs, 10	Los Angeles Coliseum
1968	Green Bay Packers, 33	Oakland Raiders, 14	Orange Bowl, Miami
1969	New York Jets, 16	Baltimore Colts, 7	Orange Bowl, Miami
1970	Kansas City Chiefs, 23	Minnesota Vikings, 7	Tulane Stadium, New Orleans
1971	Baltimore Colts, 16	Dallas Cowboys, 13	Orange Bowl, Miami
1972	Dallas Cowboys, 24	Miami Dolphins, 3	Tulane Stadium, New Orleans
1973	Miami Dolphins, 14	Washington Redskins, 7	Los Angeles Coliseum
1974	Miami Dolphins, 24	Minnesota Vikings, 7	Rice Stadium, Houston
1975	Pittsburgh Steelers, 16	Minnesota Vikings, 6	Tulane Stadium, New Orleans
1976	Pittsburgh Steelers, 21	Dallas Cowboys, 17	Orange Bowl, Miami
1977	Oakland Raiders, 32	Minnesota Vikings, 14	Rose Bowl, Pasadena
1978	Dallas Cowboys, 27	Denver Broncos, 10	Superdome, New Orleans
1979	Pittsburgh Steelers, 35	Dallas Cowboys, 31	Orange Bowl, Miami
1980	Pittsburgh Steelers, 31	Los Angeles Rams, 19	Rose Bowl, Pasadena
1981	Oakland Raiders, 27	Philadelphia Eagles, 10	Superdome, New Orleans
1982	San Francisco 49ers, 26	Cincinatti Bengals, 21	Silverdome, Pontiac, Mich.
1983	Washington Redskins, 27	Miami Dolphins, 17	Rose Bowl, Pasadena
1984	Los Angeles Raiders, 38	Washington Redskins, 9	Tampa Stadium

Super Bowl MVPs

1967 Bart Starr, Green Bay
1968 Bart Starr, Green Bay
1969 Joe Namath, N.Y. Jets
1970 Len Dawson, Kansas City
1971 Chuck Howley, Dallas
1972 Roger Staubach, Dallas

1973 Jake Scott, Miami
1974 Larry Csonka, Miami
1975 Franco Harris, Pittsburgh
1976 Lynn Swann, Pittsburgh
1977 Fred Biletnikoff, Oakland
1978 Randy White, Harvey Martin, Dallas

1979 Terry Bradshaw, Pittsburgh
1980 Terry Bradshaw, Pittsburgh
1981 Jim Plunkett, Oakland
1982 Joe Montana, San Francisco
1983 John Riggins, Washington
1984 Marcus Allen, L.A. Raiders

National Football League Champions

Year	East Winner (W.L.T.)	West Winner (W.L.T.)	Playoff
1933	New York Giants (11-3-0)	Chicago Bears (10-2-1)	Chicago Bears 23, New York 21
1934	New York Giants (8-5-0)	Chicago Bears (13-0-0)	New York 30, Chicago Bears 13
1935	New York Giants (9-3-0)	Detroit Lions (7-3-2)	Detroit 26, New York 7
1936	Boston Redskins (7-5-0)	Green Bay Packers (10-1-1)	Green Bay 21, Boston 6
1937	Washington Redskins (8-3-0)	Chicago Bears (9-1-1)	Washington 28, Chicago Bears 21
1938	New York Giants (8-2-1)	Green Bay Packers (8-3-0)	New York 23, Green Bay 17
1939	New York Giants (9-1-1)	Green Bay Packers (9-2-0)	Green Bay 27, New York 0
1940	Washington Redskins (9-2-0)	Chicago Bears (8-3-0)	Chicago Bears 73, Washington 0
1941	New York Giants (8-3-0)	Chicago Bears (10-1-1)(a)	Chicago Bears 37, New York 9
1942	Wash. Redskins (10-1-1)	Chicago Bears (11-0-0)	Washington 14, Chicago Bears 6
1943	Wash. Redskins (6-3-1)(a)	Chicago Bears (8-1-1)	Chicago Bears, 41, Washington 21
1944	New York Giants (8-1-1)	Green Bay Packers (8-2-0)	Green Bay 14, New York 7
1945	Wash. Redskins (8-2-0)	Cleveland Rams (9-1-0)	Cleveland 15, Washington 14
1946	New York Giants (7-3-1)	Chicago Bears (8-2-1)	Chicago Bears 24, New York 14
1947	Philadelphia Eagles (8-4-0)(a)	Chicago Cardinals (9-3-0)	Chicago Cardinals 28, Philadelphia 21
1948	Philadelphia Eagles (9-2-1)	Chicago Cardinals (11-1-0)	Philadelphia 7, Chicago Cardinals 0
1949	Philadelphia Eagles (11-1-0)	Los Angeles Rams (8-2-2)	Philadelphia 14, Los Angeles 0
1950	Cleveland Browns (10-2-0)(a)	Los Angeles Rams (9-3-0)(a)	Cleveland 30, Los Angeles 28
1951	Cleveland Browns (11-1-0)	Los Angeles Rams (8-4-0)	Los Angeles 24, Cleveland 17
1952	Cleveland Browns (8-4-0)	Detroit Lions (9-3-0)(a)	Detroit 17, Cleveland 7
1953	Cleveland Browns (11-1-0)	Detroit Lions (10-2-0)	Detroit 17, Cleveland 16
1954	Cleveland Browns (9-3-0)	Detroit Lions (9-2-1)	Cleveland 56, Detroit 10
1955	Cleveland Browns (9-2-1)	Los Angeles Rams (8-3-1)	Cleveland 38, Los Angeles 14
1956	New York Giants (8-3-1)	Chicago Bears (9-2-1)	New York 47, Chicago Bears 7
1957	Cleveland Browns (9-2-1)	Detroit Lions (8-4-0)(a)	Detroit 59, Cleveland 14
1958	New York Giants (9-3-0)(a)	Baltimore Colts (9-3-0)	Baltimore 23, New York 17(b)
1959	New York Giants (10-2-0)	Baltimore Colts (9-3-0)	Baltimore 31, New York 16
1960	Philadelphia Eagles (10-2-0)	Green Bay Packers (8-4-0)	Philadelphia 17, Green Bay 13
1961	New York Giants (10-3-1)	Green Bay Packers (11-3-0)	Green Bay 37, New York 0
1962	New York Giants (12-2-0)	Green Bay Packers (13-1-0)	Green Bay 16, New York 7
1963	New York Giants (11-3-0)	Chicago Bears (11-1-2)	Chicago 14, New York 10
1964	Cleveland Browns (10-3-1)	Baltimore Colts (12-2-0)	Cleveland 27, Baltimore 0
1965	Cleveland Browns (11-3-0)	Green Bay Packers (10-3-1)(a)	Green Bay 23, Cleveland 12
1966	Dallas Cowboys (10-3-1)	Green Bay Packers (12-2-0)	Green Bay 34, Dallas 27

(a) Won divisional playoff. (b) Won at 8:15 sudden death overtime period.

Year	Conference	Division	Winner (W-L-T)	Playoff
1967	East	Century	Cleveland (9-5-0)	Dallas 52, Cleveland 14
		Capitol	Dallas (9-5-0)	
	West	Central	Green Bay (9-4-1)	Green Bay 28, Los Angeles 7
		Coastal	Los Angeles (11-1-2)(a)	Green Bay 21, Dallas 17
1968	East	Century	Cleveland (10-4-0)	Cleveland 31, Dallas 20
		Capitol	Dallas (12-2-0)	
	West	Central	Minnesota (8-6-0)	Baltimore 24, Minnesota 14
		Coastal	Baltimore (13-1-0)	Baltimore 34, Cleveland 0
1969	East	Century	Cleveland (10-3-1)	Cleveland 38, Dallas 14
		Capitol	Dallas (11-2-1)	
	West	Central	Minnesota (12-2-0)	Minnesota 23, Los Angeles 20
		Coastal	Los Angeles (11-3-0)	Minnesota 27, Cleveland 7
1970	American	Eastern	Baltimore (11-2-1)	Baltimore 17, Cincinnati 0
		Central	Cincinnati (8-6-0)	Oakland 21, Miami 14
		Western	Oakland (8-4-2)	Baltimore 27, Oakland 17
	National	Eastern	Dallas (10-4-0)	Dallas 5, Detroit 0
		Central	Minnesota (12-2-0)	San Francisco 17, Minnesota 14
		Western	San Francisco (10-3-1)	Dallas 17, San Francisco 10
1971	American	Eastern	Miami (10-3-1)	Miami 27, Kansas City 24
		Central	Cleveland (9-5-0)	Baltimore 20, Cleveland 3
		Western	Kansas City (10-3-1)	Miami 21, Baltimore 0
	National	Eastern	Dallas (11-3-0)	Dallas 20, Minnesota 12
		Central	Minnesota (11-3-0)	San Francisco 24, Washington 20
		Western	San Francisco (9-5-0)	Dallas 14, San Francisco 3
1972	American	Eastern	Miami (14-0-0)	Miami 20, Cleveland 14
		Central	Pittsburgh (11-3-0)	Pittsburgh 13, Oakland 7
		Western	Oakland (10-3-1)	Miami 21, Pittsburgh 17
	National	Eastern	Washington (11-3-0)	Washington 16, Green Bay 3
		Central	Green Bay (10-4-0)	Dallas 30, San Francisco 28
		Western	San Francisco (8-5-1)	Washington 26, Dallas 3
1973	American	Eastern	Miami (12-2-0)	Miami 34, Cincinnati 16
		Central	Cincinnati (10-4-0)	Oakland 33, Pittsburgh 14
		Western	Oakland (9-4-1)	Miami 27, Oakland 10
	National	Eastern	Dallas (10-4-0)	Dallas 27, Los Angeles 16
		Central	Minnesota (12-2-0)	Minnesota 27, Washington 20
		Western	Los Angeles (12-2-0)	Minnesota 27, Dallas 10
1974	American	Eastern	Miami (11-3-0)	Oakland 28, Miami 26
		Central	Pittsburgh (10-3-1)	Pittsburgh 32, Buffalo 14
		Western	Oakland (12-2-0)	Pittsburgh 24, Oakland 13
	National	Eastern	St. Louis (10-4-0)	Minnesota 30, St. Louis 14
		Central	Minnesota (10-4-0)	Los Angeles 19, Washington 10
		Western	Los Angeles (10-4-0)	Minnesota 14, Los Angeles 10
1975	American	Eastern	Baltimore (10-4-0)	Pittsburgh 28, Baltimore 10
		Central	Pittsburgh (12-2-0)	Oakland 31, Cincinnati 28
		Western	Oakland (11-3-0)	Pittsburgh 16, Oakland 10
	National	Eastern	St. Louis (11-3-0)	Dallas 17, Minnesota 14

(continued)

(continued)

Year	Conference	Division	Winner (W-L-T)	Playoff
		Central	Minnesota (12-2-0)	Los Angeles 35, St. Louis 23
		Western	Los Angeles (12-2-0)	Dallas 37, Los Angeles 7
1976	American	Eastern	Baltimore (11-3-0)	Pittsburgh 40, Baltimore 14
		Central	Pittsburgh (10-4-0)	Oakland 24, New England 21
		Western	Oakland (13-1-0)	Oakland 24, Pittsburgh 12
	National	Eastern	Dallas (11-3-0)	Minnesota 35, Washington 20
		Central	Minnesota (11-2-1)	Los Angeles 14, Dallas 12
		Western	Los Angeles (10-3-1)	Minnesota 24, Los Angeles 13
1977	American	Eastern	Baltimore (10-4-0)	Oakland 37, Baltimore 31
		Central	Pittsburgh (9-5-0)	Denver 34, Pittsburgh 21
		Western	Denver (12-2-0)	Dallas 37, Chicago 7
	National	Eastern	Dallas (12-2-0)	Minnesota 14, Los Angeles 7
		Central	Minnesota (9-5-0)	Denver 20, Oakland 17
		Western	Los Angeles (10-4-0)	Dallas 23, Minnesota 6
1978	American	Eastern	New England (11-5-0)	Pittsburgh 33, Denver 10
		Central	Pittsburgh (14-2-0)	Houston 31, New England 14
		Western	Denver (10-6-0)	Pittsburgh 34, Houston 5
	National	Eastern	Dallas (12-4-0)	Dallas 27, Atlanta 20
		Central	Minnesota (8-7-1)	Los Angeles 34, Minnesota 10
		Western	Los Angeles (12-4-0)	Dallas 28, Los Angeles 0
1979	American	Eastern	Miami (10-6-0)	Houston 17, San Diego 14
		Central	Pittsburgh (12-4-0)	Pittsburgh 34, Miami 14
		Western	San Diego (12-4-0)	Pittsburgh 27, Houston 13
	National	Eastern	Dallas (11-5-0)	Tampa Bay 24, Philadelphia 17
		Central	Tampa Bay (10-6-0)	Los Angeles 21, Dallas 19
		Western	Los Angeles (9-7-0)	Los Angeles 9, Tampa Bay 0
1980	American	Eastern	Buffalo (11-5-0)	San Diego 20, Buffalo 14
		Central	Cleveland (11-5-0)	Oakland 14, Cleveland 12
		Western	San Diego (11-5-0)	Oakland 34, San Diego 27
	National	Eastern	Philadelphia (12-4-0)	Philadelphia 31, Minnesota 16
		Central	Minnesota (9-7-0)	Dallas 30, Atlanta 27
		Western	Atlanta (12-4-0)	Philadelphia 20, Dallas 7
1981	American	Eastern	Miami (11-4-1)	San Diego 41, Miami 38
		Central	Cincinnati (12-4-0)	Cincinnati 28, Buffalo 21
		Western	San Diego (10-6-0)	Cincinnati 27, San Diego 7
	National	Eastern	Dallas (12-4-0)	Dallas 38, Tampa Bay 0
		Central	Tampa Bay (9-7-0)	San Francisco 38, N.Y. Giants 24
		Western	San Francisco (13-3-0)	San Francisco 28, Dallas 27
1982(1)	American		L.A. Raiders (8-1-0)	
	National		Washington (8-1-0)	

AFC playoffs—Miami 28, New England 13; L.A. Raiders 27, Cleveland 10; N.Y. Jets 44, Cincinnati 17; San Diego 31, Pittsburgh 28; N.Y. Jets 17, L.A. Raiders 14; Miami 34, San Diego 13; Miami 14, N.Y. Jets 0. **NFC playoffs**—Washington 31, Detroit 7; Green Bay 41, St. Louis 16; Dallas 30, Tampa Bay 17; Minnesota 30, Atlanta 24; Washington 21, Minnesota 7; Dallas 37, Green Bay 26; Washington 31, Dallas 17.

Year	Conference	Division	Winner (W-L-T)	Playoff
1983	American	Eastern	Miami (12-4-0)	Seattle 27, Miami 20
		Central	Pittsburgh (10-6-0)	L.A. Raiders 38, Pittsburgh 10
		Western	L.A. Raiders (12-4-0)	L.A. Raiders 30, Seattle 14
	National	Eastern	Washington (14-2-0)	Washington 51, L.A. Rams 7
		Central	Detroit (9-7-0)	San Francisco 24, Detroit 23
		Western	San Francisico (10-6-0)	Washington 24, San Francisco 21

(1) Strike-shortened season

Jim Thorpe Trophy Winners

The winner of the Jim Thorpe Trophy, named after the athletic great, is picked by Murray Olderman of Newspaper Enterprise Assn. in a poll of players from the 28 NFL teams. It goes to the most valuable NFL player and is the oldest and highest professional football award.

Year	Player, team	Year	Player, team
1955	Harlon Hill, Chicago Bears	1969	Roman Gabriel, Los Angeles Rams
1956	Frank Gifford, N.Y. Giants	1970	John Brodie, San Francisco 49ers
1957	John Unitas, Baltimore Colts	1971	Bob Griese, Miami Dolphins
1958	Jim Brown, Cleveland Browns	1972	Larry Brown, Washington Redskins
1959	Charley Conerly, N.Y. Giants	1973	O.J. Simpson, Buffalo Bills
1960	Norm Van Brocklin, Philadelphia Eagles	1974	Ken Stabler, Oakland Raiders
1961	Y.A. Tittle, N.Y. Giants	1975	Fran Tarkenton, Minnesota Vikings
1962	Jim Taylor, Green Bay Packers	1976	Bert Jones, Baltimore Colts
1963	(tie) Jim Brown, Cleveland Browns,	1977	Walter Payton, Chicago Bears
	and Y.A. Tittle, N.Y. Giants	1978	Earl Campbell, Houston Oilers
1964	Lenny Moore, Baltimore Colts	1979	Earl Campbell, Houston Oilers
1965	Jim Brown, Cleveland Browns	1980	Earl Campbell, Houston Oilers
1966	Bart Starr, Green Bay Packers	1981	Ken Anderson, Cincinnati Bengals
1967	John Unitas, Baltimore Colts	1982	Dan Fouts, San Diego Chargers
1968	Earl Morrall, Baltimore Colts	1983	Joe Theismann, Washington Redskins

George Halas Trophy Winners

The Halas Trophy, named after football coach George Halas, is awarded annually to the outstanding defensive player in football in a poll conducted by Murray Olderman of Newspaper Enterprise Assn.

Year	Player, team	Year	Player, team	Year	Player, team
1966	Larry Wilson, St. Louis	1972	Joe Greene, Pittsburgh	1978	Randy Gradishar, Denver
1967	Deacon Jones, Los Angeles	1973	Alan Page, Minnesota	1979	Lee Roy Selmon, Tampa Bay
1968	Deacon Jones, Los Angeles	1974	Joe Greene, Pittsburgh	1980	Lester Hayes, Oakland
1969	Dick Butkus, Chicago	1975	Curley Culp, Houston	1981	Joe Klecko, N.Y. Jets
1970	Dick Butkus, Chicago	1976	Jerry Sherk, Cleveland	1982	Mark Gastineau, N.Y. Jets
1971	Carl Eller, Minnesota	1977	Harvey Martin, Dallas	1983	Jack Lambert, Pittsburgh

National Football Conference Leaders

(National Football League prior to 1970)

Passing

Player, team	Atts	Com	YG	TD	Year
Sonny Jurgensen, Washington	508	288	3,747	31	1967
Earl Morrall, Baltimore	317	182	2,909	26	1968
Sonny Jurgensen, Washington	422	274	3,102	22	1969
John Brodie, San Francisco	378	223	2,941	24	1970
Roger Staubach, Dallas	211	126	1,882	15	1971
Norm Snead, N.Y. Giants	325	196	2,307	17	1972
Roger Staubach, Dallas	286	179	2,428	23	1973
Sonny Jurgensen, Washington	167	107	1,185	11	1974
Fran Tarkenton, Minnesota	425	273	2,294	25	1975
James Harris, Los Angeles	158	91	1,460	8	1976
Roger Staubach, Dallas	361	210	2,620	18	1977
Roger Staubach, Dallas	413	231	3,190	25	1978
Roger Staubach, Dallas	461	267	3,586	27	1979
Ron Jaworski, Philadelphia	451	257	3,529	27	1980
Joe Montana, San Francisco	488	311	3,565	19	1981
Joe Thiesmann, Washington	252	161	2,033	13	1982
Steve Bartkowski, Atlanta	423	274	3,167	22	1983

Pass-Receiving

Player, team	Ct	YG	TD	Year
Charlie Taylor, Washington	70	990	9	1967
Clifton McNeil, San Francisco	71	944	7	1968
Dan Abramowicz, New Orleans	73	1,015	7	1969
Dick Gordon, Chicago	71	1,026	13	1970
Bob Tucker, Giants	59	791	4	1971
Harold Jackson, Philadelphia	62	1,048	4	1972
Harold Carmichael, Philadelphia	67	1,116	9	1973
Charles Young, Philadelphia	63	696	3	1974
Chuck Foreman, Minnesota	73	691	9	1975
Drew Pearson, Dallas	58	806	6	1976
Ahmad Rashad, Minnesota	51	681	2	1977
Rickey Young, Minnesota	88	704	5	1978
Ahmad Rashad, Minnesota	80	1,156	9	1979
Earl Cooper, San Francisco	83	567	4	1980
Dwight Clark, San Francisco	85	1,105	4	1981
Dwight Clark, San Francisco	60	913	5	1982
Roy Green, St. Louis	78	1,227	14	1983
Charlie Brown, Washington	78	1,225	8	
Earnest Gray, N.Y. Giants	78	1,139	5	

Scoring

Player, team	TD	PAT	FG	Pts	Year
Jim Bakken, St. Louis	0	36	27	117	1967
Leroy Kelly, Cleveland	20	0	0	120	1968
Fred Cox, Minnesota	0	43	26	121	1969
Fred Cox, Minnesota	0	35	30	125	1970
Curt Knight, Washington	0	27	29	114	1971
Chester Marcol, Green Bay	0	29	33	128	1972
David Ray, Los Angeles	0	40	30	130	1973
Chester Marcol, Green Bay	0	19	25	94	1974
Chuck Foreman, Minnesota	22	0	0	132	1975
Mark Mosoley, Washington	0	31	22	97	1976
Walter Payton, Chicago	16	0	0	96	1977
Frank Corrall, Los Angeles	0	31	29	118	1978
Mark Moseley, Washington	0	39	25	114	1979
Ed Murray, Detroit	0	35	27	116	1980
Ed Murray, Detroit	0	46	25	121	1981
Wendell Tyler, L.A. Rams	13	0	0	78	1982
Mark Moseley, Washington	0	62	33	161	1983

Rushing

Player, team	Yds	Atts	TD	Year
Leroy Kelly, Cleveland	1,205	235	11	1967
Leroy Kelly, Cleveland	1,239	248	16	1968
Gale Sayers, Chicago	1,032	236	8	1969
Larry Brown, Washington	1,125	237	5	1970
John Brockington, Green Bay	1,105	216	4	1971
Larry Brown, Washington	1,216	285	8	1972
John Brockington, Green Bay	1,144	265	3	1973
Larry McCutcheon, Los Angeles	1,109	236	3	1974
Jim Otis, St. Louis	1,076	269	5	1975
Walter Payton, Chicago	1,390	311	13	1976
Walter Payton, Chicago	1,852	339	14	1977
Walter Payton, Chicago	1,395	333	11	1978
Walter Payton, Chicago	1,610	369	14	1979
Walter Payton, Chicago	1,460	317	15	1980
George Rogers, New Orleans	1,674	378	13	1981
Tony Dorsett, Dallas	745	177	5	1982
Eric Dickerson, L.A. Rams	1,808	390	18	1983

American Football Conference Leaders

(American Football League prior to 1970)

Passing

Player, team	Atts	Com	YG	TD	Year
Daryle Lamonica, Oakland	425	220	3,228	30	1967
Len Dawson, Kansas City	224	131	2,109	17	1968
Greg Cook, Cincinnati	197	106	1,845	15	1969
Daryle Lamonica, Oakland	356	179	2,516	22	1970
Bob Griese, Miami	263	145	2,089	19	1971
Earl Morrall, Miami	150	83	1,360	11	1972
Ken Stabler, Oakland	260	163	1,997	14	1973
Ken Anderson, Cincinnati	328	213	2,667	18	1974
Ken Anderson, Cincinnati	377	228	3,169	21	1975
Ken Stabler, Oakland	291	194	2,737	27	1976
Bob Griese, Miami	307	180	2,252	22	1977
Terry Bradshaw, Pittsburgh	368	207	2,915	28	1978
Dan Fouts, San Diego	530	332	4,082	24	1979
Brian Sipe, Cleveland	554	337	4,132	30	1980
Ken Anderson, Cincinnati	479	300	3,754	29	1981
Ken Anderson, Cincinnati	309	218	2,495	12	1982
Dan Marino, Miami	296	173	2,210	20	1983

Pass-Receiving

Player, team	Ct	YG	TD	Year
George Sauer, N.Y. Jets	75	1,312	10	1967
Lance Alworth, San Diego	68	1,312	10	1968
Lance Alworth, San Diego	64	1,003	4	1969
Marlin Briscoe, Buffalo	57	1,036	8	1970
Fred Biletnikoff, Oakland	61	929	9	1971
Fred Biletnikoff, Oakland	58	802	7	1972
Fred Willis, Houston	57	371	1	1973
Lydell Mitchell, Baltimore	72	544	2	1974
Reggie Rucker, Cleveland	60	770	3	1975
Lydell Mitchell, Baltimore	60	554	4	
MacArthur Lane, Kansas City	66	686	1	1976
Lydell Mitchell, Baltimore	71	620	4	1977
Steve Largent, Seattle	71	1,168	8	1978
Joe Washington, Baltimore	82	750	3	1979
Kellen Winslow, San Diego	89	1,290	9	1980
Kellen Winslow, San Diego	88	1,075	10	1981
Kellen Winslow, San Diego	54	721	6	1982
Todd Christensen, L.A. Raiders	92	1,247	12	1983

Scoring

Player, team	TD	PAT	FG	Pts	Year
George Blanda, Oakland	0	56	20	116	1966
Jim Turner, N.Y. Jets	0	43	34	145	1968
Jim Turner, N.Y. Jets	0	33	32	129	1969
Jan Stenerud, Kansas City	0	26	30	116	1970
Garo Yepremian, Miami	0	33	28	117	1971
Bobby Howfield, N.Y. Jets	0	40	27	121	1972
Roy Gerela, Pittsburgh	0	36	29	123	1973
Roy Gerela, Pittsburgh	0	33	20	93	1974
O.J. Simpson, Buffalo	23	0	0	138	1975
Toni Linhart, Baltimore	0	49	20	109	1976
Errol Mann, Oakland	0	39	20	99	1977
Pat Leahy, N.Y. Jets	0	41	22	107	1978
John Smith, New England	0	46	23	115	1979
John Smith, New England	0	51	26	129	1980
Jim Breech, Cincinnati	0	49	22	115	1981
Marcus Allen, L.A. Raiders	14	0	0	84	1982
Gary Anderson, Pittsburgh	0	38	27	119	1983

Rushing

Player, team	Yds	Atts	TD	Year
Jim Nance, Boston	1,216	269	7	1966
Paul Robinson, Cincinnati	1,023	238	8	1968
Dick Post, San Diego	873	182	6	1969
Floyd Little, Denver	901	209	3	1970
Floyd Little, Denver	1,133	284	6	1971
O.J. Simpson, Buffalo	1,251	292	6	1972
O.J. Simpson, Buffalo	2,003	332	12	1973
Otis Armstrong, Denver	1,407	263	9	1974
O.J. Simpson, Buffalo	1,817	329	16	1975
O.J. Simpson, Buffalo	1,503	290	8	1976
Mark van Eeghen, Oakland	1,273	324	7	1977
Earl Campbell, Houston	1,450	302	13	1978
Earl Campbell, Houston	1,697	368	19	1979
Earl Campbell, Houston	1,934	373	13	1980
Earl Campbell, Houston	1,376	361	10	1981
Freeman McNeil, N.Y. Jets	786	151	6	1982
Curt Warner, Seattle	1,446	335	13	1983

Bert Bell Memorial Trophy Winners

The Bert Bell Memorial Trophy. named after the former NFL commissioner. is awarded annually to the outstanding rookies in a poll conducted by Murray Olderman of Newspaper Enterprise Assn.

1964	Charlie Taylor. Washington. WR	1974	Don Woods, San Diego. RB
1965	Gale Sayers, Chicago. RB	1975	AFC: Robert Brazile. Houston. LB
1966	Tommy Nobis, Atlanta. LB		NFC: Steve Bartkowski. Atlanta. QB
1967	Mel Farr, Detroit. RB	1976	AFC: Mike Haynes, New England. CB
1968	Earl McCullouch, Detroit. WR		NFC: Sammy White. Minnesota. WR
1969	Calvin Hill, Dallas. RB	1977	Tony Dorsett, Dallas. RB
1970	Raymond Chester, Oakland. TE	1978	Earl Campbell, Houston. RB
1971	AFC: Jim Plunkett, New England. QB	1979	Ottis Anderson, St. Louis. RB
	NFC: John Brockington. Green Bay. RB	1980	Billy Sims, Detroit. RB
1972	AFC: Franco Harris, Pittsburgh. RB	1981	Lawrence Taylor, N.Y. Giants. LB
	NFC: Willie Buchanon, Green Bay. DB	1982	Marcus Allen, L.A. Raiders, RB
1973	AFC: Boobie Clark, Cincinnati, RB	1983	Eric Dickerson, L.A. Rams, RB
	NFC: Chuck Foreman, Minnesota. RB		

1983 NFL Individual Leaders
National Football Conference

Passing[1]

	Att	Comp	Pct Comp	Yards	Avg Gain	TD	Pct TD	Int	Rating Points
Bartkowski, Atlanta	432	274	63.4	3167	7.33	22	5.1	5	97.6
Theismann, Washington	459	276	60.1	3714	8.09	29	6.3	11	97.0
Montana, San Francisco	515	332	64.5	3910	7.59	26	5.0	12	94.6
Lomax, St. Louis	354	209	59.0	2636	7.45	24	6.8	11	92.0
Dickey, Green Bay	484	289	59.7	4458	9.21	32	6.6	29	87.3
D. White, Dallas	533	334	62.7	3980	7.47	29	5.4	23	85.6
McMahon, Chicago	295	175	59.3	2184	7.40	12	4.1	13	77.6
Ferragamo, L.A. Rams	464	274	59.1	3276	7.06	22	4.7	23	75.9
Jaworski, Philadelphia	446	235	52.7	3315	7.43	20	4.5	18	75.1
J. Thompson, Tampa Bay	423	249	58.9	2906	6.87	18	4.3	21	73.3
Dils, Minnesota	444	239	53.8	2840	6.40	11	2.5	16	66.8
Hipple, Detroit	387	204	52.7	2577	6.66	12	3.1	18	64.7
Stabler, New Orleans	311	176	56.6	1988	6.39	9	2.9	18	61.4
Brunner, N.Y. Giants	386	190	49.2	2516	6.52	9	2.3	22	54.3

Rushing

	Att	Yds	Avg	TD
Dickerson, L.A. Rams	390	1808	4.6	18
Andrews, Atlanta	331	1567	4.7	7
Payton, Chicago	314	1421	4.5	6
Riggins, Washington	375	1347	3.6	24
Dorsett, Dallas	289	1321	4.6	8
Anderson, St. Louis	296	1270	4.3	5
G. Rogers, New Orleans	256	1144	4.5	5
Sims, Detroit	220	1040	4.7	7
Woolfolk, N.Y. Giants	246	857	3.5	4
Tyler, San Francisco	176	856	4.9	4

Receiving

	No	Yds	Avg	TD
Green, St. Louis	78	1227	15.7	14
Brown, Washington	78	1225	15.7	8
Gray, N.Y. Giants	78	1139	14.6	5
Springs, Dallas	73	589	8.1	1
D. Clark, San Francisco	70	840	12.0	8
Quick, Philadelphia	69	1409	20.4	13
B. Johnson, Atlanta	64	709	11.1	4
Andrews, Atlanta	59	609	10.3	4
Lofton, Green Bay	58	1300	22.4	8
Jefferson, Green Bay	57	830	14.6	7

Scoring-Touchdowns

	TD	Rush	Pass	Pts
Riggins, Washington	24	24	0	144
Dickerson, L.A. Rams	20	18	2	120
Green, St. Louis	14	0	14	84
Quick, Philadelphia	13	0	13	78
Craig, San Francisco	12	8	4	72
Andrews, Atlanta	11	7	4	66
T. Brown, Minnesota	11	10	1	66
Coffman, Green Bay	11	0	11	66
W. Wilson, New Orleans	11	9	2	66

Scoring-Kicking

	XP	XPA	FG	FGA	Pts
Moseley, Washington	62	63	33	47	161
Haji-Sheikh, N.Y. Giants	22	23	35	42	127
Wersching, San Francisco	51	51	25	30	126
Septien, Dallas	57	59	22	27	123
Stenerud, Green Bay	52	52	21	26	115
Murray, Detroit	38	38	25	32	113
Ricardo, Minnesota	33	34	25	33	108
Luckhurst, Atlanta	43	45	17	22	94
Andersen, New Orleans	37	38	18	23	91
O'Donoghue, St. Louis	45	47	15	29	90

Interceptions

	No	Yds	TD
Murphy, Washington	9	127	0
Reece, Tampa Bay	8	103	0
Washington, St. Louis	8	92	0
Wright, San Francisco	7	164	2
Poe, New Orleans	7	146	1
Frazier, Chicago	7	135	1
McNorton, Detroit	7	30	0

Kickoff Returns

	No	Yds	Avg	TD
Nelson, Minnesota	18	445	24.7	0
Morton, Tampa Bay	30	689	23.0	0
Nelms, Washington	35	802	22.9	0
Bright, N.Y. Giants	21	475	22.6	0
Redwine, Minnesota	38	838	22.1	0
Duckett, New Orleans	33	719	21.8	0
Mitchell, St. Louis	36	778	21.6	0

Punt Returns

	No	Yds	Avg	TD
Ellard, L.A. Rams	16	217	13.6	1
McLemore, San Francisco	31	331	10.7	1
B. Johnson, Atlanta	46	489	10.6	1
Jenkins, Detroit	23	230	10.0	0
McKinnon, Chicago	34	316	9.3	1

Punting

	No	Yds	Avg
Garcia, Tampa Bay	95	4008	42.2
Runager, Philadelphia	59	2459	41.7
Scribner, Green Bay	69	2869	41.6
Coleman, Minnesota	91	3780	41.5
Birdsong, St. Louis	85	3529	41.5

American Football Conference

Passing[1]

	Att	Comp	Pct Comp	Yards	Avg Gain	TD	Pct TD	Int	Rating Points
Marino, Miami	299	173	58.4	2210	7.47	20	6.8	6	96.0
Krieg, Seattle	243	147	60.5	2139	8.80	18	7.4	11	95.0
Fouts, San Diego	340	215	63.2	2975	8.75	20	5.9	15	92.5
Anderson, Cincinnati	297	198	66.7	2329	7.84	12	4.0	13	85.5
Plunkett, L.A. Raiders	379	230	60.7	2935	7.74	20	5.3	18	82.7
Grogan, New England	303	168	55.4	2411	7.96	15	5.0	12	81.4
Kenney, Kansas City	603	346	57.4	4348	7.21	24	4.0	18	80.8
DeBerg, Denver	215	119	55.3	1617	7.52	9	4.2	7	79.9
Sipe, Cleveland	496	291	58.7	3566	7.19	26	5.2	23	79.1
Todd, N.Y. Jets	518	308	59.5	3478	6.71	18	3.5	26	70.3
Ferguson, Buffalo	508	281	55.3	2995	5.90	26	5.1	25	69.3
Zorn, Seattle	205	103	50.2	1166	5.69	7	3.4	7	64.8
Pagel, Baltimore	328	163	49.7	2353	7.17	12	3.7	17	64.0
Luck, Houston	217	124	57.1	1375	6.34	8	3.7	13	63.4
Stoudt, Pittsburgh	381	197	51.7	2553	6.70	12	3.1	21	60.6
Luther, San Diego	287	151	52.6	1875	6.53	7	2.4	17	56.6
Elway, Denver	259	123	47.5	1663	6.42	7	2.7	14	54.9

(1) At least 192 passes needed to qualify. Points based on percentage of completions, TD passes, interceptions, and average yards.

Rushing

	Att	Yds	Avg	TD
Warner, Seattle	335	1449	4.3	13
Campbell, Houston	322	1301	4.0	12
Pruitt, Cleveland	293	1184	4.0	10
Cribbs, Buffalo	263	1131	4.3	3
Dickey, Baltimore	254	1122	4.4	4
Collins, New England	219	1049	4.8	10
Allen, L.A. Raiders	266	1014	3.8	9
F. Harris, Pittsburgh	279	1007	3.6	5
Muncie, San Diego	235	886	3.8	12
McMillan, Baltimore	198	802	4.1	5

Receiving

	No	Yds	Avg	TD
Christensen, L.A. Raiders	92	1247	13.6	12
Newsome, Cleveland	89	970	10.9	6
Winslow, San Diego	88	1172	13.3	8
Smith, Houston	83	1176	14.2	6
Carson, Kansas City	80	1351	16.9	7
Largent, Seattle	72	1074	14.9	11
Allen, L.A. Raiders	68	590	8.7	2
Collinsworth, Cincinnati	66	1126	17.1	5
Joiner, San Diego	65	960	14.8	3
W. Walker, N.Y. Jets	61	868	14.2	7

Scoring-Touchdowns

	TD	Rush	Pass	Pts
Johnson, Cincinnati	14	14	0	84
Warner, Seattle	14	13	1	84
Muncie, San Diego	13	12	1	78
Allen, L.A. Raiders	12(1)	9	2	72
Campbell, Houston	12	12	0	72
Christensen, L.A. Raiders	12	0	12	72
Pruitt, Cleveland	12	10	2	72
Largent, Seattle	11	0	11	66

(1) One by kickoff return

Scoring-Kicking

	XP	XPA	FG	FGA	Pts
Anderson, Pittsburgh	38	39	27	31	119
Lowery, Kansas City	44	45	24	30	116
Bahr, L.A. Raiders	51	53	21	27	114
Allegre, Baltimore	22	24	30	35	112
N. Johnson, Seattle	49	50	18	25	103
Bahr, Cleveland	38	40	21	24	101
von Schamann, Miami	45	48	18	27	99
Karlis, Denver	33	34	21	25	96
Benirschke, San Diego	43	45	15	24	88
Breech, Cincinnati	39	41	16	23	87

Interceptions

	No	Yds	TD
Riley, Cincinnati	8	89	2
McElroy, L.A. Raiders	8	68	0
Easley, Seattle	7	106	0
Cherry, Kansas City	7	100	0
Mehl, N.Y. Jets	7	57	1
Walters, San Diego	7	55	0
Sanford, New England	7	24	0

Kickoff Returns

	No	Yds	Avg	TD
Walker, Miami	36	962	26.7	0
S. Brown, Houston	31	795	25.6	1
K. Williams, Baltimore	20	490	24.5	0
Dixon, Seattle	51	1171	23.0	1
Springs, N.Y. Jets	16	364	22.8	0
V. Williams, Buffalo	22	494	22.5	0
Brown, N.Y. Jets	29	645	22.2	0

Punt Returns

	No	Yds	Avg	TD
Springs, N.Y. Jets	23	287	12.5	1
Pruitt, L.A. Raiders	58	666	11.5	1
Johns, Seattle	28	316	11.3	1
Thomas, Denver	33	368	11.2	1
R. Smith, New England	38	398	10.5	0

Punting

	No	Yds	Avg
Stark, Baltimore	91	4124	45.3
Camarillo, New England	81	3615	44.6
Buford, San Diego	63	2763	43.9
Roby, Miami	74	3189	43.1
Guy, L.A. Raiders	78	3336	42.8

American Football League

Year	Eastern Division	Western Division	Playoff
1960	Houston Oilers (10-4-0)	L.A. Chargers (10-4-0)	Houston 24, Los Angeles 16
1961	Houston Oilers (10-3-1)	San Diego Chargers (12-2-0)	Houston 10, San Diego 3
1962	Houston Oilers (11-3-0)	Dallas Texans (11-3-0)	Dallas 20, Houston 17(b)
1963	Boston Patriots (8-6-1)(a)	San Diego Chargers (11-3-0)	San Diego 51, Boston 10
1964	Buffalo Bills (12-2-0)	San Diego Chargers (8-5-1)	Buffalo 20, San Diego 7
1965	Buffalo Bills (10-3-1)	San Diego Chargers (9-2-3)	Buffalo 23, San Diego 0
1966	Buffalo Bills (9-4-1)	Kansas City Chiefs (11-2-1)	Kansas City 31, Buffalo 7
1967	Houston Oilers (9-4-1)	Oakland Raiders (13-1-0)	Oakland 40, Houston 7
1968	New York Jets (11-3-0)	Oakland Raiders (12-2-0)(a)	New York 27, Oakland 23
1969	New York Jets (10-4-0)	Oakland Raiders (12-1-1)	Kansas City 17, Oakland 7(c)

(a) won divisional playoff (b) won at 2:45 of second overtime. (c) Kansas City defeated Jets to make playoffs.

All-Time Football Records
NFL, AFL, and All-American Football Conference
(at start of 1984 season)

Leading Lifetime Rushers

Player	League	Yrs	Att	Yards	Avg	Player	League	Yrs	Att	Yards	Avg
Jim Brown	NFL	9	2,359	12,312	5.2	Leroy Kelly	NFL	10	1,727	7,274	4.2
Franco Harris	NFL	12	2,881	11,950	4.1	John Henry Johnson	NFL-AFL	13	1,571	6,803	4.3
Walter Payton	NFL	9	2,666	11,654	4.4	Chuck Muncie	NFL	8	1,547	6,651	4.3
O.J. Simpson	AFL-NFL	11	2,404	11,236	4.7	Mark van Eeghen	NFL	10	1,652	6,651	4.0
Joe Perry	AAFC-NFL	16	1,929	9,723	5.0	Lawrence McCutcheon	NFL	10	1,521	6,578	4.3
John Riggins	NFL	12	2,413	9,436	3.9	Lydell Mitchell	NFL	9	1,675	6,534	3.9
Jim Taylor	NFL	10	1,941	8,597	4.4	Floyd Little	AFL-NFL	9	1,641	6,323	3.8
Tony Dorsett	NFL	7	1,834	8,336	4.5	Don Perkins	NFL	8	1,500	6,217	4.1
Earl Campbell	NFL	6	1,883	8,296	4.4	Ottis Anderson	NFL	5	1,401	6,190	4.4
Larry Csonka	AFL-NFL	11	1,891	8,081	4.3	Ken Willard	NFL	10	1,622	6,105	3.8

Most Yards Gained, Season — 2,003, O.J. Simpson, Buffalo Bills, 1973.
Most Yards Gained, Game — 275, Walter Payton, Chicago Bears vs. Minnesota Vikings, Nov. 20, 1977.
Most Games, 100 Yards or more, Season — 11, O.J. Simpson, Buffalo Bills, 1973; Earl Campbell, Houston Oilers, 1979.
Most Games, 100 Yards or more, Career — 58, Jim Brown, Cleveland Browns, 1957-1965.
Most Games, 200 Yards or more, Career — 6, O.J. Simpson, Buffalo Bills, 1969-1977; San Francisco 49ers, 1978-1979.
Most Touchdowns Rushing, Career — 106, Jim Brown, Cleveland Browns, 1957-1965.
Most Touchdowns Rushing, Season — 24, John Riggins, Washington Redskins, 1983.
Most Touchdowns Rushing, Game — 6, Ernie Nevers, Chicago Cardinals vs. Chicago Bears, Nov. 8, 1929.
Most Rushing Attempts, Season — 390, Eric Dickerson, Los Angeles Rams, 1983.
Most Rushing Attempts, Game — 43, Butch Woolfolk, N.Y. Giants vs. Philadelphia, Nov. 20, 1983.
Longest run from Scrimmage — 99 yds., Tony Dorsett, Dallas vs. Minnesota, Jan. 3, 1983 (scored touchdown).

Leading Lifetime Passers
(Minimum 1,500 attempts)

Player	League	Yrs	Att	Comp	Yds	Pts*	Player	League	Yrs	Att	Comp	Yds	Pts*
Joe Montana	NFL	5	1,645	1,045	11,979	89.8	Johnny Unitas	NFL	18	5,186	2,830	40,239	78.2
Otto Graham	AAFC-NFL	10	2,626	1,464	23,584	86.8	Bert Jones	NFL	10	2,551	1,430	18,190	78.2
Danny White	NFL	8	1,710	1,029	13,174	84.2	Frank Ryan	NFL	13	2,133	1,090	16,042	77.7
Roger Staubach	NFL	11	2,958	1,685	22,700	83.5	Joe Theismann	NFL	10	2,824	1,594	20,041	77.4
Sonny Jurgensen	NFL	18	4,262	2,433	32,224	82.8	Bob Griese	AFL-NFL	14	3,429	1,926	25,092	77.3
Len Dawson	NFL-AFL	19	3,741	2,136	28,711	82.6	Ken Stabler	AFL-NFL	14	3,723	2,237	27,599	76.2
Ken Anderson	NFL	13	4,145	2,452	30,386	82.1	Norm Van Brocklin	NFL	12	2,895	1,553	23,611	75.3
Dan Fouts	NFL	11	3,873	2,268	30,114	81.1	Sid Luckman	NFL	12	1,744	904	14,686	75.0
Fran Tarkenton	NFL	18	6,467	3,686	47,003	80.5	Brian Sipe	NFL	10	3,439	1,944	23,713	75.0
Bart Starr	NFL	16	3,149	1,808	24,718	80.3	Don Meredith	NFL	9	2,308	1,170	17,199	74.7

*Rating points based on performances in the following categories: Percentage of completions, percentage of touchdown passes, percentage of interceptions, and average gain per pass attempt.

Most Yards Gained, Season — 4,802, Dan Fouts, San Diego Chargers, 1981.
Most Yards Gained, Game — 554, Norm Van Brocklin, Los Angeles Rams vs. New York Yankees, Sept. 18, 1951 (27 completions in 41 attempts).
Most Games, 300 or More Yards Passing, Career — 35, Dan Fouts, San Diego Chargers, 1973-83.
Most Touchdowns Passing, Career — 342, Fran Tarkenton, Minnesota Vikings, 1961-65; N.Y. Giants, 1967-71; Minnesota Vikings, 1972-78.
Most Touchdown Passing, Season — 36, George Blanda, Houston Oilers, 1961 and Y.A. Tittle, N.Y. Giants, 1963.
Most Touchdown Passing, Game — 7, Sid Luckman, Chicago Bears vs. New York Giants, Nov. 14, 1943; Adrian Burk, Philadelphia Eagles vs. Washington Redskins, Oct. 17, 1954; George Blanda, Houston Oilers vs. New York Titans, Nov. 19, 1961; Y.A. Tittle, New York Giants vs. Washington Redskins, Oct. 28, 1962; Joe Kapp, Minnesota Vikings vs. Baltimore Colts, Sept. 28, 1969.
Most Passing Attempts, Season — 609, Dan Fouts, San Diego Chargers, 1981.
Most Passing Attempts, Game — 68, George Blanda, Houston Oilers vs. Buffalo Bills, Nov. 1, 1964 (37 completions).
Most Passes Completed, Season — 360, Dan Fouts, San Diego Chargers, 1981.
Most Passes Completed, Game — 42, Richard Todd, N.Y. Jets vs. San Francisco 49ers, Sept. 21, 1980.
Most Consecutive Passes Completed — 20, Ken Anderson, Cincinnati vs. Houston, Jan. 2, 1983.

Leading Lifetime Receivers

Player	League	Yrs	No	Yds	Avg	Player	League	Yrs	No	Yds	Avg
Charley Taylor	NFL	13	649	9,110	14.0	Billy Howton	NFL	12	503	8,459	16.8
Don Maynard	AFL-NFL	15	633	11,834	18.7	Tommy McDonald	NFL	12	495	8,410	17.0
Ray Berry	NFL	13	631	9,275	14.7	Ahmad Rashad	NFL	10	495	6,831	13.8
Charlie Joiner	AFL-NFL	15	596	9,981	16.7	Drew Pearson	NFL	11	489	7,822	16.0
Harold Carmichael	NFL	13	589	8,978	15.2	Don Hutson	NFL	11	488	7,991	16.4
Fred Biletnikoff	AFL-NFL	14	589	8,974	15.2	Jackie Smith	NFL	16	488	7,991	16.4
Harold Jackson	NFL	16	579	10,372	17.9	Art Powell	AFL-NFL	10	479	8,046	16.8
Lionel Taylor	AFL	10	567	7,195	12.7	Cliff Branch	NFL	11	474	8,284	17.5
Lance Alworth	AFL-NFL	11	542	10,266	18.9	Boyd Dowler	NFL	12	474	7,270	15.4
Bobby Mitchell	NFL	11	521	7,954	15.3	Steve Largent	NFL	8	471	7,608	16.2

Most Yards Gained, Season — 1,746, Charley Hennigan, Houston Oilers, 1961.
Most Yards Gained, Game — 303, Jim Benton, Cleveland Rams vs. Detroit Lions, Nov. 22, 1945 (10 receptions).
Most Pass Receptions, Season — 101, Charley Hennigan, Houston Oilers, 1964.
Most Pass Receptions, Game — 18, Tom Fears, Los Angeles Rams vs. Green Bay Packers, Dec. 3, 1950 (189 yards).
Most Consecutive Games, Pass Receptions — 127, Harold Carmichael, Philadelphia Eagles, 1972-1980.
Most Touchdown Passes, Career — 99, Don Hutson, Green Bay Packers, 1935-1945.
Most Touchdown Passes, Season — 17, Don Hutson, Green Bay Packers, 1942; Elroy Hirsch, Los Angeles Rams, 1951; Bill Groman, Houston Oilers, 1961.
Most Touchdown Passes, Game — 5, Bob Shaw, Chicago Cardinals vs. Baltimore Colts, Oct. 2, 1950; Kellen Winslow, San Diego vs. Oakland, Nov. 22, 1981.

Leading Lifetime Scorers

Player	League	Yrs	TD	PAT	FG	Total	Player	League	Yrs	TD	PAT	FG	Total
George Blanda	NFL-AFL	26	9	943	335	2,002	Sam Baker	NFL	15	2	428	179	977
Lou Groza	AAFC-NFL	21	1	810	264	1,608	Lou Michaels	NFL	13	1	386	187	955*
Jan Stenerud	AFL-NFL	17	0	509	338	1,523	Roy Gerela	AFL-NFL	11	0	351	184	903
Jim Turner	AFL-NFL	16	1	521	304	1,439	Bobby Walston	NFL	12	46	365	80	881
Jim Bakken	NFL	17	0	534	282	1,380	Pete Gogolak	AFL-NFL	10	0	344	173	863
Fred Cox	NFL	15	0	519	282	1,365	Errol Mann	NFL	11	0	315	177	846
Gino Cappelletti	AFL	11	42	350	176	1,130	Don Hutson	NFL	11	105	172	7	823
Mark Moseley	NFL	13	0	378	242	1,104	Paul Hornung	NFL	9	62	190	66	760
Don Cockroft	NFL	13	0	432	216	1,080	Tony Fritsch	NFL	11	0	287	157	758
Garo Yepremian	AFL-NFL	14	0	444	210	1,074	*Includes safety.						
Bruce Gossett	NFL	11	0	374	219	1,031							

Most Points, Season — 176, Paul Hornung, Green Bay Packers, 1960 (15 TD's, 41 PAT's, 15 FG's).
Most Points, Game — 40, Ernie Nevers, Chicago Cardinals vs. Chicago Bears, Nov. 28, 1929 (6 TD's, 4 PAT's).
Most Touchdowns, Season — 24, John Riggins, Washington Redskins, 1984 (24 rushing).
Most Touchdowns, Game — 6, Ernie Nevers, Chicago Cardinals vs. Chicago Bears, Nov. 28, 1929 (6 rushing); Dub Jones, Cleveland Browns vs. Chicago Bears, Nov. 25, 1951 (4 rushing, 2 pass receptions); Gale Sayers, Chicago Bears vs. San Francisco 49ers, Dec. 12, 1965 (4 rushing, 1 pass reception, 1 punt return).
Most Points After Touchdown, Season — 64, George Blanda, Houston Oilers, 1961 (65 attempts).
Most Consecutive Points After Touchdown — 234, Tommy Davis, San Francisco 49ers, 1959-1969.
Most Field Goals, Game — 7, Jim Bakken, St. Louis Cardinals vs. Pittsburgh Steelers, Sept. 24, 1967.
Most Field Goals, Season — 35, Ali Haji-Sheikh, N.Y. Giants, 1983.
Most Field Goals Attempted, Season — 49, Bruce Gossett, Los Angeles Rams, 1966; Curt Knight, Washington Redskins, 1971.
Most Field Goals Attempted, Game — 9, Jim Bakken, St. Louis Cardinals vs. Pittsburgh Steelers, Sept. 24, 1967 (7 successful).
Most Consecutive Field Goals — 23, Mark Moseley, Washington Redskins, 1981-1982.
Most Consecutive Games, Field Goal — 31, Fred Cox, Minnesota Vikings, 1968-1970.
Longest Field Goal — 63 yds., Tom Dempsey, New Orleans Saints vs. Detroit Lions, Nov. 8, 1970.
Highest Field Goal Completion Percentage, Season (14 attempts) — 95.24 Mark Moseley, Washington Redskins, 1982 (20 FG's in 21 attempts).

Pass Interceptions

Most Passes Had Intercepted, Game — 8, Jim Hardy, Chicago Cardinals vs. Philadelphia Eagles, Sept. 24, 1950 (39 attempts).
Most Passes Had Intercepted, Season — 42, George Blanda, Houston Oilers, 1962 (418 attempts).
Most Passes Had Intercepted, Career — 277, George Blanda, Chicago Bears, 1949-1958; Houston Oilers, 1960-1966; Oakland Raiders, 1967-1975 (4,000 attempts).
Most Consecutive Passes Attempted Without Interception — 294, Bart Starr, Green Bay Packers, 1964-1965.
Most Interceptions By, Season — 14, Dick Lane, Los Angeles Rams, 1952.
Most Interceptions By, Career — 81, Paul Krause, Washington Redskins, 1964-67; Minnesota Vikings, 1968-79.
Most Consecutive Games, Passes Intercepted By — 8, Tom Morrow, Oakland Raiders, 1962 (4), 1963 (4).

Punting

Most Punts, Career — 1,072, Jerrel Wilson, Kansas City, 1963-77; New England, 1978.
Most Punts, Season — 114, Bob Parsons, Chicago Bears, 1981.
Highest Punting Average, Season (20 punts) — 51.40, Sam Baugh, Washington Redskins, 1940 (35 punts).
Longest Punt — 98 yds., Steve O'Neal, New York Jets vs. Denver Broncos, Sept. 21, 1969.

Kickoff Returns

Most Yardage Returning Kickoffs, Career — 6,922, Ron Smith, Chicago Bears, 1965; Atlanta Falcons, 1966-67; Los Angeles Rams, 1968-69; Chicago Bears, 1970-72; San Diego Chargers, 1973; Oakland Raiders, 1974.
Most Yardage Returning Kickoffs, Season — 1,317, Bobby Jancik, Houston Oilers, 1963.
Most Yardage Returning Kickoffs, Game — 294, Wally Triplett, Detroit Lions vs. Los Angeles Rams, Oct. 29, 1950 (4 returns).
Most Touchdowns Scored via Kickoff Returns, Career — 6, Ollie Matson, Chicago Cardinals, 1952 (2), 1954, 1956, 1958 (2); Gale Sayers, Chicago Bears, 1965, 1966 (2), 1967 (3); Travis Williams, Green Bay Packers, 1967 (4), 1969; Los Angeles Rams, 1971.
Most Touchdowns Scored via Kickoff Returns, Season — 4, Travis Williams, Green Bay Packers, 1967; Cecil Turner, Chicago Bears, 1970.
Most Touchdowns Scored via Kickoff Returns, Game — 2, Tim Brown, Philadelphia Eagles vs. Dallas Cowboys, Nov. 6, 1966; Travis Williams, Green Bay Packers vs. Cleveland Browns, Nov. 12, 1967.
Most Kickoff Returns, Career — 275, Ron Smith, Chicago Bears, 1965; Atlanta Falcons, 1966-67; Los Angeles Rams, 1968-69; Chicago Bears, 1970-72; San Diego Chargers, 1973; Oakland Raiders, 1974.
Most Kickoff Returns, Season — 60, Drew Hill, Los Angeles Rams, 1981.
Longest Kickoff Return — 106 yds., Al Carmichael, Green Bay Packers vs. Chicago Bears, October 7, 1956; Noland Smith, Kansas City vs. Denver, Dec. 17, 1967; Roy Green, St. Louis Cardinals vs. Dallas Cowboys, Oct. 21, 1979 (all scored TD).

Punt Returns

Most Yardage Returning Punts, Career — 3,008, Rick Upchurch, Denver Broncos, 1975-1983.
Most Yardage Returning Punts, Season — 666, Greg Pruitt, Los Angeles Raiders, 1983.
Most Yardage Returning Punts, Game — 207, Leroy Irvin, Los Angeles Rams vs. Atlanta Falcons, Oct. 11, 1981.
Most Touchdowns Scored via Punt Returns, Career — 8, Jack Christiansen, Detroit Lions, 1951-1958; Rick Upchurch, Denver Broncos, 1975-83.
Most Punt Returns, Career — 258, Emlen Tunnell, New York Giants, 1948-1958; Green Bay Packers, 1959-1961.
Most Punt Returns, Season — 70, Danny Reece, Tampa Bay Buccaneers, 1979.
Longest Punt Return — 98 yards, Gil LeFebvre, Cincinnati Reds vs. Brooklyn Dodgers, Dec. 3, 1933; Charles West, Minnesota Vikings vs. Washington Redskins, Nov. 3, 1968; Dennis Morgan, Dallas Cowboys vs. St. Louis Cardinals, Oct. 13, 1974 (all scored TD).

Miscellaneous Records

Most Fumbles, Season — 17, Dan Pastorini, Houston Oilers, 1973.
Most Fumbles, Game — 7, Len Dawson, Kansas City Chiefs vs. San Diego Chargers, Nov. 15, 1964.
Winning Streak (Regular Season) — 17 games, Chicago Bears, 1933-34.
Most Seasons, Active Player — 26, George Blanda, Chicago Bears, 1949-1958; Houston Oilers, 1960-1966 and Oakland, 67-75.

NEA All-NFL Team in 1983

Chosen by team captains, player representatives, and head coaches of the 28 NFL teams in a poll conducted by Newspaper Enterprise Assn.

First team	Offense	Second team
Roy Green, St. Louis	Wide receiver	James Lofton, Green Bay
Mike Quick, Philadelphia	Wide receiver	Cris Collinsworth, Cincinnati
Todd Christensen, L.A. Raiders	Tight end	Ozzie Newsome, Cleveland
Joe Jacoby, Washington	Tackle	Jackie Slater, L.A. Rams
Keith Fahnhorst, San Francisco	Tackle	Cody Risien, Cleveland
John Hannah, New England	Guard	Ed Newman, Miami
Russ Grimm, Washington	Guard	Mike Munchak, Houston
Dwight Stephenson, Miami	Center	Larry McCarren, Green Bay
Joe Theismann, Washington	Quarterback	Joe Montana, San Francisco
Eric Dickerson, L.A. Rams	Running back	John Riggins, Washington
William Andrews, Atlanta	Running back	Walter Payton, Chicago
Ali Haji Sheikh, N.Y. Giants	Placekicker	Raul Allegre, Baltimore

First team	Defense	Second team
Howie Long, L.A. Raiders	End	Jacob Green, Seattle
Doug Betters, Miami	End	Ed Jones, Dallas
Dave Butz, Washington	Tackle	Doug English, Detroit
Fred Smerlas, Buffalo	Nose tackle	Randy White, Dallas
Jack Lambert, Pittsburgh	Inside linebacker	Jerry Robinson, Philadelphia
Mike Singletary, Chicago	Inside linebacker	Tom Cousineau, Cleveland
Rod Martin, L.A. Raiders	Outside linebacker	Hugh Green, Tampa Bay
Lawrence Taylor, N.Y. Giants	Outside linebacker	Chip Banks, Cleveland
Louis Wright, Denver	Cornerback	Lester Hayes, L.A. Raiders
Gary Green, Kansas City	Cornerback	Johnny Poe, New Orleans
Ken Easley, Seattle	Strong safety	Nolan Cromwell, L.A. Rams
Johnnie Johnson, L.A. Rams	Free safety	Mark Murphy, Washington
Rich Camarillo, New England	Punter	Rohn Stark, Baltimore

1984 NFL Player Draft

The following are the first round picks of the National Football League.

Team	Player	Pos.	College	Team	Player	Pos.	College
1—New England	Irving Fryar	WR	Nebraska	15—N.Y. Jets	Ron Faurot	DE	Arkansas
2—Houston	Dean Steinkuhler	OG	Nebraska	16—Cincinnati	Pete Koch	DE	Maryland
3—N.Y. Giants	Carl Banks	LB	Michigan St.	17—St. Louis	Clyde Duncan	WR	Tennessee
4—Philadelphia	Kenny Jackson	WR	Penn St.	18—Cleveland	Don Rogers	DB	UCLA
5—Kansas City	Bill Maas	DT	Pittsburgh	19—Indianapolis	Ron Solt	OG	Maryland
6—San Diego	Mossy Cade	DB	Texas	20—Detroit	David Lewis	TE	California
7—Cincinnati	Ricky Hunley	LB	Arizona	21—Kansas City	John Alt	OT	Iowa
8—Indianapolis	Leonard Coleman	DB	Vanderbilt	22—Seattle	Terry Taylor	DB	So. Illinois
9—Atlanta	Rick Bryan	DT	Oklahoma	23—Pittsburgh	Louis Lipps	WR	So. Miss.
10—N.Y. Jets	Russell Carter	DB	SMU	24—San Francisco	Todd Shell	LB	Brigham Young
11—Chicago	Wilber Marshall	LB	Florida	25—Dallas	Billy Cannon Jr.	LB	Texas A&M
12—Green Bay	Alphonso Carreker	DE	Florida St.	26—Buffalo	Greg Bell	RB	Notre Dame
13—Minnesota	Keith Millard	DE	Washington St.	27—N.Y. Giants	Bill Roberts	OT	Ohio St.
14—Miami	Jackie Shipp	LB	Oklahoma	28—Cincinnati	Brian Blados	OT	North Carolina

Pro Football Hall of Fame

Canton, Ohio

Herb Adderley	Art Donovan	Cal Hubbard	John (Blood) McNally	Art Rooney
Lance Alworth	Paddy Driscoll	Sam Huff	Mike Michalske	Gale Sayers
Doug Atkins	Bill Dudley	Lamar Hunt	Wayne Millner	Joe Schmidt
Morris (Red) Badgro	Turk Edwards	Don Hutson	Bobby Mitchell	Bart Starr
Cliff Battles	Weeb Ewbank	Deacon Jones	Ron Mix	Ernie Stautner
Sammy Baugh	Tom Fears	Sonny Jurgensen	Lenny Moore	Ken Strong
Chuck Bednarik	Ray Flaherty	Walt Kiesling	Marion Motley	Joe Stydahar
Bert Bell	Len Ford	Frank (Bruiser) Kinard	George Musso	Charlie Taylor
Bobby Bell	Dr. Daniel Fortmann	Curly Lambeau	Bronko Nagurski	Jim Taylor
Raymond Berry	Bill George	Dick (Night Train) Lane	Greasy Neale	Jim Thorpe
Charles Bidwell	Frank Gifford	Yale Lary	Ernie Nevers	Y.A. Tittle
George Blanda	Sid Gillman	Dante Lavelli	Ray Nitschke	George Trafton
Jim Brown	Otto Graham	Bobby Layne	Leo Nomellini	Charlie Trippi
Paul Brown	Red Grange	Tuffy Leemans	Merlin Olsen	Emlen Tunnell
Roosevelt Brown	Forrest Gregg	Bob Lilly	Jim Otto	Clyde (Bulldog) Turner
Willie Brown	Lou Groza	Vince Lombardi	Steve Owen	Norm Van Brocklin
Dick Butkus	Joe Guyon	Sid Luckman	Clarence (Ace) Parker	Steve Van Buren
Tony Canadeo	George Halas	Link Lyman	Jim Parker	Johnny Unitas
Joe Carr	Ed Healey	Tim Mara	Joe Perry	Paul Warfield
Guy Chamberlin	Mel Hein	Gino Marchetti	Pete Pihos	Bob Waterfield
Jack Christiansen	Pete Henry	George Marshall	Hugh (Shorty) Ray	Arnie Weinmeister
Dutch Clark	Arnold Herber	Ollie Matson	Dan Reeves	Bill Willis
George Connor	Bill Hewitt	George McAfee	Jim Ringo	Larry Wilson
Jim Conzelman	Clarke Hinkle	Mike McCormack	Andy Robustelli	Alex Wojciechowicz
Willie Davis	Elroy Hirsch	Hugh McElhenny		

United States Football League

Final 1984 Standings

Eastern Conference

Atlantic Division

	W	L	T	Pct	Pts	Opp
Philadelphia	16	2	0	.889	479	225
New Jersey	14	4	0	.778	430	312
Pittsburgh	3	15	0	.167	256	358
Washington	3	15	0	.167	270	482

Southern Division

	W	L	T	Pct	Pts	Opp
Birmingham	14	4	0	.778	557	316
Tampa Bay	14	4	0	.778	498	347
New Orleans	8	10	0	.444	348	395
Memphis	7	11	0	.389	320	455
Jacksonville	6	12	0	.333	327	455

Western Conference

Central Division

	W	L	T	Pct	Pts	Opp
Houston	13	5	0	.722	618	400
Michigan	10	8	0	.556	400	382
San Antonio	7	11	0	.389	309	325
Oklahoma	6	12	0	.333	251	459
Chicago	5	13	0	.278	340	466

Pacific Division

	W	L	T	Pct	PF	PA
Los Angeles	10	8	0	.556	338	373
Arizona	10	8	0	.556	502	284
Denver	9	9	0	.500	356	413
Oakland	7	11	0	.389	242	348

USFL Playoffs

Eastern Conference—Philadelphia 28, New Jersey 17; Birmingham 36, Tampa Bay 17; Philadelphia 20, Birmingham 10.
Western Conference—Arizona 17, Houston 16; Los Angeles 27, Michigan 21; Arizona 35, Los Angeles 23.
Championship—Philadelphia 23, Arizona 3.

1984 USFL Individual Leaders

Eastern Conference

Passing

	Att	Comp	Pct	Yards	TD	Pct	Int	Pts
Fusina, Philadelphia	465	302	64.9	3,837	31	6.7	9	104.7
Stoudt, Birmingham	366	212	57.9	3,121	26	7.1	7	101.6
Reaves, Tampa Bay	544	313	57.5	4,092	28	5.1	16	86.3
Sipe, New Jersey	325	192	59.1	2,540	17	5.2	15	82.1
Lewis, Memphis	276	161	58.3	1,862	15	5.4	10	81.8
Mahfouz, Jacksonville	309	180	58.3	2,174	11	3.6	13	74.3
Hohensee, Washington	400	231	57.8	2,766	17	4.3	20	72.4
Walton, New Orleans	512	280	54.7	3,554	17	3.3	19	72.2
Robinson, Jacksonville	235	125	53.2	1,687	7	3.0	12	65.0

Rushing

	Att	Yds	Avg	TD
Cribbs, Birmingham	297	1,467	4.9	8
Bryant, Philadelphia	297	1,406	4.7	13
Walker, New Jersey	293	1,339	4.6	16
Jordan, New Orleans	214	1,276	6.0	8
Bledsoe, Washington	246	1,080	4.4	7
Carthon, New Jersey	238	1,042	4.4	11
Boone, Tampa Bay	193	1,009	5.2	8
G. Anderson, Tampa Bay	268	1,008	3.8	19
Rozier, Pittsburgh	223	792	3.6	3

Receiving

	No	Yds	Avg	TD
Walters, Washington	98	1,410	14.4	13
Smith, Birmingham	89	1,481	16.6	8
Truvillion, Tampa Bay	70	1,044	14.9	9
Harvey, Tampa Bay	70	938	13.4	9
G. Anderson, Tampa Bay	66	682	10.3	32
Ross, New Orleans	65	833	12.8	6
Anderson, Pittsburgh	63	994	15.8	6
Crawford, Memphis	61	703	11.5	12
Shirk, Memphis	57	604	10.6	2

Scoring

	TD	FG	Att	1XP	Att	Pts
Walker, New Jersey	21	0	0	0	0	*128
Trout, Philadelphia	0	26	40	49	53	127
G. Anderson, Tampa Bay	21	0	0	0	0	126
Miller, Jack.-Birm	0	13	20	69	74	108
Andrusyshyn, Tampa Bay	0	17	25	55	59	106

Ruzek, New Jersey	0	17	23	51	53	102
Mazzetti, New Orleans	0	21	27	35	35	98
Duncan, Memphis	0	21	28	35	36	98
Bryant, Philadelphia	15	0	0	0	0	90

*Includes one two-point conversion.

Western Conference

Passing

	Att	Comp	Pct	Yards	TD	Pct	Int	Pts
Kelly, Houston	587	370	63.0	5,219	44	7.5	26	98.2
Landry, Arizona	449	283	63.0	3,334	26	5.8	15	92.8
Young, Los Angeles	310	179	57.7	2,361	10	3.2	9	80.6
Penrose, Denver	262	158	60.3	1,984	12	4.6	14	76.9
Hebert, Michigan	500	272	54.4	5,758	24	4.8	22	76.4
Besana, Oakland	446	257	57.6	2,792	14	3.1	12	75.4
Neuheisel, San Antonio	385	211	54.8	2,544	14	3.6	15	71.2
D. Williams, Oklahoma	528	261	49.4	3,084	15	2.8	21	60.5
Evans, Chicago	411	200	48.7	2,624	14	3.4	22	58.3

Rushing	Att	Yds	Avg	TD		Receiving	No	Yds	Avg	TD
Spencer, Arizona	227	1,212	5.3	17		R. Johnson, Houston	115	1,455	12.7	15
Long, Arizona	225	1,010	4.5	15		Sanders, Houston	101	1,378	13.6	11
Fowler, Houston	170	1,003	5.9	11		T. Johnson, Arizona	90	1,268	14.1	13
J. Williams, Michigan	197	984	5.0	8		Banks, Oakland	64	937	14.6	5
Sydney, Denver	230	961	4.2	10		Holloway, Michigan	62	1,219	19.7	9
Canada, Chicago	169	915	5.4	7		Townsell, Los Angeles	58	889	15.3	7
Nelson, Los Angeles	216	828	3.8	7		Cobb, Michigan	54	573	10.6	5
Jordan, Oakland	135	744	5.5	6		Wheeler, Oklahoma	51	651	12.8	2
Harrell, Houston	120	697	5.8	14		A. Williams, Oklahoma	50	1,087	21.7	7

Scoring

	TD	FG	Att	1XP	Att	Pts			TD	FG	Att	1XP	Att	Pts
Fritsch, Houston	0	21	26	67	69	130		Corral, Arizona	0	11	21	63	65	96
Spencer, Arizona	19	0	0	0	0	114		Mike-Mayer, San Antonio	0	20	27	33	35	93
Bojovic, Michigan	0	22	29	46	47	112		Long, Arizona	15	0	0	0	0	90
Harrell, Houston	16	0	0	0	0	*100		R. Johnson, Houston	15	0	0	0	0	90
Zendejas, Los Angeles	0	21	30	33	33	96		Speelman, Denver	0	19	32	33	35	90

*Includes two two-point conversion.

Rifle and Pistol Individual Championships in 1984

Source: National Rifle Association

National Outdoor Rifle and Pistol Championships

Pistol — James R.I. Laguana, Ft. Benning, Ga., 2640.137.
Civilian Pistol — William P. Tierney, St. Petersburg, Fla., 2629.118.
Regular Service Pistol — James R.I. Laguana, 2640.137.
Police Pistol — John L. Farley, Americus, Ga., 2606.092.
Woman Pistol — Cherrie A. Shaw, Rockford, Ill., 2529.070.
Senior Pistol — Joseph C. White, Rockville, Md., 2577.081.
Collegiate Pistol — William C. Karditzas, Edgewater, Md., 2503.066.
Smallbore Rifle Prone — Ronald O. West, Zanesville, Oh., 6398.536.
Civilian Smallbore Rifle Prone — Ronald O. West, 6398.536.
Service Smallbore Rifle Prone — Lones W. Wigger Jr., Ft. Benning, Ga., 6395.495.
Woman Smallbore Rifle Prone — Marsha Beasley, Arlington, Va., 6392.495.
Senior Smallbore Rifle Prone — Joseph W. Barnes Jr., Branchville, N.J., 6388.499.
Collegiate Smallbore Rifle Prone — Erik R. Kugler, Fairfax, Va., 6385.485.

Smallbore Rifle 3-Position — Lones W. Wigger Jr., 2276.059.
Civilian Smallbore Rifle 3-Position — Deena L. Wigger, Ft. Benning, Ga. 2202.023.
Service Smallbore Rifle 3-Position — Lones W. Wigger Jr., 2276.059.
Women Smallbore Rifle 3-Position — Deena L. Wigger, 2202.023.
Collegiate Smallbore Rifle 3-Position — Mike E. Anti, Jacksonville, N.C., 2197.024.
Highpower Rifle — Patrick M. McCann, Staunton, Ill., 2377.119.
Civilian Highpower Rifle — Patrick M. McCann, 2377.119.
Service Highpower Rifle — David B. Erickson, Ft. Benning, Ga., 2369.098.
Woman Highpower Rifle — Noma J. McCullough, Newhall, Cal., 2346.099.
Senior Highpower Rifle — Robert W. Wright, Farmersville, Oh., 2318.061.
Collegiate Highpower Rifle — Lee W. Sailer, Cannon Falls, Minn., 2347.092.
Junior Highpower Rifle — Lee W. Sailer, 2347.092.

U. S. NRA International Shooting Championships

English Match — Edward F. Etzel, Morgantown, W. Va., 1793.
Air Rifle — Glenn A. Dubis, Ft. Benning, Ga., 1767.
Woman Air Rifle — Pat K. Spurgin, Billings, Mont., 1164.
Smallbore Free Rifle — Edward F. Etzel, 3502.
Woman Standard Rifle Prone — Marsha Beasley, Arlington, Va., 1770.
Woman Standard Rifle 3-Position — Wanda R. Jewell, Redstone Arsenal, Ala., 1729.

Free Pistol — Donald C. Nygord, LaCrescenta, Cal., 1677.
Rapid Fire Pistol — Allyn W. Johnson, Fremont, Cal., 1770.
Center Fire Pistol — Erich Buljung, Ft. Benning, Cal., 1767.
Standard Pistol — Eugene G. Ross, Saugus, Cal., 1714.
Air Pistol — Darius R. Young, Winterburn, Alberta, Canada, 1733.
Woman Smallbore Pistol — Kim S. Dyer, Waco, Tex., 1740.

National Indoor Rifle and Pistol Championships

Smallbore Rifle 4-Position — Lones W. Wigger Jr., Ft. Benning, Ga., 799.
Smallbore Rifle International — Glenn Dubis, Ft. Benning, Ga., 1176.
Smallbore Rifle 3-Position — Karen E. Monez, Weatherford, Tex., 1185.
Woman Smallbore Rifle 4-Position — Karen E. Monez, 799.
Woman Smallbore Rifle International — Wanda R. Jewell, Redstone Arsenal, Ala., 1164.
Conventional Pistol — Thomas R. Woods, Ft. Benning, Ga., 887.

Woman Conventional Pistol — Ruby E. Fox, Parker, Ariz., 859.
International Free Pistol — Jimmie W. McCoy, Ft. Benning, Ga., 588.
Woman International Free Pistol — Madeline B. Thompson, Lewistown, Pa., 521.
International Standard Pistol — Eugene G. Ross, Saugus, Cal., 576.
Woman International Standard Pistol — Ruby E. Fox, 561.
Air Pistol — Jan R. Brundin, Quakertown, Pa., 577.
Air Rifle — Ethel Ann Alves, New Castle, Del, 584.
Woman Air Rifle — Wanda R. Jewell, 583.

Amateur Softball Assn. National Champions in 1984

Men

Super Slow Pitch — Howard's Western Steer, Denver, N.C.
Major Slow Pitch — Lilly Air System, Chicago, Ill.
"A" Slow Pitch — Bender Plumbing, New Haven, Conn.
"A" Ind. Slow Pitch — Brown & Williamson, Macon, Ga.
Major Ind. Slow Pitch — Sikorsky Aircraft, Stratford, Conn.
Church Slow Pitch — Palatka First Baptist, Palatka, Fla.
16-Inch Major Slow Pitch — Budweiser Whips, Harvey, Ill.

Women

Ind. Slow Pitch — Cargill Gold, Mound, Minn.
Major Slow Pitch — Spooks, Anoka, Minn.
Major Fast Pitch — Los Angeles Diamonds, Los Angeles, Cal.
"A" Fast Pitch — Arrow Butane Flames, Las Cruces, N.M.
"A" Slow Pitch — Mr. A's Express, Sacramento, Cal.
Church Slow Pitch — CME Crushettes, Warner Robbins, Ga.

World Track and Field Records

As of Sept. 1984

*Indicates pending record; a number of new records await confirmation. The International Amateur Atheletic Federation, the world body of track and field, recognizes only records in metric distances except for the mile.

Men's Records

Running

Event	Record	Holder	Country	Date	Where made
100 meters	9.93 s.	Calvin Smith	U.S.	July 3, 1983	Colorado Springs
200 meters	19.72 s.	Pietro Mennea	Italy	Sept. 12, 1979	Mexico City
400 meters	43.86 s.	Lee Evans	U.S.	Oct. 18, 1968	Mexico City
800 meters	1 m., 41.73 s.	Sebastian Coe	Gr. Britain	June 10, 1981	Florence, Italy
1,000 meters	2 m., 12.18 s.	Sebastian Coe	Gr. Britain	July 11, 1981	Oslo
1,500 meters	3 m., 30.77 s.	Steve Ovett	Gr. Britain	Sept. 1983	Reiti, Italy
1 mile	3 m., 47.33 s.	Sebastian Coe	Gr. Britain	Aug. 28, 1981	Brussels
2,000 meters	4 m., 51.4 s.	John Walker	New Zealand	June 30, 1976	Oslo
3,000 meters	7 m., 32.1 s.	Henry Rono	Kenya	June 27, 1978	Oslo
5,000 meters	13 m., 00.42 s.	Dave Moorcroft	Gr. Britain	July 7, 1982	Oslo
10,000 meters	*27 m., 13.81 s.	Fernando Mamede	Portugal	July 2, 1984	Stockholm
20,000 meters	57 m., 24.2 s.	Jos Hermens	Netherlands	May 1, 1976	Netherlands
25,000 meters	1 hr., 13 m., 55.8 s.	Toshihiko Seko	Japan	Mar. 22, 1981	New Zealand
30,000 meters	1 hr., 29 m., 18.8 s.	Toshihiko Seko	Japan	Mar. 22, 1981	New Zealand
3,000 meter stpl	8 m., 05.4 s.	Henry Rono	Kenya	May 13, 1978	Seattle

Hurdles

Event	Record	Holder	Country	Date	Where made
110 meters	12.93 s.	Renaldo Nehemiah	U.S.	Aug. 19, 1981	Zurich
400 meters	47.02 s.	Edwin Moses	U.S.	Aug. 31, 1983	Koblenz, W. Ger.

Relay Races

Event	Record	Holder	Country	Date	Where made
400 mtrs.	*37.83 s.	National team (Graddy, Brown, Smith, Lewis)	U.S.	Aug. 1984	Los Angeles
800 mtrs. (4×200)	1 m., 20.3 s.	USC	U.S.	May 27, 1978	Tempe, Ariz.
1,600 mtrs. (4×400)	2 m., 56.1 s.	National team (Matthews, Freeman, James, Evans)	U.S.	Oct. 20, 1968	Mexico City
3,200 mtrs. (4×800)	7 m., 03.89 s.	National team	Gr. Britain	Aug. 31,1982	London

Field Events

Event	Record	Holder	Country	Date	Where made
High jump	*7 ft., 10 in.	Zhu Jianhua	China	June 10, 1984	W. Germany
Long jump	29 ft., 2½ in.	Bob Beamon	U.S.	Oct. 18,1968	Mexico City
Triple jump	58 ft., 8¼ in.	Joao de Oliveira	Brazil	Oct. 15, 1975	Mexico City
Pole vault	*19 ft., 5¾ in.	Sergei Bubka	USSR	Sept., 1984	Rome
16 lb. shot put.	72 ft., 10¾ in.	Udo Beyer	E. Germany	June 25, 1983	Los Angeles
Discus throw	235 ft., 9 in.	Yuriy Dumchev	USSR	May 25, 1983	Moscow
Javelin throw	*343 ft., 10 in.	Uwe Hohn	E. Germany	July, 1984	E. Berlin
16 lb. hammer throw	* 283 ft., 3 in.	Yuri Sedykh	USSR	July 4, 1984	Cork, Ireland
Decathlon	*8,798 pts.	Jurgen Hingsen	W. Germany	June 9, 1984	W. Germany

Walking

Event	Record	Holder	Country	Date	Where made
2 hours	17 mi., 881 yds.	Jose Marin	Spain	Apr. 8, 1979	Barcelona
30,000 mtrs.	2 h., 6 min., 54 s.	Ralph Kowalsky	E. Germany	Mar. 28, 1982	Berlin
50,000 mtrs.	3 hr., 41 m., 39 s.	Raul Gonzales	Mexico	May 25, 1978	Norway

Women's Records

Running

Event	Record	Holder	Country	Date	Where made
100 meters	*10.76 s.	Evelyn Ashford	U.S.	Aug. 23, 1984	Zurich
200 meters	21.71 s.	Marita Koch	E. Germany	June 10, 1979	E. Berlin
400 meters	47.99 s.	Jarmila Kratochvilova	Czech.	Aug. 10, 1983	Helsinki
800 meters	1 m., 53.28 s.	Jarmila Kratochvilova	Czech.	July 26, 1983	Munich
1,500 meters	3 m., 52.47 s.	Tatyana Kazankina	USSR	Aug. 13, 1980	Zurich
1 mile	4 m., 17.44 s.	Maricica Puica	Romania	Sept. 16,1982	Rieta, Italy
2,000 meters	*5 m., 32.7 s.	Tatyana Kazankina	USSR	Aug., 1984	Moscow
3,000 meters	*8 m., 22.62 s.	Tatyana Kazankina	USSR	Aug. 26, 1984	Leningrad
5,000 meters	*14 m., 58.89 s.	Ingrid Kristiansen	Norway	June 28, 1984	Oslo
10,000 meters	*31 m., 13.78 s.	Olga Bondarenko	USSR	June 24, 1984	Moscow

Hurdles

Event	Record	Holder	Country	Date	Where made
110 meters	12.36 s.	Grazyna Rabsztyn	Poland	June 13, 1980	Warsaw
400 meters	*54.02 s.	Anna Ambrosene	USSR	June 11, 1983	Moscow

Field Events

Event	Record	Holder	Country	Date	Where made
High jump	* 6 ft., 9½ in.	Ludmilla Andonova	Bulgaria	July, 1984	E. Germany
Shot put	73 ft., 8 in.	Ilona Slupianek	E. Germany	May 11, 1980	Potsdam
Long jump	24 ft., 4½ in.	Anisoara Cusmir	Romania	June 4, 1983	Bucharest
Discus throw	*244 ft., 11 in.	Zdena Silvaha	Czechoslovakia	Aug. 26, 1984	Prague
Javelin	245 ft., 3 in.	Tiina Lillak	Finland	June 13, 1983	Finland
Pentathlon	5,083 pts.	Nadyezhda Tkachenko	USSR	July 24, 1980	Moscow

Relay Races

400 mtrs. (4×100)	**41.53 s.**	National team	E. Germany	July 31, 1983	Berlin
800 mtrs. (4×200)	**1 m., 28.15 s.**	National team	E. Germany	Aug. 9, 1980	E. Germany
1,600 mtrs. (4×400)	***3 m., 15.92 s.**	National team	E. Germany	June, 1984	E. Germany
3,200 mtrs. (4×800)	***7 m., 50.17 s.**	National team	USSR	Aug., 1984	Moscow

U.S. Track and Field Indoor Records

As of Sept., 1984

*Indicates pending record; a number of new records await confirmation. The International Amateur Federation, the world body of track and field, does not recognize world indoor records.

Men's Records

Running

Event	Record	Holder	Date	Where made
50 yards	5.22	Stanley Floyd	Jan. 22, 1982	Los Angeles
50 meters	5.61	James Sanford	Feb. 20, 1981	San Diego
60 yards	6.02	Carl Lewis	Feb. 5, 1983	Dallas
60 meters	6.54	Houston McTear	Jan. 7, 1978	Long Beach, Cal.
100 yards	9.54	Harvey Glance	Feb. 16, 1980	Houston
200 meters	*20.84	Mel Lattany	Feb. 3, 1984	W. Germany
300 yards	29.27	Terron Wright	Feb. 7, 1981	Bloomington, Ind.
300 meters	33.19	Elliott Quow	Jan. 23, 1983	Boston
400 meters	*45.79	Antonio McKay	Feb. 11, 1984	Gainesville, Fla.
500 yards	54.4	Lee Evans	Jan. 8, 30, 1971	Idaho and Maryland
500 meters	1:01.5	Mark Enyeart	Feb. 7, 1981	Louisville
600 yards	1:07.6	Marty McGrady	Feb. 27, 1970	New York City
600 meters	1:16.91	Mark Enyeart	Jan. 16, 1983	Sherbrooke, Canada
800 meters	1:47.4	Ted Nelson	Apr. 7, 1965	Berlin
1,000 yards	2:04.7	Don Paige	Feb. 5, 1982	Inglewood, Cal.
1,000 meters	*2:18.88	Don Paige	Feb. 11, 1984	E. Rutherford, N.J.
1,500 meters	3:38.3	Steve Scott	Feb. 19, 1982	San Diego
One mile	3.51.8	Steve Scott	Feb. 15, 1980	Los Angeles
2,000 meters	4.58.6	Steve Scott	Feb. 7, 1981	Louisville
3,000 meters	7:44.9	Doug Padilla	Feb. 18, 1983	San Diego, Cal.
2 miles	8:16.5	Doug Padilla	Feb. 18, 1983	San Diego
3 miles	12:56.6	Alberto Salazar	Feb. 6, 1981	New York City
5,000 meters	13:20.55	Doug Padilla	Feb. 12, 1982	New York City
50-yd. hurdles	5.92	Renaldo Nehemiah	Jan. 29, 1982	Toronto
60-m. hurdles	6.82	Renaldo Nehemiah	Jan. 30, 1982	Dallas

Field Events

High jump	7 ft. 7 3/4 in.	Jeff Woodard	Feb. 27, 1981	New York City
Pole vault	19 ft. 1/4 in.	Billy Olson	Feb. 4, 1983	Toronto
			Feb. 10, 1984	Inglewood, Cal.
Long jump	*28 ft. 10 1/4 in.	Carl Lewis	Jan. 27, 1984	New York City
Triple jump	57 ft. 1 1/2 in.	Willie Banks	Feb. 19, 1982	San Diego
Shot put	72 ft. 2 3/4 in.	George Woods	Feb. 8, 1974	Inglewood, Cal.

Women's Records

Running

Event	Record	Holder	Date	Where made
50 yards	5.74	Evelyn Ashford	Feb. 18, 1983	San Diego
50 meters	6.13	Jeannette Bolden	Feb. 21, 1981	Edmonton
60 yards	6.54	Evelyn Ashford	Feb. 26, 1982	New York City
60 meters	*7.18	Alice Brown	Mar. 10, 1984	Tokyo
200 meters	23.27	Chandra Cheeseborough	Feb. 27, 1981	New York City
220 yards	23.25	Chandra Cheeseborough	Feb. 26, 1982	New York City
300 yards	33.83	Diane Dixon	Mar. 5, 1983	Madison, Wis.
300 meters	37.50	Diane Dixon	Feb. 19, 1983	Normal, Ill.
400 meters	53.17	Diane Dixon	Feb. 27, 1983	E. Rutherford, N.J.
440 yards	53.29	Lori McCauley	Mar. 6, 1983	Cambridge, Mass.
500 yards	1:03.3	Rosalyn Bryant	Feb. 18, 1977	San Diego
500 meters	*1:11.1	Edna Brown	Jan. 8, 1984	Hanover, N.H.
600 yards	1:17.38	Delisa Walton	Mar. 13, 1982	Cedar Falls, Ia.
600 meters	1:26.56	Delisa Walton	Mar. 14, 1981	Pocatello, Ida.
800 meters	1:58.9	Mary Decker	Feb. 22, 1980	San Diego
880 yards	1:59.7	Mary Decker	Feb. 22, 1980	San Diego
1,000 yards	2:23.8	Mary Decker	Feb. 3, 1978	Inglewood, Cal.
1,000 meters	2:40.1	Diana Richburg	Dec. 7, 1982	New London, Conn.
1,500 meters	4:00.8	Mary Decker	Feb. 8, 1980	New York City
One mile	4:20.5	Mary Decker	Feb. 19, 1982	San Diego
2,000 meters	5:51.1	Mary Decker	Feb. 5, 1982	Inglewood, Cal.
3,000 meters	8:47.3	Mary Decker	Feb. 5, 1982	Inglewood, Cal.
2 miles	9:31.7	Mary Decker	Jan. 31, 1983	Los Angeles
50-yd. hurdles	6.37	Deby La Plante	Feb. 10, 1978	Toronto
50-m. hurdles	6.85	Candy Young	Jan. 15, 1983	Rosemont, Ill.
60-yd. hurdles	7.37	Stephanie Hightower	Feb. 12, 1982	New York City
		Candy Young	Feb. 12, 1982	New York City
60-m hurdles	7.36	Stephanie Hightower	Feb. 25, 1983	New York City

Field Events

High Jump	6 ft. 6 3/4 in.	Colleen Rienstra	Feb. 13, 1982	Ottawa
Shot put	61 ft. 2 1/4 in.	Maren Seidler	Jan. 20, 1978	W. Germany
Long jump	*22 ft. 2 1/4 in.	Carol Lewis	Feb. 4, 1984	Dallas, Tex.

Track and Field Events in 1984

77th Annual Millrose Games

New York, N.Y., Jan. 27, 1984

Men

60 Yds.—Emmit King, New Balance TC. **Time—0:06.12.**
60-Yd. High Hurdles—Greg Foster, Wilt's AC. **Time—0:07.07.**
400 Meters—Michael Paul, Tiger International. **Time—0:47.60.**
500 Yds.—Tony Darden, Philadelphia Pioneer Club.
Time—0:56.73.
600 Yds.—Stanley Redwine, Arkansas. **Time—1:09.04.**
800 Meters—James Robinson, Inner City AC. **Time—1:49.69.**
1,000 Meters—Sammy Koskei, El Paso TC. **Time—2:22.68.**
One Mile—Steve Scott, Sub-4 TC. **Time—3:59.38.**
5,000 Meters—Doug Padilla, Athletics West. **Time—13:33.83.**
One-Mile Walk—Ray Sharp, unattached. **Time—5:52.59.**
Long Jump—Carl Lewis, Santa Monica TC. **28 ft. 10¼ in.**

Pole Vault—Billy Olson, Pacific Coast Club. **18 ft. 8¼ in.**
High Jump—Dwight Jones, Pacific Coast Club. **7 ft. 6½ in.**

Women

60 Yds.—Chandra Cheeseborough, Athletics West.
Time—0:06.69.
60-Yd. High Hurdles—Stephanie Hightower, Nutri-Onix TC.
Time—0:07.47.
400 Meters—Grace Jackson, Atoms TC. **Time—0:53.87.**
800 Meters—Robin Campbell, Puma Energizer T&FC.
Time—2:05.91.
One Mile—Cindy Bremser, Wisconsin United. **Time—4:35.81.**
High Jump—Ulrike Meyfarth, W. Germany. **6 ft. 2¼ in.**

USA/Mobil Indoor Championships

New York, N.Y., Feb. 24, 1984

Men

60 Yds.—Emmit King, New Balance. **Time—0:06.08.**
440 Yds.—Clinton Davis, New Image TC. **Time—0:48.10.**
600 Yds.—Mike Rowe, Tiger International. **Time—1:09.60.**
1,000 Meters—Don Paige, unattached. **Time—2:08.20.**
One Mile—Steve Scott, Sub-4 TC. **Time—4:00.06.**
3 Miles—Doug Padilla, Athletics West. **Time—13:09.01.**
60-Yd. High Hurdles—Greg Foster, World Class AC.
Time—0:06.95.
2-Mile Walk—Jim Heiring, Bud Light Track America.
Time—12:11.21.
35-Lb. Weight Throw—Jud Logan, Chicago TC. **75 ft. 3¼ in.**
Shot Put—Augie Wolf, N.Y. AC. **69 ft. ¾ in.**
Triple Jump—Alayi Agbebaku, El Paso TC. **55 ft. 7 in.**
Long Jump—Carl Lewis, Santa Monica TC. **27 ft. 10¾ in.**
Pole Vault—Sergei Bubka, USSR. **18 ft. 6 in.**

High Jump—Dennis Lewis, New Balance TC. **7 ft. 7 in.**

Women

60 Yds.—Alice Brown, World Class AC. **Time—0:06.62.**
220 Yds.—Valerie Brisco, Hooks World Class AC. **Time—0:23.97.**
440 Yds.—Diane Dixon, Atoms TC. **Time—0:53.82.**
880 Yds.—Lyubova Gurina, USSR. **Time—2:05.34.**
One Mile—Britt McRoberts, Canada. **Time—4:33.91.**
2 Miles—Cathy Branta, Wisconsin. **Time—9:49.39.**
60-Yd. Hurdles—Stephanie Hightower, Bud Light Track America. **Time— 0:07.43.**
One-Mile Walk—Teresa Vaill, Island TC. **Time— 7:12.85.**
High Jump—Tamara Bykova, USSR. **6 ft. 6¾ in.**
Long Jump—Carol Lewis, Univ. of Houston. **21 ft. 5 in.**

NCAA Outdoor Championships

Eugene, Ore. June 1-3, 1984

Men

100 Meters—Sam Graddy, Tennessee. **Time—0:10.25.**
400 Meters—Antonio McKay, Georgia Tech. **Time—0:44.83.**
1,500 Meters—Joaquim Cruz, Oregon. **Time—3:36.48.**
5,000 Meters—Julius Korir, Washington St. **Time—13:47.77.**
110-Meter Hurdles—Albert Lane, Missouri. **Time—0:13.61.**
Javelin—Einar Vilhjalmsson, Texas. **294 ft.**
Shot Put—John Brenner, UCLA. **71 ft. 11 1/4 in.**
Triple Jump—Mike Conley, Arkansas. **56 ft. 11 3/4 in.**
Pole Vault—Joe Dial, Oklahoma St. **18 ft. 2 1/2 in.**

Women

200 Meters—Randy Givens, Florida St. **Time—0:22.87.**
400 Meters—Marita Payne, Florida St. **Time—0:51.05.**
800 Meters—Joetta Clark, Tennessee. **Time—2:02.60.**
5,000 Meters—Patti Sue Plumer, Stanford. **Time—15:39.38.**
100-Meter Hurdles—Kim Turner, Texas-El Paso. **Time—0:13.02.**
High Jump—Tonya Alston, UCLA. **6 ft. 1 1/4 in.**
Long Jump—Gwen Loud, Hawaii. **22 ft. 5 3/4 in.**
Discus—Carol Cady, Stanford. **198 ft. 5 in.**

USA/Mobil Outdoor Championships

San Jose, Cal., June 7-9, 1984

Men

100 Meters—Sam Graddy, Adidas TC. **Time—0:10.28.**
200 Meters—Brady Crain, N.Y. Pioneer Club. **Time—0:20.09.**
400 Meters—Mark Rowe, Tiger International. **Time—0:45.34.**
800 Meters—James Robinson, Inner City AC. **Time—1:47.46.**
1,500 Meters—Jim Spivey, Athletics West. **Time—3:40.34.**
5,000 Meters—Sydney Maree, Reebok Racing Team.
Time—13:51.31.
10,000 Meters—Jon Sinclair, unattached. **Time—28:42.54.**
3,000-Meter Steeplechase—Henry Marsh, Athletics West.
Time—8:26.07.
110-Meter Hurdles—Tonie Campbell, Stars & Stripes TC.
Time—0:13.26.
400-Meter Hurdles—David Patrick, Adidas TC. **Time—0:48.08.**
20-Km. Walk—Ray Funkhouser, Shore AC. **Time—1:31:47.1.**
High Jump—Jimmy Howard, Pacific Coast Club. **7 ft. 7 ¼ in.**
Pole Vault—Earl Bell, Pacific Coast Club. **19 ft. ¼ in.**
Long Jump—Mike McRae, Bay Area Striders. **27 ft. 1¾ in.**
Triple Jump—Al Joyner, Bud Light. **55 ft. 6¼ in.**
Shot Put—Augie Wolf, Bud Light. **70 ft. 5¾ in.**
Discus—John Powell, Bud Light. **233 ft. 9 in.**
Hammer—Jud Logan, Chicago TC. **240 ft. 6 in.**
Javelin—Curt Ransford, Puma Energizer. **276 ft. 11 in.**
Team champion—Bud Light.

Women

100 Meters—Merlene Ottey, unattached. **Time—0:11.12.**
200 Meters—Merlene Ottey. **Time—0:22.20.**
400 Meters—Valerie Brisco-Hooks, Tiger World Class AC.
Time—0:49.83.
800 Meters—Kim Gallagher, Puma & Energizer.
Time—1:59.87.
1,500 Meters—Kim Gallagher. **Time—4:08.08.**
3,000 Meters—Jan Merrill, Age Group AA. **Time—9:01.31.**
5,000 Meters—Katie Ishmael, Wisconsin United TC.
Time—16:07.05.
10,000 Meters—Bonnie Sons, Iowa St. (unchallenged).
Time—35:03.6.
100-Meter Hurdles—Stephanie Hightower, Bud Light.
Time—0:12.99.
400-Meter Hurdles—Judy Brown, Nike TC. **Time—0:54.99.**
10 Km. Walk—Debbie Lawrence, Team Kangaroo.
Time—51:00.03
High Jump—Pam Spencer, Puma & Energizer TC. **6 ft. 4 in.**
Long Jump—Shonel Ferguson, unattached. **22 ft. ¼ in.**
Shot Put—Ria Stalman, Adidas TC. **59 ft. 1½ in.**
Discus—Ria Stalman. **221 ft. 9 in.**
Javelin—Karin Smith, Athletics West. **198 ft. 11 in.**
Team champion—Puma & Energizer TC.

National Track & Field Hall of Fame

Indianapolis. Ind.

Jesse Abramson
Dave Albritton
Horace Ashenfelter
Weems Baskins
James Bausch
Bob Beamon
Percy Beard
Dee Boeckman
Tom Botts
Ralph Boston
Bill Bowerman
Avery Brundage
Lee Calhoun
Alice Coachman (Davis)
Harold Connolly
Tom Courtney
Dean Cromwell
Glenn Cunningham
William Curtis
Willie Davenport
Glenn Davis
Harold Davis

Mildred (Babe) Didrikson
Harrison Dillard
Ken Doherty
Bill Easton
James (Jumbo) Elliott
Lee Evans
Ray Ewry
Mae Faggs (Starr)
Dan Ferris
John Flanagan
Dick Fosbury
Bob Giegengack
Fortune Gordien
John Griffith
Archie Hahn
Brutus Hamilton
Glenn Hardin
Ted Haydon
Billy Hayes
Bob Hayes
Ward Haylett
Ralph Higgins

Harry Hillman
Jim Hines
Bud Houser
DeHart Hubbard
Edward Hurt
Wilbur Hutsell
Bruce Jenner
Rafer Johnson
Hayes Jones
Thomas Jones
Payton Jordan
John Kelley
Alvin Kraenzlein
Clyde Littlefield
Bob Mathias
Randy Matson
Mildred McDaniel
Edith McGuire (DuVall)
Ted Meredith
Ralph Metcalfe
Billy Mills
Madeline Manning-Mims

Bobby Morrow
Michael Murphy
Lon Myers
Parry O'Brien
Al Oerter
Harold Osborn
Jesse Owens
Charlie Paddock
Steve Prefontaine
Joie Ray
Greg Rice
Bob Richards
Betty Robinson (Schwartz)
Ralph Rose
Wilma Rudolph
Jim Ryun
Jackson Scholz
Mel Sheppard
Dave Sime
Robert Simpson
Tommie Smith
Larry Snyder

Andy Stanfield
Les Steers
Helen Stephens
James Sullivan
Dink Templeton
Earl Thomson
Jim Thorpe
Eddie Tolan
Bill Toomey
Forrest Towns
Wyomia Tyus
LeRoy Walker
Stella Walsh
Cornelius Warmerdam
Willye White
Mal Whitfield
Fred Wilt
John Woodruff
Dave Wottle
Frank Wykoff
Joe Yancey
George Young

Evolution of the World Record for the One-Mile Run

The table below shows how the world record for the one-mile has been lowered in the past 119 years.

Year	Individual, country	Time	Year	Individual, country	Time
1864	Charles Lawes, Britain	4:56	1942	Arne Andersson, Sweden	4:06.2
1865	Richard Webster, Britain	4:36.5	1942	Gunder Haegg, Sweden	4:04.6
1868	William Chinnery, Britain	4:29	1943	Arne Andersson, Sweden	4:02.6
1868	W. C. Gibbs, Britain	4:28.8	1944	Arne Andersson, Sweden	4:01.6
1874	Walter Slade, Britain	4:26	1945	Gunder Haegg, Sweden	4:01.4
1875	Walter Slade, Britain	4:24.5	1954	Roger Bannister, Britain	3:59.4
1880	Walter George, Britain	4:23.2	1954	John Landy, Australia	3:58
1882	Walter George, Britain	4:21.4	1957	Derek Ibbotson, Britain	3:57.2
1882	Walter George, Britain	4:19.4	1958	Herb Elliott, Australia	3:54.5
1884	Walter George, Britain	4:18.4	1962	Peter Snell, New Zealand	3:54.4
1894	Fred Bacon, Scotland	4:18.2	1964	Peter Snell, New Zealand	3:54.1
1895	Fred Bacon, Scotland	4:17	1965	Michel Jazy, France	3:53.6
1895	Thomas Conneff, U.S.	4:15.6	1966	Jim Ryun, U.S.	3:51.3
1911	John Paul Jones, U.S.	4:15.4	1967	Jim Ryun, U.S.	3:51.1
1913	John Paul Jones, U.S.	4:14.6	1975	Filbert Bayi, Tanzania	3:51
1915	Norman Taber, U.S.	4:12.6	1975	John Walker, New Zealand	3:49.4
1923	Paavo Nurmi, Finland	4:10.4	1979	Sebastian Coe, Britain	3:49
1931	Jules Ladoumegue, France	4:09.2	1980	Steve Ovett, Britain	3:48.8
1933	Jack Lovelock, New Zealand	4:07.6	1981	Sebastian Coe, Britain	3:48.53
1934	Glenn Cunningham, U.S.	4:06.8	1981	Steve Ovett, Britain	3:48.40
1937	Sydney Wooderson, Britain	4:06.4	1981	Sebastian Coe, Britain	3:47.33
1942	Gunder Haegg, Sweden	4:06.2			

Davis Cup Challenge Round

Year	Result	Year	Result	Year	Result
1900	United States 5, British Isles 0	1929	France 3, United States 2	1960	Australia 4, Italy 1
1901	(not played)	1930	France 4, United States 1	1961	Australia 5, Italy 0
1902	United States 3, British Isles 2	1931	France 3, Great Britain 2	1962	Australia 5, Mexico 0
1903	British Isles 4, United States 1	1932	France 3, United States 2	1963	United States 3, Australia 2
1904	British Isles 5, Belgium 0	1933	Great Britain 3, France 2	1964	Australia 3, United States 2
1905	British Isles 5, United States 0	1934	Great Britain 4, United States 1	1965	Australia 4, Spain 1
1906	British Isles 5, United States 0	1935	Great Britain 5, United States 0	1966	Australia 4, India 1
1907	Australia 3, British Isles 2	1936	Great Britain 3, Australia 2	1967	Australia 4, Spain 1
1908	Australasia 3, United States 2	1937	United States 4, Great Britain 1	1968	United States 4, Australia 1
1909	Australasia 5, United States 0	1938	United States 3, Australia 2	1969	United States 5, Romania 0
1910	(not played)	1939	Australia 3, United States 2	1970	United States 5, W. Germany 0
1911	Australasia 5, United States 0	1940-45	(not played)	1971	United States 3, Romania 2
1912	British Isles 3, Australasia 2	1946	United States 5, Australia 0	1972	United States 3, Romania 2
1913	United States 3, British Isles 2	1947	United States 4, Australia 1	1973	Australia 5, United States 0
1914	Australasia 3, United States 2	1948	United States 5, Australia 0	1974	South Africa (default by India)
1915-18	(not played)	1949	United States 4, Australia 1	1975	Sweden 3, Czech. 2
1919	Australasia 4, British Isles 1	1950	Australia 4, United States 1	1976	Italy 4, Chile 1
1920	United States 5, Australasia 0	1951	Australia 3, United States 2	1977	Australia 3, Italy 1
1921	United States 5, Japan 0	1952	Australia 4, United States 1	1978	United States 4, Great Britain 1
1922	United States 4, Australasia 1	1953	Australia 3, United States 2	1979	United States 5, Italy 0
1923	United States 4, Australasia 1	1954	United States 3, Australia 2	1980	Czechoslovakia 4, Italy 1
1924	United States 5, Australasia 0	1955	Australia 5, United States 0	1981	United States 3, Argentina 1
1925	United States 5, France 0	1956	Australia 5, United States 0	1982	United States 3, France, 0
1926	United States 4, France 1	1957	Australia 3, United States 2	1983	Australia 3, Sweden 1
1927	France 3, United States 2	1958	United States 3, Australia 2		
1928	France 4, United States 1	1959	Australia 3, United States 2		

Tennis

USTA National Champions

Men's Singles

Year	Champion	Final opponent	Year	Champion	Final opponent
1920	Bill Tilden	William Johnston	1953	Tony Trabert	E. Victor Seixas Jr.
1921	Bill Tilden	Wallace Johnston	1954	E. Victor Seixas Jr.	Rex Hartwig
1922	Bill Tilden	William Johnston	1955	Tony Trabert	Ken Rosewall
1923	Bill Tilden	William Johnston	1956	Ken Rosewall	Lewis Hoad
1924	Bill Tilden	William Johnston	1957	Malcolm Anderson	Ashley Cooper
1925	Bill Tilden	William Johnston	1958	Ashley Cooper	Malcolm Anderson
1926	Rene Lacoste	Jean Borotra	1959	Neale A. Fraser	Alejandro Olmedo
1927	Rene Lacoste	Bill Tilden	1960	Neale A. Fraser	Rod Laver
1928	Henri Cochet	Francis Hunter	1961	Roy Emerson	Rod Laver
1929	Bill Tilden	Francis Hunter	1962	Rod Laver	Roy Emerson
1930	John Doeg	Francis Shields	1963	Rafael Osuna	F. A. Froehling 3d
1931	H. Ellsworth Vines	George Lott	1964	Roy Emerson	Fred Stolle
1932	H. Ellsworth Vines	Henri Cochet	1965	Manuel Santana	Cliff Drysdale
1933	Fred Perry	John Crawford	1966	Fred Stolle	John Newcombe
1934	Fred Perry	Wilmer Allison	1967	John Newcombe	Clark Graebner
1935	Wilmer Allison	Sidney Wood	1968	Arthur Ashe	Tom Okker
1936	Fred Perry	Don Budge	1969	Rod Laver	Tony Roche
1937	Don Budge	Baron G. von Cramm	1970	Ken Rosewall	Tony Roche
1938	Don Budge	C. Gene Mako	1971	Stan Smith	Jan Kodes
1939	Robert Riggs	S. Welby Van Horn	1972	Ilie Nastase	Arthur Ashe
1940	Don McNeill	Robert Riggs	1973	John Newcombe	Jan Kodes
1941	Robert Riggs	F. L. Kovacs	1974	Jimmy Connors	Ken Rosewall
1942	F. R. Schroeder Jr.	Frank Parker	1975	Manuel Orantes	Jimmy Connors
1943	Joseph Hunt	Jack Kramer	1976	Jimmy Connors	Bjorn Borg
1944	Frank Parker	William Talbert	1977	Guillermo Vilas	Jimmy Connors
1945	Frank Parker	William Talbert	1978	Jimmy Connors	Bjorn Borg
1946	Jack Kramer	Thomas Brown Jr.	1979	John McEnroe	Vitas Gerulaitis
1947	Jack Kramer	Frank Parker	1980	John McEnroe	Bjorn Borg
1948	Pancho Gonzales	Eric Sturgess	1981	John McEnroe	Bjorn Borg
1949	Pancho Gonzales	F. R. Schroeder Jr.	1982	Jimmy Connors	Ivan Lendl
1950	Arthur Larsen	Herbert Flam	1983	Jimmy Connors	Ivan Lendl
1951	Frank Sedgman	E. Victor Seixas Jr.	1984	John McEnroe	Ivan Lendl
1952	Frank Sedgman	Gardnar Mulloy			

Men's Doubles

Year	Champions	Year	Champions
1935	Wilmer Allison—John Van Ryn	1960	Neale A. Fraser—Roy Emerson
1936	Don Budge—C. Gene Mako	1961	Dennis Ralston—Chuck McKinley
1937	Baron G. von Cramm—Henner Henkel	1962	Rafael Osuna—Antonio Palafox
1938	Don Budge—C. Gene Mako	1963	Dennis Ralston—Chuck McKinley
1939	Adrian Quist—John Bromwich	1964	Dennis Ralston—Chuck McKinley
1940	Jack Kramer—Frederick Schroeder Jr.	1965	Roy Emerson—Fred Stolle
1941	Jack Kramer—Frederick Schroeder Jr.	1966	Roy Emerson—Fred Stolle
1942	Gardnar Mulloy—William Talbert	1967	John Newcombe—Tony Roche
1943	Jack Kramer—Frank Parker	1968	Robert Lutz—Stan Smith
1944	Don McNeill—Robert Falkenburg	1969	Fred Stolle—Ken Rosewall
1945	Gardnar Mulloy—William Talbert	1970	Pierre Barthes—Nicki Pilic
1946	Gardnar Mulloy—William Talbert	1971	John Newcombe—Roger Taylor
1947	Jack Kramer—Frederick Schroeder Jr.	1972	Cliff Drysdale—Roger Taylor
1948	Gardnar Mulloy—William Talbert	1973	John Newcombe—Owen Davidson
1949	John Bromwich—William Sidwell	1974	Bob Lutz—Stan Smith
1950	John Bromwich—Frank Sedgman	1975	Jimmy Connors—Ilie Nastase
1951	Frank Sedgman—Kenneth McGregor	1976	Marty Riessen—Tom Okker
1952	Mervyn Rose—E. Victor Seixas Jr.	1977	Bob Hewitt—Frew McMillan
1953	Rex Hartwig—Mervyn Rose	1978	Stan Smith—Bob Lutz
1954	E. Victor Seixas Jr.—Tony Trabert	1979	John McEnroe—Peter Fleming
1955	Kosei Kamo—Atsushi Miyagi	1980	Bob Lutz—Stan Smith
1956	Lewis Hoad—Ken Rosewall	1981	John McEnroe—Peter Fleming
1957	Ashley Cooper—Neale Fraser	1982	Kevin Curren—Steve Denton
1958	Hamilton Richardson—Alejandro Olmedo	1983	John McEnroe—Peter Fleming
1959	Neale A. Fraser—Roy Emerson	1984	Tomas Smid—John Fitzgerald

Mixed Doubles

Year	Champions	Year	Champions
1961	Margaret Smith—Robert Mark	1973	Billie Jean King—Owen Davidson
1962	Margaret Smith—Fred Stolle	1974	Pam Teeguarden—Geoff Masters
1963	Margaret Smith—Kenneth Fletcher	1975	Rosemary Casals—Dick Stockton
1964	Margaret Smith—John Newcombe	1976	Billie Jean King—Phil Dent
1965	Margaret Smith—Fred Stolle	1977	Betty Stove—Frew McMillan
1966	Donna Floyd Fales—Owen Davidson	1978	Betty Stove—Frew McMillan
1967	Billie Jean King—Owen Davidson	1979	Greer Stevens—Bob Hewitt
1968	Mary Ann Eisel—Peter Curtis	1980	Wendy Turnbull—Marty Riessen
1969	Margaret S. Court—Marty Riessen	1981	Anne Smith—Kevin Curren
1970	Margaret S. Court—Marty Riessen	1982	Anne Smith—Kevin Curren
1971	Billie Jean King—Owen Davidson	1983	Elizabeth Sayers—John Fitzgerald
1972	Margaret S. Court—Marty Riessen	1984	Manuela Maleeva—Tom Gullikson

Women's Singles

Year	Champion	Final opponent	Year	Champion	Final opponent
1936	Alice Marble	Helen Jacobs	1961	Darlene Hard	Ann Haydon
1937	Anita Lizana	Pauline Betz	1962	Margaret Smith	Darlene Hard
1938	Alice Marble	Louise Brough	1963	Maria Bueno	Margaret Smith
1939	Alice Marble	Louise Brough	1964	Maria Bueno	Carole Graebner
1940	Alice Marble	Margaret Osborne	1965	Margaret Smith	Billie Jean Moffitt
1941	Sarah Palfrey Cooke	Pauline Betz	1966	Maria Bueno	Nancy Richey
1942	Pauline Betz	Jadwiga Jedrzejowska	1967	Billie Jean King	Ann Haydon Jones
1943	Pauline Betz	Nancye Wynne	1968	Virginia Wade	Billie Jean King
1944	Pauline Betz	Helen Jacobs	1969	Margaret Court	Nancy Richey
1945	Sarah P. Cooke	Helen Jacobs	1970	Margaret Court	Rosemary Casals
1946	Pauline Betz	Doris Hart	1971	Billie Jean King	Rosemary Casals
1947	Louise Brough	Margaret Osborne	1972	Billie Jean King	Kerry Melville
1948	Margaret Osborne duPont	Louise Brough	1973	Margaret Court	Evonne Goolagong
1949	Margaret Osborne duPont	Doris Hart	1974	Billie Jean King	Evonne Goolagong
1950	Margaret Osborne duPont	Doris Hart	1975	Chris Evert	Evonne Goolagong
1951	Maureen Connolly	Shirley Fry	1976	Chris Evert	Evonne Goolagong
1952	Maureen Connolly	Doris Hart	1977	Chris Evert	Wendy Turnbull
1953	Maureen Connolly	Doris Hart	1978	Chris Evert	Pam Shriver
1954	Doris Hart	Louise Brough	1979	Tracy Austin	Chris Evert Lloyd
1955	Doris Hart	Patricia Ward	1980	Chris Evert Lloyd	Hana Mandlikova
1956	Shirley Fry	Althea Gibson	1981	Tracy Austin	Martina Navratilova
1957	Althea Gibson	Louise Brough	1982	Chris Evert Lloyd	Hana Mandlikova
1958	Althea Gibson	Darlene Hard	1983	Martina Navratilova	Chris Evert Lloyd
1959	Maria Bueno	Christine Truman	1984	Martina Navratilova	Chris Evert Lloyd
1960	Darlene Hard	Maria Bueno			

Women's Doubles

Year	Champions	Year	Champions
1939	Alice Marble—Mrs. Sarah P. Fabyan	1962	Maria Bueno—Darlene Hard
1940	Alice Marble—Mrs. Sarah P. Fabyan	1963	Margaret Smith—Robyn Ebbern
1941	Mrs. S. P. Cooke—Margaret Osborne	1964	Billie Jean Moffitt—Karen Susman
1942	A. Louise Brough—Margaret Osborne	1965	Carole C. Graebner—Nancy Richey
1943	A. Louise Brough—Margaret Osborne	1966	Maria Bueno—Nancy Richey
1944	A. Louise Brough—Margaret Osborne	1967	Rosemary Casals—Billie Jean King
1945	A. Louise Brough—Margaret Osborne	1968	Maria Bueno—Margaret S. Court
1946	A. Louise Brough—Margaret Osborne	1969	Francoise Durr—Darlene Hard
1947	A. Louise Brough—Margaret Osborne	1970	M. S. Court—Judy Tegart Dalton
1948	A. Louise Brough—Mrs. M. O. du Pont	1971	Rosemary Casals—Judy Tegart Dalton
1949	A. Louise Brough—Mrs. M. O. du Pont	1972	Francoise Durr—Betty Stove
1950	A. Louise Brough—Mrs. M. O. du Pont	1973	Margaret S. Court—Virginia Wade
1951	Doris Hart—Shirley Fry	1974	Billie Jean King—Rosemary Casals
1952	Doris Hart—Shirley Fry	1975	Margaret Court—Virginia Wade
1953	Doris Hart—Shirley Fry	1976	Linky Boshoff—Ilana Kloss
1954	Doris Hart—Shirley Fry	1977	Betty Stove—Martina Navratilova
1955	A. Louise Brough—Mrs. M. O. du Pont	1978	Martina Navratilova—Billie Jean King
1956	A. Louise Brough—Mrs. M. O. du Pont	1979	Betty Stove—Wendy Turnbull
1957	A. Louise Brough—Mrs. M. O. du Pont	1980	Billie Jean King—Martina Navratilova
1958	Darlene Hard—Jeanne Arth	1981	Anne Smith—Kathy Jordan
1959	Darlene Hard—Jeanne Arth	1982	Rosemary Casals—Wendy Turnbull
1960	Darlene Hard—Maria Bueno	1983	Martina Navratilova—Pam Shriver
1961	Darlene Hard—Lesley Turner	1984	Martina Navratilova—Pam Shriver

WCT Tournaments in 1984

Dates	Event, city	Singles winner	Doubles winners
Feb. 1-5	United Virginia Bank Tennis Classic, Richmond, Va.	John McEnroe	John McEnroe/Patrick McEnroe
Apr. 3-8	River Oaks, Houston, Tex.	Mark Dickson	Peter McNamee/Pat Cash
Apr. 24-29	Buick WCT Finals, Dallas, Tex.	John McEnroe	
May 6-13	Mercedes Tournament of Champions, New York, N.Y.	John McEnroe	David Dowlen/Nduka Odizor

French Open Champions

Year	Men	Women	Year	Men	Women
1967	Roy Emerson	Françoise Durr	1976	Adriano Panatta	Sue Barker
1968	Ken Rosewall	Nancy Richey	1977	Guillermo Vilas	Mima Jausovec
1969	Rod Laver	Margaret Smith Court	1978	Bjorn Borg	Virginia Ruzici
1970	Jan Kodes	Margaret Smith Court	1979	Bjorn Borg	Chris Evert Lloyd
1971	Jan Kodes	Evonne Goolagong	1980	Bjorn Borg	Chris Evert Lloyd
1972	Andres Gimeno	Billie Jean King	1981	Bjorn Borg	Hana Mandlikova
1973	Ilie Nastase	Margaret Court	1982	Mats Wilander	Martina Navratilova
1974	Bjorn Borg	Chris Evert	1983	Yannick Noah	Chris Evert Lloyd
1975	Bjorn Borg	Chris Evert	1984	Ivan Lendl	Martina Navratilova

Leading Tennis Money Winners in 1983

Men

Ivan Lendl	$1,287,128	Yannick Noah	268,394	Pam Shriver	312,21•
John McEnroe	729,844	Bill Scanlon	268,372	Andrea Jaeger	261,95•
Guillermo Vilas	645,035			Kathy Jordan	211,78•
Mats Wilander	489,650			Jo Durie	211,34•
Tomas Smid	386,886	**Women**		Wendy Turnbull	206,39•
Jimmy Connors	368,047			Andrea Temesvari	168,30•
Brian Teacher	315,948	Martina Navratilova	$1,456,030	Sylvia Hanika	154,95•
Kevin Curren	276,852	Chris Evert Lloyd	430,436	Hana Mandlikova	151,76•

British Champions, Wimbledon

Men's Singles

Year	Champion	Final opponent	Year	Champion	Final opponent
1933	Jack Crawford	Ellsworth Vines	1962	Rod Laver	Martin Mulligan
1934	Fred Perry	Jack Crawford	1963	Chuck McKinley	Fred Stolle
1935	Fred Perry	Gottfried von Cramm	1964	Roy Emerson	Fred Stolle
1936	Fred Perry	Gottfried von Cramm	1965	Roy Emerson	Fred Stolle
1937	Donald Budge	Gottfried von Cramm	1966	Manuel Santana	Dennis Ralston
1938	Donald Budge	Wilfred Austin	1967	John Newcombe	Wilhelm Bungert
1939	Bobby Riggs	Elwood Cooke	1968	Rod Lavor	Tony Roche
1940-45	not held		1969	Rod Laver	John Newcombe
1946	Yvon Petra	Geoff E. Brown	1970	John Newcombe	Ken Rosewall
1947	Jack Kramer	Tom P. Brown	1971	John Newcombe	Stan Smith
1948	Bob Falkenburg	John Bromwich	1972	Stan Smith	Ilie Nastase
1949	Ted Schroeder	Jaroslav Drobny	1973	Jan Kodes	Alex Metreveli
1950	Budge Patty	Fred Sedgman	1974	Jimmy Connors	Ken Rosewall
1951	Dick Savitt	Ken McGregor	1975	Arthur Ashe	Jimmy Connors
1952	Frank Sedgman	Jaroslav Drobny	1976	Bjorn Borg	Ilie Nastase
1953	Vic Seixas	Kurt Nielsen	1977	Bjorn Borg	Jimmy Connors
1954	Jaroslav Drobny	Ken Rosewall	1978	Bjorn Borg	Jimmy Connors
1955	Tony Trabert	Kurt Nielsen	1979	Bjorn Borg	Roscoe Tanner
1956	Lew Hoad	Ken Rosewall	1980	Bjorn Borg	John McEnroe
1957	Lew Hoad	Ashley Cooper	1981	John McEnroe	Bjorn Borg
1958	Ashley Cooper	Neale Fraser	1982	Jimmy Connors	John McEnroe
1959	Alex Olmedo	Rod Laver	1983	John McEnroe	Chris Lewis
1960	Neale Fraser	Rod Laver	1984	John McEnroe	Jimmy Connors
1961	Rod Laver	Chuck McKinley			

Women's Singles

Year	Champion	Year	Champion	Year	Champion	Year	Champion
1946	Pauline Betz	1956	Shirley Fry	1966	Billie Jean King	1976	Chris Evert
1947	Margaret Osborne	1957	Althea Gibson	1967	Billie Jean King	1977	Virginia Wade
1948	Louise Brough	1958	Althea Gibson	1968	Billie Jean King	1978	Martina Navratilova
1949	Louise Brough	1959	Maria Bueno	1969	Ann Haydon-Jones	1979	Martina Navratilova
1950	Louise Brough	1960	Maria Bueno	1970	Margaret Court	1980	Evonne Goolagong
1951	Doris Hart	1961	Angela Mortimer	1971	Evonne Goolagong	1981	Chris Evert Lloyd
1952	Maureen Connolly	1962	Karen Hantze-Susman	1972	Billie Jean King	1982	Martina Navratilova
1953	Maureen Connolly	1963	Margaret Smith	1973	Billie Jean King	1983	Martina Navratilova
1954	Maureen Connolly	1964	Maria Bueno	1974	Chris Evert	1984	Martina Navratilova
1955	Louise Brough	1965	Margaret Smith	1975	Billie Jean King		

Trotting and Pacing Records

Source: David Carr, U.S. Trotting Assn.; records to Sept. 21, 1984

Trotting Records

Asterisk (*) denotes record was made against the clock. Times—seconds in fifths.

One mile records (mile track)

All-age — 1:53.4 — Cornstalk, Springfield, Ill., Aug. 15, 1984 & Fancy Crown, Springfield, Ill., Aug. 16, 1984.
Two-year-old — 1:55.4 — Fancy Crown, Lexington, Ky., Oct. 8, 1983.
Three-year-old — 1:53.4 — Cornstalk, Springfield, Ill., Aug. 15, 1984 & Fancy Crown, Springfield, Ill., Aug. 16, 1984.

(Half-mile track)

All-age — 1:56.4 — Nevele Pride, Saratoga Springs, N.Y., Sept. 6, 1969.
Two-year-old — 2:00 — Incredible Nevele, Delaware, Oh., Sept. 22, 1981.
Three-year-old — 1:57.1 — Fancy Crown, Delaware Oh., Sept. 20, 1984

Pacing Records

One mile records (mile track)

All-age — *1:49.1 — Niatross, Lexington, Ky., Oct. 1, 1980.
Two-year-old — 1:52.4 — Nihilator, E. Rutherford, N.J., Aug. 16, 1984.
Three-year-old — *1:49.1 — Niatross, Lexington, Ky., Oct. 1, 1980.

(Half-mile track)

All age — 1:53.3 — It's Fritz, Louisville, Ky., Sept. 3, 1983 & Legal Notice, Delaware, Oh., Sept. 20, 1984.
Two-year-old — 1:56 — Cervantes Osborne, Delaware, Oh., Sept. 20, 1984.
Three-year-old — 1:53.3 — Legan Notice, Delaware, Oh., Sept. 20, 1984.

Little Brown Jug (3-year-old pacers)

Year	Winner	Driver	Purse	Year	Winner	Driver	Purse
1961	Henry T. Adios	Stanley Dancer	$70,069	1973	Melvin's Woe	Joe O'Brien	$120,000
1962	Lehigh Hanover	Stanley Dancer	75,038	1974	Ambro Omaha	Billy Haughton	132,630
1963	Overtrick	John Patterson Sr.	68,294	1975	Seatrain	Ben Webster	147,813
1964	Vicar Hanover	Billy Haughton	66,590	1976	Keystone Ore	Stanley Dancer	153,799
1965	Bret Hanover	Frank Ervin	71,447	1977	Gov. Skipper	John Chapman	150,000
1966	Romeo Hanover	George Sholty	74,616	1978	Happy Escort	Bill Popfinger	186,760
1967	Best of All	James Hackett	84,778	1979	Hot Hitter	Herve Filion	226,455
1968	Rum Customer	Billy Haughton	104,226	1980	Niatross	Clint Galbraith	207,000
1969	Laverne Hanover	Billy Haughton	109,731	1981	Fan Hanover(A)	Glen Garnsey	243,779
1970	Most Happy Fella	Stanley Dancer	100,110	1982	Merger	John Campbell	328,900
1971	Nansemond	Herve Filion	102,944	1983	Ralph Hanover	Ron Waples	358,800
1972	Strike Out	Keith Waples	104,916	1984	Colt Forty Six	Chris Boring	366,717

(A) First filly to win the Little Brown Jug.

The Hambletonian (3-year-old trotters)

Year	Winner	Driver	Purse	Year	Winner	Driver	Purse
1948	Demon Hanover	Harrison Hoyt	$59,941	1967	Speedy Streak	Del Cameron	$122,650
1949	Miss Tilly	Fred Egan	69,791	1968	Nevele Pride	Stanley Dancer	116,190
1950	Lusty Song	Del Miller	75,209	1969	Lindy's Pride	Howard Beissinger	124,910
1951	Mainliner	Guy Crippen	95,263	1970	Timothy T	John Simpson Sr..	143,630
1952	Sharp Note	Bion Shively	87,637	1971	Speedy Crown	Howard Beissinger	128,770
1953	Helicopter	Harry Harvey	117,118	1972	Super Bowl	Stanley Dancer	119,090
1954	Newport Dream	Del Cameron	106,830	1973	Flirth	Ralph Baldwin	144,710
1955	Scott Frost	Joe O'Brien	86,863	1974	Christopher T	Bill Haughton	160,150
1956	The Intruder	Ned Bower	98,591	1975	Bonefish	Stanley Dancer	232,192
1957	Hickory Smoke	John Simpson Sr..	111,126	1976	Steve Lobell	Bill Haughton	263,524
1958	Emily's Pride	Flave Nipe	106,719	1977	Green Speed	Bill Haughton	284,131
1959	Diller Hanover	Frank Ervin	125,284	1978	Speedy Somolli	Howard Beissinger	241,280
1960	Blaze Hanover	Joe O'Brien	144,590	1979	Legend Hanover	George Sholty	300,000
1961	Harlan Dean	James Arthur	131,573	1980	Burgomeister	Bill Haughton	293,570
1962	A.C. Os Viking	Sanders Russell	116,312	1981	Shiaway St. Pat	Ray Remmen	838,000
1963	Speedy Scot	Ralph Baldwin	115,549	1982	Speed Bowl	Tommy Haughton	875,750
1964	Ayres	John Simpson Sr..	115,281	1983	Duenna	Stanley Dancer	1,080,000
1965	Egyptian Candor	Del Cameron	122,245	1984	Historic Freight	Ben Webster	1,219,000
1966	Kerry Way	Frank Ervin	122,540				

Leading Drivers

Races Won

Year	Driver		Year	Driver		Year	Driver		Year	Driver	
1959	William Gilmour	165	1966	Bob Farrington	283	1972	Herve Filion	605	1978	Herve Filion	423
1960	Del Insko	156	1967	Bob Farrington	277	1973	Herve Filion	445	1979	Ron Waples	443
1961	Bob Farrington	201	1968	Herve Filion	407	1974	Herve Filion	637	1980	Herve Filion	474
1962	Bob Farrington	203	1969	Herve Filion	394	1975	Daryl Buse	360	1981	Eddie Davis	404
1963	Donald Busse	201	1970	Herve Filion	486	1976	Herve Filion	445	1982	Herve Filion	495
1964	Bob Farrington	312	1971	Herve Filion	543	1977	Herve Filion	441	1983	Eddie Davis	470
1965	Bob Farrington	310									

Money Won

Year	Driver	Dollars	Year	Driver	Dollars	Year	Driver	Dollars
1957	Bill Haughton	586,950	1966	Stanley Dancer	1,218,403	1975	Carmine Abbatiello	2,275,093
1958	Bill Haughton	816,659	1967	Bill Haughton	1,305,773	1976	Herve Filion	2,241,045
1959	Bill Haughton	711,435	1968	Bill Haughton	1,654,172	1977	Herve Filion	2,551,058
1960	Del Miller	567,282	1969	Del Insko	1,635,463	1978	Carmine Abbatiello	3,344,457
1961	Stanley Dancer	674,723	1970	Herve Filion	1,647,837	1979	John Campbell	3,308,984
1962	Stanley Dancer	760,343	1971	Herve Filion	1,915,945	1980	John Campbell	3,732,306
1963	Bill Haughton	790,086	1972	Herve Filion	2,473,265	1981	William O'Donnell	4,065,608
1964	Stanley Dancer	1,051,538	1973	Herve Filion	2,233,302	1982	William O'Donnell	5,755,067
1965	Bill Haughton	889,943	1974	Herve Filion	3,474,315	1983	John Campbell	6,104,082

Harness Horse of the Year

(Chosen by the U.S. Trotting Assn. and the U.S. Harness Writers Assn.)

Year		Year		Year		Year	
1948	Rodney	1957	Torpid	1966	Bret Hanover	1975	Savior
1949	Good Time	1958	Emily's Pride	1967	Nevele Pride	1976	Keystone Ore
1950	Proximity	1959	Bye Bye Byrd	1968	Nevele Pride	1977	Green Speed
1951	Pronto Don	1960	Adios Butler	1969	Nevele Pride	1978	Abercrombie
1952	Good Time	1961	Adios Butler	1970	Fresh Yankee	1979	Niatross
1953	Hi Lo's Forbes	1962	Su Mac Lad	1971	Albatross	1980	Niatross
1954	Stenographer	1963	Speedy Scot	1972	Albatross	1981	Fan Hanover
1955	Scott Frost	1964	Bret Hanover	1973	Sir Dalrae	1982	Cam Fella
1956	Scott Frost	1965	Bret Hanover	1974	Delmonica Hanover	1983	Cam Fella

Annual Leading Money-Winning Horses

Trotters

Year	Horse	Dollars	Year	Horse	Dollars	Year	Horse	Dollars
1960	Su Mac Lad	159,662	1968	Nevele Pride	427,440	1976	Steve Lobell	338,770
1961	Su Mac Lad	245,750	1969	Lindy's Pride	323,997	1977	Green Speed	584,405
1962	Duke Rodney	206,113	1970	Fresh Yankee	359,002	1978	Speedy Somolli	362,404
1963	Speedy Scot	144,403	1971	Fresh Yankee	293,960	1979	Chiola Hanover	553,058
1964	Speedy Scot	235,710	1972	Super Bowl	437,108	1980	Classical Way	350,040
1965	Dartmouth	252,348	1973	Spartan Hanover	262,023	1981	Shiaway St. Pat	480,095
1966	Noble Victory	210,696	1974	Delmonica Hanover	252,165	1982	Speed Bowl	672,084
1967	Carlisle	231,243	1975	Savoir	351,385	1983	Joie De Vie	1,007,705

Pacers

Year	Horse	Dollars	Year	Horse	Dollars	Year	Horse	Dollars
1960	Bye Bye Byrd	187,612	1968	Rum Customer	355,618	1976	Keystone Ore	539,762
1961	Adios Butler	180,250	1969	Overcall	373,150	1977	Governor Skipper	522,148
1962	Henry T. Adios	220,302	1970	Most Happy Fella	387,239	1978	Abercrombie	703,260
1963	Overtrick	208,833	1971	Albatross	558,009	1979	Hot Hitter	826,542
1964	Race Time	199,292	1972	Albatross	459,921	1980	Niatross	1,414,313
1965	Bret Hanover	341,784	1973	Sir Dalrae	307,354	1981	McKinzie Almahurst	936,418
1966	Bret Hanover	407,534	1974	Armbro Omaha	345,146	1982	Fortune Teller	1,313,175
1967	Romulus Hanover	277,636	1975	Silk Stockings	336,312	1983	Ralph Hanover	1,711,990

Leading Money-Winning Horses

(As of Sept. 21, 1984)

Trotters				Pacers		
Savoir	$1,365,145	Joie De Vie	$1,017,251	Cam Fella	$2,041,367	On the Road Again	$1,557,150
Fresh Yankee	1,294,252	Green Speed	953,013	Rambling Willie	2,038,219	McKinzie Almahurst	1,532,870
Duenna	1,077,551	Cold Comfort	931,386	Niatross	2,019,213	Nihilator	1,218,921
Keystone Pioneer	1,071,927	Su Mac Lad	885,095	Ralph Hanover	1,828,871	Albatross	1,201,470
Baltic Speed	1,027,639	Nevele Pride	873,350	Fortune Teller	1,683,639	Carls Bird	1,138,803

World Swimming Records

As of Sept., 1984

Effective June 1, 1969, FINA recognizes only records made over a 50-meter course.

Men's Records

Freestyle

Distance	Time	Holder	Country	Where made	Date
100 Meters	0:49.36	Rowdy Gaines	U.S.	Austin, Tex.	Apr. 3, 1981
200 Meters	1:47.55	Michael Gross	W. Germany	Munich	June 6, 1984
400 Meters	3:48.32	Vladimir Salnikov	USSR	Moscow	Feb. 19, 1983
800 Meters	7:52.33	Vladimir Salnikov	USSR	Los Angeles	July 14, 1983
1,500 Meters	14:54.76	Vladimir Salnikov	USSR	Moscow	Feb. 22, 1983

Breaststroke

100 Meters	1:02.13	John Moffet	U.S.	Indianapolis	June 25, 1984
200 Meters	2:13.34	Victor Davis	Canada	Los Angeles	Aug., 1984

Butterfly

100 Meters	0:53.08	Michael Gross	W. Germany	Los Angeles	Aug., 1984
200 Meters	1:57.04	Jon Sieben	Australia	Los Angeles	Aug., 1984

Backstroke

100 Meters	0:55.19	Rick Carey	U.S.	Caracas	Aug. 21, 1983
200 Meters	1:58.41	Sergei Zabolotnov	USSR	Moscow	Aug., 1984

Individual Medley

200 Meters	2:01.42	Alex Baumann	Canada	Los Angeles	Aug., 1984
400 Meters	4:17.41	Alex Baumann	Canada	Los Angeles	Aug., 1984

Freestyle Relays

400 M. (4 × 100)	3:19.03	Cavanaugh, Heath, Biondi, Gaines	U.S.	Los Angeles	Aug., 1984
800 M. (4 × 200)	7:15.69	Heath, Larson, Float, Hayes	U.S.	Los Angeles	Aug., 1984

Medley Relays

400 M. (4 × 100)	3:39.30	Carey, Lundquist, Morales, Gaines	U.S.	Los Angeles	Aug., 1984

Women's Records

Freestyle

100 Meters	0:54.79	Barbara Krause	E. Germany	Moscow	July, 1980
200 Meters	1:57.75	Kristin Otto	E. Germany	Magedeburg, E. Ger.	May 23, 1984
400 Meters	4:06.28	Tracey Wickham	Australia	W. Berlin	Aug. 24, 1978
800 Meters	8:24.62	Tracey Wickham	Australia	Edmonton, Canada	Aug. 5, 1978
1,500 Meters	16:04.49	Kim Linehan	U.S.	Ft. Lauderdale, Fla.	Aug. 19, 1979

Breaststroke

100 Meters	1:08.29	Sylvia Gerasch	E. Germany	Moscow	Aug. 23, 1984
200 Meters	2:28.36	Lina Kachushite	USSR	Potsdam	Mar. 6, 1979

Butterfly

100 Meters	0:57.93	Mary T. Meagher	U.S.	Brown Deer, Wis.	Aug. 16, 1981
200 Meters	2:05.96	Mary T. Meagher	U.S.	Brown Deer, Wis.	Aug. 13, 1981

Backstroke

100 Meters	1:00.59	Ina Kleber	E. Germany	Moscow	Aug. 24, 1984
200 Meters	2:09.91	Cornelia Sirch	E. Germany	Ecuador	Aug. 7, 1982

Individual Medley

200 Meters	2:10.60	Petra Schneider	E. Germany	Gainesville, Fla.	Aug. 1, 1982
400 Meters	4:36.10	Petra Schneider	E. Germany	Ecuador	Aug. 1, 1982

Freestyle Relays

400 M. (4 × 100)	3:42.41	National Team	E. Germany	Moscow	Aug., 1984

Medley Relays

400 M. (4 × 100)	4:03.69	National Team	E. Germany	Moscow	Aug. 24, 1984

Auto Racing

Indianapolis 500 Winners

Year	Winner	Chassis	Engine	MPH	Purse	Runner up
1949	Bill Holland	Deidt	Offenhauser	121.327	$179,050	Johnnie Parsons
1950	Johnnie Parsons	Kurtis Kraft	Offenhauser	124.002(a)	201,135	Bill Holland
1951	Lee Wallard	Kurtis Kraft	Offenhauser	126.244	207,650	Mike Nazaruk
1952	Troy Ruttman	Kuzma	Offenhauser	128.922	230,100	Jim Rathmann
1953	Bill Vukovich	Kurtis Kraft 500A	Offenhauser	128.740	246,300	Art Cross
1954	Bill Vukovich	Kurtis Kraft 500A	Offenhauser	130.840	269,375	Jim Bryan
1955	Bob Sweikert	Kurtis Kraft 500C	Offenhauser	128.209	270,400	Tony Bettenhausen
1956	Pat Flaherty	Watson	Offenhauser	128.490	282,052	Sam Hanks
1957	Sam Hanks	Epperly	Offenhauser	135.601	300,252	Jim Rathmann
1958	Jimmy Bryan	Epperly	Offenhauser	133.791	305,217	George Amick
1959	Rodger Ward	Watson	Offenhauser	135.857	338,100	Jim Rathmann
1960	Jim Rathmann	Watson	Offenhauser	138.767	369,150	Rodger Ward
1961	A.J. Foyt	Watson	Offenhauser	139.130	400,000	Eddie Sachs
1962	Rodger Ward	Watson	Offenhauser	140.293	426,152	Len Sutton
1963	Parnelli Jones	Watson	Offenhauser	143.137	494,031	Jim Clark
1964	A.J. Foyt	Watson	Offenhauser	147.350	506,625	Rodger Ward
1965	Jim Clark	Lotus	Ford	151.388	628,399	Parnelli Jones
1966	Graham Hill	Lola	Ford	144.317	691,809	Jim Clark
1967	A.J. Foyt	Coyote	Ford	151.207	737,109	Al Unser
1968	Bobby Unser	Eagle	Offenhauser	152.882	809,627	Dan Gurney
1969	Mario Andretti	Hawk	Ford	156.867	805,127	Dan Gurney
1970	Al Unser	P.J. Colt	Ford	155.749	1,000,002	Mark Donohue
1971	Al Unser	P.J. Colt	Ford	157.735	1,001,604	Peter Revson
1972	Mark Donohue	McLaren	Offenhauser	163.465	1,011,846	Al Unser
1973	Gordon Johncock	Eagle	Offenhauser	159.014(b)	1,011,846	Billy Vukovich
1974	Johnny Rutherford	McLaren	Offenhauser	158.589	1,015,686	Bobby Unser
1975	Bobby Unser	Eagle	Offenhauser	149.213(c)	1,101,322	Johnny Rutherford
1976	Johnny Rutherford	McLaren	Offenhauser	148.725(d)	1,037,775	A.J. Foyt
1977	A.J. Foyt	Coyote	Ford	161.331	1,116,807	Tom Sneva
1978	Al Unser	Lola	Cosworth	161.363	1,145,225	Tom Sneva
1979	Rick Mears	Penske	Cosworth	158.899	1,271,954	A.J. Foyt
1980	Johnny Rutherford	Chaparral	Cosworth	142.862	1,502,425	Tom Sneva
1981	Bobby Unser	Penske	Cosworth	139.085	1,609,375	Mario Andretti
1982	Gordon Johncock	Wildcat	Cosworth	162.026	2,067,475	Rick Mears
1983	Tom Sneva	March	Cosworth	162.117	2,411,450	Al Unser
1984	Rick Mears	March	Cosworth	163.621	2,795,399	Roberto Guerrero

(a) 345 miles. (b) 332.5 miles. (c) 435 miles. (d) 255 miles. Race record—163.621 MPH, Rick Mears, 1984.

Notable One-Mile Speed Records

Date	Driver	Car	MPH	Date	Driver	Car	MPH
1/26/06	Marriott	Stanley (Steam)	127.659	9/ 3/35	Campbell	Bluebird Special	301.13
3/16/10	Oldfield	Benz	131.724	11/19/37	Eyston	Thunderbolt 1	311.42
4/23/11	Burman	Benz	141.732	9/16/38	Eyston	Thunderbolt 1	357.5
2/12/19	DePalma	Packard	149.875	8/23/39	Cobb	Railton	368.9
4/27/20	Milton	Dusenberg	155.046	9/16/47	Cobb	Railton-Mobil	394.2
4/28/26	Parry-Thomas	Thomas Spl.	170.624	8/ 5/63	Breedlove	Spirit of America	407.45
3/29/27	Seagrave	Sunbeam	203.790	10/27/64	Arfons	Green Monster	536.71
4/22/28	Keech	White Triplex	207.552	11/15/65	Breedlove	Spirit of America	600.601
3/11/29	Seagrave	Irving-Napier	231.446	10/23/70	Gabelich	Blue Flame	622.407
2/ 5/31	Campbell	Napier-Campbell	246.086	10/9/79	Barrett	Budweiser Rocket	638.637*
2/24/32	Campbell	Napier-Campbell	253.96	10/4/83	Noble	Thrust 2	633.6
2/22/33	Campbell	Napier-Campbell	272.109		*not recognized as official by sanctioning bodies.		

World Grand Prix Champions

Year	Driver	Year	Driver	Year	Driver
1950	Nino Farina, Italy	1962	Graham Hill, England	1973	Jackie Stewart, Scotland
1951	Juan Fangio, Argentina	1963	Jim Clark, Scotland	1974	Emerson Fittipaldi, Brazil
1952	Alberto Ascari, Italy	1964	John Surtees, England	1975	Nicki Lauda, Austria
1953	Alberto Ascari, Italy	1965	Jim Clark, Scotland	1976	James Hunt, England
1954	Juan Fangio, Argentina	1966	Jack Brabham, Australia	1977	Nikki Lauda, Austria
1955	Juan Fangio, Argentina	1967	Denis Hulme, New Zealand	1978	Mario Andretti, U.S.
1956	Juan Fangio, Argentina	1968	Graham Hill, England	1979	Jody Scheckter, So. Africa
1957	Juan Fangio, Argentina	1969	Jackie Stewart, Scotland	1980	Alan Jones, Australia
1958	Mike Hawthorne, England	1970	Jochen Rindt, Austria	1981	Nelson Piquet, Brazil
1959	Jack Brabham, Australia	1971	Jackie Stewart, Scotland	1982	Keke Rosberg, Finland
1960	Jack Brabham, Australia	1972	Emerson Fittipaldi, Brazil	1983	Nelson Piquet, Brazil
1961	Phil Hill, United States				

United States Auto Club National Champions

Year	Driver	Year	Driver	Year	Driver	Year	Driver
1956	Jimmy Bryan	1963	A. J. Foyt	1970	Al Unser	1977	Tom Sneva
1957	Jimmy Bryan	1964	A. J. Foyt	1971	Joe Leonard	1978	Tom Sneva
1958	Tony Bettenhausen	1965	Mario Andretti	1972	Joe Leonard	1979	A. J. Foyt
1959	Rodger Ward	1966	Mario Andretti	1973	Roger McCluskey	1980	Johnny Rutherford
1960	A. J. Foyt	1967	A. J. Foyt	1974	Bobby Unser	1981	George Snider
1961	A. J. Foyt	1968	Bobby Unser	1975	A. J. Foyt	1982	George Snider
1962	Rodger Ward	1969	Mario Andretti	1976	Gordon Johncock	1983	Tom Sneva

Grand Prix for Formula 1 Cars in 1984

Grand Prix	Winner, car	Grand Prix	Winner, car
Austrian	Niki Lauda, McLaren Porsche	French	Niki Lauda, McLaren Porsche
Belgian	Michele Alboreto, Ferrari	German	Alain Prost, McLaren Porsche
Brazilian	Alain Prost, McLaren Porsche	Italian	Niki Lauda, McLaren Porsche
British	Niki Lauda, McLaren Porsche	Long Beach	Mario Andretti, Lola Cosworth
Canadian	Nelson Piquet, Brabham	Meadowlands	Mario Andretti, Lola Cosworth
Dallas	Keke Rosberg, Williams Honda	Monaco	Alain Prost, McLaren Porsche
Detroit	Nelson Piquet, Brabham	San Marino	Alain Prost, McLaren Porsche
Dutch	Alain Prost, McLaren Porsche	South African	Niki Lauda, McLaren Porsche

Le Mans 24-Hour Race in 1984

Henri Pescarolo of France and Klaus Ludwig of West Germany drove their Porsche 956 turbo to victory in the 1984 Le Mans 24-hour race. They covered 3,044.97 miles at an average speed of 126.87 miles per hour.

NASCAR Racing in 1984

Winston Cup Grand National Races

Date	Race, site	Winner	Car	Winnings
Feb. 19	Daytona 500, Daytona Beach, Fla.	Cale Yarborough	Chevrolet	$160,300
Mar. 4	Warner W. Hodgdon Carolina 500, Rockingham, N.C.	Bobby Allison	Buick	33,150
Mar. 18	Coca-Cola 500, Atlanta, Ga.	Benny Parsons	Chevrolet	51,110
Apr. 1	Valleydale 500, Bristol, Tenn.	Darrell Waltrip	Chevrolet	31,670
Apr. 8	Northwestern Bank 400, No. Wilkesboro, N.C.	Tim Richmond	Pontiac	24,780
Apr. 15	Transouth 500, Darlington, S.C.	Darrell Waltrip	Chevrolet	39,450
Apr. 29	Sovran Bank 500, Martinsville, Va.	Geoff Bodine	Chevrolet	29,880
May 6	Winston 500, Talladega, Ala.	Cale Yarborough	Chevrolet	42,300
May 12	Coors 420, Nashville, Tenn.	Darrell Waltrip	Chevrolet	29,300
May 20	Budweiser 500, Dover, Del.	Richard Petty	Pontiac	28,105
May 27	World 600, Harrisburg, N.C.	Bobby Allison	Buick	88,500
June 3	Budweiser 400, Riverside, Cal.	Terry Labonte	Chevrolet	31,995
June 10	Van Scoy Diamond Mine 500, Pocono, Pa.	Cale Yarborough	Chevrolet	30,850
June 17	Miller High Life 400, Brooklyn, Mich.	Bill Elliott	Ford	41,600
July 4	Firecracker 400, Daytona Beach, Fla.	Richard Petty	Pontiac	43,755
July 14	Pepsi 420, Nashville, Tenn.	Geoff Bodine	Chevrolet	25,800
July 22	Like Cola 500, Long Pond, Pa.	Harry Gant	Chevrolet	34,605
July 29	Talladega 500, Talladega, Ala.	Dale Earnhardt	Chevrolet	47,100
Aug. 12	Champion Spark Plug 400, Brooklyn, Mich.	Darrell Waltrip	Chevrolet	40,800
Aug. 25	Busch 500, Bristol, Tenn.	Terry Labonte	Chevrolet	28,480
Sept. 2	Southern 500, Darlington, S.C.	Harry Gant	Chevrolet	46,180
Sept. 9	Wrangler Sanforset 400, Richmond, Va.	Darrell Waltrip	Chevrolet	46,550
Sept. 16	Delaware 500, Dover, Del.	Harry Gant	Chevrolet	40,005
Sept. 23	Goody's 500, Martinsville, Va.	Darrell Waltrip	Chevrolet	38,300

Daytona 500 Winners

Year	Driver, car	Avg. MPH	Year	Driver, car	Avg. MPH
1962	Fireball Roberts, Pontiac	152.529	1974	Richard Petty, Dodge (c)	140.894
1963	Tiny Lund, Ford	151.566	1975	Benny Parsons, Chevrolet	153.649
1964	Richard Petty, Plymouth	154.334	1976	David Pearson, Mercury	152.181
1965	Fred Lorenzen, Ford (a)	141.539	1977	Cale Yarborough, Chevrolet	153.218
1966	Richard Petty, Plymouth (b)	160.627	1978	Bobby Allison, Ford	159.730
1967	Mario Andretti, Ford	146.926	1979	Richard Petty, Oldsmobile	143.977
1968	Cale Yarborough, Mercury	143.251	1980	Buddy Baker, Oldsmobile	177.602
1969	Lee Roy Yarborough, Ford	160.875	1981	Richard Petty, Buick	169.651
1970	Pete Hamilton, Plymouth	149.601	1982	Bobby Allison, Buick	153.991
1971	Richard Petty, Plymouth	144.456	1983	Cale Yarborough, Pontiac	155.979
1972	A. J. Foyt, Mercury	161.550	1984	Cale Yarborough, Chevrolet	150.994
1973	Richard Petty, Dodge	157.205			

(a) 322.5 miles because of rain. (b) 495 miles because of rain. (c) 450 miles.

Grand National Champions (NASCAR)

Year	Driver	Year	Driver	Year	Driver	Year	Driver
1956	Buck Baker	1963	Joe Weatherly	1970	Bobby Isaac	1977	Cale Yarborough
1957	Buck Baker	1964	Richard Petty	1971	Richard Petty	1978	Cale Yarborough
1958	Lee Petty	1965	Ned Jarrett	1972	Richard Petty	1979	Richard Petty
1959	Lee Petty	1966	David Pearson	1973	Benny Parson	1980	Dale Earnhardt
1960	Rex White	1967	Richard Petty	1974	Richard Petty	1981	Darrell Waltrip
1961	Ned Jarrett	1968	David Pearson	1975	Richard Petty	1982	Darrell Waltrip
1962	Joe Weatherly	1969	David Pearson	1976	Cale Yarborough	1983	Bobby Allison

Polo Records

U.S. Open		Silver Cup	
1975	Milwaukee 14, Tulsa-Dallas 6.	1975	Lone Oak-Bunntyco 8, Tulsa 5.
1976	Willow Bend 10, Tulsa 8.	1976	Wilson Ranch 10, Tulsa 8.
1977	Retama 11, Wilson Ranch 7.	1977	Boca Raton 6, Houston 5.
1978	Abercrombie & Kent 7, Tulsa 6.	1978	Wilson Ranch 7, Ft. Lauderdale 6.
1979	Retama 6, Huisache 5.	1979	Retama 7, Willow Bend 6.
1980	Southern Hills 9, Willow Bend 6.	1980	Retama 9, Houston 8.
1981	Rolex A & K 10, Retama 9.	1981	Retama 10, Thunder 8.
1982	Retama 11, Tulsa 6.	1982	Rio Grande 10, Valdina Farms 9.
1983	Ft. Lauderdale 8; Retama 5.	1983	Tulsa 9; San Antonio 7.

Boxing Champions by Classes

As of Oct., 1984 the only universally accepted title holders were in the light heavyweight and middleweight divisions. The following are the recognized champions of the World Boxing Association and the World Boxing Council.

	WBA	WBC
Heavyweight	Gerrie Coetzee, So. Africa	Pinklon Thomas, Wyncotte, Pa.
Cruiserweight (not over 195 lbs.)	Osvaldo Ocasio, Puerto Rico	Carlos De Leon, Puerto Rico
Light Heavyweight (not over 175 lbs.)	Michael Spinks, St. Louis, Mo.	Michael Spinks
Middleweight (not over 160 lbs.)	Marvin Hagler, Brockton, Mass.	Marvin Hagler
Jr. Middleweight (not over 154 lbs.)	Vacant	Thomas Hearns, Detroit, Mich.
Welterweight (not over 147 lbs.)	Donald Curry, Ft. Worth, Tex.	Milton McCrory, Detroit, Mich.
Jr. Welterweight (not over 140 lbs.)	Gene Hatcher, Ft. Worth, Tex.	Billy Costello, Kingston, N.Y.
Lightweight (not over 135 lbs.)	Livingstone Bramble, Passaic N.J.	Edwin Rosario, Puerto Rico
Jr. Lightweight (not over 130 lbs.)	Rocky Lockridge, Maple Shade, N.J.	Hector Camacho, New York, N.Y.
Featherweight (not over 126 lbs.)	Eusebio Pedroza, Panama	Wilfredo Gomez, Puerto Rico
Jr. Featherweight (not over 122 lbs.)	Victor Callejas, Puerto Rico	Jaime Garza, Los Angeles, Cal.
Bantamweight (not over 118 lbs.)	Richard Sandoval, Los Angeles, Cal.	Albert Davila, Pomona, Cal.
Flyweight (not over 112 lbs.)	Santos Laciar, Argentina	Gabriel Bernal, Mexico

Ring Champions by Years

*Abandoned title

Heavyweights

1882-1892	John L. Sullivan (a)
1892-1897	James J. Corbett (b)
1897-1899	Robert Fitzsimmons
1899-1905	James J. Jeffries (c)
1905-1906	Marvin Hart
1906-1908	Tommy Burns
1908-1915	Jack Johnson
1915-1919	Jess Willard
1919-1926	Jack Dempsey
1926-1928	Gene Tunney*
1928-1930	vacant
1930-1932	Max Schmeling
1932-1933	Jack Sharkey
1933-1934	Primo Carnera
1934-1935	Max Baer
1935-1937	James J. Braddock
1937-1949	Joe Louis*
1949-1951	Ezzard Charles
1951-1952	Joe Walcott
1952-1956	Rocky Marciano*
1956-1959	Floyd Patterson
1959-1960	Ingemar Johansson
1960-1962	Floyd Patterson
1962-1964	Sonny Liston
1964-1967	Cassius Clay* (Muhammad Ali) (d)
1970-1973	Joe Frazier
1973-1974	George Foreman
1974-1978	Muhammad Ali
1978-1979	Leon Spinks (e), Muhammad Ali*
1978	Ken Norton (WBC), Larry Holmes (WBC)
1979	John Tate (WBA)
1980	Mike Weaver (WBA)
1983	Michael Dokes (WBA)
1983	Gerrie Coetzee (WBA)
1984	Tim Witherspoon (WBC); Pinklon Thomas (WBC)

(a) London Prize Ring (bare knuckle champion).
(b) First Marquis of Queensberry champion.
(c) Jeffries abandoned the title (1905) and designated Marvin Hart and Jack Root as logical contenders and agreed to referee a fight between them, the winner to be declared champion. Hart defeated Root in 12 rounds (1905) and in turn was defeated by Tommy Burns (1906) who immediately laid claim to the title. Jack Johnson defeated Burns (1908) and was recognized as champion. He clinched the title by defeating Jeffries in an attempted comeback (1910).
(d) Title declared vacant by the World Boxing Assn. and other groups in 1967 after Clay's refusal to fulfill his military obligation. Joe Frazier was recognized as champion by New York, 5 other states, Mexico, and So. America. Jimmy Ellis was declared champion by the World Boxing Assn. Frazier KOd Ellis, Feb. 16, 1970.
(e) After Spinks defeated Ali, the WBC recognized Ken Norton as champion. Norton subsequently lost his title to Larry Holmes.

Light Heavyweights

1903	Jack Root, George Gardner
1903-1905	Bob Fitzsimmons
1905-1912	Philadelphia Jack O'Brien*
1912-1916	Jack Dillon
1916-1920	Battling Levinsky
1920-1922	George Carpentier
1922-1923	Battling Siki
1923-1925	Mike McTigue
1925-1926	Paul Berlenbach
1926-1927	Jack Delaney*
1927-1929	Tommy Loughran*
1930-1934	Maxey Rosenbloom
1934-1935	Bob Olin
1935-1939	John Henry Lewis*
1939	Melio Bettina
1939-1941	Billy Conn*
1941	Anton Christoforidis (won NBA title)
1941-1948	Gus Lesnevich, Freddie Mills
1948-1950	Freddie Mills
1950-1952	Joey Maxim
1952-1960	Archie Moore
1961-1962	vacant
1962-1963	Harold Johnson
1963-1965	Willie Pastrano
1965-1966	Jose Torres
1966-1968	Dick Tiger
1968-1974	Bob Foster*, John Conteh (WBA)
1975-1977	John Conteh (WBC), Miguel Cuello (WBC), Victor Galindez (WBA)
1978	Mike Rossman (WBA), Mate Parlov (WBC), Marvin Johnson (WBC)
1979	Victor Galindez (WBA), Matthew Saad Muhammad (WBC)
1980	Eddie Mustava Muhammad (WBA)
1981	Michael Spinks (WBA), Dwight Braxton (WBC)
1983	Michael Spinks

Middleweights

1884-1891	Jack "Nonpareil" Dempsey
1891-1897	Bob Fitzsimmons*
1897-1907	Tommy Ryan*
1907-1908	Stanley Ketchel, Billy Papke
1908-1910	Stanley Ketchel
1911-1913	vacant
1913	Frank Klaus, George Chip
1914-1917	Al McCoy
1917-1920	Mike O'Dowd
1920-1923	Johnny Wilson
1923-1926	Harry Greb
1926-1931	Tiger Flowers, Mickey Walker
1931-1932	Gorilla Jones (NBA)
1932-1937	Marcel Thil
1938	Al Hostak (NBA), Solly Krieger (NBA)
1939-1940	Al Hostak (NBA)
1941-1947	Tony Zale
1947-1948	Rocky Graziano
1948	Tony Zale, Marcel Cerdan
1949-1951	Jake LaMotta
1951	Ray Robinson, Randy Turpin, Ray Robinson*
1953-1955	Carl (Bobo) Olson
1955-1957	Ray Robinson
1957	Gene Fullmer, Ray Robinson, Carmen Basilio
1958	Ray Robinson
1959	Gene Fullmer (NBA); Ray Robinson (N.Y.)

1960	Gene Fullmer (NBA); Paul Pender (New York and Mass.)
1961	Gene Fullmer (NBA); Terry Downes (New York, Mass., Europe)
1962	Gene Fullmer, Dick Tiger (NBA), Paul Pender (New York and Mass.)*
1963	Dick Tiger (universal).
1963-1965	Joey Giardello
1965-1966	Dick Tiger
1966-1967	Emile Griffith
1967	Nino Benvenuti
1967-1968	Emile Griffith
1968-1970	Nino Benvenuti
1970-1977	Carlos Monzon*
1977-1978	Rodrigo Valdez
1978-1979	Hugo Corro
1979-1980	Vito Antuofermo
1980	Alan Minter, Marvin Hagler

Welterweights

1892-1894	Mysterious Billy Smith
1894-1896	Tommy Ryan
1896	Kid McCoy*
1900	Rube Ferns, Matty Matthews
1901	Rube Ferns
1901-1904	Joe Walcott
1904-1906	Dixie Kid, Joe Walcott, Honey Mellody
1907-1911	Mike Sullivan
1911-1915	vacant
1915-1919	Ted Lewis
1919-1922	Jack Britton
1922-1926	Mickey Walker
1926	Pete Latzo
1927-1929	Joe Dundee
1929	Jackie Fields
1930	Jack Thompson, Tommy Freeman
1931	Freeman, Thompson, Lou Brouillard
1932	Jackie Fields
1933	Young Corbett, Jimmy McLarnin
1934	Barney Ross, Jimmy McLarnin
1935-1938	Barney Ross
1938-1940	Henry Armstrong
1940-1941	Fritzie Zivic
1941-1946	Fred Cochrane
1946-1946	Marty Servo*; Ray Robinson (a)
1946-1950	Ray Robinson*
1951	Johnny Bratton (NBA)
1951-1954	Kid Gavilan
1954-1955	Johnny Saxton
1955	Tony De Marco, Carmen Basilio
1956	Carmen Basilio, Johnny Saxton, Carmen Basilio
1957	Carmen Basilio*
1958-1960	Virgil Akins, Don Jordan
1960	Benny Paret
1961	Emile Griffith, Benny Paret
1962	Emile Griffith
1963	Luis Rodriguez, Emile Griffith
1964-1966	Emile Griffith*
1966-1969	Curtis Cokes
1969-1970	Jose Napoles, Billy Backus
1971-1975	Jose Napoles
1975-1976	John Stracey (WBC), Angel Espada (WBA)
1976-1979	Carlos Palomino (WBC), Jose Cuevas (WBA)
1979	Wilfredo Benitez (WBC), Sugar Ray Leonard (WBC)
1980	Roberto Duran (WBC), Thomas Hearns (WBA), Sugar Ray Leonard (WBC)
1981-1982	Sugar Ray Leonard*
1983	Donald Curry (WBA); Milton McCrory (WBC)

(a) Robinson gained the title by defeating Tommy Bell in an elimination agreed to by the NY Commission and the NBA. Both claimed Robinson waived his title when he won the middleweight crown from LaMotta in 1951, Gavilan defeated Bratton in an elimination to find a successor.

Lightweights

1896-1899	Kid Lavigne
1899-1902	Frank Erne
1902-1908	Joe Gans
1908-1910	Battling Nelson
1910-1912	Ad Wolgast
1912-1914	Willie Ritchie
1914-1917	Freddie Welsh
1917-1925	Benny Leonard*

1925	Jimmy Goodrich, Rocky Kansas
1926-1930	Sammy Mandell
1930	Al Singer, Tony Canzoneri
1930-1933	Tony Canzoneri
1933-1935	Barney Ross*
1935-1936	Tony Canzoneri
1936-1938	Lou Ambers
1938	Henry Armstrong
1939	Lou Ambers
1940	Lew Jenkins
1941-1943	Sammy Angott
1944	S. Angott (NBA), J. Zurita (NBA)
1945-1951	Ike Williams (NBA; later universal)
1951-1952	James Carter
1952	Lauro Salas, James Carter
1953-1954	James Carter
1954	Paddy De Marco; James Carter
1955	James Carter; Bud Smith
1956	Bud Smith, Joe Brown
1956-1962	Joe Brown
1962-1965	Carlos Ortiz
1965	Ismael Laguna
1965-1968	Carlos Ortiz
1968-1969	Teo Cruz
1969-1970	Mando Ramos
1970	Ismael Laguna, Ken Buchanan (WBA)
1971	Mando Ramos (WBC), Pedro Carrasco (WBC)
1972-1979	Roberto Duran* (WBA)
1972	Pedro Carrasco (WBC), Mando Ramos (WBC), Chango Carmona (WBC), Rodolfo Gonzalez (WBC)
1974-1976	Guts Ishimatsu (WBC)
1976-1977	Esteban De Jesus (WBC)
1979	Jim Watt (WBC), Ernesto Espana (WBA)
1980	Hilmer Kenty (WBA)
1981	Alexis Arguello (WBC), Sean O'Grady (WBA), Arturo Frias (WBA)
1982-1984	Ray Mancini (WBA)
1983	Edwin Rosario (WBC)
1984	Livingstone Bramble (WBA)

Featherweights

1892-1900	George Dixon (disputed)
1900-1901	Terry McGovern, Young Corbett*
1901-1912	Abe Attell
1912-1923	Johnny Kilbane
1923	Eugene Criqui, Johnny Dundee
1923-1925	Johnny Dundee*
1925-1927	Kid Kaplan*
1927-1928	Benny Bass, Tony Canzoneri
1928-1929	Andre Routis
1929-1932	Battling Battalino*
1932-1934	Tommy Paul (NBA)
1933-1936	Freddie Miller
1936-1937	Petey Sarron
1937-1938	Henry Armstrong*
1938-1940	Joey Archibald (b)
1942-1948	Willie Pep
1948-1949	Sandy Saddler
1949-1950	Willie Pep
1950-1957	Sandy Saddler*
1957-1959	Hogan (Kid) Bassey
1959-1963	Davey Moore
1963-1964	Sugar Ramos
1964-1967	Vicente Saldivar*
1968-1971	Paul Rojas (WBA), Sho Saijo (WBA)
1971	Antonio Gomez (WBA), Kuniaki Shibada (WBC)
1972	Ernesto Marcel* (WBA), Clemente Sanchez* (WBC), Jose Legra (WBC)
1973	Eder Jofre (WBC)
1974	Ruben Olivares (WBA), Alexis Arguello (WBA), Bobby Chacon (WBC)
1975	Ruben Olivares (WBC), David Kotey (WBC)
1976	Danny Lopez (WBC)
1977	Rafael Ortega (WBA)
1978	Cecilio Lastra (WBA), Eusebio Pedrosa (WBA)
1980	Salvador Sanchez (WBC)
1982	Juan LaPorte (WBC)
1984	Wilfredo Gomez (WBC)

(b) After Petey Scalzo knocked out Archibald (Dec. 5, 1938) in an overweight match and was refused a title bout, the NBA named Scalzo champion. The NBA title succession was: Petey Scalzo, 1938-1941; Richard Lemos, 1941; Jackie Wilson, 1941-1943; Jackie Callura, 1943; Phil Terranova, 1943-1944; Sal Bartolo, 1944-1946.

History of Heavyweight Championship Bouts

*Title Changed Hands

1889—July 8—John L. Sullivan def. Jake Kilrain, 75, Richburg, Miss. Last championship bare knuckles bout.
*1892—Sept. 7—James J. Corbett def. John L. Sullivan, 21, New Orleans. Big gloves used for first time.
1894—Jan. 25—James J. Corbett KOd Charley Mitchell, 3, Jacksonville, Fla.
*1897—Bob Fitzsimmons def. James J. Corbett, 14, Carson City, Nev.
*1899—June 9—James J. Jeffries def. Bob Fitzsimmons, 11, Coney Island, N.Y.
1899—Nov. 3—James J. Jeffries def. Tom Sharkey, 25, Coney Island, N.Y.
1900—May 11—James J. Jeffries KOd James J. Corbett, 23, Coney Island, N.Y.
1901—Nov. 15—James J. Jeffries KOd Gus Ruhlin, 5, San Francisco.
1902—July 25—James J. Jeffries KOd Bob Fitzsimmons, 8, San Francisco.
1903—Aug. 14—James J. Jeffries KOd James J. Corbett, 10, San Francisco.
1904—Aug. 26—James J. Jeffries KOd Jack Monroe, 2, San Francisco.
*1905—James J. Jeffries retired, July 3—Marvin Hart KOd Jack Root, 12, Reno. Jeffries refereed and presented the title to the victor. Jack O'Brien also claimed the title.
*1906—Feb. 23—Tommy Burns def. Marvin Hart, 20, Los Angeles.
1906—Nov. 28—Philadelphia Jack O'Brien and Tommy Burns, 20, draw, Los Angeles.
1907—May 8—Tommy Burns def. Jack O'Brien, 20, Los Angeles.
1907—July 4—Tommy Burns KOd Bill Squires, 1, Colma, Cal.
1907—Dec. 2—Tommy Burns KOd Gunner Moir, 10, London.
1908—Feb. 10—Tommy Burns KOd Jack Palmer, 4, London.
1908—March 17—Tommy Burns KOd Jem Roche, 1, Dublin.
1908—April 18—Tommy Burns KOd Jewey Smith, 5, Paris.
1908—June 13—Tommy Burns KOd Bill Squires, 8, Paris.
1908—Aug. 24—Tommy Burns KOd Bill Squires, 13, Sydney, New South Wales.
1908—Sept. 2—Tommy Burns KOd Bill Lang, 2, Melbourne, Australia.
*1908—Dec. 26—Jack Johnson KOd Tommy Burns, 14, Sydney, Australia. Police halted contest.
1909—May 19—Jack Johnson and Jack O'Brien, 6, draw, Philadelphia.
1909—June 30—Jack Johnson and Tony Ross, 6, draw, Pittsburgh.
1909—Sept. 9—Jack Johnson and Al Kaufman, 10, draw, San Francisco.
1909—Oct. 16—Jack Johnson KOd Stanley Ketchel, 12, Colma, Cal.
1910—July 4—Jack Johnson KOd Jim Jeffries, 15, Reno, Nev. Jeffries came back from retirement.
1912—July 4—Jack Johnson def. Jim Flynn, 9, Las Vegas, N.M. Contest stopped by police.
1913—Nov. 28—Jack Johnson KOd Andre Spaul, 2, Paris.
1913—Dec. 9—Jack Johnson and Jim Johnson, 10, draw, Paris. Bout called a draw when Jack Johnson declared he had broken his arm.
1914—June 27—Jack Johnson def. Frank Moran, 20, Paris.
*1915—April 5—Jess Willard KOd Jack Johnson, 26, Havana, Cuba.
1916—March 25—Jess Willard and Frank Moran, 10, draw, New York.
*1919—July 4—Jack Dempsey def. Jess Willard, Toledo, Oh. Willard failed to answer bell for 4th round.
1920—Sept. 6—Jack Dempsey KOd Billy Miske, 3, Benton Harbor, Mich.
1920—Dec. 14—Jack Dempsey KOd Bill Brennan, 12, New York.
1921—July 2—Jack Dempsey KOd George Carpentier, 4, Boyle's Thirty Acres, Jersey City, N.J. Carpentier had held the so-called white heavyweight title since July 16, 1914, in a series established in 1913, after Jack Johnson's exile in Europe late in 1912.
1923—July 4—Jack Dempsey def. Tom Gibbons, 15, Shelby, Mont.
1923—Sept. 14—Jack Dempsey KOd Luis Firpo, 2, New York.
*1926—Sept. 23—Gene Tunney def. Jack Dempsey, 10, Philadelphia.
1927—Sept. 22—Gene Tunney def. Jack Dempsey, 10, Chicago.
1928—July 26—Gene Tunney KOd Tom Heeney, 11, New York; soon afterward he announced his retirement.

*1930—June 12—Max Schmeling def. Jack Sharkey, 4, New York. Sharkey fouled Schmeling in a bout which was generally considered to have resulted in the election of a successor to Gene Tunney, New York.
1931—July 3—Max Schmeling KOd Young Stribling, 15, Cleveland.
*1932—June 21—Jack Sharkey def. Max Schmeling, 15, New York.
*1933—June 29—Primo Carnera KOd Jack Sharkey, 6, New York.
1933—Oct. 22—Primo Carnera def. Paulino Uzcudun, 15, Rome.
1934—March 1—Primo Carnera def. Tommy Loughran, 15, Miami.
*1934—June 14—Max Baer KOd Primo Carnera, 11, New York.
*1935—June 13—James J. Braddock def. Max Baer, 15, New York.
*1937—June 22—Joe Louis KOd James J. Braddock, 8, Chicago.
1937—Aug. 30—Joe Louis def. Tommy Farr, 15, New York.
1938—Feb. 23—Joe Louis KOd Nathan Mann, 3, New York.
1938—April 1—Joe Louis KOd Harry Thomas, 5, New York.
1938—June 22—Joe Louis KOd Max Schmeling, 1, New York.
1939—Jan. 25—Joe Louis KOd John H. Lewis, 1, New York.
1939—April 17—Joe Louis KOd Jack Roper, 1, Los Angeles.
1939—June 28—Joe Louis KOd Tony Galento, 4, New York.
1939—Sept. 20—Joe Louis KOd Bob Pastor, 11, Detroit.
1940—February 9—Joe Louis def. Arturo Godoy, 15, New York.
1940—March 29—Joe Louis KOd Johnny Paycheck, 2, New York.
1940—June 20—Joe Louis KOd Arturo Godoy, 8, New York.
1940—Dec. 16—Joe Louis KOd Al McCoy, 6, Boston.
1941—Jan. 31—Joe Louis KOd Red Burman, 5, New York.
1941—Feb. 17—Joe Louis KOd Gus Dorzaio, 2, Philadelphia.
1941—March 21—Joe Louis KOd Abe Simon, 13, Detroit.
1941—April 8—Joe Louis KOd Tony Musto, 9, St. Louis.
1941—May 23—Joe Louis def. Buddy Baer, 7, Washington, D.C., on a disqualification.
1941—June 18—Joe Louis KOd Billy Conn, 13, New York.
1941—Sept. 29—Joe Louis KOd Lou Nova, 6, New York.
1942—Jan. 9—Joe Louis KOd Buddy Baer, 1, New York.
1942—March 27—Joe Louis KOd Abe Simon, 6, New York.
1946—June 19—Joe Louis KOd Billy Conn, 8, New York.
1946—Sept. 18—Joe Louis KOd Tami Mauriello, 1, New York.
1947—Dec. 5—Joe Louis def. Joe Walcott, 15, New York.
1948—June 25—Joe Louis KOd Joe Walcott, 11, New York.
*1949—June 22—Following Joe Louis' retirement Ezzard Charles def. Joe Walcott, 15, Chicago, NBA recognition only.
1949—Aug. 10—Ezzard Charles KOd Gus Lesnevich, 7, New York.
1949—Oct. 14—Ezzard Charles KOd Pat Valentino, 8, San Francisco; clinched American title.
1950—Aug. 15—Ezzard Charles KOd Freddy Beshore, 14, Buffalo.
1950—Sept. 27—Ezzard Charles def. Joe Louis in latter's attempted comeback, 15, New York; universal recognition.
1950—Dec. 5—Ezzard Charles KOd Nick Barone, 11, Cincinnati.
1951—Jan. 12—Ezzard Charles KOd Lee Oma, 10, New York.
1951—March 7—Ezzard Charles def. Joe Walcott, 15, Detroit.
1951—May 30—Ezzard Charles def. Joey Maxim, light heavyweight champion, 15, Chicago.
*1951—July 18—Joe Walcott KOd Ezzard Charles, 7, Pittsburgh.
1952—June 5—Joe Walcott def. Ezzard Charles, 15, Philadelphia.
*1952—Sept. 23—Rocky Marciano KOd Joe Walcott, 13, Philadelphia.
1953—May 15—Rocky Marciano KOd Joe Walcott, 1, Chicago.
1953—Sept. 24—Rocky Marciano KOd Roland LaStarza, 11, New York.
1954—June 17—Rocky Marciano def. Ezzard Charles, 15, New York.
1954—Sept. 17—Rocky Marciano KOd Ezzard Charles, 8, New York.
1955—May 16—Rocky Marciano KOd Don Cockell, 9, San Francisco.
1955—Sept. 21—Rocky Marciano KOd Archie Moore, 9, New York. Marciano retired undefeated, Apr. 27, 1956.

*1956—Nov. 30—Floyd Patterson KOd Archie Moore, 5, Chicago.
1957—July 29—Floyd Patterson KOd Hurricane Jackson, 10, New York.
1957—Aug. 22—Floyd Patterson KOd Pete Rademacher, 6, Seattle.
1958—Aug. 18—Floyd Patterson KOd Roy Harris, 12, Los Angeles.
1959—May 1—Floyd Patterson KOd Brian London, 11, Indianapolis.
*1959—June 26—Ingemar Johansson KOd Floyd Patterson, 3, New York.
*1960—June 20—Floyd Patterson KOd Ingemar Johansson, 5, New York. First heavyweight in boxing history to regain title.
1961—Mar. 13—Floyd Patterson KOd Ingemar Johansson, 6, Miami Beach.
1961—Dec. 4—Floyd Patterson KOd Tom McNeeley, 4, Toronto.
*1962—Sept. 25—Sonny Liston KOd Floyd Patterson, 1, Chicago.
1963—July 22—Sonny Liston KOd Floyd Patterson, 1, Las Vegas.
*1964—Feb. 25—Cassius Clay KOd Sonny Liston, 7, Miami Beach.
1965—May 25—Cassius Clay KOd Sonny Liston, 1, Lewiston, Maine.
1965—Nov. 11—Cassius Clay KOd Floyd Patterson, 12, Las Vegas.
1966—Mar. 29—Cassius Clay def. George Chuvalo, 15, Toronto.
1966—May 21—Cassius Clay KOd Henry Cooper, 6, London.
1966—Aug. 6—Cassius Clay KOd Brian London, 3, London.
1966—Sept. 10—Cassius Clay KOd Karl Mildenberger, 12, Frankfurt, Germany.
1966—Nov. 14—Cassius Clay KOd Cleveland Williams, 3, Houston.
1967—Feb. 6—Cassius Clay def. Ernie Terrell, 15, Houston.
1967—Mar. 22—Cassius Clay KOd Zora Folley, 7, New York. Clay was stripped of his title by the WBA and others for refusing military service.
*1970—Feb. 16—Joe Frazier KOd Jimmy Ellis, 5, New York.
1970—Nov. 18—Joe Frazier KOd Bob Foster, 2, Detroit.
1971—Mar. 8—Joe Frazier def. Cassius Clay (Muhammad Ali), 15, New York.
1972—Jan. 15—Joe Frazier KOd Terry Daniels, 4, New Orleans.
1972—May 25—Joe Frazier KOd Ron Stander, 5, Omaha.
*1973—Jan. 22—George Foreman KOd Joe Frazier, 2, Kingston, Jamaica.
1973—Sept. 1—George Foreman KOd Joe Roman, 1, Tokyo.
1974—Mar. 3—George Foreman KOd Ken Norton, 2, Caracas.
*1974—Oct. 30—Muhammad Ali KOd George Foreman, 8, Zaire.
1975—Mar. 24—Muhammad Ali KOd Chuck Wepner, 15, Cleveland.
1975—May 16—Muhammad Ali KOd Ron Lyle, 11, Las Vegas.
1975—June 30—Muhammad Ali def. Joe Bugner, 15, Malaysia.
1975—Oct. 1—Muhammad Ali KOd Joe Frazier, 14, Manila.
1976—Feb. 20—Muhammad Ali KOd Jean-Pierre Coopman, 5, San Juan.
1976—Apr. 30—Muhammad Ali def. Jimmy Young, 15, Landover, Md.
1976—May 25—Muhammad Ali KOd Richard Dunn, 5, Munich.
1976—Sept. 28—Muhammad Ali def. Ken Norton, 15, New York.
1977—May 16—Muhammad Ali def. Alfredo Evangelista, 15, Landover, Md.
1977—Sept. 29—Muhammad Ali def. Earnie Shavers, 15, New York.
*1978—Feb. 15—Leon Spinks def. Muhammad Ali, 15, Las Vegas.
*1978—Sept. 15—Muhammad Ali def. Leon Spinks, 15, New Orleans. Ali retired in 1979.

(Bouts when title changed hands only)

*1978—June 9—(WBC) Larry Holmes def. Ken Norton, 15, Las Vegas.
*1980—Mar. 31—(WBA) Mike Weaver KOd John Tate, 15, Knoxville.
*1982—Dec. 10—(WBA) Michael Dokes KOd Mike Weaver, 1, Las Vegas.
*1983—Sept. 23—(WBA) Gerrie Coetzee KOd Michael Dokes, 10, Richfield, Oh.
*1984—Mar. 10—(WBC) Tim Witherspoon def. Greg Page, 12, Las Vegas, Nev.
*1984—Aug. 31—(WBC) Pinklon Thomas def. Tim Witherspoon, 12, Las Vegas, Nev.

Notable Sports Personalities

Henry Aaron, b. 1934: Milwaukee-Atlanta outfielder hit record 755 home runs; led NL 4 times.
Kareem Abdul-Jabbar, b. 1947: Milwaukee, L.A. Lakers center; MVP 6 times; leading scorer twice.
Grover Cleveland Alexander, (1887-1950): pitcher won 374 NL games; pitched 16 shutouts, 1916.
Muhammad Ali, b. 1942: 3-time heavyweight champion.
Ken Anderson, b. 1949: Cinn. Bengals quarterback led AFC in passing 4 times.
Mario Andretti, b. 1940: U.S. Auto Club national champ 3 times: won Indy 500, 1969; Grand Prix champ, 1978.
Eddie Arcaro, b. 1916: jockey rode 4,779 winners including the Kentucky Derby 5 times; the Preakness and Belmont Stakes 6 times each.
Henry Armstrong, b. 1912: boxer held feather-, welter-, lightweight titles simultaneously, 1937-38.
Arthur Ashe, b. 1943: U.S. singles champ, 1968, Wimbledon champ, 1975.
Red Auerbach, b. 1917: coached Boston Celtics to 9 NBA championships.
Ernie Banks, b. 1931: Chicago Cubs slugger hit 512 NL homers; twice MVP.
Roger Bannister, b. 1929: Briton ran first sub 4-minute mile, May 6, 1954.
Rick Barry, b. 1944: NBA scoring leader, 1967; ABA, 1969.
Sammy Baugh, b. 1914: Washington Redskins quarterback held numerous records upon retirement after 16 pro seasons.
Elgin Baylor, b. 1934: L.A. Lakers forward; 1st team all-star 10 times.
Bob Beamon, b. 1946: long jumper won 1968 Olympic gold medal with record 29 ft. 2½ in.
Jean Beliveau, b. 1931: Montreal Canadiens center scored 507 goals; twice MVP.
Johnny Bench, b. 1947: Cincinnati Reds catcher; MVP twice; led league in home runs twice, RBIs 3 times.
Patty Berg, b. 1918: won over 80 golf tournaments; AP Woman Athlete-of-the-Year 3 times.
Yogi Berra, b. 1925: N.Y. Yankees catcher; MVP 3 times; played in 14 World Series.

Raymond Berry, b. 1933: Baltimore Colts receiver caught 631 passes.
Larry Bird, b. 1956: Boston Celtics forward; chosen MVP, playoff MVP, 1984.
George Blanda, b. 1927: quarterback, kicker; 26 years as active player, scoring record 2,002 points.
Bjorn Borg, b. 1956: led Sweden to first Davis Cup, 1975; Wimbledon champion, 5 times.
Julius Boros, b. 1920: won U.S. Open, 1952, 1963; PGA champ, 1968.
Mike Bossy, b.1957; N.Y. Islanders right wing scored over 50 goals 7 times.
Jack Brabham, b. 1926: Grand Prix champ 3 times.
Terry Bradshaw, b. 1948; Pittsburgh Steelers quarterback led team to 4 Super Bowl titles.
George Brett, b. 1953: Kansas City Royals 3d baseman led AL in batting, 1976, 1980; MVP, 1980.
Lou Brock, b. 1939: St. Louis Cardinals outfielder stole record 118 bases, 1974; record 937 career; led NL 8 times.
Jimmy Brown, b. 1936: Cleveland Browns fullback ran for 12,312 career yards; MVP 3 times.
Paul "Bear" Bryant, (1913-1983), college football coach with record 323 victories.
Don Budge, b. 1915: won numerous amateur and pro tennis titles, "grand slam," 1938.
Maria Bueno, b. 1939: U.S. singles champ 4 times; Wimbledon champ 3 times.
Dick Butkus, b. 1942: Chicago Bears linebacker twice chosen best NFL defensive player.
Dick Button, b. 1929: figure skater won 1948, 1952 Olympic gold medals; world titlist, 1948-52.
Walter Camp, (1859-1925): Yale football player, coach, athletic director; established many rules; promoted All-America designations.
Roy Campanella, b. 1921: Brooklyn Dodgers catcher; MVP 3 times.
Earl Campbell, b. 1955: Houston Oilers running back; NFL MVP 1978-1980.
Rod Carew, b. 1945: AL infielder won 7 batting titles; MVP,

1977.

Steve Carlton, b. 1944: NL pitcher won 20 games 5 times, Cy Young award 4 times.

Billy Casper, b. 1931: PGA Player-of-the-Year 3 times; U.S. Open champ twice.

Wilt Chamberlain, b. 1936: center scored NBA career record 31,419 points; MVP 4 times.

Bobby Clarke, b. 1949: Philadelphia Flyers center led team to 2 Stanley Cup championships; MVP 3 times.

Roberto Clemente, (1934-1972): Pittsburgh Pirates outfielder won 4 batting titles; MVP, 1966.

Ty Cobb, (1886-1961): Detroit Tigers outfielder had record .367 lifetime batting average, 4,191 hits, 12 batting titles.

Sebastian Coe, b. 1956: Briton won Olympic 1,500-meter run, 1980, 1984.

Nadia Comaneci, b. 1961: Romanian gymnast won 3 gold medals, achieved 7 perfect scores, 1976 Olympics.

Maureen Connolly, (1934-1969): won tennis "grand slam," 1953; AP Woman-Athlete-of-the-Year 3 times.

Jimmy Connors, b. 1952: U.S. singles champ 5 times; Wimbledon champ twice.

James J. Corbett, (1866-1933): heavyweight champion, 1892-97; credited with being the first "scientific" boxer.

Margaret Smith Court, b. 1942: Australian won U.S. singles championship 5 times; Wimbledon champ 3 times.

Bob Cousy, b. 1928: Boston Celtics guard led team to 6 NBA championships; MVP, 1957.

Dizzy Dean, (1911-1974): colorful pitcher for St. Louis Cardinals "Gashouse Gang" in the 30s; MVP, 1934.

Jack Dempsey, (1895-1983): heavyweight champion, 1919-26.

Joe DiMaggio, b. 1914: N.Y. Yankees outfielder hit safely in record 56 consecutive games, 1941; MVP 3 times.

Leo Durocher, b. 1906: colorful manager of Dodgers, Giants, and Cubs; won 3 NL pennants.

Gertrude Ederle, b. 1906: first woman to swim English Channel, broke existing men's record, 1926.

Julius Erving, b. 1950: MVP and leading scorer in ABA 3 times; NBA MVP, 1981.

Phil Esposito, b. 1942: NHL scoring leader 5 times.

Chris Evert Lloyd, b 1954: U.S. singles champ 6 times, Wimbledon champ 3 times.

Ray Ewry, (1873-1937): track and field star won 8 gold medals, 1900, 1904, and 1908 Olympics.

Juan Fangio, b. 1911: Argentine World Grand Prix champion 5 times.

Bob Feller, b. 1918: Cleveland Indians pitcher won 266 games; pitched 3 no-hitters, 12 one-hitters.

Peggy Fleming, b. 1948: world figure skating champion, 1966-68; gold medalist 1968 Olympics.

Whitey Ford, b. 1928: N.Y. Yankees pitcher won record 10 World Series games.

Dick Fosbury, b. 1947: high jumper won 1968 Olympic gold medal; developed the "Fosbury Flop."

Dan Fouts, b. 1951: S.D. Chargers quarterback passed for NFL record 4,802 yds., 1981.

Jimmy Foxx, (1907-1967): Red Sox, Athletics slugger; MVP 3 times; triple crown, 1933.

A.J. Foyt, b. 1935: won Indy 500 4 times; U.S. Auto Club champ 6 times.

Dawn Fraser, b. 1937: Australian swimmer won Olympics 100-meter freestyle 3 times.

Joe Frazier, b. 1944: heavyweight champion, 1970-73.

Lou Gehrig, (1903-1941): N.Y. Yankees 1st baseman played record 2,130 consecutive games, MVP, 1936.

George Gervin, b. 1952: leading NBA scorer, 1978-80, 1982.

Althea Gibson, b. 1927: twice U.S. and Wimbledon singles champ.

Bob Gibson, b. 1935: St. Louis Cardinals pitcher won Cy Young award twice; struck out 3,117 batters.

Frank Gifford, b. 1930: N.Y. Giants back; MVP 1956.

Otto Graham, b. 1921: Cleveland Browns quarterback; all-pro 4 times.

Red Grange, b 1903: All-America at Univ. of Illinois; played for Chicago Bears, 1925-35.

Joe Greene, b. 1946: Pittsburgh Steelers lineman; twice NFL outstanding defensive player.

Wayne Gretzky, b. 1961: Edmonton Oilers center scored record 92 goals, 212 pts., 1982; MVP, 1980-84.

Lefty Grove, (1900-1975): pitcher won 300 AL games; 20-game winner 8 times.

Walter Hagen, (1892-1969): won PGA championship 5 times. British Open 4 times.

George Halas, (1895-1983); founder-coach of Chicago Bears; won 5 NFL championships.

Bill Hartack, b. 1932: jockey rode 5 Kentucky Derby winners.

Doug Harvey, b. 1930: Montreal Canadiens defenseman; Norris Trophy 7 times.

Bill Haughton, b. 1923: harness racing driver won Little Brown Jug 4 times, Hambletonian 4 times.

John Havlicek, b. 1940: Boston Celtics forward scored over 26,000 NBA points.

Eric Heiden, b. 1958: speed skater won 5 1980 Olympic gold medals.

Carol Heiss, b. 1940: world champion figure skater 5 consecutive years, 1956-60; won 1960 Olympic gold medal.

Rickey Henderson, b. 1958: Oakland A's outfielder stole record 130 bases, 1982.

Sonja Henie, (1912-1969): world champion figure skater, 1927-36; Olympic gold medalist, 1928, 1932, 1936.

Ben Hogan, b. 1912: won 4 U.S. Open championships, 2 PGA, 2 Masters.

Willie Hoppe, (1887-1959): won some 50 world billiard titles.

Larry Holmes, b. 1949: WBC Heavyweight Champ 1978-84.

Rogers Hornsby, (1896-1963): NL 2d baseman batted record .424 in 1924; twice won triple crown; batting leader 7 times.

Paul Hornung, b. 1935: Green Bay Packers runner-placekicker scored record 176 points, 1960.

Gordie Howe, b. 1928: hockey forward holds NHL career records in goals, assists, and points; NHL MVP 6 times.

Carl Hubbell, b. 1903: N.Y. Giants pitcher; 20-game winner 5 consecutive years, 1933-37.

Bobby Hull, b. 1939: NHL all-star 10 times.

Catfish Hunter, b 1946: pitched perfect game, 1968; 20-game winner 5 times.

Don Hutson, b. 1913: Green Bay Packers receiver caught NFL record 99 touchdown passes.

Reggie Jackson, b. 1946: slugger led AL in home runs 4 times; MVP, 1973; hit 5 World Series home runs, 1977.

Bruce Jenner, b. 1949: decathlon gold medalist, 1976.

Jack Johnson, (1878-1946): heavyweight champion, 1910-15.

Magic Johnson, b. 1959: NBA playoff MVP 1980, 1982.

Rafer Johnson, b. 1935: decathlon gold medalist, 1960.

Walter Johnson, (1887-1946): Washington Senators pitcher won 414 games.

Bobby Jones, (1902-1971): won "grand slam of golf" 1930; U.S. Amateur champ 5 times, U.S. Open champ 4 times.

Deacon Jones, b. 1938: L.A. Rams lineman; twice NFL outstanding defensive player.

Sonny Jurgensen, b. 1934: quarterback named all-pro 5 times; completed record 288 passes, 1967.

Duke Kahanamoku, (1890-1968): swimmer won 1912, 1920 Olympic gold medals in 100-meter freestyle.

Harmon Killebrew, b. 1936: Minnesota Twins slugger led AL in home runs 6 times.

Jean Claude Killy, b. 1943: French skier won 3 1968 Olympic gold medals.

Ralph Kiner, b. 1922: Pittsburgh Pirates slugger led NL in home runs 7 consecutive years, 1946-52.

Billie Jean King, b. 1943: U.S. singles champ 4 times; Wimbledon champ 6 times.

Olga Korbut, b. 1956: Soviet gymnast won 3 1972 Olympic gold medals.

Sandy Koufax, b. 1935: Dodgers pitcher won Cy Young award 3 times; lowest ERA in NL, 1962-66; pitched 4 no-hitters, one a perfect game.

Guy Lafleur, b. 1951: Montreal Canadiens forward led NHL in scoring 3 times; MVP, 1977, 1978.

Tom Landry, b. 1924: Dallas Cowboys head coach since 1960.

Rod Laver, b. 1938: Australian won tennis "grand slam," 1962, 1969; Wimbledon champ 4 times.

Sugar Ray Leonard, b. 1956: WBC welterweight champ, 1979-82.

Carl Lewis, b. 1961: track and field star won 4 1984 Olympic gold medals.

Vince Lombardi, (1913-1970): Green Bay Packers coach led team to 5 NFL championships and 2 Super Bowl victories.

Joe Louis, (1914-1981): 1914: heavyweight champion, 1937-49.

Sid Luckman, b. 1916: Chicago Bears quarterback led team to 4 NFL championships; MVP, 1943.

Connie Mack, (1862-1956): Philadelphia Athletics manager, 1901-50; won 9 pennants, 5 championships.

Bill Madlock, b. 1951: NL batting leader 4 times.

Moses Malone, b. 1955: NBA center was MVP 1979, 1982, 1983.

Mickey Mantle, b. 1931: N.Y. Yankees outfielder; triple crown, 1956; 18 World Series home runs.

Alice Marble, b. 1913: U.S. singles champ 4 times.

Rocky Marciano, (1923-1969): heavyweight champion, 1952-56; retired undefeated.

Roger Maris, b. 1934: N.Y. Yankees outfielder hit record 61 home runs, 1961; MVP, 1960 and 1961.

Billy Martin, b. 1928: baseball manager led N.Y. Yankees to World Series title, 1977.

Eddie Mathews, b. 1931: Milwaukee-Atlanta 3d baseman hit 512 career home runs.

Christy Mathewson, (1880-1925): N.Y. Giants pitcher won 373 games.

Bob Mathias, b. 1930: decathlon gold medalist, 1948, 1952.

Willie Mays, b. 1931: N.Y.-S.F. Giants center fielder hit 660 home runs, twice MVP.

John McEnroe, b. 1959: U.S. singles champ, 1979-81, 1984; Wimbledon champ, 1981, 1983-84.

John McGraw, (1873-1934): N.Y. Giants manager led team to 10 pennants, 3 championships.

Debbie Meyer, b. 1952: swimmer won 200-, 400-, and 800- meter freestyle events, 1968 Olympics.

George Mikan, b. 1924: Minneapolis Lakers center selected in a 1950 AP poll as the greatest basketball player of the first half of the 20th century.

Stan Mikita, b. 1940: Chicago Black Hawks center led NHL in scoring 4 times; MVP twice.

Archie Moore, b. 1913: world light-heavyweight champion 1952-62.

Howie Morenz, (1902-1937): Montreal Canadiens forward chosen in a 1950 Canadian press poll as the outstanding hockey player of the first half of the 20th century.

Joe Morgan, b. 1943: National League MVP, 1975, 1976.

Thurman Munson, (1947-1979): N.Y. Yankees catcher; MVP, 1976.

Dale Murphy, b. 1956: Atlanta Braves outfielder chosen NL MVP 1982, 1983.

Stan Musial, b. 1920: St. Louis Cardinals star won 7 NL batting titles; MVP 3 times; NL record 3,630 hits.

Bronko Nagurski, b. 1908: Chicago Bears fullback and tackle; gained over 4,000 yds. rushing.

Joe Namath, b. 1943: quarterback passed for record 4,007 yds., 1967.

Martina Navratilova, b. 1956: Wimbledon champ 4 times, U.S. champ 1983, 1984.

Byron Nelson, b. 1912: won 11 consecutive golf tournaments in 1945; twice Masters and PGA titlist.

Ernie Nevers, (1903-1976): Stanford star selected the best college fullback to play between 1919-1969.

John Newcombe, b. 1943: Australian twice U.S. singles champ; Wimbledon titlist 3 times.

Jack Nicklaus, b. 1940: PGA Player of the Year, 1967, 1972; leading money winner 8 times.

Chuck Noll, b. 1931: Pittsburgh Steelers coach led team to 4 Super Bowl titles.

Paavo Nurmi, (1897-1973): Finnish distance runner won 6 Olympic gold medals, 1920, 1924, 1928.

Al Oerter, b. 1936: discus thrower won gold medal at 4 consecutive Olympics, 1956-68.

Bobby Orr, b. 1948: Boston Bruins defenseman; Norris Trophy 8 times; led NHL in scoring twice, assists 5 times.

Mel Ott, (1909-1958); N.Y. Giants outfielder hit 511 home runs; led NL 6 times.

Jesse Owens, (1913-1980): track and field star won 4 1936 Olympic gold medals.

Satchel Paige, (1906-1982): pitcher starred in Negro leagues, 1924-48; entered major leagues at age 42.

Arnold Palmer, b. 1929: golf's first $1 million winner; won 4 Masters, 2 British Opens.

Jim Palmer, b. 1945: Baltimore Orioles pitcher; Cy Young award 3 times; 20-game winner 7 times.

Floyd Patterson, b. 1935: twice heavyweight champion.

Walter Payton, 1954: Chicago Bears running back ran for game record 275 yards, 1977; leading NFC rusher, 1976-80.

Pele, b. 1940: Brazilian soccer star scored 1,281 goals during 22-year career.

Bob Pettit, b. 1932: first NBA player to score 20,000 points; twice NBA scoring leader.

Richard Petty, b. 1937: NASCAR national champ 6 times; 7-times Daytona 500 winner.

Laffit Pincay Jr., b. 1946: leading money-winning jockey, 1970-74, 1979.

Jacques Plante, b. 1929: goalie, 7 Vezina trophies; first goalie to wear a mask in a game.

Gary Player, b. 1935: South African won the Masters, U.S. Open, PGA, and twice the British Open.

Annemarie Proell Moser, b. 1953: Austrian skier won the World Cup championship 6 times.

Willis Reed, b. 1942: N.Y. Knicks center; MVP, 1970; playoff MVP, 1970, 1973.

Jim Rice, b. 1953: Boston Red Sox outfielder led AL in home runs, 1977-78, 1983; MVP 1978.

Maurice Richard, b. 1921: Montreal Canadiens forward scored 544 regular season goals, 82 playoff goals.

Branch Rickey, (1881-1965): executive instrumental in breaking baseball's color barrier, 1947; initiated farm system, 1919.

Oscar Robertson, b. 1938: guard averaged career 25.7 points per game; record 9,887 career assist; MVP, 1964.

Brooks Robinson, b. 1937: Baltimore Orioles 3d baseman played in 4 World Series; MVP, 1964.

Frank Robinson, b. 1935: slugger MVP in both NL and AL; triple crown winner, 1966; first black manager in majors.

Jackie Robinson, (1919-1972): broke baseball's color barrier with Brooklyn Dodgers, 1947; MVP, 1949.

Larry Robinson, b. 1951: Montreal Canadiens defenseman won Norris trophy, 1977, 1980.

Sugar Ray Robinson, b. 1920: middleweight champion 5 times, welterweight champion.

Knute Rockne, (1888-1931): Notre Dame football coach, 1918-31; revolutionized game by stressing forward pass.

Pete Rose, b. 1942: won 3 NL batting titles; hit safely in 44 consecutive games, 1978; set record for most NL hits, 1981.

Wilma Rudolph, b. 1940: sprinter won 3 1960 Olympic gold medals.

Bill Russell, b. 1934: Boston Celtics center led team to 11 NBA titles; MVP 5 times; first black coach of major pro sports team.

Babe Ruth, (1895-1948): N.Y. Yankees outfielder hit 60 home runs, 1927; 714 lifetime; led AL 11 times.

Johnny Rutherford, b. 1938: auto racer won Indy 500 3 times.

Nolan Ryan, b. 1947: pitcher struck out record 383 batters, 1973; pitched record 5 no-hitters.

Gene Sarazen, b. 1902: won PGA championship 3 times, U.S. Open twice; developer of sand wedge.

Gale Sayers, b. 1943: Chicago Bears back twice led NFC in rushing.

Mike Schmidt, b. 1949: Phillies 3d baseman led NL in home runs, 1974-76, 1980-81, 1983-84; NL MVP, 1980, 1981.

Tom Seaver, b. 1944: pitcher won NL Cy Young award 3 times.

Willie Shoemaker, b. 1931: jockey rode 3 Kentucky Derby and 5 Belmont Stakes winners; leading career money winner.

Eddie Shore, b. 1902: Boston Bruins defenseman; MVP 4 times, first-team all-star 7 times.

Al Simmons, (1902-1956): AL outfielder had lifetime .334 batting average.

O.J. Simpson, b. 1947: running back rushed for record 2,003 yds., 1973; AFC leading rusher 4 times.

George Sisler, (1893-1973): St. Louis Browns 1st baseman had record 257 hits, 1920; batted .340 lifetime.

Sam Snead, b. 1912: PGA and Masters champ 3 times each.

Peter Snell, b. 1938: New Zealand runner won 800-meter race, 1960, 1964 Olympics.

Warren Spahn, b. 1921: pitcher won 363 NL games; 20-game winner 13 times; Cy Young award, 1957.

Tris Speaker, (1885-1958): AL outfielder batted .344 over 22 seasons; hit record 793 career doubles.

Mark Spitz, b. 1950: swimmer won 7 1972 Olympic gold medals.

Amos Alonzo Stagg, (1862-1965): coached Univ. of Chicago football team for 41 years, including 5 undefeated seasons; introduced huddle, man-in-motion, and end-around play.

Willie Stargell, b. 1941: Pittsburgh Pirate slugger chosen NL, World Series MVP, 1979.

Bart Starr, b. 1934: Green Bay Packers quarterback led team to 5 NFL titles and 2 Super Bowl victories.

Roger Staubach, b. 1942: Dallas Cowboys quarterback; leading NFC passer 5 times.

Casey Stengel, (1890-1975): managed Yankees to 10 pennants, 7 championships, 1949-60.

Jackie Stewart, b. 1939: Scot auto racer retired with record 27 Grand Prix victories.

John L. Sullivan, (1858-1918): last bareknuckle heavyweight champion, 1882-1892.

Fran Tarkenton, b. 1940: quarterback holds career passing records for touchdowns, completions, yardage.

Gustave Thoeni, b. 1951: Italian 4-time world alpine ski champ.

Jim Thorpe, (1888-1953): football All-America, 1911, 1912; won pentathlon and decathlon, 1912 Olympics.

Bill Tilden, (1893-1953): U.S. singles champ 7 times; played on 11 Davis Cup teams.

Y.A. Tittle, b. 1926: N.Y. Giants quarterback; MVP, 1961, 1963

Lee Trevino, b. 1939: won the U.S. and British Open championships twice.

Bryan Trottier, b. 1956: N.Y. Islanders center led team to 4 consecutive Stanley Cup championships, 1980-83.

Gene Tunney, (1897-1978): heavyweight champion, 1926-28.

Wyomia Tyus, b. 1945: sprinter won 1964, 1968 Olympic 100-meter dash.

Johnny Unitas, b. 1933: Baltimore Colts quarterback passed for over 40,000 yds.; MVP, 1957, 1967.

Al Unser, b. 1939: Indy 500 winner, 3 times.

Bobby Unser, b. 1934: Indy 500 winner, 1968, 1981, twice U.S. Auto Club national champ.

Fernando Valenzuela, b. 1960: L.A. Dodgers pitcher won Cy Young award, 1981.

Norm Van Brocklin, b. (1926-1983); quarterback passed for game record 554 yds., 1951; MVP, 1960.

Honus Wagner, (1874-1955): Pittsburgh Pirates shortstop won 8 NL batting titles.

Bill Walton, b. 1952: led Portland Trail Blazers to NBA championship, 1977; MVP, 1978.

Tom Watson, b. 1949: golfer won British Open 5 times.

Johnny Weissmuller, (1903-1984); swimmer won 52 national championships, 5 Olympic gold medals; set 67 world records.

Jerry West, b. 1938: L.A. Lakers guard had career average 27 points per game; first team all-star 10 times.
Kathy Whitworth, b. 1939: women's golf leading money winner 8 times; first woman to earn over $300,000.
Ted Williams, b. 1918: Boston Red Sox outfielder won 6 batting titles; last major leaguer to hit over .400: .406 in 1941: .344 lifetime batting average.
Helen Wills, b. 1906: winner of 7 U.S., 8 British, 4 French women's singles titles.
John Wooden, b. 1910: coached UCLA basketball team to 10 national championships.

Mickey Wright, b. 1935: won LPGA championship 4 times. Vare Trophy 5 times; twice AP Woman-Athlete-of-the-Year.
Carl Yastrzemski, b. 1939: Boston Red Sox slugger won 3 batting titles, triple crown, 1967.
Cy Young, (1867-1955): pitcher won record 511 major league games.
Robin Yount, b. 1955: shortstop was AL MVP, 1982.
Babe Didrikson Zaharias, (1914-1956): track star won 2 1932 Olympic gold medals; won numerous golf tournaments.

National Baseball Hall of Fame and Museum, (Cooperstown, N.Y.)

Aaron, Hank
Alexander, Grover Cleveland
Alston, Walt
Anson, Cap
Averill, Earl
Aparicio, Luis
Appling, Luke
Baker, Home Run
Bancroft, Dave
Banks, Ernie
Barrow, Edward G.
Beckley, Jake
Bell, Cool Papa
Bender, Chief
Berra, Yogi
Bottomley, Jim
Boudreau, Lou
Bresnahan, Roger
Brouthers, Dan
Brown (Three Finger), Mordecai
Bulkeley, Morgan C.
Burkett, Jesse C.
Campanella, Roy
Carey, Max
Cartwright, Alexander
Chadwick, Henry
Chance, Frank
Chandler, Happy
Charleston, Oscar
Chesbro, John
Clarke, Fred
Clarkson, John
Clemente, Roberto
Cobb, Ty
Cochrane, Mickey
Collins, Eddie
Collins, James
Combs, Earle

Comiskey, Charles A.
Conlan, Jocko
Connolly, Thomas H.
Connor, Roger
Coveleski, Stan
Crawford, Sam
Cronin, Joe
Cummings, Candy
Cuyler, Kiki
Dean, Dizzy
Delahanty, Ed
Dickey, Bill
DiHigo, Martin
DiMaggio, Joe
Drysdale, Don
Duffy, Hugh
Evans, Billy
Evers, John
Ewing, Buck
Faber, Urban
Feller, Bob
Ferrell, Rick
Flick, Elmer H.
Ford, Whitey
Foster, Andrew
Foxx, Jimmy
Frick, Ford
Frisch, Frank
Galvin, Pud
Gehrig, Lou
Gehringer, Charles
Gibson, Bob
Gibson, Josh
Giles, Warren
Gomez, Lefty
Goslin, Goose
Greenberg, Hank
Griffith, Clark

Grimes, Burleigh
Grove, Lefty
Hafey, Chick
Haines, Jesee
Hamilton, Bill
Harridge, Will
Harris, Bucky
Hartnett, Gabby
Heilmann, Harry
Herman, Billy
Hooper, Harry
Hornsby, Rogers
Hoyt, Waite
Hubbard, Cal
Hubbell, Carl
Huggins, Miller
Irvin, Monte
Jackson, Travis
Jennings, Hugh
Johnson, Byron
Johnson, William (Rudy)
Johnson, Walter
Joss, Addie
Kaline, Al
Keefe, Timothy
Keeler, William
Kell, George
Kelley, Joe
Kelly, George
Kelly, King
Killebrew, Harmon
Kiner, Ralph
Klein, Chuck
Klem, Bill
Koufax, Sandy
Lajoie, Napoleon
Landis, Kenesaw M.
Lemon, Bob

Leonard, Buck
Lindstrom, Fred
Lloyd, Pop
Lopez, Al
Lyons, Ted
Mack, Connie
MacPhail, Larry
Mantle, Mickey
Manush, Henry
Maranville, Rabbit
Marichal, Juan
Marquard, Rube
Mathews, Eddie
Mathewson, Christy
Mays, Willie
McCarthy, Joe
McCarthy, Thomas
McGinnity, Joe
McGraw, John
McKechnie, Bill
Medwick, Joe
Mize, Johnny
Musial, Stan
Nichols, Kid
O'Rourke, James
Ott, Mel
Paige, Satchel
Pennock, Herb
Plank, Ed
Radbourne, Charlie
Reese, Pee Wee
Rice, Sam
Rickey, Branch
Rixey, Eppa
Roberts, Robin
Robinson, Brooks
Robinson, Frank
Robinson, Jackie

Robinson, Wilbert
Roush, Edd
Ruffing, Red
Rusie, Amos
Ruth, Babe
Schalk, Ray
Sewell, Joe
Simmons, Al
Sisler, George
Snider, Duke
Spahn, Warren
Spalding, Albert
Speaker, Tris
Stengel, Casey
Terry, Bill
Thompson, Sam
Tinker, Joe
Traynor, Pie
Vance, Dazzy
Waddell, Rube
Wagner, Honus
Wallace, Roderick
Walsh, Ed.
Waner, Lloyd
Waner, Paul
Ward, John
Weiss, George
Welch, Mickey
Wheat, Zach
Williams, Ted
Wilson, Hack
Wright, George
Wright, Harry
Wynn, Early
Yawkey, Tom
Young, Cy
Youngs, Ross

All-Star Baseball Games, 1933-1984

Year	Winner	Score	Location	Year	Winner	Score	Location
1933	American	4-2	Chicago	1960	National	5-3	Kansas City
1934	American	9-7	New York	1960	National	6-0	New York
1935	American	4-1	Cleveland	1961	National (3)	5-4	San Francisco
1936	National	4-3	Boston	1961	Called-rain	1-1	Boston
1937	American	8-3	Washington	1962	National (3)	3-1	Washington
1938	National	4-1	Cincinnati	1962	American	9-4	Chicago
1939	American	3-1	New York	1963	National	5-3	Cleveland
1940	National	4-0	St. Louis	1964	National	7-4	New York
1941	American	7-5	Detroit	1965	National	6-5	Minnesota
1942	American	3-1	New York	1966	National (3)	2-1	St. Louis
1943*	American	5-3	Philadelphia	1967	National (4)	2-1	Anaheim
1944*	National	7-1	Pittsburgh	1968*	National	1-0	Houston
1945	(not played)			1969	National	9-3	Washington
1946	American	12-0	Boston	1970*	National (2)	5-4	Cincinnati
1947	American	2-1	Chicago	1971*	American	6-4	Detroit
1948	American	5-2	St. Louis	1972*	National	4-3	Atlanta
1949	American	11-7	New York	1973*	National	7-1	Kansas City
1950	National (1)	4-3	Chicago	1974*	National	7-2	Pittsburgh
1951	National	8-3	Detroit	1975*	National	6-3	Milwaukee
1952	National	3-2	Philadelphia	1976*	National	7-1	Philadelphia
1953	National	5-1	Cincinnati	1977*	National	7-5	New York
1954	American	11-9	Cleveland	1978*	National	7-3	San Diego
1955	National (2)	6-5	Milwaukee	1979*	National	7-6	Seattle
1956	National	7-3	Washington	1980*	National	4-2	Los Angeles
1957	American	6-5	St. Louis	1981*	National	5-4	Cleveland
1958	American	4-3	Baltimore	1982*	National	4-1	Montreal
1959	National	5-4	Pittsburgh	1983*	American	13-3	Chicago
1959	American	5-3	Los Angeles	1984*	National	3-1	San Francisco

(1) 14 innings, (2) 12 innings, (3) 10 innings, (4) 15 innings *Night game.

Most Valuable Player
Baseball Writers' Association
National League

Year	Player, team	Year	Player, team	Year	Player, team
1931	Frank Frisch, St. Louis	1949	Jackie Robinson, Brooklyn	1967	Orlando Cepeda, St. Louis
1932	Charles Klein, Philadelphia	1950	Jim Konstanty, Philadelphia	1968	Bob Gibson, St. Louis
1933	Carl Hubbell, New York	1951	Roy Campanella, Brooklyn	1969	Willie McCovey, San Francisco
1934	Dizzy Dean, St. Louis	1952	Hank Sauer, Chicago	1970	Johnny Bench, Cincinnati
1935	Gabby Hartnett, Chicago	1953	Roy Campanella, Brooklyn	1971	Joe Torre, St. Louis
1936	Carl Hubbell, New York	1954	Willie Mays, New York	1972	Johnny Bench, Cincinnati
1937	Joe Medwick, St. Louis	1955	Roy Campanella, Brooklyn	1973	Pete Rose, Cincinnati
1938	Ernie Lombardi, Cincinnati	1956	Don Newcombe, Brooklyn	1974	Steve Garvey, Los Angeles
1939	Bucky Walters, Cincinnati	1957	Henry Aaron, Milwaukee	1975	Joe Morgan, Cincinnati
1940	Frank McCormick, Cincinnati	1958	Ernie Banks, Chicago	1976	Joe Morgan, Cincinnati
1941	Dolph Camilli, Brooklyn	1959	Ernie Banks, Chicago	1977	George Foster, Cincinnati
1942	Mort Cooper, St. Louis	1960	Dick Groat, Pittsburgh	1978	Dave Parker, Pittsburgh
1943	Stan Musial, St. Louis	1961	Frank Robinson, Cincinnati	1979	(tie) Willie Stargell, Pittsburgh
1944	Martin Marion, St. Louis	1962	Maury Wills, Los Angeles		Keith Hernandez, St. Louis
1945	Phil Cavarretta, Chicago	1963	Sandy Koufax, Los Angeles	1980	Mike Schmidt, Philadelphia
1946	Stan Musial, St. Louis	1964	Ken Boyer, St. Louis	1981	Mike Schmidt, Philadelphia
1947	Bob Elliott, Boston	1965	Willie Mays, San Francisco	1982	Dale Murphy, Atlanta
1948	Stan Musial, St. Louis	1966	Roberto Clemente, Pittsburgh	1983	Dale Murphy, Atlanta

American League

Year	Player, team	Year	Player, team	Year	Player, team
1931	Lefty Grove, Philadelphia	1949	Ted Williams, Boston	1967	Carl Yastrzemski, Boston
1932	Jimmy Foxx, Philadelphia	1950	Phil Rizzuto, New York	1968	Denny McLain, Detroit
1933	Jimmy Foxx, Philadelphia	1951	Yogi Berra, New York	1969	Harmon Killebrew, Minnesota
1934	Mickey Cochrane, Detroit	1952	Bobby Shantz, Philadelphia	1970	John (Boog) Powell, Baltimore
1935	Henry Greenberg, Detroit	1953	Al Rosen, Cleveland	1971	Vida Blue, Oakland
1936	Lou Gehrig, New York	1954	Yogi Berra, New York	1972	Dick Allen, Chicago
1937	Charley Gehringer, Detroit	1955	Yogi Berra, New York	1973	Reggie Jackson, Oakland
1938	Jimmy Foxx, Boston	1956	Mickey Mantle, New York	1974	Jeff Burroughs, Texas
1939	Joe DiMaggio, New York	1957	Mickey Mantle, New York	1975	Fred Lynn, Boston
1940	Hank Greenberg, Detroit	1958	Jackie Jensen, Boston	1976	Thurman Munson, New York
1941	Joe DiMaggio, New York	1959	Nellie Fox, Chicago	1977	Rod Carew, Minnesota
1942	Joe Gordon, New York	1960	Roger Maris, New York	1978	Jim Rice, Boston
1943	Spurgeon Chandler, New York	1961	Roger Maris, New York	1979	Don Baylor, California
1944	Hal Newhouser, Detroit	1962	Mickey Mantle, New York	1980	George Brett, Kansas City
1945	Hal Newhouser, Detroit	1963	Elston Howard, New York	1981	Rollie Fingers, Milwaukee
1946	Ted Williams, Boston	1964	Brooks Robinson, Baltimore	1982	Robin Yount, Milwaukee
1947	Joe DiMaggio, New York	1965	Zoilo Versalles, Minnesota	1983	Cal Ripken Jr., Baltimore
1948	Lou Boudreau, Cleveland	1966	Frank Robinson, Baltimore		

Rookie of the Year
Baseball Writers' Association

1947—Combined selection—Jackie Robinson, Brooklyn, 1b
1948—Combined selection—Alvin Dark, Boston, N.L. ss

National League

Year	Player, team	Year	Player, team	Year	Player, team
1949	Don Newcombe, Brooklyn, p	1962	Ken Hubbs, Chicago, 2b	1975	John Montefusco, S.F., p
1950	Sam Jethroe, Boston, of	1963	Pete Rose, Cincinnati, 2b	1976	(tie) Butch Metzger, San Diego, p
1951	Willie Mays, New York, of	1964	Richie Allen, Philadelphia, 3b		Pat Zachry, Cincinnati, p
1952	Joe Black, Brooklyn, p	1965	Jim Lefebvre, Los Angeles, 2b	1977	Andre Dawson, Montreal, of
1953	Jim Gilliam, Brooklyn, 2b	1966	Tommy Helms, Cincinnati, 2b	1978	Bob Horner, Atlanta, 3b
1954	Wally Moon, St. Louis, of	1967	Tom Seaver, New York, p	1979	Rick Sutcliffe, Los Angeles, p
1955	Bill Virdon, St. Louis, of	1968	Johnny Bench, Cincinnati c	1980	Steve Howe, Los Angeles, p
1956	Frank Robinson, Cincinnati, of	1969	Ted Sizemore, Los Angeles, 2b	1981	Fernando Valenzuela, Los
1957	Jack Sanford, Philadelphia, p	1970	Carl Morton, Montreal, p		Angeles, p
1958	Orlando Cepeda, S.F., 1b	1971	Earl Williams, Atlanta, c	1982	Steve Sax, Los Angeles, 2b
1959	Willie McCovey, S.F., 1b	1972	Jon Matlack, New York, p	1983	Darryl Strawberry, New York, of
1960	Frank Howard, Los Angeles, of	1973	Gary Matthews, S.F., of		
1961	Billy Williams, Chicago, of	1974	Bake McBride, St. Louis, of		

American League

Year	Player, team	Year	Player, team	Year	Player, team
1949	Roy Sievers, St. Louis, of	1961	Don Schwall, Boston, p	1973	Al Bumbry, Baltimore, of
1950	Walt Dropo, Boston, 1b	1962	Tom Tresh, New York, if-of	1974	Mike Hargrove, Texas, 1b
1951	Gil McDougald, New York, 3b	1963	Gary Peters, Chicago, p	1975	Fred Lynn, Boston, of
1952	Harry Byrd, Philadelphia, p	1964	Tony Oliva, Minnesota, of	1976	Mark Fidrych, Detroit, p
1953	Harvey Kuenn, Detroit, ss	1965	Curt Blefary, Baltimore, of	1977	Eddie Murray, Baltimore, dh
1954	Bob Grim, New York, p	1966	Tommie Agee, Chicago, of	1978	Lou Whitaker, Detroit, 2b
1955	Herb Score, Cleveland, p	1967	Rod Carew, Minnesota, 2b	1979	(tie) John Castino, Minnesota, 3b
1956	Luis Aparicio, Chicago, ss	1968	Stan Bahnsen, New York, p		Alfredo Griffin, Toronto, ss
1957	Tony Kubek, New York, if-of	1969	Lou Piniella, Kansas City, of	1980	Joe Charboneau, Cleveland, of
1958	Albie Pearson, Washington, of	1970	Thurman Munson, New York, c	1981	Dave Righetti, New York, p
1959	Bob Allison, Washington, of	1971	Chris Chambliss, Cleveland, 1b	1982	Cal Ripken Jr., Baltimore, ss, 3b
1960	Ron Hansen, Baltimore, ss	1972	Carlton Fisk, Boston, c	1983	Ron Kittle, Chicago, of

College World Series

The Cal State Fullerton Titans won the 1984 College World Series by defeating Texas 3-1 in the final game at Omaha, Neb. It was the Titans second College World Series title.

Major League Pennant Winners, 1901–1984

National League / American League

Year	Winner	Won	Lost	Pct	Manager	Year	Winner	Won	Lost	Pct	Manager
1901	Pittsburgh	90	49	.647	Clarke	1901	Chicago	83	53	.610	Griffith
1902	Pittsburgh	103	36	.741	Clarke	1902	Philadelphia	83	53	.610	Mack
1903	Pittsburgh	91	49	.650	Clarke	1903	Boston	91	47	.659	Collins
1904	New York	106	47	.693	McGraw	1904	Boston	95	59	.617	Collins
1905	New York	105	48	.686	McGraw	1905	Philadelphia	92	56	.622	Mack
1906	Chicago	116	36	.763	Chance	1906	Chicago	93	58	.616	Jones
1907	Chicago	107	45	.704	Chance	1907	Detroit	92	58	.613	Jennings
1908	Chicago	99	55	.643	Chance	1908	Detroit	90	63	.588	Jennings
1909	Pittsburgh	110	42	.724	Clarke	1909	Detroit	98	54	.645	Jennings
1910	Chicago	104	50	.675	Chance	1910	Philadelphia	102	48	.680	Mack
1911	New York	99	54	.647	McGraw	1911	Philadelphia	101	50	.669	Mack
1912	New York	103	48	.682	McGraw	1912	Boston	105	47	.691	Stahl
1913	New York	101	51	.664	McGraw	1913	Philadelphia	96	57	.627	Mack
1914	Boston	94	59	.614	Stallings	1914	Philadelphia	99	53	.651	Mack
1915	Philadelphia	90	62	.592	Moran	1915	Boston	101	50	.669	Carrigan
1916	Brooklyn	94	60	.610	Robinson	1916	Boston	91	63	.591	Carrigan
1917	New York	98	56	.636	McGraw	1917	Chicago	100	54	.649	Rowland
1918	Chicago	84	45	.651	Mitchell	1918	Boston	75	51	.595	Barrow
1919	Cincinnati	96	44	.686	Moran	1919	Chicago	88	52	.629	Gleason
1920	Brooklyn	93	60	.604	Robinson	1920	Cleveland	98	56	.636	Speaker
1921	New York	94	56	.614	McGraw	1921	New York	98	55	.641	Huggins
1922	New York	93	61	.604	McGraw	1922	New York	94	60	.610	Huggins
1923	New York	95	58	.621	McGraw	1923	New York	98	54	.645	Huggins
1924	New York	93	60	.608	McGraw	1924	Washington	92	62	.597	Harris
1925	Pittsburgh	95	58	.621	McKechnie	1925	Washington	96	55	.636	Harris
1926	St. Louis	89	65	.578	Hornsby	1926	New York	91	63	.591	Huggins
1927	Pittsburgh	94	60	.610	Bush	1927	New York	110	44	.714	Huggins
1928	St. Louis	95	59	.617	McKechnie	1928	New York	101	53	.656	Huggins
1929	Chicago	98	54	.645	McCarthy	1929	Philadelphia	104	46	.693	Mack
1930	St. Louis	92	62	.597	Street	1930	Philadelphia	102	52	.622	Mack
1931	St. Louis	101	53	.656	Street	1931	Philadelphia	107	45	.704	Mack
1932	Chicago	90	64	.584	Grimm	1932	New York	107	47	.695	McCarthy
1933	New York	91	61	.599	Terry	1933	Washington	99	53	.651	Cronin
1934	St. Louis	95	58	.621	Frisch	1934	Detroit	101	53	.656	Cochrane
1935	Chicago	100	54	.649	Grimm	1935	Detroit	93	58	.616	Cochrane
1936	New York	91	62	.597	Terry	1936	New York	102	51	.667	McCarthy
1937	New York	95	57	.625	Terry	1937	New York	102	52	.662	McCarthy
1938	Chicago	89	63	.586	Hartnett	1938	New York	99	53	.651	McCarthy
1939	Cincinnati	97	57	.630	McKechnie	1939	New York	106	45	.702	McCarthy
1940	Cincinnati	100	53	.654	McKechnie	1940	Detroit	90	64	.584	Baker
1941	Brooklyn	100	54	.649	Durocher	1941	New York	101	53	.656	McCarthy
1942	St. Louis	106	48	.688	Southworth	1942	New York	103	51	.669	McCarthy
1943	St. Louis	105	49	.682	Southworth	1943	New York	98	56	.636	McCarthy
1944	St. Louis	105	49	.682	Southworth	1944	St. Louis	89	65	.578	Sewell
1945	Chicago	98	56	.636	Grimm	1945	Detroit	88	65	.575	O'Neill
1946	St. Louis	98	58	.628	Dyer	1946	Boston	104	50	.675	Cronin
1947	Brooklyn	94	60	.610	Shotton	1947	New York	97	57	.630	Harris
1948	Boston	91	62	.595	Southworth	1948	Cleveland	97	58	.626	Boudreau
1949	Brooklyn	97	57	.630	Shotton	1949	New York	97	57	.630	Stengel
1950	Philadelphia	91	63	.591	Sawyer	1950	New York	98	56	.636	Stengel
1951	New York	98	59	.624	Durocher	1951	New York	98	56	.636	Stengel
1952	Brooklyn	96	57	.627	Dressen	1952	New York	95	59	.617	Stengel
1953	Brooklyn	105	49	.682	Dressen	1953	New York	99	52	.656	Stengel
1954	New York	97	57	.630	Durocher	1954	Cleveland	111	43	.721	Lopez
1955	Brooklyn	98	55	.641	Alston	1955	New York	96	58	.623	Stengel
1956	Brooklyn	93	61	.604	Alston	1956	New York	97	57	.630	Stengel
1957	Milwaukee	95	59	.617	Haney	1957	New York	98	56	.636	Stengel
1958	Milwaukee	92	62	.597	Haney	1958	New York	92	62	.597	Stengel
1959	Los Angeles	88	68	.564	Alston	1959	Chicago	94	60	.610	Lopez
1960	Pittsburgh	95	59	.617	Murtaugh	1960	New York	97	57	.630	Stengel
1961	Cincinnati	93	61	.604	Hutchinson	1961	New York	109	53	.673	Houk
1962	San Francisco	103	62	.624	Dark	1962	New York	96	66	.593	Houk
1963	Los Angeles	99	63	.611	Alston	1963	New York	104	57	.646	Houk
1964	St. Louis	93	69	.574	Keane	1964	New York	99	63	.611	Berra
1965	Los Angeles	97	65	.599	Alston	1965	Minnesota	102	60	.630	Mele
1966	Los Angeles	95	67	.586	Alston	1966	Baltimore	97	63	.606	Bauer
1967	St. Louis	101	60	.627	Schoendienst	1967	Boston	92	70	.568	Williams
1968	St. Louis	97	65	.599	Schoendienst	1968	Detroit	103	59	.636	Smith

National League

Year	Winner	East W	L	Pct	Manager	Winner	West W	L	Pct	Manager	Playoff winner
1969	N.Y. Mets	100	62	.617	Hodges	Atlanta	93	69	.574	Harris	New York
1970	Pittsburgh	89	73	.549	Murtaugh	Cincinnati	102	60	.630	Anderson	Cincinnati
1971	Pittsburgh	97	65	.599	Murtaugh	San Francisco	90	72	.556	Fox	Pittsburgh
1972	Pittsburgh	96	59	.619	Virdon	Cincinnati	95	59	.617	Anderson	Cincinnati
1973	N.Y. Mets	82	79	.509	Berra	Cincinnati	99	63	.611	Anderson	New York
1974	Pittsburgh	88	74	.543	Murtaugh	Los Angeles	102	60	.630	Alston	Los Angeles
1975	Pittsburgh	92	69	.571	Murtaugh	Cincinnati	108	54	.667	Anderson	Cincinnati
1976	Philadelphia	101	61	.623	Ozark	Cincinnati	102	60	.630	Anderson	Cincinnati
1977	Philadelphia	101	61	.623	Ozark	Los Angeles	98	64	.605	Lasorda	Los Angeles
1978	Philadelphia	90	72	.556	Ozark	Los Angeles	95	67	.586	Lasorda	Los Angeles
1979	Pittsburgh	98	64	.605	Tanner	Cincinnati	90	71	.559	McNamara	Pittsburgh

Year	Winner	East W	L	Pct	Manager	Winner	West W	L	Pct	Manager	Playoff winner
1980	Philadelphia	91	71	.562	Green	Houston	93	70	.571	Virdon	Philadelphia
1981(a)	Philadelphia	34	21	.618	Green	Los Angeles	36	21	.632	Lasorda	(c)
1981(b)	Montreal	30	23	.566	Williams, Fanning	Houston	33	20	.623	Virdon	Los Angeles
1982	St. Louis	92	70	.568	Herzog	Atlanta	89	73	.549	Torre	St. Louis
1983	Philadelphia	90	72	.556	Corrales, Owens	Los Angeles	91	71	.562	Lasorda	Philadelphia
1984	Chicago	96	65	.596	Frey	San Diego	92	70	.568	Williams	San Diego

American League

Year	Winner	East W	L	Pct	Manager	Winner	West W	L	Pct	Manager	Playoff winner
1969	Baltimore	109	53	.673	Weaver	Minnesota	97	65	.599	Martin	Baltimore
1970	Baltimore	108	54	.667	Weaver	Minnesota	98	64	.605	Rigney	Baltimore
1971	Baltimore	101	57	.639	Weaver	Oakland	101	60	.627	Williams	Baltimore
1972	Detroit	86	70	.551	Martin	Oakland	93	62	.600	Williams	Oakland
1973	Baltimore	97	65	.599	Weaver	Oakland	94	68	.580	Williams	Oakland
1974	Baltimore	91	71	.562	Weaver	Oakland	90	72	.556	Dark	Oakland
1975	Boston	95	65	.594	Johnson	Oakland	98	64	.605	Dark	Boston
1976	New York	97	62	.610	Martin	Kansas City	90	72	.556	Herzog	New York
1977	New York	100	62	.617	Martin	Kansas City	102	60	.630	Herzog	New York
1978	New York	100	63	.613	Martin, Lemon	Kansas City	92	70	.568	Herzog	New York
1979	Baltimore	102	57	.642	Weaver	California	88	74	.543	Fregosi	Baltimore
1980	New York	103	59	.636	Howser	Kansas City	97	65	.599	Frey	Kansas City
1981(a)	New York	34	22	.607	Michael	Oakland	37	23	.617	Martin	(d)
1981(b)	Milwaukee	31	22	.585	Rodgers	Kansas City	30	23	.566	Frey, Howser	New York
1982	Milwaukee	95	67	.586	Rodgers, Kuenn	California	93	69	.574	Mauch	Milwaukee
1983	Baltimore	98	64	.605	Altobelli	Chicago	99	63	.611	LaRussa	Baltimore
1984	Detroit	104	58	.642	Anderson	Kansas City	84	78	.519	Howser	Detroit

(a) First half; (b) Second half; (c) Montreal and Los Angeles won the divisional playoffs; (d) New York and Oakland won the divisional playoffs.

Baseball Stadiums

National League

Team		Surface	Home run distances (ft.) LF	Center	RF	Seating capacity
Atlanta Braves	Atlanta-Fulton County Stadium	Natural grass	330	402	330	52,785
Chicago Cubs	Wrigley Field	Natural grass	355	400	353	37,272
Cincinnati Reds	Riverfront Stadium	Artificial	330	404	330	52,392
Houston Astros	Astrodome	Artificial	340	406	340	45,000
Los Angeles Dodgers	Dodger Stadium	Natural grass	330	400	330	56,000
Montreal Expos	Olympic Stadium	Artificial	325	404	325	58,838
New York Mets	Shea Stadium	Natural grass	338	410	338	55,300
Philadelphia Phillies	Veterans Stadium	Artificial	330	408	330	66,507
Pittsburgh Pirates	Three Rivers Stadium	Artificial	335	400	335	54,490
St. Louis Cardinals	Busch Memorial Stadium	Artificial	330	414	330	50,222
San Diego Padres	Jack Murphy Stadium	Natural grass	330	405	330	51,319
San Francisco Giants	Candlestick Park	Natural grass	335	400	335	58,000

American League

Team		Surface	LF	Center	RF	Seating capacity
Baltimore Orioles	Memorial Stadium	Natural grass	309	405	309	53,208
Boston Red Sox	Fenway Park	Natural grass	315	390	302	33,465
California Angels	Anaheim Stadium	Natural grass	333	404	333	65,158
Chicago White Sox	Comiskey Park	Natural grass	341	401	341	43,695
Cleveland Indians	Cleveland Stadium	Natural grass	320	400	320	74,208
Detroit Tigers	Tiger Stadium	Natural grass	340	440	325	52,806
Kansas City Royals	Royals Stadium	Artificial	330	410	330	40,635
Milwaukee Brewers	Milwaukee County Stadium	Natural grass	315	402	315	53,192
Minnesota Twins	Hubert H. Humphrey Metrodome	Artificial	343	408	327	55,122
New York Yankees	Yankee Stadium	Natural grass	312	417	310	57,545
Oakland A's	Oakland Coliseum	Natural grass	330	397	330	50,219
Seattle Mariners	Kingdome	Artificial	316	410	316	59,438
Texas Rangers	Arlington Stadium	Natural grass	330	400	330	41,284
Toronto Blue Jays	Exhibition Stadium	Artificial grass	330	400	330	43,737

Cy Young Award Winners

Year	Player, club	Year	Player, club	Year	Player, club
1956	Don Newcombe, Dodgers	1969	(NL) Tom Seaver, Mets	1976	(NL) Randy Jones, Padres
1957	Warren Spahn, Braves		(AL) (tie) Dennis McLain, Tigers		(AL) Jim Palmer, Orioles
1958	Bob Turley, Yankees		Mike Cuellar, Orioles	1977	(NL) Steve Carlton, Phillies
1959	Early Wynn, White Sox	1970	(NL) Bob Gibson, Cardinals		(AL) Sparky Lyle, Yankees
1960	Vernon Law, Pirates		(AL) Jim Perry, Twins	1978	(NL) Gaylord Perry, Padres
1961	Whitey Ford, Yankees	1971	(NL) Ferguson Jenkins, Cubs		(AL) Ron Guidry, Yankees
1962	Don Drysdale, Dodgers		(AL) Vida Blue, A's	1979	(NL) Bruce Sutter, Cubs
1963	Sandy Koufax, Dodgers	1972	(NL) Steve Carlton, Phillies		(AL) Mike Flanagan, Orioles
1964	Dean Chance, Angels		(AL) Gaylord Perry, Indians	1980	(NL) Steve Carlton, Phillies
1965	Sandy Koufax, Dodgers	1973	(NL) Tom Seaver, Mets		(AL) Steve Stone, Orioles
1966	Sandy Koufax, Dodgers		(AL) Jim Palmer, Orioles	1981	(NL) Fernando Valenzuela, Dodgers
1967	(NL) Mike McCormick, Giants	1974	(NL) Mike Marshall, Dodgers		(AL) Rollie Fingers, Brewers
	(AL) Jim Lonborg, Red Sox		(AL) Jim (Catfish) Hunter, A's	1982	(NL) Steve Carlton, Phillies
1968	(NL) Bob Gibson, Cardinals	1975	(NL) Tom Seaver, Mets		(AL) Pete Vuckovich, Brewers
	(AL) Dennis McLain, Tigers		(AL) Jim Palmer, Orioles	1983	(NL) John Denny, Phillies
					(AL) LaMarr Hoyt, White Sox

Home Run Leaders

National League		American League	
Year	**HR**	**Year**	**HR**
1923 Cy Williams, Philadelphia	41	1923 Babe Ruth, New York	41
1924 Jacques Fournier, Brooklyn	27	1924 Babe Ruth, New York	46
1925 Rogers Hornsby, St. Louis	39	1925 Bob Meusel, New York	33
1926 Hack Wilson, Chicago	21	1926 Babe Ruth, New York	47
1927 Hack Wilson, Chicago; Cy Williams, Philadelphia	30	1927 Babe Ruth, New York	60
1928 Hack Wilson, Chicago; Jim Bottomley, St. Louis	31	1928 Babe Ruth, New York	54
1929 Charles Klein, Philadelphia	43	1929 Babe Ruth, New York	46
1930 Hack Wilson, Chicago	56	1930 Babe Ruth, New York	49
1931 Charles Klein, Philadelphia	31	1931 Babe Ruth, Lou Gehrig, New York	46
1932 Charles Klein, Philadelphia, Mel Ott, New York	38	1932 Jimmy Foxx, Philadelphia	58
1933 Charles Klein, Philadelphia	28	1933 Jimmy Foxx, Philadelphia	48
1934 Collins, St. Louis; Mel Ott, New York	35	1934 Lou Gehrig, New York	49
1935 Walter Berger, Boston	34	1935 Jimmy Foxx, Philadelphia, Hank Greenberg, Detroit	36
1936 Mel Ott, New York	33	1936 Lou Gehrig, New York	49
1937 Mel Ott, New York; Joe Medwick, St. Louis	31	1937 Joe DiMaggio, New York	46
1938 Mel Ott, New York	36	1938 Hank Greenberg, Detroit	58
1939 John Mize, St. Louis	28	1939 Jimmy Foxx, Boston	35
1940 John Mize, St. Louis	43	1940 Hank Greenberg, Detroit	41
1941 Dolph Camilli, Brooklyn	34	1941 Ted Williams, Boston	37
1942 Mel Ott, New York	30	1942 Ted Williams, Boston	36
1943 Bill Nicholson, Chicago	29	1943 Rudy York, Detroit	34
1944 Bill Nicholson, Chicago	33	1944 Nick Etten, New York	22
1945 Tommy Holmes, Boston	28	1945 Vern Stephens, St. Louis	24
1946 Ralph Kiner, Pittsburgh	23	1946 Hank Greenberg, Detroit	44
1947 Ralph Kiner, Pittsburgh; John Mize, New York	51	1947 Ted Williams, Boston	32
1948 Ralph Kiner, Pittsburgh; John Mize, New York	40	1948 Joe DiMaggio, New York	39
1949 Ralph Kiner, Pittsburgh	54	1949 Ted Williams, Boston	43
1950 Ralph Kiner, Pittsburgh	47	1950 Al Rosen, Cleveland	37
1951 Ralph Kiner, Pittsburgh	42	1951 Gus Zernial, Chicago-Philadelphia	33
1952 Ralph Kiner, Pittsburgh; Hank Sauer, Chicago	37	1952 Larry Doby, Cleveland	32
1953 Ed Mathews, Milwaukee	47	1953 Al Rosen, Cleveland	43
1954 Ted Kluszewski, Cincinnati	49	1954 Larry Doby, Cleveland	32
1955 Willie Mays, New York	51	1955 Mickey Mantle, New York	37
1956 Duke Snider, Brooklyn	43	1956 Mickey Mantle, New York	52
1957 Hank Aaron, Milwaukee	44	1957 Roy Sievers, Washington	42
1958 Ernie Banks, Chicago	47	1958 Mickey Mantle, New York	42
1959 Ed Mathews, Milwaukee	46	1959 Rocky Colavito, Cleveland,	
1960 Ernie Banks, Chicago	41	Harmon Killebrew, Washington	42
1961 Orlando Cepeda, San Francisco	46	1960 Mickey Mantle, New York	40
1962 Willie Mays, San Francisco	49	1961 Roger Maris, New York	61
1963 Hank Aaron, Milwaukee,		1962 Harmon Killebrew, Minnesota	48
Willie McCovey, San Francisco	44	1963 Harmon Killebrew, Minnesota	45
1964 Willie Mays, San Francisco	47	1964 Harmon Killebrew, Minnesota	49
1965 Willie Mays, San Francisco	52	1965 Tony Conigliaro, Boston	32
1966 Hank Aaron, Atlanta	44	1966 Frank Robinson, Baltimore	49
1967 Hank Aaron, Atlanta	39	1967 Carl Yastrzemski, Boston, Harmon Killebrew, Minn.	44
1968 Willie McCovey, San Francisco	36	1968 Frank Howard, Washington	44
1969 Willie McCovey, San Francisco	45	1969 Harmon Killebrew, Minnesota	49
1970 Johnny Bench, Cincinnati	45	1970 Frank Howard, Washington	44
1971 Willie Stargell, Pittsburgh	48	1971 Bill Melton, Chicago	33
1972 Johnny Bench, Cincinnati	40	1972 Dick Allen, Chicago	37
1973 Willie Stargell, Pittsburgh	44	1973 Reggie Jackson, Oakland	32
1974 Mike Schmidt, Philadelphia	36	1974 Dick Allen, Chicago	32
1975 Mike Schmidt, Philadelphia	38	1975 George Scott, Milwaukee; Reggie Jackson, Oakland	36
1976 Mike Schmidt, Philadelphia	38	1976 Graig Nettles, New York	32
1977 George Foster, Cincinnati	52	1977 Jim Rice, Boston	39
1978 George Foster, Cincinnati	40	1978 Jim Rice, Boston	46
1979 Dave Kingman, Chicago	48	1979 Gorman Thomas, Milwaukee	45
1980 Mike Schmidt, Philadelphia	48	1980 Reggie Jackson, New York; Ben Oglivie, Milwaukee	41
1981 Mike Schmidt, Philadelphia	31	1981 Bobby Grich, California; Tony Armas, Oakland; Dwight	
		Evans, Boston; Eddie Murray, Baltimore	22
1982 Dave Kingman, New York	37	1982 Gorman Thomas, Milwaukee; Reggie Jackson,	
		California	39
1983 Mike Schmidt, Philadelphia	40	1983 Jim Rice, Boston	39
1984 Mike Schmidt, Phil.; Dale Murphy, Atlanta	36	1984 Tony Armas, Boston	43

All-time Major League Record (154-game Season)—60—Babe Ruth, New York Yankees (A), 1927. **(162-game Season)—61**—Roger Maris, New York Yankees, 1961.

Runs Batted In Leaders

National League		American League	
Year	**RBI**	**Year**	**RBI**
1950 Del Ennis, Philadelphia	126	1950 Walt Dropo, Vern Stephens, Boston	144
1951 Monte Irvin, New York	121	1951 Gus Zernial, Chicago-Philadelphia	129
1952 Hank Sauer, Chicago	121	1952 Al Rosen, Cleveland	105
1953 Roy Campanella, Brooklyn	142	1953 Al Rosen, Cleveland	145
1954 Ted Kluszewski, Cincinnati	141	1954 Larry Doby, Cleveland	126
1955 Duke Snider, Brooklyn	136	1955 Ray Boone, Detroit, Jack Jensen, Boston	116
1956 Stan Musial, St. Louis	109	1956 Mickey Mantle, New York	130
1957 Hank Aaron, Milwaukee	132	1957 Roy Sievers, Washington	114
1958 Ernie Banks, Chicago	129	1958 Jack Jensen, Boston	122
1959 Ernie Banks, Chicago	143	1959 Jack Jensen, Boston	112
1960 Hank Aaron, Milwaukee	126	1960 Roger Maris, New York	112
1961 Orlando Cepeda, San Francisco	142	1961 Roger Maris, New York	142
1962 Tommy Davis, Los Angeles	153	1962 Harmon Killebrew, Minnesota	126

Year		RBI	Year		RBI
1963	Hank Aaron, Milwaukee	130	1963	Dick Stuart, Boston	118
1964	Ken Boyer, St. Louis	119	1964	Brooks Robinson, Baltimore	118
1965	Deron Johnson, Cincinnati	130	1965	Rocky Colavito, Cleveland	108
1966	Hank Aaron, Atlanta	127	1966	Frank Robinson, Baltimore	122
1967	Orlando Cepeda, St. Louis	111	1967	Carl Yastrzemski, Boston	121
1968	Willie McCovey, San Francisco	105	1968	Ken Harrelson, Boston	109
1969	Willie McCovey, San Francisco	126	1960	Harmon Killebrew, Minnesota	140
1970	Johnny Bench, Cincinnati	148	1970	Frank Howard, Washington	126
1971	Joe Torre, St. Louis	137	1971	Harmon Killebrew, Minnesota	119
1972	Johnny Bench, Cincinnati	125	1972	Dick Allen, Chicago	113
1973	Willie Stargell, Pittsburgh	119	1973	Reggie Jackson, Oakland	117
1974	Johnny Bench, Cincinnati	129	1974	Jeff Burroughs, Texas	118
1975	Greg Luzinski, Philadelphia	120	1975	George Scott, Milwaukee	109
1976	George Foster, Cincinnati	121	1976	Lee May, Baltimore	109
1977	George Foster, Cincinnati	149	1977	Larry Hisle, Minnesota	119
1978	George Foster, Cincinnati	120	1978	Jim Rice, Boston	139
1979	Dave Winfield, San Diego	118	1979	Don Baylor, California	139
1980	Mike Schmidt, Philadelphia	121	1980	Cecil Cooper, Milwaukee	122
1981	Mike Schmidt, Philadelphia	91	1981	Eddie Murray, Baltimore	78
1982	Dale Murphy, Atlanta; Al Oliver, Montreal	109	1982	Hal McRae, Kansas City	133
1983	Dale Murphy, Atlanta	121	1983	Cecil Cooper, Milwaukee; Jim Rice, Boston	126
1984	Mike Schmidt, Phil.; Gary Carter, Montreal	106	1984	Tony Armas, Boston	123

Batting Champions

	National League				American League		
Year	Player	Club	Pct.	Year	Player	Club	Pct.
1922	Rogers Hornsby	St. Louis	.401	1922	George Sisler	St. Louis	.420
1923	Rogers Hornsby	St. Louis	.384	1923	Harry Heilmann	Detroit	.403
1924	Rogers Hornsby	St. Louis	.424	1924	Babe Ruth	New York	.378
1925	Rogers Hornsby	St. Louis	.403	1925	Harry Heilmann	Detroit	.393
1926	Eugene Hargrave	Cincinnati	.353	1926	Henry Manush	Detroit	.378
1927	Paul Waner	Pittsburgh	.380	1927	Harry Heilmann	Detroit	.398
1928	Rogers Hornsby	Boston	.387	1928	Goose Goslin	Washington	.379
1929	Lefty O'Doul	Philadelphia	.398	1929	Lew Fonseca	Cleveland	.369
1930	Bill Terry	New York	.401	1930	Al Simmons	Philadelphia	.381
1931	Chick Hafey	St. Louis	.349	1931	Al Simmons	Philadelphia	.390
1932	Lefty O'Doul	Brooklyn	.368	1932	Dale Alexander	Detroit-Boston	.367
1933	Charles Klein	Philadelphia	.368	1933	Jimmy Foxx	Philadelphia	.356
1934	Paul Waner	Pittsburgh	.362	1934	Lou Gehrig	New York	.363
1935	Arky Vaughan	Pittsburgh	.385	1935	Buddy Myer	Washington	.349
1936	Paul Waner	Pittsburgh	.373	1936	Luke Appling	Chicago	.388
1937	Joe Medwick	St. Louis	.374	1937	Charlie Gehringer	Detroit	.371
1938	Ernie Lombardi	Cincinnati	.342	1938	Jimmy Foxx	Boston	.349
1939	John Mize	St. Louis	.349	1939	Joe DiMaggio	New York	.381
1940	Debs Garms	Pittsburgh	.355	1940	Joe DiMaggio	New York	.352
1941	Pete Reiser	Brooklyn	.343	1941	Ted Williams	Boston	.406
1942	Ernie Lombardi	Boston	.330	1942	Ted Williams	Boston	.356
1943	Stan Musial	St. Louis	.357	1943	Luke Appling	Chicago	.328
1944	Dixie Walker	Brooklyn	.357	1944	Lou Boudreau	Cleveland	.327
1945	Phil Cavarretta	Chicago	.355	1945	George Stirnweiss	New York	.309
1946	Stan Musial	St. Louis	.365	1946	Mickey Vernon	Washington	.353
1947	Harry Walker	Philadelphia	.363	1947	Ted Williams	Boston	.343
1948	Stan Musial	St. Louis	.376	1948	Ted Williams	Boston	.369
1949	Jackie Robinson	Brooklyn	.342	1949	George Kell	Detroit	.343
1950	Stan Musial	St. Louis	.346	1950	Billy Goodman	Boston	.354
1951	Stan Musial	St. Louis	.355	1951	Ferris Fain	Philadelphia	.344
1952	Stan Musial	St. Louis	.336	1952	Ferris Fain	Philadelphia	.327
1953	Carl Furillo	Brooklyn	.344	1953	Mickey Vernon	Washington	.337
1954	Willie Mays	New York	.345	1954	Roberto Avila	Cleveland	.341
1955	Richie Ashburn	Philadelphia	.338	1955	Al Kaline	Detroit	.340
1956	Hank Aaron	Milwaukee	.328	1956	Mickey Mantle	New York	.353
1957	Stan Musial	St. Louis	.351	1957	Ted Williams	Boston	.388
1958	Richie Ashburn	Philadelphia	.350	1958	Ted Williams	Boston	.328
1959	Hank Aaron	Milwaukee	.355	1959	Harvey Kuenn	Detroit	.353
1960	Dick Groat	Pittsburgh	.325	1960	Pete Runnels	Boston	.320
1961	Roberto Clemente	Pittsburgh	.351	1961	Norm Cash	Detroit	.361
1962	Tommy Davis	Los Angeles	.346	1962	Pete Runnels	Boston	.326
1963	Tommy Davis	Los Angeles	.326	1963	Carl Yastrzemski	Boston	.321
1964	Roberto Clemente	Pittsburgh	.339	1964	Tony Oliva	Minnesota	.323
1965	Roberto Clemente	Pittsburgh	.329	1965	Tony Oliva	Minnesota	.321
1966	Matty Alou	Pittsburgh	.342	1966	Frank Robinson	Baltimore	.316
1967	Roberto Clemente	Pittsburgh	.357	1967	Carl Yastrzemski	Boston	.326
1968	Pete Rose	Cincinnati	.335	1968	Carl Yastrzemski	Boston	.301
1969	Pete Rose	Cincinnati	.348	1969	Rod Carew	Minnesota	.332
1970	Rico Carty	Atlanta	.366	1970	Alex Johnson	California	.328
1971	Joe Torre	St. Louis	.363	1971	Tony Oliva	Minnesota	.337
1972	Billy Williams	Chicago	.333	1972	Rod Carew	Minnesota	.318
1973	Pete Rose	Cincinnati	.338	1973	Rod Carew	Minnesota	.350
1974	Ralph Garr	Atlanta	.353	1974	Rod Carew	Minnesota	.364
1975	Bill Madlock	Chicago	.354	1975	Rod Carew	Minnesota	.359
1976	Bill Madlock	Chicago	.339	1976	George Brett	Kansas City	.333
1977	Dave Parker	Pittsburgh	.338	1977	Rod Carew	Minnesota	.388
1978	Dave Parker	Pittsburgh	.334	1978	Rod Carew	Minnesota	.333
1979	Keith Hernandez	St. Louis	.344	1979	Fred Lynn	Boston	.333
1980	Bill Buckner	Chicago	.324	1980	George Brett	Kansas City	.390
1981	Bill Madlock	Pittsburgh	.341	1981	Carney Lansford	Boston	.336
1982	Al Oliver	Montreal	.331	1982	Willie Wilson	Kansas City	.332
1983	Bill Madlock	Pittsburgh	.323	1983	Wade Boggs	Boston	.361
1984	Tony Gwynn	San Diego	.351	1984	Don Mattingly	New York	.343

National League Records in 1984

Final standings

Eastern Division

Club	W	L	Pct	GB
Chicago	96	65	.596	—
New York	90	72	.556	6½
St. Louis	84	78	.519	12½
Philadelphia	81	81	.500	15½
Montreal	78	83	.484	18
Pittsburgh	75	87	.463	21½

Western Division

Club	W	L	Pct	GB
San Diego	92	70	.568	—
Atlanta	80	82	.494	12
Houston	80	82	.494	12
Los Angeles	79	83	.488	13
Cincinnati	70	92	.432	22
San Francisco	66	96	.407	26

National League Playoffs

Chicago 13, San Diego 0
Chicago 4, San Diego 2

San Diego 7, Chicago 1
San Diego 7, Chicago 5

San Diego 6, Chicago 3

Club Batting

Club	Pct	AB	R	H	HR	SB
Philadelphia	.266	5614	720	1494	147	186
San Francisco	.265	5650	682	1499	112	126
Houston	.264	5548	693	1465	79	105
Chicago	.260	5437	762	1415	136	154
San Diego	.259	5504	686	1425	109	152
New York	.257	5438	652	1400	107	149
Pittsburgh	.255	5537	615	1412	98	96
St. Louis	.252	5422	652	1369	75	220
Montreal	.251	5439	593	1367	96	131
Atlanta	.247	5422	632	1338	111	140
Cincinnati	.244	5498	627	1342	106	160
Los Angeles	.244	5399	580	1316	102	109

Club Pitching

Club	ERA	CG	IP	H	R	BB	SO
Pittsburgh	3.11	27	1470	1344	567	502	995
Los Angeles	3.17	39	1460	1381	600	499	1033
Montreal	3.31	19	1431	1333	585	474	861
Houston	3.32	24	1449	1350	630	502	950
San Diego	3.48	13	1460	1327	634	563	812
Atlanta	3.57	17	1447	1401	655	525	859
St. Louis	3.58	19	1449	1427	645	494	808
New York	3.60	12	1442	1371	676	573	1028
Philadelphia	3.62	11	1458	1416	690	448	904
Chicago	3.75	19	1434	1458	658	442	879
Cincinnati	4.16	25	1461	1445	747	578	946
San Francisco	4.39	9	1461	1589	807	549	854

Individual Batting

Leaders—Based on 502 plate appearances.

Player, club	Pct	AB	R	H	HR	RBI	SB
Gwynn, San Diego	.351	606	88	213	5	71	33
Lacy, Pittsburgh	.321	474	66	152	12	70	21
C. Davis, San Fran.	.315	499	87	157	21	81	12
Sandberg, Chicago	.314	636	114	200	19	84	32
Ray, Pittsburgh	.312	555	75	173	6	67	11
Cruz, Houston	.312	600	96	187	12	95	22
Hernandez, N.Y.	.311	550	83	171	15	94	2
Raines, Montreal	.309	622	106	192	8	60	75
Guerrero, Los Angeles	.303	535	85	162	16	72	9
Leonard, San Francisco	.302	514	76	155	21	86	17

Individual Pitching

Leaders—Based on 162 innings pitched.

Pitcher, club	W	L	ERA	G	IP	H	BB	SO
Pena, Los Angeles	12	6	2.48	28	199	186	46	135
Gooden, New York	17	9	2.60	31	218	161	73	276
Hershiser, Los Angeles	11	8	2.66	45	189	160	50	150
Rhoden, Pittsburgh	14	9	2.72	33	238	216	62	136
Candelaria, Pittsburgh	12	11	2.72	33	185	179	34	133
Honeycutt, Los Angeles	10	9	2.84	29	183	180	51	75
Lea, Montreal	15	10	2.89	30	224	198	68	123
McWilliams, Pittsburgh	12	11	2.93	34	227	226	78	149
Thurmond, San Diego	14	8	2.97	32	178	174	55	57
Valenzuela, Los Angeles	12	17	3.03	34	261	218	106	240

Individual Batting (at least 115 at-bats); Individual Pitching (at least 50 innings)

Atlanta Braves

Batting	Avg	AB	R	H	HR	RBI
Murphy	.290	607	94	176	36	100
Washington	.286	416	62	119	17	61
Johnson	.279	294	28	82	5	30
Oberkfell	.269	324	38	87	1	21
Ramirez	.266	591	51	157	2	48
Perry	.265	347	52	92	7	47
Hall	.261	142	25	37	1	9
Chambliss	.257	389	47	100	9	44
Trevino	.243	272	36	66	3	28
Hubbard	.234	397	53	93	9	43
Benedict	.223	300	26	67	4	25
Royster	.207	227	22	47	1	21
Komminsk	.203	301	37	61	8	36

Pitching	W	L	ERA	IP	BB	SO	Sv
Bedrosian	9	6	2.37	83	33	81	11
Moore	4	5	2.94	64	18	47	16
Garber	3	6	3.06	106	24	55	11
Mahler	13	10	3.12	222	62	106	
Camp	8	6	3.27	148	63	69	
Perez	14	8	3.74	211	51	145	
Dedmon	4	3	3.78	81	35	51	4
Barker	7	8	3.85	126	38	95	
Falcone	5	7	4.13	120	57	55	2
McMurtry	9	17	4.32	183	102	99	

Chicago Cubs

Batting	Avg	AB	R	H	HR	RBI
Sandberg	.314	636	114	200	19	84
Matthews	.291	491	101	143	14	82
Durham	.279	473	86	132	23	96
Moreland	.279	495	59	138	16	80
Dernier	.278	536	94	149	3	32
Cotto	.274	146	24	40	0	8
Davis	.256	523	55	134	19	94
Cey	.240	505	71	121	25	97
Bowa	.223	391	33	87	0	17

Pitching	W	L	ERA	IP	BB	SO	Sv
Sutcliffe	16	1	2.69	150	39	155	
Eckersley	10	8	3.03	160	36	81	
Brusstar	1	1	3.11	63	21	36	3
Sanderson	8	5	3.14	140	24	76	
Trout	13	7	3.41	190	59	81	
Bordi	5	2	3.46	83	20	41	4
Smith	9	7	3.65	101	35	86	33
Stoddard	10	6	3.82	92	57	87	7
Frazier	6	3	4.10	63	26	58	3
Ruthven	6	10	5.04	126	41	55	
Reuschel	5	5	5.17	92	23	43	

Cincinnati Reds

Batting	Avg	AB	R	H	HR	RBI
Krenchicki	.298	181	18	54	6	22
Walker	.292	195	35	57	10	28
Rose	.286	374	43	107	0	34
Parker	.285	607	73	173	16	94
Cedeno	.276	380	59	105	10	47
Redus	.254	394	69	100	7	22
Foley	.253	277	26	70	5	27
Concepcion	.245	531	46	130	4	58
Oester	.242	553	54	134	3	38
Perez	.241	137	9	33	2	15
Milner	.232	336	44	78	7	29
Gulden	.226	292	31	66	4	33
Davis	.224	174	33	39	10	30
Bilardello	.209	182	16	38	2	10
Esasky	.193	322	30	62	10	45

Pitching	W	L	ERA	IP	BB	SO	Sv
Franco	6	2	2.61	79	36	55	4
Power	9	7	2.82	108	46	81	11
Tibbs	6	2	2.86	100	33	40	
McGaffigan	3	6	3.52	69	23	57	1
Soto	18	7	3.53	237	87	185	
Owchinko	3	5	4.12	94	39	60	2
Price	7	13	4.19	171	61	129	
Russell	6	18	4.26	181	65	101	
Hume	4	13	5.64	113	41	59	3
Pastore	3	8	6.50	98	40	53	

Montreal Expos

Batting	Avg	AB	R	H	HR	RBI
Francona	.346	214	18	74	1	18
Raines	.309	622	106	192	8	60
Wohlford	.300	213	20	64	5	29
Carter	.294	596	75	175	27	106
Dilone	.278	169	28	47	1	10
Driessen	.269	387	47	104	16	60
Dawson	.248	533	73	132	17	86
Wallach	.246	582	55	143	18	72
Little	.244	266	31	65	0	9
Flynn	.243	366	23	89	0	17
Stenhouse	.183	175	14	32	4	16
Salazar	.155	174	12	27	0	12

Pitching	W	L	ERA	IP	BB	SO	Sv
Schatzeder	7	7	2.71	136	36	89	1
Lucas	0	3	2.72	53	20	42	8
Lea	15	10	2.89	224	68	123	
Reardon	7	7	2.90	87	37	79	23
Smith	12	13	3.32	179	51	101	
Gullickson	12	9	3.61	226	37	100	
James	6	6	3.66	96	45	91	10
Palmer	7	3	3.84	105	44	66	
Rogers	6	15	4.31	169	78	64	

Houston Astros

Batting	Avg	AB	R	H	HR	RBI
Cruz	.312	600	96	187	12	95
Cabell	.310	436	52	135	8	44
Puhl	.301	449	66	135	9	55
Mumphrey	.290	524	66	152	9	83
Walling	.281	249	37	70	3	31
Garner	.278	374	60	104	4	45
Ashby	.262	191	16	50	4	27
Doran	.261	548	92	143	4	41
Reynolds	.260	527	61	137	6	60
Bass	.260	331	33	86	2	29
Bailey	.212	344	38	73	9	34

Pitching	W	L	ERA	IP	BB	SO	Sv
Dawley	11	4	1.93	98	35	47	5
Solano	1	3	1.95	50	18	33	
Smith	5	4	2.21	77	20	45	5
Ryan	12	11	3.04	183	69	197	
Niekro	16	12	3.04	248	89	127	
Knepper	15	10	3.20	233	55	140	
DiPino	4	9	3.35	75	36	65	14
LaCoss	7	5	4.02	132	55	86	3
Ruhle	1	9	4.58	90	29	60	2
Scott	5	11	4.68	154	43	83	

Los Angeles Dodgers

Batting	Avg	AB	R	H	HR	RBI
Guerrero	.303	535	85	162	16	72
Bailor	.275	131	11	36	0	8
Scioscia	.273	341	29	93	5	38
Maldonado	.268	254	25	68	5	28
Russell	.267	262	25	70	0	19
Rivera	.260	227	20	59	2	17
Reynolds	.258	240	23	62	2	24
Marshall	.257	495	69	127	21	65
Anderson	.251	374	51	94	3	34
Landreaux	.251	438	39	110	11	47
Whitfield	.244	180	15	44	4	18
Sax	.243	569	70	138	1	35
Yeager	.228	197	16	45	4	29
Brock	.225	271	33	61	14	34

Pitching	W	L	ERA	IP	BB	SO	Sv
Pena	12	6	2.48	199	46	135	
Hershiser	11	8	2.66	189	50	150	2
Honeycutt	10	9	2.84	183	51	75	
Valenzuela	12	17	3.03	261	106	240	
Howell	5	5	3.33	51	9	54	6
Hooton	3	6	3.44	110	43	62	4
Welch	13	13	3.78	178	58	126	
Zachry	5	6	3.81	82	51	55	2
Reuss	5	7	3.82	99	31	44	1

New York Mets

Batting	Avg	AB	R	H	HR	RBI
Hernandez	.311	550	83	171	15	94
Chapman	.289	197	27	57	3	23
Brooks	.283	561	61	159	16	73
Backman	.280	436	68	122	1	26
Santana	.276	152	14	42	1	12
Wilson	.276	587	88	162	10	54
Foster	.269	553	67	149	24	86
Strawberry	.251	522	75	131	26	97
Gardenhire	.246	207	20	51	1	10
Fitzgerald	.242	360	20	87	2	33
Knight	.237	371	28	88	3	35
Heep	.231	199	36	46	1	12
Oquendo	.222	189	23	42	0	10

Pitching	W	L	ERA	IP	BB	SO	Sv
Sisk	1	3	2.09	77	54	32	15
Orosco	10	6	2.59	87	34	85	31
Gooden	17	9	2.60	218	73	276	
Gorman	6	0	2.97	57	13	40	
Fernandez	6	6	3.50	90	34	62	
Terrell	11	12	3.52	215	80	114	
Gaff	3	2	3.63	84	36	42	1
Darling	12	9	3.81	205	104	136	
Berenyi	12	13	4.45	166	95	134	
Lynch	9	8	4.50	124	24	62	2

Philadelphia Phillies

Batting	Avg	AB	R	H	HR	RBI
Stone	.362	185	27	67	1	15
Corcoran	.341	208	30	71	5	36
G. Gross	.322	202	19	65	0	16
Oliver	.301	432	36	130	0	48
Hayes	.292	561	85	164	16	67
Wockenfuss	.289	180	20	52	6	24
Maddox	.282	241	29	68	5	19
Lezcano	.277	256	36	71	14	40
Schmidt	.277	528	93	146	36	106
Samuel	.272	701	105	191	15	69
Virgil	.261	456	61	119	18	68
DeJesus	.257	435	40	112	0	35
Lefebvre	.250	160	22	40	3	18
Matuszek	.248	262	40	65	12	43
Wilson	.240	341	28	82	6	31

Pitching	W	L	ERA	IP	BB	SO	Sv
Andersen	3	7	2.38	90	25	54	4
Denny	7	7	2.45	154	29	94	
Koosman	14	15	3.25	224	60	137	
Holland	5	10	3.39	98	30	61	29
Campbell	6	5	3.43	81	35	52	1
Carlton	13	7	3.58	229	79	163	
Rawley	10	6	3.81	120	27	58	
Hudson	9	11	4.04	173	52	94	
K. Gross	8	5	4.12	129	44	84	1

Pittsburgh Pirates

Batting	Avg	AB	R	H	HR	RBI
Lacy	.321	474	66	152	12	70
Ray	.312	555	75	173	6	67
Morrison	.286	304	38	87	11	45
Pena	.286	546	77	156	15	78
Wynne	.266	653	77	174	0	39
Thompson	.254	543	61	138	17	74
Madlock	.253	403	38	102	4	44
Mazzilli	.237	266	37	63	4	21
Berra	.222	450	31	100	9	52
Frobel	.203	276	33	56	12	28

Pitching	W	L	ERA	IP	BB	SO	Sv
Tekulve	3	9	2.66	88	33	36	13
Rhoden	14	9	2.72	238	62	136	
Candelaria	12	11	2.72	185	34	133	2
McWilliams	12	11	2.93	227	78	149	1
Robinson	5	6	3.02	122	49	110	10
Tudor	12	11	3.27	212	56	117	
DeLeon	7	13	3.74	192	92	153	
Tunnell	1	7	5.27	68	40	51	1

San Diego Padres

Batting	Avg	AB	R	H	HR	RBI
Gwynn	.351	606	88	213	5	71
Garvey	.284	617	72	175	8	86
McReynolds	.278	525	68	146	20	75
Flannery	.273	128	24	35	2	10
Wiggins	.258	596	106	154	3	34
Templeton	.258	493	40	127	2	35
Brown	.251	171	28	43	3	29
Martinez	.250	488	64	122	13	66
Salazar	.241	228	20	55	3	17
Kennedy	.240	530	54	127	14	57
Nettles	.228	395	56	90	20	65

Pitching	W	L	ERA	IP	BB	SO	Sv
Lefferts	3	4	2.13	105	24	56	10
Harris	2	2	2.48	54	25	45	3
Gossage	10	6	2.90	102	36	84	25
Dravecky	9	8	2.93	156	51	71	8
Thurmond	14	8	2.97	178	55	57	
Whitson	14	8	3.24	189	42	103	
Booker	1	1	3.30	57	27	28	
Show	15	9	3.40	206	88	104	
Lollar	11	13	3.91	195	105	131	
Hawkins	8	9	4.68	146	72	77	

St. Louis Cardinals

Batting	Avg	AB	R	H	HR	RBI
Pendleton	.324	262	37	85	1	33
McGee	.291	571	82	166	6	50
Hendrick	.277	441	57	122	9	69
Herr	.276	558	67	154	4	49
Landrum	.272	173	21	47	3	26
Green	.268	452	49	121	15	65
O. Smith	.257	412	53	106	1	44
Jorgensen	.250	124	9	31	1	17
L. Smith	.250	504	77	126	6	49
Van Slyke	.244	361	45	88	7	50
Porter	.232	422	56	98	11	68
Howe	.216	139	17	30	2	12

Pitching	W	L	ERA	IP	BB	SO	Sv
Sutter	5	7	1.54	122	23	77	45
Rucker	2	3	2.10	73	34	38	
Kepshire	6	5	3.30	109	44	71	
Andujar	20	14	3.34	261	70	147	
Horton	9	4	3.44	125	39	76	1
Allen	9	6	3.55	119	49	66	3
Lahti	4	2	3.72	84	34	45	1
LaPoint	12	10	3.96	193	77	130	
Cox	9	11	4.03	156	54	70	
Forsch	2	5	6.02	52	19	21	

San Francisco Giants

Batting	Avg	AB	R	H	HR	RBI
Gladden	.351	342	71	120	4	31
Clark	.320	203	33	65	11	44
C. Davis	.315	499	87	157	21	81
Thompson	.306	245	30	75	1	31
Nicosia	.303	132	9	40	2	19
Leonard	.302	514	76	155	21	86
Baker	.292	243	31	71	3	32
Brenly	.291	506	74	147	20	80
Trillo	.254	401	45	102	4	36
Youngblood	.254	469	50	119	10	51
Richards	.252	135	18	34	0	4
Wellman	.226	265	23	60	2	25
LeMaster	.217	451	46	98	4	32
Kuiper	.200	115	8	23	0	11

Pitching	W	L	ERA	IP	BB	SO	Sv
Lavelle	5	4	2.76	101	42	71	12
Williams	9	4	3.55	106	51	91	3
Minton	4	9	3.76	124	57	48	19
Lacey	1	3	3.88	51	13	26	
Lerch	5	3	4.23	72	36	48	2
Laskey	9	14	4.33	207	50	71	
Krukow	11	12	4.56	199	78	141	1
Robinson	7	15	4.56	171	52	102	
M. Davis	5	17	5.36	174	54	124	
Grant	1	4	6.37	53	19	32	1

Leading Pitchers, Earned-Run Average

	National League						American League			
Year	Player, club	G	IP	ERA		Year	Player, club	G	IP	ERA
1965	Sandy Koufax, Los Angeles	43	336	2.04		1965	Sam McDowell, Cleveland	42	274	2.17
1966	Sandy Koufax, Los Angeles	41	323	1.73		1966	Gary Peters, Chicago	29	204	2.03
1967	Phil Niekro, Atlanta	46	207	1.87		1967	Joe Horlen, Chicago	35	258	2.06
1968	Bob Gibson, St. Louis	34	305	1.12		1968	Luis Tiant, Cleveland	34	258	1.60
1969	Juan Marichal, San Francisco	37	300	2.10		1969	Dick Bosman, Washington	31	193	2.19
1970	Tom Seaver, New York	37	291	2.81		1970	Diego Segui, Oakland	47	162	2.56
1971	Tom Seaver, New York	36	286	1.76		1971	Vida Blue, Oakland	39	312	1.82
1972	Steve Carlton, Philadelphia	41	346	1.98		1972	Luis Tiant, Boston	43	179	1.91
1973	Tom Seaver, New York	36	290	2.07		1973	Jim Palmer, Baltimore	38	296	2.40
1974	Buzz Capra, Atlanta	39	217	2.28		1974	Catfish Hunter, Oakland	41	318	2.49
1975	Randy Jones, San Diego	37	285	2.24		1975	Jim Palmer, Baltimore	39	323	2.09
1976	John Denny, St. Louis	30	207	2.52		1976	Mark Fidrych, Detroit	31	250	2.34
1977	John Candelaria, Pittsburgh	33	231	2.34		1977	Frank Tanana, California	31	241	2.54
1978	Craig Swan, New York	29	207	2.43		1978	Ron Guidry, New York	35	274	1.74
1979	J. R. Richard, Houston	38	292	2.71		1979	Ron Guidry, New York	33	236	2.78
1980	Don Sutton, Los Angeles	32	212	2.21		1980	Rudy May, New York	41	175	2.47
1981	Nolan Ryan, Houston	21	149	1.69		1981	Steve McCatty, Oakland	22	186	2.32
1982	Steve Rogers, Montreal	35	277	2.40		1982	Rick Sutcliffe, Cleveland	34	216	2.96
1983	Atlee Hammaker, San Fran.	23	172	2.25		1983	Rick Honeycutt, Texas	25	174	2.42
1984	Alejandro Pena, Los Angeles	28	199	2.48		1984	Mike Boddicker, Baltimore	34	261	2.79

ERA is computed by multiplying earned runs allowed by 9, then dividing by innings pitched.

Little League World Series in 1984

The team from South Korea won the 1984 Little League World Series by defeating the team from Altamonte Springs, Fla. 6-2 at Williamsport, Pa. on Aug. 26.

American League Records in 1984

Final standings

Eastern Division

Club	W	L	Pct	GB
Detroit	104	58	.642	—
Toronto	89	73	.549	15
New York	87	75	.537	17
Boston	86	76	.531	18
Baltimore	85	77	.525	19
Cleveland	75	87	.463	29
Milwaukee	67	94	.416	36½

Western Division

Club	W	L	Pct	GB
Kansas City	84	78	.519	—
California	81	81	.500	3
Minnesota	81	81	.500	3
Oakland	77	85	.475	7
Chicago	74	88	.457	10
Seattle	74	88	.457	10
Texas	69	92	.429	14½

American League Playoffs

Detroit 8, Kansas City 1   Detroit 5, Kansas City 3   Detroit 1, Kansas City 0

Club Batting

Club	Pct	AB	R	H	HR	SB
Boston	.283	5648	810	1598	181	38
New York	.276	5661	758	1560	130	62
Toronto	.273	5687	750	1555	143	192
Detroit	.271	5644	829	1529	187	106
Kansas City	.268	5543	673	1487	117	106
Cleveland	.265	5643	761	1498	123	126
Minnesota	.265	5562	673	1473	114	39
Milwaukee	.262	5511	641	1446	96	52
Texas	.261	5569	656	1452	120	81
Oakland	.259	5457	738	1415	158	145
Seattle	.258	5546	692	1429	129	116
Baltimore	.252	5456	681	1374	160	51
California	.249	5470	696	1363	150	80
Chicago	.247	5513	679	1360	172	109

Club Pitching

Club	ERA	CG	IP	H	R	BB	SO
Detroit	3.49	19	1464	1358	643	489	914
Baltimore	3.71	48	1439	1393	667	512	714
New York	3.78	15	1465	1485	679	518	992
Minnesota	3.85	32	1437	1429	675	463	713
Toronto	3.86	34	1464	1433	696	528	875
Texas	3.91	38	1438	1443	714	518	863
Kansas City	3.92	18	1444	1426	686	433	724
California	3.96	36	1458	1526	697	474	754
Milwaukee	4.06	13	1433	1532	734	480	785
Chicago	4.13	43	1454	1416	736	483	840
Boston	4.18	40	1442	1524	764	517	927
Cleveland	4.26	21	1467	1523	766	545	803
Seattle	4.31	26	1442	1497	774	619	971
Oakland	4.48	15	1430	1554	796	592	695

Individual Batting

Leaders—Based on 502 plate appearances.

Player, club	Pct	AB	R	H	HR	RBI	SB
Mattingly, New York	.343	603	91	207	23	110	1
Winfield, New York	.340	567	106	193	19	100	6
Boggs, Boston	.325	625	109	203	6	55	3
Bell, Texas	.315	553	88	174	11	83	2
Trammell, Detroit	.314	555	85	174	14	69	19
Easler, Boston	.313	601	87	188	27	91	1
Hrbek, Minnesota	.311	559	80	174	27	107	1
Murray, Baltimore	.306	588	97	180	29	110	10
Ripken, Baltimore	.304	641	103	195	27	86	2
Baines, Chicago	.304	569	72	173	29	94	1

Individual Pitching

Leaders—Based on 162 innings pitched.

Pitcher, club	W	L	ERA	G	IP	H	BB	SO
Boddicker, Baltimore	20	11	2.79	34	261	218	81	128
Stieb, Toronto	16	8	2.83	35	267	215	88	198
Blyleven, Cleveland	19	7	2.87	33	245	204	74	170
Niekro, New York	16	8	3.09	32	215	219	76	136
Zahn, California	13	10	3.12	28	199	200	48	61
Black, Kansas City	17	12	3.12	35	257	226	64	140
Davis, Baltimore	14	9	3.12	35	225	205	71	105
Alexander, Toronto	17	6	3.13	36	261	238	59	139
Burris, Oakland	13	10	3.15	34	211	193	90	93
Viola, Minnesota	18	12	3.21	35	257	225	73	149

Individual Batting (at least 115 at-bats); Individual Pitching (at least 50 innings)

Baltimore Orioles

Batting	Avg	AB	R	H	HR	RBI
Murray	.306	588	97	180	29	110
Ripken	.304	641	103	195	27	86
Bumbry	.270	344	47	93	3	24
Rayford	.256	250	24	64	4	27
Dwyer	.255	161	22	41	2	21
Dauer	.254	397	29	101	2	24
Young	.252	401	59	101	17	52
Lowenstein	.237	270	34	64	8	28
Dempsey	.230	330	37	76	11	34
Roenicke	.224	326	36	73	10	44
Cruz	.218	142	15	31	3	9
Gross	.216	342	53	74	22	64
Singleton	.215	363	28	78	6	36
Ayala	.212	118	9	25	4	24
Shelby	.209	383	44	80	6	30
Jackson	.193	119	5	23	0	7
Sakata	.191	157	23	30	3	11

Pitching	W	L	ERA	IP	BB	SO	Sv
Boddicker	20	11	2.79	261	81	128	
Davis	14	9	3.12	225	71	105	1
Stewart	7	4	3.29	93	47	56	13
Underwood	1	0	3.52	71	31	39	1
Flanagan	13	13	3.53	226	81	115	
T. Martinez	4	9	3.91	89	51	72	17
McGregor	15	12	3.94	196	54	67	
D. Martinez	6	9	5.02	141	37	77	
Swaggerty	3	2	5.21	57	21	18	

Boston Red Sox

Batting	Avg	AB	R	H	HR	RBI
Boggs	.325	625	109	203	6	55
Easler	.313	601	87	188	27	91
Barrett	.303	475	56	144	3	45
Evans	.295	630	121	186	32	104
Rice	.280	657	98	184	28	122
Buckner	.278	439	51	122	11	67
Gedman	.269	449	54	121	24	72
Armas	.268	639	107	171	43	123
Gutierrez	.263	449	55	118	2	29
Miller	.260	123	17	32	0	12
Nichols	.226	124	14	28	1	14

Pitching	W	L	ERA	IP	BB	SO	Sv
Crawford	5	0	3.34	62	21	21	1
Johnson	1	2	3.53	63	27	57	1
Stanley	9	10	3.54	106	23	52	22
Nipper	11	6	3.89	182	52	84	
Hurst	12	12	3.92	218	88	136	
Ojeda	12	12	3.99	216	96	137	
Clear	8	3	4.03	67	70	76	8
Clemens	9	4	4.32	133	29	126	
Boyd	12	12	4.37	197	53	134	
Brown	1	8	6.85	67	19	32	

California Angels

Batting

Batting	Avg	AB	R	H	HR	RBI
Beniquez	.336	354	60	119	8	39
Carew	.295	329	42	97	3	31
M. Brown	.284	148	19	42	7	22
Downing	.275	539	65	148	23	91
Lynn	.271	517	84	140	23	79
DeCinces	.269	547	77	147	20	82
Grich	.256	363	60	93	18	58
Wilfong	.248	307	31	76	6	33
Narron	.247	150	9	37	3	17
Sconiers	.244	160	14	39	4	17
Pettis	.227	397	63	90	2	29
Jackson	.223	525	67	117	25	81
Boone	.202	450	33	91	3	32
Picciolo	.202	119	18	24	1	9
Schofield	.192	400	39	77	4	21

Pitching

Pitching	W	L	ERA	IP	BB	SO	Sv
Corbett	5	1	2.12	85	30	48	4
Zahn	13	10	3.12	199	48	61	
Sanchez	9	7	3.33	83	33	62	11
Witt	15	11	3.47	246	84	196	
Romanick	12	12	3.76	229	61	87	
John	7	13	4.52	181	56	47	
Kaufman	2	3	4.57	69	20	41	1
Slaton	7	10	4.97	163	56	67	
Kison	4	5	5.37	65	28	66	2

Detroit Tigers

Batting

Batting	Avg	AB	R	H	HR	RBI
Trammell	.314	555	85	174	14	69
Whitaker	.289	558	90	161	13	56
Garbey	.287	327	45	94	5	52
Lemon	.287	509	77	146	20	76
Kuntz	.286	140	32	40	2	22
Jones	.284	215	26	61	12	37
Gibson	.282	531	92	150	27	91
Herndon	.280	407	52	114	7	43
Bergman	.273	271	42	74	7	44
Grubb	.267	176	25	47	8	17
Johnson	.248	355	43	88	12	50
Brookens	.246	224	32	55	5	26
Parrish	.237	578	75	137	33	98
Castillo	.234	141	16	33	4	17
Evans	.232	401	60	93	16	63

Pitching

Pitching	W	L	ERA	IP	BB	SO	Sv
Hernandez	9	3	1.92	140	36	112	32
Lopez	10	1	2.94	137	52	94	14
Petry	18	8	3.24	233	66	144	
Berenguer	11	10	3.48	168	79	118	
Morris	19	11	3.60	240	87	148	
Rozema	7	6	3.74	101	18	48	
Bair	5	3	3.75	93	36	57	4
Wilcox	17	8	4.00	193	66	119	

Chicago White Sox

Batting

Batting	Avg	AB	R	H	HR	RBI
Baines	.304	569	72	173	29	94
Walker	.294	442	62	130	24	75
Hairston	.260	227	41	59	5	19
Paciorek	.256	363	35	93	4	29
V. Law	.252	481	60	121	17	59
R. Law	.251	487	68	122	6	37
Fletcher	.250	456	46	114	3	35
Luzinski	.238	412	47	98	13	58
Dybzinski	.235	132	17	31	1	10
Hill	.233	193	15	45	5	20
Fisk	.231	359	54	83	21	43
Cruz	.222	415	42	92	5	43
Kittle	.215	466	67	100	32	74
Smalley	.212	344	32	73	11	39

Pitching

Pitching	W	L	ERA	IP	BB	SO	Sv
Reed	0	6	3.08	73	14	57	12
Agosto	2	1	3.09	55	34	26	7
Dotson	14	15	3.59	245	103	120	
Seaver	15	11	3.95	236	61	131	
Nelson	3	5	4.46	74	17	36	1
Hoyt	13	18	4.47	235	43	126	
Bannister	14	11	4.83	218	80	152	
Spillner	1	5	4.89	99	36	49	2
Burns	4	12	5.00	117	45	85	3

Kansas City Royals

Batting

Batting	Avg	AB	R	H	HR	RBI
McRae	.303	317	30	96	3	42
Wilson	.301	541	81	163	2	44
Orta	.298	403	50	120	9	50
Brett	.284	377	42	107	13	69
Motley	.284	522	64	148	15	70
Sheridan	.283	481	64	136	8	53
Concepcion	.282	287	36	81	1	23
White	.271	479	58	130	17	56
Slaught	.264	409	48	108	4	42
Pryor	.263	270	32	71	4	25
Iorg	.255	235	27	60	5	30
Balboni	.244	438	58	107	28	77
Washington	.224	170	18	38	1	10
Biancalana	.194	134	18	26	2	9
Wathan	.181	171	17	31	2	10

Pitching

Pitching	W	L	ERA	IP	BB	SO	Sv
Quisenberry	6	3	2.64	129	12	41	44
Black	17	12	3.12	257	64	140	
Beckwith	8	4	3.40	100	25	75	2
Saberhagen	10	11	3.48	157	36	73	1
Leibrandt	11	7	3.63	143	38	53	
Gubicza	10	14	4.05	189	75	111	
Huismann	3	3	4.20	75	21	54	3
Jackson	2	6	4.26	76	35	40	
M. Jones	2	3	4.89	81	36	43	
Gura	12	9	5.18	168	67	68	

Cleveland Indians

Batting

Batting	Avg	AB	R	H	HR	RBI
Vukovich	.304	437	38	133	9	60
Bando	.291	220	38	64	12	41
Tabler	.290	473	66	137	10	68
Franco	.286	658	82	188	3	79
Carter	.275	244	32	67	13	41
Thornton	.271	587	91	159	33	99
Butler	.269	602	108	162	3	49
Hargrove	.267	352	44	94	2	44
Jacoby	.264	439	64	116	7	40
Castillo	.261	211	36	55	10	36
Hall	.257	257	43	66	7	30
Fischlin	.226	133	17	30	1	14
Willard	.224	246	21	55	10	37
Bernazard	.221	439	44	97	2	38

Pitching

Pitching	W	L	ERA	IP	BB	SO	Sv
Camacho	5	9	2.43	100	37	48	23
Blyleven	19	7	2.87	245	74	170	
Jeffcoat	5	2	2.99	75	24	41	1
Waddell	7	4	3.06	97	37	59	6
Easterly	3	1	3.38	69	23	42	2
Farr	3	11	4.58	116	46	83	1
Smith	5	5	4.59	86	40	55	
Schulze	3	6	4.83	85	27	39	
Heaton	12	15	5.21	198	75	75	
Comer	4	8	5.68	117	39	39	

Milwaukee Brewers

Batting

Batting	Avg	AB	R	H	HR	RBI
Yount	.298	624	105	186	16	80
James	.295	387	52	114	1	30
Gantner	.282	613	61	173	3	56
Cooper	.275	603	63	166	11	67
Oglivie	.262	461	49	121	12	60
Sundberg	.261	348	43	91	7	43
Clark	.260	169	17	44	2	16
Schroeder	.257	210	29	54	14	25
Romero	.252	357	36	90	1	31
Manning	.249	341	53	85	7	31
Brouhard	.239	197	20	47	6	22
Moore	.234	188	13	44	2	17
Howell	.232	164	12	38	4	17
Simmons	.221	497	44	110	4	52

Pitching

Pitching	W	L	ERA	IP	BB	SO	Sv
Tellmann	6	3	2.78	81	31	28	4
Waits	2	4	3.58	73	24	49	3
Sutton	14	12	3.77	212	51	143	
Porter	6	4	3.87	81	12	48	
Haas	9	11	3.99	189	43	84	
Cocanower	8	16	4.02	174	78	65	
McClure	4	8	4.38	139	52	68	1
Caldwell	6	13	4.64	126	21	34	
Gibson	2	5	4.96	69	47	54	
Ladd	4	9	5.24	91	38	75	3

Minnesota Twins

Batting	Avg	AB	R	H	HR	RBI
Hrbek	.311	559	80	174	27	107
Hatcher	.302	576	61	174	5	69
Puckett	.296	557	63	165	0	31
Washington	.294	197	25	58	3	23
Brown	.273	260	36	71	1	19
Engle	.266	391	56	104	4	38
Teufel	.262	568	76	149	14	61
Gaetti	.262	588	55	154	5	65
Brunansky	.254	567	75	144	32	85
Meier	.238	147	18	35	0	13
Bush	.222	311	46	69	11	43
Laudner	.206	262	31	54	10	35
Jimenez	.201	298	28	60	0	19
Putnam	.176	193	12	34	2	20

Pitching	W	L	ERA	IP	BB	SO	Sv
Viola	18	12	3.21	257	73	149	
Butcher	13	11	3.44	225	53	83	
Lysander	4	3	3.49	56	27	22	5
Smithson	15	13	3.68	252	54	144	
Filson	6	5	4.10	118	54	59	1
Schrom	5	11	4.47	137	41	49	
Davis	7	11	4.55	83	41	74	29
Hodge	4	3	4.77	100	29	59	
Williams	3	5	5.77	68	22	22	

Seattle Mariners

Batting	Avg	AB	R	H	HR	RBI
Bradley	.301	322	49	97	0	24
Perconte	.294	612	93	180	0	31
Davis	.284	567	80	161	27	116
D. Henderson	.280	350	42	98	14	43
Cowens	.277	524	60	145	15	78
Milbourne	.265	211	22	56	1	22
Bonnell	.264	363	42	96	8	48
S. Henderson	.262	325	42	85	10	35
Owen	.245	530	67	130	3	43
Phelps	.241	290	52	70	24	51
Presley	.227	251	27	57	10	36
Kearney	.225	431	39	97	7	43

Pitching	W	L	ERA	IP	BB	SO	Sv
Nunez	2	2	3.19	67	21	57	7
Langston	17	10	3.40	225	118	204	
Beattie	12	16	3.41	211	75	119	
Stanton	4	4	3.54	61	22	55	8
Barojas	9	7	4.14	134	60	55	2
Mirabella	2	5	4.37	68	32	41	3
Vande Berg	8	12	4.76	130	50	71	7
Moore	7	17	4.97	212	85	158	
Stoddard	2	3	5.13	79	37	39	
Young	6	8	5.72	113	57	73	
Beard	3	2	5.80	76	33	40	5

New York Yankees

Batting	Avg	AB	R	H	HR	RBI
Mattingly	.343	603	91	207	23	110
Winfield	.340	567	106	193	19	100
Kemp	.291	313	37	91	7	41
Randolph	.287	564	86	162	2	31
Griffey	.273	399	44	109	7	56
Wynegar	.267	442	48	118	6	45
Baylor	.262	493	84	129	27	89
Moreno	.259	355	37	92	4	38
Meacham	.253	360	62	91	2	25
Foli	.252	163	8	41	0	16
Dayett	.244	127	14	31	4	23
Pagliarulo	.239	201	24	48	7	34
Harrah	.217	253	40	55	1	26
Robertson	.214	140	10	30	0	6
Cerone	.208	120	8	25	2	13
Gamble	.184	125	17	23	10	27

Pitching	W	L	ERA	IP	BB	SO	Sv
Righetti	5	6	2.34	96	37	90	31
Howell	9	4	2.69	103	34	109	7
Niekro	16	8	3.09	215	76	136	
Shirley	3	3	3.38	114	38	48	
Armstrong	3	2	3.48	54	26	43	1
Cowley	9	2	3.56	83	31	71	
Montefusco	5	3	3.58	55	13	23	
Fontenot	8	9	3.61	169	58	85	
Guidry	10	11	4.51	195	44	127	
Rasmussen	9	6	4.57	147	60	110	

Texas Rangers

Batting	Avg	AB	R	H	HR	RBI
Bell	.315	553	88	174	11	83
Rivers	.300	313	40	94	4	33
O'Brien	.287	520	57	149	18	80
Parrish	.285	613	72	175	22	101
Ward	.284	602	97	171	21	79
B. Jones	.259	143	14	37	4	22
Wilkerson	.248	484	47	120	1	26
Sample	.247	489	67	121	5	33
G. Wright	.243	383	40	93	9	48
Scott	.221	235	16	52	3	20
Foley	.217	115	13	25	6	19
Tolleson	.213	338	35	72	0	9
Kunkel	.204	142	13	29	3	7
Yost	.182	242	15	44	6	25

Pitching	W	L	ERA	IP	BB	SO	Sv
Schmidt	6	6	2.56	70	20	46	12
Tanana	15	15	3.25	246	81	141	
Mason	9	13	3.61	184	51	113	
O. Jones	2	4	3.64	59	23	28	2
Hough	16	14	3.76	266	94	164	
Darwin	8	12	3.94	223	54	123	
Stewart	7	14	4.73	192	87	119	
Noles	2	3	5.15	57	30	39	

Oakland A's

Batting	Avg	AB	R	H	HR	RBI
Lansford	.300	597	70	179	14	74
Henderson	.293	502	'13	147	16	58
Kingman	.268	549	68	147	35	118
Phillips	.266	451	62	120	4	37
Bochte	.264	469	58	124	5	52
Murphy	.256	559	93	143	33	88
Heath	.248	475	49	118	13	64
Morgan	.244	365	50	89	6	43
Essian	.235	136	17	32	2	10
Davis	.230	382	47	88	9	46
Hill	.230	174	21	40	2	16
Almon	.223	211	24	47	7	15

Pitching	W	L	ERA	IP	BB	SO	Sv
Caudill	9	7	2.71	96	31	89	36
Burris	13	10	3.15	211	90	93	
Young	9	4	4.06	108	31	41	
Atherton	7	6	4.33	104	39	58	2
Krueger	10	10	4.75	142	85	61	
McCatty	8	14	4.76	179	71	63	
Warren	3	6	4.90	90	44	61	
Sorensen	6	13	4.91	183	44	63	1
Conroy	1	6	5.23	93	63	69	
Codiroli	6	4	5.84	89	34	44	1

Toronto Blue Jays

Batting	Avg	AB	R	H	HR	RBI
Mulliniks	.324	343	41	111	3	42
Collins	.308	441	59	136	2	44
Johnson	.304	359	51	109	16	61
Bell	.292	606	85	177	26	88
Barfield	.284	320	51	91	14	49
Garcia	.284	633	79	180	5	46
Moseby	.280	592	97	166	18	92
Upshaw	.278	569	79	158	19	84
Fernandez	.269	234	29	63	3	19
Griffin	.242	418	53	101	4	30
Whitt	.238	315	35	75	15	46
Iorg	.227	247	24	56	1	25
Martinez	.220	232	24	51	5	37
Aikens	.205	234	21	48	11	26

Pitching	W	L	ERA	IP	BB	SO	Sv
Stieb	16	8	2.83	267	88	198	
Alexander	17	6	3.13	261	59	139	
Jackson	7	8	3.56	86	31	58	10
Leal	13	8	3.89	222	77	134	
Gott	7	6	4.02	109	49	73	2
Acker	3	5	4.38	72	25	33	1
Lamp	8	8	4.55	85	38	45	9
Key	4	5	4.65	62	32	44	10
Clancy	13	15	5.12	219	88	118	

1984 World Series

First Game

Detroit	ab	r	h	bi	San Diego	ab	r	h	bi
Whitaker, 2b	4	1	1	0	Wiggins, 2b	4	0	1	0
Trammell, ss	5	0	2	1	Gwynn, rf	2	0	1	0
Gibson, rf	4	0	0	0	Garvey, 1b	4	1	1	0
Parrish, c	3	1	2	0	Nettles, 3b	2	1	2	0
Herndon, lf	3	1	2	2	Salazer, 3b	1	0	0	0
Garbey, dh	4	0	0	0	Kennedy, c	4	0	2	2
Lemon, cf	4	0	1	0	Brown, cf	4	0	0	0
Evans, 1b	3	0	0	0	Martinez, lf	4	0	0	0
Bergman, 1b	0	0	0	0	Templeton, ss	4	0	0	0
Castillo, 3b	2	0	0	0	Bevacqua, dh	3	0	1	0
Grubb, ph	0	0	0	0	Thurmond, p	0	0	0	0
Brookens, ph	1	0	0	0	Hawkins, p	0	0	0	0
Morris, p	0	0	0	0	Dravecky, p	0	0	0	0
Totals	33	3	8	3	Totals	32	2	8	2

```
Detroit . . . . . . . . . . 1 0 0 0 2 0 0 0 0—3
San Diego . . . . . . . . . 2 0 0 0 0 0 0 0 0—2
```

E - Martinez, DP - Detroit 1, San Diego 1. LOB - Detroit 9, San Diego 6. 2B - Whitaker, Kennedy, Parrish, Bevacqua. HR - Herndon (1). SB - Trammell (1), Gwynn (1).

Detroit	ip	h	r	er	bb	so
Morris W, 1-0	9	8	2	2	3	9
San Diego						
Thurmond L, 0-1	5	7	3	3	3	2
Hawkins	2 2/3	1	0	0	3	0
Dravecky	1 1/3	0	0	0	0	1

T - 3:18. A - 57,908.

How runs were scored—One in Tigers first: Whitaker doubled. Trammell singled scoring Whitaker.

Two in Padres first: Garvey and Nettles singled. Kennedy doubled scoring Garvey and Nettles.

Two in Tigers fifth: Parrish doubled. Herndon hit a home run.

Second Game

Detroit	ab	r	h	bi	San Diego	ab	r	h	bi
Whitaker, 2b	4	1	1	0	Wiggins, 2b	5	1	3	0
Trammell, ss	4	1	2	0	Gwynn, rf	3	0	1	0
Gibson, rf	4	1	2	1	Garvey, 1b	3	0	0	0
Parrish, c	3	0	0	1	Nettles, 3b	1	1	0	1
Evans, 3b-1b	4	0	1	1	Kennedy, c	4	1	1	0
Jones, lf	2	0	0	0	Bevacqua, dh	4	2	3	3
Herndon, lf	2	0	0	0	Martinez, lf	3	0	0	0
Grubb, dh	2	0	1	0	Templeton, ss	4	0	3	0
Kuntz, ph	1	0	0	0	Brown, cf	3	0	0	1
Lemon, cf	3	0	0	0	Salazar, cf	1	0	0	0
Bergman, 1b	2	0	0	0	Whitson, p	0	0	0	0
Brookens, 3b	1	0	0	0	Hawkins, p	0	0	0	0
Petry, p	0	0	0	0	Lefferts, p	0	0	0	0
Lopez, p	0	0	0	0					
Scherrer, p	0	0	0	0					
Bair, p	0	0	0	0					
Hernandez, p	0	0	0	0					
Totals	32	3	7	3	Totals	31	5	11	5

```
Detroit . . . . . . . . . . 3 0 0 0 0 0 0 0 0—3
San Diego . . . . . . . . . 1 0 0 1 3 0 0 0 x—5
```

E - Trammell, Gibson. DP - Detroit 1, San Diego 1. LOB - Detroit 3, San Diego 8. HR - Bevacqua (1). SB - Gibson (1). S - Garvey. SF - Parrish, Nettles.

Detroit	ip	h	r	er	bb	so
Petry L, 0-1	4 1/3	8	5	5	3	2
Lopez	2/3	1	0	0	1	0
Scherrer	1 1/3	2	0	0	0	0
Bair	2/3	0	0	0	0	1
Hernandez	1	0	0	0	0	0
San Diego						
Whitson	2/3	5	3	3	0	0
Hawkins W, 1-0	5 1/3	1	0	0	3	0
Lefferts S, 1	3	1	0	0	0	5

Balk - Petry. T - 2:44. A - 57,911.

How runs were scored—Three in Tigers first: Whitaker and Trammell singled. Gibson singled scoring Whitaker. Parrish hit a sacrifice fly scoring Trammell. Evans singled scoring Gibson.

One in Padres first: Wiggins singled. Gwynn walked. Garvey sacrificed Wiggins to third. Nettles hit a sacrifice fly scoring Wiggins.

One in Padres fourth: Bevacqua and Templeton singled. Brown grounded out scoring Bevacqua.

Three in Padres fifth: Nettles walked. Kennedy singled. Bevacqua hit a home run.

Third Game

San Diego	ab	r	h	bi	Detroit	ab	r	h	bi
Wiggins, 2b	5	1	2	0	Whitaker, 2b	3	1	0	0
Gwynn, rf	5	1	2	0	Trammell, ss	3	1	2	1
Garvey, 1b	5	0	1	1	Gibson, rf	2	0	0	1
Nettles, 3b	2	0	0	1	Parrish, c	3	0	1	0
Kennedy, c	3	0	0	0	Herndon, lf	4	0	1	1
Bevacqua, dh	4	0	1	0	Garbey, dh	5	0	0	0
Martinez, lf	4	0	1	0	Lemon, cf	5	1	2	0
Templeton, ss	4	0	2	0	Evans, 1b	2	1	0	0
Brown, cf	3	0	0	0	Bergman, 1b	0	0	0	0
Salazar, ph	1	0	1	0	Castillo, 3b	4	1	1	2
Lollar, p	0	0	0	0	Wilcox, p	0	0	0	0
Booker, p	0	0	0	0	Scherrer, p	0	0	0	0
Harris, p	0	0	0	0	Hernandez, p	0	0	0	0
Totals	36	2	10	2	Totals	31	5	7	5

```
San Diego . . . . . . . . . 0 0 1 0 0 0 1 0 0—2
Detroit . . . . . . . . . . 0 4 1 0 0 0 0 0 x—5
```

LOB - San Diego 10, Detroit 14. 2B - Wiggins, Trammell, Garvey. HR - Castillo (1). SB - Gibson (2). SF - Nettles.

San Diego	ip	h	r	er	bb	so
Lollar L, 0-1	1 2/3	4	4	4	4	0
Booker	1	0	1	1	4	0
Harris	5 1/3	3	0	0	3	5
Detroit						
Wilcox W, 1-0	6	7	1	1	2	4
Scherrer	2/3	2	1	1	0	0
Hernandez S, 1	2 1/3	1	0	0	0	0

HPB - Gibson by Harris. WP - Lollar. A - 51,970.

How runs were scored—Four in Tigers second: Lemon singled. Castillo hit a home run. Whitaker walked. Trammell doubled scoring Whitaker. Gibson walked. Parrish singled. Herndon walked scoring Trammell.

One in Padres third: Wiggins and Gwynn singled. Garvey grounded out scoring Wiggins.

One in Tigers third: Evans, Whitaker, and Trammell walked. Gibson was hit by a pitch scoring Evans.

One in Padres seventh: Gwynn singled. Garvey doubled. Nettles hit a sacrifice fly scoring Gwynn.

Fourth Game

San Diego	ab	r	h	bi	Detroit	ab	r	h	bi
Wiggins, 2b	3	0	0	0	Whitaker, 2b	4	2	2	0
Summers, ph	1	0	0	0	Trammell, ss	4	2	3	4
Roenicke, lf	0	0	0	0	Gibson, rf	4	0	0	0
Gwynn, rf	4	0	1	0	Parrish, c	4	0	0	0
Garvey, 1b	4	1	1	0	Evans, 3b	2	0	0	0
Nettles, 3b	3	0	0	0	Brookens, 3b	1	0	0	0
Kennedy, c	4	1	1	1	Grubb, dh	1	0	0	0
Bevacqua, dh	3	0	1	0	Garbey, dh	2	0	0	0
Martinez, lf	2	0	0	0	Jones, lf	1	0	0	0
Flannery, 2b	1	0	1	0	Herndon, lf	2	0	1	0
Templeton, ss	3	0	0	0	Lemon, cf	2	0	0	0
Brown, cf	3	0	0	0	Bergman, 1b	3	0	0	0
Show, p	0	0	0	0	Morris, p	0	0	0	0
Dravecky, p	0	0	0	0					
Lefferts, p	0	0	0	0					
Gossage, p	0	0	0	0					
Totals	36	2	10	2	Totals	31	5	7	5

```
San Diego . . . . . . . . . 0 1 0 0 0 0 0 0 1—2
Detroit . . . . . . . . . . 2 0 2 0 0 0 0 0 x—4
```

E - Wiggins, Gwynn. DP - San Diego 2. LOB - San Diego 3, Detroit 4. 2B - Bevacqua, Whitaker, Garvey. HR - Trammell 2 (2), Kennedy (1). SB - Gibson (3), Lemon (1).

San Diego	ip	h	r	er	bb	so
Show L, 0-1	2 2/3	4	4	3	1	2
Dravecky	3 1/3	3	0	0	1	4
Lefferts	1	0	0	0	0	0
Gossage	1	0	0	0	0	0
Detroit						
Morris W, 2-0	9	5	2	2	0	4

Wild pitch - Morris 2. Attendance - 52,130.

How runs were scored—Two in Tigers first: Whitaker reached first on an error. Trammell hit a home run.

One in Padres second: Kennedy hit a home run.

Two in Tigers third: Whitaker singled. Trammell hit a home run.

Two in Padres ninth: Garvey doubled and went to third on a ground out. Garvey scored on a wild pitch.

Fifth Game

San Diego	ab	r	h	bi	Detroit	ab	r	h	bi
Wiggins, 2b	5	0	2	1	Whitaker, 2b	4	1	1	0
Gwynn, rf	5	0	0	0	Trammell, ss	4	1	0	0
Garvey, 1b	4	0	1	1	Gibson, rf	4	3	3	5
Nettles, 3b	3	0	1	0	Parrish, c	5	2	2	1
Kennedy, c	4	0	0	0	Herndon, lf	4	0	1	0
Bevacqua, dh	3	2	1	1	Lemon, cf	3	0	2	1
Martinez, lf	4	0	2	0	Garbey, dh	1	0	0	0
Salazar, pr-lf	0	0	0	0	Grubb, dh	0	0	0	1
Templeton, ss	4	1	1	0	Kuntz, dh	0	0	0	0
Brown, cf	2	1	1	1	Johnson, dh	1	0	0	0
Bochy, ph	1	0	1	0	Evans, 1b	4	0	0	0
Roenicke, pr	0	0	0	0	Bergman, 1b	0	0	0	0
Thurmond, p	0	0	0	0	Castillo, 3b	3	1	2	0
Hawkins, p	0	0	0	0	Petry, p	0	0	0	0
Lefferts, p	0	0	0	0	Scherrer	0	0	0	0
Gossage, p	0	0	0	0	Lopez, p	0	0	0	0
					Hernandez, p	0	0	0	0
Totals	**35**	**4**	**10**	**4**	**Totals**	**33**	**8**	**11**	**8**

San Diego	ip	h	r	er	bb	so
Thurmond	1_3	5	3	3	0	0
Hawkins L, 1-1	4	2	1	1	3	1
Lefferts	2	1	0	0	1	2
Gossage	1_3^2	3	4	4	1	2
Detroit						
Petry	3_3^2	6	3	3	2	2
Scherrer	1	1	0	0	0	0
Lopez W, 1-0	2_3^1	0	0	0	0	4
Hernandez S, 2	2	3	1	1	0	0

HPB - by Hawkins (Grubb). Wild pitch - Hawkins. T - 2:55. A - 51,901.

San Diego . . . . 0 0 1 2 0 0 0 1 0—4
Detroit . . . . 3 0 0 0 1 0 1 3 x—8

E - Parrish, Wiggins. DP - San Diego 1. LOB - San Diego 7, Detroit 9. 2B - Templeton. HR - Gibson 2 (2), Parrish (1), Bevacqua (2). SB - Wiggins (1), Parrish (1), Lemon (1). S - Trammell. SF - Brown, Kuntz.

How runs were scored—Three in Tigers first: Whitaker singled. Gibson hit a home run. Parrish and Herndon singled. Lemon singled scoring Parrish.

One in Padres third: Brown singled. Garvey singled scoring Brown.

Two in Padres fourth: Bevacqua walked. Templeton doubled. Brown hit a sacrifice fly scoring Bevacqua. Wiggins singled scoring Templeton.

One in Tigers fifth: Gibson singled. Herndon and Lemon walked. Kuntz hit a sacrifice fly scoring Gibson.

One in Tigers seventh: Parrish hit a home run.

One in Padres eighth: Bevacqua hit a home run.

Three in Tigers eighth: Castillo walked. Whitaker reached first on a fielders choice. Gibson hit a home run.

World Series Results, 1903-1984

1903 Boston AL 5, Pittsburgh NL 3
1904 No series
1905 New York NL 4, Philadelphia AL 1
1906 Chicago AL 4, Chicago NL 2
1907 Chicago AL 4, Detroit AL 0, 1 tie
1908 Chicago AL 4, Detroit AL 1
1909 Pittsburgh NL 4, Detroit AL 3
1910 Philadelphia AL 4, Chicago NL 1
1911 Philadelphia AL 4, New York NL 2
1912 Boston AL 4, New York NL 3, 1 tie
1913 Philadelphia AL 4, New York NL 1
1914 Boston NL 4, Philadelphia AL 0
1915 Boston AL 4, Philadelphia NL 1
1916 Boston AL 4, Brooklyn NL 1
1917 Chicago AL 4, New York NL 2
1918 Boston AL 4, Chicago NL 2
1919 Cincinnati NL 5, Chicago AL 3
1920 Cleveland AL 5, Brooklyn NL 2
1921 New York NL 5, New York AL 3
1922 New York NL 4, New York AL 0, 1 tie
1923 New York AL 4, New York NL 2
1924 Washington AL 4, New York NL 3
1925 Pittsburgh NL 4, Washington AL 3
1926 St. Louis NL 4, New York AL 3
1927 New York AL 4, Pittsburgh NL 0
1928 New York AL 4, St. Louis NL 0
1929 Philadelphia AL 4, Chicago NL 1
1930 Philadelphia AL 4, St. Louis NL 2

1931 St. Louis NL 4, Philadelphia AL 3
1932 New York AL 4, Chicago NL 0
1933 New York NL 4, Washington AL 1
1934 St. Louis NL 4, Detroit AL 3
1935 Detroit AL 4, Chicago NL 2
1936 New York AL 4, New York NL 2
1937 New York AL 4, New York NL 1
1938 New York AL 4, Chicago NL 0
1939 New York AL 4, Cincinnati NL 0
1940 Cincinnati NL 4, Detroit AL 3
1941 New York AL 4, Brooklyn NL 1
1942 St. Louis NL 4, New York AL 1
1943 New York AL 4, St. Louis NL 1
1944 St. Louis NL 4, St. Louis AL 2
1945 Detroit AL 4, Chicago NL 3
1946 St. Louis NL 4, Boston AL 3
1947 New York AL 4, Brooklyn NL 3
1948 Cleveland AL 4, Boston NL 2
1949 New York AL 4, Brooklyn NL 1
1950 New York AL 4, Philadelphia NL 0
1951 New York AL 4, New York NL 2
1952 New York AL 4, Brooklyn NL 3
1953 New York AL 4, Brooklyn NL 2
1954 New York NL 4, Cleveland AL 0
1955 Brooklyn NL 4, New York AL 3
1956 New York AL 4, Brooklyn NL 3
1957 Milwaukee NL 4, New York AL 3

1958 New York AL 4, Milwaukee NL 3
1959 Los Angeles NL 4, Chicago AL 2
1960 Pittsburgh NL 4, New York AL 3
1961 New York AL 4, Cincinnati NL 1
1962 New York AL 4, San Francisco NL 3
1963 Los Angeles NL 4, New York AL 0
1964 St. Louis NL 4, New York AL 3
1965 Los Angeles NL 4, Minnesota AL 3
1966 Baltimore AL 4, Los Angeles NL 0
1967 St. Louis NL 4, Boston AL 3
1968 Detroit AL 4, St. Louis NL 3
1969 New York NL 4, Baltimore AL 1
1970 Baltimore AL 4, Cincinnati NL 1
1971 Pittsburgh NL 4, Baltimore AL 3
1972 Oakland AL 4, Cincinnati NL 3
1973 Oakland AL 4, New York NL 3
1974 Oakland AL 4, Los Angeles NL 1
1975 Cincinnati NL 4, Boston AL 3
1976 Cincinnati NL 4, New York AL 0
1977 New York AL 4, Los Angeles NL 2
1978 New York AL 4, Los Angeles NL 2
1979 Pittsburgh NL 4, Baltimore AL 3
1980 Philadelphia NL 4, Kansas City AL 2
1981 Los Angeles NL 4, New York AL 2
1982 St. Louis NL 4, Milwaukee AL 3
1983 Baltimore AL 4, Philadelphia NL 1
1984 Detroit AL 4, San Diego NL 1

World Series MVPs

1955 Johnny Podres, Brooklyn (NL)
1956 Don Larsen, New York (AL)
1957 Lew Burdette, Milwaukee (NL)
1958 Bob Turley, New York (AL)
1959 Larry Sherry, Los Angeles (NL)
1960 Bobby Richardson, New York (AL)
1961 Whitey Ford, New York (AL)
1962 Ralph Terry, New York (AL)
1963 Sandy Koufax, Los Angeles (NL)
1964 Bob Gibson, St. Louis (NL)
1965 Sandy Koufax, Los Angeles (NL)

1966 Frank Robinson, Baltimore (AL)
1967 Bob Gibson, St. Louis (NL)
1968 Mickey Lolich, Detroit (AL)
1969 Donn Clendenon, New York (NL)
1970 Brooks Robinson, Baltimore (AL)
1971 Roberto Clemente, Pittsburgh (NL)
1972 Gene Tenace, Oakland (AL)
1973 Reggie Jackson, Oakland (AL)
1974 Rollie Fingers, Oakland (AL)
1975 Pete Rose, Cincinnati (NL)

1976 Johnny Bench, Cincinnati (NL)
1977 Reggie Jackson, New York (AL)
1978 Bucky Dent, New York (AL)
1979 Willie Stargell, Pittsburgh (NL)
1980 Mike Schmidt, Philadelphia (NL)
1981 Ron Cey, Pedro Guerrero, Steve Yeager, Los Angeles (NL)
1982 Darrell Porter, St. Louis (NL)
1983 Rick Dempsey, Baltimore (AL)
1984 Alan Trammell, Detroit (AL)

All-Time Home Run Leaders

Player	HR	Player	HR	Player	HR	Player	HR	Player	HR
Hank Aaron	755	Reggie Jackson	503	Norm Cash	377	Ron Santo	342	Rogers Hornsby	302
Babe Ruth	714	Lou Gehrig	493	Dave Kingman	375	John (Boog) Powell	339	Chuck Klein	300
Willie Mays	660	Stan Musial	475	Rocky Colavito	374	Joe Adcock	336	Jim Wynn	291
Frank Robinson	586	Willie Stargell	475	Tony Perez	371	Bobby Bonds	332	Rusty Staub	291
Harmon Killebrew	573	Carl Yastrzemski	452	Gil Hodges	370	Hank Greenberg	331	Robert Johnson	288
Mickey Mantle	536	Billy Williams	426	Ralph Kiner	369	Willie Horton	325	Hank Sauer	288
Jimmy Foxx	534	Mike Schmidt	425	Joe DiMaggio	361	Roy Sievers	318	Del Ennis	288
Ted Williams	521	Duke Snider	407	John Mize	359	Reggie Smith	315	Frank Thomas	286
Willie McCovey	521	Al Kaline	399	Yogi Berra	358	George Foster	313	Ken Boyer	282
Ed Mathews	512	Johnny Bench	389	Lee May	354	Greg Luzinski	307	Ted Kluszewski	279
Ernie Banks	512	Frank Howard	382	Graig Nettles	353	Al Simmons	307	Darrell Evans	278
Mel Ott	511	Orlando Cepeda	379	Dick Allen	351	Jim Rice	304		

Major League Leaders in 1984

National League

Home Runs

Murphy, Atlanta, 36; Schmidt, Philadelphia, 36; Carter, Montreal, 27; Strawberry, New York, 26; Cey, Chicago, 25.

Runs Batted In

Carter, Montreal, 106; Schmidt, Philadelphia, 106; Murphy, Atlanta, 100; Cey, Chicago, 97; Strawberry, New York, 97.

Stolen Bases

Raines, Montreal, 75; Samuel, Philadelphia, 72; Wiggins, San Diego, 70; L. Smith, St. Louis, 50; Redus, Cincinnati, 48; Hayes, Philadelphia, 48.

Runs

Sandberg, Chicago, 114; Raines, Montreal, 106; Samuel, Philadelphia, 106; Wiggins, San Diego, 106; Matthews, Chicago, 101.

Hits

Gwynn, San Diego, 213; Sandberg, Chicago, 200; Raines, Montreal, 192; Samuel, Philadelphia, 191; Cruz, Houston, 187.

Doubles

Raines, Montreal, 38; Ray, Pittsburgh, 38; Samuel, Philadelphia, 36; Sandberg, Chicago, 36; Carter, Montreal, 32; Murphy, Atlanta, 32.

Triples

Samuel, Philadelphia, 19; Sandberg, Chicago, 19; Cruz, Houston,13; Reynolds, Houston, 11; Doran, Houston, 11; McGee, St. Louis, 11; Wynne, Pittsburgh, 11.

Pitching (15 Decisions)

Sutcliffe, Chicago, 16-1, .941; Dawley, Houston, 11-4, .733, 1.93; Soto, Cincinnati, 18-7, .720, 3.53; A. Pena, Los Angeles, 12-6, .667, 2.48; Gooden, New York, 17-9, .654, 2.60.

Strikeouts

Gooden, New York, 276; Valenzuela, Los Angeles, 240; Ryan, Houston, 197; Soto, Cincinnati, 185; Carlton, Philadelphia, 163.

Saves

Sutter, St. Louis, 45; Le. Smith, Chicago, 33; Orosco, New York, 31; Holland, Philadelphia, 29; Gossage, San Diego, 25.

American League

Home Runs

Armas, Boston, 43; Kingman, Oakland, 35; L.N. Parrish, Detroit, 33; Murphy, Oakland, 33; Thornton, Cleveland, 33.

Runs Batted In

Armas, Boston 123; Rice, Boston, 122; Kingman, Oakland, 118; A. Davis, Seattle, 116; Murray, Baltimore, 110; Mattingly, New York, 110.

Stolen Bases

Henderson, Oakland, 66; Collins, Toronto, 60; Butler, Cleveland, 52; Pettis, California, 48; Wilson, Kansas City, 47.

Runs

Evans, Boston, 121; Henderson, Oakland, 113; Boggs, Boston, 109; Butler, Cleveland, 108; Armas, Boston, 107.

Hits

Mattingly, New York, 207; Boggs, Boston, 203; Ripken, Baltimore, 195; Winfield, New York, 193; Easler, Boston, 188; Franco, Cleveland, 188.

Doubles

Mattingly, New York, 44; L.A. Parrish, Texas, 42; G. Bell, Toronto, 39; Evans, Boston, 37; Ripkin, Baltimore, 37.

Triples

Collins, Toronto, 15; Moseby, Toronto, 15; Baines, Chicago, 10; K. Gibson, Detroit, 10; Butler, Cleveland, 9; Upshaw, Toronto, 9; Wilson, Kansas City, 9.

Pitching (15 Decisions)

Alexander, Toronto, 17-6, .739, 3.13; Blyleven, Cleveland, 19-7, .731, 2.87; Petry, Detroit, 18-8, .692, 3.24; Wilcox, Detroit, 17-8, .680, 4.00; Niekro, New York, 16-8, .667, 3.00; Stieb, Toronto, 16-8, .667, 2.83.

Strikeouts

Langston, Seattle, 204; Stieb, Toronto, 198; Witt, California, 196; Blyleven, Cleveland, 169; Hough, Texas, 164.

Saves

Quisenberry, Kansas City, 44; Caudill, Oakland, 36; Hernandez, Detroit, 32; Righetti, New York, 31; R. Davis, Minnesota, 29.

Major League Perfect Games Since 1900

Year	Player	Clubs	Score	Year	Player	Clubs	Score
1904	Cy Young	Boston vs. Phil. (AL)	3-0	1964	Jim Bunning	Phil. vs. N.Y. Mets (NL)	6-0
1908	Addie Joss	Cleveland vs. Chicago (AL)	1-0	1965	Sandy Koufax	Los Angeles vs. Chic. (NL)	1-0
1917	Ernie Shore (a)	Boston vs. Wash. (AL)	4-0	1968	Jim Hunter	Oakland vs. Minn. (AL)	4-0
1922	Charles Robertson	Chicago vs. Detroit (AL)	2-0	1981	Len Barker	Cleveland vs. Toronto (AL)	3-0
1956	Don Larsen (b)	N.Y. Yankees vs. Brooklyn	2-0	1984	Mike Witt	California vs. Texas (AL)	1-0

(a) Babe Ruth, the starting pitcher, was ejected from the game after walking the first batter. Shore replaced him and the base-runner was out stealing. Shore retired the next 26 batters. (b) World Series.

The America's Cup

The Australian yacht *Australia II* defeated the United States yacht *Liberty* for the fourth time in the best-of-seven series of races to win the America's Cup on Sept. 26, 1983. It was the first time that the United States had lost the America's Cup series after having successfully defended the cup against 24 challengers dating back to 1851. Businessman Alan Bond headed the victorious *Australia II* syndicate and John Bertrand was the yacht's skipper.

Competition for the America's Cup grew out of the first contest to establish a world yachting championship, one of the carnival features of the London Exposition of 1851. The race, open to all classes of yachts from all over the world, covered a 60-mile course around the Isle of Wight; the prize was a cup worth about $500, donated by the Royal Yacht Squadron of England, known as the "America's Cup" because it was first won by the United States yacht *America*. Successive efforts of British and Australian yachtsmen had failed to win the famous trophy until 1983.

Winners of the America's Cup

1851	America	1920	Resolute defeated Shamrock IV, England, (3-2)
1870	Magic defeated Cambria, England, (1-0)	1930	Enterprise defeated Shamrock V, England, (4-0)
1871	Columbia (first three races) and Sappho (last two races) defeated Livonia, England, (4-1)	1934	Rainbow defeated Endeavour, England, (4-2)
1876	Madeline defeated Countess of Dufferin, Canada, (2-0)	1937	Ranger defeated Endeavour II, England, (4-0)
1881	Mischief defeated Atalanta, Canada, (2-0)	1958	Columbia defeated Sceptre, England, (4-0)
1885	Puritan defeated Genesta, England, (2-0)	1962	Weatherly defeated Gretel, Australia, (4-1)
1886	Mayflower defeated Galatea, England, (2-0)	1964	Constellation defeated Sovereign, England, (4-0)
1887	Volunteer defeated Thistle, Scotland, (2-0)	1967	Intrepid defeated Dame Pattie, Australia, (4-0)
1893	Vigilant defeated Valkyrie II, England, (3-0)	1970	Intrepid defeated Gretel II, Australia, (4-1)
1895	Defender defeated Valkyrie III, England, (3-0)	1974	Courageous defeated Southern Cross, Australia, (4-0)
1899	Columbia defeated Shamrock, England, (3-0)	1977	Courageous defeated Australia, Australia, (4-0)
1901	Columbia defeated Shamrock II, England, (3-0)	1980	Freedom defeated Australia, Australia, (4-1)
1903	Reliance defeated Shamrock III, England, (3-0)	1983	Australia II defeated Liberty, (4-3)

Golf Records

United States Open

Year	Winner	Year	Winner	Year	Winner	Year	Winner
1901	Willie Anderson	1922	Gene Sarazen	1942-45	(Not played)	1965	Gary Player
1902	L. Auchterlonie	1923	Bobby Jones*	1946	Lloyd Mangrum	1966	Billy Casper
1903	Willie Anderson	1924	Cyril Walker	1947	L. Worsham	1967	Jack Nicklaus
1904	Willie Anderson	1925	Willie MacFarlane	1948	Ben Hogan	1968	Lee Trevino
1905	Willie Anderson	1926	Bobby Jones*	1949	Cary Middlecoff	1969	Orville Moody
1906	Alex Smith	1927	Tommy Armour	1950	Ben Hogan	1970	Tony Jacklin
1907	Alex Ross	1928	John Farrell	1951	Ben Hogan	1971	Lee Trevino
1908	Fred McLeod	1929	Bobby Jones*	1952	Julius Boros	1972	Jack Nicklaus
1909	George Sargent	1930	Bobby Jones*	1953	Ben Hogan	1973	Johnny Miller
1910	Alex Smith	1931	Wm. Burke	1954	Ed Furgol	1974	Hale Irwin
1911	John McDermott	1932	Gene Sarazen	1955	Jack Fleck	1975	Lou Graham
1912	John McDermott	1933	John Goodman*	1956	Cary Middlecoff	1976	Jerry Pate
1913	Francis Ouimet*	1934	Olin Dutra	1957	Dick Mayer	1977	Hubert Green
1914	Walter Hagen	1935	Sam Parks Jr.	1958	Tommy Bolt	1978	Andy North
1915	Jerome Travers*	1936	Tony Manero	1959	Billy Casper	1979	Hale Irwin
1916	Chick Evans*	1937	Ralph Guldahl	1960	Arnold Palmer	1980	Jack Nicklaus
1917-18	(Not played)	1938	Ralph Guldahl	1961	Gene Littler	1981	David Graham
1919	Walter Hagen	1939	Byron Nelson	1962	Jack Nicklaus	1982	Tom Watson
1920	Edward Ray	1940	Lawson Little	1963	Julius Boros	1983	Larry Nelson
1921	Jim Barnes	1941	Craig Wood	1964	Ken Venturi	1984	Fuzzy Zoeller

*Amateur

U.S. Women's Open Golf Champions

Year	Winner	Year	Winner	Year	Winner	Year	Winner
1948	"Babe" Zaharias	1957	Betsy Rawls	1966	Sandra Spuzich	1975	Sandra Palmer
1949	Louise Suggs	1958	Mickey Wright	1967	Catherine Lacoste*	1976	JoAnne Carner
1950	"Babe" Zaharias	1959	Mickey Wright	1968	Susie Maxwell Berning	1977	Hollis Stacy
1951	Betsy Rawls	1960	Betsy Rawls	1969	Donna Caponi	1978	Hollis Stacy
1952	Louise Suggs	1961	Mickey Wright	1970	Donna Caponi	1979	Jerilyn Britz
1953	Betsy Rawls	1962	Marie Lindstrom	1971	JoAnne Carner	1980	Amy Alcott
1954	"Babe" Zaharias	1963	Mary Mills	1972	Susie Maxwell Berning	1981	Pat Bradley
1955	Fay Crocker	1964	Mickey Wright	1973	Susie Maxwell Berning	1982	Janet Alex
1956	Mrs. K. Cornelius	1965	Carol Mann	1974	Sandra Haynie	1983	Jan Stephenson
						1984	Hollis Stacy

*Amateur

Masters Golf Tournament Champions

Year	Winner	Year	Winner	Year	Winner	Year	Winner
1934	Horton Smith	1948	Claude Harmon	1960	Arnold Palmer	1972	Jack Nicklaus
1935	Gene Sarazen	1949	Sam Snead	1961	Gary Player	1973	Tommy Aaron
1936	Horton Smith	1950	Jimmy Demaret	1962	Arnold Palmer	1974	Gary Player
1937	Byron Nelson	1951	Ben Hogan	1963	Jack Nicklaus	1975	Jack Nicklaus
1938	Henry Picard	1952	Sam Snead	1964	Arnold Palmer	1976	Ray Floyd
1939	Ralph Guldahl	1953	Ben Hogan	1965	Jack Nicklaus	1977	Tom Watson
1940	Jimmy Demaret	1954	Sam Snead	1966	Jack Nicklaus	1978	Gary Player
1941	Craig Wood	1955	Cary Middlecoff	1967	Gay Brewer Jr.	1979	Fuzzy Zoeller
1942	Byron Nelson	1956	Jack Burke	1968	Bob Goalby	1980	Severiano Ballesteros
1943-1945	(Not played)	1957	Doug Ford	1969	George Archer	1981	Tom Watson
1946	Herman Keiser	1958	Arnold Palmer	1970	Billy Casper	1982	Craig Stadler
1947	Jimmy Demaret	1959	Art Wall Jr.	1971	Charles Coody	1983	Severiano Ballesteros
						1984	Ben Crenshaw

Professional Golfer's Association Championships

Year	Winner	Year	Winner	Year	Winner	Year	Winner
1920	Jock Hutchison	1936	Denny Shute	1953	Walter Burkemo	1969	Ray Floyd
1921	Walter Hagen	1937	Denny Shute	1954	Melvin Harbert	1970	Dave Stockton
1922	Gene Sarazen	1938	Paul Runyan	1955	Doug Ford	1971	Jack Nicklaus
1923	Gene Sarazen	1939	Henry Picard	1956	Jack Burke	1972	Gary Player
1924	Walter Hagen	1940	Byron Nelson	1957	Lionel Hebert	1973	Jack Nicklaus
1925	Walter Hagen	1941	Victor Ghezzi	1958	Dow Finsterwald	1974	Lee Trevino
1926	Walter Hagen	1942	Sam Snead	1959	Bob Rosburg	1975	Jack Nicklaus
1927	Walter Hagen	1944	Bob Hamilton	1960	Jay Hebert	1976	Dave Stockton
1928	Leo Diegel	1945	Byron Nelson	1961	Jerry Barber	1977	Lanny Wadkins
1929	Leo Diegel	1946	Ben Hogan	1962	Gary Player	1978	John Mahaffey
1930	Tommy Armour	1947	Jim Ferrier	1963	Jack Nicklaus	1979	David Graham
1931	Tom Creavy	1948	Ben Hogan	1964	Bob Nichols	1980	Jack Nicklaus
1932	Olin Dutra	1949	Sam Snead	1965	Dave Marr	1981	Larry Nelson
1933	Gene Sarazen	1950	Chandler Harper	1966	Al Geiberger	1982	Ray Floyd
1934	Paul Runyan	1951	Sam Snead	1967	Don January	1983	Hal Sutton
1935	Johnny Revolta	1952	James Turnesa	1968	Julius Boros	1984	Lee Trevino

Canadian Open Golf Champions

Year	Winner	Year	Winner	Year	Winner	Year	Winner
1953	Dave Douglas	1961	Jacky Cupit	1969	Tommy Aaron	1977	Lee Trevino
1954	Pat Fletcher	1962	Ted Kroll	1970	Kermit Zarley	1978	Bruce Lietzke
1955	Arnold Palmer	1963	Doug Ford	1971	Lee Trevino	1979	Lee Trevino
1956	Doug Sanders	1964	Kel Nagle	1972	Gay Brewer	1980	Bob Gilder
1957	George Bayer	1965	Gene Littler	1973	Tom Weiskopf	1981	Peter Oosterhuis
1958	Wes Ellis Jr.	1966	Don Massengale	1974	Bobby Nichols	1982	Bruce Lietzke
1959	Doug Ford	1967	Billy Casper	1975	Tom Weiskopf	1983	John Cook
1960	Art Wall, Jr.	1968	Bob Charles	1976	Jerry Pate	1984	Greg Norman

Professional Golf Tournaments in 1984

Date	Event	Winner	Score	Prize
Jan. 15	Bob Hope Desert Classic, Palm Springs	John Mahaffey	*240	$72,000
Jan. 22	Phoenix Open	Tom Purtzer	268	72,000
Jan. 29	Isuzu-Andy Williams San Diego Open	Gary Koch	272	72,000
Feb. 5	Bing Crosby National Pro-Am, Pebble Beach, Cal.	Hale Irwin	*278	72,000
Feb. 12	Hawaiian Open, Honolulu	Jack Renner	*271	90,000
Feb. 19	Los Angeles Open	David Edwards	279	72,000
Mar. 4	Honda Classic, Coral Springs, Fla.	Bruce Lietzke	*280	90,000
Mar. 11	Doral-Eastern Open, Miami, Fla.	Tom Kite	272	72,000
Mar. 18	Bay Hill Classic, Orlando, Fla.	Gary Koch	*272	72,000
Mar. 25	New Orleans Open	Bob Eastwood	272	72,000
Apr. 1	Tournament Players Championship, Ponte Vedra, Fla.	Fred Couples	277	144,000
Apr. 8	Greater Greensboro Open, N.C.	Andy Bean	280	72,000
Apr. 15	Masters Tournament, Augusta, Ga.	Ben Crenshaw	277	108,000
Apr. 22	Sea Pines Heritage Classic, Hilton Head, S.C.	Nick Faldo	270	72,000
May 6	Tournament of Champions, Carlsbad, Cal.	Tom Watson	274	72,000
May 13	Byron Nelson Classic, Dallas, Tex.	Craig Stadler	276	90,000
May 20	Colonial National Tournament, Ft. Worth, Tex.	Peter Jacobsen	*270	90,000
May 27	Memorial Tournament, Dublin, Oh.	Jack Nicklaus	*280	90,000
June 3	Kemper Open, Bethesda, Md.	Greg Norman	280	72,000
June 10	Westchester Classic, Harrison, N.Y.	Scott Simpson	269	90,000
June 18	U.S. Open, Mamaroneck, N.Y.	Fuzzy Zoeller	*276	94,000
June 24	Atlanta Classic, Atlanta, Ga.	Tom Kite	269	72,000
July 1	Canadian Open, Oakville, Ont.	Greg Norman	278	72,000
July 8	Western Open, Oak Brook, Ill.	Tom Watson	280	72,000
July 15	Anheuser-Busch Classic, Williamsburg, Va.	Ronnie Black	267	63,000
July 29	Sammy Davis Jr. Greater Hartford Open, Conn.	Peter Jacobsen	269	72,000
Aug. 5	Memphis Classic, Tenn.	Bob Eastwood	280	90,000
Aug. 12	Buick Open, Grand Blanc, Mich.	Denis Watson	271	72,000
Aug. 19	PGA Championship, Shoal Creek, Ala.	Lee Trevino	273	125,000
Aug. 26	World Series of Golf, Akron, Oh.	Denis Watson	271	126,000
Sept. 2	B.C. Open, Endicott, N.Y.	Wayne Levi	275	54,000
Sept. 9	Boston Classic, Sutton, Mass.	George Archer	270	63,000
Sept. 16	Greater Milwaukee Open, Wis.	Mark O'Meara	272	54,000
Sept. 23	Panasonic Las Vegas Invitational, Nev.	Denis Watson	341	162,000

Women

Date	Event	Winner	Score	Prize
Jan. 29	Mazda Classic, Deerfield Beach, Fla.	Silvia Bertolaccini	280	$30,000
Feb. 5	Elizabeth Arden Classic, Miami, Fla.	Patty Sheehan	280	26,250
Feb. 12	Sarasota Classic, Sarasota, Fla.	Alice Miller	280	26,000
Mar. 4	Uniden Invitational, Costa Mesa, Cal.	Nancy Lopez	284	45,000
Mar. 11	Samaritan Turquoise Classic, Phoenix, Ariz.	Chris Johnson	276	22,500
Mar. 18	Tucson Open, Tucson, Ariz.	Chris Johnson	272	22,500
Apr. 8	Dinah Shore Invitational, Rancho Mirage, Cal.	Juli Inkster	280	55,500
Apr. 15	J & B Pro-Am, Las Vegas, Nev.	Ayako Okamoto	275	30,000
Apr. 29	Orlando Classic, Orlando, Fla.	Betsy King	202	22,000
May 20	Chrysler-Plymouth Classic, Clifton, N.J.	Barbara Bunkowsky	209	26,250
May 27	Corning Classic, Corning, N.Y.	JoAnne Carner	281	22,500
June 3	LPGA Championship, Kings Island, Oh.	Patty Sheehan	272	37,000
June 10	McDonald's Kids Classic, Malvern, Pa.	Patty Sheehan	281	52,500
June 17	Mayflower Classic, Indianapolis, Ind.	Ayako Okamoto	281	37,500
June 24	Boston Five Classic, Danvers, Mass.	Laurie Rinker	286	33,700
July 1	Lady Keystone Open, Hershey, Pa.	Amy Alcott	208	30,000
July 8	Jamie Farr Toledo Classic, Toledo, Oh.	Lauri Peterson	278	26,250
July 15	U.S. Women's Open, Peabody, Mass.	Hollis Stacy	290	36,000
June 22	Rochester International, Rochester, N.Y.	Kathy Whitworth	*281	30,000
July 29	Du Maurier Classic, Toronto, Ont.	Juli Inkster	279	41,250
Aug. 5	West Virginia Classic, Wheeling, W. Va.	Alice Miller	209	22,500
Aug. 12	Henredon Classic, High Point, N.C.	Patty Sheehan	277	27,000
Aug. 19	World Championship of Women's Golf, Shaker Heights, Oh.	Nancy Lopez	281	65,000
Aug. 26	Columbia Savings Classic, Denver, Col.	Betsy King	281	30,000
Sept. 9	Portland Ping Championship, Portland, Ore.	Amy Alcott	212	22,500
Sept. 16	Safeco Classic, Kent, Wash.	Kathy Whitworth	279	22,500

*Won playoff.

British Open Golf Champions

Year	Winner	Year	Winner	Year	Winner	Year	Winner
1920	George Duncan	1935	Alf Perry	1955	Peter Thomson	1970	Jack Nicklaus
1921	Jock Hutchison	1936	Alf Padgham	1956	Peter Thomson	1971	Lee Trevino
1922	Walter Hagen	1937	T.H. Cotton	1957	Bobby Locke	1972	Lee Trevino
1923	Arthur Havers	1938	R.A. Whitcombe	1958	Peter Thomson	1973	Tom Weiskopf
1924	Walter Hagen	1939	Richard Burton	1959	Gary Player	1974	Gary Player
1925	Jim Barnes	1940-45	(Not played)	1960	Kel Nagle	1975	Tom Watson
1926	Bobby Jones	1946	Sam Snead	1961	Arnold Palmer	1976	Johnny Miller
1927	Bobby Jones	1947	Fred Daly	1962	Arnold Palmer	1977	Tom Watson
1928	Walter Hagen	1948	Henry Cotton	1963	Bob Charles	1978	Jack Nicklaus
1929	Walter Hagen	1949	Bobby Locke	1964	Tony Lema	1979	Seve Ballesteros
1930	Bobby Jones	1950	Bobby Locke	1965	Peter Thomson	1980	Tom Watson
1931	Tommy Armour	1951	Max Faulkner	1966	Jack Nicklaus	1981	Bill Rogers
1932	Gene Sarazen	1952	Bobby Locke	1967	Roberto de Vicenzo	1982	Tom Watson
1933	Denny Shute	1953	Ben Hogan	1968	Gary Player	1983	Tom Watson
1934	Henry Cotton	1954	Peter Thomson	1969	Tony Jacklin	1984	Seve Ballesteros

U.S. Amateur

Year	Winner	Year	Winner	Year	Winner	Year	Winner
1921	Jesse Guilford	1937	John Goodman	1955	Harvie Ward	1970	Lanny Wadkins
1922	Jess Sweetser	1938	Willie Turnesa	1956	Harvie Ward	1971	Gary Cowan
1923	Max Marston	1939	Bud Ward	1957	Hillman Robbins	1972	Vinnie Giles
1924	Bobby Jones	1940	Dick Chapman	1958	Charles Coe	1973	Craig Stadler
1925	Bobby Jones	1941	Bud Ward	1959	Jack Nicklaus	1974	Jerry Pate
1926	George Von Elm	1942-45	(not played)	1960	Deane Beman	1975	Fred Ridley
1927	Bobby Jones	1946	Ted Bishop	1961	Jack Nicklaus	1976	Bill Sander
1928	Bobby Jones	1947	Skee Riegel	1962	Labron Harris Jr.	1977	John Fought
1929	Harrison Johnston	1948	Willie Turnesa	1963	Deane Beman	1978	John Cook
1930	Bobby Jones	1949	Charles Coe	1964	Bill Campbell	1979	Mark O'Meara
1931	Francis Ouimet	1950	Sam Urzetta	1965	Robert Murphy Jr.	1980	Hal Sutton
1932	Ross Somerville	1951	Billy Maxwell	1966	Gary Cowan	1981	Nathaniel Crosby
1933	George Dunlap Jr.	1952	Jack Westland	1967	Bob Dickson	1982	Jay Sigel
1934	Lawson Little	1953	Gene Littler	1968	Bruce Fleisher	1983	Jay Sigel
1935	Lawson Little	1954	Arnold Palmer	1969	Steve Melnyk	1984	Scott Verplank
1936	John Fischer						

Women's U.S. Amateur

Year	Winner	Year	Winner	Year	Winner	Year	Winner
1921	Marion Hollins	1937	Mrs. J. A. Page	1955	Pat Lesser	1970	Martha Wilkinson
1922	Glenna Collett	1938	Patty Berg	1956	Marlene Stewart	1971	Laura Baugh
1923	Edith Cummings	1939	Betty Jameson	1957	JoAnne Gunderson	1972	Mary Budke
1924	Mrs. D.C. Hurd	1940	Betty Jameson	1958	Anne Quast	1973	Carol Semple
1925	Glenna Collett	1941	Mrs. Frank New	1959	Barbara McIntire	1974	Cynthia Hill
1926	Mrs. G. Stetson	1942-45	(not played)	1960	JoAnne Gunderson	1975	Beth Daniel
1927	Mrs. M. Horn	1946	"Babe" Zaharias	1961	Anne Q. Decker	1976	Donna Horton
1928	Glenna Collett	1947	Louise Suggs	1962	JoAnne Gunderson	1977	Beth Daniel
1929	Glenna Collett	1948	Grace Lenczyk	1963	Anne Q. Welts	1978	Cathy Sherk
1930	Glenna Collett	1949	Dorothy Porter	1964	Barbara McIntire	1979	Carolyn Hill
1931	Helen Hicks	1950	Beverly Hanson	1965	Jean Ashley	1980	Juli Inkster
1932	Virginia Van Wie	1951	Dorothy Kirby	1966	JoAnne Carner	1981	Juli Inkster
1933	Virginia Van Wie	1952	Jackie Pung	1967	Lou Dill	1982	Juli Inkster
1934	Virginia Van Wie	1953	Mary Faulk	1968	JoAnne Carner	1983	Joanne Pacillo
1935	Glenna C. Vare	1954	Barbara Romack	1969	Catherine Lacoste	1984	Deb Richard
1936	Pamela Barton						

PGA Hall of Fame

Established in 1940 to honor those who have made outstanding contributions to the game by their lifetime playing ability.

Anderson, Willie	Dudley, Edward	Jones, Bob	Sarazen, Gene
Armour, Tommy	Dutra, Olin	Little, W. Lawson	Shute, Denny
Barnes, Jim	Evans, Chick	Littler, Gene	Smith, Alex
Berg, Patty	Farrell, Johnny	Mangrum, Lloyd	Smith, Horton
Boros, Julius	Ford, Doug	McDermott, John	Smith, MacDonald
Brady, Mike	Ghezzi, Vic	McLeod, Fred	Snead, Sam
Burke, Billy	Guldahl, Ralph	Middlecoff, Cary	Travers, Jerry
Burke Jr., Jack	Hagen, Walter	Nelson, Byron	Travis, Walter
Casper, Billy	Harbert, M. R. (Chick)	Ouimet, Francis	de Vicenzo, Roberto
Cooper, Harry	Harper, Chandler	Palmer, Arnold	Wood, Craig
Cruickshank, Bobby	Harrison, E. J.	Picard, Henry	Zaharias, Mildred (Babe)
Demaret, Jimmy	Hogan, Ben	Revolta, Johnny	
Diegel, Leo	Hutchison Sr., Jock	Runyan, Paul	

PGA Leading Money Winners

Year	Player	Dollars	Year	Player	Dollars	Year	Player	Dollars
1945	Byron Nelson	52,511	1958	Arnold Palmer	42,407	1971	Jack Nicklaus	244,490
1946	Ben Hogan	42,556	1959	Art Wall Jr.	53,167	1972	Jack Nicklaus	320,542
1947	Jimmy Demaret	27,936	1960	Arnold Palmer	75,262	1973	Jack Nicklaus	308,362
1948	Ben Hogan	36,812	1961	Gary Player	64,540	1974	Johnny Miller	353,201
1949	Sam Snead	31,593	1962	Arnold Palmer	81,448	1975	Jack Nicklaus	323,149
1950	Sam Snead	35,758	1963	Arnold Palmer	128,230	1976	Jack Nicklaus	266,438
1951	Lloyd Mangrum	26,088	1964	Jack Nicklaus	113,284	1977	Tom Watson	310,653
1952	Julius Boros	37,032	1965	Jack Nicklaus	140,752	1978	Tom Watson	362,429
1953	Lew Worsham	34,002	1966	Billy Casper	121,944	1979	Tom Watson	462,636
1954	Bob Toski	65,819	1967	Jack Nicklaus	188,988	1980	Tom Watson	530,808
1955	Julius Boros	65,121	1968	Billy Casper	205,168	1981	Tom Kite	375,699
1956	Ted Kroll	72,835	1969	Frank Beard	175,223	1982	Craig Stadler	446,462
1957	Dick Mayer	65,835	1970	Lee Trevino	157,037	1983	Hal Sutton	426,668

LPGA Leading Money Winners

Year	Winner	Dollars	Year	Winner	Dollars	Year	Winner	Dollars
1954	Patty Berg	16,011	1964	Mickey Wright	29,800	1974	JoAnne Carner	87,094
1955	Patty Berg	16,492	1965	Kathy Whitworth	28,658	1975	Sandra Palmer	94,805
1956	Marlene Hagge	20,235	1966	Kathy Whitworth	33,517	1976	Judy Rankin	150,734
1957	Patty Berg	16,272	1967	Kathy Whitworth	32,937	1977	Judy Rankin	122,890
1958	Beverly Hanson	12,629	1968	Kathy Whitworth	48,379	1978	Nancy Lopez	189,813
1959	Betsy Rawls	26,774	1969	Carol Mann	49,152	1979	Nancy Lopez	215,987
1960	Louise Suggs	16,892	1970	Kathy Whitworth	30,235	1980	Beth Daniel	231,000
1961	Mickey Wright	22,236	1971	Kathy Whitworth	41,181	1981	Beth Daniel	206,977
1962	Mickey Wright	21,641	1972	Kathy Whitworth	65,063	1982	JoAnne Carner	310,399
1963	Mickey Wright	31,269	1973	Kathy Whitworth	82,854	1983	JoAnne Carner	291,404

North American Soccer League in 1984

Final Standings

Eastern Division

	W	L	GF	GA	Bonus points	Total points
Chicago	13	11	50	49	44	120
Toronto	14	10	46	33	35	117
New York	13	11	43	42	39	115
Tampa Bay	9	15	43	61	35	87

Western Division

	W	L	GF	GA	Bonus points	Total points
San Diego	14	10	51	42	40	118
Vancouver	13	11	51	48	43	117
Minnesota	14	10	40	44	35	115
Tulsa	10	14	42	46	38	98
Golden Bay	8	16	61	62	49	95

Total Points: Win = 6 points, Loss = 0 points, Shootout Win = 4 points. Bonus points: one point is awarded for each goal scored up to a maximum of 3 per team per game. No bonus points are given for goal scored in overtime or the Shootout.

NASL Champions

Year	Champion	Year	Champion	Year	Champion	Year	Champion
1967	Oakland Clippers (NPSL)	1971	Dallas Tornado	1976	Toronto Metros	1981	Chicago Sting
1967	Los Angeles Wolves (USA)	1972	New York Cosmos	1977	New York Cosmos	1982	New York Cosmos
1968	Atlanta Chiefs	1973	Philadelphia Atoms	1978	New York Cosmos	1983	Tulsa Roughnecks
1969	Kansas City Spurs	1974	Los Angeles Aztecs	1979	Vancouver Whitecaps	1984	Chicago Sting
1970	Rochester Lancers	1975	Tampa Bay Rowdies	1980	New York Cosmos		

NASL Leading Scorers

Year	Player, team	G	A	Pts	Year	Player, team	G	A	Pts
1973	Kyle Rote Jr., Dallas	10	10	30	1979	Oscar Fabbiani, Tampa Bay	25	8	58
1974	Paul Child, San Jose	15	6	36	1980	Giorgio Chinaglia, New York	32	13	77
1975	Steven David, Miami	23	6	52	1981	Giorgio Chinaglia, New York	29	16	74
1976	Giorgio Chinaglia, New York	19	11	49	1982	Giorgio Chinaglia, New York	20	15	55
1977	Steven David, Los Angeles	26	6	58	1983	Roberto Cabanas, New York	25	16	66
1978	Giorgio Chinaglia, New York	34	11	79	1984	Steve Zungul, Golden Bay	20	10	50

NASL Leading Goalkeepers

Year	Player, team	Minutes	G	Avg	Year	Player, team	Minutes	G	Avg
1973	Bob Rigby, Philadelphia	1,157	8	0.62	1979	Phil Parkes, Vancouver	2,705	29	0.96
1974	Barry Watling, Seattle	1,800	16	0.80	1980	Jack Brand, Seattle	2,975	30	0.91
1975	Shep Messing, Boston	1,639	17	0.93	1981	Arnie Mausser, Jacksonville	2,906	39	1.21
1976	Tony Chursky, Seattle	1,981	20	0.91	1982	Tino Lettieri, Vancouver	2,496	34	1.23
1977	Ken Cooper, Dallas	2,100	21	0.90	1983	Tino Lettieri, Vancouver	2,594	25	0.86
1978	Phil Parkes, Vancouver	2,650	28	0.95	1984	Paul Hammond, Toronto	1,937	25	1.16

The World Cup

The World Cup, emblematic of International soccer supremacy, was won by Italy on July 11, 1982, with a 3-1 victory over W. Germany. It was the 3d time Italy has won the event. Colombia is scheduled to host the 1986 tournament. Winners and sites of previous World Cup play follow:

Year	Winner	Site	Year	Winner	Site
1930	Uruguay	Uruguay	1962	Brazil	Chile
1934	Italy	Italy	1966	England	England
1938	Italy	France	1970	Brazil	Mexico City
1950	Uruguay	Brazil	1974	W. Germany	W. Germany
1954	W. Germany	Switzerland	1978	Argentina	Argentina
1958	Brazil	Sweden	1982	Italy	Spain

Water Ski Champions in 1984

42d Annual National Water Ski Championships

Men's Open Slalom—Bob LaPoint, Sacramento, Cal., 58 buoys.
Men's Open Tricks—Cory Pickos, Eagle Lake, Fla., 9,840 pts.
Men's Open Jump—Mike Morgan, Lake Wales, Fla., 184 feet.
Men's Open Overall—Sammy Duvall, Windermere, Fla., 3,267 pts.
Women's Open Slalom—Deena Brush, Leesburg, Fla., 61¼ buoys.
Women's Open Tricks—Britt Larsen, Madison, Wis., 7,740 pts.
Women's Open Jump—Deena Brush, 131 feet.
Women's Open Overall—Deena Brush, 3,742 pts.
Senior Men's Slalom—Ken White, Bynum, Tex., 53 buoys.
Senior Men's Tricks—Bill Peterson, Windermere, Fla., 4,950 pts.
Senior Men's Jump—Ken White, 130 feet.

Senior Men's Overall—Ken White, 3,015 pts.
Senior Women's Slalom—Barbara Cleveland, Hawthorne, Fla., 50½ buoys.
Senior Women's Tricks—Barbara Cleveland, 4,640 pts.
Senior Women's Jump—Thelma Salmas, Lantana, Fla., 98 feet.
Senior Women's Overall—Barbara Cleveland, 3,763 pts.
Boys' Slalom—Jeff Rodgers, Greenwood, S.C., 51½ buoys.
Boys' Tricks—Tory Baggiano, Montgomery, Ala., 8,210 pts.
Boys' Jump—Kirby Whetsel, Winchester, Tenn., 129 feet.
Boys' Overall—Mark Masiello, Coventry, R.I., 2,954 pts.
Girl's Slalom—Melanie Maxfield, Canton, Ill., 50 buoys.
Girl's Tricks—Michelle Mason, Boynton Beach, Fla., 4,430 pts.
Girl's Jump—Renee Aurich, Clemson, S.C., 105 feet.
Girl's Overall—Kristi Overton, Greenville, S.C., 3,265 pts.

26th Annual Masters Water Ski Tournament

Men's Overall—Sammy Duvall, Windermere, Fla., 2,714 pts.
Men's Slalom—Andy Mapple, Great Britain, 62 buoys.
Men's Tricks—Cory Pickos, Eagle Lake, Fla., 9,940 pts.
Men's Jumping—Mike Hazelwood, Great Britain, 187 feet.
Women's Overall—Ana Maria Carrasco, Venezuela, 2,515 pts.

Women's Slalom—Camille Duvall, Windermere, Fla., 57½ buoys.
Women's Tricks—Karin Roberge, Orlando, Fla., 5,990 pts.
Women's Jumping—Sue Lipplegoes, Australia, 130 feet.

CHRONOLOGY OF THE YEAR'S EVENTS

Reported Month by Month in 3 Categories: National, International, and General—Oct. 15, 1983 to Nov. 1, 1984

OCTOBER/NOVEMBER

241 Killed in Bombing of U.S. Marine Headquarters Building in Beirut

A powerful bomb, detonated by the driver of a truck, exploded at the headquarters building occupied by U.S. troops in Beirut, Lebanon, on Oct. 23, resulting in the deaths of 241 men, mostly Marines. The terrorist behind the wheel, apparently affiliated with a fundamentalist Islamic sect, drove into the loosely-guarded compound in a Mercedes truck. The bomb exploded at 6:22 a.m., while most of the occupants of the building were still asleep. Two minutes later, a second bomb exploded at the French paratroop barracks two miles away, killing 58 French soldiers in the multinational peacekeeping force. The two terrorists were also killed.

Demands quickly grew in Congress and throughout the United States for the withdrawal of the U.S. peacekeeping force from Lebanon. Investigations into the tragedy at the Marine headquarters placed primary responsibility for lax security on the Marine commanders in Beirut.

The truck delivering its lethal cargo to the U.S. compound passed through Lebanese and Marine checkpoints on the airport highway just after dawn. It turned onto the access road leading to the compound and circled a parking lot. The driver then gunned his engine, crashed through a barbed-wire fence into the compound parking lot, passed between two sentry posts, crashed through a gate, and barreled into the lobby of the headquarters building, where he set off the TNT. The force of the explosion collapsed the 4-story cinder-block building into rubble. Many of the victims were crushed by tons of debris.

In the nearly identical attack on the French barracks, a truck drove down the ramp into the building's underground garage and exploded, destroying the structure.

Heroic efforts to save the injured continued for days. Occasional sniper fire from Muslim strongholds hindered the U.S. rescue operations. Some 300 men had been in the building at the time, and recovery and identification of the victims proceeded slowly. Most of the injured were taken to U.S. ships offshore, and others were flown to Cyprus and West Germany.

Pres. Reagan, returning to Washington, Oct. 23, from a golfing vacation in Georgia, denounced the "despicable act" and said that such terrorists must not be permitted to take power in Lebanon. Defense Secretary Caspar Weinberger said, Oct. 23, that there would be no major change in U.S. policy in Lebanon. Questioned about security at the base, he said "Nothing can work against a suicidal attack like that." French Pres. François Mitterand visited the French and American barracks in Beirut, Oct. 24, and met with Lebanese Pres. Amin Gemayel. He later said that France would remain faithful to its commitments in Lebanon.

Instigators of the attack could not be identified. Some U.S. officials speculated that Iran or Syria were to blame, and Weinberger said, Oct. 23, that circumstantial evidence "points in the direction of Iran." Reagan said, Oct. 24, that "strong circumstantial evidence" linked the bombing to earlier acts against the United States, including the bombing of the U.S. Embassy in Beirut in April 1983. Syria and Iran promptly denied any involvement in the bombings. Press reports that two Shiite Muslim splinter groups were suspected prompted the leader of one of them, Hussein Mussawi of the Islamic Amal, to deny any role. However, when meeting reporters, Oct. 27, he praised "this good act."

Congress was divided on what the United States should do in Lebanon. House Speaker Thomas P. O'Neill (D, Mass.) and Howard Baker (R, Tenn.), the Senate majority leader, both said, Oct. 24, that the United States should keep its forces in Beirut. Members of Congress who favored a pullout described the Marines as "sitting ducks" and "targets in a shooting gallery."

Inquiries into the adequacy of the security at the Marine base began almost immediately. A Marine spokesman said,

Oct. 23, that few special measures had been taken to protect the building. The one sentry guarding a post in front of the building had only an unloaded gun, in compliance with orders, and he had not been able to load in time to fire effectively at the truck. The Marine Corps commandant, Gen. Paul X. Kelley, toured the compound, Oct. 25, and said that he had been totally satisfied with security arrangements on previous visits to Beirut. After the Senate Armed Services Committee met with Weinberger, Oct. 25, Sen. John Tower (R, Texas) said the the committee's consensus was that security was not adequate. A Lebanese liaison with the Marine Corps said, Oct. 26, that he had repeatedly warned of lax security and that terrorists would attack the base. Vice Pres. George Bush toured the base, Oct. 26. Weinberger announced, Oct. 29, that a formal board of inqury would investigate all circumstances surrounding the bombing. Gen. Kelley completed 3 days of testimony before Senate and House armed services committees on Nov. 2. He conceded that security at the base had not been adequate to stop the speeding truck. Kelley said that "extraordinary measures" had now been taken to safeguard the Marine position. Commenting on a news report that the CIA had warned of a possible terrorist attack on the Marines, Kelley said no specific warning had been received that could have prepared the Marines for a truck-bomb attack.

The Pentagon, Nov. 10, put the death toll in the bombings at 239—218 Marines, 18 Navy personnel, and 3 Army soldiers. Two more men died later. FBI Director William Webster said, Nov. 10, that FBI forensic experts had concluded that the blast had been caused by 12,000 pounds of dynamite.

The investigations subcommittee of the House Armed Services Committee, in a report issued Dec. 19, found "very serious errors in judgment" by Marine commanders before the Oct. 23 attack. The report placed "principal responsibility" on Col. Timothy J. Geraghty, the Marine commander in Beirut, "for failing to provide better protection for his troops." It also charged that Gen. Kelley had given "often inaccurate, erroneous and misleading" testimony about the bombing. The House report said Kelley and others in the chain of command had "failed to exercise sufficient oversight" of the Marines in Beirut. The panel pointed out that the shelling of Druse Muslim positions by the Marines in September had resulted in a "significant change" in the way Lebanese Muslims saw the Marines, and should have been followed by increased security measures. The investigators found that the gate outside the compound was "most assuredly open" that morning, and that the sewer pipe cited by Kelley and others as a barrier in fact consisted of 2 pipes so far apart that the truck had been driven between them. The Marine Corps denied, Dec. 20, that Kelley had provided misleading testimony. Reagan, Dec. 20, defended Kelley and the Marine command and said that the Marines must remain in Lebanon to prevent a wider war.

The Defense Department issued a declassification version of its own report on the bombing, Dec. 23. The report, by a commission headed by retired Adm. Robert L. J. Long, found that failure of command, intelligence, and U.S. policy had all contributed to the Marine's vulnerable position. The commission blamed the inadequate security at the compound on Col. Geraghty and on Lt. Col. Howard Gerlach. The commission criticized the chain of command for failures in intelligence and oversight. It also noted that U.S. commanders in Europe and Lebanon were uncertain as to the nature of the U.S. mission. In something of a surprise, the commission criticized civilian policy-making. The report asserted that U.S. policies in Lebanon over the previous 15 months had been characterized by an "emphasis on military options and the expansion of the U.S. military role," and it recommended that "alternative means" be considered for "achieving U.S. objectives in Lebanon."

In a dramatic response to the commission's report, Reagan, **Dec. 27**, said he accepted full responsibility for the lack of security measures at the compound. He said, "If there is to be blame, it properly rests here in this office and with this President. I accept responsibility for the bad as well as the good." He said he did not believe U.S. commanders "should be punished for not fully comprehending the nature of today's terrorist threat."

U.S. Invades Grenada; Marxist Regime Ousted

Striking swiftly and unexpectedly, Pres. Reagan, **Oct. 25**, sent U.S. armed forces onto the island nation of Grenada in the Caribbean Sea. After a few days of intense fighting, Marine and Army units overcame the resistance of the Grenadian militia and Cuban "construction workers." Hundreds of U.S. citizens were evacuated safely, and the hardline Marxist regime that had seized power a few days earlier was deposed. The extremists had killed Prime Minister Maurice Bishop, a more moderate communist, who had led the country since 1979.

Bishop had been placed under house arrest, **Oct. 13**, reportedly after refusing to share power with his deputy prime minister, Bernard Coard. Several thousand of Bishop's supporters rallied at his home, **Oct. 19**, and freed him from arrest. Bishop led the crowd through the streets of St. George's, the capital, to the army headquarters. Although reports differed on what happened next, it appeared that Bishop and several of his ministers were separated from the crowd by soldiers and shot. A 16-member military council under the army commander, Gen. Hudson Austin, took over the government, **Oct. 20**. Jamaica's prime minister, Edward Seaga, warned that the new rulers were Cuban-trained Marxists.

After Bishop's overthrow, a 10-ship U.S. Navy task force that left Norfolk, Va., **Oct. 19**, for Lebanon was diverted, **Oct. 21**, to Grenada. The Grenadian regime predicted, **Oct. 23**, that the island would be invaded by its neighbors in the eastern Caribbean. The U.S. invasion began at 5:30 a.m. eastern daylight time, **Oct. 25**, when 600 Marines flew by helicopter from the aircraft carrier *Independence* and landed at Pearls Airport on the eastern shore of the island. Army Rangers parachuted onto Point Salinas airport in the southwestern part of the island from Air Force jet transports. In all, 1,900 American troops came ashore during the initial invasion. Local militias and armed Cuban construction workers put up stiff resistance. U.S. troops quickly spread throughout the island and occupied the St. George's University School of Medicine campus, where many students from the United States were enrolled. By late morning, 300 members of a task force representing eastern Caribbean nations, mostly policemen, had landed. By late in the day, U.S. troops had captured Fort Frederick, believed to be the headquarters of the military council. Troops from the U.S. 82nd Airborne Division joined the action.

Reagan announced the invasion at a news conference at 9 a.m., **Oct. 25**. He said that on **Oct. 23**, the United States had received an "urgent, formal request" from the Organization of Eastern Caribbean States (OECS) to help "restore order and democracy" in Grenada, where, he said "a brutal group of leftist thugs violently seized power." He said the United States agreed to join a multinational effort with contingents from Antigua, Barbados, Dominica, Jamaica, St. Lucia, and St. Vincent. The United States had also acted to protect American citizens, according to Reagan. The 1981 OECS treaty permitted collective action against external aggression provided members acted unanimously. Three OECS members, including Grenada, had not voted for the invasion. At a news conference, **Oct. 25**, Secretary of State George Shultz denied that the invasion violated the Organization of American States (OAS) charter, which prohibited intervention in the affairs of member states. He pointed out that the OECS nations had not signed the OAS treaty. At a press briefing, **Oct. 25**, White House spokesman Larry Speakes said that the invasion sent a clear message to Soviet and Cuban expansionists in the Caribbean. The Cubans had been building an airfield, but the administration did not clearly establish that the Russians or Cubans intended to make Grenada an outpost for their military or political activities.

World reaction to the invasion was broadly critical. British Prime Minister Margaret Thatcher told Parliament, **Oct.** 25, that she had expressed "very considerable doubts" to Reagan. The French government, **Oct. 25**, called the action "surprising . . . in relation to international law." The Soviet news agency Tass, **Oct. 25**, condemned what it called an "act of undisguised banditry and international terrorism." Victor Hugh Tinoco, deputy foreign minister for the leftist government of Nicaragua, said, **Oct. 25**, that Reagan could use his same reasoning to attack Nicaragua. Immediate congressional reaction was divided. Sen. Daniel Moynihan (D, N.Y.), **Oct. 25**, called the invasion "an act of war," adding, "I don't know that you restore democracy at the point of a bayonet." But Sen. Steve Symms (R, Idaho) compared Reagan's action with Britain's victory over Argentina in the Falkland Islands war of 1982.

Defense Secretary Caspar Weinberger said, **Oct. 26**, that Grenadian and Cuban resistance continued, primarily at Richmond Hill, east of St. George's. Weinberger and Gen. John Vessey, chairman of the joint chiefs of staff, acknowledged that opposition had been stronger than expected. Asked how long U.S. forces would remain on the island, Weinberger replied, "I hope we're talking about days and weeks." He said 600 Cubans had been captured and that caches of Soviet-made arms had been found. He said that Gov. Gen. Sir Paul Scoon had been rescued on **Oct. 25**. At an OAS meeting in Washington, **Oct. 26**, a majority of the delegates condemned the invasion. U.S. casualties were put at 8 dead, 8 missing, and 39 wounded on **Oct. 27**. The Pentagon, **Oct. 27**, showed videotapes of what it said were warehouses full of Soviet-made small arms, ammunition and weapons found near the Point Salinas Airport. The House Foreign Affairs Committee, **Oct. 27**, voted 32-2 to support a declaration that the invasion was subject to the War Powers Resolution, which would require U.S. troops to leave Grenada by Dec. 24.

During the first few days of the conflict, some 700 U.S. citizens and other persons, most of whom were medical students at St. George's University, were evacuated from the island. Some of them said they believed they had been in danger from the revolutionary government. The chancellor of the university, Charles Modica, had said, **Oct. 25**, that the students' safety had been assured and that the invasion was unnecessary, but he reversed himself after a briefing by the State Department. The White House confirmed, **Oct. 26**, that it had rejected messages received before the invasion from the military regime, guaranteeing the safety of U.S. citizens. The White House stated, inaccurately, that no aircraft had been allowed in or out of Grenada on Oct. 24. The State Department denied, **Oct. 27**, an assertion by Tom Adams, prime minister of Barbados, that the United States had been involved in a discussion of a possible invasion of Grenada as early as Oct. 15.

During a debate at the United Nations, U.S. Ambassador Jeane Kirkpatrick said that the invasion had been a necessary defensive action against the "madmen" who had seized power in Grenada. The U.N. Security Council, **Oct. 28**, voted, 11-1, with three abstentions, in favor of a resolution condemning the invasion. The only negative vote, cast by the United States, constituted a veto of the resolution. The U.N. General Assembly, **Nov. 2**, adopted 108-9 a resolution "deeply deploring" the intervention.

Direct U.S. press coverage of the fighting in Grenada began on **Oct. 27**. Refusal by the Defense Department to permit U.S. news personnel to cover the initial invasion provoked controversy. The White House said the Defense Department had "strong views" on what news it wanted released. Four reporters were held incommunicado for 2 days, and Vice Adm. Joseph Metcalf 3d, said, **Oct. 29**, he had ordered naval patrol boats to shoot at unauthorized craft attempting to land members of the press. White House Deputy Press Secretary Les Janka resigned, **Oct. 31**, in protest against official handling of news coverage.

International

First U.S. Cruise Missiles Deployed in Britain — The long-anticipated deployment of U.S. intermediate-range missiles in Western Europe began in England in November, causing harsh reactions from the Soviet Union. Scientists from the United States, the Soviet Union, and other nations met in Washington, D.C., **Oct. 31** and **Nov. 1**, to discuss "The World After Nuclear War." The findings included an estimated death toll of 1.1 billion, with another 1.1 billion likely to be injured in a nuclear war. Based on a computer study, 5 U.S. scientists concluded that dense clouds of dust and soot sent aloft by the explosions would obscure the sun and plunge the northern hemisphere into subzero temperatures for months. Prime Minister Pierre Trudeau of Canada visited 6 European capitals, **Nov. 7-11**, and discussed ways to reduce international tensions and achieve a nuclear arms control agreement. He proposed to French President François Mitterand, **Nov. 8**, that the 5 nuclear powers—the United States, USSR, France, Britain, and China—meet at a disarmament summit. The United States made a new proposal on the limitation of medium-range missiles, **Nov. 14**. The plan, which would limit each side to 420 warheads, was issued to coincide with the delivery, **Nov. 14**, of the first U.S. ground-launched Cruise missiles to Britain's Greenham Common Air Base. These were the first of a projected total of 572 U.S. missiles that were scheduled for deployment in Western Europe over a 5-year period. The arrival of the missiles triggered anti-missile demonstrations in England. Some 100 million Americans, **Nov. 20**, watched a controversial motion picture, *The Day After*, on the ABC television network. It depicted the impact of nuclear war on the citizens of Lawrence, Kan., and seemed to suggest that the policy of nuclear deterrence could lead to war. Many political conservatives denounced the film as leftist propaganda. The West German Bundestag, **Nov. 22**, affirmed, 286-226, its support of the deployment of U.S. medium-range missiles in West Germany. The Christian Democrats and their allies in the ruling coalition held firm for deployment. However, the Social Democratic Party (SDP) came out against deployment. Two former SDP chancellors were divided on the issue: Willy Brandt opposed deployment, but Helmut Schmidt supported it. The Soviet Union, **Nov. 23**, withdrew from the talks in Geneva with the United States on reducing the number of intermediate-range nuclear missiles. The USSR had repeatedly threatened to do so if NATO proceeded with its deployment of U.S. missiles. Soviet President Yuri Andropov, **Nov. 24**, issued a statement announcing countermeasures that would follow the beginning of deployment. He cancelled the moratorium on the deployment of Soviet medium-range nuclear weapons in the western USSR, accelerated the timetable for Soviet missile deployment in East Germany and Czechoslovakia, and said Soviet missile systems would be deployed "in ocean areas and seas." Romania's communist leaders, **Nov. 25**, criticized the planned deployments by both NATO and the Warsaw Pact.

Violence Continues in Lebanon on Several Fronts — The aftermath of the disastrous bombing of a Marine barracks in Beirut, and the last stand of Yasir Arafat in Tripoli dominated the news from strife-torn Lebanon in November. Gen. Paul X. Kelley, the Marine Corps commandant, completed 3 days of testimony before Senate and House armed services committees on **Nov. 2**. He conceded that security at the Marine base in Beirut had not been adequate to stop the speeding truck that delivered the bomb that destroyed the headquarters building, **Oct. 23**. Kelley said, **Nov. 2**, that the death toll in the bombing was at least 234. The death count in the French peace-keeping force as a result of a similar explosion the same day stood at 58. In his testimony, Kelley said that "extraordinary measures" had now been taken to safeguard the Marine position. Commenting on a news report that the CIA had warned of a possible terrorist attack on the Marines, Kelley said no specific warning had been received that could have prepared the Marines for a truck-bomb attack. The House, **Nov. 2**, rejected, 274-153, a move to cut off funding for the Marines in Lebanon by March

---

Adm. Wesley McDonald, commander of U.S. forces in the Atlantic, said, **Oct. 28**, that 500 or more Cubans were still at large on the island and might have fled to the hills. He said 638 Cubans and 17 Grenadians were being held prisoner and that 36 Cuban and Grenadian fighters had been killed and 56 wounded. Some 700 Army Rangers began to withdraw, **Oct. 28**. By **Oct. 29**, most of the original force of Marines and Rangers had been replaced by some 5,000 82nd Airborne soldiers. Bernard Coard and Hudson Austin, leaders of the anti-Bishop coup, were captured, **Oct. 29** and **30**, respectively. The Defense Department admitted, **Oct. 31**, that a Navy plane had bombed a civilian mental hospital by mistake, **Oct. 25**, killing at least 12 persons. Other reports of deaths in the bombing ran as high as 50. Kenneth Dam, U.S. deputy secretary of state, said, **Oct. 30**, that a "treasure trove" of documents, including treaties involving Grenada, Cuba, the Soviet Union, and North Korea, had been found.

Scoon, **Oct. 29**, announced plans for an interim government to rule until elections could be held. He signed a proclamation, **Nov. 1**, asserting his right to govern in the name of Queen Elizabeth II of England. Grenada had been a British possession before independence. Scoon, **Nov. 1**, ended diplomatic relations with the Soviet Union and Libya. He ordered all Cuban diplomatic personnel to leave, but Cuba said, **Nov. 1**, it would not withdraw its diplomatic personnel until all Cuban dead and wounded had been returned to Cuba. The first Cubans were returned to Cuba, **Nov. 2**, and were hailed as heros by Prime Minister Fidel Castro. The U.S. Senate, **Oct. 28**, 64-20, and the House, **Nov. 1**, 403-23, approved resolutions applying the War Powers Resolution to the Grenadian conflict. The Defense Department said, **Nov. 2**, that hostilities in Grenada had ceased. American dead totaled 18, with 91 wounded. Reagan, **Nov. 3**, said that the U.S. operation should be described as a "rescue mission" rather than an invasion. The U.S., **Nov. 4**, promised Grenada more than $3 million in economic aid. Occupants of the Russian embassy, including Cubans and North Koreans, left the island **Nov. 4**. The last of the Cuban prisoners left, **Nov. 9**, for Havana.

In another mix-up by the United States, the State Department said, **Nov. 7**, that a mass grave containing up to 150 bodies had been discovered, but a few hours later the report was withdrawn and attributed to a "lack of communication." Fourteen members of the House returned from Grenada, **Nov. 7**, and a majority reported that a real potential threat to U.S. citizens had existed on the island. The report prompted Speaker Thomas P. O'Neill (D, Mass.) to endorse the invasion he had previously criticized. At the White House, **Nov. 7**, Reagan welcomed American students and service personnel from Grenada. Public opinion polls showed that most Americans supported the president's actions.

Scoon, **Nov. 9**, named 9 Grenadians to an advisory council to run the government. Defense Secretary Weinberger said, **Nov. 10**, that he could not give a "target date" for withdrawal of all U.S. forces. Castro, **Nov. 14**, condemned both the United States and the hard-line Marxists who had overthrown Bishop. A U.S. spokesman said, **Nov. 15**, that a camp on Grenada where some 1,130 persons had been interrogated would be closed within a few days. The White House said, **Nov. 16**, that all U.S. combat troops would be withdrawn by Dec. 23.

The Reagan administration said, **Nov. 23**, that it would provide Grenada with $30 million in military and economic aid. Maj. Gen. Jack B. Farris, commander of the last U.S. troops to leave Grenada, said, **Dec. 13**, that final figures for U.S. casualties were 18 killed, 115 wounded in action, and 36 nonbattle injuries. Other revised casualty totals included 45 Grenadians and 24 Cubans killed. Farris said U.S. troop strength had reached a peak of 7,355 on Oct. 31. The last 190 U.S. combat troops left Grenada, **Dec. 15**, but some 300 noncombat troops remained on the island. Defending the decision to prevent journalists from covering the first days of the invasion, Secretary of State George Shultz said, **Dec. 15**, that reporters "are always against us and so they're always seeking to report something that's going to screw things up."

1984. A spokesman for Israeli Prime Minister Yitzhak Shamir said, **Nov. 2**, that the United States and Israel would soon step up their strategic cooperation. Undersecretary of State Lawrence Eagleburger was meeting with Israeli leaders at the time. Pres. Reagan, **Nov. 3**, named Donald Rumsfeld, a former secretary of defense, as his new special envoy to the Middle East. Syrian-supported rebels, seeking to overthrow Yasir Arafat as leader of the Palestine Liberation Organization, launched a tank and artillery attack, **Nov. 3**, on his strongholds on the outskirts of Tripoli, Lebanon. International Red Cross officials reported, **Nov. 4**, that hundreds of civilians in the Palestinian camps were being killed and wounded in the shelling. Another truck delivered a deadly cargo, **Nov. 4**, as it crashed into the Israeli headquarters compound in Tyre, in southern Lebanon, exploded, and killed 28 Israeli soldiers and 32 Arabs. A mysterious Iranian organization, Muslim Jihad ("Muslim Holy War") claimed responsibility. In retaliation, Israeli jets attacked Palestinian positions along the Beirut-Damascus highway. The White House, **Nov. 5**, reported that the U.S. naval presence in the eastern Mediterranean was increasing to some 30 ships, includng 3 aircraft carriers. PLO rebels, attacking Yasir Arafat's forces, overran a refugee camp, **Nov. 6**, and began to shell Tripoli, **Nov. 7**. A cease-fire was agreed to, **Nov. 9**. Syrian antiaircraft batteries fired on U.S. reconnaissance planes, **Nov. 10** and **11**, as they flew over Syrian positions in eastern Lebanon. The week-long session of the Lebanese national reconciliation talks ended in Geneva, **Nov. 11**, amid signs of progress; delegates said that the factions had discussed a formula for increasing representation in government for the nation's Muslim majority. The Soviet Union, **Nov. 11**, told Syria that factional fighting within the PLO must be ended. Arafat said he would not abandon Tripoli without guarantees of safety for his supporters. An aide to Arafat was reported to be negotiating with King Hussein of Jordan on possible resumption of joint PLO-Jordanian talks with Israel. PLO rebels overran a second refugee camp, Arafat's last military stronghold, on **Nov. 16**, and Arafat's men moved their equipment into the streets of Tripoli. Israel, **Nov. 16**, bombed a Shiite Muslim militia base in eastern Lebanon that was suspected of having links to recent truck bombings in Lebanon. French jets bombed Iranian-occupied barracks near Baalbek, Lebanon, **Nov. 17**, and the Israelis bombed pro-Syrian Palestinians east of Beirut, **Nov. 20**. U.S. Defense Secretary Caspar Weinberger charged, **Nov. 23**, that the Oct. 23 bombing of Marine headquarters had occurred with the "sponsorship and knowledge" of Syria. Arafat gained a small victory, **Nov. 24**, when he exchanged 6 Israeli prisoners for some 4,500 Palestinians and Lebanese guerillas held prisoner by the Israelis. With anti-Arafat rebels at the outskirts of Tripoli, PLO representatives in Damascus said, **Nov. 25**, they had accepted a Saudi Arabian plan that would avert Tripoli's destruction. The agreement would permit Arafat and his supporters to evacuate the city. Prime Minister Shamir met with Reagan in Washington, **Nov. 28** and **29**, and took major steps to establish a closer relationship. They announced that a joint military command would be established to coordinate planning and maneuvers. Israel would be allowed to use $550 million in U.S. military aid to develop a new combat aircraft. Reagan endorsed exempting from repayment Israeli military aid for fiscal 1984.

South African Whites Yield a Little Power — By a 2 to 1 margin, white voters in South Africa, **Nov. 2**, approved a new constitution that granted limited powers to "coloreds" (persons of mixed race) and Asians. The plan, supported by Prime Minister Pieter Botha, provided for a tricameral legislature, one branch each for whites, coloreds, and Asians, most of whom are of Indian descent. The office of prime minister was replaced with a strong presidency. The president would be chosen by an electoral college consisting of 50 whites, 25 coloreds, and 13 Asians. The allocation of votes seemed to assure that the presidency would remain in white hands. Many supporters of apartheid, the nation's system of racial segregation, opposed the reforms, fearing they would be the first steps toward the loss of power by whites. Those who advocated political rights for the nation's black majority also opposed the constitution, which made no provision for participation by blacks in the affairs of the nation. Botha, **Nov. 3**, hailed the result as "a vote for evolutionary reform." The U.S. State Department, **Nov. 3**, welcomed the result as a prelude to broader reforms.

Reagan Visits Japan and South Korea — Pres. Reagan dealt primarily with economic and security matters during visits to Japan and South Korea, **Nov. 8–14**. An agreement announced in Tokyo, **Nov. 9**, sought to strengthen the yen against the dollar, and allow the yen to be used more widely in international transactions. One object of the agreement was to reduce the large U.S. trade deficit with Japan. Reagan met separately with Prime Minister Yasuhiro Nakasone and Emperor Hirohito. Addressing the Japanese parliament, **Nov. 11**, Reagan declared his opposition to protectionism, but warned that Congress might shift toward protectionism if America's trading partners did the same. In the only country ever to suffer an atomic attack, Reagan said, "A nuclear war can never be won and must never be fought." In an address to South Korean National Assembly, Reagan, **Nov. 12**, reaffirmed the American commitment to South Korea's defense. The president, **Nov. 13**, toured the demilitarized zone separating the two Koreas.

"Death Squads" Worry Two Governments — Right-wing "death squads" in El Salvador continued to pose problems for the Salvadoran and U.S. governments in November. The embattled Salvadoran regime cracked down, **Nov. 26**, on 21 military and security men, who were suspected of having ties to the killer teams that had murdered thousands of leftists, labor leaders, advocates of land reform, and other Salvadoran civilians. The suspect officials, including 2 police intelligence officers responsible for investigating abuses against civilians, were reassigned to new posts. Pres. Reagan, **Nov. 30**, rejected, by pocket veto, legislation that would link continued military aid to El Salvador to semiannual certification, by the State Department, that the country was making progress on human rights. Both houses of Congress had unanimously approved the legislation to replace an expiring law. It was expected that the State Department would have found it difficult to certify Salvadoran progress in light of the rising civilian death toll.

Economic Statistics Still Encouraging — Data released during November indicated that the economic recovery was continuing. The Japanese government said, **Nov. 1**, that it would extend voluntary curbs on the number of cars it would export to the United States. The total, for the 12 months beginning April 1, 1984, would be increased from 1.68 million to 1.85 million, based on negotiations with U.S. Special Trade Representative William Brock. The unemployment rate fell 8.7 percent in October, the Labor Department announced, **Nov. 4**. The Federal Reserve Board said, **Nov. 15**, that industrial production advanced by 0.8 percent in October. The Commerce Department reported, **Nov. 22**, that corporate profits rose 11.6 percent during the third quarter. The Consumer Price Index edged upward 0.4 percent in October, the Labor Department reported, **Nov. 23**. The Commerce Department said, **Nov. 29**, that the U.S. trade deficit set another all-time one-month record of $8.97 billion in October. The Dow Jones Industrial Average hit another all-time high of 1287.20 on **Nov. 29**.

Federal Holiday Honors Dr. King — Pres. Reagan, **Nov. 2**, signed a bill designating the third Monday in January as a national holiday in honor of the Rev. Martin Luther King, Jr. King, who was born Jan. 15, 1929, was assassinated in Memphis, Tenn., April 4, 1968. In the last decade of his life, he had emerged as the unofficial leader and most articulate spokesman for the black civil-rights movement in the United States. He received the Nobel Peace Prize in 1964. The House, in August, and the Senate, in October, had approved the holiday. Reagan had agreed to sign the bill after blacks and their supporters in Congress conveyed the intensity of their desire for the holiday.

Blacks Gain in Elections; Jackson in '84 Race — The Rev. Jesse Jackson, a black civil-rights leader, entered the race for the Democratic presidential nomination in November. The results of off-year voting, a few days after the announcement, indicated the potential for his candidacy. In declaring his candidacy, **Nov. 3**, Jackson became the first black male to make a serious bid for a major-party presidential nomination. A black congresswoman, Shirley Chisholm, sought the Democratic nomination in 1972. As a young man, Jackson had worked closely with Dr. Martin Luther King, Jr. In recent years, he had headed Operation PUSH, a Chicago-based organization that sought to advance economic opportunities for blacks. Jackson said he would put together a "rainbow coalition" of blacks, Hispanics, women, and others who he said suffered as a result of Reagan administration policies. Elections held **Nov. 8,** encouraged blacks and women. Winning 55 percent of the vote against 2 white candidates, City Manager W. Wilson Goode, a Democrat, became the first black to be elected mayor of Philadelphia. The campaign was largely free of racial controversy. Martha Layne Collins, a Democrat, became the first woman to win the governorship of Kentucky. Two women mayors, Kathy Whitmire and Dianne Feinstein, both Democrats, were reelected in Houston and San Francisco, respectively. Richard Hatcher, a black Democrat, won a 5th term as a mayor of Gary, Indiana. Bill Allain held the Mississippi governorship for the Democrats. In the only U.S. Senate race, Daniel Evans, a Republican, appointed to the Senate after the death of Henry Jackson in September, won the election to fill the rest of Jackson's term. Kathryn McDonald, whose husband, Rep. Larry McDonald, was killed when the Soviet Union shot down Korean Air Lines flight 007 in September, lost her bid to succeed him to George Darden, a Democrat. A woman won the Toledo mayoralty race, and blacks captured similar positions in Charlotte, N.C. and Flint, Mich. Raymond Flynn, a member of the city council, was elected mayor of Boston, **Nov. 15,** defeating a black candidate, Melvin King.

Congress OKs MX, B-1 Funds, Rejects Nerve Gas — In its rush to adjourn for the year, Congress approved and rejected a large number of legislative proposals. Pres. Reagan, **Nov. 14,** signed stopgap funding legislation permitting several agencies to continue to function. Congress had not yet enacted 5 of 13 appropriation bills for the 1984 fiscal year. Defense spending was authorized at an annual rate of $247 billion, less than Reagan wanted, but enough for initial spending on MX missile production and advance procurement for the B-1 bomber. The Senate, **Nov. 16,** defeated legislation granting tuition tax credits to parents whose children attended private schools. Congress, **Nov. 16,** completed action on legislation to reconstitute the U.S. Civil Rights Commission. Congress and the president, who agreed to the compromise legislation, would each appoint 4 members who could be dismissed only for cause. Earlier in the year, Reagan had sought to fire three commissioners in an attempt to end criticism by the commission of his civil rights policies. Congress adjourned for the year, **Nov. 18,** after a last-minute rush. The national debt limit was increased to $1.49 trillion from $1.389 trillion. An increase of $8.4 billion in the U.S. contribution to the International Monetary Fund was also approved. The renewed production of nerve gas, which had been approved by the Senate, **Nov. 8,** when Vice Pres. George Bush broke a tie vote, but which had been rejected by the House, was killed by the Senate-House conference committee.

Equal Rights Amendment Fails in House — An attempt to revive the Equal Rights Amendment to the U.S. Constitution was set back by a vote in the House, **Nov. 15.** With a two-thirds majority vote required to clear the amendment for ratification by the states, supporters fell 6 votes short in a count of 278 to 147. Some negative votes were cast by Republicans who said they favored the amendment, but objected to tactics used by Speaker Thomas P. O'Neill, Jr. (D, Mass.), who brought the measure to the floor under special rules that restricted debate and prevented amendments to the amendment.

General

U.S. Intervenes in "Baby Jane Doe" Case — The U.S. Justice Department sued in federal district court in Brooklyn, N.Y., **Nov. 2,** to obtain medical records of a severely handicapped infant known in court records only as Baby Jane Doe. The girl was born on Long Island on Oct. 11 with 3 major birth defects: an abnormally small head, excess fluid on the brain, and incomplete closure of the spine. Her parents had decided on a limited treatment, including antibiotics. Doctors had advised them that without surgery the baby would die within 2 years, but that even with surgery she would be severely retarded and bedridden. A lawyer associated with the right-to-life movement had sought to force doctors to perform surgery. A court order, **Oct. 20,** that the infant undergo surgery was blocked the same day by a New York state appeals court, which in turn was upheld by a

state appellate court. In the **Nov. 2** suit, Justice Department attorneys argued that the Stony Brook (N.Y.) hospital's refusal to provide medical records to government investigators constituted violation of the law guaranteeing equal rights to disabled persons. Federal District Judge Leonard Wexler, **Nov. 16,** denied the Reagan administration's request for access and asserted that the parents' decision "to refuse to the surgical procedure was a reasonable one based on due consideration of the medical options available and on a genuine concern for the best interests of the child."

Disasters — An Angolan Boeing 737 crashed on takeoff from Lubango Airport, **Nov. 8,** killing all 126 aboard . . . The crash of a Columbian Boeing 747 near Madrid, Spain, **Nov. 27,** took 183 lives, one of the 10 highest tolls in aviation history . . . A Nigerian Airways airliner, a Fokker-28, crashed 300 miles east of Lagos, killing 65 persons, **Nov. 28.**

DECEMBER

National

Former EPA Official Guilty of Perjury — Rita Lavelle, a former official in the Environmental Protection Agency, was found guilty, **Dec. 1,** of having committed perjury and of obstructing a congressional investigation. Lavelle had headed EPA's toxic waste program until her dismissal on Feb. 7, 1983. She was convicted on 4 counts by a U.S. district court jury in Washington, D.C. In sworn testimony at congressional hearings, Lavelle said she did not know before June 17, 1982, that her former employer, Aerojet-General Corp., had dumped hazardous wastes at a California disposal site. She also testified that she had not dealt with the cleanup of the California site after she learned that Aerojet was involved. At the trial, witnesses contradicted these assertions. Lavelle was also found guilty of perjury for claiming that the cleanup projects in 3 states had not been influenced by political considerations. On **Jan. 9,** Lavelle was sentenced to 6 months in prison and fined $10,000.

Leading Economic Indicators Decline Slightly — Economic statistics released during December remained generally encouraging, but it was announced at the end of the month that the leading indicators had signaled a possible decline for the future. The Labor Department reported, **Dec. 2,** that unemployment had continued to fall in November, from 8.7 percent to 8.2 percent. The Labor Department said, **Dec. 15,** that the U.S. balance of payments showed a record deficit of $11.98 billion in the third quarter. This was greater than the entire deficit for 1982. The Federal Reserve Board announced, **Dec. 15,** that industrial production had risen by 0.8 percent in November. New housing starts rose 6.4 percent in November, the Commerce Department announced, **Dec. 20,** The Labor Department said, **Dec. 21,** that the Consumer Price Index edged upward 0.3 percent in November. U.S. Steel Corp. announced, **Dec. 27,** that it planned to reduce its production capacity by about 20 percent. The cutback would result in the loss of 15,400 jobs. The Commerce Department reported, **Dec. 29,** that the leading economic indicators had fallen 0.4 percent in November, the first monthly decline in 15 months.

Controversies Envelop Administration Officials — Several administration officials found themselves in hot water on the eve of the presidential-election year. Presidential counselor Edwin Meese told reporters, **Dec. 8,** that he had not seen any authoritative evidence that there were any hungry children in the United States, and that some allegations of hunger were "purely political." He added, "I think some people are going to soup kitchens voluntarily . . . because the food is free . . . That's easier than paying for it." Several Democratic presidential candidates responded with denunciations of Meese. J. Lynn Helms resigned, **Dec. 23,** as head of the Federal Aviation Administration during investigations of his private business dealings by 2 federal grand juries. *The Wall Street Journal* had reported, **Oct. 7,** that Helms and an associate had taken over several small businesses and manipulated their assets, resulting in several bankruptcies and defaults on millions of dollars of debt, much of it backed by government agencies. The newspaper said Helms had engaged in questionable business practices. *The New York Times* reported, **Dec. 27,** that Charles Z. Wick, director of the U.S. Information Agency, had tape-recorded telephone conversations without telling the other parties. Wick acknowledged having done so, but made contradictory statements concerning the tapings. An investigation, begun in 1983, led to the resignation, **Jan. 4**, of Paul Thayer as deputy secretary of defense. On **Jan. 5**, the Securities and Exchange Commission charged in a civil suit that Thayer had used business positions in 1981 and 1982 to supply other individuals with inside information that helped them make $1.9 million in the stock market. Eight other persons were charged in the suit.

International

Arafat and His Men Evacuated From Tripoli — The evacuation of Yasir Arafat and his loyalist guerrillas in the Palestine Liberation Organization (PLO) from Lebanon ended one source of conflict in the Middle East in December, but violence in Lebanon and elsewhere kept tensions high. The agreement on strategic cooperation between the United States and Israel, which was announced **Nov. 29**, quickly came under fire from Arab states. King Hussein of Jordan warned, **Dec. 1**, that the Reagan administration's action, without obtaining concessions from Israel on Middle Eastern issues, would handicap efforts by the United States to appear fair-minded. Pres. Hosni Mubarak of Egypt, **Dec. 3**, called the agreement "an obstacle" to the peace process in the Middle East. Meanwhile, Pres. Amin Gemayel of Lebanon met with Pres. Reagan in Washington, **Dec. 1** and **2**. Reagan and Secretary of State George Shultz reportedly urged Gemayel to widen his political base and to extend the army's control in southern Lebanon, possibly by replacing some Israeli forces and thus encouraging Syria to negotiate their own withdrawal from Lebanon. On **Dec. 4**, for the first time since August 1982, when the United States became militarily involved in Lebanon, U.S. planes struck at Syrian antiaircraft batteries in the mountains east of Beirut. Two U.S. planes were shot down. One pilot was rescued, and in the other plane, one crewman was killed and the other captured by Syrians. Syria said 2 of its soldiers had been killed in the raids. Pres. Reagan said that the U.S. air attacks were responses to the attack by Syria on U.S. reconnaissance planes, **Dec. 3**. Later, on **Dec. 4**, 8 Marines were killed at Beirut airport when their observation bunker was hit by artillery fire from Syrian-backed militia. Sen. Barry Goldwater (R, Ariz.) said, **Dec. 4**, "I think the President ought to bring everybody that's in an American uniform back and do it now, because we're headed for war." A bomb exploded in west Beirut, **Dec. 5**, killing at least 14 persons and wounding 83. Another bomb destroyed a bus in Jerusalem, **Dec. 6**, killing 5 Israelis and wounding 45, the first terrorist bombing in Israel in 4 years. Six bombings in Kuwait on **Dec. 12**, killed 7 persons and injured more than 60. Six persons, none of them Americans, were killed when a truck carrying explosives crashed into the U.S. Embassy compound and exploded. At a news conference, **Dec. 14**, Reagan said that Marines might be withdrawn from Lebanon as a result of either of 2 circumstances: the resolution of the Lebanese political crisis, or a "collapse of order" signaling that no solution could be found. On **Dec. 14**, after Navy F-14 reconnaissance jets had been fired on by Syrian batteries, the U.S. battleship *New Jersey* fired on Syrian positons east of Beirut. The battleship fired, **Dec. 15**, in support of U.S Marines under attack from Druse positions in hills near Beirut. The next round of national reconciliation talks among Lebanese factions was postponed after Lebanese, Syrian, and Saudi Arabian foreign ministers failed, **Dec. 18**, to resolve their differences over the May 17 troop withdrawal agreement between Lebanon and Israel. Arafat, chairman of the PLO, and 4,000 of his men left Tripoli on 5 Greek ships, **Dec. 20**, ending a 6-week seige during which Arafat's forces had been trapped by rival Palestinians supported by Syria. During weeks of negotiation preceding the evacuation, the United Nations had agreed to permit Arafat to fly the U.N. flag over the evacuation ships. Greece agreed to provide the ships, and Israel ended 10 days of bombardment of Arafat's forces and consented to the evacuation. The ships transported Arafat's men to Tunis. Two bombings in Beirut, **Dec. 21**, apparently aimed at the Western peacekeeping forces, killed at least 19 persons. Arafat met in Cairo, **Dec. 22**, with Mubarak, ending a rift between Arafat and Egypt dating from 1977, when former Pres. Anwar Sadat of Egypt initi-

ated a dialogue with Israel. The United States endorsed the meeting, but Israel expressed dismay. French peacekeeping forces in southern Lebanon pulled back from positions in southern Beirut, **Dec. 24**, and turned them over to the Lebanese army. The Rev. Jesse Jackson, a candidate for the Democratic presidential nomination, flew to Damascus, **Dec. 29**, to seek the release of Navy Lt. Robert Goodman, whose plane had been shot down, **Dec. 4**. Jackson had charged that the Reagan administration was doing little to free Goodman. Jackson met Goodman, **Dec. 31**, in a Syrian army headquarters.

USSR Declines to Set New Date for START Talks — The current round of Strategic Arms Reduction Talks (START) between the United States and the Soviet Union ended on **Dec. 8**, with no date set for their resumption. The United States sought to dispel the suspicion that the Russians had broken off the talks as a protest against the deployment of the first of 572 U.S. intermediate-range nuclear missiles in Western Europe. Pres. Reagan said, **Dec. 8**, that the Russians had been careful not to say that they were walking out, although Marshal Nikolai Ogarkov, chief of the Soviet general staff, had said, **Dec. 5**, that the USSR was considering a walkout. Mutual and Balanced Force Reduction talks between the North Atlantic Treaty Organization and the Warsaw Pact recessed, **Dec. 15**, with no date set for new negotiations. The Warsaw Pact nations declined to set a new date for continuing the decade-long discussions on reducing conventional forces in Central Europe.

Democratic Regime Takes Over in Argentina — Eight years of military rule, often stained with scandal and violence, came to an end in Argentina, **Dec. 10**, when Raúl Ricardo Alfonsín was sworn in as president. Alfonsín, candidate of the Radical Civic Union, had been the surprise winner of an election held **Oct. 30**. The 3-man ruling junta, consisting of the chiefs of the armed services, dissolved itself, **Dec. 5**. Former Pres. Isabel Martínez de Perón returned to Argentina, **Dec. 9**, to attend the inauguration ceremony. The widow of former Pres. Juan Domingo Perón, she had been in exile in Spain following her ouster as president in 1976. As the elected titular leader of the Perónist movement, Mrs. Perón could still play a role in Argentine politics. In his inaugural address, Alfonsín promised "a decent government" and an end to "public immorality." He asked Congress to abrogate an amnesty granted in September to those who had committed human-rights abuses. Principal victims had been thousands of leftists who had disappeared after being seized by the military during the 1970s. The U.S. State Department, **Dec. 10**, lifted a ban on military aid and arms sales to Argentina, based on an improvement in Argentina's record on human rights. Alfonsín, **Dec. 13**, issued a decree ordering that 3 juntas that had ruled from 1976 to 1982 be court-martialed on charges of murder and torture. A similar decree ordered a trial for 7 leftist terrorist leaders for murder and disturbing public order in the 1970s. Seeking to lower an inflation rate of 400 percent, the government froze prices, **Dec. 14**. Alfonsín, **Dec. 16**, created a commission to investigate the disappearance of more than 6,000 people in the 1970s. On **Dec. 27**, he signed a law repealing amnesty for both former security personnel and leftist guerrillas. Two former presidents and other former junta members went on trial, **Dec. 29**.

Japan's Ruling Party Loses Ground in Election — The Liberal Democratic Party (LDP) suffered a setback in elections, **Dec. 18**, losing its majority in the lower house of the Diet (parliament). Premier Yasuhiro Nakasone had dissolved the House of Representatives, **Nov. 28**, and called the election after a brief boycott of the parliamentary proceedings by opposition parties. The opposition had been protesting the refusal of former Premier Kakuei Tanaka to give up his seat after his conviction for accepting a bribe from the Lockheed Corp. Although a compromise had been worked out in which the LDP agreed to form an ethics committee to guard against future corruption, Tanaka became an issue in the election. The results showed that the LDP captured only 250 of the 511 seats, a decline of 36 in their total. Tanaka, leader of the largest faction within the LDP, easily retained his own seat. The Socialist Party, with 112 seats, remained the principal opposition. The LDP was able to form a majority when 8 independent members of the Diet, **Dec. 19**, agreed to join its ranks. Premier Nakasone, a conservative with close ties to the Reagan administration, said, **Dec. 19**, that he would remain in office.

Military Seizes Power in Nigeria — Four years of civilian control ended in Nigeria, **Dec. 31,** when a military coup ousted Pres. Shehu Shagari as head of Africa's most populous country. Shagari had been inaugurated, **Oct. 1,** for a second term following an election victory. On **Dec. 29,** he had presented an austerity budget to the National Assembly that called for cuts in capital spending and imports in an attempt to balance the budget. Maj. Gen. Mohammed Buhari, who replaced Shagari following the bloodless coup, suspended the constitution and banned political parties. Buhari said that deteriorating economic conditions had made the coup necessary. Nigeria, a major oil producer, had suffered economically after the price of oil declined on world markets. Buhari, **Jan. 3,** announced the formation of a Supreme Military Council to run the government under his leadership.

Small Fire Breaks Out as Shuttle Lands — The space shuttle *Columbia* landed safely at Edwards Air Force Base in California, **Dec. 8,** ending 10-day flight that had begun at Cape Canaveral, Fla., **Nov. 28.** The Space Lab, a portable science laboratory built in West Germany, was carried aloft for the first time and was used to conduct 70 experiments in medicine, astronomy, and physics. The Tracking and Data Relay Satellite System was used operationally for the first time. Ulf Merbold, a West German physicist, became the first foreigner to participate in an American space flight. The 6-man crew was the largest ever for a U.S. mission. On **Dec. 13,** the National Aeronautics and Space Administration (NASA) revealed that a small fire and an explosion had occurred in a rear compartment as the shuttle made its landing approach. The mishap, not discovered at the time of the landing, was attributed to contact between leaking fuel and the hot surface of a power unit. NASA said that the astronauts had not been in danger.

Joint G.M.-Toyota Venture is Approved — By a 3-2 vote, the Federal Trade Commission, **Dec. 22,** approved a joint venture between General Motors Corp. and Japan's Toyota Motor Corp. As a condition of approval, the 2 companies agreed not to expand their operation beyond its proposed limits. G.M. is the world's largest auto maker, and Toyota ranks third. The companies planned to build 200,000 to 250,000 small cars each year at an idle G.M. plant in California. The operation would be run by Toyota executives, with production beginning in 1985. The commission majority believed that the venture would help consumers by providing a new choice in the small-car market, and would help G.M. to learn Toyota's management and production techniques.

Cold Wave Breaks Records — A severe cold wave swept across the United States for a 2-week period beginning **Dec. 17.** More than 400 deaths were attributed to the severe weather. The National Severe Storms Forecast Center reported that temperature records in 60 cities in 21 states had been broken. In the northern Great Plains, wind-chill factor temperatures were as low as −100° Fahrenheit. Some 80 tugboats and 800 barges on the Mississippi River were frozen in place by 8-inch-thick ice. Citrus crops in Florida and Texas were severely damaged.

Disasters — The collision of 2 Spanish jetliners, **Dec. 7,** on a runway at Madrid's Barajas Airport killed 92 persons . . . A fire in a Madrid discotheque, **Dec. 17,** took the lives of 83 people, most of them teenagers . . . An earthquake in Guinea, **Dec. 21,** killed more than 300 people. A second quake in Guinea, **Dec. 24,** killed about 150.

JANUARY

National

Statistics Show Sharp Economic Rebound in 1983 — Data released in January established that the American economy, on the whole, recovered dramatically from the recession during 1983. On the negative side, the Federal Deposit Insurance Corp. reported, **Jan. 3,** that 48 federally insured banks failed in 1983, the highest total since 1939. Figures issued **Jan. 5,** showed that all but one of the nation's largest retailers gained 10 percent or more in sales in December 1983 compared with December 1982. Sears Roebuck & Co., the largest retailer, reported an increase of 17.5 percent. Sales of automobiles in the United States, including imports, increased by 15.1 percent over 1982 to a total of 9,155,741. Imports accounted for 26 percent of the total. The unemployment rate continued to edge downward to 8.1 percent in December, the Labor Department announced, **Jan. 6.** Dun & Bradstreet Corp. reported, **Jan. 9,** that 31,334 businesses failed during 1983, up 24 percent from 1982 and the highest total since 1932. Prices paid by producers for finished goods rose only 0.6 percent in 1983, the Labor Department said, **Jan. 13.** A sharp decline in energy prices helped produce the smallest increase since 1964. The Federal Reserve Board reported, **Jan. 13,** that industrial production averaged 6.5 percent higher in 1983 than in 1982. The Commerce Department announced, **Jan. 18,** that housing starts in 1983 increased 60.3 percent, to 1,703,100, from 1982's depressed level. Real personal income, adjusted for inflation, rose 3.2 percent in 1983, the Commerce Department announced, **Jan. 19.** Real gross national product rose at an annual rate of 4.5 percent during the fourth quarter of 1983, the Commerce Department said, **Jan. 20.** The department said the GNP stood 6.1 percent higher than a year earlier. The consumer price index rose 3.8 percent during 1983, the Labor Department reported, **Jan. 24.** This was the smallest annual increase since 1972. The U.S. deficit on merchandise trade totaled $69.4 billion in 1983, easily breaking the of $42.7 billion reported in 1982, according to the Commerce Department, **Jan. 27.** The government's Index of Leading Economic Indicators rose 0.6 percent in December, the Commerce Department reported, **Dec. 31,** thus reversing the one-month dip in November.

Civil Rights Commission Changes Course — The new U.S. Civil Rights commission, in a reversal of the previous panel's stand, renounced the use of racial quotas for the promotion of blacks. The commission had been reconstituted late in 1983 after a compromise between Congress and Pres. Reagan. The compromise, following charges that Reagan had sought to gain control of the traditionally independent commission, resulted in an 8-member commission with 4 members each appointed by Congress and the President. By January, it was apparent that Reagan had an ideological majority on the commission. In a memorandum, **Jan. 5,** Reagan's appointee as staff director of the commission, Linda Chavez, proposed that the commission identify potential adverse aspects of affirmative action, racial quotas, bilingual education, and court-ordered busing of school children. All of these devices had been supported by liberals as means of furthering the attainment of civil rights for minorities. On **Jan. 17,** the commission adopted, 6-2, a statement on racial quotas asserting that "such racial preferences merely constitute another form of unjustified discrimination, create a new class of victims and, when used in public employment, offend the constitutional principle of equal protection of the law for all citizens." In its annual report, "State of Black America," the National Urban League found, **Jan. 19,** that the economic circumstances of black Americans declined in 1983. The report said that black unemployment was more than twice as much as white unemployment, that 42 percent of black families were headed by single mothers, and that a third of all blacks were living in poverty.

Reagan Announces Bid for Second Term — Pres. Reagan announced in January that he would seek reelection in 1984. The 8 Democrats seeking the chance to run against him participated in a nationally televised debate in New Hampshire, **Jan. 15.** Former Vice Pres. Walter Mondale, widely assumed to be the front runner for the presidential nomination, became the target of several of his rivals. Sen. John Glenn (Ohio) said that Mondale's economic program was "vague gobbledygook" that would add $170 billion to the deficit. Mondale said that Glenn bore part of the blame for the high deficits because he voted for Reagan's 1981 tax-reduction bill. Attorney General William French Smith, who said he wanted to participate in Reagan's reelection campaign, resigned, **Jan. 23.** Reagan nominated Edwin Meese, his counselor, to succeed Smith. Reagan's State of the Union address, delivered to Congress, **Jan. 25,** was seen as his attempt to define the issues for 1984. He asserted that there was "renewed energy and optimism throughout the land" and that "America is back—standing tall, looking to the 80s with courage, confidence and hope." The President called for a "down payment" on the deficit—budget cuts of $100 billion over 3 years—but he opposed increased taxes, and proposed that he have the authority to veto individual items in money bills. He endorsed the idea of a U.S. space station. In announcing his candidacy, **Jan. 29,** in a paid political telecast, Reagan also called for the renomination of Vice Pres. George Bush. He cited his administration's achievements in rebuilding the nation's defenses, and in reviving the economy and the nation's spirits, and concluded by saying that "our work is not finished."

Panel Proposes Savings of $424.4 Billion — A commission appointed by Pres. Reagan to find ways to eliminate waste, inefficiency, and unnecessary spending came up with sweeping proposals in January. The panel, headed by J. Peter Grace, chairman of W. R. Grace & Co., issued its report, **Jan. 12.** The proposals, which allegedly would save $424.4 billion over 3 years, entered into the area of policy. For example, the panel called for a revision of the federal pension system. Grace pointed out that the Civil Service and military retirement systems provided participants with 3 to 6 times the benefits offered by private industry. The commission called for cutbacks in a wide range of programs, including food stamps, Medicare, housing subsidies, and loans to farmers. Grace told the press, **Jan. 12,** "The government is run horribly" and that annual deficits of $1 trillion or more were in the prospect by the year 2000. Ralph Nader, the consumer advocate, said, **Jan. 12,** that the commission's proposals reflected the bias of the corporate executives who constituted most of its membership.

International

Commission Asks More Aid for Central America — Pres. Reagan's National Bipartisan Commission on Central America, headed by Dr. Henry Kissinger, called in January for a sharp increase in economic and military aid for the region. Leftist guerrillas, **Jan. 1,** blew up the largest bridge in El Salvador and routed several hundred national guardsmen in the process. The rebel-operated radio said the attack marked the beginning of a new offensive. The army said, **Jan. 3,** that more than 100 government soldiers were killed, **Dec. 30,** in an attack on a brigade headquarters, the highest total in any single clash with the guerrillas. On **Jan. 8,** 5 Central American nations agreed to a peace plan proposed by the nations of the Contadora Group—Mexico, Panama, Colombia, and Venezuela. Foreign ministers of Costa Rica, Honduras, Nicaragua, Guatamala, and El Salvador accepted the proposals. The provisions of the plan included an inventory of arms, bases, and soldiers in each country; a timetable for reducing and removing foreign military advisers; free elections; respect for human rights; and an end to the use of one country's territory as a base for attacks against another. The Kissinger Commission, submitting its report on **Jan. 11,** endorsed most of the elements of the Reagan policy for Central America. The report called for a comprehensive approach to economic development of the region involving both the Central American republics and the United States. The commission favored both an outlay of $8 billion in economic aid over 5 years and a big increase in military aid to El Salvador. The report saw a serious threat to U.S. security in the involvement of Cuba and the Soviet Union in the region. Kissinger was among 3 members of the commission who dissented from the majority view that aid to El Salvador should be contingent on improvement in the nation's human-rights record. The commission favored military aid for Honduras and, possibly, for Guatamala. It called for "the development of an open political system in Nicaragua." Reagan praised the report, but some Democrats in Congress questioned the outlay of $8 billion at a time of high budget deficits. A U.S. helicopter pilot was killed along the Honduran-Nicaraguan border, **Jan. 11,** by fire from Nicaraguan military units that downed the helicopter. Nicaragua announced, **Jan. 14,** that presidential and legislative elections would be held in 1985.

Rev. Jackson Obtains Flier's Release — Syria freed a captured Navy flier in January after the personal intervention of the Rev. Jesse Jackson in his behalf. Jackson had flown to Damascus, **Dec. 29,** to seek the freedom of Lt. Robert Goodman, Jr., whose plane had been shot down, **Dec. 4,** over Syrian-controlled territory in Lebanon. Jackson, in the unusual position of being not only a private citizen, but also a candidate for the Democratic presidential nomination,

met with Pres. Hafez al-Assad on **Jan. 2.** After a meeting with the Syrian foreign minister, **Jan. 3,** Jackson told the press that "our prayers have been answered," and that Goodman was to be freed that morning on the orders of Assad. Abdel Halim Khaddam, the Syrian foreign minister, said the release was in response to Jackson's personal appeal and the demands of the U.S. government. The minister suggested that the release would "facilitate the withdrawal of American troops from Lebanon." Jackson, Goodman, and Jackson's entourage left Syria, **Jan. 3,** and arrived at Andrews Air Force Base in Maryland, **Jan. 4.** Goodman said his captors had beaten him several times before Red Cross members had visited him. Pres. Reagan thanked Assad for freeing Goodman and said of Jackson's intervention, "You can't argue with success." Reagan welcomed Goodman, his family, and Jackson at a White House ceremony, **Jan. 4.**

Hussein Appears Ready to Reenter Peace Process — King Hussein of Jordan, a key player in the search for a solution to the Palestinian deadlock, indicated by his actions in January that he was prepared to become more active in trying to bring the disputants together. France said, **Jan. 2,** that it would remove 482 troops from the multinational peacekeeping force in Beirut and would rejoin the U.N. peacekeeping force in southern Lebanon. British Prime Minister Margaret Thatcher said, **Jan. 4,** there could be no pullout of the multinational force from Beirut unless the United Nations provided an alternative force. Israel, **Jan. 4,** bombed Shiite Muslim positions in eastern Lebanon. Lebanese police said many civilians were among more than 100 persons killed, a report confirmed by the International Red Cross, **Jan. 5.** On the call of King Hussein, the Jordanian parliament convened, **Jan. 9.** Because the parliament included representatives of the West Bank Palestinians, this move was seen as a means of getting Yasir Arafat, chairman of the Palestine Liberation Organization, to negotiate with Jordan on a Palestinian settlement. Reorganizing his government, **Jan. 10,** Hussein increased the number of Palestinians in his cabinet. Gen. Saad Haddad, leader of an Israeli-backed militia in southern Lebanon, died, **Jan. 14,** of cancer. Addressing his parliament, **Jan. 16,** Hussein appealed to the PLO for help in finding a formula for Middle East peace negotiations. He called for an end to the requirement for unanimity in reaching decisions among Arab nations, which had given veto power to hard-line opponents of Israel. He also urged that Egypt be readmitted to the Arab League. This speech was seen as an attempt to revive Pres. Reagan's 1982 Middle East peace plan, which contemplated a semiautonomous Palestinian entity in the West Bank "in association with Jordan." Malcolm H. Kerr, president of the American University of Beirut, was shot to death by 2 gunmen, **Jan. 18,** near his office. A pro-Iranian guerrilla group, Islamic Holy War, claimed responsibility. The Organization of the Islamic Conference, **Jan. 19,** voted to readmit Egypt to membership. After signing a peace treaty with Israel in 1979, Egypt's membership had been suspended. To reduce pressure in Congress for the withdrawal of U.S. troops from Beirut, Reagan went to Capitol Hill, **Jan. 24,** to lobby for his position. After the meeting, Sen. Howard Baker (R, Tenn.), the Senate Republican leader, said GOP senators would stand behind the October 1983 resolution allowing Reagan to keep troops in Beirut for 18 months. But House Speaker Thomas P. O'Neill, Jr. (D, Mass.) said Reagan had misled Congress about the likelihood of a political solution in Lebanon. He said he now favored a U.S. withdrawal.

Superpowers Continue Rhetorical Sparring — The United States and the USSR continued to seek rhetorical advantage in January as part of the fight for public opinion. The Soviet Union called, **Jan. 10,** for a ban on chemical weapons in Europe. Western diplomats, responding cautiously, noted that previous negotiations on the subject had failed because of Soviet reluctance to agree to verification procedures. In a major statement, **Jan. 16,** Reagan spoke with unusual restraint about the state of U.S.-Soviet relations. In an apparent effort to project a more conciliatory image at the beginning of the presidential campaign, he called for resumption of the discontinued arms talks. The 35-nation Conference on Confidence- and Security-Building Measures and Disarmament in Europe opened, **Jan. 17,** in Stockholm. The first objective of the conference was to find ways to reduce the risk of war in Europe. In his speech to the delegates, **Jan. 18,** Soviet Foreign Minister Andrei Gromyko bitterly attacked the United States as a threat to world peace and rejected Reagan's **Jan. 16** speech as propaganda. Gromyko met with Secretary of State George Shultz, **Jan. 18,** but Shultz, **Jan. 19,** reported "absolutely no movement" toward resuming nuclear arms reduction talks. However, Shultz said, **Jan. 22,** that U.S.-Soviet talks on reducing conventional armed forces in Europe would resume March 16. Reagan, **Jan. 23,** sent to Congress a report alleging 7 Soviet violations or probable violations of arms-control agreements. They included the use of chemical weapons in Afghanistan and Southeast Asia, electronic encoding of signals from missile test flights, and development of a second intercontinental ballistic missile beyond the one permitted by Salt II. The USSR responded, **Jan. 29,** by accusing the United States of violating arms control agreements. A study by the North Atlantic Treaty Organization, released **Jan. 29,** showed that the rate of growth of Soviet military spending had slowed between 1976 and 1982.

Chinese Premier Visits U.S. — China and the United States signed agreements on industrial cooperation and on science and technology during a U.S. visit by Premier Zhao Ziyang in January. At a White House dinner, **Jan. 10,** Zhao pledged to oppose the spread of nuclear weapons. He reportedly expressed concern to Pres. Reagan about the close U.S. ties with Taiwan. Zhao met with Cabinet members and congressional leaders, **Jan. 11,** and asked the latter to permit communist Third World countries to receive most favorable trade and economic aid conditions. Zhao and Reagan signed the accords, **Jan. 12.**

General

Cholesterol Linked to Heart Disease — The relationship between heart attacks and high levels of cholesterol in the bloodstream was established in a report issued **Jan. 12.** The results of the 10-year, $150 million project were reported by the National Heart, Lung, and Blood Institute. The study of 3,806 middle-aged men showed that diet and medication reduced cholesterol levels, but the researchers emphasized that a change in diet, by itself, could reduce the threat of heart disease. High consumption of saturated fats found in meats and dairy products was identified as a source of high levels of cholesterol in the bloodstream.

Disasters — A fire in an undersea coal mine 550 miles southwest of Tokyo killed 83 miners, **Jan. 18.**

FEBRUARY

National

Big Budget Deficit Stirs Debate — Pres. Reagan, **Feb. 1,** submitted a $925.5 billion budget to Congress that was $180.4 billion out of balance. The budget, for the 1985 fiscal year beginning Oct. 1, 1984, included a proposed increase in military spending of $33 billion, or 14.5 percent above the defense outlays for the 1984 fiscal year. The president called for no new major tax increases. The projected deficit represented a slight decline from the $183.7 billion expected for fiscal year 1984. Projections indicated that the national debt after 4 years of the Reagan presidency would rise 74 percent. House Majority Leader Jim Wright (D, Tex.) said, **Feb. 1,** that the Democrats would come up with "at least $200 billion" in deficit reductions over a 3-year period. A division within the administration over the possible danger posed by the deficits was dramatized, **Feb. 3,** in testimony by Treasury Secretary Donald Regan before the Senate Budget Committee. Commenting on a report by Martin Feldstein, chairman of the president's council of economic advisers, that expressed concern about the deficits, Regan said the senators could throw away Feldstein's report. Reagan and Regan held that the economic recovery would generate enough tax revenues to cut the annual deficits to manageable levels. Testifying before the House Budget Committee, **Feb. 6,** Feldstein said the deficits could reach $300 billion a year if the economy did not expand. Paul Volcker, chairman of the Federal Reserve Board, warned the House Banking Committee, **Feb. 7,** that the deficits "pose a clear and present danger" to economic growth. His comments helped trigger a sharp drop on Wall Street, where the Dow-Jones Industrial Average, which had already been slipping, fell to

1156 on **Feb. 8,** a 10 percent decline in just 5 weeks. As advocated in Reagan's State of the Union address in January, a bipartisan congressional delegation met with White House officials, **Feb. 8,** to seek ways to cut the deficits. However, Democrats indicated that progress was impossible unless the administration cut the proposed increase in military spending. The Congressional Budget Office (CBO), **Feb. 22,** made higher deficits projections than the administration had forecast. Although the estimates for 1985 were close, the CBO said that by fiscal 1989, the deficit could be $248 billion, twice that estimated by the administration. At their convention, **Feb. 28,** the nation's governors, by a 28-10 vote, called for higher taxes and reduced defense outlays as means of reducing the deficits.

Hart Upsets Mondale in New Hampshire — Sen. Gary Hart (Colo.) emerged as a strong contender for the Democratic presidential nomination, **Feb. 28,** when he upset former Vice Pres. Walter Mondale (Minn.) in the New Hampshire primary. Mondale had been regarded as the overwhelming favorite for the nomination. He had gotten a good start in late January, when, during a week of caucuses, Democrats in the House of Representatives had selected 164 delegates. Although all were officially uncommitted, almost half were believed to favor Mondale. In the first state caucus in Iowa, **Feb. 20,** Mondale won 45 percent of the preference vote, far outdistancing his rivals. Hart was second with 15 percent and former Sen. George McGovern (S.D.), the 1972 nominee for president, received 13 percent. Sen. John Glenn (Ohio), once considered a strong possibility for the nomination, got only 5 percent. Mondale benefited from his strong support by organized labor. The Rev. Jesse Jackson, another contender, apologized, **Feb. 26,** to Jewish voters for having referred earlier to Jews as "Hymies" and to New York City as "Hymietown." A New York Times/CBS poll, made public, **Feb. 28,** showed that Mondale was the lopsided choice, nationwide, for the nomination. But within a few hours, New Hampshire voters, participating in the nation's first 1984 primary, gave a big plurality of 37 percent to Hart. Mondale received 28 percent and Glenn 12 percent. Hart had said that the choice between him and Mondale was one between "the party's future and its past," and his campaign stressed his "new ideas." Hart, lesser known than Mondale, seemed to draw his support about equally in New Hampshire from voters who described themselves as conservatives, moderates, and liberals. Pres. Reagan got 86 percent of the vote in the Republican primary. Sen. Alan Cranston (Calif.), on **Feb. 29,** and Sen. Ernest Hollings (S.C.) and former Gov. Reuben Askew (Fla.), on **March 1,** withdrew from the race for the Democratic nomination after their poor showings in New Hampshire.

Statistics Reflect Continued Surge in Economy — Data made public in February showed that the economic recovery remained robust. The Labor Department reported, **Feb. 3,** that the unemployment rate in January had fallen to 7.9 percent. Increases in food prices during January were primarily responsible for an 0.6 percent jump in prices paid by producers for finished goods, the Labor Department reported, **Feb. 10.** During February, the nation's "Big 3" automakers announced record profits, totaling $6.3 billion, for 1983. General Motors, reporting **Feb. 7,** led the others with $3.73 billion in profits on total sales of almost $75 billion. New housing starts rose 15 percent in January, the Commerce Department reported, **Feb. 16.** The department also said, **Feb. 16,** that personal income advanced 1.1 percent in January. The Consumer Price Index jumped 0.6 percent in January, its largest advance since April 1983, the Labor Department reported, **Feb. 24.** The Commerce Department said, **Feb. 29,** that the U.S. deficit on merchandise trade had increased by a record $9.47 billion. The department also reported, **Feb. 29,** that the Index of Leading Economic Indicators had risen 1.1 percent in January.

EPA Limits Use of Pesticide — The U.S. Environmental Protection Agency, **Feb. 3,** prohibited use of ethylene dibromide (EDB) on grain products. The pesticide had been identified as a cause of cancer in animals. The EPA also set guidelines for maximum safe levels on EDB in grain and foods already contaminated. EDB had been detected in many products, especially in cake, muffin, and pancake mixes. Independently, several states had begun to move against products linked to EDB.

FTC Approves Texaco-Getty Merger — The Federal Trade Commission gave its tentative approval, **Feb.13,** to the purchase of Getty Oil Co. by Texaco Inc. The merger would be the largest in U.S. history. Texaco and Getty were the nation's 3rd and 14th largest U.S. oil companies. The FTC, in approving the merger by a 4-1 vote, imposed safeguards aimed at preventing possible anticompetitive effects of the merger. After the decision, Texaco bought 56 percent of Getty's stock for $128 a share.

Justice Department Opposes Steel Firms' Merger — The U.S. Justice Department said, **Feb. 15,** it would sue to block the proposed merger of LTV and Republic Steel Corp., the nation's 3rd and 4th largest steel companies. The announcement also cast doubt on plans announced, **Feb. 1,** by U.S. Steel, the nation's largest steel maker, to buy National Steel Corp., the 7th largest producer. Under the arrangement, U.S. Steel would pay National Intergroup Inc. $575 million for National Steel Corp. and assume $400 million of National's long-term debt. But that plan seemed less likely to survive Justice Department scrutiny after **Feb. 15,** when the department said it would oppose the LTV-Republic merger on antitrust grounds. J. Paul McGrath, chief of the antitrust division, said that the combined operation would control an "unacceptably high" share of production in several sectors of the market. He acknowledged, however, that the domestic steel industry was in a state of crisis. Commerce Secretary Malcolm Baldrige criticized the decision, saying it would prevent the industry from doing what it could to remain competitive in the world market. After several weeks of negotiation, the Justice Department, **Mar. 21,** announced that it had approved a revised plan for the merger. The companies agreed to sell 2 plants owned by Republic in order to win approval for the merger.

International

Reagan Pulls Marines Out of Beirut — Pres. Reagan removed U.S. Marines from Beirut and placed them on U.S. ships offshore. He acted as the position of Pres. Amin Gemayel of Lebanon deteriorated and his army crumbled. The leader of Lebanon's Druse Muslims, Walid Jumblat, said, **Feb. 1,** that peace talks with Gemayel were a waste of time and that a decisive battle in Lebanon was inevitable. House Democrats, **Feb. 1,** approved a resolution calling for "prompt and orderly" withdrawal of the Marines from Lebanon. White House spokesman Larry Speakes said, **Feb. 1,** that the action "aids and abets" the enemies of peace in Lebanon. Reagan said he would ignore the resolution. He told the Wall Street Journal, **Feb. 3,** that Speaker Thomas P. O'Neill (D, Mass.) "may be ready to surrender, but I'm not." On **Feb. 4,** Reagan said that if the United States "cut and run," it would be a signal to terrorists everywhere to

wage war against innocent people. The Lebanese premier, a Muslim, and his 9-member cabinet resigned, **Feb. 5.** Meanwhile, the Lebanese army was weakened by defections of Muslim soldiers, and on **Feb. 6,** Shiite and Druse militiamen began attacking army outposts in west Beirut, the Muslim sector of the city. U.S. warships, **Feb. 6,** fired at Muslim positions above the city and U.S. jets flew air strikes. But by **Feb. 7,** the Muslim forces had consolidated their control over west Beirut. In a move that surprised Washington, Reagan, **Feb. 7,** ordered the 1,400-man Marine contingent to begin withdrawing. He also authorized U.S. military commanders to launch bombardments and air strikes against Syrian positions that fired on Beirut. Reagan said he was "concentrating our forces," but that after Lebanon reorganized and broadened its government, the United States would again train and supply the Lebanese army. The withdrawal was to proceed "shortly" in stages. Congressional leaders of both parties gave broad approval to Reagan's action. On **Feb. 8** and **9,** U.S. ships launched artillery barrages against Syrian positions. O'Neill said, **Feb. 8,** that this went beyond the war powers authorized in a congressional resolution on Lebanon adopted on October 1983. Jumblat warned, **Feb. 8,** that if the shelling of Druse villages continued, his forces would retaliate against U.S. diplomats and other civilians. Two partners in the peacekeeping force, Britain and Italy, made plans to withdraw their forces from Beirut, but the French decided to stay for the time being. Evacuation of U.S. and British civilians began, **Feb. 10,** and by **Feb. 12,** some 2,400 foreign nationals, including 884 Americans, had been removed from Lebanon. Israel, **Feb. 10,** resumed its bombing of suspected Palestinian guerrilla positions in Lebanon. By **Feb. 15,** the advancing Muslim forces had virtually surrounded the Marines, and on that day Reagan formally notified Congress of plans to remove most Marines from Beirut "within 30 days." Many defeated Lebanese army soldiers fled south to the Israeli lines in southern Lebanon. Gemayel, **Feb. 15,** reportedly had decided to abandon the May 17, 1983 treaty with Israel, providing for withdrawal of Israeli and Syrian forces in Lebanon. Syria had said that cancellation of the treaty was essential if Gemayel was to survive in office. Gemayel reportedly had accepted this and other provisions of a Saudi Arabian peace plan, which also included a simultaneous phased withdrawal of Israelis and Syrians, power-sharing talks between the government and its Muslim opponents, and the replacement of the Western peacekeepers with neutral U.N. troops. Gemayel said, **Feb. 16,** he would cancel the agreement with Israel if opposition groups entered peace talks, but all other Muslim and Christian factions, plus Israel, rejected that proposal. Israeli Defense Minster Moshe Arens said, **Feb. 16,** that Israel would remain in southern Lebanon for security reasons. Sporadic fighting began, **Feb. 17,** across the line separating Muslim

---

Soviet Leader Andropov Dies; Chernenko Succeeds to Top Party Post

Soviet leader Yuri V. Andropov, 69, died in Moscow, **Feb. 9,** after a lengthy illness. The Communist party's ruling Politburo chose Konstantin U. Chernenko to replace him as general secretary of the party. Andropov's death came only 15 months after he had risen to power following the death of Leonid Brezhnev. No one was immediately named to Andropov's position as titular head of state, or chairman of the Presidium of the Supreme Soviet (parliament). Andropov, who for many years had run the Soviet secret police, or KGB, had not had enough time as party leader to leave a heavy imprint on Soviet society or government. He had sought to get rid of incompetence, corruption, and inefficiency, and had removed many members of the bureaucracy, including some Brezhnev cronies. His brief tenure had been marked by sharp exchanges with Pres. Reagan, increasing international tensions, and a breakdown of arms talks with the United States. After he disappeared from view in August 1983, Soviet authorities denied he was seriously ill. But the medical bulletin issued after his death was announced, **Feb. 10,** said he had "suffered nephritis, nephrosclerosis, secondary hypertension and sugar diabetes, which were worsened by chronic kidney insufficiency." The bulletin said he had been receiving kidney dialysis therapy for a year. At a meeting of the party's Central Committee, **Feb. 13,** Chernenko was nominated as general secretary by Premier Nikolai Tik-

honov, who said he had been the unanimous choice of the Politburo. Chernenko, a close ally of Brezhnev for many years, had served as chief of staff for the Supreme Soviet and as head of administration and security for the Central Committee. He had become a full member of the Politburo in 1978, and was believed to be Brezhnev's choice as a successor. After Brezhnev's death, he was passed over for Andropov, but escaped the subsequent housecleaning of Brezhnev's loyalists. At age 72, he was the oldest man to assume power in the Soviet Union. Western experts on the USSR regarded him as limited intellectually and as inexperienced in foreign and domestic policy. In accepting his nomination, **Feb. 13,** Chernenko seemed conciliatory toward the West, but warned that no one would be permitted to upset the "military equilibrium that had been achieved." After Andropov was buried in Red Square, **Feb. 14,** Chernenko met with visiting dignitaries, including Vice Pres. George Bush, who headed the U.S. delegation. Bush said later that the mood and spirit of the meeting were good and that he and delivered a letter from Reagan conveying his interest in productive talks with the new Soviet leadership. It was reported, **Feb. 23,** by Marshal Nikolai Ogarkov, chief of the Soviet general staff, that Chernenko had assumed another Andropov office, chairman of the Defense Council, which was believed to be in charge of military policy.

and Christian sections of Beirut. The Marine withdrawal finally began, **Feb. 21.** Saudi Arabia, **Feb. 23,** announced an agreement on a cease-fire that brought a brief lull to the fighting. The Marine withdrawal was completed, **Feb. 26,** and the empty bunkers were occupied by Lebanese units that opposed Gemayel. The Soviet Union, **Feb. 29,** vetoed a U.N. Security Council resolution, proposed by France, that would have sent an international peace-keeping force to Beirut.

Reagan Asks More Aid for Central America — Pres. Reagan made new proposals in February for aid to U.S.-supported regimes in Central America. Leftist opponents of the Salvadoran government said, **Feb. 9,** that they would boycott, but not interfere militarily with the March elections, and also called for a broad-based provisional government. The rebels said there would be room for "private ownership and foreign investments" under the government they envisioned. The U.S. envoy to Central America, Richard Stone, resigned, **Feb. 17,** and Harry Shlaudeman, former ambassador to Argentina, was chosen to succeed him. Stone reportedly resigned because of differences with Langhorne Motley, assistant secretary of state for inter-American affairs. Reagan, **Feb. 17,** submitted legislation calling for new outlays to Guatemala, El Salvador, and Honduras. He said aid would be provided under conditions aimed at fostering human rights and political and economic development. The New York Times reported, **Feb. 19,** that State Department audits showed that funds sent to Central America were often diverted into private hands and often did not benefit the intended individuals. Nicaragua announced, **Feb. 21,** that its national election would be moved up to Nov. 4. Secretary of State George Shultz said, **Feb. 22,** that the United States might continue to aid Nicaraguan "contras" even if the leftist regime conducted an honest election, providing Nicaragua continued to "upset" neighboring governments.

War Between Iran and Iraq Escalates — The prolonged war between Iran and Iraq grew bloodier in February. The conflicting claims proved difficult to verify. In what may have been the first deliberate bombardment of a civilian center during the war, Iraqi missiles hit the Iran city of Dizful, **Feb. 11.** Iran attacked several Iraqi towns, **Feb. 12.** Iran said, **Feb. 13,** that on Feb. 11 it had launched a major offensive into northeast Iraq. Iraq denied any invasion. Iran claimed, **Feb. 16,** that it had begun a new offensive on the central front, which Iraq said it was containing. Iraq said, **Feb. 22,** that it had crushed another Iran drive launched, **Feb. 21,** and that Iran had sent many young boys into the battle. Iraq said, **Feb. 27,** that it had begun to blockade Kharg Island, Iran's principal oil export terminal, and claimed to have attacked oil tankers at Kharg by air. The United States said, **Feb. 27,** that it could not verify the air attacks, and Iran denied, **Feb. 28,** that the terminal or any tankers had been hit.

Three Leaders Meet on Middle East Impasse — Pres. Reagan met in Washington, **Feb. 13** and **14,** with King Hussein of Jordan and Pres. Hosni Mubarak of Egypt. Reagan reaffirmed his commitment to his 1982 peace initiative proposing Palestinian self-government in the occupied West Bank and Gaza "in association with Jordon." After the 3 men met, **Feb. 14,** Mubarak openly contraindicated U.S. policy. He called for talks with the Palestine Liberation Organization (PLO), saying there was no substitute for "a direct dialogue" with the Palestinian people through "their chosen representatives." The New York Times reported, **Feb. 18,** that for 9 months in 1981 and 1982, the Reagan administration had conducted indirect talks with Yasir Arafat, the PLO chairman. An American, John Edwin Mroz, a specialist on the Middle East, reportedly met with Arafat more than 50 times to discuss PLO recognition of Israel's right to exist in exchange for U.S. recognition of the PLO. The talks were inconclusive. After the Jordanian embassy in Tripoli, Libya, was burned by protestors, **Feb. 18,** Jordon blamed the Libyan government, and on **Feb. 22,** severed diplomatic relations with Libya. The official Libyan news agency said the protestors objected to Hussein's meeting with Reagan and Mubarak because it might lead to the undermining of the Palestinian cause.

Prime Minister Trudeau to Retire — Prime Minister Pierre Elliott Trudeau, who had headed Canada's Liberal party for more than 15 years, and who had been prime minister for almost all of that time, announced, **Feb. 19,** that he would step down as party leader and prime minister. Saying it was time "for someone else to assume this challenge," he said he would remain in office until a successor was chosen by the party. Trudeau, who was trailing in polls, would have had to face the voters by the spring of 1985. First elected prime minister in 1968, he had remained in office except for 9 months in 1979-80, when the Progressive Conservatives gained power briefly. Trudeau would be remembered for his efforts to advance the cause of disarmament and to assist the Third World, and for repatriation from Britain of the Canadian constitution and enactment of the Charter of Rights and Freedoms. He had prevented his native Quebec from seceding, and had successfully supported the adoption of French as an official language along with English.

General

U.S. Astronauts Fly Freely in Space — The space shuttle Challenger was launched on its 4th trip into space, **Feb. 3,** with both historic and disappointing results. The 10th mission of the shuttle program began at Cape Canaveral, Fla., but trouble began 8 hours later. The 5-man crew released Western Union Corporation's Westar 6 communications satellite, built by Hughes Aircraft Co. Apparently exploding, the satellite trailed debris in its wake and failed to reach its intended orbit. Next, a target balloon released, **Feb. 5,** exploded when inflated. The launch of a second satellite, Indonesia's Palapa-B, also failed, **Feb. 6.** But on **Feb. 7,** Navy Capt. Bruce McCandless, followed by Army Lieut. Col. Robert Stewart, flew free of the spacecraft, the first humans to do so without a tether. They were driven by jet propulsion backpacks designed by McCandless. Though flying at 17,500 miles an hour, as far as 320 feet from the spacecraft, the astronauts had no sense of motion because there was no atmospheric resistance. The Soviet Union, **Feb. 8,** launched 3 men into space in a Soyuz-10 spaceship. The 8 humans in space at one time was a record. The shuttle landed at Cape Canaveral, **Feb. 11.** It was the first time a shuttle had landing at its launching base.

Baby Born from Donated Embryo — Doctors in Long Beach, Calif., announced, **Feb. 3,** that a baby boy had been born to an infertile woman who had received an embryo from a second woman in whom it had been conceived. The baby had been born in Los Angeles in January. Sperm used in the artificial insemination had come from the husband of the infertile woman. The transfer of the embryo, which had begun to develop, involved no surgery and, according to the doctors, could be performed in a doctor's office. The technique differed from the "in vitro," or "test-tube" fertilization, in which eggs were removed surgically from one woman and fertilized in a laboratory.

"Bubble Boy" Dies After 15 Days of Freedom — A Texas boy known publicly only as David, who had spent almost all of his 12 years inside a plastic bubble, died in February in Houston. He had been born with severe combined immune deficiency syndrome and had been placed in an enclosed sterile crib seconds after his birth. David, for whom a common cold could have proved fatal, remained in the bubble thereafter, never experiencing so much as the touch of another human. His health had remained good, and in October 1983, he had received a bone marrow transplant from his sister, which doctors hoped would help produce the antibodies that give the body the ability to defend itself against infection. But after David developed fever and diarrhea early in 1984, Dr. William Shearer, head of the Baylor College of Medicine's pediatrics department, took him out of the bubble, **Feb. 7.** For the first time, David was able to kiss his mother. At first he seemed to respond well, but he developed fluid in his lungs and around his heart, and he died, **Feb. 22.**

Disasters — The explosion of an oil pipeline and the subsequent fire on the outskirts of Cubatao, Brazil, **Feb. 25,** killed at least 508 persons.

MARCH

National

Meese Faces Independent Investigation — Pres. Reagan's nomination of Edwin Meese 3d to be U.S. attorney general came under fire in March, and the controversy quickly evolved into an investigation. Meese, the White House counselor and a key advisor to Reagan since the 1960s, was challenged in several areas during his confirmation hearings, **Mar. 1-6**, before the Senate Judiciary Committee. Sen. Howard Metzenbaum (D, Ohio) raised a number of questions about Meese's finances, including what he called "special treatment" that Meese may have received from the Great American Federal Bank in California. The bank loaned Meese more than $400,000, and at one time he was 15 months behind in his mortgage payments on his California home and 4 months behind on his Virginia home. Several persons who worked at the bank and others who helped Meese later received federal appointments. Meese acknowledged that he had had financial difficulties and that he had been helped by "sympathetic" friends, but he denied any improprieties. Asked about what he may have known of the transfer of campaign documents from the Carter to the Reagan campaign in 1980, Meese replied in writing, **Mar. 8**, that he had "no knowledge of any effort" to get information. Meese was also challenged by Democratic liberals on his civil-rights record and on his ability as attorney general to remain independent of the White House. On **Mar. 13**, it was learned that Meese has failed to report on financial-disclosure forms, as required by law, that in 1981 his wife had received a $15,000 interest-free loan from a friend, Edwin Thomas, who went to work for Meese in the White House at about the same time. Thomas later got another federal job, as did his wife and son. Meese said the omission on the forms was inadvertent. Reagan said, **Mar. 21**, he had complete confidence in Meese. Meese, on **Mar. 22**, asked for the appointment of an independent counsel, formerly called a special prosecutor, to investigate the allegations against him. On **Mar. 27**, Attorney General Willaim French Smith asked a 3-member federal court panel to appoint such an investigator, who would look into other allegations, including Meese's promotion to colonel in the Army Reserve and his switch from retired to active status, which the Army's inspector general had found to be improper. Jacob Stein, a professor of law at George Washington University, was named as the independent counsel on **Apr. 2**. Action on the Meese nomination by the Judiciary Committee was left in abeyance.

Mondale Rebounds to Lead Hart for Nomination — The contest for the Democratic presidential nomination seesawed in March, with former Vice Pres. Walter Mondale maintaining the lead in the chase for delegates. Mondale's loss in New Hampshire in late February was followed by a second defeat by Colorado Sen. Gary Hart in the Maine caucuses **Mar. 4**. Once considered a virtual shoo-in for the nomination, Mondale said, **Mar. 5**, "I'm in trouble. I need help." In the following weeks, Hart continued to argue that Mondale was a part of the party's past that had been rejected by the voters in 1980. Addressing Hart's claim to new ideas, Mondale said in paid advertisements, "The question isn't whether an idea is new or old. The question is whether it's right or wrong." Mondale continued to sharpen his criticism of Hart. Speaking to the Alabama legislature, **Mar. 7**, he said, "Don't hold experience and qualifications against a person. Pick someone who just might know what he is doing." He called Hart a candidate of tinsel and public relations. Hart, speaking to the same audience, **Mar. 8**, said that the parties "must free themselves from the grasp of special interests and once again address the country's national interest." On the so-called Super Tuesday, **Mar. 13**, Hart won primaries in Massachusetts, Rhode Island, and Florida, and Mondale won primaries in Georgia and Alabama. The results knocked two contenders, Ohio Sen. John Glenn and former Sen. George McGovern (S.D.) out of the race. The Rev. Jesse Jackson, ran well in the South, finishing third in Georgia and Florida, and remained in the race, saying he would be the "conscience" of the campaign. The scene then shifted to the Midwest, with Mondale winning the Michigan caucuses, **Mar. 17**, and the Illinois primary, **Mar. 20**, where he got 41 percent, while Hart got 35 percent, and Jackson got 21 percent in his home state. It was believed that Hart hurt his cause in Illinois by his attacks on the Chicago Democratic organization for its support of Mondale, which may have spurred it to greater effort. The campaign between the 2 front-runners continued at a highly personal level, with both seeking to exploit relatively minor differences in their generally liberal positions. In a more substantive difference, Hart favored a complete U.S. military withdrawal from Central America, while Mondale favored keeping some U.S. troops there. Hart won the Connecticut primary **Mar. 27**. A number of states chose their delegates at caucuses, some of which extended over days or even weeks. These were sometimes inconclusive, with many uncommitted delegates being chosen. At the end of March, with 1,967 delegates needed for the nomination, Mondale had about 700, Hart about 400, Jackson about 100, and some 400 were uncommitted.

Standard Oil of California Buys Gulf — Merger mania within the oil industry continued in March, when Standard Oil Co. of California (Socal) and Gulf Corp. reached an agreement, **Mar. 5**, by which Socal would purchase Gulf for $80 a share. The merger would be the largest in U.S. history at $13.3 billion, topping the $10.1 billion purchase of Getty Oil by Texaco Inc. earlier in 1984. Gulf's board of directors accepted Socal's bid in preference to 2 other formal offers. The agreement, however, was subject to the approval of the Federal Trade Commission (FTC). Because the merged companies would control more than 20 percent of the gasoline markets in 4 states, there was speculation that Socal would have to drop some Gulf marketing outlets to meet antitrust concerns by the FTC. The recent trend in oil-company mergers had been spurred by belief within the industry that it was less expensive to build oil reserves through mergers than by exploring. Mobil Corp., the nation's second largest oil company, announced, **Mar. 11**, that it had agreed to buy Superior Oil Co. for $5.7 billion.

Senate Rejects School Prayer Amendments — The U. S. Senate rejected 2 constitutional amendments during March that would have permitted prayer in the public schools. Pres. Reagan, a leading advocate of one of the amendments, said in a speech, **Mar. 6**, to the National Association of Evangelicals, "Hasn't something gone haywire" when the Constitution permits radical groups "to march on public property" and spread doctrines of hate, but "it supposedly prevents our children from Bible study or the saying of a simple prayer in their schools?" The Senate, **Mar. 15**, rejected 81-15 an amendment that would have permitted silent prayer in the public schools. Sen. Lowell Weicker (R, Conn.), leader of the fight against the prayer amendments, argued that any form of organized prayer would violate the basic rights of free speech and religion guaranteed by the First Amendment. On **Mar. 20**, a 56-44 majority of the Senate supported an amendment that would have permitted organized spoken prayer in the public schools. However, this fell short of the two-thirds majority required for approval.

Jump in Prime Rate Is Only Cloud on Economy — An increase in the key interest rate provided the only serious concern about the U.S. economy during March. The unemployment rate continued its steady decline in February to 7.7 percent, the Labor Department announced, **Mar. 9**. The Federal Reserve Board said, **Mar. 15**, that industrial production had risen by 1.2 percent in February. Housing starts jumped 11.2 percent in February, the Commerce Department announced, **Mar. 16**. The index of prices that producers pay for finished goods rose 0.4 percent in February, the Labor Department said, **Mar. 16**. On **Mar. 19**, major banks raised their prime lending rates from 11 to 11.5 percent, the first increase in that interest-rate indicator since August 1983. The U.S. balance of payments, a measure of the nation's trade with other countries, showed a record deficit of $40.78 billion in 1983, the Commerce Department reported **Mar. 19**. Commerce Secretary Malcolm Baldrige said that the gap could double in 1984. The Labor Department said, **Mar. 23**, that the Consumer Price Index rose 0.4 percent in February. The Commerce Department reported, **Mar. 29**, that the Index of Leading Economic Indicators rose 0.7 percent in February.

Reagan, GOP Leaders Agree on Budget Cuts — After bipartisan discussions on reducing the budget deficit broke down at the end of February, Pres. Reagan and Republican leaders in Congress worked out a deficit-reducing package, which was announced on **Mar. 15**. As compared with the budget submitted by Reagan to Congress in February, the new agreement would reduce military and domestic spending by about $40 billion each and would increase taxes by $48 billion. Including savings on interest, the total deficit-reduction over 3 years would come to $150 billion. On **Mar.**

19, however, the Congressional Budget office said that the projected reductions claimed in the agreement had been exaggerated. House Democrats, **Mar. 20,** came up with their own $185 billion 3-year deficit-reduction plan that put much more emphasis on reducing military outlays.

International

Hussein Rebukes U.S. on Ties With Israel — The peace process in the Middle East was abruptly set back in March when King Hussein of Jordan sharply criticized the close relationship between the United States and Israel. Hussein and Yasir Arafat, chairman of the Palestine Liberation Organization, ended 5 days of discussions on **Mar. 1,** on how to coordinate their approach to the Middle East peace negotiations. The issue before them was Pres. Reagan's 1982 proposal for a Palestinian "entity" on the West Bank "in association with Jordan." In their statement, the 2 leaders agreed to continue talking and they reaffirmed their support for the 1982 Arab summit declaration that called for Palestinian statehood. A Reagan administration proposal to sell 1,600 antiaircraft missiles to Jordan provoked debate on Capitol Hill, where, by **Mar. 9,** opponents of the sale in both houses had drafted legislation to prevent it. Reagan, addressing a Jewish group, **Mar. 13,** appealed for support for his policy toward Jordan, which he described as "crucial to the peace process." Then, on March 14, the New York Times published an interview with Hussein in which he said that the United States was not a credible mediator in the Middle East because of its one-sided support of Israel. He cited the U.S.-Israeli strategic cooperation agreement. He said, "Israel is on our land. . .by virtue of American military assistance and economic aid. . .(and) by American moral and political support. . . ." He said principles meant nothing to the United States, especially in presidential election years. The U.S. State Department described Hussein's criticism as "just another monkey wrench." Reagan decided, **Mar. 21,** to cancel the sale of the antiaircraft missiles to Jordan and the sale of 1,200 of the missiles to Saudi Arabia.

Lebanese Peace Talks Show No Progress — Again, in March, the leaders of Lebanon's warring factions met to discuss a political settlement, but without any apparent progress. U.S. Secretary of State George Shultz complained, **Mar. 1,** that congressional debate had made it impossible for the Reagan administration to conduct a "sensible" policy in Lebanon. The Syrian press agency, **Mar. 1,** issued a communique on the meeting in Damascus between Lebanese Pres. Amin Gemayel and Syrian Pres. Hafez al-Assad. It was reported that the leaders were in "complete agreement" on ways of "reinforcing Lebanon's Arab identity, unity, and independence." On **Mar. 2,** apparently as a result of these discussions, Druse Muslim leader Walid Jumblat softened his tone toward Gemayel. On **Mar. 5,** the Lebanese cabinet formally abrogated the May 17, 1983, troop withdrawal agreement with Israel. The agreement had been worked out with the held of Shultz, but Syria had never agreed to withdraw its troops from Lebanon, and Israeli forces remained in southern Lebanon. The Israeli government, **Mar. 5,** called the abrogation the "death sentence for Lebanese independence and sovereignty." The abrogation cleared the way for the Lebanese government, **Mar. 6,** to formally invite opposition leaders to meet in Lausanne, Switzerland, for a new round of reconciliation talks. Meanwhile, Assad restructured his government, **Mar. 11,** apparently, in part, as a result of disagreements with his brother, whom Assad made a vice president. The Lebanese reconciliation talks opened **Mar. 12,** and Gemayel appealed to those present to end "nine years of insane and continuous war." Mohammed Ibrahim Massoud, another of Syria's new vice presidents and a key player in the reconciliation talks, came as an observer. The participants, **Mar. 13,** announced a nationwide ceasefire and the revival of a military committee to enforece it. However, the cease-fire had broken down by **Mar. 16,** and Lausanne conference itself ended on **Mar. 20,** with little to show except the appointment of a comittee to draft a new constitution. France, **Mar. 25,** began withdrawing its last 1,250 troops from Beirut. Pres. Reagan, **Mar. 30,** formally ended U.S. participation in the multinational peacekeeping force.

Chernenko Takes Softer Approach Toward U.S. — In his first major policy address since becoming leader of the So-

viet Union, Konstantin Chernenko, **Mar. 2,** employed more restrained rhetoric than his predecessor, Yuri Andropov, in discussing U.S.-U.S.S.R. relations. Addressing 5,000 party members in the Kremlin, in advance of the **Mar. 4** elections for a Supreme Soviet, Chernenko urged a "drastic change" for the better in relations between the super-powers. He noted that Pres. Reagan had "begun to make peaceable sounding statements," but that they must be followed by actions. He seemed to indicate that intermediate-range and strategic nuclear-weapons talks could not resume until NATO reversed its deployment of missiles in Europe. Chernenko also made cautious overtures toward China and endorsed Andropov's plans to revive the economy and end corruption and inefficiency. The U.S. State Department said, **Mar. 2,** that it welcomed Chernenko's statements, including his expressed interest in a complete ban on chemical weapons. The high level of tension between the United States and Russia was underscored, **Mar. 21,** when a Soviet nuclear-powered submarine collided in the dark with the U.S. aircraft carrier *Kittyhawk* in the sea of Japan. Close surveillance by Soviet submarines is routine, according to U.S. naval officers, and the carrier was not seriously damaged, nor was the submarine. On **Mar. 16,** talks on reducing conventional armed forces in Europe resumed in Vienna, three months after the Warsaw Pact nations broke off discussions in protest against U.S. missile deployment. Also on **Mar. 16,** the 35-nation conference on Confidence- and Security-Building Measures and Disarmament in Europe ended its first round of meetings, with no report of progress. Administration officials revealed, **Mar. 23,** that earlier in the month, Soviet officials had refused to accept a note from Reagan carried to Moscow by retired Gen. Brent Scowcroft.

Moderate, Rightist in El Salvador Runoff — A moderate candidate and a right-winger linked to the notorious death squads survived the first round of the presidential election in El Salvador and were scheduled to face each other in a runoff. Roberto D'Aubuisson, the right-wing candidate, was accused by a former Salvadoran military official in the *New York Times,* **Mar. 3,** of having organized and directed the death squads. The unnamed official, who said he had known D'Aubuisson for many years, described him as an "anarchic psychopath." The informant also briefed leading members of Congress. He charged that Col. Ocsar Edgardo Casanova, cousin of the Salvadoran defense minister, had ordered the slaying in 1980 of 3 U.S. nuns and a U.S. lay worker. The men accused by the informant denied the allegations. The U.S. Senate Appropriations Committee, **Mar. 8,** rejected, 15-14, more money for "Contras" fighting against the leftist Nicaraguan regime. The money, requested by the Reagan administration, was turned down when key senators objected to the administration's attempt to tie the aid to a bill providing low-income fuel assistance. But the committee, on **Mar. 14,** approved $92.8 million for El Salvador and $21 million for the U.S. Central Intelligence Agency to assist the opponents of the Nicaraguan regime. On **Mar. 20,** a Soviet oil tanker struck a mine outside a Nicaraguan port, and 5 crewmen were injured. The Nicaraguan rebels had previously announced that other Nicaraguan ports had been mined. Other ships had also struck mines, but without fatalities. The Soviet Union, **Mar. 21,** charged U.S. complicity in the mining. The U.S. State Department, **Mar. 21,** rejected the charges, saying the rebels had already claimed responsibility. Amid much confusion, the first round in the Salvadoran presidential election was held **Mar. 25.** With an absolute majority required for victory, José Napoleón Duarte of the centrist Christian Democratic Party received 43 percent and D'Aubusson was second with 30 percent. Rebels succeeded in preventing voting in areas under their control. The *Washington Post* reported, **Mar. 28,** that U.S. planes were flying reconnaissance missions during Salvadoran military operations to give information on guerrilla movements. Gen. Gustavo Alvarez Martínez, commander of the Honduran armed forces and a key U.S. ally in Central America, was forced to resign, **Mar. 31,** a move apparently related to corruption and to his threat to the regime.

U.S. Says Iraq Is Using Chemical Weapons — The U.S. State Department said that Iraq appeared to be using chemical weapons in its war against Iran. The Speaker of the Iranian Parliament charged, **Mar. 4,** that Iraqi chemical attacks had killed 400 Iranian soldiers and injured 1,100 more within the previous week. The U.S. State Department said, **Mar. 5,** that "available evidence" indicated that Iraq was using "lethal chemical weapons." *The New York Times* reported, **Mar. 5,** that an administration official believed Iraq was using mustard gas, which blisters any tissue exposed to it. Both Iraq and Iran had signed the 1925 Geneva Protocol barring the use of such weapons. Without actually denying the charge, Iraq said, **Mar. 6,** that the U.S. statement was "full of lies." The Red Cross announced, **Mar. 7,** that 160 Iranian soldiers examined by a Red Cross medical team in Teheran had been affected by "substances prohibited by international law." The United States, **Mar. 30,** restricted the sale to Iraq of 5 chemical compounds that could be used to make poison gases.

Polish Students Protest Crucifix Removal — Unrest swept Poland in March over the issue of the display of crucifixes in schools. On **Mar. 7,** 400 students at Stanislaw Staszic Agricultural College protested the removal of crucifixes from their classrooms. The director of the school, Ryszard Debrynski, had ordered the action in response to a government directive barring the crucifixes in hospitals and schools. This policy reflected the constitutional separation of church and state. Police broke up the **Mar. 7** sit-in demonstration, and the college was closed. Parents of the students refused, **Mar. 8,** to sign statements approving the removal. On that day, protest spread to three other schools. National opposition to the removal of crucifixes was fanned, **Mar. 14,** when Jozef Cardinal Glemp, the primate of Poland, protested the ban on the crucifixes. In a compromise announced **Apr. 6,** the government and the Roman Catholic Church agreed that crucifixes would be allowed in reading rooms and dormitories of the school where the trouble started, but not in the classrooms.

Mozambique, South Africa Sign Pact — For the first time, **Mar. 16,** the white regime in South Africa signed a nonaggression pact with one of its neighbors. The agreement with Mozambique, called the "accord of Nkomati," provided that neither nation would permit armed groups, including mercenaries, to use its territory to mount attacks across the border. Prime Minister Pieter Botha of South Africa said that the agreement was based on economic and geographic realities. The agreement was a setback to the African national Congress, whic used bases inside Mozambique to attack South Africa, and to the Mozambique National Resistance, a guerilla movement operating in Mozambique with South African support.

Five Nations Help Argentina Pay Interest — The United States and 4 Latin nations came to the rescue of Argentina, **Mar. 30,** agreeing on a package of assistance that would permit Argentina to make a long-overdue interest payment to American banks. Had Argentina failed to pay by **Mar. 31,** the banks would have suffered sharply reduced first-quarter earnings. The $500 million aid package was put together by Brazil, Mexico, Venezuela, Colombia, and by a group of commercial banks. The sum also included $100 million of Argentina's own reserves. Argentina had been weakened economically by the 1983 Falkland Islands war and other extravagances of the recent military dictatorship. Argentina's international debt totaled $43.6 billion. The new government of Pres. Raúl Alfonsín sought to use most of its available capital to strengthen the domestic economy. Until the agreement of **Mar. 30** was reached, many bankers feared Argentina would repudiate its debts altogether. Treasury Secretary Donald Regan said, **Mar. 31,** that the United States had agreed to help to prevent "a crisis of government" in Argentina.

General

Four Men Convicted in Barroom Rape Trial — In separate trials that ran concurrently in morning and afternoon sessions, 4 men were convicted **Mar. 17** and **22** of raping a woman in a bar in New Bedford, Mass., in 1983. Two men, who had been accused of complicity, were found not guilty. For the convictions on aggravated rape, Judge William Young, **Mar. 26,** handed down prison sentences of 6 to 8 and 9 to 12 years. The trial, which was conducted in Fall River, Mass., attracted national attention because of the number of defendants and because it was televised nationally almost in its entirety by Cable News Network. Women's groups deplored attempts by the defense to discredit the character of the victim. Those who sympathized with the defendants charged that the guilty verdicts reflected prejudice against persons of Portuguese descent. All of the accused were of Portuguese descent—two of them spoke no English—as was the victm. On **Mar. 22** and **23,** crowds as large as 10,000, mostly of Portuguese descent, marched in New Bedford and Fall River to protest the convictions.

Tornadoes Kill 61 in Carolinas — A series of 24 early spring tornadoes killed 61 persons in North and South Carolina on **Mar. 28.** The paths of destruction, cutting through small towns and countryside, injured 1,000 persons and left 3,000 homeless. Damage was estimated at more than $100 million. It was the heaviest death toll from tornadoes in the United States in 10 years. A general storm system swept the East Coast in the last days of March, causing widespread damage. Sixteen inches of snow were reported in Worcester, Mass., and winds of 115 miles an hour were recorded atop Mt. Washington, N.H. Some 300,000 Massachusetts residents were without electricity, and flooding was widespread, particularly in northeastern New Jersey.

APRIL

National

Mondale Wins New York, Pennsylvania Primaries — Former Vice President Walter Mondale widened his lead in the contest for the Democratic presidential nomination in April by winning big victories in New York, Pennsylvania, and other states. After a personal, sometimes bitter, campaign between Mondale and Sen. Gary Hart (Col.), Mondale won 45 percent of the popular vote in the New York primary, **Apr. 3.** Hart received 27 percent, barely ahead of the Rev. Jesse Jackson, who won 26 percent. Jackson, who got more than four-fifths of the black vote, made his best showing yet in a major industrial state. Mondale had the support of Gov. Mario Cuomo, New York City Mayor Edward Koch, and the state's labor unions. At a press conference, **Apr. 4,** Pres. Ronald Reagan touched on themes he was expected to develop in the fall campaign. In particular, he criticized Congress for interfering with foreign policy, saying it "must take responsibility" for the problems in Lebanon. He suggested that the many calls for the withdrawal of American troops might have helped stimulate terrorists, who had killed 260 U.S. servicemen, mostly Marines. House Speaker Thomas P. O'Neill (D, Mass.), **Apr. 5,** rejected Reagan's criticism, saying, "The deaths of the U.S. Marines are the responsibility of the president. . . ." Reagan said, **Apr. 6,** that Congress had undermined administration efforts in Lebanon and Central America, and he called for a return to a "bipartisan consensus in support of U.S. foreign policy." Mondale won a big victory in the Wisconsin caucuses, **Apr. 7,** reversing the results of a nonbinding preference vote won by Hart. Jackson, **Apr. 8,** deplored statements made by Louis Farrakhan, a Black Muslim leader, against a black newspaper reporter, but he refused to repudiate Farrakhan's political support. Farrakhan had said, March 11, that Milton Coleman, a reporter for the Washington Post, was a traitor for having reported Jackson's remarks about Jews. In a radio broadcast, Farrakhan had warned Coleman, "One day soon we will punish you with death." Vice Pres. George Bush said, **Apr. 9,** that Jackson's failure to repudiate Farrakhan more strongly was shocking. Farrakhan renewed his criticism of Coleman, **Apr. 11,** but said that the lives of Coleman and his family "are sacred to me." Mondale, meanwhile, rolled up another victory in Pennsylvania, **Apr. 10,** winning 47 percent of the vote to 35 percent for Hart and 17 percent for Jackson, who carried Philadelphia. Mondale also won the Missouri caucuses, **Apr. 18.** Jackson reached an agreement, **Apr. 23,** with party chairman Charles Manatt on party rules that removed the possibility that Jackson might walk out of the national convention. Reacting to pressure from the Hart campaign, Mondale, **Apr. 25,** told ostensibly independent committees that had been set up in his behalf to terminate their activities. The committees, funded by organized labor, supported candidates for delegates pledged to Mondale. Hart had charged that they might be an illegal means of getting around the limits on campaign spending. Mondale went further, **Apr. 27,** saying he would return about $300,000 that had been contributed to the committees, and that money already spent by the committees would be counted toward his legal pre-convention limit of $20.2 million. At the end of April, with 1,967 votes needed to nominate, Mondale had about 1,075 delegates, Hart about 575, Jackson about 150, and some 275 supported others or were uncommitted.

Congress Steps Up Efforts to Cut Deficits — Responding to warnings from economists and business leaders, Congress moved forward in April with legislation to reduce projected deficits in the federal budget. The House, **Apr. 5,** approved, 250 to 168, a plan to cut the deficit by $182 billion over 3 years. By approving smaller increases in defense spending, the House plan surpassed a proposal put forth by Pres. Reagan that would cut the deficit by $150 billion over 3 years. Implementing the plan, the House, **Apr. 11,** approved a tax-increase bill, and it then passed a bill, **Apr. 12,** to reduce spending by nearly $5 billion. The Senate, **Apr. 13,** approved a 3-year $47 billion tax bill, slightly smaller than the $49.2 billion in new taxes previously approved by the House. The Senate bill would reduce spending by $14.8 billion.

Key Interest Rates Edge Upward — Two interest rates watched closely as economic barometers moved higher in April. Major banks, **Apr. 5,** increased their prime lending rates from 11.5 percent to 12 percent, the highest level for the prime rate since October 1982. The Federal Reserve Board, **Apr. 6,** voted to raise the interest rate it charged on loans to financial institutions from 8.5 percent to 9 percent. The increase in the rate, which had been unchanged since December 1982, could restrict the amount of money available in the economy. The Labor Department reported, **Apr. 6,** that unemployment was 7.7 percent, virtually unchanged from recent months. The surge in the economy was reflected, **Apr. 10,** in an estimate by the administration that the real gross national product would grow by 5 percent in 1984. The previous estimate had been 4.5 percent. Housing starts fell 26.6 percent in March, the largest one-month decline ever, the Commerce Department said, **Apr. 17.** The drop was attributed to bad weather. The Commerce Department reported, **Apr. 19,** that the economy had grown at an annual rate of 8.3 percent during the first quarter, a sharp increase from the 5 percent rate in the previous quarter. Consumer prices rose 0.2 percent in March, the Labor Department reported, **Apr. 24.** The index of leading economic indicators fell 1.1 percent in March, the Commerce Department reported, **Apr. 30.**

Social Security Disability Reviews Dropped — Margaret Heckler, secretary of Health and Human Services, announced, **Apr. 13,** that the Reagan administration was dropping its controversial program of reviewing Social Security disability rolls to verify that those receiving benefits were eligible. She said the suspension would remain in effect until new disability legislation was enacted. Congress, suspecting widespread abuse of the disability payments program, had ordered a review of the rolls in 1980. Since 1981, almost 500,000 persons had been told they were being dropped as recipients of payments. Many of these were restored to the rolls on appeal, and the reviews were criticized in Congress and elsewhere. The House, on March 27, had voted 410 to 1 to ease the tough administrative reviews and assure continued payment of legitimate benefits.

Klansmen, Nazis Acquitted in Shooting Deaths — Six members of the Ku Klux Klan and 3 members of the American Nazi Party were found not guilty, **Apr. 13,** of federal civil rights charges growing out of the deaths of five persons in Greensboro, N. C., in 1979. An all-white jury deliberated 3 days before reaching a verdict in federal district court in Winston-Salem, N.C. Four white men and a black woman, all members of the Communist Workers Party, had been killed at the "Death to the Klan" rally in Greensboro on Nov. 3, 1979. Five of the defendants had also been acquitted of state murder and rioting charges in 1980. The government claimed that the defendants had gone to the rally to provoke a fight and that they had fired the first 11 shots in the subsequent outburst of violence. Defense lawyers argued that the defendants had gone to the rally because of their patriotic, anticommunist feelings and that they had been provoked by the other side. The government was required to prove that the defendants were motivated by racial hatred.

International

CIA Role in Nicaragua Mining Revealed — The U.S.

Central Intelligence Agency (CIA) acknowledged in April that it had participated in the mining of Nicaraguan harbors. The revelation touched off an explosion of controversy in Congress, and endangered the administration-supported packages of military aid to the government of El Salvador and to "contras" opposing the Nicaraguan regime. On **Apr. 4,** before the full role of the United States was known, the U.S. vetoed a U.N. Security Council resolution condemning the mining. On **Apr. 5,** France offered to help clear the mines. The Senate, **Apr. 5,** approved 76-19 an additional $61.75 million in military aid to El Salvador and $21 million for the anti-Sandinista rebels in Nicaragua. Pres. Reagan had originally asked for $92.8 million for El Salvador in the 1984 fiscal year. Opposing the compromise figure, Sen. Edward Kennedy (D, Mass.) had warned that the aid to El Salvador risked giving a "blank check to death squads and despotism." Reports began to appear in the press, **Apr. 6,** that CIA personnel on a ship operating in the Pacific Ocean off the Nicaraguan coast had helped Latin American nationals plant mines in the ports of Corinto and Puerto Sandino. The mining, which had begun in February, had resulted in damage to at least 8 ships, including a Soviet tanker, from 6 nations. Nicaragua, **Apr. 9,** asked the International Court of Justice to order the United States to halt the mining. The suit asked for reparations for loss of life and property and for economic disruption caused by the mining. Anticipating the move, the Reagan administration, **Apr. 8,** had announced that it would not accept the court's jurisdiction on disputes involving Latin America for 2 years. In a letter to CIA Director William Casey, written on **Apr. 9,** and made public **Apr. 11,** Sen. Barry Goldwater (R, Ariz.), chairman of the Senate Intelligence Committee, said it would be difficult to back Reagan's foreign policy "when we don't know what the hell he is doing." Calling the mining "an act of war," Goldwater added, "I don't see how we are going to explain it." Casey said, **Apr. 10,** that he had alluded to the CIA role in the mining during briefings to congressional intelligence committees. But some other senators said they had been unaware of the CIA role. The Senate, **Apr. 10,** adopted 84-12 a nonbinding resolution condemning the U.S. participation in the mining. Adolfo Calero Portocarrero, leader of one of the anti-Nicaraguan groups, said, **Apr. 11,** that the mining would continue, but he denied that the United States was involved. The Reagan administration said, **Apr. 11,** that the mining had been halted. Published reports appearing, **Apr. 11,** and thereafter said that Reagan had approved the decision to mine the ports on the recommendation of Robert McFarlane, the national security adviser. Deputy Secretary of State Kenneth Dam told the House Foreign Affairs Committee, **Apr. 11,** that collective self-defense would be the justification for the mining, but he refused to acknowledge that the United States was directly involved. The House, **Apr. 12,** by a vote of 281 to 111, joined the Senate in condemning the mining. Edward P. Boland (D, Mass.), chairman of the House Intelligence Committee, said **Apr. 12,** that the CIA had briefed the committee on the mining Jan. 31. Reagan, **Apr. 13,** invoked emergency powers under the Arms Export Control Act to give El Salvador an additional $32 million in military aid. Anti-Sandinista guerrillas based in Costa Rica and supported by the United States claimed, **Apr. 14,** that they had captured a town in Nicaragua for the first time. Senators Lawton Chiles (D, Fla.) and J. Bennett Johnston (D, La.) were on a helicopter hit by rebel gunfire near the border between Honduras and El Salvador, **Apr. 18,** but they were not injured. Newspaper reports, **Apr. 18,** confirmed that the United States had rejected Nora Astorga, who Nicaragua had proposed as ambassador to the United States. She had been linked to the killing in 1978 of an officer in the Nicaraguan National Guard who reportedly had worked with the CIA.

Reagan Backs Ban on Chemical Weapons — Pres. Reagan announced, **Apr. 4,** that the United States would soon propose a "comprehensive worldwide ban on chemical weapons." He said the USSR and Iraq had been using chemical weapons against Afghanistan and Iran, respectively, and that the United States had been forced to "maintain a limited retaliatory capability of its own" to counter the Soviet chemical-weapons arsenal. He called for strict verification measures. Reagan's announcement followed, by 6 weeks, an offer by the Soviet Union to permit inspection of the destruction of its chemical-arms facilities if a treaty banning the weapons went into effect. The Soviet news agency Tass, **Apr. 8,** published an interview with Konstantin Chernenko, general secretary of the Soviet Communist party, in which he charged that the United States used "sometimes peace-loving rhetoric" to mask its efforts to block arms control agreements and to press its bid for "military superiority." He said the world situation was "very dangerous." The U.S. Defense Department, **Apr. 10,** released the third edition of *Soviet Military Power,* which purported to show an ongoing buildup of weaponry by the USSR. In reference to the report, Defense Secretary Caspar Weinberger said that Russia was seeking "world domination." At a meeting of the Committee on Disarmament in Geneva, **Apr. 18,** Vice Pres. George Bush presented the proposed U.S. treaty providing for a comprehensive ban on chemical weapons.

U.S., Japan Agree on Beef, Citrus Imports — Long and sometimes bitter negotiations between the United States and Japan ended amicably, **Apr. 7,** when Japan agreed to increase the amounts of beef and citrus products that could be imported from the United States. The agreement was reached in Washington, D. C., between U.S. Special Trade Representative William Brock and Japanese Agriculture Minister Shinjiro Yamamura. The pacts, which replaced agreements that had expired at the end of March, would permit a gradual increase in the imports of high-grade beef and citrus fruit over a 4-year period. The United States had insisted strongly on the concessions, but the opposition of Japanese farmers had restrained the Japanese government from acting.

Chernenko Elected President of USSR — Konstantin Chernenko, general secretary of the Communist Party of the Soviet Union, added another title, **Apr. 11.** In a unanimous vote by the Supreme Soviet, Chernenko was named head of state. Officially the title was chairman of the Presidium of the Supreme Soviet. Chernenko thus followed as secretary, his two predecessors Leonid Brezhnev and Yuri Andropov, in adding the second honor. Mikhail Gorbachev, youngest member of the ruling Politburo at age 53, nominated Chernenko for the post, prompting some speculation that Gorbachev was in line to succeed the 72-year-old Chernenko.

Britain Ends Libya Ties After Shooting — Britain broke diplomatic relations with Libya in April following a violent episode at the Libyan Embassy in London. During a demonstration, **Apr. 17,** by Libyans opposed to Libyan ruler Muammar el Qaddafi, a burst of machine-gun fire from an embassy window wounded 10 of the dissidents and killed a British policewoman. British police surrounded the embassy, which the Libyans had renamed the People's Bureau, but made no attempt to attack it. Under international law, the occupants were immune from intrusion even though not all were diplomats. In Tripoli, Libya, troops and demonstrators surrounded the British Embassy. Britain, **Apr. 22,** announced its intention to break diplomatic relations with Libya and ordered the occupants of the London Embassy to leave within a week. The British acted after Qaddafi refused to cooperate in an investigation into the shootings. On **Apr. 27, 30** diplomats and other occupants of the Libyan Embassy filed out of the building and returned to Libya. On the same day, most of the remaining British officials in Tripoli returned to Britain. Diplomatic relations officially ended, **Apr. 30.**

Reagan Visits China — Pres. Reagan, who had been an outspoken critic of Chinese policies for many years, but who had shifted his position gradually during his presidency, visited China for the first time in April. He was cordially received. Reagan arrived in Peking, **Apr. 26,** to a 21-gun salute and immediately entered a series of discussions with Chinese leaders. In meetings, **Apr. 27,** between Reagan and Prime Minister Zhao Ziyang and Hu Yaobang, general secretary of the Communist Party, Reagan heard of China's concern about the deployment of U.S. missiles in Europe, and about the interventionist U.S. policy in Central America. Reagan's address on Chinese television, **Apr. 27,** was censored, to eliminate his implied criticism of the Soviet Union. The Chinese also deleted implied criticism of the Soviets from a televised interview of the president, **Apr. 28.** At a meeting between Reagan and Chinese leader Deng Ziaoping, **Apr. 29,** Deng asked Reagan to use his influence with the Republic of China (Taiwan) to speed up reunification talks, but

Reagan indicated that he did not wish to intercede in what he believed was a matter for the 2 Chinas to resolve. Reagan or his aides and the Chinese signed agreements, **Apr. 30,** that would guarantee against double taxation for American corporations operating in China, provide for new exchanges of cultural programs, and enable American companies to help build Chinese nuclear reactors. The sightseeing schedule for President and Mrs. Reagan included a visit, **Apr. 30,** to the ancient capital of Xian, where archaeologists in recent years had unearthed thousands of terra-cotta figures of soldiers at the tomb of the first emperor of China. Hundreds of thousands of people lined the streets of Shanghai to cheer the president as he concluded his visit to China, **May 1.** Returning to the United States, Reagan, **May 2,** met briefly in Fairbanks, Alaska, with Pope John Paul II, who was beginning a trip to several Asian countries, including South Korea.

General

Shuttle Crew Repairs Satellite — The crew of the U.S. space shuttle *Challenger* achieved another first in April with the repair of a damaged satellite in space. The Challenger was launched on its fifth mission, **Apr. 6,** from Cape Canaveral in Florida. On **Apr. 7,** the mission deployed a module designed to test the durability of materials in space. Attention then turned to the damaged satellite, the Solar Maximum Mission, or Solar Max, launched in 1980 to study a variety of solar phenomena. The satellite's sensors were no longer oriented properly. After one unsuccessful effort, the crew, on **Apr. 10,** caught the satellite with a robot arm and brought it into the cargo bay. George Nelson, an astronomer, and James Van Hoften, a physicist, replaced the satellite's attitude control module, which was responsible for keeping the satellite oriented properly. The satellite was returned to orbit, **Apr. 12.** The shuttle landed at Edwards Air Force base in California on **Apr. 13.**

French, Americans Link Viruses to AIDS — French and American researchers, working separately, reported in April that they had identified viruses that appeared to be the cause of acquired immune deficiency syndrome (AIDS), the disease that had stricken several thousand persons in the past few years. It was believed possible that the LAV virus, found by the French, and the American virus, HTLV-3, would prove to be the same. Physicians, responding, **Apr. 19,** to the news of the French breakthrough, were cautiously optimistic, noting that the virus had been found in blood samples of 80 to 90 percent of AIDS patients whose blood had been tested. Margaret Heckler, U.S. Secretary of Health and Human Services, announced, **Apr. 23,** that federal researchers had identified HTLV-3, and had developed a test that could reliably detect it in blood donated for various uses, including the treatment of hemophilia. The disease, which primarily affected male homosexuals and intravenous drug users, had also struck some hemophiliacs who had received blood transfusions. The American researchers thought that a vaccine would be ready for testing within 2 years.

MAY

National

Hart's Victories Keep His Hopes Alive — Sen. Gary Hart (Col.) stayed in contention for the Democratic presidential nomination in May by scoring some surprising victories over former Vice Pres. Walter Mondale. The Rev. Jesse Jackson won his first primary, **May 1,** sweeping the District of Columbia with 67 percent of the vote. Mondale won the Tennessee primary, **May 1.** Jackson won his first state primary, **May 5,** taking Louisiana in a light vote. On the same day, Mondale scored a big victory in the Texas caucuses, setting back Hart's hopes for a resurgence in the Southwest and West. But Hart recovered, winning the caucuses in his home state of Colorado, **May 7,** and defeating Mondale by narrow margins in Ohio and Indiana, **May 8,** for his first breakthroughs in northern industrial states. Mondale won, **May 8,** in North Carolina and Maryland, but the momentum gained by Hart kept the contest in doubt despite Mondale maintaining his large lead in delegates. Hart won decisively in Nebraska and Oregon **May 15.**

Senate Acts on Budget Deficits — The U.S. Senate supported the Reagan administration plan to cut federal budget deficits. A group called the Bipartisan Budget Appeal warned, **May 3,** that the nation would soon face annual deficits of $300 billion or more. The group, headed by former Commerce Secretary Peter Peterson and former Treasury Secretary C. Douglas Dillon, said that the United States was drifting toward "economic calamity." Defense Secretary Caspar Weinberger, **May 3,** gave Congress the specifics of the Pentagon's plan for cutting $13.9 billion from the defense budget. This was in response to an agreement between the White House and GOP congressional leaders on a package to reduce the deficit. By narrow margins, the Senate, **May 8 and 10,** rejected plans offered by the minority Democrats and by a group of Republican moderates that would have reduced military spending, in particular, and the federal deficit, in general, by greater amounts than the White House favored. The Senate, **May 17,** approved the administration's budget reduction plan. Providing for deficit cuts of about $142 billion through 1987, it differed with the House-approved bill, which would cut military spending more and social spending less, and which provided for reductions in deficits totaling $182 million. The Senate, **May 18,** adopted its budget resolution for fiscal 1985, 41-34. The projected deficit was $181.7 billion.

Feldstein to Step Down as Economic Adviser — Martin Feldstein announced that he was planning to resign as chairman of the President's Council of Economic Advisers. The Labor Department reported, **May 4,** that the nation's unemployment rate had held steady to 7.7 percent in April. Major banks, **May 8,** boosted their prime lending rates from 12 to 12.5 percent. Fearing that rising interest rates could have a negative impact on the electorate, administration spokesmen criticized Federal Reserve Board policies. Secretary of the Treasury Donald Regan, **May 9,** challenged as misguided the board's concern about a possible upswing in inflation. Feldstein, another lightening rod for administration criticism, announced **May 9,** that he would soon resume his teaching career at Harvard. In keeping with his previously expressed concerns about high deficits and his other public departures from administration points of view, Feldstein in stepping down endorsed the restrictive monetary policies of the Federal Reserve Board. He said his departure was not due to differences between himself and the administration. Pres. Raúl Alfonsín of Argentina said, **May 10,** that rising U.S. interest rates were "madness" and could "jeopardize Argentina's social peace." Bouncing back from a sharply depressed state in March, housing starts rose in April by 19.3 percent, the Commerce Department said, **May 16.** The Labor Department reported, **May 22,** that the consumer price index had risen 0.5 percent in April. The Commerce Department said, **May 30,** that the U.S. trade deficit set another record in April at $12.2 billion. The department said, **May 31,** that the Index of Leading Economic Indicators had risen only 0.5 percent in April, evidence that the economic recovery was slowing.

Veterans, Companies Settle Agent Orange Suit — American veterans of the Vietnam war reached an out-of-court settlement, **May 7,** with 7 chemical companies in their class-action suit relating to the herbicide called Agent Orange. Although the suit involved some 15,000 veterans and members of their families, many more persons might ultimately get a share of the $180 billion made available for compensation by the companies under the agreement. The veterans, in bringing suit, claimed that dioxin, a by-product of the herbicide that had been used as a defoliant in Vietnam, had caused cancer as well as nerve, liver, and skin damage, and had also resulted in miscarriages and birth defects. In the settlement, the companies made no acknowledgement of culpability. A court-approved panel was to authorize disbursements to claimants from a trust fund that was established immediately. The settlement, believed to be the largest in the history of product-liability law, left open the question of culpability by the federal government.

U.S. Props Up Continental Illinois Bank — U.S. banking regulators acted in May to restore public faith in Continental Illinois Corp., a Chicago bank holding company. Rumors of financial difficulties had started a run on the bank's deposits on **May 10.** The bank had large loans outstanding to financially troubled Latin American countries, and some of its domestic loans had been adversely affected by the re-

cent economic recession. In announcing the federal package on **May 17,** bank chairman David Taylor said that the bank was not on the verge of failure. He said it would seek a merger partner to help build confidence in its ability to attract deposits. As part of the confidence-building arrangement, the Federal Deposit Insurance Corp. announced that it would guarantee all bank deposits, not just those up to $100,000. The FDIC said it would also lend the bank $1.5 billion. The Federal Reserve Board said it would become a lender of last resort to meet any "extraordinary liquidity requirements" at the bank.

U.S. Found Negligent in Atomic-Tests Case — A federal judge in Salt Lake City held, **May 10,** that the U.S. government had been negligent in its above-ground testing of nuclear weapons in Nevada from 1951 to 1962. He awarded compensation of $2.66 million to one living cancer victim and to the families of 8 others who had contracted cancer and died. In a 10th case, damages were yet to be determined. The U.S. district judge, Bruce Jenkins, dismissed 14 similar claims. Several hundred more suits have been filed. Jenkins held that the Tort Claims Act, which grants the government immunity from actions of high-level officials, did not protect the government from damages in this situation because it had failed to meets its stated aim of protecting the public from excessive radioactive contamination. He said that the government had not given adequate warning to residents, mostly in southwestern Utah, who lived downwind from the explosion sites. He also found that the government had not adequately measured the amount of radioactivity in the area after the tests. Federal lawyers had previously said they would appeal any adverse rulings.

MX Barely Survives Vote in House — The U.S. House nearly killed the MX missile program in May, and then approved a scaled-down version for the controversial weapon. On **May 10 and 11,** the General Accounting Office issued 2 reports questioning the ability of the MX to reach targets in the Soviet Union and to destroy newly-hardened silos containing Soviet missiles. The GAO said the ability of the MX to accomplish its mission "may have been impaired." The GAO also said that decisions on basing the missile had been influenced by shortcomings in its range. The House, **May 16,** defeated, 218-212, a move to eliminate all financing for construction of new MX missiles in the fiscal year beginning Oct. 1. The House then approved, 229-199, the financing of 15 missiles, half the total approved by the Armed Services Committee. Furthermore, the money could not be spent until April 1985, and even then only if the Russians had not returned to the arms-control talks in Geneva. The Senate had not yet voted on the missile.

House Unit Reports on Briefing Papers — A U.S. House subcommittee issued a report that linked William Casey, director of the Central Intelligence Agency, to documents taken from the Carter White House during the 1980 presidential campaign. Earlier, U.S. District Court Judge Harold Greene, **May 14,** ordered Attorney General William French Smith to name an independent counsel (formerly called a special prosecutor) to investigate the removal of the documents. Some of the documents had been used to brief Ronald Reagan before his debate with Pres. Jimmy Carter in 1980. Other White House documents had also been found in the Reagan campaign files. The Justice Department reported in February that it had found no "credible evidence" of wrongdoing in its own investigation. Greene said, however, that allegations of possible crimes warranted further investigation. A 3-judge panel of the U.S. Court of Appeals issued a temporary stay of Greene's order, **May 18.** The report of the Democratic majority on the House subcommittee said, **May 23,** that the "better evidence" indicated that Casey, then manager of the Reagan campaign, was the conduit for entry of the Carter documents into the campaign. In also urging the appointment of an independent counsel, the subcommittee majority said that it had not been possible to determine who had taken the documents from the White House. Republicans on the subcommittee refused to sign the majority report. The U.S. Court of Appeals in the District of Columbia ruled, **June 25,** that the courts could not require the attorney general to name an independent counsel to investigate the incident.

Senate Committee Rejects Reagan Nominee — The Senate Foreign Relations Committee, **May 15,** took the rare step of rejecting a presidential nominee. By a vote of 11 to 6, it refused to approve the nomination of Leslie Lenkowsky to be deputy director of the U.S. Information Agency. Lenkowsky, who had been acting deputy director of the agency since September 1983, had testified to the committee that he had been unaware, until it was made public, of a "blacklist" containing names of people who were not to be considered as overseas speakers. A report by the committee staff said, however, that Lenkowsky had "been actively involved" in reviewing the blacklist. Several former and present officials of the agency disputed Lenkowsky's statements on the blacklist and on other matters. Sen. Charles Percy (R, Ill.), chairman of the committee and one of 3 Republicans who joined all the Democrats in voting against the nomination, said, "I am convinced that Mr. Lenkowsky was an active participant in the blacklisting process."

Unknown Vietnam Casualty Honored — Pres. Reagan led a tribute, **May 28**, Memorial Day, to the only unidentified U.S. serviceman to die in the Vietnam War. He was buried in a state funeral at Arlington National Cemetery alongside fallen soldiers from World Wars I and II and Korea. Reagan awarded the soldier the Medal of Honor. Advances in forensic medicine had resulted in the identification of almost all casualties of the war, and the Pentagon destroyed all records that might have provided clues to the identity of the man buried at Arlington.

International

Syria Holds 3 Israeli "Saboteurs" in Lebanon — Syrian forces, **May 1**, seized 3 Israeli officials who had crossed Syrian lines in northern Lebanon. Syria, in confirming the incident, **May 2**, charged that they were "saboteurs who tried to infiltrate the area held by our forces. . . ." Israeli Prime Minister Yitzhak Shamir warned Syria, **May 2**, that Israel would "regard with great severity any Syrian attempt to make false accusations against them." The 3 were members of Israel's informal embassy in Lebanon. A Syrian official said, **May 3**, that the 3 had admitted being on a spying mission. A new unity cabinet met in Lebanon for the first time, **May 10**. Named by premier-designate Rashid Karami, it consisted of 5 Christians and 5 Muslims, and reflected all the major sectarian divisions and warring factions.

Duarte Elected President of El Salvador — José Napoleón Duarte, the candidate of the Christian Democratic party and a political moderate, was elected president of strife-torn El Salvador. In the runoff election, he defeated Roberto d'Aubuisson of the right-wing National Republican Alliance (Arena). The latter had been implicated in deathsquad killings, a charge that he denied. Sen. Jesse Helms (R, N.C.) wrote to Pres. Reagan, **May 2**, demanding the dismissal of Thomas Pickering, the U.S. ambassador to El Salvador. Helms asserted that Pickering had become involved in the election on behalf of Duarte, which Helms called "an unwarranted interference in the internal affairs of a sovereign nation." Reagan and members of Congress, **May 3**, defended Pickering, and White House spokesman Larry Speakes said that the administration was not taking sides in the election. The Washington Post, in a story datelined **May 3**, said that the United States had worked in Duarte's behalf, funneling money through a West German organization. Duarte, in claiming victory on **May 7**, the day after the voting, called on Salvadorans of both the left and the right to help him bring peace to the nation. He said he would not accept assistance from U.S. troops to help put down the leftist-led rebellion. Helms charged **May 8**, that the United States had impugned d'Aubuisson's character to help Duarte, and d'Aubuisson charged, **May 9**, that Duarte was a "puppet" of the U.S. Central Intelligence Agency. The Arena party claimed irregularities in the voting and refused to continue to participate in the vote count. In a speech, **May 9**, Reagan defended his Central American policies; he warned that Cuba and Nicaragua would win the civil war in El Salvador unless the United States provided more military aid. Defending the administration's covert war against the Sandinista regime in Nicaragua, he characterized the U.S.-backed "Contras" as freedom fighters. Rep. Michael Barnes (D, Md.), responding to Reagan, said that administration policies relied too much on military solutions at the expense of diplomacy. The House of Representatives, **May 10**, approved 212-208 further military aid to El Salvador with no

conditions attached relating to abuses of human rights. The International Court of Justice, **May 10**, voted 15-0 to order the United States to stop any actions to blockade or mine the Nicaraguan ports. When U.S. involvement in the mining became generally known in April, leaders of both parties were sharply critical. The interim decision, like the final decision yet to come, was nonbinding. The U.S. judge joined in the unanimous decision. El Salvador's election council declared, **May 11**, that Duarte had won the election with 54 percent of the vote. Arena refused to accept the results. In an article datelined **May 11**, *The New York Times* said the CIA had spent $2.1 million on the Salvadoran election, with almost $1 million going to Duarte. An unnamed administration official said that the effort was made because of the fear that a d'Aubuisson victory would prompt Congress to cut off military aid to the country. Mexican President Miguel de la Madrid Hurtado visited the United States, **May 14-17**, and warned both Reagan and Congress that U.S. military involvement in Central America increased the danger of a general war in the region. Costa Rica, Nicaragua's southern neighbor, signed a border agreement with the Sandinista regime, **May 15**, aimed at reducing tensions between the 2 countries, and reducing the number of anti-Sandinista "Contras" who had been crossing the border. Amnesty International, **May 21**, accused the Salvadoran government of "blatant failure" to investigate the deaths of thousands of persons. Duarte visited the United States, **May 19-22**, to meet with Reagan and members of Congress. He appealed to the latter for more military aid. Duarte pledged to end deathsquad activity, but said he would not accept aid tied to improvement in the human-rights area, saying such conditions would be "degrading." In a news conference, **May 22**, Reagan said that he was not considering sending U.S. troops to Central America. A Salvadoran court, **May 24**, found 5 former national guardsmen guilty of the 1980 murders of 3 U.S. nuns and a U.S. lay worker. The House, **May 24**, reaffirmed its support for El Salvador, approving $61.75 million in emergency military aid, but rejected further financing through the CIA of Nicaraguan rebel groups. A move toward unity among "Contras" opposing the Nicaraguan regime was reported, **May 30**. The group based in Costa Rica voted to unite with one in Honduras, but Edén Pastora Gómez, military leader of the Costa Rican group, opposed the union, which was supported by the CIA, because of the influence of supporters of former Nicaraguan dictator Anastasio Somoza in the other group.

Soviet Dissident Sakharov Begins Hunger Strike — Andrei Sakharov, a Soviet dissident, began a hunger strike, **May 2**, to publicize his demand for medical treatment abroad for his wife, Dr. Yelena Bonner. Both suffered from heart ailments, but they objected to receiving medical treatment in Gorky, where Sakharov was confined. Sakharov, a nuclear physicist, received the Nobel Peace Prize in 1975. Tass, the official Soviet news agency, charged, **May 4**, that Sakharov and his wife had planned a "provocative operation" as part of an anti-Soviet campaign in the West. Bonner said that on **May 7**, her husband had been taken from his apartment to an unknown location. Governments, academic leaders, and human-rights groups in the West protested against the treatment of the Sakharovs. The U.S. State Department, **May 16**, called the Soviet government's attitude toward them "inhumane and virtually incomprehensible." The Soviet government newspaper *Izvestia* hinted, **May 20**, that criminal charges might be filed against Bonner for anti-Soviet activities.

Iran, Iraq Attack Ships in Persian Gulf — The war between Iran and Iraq took a dangerous turn in May as both countries attacked ships in the Persian Gulf. The escalation threatened to embroil other nations in the war and endangered the flow of oil to the rest of the world. In an interview, **May 3**, Iraqi President Saddam Hussein, apparently referring to the mysterious explosion on a Saudi tanker a week earlier, urged "my Arab brothers to avoid chartering their ships to foreign companies that load oil at Kharg Island." The island is Iran's oil-loading terminal, situated near the head of the gulf. Another Saudi tanker leaving the island was hit by an Iraqi missile, **May 7**. Unidentified planes attacked 2 Kuwaiti oil tankers, **May 12** and **13**, and a Saudi tanker, **May 16**. Meanwhile, shipping insurance rates were rising in response to the attacks. *The New York Times* reported, **May 16**, that the United States had offered air cover to the ships of friendly gulf-area nations. The 6-member Gulf Cooperation Council decided, **May 17**, not to seek direct U.S. assistance for the time being. They condemned "Iranian aggression" against their shipping. A Greek cargo ship was sunk, **May 19**, after being attacked by Iraqi jets. The Arab League, **May 20**, condemned Iran for its attacks. Pres. Reagan, **May 21**, wrote to King Fahd of Saudi Arabia affirming U.S. support in the event of a military conflict with Iran. The State Department said, **May 23**, that the administration intended to revive a plan to sell shoulder-fired Stinger antiaircraft missiles to Saudi Arabia. After a 5-day lull, Iraq and Iran renewed their attacks on shipping. The administration said, **May 28**, that 400 Stingers had been sent to Saudi Arabia.

Panama Elects President — By a narrow margin, Panama's voters in May chose Nicolás Ardito Barletta as their next president. The nation's first presidential election in .16 years took place, **May 6**, after a bitter campaign. The leading contenders were Barletta, a former vice president of the World Bank, and Anulfo Arias Madrid, 83 years old, a 3-time former president who had been overthrown by coups all 3 times. Barletta was viewed as the candidate of the nation's military forces. After some confusion and charges of fraud, Barletta was declared the winner, **May 16**, by only 1,713 votes out of some 600,000 cast.

USSR Refuses to Compete in Olympic Games — The Soviet Union, **May 8**, announced that it would not participate in the summer Olympic games in Los Angeles. In an announcement, the Soviet National Olympic Committee referred to a "cavalier attitude of the U.S. authorities to the Olympic Charter," and said that the U.S. government "does not intend to insure the security of all sportsmen. . . ." The committee also said that "extremist organizations" in the United States had made "undisguised threats" against Russian officials and athletes and were planning anti-Soviet demonstrations in Los Angeles. An organization in California had planned to protest the Russian participation and had predicted that many Soviet-bloc athletes would defect. The U.S. State Department, **May 8**, said the Soviet decision was "a blatant political action for which there is no justification." William Simon, president of the U.S. Olympic Committee, said, **May 8**, that the decision was a "tragedy for all the athletes who worked so hard." Within the next few weeks, other Soviet-bloc nations, including such athletic powerhouses as East Germany and Cuba, followed the Russian lead, but other nations with communist systems, including China and Yugoslavia, said they would compete. Speculation as to the Soviet motives included the possibility that the nonparticipation was in response to the U.S. withdrawal from the 1980 games in Moscow in protest against the Soviet invasion of Afghanistan. It was also suggested that the Soviet Union wished to embarrass Pres. Reagan during his reelection campaign. Despite efforts to persuade the Russians to change their minds, the chairman of the Soviet Olympic committee said, **May 14**, that the decision was "irrevocable." He repeated earlier allegations and added that the Reagan administration was planning to use "psychotropic chemicals to affect the nervous system"to induce athletes to defect.

Filipinos Opposing Marcos Gain in Election — Opponents of President Ferdinand Marcos gained ground in the election of members of the National Assembly, **May 14**. Marcos had been under intense criticism throughout the country because of alleged abuses of power and because of the mysterious circumstances surrounding the killing of opposition leader Benigno Aquino in August 1983. In the outgoing assembly, Marcos controlled all but 13 of the 200 seats. As returns came in slowly, it appeared that his opponents would henceforth control about one third of the seats. The Marcos forces did badly in Manila, where Imelda Marcos, wife of the president and a possible successor, was governor. The military reported, **May 16**, that at least 91 people had been killed in election-related violence. Opponents accused Marcos of using public funds to finance his campaign. Marcos claimed, **May 20**, that the election had given his government a "new mandate."

USSR Reports More Armed Subs Off U.S. Coasts — Marshall Dmitri Ustinov, the defense minister of the Soviet Union, announced, **May 20**, that the USSR had increased the number of submarines carrying nuclear missiles off the coasts of the United States. He said the missiles could hit U.S. targets within 8 to 10 minutes. Ustinov said the subs were one of the countermeasures taken in response to the deployment of U.S. intermediate-range nuclear missiles in Europe. He added that the Soviet Union would also increase its European arsenal of nuclear weapons in response to the NATO buildup. At a White House press conference, **May 22**, Pres. Reagan discounted the importance of the added submarines, saying, "If I thought there was some reason to be concerned about them, I wouldn't be sleeping in this house tonight."

General

Mayan Burial Chamber Found — The discovery of an undamaged Mayan tomb is expected to add much new knowledge about the great civilization that flourished in Middle America 1,500 years ago. A team from the University of Texas and the government of Guatamala discovered the tomb at Río Azul in Guatamala on **May 15**. The painted burial chamber dates from about A.D. 450, during the Early Classic period of Mayan civilization. The skeleton, believed to be that of a member of the ruling class, was surrounded by many objects, including 15 intact ceramic vessels. One of these had a screw-on top, the first of its kind found among pre-Columbian artifacts. Hieroglyphics on the walls may reveal the social conditions of the period. The Río Azul site also contains previously-excavated temples, palaces, and a ball court.

Disasters — Indian officials reported, **May 2**, that a dysentary epidemic caused by contaminated drinking water in the state of West Bengal had killed 911 persons, and that 20,780 had been reported as ill . . . A disease possibly caused by a virus had proved fatal to 252 young children in Feira de Santana, Brazil, local health officials said, **May 13**.

JUNE

National

Unemployment Rate Continues to Fall — The Labor Department reported, **June 1**, that the unemployment rate had continued to fall in May, to 7.4 percent. The Federal Reserve Board reported, **June 15**, that industrial production advanced 0.4 percent in May. The U.S. balance of payments of deficit for the first quarter, $19.41 billion, set a record, the Commerce Department reported, **June 18**. The department said, **June 19**, that housing starts fell 10.5 percent in May. The Labor Department reported, **June 22**, that the consumer price index edged upward 0.2 percent in May. The country's major banks, **June 25**, raised their prime interest rate from 12.5 percent to 13 percent, the highest level since October 1982. Pres Reagan said he could see "no excuse" for the increase. During the last week in June, the U.S. dollar set or approached record highs in relation to major foreign currencies. The Index of Leading Economic Indicators fell 0.1 percent in May, the Commerce Department said, **June 29**.

Mondale Wins Enough Delegates for Nomination — Former Vice Pres. Walter Mondale claimed victory in June in his long struggle with Sen. Gary Hart (Col.) for the Democratic presidential nomination. Mondale, who was already far ahead in total delegates, easily won the key New Jersey primary on **June 5**. He also won in West Virginia the same day, while Hart was winning in California, New Mexico, and South Dakota. When, on the morning of **June 6**, Mondale appeared to be short of the 1,967 votes required for the nomination, he called a number of uncommitted delegates and won over enough, he said, to declare victory at a press conference in St. Paul, Minn., at noon. Independent tabulations supported his claim. United Press International reported that Mondale had 1,969 delegates, Hart 1,220, and the Rev. Jesse Jackson 373. Neither Hart nor Jackson withdrew from the race. A compilation by *Congressional Quarterly* showed that in the primary voting Mondale had captured 39 percent of the popular vote, Hart 36 percent, and Jackson 18 percent. Mondale began meeting with prospective vice presidential running mates at his home in North Oaks, Minn., on **June 21**, when Mayor Tom Bradley of Los Angeles came to see him. On **June 23**, Mondale met with

Sen. Lloyd Bentsen (Tex.) and San Francisco Mayor Dianne Feinstein. In St. Paul, **June 25,** Sen. Edward Kennedy (D, Mass.) endorsed Mondale for president, and Kennedy was instrumental in arranging a meeting between Mondale and Hart in New York City, **June 26.** They affirmed that they were united in their determination to defeat Pres. Ronald Reagan in November. The party's Rules Committee, **June 26,** rejected a plea by Jackson that he be granted more delegates to reflect his share of the popular vote in the primaries. But the committee agreed to ask the convention to create a commission to promoted fairness in delegate-selection procedures. Jackson, **June 28,** repudiated anti-Semitic remarks by the Rev. Louis Farrakhan, a Black Muslim leader, who had said, **June 24,** that Judaism was a "gutter religion" and that Israel was an "outlaw" state. On **June 28,** Mondale interviewed Mayor W. Wilson Goode of Philadelphia, another possible running mate.

Congress Backs Plan to Raise Drinking Age — Responding to a public outcry against deaths caused by drunk drivers, Congress acted to bring pressure on the states to raise, to 21, the age at which their residents could drink alcoholic beverages legally. The House, **June 7,** and the Senate, **June 27,** approved a bill that would penalize, by withholding some federal highway construction funds, those states that failed to set their legal drinking age at 21. The bill went to conference committee for resolution of differences between the House and Senate versions. Statistics had shown that a disproportionate share of highway fatalities and injuries were caused by young drivers who had been drinking. Pres. Ronald Reagan supported the bill, but some conservatives regarded it as an intrusion into the prerogatives of the states. The House, **June 28,** approved the Senate version of the bill. Reagan signed the bill **July 17.**

Immigration Bill Approved in House — The U.S. House approved an immigration bill that would seek to control the flow of immigrants, chiefly Hispanics, across the nation's southern borders. Pres. Reagan, **June 14,** endorsed the bill before Congress, saying that "we've lost control of our own borders, and no nation can do that and survive." The House, **June 20,** approved a compromise bill, but by only 216-211. The bill, which would have to be reconciled in conference committee with the one passed by the Senate in 1983, would provide legal status, or amnesty, to millions of aliens who had established U.S. residence before 1982. The Senate bill put the date at Jan. 1, 1980. Both Senate and House bills required employers to demand documents from job applicants to verify citizenship or authorization to work in the United States. Hispanics opposed the bill, fearing the sanctions against employers would discourage them from hiring any Hispanics, legal residents or not. The AFL-CIO turned against the bill when an amendment was approved that would permit farmers to bring aliens into the United States as temporary workers to harvest fruit and vegetables.

Congress Approves Tax-Increase Package — Congress, **June 27,** approved a package of budget cuts and tax increases designed to make a "down payment" against the enormous budget deficits projected for the next few years. The Senate, 83-15, and the House 268-155, endorsed a package worked out by congressional leaders in conference committee. The complex bill, containing hundreds of provisions, was expected to raise $50 billion in taxes and reduce spending by $11 billion. The bill diminished the value of income averaging, increased from 15 to 18 years the write-off period for real estate, barred the use of certain housing bonds to avoid estate and gift taxes, extended the 3 percent telephone-services tax, and increased liquor taxes. On the other hand, the federal cigarette tax was reduced from 16 to 8 cents. Fees paid to doctors under Medicare were frozen for 15 months.

International

Saudis Down Iranian Jets — Saudi Arabia took a step toward involvement in the long war between Iran and Iraq when it shot down 2 Iranian jet fighters. The U.N. Security Council, **June 1,** adopted 13-0 an Arab sponsored resolution than condemned Iranian attacks on commercial shipping in the Persian Gulf. The Saudis, using U.S.-made F-15s, downed the 2 Iranian planes near the Saudi port of Jubail, **June 5.** The official Saudi news agency said that the Iranian planes had ignored a warning to turn back. A lull in the at-

tacks on shipping ended, **June 24,** when Iraqi planes struck a Greek tanker at Iran's Kharg Island oil-loading terminal. The tanker received only light damage, but a Swiss tanker was hit and severely damaged by Iraqi planes, **June 27.** Eight crewmen were killed, 3 were wounded, and 7 were missing.

Reagan Eases Position on Soviet Summit — Pres. Reagan modified his position with respect to meeting with Soviet leaders to discuss arms control and other issues. The delicate issue of U.S. missiles in Europe was further complicated, **June 1,** when the Dutch cabinet voted to postpone until Nov. 1, 1985, a decision on whether to deploy U.S. cruise missiles. The Dutch had made a commitment to allow deployment of 48 missiles on their soil. Failure by the Dutch to deploy could further encourage the USSR not to resume arms-control talks. The U.S. Army, **June 10,** successfully tested a missile system designed to destroy incoming intercontinental ballistic warheads. Soviet leader Konstantin Chernenko, **June 11,** urged the United States "without delay" to negotiate a treaty that would ban the development and use of anti-satellite weapons. Sens. Howard Baker, (R, Tenn.) and Charles Percy (R, Ill.) **June 12,** urged Reagan to meet regularly with Chernenko. At a news conference, **June 14,** Reagan eased his conditions for holding a summit. He no longer would insist, he said, that a summit must be preceded by careful preparations and deal with specific issues. He said he was "willing to meet and talk any time" with the Soviets. Reagan denied that he had softened his opposition because of the approach of the presidential election. A spokesman for the Kremlin said, **June 14,** that the Soviet Union favored a summit conference on important issues dividing the two countries. The USSR offered, **June 29,** to begin talks with the United States in the fall on banning weapons in outer space. The U.S. State Department said it was willing but wanted the talks broadened to include other weapons systems.

U.S. Envoy Reported to be Murder Target — An alleged plot to kill the U.S. ambassador to El Salvador added to the intrigue in Central America in June. José Napoleón Duarte, after being sworn in as president of El Salvador, **June 1,** declared his support for human rights and his opposition to abuses of authority and death-squad activity. He said his nation was a "focal point in the struggle between the big world power blocs." U.S. Secretary of State George Shultz attended the inauguration and then flew to Managua for a surprise meeting with Daniel Ortega, a leader of the leftist regime in Nicaragua. Nicaragua's foreign minister, Miguel d'Escoto Brockmann, said, **June 2,** that his government was eager to begin talks with the United States, but he expressed concern that Shultz's visit was a "publicity stunt." Five former national guardsmen were sentenced, **June 18,** to 30 years in prison for the murders in 1980 of 4 U.S. churchwomen. On **June 20,** the Sandinista government in Nicaragua charged that a Roman Catholic priest, the Rev. Luis Amado Pena, had supplied explosives to rebels fighting the regime. It said that Pena was part of a plot to establish an "internal front" inside Nicaragua. The *New York Times* reported, **June 23,** that right-wing Salvadorans, including Arena party leader Roberto D'Aubuisson, had plotted to murder U.S. Ambassador Thomas Pickering. The story said that ambassador at large Vernon Walters had been sent to El Salvador to warn the plotters not to carry out their plan. The plot reportedly developed after Sen. Jesse Helms (R, N.C.) made it known in May that the United States was backing moderate opponents of D'Aubuisson in the presidential election. D'Aubuisson came to the United States, **June 25,** and in a meeting with 12 U.S. senators, **June 27,** denied involvement in any such plot. The Senate, meanwhile, voted 88-1, **June 25,** to delete $21 million in additional military aid for rebels seeking to overthrow the Nicaraguan government. That settled the issue for the current fiscal year, the House having already taken similar action. House Speaker Thomas P. O'Neill (D, Mass.) said that the Senate's action "should bring to a close U.S. support for the war in Nicaragua."

Reagan Visits Ancestral Irish Home — Pres. Reagan came to Ireland in June, and was welcomed by modest crowds and by protestors. He received an honorary doctorate of law from the University College in Galway, **June 2.** He visited Ballyporeen, where his great-grandfather Michael

Regan was baptized in 1829. At a state banquet, Prime Minister Garret FitzGerald of Ireland said that the Irish people wanted the problems of Central America to be resolved peacefully by the people of the region. Addressing the Irish Parliament in Dublin, **June 4**, Reagan indicated his desire to discuss the renunciation of force with the Soviet Union. Crowds who turned out to see Reagan fell short of organizers' expectations at each stop. Protestors, numbering as many as 5,000 in Dublin, also came out to demonstrate against U.S. policies in Central America. Security measures taken by the Irish to protect Reagan included the deployment of surface-to-air missiles.

Hundreds Die in Assault in Sikh Shrine — A long period of rising tensions between Sikh extremists and the government of India culminated in a day of violent bloodletting, **June 6**. The tragedy evolved from a complex rivalry among Sikh factions in their stronghold, the state of Punjab. The slaying of a Sikh extremist in April had been followed by a series of reprisal killings. Attempts by the Indian government to control the violence led to threats by Sikh militants to blockade all water, power, and grain supplies from Punjab to the rest of India. The Sikhs believed that Punjab was being exploited economically by the rest of the country. Eleven people died, **June 1**, in a gun battle between police and militants at the Golden Temple in Amritsar, Punjab, the holiest Sikh shrine. The police, **June 2**, surrounded the temple, and Prime Minister Indira Gandhi warned that the government would not yield to violence and terrorism. Jarnail Singh Bhindranwale, leader of the Sikh extremists, said, **June 3**, that his followers would "fight to the death" if the army tried to enter the temple. But the army, using mortars, antitank rockets, and machine guns, moved into the temple on **June 6**. After a daylong battle, the army ended all resistance, but at a cost of more than 300 lives, including those of 48 soldiers. Bhindranwale was among the dead. About 240 persons were injured, and the army took 450 prisoners. Such sectarian violence was not new to India, and in fact it followed by only a few weeks a period in which 228 persons died in fighting between Hindus and Muslims in Bombay and in the state of Maharashtra. In the week after the attack on the Golden Temple, about 1,200 Sikhs in the army mutinied or deserted. Estimates of the death toll during the rebellion ranged from 450 to 1,200.

Leaders Mark 40th Anniversary of D-Day — Leaders of 8 nations participated, **June 6**, in ceremonies commemorating the 40th anniversary of D-Day—June 6, 1944—when Allied armies landed on the beaches of Normandy in Nazi-held France during World War II. Pres. Ronald Reagan spoke at Pointe du Hoc, where 225 U.S. Rangers—135 of whom died—scaled cliffs to knock out a German battery. He acknowledged the importance of the Soviet contribution to the war effort, but he noted that the USSR, which did not participate in the ceremonies, had kept its troops in "the center of this continent. . . They are still there, uninvited, unwanted, unyielding. . ." Reagan also spoke at Omaha Beach, site of an American cemetery. At Utah Beach, French President François Mitterand paid tribute to the 3,500 soldiers who died on D-Day and to the 30,000 killed and 20,000 wounded during the Normandy campaign. Many veterans of the invasion attended the observation. Mitterand also honored the Germans who died, adding, "The enemies of yesterday are now reconciled."

Questions on Sakharov's Health Persist — It was reported by a senior U.S. official, **June 7**, that the Soviet Union had assured the United States that dissident physicist Andrei Sakharov had not died. Assurances were also given that his wife, Dr. Yelena Bonner, was well. The USSR had previously rejected rumors of Sakharov's death as anti-Soviet propaganda. Concern over the condition of the couple had become widespread in the West after Sakharov began a hunger strike in May to underscore his wish that his wife receive medical attention in the West. Arriving in the Soviet Union, **June 20**, French Pres. François Mitterand asked about Sakharov, but the Soviet leader Konstantin Chernenko refused to discuss the subject. At a dinner for Mitterand, **June 21**, Chernenko said, "We shall not allow anyone to interfere in our internal affairs."

Leaders of Industrial Nations Meet — Presidents and prime ministers of 7 major industrial nations met in London, **June 7-9**. The 10th annual summit produced little of substance and some discord over interest rates. Leaders of other nations indicated their belief that high U.S. interest rates could abort the international economic recovery, but the final communique did not fix any blame on the United States. The leaders pledged to help poor countries pay their debts. During the meeting, Canada's Prime Minister Pierre Trudeau reportedly clashed with Pres. Ronald Reagan over whether the United States was doing enough to promote détente with the Soviet Union.

Bulgarians Tied to Plot Against Pope — A report written by Italian State Prosecutor Antonio Albano and made public in June linked the Bulgarian secret service to the plot to assassinate Pope John Paul II in 1981. Excerpts from the report, published in the *New York Times*, **June 10**, included recommendations that 3 Bulgarians and 6 Turks be indicted in the alleged conspiracy. The Turks included Mehmet Ali Agca, who had shot the pope, and whose testimony provided much of the basis for the proposed indictments. The report was believed to reflect the views of Judge Ilario Martella, who had conducted the inquiry into the assassination attempt. The report stopped short of suggesting involvement by the Soviet Union in the plot. The *Times* article said that the report contained evidence of another plot to kill Polish union leader Lech Walesa.

Lebanese Parliament Approves New Cabinet — Lebanon put its new government in place in June, but not before another violent day on **June 11**, when more than 100 persons were killed and some 250 were wounded in an exchange of shelling and gunfire between Christian and Muslim militiamen. On **June 12**, the parliament approved Premier Rashid Karami and his "national unity" cabinet. Although the parliament refused Karami's request to govern by decree, he was granted emergency powers for 9 months. On **June 23**, Karami announced that the army would be reorganized under a new commander and would be overseen by a 6-member military council representing leading religious groups. The plan sought to create parity between Christians and Muslims within the army. In a prisoner exchange, **June 28**, Syria delivered to Israel 3 soldiers captured in Lebanon and 3 diplomats seized May 1 after they drove into Syrian-controlled territory in Lebanon. Israel returned 291 Syrian soldiers.

Turner Becomes Prime Minister of Canada — John Napier Turner, the new leader of the Liberal Party, became Canada's 17th prime minister in June. He succeeded Pierre Elliott Trudeau, who had served as prime minister, with one short interruption, since 1968. Trudeau had previously announced his decision to step down. At the Liberal leadership convention in Ottawa, **June 16**, Turner was chosen as the new leader of the party on the second ballot. Between 1968 and 1975, he had served as solicitor general, justice minister, and finance minister. He subsequently became a corporate lawyer in Toronto. After being chosen as the Liberal leader, Turner, in a press conference, expressed concern over moves toward protectionism in the United States, and called for a bilateral agreement with the United States to reduce acid-rain pollution. Turner was sworn in, **June 30**. On **July 9**, Turner called a general election for September 4.

Jackson Wins Freedom for 48 Prisoners — Jesse Jackson, a candidate for the Democratic presidential nomination, succeeded in persuading Cuban Premier Fidel Castro to free 48 prisoners from Cuban jails in June. During his Central American and Caribbean trip, Jackson met in Panama, **June 23**, with Panamanian President Jorge Illueca. In Panama, **June 24**, he met with 4 representatives of the Salvadoran rebels, and on **June 25** he flew to San Salvador to meet with Salvadoran President José Napoleón Duarte. Jackson went to Cuba, **June 25**, where he was greeted at the Havana airport by Castro. After 8 hours of discussions with Castro, Jackson, **June 27**, announced the release of 22 Americans and 26 Cubans. It was believed that most of the Americans were being held on drug charges. Jackson and Castro called for normalization of relations between the United States and Cuba and endorsed peace negotiations to end military conflicts in Central America. Castro indicated willingness to discuss the return to Cuba of hundreds of Cubans being held in the United States since Castro permitted them to migrate to Florida from the Cuban port of Mariel in 1980. Jackson went to Nicaragua, **June 27**, and on **June 28**, he praised the leftist Sandinista regime and predicted that it would win "final victory" over insurgents supported by the United States. Jackson returned to Havanna, **June 28**, and then came to the United States with the freed prisoners.

General

U.S. Death Toll in Tornadoes Heavy — At least 120 persons had been killed by tornadoes in the United States by mid-June, according to the National Severe Storms Forecast Center. The tornado toll for all of 1983 had been 34. Some 50 tornadoes struck the Midwest, **June 8**, killing at least 16 persons. Nine died in the small town of Barneveld, Wis.

Shuttle Launching Aborted — The maiden flight of the space shuttle *Discovery* was aborted 4 seconds before its scheduled takeoff, **June 26**. The malfunctioning of an engine fuel valve stopped the countdown and prevented the launch even after the main rocket engines had begun to ignite. The *Discovery*, the third shuttle in the U.S. fleet, had been scheduled to lift off from Cape Canaveral, Fla., on **June 25**, but a failure in its backup navigating computer forced a one-day postponement just about 30 minutes short of the takeoff time. The last-minute shutdown on **June 26**, was only the third in the history of the U.S. manned space program. A few minutes later, while the 6 astronauts were still in the craft, a fire broke out near the faulty engine. Jets of water, ejected from within the launch pad, extinguished the fire quickly, and the astronauts left the spacecraft unharmed.

Disasters — At least 50 persons were killed southeast of Luanda, Angola, **June 18**, when a train traveling at great speed crashed.

JULY

National

Democrats Nominate Mondale, Ferraro — The Democratic Party nominated former Vice President Walter F. Mondale (Minn.) for president in July. Mondale, in a historic move, chose a woman, Rep. Geraldine Ferraro (N.Y.) to run with him as the candidate for vice president. The National Organization for Women passed a resolution, **July 1**, calling for the nomination of a woman for vice president. Altogether, Mondale interviewed seven persons during his search for a running mate, including Ferraro, **July 2**, San Antonio Mayor Henry Cisneros, **July 4**, and Gov. Martha Layne Collins of Kentucky, **July 6**. Noting that Mondale had interviewed blacks, women, and a Hispanic, Sen. Gary Hart (Col.), who was still seeking the presidential nomination, said, **July 6**, that his search was "a little like pandering." Pres. Ronald Reagan caused a stir, **July 6**, by suggesting the "probability" that many young people would never get back all they put into Social Security. Experts on the system said they did not share Reagan's concerns about its viability. Reagan, **July 10–12**, sought to underscore his interest in the environment by visiting the Chesapeake Bay area, where pollution was a growing problem; Theodore Roosevelt Island in the Potomac River; and Mammoth Cave, in Kentucky. Mondale, **July 12**, stunned the political world by announcing that he had asked Ferraro to be the candidate for vice president. Never before had a major party nominated a woman for the ticket, and such a selection had been viewed as a serious possibility for only the previous few months. By announcing his choice before the convention, Mondale broke another precedent. Ferraro, who joined him at the state capitol in St. Paul, Minn., for the announcement, had been an assistant district attorney in Queens, a borough of New York City, between 1974 and 1978, and had served in the U.S. House since 1979. Despite a liberal voting record, she had enjoyed strong electoral support from the voters in her conservative, working-class district. Ferraro, the wife of a real-estate developer, John Zaccaro, and the mother of three children, had retained her maiden name in her professional life to honor her mother. Geraldine Ferraro's father, an Italian immigrant, had died when she was 8. In announcing that he had chosen Ferraro, Mondale said the message was that "America is for everyone who works hard and contributes to our blessed country." The choice of Ferraro excited Democrats gathering for the national convention in San Francisco and gave new hope to their uphill fight against Reagan. Ferraro, **July 13**, said she did not believe Reagan was a "good Christian" because his policies were unfair to the poor. It was reported, **July 14**, that Mon-

dale would force party chairman Charles Manatt to resign. Mondale had reportedly chosen Georgia state chairman Bert Lance to replace Manatt, but he then backed down amid protests. Lance had served in the Carter administration and had resigned amid allegations, later unproved, that he had engaged in illegal banking practices. Mondale, **July 14**, compromised on Lance, naming him general chairman of the campaign and on **July 15** said he wanted Manatt to stay as party chairman. The convention, which opened on **July 16**, was marked by stirring oratory. Gov. Mario Cuomo (N.Y.), the keynoter, spoke with emotion about "the family of America" and said that the nation, often called "a shining city on a hill" by Reagan, should instead be seen as "a tale of 2 cities," rich and poor, with the latter being excluded by Reagan's policies. Jesse Jackson, speaking, **July 17**, roused the convention with an emotional appeal in behalf of "the desperate, the damned, the disinherited, the disrespected, and the despised." Apologizing for some statements during the campaign for the nomination, Jackson said that if "I have caused anyone discomfort, created pain or revived someone's fears, that was not my truest self." On the same night, Jackson's platform planks, calling for reductions in military spending and for an end to runoff primaries in the South, had been defeated by the delegates. Hart, speaking to the convention, **July 18**, appeared to leave the door open to another bid for the nomination in the future. Mondale, nominated for president, **July 18**, received 2,191 of the 3,933 convention votes. Hart, who asked that the nomination be made unanimous, received 1,200.5 and Jackson 465.5. Ferraro was nominated for vice president, **July 19**, by acclamation. Accepting the nomination, **July 19**, she spoke of the honor: "America is a land where dreams can come true for all our citizens. ... There are no doors we cannot unlock. We will place no limit on achievement. If we can do this, we can do anything." Mondale, accepting his nomination, castigated the Reagan administration on a wide range of issues. He called for a "new realism" in public life, and took another bold step by warning that taxes would have to go up: "Mr. Reagan will raise taxes, and so will I. He won't tell you. I just did." Mondale, **July 20**, challenged Reagan to 6 debates. On **July 21**, he said Reagan had a "secret plan" to raise taxes after the election. Reagan said, **July 24**, that he had no plans to raise taxes in 1985. Reagan, at a campaign rally, **July 25**, in Austin, Tex., said the Democratic ticket was "so far left they've left America." He charged that the Democrats were planning billions in new spending and taxes. Reagan, **July 27**, rejected the idea of 6 debates and said that 2 debates "would be as many as the public should stand for."

Burford Resigns Again After Protests — Anne Burford, former administrator of the Environmental Protection Agency, was appointed to a new position in the Reagan administration in July, but resigned amid a flurry of criticism within a month. Burford left her EPA post in March 1983 following accusations that the agency had shown political favoritism and had mismanaged the cleanup of toxic wastes. On **July 2**, Pres. Ronald Reagan named her to head the National Advisory Committee on Oceans and Atmosphere. Several environmental organizations denounced the appointment. At a previously-scheduled luncheon at the White House, **July 3**, for several pro-environment leaders, Reagan was roundly criticized for making the appointment. The Senate, **July 24**, 74-19, called on Reagan to withdraw the appointment. Burford, **July 27**, remarked that the job was a "nothingburger" because "They don't do anything." Reagan, **July 27**, defended Burford and said she had been forced out in 1983 by a "lynch mob." The House, **July 31**, 363-51, also called on Burford to leave. The White House, **Aug. 1**, announced that the appointment would be withdrawn at Burford's request because of the furor she said it had caused.

Unemployment Continues to Fall — The U.S. unemployment rate fell to 7.0 percent in June, the Labor Department reported, **July 6**. This was the lowest level since the spring of 1980. The department said, **July 13**, that in June, for the third straight month, the index of prices paid by producers for finished goods had remained stable. Between **July 19** and **27** the "Big 3" automakers—General Motors, Ford, and Chrysler—reported record earnings. GM led the way with second-quarter profits of $1.6 billion on sales of $21.6 billion. The Commerce Department said, **July 23**, that the real gross national product rose by an impressive 7.5 percent during the second quarter of 1984. The Consumer Price Index edged upward 0.2 percent in June, the Labor Department reported, **July 24**. The Commerce Department said, **July 27**, that the U.S. deficit in merchandise trade had risen to $8.9 billion in June. The department said, **July 31**, that the Index of Leading Economic Indicators fell 0.9 percent in June, a strong sign that the economic growth was slowing.

U.S. Sets Rules on Auto Air Bags — Transportation Secretary Elizabeth Dole announced, **July 11**, that air bags or automatic seat belts would be mandatory equipment on all automobiles made in the United States by 1989. But she said the requirement would be nullified if states representing two thirds of the U.S. population voted to make the use of seat belts compulsory. The percentage of vehicles required to have air bags or belts would be increased each year until 1989. The auto industry approved of the new regulation, but consumer and insurance groups said that the seat-belt law provision was a potential "escape route" for the auto industry. New York, **July 12**, became the first state to require drivers, front-seat passengers, and children under age 10 to wear seat belts.

U.S. Buys Loans of Ailing Illinois Bank — A rescue package for the shaky Continental Illinois Corp., the nation's 8th largest bank holding company, was unveiled, **July 26**. U.S. bank regulators said that the U.S. Federal Deposit Insurance Corp. would buy most of the bank's "problem" loans and would provide $1 billion in aid to the bank, for a total outlay of $4.5 billion in support. Although it would, in effect, own 80 percent of Continental, the FDIC emphasized that the bank was not being nationalized. Regulators said they had acted "to avoid general instability in the financial system." The Chicago-based bank had made a number of bad loans, and had even bought some from the failed Penn Square Bank of Oklahoma. Two months after a temporary U.S. rescue operation in May, Continental was still borrowing heavily to stay afloat, and on **July 26**, it reported a 2d-quarter loss of $1.1 billion. The new plan was subject to approval of the bank's stockholders. Any losses suffered by the FDIC on the loans it assumed would be offset by the assumption of an increased holding in the bank. The FDIC said it would put new officers in command of the bank. On the day before the new plan was announced, Treasury Secretary Donald Regan said it represented "bad public policy" and an "unauthorized and unlegislated expansion of federal guarantees."

International

U.S.-Soviet Debate on Proposed Talks Continues — The United States and Russia continued to debate in July over what would be included in talks proposed for Vienna in September. The Soviet Union, **July 1**, rejected the administration's attempt to tie space weapons talks to the talks on nuclear missiles. The news agency Tass reported that the USSR opposed any preconditions for the talks. On **July 1** and **3**, Pres. Ronald Reagan and Secretary of State George Shultz, in meetings with Soviet Ambassador Anatoly Dobrynin, sought to reassure him that the United States had accepted the Soviet proposal to open space weapons talks in Vienna in September, and that no preconditions had been set. On **July 7** in Stockholm, the 35-nation Conference on Confidence- and Security Building Measures and Disarmament in Europe adjourned for the summer after failing to agree on a format for further talks. Acknowledging the possibility that the Russians might see the prospective meeting in Vienna as a pre-election ploy, Reagan had written Soviet Pres. Konstantin Chernenko and offered to postpone the talks, according to administration officials, **July 14**. The superpowers, **July 17**, initialed an agreement to modernize the "hot line" between their two capitals. The agreement provided for a high-speed facsimile transmission system that would triple the speed of word transmissions and could transmit graphic material such as maps and charts. A study by the U.S. House, made public, **July 21**, asserted that the U.S. military was unprepared for major conventional warfare despite sharp increases in defense spending. Defense Secretary Caspar Weinberger, rejecting the report's major conclusion that combat readiness had declined, said the findings were "dangerously wrong" and perhaps politically motivated. In an appeal made public, **July 23**, the USSR, **July 21**, called on the United States to join in a formal statement pledging both countries to begin talks on banning space weapons. The United States, **July 24**, responded privately with its own draft of a joint statement, which the Soviets rejected, **July 27**. Appearing to run counter to recent statements from Washington, Weinberger, **July 26** and **29** said that the United States intended to bring up nuclear weapons issues at bilateral space weapons talks. The United States, **July 28**, sent a new draft for a joint statement on the proposed talks to Moscow.

Pre-Election Activity Builds in Nicaragua — Eden Pastora Gomez, one of the "contras" opposing the leftist Sandinista regime in Nicaragua, said, **July 2**, that he and his allies would end their military fight against the government and participate in the elections if the government would assure that the election would be fair. The announcement followed reports of a split between Pastora's faction of the anti-Sandinista effort and other contras. On **July 9**, the Roman Catholic archbishop of Managua, Miguel Obando y Bravo, led a church-sponsored march to show support for the Rev. Luis Amado Pena, a priest arrested in June and charged with a plot against the government. About 27 priests and 300 other persons joined the procession. Later that day, the government ordered 10 foreign priests who had participated to leave Nicaragua. Pope John Paul II called on the government, **July 11**, not to expel the priests. The government announced, **July 14**, that Pena would be tried before a special tribunal. The Social Democratic Party said, **July 16**, that its presidential candidate in the Nicaragua election would be its party leader, Adan Fletes. The Sandinistas announced, **July 17**, that Daniel Saavedra Ortega, coordinator of the government junta, would be its candidate. In Germany during a week-long, 6-nation tour to build support for his government, Salvadoran Pres. José Napoleón Duarte, **July 17**, obtained the German government's agreement to lift its 5-year ban on aid to El Salvador. In Washington on **July 23**, Duarte met with Pres. Ronald Reagan and leaders of the U.S. House.

Lebanon Implements Security Plan — Lebanon's new government took the first steps in July toward implementing the security plan adopted by its new national-unity cabinet. Units of the reconstituted Lebanese army moved through Beirut, **July 4-7**, to take over positions from the rival militia units that had taken control of the city in February. Lebanese troops, **July 5**, began to dismantle the "green line," a barricade of rubble and burned-out cars, which had separated the Christian and Muslim halves of the city. An army brigade comprising both Christians and Muslims was to be deployed between the halves of the city. Closed down 5 months by fighting, the Beirut international airport was reopened, **July 9**. It was temporarily shut down after a few hours by citizens demanding the return of several thousand relatives kidnapped during the civil war.

Ex-Nigerian Official Found in Crate — A bizarre kidnapping in London in July resulted in strained relations between Nigeria and Great Britain. Umaru Dikko, former transport and aviation minister in the Nigerian government, was kidnapped, **July 5**. Dikko, who fled Nigeria after a military coup in December 1983, had been wanted in his country on charges of corruption. Later on **July 5**, British police broke into a crate at Stansted Airport, 30 miles north of London, and found Dikko, who had been drugged. A man with drugs and syringes also occupied the crate, and another crate contained 2 more men. The crates had been marked "diplomatic baggage." The British held the aircraft that was to have flown the crates to Nigeria, and Nigeria retaliated, **July 6**, by detaining a British plane. The planes were freed, **July 7**. Four men, including the 3 men in the crates, were charged with kidnapping. Three of these were Israelis. Altogether, Britain arrested 17 persons in the plot, but 13 were released. Dikko, who was taken to an undisclosed location, **July 8**, after being examined in a hospital, had been accused by the new Nigerian government of stealing millions of dollars.

Israeli Election Inconclusive — The voting in Israel's parliamentary election in July seemed likely to lead to the eventual formation of a weak coalition government. The principal figures in the election had been Prime Minister Yitzhak Shamir of the Likud bloc and Shimon Peres, leader of the Labor Party. Likud had appeared vulnerable in the election because inflation had been running at more than 300 percent a year and because of dissatisfaction with the prolonged Israeli involvement in Lebanon's civil war. Peres emphasized these issues and said that he would end construction of controversial Jewish settlements near densely populated Arab areas. In a debate with Shamir, **July 10**, Peres called the war in Lebanon a "very bad joke." Shamir warned that Peres's proposal to set a timetable for Israeli withdrawal from Lebanon was dangerous. Former Prime Minister Menachem Begin, still popular, remained in seclusion and declined to campaign for Likud. The voting took place, **July 23**. Results announced, **July 26**, showed Labor with 44 seats and Likud with 41, both far short of a majority in the 120-seat parliament. Peres and Shamir began to negotiate with potential allies among the many minority parties, but neither was immediately successful in building a majority coalition.

Mitterand Appoints New French Premier — French Premier Pierre Mauroy stepped down in July and was succeeded by Laurent Fabius, the minister of industry, who at 37 was the nation's youngest premier in more than a century. Two days after Mauroy resigned on **July 17**, the Communist Party withdrew from the Socialist-led coalition government. Fabius named a new cabinet, **July 19**. Popular support for the Communists had declined in recent months, and in the face of continuing economic troubles, Mauroy's popularity had also fallen sharply.

Poland to Free Political Prisoners — Declaring an amnesty, the Polish government proclaimed, **July 21**, that it would release 652 political prisoners within 30 days. The amnesty, approved by the parliament, was also to apply to 35,000 criminals serving short sentences. Polish Premier Wojciech Jaruzelski called the amnesty both "a humanitarian act" and an "expression of the strength of the state." He warned political prisoners not to engage in anti-state activities in the future. Eugenia Kempara, who introduced the bill, said that the amnesty would also cover underground activists and exiles abroad who confessed "their crimes" and produced "as evidence the tools or output of their clandestine activities." The U.S. State Department said, **July 21**, that it would study the terms of the amnesty before deciding whether to lift sanctions established after the imposition of martial law in 1981.

General

4 Amtrak Crashes Take 10 Lives — Ten persons died in accidents involving National Railroad Passenger Corp. (Amtrak), trains during July. One train hit a truck, **July 4**, at a crossing in Elgin, S.C., killing 2 people in the truck. A northbound train derailed near Williston, Vt., **July 7**, and crashed into a ravine, killing 5 persons and causing injuries to 153. The accident was attributed to a washed-out culvert. On **July 11**, at a crossing without signals near McBee, S.C., a train struck a diesel truck. The truckdriver and the train engineer died. Two trains collided head-on in Queens, N.Y., **July 23**, causing the death of one passenger and injuries to more than 100 persons. John Riley, head of the Federal Railroad Administration, said, **July 26**, that Amtrak had an outstanding safety record, with 20 passenger fatalities for Amtrak's first 13 years prior to July. However, fatalities among pedestrians and occupants of other vehicles were much higher, totaling 188 during the 1981-1983 period alone.

Gunman Kills 21 in Restaurant — James Humberty, a gun collector who had recently lost his job, shot 21 persons to death in and near a McDonald's restaurant in San Ysidro, Calif., **July 18**, before police sharpshooter killed Huberty. The mass murder may have been the worst in U.S. history. Eighteen other persons were wounded. Huberty's motivation was not known. He carried 3 guns into the restaurant about 4 p.m., and ordered everyone to lie down. He shot anyone who moved inside the restaurant and shot others who were outside. Many of the victims were children. The nightmare lasted about 77 minutes before Huberty was felled by a single shot fired by Charles Foster, a member of the police SWAT team. McDonald's, **July 19**, contributed $1 million to pay burial costs and assist the survivors.

Miss America Resigns — Vanessa Williams, the first black Miss America, resigned in July, just 2 months before the end of her "reign." After several days of controversy related to some nude photographs of her that were about to be published, she gave up her title, **July 23**. The photographs,

scheduled for publication in Penthouse Magazine, showed Williams and another woman simulating sexual activities. Officials of the Miss America Pageant said that Williams, who was from New York, would be permitted to keep her scholarship and personal-appearance fees. Suzette Charles of New Jersey, who is also black and who had been the first runner-up in the September 1983 pageant in Atlantic City, succeeded Williams.

Retiree Wins $20 Million in Lottery — A retired carpenter won $20 million in a New York Lotto drawing, **July 25**. Venero Pagano, a 63-year-old former carpenter who lived with his wife in a 2-family home in the Bronx, may have won the biggest jackpot in the history of lottery contests. He said his income had been less than $1,000 a month. Pagano, whose pastime was growing tomatoes, said he had no plans for changes in his life.

AUGUST

National

Reagan and Bush Renominated — Pres. Ronald Reagan and Vice Pres. George Bush were renominated in August at the 33rd Republican National Convention. Former Vice Pres. Water Mondale and Rep. Geraldine Ferraro (N.Y.), the Democratic standard bearers, campaigned together in Mississippi and Texas, **Aug. 1** and **2**. Mondale said, **Aug. 1**, "What Americans want is common sense, not salesmanship," and he added that the campaign "shouldn't be a contest between advertising agencies, it should be about ideas and plans for the American people." Bert Lance resigned as general chairman of the Mondale campaign, **Aug. 2**, as a result of concern within the party over old charges—of which he had been found not guilty—that he had violated banking laws. The tax-increase issue initiated in July by Mondale heated up, with Reagan charging, **Aug. 4**, that Mondale planned spending increases that would raise taxes by $1,500 a household. Reagan said he would propose no personal tax increases if reelected, in order, he said, "to keep the economic recovery going." Bush said, **Aug. 5**, however, that the administration would consider reducing the deficit through "revenue increases." After meeting with Reagan, **Aug. 6**, Bush refused to rule out a tax hike in 1985. Mondale, **Aug. 6**, denounced the federal budget deficits as "obscene," and suggested, **Aug. 7**, that Reagan and Bush debate each other on the question of a tax increase. A new controversy emerged, **Aug. 7**, when the Washington (D.C.) Legal Foundation asked the House Ethics Committee to investigate Ferraro for her allegedly improper failure to provide details of her husband's finances as prescribed by the Ethics in Government Act. While testing a radio microphone, **Aug. 11**, Reagan joked about outlawing Russia and said, "We begin bombing in 5 minutes." Mondale deplored the choice of subject matter for a joke, and the Soviet Union professed to be offended. Reagan said, **Aug. 12**, that raising taxes would be a last resort for him but a first resort for Mondale. The controversy over Ferraro's finances came to a climax, **Aug. 20**, when she released a mass of personal financial records showing that she and her husband, John Zaccaro, had paid taxes equivalent to about 40 percent of their income from 1979 to 1983. By releasing her husband's tax data, Ferraro sought to end speculation that the couple might have something to hide. In fact, because of what Ferraro called an accounting error, they did owe $53,459, including interest, on the profit from sale of property. This was paid by check, **Aug. 20**. The documents showed that Ferraro and Zaccaro had a net worth of $3.78 million, and they revealed many details of Zaccaro's real-estate business. In a 90-minute news conference before 200 reporters, **Aug. 21**, Ferraro denied any wrongdoing with respect to her financial disclosure statements. Later, Mondale praised his running mate for having "passed a test of leadership that will strengthen public respect for her . . . ." Meanwhile, the Republican convention, which opened in Dallas, **Aug. 20**, had heard U.N. Ambassador Jeane Kirkpatrick assert that the election of Reagan in 1980 had "marked the end of a dismal period of retreat and decline" for the United States on the world stage. The platform adopted, **Aug. 21**, had a strong conservative cast. It rejected any question of a tax increase, opposed passage of the Equal Rights Amendment, and declared that prospective judges should be nominated for the federal bench only if they opposed abortion. Reagan and Bush were renominated, **Aug. 22,** in nearly unanimous votes. Reagan planted the seeds of a new controversy on **Aug. 23,** when he addressed an ecumenical prayer breakfast in Dallas and declared that "religion and politics are necessarily related." That evening, accepting his nomination, the president told an ecstatic convention that he had fulfilled his promises to reduce the growth of the federal government and to cut interest rates, taxes, and inflation. He noted that during his administration "not one inch of soil has fallen to the communists," and he said that "We are in the midst of a springtime of hope for America." Mondale said, **Aug. 24,** that a reelected Reagan would raise taxes for the workers and "leave his rich friends alone." On **Aug. 26,** he claimed that Reagan regarded arms control as "weakness." On **Aug. 28,** Mondale won the endorsements of the Rev. Jesse Jackson and three dozen other black leaders, after agreeing to bring more blacks into his campaign. John Anderson, an independent candidate for president in 1980, endorsed Mondale, **Aug. 28.**

Stocks Soar as Economy Slows — The stock market rocketed in August in the heaviest trading volume ever, even as signs grew that the economic recovery was slowing down. The Census Bureau said, **Aug. 2,** that the nation's poverty rate had edged upward to 15.2 percent in 1983, the highest level since 1965, and that the number of poor people totaled 35.3 million. The jobless rate rose in July to 7.4 percent, the Labor Department reported, **Aug. 3,** the first jump in that figure since the depths of the 1982 recession. The stock market concluded a phenomenal week, **Aug. 3,** with record trading on the New York Stock Exchange of 236.57 million shares. The Dow Jones Industrial Average rose 36.0 points to 1,202.08. The Dow's gain for the week, 87.46 points, set another record. Analysts said that evidence of lower economic activity meant that pressure on interest rates would be reduced. The market also took heart from a July 25 statement by Paul Volcker, chairman of the Federal Reserve Board, that the "Fed" would not seek to tighten the growth in the money supply to control inflation. The Commerce Department reported, **Aug. 20,** that after-tax profits of U.S. corporations rose 1.5 percent in the second quarter of 1984. The Labor Department announced, **Aug. 22,** that the consumer price index had advanced only 0.3 percent in July. The Commerce Department said, **Aug. 29,** that the index of leading economic indicators fell 0.8 percent in July, the second straight monthly decline. The department reported, **Aug. 29,** that the U.S. trade deficit in July had been a record $14.06 billion.

John De Lorean Not Guilty in Drug Case — A sensational trial in Los Angeles ended, **Aug. 16,** with the acquittal of John De Lorean on charges that he had conspired to distribute cocaine worth $24 million. The prosecution, using tapes that showed De Lorean meeting with government agents posing as drug dealers, sought to establish that De Lorean had entered into an illicit deal to save his failing automobile company in Ireland. Some jurors said after the trial that they thought that De Lorean had been entrapped and other said that the case against him had not been proved.

B-1 Crashes on Test Flight — A prototype of the controversial B-1 bomber crashed into the Mojave Desert in California, **Aug. 29.** The pilot was killed and the two other crewmen were injured. Although the Air Force offered no immediate explanation for the accident, there were reports that the B-1 had veered to avoid a plane filming the test, lost power, and crashed. The three members of the crew ejected in an escape capsule, which struck the ground hard, causing the death of retired Col. Tommie Douglas (Doug) Benefield, the chief test pilot for Rockwell International Corp., the plane's manufacturer. The crash, first ever in 127 test flights of B-1 prototypes, was not expected to delay the bomber program, although the production of the plane was expected to continue to face opposition from some members of Congress.

Law Opens Schools to Religious Worship — Pres. Reagan, **Aug. 11,** signed into law an act of Congress that would prohibit public high schools from barring students who wished to assemble for religious or political activities outside school hours. He said it would "allow student religious groups to begin enjoying a right they've too long been denied, the freedom to meet in public high schools . . . just as other student groups are allowed to do." The sponsors of the bill had in mind that students would be able to join in prayer, but some lawyers who analyzed the language of the bill anticipated that cults and extremist groups could also ask to meet. Because of the touchy issue of introducing religion into schools, the law was expected to face challenges as to its constitutionality.

International

Events Suggest Power Struggle in Iran — Several unusual occurrences in August seemed to suggest the possibility that a struggle for power was continuing behind the scenes in Iran. First came a confused response to the hijacking by 3 Iranians of a Paris-bound jet from Frankfurt, West Germany. The hijackers, who forced the plane to fly to Teheran, **Aug. 1,** demanded the release of 5 Iranians held in Paris in connection with an attempted assassination of an opponent of Ayatollah Ruhollah Khomeini. The hijackers threatened to kill the hostages, but eventually released them, **Aug. 2,** though they damaged the plane with a bomb. Some diplomats thought that the settlement worked out by Iranian authorities reflected a compromise between hardliners and moderates seeking to preserve Iran's ties to the outside world. Early in August, the United States, Egypt, and Britain sent ships into the Red Sea to search for evidence, after explosions had damaged as many as 15 ships. Teheran radio, **Aug. 7,** praised the explosions, which it said were directed against the United States, Britain, and France. On **Aug. 9,** however, Khomeini denounced the mining and criticized the state radio for its statements. The Iranian parliament, **Aug. 15,** dismissed 5 cabinet ministers, including the defense minister, possibly because of dissatisfaction with the progress of the war against Iraq. The dismissed ministers were accused of financial mismanagement, inefficiency, and nepotism. Later in August, the Soviet Union, Italy, and France joined the effort to clear the Red Sea of mines. On **Aug. 21,** an Egyptian official said that a Libyan ship was the chief suspect in the distribution of the mines, which had killed no one and which were apparently intended to damage ships and not sink them.

Accord Reached on Hong Kong's Future — Britain announced, **Aug. 1,** that it had reached an agreement with China on the future of Hong Kong. Britain's leases on most of the colony, which lies on and adjacent to the Chinese mainland, are due to expire in 1997. British Foreign Secretary Sir Geoffrey Howe, who had met with Chinese leaders in Peking in late July, made the announcement in Hong Kong. He said that the draft agreement provided for "the preservation of all the rights and freedom which the people of Hong Kong now enjoy." Legal, judicial, and educational systems would be maintained for 50 years after 1997. He said China planned to incorporate Hong Kong into a special administrative region.

U.S. Lifts Some Sanctions Against Poland — The United States said, **Aug. 3,** that it was lifting some of the sanctions it imposed on Poland after the government established martial law in 1981. Poland had announced, **July 21,** that it was declaring amnesty for political prisoners. The United States said that it would take one step at a time, with priority going to removing a ban on U.S. landing rights for the Polish airline, and to an end to U.S. opposition to Polish membership in the International Monetary Fund. By **Aug. 9,** Poland had freed more than 20,000 convicted criminals and most of the 652 political prisoners included in the amnesty. Some top leaders of the outlawed union Solidarity were included among those released. In a diplomatic note, **Aug. 16,** Poland asked the United States to begin direct talks on the lifting of sanctions, which the note said had "harmed the entire people of Poland."

Israeli Parties OK Unity Government — Israel's 2 largest parties agreed in August to a national unity government with alternating prime ministers to lead the country for the next 4 years. Following the indecisive July election, Pres. Chaim Herzog, **Aug. 5,** called on Shimon Peres, leader of the Labor Party, to try to form a new government. While his efforts continued, the new Knesset (parliament) was sworn in, **Aug. 13.** One new member who received a lot of nervous attention was the outspoken Rabbi Meir Kahane, who had demanded that all Arabs be expelled from Israel and the occupied territories. The U.S. State Department, **Aug. 14,** formally opened a study of Kahane's U.S. citizenship, which was jeopardized by his membership in a foreign government. After it became apparent that Peres would be unable to form a majority coalition in the Knesset, it was reported, **Aug. 31,** that he and Prime Minister Yitzhak Shamir, leader of the Likud bloc, had agreed on a national unity government in which first Peres and then Shamir would serve as prime minister for 25 months. Under the plan, Labor and Likud would have 12 ministers each in the 24-member cabinet.

Aid for Central America Approved — A half-billion dollar package of military and economic aid to Central America was approved by Congress in August. The key issue, military aid for El Salvador, was acted on **Aug. 8** in the Senate, which voted 69-29 in favor of the Reagan administration request for $117 million in additional military aid to the embattled nation. The House bill, which had been approved, **Aug. 1,** contained no military aid for El Salvador, but a conference committee reconciling differences in the omnibus aid bill approved an outlay of $70 million. This figure was approved in the House 234-161 and by a voice vote in the Senate. The aid package also included $120 million in economic aid for El Salvador.

One-Party Marxist State Voted in Zimbabwe — Zimbabwe's ruling African National Union-Patriotic Front, **Aug. 8–12,** adopted a charter calling for one-party Marxist rule. The draft charter, adopted at a party congress, provided that the socialist state would be achieved "in the fullness of time" under the "vanguard leadership" of the Union and Front. The party approved expanded power for Prime Minister Robert Mugabe through the creation of an executive presidency that would permit Mugabe to become head of state. The party delegates also approved a strict moral code for party officials.

Uganda Criticized on Human Rights — Uganda and the United States argued in August over whether the African country was guilty of massive abuses of human rights. Assistant Secretary of State Elliott Abrams called the situation in Uganda "horrendous." In an interview published **Aug. 5,** he said U.S. officials and international relief agencies had determined that between 100,000 and 200,000 persons had been killed in the past 3 years in the area occupied by the Baganda tribe, which the Ugandan army allegedly believed was supporting an insurgent movement. An official of the Ugandan embassy, **Aug. 9,** called the charges "totally untrue." Abrams, testifying before 2 House subcommittees, **Aug. 9,** said that the United States had received "repeated reports of large-scale civilian massacres, forced starvation and impeded humanitarian relief operations." A Ugandan government spokesman acknowledged, **Aug. 19,** that 15,000 persons had been killed in political and tribal violence in Uganda since Pres. Milton Obote came to power in 1980.

General

Olympic Games Lift U.S. Spirits — The games of the XXIII Olympiad provided two weeks of midsummer celebration for the American people. The games ran smoothly, showed a financial profit, and resulted in a harvest of gold medals for American athletes. From the moment Pres. Ronald Reagan officially opened the games at the Los Angeles Memorial Coliseum, **July 28,** they were conducted without any of the feared consequences—acts of terrorism, traffic jams, or choking smog—that could have marred the competition. Some 5.5 million persons attended events in which 7,800 athletes from 140 countries competed. Fifty thousand persons served as unpaid volunteers during the games. The boycott by the Soviet Union and some of its allies did not go unnoticed as competition in many event was evidently affected. Americans won a record total of 174 medals, including 83 gold, 61 silver, and 30 bronze. West Germany and Romania won a total of 59 and 53 medals, respectively. China, competing seriously for the first time, won 32 medals. Carl Lewis led the American domination with 4 gold medals in track and field—in the 100 and 200 meters, long jump, and 400 meter relay. Mary Lou Retton became a popular favorite by winning 4 medals in gymnastics, including a gold in the all-around competition. Other outstanding performers for the United States included Greg Louganis, who won two diving events, and Joan Benoit, winner of the first

Olympic marathon for women. The U.S. men won team titles in basketball, gymnastics, and volleyball. U.S. boxers captured 9 of 12 titles. Britain's Daley Thompson and Sebastian Cole won two major track events, the decathlon and the 1,500 meters, repeating their victories at Moscow in 1980. Carlos Lopes of Portugal took the men's marathon. In perhaps the most heartbreaking moment, the U.S. favorite, Mary Decker, and Zola Budd, a barefoot competitor from South Africa who was running for Britain, collided in the 3,000-meter run, causing Decker to fall; the gold medal went to Maricica Puica of Romania. The closing ceremonies on **Aug. 12,** featured a massive fireworks display and, like the opening ceremonies, included Hollywood-style entertainment by thousands of musicians, dancers, and singers.

Montana Swept by Fires — The state of Montana—dry, windy, and hot—was "literally . . . on fire", in the words of Gov. Ted Schwinden, during the last days of August. A dry winter, followed by a dry summer, electrical storms, and high winds helped account for the flames all over the state. Some 250,000 acres were affected as more than a dozen fires, propelled by winds gusting to 80 miles an hour, leaped such natural barriers as the Missouri River, 100 yards wide. The flames claimed $10.5 million in damages, and Pres. Reagan provided disaster relief. Some 1,000 volunteers from 7 states fought a fire on Houghton Creek in the extreme northwestern corner of the state.

Disasters — All 49 persons aboard a Bangladesh plane died when it attempted to land, **Aug. 5,** at Dhaka in a driving rainstorm . . . Nearly 200 persons were missing and believed drowned, **Aug. 13,** after a ferry capsized off the state of Sabah in Malaysia.

SEPTEMBER

National

Presidential Campaign Intensifies — The 1984 campaign for the White House got into full swing in September, with the candidates exchanging sharp attacks on a number of issues. Walter Mondale and his running mate Geraldine Ferraro kicked off their campaign with a Labor Day **(Sept. 3)** march up New York City's Fifth Avenue, only to be greeted by mostly empty sidewalks at an early hour. In a Labor Day rally in Southern California, Reagan said that if he was reelected, America's message to the world would be "You ain't seen nothing yet." Mondale said, **Sept. 4,** that he was "damned mad" about administration tax policies which, he said, favored the rich. Reagan, speaking, **Sept. 5,** said that the federal deficits that Mondale had deplored were being reduced "right now" because of enhanced revenues produced by the economic recovery. In an address to B'nai B'rith, a Jewish organization, Mondale, **Sept. 6,** warned of dangers in Reagan's remarks linking religion and politics. He reproached Reagan for saying that those opposed to a school-prayer amendment to the U.S. Constitution were "intolerant" of religion. Not responding directly to Mondale in his own address to B'nai B'rith, Reagan affirmed his belief in the separation of church and state, and his opposition to a state-approved religion. Mondale, **Sept. 10,** unveiled his proposal for cutting the federal deficits by two thirds by the 1989 fiscal year. The instrument would be tax increases rising to $85 billion by 1989. Mondale said he would limit circumstances under which tax rates would be "indexed" to protect taxpayers forced into higher brackets by inflation. He said he would also cap the third year of the Reagan tax cut for wealthy Americans, impose a surtax on those with high incomes, and set a minimum 15 percent tax rate for corporations. Most spending cuts would fall on the defense budget. Ferraro, **Sept. 10,** sought to settle a controversy with New York Archbishop John O'Connor, who had said that she had misrepresented the position of the Roman Catholic Church on abortion. He had said the teaching of the church on abortion was not divided, as he said Ferraro had asserted, but united in its opposition. A Ferraro aide said, that in a letter she had written, she only meant to state that opinion among individual Catholics was divided. The House Ethics Committee, **Sept. 12,** voted unanimously to investigate charges that Ferraro had violated congressional standards by improperly claiming an exemption from the requirement that she disclose her spouse's finances. Reagan,

Sept. 12, said that Mondale's plan to cut the budget deficits would increase taxes for "working families all across America," and added that whereas "we see an America where every day is the Fourth of July, they see an America where every day is April 15." Reagan, touring a Buffalo (N.Y.) housing project, **Sept. 12,** proclaimed it a "great thing" even though he had sought to cut funds for the programs that had helped to build it. Four public opinion surveys released between **Sept. 12** and **15,** showed Reagan leading Mondale by 15 to 18 percentage points, and an Associated Press survey put Reagan ahead in 41 states with 420 electoral votes, far more than the 270 required for victory. Mondale said, **Sept. 14,** that Reagan was an isolated president operating in a "question-free zone" and conducting a "happy-talk campaign." He said, **Sept. 17,** that he would make war and peace a major issue and charged that Reagan had made the world more dangerous. In an interview published, **Sept. 18,** he said that he would quarantine Nicaragua if it refused to negotiate with its neighbors or used force against them. Accepting the endorsement of the Sierra Club, **Sept. 19,** Mondale said he would "take polluters to court, not to lunch." Reagan, campaigning in Connecticut, **Sept. 19,** called on "good and decent Democrats of the JFK, FDR, and Harry Truman tradition—people who believe in the interests of working people" to cross party lines and support him. Mondale, **Sept. 25,** said Reagan was moderating some of his positions, including renewed expression of interest in arms control, only because the election was at hand.

Meese Cleared of Wrongdoing — Presidential counselor Edwin Meese III, Pres. Reagan's nominee for attorney general, was cleared of accusations against him by an independent investigator in September. Sen. Strom Thurmond (R, S.C.), chairman of the Judiciary Committee, announced, **Sept. 7,** that the committee had put aside further consideration of Meese's nomination until after the election to prevent it from becoming "overly politicized." Jacob Stein, the independent counsel who had conducted a 5-month investigation of allegations against Meese, reported, **Sept. 20,** that there was "no basis" for bringing criminal charges against Meese on questions relating to his personal finances and to whether he had reported them accurately on financial-disclosure forms. Reagan hailed the "vindication" of his aide of many years. Stein did note that Meese had not paid close attention to his finances and that his disclosure forms had often been "false" because of omitted data, but he added that evidence was persuasive that the omissions were not deliberate.

Economic Statistics Show Slower Growth — Data released in August showed that the economy was expanding at a slower pace. The unemployment rate continued at a steady 7.4 percent in August, the Labor Department reported, **Sept. 7.** Industrial production was up only 0.2 percent in August, the Federal Reserve announced, **Sept. 14.** The Labor Department said, **Sept. 14,** that the prices paid by producers for finished goods edged downward 0.1 percent in August. The balance of payments showed a record deficit of $24.4 billion in the second quarter, according to the Commerce Department, **Sept. 17.** Housing starts fell 12.8 percent, and personal income advanced 0.5 percent in August, the department reported, **Sept. 19.** The Commerce Department said, **Sept. 20,** that third-quarter gross national product rose 3.6 percent, about half the rate for the second quarter. The Labor Department said, **Sept. 21,** that the consumer price index had risen 0.5 percent in August.

Stronger Warnings Approved for Cigarettes — The House of Representatives, **Sept. 10,** approved compromise legislation providing for stronger health warnings on cigarette packages and advertising. The new warnings would cite dangers posed by cigarettes both to smokers and their unborn children. The bill was the result of long negotiations among the House members, health groups, and the tobacco industry. The warnings included such information as "Cigarette smoke contains carbon monoxide." Rep. Albert Gore (D, Tenn.) worked out the compromise. Prospects for passage remained uncertain in the Senate, where tobacco-state senators led the opposition. However, a threatened filibuster failed to materialize in the Senate, and Congress completed action on the bill, **Sept. 26.**

Reagan Seeks Steel Industry Rescue — Pres. Ronald Reagan announced, **Sept. 18,** that he would seek to negotiate "voluntary" agreements with other nations that would protect U.S. steel producers from foreign imports. Brazil, South Korea, and Spain were among the principal targets of Reagan's plan. In the first 7 months of 1984, imported steel had accounted for about 25 percent of the U.S. market, but that share could drop to 18 percent if the voluntary agreements were accepted by other countries. Under the plan, nations would be expected to limit their imports for 5 years. Those refusing to do so might be cut off from their U.S. markets altogether.

GM and Auto Workers Reach Settlement — General Motors Corp. and the United Automobile Workers reached a tentative contract settlement, **Sept. 21,** which averted a strike that could have crippled the already-shaky automotive industry. The union had already begun selective strikes that had idled some 110,000 workers. The settlement covered 350,000 workers. The terms provided for a first-year pay raise averaging about 2.5 percent, with lump-sum payments of about 2.5 percent for the next 2 years. GM also agreed to improvements in pension benefits. Though a settlement by one company often sets a pattern for the rest of the industry, a spokesmen for Ford Motor Company said that Ford would not "walk in lockstep" with GM.

International

Two Americans Killed in Nicaragua — Two U.S. citizens, who were members of an anticommunist group, were killed, **Sept. 1,** when their helicopter was shot down by Nicaraguan forces during a rebel raid on a military camp at Santa Clara, in Nicaragua. The U.S.-made helicopter was apparently providing support for ground forces involved in the raid. The Reagan administration denied, **Sept. 3,** that any U.S. government personnel had been involved in the attack. The men, as it turned out, belonged to Civilian Military Assistance, which had been formed to support opponents of the leftist Nicaraguan regime. Members of the small group, consisting of former U.S. servicemen, had gone to Honduras to join the Nicaraguan Democratic Force. Tom Posey, head of the CMA, said the 2 men who died had been training rebel pilots. Foreign ministers of the 4 Contadora countries—Colombia, Mexico, Panama, and Venezuela—ended 2 days of meetings, **Sept. 7,** with a call for disarmament in Central America. The appeal was included in a revised version of the group's peace plan for the region, but Nicaragua's foreign minister said it was unacceptable while Nicaragua was under attack. However, Nicaragua, **Sept. 22,** announced that it would sign the peace plan. Nicaraguan leaders, **Sept. 23,** said they would not postpone the Nov. 4 presidential election despite pressure from the Reagan administration to do so in order to permit opposition parties to mount a stronger campaign.

Mulroney Elected Prime Minister of Canada — The Progressive Conservative Party rolled to a landslide victory in the Canadian national election, **Sept. 4.** The results elevated the party's leader, Brian Mulroney, to the office of prime minister. Mulroney led the Conservatives to victory over the Liberal incumbent prime minister, John M. Turner, who had succeeded Pierre Elliott Trudeau in June. The Conservatives captured 211 of the 282 seats in the House of Commons, the largest total ever won by a single party. The Liberals, who had led Canada for 42 of the last 50 years, won only 40 seats. The New Democratic Party won 30 seats. The Conservatives received 50 percent of the popular vote, the Liberals an embarrassing 28 percent, and the New Democrats 19 percent. The magnitude of the Liberal defeat was revealed in the province of Quebec, their traditional stronghold, where they won only 17 of 76 seats. Mulroney, a resident of the province, had strongly defended minority-language rights, endearing himself to many voters of French descent. He had also made a number of promises, including commitments to reduce regulation of the energy industry, create jobs, impose a minimum income tax on the wealthy, and improve relations with the United States, which had been strained under Trudeau. Mulroney, 45 years old, had long been active in Conservative Party affairs and was also president of Iron Ore Company of Canada. He did not hold elective office until he won a seat in the House of Commons in 1983, the same year in which he was chosen party leader. Taking office as Canada's 18th prime minister, **Sept. 17,** Mulroney appointed a 40-member cabinet, the largest in Canadian history.

Meeting of 2 German Leaders Postponed — Erich Honecker, head of state of East Germany, disappointed many Germans, **Sept. 4,** when he postponed a visit to West Germany. He apparently bowed to pressures from the Soviet Union. The visit would have been the first by an East German leader to West Germany. The USSR, clearly displeased by hints of a thaw in relations between the two Germanys, had stepped up its denunciations of West Germany for its alleged desire to unite all Germans under noncommunist rule. Hungary and Romania had given cautious support to Honecker's visit, but 2 other Soviet allies in Eastern Europe, Poland and Czechoslovakia, had criticized it. The East Germans attributed the postponement to a flurry of statements critical of East Germany by West German political leaders. The Bulgarian head of state, Todor Zhivkov, announced, **Sept. 9,** that he, too, had postponed a scheduled visit to West Germany.

Chernenko Reappears After Rumors of Illness — Pres. Konstantin Chernenko appeared on Soviet television, **Sept. 5,** after being out of public view for 7 weeks. Rumors had spread that he was seriously ill. Chernenko moved slowly and seemed to have some difficulty breathing as he presented medals to 3 cosmonauts. Other events stirred speculation that a contest for power might be in progress in the USSR. On **Sept. 6,** Marshal Nikolai Ogarkov, chief of the Soviet general staff, was removed from his post and replaced by his deputy, Marshal Sergei Akhromeyev. Tass, the Soviet news agency, said Ogarkov would be assigned other unspecified duties. Speculation in the West focused on the possibilities that Ogarkov had opposed defense policy or that he had been embroiled in the jockeying for position in the contest to succeed Chernenko. An elaborate funeral, **Sept. 7,** in Red Square for a deputy prime minister, Leonid Kostandov, also struck some observers as odd. The funeral, shown on national television, may have been used as an occasion to give attention to some of the pallbearers. If so, it appeared that Politburo member Mikhail Gorbachov was placed in the most prominent position.

Pope Tours Canada — Pope John Paul II toured Canada for 12 days, coast-to-coast, **Sept. 9-20.** The first pope to visit Canada and its 11 million Roman Catholics, he stopped in almost every major city, including Quebec, Ottawa, Montreal, Toronto, Winnipeg, Edmonton, and Vancouver. He spoke out on a number of issues, emphasizing familiar church positions on divorce and abortion. He supported the right of Eskimos and Indians to control their own lands and resources, and praised the nation's tradition of cultural pluralism—a reference to Canada's French-speaking minority.

Reagan Meets With Gromyko — For the first time as president, Ronald Reagan met in September with a major Soviet leader. Foreign Minister Andrei Gromyko, in the United States to attend the opening of the U.N. General Assembly, came to Washington to confer with the president, who had been criticized frequently for not having sought personal contacts with Soviet leaders. Reagan said, **Sept. 11,** that he had invited Gromyko to the White House in an effort to ease U.S.-Soviet tensions. Gromyko, who had been foreign minister since 1957, was believed to have gained in power in recent years at a time when other Soviet leaders were in poor health. Walter Mondale, the Democratic presidential candidate, said, **Sept. 11,** that he was pleased that the meeting would take place, but added that it was "pathetic" that it was happening for the first time in the middle of the president's campaign for reelection. Reagan, addressing the General Assembly, **Sept. 24,** appealed for "a better working relationship" between the superpowers and he asked that nations work together to lift "the dread of nuclear war" from the earth. Gromyko and U.S. Secretary of State George Shultz met in New York, **Sept. 26,** as a curtain-raiser for Gromyko's White House visit. Gromyko also met with Mondale, **Sept. 27.** In a harsh speech to the General Assembly, **Sept. 27,** Gromyko said that the United States would have to show through its deeds, not just its words, that it wanted better relations with the Soviet Union. The Reagan-Gromyko meeting took place, **Sept. 28,** and was described in diplomatic language as "forceful and direct." Reagan reportedly called for more top-level meetings between U.S. and Soviet leaders, but no known progress was made on issues dividing the superpowers.

Peres Sworn In As Israeli Prime Minister — Shimon Peres, leader of the Labor Party, was sworn in, **Sept. 14,** as prime minister of Israel. On the same day, the outgoing prime minister, Yitzhak Shamir, leader of the Likud bloc in the parliament, stepped down to the positions of deputy prime minister and foreign minister. The agreement between the two leading factions to share power for the next 4 years was thus implemented. Neither side had been able to form a government on its own after the close election of July 23. The agreement called for Peres and Shamir to serve as prime minister for 25 months each. An 89-18 vote of approval in the Knesset (parliament), **Sept. 14,** cleared the way for the new government. The most important national decisions were to be made by an "inner cabinet" consisting of 5 ministers from each side. Peres had held several ministerial posts in previous Labor governments, including defense minister. He had headed the Labor Party since 1977. In austerity measures, the new government, **Sept. 16,** devalued the shekel by 9 percent and announced plans to make big cuts in the national budget. The Reagan administration had indicated that future economic aid would be tied to the taking of such steps. Shamir, **Sept. 22,** said his government would ask the United States to serve as a go-between with Syria to arrange for the withdrawal of Israeli forces from southern Lebanon.

Bomb Kills 2 Americans at Beirut Embassy — A suicide bomber drove an American-made station wagon to the front of the U.S. Embassy annex in Beirut, **Sept. 20,** and detonated about 400 pounds of TNT. The resulting explosion killed 2 American servicemen and an unknown number of Lebanese, and demolished part of the front of the 5-story building. The attack was the third of its kind on U.S. installations in Beirut in 17 months. In 1983, bombs transported in vehicles ripped through the U.S. Embassy and the Marine compound. In the latest incident, the driver maneuvered around concrete-block barriers and through a barrage of bullets fired by Lebanese guards and British bodyguards who had accompanied the British ambassador to the building. Both the U.S. and British ambassadors were slightly injured. Someone saying he represented a shadowy extremist group Islamic Jihad (Holy War) phoned a French press agency to claim responsibility. Another caller had warned, **Sept. 8,** that an attack would occur somewhere. This came 2 days after the United States, **Sept. 6,** vetoed a U.S. resolution calling on Israel to "immediately lift all restrictions and obstacles" imposed on Lebanese civilians. The resolution had also asked Israel to withdraw from southern Lebanon. Lebanese Premier Hashid Karami had criticized the United States, **Sept. 7,** for its vote. After the bombing, questions as to how it could have happened again centered on the fact that security arrangements at the annex had not been completed and on the fact that the U.S. Marine guards had been withdrawn. Pres. Ronald Reagan, campaigning in Iowa, **Sept. 20,** said, "I think if someone is determined to do what they did, it is pretty difficult to prevent it." Reagan, **Sept. 23,** acknowledged that security had not been complete at the Embassy building, observing "Anyone that's ever had their kitchen done over knows that it never gets done as soon as you wish it would." Walter Mondale, the Democratic presidential nominee, **Sept. 24,** accused Reagan of letting terrorists "humiliate us and push us around and kill our people." Reagan said, **Sept. 26,** that "the near destruction of our intelligence capability" in the years preceding his administration had been in part to blame for the bombing of the embassy. After former Pres. Jimmy Carter complained about this remark, Reagan, **Sept. 28,** phoned his predecessor and said he had not meant to suggest that Carter or his administration was responsible for the bombing.

General

Discovery Completes Maiden Flight — The space shuttle *Discovery* completed its first flight, **Sept. 5,** a successful journey, in sharp contrast to its initial inability to get off the launching pad. The flight of the *Discovery,* third in a projected fleet of 4 space shuttles, had been postponed twice in June, the second time only 4 seconds before lift-off by an unexpected shutdown of the engine. After a one-day postponement caused by a problem in an electronic system, the flight finally got underway from Cape Canaveral, Fla., on Aug. 30. The flight went fairly smoothly, with 3 communications satellites being launched from the shuttle. The shuttle carried a crew of 6, including Judith Resnick, the second

U.S. woman in space. The only serious problem was overcome when the crew, **Sept. 4,** used the robot arm in the cargo bay to knock off a block of ice that had formed ouside one of the waste-water vents.

Florida Citrus Crop Imperiled — The Florida citrus industry encountered a small but deadly problem in late August, and by September the state's annual crop, valued as high as $2.5 billion, was in serious danger. The culprit was the citrus canker, a bacterium harmless to humans and animals but deadly to citrus trees. The U.S. government, **Sept. 13,** halted all shipments of citrus from Florida. Within a week, some 160 state and federal agents were inspecting the citrus groves. Florida, **Sept. 19,** approved an emergency measure that empowered state agents to decide, on the spot, whether to destroy crops or burn trees. By the end of September, growers and agents had destroyed millions of trees.

Disasters — A typhoon, carrying winds of 137 miles per hour, struck the Philippines, **Sept. 2,** and took at least 1,363 lives, the relief agencies reported, **Sept. 6.** It was the nation's worst storm of the century . . . The crash of a jet airplane at Quito, Ecuador, **Sept. 18,** killed at least 60 persons, almost all of them residents of a neighborhood into which the plane fell.

OCTOBER

National

Candidates Clash in Televised Debates — The major-party nominees for president and vice president slugged it out in three debates on national television in October. Although almost everyone argued about who won, all national polls showed the Republican ticket retaining its wide lead over the Democrats. Geraldine Ferraro, the Democratic vice-presidential candidate, broke with convention, **Oct. 2,** challenging auto workers at a Rockford, Ill., plant to explain why some were supporting Pres. Ronald Reagan. She rejected their claims that the Democrats were weak on national defense. On Iran, she asserted that the hostages had come home alive, unlike 300 Americans killed in bombings in Lebanon during the Reagan administration. Vice Pres. George Bush revealed, **Oct. 3,** that in June he had paid the Internal Revenue Service $198,000 in back taxes and interest after the IRS held that he had failed to report $500,000 in income from the sale of a house on his 1981 returns, and had improperly used $29,000 in leftover campaign funds. Bush's attorneys said he had believed that he did not have to report the income from the house. Reagan and Walter Mondale, the Democratic presidential nominee, met in debate for the first time, **Oct. 7,** in Louisville. The "debate" consisted of responses to questions posed by journalists. Reagan contended that America and its people were better off than in 1980, when he was elected. Mondale said only the wealthy were better off, and that new leadership was needed. Mondale deplored the high deficits of the Reagan years, but the president blamed the deficits on "excessive government spending," which he said he opposed. He suggested that Mondale's plan to balance the budget really amounted to a plan to raise taxes. Mondale warned that high deficits would lead to high interest rates, but Reagan said there was "no connection" between the two. They argued over whether Reagan had sought to cut Social Security benefits. Mondale also said that Reagan had sought to cut Medicare after saying in a debate in 1980 with Pres. Jimmy Carter that he would not. Polls taken after the debate showed Mondale had "won," in part because he was more assertive and alert. Reagan, **Oct. 9,** clarified a statement from the debate, saying he would oppose cuts in Social Security for future as well as current retirees. When speculation after the debate began to grow that Reagan was too old to be president, the White House released findings of his most recent physical examination, in May, which concluded that he was robust and mentally alert. Reagan's record was the focus of attention, **Oct. 11,** when Bush and Ferraro debated in Philadelphia. Asked about previous differences with Reagan, Bush said, "I've been with him every step of the way," and he said he would support all of his policies. Ferraro criticized Reagan across the board, emphasizing alleged failures in Lebanon and negligence in the deaths of Marines killed in the October 1983 bombing. Bush was intense, Ferraro subdued, though at one point she admonished him not to be patronizing toward her.

Mondale, **Oct. 12,** demanded that Bush apologize for saying in the debate that the Democrats had suggested that the Marines killed in Lebanon had "died in shame." The Roman Catholic archbishop of New York, John J. O'Connor, said, **Oct. 15,** that bishops of the church expected public officials and candidates for election to oppose "abortion on demand" and to seek "modification" of legalized abortion. Reagan and Mondale debated for the second time in Kansas City, **Oct. 21.** Foreign affairs was the subject, and Mondale's main theme was that Reagan was not in command of the facts that he had to know to provide strong leadership. He cited alleged mistakes Reagan had made in discussing arms-control issues, and asked, "Who's in charge?" Reagan vigorously defended his policies and argued that he had built up America's strength while Mondale was advocating arms cuts that would weaken the nation. Reagan restated his support for a space-based antimissile system, or "star wars" defense. Mondale warned of the dangers of extending the rivalry with the Soviet Union into space, and disagreed with Reagan's suggestion that defensive technology might be shared with the USSR. Mondale argued that national security would be enhanced by reducing the number of missiles on each side. Reagan, rebutting the "age issue," got off the best line of the debate, saying "I'm not going to exploit for political purposes my opponent's youth and inexperience." Campaigning in California, **Oct. 22,** Reagan stood next to a B-1 bomber to emphasize his support for a weapon Mondale opposed. Polls taken after the second debate showed Reagan widening a lead that had slipped a bit after the first debate. Reagan turned his attention to trying to bring congressional candidates in on his coattails.

Labor Secretary Donovan Indicted — Raymond Donovan, Secretary of Labor in the Reagan administration, pleaded not guilty, **Oct. 2,** to a 137-count indictment charging him with involvement in an attempt to defraud the New York City Transit Authority. He pleaded not guilty on arraignment in the State Supreme Court in the Bronx, N.Y. Donovan, who requested and was granted a leave of absence from his cabinet position, charged that he was the victim of a politically motivated "inquisition" by Mario Merola, the Bronx District Attorney. Donovan was the first cabinet officer to be indicted while in office. Altogether, 2 companies and 10 individuals—all of whom pleaded not guilty—were named in the indictment. Those charged included the Schiavone Construction Company of Seacaucus, New Jersey, which Donovan had served as vice president before entering the cabinet in 1981, and 6 of its present officers. The Jopel Contracting and Trucking Corporation was also cited. The indictment asserted that Donovan had participated in a plan to inflate the value of Jopel's work as a subcontractor in the $186 million construction of a subway tunnel for the Transit Authority. The indictment did not state how much Schiavone was supposed to have overcharged the transit authority. Merola, a Democrat, denied that the indictment of Donovan was timed to coincide with the election campaign, saying that the statute of limitations was about to expire on several of the alleged crimes. In 1982, an independent counsel had found insufficient evidence to indict Donovan on federal allegations.

FBI Agent Arrested for Espionage — Richard Miller, a 20-year veteran of the FBI who had been assigned to the bureau's counterintelligence squad in Los Angeles, was arrested for espionage, **Oct. 3.** Two Russian immigrants, Svetlana Ogorodnikova and her estranged husband Nikolay, were also arrested. It was alleged that Miller had offered to sell FBI documents to the couple for $65,000. Reportedly, one document that had gone to the Russians was a classified manual describing U.S. intelligence activities. The FBI said that Miller, who was reportedly in financial need, had had a "personal relationship" with the woman. Miller was the first FBI agent ever charged with espionage.

Economy Appears Becalmed — Data released in October showed that the economy was essentially stable. The unemployment rate in September remained at 7.3 percent, the Labor Department reported, **Oct. 5.** Prices paid to producers for finished goods edged downward 0.2 percent in September, the Labor Department said, **Oct. 12,** the first time the index had declined for two consecutive months in 8 years. The Federal Reserve Board announced, **Oct. 16,** that industrial production had edged downward in September by 0.6

percent, its first decline since the recession bottomed out in November 1982. Leading banks, **Oct. 16,** lowered their prime lending rate by a quarter of a percentage point to 12.5 percent, another sign of a cooling economy. The Commerce Department said, **Oct. 19,** that the economy had grown at an annual rate of only 2.7 percent in the third quarter, lower than an earlier estimate, and the slowest rate since the recovery had begun to gather momentum. The Department of Labor reported, **Oct. 24,** that the consumer price index had risen 0.4 percent in September. The total advance for the 12 preceding months was 4.2 percent, and this triggered an automatic adjustment in tax brackets for 1983 called indexing —designed to prevent taxpayers from being forced into higher brackets through inflation alone. The administration reported, **Oct. 25,** that the federal budget deficit for the 1984 fiscal year was $175.3 billion, $20.1 billion less than the record deficit of the previous year. The government's index of leading economic indicators rose 0.4 percent in September, the Commerce Department said, **Oct. 31.** Revised figures showed that the index had fallen for 3 straight months previous to September. The nation's trade deficit widened to $12.6 billion in September, the second-biggest monthly total on record, according to the Commerce Department, **Oct. 31.**

98th Congress Adjourns — Amid the usual chaos and controversy, the 98th Congress closed its last session, **Oct. 12,** and most of its members turned their attention to electioneering. In its final rush, Congress approved a catchall spending bill of $370 billion for the 1985 fiscal year and, after one failure, raised the debt limit. Attached to the spending bill was a major piece of anticrime legislation that sought to restrict bail for "dangerous" suspects, standardize prison sentences, increase penalties for drug convictions, and limit use of the insanity defense. Pres. Ronald Reagan had strongly supported the legislation. In the new spirit of cutting costs, some $100 million in "pork-barrel" water projects were eliminated from the spending bill. A civil rights bill approved in the House, failed when the Senate was unable to find a compromise; the bill would have required any institution receiving federal aid for any of its programs to obey federal civil-rights laws in all of its programs and activities. The Simpson-Mazzoli immigration bill also lost when the 2 houses were unable to work out their differences under strong criticism from Hispanic groups and others. Conservatives succeeded in blocking Senate approval of the 35-year-old U.N. treaty outlawing genocide. Howard Baker (R, Tenn.), the Senate majority leader, was among those retiring from Congress.

International

CIA Guerrilla Manual Causes Furor — In the Central American crisis, acrimony and tragedy overshadowed peace talks in El Salvador in October. Daniel Ortega Saavedra, Nicaragua's head of state, charged in a speech to the U.N. General Assembly, **Oct. 2,** that the United States was planning to mount a military attack on Nicaragua to prevent the Nicaraguan national election scheduled for Nov. 4. El Salvador's Pres. Jóse Napoleón Duarte told the General Assembly, **Oct. 9,** that he would be willing to hold peace talks with guerrilla leaders starting in a week. The guerrillas, **Oct. 9,** accepted the invitation. Both houses of Congress, **Oct. 11,** voted to continue a ban on financial support for "contras" fighting against the Nicaraguan government. Reports surfaced, **Oct. 14,** concerning the existence of a manual written in Spanish and distributed among rebels opposing the leftist regime in Nicaragua. It was reported to be the work of the Central Intelligence Agency. It described how some government officials could be "neutralized"—a term that might mean "assassinated." The manual described various techniques for waging guerrilla warfare. An executive order signed by Pres. Reagan in 1981 forbade any U.S. government employee from engaging or conspiring to engage in assassinations. Duarte met with the Salvadoran rebel leaders in a church in La Palma, **Oct. 15,** and the 2 sides agreed to form a joint commission to seek an end to the 5-year-old civil war that had caused the deaths of more than 50,000 civilians. However, Duarte and the rebels did not agree to a formal cease-fire. The 4 nations of the Contradora group said, **Oct. 12,** that they would revise their draft peace plan for Central America to meet U.S. concerns about adequate verification and control mechanisms to insure Nicaraguan compliance. Reagan, **Oct. 18,** ordered the CIA to investigate the guerrilla manual to determine who was responsible and whether U.S. law had been violated. An administration official said that the manual appeared to be the work of a "low-level contract employee" of the CIA in the region. The war resumed in El Salvador, **Oct. 18,** as the army opened an offensive against the leftist guerrillas. Four employees of the CIA died, **Oct. 19,** when their airplane crashed during a surveillance mission over El Salvador. They were the first agency employees known to have died in the conflicts in Central America. In an interview, **Oct. 20,** Edward Chamorro, one of the Nicaraguan rebel leaders, admitted that his forces had carried out assassinations of the type implied in the CIA manual. He said Sandinista "tyrants" had been killed "when we have found them guilty of crimes." Robert McFarlane, Reagan's adviser for national security affairs, said, **Oct. 21,** that Reagan would dismiss any U.S. official who developed or approved the manual. CIA officials, **Oct. 22,** denied Reagan's assertion, made during an Oct. 21 debate with Walter Mondale, that most copies of the manual had been edited to remove advice on "neutralizing" Nicaraguan officials. The Salvadoran government suffered a blow, **Oct. 3,** when a helicopter crash took the lives of Lt. Col. Domingo Monterrosa, the army's leading combat commander, and 3 other senior officers.

Concern Grows on Threats to Embassies — The House Select Committee on Intelligence said in a report, **Oct. 3,** that officials responsible for security at the U.S. Embassy near East Beirut had paid insufficient attention to warnings of potential terrorist attacks prior to the bombing of Sept. 20. Reagan administration officials said, **Oct. 4,** that U.S. intelligence agencies had evidence that a Muslim militant group called the Party of God was responsible for the bombing as well as for terrorist attacks in 1983 on the U.S. Embassy and the Marine barracks in Beirut. As more threats from terrorists were received by the U.S. Embassy in Beirut, the embassy began to evacuate dependents and nonessential personnel. Pres. Ronald Reagan, **Oct. 20,** signed a law allocating $336 million to enhance security at U.S. embassies around the world. Secretary of State George Shultz said, **Oct. 25,** that the United States should adopt a policy of responding militarily to future acts of terrorism. He warned that such responses could involve the deaths of American servicemen and innocent civilians. A report by the staff of the Senate Foreign Relations Committee blamed the bombing in East Beirut on the "tragically simple mistake" of not blocking access to the road leading to the building.

Prime Minister Gandhi Assassinated

Indira Gandhi, the prime minister of India, was slain by 2 of her own bodyguards in New Delhi, **Oct. 31.** Her assassins were reported to be members of the Sikh religious minority. The Sikhs had been in violent confrontation with the Gandhi government for months, and many of them had died when the army attacked extremists in a Sikh shrine earlier this year. Mrs. Gandhi was shot a number of times as she walked from her residence through a garden to an interview with the British actor Peter Ustinov. Early reports indicated that one of the assassins was killed immediately, and the other was wounded. Gandhi was succeeded by her son Rajiv, 40 years old, who was the ranking general secretary of his mother's party. To suppress any further violence, he put the army on full alert and imposed curfews in several cities. Many Sikhs, in India and elsewhere, rejoiced at the news of the assassination, and Hindu followers of Mrs. Gandhi responded with attacks on Sikhs in India. It was feared that India's fragile unity would collapse amid the sectarian hatreds. Mrs. Gandhi, a Hindu, had, at age 66, led India for all but 3 of the last 18 years. She became Prime Minister in 1966, 2 years after the death of her father, Jawaharlal Nehru, the nation's first Prime Minister.

Thatcher Unhurt in Bombing Fatal to 4 — British Prime Minister Margaret Thatcher escaped unhurt, **Oct. 12,** when a bomb ripped through a hotel in Brighton where the Conservative Party was conducting its annual conference. Four persons, including a member of Parliament, were killed and 32 were injured. Thatcher had left an area that was seriously damaged by the bomb just minutes before it went off. The Irish Republican Army claimed responsibility for the bombing, **Oct. 13.** The IRA acknowledged that the bomb had been aimed at Thatcher, whose policies in Northern Ireland it opposed. Thatcher, **Oct. 13,** said "All attempts to destroy democracy by terrorism will fail." Bill Hucklesby, head of Scotland Yard's antiterrorist squad, said, **Oct. 13,** that the device may have been a highly sophisticated time bomb planted weeks in advance.

Oil Prices Begin to Fall — Britain, **Oct. 17,** announced it would reduce the price of its North Sea oil by $1.35 a barrel. Nigeria, a member of the Organization of Petroleum Exporting Countries, followed suit, **Oct. 18,** slashing the price of its principal grades of oil by $2 a barrel. As prospects for more price reductions grew, ministers of 8 oil-producing nations met informally in Geneva, **Oct. 22,** in advance of a formal emergency session of OPEC, but Nigeria declined to take part. An OPEC committee drew up a recommendation, **Oct. 28,** that the 13-member organization cut oil production to prevent prices from falling further. Once again, Nigeria was a holdout, refusing to cut production or raise its discounted prices. The other OPEC countries approved the recommendation, **Oct. 29.**

China Edges Toward Capitalism — The government of China, **Oct. 20,** announced plans to cut back on its control over the nation's economy. Under the new program, a million state-owned enterprises would have greater independence and would be obliged to compete with each other. The intention was to let prices in the market place be determined by supply and demand. The new environment would be created in the urban areas, and would follow the introduction of incentives for China's 800 million peasants. Under that approach, begun in 1978, those who produced more were rewarded, and the result was a sharp rise in agricultural output. Mindful of the abrupt upheavals of the years under Mao Zedong, the Communist Central Committee said that the changes would be introduced gradually under the supervision of the Cabinet.

Philippine Military Accused in Assassination — A 5-member panel investigating the assassination of Benigno Aquino, the opposition political leader in the Philipines, concluded in October that he was the victim of a military plot. Aquino was shot as he left a plane at Manila airport in August 1983. The official version of the incident was that Aquino had been shot by a lone gunman who in turn was shot dead on the spot. The panel, after conducting an extensive investigation under tense circumstances, was not unanimous in its conclusions. Corazon Agrava, head of the commission, in a report given to Pres. Ferdinand Marcos, **Oct. 23,** implicated an air force general and 6 soldiers in the murder. The 4 remaining investigators, in a report given to Marcos, **Oct. 24,** found a wider conspiracy that included Gen. Fabian Ver, the chief of staff of the armed forces and a cousin and close associate of Marcos. Marcos had said that he would prosecute whomever the panel named. Ver, **Oct. 24,** was granted a temporary leave of absence from his duties.

Aid Rushed to Starving Ethiopians — As starvation threatened to engulf millions of people in Ethiopia, the Reagan administration announced, **Oct. 24,** that it was sending $45 million in wheat and other foodstuffs. The food was to be delivered to private relief organizations for distribution in Ethiopia. Ethiopia and other countries had suffered from a protracted drought throughout much of Africa. A. Peter McPherson, administrator of the Agency for International Development, criticized the Ethiopian government for having spent $100 million on its tenth anniversary celebration and for showing insufficient concern about its hungry people. Critics of the Reagan administration said it had moved too slowly to provide aid to a nation allied with the Soviet Union. As Ethiopia's plight became known, other countries and thousands of individuals rushed to offer assistance.

7 to Be Tried in Attempt on Pope's Life — Italian officials said, **Oct. 25,** that 3 Bulgarians and 4 Turks would be tried in the attempt in 1981 to assassinate Pope John Paul II. It was reported that Judge Ilario Martella would also order Mehmet Ali Agca, who fired at the pope, to stand trial on new charges. Agca would also be the principal prosecution witness, and his credibility was expected to be challenged by the defense in view of the frequent contradictions in his story of what happened. Antonio Albano, the state prosecutor, had said in June that he doubted Bulgarians would have become involved without the approval of the Soviet Union. The presumed motive of the alleged plotters was the fear that the first Polish pope would continue to rekindle religious fervor in Eastern Europe so as to pose a threat to the communist regimes there. Only 3 of the accused men were actually in Italian custody. Martella said at a news conference, **Oct. 26,** that the pope had been shot by 2 gunmen in St. Peter's Square. The second man, identified as Oral Celik, a Turk, was in custody and among those facing trial.

General

Thousands of Caribou Drown — Officials in Quebec reported, **Oct. 3,** that more than 7,000 migrating caribou had drowned in northern Quebec while crossing 2 rivers. There were fears that the toll might be even higher. The large mammals, which are members of the deer family, were overwhelmed by high water or swept over waterfalls. Inuit (Eskimo) leaders charged that a public utility had caused the disaster by letting too much water spill over a dam. Aside from the danger to the water supply posed by the rotting carcasses, the deaths were regarded as a major environmental catastrophe. Quebec officials chartered aircraft to create a "wall of sound" and began constructing a fence to discourage more caribou from crossing the rivers at dangerous spots.

Crew of 7 Travels on Shuttle — Five men and 2 women constituting the largest crew in the history of space flight, rode the shuttle *Challenger* into space, **Oct. 5.** The crew included Canada's first astronaut, Marc Garneau of the Canadian navy. The shuttle, **Oct. 5,** deployed a satellite to measure the amount of solar energy reaching the earth. The *Challenger* astronauts lost much of their communications, **Oct. 8,** when cosmic radiation disabled a relay satellite, but an alternative network was activated to permit resumption of human messages and transmittal of scientific data. Kathryn Sullivan, **Oct. 11,** became the first American woman to walk in space. *Challenger* landed, **Oct. 13,** at Cape Canaveral, successfully concluding the first of a "launch a month" series of shuttle flights.

Heart of Baboon Implanted in Infant — The heart of a baboon was implanted in a 15-day-old girl, **Oct. 26,** in a 5-hour operation performed at Loma Linda University Medical Center in California. Doctors said the baby, identified only as Baby Fae, was "doing fine," but was still listed in critical condition. Dr. Leonard Bailey headed the surgical team that performed the operation. The child had been born with a severe birth defect, hypoplastic heart syndrome; the left side of her heart was much smaller than the right side. As a result, she had almost died. A young baboon was chosen as the donor because, it was reported, a compatible human heart was not available. Doctors said they expected that the heart would grow with the child. The baby was removed from the critical list, **Oct. 29.** Dr. Bailey, responding to criticism of the operation on ethical grounds, said, **Oct. 29,** that in fact, a human heart had not been sought, and that "Our entire research endeavor has been aimed" at transplanting animal hearts in humans.

Major Decisions of the U.S. Supreme Court, 1983-84

The 1983-84 Supreme Court term opened October 3, 1983 and ended July 5, 1984. Some 151 cases were decided with full opinions, 66 unanimously and 29 by one-vote margins. Among the notable actions, the Supreme Court:

Refused to review, thus let stand, a ruling favoring a handgun ban. In 1981 the Chicago suburb of Morton Grove passed an ordinance prohibiting the sale and possession of handguns within town limits. The ban was challenged by individuals and state groups in state and federal courts. In a 1982 decision, a 3-judge panel of the U.S. 7th Circuit Court of Appeals ruled that the ban did not infringe on the Second Amendment right to bear arms, since the Amendment referred only to "the preservation of a militia." The Supreme Court has never handed down a definitive interpretation of the Second Amendment. (Oct. 3)

Refused to review, thus let stand, a decision favoring a Pan American World Airways policy requiring pregnant flight attendants to take unpaid leaves of absence. (Oct. 31)

Ruled, unanimously, that the Racketeer Influenced and Corrupt Organizations Act (RICO) permitted the government to seize the profits and income from all corrupt enterprises. (Nov. 28)

Ruled, unanimously, to interpret narrowly an Immigration and Nationality Act provision requiring seven years of "continuous physical presence" in the U.S. as a precondition for the suspension of deportation procedures. The case concerned an attempt to deport a Thai woman who had met the seven-year test except for a three-month trip to Thailand. The U.S. 9th Circuit Court of Appeals ruled against the INS, maintaining that the government's interpretation was overly strict. The Supreme Court reversed the appeals court, stating that in 1952 Congress had changed the wording of the provision from the more permissive "continuous residence" to the stricter "continuous physical presence." (Jan. 10)

Ruled, 5-4, that arson investigators needed a warrant to search a private residence several hours after a fire. The majority agreed with a lower court that the warrantless search in question was unconstitutional. However, a four-member plurality maintained that investigators could conduct a search with an "administrative" warrant, which did not require the support of probable cause. (Jan. 11)

Ruled, 5-4, that courts could impose punitive damages on the nuclear power industry for safety violations. Karen Silkwood, killed in a 1974 car crash, had been contaminated by plutonium while a lab technician at a Kerr-McGee Corp. processing plant in Oklahoma. Her estate won $10 million in punitive damages, but the award was overturned by the U.S. 10th Circuit Court of Appeals. The Supreme Court reversed the appeals court, all 9 judges agreeing that punitive damages were a form of regulation, but divided as to whether federal laws shielded the nuclear power industry from state laws protecting workers' safety. (Jan. 11)

Ruled, 5-4, that states could not stop the federal government's attempts to sell offshore oil and natural gas leases. The Coastal Zone Management Act of 1982 required the government to insure that its actions "directly affecting the coastal zone" were consistent with the policies of the coastal states. In 1981, California used the law to successfully sue the Interior Dept., blocking the lease sale of 29 offshore tracts. A federal district judge and the U.S. 9th Circuit Court of Appeals backed the state's argument that the Dept. had violated the law by not adequately investigating California's environmental concerns. Overturning these rulings, the Supreme Court concluded that since a lease sale was only the first step of a process that involved obtaining federal permits before exploratory drilling or actual production, it did not require review provisions. (Jan. 11)

Ruled, 5-4, that the noncommercial home use of video cassette recorders was not in violation of the federal Copyright Act of 1976. The case concerned Sony v. Universal City Studios, the latter arguing that the home taping of copyrighted films and television shows violated their property rights and deprived them of revenues. The court reversed a 1981 ruling by the U.S. 9th Circuit Court of Appeals, maintaining that home taping did not infringe on the copyright law unless the material was used for "commercial or profit-making purpose." Writing for the majority, Justice John Paul Stevens held that the court had no choice but to rule as it did, since Congress had failed to include video technology in the copyright laws. (Jan. 17)

Ruled, 8-1, that there was no time limit on the collection of taxes owed on a fraudulent or false federal tax return, even if the taxpayer subsequently submitted an amended, nonfraudulent return. (Jan. 17)

Ruled, unanimously, that under most circumstances the public and press were entitled to be present during the selection of trial jurors. The case concerned a California judge's pretrial order keeping the press and public from most of a murder case's jury selection in order to protect the privacy of the potential jurors questioned as to their willingness to impose the death penalty. Reversing the California Court of Appeals, the Supreme Court maintained that the trial judge could close the jury selection only when it was "essential to protect higher values," with the "privacy interests" of potential jurors balanced against the "historical values" of an open judicial system. (Jan. 18)

Ruled, 7-2, that a state need not review a death sentence to determine whether it was comparable to punishments given in similar cases in that state. The ruling affected a convicted muderer who challenged his death sentence on the ground that his state had violated the Eighth Amendment prohibition of cruel and unusual punishment by failing to conduct a "proportionality" sentence review. It indirectly affected another convicted murder whose execution was delayed pending the outcome of the case. The court held that neither the Eighth Amendment nor previous high court rulings required proportionality reviews. (Jan. 23)

Ruled, 5-4, that a failing company could free itself from its labor obligations. The court held that the federal Bankruptcy Code took precedence over the labor law. (Feb. 22)

Refused to review, thus let stand, a ruling that the federal government had adequately studied the risks of permitting nuclear waste to be transported on the nation's highways. (Feb. 27)

Ruled, 6-3, that a murder confession made by a probationer in a conversation with a probation officer was valid evidence, even if the probationer had not been given the "Miranda warning" that he had the right to remain silent. The court concluded that no warning was necessary since the person had not been in custody at the time of the confession. (Feb. 22)

Ruled, 7-2, that family members' interest-free loans to one another were subject to the federal gift tax. This decision eliminated a loophole under which wealthy parents gave interest-free loans to their offspring for high-yield investments. The offspring were taxed at a lower rate than the parents would have been if they themselves had invested. (Feb. 22)

Ruled, 6-3, that Title IX of the Education Amendments of 1972 was enforceable only on programs specifically receiving federal funds. Title IX prohibited sex discrimination in education programs receiving federal funds. Using the broadest interpretation, a college or university that violated the law risked a cutoff of federal funds to the entire institution. However, the majority accepted the narrow view of the Reagan administration that Title IX applied only to that function of a school receiving federal funds. This decision gave the Reagan administration its first victory in a significant civil rights case brought before the Supreme Court. (Feb. 28)

Ruled, 6-3, that a court could not apply retroactively a 1981 decision that had expanded the Fifth Amendment protection against self-incrimination. In the important 1981 ruling, the Supreme Court had held that a criminal suspect who requested an attorney was "not subject to further interrogation by the authorities until counsel has been made available to him, unless the accused himself initiates further communications." This ruling was handed down as the U.S. 8th Circuit Court of Appeals was considering an appeal of a manslaughter conviction, the arrest and interrogation for which took place in 1973. The appeals court overturned the conviction, citing a violation of the Supreme Court's expansion of the Fifth Amendment protection. The Supreme Court reversed the appeals court, deciding that although retroactive application of judicial rulings was routine, it was not compulsory. (Feb. 29)

Ruled, 5-4, that a city could constitutionally use public funds for a Christmas Nativity scene. Deciding that a Christmas display, sponsored by Pawtucket, R.I., did not violate the First Amendment doctrine of separation of Church and State, the high court held that the determining factor was whether a public-funded religious practice created "real danger of establishment of a state church." However, since the Pawtucket display included such secular symbols as reindeer and a Christmas tree, as well as a life-size Nativity scene, the ruling did not decide on the constitutionality of tax-supported Christmas displays that included only religious symbols. Cases concerning such displays were in the lower federal courts. The Pawtucket display had been challenged by the American Civil Liberties Union with the support of the National Council of Churches and the American Jewish Committee. (Mar. 5)

Agreed to rule on the constitutionality of a state law permitting school teachers to set aside a moment of silence for student prayer or meditation. The action came less than a month after the Senate had defeated proposed constitutional amendments sanctioning voluntary silent prayer or oral prayer in public schools. (Apr. 2)

Ruled, 7-2, that the Immigration and Naturalization Service could raid factories and other workplaces suspected of employing illegal aliens. (Apr. 17)

Ruled, unanimously, that state courts could not use race to decide child custody rulings. The case concerned a ruling by a Florida judge to refuse a divorced white woman the custody of her child after the woman married a black man. The judge concluded that the child would be stigmatized by a black stepfather. Overturning the Florida Court of Appeals, the Supreme Court maintained that the judge's decision violated the Constitution's equal protection law. (Apr. 25)

Ruled, unanimously, that a publication or its employees could be sued for libel in any state in which the publication was circulated. The decision gave libel plaintiffs the latitude to seek favorable jurisdictions for their suits, and compelled the media to pay the increased costs of legal defense in distant states. (Mar. 20)

Ruled, unanimously, that the lawyers of nonprofit "public interest" groups in civil rights cases were entitled to the same awards of legal fees as private lawyers. (Mar. 21)

Ruled, unanimously, that an exclusive contract between a hospital and a group of doctors for medical services was not automatically a violation of federal antitrust law. (Mar. 27)

Defined for the first time, in an 8-1 vote, the standards for criminal appeals on the ground of ineffective assistance of counsel: The defendant must demonstrate that his lawyer's performance "fell below an objective standard of reasonableness" based on "identified acts or omissions," and must show that "there is a reasonable probability that, but for the counsellor's unprofessional errors, the result of the proceeding would have been different." (May 14)

Ruled, unanimously, that the Federal Energy Regulatory Commission was required to accept whatever conditions the Interior Department imposed on the licensing of hydroelectric power plants on Indian reservation lands. (May 15)

Ruled, 6-3, that cities could prohibit signs, including political campaign posters, from public property. (May 15)

Ruled, 6-2, to broaden protection against warrantless home arrests. In an earlier ruling the justices had held that police could make a home arrest without a warrant only if they had probable cause and only under "exigent circumstances"—those circumstances not specified. The current case arose from an arrest by police of a man on suspicion of drunk driving. Acting on a witness's tip, police made the arrest in the defendant's home without a warrant. The state supreme court rejected the defendant's claim that police had violated his Fourth Amendment protection against unreasonable searches and seizures, holding that the police are

justified because if they'd obtained a warrant the alcohol in the defendant's system might have been metabolized before the police reached his home. The Supreme Court reversed the ruling, arguing that the severity of the offense was an important factor in whether exigent circumstance allowed a warrantless home arrest, and noting that under the state law, first-offense drunk driving was a civil infraction punished by a fine, not a jail term. (May 15)

Ruled, unanimously, that a federal law banning employment discrimination covered partnership decisions in law firms. The ruling came from a suit by Elizabeth A. Hishon against the Atlanta law firm of King & Spalding. Hishon, a former associate at the firm, sued for sex bias under Title VII of the 1964 Civil Rights Act, charging that she had been denied a partnership because she was a woman. King & Spalding held that business partnerships were outside the scope of the bias law. Overturning a U.S. 11th Circuit Court of Appeals decision, the Supreme Court maintained that Title VII did cover law firms with respect to the promotion of associates to partners. Chief Justice Warren E. Burger said that the key to the ruling was Hishon's claim that when she was hired in 1972 she received verbal assurance that she would be considered for a partnership. (May 22)

Rule, 8-0, to uphold a sweeping land-reform program in Hawaii. The court thus broadened the states' power to transfer the ownership of vast tracts of land through the doctrine of eminent domain. The high court concluded: "Where the exercise of eminent domain power is rationally related to a conceivable public purpose, the court has never held a compensated taking to be proscribed by the public use clause." (May 30)

Ruled, 6-3, that states could constitutionally hold juvenile criminal suspects in preventive detention before bringing them to trial. All 50 states already sanctioned juvenile pretrial confinement of one kind or another. Writing for the majority, Justice William H. Rehnquist concluded that preventive detention served "a legitimate regulatory purpose compatible with the 'fundamental fairness' demanded by the due process clause in juvenile proceedings." (June 4)

Rule, 6-3 and 7-2 in two separate cases, for a "good-faith" exception to the "exclusionary rule" under which evidence gained by police in violation of the constitutional rights of suspects was inadmissible at trial. Both cases dealt with search warrants later ruled invalid. One was issued without probable cause; the second was not the right type of warrant for that crime and did not properly identify the location searched. The court held that in both cases it was the magistrate, not the police, who had erred, thus there was no police illegality. (June 5)

Ruled, 6-3, that courts could not upset valid seniority systems to protect the jobs of minority workers hired under affirmative action. The decision was the most significant victory for the Reagan administration in a civil rights case. Most proponents of affirmative action viewed it as a major setback for minorities and women. The case developed from a 1980 consent decree between Memphis and the Justice Dept., under which the city agreed to raise the percentage of black firefighters to 11.5 from 4. During a 1981 fiscal crisis, a federal judge ordered the city to preserve the jobs of newly-hired blacks; white firefighters with many years seniority were instead laid off. The city and the mainly white firefighters union unsuccessfully challenged the order in the U.S. 6th Circuit Court of Appeals. The Supreme Court majority reversed the appeals court, based on Title VII of the 1964 Civil Rights Act and on the high court's 1977 Teamsters v. Teamsters decision. Title VII prohibited employment discrimination based on race or sex but exempted from interference "bona fide" seniority systems that had not been set up to discriminate. The 1977 ruling established that only workers who could prove they were discrimination victims were entitled to retroactive seniority. (June 12)

Ruled, unanimously, that criminal evidence police had gathered illegally was admissible at trial if the police could prove that the evidence would have been inevitably discovered by lawful means. Overturning a lower court ruling, this ruling established an "inevitable-discovery" exception to the "exclusionary rule" under which judges must disallow evidence gathered in violation of the constitutional rights of criminal suspects. (June 11)

Ruled, unanimously, that criminal prosecutors need not honor plea-bargain agreements with suspects. The high court maintained that as long as a plea-bargain agreement was "voluntary and intelligent" and accepted by a suspect "with full awareness of the consequences," prosecutors were not constitutionally bound to abide by it. (June 11)

Ruled, 5-4, that police need not advise a criminal suspect of his constitutional rights if doing so would compromise public safety. This was the first time a "public safety exception" was made to the Miranda ruling. (June 12)

Ruled, unanimously, that the Federal Aviation Administration could not be sued for damaged coming from aircraft accidents. The two cases in question involved suits as a result of two aircraft accidents stemming from in-flight fires. 124 people were killed in one case, 4 in the other. In both cases, survivors and families of the victims accused the FAA of negligence in certifying that the planes were air-worthy. The high court maintained that it was the aircraft manufacturers responsibility to meet the safety standards set by the FAA, since the agency itself could not inspect every plane for violations. This was one of the most important recent rulings on the legal liability of federal government agencies. (June 19)

Ruled, 6-0, that the Environmental Protection Agency could expand its "bubble policy" to areas of the country that had not yet met federal clean-air standards. Under the bubble policy, industrial pollutants emitted by a factory were regarded as being within a "bubble," and the plant could add new facilities, including boilers and smokestacks, as long as there was no increase in the pollution level within the bubble. In 1982 the U.S. Court of Appeals in Washington, D.C. had blocked the EPA's attempt to extend the bubble concept to already-polluted regions. The Supreme Court overturned the ruling. (June 25)

Ruled, 8-0, that chemical manufacturers could not withhold health and safety information on new pesticides on the ground of protecting trade secrets. (June 26)

Ruled, 5-4, that the Reagan administration could impose restrictions on U.S. citizens' travel to Cuba. The court accepted the Treasury Dept.'s argument that the travel limits were needed to stop the flow of U.S. currency to a belligerent nation. (June 26)

Ruled, 7-2, that the National Collegiate Athletic Assn. violated federal antitrust law by preventing individual schools from negotiating the rights to football telecasts. (June 27)

Ruled, 5-4, that prison inmates had no constitutional right of privacy in their cells; and, 6-3, that jail officials could restrict physical contact between inmates and visitors. (July 3)

Ruled, 7-0, that the U.S. Jaycees—a civic organization with 300,000 members nationwide—could not exclude women from full membership. The organization had allowed women to join only as associate members without voting rights or the possibility of holding office. (July 3)

Ruled, unanimously, that public school districts were required to give quasi-medical services to handicapped students; but held, 6-3, that the parents of such students who successfully sued school officials could not recover lawyers' fees. (July 5)

Ruled, 6-2, to uphold a law allowing the denial of federal student aid to young men who had failed to register for the military draft. (July 5)

Major Actions During the 98th Congress, 1983-84

The 98th Congress adjourned Nov. 18, 1983, and reconvened Jan. 23, 1984. Bills passed and signed and other major actions during the latter part of the 1983 session and the first three-fourths of the 1984 session include the following:

Immigration Reform. House Speaker Thomas P. O'Neill (D., Mass.) withdrew, Oct. 4, 1983, an immigration reform bill. The bill was designed to decrease the flow of illegal aliens into the U.S., by establishing a system of civil and criminal penalties against employers who knowingly hired such aliens. It would also grant legal status to millions of illegal aliens already in the U.S.—since 1979 in the Senate version and 1981 in the House version. The withdrawal was prompted by opposition from Hispanic Americans, who were concerned that the threatened sanctions would mean increased bias against hiring any Hispanics.

Martin Luther King Day. The Senate voted, Oct. 19, to make the third Monday in January of each year a federal holiday to honor the Rev. Martin Luther King, Jr. The House had approved similar legislation in August. The only other American to be honored by a federal holiday was George Washington. Pres. Reagan signed the legislation, Nov. 2.

Clinch River Reactor. The Senate voted, Oct. 26, against authorizing further funding for the controversial Clinch River Breeder Reactor project, near Oak Ridge, Tenn. The Energy Dept. had failed to develop an acceptable cost-sharing arrangement with private industry by the deadline of Sept. 30. No further funds meant that the reactor would probably not be built.

Government Spending. Pres. Reagan signed stopgap funding legislation, Nov. 14, permitting continued government spending for several agencies for the rest of fiscal 1984, ending Sept. 30, 1984. Both Houses cleared the measure, Nov. 12. The final version added $98.7 million in funding for domestic programs. House Democrats had sought nearly $1 billion in such funds. Most of the additional funds were going to emergency housing for the homeless, and education programs for immigrant children and the handicapped. Defense spending was authorized at $247 billion annually, allowing initial spending for MX missile production and advance procurement for the B-1 bomber, naval vessels and several other weapons. The bill also provided for $11.5 billion in foreign aid, including $64.8 million to El Salvador. Several policy amendments were carried in the legislation. One prohibited the Interior Dept. from issuing leases for oil and gas development on national wildlife refuges, unless a formal rule-making process was initiated; another forbade insurance coverage for abortions for federal workers unless the woman's life was endangered.

ERA. The House, Nov. 15, narrowly defeated the proposed Equal Rights Amendment to the U.S. Constitution. The vote fell six votes short of the two-thirds majority required to send it to the states for ratification. The wording was exactly the same as that of the ERA proposed in 1972 and dropped in June, 1982 after failing to receive ratification by 38 of the state legislatures. House Speaker Thomas P. O'Neill, Jr. had brought the measure to the floor under special rules usually reserved for noncontroversial or minor legislation—all amendments forbidden and each side allowed only twenty minutes debate before the vote. In protest, a dozen representatives who had sponsored the bill voted against it.

Gas Deregulation. The Senate defeated, Nov. 15, two proposed—and opposing—changes in the country's natural gas deregulation policy. This effectively ended the chances that meaningful new natural gas legislation would be passed in 1983. One measure, supported by the Reagan administration, would have resulted in the decontrol of all gas prices by 1987; the other, favored by consumer groups, would have rolled back some natural gas prices and reinstituted controls on other classifications of gas.

National Debt Ceiling. The Senate agreed, Nov. 16, to increase the national debt ceiling to $1.49 trillion, permitting the Treasury to continue borrowing money through April, 1984.

State, Commerce, Justice Clearing. Congress cleared, Nov. 16, a fiscal 1984 $10.5 billion appropriations bill for the State, Commerce, and Justice Depts. and the federal judiciary. These agencies had not been cleared since fiscal 1980, because all had been involved with controversial legislation.

Civil Rights Commission. Congress cleared a bill restructuring and extending the Civil Rights Commission, Nov. 16. The new commission would have 8 members—4 appointed by the president and 4 by Congress, 2 by Senate leadership and two by the Speaker of the House. The commissioners could be dismissed only for cause. The panel was authorized for a 6-year period, after which Congress would have to renew the authorization for the panel to continue its operation. The Senate approved the panel Nov. 14, the House Nov. 16.

Private School Tax Credits. The Senate defeated, Nov. 16, a proposal that would have granted as much as $300 in tax credits to parents of children enrolled in private schools. Pres. Reagan had attempted to gain support for the measure. Only families whose annual income was less than $40,000 would have received the full credit, and those with incomes over $60,000 would not have qualified for any credit.

Dairy Farmers. The Senate, Nov. 17, and House, Nov. 18, approved a bill freezing tobacco price supports and authorizing payments for dairy farmers for producing less milk. The freeze in tobacco price supports was designed to make U.S. tobacco products more competitive in world markets. The dairy bill was designed to reduce U.S. dairy output, which had been running about 10% above demands. It was the first such federal payment plan for dairy products.

Revenue Sharing. Both Houses adopted, Nov. 17, a conference report extending revenue sharing to local governments.

International Monetary Fund/Federal Housing. Congress passed, Nov. 18, a legislative package increasing by $8.4 billion the U.S. contribution to the International Monetary Fund, and also authorizing a $15.6 billion federal housing program—the first under the Reagan administration.

War Powers Resolution. The House, Nov. 1, and Senate, Oct. 28, each invoked the War Powers Resolution regarding Grenada, but the Senate later dropped the debt ceiling bill to which it had attached the amendment. Congress did not pass any legislation to prevent Pres. Reagan from retaining U.S. troops in Grenada while Congress was adjourned, but both Houses passed resolutions allowing congressional leaders to call Congress back into session to deal with foreign crises.

Federal Deficit. Congress failed to implement reduction of the federal deficit, which was expected to remain around $200 billion a year through the rest of the decade. This was the first time since passage of the 1974 Congressional Budget Act that Congress did not take steps to meet the requirements of its budget resolutions.

Wheat Farmers. Pres. Reagan signed, Apr. 10, 1984, a bill providing payments to wheat farmers who idled 10% of their land in addition to the 20% idled to participate in the federal price support program. The bill covered the 1984 and 1985 growing seasons.

Student Religious Groups. The House of Representatives passed, July 25, a Senate-approved measure allowing student religious groups the same access to public high school buildings as nonreligious groups, providing their meetings were held before or after regular school hours.

"Inside" Trading. Pres. Reagan signed, Aug. 10, a bill to authorize tripling penalties against any person profiting from trading stocks on the basis of "inside" information. The Senate had passed the measure by a voice vote June 28, the House by voice vote July 25.

Child Support Payments. Pres. Reagan signed, Aug. 16, a bill that required states to pass laws obliging employers to withhold wages from parents who fell one month behind in making court-ordered child support payments. It would also allow seizure of the delinquent parent's property, dividends, pensions and tax refunds. The House had approved Aug. 8 and the Senate Aug. 6.

Women's Retirement Benefits. Pres. Reagan signed, Aug. 23, a bill to make it easier for women to earn retirement benefits under private pension plans. Most pension plans would have to meet the new standards by Jan. 1, 1985.

Deaths, Nov. 1, 1983—Oct. 31, 1984

A

Adams, Ansel, 82; photographer of the American West; Carmel, Cal., Apr. 22.

Aldrich, Robert, 65; Hollywood film director, *The Dirty Dozen;* Los Angeles, Dec. 5.

Alston, Walter, 72; manager of the Dodgers for 23 years; led team to 7 pennants and 4 world series titles; Oxford, Oh., Oct. 1.

Andropov, Yuri V., 69; leader of the Soviet Union since 1982; USSR, Feb. 9.

Atkinson, Brooks, 89; drama critic for the *N.Y. Times,* 1925-60; Huntsville, Ala., Jan. 13.

B

Baldwin, Billy, 80; interior decorator who greatly influenced post World War II designers; Nantucket, Mass., Nov. 25.

Barry, Jack, 66; producer and star of television game shows, *The Joker's Wild;* New York, May 2.

Barzini, Luigi, 75; Italian author and journalist; Rome, Mar. 31.

Basehart, Richard, 70; stage and screen actor; Los Angeles, Sept. 17.

Basie, Count, 79; jazz pianist and band leader who was one of the major influences of the big band era of the 1930s and 40s; Hollywood, Fla., Apr. 26.

Bentley, Max, 63; hockey hall of famer who scored 245 NHL goals; Saskatoon, Sask., Jan. 19.

Bergeron, Victor J., 81; founder of the "Trader Vic" restaurant chain; Hillsborough, Cal., Oct. 11.

Berlinguer, Enrico, 62; leader of the Italian Communist Party; Padua, Italy, June 11.

Betjeman, Sir John, 77; poet laureate of Britain since 1972; Cornwall, England, May 19.

Boylston, Helen Dore, 89; author of the *Sue Barton* series of books; Trumbull, Conn., Sept. 30.

Brandt, Bill, 78; British photographer who was noted for his foreboding images; London, Dec. 20.

Brassaï, 84; photographer famed for his portraits of Paris nightlife; Cote d'Azur, Nice, France, July 8.

Brautigan, Richard, 49; poet and author who was popular in the 1960s, *Trout Fishing in America;* Bolinas, Cal., Oct. 25.

Bricktop, 89; legendary night club owner and entertainer; New York, Jan. 31.

Brisson, Frederick, 71; theater and film producer; New York, Oct. 8.

Bunker, Ellsworth, 90; diplomat who served 7 presidents; Dummerston, Vt., Sept. 27.

Burton, Richard, 58; Welsh-born actor of the theater and films who was nominated for 7 Oscars; Geneva, Switzerland, Aug. 5.

C

Cameron, Rod, 73; actor who starred in action films in the 1940s and 1950s; Gainesville, Ga., Dec 21.

Campbell, Clarence, 78; president of the National Hockey League, 1946-77; Montreal, June 24.

Capote, Truman, 59; television personality and author, "In Cold

Blood"; Los Angeles, Aug. 25.

Case, Anna, 95; operatic soprano who made her Metropolitan Opera debut in 1909; New York, Jan. 7.

Christensen, Lew, 75; ballet dancer and choreographer; Burlingham, Cal., Oct. 9.

Christopher, Milbourne, 70; magician and author of 24 books about magic; New York, June 17.

Church, Frank, 59; U.S. senator from Idaho, 1957-81; Bethesda, Md., Apr. 7.

Clark, Gen. Mark, 87; commander of the 5th Army in Italy during World War II; Charleston, S.C., Apr. 17.

Collins, Kirk, 25; cornerback for the L.A. Rams football team; Anaheim, Cal., Feb. 22.

Conrad, Michael, 58; actor who won 2 Emmys portraying Sgt. Esterhaus on the *Hill Street Blues* TV drama; Los Angeles, Nov. 22.

Coogan, Jackie, 69; actor who was a major child star of the silent screen; Palm Springs, Cal., Mar. 1.

Cooper, Chuck, 57; first black player in the National Basketball Assn., 1950; Pittsburgh, Feb. 5.

Cori, Dr. Carl Ferdinand, 87; winner with his wife, Gerty Theresa Radnitz, of 1947 Nobel Prize in medicine; Cambridge, Mass., Oct. 20.

Coveleski, Stan, 94; pitcher who was elected to the baseball hall of fame in 1969; South Bend, Ind., Mar. 20.

Coxe Jr., George Harmon, 82; author of more than 60 mystery novels; Hilton Head, S.C., Jan. 30.

Cronin, Joe, 77; former baseball player, manager, general manager and American League president; Osterville, Mass., Sept. 7.

Culver, Ronald, 83; British actor of stage and screen; London, Feb. 29.

D

Dana, Leora, 60; actress who appeared on Broadway and in films; New York, Dec. 13.

David, 12; immune-deficient "bubble boy"; Houston, Feb. 22.

Davis, Allison, 81; psychologist and social anthropologist who wrote of the black experience and black leaders; Chicago, Nov. 21.

Deacon, Richard, 62; character actor in films and TV, Mel Cooley on *The Dick Van Dyke Show;* Los Angeles, Aug. 8.

Delmar, Kenny, 73; actor who played Senator Claghorn on Fred Allen's radio show; Stanford, Conn., July 14.

Demarest, William, 91; actor who appeared in over 100 movies and in the *My Three Sons* TV series; Palm Springs, Cal.,

Demaret, Jimmy, 73; golfer who won the Masters Tournament 3 times; Houston, Dec. 28.

Dirac, Paul, 82; physicist who won the 1933 Nobel Prize in Physics; Tallahassee, Fla., Oct. 20.

Dockery, Rex, 41; football coach at Memphis State Univ.; in plane crash; Dec. 12.

Dolin, Sir Anton, 79; British ballet star and choreographer; Paris, Nov. 25.

Donohue, Jack, 75; film and television director; Los Angeles, Mar. 27.

Dors, Diana, 52; British film actress who was popular in the 1950s; Windsor, England, May 4.

Dragon, Carmen, 69; composer and conductor; Santa Monica, Cal., Mar. 28.

E

Eckstein, Otto, 56; economist and educator; Boston, Mar. 22.

Egan, William, 69; first governor of Alaska after statehood, 1959-75; Anchorage, May 6.

Elliott, Don, 57; jazz singer, vibraphonist,

and composer; Weston, Conn., July 5.

Evins, Joe L., 73; U.S. representative from Tenn., 1946-77; Nashville, Mar. 31.

F

Farrar, Margaret, 87; pioneer crossword-puzzle editor; New York, June 11.

Fixx, James F., 52; lecturer and author of books on running; Hardwick, Vt., July 20.

Flowers, Walter, 51; U.S. representative from Alabama, 1969-79; Falls Church, Va., Apr. 12.

Foreman, Carl, 69; film producer and screenwriter; Beverly Hills, Cal., June 26.

Forsythe, Edwin, 68; U.S. representative from New Jersey since 1971; Moorestown, N.J., Mar. 29.

Foucault, Michel, 57; French philosopher and historian; Paris, June 25.

Friedrich, Carl J., 83; author and educator who taught at Harvard Univ. for 50 years; Lexington, Mass., Sept. 19.

Friendly, Alfred, 71; journalist who won a Pulitzer prize for coverage of the 1967 Arab-Israeli war; Washington, D.C., Nov. 7.

G

Gallup, George H., 82; public opinion polling pioneer; Tschingel, Switzerland, July 26.

Gandhi, Indira, 66; prime minister of India; New Delhi, India, Oct. 31.

Garland, Red, 60; jazz pianist in Miles Davis quintet; Dallas, Apr. 23.

Garner, Peggy Ann, 53; child actress who is best known for the 1945 film *A Tree Grows in Brooklyn;* Woodland Hills, Cal., Oct. 16.

Gaye, Marvin, 44; pop singer, *Sexual Healing;* Los Angeles, Apr. 1.

Glass, Ned, 75; character actor whose career in the theater, films, and TV spanned 50 years; Los Angeles, June 15.

Gobbi, Tito, 68; Italian operatic baritone who was famed for his Scarpia in Puccini's *Tosca;* Rome, Mar. 5.

Goldstein, Ruby, 76; boxing referee who worked 39 championship fights; Miami Beach, Apr. 22.

Goodman, Billy, 58; baseball player who led the American League in batting in 1950; Sarasota, Fla., Oct. 1.

Grimm, Charlie, 85; major league baseball player and manager for some 40 years, mostly with the Chicago Cubs; Scottsdale, Ariz., Nov. 15.

H

Haddad, Maj. Saad, 47; Lebanese army officer who led militia force in southern Lebanon with Israeli support; Merj 'Uyun, Lebanon, Jan. 14.

Harris, Sir Arthur Travers, 91; leader of Britain's bomber command during World War II; Goring-on-Thames, England, Apr. 5.

Hegan, Jim, 63; former major league catcher and coach; Swampscott, Mass., June 17.

Hellman, Lillian, 79; playwright, *The Children's Hour, The Little Foxes;* Martha's Vineyard, Mass., June 30.

Hextall, Bryan, 70; hockey hall of famer who played for the N.Y. Rangers; Portage La Prairie, Manitoba, July 24.

Hexum, Jon-Erik, 26; actor who starred in the *Cover Up* TV series; San Francisco, Oct. 19.

Hinkle, Samuel F., 83; chemist and businessman who developed the K, C, and D. rations first used by U.S. soldiers in World War II; Hershey, Pa., Apr. 19.

Holyoake, Sir Keith Jacka, 79; New Zealand prime minister, 1960-72;

Wellington, New Zealand, Dec. 8.

Hoyt, Waite, 84; baseball hall of fame pitcher who won 237 major league games; broadcaster of the Cincinnati Reds games for 25 years; Cincinnati, Aug. 25.

Hunter, Alberta, 89; blues singer and cabaret star of the 1920s and 1930s; New York, Oct. 17.

Hutton, Ina Ray, 67; band leader who was popular in the 1940s and 50s; Ventura, Cal., Feb. 19.

J

Jacoby, Oswald, 81; bridge champion, columnist, and author; Dallas, June 27.

Jaffe, Sam, 93; character actor who appeared in films, television, and the theater; Beverly Hills, Cal., Mar. 24.

Jenkins, Gordon, 73; composer, conductor, and Grammy-winning arranger; Malibu, Cal., May 1.

Johnson, Sonny, 30; actress who gained prominence in the film *Flashdance;* Los Angeles, June 20.

K

Kapitsa, Pyotr, L., 89; Soviet physicist who won the 1978 Nobel Prize in physics; Moscow, Apr. 8.

Kastler, Dr. Alfred, 81; scientist whose work helped set the stage for the invention of the laser; won 1966 Nobel Prize; Bandol, France, Jan. 7.

Kaufman, Andy, 35; comedian who starred on TV in *Taxi* and *Saturday Night Live;* Los Angeles, May 16.

Kelly, George "High Pockets", 89; baseball hall of famer who played for the N.Y. Giants in the 1920s; Burlingame, Cal., Oct. 13.

Kennedy, David, 28; son of the late Sen. Robert F. Kennedy; Palm Beach, Fla., Apr. 26.

King, Walter Woolf, 88; actor who starred in films in the 1930s; Beverly Hills, Cal., Oct. 24.

Knopf, Alfred A., 91; book publisher; Purchase, N.Y., Aug. 11.

Kotar, Doug, 32; former N.Y. Giants running back; Pittsburgh, Dec. 16.

Krasner, Lee, 75; abstract impressionist painter; widow of Jackson Pollock; New York, June 19.

Kroc, Ray A., 81; builder of the McDonald's fast food empire; owner of the San Diego Padres baseball team; San Diego, Jan. 14.

Kubic, Gail T., 69; composer who won a 1950 Oscar as well as a 1952 Pulitzer prize; Claremont, Cal., July 20.

L

LaRue, Jack, 80; supporting actor who appeared in some 200 films, often as a villain; Santa Monica, Cal., Jan. 11.

Laskin, Bora, 71; chief justice of the Supreme Court of Canada; Ottawa, Mar. 26.

Lau, Charlie, 50; former major league player and renowned batting instructor; Marathon, Fla., Mar. 18.

Leigh, Carolyn, 57; lyricist, *Hey Look Me Over, Young at Heart;* New York, Nov. 19.

Llewellyn, Richard, 76; Welsh playwright and author, *How Green Was My Valley;* Dublin, Nov. 30.

Loo, Richard, 80; Chinese-American actor who appeared in 150 films during his 50-year career; Los Angeles, Nov. 20.

Losey, Joseph, 75; film director; London, June 22.

Low, George M., 58; educator and engineer who headed the Apollo Space Project; Troy, N.Y., July 17.

M

Machito, 76; Cuban-born bandleader who helped revolutionize Latin dance music; London, Apr. 15.

Manahan, Anna, 82; woman who failed in her lifetime quest to prove that she was

Anastasia, daughter of Czar Nicholas II; Charlottesville, Va., Feb. 12.

Manne, Shelly, 64; jazz drummer and composer; Los Angeles, Sept. 26.

Marley, John, 77; character actor in the theater and in films; Los Angeles, May 22.

Mason, James, 75; British-born actor who starred in some 100 films; Lausanne, Switzerland, July 27.

Mayfield Julian, 56; actor and writer on black themes; Takoma Park, Md., Oct. 20.

Mays, Benjamin, 89; educator and civil rights leader; headed Morehouse College, 1940-67; Atlanta, Mar. 28.

McAvoy, May, 82; silent-screen actress, *The Jazz Singer;* Los Angeles, Apr. 26.

McBride, Lloyd, 67; president of the United Steelworkers of America since 1977; Whitehall, Pa., Nov. 6.

Marland, Ernest W., 89; U.S. senator from Arizona, 1941-53; Phoenix, June 9.

Mercer, Mabel, 84; cabaret singer much admired by other entertainers and songwriters; Pittsfield, Mass., Apr. 20.

Merman, Ethel, 76; the leading Broadway musical-comedy star for over 40 years; New York, Feb. 15.

Merrill, Dr. John, 67; physician who led 1954 medical team which did the first successful organ transplant from one human to another; Bahamas, Apr. 4.

Middleton, Ray, 77; baritone who starred in Broadway musicals in the 1930s and 1940s; Panorama City, Cal., Apr. 10.

Minter, Mary Miles, 82; silent screen star; Santa Monica, Cal., Aug. 4.

Mohieddin, Fuad, 58; prime minister of Egypt since 1982; Cairo, June 5.

Moore, Ray S., 78; cartoonist who created "The Phantom" comic strip; Kirkwood, Mo., Jan. 13.

Moore, Robert, 56; film and theater director; New York, May 10.

N

Nadler, Teddy, 74; clerk who won $264,000 on TV quiz shows in the 1950s; St. Louis, May 23.

Nagano, Shigeo, 83; Japanese industrialist, diplomat; Tokyo, May 4.

Naguib, Mohammed, 83; first president of Egypt, 1952; Egypt, Aug. 28.

Nelson, Nate, 52; lead singer for the Flamingos and the Platters; Boston, June 1.

Nemtchinova, Vera, 84; Russian-born ballerina who starred for the Ballets Russes in the 1920s; New York, July 22.

O

O'Flaherty, Liam, 88; Irish novelist, *The Informer;* Dublin, Sept. 8.

Oppen, George, 76; poet who won the 1969 Pulitzer prize; Sunnyvale, Cal., July 7.

Overstreet, David, 25; running back for the Miami Dolphins; Winona, Tex., June 24.

P

Parsons, Johnnie, 66; auto racer who won the 1950 Indy 500; Los Angeles, Sept. 8.

Partch, Virgil, 67; cartoonist best known for comic strip "Big George"; Valencia, Cal., Aug. 10.

Perkins, Rep. Carl D., 71; U.S. representative from Kentucky since 1949; Lexington, Aug. 3.

Petrillo, James C., 92; former president of the American Federation of Musicians; Chicago, Oct. 23.

Petrosian, Tigran, 55; Soviet world chess champion in the 1960s; Moscow, reported Aug. 13.

Phillips, Esther, 48; blues singer; Torrance, Cal., Aug. 7.

Pickens, Slim, 64; actor who appeared in numerous films in cowboy sidekick roles; Modesto, Cal., Dec. 8.

Pidgeon, Walter, 87; actor who appeared in films for more than 5 decades, *Mrs. Miniver, How Green Was My Valley;* Santa Monica, Cal., Sept. 25.

Pinelli, Babe, 89; major league umpire for 21 years; Daly City, Cal., Oct. 22.

Powell, William, 91; film actor who was best known as the star of the "Thin Man" series in the 1930s and 40s; Palm Springs, Cal., Mar. 5.

Priestley, J.B., 89; British essayist, novelist, and playwright; Stratford-on-Avon, England, Aug. 14.

Provost, Claude, 51; hockey star with the Montreal Canadiens in the 1960s; played on 9 Stanley Cup championship teams; Hallandale, Fla., Apr. 17.

R

Rahner, Karl, 80; German-born Jesuit theologian and author; Innsbruck, Austria, Mar. 30.

Renault, Mary, 78; British author whose best-selling novels were based on the history of the Grecian age; Cape Town, South Africa, Dec. 13.

Robson, Dame Flora, 82; British actress whose career in films and on the stage spanned 50 years; Brighton, England, July 7.

Rogers, Byron G., 83; U.S. representative from Colorado, 1951-71; Denver, Dec. 31.

Rossiter, Leonard, 57; British comic actor; London, Oct. 5.

Rowe, James, 75; lawyer who was a special advisor to FDR; Washington, D.C., June 17.

Ryle, Sir Martin, 66; British astronomer who shared the 1974 Nobel Prize in physics; Cambridge, England, Oct. 14.

S

Samples, Junior, 56; comedian who appeared on the *Hee Haw* television show since 1969; Cumming, Ga., Nov. 13.

Samuels, Howard, 64; industrialist, politician, and sports executive; New York, Oct. 26.

Schacht, Al, 91; entertainer who was known as the "crown prince of baseball"; Waterbury, Conn., July 14.

Schneider, Alan, 66; stage director; London, May 3.

Shaw, Irwin, 71; novelist and short-story writer, *The Young Lions;* Davos, Switzerland, May 16.

Schwartz, Arthur, 83; composer of musicals for movies and Broadway, *The Band Wagon;* Kintnersville, Pa., Sept. 3.

Shehan, Lawrence Cardinal, 86; retired Roman Catholic archbishop of Baltimore; Baltimore, Aug. 26.

Sholokhov, Mikhail A., 78; Soviet author who was awarded the 1965 Nobel Prize, *And Quiet Flows the Don;* USSR, Feb 21.

Sinclair, Gordon, 83; Canadian newsman who gained fame by defending the U.S. in 1973; Toronto, May 17.

Prince Souvanna Phouma, 82; prime minister of Laos who was ousted by the communists in 1975; Vientiane, Laos, Jan. 10.

Stern, Philip Van Doren, 83; novelist, editor, and Civil War historian; wrote novel which became film *It's A Wonderful Life;* Sarasota, Fla., July 31.

Stevens, Julie, 66; actress who portrayed Helen Trent on radio, 1944-60; Wellfleet, Mass., Aug. 26.

Stuart, Jesse, 78; poet, novelist, and short-story writer; Ironton, Oh., Feb. 17.

Swale, 3; colt who won the 1984 Kentucky Derby and Belmont Stakes; New York, June 17.

T

Taylor, Glen H., 80; U.S. senator from Idaho, 1945-51; Henry Wallace's running mate in 1948; Burlingame, Cal., Apr. 28.

Taylor, Henry J., 81; author, journalist, and diplomat; New York, Feb. 26.

Tevis, Walter, 56; novelist, *The Hustler;* New York, Aug. 9.

Thornton, Willie Mae, 57; blues singer who influenced Elvis Presley, Aretha Franklin; Los Angeles, July 25.

Tidyman, Ernest R., 56; author and screenwriter, *The French Connection;* London, July 15.

Tizol, Juan, 84; jazz trombonist who was long associated with the Duke Ellington orchestra; Inglewood, Cal., Apr. 23.

Toure, Ahmed Sekou, 62; president of Guinea for 26 years; Cleveland, Oh., Mar. 26.

Truffaut, Francois, 52; French film director, *The 400 Blows, Day For Night;* Neuilly-Sur-Seine, France, Oct. 14.

Tubb, Ernest, 70; country music singer noted for his honky tonk sound with songs like *I'm Walking the Floor Over You;* Nashville, Sept. 6.

Tully, Grace G., 83; personal secretary of FDR; Washington, D.C., June 15.

V

Varipapa, Andy, 93; bowler who won national championships in the 1940s; Huntington, N.Y., Aug. 25.

W

Wallace, Lila, 94; philanthropist and co-founder of the *Reader's Digest;* Mt. Kisco, N.Y., May 8.

Waring, Fred, 84; big band leader whose "Pennsylvanians" were popular for almost 7 decades; invented the Waring blender; Danville, Pa., July 29.

Webster, Paul, 77; lyricist who wrote over 500 songs, *The Shadow of Your Smile;* Beverly Hills, Cal., Mar. 22.

Weissmuller, Johnny, 79; Olympic swimming gold medalist who played Tarzan in some 20 films; Acapulco, Mexico, Jan. 20.

Werner, Oskar, 61; Austrian actor, *Ship of Fools, Jules and Jim;* Marburg, W. Germany, Oct. 23.

West, Jessamyn, 81; author of short stories and novels about Quakers; Napa, Cal., Feb. 25.

Wibberley, Leonard, 68; journalist and author of over 100 books, *The Mouse That Roared;* Santa Monica, Cal., Nov. 22.

Widnall, William B., 77; U.S. representative from New Jersey, 1951-75; Ridgewood, N.J., Dec. 29.

Wilcoxon, Henry, 78; British film actor and producer; Burbank, Cal., Mar. 6.

Willson, Meredith, 82; composer of Broadway musicals *The Music Man, The Unsinkable Molly Brown;* Santa Monica, Cal., June 15.

Wilson, Charles H., 67; U.S. representative from California, 1963-80; Clinton, Md., July 21.

Wilson, Dennis, 39; member of the Beach Boys singing group; Marina del Rey, Cal., Dec. 28.

Wilson, Jackie, 49; rock-and-roll singer who was popular in the 1950s; Mt. Holly, N.J., Jan. 21.

Winwood, Estelle, 101; stage and film actress whose career began in 1888; Los Angeles, June 20.

Z

Zablicki, Rep. Clement J., 71; U.S. representative from Wisconsin since 1949; sponsor of the 1973 War Powers Act; Washington, D.C., Dec. 3.

Zivic, Fritzie, 71; boxer who was a leading welterweight of the 1940s; Aspinwall, Pa., May 16.

QUICK REFERENCE INDEX